Racehorse Record

FLAT 2002

Raceform's A-Z Guide to horses which ran in Britain during the 2001 Flat Season (January 1st - November 10th 2001)

Sponsored by:

Editor Ashley Rumney
Comments by David Bellingham, Nicki Bowen, Steffan Edwards, Iona Hughes, Richard Lowther, Ashley Rumney, Ronald Wood
Raceform Ratings Walter Glynn, Simon Turner
Development Phillip Lamphee, Dan Di Pol

Typeset and Published by Raceform Ltd,
Compton, Newbury, Berkshire, RG20 6NL
Tel: 01635 578080
Fax: 01635 578101
Web http://www.raceform.co.uk
EMail: raceform@raceform.co.uk
Printed by Polestar Wheatons Ltd, Exeter

ISBN 1 901100 58 8

CONTENTS

Full details of all Raceform services and publications are available from
Raceform, Compton, Newbury, Berkshire RG20 6NL.
Tel: 01635 578080 Fax: 01635 578101.
Web http://www.raceform.co.uk
Email: raceform@raceform.co.uk

Cover Photo: Allsport
Fantastic Light (L. Dettori) narrowly beats Galileo (M. Kinane)
in a terrific race for the Irish Champion Stakes at Leopardstown

INTRODUCTION

Raceform's *Racehorse Record* has been designed not only as an historical reference, but also as a guide to the future, with the aim being to provide factual information about individual horses that ran on the Flat in Britain during the 2001 season, and also to pinpoint conditions that are likely to prove conducive to future success.

Raceform Ratings and Split Second Speed Ratings are as at November 10, 2001. For full season's results and ratings, refer to the *Raceform 2002 Annual*.

The horses are listed in alphabetical order, with a space ordered before 'a', so that, for example, A Day On The Dub comes *before* Abajany

KEY TO HORSE RECORDS

Arpeggio

106(104) (76)**79**

6-y-o b g Polar Falcon (USA)-Hilly (Town Crier)

D Nicholls H E Lhendup Dorji

Placings:224/30040/1000/**0**00410313000-**5150006**2666130003 **(5344)**

2001: **8**^{5}SD, **7**^{1}SD, **7**^{5}SW, **7**^{0}SW, **8**^{0}SD, 9^{0}S, **7**^{6}SD, **8**^{2}SD, 10^{6}G, 10^{6}GF, 8^{6}G, 8^{1}GS, 8^{3}GS, 8^{0}G, 8^{0}GS, 8^{3}GS

	Starts	1st	2nd	3rd	Win & Pl
Career Total (Turf)	**32**	**4**	**2**	**5**	**30180**
Career Total (AW)	**8**	**1**	**1**	**0**	**4711**

76	7/01	NmkJ	1m	D(0-80)H	G-S	£8502
76	1/01	Sthl	7f	D(0-85)H	STD	£3844
74	9/00	Ling	7f140y	D(0-80)H	G-F	£7605
64	7/00	Catt	7f	E(0-65)	G-F	£2769
72	5/99	Thsk	6f	D	SFT	£3535

Total win prize-money £26256

Going (Turf): Sf: 1-5 GS: 1-7 Gd: 0-11 **GF: 2-8** Fm: 0-1

Distance: 5f/6f: 1-8 **7f-8f: 4-26** 9f-13f: 0-6 14f+: 0-0

Track : **LH: 2-17** RH: 0-3 **Tight: 1-5** Gall: 0-2

Aids: Bl: 0-1 Vi: 0-0 Tstrap: 0-0

Best Rating: **79** 7/01 Ayr 1m gd-sft

A useful handicapper who stays a mile plus, he is effective on the All-Weather but has been a bit excitable in the past. Acts on any going on turf. Needs a fast pace to help him settle.

Name of horse, plus country of origin suffix in brackets

Current master Split Second speed rating on left, Raceform rating on right (all-weather ratings in brackets)

Age, colour, sex and pedigree. The sire's name is followed by the dam's name, then the dam's sire's name in brackets

Trainer's name in bold (plus date of transfer and previous trainer's name if the horse changed stables during the season), followed by the owner's name

Complete list of the horse's placings, starting with its first recorded race. All-weather or sand outings in bold type. A slash '/' or dash '-' indicates a change of season. This is followed in brackets by the Raceform number of the last race in the Form Book in which the horse competed

2001 record, showing each outing by distance (in furlongs), finishing position (superscript figure) and going

Career record, broken down into turf and all-weather appearances

Career wins, showing (left to right) winning Raceform rating, date of win (month/year), course, distance, race conditions, going, win prize money

Career Going record (wins-runs), best figures in bold

Career Distance record

Track type record

Aids record for the season (blinkers, visor, tongue strap)

Best Raceform rating achieved during the 2001 season, followed by the relevant date, course, distance, and going

Raceform master comment on selected horses only

REVIEW OF THE SEASON

By Richard Lowther

2001 was another vintage year on the Flat. The twin powers of Coolmore and Godolphin dominated events on the racecourse and provided racefans with some outstanding equine performers, while there was another compelling battle for the jockeys' championship.

Aidan O'Brien, the brilliant young master of Ballydoyle, enjoyed a sensational season. He saddled the winners of no fewer than 23 Group or Grade One races worldwide, beating the previous record held by American Bob Baffert. O'Brien horses won both Epsom Classics and three at home in Ireland, but it was with the two-year-olds with which O'Brien excelled. His runners won nine of the ten Group One events open to juvenile colts in Europe, the only one to get away being the Criterium International at Saint-Cloud. Throw in the Breeders' Cup Juvenile, in which Johannesburg beat the best of the Americans, and Ireland's top event for fillies the Moyglare Stud Stakes, won by Quarter Moon, and O'Brien enjoyed an unprecedented season of dominance. He was the first foreign-based trainer to win the trainers' championship in Britain since namesake Vincent O'Brien in 1977, and only the fourth in all. Vincent O'Brien, of course, was Aidan O'Brien's predecessor at the famous Ballydoyle stables in County Tipperary, and Vincent's daughter Susan is co-owner with her husband John Magnier and businessman Michael Tabor of most of the stars in Aidan's string . John Magnier has built up a personal fortune estimated at £150 million, mainly through stallion earnings at his Coolmore Stud, and has provided the funds to allow enable O'Brien's brilliance to prosper.

TRIUMPH FOR FALLON

When Kieren Fallon broke his left shoulder at Royal Ascot in 2000, many doubted that he would ever ride again. The Irishman suffered extensive damage to the nerves and muscle tissues, and may have even lost the use of the arm had surgery been delayed any longer. Fallon set out to prove the doubters wrong, and after a long and painful process of rehabilitation he made a successful comeback in Dubai in December, astounding those who had doubted whether he would ever return to the saddle. The acid test, however, would come when he returned to the track in Britain. On his first ride back, riding Wintertide at Wolverhampton on March 27, he was unable to give his mount the necessary help in a close finish and the partnership went down by a head. There was no doubt that the left arm looked weak, and there were plenty of critics ready to write him off. Fallon had other ideas, predicting 'the only way I won't be champion again is if I have another injury'. He was to be proved right. Getting off the mark in Britain with a double at Musselburgh on April 7 – Grand National day – Fallon trailed Pat Eddery in the early months of the season, with Richard Quinn and reigning Champion Kevin Darley also in contention. Eleven-times Champion Eddery still led the race at the end of June, but Fallon soon moved ahead and never relinquished his lead, although not without withstanding a spirited challenge from Darley who enjoyed another fine season. The campaign was a triumph for Fallon, but it ended with the surprising news that he would not be retained as stable jockey to Sir Michael Stoute next season, some of Stoute's owners preferring to use other riders. Fallon is sure to be in demand, however, although he has announced that he will not be going all out to retain his title.

There was an even closer outcome to the apprentice jockeys' championship. Victory went to Chris Catlin, a 19-year-old from Barnet. Attached to Ken Ivory's stable, Catlin finished just one winner ahead of young Scot Keith Dalgleish, with the battle going right to the wire.

The first important event of the British season, the Randombet.com Lincoln at Doncaster on March 24, went to the favourite Nimello from the Paul Cole yard. The gelding was to supplement this win with victory in the Doubleprint Handicap at Kempton, a race regrettably no longer run under its traditional title of the Jubilee Handicap. On the same day as the Lincoln much attention was centred on Nad Al Sheba, where the American colt Captain Steve won the sixth running of the Dubai World Cup. Best Of The Bests, carrying the hopes of the race's founder Sheikh Mohammed, could finish no nearer than eighth, and rider Frankie Dettori was heckled by a section of the crowd on returning to unsaddle.

GUINEAS REPEAT

With thoughts turning to the first Classics of the season, the seasonal reappearance of Nayef in the Macau Jockey Club Craven Stakes at Newmarket on April 19 was eagerly anticipated. The colt, winter favourite for the 2000 Guineas after an unbeaten juvenile campaign, was almost withdrawn from the Craven on account of the soft ground, but he took his chance only to find King's Ironbridge and Red Carpet too strong. The defeat of Nayef further undermined the standing of the traditional Guineas trials, as Newmarket's fillies' feature, the Nell Gwyn Stakes, as well as the Greenham and Fred Darling Stakes at the Newbury Spring Meeting, appeared to have shed little light on the Classic picture.

Much more prominence was given to the results of the Godolphin private trials earlier in the month, and the winner of the colts' version, Tobougg, was sent off favourite for the Sagitta 2000 Guineas at Newmarket on May 5. He could finish only ninth, however, as victory went to Kieren Fallon aboard Golan for Sir Michael Stoute, the same jockey-trainer combination having won the Guineas with King's Best twelve months earlier. Nayef, sent off a 10/1 shot on the day, was eighth.

The following day's Sagitta 1000 Guineas saw a highly popular winner in Ameerat, another seasonal debutant. The filly, ridden by Philip Robinson in the colours of Sheikh Ahmed Al Maktoum, gave Newmarket trainer Michael Jarvis his first English Classic in his 34th year with a licence. Jarvis, greatly respected by his fellow professionals, had enjoyed success in the Prix de l'Arc de Triomphe with Carroll House in 1989, but said after Ameerat's win 'if you're English and you've been training in England a long time, it's a big thrill to win one of our Classics. I think it's better than winning the Arc because it's at home'. The Guineas was to be the highlight of Ameerat's career, as she was retired to the paddocks after failing to reproduce her best in three subsequent starts.

The feature of the Chester May Meeting, the Tote Chester Cup, saw a fine weight-carrying performance from Rainbow High. Following up his win in the race of two years earlior, the six year-old defied a record 9st 13lb under a typically cool ride from Richard Hughes. Trainer Barry Hills numbers this meeting among his favourites, and another of his raiding party, Mr Combustible, captured the Victor Chandler Chester Vase to earn himself a crack at the Derby.

There was controversy in the SIS Huxley Stakes on the final day of the Chester meeting when Darryll Holland dropped his hands on Island House in the dying strides, allowing Adilabad and Kieren Fallon to snatch the prize right on the line. For his lapse of concentration Holland was handed a fourteen-day ban, although that was scant consolation to those who had backed his mount.

Barry Hills gave himself another option for the Vodafone Derby when Perfect Sunday, in the colours of Khalid Abdulla, made all the running in the Arena Racing Derby Trial at Lingfield on May 12. The Oaks trial on the same card was a most unsatisfactory affair. Just three fillies took part, and two of them came very close together below the distance. Double Crossed, who passed the post a neck to the good, was thrown out by the Stewards in favour of Silver Grey Lady, but many observers believed that was a harsh decision. Following an appeal by the demoted filly's connections, the decision was eventually reversed.

York's Oaks trial, the Tattersalls Musidora Stakes on May 15, was won by Time Away from the John Dunlop yard, the filly being a granddaughter of her owner-breeder

Robert Barnett's 1982 Oaks winner Time Charter. Time Away's performance was somewhat overshadowed by the post-race reaction of Lord Carnarvon, racing manager to the Queen whose runner Flight Of Fancy was a fast-finishing fourth. Lord Carnarvon was less than charitable about jockey Kieren Fallon, describing his ride as 'awful'. Trainer Sir Michael Stoute seemed to concur, saying 'I wasn't disappointed with the horse'.

Fallon let his riding do the talking in the following afternoon's feature event, the Convergent Communications Dante Stakes, partnering Dilshaan to a decisive victory. With Golan already earmarked for the Derby, Sir Michael Stoute and Fallon now had two leading candidates for Epsom.

The Godolphin team had endured some setbacks in the early weeks of the campaign, but they got off the mark in Britain when Marienbard took the Merewood Homes Yorkshire Cup under Frankie Dettori. Half an hour later Godolphin notched winner number two, Musha Merr landing the odds in the Michael Seely Memorial Glasgow Stakes.

The Stoute-Fallon partnership enjoyed another high-profile victory on May 19 when Medicean battled home in the Juddmonte Lockinge Stakes at Newbury. For a Group One, the race lacked strength in depth, Observatory, for one, running in the Prix d'Ispahan instead.

CLASSIC COLLECTION

Aidan O'Brien was in fine Classic-winning form in May. His filly Rose Gypsy landed the French 1000 Guineas, while later in the month Ballydoyle runners won both Irish Guineas at the Curragh. Black Minnaloushe, ridden by Johnny Murtagh, beat stablemate and fellow 20/1 shot Mozart in the colts' version, with first string Minardi back in third. This 1-2-3 by O'Brien was followed by a 1-3-4 in the 1,000 the next day, victory going to Imagine under Seamus Heffernan.

Twelve days later Imagine added another Classic when justifying favouritism in the Vodafone Oaks at Epsom, this time in the hands of stable jockey Michael Kinane. Flight Of Fancy again endured a troubled passage in finishing second. Neither filly was to race again, but Imagine's value as a Group One-winning half-sister to Derby winner Generous was inestimable.

The Ballydoyle team completed the Oaks-Derby double the following day when their representative Galileo careered away from fellow joint-favourite Golan to win by three and a half lengths. Galileo went to Epsom unbeaten, having shown off his Derby credentials with two wins at Leopardstown. Tobougg was third in the Classic, followed by the Barry Hills triumvirate of Mr Combustible, Storming Home and Perfect Sunday. Dilshaan was next. This was Aidan O'Brien's first Derby winner, and also a first for Galileo's sire Sadler's Wells, the stallion who has proved such a goldmine for the Coolmore team. Kieren Fallon had chosen Golan in preference to Dilshaan, but picked up a riding ban at Ayr nine days before the Derby and was forced to watch from the sidelines as Pat Eddery deputised on the runner-up. The Derby was back on BBC Television for the first time since 1979, and an estimated three million viewers enjoyed excellent coverage of the race.

On the opening day of Royal Ascot on June 19 Black Minnaloushe recorded his second Group One when coming late in the St James's Palace Stakes. Johnny Murtagh was again on board, Michael Kinane having remained loyal to Minardi, who was sent off favourite but finished only eighth. Runner-up was the Godolphin colt Noverre. He had been first past the post in the French 2000 Guineas at Longchamp on his previous start, but was to be disqualified later in the year when testing positive to Methyprednisolone, a widely used meditation for horses with an arthritic complaint. Vahorimix, recipient of the Longchamp prize, finished fourth in the Ascot race.

Mark Johnston enjoyed an excellent first day at Ascot. He sent out the first and second in the Duke of Edinburgh Handicap, Takamaka Bay short-heading Akbar, and completed a double with And Beyond in the Queen's Vase.

There was a rough race for the Coventry Stakes, which went to the Aidan O'Brien-trained Landseer. Winning jockey Jamie Spencer and fifth-placed Johnny Murtagh both received riding bans, while Frankie Dettori endured a nightmare passage on Meshaheer who flew home in third.

A huge gamble was landed in the Jersey Stakes on day two of the Royal Meeting. Mozart, backed from 9/2 in the morning to a starting price of 7/4, held on in the colours of Michael Tabor to cost the bookmakers an estimated £2million.

There was an outstanding display from Fantastic Light in the Prince of Wales's Stakes, which earned the Godolphin flagbearer Raceform's highest speed figure of the season. Unfortunately both runner-up Kalanisi and fourth-placed Observatory incurred injuries during the race which ended their careers.

Mark Johnston sent out his third winner of the meeting when Royal Rebel battled home from the gallant Persian Punch in a memorable renewal of the Gold Cup. This was the middle leg of a treble for Johnny Murtagh, his other wins coming on Sahara Slew in the Ribblesdale and Beekeeper in the King George V Handicap. Royal Rebel's owner Peter Savill, chairman of the BHB, was embroiled all week in delicate discussions on media rights. A consortium known as Go Racing, consisting of the BBC, Channel 4, Sky and Arena Leisure, had agreed in principle to a deal worth £307 million, a sum which would put racing's finances on a sound footing, but in the week before Ascot negotiations appeared on the brink of collapse as a number of factions within the industry voiced their concerns. It took a great deal of fine-tuning to the package, and tense discussions lasting through the night, before the deal was finally sealed.

Henry Cecil salvaged something from a disappointing week when Sandmason won the Hardwicke Stakes on the final day. The colt was Cecil's second string, favourite Wellbeing finishing only fifth. After the race Cecil hinted at his disillusionment with training, revealing 'sometimes it's in my mind that I can't go on forever'.

Jamie Osborne's training career, on the other hand, has only just begun. The former top jump jockey enjoyed his biggest success to date courtesy of the grey juvenile Irony in the Windsor Castle Stakes. 'This is the first time in my life I've lost sleep over a horserace', said Osborne.

Nice One Clare was another winner for Johnny Murtagh, earning him the London Clubs Trophy for the meeting's leading rider, when swooping late to land the Wokingham Handicap. For trainer Pip Payne it was his first winner for six months. The mare is named after her owner-breeder Clare McGinn.

The sole three-year-old in the line-up, Archduke Ferdinand, came out on top in the Foster's Lager Northumberland Plate at Newcastle on June 30. Trained by Paul Cole and ridden by Franny Norton, Archduke Ferdinand foiled a big gamble on favourite Cover Up, beating him by a neck.

OUTSTANDING

By this stage Galileo was being feted as an outstanding Derby winner, and his next appearance in the Budweiser Irish Derby at the Curragh on July 1 was eagerly awaited. He did not let his followers down, slamming his rivals in effortless style. Runner-up Morshdi, winner of the Italian Derby on his previous start, was supplemented for the Curragh race at a cost of £90,000, but earned almost double that for finishing second. Golan, reunited with Kieren Fallon, was a lacklustre third.

Medicean recorded his second Group One success of the year in the Coral Eurobet Eclipse Stakes at a rain-lashed Sandown on July 7. He had to make up a lot of ground in the straight as Godolphin pacemaker Broche set a blistering pace up front, but his reserves of courage got him home by half a length in a blanket finish. Tobougg and Black Minnaloushe, who filled fourth and fifth spots, were perhaps given too much to do by their riders.

The Newmarket July meeting was a triumph for David Loder. The talented young trainer had enjoyed two frustrating seasons at Evry in France before Godolphin pulled the plug on that venture and brought Loder back to headquarters. Three of his juveniles scored at the meeting, Dubai Destination taking a maiden, Silent Honor scrambling home in the Cherry Hinton Stakes and Meshaheer atoning for his unlucky run at Ascot with a comfortable win in the TNT July Stakes. 'Although there is pressure to get results', said Loder, I would much rather have that than the pressure of training no winners'.

Mutamam was produced bursting with health by Alec Stewart to win the Princess of Wales's Pearl and Coutts Stakes on day one of the July Meeting. Back in April, the six-year-old's life had been threatened as he battled a serious stomach infection.

German racing has become an increasingly potent force in recent years, further proof coming with the victory of Proudwings in the Group Two Falmouth Stakes. Trained by Ralf Suerland, the mare was the first German raider to win a British pattern race since Star Appeal in the 1975 Eclipse Stakes.

Mozart, whose stamina had been ebbing over seven furlongs at Royal Ascot, emerged as a new sprint star with a scintillating display in the Darley July Cup. Runner-up Cassandra Go, winner of the King's Stand Stakes on her previous start, was having her racecourse swansong as she was in foal to Green Desert.

The procedures for starting races came under scrutiny following the John Smith's Cup at York on July 14. Three horses had to be withdrawn at the start, delaying proceedings by eleven minutes, among them Riberac. Her trainer Mark Johnston and rider Kevin Darley both professed their dissatisfaction at the shortage of stalls handlers, something which the BHB hopes to rectify in the new season. The race went to the well-backed favourite Foreign Affairs, whose trainer Sir Mark Prescott has such a fine record with handicappers.

Newmarket trainer Ed Dunlop enjoyed a notable 1-2 in the Kildangan Stud Irish Oaks at the Curragh on July 15, Lailani getting the better of Mot Juste by a neck. Lailani, a supplementary entry, had begun her season in a Windsor maiden before progressing to handicaps off an initial mark of 80.

Anticipation was high prior to the King George VI and Queen Elizabeth Diamond Stakes at Ascot on July 28, with Galileo pitching his unbeaten record against Fantastic Light. A huge crowd at Ascot was not to be disappointed as the pair engaged in a terrific duel in the final quarter-mile, the younger horse pulling away near the finish to prevail by two lengths. Michael Kinane had been due serve a ban imposed by the Leopardstown stewards, but he successfully took out an injunction in the High Court in Dublin to enable him to ride the dual the dual Derby hero.

Noverre gained reward for his disqualification from the French Guineas when taking the Champagne Lanson Sussex Stakes at Glorious Goodwood on August 1. Owner Sheikh Mohammed hailed the colt as the 'best miler in Europe' following his two-length win over No Excuse Needed.

Persian Punch, so courageous in defeat at Royal Ascot, was a hugely popular winner of the JPMorgan Private Bank Goodwood Cup. In a race run in heavy rain, the three-year-old Double Honour looked to be going the better when leading early in the home straight, but Persian Punch battled back bravely to score by a length and a half. Ascot winner Royal Rebel was only sixth.

The valuable William Hill Mile Handicap had a pillar-to-post winner in the shape of Riberac. The mare showed no ill effects from her unfortunate experience at York the previous month, where she had reared over backwards in the starting stalls.

NAILBITING

The Vodafone Stewards' Cup on Glorious Goodwood's final day saw 33/1 chance Guinea Hunter edge home in a typical blanket finish, but the nailbiting was by no means over for connections. The Stewards inquired into no fewer than four incidents of interference before announcing that the result was to stand more than half an hour after the runners had passed the post. Guinea Hunter, trained by Tim Easterby for Martyn Burke, was sold to race in Malaysia at the end of the season.

Racing's team event, The Blue Square Shergar Cup at Ascot on August 11, was revamped as a jockeys' challenge. The Rest of the World team, managed by former Australian fast bowler Jeff Thompson, pipped soccer hardman Vinnie Jones's Europeans to snatch the trophy, and the event was generally held to be a great success.

Newmarket trainer George Margarson enjoyed the biggest success of his career when Atavus won the Stan James Hungerford Stakes at Newbury on August 18. 33/1-shot Atavus, given a fine ride from the front by apprentice Jamie Mackay, was venturing into pattern company for the first time having won prestigious handicaps at Newmarket and Ascot earlier in the summer.

Godolphin struck at the top level at York on August 21 when Sakhee ran away with the Juddmonte International Stakes by seven lengths. Runner-up to Sinndar in the 2000 Derby when trained by John Dunlop, Sakhee suffered knee trouble afterwards but had looked over his problems when making an impressive debut for Godolphin in a listed race at Newbury.

There was an Italian winner of the Group One Aston Upthorpe Yorkshire Oaks in Super Tassa, an outsider partnered by Kevin Darley for trainer Valfredo Valiani. Super Tassa was the first Italian-trained winner in Britain since Marguerite Vernaut in the Champion Stakes of 1960.

Aidan O'Brien, naturally, was in sparkling form at the Ebor meeting with four winners. The Great Voltigeur Stakes fell to Milan, whose defeat of Storming Home stamped him as a leading candidate for the St Leger, while O'Brien enjoyed a second-day double, initiated by Mediterranean in the Tote Ebor itself and completed by Rock Of Gibraltar in the Scottish Equitable Gimcrack Stakes.

The victory of Mozart in the Victor Chandler Nunthorpe Stakes was a good example of the attention to detail that sets O'Brien apart. With the runners already at the post, the trainer got a lift to the start just in time to warn Michael Kinane to be on his guard as the colt had become lazy at home. O'Brien need not have worried as Mozart stormed clear for an easy victory, but Kinane still had an anxious ride as the saddle had slipped back slightly leaving the stalls.

Runner-up in the Nunthorpe was the previous year's winner Nuclear Debate, who gained compensation next time when quickening away with the Stanley Leisure Sprint Cup at Haydock on September 8. The six-year-old gelding, trained in France by John Hammond, fetched 180,000 guineas at the autumn sales and is to continue his career in the United States.

The keenly awaited rematch between Galileo and Fantastic Light took place in the Ireland the Food Island Champion Stakes at Leopardstown on September 8. In front of a record crowd, the Godolphin runner exacted revenge by a head after a pulsating battle, Galileo losing his unbeaten record. There was no doubt that tactics had played a major part in the outcome, and the pair were set for a deciding clash in the Breeders' Cup Classic.

HISTORIC ACHIEVEMENT

Racing history was made at Nottingham on September 10 when Madame Jones won her tenth handicap of the year. She was the first horse to achieve this feat since 1874, although seven horses had won nine handicaps, among them Nineacres in 2000. Trained in South Wales by David Evans, Madame Jones is incredibly tough, but she needed to be as she appeared on the racetrack more than 50 times in 2001.

Aidan O'Brien made it European Classic winner number seven for the season when Milan ran clean away with the Rothmans Royals St Leger on September 15. Milan looked one of the best Leger winners of recent years, although the Ballydoyle team's joy was tempered as another of their runners, Ebor winner Mediterranean, suffered a career-ending injury. Milan was the first Irish-trained winner of the Doncaster showpiece since Boucher, from the Vincent O'Brien yard, in 1972.

Two of racing's less-familiar players enjoyed a spell in the limelight on the opening day of the Leger Meeting, courtesy of Smokin Beau's win in the Tote Trifecta Portland Handicap. The gelding, who was taking his seasonal earnings to more than £100,000, was the best horse in the Buckinghamshire stable of John Cullinan and was ridden by Matt

Henry who had endured some lean times since coming out of his apprenticeship.

The victory of Half Glance in the May Hill Stakes gave Henry Cecil his eleventh win in this Group Two event for juvenile fillies, but was a rare high spot in a very moderate season by Cecil's standards. After the race the trainer played down strong speculation that the 2002 season would be his last.

Highlight of the Friday of Doncaster was the scintillating success of Dubai Destination, ridden by Frankie Dettori for David Loder, in the Champagne Stakes. The colt quickened past Aidan O'Brien's Gimcrack winner Rock Of Gibraltar to win most impressively, but was denied the chance to confirm the form when picking up an injury on the eve of the Dewhurst Stakes.

There was embarrassment for racing's authorites when a nursery handicap on the opening day of the St Leger meeting was run over half a furlong shorter than the advertised distance. Not everyone was happy that the result was allowed to stand. There were several other 'cock-ups' during the season, notably at Epsom on August 27 when half a dozen stalls opened a fraction late at the start of a five-furlong handicap. Controversially, the result stood as the Stewards ruled that insufficient runners had been 'materially prejudiced'.

The Jefferson Smurfit Irish St Leger at the Curragh took place on the same afternoon as the Doncaster version. Victory went to Vinnie Roe, whose co-owner Seamus Sheridan, better known as Jim Sheridan, is director of the acclaimed feature films In the Name of the Father and My Left Foot.

David Nicholls has few peers when it comes to training sprint handicappers, and he completed a notable double in the Ayr Silver and Gold Cups at the Western Meeting on September 21 and 22. Tayif, under Kieren Fallon, won the consolation race, while the following day the big one went to Continent and Darryll Holland. Runner-up Brevity, trained by another sprint specialist in Milton Bradley, was one of the season's success stories with eight victories.

The Ascot Festival at the end of September was officially extended to three days, but none of the winners was more popular than Gossamer in the Meon Valley Stud Fillies' Mile. The two-year-old's owner-breeder Gerald Leigh had generously pledged to donate all the prizemoney he won during the season to CancerBACUP, and Gossamer's impressive success meant that the charity benefited to the tune of £116,000. Mr Leigh is fighting cancer himself. Gossamer, from the Luca Cumani yard, is a leading contender for next year's 1000 Guineas. Cumani's stable jockey Jamie Spencer, incidentally, enjoyed a fine season. Under contract to Cumani for one more year, he looks sure to be snapped up by either Godolphin or Ballydoyle before long.

GODOLPHIN SHOCK

There was a shock winner of the Group One Queen Elizabeth II Stakes when 33/1 shot Summoner, who had been supplemented for the race to act as pacemaker for Noverre, held off his Godolphin stablemate to win by a length and a half. Successful jockey Richard Hills had ridden Maroof to victory at 66/1 in similar circumstances in 1994. Summoner's win came just a few days after the Stewards of the Jockey Club, unhappy with the ride Give The Slip had received when acting as pacemaker in the Irish Champion Stakes, had issued a gentle reminder that all horses had to run on their merits.

Marcus Tregoning had given stable star Nayef a relatively low-key campaign since the Guineas, and the colt repaid the kindness by compiling a hat-trick, completed in the Royal Court Theatre Cumberland Lodge Stakes at Ascot. Tregoning had resisted the temptation to run Nayef in the St Leger, being of the opinion that a hard race over fourteen furlongs would be detrimental to the colt's progress.

There were a couple of outstanding juvenile performances at the Newmarket Cambridgeshire meeting in early October. Queen's Logic had already established herself among the best of her sex with wins in the Queen Mary at Royal Ascot and the Lowthor at York, but her performance in the Shadwell Stud Cheveley Park Stakes was particularly impressive as she went in by seven lengths. For rider Steven Drowne it was a first Group

One winner, while trainer Mick Channon can dream of Classic glory with the filly who will remain in his care in 2002.

The line-up for the Group One Middle Park Stakes lacked strength in depth, but the winner Johannesburg, from the Aidan O'Brien camp, took his unbeaten run to six with a thoroughly professional display.

James Given, a former assistant to Mark Johnston, sent out the biggest winner of his training career when I Cried For You was too good for 34 rivals in the Tote Scoop6 Cambridgeshire Handicap. The gelding had also provided Given with his first winner in 1999.

Sakhee had been impressive at York, but his performance in the Prix de l'Arc de Triomphe at Longchamp on October 7 was a revelation. In the hands of Frankie Dettori, the Saeed bin Suroor colt stretched six lengths clear of French Oaks winner Aquarelliste and, a relatively fresh horse, would head to the Breeders' Cup with outstanding claims. There were another four British-trained winners on Arc weekend, principally John Gosden's filly Sulk who showed commendable gameness in the Prix Marcel Boussac.

The Dubai Champion Stakes at Newmarket on October 20 suffered from its proximity to the following week's Breeders' Cup and the field was not a vintage one. There was still a top-class winner, however, with favourite Nayef outgunning Tobougg by three parts of a length.

Aidan O'Brien's dominance in the two-year-old division was underlined when his colts Rock Of Gibraltar, Landseer and Tendulkar fought out the finish of the Darley Dewhurst Stakes, the former holding on by the minimum margin. Rock Of Gibraltar carries the red and white colours of Sir Alex Ferguson, manager of Manchester United.

The victory of Distant Prospect in the Tote Cesarewitch Handicap was a notable one for trainer Ian Balding, who also saddled runner-up Palua. Balding's son Andrew deserved much of the credit however, as both horses are effectively trained by him even though it is Balding senior whose name is on the licence.

The Racing Post Trophy at Doncaster on October 27 attracted a small field and and it was no surprise when the race went to the Aidan O'Brien team, although not to the first string as far as punters were concerned. Castle Gandolfo started odds-on, but was cut down in the closing stages by stablemate High Chapparal under Kevin Darley.

INTERNATIONAL GLORY

The same evening featured the Breeders' Cup at Belmont Park in New York, a city still recovering from the trauma of the terrorist attacks on the World Trade Center on September 11. Rebranded as the World Thoroughbred Championships, the Breeders' Cup lived up to its name with some outstanding racing. The scene appeared set for a final show-down between Fantastic Light and Galileo in the Classic, but Godolphin took everyone by surprise by rerouting Fantastic Light to the Turf, with Sakhee switching to the Classic instead. Fantastic Light wrapped up a fine career with a comfortable victory, beating Milan by three-quarters of a length, but Sakhee could not quite complete the double, going down narrowly to Tiznow who was winning the meeting's showpiece event for the second time. Galileo's reputation was slightly dented as he finished only sixth, but he will long be remem-bered for his outstanding display on Derby Day. The Ballydoyle team had another setback when Mozart was always trailing in the Sprint, but enjoyed an exciting success with Johannesburg in the Juvenile. The colt had now won at the highest level in four different countries, and was installed as favourite for the 2002 Kentucky Derby.

Godolphin made a brave assault on the Melbourne Cup at Flemington on November 6. Their second string Give The Slip very nearly made all the running, but was caught close home by the New Zealand mare Ethereal. Persian Punch, for David Elsworth, finished third, with Godolphin's number one hope Marienbard seventh. Give The Slip's rider Richard Hills came in for criticism in the Australian press, one columnist writing 'the one sour note was the dopey ride of the Englishman Richard Hills. He was as big a clod as what his horse was kicking up. The foreigners had the best cattle, but the worst cowboys on the day'.

Among the jockeys to hang up their boots in 2001, the most successful was John Reid who announced his retirement in September. At the top of his profession for more than 20 years, Reid won the Derby on Dr Devious in 1992 and the Prix de l'Arc de Triomphe on Carroll House in 1988, as well as the King George VI and Queen Elizabeth Diamond Stakes twice on Ile de Bourbon and Swain.

John Lowe, who decided against renewing his licence at the start of the season, won 1,138 races in Britain in a 32-year career. More than just a lightweight jockey, Lowe had an excellent record in the top handicaps.

Doug Marks was the longest-serving trainer with a licence at the time of his retirement. A popular character in the Lambourn area, Marks had won both fillies' Classics on Godiva in 1940 when an apprentice jockey.

A number of prominent Flat racing figures passed away in 2000. Cyril Mitchell was 85 when he died in January. Father of Epsom trainer Philip Mitchell, he was best known for his handling of top sprinter Be Friendly and useful hurdler and staying handicapper Attivo, both owned by Peter O'Sullevan.

Dick Hollingsworth was 82 when he died in February. A successful owner-breeder whose horses' names had a nautical connection, he won the 1980 Oaks with Bireme and the 1986 Ascot Gold Cup with Longboat.

Fahd Salman died suddenly in July aged 46. A member of the Saudi Royal family, he saw his dark green colours carried to victory in the 1991 Derby, Irish Derby and King George by Generous, and by Ramruma in the English and Irish Oaks of 1999.

Lord Carnarvon died in September at the age of 1977. The Queen's Racing Manager for many years, he saw his own colours carried with distinction by the flying filly Lyric Fantasy, winner of the Nunthorpe Stakes in 1992.

Daniel Wildenstein, a hugely successful owner-breeder, died in October at the age of 84. He won the Arc de Triomphe four times with Allez France in 1974, All Along (1983), Sagace (1984) and Peintre Celebre (1997). Wildenstein, an outspoken figure, always claimed to have won five Arcs as he never accepted that Sagace should have been disqualified after passing the post first in 1985.

Graham Rock was only 56 when he died in November. Founding editor of the Racing Post in 1985, Rock was a leading journalist, jockey's agent and TV analyst, and owned 1997 Cambridgeshire winner Pasternak.

Several equine stars of yesteryear died during 2001, most tragically Dubai Millennium, who succumbed to grass sickness in May. Only a five-year-old, Sheikh Mohammed's brilliant flagbearer surely had a glittering career at stud in front of him.

Among other equine losses, Affirmed was the last horse to win the American Triple Crown, achieving the feat in 1978. Shaamit, trained by William Haggas to win the 1996 Derby, was only eight when he died. Dahlia won back-to-back King Georges at Ascot in 1973 and 1974. Darshaan won the French Derby in 1984 before becoming a top sire. Further Flight, Barry Hills' popular grey, won five consecutive Jockey Club Cups between 1991 and 1995. Nureyev, disqualified from the 2000 Guineas of 1980, sired champions Miesque and Peintre Celebre in a long stallion career. Master Willie, runner-up in the 1980 Derby, won the Coronation Cup and the Eclipse the following year, while Oh So Sharp was the last winner of the fillies' Triple Crown in 1985.

RACEFORM
TOP RATED HORSES OF 2001

Point Given (USA)	136
Sakhee (USA)	133
Fantastic Light (USA)	132
Galileo (IRE)	132
Tiznow (USA)	129
Milan	128
Lido Palace (CHI)	128
Kalanisi (IRE)	127
Hightori (FR)	127
Mozart (IRE)	127
Caller One (USA)	127
Monarchos (USA)	127
China Visit (USA)	126
Medicean	126
Meisho Doto (IRE)	126
Storming Home	126
Albert The Great (USA)	126
Endless Hall	125
Captain Steve (USA)	125
Noverre (USA)	125
Banks Hill	125
Northerly (AUS)	125
Squirtle Squirt (USA)	125

RACEFORM RATINGS

Raceform Ratings for each horse are listed after the Starting Price and indicate the actual level of performance attained in that race. The figure in the back index represents the BEST public form that Raceform's Handicappers still believe the horse capable of reproducing.

To use the ratings constructively in determining those horses best-in in future events, the following procedure should be followed:

(i) In races where all runners are the same age and are set to carry the same weight, no calculations are necessary. The horse with the highest rating is best-in.

(ii) In races where all runners are the same age but are set to carry different weights, add one point to the Raceform Rating for every poundless than 10 stone to be carried; deduct one point for every pound more than 10 stone.

For example,

Horse	Adjustment Age & Weight	RR from 10st	base rating	Adjusted rating
Swynford	3-10-1	-1	78	77
Tracery	3-9-13	+1	80	81
Night Hawk	3-9-7	+7	71	78
Black Jester	3-8-11	+17	60	77

Therefore Tracery is top-rated (best-in)

(iii) In races concerning horses of different ages the procedure in example (ii) should again be followed, but reference must also be made to the Official Scale of Weight-For-Age.

For example,

12 furlongs July 20th

Horse	Age & Weight	Adjusted from 10st	RR base rating	Adjusted rating	W-F-A deduct	Final rating
Cherimoya	5-10-0	0	90	90	Nil	90
Mirska	4-9-9	+5	83	88	Nil	88
Jest	3-9-4	+10	85	95	-12	83
Princess Dorrie	4-8-7	+21	73	94	Nil	94

Therefore Princess Dorrie is top-rated (best-in)

(A 3-y-o is deemed 12lb less mature than a 4-y-o or older horse on 20th July over 12f. Therefore, the deduction of 12 points is necessary.)

The following symbols are used in conjunction with the ratings:

++ almost certain to prove better
\+ likely to prove better
d disappointing (has run well below best recently)
? form hard to evaluate - rating may prove unreliable
t tentative rating based on race-time

Weight adjusted ratings for every race are published daily in Raceform Private Handicap. For subscription terms please contact the Subscription Department on (01635) 578080.

The Official Scale of Weight, Age & Distance (Flat)

The following scale should only be used in conjunction with the Official ratings published in this book. Use of any other scale will introduce errors into calculations. The allowances are expressed as the number of pounds that is deemed the average horse in each group falls short of maturity at different dates and

Dist		Jan		Feb		Mar		Apr		May		Jun		Jul		Aug		Sep		Oct		Nov		Dec	
(fur)	Age	1-15	16-31	1-14	15-28	1-15	16-31	1-15	16-30	1-15	16-31	1-15	16-30	1-15	16-31	1-15	16-31	1-15	16-30	1-15	16-31	1-15	16-30	1-15	16-31
5	2	-	-	-	-	-	47	44	41	38	36	34	32	30	28	26	24	22	20	19	18	17	17	16	16
	3	15	15	14	14	13	12	11	10	9	8	7	6	5	4	3	2	1	1	-	-	-	-	-	-
6	2	-	-	-	-	-	-	-	-	44	41	38	36	33	31	28	26	24	22	21	20	19	18	17	17
	3	16	16	15	15	14	13	12	11	10	9	8	7	6	5	4	3	2	2	1	1	-	-	-	-
7	2	-	-	-	-	-	-	-	-	-	-	-	-	38	35	32	30	27	25	23	22	21	20	19	19
	3	18	18	17	17	16	15	14	13	12	11	10	9	8	7	6	5	4	3	2	2	1	1	-	-
8	2	-	-	-	-	-	-	-	-	-	-	-	-	-	-	37	34	31	28	26	24	23	22	21	20
	3	20	20	19	19	18	17	15	14	13	12	11	10	9	8	7	6	5	4	3	3	2	2	1	1
9	3	22	22	21	21	20	19	17	15	14	13	12	11	10	9	8	7	6	5	4	4	3	3	2	2
	4	1	1	-	-	-	-	-	-	-	-	-	-	-	-	-	-	-	-	-	-	-	-	-	-
10	3	23	23	22	22	21	20	19	17	15	14	13	12	11	10	9	8	7	6	5	5	4	4	3	3
	4	2	2	1	1	-	-	-	-	-	-	-	-	-	-	-	-	-	-	-	-	-	-	-	-
11	3	24	24	23	23	22	21	20	19	17	15	14	13	12	11	10	9	8	7	6	6	5	5	4	4
	4	3	3	2	2	1	1	-	-	-	-	-	-	-	-	-	-	-	-	-	-	-	-	-	-
12	3	25	25	24	24	23	22	21	20	19	17	15	14	13	12	11	10	9	8	7	7	6	6	5	5
	4	4	4	3	3	2	2	1	1	-	-	-	-	-	-	-	-	-	-	-	-	-	-	-	-
13	3	26	26	25	25	24	23	22	21	20	19	17	15	14	13	12	11	10	9	8	8	7	7	6	6
	4	5	5	4	4	3	3	2	1	-	-	-	-	-	-	-	-	-	-	-	-	-	-	-	-
14	3	27	27	26	26	25	24	23	22	21	20	19	17	15	14	13	12	11	10	9	9	8	8	7	7
	4	6	6	5	5	4	4	3	2	1	-	-	-	-	-	-	-	-	-	-	-	-	-	-	-
15	3	28	28	27	27	26	25	24	23	22	21	20	19	17	15	14	13	12	11	10	9	8	8	7	7
	4	6	6	5	5	4	4	3	3	2	1	-	-	-	-	-	-	-	-	-	-	-	-	-	-
16	3	29	29	28	28	27	26	25	24	23	22	21	20	19	17	15	14	13	12	11	10	9	9	8	8
	4	7	7	6	6	5	5	4	4	3	2	1	-	-	-	-	-	-	-	-	-	-	-	-	-
18	3	31	31	30	30	29	28	27	26	25	24	23	22	21	20	18	16	14	13	12	11	10	10	9	9
	4	8	8	7	7	6	6	5	5	4	3	2	1	-	-	-	-	-	-	-	-	-	-	-	-
20	3	33	33	32	32	31	30	29	28	27	26	25	24	23	22	20	18	16	14	13	12	11	11	10	10
	4	9	9	8	8	7	7	6	6	5	4	3	2	1	-	-	-	-	-	-	-	-	-	-	-

A B My Boy

3-y-o ch g Young Ern-Whitstar (Whitstead)
J R Best C Hales

Placings:60060-000 **(5503)**
2001: 11^{0}F, 8^{0}GF, 7^{0}HY

	Starts	1st	2nd	3rd	Win & Pl
Career Total (Turf)	8	0	0	0	0

Going (Turf): Sf: 0-2 GS: 0-2 Gd: 0-1 GF: 0-2 Fm: 0-1
Distance: 5f/6f: 0-4 7f-8f: 0-2 9f-13f: 0-2 14f+: 0-0
Track : LH: 0-5 RH: 0-0 Tight: 0-1 Gall: 0-0
Aids: Bl: 0-1 Vi: 0-0 Tstrap: 0-0
Best Rating: 12 10/01 Donc 7f heavy

A Bit Special

105 **86**
3-y-o b f Rahy (USA)-Speedybird (IRE) (Danehill (USA))
H R A Cecil The Thoroughbred Corporation

Placings:3-221 **(2271)**
2001: 7^{2}G, 9^{2}GF, 7^{1}G

	Starts	1st	2nd	3rd	Win & Pl
Career Total (Turf)	4	1	2	1	8197

76	6/01	Thsk	7f	D	GD	£4192

Total win prize-money £4193

Going (Turf): Sf: 0-1 GS: 0-0 **Gd: 1-2** GF: 0-1 Fm: 0-0
Distance: 5f/6f: 0-0 **7f-8f: 1-3** 9f-13f: 0-1 14f+: 0-0
Track : **LH: 1-1** RH: 0-1 **Tight: 1-1** Gall: 0-0
Aids: Bl: 0-0 Vi: 0-0 Tstrap: 0-0
Best Rating: 86 5/01 NmkR 7f good

Faces disqualification from the Thirsk race after failing a dope test.

A C Azure (IRE)

(95) (77)**72**
3-y-o br g Dolphin Street (FR)-Kelvedon (General Assembly (USA))
P M Mooney Hangover Syndicate

Placings:6530223-6000 **(3772a)**
2001: 6^{6}HY, 8^{0}G, 7^{0}GY, 8^{0}S

	Starts	1st	2nd	3rd	Win & Pl
Career Total (Turf)	8	0	0	1	597
Career Total (AW)	3	0	2	1	1579

Going (Turf): Sf: 0-3 GS: 0-1 Gd: 0-2 GF: 0-1 Fm: 0-0
Distance: 5f/6f: 0-4 7f-8f: 0-6 9f-13f: 0-1 14f+: 0-0
Track : LH: 0-4 RH: 0-0 Tight: 0-3 Gall: 0-0
Aids: Bl: 0-0 Vi: 0-0 Tstrap: 0-0
Best Rating: 64 7/01 Curr 7f gd-yld

A Chef Too Far

(79) (21)
8-y-o b g Be My Chief (USA)-Epithet (Mill Reef (USA))
R G Frost Merlin Pippa Partnership

Placings:541000/040/0 **(0270)**
2001: 16^{0}SW

	Starts	1st	2nd	3rd	Win & Pl
Career Total (Turf)	8	1	0	0	5969
Career Total (AW)	2	0	0	0	

70	5/96	Newb	7f64y	D	SFT	£5407

Total win prize-money £5407

Going (Turf): Sf: 1-2 GS: 0-1 Gd: 0-2 GF: 0-2 Fm: 0-1
Distance: 5f/6f: 0-0 **7f-8f: 1-6** 9f-13f: 0-3 14f+: 0-1
Track : **LH: 1-3** RH: 0-4 Tight: 0-1 **Gall: 1-3**
Aids: Bl: 0-0 Vi: 0-0 Tstrap: 0-3
Best Rating: 4 2/01 Sthl 2m slow

A Day On The Dub

101(39) (39)**42**
8-y-o b g Presidium-Border Mouse (Border Chief)
D Eddy Revblayd

Placings:4/14640021125/644014005050-10230005050 **(5382)**
2001: 9^{1}S, 11^{0}S, 8^{2}GF, 10^{3}GF, 12^{0}G, 10^{0}GF, 11^{0}S, 12^{5}GF, 11^{0}G, 16^{5}F, 11^{0}S

	Starts	1st	2nd	3rd	Win & Pl
Career Total (Turf)	33	4	3	1	14825
Career Total (AW)	2	1	0	0	2169

48	3/01	Muss	1m1f	F(0-60)H	SFT	£2758
54	5/00	Nott	1m1f213y	E(0-70)H	G-S	£3080
50	10/99	Rdcr	1m3f	F	SFT	£2547
40	10/99	Newc	1m	F(0-60)H	G-S	£2421
39	1/99	Sthl	1m4f	F	STD	£2169

Total win prize-money £12976

Going (Turf): Sf: 2-13 GS: 2-4 Gd: 0-5 GF: 0-7 Fm: 0-4
Distance: 5f/6f: 0-0 7f-8f: 1-6 **9f-13f: 4-28** 14f+: 0-1
Track : **LH: 4-21** RH: 0-10 Tight: 1-11 Gall: 1-10
Aids: Bl: 0-0 Vi: 0-0 Tstrap: 0-0
Best Rating: 48 6/01 Newc 1m gd-fm

Versatile sort who appreciates nine to ten furlongs and easy ground on the Flat, although has been running over further in 2001.

A One (IRE)

98 **74**
2-y-o b c Alzao (USA)-Anita's Contessa (IRE) (Anita's Prince)
B Palling Albert Yemm

Placings:6324550 **(5379)**
2001: 5^{6}GS, 6^{3}F, 6^{2}GF, 6^{4}GF, 6^{5}G, 6^{5}GS, 7^{0}S

	Starts	1st	2nd	3rd	Win & Pl
Career Total (Turf)	7	0	1	1	1705

Going (Turf): Sf: 0-1 GS: 0-2 Gd: 0-1 GF: 0-2 Fm: 0-1
Distance: 5f/6f: 0-3 7f-8f: 0-4 9f-13f: 0-0 14f+: 0-0
Track : LH: 0-2 RH: 0-0 Tight: 0-1 Gall: 0-1
Aids: Bl: 0-0 Vi: 0-0 Tstrap: 0-0
Best Rating: 74 10/01 Sals 6f212y gd-sft

Has shown ability on all starts, was a game second to Foxcote at Windsor in July, and capable of finding a race.

A Teen

101(95) (54)**52**
3-y-o ch c Presidium-Very Good (Noalto)
P Howling Mrs A K Petersen

Placings:0034-23056600050 **(3394)**
2001: 5^{2}SD, 6^{3}SD, 5^{0}SD, 5^{5}SD, 5^{6}SD, 5^{6}GF, 6^{0}G, 5^{0}F, 5^{0}GF, 5^{5}GF, 5^{0}GF

	Starts	1st	2nd	3rd	Win & Pl
Career Total (Turf)	6	0	0	0	0
Career Total (AW)	9	0	1	2	1488

Going (Turf): Sf: 0-0 GS: 0-0 Gd: 0-1 GF: 0-4 Fm: 0-1
Distance: 5f/6f: 0-13 7f-8f: 0-1 9f-13f: 0-1 14f+: 0-0
Track : LH: 0-7 RH: 0-0 Tight: 0-7 Gall: 0-0
Aids: Bl: 0-1 Vi: 0-0 Tstrap: 0-0
Best Rating: 69 1/01 Ling 5f stand

A Touch Of Frost

111 **94**
6-y-o gr m Distant Relative-Pharland (FR) (Bellypha)
G G Margarson Mrs Patricia J Williams

Placings:0100/001210150/1400-5060331154033 **(5391)**
2001: 6^{5}S, 7^{0}G, 7^{6}S, 8^{0}GF, 6^{3}G, 6^{3}GF, 7^{1}G, 7^{1}GF, 6^{5}GF, 7^{4}G, 7^{0}S, 7^{3}GS, 7^{3}GS

	Starts	1st	2nd	3rd	Win & Pl
Career Total (Turf)	30	7	1	4	69496

85	8/01	Newb	7f	C(0-95)H	G-F	£7934
78	8/01	NmkJ	7f	B(0-105)H	GD	£19500
84	6/00	Thsk	7f	D(0-80)	SFT	£4445
79	9/99	Sals	6f212y	C(0-95)H	G-F	£12689
74	7/99	York	6f214y	C(0-90)H	G-F	£8220
64	6/99	Sals	6f212y	F(0-65)H	GD	£3037
68	8/98	Sals	1m	D	G-F	£3746

Total win prize-money £59573

Going (Turf): Sf: 1-8 GS: 0-4 Gd: 2-9 **GF: 4-9** Fm: 0-0
Distance: 5f/6f: 0-0 **7f-8f: 7-25** 9f-13f: 0-5 14f+: 0-0
Track : **LH: 2-6** RH: 0-6 Tight: 1-3 Gall: 1-5
Aids: **Bl: 6-24** Vi: 0-0 Tstrap: 0-0
Best Rating: 94 9/01 Donc 7f good

Versatile six and seven furlong handicapper who goes particularly well at Salisbury. Seemingly effective on all ground. Occasionally misses the break, but that habit appeared to have been overcome when she got off the mark in a competitive handicap at Newmarket in August and followed up at Newbury. Some decent efforts since including in Listed company. Likes to come from behind off a fast pace.

A Two (IRE)

83 **32**
2-y-o b f Ali-Royal (IRE)-Rainelle (Rainbow Quest (USA))
B Palling Albert Yemm

Placings:0 **(4287)**
2001: 8^{0}GF

	Starts	1st	2nd	3rd	Win & Pl
Career Total (Turf)	1	0	0	0	

Going (Turf): Sf: 0-0 GS: 0-0 Gd: 0-0 GF: 0-1 Fm: 0-0
Distance: 5f/6f: 0-0 7f-8f: 0-0 9f-13f: 0-1 14f+: 0-0
Track : LH: 0-0 RH: 0-0 Tight: 0-0 Gall: 0-0
Aids: Bl: 0-0 Vi: 0-0 Tstrap: 0-0
Best Rating: 32 8/01 Chep 1m14y gd-fm

Aa-Youknownothing

(102) (58)
5-y-o b g Superpower-Bad Payer (Tanfirion)
Miss J F Craze T Marshall

Placings:02116020/**320055000300003341**/6204230-004610 **(0633)**
2001: 6^{0}SD, 5^{0}SD, 5^{4}SW, 5^{6}SD, 5^{1}SD, 5^{0}SD

	Starts	1st	2nd	3rd	Win & Pl
Career Total (Turf)	19	2	3	2	9885
Career Total (AW)	19	2	2	3	7742

54	3/01	Wolv	5f	G	STD	£1827
64	12/99	Ling	5f	E(0-75)H	STD	£2615
68	5/98	Thsk	5f	E	GD	£3322
68	4/98	Muss	5f	F	G-S	£2757

Total win prize-money £10522

Going (Turf): Sf: 0-2 **GS: 1-2 Gd: 1-7** GF: 0-8 Fm: 0-0
Distance: **5f/6f: 4-37** 7f-8f: 0-1 9f-13f: 0-0 14f+: 0-0
Track : **LH: 2-19** RH: 0-1 **Tight: 2-17** Gall: 0-2
Aids: Bl: 1-9 Vi: 1-12 **Tstrap: 2-21**
Best Rating: 58 2/01 Wolv 5f slow

Pacey sprint handicapper who wins in his turn.

Aahgowangowan (IRE)

99(88) (55)**73**
2-y-o b f Tagula (IRE)-Cabcharge Princess (IRE) (Rambo Dancer (CAN))
M R Channon M Channon

Placings:0014211021 **(5660)**

2001: 5^{0}GF, 5^{0}G, 6^{1}G, 5^{4}GS, 6^{2}HY, 5^{1}S, 5^{1}GS, 6^{0}SD, 5^{2}GS, 5^{1}G

	Starts	1st	2nd	3rd	Win & Pl
Career Total (Turf)	9	4	2	0	20961
Career Total (AW)	1	0	0	0	

73	11/01	Muss	5f	E	GD	£5525
73	10/01	NmkR	5f	C(0-95)H	G-S	£6971
66	10/01	Brig	5f213y	D(0-85)	SFT	£3627
57	8/01	Ripn	6f	F	GD	£2618

Total win prize-money £18741

Going (Turf): Sf: 1-2 GS: 1-3 **Gd: 2-3** GF: 0-1 Fm: 0-0
Distance: **5f/6f: 4-10** 7f-8f: 0-0 9f-13f: 0-0 14f+: 0-0
Track : **LH: 1-3** RH: 0-0 Tight: 0-0 Gall: 0-1
Aids: Bl: 0-0 Vi: 0-0 Tstrap: 0-0
Best Rating: 73 11/01 Muss 5f good

She had to be dropped into selling company to get off the mark before winning back-to-back nurseries on consecutive days at Brighton and Newmarket in October. Won another seller at Musselburgh in November despite hanging under pressure. Suited by cut in the ground.

Abajany

108(97) (56)**67**

7-y-o b g Akarad (FR)-Miss Ivory Coast (USA) (Sir Ivor)
M R Channon John White And Partners

Placings:5/30325515150/4200401031204030/4640000 5603345033524/0000020-000250050602130 **(5681)**

2001: 10^{0}F, 9^{0}GF, 8^{0}G, 8^{2}GF, 8^{5}HD, 8^{0}GF, 8^{0}GF, 8^{5}S, 8^{0}G, 8^{6}G, 8^{0}GF, 8^{2}G, 8^{1}G, 10^{3}G, 8^{0}S

	Starts	1st	2nd	3rd	Win & Pl
Career Total (Turf)	69	5	7	9	54312
Career Total (AW)	1	0	0	0	

67	10/01	Rdcr	1m	D(0-85)H	GD	£6474
85	8/98	Ayr	1m	C(0-90)H	G-S	£7249
78	7/98	Bath	1m2f46y	D(0-80)	GD	£3387
77	9/97	Sand	1m14y	D(0-80)H	G-F	£4533
72	8/97	Leic	1m8y	E(0-70)H	GD	£3275

Total win prize-money £24919

Going (Turf): Sf: 0-14 GS: 1-4 **Gd: 3-30** GF: 1-18 Fm: 0-2
Distance: 5f/6f: 0-0 7f-8f: 2-31 **9f-13f: 3-39** 14f+: 0-0
Track : **LH: 2-27** RH: 1-24 **Tight: 1-23** Gall: 0-8
Aids: Bl: 0-0 Vi: 0-4 Tstrap: 0-0
Best Rating: 71 6/01 Gdwd 1m gd-fm

Had not won since the summer of 1998 and did not seem to improve for the fitting of a visor during the summer. Had the benefit of a good draw when running better at Beverley, and then went one better next time at Redcar. Suited by a mile. Acts on good ground. Has handled heavy earlier in his career.

Abbajabba

107(58) (44)**94**

5-y-o b g Barrys Gamble-Bo' Babbity (Strong Gale)
C W Fairhurst North Cheshire Trading & Storage Ltd

Placings:62054/000606660/3131204-52203001 **(5266)**

2001: 6^{5}S, 5^{2}S, 6^{2}S, 6^{0}G, 6^{3}G, 5^{0}GF, 6^{0}GF, 6^{1}GS

	Starts	1st	2nd	3rd	Win & Pl
Career Total (Turf)	29	4	4	3	58392
Career Total (AW)	1	0	0	0	

94	10/01	York	6f	C(0-100)H	G-S	£25496
65	8/00	Ayr	6f	D(0-80)	GD	£3828
81	4/00	Epsm	6f	C(0-95)H	HVY	£7052
76	4/00	Haml	6f5y	D(0-85)H	GD	£6032

Total win prize-money £42410

Going (Turf): Sf: 1-7 GS: 1-6 **Gd: 2-8** GF: 0-7 Fm: 0-1
Distance: **5f/6f: 3-24** 7f-8f: 1-6 9f-13f: 0-0 14f+: 0-0
Track : **LH: 1-4** RH: 0-0 **Tight: 1-2** Gall: 0-0
Aids: Bl: 0-0 Vi: 0-0 Tstrap: 0-0
Best Rating: 94 10/01 York 6f gd-sft

He enjoyed a good season in 2000, winning three times over six furlongs and hads run some fine races this season before to his tally at York in the autumn. Suited bysix furlongs and cut in the ground.

Abbey Bridge (USA)

103 **66+**

3-y-o b f Irish River (FR)-Francisco Road (USA) (Strawberry Road (AUS))
J Noseda Sanford R Robertson

Placings:310 **(2667)**

2001: 7^{3}GS, 6^{1}GF, 7^{0}G

	Starts	1st	2nd	3rd	Win & Pl
Career Total (Turf)	3	1	0	1	3732

66	6/01	Rdcr	6f	D	G-F	£3094

Total win prize-money £3094

Going (Turf): Sf: 0-0 GS: 0-1 Gd: 0-1 **GF: 1-1** Fm: 0-0
Distance: **5f/6f: 1-1** 7f-8f: 0-2 9f-13f: 0-0 14f+: 0-0
Track : LH: 0-0 RH: 0-0 Tight: 0-0 Gall: 0-0
Aids: Bl: 0-0 Vi: 0-0 Tstrap: 0-0
Best Rating: 66 6/01 Rdcr 6f gd-fm

Abbey Park (USA)

87(70) (25)**73**

2-y-o b/br f Known Fact (USA)-Taylor Park (USA) (Sir Gaylord)
J W Hills D J Deer

Placings:420 **(5415)**

2001: 6^{4}GF, 7^{2}F, 6^{0}SD

	Starts	1st	2nd	3rd	Win & Pl
Career Total (Turf)	2	0	1	0	952
Career Total (AW)	1	0	0	0	

Going (Turf): Sf: 0-0 GS: 0-0 Gd: 0-0 GF: 0-1 Fm: 0-1
Distance: 5f/6f: 0-2 7f-8f: 0-1 9f-13f: 0-0 14f+: 0-0
Track : LH: 0-1 RH: 0-0 Tight: 0-1 Gall: 0-0
Aids: Bl: 0-0 Vi: 0-0 Tstrap: 0-0
Best Rating: 73 9/01 Chep 7f16y firm

Abbot

99 **74**

3-y-o b g Bishop Of Cashel-Gifted (Shareef Dancer (USA))
B J Meehan Abbott Racing Limited

Placings:0-036656 **(3083)**

2001: 8^{0}HY, 11^{3}S, 11^{6}G, 12^{6}GF, 16^{5}G, 11^{6}GF

	Starts	1st	2nd	3rd	Win & Pl
Career Total (Turf)	7	0	0	1	639

Going (Turf): Sf: 0-3 GS: 0-0 Gd: 0-2 GF: 0-2 Fm: 0-0
Distance: 5f/6f: 0-1 7f-8f: 0-0 9f-13f: 0-5 14f+: 0-1
Track : LH: 0-3 RH: 0-2 Tight: 0-1 Gall: 0-1
Aids: Bl: 0-1 Vi: 0-0 Tstrap: 0-0
Best Rating: 74 6/01 Newb 1m4f5y gd-fm

He has run one fair race in maiden company, but does not look anything special.

Abby Goa (IRE)

91 **28**

3-y-o b f Dr Devious (IRE)-Spring Reel (Mill Reef (USA))
M W Easterby B Bargh, T Swain, P Parker & D Smith

Placings:45030-0000 **(4542)**

2001: 7^{0}GF, 5^{0}GF, 9^{0}GF, 10^{0}GF

	Starts	1st	2nd	3rd	Win & Pl
Career Total (Turf)	9	0	0	1	821

Going (Turf): Sf: 0-2 GS: 0-0 Gd: 0-0 GF: 0-7 Fm: 0-0
Distance: 5f/6f: 0-2 7f-8f: 0-4 9f-13f: 0-3 14f+: 0-0
Track : LH: 0-3 RH: 0-1 Tight: 0-1 Gall: 0-1
Aids: Bl: 0-3 Vi: 0-0 Tstrap: 0-0
Best Rating: 28 8/01 Muss 1m1f gd-fm

Abercorn (IRE)

74 **49**

2-y-o b g Woodborough (USA)-Ravensdale Rose (IRE) (Henbit (USA))
B J Meehan Thurloe Thoroughbreds Iv

Placings:0000 **(5280)**

2001: 7^{0}G, 7^{0}GF, 7^{0}GF, 9^{0}S

	Starts	1st	2nd	3rd	Win & Pl
Career Total (Turf)	4	0	0	0	

Going (Turf): Sf: 0-1 GS: 0-0 Gd: 0-1 GF: 0-2 Fm: 0-0
Distance: 5f/6f: 0-0 7f-8f: 0-3 9f-13f: 0-1 14f+: 0-0
Track : LH: 0-1 RH: 0-2 Tight: 0-0 Gall: 0-0
Aids: Bl: 0-1 Vi: 0-0 Tstrap: 0-0
Best Rating: 49 9/01 Leic 7f9y gd-fm

Abercrombie

85 **50**

2-y-o ch c Dancing Spree (USA)-Coleford (USA) (Secreto (USA))
C A Dwyer S B Components (international) Ltd

Placings:0200 **(2948)**

2001: 6^{0}G, 7^{2}GF, 6^{0}G, 7^{0}G

	Starts	1st	2nd	3rd	Win & Pl
Career Total (Turf)	4	0	1	0	530

Going (Turf): Sf: 0-0 GS: 0-0 Gd: 0-3 GF: 0-1 Fm: 0-0
Distance: 5f/6f: 0-0 7f-8f: 0-4 9f-13f: 0-0 14f+: 0-0
Track : LH: 0-0 RH: 0-0 Tight: 0-0 Gall: 0-0
Aids: Bl: 0-1 Vi: 0-3 Tstrap: 0-0
Best Rating: 50 6/01 Yarm 7f3y gd-fm

Aberkeen

89(103) (63d)**48**

6-y-o ch g Keen-Miss Aboyne (Lochnager)
M Dods N A Riddell

Placings:41522/040003000/3361004520603/21221200-663500 **(3592)**

2001: 7^{6}S, 7^{6}SD, 8^{3}SD, 7^{5}SD, 8^{0}SD, 7^{0}GS

	Starts	1st	2nd	3rd	Win & Pl
Career Total (Turf)	30	3	4	3	15950
Career Total (AW)	11	1	3	2	5506

67	3/00	Sthl	7f	E(0-70)H	GD	£2996
63	1/00	Sthl	7f	E(0-70)H	STD	£2899
60	5/99	Donc	7f	F(0-70)H	G-F	£2252
57	6/97	Pont	6f	D	G-F	£3223

Total win prize-money £11372

Going (Turf): Sf: 0-4 GS: 0-6 Gd: 1-9 **GF: 2-11** Fm: 0-0
Distance: 5f/6f: 1-8 **7f-8f: 3-29** 9f-13f: 0-4 14f+: 0-0
Track : **LH: 3-23** RH: 0-4 Tight: 0-9 Gall: 0-2
Aids: Bl: 0-0 Vi: 0-1 Tstrap: 0-0
Best Rating: 43 6/01 Sthl 7f stand

He had a busy time of it in 1999, but only scored a solitary victory at Doncaster. Better form last season, winning on turf and Fibresand at Southwell. He looks a seven-furlong specialist.

Aberthatch (FR)

86 **67**

2-y-o b f Thatching-Academy Angel (FR) (Royal Academy (USA))
M J Ryan Bernard H Bosomworth

Placings:020 (5602)
2001: 7^{0}GS, 7^{2}HY, 7^{0}GS

	Starts	1st	2nd	3rd	Win & Pl
Career Total (Turf)	3	0	1	0	868

Going (Turf): Sf: 0-1 GS: 0-2 Gd: 0-0 GF: 0-0 Fm: 0-0
Distance: 5f/6f: 0-0 7f-8f: 0-3 9f-13f: 0-0 14f+: 0-0
Track: LH: 0-0 RH: 0-0 Tight: 0-0 Gall: 0-0
Aids: Bl: 0-0 Vi: 0-0 Tstrap: 0-0
Best Rating: 67 11/01 NmkR 7f gd-sft

Able Ayr

103 **47**
4-y-o ch g Formidable (USA)-Ayr Classic (Local Suitor (USA))
J S Goldie Frank Brady

Placings:34410450/000500000000-44324000005000 (5288)
2001: 6^{4}G, 6^{4}F, 6^{3}GF, 5^{2}G, 6^{4}GS, 5^{0}GF, 5^{0}S, 6^{0}G, 6^{0}GS, 6^{0}G, 6^{5}G, 6^{0}F, 5^{0}GS, 6^{0}HY

	Starts	1st	2nd	3rd	Win & Pl
Career Total (Turf)	34	1	1	2	7249

74 6/99 Carl 5f E GD £2771
Total win prize-money £2771

Going (Turf): Sf: 0-6 GS: 0-4 **Gd: 1-13** GF: 0-9 Fm: 0-2
Distance: 5f/6f: 1-26 7f-8f: 0-8 9f-13f: 0-0 14f+: 0-0
Track: LH: 0-4 **RH: 1-2** Tight: 0-0 **Gall: 1-3**
Aids: Bl: 0-2 Vi: 0-3 Tstrap: 0-0
Best Rating: 57 6/01 Hayd 5f good

Has not won for over two years. Has speed to win over five furlongs. Does not want the ground too soft.

Able Baker Charlie (IRE)

93 **80**
2-y-o b c Sri Pekan (USA)-Lavezzola (IRE) (Salmon Leap (USA))
J R Fanshawe David Croft & Partners

Placings:33 (5087)
2001: 7^{3}GS, 7^{3}GS

	Starts	1st	2nd	3rd	Win & Pl
Career Total (Turf)	2	0	0	2	796

Going (Turf): Sf: 0-0 GS: 0-2 Gd: 0-0 GF: 0-0 Fm: 0-0
Distance: 5f/6f: 0-0 7f-8f: 0-2 9f-13f: 0-0 14f+: 0-0
Track: LH: 0-0 RH: 0-1 Tight: 0-0 Gall: 0-0
Aids: Bl: 0-0 Vi: 0-0 Tstrap: 0-0
Best Rating: 80 10/01 Newc 7f gd-sft

Placed in ordinary maiden company.

Able Millenium (IRE)

106(92) (50)**40**
5-y-o ch g Be My Guest (USA)-Miami Life (Miami Springs)
Mrs Lydia Pearce (J Pearce 9/2) & Mrs S Fernandes

Placings:3330/0000-60010300000 (4908)
2001: 7^{6}SW, 8^{0}SW, 10^{0}SW, 8^{1}GS, 8^{0}G, 10^{3}GF, 10^{0}G, 9^{0}G, 10^{0}GF, 8^{0}F, 9^{0}G

	Starts	1st	2nd	3rd	Win & Pl
Career Total (Turf)	10	1	0	1	3434
Career Total (AW)	9	0	0	3	1184

50 5/01 Pont 1m4y F(0-60)H G-S £2849
Total win prize-money £2849

Going (Turf): Sf: 0-1 **GS: 1-1** Gd: 0-4 GF: 0-3 Fm: 0-1
Distance: 5f/6f: 0-0 7f-8f: 0-5 **9f-13f: 1-14** 14f+: 0-0
Track: LH: 1-16 RH: 0-2 Tight: 0-11 Gall: 0-0
Aids: Bl: 0-1 **Vi: 1-8** Tstrap: 0-0
Best Rating: 50 5/01 Pont 1m4y gd-sft

Able Native (IRE)

(97) (50d)**50d**
4-y-o b f Thatching-Native Joy (IRE) (Be My Native (USA))
N B Mason (G M Moore 21/5) N B Mason

Placings:025/021004060-050 (1470)
2001: 14^{0}HY, 14^{5}SD, 16^{0}SD

	Starts	1st	2nd	3rd	Win & Pl
Career Total (Turf)	8	0	2	0	2194
Career Total (AW)	7	1	0	0	2821

66 6/00 Ling 1m4f E(0-70)H STD £2821
Total win prize-money £2821

Going (Turf): Sf: 0-2 GS: 0-2 Gd: 0-2 GF: 0-2 Fm: 0-0
Distance: 5f/6f: 0-0 7f-8f: 0-3 **9f-13f: 1-8** 14f+: 0-4
Track: LH: 1-9 RH: 0-4 **Tight: 1-6** Gall: 0-2
Aids: Bl: 0-7 Vi: 0-0 Tstrap: 0-0
Best Rating: 50 5/01 Sthl 1m6f stand

Able Pete

(103) (33)**24**
5-y-o b g Formidable (USA)-An Empress (USA) (Affirmed (USA))
A G Newcombe A G Newcombe

Placings:00/000000/05021460000-3332040054 (4553)
2001: 11^{3}SD, 12^{3}SD, 12^{3}SW, 12^{2}SD, 11^{0}GS, 12^{4}SD, 14^{0}SD, 11^{0}G, 14^{5}SD, 14^{4}SW

	Starts	1st	2nd	3rd	Win & Pl
Career Total (Turf)	10	0	0	0	
Career Total (AW)	19	1	2	3	3426

36 2/00 Wolv 1m4f G(0-60)H STD £1456
Total win prize-money £1456

Going (Turf): Sf: 0-2 GS: 0-2 Gd: 0-2 GF: 0-3 Fm: 0-1
Distance: 5f/6f: 0-1 7f-8f: 0-4 **9f-13f: 1-21** 14f+: 0-3
Track: LH: 1-24 RH: 0-2 **Tight: 1-10** Gall: 0-1
Aids: Bl: 0-0 Vi: 0-0 Tstrap: 0-1
Best Rating: 35 2/01 Wolv 1m4f stand

Able Seaman (USA)

(103) (65+)**68**
4-y-o b/br g Northern Flagship (USA)-Love At Dawn (USA) (Grey Dawn Ii)
C E Brittain C E Brittain

Placings:0453334364020-3214 (0317)
2001: 16^{3}SD, 16^{2}SD, 16^{1}SW, 16^{4}SW

	Starts	1st	2nd	3rd	Win & Pl
Career Total (Turf)	13	0	1	4	4250
Career Total (AW)	4	1	1	1	4498

65 2/01 Sthl 2m E(0-70)H SLW £3017
Total win prize-money £3017

Going (Turf): Sf: 0-1 GS: 0-2 Gd: 0-5 GF: 0-4 Fm: 0-1
Distance: 5f/6f: 0-0 7f-8f: 0-1 9f-13f: 0-9 **14f+: 1-7**
Track: LH: 1-12 RH: 0-4 Tight: 0-10 Gall: 0-1
Aids: Bl: 1-2 Vi: 0-3 Tstrap: 0-0
Best Rating: 65 2/01 Sthl 2m slow

Above Board

(96) (43)**28**
6-y-o b g Night Shift (USA)-Bundled Up (USA) (Sharpen Up)
R F Marvin R A B Saville

Placings:03/00000/005400600556/500022033060-00005300 (3428)
2001: 6^{0}SD, 7^{0}SW, 6^{0}SD, 5^{0}SD, 6^{5}SD, 7^{3}SD, 6^{0}SD, 8^{0}SD

	Starts	1st	2nd	3rd	Win & Pl
Career Total (Turf)	11	0	0	1	514
Career Total (AW)	28	0	2	3	3106

Going (Turf): Sf: 0-3 GS: 0-2 Gd: 0-3 GF: 0-3 Fm: 0-0
Distance: 5f/6f: 0-25 7f-8f: 0-12 9f-13f: 0-2 14f+: 0-0
Track: LH: 0-29 RH: 0-2 Tight: 0-4 Gall: 0-0
Aids: Bl: 0-11 Vi: 0-0 Tstrap: 0-1
Best Rating: 36 7/01 Sthl 7f stand

Above The Cut (USA)

(67) (9)**63**
9-y-o ch g Topsider (USA)-Placer Queen (Habitat)
C P Morlock J P M & J W Cook

Placings:11/40/0400/0 (0376)
2001: 12^{0}SD

	Starts	1st	2nd	3rd	Win & Pl
Career Total (Turf)	8	2	0	0	12721
Career Total (AW)	1	0	0	0	

84 7/94 Newb 7f B G-F £8252
75 6/94 Kemp 7f D G-F £3494
Total win prize-money £11746

Going (Turf): Sf: 0-0 GS: 0-0 Gd: 0-2 **GF: 2-5** Fm: 0-1
Distance: 5f/6f: 0-0 **7f-8f: 2-5** 9f-13f: 0-4 14f+: 0-0
Track: LH: 0-3 **RH: 1-4** Tight: 0-3 **Gall: 1-3**
Aids: Bl: 0-3 Vi: 0-0 Tstrap: 0-0
Best Rating: 9 2/01 Wolv 1m4f stand

Abracadabjar

(96) (57d)**48**
3-y-o b g Royal Abjar (USA)-Celt Song (IRE) (Unfuwain (USA))
G A Butler Five Horses Ltd

Placings:050-205050 (5397)
2001: 8^{2}SD, 10^{0}GF, 8^{5}G, 7^{0}G, 10^{5}GF, 8^{0}SD

	Starts	1st	2nd	3rd	Win & Pl
Career Total (Turf)	7	0	0	0	0
Career Total (AW)	2	0	1	0	664

Going (Turf): Sf: 0-1 GS: 0-0 Gd: 0-3 GF: 0-3 Fm: 0-0
Distance: 5f/6f: 0-0 7f-8f: 0-4 9f-13f: 0-5 14f+: 0-0
Track: LH: 0-7 RH: 0-0 Tight: 0-5 Gall: 0-0
Aids: Bl: 0-2 Vi: 0-0 Tstrap: 0-0
Best Rating: 57 4/01 Ling 1m stand

Abraxas

92(98) (56)**56**
3-y-o b c Emperor Jones (USA)-Snipe Hall (Crofthall)
J Akehurst Canisbay Bloodstock Ltd

Placings:20004 (2933)
2001: 5^{2}SD, 6^{0}GS, 6^{0}G, 6^{0}GF, 5^{4}GF

	Starts	1st	2nd	3rd	Win & Pl
Career Total (Turf)	4	0	0	0	353
Career Total (AW)	1	0	1	0	848

Going (Turf): Sf: 0-0 GS: 0-1 Gd: 0-1 GF: 0-2 Fm: 0-0
Distance: 5f/6f: 0-5 7f-8f: 0-0 9f-13f: 0-0 14f+: 0-0
Track: LH: 0-1 RH: 0-0 Tight: 0-1 Gall: 0-0
Aids: Bl: 0-0 Vi: 0-0 Tstrap: 0-0
Best Rating: 56 5/01 Sals 6f gd-sft

Bred for speed. Ran well on All-Weather debut, but a bit disappointing since over six furlongs. Dropped back to the minimum trip in July 2001 and showed a bit more sparkle. Acts on fast ground.

Absent Friends

106(81) (25)**74**
4-y-o b g Rock City-Green Supreme (Primo Dominie)

J Balding Mrs Jo Hardy

Placings:0300/04005300-5213300 **(3021)**
2001: 6^{5}GS, 5^{2}G, 5^{1}F, 5^{3}F, 5^{3}G, 5^{0}GF, 5^{0}G

	Starts	1st	2nd	3rd	Win & Pl
Career Total (Turf)	18	1	1	4	12467
Career Total (AW)	1	0	0	0	

70 5/01 Rdcr 5f C(0-90)H FRM £7085
Total win prize-money £7085

Going (Turf): Sf: 0-4 GS: 0-4 Gd: 0-5 GF: 0-3 **Fm: 1-2**
Distance: **5f/6f: 1-17** 7f-8f: 0-2 9f-13f: 0-0 14f+: 0-0
Track : LH: 0-4 RH: 0-1 Tight: 0-1 Gall: 0-2
Aids: Bl: 0-0 Vi: 0-0 Tstrap: 0-0
Best Rating: 74 6/01 York 5f good

He is a fair sprint handicapper, but has only won once in his career so far. Suited by the minimum trip and fast ground, he has tended to lose ground at the start.

Absinther

103(100) (63d)**61**
4-y-o b g Presidium-Heavenly Queen (Scottish Reel)
M R Bosley (E J Alston 18/1) Mrs Richard Pilkington

Placings:0300/020053125**256624-2004**05221000 **(5407)**
2001: 9^{2}SW, 12^{0}SD, 8^{0}SD, 8^{4}GF, 9^{0}GF, 10^{5}GF, 11^{2}F, 10^{2}HY, 12^{1}GF, 12^{0}G, 14^{0}HY, 12^{0}SD

	Starts	1st	2nd	3rd	Win & Pl
Career Total (Turf)	21	2	4	2	11259
Career Total (AW)	10	0	3	0	2319

61 8/01 Folk 1m4f E(0-70)H G-F £2905
46 8/00 Muss 1m1f E(0-65) G-F £3445
Total win prize-money £6350

Going (Turf): Sf: 0-6 GS: 0-1 Gd: 0-3 **GF: 2-7** Fm: 0-3
Distance: 5f/6f: 0-3 7f-8f: 0-7 **9f-13f: 2-19** 14f+: 0-1
Track : LH: 0-19 **RH: 2-6 Tight: 2-16** Gall: 0-1
Aids: Bl: 0-0 Vi: 0-0 Tstrap: 0-0
Best Rating: 63 1/01 Wolv 1m1f79y slow

Fair handicapper, suited by fast ground on turf but acts on Fibresand. He ended a fairly long losing run at Folkestone in August and looks suited by 12 furlongs these days.

Absolute Charmer (IRE)

93 **89**
2-y-o ch f Entrepreneur-Diavolina (USA) (Lear Fan (USA))
R Charlton Marston Stud

Placings:244 **(4629)**
2001: 6^{2}GF, 6^{4}GF, 8^{4}GF

	Starts	1st	2nd	3rd	Win & Pl
Career Total (Turf)	3	0	1	0	1860

Going (Turf): Sf: 0-0 GS: 0-0 Gd: 0-0 GF: 0-3 Fm: 0-0
Distance: 5f/6f: 0-1 7f-8f: 0-1 9f-13f: 0-1 14f+: 0-0
Track : LH: 0-0 RH: 0-0 Tight: 0-0 Gall: 0-0
Aids: Bl: 0-0 Vi: 0-0 Tstrap: 0-0
Best Rating: 89 8/01 Sals 6f212y gd-fm

Absolute Fantasy

(102) (72)**72**
5-y-o b m Beveled (USA)-Sharp Venita (Sharp Edge)
E A Wheeler The Red Square Partnership

Placings:0004/**6260**2014034202421205102401 4-630231100422042 **(5629)**
2001: 6^{6}SD, 5^{3}GF, 6^{0}GF, 5^{2}F, 5^{3}F, 5^{1}GF, 5^{1}GS, 5^{0}GF, 5^{0}GF, 5^{4}GF, 5^{2}GF, 5^{2}GF, 5^{0}G, 5^{4}GS, 5^{2}G

	Starts	1st	2nd	3rd	Win & Pl
Career Total (Turf)	36	5	10	3	28529
Career Total (AW)	10	1	1	0	2955

70 7/01 Hayd 5f E(0-70)H G-S £3472
68 6/01 Gdwd 5f D(0-80)H G-F £4153
61 12/00 Ling 6f F(0-65)H STD £1767
60 9/00 Gdwd 5f E(0-70)H HVY £3250
53 8/00 Newb 6f8y E(0-75)H G-F £3152
45 5/00 Brig 5f213y E(0-70)H FRM £2884
Total win prize-money £18681

Going (Turf): Sf: 1-5 GS: 1-6 Gd: 0-5 **GF: 2-13** Fm: 1-6
Distance: **5f/6f: 5-37** 7f-8f: 1-6 9f-13f: 0-2 14f+: 0-0
Track : **LH: 2-20** RH: 0-5 **Tight: 1-10** Gall: 0-4
Aids: **Bl: 6-42** Vi: 0-0 Tstrap: 0-0
Best Rating: 72 9/01 Sals 5f gd-fm

Fair sprint handicapper who won four times in 2000 and in good form the following term, winning twice over five furlongs.Versatile with regard to ground conditions and effective on Equitrack, likes a sharp track and suited by being held up.

Absolute Utopia (USA)

99 **55**
8-y-o b g Mr Prospector (USA)-Magic Gleam (USA) (Danzig (USA))
N E Berry M T Lawrance

Placings:56065400/04021451/4025144/032420/60005 **(4946)**
2001: 9^{6}F, 12^{0}GF, 9^{0}GF, 12^{0}G, 12^{5}G

	Starts	1st	2nd	3rd	Win & Pl
Career Total (Turf)	34	3	4	1	21828

67 8/98 Kemp 1m4f D(0-85)H G-F £4240
62 10/97 Sals 1m1f209yE(0-70)H G-F £3463
60 8/97 Bath 1m5y F(0-65)H GD £2915
Total win prize-money £10620

Going (Turf): Sf: 0-2 GS: 0-3 Gd: 1-11 **GF: 2-16** Fm: 0-2
Distance: 5f/6f: 0-0 7f-8f: 0-5 **9f-13f: 3-29** 14f+: 0-0
Track : LH: 1-14 **RH: 2-17 Tight: 2-16** Gall: 0-3
Aids: Bl: 0-1 Vi: 0-0 Tstrap: 0-0
Best Rating: 62 5/01 Leic 1m1f218y firm

He gained his only victory when stepped up to twelve furlongs for the first time at Kempton back in 1998. Likes a decent surface on turf. Ran well enough on his reappearance after an absence of over 18 months, but has failed to build on that promise.

Absolutelymarvelos

(70) (25)**28**
2-y-o b g Royal Applause-Snipe Hall (Crofthall)
N Tinkler Stella Pennington And Anne Marie Davison

Placings:6006 **(4067)**
2001: 5^{6}F, 6^{0}GF, 5^{0}GF, 7^{6}SD

	Starts	1st	2nd	3rd	Win & Pl
Career Total (Turf)	3	0	0	0	0
Career Total (AW)	1	0	0	0	0

Going (Turf): Sf: 0-0 GS: 0-0 Gd: 0-0 GF: 0-2 Fm: 0-1
Distance: 5f/6f: 0-3 7f-8f: 0-1 9f-13f: 0-0 14f+: 0-0
Track : LH: 0-1 RH: 0-0 Tight: 0-1 Gall: 0-0
Aids: Bl: 0-0 Vi: 0-0 Tstrap: 0-0
Best Rating: 28 6/01 Nott 5f13y firm

Abuelos

90 **73**
2-y-o b c Sabrehill (USA)-Miss Oasis (Green Desert (USA))
S Dow J Noonan

Placings:000 **(5491)**
2001: 6^{0}GF, 6^{0}HY, 6^{0}HY

	Starts	1st	2nd	3rd	Win & Pl
Career Total (Turf)	3	0	0	0	

Going (Turf): Sf: 0-2 GS: 0-0 Gd: 0-0 GF: 0-1 Fm: 0-0
Distance: 5f/6f: 0-1 7f-8f: 0-2 9f-13f: 0-0 14f+: 0-0
Track : LH: 0-0 RH: 0-0 Tight: 0-0 Gall: 0-0
Aids: Bl: 0-0 Vi: 0-0 Tstrap: 0-0
Best Rating: 73 9/01 Newb 6f8y gd-fm

Abyssinian Wolf

107 **86**
3-y-o ch g Dr Devious (IRE)-Guilty Secret (IRE) (Kris)
J R Fanshawe Abdulla Al Khalifa

Placings:0-301300 **(5143)**
2001: 12^{3}GS, 12^{0}GF, 12^{1}GF, 13^{3}GF, 14^{0}HY, 14^{0}G

	Starts	1st	2nd	3rd	Win & Pl
Career Total (Turf)	7	1	0	2	6595

82 6/01 NmkJ 1m4f D(0-85)H G-F £4771
Total win prize-money £4771

Going (Turf): Sf: 0-1 GS: 0-1 Gd: 0-2 **GF: 1-3** Fm: 0-0
Distance: 5f/6f: 0-0 7f-8f: 0-1 **9f-13f: 1-3** 14f+: 0-3
Track : LH: 0-2 **RH: 1-3** Tight: 0-1 **Gall: 1-2**
Aids: Bl: 0-0 Vi: 0-0 Tstrap: 0-0
Best Rating: 86 7/01 Newb 1m5f61y gd-fm

Shaped with enough promise on second start in a 12 furlong Thirsk maiden, and won a Newmarket handicap over the same trip. Beaten off a higher mark. Acts on fast ground.

Academic Accuracy

95 **40**
3-y-o b f Environment Friend-Branitska (Mummy's Pet)
R Hannon R Hannon

Placings:06-0234460060 **(5084)**
2001: 7^{0}S, 8^{2}G, 8^{3}F, 7^{4}GF, 9^{4}GF, 8^{6}GF, 8^{0}GF, 7^{0}GF, 8^{6}G, 9^{0}S

	Starts	1st	2nd	3rd	Win & Pl
Career Total (Turf)	12	0	1	1	1005

Going (Turf): Sf: 0-2 GS: 0-0 Gd: 0-2 GF: 0-7 Fm: 0-1
Distance: 5f/6f: 0-1 7f-8f: 0-4 9f-13f: 0-7 14f+: 0-0
Track : LH: 0-5 RH: 0-2 Tight: 0-3 Gall: 0-1
Aids: Bl: 0-0 Vi: 0-0 Tstrap: 0-0
Best Rating: 63 6/01 Brig 7f214y gd-fm

Academic Gold (IRE)

94(93) (55)**69d**
3-y-o ch g Royal Academy (USA)-Penultimate (USA) (Roberto (USA))
K R Burke Nigel Shields

Placings:3-2000 **(4305)**
2001: 8^{2}SD, 8^{0}GF, 10^{0}GS, 12^{0}GF

	Starts	1st	2nd	3rd	Win & Pl
Career Total (Turf)	4	0	0	1	538
Career Total (AW)	1	0	1	0	806

Going (Turf): Sf: 0-0 GS: 0-1 Gd: 0-1 GF: 0-2 Fm: 0-0
Distance: 5f/6f: 0-0 7f-8f: 0-2 9f-13f: 0-3 14f+: 0-0
Track : LH: 0-3 RH: 0-1 Tight: 0-1 Gall: 0-0
Aids: Bl: 0-0 Vi: 0-0 Tstrap: 0-1
Best Rating: 60 7/01 Donc 1m gd-fm

Academic Record

94(93) (38)**47**
3-y-o b g Royal Academy (USA)-Bala Monaafis (IRE) (In The Wings)
N M Babbage (Gerard Cully 24/9) B Babbage

Placings:0053114-6030206010 **(2375)**
2001: 10^{6}SD, 9^{0}SD, 10^{3}SW, 11^{0}SD, 9^{2}G, 9^{0}GF, 11^{6}SD, 11^{0}GF, 11^{1}GF, 10^{0}GF

	Starts	1st	2nd	3rd	Win & Pl
Career Total (Turf)	8	1	1	0	4209
Career Total (AW)	9	2	0	2	4394

47 6/01 Haml 1m3f16y E(0-70) G-F £3428
60 12/00 Wolv 1m1f79y G STD £1876
55 11/00 Ling 1m G STD £1886
Total win prize-money £7192

Going (Turf): Sf: 0-1 GS: 0-0 Gd: 0-3 **GF: 1-4** Fm: 0-0
Distance: 5f/6f: 0-1 7f-8f: 1-4 **9f-13f: 2-12** 14f+: 0-0
Track : **LH: 2-12** RH: 1-4 **Tight: 3-12** Gall: 0-0
Aids: **Bl: 2-12** Vi: 0-0 Tstrap: 0-0
Best Rating: 54 5/01 Bevl 1m1f207y good

Accepting

104 **86**

4-y-o b c Mtoto-D'Azy (Persian Bold)
J Mackie Ms Caroline F Breay

Placings:02/64-30103200 **(5661)**
2001: 14^{3}GS, 13^{0}GF, 16^{1}GF, 16^{0}F, 16^{3}G, 15^{2}G, 16^{0}S, 16^{0}G

	Starts	1st	2nd	3rd	Win & Pl
Career Total (Turf)	12	1	2	2	13239

86 6/01 Muss 2m D(0-85)H G-F £8112
Total win prize-money £8112

Going (Turf): Sf: 0-1 GS: 0-2 Gd: 0-4 **GF: 1-4** Fm: 0-1
Distance: 5f/6f: 0-0 7f-8f: 0-1 9f-13f: 0-3 **14f+: 1-8**
Track : LH: 0-5 **RH: 1-5 Tight: 1-6** Gall: 0-4
Aids: Bl: 0-0 Vi: 0-0 Tstrap: 0-0
Best Rating: 86 6/01 Muss 2m gd-fm

A sister to the smart Presenting, had two races in the spring of 2000 without success. With John Gosden last season, he has changed stables since. Scored over two miles when raced prominently at Musselburgh in June. Acts on fast ground.

Access Denied (FR)

104 **94+**

2-y-o b c Revoque (IRE)-Forentia (Formidable (USA))
D R Loder Sheikh Mohammed

Placings:214 **(5264)**
2001: 6^{2}F, 6^{1}S, 6^{4}GS

	Starts	1st	2nd	3rd	Win & Pl
Career Total (Turf)	3	1	1	0	5932

94 9/01 Pont 6f D SFT £4013
Total win prize-money £4014

Going (Turf): **Sf: 1-1** GS: 0-1 Gd: 0-0 GF: 0-0 Fm: 0-1
Distance: **5f/6f: 1-3** 7f-8f: 0-0 9f-13f: 0-0 14f+: 0-0
Track : **LH: 1-1** RH: 0-0 Tight: 0-0 Gall: 0-0
Aids: Bl: 0-0 Vi: 0-0 Tstrap: 0-0
Best Rating: 94 9/01 Pont 6f soft

A FF2.5m yearling out of a half-sister to Bahamian Bounty, he came across a very useful sort when odds on for his Newcastle debut, but made no mistake next time at Pontefract over six furlongs on soft ground. On the face of it his fourth in a listed race was somewhat disappointing.

Acclamation

101 **100**

2-y-o b c Royal Applause-Princess Athena (Ahonoora)
L G Cottrell Dulford Cavaliers

Placings:21211 **(4650)**
2001: 5^{2}S, 5^{1}GF, 5^{2}G, 5^{1}GF, 6^{1}GF

	Starts	1st	2nd	3rd	Win & Pl
Career Total (Turf)	5	3	2	0	164980

100 9/01 Donc 6f B G-F £151800
91 8/01 Newb 5f34y D G-F £4309
73 6/01 Sand 5f6y D G-F £3510
Total win prize-money £159620

Going (Turf): Sf: 0-1 GS: 0-0 Gd: 0-1 **GF: 3-3** Fm: 0-0
Distance: **5f/6f: 3-5** 7f-8f: 0-0 9f-13f: 0-0 14f+: 0-0
Track : LH: 0-0 RH: 0-0 Tight: 0-0 Gall: 0-0
Aids: Bl: 0-0 Vi: 0-0 Tstrap: 0-0
Best Rating: 100 9/01 Donc 6f gd-fm

33,000gns half brother to three winners out of a sprinter. Followed up a promising debut by beating a fair sort at Sandown, then was narrowly beaten in a listed event before gaining compensation at Newbury and taking a valuable sales race at Doncaster. Acts on fast ground and usually races prominently.

Accystan

85(105) (54)**23**

6-y-o ch g Efisio-Amia (CAN) (Nijinsky (CAN))
A Crook (M D Hammond 21/2) Middleham Racing Bureau/g Heap

Placings:005/613315433/010/06201633500-00000 **(2188)**
2001: 12^{0}SW, 12^{0}SW, 11^{0}G, 10^{0}F, 14^{0}GF

	Starts	1st	2nd	3rd	Win & Pl
Career Total (Turf)	10	0	0	1	638
Career Total (AW)	21	4	1	5	10524

54 3/00 Sthl 1m4f F(0-65)H STD £1949
45 7/99 Sthl 1m4f G STD £2018
67 2/98 Sthl 1m3f F(0-60)H STD £1735
66 1/98 Wolv 1m1f79y F(0-65) STD £2221
Total win prize-money £7926

Going (Turf): Sf: 0-1 GS: 0-1 Gd: 0-4 GF: 0-2 Fm: 0-2
Distance: 5f/6f: 0-1 7f-8f: 0-3 **9f-13f: 4-23** 14f+: 0-4
Track : **LH: 4-26** RH: 0-4 **Tight: 1-14** Gall: 0-0
Aids: Bl: 0-2 Vi: 0-0 Tstrap: 0-0
Best Rating: 16 6/01 Pont 1m2f6y firm

He managed to win a couple of very poor events on Fibresand at the start of '98, and regained winning form on the Flat with an easy win in a seller at Southwell in July 2000. No form this season.

Ace Of Trumps

108 **60**

5-y-o ch g First Trump-Elle Reef (Shareef Dancer (USA))
Miss L A Perratt (J Hetherton 15/8) C D Barber-Lomax

Placings:6502621200601100003533500/10000120300 25643523210-332035420016036111O346 **(5272)**
2001: 9^{3}S, 10^{3}HY, 8^{2}GS, 8^{0}GS, 9^{3}GS, 9^{5}GF, 8^{4}G, 8^{2}GF, 10^{0}F, 9^{0}G, 9^{1}G, 8^{6}F, 9^{0}GF, 9^{3}GS, 9^{6}G, 9^{1}GS, 8^{1}S, 10^{1}G, 9^{0}G, 9^{3}G, 8^{4}GF, 10^{6}HY

	Starts	1st	2nd	3rd	Win & Pl
Career Total (Turf)	67	10	9	11	39294
Career Total (AW)	2	0	0	0	

59 8/01 Ayr 1m2f E(0-70)H GD £3318
55 8/01 Haml 1m65y G(0-60)H SFT £2520
45 8/01 Haml 1m1f36y F(0-60) G-S £2828
45 6/01 Haml 1m1f36y E GD £3066
47 10/00 Muss 1m1f F(0-65)H SFT £1778
50 5/00 Haml 1m1f36y E G-F £2444
51 3/00 Muss 1m1f F(0-60)H GD £2492
59 5/99 Wwck 1m2f110yF SFT £2238
59 5/99 Nott 1m54y G(0-60)H FRM £2250
68 8/98 NmkJ 7f E FRM £3720
Total win prize-money £26654

Going (Turf): Sf: 3-18 GS: 1-9 **Gd: 3-17** GF: 1-15 Fm: 2-8
Distance: 5f/6f: 0-3 7f-8f: 1-13 **9f-13f: 9-53** 14f+: 0-0
Track : LH: 3-28 **RH: 6-29 Tight: 6-31** Gall: 0-2
Aids: Bl: 0-6 Vi: 0-3 **Tstrap: 9-58**
Best Rating: 60 9/01 Haml 1m65y gd-fm

He has been in good form this season, winning four times. Most of his wins were in plating company, but he won a much better race at Ayr. Usually goes well at Hamilton and effective from a mile to ten furlongs.

Ace-Ma-Vahra

(95) (46)**34**

3-y-o b f Savahra Sound-Asmarina (Ascendant)
S R Bowring Ace Racing One

Placings:5022500 **(5503)**
2001: 7^{5}SW, 6^{0}SD, 7^{2}SD, 7^{2}SD, 7^{5}GF, 10^{0}GF, 7^{0}HY

	Starts	1st	2nd	3rd	Win & Pl
Career Total (Turf)	3	0	0	0	0
Career Total (AW)	4	0	2	0	522

Going (Turf): Sf: 0-1 GS: 0-0 Gd: 0-0 GF: 0-2 Fm: 0-0
Distance: 5f/6f: 0-1 7f-8f: 0-5 9f-13f: 0-1 14f+: 0-0
Track : LH: 0-5 RH: 0-1 Tight: 0-1 Gall: 0-0
Aids: Bl: 0-0 Vi: 0-0 Tstrap: 0-0
Best Rating: 46 4/01 Sthl 7f stand

Seems suited by Fibresand and has been staying on over seven. Should be effective at a mile.

Acebo Lyons (IRE)

(69) (18)

6-y-o b m Waajib-Etage (Ile De Bourbon (USA))
A P Jarvis Terence P Lyons Ii

Placings:5642/030105/06030260400/1665040320140-
2001:

	Starts	1st	2nd	3rd	Win & Pl
Career Total (Turf)	31	3	3	3	13109
Career Total (AW)	3	0	0	0	

38 10/00 Yarm 1m6f17y F SFT £2289
59 3/00 Donc 1m2f60y F(0-75)H G-F £2509
70 8/98 Hayd 1m2f120yE(0-70) GD £2810
Total win prize-money £7609

Going (Turf): Sf: 1-4 GS: 0-4 **Gd: 1-9 GF: 1-13** Fm: 0-1
Distance: 5f/6f: 0-1 7f-8f: 0-2 **9f-13f: 2-27** 14f+: 1-4
Track : **LH: 3-20** RH: 0-10 Tight: 1-12 Gall: 1-9
Aids: Bl: 0-0 Vi: 0-3 Tstrap: 0-0
Best Rating: 70 8/98 Hayd 1m2f120y G

She has shown ability in moderate handicap company, but was dropped to claiming company when scoring last backend. Has swished her tail under pressure.

Achilles Sky

(81) (29)**66**

5-y-o b g Hadeer-Diva Madonna (Chief Singer)
Jamie Poulton Achilles International

Placings:400/016/10023000-00021060 **(5191)**
2001: 10^{0}GS, 14^{0}HY, 12^{0}S, 11^{2}GF, 11^{1}F, 12^{0}G, 12^{6}G, 12^{0}SD

	Starts	1st	2nd	3rd	Win & Pl
Career Total (Turf)	21	3	2	1	15177
Career Total (AW)	1	0	0	0	

42 6/01 Brig 1m3f196yE(0-65) FRM £2772
73 3/00 Sthl 1m4f D(0-85)H GD £3692
71 7/99 Nott 1m1f213yE(0-70)H G-F £4757
Total win prize-money £11221

Going (Turf): Sf: 0-4 GS: 0-2 **Gd: 1-9 GF: 1-4 Fm: 1-2**
Distance: 5f/6f: 0-0 7f-8f: 0-2 **9f-13f: 3-18** 14f+: 0-2
Track : **LH: 3-16** RH: 0-4 Tight: 0-8 Gall: 0-5
Aids: **Bl: 1-4** Vi: 0-1 Tstrap: 0-0
Best Rating: 66 6/01 Wind 1m3f135y gd-fm

He won on turf at Southwell in March 2000, and ran the odd good race before winning at Brighton. Seems to prefer a slowly-run race.

Achilles Spirit (IRE)

103 **81**

3-y-o b g Deploy-Scenic Spirit (IRE) (Scenic)
J A Osborne Achilles International

Placings:01360-0122200 **(4952)**
2001: 10^{0}G, 10^{1}GF, 10^{2}GS, 12^{2}G, 11^{2}GF, 13^{0}GF, 11^{0}G

	Starts	1st	2nd	3rd	Win & Pl
Career Total (Turf)	12	2	3	1	15353

81	7/01	Pont	1m2f6y	D(0-75)	G-F	£4212
76	7/00	Epsm	6f	E	G-S	£4153

Total win prize-money £8366

Going (Turf): Sf: 0-1 **GS: 1-3** Gd: 0-4 **GF: 1-4** Fm: 0-0
Distance: 5f/6f: 1-2 7f-8f: 0-2 9f-13f: 1-7 14f+: 0-1
Track : **LH: 2-5** RH: 0-3 **Tight: 1-4** Gall: 0-3
Aids: Bl: 0-0 Vi: 0-0 Tstrap: 0-0
Best Rating: 81 7/01 Pont 1m2f6y gd-fm

A winner on easy ground at Epsom as a juvenile, he returned to form on faster going at Pontefract this season when he had the run of the race. Running well since, he appears to handle most ground and seems well suited by making the running.

Achilles Sun

97(92) (57)**55**
3-y-o b g Deploy-Tsungani (Cure The Blues (USA))
Jamie Poulton Achilles International

Placings:U40000-000020 **(5525)**
2001: 11^{0}GF, 12^{0}GF, 10^{0}GF, 10^{0}G, 11^{2}S, 11^{0}HY

	Starts	1st	2nd	3rd	Win & Pl
Career Total (Turf)	11	0	1	0	1386
Career Total (AW)	1	0	0	0	

Going (Turf): Sf: 0-3 GS: 0-1 Gd: 0-4 GF: 0-3 Fm: 0-0
Distance: 5f/6f: 0-1 7f-8f: 0-4 9f-13f: 0-7 14f+: 0-0
Track : LH: 0-4 RH: 0-3 Tight: 0-4 Gall: 0-1
Aids: Bl: 0-0 Vi: 0-0 Tstrap: 0-0
Best Rating: 59 6/01 Gdwd 1m3f gd-fm

Very moderate performer, runner-up in a bad maiden on soft ground.

Achilles Wings (USA)

106(97) (48)**61**
5-y-o b g Irish River (FR)-Shirley Valentine (Shirley Heights)
Miss K M George Stableline

Placings:3442020-4404465 **(5098)**
2001: 10^{4}GF, 10^{4}GS, 14^{0}GF, 12^{4}S, 12^{4}SD, 14^{6}SW, 14^{5}GS

	Starts	1st	2nd	3rd	Win & Pl
Career Total (Turf)	10	0	2	0	2448
Career Total (AW)	4	0	0	1	612

Going (Turf): Sf: 0-1 GS: 0-4 Gd: 0-2 GF: 0-3 Fm: 0-0
Distance: 5f/6f: 0-0 7f-8f: 0-0 9f-13f: 0-9 14f+: 0-5
Track : LH: 0-11 RH: 0-2 Tight: 0-7 Gall: 0-3
Aids: Bl: 0-0 Vi: 0-0 Tstrap: 0-0
Best Rating: 61 7/01 Wwck 1m2f188y gd-fm

Still a maiden, but has run some fair races on most surfaces, including Fibresand, and also run some good races over hurdles. Effective from 12 furlongs upwards.

Acid Test

(103) (53)**54**
6-y-o ch g Sharpo-Clunk Click (Star Appeal)
M A Buckley Fair Price Racing

Placings:0001012520/00051000002000**1031/0120246**
1100400/**066**30003000506003**6352-2605** **(0265)**
2001: 8^{2}SD, 8^{6}SD, 8^{0}SD, 8^{5}SW

	Starts	1st	2nd	3rd	Win & Pl
Career Total (Turf)	41	5	3	2	30801
Career Total (AW)	27	3	4	3	12257

78	6/99	Ches	7f2y	C(0-95)H	SFT	£10455
72	5/99	Catt	7f	D(0-85)H	FRM	£5182
67	1/99	Ling	6f	E(0-70)H	STD	£2595
64	1/99	Ling	6f	F(0-60)H	STD	£2476
60	12/98	Ling	6f	F(0-60)H	STD	£1735
72	6/98	Ling	7f	E(0-70)	GD	£3131
69	8/97	NmkJ	7f	D	G-F	£4620
63	7/97	Ling	6f	G	G-F	£1984

Total win prize-money £32182

Going (Turf): Sf: 1-5 GS: 0-3 Gd: 1-16 **GF: 2-14** Fm: 1-3
Distance: 5f/6f: 4-20 7f-8f: 4-43 9f-13f: 0-5 14f+: 0-0
Track : **LH: 5-47** RH: 0-4 **Tight: 5-35** Gall: 0-7
Aids: Bl: 0-1 Vi: 0-1 Tstrap: 0-0
Best Rating: 52 1/01 Ling 1m stand

Changed stables in '98, and showed pretty good form in sprint handicap company on Equitrack before scoring twice on turf last term at Catterick and Chester over seven furlongs. Out of form since however.

Aconite

54
2-y-o b f Primo Dominie-Laugharne (Known Fact (USA))
C N Allen G S Shropshire

Placings:6 **(2665)**
2001: 7^{6}G

	Starts	1st	2nd	3rd	Win & Pl
Career Total (Turf)	1	0	0	0	0

Going (Turf): Sf: 0-0 GS: 0-0 Gd: 0-1 GF: 0-0 Fm: 0-0
Distance: 5f/6f: 0-0 7f-8f: 0-1 9f-13f: 0-0 14f+: 0-0
Track : LH: 0-0 RH: 0-0 Tight: 0-0 Gall: 0-0
Aids: Bl: 0-0 Vi: 0-0 Tstrap: 0-0

Acorazado (IRE)

97 **84**
2-y-o b c Petorius-Jaldi (IRE) (Nordico (USA))
S P C Woods B Allen/r Hine/r Dawson/a Duke

Placings:31 **(5526)**
2001: 6^{3}S, 5^{1}S

	Starts	1st	2nd	3rd	Win & Pl
Career Total (Turf)	2	1	0	1	4928

84	10/01	Nott	5f13y	D	SFT	£3737

Total win prize-money £3738

Going (Turf): Sf: 1-2 GS: 0-0 Gd: 0-0 GF: 0-0 Fm: 0-0
Distance: **5f/6f: 1-2** 7f-8f: 0-0 9f-13f: 0-0 14f+: 0-0
Track : LH: 0-0 RH: 0-0 Tight: 0-0 Gall: 0-0
Aids: Bl: 0-0 Vi: 0-0 Tstrap: 0-0
Best Rating: 84 10/01 Nott 5f13y soft

A half-brother to a sprint winner, he was green when making an encouraging debut at York in October and got off the mark at Nottingham. He looks to have a future but has only raced on soft ground so far.

Acorn Catcher

(101) (54d)**53**
3-y-o b f Emarati (USA)-Anytime Baby (Bairn (USA))
B Palling N C Phillips & T Davies

Placings:01300**13350-602** **(0435)**
2001: 5^{6}SW, 5^{0}SW, 5^{2}SD

	Starts	1st	2nd	3rd	Win & Pl
Career Total (Turf)	5	1	0	1	2445
Career Total (AW)	8	1	1	2	3207

63	9/00	Wolv	5f	G	STD	£1970
53	7/00	Leic	5f2y	G	G-F	£1876

Total win prize-money £3847

Going (Turf): Sf: 0-1 GS: 0-0 Gd: 0-0 **GF: 1-4** Fm: 0-0
Distance: **5f/6f: 2-13** 7f-8f: 0-0 9f-13f: 0-0 14f+: 0-0
Track : **LH: 1-8** RH: 0-0 **Tight: 1-6** Gall: 0-2
Aids: Bl: 0-0 Vi: 0-1 Tstrap: 0-0
Best Rating: 46 2/01 Ling 5f slow

Acquittal (IRE)

104 (36)**38**
9-y-o b g Danehill (USA)-Perfect Alibi (Law Society (USA))
P L Clinton In The Clear Racing

Placings:00/4236136430/**05**0040002/32000/62600/324
3U000/004453006-62650351300 **(4404)**
2001: 10^{6}G, 14^{2}F, 14^{6}GF, 12^{5}GF, 12^{0}GF, 14^{3}GF, 13^{5}G, 11^{1}G, 14^{3}GF, 11^{0}GF, 12^{0}GS

	Starts	1st	2nd	3rd	Win & Pl
Career Total (Turf)	56	2	6	9	14395
Career Total (AW)	3	0	0	0	256

38	8/01	Catt	1m3f214y	F(0-75)H	GD	£2516
61	6/95	Muss	1m3f32y	G(0-60)H	G-F	£2668

Total win prize-money £5185

Going (Turf): Sf: 0-3 GS: 0-4 **Gd: 1-10 GF: 1-32** Fm: 0-7
Distance: 5f/6f: 0-0 7f-8f: 0-3 **9f-13f: 2-45** 14f+: 0-11
Track : LH: 1-37 RH: 1-18 **Tight: 2-31** Gall: 0-1
Aids: Bl: 0-1 **Vi: 1-41** Tstrap: 0-0
Best Rating: 38 8/01 Catt 1m3f214y good

Action Jackson

95(95) (25)**23**
9-y-o ch g Hadeer-Water Woo (USA) (Tom Rolfe)
A W Carroll D Morgan

Placings:606/5226**4**00**55**/042104100/0223405320/0020
004204265/**0**204604/0500-**530055**000 **(4048)**
2001: 11^{5}SW, 13^{0}SD, 13^{0}SW, 16^{0}SD, 10^{5}SD, 11^{5}F, 14^{0}GF, 9^{0}G, 10^{0}F

	Starts	1st	2nd	3rd	Win & Pl
Career Total (Turf)	52	2	9	2	25501
Career Total (AW)	12	0	1	1	930

45	9/96	Pont	1m2f6y	G	GD	£2784
55	7/96	Nott	1m1f213y	G	G-F	£2070

Total win prize-money £4854

Going (Turf): Sf: 0-2 GS: 0-6 **Gd: 1-15 GF: 1-21** Fm: 0-8
Distance: 5f/6f: 0-1 7f-8f: 0-7 **9f-13f: 2-41** 14f+: 0-15
Track : **LH: 2-41** RH: 0-15 Tight: 0-23 Gall: 0-4
Aids: Bl: 0-5 Vi: 0-0 Tstrap: 0-6
Best Rating: 25 2/01 Ling 1m5f stand

Activist

101 **70**
3-y-o ch g Diesis-Shicklah (USA) (The Minstrel (CAN))
G M Moore (M L W Bell 30/8) John Robson

Placings:0-04224 **(4382)**
2001: 8^{0}GF, 7^{4}G, 11^{2}GF, 12^{2}G, 12^{4}GF

	Starts	1st	2nd	3rd	Win & Pl
Career Total (Turf)	6	0	2	0	2065

Going (Turf): Sf: 0-1 GS: 0-0 Gd: 0-2 GF: 0-3 Fm: 0-0
Distance: 5f/6f: 0-0 7f-8f: 0-3 9f-13f: 0-3 14f+: 0-0
Track : LH: 0-3 RH: 0-1 Tight: 0-2 Gall: 0-1
Aids: Bl: 0-0 Vi: 0-0 Tstrap: 0-0
Best Rating: 70 8/01 Newc 1m4f93y good

By Diesis and from a useful family, was runner-up twice in moderate events in August on a sound surface.

Activity (IRE)

83 **74**
2-y-o ch c Pennekamp (USA)-Actoris (USA) (Diesis)
D R Loder Sheikh Mohammed

Placings:0 **(5107)**
2001: 7^{0}GS

	Starts	1st	2nd	3rd	Win & Pl
Career Total (Turf)	1	0	0	0	

Going (Turf): Sf: 0-0 GS: 0-1 Gd: 0-0 GF: 0-0 Fm: 0-0
Distance: 5f/6f: 0-0 7f-8f: 0-1 9f-13f: 0-0 14f+: 0-0
Track : LH: 0-0 RH: 0-0 Tight: 0-0 Gall: 0-0
Aids: Bl: 0-0 Vi: 0-0 Tstrap: 0-0
Best Rating: 74 10/01 NmkR 7f gd-sft

Adaleel

82 **70**

2-y-o b c Polar Falcon (USA)-Ameerat Jumaira (USA) (Alydar (USA))
A C Stewart Sheikh Ahmed Al Maktoum

Placings:000 **(5466)**
2001: 7^{0}G, 7^{0}S, 6^{0}S

	Starts	1st	2nd	3rd	Win & Pl
Career Total (Turf)	3	0	0	0	

Going (Turf): Sf: 0-2 GS: 0-0 Gd: 0-1 GF: 0-0 Fm: 0-0
Distance: 5f/6f: 0-0 7f-8f: 0-3 9f-13f: 0-0 14f+: 0-0
Track : LH: 0-2 RH: 0-0 Tight: 0-0 Gall: 0-1
Aids: Bl: 0-0 Vi: 0-0 Tstrap: 0-0
Best Rating: 70 9/01 NmkR 7f good

Adalpour (IRE)

99 **70**

3-y-o b c Kahyasi-Adalya (IRE) (Darshaan)
Sir Michael Stoute H H Aga Khan

Placings:30 **(5180)**
2001: 9^{3}GS, 10^{0}HY

	Starts	1st	2nd	3rd	Win & Pl
Career Total (Turf)	2	0	0	1	740

Going (Turf): Sf: 0-1 GS: 0-1 Gd: 0-0 GF: 0-0 Fm: 0-0
Distance: 5f/6f: 0-0 7f-8f: 0-0 9f-13f: 0-2 14f+: 0-0
Track : LH: 0-0 RH: 0-1 Tight: 0-2 Gall: 0-0
Aids: Bl: 0-0 Vi: 0-0 Tstrap: 0-0
Best Rating: 70 9/01 Gdwd 1m1f192y gd-sft

Adamas (IRE)

98 **52**

4-y-o b f Fairy King (USA)-Corynida (USA) (Alleged (USA))
Andrew Turnell Mrs Claire Hollowood

Placings:2/0410043U00-0056044U0 **(5288)**
2001: 9^{0}GF, 12^{0}G, 9^{5}F, 10^{6}GF, 9^{0}GF, 10^{4}GF, 6^{4}F, 7^{U}GF, 6^{0}HY

	Starts	1st	2nd	3rd	Win & Pl
Career Total (Turf)	20	1	1	1	6114

57 6/00 Bevl 1m100y D G-F £3850
Total win prize-money £3850

Going (Turf): Sf: 0-2 GS: 0-2 Gd: 0-2 **GF: 1-10** Fm: 0-4
Distance: 5f/6f: 0-3 7f-8f: 0-3 **9f-13f: 1-14** 14f+: 0-0
Track : LH: 0-12 **RH: 1-3** Tight: 0-5 Gall: 0-3
Aids: Bl: 0-0 Vi: 0-0 Tstrap: 0-0
Best Rating: 62 6/01 Bevl 1m1f207y gd-fm

Had got off the mark in cosy style at Beverley in June 2000, but failed to build on that. She has dropped considerably in the handicap as a result, and ran her best race for a while dropped to six furlongs at Newcastle in September.

Adamatic (IRE)

10-y-o b g Henbit (USA)-Arpal Magic (Master Owen)
R Allan Ian R Flannigan

Placings:0 **(2866)**
2001: 16^{0}GF

	Starts	1st	2nd	3rd	Win & Pl
Career Total (Turf)	1	0	0	0	

Going (Turf): Sf: 0-0 GS: 0-0 Gd: 0-0 GF: 0-1 Fm: 0-0
Distance: 5f/6f: 0-0 7f-8f: 0-0 9f-13f: 0-0 14f+: 0-1
Track : LH: 0-0 RH: 0-1 Tight: 0-1 Gall: 0-0
Aids: Bl: 0-0 Vi: 0-0 Tstrap: 0-0

Adams Ale

80 **41**

2-y-o b f Mistertopogigo (IRE)-Knayton Lass (Presidium)
J M Jefferson Mr & Mrs J M Davenport

Placings:00 **(4367)**
2001: 5^{0}GS, 5^{0}GF

	Starts	1st	2nd	3rd	Win & Pl
Career Total (Turf)	2	0	0	0	

Going (Turf): Sf: 0-0 GS: 0-1 Gd: 0-0 GF: 0-1 Fm: 0-0
Distance: 5f/6f: 0-2 7f-8f: 0-0 9f-13f: 0-0 14f+: 0-0
Track : LH: 0-0 RH: 0-0 Tight: 0-0 Gall: 0-0
Aids: Bl: 0-0 Vi: 0-0 Tstrap: 0-0
Best Rating: 41 8/01 Thsk 5f gd-sft

Adantino

88 **76**

2-y-o b c Glory Of Dancer-Sweet Whisper (Petong)
B R Millman Tarka Two Racing

Placings:000 **(5038)**
2001: 6^{0}G, 7^{0}F, 5^{0}G

	Starts	1st	2nd	3rd	Win & Pl
Career Total (Turf)	3	0	0	0	

Going (Turf): Sf: 0-0 GS: 0-0 Gd: 0-2 GF: 0-0 Fm: 0-1
Distance: 5f/6f: 0-1 7f-8f: 0-2 9f-13f: 0-0 14f+: 0-0
Track : LH: 0-1 RH: 0-0 Tight: 0-0 Gall: 0-1
Aids: Bl: 0-0 Vi: 0-0 Tstrap: 0-0
Best Rating: 76 10/01 Bath 5f161y good

Slowly away on Nottingham debut.

Addeyll

95 **96**

2-y-o ch c Efisio-Rohita (IRE) (Waajib)
M R Channon Sheikh Ahmed Al Maktoum

Placings:215225 **(5260)**
2001: 6^{2}GF, 6^{1}GF, 6^{5}GY, 6^{2}G, 6^{2}GS, 7^{5}GS

	Starts	1st	2nd	3rd	Win & Pl
Career Total (Turf)	6	1	3	0	9678

96 6/01 Ayr 6f E G-F £3164
Total win prize-money £3164

Going (Turf): Sf: 0-0 GS: 0-2 Gd: 0-1 **GF: 1-2** Fm: 0-0
Distance: **5f/6f: 1-4** 7f-8f: 0-2 9f-13f: 0-0 14f+: 0-0
Track : LH: 0-0 RH: 0-0 Tight: 0-0 Gall: 0-0
Aids: Bl: 0-0 Vi: 0-0 Tstrap: 0-0
Best Rating: 96 9/01 Gdwd 6f gd-sft

Ran a fine race on his debut when chasing home Western Verse over six furlongs at York. Off the mark at Ayr in lesser event on next start and produced decent efforts afterwards.

Addition

97 **35**

5-y-o b m Dilum (USA)-Cedar Lady (Telsmoss)
R J Hodges J W Mursell

Placings:44366/6002310060/00460-040040 **(4733)**
2001: 6^{0}GF, 8^{4}GF, 7^{0}G, 7^{0}G, 7^{4}GF, 7^{0}F

	Starts	1st	2nd	3rd	Win & Pl
Career Total (Turf)	26	1	1	2	6877

60 7/99 Wwck 6f168y D(0-80)H G-F £4199
Total win prize-money £4199

Going (Turf): Sf: 0-2 GS: 0-4 Gd: 0-8 **GF: 1-8** Fm: 0-4
Distance: 5f/6f: 0-9 **7f-8f: 1-15** 9f-13f: 0-2 14f+: 0-0
Track : **LH: 1-8** RH: 0-2 Tight: 0-2 Gall: 0-5
Aids: Bl: 0-0 Vi: 0-0 Tstrap: 0-0
Best Rating: 48 7/01 Sals 1m gd-fm

Addo (IRE)

(79) (48)**77**

2-y-o b f Mujadil (USA)-Miss Siham (IRE) (Green Forest (USA))
G C Bravery The Tt Partnership

Placings:46100300 **(5408)**
2001: 5^{4}GF, 6^{6}Y, 5^{1}GF, 5^{0}GF, 5^{0}F, 5^{3}G, 5^{0}GS, 6^{0}SD

	Starts	1st	2nd	3rd	Win & Pl
Career Total (Turf)	7	1	0	1	5195
Career Total (AW)	1	0	0	0	

77 7/01 Bevl 5f E G-F £3346
Total win prize-money £3346

Going (Turf): Sf: 0-0 GS: 0-1 Gd: 0-1 **GF: 1-3** Fm: 0-1
Distance: **5f/6f: 1-7** 7f-8f: 0-1 9f-13f: 0-0 14f+: 0-0
Track : LH: 0-1 RH: 0-0 Tight: 0-0 Gall: 0-0
Aids: Bl: 0-0 Vi: 0-0 Tstrap: 0-0
Best Rating: 77 7/01 Bevl 5f gd-fm

Bred for speed. Sixth at the Curragh on only second outing. Scored over minimum trip at Beverley on next outing, but has struggled in Listed and nursery company since. Acts on fast ground and is suited by five furlongs.

Adelphi Boy (IRE)

(107) (95)**60**

5-y-o ch g Ballad Rock-Toda (Absalom)
M C Chapman Darry Drown

Placings:05542111/2343040003005024/03146002104-00500660000206 **(5376)**
2001: 7^{0}SD, 8^{0}SD, 7^{5}SD, 8^{0}S, 10^{0}G, 8^{6}G, 8^{6}G, 10^{0}GF, 5^{0}G, 7^{0}G, 7^{0}GF, 11^{2}GF, 12^{0}GS, 9^{6}G

	Starts	1st	2nd	3rd	Win & Pl
Career Total (Turf)	35	1	3	2	14199
Career Total (AW)	14	4	2	2	20224

71 9/00 Yarm 1m3y D(0-80)H G-F £5850
95 2/00 Wolv 1m1f79y C STD £6107
82 12/98 Ling 5f E H STD £2752
84 12/98 Sthl 5f E(0-85)H STD £2815
71 12/98 Sthl 5f D STD £2801
Total win prize-money £20325

Going (Turf): Sf: 0-6 GS: 0-6 Gd: 0-11 **GF: 1-12** Fm: 0-0
Distance: **5f/6f: 3-12** 7f-8f: 0-19 9f-13f: 2-18 14f+: 0-0
Track : **LH: 2-28** RH: 0-1 **Tight: 2-12** Gall: 0-7
Aids: Bl: 0-0 Vi: 0-0 Tstrap: 0-0
Best Rating: 88 3/01 Sthl 7f stand

Effective on both the All-Weather, and turf, winning five times, once on the Equitrack, three times on the Fibresand, and once on good to firm, although he has not won for over a year. Best watched until back on the All-Weather during the winter.

Adelphi Theatre (USA)

105 **87**

4-y-o b g Sadler's Wells (USA)-Truly Bound (USA) (In Reality)

R Rowe The Encore Partnership

Placings:610/6-0140 **(5020)**
2001: 11^{0}GF, 9^{1}GF, 12^{4}G, 12^{0}HY

	Starts	1st	2nd	3rd	Win & Pl
Career Total (Turf)	**8**	**2**	**0**	**0**	**13496**

73	7/01	Folk	1m1f149yC(0-85)	G-F	£7633
83	8/99	Tral	1m	G-Y	£5175

Total win prize-money £12809

Going (Turf): Sf: 0-1 GS: 0-0 Gd: 0-2 **GF: 1-2** Fm: 0-0
Distance: 5f/6f: 0-0 7f-8f: 1-3 9f-13f: 1-5 14f+: 0-0
Track : LH: 1-4 RH: 1-3 **Tight: 1-2** Gall: 0-1
Aids: Bl: 0-1 Vi: 0-0 Tstrap: 0-0
Best Rating: 87 9/01 Kemp 1m4f good

Won a mile maiden in Ireland in 1999. Off the track for a year before his reappearance at Windsor in July 2001. Scored on his next outing over nine and a half furlongs at Folkestone in a classified stakes and put up a good show next time when back in handicap company. Handles fast ground. Has won on good to soft in Ireland.

Adept

95 **77**

2-y-o b f Efisio-Prancing (Prince Sabo)
Sir Mark Prescott Cheveley Park Stud

Placings:336 **(5183)**
2001: 5^{3}S, 6^{3}HY, 5^{6}GS

	Starts	1st	2nd	3rd	Win & Pl
Career Total (Turf)	**3**	**0**	**0**	**2**	**999**

Going (Turf): Sf: 0-2 GS: 0-1 Gd: 0-0 GF: 0-0 Fm: 0-0
Distance: 5f/6f: 0-2 7f-8f: 0-1 9f-13f: 0-0 14f+: 0-0
Track : LH: 0-0 RH: 0-0 Tight: 0-0 Gall: 0-0
Aids: Bl: 0-0 Vi: 0-0 Tstrap: 0-0
Best Rating: 77 8/01 Chep 5f16y soft

Ran well on debut but was disappointing next time, and is best watched until tackling handicap company.

Adiemus

101 **70**

3-y-o b c Green Desert (USA)-Anodyne (Dominion)
J Noseda G Lansbury

Placings:431 **(5670)**
2001: 7^{4}GF, 6^{3}HY, 8^{1}HY

	Starts	1st	2nd	3rd	Win & Pl
Career Total (Turf)	**3**	**1**	**0**	**1**	**3916**

59	11/01	Wind	1m67y	D	HVY	£3122

Total win prize-money £3122

Going (Turf): Sf: 1-2 GS: 0-0 Gd: 0-0 GF: 0-1 Fm: 0-0
Distance: 5f/6f: 0-1 7f-8f: 0-1 **9f-13f: 1-1** 14f+: 0-0
Track : LH: 0-0 **RH: 1-1 Tight: 1-1** Gall: 0-0
Aids: Bl: 0-0 Vi: 0-0 Tstrap: 0-0
Best Rating: 70 6/01 Newb 7f gd-fm

He got off the mark in heavy ground at Windsor on his third start despite veering all over the track.

Adilabad (USA)

109 **114**

4-y-o b h Gulch (USA)-Adaiyka (IRE) (Doyoun)
Sir Michael Stoute H H Aga Khan

Placings:11/5113-513441 **(4263)**
2001: 10^{5}S, 10^{1}GF, 10^{3}GF, 12^{4}GF, 10^{4}GF, 10^{1}GF

	Starts	1st	2nd	3rd	Win & Pl
Career Total (Turf)	**12**	**6**	**0**	**2**	**111324**

111	8/01	Wind	1m2f7y	A	G-F	£23400
114	5/01	Ches	1m2f75y	A	G-F	£14943
118	8/00	Wind	1m2f7y	A	GD	£23400
112	8/00	Gdwd	1m	A	GD	£17269
82	10/99	NmkJ	7f	B	GD	£7873
91	9/99	Sand	7f16y	D	GD	£4104

Total win prize-money £90991

Going (Turf): Sf: 0-1 GS: 0-1 **Gd: 4-5** GF: 2-5 Fm: 0-0
Distance: 5f/6f: 0-0 7f-8f: 3-4 9f-13f: 3-8 14f+: 0-0
Track : LH: 1-1 **RH: 2-6 Tight: 3-3** Gall: 0-1
Aids: Bl: 0-0 Vi: 0-0 Tstrap: 0-0
Best Rating: 114 5/01 Ches 1m2f75y gd-fm

Well beaten on soft ground in the Craven on his return at three, he returned to land a Listed race in August and stepped up on that form in Windsor's Winter Hill Stakes. He was fortunate to win a Listed event at Chester in May, but would have been an unlucky loser, but has been disappointing in Group company until winning a second Winter Hill in August 2001.

Adjawar (IRE)

108 **88**

3-y-o b c Ashkalani (IRE)-Adjriyna (Top Ville)
Sir Michael Stoute H H Aga Khan

Placings:0-0310200 **(4409)**
2001: 6^{0}HY, 8^{3}HY, 11^{1}G, 11^{0}GS, 12^{2}GF, 11^{0}G, 10^{0}GS

	Starts	1st	2nd	3rd	Win & Pl
Career Total (Turf)	**8**	**1**	**1**	**1**	**8849**

79	5/01	Wind	1m3f135yD(0-85)H	GD	£4069

Total win prize-money £4069

Going (Turf): Sf: 0-3 GS: 0-2 **Gd: 1-2** GF: 0-1 Fm: 0-0
Distance: 5f/6f: 0-0 7f-8f: 0-2 **9f-13f: 1-6** 14f+: 0-0
Track : LH: 0-4 RH: 0-2 **Tight: 1-4** Gall: 0-2
Aids: Bl: 0-0 Vi: 0-2 Tstrap: 0-3
Best Rating: 88 6/01 Sals 1m4f gd-fm

He had the arbitrary three runs in maidens on heavy ground and made a successful winning debut in handicap company when stepped up to the extended 11 furlongs at Windsor. Had little chance from his draw at York and ran into an improving sort at Salisbury. He should continue to improve. Stays a mile and a half.

Adjiram (IRE)

91(62) (7)**39**

5-y-o b g Be My Guest (USA)-Adjriyna (Top Ville)
D C O'Brien K Marshall

Placings:1/0-0400 **(4181)**
2001: 7^{0}F, 10^{4}F, 8^{0}G, 12^{0}GF

	Starts	1st	2nd	3rd	Win & Pl
Career Total (Turf)	**5**	**1**	**0**	**0**	**10223**
Career Total (AW)	**1**	**0**	**0**	**0**	

	5/99	Lonc	1m3f	GD	£9688

Total win prize-money £9688

Going (Turf): Sf: 0-0 GS: 0-0 Gd: 0-1 GF: 0-1 Fm: 0-2
Distance: 5f/6f: 0-0 7f-8f: 0-1 9f-13f: 0-4 14f+: 0-0
Track : LH: 0-2 RH: 0-2 Tight: 0-3 Gall: 0-1
Aids: Bl: 0-0 Vi: 0-0 Tstrap: 0-0
Best Rating: 39 5/01 Leic 7f9y firm

Adjudicator (IRE)

(96) (60)**48**

3-y-o br g Barathea (IRE)-Mnaafa (IRE) (Darshaan)
P F I Cole W J Smith And M D Dudley

Placings:3040 **(4874)**
2001: 7^{3}SD, 7^{0}GF, 6^{4}GF, 8^{0}SD

	Starts	1st	2nd	3rd	Win & Pl
Career Total (Turf)	**2**	**0**	**0**	**0**	**378**
Career Total (AW)	**2**	**0**	**0**	**1**	**353**

Going (Turf): Sf: 0-0 GS: 0-0 Gd: 0-0 GF: 0-2 Fm: 0-0
Distance: 5f/6f: 0-1 7f-8f: 0-2 9f-13f: 0-1 14f+: 0-0
Track : LH: 0-3 RH: 0-0 Tight: 0-1 Gall: 0-0
Aids: Bl: 0-0 Vi: 0-0 Tstrap: 0-0
Best Rating: 60 3/01 Sthl 7f stand

Admiral's Guest (IRE)

(83) (20)

9-y-o ch g Be My Guest (USA)-Watership (USA) (Foolish Pleasure (USA))
W Clay Mrs M Robertson

Placings:0/000560/0/**00** **(1016)**
2001: 12^{0}SW, 12^{0}SD

	Starts	1st	2nd	3rd	Win & Pl
Career Total (Turf)	**8**	**0**	**0**	**0**	
Career Total (AW)	**2**	**0**	**0**	**0**	

Going (Turf): Sf: 0-1 GS: 0-0 Gd: 0-2 GF: 0-4 Fm: 0-1
Distance: 5f/6f: 0-1 7f-8f: 0-1 9f-13f: 0-6 14f+: 0-2
Track : LH: 0-3 RH: 0-4 Tight: 0-4 Gall: 0-1
Aids: Bl: 0-0 Vi: 0-2 Tstrap: 0-1
Best Rating: 20 4/01 Sthl 1m4f stand

Admirals Flame (IRE)

93 (50)**58**

10-y-o b g Doulab (USA)-Fan The Flame (Grundy)
C F Wall Mrs C A Wall

Placings:14000420/**060**04061510302/02443100/05040/00001300300/01400/01330-06 **(3221)**
2001: 7^{0}GS, 8^{6}GS

	Starts	1st	2nd	3rd	Win & Pl
Career Total (Turf)	**55**	**7**	**3**	**6**	**32957**
Career Total (AW)	**3**	**0**	**0**	**0**	

58	6/00	Nott	1m54y	G(0-70)H	SFT	£1858
62	6/99	Leic	1m8y	F(0-65)H	G-S	£3057
60	6/98	Wind	1m67y	E(0-70)H	SFT	£3273
80	8/96	Wind	1m67y	C(0-90)H	SFT	£4874
72	7/95	Kemp	1m	D(0-80)H	G-F	£4338
64	6/95	Wind	1m67y	E(0-70)H	G-F	£3806
56	3/94	Leic	5f218y	G	SFT	£2406

Total win prize-money £23616

Going (Turf): Sf: 4-8 GS: 1-11 Gd: 0-16 GF: 2-17 Fm: 0-3
Distance: 5f/6f: 1-2 7f-8f: 1-30 **9f-13f: 5-26** 14f+: 0-0
Track : LH: 1-17 **RH: 4-17 Tight: 3-14** Gall: 0-1
Aids: Bl: 0-0 Vi: 0-0 Tstrap: 0-0
Best Rating: 43 5/01 Brig 7f214y gd-sft

Not as good as he was, he returned to a winning mark when scoring at Nottingham in 2000. He likes cut in the ground.

Admirals Place (IRE)

109(107) (78)**79**

5-y-o ch h Perugino (USA)-Royal Daughter (High Top)
H J Collingridge C G Donovan

Placings:00/3312261205/**122**314205322041-135143100 **(3258)**
2001: 12^{1}SD, 12^{3}SD, 12^{5}SW, 12^{1}GS, 12^{4}S, 12^{3}GF, 12^{1}GF, 12^{0}GF, 12^{0}GF

	Starts	1st	2nd	3rd	Win & Pl
Career Total (Turf)	**21**	**4**	**5**	**3**	**39343**
Career Total (AW)	**15**	**4**	**3**	**3**	**22201**

79	6/01	Newc	1m4f93y	D(0-80)H	G-F	£15015
74	5/01	Kemp	1m4f	C(0-90)H	G-S	£7085
76	1/01	Ling	1m4f	D(0-85)H	STD	£6695
69	12/00	Ling	1m4f	D(0-80)H	STD	£3753
67	4/00	Folk	1m1f149yE(0-70)H		SFT	£3395
57	1/00	Ling	1m2f	F(0-60)	STD	£2383
60	9/99	Bevl	1m1f207yF(0-60)H		SFT	£2355
58	6/99	Ling	1m	E(0-70)H	STD	£2709

Total win prize-money £43392

Going (Turf): Sf: 2-7 GS: 1-2 Gd: 0-6 GF: 1-6 Fm: 0-0
Distance: 5f/6f: 0-3 7f-8f: 1-2 **9f-13f: 7-31** 14f+: 0-0
Track : **LH: 5-25** RH: 3-9 **Tight: 5-18** Gall: 1-10

Aids:	Bl: 0-0 Vi: 0-0 Tstrap: 0-0
Best Rating: 79	6/01 Newc 1m4f93y gd-fm

A useful handicapper, he won twice on Equitrack in the winter of 2000 and transferred that ability to turf with further victories at Kempton and Newcastle. Suited by a decent pace and, although most of his wins have come with cut, he acts on fast ground. Suited by 12 furlongs.

Adobe

106(106) (55)**82**

6-y-o b g Green Desert (USA)-Shamshir (Kris)

W M Brisbourne P R Kirk

Placings:0000/303000210210400533000/10242111133 41211050000-004255352001031000 **(5366)**

2001: 7^0SD, 7^0GF, 8^4GF, 8^2F, 8^5GF, 8^5GF, 8^3GF, 9^5GF, 8^2GF, 8^0G, 8^0GF, 8^1F, 8^0G, 8^3GF, 8^1G, 8^0G, 8^0S, 8^0GS

	Starts	1st	2nd	3rd	Win & Pl
Career Total (Turf)	58	11	6	7	69984
Career Total (AW)	7	1	1	1	3922

82	8/01	Ripn	1m	C(0-100)H	GD	£8580
79	8/01	Thsk	1m	C(0-95)H	FRM	£7085
83	8/00	Hayd	1m30y	C(0-90)H	GD	£6192
78	8/00	Thsk	1m	C(0-95)H	G-F	£6890
71	7/00	Donc	1m	D(0-85)H	G-F	£4290
61	6/00	Gdwd	1m	D(0-85)H	G-F	£4387
60	6/00	Bath	1m5y	E(0-75)H	G-F	£2884
55	6/00	Haml	1m65y	F(0-60)	GD	£2632
53	5/00	Haml	1m65y	E(0-75)H	G-F	£3705
54	3/00	Wolv	7f	F(0-60)H	STD	£2383
55	7/99	Nott	1m54y	E(0-70)H	G-F	£3792
54	6/99	Bath	1m5y	F(0-65)H	GD	£2528

Total win prize-money £55351

Going (Turf):	Sf: 0-11 GS: 0-3 Gd: 4-18 **GF: 6-21** Fm: 1-5
Distance:	5f/6f: 0-3 7f-8f: 6-27 9f-13f: 6-35 14f+: 0-0
Track :	**LH: 8-29** RH: 4-25 **Tight: 8-27** Gall: 1-4
Aids:	Bl: 0-0 Vi: 0-0 **Tstrap: 2-21**
Best Rating: 82	8/01 Ripn 1m good

Like most of his stablemates, he was in fantastic form in 2000, winning no fewer than eight times. He had been running well this term before scoring at Thirsk in August and added a victory at Ripon later the same month, although he has been very disappointing since. He is suited by a mile on fast ground and a decent pace.

Adorara (USA)

106 **77+**

3-y-o b f Silver Hawk (USA)-Adored Slew (USA) (Seattle Slew (USA))

Saeed Bin Suroor Godolphin

Placings:1 **(2934)**

2001: 10^1GF

	Starts	1st	2nd	3rd	Win & Pl
Career Total (Turf)	1	1	0	0	4427

77	7/01	Kemp	1m2f	D	G-F	£4426

Total win prize-money £4427

Going (Turf):	Sf: 0-0 GS: 0-0 Gd: 0-0 **GF: 1-1** Fm: 0-0
Distance:	5f/6f: 0-0 7f-8f: 0-0 **9f-13f: 1-1** 14f+: 0-0
Track :	LH: 0-0 **RH: 1-1** Tight: 0-0 **Gall: 1-1**
Aids:	Bl: 0-0 Vi: 0-0 Tstrap: 0-0
Best Rating: 77	7/01 Kemp 1m2f gd-fm

Late developing filly, out of a 12-furlong Group Two winner. Made all to win fillies' maiden over ten furlongs at Kempton in July.

Adriana

97(85) (18)**31**

4-y-o b f Tragic Role (USA)-Beatle Song (Song)

C E Brittain R A Pledger

Placings:000010140-000060200 **(5469)**

2001: 9^0SW, 8^0SD, 11^0GF, 10^0F, 9^6GF, 10^0GF, 11^2GF, 11^0S, 9^0S

	Starts	1st	2nd	3rd	Win & Pl
Career Total (Turf)	15	2	1	0	5300
Career Total (AW)	3	0	0	0	

46	7/00	Brig	1m1f209yF(0-60)H		FRM	£2383
46	6/00	Ling	1m3f106yF(0-60)H		FRM	£2362

Total win prize-money £4747

Going (Turf):	Sf: 0-3 GS: 0-0 Gd: 0-2 GF: 0-7 **Fm: 2-3**
Distance:	5f/6f: 0-1 7f-8f: 0-2 **9f-13f: 2-15** 14f+: 0-0
Track :	**LH: 2-14** RH: 0-2 **Tight: 1-11** Gall: 0-0
Aids:	Bl: 0-0 Vi: 0-0 Tstrap: 0-0
Best Rating: 36	6/01 Ling 1m2f firm

Adrock Boy

100 **66**

2-y-o b g Rock City-Riva La Belle (Ron's Victory (USA))

M W Easterby Anne Dawson & David Dudley

Placings:2403 **(3184)**

2001: 5^2S, 5^4S, 5^0GF, 5^3GS

	Starts	1st	2nd	3rd	Win & Pl
Career Total (Turf)	4	0	1	1	1446

Going (Turf):	**Sf: 0-2 GS: 0-1 Gd: 0-0 GF: 0-1 Fm: 0-0**
Distance:	5f/6f: 0-4 7f-8f: 0-0 9f-13f: 0-0 14f+: 0-0
Track :	LH: 0-0 RH: 0-0 Tight: 0-0 Gall: 0-0
Aids:	Bl: 0-0 Vi: 0-0 Tstrap: 0-0
Best Rating: 66	7/01 Leic 5f218y gd-sft

Ads-Sixty-Five

(57) **11**

4-y-o b g Casteddu-Come On Lucy (Reesh)

D J Wintle A D Bennett

Placings:000 **(4070)**

2001: 11^0GF, 10^0S, 9^0SD

	Starts	1st	2nd	3rd	Win & Pl
Career Total (Turf)	2	0	0	0	
Career Total (AW)	1	0	0	0	

Going (Turf):	**Sf: 0-1 GS: 0-0 Gd: 0-0 GF: 0-1 Fm: 0-0**
Distance:	5f/6f: 0-0 7f-8f: 0-0 9f-13f: 0-3 14f+: 0-0
Track :	LH: 0-2 RH: 0-0 Tight: 0-2 Gall: 0-0
Aids:	Bl: 0-0 Vi: 0-0 Tstrap: 0-0
Best Rating: 11	8/01 Chep 1m2f36y soft

Adstone Blaze

(85) (55)**55**

2-y-o ch f Selkirk (USA)-Galine (Most Welcome)

J G Smyth-Osbourne R Smith, M White, M Barlow, C James

Placings:00004 **(5197)**

2001: 6^0GF, 6^0GF, 5^0G, 8^0GF, 8^4SD

	Starts	1st	2nd	3rd	Win & Pl
Career Total (Turf)	4	0	0	0	
Career Total (AW)	1	0	0	0	0

Going (Turf):	**Sf: 0-0 GS: 0-0 Gd: 0-1 GF: 0-3 Fm: 0-0**
Distance:	5f/6f: 0-3 7f-8f: 0-0 9f-13f: 0-2 14f+: 0-0
Track :	LH: 0-2 RH: 0-0 Tight: 0-1 Gall: 0-0
Aids:	Bl: 0-0 Vi: 0-0 Tstrap: 0-0
Best Rating: 55	10/01 Wolv 1m100y stand

Advance Party (IRE)

101 **98**

2-y-o b c Mujadil (USA)-Battle Queen (Kind Of Hush)

J Noseda Mrs A M Burns

Placings:11043 **(5493)**

2001: 6^1GF, 6^1GS, 6^0G, 7^4GS, 7^3HY

	Starts	1st	2nd	3rd	Win & Pl
Career Total (Turf)	5	2	0	1	35483

95	9/01	Donc	6f	B	G-S	£27000
79	8/01	Wind	6f	E	G-F	£3932

Total win prize-money £30933

Going (Turf):	Sf: 0-1 **GS: 1-2** Gd: 0-1 **GF: 1-1** Fm: 0-0
Distance:	**5f/6f: 2-3** 7f-8f: 0-2 9f-13f: 0-0 14f+: 0-0
Track :	LH: 0-0 RH: 0-0 Tight: 0-0 Gall: 0-0
Aids:	Bl: 0-0 Vi: 0-0 Tstrap: 0-0
Best Rating: 98	10/01 Newb 7f heavy

Ran out a comfortable winner on his Windsor debut despite showing signs of inexperience once in front. Came from almost last to first to take the St Leger Yearling Sales consolation race, but was very disappointing at Redcar next time. Looked a hard ride when staying on late over seven in a decent event at Newmarket on his fourth start and did not get home in the Horris Hill run in a bog. Sold to race in Norway.

Adweb

105 **78**

3-y-o b f Muhtarram (USA)-What A Present (Pharly (FR))

J Cullinan Adweb Ltd

Placings:004100-12042000 **(5462)**

2001: 5^1GF, 5^2GF, 5^0GF, 5^4G, 6^2GF, 6^0G, 5^0GS, 5^0G

	Starts	1st	2nd	3rd	Win & Pl
Career Total (Turf)	14	2	2	0	13096

71	7/01	Sand	5f6y	D(0-80)H	G-F	£5369
67	9/00	Sand	5f6y	D(0-85)	SFT	£4660

Total win prize-money £10030

Going (Turf):	**Sf: 1-3** GS: 0-1 Gd: 0-4 **GF: 1-6** Fm: 0-0
Distance:	**5f/6f: 2-13** 7f-8f: 0-1 9f-13f: 0-0 14f+: 0-0
Track :	LH: 0-1 RH: 0-1 Tight: 0-0 Gall: 0-2
Aids:	Bl: 0-0 Vi: 0-0 Tstrap: 0-0
Best Rating: 78	9/01 Kemp 6f gd-fm

Useful sprint handicapper. Was making her first appearance since October when winning well over five furlongs at Sandown in July. Nearly followed up at the same track before being hampered at Newbury. Went close at Kempton over six furlongs. Suited by five to six furlongs on soft and good to firm.

Aegean Daisy

97 **60**

2-y-o ch f Bal Harbour-Dizzydaisy (Sharpo)

K T Ivory (R Hannon 23/7) Theobalds Stud

Placings:540260405 **(5458)**

2001: 5^5GF, 6^4GF, 6^0GF, 6^2GF, 5^6GF, 6^0G, 6^4GF, 5^0S, 5^5G

	Starts	1st	2nd	3rd	Win & Pl
Career Total (Turf)	9	0	1	0	1114

Going (Turf):	**Sf: 0-1 GS: 0-0 Gd: 0-2 GF: 0-6 Fm: 0-0**
Distance:	5f/6f: 0-6 7f-8f: 0-3 9f-13f: 0-0 14f+: 0-0
Track :	LH: 0-3 RH: 0-0 Tight: 0-1 Gall: 0-1
Aids:	Bl: 0-1 Vi: 0-0 Tstrap: 0-0
Best Rating: 71	8/01 Epsm 6f gd-fm

Showed ability in three runs for Richard Hannon before being switched to Ken Ivory. Has looked a bit temperamental under pressure. Best efforts at around six furlongs at present.

Aegean Dream (IRE)

109 **90**

5-y-o b m Royal Academy (USA)-L'Ideale (USA) (Alysheba (USA))

R Hannon Theobalds Stud

Placings:02225105/23443311040-663631261 (5686)
2001: 12^{6}GF, 10^{6}GF, 10^{3}GF, 12^{6}GF, 11^{3}GF, 10^{1}G, 10^{2}G, 10^{6}GF, 10^{1}S

	Starts	1st	2nd	3rd	Win & Pl
Career Total (Turf)	28	5	5	5	52877

71	11/01	Donc	1m2f60y	C	SFT	£7052
90	8/01	Epsm	1m2f18y	C(0-90)H	GD	£7150
86	8/00	Gdwd	1m1f	C(0-90)H	G-F	£11180
80	7/00	Newb	1m1f	C(0-90)H	G-F	£6760
81	9/99	Epsm	1m114y	D	GD	£3777

Total win prize-money £35921

Going (Turf): Sf: 1-2 GS: 0-3 **Gd: 2-7 GF: 2-16** Fm: 0-0
Distance: 5f/6f: 0-0 7f-8f: 0-0 **9f-13f: 5-28** 14f+: 0-0
Track : **LH: 4-13** RH: 1-10 **Tight: 3-10** Gall: 2-13
Aids: Bl: 0-0 Vi: 0-0 Tstrap: 0-0
Best Rating: 90 9/01 Newb 1m2f6y gd-fm

She likes to come from behind off a strong pace and can look good when things go her way, as when winning at Epsom and Doncaster. Suited by ten furlongs and fast ground.

Aegean Flower

70 **45**

4-y-o b g Robellino (USA)-Bercheba (Bellypha)
R M Flower K Panos

Placings:0400003403-000 (3840)
2001: 7^{0}GS, 8^{0}GF, 7^{0}G

	Starts	1st	2nd	3rd	Win & Pl
Career Total (Turf)	13	0	0	2	1312

Going (Turf): Sf: 0-0 GS: 0-2 Gd: 0-2 GF: 0-7 Fm: 0-2
Distance: 5f/6f: 0-0 7f-8f: 0-8 9f-13f: 0-5 14f+: 0-0
Track : LH: 0-2 RH: 0-2 Tight: 0-3 Gall: 0-0
Aids: Bl: 0-10 Vi: 0-0 Tstrap: 0-0
Best Rating: 90 9/01 Newb 1m2f6y gd-fm

Aegean Glory

5-y-o b m Shareef Dancer (USA)-Sayulita (Habitat)
J G M O'Shea Gary Roberts

Placings:0/0502033340/0 (3741)
2001: 10^{0}S

	Starts	1st	2nd	3rd	Win & Pl
Career Total (Turf)	10	0	1	2	1811
Career Total (AW)	2	0	0	1	289

Going (Turf): Sf: 0-2 GS: 0-0 Gd: 0-4 GF: 0-2 Fm: 0-2
Distance: 5f/6f: 0-0 7f-8f: 0-4 9f-13f: 0-8 14f+: 0-0
Track : LH: 0-9 RH: 0-0 Tight: 0-4 Gall: 0-1
Aids: Bl: 0-0 Vi: 0-0 Tstrap: 0-1

Aegean Heights

95 **75?**

3-y-o b c Ezzoud (IRE)-Perdicula (IRE) (Persian Heights)
R Hannon Theobalds Stud

Placings:366 (4522)
2001: 10^{3}GF, 10^{6}S, 11^{6}GF

	Starts	1st	2nd	3rd	Win & Pl
Career Total (Turf)	3	0	0	1	651

Going (Turf): Sf: 0-1 GS: 0-0 Gd: 0-0 GF: 0-2 Fm: 0-0
Distance: 5f/6f: 0-0 7f-8f: 0-0 9f-13f: 0-3 14f+: 0-0
Track : LH: 0-3 RH: 0-0 Tight: 0-3 Gall: 0-0
Aids: Bl: 0-0 Vi: 0-0 Tstrap: 0-0
Best Rating: 75 9/01 Ling 1m3f106y gd-fm

Aegean Sunrise

99(93) (60)**48**

3-y-o ch g Deploy-Dizzydaisy (Sharpo)
R M Flower K Panos

Placings:6-001000504000 (4523)
2001: 8^{0}SD, 8^{0}SD, 12^{1}SD, 14^{0}GF, 12^{0}GF, 12^{0}GF, 11^{5}G, 16^{0}SD, 14^{4}F, 12^{0}GF, 11^{0}GF, 16^{0}GF

	Starts	1st	2nd	3rd	Win & Pl
Career Total (Turf)	8	0	0	0	0
Career Total (AW)	5	1	0	0	2933

60	2/01	Ling	1m4f	D	STD	£2933

Total win prize-money £2933

Going (Turf): **Sf: 0-0 GS: 0-0 Gd: 0-1 GF: 0-6 Fm: 0-1**
Distance: 5f/6f: 0-0 7f-8f: 0-2 **9f-13f: 1-7** 14f+: 0-4
Track : **LH: 1-9** RH: 0-4 **Tight: 1-7** Gall: 0-1
Aids: Bl: 0-3 Vi: 0-0 Tstrap: 0-0
Best Rating: 60 2/01 Ling 1m4f stand

Aegean Wind

78 **53**

4-y-o b g Dolphin Street (FR)-Perdicula (IRE) (Persian Heights)
D R C Elsworth Theobalds Stud

Placings:0/5000-00 (2250)
2001: 12^{0}S, 16^{0}GF

	Starts	1st	2nd	3rd	Win & Pl
Career Total (Turf)	7	0	0	0	0

Going (Turf): **Sf: 0-2 GS: 0-0 Gd: 0-0 GF: 0-5 Fm: 0-0**
Distance: 5f/6f: 0-0 7f-8f: 0-1 9f-13f: 0-3 14f+: 0-3
Track : LH: 0-2 RH: 0-4 Tight: 0-4 Gall: 0-0
Aids: Bl: 0-0 Vi: 0-0 Tstrap: 0-0
Best Rating: 17 5/01 Sals 1m4f soft

Afaan (IRE)

109(112) (83)**91**

8-y-o ch h Cadeaux Genereux-Rawaabe (USA) (Nureyev (USA))
R F Marvin R A B Saville

Placings:5222302310200001102 1/003112502/6000505 504330/0640204000500051-0034360521305 5000 (5105)
2001: 5^{0}SD, 6^{0}SD, 5^{3}SD, 5^{4}SD, 5^{3}GS, 5^{6}GF, 5^{0}GS, 5^{5}GF, 5^{2}GF, 5^{1}GF, 6^{3}GS, 5^{0}G, 5^{5}G, 5^{5}GF, 5^{0}GF, 5^{0}S, 5^{0}GS

	Starts	1st	2nd	3rd	Win & Pl
Career Total (Turf)	54	6	6	4	61710
Career Total (AW)	21	2	4	4	12370

88	8/01	Newb	5f34y	C(0-95)H	G-F	£7247
83	12/00	Wolv	5f	D(0-85)H	STD	£3731
91	7/98	NmkJ	5f	C(0-100)H	GD	£6004
79	7/98	Catt	5f	D(0-75)H	FRM	£3548
72	12/97	Sthl	5f	G(0-85)H	STD	£1998
79	11/97	Rdcr	5f	D(0-75)	GD	£3350
67	10/97	Pont	5f	D(0-80)H	G-S	£4207
64	5/97	Rdcr	6f	G(0-60)H	G-F	£2440

Total win prize-money £32529

Going (Turf): Sf: 0-5 GS: 1-13 **Gd: 2-17 GF: 2-16** Fm: 1-3
Distance: **5f/6f: 8-67** 7f-8f: 0-8 9f-13f: 0-0 14f+: 0-0
Track : **LH: 2-17** RH: 0-1 **Tight: 1-11** Gall: 0-1
Aids: **Bl: 3-34** Vi: 2-8 Tstrap: 0-0
Best Rating: 97 7/01 Gdwd 5f gd-fm

Exceptionally speedy, he is best at the minimum trip on turf or sand, but was proving very difficult to place until striking form in early August, finishing second at 100/1 in a Group Three at Goodwood before winning at Newbury. His best form on turf has been on good ground and he usually blazes a trail.

Afeef (USA)

88 **72**

2-y-o br c Dayjur (USA)-Jah (USA) (Relaunch (USA))
E A L Dunlop Hamdan Al Maktoum

Placings:05 (5561)
2001: 8^{0}GS, 7^{5}S

	Starts	1st	2nd	3rd	Win & Pl
Career Total (Turf)	2	0	0	0	0

Going (Turf): **Sf: 0-1 GS: 0-1 Gd: 0-0 GF: 0-0 Fm: 0-0**
Distance: 5f/6f: 0-0 7f-8f: 0-2 9f-13f: 0-0 14f+: 0-0
Track : LH: 0-0 RH: 0-0 Tight: 0-0 Gall: 0-0
Aids: Bl: 0-0 Vi: 0-0 Tstrap: 0-2
Best Rating: 72 10/01 NmkR 1m gd-sft

Affaire D'Amour

87 **58**

2-y-o ch f Hernando (FR)-Entente Cordiale (USA) (Affirmed (USA))
Sir Mark Prescott Miss K Rausing

Placings:030 (5627)
2001: 7^{0}GS, 7^{3}S, 7^{0}G

	Starts	1st	2nd	3rd	Win & Pl
Career Total (Turf)	3	0	0	1	444

Going (Turf): **Sf: 0-1 GS: 0-1 Gd: 0-1 GF: 0-0 Fm: 0-0**
Distance: 5f/6f: 0-0 7f-8f: 0-3 9f-13f: 0-0 14f+: 0-0
Track : LH: 0-1 RH: 0-0 Tight: 0-1 Gall: 0-0
Aids: Bl: 0-0 Vi: 0-0 Tstrap: 0-0
Best Rating: 58 10/01 Leic 7f9y gd-sft

Affaire Royale (IRE)

104 **100**

3-y-o b f Royal Academy (USA)-Fleet Amour (USA) (Afleet (CAN))
J R Fanshawe Mrs Denis Haynes

Placings:1004 (4487)
2001: 7^{1}GF, 8^{0}G, 7^{0}GF, 7^{4}S

	Starts	1st	2nd	3rd	Win & Pl
Career Total (Turf)	4	1	0	0	4086

86	6/01	Yarm	7f3y	D	G-F	£3558

Total win prize-money £3559

Going (Turf): Sf: 0-1 GS: 0-0 Gd: 0-1 **GF: 1-2** Fm: 0-0
Distance: 5f/6f: 0-0 **7f-8f: 1-4** 9f-13f: 0-0 14f+: 0-0
Track : LH: 0-0 RH: 0-1 Tight: 0-0 Gall: 0-0
Aids: Bl: 0-0 Vi: 0-0 Tstrap: 0-0
Best Rating: 100 7/01 NmkJ 1m good

Looked a promising sort when bolting up on her Yarmouth debut, but was well beaten in the Group Two Falmouth Stakes at Newmarket next time. Acts on fast ground.

Affarati

103(81) (24)**58d**

3-y-o b g Emarati (USA)-Affairiste (IRE) (Simply Great (FR))
J L Eyre David Scott

Placings:216050-3050506004000 (5292)
2001: 7^{3}S, 7^{0}GS, 8^{5}S, 8^{0}G, 8^{5}G, 9^{0}GF, 10^{6}GF, 7^{0}G, 8^{0}GS, 7^{4}F, 8^{0}GS, 6^{0}SD, 7^{0}S

	Starts	1st	2nd	3rd	Win & Pl
Career Total (Turf)	18	1	1	1	8088
Career Total (AW)	1	0	0	0	

70	5/00	Pont	6f	C	GD	£5974

Total win prize-money £5974

Going (Turf): Sf: 0-4 GS: 0-4 **Gd: 1-6** GF: 0-3 Fm: 0-1
Distance: **5f/6f: 1-5** 7f-8f: 0-11 9f-13f: 0-3 14f+: 0-0
Track : **LH: 1-8** RH: 0-4 Tight: 0-4 Gall: 0-1
Aids: Bl: 0-0 Vi: 0-0 Tstrap: 0-0

Best Rating: 72 3/01 Donc 7f soft

Made a good start as a juvenile but failed to progress. Seems to appreciate cut in the ground. Started well again in 2001.

Affray (USA)

99 **83**

2-y-o b c Affirmed (USA)-Wee Miss Bee (USA) (Shelter Half (USA))

M Johnston Abdullah Saeed Belhab

Placings:241 **(4837)**

2001: 8^2G, 8^4G, 8^1G

	Starts	1st	2nd	3rd	Win & Pl
Career Total (Turf)	3	1	1	0	5537

83 9/01 Nott 1m54y D GD £3948

Total win prize-money £3949

Going (Turf): Sf: 0-0 GS: 0-0 **Gd: 1-3** GF: 0-0 Fm: 0-0
Distance: 5f/6f: 0-0 7f-8f: 0-1 **9f-13f: 1-2** 14f+: 0-0
Track : **LH: 1-1** RH: 0-1 Tight: 0-1 Gall: 0-0
Aids: Bl: 0-0 Vi: 0-0 Tstrap: 0-0
Best Rating: 83 9/01 Nott 1m54y good

A $160,000 yearling, won the first race of his career over a mile on good ground at Nottingham in September. He is bred to get further next season.

Afkaar (USA)

105 **50+**

3-y-o b f Unbridled (USA)-Barakat (Bustino)

A C Stewart Hamdan Al Maktoum

Placings:2 **(5041)**

2001: 10^2G

	Starts	1st	2nd	3rd	Win & Pl
Career Total (Turf)	1	0	1	0	864

Going (Turf): Sf: 0-0 GS: 0-0 Gd: 0-1 GF: 0-0 Fm: 0-0
Distance: 5f/6f: 0-0 7f-8f: 0-0 9f-13f: 0-1 14f+: 0-0
Track : LH: 0-1 RH: 0-0 Tight: 0-1 Gall: 0-0
Aids: Bl: 0-0 Vi: 0-0 Tstrap: 0-0
Best Rating: 50 10/01 Bath 1m2f46y good

Africa (IRE)

90(97) (44)**34**

4-y-o b f Namaqualand (USA)-Tannerrun (IRE) (Runnett)

A Streeter Malt 'N' Hops

Placings:0U0514260330/1604160400-51600 **(3454)**

2001: 12^5SD, 14^1SD, 16^6SD, 16^0GF, 14^0GF

	Starts	1st	2nd	3rd	Win & Pl
Career Total (Turf)	20	2	1	2	7000
Career Total (AW)	7	2	0	0	4151

35 2/01 Wolv 1m6f166yG STD £1890
47 7/00 Bevl 7f100y E G-F £2852
62 5/00 Sthl 7f F(0-65)H STD £2261
57 7/99 Catt 7f G GD £2038

Total win prize-money £9042

Going (Turf): Sf: 0-1 GS: 0-3 **Gd: 1-5 GF: 1-7** Fm: 0-4
Distance: 5f/6f: 0 4 **7f-8f: 3-17** 9f-13f: 0-2 14f+: 1-4
Track : **LH: 3-13** RH: 1-8 **Tight: 2-9** Gall: 0-1
Aids: Bl: 0-1 Vi: 0-0 Tstrap: 0-0
Best Rating: 39 2/01 Wolv 2m46y stand

African Dawn

(101) (56+)**57**

3-y-o b c Spectrum (IRE)-Lamu Lady (IRE) (Lomond (USA))

J H M Gosden David J Simpson

Placings:36 **(5631)**

2001: 10^3F, 10^6G,

	Starts	1st	2nd	3rd	Win & Pl
Career Total (Turf)	2	0	0	1	603

Going (Turf): Sf: 0-0 GS: 0-0 Gd: 0-1 GF: 0-0 Fm: 0-1
Distance: 5f/6f: 0-0 7f-8f: 0-0 9f-13f: 0-2 14f+: 0-0
Track : LH: 0-2 RH: 0-0 Tight: 0-1 Gall: 0-0
Aids: Bl: 0-0 Vi: 0-0 Tstrap: 0-0
Best Rating: 57 9/01 Pont 1m2f6y firm

Lightly-raced, has shown some ability on turf, but got off the mark with a clear-cut win on the Lingfield Polytrack in November.

African Sahara (USA)

88 **78**

2-y-o br c El Gran Senor (USA)-Able Money (USA) (Distinctive (USA))

E A L Dunlop Abdulla Buhaleeba

Placings:464 **(4961)**

2001: 6^4GS, 7^6GF, 6^4S

	Starts	1st	2nd	3rd	Win & Pl
Career Total (Turf)	3	0	0	0	623

Going (Turf): Sf: 0-1 GS: 0-1 Gd: 0-0 GF: 0-1 Fm: 0-0
Distance: 5f/6f: 0-2 7f-8f: 0-1 9f-13f: 0-0 14f+: 0-0
Track : LH: 0-1 RH: 0-0 Tight: 0-0 Gall: 0-0
Aids: Bl: 0-0 Vi: 0-0 Tstrap: 0-3
Best Rating: 78 9/01 Leic 7f9y gd-fm

Afterjacko (IRE)

85 **99**

5-y-o ch g Seattle Dancer (USA)-Shilka (Soviet Star (USA))

D R C Elsworth Mcdowell Racing

Placings:00153/5120056421-0 **(5600)**

2001: 16^0GS

	Starts	1st	2nd	3rd	Win & Pl
Career Total (Turf)	16	3	2	1	51055

99 9/00 Newb 1m5f61y C(0-100)H G-F £18443
85 5/00 Sals 1m6f15y C(0-90)H G-F £7572
84 9/99 Bath 1m3f144yD G-F £3974

Total win prize-money £29991

Going (Turf): Sf: 0-0 GS: 0-5 Gd: 0-1 **GF: 3-8** Fm: 0-2
Distance: 5f/6f: 0-0 7f-8f: 0-0 9f-13f: 1-7 **14f+: 2-9**
Track : **LH: 2-6** RH: 1-10 **Tight: 2-3** Gall: 1-10
Aids: Bl: 0-0 Vi: 0-0 Tstrap: 0-0
Best Rating: 63 11/01 NmkR 2m gd-sft

#F#He gained reward for some good efforts when landing Newbury's Autumn Cup on his final start in 2000. Only one run this season.

Agent Mulder

94(75) (55)**60d**

7-y-o b g Kylian (USA)-Precious Caroline (IRE) (The Noble Player (USA))

P D Cundell P D Cundell

Placings:0/50214/032400110/51461000/23302-000 **(5497)**

2001: 6^0G, 5^0SD, 5^0HY

	Starts	1st	2nd	3rd	Win & Pl
Career Total (Turf)	27	5	4	3	26078
Career Total (AW)	4	0	0	0	0

77 6/99 Sals 6f C(0-90)H GD £7522
70 4/99 Nott 6f15y E(0-70)H SFT £3150
58 10/98 Nott 6f15y F(0-60) SFT £2889
62 10/98 Nott 6f15y F(0-60) SFT £2826
61 6/97 Wind 1m67y E(0-70)H G-F £3078

Total win prize-money £19467

Going (Turf): Sf: 3-9 GS: 0-8 Gd: 1-6 GF: 1-4 Fm: 0-0
Distance: 5f/6f: 1-9 **7f-8f: 3-16** 9f-13f: 1-6 14f+: 0-0
Track : LH: 0-9 **RH: 1-4 Tight: 1-3** Gall: 0-1
Aids: **Bl: 4-19** Vi: 0-0 Tstrap: 0-0
Best Rating: 36 5/01 Donc 6f good

Lightly-raced of late, he has a fine winning record at Nottingham. Six furlongs and cut in the ground seem to suit.

Agile Dancer (IRE)

(86) (47)**49**

3-y-o ch f Eagle Eyed (USA)-Be Nimble (Wattlefield)

N A Graham Second Millennium Racing

Placings:005045-0 **(0111)**

2001: 8^0SD

	Starts	1st	2nd	3rd	Win & Pl
Career Total (Turf)	4	0	0	0	0
Career Total (AW)	3	0	0	0	0

Going (Turf): Sf: 0-1 GS: 0-0 Gd: 0-0 GF: 0-2 Fm: 0-1
Distance: 5f/6f: 0-2 7f-8f: 0-5 9f-13f: 0-0 14f+: 0-0
Track : LH: 0-4 RH: 0-0 Tight: 0-3 Gall: 0-0
Aids: Bl: 0-1 Vi: 0-0 Tstrap: 0-0
Best Rating: 10 1/01 Ling 1m stand

Agitando (IRE)

103 **69**

5-y-o b g Tenby-Crown Rose (Dara Monarch)

R Charlton W Hungerford, Bromilow, Keane

Placings:0610226/03000005 **(5463)**

2001: 10^0GF, 12^3GF, 11^0GS, 12^0GF, 10^0G, 8^0G, 9^0S, 11^5G

	Starts	1st	2nd	3rd	Win & Pl
Career Total (Turf)	15	1	2	1	6819

81 6/99 Gdwd 1m1f192yE G-F £3926

Total win prize-money £3927

Going (Turf): Sf: 0-3 GS: 0-1 Gd: 0-4 **GF: 1-6** Fm: 0-1
Distance: 5f/6f: 0-0 7f-8f: 0-2 **9f-13f: 1-13** 14f+: 0-0
Track : LH: 0-5 **RH: 1-9 Tight: 1-5** Gall: 0-5
Aids: Bl: 0-0 Vi: 0-2 Tstrap: 0-0
Best Rating: 86 6/01 Gdwd 1m4f gd-fm

He did not race at two, but ran some decent races at three in 1999 including winning a Goodwood maiden. He missed the whole of 2000 and was racing for the first time in 20 months when reappearing at Kempton in May. He ran very well at Goodwood next time but has been disappointing since. He stays 12 furlongs.

Aglow

95 **89**

2-y-o b f Spinning World (USA)-Flame Valley (USA) (Gulch (USA))

Sir Michael Stoute Cheveley Park Stud

Placings:214 **(5609)**

2001: 7^2GF, 8^1GF, 8^4GS

	Starts	1st	2nd	3rd	Win & Pl
Career Total (Turf)	3	1	1	0	6446

76 9/01 Leic 1m9y D G-F £3926

Total win prize-money £3926

Going (Turf): Sf: 0-0 GS: 0-1 Gd: 0-0 **GF: 1-2** Fm: 0-0
Distance: 5f/6f: 0-0 7f-8f: 0-2 **9f-13f: 1-1** 14f+: 0-0
Track : LH: 0-0 RH: 0-0 Tight: 0-0 Gall: 0-0
Aids: Bl: 0-0 Vi: 0-0 Tstrap: 0-0
Best Rating: 89 11/01 NmkR 1m gd-sft

Out of a ten-furlong winner who scored at Listed level and was placed in Group Twos, benefited from her debut to score comfortably at Leicester. May have found the easy ground against her in a back-end Listed race.

Agnes For Ransom (USA)

98 **62**

3-y-o b/br f Red Ransom (USA)-Golden Rhyme (Dom Racine (FR))

J L Dunlop Mrs Maria Mai Goransson

Placings:0-250000500 **(5532)**

2001: 8^{2}GS, 9^{0}GF, 10^{0}G, 11^{0}GF, 11^{0}GF, 11^{5}G, 9^{0}HY, 9^{0}HY

	Starts	1st	2nd	3rd	Win & Pl
Career Total (Turf)	10	0	1	0	1060

Going (Turf): Sf: 0-3 GS: 0-1 Gd: 0-2 GF: 0-4 Fm: 0-0
Distance: 5f/6f: 0-1 7f-8f: 0-0 9f-13f: 0-9 14f+: 0-0
Track : LH: 0-6 RH: 0-3 Tight: 0-5 Gall: 0-0
Aids: Bl: 0-3 Vi: 0-0 Tstrap: 0-0
Best Rating: 71 4/01 Wind 1m67y gd-sft

Ago

98 **67**

3-y-o ch f Rudimentary (USA)-Amidst (Midyan (USA))

R F Johnson Houghton Mrs P Robeson

Placings:0-0001 **(3424)**

2001: 7^{0}GF, 8^{0}GF, 8^{0}GF, 8^{1}GF

	Starts	1st	2nd	3rd	Win & Pl
Career Total (Turf)	5	1	0	0	3528
67 7/01 Sals 1m E(0-70)H	G-F	£3528			

Total win prize-money £3528

Going (Turf): Sf: 0-0 GS: 0-0 Gd: 0-0 **GF: 1-5** Fm: 0-0
Distance: 5f/6f: 0-1 **7f-8f: 1-4** 9f-13f: 0-0 14f+: 0-0
Track : LH: 0-0 RH: 0-2 Tight: 0-0 Gall: 0-0
Aids: Bl: 0-0 Vi: 0-0 Tstrap: 0-0
Best Rating: 67 7/01 Sals 1m gd-fm

Sprung a surprise in a weak handicap at Salisbury in July, and could have improvement in her.

Agostini

92 **62**

2-y-o b g Octagonal (NZ)-Majestic Image (Niniski (USA))

T D Easterby M J Dawson

Placings:0460 **(5229)**

2001: 6^{0}G, 8^{4}GF, 5^{6}GF, 7^{0}S

	Starts	1st	2nd	3rd	Win & Pl
Career Total (Turf)	4	0	0	0	341

Going (Turf): Sf: 0-1 GS: 0-0 Gd: 0-1 GF: 0-2 Fm: 0-0
Distance: 5f/6f: 0-1 7f-8f: 0-3 9f-13f: 0-0 14f+: 0-0
Track : LH: 0-4 RH: 0-0 Tight: 0-2 Gall: 0-2
Aids: Bl: 0-0 Vi: 0-0 Tstrap: 0-0
Best Rating: 62 9/01 Thsk 1m gd-fm

Agrippina

104 **78**

4-y-o b f Timeless Times (USA)-Boadicea's Chariot (Commanche Run)

A Bailey Mrs Fiona Williams

Placings:211/00-0556 **(5694)**

2001: 7^{0}G, 7^{5}HY, 8^{5}GS, 6^{6}S

	Starts	1st	2nd	3rd	Win & Pl
Career Total (Turf)	9	2	1	0	17699
95 10/99 NmkJ 7f A	SFT	£11363			
77 9/99 Ayr 7f D	G-S	£4588			

Total win prize-money £15951

Going (Turf): Sf: 1-3 GS: 1-2 Gd: 0-2 GF: 0-2 Fm: 0-0
Distance: 5f/6f: 0-2 **7f-8f: 2-6** 9f-13f: 0-1 14f+: 0-0
Track : **LH: 1-2** RH: 0-0 Tight: 0-0 Gall: 0-1
Aids: Bl: 0-0 Vi: 0-0 Tstrap: 0-0
Best Rating: 87 11/01 Donc 6f soft

A Listed winner at two in 1999, she made no impression in either the 1000 Guineas or the Musidora in the spring of 2000. Has had her problems and yet to recapture her two-year-old form. Best with give.

Aguila Loco (IRE)

(86) (56)**60**

2-y-o ch g Eagle Eyed (USA)-Go Likecrazy (Dowsing (USA))

E J Alston The Steady Eddie Partnership

Placings:03044034 **(4041)**

2001: 5^{0}GS, 5^{3}GS, 5^{0}GF, 5^{4}G, 5^{4}G, 6^{0}GF, 5^{3}GS, 5^{4}HY

	Starts	1st	2nd	3rd	Win & Pl
Career Total (Turf)	8	0	0	2	1152

Going (Turf): Sf: 0-1 GS: 0-3 Gd: 0-2 GF: 0-2 Fm: 0-0
Distance: 5f/6f: 0-8 7f-8f: 0-0 9f-13f: 0-0 14f+: 0-0
Track : LH: 0-2 RH: 0-0 Tight: 0-1 Gall: 0-0
Aids: Bl: 0-1 Vi: 0-0 Tstrap: 0-0
Best Rating: 60 8/01 Hayd 5f gd-sft

A speedy type. Still a maiden. Ran too keenly in blinkers at Haydock in August.

Ahraar (USA)

109 **102**

3-y-o b c Gulch (USA)-Saffaanh (USA) (Shareef Dancer (USA))

M P Tregoning Hamdan Al Maktoum

Placings:0-04311120 **(5020)**

2001: 8^{0}GF, 8^{4}GF, 9^{3}GF, 10^{1}G, 12^{1}G, 11^{1}GF, 12^{2}G, 12^{0}HY

	Starts	1st	2nd	3rd	Win & Pl
Career Total (Turf)	9	3	1	1	22946
90 8/01 Bevl 1m3f216yD(0-80)	G-F	£5694			
86 8/01 Ripn 1m4f60y C(0-90)H	GD	£7052			
83 8/01 Ripn 1m2f D	GD	£3458			

Total win prize-money £16205

Going (Turf): Sf: 0-2 GS: 0-0 **Gd: 2-3** GF: 1-4 Fm: 0-0
Distance: 5f/6f: 0-0 7f-8f: 0-2 **9f-13f: 3-7** 14f+: 0-0
Track : LH: 0-2 **RH: 3-6 Tight: 3-4** Gall: 0-2
Aids: Bl: 0-1 Vi: 0-0 Tstrap: 0-0
Best Rating: 102 9/01 Donc 1m4f good

Got off the mark with any easy win in a poor ten-furlong maiden at Ripon in August and went on to complete a hat-trick with another win at Ripon and one at Beverley. Suited by fast ground, he looks better the further he goes.

Ailincala (IRE)

98 **61**

3-y-o b f Pursuit Of Love-Diabaig (Precocious)

C F Wall M Sinclair

Placings:U056-444026240 **(4900)**

2001: 8^{4}GS, 7^{4}F, 7^{4}GF, 6^{0}GF, 8^{2}GF, 9^{6}G, 7^{2}G, 6^{4}GF, 8^{0}GS

	Starts	1st	2nd	3rd	Win & Pl
Career Total (Turf)	13	0	2	0	1608

Going (Turf): Sf: 0-1 GS: 0-3 Gd: 0-2 GF: 0-6 Fm: 0-1
Distance: 5f/6f: 0-3 7f-8f: 0-7 9f-13f: 0-3 14f+: 0-0
Track : LH: 0-5 RH: 0-0 Tight: 0-0 Gall: 0-0
Aids: Bl: 0-0 Vi: 0-0 Tstrap: 0-0
Best Rating: 62 5/01 Sals 1m gd-sft

Aintnecessarilyso

103 **71**

3-y-o ch g So Factual (USA)-Ovideo (Domynsky)

D R C Elsworth Richard Marker

Placings:006023004-0010142460 **(4448)**

2001: 6^{0}GS, 5^{0}G, 5^{1}F, 6^{0}GF, 5^{1}GF, 6^{4}GF, 6^{2}GF, 6^{4}GF, 5^{6}G, 5^{0}G

	Starts	1st	2nd	3rd	Win & Pl
Career Total (Turf)	19	2	2	1	10189
68 7/01 Kemp 5f E(0-75)H	G-F	£4582			
59 6/01 Bath 5f11y F	FRM	£2296			

Total win prize-money £6879

Going (Turf): Sf: 0-3 GS: 0-1 Gd: 0-5 **GF: 1-9 Fm: 1-1**
Distance: **5f/6f: 2-15** 7f-8f: 0-4 9f-13f: 0-0 14f+: 0-0
Track : **LH: 1-5** RH: 0-1 Tight: 0-2 **Gall: 1-4**
Aids: Bl: 0-1 Vi: 0-0 Tstrap: 0-0
Best Rating: 71 8/01 Epsm 6f gd-fm

Fair sprint handicapper, twice successful in modest company in 2001. Suited by a sound surface.

Air Mail

106(112) (93)**66**

4-y-o b g Night Shift (USA)-Wizardry (Shirley Heights)

Mrs N Macauley West Indies Capital Company Limited

Placings:2105000010205032321-241203222630300054 **(5685)**

2001: 5^{2}SD, 6^{4}SW, 6^{1}SD, 7^{2}SW, 6^{0}SD, 6^{3}SD, 7^{2}SD, 8^{2}SD, 7^{2}SD, 8^{6}SD, 7^{3}SD, 5^{0}GF, 5^{3}F, 7^{0}F, 6^{0}G, 5^{0}GF, 6^{5}HY, 5^{4}S

	Starts	1st	2nd	3rd	Win & Pl
Career Total (Turf)	15	0	1	1	2160
Career Total (AW)	22	4	8	4	36699
86 1/01 Sthl 6f D(0-80)H	STD	£3191			
81 12/00 Sthl 6f C(0-95)H	STD	£6825			
61 9/00 Wolv 7f F	STD	£2436			
67 3/00 Ling 7f D	STD	£2808			

Total win prize-money £15261

Going (Turf): Sf: 0-3 GS: 0-2 Gd: 0-3 GF: 0-5 Fm: 0-2
Distance: 5f/6f: 2-15 7f-8f: 2-18 9f-13f: 0-4 14f+: 0-0
Track : **LH: 4-24** RH: 0-2 **Tight: 2-14** Gall: 0-3
Aids: Bl: 0-1 Vi: 0-2 Tstrap: 0-0
Best Rating: 93 2/01 Wolv 1m100y stand

A genuine gelding, he had a busy time over the winter of 2000/2001, generally running well and winning twice on the Southwell Fibresand.

Air Marshall (IRE)

119

4-y-o ch h In The Wings-Troyanna (Troy)

Sir Michael Stoute Lord Weinstock

Placings:214/2212-0 **(1098)**

2001: 12^{0}G

	Starts	1st	2nd	3rd	Win & Pl
Career Total (Turf)	8	2	4	0	204161
117 8/00 York 1m3f195yA	GD	£89250			
91 9/99 Gdwd 1m D	G-F	£4410			

Total win prize-money £93661

Going (Turf): Sf: 0-1 GS: 0-0 **Gd: 1-2 GF: 1-5** Fm: 0-0
Distance: 5f/6f: 0-0 7f-8f: 1-3 9f-13f: 1-4 14f+: 0-1
Track : LH: 1-4 RH: 1-3 Tight: 0-1 **Gall: 1-4**
Aids: Bl: 0-0 Vi: 0-0 Tstrap: 0-0
Best Rating: 91 9/99 Gdwd 1m GF

He ran out an authoritative winner of the 2000 Great Voltigeur to set himself up for a crack at the Leger, in which he was outbattled by Millenary after his stamina seemed to give way. Lost his action on his reappearance and was not seen again, and has joined John Hammond in France.

Air Of Esteem

(105) (60d)**61**
5-y-o b g Forzando-Shadow Bird (Martinmas)
P C Haslam G Ward

Placings:5/21201300260/3504525-206500002 **(5397)**
2001: 8^{2}SD, 8^{0}SD, 8^{6}SD, 9^{5}HY, 8^{0}S, 8^{0}GS, 7^{0}SD, 8^{0}SD, 8^{2}SD

	Starts	1st	2nd	3rd	Win & Pl
Career Total (Turf)	15	1	1	2	5739
Career Total (AW)	13	1	5	0	7420

80 6/99 Hayd 1m30y E(0-70)H SFT £3004
60 1/99 Ling 1m D STD £3572
Total win prize-money £6576

Going (Turf): Sf: 1-6 GS: 0-3 Gd: 0-4 GF: 0-2 Fm: 0-0
Distance: 5f/6f: 0-1 7f-8f: 1-13 9f-13f: 1-14 14f+: 0-0
Track : LH: 2-21 RH: 0-6 Tight: 1-9 Gall: 0-2
Aids: Bl: 0-0 Vi: 0-1 Tstrap: 0-0
Best Rating: 60 2/01 Sthl 1m stand

He has not won since his 3yo days, but gives the impression that he is still capable of winning a race on turf or Fibresand. Has dropped in the ratings and showed something of a revival when second-best on the All-Weather in October over a mile.

Aira Force (USA)

93(95) (80)**50**
4-y-o ch g Dehere (USA)-Cinnamon Splendor (USA) (Trempolino (USA))
A G Newcombe Alex Gorrie Combi (uk)

Placings:03310/20000-0540 **(4677)**
2001: 6^{0}GF, 7^{5}GS, 6^{4}GF, 7^{0}G

	Starts	1st	2nd	3rd	Win & Pl
Career Total (Turf)	12	1	0	2	4667
Career Total (AW)	2	0	1	0	1140

81 9/99 Hayd 5f D G-F £3805
Total win prize-money £3805

Going (Turf): Sf: 0-1 GS: 0-1 Gd: 0-4 GF: 1-5 Fm: 0-1
Distance: 5f/6f: 1-11 7f-8f: 0-3 9f-13f: 0-0 14f+: 0-0
Track : LH: 0-3 RH: 0-0 Tight: 0-3 Gall: 0-0
Aids: Bl: 0-0 Vi: 0-0 Tstrap: 0-0
Best Rating: 50 8/01 Ling 6f gd-fm

Aisle

(99) (42)**22**
4-y-o b g Arazi (USA)-Chancel (USA) (Al Nasr (FR))
S R Bowring S R Bowring

Placings:063001160/52255050000400-60624643020660000 **(5539)**
2001: 6^{6}SD, 8^{0}SD, 6^{6}SD, 7^{2}SD, 6^{4}SD, 6^{6}SD, 6^{4}SD, 7^{3}SD, 8^{0}G, 7^{2}SD, 7^{0}F, 6^{6}GF, 6^{6}SD, 6^{0}F, 6^{0}G, 7^{0}HY, 8^{0}S

	Starts	1st	2nd	3rd	Win & Pl
Career Total (Turf)	18	1	0	0	3585
Career Total (AW)	22	1	4	2	6363

58 11/99 Nott 6f15y E(0-75)H SFT £3224
61 10/99 Sthl 6f E(0-85)H STD £2853
Total win prize-money £6078

Going (Turf): Sf: 1-6 GS: 0-1 Gd: 0-7 GF: 0-2 Fm: 0-2
Distance: 5f/6f: 1-17 7f-8f: 1-20 9f-13f: 0-3 14f+: 0-0
Track : LH: 1-23 RH: 0-3 Tight: 0-6 Gall: 0-1
Aids: Bl: 0-28 Vi: 0-0 Tstrap: 0-4
Best Rating: 49 2/01 Wolv 7f stand

Modest sprinter. Mixes turf and All-Weather but is better on the All-Weather.

Aisling's Dream (IRE)

80 **63**
2-y-o ch f Desert King (IRE)-Daftiyna (IRE) (Darshaan)
S Kirk M Cooke And D Potter

Placings:6000 **(4730)**
2001: 5^{6}GF, 6^{0}GF, 6^{0}GF, 5^{0}F

	Starts	1st	2nd	3rd	Win & Pl
Career Total (Turf)	4	0	0	0	0

Going (Turf): Sf: 0-0 GS: 0-0 Gd: 0-0 GF: 0-3 Fm: 0-1
Distance: 5f/6f: 0-3 7f-8f: 0-1 9f-13f: 0-0 14f+: 0-0
Track : LH: 0-0 RH: 0-0 Tight: 0-0 Gall: 0-0
Aids: Bl: 0-0 Vi: 0-0 Tstrap: 0-0
Best Rating: 63 8/01 Sals 6f212y gd-fm

Aiwai (IRE)

(94) (36)**77**
4-y-o b c Thatching-Peach Melba (So Blessed)
G C H Chung The Happy Valley Leisure Club

Placings:020/0000 **(0546)**
2001: 8^{0}SD, 7^{0}SD, 6^{0}SD, 11^{0}SD

	Starts	1st	2nd	3rd	Win & Pl
Career Total (Turf)	3	0	1	0	1198
Career Total (AW)	4	0	0	0	

Going (Turf): Sf: 0-0 GS: 0-1 Gd: 0-0 GF: 0-2 Fm: 0-0
Distance: 5f/6f: 0-3 7f-8f: 0-3 9f-13f: 0-1 14f+: 0-0
Track : LH: 0-5 RH: 0-0 Tight: 0-2 Gall: 0-1
Aids: Bl: 0-0 Vi: 0-0 Tstrap: 0-1
Best Rating: 36 3/01 Sthl 1m3f stand

Aix En Provence (USA)

56(44) (39)**42**
6-y-o b g Geiger Counter (USA)-Low Hill (Rousillon (USA))
C A Dwyer Mrs Shelley Dwyer

Placings:104130/6/000000105000/5-0 **(1735)**
2001: 7^{0}GF

	Starts	1st	2nd	3rd	Win & Pl
Career Total (Turf)	18	3	0	1	10953
Career Total (AW)	3	0	0	0	

62 8/99 Yarm 1m3y G(0-60)H FRM £2232
84 8/97 Ripn 6f D G-F £3308
85 6/97 Ayr 6f E GD £3054
Total win prize-money £8595

Going (Turf): Sf: 0-1 GS: 0-3 Gd: 1-5 GF: 1-7 Fm: 1-2
Distance: 5f/6f: 2-3 7f-8f: 0-10 9f-13f: 1-8 14f+: 0-0
Track : LH: 0-9 RH: 0-3 Tight: 0-5 Gall: 0-0
Aids: Bl: 0-0 Vi: 0-0 Tstrap: 0-2
Best Rating: 85 6/97 Ayr 6f G

He has been out of form for a couple of years now.

Ajeel (IRE)

92 **74+**
2-y-o b c Green Desert (USA)-Samheh (USA) (Private Account (USA))
J L Dunlop Hamdan Al Maktoum

Placings:06 **(5594)**
2001: 6^{0}GS, 6^{6}GS

	Starts	1st	2nd	3rd	Win & Pl
Career Total (Turf)	2	0	0	0	0

Going (Turf): Sf: 0-0 GS: 0-2 Gd: 0-0 GF: 0-0 Fm: 0-0
Distance: 5f/6f: 0-2 7f-8f: 0-0 9f-13f: 0-0 14f+: 0-0
Track : LH: 0-0 RH: 0-0 Tight: 0-0 Gall: 0-0
Aids: Bl: 0-0 Vi: 0-0 Tstrap: 0-0
Best Rating: 74 11/01 NmkR 6f gd-sft

Ajwaa (IRE)

95 **92**
3-y-o ch c Mujtahid (USA)-Nouvelle Star (AUS) (Luskin Star (AUS))
M P Tregoning Hamdan Al Maktoum

Placings:214-00 **(3675)**
2001: 6^{0}GF, 6^{0}G

	Starts	1st	2nd	3rd	Win & Pl
Career Total (Turf)	5	1	1	0	9461

92 10/00 NmkR 6f D SFT £7397
Total win prize-money £7397

Going (Turf): Sf: 1-2 GS: 0-0 Gd: 0-2 GF: 0-1 Fm: 0-0
Distance: 5f/6f: 1-5 7f-8f: 0-0 9f-13f: 0-0 14f+: 0-0
Track : LH: 0-0 RH: 0-0 Tight: 0-0 Gall: 0-0
Aids: Bl: 0-0 Vi: 0-1 Tstrap: 0-0
Best Rating: 77 8/01 Ripn 6f good

He looked a decent prospect when beating a big field in a Newmarket maiden towards the end of last season, but has disappointed on subsequent starts.

Akalim

95 (60)**51**
8-y-o b g Petong-Tiszta Sharok (Song)
L G Cottrell Mrs Lucy Halloran

Placings:651061/0600/00443033/420050122/05200210/0500-00 **(4677)**
2001: 7^{0}G, 7^{0}G

	Starts	1st	2nd	3rd	Win & Pl
Career Total (Turf)	38	4	5	2	19415
Career Total (AW)	3	0	0	1	297

69 10/99 Newb 7f E(0-80)H SFT £3191
60 9/98 Chep 7f16y F(0-65)H G-S £2794
78 10/95 Nott 6f15y E(0-85) G-F £3559
77 7/95 NmkJ 6f D G-F £4620
Total win prize-money £14165

Going (Turf): Sf: 1-10 GS: 1-4 Gd: 0-10 GF: 2-12 Fm: 0-2
Distance: 5f/6f: 1-14 7f-8f: 3-26 9f-13f: 0-1 14f+: 0-0
Track : LH: 0-10 RH: 0-5 Tight: 0-4 Gall: 0-3
Aids: Bl: 0-1 Vi: 0-1 Tstrap: 0-0
Best Rating: 48 9/01 Chep 7f16y good

Last win back in 1999, has shown nothing since then, although he does tend to pick up a race when least expected.

Akatib (IRE)

69(78) (9)**19**
3-y-o b f Lahib (USA)-Daltak (Night Shift (USA))
B S Rothwell A Cute Group

Placings:00-0055 **(3162)**
2001: 8^{0}F, 8^{0}SD, 7^{5}SD, 7^{5}G

	Starts	1st	2nd	3rd	Win & Pl
Career Total (Turf)	4	0	0	0	0
Career Total (AW)	2	0	0	0	0

Going (Turf): Sf: 0-0 GS: 0-1 Gd: 0-2 GF: 0-0 Fm: 0-1
Distance: 5f/6f: 0-2 7f-8f: 0-3 9f-13f: 0-1 14f+: 0-0
Track : LH: 0-3 RH: 0-0 Tight: 0-0 Gall: 0-0
Aids: Bl: 0-0 Vi: 0-0 Tstrap: 0-0
Best Rating: 19 6/01 Nott 1m54y firm

Akbar (IRE)

111(100) (84)**111**
5-y-o b/br h Doyoun-Akishka (Nishapour (FR))
M Johnston Markus Graff

Placings:13/52203230/1106411-40121333 **(5691)**
2001: 10^{4}GF, 12^{0}SD, 14^{1}GF, 12^{2}G, 13^{1}G, 14^{3}GF, 12^{3}HY, 12^{3}S

	Starts	1st	2nd	3rd	Win & Pl
Career Total (Turf)	24	7	4	6	136897
Career Total (AW)	1		0	0	0

111 7/01 York 1m5f194yA(0-105)H GD £18722
103 5/01 Gdwd 1m6f B(0-100)H G-F £29000
100 9/00 Diel 1m4f82y GD £18824

100	8/00	Diel	2m	GD	£5647
106	6/00	Frau	1m4f	GD	£5647
106	4/00	Diel	1m4f83y	GD	£7529
57	10/98	Tipp	7f	SH	£3781

Total win prize-money £89150

Going (Turf): Sf: 0-5 GS: 0-1 **Gd: 5-9** GF: 1-6 Fm: 0-0
Distance: 5f/6f: 0-0 7f-8f: 1-3 9f-13f: 3-17 14f+: 3-5
Track : **LH: 4-12** RH: 2-10 Tight: 1-3 Gall: 1-6
Aids: Bl: 0-0 Vi: 0-0 Tstrap: 0-0
Best Rating: 111 8/01 Gdwd 1m6f gd-fm

He scored four times in Switzerland last year and clearly likes Dielsdorf's sharp track. He has not quite enjoyed the same success domestically, but has won at Goodwood and a Listed handicap at York this season. Fourteen furlongs looks his best trip these days.

Akeed (USA)

90 **83**
4-y-o ch c Affirmed (USA)-Victorious Lil (CAN) (Vice Regent (CAN))
P F I Cole H R H Prince Fahd Salman

Placings:144/550-0 **(0805)**
2001: 7^{0}S

	Starts	1st	2nd	3rd	Win & Pl
Career Total (Turf)	7	1	0	0	11742

85 9/99 York 6f214y D G-F £6758
Total win prize-money £6758

Going (Turf): Sf: 0-3 GS: 0-0 Gd: 0-2 **GF: 1-1** Fm: 0-0
Distance: 5f/6f: 0-0 **7f-8f: 1-4** 9f-13f: 0-3 14f+: 0-0
Track : **LH: 1-2** RH: 0-1 Tight: 0-1 **Gall: 1-2**
Aids: Bl: 0-0 Vi: 0-0 Tstrap: 0-0
Best Rating: 61 4/01 NmkR 7f soft

Bolted up over seven furlongs on his York debut at two. Lightly raced since then, he has failed to live up to expectations somewhat.

Akeesha

(80) (32)**63**
2-y-o b f Mukaddamah (USA)-Butterwick Belle (IRE) (Distinctly North (USA))
R A Fahey R A Fahey

Placings:00150 **(4554)**
2001: 6^{0}GF, 6^{0}GF, 6^{1}G, 5^{5}HY, 6^{0}SW

	Starts	1st	2nd	3rd	Win & Pl
Career Total (Turf)	4	1	0	0	2415
Career Total (AW)	1	0	0	0	

63 8/01 Rdcr 6f G GD £2415
Total win prize-money £2415

Going (Turf): Sf: 0-1 GS: 0-0 **Gd: 1-1** GF: 0-2 Fm: 0-0
Distance: **5f/6f: 1-5** 7f-8f: 0-0 9f-13f: 0-0 14f+: 0-0
Track : LH: 0-2 RH: 0-0 Tight: 0-1 Gall: 0-0
Aids: Bl: 0-0 Vi: 0-0 Tstrap: 0-0
Best Rating: 63 8/01 Rdcr 6f good

A sprint-bred juvenile, won a seller at Redcar in August over six furlongs. Suited to good ground.

Aker Wood

(90) (58)**70**
3-y-o b f Bin Ajwaad (IRE)-Wannaplantatree (Niniski (USA))
A P Jarvis A M Tombs

Placings:020500-32140042306 **(5611)**
2001: 10^{3}GS, 9^{2}GS, 10^{1}GF, 12^{4}GF, 10^{0}GF, 10^{0}GF, 10^{4}GF, 10^{2}GF, 10^{3}G, 12^{0}SD, 8^{6}SD

	Starts	1st	2nd	3rd	Win & Pl
Career Total (Turf)	15	1	3	2	12010
Career Total (AW)	2	0	0	0	0

58 5/01 Ayr 1m2f192yD G-F £3783
Total win prize-money £3783

Going (Turf): Sf: 0-0 GS: 0-4 Gd: 0-3 **GF: 1-8** Fm: 0-0
Distance: 5f/6f: 0-1 7f-8f: 0-5 **9f-13f: 1-11** 14f+: 0-0
Track : **LH: 1-11** RH: 0-3 Tight: 0-4 Gall: 0-6
Aids: Bl: 0-0 Vi: 0-0 Tstrap: 0-0
Best Rating: 75 4/01 Newb 1m2f6y gd-sft

Bred to stay well is likely to need middle-distances this year. Ran with credit on seasonal bow at Newbury,. and then won at Ayr, but has since looked well held.

Akhira

102(95) (60)**72**
4-y-o b f Emperor Jones (USA)-Fakhira (IRE) (Jareer (USA))
S P C Woods Dennis Yardy

Placings:45/02-30230104 **(3735)**
2001: 8^{3}SD, 8^{0}SD, 6^{2}F, 6^{3}GF, 6^{0}F, 7^{1}G, 6^{0}GF, 6^{4}G

	Starts	1st	2nd	3rd	Win & Pl
Career Total (Turf)	10	1	2	1	20501
Career Total (AW)	2	0	0	1	403

72 7/01 Yarm 7f3y D(0-80)H GD £4192
Total win prize-money £4193

Going (Turf): Sf: 0-1 GS: 0-3 **Gd: 1-2** GF: 0-2 Fm: 0-2
Distance: 5f/6f: 0-0 **7f-8f: 1-12** 9f-13f: 0-0 14f+: 0-0
Track : LH: 0-5 RH: 0-1 Tight: 0-1 Gall: 0-0
Aids: Bl: 0-0 Vi: 0-0 Tstrap: 0-0
Best Rating: 72 7/01 Yarm 7f3y good

Got off the mark on tenth attempt at Yarmouth over seven furlongs, in decisive fashion. Acts on a sound surface.

Akina (NZ)

69 **2**
10-y-o b g Ivory Hunter (USA)-Wairoa Belle (NZ) (Bold Venture (NZ))
J Neville N Brookes

Placings:0 **(5492)**
2001: 16^{0}HY

	Starts	1st	2nd	3rd	Win & Pl
Career Total (Turf)	1	0	0	0	

Going (Turf): Sf: 0-1 GS: 0-0 Gd: 0-0 GF: 0-0 Fm: 0-0
Distance: 5f/6f: 0-0 7f-8f: 0-0 9f-13f: 0-0 14f+: 0-1
Track : LH: 0-1 RH: 0-0 Tight: 0-0 Gall: 0-0
Aids: Bl: 0-0 Vi: 0-0 Tstrap: 0-0
Best Rating: 2 10/01 Newb 2m heavy

Al Aali

101 **86+**
3-y-o b c Lahib (USA)-Maraatib (IRE) (Green Desert (USA))
J L Dunlop Hamdan Al Maktoum

Placings:011 **(3636)**
2001: 6^{0}GS, 7^{1}G, 7^{1}GS

	Starts	1st	2nd	3rd	Win & Pl
Career Total (Turf)	3	2	0	0	8392

86 8/01 NmkJ 7f D(0-80)H G-S £4173
73 6/01 Thsk 7f D GD £4218
Total win prize-money £8392

Going (Turf): Sf: 0-0 **GS: 1-2 Gd: 1-1** GF: 0-0 Fm: 0-0
Distance: 5f/6f: 0-1 **7f-8f: 2-2** 9f-13f: 0-0 14f+: 0-0
Track : **LH: 1-1** RH: 0-0 **Tight: 1-1** Gall: 0-0
Aids: Bl: 0-0 Vi: 0-0 Tstrap: 0-0
Best Rating: 86 8/01 NmkJ 7f gd-sft

Got off the mark in an ordinary maiden having shown promise on his debut before winning aNewmarket handicap. Yet to encounter fast ground. Progressive.

Al Awaalah

102(97) (44)**46**
4-y-o b f Mukaddamah (USA)-Zippy Zoe (Rousillon (USA))
M Salaman J P M & J W Cook

Placings:000035-4463000 **(2935)**
2001: 9^{4}SD, 8^{4}SD, 8^{6}F, 7^{3}GF, 8^{0}HD, 8^{0}GF, 9^{0}GF

	Starts	1st	2nd	3rd	Win & Pl
Career Total (Turf)	10	0	0	2	970
Career Total (AW)	3	0	0	0	0

Going (Turf): Sf: 0-1 GS: 0-0 Gd: 0-2 GF: 0-5 Fm: 0-2
Distance: 5f/6f: 0-0 7f-8f: 0-5 9f-13f: 0-8 14f+: 0-0
Track : LH: 0-8 RH: 0-2 Tight: 0-5 Gall: 0-0
Aids: Bl: 0-0 Vi: 0-0 Tstrap: 0-0
Best Rating: 44 7/01 Kemp 1m1f gd-fm

Al Azhar

105 **68**
7-y-o b g Alzao (USA)-Upend (Main Reef)
M Dods Mrs Karen S Pratt

Placings:211/6023015/265430/50660-62502630400 **(5632)**
2001: 9^{6}S, 10^{2}S, 10^{5}G, 10^{0}G, 12^{2}G, 11^{6}G, 10^{3}GS, 14^{0}G, 12^{4}GS, 13^{0}HY, 10^{0}G

	Starts	1st	2nd	3rd	Win & Pl
Career Total (Turf)	32	3	5	3	52061

96	10/97	Donc	1m4f	C(0-100)H	GD	£13012
98	9/96	Donc	1m	C	G-F	£18310
86	8/96	Chep	1m14y	D	GD	£3533

Total win prize-money £34857

Going (Turf): Sf: 0-9 GS: 0-5 **Gd: 2-12** GF: 1-6 Fm: 0-0
Distance: 5f/6f: 0-0 7f-8f: 1-3 **9f-13f: 2-27** 14f+: 0-2
Track : **LH: 1-16** RH: 0-10 Tight: 0-6 **Gall: 1-11**
Aids: Bl: 0-0 Vi: 0-0 Tstrap: 0-0
Best Rating: 75 7/01 Ayr 1m2f gd-sft

He is an effective performer over ten to 12 furlongs on any ground and has run some decent races in recent seasons, but has not won since 1997.

Al Ghabraa

105(97) (66)**58**
4-y-o ch f Pursuit Of Love-Tenderetta (Tender King)
D Shaw (J W Hills 3/2) K Nicholls

Placings:1/6500004-260105000406263600 **(4804)**
2001: 12^{2}SD, 14^{6}SD, 9^{0}SD, 8^{1}SD, 8^{0}SD, 8^{5}SD, 8^{0}F, 7^{0}GF, 8^{0}GF, 9^{4}GF, 7^{0}GF, 8^{6}GF, 6^{2}GS, 7^{6}GF, 6^{3}G, 7^{6}G, 6^{0}GF, 6^{0}F

	Starts	1st	2nd	3rd	Win & Pl
Career Total (Turf)	18	1	1	1	5665
Career Total (AW)	8	1	1	0	3518

61 4/01 Sthl 1m F(0-65)H STD £2982
81 10/99 Rdcr 1m E GD £3414
Total win prize-money £6396

Going (Turf): Sf: 0-1 GS: 0-1 **Gd: 1-4** GF: 0-10 Fm: 0-2
Distance: 5f/6f: 0-4 **7f-8f: 2-12** 9f-13f: 0-9 14f+: 0-1
Track : **LH: 1-15** RH: 0-4 Tight: 0-5 Gall: 0-2
Aids: Bl: 0-1 Vi: 0-9 Tstrap: 0-3
Best Rating: 61 4/01 Sthl 1m stand

Al Ihsas (IRE)

107 **102**
3-y-o b f Danehill (USA)-Simaat (USA) (Mr Prospector (USA))
J H M Gosden Hamdan Al Maktoum

Placings:22-11040 **(4683)**
2001: 7^{1}GF, 7^{1}GF, 7^{0}GF, 7^{4}GF, 5^{0}GS

	Starts	1st	2nd	3rd	Win & Pl

	Starts	1st	2nd	3rd	Win & Pl
Career Total (Turf)	7	2	2	0	27330

102	6/01	Leic	7f9y	C	G-F	£6049
98	5/01	Gdwd	7f	D	G-F	£5785

Total win prize-money £11834

Going (Turf): Sf: 0-0 GS: 0-2 Gd: 0-0 **GF: 2-5** Fm: 0-0
Distance: 5f/6f: 0-3 **7f-8f: 2-4** 9f-13f: 0-0 14f+: 0-0
Track : LH: 0-1 **RH: 1-2** Tight: 0-0 Gall: 0-1
Aids: Bl: 0-0 Vi: 0-1 Tstrap: 0-1
Best Rating: 102 6/01 Leic 7f9y gd-fm

Second in the Queen Mary at two, she was absent for the rest of the season after suffering from colic. Returned to action this term and ran away with a maiden at Goodwood before treating the opposition with disdain in a conditions event at Leicester. Well beaten in the Jersey Stakes at Royal Ascot when done no favours by the draw, but ran to form at Goodwood next time.

Al Maali (IRE)

94 **84**

2-y-o b c Polar Falcon (USA)-Amwag (USA) (El Gran Senor (USA))
A C Stewart Hamdan Al Maktoum

Placings:22 **(4838)**
2001: 6^{2}GF, 6^{2}G

	Starts	1st	2nd	3rd	Win & Pl
Career Total (Turf)	2	0	2	0	2254

Going (Turf): Sf: 0-0 GS: 0-0 Gd: 0-1 GF: 0-1 Fm: 0-0
Distance: 5f/6f: 0-1 7f-8f: 0-1 9f-13f: 0-0 14f+: 0-0
Track : LH: 0-0 RH: 0-0 Tight: 0-0 Gall: 0-0
Aids: Bl: 0-0 Vi: 0-0 Tstrap: 0-0
Best Rating: 84 9/01 Nott 6f15y good

Al Mabrook (IRE)

83(104)

6-y-o b g Rainbows For Life (CAN)-Sky Lover (Ela-Mana-Mou)
Ferdy Murphy (K A Ryan 6/5) The Gloria Darley Racing Partnership

Placings:0652/06300016/4050500/100003500504-0500303000 **(1133)**
2001: 8^{0}SD, 8^{5}SW, 11^{0}SW, 8^{0}SW, 9^{3}SD, 8^{0}SW, 8^{3}SD, 9^{0}S, 11^{0}SD, 8^{0}GS

	Starts	1st	2nd	3rd	Win & Pl
Career Total (Turf)	21	0	1	2	1935
Career Total (AW)	20	2	0	2	6664

61	1/00	Wolv	1m1f79y	D(0-80)H	STD	£3354
66	11/98	Ling	6f	D	STD	£2741

Total win prize-money £6095

Going (Turf): Sf: 0-3 GS: 0-2 **Gd: 0-10** GF: 0-4 Fm: 0-2
Distance: 5f/6f: 1-8 7f-8f: 0-17 9f-13f: 1-16 14f+: 0-0
Track : **LH: 2-28** RH: 0-5 **Tight: 2-15** Gall: 0-3
Aids: Bl: 0-9 Vi: 0-0 Tstrap: 0-0
Best Rating: 39 3/01 Sthl 1m stand

He has shown bits and pieces of form and has been set some stiff tasks in handicaps, but has become disappointing.

Al Mohallab (FR)

109 **101+**

2-y-o b c Marju (IRE)-Deyaajeer (USA) (Dayjur (USA))
B W Hills Hamdan Al Maktoum

Placings:31 **(4864)**
2001: 6^{3}GF, 7^{1}GF

	Starts	1st	2nd	3rd	Win & Pl
Career Total (Turf)	2	1	0	1	6789

101	9/01	Newb	7f	D	G-F	£5772

Total win prize-money £5772

Going (Turf): Sf: 0-0 GS: 0-0 Gd: 0-0 **GF: 1-2** Fm: 0-0
Distance: 5f/6f: 0-0 **7f-8f: 1-2** 9f-13f: 0-0 14f+: 0-0
Track : LH: 0-1 RH: 0-0 Tight: 0-0 Gall: 0-1
Aids: Bl: 0-0 Vi: 0-0 Tstrap: 0-0
Best Rating: 101 9/01 Newb 7f gd-fm

Out of a half-sister to Nashwan ansd Unfuwain, he shaped with considerable promise on his debut at York and made no mistake in a maiden at Newbury next time. Should go on to better things. His win came over seven furlongs on a sound surface.

Al Moughazel (USA)

103 **94**

2-y-o b c Royal Academy (USA)-Wild Vintage (USA) (Alysheba (USA))
J W Payne C Cotran

Placings:114 **(5255)**
2001: 6^{1}GF, 7^{1}G, 8^{4}GS

	Starts	1st	2nd	3rd	Win & Pl
Career Total (Turf)	3	2	0	0	12397

94	9/01	Ayr	7f50y	C	GD	£6438
88	6/01	NmkJ	6f	D	G-F	£4901

Total win prize-money £11339

Going (Turf): Sf: 0-0 GS: 0-1 **Gd: 1-1 GF: 1-1** Fm: 0-0
Distance: 5f/6f: 1-1 7f-8f: 1-2 9f-13f: 0-0 14f+: 0-0
Track : LH: 0-0 RH: 0-1 Tight: 0-0 Gall: 0-1
Aids: Bl: 0-0 Vi: 0-0 Tstrap: 0-0
Best Rating: 94 9/01 Ayr 7f50y good

Promising sort, successful at Newmarket on his debut and at Ayr three months later. Out of his depth in Listed company on easy ground on his last outing.

Al Muallim (USA)

111 **85**

7-y-o b g Theatrical-Gerri N Jo Go (USA) (Top Command (USA))
D Nicholls Neil Smith

Placings:41/41321/0232/5020/300000401000040-005502611411 **(4715)**
2001: 6^{0}S, 6^{0}S, 7^{0}G, 6^{0}GF, 7^{0}GF, 7^{2}GF, 6^{0}G, 6^{1}G, 6^{1}GF, 7^{4}G, 6^{1}G, 6^{1}G

	Starts	1st	2nd	3rd	Win & Pl
Career Total (Turf)	42	8	5	3	61181

73	9/01	Epsm	6f	E	GD	£3835
64	8/01	Epsm	6f	E	GD	£3575
74	8/01	Kemp	6f	E	G-F	£3136
85	7/01	Kemp	6f	E	GD	£3623
91	8/00	Epsm	7f	C(0-90)H	G-F	£6955
94	10/97	NmkR	7f	B(0-100)	G-F	£8468
87	8/97	Ling	6f	D(0-85)H	G-F	£3550
78	10/96	Catt	5f212y	D	GD	£3242

Total win prize-money £36387

Going (Turf): Sf: 0-6 GS: 0-4 **Gd: 4-15 GF: 4-15** Fm: 0-2
Distance: **5f/6f: 6-19** 7f-8f: 2-23 9f-13f: 0-0 14f+: 0-0
Track : **LH: 4-11** RH: 0-3 **Tight: 4-6** Gall: 0-4
Aids: Bl: 0-0 Vi: 0-0 **Tstrap: 5-19**
Best Rating: 85 7/01 Kemp 6f good

Formerly useful handicapper at six or seven furlongs with a poor win ratio in recent years. Most of his wins have come on fast ground. In sparkling form this term in claiming company, winning four times.

Al Towd (USA)

104 **71**

4-y-o b c Kingmambo (USA)-Toujours Elle (USA) (Lyphard (USA))
S Dow Mrs Mandy Hall

Placings:3123/05460-000560 **(3064)**
2001: 10^{0}S, 13^{0}GF, 14^{0}GF, 20^{5}GF, 16^{6}GF, 17^{0}G

	Starts	1st	2nd	3rd	Win & Pl
Career Total (Turf)	15	1	1	2	9088

75	9/99	Newc	7f	D	G-F	£3761

Total win prize-money £3761

Going (Turf): Sf: 0-3 GS: 0-3 Gd: 0-4 **GF: 1-5** Fm: 0-0
Distance: 5f/6f: 0-0 **7f-8f: 1-4** 9f-13f: 0-6 14f+: 0-5
Track : LH: 0-6 RH: 0-5 Tight: 0-4 Gall: 0-4
Aids: Bl: 0-0 Vi: 0-0 Tstrap: 0-0
Best Rating: 71 6/01 Asct 2m4f gd-fm

Got off the mark in a Newcastle maiden on his second start at two, but has not won since and has changed stables. Ran a blinder for a 100/1 shot when fifth in the Ascot Stakes, but even the two and a half miles there looked an insufficient test of stamina.

Al's Alibi

(106) (47d)**61**

8-y-o b g Alzao (USA)-Lady Kris (IRE) (Kris)
W R Muir J Haim

Placings:63025/65105/4026010400/01061/0002142045 20-30145 **(0511)**
2001: 12^{3}SW, 12^{0}SD, 12^{1}SD, 14^{4}SD, 12^{5}SD

	Starts	1st	2nd	3rd	Win & Pl
Career Total (Turf)	30	4	3	1	27816
Career Total (AW)	12	2	2	1	6155

34	2/01	Wolv	1m4f	G	STD	£1841
72	6/00	Sthl	1m4f	F	STD	£2219
75	8/98	Bath	1m3f144y	D(0-80)H	FRM	£3355
75	5/98	Newb	1m4f5y	C(0-90)H	GD	£5605
76	8/97	Carl	1m4f	D(0-80)H	G-F	£3420
75	4/96	Newb	1m4f5y	C(0-90)H	G-S	£5377

Total win prize-money £21818

Going (Turf): Sf: 0-4 **GS: 1-5 Gd: 1-14 GF: 1-6 Fm: 1-1**
Distance: 5f/6f: 0-1 7f-8f: 0-4 **9f-13f: 6-33** 14f+: 0-4
Track : **LH: 5-30** RH: 1-11 Tight: 2-10 Gall: 2-11
Aids: Bl: 0-0 Vi: 0-0 Tstrap: 0-0
Best Rating: 47 1/01 Wolv 1m4f slow

A veteran plater these days, does most of his racing on Fibresand. Suited by a mile and a half.

Al's Fella (IRE)

(84) (14)

6-y-o br g Alzao (USA)-Crystal Cross (USA) (Roberto (USA))
Miss K M George Exterior Profiles Ltd

Placings:34660026/3422001/6504141/5 **(2580)**
2001: 12^{5}SD

	Starts	1st	2nd	3rd	Win & Pl
Career Total (Turf)	16	3	1	1	10133
Career Total (AW)	7	0	2	1	2113

64	8/99	Wind	1m3f135yG		HVY	£1884
63	7/99	Leic	1m3f183yF		G-F	£2406
69	11/98	Rdcr	1m3f	D(0-80)H	G-S	£3610

Total win prize-money £7900

Going (Turf): Sf: 1-3 GS: 1-5 Gd: 0-3 **GF: 1-3** Fm: 0-2
Distance: 5f/6f: 0-1 7f-8f: 0-6 **9f-13f: 3-13** 14f+: 0-3
Track : LH: 1-16 RH: 1-3 **Tight: 2-12** Gall: 0-2
Aids: **Bl: 2-6** Vi: 0-0 Tstrap: 0-1
Best Rating: 14 6/01 Sthl 1m4f stand

Al's Me Trainer

(92) (62)**68**

3-y-o b g Emarati (USA)-Ray Of Hope (Rainbow Quest (USA))
A Dickman Mike Smallman

Placings:405-001140 **(4876)**
2001: 6^{0}GF, 6^{0}G, 6^{1}SD, 5^{1}GS, 5^{4}G, 6^{0}SD

Starts 1st 2nd 3rd Win & Pl

	Starts	1st	2nd	3rd	Win & Pl
Career Total (Turf)	7	1	0	0	5501
Career Total (AW)	2	1	0	0	2303

68	8/01	Thsk	5f	D(0-80)H	G-S	£4758
62	7/01	Sthl	6f	F	STD	£2303

Total win prize-money £7061

Going (Turf): Sf: 0-2 **GS: 1-1** Gd: 0-2 GF: 0-1 Fm: 0-1
Distance: **5f/6f: 2-8** 7f-8f: 0-1 9f-13f: 0-0 14f+: 0-0
Track : **LH: 1-3** RH: 0-0 Tight: 0-2 Gall: 0-0
Aids: Bl: 0-0 **Vi: 2-4** Tstrap: 0-0
Best Rating: 68 8/01 Thsk 5f gd-sft

He got off the mark in a maiden on the Southwell Fibresand in July and followed up on turf at Thirsk. Suited by forcing tactics.

Al-King Slayer

(96) (55)**75**
4-y-o b c Batshoof-Top Sovereign (High Top)
T P McGovern Ahmed Abdel-Khaleq

Placings:02-30 **(0289)**
2001: 7^{3}SD, 8^{0}SW

	Starts	1st	2nd	3rd	Win & Pl
Career Total (Turf)	1	0	1	0	756
Career Total (AW)	3	0	0	1	430

Going (Turf): Sf: 0-1 GS: 0-0 Gd: 0-0 GF: 0-0 Fm: 0-0
Distance: 5f/6f: 0-0 7f-8f: 0-3 9f-13f: 0-1 14f+: 0-0
Track : LH: 0-3 RH: 0-0 Tight: 0-2 Gall: 0-0
Aids: Bl: 0-0 Vi: 0-0 Tstrap: 0-0
Best Rating: 55 1/01 Ling 7f stand

Alabama Wurley

94(72) (53d)**26**
4-y-o b f Environment Friend-Logarithm (King Of Spain)
J Balding Wacky Racing

Placings:306242103/000060010400-000000 **(4898)**
2001: 5^{0}GF, 5^{0}GF, 6^{0}F, 6^{0}GF, 6^{0}G, 5^{0}GS

	Starts	1st	2nd	3rd	Win & Pl
Career Total (Turf)	25	2	1	2	7035
Career Total (AW)	2	0	1	0	542

45	7/00	Yarm	7f3y	G	G-F	£1939
70	8/99	NmkJ	7f	E	GD	£3785

Total win prize-money £5724

Going (Turf): Sf: 0-2 GS: 0-4 **Gd: 1-6 GF: 1-10** Fm: 0-3
Distance: 5f/6f: 0-8 **7f-8f: 2-12** 9f-13f: 0-7 14f+: 0-0
Track : LH: 0-5 RH: 0-1 Tight: 0-2 Gall: 0-1
Aids: Bl: 0-0 **Vi: 1-7** Tstrap: 0-0
Best Rating: 31 6/01 Bevl 5f gd-fm

Alabamy Sound (IRE)

86(88) (32)**13**
5-y-o ch m Superlative-Salt Peanuts (IRE) (Salt Dome (USA))
K A Morgan S Giles & M Hawkins

Placings:441/40400500-000 **(3317)**
2001: 7^{0}GF, 7^{0}GF, 7^{0}G

	Starts	1st	2nd	3rd	Win & Pl
Career Total (Turf)	10	1	0	0	9445
Career Total (AW)	4	0	0	0	0

5/99	Chan	1m		GD	£5920

Total win prize-money £5920

Going (Turf): Sf: 0-1 GS: 0-1 Gd: 0-2 GF: 0-3 Fm: 0-0
Distance: 5f/6f: 0-2 7f-8f: 0-6 9f-13f: 0-3 14f+: 0-0
Track : LH: 0-7 RH: 0-1 Tight: 0-4 Gall: 0-1
Aids: Bl: 0-0 Vi: 0-3 Tstrap: 0-0
Best Rating: 13 7/01 Yarm 7f3y good

Alabang

(103) (70)**68**
10-y-o ch g Valiyar-Seleter (Hotfoot)
C G Cox (C R Egerton 17/2) Elite Racing Club

Placings:0050020/305/012414215/21551 **(0691)**
2001: 11^{2}SD, 16^{1}SD, 12^{5}SW, 16^{5}SW, 16^{1}SD

	Starts	1st	2nd	3rd	Win & Pl
Career Total (Turf)	19	3	3	1	13203
Career Total (AW)	5	2	1	0	5685

70	4/01	Sthl	2m	F(0-65)H	STD	£2331
67	1/01	Ling	2m	E(0-75)H	STD	£2940
68	7/96	Nott	1m1f213yF(0-60)		G-F	£2381
62	6/96	Newc	1m2f32y	D(0-75)H	FRM	£3793
52	5/96	Rdcr	1m1f	E(0-70)H	G-F	£3309

Total win prize-money £14755

Going (Turf): Sf: 0-0 GS: 0-1 Gd: 0-5 **GF: 2-8** Fm: 1-5
Distance: 5f/6f: 0-2 7f-8f: 0-6 **9f-13f: 3-13** 14f+: 2-3
Track : **LH: 5-16** RH: 0-4 **Tight: 2-12** Gall: 1-3
Aids: Bl: 0-0 Vi: 0-0 Tstrap: 0-0
Best Rating: 70 4/01 Sthl 2m stand

He was a very useful performer on the Flat a few seasons ago and went on to become a decent hurdler. He also won over fences, but recently his victories have come in modest staying events on sand. He is not the horse he was and is not the easiest of rides these days. Made a successful debut for the Clive Cox stable at Southwell.

Alafzar (IRE)

95 **69**
3-y-o b c Green Desert (USA)-Alasana (IRE) (Darshaan)
Sir Michael Stoute H H Aga Khan

Placings:004 **(5174)**
2001: 8^{0}S, 8^{0}HY, 8^{4}GS

	Starts	1st	2nd	3rd	Win & Pl
Career Total (Turf)	3	0	0	0	278

Going (Turf): Sf: 0-2 GS: 0-1 Gd: 0-0 GF: 0-0 Fm: 0-0
Distance: 5f/6f: 0-0 7f-8f: 0-1 9f-13f: 0-2 14f+: 0-0
Track : LH: 0-2 RH: 0-0 Tight: 0-0 Gall: 0-0
Aids: Bl: 0-0 Vi: 0-0 Tstrap: 0-0
Best Rating: 69 4/01 NmkR 1m soft

Alagazam

93 **31**
3-y-o ch g Alhijaz-Maziere (Mazilier (USA))
B I Case Paul Rackham

Placings:000-00600 **(4183)**
2001: 11^{0}G, 8^{0}GF, 11^{6}GF, 14^{0}GF, 16^{0}GF

	Starts	1st	2nd	3rd	Win & Pl
Career Total (Turf)	8	0	0	0	0

Going (Turf): Sf: 0-0 GS: 0-0 Gd: 0-3 GF: 0-5 Fm: 0-0
Distance: 5f/6f: 0-1 7f-8f: 0-2 9f-13f: 0-3 14f+: 0-2
Track : LH: 0-0 RH: 0-3 Tight: 0-3 Gall: 0-1
Aids: Bl: 0-0 Vi: 0-0 Tstrap: 0-0
Best Rating: 31 7/01 Wind 1m3f135y gd-fm

Alakananda

110 **84+**
3-y-o b f Hernando (FR)-Alouette (Darshaan)
Sir Mark Prescott Miss K Rausing

Placings:222-3411 **(5525)**
2001: 12^{3}G, 11^{4}HY, 11^{1}G, 11^{1}HY, 12^{0}HY

	Starts	1st	2nd	3rd	Win & Pl
Career Total (Turf)	7	2	3	1	11342

84	10/01	Wind	1m3f135yD(0-80)H	HVY	£4069
83	10/01	Bath	1m3f144yD	GD	£3052

Total win prize-money £7121

Going (Turf): Sf: 1-4 GS: 0-0 **Gd: 1-3** GF: 0-0 Fm: 0-0
Distance: 5f/6f: 0-0 7f-8f: 0-3 **9f-13f: 2-4** 14f+: 0-0
Track : **LH: 1-3** RH: 0-2 **Tight: 2-6** Gall: 0-1
Aids: **Bl: 2-2** Vi: 0-0 Tstrap: 0-0
Best Rating: 84 10/01 Wind 1m3f135y heavy

She finished runner-up in all three of her starts at two and was off the track for a long time afterwards. She is suited by middle distances and appreciated forcing tactics when scoring in first-time blinkers at Bath in October, and those blinkers worked to similar effect when she scored at Windsor also in October.

Alam (USA)

86 **81+**
2-y-o b c Silver Hawk (USA)-Ghashtah (USA) (Nijinsky (CAN))
E A L Dunlop Hamdan Al Maktoum

Placings:5 **(4484)**
2001: 7^{5}S

	Starts	1st	2nd	3rd	Win & Pl
Career Total (Turf)	1	0	0	0	0

Going (Turf): Sf: 0-1 GS: 0-0 Gd: 0-0 GF: 0-0 Fm: 0-0
Distance: 5f/6f: 0-0 7f-8f: 0-1 9f-13f: 0-0 14f+: 0-0
Track : LH: 0-0 RH: 0-0 Tight: 0-0 Gall: 0-0
Aids: Bl: 0-0 Vi: 0-0 Tstrap: 0-0
Best Rating: 81 9/01 Yarm 7f3y soft

Alamein (USA)

97(95) (57)**33**
8-y-o ch g Roi Danzig (USA)-Pollination (Pentotal)
W Storey R J H Limited

Placings:0334/31163/620400/100623360/3114602440/000023010403-0000265000 **(4662)**
2001: 8^{0}SD, 10^{0}S, 9^{0}GS, 11^{0}G, 12^{0}GF, 10^{2}GF, 10^{6}GF, 11^{5}GF, 12^{0}G, 8^{0}GF, 10^{0}GF

	Starts	1st	2nd	3rd	Win & Pl
Career Total (Turf)	48	3	5	7	20211
Career Total (AW)	9	3	0	2	7162

42	8/00	Haml	1m1f36y	F(0-60)	SFT	£2744
66	2/99	Ling	7f	F(0-70)H	STD	£2175
57	2/99	Ling	7f	F	STD	£2126
72	3/98	Sthl	7f	F	STD	£2242
78	6/96	Thsk	7f	D	FRM	£3613
73	6/96	Catt	7f	E	GD	£3158

Total win prize-money £16061

Going (Turf): Sf: 1-4 GS: 0-5 **Gd: 1-11** GF: 0-24 **Fm: 1-4**
Distance: 5f/6f: 0-4 **7f-8f: 5-29** 9f-13f: 1-24 14f+: 0-0
Track : **LH: 5-25** RH: 1-21 **Tight: 5-22** Gall: 0-8
Aids: **Bl: 2-20** Vi: 0-0 Tstrap: 1-22
Best Rating: 33 7/01 Hayd 1m3f200y gd-fm

A modest handicapper with a poor strike rate on turf but a better one on sand.

Alan's Prince (IRE)

(53)
3-y-o b c Anita's Prince-Fandangerina (USA) (Grey Dawn Ii)
B Palling Merthyr Motor Auctions

Placings:0 **(3427)**
2001: 6^{0}SD

	Starts	1st	2nd	3rd	Win & Pl
Career Total (Turf)	0	0	0	0	
Career Total (AW)	1	0	0	0	

Going (Turf): Sf: 0-0 GS: 0-0 Gd: 0-0 GF: 0-0 Fm: 0-0
Distance: 5f/6f: 0-1 7f-8f: 0-0 9f-13f: 0-0 14f+: 0-0

Track : LH: 0-1 RH: 0-0 Tight: 0-0 Gall: 0-0
Aids: Bl: 0-0 Vi: 0-0 Tstrap: 0-0

Alasha (IRE)

101 **98+**
2-y-o ch f Barathea (IRE)-Alasana (IRE) (Darshaan)
Sir Michael Stoute H H Aga Khan

Placings:31 **(4544)**
2001: 7^{3}GF, 6^{1}GF

	Starts	1st	2nd	3rd	Win & Pl
Career Total (Turf)	2	1	0	1	6471

98 9/01 Sals 6f212y D G-F £5707
Total win prize-money £5707

Going (Turf): Sf: 0-0 GS: 0-0 Gd: 0-0 **GF: 1-2** Fm: 0-0
Distance: 5f/6f: 0-0 **7f-8f: 1-2** 9f-13f: 0-0 14f+: 0-0
Track : LH: 0-0 RH: 0-0 Tight: 0-0 Gall: 0-0
Aids: Bl: 0-0 Vi: 0-0 Tstrap: 0-0
Best Rating: 98 9/01 Sals 6f212y gd-fm

Won a six-furlong maiden in decent company on her second outing. Her pedigree suggests she will be suited by at least a mile in the future. Favours a sound surface.

Alastair Smellie

101(75) (17)**58**
5-y-o ch g Sabrehill (USA)-Reel Foyle (USA) (Irish River (FR))
D Nicholls Ian Guise

Placings:6003163/354004/005040000-**0L0**34000 **(5287)**
2001: 6^{0}SD, 6^{L}G, **6**^{0}SD, 6^{3}G, 5^{4}GF, 5^{0}G, 6^{0}HY, 6^{0}HY

	Starts	1st	2nd	3rd	Win & Pl
Career Total (Turf)	28	1	0	4	11587
Career Total (AW)	2	0	0	0	

79 9/98 Ayr 6f D H G-S £5394
Total win prize-money £5394

Going (Turf): Sf: 0-6 **GS: 1-5** Gd: 0-10 GF: 0-4 Fm: 0-3
Distance: **5f/6f: 1-22** 7f-8f: 0-8 9f-13f: 0-0 14f+: 0-0
Track : LH: 0-7 RH: 0-1 Tight: 0-4 Gall: 0-0
Aids: Bl: 0-0 Vi: 0-6 Tstrap: 0-0
Best Rating: 58 9/01 Ayr 5f good

Useful handicapper at six or seven furlongs, but a tricky customer who tends to find trouble in running.

Alawar

(94) (38)**46**
4-y-o ch c Wolfhound (USA)-Ghassanah (Pas De Seul)
C G Cox Sheikh Amin Dahlawi

Placings:030/00044450-0066 **(2650)**
2001: 8^{0}S, 8^{0}G, 7^{6}GF, 8^{6}SD

	Starts	1st	2nd	3rd	Win & Pl
Career Total (Turf)	14	0	0	1	1365
Career Total (AW)	1	0	0	0	0

Going (Turf): Sf: 0-5 GS: 0-1 Gd: 0-4 GF: 0-4 Fm: 0-0
Distance: 5f/6f: 0-4 7f-8f: 0-8 9f-13f: 0-3 14f+: 0-0
Track : LH: 0-4 RH: 0-3 Tight: 0-0 Gall: 0-1
Aids: Bl: 0-2 Vi: 0-0 Tstrap: 0-13
Best Rating: 39 6/01 Bevl 7f100y gd-fm

Alazan

92(57) **18**
6-y-o ch g Risk Me (FR)-Gunnard (Gunner B)
W De Best-Turner The Spanish Connection

Placings:055/4/00P/000-000000 **(3865)**
2001: 12^{0}SD, 11^{0}F, 8^{0}GF, 7^{0}F, 7^{0}GS, 8^{0}GF

	Starts	1st	2nd	3rd	Win & Pl
Career Total (Turf)	15	0	0	0	740

	Starts	1st	2nd	3rd	Win & Pl
Career Total (AW)	1	0	0	0	

Going (Turf): Sf: 0-0 GS: 0-3 Gd: 0-3 GF: 0-6 Fm: 0-3
Distance: 5f/6f: 0-0 7f-8f: 0-8 9f-13f: 0-8 14f+: 0-0
Track : LH: 0-4 RH: 0-4 Tight: 0-3 Gall: 0-1
Aids: Bl: 0-0 Vi: 0-0 Tstrap: 0-0
Best Rating: 49 6/01 Wind 1m67y gd-fm

Albadou

97 **81**
3-y-o ch c Wolfhound (USA)-Ameerat Jumaira (USA) (Alydar (USA))
M P Tregoning Sheikh Ahmed Al Maktoum

Placings:255 **(2017)**
2001: 6^{2}HY, 8^{5}GS, 8^{5}GF

	Starts	1st	2nd	3rd	Win & Pl
Career Total (Turf)	3	0	1	0	728

Going (Turf): Sf: 0-1 GS: 0-1 Gd: 0-0 GF: 0-1 Fm: 0-0
Distance: 5f/6f: 0-0 7f-8f: 0-1 9f-13f: 0-2 14f+: 0-0
Track : LH: 0-1 RH: 0-2 Tight: 0-2 Gall: 0-0
Aids: Bl: 0-0 Vi: 0-0 Tstrap: 0-0
Best Rating: 81 6/01 Hayd 1m30y gd-fm

Albania

97 **72**
2-y-o ch c Selkirk (USA)-Elaine's Honor (USA) (Chief's Crown (USA))
M R Channon Sheikh Ahmed Al Maktoum

Placings:5331400 **(4196)**
2001: 5^{5}GS, 5^{3}G, 5^{3}G, 5^{1}GF, 6^{4}GF, 7^{0}G, 6^{0}G

	Starts	1st	2nd	3rd	Win & Pl
Career Total (Turf)	7	1	0	2	5603

66 6/01 Ches 5f16y D G-F £3493
Total win prize-money £3494

Going (Turf): Sf: 0-0 GS: 0-1 Gd: 0-4 **GF: 1-2** Fm: 0-0
Distance: **5f/6f: 1-5** 7f-8f: 0-2 9f-13f: 0-0 14f+: 0-0
Track : **LH: 1-3** RH: 0-1 **Tight: 1-1** Gall: 0-2
Aids: Bl: 0-0 Vi: 0-1 Tstrap: 0-0
Best Rating: 72 8/01 York 6f214y good

An 82,000gns half-brother to a couple of winners inculding a successful juvenile, he got off the mark at Chester on his fourth start despite not handling the track, but was firmly put in his place on his first attempt at six furlongs at Goodwood.

Albanova

104 **84+**
2-y-o gr f Alzao (USA)-Alouette (Darshaan)
Sir Mark Prescott Miss K Rausing

Placings:1 **(5015)**
2001: 7^{1}HY

	Starts	1st	2nd	3rd	Win & Pl
Career Total (Turf)	1	1	0	0	4339

84 9/01 Hayd 7f30y D HVY £4338
Total win prize-money £4339

Going (Turf): Sf: 1-1 GS: 0-0 Gd: 0-0 GF: 0-0 Fm: 0-0
Distance: 5f/6f: 0-0 **7f-8f: 1-1** 9f-13f: 0-0 14f+: 0-0
Track : **LH: 1-1** RH: 0-0 Tight: 0-0 Gall: 0-0
Aids: Bl: 0-0 Vi: 0-0 Tstrap: 0-0
Best Rating: 84 9/01 Hayd 7f30y heavy

A full-sister to Champion Stakes winner Alborada, she made a successful debut on bottomless ground in a fair maiden at Haydock in September. Likely to go on to better things.

Albarahin (USA)

119 **114**
6-y-o b h Silver Hawk (USA)-My Dear Lady (USA) (Mr Prospector (USA))
M P Tregoning Hamdan Al Maktoum

Placings:22/34/11612/2121211-22421110 **(5389)**
2001: 8^{2}GS, 9^{2}S, 8^{4}S, 10^{2}GS, 10^{1}G, 10^{1}GF, 9^{1}VS, 10^{0}GS

	Starts	1st	2nd	3rd	Win & Pl
Career Total (Turf)	24	10	9	1	205108

114	10/01	Lonc	1m1f165y		VS	£29028
112	9/01	Ayr	1m2f192y	A	G-F	£14089
87	8/01	NmkJ	1m2f	C	GD	£6061
120	10/00	NmkR	1m	A	SFT	£14210
120	10/00	NmkR	1m1f	A	SFT	£15892
118	9/00	Gdwd	1m1f192y	A	HVY	£17810
108	8/00	Sand	1m1f	C	GD	£6515
108	10/99	Newb	1m1f	B(0-100)H	HVY	£9649
93	8/99	Sand	1m2f7y	C(0-90)H	GD	£9675
90	8/99	Leic	1m1f218y	D(0-80)H	GD	£4825

Total win prize-money £127756

Going (Turf): Sf: 4-9 GS: 0-4 **Gd: 4-8** GF: 1-2 Fm: 0-0
Distance: 5f/6f: 0-0 7f-8f: 1-5 **9f-13f: 9-19** 14f+: 0-0
Track : LH: 2-6 **RH: 6-10** Tight: 1-2 **Gall: 2-6**
Aids: Bl: 0-0 Vi: 0-0 Tstrap: 0-0
Best Rating: 114 10/01 Lonc 1m1f165y v soft

A genuine and consistent sort with a high strike-rate since returning from injury in 1999, he returned to winning form in a conditions event at Newmarket in August, and followed that up with another Listed success at Ayr. Completed the hat-trick when gaining his first Group-race victory in the Prix Dollar Effective from eight to ten furlongs, he goes well from the front and appreciates give.

Albashoosh

107 **87**
3-y-o b g Cadeaux Genereux-Annona (USA) (Diesis)
E A L Dunlop Khalifa Sultan

Placings:032-0506152 **(4486)**
2001: 10^{0}S, 7^{5}GF, 8^{0}GF, 8^{6}G, 7^{1}S, 7^{5}GF, 7^{2}S

	Starts	1st	2nd	3rd	Win & Pl
Career Total (Turf)	10	1	2	1	6040

71 8/01 Chop 7f16y D SFT £2821
Total win prize-money £2821

Going (Turf): Sf: 1-3 GS: 0-0 Gd: 0-1 GF: 0-6 Fm: 0-0
Distance: 5f/6f: 0-0 **7f-8f: 1-7** 9f-13f: 0-3 14f+: 0-0
Track : LH: 0-3 RH: 0-0 Tight: 0-0 Gall: 0-2
Aids: Bl: 0-1 **Vi: 1-2** Tstrap: 0-0
Best Rating: 87 5/01 York 7f202y gd-fm

A free-running handicapper suited by seven furlongs and easy ground. has worn a visor..

Albemarle Street

91 **70d**
2-y-o b f Alhaarth (IRE)-Pigeon Hole (Green Desert (USA))
J A Osborne Mountgrange Stud

Placings:55000 **(5128)**
2001: 6^{5}GF, 6^{5}GF, 6^{0}F, 5^{0}GS, 6^{0}HY

	Starts	1st	2nd	3rd	Win & Pl
Career Total (Turf)	5	0	0	0	0

Going (Turf): Sf: 0-1 GS: 0-1 Gd: 0-0 GF: 0-2 Fm: 0-1
Distance: 5f/6f: 0-2 7f-8f: 0-3 9f-13f: 0-0 14f+: 0-0
Track : LH: 0-1 RH: 0-0 Tight: 0-0 Gall: 0-0
Aids: Bl: 0-1 Vi: 0-0 Tstrap: 0-0
Best Rating: 70 8/01 Brig 6f209y gd-fm

Alberkinnie

102(101) (21)**32**

6-y-o b m Ron's Victory (USA)-Trojan Desert (Troy)
John A Harris (J L Harris 4/6) Paddy Barrett

Placings:40006U0650/0000502644020/0253321000-0000535000500000 **(5599)**
2001: 9^{0}SW, 12^{0}SD, 11^{0}SD, 8^{0}SD, 8^{5}SD, 9^{3}HY, 10^{5}G, 10^{0}S, 10^{0}GF, 11^{0}GF, 10^{5}G, 10^{0}HY, 9^{0}GF, 8^{0}F, 10^{0}S, 12^{0}GS

	Starts	1st	2nd	3rd	Win & Pl
Career Total (Turf)	34	1	2	1	6883
Career Total (AW)	15	0	2	2	2081

45	5/00	Nott	1m1f213y	D(0-80)H	G-S	£4101

Total win prize-money £4102

Going (Turf): Sf: 0-7 **GS: 1-4** Gd: 0-8 GF: 0-11 Fm: 0-4
Distance: 5f/6f: 0-0 7f-8f: 0-6 **9f-13f: 1-43** 14f+: 0-0
Track : **LH: 1-36** RH: 0-8 Tight: 0-20 Gall: 0-5
Aids: Bl: 0-0 Vi: 0-0 Tstrap: 0-0
Best Rating: 42 5/01 Ripn 1m2f good

Albero (IRE)

89(65) (19)**57**
2-y-o b g Priolo (USA)-Woody's Colours (USA) (Caro)
P R Chamings Twenty Twenty Research

Placings:0025000 **(5667)**
2001: 6^{0}GF, 7^{0}GS, 6^{2}GF, 6^{5}GF, 7^{0}S, 8^{0}SD, 8^{0}HY

	Starts	1st	2nd	3rd	Win & Pl
Career Total (Turf)	6	0	1	0	542
Career Total (AW)	1	0	0	0	

Going (Turf): Sf: 0-2 GS: 0-1 Gd: 0-0 GF: 0-3 Fm: 0-0
Distance: 5f/6f: 0-1 7f-8f: 0-4 9f-13f: 0-2 14f+: 0-0
Track : LH: 0-3 RH: 0-1 Tight: 0-2 Gall: 0-0
Aids: Bl: 0-1 Vi: 0-0 Tstrap: 0-0
Best Rating: 62 8/01 Brig 6f209y gd-fm

Albert The Bear

100 (45)**46**
8-y-o b g Puissance-Florentynna Bay (Aragon)
A Berry Chris & Antonia Deuters

Placings:0050111420/021253/310105462000520/00056300/00541123004600/060030026006-40002560600003 **(5287)**
2001: 6^{4}HY, 7^{0}GF, 6^{0}GF, 6^{0}GF, 6^{2}GS, 6^{5}G, 6^{6}GF, 5^{0}GF, 5^{6}G, 6^{0}GF, 5^{0}G, 6^{0}GS, 6^{0}G, 6^{3}HY

	Starts	1st	2nd	3rd	Win & Pl
Career Total (Turf)	77	8	8	6	59860
Career Total (AW)	2	0	0	0	

64	7/99	Pont	6f	D(0-80)H	G-S	£7960
52	6/99	Carl	5f207y	F	G-F	£2458
87	6/97	Ches	7f2y	C(0-95)H	G-F	£8481
87	5/97	Ches	7f122y	C(0-90)H	HVY	£9280
77	6/96	Ches	7f2y	D(0-80)H	G-F	£4380
65	8/95	Catt	5f212y	E	G-F	£3106
65	8/95	Bath	5f161y	E	HRD	£3142
60	6/95	Carl	5f	G	FRM	£2465

Total win prize-money £41272

Going (Turf): Sf: 1-8 GS: 1-13 Gd: 0-16 **GF: 4-34** Fm: 2-6
Distance: **5f/6f: 5-39** 7f-8f: 3-40 9f-13f: 0-0 14f+: 0-0
Track : **LH: 6-38** RH: 2-10 **Tight: 4-19** Gall: 3-11
Aids: Bl: 0-8 **Vi: 2-33** Tstrap: 0-0
Best Rating: 47 6/01 Haml 6f5y gd-sft

Albert's Lad

(71)
3-y-o br g Alhijaz-Nikiya (IRE) (Lead On Time (USA))
M W Easterby T Swain, B Bargh, Mrs A Geraghty & J Walsh

Placings:0000 **(0797)**
2001: 7^{0}SD, 5^{0}SW, 6^{0}SD, 12^{0}SD

	Starts	1st	2nd	3rd	Win & Pl
Career Total (Turf)	0	0	0	0	
Career Total (AW)	4	0	0	0	

Going (Turf): Sf: 0-0 GS: 0-0 Gd: 0-0 GF: 0-0 Fm: 0-0
Distance: 5f/6f: 0-2 7f-8f: 0-1 9f-13f: 0-1 14f+: 0-0
Track : LH: 0-3 RH: 0-0 Tight: 0-0 Gall: 0-0
Aids: Bl: 0-0 Vi: 0-0 Tstrap: 0-0

Albuhera (IRE)

110 **109+**
3-y-o b g Desert Style (IRE)-Morning Welcome (IRE) (Be My Guest (USA))
M Johnston D J & F A Jackson

Placings:261-23010134100 **(5362)**
2001: 8^{2}GS, 9^{3}GS, 6^{0}F, 8^{1}GF, 8^{0}GF, 10^{1}GF, 10^{3}G, 8^{4}GF, 10^{1}GF, 9^{0}G, 9^{0}GS

	Starts	1st	2nd	3rd	Win & Pl
Career Total (Turf)	14	4	2	2	82857

109	9/01	Newb	1m2f6y	B(0-105)H	G-F	£43500
99	7/01	NmkJ	1m2f	C(0-95)H	G-F	£17238
91	5/01	Ayr	1m	C(0-90)	G-F	£7621
85	11/00	Muss	7f30y	E	G-S	£2323

Total win prize-money £70683

Going (Turf): Sf: 0-2 GS: 1-4 Gd: 0-2 **GF: 3-5** Fm: 0-1
Distance: 5f/6f: 0-1 7f-8f: 2-6 9f-13f: 2-7 14f+: 0-0
Track : LH: 2-5 RH: 2-3 Tight: 1-2 **Gall: 2-5**
Aids: Bl: 0-0 Vi: 0-0 Tstrap: 0-0
Best Rating: 109 9/01 Newb 1m2f6y gd-fm

A progressive sort, he won handicaps at Ayr and Newmarket earlier in the season and was eventually tried in Listed company. He failed to shine there, but got back to winning ways with a very easy win in a very valuable handicap at Newbury in September 2001, but has been disappointing twice since. Suited by ten furlongs and fast ground.

Albundy (IRE)

72 **30**
2-y-o b c Alzao (USA)-Grove Daffodil (IRE) (Salt Dome (USA))
M H Tompkins P H Betts

Placings:000 **(5125)**
2001: 6^{0}GS, 6^{0}GF, 5^{0}HY

	Starts	1st	2nd	3rd	Win & Pl
Career Total (Turf)	3	0	0	0	

Going (Turf): Sf: 0-1 GS: 0-1 Gd: 0-0 GF: 0-1 Fm: 0-0
Distance: 5f/6f: 0-2 7f-8f: 0-1 9f-13f: 0-0 14f+: 0-0
Track : LH: 0-1 RH: 0-0 Tight: 0-0 Gall: 0-1
Aids: Bl: 0-1 Vi: 0-0 Tstrap: 0-0
Best Rating: 30 9/01 York 6f214y gd-fm

Alburack

94(78) (33)**36**
3-y-o b g Rock City-Suzannah's Song (Song)
G G Margarson G G Margarson

Placings:000-0000000 **(4360)**
2001: 7^{0}SD, 8^{0}S, 6^{0}G, 5^{0}F, 5^{0}F, 10^{0}G, 9^{0}GF

	Starts	1st	2nd	3rd	Win & Pl
Career Total (Turf)	9	0	0	0	
Career Total (AW)	1	0	0	0	

Going (Turf): Sf: 0-1 GS: 0-1 Gd: 0-3 GF: 0-2 Fm: 0-2
Distance: 5f/6f: 0-4 7f-8f: 0-4 9f-13f: 0-2 14f+: 0-0
Track : LH: 0-5 RH: 0-2 Tight: 0-2 Gall: 0-2
Aids: Bl: 0-2 Vi: 0-0 Tstrap: 0-0
Best Rating: 44 5/01 Nott 6f15y good

Alcayde

105 **59**
6-y-o ch g Alhijaz-Lucky Flinders (Free State)
J Akehurst A D Spence

Placings:4/2321425/0053502-5611364543 **(4953)**
2001: 14^{5}S, 14^{6}HY, 17^{1}GF, 17^{1}G, 17^{3}GF, 16^{6}GF, 21^{4}GF, 17^{5}GF, 16^{4}G, 16^{3}GS

	Starts	1st	2nd	3rd	Win & Pl
Career Total (Turf)	25	3	4	4	20218

51	6/01	Bath	2m1f34y	D(0-80)H	GD	£3786
48	5/01	Bath	2m1f34y	E(0-75)H	G-F	£3454
77	7/98	Newc	1m2f32y	D(0-85)H	G-F	£3420

Total win prize-money £10661

Going (Turf): Sf: 0-8 GS: 0-3 Gd: 1-5 **GF: 2-9** Fm: 0-0
Distance: 5f/6f: 0-0 7f-8f: 0-2 9f-13f: 1-9 **14f+: 2-14**
Track : **LH: 3-17** RH: 0-7 **Tight: 2-6** Gall: 1-4
Aids: Bl: 0-0 Vi: 0-0 Tstrap: 0-0
Best Rating: 59 6/01 Pont 2m1f216y gd-fm

Successful twice over 17 furlongs at Bath this term but held off a higher mark.

Alcazar (IRE)

111 **102**
6-y-o b g Alzao (USA)-Sahara Breeze (Ela-Mana-Mou)
H Morrison Jrepard,Fmelrose,Opawle,Mstokes,Rblack

Placings:510414113/1 **(4869)**
2001: 14^{1}G

	Starts	1st	2nd	3rd	Win & Pl
Career Total (Turf)	10	5	0	1	50407

102	9/01	NmkR	1m6f	B(0-100)H	GD	£15196
105	11/98	Donc	1m4f	A	SFT	£11650
103	10/98	Hayd	1m3f200y	C	SFT	£4733
103	9/98	Hayd	1m3f200y	B(0-105)H	GD	£8211
92	6/98	Ripn	1m	D	HVY	£3598

Total win prize-money £43390

Going (Turf): Sf: 3-4 GS: 0-0 Gd: 2-4 GF: 0-1 Fm: 0-0
Distance: 5f/6f: 0-0 7f-8f: 1-2 **9f-13f: 3-7** 14f+: 1-1
Track : **LH: 3-5** RH: 2-4 Tight: 1-1 **Gall: 2-4**
Aids: Bl: 0-0 Vi: 0-0 Tstrap: 0-0
Best Rating: 102 9/01 NmkR 1m6f good

A listed winner for John Dunlop in November 1998, he was having his first run since when landing a Newmarket handicap in September 2001. Likes soft ground.

Alconbury

(96) (68)**61**
3-y-o b c Green Desert (USA)-Allegra (Niniski (USA))
Patrick J Flynn (Sir Mark Prescott 20/2) Ms Geraldine M Reilly

Placings:104500000 **(5642a)**
2001: 6^{1}SD, 6^{0}SD, 8^{4}SD, 7^{5}S, 7^{0}G, 8^{0}G, 9^{0}GF, 7^{0}G, 6^{0}Y

	Starts	1st	2nd	3rd	Win & Pl
Career Total (Turf)	6	0	0	0	
Career Total (AW)	3	1	0	0	3216

62	1/01	Sthl	6f	D	STD	£2926

Total win prize-money £2926

Going (Turf): Sf: 0-1 GS: 0-0 Gd: 0-3 GF: 0-1 Fm: 0-0
Distance: **5f/6f: 1-3** 7f-8f: 0-3 9f-13f: 0-3 14f+: 0-0
Track : **LH: 1-3** RH: 0-0 Tight: 0-1 Gall: 0-0
Aids: Bl: 0-0 Vi: 0-0 Tstrap: 0-0
Best Rating: 68 2/01 Wolv 1m100y stand

Alconleigh

96 (53d)**36**
6-y-o ch g Pursuit Of Love-Serotina (IRE) (Mtoto)
B Ellison Alconleigh Partnership

Placings:312212042/040/00350535250000000/0-0040 **(1907)**
2001: 5^{0}GF, 8^{0}GF, 8^{4}GF, 8^{0}GF

	Starts	1st	2nd	3rd	Win & Pl
Career Total (Turf)	33	2	5	2	21183
Career Total (AW)	1	0	0	1	537

90 7/97 Thsk 7f C GD £5209
77 5/97 Ripn 6f D G-S £3391
Total win prize-money £8601

Going (Turf): Sf: 0-3 **GS: 1-5 Gd: 1-13** GF: 0-12 Fm: 0-0
Distance: 5f/6f: 1-6 7f-8f: 1-12 9f-13f: 0-16 14f+: 0-0
Track : **LH: 1-20** RH: 0-8 **Tight: 1-7** Gall: 0-9
Aids: Bl: 0-1 Vi: 0-0 Tstrap: 0-1
Best Rating: 36 6/01 Newc 1m gd-fm

Aldafra

99 **92**

2-y-o b f Spectrum (IRE)-Abeyr (Unfuwain (USA))
M R Channon Sheikh Ahmed Al Maktoum

Placings:516300 **(5052)**
2001: 6^{5}F, 6^{1}GF, 7^{6}G, 6^{3}GF, 6^{0}GF, 7^{0}S

	Starts	1st	2nd	3rd	Win & Pl
Career Total (Turf)	6	1	0	1	6215

80 7/01 Nott 6f15y D G-F £4176
Total win prize-money £4176

Going (Turf): Sf: 0-1 GS: 0-0 Gd: 0-1 **GF: 1-3** Fm: 0-1
Distance: 5f/6f: 0-3 **7f-8f: 1-3** 9f-13f: 0-0 14f+: 0-0
Track : LH: 0-0 RH: 0-0 Tight: 0-0 Gall: 0-0
Aids: Bl: 0-0 Vi: 0-0 Tstrap: 0-0
Best Rating: 92 9/01 Sals 6f gd-fm

Improved from her debut to take a six-furlong fillies' maiden at Nottingham in July, but has found things difficult since being stepped up in class.

Aldebaran (USA)

113 **108**

3-y-o b c Mr Prospector (USA)-Chimes Of Freedom (USA) (Private Account (USA))
H R A Cecil Niarchos Family

Placings:1-222223 **(5103)**
2001: 8^{2}G, 8^{2}GF, 7^{2}GF, 7^{2}GF, 10^{2}GS, 8^{3}GS

	Starts	1st	2nd	3rd	Win & Pl
Career Total (Turf)	7	1	5	1	39449

100 10/00 Donc 7f D GD £3477
Total win prize-money £3478

Going (Turf): Sf: 0-0 GS: 0-2 **Gd: 1-2** GF: 0-3 Fm: 0-0
Distance: 5f/6f: 0-0 **7f-8f: 1-6** 9f-13f: 0-1 14f+: 0-0
Track : LH: 0-3 RH: 0-1 Tight: 0-0 Gall: 0-3
Aids: Bl: 0-0 Vi: 0-0 Tstrap: 0-0
Best Rating: 108 6/01 Asct 7f gd-fm

A promising colt, who is probably on the upgrade. He chased Dandoun home on his first two outings this season. After trying to stretch the favourite at Kempton, he was unable to cope with Dandoun's burst of speed. Ran a cracker when runner-up in the Jersey at Ascot and has continued to run well. Stays a mile to ten furlongs. Acts on a sound surface.

Aldenham (IRE)

75

4-y-o b f Namaqualand (USA)-Lamp Of Phoebus (USA) (Sunshine Forever (USA))
Andrew Reid A S Reid

Placings:0 **(2057)**
2001: 6^{0}GF

	Starts	1st	2nd	3rd	Win & Pl
Career Total (Turf)	1	0	0	0	

Going (Turf): Sf: 0-0 GS: 0-0 Gd: 0-0 GF: 0-1 Fm: 0-0
Distance: 5f/6f: 0-0 7f-8f: 0-1 9f-13f: 0-0 14f+: 0-0
Track : LH: 0-0 RH: 0-0 Tight: 0-0 Gall: 0-0
Aids: Bl: 0-0 Vi: 0-0 Tstrap: 0-0

Aldora

93 **77**

2-y-o ch f Magic Ring (IRE)-Sharp Top (Sharpo)
M J Ryan D Bell

Placings:031 **(5533)**
2001: 7^{0}GF, 6^{3}GS, 5^{1}S

	Starts	1st	2nd	3rd	Win & Pl
Career Total (Turf)	3	1	0	1	3731

74 10/01 Rdcr 5f F SFT £2838
Total win prize-money £2839

Going (Turf): Sf: 1-1 GS: 0-1 Gd: 0-0 GF: 0-1 Fm: 0-0
Distance: **5f/6f: 1-2** 7f-8f: 0-1 9f-13f: 0-0 14f+: 0-0
Track : LH: 0-0 RH: 0-0 Tight: 0-0 Gall: 0-0
Aids: Bl: 0-0 Vi: 0-0 Tstrap: 0-0
Best Rating: 77 10/01 NmkR 6f gd-sft

Half-sister to the useful ten-furlong winner Polar Red, improved from her debut in a race that has worked out well with a bold effort in a maiden at Newmarket in October.

Aldwych

111 **111**

3-y-o ch c In The Wings-Arderelle (FR) (Pharly (FR))
R Charlton Newgate Stud

Placings:01-142520 **(4201a)**
2001: 10^{1}GS, 10^{4}GF, 10^{2}GF, 12^{5}GF, 10^{2}GF, 10^{0}Y

	Starts	1st	2nd	3rd	Win & Pl
Career Total (Turf)	8	2	2	0	34993

107 5/01 Bath 1m2f46y B(0-95) G-S £10010
91 10/00 Newb 1m C SFT £6612
Total win prize-money £16622

Going (Turf): Sf: 1-1 GS: 1-1 Gd: 0-1 GF: 0-4 Fm: 0-0
Distance: 5f/6f: 0-0 7f-8f: 1-2 9f-13f: 1-6 14f+: 0-0
Track : **LH: 1-2** RH: 0-1 **Tight: 1-1** Gall: 0-2
Aids: Bl: 0-1 Vi: 0-0 Tstrap: 0-0
Best Rating: 111 6/01 Asct 1m4f gd-fm

A half-brother to Spout amongst others, he improved on his Newmarket juvenile debut when scoring in good style at Newbury, but was not particularly impressive in winning a Bath conditions event on his return. Finished a fair fourth in the Dante, but did not look to go through with his effort when beaten a neck by Potemkin in Listed event at Newmarket. Subsequent races reinforced that view and he has reportedly been sold to race in America.

Aldwych Arrow (IRE)

(99) (48)**41**

6-y-o ch g Rainbows For Life (CAN)-Shygate (Shy Groom (USA))
M A Buckley M A Buckley

Placings:60600/**3224**022112030354/**5042**023120000/0 0006025**402**-20330 **(5044)**
2001: 12^{2}SD, 14^{0}HY, 12^{3}G, 11^{3}G, 14^{0}SD

	Starts	1st	2nd	3rd	Win & Pl
Career Total (Turf)	35	3	6	5	20480
Career Total (AW)	15	0	5	1	4297

66 4/99 Catt 1m3f214yD(0-85)H SFT £5004
66 6/98 Muss 1m6f D(0-80)H SFT £3434
67 6/98 Ayr 1m5f13y E(0-70)H GD £3036
Total win prize-money £11475

Going (Turf): Sf: 2-13 GS: 0-2 Gd: 1-10 GF: 0-8 Fm: 0-2
Distance: 5f/6f: 0-2 7f-8f: 0-1 9f-13f: 1-26 **14f+: 2-21**
Track : **LH: 2-38** RH: 1-9 **Tight: 2-26** Gall: 0-4
Aids: Bl: 0-1 Vi: 0-0 Tstrap: 0-0
Best Rating: 48 3/01 Wolv 1m4f stand

Alegranza (IRE)

112 **100**

3-y-o b f Lake Coniston (IRE)-Angelic Sounds (IRE) (The Noble Player (USA))
Declan Gillespie (David Wachman 17/4) G Callanan

Placings:215250 **(4861)**
2001: 6S, 5^{2}GF, 5^{1}Y, 5^{5}Y, 5^{2}GF, 5^{5}G, 5^{0}GF

	Starts	1st	2nd	3rd	Win & Pl
Career Total (Turf)	8	1	2	0	16890

99 5/01 Tipp 5f YLD £8970
Total win prize-money £8970

Going (Turf): Sf: 0-1 GS: 0-0 Gd: 0-1 GF: 0-3 Fm: 0-0
Distance: **5f/6f: 1-8** 7f-8f: 0-0 9f-13f: 0-0 14f+: 0-0
Track : LH: 0-0 RH: 0-0 Tight: 0-0 Gall: 0-0
Aids: Bl: 0-0 Vi: 0-0 Tstrap: 0-0
Best Rating: 100 9/01 Leop 5f good

Irish sprinter, successful at Tipperary in May, and a good second to Misraah in five-furlong Listed event at Sandown in July (forcing the pace after a quick start). Fifth when upped to a group Three at Leopardstown, she does not look quite up to that class.

Alegria

107(100) (79)**70**

5-y-o b m Night Shift (USA)-High Habit (Slip Anchor)
J M P Eustace J C Smith

Placings:51/20364530/0106000-00344463430000 **(5027)**
2001: 5^{0}GS, 6^{0}SD, 5^{3}GF, 5^{4}F, 6^{4}GF, 5^{4}GF, 5^{6}GF, 6^{3}GF, 6^{4}G, 5^{3}GF, 7^{0}G, 5^{0}GF, 6^{0}G, 5^{0}S

	Starts	1st	2nd	3rd	Win & Pl
Career Total (Turf)	30	2	1	5	22551
Career Total (AW)	1	0	0	0	

85 6/00 Wind 6f C(0-90) GD £6418
84 7/98 Wind 5f217y D GD £3436
Total win prize-money £9855

Going (Turf): Sf: 0-3 GS: 0-2 **Gd: 2-11** GF: 0-11 Fm: 0-3
Distance: **5f/6f: 2-27** 7f-8f: 0-4 9f-13f: 0-0 14f+: 0-0
Track : LH: 0-4 **RH: 2-2** Tight: 0-0 **Gall: 2-3**
Aids: Bl: 0-6 Vi: 0-1 Tstrap: 0-3
Best Rating: 82 8/01 Gdwd 6f good

Best at six furlongs on a sound surface, she has worn blinkers and a tongue tie in the past, but has gained only one win since 1998. Looks to need more leniency from the Handicapper.

Alessandro Severo

(83) (55)**85**

2-y-o gr c Brief Truce (USA)-Altaia (FR) (Sicyos (USA))
N P Littmoden G Mazza

Placings:3625 **(5197)**
2001: 7^{3}HY, 6^{6}GS, 7^{2}GS, 8^{5}SD

	Starts	1st	2nd	3rd	Win & Pl
Career Total (Turf)	3	0	1	1	3623
Career Total (AW)	1	0	0	0	0

Going (Turf): Sf: 0-1 GS: 0-2 Gd: 0-0 GF: 0-0 Fm: 0-0
Distance: 5f/6f: 0-1 7f-8f: 0-2 9f-13f: 0-1 14f+: 0-0
Track : LH: 0-1 RH: 0-0 Tight: 0-1 Gall: 0-0
Aids: Bl: 0-0 Vi: 0-0 Tstrap: 0-0
Best Rating: 85 10/01 Newc 7f gd-sft

Looks a staying type.

Alexander Academy (USA)

(84) (47)**79**

2-y-o b/br f Royal Academy (USA)-Fantastic Bid (USA) (Auction Ring (USA))
R Hannon Mrs N O'Callaghan

Placings:036 **(4663)**
2001: 6^{0}GF, 6^{3}GS, 6^{6}GF

	Starts	1st	2nd	3rd	Win & Pl
Career Total (Turf)	3	0	0	1	666

Going (Turf): Sf: 0-0 GS: 0-1 Gd: 0-0 GF: 0-2 Fm: 0-0
Distance: 5f/6f: 0-2 7f-8f: 0-1 9f-13f: 0-0 14f+: 0-0
Track : LH: 0-0 RH: 0-0 Tight: 0-0 Gall: 0-0
Aids: Bl: 0-0 Vi: 0-0 Tstrap: 0-0
Best Rating: 79 8/01 Gdwd 6f gd-sft

A half-sister to seven-furlong three-year-old winner Fantastic Dance. Dam won mile Listed race in France.

Alexander Allstars (IRE)

87(69) (19)**37**
2-y-o ch f Petardia-Katherine Gorge (USA) (Hansel (USA))
T D Easterby Mrs N O'Callaghan

Placings:503 **(2750)**
2001: 5^{5}SD, 5^{0}GS, 6^{3}GF

	Starts	1st	2nd	3rd	Win & Pl
Career Total (Turf)	2	0	0	1	376
Career Total (AW)	1	0	0	0	0

Going (Turf): Sf: 0-0 GS: 0-1 Gd: 0-0 GF: 0-1 Fm: 0-0
Distance: 5f/6f: 0-3 7f-8f: 0-0 9f-13f: 0-0 14f+: 0-0
Track : LH: 0-0 RH: 0-0 Tight: 0-0 Gall: 0-0
Aids: Bl: 0-0 Vi: 0-0 Tstrap: 0-0
Best Rating: 37 7/01 Hayd 6f gd-fm

Alexander Star (IRE)

96 **59**
3-y-o b/br f Inzar (USA)-Business Centre (IRE) (Digamist (USA))
Miss D A McHale (J A R Toller 11/7) Mark Venus

Placings:430-260200 **(5181)**
2001: 6^{2}GF, 6^{6}GF, 8^{0}G, 6^{2}G, 6^{0}GF, 6^{0}HY

	Starts	1st	2nd	3rd	Win & Pl
Career Total (Turf)	9	0	2	1	2771

Going (Turf): Sf: 0-2 GS: 0-0 Gd: 0-3 GF: 0-4 Fm: 0-0
Distance: 5f/6f: 0-5 7f-8f: 0-3 9f-13f: 0-1 14f+: 0-0
Track : LH: 0-2 RH: 0-1 Tight: 0-1 Gall: 0-2
Aids: Bl: 0-0 Vi: 0-0 Tstrap: 0-0
Best Rating: 59 8/01 Yarm 6f3y good

Alexander Three D (IRE)

106 **92+**
2-y-o b f Pennekamp (USA)-Loon (FR) (Kaldoun (FR))
B W Hills Mrs N O'Callaghan

Placings:032421 **(5606)**
2001: 7^{0}GS, 7^{3}G, 8^{2}GF, 8^{4}G, 7^{2}S, 10^{1}GS

	Starts	1st	2nd	3rd	Win & Pl
Career Total (Turf)	6	1	2	1	16248

92 11/01 NmkR 1m2f A G-S £12342
Total win prize-money £12342

Going (Turf): Sf: 0-1 **GS: 1-2** Gd: 0-2 GF: 0-1 Fm: 0-0
Distance: 5f/6f: 0-0 7f-8f: 0-3 **9f-13f: 1-3** 14f+: 0-0
Track : LH: 0-1 RH: 0-0 Tight: 0-0 Gall: 0-1
Aids: Bl: 0-0 Vi: 0-0 Tstrap: 0-0
Best Rating: 92 11/01 NmkR 1m2f gd-sft

Rann some good races, in both maidens and a competitive York nursery, before winning a Newmarket Listed race over ten furlongs.

Alexandra S (IRE)

87 **45**
3-y-o b f Sadler's Wells (USA)-Heaven Only Knows (High Top)
P F I Cole Mrs Belinda Strudwick

Placings:4P **(1151)**
2001: 12^{4}HY, 12^{P}GS

	Starts	1st	2nd	3rd	Win & Pl
Career Total (Turf)	2	0	0	0	0

Going (Turf): Sf: 0-1 GS: 0-1 Gd: 0-0 GF: 0-0 Fm: 0-0
Distance: 5f/6f: 0-0 7f-8f: 0-0 9f-13f: 0-2 14f+: 0-0
Track : LH: 0-0 RH: 0-2 Tight: 0-2 Gall: 0-0
Aids: Bl: 0-0 Vi: 0-0 Tstrap: 0-0
Best Rating: 45 4/01 Folk 1m4f heavy

Alexius (IRE)

114 **116+**
3-y-o b c Rainbow Quest (USA)-Alexandrie (USA) (Val De L'Orne (FR))
Sir Michael Stoute Sheikh Mohammed

Placings:11 **(3512)**
2001: 10^{1}G, 12^{1}GF

	Starts	1st	2nd	3rd	Win & Pl
Career Total (Turf)	2	2	0	0	34434

116 7/01 Gdwd 1m4f A G-F £29000
95 7/01 NmkJ 1m2f D GD £5434
Total win prize-money £34434

Going (Turf): Sf: 0-0 GS: 0-0 **Gd: 1-1 GF: 1-1** Fm: 0-0
Distance: 5f/6f: 0-0 7f-8f: 0-0 **9f-13f: 2-2** 14f+: 0-0
Track : LH: 0-0 **RH: 2-2** Tight: 1-1 Gall: 1-1
Aids: Bl: 0-0 Vi: 0-0 Tstrap: 0-0
Best Rating: 116 7/01 Gdwd 1m4f gd-fm

Made a good impression when landing a maiden at the Newmarket July meeting on his debut, then took the Group three Gordon Stakes in tremendous style after being very slowly away. Looked a live contender for the St Leger before sustaining a tendon injury. Remains a colt of potential if recovering, and may race for Godolphin next year.

Alfalfa

86 **39**
3-y-o b g Rudimentary (USA)-Zalfa (Luthier)
G B Balding Mrs P Gulliver Mrs K Perrin G Balding

Placings:000-2005 **(3670)**
2001: 8^{2}HY, 10^{0}GF, 8^{0}GF, 8^{5}S

	Starts	1st	2nd	3rd	Win & Pl
Career Total (Turf)	7	0	1	0	872

Going (Turf): Sf: 0-4 GS: 0-1 Gd: 0-0 GF: 0-2 Fm: 0-0
Distance: 5f/6f: 0-1 7f-8f: 0-3 9f-13f: 0-3 14f+: 0-0
Track : LH: 0-3 RH: 0-0 Tight: 0-0 Gall: 0-2
Aids: Bl: 0-0 Vi: 0-0 Tstrap: 0-0
Best Rating: 39 8/01 Nott 1m54y soft

Alfano (IRE)

99(65) (12)**60**
3-y-o b g Priolo (USA)-Sartigila (Efisio)
P Mitchell Alleynian Racing Partnership

Placings:550-00061404021 **(5601)**
2001: 9^{0}GS, 9^{0}GS, 11^{0}G, 11^{6}F, 10^{1}GS, 12^{4}GS, 12^{0}GF, 11^{4}G, 10^{0}HY, 8^{2}G, 8^{1}GS

	Starts	1st	2nd	3rd	Win & Pl
Career Total (Turf)	13	2	1	0	9254
Career Total (AW)	1	0	0	0	

60 11/01 NmkR 1m E(0-70)H G-S £3698
58 7/01 Wwck 1m2f188yD(0-80)H G-S £4078
Total win prize-money £7778

Going (Turf): Sf: 0-3 **GS: 2-5** Gd: 0-3 GF: 0-1 Fm: 0-1
Distance: 5f/6f: 0-0 7f-8f: 1-4 9f-13f: 1-10 14f+: 0-0
Track : LH: 0-5 RH: 0-4 Tight: 0-6 Gall: 0-1
Aids: Bl: 0-0 Vi: 1-3 Tstrap: 1-3
Best Rating: 60 11/01 NmkR 1m gd-sft

Caused a surprise when winning a Warwick handicap in a first-time visor and a tongue tie, but won without the aids at Newmarket in November. Suited by good to soft and eight to 11 furlongs.

Alfie Lee (IRE)

95(103) (69)**65**
4-y-o ch c Case Law-Nordic Living (IRE) (Nordico (USA))
C N Allen Shadowfax Racing.Com

Placings:54100/005005-**00000**400 **(2165)**
2001: 6^{0}SD, 6^{0}SD, 7^{0}SD, 6^{0}SD, 6^{0}SD, 5^{4}SD, 5^{0}GF, 5^{0}G

	Starts	1st	2nd	3rd	Win & Pl
Career Total (Turf)	13	1	0	0	5474
Career Total (AW)	6	0	0	0	292

74 5/99 Gdwd 5f D GD £4123
Total win prize-money £4124

Going (Turf): Sf: 0-0 GS: 0-0 **Gd: 1-5** GF: 0-7 Fm: 0-1
Distance: **5f/6f: 1-15** 7f-8f: 0-4 9f-13f: 0-0 14f+: 0-0
Track : LH: 0-6 RH: 0-1 Tight: 0-3 Gall: 0-1
Aids: Bl: 0-1 Vi: 0-0 Tstrap: 0-7
Best Rating: 69 3/01 Wolv 6f stand

Fairly useful sprint handicapper at best. Enjoyed a profitable three-year-old campaign but lost his way earlier this year on sand. Very well treated on best form but is best watched until hinting at a return. Best on a sound surface.

Algunas Veces

(100) (58)**70**
2-y-o b g Timeless Times (USA)-Nuthatch (IRE) (Thatching)
T D Barron J G Brown

Placings:516420003 **(5193)**
2001: 5^{5}S, 5^{1}SD, 5^{6}GF, 6^{4}GS, 5^{2}G, 5^{0}GF, 5^{0}F, 7^{0}GF, 6^{3}SD

	Starts	1st	2nd	3rd	Win & Pl
Career Total (Turf)	7	0	1	0	1572
Career Total (AW)	2	1	0	1	2075

4/01 Sthl 5f F STD £1743
Total win prize-money £1743

Going (Turf): Sf: 0-1 GS: 0-1 Gd: 0-1 GF: 0-3 Fm: 0-1
Distance: **5f/6f: 1-8** 7f-8f: 0-1 9f-13f: 0-0 14f+: 0-0
Track : LH: 0-2 RH: 0-0 Tight: 0-2 Gall: 0-0
Aids: Bl: 0-1 Vi: 0-0 Tstrap: 0-0
Best Rating: 70 8/01 Muss 5f good

Proven over five furlongs on the sand, this gelding has gone off the boil on the turf, and has a stiff handicap mark for what he has achieved.

Alhesn (USA)

100(104) (61)**36**
6-y-o b/br g Woodman (USA)-Deceit Princess (CAN) (Vice Regent (CAN))
C N Allen Shadowfax Racing.Com

Placings:032454/0001160**161**2**5015/4132360**05-**2210314**50060 **(3497)**
2001: 16^{2}SD, 16^{2}SW, 16^{1}SW, 16^{0}SD, 16^{3}SD, 16^{1}SD, 16^{4}SD, 16^{5}SD, 17^{0}GF, 14^{0}GF, 16^{6}GF, 16^{0}GF

	Starts	1st	2nd	3rd	Win & Pl
Career Total (Turf)	19	2	1	1	8345
Career Total (AW)	23	6	4	3	23439

61	3/01	Wolv	2m46y	D(0-85)H	STD	£3786
60	1/01	Wolv	2m46y	D(0-85)H	SLW	£2863
71	1/00	Wolv	2m46y	E(0-75)H	STD	£2601
70	12/99	Wolv	2m46y	D(0-85)H	STD	£3720
63	9/99	Wolv	2m46y	E(0-70)H	STD	£2915
52	8/99	Ling	2m	E(0-70)H	STD	£2811
41	7/99	Yarm	2m	E(0-70)H	G-F	£3377
43	7/99	Yarm	1m6f17y	E(0-70)H	FRM	£3028

Total win prize-money £25103

Going (Turf): Sf: 0-0 GS: 0-1 Gd: 0-3 **GF: 1-11 Fm: 1-4**
Distance: 5f/6f: 0-0 7f-8f: 0-0 9f-13f: 0-8 **14f+: 8-34**
Track : **LH: 8-37** RH: 0-5 **Tight: 8-30** Gall: 0-4
Aids: Bl: 0-0 Vi: 0-2 Tstrap: 0-2
Best Rating: 61 3/01 Wolv 2m46y stand

Won a couple of modest fast-ground staying events at Yarmouth in the summer of 1999. Has since shown himself to be well suited by All-Weather surfaces of Lingfield and Wolverhampton. Very disappointing when tried at Southwell. Ideally needs two miles and a truly-run race.

Alhitrate

87 **52**

3-y-o ch f Alhijaz-Infiltrate (IRE) (Bering)
C A Dwyer (Mrs Lydia Pearce 2/7) Black Horse Racing Club

Placings:00000 **(3637)**
2001: 8^0G, 10^0GF, 10^0GF, 12^0GF, 12^0GS

	Starts	1st	2nd	3rd	Win & Pl
Career Total (Turf)	5	0	0	0	

Going (Turf): Sf: 0-0 GS: 0-1 Gd: 0-1 GF: 0-3 Fm: 0-0
Distance: 5f/6f: 0-0 7f-8f: 0-0 9f-13f: 0-5 14f+: 0-0
Track : LH: 0-3 RH: 0-1 Tight: 0-1 Gall: 0-1
Aids: Bl: 0-0 Vi: 0-0 Tstrap: 0-0
Best Rating: 52 5/01 Ling 1m2f gd-fm

Little form so far.

Alhuwbill

94(88) (21)**36**

6-y-o b g Full Extent (USA)-Hale Lane (Comedy Star (USA))
J J Bridger W R Shere

Placings:00000500000/6004300-50000000 **(5664)**
2001: 8^5GF, 7^0GF, 7^0GF, 8^0GF, 7^0GF, 8^0GF, 9^0GF, 8^0HY

	Starts	1st	2nd	3rd	Win & Pl
Career Total (Turf)	23	0	0	1	936
Career Total (AW)	3	0	0	0	

Going (Turf): Sf: 0-3 GS: 0-2 Gd: 0-5 GF: 0-13 Fm: 0-0
Distance: 5f/6f: 0-3 7f-8f: 0-14 9f-13f: 0-9 14f+: 0-0
Track : LH: 0-7 RH: 0-10 Tight: 0-9 Gall: 0-0
Aids: Bl: 0-1 Vi: 0-0 Tstrap: 0-0
Best Rating: 36 7/01 Newb 7f gd-fm

Ali Can (IRE)

88 **56**

2-y-o b c Ali-Royal (IRE)-Desert Native (Formidable (USA))
A P Jarvis Jarvis Associates

Placings:05 **(3704)**
2001: 7^0GF, 5^5G

	Starts	1st	2nd	3rd	Win & Pl
Career Total (Turf)	2	0	0	0	0

Going (Turf): Sf: 0-0 GS: 0-0 Gd: 0-1 GF: 0-1 Fm: 0-0
Distance: 5f/6f: 0-1 7f-8f: 0-1 9f-13f: 0-0 14f+: 0-0
Track : LH: 0-0 RH: 0-0 Tight: 0-0 Gall: 0-0
Aids: Bl: 0-0 Vi: 0-0 Tstrap: 0-0
Best Rating: 56 8/01 Leic 5f218y good

Ali D

101 **63**

3-y-o b c Alhijaz-Doppio (Dublin Taxi)
A B Mulholland Andrew Lloyd

Placings:045303 **(4844)**
2001: 6^0GF, 7^4G, 5^5GF, 7^3GF, 8^0GF, 9^3G

	Starts	1st	2nd	3rd	Win & Pl
Career Total (Turf)	6	0	0	2	1169

Going (Turf): Sf: 0-0 GS: 0-0 Gd: 0-2 GF: 0-4 Fm: 0-0
Distance: 5f/6f: 0-2 7f-8f: 0-3 9f-13f: 0-1 14f+: 0-0
Track : LH: 0-2 RH: 0-0 Tight: 0-1 Gall: 0-0
Aids: Bl: 0-0 Vi: 0-0 Tstrap: 0-0
Best Rating: 63 7/01 Newc 7f gd-fm

Ali Gee Gee (IRE)

77 **45**

2-y-o b g Desert Style (IRE)-Molvina (ITY) (Final Straw)
J L Eyre Wetherby Racing Bureau 52

Placings:0 **(3842)**
2001: 6^0G

	Starts	1st	2nd	3rd	Win & Pl
Career Total (Turf)	1	0	0	0	

Going (Turf): Sf: 0-0 GS: 0-0 Gd: 0-1 GF: 0-0 Fm: 0-0
Distance: 5f/6f: 0-1 7f-8f: 0-0 9f-13f: 0-0 14f+: 0-0
Track : LH: 0-0 RH: 0-0 Tight: 0-0 Gall: 0-0
Aids: Bl: 0-0 Vi: 0-0 Tstrap: 0-0
Best Rating: 45 8/01 Rdcr 6f good

Ali Oop

72 **19**

4-y-o b g Shareef Dancer (USA)-Happydrome (Ahonoora)
P Beaumont (J D Bethell 21/5) Mrs J M Plummer

Placings:640-000 **(1468)**
2001: 9^0GS, 10^0S, 14^0GF

	Starts	1st	2nd	3rd	Win & Pl
Career Total (Turf)	6	0	0	0	321

Going (Turf): Sf: 0-1 GS: 0-2 Gd: 0-2 GF: 0-1 Fm: 0-0
Distance: 5f/6f: 0-0 7f-8f: 0-0 9f-13f: 0-5 14f+: 0-1
Track : LH: 0-0 RH: 0-5 Tight: 0-5 Gall: 0-0
Aids: Bl: 0-1 Vi: 0-0 Tstrap: 0-0
Best Rating: 19 5/01 Muss 1m6f gd-fm

Ali Pasha

89 **66**

2-y-o b c Ali-Royal (IRE)-Edge Of Darkness (Vaigly Great)
D W P Arbuthnot M J Peters

Placings:000 **(3410)**
2001: 6^0GF, 6^0GF, 6^0GF

	Starts	1st	2nd	3rd	Win & Pl
Career Total (Turf)	3	0	0	0	

Going (Turf): Sf: 0-0 GS: 0-0 Gd: 0-0 GF: 0-3 Fm: 0-0
Distance: 5f/6f: 0-0 7f-8f: 0-3 9f-13f: 0-0 14f+: 0-0
Track : LH: 0-0 RH: 0-0 Tight: 0-0 Gall: 0-0
Aids: Bl: 0-0 Vi: 0-0 Tstrap: 0-0
Best Rating: 66 7/01 Chep 6f16y gd-fm

Ali Rose

86 **42**

3-y-o b f Cigar-Hurricane Rose (Windjammer (USA))
H Morrison Impulse Racing

Placings:000 **(5528)**
2001: 8^0HY, 7^0S, 8^0HY

	Starts	1st	2nd	3rd	Win & Pl
Career Total (Turf)	3	0	0	0	

Going (Turf): Sf: 0-3 GS: 0-0 Gd: 0-0 GF: 0-0 Fm: 0-0
Distance: 5f/6f: 0-0 7f-8f: 0-1 9f-13f: 0-2 14f+: 0-0
Track : LH: 0-2 RH: 0-0 Tight: 0-0 Gall: 0-0
Aids: Bl: 0-0 Vi: 0-0 Tstrap: 0-0
Best Rating: 42 10/01 Nott 1m54y heavy

Aliabad (IRE)

103(102) (45)**50**

6-y-o b/br g Doyoun-Alannya (FR) (Relko)
J G M O'Shea (D Haydn Jones 8/6) N G H Ayliffe

Placings:02205/0/**500-640234211**350 **(2743)**
2001: **12**^{0}SD, **14**^{4}SW, **16**^{0}SD, **14**^{2}SD, **16**^{3}SD, **14**^{4}SD, **12**^{2}SD, **14**^{1}SD, **14**^{1}SD, 17^3G, 16^5GF, 18^0GF

	Starts	1st	2nd	3rd	Win & Pl
Career Total (Turf)	9	0	2	1	2903
Career Total (AW)	12	2	2	1	6128

38	6/01	Sthl	1m6f	F	STD	£2254
41	5/01	Sthl	1m6f	F(0-60)H	STD	£2429

Total win prize-money £4683

Going (Turf): Sf: 0-0 GS: 0-1 Gd: 0-3 GF: 0-4 Fm: 0-1
Distance: 5f/6f: 0-0 7f-8f: 0-1 9f-13f: 0-7 **14f+: 2-13**
Track : **LH: 2-18** RH: 0-2 Tight: 0-12 Gall: 0-0
Aids: Bl: 0-1 Vi: 0-1 Tstrap: 0-0
Best Rating: 50 6/01 Wwck 2m39y gd-fm

Has only ever won on All-Weather at Southwell over fourteen furlongs. Stays two miles on turf.

Aligatou

(84) (60)**72**

2-y-o b c Distant Relative-Follow The Stars (Sparkler)
C E Brittain Bernard Butt

Placings:3600056 **(5192)**
2001: 7^3S, 7^6GF, 7^0GF, 7^0GS, 7^0G, 8^5SD, 8^6SD

	Starts	1st	2nd	3rd	Win & Pl
Career Total (Turf)	5	0	0	1	666
Career Total (AW)	2	0	0	0	0

Going (Turf): Sf: 0-1 GS: 0-1 Gd: 0-1 GF: 0-2 Fm: 0-0
Distance: 5f/6f: 0-0 7f-8f: 0-6 9f-13f: 0-1 14f+: 0-0
Track : LH: 0-3 RH: 0-3 Tight: 0-1 Gall: 0-0
Aids: Bl: 0-1 Vi: 0-0 Tstrap: 0-0
Best Rating: 72 7/01 Wwck 7f26y gd-fm

A half-brother to numerous winners, he made a promising debut on soft ground but has subsequently disappointed. His dam stayed ten furlongs and he looks to need a trip.

Alijo

62

3-y-o b f Alhijaz-Hen Night (Mummy's Game)
J Balding J M Lacey

Placings:0 **(1081)**
2001: 7^0S

	Starts	1st	2nd	3rd	Win & Pl
Career Total (Turf)	1	0	0	0	

Going (Turf): Sf: 0-1 GS: 0-0 Gd: 0-0 GF: 0-0 Fm: 0-0
Distance: 5f/6f: 0-0 7f-8f: 0-1 9f-13f: 0-0 14f+: 0-0
Track : LH: 0-0 RH: 0-0 Tight: 0-0 Gall: 0-0
Aids: Bl: 0-0 Vi: 0-0 Tstrap: 0-0

Alithini (IRE)

93 **61**

3-y-o b f Darshaan-Quiet Counsel (IRE) (Law Society (USA))

J Noseda Mrs Charlotte Musgrave

Placings:04 **(1114)**

2001: 10^{0}GS, 10^{4}S

	Starts	1st	2nd	3rd	Win & Pl
Career Total (Turf)	2	0	0	0	305

Going (Turf): Sf: 0-1 GS: 0-1 Gd: 0-0 GF: 0-0 Fm: 0-0
Distance: 5f/6f: 0-0 7f-8f: 0-0 9f-13f: 0-2 14f+: 0-0
Track : LH: 0-1 RH: 0-0 Tight: 0-0 Gall: 0-0
Aids: Bl: 0-0 Vi: 0-0 Tstrap: 0-0
Best Rating: 61 5/01 Hayd 1m2f120y soft

Alizarin (IRE)

90 **51**

2-y-o b f Tagula (IRE)-Persian Empress (IRE) (Persian Bold)

J L Eyre M Gleason

Placings:340 **(4029)**

2001: 6^{3}GF, 6^{4}GF, 7^{0}G

	Starts	1st	2nd	3rd	Win & Pl
Career Total (Turf)	3	0	0	1	704

Going (Turf): Sf: 0-0 GS: 0-0 Gd: 0-1 GF: 0-2 Fm: 0-0
Distance: 5f/6f: 0-1 7f-8f: 0-2 9f-13f: 0-0 14f+: 0-0
Track : LH: 0-1 RH: 0-0 Tight: 0-0 Gall: 0-0
Aids: Bl: 0-0 Vi: 0-0 Tstrap: 0-0
Best Rating: 51 7/01 Haml 6f5y gd-fm

19,000Irgns half-sister to two winning juveniles and should stay a mile in time.

Aljard (USA)

90 **62**

3-y-o ch c Gilded Time (USA)-Diaspora (USA) (Vice Regent (CAN))

D W Barker (E A L Dunlop 25/6) Keith Nicholson

Placings:03400 **(4571)**

2001: 8^{0}GF, 9^{3}GF, 8^{4}GF, 10^{0}G, 8^{0}HY

	Starts	1st	2nd	3rd	Win & Pl
Career Total (Turf)	5	0	0	1	673

Going (Turf): Sf: 0-1 GS: 0-0 Gd: 0-1 GF: 0-3 Fm: 0-0
Distance: 5f/6f: 0-0 7f-8f: 0-1 9f-13f: 0-4 14f+: 0-0
Track : LH: 0-3 RH: 0-2 Tight: 0-2 Gall: 0-0
Aids: Bl: 0-0 Vi: 0-0 Tstrap: 0-0
Best Rating: 62 6/01 Ripn 1m1f gd-fm

Aljaz

(102) (38) **17**

11-y-o b g Al Nasr (FR)-Santa Linda (USA) (Sir Ivor)

Mrs N Macauley Mrs N Macauley

Placings:135/060000/43036301000600/04150025/3266 200202/21123022024212/00360004301002022З/40206 464026004-10040006600 **(2644)**

2001: 6^{1}SD, 5^{0}SD, 6^{0}SW, 6^{4}SD, 7^{0}SD, 6^{0}SD, 6^{0}SD, 6^{6}SD, 5^{6}SD, 5^{0}SD, 6^{0}SD

	Starts	1st	2nd	3rd	Win & Pl
Career Total (Turf)	12	1	0	1	5475
Career Total (AW)	86	7	17	8	34094

47	1/01	Sthl	6f	F	STD	£2219
61	5/99	Sthl	6f	F(0-60)H	STD	£2444
67	6/98	Wolv	6f	F(0-65)H	STD	£2616
52	1/98	Wolv	5f	F	STD	£1738
52	1/98	Wolv	5f	E(0-70)H	STD	£2372
43	8/96	Wolv	5f	F(0-65)H	STD	£2381
62	3/95	Haml	6f5y	D(0-75)H	HVY	£5020
63	7/93	Sthl	6f	D	STD	£3348

Total win prize-money £22138

Going (Turf): Sf: 1-3 GS: 0-1 Gd: 0-5 GF: 0-3 Fm: 0-0
Distance: 5f/6f: 7-80 7f-8f: 1-18 9f-13f: 0-0 14f+: 0-0
Track : LH: 7-80 RH: 0-1 **Tight: 4-49** Gall: 0-1
Aids: Bl: 0-1 **Vi: 1-9** Tstrap: 0-0
Best Rating: 53 1/01 Sthl 6f stand

He has been a decent sprint handicapper in the past, but is rather long in the tooth now and if he is to win again, it will be in the very lowest grade.

Aljazir

86(97) (44) **12**

4-y-o b g Alhijaz-Duxyana (IRE) (Cyrano De Bergerac)

E J Alston Liam & Tony Ferguson

Placings:3060054/020505000000-544366000 **(2244)**

2001: 6^{5}SW, 5^{4}SD, 6^{4}SD, 6^{3}SD, 6^{6}SD, 5^{6}SD, 5^{0}G, 6^{0}F, 7^{0}G

	Starts	1st	2nd	3rd	Win & Pl
Career Total (Turf)	20	0	1	1	1623
Career Total (AW)	8	0	0	1	416

Going (Turf): Sf: 0-6 GS: 0-1 Gd: 0-5 GF: 0-6 Fm: 0-2
Distance: 5f/6f: 0-16 7f-8f: 0-11 9f-13f: 0-1 14f+: 0-0
Track : LH: 0-13 RH: 0-3 Tight: 0-7 Gall: 0-1
Aids: Bl: 0-7 Vi: 0-1 Tstrap: 0-0
Best Rating: 44 2/01 Sthl 6f stand

Aljohoncha

82(69) **13**

3-y-o b f Bigstone (IRE)-Ibda (Mtoto)

C N Kellett Sean A Taylor

Placings:0-0000 **(3297)**

2001: 7^{0}SD, 6^{0}SD, 8^{0}GF, 6^{0}GF

	Starts	1st	2nd	3rd	Win & Pl
Career Total (Turf)	3	0	0	0	
Career Total (AW)	2	0	0	0	

Going (Turf): Sf: 0-0 GS: 0-0 Gd: 0-0 GF: 0-3 Fm: 0-0
Distance: 5f/6f: 0-1 7f-8f: 0-3 9f-13f: 0-1 14f+: 0-0
Track : LH: 0-4 RH: 0-0 Tight: 0-0 Gall: 0-0
Aids: Bl: 0-0 Vi: 0-1 Tstrap: 0-0
Best Rating: 13 7/01 Pont 1m4y gd-fm

Aljomar

(87) (56) **54**

2-y-o b g College Chapel-Running For You (FR) (Pampabird)

R Hollinshead John L Marriott

Placings:605050004 **(5618)**

2001: 5^{6}SD, 5^{0}SD, 5^{5}SD, 7^{0}F, 7^{5}GS, 6^{0}G, 8^{0}GF, 6^{0}S, 8^{4}SD

	Starts	1st	2nd	3rd	Win & Pl
Career Total (Turf)	5	0	0	0	0
Career Total (AW)	4	0	0	0	0

Going (Turf): Sf: 0-1 GS: 0-1 Gd: 0-1 GF: 0-1 Fm: 0-1
Distance: 5f/6f: 0-5 7f-8f: 0-2 9f-13f: 0-2 14f+: 0-0
Track : LH: 0-2 RH: 0-0 Tight: 0-2 Gall: 0-0
Aids: Bl: 0-0 Vi: 0-0 Tstrap: 0-0
Best Rating: 56 11/01 Wolv 1m100y stand

Alka International

84 **29**

9-y-o b g Northern State (USA)-Cachucha (Gay Fandango (USA))

Mrs P Townsley Paul Townsley

Placings:0004/063005/5 **(0733)**

2001: 11^{5}GS

	Starts	1st	2nd	3rd	Win & Pl
Career Total (Turf)	7	0	0	0	0
Career Total (AW)	4	0	0	1	579

Going (Turf): Sf: 0-0 GS: 0-2 Gd: 0-1 GF: 0-4 Fm: 0-0
Distance: 5f/6f: 0-1 7f-8f: 0-5 9f-13f: 0-5 14f+: 0-0
Track : LH: 0-5 RH: 0-3 Tight: 0-6 Gall: 0-1
Aids: Bl: 0-0 Vi: 0-0 Tstrap: 0-0
Best Rating: 29 4/01 Brig 1m3f196y gd-sft

Alkateb

94(86) (27) **49**

9-y-o ch g Rock City-Corley Moor (Habitat)

A E Jones Mrs J Whitburn

Placings:131245/3/0333000020/5004 **(4077)**

2001: 11^{5}SD, 13^{0}GF, 12^{0}GF, 13^{4}G

	Starts	1st	2nd	3rd	Win & Pl
Career Total (Turf)	20	2	2	5	22126
Career Total (AW)	1	0	0	0	0

87	8/95	Sand	1m14y	C(0-90)H	G-F	£5810
82	6/95	Gdwd	1m1f	D	G-F	£4207

Total win prize-money £10018

Going (Turf): Sf: 0-3 GS: 0-0 Gd: 0-9 **GF: 2-8** Fm: 0-0
Distance: 5f/6f: 0-0 7f-8f: 0-0 **9f-13f: 2-19** 14f+: 0-2
Track : LH: 0-9 **RH: 2-9 Tight: 1-3** Gall: 0-9
Aids: Bl: 0-1 Vi: 0-1 Tstrap: 0-0
Best Rating: 49 7/01 Newb 1m5f61y gd-fm

All Business

96 **79**

2-y-o b f Entrepreneur-Belle Esprit (Warning)

J Noseda B McAllister

Placings:3 **(5682)**

2001: 7^{3}S

	Starts	1st	2nd	3rd	Win & Pl
Career Total (Turf)	1	0	0	1	729

Going (Turf): Sf: 0-1 GS: 0-0 Gd: 0-0 GF: 0-0 Fm: 0-0
Distance: 5f/6f: 0-0 7f-8f: 0-1 9f-13f: 0-0 14f+: 0-0
Track : LH: 0-0 RH: 0-0 Tight: 0-0 Gall: 0-0
Aids: Bl: 0-0 Vi: 0-0 Tstrap: 0-0
Best Rating: 79 11/01 Donc 7f soft

Her dam is an unraced sister to German Group Two-winning miler Torch Rouge, from the outstanding family of Kayf Tara and Opera House. Shaped with plenty of promise on her debut in a back-end maiden and is sure to break her duck at three.

All Good Things (IRE)

96(96) (62) **57**

4-y-o b c Marju (IRE)-Garah (Ajdal (USA))

R Ingram A Rosenberg

Placings:00/46510-60000100 **(3373)**

2001: 12^{6}SD, 8^{0}SD, 10^{0}G, 9^{0}GF, 8^{0}G, 12^{1}GF, 12^{0}GF, 11^{0}F

	Starts	1st	2nd	3rd	Win & Pl
Career Total (Turf)	9	1	0	0	3150
Career Total (AW)	6	1	0	0	2256

52	6/01	Folk	1m4f	F(0-65)H	G-F	£2810
51	11/00	Sthl	1m4f	D	STD	£2255

Total win prize-money £5067

Going (Turf): Sf: 0-1 GS: 0-1 Gd: 0-3 **GF: 1-3** Fm: 0-1
Distance: 5f/6f: 0-0 7f-8f: 0-3 **9f-13f: 2-12** 14f+: 0-0
Track : LH: 1-8 RH: 1-4 **Tight: 1-8** Gall: 0-0
Aids: Bl: 0-0 Vi: 0-0 Tstrap: 0-1
Best Rating: 52 6/01 Folk 1m4f gd-fm

All Grain

109 **100**

3-y-o b f Polish Precedent (USA)-Mill Line (Mill Reef (USA))

Sir Michael Stoute R Barnett

Placings:6-3130 (4984)

2001: 9³S, 12¹GF, 11³GS, 12⁰G

	Starts	1st	2nd	3rd	Win & Pl
Career Total (Turf)	5	1	0	2	8696
83 6/01 Wwck 1m4f134yD G-F					£3626
Total win prize-money £3626					

Going (Turf): Sf: 0-1 GS: 0-1 Gd: 0-1 **GF: 1-2** Fm: 0-0
Distance: 5f/6f: 0-0 7f-8f: 0-1 **9f-13f: 1-4** 14f+: 0-0
Track : **LH: 1-2** RH: 0-2 Tight: 0-1 Gall: 0-1
Aids: Bl: 0-0 Vi: 0-0 Tstrap: 0-0
Best Rating: 100 7/01 Hayd 1m3f200y gd-sft

Full-sister to the Irish Oaks and Yorkshire Oaks winner Pure Grain. She was a six-length third to Sacred Song in the Lancashire Oaks over 12 furlongs at Haydock in July, shaping as if further would suit. Tubed after suffering breathing problems, she finished distressed at Ascot next time. Suited by 12 furlongs and good to firm going.

All I Ask

100 **70**

3-y-o b c Spectrum (IRE)-Christine Daae (Sadler's Wells (USA))

P W Harris Mrs P W Harris

Placings:34 (4842)

2001: 8³GF, 8⁴G

	Starts	1st	2nd	3rd	Win & Pl
Career Total (Turf)	2	0	0	1	884

Going (Turf): Sf: 0-0 GS: 0-0 Gd: 0-1 GF: 0-1 Fm: 0-0
Distance: 5f/6f: 0-0 7f-8f: 0-1 9f-13f: 0-1 14f+: 0-0
Track : LH: 0-1 RH: 0-0 Tight: 0-0 Gall: 0-0
Aids: Bl: 0-0 Vi: 0-0 Tstrap: 0-0
Best Rating: 70 9/01 Nott 1m54y good

All In All

87 **76**

2-y-o ch f Halling (USA)-Alligram (USA) (Alysheba (USA))

L M Cumani Helena Springfield Ltd

Placings:00 (5609)

2001: 7⁰GF, 8⁰GS

	Starts	1st	2nd	3rd	Win & Pl
Career Total (Turf)	2	0	0	0	

Going (Turf): Sf: 0-0 GS: 0-1 Gd: 0-0 GF: 0-1 Fm: 0-0
Distance: 5f/6f: 0-0 7f-8f: 0-2 9f-13f: 0-0 14f+: 0-0
Track : LH: 0-0 RH: 0-0 Tight: 0-0 Gall: 0-0
Aids: Bl: 0-0 Vi: 0-0 Tstrap: 0-0
Best Rating: 76 11/01 NmkR 1m gd-sft

A half-sister to Kissogram, was disappointing when gambled on on her debut. Likely to do better given time.

All Points North (IRE)

80 **51**

2-y-o b g Distinctly North (USA)-Winscarlet North (Garland Knight)

M W Easterby Paul G Jacobs

Placings:50500 (4630)

2001: 5⁵S, 5⁰S, 5⁵GF, 7⁰F, 8⁰GF

	Starts	1st	2nd	3rd	Win & Pl
Career Total (Turf)	5	0	0	0	0

Going (Turf): Sf: 0-2 GS: 0-0 Gd: 0-0 GF: 0-2 Fm: 0-1
Distance: 5f/6f: 0-3 7f-8f: 0-1 9f-13f: 0-1 14f+: 0-0
Track : LH: 0-1 RH: 0-0 Tight: 0-1 Gall: 0-0
Aids: Bl: 0-0 Vi: 0-0 Tstrap: 0-0
Best Rating: 51 9/01 Leic 1m9y gd-fm

All Smiles

85 **33**

3-y-o ch f Halling (USA)-Fairy Flax (IRE) (Dancing Brave (USA))

Mrs J R Ramsden Mrs J R Ramsden

Placings:00 (5374)

2001: 8⁰G, 6⁰G

	Starts	1st	2nd	3rd	Win & Pl
Career Total (Turf)	2	0	0	0	

Going (Turf): Sf: 0-0 GS: 0-0 Gd: 0-2 GF: 0-0 Fm: 0-0
Distance: 5f/6f: 0-1 7f-8f: 0-0 9f-13f: 0-1 14f+: 0-0
Track : LH: 0-1 RH: 0-0 Tight: 0-0 Gall: 0-0
Aids: Bl: 0-0 Vi: 0-0 Tstrap: 0-0
Best Rating: 33 10/01 Rdcr 6f good

Not much to speak about her runs in maidens, so is probably best watched until running in handicaps.

All Trumps

(85) (48)**58**

2-y-o b c First Trump-So Bold (Never So Bold)

G L Moore Bryan Pennick

Placings:0 (5620)

2001: 8⁰GS, 8⁰SD

	Starts	1st	2nd	3rd	Win & Pl
Career Total (Turf)	1	0	0	0	

Going (Turf): Sf: 0-0 GS: 0-1 Gd: 0-0 GF: 0-0 Fm: 0-0
Distance: 5f/6f: 0-0 7f-8f: 0-0 9f-13f: 0-1 14f+: 0-0
Track : LH: 0-1 RH: 0-0 Tight: 0-0 Gall: 0-0
Aids: Bl: 0-0 Vi: 0-0 Tstrap: 0-0
Best Rating: 58 11/01 Nott 1m54y gd-sft

Allegedly Red

65 **8**

2-y-o ch f Sabrehill (USA)-Tendency (Ballad Rock)

Mrs A Duffield Mrs Ann Swinbank

Placings:0 (5168)

2001: 10⁰GS

	Starts	1st	2nd	3rd	Win & Pl
Career Total (Turf)	1	0	0	0	

Going (Turf): Sf: 0-0 GS: 0-1 Gd: 0-0 GF: 0-0 Fm: 0-0
Distance: 5f/6f: 0-0 7f-8f: 0-0 9f-13f: 0-1 14f+: 0-0
Track : LH: 0-1 RH: 0-0 Tight: 0-0 Gall: 0-0
Aids: Bl: 0-0 Vi: 0-0 Tstrap: 0-0
Best Rating: 8 10/01 Pont 1m2f6y gd-sft

Allegresse (IRE)

92 **52**

4-y-o b f Alzao (USA)-Millie Musique (Miller's Mate)

H Candy Mrs S L Richardson

Placings:36/3504-6 (1460)

2001: 13⁶G

	Starts	1st	2nd	3rd	Win & Pl
Career Total (Turf)	7	0	0	2	1287

Going (Turf): Sf: 0-1 GS: 0-1 Gd: 0-1 GF: 0-4 Fm: 0-0
Distance: 5f/6f: 0-0 7f-8f: 0-2 9f-13f: 0-4 14f+: 0-1
Track : LH: 0-4 RH: 0-2 Tight: 0-2 Gall: 0-1
Aids: Bl: 0-1 Vi: 0-0 Tstrap: 0-0
Best Rating: 49 5/01 Bath 1m5f22y good

Alleluia

113 **111**

3-y-o b f Caerleon (USA)-Alruccaba (Crystal Palace (FR))

Sir Mark Prescott Mrs Sonia Rogers

Placings:360-11211116 (5387)

2001: 9¹F, 10¹GF, 12²G, 12¹G, 15¹GF, 16¹G, 18¹G, 18⁶GS

				Starts	1st	2nd	3rd	Win & Pl
Career Total (Turf)				11	6	1	1	47545
111 9/01	Donc	2m2f	A				GD	£30000
87 8/01	Thsk	2m	D(0-85)H				GD	£4280
86 7/01	Folk	1m7f92y	E(0-70)H				G-F	£3094
77 7/01	Chep	1m4f23y	E(0-70)				GD	£2982
44 6/01	Ripn	1m2f	E(0-70)				G-F	£3209
58 6/01	Nott	1m1f213yF(0-70)					FRM	£2331
Total win prize-money £45897								

Going (Turf): Sf: 0-3 GS: 0-1 **Gd: 3-4** GF: 2-2 Fm: 1-1
Distance: 5f/6f: 0-0 7f-8f: 0-2 9f-13f: 3-5 14f+: 3-4
Track : **LH: 4-5** RH: 2-4 **Tight: 3-5** Gall: 1-2
Aids: Bl: 0-0 Vi: 0-0 Tstrap: 0-0
Best Rating: 111 9/01 Donc 2m2f good

A half-sister to Last Second, she progressed superbly, winning six times between ten furlongs and two and a quarter miles. Made the big step up in class to land the Doncaster Cup before failing in the Cesarewitch, in which she suffered a pelvic injury. Effective on good or fast ground, she has an excellent attitude.

Allenby

95 **85**

2-y-o b c Inchinor-Lady Lydia (Ela-Mana-Mou)

R Hannon Alessandro Gaucci

Placings:611 (5504)

2001: 7⁶GS, 7¹S, 7¹HY

				Starts	1st	2nd	3rd	Win & Pl
Career Total (Turf)				3	2	0	0	10676
85 10/01	Donc	7f	C(0-95)				HVY	£6581
76 10/01	Leic	7f9y	D				SFT	£4095
Total win prize-money £10676								

Going (Turf): Sf: 2-2 GS: 0-1 Gd: 0-0 GF: 0-0 Fm: 0-0
Distance: 5f/6f: 0-0 **7f-8f: 2-3** 9f-13f: 0-0 14f+: 0-0
Track : LH: 0-0 RH: 0-0 Tight: 0-0 Gall: 0-0
Aids: Bl: 0-0 Vi: 0-0 Tstrap: 0-0
Best Rating: 85 10/01 Donc 7f heavy

Showed promise on his Newmarket debut and went on to land a Leicester maiden next time. Won a nursery at Doncaster in comfortable fashion. Appreciates soft going and should be suited by middle distances at three.

Allerton Boy

88 **69**

2-y-o ch g Beveled (USA)-Darakah (Doulab (USA))

R J Hodges Andrew Midgley

Placings:5230 (4730)

2001: 5⁵GF, 5²G, 5³G, 5⁰F

	Starts	1st	2nd	3rd	Win & Pl
Career Total (Turf)	4	0	1	1	1286

Going (Turf): Sf: 0-0 GS: 0-0 Gd: 0-2 GF: 0-1 Fm: 0-1
Distance: 5f/6f: 0-4 7f-8f: 0-0 9f-13f: 0-0 14f+: 0-0
Track : LH: 0-2 RH: 0-0 Tight: 0-0 Gall: 0-2
Aids: Bl: 0-0 Vi: 0-0 Tstrap: 0-0
Best Rating: 75 7/01 Chep 5f16y good

A half-brother to Bodfari Signet. Second in a Chepstow maiden over five, should appreciate a step up in trip.

Allez Mousson

106 **77**

3-y-o b c Hernando (FR)-Rynechra (Blakeney)
A Bailey Dr K Kaye

Placings:34415206131602 **(5692)**
2001: 10^{3}GS, 12^{4}G, 12^{4}GF, 16^{1}G, 13^{5}GS, 16^{2}HY, 15^{0}G, 15^{6}G, 17^{1}G, 16^{3}GS, 17^{1}GS, 17^{6}S, 16^{0}G, 16^{2}S

	Starts	1st	2nd	3rd	Win & Pl
Career Total (Turf)	14	3	2	2	17471

72 10/01 Pont 2m1f22y E(0-70)H G-S £3851
68 9/01 Ayr 2m1f105yD(0-80)H GD £5115
66 7/01 Chep 2m49y E(0-75)H GD £2800
Total win prize-money £11767

Going (Turf): Sf: 0-3 GS: 1-4 **Gd: 2-6** GF: 0-1 Fm: 0-0
Distance: 5f/6f: 0-0 7f-8f: 0-0 9f-13f: 0-3 **14f+: 3-11**
Track : **LH: 3-11** RH: 0-3 Tight: 0-3 Gall: 0-3
Aids: Bl: 0-2 Vi: 0-0 Tstrap: 0-0
Best Rating: 77 11/01 Donc 2m110y soft

He stays well, and has scored at Chepstow, Ayr and Pontefract this term, but was disappointing at Pontefract when trying to follow up in October, before bouncing right back to form at Doncaster in November when a good second. Goes well with some ease in the ground.

Allinjim (IRE)

94 **71**

2-y-o b c Turtle Island (IRE)-Bounayya (USA) (Al Nasr (FR))
J A Glover Advance Brickwork Ltd

Placings:0042 **(5176)**
2001: 7^{0}GS, 6^{0}GF, 5^{4}GF, 8^{2}HY

	Starts	1st	2nd	3rd	Win & Pl
Career Total (Turf)	4	0	1	0	952

Going (Turf): Sf: 0-1 GS: 0-1 Gd: 0-0 GF: 0-2 Fm: 0-0
Distance: 5f/6f: 0-2 7f-8f: 0-1 9f-13f: 0-1 14f+: 0-0
Track : LH: 0-2 RH: 0-1 Tight: 0-3 Gall: 0-0
Aids: Bl: 0-0 Vi: 0-0 Tstrap: 0-0
Best Rating: 71 10/01 Wind 1m67y heavy

Showed ability in maidens before finishing second when stepping up to a mile nursery on his fourth start. Handles heavy ground.

Allotrope (IRE)

88 **14**

6-y-o b g Nashwan (USA)-Graphite (USA) (Mr Prospector (USA))
Mrs M Reveley Mrs M Reveley

Placings:2510/0460/0000-000006 **(4803)**
2001: 17^{0}F, 16^{0}F, 14^{0}G, 16^{0}GF, 17^{0}GF, 17^{6}F

	Starts	1st	2nd	3rd	Win & Pl
Career Total (Turf)	18	1	1	0	4504

78 8/98 Tral 1m6f GD £3437
Total win prize-money £3438

Going (Turf): Sf: 0-1 GS: 0-1 **Gd: 1-3** GF: 0-6 Fm: 0-6
Distance: 5f/6f: 0-0 7f-8f: 0-0 9f-13f: 0-2 **14f+: 1-16**
Track : **LH: 1-16** RH: 0-2 Tight: 0-7 Gall: 0-2
Aids: Bl: 0-2 Vi: 0-0 Tstrap: 0-0
Best Rating: 14 9/01 Pont 2m1f216y firm

Allthedotcoms

101 **50**

3-y-o ch g Elmaamul (USA)-North Wind (IRE) (Lomond (USA))
N A Callaghan N A Callaghan

Placings:04600-002520 **(5043)**
2001: 8^{0}GF, 12^{0}GS, 10^{2}G, 9^{5}G, 8^{2}G, 8^{0}G

	Starts	1st	2nd	3rd	Win & Pl
Career Total (Turf)	11	0	2	0	2881

Going (Turf): Sf: 0-0 GS: 0-1 Gd: 0-5 GF: 0-4 Fm: 0-0
Distance: 5f/6f: 0-0 7f-8f: 0-4 9f-13f: 0-6 14f+: 0-0
Track : LH: 0-4 RH: 0-3 Tight: 0-2 Gall: 0-2
Aids: Bl: 0-0 Vi: 0-0 Tstrap: 0-0
Best Rating: 50 8/01 NmkJ 1m2f good

Allude (IRE)

95 **77**

2-y-o b c Darshaan-Ahliyat (USA) (Irish River (FR))
N P Littmoden Mrs Sonia Rogers

Placings:50 **(5056)**
2001: 8^{5}G, 8^{0}S

	Starts	1st	2nd	3rd	Win & Pl
Career Total (Turf)	2	0	0	0	0

Going (Turf): Sf: 0-1 GS: 0-0 Gd: 0-1 GF: 0-0 Fm: 0-0
Distance: 5f/6f: 0-0 7f-8f: 0-2 9f-13f: 0-0 14f+: 0-0
Track : LH: 0-0 RH: 0-0 Tight: 0-0 Gall: 0-0
Aids: Bl: 0-0 Vi: 0-0 Tstrap: 0-0
Best Rating: 77 8/01 NmkJ 1m good

Almashrouk (IRE)

98(50) **55**

4-y-o b c Common Grounds-Red Note (Rusticaro (FR))
Miss Gay Kelleway Kevin Hudson

Placings:040/6640650000-55500 **(4951)**
2001: 5^{5}GS, 5^{5}GF, 5^{5}GF, 6^{0}SW, 8^{0}G

	Starts	1st	2nd	3rd	Win & Pl
Career Total (Turf)	17	0	0	0	705
Career Total (AW)	1	0	0	0	

Going (Turf): Sf: 0-4 GS: 0-4 Gd: 0-3 GF: 0-5 Fm: 0-1
Distance: 5f/6f: 0-13 7f-8f: 0-5 9f-13f: 0-0 14f+: 0-0
Track : LH: 0-3 RH: 0-2 Tight: 0-1 Gall: 0-0
Aids: Bl: 0-2 Vi: 0-0 Tstrap: 0-0
Best Rating: 55 8/01 Folk 5f gd-fm

Still a maiden. Changed stables in the summer of 2001. Tried from five to seven furlongs. Seems to act on any going.

Almaydan

102 **65**

3-y-o b c Marju (IRE)-Cunning (Bustino)
R Lee (S R Bowring 11/9) George Brookes & Family

Placings:4-32 **(5634)**
2001: 9^{3}GF, 11^{2}G

	Starts	1st	2nd	3rd	Win & Pl
Career Total (Turf)	3	0	1	1	1761

Going (Turf): Sf: 0-1 GS: 0-0 Gd: 0-1 GF: 0-1 Fm: 0-0
Distance: 5f/6f: 0-0 7f-8f: 0-1 9f-13f: 0-2 14f+: 0-0
Track : LH: 0-1 RH: 0-1 Tight: 0-1 Gall: 0-0
Aids: Bl: 0-0 Vi: 0-0 Tstrap: 0-0
Best Rating: 65 11/01 Catt 1m3f214y good

He has had three trainers already, is bred to stay, and improved when stepped up to 12 furlongs.

Almiddina (IRE)

107 **81**

4-y-o b f Selkirk (USA)-Arbela (IRE) (Persian Bold)
R Charlton James D Wolfensohn

Placings:4010-051210300 **(5145)**
2001: 8^{0}GF, 7^{5}F, 7^{1}GF, 7^{2}GF, 7^{1}GF, 7^{0}GF, 6^{3}GF, 7^{0}GF, 7^{0}G

	Starts	1st	2nd	3rd	Win & Pl
Career Total (Turf)	13	3	1	1	15710

81 7/01 Newb 7f D(0-80)H G-F £4459
55 6/01 Rdcr 7f E(0-70) G-F £3710
77 9/00 Hayd 7f30y D HVY £4199
Total win prize-money £12368

Going (Turf): Sf: 1-2 GS: 0-0 Gd: 0-1 **GF: 2-9** Fm: 0-1
Distance: 5f/6f: 0-0 **7f-8f: 3-11** 9f-13f: 0-2 14f+: 0-0
Track : **LH: 1-3** RH: 0-0 Tight: 0-0 Gall: 0-0
Aids: Bl: 0-0 Vi: 0-0 Tstrap: 0-0
Best Rating: 81 7/01 Newb 7f gd-fm

Suited by seven furlongs as he has shown this season with wins at Redcar and Newbury, although he later looked well held. He handles both fast and heavy ground and is best held up

Alminstar

86(80) (14) **14**

5-y-o br m Minshaanshu Amad (USA)-Joytime (John De Coombe)
Mrs L Richards Mrs G M Gooderham

Placings:0/0600550/000-00 **(3381)**
2001: 13^{0}SW, 8^{0}GF

	Starts	1st	2nd	3rd	Win & Pl
Career Total (Turf)	10	0	0	0	0
Career Total (AW)	3	0	0	0	

Going (Turf): Sf: 0-0 GS: 0-3 Gd: 0-1 GF: 0-6 Fm: 0-0
Distance: 5f/6f: 0-0 7f-8f: 0-1 9f-13f: 0-10 14f+: 0-2
Track : LH: 0-9 RH: 0-3 Tight: 0-6 Gall: 0-1
Aids: Bl: 0-0 Vi: 0-0 Tstrap: 0-0
Best Rating: 14 7/01 Sand 1m14y gd-fm

Almnadia (IRE)

83 **57**

2-y-o b f Alhaarth (IRE)-Mnaafa (IRE) (Darshaan)
G A Butler Abdulla Al Khalifa

Placings:000 **(5666)**
2001: 6^{0}HY, 6^{0}G, 6^{0}HY

	Starts	1st	2nd	3rd	Win & Pl
Career Total (Turf)	3	0	0	0	

Going (Turf): Sf: 0-2 GS: 0-0 Gd: 0-1 GF: 0-0 Fm: 0-0
Distance: 5f/6f: 0-2 7f-8f: 0-1 9f-13f: 0-0 14f+: 0-0
Track : LH: 0-0 RH: 0-0 Tight: 0-0 Gall: 0-0
Aids: Bl: 0-0 Vi: 0-0 Tstrap: 0-0
Best Rating: 57 10/01 Rdcr 6f good

Well beaten to date, and is best watched until tackling handicaps.

Almohad

85(73) **19**

6-y-o ch g Belmez (USA)-Anna Paola (GER) (Prince Ippi (GER))
Dr J D Scargill Mrs Janet Mudd

Placings:20155000/00030160/00000 **(5448)**
2001: 11^{0}SD, 10^{0}GS, 10^{0}G, 12^{0}GS, 10^{0}HY

	Starts	1st	2nd	3rd	Win & Pl
Career Total (Turf)	15	2	1	1	5617
Career Total (AW)	6	0	0	0	

49 8/99 Wind 1m3f135yE(0-70)H HVY £2878
7/98 Colo 1m1f55y GD £2027
Total win prize-money £4905

Going (Turf): Sf: 1-5 GS: 0-3 Gd: 0-3 GF: 0-1 Fm: 0-0
Distance: 5f/6f: 0-0 7f-8f: 0-1 9f-13f: 1-14 14f+: 0-3
Track : LH: 0-11 RH: 0-3 Tight: 1-9 Gall: 0-2
Aids: Bl: 0-1 Vi: 0-1 Tstrap: 0-4
Best Rating: 19 8/01 Yarm 1m2f21y good

Alnahaam (IRE)

103 **89+**

3-y-o ch c Hamas (IRE)-Abir (Soviet Star (USA))
B Hanbury Hamdan Al Maktoum

Placings:62-1050 (3837)
2001: 7¹G, 8⁰GF, 8⁵G, 7⁰G

	Starts	1st	2nd	3rd	Win & Pl
Career Total (Turf)	6	1	1	0	5596

87 5/01 Donc 7f D GD £4436
Total win prize-money £4436

Going (Turf): Sf: 0-0 GS: 0-0 Gd: 1-3 GF: 0-3 Fm: 0-0
Distance: 5f/6f: 0-1 7f-8f: 1-4 9f-13f: 0-1 14f+: 0-0
Track : LH: 0-1 RH: 0-0 Tight: 0-0 Gall: 0-0
Aids: Bl: 0-0 Vi: 0-0 Tstrap: 0-0
Best Rating: 87 5/01 Donc 7f good

Landed a Doncaster maiden on his first start of this season, but has been held in warm company since. Gives the impression that he does want the ground too lively.

Alowmdah (USA)

104 **82**

3-y-o b c Gone West (USA)-Halholah (USA) (Secreto (USA))
B Hanbury Hamdan Al Maktoum

Placings:0-510052 (3247)
2001: 8⁵S, 10¹GF, 9⁰GF, 12⁰GF, 9⁵GF, 10²GS

	Starts	1st	2nd	3rd	Win & Pl
Career Total (Turf)	7	1	1	0	8791

82 5/01 Ches 1m2f75y D G-F £7150
Total win prize-money £7150

Going (Turf): Sf: 0-2 GS: 0-1 Gd: 0-0 GF: 1-4 Fm: 0-0
Distance: 5f/6f: 0-1 7f-8f: 0-0 9f-13f: 1-6 14f+: 0-0
Track : LH: 1-2 RH: 0-3 Tight: 1-4 Gall: 0-1
Aids: Bl: 0-0 Vi: 0-0 Tstrap: 0-0
Best Rating: 82 5/01 Ches 1m2f75y gd-fm

Only had the one outing as a juvenile. Reappeared at Epsom in April in 2001 over a mile before scoring next time out when stepped up to ten furlongs in a Chester maiden. Should stay a mile and a half. Has won on good to firm ground.

Alpen Wolf (IRE)

(98) (70)**77**

6-y-o ch g Wolfhound (USA)-Oatfield (Great Nephew)
W R Muir R Haim

Placings:56050300/04350401111 0/0136320105/31021 0130000-06065200000 (4612)
2001: 6⁰GS, 6⁶GF, 6⁰GF, 5⁶G, 6⁵GF, 6²GF, 6⁰G, 7⁰GF, 6⁰G, 7⁰GF, 5⁰F

	Starts	1st	2nd	3rd	Win & Pl
Career Total (Turf)	53	9	3	6	45835

87 7/00 Newb 6f8y C(0-95)H G-F £7052
81 6/00 Wwck 6f168y D(0-80) G-F £3753
77 5/00 Bath 5f11y D(0-80) G-F £3721
79 8/99 Bath 5f161y C(0-90)H GD £7392
69 4/99 Brig 5f213y D(0-80)H G-F £4526
68 9/98 Brig 6f209y F(0-60) FRM £2263
68 8/98 Folk 6f F(0-60) G-F £2070
64 8/98 Brig 5f213y E(0-70)H G-F £2801
41 8/98 Brig 5f213y G FRM £1924
Total win prize-money £35507

Going (Turf): Sf: 0-4 GS: 0-2 Gd: 1-13 GF: 6-30 Fm: 2-4
Distance: 5f/6f: 6-40 7f-8f: 3-13 9f-13f: 0-0 14f+: 0-0

Track : LH: 7-22 RH: 0-3 Tight: 0-4 Gall: 2-12
Aids: Bl: 0-1 Vi: 0-3 Tstrap: 0-0
Best Rating: 83 5/01 Gdwd 6f gd-fm

Scored three times in 2000 and is suited by turning tracks like Brighton and Bath. Best at six furlongs, though he can go well over five and is suited by a fast surface. Showed little this season, but is back on a winning mark.

Alpha Heights (IRE)

95(80) (17)**25**

4-y-o b f Namaqualand (USA)-Mnaafa (IRE) (Darshaan)
D W Barker D W Barker

Placings:30500/00500-000003 (5534)
2001: 6⁰SD, 8⁰SW, 8⁰SD, 8⁰GF, 9⁰HY, 11³S

	Starts	1st	2nd	3rd	Win & Pl
Career Total (Turf)	13	0	0	2	2841
Career Total (AW)	3	0	0	0	

Going (Turf): Sf: 0-3 GS: 0-0 Gd: 0-3 GF: 0-7 Fm: 0-0
Distance: 5f/6f: 0-3 7f-8f: 0-6 9f-13f: 0-7 14f+: 0-0
Track : LH: 0-7 RH: 0-1 Tight: 0-5 Gall: 0-2
Aids: Bl: 0-0 Vi: 0-0 Tstrap: 0-0
Best Rating: 25 10/01 Rdcr 1m3f soft

Alpha Rose

104(103) (60)**72**

4-y-o ch f Inchinor-Philgwyn (Milford)
M L W Bell Richard I Morris Jr

Placings:6/55411253114 2101-5040333202 (5599)
2001: 12⁵S, 11⁰GS, 14⁴GF, 12⁰GF, 10³GF, 11³GF, 10³GF, 11²GF, 12⁰SD, 12²GS

	Starts	1st	2nd	3rd	Win & Pl
Career Total (Turf)	22	5	4	4	25482
Career Total (AW)	4	1	0	0	2695

79 10/00 NmkR 1m4f D(0-80)H SFT £6942
72 8/00 Brig 1m3f196yE(0-70)H FRM £2834
66 7/00 Brig 1m3f196yE(0-75)H FRM £2925
60 7/00 Ling 1m4f E(0-70)H STD £2695
59 6/00 Ayr 1m5f13y F(0-60) G-F £2341
57 5/00 Muss 1m6f F(0-60) FRM £3461
Total win prize-money £21199

Going (Turf): Sf: 1-3 GS: 0-2 Gd: 0-3 GF: 1-9 Fm: 3-5
Distance: 5f/6f: 0-2 7f-8f: 0-1 9f-13f: 4-17 14f+: 2-6
Track : LH: 4-15 RH: 2-10 Tight: 2-10 Gall: 1-6
Aids: Bl: 0-0 Vi: 0-0 Tstrap: 0-0
Best Rating: 72 6/01 Kemp 1m6f92y gd-fm

Showed improvement when stepped up in trip and won six times in 2000, one on Equitrack. Suited by fast ground and trips of at least 12 furlongs. Does not seem to handle Fibresand.

Alphacall

99 **51**

3-y-o b f Forzando-Second Call (Kind Of Hush)
T D Walford (T D Easterby 6/8) J W Nellis

Placings:450-0404620524 (3670)
2001: 9⁰S, 9⁴GF, 11⁰GF, 10⁴GF, 10⁶GF, 8²GF, 8⁰GF, 8⁵GF, 8²GF, 8⁴S

	Starts	1st	2nd	3rd	Win & Pl
Career Total (Turf)	13	0	2	0	1782

Going (Turf): Sf: 0-2 GS: 0-1 Gd: 0-0 GF: 0-10 Fm: 0-0
Distance: 5f/6f: 0-2 7f-8f: 0-3 9f-13f: 0-8 14f+: 0-0
Track : LH: 0-6 RH: 0-4 Tight: 0-5 Gall: 0-0
Aids: Bl: 0-5 Vi: 0-0 Tstrap: 0-0
Best Rating: 54 5/01 Bevl 1m1f207y gd-fm

Alphaeus

115(99) (83+)**95+**

3-y-o b g Sillery (USA)-Aethra (USA) (Trempolino (USA))
Sir Mark Prescott Hesmonds Stud

Placings:5512-110 (5142)
2001: 10¹G, 10¹GS, 9⁰G

	Starts	1st	2nd	3rd	Win & Pl
Career Total (Turf)	6	3	0	0	38942
Career Total (AW)	1	0	1	0	888

91 7/01 NmkJ 1m2f B(0-100)H G-S £9204
95 7/01 NmkJ 1m2f B(0-105)H GD £26000
78 8/00 Bevl 1m100y E G-F £3737
Total win prize-money £38943

Going (Turf): Sf: 0-0 GS: 1-1 Gd: 1-2 GF: 1-3 Fm: 0-0
Distance: 5f/6f: 0-2 7f-8f: 0-1 9f-13f: 3-4 14f+: 0-0
Track : LH: 0-2 RH: 3-3 Tight: 0-0 Gall: 2-2
Aids: Bl: 0-0 Vi: 0-0 Tstrap: 0-0
Best Rating: 95 7/01 NmkJ 1m2f good

A big gelding, who reappeared to make all in a competitive handicap over ten furlongs at the Newmarket July Meeting. Followed up over course and distance. He stays ten furlongs well, and may be just as effective over further. Looks ahead of the handicapper, and could be set for a sequence.

Alphonse (IRE)

66 **7**

3-y-o b g Common Grounds-Windini (Windjammer (USA))
D Nicholls Lucayan Stud

Placings:00 (4537)
2001: 10⁰GF, 9⁰G

	Starts	1st	2nd	3rd	Win & Pl
Career Total (Turf)	2	0	0	0	

Going (Turf): Sf: 0-0 GS: 0-0 Gd: 0-0 GF: 0-2 Fm: 0-0
Distance: 5f/6f: 0-0 7f-8f: 0-0 9f-13f: 0-2 14f+: 0-0
Track : LH: 0-2 RH: 0-0 Tight: 0-1 Gall: 0-1
Aids: Bl: 0-0 Vi: 0-0 Tstrap: 0-0
Best Rating: 7 9/01 York 1m2f85y gd-fm

Alpine Hideaway (IRE)

102(87) (44)**34**

8-y-o b g Tirol-Arbour (USA) (Graustark)
J S Wainwright (K A Ryan 5/1) Peter Easterby

Placings:00/22020325610/30300130610023 0/0024/600 00163/600-00405300050 (4662)
2001: 16⁰SD, 10⁰S, 8⁴GS, 9⁰F, 8⁵GF, 8³G, 8⁰GF, 8⁰GF, 9⁰GF, 8⁵G, 10⁰GF

	Starts	1st	2nd	3rd	Win & Pl
Career Total (Turf)	47	3	6	7	17823
Career Total (AW)	7	1	0	0	2277

51 8/99 Bevl 1m100y E GD £2994
61 8/97 Ripn 1m F G-F £2778
66 7/97 Sthl 7f F STD £2277
71 10/96 Leic 7f9y G G-F £2224
Total win prize-money £10273

Going (Turf): Sf: 0-4 GS: 0-3 Gd: 1-19 GF: 2-18 Fm: 0-3
Distance: 5f/6f: 0-5 7f-8f: 3-35 9f-13f: 1-13 14f+: 0-1
Track : LH: 1-20 RH: 2-13 Tight: 1-12 Gall: 0-3
Aids: Bl: 0-2 Vi: 0-0 Tstrap: 0-0
Best Rating: 49 6/01 Ripn 1m good

A winner at Beverley over a mile in a claimer in August 1999, showed signs of finding his form in 2001, and is on a fair mark.

Alpine Love (IRE)

41

2-y-o ch f Pursuit Of Love-Alpina (USA) (El Prado (IRE))
E J O'Neill Mrs Patrick O'Neill

Placings:0 (5022)
2001: 7^{0}S

	Starts	1st	2nd	3rd	Win & Pl
Career Total (Turf)	1	0	0	0	

Going (Turf): Sf: 0-1 **GS:** 0-0 **Gd:** 0-0 **GF:** 0-0 **Fm:** 0-0
Distance: 5f/6f: 0-0 7f-8f: 0-1 9f-13f: 0-0 14f+: 0-0
Track : LH: 0-1 RH: 0-0 Tight: 0-0 Gall: 0-0
Aids: Bl: 0-0 Vi: 0-0 Tstrap: 0-0

Alpine Racer (IRE)

99 **70**
2-y-o b g Lake Coniston (IRE)-Cut No Ice (Great Nephew)
B J Meehan J S Threadwell

Placings:602 (5667)
2001: 8^{6}S, 8^{0}HY, 8^{2}HY

	Starts	1st	2nd	3rd	Win & Pl
Career Total (Turf)	3	0	1	0	692

Going (Turf): Sf: 0-3 GS: 0-0 Gd: 0-0 GF: 0-0 Fm: 0-0
Distance: 5f/6f: 0-0 7f-8f: 0-0 9f-13f: 0-3 14f+: 0-0
Track : LH: 0-1 RH: 0-1 Tight: 0-1 Gall: 0-0
Aids: Bl: 0-1 Vi: 0-0 Tstrap: 0-0
Best Rating: 70 10/01 Leic 1m9y soft

Plating-class maiden, has raced only on soft.

Alqabas (IRE)

89 **9**
3-y-o b g Nashwan (USA)-Harayir (USA) (Gulch (USA))
M R Ewer-Hoad (M P Tregoning 8/7) Mrs J E Taylor

Placings:045000 (5330)
2001: 10^{0}G, 10^{4}F, 10^{5}G, 12^{0}G, 12^{0}GS, 16^{0}HY

	Starts	1st	2nd	3rd	Win & Pl
Career Total (Turf)	6	0	0	0	0

Going (Turf): Sf: 0-1 GS: 0-1 Gd: 0-3 GF: 0-0 Fm: 0-1
Distance: 5f/6f: 0-0 7f-8f: 0-0 9f-13f: 0-5 14f+: 0-1
Track : LH: 0-2 RH: 0-3 Tight: 0-4 Gall: 0-1
Aids: Bl: 0-1 Vi: 0-0 Tstrap: 0-0
Best Rating: 74 6/01 Ling 1m2f firm

Alqawaaser (USA)

83 **21**
4-y-o b/br g Dayjur (USA)-Alghuzaylah (Habitat)
J G Portman R C C Villers

Placings:30/56450-0000 (2726)
2001: 8^{0}GF, 13^{0}GF, 9^{0}G, 8^{0}GF

	Starts	1st	2nd	3rd	Win & Pl
Career Total (Turf)	11	0	0	1	770

Going (Turf): Sf: 0-1 GS: 0-1 Gd: 0-5 GF: 0-3 Fm: 0-1
Distance: 5f/6f: 0-1 7f-8f: 0-4 9f-13f: 0-4 14f+: 0-2
Track : LH: 0-3 RH: 0-3 Tight: 0-3 Gall: 0-1
Aids: Bl: 0-2 Vi: 0-0 Tstrap: 0-1
Best Rating: 21 6/01 Nott 1m1f213y good

Alrafid (IRE)

94 **75**
2-y-o ch c Halling (USA)-Ginger Tree (USA) (Dayjur (USA))
A C Stewart Sheikh Ahmed Al Maktoum

Placings:02 (5290)
2001: 6^{0}S, 7^{2}S

	Starts	1st	2nd	3rd	Win & Pl
Career Total (Turf)	2	0	1	0	1260

Going (Turf): Sf: 0-2 GS: 0-0 Gd: 0-0 GF: 0-0 Fm: 0-0
Distance: 5f/6f: 0-1 7f-8f: 0-1 9f-13f: 0-0 14f+: 0-0
Track : LH: 0-1 RH: 0-0 Tight: 0-0 Gall: 0-0
Aids: Bl: 0-0 Vi: 0-0 Tstrap: 0-0
Best Rating: 75 10/01 Leic 7f9y soft

Showed promise on his second start at Leicester and should win a maiden.

Alrida (IRE)

94 **80**
2-y-o b g Ali-Royal (IRE)-Ride Bold (USA) (J O Tobin (USA))
W Jarvis Nigel Rich

Placings:5046333 (5404)
2001: 6^{5}GF, 6^{0}GF, 7^{4}G, 7^{6}G, 8^{3}G, 9^{3}HY, 8^{3}S

	Starts	1st	2nd	3rd	Win & Pl
Career Total (Turf)	7	0	0	3	1775

Going (Turf): Sf: 0-2 GS: 0-0 Gd: 0-3 GF: 0-2 Fm: 0-0
Distance: 5f/6f: 0-1 7f-8f: 0-3 9f-13f: 0-3 14f+: 0-0
Track : LH: 0-3 RH: 0-1 Tight: 0-1 Gall: 0-0
Aids: Bl: 0-0 Vi: 0-0 Tstrap: 0-0
Best Rating: 80 10/01 Pont 1m4y soft

Still a maiden but has ran with credit in both maidens and nurseries, and should be winning before long.

Alrisha (IRE)

108 **82**
4-y-o b f Persian Bold-Rifaya (IRE) (Lashkari)
D R C Elsworth Mrs R F Lowe

Placings:0212430-00013304 (4669)
2001: 14^{0}GS, 16^{0}GF, 14^{0}S, 14^{1}GF, 16^{3}G, 14^{3}GS, 21^{0}GF, 16^{4}GF

	Starts	1st	2nd	3rd	Win & Pl
Career Total (Turf)	15	2	2	3	17646

80	6/01	Sals	1m6f15y	D(0-80)H	G-F	£4348
74	7/00	NmkJ	1m6f175yD		GD	£4036

Total win prize-money £8386

Going (Turf): Sf: 0-1 GS: 0-3 **Gd: 1-3 GF: 1-8** Fm: 0-0
Distance: 5f/6f: 0-0 7f-8f: 0-0 9f-13f: 0-2 **14f+: 2-13**
Track : LH: 0-2 **RH: 2-11** Tight: 1-4 Gall: 1-4
Aids: Bl: 0-0 Vi: 0-0 Tstrap: 0-0
Best Rating: 82 7/01 NmkJ 1m6f175y gd-sft

Her trainer once considered her a Gold Cup hope, but she disappointed before winning a moderate event at Salisbury off top weight in summer of 2001. Appreciates fast ground and stays two miles.

Alsahib (USA)

(102) (54)
8-y-o b g Slew O'Gold (USA)-Khwlah (USA) (Best Turn (USA))
W R Muir Mrs J M Muir

Placings:4/054020/606**16300**02/**3105**00400014**2**/43131 553**4**3544/**131260601224662** (4552)
2001: 16^{1}SD, 16^{3}SD, 16^{1}SD, 16^{2}SD, 16^{6}SD, 14^{0}S, 14^{6}SD, 16^{0}SD, 14^{1}SD, 16^{2}SD, 12^{2}SD, 16^{4}SD, 16^{6}SD, 14^{6}SD, 14^{2}SW

	Starts	1st	2nd	3rd	Win & Pl
Career Total (Turf)	27	0	1	3	4701
Career Total (AW)	31	8	6	4	29191

48	6/01	Sthl	1m6f	F	STD	£2261
69	2/01	Wolv	2m46y	E(0-70)H	STD	£2660
41	1/01	Ling	2m	G	STD	£1834
73	4/99	Sthl	1m4f	F	STD	£2141
70	2/99	Sthl	1m4f	F	STD	£2083
81	10/98	Wolv	1m4f	F	STD	£2469
80	1/98	Sthl	1m3f	D(0-80)H	STD	£3811
76	6/97	Wolv	1m1f79y	C(0-100)H	STD	£5447

Total win prize-money £22706

Going (Turf): Sf: 0-5 GS: 0-4 Gd: 0-8 GF: 0-7 Fm: 0-3
Distance: 5f/6f: 0-0 7f-8f: 0-7 **9f-13f: 5-36** 14f+: 3-15
Track : **LH: 8-45** RH: 0-3 **Tight: 4-24** Gall: 0-3
Aids: Bl: 0-2 Vi: 0-1 Tstrap: 0-0
Best Rating: 71 3/01 Wolv 2m46y stand

A very effective performer over middle distances on Fibresand a few years back, he had the distinction of managing to beat China Castle in the month of January, and not many achieve that. Below form on turf and sand subsequently, but has come back to gain some success in modest staying events on sand, though he is nothing like as good as he was.

Alsaleet (USA)

91 **70**
3-y-o ch c Mr Prospector (USA)-Bint Salsabil (USA) (Nashwan (USA))
Saeed Bin Suroor Godolphin

Placings:44 (3254)
2001: 9^{4}F, 7^{4}GS

	Starts	1st	2nd	3rd	Win & Pl
Career Total (Turf)	2	0	0	0	618

Going (Turf): Sf: 0-0 GS: 0-1 Gd: 0-0 GF: 0-0 Fm: 0-1
Distance: 5f/6f: 0-0 7f-8f: 0-1 9f-13f: 0-1 14f+: 0-0
Track : LH: 0-1 RH: 0-0 Tight: 0-1 Gall: 0-0
Aids: Bl: 0-0 Vi: 0-2 Tstrap: 0-1
Best Rating: 70 7/01 NmkJ 7f gd-sft

Alsanutter

(41)
2-y-o b f Royal Applause-Andbell (Trojan Fen)
Mrs C A Dunnett O Nugent

Placings:0 (5193)
2001: 6^{0}SD

	Starts	1st	2nd	3rd	Win & Pl
Career Total (Turf)	0	0	0	0	
Career Total (AW)	1	0	0	0	

Going (Turf): Sf: 0-0 GS: 0-0 Gd: 0-0 GF: 0-0 Fm: 0-0
Distance: 5f/6f: 0-1 7f-8f: 0-0 9f-13f: 0-0 14f+: 0-0
Track : LH: 0-1 RH: 0-0 Tight: 0-1 Gall: 0-0
Aids: Bl: 0-0 Vi: 0-0 Tstrap: 0-0

A half-sister to mile winner Willoughby's Boy. Slowly away on her debut on the All-Weather at Wolverhampton over six furlongs.

Alshadiyah (USA)

112 **96**
3-y-o gr f Danzig (USA)-Shadayid (USA) (Shadeed (USA))
J L Dunlop Hamdan Al Maktoum

Placings:1315-32402 (4682)
2001: 7^{3}GS, 6^{2}G, 6^{4}GS, 5^{0}GS, 7^{2}G

	Starts	1st	2nd	3rd	Win & Pl
Career Total (Turf)	9	2	2	2	26143

94	9/00	Ayr	6f	A	SFT	£12992
75	8/00	Ling	6f	D	G-F	£2925

Total win prize-money £15917

Going (Turf): Sf: 1-2 GS: 0-3 Gd: 0-2 **GF: 1-2** Fm: 0-0
Distance: **5f/6f: 2-6** 7f-8f: 0-3 9f-13f: 0-0 14f+: 0-0
Track : LH: 0-0 RH: 0-0 Tight: 0-0 Gall: 0-0

Aids: Bl: 0-0 Vi: 0-0 Tstrap: 0-0
Best Rating: 96 9/01 Donc 7f good

A daughter of the 1000 Guineas winner Shadayid, she won two of her four juvenile starts including an Ayr Listed event. Failed to settle in the Fred Darling, where she needed the run, and was off for two months after. She came back to take second to Mujado in five-runner classified stakes at Yarmouth in June and ran with credit in a Newmarket handicap.

Alsyati

102 **68**

3-y-o ch c Salse (USA)-Rubbiyati (Cadeaux Genereux)
C E Brittain R A Pledger

Placings:60-6526500 **(4413)**
2001: 7^{6}S, 7^{5}GS, 10^{2}GF, 9^{6}S, 11^{5}F, 10^{0}GF, 10^{0}S

	Starts	1st	2nd	3rd	Win & Pl
Career Total (Turf)	9	0	1	0	2219

Going (Turf): Sf: 0-3 GS: 0-1 Gd: 0-1 GF: 0-3 Fm: 0-1
Distance: 5f/6f: 0-0 7f-8f: 0-4 9f-13f: 0-5 14f+: 0-0
Track : LH: 0-6 RH: 0-2 Tight: 0-3 Gall: 0-1
Aids: Bl: 0-2 Vi: 0-0 Tstrap: 0-0
Best Rating: 70 5/01 Bath 1m2f46y gd-fm

Moderate middle-distance maiden. Suited by fast ground.

Altay

101 **63**

4-y-o b g Erin's Isle-Aliuska (IRE) (Fijar Tango (FR))
R A Fahey John T Robson

Placings:506/03635110-541 **(2093)**
2001: 8^{5}GF, 8^{4}GF, 9^{1}GF

	Starts	1st	2nd	3rd	Win & Pl
Career Total (Turf)	14	3	0	2	15490

63	6/01	Bevl	1m1f207yE(0-70)H		G-F	£6165
60	9/00	Epsm	1m114y	E(0-75)H	GD	£4485
60	8/00	Ripn	1m2f	E(0-70)H	GD	£3796

Total win prize-money £14446

Going (Turf): Sf: 0-1 GS: 0-1 **Gd: 2-4** GF: 1-7 Fm: 0-1
Distance: 5f/6f: 0-2 7f-8f: 0-3 **9f-13f: 3-8** 14f+: 0-1
Track : LH: 1-5 **RH: 2-6 Tight: 2-7** Gall: 0-1
Aids: Bl: 0-0 Vi: 0-0 Tstrap: 0-0
Best Rating: 63 6/01 Bevl 1m1f207y gd-fm

Fair ten-furlong handicapper, best on decent ground.

Alunissage (USA)

107 **107**

3-y-o b c Rainbow Quest (USA)-Moonshell (IRE) (Sadler's Wells (USA))
Saeed Bin Suroor Godolphin

Placings:22126 **(4711)**
2001: 9^{2}GF, 12^{2}GF, 14^{1}F, 14^{2}GF, 14^{6}G

	Starts	1st	2nd	3rd	Win & Pl
Career Total (Turf)	5	1	3	0	8270

91	8/01	Ling	1m6f	D	FRM	£3510

Total win prize-money £3510

Going (Turf): Sf: 0-0 GS: 0-0 Gd: 0-1 GF: 0-3 **Fm: 1-1**
Distance: 5f/6f: 0-0 7f-8f: 0-0 9f-13f: 0-2 **14f+: 1-3**
Track : **LH: 1-3** RH: 0-2 **Tight: 1-3** Gall: 0-2
Aids: Bl: 0-0 **Vi. 1-3** Tstrap. 0-0
Best Rating: 107 9/01 Donc 1m6f132y good

Appreciated the first-time visor when running away with a 14-furlong Lingfield maiden in August and put up a better performance to shake up stable-companion Hatha Anna in a conditions event at Salisbury. Sixth in the Leger, he is suited by fast ground.

Alunite (USA)

102 **99**

3-y-o b c Red Ransom (USA)-Allusion (USA) (Mr Prospector (USA))
Saeed Bin Suroor Godolphin

Placings:2-12 **(4866)**
2001: 8^{1}F, 9^{2}GF

	Starts	1st	2nd	3rd	Win & Pl
Career Total (Turf)	3	1	2	0	11260

93	6/01	Thsk	1m	D	FRM £4270

Total win prize-money £4271

Going (Turf): Sf: 0-0 GS: 0-0 Gd: 0-0 GF: 0-1 **Fm: 1-1**
Distance: 5f/6f: 0-0 **7f-8f: 1-1** 9f-13f: 0-1 14f+: 0-0
Track : **LH: 1-2** RH: 0-0 **Tight: 1-1** Gall: 0-1
Aids: Bl: 0-0 Vi: 0-0 Tstrap: 0-0
Best Rating: 99 9/01 Newb 1m1f gd-fm

Runner-up on his only start for Andre Fabre last term, he finichud just over eight lengths behind Rumpold in a trial in Dubai in April 2001. Scored at Thirsk over a mile on his reappearance and narrowly beaten in a conditions event after a break. Acts on fast ground.

Alvaro (IRE)

93(89) (44)**34**

4-y-o ch g Priolo (USA)-Gezalle (Shareef Dancer (USA))
M C Chapman Sir Clement Freud

Placings:00/0620640000-04000 **(3682)**
2001: 10^{0}GF, 12^{4}GF, 10^{0}GF, 10^{0}GF, 5^{0}G

	Starts	1st	2nd	3rd	Win & Pl
Career Total (Turf)	14	0	1	0	1710
Career Total (AW)	3	0	0	0	

Going (Turf): Sf: 0-1 GS: 0-0 Gd: 0-2 GF: 0-6 Fm: 0-0
Distance: 5f/6f: 0-1 7f-8f: 0-3 9f-13f: 0-12 14f+: 0-1
Track : LH: 0-10 RH: 0-5 Tight: 0-4 Gall: 0-4
Aids: Bl: 0-1 Vi: 0-0 Tstrap: 0-0
Best Rating: 56 6/01 Newc 1m4f93y gd-fm

Always

98 **82**

2-y-o b c Dynaformer (USA)-Love And Affection (USA) (Exclusive Era (USA))
J L Dunlop Newgate Stud

Placings:4326 **(5590)**
2001: 7^{4}G, 7^{3}GF, 8^{2}G, 9^{6}GS

	Starts	1st	2nd	3rd	Win & Pl
Career Total (Turf)	4	0	1	1	2083

Going (Turf): Sf: 0-0 GS: 0-1 Gd: 0-2 GF: 0-1 Fm: 0-0
Distance: 5f/6f: 0-0 7f-8f: 0-2 9f-13f: 0-2 14f+: 0-0
Track : LH: 0-2 RH: 0-0 Tight: 0-0 Gall: 0-0
Aids: Bl: 0-0 Vi: 0-0 Tstrap: 0-0
Best Rating: 82 9/01 Nott 1m54y good

Always Daring

92 **68**

2-y-o b f Atraf-Steamy Windows (Dominion)
K R Burke M Nelmes-Crocker

Placings:2524644 **(5185)**
2001: 5^{2}F, 5^{5}GF, 5^{2}GF, 5^{4}G, 5^{6}F, 7^{4}GF, 7^{4}GS

	Starts	1st	2nd	3rd	Win & Pl
Career Total (Turf)	7	0	2	0	2120

Going (Turf): Sf: 0-0 GS: 0-1 Gd: 0-1 GF: 0-3 Fm: 0-2
Distance: 5f/6f: 0-5 7f-8f: 0-2 9f-13f: 0-0 14f+: 0-0

Track : LH: 0-3 RH: 0-0 Tight: 0-2 Gall: 0-1
Aids: Bl: 0-0 Vi: 0-0 Tstrap: 0-0
Best Rating: 69 6/01 Newc 5f firm

Has shown enough in ordinary maidens and nurseries to suggest that he can pick uo a small event.

Alyportent

(83) (16)**14**

7-y-o b g Warning-Alilisa (USA) (Alydar (USA))
N Bycroft J E Hulme

Placings:00/00000/00-0 **(0037)**
2001: 16^{0}SD

	Starts	1st	2nd	3rd	Win & Pl
Career Total (Turf)	7	0	0	0	
Career Total (AW)	3	0	0	0	

Going (Turf): Sf: 0-1 GS: 0-0 Gd: 0-4 GF: 0-0 Fm: 0-2
Distance: 5f/6f: 0-4 7f-8f: 0-4 9f-13f: 0-1 14f+: 0-1
Track : LH: 0-4 RH: 0-1 Tight: 0-1 Gall: 0-1
Aids: Bl: 0-0 Vi: 0-2 Tstrap: 0-0
Best Rating: 69 6/01 Newc 5f firm

Alzola (IRE)

95 **48**

4-y-o b f Alzao (USA)-Polistatic (Free State)
C A Horgan Mrs B Sumner

Placings:0/004 **(5670)**
2001: 7^{0}GS, 8^{0}G, 8^{4}HY

	Starts	1st	2nd	3rd	Win & Pl
Career Total (Turf)	4	0	0	0	0

Going (Turf): Sf: 0-1 GS: 0-1 Gd: 0-2 GF: 0-0 Fm: 0-0
Distance: 5f/6f: 0-0 7f-8f: 0-2 9f-13f: 0-2 14f+: 0-0
Track : LH: 0-0 RH: 0-2 Tight: 0-2 Gall: 0-0
Aids: Bl: 0-0 Vi: 0-0 Tstrap: 0-0
Best Rating: 48 5/01 Wind 1m67y good

Lightly-raced and no form so far.

Amacita

97 **29**

3-y-o b f Shareef Dancer (USA)-Kina (USA) (Bering)
Miss E C Lavelle Investment Ab Rustningen

Placings:0-402000040 **(5278)**
2001: 8^{4}GS, 10^{0}G, 11^{2}F, 14^{0}GF, 10^{0}GF, 11^{0}GF, 12^{0}S, 11^{4}GF, 9^{0}GS

	Starts	1st	2nd	3rd	Win & Pl
Career Total (Turf)	10	0	1	0	1170

Going (Turf): Sf: 0-2 GS: 0-2 Gd: 0-1 GF: 0-4 Fm: 0-1
Distance: 5f/6f: 0-0 7f-8f: 0-1 9f-13f: 0-8 14f+: 0-1
Track : LH: 0-3 RH: 0-4 Tight: 0-5 Gall: 0-0
Aids: Bl: 0-0 Vi: 0-1 Tstrap: 0-0
Best Rating: 62 5/01 Leic 1m3f183y firm

Amamackemmush (IRE)

(99) (34)**51**

3-y-o b g General Monash (USA)-Paganina (FR) (Galetto (FR))
K A Ryan Roses Racing Club

Placings:022352004-0064360540000 **(2978)**
2001: 5^{0}SW, 5^{0}SD, 5^{6}SW, 5^{4}SD, 6^{3}HY, 5^{6}SD, 6^{0}SD, 6^{5}GF, 6^{4}F, 5^{0}G, 5^{0}F, 6^{0}GF, 6^{0}SD

	Starts	1st	2nd	3rd	Win & Pl
Career Total (Turf)	13	0	3	2	3617
Career Total (AW)	9	0	0	0	0

Going (Turf): Sf: 0-1 GS: 0-1 Gd: 0-2 GF: 0-6 Fm: 0-3
Distance: 5f/6f: 0-21 7f-8f: 0-1 9f-13f: 0-0 14f+: 0-0
Track : LH: 0-9 RH: 0-0 Tight: 0-6 Gall: 0-0
Aids: Bl: 0-2 Vi: 0-0 Tstrap: 0-0
Best Rating: 51 6/01 Ling 6f firm

Moderate sprinter, likes to race prominently, probably does not want the ground too fast.

Amandari (FR)

(58)
5-y-o ch g Petit Loup (USA)-Baby Sitting (FR) (Son Of Silver)
A Berry Walt Sylvester

Placings:06501003000252/000005-0000 **(1992)**
2001: 12^{0}S, 12^{0}S, 8^{0}GF, 14^{0}SD

	Starts	1st	2nd	3rd	Win & Pl
Career Total (Turf)	23	1	2	1	13455
Career Total (AW)	1	0	0	0	

6/99	Fntb	1m4f110y		SFT	£5382

Total win prize-money £5382

Going (Turf): Sf: 1-4 GS: 0-0 Gd: 0-2 GF: 0-1 Fm: 0-0
Distance: 5f/6f: 0-0 7f-8f: 0-0 **9f-13f: 1-10** 14f+: 0-2
Track : LH: 0-3 RH: 0-1 Tight: 0-1 Gall: 0-1
Aids: **Bl: 1-2** Vi: 0-0 Tstrap: 0-0

Amandolo (IRE)

67 **30**
2-y-o ch c Grand Lodge (USA)-Marqueterie (USA) (Well Decorated (USA))
A Bailey (M Quinn 21/7) Mrs Tina-Gunn Hamann

Placings:5000 **(5268)**
2001: 6^{5}GF, 7^{0}GS, 6^{0}S, 7^{0}HY

	Starts	1st	2nd	3rd	Win & Pl
Career Total (Turf)	4	0	0	0	266

Going (Turf): Sf: 0-2 GS: 0-1 Gd: 0-0 GF: 0-1 Fm: 0-0
Distance: 5f/6f: 0-2 7f-8f: 0-2 9f-13f: 0-0 14f+: 0-0
Track : LH: 0-1 RH: 0-0 Tight: 0-0 Gall: 0-0
Aids: Bl: 0-0 Vi: 0-0 Tstrap: 0-0
Best Rating: 30 7/01 Wwck 7f26y gd-sft

Amaranth (IRE)

(108) (85+)**93**
5-y-o b g Mujadil (USA)-Zoes Delight (IRE) (Hatim (USA))
J L Eyre M Gleason

Placings:21/00231060016/00001265014461602-4040010305600010 **(5228)**
2001: 8^{4}SD, 8^{0}S, 6^{4}GF, 5^{0}GF, 6^{0}GF, 7^{1}F, 7^{0}GF, 6^{3}G, 7^{0}GF, 6^{5}G, 7^{6}GS, 6^{0}GF, 7^{0}GS, 7^{0}S, 7^{1}GS, 6^{0}S

	Starts	1st	2nd	3rd	Win & Pl
Career Total (Turf)	39	7	3	2	51101
Career Total (AW)	7	1	1	0	5539

77	10/01	Newc	7f	C(0-90)	G-S	£7412
93	6/01	Newc	7f	C(0-100)H	FRM	£14007
84	11/00	Sthl	6f	D(0-85)H	STD	£3341
85	8/00	NmkJ	5f	E(0-85)H	G-F	£3474
80	6/00	Ayr	6f	D(0-85)H	G-F	£4017
80	8/99	NmkJ	5f	E(0-85)H	G-F	£3785
83	6/99	Newc	6f	D(0-85)H	G-F	£3777
79	10/98	Rdcr	5f	F	SFT	£2192

Total win prize-money £42007

Going (Turf): Sf: 1-8 GS: 1-7 Gd: 0-7 **GF: 4-15** Fm: 1-2
Distance: **5f/6f: 6-33** 7f-8f: 2-12 9f-13f: 0-1 14f+: 0-0
Track : **LH: 1-11** RH: 0-0 Tight: 0-4 Gall: 0-1
Aids: Bl: 0-0 Vi: 0-0 **Tstrap: 4-31**
Best Rating: 93 8/01 Ripn 6f good

A versatile performer, he had only won over five and six furlongs before this season, but gained his first win over seven at Newcastle in June and added to that in a classified event at Newcastle. He does stay as far as a mile and acts on sand and most types of ground on turf. Can get worked up beforehand.

Amaretto Express (IRE)

83(84) (62)**53**
2-y-o b g Blues Traveller (IRE)-Cappuchino (IRE) (Roi Danzig (USA))
B J Meehan The Harlequin Partnership

Placings:050 **(4722)**
2001: 6^{0}G, 8^{5}SW, 7^{0}GF

	Starts	1st	2nd	3rd	Win & Pl
Career Total (Turf)	2	0	0	0	0
Career Total (AW)	1	0	0	0	0

Going (Turf): Sf: 0-0 GS: 0-0 Gd: 0-1 GF: 0-1 Fm: 0-0
Distance: 5f/6f: 0-0 7f-8f: 0-2 9f-13f: 0-1 14f+: 0-0
Track : LH: 0-2 RH: 0-0 Tight: 0-1 Gall: 0-0
Aids: Bl: 0-0 Vi: 0-0 Tstrap: 0-0
Best Rating: 62 9/01 Wolv 1m100y slow

Amaro

(94) (30)**37**
5-y-o b m Emarati (USA)-Redcross Miss (Tower Walk)
J L Harris J Rose

Placings:5452204005/5636000000403-5 **(0023)**
2001: 7^{5}SD

	Starts	1st	2nd	3rd	Win & Pl
Career Total (Turf)	11	0	2	0	970
Career Total (AW)	13	0	0	2	696

Going (Turf): Sf: 0-2 GS: 0-1 Gd: 0-3 GF: 0-5 Fm: 0-0
Distance: 5f/6f: 0-16 7f-8f: 0-7 9f-13f: 0-1 14f+: 0-0
Track : LH: 0-15 RH: 0-0 Tight: 0-5 Gall: 0-1
Aids: Bl: 0-0 Vi: 0-0 Tstrap: 0-0
Best Rating: 30 1/01 Sthl 7f stand

Amarone

(93) (30)**27**
3-y-o b g Young Ern-Tendresse (IRE) (Tender King)
M J Ryan M J Ryan

Placings:0600-05040 **(3234)**
2001: 6^{0}S, 9^{5}F, 7^{0}GF, 7^{4}SD, 8^{0}SD

	Starts	1st	2nd	3rd	Win & Pl
Career Total (Turf)	7	0	0	0	0
Career Total (AW)	2	0	0	0	0

Going (Turf): Sf: 0-2 GS: 0-0 Gd: 0-1 GF: 0-3 Fm: 0-1
Distance: 5f/6f: 0-3 7f-8f: 0-5 9f-13f: 0-1 14f+: 0-0
Track : LH: 0-3 RH: 0-0 Tight: 0-0 Gall: 0-0
Aids: Bl: 0-2 Vi: 0-4 Tstrap: 0-0
Best Rating: 30 7/01 Sthl 7f stand

Amazed

86 **58**
4-y-o ch f Clantime-Indigo (Primo Dominie)
Mrs J R Ramsden D R Brotherton

Placings:6/4200-00 **(3453)**
2001: 5^{0}G, 5^{0}GF

	Starts	1st	2nd	3rd	Win & Pl
Career Total (Turf)	7	0	1	0	1068

Going (Turf): Sf: 0-1 GS: 0-1 Gd: 0-1 GF: 0-4 Fm: 0-0
Distance: 5f/6f: 0-7 7f-8f: 0-0 9f-13f: 0-0 14f+: 0-0
Track : LH: 0-1 RH: 0-0 Tight: 0-0 Gall: 0-0
Aids: Bl: 0-0 Vi: 0-1 Tstrap: 0-0
Best Rating: 32 7/01 Newc 5f gd-fm

She showed some promise in maiden company last season, but then became disappointing,.

Ambassador Lady (IRE)

93(88) (20)**41**
3-y-o b f General Monash (USA)-La Fandango (IRE) (Taufan (USA))
A G Newcombe Alex Gorrie Combi (uk)

Placings:060-00040 **(4385)**
2001: 6^{0}F, 6^{0}SD, 5^{0}GF, 6^{4}GF, 6^{0}GF

	Starts	1st	2nd	3rd	Win & Pl
Career Total (Turf)	7	0	0	0	0
Career Total (AW)	1	0	0	0	

Going (Turf): Sf: 0-0 GS: 0-0 Gd: 0-0 GF: 0-5 Fm: 0-1
Distance: 5f/6f: 0-5 7f-8f: 0-2 9f-13f: 0-0 14f+: 0-0
Track : LH: 0-3 RH: 0-0 Tight: 0-0 Gall: 0-0
Aids: Bl: 0-0 Vi: 0-0 Tstrap: 0-0
Best Rating: 41 8/01 Brig 6f209y gd-fm

Amber Brown

97(102) (61)**60**
5-y-o b m Thowra (FR)-High Velocity (Frimley Park)
K T Ivory K T Ivory

Placings:6066050/0100140060202556-6200104363000 **(2655)**
2001: 6^{6}SD, 7^{2}SD, 6^{0}SD, 8^{0}SD, 7^{1}SW, 8^{0}SW, 7^{4}SW, 7^{3}SD, 6^{6}HY, 7^{3}G, 7^{0}GF, 7^{0}GF, 6^{0}GF

	Starts	1st	2nd	3rd	Win & Pl
Career Total (Turf)	23	2	1	1	9158
Career Total (AW)	13	1	2	1	4290

59	2/01	Ling	7f	F(0-60)	SLW	£2170
61	5/00	Ling	7f	E(0-75)H	HVY	£3178
57	4/00	Thsk	6f	E(0-75)H	SFT	£3900

Total win prize-money £9248

Going (Turf): Sf: 2-5 GS: 0-4 Gd: 0-6 GF: 0-7 Fm: 0-1
Distance: 5f/6f: 1-21 **7f-8f: 2-15** 9f-13f: 0-0 14f+: 0-0
Track : **LH: 1-14** RH: 0-6 **Tight: 1-7** Gall: 0-6
Aids: **Bl: 2-23** Vi: 0-0 Tstrap: 0-0
Best Rating: 61 1/01 Ling 7f stand

Amber Fort

107(90) (60)**62**
8-y-o gr g Indian Ridge-Lammastide (Martinmas)
J M Bradley I'm Out Of Here Racing

Placings:600203/550451022316/00520031/004511003 3350/05533040032000/325405553450044030500-0014000604360030 **(5681)**
2001: 7^{0}HY, 6^{0}GF, 6^{1}S, 6^{4}F, 7^{0}GF, 7^{0}GF, 6^{0}G, 7^{6}GS, 7^{0}GF, 7^{4}GF, 6^{3}GF, 7^{6}GF, 7^{0}G, 7^{0}S, 7^{3}G, 8^{0}S

	Starts	1st	2nd	3rd	Win & Pl
Career Total (Turf)	83	5	6	13	44618
Career Total (AW)	7	1	0	1	3332

75	5/01	Sals	6f212y	D(0-80)H	SFT	£4621
82	7/98	Kemp	7f	D(0-85)H	G-S	£3745
81	6/98	Gdwd	7f	E(0-80)H	G-F	£3850
77	6/97	Gdwd	7f	E(0-80)H	SFT	£3915
74	10/96	Newb	7f	F(0-80)H	SFT	£3457
60	6/96	Ling	7f	F	STD	£2880

Total win prize-money £22471

Going (Turf): Sf: 3-15 GS: 1-5 Gd: 0-23 GF: 1-36 Fm: 0-4
Distance: 5f/6f: 0-7 **7f-8f: 6-73** 9f-13f: 0-10 14f+: 0-0
Track : LH: 1-34 **RH: 3-19** Tight: 1-14 Gall: 1-12
Aids: Bl: 2-53 **Vi: 4-26** Tstrap: 0-0
Best Rating: 75 5/01 Sals 6f212y soft

Scored his first win in almost three years at Salisbury in

May. Suited by seven furlongs, he acts on soft ground and needs to come late off a strong pace.

Amber Rose (IRE)

(89) (48)**69**

3-y-o ch f Royal Academy (USA)-La Fille De Cirque (Cadeaux Genereux)

M Johnston Greenland Park Ltd

Placings:3-03460 **(5347)**

2001: 6^{0}GF, 9^{3}GF, 8^{4}G, 9^{6}G, 8^{0}SD

	Starts	1st	2nd	3rd	Win & Pl
Career Total (Turf)	5	0	0	2	1828
Career Total (AW)	1	0	0	0	

Going (Turf): Sf: 0-0 GS: 0-0 Gd: 0-2 GF: 0-3 Fm: 0-0
Distance: 5f/6f: 0-2 7f-8f: 0-1 9f-13f: 0-3 14f+: 0-0
Track : LH: 0-1 RH: 0-3 Tight: 0-2 Gall: 0-0
Aids: Bl: 0-0 Vi: 0-0 Tstrap: 0-2
Best Rating: 68 5/01 Bevl 1m1f207y gd-fm

Has shown promise, but improvement needed to win a race.

Amber Tide (IRE)

101 **69**

3-y-o ch f Pursuit Of Love-Tochar Ban (USA) (Assert)

M L W Bell A Buxton

Placings:340-303442224 **(4468)**

2001: 6^{3}G, 8^{0}GF, 8^{3}F, 8^{4}GF, 8^{4}G, 7^{2}G, 7^{2}F, 10^{2}G, 9^{4}G

	Starts	1st	2nd	3rd	Win & Pl
Career Total (Turf)	12	0	3	3	5585

Going (Turf): Sf: 0-2 GS: 0-1 Gd: 0-5 GF: 0-2 Fm: 0-2
Distance: 5f/6f: 0-3 7f-8f: 0-4 9f-13f: 0-5 14f+: 0-0
Track : LH: 0-5 RH: 0-2 Tight: 0-3 Gall: 0-0
Aids: Bl: 0-0 Vi: 0-0 Tstrap: 0-0
Best Rating: 69 8/01 Brig 7f214y firm

Amber's Bluff

94 **88+**

2-y-o b f Mind Games-Amber Mill (Doulab (USA))

A C Stewart Racing For Gold

Placings:2 **(4573)**

2001: 6^{2}G

	Starts	1st	2nd	3rd	Win & Pl
Career Total (Turf)	1	0	1	0	1416

Going (Turf): Sf: 0-0 GS: 0-0 Gd: 0-1 GF: 0-0 Fm: 0-0
Distance: 5f/6f: 0-1 7f-8f: 0-0 9f-13f: 0-0 14f+: 0-0
Track : LH: 0-0 RH: 0-0 Tight: 0-0 Gall: 0-0
Aids: Bl: 0-0 Vi: 0-0 Tstrap: 0-0
Best Rating: 88 9/01 Kemp 6f good

Speedily-bred, finished well after a slow atart on her Kempton debut.

Ambersong

102 **45**

3-y-o ch c Hernando (FR)-Stygian (USA) (Irish River (FR))

J W Hills C New

Placings:00-5020000 **(4773)**

2001. 6^{0}GS, 7^{0}G, 8^{0}G, 8^{0}GF, 8^{0}G, 8^{0}G, 8^{0}G

	Starts	1st	2nd	3rd	Win & Pl
Career Total (Turf)	9	0	1	0	2100

Going (Turf): Sf: 0-1 GS: 0-2 Gd: 0-5 GF: 0-1 Fm: 0-0
Distance: 5f/6f: 0-1 7f-8f: 0-3 9f-13f: 0-5 14f+: 0-0
Track : LH: 0-3 RH: 0-2 Tight: 0-2 Gall: 0-1
Aids: Bl: 0-0 Vi: 0-0 Tstrap: 0-0
Best Rating: 71 6/01 Bath 1m5y good

Modest maiden, had two outings at two over seven furlongs. Dropped back to six on reappearance in 2001, but seemed to appreciate a step up in trip and a faster surface at Bath.

Ambitious

110(102) (81)**89**

6-y-o b m Ardkinglass-Ayodhya (IRE) (Astronef)

K T Ivory Dean Ivory

Placings:024/024/6215520201002130661120/0104014 10100040-0532030030006 **(5502)**

2001: 5^{0}GF, 5^{5}GF, 5^{3}GF, 5^{2}GF, 5^{0}GF, 5^{3}GF, 5^{0}G, 6^{0}G, 6^{3}G, 5^{0}G, 5^{0}GF, 6^{0}GF, 5^{6}HY

	Starts	1st	2nd	3rd	Win & Pl
Career Total (Turf)	48	7	6	4	57853
Career Total (AW)	8	2	2	0	7938

90	8/00	Newb	5f34y	C(0-95)H	G-F	£7085
87	7/00	Sand	5f6y	C(0-95)H	GD	£10822
81	6/00	Sthl	5f	E(0-70)H	STD	£2737
81	4/00	Thsk	5f	D(0-80)	SFT	£4127
76	10/99	York	5f	D(0-80)H	G-S	£7694
69	10/99	Rdcr	5f	E(0-70)	GD	£2951
65	8/99	Sand	5f6y	E(0-75)H	G-S	£3582
57	6/99	Sand	5f6y	E	GD	£2879
65	2/99	Sthl	6f	D(0-80)H	STD	£3543

Total win prize-money £45424

Going (Turf): Sf: 1-6 GS: 2-6 Gd: 3-17 GF: 1-16 Fm: 0-3
Distance: 5f/6f: 9-52 7f-8f: 0-4 9f-13f: 0-0 14f+: 0-0
Track : LH: 1-11 RH: 0-7 Tight: 0-5 Gall: 0-8
Aids: Bl: 0-2 Vi: 1-4 Tstrap: 0-0
Best Rating: 91 7/01 Donc 5f gd-fm

A useful, consistent sprint handicapper, she is most effective when the ground is good or on the easy side, but has run well without winning under faster conditions this season.

Ambitious Alliance (IRE)

69(86) (47)**26**

2-y-o b g General Monash (USA)-Northern Amber (Shack (USA))

M Quinn Open Warfare Partners

Placings:560000 **(3367)**

2001: 5^{5}S, 5^{6}SD, 5^{0}GF, 6^{0}G, 5^{0}GS, 7^{0}GF

	Starts	1st	2nd	3rd	Win & Pl
Career Total (Turf)	5	0	0	0	0
Career Total (AW)	1	0	0	0	0

Going (Turf): Sf: 0-1 GS: 0-1 Gd: 0-1 GF: 0-2 Fm: 0-0
Distance: 5f/6f: 0-5 7f-8f: 0-1 9f-13f: 0-0 14f+: 0-0
Track : LH: 0-2 RH: 0-0 Tight: 0-1 Gall: 0-1
Aids: Bl: 0-1 Vi: 0-0 Tstrap: 0-0
Best Rating: 53 5/01 Wolv 5f stand

Ambry

104(93) (60+)**78**

4-y-o br g Machiavellian (USA)-Alkaffeyeh (IRE) (Sadler's Wells (USA))

G L Moore Raymond Gross, Ms Adrienne Gross

Placings:42032530204-3236 **(5330)**

2001: 16^{0}SD, 14^{0}GS, 16^{0}GF, 16^{0}HY

	Starts	1st	2nd	3rd	Win & Pl
Career Total (Turf)	14	0	4	3	8770
Career Total (AW)	1	0	0	1	316

Going (Turf): Sf: 0-4 GS: 0-1 Gd: 0-2 GF: 0-3 Fm: 0-0
Distance: 5f/6f: 0-0 7f-8f: 0-1 9f-13f: 0-9 14f+: 0-5
Track : LH: 0-6 RH: 0-7 Tight: 0-3 Gall: 0-1
Aids: Bl: 0-3 Vi: 0-0 Tstrap: 0-0
Best Rating: 67 6/01 Folk 2m93y gd-fm

Ex-Irish, he has been placed in staying events on the Flat and is a winning hurdler.

Ambushed (IRE)

97(98) (36)**62**

5-y-o b g Indian Ridge-Surprise Move (IRE) (Simply Great (FR))

P Monteith Allan W Melville

Placings:00/001052106315-510564400 **(3595)**

2001: 8^{5}GS, 9^{1}GF, 8^{0}G, 8^{5}GF, 6^{6}GF, 9^{4}G, 9^{4}F, 9^{0}GF, 9^{0}GS

	Starts	1st	2nd	3rd	Win & Pl
Career Total (Turf)	17	3	1	1	13430
Career Total (AW)	6	1	0	0	1806

63	5/01	Ayr	1m1f20y	E(0-70)H	G-F	£3570
58	10/00	Muss	1m1f	F(0-65)H	SFT	£1788
55	9/00	Haml	1m65y	C(0-90)H	SFT	£6955
36	2/00	Sthl	1m	F(0-60)H	STD	£1806

Total win prize-money £14120

Going (Turf): Sf: 2-5 GS: 0-3 Gd: 0-3 GF: 1-4 Fm: 0-2
Distance: 5f/6f: 0-2 7f-8f: 1-7 9f-13f: 3-14 14f+: 0-0
Track : LH: 1-8 RH: 2-7 Tight: 2-10 Gall: 0-1
Aids: Bl: 1-2 Vi: 0-0 Tstrap: 0-0
Best Rating: 63 5/01 Ayr 1m1f20y gd-fm

Ameerat

111 **119**

3-y-o b f Mark Of Esteem (IRE)-Walimu (IRE) (Top Ville)

M A Jarvis Sheikh Ahmed Al Maktoum

Placings:126-1500 **(5141)**

2001: 8^{1}G, 8^{5}GF, 8^{0}GF, 8^{0}G

	Starts	1st	2nd	3rd	Win & Pl
Career Total (Turf)	7	2	1	0	201620

119	5/01	NmkR	1m	A	GD	£174000
88	8/00	Gdwd	7f	D	GD	£10920

Total win prize-money £184920

Going (Turf): Sf: 0-0 GS: 0-1 Gd: 2-3 GF: 0-3 Fm: 0-0
Distance: 5f/6f: 0-0 7f-8f: 2-7 9f-13f: 0-0 14f+: 0-0
Track : LH: 0-1 RH: 1-3 Tight: 0-0 Gall: 0-2
Aids: Bl: 0-0 Vi: 0-0 Tstrap: 0-0
Best Rating: 119 5/01 NmkR 1m good

Improved on her already useful juvenile form when landing the 1000 Guineas from Muwakleh, staying on well for pressure up the hill. A respectable fifth in the Coronation Stakes next time, after racing freely, she disappointed in Group races afterwards and has reportedly retired to stud.

Amelia (IRE)

103 **67**

3-y-o b f General Monash (USA)-Rose Tint (IRE) (Salse (USA))

J Cullinan Alan Spargo Ltd Toolmakers

Placings:4233431120-000000 **(5275)**

2001: 6^{0}S, 5^{0}S, 6^{0}G, 5^{0}G, 6^{0}GF, 8^{0}GS, 6^{0}SD

	Starts	1st	2nd	3rd	Win & Pl
Career Total (Turf)	14	1	2	3	9011
Career Total (AW)	2	1	0	0	19140

76	9/00	Ling	5f	D(0-85)	GD	£4374
73	8/00	Wolv	6f	B	STD	£19140

Total win prize-money £23515

Going (Turf): Sf: 0-4 GS: 0-1 Gd: 1-5 GF: 0-4 Fm: 0-0
Distance: 5f/6f: 2-14 7f-8f: 0-1 9f-13f: 0-1 14f+: 0-0
Track : LH: 1-1 RH: 0-0 Tight: 1-1 Gall: 0-0
Aids: Bl: 0-0 Vi: 0-0 Tstrap: 0-0
Best Rating: 75 4/01 NmkR 6f soft

Consistent form on both turf and sand last season, winning the Weatherbys Dash at Wolverhampton and following up in a Lingfield nursery on turf. Failed to fire this season.

Amen Corner (USA)

89(94) (79d)**77**

3-y-o ch g Mt. Livermore (USA)-For All Seasons (USA) (Crafty Prospector (USA))

M Johnston M Doyle

Placings:41350230-005 **(2814)**

2001: 6^{0}SD, 6^{0}SW, 8^{5}GF

	Starts	1st	2nd	3rd	Win & Pl
Career Total (Turf)	7	1	0	2	5171
Career Total (AW)	4	0	1	0	874

67 7/00 Ayr 6f D G-F £3679

Total win prize-money £3679

Going (Turf): Sf: 0-2 GS: 0-0 Gd: 0-1 **GF: 1-4** Fm: 0-0
Distance: **5f/6f: 1-8** 7f-8f: 0-2 9f-13f: 0-1 14f+: 0-0
Track : LH: 0-5 RH: 0-1 Tight: 0-2 Gall: 0-1
Aids: Bl: 0-0 Vi: 0-0 Tstrap: 0-0
Best Rating: 63 7/01 Bevl 1m100y gd-fm

Scored once at two over six furlongs and likes to dominate. Best suited to fast ground, but has mostly been running on the All-Weather since last autumn to little effect.

America Calling (USA)

105(94) (58)**78**

3-y-o b f Quiet American (USA)-Allison's Dance (USA) (Storm Bird (CAN))

G A Butler Mrs C J O'Reilly

Placings:23423-5536130 **(5148)**

2001: 6^{5}SD, 6^{5}S, 5^{3}GS, 5^{6}G, 6^{1}F, 6^{3}GF, 5^{0}G

	Starts	1st	2nd	3rd	Win & Pl
Career Total (Turf)	13	1	3	4	13102
Career Total (AW)	1	0	0	0	0

69 9/01 Chep 6f16y F(0-65)H FRM £2436

Total win prize-money £2436

Going (Turf): Sf: 0-2 GS: 0-1 Gd: 0-5 GF: 0-1 **Fm: 1-1**
Distance: 5f/6f: 0-10 **7f-8f: 1-4** 9f-13f: 0-0 14f+: 0-0
Track : LH: 0-3 RH: 0-2 Tight: 0-1 Gall: 0-0
Aids: **Bl: 1-1** Vi: 0-0 Tstrap: 0-7
Best Rating: 78 9/01 Kemp 6f gd-fm

Placed in all her runs in maidens in Ireland in 2000, she has proved a modest sprinter on fast ground.

American Cousin

107(87) (58)**73**

6-y-o b g Distant Relative-Zelda (USA) (Sharpen Up)

D Nicholls Middleham Park Racing Xiv

Placings:03330/002500/000214215240/0000005011 10-54040612501000000 **(4897)**

2001: 5^{5}S, 5^{4}S, 6^{0}SD, 6^{4}G, 5^{0}GF, 5^{6}GF, 5^{1}G, 6^{2}GF, 5^{5}F, 5^{0}GF, 5^{1}G, 5^{0}GF, 6^{0}G, 5^{0}GF, 6^{0}GF, 5^{0}GS, 5^{0}GS

	Starts	1st	2nd	3rd	Win & Pl
Career Total (Turf)	52	7	5	2	33133
Career Total (AW)	2	0	0	1	439

73 7/01 York 5f C(0-95)H GD £9529
65 6/01 Muss 5f E(0-70)H GD £3587
58 9/00 Yarm 6f3y F(0-60)H G-F £2135
53 9/00 Chep 5f16y E(0-70)H G-S £2990
54 8/00 Sals 5f E(0-80)H G-F £2827
58 7/99 Donc 5f F(0-65)H G-F £2400
48 6/99 Donc 6f E(0-70)H G-F £2892

Total win prize-money £26362

Going (Turf): Sf: 0-6 GS: 1-8 Gd: 2-10 **GF: 4-24** Fm: 0-4
Distance: **5f/6f: 6-49** 7f-8f: 1-5 9f-13f: 0-0 14f+: 0-0
Track : LH: 0-7 RH: 0-4 Tight: 0-3 Gall: 0-6

Aids: Bl: 0-2 Vi: 0-0 Tstrap: 0-0
Best Rating: 73 7/01 York 5f good

He took advantage of a lenient handicap mark to complete a hat-trick late last summer and has run well since from a much higher mark, including victories at Musselburgh in June and York in July. Equally effective over five and six furlongs.

Amezola

100 **35**

5-y-o gr g Northern Park (USA)-Yamamah (Siberian Express (USA))

J C McConnochie (Mrs A J Perrett 1/5) Mrs R E Stocks

Placings:01/43206/06600-00000006 **(5557)**

2001: 14^{0}HY, 10^{0}GF, 16^{0}GF, 14^{0}GS, 14^{0}G, 16^{0}G, 16^{0}G, 14^{6}S

	Starts	1st	2nd	3rd	Win & Pl
Career Total (Turf)	20	1	1	1	5274

74 10/98 Bath 1m5y E HVY £2479

Total win prize-money £2479

Going (Turf): **Sf: 1-4** GS: 0-5 Gd: 0-5 GF: 0-6 Fm: 0-0
Distance: 5f/6f: 0-0 7f-8f: 0-1 **9f-13f: 1-5** 14f+: 0-14
Track : **LH: 1-9** RH: 0-11 **Tight: 1-7** Gall: 0-2
Aids: Bl: 0-1 Vi: 0-0 Tstrap: 0-7
Best Rating: 44 8/01 Yarm 1m6f17y gd-sft

He is very moderate these days.

Ami's Angel (IRE)

83(90) (40)**36**

3-y-o b f Fayruz-Khunasira (FR) (Nishapour (FR))

A G Newcombe Mr A Newby

Placings:21600-0000000 **(4609)**

2001: 5^{0}SD, 5^{0}SD, 5^{0}SD, 6^{0}GF, 7^{0}GF, 6^{0}GF, 8^{0}F

	Starts	1st	2nd	3rd	Win & Pl
Career Total (Turf)	9	1	1	0	8277
Career Total (AW)	3	0	0	0	0

64 8/00 Pont 5f D G-F £6032

Total win prize-money £6032

Going (Turf): Sf: 0-1 GS: 0-1 Gd: 0-1 **GF: 1-5** Fm: 0-1
Distance: **5f/6f: 1-8** 7f-8f: 0-3 9f-13f: 0-1 14f+: 0-0
Track : **LH: 1-5** RH: 0-0 Tight: 0-3 Gall: 0-1
Aids: Bl: 0-1 Vi: 0-0 Tstrap: 0-0
Best Rating: 40 3/01 Wolv 5f stand

Amiabla (IRE)

87 **59**

2-y-o gr f Dr Devious (IRE)-Safkana (IRE) (Doyoun)

C E Brittain R A Pledger

Placings:40 **(3215)**

2001: 7^{4}G, 7^{0}GF

	Starts	1st	2nd	3rd	Win & Pl
Career Total (Turf)	2	0	0	0	290

Going (Turf): **Sf: 0-0 GS: 0-0 Gd: 0-1 GF: 0-1** Fm: 0-0
Distance: 5f/6f: 0-0 7f-8f: 0-2 9f-13f: 0-0 14f+: 0-0
Track : LH: 0-0 RH: 0-0 Tight: 0-0 Gall: 0-0
Aids: Bl: 0-0 Vi: 0-0 Tstrap: 0-0
Best Rating: 59 7/01 Yarm 7f3y good

Amicable (IRE)

106 **103**

3-y-o b c Common Grounds-Bahia Laura (FR) (Bellypha)

B W Hills Lady Harrison

Placings:42-11020440 **(5391)**

2001: 7^{1}S, 7^{1}GF, 8^{0}GY, 7^{2}GF, 8^{0}GF, 8^{4}GS, 8^{4}G, 7^{0}GS

	Starts	1st	2nd	3rd	Win & Pl
Career Total (Turf)	10	2	2	0	34195

101 5/01 Ches 7f122y C(0-100)H G-F £18102
83 3/01 Donc 7f D SFT £4407

Total win prize-money £22510

Going (Turf): **Sf: 1-1** GS: 0-2 Gd: 0-2 **GF: 1-4** Fm: 0-0
Distance: 5f/6f: 0-0 **7f-8f: 2-9** 9f-13f: 0-1 14f+: 0-0
Track : **LH: 1-3** RH: 0-0 **Tight: 1-3** Gall: 0-0
Aids: Bl: 0-0 Vi: 0-0 Tstrap: 0-0
Best Rating: 103 6/01 Asct 1m gd-fm

Showed some ability in two starts as a juvenile and battled on well to narrowly land a Doncaster maiden on bad ground on his reappearance. Followed up in a decent Chester handicap, but was taking on a bit too much when down the field in the Irish 2000 Guineas. Better effort to finish runner-up to Jentzen in an Epsom Listed event next time and was not beaten far in the Britannia although has been held in handicaps and conditions races since.

Amigo (IRE)

92(88) (45)**55**

3-y-o b c Spectrum (IRE)-Eleanor Antoinette (IRE) (Double Schwartz)

P Mitchell Sir Peter O'Sullevan

Placings:066-0000 **(5055)**

2001: 8^{0}G, 9^{0}GF, 10^{0}G, 10^{0}S

	Starts	1st	2nd	3rd	Win & Pl
Career Total (Turf)	6	0	0	0	0
Career Total (AW)	1	0	0	0	0

Going (Turf): **Sf: 0-2 GS: 0-1 Gd: 0-2 GF: 0-1 Fm: 0-0**
Distance: 5f/6f: 0-0 7f-8f: 0-3 9f-13f: 0-4 14f+: 0-0
Track : LH: 0-2 RH: 0-1 Tight: 0-3 Gall: 0-0
Aids: Bl: 0-0 Vi: 0-0 Tstrap: 0-0
Best Rating: 55 5/01 NmkR 1m good

Amington Lady

3-y-o ch f Superlative-Amington Lass (Cree Song)

P D Evans M J Higgins

Placings:P **(4179)**

2001: 5^{P}GF

	Starts	1st	2nd	3rd	Win & Pl
Career Total (Turf)	1	0	0	0	

Going (Turf): **Sf: 0-0 GS: 0-0 Gd: 0-0 GF: 0-1 Fm: 0-0**
Distance: 5f/6f: 0-1 7f-8f: 0-0 9f-13f: 0-0 14f+: 0-0
Track : LH: 0-0 RH: 0-0 Tight: 0-0 Gall: 0-0
Aids: Bl: 0-0 Vi: 0-0 Tstrap: 0-0

Amir Zaman

98 **67**

3-y-o ch c Salse (USA)-Colorvista (Shirley Heights)

J W Payne C Cotran

Placings:00-404631 **(3318)**

2001: 8^{4}S, 8^{0}S, 11^{4}F, 11^{6}G, 16^{3}G, 14^{1}G

	Starts	1st	2nd	3rd	Win & Pl
Career Total (Turf)	8	1	0	1	4349

67 7/01 Yarm 1m6f17y E(0-70)H GD £3290

Total win prize-money £3290

Going (Turf): Sf: 0-2 GS: 0-1 **Gd: 1-3** GF: 0-1 Fm: 0-1
Distance: 5f/6f: 0-0 7f-8f: 0-3 9f-13f: 0-3 **14f+: 1-2**
Track : **LH: 1-5** RH: 0-1 **Tight: 1-2** Gall: 0-1
Aids: Bl: 0-0 Vi: 0-0 Tstrap: 0-0
Best Rating: 67 7/01 Yarm 1m6f17y good

Has improved since faced with an extended trip and fast ground. Opened his account in a maiden handicap at Yarmouth in July.

Amjad

91 (106) (70) **41**

4-y-o ch g Cadeaux Genereux-Babita (Habitat)

P C Haslam Mrs B Hawkins

Placings:5045502006-160430 **(4218)**

2001: 8^{1}SD, 9^{6}SD, 8^{0}HY, 12^{4}SD, 8^{3}GS, 9^{0}G

	Starts	1st	2nd	3rd	Win & Pl
Career Total (Turf)	13	0	1	1	1684
Career Total (AW)	4	1	0	0	2464

70 1/01 Sthl 1m E(0-70)H STD £2464

Total win prize-money £2464

Going (Turf): Sf: 0-1 GS: 0-1 Gd: 0-4 GF: 0-7 Fm: 0-0
Distance: 5f/6f: 0-2 **7f-8f: 1-6** 9f-13f: 0-9 14f+: 0-0
Track : **LH: 1-8** RH: 0-4 Tight: 0-3 Gall: 0-3
Aids: Bl: 0-5 Vi: 0-1 Tstrap: 0-0
Best Rating: 70 1/01 Sthl 1m stand

Amnesty

95 **73**

2-y-o ch g Salse (USA)-Amaranthus (Shirley Heights)

H Candy Kingstone Warren Partners

Placings:005 **(5080)**

2001: 6^{0}GF, 6^{0}GF, 6^{5}S

	Starts	1st	2nd	3rd	Win & Pl
Career Total (Turf)	3	0	0	0	0

Going (Turf): Sf: 0-1 GS: 0-0 Gd: 0-0 GF: 0-2 Fm: 0-0
Distance: 5f/6f: 0-1 7f-8f: 0-2 9f-13f: 0-0 14f+: 0-0
Track : LH: 0-1 RH: 0-0 Tight: 0-0 Gall: 0-0
Aids: Bl: 0-0 Vi: 0-0 Tstrap: 0-0
Best Rating: 73 10/01 Brig 6f209y soft

Among Equals

98 **88**

4-y-o b g Sadler's Wells (USA)-Epicure's Garden (USA) (Affirmed (USA))

M Meade Ladyswood Stud

Placings:422215-60 **(5008)**

2001: 13^{6}GF, 16^{0}S

	Starts	1st	2nd	3rd	Win & Pl
Career Total (Turf)	8	1	3	0	10662

84 9/00 List 1m2f HVY £6900

Total win prize-money £6900

Going (Turf): Sf: 1-2 GS: 0-0 Gd: 0-0 GF: 0-3 Fm: 0-0
Distance: 5f/6f: 0-0 7f-8f: 0-0 **9f-13f: 1-6** 14f+: 0-2
Track : **LH: 1-3** RH: 0-5 Tight: 0-0 Gall: 0-1
Aids: **Bl: 1-2** Vi: 0-0 Tstrap: 0-0
Best Rating: 80 9/01 Ayr 1m5f13y gd-fm

Among Women

(95) (56) **60**

3-y-o b f Common Grounds-Key West (FR) (Highest Honor (FR))

J R Best (N A Callaghan 18/7) Tendorra

Placings:001-46400100430 **(5611)**

2001: 7^{4}GS, 8^{6}GS, 8^{4}G, 9^{0}GF, 8^{0}GF, 7^{1}GS, 8^{0}G, 10^{0}G, 8^{4}S, 8^{3}SD, 8^{0}SD

	Starts	1st	2nd	3rd	Win & Pl
Career Total (Turf)	12	2	0	0	5878
Career Total (AW)	2	0	0	1	330

36 7/01 Ling 7f F G-S £2464
70 10/00 Brig 7f214y D SFT £2886

Total win prize-money £5350

Going (Turf): Sf: 1-4 GS: 1-3 Gd: 0-3 GF: 0-2 Fm: 0-0
Distance: 5f/6f: 0-2 **7f-8f: 2-4** 9f-13f: 0-8 14f+: 0-0
Track : **LH: 1-5** RH: 0-3 Tight: 0-6 Gall: 0-0
Aids: Bl: 0-0 Vi: 0-0 Tstrap: 0-0

Best Rating: 68 4/01 Brig 7f214y gd-sft

Scored as a juvenile when dropped in class at Brighton, but did not win again this term until easily landing a Lingfield claimer. Appreciates an easy surface, and ran well on her All-Weather debut in October.

Amoras (IRE)

(105) (69) **71**

4-y-o b f Hamas (IRE)-Red Lory (Bay Express)

J W Hills Espresso Racing

Placings:06253154/4004251-23054 **(4279)**

2001: 7^{2}GF, 7^{3}S, 8^{0}GF, 8^{5}G, 7^{4}GF

	Starts	1st	2nd	3rd	Win & Pl
Career Total (Turf)	20	2	3	2	17039

71 8/00 Wind 1m67y D(0-85)H GD £4062
74 9/99 Bath 1m5y C(0-90)H G-F £7197

Total win prize-money £11261

Going (Turf): Sf: 0-3 GS: 0-0 **Gd: 1-6 GF: 1-9** Fm: 0-2
Distance: 5f/6f: 0-3 7f-8f: 0-10 **9f-13f: 2-7** 14f+: 0-0
Track : LH: 1-7 RH: 1-7 **Tight: 2-4** Gall: 0-4
Aids: Bl: 0-0 Vi: 0-0 Tstrap: 0-0
Best Rating: 75 6/01 Kemp 7f gd-fm

A consistent handicapper, she ran very well at Kempton on her belated reappearance and may not have been suited by the softer ground at Haydock next time. Suited by a mile and fast ground.

Amorous Sarita

94 **51**

3-y-o b f Pursuit Of Love-Hug Me (Shareef Dancer (USA))

P W Harris Cage, Derry, Fox & Wort

Placings:0-004000 **(5497)**

2001: 8^{0}G, 6^{0}GF, 5^{4}GF, 6^{0}S, 6^{0}F, 5^{0}HY

	Starts	1st	2nd	3rd	Win & Pl
Career Total (Turf)	7	0	0	0	0

Going (Turf): Sf: 0-3 GS: 0-0 Gd: 0-1 GF: 0-2 Fm: 0-1
Distance: 5f/6f: 0-3 7f-8f: 0-3 9f-13f: 0-1 14f+: 0-0
Track : LH: 0-1 RH: 0-1 Tight: 0-1 Gall: 0-0
Aids: Bl: 0-0 Vi: 0-0 Tstrap: 0-0
Best Rating: 51 7/01 Brig 5f213y gd-fm

Amour Sans Fin (FR)

(94) (74) **94**

2-y-o b c Kendor (FR)-Nult Sans Fin (FR) (Lead On Time (USA))

B J Meehan Abbott Racing Limited

Placings:413600 **(5255)**

2001: 5^{4}G, 6^{1}S, 8^{3}GF, 7^{6}GS, 8^{0}S, 8^{0}GS

	Starts	1st	2nd	3rd	Win & Pl
Career Total (Turf)	6	1	0	1	6418

81 5/01 Newb 6f8y D SFT £4823

Total win prize-money £4823

Going (Turf): Sf: 1-2 GS: 0-2 Gd: 0-1 GF: 0-1 Fm: 0-0
Distance: 5f/6f: 0-1 **7f-8f: 1-5** 9f-13f: 0-0 14f+: 0-0
Track : LH: 0-0 RH: 0-2 Tight: 0-0 Gall: 0-2
Aids: Bl: 0-1 Vi: 0-0 Tstrap: 0-0
Best Rating: 94 9/01 Sals 1m gd-fm

He was given a break after winning a soft-ground maiden at Newbury on his second start and ran with credit in a Salisbury conditions event on his return. Looked out of his depth in Group Twos at Doncaster and Ascot.

Amoure King (IRE)

91 **68**

2-y-o b c Desert King (IRE)-Ange Rouge (Priolo (USA))

B W Hills Mrs Drusilla Thomas

Placings:050 **(5175)**

2001: 6^{0}GF, 7^{5}GF, 6^{0}HY

	Starts	1st	2nd	3rd	Win & Pl
Career Total (Turf)	3	0	0	0	0

Going (Turf): Sf: 0-1 GS: 0-0 Gd: 0-0 GF: 0-2 Fm: 0-0
Distance: 5f/6f: 0-1 7f-8f: 0-2 9f-13f: 0-0 14f+: 0-0
Track : LH: 0-2 RH: 0-0 Tight: 0-0 Gall: 0-1
Aids: Bl: 0-0 Vi: 0-0 Tstrap: 0-0
Best Rating: 68 9/01 Wwck 7f26y gd-fm

Ampulla

100 **52**

3-y-o b g Primo Dominie-Lead Them Lady (FR) (Lead On Time (USA))

G B Balding The Bogie Boys

Placings:0-0000000 **(4736)**

2001: 6^{0}HY, 6^{0}GS, 5^{0}G, 6^{0}GF, 5^{0}GF, 7^{0}G, 6^{0}F

	Starts	1st	2nd	3rd	Win & Pl
Career Total (Turf)	8	0	0	0	

Going (Turf): Sf: 0-1 GS: 0-2 Gd: 0-2 GF: 0-2 Fm: 0-1
Distance: 5f/6f: 0-5 7f-8f: 0-3 9f-13f: 0-0 14f+: 0-0
Track : LH: 0-1 RH: 0-2 Tight: 0-0 Gall: 0-3
Aids: Bl: 0-0 Vi: 0-0 Tstrap: 0-0
Best Rating: 52 5/01 Wind 5f10y good

Amrak Ajeeb (IRE)

105 **57**

9-y-o b h Danehill (USA)-Noble Dust (USA) (Dust Commander (USA))

R J Baker B P Jones

Placings:0/251041220050/006120501016/435030055/1466004000/03143020-00040044505 **(4635)**

2001: 10^{0}GS, 9^{0}G, 13^{0}GF, 11^{4}GF, 10^{0}F, 12^{0}GF, 11^{4}G, 11^{4}F, 12^{5}S, 9^{0}GF, 9^{5}GF

	Starts	1st	2nd	3rd	Win & Pl
Career Total (Turf)	61	7	5	4	92944
Career Total (AW)	2	0	0	0	1146

70 6/00 Chep 1m2f36y D(0-80)H FRM £3835
1/99 Abud 1m H G-F £3682
105 9/96 Asct 1m B H GD £29700
98 8/96 York 1m2f85y B(0-105)H GD £14207
95 5/96 Newb 1m D(0-85)H SFT £7360
85 8/95 Hayd 1m2f120yD(0-85)H G-F £3787
79 6/95 Kemp 7f D GD £3928

Total win prize-money £66500

Going (Turf): Sf: 1-5 GS: 0-5 **Gd: 3-19** GF: 1-27 Fm: 1-4
Distance: 5f/6f: 0-0 7f-8f: 3-15 9f-13f: 3-43 14f+: 0-2
Track : **LH: 3-24** RH: 1-20 Tight: 0-8 **Gall: 2-21**
Aids: Bl: 0-2 Vi: 0-0 Tstrap: 0-0
Best Rating: 57 7/01 Ling 1m3f106y firm

A former smart handicapper, he has deteriorated since he returned from a spell in Dubai, but is still capable of winning an ordinary handicap on fast ground.

Amritsar

97 (87) (53) **70**

4-y-o ch c Indian Ridge-Trying For Gold (USA) (Northern Baby (CAN))

P Howling Arkland International (uk) Ltd

Placings:0543233600-000 **(2846)**

2001: 9^{0}G, 10^{0}GF, 10^{0}F

	Starts	1st	2nd	3rd	Win & Pl
Career Total (Turf)	11	0	1	3	3456
Career Total (AW)	2	0	0	0	

Going (Turf): Sf: 0-1 GS: 0-3 Gd: 0-3 GF: 0-3 Fm: 0-1
Distance: 5f/6f: 0-0 7f-8f: 0-3 9f-13f: 0-10 14f+: 0-0
Track : LH: 0-8 RH: 0-2 Tight: 0-7 Gall: 0-1
Aids: Bl: 0-0 Vi: 0-0 Tstrap: 0-0
Best Rating: 61 6/01 Nott 1m1f213y good

Amron

92 **18**

14-y-o b g Bold Owl-Sweet Minuet (Minshaanshu Amad (USA))
A Berry Roy Peebles

Placings:15653/00002110534**4**000/1011000364 0/1160 00602000/1410060015/106240400/006000000/0602000 3005302/1626202630400/0004033010/451000060120 000/00600000-4600000 **(5272)**
2001: 9^{4}GF, 8^{6}GF, 8^{0}GF, 10^{0}GF, 10^{0}F, 7^{0}GS, 10^{0}HY

	Starts	1st	2nd	3rd	Win & Pl
Career Total (Turf)	135	16	8	7	108488
Career Total (AW)	4	0	1	1	1000

53	8/99	Ayr	1m2f	E(0-75)H	G-F	£4029
59	5/99	Rdcr	1m	E(0-70)H	SFT	£3722
48	10/98	Rdcr	1m	D(0-75)H	SFT	£3766
63	3/97	Newc	5f	D(0-85)H	GD	£3436
98	3/94	Donc	6f	A	G-F	£10867
91	9/93	Donc	5f140y	B(0-110)H	SFT	£17432
77	5/93	Donc	6f	C(0-100)H	GD	£5071
78	3/93	Donc	5f	D(0-85)H	G-F	£3817
80	3/92	Newc	5f	F(0-90)H	SFT	£2820
77	3/92	Donc	5f	D(0-100)H	GD	£3840
71	4/91	Ripn	6f	D(0-80)H	G-F	£4077
68	4/91	Ayr	6f	D(0-105)H	G-S	£3622
57	3/91	Donc	5f	D(0-100)H	SFT	£4480
	6/90	Ayr	6f	(0-70)H	GD	£2469
	6/90	Carl	6f	(0-70)H	GD	£2469
	4/89	Haml	5f		HVY	£1338

Total win prize-money £77260

Going (Turf): Sf: **5-24** GS: 1-14 **Gd: 5-45** GF: 4-36 Fm: 0-12
Distance: **5f/6f: 12-94** 7f-8f: 2-21 9f-13f: 1-19 14f+: 0-0
Track : LH: 1-21 RH: 1-20 Tight: 0-12 **Gall: 1-11**
Aids: Bl: 0-1 Vi: 0-0 Tstrap: 0-0
Best Rating: 29 5/01 Ayr 1m1f20y gd-fm

Amsara (IRE)

94(79) **18**

5-y-o b m Taufan (USA)-Legend Of Spain (USA) (Alleged (USA))
D W Chapman David W Chapman

Placings:00/61**0040525**000/**06**0000**2**00-00006043 **(3966)**
2001: 11^{0}SD, 13^{0}GF, 14^{0}GF, 12^{0}GF, 12^{6}GS, 12^{0}G, 16^{4}GS, 16^{3}GS

	Starts	1st	2nd	3rd	Win & Pl
Career Total (Turf)	18	1	1	1	3441
Career Total (AW)	13	0	1	0	675

52	4/99	Pont	1m4f8y	F	G-S	£2301

Total win prize-money £2301

Going (Turf): Sf: 0-3 **GS: 1-5** Gd: 0-6 GF: 0-4 Fm: 0-0
Distance: 5f/6f: 0-0 7f-8f: 0-1 **9f-13f: 1-16** 14f+: 0-14
Track : **LH: 1-21** RH: 0-7 Tight: 0-12 Gall: 0-2
Aids: Bl: 0-2 Vi: 0-0 Tstrap: 0-0
Best Rating: 18 8/01 Thsk 2m gd-sft

Amused

92 **61+**

2-y-o ch f Prince Sabo-Indigo (Primo Dominie)
R A Fahey D R Brotherton

Placings:5 **(4777)**
2001: 5^{5}G

	Starts	1st	2nd	3rd	Win & Pl
Career Total (Turf)	1	0	0	0	0

Going (Turf): Sf: 0-0 GS: 0-0 Gd: 0-1 GF: 0-0 Fm: 0-0
Distance: 5f/6f: 0-1 7f-8f: 0-0 9f-13f: 0-0 14f+: 0-0
Track : LH: 0-0 RH: 0-0 Tight: 0-0 Gall: 0-0
Aids: Bl: 0-0 Vi: 0-0 Tstrap: 0-0
Best Rating: 61 9/01 Bevl 5f good

Amwell Star (USA)

100(89) (30)**40**

3-y-o gr f Silver Buck (USA)-Markham Fair (CAN) (Woodman (USA))
J R Jenkins Amwell Racing

Placings:000-5U200043402 **(5637)**
2001: 11^{5}SD, 11^{U}GS, 14^{2}G, 14^{0}G, 11^{0}F, 16^{0}GF, 16^{4}G, 14^{3}S, 16^{4}GF, 14^{0}S, 11^{2}G

	Starts	1st	2nd	3rd	Win & Pl
Career Total (Turf)	11	0	2	1	2356
Career Total (AW)	3	0	0	0	0

Going (Turf): Sf: 0-3 GS: 0-1 Gd: 0-4 GF: 0-2 Fm: 0-1
Distance: 5f/6f: 0-1 7f-8f: 0-2 9f-13f: 0-4 14f+: 0-7
Track : LH: 0-10 RH: 0-2 Tight: 0-6 Gall: 0-0
Aids: Bl: 0-0 Vi: 0-0 Tstrap: 0-0
Best Rating: 46 5/01 Nott 1m6f15y good

Exposed maiden stayer.

Amy Dee

87 **33**

3-y-o b f Be My Chief (USA)-Bailey's By Name (Nomination)
N Tinkler R Midgley

Placings:6000-0000 **(2763)**
2001: 6^{0}F, 6^{0}GF, 8^{0}GF, 6^{0}GF

	Starts	1st	2nd	3rd	Win & Pl
Career Total (Turf)	8	0	0	0	0

Going (Turf): Sf: 0-2 GS: 0-0 Gd: 0-2 GF: 0-3 Fm: 0-1
Distance: 5f/6f: 0-7 7f-8f: 0-0 9f-13f: 0-1 14f+: 0-0
Track : LH: 0-2 RH: 0-0 Tight: 0-0 Gall: 0-0
Aids: Bl: 0-2 Vi: 0-0 Tstrap: 0-0
Best Rating: 33 6/01 Nott 1m54y gd-fm

Amy G (IRE)

74 **47**

3-y-o b f Common Grounds-Queen Canute (IRE) (Ahonoora)
N Tinkler Mike Gosse

Placings:06-02350 **(5503)**
2001: 5^{0}GF, 5^{2}G, 6^{3}GF, 6^{5}GF, 7^{0}HY

	Starts	1st	2nd	3rd	Win & Pl
Career Total (Turf)	7	0	1	1	860

Going (Turf): Sf: 0-1 GS: 0-0 Gd: 0-2 GF: 0-4 Fm: 0-0
Distance: 5f/6f: 0-6 7f-8f: 0-1 9f-13f: 0-0 14f+: 0-0
Track : LH: 0-0 RH: 0-0 Tight: 0-0 Gall: 0-0
Aids: Bl: 0-0 Vi: 0-0 Tstrap: 0-0
Best Rating: 47 9/01 Ling 6f gd-fm

An Jolien

91(70) **32**

4-y-o b f Aragon-Joli's Girl (Mansingh (USA))
M J Ryan Mr & Mrs W J Foley

Placings:0050/400000-0000 **(2991)**
2001: 7^{0}GF, 7^{0}SD, 8^{0}GF, 8^{0}G

	Starts	1st	2nd	3rd	Win & Pl
Career Total (Turf)	13	0	0	0	0
Career Total (AW)	1	0	0	0	

Going (Turf): Sf: 0-4 GS: 0-1 Gd: 0-3 GF: 0-5 Fm: 0-0
Distance: 5f/6f: 0-5 7f-8f: 0-6 9f-13f: 0-3 14f+: 0-0
Track : LH: 0-5 RH: 0-3 Tight: 0-1 Gall: 0-3
Aids: Bl: 0-3 Vi: 0-0 Tstrap: 0-0
Best Rating: 32 5/01 Sthl 7f gd-fm

Anabaa Blue

109 **121**

3-y-o b c Anabaa (USA)-Allez Les Trois (USA) (Riverman (USA))
C Lerner C Mimouni

Placings:33-1121020 **(5247a)**
2001: 10^{1}HY, 11^{1}HY, 10^{2}G, 12^{1}G, 12^{0}GF, 12^{2}G, 12^{0}HO

	Starts	1st	2nd	3rd	Win & Pl
Career Total (Turf)	9	3	2	2	466100

120	6/01	Chan	1m4f	GD	£387973
103	4/01	Lonc	1m3f	HVY	£29098
	3/01	MsnL	1m2f	HVY	£8923

Total win prize-money £425994

Going (Turf): Sf: 2-2 GS: 0-0 Gd: 1-3 GF: 0-1 Fm: 0-0
Distance: 5f/6f: 0-0 7f-8f: 0-0 **9f-13f: 3-7** 14f+: 0-0
Track : LH: 0-0 RH: 0-3 Tight: 0-0 Gall: 0-1
Aids: Bl: 0-0 Vi: 0-0 Tstrap: 0-0
Best Rating: 121 9/01 Lonc 1m4f good

He has been gradually improving this season, starting off with an easy victory in the Prix Noailles and going down narrowly to Chichicastenango in the Prix Lupin. Reversed the from with that horse when well ridden to win the Prix du Jockey Club. Well behind in the King George when the ground was probably against him, he ran much better when chasing home Golan in the Prix Niel before finding the ground too heavy in the Arc. Suited by good ground or better, stays 12 furlongs .

Anada (FR)

103 **73**

3-y-o b f Exit To Nowhere (USA)-Anafi (Slip Anchor)
L M Cumani L Marinopoulos

Placings:0402 **(3207)**
2001: 8^{0}S, 8^{4}HY, 9^{0}GF, 12^{2}G

	Starts	1st	2nd	3rd	Win & Pl
Career Total (Turf)	4	0	1	0	1146

Going (Turf): Sf: 0-2 GS: 0-0 Gd: 0-1 GF: 0-1 Fm: 0-0
Distance: 5f/6f: 0-0 7f-8f: 0-1 9f-13f: 0-3 14f+: 0-0
Track : LH: 0-2 RH: 0-1 Tight: 0-1 Gall: 0-0
Aids: Bl: 0-0 Vi: 0-0 Tstrap: 0-0
Best Rating: 73 7/01 Chep 1m4f23y good

Anadonis

98 **72**

3-y-o b c Anabaa (USA)-Stiletta (Dancing Brave (USA))
H R A Cecil K Abdulla

Placings:32 **(5528)**
2001: 7^{3}S, 8^{2}HY

	Starts	1st	2nd	3rd	Win & Pl
Career Total (Turf)	2	0	1	1	2072

Going (Turf): Sf: 0-2 GS: 0-0 Gd: 0-0 GF: 0-0 Fm: 0-0
Distance: 5f/6f: 0-0 7f-8f: 0-1 9f-13f: 0-1 14f+: 0-0
Track : LH: 0-1 RH: 0-0 Tight: 0-0 Gall: 0-0
Aids: Bl: 0-0 Vi: 0-0 Tstrap: 0-0
Best Rating: 72 10/01 Nott 1m54y heavy

A well-bred colt who has shown form in soft ground maidens, should appreciate a step up to a mile.

Analyser (IRE)

108 **99**

3-y-o ch c Royal Academy (USA)-Mountain Ash (Dominion)
J H M Gosden R E Sangster & A K Collins

Placings:40-021120 **(3583)**
2001: 7^{0}GS, 7^{2}G, 7^{1}GF, 8^{1}GF, 8^{2}GF, 8^{0}G

	Starts	1st	2nd	3rd	Win & Pl
Career Total (Turf)	**8**	**2**	**2**	**0**	**50542**

94	6/01	Asct	1m	B(0-105)H	G-F	£35750
90	6/01	Newb	7f	E(0-75)H	G-F	£3867

Total win prize-money £39618

Going (Turf): Sf: 0-2 GS: 0-1 Gd: 0-2 **GF: 2-3** Fm: 0-0
Distance: 5f/6f: 0-1 **7f-8f: 2-7** 9f-13f: 0-0 14f+: 0-0
Track : LH: 0-0 RH: 0-2 Tight: 0-0 Gall: 0-0
Aids: Bl: 0-0 **Vi: 2-5** Tstrap: 0-0
Best Rating: 99 7/01 Newb 1m gd-fm

Progressive, he got off the mark under top weight in a Newbury handicap in June and followed up with a fine win in the Britannia at Royal Ascot. Just beaten off a much higher mark at Newbury next time, he has been sold to race in the United States.

Analytical

102 **65**

5-y-o b g Pursuit Of Love-Risha Flower (Kris)
R Charlton Martin Myers

Placings:31300/00030-020 **(4632)**
2001: 7^{0}GF, 6^{2}GF, 7^{0}GF

	Starts	1st	2nd	3rd	Win & Pl
Career Total (Turf)	**13**	**1**	**1**	**3**	**6025**

67	7/99	Nott	1m54y	E	G-F	£3260

Total win prize-money £3260

Going (Turf): Sf: 0-2 GS: 0-1 Gd: 0-1 **GF: 1-8** Fm: 0-0
Distance: 5f/6f: 0-0 7f-8f: 0-10 **9f-13f: 1-2** 14f+: 0-0
Track : **LH: 1-4** RH: 0-2 Tight: 0-2 Gall: 0-2
Aids: Bl: 0-0 Vi: 0-0 Tstrap: 0-0
Best Rating: 65 8/01 Sals 6f212y gd-fm

Analyze (FR)

106 **70**

3-y-o b g Anabaa (USA)-Bramosia (Forzando)
M R Channon Mrs A M Jones

Placings:03502-05063464133430600 **(5171)**
2001: 9^{0}S, 8^{5}S, 7^{0}G, 8^{0}GS, 10^{3}GF, 8^{4}GF, 9^{0}GF, 8^{4}GF, 9^{1}GF, 10^{3}GS, 9^{3}GF, 10^{4}GF, 9^{3}GF, 10^{0}S, 9^{6}GF, 10^{0}S, 8^{0}GS

	Starts	1st	2nd	3rd	Win & Pl
Career Total (Turf)	**22**	**1**	**1**	**5**	**7939**

70	7/01	Nott	1m1f213yE(0-70)H	G-F	£3542

Total win prize-money £3542

Going (Turf): Sf: 0-4 GS: 0-4 Gd: 0-3 **GF: 1-11** Fm: 0-0
Distance: 5f/6f: 0-2 7f-8f: 0-5 **9f-13f: 1-15** 14f+: 0-0
Track : **LH: 1-11** RH: 0-5 Tight: 0-9 Gall: 0-1
Aids: Bl: 0-0 Vi: 0-0 Tstrap: 0-0
Best Rating: 70 8/01 Folk 1m1f149y gd-fm

Seems best at around ten furlongs on a sound surface. Usually held up.

Anastasia Venture

(100) (23)**42**

4-y-o b f Lion Cavern (USA)-Our Shirley (Shirley Heights)
J Akehurst Canisbay Bloodstock Ltd

Placings:5324530-0056 **(2976)**
2001: 10^{0}GS, 9^{0}GF, 9^{5}GF, 8^{6}SD

	Starts	1st	2nd	3rd	Win & Pl
Career Total (Turf)	**8**	**0**	**0**	**1**	**1112**
Career Total (AW)	**3**	**0**	**1**	**1**	**1195**

Going (Turf): Sf: 0-0 GS: 0-2 Gd: 0-0 GF: 0-4 Fm: 0-2
Distance: 5f/6f: 0-0 7f-8f: 0-1 9f-13f: 0-10 14f+: 0-0
Track : LH: 0-7 RH: 0-3 Tight: 0-8 Gall: 0-2
Aids: Bl: 0-0 Vi: 0-1 Tstrap: 0-0
Best Rating: 42 6/01 Kemp 1m1f gd-fm

Anastasia's Shadow

88(82) (22)**26**

5-y-o b m Theatrical Charmer-Lamloum (IRE) (Vacarme (USA))
Ms A E Embiricos (H Akbary 25/5) Mrs Jacquie Mikhailides

Placings:6/0020300/0000010105000-0000 **(5539)**
2001: 8^{0}SW, 7^{0}F, 8^{0}GS, 8^{0}S

	Starts	1st	2nd	3rd	Win & Pl
Career Total (Turf)	**23**	**2**	**1**	**1**	**15419**
Career Total (AW)	**2**	**0**	**0**	**0**	

8/00	Deau	1m2f	H	G-S	£7685
7/00	Chan	1m1f	H	SFT	£4803

Total win prize-money £12488

Going (Turf): Sf: 0-1 GS: 0-1 Gd: 0-2 GF: 0-0 Fm: 0-1
Distance: 5f/6f: 0-0 7f-8f: 0-8 9f-13f: 0-3 14f+: 0-0
Track : LH: 0-3 RH: 0-0 Tight: 0-1 Gall: 0-0
Aids: Bl: 0-0 Vi: 0-0 Tstrap: 0-0
Best Rating: 26 8/01 Thsk 1m gd-sft

Ancient Quest

100 **63**

8-y-o b g Rainbow Quest (USA)-Racquette (Ballymore)
T D Easterby J O Eddery

Placings:0226/045114/665 **(1852)**
2001: 12^{6}G, 14^{6}GF, 12^{5}GF

	Starts	1st	2nd	3rd	Win & Pl
Career Total (Turf)	**13**	**2**	**2**	**0**	**10569**

82	6/97	Epsm	1m4f10y	D(0-75)H	G-S	£3517
75	6/97	NmkJ	1m4f	E(0-70)H	G-S	£4045

Total win prize-money £7563

Going (Turf): Sf: 0-0 **GS: 2-3** Gd: 0-7 GF: 0-3 Fm: 0-0
Distance: 5f/6f: 0-0 7f-8f: 0-0 **9f-13f: 2-9** 14f+: 0-4
Track : LH: 1-6 RH: 1-6 Tight: 1-5 Gall: 1-6
Aids: Bl: 0-2 Vi: 0-0 Tstrap: 0-0
Best Rating: 63 5/01 Hayd 1m6f gd-fm

And Beyond (IRE)

109 **103**

3-y-o b c Darshaan-Al Najah (USA) (Topsider (USA))
M Johnston Maktoum Al Maktoum

Placings:15110 **(4711)**
2001: 12^{1}S, 12^{5}G, 13^{1}F, 16^{1}GF, 14^{0}G

	Starts	1st	2nd	3rd	Win & Pl
Career Total (Turf)	**5**	**3**	**0**	**0**	**48839**

101	6/01	Asct	2m45y	A	G-F	£36000
96	5/01	York	1m5f194yB		FRM	£9178
67	4/01	Muss	1m4f	D	SFT	£3402

Total win prize-money £48580

Going (Turf): Sf: 1-1 GS: 0-0 Gd: 0-2 **GF: 1-1 Fm: 1-1**
Distance: 5f/6f: 0-0 7f-8f: 0-0 9f-13f: 1-2 **14f+: 2-3**
Track : LH: 1-2 RH: 1-2 Tight: 0-0 **Gall: 2-4**
Aids: Bl: 0-0 Vi: 0-0 Tstrap: 0-0
Best Rating: 103 9/01 Donc 1m6f132y good

Lightly-raced, he has progressed steadily with racing, winning at Musselburgh on his debut and a conditions event at York and going on to win the Queen's Vase in game style. A potential top-class stayer.

Andrew Doble

89 **72**

2-y-o ch c Sabrehill (USA)-Verchinina (Star Appeal)
M A Jarvis W J Gredley

Placings:0 **(3813)**
2001: 7^{0}G

	Starts	1st	2nd	3rd	Win & Pl
Career Total (Turf)	**1**	**0**	**0**	**0**	

Going (Turf): Sf: 0-0 GS: 0-0 Gd: 0-1 GF: 0-0 Fm: 0-0
Distance: 5f/6f: 0-0 7f-8f: 0-1 9f-13f: 0-0 14f+: 0-0
Track : LH: 0-0 RH: 0-0 Tight: 0-0 Gall: 0-0
Aids: Bl: 0-0 Vi: 0-0 Tstrap: 0-0
Best Rating: 72 8/01 NmkJ 7f good

Andreyev (IRE)

100 (101)**99**

7-y-o ch g Presidium-Missish (Mummy's Pet)
R Hannon J Palmer-Brown

Placings:4114016/4100/1031341466/403025002440/100504136216-006000 **(5494)**
2001: 6^{0}FT, 6^{0}F, 6^{6}GS, 6^{0}G, 5^{0}GS, 6^{0}HY

	Starts	1st	2nd	3rd	Win & Pl
Career Total (Turf)	**50**	**10**	**3**	**4**	**176073**
Career Total (AW)	**1**	**0**	**0**	**0**	

109	11/00	Donc	6f	A	HVY	£14950
109	8/00	York	6f	B(0-105)H	GD	£15848
108	3/00	Donc	6f	A	GD	£17410
119	8/98	Deau	6f		GD	£22222
117	6/98	Newc	6f	A	SFT	£12544
107	4/98	Kemp	6f	C	SFT	£4924
100	5/97	NmkR	7f	A	GD	£10842
102	10/96	Asct	7f	B	GD	£7178
104	8/96	Ches	6f18y	C	G-S	£4909
88	6/96	Wind	5f10y	D	G-F	£3160

Total win prize-money £113989

Going (Turf): Sf: 3-10 GS: 1-10 **Gd: 5-18** GF: 1-10 Fm: 0-1
Distance: **5f/6f: 7-36** 7f-8f: 3-15 9f-13f: 0-0 14f+: 0-0
Track : LH: 1-4 RH: 1-4 Tight: 1-2 Gall: 1-3
Aids: Bl: 0-4 Vi: 0-1 Tstrap: 0-0
Best Rating: 101 3/01 Ndas 6f fast

A useful sprinter on his day, but he has not shown his best in a light campaign in 2001. Six furlongs is his trip and he is best suited by the ground good or softer.

Andromache

92 **65**

2-y-o ch f Hector Protector (USA)-South Sea Bubble (IRE) (Bustino)
L M Cumani Lady Juliet Tadgell

Placings:650 **(5112)**
2001: 6^{6}GS, 6^{5}GF, 8^{0}HY

	Starts	1st	2nd	3rd	Win & Pl
Career Total (Turf)	**3**	**0**	**0**	**0**	**0**

Going (Turf): Sf: 0-1 GS: 0-1 Gd: 0-0 GF: 0-1 Fm: 0-0
Distance: 5f/6f: 0-2 7f-8f: 0-0 9f-13f: 0-1 14f+: 0-0
Track : LH: 0-1 RH: 0-0 Tight: 0-0 Gall: 0-0
Aids: Bl: 0-0 Vi: 0-0 Tstrap: 0-0
Best Rating: 65 8/01 Ling 6f gd-fm

Andromeda (IRE)

92 **78**

2-y-o b f Barathea (IRE)-Royal York (Bustino)
J Noseda Sir Robert Ogden

Placings:0 **(5602)**

2001: 7^{0}GS

	Starts	1st	2nd	3rd	Win & Pl
Career Total (Turf)	1	0	0	0	

Going (Turf): Sf: 0-0 GS: 0-1 Gd: 0-0 GF: 0-0 Fm: 0-0
Distance: 5f/6f: 0-0 7f-8f: 0-1 9f-13f: 0-0 14f+: 0-0
Track : LH: 0-0 RH: 0-0 Tight: 0-0 Gall: 0-0
Aids: Bl: 0-0 Vi: 0-0 Tstrap: 0-0
Best Rating: 78 11/01 NmkR 7f gd-sft

Andromeda's Way

75 61

3-y-o b f Kris-Titania's Way (Fairy King (USA))
P R Chamings Mrs Alexandra J Chandris

Placings:64000-0 (4162)
2001: 10^{0}GF

	Starts	1st	2nd	3rd	Win & Pl
Career Total (Turf)	6	0	0	0	214

Going (Turf): Sf: 0-1 GS: 0-0 Gd: 0-0 GF: 0-5 Fm: 0-0
Distance: 5f/6f: 0-3 7f-8f: 0-2 9f-13f: 0-1 14f+: 0-0
Track : LH: 0-2 RH: 0-2 Tight: 0-2 Gall: 0-1
Aids: Bl: 0-0 Vi: 0-0 Tstrap: 0-0
Best Rating: 9 8/01 Ling 1m2f gd-fm

Andy's Elective

103(80) (42)63

4-y-o b g Democratic (USA)-English Mint (Jalmood (USA))
J R Jenkins Mrs Stella Peirce

Placings:054/36051000-00330100 (4891)
2001: 6^{0}GF, 6^{0}F, 7^{3}F, 8^{3}GF, 7^{0}G, 7^{1}G, 7^{0}GF, 8^{0}GF

	Starts	1st	2nd	3rd	Win & Pl
Career Total (Turf)	18	2	0	3	8316
Career Total (AW)	1	0	0	0	0

63 8/01 Folk 7f E(0-75)H GD £3290
62 6/00 Brig 6f209y E(0-70)H FRM £3178
Total win prize-money £6468

Going (Turf): Sf: 0-1 GS: 0-1 **Gd: 1-5** GF: 0-8 **Fm: 1-3**
Distance: 5f/6f: 0-3 **7f-8f: 2-15** 9f-13f: 0-1 14f+: 0-0
Track : **LH: 1-7** RH: 0-4 Tight: 0-3 Gall: 0-2
Aids: Bl: 0-0 **Vi: 2-9** Tstrap: 0-0
Best Rating: 63 8/01 Folk 7f good

Anemos (IRE)

71(109) (75d)68

6-y-o ch g Be My Guest (USA)-Frendly Persuasion (General Assembly (USA))
Ian Williams Andreas Michael

Placings:03/33023/00301006201**2**/3426340-00450 (2811)
2001: 9^{0}SW, 9^{0}SD, 10^{4}SW, 10^{5}SD, 12^{0}GF

	Starts	1st	2nd	3rd	Win & Pl
Career Total (Turf)	22	1	2	6	10349
Career Total (AW)	9	1	2	1	11071

78 12/99 Ling 1m2f D(0-80)H STD £3401
75 8/99 Nott 1m1f213yE(0-70) G-F £2937
Total win prize-money £6339

Going (Turf): Sf: 0-2 GS: 0-2 Gd: 0-10 **GF: 1-8** Fm: 0-0
Distance: 5f/6f: 0-0 7f-8f: 0-5 **9f-13f: 2-26** 14f+: 0-0
Track : **LH: 2-19** RH: 0-10 **Tight: 1-16** Gall: 0-2
Aids: **Bl: 1-8** Vi: 0-0 Tstrap: 0-0
Best Rating: 69 2/01 Ling 1m2f slow

Angel Hill

99(101) (63)56

6-y-o ch m King's Signet (USA)-Tawny (Grey Ghost)
K A Ryan Keith Taylor

Placings:12343540/36200/03300160400/0000610040 140-100006000 (4859)
2001: 5^{1}S, 5^{0}F, 7^{0}GF, 5^{0}GF, 6^{0}GF, 6^{6}G, 6^{0}G, 6^{0}F, 7^{0}GF

	Starts	1st	2nd	3rd	Win & Pl
Career Total (Turf)	45	5	2	5	28745
Career Total (AW)	2	0	0	0	0

63 5/01 Rdcr 5f D(0-80)H SFT £5050
63 9/00 Catt 7f F(0-60)H SFT £2880
52 6/00 Newc 6f E(0-75)H FRM £3916
76 7/99 Newc 6f D(0-85)H G-F £3777
63 5/97 Newc 5f F GD £2599
Total win prize-money £18226

Going (Turf): **Sf: 2-7** GS: 0-3 Gd: 1-12 GF: 1-17 Fm: 1-6
Distance: **5f/6f: 4-40** 7f-8f: 1-6 9f-13f: 0-1 14f+: 0-0
Track : **LH: 1-6** RH: 0-2 **Tight: 1-3** Gall: 0-0
Aids: **Bl: 1-6** Vi: 0-2 Tstrap: 0-0
Best Rating: 63 5/01 Rdcr 5f soft

Fair handicapper, effective 5-7 furlongs, acts on any ground.

Angel Lane

98(52) 15

4-y-o b f Merdon Melody-Young Whip (Bold Owl)
A W Carroll Aramis Racing Syndicate

Placings:00000/00400-00003600 (4472)
2001: 8^{0}GS, 6^{0}GF, 7^{0}GF, 8^{0}SD, 8^{3}GF, 8^{6}GF, 10^{0}GF, 9^{0}GF

	Starts	1st	2nd	3rd	Win & Pl
Career Total (Turf)	17	0	0	1	653
Career Total (AW)	1	0	0	0	

Going (Turf): Sf: 0-1 GS: 0-4 Gd: 0-3 GF: 0-9 Fm: 0-0
Distance: 5f/6f: 0-3 7f-8f: 0-4 9f-13f: 0-11 14f+: 0-0
Track : LH: 0-6 RH: 0-7 Tight: 0-5 Gall: 0-1
Aids: Bl: 0-0 Vi: 0-0 Tstrap: 0-1
Best Rating: 39 5/01 Wind 1m67y gd-sft

Angelicus (IRE)

75 38

2-y-o b f Pennekamp (USA)-Merry Devil (IRE) (Sadler's Wells (USA))
J S Moore Alan J Speyer

Placings:00 (4072)
2001: 5^{0}G, 5^{0}G

	Starts	1st	2nd	3rd	Win & Pl
Career Total (Turf)	2	0	0	0	

Going (Turf): Sf: 0-0 GS: 0-0 Gd: 0-2 GF: 0-0 Fm: 0-0
Distance: 5f/6f: 0-2 7f-8f: 0-0 9f-13f: 0-0 14f+: 0-0
Track : LH: 0-1 RH: 0-0 Tight: 0-0 Gall: 0-1
Aids: Bl: 0-0 Vi: 0-0 Tstrap: 0-0
Best Rating: 38 8/01 Bath 5f11y good

Angels Venture

103(101) (57)72

5-y-o ch g Unfuwain (USA)-City Of Angels (Woodman (USA))
J R Jenkins Tony Hayward

Placings:4/334333120321/00043264-1056 (3653)
2001: 12^{1}GF, 12^{0}GF, 11^{5}G, 12^{6}G

	Starts	1st	2nd	3rd	Win & Pl
Career Total (Turf)	24	3	3	7	16901
Career Total (AW)	1	0	0	0	0

84 10/99 Brig 1m3f196yE(0-80)H GD £2762
79 7/99 Yarm 1m3f101yD FRM £3949
Total win prize-money £6711

Going (Turf): Sf: 0-1 GS: 0-2 **Gd: 1-10 GF: 1-9 Fm: 1-2**
Distance: 5f/6f: 0-0 7f-8f: 0-3 **9f-13f: 3-21** 14f+: 0-1
Track : **LH: 3-11** RH: 0-13 **Tight: 1-12** Gall: 0-4
Aids: Bl: 0-0 Vi: 0-3 Tstrap: 0-8
Best Rating: 72 5/01 Sthl 1m4f gd-fm

Angelus Domini (IRE)

(84) (54)47

2-y-o b f Blues Traveller (IRE)-Lyphards Goddess (IRE) (Lyphard's Special (USA))
B A McMahon Mrs J McMahon

Placings:0U3 (5345)
2001: 5^{0}GF, 6^{U}HY, 6^{3}SD

	Starts	1st	2nd	3rd	Win & Pl
Career Total (Turf)	2	0	0	0	
Career Total (AW)	1	0	0	1	426

Going (Turf): Sf: 0-1 GS: 0-0 Gd: 0-0 GF: 0-1 Fm: 0-0
Distance: 5f/6f: 0-2 7f-8f: 0-1 9f-13f: 0-0 14f+: 0-0
Track : LH: 0-1 RH: 0-0 Tight: 0-0 Gall: 0-0
Aids: Bl: 0-0 Vi: 0-0 Tstrap: 0-0
Best Rating: 54 10/01 Sthl 6f stand

Modest form in maidens.

Angelus Sunset (USA)

99 107?

2-y-o b c Numerous (USA)-Angelic Note (USA) (The Minstrel (CAN))
B J Meehan Total (bloodstock) Ltd

Placings:3011 (5495)
2001: 7^{3}G, 8^{0}GF, 6^{1}GS, 8^{1}HY, 10^{0}HY

	Starts	1st	2nd	3rd	Win & Pl
Career Total (Turf)	4	2	0	1	13737

90 10/01 Newb 1m C HVY £8723
90 10/01 Sals 6f212y D G-S £4465
Total win prize-money £13189

Going (Turf): **Sf: 1-1 GS: 1-1** Gd: 0-1 GF: 0-1 Fm: 0-0
Distance: 5f/6f: 0-0 **7f-8f: 2-4** 9f-13f: 0-0 14f+: 0-0
Track : LH: 0-0 RH: 0-1 Tight: 0-0 Gall: 0-0
Aids: Bl: 0-0 Vi: 0-0 Tstrap: 0-0
Best Rating: 90 10/01 Newb 1m heavy

Scored at the third time of asking in a novice event at Salisbury and followed up in a three-runner event at Newbury run in a bog. Should stay middle distances at three.

Angie Marinie

66 (37)60

5-y-o b m Sabrehill (USA)-Lambast (Relkino)
C J Price A E Price

Placings:6/000132305/060-0 (4212)
2001: 13^{0}GF

	Starts	1st	2nd	3rd	Win & Pl
Career Total (Turf)	10	1	1	2	5322
Career Total (AW)	4	0	0	0	

53 4/99 Nott 1m54y G SFT £2110
Total win prize-money £2110

Going (Turf): **Sf: 1-4** GS: 0-1 Gd: 0-1 GF: 0-4 Fm: 0-0
Distance: 5f/6f: 0-2 7f-8f: 0-2 **9f-13f: 1-9** 14f+: 0-1
Track : **LH: 1-13** RH: 0-1 Tight: 0-8 Gall: 0-0
Aids: Bl: 0-0 Vi: 0-0 Tstrap: 0-0
Best Rating: 53 4/99 Nott 1m54y S

Angies Quest

(95) (40)68

4-y-o b f Inchinor-Chanson D'Avril (Chief Singer)
P W D'Arcy Mrs A Lovat

Placings:630/24-260 (0446)
2001: 13^{2}SW, 12^{6}SW, 12^{0}SD

	Starts	1st	2nd	3rd	Win & Pl

Career Total (Turf) 5 0 1 1 2230
Career Total (AW) 3 0 1 0 622

Going (Turf): Sf: 0-0 GS: 0-0 Gd: 0-2 GF: 0-3 Fm: 0-0
Distance: 5f/6f: 0-1 7f-8f: 0-3 9f-13f: 0-4 14f+: 0-0
Track : LH: 0-6 RH: 0-0 Tight: 0-2 Gall: 0-0
Aids: Bl: 0-0 Vi: 0-0 Tstrap: 0-1
Best Rating: 40 2/01 Ling 1m5f slow

Angus-G

106 **78**

9-y-o br g Chief Singer-Horton Line (High Line)
Mrs M Reveley W Ginzel

Placings:45/530311223/11/0/02305/00001-12410 **(3257)**
2001: 10^{1}GF, 10^{2}GF, 12^{4}GF, 10^{1}GF, 10^{0}GF

	Starts	1st	2nd	3rd	Win & Pl
Career Total (Turf)	**29**	**7**	**4**	**4**	**71159**

78	7/01	Donc	1m2f60y	B(0-105)H	G-F	£10383
71	6/01	Ayr	1m2f	C(0-95)H	G-F	£6948
66	10/00	Rdcr	1m2f	E(0-65)	SFT	£2873
93	5/97	York	1m3f195y	C(0-95)H	GD	£7375
87	4/97	NmkR	1m4f	C(0-95)H	GD	£6116
78	8/96	NmkJ	1m2f	C(0-95)H	G-F	£6472
74	7/96	NmkJ	1m2f	D(0-80)H	G-F	£4581

Total win prize-money £44750

Going (Turf): Sf: 1-1 GS: 0-3 Gd: 2-9 **GF: 4-15** Fm: 0-1
Distance: 5f/6f: 0-0 7f-8f: 0-2 **9f-13f: 7-25** 14f+: 0-2
Track : **LH: 4-17** RH: 3-8 Tight: 1-5 **Gall: 5-13**
Aids: Bl: 0-0 Vi: 0-0 Tstrap: 0-0
Best Rating: 78 7/01 Donc 1m2f60y gd-fm

He has had injury problems and, although not the performer he was, is still capable of winning decent handicaps at ten furlongs as he has shown twice this season. Stays 12 furlongs and acts on soft, but prefers top of the ground.

Anikitos

96 **78**

3-y-o ch c Nashwan (USA)-Tamassos (Dance In Time (CAN))
Mrs A J Perrett Athos Christodoulou

Placings:0531 **(3149)**
2001: 11^{0}GS, 12^{5}GS, 12^{3}G, 12^{1}G

	Starts	1st	2nd	3rd	Win & Pl
Career Total (Turf)	**4**	**1**	**0**	**1**	**4911**

78	7/01	Kemp	1m4f	D	GD	£4192

Total win prize-money £4193

Going (Turf): Sf: 0-0 GS: 0-2 **Gd: 1-2** GF: 0-0 Fm: 0-0
Distance: 5f/6f: 0-0 7f-8f: 0-0 **9f-13f: 1-4** 14f+: 0-0
Track : LH: 0-1 **RH: 1-3** Tight: 0-1 Gall: 0-2
Aids: Bl: 0-0 Vi: 0-0 Tstrap: 0-0
Best Rating: 78 7/01 Kemp 1m4f good

He was a disappointing well-backed favourite on his debut but, after looking ordinary, hit form at Kempton. He is open to more improvement.

Anima Mundi (IRE)

101 **79**

2-y-o b f Namaqualand (USA)-Dieci Anno (IRE) (Classic Music (USA))
Mrs P N Dutfield Mrs Nerys Dutfield

Placings:6150102345 **(4930a)**
2001: 5^{6}S, 5^{1}S, 5^{5}GF, 5^{0}GF, 5^{1}GF, 5^{0}GF, 5^{2}S, 6^{3}GF, 6^{4}GF, 7^{5}GF

	Starts	1st	2nd	3rd	Win & Pl
Career Total (Turf)	**10**	**2**	**1**	**1**	**12916**

79	7/01	Wind	5f10y	E	G-F	£3480
64	5/01	Rdcr	5f	E	SFT	£3192

Total win prize-money £6673

Going (Turf): Sf: 1-3 GS: 0-0 Gd: 0-0 **GF: 1-7** Fm: 0-0
Distance: 5f/6f: 2-9 7f-8f: 0-1 9f-13f: 0-0 14f+: 0-0
Track : LH: 0-1 **RH: 1-1** Tight: 0-0 **Gall: 1-2**
Aids: Bl: 0-0 Vi: 0-0 Tstrap: 0-0
Best Rating: 79 9/01 Cork 7f gd-fm

From a yard that specialises with juvenile fillies, she has paid her way this season with victories on varying ground at Redcar and Windsor. Seemed better suited by being held up for a late run on the second occasion.

Animal Cracker

85(93) (64)**58**

3-y-o gr f Primo Dominie-Child Star (FR) (Bellypha)
Mrs Merrita Jones (D Marks 16/6) D Marks

Placings:05155-000400 **(5131)**
2001: 5^{0}SD, 5^{0}S, 6^{0}GF, 5^{4}S, 6^{0}GF, 7^{0}HY

	Starts	1st	2nd	3rd	Win & Pl
Career Total (Turf)	**10**	**1**	**0**	**0**	**5536**
Career Total (AW)	**1**	**0**	**0**	**0**	

72	5/00	Newb	5f34y	D	G-S	£4446

Total win prize-money £4446

Going (Turf): Sf: 0-3 **GS: 1-2** Gd: 0-1 GF: 0-4 Fm: 0-0
Distance: 5f/6f: 1-9 7f-8f: 0-2 9f-13f: 0-0 14f+: 0-0
Track : LH: 0-1 RH: 0-0 Tight: 0-1 Gall: 0-0
Aids: Bl: 0-0 Vi: 0-0 Tstrap: 0-0
Best Rating: 64 3/01 Wolv 5f stand

Ankasamen

93 **46**

3-y-o b f Muhtarram (USA)-Arusha (IRE) (Dance Of Life (USA))
M L W Bell Raymond Tooth

Placings:000-55 **(1614)**
2001: 14^{5}G, 11^{5}GF

	Starts	1st	2nd	3rd	Win & Pl
Career Total (Turf)	**5**	**0**	**0**	**0**	**0**

Going (Turf): Sf: 0-1 GS: 0-0 Gd: 0-2 GF: 0-2 Fm: 0-0
Distance: 5f/6f: 0-1 7f-8f: 0-2 9f-13f: 0-1 14f+: 0-1
Track : LH: 0-4 RH: 0-0 Tight: 0-2 Gall: 0-0
Aids: Bl: 0-0 Vi: 0-0 Tstrap: 0-0
Best Rating: 46 5/01 Nott 1m6f15y good

Ann's Mill

97(79) (11)**26**

4-y-o b f Pelder (IRE)-Honey Mill (Milford)
N E Berry (J S Moore 9/1) Mrs A Anidjah

Placings:00100/0400000-000000 **(4471)**
2001: 12^{0}SW, 7^{0}F, 7^{0}GS, 7^{0}GF, 5^{0}G, 6^{0}GF

	Starts	1st	2nd	3rd	Win & Pl
Career Total (Turf)	**16**	**1**	**0**	**0**	**2810**
Career Total (AW)	**2**	**0**	**0**	**0**	

64	8/99	Thsk	7f	F	G-F	£2810

Total win prize-money £2810

Going (Turf): Sf: 0-1 GS: 0-2 Gd: 0-4 **GF: 1-6** Fm: 0-3
Distance: 5f/6f: 0-3 **7f-8f: 1-11** 9f-13f: 0-4 14f+: 0-0
Track : **LH: 1-9** RH: 0-1 **Tight: 1-3** Gall: 0-1
Aids: Bl: 0-0 Vi: 0-0 Tstrap: 0-0
Best Rating: 26 7/01 Chep 7f16y gd-fm

Anna Walhaan (IRE)

101 **94**

2-y-o b c Green Desert (USA)-Queens Music (USA) (Dixieland Band (USA))
M R Channon Jaber Abdullah

Placings:1360 **(5053)**
2001: 6^{1}GF, 6^{3}GF, 6^{6}G, 7^{0}S

	Starts	1st	2nd	3rd	Win & Pl
Career Total (Turf)	**4**	**1**	**0**	**1**	**13765**

83	6/01	Nott	6f15y	D	G-F	£3640

Total win prize-money £3640

Going (Turf): Sf: 0-1 GS: 0-0 Gd: 0-1 **GF: 1-2** Fm: 0-0
Distance: 5f/6f: 0-2 **7f-8f: 1-2** 9f-13f: 0-0 14f+: 0-0
Track : LH: 0-0 RH: 0-0 Tight: 0-0 Gall: 0-0
Aids: Bl: 0-0 Vi: 0-0 Tstrap: 0-0
Best Rating: 94 7/01 Gdwd 6f gd-fm

A 70,000 gns yearling, he made an impressive winning debut in a Nottingham maiden in June and ran well in the Richmond Stakes next time. Disappointed, along with his Goodwood conquerors, in the Gimcrack, and may not have handled the soft ground at Newmarket. Acts on fast ground, and should have little difficulty staying seven furlongs, but a drop in class may be needed to add to his score.

Annabelle

101 **64**

3-y-o ch f Most Welcome-Saluti Tutti (Trojan Fen)
C F Wall S Fustok

Placings:0520 **(4571)**
2001: 7^{0}GS, 8^{5}GF, 9^{2}GS, 8^{0}HY

	Starts	1st	2nd	3rd	Win & Pl
Career Total (Turf)	**4**	**0**	**1**	**0**	**721**

Going (Turf): Sf: 0-1 GS: 0-2 Gd: 0-0 GF: 0-1 Fm: 0-0
Distance: 5f/6f: 0-0 7f-8f: 0-1 9f-13f: 0-3 14f+: 0-0
Track : LH: 0-1 RH: 0-2 Tight: 0-1 Gall: 0-0
Aids: Bl: 0-0 Vi: 0-0 Tstrap: 0-0
Best Rating: 64 7/01 Wind 1m67y gd-fm

Improved when stepped up to ten furlongs on easy ground at Leicester. Now qualified for handicaps.

Annadawi

108(95) (32)**62**

6-y-o b g Sadler's Wells (USA)-Prayers'n Promises (USA) (Foolish Pleasure (USA))
C N Kellett Sean A Taylor

Placings:060044/440546322210223633102050040400000430360060 **(5624)**
2001: 11^{0}SW, 12^{0}S, 10^{4}HY, 10^{0}S, 12^{4}S, 10^{0}GF, 12^{0}GF, 8^{0}GF, 12^{0}GF, 10^{0}GF, 10^{4}G, 11^{3}GS, 12^{0}G, 10^{3}S, 9^{6}HY, 11^{0}S, 10^{0}S, 10^{6}S, 9^{0}GS

	Starts	1st	2nd	3rd	Win & Pl
Career Total (Turf)	**40**	**2**	**6**	**6**	**23719**
Career Total (AW)	**8**	**0**	**0**	**0**	**620**

80	9/00	Pont	1m2f6y	C(0-95)H	G-S	£6478
49	5/00	Leic	1m1f218y	E(0-70)H	G-S	£3263

Total win prize-money £9742

Going (Turf): Sf: 0-15 **GS: 2-9** Gd: 0-6 GF: 0-10 Fm: 0-0
Distance: 5f/6f: 0-1 7f-8f: 0-3 **9f-13f: 2-44** 14f+: 0-0
Track : LH: 1-38 RH: 1-7 Tight: 0-16 Gall: 0-9
Aids: Bl: 0-3 Vi: 0-1 Tstrap: 0-1
Best Rating: 80 4/01 Ripn 1m4f60y soft

On the downgrade since 2000. Best trip probably around ten furlongs. Goes well with cut in the ground.

Annatto (USA)

94(92) (41)**81**

3-y-o b/br f Mister Baileys-Miss Rossi (Artaius (USA))
I A Balding George Strawbridge

Placings:24230-56 **(1068)**
2001: 8^{5}SW, 6^{6}GS

	Starts	1st	2nd	3rd	Win & Pl

	Starts	1st	2nd	3rd	Win & Pl
Career Total (Turf)	6	0	2	1	4252
Career Total (AW)	1	0	0	0	0

Going (Turf): Sf: 0-0 GS: 0-2 Gd: 0-1 GF: 0-3 Fm: 0-0
Distance: 5f/6f: 0-3 7f-8f: 0-4 9f-13f: 0-0 14f+: 0-0
Track : LH: 0-2 RH: 0-0 Tight: 0-0 Gall: 0-0
Aids: Bl: 0-1 Vi: 0-0 Tstrap: 0-0
Best Rating: 56 5/01 Pont 6f gd-sft

Anne Tudor (IRE)

100 **90**

2-y-o b f Anabaa (USA)-Alikhlas (Lahib (USA))
B W Hills E D Kessly

Placings:22 **(5372)**
2001: 5^{2}G, 6^{2}G

	Starts	1st	2nd	3rd	Win & Pl
Career Total (Turf)	2	0	2	0	2219

Going (Turf): Sf: 0-0 GS: 0-0 Gd: 0-2 GF: 0-0 Fm: 0-0
Distance: 5f/6f: 0-2 7f-8f: 0-0 9f-13f: 0-0 14f+: 0-0
Track : LH: 0-1 RH: 0-0 Tight: 0-0 Gall: 0-1
Aids: Bl: 0-0 Vi: 0-0 Tstrap: 0-0
Best Rating: 90 10/01 Rdcr 6f good

Promising debut at Bath, and again ran well when second at Redcar in October behind a useful sort.

Anne's Birthday

(43) **54**

2-y-o ch f Emarati (USA)-Kinraddie (Wuzo (USA))
M G Quinlan Grant Harper

Placings:660 **(5125)**
2001: 5^{6}GF, 6^{6}GF, 5^{0}HY, 6^{0}SD

	Starts	1st	2nd	3rd	Win & Pl
Career Total (Turf)	3	0	0	0	0

Going (Turf): Sf: 0-1 GS: 0-0 Gd: 0-0 GF: 0-2 Fm: 0-0
Distance: 5f/6f: 0-3 7f-8f: 0-0 9f-13f: 0-0 14f+: 0-0
Track : LH: 0-0 RH: 0-0 Tight: 0-0 Gall: 0-0
Aids: Bl: 0-0 Vi: 0-0 Tstrap: 0-0
Best Rating: 54 9/01 Ling 6f gd-fm

Anne-Lise

100 **51**

3-y-o ch f Inchinor-Red Gloves (Red God)
D J S Cosgrove Paul V Jackson & Ms Ann Cully

Placings:0002500 **(5552a)**
2001: 7^{0}S, 8^{0}GS, 8^{0}G, 8^{2}GF, 10^{5}GF, 8^{0}S, 9^{0}YS

	Starts	1st	2nd	3rd	Win & Pl
Career Total (Turf)	7	0	1	0	1008

Going (Turf): Sf: 0-2 GS: 0-1 Gd: 0-1 GF: 0-2 Fm: 0-0
Distance: 5f/6f: 0-0 7f-8f: 0-3 9f-13f: 0-4 14f+: 0-0
Track : LH: 0-2 RH: 0-2 Tight: 0-2 Gall: 0-1
Aids: Bl: 0-0 Vi: 0-0 Tstrap: 0-0
Best Rating: 51 6/01 Nott 1m54y gd-fm

Anne-Sophie

(103) (60)**60**

3-y-o ch f First Trump-Hardiprincess (Keen)
M L W Bell Mrs Anne Yearley

Placings:000-601124454 **(5407)**
2001: 8^{6}G, 8^{0}F, 10^{1}GF, 10^{1}GF, 11^{2}GF, 10^{4}GF, 9^{4}G, 10^{5}G, 12^{4}SD

	Starts	1st	2nd	3rd	Win & Pl
Career Total (Turf)	11	2	1	0	7650
Career Total (AW)	1	0	0	0	0
52	6/01	Wind	1m2f7y	E(0-70)H	G-F £3122
49	6/01	Yarm	1m2f21y	E(0-70)H	G-F £3248

Total win prize-money £6370

Going (Turf): Sf: 0-0 GS: 0-0 Gd: 0-4 GF: 2-6 Fm: 0-1
Distance: 5f/6f: 0-3 7f-8f: 0-1 **9f-13f: 2-8** 14f+: 0-0
Track : **LH: 1-7** RH: 0-0 **Tight: 2-4** Gall: 0-2
Aids: Bl: 0-0 Vi: 0-0 Tstrap: 0-0
Best Rating: 60 7/01 Ling 1m3f106y gd-fm

Annette Vallon (IRE)

107 **87**

4-y-o b f Efisio-Christine Daae (Sadler's Wells (USA))
P W Harris Mrs P W Harris

Placings:2132-00204 **(4432)**
2001: 6^{0}G, 5^{0}GF, 5^{2}GF, 5^{0}GF, 5^{4}G

	Starts	1st	2nd	3rd	Win & Pl
Career Total (Turf)	9	1	3	1	10087
75	6/00	Folk	5f	D	FRM £2884

Total win prize-money £2884

Going (Turf): Sf: 0-0 GS: 0-1 Gd: 0-3 GF: 0-4 **Fm: 1-1**
Distance: **5f/6f: 1-9** 7f-8f: 0-0 9f-13f: 0-0 14f+: 0-0
Track : LH: 0-0 RH: 0-0 Tight: 0-0 Gall: 0-0
Aids: Bl: 0-0 Vi: 0-0 Tstrap: 0-0
Best Rating: 87 8/01 Newb 5f34y gd-fm

A lightly-raced sprinter. After disappointing in the spring of 2001 she returned with a much better effort in a Newbury handicap. Handles soft, but well suited by fast ground.

Annie Apple (IRE)

(102) (54)**41**

5-y-o ch m Petardia-Art Duo (Artaius (USA))
N Hamilton Epsom Downs Racing Club

Placings:00510/03144000042242300/00050450014230 20231-60U65000 **(4672)**
2001: 8^{6}SD, 8^{0}SD, 7^{U}SD, 6^{6}G, 7^{5}F, 7^{0}GF, 7^{0}S, 8^{0}G

	Starts	1st	2nd	3rd	Win & Pl
Career Total (Turf)	30	2	4	1	8430
Career Total (AW)	19	2	2	3	6074
54	12/00	Sthl	1m	F(0-60)H	STD £1960
44	8/00	Brig	6f209y	F	FRM £2352
60	1/99	Ling	1m	G	STD £1809
60	8/98	Folk	7f	G	G-F £1725

Total win prize-money £7847

Going (Turf): Sf: 0-5 GS: 0-2 Gd: 0-7 **GF: 1-6 Fm: 1-10**
Distance: 5f/6f: 0-5 **7f-8f: 4-36** 9f-13f: 0-8 14f+: 0-0
Track : **LH: 3-35** RH: 0-4 **Tight: 1-19** Gall: 0-2
Aids: Bl: 0-0 Vi: 0-4 Tstrap: 0-0
Best Rating: 45 1/01 Sthl 1m stand

Annie Ruan

(93) (54)**56**

3-y-o b f So Factual (USA)-Sans Diablo (IRE) (Mac's Imp (USA))
D Haydn Jones G D Rosser

Placings:03440-5000220000 **(5619)**
2001: 5^{5}SD, 6^{0}SW, 5^{0}GF, 5^{0}GF, 5^{2}GF, 5^{2}G, 5^{0}GF, 5^{0}G, 6^{0}G, 6^{0}SD

	Starts	1st	2nd	3rd	Win & Pl
Career Total (Turf)	12	0	2	1	2670
Career Total (AW)	3	0	0	0	0

Going (Turf): Sf: 0-0 GS: 0-1 Gd: 0-4 GF: 0-6 Fm: 0-1
Distance: 5f/6f: 0-14 7f-8f: 0-1 9f-13f: 0-0 14f+: 0-0
Track : LH: 0-7 RH: 0-0 Tight: 0-2 Gall: 0-3
Aids: Bl: 0-0 Vi: 0-0 Tstrap: 0-0
Best Rating: 63 7/01 Leic 5f2y good

Annie's Song

99(97) (66)**43**

3-y-o b f Farfelu-Arasong (Aragon)
Mrs H Dalton (M Mullineaux 19/5) Ray Harrison

Placings:031-100000 **(5490)**
2001: 7^{1}S, 8^{0}S, 6^{0}S, 7^{0}G, 7^{0}SD, 7^{0}HY

	Starts	1st	2nd	3rd	Win & Pl
Career Total (Turf)	5	1	0	0	4602
Career Total (AW)	4	1	0	1	2495
69	3/01	Donc	7f	D(0-85)H	SFT £4602
65	12/00	Wolv	7f	F	STD £2247

Total win prize-money £6849

Going (Turf): Sf: 1-4 GS: 0-0 Gd: 0-1 GF: 0-0 Fm: 0-0
Distance: 5f/6f: 0-2 **7f-8f: 2-7** 9f-13f: 0-0 14f+: 0-0
Track : **LH: 1-5** RH: 0-1 **Tight: 1-3** Gall: 0-0
Aids: Bl: 0-0 Vi: 0-0 Tstrap: 0-0
Best Rating: 69 3/01 Donc 7f soft

Got off the mark on Fibresand on her third and final start at two, but caused a bit of a shock by winning a competitive Doncaster handicap on her return, but failed to go on from that.

Anniegetyourgun (USA)

103 **78**

3-y-o b f Gone West (USA)-Encorelle (FR) (Arctic Tern (USA))
E A L Dunlop Maktoum Al Maktoum

Placings:004-24 **(3267)**
2001: 7^{2}F, 8^{4}GS

	Starts	1st	2nd	3rd	Win & Pl
Career Total (Turf)	3	0	1	0	2988
Career Total (AW)	2	0	0	0	0

Going (Turf): Sf: 0-0 GS: 0-1 Gd: 0-0 GF: 0-0 Fm: 0-2
Distance: 5f/6f: 0-2 7f-8f: 0-2 9f-13f: 0-1 14f+: 0-0
Track : LH: 0-1 RH: 0-0 Tight: 0-0 Gall: 0-0
Aids: Bl: 0-0 Vi: 0-0 Tstrap: 0-0
Best Rating: 78 7/01 Brig 7f214y firm

Anniegram

48

5-y-o br m Petong-Pinkerton's Pet (Dominion)
A R Dicken D W Shaw

Placings:00 **(2240)**
2001: 5^{0}GS, 7^{0}G

	Starts	1st	2nd	3rd	Win & Pl
Career Total (Turf)	2	0	0	0	

Going (Turf): Sf: 0-0 GS: 0-1 Gd: 0-1 GF: 0-0 Fm: 0-0
Distance: 5f/6f: 0-1 7f-8f: 0-1 9f-13f: 0-0 14f+: 0-0
Track : LH: 0-0 RH: 0-0 Tight: 0-0 Gall: 0-0
Aids: Bl: 0-0 Vi: 0-0 Tstrap: 0-0

Annijaz

101(98) (51)**61**

4-y-o b f Alhijaz-Figment (Posse (USA))
J M Bradley (J G Portman 10/9) Ye Olde Monken Holt

Placings:4232/5000463301035234-4004406201346034 **(5027)**
2001: 8^{4}SW, 9^{0}SD, 7^{0}SD, 8^{4}SW, 10^{4}SD, 7^{0}HY, 10^{6}GS, 10^{2}SD, 9^{0}F, 6^{1}GF, 7^{3}GF, 7^{4}G, 7^{6}GF, 8^{0}F, 8^{3}GS, 5^{4}S

	Starts	1st	2nd	3rd	Win & Pl
Career Total (Turf)	28	2	3	7	15226
Career Total (AW)	8	0	1	0	804
60	6/01	Folk	6f189y	E(0-70)H	G-F £2919
60	7/00	Epsm	7f	E(0-70)H	G-F £5255

Total win prize-money £8174

Going (Turf): Sf: 0-5 GS: 0-2 Gd: 0-6 **GF: 2-8** Fm: 0-6
Distance: 5f/6f: 0-5 **7f-8f: 2-21** 9f-13f: 0-9 14f+: 0-0
Track : LH: 1-17 RH: 1-4 **Tight: 2-12** Gall: 0-0
Aids: Bl: 0-0 Vi: 0-0 Tstrap: 0-0
Best Rating: 61 8/01 Ling 7f gd-fm

Anniversary

105 **95**
3-y-o b f Salse (USA)-Applecross (Glint Of Gold)
H R A Cecil Dr Catherine Wills

Placings:1303 **(5600)**
2001: 12^{1}GF, 14^{3}HY, 12^{0}GS, 16^{3}GS

	Starts	1st	2nd	3rd	Win & Pl
Career Total (Turf)	4	1	0	2	8093

95 8/01 Donc 1m4f D G-F £4290
Total win prize-money £4290

Going (Turf): Sf: 0-1 GS: 0-2 Gd: 0-0 **GF: 1-1** Fm: 0-0
Distance: 5f/6f: 0-0 7f-8f: 0-0 **9f-13f: 1-2** 14f+: 0-2
Track : **LH: 1-2** RH: 0-2 Tight: 0-0 **Gall: 1-3**
Aids: Bl: 0-1 Vi: 0-0 Tstrap: 0-0
Best Rating: 95 8/01 Donc 1m4f gd-fm

She managed to make a winning debut at Doncaster in August despite running as green as grass. She failed to build on that subsequently.

Anniversary Guest (IRE)

90 **60**
2-y-o b/br f Desert King (IRE)-Polynesian Goddess (IRE) (Salmon Leap (USA))
M R Channon John Guest

Placings:060 **(4485)**
2001: 7^{0}GF, 8^{6}GF, 8^{0}S

	Starts	1st	2nd	3rd	Win & Pl
Career Total (Turf)	3	0	0	0	0

Going (Turf): Sf: 0-1 GS: 0-0 Gd: 0-0 GF: 0-2 Fm: 0-0
Distance: 5f/6f: 0-0 7f-8f: 0-1 9f-13f: 0-2 14f+: 0-0
Track : LH: 0-0 RH: 0-1 Tight: 0-0 Gall: 0-1
Aids: Bl: 0-0 Vi: 0-0 Tstrap: 0-0
Best Rating: 60 9/01 Yarm 1m3y soft

Annonce (GER)

(91) (21)
4-y-o b f Daun (GER)-Alenka (GER) (Akari (GER))
M G Quinlan P J McBride

Placings:400000-000 **(0418)**
2001: 13^{0}SD, 9^{0}SD, 12^{0}SD

	Starts	1st	2nd	3rd	Win & Pl
Career Total (Turf)	4	0	0	0	217
Career Total (AW)	5	0	0	0	

Going (Turf): Sf: 0-2 GS: 0-0 Gd: 0-0 GF: 0-0 Fm: 0-0
Distance: 5f/6f: 0-0 7f-8f: 0-1 9f-13f: 0-7 14f+: 0-1
Track : LH: 0-5 RH: 0-0 Tight: 0-4 Gall: 0-0
Aids: Bl: 0-0 Vi: 0-0 Tstrap: 0-0
Best Rating: 21 2/01 Ling 1m5f stand

Anoof

89 **77**
2-y-o b f Marju (IRE)-Waqood (USA) (Riverman (USA))
M P Tregoning Hamdan Al Maktoum

Placings:534 **(5282)**
2001: 7^{5}GF, 7^{3}GS, 8^{4}HY

	Starts	1st	2nd	3rd	Win & Pl
Career Total (Turf)	3	0	0	1	933

Going (Turf): Sf: 0-1 GS: 0-1 Gd: 0-0 GF: 0-1 Fm: 0-0
Distance: 5f/6f: 0-0 7f-8f: 0-3 9f-13f: 0-0 14f+: 0-0
Track : LH: 0-2 RH: 0-1 Tight: 0-1 Gall: 0-1
Aids: Bl: 0-0 Vi: 0-0 Tstrap: 0-0
Best Rating: 77 10/01 Ayr 1m heavy

Half-sister to 2001 four-year-old, Rezif, has not been disgraced in her only three starts. Bred to stay a mile at least.

Another Aspect (IRE)

(80) (43)**68**
2-y-o b c Inzar (USA)-The Aspecto Girl (IRE) (Alzao (USA))
M R Channon Equality Racing

Placings:500003040101 **(5667)**
2001: 6^{5}GF, 6^{0}GF, 6^{0}GF, 6^{0}GF, 7^{0}GF, 6^{3}GF, 7^{0}GF, 7^{4}HY, 6^{0}S, 8^{1}HY, 8^{0}G, 8^{1}HY

	Starts	1st	2nd	3rd	Win & Pl
Career Total (Turf)	12	2	0	1	4685

68 11/01 Wind 1m67y F HVY £2422
65 10/01 Nott 1m54y G HVY £1968
Total win prize-money £4390

Going (Turf): Sf: 2-4 GS: 0-0 Gd: 0-1 GF: 0-7 Fm: 0-0
Distance: 5f/6f: 0-2 7f-8f: 0-8 **9f-13f: 2-2** 14f+: 0-0
Track : LH: 1-3 RH: 1-1 **Tight: 1-1** Gall: 0-0
Aids: Bl: 0-0 Vi: 0-0 Tstrap: 0-0
Best Rating: 81 7/01 Chep 6f16y gd-fm

A winner of two sellers in the mud, he has struggled otherwise.

Another Diamond (IRE)

94 **54**
3-y-o b f First Trump-Rockin' Rosie (Song)
P Howling P A & M J Reditt

Placings:0-06002300 **(5330)**
2001: 7^{0}G, 7^{6}GF, 10^{0}GF, 9^{0}GF, 9^{2}G, 14^{3}GF, 13^{0}F, 16^{0}HY

	Starts	1st	2nd	3rd	Win & Pl
Career Total (Turf)	9	0	1	1	1410

Going (Turf): Sf: 0-2 GS: 0-0 Gd: 0-2 GF: 0-4 Fm: 0-1
Distance: 5f/6f: 0-0 7f-8f: 0-3 9f-13f: 0-3 14f+: 0-3
Track : LH: 0-5 RH: 0-1 Tight: 0-5 Gall: 0-0
Aids: Bl: 0-0 Vi: 0-0 Tstrap: 0-0
Best Rating: 54 8/01 Rdcr 1m6f19y gd-fm

Another Glimpse

91 **63**
3-y-o b c Rudimentary (USA)-Running Glimpse (IRE) (Runnett)
Miss B Sanders Copy Xpress Ltd

Placings:0000 **(2432)**
2001: 7^{0}GS, 8^{0}GF, 10^{0}GF, 11^{0}GF

	Starts	1st	2nd	3rd	Win & Pl
Career Total (Turf)	4	0	0	0	

Going (Turf): Sf: 0-0 GS: 0-1 Gd: 0-0 GF: 0-3 Fm: 0-0
Distance: 5f/6f: 0-0 7f-8f: 0-2 9f-13f: 0-2 14f+: 0-0
Track : LH: 0-0 RH: 0-1 Tight: 0-2 Gall: 0-0
Aids: Bl: 0-0 Vi: 0-0 Tstrap: 0-0
Best Rating: 63 5/01 Gdwd 1m gd-fm

Little worthwhile form so far.

Another Secret

102 **77**
3-y-o b f Efisio-Secrets Of Honour (Belmez (USA))
R Hannon Jubert Family

Placings:4040-0240310 **(5669)**
2001: 8^{0}GS, 8^{2}GS, 7^{4}F, 9^{0}F, 7^{3}HY, 8^{1}GS, 10^{0}HY

	Starts	1st	2nd	3rd	Win & Pl
Career Total (Turf)	11	1	1	1	5454

77 10/01 Leic 1m9y E(0-70)H G-S £3241
Total win prize-money £3241

Going (Turf): Sf: 0-3 **GS: 1-4** Gd: 0-1 GF: 0-1 Fm: 0-2
Distance: 5f/6f: 0-2 7f-8f: 0-5 **9f-13f: 1-4** 14f+: 0-0
Track : LH: 0-2 RH: 0-3 Tight: 0-3 Gall: 0-2
Aids: Bl: 0-0 Vi: 0-0 Tstrap: 0-0
Best Rating: 77 10/01 Leic 1m9y gd-sft

She took time in getting off the mark, but did so in a fillies' handicap over a mile at Leicester in October. Best on soft ground.

Another Time

104 (64)**76**
9-y-o ch g Clantime-Another Move (Farm Walk)
S P C Woods One Dream Partnership

Placings:006/5561F121/0261510345/15500124000/005 4410360100/5536004012000/05043520-0061243066 **(4597)**
2001: 10^{0}G, 10^{0}GF, 9^{6}F, 10^{1}G, 10^{2}GF, 10^{4}GF, 10^{3}GF, 10^{0}GF, 10^{6}G, 12^{6}GF

	Starts	1st	2nd	3rd	Win & Pl
Career Total (Turf)	76	11	6	5	100124
Career Total (AW)	1	0	0	0	0

80 6/01 Ripn 1m2f D(0-85)H GD £5398
82 8/99 Leic 1m1f218yD(0-85)H G-F £4102
93 8/98 Ling 1m2f C(0-90) G-F £5231
90 6/98 Asct 1m2f B(0-105)H GD £21950
89 7/97 Newb 1m1f C(0-90)H G-F £5393
84 4/97 Pont 1m4y D(0-85)H G-F £3785
77 8/96 Ling 1m2f D(0-80)H G-F £3501
73 6/96 Ripn 1m2f E(0-70) G-F £2918
72 10/95 Rdcr 1m2f F(0-65) FRM £2966
68 9/95 Brig 7f214y F GD £3073
58 9/95 Thsk 1m G G-F £3164
Total win prize-money £61485

Going (Turf): Sf: 0-4 GS: 0-5 Gd: 3-25 **GF: 7-39** Fm: 1-3
Distance: 5f/6f: 0-3 7f-8f: 2-5 **9f-13f: 9-69** 14f+: 0-0
Track : **LH: 7-36** RH: 4-27 **Tight: 6-29** Gall: 2-20
Aids: Bl: 0-0 Vi: 0-0 Tstrap: 0-0
Best Rating: 80 6/01 Ripn 1m2f good

A rather in-and-out ten-furlong handicapper, he is suited by fast ground and coming off a fast pace and ended a long losing run at Ripon in June. He needs things to go his way.

Another Victim

107 **49**
7-y-o ch g Beveled (USA)-Ragtime Rose (Ragstone)
M R Bosley John Hughes

Placings:0/6/00300020-00214002 **(5451)**
2001: 5^{0}GS, 5^{0}GF, 6^{2}GF, 5^{1}G, 5^{4}GS, 5^{0}GF, 5^{0}S, 5^{2}HY

	Starts	1st	2nd	3rd	Win & Pl
Career Total (Turf)	17	1	3	1	6908
Career Total (AW)	1	0	0	0	0

46 6/01 Wind 5f10y E(0-70)H GD £3342
Total win prize-money £3343

Going (Turf): Sf: 0-3 GS: 0-4 **Gd: 1-2** GF: 0-8 Fm: 0-0
Distance: **5f/6f: 1-13** 7f-8f: 0-3 9f-13f: 0-2 14f+: 0-0
Track : LH: 0-7 **RH: 1-1** Tight: 0-2 **Gall: 1-2**
Aids: Bl: 0-0 Vi: 0-0 Tstrap: 0-0
Best Rating: 49 10/01 Newc 5f heavy

Ansar (IRE)

97 **92**

5-y-o b g Kahyasi-Anaza (Darshaan)

D K Weld Mrs K Devlin

Placings:06/21323/020110-50454 **(4510a)**

2001: 10^{5}HY, 18^{0}GF, 12^{4}G, 12^{5}F, 14^{4}GY, 16^{0}S

	Starts	1st	2nd	3rd	Win & Pl
Career Total (Turf)	18	3	3	2	47706

92	8/00	Tral	2m1f		Y-S	£8280
94	8/00	Gway	1m6f		GD	£5865
84	7/99	Dund	1m4f		FRM	£2655

Total win prize-money £16800

Going (Turf): Sf: 0-3 GS: 0-1 **Gd: 1-5** GF: 0-2 **Fm: 1-3**
Distance: 5f/6f: 0-0 7f-8f: 0-2 9f-13f: 1-6 **14f+: 2-10**
Track : **LH: 2-7** RH: 1-6 Tight: 0-2 Gall: 0-2
Aids: Bl: 0-1 Vi: 0-0 Tstrap: 0-0
Best Rating: 89 8/01 Tral 1m6f gd-yld

A decent staying handicapper, he just failed to land the Chester Cup of 2000 but disappointed in this year's renewal. He is also very useful over timber. Best on good or yielding ground.

Ansellad (IRE)

94(106) (74)**66**

4-y-o b g Dancing Dissident (USA)-Dutch Queen (Ahonoora)

Andrew Reid (A Berry 31/1) A S Reid

Placings:3120330/00250**00-201040**000 **(1770)**

2001: 6^{2}SD, 6^{0}SW, 5^{1}SW, 5^{0}SW, 6^{4}SW, 5^{0}S, 5^{0}GS, 5^{0}GF, 5^{0}F

	Starts	1st	2nd	3rd	Win & Pl
Career Total (Turf)	17	1	2	3	8847
Career Total (AW)	7	1	1	0	3660

73	1/01	Ling	5f	F	SLW	£2128
84	6/99	Bath	5f11y	D	GD	£3533

Total win prize-money £5662

Going (Turf): Sf: 0-3 GS: 0-2 **Gd: 1-5** GF: 0-5 Fm: 0-2
Distance: **5f/6f: 2-23** 7f-8f: 0-1 9f-13f: 0-0 14f+: 0-0
Track : **LH: 2-13** RH: 0-0 Tight: 1-8 Gall: 1-5
Aids: Bl: 0-0 Vi: 0-1 Tstrap: 0-0
Best Rating: 74 1/01 Ling 6f stand

Ansellman

99(88) (63)**55**

11-y-o gr g Absalom-Grace Poole (Sallust)

A Berry Ansells Of Watford

Placings:0531325241/0000006/00610005000/0562301 23005/00160120005205**3/41402005232012230/054412 32022300/04000440000100003**00/025400145332050-00060363 **(3391)**

2001: 5^{0}SD, 5^{0}GS, 6^{0}G, 5^{6}GF, 5^{0}GS, 5^{3}GF, 6^{6}G, 5^{3}F

	Starts	1st	2nd	3rd	Win & Pl
Career Total (Turf)	122	11	16	13	102291
Career Total (AW)	6	0	1	1	1566

56	7/00	Bath	5f11y	F	FRM	£2401
72	8/99	Bath	5f11y	D(0-85)H	HRD	£3759
84	5/98	Rdcr	6f	F	GD	£2302
80	9/97	Leic	5f2y	D(0-80)H	G-F	£3691
77	4/97	Ripn	5f	F	G-F	£2563
77	7/96	Chep	5f16y	C(0-100)H	G-F	£5215
78	4/96	Bath	5f11y	E(0-70)H	GD	£3226
74	8/95	Catt	5f	F	G-F	£2863
84	5/94	NmkR	5f	C(0-100)H	G-S	£5481
95	10/92	Donc	5f	A	G-S	£7375
68	7/92	Sals	5f	F	G-S	£2092

Total win prize-money £40973

Going (Turf): Sf: 0-13 GS: 3-29 Gd: 2-41 **GF: 4-31** Fm: 2-8
Distance: **5f/6f: 11-122** 7f-8f: 0-6 9f-13f: 0-0 14f+: 0-0
Track : **LH: 3-21** RH: 0-0 Tight: 0-6 **Gall: 3-14**
Aids: **Bl: 5-76** Vi: 2-8 Tstrap: 0-0
Best Rating: 55 7/01 Bath 5f11y firm

A veteran sprinter, went into deserved retirement in July.

Anstand

(107) (67)**60**

6-y-o b g Anshan-Pussy Foot (Red Sunset)

M S Saunders M S Saunders

Placings:056/05103004041/00500/006000000-51123120 **(0607)**

2001: 6^{5}SW, 7^{1}SW, 7^{1}SD, 7^{2}SD, 7^{3}SD, 7^{1}SD, 7^{2}SD, 7^{0}SD

	Starts	1st	2nd	3rd	Win & Pl
Career Total (Turf)	28	2	0	1	11429
Career Total (AW)	8	3	2	1	9204

67	3/01	Wolv	7f	D(0-85)H	STD	£3727
49	3/01	Wolv	7f	E(0-70)H	STD	£2387
45	2/01	Sthl	7f	G(0-75)H	SLW	£1358
76	10/98	York	6f	D(0-75)	GD	£7174
86	5/98	Ripn	6f	E(0-70)H	GD	£3035

Total win prize-money £17682

Going (Turf): Sf: 0-3 GS: 0-4 **Gd: 2-7** GF: 0-11 Fm: 0-3
Distance: 5f/6f: 2-20 **7f-8f: 3-16** 9f-13f: 0-0 14f+: 0-0
Track : **LH: 3-13** RH: 0-2 **Tight: 2-8** Gall: 0-5
Aids: Bl: 0-4 Vi: 0-0 Tstrap: 0-0
Best Rating: 67 3/01 Wolv 7f stand

Answered Promise (FR)

87 **65+**

2-y-o b g Highest Honor (FR)-Answered Prayer (Green Desert (USA))

E A L Dunlop Maktoum Al Maktoum

Placings:05 **(5620)**

2001: 7^{0}GS, 8^{5}GS

	Starts	1st	2nd	3rd	Win & Pl
Career Total (Turf)	2	0	0	0	

Going (Turf): Sf: 0-0 GS: 0-2 Gd: 0-0 GF: 0-0 Fm: 0-0
Distance: 5f/6f: 0-0 7f-8f: 0-1 9f-13f: 0-1 14f+: 0-0
Track : LH: 0-1 RH: 0-0 Tight: 0-0 Gall: 0-0
Aids: Bl: 0-0 Vi: 0-0 Tstrap: 0-0
Best Rating: 65 11/01 Nott 1m54y gd-sft

Anthony Mon Amour (USA)

104(76) (62)**65d**

6-y-o b g Nicholas (USA)-Reine De La Ciel (USA) (Conquistador Cielo (USA))

D Nicholls Tony Fawcett

Placings:03441315/2230040/0041013560000-000320006100000 **(4965)**

2001: 5^{0}S, 6^{0}G, 5^{0}GF, 5^{3}F, 5^{2}F, 5^{0}G, 5^{0}G, 5^{0}G, 5^{6}GF, 5^{1}GF, 6^{0}F, 5^{0}GF, 5^{0}GS, 5^{0}G, 5^{0}S

	Starts	1st	2nd	3rd	Win & Pl
Career Total (Turf)	37	4	2	5	26781
Career Total (AW)	6	1	1	0	3601

65	7/01	Newc	5f	C(0-90)H	G-F	£6938
70	7/00	Pont	5f	D(0-80)H	G-F	£7345
71	7/00	Catt	5f	E(0-75)H	G-F	£3298
69	7/98	Sthl	6f	F(0-60)	STD	£2301
74	7/98	Chep	6f16y	E(0-70)H	GD	£3081

Total win prize-money £22965

Going (Turf): Sf: 0-6 GS: 0-4 Gd: 1-13 **GF: 3-10** Fm: 0-4
Distance: **5f/6f: 4-39** 7f-8f: 1-4 9f-13f: 0-0 14f+: 0-0
Track : **LH: 2-14** RH: 0-2 Tight: 0-5 Gall: 0-3
Aids: Bl: 0-0 Vi: 0-0 **Tstrap: 3-24**
Best Rating: 65 7/01 Newc 5f gd-fm

He went up the handicap after winning twice last summer and struggled as a result, but has dropped now and is running better. Equally effective over five and six furlongs, all of his wins to date have come in the month of July.

Anthony Royle

86(87) (41)**39**

3-y-o ch g King's Signet (USA)-La Thuile (Statoblest)

A Berry Galaxy Moss Side Racing Clubs Limited

Placings:66550**000-00430050**0000050 **(5629)**

2001: 8^{0}SD, 6^{0}SD, 6^{4}SD, 6^{3}SD, 6^{0}SD, 7^{0}GS, 5^{5}SD, 5^{0}SD, 8^{0}GF, 7^{0}GF, 7^{0}G, 5^{0}GF, 5^{0}GF, 6^{5}SD, 5^{0}G

	Starts	1st	2nd	3rd	Win & Pl
Career Total (Turf)	13	0	0	0	885
Career Total (AW)	10	0	0	1	390

Going (Turf): Sf: 0-1 GS: 0-2 Gd: 0-4 GF: 0-5 Fm: 0-1
Distance: 5f/6f: 0-17 7f-8f: 0-5 9f-13f: 0-1 14f+: 0-0
Track : LH: 0-11 RH: 0-2 Tight: 0-8 Gall: 0-0
Aids: Bl: 0-2 Vi: 0-0 Tstrap: 0-0
Best Rating: 52 4/01 Muss 7f30y gd-sft

Anticipate

103 **84+**

3-y-o ch c Nashwan (USA)-De Stael (USA) (Nijinsky (CAN))

R Charlton K Abdulla

Placings:32321 **(4613)**

2001: 8^{3}GF, 9^{2}GF, 10^{3}GF, 11^{2}G, 11^{1}F

	Starts	1st	2nd	3rd	Win & Pl
Career Total (Turf)	5	1	2	2	7271

81	9/01	Bath	1m3f144yD	FRM	£3520

Total win prize-money £3520

Going (Turf): Sf: 0-0 GS: 0-0 Gd: 0-1 GF: 0-3 **Fm: 1-1**
Distance: 5f/6f: 0-0 7f-8f: 0-0 **9f-13f: 1-5** 14f+: 0-0
Track : **LH: 1-3** RH: 0-1 **Tight: 1-3** Gall: 0-0
Aids: Bl: 0-0 Vi: 0-0 Tstrap: 0-0
Best Rating: 84 6/01 Hayd 1m30y gd-fm

Anticles (FR)

97 **65**

4-y-o ch g Barathea (IRE)-Alexandra Fair (USA) (Green Dancer (USA))

R Chotard (Ian Williams 15/7) A Stennett

Placings:331560-00030240

2001: 12^{0}S, 8^{0}GS, 10^{0}GF, 9^{3}G, 10^{0}S, 11^{2}S, 12^{4}S, 12^{0}HY

	Starts	1st	2nd	3rd	Win & Pl
Career Total (Turf)	14	1	1	3	14903

6/00	Chan	1m2f		VS	£6724

Total win prize-money £6724

Going (Turf): Sf: 0-5 GS: 0-1 Gd: 0-3 GF: 0-1 Fm: 0-0
Distance: 5f/6f: 0-0 7f-8f: 0-1 9f-13f: 0-10 14f+: 0-0
Track : LH: 0-3 RH: 0-6 Tight: 0-0 Gall: 0-2
Aids: Bl: 0-0 Vi: 0-1 Tstrap: 0-0
Best Rating: 65 5/01 York 1m2f85y gd-fm

A winner in France over ten furlongs in heavy ground, put in his best effort for some time at Leicester in summer of 2001. Stays ten furlongs. Probably would not want the ground any faster than good.

Antipodes (USA)

94 **74**

3-y-o gr f Pleasant Colony (USA)-La Grande Epoque (USA) (Lyphard (USA))

J L Dunlop Robin F Scully

Placings:0-30400 **(4626)**

2001: 8^{3}GS, 8^{0}G, 9^{4}GF, 10^{0}GF, 9^{0}GF

	Starts	1st	2nd	3rd	Win & Pl

	Starts	1st	2nd	3rd	Win & Pl
Career Total (Turf)	6	0	0	1	1091

Going (Turf): Sf: 0-0 GS: 0-1 Gd: 0-1 GF: 0-4 Fm: 0-0
Distance: 5f/6f: 0-0 7f-8f: 0-2 9f-13f: 0-4 14f+: 0-0
Track : LH: 0-2 RH: 0-3 Tight: 0-2 Gall: 0-1
Aids: Bl: 0-0 Vi: 0-0 Tstrap: 0-0
Best Rating: 76 5/01 Kemp 1m gd-sft

Antonia's Dilemma

92 **53**

3-y-o ch f Primo Dominie-Antonia's Folly (Music Boy)
A Berry Slatch Farm Stud

Placings:013-00000 **(5148)**
2001: 5^{0}GF, 5^{0}GF, 5^{0}G, 5^{0}G, 5^{0}G

	Starts	1st	2nd	3rd	Win & Pl
Career Total (Turf)	8	1	0	1	4658

64	7/00	Ling	5f	D	G-F	£3477

Total win prize-money £3478

Going (Turf): Sf: 0-1 GS: 0-0 Gd: 0-4 **GF: 1-3** Fm: 0-0
Distance: 5f/6f: 1-8 7f-8f: 0-0 9f-13f: 0-0 14f+: 0-0
Track : LH: 0-2 RH: 0-0 Tight: 0-1 Gall: 0-1
Aids: Bl: 0-1 Vi: 0-0 Tstrap: 0-0
Best Rating: 53 8/01 Gdwd 5f good

Lightly-raced winner of ordinary fast-ground Lingfield maiden as a juvenile. No formin 2001.

Antonio Canova

111 **92**

5-y-o ch g Komaite (USA)-Joan's Venture (Beldale Flutter (USA))
Bob Jones The Antonio Canova Partnership

Placings:6223/30012-14114 **(4849)**
2001: 6^{1}GF, 6^{4}F, 6^{1}GS, 6^{1}G, 6^{4}GF

	Starts	1st	2nd	3rd	Win & Pl
Career Total (Turf)	14	4	3	2	62549

90	8/01	Ripn	6f	B(0-105)H	GD	£23200
84	8/01	NmkJ	6f	C(0-90)H	G-S	£6971
84	5/01	Kemp	6f	C(0-90)H	G-F	£7000
76	7/00	NmkJ	6f	C(0-90)H	GD	£7670

Total win prize-money £45641

Going (Turf): Sf: 0-1 GS: 1-1 **Gd: 2-7** GF: 1-4 Fm: 0-1
Distance: 5f/6f: 4-13 7f-8f: 0-1 9f-13f: 0-0 14f+: 0-0
Track : LH: 0-1 RH: 0-1 Tight: 0-0 Gall: 0-2
Aids: Bl: 0-0 Vi: 0-0 Tstrap: 0-0
Best Rating: 92 9/01 Ayr 6f gd-fm

A good winner at Kempton on his reappearance and added another victory at Newmarket in August before gaining his biggest win so far in the Great St Wilfrid at Ripon, and followed up with a good fourth in the Ayr Gold Cup. He has won on fast ground, but looks better with some cut. Suited by six furlongs.

Antonio Mariano (SWE)

10-y-o b g Mango Express-Mango Sampaquita (SWE) (Colombian Friend (USA))
Lady Herries Mrs Mette Campbell

Placings:000/0 **(2061)**
2001: 12^{0}GF

	Starts	1st	2nd	3rd	Win & Pl
Career Total (Turf)	4	0	0	0	

Going (Turf): Sf: 0-1 GS: 0-1 Gd: 0-0 GF: 0-2 Fm: 0-0
Distance: 5f/6f: 0-0 7f-8f: 0-2 9f-13f: 0-2 14f+: 0-0
Track : LH: 0-0 RH: 0-1 Tight: 0-2 Gall: 0-0
Aids: Bl: 0-0 Vi: 0-0 Tstrap: 0-0

Antony Ebeneezer

95 **58?**

2-y-o ch c Hurricane Sky (AUS)-Captivating (IRE) (Wolfhound (USA))
I A Wood John Purcell

Placings:00050 **(5690)**
2001: 6^{0}GF, 6^{0}GF, 7^{0}G, 6^{5}S, 7^{0}S

	Starts	1st	2nd	3rd	Win & Pl
Career Total (Turf)	5	0	0	0	0

Going (Turf): Sf: 0-2 GS: 0-0 Gd: 0-1 GF: 0-2 Fm: 0-0
Distance: 5f/6f: 0-1 7f-8f: 0-4 9f-13f: 0-0 14f+: 0-0
Track : LH: 0-1 RH: 0-1 Tight: 0-0 Gall: 0-0
Aids: Bl: 0-0 Vi: 0-0 Tstrap: 0-0
Best Rating: 58 9/01 Gdwd 7f good

Ran his best race to date on his handicap debut over six furlongs on soft ground, but was well beaten after that.

Anyhow (IRE)

104(97) (48)**57**

4-y-o b f Distant Relative-Fast Chick (Henbit (USA))
Andrew Reid A S Reid

Placings:3/04100044-060040651000 **(5275)**
2001: 7^{0}SD, 9^{6}SW, 8^{0}SD, 6^{0}SD, 6^{4}G, 7^{0}G, 7^{6}GF, 8^{5}GF, 9^{1}F, 7^{0}GF, 9^{0}HY, 8^{0}GS

	Starts	1st	2nd	3rd	Win & Pl
Career Total (Turf)	13	2	0	0	6537
Career Total (AW)	8	0	0	1	539

66	6/01	Ling	1m1f	D(0-80)H	FRM	£4108
74	7/00	Ling	7f	F(0-65)H	GD	£1893

Total win prize-money £6002

Going (Turf): Sf: 0-3 GS: 0-1 **Gd: 1-5** GF: 0-3 **Fm: 1-1**
Distance: 5f/6f: 0-2 7f-8f: 1-11 9f-13f: 1-8 14f+: 0-0
Track : LH: 1-12 RH: 0-1 **Tight: 1-7** Gall: 0-0
Aids: Bl: 0-0 Vi: 0-0 Tstrap: 0-0
Best Rating: 68 6/01 Wind 1m67y gd-fm

Modest handicapper, goes well at Lingfield.

Anywhichway

(86) (44)**62**

2-y-o b f Bijou D'Inde-Risk The Witch (Risk Me (FR))
C E Brittain Michael Clarke

Placings:0000000 **(5618)**
2001: 6^{0}GF, 6^{0}GF, 5^{0}GF, 5^{0}GS, 6^{0}SD, 8^{0}HY, 8^{0}SD

	Starts	1st	2nd	3rd	Win & Pl
Career Total (Turf)	5	0	0	0	
Career Total (AW)	2	0	0	0	

Going (Turf): Sf: 0-1 GS: 0-1 Gd: 0-0 GF: 0-3 Fm: 0-0
Distance: 5f/6f: 0-4 7f-8f: 0-1 9f-13f: 0-2 14f+: 0-0
Track : LH: 0-4 RH: 0-1 Tight: 0-3 Gall: 0-0
Aids: Bl: 0-0 Vi: 0-0 Tstrap: 0-0
Best Rating: 62 8/01 Brig 5f213y gd-fm

Apache Point (IRE)

105 **56**

4-y-o ch g Indian Ridge-Ausherra (USA) (Diesis)
N Tinkler The Penniless Partnership

Placings:0-140603005625 **(5539)**
2001: 7^{1}S, 8^{4}GF, 8^{0}GF, 8^{6}GF, 8^{0}GF, 9^{3}GS, 8^{0}G, 8^{0}GF, 8^{5}G, 8^{6}F, 8^{2}GS, 8^{5}S

	Starts	1st	2nd	3rd	Win & Pl
Career Total (Turf)	13	1	1	1	4245

52	5/01	Rdcr	7f	F	SFT	£2485

Total win prize-money £2485

Going (Turf): Sf: 1-2 GS: 0-3 Gd: 0-2 GF: 0-5 Fm: 0-1
Distance: 5f/6f: 0-0 **7f-8f: 1-7** 9f-13f: 0-6 14f+: 0-0
Track : LH: 0-3 RH: 0-3 Tight: 0-2 Gall: 0-1
Aids: Bl: 0-0 Vi: 0-0 Tstrap: 0-0
Best Rating: 58 7/01 Ripn 1m gd-fm

Lightly-raced, ex-Henry Cecil inmate. Won moderate maiden before a fair effort on his handicap debut at Beverley. Bits of form since.

Apadi (USA)

96(83) (77)**46**

5-y-o ch g Diesis-Ixtapa (USA) (Chief's Crown (USA))
M C Chapman (K Bell 22/7) Barry Brown & Kenny Blanch

Placings:216/00006600/00-000 **(4858)**
2001: 8^{0}SD, 11^{0}G, 15^{0}GF

	Starts	1st	2nd	3rd	Win & Pl
Career Total (Turf)	12	1	1	0	12727
Career Total (AW)	4	0	0	0	0

6/98	MsnL	5f110y		SFT	£9091

Total win prize-money £9091

Going (Turf): Sf: 0-0 GS: 0-1 Gd: 0-3 GF: 0-1 Fm: 0-0
Distance: 5f/6f: 0-0 7f-8f: 0-4 9f-13f: 0-4 14f+: 0-1
Track : LH: 0-6 RH: 0-1 Tight: 0-5 Gall: 0-0
Aids: Bl: 0-0 Vi: 0-0 Tstrap: 0-0
Best Rating: 46 9/01 Catt 1m7f177y gd-fm

Aphelion

66(62) **6**

3-y-o b c Superlative-Starchy Cove (Starch Reduced)
N M Babbage Colin Rashbrook

Placings:000 **(3855)**
2001: 7^{0}GF, 6^{0}SD, 7^{0}GS

	Starts	1st	2nd	3rd	Win & Pl
Career Total (Turf)	2	0	0	0	
Career Total (AW)	1	0	0	0	

Going (Turf): Sf: 0-0 GS: 0-1 Gd: 0-0 GF: 0-1 Fm: 0-0
Distance: 5f/6f: 0-1 7f-8f: 0-2 9f-13f: 0-0 14f+: 0-0
Track : LH: 0-2 RH: 0-0 Tight: 0-1 Gall: 0-0
Aids: Bl: 0-0 Vi: 0-0 Tstrap: 0-0
Best Rating: 6 6/01 Hayd 7f30y gd-fm

Apollo Red

90(105) (26)**36**

12-y-o ch g Dominion-Woolpack (Golden Fleece (USA))
G L Moore Exors Of The Late Mr A Moore

Placings:00500/5335026/13440130403606/536003200 0302/034303110011/4431323212310300255101/00050 13050040/00504323020613/1261104-0206040 **(1371)**
2001: 6^{0}SD, 8^{2}SW, 8^{0}SW, 6^{6}SD, 7^{0}SW, 6^{4}SD, 6^{0}G

	Starts	1st	2nd	3rd	Win & Pl
Career Total (Turf)	51	5	5	7	22204
Career Total (AW)	63	11	6	13	41760

61	2/00	Ling	7f	E	STD	£2601
77	2/00	Ling	7f	F(0-70)H	STD	£1809
56	1/00	Ling	1m	G	STD	£1951
49	12/99	Ling	7f	G	STD	£1532
72	7/98	Brig	6f209y	E(0-70)H	GD	£3009
87	12/97	Ling	6f	D(0-85)H	STD	£3403
83	11/97	Ling	6f	D(0-85)H	STD	£3452
76	5/97	Brig	6f209y	E(0-70)H	G-F	£3148
79	4/97	Ling	6f	D(0-80)H	STD	£3677
65	2/97	Ling	6f	D(0-75)H	STD	£3420
62	12/96	Ling	7f	E(0-70)H	STD	£2643
59	11/96	Ling	7f	F	STD	£2297
57	5/96	Ling	7f	E(0-80)H	G-F	£3261
53	4/96	Brig	5f59y	E(0-70)H	FRM	£2933
45	4/94	Brig	5f213y	F	SFT	£2243
56	1/94	Ling	7f	F(0-60)H	STD	£2758

Total win prize-money £44144

Going (Turf): Sf: 1-2 GS: 0-5 Gd: 1-17 **GF: 2-17** Fm: 1-10
Distance: 5f/6f: 6-44 **7f-8f: 10-64** 9f-13f: 0-6 14f+: 0-0
Track : **LH: 15-88** RH: 0-6 **Tight: 11-63** Gall: 0-2
Aids: Bl: 0-1 **Vi: 1-10** Tstrap: 0-0
Best Rating: 43 2/01 Ling 1m slow

Aporto

101(68) (13)40

3-y-o ch g Clantime-Portvally (Import)
D W Barker D W Barker

Placings:003041040-006503500040060 (4896)
2001: 7^{0}SD, 8^{0}SD, 6^{0}HY, 8^{5}S, 8^{0}F, 8^{3}GF, 7^{5}GF, 8^{0}GF, 7^{0}GF, 8^{0}GF, 8^{4}F, 11^{0}G, 9^{0}G, 8^{0}GF, 9^{0}GS

	Starts	1st	2nd	3rd	Win & Pl
Career Total (Turf)	21	1	0	2	4016
Career Total (AW)	3	0	0	0	

55 9/00 Catt 7f E(0-75) SFT £3094
Total win prize-money £3094

Going (Turf): **Sf: 1-4** GS: 0-2 Gd: 0-3 GF: 0-10 Fm: 0-2
Distance: 5f/6f: 0-5 **7f-8f: 1-16** 9f-13f: 0-3 14f+: 0-0
Track : **LH: 1-12** RH: 0-6 **Tight: 1-7** Gall: 0-2
Aids: Bl: 0-0 Vi: 0-0 Tstrap: 0-0
Best Rating: 57 5/01 Newc 1m soft

Appellation

103 92

3-y-o b c Clantime-Chablisse (Radetzky)
W Jarvis Mrs Jane Chapple-Hyam

Placings:6411-0620 (1976)
2001: 6^{0}S, 6^{0}GS, 5^{2}F, 7^{0}GF

	Starts	1st	2nd	3rd	Win & Pl
Career Total (Turf)	8	2	1	0	11778

92 9/00 Gdwd 6f D SFT £4189
92 9/00 Gdwd 6f D GD £4927
Total win prize-money £9116

Going (Turf): **Sf: 1-2** GS: 0-1 **Gd: 1-2** GF: 0-1 Fm: 0-1
Distance: **5f/6f: 2-6** 7f-8f: 0-1 9f-13f: 0-0 14f+: 0-0
Track : LH: 0-1 RH: 0-1 Tight: 0-1 Gall: 0-1
Aids: Bl: 0-0 Vi: 0-0 Tstrap: 0-0
Best Rating: 84 5/01 Leic 5f218y firm

A dual Goodwood winner in 2000. Modest form in 2001.

Appian Way

99 81

3-y-o b g Shareef Dancer (USA)-Ambassadress (USA) (Alleged (USA))
J Noseda Hesmonds Stud

Placings:35 (0758)
2001: 7^{3}S, 7^{5}S

	Starts	1st	2nd	3rd	Win & Pl
Career Total (Turf)	2	0	0	1	678

Going (Turf): Sf: 0-2 GS: 0-0 Gd: 0-0 GF: 0-0 Fm: 0-0
Distance: 5f/6f: 0-0 7f-8f: 0-2 9f-13f: 0-0 14f+: 0-0
Track : LH: 0-0 RH: 0-1 Tight: 0-0 Gall: 0-1
Aids: Bl: 0-0 Vi: 0-0 Tstrap: 0-0
Best Rating: 81 3/01 Donc 7f soft

Apple Zed

95 45

3-y-o b f Catrail (USA)-Mrs Croesus (USA) (Key To The Mint (USA))
G C Bravery Me And Them

Placings:420000 (4675)
2001: 7^{4}GF, 6^{2}GF, 8^{0}GF, 5^{0}GF, 7^{0}G, 7^{0}G

	Starts	1st	2nd	3rd	Win & Pl
Career Total (Turf)	6	0	1	0	1184

Going (Turf): Sf: 0-0 GS: 0-0 Gd: 0-2 GF: 0-4 Fm: 0-0
Distance: 5f/6f: 0-1 7f-8f: 0-4 9f-13f: 0-1 14f+: 0-0
Track : LH: 0-1 RH: 0-3 Tight: 0-2 Gall: 0-0
Aids: Bl: 0-0 Vi: 0-0 Tstrap: 0-0
Best Rating: 45 6/01 Bevl 7f100y gd-fm

Appleacre

77 63

2-y-o b f Polar Falcon (USA)-Absaloute Service (Absalom)
J M P Eustace Major M G Wyatt

Placings:00 (5483)
2001: 6^{0}HY, 7^{0}HY

	Starts	1st	2nd	3rd	Win & Pl
Career Total (Turf)	2	0	0	0	

Going (Turf): **Sf: 0-2** GS: 0-0 Gd: 0-0 GF: 0-0 Fm: 0-0
Distance: 5f/6f: 0-0 7f-8f: 0-2 9f-13f: 0-0 14f+: 0-0
Track : LH: 0-0 RH: 0-0 Tight: 0-0 Gall: 0-0
Aids: Bl: 0-0 Vi: 0-0 Tstrap: 0-0
Best Rating: 63 10/01 Nott 6f15y heavy

Approachable (USA)

(102) (51)13

6-y-o b/br g Known Fact (USA)-Western Approach (USA) (Gone West (USA))
K A Morgan R G Marriott

Placings:000/3510031166240/2544232422543202336-43346060010 (5615)
2001: 12^{4}SW, 8^{3}SD, 9^{3}SD, 11^{4}SD, 11^{6}SD, 10^{0}GF, 11^{6}SD, 10^{0}GF, 7^{0}G, 11^{1}SD, 12^{0}SD

	Starts	1st	2nd	3rd	Win & Pl
Career Total (Turf)	8	0	0	0	
Career Total (AW)	38	4	8	8	15971

51 10/01 Sthl 1m3f F(0-60) STD £2345
65 7/99 Wolv 1m100y F STD £1966
61 7/99 Wolv 1m1f79y F(0-60) STD £2126
57 3/99 Wolv 7f F(0-60)H SLW £2326
Total win prize-money £8765

Going (Turf): Sf: 0-0 GS: 0-1 Gd: 0-4 GF: 0-3 Fm: 0-0
Distance: 5f/6f: 0-0 7f-8f: 1-12 **9f-13f: 3-34** 14f+: 0-0
Track : **LH: 4-41** RH: 0-3 **Tight: 3-24** Gall: 0-1
Aids: Bl: 0-2 Vi: 0-1 Tstrap: 0-0
Best Rating: 51 10/01 Sthl 1m3f stand

A regular on Fibresand, he ended a long losing run in a claimer at Southwell in October. Middle distances on that surface suit him best.

Approval

96 93

2-y-o b c Royal Applause-Gentle Persuasion (Bustino)
R Hannon The Queen

Placings:125 (4578)
2001: 6^{1}GF, 6^{2}GF, 6^{5}G

	Starts	1st	2nd	3rd	Win & Pl
Career Total (Turf)	3	1	1	0	8287

83 7/01 Sals 6f D G-F £4010
Total win prize-money £4011

Going (Turf): Sf: 0-0 GS: 0-0 Gd: 0-1 **GF: 1-2** Fm: 0-0
Distance: **5f/6f: 1-2** 7f-8f: 0-1 9f-13f: 0-0 14f+: 0-0
Track : LH: 0-0 RH: 0-0 Tight: 0-0 Gall: 0-0
Aids: Bl: 0-0 Vi: 0-0 Tstrap: 0-0
Best Rating: 93 7/01 Newb 6f8y gd-fm

Speedily bred, a half-brother to Sharp Prod, he made a good impression winning his debut over six furlongs at Salisbury in July before a better effort in defeat next time.

April Ace

89 (56d)40

5-y-o ch g First Trump-Champ D'Avril (Northfields (USA))
R J Baker Graham Brown

Placings:041564406/06500362310214323/000000-00 (2808)
2001: 9^{0}F, 8^{0}GF

	Starts	1st	2nd	3rd	Win & Pl
Career Total (Turf)	31	3	3	4	18065
Career Total (AW)	3	0	0	0	0

56 8/99 Brig 7f214y D(0-80)H G-F £4084
49 7/99 Nott 1m54y D(0-85)H FRM £5540
70 6/98 Bath 5f161y E G-S £2969
Total win prize-money £12594

Going (Turf): Sf: 0-4 **GS: 1-4** Gd: 0-7 **GF: 1-12 Fm: 1-4**
Distance: 5f/6f: 1-7 7f-8f: 1-16 9f-13f: 1-11 14f+: 0-0
Track : **LH: 3-14** RH: 0-3 Tight: 0-7 **Gall: 1-1**
Aids: Bl: 0-0 Vi: 0-1 Tstrap: 0-0
Best Rating: 22 5/01 Brig 1m1f209y firm

April Lee

101(93) (60)60

3-y-o b f Superpower-Petitesse (Petong)
K McAuliffe E P Jameson

Placings:605525203000146-36530202300505 (4370)
2001: 8^{3}SD, 7^{6}SD, 8^{5}SD, 7^{3}SW, 7^{0}SD, 7^{2}G, 7^{0}SD, 7^{2}F, 7^{3}GF, 6^{0}GF, 8^{0}GF, 7^{5}GF, 7^{0}GF, 7^{5}GF

	Starts	1st	2nd	3rd	Win & Pl
Career Total (Turf)	18	0	4	2	5008
Career Total (AW)	11	1	0	2	2495

72 11/00 Wolv 7f F STD £1736
Total win prize-money £1736

Going (Turf): Sf: 0-3 GS: 0-2 Gd: 0-2 GF: 0-8 Fm: 0-2
Distance: 5f/6f: 0-4 **7f-8f: 1-22** 9f-13f: 0-2 14f+: 0-0
Track : **LH: 1-17** RH: 0-0 **Tight: 1-6** Gall: 0-0
Aids: Bl: 0-2 Vi: 0-7 Tstrap: 0-0
Best Rating: 64 6/01 Ling 7f firm

April Louise

76 6

5-y-o b m Meqdaam (USA)-California Dreamin (Slip Anchor)
T Wall D Bunn

Placings:0 (4268)
2001: 9^{0}GF

	Starts	1st	2nd	3rd	Win & Pl
Career Total (Turf)	1	0	0	0	

Going (Turf): Sf: 0-0 GS: 0-0 Gd: 0-0 GF: 0-1 Fm: 0-0
Distance: 5f/6f: 0-0 7f-8f: 0-0 9f-13f: 0-1 14f+: 0-0
Track : LH: 0-0 RH: 0-1 Tight: 0-0 Gall: 0-0
Aids: Bl: 0-0 Vi: 0-0 Tstrap: 0-0
Best Rating: 6 8/01 Bevl 1m1f207y gd-fm

April Star

(86) (25)13

4-y-o ch f Deploy-Cabaret Artiste (Shareef Dancer (USA))
B A Pearce M O'Malley

Placings:050000-0 (4522)
2001: 11^{0}GF

	Starts	1st	2nd	3rd	Win & Pl
Career Total (Turf)	6	0	0	0	0
Career Total (AW)	1	0	0	0	

Going (Turf): Sf: 0-1 GS: 0-0 Gd: 0-3 GF: 0-2 Fm: 0-0
Distance: 5f/6f: 0-1 7f-8f: 0-3 9f-13f: 0-3 14f+: 0-0
Track : LH: 0-2 RH: 0-2 Tight: 0-3 Gall: 0-0
Aids: Bl: 0-0 Vi: 0-0 Tstrap: 0-0
Best Rating: 8 9/01 Ling 1m3f106y gd-fm

April Stock

107 89
6-y-o ch m Beveled (USA)-Stockline (Capricorn Line)
G A Butler Stock Hill Racing

Placings:242233/100410/510-311030 (5693)
2001: 12^3S, 11^1GS, 12^1S, 13^0G, 10^3GS, 12^0S

	Starts	1st	2nd	3rd	Win & Pl
Career Total (Turf)	21	5	3	4	43395

87 5/01 Newb 1m4f5y C(0-90)H SFT £13456
84 5/01 Bath 1m3f144yD(0-80)H G-S £6857
86 5/00 Chep 1m4f23y D(0-80)H HVY £7150
74 10/99 Wind 1m3f135yD(0-75) G-S £4013
68 4/99 Folk 1m4f D HVY £3833
Total win prize-money £35311

Going (Turf): Sf: 3-8 GS: 2-4 Gd: 0-6 GF: 0-2 Fm: 0-1
Distance: 5f/6f: 0-0 7f-8f: 0-0 9f-13f: 5-15 14f+: 0-6
Track : LH: 3-12 RH: 1-8 Tight: 3-6 Gall: 1-8
Aids: Bl: 0-0 Vi: 0-0 Tstrap: 2-7
Best Rating: 88 10/01 Asct 1m2f gd-sft

A decent handicapper, she needs 12 furlongs and soft ground in order to show her best.

April's Comait

91(93) (47)27
4-y-o br f Komaite (USA)-Sweet Caroline (Squill (USA))
T T Clement Mrs Patricia Appleby

Placings:04400003/6053300056000-00 (4283)
2001: 9^0G, 7^0G

	Starts	1st	2nd	3rd	Win & Pl
Career Total (Turf)	16	0	0	1	322
Career Total (AW)	7	0	0	2	511

Going (Turf): Sf: 0-0 GS: 0-2 Gd: 0-5 GF: 0-5 Fm: 0-4
Distance: 5f/6f: 0-19 7f-8f: 0-3 9f-13f: 0-1 14f+: 0-0
Track : LH: 0-5 RH: 0-1 Tight: 0-5 Gall: 0-0
Aids: Bl: 0-5 Vi: 0-0 Tstrap: 0-0
Best Rating: 22 8/01 Yarm 7f3y good

Aqaba

83 79
2-y-o b f Lake Coniston (IRE)-Sahara Breeze (Ela-Mana-Mou)
S Kirk J P Repard

Placings:20 (5250)
2001: 6^2HY, 6^0S

	Starts	1st	2nd	3rd	Win & Pl
Career Total (Turf)	2	0	1	0	1205

Going (Turf): Sf: 0-2 GS: 0-0 Gd: 0-0 GF: 0-0 Fm: 0-0
Distance: 5f/6f: 0-1 7f-8f: 0-1 9f-13f: 0-0 14f+: 0-0
Track : LH: 0-0 RH: 0-0 Tight: 0-0 Gall: 0-0
Aids: Bl: 0-0 Vi: 0-0 Tstrap: 0-0
Best Rating: 79 10/01 Nott 6f15y heavy

A half-sister to Group One winner Lady Of Chad, she showed promise on her debut.

Aquae Sulis

86 44
2-y-o ch f Greensmith-Stealthy (Kind Of Hush)
W M Brisbourne John Wills

Placings:000 (5487)
2001: 5^0HY, 6^0HY, 6^0HY

	Starts	1st	2nd	3rd	Win & Pl
Career Total (Turf)	3	0	0	0	

Going (Turf): Sf: 0-3 GS: 0-0 Gd: 0-0 GF: 0-0 Fm: 0-0
Distance: 5f/6f: 0-2 7f-8f: 0-1 9f-13f: 0-0 14f+: 0-0
Track : LH: 0-0 RH: 0-0 Tight: 0-0 Gall: 0-0
Aids: Bl: 0-0 Vi: 0-0 Tstrap: 0-0
Best Rating: 44 9/01 Hayd 5f heavy

Aquarius (IRE)

108 101
3-y-o b c Royal Academy (USA)-Rafha (Kris)
J L Dunlop Prince A A Faisal

Placings:5-1423456 (4689a)
2001: 11^1S, 12^4G, 13^2F, 16^3GF, 15^4G, 15^5S, 15^6GS

	Starts	1st	2nd	3rd	Win & Pl
Career Total (Turf)	8	1	1	1	20097

81 4/01 Kemp 1m3f30y D SFT £4153
Total win prize-money £4154

Going (Turf): Sf: 1-2 GS: 0-1 Gd: 0-2 GF: 0-2 Fm: 0-1
Distance: 5f/6f: 0-0 7f-8f: 0-1 9f-13f: 1-2 14f+: 0-5
Track : LH: 0-1 RH: 1-4 Tight: 0-0 Gall: 0-3
Aids: Bl: 0-0 Vi: 0-2 Tstrap: 0-0
Best Rating: 101 6/01 Asct 2m45y gd-fm

A half-brother to Sadian, he has won over a mile and three and should have no trouble staying an additional couple of furlongs. Suited to a strong pace.

Aquiline

84 42
3-y-o ch g Sanglamore (USA)-Fantasy Flyer (USA) (Lear Fan (USA))
John A Harris Mrs Annette Harris

Placings:6 (4455)
2001: 10^6GF

	Starts	1st	2nd	3rd	Win & Pl
Career Total (Turf)	1	0	0	0	0

Going (Turf): Sf: 0-0 GS: 0-0 Gd: 0-0 GF: 0-1 Fm: 0-0
Distance: 5f/6f: 0-0 7f-8f: 0-0 9f-13f: 0-1 14f+: 0-0
Track : LH: 0-1 RH: 0-0 Tight: 0-0 Gall: 0-1
Aids: Bl: 0-0 Vi: 0-0 Tstrap: 0-0
Best Rating: 42 9/01 York 1m2f85y gd-fm

Arabian Goggles

75 36
2-y-o ch f Cosmonaut-Jarrettelle (All Systems Go)
H S Howe Blow Your Dough Syndicate

Placings:000 (5491)
2001: 7^0GF, 8^0GS, 6^0HY

	Starts	1st	2nd	3rd	Win & Pl
Career Total (Turf)	3	0	0	0	

Going (Turf): Sf: 0-1 GS: 0-1 Gd: 0-0 GF: 0-1 Fm: 0-0
Distance: 5f/6f: 0-0 7f-8f: 0-3 9f-13f: 0-0 14f+: 0-0
Track : LH: 0-0 RH: 0-1 Tight: 0-0 Gall: 0-1
Aids: Bl: 0-0 Vi: 0-0 Tstrap: 0-0
Best Rating: 36 10/01 Salo 1m gd-sft

Arabian Moon (IRE)

104(98) (80)86
5-y-o ch h Barathea (IRE)-Excellent Alibi (USA) (Exceller (USA))
S Dow Byerley Bloodstock

Placings:00/0004211300/0351346-5062044 (3246)
2001: 12^5SD, 12^0S, 14^6GF, 13^2GF, 16^0F, 14^4GF, 13^4GF

	Starts	1st	2nd	3rd	Win & Pl
Career Total (Turf)	24	3	2	3	32990
Career Total (AW)	2	0	0	0	0

91 6/00 Pont 1m2f6y C(0-90) G-F £8190
84 7/99 Wind 1m3f135yD(0-85)H G-F £4263
80 6/99 Ripn 1m4f60y D(0-80)H G-F £4240
Total win prize-money £16694

Going (Turf): Sf: 0-3 GS: 0-1 Gd: 0-8 GF: 3-11 Fm: 0-1
Distance: 5f/6f: 0-1 7f-8f: 0-4 9f-13f: 3-13 14f+: 0-8
Track : LH: 1-10 RH: 1-10 Tight: 2-7 Gall: 0-7
Aids: Bl: 0-0 Vi: 0-0 Tstrap: 0-0
Best Rating: 86 6/01 Newb 1m5f61y gd-fm

Arabian Waters

(91) (47)59
3-y-o b f Muhtarram (USA)-Secret Waters (Pharly (FR))
R F Johnson Houghton Anthony Harrison

Placings:00-50506 (4879)
2001: 8^5GS, 9^0G, 11^5G, 14^0S, 12^6SD

	Starts	1st	2nd	3rd	Win & Pl
Career Total (Turf)	6	0	0	0	0
Career Total (AW)	1	0	0	0	0

Going (Turf): Sf: 0-1 GS: 0-1 Gd: 0-2 GF: 0-2 Fm: 0-0
Distance: 5f/6f: 0-1 7f-8f: 0-1 9f-13f: 0-4 14f+: 0-1
Track : LH: 0-2 RH: 0-4 Tight: 0-3 Gall: 0-1
Aids: Bl: 0-0 Vi: 0-0 Tstrap: 0-0
Best Rating: 59 8/01 Leic 1m3f183y good

Arabie

113 97
3-y-o b c Polish Precedent (USA)-Always Friendly (High Line)
H R A Cecil Newgate Stud

Placings:0421361 (4286)
2001: 10^0GS, 9^4GS, 12^2GF, 10^1GF, 12^3GF, 10^6G, 10^1G

	Starts	1st	2nd	3rd	Win & Pl
Career Total (Turf)	7	2	1	1	21385

97 8/01 Yarm 1m2f21y C(0-90) GD £7199
88 6/01 Wind 1m2f7y C(0-100)H G-F £6825
Total win prize-money £14025

Going (Turf): Sf: 0-0 GS: 0-2 Gd: 1-2 GF: 1-3 Fm: 0-0
Distance: 5f/6f: 0-0 7f-8f: 0-0 9f-13f: 2-7 14f+: 0-0
Track : LH: 1-3 RH: 0-2 Tight: 2-3 Gall: 0-2
Aids: Bl: 0-0 Vi: 0-0 Tstrap: 0-0
Best Rating: 97 8/01 Yarm 1m2f21y good

He was supplemented for the Derby but did not live up to expectations. Got off the mark in a ten-furlong handicap at Windsor in June, and ran well at Royal Ascot next time. Looked good when adding a minor event at Yarmouth in August. Stays a mile and a half and acts on fast ground.

Arabin

81 64
2-y-o b c Bin Ajwaad (IRE)-Just Julia (Natroun (FR))
K O Cunningham-Brown H R Moszkowicz

Placings:00 (4732)
2001: 7^0GF, 7^0F

	Starts	1st	2nd	3rd	Win & Pl
Career Total (Turf)	2	0	0	0	

Going (Turf): Sf: 0-0 GS: 0-0 Gd: 0-0 GF: 0-1 Fm: 0-1
Distance: 5f/6f: 0-0 7f-8f: 0-2 9f-13f: 0-0 14f+: 0-0
Track : LH: 0-0 RH: 0-0 Tight: 0-0 Gall: 0-0
Aids: Bl: 0-0 Vi: 0-0 Tstrap: 0-0
Best Rating: 64 9/01 Chep 7f16y firm

Arachine

83(77) (51)**53**

2-y-o ch c Indian Ridge-Hill Hopper (IRE) (Danehill (USA))

Sir Mark Prescott Mrs S L Warman

Placings:050 **(5635)**

2001: 7^{0}S, 7^{5}SD, 7^{0}G

	Starts	1st	2nd	3rd	Win & Pl
Career Total (Turf)	2	0	0	0	
Career Total (AW)	1	0	0	0	0

Going (Turf): Sf: 0-1 GS: 0-0 Gd: 0-1 GF: 0-0 Fm: 0-0
Distance: 5f/6f: 0-0 7f-8f: 0-3 9f-13f: 0-0 14f+: 0-0
Track : LH: 0-2 RH: 0-0 Tight: 0-2 Gall: 0-0
Aids: Bl: 0-0 Vi: 0-0 Tstrap: 0-0
Best Rating: 53 10/01 Leic 7f9y soft

Araf

(72) (31)

2-y-o b g Millkom-Euphyllia (Superpower)

A G Newcombe A G Newcombe

Placings:0 **(4878)**

2001: 7^{0}SD

	Starts	1st	2nd	3rd	Win & Pl
Career Total (Turf)	0	0	0	0	
Career Total (AW)	1	0	0	0	

Going (Turf): Sf: 0-0 GS: 0-0 Gd: 0-0 GF: 0-0 Fm: 0-0
Distance: 5f/6f: 0-0 7f-8f: 0-1 9f-13f: 0-0 14f+: 0-0
Track : LH: 0-1 RH: 0-0 Tight: 0-1 Gall: 0-0
Aids: Bl: 0-0 Vi: 0-0 Tstrap: 0-0
Best Rating: 31 9/01 Wolv 7f stand

Aragant (FR)

98 **30**

5-y-o b/br g Aragon-Soolaimon (IRE) (Shareef Dancer (USA))

R J Hodges Joli Racing

Placings:445330/000006-65040 **(3297)**

2001: 9^{6}GF, 9^{5}G, 9^{0}F, 7^{4}GF, 6^{0}GF

	Starts	1st	2nd	3rd	Win & Pl
Career Total (Turf)	17	0	0	2	2126

Going (Turf): Sf: 0-1 GS: 0-1 Gd: 0-3 GF: 0-7 Fm: 0-5
Distance: 5f/6f: 0-0 7f-8f: 0-5 9f-13f: 0-12 14f+: 0-0
Track : LH: 0-11 RH: 0-4 Tight: 0-3 Gall: 0-2
Aids: Bl: 0-1 Vi: 0-0 Tstrap: 0-0
Best Rating: 30 6/01 Brig 7f214y gd-fm

Araglin

(93) (80+)**83**

2-y-o b c Sadler's Wells (USA)-River Caro (USA) (Irish River (FR))

Miss S J Wilton (J H M Gosden 25/10) John Pointon And Sons

Placings:02234 **(5690)**

2001: 7^{0}GF, 8^{2}GS, 8^{2}S, 7^{3}S, 7^{4}S

	Starts	1st	2nd	3rd	Win & Pl
Career Total (Turf)	5	0	2	1	3593

Going (Turf): Sf: 0-3 GS: 0-1 Gd: 0-0 GF: 0-1 Fm: 0-0
Distance: 5f/6f: 0-0 7f-8f: 0-4 9f-13f: 0-1 14f+: 0-0
Track : LH: 0-1 RH: 0-0 Tight: 0-0 Gall: 0-0
Aids: Bl: 0-2 Vi: 0-0 Tstrap: 0-0
Best Rating: 83 11/01 Donc 7f soft

By Sadler's Wells, he improved on his debut when second in maidens at Salisbury and Leicester in October, and has since run well in competitive events at Brighton and Doncaster, although he is still a maiden. Should be able to win over further next season.

Arajambo

(78) (24)**53**

2-y-o b f Aragon-Jambo (Rambo Dancer (CAN))

J R Weymes John Weymes Racing Club

Placings:04000 **(5633)**

2001: 5^{0}SD, 5^{4}F, 7^{0}GF, 6^{0}G, 7^{0}G

	Starts	1st	2nd	3rd	Win & Pl
Career Total (Turf)	4	0	0	0	
Career Total (AW)	1	0	0	0	

Going (Turf): Sf: 0-0 GS: 0-0 Gd: 0-2 GF: 0-1 Fm: 0-1
Distance: 5f/6f: 0-3 7f-8f: 0-2 9f-13f: 0-0 14f+: 0-0
Track : LH: 0-3 RH: 0-0 Tight: 0-2 Gall: 0-0
Aids: Bl: 0-0 Vi: 0-0 Tstrap: 0-0
Best Rating: 53 7/01 Brig 5f213y firm

Arana

69 (15)

6-y-o b m Noble Patriarch-Pod's Daughter (IRE) (Tender King)

W De Best-Turner The Spanish Connection

Placings:00/0000000/0006000-000 **(5670)**

2001: 14^{0}G, 8^{0}GS, 8^{0}HY

	Starts	1st	2nd	3rd	Win & Pl
Career Total (Turf)	16	0	0	0	144
Career Total (AW)	4	0	0	0	

Going (Turf): Sf: 0-2 GS: 0-5 Gd: 0-4 GF: 0-5 Fm: 0-0
Distance: 5f/6f: 0-3 7f-8f: 0-3 9f-13f: 0-11 14f+: 0-3
Track : LH: 0-9 RH: 0-4 Tight: 0-10 Gall: 0-0
Aids: Bl: 0-4 Vi: 0-0 Tstrap: 0-1
Best Rating: 53 7/01 Brig 5f213y firm

Aranui (IRE)

91(83) (20)**54**

4-y-o b g Pursuit Of Love-Petite Rosanna (Ile De Bourbon (USA))

J Gallagher Horses Away Racing Club

Placings:0/0350-000 **(2625)**

2001: 9^{0}GF, 8^{0}G, 9^{0}GF

	Starts	1st	2nd	3rd	Win & Pl
Career Total (Turf)	6	0	0	0	500
Career Total (AW)	2	0	0	0	

Going (Turf): Sf: 0-0 GS: 0-0 Gd: 0-3 GF: 0-3 Fm: 0-0
Distance: 5f/6f: 0-1 7f-8f: 0-1 9f-13f: 0-6 14f+: 0-0
Track : LH: 0-1 RH: 0-4 Tight: 0-5 Gall: 0-0
Aids: Bl: 0-0 Vi: 0-0 Tstrap: 0-6
Best Rating: 36 6/01 Gdwd 1m1f gd-fm

Aravonian

102 **83**

3-y-o ch f Night Shift (USA)-Age Of Reality (USA) (Alleged (USA))

R Hannon Mrs Perle O'Rourke

Placings:563-0163020250 **(5529)**

2001: 8^{0}GS, 8^{1}G, 10^{6}G, 8^{3}G, 7^{0}G, 8^{2}G, 8^{0}G, 8^{2}GF, 8^{5}G, 8^{0}HY

	Starts	1st	2nd	3rd	Win & Pl
Career Total (Turf)	13	1	2	2	6592

66 5/01 Wwck 1m22y D GD £3045
Total win prize-money £3045

Going (Turf): Sf: 0-4 GS: 0-1 **Gd: 1-7** GF: 0-1 Fm: 0-0
Distance: 5f/6f: 0-0 7f-8f: 0-4 **9f-13f: 1-9** 14f+: 0-0
Track : LH: 0-2 RH: 0-5 Tight: 0-5 Gall: 0-1
Aids: Bl: 0-0 Vi: 0-0 Tstrap: 0-0
Best Rating: 83 8/01 Wind 1m67y gd-fm

Made all to win a maiden at Warwick in May and ran well in ordinary handicaps after that. Suited by a mile, and acts on good ground.

Arawak Prince (IRE)

(101) (51)**50**

5-y-o ch g College Chapel-Alpine Symphony (Northern Dancer)

G Prodromou (D G Bridgwater 5/5) C Karavias

Placings:516/0-304500 **(2731)**

2001: 13^{3}SW, 16^{0}SD, 12^{4}SD, 8^{5}G, 10^{0}F, 14^{0}GF

	Starts	1st	2nd	3rd	Win & Pl
Career Total (Turf)	6	1	0	0	3037
Career Total (AW)	4	0	0	1	315

70 8/99 Wind 1m2f7y D GD £2866
Total win prize-money £2866

Going (Turf): Sf: 0-1 GS: 0-1 **Gd: 1-2** GF: 0-1 Fm: 0-1
Distance: 5f/6f: 0-0 7f-8f: 0-1 **9f-13f: 1-7** 14f+: 0-2
Track : LH: 0-7 RH: 0-1 **Tight: 1-5** Gall: 0-0
Aids: Bl: 0-1 Vi: 0-2 Tstrap: 0-0
Best Rating: 51 2/01 Ling 1m5f slow

Arbenig (IRE)

100(93) (35)**54**

6-y-o b m Anita's Prince-Out On Her Own (Superlative)

B Palling Andrew Smallwood

Placings:5301545/05132653000430/36230026600/03 105204026-232000 **(2874)**

2001: 10^{2}GS, 9^{3}F, 11^{2}GF, 10^{0}GF, 10^{0}GF, 10^{0}GF

	Starts	1st	2nd	3rd	Win & Pl
Career Total (Turf)	41	2	7	6	12514
Career Total (AW)	9	1	0	2	2751

47 6/00 Leic 1m8y F G-S £2016
60 5/98 Sals 6f212y F FRM £2547
77 10/97 Wolv 6f F STD £2070
Total win prize-money £6634

Going (Turf): Sf: 0-3 **GS: 1-6** Gd: 0-10 GF: 0-18 **Fm: 1-4**
Distance: 5f/6f: 1-6 7f-8f: 1-23 9f-13f: 1-21 14f+: 0-0
Track : **LH: 1-19** RH: 0-8 **Tight: 1-23** Gall: 0-2
Aids: Bl: 0-6 Vi: 0-0 Tstrap: 0-0
Best Rating: 54 6/01 Wind 1m3f135y gd-fm

Arbie (CAN)

83 **63**

2-y-o b c Mountain Cat (USA)-Empress Of Love (USA) (Czaravich (USA))

C F Wall Sir Stanley And Lady Grinstead

Placings:000 **(5089)**

2001: 5^{0}G, 7^{0}G, 8^{0}GS

	Starts	1st	2nd	3rd	Win & Pl
Career Total (Turf)	3	0	0	0	

Going (Turf): Sf: 0-0 GS: 0-1 Gd: 0-2 GF: 0-0 Fm: 0-0
Distance: 5f/6f: 0-1 7f-8f: 0-2 9f-13f: 0-0 14f+: 0-0
Track : LH: 0-1 RH: 0-0 Tight: 0-0 Gall: 0-1
Aids: Bl: 0-0 Vi: 0-0 Tstrap: 0-0
Best Rating: 63 8/01 Folk 7f good

Arc (IRE)

106(108) (70)**72**

7-y-o b g Archway (IRE)-Columbian Sand (IRE) (Salmon Leap (USA))

G M Moore Mrs A Roddis

Placings:605/5330060/06066220/32100400226221024/242412010-603251001300100 (5151)
2001: 8[6]SW, 8[0]SD, 8[3]SW, 8[2]SD, 8[5]SW, 9[1]SD, 9[0]SD, 8[0]HY, 8[1]GF, 8[3]G, 8[0]F, 8[0]GF, 9[1]G, 10[0]G, 10[0]G

	Starts	1st	2nd	3rd	Win & Pl
Career Total (Turf)	33	5	5	3	21000
Career Total (AW)	26	2	7	2	14171

72	8/01	Newc	1m1f9y	E(0-70)H	GD	£3094
65	6/01	Muss	1m	E(0-70)	G-F	£4290
70	3/01	Wolv	1m1f79y	D(0-85)H	STD	£3796
68	6/00	Carl	7f214y	E(0-75)H	SFT	£2912
65	4/00	Muss	1m	E(0-75)H	G-S	£3201
61	7/99	Carl	7f214y	F(0-60)	GD	£2542
65	2/99	Wolv	7f	E(0-70)H	STD	£2424

Total win prize-money £22259

Going (Turf): Sf: 1-4 GS: 1-1 **Gd: 2-7** GF: 1-10 Fm: 0-4
Distance: 5f/6f: 0-13 **7f-8f: 5-19** 9f-13f: 2-27 14f+: 0-0
Track : LH: 3-38 **RH: 4-12 Tight: 4-27** Gall: 1-2
Aids: Bl: 0-2 Vi: 0-0 Tstrap: 0-0
Best Rating: 72 8/01 Newc 1m1f9y good

A fair handicapper on turf and sand, he scored at Wolverhampton, Musselburgh and Newcastle this season. Nine furlongs looks his optimum trip.

Arc El Ciel (ARG)

93 **61**

3-y-o b f Fitzcarraldo (ARG)-Ardoise (USA) (Diamond Prospect (USA))
B R Millman Lau Po Man, James & Woo Wai See, Alice

Placings:340 (4842)
2001: 6[3]F, 7[4]GF, 8[0]G

	Starts	1st	2nd	3rd	Win & Pl
Career Total (Turf)	3	0	0	1	884

Going (Turf): Sf: 0-0 GS: 0-0 Gd: 0-1 GF: 0-1 Fm: 0-1
Distance: 5f/6f: 0-0 7f-8f: 0-2 9f-13f: 0-1 14f+: 0-0
Track : LH: 0-2 RH: 0-0 Tight: 0-0 Gall: 0-0
Aids: Bl: 0-0 Vi: 0-0 Tstrap: 0-0
Best Rating: 61 8/01 Sals 6f212y firm

Arc En Ciel

104 **78**

3-y-o b g Rainbow Quest (USA)-Nadia Nerina (CAN) (Northern Dancer)
J L Dunlop Philip Wroughton

Placings:0640-24031100 (4721)
2001: 10[2]GS, 11[4]G, 11[0]G, 11[3]F, 12[1]F, 11[1]GF, 13[0]G, 12[0]G

	Starts	1st	2nd	3rd	Win & Pl
Career Total (Turf)	12	2	1	1	9252

78	8/01	Bath	1m3f144y	E(0-75)H	G-F	£3003
73	7/01	Thsk	1m4f	D(0-80)H	FRM	£4348

Total win prize-money £7352

Going (Turf): Sf: 0-0 GS: 0-2 Gd: 0-5 **GF: 1-3 Fm: 1-2**
Distance: 5f/6f: 0-0 7f-8f: 0-2 **9f-13f: 2-9** 14f+: 0-1
Track : **LH: 2-7** RH: 0-1 **Tight: 2-9** Gall: 0-0
Aids: Bl: 0-0 Vi: 0-1 Tstrap: 0-0
Best Rating: 78 8/01 Bath 1m3f144y gd-fm

Fair handicapper, suited by good to firm ground, stays a mile and a half.

Arcadian Chief

(81)

4-y-o b g Be My Chief (USA)-May Hinton (Main Reef)
B A Pearce J Salter

Placings:06404/05500000000-
2001:

	Starts	1st	2nd	3rd	Win & Pl
Career Total (Turf)	12	0	0	0	0
Career Total (AW)	4	0	0	0	

Going (Turf): Sf: 0-1 GS: 0-1 Gd: 0-3 GF: 0-4 Fm: 0-3
Distance: 5f/6f: 0-10 7f-8f: 0-4 9f-13f: 0-1 14f+: 0-1
Track : LH: 0-8 RH: 0-0 Tight: 0-4 Gall: 0-1
Aids: Bl: 0-1 Vi: 0-0 Tstrap: 0-0
Best Rating: 78 8/01 Bath 1m3f144y gd-fm

Archduke Ferdinand (FR)

109 **104**

3-y-o ch c Dernier Empereur (USA)-Lady Norcliffe (USA) (Norcliffe (CAN))
P F I Cole C Wright & The Hon Mrs J M Corbett

Placings:0155-3630100 (5387)
2001: 10[3]GS, 12[6]GF, 13[3]F, 16[0]GF, 16[1]F, 13[0]G, 18[0]GS

	Starts	1st	2nd	3rd	Win & Pl
Career Total (Turf)	11	2	0	2	97897

104	6/01	Newc	2m19y	B H	FRM	£83578
85	8/00	Gdwd	7f	D	GD	£7020

Total win prize-money £90598

Going (Turf): Sf: 0-0 GS: 0-2 **Gd: 1-3** GF: 0-4 **Fm: 1-2**
Distance: 5f/6f: 0-0 7f-8f: 1-4 9f-13f: 0-2 14f+: 1-5
Track : LH: 1-5 RH: 1-5 Tight: 0-1 **Gall: 1-6**
Aids: Bl: 0-0 Vi: 0-0 Tstrap: 0-0
Best Rating: 104 6/01 Newc 2m19y firm

A big, rangy type, he became only the third three-year-old to win the Northumberland Plate in the last 100 years. Acts on a sound surface. Stays two miles.

Archello (IRE)

(71) **44**

7-y-o b m Archway (IRE)-Golden Room (African Sky)
D W Barker Robert E Cook

Placings:23/33222431006/05050600/000000004000/1000030-00 (3020)
2001: 5[0]GF, 7[0]SD

	Starts	1st	2nd	3rd	Win & Pl
Career Total (Turf)	40	2	4	5	12770
Career Total (AW)	2	0	0	0	

53	5/00	Carl	5f207y	E(0-70)H	FRM	£3029
46	8/97	Ripn	5f	D	G-F	£3452

Total win prize-money £6482

Going (Turf): Sf: 0-3 GS: 0-2 Gd: 0-14 **GF: 1-16 Fm: 1-5**
Distance: **5f/6f: 2-22** 7f-8f: 0-19 9f-13f: 0-1 14f+: 0-0
Track : LH: 0-8 **RH: 1-5** Tight: 0-4 **Gall: 1-3**
Aids: Bl: 0-0 Vi: 0-2 Tstrap: 0-0
Best Rating: 32 6/01 Bevl 5f gd-fm

Archer For Four (USA)

85 **46**

2-y-o b/br g Royal Academy (USA)-Depelchin (USA) (Star De Naskra (USA))
N Tinkler Tim Archer & Gaynor Archer

Placings:000 (4565)
2001: 6[0]G, 6[0]G, 5[0]HY

	Starts	1st	2nd	3rd	Win & Pl
Career Total (Turf)	3	0	0	0	

Going (Turf): Sf: 0-1 GS: 0-0 Gd: 0-2 GF: 0-0 Fm: 0-0
Distance: 5f/6f: 0-3 7f-8f: 0-0 9f-13f: 0-0 14f+: 0-0
Track : LH: 0-1 RH: 0-0 Tight: 0-0 Gall: 0-0
Aids: Bl: 0-0 Vi: 0-0 Tstrap: 0-0
Best Rating: 46 9/01 Hayd 5f heavy

Archie Babe (IRE)

100 **79d**

5-y-o ch g Archway (IRE)-Frensham Manor (Le Johnstan)
J J Quinn Mrs K Mapp

Placings:36010060/051132542531/6501010102500301-000005235 (3714)
2001: 13[0]S, 12[0]S, 12[0]GF, 14[0]GF, 14[0]G, 10[5]G, 11[2]GS, 12[3]GF, 10[5]G

	Starts	1st	2nd	3rd	Win & Pl
Career Total (Turf)	45	8	4	5	39881

79	10/00	Newc	1m2f32y	E(0-75)H	HVY	£2870
80	7/00	Pont	1m2f6y	D(0-75)	GD	£3851
73	6/00	Newc	1m2f32y	E(0-75)H	SFT	£2804
67	5/00	Pont	1m4f8y	E(0-70)H	GD	£3120
66	11/99	Rdcr	1m3f	D(0-80)H	G-S	£4337
61	5/99	Pont	1m2f6y	C(0-90)H	GD	£7824
63	5/99	Rdcr	1m2f	E(0-70)H	SFT	£3218
75	9/98	Thsk	7f	F	GD	£2512

Total win prize-money £30539

Going (Turf): Sf: 3-15 GS: 1-4 **Gd: 4-15** GF: 0-11 Fm: 0-0
Distance: 5f/6f: 0-3 7f-8f: 1-4 **9f-13f: 7-36** 14f+: 0-2
Track : **LH: 8-30** RH: 0-9 **Tight: 3-19** Gall: 2-7
Aids: Bl: 0-0 Vi: 0-0 Tstrap: 0-0
Best Rating: 71 5/01 Hayd 1m6f gd-fm

Did not show his best form this season, he is suited by ten to 12 furlongs on a stiff track and goes well at Pontefract and Newcastle. Likes to get his toe in.

Archirondel

105 **57**

3-y-o b g Bin Ajwaad (IRE)-Penang Rose (NZ) (Kingdom Bay (NZ))
John Berry D J Huelin

Placings:000-016411 (3484)
2001: 8[0]HY, 10[1]GF, 10[6]GF, 9[4]GF, 9[1]GF, 9[1]GF

	Starts	1st	2nd	3rd	Win & Pl
Career Total (Turf)	9	3	0	0	8517

57	7/01	Folk	1m1f149y	E(0-75)H	G-F	£3052
50	7/01	Brig	1m1f209y	F(0-60)H	G-F	£2674
49	6/01	Rdcr	1m2f	F(0-65)H	G-F	£2453

Total win prize-money £8180

Going (Turf): Sf: 0-3 GS: 0-1 Gd: 0-0 **GF: 3-5** Fm: 0-0
Distance: 5f/6f: 0-2 7f-8f: 0-1 **9f-13f: 3-6** 14f+: 0-0
Track : **LH: 2-4** RH: 1-2 **Tight: 2-3** Gall: 0-0
Aids: Bl: 0-0 Vi: 0-0 Tstrap: 0-0
Best Rating: 57 7/01 Folk 1m1f149y gd-fm

A fair handicapper. Won three times in 2001 at around ten furlongs. Suited by strong pace. Acts on fast ground.

Archon (IRE)

95 **65**

4-y-o ch g Archway (IRE)-Lindas Delight (Batshoof)
Mrs P N Dutfield Simon Dutfield

Placings:3030 (4983)
2001: 8[3]G, 8[0]GF, 9[3]GF, 12[0]G

	Starts	1st	2nd	3rd	Win & Pl
Career Total (Turf)	4	0	0	2	1156

Going (Turf): Sf: 0-0 GS: 0-0 Gd: 0-2 GF: 0-2 Fm: 0-0
Distance: 5f/6f: 0-0 7f-8f: 0-1 9f-13f: 0-3 14f+: 0-0
Track : LH: 0-1 RH: 0-2 Tight: 0-0 Gall: 0-1
Aids: Bl: 0-0 Vi: 0-0 Tstrap: 0-4
Best Rating: 65 8/01 Pont 1m4y good

Arctic Falcon (IRE)

96 **73**

2-y-o b f Polar Falcon (USA)-Chandni (IRE) (Ahonoora)

R Hannon Mrs M D Stewart

Placings:4100 **(5340)**
2001: 6^{4}GF, 5^{1}GF, 6^{0}G, 6^{0}GS

	Starts	1st	2nd	3rd	Win & Pl
Career Total (Turf)	4	1	0	0	4639

73 8/01 Ling 5f D G-F £4355
Total win prize-money £4355

Going (Turf): Sf: 0-0 GS: 0-1 Gd: 0-1 **GF: 1-2** Fm: 0-0
Distance: **5f/6f: 1-3** 7f-8f: 0-1 9f-13f: 0-0 14f+: 0-0
Track : LH: 0-0 RH: 0-0 Tight: 0-0 Gall: 0-0
Aids: Bl: 0-0 Vi: 0-0 Tstrap: 0-0
Best Rating: 73 8/01 Ling 5f gd-fm

A half-sister to Irish nine to 12 furlong winner Channoud, is bred to appreciate further in time. Showed good speed to get off the mark over the minimum trip at Lingfield in summer of 2001. Acts on fast ground.

Arctic Fancy (USA)

(94)
8-y-o ch g Arctic Tern (USA)-Fit And Fancy (USA) (Vaguely Noble)
J G Smyth-Osbourne The Cool Customers

Placings:023/3210200/0350030/330201136/622/0 **(0488)**
2001: 12^{0}SD

	Starts	1st	2nd	3rd	Win & Pl
Career Total (Turf)	29	3	6	7	22878
Career Total (AW)	1	0	0	0	

75 10/98 Brig 1m3f196yE(0-80)H SFT £2685
70 9/98 Newb 1m4f5y F(0-70)H GD £2626
73 6/96 Hayd 1m6f D GD £3538
Total win prize-money £8850

Going (Turf): Sf: 1-5 GS: 0-6 **Gd: 2-7** GF: 0-10 Fm: 0-1
Distance: 5f/6f: 0-0 7f-8f: 0-0 **9f-13f: 2-13** 14f+: 1-17
Track : **LH: 3-20** RH: 0-10 Tight: 0-5 **Gall: 1-11**
Aids: Bl: 0-0 Vi: 0-0 Tstrap: 0-0
Best Rating: 49 3/01 Sthl 1m4f stand

Arctic Flight

99 **68**
3-y-o ch f Polar Falcon (USA)-Laugharne (Known Fact (USA))
P W Harris Arctic Circle

Placings:00051 **(4632)**
2001: 8^{0}GF, 8^{0}GF, 8^{0}G, 7^{5}S, 7^{1}GF

	Starts	1st	2nd	3rd	Win & Pl
Career Total (Turf)	5	1	0	0	3535

68 9/01 Leic 7f9y E(0-70)H G-F £3535
Total win prize-money £3535

Going (Turf): Sf: 0-1 GS: 0-0 Gd: 0-1 **GF: 1-3** Fm: 0-0
Distance: 5f/6f: 0-0 **7f-8f: 1-3** 9f-13f: 0-2 14f+: 0-0
Track : LH: 0-1 RH: 0-3 Tight: 0-3 Gall: 0-0
Aids: Bl: 0-0 Vi: 0-0 Tstrap: 0-0
Best Rating: 68 9/01 Leic 7f9y gd-fm

Modest handicapper, suited by firm ground.

Arctic High

(97) (44)**33**
4-y-o b f Polar Falcon (USA)-Oublier L'Ennui (FR) (Bellman (FR))
I A Wood (M S Saunders 27/3) D T Horn

Placings:3230300000-335500 **(5519)**
2001: 9^{3}SW, 8^{3}SD, 9^{5}SD, 8^{5}SD, 9^{0}SD, 6^{0}HY

	Starts	1st	2nd	3rd	Win & Pl
Career Total (Turf)	6	0	0	0	
Career Total (AW)	10	0	1	5	2760

Going (Turf): Sf: 0-2 GS: 0-1 Gd: 0-0 GF: 0-2 Fm: 0-1
Distance: 5f/6f: 0-1 7f-8f: 0-3 9f-13f: 0-12 14f+: 0-0
Track : LH: 0-12 RH: 0-2 Tight: 0-12 Gall: 0-0
Aids: Bl: 0-0 Vi: 0-0 Tstrap: 0-0
Best Rating: 44 1/01 Wolv 1m100y stand

Ardanza (IRE)

68(80) (21)**60**
4-y-o b f Hernando (FR)-Arrastra (Bustino)
T Stack (Miss J Feilden 18/5) Mrs T Stack

Placings:24652-00060 **(4498a)**
2001: 8^{0}SD, 12^{0}SD, 7^{0}G, 10^{6}S, 12^{0}GF

	Starts	1st	2nd	3rd	Win & Pl
Career Total (Turf)	8	0	2	0	2330
Career Total (AW)	2	0	0	0	

Going (Turf): Sf: 0-2 GS: 0-0 Gd: 0-4 GF: 0-2 Fm: 0-0
Distance: 5f/6f: 0-0 7f-8f: 0-4 9f-13f: 0-6 14f+: 0-0
Track : LH: 0-4 RH: 0-3 Tight: 0-2 Gall: 0-1
Aids: Bl: 0-0 Vi: 0-0 Tstrap: 0-0
Best Rating: 30 5/01 NmkR 7f good

Ardent

93(99) (46)**45**
7-y-o b g Aragon-Forest Of Arden (Tap On Wood)
Miss B Sanders R Lamb

Placings:0/500660/**652**10000002352/21001306620**220**
6/**6**4000513**41030-4**00 **(1979)**
2001: 10^{4}SD, 7^{0}F, 9^{0}GF

	Starts	1st	2nd	3rd	Win & Pl
Career Total (Turf)	37	4	3	3	16650
Career Total (AW)	15	1	4	1	5435

46 11/00 Ling 1m2f E(0-70)H STD £2320
45 8/00 Brig 1m1f209yE(0-70)H FRM £2834
49 6/99 Wind 1m67y E(0-70)H G-F £3020
50 5/99 Kemp 1m1f E(0-75)H G-F £3607
54 4/98 Brig 7f214y E(0-70)H GD £2957
Total win prize-money £14739

Going (Turf): Sf: 0-4 GS: 0-4 Gd: 1-9 **GF: 2-15** Fm: 1-5
Distance: 5f/6f: 0-0 7f-8f: 1-20 **9f-13f: 4-32** 14f+: 0-0
Track : **LH: 3-33** RH: 2-13 **Tight: 2-27** Gall: 0-3
Aids: Bl: 0-1 Vi: 0-0 Tstrap: 0-0
Best Rating: 37 2/01 Ling 1m2f stand

Ardgowan

93 **32**
4-y-o b g Ardkinglass-Final Fling (Last Tycoon)
Denys Smith Evelyn Duchess Of Sutherland

Placings:0004000 **(3946)**
2001: 12^{0}S, 12^{0}GS, 16^{0}GF, 11^{4}GF, 9^{0}GS, 10^{0}GS, 9^{0}GS

	Starts	1st	2nd	3rd	Win & Pl
Career Total (Turf)	7	0	0	0	0

Going (Turf): Sf: 0-1 GS: 0-4 Gd: 0-0 GF: 0-2 Fm: 0-0
Distance: 5f/6f: 0-0 7f-8f: 0-0 9f-13f: 0-6 14f+: 0-1
Track : LH: 0-3 RH: 0-3 Tight: 0-5 Gall: 0-0
Aids: Bl: 0-0 Vi: 0-1 Tstrap: 0-0
Best Rating: 41 5/01 Thsk 1m4f gd-sft

Arella Rabbit

(60)
5-y-o b m Presidium-Musical Star (Music Boy)
A Smith Hampston Hillbillies

Placings:060 **(0307)**
2001: 6^{0}SD, 6^{6}SD, 6^{0}SD

	Starts	1st	2nd	3rd	Win & Pl
Career Total (Turf)	0	0	0	0	
Career Total (AW)	3	0	0	0	0

Going (Turf): Sf: 0-0 GS: 0-0 Gd: 0-0 GF: 0-0 Fm: 0-0
Distance: 5f/6f: 0-3 7f-8f: 0-0 9f-13f: 0-0 14f+: 0-0
Track : LH: 0-3 RH: 0-0 Tight: 0-1 Gall: 0-0
Aids: Bl: 0-0 Vi: 0-0 Tstrap: 0-0

Aretino (IRE)

113 **83**
4-y-o ch g Common Grounds-Inonder (Belfort (FR))
P W Harris Mrs A M Palmer

Placings:12203/050500264-00221335 **(4526)**
2001: 6^{0}G, 6^{0}GF, 6^{2}F, 7^{2}GF, 7^{1}GF, 7^{3}GF, 7^{3}GF, 7^{5}GF

	Starts	1st	2nd	3rd	Win & Pl
Career Total (Turf)	22	2	5	3	21978

82 7/01 Epsm 7f D(0-85)H G-F £7247
83 7/99 Pont 6f E G-F £3321
Total win prize-money £10569

Going (Turf): Sf: 0-2 GS: 0-2 Gd: 0-4 **GF: 2-12** Fm: 0-1
Distance: 5f/6f: 1-6 7f-8f: 1-15 9f-13f: 0-0 14f+: 0-0
Track : **LH: 2-5** RH: 0-5 **Tight: 1-3** Gall: 0-2
Aids: Bl: 0-0 Vi: 0-0 Tstrap: 0-0
Best Rating: 83 7/01 Folk 7f gd-fm

Moderate handicapper who picked up a handicap at Epsom in July. Suited by front-running tactics, acts on fast ground and a sharp track.

Argamia (GER)

109(108) (53)**55**
5-y-o b m Orfano (GER)-Arkona (GER) (Aspros (GER))
M G Quinlan P J McBride

Placings:10/56002/5450-**22104**3135**0**50**1**3540 **(5599)**
2001: **11**^{2}SD, **12**^{2}SD, **12**^{1}SD, **16**^{0}SD, 14^{4}HY, **11**^{3}SD, 14^{1}S, 16^{3}S, 13^{5}GF, **14**^{0}SD, 14^{5}G, 16^{0}GF, **14**^{1}SD, 14^{3}HY, 11^{5}S, 16^{4}HY, 12^{0}GS

	Starts	1st	2nd	3rd	Win & Pl
Career Total (Turf)	21	2	1	2	9940
Career Total (AW)	7	2	2	1	4930

53 9/01 Wolv 1m6f166yF(0-60) STD £2317
55 4/01 Nott 1m6f15y D(0-80)H SFT £3818
48 2/01 Wolv 1m4f G(0-60)H STD £1386
7/98 Hopp 7f GD £2027
Total win prize-money £9549

Going (Turf): Sf: 1-10 GS: 0-1 **Gd: 1-4** GF: 0-2 Fm: 0-0
Distance: 5f/6f: 0-0 7f-8f: 1-3 9f-13f: 1-13 **14f+: 2-11**
Track : **LH: 3-15** RH: 0-3 **Tight: 2-7** Gall: 0-3
Aids: Bl: 0-1 Vi: 0-0 Tstrap: 0-0
Best Rating: 55 10/01 Newb 2m heavy

He has won on turf both here and in Germany, but looks especially suited by staying trips on Fibresand.

Argent Facile (IRE)

104 **88**
4-y-o b g Midhish-Rosinish (IRE) (Lomond (USA))
D J S Cosgrove Winning Circle Racing Club Ltd

Placings:56620410/220223055-0640105 **(2799)**
2001: 6^{0}GS, 6^{6}G, 5^{4}GF, 6^{0}GF, 6^{1}GF, 6^{0}GF, 5^{5}GF

	Starts	1st	2nd	3rd	Win & Pl
Career Total (Turf)	24	2	5	1	22985

87 6/01 Wind 6f C(0-90) G-F £6581
87 7/99 Leic 5f2y E H G-F £2882
Total win prize-money £9463

Going (Turf): Sf: 0-3 GS: 0-4 Gd: 0-7 **GF: 2-10** Fm: 0-0
Distance: **5f/6f: 2-24** 7f-8f: 0-0 9f-13f: 0-0 14f+: 0-0
Track : LH: 0-4 RH: 0-1 Tight: 0-1 Gall: 0-1
Aids: Bl: 0-1 Vi: 0-0 **Tstrap: 1-14**
Best Rating: 88 7/01 Sand 5f6y gd-fm

Took advantage of a drop in class to score at Windsor in

June. Six furlongs is his optimum.

Argostoli

76 **40**

2-y-o b f Marju (IRE)-Barque Bleue (USA) (Steinlen)
P C Haslam J Roundtree

Placings:640 **(5370)**
2001: 5^{6}GF, 8^{4}S, 7^{0}G

	Starts	1st	2nd	3rd	Win & Pl
Career Total (Turf)	3	0	0	0	315

Going (Turf): Sf: 0-1 GS: 0-0 Gd: 0-1 GF: 0-1 Fm: 0-0
Distance: 5f/6f: 0-1 7f-8f: 0-1 9f-13f: 0-1 14f+: 0-0
Track : LH: 0-2 RH: 0-0 Tight: 0-1 Gall: 0-0
Aids: Bl: 0-0 Vi: 0-0 Tstrap: 0-0
Best Rating: 40 9/01 Catt 5f212y gd-fm

Argue

(81) (43)**59**

2-y-o b c College Chapel-Cache (Bustino)
N A Callaghan N A Callaghan

Placings:005 **(5410)**
2001: 7^{0}G, 7^{0}GS, 7^{5}SD

	Starts	1st	2nd	3rd	Win & Pl
Career Total (Turf)	2	0	0	0	
Career Total (AW)	1	0	0	0	0

Going (Turf): Sf: 0-0 GS: 0-1 Gd: 0-1 GF: 0-0 Fm: 0-0
Distance: 5f/6f: 0-0 7f-8f: 0-3 9f-13f: 0-0 14f+: 0-0
Track : LH: 0-1 RH: 0-0 Tight: 0-0 Gall: 0-0
Aids: Bl: 0-0 Vi: 0-0 Tstrap: 0-0
Best Rating: 59 10/01 NmkR 7f gd-sft

Arhaaff (IRE)

104 **111**

3-y-o b f Danehill (USA)-Mosaique Bleue (Shirley Heights)
M R Channon Sheikh Ahmed Al Maktoum

Placings:2-262014 **(3413)**
2001: 7^{2}S, 8^{6}G, 9^{2}GF, 10^{0}G, 8^{1}F, 10^{4}GF

	Starts	1st	2nd	3rd	Win & Pl
Career Total (Turf)	7	1	3	0	18984

55	7/01	Newc	1m	D	FRM	£4153

Total win prize-money £4154

Going (Turf): Sf: 0-1 GS: 0-0 Gd: 0-2 GF: 0-3 **Fm: 1-1**
Distance: 5f/6f: 0-1 **7f-8f: 1-3** 9f-13f: 0-3 14f+: 0-0
Track : **LH: 1-2** RH: 0-1 Tight: 0-1 **Gall: 1-1**
Aids: Bl: 0-0 Vi: 0-0 Tstrap: 0-0
Best Rating: 111 6/01 Chan 1m2f110y good

She took on the best early on this season, running well in the 1000 Guineas, Lupe Stakes and Prix de Diane, but scored her only win in a Newcastle maiden.

Ariala

95 **23**

4-y-o b f Arazi (USA)-Kashtala (Lord Gayle (USA))
G L Moore (K R Burke 3/5) Leydens Farm Stud

Placings:600302-00460 **(3734)**
2001: 14^{0}GS, 10^{0}S, 9^{1}S, 11^{6}GF, 11^{0}G

	Starts	1st	2nd	3rd	Win & Pl
Career Total (Turf)	11	0	1	1	995

Going (Turf): Sf: 0-7 GS: 0-2 Gd: 0-1 GF: 0-1 Fm: 0-0
Distance: 5f/6f: 0-0 7f-8f: 0-0 9f-13f: 0-10 14f+: 0-1
Track : LH: 0-3 RH: 0-6 Tight: 0-6 Gall: 0-0
Aids: Bl: 0-0 Vi: 0-0 Tstrap: 0-0

Best Rating: 25 4/01 Muss 1m6f gd-sft

Aristaeus

77(74) (32)**22**

3-y-o b g Mistertopogigo (IRE)-Zealous (Hard Fought)
Mrs Lydia Pearce (J Pearce 23/1) Miss B Garnham

Placings:0-**000**0060 **(1872)**
2001: 7^{0}SD, 9^{0}SW, 10^{0}SD, 8^{0}HY, 9^{0}G, 8^{6}F, 7^{0}F

	Starts	1st	2nd	3rd	Win & Pl
Career Total (Turf)	5	0	0	0	0
Career Total (AW)	3	0	0	0	

Going (Turf): Sf: 0-1 GS: 0-0 Gd: 0-1 GF: 0-0 Fm: 0-3
Distance: 5f/6f: 0-0 7f-8f: 0-3 9f-13f: 0-5 14f+: 0-0
Track : LH: 0-3 RH: 0-1 Tight: 0-2 Gall: 0-0
Aids: Bl: 0-0 Vi: 0-4 Tstrap: 0-0
Best Rating: 32 1/01 Sthl 7f stand

Arizona (IRE)

86 **48**

3-y-o b c Sadler's Wells (USA)-Marie De Beaujeu (FR) (Kenmare (FR))
S Gollings F S W Partnership

Placings:0060 **(4014)**
2001: 8^{0}HY, 7^{0}GF, 10^{6}GF, 15^{0}G

	Starts	1st	2nd	3rd	Win & Pl
Career Total (Turf)	4	0	0	0	0

Going (Turf): Sf: 0-1 GS: 0-0 Gd: 0-1 GF: 0-2 Fm: 0-0
Distance: 5f/6f: 0-0 7f-8f: 0-1 9f-13f: 0-2 14f+: 0-1
Track : LH: 0-3 RH: 0-1 Tight: 0-1 Gall: 0-0
Aids: Bl: 0-0 Vi: 0-0 Tstrap: 0-0
Best Rating: 48 5/01 Bevl 7f100y gd-fm

Arizona Lady

(105) (68)**52**

4-y-o ch f Lion Cavern (USA)-Unfuwaanah (Unfuwain (USA))
I Semple Ian Crawford

Placings:43040/100321500**24032-0**04040003005**0** **(5615)**
2001: 9^{0}SW, 12^{0}GS, 9^{4}GF, 10^{0}GF, 9^{4}GF, 9^{0}GF, 9^{0}F, 9^{0}GF, 11^{3}G, 8^{0}G, 8^{0}GF, 12^{5}SD, 12^{0}SD

	Starts	1st	2nd	3rd	Win & Pl
Career Total (Turf)	24	2	1	3	10549
Career Total (AW)	8	0	2	1	2445

66	7/00	Haml	1m1f36y	E(0-75)H	G-F	£3607
66	4/00	Muss	1m1f	D	G-S	£2758

Total win prize-money £6366

Going (Turf): Sf: 0-2 **GS: 1-4** Gd: 0-5 **GF: 1-10** Fm: 0-3
Distance: 5f/6f: 0-0 7f-8f: 0-7 **9f-13f: 2-25** 14f+: 0-0
Track : LH: 0-14 **RH: 2-12 Tight: 2-19** Gall: 0-1
Aids: Bl: 0-1 Vi: 0-0 Tstrap: 0-0
Best Rating: 61 5/01 Haml 1m1f36y gd-fm

Arjay

103 **81**

3-y-o b g Shaamit (IRE)-Jenny's Call (Petong)
Andrew Turnell Dr John Hollowood

Placings:5021-00054410 **(5207)**
2001: 8^{0}S, 10^{6}GF, 10^{6}GF, 8^{5}GF, 9^{4}G, 7^{4}GF, 7^{1}GF, 6^{0}GS

	Starts	1st	2nd	3rd	Win & Pl
Career Total (Turf)	12	2	1	0	14035

81	9/01	Ayr	7f50y	C(0-90)H	G-F	£8060
82	10/00	Newc	6f	D	HVY	£3334

Total win prize-money £11395

Going (Turf): Sf: 1-2 GS: 0-3 Gd: 0-2 **GF: 1-5** Fm: 0-0
Distance: 5f/6f: 1-2 7f-8f: 1-7 9f-13f: 0-3 14f+: 0-0
Track : LH: 0-5 RH: 0-3 Tight: 0-3 Gall: 0-2
Aids: Bl: 0-0 Vi: 0-0 Tstrap: 0-0
Best Rating: 81 9/01 Ayr 7f50y gd-fm

He got off the mark in heavy ground on his final start at two and a drop in the handicap helped him get back to winning ways on fast ground at Ayr in September. Seven furlongs looks his best trip.

Arjaypear (IRE)

87(81) (55)**39**

2-y-o b g Petardia-Lila Pedigo (IRE) (Classic Secret (USA))
W R Muir (K A Ryan 21/5) T R Pearson

Placings:00200 **(3703)**
2001: 5^{0}GS, 5^{0}GF, 6^{2}SD, 6^{0}GF, 5^{0}G

	Starts	1st	2nd	3rd	Win & Pl
Career Total (Turf)	4	0	0	0	
Career Total (AW)	1	0	1	0	518

Going (Turf): Sf: 0-0 GS: 0-1 Gd: 0-1 GF: 0-2 Fm: 0-0
Distance: 5f/6f: 0-5 7f-8f: 0-0 9f-13f: 0-0 14f+: 0-0
Track : LH: 0-3 RH: 0-0 Tight: 0-0 Gall: 0-0
Aids: Bl: 0-0 Vi: 0-0 Tstrap: 0-0
Best Rating: 55 5/01 Sthl 6f stand

Arkadian Hero (USA)

109 **119**

6-y-o ch h Trempolino (USA)-Careless Kitten (USA) (Caro)
L M Cumani Lindy Regis & M J Dawson

Placings:51114/402400/641130/40416120-56302 **(4560a)**
2001: 8^{5}G, 8^{6}S, 8^{3}G, 7^{0}GF, 8^{2}G

	Starts	1st	2nd	3rd	Win & Pl
Career Total (Turf)	30	7	3	2	317331

119	8/00	Newb	7f64y	A	G-F	£21000
114	7/00	NmkJ	7f	A	G-F	£20300
114	8/99	NmkJ	6f	A	GD	£13393
116	7/99	Newb	6f8y	A	G-F	£15584
99	9/97	Newb	6f8y	A	G-S	£33144
104	8/97	Ripn	6f	A	G-F	£13451
102	7/97	Gdwd	6f	D	G-F	£7067

Total win prize-money £123941

Going (Turf): Sf: 0-3 GS: 1-3 Gd: 1-9 **GF: 5-10** Fm: 0-5
Distance: 5f/6f: 3-15 **7f-8f: 4-14** 9f-13f: 0-1 14f+: 0-0
Track : **LH: 1-4** RH: 0-1 Tight: 0-1 **Gall: 1-2**
Aids: Bl: 0-0 Vi: 0-0 Tstrap: 0-0
Best Rating: 118 6/01 Asct 1m good

Very useful performer. Was very slowly away when running second in Grade One over a mile at Woodbine in 2000. Had earlier landed a pair of Group Threes over seven furlongs in Britain. Needs top of the ground, gets a mile on an easy track, but perhaps not at the very top level. Has been retired to stud.

Arkatme

72(100) (58)**4**

3-y-o b g Then Again-Watheeqah (USA) (Topsider (USA))
T D Barron J Baggott

Placings:465520 **(1170)**
2001: 7^{4}SD, 7^{6}SD, 6^{5}SD, 5^{5}SD, 6^{2}SD, 6^{0}S

	Starts	1st	2nd	3rd	Win & Pl
Career Total (Turf)	1	0	0	0	
Career Total (AW)	5	0	1	0	858

Going (Turf): Sf: 0-1 GS: 0-0 Gd: 0-0 GF: 0-0 Fm: 0-0
Distance: 5f/6f: 0-4 7f-8f: 0-2 9f-13f: 0-0 14f+: 0-0

Track : LH: 0-4 RH: 0-0 Tight: 0-0 Gall: 0-0
Aids: Bl: 0-0 Vi: 0-0 Tstrap: 0-0
Best Rating: 58 4/01 Sthl 6f stand

Armagnac

110 **91**

3-y-o b g Young Ern-Arianna Aldini (Habitat)
M A Buckley C C Buckley

Placings:64042551200-0360210444006 **(5266)**
2001: 6^{0}S, 6^{3}GF, 6^{6}G, 6^{0}GF, 6^{2}GS, 6^{1}G, 6^{0}GS, 6^{4}GF, 5^{4}GS, 6^{4}G, 6^{0}HY, 6^{0}GF, 6^{6}GS

	Starts	1st	2nd	3rd	Win & Pl
Career Total (Turf)	24	2	3	1	35827

91	6/01	Ripn	6f	C(0-95)H	GD £7306
87	9/00	Ayr	6f	E	SFT £3893

Total win prize-money £11200

Going (Turf): Sf: 1-5 GS: 0-5 **Gd: 1-7** GF: 0-7 Fm: 0-0
Distance: **5f/6f: 2-22** 7f-8f: 0-2 9f-13f: 0-0 14f+: 0-0
Track : LH: 0-3 RH: 0-0 Tight: 0-2 Gall: 0-0
Aids: Bl: 0-0 Vi: 0-0 Tstrap: 0-0
Best Rating: 91 6/01 Ripn 6f good

Returned to his best when touched off in the William Hill Trophy at York in June and just got home at Ripon four days later. Decent runs in competitive handicaps since. Goes well with some cut, but acts on good to firm. best at six furlongs.

Armen (FR)

92 **82**

4-y-o b g Kaldoun (FR)-Anna Edes (FR) (Fabulous Dancer (USA))
M C Pipe T M Hely-Hutchinson

Placings:0/220-0 **(1483)**
2001: 17^{0}GF

	Starts	1st	2nd	3rd	Win & Pl
Career Total (Turf)	5	0	2	0	2434

Going (Turf): Sf: 0-1 GS: 0-0 Gd: 0-2 GF: 0-2 Fm: 0-0
Distance: 5f/6f: 0-0 7f-8f: 0-0 9f-13f: 0-2 14f+: 0-3
Track : LH: 0-2 RH: 0-2 Tight: 0-2 Gall: 0-0
Aids: Bl: 0-0 Vi: 0-0 Tstrap: 0-0
Best Rating: 52 5/01 Bath 2m1f34y gd-fm

Armenia (IRE)

(98) (40)**57**

4-y-o ch f Arazi (USA)-Atlantic Flyer (USA) (Storm Bird (CAN))
A G Newcombe Mr A Newby

Placings:5403/**2143200000002060-0** **(0080)**
2001: 11^{0}SD

	Starts	1st	2nd	3rd	Win & Pl
Career Total (Turf)	10	0	1	1	1654
Career Total (AW)	11	1	2	1	4759

65	1/00	Sthl	1m	D	STD £2847

Total win prize-money £2847

Going (Turf): Sf: 0-4 GS: 0-2 Gd: 0-3 GF: 0-0 Fm: 0-0
Distance: 5f/6f: 0-0 **7f-8f: 1-8** 9f-13f: 0-13 14f+: 0-0
Track : **LH: 1-16** RH: 0-2 Tight: 0-10 Gall: 0-1
Aids: Bl: 0-0 Vi: 0-0 Tstrap: 0-0
Best Rating: 19 1/01 Sthl 1m3f stand

Armida

93 **26**

3-y-o b f Lycius (USA)-Ma Petite Cherie (USA) (Caro)
G G Margarson Stableside Racing Partnership 3

Placings:000000-4005055 **(2572)**
2001: 12^{4}S, 9^{0}GS, 6^{0}GF, 8^{5}F, 10^{0}GF, 8^{5}GF, 10^{5}GF

	Starts	1st	2nd	3rd	Win & Pl
Career Total (Turf)	13	0	0	0	0

Going (Turf): Sf: 0-2 GS: 0-2 Gd: 0-0 GF: 0-8 Fm: 0-1
Distance: 5f/6f: 0-4 7f-8f: 0-3 9f-13f: 0-6 14f+: 0-0
Track : LH: 0-4 RH: 0-2 Tight: 0-1 Gall: 0-3
Aids: Bl: 0-2 Vi: 0-0 Tstrap: 0-5
Best Rating: 26 6/01 NmkJ 1m gd-fm

Arms Acrossthesea

(91) (63)**66**

2-y-o b g Namaqualand (USA)-Zolica (Beveled (USA))
R A Fahey Clayton Bigley Partnership Ltd

Placings:0313443500 **(5195)**
2001: 5^{0}S, 5^{3}GF, 6^{1}F, 6^{3}GF, 7^{4}GF, 7^{4}F, 7^{3}SD, 7^{5}GS, 7^{0}GF, 6^{0}SD

	Starts	1st	2nd	3rd	Win & Pl
Career Total (Turf)	8	1	0	2	4422
Career Total (AW)	2	0	0	1	403

66	5/01	Newc	6f	F	FRM £2604

Total win prize-money £2604

Going (Turf): Sf: 0-1 GS: 0-1 Gd: 0-0 GF: 0-4 **Fm: 1-2**
Distance: **5f/6f: 1-5** 7f-8f: 0-5 9f-13f: 0-0 14f+: 0-0
Track : LH: 0-3 RH: 0-1 Tight: 0-2 Gall: 0-0
Aids: Bl: 0-0 Vi: 0-2 Tstrap: 0-0
Best Rating: 66 7/01 Pont 6f gd-fm

Modest sprinter. Suited by a firm surface.

Arnbi Dancer

80 **52**

2-y-o b g Presidium-Travel Myth (Bairn (USA))
P C Haslam Brian Pearson

Placings:000 **(4064)**
2001: 5^{0}GF, 5^{0}GF, 6^{0}G

	Starts	1st	2nd	3rd	Win & Pl
Career Total (Turf)	3	0	0	0	

Going (Turf): Sf: 0-0 GS: 0-0 Gd: 0-1 GF: 0-2 Fm: 0-0
Distance: 5f/6f: 0-3 7f-8f: 0-0 9f-13f: 0-0 14f+: 0-0
Track : LH: 0-0 RH: 0-0 Tight: 0-0 Gall: 0-0
Aids: Bl: 0-0 Vi: 0-0 Tstrap: 0-0
Best Rating: 52 8/01 Ripn 6f good

Arniston Lover

85 **22**

3-y-o ch g Tigani-Chelwood (Kala Shikari)
B Ellison Mrs Cheryl L Owen

Placings:00 **(4600)**
2001: 5^{0}GF, 6^{0}GF

	Starts	1st	2nd	3rd	Win & Pl
Career Total (Turf)	2	0	0	0	

Going (Turf): Sf: 0-0 GS: 0-0 Gd: 0-0 GF: 0-2 Fm: 0-0
Distance: 5f/6f: 0-2 7f-8f: 0-0 9f-13f: 0-0 14f+: 0-0
Track : LH: 0-1 RH: 0-0 Tight: 0-1 Gall: 0-0
Aids: Bl: 0-0 Vi: 0-0 Tstrap: 0-0
Best Rating: 21 9/01 Thsk 6f gd-fm

Arogant Prince

102(89) (38)**51**

4-y-o ch g Aragon-Versaillesprincess (Legend Of France (USA))
B W Hills (J J Bridger 15/6) Mrs B W Hills

Placings:30460/04316000403000-**0060**5300324000300 **(4543)**
2001: 5^{0}SD, 5^{0}SD, 5^{6}SW, 6^{0}SW, 5^{5}GS, 5^{3}HY, 5^{0}GS, 5^{0}GF, 5^{3}G, 5^{2}F, 7^{4}GF, 6^{0}G, 5^{0}GF, 6^{0}G, 6^{3}GF, 6^{0}GF, 5^{0}GF

	Starts	1st	2nd	3rd	Win & Pl
Career Total (Turf)	32	1	1	6	11800
Career Total (AW)	4	0	0	0	

64	5/00	Wind	5f10y	D(0-85)H	G-S £7592

Total win prize-money £7592

Going (Turf): Sf: 0-2 **GS: 1-5** Gd: 0-8 GF: 0-13 Fm: 0-4
Distance: **5f/6f: 1-32** 7f-8f: 0-4 9f-13f: 0-0 14f+: 0-0
Track : LH: 0-12 **RH: 1-5** Tight: 0-5 **Gall: 1-5**
Aids: Bl: 0-1 Vi: 0-0 Tstrap: 0-0
Best Rating: 56 7/01 Brig 5f59y firm

Arona (IRE)

83 **46**

3-y-o b f Spectrum (IRE)-Divine Valse (FR) (Groom Dancer (USA))
J G Given Mr & Mrs G Middlebrook

Placings:0050-006 **(2101)**
2001: 11^{0}GF, 14^{0}F, 11^{6}GF

	Starts	1st	2nd	3rd	Win & Pl
Career Total (Turf)	7	0	0	0	0

Going (Turf): Sf: 0-3 GS: 0-1 Gd: 0-0 GF: 0-2 Fm: 0-1
Distance: 5f/6f: 0-1 7f-8f: 0-3 9f-13f: 0-2 14f+: 0-1
Track : LH: 0-1 RH: 0-2 Tight: 0-3 Gall: 0-0
Aids: Bl: 0-1 Vi: 0-0 Tstrap: 0-0
Best Rating: 33 6/01 Haml 1m3f16y gd-fm

Arpeggio

106(104) (76)**79**

6-y-o b g Polar Falcon (USA)-Hilly (Town Crier)
D Nicholls H E Lhendup Dorji

Placings:224/30040/1000/000410313000-5150006266613003 **(5344)**
2001: 8^{5}SD, 7^{1}SD, 7^{5}SW, 7^{0}SW, 8^{0}SD, 9^{0}S, 7^{6}SD, 8^{2}SD, 10^{6}G, 10^{6}GF, 8^{6}G, 8^{1}GS, 8^{3}GS, 8^{0}G, 8^{0}GS, 8^{3}GS

	Starts	1st	2nd	3rd	Win & Pl
Career Total (Turf)	32	4	2	5	30180
Career Total (AW)	8	1	1	0	4711

76	7/01	NmkJ	1m	D(0-80)H	G-S £8502
76	1/01	Sthl	7f	D(0-85)H	STD £3844
74	9/00	Ling	7f140y	D(0-80)H	G-F £7605
64	7/00	Catt	7f	E(0-65)	G-F £2769
72	5/99	Thsk	6f	D	SFT £3535

Total win prize-money £26256

Going (Turf): Sf: 1-5 GS: 1-7 Gd: 0-11 **GF: 2-8** Fm: 0-1
Distance: 5f/6f: 1-8 **7f-8f: 4-26** 9f-13f: 0-6 14f+: 0-0
Track : **LH: 2-17** RH: 0-3 **Tight: 1-5** Gall: 0-2
Aids: Bl: 0-1 Vi: 0-0 Tstrap: 0-0
Best Rating: 79 7/01 Ayr 1m gd-sft

A useful handicapper who stays a mile plus, he is effective on the All-Weather but has been a bit excitable in the past. Acts on any going on turf. Needs a fast pace to help him settle.

Arpello

(107) (55)

4-y-o b f Unfuwain (USA)-Arpero (Persian Bold)
Sir Mark Prescott Hesmonds Stud

Placings:000/5112 **(0361)**
2001: 9^{5}SW, 12^{1}SW, 11^{1}SD, 14^{2}SW

	Starts	1st	2nd	3rd	Win & Pl
Career Total (Turf)	0	0	0	0	
Career Total (AW)	7	2	1	0	4383

54	2/01	Sthl	1m3f	F(0-65)H	STD £1771
46	2/01	Wolv	1m4f	F(0-60)H	SLW £1764

Total win prize-money £3535

Going (Turf): Sf: 0-0 GS: 0-0 Gd: 0-0 GF: 0-0 Fm: 0-0
Distance: 5f/6f: 0-2 7f-8f: 0-1 **9f-13f: 2-3** 14f+: 0-1
Track : **LH: 2-7** RH: 0-0 **Tight: 1-5** Gall: 0-0

Aids: Bl: 0-0 Vi: 0-0 Tstrap: 0-0
Best Rating: 54 2/01 Sthl 1m6f slow

Arran Mist

(92) (37)**40**

3-y-o b f Alhijaz-Saraswati (Mansingh (USA))
D W Barker L H Gilmurray & T J Docherty

Placings:03060-000005205 **(5186)**
2001: 6^{0}GF, 6^{0}F, 6^{0}GF, 6^{0}SD, 5^{0}G, 5^{5}G, 5^{2}S, 5^{0}G, 5^{5}GS

	Starts	1st	2nd	3rd	Win & Pl
Career Total (Turf)	13	0	1	1	1205
Career Total (AW)	1	0	0	0	

Going (Turf): Sf: 0-1 GS: 0-2 Gd: 0-5 GF: 0-4 Fm: 0-1
Distance: 5f/6f: 0-14 7f-8f: 0-0 9f-13f: 0-0 14f+: 0-0
Track: LH: 0-2 RH: 0-0 Tight: 0-1 Gall: 0-0
Aids: Bl: 0-0 Vi: 0-0 Tstrap: 0-0
Best Rating: 47 5/01 Ripn 6f gd-fm

Still a maiden and improvement needed to win a race.

Arribilo (GER)

98(95) (68)**46**

7-y-o b g Top Ville-Arborea (GER) (Priamos (GER))
G M McCourt P J Dixon

Placings:160454/16046/11001566624 0/60260021-60004660000 **(4727)**
2001: 12^{6}SD, 7^{0}GS, 10^{0}GF, 12^{0}F, 11^{4}F, 8^{6}G, 10^{6}G, 10^{0}GF, 12^{0}GF, 16^{0}GF, 10^{0}GF

	Starts	1st	2nd	3rd	Win & Pl
Career Total (Turf)	41	6	3	0	25144
Career Total (AW)	1	0	0	0	0

9/00 Hanv 1m2f SFT £3774
6/99 Brem 1m2f110y H GD £5306
5/99 Colo 1m1f55y H GD £4332
4/99 Gels 1m2f H HVY £2727
Total win prize-money £20134

Going (Turf): Sf: 2-5 GS: 0-1 **Gd: 2-11** GF: 0-5 Fm: 0-2
Distance: 5f/6f: 0-0 7f-8f: 0-1 **9f-13f: 6-34** 14f+: 0-1
Track: LH: 0-8 RH: 0-1 Tight: 0-7 Gall: 0-0
Aids: Bl: 0-1 Vi: 0-0 Tstrap: 0-0
Best Rating: 68 5/01 Ches 1m2f75y gd-fm

Arrive

114 **101+**

3-y-o b f Kahyasi-Kerali (High Line)
R Charlton K Abdulla

Placings:12110 **(3763a)**
2001: 9^{1}S, 11^{2}GF, 12^{1}GF, 14^{1}G, 13^{0}S

	Starts	1st	2nd	3rd	Win & Pl
Career Total (Turf)	5	3	1	0	34105

101 7/01 NmkJ 1m6f175yA GD £15312
96 6/01 Sals 1m4f C(0-95)H G-F £13624
76 5/01 Sals 1m1f198yD SFT £3055
Total win prize-money £31991

Going (Turf): Sf: 1-2 GS: 0-0 **Gd: 1-1 GF: 1-2** Fm: 0-0
Distance: 5f/6f: 0-0 7f-8f: 0-0 **9f-13f: 2-3** 14f+: 1-2
Track: LH: 0-0 **RH: 3-3 Tight: 2-3** Gall: 1-1
Aids: Bl: 0-0 Vi: 0-0 Tstrap: 0-0
Best Rating: 101 7/01 NmkJ 1m6f175y good

Big filly with plenty of scope, broke the course record when landing. Acts on good to firm and good to soft ground. Progressive.

Art Expert (FR)

(94) (56)**52**

3-y-o b g Pursuit Of Love-Celtic Wing (Midyan (USA))
Mrs N Macauley (P F I Cole 7/7) Classic Glass & Dishwashing Systems Ltd

Placings:0225-05535355526 **(5348)**
2001: 8^{0}HY, 8^{5}SD, 10^{5}GF, 10^{3}GF, 9^{5}G, 12^{3}GF, 18^{5}GF, 16^{5}G, 9^{5}GF, 14^{2}SD, 12^{6}SD

	Starts	1st	2nd	3rd	Win & Pl
Career Total (Turf)	12	0	2	2	3767
Career Total (AW)	3	0	1	0	576

Going (Turf): Sf: 0-4 GS: 0-1 Gd: 0-2 GF: 0-5 Fm: 0-0
Distance: 5f/6f: 0-0 7f-8f: 0-4 9f-13f: 0-8 14f+: 0-3
Track: LH: 0-13 RH: 0-1 Tight: 0-0 Gall: 0-2
Aids: Bl: 0-2 Vi: 0-3 Tstrap: 0-0
Best Rating: 58 5/01 Wwck 1m2f188y gd-fm

Looks a hard ride, but has a little bit of ability and could nick a small race.

Artful Dane (IRE)

94(99) (56)**34**

9-y-o b g Danehill (USA)-Art Age (Artaius (USA))
C G Cox S P Lansdown Racing

Placings:325/2031006/0400010001536/1050200004/00 000000/540020004/050300110440-060050 **(4672)**
2001: 8^{0}GF, 8^{6}GF, 8^{0}G, 8^{0}S, 8^{5}GF, 8^{0}G

	Starts	1st	2nd	3rd	Win & Pl
Career Total (Turf)	64	6	4	4	61571
Career Total (AW)	4	0	0	0	0

52 9/00 Chep 1m14y F G-S £2359
43 8/00 Ripn 1m F GD £2632
79 3/97 Donc 1m B H G-F £15790
72 9/96 Newb 1m7y C(0-100)H G-F £17750
66 8/96 Bath 1m5y D(0-75)H G-F £4276
74 7/95 Wind 1m67y D G-F £4377
Total win prize-money £47184

Going (Turf): Sf: 0-8 GS: 1-8 Gd: 1-21 **GF: 4-23** Fm: 0-4
Distance: 5f/6f: 0-3 7f-8f: 2-29 **9f-13f: 4-36** 14f+: 0-0
Track: LH: 2-24 RH: 2-15 **Tight: 3-19** Gall: 1-8
Aids: Bl: 2-20 Vi: 2-25 Tstrap: 0-0
Best Rating: 34 8/01 Ripn 1m gd-fm

Arthur Symons

(44) **26**

3-y-o b g River Falls-Anchor Inn (Be My Guest (USA))
J M Jefferson Mrs Jean Key

Placings:0000 **(5046)**
2001: 5^{0}GF, 8^{0}G, 5^{0}GF, 11^{0}SD

	Starts	1st	2nd	3rd	Win & Pl
Career Total (Turf)	3	0	0	0	
Career Total (AW)	1	0	0	0	

Going (Turf): Sf: 0-0 GS: 0-0 Gd: 0-1 GF: 0-2 Fm: 0-0
Distance: 5f/6f: 0-2 7f-8f: 0-0 9f-13f: 0-2 14f+: 0-0
Track: LH: 0-2 RH: 0-1 Tight: 0-2 Gall: 0-0
Aids: Bl: 0-0 Vi: 0-0 Tstrap: 0-0
Best Rating: 26 8/01 Wind 1m67y good

Arthurs Kingdom (IRE)

84 (61)**56**

5-y-o b g Roi Danzig (USA)-Merrie Moment (IRE) (Taufan (USA))
Miss Kate Milligan Dr Roy Palmer

Placings:0053/203006/0304463-50 **(2815)**
2001: 14^{5}GF, 16^{0}GF

	Starts	1st	2nd	3rd	Win & Pl
Career Total (Turf)	17	0	0	4	2661
Career Total (AW)	2	0	1	0	616

Going (Turf): Sf: 0-1 GS: 0-1 Gd: 0-10 GF: 0-5 Fm: 0-0
Distance: 5f/6f: 0-0 7f-8f: 0-4 9f-13f: 0-11 14f+: 0-4
Track: LH: 0-8 RH: 0-8 Tight: 0-9 Gall: 0-0
Aids: Bl: 0-0 Vi: 0-2 Tstrap: 0-0
Best Rating: 42 5/01 Muss 1m6f gd-fm

Artie

98 **79**

2-y-o b c Whittingham (IRE)-Calamanco (Clantime)
T D Easterby A Arton

Placings:2120 **(4695)**
2001: 5^{2}S, 5^{1}GF, 5^{2}F, 6^{0}GS

	Starts	1st	2nd	3rd	Win & Pl
Career Total (Turf)	4	1	2	0	10437

74 5/01 Ches 5f16y D G-F £7247
Total win prize-money £7248

Going (Turf): Sf: 0-1 GS: 0-1 Gd: 0-0 **GF: 1-1** Fm: 0-1
Distance: 5f/6f: 1-4 7f-8f: 0-0 9f-13f: 0-0 14f+: 0-0
Track: LH: 1-1 RH: 0-0 **Tight: 1-1** Gall: 0-0
Aids: Bl: 0-0 Vi: 0-0 Tstrap: 0-0
Best Rating: 79 9/01 Muss 5f firm

Bred to be a sprinter, he showed plenty of promise on his debut. Proved effective on fast ground when scoring next time.

Artifact

(100) (65)**35**

3-y-o b f So Factual (USA)-Ancient Secret (Warrshan (USA))
J A Pickering S Kitching

Placings:300063-2116000005643 **(5611)**
2001: 7^{2}SD, 6^{1}SD, 6^{1}SW, 7^{6}SD, 8^{0}GS, 9^{0}G, 8^{0}HY, 6^{0}G, 8^{0}GS, 7^{5}SD, 9^{6}SD, 8^{4}SD, 8^{3}SD

	Starts	1st	2nd	3rd	Win & Pl
Career Total (Turf)	9	0	0	1	450
Career Total (AW)	10	2	1	2	5863

64 1/01 Wolv 6f F(0-65)H SLW £2191
58 1/01 Sthl 6f F(0-65)H STD £2247
Total win prize-money £4438

Going (Turf): Sf: 0-3 GS: 0-2 Gd: 0-2 GF: 0-2 Fm: 0-0
Distance: 5f/6f: 2-4 7f-8f: 0-9 9f-13f: 0-0 14f+: 0-0
Track: LH: 2-12 RH: 0-1 **Tight: 1-5** Gall: 0-1
Aids: Bl: 0-0 Vi: 0-0 Tstrap: 0-0
Best Rating: 64 1/01 Wolv 6f slow

Twice a winner on Fibresand, she is at her best over trips short of a mile.

Artifice

105 **77**

3-y-o b f Green Desert (USA)-Reuval (Sharpen Up)
J R Fanshawe Dr Catherine Wills

Placings:3222140 **(5138)**
2001: 7^{3}GF, 6^{2}GF, 8^{2}F, 6^{2}GF, 6^{1}GF, 6^{4}GF, 6^{0}G

	Starts	1st	2nd	3rd	Win & Pl
Career Total (Turf)	7	1	3	1	9550

52 9/01 Thsk 6f D G-F £4914
Total win prize-money £4914

Going (Turf): Sf: 0-0 GS: 0-0 Gd: 0-1 **GF: 1-5** Fm: 0-1
Distance: 5f/6f: 1-4 7f-8f: 0-3 9f-13f: 0-0 14f+: 0-0
Track: LH: 0-1 RH: 0-0 Tight: 0-1 Gall: 0-0
Aids: Bl: 0-0 Vi: 0-0 Tstrap: 0-0
Best Rating: 79 6/01 Yarm 7f3y gd-fm

Artillery (IRE)

103 **105+**

3-y-o b c Darshaan-Alimana (Akarad (FR))
Sir Michael Stoute Sheikh Mohammed

Placings:31013 **(4549)**
2001: 10^{3}GF, 11^{1}GF, 16^{0}GF, 13^{1}G, 14^{3}GF

	Starts	1st	2nd	3rd	Win & Pl
Career Total (Turf)	5	2	0	2	29943

105 8/01 York 1m5f194yB(0-100)H GD £23949
75 6/01 Leic 1m3f183yD G-F £4273
Total win prize-money £28223

Going (Turf): Sf: 0-0 GS: 0-0 **Gd: 1-1 GF: 1-4** Fm: 0-0
Distance: 5f/6f: 0-0 7f-8f: 0-0 9f-13f: 1-2 14f+: 1-3
Track : LH: 1-2 RH: 1-3 Tight: 0-2 **Gall: 1-2**
Aids: Bl: 0-0 Vi: 0-0 Tstrap: 0-0
Best Rating: 105 8/01 York 1m5f194y good

Bred to stay. He won a Leicester maidenover a mile and a half, and at York over a mile and six. Acts on fast ground. Could make a Cup horse next year.

Artists Retreat

85 **62**
2-y-o ch f Halling (USA)-Jumairah Sunset (Be My Guest (USA))
D J S Ffrench Davis Badgers Holt 2

Placings:0400 **(4985)**
2001: 5^0GS, 6^4GF, 6^0G, 6^0G

	Starts	1st	2nd	3rd	Win & Pl
Career Total (Turf)	4	0	0	0	324

Going (Turf): Sf: 0-0 GS: 0-1 Gd: 0-2 GF: 0-1 Fm: 0-0
Distance: 5f/6f: 0-3 7f-8f: 0-1 9f-13f: 0-0 14f+: 0-0
Track : LH: 0-0 RH: 0-0 Tight: 0-0 Gall: 0-0
Aids: Bl: 0-0 Vi: 0-0 Tstrap: 0-0
Best Rating: 62 6/01 Gdwd 6f gd-fm

Arzamas

82
2-y-o b f Cadeaux Genereux-Belle Argentine (FR) (Fijar Tango (FR))
M P Tregoning Sheikh Ahmed Al Maktoum

Placings:2 **(3303)**
2001: 6^2GF

	Starts	1st	2nd	3rd	Win & Pl
Career Total (Turf)	1	0	1	0	1135

Going (Turf): Sf: 0-0 GS: 0-0 Gd: 0-0 GF: 0-1 Fm: 0-0
Distance: 5f/6f: 0-1 7f-8f: 0-0 9f-13f: 0-0 14f+: 0-0
Track : LH: 0-0 RH: 0-0 Tight: 0-0 Gall: 0-0
Aids: Bl: 0-0 Vi: 0-0 Tstrap: 0-0
Best Rating: 82 7/01 Wind 6f gd-fm

Arzillo

92(101) (51)**56**
5-y-o b g Forzando-Titania's Dance (IRE) (Fairy King (USA))
J M Bradley M G Ridley & Partners

Placings:000/040030/0340403050026**000230243-46000** **(4386)**
2001: 7^4SW, 6^6SW, 7^0SD, 8^0S, 6^0GF

	Starts	1st	2nd	3rd	Win & Pl
Career Total (Turf)	24	0	1	3	2136
Career Total (AW)	12	0	2	2	2064

Going (Turf): Sf: 0-3 GS: 0-1 Gd: 0-5 GF: 0-12 Fm: 0-3
Distance: 5f/6f: 0-10 7f-8f: 0-19 9f-13f: 0-7 14f+: 0-0
Track : LH: 0-17 RH: 0-5 Tight: 0-15 Gall: 0-2
Aids: Bl: 0-2 Vi: 0-0 Tstrap: 0-0
Best Rating: 40 1/01 Wolv 6f slow

As Good As It Gets

82 **35**
3-y-o b f Alhijaz-Iota (Niniski (USA))
C Smith Mrs Jennie M Raymond

Placings:0-000 **(4858)**
2001: 10^0GS, 9^0GF, 15^0GF

	Starts	1st	2nd	3rd	Win & Pl
Career Total (Turf)	4	0	0	0	

Going (Turf): Sf: 0-1 GS: 0-1 Gd: 0-0 GF: 0-2 Fm: 0-0
Distance: 5f/6f: 0-0 7f-8f: 0-1 9f-13f: 0-2 14f+: 0-1
Track : LH: 0-3 RH: 0-1 Tight: 0-1 Gall: 0-1
Aids: Bl: 0-0 Vi: 0-0 Tstrap: 0-0
Best Rating: 35 5/01 Bevl 1m1f207y gd-fm

As Time Goes By

66(79) (39)**21**
3-y-o ch g Timeless Times (USA)-Parfait Amour (Clantime)
B S Rothwell Brian Rothwell

Placings:00-03 **(0581)**
2001: 7^0SD, 8^3HY

	Starts	1st	2nd	3rd	Win & Pl
Career Total (Turf)	1	0	0	1	272
Career Total (AW)	3	0	0	0	

Going (Turf): Sf: 0-1 GS: 0-0 Gd: 0-0 GF: 0-0 Fm: 0-0
Distance: 5f/6f: 0-0 7f-8f: 0-3 9f-13f: 0-1 14f+: 0-0
Track : LH: 0-4 RH: 0-0 Tight: 0-1 Gall: 0-0
Aids: Bl: 0-0 Vi: 0-0 Tstrap: 0-0
Best Rating: 21 3/01 Nott 1m54y heavy

Asareer (USA)

98 **75**
3-y-o b f Gone West (USA)-Leo's Lucky Lady (USA) (Seattle Slew (USA))
M P Tregoning Hamdan Al Maktoum

Placings:0-05 **(2438)**
2001: 10^0GF, 8^5G

	Starts	1st	2nd	3rd	Win & Pl
Career Total (Turf)	3	0	0	0	0

Going (Turf): Sf: 0-0 GS: 0-0 Gd: 0-2 GF: 0-1 Fm: 0-0
Distance: 5f/6f: 0-0 7f-8f: 0-1 9f-13f: 0-2 14f+: 0-0
Track : LH: 0-1 RH: 0-0 Tight: 0-0 Gall: 0-1
Aids: Bl: 0-0 Vi: 0-0 Tstrap: 0-0
Best Rating: 70 6/01 NmkR 1m2f gd-fm

Aseelah

95 **67**
2-y-o b f Nashwan (USA)-Mawhiba (USA) (Dayjur (USA))
J L Dunlop Hamdan Al Maktoum

Placings:03 **(5620)**
2001: 7^0G, 8^3GS

	Starts	1st	2nd	3rd	Win & Pl
Career Total (Turf)	2	0	0	1	573

Going (Turf): Sf: 0-0 GS: 0-1 Gd: 0-1 GF: 0-0 Fm: 0-0
Distance: 5f/6f: 0-0 7f-8f: 0-1 9f-13f: 0-1 14f+: 0-0
Track : LH: 0-1 RH: 0-0 Tight: 0-0 Gall: 0-0
Aids: Bl: 0-0 Vi: 0-0 Tstrap: 0-0
Best Rating: 67 11/01 Nott 1m54y gd-sft

She finished third in a Nottingham maiden on her second start, but looked very one-paced.

Ash

85 **51**
3-y-o b f Salse (USA)-Thundercloud (Electric)
L M Cumani L Marinopoulos

Placings:0-00000 **(4371)**
2001: 7^0S, 7^0GS, 16^0GF, 14^0GS, 11^0GF

	Starts	1st	2nd	3rd	Win & Pl
Career Total (Turf)	6	0	0	0	

Going (Turf): Sf: 0-2 GS: 0-2 Gd: 0-0 GF: 0-2 Fm: 0-0
Distance: 5f/6f: 0-1 7f-8f: 0-2 9f-13f: 0-1 14f+: 0-2
Track : LH: 0-2 RH: 0-1 Tight: 0-3 Gall: 0-0
Aids: Bl: 0-1 Vi: 0-0 Tstrap: 0-0
Best Rating: 51 8/01 Yarm 1m6f17y gd-sft

Ran in sprint maidens before stepping up to two miles for her first handicap. That trip looked too far.

Ash Hab (USA)

100 **65**
3-y-o b c A.P. Indy (USA)-Histoire (FR) (Riverman (USA))
Luke Comer (J L Dunlop 7/7) Brian Comer

Placings:000-0013000 **(3796a)**
2001: 11^0GS, 14^0GF, 16^1F, 16^3GF, 12^0GY, 12^0GY, 8^0GY

	Starts	1st	2nd	3rd	Win & Pl
Career Total (Turf)	10	1	0	1	3368

63 6/01 Thsk 2m F(0-60)H FRM £2660
Total win prize-money £2660

Going (Turf): Sf: 0-0 GS: 0-1 Gd: 0-1 GF: 0-4 **Fm: 1-1**
Distance: 5f/6f: 0-0 7f-8f: 0-3 9f-13f: 0-4 **14f+: 1-3**
Track : **LH: 1-2** RH: 0-3 **Tight: 1-4** Gall: 0-2
Aids: **Bl: 1-3** Vi: 0-0 Tstrap: 0-0
Best Rating: 65 7/01 Bevl 2m35y gd-fm

A half-brother to several winners, most notably the 1994 Derby and Dante winner, Erhaab, this colt appreciated the step up in trip and the drop in class to win a weak race in June. He is suited by firm ground.

Ash Moon (IRE)

(101) (85)**91**
3-y-o ch f General Monash (USA)-Jarmar Moon (Unfuwain (USA))
K R Burke David H Morgan

Placings:1103020-0050020000 **(5688)**
2001: 7^0GS, 6^0G, 6^5GF, 6^0GF, 6^0SD, 7^2S, 7^0HY, 7^0G, 6^0GS, 7^0S

	Starts	1st	2nd	3rd	Win & Pl
Career Total (Turf)	16	2	2	1	17603
Career Total (AW)	1	0	0	0	

72 6/00 Carl 5f207y E FRM £3542
75 5/00 Hayd 5f D SFT £4212
Total win prize-money £7755

Going (Turf): Sf: 1-6 GS: 0-2 Gd: 0-4 GF: 0-3 **Fm: 1-1**
Distance: **5f/6f: 2-12** 7f-8f: 0-5 9f-13f: 0-0 14f+: 0-0
Track : LH: 0-1 **RH: 1-1** Tight: 0-0 **Gall: 1-1**
Aids: Bl: 0-1 Vi: 0-0 Tstrap: 0-0
Best Rating: 92 6/01 Hayd 6f gd-fm

A winner of some ordinary events in the spring of 2000, she has struggled since taking on better company. Decent run at Yarmouth in September and over ten furlongs on the Lingfield Polytrack in November. Has won on good and good to soft.

Asha'Th

97 **83**
2-y-o b c Barathea (IRE)-Elrayahin (Riverman (USA))
M P Tregoning Hamdan Al Maktoum

Placings:03204 **(5080)**
2001: 6^0GF, 7^3G, 7^2GF, 8^0G, 6^4S
Starts 1st 2nd 3rd Win & Pl

Career Total (Turf) 5 0 1 1 1737

Going (Turf): Sf: 0-1 GS: 0-0 Gd: 0-2 GF: 0-2 Fm: 0-0
Distance: 5f/6f: 0-0 7f-8f: 0-4 9f-13f: 0-1 14f+: 0-0
Track : LH: 0-1 RH: 0-0 Tight: 0-0 Gall: 0-0
Aids: Bl: 0-0 Vi: 0-0 Tstrap: 0-0
Best Rating: 83 8/01 Newc 7f gd-fm

Ashaka (IRE)

102 **53+**

3-y-o b f Mujtahid (USA)-Ashkara (IRE) (Chief Singer)
Sir Michael Stoute H H Aga Khan

Placings:510 (4318)
2001: 8⁵F, 8¹G, 10⁰G

	Starts	1st	2nd	3rd	Win & Pl
Career Total (Turf)	3	1	0	0	4173
51 7/01 Haml 1m65y D				GD	£4173
					Total win prize-money £4173

Going (Turf): Sf: 0-0 GS: 0-0 **Gd: 1-2** GF: 0-0 Fm: 0-1
Distance: 5f/6f: 0-0 7f-8f: 0-0 **9f-13f: 1-3** 14f+: 0-0
Track : LH: 0-0 **RH: 1-2 Tight: 1-2** Gall: 0-0
Aids: Bl: 0-0 Vi: 0-0 Tstrap: 0-0
Best Rating: 53 8/01 Ripn 1m2f good

This moderate mover, whose dam was a half-sister to French 2,000 Guineas and Prix Moulin winner, Ashkalani, won a maiden run over a mile at Hamilton to get off the mark in July. Proven on good ground.

Ashantiana

(87) (52)**57**

2-y-o ch f Ashkalani (IRE)-Fast Chick (Henbit (USA))
E L James S Nunn & A Amin

Placings:045 (5420)
2001: 6⁰G, 7⁴S, 7⁵SD

	Starts	1st	2nd	3rd	Win & Pl
Career Total (Turf)	2	0	0	0	0
Career Total (AW)	1	0	0	0	0

Going (Turf): Sf: 0-1 GS: 0-0 Gd: 0-1 GF: 0-0 Fm: 0-0
Distance: 5f/6f: 0-1 7f-8f: 0-2 9f-13f: 0-0 14f+: 0-0
Track : LH: 0-2 RH: 0-0 Tight: 0-1 Gall: 0-0
Aids: Bl: 0-0 Vi: 0-0 Tstrap: 0-0
Best Rating: 57 9/01 Brig 7f214y soft

Ashdown Express (IRE)

100 **99**

2-y-o ch c Ashkalani (IRE)-Indian Express (Indian Ridge)
S P C Woods W J P Jackson

Placings:311201 (5596)
2001: 6³GF, 7¹F, 7¹GF, 8²GF, 8⁰S, 8¹GS

	Starts	1st	2nd	3rd	Win & Pl
Career Total (Turf)	6	3	1	1	17305
95 11/01 NmkR 1m C				G-S	£5563
93 7/01 Bevl 7f100y D				G-F	£5018
71 7/01 Newc 7f D				FRM	£4065
					Total win prize-money £14647

Going (Turf): Sf: 0-1 **GS: 1-1** Gd: 0-0 **GF: 1-3 Fm: 1-1**
Distance: 5f/6f: 0-0 **7f-8f: 3-6** 9f-13f: 0-0 14f+: 0-0
Track : LH: 0-0 **RH: 1-2** Tight: 0-0 Gall: 0-1
Aids: Bl: 0-0 Vi: 0-0 Tstrap: 0-0
Best Rating: 99 9/01 Sals 1m gd-fm

Showed some promise on his Nottingham debut and duly scored in a weak Newcastle maiden next time. Won twice more on varying ground but yet to prove he is Pattern class.

Asheer

108 **104**

2-y-o ch c Inchinor-Shoshone (Be My Chief (USA))
J W Payne C Cotran

Placings:31234 (5002)
2001: 5³GF, 6¹GS, 6²G, 7³G, 8⁴S

	Starts	1st	2nd	3rd	Win & Pl
Career Total (Turf)	5	1	1	2	21396
75 7/01 Ling 6f D				G-S	£3549
					Total win prize-money £3549

Going (Turf): Sf: 0-1 **GS: 1-1** Gd: 0-2 GF: 0-1 Fm: 0-0
Distance: 5f/6f: 1-2 7f-8f: 0-3 9f-13f: 0-0 14f+: 0-0
Track : LH: 0-1 RH: 0-2 Tight: 0-0 Gall: 0-2
Aids: Bl: 0-0 Vi: 0-0 Tstrap: 0-0
Best Rating: 104 8/01 York 6f214y good

Improved from his debut to gain a battling victory at Lingfield in July with the first two well clear. Showed he stayed seven furlongs with good efforts in a Listed event at York and the Solario. Should get further and open to improvement.

Ashgar Sayyad (USA)

99 **88**

2-y-o b c Kingmambo (USA)-Quelle Affaire (USA) (Riverman (USA))
M R Channon Jaber Abdullah

Placings:32344 (5053)
2001: 6³S, 6²GF, 7³GF, 6⁴GF, 7⁴S

	Starts	1st	2nd	3rd	Win & Pl
Career Total (Turf)	5	0	1	2	23487

Going (Turf): Sf: 0-2 GS: 0-0 Gd: 0-0 GF: 0-3 Fm: 0-0
Distance: 5f/6f: 0-1 7f-8f: 0-4 9f-13f: 0-0 14f+: 0-0
Track : LH: 0-1 RH: 0-0 Tight: 0-0 Gall: 0-1
Aids: Bl: 0-0 Vi: 0-0 Tstrap: 0-0
Best Rating: 88 10/01 NmkR 7f soft

A 60,000gns half-brother to Ma Yoram, he has shown plenty of ability in four decent maidens and a Newmarket sales event to date. A ready-made winner of a maiden, he handles fast ground, but may be suited by an easier surface.

Ashkalani Star (IRE)

(97) (77+)**66**

2-y-o ch c Ashkalani (IRE)-Atacama (Green Desert (USA))
M Johnston The Always Trying Partnership

Placings:051 (5420)
2001: 5⁰GS, 5⁵GF, 7¹SD,

	Starts	1st	2nd	3rd	Win & Pl
Career Total (Turf)	2	0	0	0	0
Career Total (AW)	1	1	0	0	2898
77 10/01 Wolv 7f E				STD	£2898
					Total win prize-money £2898

Going (Turf): Sf: 0-0 GS: 0-1 Gd: 0-0 GF: 0-1 Fm: 0-0
Distance: 5f/6f: 0-2 **7f-8f: 1-1** 9f-13f: 0-0 14f+: 0-0
Track : LH: 1-2 RH: 0-0 **Tight: 1-1** Gall: 0-0
Aids: Bl: 0-0 Vi: 0-0 **Tstrap: 1-3**
Best Rating: 77 10/01 Wolv 7f stand

He has made no impression on the turf, but proved partial to the sand when deservedly winning a modest event at Wolverhampton.

Ashkelon

101 **85**

2-y-o ch c Ashkalani (IRE)-Subtle Blush (Nashwan (USA))
Mrs A J Perrett Seymour Cohn

Placings:10 (4895)
2001: 6¹F, 7⁰GS

	Starts	1st	2nd	3rd	Win & Pl
Career Total (Turf)	2	1	0	0	3738
85 8/01 Sals 6f212y E				FRM	£3737
					Total win prize-money £3738

Going (Turf): Sf: 0-0 GS: 0-1 Gd: 0-0 GF: 0-0 **Fm: 1-1**
Distance: 5f/6f: 0-0 **7f-8f: 1-2** 9f-13f: 0-0 14f+: 0-0
Track : LH: 0-0 RH: 0-0 Tight: 0-0 Gall: 0-0
Aids: Bl: 0-0 Vi: 0-0 Tstrap: 0-0
Best Rating: 85 8/01 Sals 6f212y firm

Whose dam is a half-sister to several useful performers, including Group One winning miler Indian Lodge, won a decent maiden on his debut on firm ground.

Ashleigh Baker (IRE)

105 (45)**52**

6-y-o b/br m Don't Forget Me-Gayla Orchestra (Lord Gayle (USA))
A Bailey The David James Partnership

Placings:056010060000/340053/64030161244056-600220 (5632)
2001: 14⁶GF, 16⁰F, 14⁰HY, 10²HY, 10²HY, 10⁰G

	Starts	1st	2nd	3rd	Win & Pl
Career Total (Turf)	36	3	3	3	13681
Career Total (AW)	2	0	0	0	
49 7/00 Haml 1m4f17y F(0-60)H				G-F	£2814
44 7/00 Muss 1m4f F(0-65)H				G-S	£2702
66 7/98 Ayr 1m2f192yE(0-70)H				SFT	£2851
					Total win prize-money £8367

Going (Turf): Sf: 1-10 GS: 1-7 Gd: 0-12 **GF: 1-4** Fm: 0-3
Distance: 5f/6f: 0-0 7f-8f: 0-2 **9f-13f: 3-28** 14f+: 0-8
Track : LH: 1-23 **RH: 2-13 Tight: 2-18** Gall: 0-3
Aids: Bl: 0-2 Vi: 0-0 Tstrap: 0-0
Best Rating: 52 10/01 Ayr 1m2f heavy

A fair handicapper, she scored twice in the summer of 2000 over a mile and a half. Lightly raced this term.She is suited by soft ground.

Ashlinn (IRE)

105 **80**

3-y-o ch f Ashkalani (IRE)-Always Far (USA) (Alydar (USA))
R Hannon R E Anderson, J M Connolly & W Thornton

Placings:2100-606300505203 (5470)
2001: 7⁶GS, 8⁰G, 8⁶GF, 7³GF, 8⁰GF, 7⁰GS, 7⁵GS, 7⁰G, 9⁵GF, 7²G, 7⁰GS, 7³S

	Starts	1st	2nd	3rd	Win & Pl
Career Total (Turf)	16	1	2	2	8231
83 8/00 NmkJ 7f D				G-F	£4065
					Total win prize-money £4066

Going (Turf): Sf: 0-1 GS: 0-5 Gd: 0-4 **GF: 1-6** Fm: 0-0
Distance: 5f/6f: 0-1 **7f-8f: 1-14** 9f-13f: 0-1 14f+: 0-0
Track : LH: 0-2 RH: 0-4 Tight: 0-2 Gall: 0-0
Aids: Bl: 0-7 Vi: 0-1 Tstrap: 0-0
Best Rating: 96 5/01 Gdwd 1m gd-fm

She won a Newmarket maiden on her second start at two, but it was a moderate event for the track and she hac ctrugglod in bottor company cinco thon though a drop in grade saw better performances at Epsom in September andt Brighton in October. Acts on most types of ground.

Ashnaya (FR)

101 **66**

3-y-o b f Ashkalani (IRE)-Upend (Main Reef)
J L Dunlop George Galazka & Robert Scott

Placings:0-4600502100 **(5402)**
2001: 10^{4}GS, 12^{6}GS, 14^{0}GF, 14^{0}S, 16^{5}HY, 16^{0}G, 16^{2}G, 16^{1}HY, 17^{0}GS, 17^{0}S

	Starts	1st	2nd	3rd	Win & Pl
Career Total (Turf)	11	1	1	0	5258

66 10/01 Nott 2m9y D(0-80)H HVY £4046
Total win prize-money £4046

Going (Turf): Sf: 1-5 GS: 0-3 Gd: 0-2 GF: 0-1 Fm: 0-0
Distance: 5f/6f: 0-0 7f-8f: 0-1 9f-13f: 0-2 **14f+: 1-8**
Track : **LH: 1-7** RH: 0-3 Tight: 0-2 Gall: 0-1
Aids: **Bl: 1-5** Vi: 0-0 Tstrap: 0-0
Best Rating: 67 5/01 Sals 1m4f gd-sft

Found her form at the back-end, looking a thorough stayer when winning at Nottingham.

Ashtoreth (IRE)

69 **39**
2-y-o ch f Ashkalani (IRE)-Sally Chase (Sallust)
Mrs A J Perrett Major-Gen G H Watkins

Placings:0 **(5491)**
2001: 6^{0}HY

	Starts	1st	2nd	3rd	Win & Pl
Career Total (Turf)	1	0	0	0	

Going (Turf): Sf: 0-1 GS: 0-0 Gd: 0-0 GF: 0-0 Fm: 0-0
Distance: 5f/6f: 0-0 7f-8f: 0-1 9f-13f: 0-0 14f+: 0-0
Track : LH: 0-0 RH: 0-0 Tight: 0-0 Gall: 0-0
Aids: Bl: 0-0 Vi: 0-0 Tstrap: 0-0
Best Rating: 39 10/01 Newb 6f8y heavy

Ashtree Belle

(92) (67)**66**
2-y-o b f Up And At 'Em-Paris Babe (Teenoso (USA))
J G Smyth-Osbourne Mason Gill Racing

Placings:4341 **(5415)**
2001: 5^{4}GF, 5^{3}GS, 6^{4}SD, 6^{1}SD

	Starts	1st	2nd	3rd	Win & Pl
Career Total (Turf)	2	0	0	1	535
Career Total (AW)	2	1	0	0	3038

67 10/01 Wolv 6f E STD £3038
Total win prize-money £3038

Going (Turf): Sf: 0-0 GS: 0-1 Gd: 0-0 GF: 0-1 Fm: 0-0
Distance: 5f/6f: 1-4 7f-8f: 0-0 9f-13f: 0-0 14f+: 0-0
Track : LH: 1-2 RH: 0-0 **Tight: 1-2** Gall: 0-0
Aids: Bl: 0-0 Vi: 0-0 Tstrap: 0-0
Best Rating: 67 10/01 Wolv 6f stand

Got off the mark in a maiden on the Wolverhampton Fibresand in October. Suited by six furlongs.

Ashville Lad

99(101) (52)**53**
4-y-o b c Bigstone (IRE)-Hooray Lady (Ahonoora)
B A McMahon Mrs Rita Gibson

Placings:0000-4220024 **(2191)**
2001: 6^{4}SD, 6^{2}SD, 7^{2}SD, 8^{0}SD, 8^{0}G, 8^{2}F, 9^{4}G

	Starts	1st	2nd	3rd	Win & Pl
Career Total (Turf)	4	0	1	0	613
Career Total (AW)	7	0	2	0	1320

Going (Turf): Sf: 0-0 GS: 0-0 Gd: 0-2 GF: 0-1 Fm: 0-1
Distance: 5f/6f: 0-2 7f-8f: 0-3 9f-13f: 0-6 14f+: 0-0
Track : LH: 0-10 RH: 0-0 Tight: 0-5 Gall: 0-0
Aids: Bl: 0-6 Vi: 0-0 Tstrap: 0-7
Best Rating: 53 6/01 Nott 1m54y firm

Asian Heights

107 **115**
3-y-o b c Hernando (FR)-Miss Rinjani (Shirley Heights)
G Wragg J L C Pearce

Placings:1-21 **(1498)**
2001: 10^{2}HY, 11^{1}GF

	Starts	1st	2nd	3rd	Win & Pl
Career Total (Turf)	3	2	1	0	40099

115 5/01 Gdwd 1m3f A G-F £22750
83 10/00 Ling 7f D HVY £3549
Total win prize-money £26299

Going (Turf): Sf: 1-2 GS: 0-0 Gd: 0-0 **GF: 1-1** Fm: 0-0
Distance: 5f/6f: 0-0 7f-8f: 1-1 9f-13f: 1-2 14f+: 0-0
Track : LH: 0-0 RH: 0-1 Tight: 0-0 Gall: 0-0
Aids: Bl: 0-0 Vi: 0-0 Tstrap: 0-0
Best Rating: 115 5/01 Gdwd 1m3f gd-fm

A half-brother to the Ormonde winner St Expedit, he took a back-end maiden on heavy ground on his debut in 2000, and reappeared to run a good second in the Classic Trial at Sandown before winning the Predominate. Fancied for the Derby, he sustained an injurywhich forced him to miss the rest of the season.

Asian Persuasion (IRE)

96 **72**
2-y-o gr g Danehill Dancer (IRE)-Kaitlin (IRE) (Salmon Leap (USA))
E L James Tantivy Racing Partnership

Placings:40 **(4454)**
2001: 5^{4}G, 6^{0}GF

	Starts	1st	2nd	3rd	Win & Pl
Career Total (Turf)	2	0	0	0	0

Going (Turf): Sf: 0-0 GS: 0-0 Gd: 0-1 GF: 0-1 Fm: 0-0
Distance: 5f/6f: 0-2 7f-8f: 0-0 9f-13f: 0-0 14f+: 0-0
Track : LH: 0-0 RH: 0-0 Tight: 0-0 Gall: 0-0
Aids: Bl: 0-0 Vi: 0-0 Tstrap: 0-0
Best Rating: 72 8/01 Folk 5f good

Ask The Accountant (IRE)

(91) (49)**58**
4-y-o ch f Septieme Ciel (USA)-Strike Alight (USA) (Gulch (USA))
M Halford D Brennan Accountants Synd

Placings:000034-004 **(3919a)**
2001: 10^{0}GY, 13^{0}G, 13^{4}GY

	Starts	1st	2nd	3rd	Win & Pl
Career Total (Turf)	8	0	0	1	980
Career Total (AW)	1	0	0	0	283

Going (Turf): Sf: 0-1 GS: 0-0 Gd: 0-2 GF: 0-1 Fm: 0-0
Distance: 5f/6f: 0-0 7f-8f: 0-2 9f-13f: 0-5 14f+: 0-1
Track : LH: 0-3 RH: 0-2 Tight: 0-1 Gall: 0-0
Aids: Bl: 0-0 Vi: 0-0 Tstrap: 0-0
Best Rating: 58 8/01 Wxfd 1m5f gd-yld

Askham (USA)

113 **111**
3-y-o b c El Gran Senor (USA)-Konvincha (USA) (Cormorant (USA))
L M Cumani M J Dawson

Placings:3-2121220 **(5103)**
2001: 8^{2}G, 8^{1}G, 10^{2}G, 9^{1}G, 10^{2}GF, 9^{2}GF, 8^{0}GS

	Starts	1st	2nd	3rd	Win & Pl
Career Total (Turf)	8	2	4	1	67099

111 8/01 Gdwd 1m1f192yB(0-110)H GD £32500
77 6/01 Ripn 1m D GD £4176
Total win prize-money £36676

Going (Turf): Sf: 0-1 GS: 0-1 **Gd: 2-4** GF: 0-2 Fm: 0-0
Distance: 5f/6f: 0-0 7f-8f: 1-4 9f-13f: 1-4 14f+: 0-0
Track : LH: 0-0 **RH: 2-4 Tight: 2-4** Gall: 0-1
Aids: Bl: 0-0 Vi: 0-0 Tstrap: 0-0
Best Rating: 111 8/01 Gdwd 1m1f192y good

A useful type, he was beaten five lengths by Mugharreb in maiden at Newmarket on his reappearance. Accomplished an easy task at Ripon and ran very well behind a very decent sort in a valuable handicap at the Newmarket July meeting. Made no mistake with an easy win in a valuable ten-furlong handicap at Glorious Goodwood and has run some very good races in hot company since. Suited by a strong pace. Acts on a sound surface.

Aspirant Dancer

105 (62)**62**
6-y-o b g Marju (IRE)-Fairy Ballerina (Fairy King (USA))
M L W Bell (Mrs L Wadham 16/4) Peter Coe

Placings:000/211102400/042133213016/004-0361 **(5383)**
2001: 9^{0}GF, 15^{3}S, 17^{6}GS, 13^{1}S

	Starts	1st	2nd	3rd	Win & Pl
Career Total (Turf)	27	6	2	4	37151
Career Total (AW)	4	1	2	0	4132

54 10/01 Catt 1m5f175yF(0-60) SFT £2432
71 9/99 Pont 1m2f6y E(0-70) GD £2918
71 7/99 Pont 1m2f6y E(0-70) G-S £3217
69 4/99 Pont 1m2f6y E(0-75)H G-S £4467
69 5/98 Hayd 1m2f120yC(0-90)H GD £14460
63 4/98 Folk 1m1f149yF(0-65)H SFT £2679
63 4/98 Sthl 1m3f F(0-65)H STD £2448
Total win prize-money £32623

Going (Turf): Sf: 2-6 GS: 2-6 Gd: 2-11 GF: 0-3 Fm: 0-1
Distance: 5f/6f: 0-1 7f-8f: 0-2 **9f-13f: 6-24** 14f+: 1-4
Track : LH: 6-24 RH: 1-4 **Tight: 2-8** Gall: 0-3
Aids: Bl: 0-0 Vi: 0-0 Tstrap: 0-0
Best Rating: 62 9/01 Ches 1m7f195y soft

A winner three times over ten furlongs at Pontefract in 1999, he is better known as a hurdler these days, although he did return to the flat in September and October, winning over 14 furlongs at Catterick.

Assaaf (IRE)

104 **99**
2-y-o ch c Night Shift (USA)-Wannabe (Shirley Heights)
D R Loder Sheikh Mohammed

Placings:113 **(5255)**
2001: 8^{1}G, 8^{1}GF, 8^{3}GS

	Starts	1st	2nd	3rd	Win & Pl
Career Total (Turf)	3	2	0	1	11620

99 9/01 Sals 1m C G-F £5783
86 8/01 Nott 1m54y D GD £3721
Total win prize-money £9504

Going (Turf): Sf: 0-0 GS: 0-1 **Gd: 1-1 GF: 1-1** Fm: 0-0
Distance: 5f/6f: 0-0 7f-8f: 1-2 9f-13f: 1-1 14f+: 0-0
Track : LH: 1-1 RH: 0-1 Tight: 0-0 Gall: 0-1
Aids: Bl: 0-0 Vi: 0-1 Tstrap: 0-0
Best Rating: 99 9/01 Sals 1m gd-fm

He was the stable's second string when winning a Nottingham novice stakes on his debut, but proved it was no fluke with a clear-cut win in a Salisbury conditions event. He could only manage third in an Ascot Listed event next time and that is probably as good as he is. He should eventually be suited by distances beyond a mile.

Assailable

86 **34**

7-y-o b g Salse (USA)-Unsuitable (Local Suitor (USA))

P Howling Keith F J Loads

Placings:54/00 **(2726)**

2001: 10^{0}GF, 8^{0}GF

	Starts	1st	2nd	3rd	Win & Pl
Career Total (Turf)	4	0	0	0	255

Going (Turf): Sf: 0-0 GS: 0-0 Gd: 0-2 GF: 0-2 Fm: 0-0

Distance: 5f/6f: 0-0 7f-8f: 0-1 9f-13f: 0-3 14f+: 0-0

Track : LH: 0-1 RH: 0-0 Tight: 0-0 Gall: 0-0

Aids: Bl: 0-0 Vi: 0-0 Tstrap: 0-0

Best Rating: 34 7/01 Yarm 1m3y gd-fm

Assured Gamble

82 **27**

7-y-o b g Rock Hopper-Willowbank (Gay Fandango (USA))

R J Baker P Slade

Placings:31000050/100030/30/0 **(2811)**

2001: 12^{0}GF

	Starts	1st	2nd	3rd	Win & Pl
Career Total (Turf)	17	2	0	3	13921
80 4/98 Epsm 1m4f10y C(0-95)H				SFT	£8325
82 5/97 NmkR 1m4f D				GD	£3557

Total win prize-money £11883

Going (Turf): Sf: 1-2 GS: 0-1 **Gd: 1-8** GF: 0-6 Fm: 0-0

Distance: 5f/6f: 0-0 7f-8f: 0-0 **9f-13f: 2-13** 14f+: 0-4

Track : LH: 1-7 RH: 1-10 Tight: 1-4 Gall: 1-9

Aids: Bl: 0-0 Vi: 0-0 Tstrap: 0-0

Best Rating: 27 7/01 Wwck 1m4f134y gd-fm

Assured Physique

90(93) (41)**48**

4-y-o b g Salse (USA)-Metaphysique (FR) (Law Society (USA))

R J Baker Graham Brown

Placings:0600/053665560460-006 **(4613)**

2001: 11^{0}F, 12^{0}S, 11^{6}F

	Starts	1st	2nd	3rd	Win & Pl
Career Total (Turf)	18	0	0	1	595
Career Total (AW)	1	0	0	0	0

Going (Turf): Sf: 0-3 GS: 0-2 Gd: 0-3 GF: 0-6 Fm: 0-3

Distance: 5f/6f: 0-0 7f-8f: 0-4 9f-13f: 0-14 14f+: 0-0

Track : LH: 0-10 RH: 0-5 Tight: 0-5 Gall: 0-0

Aids: Bl: 0-0 Vi: 0-4 Tstrap: 0-5

Best Rating: 48 9/01 Bath 1m3f144y firm

Astafort (FR)

67 **32t**

2-y-o ch g Kendor (FR)-Tres Chic (USA) (Northern Fashion (USA))

Mrs J R Ramsden Swisspartners

Placings:3 **(4964)**

2001: 8^{3}S

	Starts	1st	2nd	3rd	Win & Pl
Career Total (Turf)	1	0	0	1	630

Going (Turf): Sf: 0-1 GS: 0-0 Gd: 0-0 GF: 0-0 Fm: 0-0

Distance: 5f/6f: 0-0 7f-8f: 0-0 9f-13f: 0-1 14f+: 0-0

Track : LH: 0-1 RH: 0-0 Tight: 0-0 Gall: 0-0

Aids: Bl: 0-0 Vi: 0-0 Tstrap: 0-0

Best Rating: 32 9/01 Pont 1m4y soft

Astairedotcom (IRE)

81(93) (49)**52**

3-y-o b f Lake Coniston (IRE)-Romantic Overture (USA) (Stop The Music (USA))

K R Burke Astaire & Partners (holdings) Ltd

Placings:450402100-020540 **(2421)**

2001: 6^{0}SD, 8^{2}SW, 7^{0}SW, 7^{5}SD, 7^{4}SD, 6^{0}GF

	Starts	1st	2nd	3rd	Win & Pl
Career Total (Turf)	7	0	1	0	1014
Career Total (AW)	8	1	1	0	2815
53 10/00 Wolv 6f F				STD	£2275

Total win prize-money £2275

Going (Turf): Sf: 0-1 GS: 0-1 Gd: 0-2 GF: 0-2 Fm: 0-1

Distance: 5f/6f: 1-9 7f-8f: 0-6 9f-13f: 0-0 14f+: 0-0

Track : LH: 1-9 RH: 0-1 **Tight: 1-3** Gall: 0-0

Aids: Bl: 0-1 Vi: 0-1 Tstrap: 0-0

Best Rating: 53 2/01 Sthl 1m slow

Aster Fields (IRE)

92 **31**

3-y-o b f Common Grounds-North Telstar (Sallust)

D Shaw J C Fretwell

Placings:0605-0000 **(4778)**

2001: 6^{0}G, 5^{0}G, 5^{0}GF, 5^{0}G

	Starts	1st	2nd	3rd	Win & Pl
Career Total (Turf)	8	0	0	0	227

Going (Turf): Sf: 0-2 GS: 0-1 Gd: 0-3 GF: 0-1 Fm: 0-1

Distance: 5f/6f: 0-7 7f-8f: 0-1 9f-13f: 0-0 14f+: 0-0

Track : LH: 0-1 RH: 0-0 Tight: 0-0 Gall: 0-1

Aids: Bl: 0-0 Vi: 0-0 Tstrap: 0-0

Best Rating: 31 8/01 Thsk 5f good

Astle (IRE)

(102) (86)**53**

3-y-o ch g Spectrum (IRE)-Very Sophisticated (USA) (Affirmed (USA))

Mrs N Macauley (W Jarvis 18/6) West Indies Capital Company Limited

Placings:32112006 **(3822)**

2001: 7^{3}SD, 6^{2}SD, 7^{1}SD, 8^{1}SD, 8^{2}SD, 8^{0}G, 7^{0}GF, 8^{6}SD

	Starts	1st	2nd	3rd	Win & Pl
Career Total (Turf)	2	0	0	0	
Career Total (AW)	6	2	2	1	9033
80 2/01 Wolv 1m100y D(0-80)H				STD	£3766
68 2/01 Wolv 7f D				STD	£2898

Total win prize-money £6665

Going (Turf): Sf: 0-0 GS: 0-0 Gd: 0-1 GF: 0-1 Fm: 0-0

Distance: 5f/6f: 0-1 **7f-8f: 1-5 9f-13f: 1-2** 14f+: 0-0

Track : LH: 2-7 RH: 0-0 **Tight: 2-4** Gall: 0-0

Aids: Bl: 0-0 Vi: 0-0 Tstrap: 0-0

Best Rating: 86 4/01 Sthl 1m stand

Aston Mara

97 **43**

4-y-o b g Bering-Coigach (Niniski (USA))

Mrs M Reveley Mrs D J Buckley

Placings:154/000000-54 **(2632)**

2001: 14^{5}G, 16^{4}F

	Starts	1st	2nd	3rd	Win & Pl
Career Total (Turf)	10	1	0	0	3878
Career Total (AW)	1	0	0	0	
75 6/99 Newc 7f D				GD	£3468

Total win prize-money £3469

Going (Turf): Sf: 0-2 GS: 0-0 **Gd: 1-4** GF: 0-3 Fm: 0-1

Distance: 5f/6f: 0-0 **7f-8f: 1-2** 9f-13f: 0-5 14f+: 0-4

Track : LH: 0-6 RH: 0-4 Tight: 0-3 Gall: 0-2

Aids: Bl: 0-4 Vi: 0-0 Tstrap: 0-0

Best Rating: 42 7/01 Muss 2m firm

Astonished

116 **111**

5-y-o ch g Weldnaas (USA)-Indigo (Primo Dominie)

Mrs J R Ramsden D R Brotherton

Placings:31136/25110/114102-003034110 **(5105)**

2001: 6^{0}GS, 5^{0}G, 6^{3}GF, 5^{0}G, 5^{3}GF, 6^{4}G, 5^{1}G, 5^{1}GS, 5^{0}GS

	Starts	1st	2nd	3rd	Win & Pl
Career Total (Turf)	25	9	2	4	139829
105 9/01 Donc 5f A				G-S	£17712
106 8/01 Nott 5f13y C				GD	£6467
8/00 Deau 5f				GD	£13449
113 6/00 Epsm 5f A(0-110)H				GD	£29000
5/00 Colo 5f				G-F	£6452
110 9/99 Donc 5f140y B(0-110)H				G-F	£22080
7/99 Deau 6f				GD	£10764
89 9/98 Donc 6f D(0-85)H				GD	£5439
85 8/98 Carl 5f F				G-S	£2794

Total win prize-money £114158

Going (Turf): Sf: 0-1 GS: 2-6 **Gd: 3-8** GF: 1-5 Fm: 0-0

Distance: 5f/6f: 6-19 7f-8f: 0-1 9f-13f: 0-0 14f+: 0-0

Track : LH: 0-1 **RH: 1-1** Tight: 0-1 **Gall: 1-1**

Aids: Bl: 0-0 **Vi: 2-4** Tstrap: 0-0

Best Rating: 111 5/01 York 6f gd-fm

He was trained by John Hammond in France in 2000 but is now back with Lynda Ramsden who had him as a juvenile. He ran some decent races early this season, but for various reasons did not get his head in front, but eventually the visor was applied and it had the desired effect at Nottingham in August and in a Listed event at Doncaster the following month. Best coming late off a fast pace, he has been sold to race in the USA.

Astoria

80 **59**

2-y-o ch f Primo Dominie-Ciboure (Norwick (USA))

M Johnston Mr & Mrs G Middlebrook

Placings:60000 **(5636)**

2001: 6^{6}F, 6^{0}G, 7^{0}G, 7^{0}GS, 5^{0}G

	Starts	1st	2nd	3rd	Win & Pl
Career Total (Turf)	5	0	0	0	0

Going (Turf): Sf: 0-0 GS: 0-1 Gd: 0-3 GF: 0-0 Fm: 0-1

Distance: 5f/6f: 0-3 7f-8f: 0-2 9f-13f: 0-0 14f+: 0-0

Track : LH: 0-2 RH: 0-0 Tight: 0-2 Gall: 0-0

Aids: Bl: 0-0 Vi: 0-0 Tstrap: 0-0

Best Rating: 59 9/01 Ayr 7f50y good

Astormydayiscoming

88(71) (18)**37**

3-y-o b g Alhaarmi-Valentine Song (Pas De Seul)

Mrs A L M King Out Of The Frying Pan Partnership

Placings:0000 **(5024)**

2001: 9^{0}SD, 10^{0}G, 9^{0}GF, 11^{0}S

	Starts	1st	2nd	3rd	Win & Pl
Career Total (Turf)	3	0	0	0	
Career Total (AW)	1	0	0	0	

Going (Turf): Sf: 0-1 GS: 0-0 Gd: 0-1 GF: 0-1 Fm: 0-0
Distance: 5f/6f: 0-0 7f-8f: 0-0 9f-13f: 0-4 14f+: 0-0
Track : LH: 0-2 RH: 0-1 Tight: 0-2 Gall: 0-0
Aids: Bl: 0-0 Vi: 0-0 Tstrap: 0-0
Best Rating: 37 7/01 Leic 1m1f218y gd-fm

Astrac (IRE)

(109) (64) **53**

10-y-o b g Nordico (USA)-Shirleen (Daring Display (USA))
Mrs A L M King Clive Titcomb

Placings:6403211/0010035231/510063/6005064111/06 0030005**500**/001500316/000065300031640**0335/13**000 000000-000414006 **(5161)**
2001: 6^{0}HY, 7^{0}GF, 6^{0}GF, 7^{4}GF, 7^{1}GS, 7^{4}G, 7^{0}SD, 7^{0}G, 6^{6}SD

	Starts	1st	2nd	3rd	Win & Pl
Career Total (Turf)	80	10	2	8	132836
Career Total (AW)	13	3	0	3	11312

51	7/01	Wwck	7f26y	G(0-70)H	G-S	£1886
77	1/00	Wolv	6f	F	STD	£2124
83	10/99	Catt	5f212y	F(0-85)	SFT	£2162
95	9/98	Haml	6f5y	C	SFT	£5180
93	5/98	Ayr	6f	D(0-85)H	GD	£3496
113	11/96	Evry	6f		VS	£18445
111	11/96	Donc	6f	A	SFT	£11798
92	10/96	Nott	6f15y	C	G-S	£5038
96	6/95	Asct	6f	B(0-110)H	FRM	£50118
84	10/94	York	6f	C(0-100)H	G-S	£15970
72	5/94	Ling	7f	(0-80)H	G-S	£3757
79	12/93	Sthl	7f	D	STD	£3260
69	11/93	Sthl	6f	D	STD	£3289

Total win prize-money £126529

Going (Turf): Sf: 3-17 **GS: 4-16** Gd: 1-27 GF: 0-18 Fm: 1-1
Distance: **5f/6f: 8-54** 7f-8f: 5-39 9f-13f: 0-0 14f+: 0-0
Track : **LH: 4-25** RH: 0-9 **Tight: 2-14** Gall: 0-5
Aids: Bl: 0-1 Vi: 0-0 Tstrap: 0-0
Best Rating: 56 8/01 Wolv 7f stand

An admirable veteran sprint handicapper, he appreciates cut in the ground and goes on Fibresand.

Astral Prince

103(100) (77)**64**

3-y-o ch g Efisio-Val D'Erica (Ashmore (FR))
B J Meehan Matham Investments

Placings:005-00140505000 **(5592)**
2001: 7^{0}GS, 9^{0}GS, 7^{1}SD, 7^{4}G, 7^{0}GF, 6^{5}GF, 7^{0}SD, 7^{5}G, 6^{0}GF, 6^{0}SD, 6^{0}GS

	Starts	1st	2nd	3rd	Win & Pl
Career Total (Turf)	11	0	0	0	424
Career Total (AW)	3	1	0	0	2926

77	5/01	Wolv	7f	E(0-70)H	STD	£2926

Total win prize-money £2926

Going (Turf): Sf: 0-1 GS: 0-3 Gd: 0-3 GF: 0-4 Fm: 0-0
Distance: 5f/6f: 0-3 **7f-8f: 1-10** 9f-13f: 0-1 14f+: 0-0
Track : **LH: 1-6** RH: 0-2 **Tight: 1-3** Gall: 0-0
Aids: **Bl: 1-9** Vi: 0-0 Tstrap: 0-0
Best Rating: 77 5/01 Wolv 7f stand

Astrocharm (IRE)

99 **73**

2-y-o b f Charnwood Forest (IRE)-Charm The Stars (Roi Danzig (USA))
M H Tompkins Mystic Meg Limited

Placings:004104 **(5364)**
2001: 6^{0}GF, 6^{0}G, 7^{4}GF, 7^{1}GF, 6^{0}G, 6^{4}GS

	Starts	1st	2nd	3rd	Win & Pl
Career Total (Turf)	6	1	0	0	10515

73	9/01	Ling	7f	E(0-75)	G-F	£3570

Total win prize-money £3570

Going (Turf): Sf: 0-0 GS: 0-1 Gd: 0-2 **GF: 1-3** Fm: 0-0
Distance: 5f/6f: 0-3 **7f-8f: 1-3** 9f-13f: 0-0 14f+: 0-0
Track : LH: 0-1 RH: 0-0 Tight: 0-0 Gall: 0-0
Aids: Bl: 0-0 Vi: 0-0 Tstrap: 0-0
Best Rating: 73 9/01 Ling 7f gd-fm

She made a successful nursery debut over seven furlongs at Lingfield in September and ran a fine race when fourth in the Tattersalls Autumn Auction Stakes at Newmarket where her stamina came into play. Should stay further.

Astrolove (IRE)

56(74) (35)**35**

3-y-o ch f Bigstone (IRE)-Pizzazz (Unfuwain (USA))
M H Tompkins Mystic Meg Limited

Placings:000-04 **(2767)**
2001: 14^{0}G, 16^{4}GF

	Starts	1st	2nd	3rd	Win & Pl
Career Total (Turf)	3	0	0	0	0
Career Total (AW)	2	0	0	0	

Going (Turf): Sf: 0-1 GS: 0-0 Gd: 0-1 GF: 0-1 Fm: 0-0
Distance: 5f/6f: 0-0 7f-8f: 0-1 9f-13f: 0-2 14f+: 0-2
Track : LH: 0-4 RH: 0-0 Tight: 0-1 Gall: 0-0
Aids: Bl: 0-1 Vi: 0-0 Tstrap: 0-0
Best Rating: 35 7/01 Sthl 2m gd-fm

Aswan (IRE)

106 **83+**

3-y-o ch c Ashkalani (IRE)-Ghariba (Final Straw)
Sir Michael Stoute James Wigan

Placings:53110 **(5344)**
2001: 8^{5}GF, 8^{3}GF, 8^{1}GF, 8^{1}GF, 8^{0}GS

	Starts	1st	2nd	3rd	Win & Pl
Career Total (Turf)	5	2	0	1	10645

83	9/01	Kemp	1m	D(0-80)H	G-F	£4855
59	8/01	Newc	1m	D	G-F	£5109

Total win prize-money £9965

Going (Turf): Sf: 0-0 GS: 0-1 Gd: 0-0 **GF: 2-4** Fm: 0-0
Distance: 5f/6f: 0-0 **7f-8f: 2-5** 9f-13f: 0-0 14f+: 0-0
Track : LH: 1-1 RH: 1-2 Tight: 0-0 **Gall: 1-1**
Aids: Bl: 0-0 Vi: 0-0 Tstrap: 0-0
Best Rating: 83 9/01 Kemp 1m gd-fm

Showed some ability before easily landing long odds-on in a four-runner maiden at Newcastle in August. Followed up in a competitive Kempton handicap and looks progressive. Suited by good to firm and a mile.

At'Em Donut (IRE)

(92) (40)**35**

4-y-o ch g Up And At 'Em-Florentink (USA) (The Minstrel (CAN))
C N Kellett Willwewontwe Club

Placings:00000000650 **(4944)**
2001: 6^{0}SD, 5^{0}SD, 6^{0}GS, 6^{0}F, 5^{0}SD, 6^{0}SD, 6^{0}GF, 7^{0}GS, 5^{6}G, 5^{5}G, 5^{0}S

	Starts	1st	2nd	3rd	Win & Pl
Career Total (Turf)	7	0	0	0	0
Career Total (AW)	4	0	0	0	

Going (Turf): Sf: 0-1 GS: 0-2 Gd: 0-2 GF: 0-1 Fm: 0-1
Distance: 5f/6f: 0-9 7f-8f: 0-2 9f-13f: 0-0 14f+: 0-0
Track : LH: 0-4 RH: 0-0 Tight: 0-1 Gall: 0-0
Aids: Bl: 0-2 Vi: 0-1 Tstrap: 0-0
Best Rating: 40 3/01 Sthl 5f stand

A very poor sprint handicapper.

Atacat (IRE)

97 **45**

5-y-o b g Catrail (USA)-Atsuko (IRE) (Mtoto)
Miss L C Siddall Mrs Ann Morgan

Placings:213-0000000065 **(5683)**
2001: 10^{0}G, 10^{0}GF, 11^{0}GS, 10^{0}S, 10^{0}G, 10^{0}S, 13^{0}GS, 10^{0}HY, 11^{6}S, 14^{5}S

	Starts	1st	2nd	3rd	Win & Pl
Career Total (Turf)	13	1	1	1	7005

85	6/00	Dund	1m1f	G-Y	£3795

Total win prize-money £3795

Going (Turf): Sf: 0-5 GS: 0-2 Gd: 0-3 GF: 0-2 Fm: 0-0
Distance: 5f/6f: 0-0 7f-8f: 0-0 **9f-13f: 1-11** 14f+: 0-2
Track : **LH: 1-11** RH: 0-1 Tight: 0-1 Gall: 0-6
Aids: Bl: 0-0 Vi: 0-0 Tstrap: 0-0
Best Rating: 70 5/01 York 1m2f85y gd-fm

The winner of a maiden in Ireland, he has yet to show much since moving to this country. Stays nine furlongs. Acts on good ground.

Atall's Flyer

71

3-y-o b f Atall Atall-Branston Kristy (Hallgate)
M A Barnes Pointerfarm Racing Partnership

Placings:000 **(4616)**
2001: 7^{0}GS, 7^{0}G, 8^{0}F

	Starts	1st	2nd	3rd	Win & Pl
Career Total (Turf)	3	0	0	0	

Going (Turf): Sf: 0-0 GS: 0-1 Gd: 0-1 GF: 0-0 Fm: 0-1
Distance: 5f/6f: 0-0 7f-8f: 0-3 9f-13f: 0-0 14f+: 0-0
Track : LH: 0-2 RH: 0-0 Tight: 0-0 Gall: 0-1
Aids: Bl: 0-0 Vi: 0-0 Tstrap: 0-2

Atamana (IRE)

103 **82**

3-y-o b f Lahib (USA)-Dance Ahead (Shareef Dancer (USA))
M P Tregoning Sheikh Ahmed Al Maktoum

Placings:22-150 **(4547)**
2001: 8^{1}GF, 8^{5}G, 6^{0}GF

	Starts	1st	2nd	3rd	Win & Pl
Career Total (Turf)	5	1	2	0	6701

82	7/01	Sand	1m14y	D	G-F	£4270

Total win prize-money £4271

Going (Turf): Sf: 0-0 GS: 0-0 Gd: 0-2 **GF: 1-3** Fm: 0-0
Distance: 5f/6f: 0-1 7f-8f: 0-3 **9f-13f: 1-1** 14f+: 0-0
Track : LH: 0-0 **RH: 1-2** Tight: 0-0 Gall: 0-0
Aids: Bl: 0-1 Vi: 0-0 Tstrap: 0-0
Best Rating: 82 7/01 Sand 1m14y gd-fm

Runner-up on both her starts as a juvenile, she took a Sandown maiden on her belated reappearance. She stays a mile and acts on fast ground.

Atarama (IRE)

96 **91**

2-y-o b f Sadler's Wells (USA)-Regal Portrait (IRE) (Royal Academy (USA))
J L Dunlop The Thoroughbred Corporation

Placings:0213 **(5609)**
2001: 7^0G, 7^2G, 7^1G, 8^3GS

	Starts	1st	2nd	3rd	Win & Pl
Career Total (Turf)	4	1	1	1	7560

87 10/01 Rdcr 7f D GD £3906
Total win prize-money £3906

Going (Turf): Sf: 0-0 GS: 0-1 **Gd: 1-3** GF: 0-0 Fm: 0-0
Distance: 5f/6f: 0-0 **7f-8f: 1-4** 9f-13f: 0-0 14f+: 0-0
Track : LH: 0-1 RH: 0-0 Tight: 0-1 Gall: 0-0
Aids: Bl: 0-0 Vi: 0-0 Tstrap: 0-0
Best Rating: 91 11/01 NmkR 1m gd-sft

Made a promising debut after a slow start and progressed from that to land the odds in a Redcar maiden over seven furlongs on good ground.

Atavus

118 **115?**
4-y-o b h Distant Relative-Elysian (Northfields (USA))
G G Margarson Stableside Racing Partnership Ii

Placings:531/4103500000-0124114100 **(5386)**
2001: 8^0GS, 8^1GS, 7^2GF, 8^4GF, 7^1G, 7^1GF, 8^4G, 7^1GF, 6^0S, 7^0GS

	Starts	1st	2nd	3rd	Win & Pl
Career Total (Turf)	23	6	1	2	193591

115 8/01 Newb 7f64y A G-F £20300
98 7/01 Asct 7f B H G-F £87000
96 7/01 NmkJ 7f B(0-105)H GD £32500
88 5/01 NmkR 1m C(0-90)H G-S £7052
84 5/00 NmkR 1m C(0-90)H GD £15665
75 10/99 Ling 7f E G-F £3509
Total win prize-money £166027

Going (Turf): Sf: 0-4 GS: 1-3 Gd: 2-8 **GF: 3-8** Fm: 0-0
Distance: 5f/6f: 0-2 **7f-8f: 6-16** 9f-13f: 0-5 14f+: 0-0
Track : **LH: 1-3** RH: 0-6 Tight: 0-1 **Gall: 1-2**
Aids: Bl: 0-0 Vi: 0-0 Tstrap: 0-0
Best Rating: 115 8/01 Newb 7f64y gd-fm

After running well at Goodwood and in the Royal Hunt Cup, he gained a fine victory when making all in the Bunbury Cup on the July course, then followed up at Ascot in the Tote International Stakes. Made all to gain a first Group win in the Hungerford Stakes at Newbury in August. He is reportedly suited by seeing plenty of daylight and seems best on a sound surface. Effective at seven furlongs or a mile, most of his best form has come on straight tracks.

Athenian

95 **70**
2-y-o b g Distant Relative-Confection (Formidable (USA))
D Morris John Khan

Placings:30400 **(5628)**
2001: 8^3G, 7^0GF, 8^4GS, 8^0GS, 8^0G

	Starts	1st	2nd	3rd	Win & Pl
Career Total (Turf)	5	0	0	1	895

Going (Turf): Sf: 0-0 GS: 0-2 Gd: 0-2 GF: 0-1 Fm: 0-0
Distance: 5f/6f: 0-0 7f-8f: 0-4 9f-13f: 0-1 14f+: 0-0
Track : LH: 0-1 RH: 0-0 Tight: 0-0 Gall: 0-1
Aids: Bl: 0-0 Vi: 0-0 Tstrap: 0-0
Best Rating: 74 8/01 Yarm 1m3y good

Showed ability in maidens on various surfaces in the second half of 2001. Stays a mile.

Athletic Sam (IRE)

(103) (70)**48**
3-y-o b c Definite Article-No Hard Feelings (IRE) (Alzao (USA))
T G Mills J E Harley

Placings:0-1 **(0509)**
2001: 12^1SD

	Starts	1st	2nd	3rd	Win & Pl
Career Total (Turf)	1	0	0	0	
Career Total (AW)	1	1	0	0	2877

70 3/01 Wolv 1m4f D STD £2877
Total win prize-money £2877

Going (Turf): Sf: 0-1 GS: 0-0 Gd: 0-0 GF: 0-0 Fm: 0-0
Distance: 5f/6f: 0-0 7f-8f: 0-1 **9f-13f: 1-1** 14f+: 0-0
Track : **LH: 1-1** RH: 0-0 **Tight: 1-1** Gall: 0-0
Aids: Bl: 0-0 Vi: 0-0 Tstrap: 0-0
Best Rating: 70 3/01 Wolv 1m4f stand

Atlantic Ace

111(97) (75)**80**
4-y-o b g First Trump-Risalah (Marju (IRE))
B Smart Richard Page

Placings:0/100-30131 **(5535)**
2001: 8^3SD, 9^0SW, 7^1GF, 8^3GF, 7^1S

	Starts	1st	2nd	3rd	Win & Pl
Career Total (Turf)	7	3	0	1	19815
Career Total (AW)	2	0	0	1	596

80 10/01 Rdcr 7f D(0-85)H SFT £4777
77 6/01 Gdwd 7f C(0-90)H G-F £11310
80 10/00 Pont 1m4y D HVY £2912
Total win prize-money £19000

Going (Turf): Sf: 2-4 GS: 0-0 Gd: 0-0 GF: 1-3 Fm: 0-0
Distance: 5f/6f: 0-1 **7f-8f: 2-6** 9f-13f: 1-2 14f+: 0-0
Track : LH: 1-4 RH: 1-2 Tight: 0-1 Gall: 0-0
Aids: Bl: 0-0 Vi: 0-0 Tstrap: 0-0
Best Rating: 80 10/01 Rdcr 7f soft

He got off the mark when winning in heavy ground at Pontefract last season before becoming disappointing, but caused a 50-1 shock in a valuable handicap on much faster ground at Goodwood in June. Best caught fresh, he added another win in the autumn after a break.

Atlantic Eagle (USA)

89 **72d**
3-y-o b g Mt. Livermore (USA)-Lyphdum (USA) (Lyphard (USA))
M Johnston Atlantic Racing Limited

Placings:00-0040 **(2055)**
2001: 8^0GF, 8^0F, 9^4GF, 10^0GF

	Starts	1st	2nd	3rd	Win & Pl
Career Total (Turf)	6	0	0	0	0

Going (Turf): Sf: 0-1 GS: 0-0 Gd: 0-1 GF: 0-3 Fm: 0-1
Distance: 5f/6f: 0-1 7f-8f: 0-3 9f-13f: 0-2 14f+: 0-0
Track : LH: 0-3 RH: 0-0 Tight: 0-2 Gall: 0-1
Aids: Bl: 0-1 Vi: 0-0 Tstrap: 0-0
Best Rating: 64 5/01 Ayr 1m1f20y gd-fm

Atlantic Mystery (IRE)

96(51) (?)**67**
3-y-o ch f Cadeaux Genereux-Nottash (IRE) (Royal Academy (USA))
M Johnston Atlantic Racing Limited

Placings:3530-300 **(2871)**
2001: 6^3GF, 7^0G, 6^0GF

	Starts	1st	2nd	3rd	Win & Pl
Career Total (Turf)	6	0	0	3	1447
Career Total (AW)	1	0	0	0	

Going (Turf): Sf: 0-3 GS: 0-0 Gd: 0-1 GF: 0-2 Fm: 0-0
Distance: 5f/6f: 0-5 7f-8f: 0-2 9f-13f: 0-0 14f+: 0-0
Track : LH: 0-2 RH: 0-0 Tight: 0-1 Gall: 0-0
Aids: Bl: 0-0 Vi: 0-0 Tstrap: 0-0
Best Rating: 67 6/01 Yarm 6f3y gd-fm

Atlantic Rhapsody (FR)

111(103) (90)**91**
4-y-o b g Machiavellian (USA)-First Waltz (FR) (Green Dancer (USA))
M Johnston Atlantic Racing Limited

Placings:2232/1044125605462042-003040345 **(3510)**
2001: 8^0S, 8^0GS, 12^3S, 12^0G, 12^4F, 10^0G, 11^3GF, 10^4GF, 9^5GF

	Starts	1st	2nd	3rd	Win & Pl
Career Total (Turf)	28	1	6	3	80369
Career Total (AW)	1	1	0	0	2821

95 5/00 Hayd 1m30y B(0-110)H SFT £43875
90 3/00 Sthl 1m D STD £2821
Total win prize-money £46696

Going (Turf): Sf: 1-7 GS: 0-2 Gd: 0-13 GF: 0-5 Fm: 0-1
Distance: 5f/6f: 0-2 7f-8f: 1-11 9f-13f: 1-16 14f+: 0-0
Track : **LH: 2-9** RH: 0-10 Tight: 0-8 Gall: 0-3
Aids: **Bl: 1-3** Vi: 0-0 Tstrap: 0-0
Best Rating: 91 6/01 Thsk 1m4f firm

Won a valuable handicap at Haydock in the spring of 2000, and ran a series of good races in the top handicaps later without getting his head in front. Held by the handicapper this term. Effective from seven to nine furlongs, probably best with cut but acts on faster ground. Has hung on occasions.

Atlantic Viking (IRE)

109 **91**
6-y-o b g Danehill (USA)-Hi Bettina (Henbit (USA))
D Nicholls David Faulkner

Placings:01623/000305000/202060141/0004040-61605400300 **(5012)**
2001: 5^6GF, 5^1GF, 5^6GF, 5^0GF, 5^5G, 5^4GF, 6^0G, 7^0GS, 5^3HY, 5^0G, 5^0HY

	Starts	1st	2nd	3rd	Win & Pl
Career Total (Turf)	41	4	3	3	35869

85 6/01 Ripn 5f D(0-80)H G-F £4517
86 8/99 Ripn 6f C(0-95)H G-F £6109
82 7/99 Pont 5f D(0-80)H G-F £7570
97 6/97 Newc 5f D FRM £3067
Total win prize-money £21266

Going (Turf): Sf: 0-4 GS: 0-3 Gd: 0-16 **GF: 3-14** Fm: 1-4
Distance: **5f/6f: 4-35** 7f-8f: 0-6 9f-13f: 0-0 14f+: 0-0
Track : **LH: 1-4** RH: 0-1 Tight: 0-2 Gall: 0-1
Aids: **Bl: 1-8** Vi: 0-0 Tstrap: 0-0
Best Rating: 91 9/01 Hayd 5f heavy

A useful sprint handicapper, he retains his enthusiasm for the game and scored at Ripon in June. He had a wind operation last winter and is best suited to five furlongs on fast ground, but does handles soft ground as well.

Atomic Flair (IRE)

(92) (70)**72**
2-y-o ch c Up And At 'Em-Gold Flair (Tap On Wood)
P R Chamings Twenty Twenty Research

Placings:535023434 **(5610)**
2001: 5^5HD, 7^3GF, 7^5G, 6^0S, 6^2GF, 6^3GF, 7^4G, 8^3SD, 8^4SD

	Starts	1st	2nd	3rd	Win & Pl
Career Total (Turf)	7	0	1	2	2243

Career Total (AW)	2	0	0	1	415

Going (Turf): Sf: 0-1 GS: 0-0 Gd: 0-2 GF: 0-3 Fm: 0-1
Distance: 5f/6f: 0-1 7f-8f: 0-6 9f-13f: 0-2 14f+: 0-0
Track : LH: 0-3 RH: 0-1 Tight: 0-2 Gall: 0-1
Aids: Bl: 0-0 Vi: 0-0 Tstrap: 0-0
Best Rating: 78 7/01 Ling 7f gd-fm

A half-brother to five winners, including seven-furlong winner Atylan Boy. Has shown ability without winning.

Atractive Girl

75(48) **34**
2-y-o ch f Atraf-Harold's Girl (FR) (Northfields (USA))
J L Spearing B Mathieson, D Oseman & D Redvers

Placings:5000 **(4671)**
2001: 5^{5}G, 6^{0}SD, 5^{0}G, 8^{0}G

	Starts	1st	2nd	3rd	Win & Pl
Career Total (Turf)	3	0	0	0	0
Career Total (AW)	1	0	0	0	

Going (Turf): Sf: 0-0 GS: 0-0 Gd: 0-3 GF: 0-0 Fm: 0-0
Distance: 5f/6f: 0-3 7f-8f: 0-0 9f-13f: 0-1 14f+: 0-0
Track : LH: 0-2 RH: 0-0 Tight: 0-0 Gall: 0-0
Aids: Bl: 0-1 Vi: 0-0 Tstrap: 0-0
Best Rating: 34 8/01 Brig 5f213y good

Attache

106 **94**
3-y-o ch c Wolfhound (USA)-Royal Passion (Ahonoora)
Mrs J R Ramsden (M Johnston 23/8) J R Good

Placings:2115-01565060000 **(5607)**
2001: 8^{0}S, 10^{1}GF, 10^{5}GF, 11^{6}S, 10^{5}G, 7^{0}G, 8^{6}G, 8^{0}GF, 10^{0}G, 8^{0}GS, 8^{0}GS

	Starts	1st	2nd	3rd	Win & Pl
Career Total (Turf)	15	3	1	0	20701

104 5/01 Donc 1m2f60y B G-F £9639
98 9/00 Sand 7f16y D G-F £4914
83 8/00 Rdcr 7f E FRM £3656
Total win prize-money £18209

Going (Turf): Sf: 0-3 GS: 0-2 Gd: 0-5 **GF: 2-4** Fm: 1-1
Distance: 5f/6f: 0-0 **7f-8f: 2-10** 9f-13f: 1-5 14f+: 0-0
Track : LH: 1-5 RH: 1-3 Tight: 0-1 **Gall: 1-3**
Aids: Bl: 0-0 Vi: 0-0 Tstrap: 0-0
Best Rating: 104 5/01 Donc 1m2f60y gd-fm

A half-brother to the good sprinter Tadeo, he followed up a narrow debut defeat in 2000 by winning twice on fast ground, beating subsequent Racing Post Trophy winner Dilshaan on the second occasion. Reported to have coughed at the start before his final run. He was a very game winner when stepped up in trip on his second run of this season, but has since rather disappointed in Pattern and handicap company. Stays ten furlongs.

Attacker (USA)

93 **32**
4-y-o b g Defensive Play (USA)-Bold Ballerina (Sadler's Wells (USA))
Miss L C Siddall Mrs Ann Morgan

Placings:06000-50500 **(5634)**
2001: 10^{5}F, 12^{0}GF, 10^{5}S, 10^{0}G, 11^{0}G

	Starts	1st	2nd	3rd	Win & Pl
Career Total (Turf)	10	0	0	0	0

Going (Turf): Sf: 0-4 GS: 0-0 Gd: 0-4 GF: 0-1 Fm: 0-1
Distance: 5f/6f: 0-0 7f-8f: 0-1 9f-13f: 0-8 14f+: 0-1
Track : LH: 0-8 RH: 0-2 Tight: 0-2 Gall: 0-3
Aids: Bl: 0-0 Vi: 0-0 Tstrap: 0-1
Best Rating: 32 7/01 Hayd 1m2f120y soft

Attention Seeker (USA)

(95) (36)**55**
4-y-o b/br f Exbourne (USA)-Popularity (USA) (Blushing Groom (FR))
S C Williams D G Burge

Placings:100-0006060400 **(5471)**
2001: 12^{0}S, 12^{0}G, 10^{0}F, 12^{6}GF, 9^{0}GF, 9^{6}GF, 12^{0}G, 11^{4}GF, 9^{0}S, 11^{0}S

	Starts	1st	2nd	3rd	Win & Pl
Career Total (Turf)	13	1	0	0	8646

6/00 MsnL 1m2f110y GD £8646
Total win prize-money £8646

Going (Turf): Sf: 0-4 GS: 0-0 Gd: 0-2 GF: 0-4 Fm: 0-1
Distance: 5f/6f: 0-0 7f-8f: 0-1 9f-13f: 0-10 14f+: 0-0
Track : LH: 0-4 RH: 0-7 Tight: 0-1 Gall: 0-3
Aids: Bl: 0-0 Vi: 0-0 Tstrap: 0-0
Best Rating: 73 5/01 NmkR 1m4f good

Attlee (USA)

79 **62**
2-y-o b/br c Atticus (USA)-No Rego (USA) (Riverman (USA))
E A L Dunlop Jumeirah Racing

Placings:4 **(2729)**
2001: 6^{4}GF

	Starts	1st	2nd	3rd	Win & Pl
Career Total (Turf)	1	0	0	0	268

Going (Turf): Sf: 0-0 GS: 0-0 Gd: 0-0 GF: 0-1 Fm: 0-0
Distance: 5f/6f: 0-0 7f-8f: 0-1 9f-13f: 0-0 14f+: 0-0
Track : LH: 0-0 RH: 0-0 Tight: 0-0 Gall: 0-0
Aids: Bl: 0-0 Vi: 0-0 Tstrap: 0-0
Best Rating: 62 7/01 Yarm 6f3y gd-fm

Atto (IRE)

78
7-y-o b g Mandalus-Deep Cristina (Deep Run)
P R Webber (J S King 19/7) S Clough

Placings:060-00 **(3187)**
2001: 10^{0}GF, 11^{0}GS

	Starts	1st	2nd	3rd	Win & Pl
Career Total (Turf)	5	0	0	0	0

Going (Turf): Sf: 0-0 GS: 0-1 Gd: 0-2 GF: 0-1 Fm: 0-1
Distance: 5f/6f: 0-0 7f-8f: 0-1 9f-13f: 0-4 14f+: 0-0
Track : LH: 0-3 RH: 0-2 Tight: 0-2 Gall: 0-0
Aids: Bl: 0-0 Vi: 0-0 Tstrap: 0-0
Best Rating: 7 7/01 Wwck 1m2f188y gd-fm

Attorney

(91) (68)**79**
3-y-o ch g Wolfhound (USA)-Princess Sadie (Shavian)
M A Jarvis J R Good

Placings:0222-2103360055 **(5414)**
2001: 5^{2}S, 5^{1}GS, 6^{0}G, 5^{3}GF, 6^{3}G, 6^{6}GS, 5^{0}G, 5^{0}HY, 6^{5}SD, 6^{5}SD

	Starts	1st	2nd	3rd	Win & Pl
Career Total (Turf)	12	1	4	2	8741
Career Total (AW)	2	0	0	0	0

75 4/01 Muss 5f D G-S £3542
Total win prize-money £3543

Going (Turf): Sf: 0-3 **GS: 1-3** Gd: 0-3 GF: 0-3 Fm: 0-0
Distance: **5f/6f: 1-14** 7f-8f: 0-0 9f-13f: 0-0 14f+: 0-0
Track : LH: 0-3 RH: 0-0 Tight: 0-2 Gall: 0-0
Aids: Bl: 0-0 Vi: 0-0 Tstrap: 0-0
Best Rating: 79 6/01 Ripn 6f good

After several near misses, he finally got off the mark in a Musselburgh maiden in April. Some fair efforts in handicap company since, but needs to drop a few pounds more.

Atylan Boy (IRE)

(100) (70d)**69**
4-y-o b g Efisio-Gold Flair (Tap On Wood)
B J Meehan Mrs Sheila Tucker

Placings:0650/00315246005000-13 **(0096)**
2001: 7^{1}SD, 7^{3}SD

	Starts	1st	2nd	3rd	Win & Pl
Career Total (Turf)	13	0	0	1	858
Career Total (AW)	7	2	1	1	5683

57 1/01 Sthl 7f G STD £1358
79 6/00 Ling 7f E(0-65) STD £2816
Total win prize-money £4175

Going (Turf): Sf: 0-6 GS: 0-0 Gd: 0-4 GF: 0-2 Fm: 0-1
Distance: 5f/6f: 0-3 **7f-8f: 2-14** 9f-13f: 0-3 14f+: 0-0
Track : **LH: 2-10** RH: 0-4 **Tight: 1-6** Gall: 0-2
Aids: Bl: 0-6 **Vi: 1-2** Tstrap: 0-0
Best Rating: 58 1/01 Sthl 7f stand

Aubrieta (USA)

(103) (52)**50**
5-y-o b m Dayjur (USA)-Fennel (Slew O'Gold (USA))
Andrew Reid (D Haydn Jones 10/4) A S Reid

Placings:6033030/00603000601/05204501140054054-2163135202600004 **(5350)**
2001: 7^{2}SD, 6^{1}SD, 7^{6}SW, 7^{3}SD, 6^{1}SD, 7^{3}SW, 7^{5}SD, 6^{2}SD, 7^{0}SD, 5^{2}GF, 5^{6}GF, 5^{0}G, 6^{0}GF, 5^{0}F, 6^{0}SD, 6^{0}SD, 5^{4}SD

	Starts	1st	2nd	3rd	Win & Pl
Career Total (Turf)	26	0	1	4	4835
Career Total (AW)	26	5	3	2	14630

52 1/01 Wolv 6f F STD £2205
56 1/01 Ling 6f F(0-60) STD £2142
60 6/00 Ling 6f F STD £2341
50 6/00 Ling 7f E STD £2403
58 11/99 Ling 6f D STD £3146
Total win prize-money £12239

Going (Turf): Sf: 0-4 GS: 0-1 Gd: 0-9 GF: 0-11 Fm: 0-1
Distance: **5f/6f: 4-26** 7f-8f: 1-23 9f-13f: 0-3 14f+: 0-0
Track : **LH: 5-29** RH: 0-3 **Tight: 5-23** Gall: 0-3
Aids: **Bl: 5-34** Vi: 0-2 Tstrap: 0-0
Best Rating: 58 3/01 Wolv 7f stand

Audacity

79(96) (26)**21**
5-y-o b g Minshaanshu Amad (USA)-Glory Isle (Hittite Glory)
N Hamilton City Industrial Supplies Ltd

Placings:000/00500/50000-20030 **(2523)**
2001: 12^{2}SD, 11^{0}SD, 16^{0}SD, 14^{3}SD, 12^{0}GF

	Starts	1st	2nd	3rd	Win & Pl
Career Total (Turf)	10	0	0	0	0
Career Total (AW)	8	0	1	1	797

Going (Turf): Sf: 0-2 GS: 0-0 Gd: 0-0 GF: 0-8 Fm: 0-0
Distance: 5f/6f: 0-3 7f-8f: 0-1 9f-13f: 0-11 14f+: 0-3
Track : LH: 0-11 RH: 0-3 Tight: 0-5 Gall: 0-1

Aids: Bl: 0-4 Vi: 0-0 Tstrap: 0-0
Best Rating: 26 6/01 Sthl 1m6f stand

Audrey's Dilemma

96 **63**
2-y-o b f Piccolo-Yesterday's Song (Shirley Heights)
S Dow Investor Information Limited

Placings:050 **(5588)**
2001: 6^0HY, 6^5S, 5^0GS

	Starts	1st	2nd	3rd	Win & Pl
Career Total (Turf)	3	0	0	0	0

Going (Turf): Sf: 0-2 GS: 0-1 Gd: 0-0 GF: 0-0 Fm: 0-0
Distance: 5f/6f: 0-2 7f-8f: 0-1 9f-13f: 0-0 14f+: 0-0
Track : LH: 0-2 RH: 0-0 Tight: 0-0 Gall: 0-0
Aids: Bl: 0-0 Vi: 0-0 Tstrap: 0-0
Best Rating: 63 10/01 Brig 6f209y soft

Aunt Doris

89 **40**
4-y-o b f Distant Relative-Nevis (Connaught)
D Eddy Dr P And Mrs D M Johnson

Placings:0130/600425-000400 **(5287)**
2001: 5^0F, 6^0G, 6^0GF, 6^4G, 6^0F, 6^0HY

	Starts	1st	2nd	3rd	Win & Pl
Career Total (Turf)	16	1	1	1	4484

66 8/99 Leic 5f2y G GD £2094
Total win prize-money £2094

Going (Turf): Sf: 0-2 GS: 0-0 **Gd: 1-5** GF: 0-7 Fm: 0-2
Distance: 5f/6f: 1-13 7f-8f: 0-3 9f-13f: 0-0 14f+: 0-0
Track : LH: 0-3 RH: 0-1 Tight: 0-0 Gall: 0-2
Aids: Bl: 0-0 Vi: 0-0 Tstrap: 0-0
Best Rating: 40 9/01 Haml 6f5y good

Aunt Hilda

91 **77**
2-y-o b f Distant Relative-Aloha Jane (USA) (Hawaii)
J L Dunlop Paul H Locke

Placings:50 **(5602)**
2001: 7^5GF, 7^0GS

	Starts	1st	2nd	3rd	Win & Pl
Career Total (Turf)	2	0	0	0	0

Going (Turf): Sf: 0-0 GS: 0-1 Gd: 0-0 GF: 0-1 Fm: 0-0
Distance: 5f/6f: 0-0 7f-8f: 0-2 9f-13f: 0-0 14f+: 0-0
Track : LH: 0-0 RH: 0-1 Tight: 0-0 Gall: 0-1
Aids: Bl: 0-0 Vi: 0-0 Tstrap: 0-0
Best Rating: 77 9/01 Kemp 7f gd-fm

Aunt Ruby (USA)

95(94) (54)**56**
3-y-o ch f Rubiano (USA)-Redress (USA) (Storm Cat (USA))
T P McGovern (M L W Bell 26/3) Heart Of The South Racing

Placings:02606-4510000 **(2059)**
2001: 8^4SW, 7^5SD, 7^1SD, 7^0GS, 6^0GF, 8^0GF, 6^0GF

	Starts	1st	2nd	3rd	Win & Pl
Career Total (Turf)	9	0	1	0	1320
Career Total (AW)	3	1	0	0	1827

49 3/01 Sthl 7f G STD £1827
Total win prize-money £1827

Going (Turf): Sf: 0-1 GS: 0-1 Gd: 0-2 GF: 0-5 Fm: 0-0
Distance: 5f/6f: 0-3 **7f-8f: 1-8** 9f-13f: 0-1 14f+: 0-0
Track : LH: 1-5 RH: 0-1 Tight: 0-2 Gall: 0-0
Aids: Bl: 0-0 Vi: 0-0 Tstrap: 0-0
Best Rating: 56 4/01 Brig 7f214y gd-sft

Out of a dam whose half-sister, Splendent, won the Gimcrack Stakes, appreciated both the drop in trip and in class to take a seller on the sand over seven furlongs.

Aunt Susan

68(49) **41**
3-y-o b f Distant Relative-Lawn Order (Efisio)
K McAuliffe Miss J Hall

Placings:0-000 **(4210)**
2001: 8^0S, 8^0SD, 11^0GF

	Starts	1st	2nd	3rd	Win & Pl
Career Total (Turf)	2	0	0	0	
Career Total (AW)	2	0	0	0	

Going (Turf): Sf: 0-1 GS: 0-0 Gd: 0-0 GF: 0-1 Fm: 0-0
Distance: 5f/6f: 0-1 7f-8f: 0-2 9f-13f: 0-1 14f+: 0-0
Track : LH: 0-3 RH: 0-0 Tight: 0-2 Gall: 0-0
Aids: Bl: 0-0 Vi: 0-0 Tstrap: 0-0
Best Rating: 41 5/01 Newb 1m soft

Auntie Dot Com

96(87) (54)**69**
2-y-o ch f Tagula (IRE)-Jadebelle (Beldale Flutter (USA))
W G M Turner Tony Smith

Placings:6130630 **(3628)**
2001: 5^6SW, 5^1S, 6^3F, 5^0GF, 6^6GF, 7^3GF, 7^0G

	Starts	1st	2nd	3rd	Win & Pl
Career Total (Turf)	6	1	0	2	5170
Career Total (AW)	1	0	0	0	0

68 4/01 Pont 5f E SFT £3472
Total win prize-money £3472

Going (Turf): Sf: 1-1 GS: 0-0 Gd: 0-1 GF: 0-3 Fm: 0-1
Distance: 5f/6f: 1-5 7f-8f: 0-2 9f-13f: 0-0 14f+: 0-0
Track : LH: 1-3 RH: 0-1 Tight: 0-0 Gall: 0-0
Aids: Bl: 0-0 Vi: 0-0 Tstrap: 0-0
Best Rating: 78 5/01 Pont 6f firm

She got off the mark on soft ground at Pontefract on her second start, but did not look the same horse on fast ground.

Aunty Mary

99 **79**
2-y-o b f Common Grounds-Flirtation (Pursuit Of Love)
T D Easterby And Mrs J D Cotton

Placings:0102200 **(4903)**
2001: 6^0GF, 5^1G, 5^0GF, 5^2G, 5^2F, 6^0G, 5^0G

	Starts	1st	2nd	3rd	Win & Pl
Career Total (Turf)	7	1	2	0	10151

79 6/01 York 5f D GD £5239
Total win prize-money £5239

Going (Turf): Sf: 0-0 GS: 0-0 **Gd: 1-4** GF: 0-2 Fm: 0-1
Distance: 5f/6f: 1-7 7f-8f: 0-0 9f-13f: 0-0 14f+: 0-0
Track : LH: 0-0 RH: 0-0 Tight: 0-0 Gall: 0-0
Aids: Bl: 0-0 Vi: 0-0 Tstrap: 0-0
Best Rating: 79 8/01 Thsk 5f firm

A lightly-made filly, she impressed on her debut at York with a gutsy performance in a hot maiden, and followed this up with a win over course and distance. Nurseries have proved elusive. Suited by five furlongs on good ground.

Aunty Rose (IRE)

105 **99**
4-y-o b f Caerleon (USA)-Come On Rosi (Valiyar)
J L Dunlop Wafic Said

Placings:130/300-643005 **(5479a)**
2001: 9^6G, 8^4GF, 8^3GF, 7^0G, 8^0GS, 8^5HY

	Starts	1st	2nd	3rd	Win & Pl
Career Total (Turf)	12	1	0	3	17825

78 7/99 NmkJ 7f D G-F £5061
Total win prize-money £5061

Going (Turf): Sf: 0-1 GS: 0-2 Gd: 0-5 **GF: 1-4** Fm: 0-0
Distance: 5f/6f: 0-0 **7f-8f: 1-10** 9f-13f: 0-2 14f+: 0-0
Track : LH: 0-2 RH: 0-2 Tight: 0-1 Gall: 0-1
Aids: Bl: 0-0 Vi: 0-0 Tstrap: 0-0
Best Rating: 99 5/01 Gdwd 1m gd-fm

A half-sister to Bin Rosie and closely related to Generous Libra and Generous Rosie, was highly tried in Group company as a juvenile in 1999. Injury ruined her three-year-old campaign, but she put in a much improved effort on her second start of the 2001 season in a Listed race over a mile, and ran well at Epsom subsequently. Has shown signs of temperament in the past, stays a mile and acts on a sound surface.

Aura Of Grace (USA)

99 **73**
4-y-o b/br f Southern Halo (USA)-Avarice (USA) (Manila (USA))
M Johnston R N Bracher

Placings:0/6501-2 **(1240)**
2001: 10^2G

	Starts	1st	2nd	3rd	Win & Pl
Career Total (Turf)	6	1	1	0	4259

73 10/00 Muss 1m D SFT £2726
Total win prize-money £2727

Going (Turf): Sf: 1-1 GS: 0-2 Gd: 0-2 GF: 0-1 Fm: 0-0
Distance: 5f/6f: 0-1 **7f-8f: 1-3** 9f-13f: 0-2 14f+: 0-0
Track : LH: 0-0 RH: 1-3 Tight: 1-2 Gall: 0-0
Aids: Bl: 0-0 Vi: 0-0 Tstrap: 0-0
Best Rating: 73 5/01 Ripn 1m2f good

Auriferous (USA)

78 **61**
2-y-o b c Seeking The Gold (USA)-Minigroom (USA) (Mt. Livermore (USA))
D R Loder Sheikh Mohammed

Placings:6 **(2947)**
2001: 6^6G

	Starts	1st	2nd	3rd	Win & Pl
Career Total (Turf)	1	0	0	0	0

Going (Turf): Sf: 0-0 GS: 0-0 Gd: 0-1 GF: 0-0 Fm: 0-0
Distance: 5f/6f: 0-1 7f-8f: 0-0 9f-13f: 0-0 14f+: 0-0
Track : LH: 0-0 RH: 0-0 Tight: 0-0 Gall: 0-0
Aids: Bl: 0-0 Vi: 0-0 Tstrap: 0-0
Best Rating: 61 7/01 NmkJ 6f good

Autumn Fantasy (USA)

87 **68**
2-y-o b/br c Lear Fan (USA)-Autumn Glory (USA) (Graustark)
J H M Gosden K Abdulla

Placings:6 **(5559)**
2001: 8^6S

	Starts	1st	2nd	3rd	Win & Pl
Career Total (Turf)	1	0	0	0	0

Going (Turf): Sf: 0-1 **GS:** 0-0 **Gd:** 0-0 **GF:** 0-0 **Fm:** 0-0
Distance: 5f/6f: 0-0 7f-8f: 0-0 9f-13f: 0-1 14f+: 0-0
Track : LH: 0-0 RH: 0-0 Tight: 0-0 Gall: 0-0
Aids: Bl: 0-0 Vi: 0-0 Tstrap: 0-0
Best Rating: 68 10/01 Yarm 1m3y soft

Autumn Rain (USA)

(108) (67)**63**
4-y-o br g Dynaformer (USA)-Edda (USA) (Ogygian (USA))
N A Callaghan (L Montague Hall 18/10) K Ovenden And M C Lane

Placings:55/20130-00 **(5608)**
2001: 8^{0}GS, 7^{0}GS

	Starts	1st	2nd	3rd	Win & Pl
Career Total (Turf)	9	1	1	1	5047

78 5/00 Ling 7f D G-S £3282
Total win prize-money £3283

Going (Turf): Sf: 0-4 **GS: 1-4** Gd: 0-0 GF: 0-1 Fm: 0-0
Distance: 5f/6f: 0-0 **7f-8f: 1-7** 9f-13f: 0-2 14f+: 0-0
Track : LH: 0-3 RH: 0-1 Tight: 0-1 Gall: 0-1
Aids: Bl: 0-0 Vi: 0-0 Tstrap: 0-0
Best Rating: 63 11/01 NmkR 7f gd-sft

Autumn Rhythm

93 **85**
3-y-o b f Hernando (FR)-Fextal (USA) (Alleged (USA))
H R A Cecil Niarchos Family

Placings:1-6 **(0813)**
2001: 9^{6}S

	Starts	1st	2nd	3rd	Win & Pl
Career Total (Turf)	2	1	0	0	3580

84 10/00 Yarm 1m3y D HVY £3233
Total win prize-money £3234

Going (Turf): Sf: 1-2 GS: 0-0 Gd: 0-0 GF: 0-0 Fm: 0-0
Distance: 5f/6f: 0-0 7f-8f: 0-0 **9f-13f: 1-2** 14f+: 0-0
Track : LH: 0-0 RH: 0-0 Tight: 0-0 Gall: 0-0
Aids: Bl: 0-0 Vi: 0-0 **Tstrap: 1-2**
Best Rating: 85 4/01 NmkR 1m1f soft

A tall filly, she was impressive when winning her one and only start as a juvenile. Broke a blood-vessel on her return and was not seen again.

Autumnal (IRE)

109 **100**
3-y-o b f Indian Ridge-Please Believe Me (Try My Best (USA))
B J Meehan Paul & Jenny Green

Placings:3112340-004601260 **(5244a)**
2001: 7^{0}GS, 8^{0}G, 6^{4}S, 7^{6}GF, 6^{0}GF, 6^{1}GF, 5^{2}GS, 5^{6}GF, 5^{0}HO

	Starts	1st	2nd	3rd	Win & Pl
Career Total (Turf)	16	3	2	2	62276

91 6/01 NmkJ 6f C G-F £6017
96 6/00 Asct 5f B G-F £20300
74 6/00 Hayd 5f D G-S £3526
Total win prize-money £29843

Going (Turf): Sf: 0-1 GS: 1-6 Gd: 0-2 **GF: 2-6** Fm: 0-0
Distance: 5f/6f: 3-11 7f-8f: 0-5 9f-13f: 0-0 14f+: 0-0
Track : LH: 0-0 RH: 0-1 Tight: 0-0 Gall: 0-1
Aids: Bl: 1-3 Vi: 0-0 Tstrap: 0-0
Best Rating: 100 5/01 NmkR 1m good

Very useful sprint form as a juvenile but has not looked quite the same horse this season having failed to stay beyond sprint distances. Returned to winning ways at Newmarket in July over her favoured six furlongs and in blinkers, and a good second in Listed company next time. Acts on fast ground.

Avalanche (FR)

77 **67**
4-y-o gr g Highest Honor (FR)-Fairy Gold (Golden Fleece (USA))
J R Best The Downhill Partnership

Placings:0/60356-0 **(0897)**
2001: 9^{0}HY

	Starts	1st	2nd	3rd	Win & Pl
Career Total (Turf)	7	0	0	1	350

Going (Turf): Sf: 0-3 GS: 0-0 Gd: 0-0 GF: 0-1 Fm: 0-1
Distance: 5f/6f: 0-0 7f-8f: 0-4 9f-13f: 0-2 14f+: 0-0
Track : LH: 0-1 RH: 0-4 Tight: 0-1 Gall: 0-1
Aids: Bl: 0-0 Vi: 0-0 Tstrap: 0-1
Best Rating: 12 4/01 Folk 1m1f149y heavy

Avanti

99(87) (50)**73**
5-y-o gr h Reprimand-Dolly Bevan (Another Realm)
Dr J R J Naylor A R M Galbraith

Placings:0/04120/00-00 **(3426)**
2001: 9^{0}SD, 14^{0}GF

	Starts	1st	2nd	3rd	Win & Pl
Career Total (Turf)	8	1	1	0	5665
Career Total (AW)	2	0	0	0	

72 5/99 Sand 7f16y D(0-80)H GD £4474
Total win prize-money £4475

Going (Turf): Sf: 0-1 GS: 0-0 **Gd: 1-3** GF: 0-4 Fm: 0-0
Distance: 5f/6f: 0-1 **7f-8f: 1-5** 9f-13f: 0-3 14f+: 0-1
Track : LH: 0-3 **RH: 1-3** Tight: 0-4 Gall: 0-1
Aids: Bl: 0-1 Vi: 0-0 Tstrap: 0-0
Best Rating: 54 7/01 Sals 1m6f15y gd-fm

Avebury

(99) (65)**60**
5-y-o b g Fairy King (USA)-Circle Of Chalk (FR) (Kris)
S E Kettlewell (T D Easterby 4/7) The Tupgill Partnership

Placings:54023353461 **(4874)**
2001: 11^{5}SD, 9^{4}GS, 11^{0}SD, 9^{2}F, 8^{3}GF, 9^{3}G, 7^{5}GF, 7^{3}GF, 9^{4}G, 8^{6}G, 8^{1}SD

	Starts	1st	2nd	3rd	Win & Pl
Career Total (Turf)	8	0	1	3	2466
Career Total (AW)	3	1	0	0	3007

65 9/01 Wolv 1m100y E(0-70)H STD £3006
Total win prize-money £3007

Going (Turf): Sf: 0-0 GS: 0-1 Gd: 0-3 GF: 0-3 Fm: 0-1
Distance: 5f/6f: 0-0 7f-8f: 0-3 **9f-13f: 1-8** 14f+: 0-0
Track : LH: 1-7 RH: 0-2 **Tight: 1-3** Gall: 0-2
Aids: Bl: 0-0 Vi: 0-0 Tstrap: 0-2
Best Rating: 65 9/01 Wolv 1m100y stand

Lightly raced. Does not find a lot at the business end. Best at around a mile. Has worn a tongue tie.

Aveiro (IRE)

(100) (41)**49**
5-y-o b g Darshaan-Avila (Ajdal (USA))
C P Morlock The Dream Connection

Placings:05300/**50202**303113540306 **(5411)**
2001: 9^{5}SW, 16^{0}SD, 13^{2}SD, 12^{0}SW, 13^{2}SD, 16^{3}SD, 14^{0}S, 11^{3}GS, 11^{1}F, 11^{1}GF, 12^{3}GF, 14^{5}GF, 12^{4}GF, 11^{0}GF, 12^{3}GF, 16^{0}GF, 14^{6}SD

	Starts	1st	2nd	3rd	Win & Pl
Career Total (Turf)	15	2	0	4	7112
Career Total (AW)	7	0	2	1	1457

46 5/01 Yarm 1m3f101yE(0-70)H G-F £3052
46 5/01 Brig 1m3f196yG(0-60)H FRM £2009
Total win prize-money £5061

Going (Turf): Sf: 0-1 GS: 0-1 Gd: 0-2 **GF: 1-10 Fm: 1-1**
Distance: 5f/6f: 0-0 7f-8f: 0-1 **9f-13f: 2-15** 14f+: 0-6
Track : LH: 2-16 RH: 0-3 **Tight: 1-12** Gall: 0-1
Aids: Bl: 2-19 Vi: 0-0 Tstrap: 0-0
Best Rating: 49 6/01 Rdcr 1m6f19y gd-fm

Averham Star

89(78) (15)**28**
6-y-o ch g Absalom-Upper Sister (Upper Case (USA))
W Clay Lee Heath

Placings:0050/4546430500/60060600050/00060000-000 **(1594)**
2001: 7^{0}SW, 6^{0}S, 6^{0}GF

	Starts	1st	2nd	3rd	Win & Pl
Career Total (Turf)	18	0	0	0	0
Career Total (AW)	18	0	0	1	620

Going (Turf): Sf: 0-2 GS: 0-2 Gd: 0-4 GF: 0-9 Fm: 0-1
Distance: 5f/6f: 0-9 7f-8f: 0-10 9f-13f: 0-17 14f+: 0-0
Track : LH: 0-28 RH: 0-1 Tight: 0-7 Gall: 0-0
Aids: Bl: 0-9 Vi: 0-4 Tstrap: 0-0
Best Rating: 41 5/01 Hayd 6f soft

Averted View (USA)

100 **82**
4-y-o ch f Distant View (USA)-Averti (USA) (Known Fact (USA))
R T Phillips Flying Tiger Partnership

Placings:24431-03250 **(5669)**
2001: 10^{0}GF, 10^{3}GF, 11^{2}GF, 12^{5}G, 10^{0}HY

	Starts	1st	2nd	3rd	Win & Pl
Career Total (Turf)	10	1	2	2	16398

11/00 Bord 1m HVY £3362
Total win prize-money £3362

Going (Turf): Sf: 1-2 GS: 0-0 Gd: 0-1 GF: 0-3 Fm: 0-0
Distance: 5f/6f: 0-0 **7f-8f: 1-1** 9f-13f: 0-5 14f+: 0-0
Track : LH: 0-2 RH: 0-2 Tight: 0-1 Gall: 0-2
Aids: Bl: 1-1 Vi: 0-0 Tstrap: 0-0
Best Rating: 82 6/01 Newb 1m2f6y gd-fm

Wore blinkers when scoring his only success to date over a mile in heavy ground in the French Provinces when trained by Mme C Head-Maarek. Has run well without the headgear for new connections this term. Appears to stay 12 furlongs.

Avery Ring

98(101) (68)**66**

3-y-o b g Magic Ring (IRE)-Thatcherella (Thatching)

A P Jarvis Avery Ring Partnership

Placings:62340-215000653 **(4226)**

2001: 7^{2}SD, 7^{1}SD, 8^{5}SD, 7^{0}SD, 6^{0}GS, 6^{0}S, 7^{6}GF, 7^{5}G, 7^{3}GF

						Starts	1st	2nd	3rd	Win & Pl
Career Total (Turf)						10	0	1	2	2432
Career Total (AW)						4	1	1	0	3712
68	2/01	Wolv	7f	D	STD					£2884

Total win prize-money £2884

Going (Turf): Sf: 0-1 GS: 0-1 Gd: 0-2 GF: 0-5 Fm: 0-0
Distance: 5f/6f: 0-3 **7f-8f: 1-9** 9f-13f: 0-1 14f+: 0-0
Track : **LH: 1-6** RH: 0-1 **Tight: 1-3** Gall: 0-1
Aids: Bl: 0-0 Vi: 0-0 Tstrap: 0-0
Best Rating: 68 2/01 Wolv 7f stand

It appeared he responded well to being gelded over the winter, when he took a seven-furlong maiden on the sand, but has failed to add to that.

Awake

100 **90**

4-y-o ch g First Trump-Pluvial (Habat)

D Nicholls (N P Littmoden 1/7) Lucayan Stud

Placings:2114/042031400-00000000 **(5502)**

2001: 6^{0}S, 6^{0}GS, 5^{0}G, 5^{0}GF, 5^{0}G, 5^{0}GF, 5^{0}GS, 5^{0}HY

							Starts	1st	2nd	3rd	Win & Pl
Career Total (Turf)							21	3	2	1	41755
99	7/00	Newb	6f8y	B(0-105)H	G-F						£8914
91	10/99	Newb	6f8y	C(0-95)H	HVY						£6287
73	8/99	Epsm	6f	D	GD						£3420

Total win prize-money £18623

Going (Turf): Sf: 1-7 GS: 0-3 **Gd: 1-5 GF: 1-6** Fm: 0-0
Distance: 5f/6f: 1-19 **7f-8f: 2-2** 9f-13f: 0-0 14f+: 0-0
Track : **LH: 1-2** RH: 0-0 **Tight: 1-2** Gall: 0-0
Aids: Bl: 0-0 Vi: 0-0 Tstrap: 0-0
Best Rating: 87 4/01 NmkR 6f gd-sft

Useful handicapper, best at six furlongs, acts on any ground and has two wins from two runs at Newbury. Tends to race prominently. Out of form this year for new connections, but gradually dropping down the handicap.

Away Win

98 **47**

3-y-o b f Common Grounds-Cafe Glace (Beldale Flutter (USA))

B Palling Albert Yemm

Placings:50-000 **(4459)**

2001: 5^{0}G, 8^{0}GF, 7^{0}G

	Starts	1st	2nd	3rd	Win & Pl
Career Total (Turf)	5	0	0	0	0

Going (Turf): Sf: 0-0 GS: 0-0 Gd: 0-2 GF: 0-3 Fm: 0-0
Distance: 5f/6f: 0-1 7f-8f: 0-2 9f-13f: 0-2 14f+: 0-0
Track : LH: 0-1 RH: 0-2 Tight: 0-1 Gall: 0-1
Aids: Bl: 0-0 Vi: 0-0 Tstrap: 0-0
Best Rating: 47 6/01 Wind 1m67y gd-fm

Ayem (IRE)

83 **39**

6-y-o ch g Sharp Victor (USA)-Morning Crown (USA) (Chief's Crown (USA))

C Weedon Mrs M A Peet

Placings:506/044/0 **(1076)**

2001: 11^{0}GS

	Starts	1st	2nd	3rd	Win & Pl
Career Total (Turf)	6	0	0	0	510
Career Total (AW)	1	0	0	0	203

Going (Turf): Sf: 0-1 GS: 0-1 Gd: 0-1 GF: 0-2 Fm: 0-0
Distance: 5f/6f: 0-0 7f-8f: 0-3 9f-13f: 0-1 14f+: 0-3
Track : LH: 0-4 RH: 0-2 Tight: 0-1 Gall: 0-2
Aids: Bl: 0-0 Vi: 0-0 Tstrap: 0-3
Best Rating: 39 5/01 Brig 1m3f196y gd-sft

Ayzal

99 **75**

2-y-o br f Zilzal (USA)-Ayunli (Chief Singer)

W J Haggas I A Southcott

Placings:1123 **(5364)**

2001: 5^{1}GF, 5^{1}GF, 6^{2}G, 6^{3}GS

						Starts	1st	2nd	3rd	Win & Pl
Career Total (Turf)						4	2	1	1	19782
70	6/01	Bevl	5f	D	G-F					£3461
60	6/01	Yarm	5f43y	F	G-F					£2296

Total win prize-money £5757

Going (Turf): Sf: 0-0 GS: 0-1 Gd: 0-1 **GF: 2-2** Fm: 0-0
Distance: **5f/6f: 2-4** 7f-8f: 0-0 9f-13f: 0-0 14f+: 0-0
Track : LH: 0-0 RH: 0-0 Tight: 0-0 Gall: 0-0
Aids: Bl: 0-0 Vi: 0-0 Tstrap: 0-0
Best Rating: 75 10/01 NmkR 6f gd-sft

Won her first two starts at Yarmouth and Beverley, both of which came in June, and got six furlongs well when second in a competitive event at Ayr. Should stay further. Has won on good to firm.

Azillion (IRE)

(99) (85+)**86**

2-y-o b c Alzao (USA)-Olivia (IRE) (Ela-Mana-Mou)

J W Hills M Kerr-Dineen, W Eason, M Smith

Placings:02 **(4671)**

2001: 7^{0}GF, 8^{2}G

	Starts	1st	2nd	3rd	Win & Pl
Career Total (Turf)	2	0	1	0	832

Going (Turf): Sf: 0-0 GS: 0-0 Gd: 0-1 GF: 0-1 Fm: 0-0
Distance: 5f/6f: 0-0 7f-8f: 0-1 9f-13f: 0-1 14f+: 0-0
Track : LH: 0-0 RH: 0-0 Tight: 0-0 Gall: 0-0
Aids: Bl: 0-0 Vi: 0-0 Tstrap: 0-0
Best Rating: 86 9/01 Chep 1m14y good

Aziz Presenting (IRE)

84 **89**

3-y-o br f Charnwood Forest (IRE)-Khalatara (IRE) (Kalaglow)

M R Channon Coriolan Partnership

Placings:201023-0 **(0815)**

2001: 6^{0}S

						Starts	1st	2nd	3rd	Win & Pl
Career Total (Turf)						7	1	2	1	8440
76	6/00	Sals	5f	D	G-F					£3120

Total win prize-money £3120

Going (Turf): Sf: 0-3 GS: 0-1 Gd: 0-1 **GF: 1-2** Fm: 0-0
Distance: **5f/6f: 1-7** 7f-8f: 0-0 9f-13f: 0-0 14f+: 0-0
Track : LH: 0-1 RH: 0-0 Tight: 0-1 Gall: 0-0
Aids: Bl: 0-0 Vi: 0-0 Tstrap: 0-0
Best Rating: 58 4/01 NmkR 6f soft

A winner at the minimum trip, she took the step up to six in her stride and should get further in time. Best on a sound surface.

Azur (IRE)

103 **60**

4-y-o b f Brief Truce (USA)-Bayadere (USA) (Green Dancer (USA))

Mrs A L M King All The Kings Horses

Placings:01/00000-0003311450 **(4635)**

2001: 9^{0}G, 11^{0}F, 9^{0}GF, 10^{3}F, 10^{3}GF, 10^{1}F, 9^{1}GF, 10^{4}G, 10^{5}GF, 9^{0}GF

						Starts	1st	2nd	3rd	Win & Pl
Career Total (Turf)						17	3	0	2	12061
60	8/01	Leic	1m1f218y	D(0-80)H	G-F					£4176
52	7/01	Bath	1m2f46y	E(0-70)H	FRM					£3101
75	10/99	Ling	7f	E	G-F					£3509

Total win prize-money £10786

Going (Turf): Sf: 0-1 GS: 0-1 Gd: 0-6 **GF: 2-6** Fm: 1-3
Distance: 5f/6f: 0-0 7f-8f: 1-4 **9f-13f: 2-13** 14f+: 0-0
Track : LH: 1-6 RH: 1-8 **Tight: 1-4** Gall: 0-3
Aids: Bl: 0-0 Vi: 0-2 Tstrap: 0-0
Best Rating: 60 8/01 Leic 1m1f218y gd-fm

Landed an ordinary fillies' handicap at Bath in July and followed up in a better race at Leicester. She acts well on fast ground, and suited by a strong pace.

Azzan (USA)

71(81) (39)

5-y-o b/br g Gulch (USA)-Dixieland Dream (USA) (Dixieland Band (USA))

T Keddy Brensway Partnership

Placings:005/404006/00-00 **(1620)**

2001: 12^{0}S, 16^{0}GF

	Starts	1st	2nd	3rd	Win & Pl
Career Total (Turf)	11	0	0	0	846
Career Total (AW)	2	0	0	0	0

Going (Turf): Sf: 0-4 GS: 0-0 Gd: 0-2 GF: 0-4 Fm: 0-1
Distance: 5f/6f: 0-3 7f-8f: 0-3 9f-13f: 0-6 14f+: 0-1
Track : LH: 0-5 RH: 0-2 Tight: 0-4 Gall: 0-0
Aids: Bl: 0-2 Vi: 0-0 Tstrap: 0-3

B Beautiful (IRE)

73 **59**

2-y-o ch f Be My Guest (USA)-Lady Donna (Dominion)
M L W Bell Mrs Caroline Parker

Placings:00 **(5666)**
2001: 8^{0}HY, 6^{0}HY

	Starts	1st	2nd	3rd	Win & Pl
Career Total (Turf)	2	0	0	0	

Going (Turf): Sf: 0-2 GS: 0-0 Gd: 0-0 GF: 0-0 Fm: 0-0
Distance: 5f/6f: 0-1 7f-8f: 0-0 9f-13f: 0-1 14f+: 0-0
Track : LH: 0-1 RH: 0-0 Tight: 0-0 Gall: 0-0
Aids: Bl: 0-0 Vi: 0-0 Tstrap: 0-0
Best Rating: 59 11/01 Wind 6f heavy

B Major (IRE)

(96) (72)**67**

2-y-o b g Key Of Luck (USA)-Lingering Melody (IRE) (Nordico (USA))
M A Jarvis Mr & Mrs Raymond Anderson Green

Placings:00 **(3960)**
2001: 6^{0}G, 6^{0}G

	Starts	1st	2nd	3rd	Win & Pl
Career Total (Turf)	2	0	0	0	

Going (Turf): Sf: 0-0 GS: 0-0 Gd: 0-2 GF: 0-0 Fm: 0-0
Distance: 5f/6f: 0-1 7f-8f: 0-1 9f-13f: 0-0 14f+: 0-0
Track : LH: 0-1 RH: 0-0 Tight: 0-0 Gall: 0-0
Aids: Bl: 0-0 Vi: 0-0 Tstrap: 0-0
Best Rating: 67 8/01 Yarm 6f3y good

B W Leader

58(81) (20)**30**

4-y-o b g Owington-Showery (Rainbow Quest (USA))
Miss D A McHale Watmore/davis/amon Racing

Placings:0/00-0050 **(0735)**
2001: 8^{0}SD, 7^{0}SD, 5^{5}SW, 5^{0}GS

	Starts	1st	2nd	3rd	Win & Pl
Career Total (Turf)	3	0	0	0	
Career Total (AW)	4	0	0	0	0

Going (Turf): Sf: 0-0 GS: 0-2 Gd: 0-0 GF: 0-1 Fm: 0-0
Distance: 5f/6f: 0-5 7f-8f: 0-2 9f-13f: 0-0 14f+: 0-0
Track : LH: 0-5 RH: 0-1 Tight: 0-3 Gall: 0-1
Aids: Bl: 0-1 Vi: 0-0 Tstrap: 0-2
Best Rating: 19 1/01 Wolv 7f stand

B'Elanna Torres

87 **63+**

2-y-o b f Entrepreneur-Miss Kemble (Warning)
W R Muir M J Caddy

Placings:30 **(5277)**
2001: 5^{3}GF, 7^{0}GS

	Starts	1st	2nd	3rd	Win & Pl
Career Total (Turf)	2	0	0	1	675

Going (Turf): Sf: 0-0 GS: 0-1 Gd: 0-0 GF: 0-1 Fm: 0-0
Distance: 5f/6f: 0-1 7f-8f: 0-1 9f-13f: 0-0 14f+: 0-0
Track : LH: 0-0 RH: 0-0 Tight: 0-0 Gall: 0-0
Aids: Bl: 0-0 Vi: 0-0 Tstrap: 0-0
Best Rating: 63 6/01 Sals 5f gd-fm

Baaridd

98 **108**

3-y-o b c Halling (USA)-Millstream (USA) (Dayjur (USA))
M A Jarvis Sheikh Ahmed Al Maktoum

Placings:12516-600 **(3443)**
2001: 6^{6}GF, 6^{0}GF, 7^{0}GF

	Starts	1st	2nd	3rd	Win & Pl		
Career Total (Turf)	8	2	1	0	28210		
101	8/00	Ripn	6f	A		GD	£13888
88	5/00	Gdwd	5f	D		G-S	£4114

Total win prize-money £18003

Going (Turf): Sf: 0-0 **GS: 1-1 Gd: 1-2** GF: 0-5 Fm: 0-0
Distance: **5f/6f: 2-5** 7f-8f: 0-3 9f-13f: 0-0 14f+: 0-0
Track : LH: 0-0 RH: 0-1 Tight: 0-0 Gall: 0-0
Aids: Bl: 0-0 Vi: 0-0 Tstrap: 0-0
Best Rating: 102 5/01 Hayd 6f gd-fm

He was a smart juvenile, finishing runner-up in the Chesham Stakes and winning a good prize at Ripon, before running a creditable fifth in the Middle Park. He made little impression in 2001.

Baba Au Rhum (IRE)

98 **58**

9-y-o b g Baba Karam-Spring About (Hard Fought)
Ian Williams Horses For Courses Partnership

Placings:06043/201401/4500/00-6 **(2246)**
2001: 10^{6}GF

	Starts	1st	2nd	3rd	Win & Pl		
Career Total (Turf)	18	2	1	1	8529		
71	8/97	Hayd	1m30y	E(0-70)H		G-F	£3143
67	6/97	Sand	1m14y	D(0-75)H		G-F	£3582

Total win prize-money £6727

Going (Turf): Sf: 0-0 GS: 0-1 Gd: 0-8 **GF: 2-9** Fm: 0-0
Distance: 5f/6f: 0-0 7f-8f: 0-5 **9f-13f: 2-13** 14f+: 0-0
Track : LH: 1-6 RH: 1-7 Tight: 0-3 Gall: 0-0
Aids: Bl: 0-0 Vi: 0-0 Tstrap: 0-0
Best Rating: 58 6/01 Wwck 1m2f188y gd-fm

Baby Barry

109 (79)**76**

4-y-o b g Komaite (USA)-Malcesine (IRE) (Auction Ring (USA))
Mrs G S Rees John W Barry

Placings:02236233401 2/003430335000000-3001310140 **(5630)**
2001: 7^{3}F, 7^{0}F, 6^{0}GF, 6^{1}GF, 6^{3}GF, 6^{1}G, 6^{0}G, 6^{1}G, 6^{4}G, 6^{0}G

	Starts	1st	2nd	3rd	Win & Pl		
Career Total (Turf)	35	4	3	8	39526		
Career Total (AW)	2	0	1	1	911		
76	9/01	Gdwd	6f	C(0-95)H		GD	£9506
69	8/01	Newc	6f	E(0-75)H		GD	£3143
69	7/01	Pont	6f	E(0-65)		G-F	£3753
77	10/99	Rdcr	5f	F		GD	£2547

Total win prize-money £18951

Going (Turf): Sf: 0-7 GS: 0-5 **Gd: 3-12** GF: 1-7 Fm: 0-4
Distance: **5f/6f: 4-28** 7f-8f: 0-9 9f-13f: 0-0 14f+: 0-0
Track : **LH: 1-8** RH: 0-2 Tight: 0-4 Gall: 0-3
Aids: Bl: 1-3 **Vi: 3-9** Tstrap: 0-0
Best Rating: 76 10/01 NmkR 6f good

He had a poor strike rate despite running some fine races, but needed a big drop in the handicap to help him get back to winning ways and has done so at Pontefract, Newcastle and Goodwood this season. Suited by six furlongs and the ground good or faster.

Baby Be

70 **11**

7-y-o b m Bold Arrangement-B Grade (Lucky Wednesday)
T P Tate M Grant

Placings:00006 **(2818)**
2001: 6^{0}GS, 6^{0}GF, 6^{0}GF, 7^{0}GF, 5^{6}GF

	Starts	1st	2nd	3rd	Win & Pl
Career Total (Turf)	5	0	0	0	0

Going (Turf): Sf: 0-0 GS: 0-1 Gd: 0-0 GF: 0-4 Fm: 0-0
Distance: 5f/6f: 0-4 7f-8f: 0-1 9f-13f: 0-0 14f+: 0-0
Track : LH: 0-2 RH: 0-1 Tight: 0-0 Gall: 0-0
Aids: Bl: 0-0 Vi: 0-0 Tstrap: 0-0
Best Rating: 11 7/01 Bevl 5f gd-fm

Baby Bunting

98(94) (41)**64**

3-y-o b f Wolfhound (USA)-Flitteriss Park (Beldale Flutter (USA))
M L W Bell Lady O'Brien, H Farr, Mrs P Gray

Placings:444-606030 **(4302)**
2001: 5^{6}SD, 5^{0}GF, 5^{6}GF, 6^{0}GF, 5^{3}G, 6^{0}GF

	Starts	1st	2nd	3rd	Win & Pl
Career Total (Turf)	8	0	0	1	1419
Career Total (AW)	1	0	0	0	0

Going (Turf): Sf: 0-0 GS: 0-1 Gd: 0-3 GF: 0-4 Fm: 0-0
Distance: 5f/6f: 0-9 7f-8f: 0-0 9f-13f: 0-0 14f+: 0-0
Track : LH: 0-3 RH: 0-1 Tight: 0-1 Gall: 0-1
Aids: Bl: 0-0 Vi: 0-0 Tstrap: 0-0
Best Rating: 62 6/01 NmkJ 5f gd-fm

Baby Maybe (USA)

91 **18**

3-y-o b f Known Fact (USA)-Bai Shun (USA) (Fappiano (USA))
T H Caldwell R S G Jones

Placings:005-0500000 **(4236)**
2001: 5^{0}S, 5^{5}G, 5^{0}G, 5^{0}G, 5^{0}GF, 5^{0}GS, 5^{0}GF

	Starts	1st	2nd	3rd	Win & Pl
Career Total (Turf)	10	0	0	0	0

Going (Turf): Sf: 0-3 GS: 0-1 Gd: 0-3 GF: 0-3 Fm: 0-0
Distance: 5f/6f: 0-10 7f-8f: 0-0 9f-13f: 0-0 14f+: 0-0
Track : LH: 0-0 RH: 0-0 Tight: 0-0 Gall: 0-0
Aids: Bl: 0-3 Vi: 0-0 Tstrap: 0-0
Best Rating: 43 5/01 Bevl 5f good

She has shown little in her races to date.

Bacchanalia (IRE)

96 **75**

2-y-o b f Blues Traveller (IRE)-Daffodil Dale (IRE) (Cyrano De Bergerac)
J L Eyre R Peel M Hpkinson J Binney G Frankland

Placings:0510 **(5185)**
2001: 7^{0}G, 8^{5}GF, 7^{1}S, 7^{0}GS

	Starts	1st	2nd	3rd	Win & Pl		
Career Total (Turf)	4	1	0	0	4544		
75	9/01	Ches	7f2y	D		SFT	£4543

Total win prize-money £4544

Going (Turf): **Sf: 1-1** GS: 0-1 Gd: 0-1 GF: 0-1 Fm: 0-0
Distance: 5f/6f: 0-0 **7f-8f: 1-3** 9f-13f: 0-1 14f+: 0-0
Track : **LH: 1-2** RH: 0-1 **Tight: 1-2** Gall: 0-0
Aids: Bl: 0-0 Vi: 0-0 Tstrap: 0-0
Best Rating: 75 9/01 Ches 7f2y soft

Improved with racing to take a Chester maiden on soft in September, but was well beaten next time when not looking very keen.

Bacchus

102(96) (69)**69d**

7-y-o b g Prince Sabo-Bonica (Rousillon (USA))
K A Ryan Uncle Jacks Pub

Placings:416000/00/0015015/2322156020300-00011000 **(1985)**

2001: 8^{0}S, 10^{0}HY, 10^{0}S, 9^{1}GS, 9^{1}G, 9^{0}F, 10^{0}GF, 10^{0}G

	Starts	1st	2nd	3rd	Win & Pl
Career Total (Turf)	33	6	4	1	32080
Career Total (AW)	3	0	0	1	487

64	5/01	Bevl	1m1f207y	E(0-70)H	GD	£3647
42	5/01	Haml	1m1f36y	E	G-S	£3206
74	7/00	Ches	1m2f75y	D(0-80)H	G-S	£5798
63	8/99	Bevl	7f100y	E(0-70)H	GD	£4874
58	7/99	Bevl	7f100y	F(0-60)H	G-F	£2810
80	7/97	NmkJ	6f	D	G-S	£3913

Total win prize-money £24248

Going (Turf): Sf: 0-8 **GS: 3-5** Gd: 2-12 GF: 1-7 Fm: 0-1
Distance: 5f/6f: 1-6 7f-8f: 2-12 **9f-13f: 3-18** 14f+: 0-0
Track : LH: 1-14 **RH: 4-11 Tight: 2-8** Gall: 0-3
Aids: Bl: 0-2 **Vi: 1-7** Tstrap: 0-0
Best Rating: 64 5/01 Bevl 1m1f207y good

Bit of a character these days who needs holding up for a late run. Goes very well at Beverley.

Baccura (IRE)

108(104) (81)98

3-y-o b g Dolphin Street (FR)-Luzzara (IRE) (Tate Gallery (USA))

A P Jarvis Christopher Shankland

Placings:0212-040222 (1535)

2001: 7^{0}SD, 7^{4}SD, 8^{0}GS, 7^{2}G, 7^{2}GF, 7^{2}GF

	Starts	1st	2nd	3rd	Win & Pl
Career Total (Turf)	8	1	5	0	22226
Career Total (AW)	2	0	0	0	798

74	7/00	Pont	6f	E	G-F	£3302

Total win prize-money £3302

Going (Turf): Sf: 0-0 GS: 0-1 Gd: 0-1 **GF: 1-5** Fm: 0-1
Distance: **5f/6f: 1-4** 7f-8f: 0-6 9f-13f: 0-0 14f+: 0-0
Track : **LH: 1-4** RH: 0-1 Tight: 0-0 Gall: 0-1
Aids: Bl: 0-0 Vi: 0-0 Tstrap: 0-0
Best Rating: 98 5/01 York 7f202y gd-fm

He shaped well at two, winning at Pontefract over six furlongs on a sound surface. Has run well on fast ground in 2001.

Bach (IRE)

117 121

4-y-o b c Caerleon (USA)-Producer (USA) (Nashua)

A P O'Brien Satish K Sanan & Mrs John Magnier

Placings:11/122-25201301343 (5575a)

2001: 10^{2}G, 10^{5}G, 8^{2}GY, 10^{0}GF, 8^{1}Y, 10^{3}GF, 8^{0}GF, 10^{1}YS, 10^{3}G, 8^{4}S, 8^{3}F

	Starts	1st	2nd	3rd	Win & Pl
Career Total (Turf)	16	5	4	3	423445

114	8/01	Curr	1m2f		Y-S	£65000
110	7/01	Curr	1m		YLD	£52000
100	4/00	Leop	1m		SFT	£16250
92	6/99	Asct	7f	A	G-F	£24200
80	5/99	Gowr	7f		GD	£4125

Total win prize-money £161575

Going (Turf): **Sf: 1-2** GS: 0-0 **Gd: 1-4 GF: 1-5** Fm: 0-1
Distance: 5f/6f: 0-0 **7f-8f: 4-8** 9f-13f: 1-8 14f+: 0-0
Track : LH: 1-4 RH: 1-6 Tight: 0-0 Gall: 0-2
Aids: Bl: 0-0 Vi: 0-0 Tstrap: 0-0
Best Rating: 121 9/01 Leop 1m2f good

He showed very useful form at three before his season was cut short by a pelvic injury. After some fair runs at the top level, he landed a listed event at the Curragh, and improved again to take third in the Eclipse Stakes at Sandown in July. Took the Royal Whip back at the Curragh, when the easy surface once again seemed to suit, and finished a distant third behind Fantastic light and Galileo in the Irish Champion. Ran really well to be third in the Breeders' Cup Mile on very fast ground at the end of the season.

Bachelors Pad

99(107) (61)54

7-y-o b g Pursuit Of Love-Note Book (Mummy's Pet)

Miss S J Wilton John Pointon And Sons

Placings:215/640306/005300420/06324000502520/021 1214142346100043035-423206233000 (5382)

2001: 16^{4}SD, 12^{2}SW, 12^{3}SD, 12^{2}SD, 12^{0}SD, 11^{6}SD, 9^{2}G, 12^{3}GF, 12^{3}GS, 9^{0}GF, 12^{0}SD, 11^{0}S

	Starts	1st	2nd	3rd	Win & Pl
Career Total (Turf)	47	3	7	6	25064
Career Total (AW)	19	3	4	3	10476

60	8/00	Ches	1m4f66y	E(0-80)H	GD	£3055
60	4/00	Sthl	1m3f	G(0-70)H	G-S	£1883
47	2/00	Wolv	1m1f79y	G	STD	£1732
61	2/00	Wolv	1m1f79y	F	STD	£2061
61	1/00	Wolv	1m1f79y	F	STD	£2236
96	9/96	Gdwd	6f	D	G-F	£4413

Total win prize-money £15384

Going (Turf): Sf: 0-6 **GS: 1-8 Gd: 1-16 GF: 1-15** Fm: 0-2
Distance: 5f/6f: 1-2 7f-8f: 0-21 **9f-13f: 5-40** 14f+: 0-3
Track : **LH: 5-46** RH: 0-11 **Tight: 4-23** Gall: 0-4
Aids: Bl: 0-8 Vi: 0-0 Tstrap: 0-0
Best Rating: 61 1/01 Wolv 1m4f slow

Back From Heaven (BEL)

80 43

2-y-o b f Septieme Ciel (USA)-Green Gem (BEL) (Pharly (FR))

S C Williams Mrs V Vilain

Placings:00 -(4637)

2001: 7^{0}GS, 7^{0}GF

	Starts	1st	2nd	3rd	Win & Pl
Career Total (Turf)	2	0	0	0	

Going (Turf): Sf: 0-0 GS: 0-1 Gd: 0-0 GF: 0-1 Fm: 0-0
Distance: 5f/6f: 0-0 7f-8f: 0-2 9f-13f: 0-0 14f+: 0-0
Track : LH: 0-0 RH: 0-0 Tight: 0-0 Gall: 0-0
Aids: Bl: 0-0 Vi: 0-0 Tstrap: 0-0
Best Rating: 43 8/01 Leic 7f9y gd-sft

Back Pass (USA)

96 67

3-y-o b/br f Quest For Fame-Skiable (IRE) (Niniski (USA))

B W Hills K Abdulla

Placings:0-2335 (4614)

2001: 10^{2}GF, 10^{3}GF, 14^{3}F, 13^{6}F

	Starts	1st	2nd	3rd	Win & Pl
Career Total (Turf)	5	0	1	2	2033

Going (Turf): Sf: 0-0 GS: 0-0 Gd: 0-1 GF: 0-2 Fm: 0-2
Distance: 5f/6f: 0-0 7f-8f: 0-1 9f-13f: 0-2 14f+: 0-2
Track : LH: 0-3 RH: 0-1 Tight: 0-4 Gall: 0-0
Aids: Bl: 0-0 Vi: 0-0 Tstrap: 0-0
Best Rating: 67 8/01 Ling 1m6f firm

Backwoods

100 46

8-y-o ch g In The Wings-Kates Cabin (Habitat)

W M Brisbourne P R Kirk

Placings:0/0000451011040/6/0-01206203 (5402)

2001: 10^{0}GF, 11^{1}GF, 16^{2}GS, 13^{0}G, 16^{6}G, 17^{2}G, 15^{0}GS, 17^{3}S

	Starts	1st	2nd	3rd	Win & Pl
Career Total (Turf)	20	3	2	1	14222
Career Total (AW)	4	1	0	0	2070

42	7/01	Hayd	1m3f200y	E(0-70)	G-F	£2940
65	10/96	Nott	2m9y	D(0-80)H	GD	£4305
64	10/96	Catt	1m7f177y	D(0-80)H	GD	£3785
52	8/96	Wolv	1m6f166y	F(0-65)H	STD	£2070

Total win prize-money £13100

Going (Turf): Sf: 0-4 GS: 0-3 **Gd: 2-10** GF: 1-3 Fm: 0-0
Distance: 5f/6f: 0-1 7f-8f: 0-1 9f-13f: 1-8 **14f+: 3-14**
Track : **LH: 4-20** RH: 0-3 **Tight: 2-11** Gall: 0-0
Aids: Bl: 0-0 Vi: 0-0 Tstrap: 0-0
Best Rating: 46 10/01 Pont 2m1f216y soft

A modest handicapper, he won his first race in five years at Haydock in July, but has been well held since. Stays two miles.

Baderna

33

3-y-o b c Rainbow Quest (USA)-Baaderah (IRE) (Cadeaux Genereux)

M R Channon Sheikh Ahmed Al Maktoum

Placings:0-P (0515)

2001: 10^{P}S

	Starts	1st	2nd	3rd	Win & Pl
Career Total (Turf)	2	0	0	0	

Going (Turf): Sf: 0-2 GS: 0-0 Gd: 0-0 GF: 0-0 Fm: 0-0
Distance: 5f/6f: 0-0 7f-8f: 0-0 9f-13f: 0-2 14f+: 0-0
Track : LH: 0-2 RH: 0-0 Tight: 0-0 Gall: 0-1
Aids: Bl: 0-0 Vi: 0-0 Tstrap: 0-0
Best Rating: 46 10/01 Pont 2m1f216y soft

Only had one run at two and finished distressed in soft conditions at Doncaster on his reappearance at three.

Badrinath (IRE)

99(103) (48)56

7-y-o b g Imperial Frontier (USA)-Badedra (King's Lake (USA))

H J Collingridge D Burke

Placings:00400231/2030100120/000420350/6320025 00-3103120360 (3505)

2001: 10^{3}SD, 10^{1}SD, 8^{0}SW, 10^{3}SD, 9^{1}F, 9^{2}GF, 8^{0}GF, 9^{3}GF, 10^{6}GF, 9^{0}GF

	Starts	1st	2nd	3rd	Win & Pl
Career Total (Turf)	24	3	4	2	13652
Career Total (AW)	23	2	3	5	9453

52	5/01	Leic	1m1f218y	G(0-60)H	FRM	£2198
48	2/01	Ling	1m2f	E(0-70)H	STD	£2408
53	9/98	Rdcr	1m2f	G(0-60)H	G-F	£2206
48	6/98	NmkJ	1m	E(0-70)H	GD	£3793
55	1/98	Ling	1m2f	D	STD	£3566

Total win prize-money £14172

Going (Turf): Sf: 0-0 GS: 0-5 **Gd: 1-6 GF: 1-10 Fm: 1-3**
Distance: 5f/6f: 0-3 7f-8f: 1-13 **9f-13f: 4-31** 14f+: 0-0
Track : **LH: 3-35** RH: 1-6 **Tight: 3-22** Gall: 0-4
Aids: Bl: 0-0 Vi: 0-0 Tstrap: 0-0
Best Rating: 56 6/01 Bevl 1m1f207y gd-fm

Bahamas (IRE)

97(97) (70)56

4-y-o b g Barathea (IRE)-Rum Cay (USA) (Our Native (USA))

J A B Old W E Sturt

Placings:0000/1233110624-00000 (5098)

2001: 12^{0}GS, 10^{0}S, 11^{0}GF, 12^{0}G, 14^{0}GS

	Starts	1st	2nd	3rd	Win & Pl
Career Total (Turf)	16	1	2	1	4645
Career Total (AW)	3	2	0	1	5551

75	7/00	Sthl	1m3f	E(0-70)H	STD	£2863
66	7/00	Sthl	1m4f	F(0-65)H	STD	£2261
65	6/00	Rdcr	1m2f	F(0-65)H	GD	£2457

Total win prize-money £7581

Going (Turf): Sf: 0-6 GS: 0-2 **Gd: 1-5** GF: 0-3 Fm: 0-0
Distance: 5f/6f: 0-1 7f-8f: 0-3 **9f-13f: 3-13** 14f+: 0-2
Track : **LH: 3-13** RH: 0-3 **Tight: 1-9** Gall: 0-1

Aids: Bl: 2-12 Vi: 0-0 Tstrap: 0-0
Best Rating: 63 5/01 Newb 1m2f6y soft

Bahamian Heir (IRE)

(71) (33)**47**
2-y-o b c Lake Coniston (IRE)-Bally Souza (IRE) (Alzao (USA))
D Nicholls Lucayan Stud

Placings:000 (5345)
2001: 6^0G, 7^0S, 6^0SD

	Starts	1st	2nd	3rd	Win & Pl
Career Total (Turf)	2	0	0	0	
Career Total (AW)	1	0	0	0	

Going (Turf): Sf: 0-1 GS: 0-0 Gd: 0-1 GF: 0-0 Fm: 0-0
Distance: 5f/6f: 0-2 7f-8f: 0-1 9f-13f: 0-0 14f+: 0-0
Track : LH: 0-2 RH: 0-0 Tight: 0-0 Gall: 0-1
Aids: Bl: 0-0 Vi: 0-0 Tstrap: 0-0
Best Rating: 47 9/01 Ayr 6f good

Has been well beaten on all starts this season, but is now qualified for handicaps.

Bahamian Minstrel

(92) (65)**73**
2-y-o b g Bahamian Bounty-Penny Ghent (Dominion)
Mrs L Stubbs Mrs P J Sands

Placings:020 (5038)
2001: 5^0GF, 5^2G, 5^0G

	Starts	1st	2nd	3rd	Win & Pl
Career Total (Turf)	3	0	1	0	1300

Going (Turf): Sf: 0-0 GS: 0-0 Gd: 0-2 GF: 0-1 Fm: 0-0
Distance: 5f/6f: 0-3 7f-8f: 0-0 9f-13f: 0-0 14f+: 0-0
Track : LH: 0-1 RH: 0-0 Tight: 0-0 Gall: 0-1
Aids: Bl: 0-0 Vi: 0-0 Tstrap: 0-0
Best Rating: 73 9/01 Bevl 5f good

Bahamian Pirate (USA)

115(109) (78+)**120**
6-y-o ch g Housebuster (USA)-Shining Through (USA) (Deputy Minister (CAN))
D Nicholls H E Lhendup Dorji

Placings:50026/**4321**/011222130151-066002013323 (5365)
2001: 6^0S, 6^6GS, 5^6G, 6^0GF, 6^0GF, 6^2F, 5^0GF, 6^1Y, 6^3GY, 6^3S, 5^2HO, 6^3GS

	Starts	1st	2nd	3rd	Win & Pl
Career Total (Turf)	29	6	6	4	181253
Career Total (AW)	4	1	1	1	3801

110	8/01	Leop	6f		YLD	£35750
109	10/00	NmkR	6f	A	SFT	£16124
91	9/00	Ayr	6f	B H	SFT	£65000
85	8/00	NmkJ	6f	D(0-85)H	G-F	£4182
78	7/00	Sthl	6f	F(0-60)H	STD	£2338
69	5/00	Carl	5f207y	E(0-70)H	FRM	£3029
68	8/99	Ripn	5f	D	GD	£3485

Total win prize-money £129909

Going (Turf): Sf: 2-4 GS: 0-3 Gd: 1-7 GF: 1-9 Fm: 1-2
Distance: 5f/6f: 7-29 7f-8f: 0-4 9f-13f: 0-0 14f+: 0-0
Track : LH: 1-5 RH: 1-2 Tight: 0-0 **Gall: 1-1**
Aids: Bl: 0-0 Vi: 0-0 Tstrap: 0-0
Best Rating: 120 10/01 Lonc 5f holding

He improved considerably in 2000, winning five times including the Ayr Gold Cup and a Listed race at Newmarket. Enjoyed a fine autumn last season and repeated the trick this year, following a third place in the Diadem Stakes with runner-up placings in the Prix de l'Abbaye and a third in a Listed event at Newmarket in October.

Bahamian Rhapsody (IRE)

100 **67**
3-y-o b f Fairy King (USA)-Lupescu (Dixieland Band (USA))
S P C Woods (M R Channon 5/8) Lucayan Stud

Placings:3205602425 (5330)
2001: 10^3S, 14^2G, 12^0GF, 12^5GF, 14^6GF, 10^0GF, 13^2F, 16^4GS, 16^2HY, 16^5HY

	Starts	1st	2nd	3rd	Win & Pl
Career Total (Turf)	10	0	3	1	4364

Going (Turf): Sf: 0-3 GS: 0-1 Gd: 0-1 GF: 0-4 Fm: 0-1
Distance: 5f/6f: 0-0 7f-8f: 0-0 9f-13f: 0-4 14f+: 0-6
Track : LH: 0-6 RH: 0-4 Tight: 0-5 Gall: 0-2
Aids: Bl: 0-0 Vi: 0-0 Tstrap: 0-0
Best Rating: 81 6/01 Asct 1m4f gd-fm

Unraced at two, she has faced some stiff tasks, but is only a modest maiden and looks a stayer.

Bahia

86 **57**
2-y-o ch f Grand Lodge (USA)-Helens Dreamgirl (Caerleon (USA))
Bob Jones Dachel Stud

Placings:6660 (5690)
2001: 8^6GF, 7^6GS, 8^6HY, 7^0S

	Starts	1st	2nd	3rd	Win & Pl
Career Total (Turf)	4	0	0	0	0

Going (Turf): Sf: 0-2 GS: 0-1 Gd: 0-0 GF: 0-1 Fm: 0-0
Distance: 5f/6f: 0-0 7f-8f: 0-4 9f-13f: 0-0 14f+: 0-0
Track : LH: 0-2 RH: 0-1 Tight: 0-0 Gall: 0-2
Aids: Bl: 0-0 Vi: 0-0 Tstrap: 0-0
Best Rating: 57 10/01 Donc 1m heavy

She has shown little in maidens.

Bahirah

96 **67**
3-y-o b f Ashkalani (IRE)-Top Of The League (High Top)
M A Jarvis Sheikh Ahmed Al Maktoum

Placings:34230 (5591)
2001: 11^3GF, 12^4GF, 9^2GF, 9^3GF, 9^0GS

	Starts	1st	2nd	3rd	Win & Pl
Career Total (Turf)	5	0	1	2	2771

Going (Turf): Sf: 0-0 GS: 0-1 Gd: 0-0 GF: 0-4 Fm: 0-0
Distance: 5f/6f: 0-0 7f-8f: 0-0 9f-13f: 0-5 14f+: 0-0
Track : LH: 0-2 RH: 0-3 Tight: 0-1 Gall: 0-0
Aids: Bl: 0-0 Vi: 0-0 Tstrap: 0-0
Best Rating: 78 5/01 Hayd 1m3f200y gd-fm

A half-sister to Noushkey, is a fair maiden on fast ground, has gradually dropped in trip from 12 to nine furlongs, but looks a little short on acceleration..

Bahrain (IRE)

(104) (32)**57**
5-y-o ch g Lahib (USA)-Twin Island (IRE) (Standaan (FR))
J M Bradley E A Hayward

Placings:0/50/400062310-00104020000000 (5613)
2001: 7^0HY, 8^0G, 7^1F, 8^0GF, 7^4GF, 8^0GF, 8^2GF, 8^0G, 7^0G, 8^0G, 7^0GF, 8^0SD, 8^0SD, 9^0SD

	Starts	1st	2nd	3rd	Win & Pl
Career Total (Turf)	20	1	2	0	5841
Career Total (AW)	6	1	0	1	3442

56	5/01	Brig	7f214y	F(0-60)H	FRM	£2422
60	9/00	Wolv	1m100y	E(0-70)H	STD	£3080

Total win prize-money £5502

Going (Turf): Sf: 0-4 GS: 0-1 Gd: 0-6 GF: 0-6 **Fm: 1-3**
Distance: 5f/6f: 0-0 7f-8f: 1-12 9f-13f: 1-14 14f+: 0-0
Track : **LH: 2-13** RH: 0-6 **Tight: 1-11** Gall: 0-2
Aids: Bl: 0-0 Vi: 0-0 Tstrap: 0-4
Best Rating: 57 7/01 Bevl 1m100y gd-fm

Fibresand winner in the autumn of 2000, he took a ladies event on fast ground at Brighton. Likes to race prominently, and a sharp track seems to suit.

Bahrqueen (USA)

99 **95**
2-y-o b f Bahri (USA)-April In Kentucky (USA) (Palace Music (USA))
H R A Cecil Raymond Tooth

Placings:3 (5274)
2001: 7^3GS

	Starts	1st	2nd	3rd	Win & Pl
Career Total (Turf)	1	0	0	1	626

Going (Turf): Sf: 0-0 GS: 0-1 Gd: 0-0 GF: 0-0 Fm: 0-0
Distance: 5f/6f: 0-0 7f-8f: 0-1 9f-13f: 0-0 14f+: 0-0
Track : LH: 0-0 RH: 0-0 Tight: 0-0 Gall: 0-0
Aids: Bl: 0-0 Vi: 0-0 Tstrap: 0-0
Best Rating: 95 10/01 Leic 7f9y gd-sft

Half-sister to a winner in the States, made a highly satisfactory debut over seven furlongs on yielding ground.

Baileys Black Tie

(74) (11)
5-y-o b g Suave Dancer (USA)-Three Stars (Star Appeal)
M Johnston G R Bailey Ltd (baileys Horse Feeds)

Placings:6010010/0-
2001:

	Starts	1st	2nd	3rd	Win & Pl
Career Total (Turf)	7	2	0	0	4918
Career Total (AW)	1	0	0	0	

62	8/99	Ripn	1m2f	F(0-60)H	GD	£2570
55	7/99	Ripn	1m2f	F	GD	£2347

Total win prize-money £4918

Going (Turf): Sf: 0-1 GS: 0-1 **Gd: 2-2** GF: 0-2 Fm: 0-1
Distance: 5f/6f: 0-0 7f-8f: 0-0 **9f-13f: 2-7** 14f+: 0-1
Track : LH: 0-5 **RH: 2-3 Tight: 2-4** Gall: 0-1
Aids: Bl: 0-0 Vi: 0-0 Tstrap: 0-0
Best Rating: 55 7/99 Ripn 1m2f G

Baileys Prize (USA)

105(98) (62)**81**
4-y-o ch g Mister Baileys-Mar Mar (USA) (Forever Casting (USA))
M Johnston G R Bailey Ltd (baileys Horse Feeds)

Placings:45/201462223140-40400531 (5382)
2001: 9^4G, 10^0GF, 10^4GF, 10^0GF, 11^0G, 10^5G, 10^3S, 11^1S

	Starts	1st	2nd	3rd	Win & Pl
Career Total (Turf)	21	3	3	2	23125
Career Total (AW)	1	0	1	0	808

56	10/01	Catt	1m3f214yF		SFT	£2590
86	7/00	NmkJ	1m2f	C(0-95)H	G-F	£7241
72	5/00	Rdcr	1m2f	E(0-70)H	G-F	£2926

Total win prize-money £12757

Going (Turf): Sf: 1-2 GS: 0-4 Gd: 0-6 **GF: 2-8** Fm: 0-1
Distance: 5f/6f: 0-1 7f-8f: 0-2 **9f-13f: 3-19** 14f+: 0-0
Track : **LH: 2-11** RH: 1-10 **Tight: 2-10** Gall: 1-5
Aids: Bl: 0-0 Vi: 0-0 Tstrap: 0-0
Best Rating: 81 6/01 Ayr 1m2f gd-fm

A come-from-behind handicapper, he showed good consistent form at three, but did not find his form this season until winning a soft-ground claimer over 12 furlongs at Catterick in October after which he was claimed.

Bailieborough (IRE)

96 **86**

2-y-o b c Charnwood Forest (IRE)-Sheranndа (USA) (Trempolino (USA))
T D Easterby M P Burke

Placings:0146 **(5368)**
2001: 5^{0}G, 6^{1}G, 6^{4}GS, 8^{6}GS

	Starts	1st	2nd	3rd	Win & Pl
Career Total (Turf)	4	1	0	0	7208

69 8/01 Thsk 6f D GD £4507
Total win prize-money £4508

Going (Turf): Sf: 0-0 GS: 0-2 **Gd: 1-2** GF: 0-0 Fm: 0-0
Distance: **5f/6f: 1-3** 7f-8f: 0-1 9f-13f: 0-0 14f+: 0-0
Track : LH: 0-0 RH: 0-0 Tight: 0-0 Gall: 0-0
Aids: Bl: 0-0 Vi: 0-0 Tstrap: 0-0
Best Rating: 86 9/01 Donc 6f gd-sft

Absent with sore shins since his Newmarket debut in may, he made a winning reappearance in August over six furlongs and followed up with a good fourth in a competitive sales race. Has won on good ground.

Bajan Blue

101 **50**

3-y-o b f Lycius (USA)-Serotina (IRE) (Mtoto)
M Johnston Mrs Louise Boggs

Placings:63330-0010 **(3570)**
2001: 12^{0}GF, 8^{0}GF, 11^{1}GF, 12^{0}G

	Starts	1st	2nd	3rd	Win & Pl
Career Total (Turf)	9	1	0	3	4329

49 7/01 Wind 1m3f135yF(0-60)H G-F £2744
Total win prize-money £2744

Going (Turf): Sf: 0-1 GS: 0-0 Gd: 0-2 **GF: 1-5** Fm: 0-0
Distance: 5f/6f: 0-1 7f-8f: 0-3 **9f-13f: 1-4** 14f+: 0-0
Track : LH: 0-3 RH: 0-3 **Tight: 1-3** Gall: 0-0
Aids: Bl: 0-0 Vi: 0-0 Tstrap: 0-0
Best Rating: 50 6/01 Wwck 1m4f134y gd-fm

Modest form before getting off the mark in a selling handicap at Windsor in July.

Bajan Broker (IRE)

86 **39**

4-y-o br f Turtle Island (IRE)-Foxrock (Ribero)
E Stanners P D Burnett

Placings:43/0405604-005 **(5292)**
2001: 8^{0}HY, 8^{0}HY, 7^{5}S

	Starts	1st	2nd	3rd	Win & Pl
Career Total (Turf)	12	0	0	1	717

Going (Turf): Sf: 0-5 GS: 0-1 Gd: 0-2 GF: 0-4 Fm: 0-0
Distance: 5f/6f: 0-0 7f-8f: 0-4 9f-13f: 0-8 14f+: 0-0
Track : LH: 0-7 RH: 0-1 Tight: 0-3 Gall: 0-0
Aids: Bl: 0-0 Vi: 0-0 Tstrap: 0-0
Best Rating: 39 10/01 Leic 7f9y soft

Bajan Sunset (IRE)

87(98) (35)**30**

4-y-o ch g Mujtahid (USA)-Dubai Lady (Kris)
J D Bethell Mrs John Lee

Placings:0/0622000-035500 **(2360)**
2001: 11^{0}SD, 12^{3}SW, 12^{5}SD, 11^{5}SD, 9^{0}F, 10^{0}GF

	Starts	1st	2nd	3rd	Win & Pl
Career Total (Turf)	10	0	2	0	1980
Career Total (AW)	4	0	0	1	416

Going (Turf): Sf: 0-0 GS: 0-2 Gd: 0-3 GF: 0-3 Fm: 0-2
Distance: 5f/6f: 0-0 7f-8f: 0-2 9f-13f: 0-12 14f+: 0-0
Track : LH: 0-9 RH: 0-1 Tight: 0-1 Gall: 0-1
Aids: Bl: 0-0 Vi: 0-4 Tstrap: 0-4
Best Rating: 35 3/01 Sthl 1m3f stand

Bakiri (IRE)

107 **90**

3-y-o b c Doyoun-Bakiya (USA) (Trempolino (USA))
Sir Michael Stoute H H Aga Khan

Placings:441042 **(3674)**
2001: 8^{4}GS, 8^{4}S, 8^{1}GF, 8^{0}GF, 10^{4}GS, 9^{2}G

	Starts	1st	2nd	3rd	Win & Pl
Career Total (Turf)	6	1	1	0	8431

84 5/01 Kemp 1m D G-F £4699
Total win prize-money £4700

Going (Turf): Sf: 0-1 GS: 0-2 Gd: 0-1 **GF: 1-2** Fm: 0-0
Distance: 5f/6f: 0-0 **7f-8f: 1-4** 9f-13f: 0-2 14f+: 0-0
Track : LH: 0-0 **RH: 1-4** Tight: 0-1 Gall: 0-1
Aids: Bl: 0-0 Vi: 0-0 Tstrap: 0-0
Best Rating: 90 8/01 Ripn 1m1f good

Bred to stay. Won his maiden in good style at Kempton in May 2001. Showed up well when stepped up ten furlongs and should be able to score over that trip in time.

Baladeur (IRE)

98 **53**

3-y-o b g Doyoun-Singing Filly (Relkino)
T D Barron Alex Gorrie Combi (uk)

Placings:2135460-000000 **(5681)**
2001: 8^{0}S, 7^{0}G, 8^{0}GF, 8^{0}HY, 8^{0}G, 8^{0}S

	Starts	1st	2nd	3rd	Win & Pl
Career Total (Turf)	13	1	1	1	11025

79 4/00 Navn 5f182y HVY £5865
Total win prize-money £5865

Going (Turf): Sf: 1-5 GS: 0-0 Gd: 0-5 GF: 0-1 Fm: 0-0
Distance: **5f/6f: 1-6** 7f-8f: 0-6 9f-13f: 0-1 14f+: 0-0
Track : **LH: 1-6** RH: 0-1 Tight: 0-2 Gall: 0-0
Aids: Bl: 0-0 Vi: 0-0 Tstrap: 0-0
Best Rating: 53 11/01 Donc 1m soft

He started his career in Ireland but was harshly handicapped following efforts in Pattern company, and he is taking a while to drop to a winning mark. He has shown little as yet for his present trainer.

Balakheri (IRE)

97 **82+**

2-y-o b c Theatrical-Balanka (IRE) (Alzao (USA))
Sir Michael Stoute H H Aga Khan

Placings:021 **(5527)**
2001: 7^{0}S, 7^{2}GS, 8^{1}HY

	Starts	1st	2nd	3rd	Win & Pl
Career Total (Turf)	3	1	1	0	5395

82 10/01 Nott 1m54y D HVY £3965
Total win prize-money £3965

Going (Turf): Sf: 1-2 GS: 0-1 Gd: 0-0 GF: 0-0 Fm: 0-0
Distance: 5f/6f: 0-0 7f-8f: 0-2 **9f-13f: 1-1** 14f+: 0-0
Track : **LH: 1-1** RH: 0-0 Tight: 0-0 Gall: 0-0
Aids: Bl: 0-0 Vi: 0-0 Tstrap: 0-0
Best Rating: 82 10/01 Nott 1m54y heavy

Out of a half-sister to the dam of Bering, he progressed with racing to win a Nottingham maiden at the backend of 2001. Well bred and likely to make up into a decent middle-distance colt.

Balakiref

94 **86**

2-y-o b c Royal Applause-Pluck (Never So Bold)
W Jarvis D Heath

Placings:0524 **(5021)**
2001: 5^{0}G, 6^{5}G, 7^{2}G, 7^{4}HY

	Starts	1st	2nd	3rd	Win & Pl
Career Total (Turf)	4	0	1	0	2435

Going (Turf): Sf: 0-1 GS: 0-0 Gd: 0-3 GF: 0-0 Fm: 0-0
Distance: 5f/6f: 0-2 7f-8f: 0-2 9f-13f: 0-0 14f+: 0-0
Track : LH: 0-1 RH: 0-0 Tight: 0-1 Gall: 0-0
Aids: Bl: 0-0 Vi: 0-0 Tstrap: 0-0
Best Rating: 86 9/01 Epsm 7f good

Fair form in maidens..

Balanou

(97) (55)**57**

3-y-o b/br f Valanour (IRE)-Batalya (BEL) (Boulou)
S C Williams Mrs V Vilain

Placings:560005-354130126023000 **(5046)**
2001: 10^{3}SD, 8^{5}SD, 8^{4}SD, 9^{1}SD, 9^{3}GS, 8^{0}G, 9^{1}F, 10^{2}GF, 10^{6}GF, 9^{0}GF, 9^{2}GF, 10^{3}GF, 10^{0}GF, 11^{0}G, 11^{0}SD

	Starts	1st	2nd	3rd	Win & Pl
Career Total (Turf)	15	1	2	2	6390
Career Total (AW)	6	1	0	1	3234

55 6/01 Brig 1m1f209yE(0-75)H FRM £3406
55 3/01 Wolv 1m1f79y E(0-75)H STD £2919
Total win prize-money £6325

Going (Turf): Sf: 0-2 GS: 0-1 Gd: 0-2 GF: 0-6 **Fm: 1-1**
Distance: 5f/6f: 0-0 7f-8f: 0-5 **9f-13f: 2-13** 14f+: 0-0
Track : **LH: 2-12** RH: 0-2 **Tight: 1-9** Gall: 0-1
Aids: Bl: 0-0 Vi: 0-0 Tstrap: 0-0
Best Rating: 58 6/01 Yarm 1m2f21y gd-fm

Baldour (IRE)

89 **89**

2-y-o b c Green Desert (USA)-Baldemara (FR) (Sanglamore (USA))
E A L Dunlop Khalifa Sultan

Placings:22 **(4423)**
2001: 6^{2}G, 6^{2}GF

	Starts	1st	2nd	3rd	Win & Pl
Career Total (Turf)	2	0	2	0	2444

Going (Turf): Sf: 0-0 GS: 0-0 Gd: 0-1 GF: 0-1 Fm: 0-0
Distance: 5f/6f: 0-1 7f-8f: 0-1 9f-13f: 0-0 14f+: 0-0
Track : LH: 0-0 RH: 0-0 Tight: 0-0 Gall: 0-0
Aids: Bl: 0-0 Vi: 0-0 Tstrap: 0-0
Best Rating: 89 8/01 Yarm 6f3y good

Bali

104 **82**

3-y-o br f Darshaan-Bonne Ile (Ile De Bourbon (USA))
Sir Michael Stoute Faisal Salman

Placings:0024 **(5024)**
2001: 8^{0}G, 10^{0}GF, 10^{2}GF, 11^{4}S

	Starts	1st	2nd	3rd	Win & Pl
Career Total (Turf)	4	0	1	0	1070

Going (Turf): Sf: 0-1 GS: 0-0 Gd: 0-1 GF: 0-2 Fm: 0-0
Distance: 5f/6f: 0-0 7f-8f: 0-1 9f-13f: 0-3 14f+: 0-0
Track : LH: 0-2 RH: 0-1 Tight: 0-0 Gall: 0-1
Aids: Bl: 0-0 Vi: 0-0 Tstrap: 0-0
Best Rating: 82 7/01 Pont 1m2f6y gd-fm

Bali Royal

107(98) (65+)**88**

3-y-o b f King's Signet (USA)-Baligay (Balidar)
J M Bradley Mrs R J Manning

Placings:2000024-4211211312165 (5502)
2001: 5[4]SD, 5[2]S, 5[1]GS, 6[1]SD, 5[2]G, 5[1]F, 5[1]GF, 5[3]GF, 5[1]G, 5[2]F, 5[1]G, 5[6]GS, 5[5]HY

	Starts	1st	2nd	3rd	Win & Pl
Career Total (Turf)	18	5	5	1	33206
Career Total (AW)	2	1	0	0	3003

88	8/01	Gdwd	5f	C(0-90)H	GD	£7670
82	7/01	Ches	5f16y	C(0-95)H	GD	£8619
81	6/01	Newc	5f	E(0-75)H	G-F	£3318
69	5/01	Brig	5f59y	E(0-75)H	FRM	£2933
65	4/01	Sthl	6f	E(0-70)H	STD	£3003
58	4/01	Muss	5f	E(0-70)H	G-S	£3052

Total win prize-money £28595

Going (Turf): Sf: 0-4 GS: 1-4 **Gd: 2-4** GF: 1-4 Fm: 1-2
Distance: **5f/6f: 6-18** 7f-8f: 0-2 9f-13f: 0-0 14f+: 0-0
Track : **LH: 3-7** RH: 0-1 **Tight: 1-2** Gall: 0-3
Aids: Bl: 0-0 Vi: 0-0 Tstrap: 0-0
Best Rating: 88 8/01 Gdwd 5f good

A speedy sprinter, she has been in fine form having won six times so far this season despite a 31lb rise in the handicap. All of her wins on turf have been over the minimum trip though she has won over six furlongs on sand. Best when able to dominate.

Bali-Star

96 **45**

6-y-o b g Alnasr Alwasheek-Baligay (Balidar)
M J Weeden E W Carnell

Placings:000/200002-300450 (4543)
2001: 6[3]GS, 5[0]G, 5[0]GF, 6[4]GF, 5[5]GF, 5[0]GF

	Starts	1st	2nd	3rd	Win & Pl
Career Total (Turf)	15	0	2	1	2156

Going (Turf): Sf: 0-2 GS: 0-1 Gd: 0-5 GF: 0-7 Fm: 0-0
Distance: 5f/6f: 0-12 7f-8f: 0-3 9f-13f: 0-0 14f+: 0-0
Track : LH: 0-2 RH: 0-1 Tight: 0-0 Gall: 0-2
Aids: Bl: 0-0 Vi: 0-0 Tstrap: 0-0
Best Rating: 56 5/01 Sals 6f gd-sft

Balidare

88 **42**

4-y-o b f King's Signet (USA)-Baligay (Balidar)
M J Weeden Just Racing

Placings:00/0000000-000 (4543)
2001: 6[0]F, 6[0]GF, 5[0]GF

	Starts	1st	2nd	3rd	Win & Pl
Career Total (Turf)	12	0	0	0	

Going (Turf): Sf: 0-2 GS: 0-0 Gd: 0-1 GF: 0-6 Fm: 0-3
Distance: 5f/6f: 0-9 7f-8f: 0-3 9f-13f: 0-0 14f+: 0-0
Track : LH: 0-3 RH: 0-0 Tight: 0-0 Gall: 0-0
Aids: Bl: 0-0 Vi: 0-0 Tstrap: 0-0
Best Rating: 42 8/01 Sals 6f firm

Ball Games

104 **66**

3-y-o b g Mind Games-Deb's Ball (Glenstal (USA))
D Moffatt Cartmel Bloodstock

Placings:6460404-35300 (5538)
2001: 8[3]S, 8[5]GF, 9[3]GF, 7[0]GS, 10[0]S

	Starts	1st	2nd	3rd	Win & Pl
Career Total (Turf)	12	0	0	2	1597

Going (Turf): Sf: 0-4 GS: 0-3 Gd: 0-2 GF: 0-3 Fm: 0-0
Distance: 5f/6f: 0-4 7f-8f: 0-6 9f-13f: 0-2 14f+: 0-0
Track : LH: 0-4 RH: 0-3 Tight: 0-4 Gall: 0-1
Aids: Bl: 0-0 Vi: 0-0 Tstrap: 0-0
Best Rating: 66 3/01 Muss 1m soft

Ball King (IRE)

96(95) (77+)**79**

3-y-o ch c Ball Park (NZ)-Firey Encounter (IRE) (Kris)
P J Makin (G A Butler 22/7) S Chan, M Fung, W P Chan

Placings:1-526440 (4161)
2001: 6[5]GS, 8[2]F, 7[6]G, 5[4]GF, 6[4]GF, 7[0]GF

	Starts	1st	2nd	3rd	Win & Pl
Career Total (Turf)	6	0	1	0	2440
Career Total (AW)	1	1	0	0	2340

77	11/00	Ling	1m	D	STD	£2340

Total win prize-money £2340

Going (Turf): Sf: 0-0 GS: 0-1 Gd: 0-1 GF: 0-3 Fm: 0-1
Distance: 5f/6f: 0-2 **7f-8f: 1-4** 9f-13f: 0-1 14f+: 0-0
Track : **LH: 1-3** RH: 0-1 **Tight: 1-1** Gall: 0-0
Aids: Bl: 0-0 Vi: 0-0 **Tstrap: 1-4**
Best Rating: 79 7/01 Sand 5f6y gd-fm

He made a winning debut on Equitrack last November and has shown enough promise on turf this season to suggest he can win a race or two on that surface. Acts on fast ground.

Balla D'Aire (IRE)

(91) (24)**32**

6-y-o b/br g Balla Cove-Silius (Junius (USA))
C N Kellett Ms L Whitehorn

Placings:400/04000000**4**/40/5-0 (0376)
2001: 12[0]SD

	Starts	1st	2nd	3rd	Win & Pl
Career Total (Turf)	9	0	0	0	243
Career Total (AW)	6	0	0	0	0

Going (Turf): Sf: 0-0 GS: 0-3 Gd: 0-0 GF: 0-5 Fm: 0-1
Distance: 5f/6f: 0-2 7f-8f: 0-1 9f-13f: 0-8 14f+: 0-4
Track : LH: 0-10 RH: 0-2 Tight: 0-9 Gall: 0-0
Aids: Bl: 0-2 Vi: 0-0 Tstrap: 0-0

Balladeer (IRE)

(105) (81)**85**

3-y-o b c King's Theatre (IRE)-Carousel Music (On Your Mark)
J W Hills Scott Hardy Partnership

Placings:043-101054401 (5164)
2001: 8[1]HY, 10[0]F, 11[1]GF, 12[0]GF, 14[5]G, 13[4]GF, 14[4]HY, 13[0]GF, 12[1]SD

	Starts	1st	2nd	3rd	Win & Pl
Career Total (Turf)	10	2	0	0	13972
Career Total (AW)	2	1	0	1	4473

81	10/01	Wolv	1m4f	D(0-85)H	STD	£4114
72	6/01	Wind	1m3f135y	C(0-85)	G-F	£6870
82	4/01	Wwck	1m22y	D(0-80)	HVY	£4251

Total win prize-money £15237

Going (Turf): Sf: 1-2 GS: 0-0 Gd: 0-1 **GF: 1-6** Fm: 0-1
Distance: 5f/6f: 0-0 7f-8f: 0-3 **9f-13f: 3-5** 14f+: 0-4
Track : **LH: 1-6** RH: 0-3 **Tight: 2-4** Gall: 0-4
Aids: Bl: 0-0 Vi: 0-0 Tstrap: 0-0
Best Rating: 85 8/01 Gdwd 1m6f good

He won his maiden on heavy ground, where the emphasis was on stamina, and has since proved himself well suited by middle distances. He had the run of the race when winning on ground which was easier than the official good to firm at Windsor, and subsequently disappointed at the Royal Meeting. Decent efforts upped in trip before winning at wolverhampton in October. Suited by Fibresand, and acts on any ground on turf.

Balladonia

109 **98**

5-y-o b m Primo Dominie-Susquehanna Days (USA) (Chief's Crown (USA))
Lady Herries D K R & Mrs J B C Oliver

Placings:22/21434024/65450-325 (3244)
2001: 10[3]G, 10[2]F, 10[5]GF

	Starts	1st	2nd	3rd	Win & Pl
Career Total (Turf)	18	1	5	2	26953

82	5/99	Gdwd	1m1f	D	GD	£4381

Total win prize-money £4382

Going (Turf): Sf: 0-2 GS: 0-2 **Gd: 1-7** GF: 0-5 Fm: 0-1
Distance: 5f/6f: 0-0 7f-8f: 0-2 **9f-13f: 1-16** 14f+: 0-0
Track : LH: 0-6 **RH: 1-9 Tight: 1-5** Gall: 0-6
Aids: Bl: 0-0 Vi: 0-0 Tstrap: 0-0
Best Rating: 98 7/01 Newb 1m2f6y gd-fm

She is genuine, but lacks the basic speed to win Listed races. Best on a sound surface.

Ballard Connection

57 **28**

2-y-o ch f Danzig Connection (USA)-Ballard Lady (IRE) (Ballad Rock)
J S Wainwright Mrs P Wake

Placings:0 (5109)
2001: 6[0]HY

	Starts	1st	2nd	3rd	Win & Pl
Career Total (Turf)	1	0	0	0	

Going (Turf): Sf: 0-1 GS: 0-0 Gd: 0-0 GF: 0-0 Fm: 0-0
Distance: 5f/6f: 0-0 7f-8f: 0-1 9f-13f: 0-0 14f+: 0-0
Track : LH: 0-0 RH: 0-0 Tight: 0-0 Gall: 0-0
Aids: Bl: 0-0 Vi: 0-0 Tstrap: 0-0
Best Rating: 28 10/01 Nott 6f15y heavy

Ballet Fame (USA)

98 **89+**

2-y-o br f Quest For Fame-Bold Ballerina (Sadler's Wells (USA))
B W Hills K Abdulla

Placings:1 (5602)
2001: 7[1]GS

	Starts	1st	2nd	3rd	Win & Pl
Career Total (Turf)	1	1	0	0	4222

89	11/01	NmkR	7f	D	G-S	£4221

Total win prize-money £4222

Going (Turf): Sf: 0-0 **GS: 1-1** Gd: 0-0 GF: 0-0 Fm: 0-0
Distance: 5f/6f: 0-0 **7f-8f: 1-1** 9f-13f: 0-0 14f+: 0-0
Track : LH: 0-0 RH: 0-0 Tight: 0-0 Gall: 0-0
Aids: Bl: 0-0 Vi: 0-0 Tstrap: 0-0
Best Rating: 89 11/01 NmkR 7f gd-sft

A half-sister to the Lowther Stakes winner Kingscote, she won a Newmarket maiden on her debut in November 2001. Should be suited by further and may well make up into a decent three-year-old.

Ballet Girl (USA)

94 **76**

2-y-o b f Theatrical-Atelier (Warning)
B W Hills K Abdulla

Placings:0 (5603)
2001: 7[0]GS

	Starts	1st	2nd	3rd	Win & Pl
Career Total (Turf)	1	0	0	0	

Going (Turf): Sf: 0-0 GS: 0-1 Gd: 0-0 GF: 0-0 Fm: 0-0
Distance: 5f/6f: 0-0 7f-8f: 0-1 9f-13f: 0-0 14f+: 0-0
Track : LH: 0-0 RH: 0-0 Tight: 0-0 Gall: 0-0
Aids: Bl: 0-0 Vi: 0-0 Tstrap: 0-0
Best Rating: 76 11/01 NmkR 7f gd-sft

Ballet High (IRE)

96 **61**

8-y-o b g Sadler's Wells (USA)-Marie D'Argonne (FR) (Jefferson)

R Dickin Wholebuild Ltd

Placings:3423/3/0-650 (2821)

2001: 13^{6}GF, 16^{5}GF, 18^{0}GF

	Starts	1st	2nd	3rd	Win & Pl
Career Total (Turf)	9	0	1	3	3813

Going (Turf): Sf: 0-1 GS: 0-0 Gd: 0-1 GF: 0-7 Fm: 0-0
Distance: 5f/6f: 0-0 7f-8f: 0-0 9f-13f: 0-3 14f+: 0-6
Track : LH: 0-7 RH: 0-2 Tight: 0-2 Gall: 0-2
Aids: Bl: 0-0 Vi: 0-0 Tstrap: 0-0
Best Rating: 61 6/01 Wwck 2m39y gd-fm

Ballet Master (USA)

(105) (86)**67**

5-y-o ch h Kingmambo (USA)-Danse Royale (IRE) (Caerleon (USA))

J D Czerpak (M W Easterby 27/9) Faisal Al Sheikh

Placings:1/4/0-6163440005021 (5616)

2001: 8^{6}SW, 7^{1}SD, 7^{6}GF, 8^{3}GS, 8^{4}F, 10^{4}G, 10^{0}GF, 8^{0}G, 7^{0}GF, 10^{5}S, 8^{0}GS, 8^{2}SD, 7^{1}SD

	Starts	1st	2nd	3rd	Win & Pl
Career Total (Turf)	12	1	0	1	12274
Career Total (AW)	4	2	1	0	6994

86	11/01	Wolv	7f	E(0-70)H	STD	£3517
69	3/01	Sthl	7f	E(0-70)H	STD	£2828
78	10/98	Yarm	7f3y	D	SFT	£3157

Total win prize-money £9503

Going (Turf): Sf: 1-3 GS: 0-3 Gd: 0-2 GF: 0-3 Fm: 0-1
Distance: 5f/6f: 0-0 7f-8f: 3-11 9f-13f: 0-5 14f+: 0-0
Track : LH: 2-12 RH: 0-2 Tight: 1-4 Gall: 0-4
Aids: Bl: 0-4 Vi: 0-0 Tstrap: 0-0
Best Rating: 86 11/01 Wolv 7f stand

Originally with Henry Cecil, he won on the Southwell Fibresand for Mick Easterby in March and has run some fair races on turf since then. He changed stables again in the autumn and ran well when put back on sand, especially when adopting front-running tactics for the first time.

Ballet Score (IRE)

97 **80+**

2-y-o b f Sadler's Wells (USA)-Puzzled Look (USA) (Gulch (USA))

J H M Gosden R E Sangster

Placings:1 (5682)

2001: 7^{1}S

	Starts	1st	2nd	3rd	Win & Pl
Career Total (Turf)	1	1	0	0	4739

80	11/01	Donc	7f	D	SFT	£4738

Total win prize-money £4739

Going (Turf): Sf: 1-1 GS: 0-0 Gd: 0-0 GF: 0-0 Fm: 0-0
Distance: 5f/6f: 0-0 7f-8f: 1-1 9f-13f: 0-0 14f+: 0-0
Track : LH: 0-0 RH: 0-0 Tight: 0-0 Gall: 0-0
Aids: Bl: 0-0 Vi: 0-0 Tstrap: 0-0
Best Rating: 80 11/01 Donc 7f soft

A February foal, she showed a round action when winning on her debut and will need middle-distances at three. Acts on soft.

Ballet Suite

103 **83+**

3-y-o b f Sadler's Wells (USA)-Houseproud (USA) (Riverman (USA))

H R A Cecil K Abdulla

Placings:31 (1795)

2001: 9^{3}GS, 11^{1}GF

	Starts	1st	2nd	3rd	Win & Pl
Career Total (Turf)	2	1	0	1	3564

83	6/01	Yarm	1m3f101yD	G-F	£3094

Total win prize-money £3094

Going (Turf): Sf: 0-0 GS: 0-1 Gd: 0-0 GF: 1-1 Fm: 0-0
Distance: 5f/6f: 0-0 7f-8f: 0-0 9f-13f: 1-2 14f+: 0-0
Track : LH: 1-1 RH: 0-1 Tight: 1-2 Gall: 0-0
Aids: Bl: 0-0 Vi: 0-0 Tstrap: 0-0
Best Rating: 83 6/01 Yarm 1m3f101y gd-fm

Beautifully bred filly, out of a winner of the Poule d'Essai des Pouliches. Was a most impressive seven length winner of a maiden at Yarmouth in June but failed to reappear.

Ballet-K

94 **76**

7-y-o ch m Gunner B-Nicolene (Nice Music)

J Neville Gallagher Enterprises Ltd

Placings:03410/0 (5692)

2001: 16^{0}S

	Starts	1st	2nd	3rd	Win & Pl
Career Total (Turf)	6	1	0	1	4616

76	6/99	Bath	2m1f34y	D(0-80)H	GD	£3772

Total win prize-money £3773

Going (Turf): Sf: 0-1 GS: 0-1 Gd: 1-2 GF: 0-2 Fm: 0-0
Distance: 5f/6f: 0-0 7f-8f: 0-0 9f-13f: 0-3 14f+: 1-3
Track : LH: 1-5 RH: 0-1 Tight: 1-3 Gall: 0-2
Aids: Bl: 0-0 Vi: 0-0 Tstrap: 0-0
Best Rating: 56 11/01 Donc 2m110y soft

Ballets Russes (IRE)

98(62) **37**

4-y-o b f Marju (IRE)-Elminya (IRE) (Sure Blade (USA))

John Berry John Berry

Placings:500/4300006000-06442550 (4361)

2001: 8^{0}GF, 11^{6}GF, 11^{4}GF, 10^{4}GF, 14^{2}GS, 15^{5}G, 14^{5}GF, 11^{0}GF

	Starts	1st	2nd	3rd	Win & Pl
Career Total (Turf)	19	0	1	1	1330
Career Total (AW)	2	0	0	0	

Going (Turf): Sf: 0-2 GS: 0-3 Gd: 0-2 GF: 0-10 Fm: 0-1
Distance: 5f/6f: 0-2 7f-8f: 0-7 9f-13f: 0-8 14f+: 0-3
Track : LH: 0-10 RH: 0-2 Tight: 0-8 Gall: 0-0
Aids: Bl: 0-0 Vi: 0-1 Tstrap: 0-0
Best Rating: 37 8/01 Yarm 1m6f17y gd-sft

Ballina Lad (IRE)

(104) (39)**40**

5-y-o b g Mac's Imp (USA)-Nationalartgallery (IRE) (Tate Gallery (USA))

D Nicholls The James Nicholls Partnership

Placings:1054000/130000/005060-0400 (0187)

2001: 6^{0}SD, 5^{4}SD, 6^{0}SW, 5^{0}SD

	Starts	1st	2nd	3rd	Win & Pl
Career Total (Turf)	18	2	0	1	6152
Career Total (AW)	5	0	0	0	0

60	5/99	Ripn	6f	E(0-70)H	G-F	£3399
81	5/98	Newc	5f	F	G-S	£1945

Total win prize-money £5344

Going (Turf): Sf: 0-0 GS: 1-1 Gd: 0-6 GF: 1-10 Fm: 0-1
Distance: 5f/6f: 2-19 7f-8f: 0-4 9f-13f: 0-0 14f+: 0-0
Track : LH: 0-7 RH: 0-0 Tight: 0-4 Gall: 0-0
Aids: Bl: 0-2 Vi: 0-0 Tstrap: 0-0
Best Rating: 39 1/01 Wolv 5f stand

Ballinger Ridge

71 **48**

2-y-o b c Sabrehill (USA)-Branston Ridge (Indian Ridge)

B Hanbury Mrs Hazel Barber

Placings:5 (3952)

2001: 6^{5}GF

	Starts	1st	2nd	3rd	Win & Pl
Career Total (Turf)	1	0	0	0	0

Going (Turf): Sf: 0-0 GS: 0-0 Gd: 0-0 GF: 0-1 Fm: 0-0
Distance: 5f/6f: 0-1 7f-8f: 0-0 9f-13f: 0-0 14f+: 0-0
Track : LH: 0-0 RH: 0-0 Tight: 0-0 Gall: 0-0
Aids: Bl: 0-0 Vi: 0-0 Tstrap: 0-0
Best Rating: 48 8/01 Sals 6f gd-fm

Ballistic Boy

58 **62**

4-y-o ch g First Trump-Be Discreet (Junius (USA))

J J O'Neill A & G Oliver

Placings:00/0030-0 (0702)

2001: 10^{0}HY

	Starts	1st	2nd	3rd	Win & Pl
Career Total (Turf)	9	0	0	1	400

Going (Turf): Sf: 0-2 GS: 0-3 Gd: 0-0 GF: 0-4 Fm: 0-0
Distance: 5f/6f: 0-0 7f-8f: 0-4 9f-13f: 0-5 14f+: 0-0
Track : LH: 0-5 RH: 0-2 Tight: 0-1 Gall: 0-0
Aids: Bl: 0-0 Vi: 0-0 Tstrap: 0-0
Best Rating: 48 8/01 Sals 6f gd-fm

Ballybunion (IRE)

(98) (73)**81**

2-y-o ch c Entrepreneur-Clarentia (Ballad Rock)

P F I Cole Mr & Mrs John Poynton

Placings:0011 (5140)

2001: 6^{0}G, 5^{0}HY, 5^{1}GF, 6^{1}G

	Starts	1st	2nd	3rd	Win & Pl
Career Total (Turf)	4	2	0	0	10792

81	10/01	NmkR	6f	C(0-95)	GD	£7166
73	9/01	Catt	5f212y	D	G-F	£3626

Total win prize-money £10792

Going (Turf): Sf: 0-1 GS: 0-0 Gd: 1-2 GF: 1-1 Fm: 0-0
Distance: 5f/6f: 2-4 7f-8f: 0-0 9f-13f: 0-0 14f+: 0-0
Track : LH: 1-1 RH: 0-0 Tight: 1-1 Gall: 0-0
Aids: Bl: 0-0 Vi: 0-0 Tstrap: 0-0
Best Rating: 81 10/01 NmkR 6f good

Appreciated the faster ground when getting off the mark at Catterick, and handled the step up in class to take a Newmarket nursery in October. Suited by six furlongs, does not want the ground too soft.

Ballyhurry (USA)

92 **66**

4-y-o b g Rubiano (USA)-Balakhna (FR) (Tyrant (USA))

J S Goldie John Breslin

Placings:05000/00003110-0000 (5538)

2001: 11^{0}F, 9^{0}FT, 8^{0}GS, 10^{0}S

	Starts	1st	2nd	3rd	Win & Pl
Career Total (Turf)	15	2	0	1	10770
Career Total (AW)	2	0	0	0	

66	8/00	Cork	1m2f	(0-70)H	Y-S	£5175
63	8/00	Tram	1m1f	(0-65)H	G-F	£5175

Total win prize-money £10350

Going (Turf): Sf: 0-1 GS: 0-1 Gd: 0-3 GF: 1-1 Fm: 0-2
Distance: 5f/6f: 0-2 7f-8f: 0-6 9f-13f: 2-8 14f+: 0-0
Track : LH: 0-4 RH: 2-5 Tight: 0-1 Gall: 0-2
Aids: Bl: 2-4 Vi: 0-0 Tstrap: 0-0
Best Rating: 45 10/01 Rdcr 1m2f soft

An ex-Irish gelding, he won a couple of handicaps back

to back in the summer of 2000. Raced in Dubai over the winter.

Ballyhurst (IRE)

63 **30**

2-y-o b g Charnwood Forest (IRE)-La Belle Katherine (USA) (Lyphard (USA))
M W Easterby The Shooting Syndicate

Placings:060 **(2812)**
2001: 6^{0}G, 5^{6}GF, 7^{0}GF

	Starts	1st	2nd	3rd	Win & Pl
Career Total (Turf)	3	0	0	0	0

Going (Turf): Sf: 0-0 GS: 0-0 Gd: 0-1 GF: 0-2 Fm: 0-0
Distance: 5f/6f: 0-2 7f-8f: 0-1 9f-13f: 0-0 14f+: 0-0
Track : LH: 0-0 RH: 0-1 Tight: 0-0 Gall: 0-0
Aids: Bl: 0-0 Vi: 0-0 Tstrap: 0-0
Best Rating: 30 6/01 Newc 5f gd-fm

Ballyjazz

(98) (55)

3-y-o b c Alhijaz-All The Girls (IRE) (Alzao (USA))
J A Osborne Mrs P M Downham

Placings:531 **(0190)**
2001: 7^{5}SD, 8^{3}SD, 7^{1}SD

	Starts	1st	2nd	3rd	Win & Pl
Career Total (Turf)	0	0	0	0	
Career Total (AW)	3	1	0	1	2659

55 1/01 Sthl 7f F STD £2233
Total win prize-money £2233

Going (Turf): Sf: 0-0 GS: 0-0 Gd: 0-0 GF: 0-0 Fm: 0-0
Distance: 5f/6f: 0-0 **7f-8f: 1-3** 9f-13f: 0-0 14f+: 0-0
Track : **LH: 1-3** RH: 0-0 Tight: 0-0 Gall: 0-0
Aids: Bl: 0-0 Vi: 0-0 Tstrap: 0-0
Best Rating: 55 1/01 Sthl 7f stand

Ballykissann

72(77) (6)**17**

6-y-o ch g Ballacashtal (CAN)-Mybella Ann (Anfield)
J C Tuck Paul De Weck

Placings:05/00600030/0000-0000 **(1529)**
2001: 9^{0}SW, 7^{0}SW, 12^{0}SD, 11^{0}F

	Starts	1st	2nd	3rd	Win & Pl
Career Total (Turf)	14	0	0	1	336
Career Total (AW)	4	0	0	0	

Going (Turf): Sf: 0-1 GS: 0-1 Gd: 0-2 GF: 0-7 Fm: 0-3
Distance: 5f/6f: 0-0 7f-8f: 0-8 9f-13f: 0-10 14f+: 0-0
Track : LH: 0-13 RH: 0-0 Tight: 0-9 Gall: 0-0
Aids: Bl: 0-4 Vi: 0-1 Tstrap: 0-0
Best Rating: 6 1/01 Ling 7f slow

Ballymagan (IRE)

(103) (78+)

3-y-o b c Charnwood Forest (IRE)-Bold Miss (Bold Lad (IRE))
B W Hills John C Grant

Placings:5-112 **(0166)**
2001: 7^{1}SD, 9^{1}SW, 8^{2}SD

	Starts	1st	2nd	3rd	Win & Pl
Career Total (Turf)	0	0	0	0	
Career Total (AW)	4	2	1	0	7055

78 1/01 Wolv 1m1f79y E(0-75)H SLW £2975
66 1/01 Sthl 7f D STD £2408
Total win prize-money £5383

Going (Turf): Sf: 0-0 GS: 0-0 Gd: 0-0 GF: 0-0 Fm: 0-0
Distance: 5f/6f: 0-1 7f-8f: 1-1 9f-13f: 1-2 14f+: 0-0
Track : **LH: 2-4** RH: 0-0 **Tight: 1-2** Gall: 0-0
Aids: Bl: 0-0 Vi: 0-0 Tstrap: 0-0
Best Rating: 78 1/01 Wolv 1m1f79y slow

Half-brother to Lomas, this big, scopey colt won twice on the sand. Improving sort.

Balmacara

75 **46**

2-y-o b f Lake Coniston (IRE)-Diabaig (Precocious)
Miss K B Boutflower Silver 2 Racing

Placings:000 **(5037)**
2001: 6^{0}GF, 6^{0}GF, 5^{0}G

	Starts	1st	2nd	3rd	Win & Pl
Career Total (Turf)	3	0	0	0	

Going (Turf): Sf: 0-0 GS: 0-0 Gd: 0-1 GF: 0-2 Fm: 0-0
Distance: 5f/6f: 0-2 7f-8f: 0-1 9f-13f: 0-0 14f+: 0-0
Track : LH: 0-1 RH: 0-0 Tight: 0-0 Gall: 0-1
Aids: Bl: 0-0 Vi: 0-0 Tstrap: 0-0
Best Rating: 46 10/01 Bath 5f161y good

Bamalko (IRE)

98(97) (79)**88**

2-y-o b c Royal Applause-Shadowglow (Shaadi (USA))
B W Hills Abdulla Buhaleeba

Placings:3225213 **(4716)**
2001: 5^{3}GF, 5^{2}G, 5^{2}GF, 6^{5}GS, 7^{2}SD, 7^{1}G, 7^{3}G

	Starts	1st	2nd	3rd	Win & Pl
Career Total (Turf)	6	1	2	2	10938
Career Total (AW)	1	0	1	0	1077

83 8/01 Epsm 7f C GD £7020
Total win prize-money £7020

Going (Turf): Sf: 0-0 GS: 0-1 **Gd: 1-3** GF: 0-2 Fm: 0-0
Distance: 5f/6f: 0-4 **7f-8f: 1-3** 9f-13f: 0-0 14f+: 0-0
Track : **LH: 1-4** RH: 0-0 **Tight: 1-3** Gall: 0-1
Aids: Bl: 0-0 Vi: 0-0 Tstrap: 0-0
Best Rating: 88 9/01 Epsm 7f good

A tough front-runner, he made all in an Epsom nursery in August. Seems best suited by good ground or faster.

Banaadir (USA)

96 **35**

3-y-o b f Diesis-Treble (USA) (Riverman (USA))
J L Dunlop Hamdan Al Maktoum

Placings:020 **(4673)**
2001: 10^{0}S, 9^{2}GF, 12^{0}G

	Starts	1st	2nd	3rd	Win & Pl
Career Total (Turf)	3	0	1	0	1340

Going (Turf): Sf: 0-1 GS: 0-0 Gd: 0-1 GF: 0-1 Fm: 0-0
Distance: 5f/6f: 0-0 7f-8f: 0-0 9f-13f: 0-3 14f+: 0-0
Track : LH: 0-2 RH: 0-1 Tight: 0-0 Gall: 0-0
Aids: Bl: 0-0 Vi: 0-0 Tstrap: 0-0
Best Rating: 35 7/01 Hayd 1m2f120y soft

Banasan (IRE)

104 **91**

3-y-o b c Marju (IRE)-Banaja (IRE) (Sadler's Wells (USA))
Sir Michael Stoute H H Aga Khan

Placings:05314 **(4597)**
2001: 8^{0}GS, 10^{5}GF, 10^{3}GF, 10^{1}G, 12^{4}GF

	Starts	1st	2nd	3rd	Win & Pl
Career Total (Turf)	5	1	0	1	4583

79 6/01 Wind 1m2f7y D GD £3290
Total win prize-money £3290

Going (Turf): Sf: 0-0 GS: 0-1 **Gd: 1-1** GF: 0-3 Fm: 0-0
Distance: 5f/6f: 0-0 7f-8f: 0-0 **9f-13f: 1-5** 14f+: 0-0
Track : LH: 0-2 RH: 0-1 **Tight: 1-5** Gall: 0-0
Aids: Bl: 0-0 **Vi: 1-2** Tstrap: 0-0
Best Rating: 91 9/01 Thsk 1m4f gd-fm

Got off the mark in a Windsor maiden, but looked a tricky ride. Hung left when fourth in a Thirsk handicap.

Banco Suivi (IRE)

96(97) (71)**86**

4-y-o b f Nashwan (USA)-Pay The Bank (High Top)
B W Hills Wafic Said

Placings:5/20231300-05 **(1100)**
2001: 12^{0}S, 9^{5}G

	Starts	1st	2nd	3rd	Win & Pl
Career Total (Turf)	10	1	2	2	11002
Career Total (AW)	1	0	0	0	

86 8/00 Donc 1m4f D G-F £4192
Total win prize-money £4193

Going (Turf): Sf: 0-5 GS: 0-1 Gd: 0-1 **GF: 1-3** Fm: 0-0
Distance: 5f/6f: 0-0 7f-8f: 0-1 **9f-13f: 1-9** 14f+: 0-1
Track : **LH: 1-5** RH: 0-4 Tight: 0-2 **Gall: 1-4**
Aids: Bl: 0-0 Vi: 0-0 Tstrap: 0-0
Best Rating: 84 5/01 NmkR 1m1f good

Band Of Colour (IRE)

53

3-y-o b f Spectrum (IRE)-Regal Scintilla (King Of Spain)
C R Egerton Band Of Colour Partnership

Placings:0 **(3744)**
2001: 7^{0}S

	Starts	1st	2nd	3rd	Win & Pl
Career Total (Turf)	1	0	0	0	

Going (Turf): Sf: 0-1 GS: 0-0 Gd: 0-0 GF: 0-0 Fm: 0-0
Distance: 5f/6f: 0-0 7f-8f: 0-1 9f-13f: 0-0 14f+: 0-0
Track : LH: 0-0 RH: 0-0 Tight: 0-0 Gall: 0-0
Aids: Bl: 0-0 Vi: 0-0 Tstrap: 0-0

Band Substance

5-y-o b m Bandmaster (USA)-Bold Dancer (FR) (Bold Arrangement)
A T Murphy Dulverton Racing Partnership

Placings:0 **(0146)**
2001: 12^{0}SW

	Starts	1st	2nd	3rd	Win & Pl
Career Total (Turf)	0	0	0	0	
Career Total (AW)	1	0	0	0	

Going (Turf): Sf: 0-0 GS: 0-0 Gd: 0-0 GF: 0-0 Fm: 0-0
Distance: 5f/6f: 0-0 7f-8f: 0-0 9f-13f: 0-1 14f+: 0-0
Track : LH: 0-1 RH: 0-0 Tight: 0-0 Gall: 0-0
Aids: Bl: 0-0 Vi: 0-0 Tstrap: 0-0

Bandanna

109 **73**

4-y-o gr f Bandmaster (USA)-Gratclo (Belfort (FR))
R J Hodges Miss R Dobson

Placings:142350/006516354-6562205504002044 **(5523)**
2001: 5^{6}GS, 6^{5}GS, 5^{6}GF, 5^{2}F, 6^{2}GF, 5^{0}GF, 5^{5}GF, 6^{5}GF, 6^{0}G, 5^{4}G, 5^{0}G, 6^{0}G, 6^{2}S, 6^{0}G, 5^{4}G, 5^{4}HY

	Starts	1st	2nd	3rd	Win & Pl
Career Total (Turf)	31	2	4	2	25179

83 7/00 Bath 5f11y C(0-90)H FRM £6922
68 5/99 Chep 6f16y F GD £2276
Total win prize-money £9199

Going (Turf): Sf: 0-4 GS: 0-5 **Gd: 1-9** GF: 0-11 **Fm: 1-2**
Distance: 5f/6f: 1-28 7f-8f: 1-3 9f-13f: 0-0 14f+: 0-0
Track : **LH: 1-8** RH: 0-1 Tight: 0-1 **Gall: 1-8**

Aids: Bl: 0-0 Vi: 0-0 Tstrap: 0-0
Best Rating: 83 7/01 Asct 6f gd-fm

Suited by six furlongs and a sound surface, she also handles easier ground. She ran well in the summer of 2001 and, slipping down the handicap, deserves a change of luck.

Bandarello

94(86) (51)**48**
3-y-o b f Distant Relative-Bangles (Chilibang)
John A Harris (J L Harris 29/6) Mrs Susan Lee

Placings:6-305540 **(5186)**
2001: 6^{3}SD, 6^{0}SD, 5^{5}G, 6^{5}G, 5^{4}GF, 5^{0}GS

	Starts	1st	2nd	3rd	Win & Pl
Career Total (Turf)	5	0	0	0	339
Career Total (AW)	2	0	0	1	398

Going (Turf): Sf: 0-0 GS: 0-1 Gd: 0-2 GF: 0-2 Fm: 0-0
Distance: 5f/6f: 0-6 7f-8f: 0-1 9f-13f: 0-0 14f+: 0-0
Track : LH: 0-3 RH: 0-0 Tight: 0-2 Gall: 0-0
Aids: Bl: 0-0 Vi: 0-0 Tstrap: 0-0
Best Rating: 51 6/01 Sthl 6f stand

Bandari (IRE)

114 **115+**
2-y-o b c Alhaarth (IRE)-Miss Audimar (USA) (Mr. Leader (USA))
M Johnston A Al-Rostamani

Placings:1011 **(5401)**
2001: 7^{1}G, 7^{0}G, 8^{1}GF, 8^{1}S

	Starts	1st	2nd	3rd	Win & Pl
Career Total (Turf)	4	3	0	0	25204

115 10/01 Pont 1m4y A SFT £16240
95 9/01 Ayr 1m D G-F £4309
90 8/01 Bevl 7f100y D GD £4654
Total win prize-money £25204

Going (Turf): Sf: 1-1 GS: 0-0 **Gd: 1-2 GF: 1-1** Fm: 0-0
Distance: 5f/6f: 0-0 **7f-8f: 2-3** 9f-13f: 1-1 14f+: 0-0
Track : **LH: 2-2 RH: 1-2** Tight: 0-0 Gall: 0-0
Aids: Bl: 0-0 Vi: 0-0 Tstrap: 0-0
Best Rating: 115 10/01 Pont 1m4y soft

Related to a number of winners, he won well on his Beverley debut but ran too free in a Sandown Group Three. Bounced back with an all-the-way win at Ayr, followed up with success in a Listed event at Pontrfract. He should appreciate middle distances as a three-year-old.

Bandbox (IRE)

107(104) (63)**67**
6-y-o ch g Imperial Frontier (USA)-Dublah (USA) (Private Account (USA))
M Salaman R H Brookes

Placings:0530242221/000020030260/0006032331030 0/1200030603062361255-0035265246025 **(4075)**
2001: 7^{0}G, 5^{0}G, 6^{3}GF, 6^{5}GF, 5^{2}HD, 6^{6}GF, 7^{5}GF, 6^{2}GF, 5^{4}GS, 6^{6}GF, 6^{0}GS, 6^{2}GF, 5^{5}G

	Starts	1st	2nd	3rd	Win & Pl
Career Total (Turf)	66	3	13	10	25331
Career Total (AW)	3	1	1	0	2518

61 8/00 Folk 6f E(0-65) G-F £3038
60 2/00 Sthl 7f F STD £2081
66 8/99 Leic 5f218y E(0-65) GD £2826
78 10/97 Leic 5f218y F GD £2952
Total win prize-money £10898

Going (Turf): Sf: 0-6 GS: 0-14 **Gd: 2-17** GF: 1-26 Fm: 0-3
Distance: **5f/6f: 3-49** 7f-8f: 1-19 9f-13f: 0-1 14f+: 0-0
Track : **LH: 1-13** RH: 0-6 Tight: 0-2 Gall: 0-11
Aids: **Bl: 1-10** Vi: 0-5 Tstrap: 0-1
Best Rating: 67 7/01 Leic 5f218y gd-sft

A fair sprint handicapper, he often runs well and has been placed umpteen times, but has a moderate strike-rate overall. Suited by six furlongs and needs to be brought late.

Bandler Ching (IRE)

103 **66**
4-y-o b g Sri Pekan (USA)-Stanerra's Wish (IRE) (Caerleon (USA))
C N Allen Newmarketconnections.Com

Placings:32533/521340-000646040 **(5376)**
2001: 9^{0}GF, 10^{0}G, 9^{0}GF, 11^{6}GF, 9^{4}GF, 9^{6}GF, 8^{0}G, 7^{4}S, 9^{0}G

	Starts	1st	2nd	3rd	Win & Pl
Career Total (Turf)	20	1	2	4	11332

78 8/00 Leic 1m1f218yE(0-70)H G-F £5044
Total win prize-money £5044

Going (Turf): Sf: 0-1 GS: 0-1 Gd: 0-6 **GF: 1-11** Fm: 0-0
Distance: 5f/6f: 0-0 7f-8f: 0-4 **9f-13f: 1-15** 14f+: 0-0
Track : LH: 0-9 **RH: 1-7** Tight: 0-6 Gall: 0-2
Aids: Bl: 0-0 Vi: 0-0 Tstrap: 0-0
Best Rating: 67 7/01 Gdwd 1m1f192y gd-fm

Ten furlongs and fast ground are his conditions but he has only managed one success so far at Leicester.

Bangled

(99) (52)**42**
4-y-o ch g Beveled (USA)-Bangles (Chilibang)
D J Coakley Chris Van Hoorn

Placings:30450/000030420-10000 **(4159)**
2001: 6^{1}SD, 6^{0}SD, 5^{0}GS, 6^{0}F, 6^{0}GF, 6^{0}SD

	Starts	1st	2nd	3rd	Win & Pl
Career Total (Turf)	13	0	0	1	778
Career Total (AW)	6	1	1	1	3273

52 3/01 Sthl 6f E(0-75)H STD £2268
Total win prize-money £2268

Going (Turf): Sf: 0-0 GS: 0-2 Gd: 0-4 GF: 0-6 Fm: 0-1
Distance: **5f/6f: 1-16** 7f-8f: 0-3 9f-13f: 0-0 14f+: 0-0
Track : **LH: 1-10** RH: 0-0 Tight: 0-4 Gall: 0-2
Aids: Bl: 0-0 Vi: 0-1 Tstrap: 0-0
Best Rating: 52 3/01 Sthl 6f stand

Baniyar (IRE)

87 **104**
4-y-o ch c Alzao (USA)-Banaja (IRE) (Sadler's Wells (USA))
Sir Michael Stoute H H Aga Khan

Placings:0/415-0 **(1534)**
2001: 12^{0}GF

	Starts	1st	2nd	3rd	Win & Pl
Career Total (Turf)	5	1	0	0	5252

72 5/00 Haml 1m3f16y D G-F £4914
Total win prize-money £4914

Going (Turf): Sf: 0-1 GS: 0-1 Gd: 0-0 **GF: 1-3** Fm: 0-0
Distance: 5f/6f: 0-0 7f-8f: 0-1 **9f-13f: 1-4** 14f+: 0-0
Track : LH: 0-0 **RH: 1-4 Tight: 1-2** Gall: 0-1
Aids: Bl: 0-0 Vi: 0-0 Tstrap: 0-0
Best Rating: 69 5/01 Gdwd 1m4f gd-fm

An interesting, lightly raced colt. Broke little sweat in winning his maiden at Hamilton in May 2000, and was upped considerably in class when beaten just over six lengths into fifth behind Subtle Power in the King Edward VII Stakes at Royal Ascot. Reappeared at Goodwood in May 2001, but was well beaten.

Banjo Bay (IRE)

111 **92**
3-y-o b c Common Grounds-Thirlmere (Cadeaux Genereux)
B A McMahon Mrs C P Lees-Jones

Placings:53050-16120250 **(5005)**
2001: 6^{1}GS, 7^{6}GF, 7^{1}G, 8^{2}G, 7^{0}G, 6^{2}G, 6^{5}GF, 7^{0}S

	Starts	1st	2nd	3rd	Win & Pl
Career Total (Turf)	13	2	2	1	23137

86 6/01 Leic 7f9y D(0-80)H GD £7696
69 5/01 Pont 6f D G-S £2941
Total win prize-money £10637

Going (Turf): Sf: 0-2 **GS: 1-2 Gd: 1-5** GF: 0-4 Fm: 0-0
Distance: 5f/6f: 1-7 7f-8f: 1-6 9f-13f: 0-0 14f+: 0-0
Track : **LH: 1-3** RH: 0-1 Tight: 0-1 Gall: 0-1
Aids: Bl: 0-0 Vi: 0-0 Tstrap: 0-0
Best Rating: 92 8/01 Ripn 6f good

Strengthened up during the winter and made a winning reappearance at Pontefract in May over six furlongs. Unlucky next time, but scored at Leicester over seven furlongs in June. Good efforts since, runner-up in the Great St Wilfrid at Ripon in August and fifth in the Ayr Gold Cup. He looks best suited by ground no faster than good.

Bank On Him

(94) (65)**49**
6-y-o b g Elmaamul (USA)-Feather Flower (Relkino)
G L Moore Allen House Partnership

Placings:066/32432412253/110404/6-0020 **(4463)**
2001: 12^{0}SD, 10^{0}G, 8^{2}G, 9^{0}GS, 10^{3}SD

	Starts	1st	2nd	3rd	Win & Pl
Career Total (Turf)	8	0	1	0	1060
Career Total (AW)	17	3	4	3	17061

75 2/99 Ling 1m2f C(0-90)H STD £6214
75 1/99 Ling 1m2f D(0-85)H STD £3683
63 9/98 Wolv 1m100y F(0-65)H STD £2637
Total win prize-money £12536

Going (Turf): Sf: 0-0 GS: 0-3 Gd: 0-4 GF: 0-1 Fm: 0-0
Distance: 5f/6f: 0-0 7f-8f: 0-7 **9f-13f: 3-18** 14f+: 0-0
Track : **LH: 3-20** RH: 0-4 **Tight: 3-19** Gall: 0-0
Aids: Bl: 0-0 Vi: 0-0 Tstrap: 0-0
Best Rating: 49 8/01 Sand 1m14y good

He has shown rather better form on sand than on turf in the last couple of years. Probably best suited by ten fur longs.

Banks Hill

113 **125+**
3-y-o b f Danehill (USA)-Hasili (IRE) (Kahyasi)
A Fabre K Abdulla

Placings:1-4211221 **(5577a)**
2001: 8^{4}HY, 8^{2}G, 8^{1}G, 8^{1}GF, 8^{2}GS, 8^{2}GS, 10^{1}F

	Starts	1st	2nd	3rd	Win & Pl
Career Total (Turf)	8	4	3	0	810450

125 10/01 Belm 1m2f FRM £481867
119 6/01 Asct 1m A G-F £156600
117 6/01 Chan 1m GD £29098
10/00 MsnL 7f HVY £8646
Total win prize-money £676211

Going (Turf): Sf: 0-1 GS: 0-2 **Gd: 1-2 GF: 1-1 Fm: 1-1**
Distance: 5f/6f: 0-0 **7f-8f: 2-6** 9f-13f: 1-1 14f+: 0-0
Track : LH: 1-1 RH: 1-2 Tight: 0-0 **Gall: 1-1**
Aids: Bl: 0-0 Vi: 0-0 Tstrap: 0-0
Best Rating: 125 10/01 Belm 1m2f firm

A progressive French filly, she finished runner-up in the Poule d'Essai des Pouliches before winning a Group Two in France. She was an impressive winner of the Coronation Stakes at Royal Ascot, and finished runner-up in the Jacques le Marois and the Moulin. Stepped up to ten furlongs, she bolted up in the Breeders' Cup Filly and Mare Turf. She has won on heavy, but is well suited by by fast ground. She looks likely to be a major threat to the colts in the top ten-furlong races in 2002.

Banneret (USA)

(100) (41)**19**

8-y-o b g Imperial Falcon (CAN)-Dashing Partner (Formidable (USA))

A G Juckes A C W Price

Placings:04/00000/**16021135/2011534/210532646-050** **(1585)**

2001: 12^{0}SD, 12^{5}SD, 14^{0}SD

	Starts	1st	2nd	3rd	Win & Pl
Career Total (Turf)	9	0	0	0	0
Career Total (AW)	25	6	4	3	15735

48	1/00	Wolv	1m4f	F	STD	£2257
63	10/99	Wolv	1m4f	F(0-60)H	STD	£2444
60	9/99	Sthl	1m3f	F(0-60)	STD	£1849
64	7/98	Sthl	1m4f	G	STD	£1882
64	7/98	Wolv	1m4f	G	STD	£1952
72	3/98	Wolv	1m1f79y	E	STD	£2336

Total win prize-money £12722

Going (Turf): Sf: 0-1 GS: 0-2 Gd: 0-2 GF: 0-4 Fm: 0-0
Distance: 5f/6f: 0-0 7f-8f: 0-1 **9f-13f: 6-30** 14f+: 0-3
Track : **LH: 6-30** RH: 0-2 **Tight: 4-21** Gall: 0-1
Aids: Bl: 0-2 **Vi: 1-9** Tstrap: 0-0

A fair handicapper on Fibresand he is an effective sort in modest company over middle distances on that surface.

Banningham Bliz

94(75) (19)**48**

3-y-o ch f Inchinor-Mary From Dunlow (Nicholas Bill)

D Shaw Crown Select

Placings:0065430223-05065 **(2225)**

2001: 7^{0}SW, 6^{5}GF, 6^{0}GF, 6^{6}GF, 7^{5}G

	Starts	1st	2nd	3rd	Win & Pl
Career Total (Turf)	14	0	2	2	1616
Career Total (AW)	1		0	0	0

Going (Turf): Sf: 0-1 GS: 0-1 Gd: 0-4 GF: 0-5 Fm: 0-2
Distance: 5f/6f: 0-8 7f-8f: 0-6 9f-13f: 0-0 14f+: 0-0
Track : LH: 0-3 RH: 0-0 Tight: 0-0 Gall: 0-0
Aids: Bl: 0-3 Vi: 0-5 Tstrap: 0-0
Best Rating: 48 5/01 Hayd 6f gd-fm

Bannister

99 **97**

3-y-o ch c Inchinor-Shall We Run (Hotfoot)

R Hannon The Royal Ascot Racing Club

Placings:2210-500 **(3240)**

2001: 8^{5}GF, 6^{0}F, 6^{0}GF

	Starts	1st	2nd	3rd	Win & Pl
Career Total (Turf)	7	1	2	0	75146

105	8/00	York	6f	A	GD	£72500

Total win prize-money £72500

Going (Turf): Sf: 0-0 GS: 0-0 **Gd: 1-4** GF: 0-2 Fm: 0-1
Distance: **5f/6f: 1-5** 7f-8f: 0-2 9f-13f: 0-0 14f+: 0-0
Track : LH: 0-0 RH: 0-1 Tight: 0-0 Gall: 0-0
Aids: Bl: 0-1 Vi: 0-0 Tstrap: 0-0
Best Rating: 97 5/01 Kemp 1m gd-fm

Last year's Gimcrack winner, he was disappointing in the Middle Park Stakes on his final outing at two. Lightly raced. Stepped up to a mile on first start of 2001 but was conceding weight all round, and was well beaten when dropped back to five furlongs at Sandown in July.

Banstead (USA)

87 **59**

3-y-o b c Known Fact (USA)-Rapid Raja (USA) (Darby Creek Road (USA))

T G Mills M J Joyce

Placings:5-0 **(1268)**

2001: 7^{0}GS

	Starts	1st	2nd	3rd	Win & Pl
Career Total (Turf)	2	0	0	0	0

Going (Turf): Sf: 0-1 GS: 0-1 Gd: 0-0 GF: 0-0 Fm: 0-0
Distance: 5f/6f: 0-0 7f-8f: 0-2 9f-13f: 0-0 14f+: 0-0
Track : LH: 0-0 RH: 0-0 Tight: 0-0 Gall: 0-0
Aids: Bl: 0-0 Vi: 0-0 Tstrap: 0-0
Best Rating: 40 5/01 Ling 7f gd-sft

Baptismal Rock (IRE)

98(99) (45)**51**

7-y-o ch g Ballad Rock-Flower From Heaven (Baptism)

A G Newcombe M Patel

Placings:0055020/**0**00000/**002/11134**6235232226366**3**
00/0500-1306 **(1770)**

2001: 5^{1}SD, 6^{3}SD, 5^{0}GS, 5^{6}F

	Starts	1st	2nd	3rd	Win & Pl
Career Total (Turf)	27	0	5	3	9165
Career Total (AW)	18	4	1	3	13800

44	3/01	Sthl	5f	F(0-65)H	STD	£1778
57	1/99	Sthl	6f	D(0-80)H	STD	£7035
54	1/99	Ling	6f	F(0-60)H	STD	£1688
37	1/99	Wolv	6f	G(0-70)H	STD	£1488

Total win prize-money £11990

Going (Turf): Sf: 0-4 GS: 0-2 Gd: 0-6 GF: 0-12 Fm: 0-2
Distance: **5f/6f: 4-41** 7f-8f: 0-3 9f-13f: 0-1 14f+: 0-0
Track : **LH: 3-25** RH: 0-2 **Tight: 2-11** Gall: 0-3
Aids: Bl: 0-0 Vi: 0-0 Tstrap: 0-0
Best Rating: 45 3/01 Sthl 6f stand

Completed a hat-trick on all three All-Weather tracks in 1999. Followed that with a string of solid efforts in competitive sprint handicaps on turf. Gained his first win for over two years in March 2001.

Barabaschi

99 **68**

5-y-o b g Elmaamul (USA)-Hills' Presidium (Presidium)

J White Miss Sally Thomas

Placings:35/20240322/2261200-0000 **(3957)**

2001: 8^{0}G, 7^{0}GF, 8^{0}GF, 9^{0}GF

	Starts	1st	2nd	3rd	Win & Pl
Career Total (Turf)	21	1	7	2	11046

64	8/00	Ayr	1m	D	G-F	£3412

Total win prize-money £3413

Going (Turf): Sf: 0-3 GS: 0-4 Gd: 0-3 **GF: 1-11** Fm: 0-0
Distance: 5f/6f: 0-2 **7f-8f: 1-14** 9f-13f: 0-5 14f+: 0-0
Track : **LH: 1-5** RH: 0-7 Tight: 0-4 Gall: 0-2
Aids: Bl: 0-1 Vi: 0-0 Tstrap: 0-0
Best Rating: 66 6/01 Wind 1m67y good

Baranova (IRE)

101 **98**

3-y-o b f Caerleon (USA)-Lacandona (USA) (Septieme Ciel (USA))

J H M Gosden R E Sangster

Placings:51-040 **(2325)**

2001: 9^{0}GF, 12^{4}G, 12^{0}GF

	Starts	1st	2nd	3rd	Win & Pl
Career Total (Turf)	5	1	0	0	7767

76	9/00	Leic	1m8y	D	G-F	£3887

Total win prize-money £3887

Going (Turf): Sf: 0-0 GS: 0-0 Gd: 0-1 **GF: 1-4** Fm: 0-0
Distance: 5f/6f: 0-0 7f-8f: 0-1 **9f-13f: 1-4** 14f+: 0-0
Track : LH: 0-0 RH: 0-2 Tight: 0-1 Gall: 0-1
Aids: Bl: 0-1 Vi: 0-0 Tstrap: 0-0
Best Rating: 98 6/01 StCl 1m4f good

Useful maiden winner (mile, good to firm) as a juvenile, improved form this term over longer trips, latest when fourth in the Prix de Rouyaumont over a mile and a half at Saint-Cloud. Has only raced on a sound surface.

Barathea Blazer

95 **83+**

2-y-o b c Barathea (IRE)-Empty Purse (Pennine Walk)

P W Harris Mrs Tina Evans

Placings:11 **(5280)**

2001: 7^{1}GS, 9^{1}S

	Starts	1st	2nd	3rd	Win & Pl
Career Total (Turf)	2	2	0	0	8282

83	10/01	Leic	1m1f218yC		SFT	£5846
81	10/01	Newc	7f	F	G-S	£2436

Total win prize-money £8282

Going (Turf): Sf: 1-1 GS: 1-1 Gd: 0-0 GF: 0-0 Fm: 0-0
Distance: 5f/6f: 0-0 7f-8f: 1-1 9f-13f: 1-1 14f+: 0-0
Track : LH: 0-0 **RH: 1-1** Tight: 0-0 Gall: 0-0
Aids: Bl: 0-0 Vi: 0-0 Tstrap: 0-0
Best Rating: 83 10/01 Leic 1m1f218y soft

Bettered his debut victory, with a win in a conditions stakes at Leicester. He stays 10 furlongs in testing ground.

Baratheastar

109 **73**

3-y-o ch f Barathea (IRE)-Sueboog (IRE) (Darshaan)

C E Brittain Mohamed Obaida

Placings:56-53626106 **(5638)**

2001: 8^{5}GF, 8^{3}G, 10^{6}GF, 7^{2}GS, 8^{6}GS, 7^{1}G, 7^{0}HY, 7^{6}G

	Starts	1st	2nd	3rd	Win & Pl
Career Total (Turf)	10	1	1	1	6098

73	10/01	Rdcr	7f	E(0-70)H	GD	£3458

Total win prize-money £3458

Going (Turf): Sf: 0-1 GS: 0-2 **Gd: 1-5** GF: 0-2 Fm: 0-0
Distance: 5f/6f: 0-0 **7f-8f: 1-7** 9f-13f: 0-3 14f+: 0-0
Track : LH: 0-1 RH: 0-5 Tight: 0-3 Gall: 0-2
Aids: Bl: 0-0 Vi: 0-0 Tstrap: 0-0
Best Rating: 73 10/01 Rdcr 7f good

Half-sister to the high-class Best Of The Bests, a rangy filly who shows plenty of knee action. She made an encouraging debut at Kempton at two and was not disgraced when stepped up in class subsequently. However, she did need a substantial drop in class to land the spoils at Redcar over seven furlongs in October.

Barathiki

85(91) (69)**79d**

3-y-o gr f Barathea (IRE)-Tagiki (IRE) (Doyoun)

P F I Cole Axom Barathiki Partnership

Placings:146201-500 **(4717)**

2001: 6^{5}SD, 7^{0}S, 8^{0}G

	Starts	1st	2nd	3rd	Win & Pl
Career Total (Turf)	8	2	1	0	14992
Career Total (AW)	1	0	0	0	0

79	10/00	Wind	6f	D(0-85)	HVY	£3445
80	5/00	York	6f	D	G-F	£7670

Total win prize-money £11115

Going (Turf): Sf: 1-4 GS: 0-0 Gd: 0-1 **GF: 1-3** Fm: 0-0
Distance: **5f/6f: 2-5** 7f-8f: 0-3 9f-13f: 0-1 14f+: 0-0
Track : LH: 0-3 **RH: 1-2** Tight: 0-2 **Gall: 1-1**
Aids: Bl: 0-1 Vi: 0-0 Tstrap: 0-0
Best Rating: 69 5/01 Wolv 6f stand

She won the first and last races of her two-year-old campaign, both over six furlongs but on totally opposite ground. Did not show much this season.

Barba Papa (IRE)

100 **96**

7-y-o b g Mujadil (USA)-Baby's Smile (Shirley Heights)

A J Martin Glen Devlin

Placings:2/13115050/00204/13-000 **(5387)**
2001: 12^{0}G, 20^{0}GF, 18^{0}GS

	Starts	1st	2nd	3rd	Win & Pl
Career Total (Turf)	**19**	**4**	**2**	**2**	**81902**

93	6/00	Asct	2m4f	C(0-95)H	G-F	£29900
102	6/97	Siro	1m2f		GD	£11571
80	5/97	Siro	1m1f		VS	£11571
77	4/97	Folk	6f189y	F	G-F	£2277

Total win prize-money £55319

Going (Turf): Sf: 0-1 GS: 0-4 Gd: 1-5 **GF: 2-6** Fm: 0-0
Distance: 5f/6f: 0-0 7f-8f: 1-3 **9f-13f: 2-11** 14f+: 1-5
Track : LH: 0-3 **RH: 4-13** Tight: 1-3 Gall: 1-4
Aids: Bl: 0-0 Vi: 0-0 **Tstrap: 1-9**
Best Rating: 90 6/01 Asct 2m4f gd-fm

A decent stayer, he won the Ascot Stakes in 2000 but was well held in that race this year.

Barbason

102(102) (57)**57**
9-y-o ch g Polish Precedent (USA)-Barada (USA) (Damascus (USA))
G L Moore Exors Of The Late Mr A Moore

Placings:00/3105053443/340111115316433 5/2162350 16022306322/36100160141060313 0/2551553420-005100230 **(5023)**
2001: 9^{0}SD, 10^{0}SD, 9^{5}GF, 9^{1}G, 9^{0}GF, 8^{0}GF, 10^{2}S, 9^{3}G, 7^{0}S

	Starts	1st	2nd	3rd	Win & Pl
Career Total (Turf)	**39**	**9**	**3**	**4**	**33775**
Career Total (AW)	**44**	**7**	**6**	**11**	**29762**

38	5/01	Brig	1m1f209yG		GD	£1939
70	6/00	Gdwd	1m1f	E(0-70)H	GD	£3753
66	12/99	Ling	1m2f	G(0-70)	STD	£1864
64	9/99	Brig	7f214y	E	G-F	£2276
67	7/99	Sand	1m14y	E	G-F	£2892
71	6/99	Newb	1m2f6y	E(0-75)H	GD	£2979
71	2/99	Ling	1m	E	STD	£2583
71	6/98	Brig	7f214y	D(0-80)H	FRM	£3728
72	1/98	Ling	1m	D(0-80)H	STD	£3517
68	7/97	Brig	6f209y	E(0-70)H	FRM	£3252
67	4/97	Brig	6f209y	D(0-85)H	FRM	£3804
62	4/97	Ling	7f	D(0-80)H	FRM	£3964
60	3/97	Ling	1m	F(0-65)H	STD	£2277
60	3/97	Ling	7f	F	STD	£2277
56	2/97	Ling	7f	E(0-70)H	STD	£2791
52	2/96	Ling	7f	D	STD	£3468

Total win prize-money £47370

Going (Turf): Sf: 0-5 GS: 0-1 Gd: 3-10 GF: 2-14 **Fm: 4-9**
Distance: 5f/6f: 0-3 **7f-8f: 11-50** 9f-13f: 5-30 14f+: 0-0
Track : **LH: 13-66** RH: 2-11 **Tight: 8-52** Gall: 1-3
Aids: **Bl: 1-4** Vi: 0-0 Tstrap: 0-0
Best Rating: 57 6/01 Gdwd 1m1f gd-fm

This seasoned campaigner has notched up 16 victories, seven of them on the All-Weather. He is now plating class, and is best on a sound surface.

Barberello (IRE)

91 **38**
3-y-o b f Bigstone (IRE)-Missish (Mummy's Pet)
G C Bravery (Miss E C Lavelle 29/6) Crandon Park Stud

Placings:05-006000 **(5129)**
2001: 7^{0}GS, 6^{0}F, 6^{0}GF, 6^{0}GF, 6^{0}GF, 7^{0}HY

	Starts	1st	2nd	3rd	Win & Pl
Career Total (Turf)	**8**	**0**	**0**	**0**	**0**

Going (Turf): Sf: 0-2 GS: 0-1 Gd: 0-0 GF: 0-4 Fm: 0-1
Distance: 5f/6f: 0-5 7f-8f: 0-3 9f-13f: 0-0 14f+: 0-0
Track : LH: 0-0 RH: 0-0 Tight: 0-0 Gall: 0-0
Aids: Bl: 0-0 Vi: 0-0 Tstrap: 0-0
Best Rating: 38 5/01 Ling 7f gd-sft

Barcelona

104(88) (57)**65**
4-y-o b c Barathea (IRE)-Pipitina (Bustino)
G L Moore Mike Charlton And Rodger Sargent

Placings:003/311631-500003 **(5098)**
2001: 14^{5}GF, 16^{0}GF, 16^{0}GF, 14^{0}G, 13^{0}GF, 14^{3}GS

	Starts	1st	2nd	3rd	Win & Pl
Career Total (Turf)	**14**	**3**	**0**	**3**	**12456**
Career Total (AW)	**1**	**0**	**0**	**1**	**420**

81	8/00	Newc	1m6f97y	D(0-80)H	SFT	£3662
78	6/00	Kemp	1m6f92y	D(0-75)	G-F	£4075
73	5/00	Nott	1m6f15y	E(0-70)H	G-F	£2854

Total win prize-money £10594

Going (Turf): Sf: 1-1 GS: 0-3 Gd: 0-3 **GF: 2-7** Fm: 0-0
Distance: 5f/6f: 0-0 7f-8f: 0-1 9f-13f: 0-3 **14f+: 3-11**
Track : **LH: 2-6** RH: 1-6 Tight: 0-3 **Gall: 1-3**
Aids: Bl: 0-0 Vi: 0-0 Tstrap: 0-6
Best Rating: 78 7/01 Sand 2m78y gd-fm

An improving stayer at three, he had been well held this term until meeting a soft surface at Salisbury where he was a good third. Stays 14 furlongs. Has worn a tongue-strap recently.

Barefooted Flyer (USA)

101(96) (64)**48**
3-y-o ch f Fly So Free (USA)-Carmelita (USA) (Mogambo (USA))
T D Barron Peter Jones

Placings:02430-5216243300600 **(5375)**
2001: 8^{5}S, 7^{2}SW, 7^{1}SD, 7^{6}SD, 7^{2}G, 8^{4}GF, 5^{3}GF, 6^{3}GF, 7^{0}G, 7^{0}GF, 7^{6}GF, 7^{0}SD, 7^{0}G

	Starts	1st	2nd	3rd	Win & Pl
Career Total (Turf)	**13**	**0**	**2**	**2**	**3264**
Career Total (AW)	**5**	**1**	**1**	**1**	**4086**

64	4/01	Sthl	7f	E(0-70)H	STD	£2989

Total win prize-money £2989

Going (Turf): Sf: 0-2 GS: 0-1 Gd: 0-4 GF: 0-6 Fm: 0-0
Distance: 5f/6f: 0-5 **7f-8f: 1-13** 9f-13f: 0-0 14f+: 0-0
Track : **LH: 1-9** RH: 0-1 Tight: 0-3 Gall: 0-1
Aids: Bl: 0-0 Vi: 0-0 Tstrap: 0-0
Best Rating: 66 7/01 Leic 5f218y gd-fm

Went up 5lbs for her win at Southwell in April, but is yet to recapture that form. Stays seven furlongs.

Baringo (USA)

95 **62**
2-y-o b c Miswaki (USA)-Galega (Sure Blade (USA))
R Charlton K Abdulla

Placings:0 **(2757)**
2001: 7^{0}GF

	Starts	1st	2nd	3rd	Win & Pl
Career Total (Turf)	**1**	**0**	**0**	**0**	

Going (Turf): Sf: 0-0 GS: 0-0 Gd: 0-0 GF: 0-1 Fm: 0-0
Distance: 5f/6f: 0-0 7f-8f: 0-1 9f-13f: 0-0 14f+: 0-0
Track : LH: 0-0 RH: 0-0 Tight: 0-0 Gall: 0-0
Aids: Bl: 0-0 Vi: 0-0 Tstrap: 0-0
Best Rating: 62 7/01 Newb 7f gd-fm

Baritone

(102) (61)**29**
7-y-o b g Midyan (USA)-Zinzi (Song)
J Balding (S E Kettlewell 10/2) Hollinbridge Racing

Placings:3330/6200055/435500603043 00032/00241050 05000/04341536000-500660021320150 **(4607)**
2001: 6^{5}SD, 7^{0}SD, 6^{0}SW, 5^{6}SD, 5^{6}SD, 7^{0}SW, 6^{0}SD, 5^{2}SD, 6^{1}SD, 6^{3}SD, 5^{2}SD, 6^{0}SD, 5^{1}SD, 5^{5}S, 6^{0}SD

	Starts	1st	2nd	3rd	Win & Pl
Career Total (Turf)	**27**	**0**	**1**	**5**	**3713**
Career Total (AW)	**39**	**4**	**4**	**5**	**14814**

61	8/01	Wolv	5f	F(0-65)H	STD	£2401
57	6/01	Sthl	6f	F(0-60)	STD	£2331
43	2/00	Wolv	5f	F(0-60)H	STD	£2268
57	2/99	Sthl	6f	E(0-75)H	STD	£3081

Total win prize-money £10081

Going (Turf): Sf: 0-5 GS: 0-5 Gd: 0-9 GF: 0-7 Fm: 0-1
Distance: **5f/6f: 4-41** 7f-8f: 0-24 9f-13f: 0-1 14f+: 0-0
Track : **LH: 4-43** RH: 0-7 **Tight: 2-27** Gall: 0-1
Aids: Bl: 0-2 **Vi: 2-29** Tstrap: 0-0
Best Rating: 61 8/01 Wolv 5f stand

He has a modest strike rate and has only ever won on Fibresand. Probably best suited by six furlongs these days though he has won over five.

Barkby (IRE)

79 **59**
2-y-o b c Lahib (USA)-Portree (Slip Anchor)
M H Tompkins Mrs Beryl Lockey

Placings:000 **(4037)**
2001: 5^{0}GF, 6^{0}GF, 8^{0}G

	Starts	1st	2nd	3rd	Win & Pl
Career Total (Turf)	**3**	**0**	**0**	**0**	

Going (Turf): Sf: 0-0 GS: 0-0 Gd: 0-1 GF: 0-2 Fm: 0-0
Distance: 5f/6f: 0-2 7f-8f: 0-1 9f-13f: 0-0 14f+: 0-0
Track : LH: 0-2 RH: 0-0 Tight: 0-0 Gall: 0-0
Aids: Bl: 0-0 Vi: 0-0 Tstrap: 0-0
Best Rating: 59 7/01 Pont 5f gd-fm

Barking Mad (USA)

101 **102**
3-y-o b/br c Dayjur (USA)-Avian Assembly (USA) (General Assembly (USA))
M L W Bell Christopher Wright

Placings:31621360-00 **(1231)**
2001: 7^{0}S, 10^{0}GF

	Starts	1st	2nd	3rd	Win & Pl
Career Total (Turf)	**10**	**2**	**1**	**2**	**27530**

88	7/00	Thsk	7f	C	FRM	£5829
83	5/00	York	6f	D	FRM	£7475

Total win prize-money £13304

Going (Turf): Sf: 0-3 GS: 0-0 Gd: 0-1 GF: 0-4 **Fm: 2-2**
Distance: 5f/6f: 1-4 7f-8f: 1-5 9f-13f: 0-1 14f+: 0-0
Track : **LH: 1-2** RH: 0-2 **Tight: 1-2** Gall: 0-0
Aids: Bl: 0-0 Vi: 0-0 Tstrap: 0-0
Best Rating: 91 4/01 NmkR 7f soft

Just below Group class as a juvenile, both his wins were on really fast ground. Like his sire Dayjur he seems to like to lead. Has struggled this term.

Barman (USA)

97 **91+**
2-y-o ch c Atticus (USA)-Blue Tip (FR) (Tip Moss (FR))
P F I Cole Sir George Meyrick

Placings:2 **(5623)**
2001: 8^{2}GS

	Starts	1st	2nd	3rd	Win & Pl
Career Total (Turf)	**1**	**0**	**1**	**0**	**1140**

Going (Turf): Sf: 0-0 GS: 0-1 Gd: 0-0 GF: 0-0 Fm: 0-0
Distance: 5f/6f: 0-0 7f-8f: 0-0 9f-13f: 0-1 14f+: 0-0
Track : LH: 0-1 RH: 0-0 Tight: 0-0 Gall: 0-0
Aids: Bl: 0-0 Vi: 0-0 Tstrap: 0-0
Best Rating: 91 11/01 Nott 1m54y gd-sft

He showed ability on his Nottingham debut and should improve.

Barna Woods (IRE)

89 **53**

2-y-o b/br f Charnwood Forest (IRE)-Bardia (Jalmood (USA))

S Kirk D A Potter

Placings:0000 **(2056)**

2001: 5^{0}GS, 5^{0}GS, 6^{0}GF, 6^{0}GF

	Starts	1st	2nd	3rd	Win & Pl
Career Total (Turf)	4	0	0	0	

Going (Turf): Sf: 0-0 GS: 0-2 Gd: 0-0 GF: 0-2 Fm: 0-0
Distance: 5f/6f: 0-4 7f-8f: 0-0 9f-13f: 0-0 14f+: 0-0
Track : LH: 0-1 RH: 0-0 Tight: 0-0 Gall: 0-0
Aids: Bl: 0-0 Vi: 0-0 Tstrap: 0-0
Best Rating: 53 6/01 Sals 6f gd-fm

Barnie Rubble

(103) (64)**65**

5-y-o ch g Pharly (FR)-Sharp Fairy (Sharpo)

P W D'Arcy A H Bennett

Placings:0/642-24003 **(5608)**

2001: 7^{2}GF, 7^{4}GS, 6^{0}GF, 7^{0}GF, 7^{3}GS

	Starts	1st	2nd	3rd	Win & Pl
Career Total (Turf)	9	0	2	1	3997

Going (Turf): Sf: 0-1 GS: 0-3 Gd: 0-2 GF: 0-3 Fm: 0-0
Distance: 5f/6f: 0-2 7f-8f: 0-7 9f-13f: 0-0 14f+: 0-0
Track : LH: 0-3 RH: 0-0 Tight: 0-0 Gall: 0-0
Aids: Bl: 0-0 Vi: 0-0 Tstrap: 0-0
Best Rating: 72 7/01 Yarm 7f3y gd-fm

Barningham

(84) (17)**59d**

3-y-o b g Emperor Jones (USA)-Lady Anchor (Slip Anchor)

J D Bethell Wwwclarendon Racingcom

Placings:645-56460300 **(5411)**

2001: 11^{5}GF, 11^{6}GF, 14^{4}GF, 14^{6}GF, 16^{0}GF, 11^{3}G, 12^{0}G, 14^{0}SD

	Starts	1st	2nd	3rd	Win & Pl
Career Total (Turf)	10	0	0	1	670
Career Total (AW)	1	0	0	0	

Going (Turf): Sf: 0-0 GS: 0-0 Gd: 0-2 GF: 0-8 Fm: 0-0
Distance: 5f/6f: 0-0 7f-8f: 0-3 9f-13f: 0-4 14f+: 0-4
Track : LH: 0-4 RH: 0-5 Tight: 0-5 Gall: 0-0
Aids: Bl: 0-7 Vi: 0-1 Tstrap: 0-0
Best Rating: 59 6/01 Rdcr 1m6f19y gd-fm

Barolo

86 **75**

2-y-o b c Danehill (USA)-Lydia Maria (Dancing Brave (USA))

P W Harris Mrs P W Harris

Placings:5 **(4222)**

2001: 7^{5}GF

	Starts	1st	2nd	3rd	Win & Pl
Career Total (Turf)	1	0	0	0	0

Going (Turf): Sf: 0-0 GS: 0-0 Gd: 0-0 GF: 0-1 Fm: 0-0
Distance: 5f/6f: 0-0 7f-8f: 0-1 9f-13f: 0-0 14f+: 0-0
Track : LH: 0-0 RH: 0-0 Tight: 0-0 Gall: 0-0
Aids: Bl: 0-0 Vi: 0-0 Tstrap: 0-0
Best Rating: 75 8/01 NmkJ 7f gd-fm

Baron Crocodile

101(71) (25)**63**

3-y-o b g Puissance-Glow Again (The Brianstan)

Mrs Dianne Sayer (A Berry 24/9) A Slack

Placings:224502402103-0000006646201631000 **(5659)**

2001: 6^{0}SW, 6^{0}GF, 5^{0}GF, 6^{0}GF, 6^{0}G, 5^{0}GS, 5^{6}GF, 5^{6}F, 5^{4}GF, 5^{6}G, 5^{2}G, 5^{0}GF, 5^{1}GF, 6^{6}G, 6^{3}F, 5^{1}GS, 6^{0}GS, 5^{0}HY, 8^{0}G

	Starts	1st	2nd	3rd	Win & Pl
Career Total (Turf)	30	3	5	2	13227
Career Total (AW)	1	0	0	0	

63	9/01	Leic	5f218y	F	G-S	£2796
55	8/01	Wwck	5f	F	G-F	£2390
73	9/00	Ling	5f	F	GD	£1974

Total win prize-money £7162

Going (Turf): Sf: 0-4 **GS: 1-4 Gd: 1-10 GF: 1-10** Fm: 0-2
Distance: **5f/6f: 3-27** 7f-8f: 0-4 9f-13f: 0-0 14f+: 0-0
Track : **LH: 1-10** RH: 0-2 Tight: 0-5 **Gall: 1-5**
Aids: Bl: 0-3 Vi: 0-2 Tstrap: 0-0
Best Rating: 63 9/01 Leic 5f218y gd-sft

Out of a five/six furlong winner as a juvenile, this keen sort got off the mark at the tenth attempt. He has won twice over five furlongs this term, and acts on any ground.

Baron De Pichon (IRE)

(109) (50)**58**

5-y-o b g Perugino (USA)-Ariadne (Bustino)

Miss S J Wilton (Andrew Reid 30/1) John Pointon And Sons

Placings:000022/111121004620б/05100143143-64313362120000 **(5622)**

2001: 8^{6}SD, 9^{4}SW, 8^{3}SW, 9^{1}SD, 9^{3}SW, 8^{3}SD, 8^{6}SD, 9^{2}SD, 12^{1}SD, 12^{2}SD, 12^{0}SD, 14^{0}SD, 12^{0}SD, 14^{0}GS

	Starts	1st	2nd	3rd	Win & Pl
Career Total (Turf)	8	0	0	0	0
Career Total (AW)	36	10	6	5	46350

72	3/01	Wolv	1m4f	C(0-100)H	STD	£6753
69	1/01	Wolv	1m1f79y	F	STD	£2275
76	11/00	Wolv	1m100y	E(0-70)H	STD	£2884
63	9/00	Wolv	7f	F	STD	£2534
70	7/00	Sthl	1m	F	STD	£1729
84	2/99	Ling	1m	D(0-80)H	STD	£3572
70	1/99	Sthl	7f	D(0-85)H	STD	£3692
74	1/99	Wolv	1m100y	D(0-85)H	STD	£4065
66	1/99	Wolv	7f	E(0-70)H	STD	£2775
67	1/99	Wolv	1m100y	D(0-85)H	STD	£5918

Total win prize-money £36200

Going (Turf): Sf: 0-3 GS: 0-1 Gd: 0-3 GF: 0-1 Fm: 0-0
Distance: 5f/6f: 0-2 7f-8f: 5-16 9f-13f: 5-22 14f+: 0-2
Track : **LH: 10-36** RH: 0-1 **Tight: 8-25** Gall: 0-1
Aids: Bl: 0-0 Vi: 0-1 Tstrap: 0-0
Best Rating: 72 3/01 Wolv 1m4f stand

Barrantes

101 **60**

4-y-o b f Distant Relative-Try The Duchess (Try My Best (USA))

Miss Sheena West W F Sandercock

Placings:0100 **(4950)**

2001: 10^{0}G, 5^{1}GF, 6^{0}F, 5^{0}G

	Starts	1st	2nd	3rd	Win & Pl
Career Total (Turf)	4	1	0	0	2650

60	7/01	Ling	5f	F	G-F	£2649

Total win prize-money £2650

Going (Turf): Sf: 0-0 GS: 0-0 Gd: 0-2 **GF: 1-1** Fm: 0-1
Distance: **5f/6f: 1-3** 7f-8f: 0-0 9f-13f: 0-1 14f+: 0-0
Track : LH: 0-0 RH: 0-0 Tight: 0-1 Gall: 0-0
Aids: Bl: 0-0 Vi: 0-0 Tstrap: 0-0
Best Rating: 60 7/01 Ling 5f gd-fm

Barresbo

95 (24)**42**

7-y-o b g Barrys Gamble-Bo' Babbity (Strong Gale)

A C Whillans E Waugh

Placings:06400**500**/43502020140/4432403046400/005 450 **(5663)**

2001: 9^{0}S, 13^{0}GF, 13^{5}GF, 16^{4}GF, 16^{5}F, 12^{0}G

	Starts	1st	2nd	3rd	Win & Pl
Career Total (Turf)	34	1	3	3	8056
Career Total (AW)	4	0	0	0	0

67	7/97	Newc	7f	F(0-65)H	GD	£2536

Total win prize-money £2537

Going (Turf): Sf: 0-5 GS: 0-5 **Gd: 1-11** GF: 0-10 Fm: 0-3
Distance: 5f/6f: 0-7 **7f-8f: 1-14** 9f-13f: 0-13 14f+: 0-4
Track : LH: 0-18 RH: 0-13 Tight: 0-14 Gall: 0-2
Aids: Bl: 0-1 Vi: 0-3 Tstrap: 0-0
Best Rating: 45 6/01 Ayr 1m5f13y gd-fm

Barrettstown

84 (40)**40**

6-y-o ch g Cadeaux Genereux-Sagar (Habitat)

R M Stronge Ralph P Peters

Placings:3204/2-000 **(4580)**

2001: 10^{0}GF, 10^{0}GF, 16^{0}G

	Starts	1st	2nd	3rd	Win & Pl
Career Total (Turf)	6	0	2	1	2020
Career Total (AW)	2	0	0	0	0

Going (Turf): Sf: 0-0 GS: 0-1 Gd: 0-2 GF: 0-2 Fm: 0-0
Distance: 5f/6f: 0-0 7f-8f: 0-0 9f-13f: 0-6 14f+: 0-1
Track : LH: 0-4 RH: 0-1 Tight: 0-4 Gall: 0-0
Aids: Bl: 0-0 Vi: 0-0 Tstrap: 0-0
Best Rating: 40 7/01 Wind 1m2f7y gd-fm

Barrosa

86 **61**

2-y-o b f Sabrehill (USA)-Shehana (USA) (The Minstrel (CAN))

A Berry Slatch Farm Stud

Placings:65600 **(4234)**

2001: 5^{6}G, 6^{5}F, 6^{6}GF, 7^{0}GS, 7^{0}GF

	Starts	1st	2nd	3rd	Win & Pl
Career Total (Turf)	5	0	0	0	0

Going (Turf): Sf: 0-0 GS: 0-1 Gd: 0-1 GF: 0-2 Fm: 0-1
Distance: 5f/6f: 0-2 7f-8f: 0-3 9f-13f: 0-0 14f+: 0-0
Track : LH: 0-1 RH: 0-1 Tight: 0-0 Gall: 0-0
Aids: Bl: 0-0 Vi: 0-0 Tstrap: 0-0
Best Rating: 61 5/01 Rdcr 6f firm

Barry Island

78 **63**

2-y-o b c Turtle Island (IRE)-Pine Ridge (High Top)

D R C Elsworth K J Mercer

Placings:00 **(5095)**

2001: 6^{0}GF, 8^{0}GS

	Starts	1st	2nd	3rd	Win & Pl
Career Total (Turf)	2	0	0	0	

Going (Turf): Sf: 0-0 GS: 0-1 Gd: 0-0 GF: 0-1 Fm: 0-0
Distance: 5f/6f: 0-1 7f-8f: 0-1 9f-13f: 0-0 14f+: 0-0
Track : LH: 0-0 RH: 0-0 Tight: 0-0 Gall: 0-0
Aids: Bl: 0-0 Vi: 0-0 Tstrap: 0-0
Best Rating: 63 10/01 Sals 1m gd-sft

A half-brother to top-class eight-12 furlong filly In The Groove and to six other winners, including Pineapple (dam of Harmonic Way), he missed the break on his debut but looks sure to improve.

Barrys Double

94(91) (44)**33**
4-y-o gr g Barrys Gamble-Pennine Star (IRE) (Pennine Walk)
Jean-Rene Auvray Lambourn Racing Limited

Placings:40030040/4000-300030 (4800)
2001: 7^{3}SD, 11^{0}SD, 6^{0}G, 7^{0}F, 8^{3}GS, 10^{0}F

	Starts	1st	2nd	3rd	Win & Pl
Career Total (Turf)	11	0	0	1	545
Career Total (AW)	7	0	0	2	751

Going (Turf): Sf: 0-1 GS: 0-1 Gd: 0-4 GF: 0-2 Fm: 0-3
Distance: 5f/6f: 0-7 7f-8f: 0-7 9f-13f: 0-4 14f+: 0-0
Track : LH: 0-12 RH: 0-1 Tight: 0-1 Gall: 0-0
Aids: Bl: 0-1 Vi: 0-4 Tstrap: 0-0
Best Rating: 41 3/01 Sthl 7f stand

Barsaya

94 **48**
3-y-o b f Wolfhound (USA)-Zeffirella (Known Fact (USA))
P R Chamings Twenty Twenty Research

Placings:05000000 (5043)
2001: 8^{0}GS, 8^{5}G, 8^{0}GF, 7^{0}G, 7^{0}G, 7^{0}GF, 6^{0}GF, 8^{0}G

	Starts	1st	2nd	3rd	Win & Pl
Career Total (Turf)	8	0	0	0	0

Going (Turf): Sf: 0-0 GS: 0-1 Gd: 0-4 GF: 0-3 Fm: 0-0
Distance: 5f/6f: 0-0 7f-8f: 0-4 9f-13f: 0-4 14f+: 0-0
Track : LH: 0-3 RH: 0-2 Tight: 0-5 Gall: 0-0
Aids: Bl: 0-1 Vi: 0-0 Tstrap: 0-0
Best Rating: 60 5/01 Bath 1m5y good

Barton Lea (IRE)

(84) (21)
4-y-o b f Distinctly North (USA)-La Mazya (IRE) (Mazaad)
R A Fahey Miss M J Barber

Placings:00/30 (0470)
2001: 12^{0}SD, 12^{0}SD

	Starts	1st	2nd	3rd	Win & Pl
Career Total (Turf)	0	0	0	0	
Career Total (AW)	4	0	0	1	302

Going (Turf): Sf: 0-0 GS: 0-0 Gd: 0-0 GF: 0-0 Fm: 0-0
Distance: 5f/6f: 0-0 7f-8f: 0-2 9f-13f: 0-2 14f+: 0-0
Track : LH: 0-4 RH: 0-0 Tight: 0-1 Gall: 0-0
Aids: Bl: 0-0 Vi: 0-0 Tstrap: 0-0
Best Rating: 21 3/01 Sthl 1m4f stand

Barton Miss

(79) (2)**26**
4-y-o ch f Whittingham (IRE)-Miss Derby (USA) (Master Derby (USA))
T E Powell R Rayfield

Placings:00/000-0 (0202)
2001: 7^{0}SW

	Starts	1st	2nd	3rd	Win & Pl
Career Total (Turf)	3	0	0	0	
Career Total (AW)	3	0	0	0	

Going (Turf): Sf: 0-1 GS: 0-0 Gd: 0-0 GF: 0-2 Fm: 0-0
Distance: 5f/6f: 0-2 7f-8f: 0-3 9f-13f: 0-1 14f+: 0-0
Track : LH: 0-3 RH: 0-1 Tight: 0-4 Gall: 0-0
Aids: Bl: 0-0 Vi: 0-0 Tstrap: 0-0

Barton Sands (IRE)

104 **89**
4-y-o b c Tenby-Hetty Green (Bay Express)
L M Cumani Stanley W Clarke

Placings:21260-005 (2509)
2001: 10^{0}GS, 10^{0}G, 8^{5}GF

	Starts	1st	2nd	3rd	Win & Pl
Career Total (Turf)	8	1	2	0	6916

82 5/00 Haml 1m1f36y E FRM £2808
Total win prize-money £2808

Going (Turf): Sf: 0-2 GS: 0-2 Gd: 0-2 GF: 0-1 **Fm: 1-1**
Distance: 5f/6f: 0-0 7f-8f: 0-1 **9f-13f: 1-7** 14f+: 0-0
Track : LH: 0-4 **RH: 1-1 Tight: 1-1** Gall: 0-3
Aids: Bl: 0-0 Vi: 0-0 Tstrap: 0-0
Best Rating: 86 6/01 Sals 1m gd-fm

Showed plenty of ability last season at up to ten furlongs. Fairly lightly-raced, he has failedt to recapture that form this term. Best on fast ground.

Barzah (IRE)

95 **82+**
2-y-o b f Darshaan-Lepikha (USA) (El Gran Senor (USA))
Sir Michael Stoute Hamdan Al Maktoum

Placings:1 (1825)
2001: 6^{1}GF

	Starts	1st	2nd	3rd	Win & Pl
Career Total (Turf)	1	1	0	0	3494

82 6/01 Pont 6f D G-F £3493
Total win prize-money £3494

Going (Turf): Sf: 0-0 GS: 0-0 Gd: 0-0 **GF: 1-1** Fm: 0-0
Distance: **5f/6f: 1-1** 7f-8f: 0-0 9f-13f: 0-0 14f+: 0-0
Track : **LH: 1-1** RH: 0-0 Tight: 0-0 Gall: 0-0
Aids: Bl: 0-0 Vi: 0-0 Tstrap: 0-0
Best Rating: 82 6/01 Pont 6f gd-fm

A well put-together filly, this Ir£300,000 half-sister to Derby runner-up Glacial Storm, she showed a maturity beyond her years to outclass her opposition on her debut. She is suited by a sound surface, and stays six furlongs.

Basbousate Nadia

95 **81**
2-y-o b f Wolfhound (USA)-Sarabah (IRE) (Ela-Mana-Mou)
W R Muir Sheikh Amin Dahlawi

Placings:6130000 (4657)
2001: 6^{6}GF, 5^{1}GF, 5^{3}G, 5^{0}GF, 5^{0}GF, 6^{0}GF, 6^{0}GF

	Starts	1st	2nd	3rd	Win & Pl
Career Total (Turf)	7	1	0	1	5110

78 6/01 Newc 5f E G-F £3010
Total win prize-money £3010

Going (Turf): Sf: 0-0 GS: 0-0 Gd: 0-1 **GF: 1-6** Fm: 0-0
Distance: **5f/6f: 1-7** 7f-8f: 0-0 9f-13f: 0-0 14f+: 0-0
Track : LH: 0-0 RH: 0-0 Tight: 0-0 Gall: 0-0
Aids: Bl: 0-0 Vi: 0-0 Tstrap: 0-0
Best Rating: 81 9/01 Donc 6f gd-fm

Showed the benefit of her debut run by following up on her second start at Newcastle. Fair effort to finish third in a Sandown Listed event but has been out of her depth since. Has won on good to firm.

Base Line

95(95) (52)**35**
3-y-o b g Rudimentary (USA)-Hemline (Sharpo)
R M Flower Atlas Public Relations Ltd

Placings:0-0501100040000 (5100)
2001: 8^{0}SD, 8^{5}SD, 7^{0}SW, 8^{1}SD, 10^{1}SW, 10^{0}GF, 9^{0}GF, 8^{0}GF, 11^{4}SD, 12^{0}GS, 10^{0}S, 10^{0}G, 9^{0}GS

	Starts	1st	2nd	3rd	Win & Pl
Career Total (Turf)	8	0	0	0	
Career Total (AW)	6	2	0	0	5173

52 2/01 Ling 1m2f E(0-70)H SLW £2919
52 2/01 Sthl 1m F(0-60)H STD £2254
Total win prize-money £5173

Going (Turf): Sf: 0-1 GS: 0-2 Gd: 0-1 GF: 0-4 Fm: 0-0
Distance: 5f/6f: 0-1 7f-8f: 0-1 9f-13f: 0-1 14f+: 0-0
Track : LH: 0-8 RH: 0-4 Tight: 0-7 Gall: 0-1
Aids: Bl: 0-0 Vi: 0-0 Tstrap: 0-0
Best Rating: 52 2/01 Ling 1m2f slow

A dual All-Weather winner at a mile and ten furlongs early in the year, he does not seem as effective on turf.

Basinet

(99) (69)**62**
3-y-o b g Alzao (USA)-Valiancy (Grundy)
Mrs J R Ramsden P R C Morrison

Placings:034-000000124361 (5397)
2001: 7^{0}S, 7^{0}GS, 8^{0}HY, 8^{0}GF, 7^{0}GF, 10^{0}GF, 8^{1}GF, 8^{2}F, 8^{4}GF, 9^{3}G, 10^{6}GF, 8^{1}SD

	Starts	1st	2nd	3rd	Win & Pl
Career Total (Turf)	13	1	1	2	5659
Career Total (AW)	2	1	0	0	2352

67 10/01 Wolv 1m100y F(0-60)H STD £2352
58 6/01 Newc 1m E(0-70)H G-F £3388
Total win prize-money £5740

Going (Turf): Sf: 0-2 GS: 0-3 Gd: 0-1 **GF: 1-6** Fm: 0-1
Distance: 5f/6f: 0-2 7f-8f: 1-7 9f-13f: 1-6 14f+: 0-0
Track : **LH: 2-10** RH: 0-2 Tight: 1-4 Gall: 1-3
Aids: Bl: 0-0 Vi: 0-0 Tstrap: 0-0
Best Rating: 67 10/01 Wolv 1m100y stand

Showed ability in maidens in 2000. Now trained by Mrs Ramsden, he scored over a mile at Newcastle in June 2001. Benefited from strong handling when scoring easily on the All-Weather in October. Acts on fast ground.

Basset

(89) (33)**55**
3-y-o b c Salse (USA)-Bempton (Blakeney)
J A Osborne Mrs A D Bourne

Placings:60 (4673)
2001: 8^{6}G, 12^{0}G

	Starts	1st	2nd	3rd	Win & Pl
Career Total (Turf)	2	0	0	0	0

Going (Turf): Sf: 0-0 GS: 0-0 Gd: 0-2 GF: 0-0 Fm: 0-0
Distance: 5f/6f: 0-0 7f-8f: 0-0 9f-13f: 0-2 14f+: 0-0
Track : LH: 0-1 RH: 0-1 Tight: 0-1 Gall: 0-0
Aids: Bl: 0-0 Vi: 0-0 Tstrap: 0-0
Best Rating: 55 8/01 Wind 1m67y good

Batchworth Breeze

82 **27**
3-y-o ch f Beveled (USA)-Batchworth Dancer (Ballacashtal (CAN))
E A Wheeler Mrs Diana Price

Placings:00-000 (3254)
2001: 6^{0}GS, 6^{0}GF, 7^{0}GS

	Starts	1st	2nd	3rd	Win & Pl
Career Total (Turf)	5	0	0	0	

Going (Turf): Sf: 0-1 GS: 0-2 Gd: 0-0 GF: 0-2 Fm: 0-0
Distance: 5f/6f: 0-3 7f-8f: 0-2 9f-13f: 0-0 14f+: 0-0
Track : LH: 0-0 RH: 0-2 Tight: 0-0 Gall: 0-2
Aids: Bl: 0-1 Vi: 0-0 Tstrap: 0-0
Best Rating: 27 6/01 Sals 6f212y gd-fm

Batchworth Lock

81 **47**
3-y-o b g Beveled (USA)-Treasurebound (Beldale Flutter

(USA))
E A Wheeler Austin Stroud & Co Ltd

Placings:000-00 **(2062)**
2001: 5^{0}GF, 6^{0}GF

	Starts	1st	2nd	3rd	Win & Pl
Career Total (Turf)	5	0	0	0	

Going (Turf): Sf: 0-0 GS: 0-0 Gd: 0-1 GF: 0-3 Fm: 0-0
Distance: 5f/6f: 0-3 7f-8f: 0-1 9f-13f: 0-0 14f+: 0-0
Track : LH: 0-1 RH: 0-1 Tight: 0-0 Gall: 0-2
Aids: Bl: 0-0 Vi: 0-0 Tstrap: 0-0
Best Rating: 47 6/01 Sals 6f212y gd-fm

Bathwick Babe (IRE)

102(97) (47)**62**
4-y-o b f Sri Pekan (USA)-Olean (Sadler's Wells (USA))
E J O'Neill Mrs S Clifford

Placings:00/2056-34100505 **(3426)**
2001: 11^{3}GS, 11^{4}G, 13^{1}G, 13^{0}GF, 12^{0}GF, 11^{5}GF, 17^{0}G, 14^{5}GF

	Starts	1st	2nd	3rd	Win & Pl
Career Total (Turf)	12	1	1	1	5384
Career Total (AW)	2	0	0	0	0

62	5/01	Bath	1m5f22y	D(0-80)H	GD	£3776

Total win prize-money £3777

Going (Turf): Sf: 0-2 GS: 0-1 **Gd: 1-4** GF: 0-5 Fm: 0-0
Distance: 5f/6f: 0-0 7f-8f: 0-0 9f-13f: 0-9 **14f+: 1-5**
Track : **LH: 1-9** RH: 0-4 **Tight: 1-9** Gall: 0-2
Aids: Bl: 0-0 Vi: 0-0 Tstrap: 0-0
Best Rating: 62 5/01 Bath 1m5f22y good

Bathwick Bruce (IRE)

102 **81d**
3-y-o b g College Chapel-Naivity (IRE) (Auction Ring (USA))
B R Millman W Clifford

Placings:62100 **(4959)**
2001: 7^{6}GF, 6^{2}GF, 7^{1}S, 8^{0}G, 7^{0}GS

	Starts	1st	2nd	3rd	Win & Pl
Career Total (Turf)	5	1	1	0	3941

81	8/01	Chep	7f16y	D	SFT	£2821

Total win prize-money £2821

Going (Turf): Sf: 1-1 GS: 0-1 Gd: 0-1 GF: 0-2 Fm: 0-0
Distance: 5f/6f: 0-0 **7f-8f: 1-4** 9f-13f: 0-1 14f+: 0-0
Track : LH: 0-1 RH: 0-2 Tight: 0-1 Gall: 0-0
Aids: Bl: 0-0 Vi: 0-0 Tstrap: 0-0
Best Rating: 81 8/01 Chep 7f16y soft

Unraced at two and improved from his belated debut to win a modest Chepstow maiden on his third start. Suited by seven and his win was on soft, but he may prove better suited by faster.

Bathwick Dream

98(101) (42)**29**
4-y-o b f Tragic Role (USA)-Trina (Malaspina)
Dr J R J Naylor W Clifford

Placings:000-55230106 **(2184)**
2001: 12^{5}SD, 16^{5}SW, 16^{2}SD, 14^{3}SD, 16^{0}SD, 16^{1}SD, 16^{0}GF, 17^{6}G

	Starts	1st	2nd	3rd	Win & Pl
Career Total (Turf)	3	0	0	0	0
Career Total (AW)	8	1	1	1	2975

42	3/01	Ling	2m	F(0-70)H	STD	£2180

Total win prize-money £2181

Going (Turf): Sf: 0-0 GS: 0-0 Gd: 0-1 GF: 0-2 Fm: 0-0
Distance: 5f/6f: 0-0 7f-8f: 0-2 9f-13f: 0-2 **14f+: 1-7**
Track : **LH: 1-10** RH: 0-0 **Tight: 1-9** Gall: 0-0
Aids: Bl: 0-0 Vi: 0-0 Tstrap: 0-0
Best Rating: 42 3/01 Ling 2m stand

Batoutoftheblue

85(101) (64)**45**
8-y-o br g Batshoof-Action Belle (Auction Ring (USA))
G A Swinbank (W W Haigh 20/1) Mrs I Gibson

Placings:00/454340115/000002/24304616/010244443/1340-4310 **(0594)**
2001: 16^{4}SW, 16^{3}SD, 16^{1}SD, 16^{0}S

	Starts	1st	2nd	3rd	Win & Pl
Career Total (Turf)	33	3	1	4	15795
Career Total (AW)	9	3	2	1	9092

64	3/01	Sthl	2m	E(0-75)H	STD	£2793
45	3/00	Muss	2m	E(0-75)H	GD	£3526
47	4/99	Muss	2m	E(0-75)H	GD	£3420
43	8/98	Pont	2m1f22y	F(0-65)H	G-F	£3745
67	9/96	Wolv	1m6f166y	F(0-60)	STD	£2070
62	9/96	Sthl	1m6f	F(0-65)H	STD	£2381

Total win prize-money £17935

Going (Turf): Sf: 0-3 GS: 0-5 **Gd: 2-14** GF: 1-6 Fm: 0-5
Distance: 5f/6f: 0-0 7f-8f: 0-3 9f-13f: 0-5 **14f+: 6-34**
Track : **LH: 4-27** RH: 2-14 **Tight: 3-19** Gall: 0-8
Aids: Bl: 0-2 Vi: 0-0 Tstrap: 0-0
Best Rating: 64 3/01 Sthl 2m stand

Batswing

98 **85**
6-y-o b g Batshoof-Magic Milly (Simply Great (FR))
B Ellison Ashley Carr

Placings:0201640020/000/030406/0020120021-0000 **(5693)**
2001: 11^{0}F, 11^{0}GS, 10^{0}GS, 12^{0}S

	Starts	1st	2nd	3rd	Win & Pl
Career Total (Turf)	33	3	5	1	43411

85	11/00	Donc	1m4f	B H	HVY	£23627
74	6/00	Ches	1m2f75y	D(0-80)H	G-S	£4348
66	6/97	Ling	5f	D	SFT	£3315

Total win prize-money £31293

Going (Turf): Sf: 2-6 GS: 1-5 Gd: 0-7 GF: 0-14 Fm: 0-1
Distance: 5f/6f: 1-5 7f-8f: 0-6 **9f-13f: 2-19** 14f+: 0-3
Track : **LH: 2-17** RH: 0-8 Tight: 1-7 Gall: 1-15
Aids: **Bl: 1-5** Vi: 0-0 Tstrap: 0-0
Best Rating: 79 5/01 York 1m3f195y firm

Loves soft ground and had his ideal conditions when winning the November Handicap in 2000, and was successful over hurdles afterwards. Failed to show anything this season.

Battle Cruiser (USA)

80 **82**
3-y-o b g Sea Hero (USA)-Wholey Ghost (USA) (Rare Performer (USA))
Miss S J Wilton (Charles O'Brien 9/10) John Pointon And Sons

Placings:5650-3022240210 **(5688)**
2001: 7^{3}G, 7^{0}Y, 9^{2}F, 8^{2}G, 10^{2}GF, 9^{4}GF, 8^{0}GF, 7^{2}G, 6^{1}G, 7^{0}S

	Starts	1st	2nd	3rd	Win & Pl
Career Total (Turf)	14	1	4	1	14255

79	10/01	Fair	6f		GD	£4830

Total win prize-money £4830

Going (Turf): Sf: 0-3 GS: 0-0 **Gd: 1-4** GF: 0-3 Fm: 0-1
Distance: **5f/6f: 1-2** 7f-8f: 0-8 9f-13f: 0-3 14f+: 0-0
Track : LH: 0-1 RH: 0-1 Tight: 0-0 Gall: 0-1
Aids: **Bl: 1-2** Vi: 0-0 Tstrap: 0-0
Best Rating: 82 8/01 Cork 1m2f gd-fm

Good form in Ireland, including a six length success in a maiden in October, now with Sue Wilton, he was disappointing on his British debut at Doncaster in November.

Battle Green Lad

82(80) (8)**20**
4-y-o b g Presidium-Antouna (Clantime)
J Balding G D And Mrs M Brumby

Placings:0000-0000 **(2004)**
2001: 5^{0}SD, 5^{0}SD, 7^{0}S, 5^{0}F

	Starts	1st	2nd	3rd	Win & Pl
Career Total (Turf)	3	0	0	0	
Career Total (AW)	5	0	0	0	

Going (Turf): Sf: 0-2 GS: 0-0 Gd: 0-0 GF: 0-0 Fm: 0-1
Distance: 5f/6f: 0-4 7f-8f: 0-3 9f-13f: 0-1 14f+: 0-0
Track : LH: 0-4 RH: 0-0 Tight: 0-2 Gall: 0-0
Aids: Bl: 0-1 Vi: 0-0 Tstrap: 0-1
Best Rating: 20 6/01 Donc 5f firm

Battle Line

88 **56**
2-y-o b g Brief Truce (USA)-Forest Heights (Slip Anchor)
K McAuliffe (E Stanners 7/7) The Hare And Hounds Partnership

Placings:00500 **(5667)**
2001: 6^{0}GF, 6^{0}GF, 8^{5}G, 8^{0}HY, 8^{0}HY

	Starts	1st	2nd	3rd	Win & Pl
Career Total (Turf)	5	0	0	0	0

Going (Turf): Sf: 0-2 GS: 0-0 Gd: 0-1 GF: 0-2 Fm: 0-0
Distance: 5f/6f: 0-0 7f-8f: 0-3 9f-13f: 0-2 14f+: 0-0
Track : LH: 0-1 RH: 0-2 Tight: 0-1 Gall: 0-0
Aids: Bl: 0-1 Vi: 0-0 Tstrap: 0-0
Best Rating: 56 7/01 Chep 6f16y gd-fm

Battle Warning

(109) (67)**56**
6-y-o b g Warning-Royal Ballet (IRE) (Sadler's Wells (USA))
A Crook (M D Hammond 10/4) M D Hammond

Placings:0/0/0500/200-062114520 **(1993)**
2001: 11^{0}SD, 12^{6}SD, 16^{2}SD, 14^{1}SW, 16^{1}SD, 14^{4}SD, 14^{5}HY, 16^{2}SD, 12^{0}SD

	Starts	1st	2nd	3rd	Win & Pl
Career Total (Turf)	10	0	1	0	1244
Career Total (AW)	8	2	2	0	6392

61	3/01	Sthl	2m	F(0-60)H	STD	£1813
59	2/01	Sthl	1m6f	E(0-70)H	SLW	£2968

Total win prize-money £4781

Going (Turf): Sf: 0-2 GS: 0-1 Gd: 0-2 GF: 0-4 Fm: 0-1
Distance: 5f/6f: 0-0 7f-8f: 0-1 9f-13f: 0-11 **14f+: 2-6**
Track : **LH: 2-12** RH: 0-3 Tight: 0-5 Gall: 0-1
Aids: Bl: 0-0 Vi: 0-0 Tstrap: 0-0
Best Rating: 67 5/01 Sthl 2m stand

Batwink

(88) (26)**23**
4-y-o b f Batshoof-Quick As A Wink (Glint Of Gold)
P D Cundell I J Heseltine

Placings:00005-500 **(0266)**
2001: 12^{5}SD, 12^{0}SD, 12^{0}SW

	Starts	1st	2nd	3rd	Win & Pl
Career Total (Turf)	5	0	0	0	268
Career Total (AW)	3	0	0	0	0

Going (Turf): Sf: 0-0 GS: 0-1 Gd: 0-0 GF: 0-4 Fm: 0-0
Distance: 5f/6f: 0-0 7f-8f: 0-1 9f-13f: 0-7 14f+: 0-0
Track : LH: 0-6 RH: 0-2 Tight: 0-2 Gall: 0-3
Aids: Bl: 0-0 Vi: 0-0 Tstrap: 0-0
Best Rating: 26 1/01 Sthl 1m4f stand

Bawsian

108(111) (90d)**87**
6-y-o b g Persian Bold-Bawaeth (USA) (Blushing Groom

(FR))
J L Eyre David Scott

Placings:3000612/**1**1412506040/**2**4404304B/40002-01124004352000 (5693)
2001: 11^{0}SD, 12^{1}GS, 9^{1}HY, 12^{2}S, 10^{4}GF, 11^{0}GS, 12^{0}GF, 9^{4}GS, 11^{3}G, 12^{5}GF, 14^{2}HY, 12^{0}G, 12^{0}HY, 12^{0}S

	Starts	1st	2nd	3rd	Win & Pl
Career Total (Turf)	40	5	3	3	59850
Career Total (AW)	7	2	3	0	11883

79	3/01	Nott	1m1f213yD(0-85)H		HVY	£4790
76	3/01	Donc	1m4f	E(0-80)H	G-S	£3318
96	5/98	York	1m2f85y	B(0-100)H	GD	£16425
90	3/98	Donc	1m2f60y	D(0-85)H	GD	£4012
82	1/98	Wolv	1m100y	D(0-85)H	STD	£3403
77	1/98	Wolv	1m100y	D(0-85)H	STD	£3468
72	11/97	Rdcr	1m	E(0-75)	GD	£3424

Total win prize-money £38845

Going (Turf): Sf: 1-12 GS: 1-7 **Gd: 3-10** GF: 0-11 Fm: 0-0
Distance: 5f/6f: 0-1 7f-8f: 1-5 **9f-13f: 6-40** 14f+: 0-1
Track : **LH: 6-38** RH: 0-5 Tight: 2-9 **Gall: 3-21**
Aids: Bl: 0-0 Vi: 0-0 **Tstrap: 2-13**
Best Rating: 91 4/01 Epsm 1m4f10y soft

A spring horse, he recorded his first win since May 1998 on the first day of the 2001 season at Doncaster having had his tongue tied down. Followed up at Nottingham and finished a good third in the Great Metropolitan. Not disgraced on much faster ground, but ideally needs testing conditions and a flat, left-handed track, as at Haydock in September. Effective ten to 14 furlongs.

Baxters Holly

79 **14**
3-y-o b f Puissance-Sveltissima (Dunphy)
I Semple Baxter Ferguson

Placings:0060 (1853)
2001: 12^{0}S, 11^{0}G, 12^{6}G, 10^{0}GF

	Starts	1st	2nd	3rd	Win & Pl
Career Total (Turf)	4	0	0	0	0

Going (Turf): Sf: 0-1 GS: 0-0 Gd: 0-2 GF: 0-1 Fm: 0-0
Distance: 5f/6f: 0-0 7f-8f: 0-0 9f-13f: 0-4 14f+: 0-0
Track : LH: 0-1 RH: 0-2 Tight: 0-2 Gall: 0-1
Aids: Bl: 0-0 Vi: 0-0 Tstrap: 0-0
Best Rating: 14 5/01 Haml 1m4f17y good

Bay Breeze (IRE)

56 **11**
3-y-o b g Pennekamp (USA)-Prairie Neba (GER) (Nebos (GER))
P W Harris Ayton, Shaw & Willis

Placings:00 (1847)
2001: 10^{0}GF, 11^{0}GF

	Starts	1st	2nd	3rd	Win & Pl
Career Total (Turf)	2	0	0	0	

Going (Turf): Sf: 0-0 GS: 0-0 Gd: 0-0 GF: 0-2 Fm: 0-0
Distance: 5f/6f: 0-0 7f-8f: 0-0 9f-13f: 0-2 14f+: 0-0
Track : LH: 0-1 RH: 0-1 Tight: 0-1 Gall: 0-0
Aids: Bl: 0-0 Vi: 0-0 Tstrap: 0-0
Best Rating: 11 5/01 Bath 1m2f46y gd-fm

Bay Of Bengal (IRE)

94(65) **35**
5-y-o ch m Persian Bold-Adjamiya (USA) (Shahrastani (USA))
J S Wainwright Barry J Ross

Placings:00300/11040/03206030400-**0**0006053006 (3467)
2001: 8^{0}SW, 11^{0}SD, 10^{0}HY, 9^{0}G, 10^{0}GF, 9^{6}GF, 8^{0}GF, 12^{5}GF, 8^{3}G, 8^{0}GF, 8^{0}F, 10^{6}GF

	Starts	1st	2nd	3rd	Win & Pl
Career Total (Turf)	31	2	1	4	9043
Career Total (AW)	2	0	0	0	

50	6/99	Pont	1m4f8y	F(0-60)H	GD	£2406
44	5/99	Nott	1m1f213yG(0-60)H		FRM	£2372

Total win prize-money £4779

Going (Turf): Sf: 0-1 GS: 0-4 **Gd: 1-8** GF: 0-14 **Fm: 1-3**
Distance: 5f/6f: 0-2 7f-8f: 0-4 **9f-13f: 2-25** 14f+: 0-1
Track : **LH: 2-16** RH: 0-11 Tight: 0-13 Gall: 0-2
Aids: Bl: 0-0 Vi: 0-0 Tstrap: 0-0
Best Rating: 35 7/01 Asct 1m2f gd-fm

She has not won since June 1999. Best over ten furlongs. Has contested classier events for appearance money.

Bay Of Dreams

82 **48**
2-y-o ch g Salse (USA)-Cantico (Green Dancer (USA))
I A Balding J C Smith

Placings:0 (5604)
2001: 7^{0}GS

	Starts	1st	2nd	3rd	Win & Pl
Career Total (Turf)	1	0	0	0	

Going (Turf): Sf: 0-0 GS: 0-1 Gd: 0-0 GF: 0-0 Fm: 0-0
Distance: 5f/6f: 0-0 7f-8f: 0-1 9f-13f: 0-0 14f+: 0-0
Track : LH: 0-0 RH: 0-0 Tight: 0-0 Gall: 0-0
Aids: Bl: 0-0 Vi: 0-0 Tstrap: 0-0
Best Rating: 48 11/01 NmkR 7f gd-sft

Bay Of Islands

106 **100**
9-y-o b g Jupiter Island-Lawyer's Wave (USA) (Advocator)
D Morris Bloomsbury Stud

Placings:431/0551304/01230000/0123/0031303-0303 (3055)
2001: 10^{0}G3, 13^{3}GF, 16^{0}F, 13^{0}G

	Starts	1st	2nd	3rd	Win & Pl
Career Total (Turf)	33	5	2	9	145362

97	7/00	Newc	2m19y	B H	FRM	£75400
82	5/99	Nott	1m6f15y	D(0-80)H	FRM	£5052
84	6/98	Donc	1m4f	C(0-90)H	GD	£6264
81	6/97	Ches	1m2f75y	D(0-80)H	G-F	£3473
74	8/95	York	1m2f85y	D	G-F	£5071

Total win prize-money £95263

Going (Turf): Sf: 0-2 GS: 0-3 Gd: 1-12 **GF: 2-13 Fm: 2-3**
Distance: 5f/6f: 0-0 7f-8f: 0-0 **9f-13f: 3-18** 14f+: 2-15
Track : **LH: 5-27** RH: 0-5 Tight: 1-5 **Gall: 3-22**
Aids: Bl: 0-0 **Vi: 2-13** Tstrap: 0-0
Best Rating: 100 5/01 Ches 1m5f89y gd-fm

He put in some decent efforts in 2000, notably when winning the Northumberland Plate. Good efforts since including when tried in Group company. Needs distances well beyond 12 furlongs nowadays and a true-run race. Reported to have suspensory problems.

Bayonet

97 **53**
5-y-o b m Then Again-Lambay (Lorenzaccio)
Jane Southcombe Mark Savill

Placings:422/0000400**0**/02100-00052032020 (4840)
2001: 5^{0}GS, 5^{0}G, 6^{0}GF, 6^{5}GF, 6^{2}GF, 7^{0}G, 6^{3}GF, 7^{2}GF, 6^{0}F, 7^{2}G, 6^{0}G

	Starts	1st	2nd	3rd	Win & Pl
Career Total (Turf)	26	1	6	1	8830
Career Total (AW)	1	0	0	0	

51	6/00	Chep	6f16y	E(0-70)H	G-F	£2940

Total win prize-money £2940

Going (Turf): Sf: 0-0 GS: 0-2 Gd: 0-9 **GF: 1-13** Fm: 0-2
Distance: 5f/6f: 0-17 **7f-8f: 1-10** 9f-13f: 0-0 14f+: 0-0
Track : LH: 0-6 RH: 0-2 Tight: 0-0 Gall: 0-5
Aids: Bl: 0-2 Vi: 0-0 Tstrap: 0-0
Best Rating: 53 9/01 Chep 7f16y good

In the frame several times this term, she is probably better over six furlongs than seven.

Bayrami

71(53) **41**
3-y-o ch f Emarati (USA)-Music Mistress (IRE) (Classic Music (USA))
R E Barr (S E Kettlewell 14/6) Middleham Park Racing Xi

Placings:65000440-000 (3466)
2001: 5^{0}GF, 5^{0}F, 7^{0}F

	Starts	1st	2nd	3rd	Win & Pl
Career Total (Turf)	9	0	0	0	0
Career Total (AW)	2	0	0	0	0

Going (Turf): Sf: 0-1 GS: 0-1 Gd: 0-1 GF: 0-4 Fm: 0-2
Distance: 5f/6f: 0-10 7f-8f: 0-1 9f-13f: 0-0 14f+: 0-0
Track : LH: 0-4 RH: 0-0 Tight: 0-2 Gall: 0-1
Aids: Bl: 0-0 Vi: 0-0 Tstrap: 0-0
Best Rating: 5 6/01 Bevl 5f gd-fm

Baytown Grace

81(77) (20)**45**
2-y-o b f Presidium-Thalya (Crofthall)
P S McEntee Mrs B A McEntee

Placings:00504425066 (4488)
2001: 5^{0}S, 5^{0}GS, 5^{5}SD, 6^{0}GF, 5^{4}G, 6^{4}G, 5^{2}GF, 5^{5}SD, 5^{0}F, 6^{6}GF, 6^{6}S

	Starts	1st	2nd	3rd	Win & Pl
Career Total (Turf)	9	0	1	0	636
Career Total (AW)	2	0	0	0	0

Going (Turf): Sf: 0-2 GS: 0-1 Gd: 0-2 GF: 0-3 Fm: 0-1
Distance: 5f/6f: 0-8 7f-8f: 0-3 9f-13f: 0-0 14f+: 0-0
Track : LH: 0-2 RH: 0-1 Tight: 0-1 Gall: 0-1
Aids: Bl: 0-0 Vi: 0-0 Tstrap: 0-0
Best Rating: 45 7/01 Brig 5f213y firm

Baytown Rhapsody

96(98) (41)**45**
4-y-o b f Emperor Jones (USA)-Sing A Rainbow (IRE) (Rainbow Quest (USA))
P S McEntee P S J Croft

Placings:265500/**3**2**1**3**1**3100-0060030 (1185)
2001: 6^{0}SD, 7^{0}SW, 6^{6}SD, 6^{0}SD, 7^{0}SW, 6^{3}HY, 6^{0}GF

	Starts	1st	2nd	3rd	Win & Pl
Career Total (Turf)	8	0	1	1	1525
Career Total (AW)	14	3	1	3	7865

60	3/00	Sthl	7f	G	STD	£1892
60	2/00	Sthl	6f	F(0-60)H	STD	£2205
52	1/00	Wolv	6f	F(0-65)H	STD	£2205

Total win prize-money £6303

Going (Turf): Sf: 0-3 GS: 0-0 Gd: 0-2 GF: 0-2 Fm: 0-1
Distance: **5f/6f: 2-9** 7f-8f: 1-13 9f-13f: 0-0 14f+: 0-0
Track : **LH: 3-18** RH: 0-2 **Tight: 1-8** Gall: 0-1
Aids: Bl: 0 0 Vi: 0 0 Tstrap: 0-0
Best Rating: 42 5/01 Nott 6f15y heavy

Baytown Robin

(61) (18)**22**
2-y-o ch f Dancing Spree (USA)-Homebeforemidnight (Fool's Holme (USA))
P S McEntee Mrs S Van Der Meulen

Placings:00040 (5396)

2001: 5^{0}S, 5^{0}GS, 6^{0}GF, 5^{4}F, 8^{0}SD

	Starts	1st	2nd	3rd	Win & Pl
Career Total (Turf)	4	0	0	0	0
Career Total (AW)	1	0	0	0	

Going (Turf): Sf: 0-1 GS: 0-1 Gd: 0-0 GF: 0-1 Fm: 0-1
Distance: 5f/6f: 0-4 7f-8f: 0-0 9f-13f: 0-1 14f+: 0-0
Track : LH: 0-2 RH: 0-1 Tight: 0-1 Gall: 0-1
Aids: Bl: 0-1 Vi: 0-0 Tstrap: 0-0
Best Rating: 22 6/01 NmkR 6f gd-fm

Is only small and has shown little so far.

Be Decisive

101 **71**

3-y-o b f Diesis-Robellino Miss (USA) (Robellino (USA))
G Wragg The Eclipse Partnership

Placings:5010 **(5529)**

2001: 7^{5}G, 8^{0}GS, 8^{1}HY, 8^{0}HY

	Starts	1st	2nd	3rd	Win & Pl
Career Total (Turf)	4	1	0	0	4599

70 10/01 Nott 1m54y D HVY £4598
Total win prize-money £4599

Going (Turf): Sf: 1-2 GS: 0-1 Gd: 0-1 GF: 0-0 Fm: 0-0
Distance: 5f/6f: 0-0 7f-8f: 0-2 **9f-13f: 1-2** 14f+: 0-0
Track : **LH: 1-2** RH: 0-0 Tight: 0-0 Gall: 0-0
Aids: Bl: 0-0 Vi: 0-0 Tstrap: 0-0
Best Rating: 71 5/01 NmkR 7f good

Having her first run since June when landing a backend Nottingham maiden in heavy ground.

Be My Buddy

(74) (25)**59**

2-y-o b g Be My Chief (USA)-Trull (Lomond (USA))
J G Smyth-Osbourne S G Weber-Brown

Placings:00 **(5466)**

2001: 8^{0}S, 6^{0}S

	Starts	1st	2nd	3rd	Win & Pl
Career Total (Turf)	2	0	0	0	

Going (Turf): Sf: 0-2 GS: 0-0 Gd: 0-0 GF: 0-0 Fm: 0-0
Distance: 5f/6f: 0-0 7f-8f: 0-2 9f-13f: 0-0 14f+: 0-0
Track : LH: 0-1 RH: 0-0 Tight: 0-0 Gall: 0-0
Aids: Bl: 0-0 Vi: 0-0 Tstrap: 0-0
Best Rating: 59 10/01 Brig 6f209y soft

Be My Tinker

93(93) (52)**48**

3-y-o ch f Be My Chief (USA)-Tinkerbird (Music Boy)
G Brown J Cleeve

Placings:622-0450650003 **(4422)**

2001: 5^{0}SD, 7^{4}SW, 6^{5}SD, 5^{0}GF, 5^{6}F, 8^{5}GF, 9^{0}G, 6^{0}S, 7^{0}GF, 10^{3}GF

	Starts	1st	2nd	3rd	Win & Pl
Career Total (Turf)	10	0	2	1	2643
Career Total (AW)	3	0	0	0	0

Going (Turf): Sf: 0-1 GS: 0-0 Gd: 0-2 GF: 0-5 Fm: 0-2
Distance: 5f/6f: 0-7 7f-8f: 0-3 9f-13f: 0-3 14f+: 0-0
Track : LH: 0-6 RH: 0-2 Tight: 0-2 Gall: 0-2
Aids: Bl: 0-1 Vi: 0-0 Tstrap: 0-0
Best Rating: 52 4/01 Sthl 7f slow

Be Swift

89 **63**

2-y-o ch c Millkom-Conwy (Rock City)
S Dow Investor Information Limited

Placings:500 **(3940)**

2001: 7^{5}G, 8^{0}GS, 6^{0}GF

	Starts	1st	2nd	3rd	Win & Pl
Career Total (Turf)	3	0	0	0	0

Going (Turf): Sf: 0-0 GS: 0-1 Gd: 0-1 GF: 0-1 Fm: 0-0
Distance: 5f/6f: 0-1 7f-8f: 0-2 9f-13f: 0-0 14f+: 0-0
Track : LH: 0-2 RH: 0-0 Tight: 0-2 Gall: 0-0
Aids: Bl: 0-0 Vi: 0-0 Tstrap: 0-0
Best Rating: 63 8/01 Epsm 6f gd-fm

Be Warned

(100) (57)**57**

10-y-o b g Warning-Sagar (Habitat)
R Brotherton Mrs S Arcourt-Rippingale

Placings:004134022213325/0063000100214/00300405000/644200000402510504302/2131011500354215422 3/340023050004 1/04050120010051-241153013016 **(5613)**

2001: 9^{2}SW, 8^{4}SW, 12^{1}SD, 11^{1}SD, 12^{5}SD, 12^{3}SD, 8^{0}G, 12^{1}SD, 11^{3}SD, 12^{0}GS, 8^{1}SD, 9^{6}SD

	Starts	1st	2nd	3rd	Win & Pl
Career Total (Turf)	62	5	6	7	43425
Career Total (AW)	57	13	9	6	43202

57	10/01	Wolv	1m100y	F(0-60)H	STD	£2352
46	5/01	Wolv	1m4f	F(0-60)	STD	£2317
56	2/01	Sthl	1m3f	G	STD	£1372
55	1/01	Wolv	1m4f	G(0-60)H	STD	£1386
43	12/00	Wolv	1m4f	G	STD	£1876
47	9/00	Sthl	1m3f	F(0-60)	STD	£1841
60	3/00	Sthl	1m	F(0-60)	STD	£1722
68	10/99	Wolv	1m4f	F	STD	£2339
66	10/98	Newb	7f	F(0-80)H	HVY	£3177
79	3/98	Sthl	1m	D(0-80)H	STD	£3517
73	3/98	Wolv	1m1f79y	E(0-70)H	STD	£2833
69	2/98	Wolv	1m1f79y	E(0-70)H	STD	£2671
55	1/98	Sthl	7f	E(0-70)H	STD	£2424
49	9/97	Yarm	6f3y	F(0-60)H	FRM	£3223
76	11/95	Sthl	7f	C(0-90)H	STD	£5680
72	9/95	Yarm	6f3y	C(0-90)H	GD	£6992
73	9/94	Hayd	6f	D(0-80)H	GD	£5979
67	6/94	Kemp	7f	D(0-80)H	G-F	£3882

Total win prize-money £55587

Going (Turf): Sf: 1-7 GS: 0-12 **Gd: 2-18** GF: 1-23 Fm: 1-2
Distance: 5f/6f: 1-25 7f-8f: 8-55 **9f-13f: 9-39** 14f+: 0-0
Track : **LH: 13-66** RH: 1-4 **Tight: 7-31** Gall: 0-2
Aids: Bl: 3-33 **Vi: 14-66** Tstrap: 0-0
Best Rating: 57 10/01 Wolv 1m100y stand

Plating-class handicapper who races mostly on Fibresand these days. A winner four times this year, he stays 12 furlongs but is effective at shorter, usually wears a visor.

Beach Hut (IRE)

91 **62**

3-y-o b g Pennekamp (USA)-Kates Cabin (Habitat)
J L Dunlop The Earl Cadogan

Placings:065000 **(4844)**

2001: 8^{0}G, 7^{6}GS, 8^{5}GF, 9^{0}GF, 12^{0}GF, 9^{0}G

	Starts	1st	2nd	3rd	Win & Pl
Career Total (Turf)	6	0	0	0	0

Going (Turf): Sf: 0-0 GS: 0-1 Gd: 0-2 GF: 0-3 Fm: 0-0
Distance: 5f/6f: 0-0 7f-8f: 0-3 9f-13f: 0-3 14f+: 0-0
Track : LH: 0-3 RH: 0-2 Tight: 0-2 Gall: 0-1
Aids: Bl: 0-1 Vi: 0-0 Tstrap: 0-0
Best Rating: 69 5/01 NmkR 1m good

Beacon Hill Gem

84 **38**

3-y-o b c Mtoto-Emeraude (Kris)
C W Fairhurst David Hawes

Placings:6000 **(2399)**

2001: 10^{6}HY, 10^{0}GS, 7^{0}GF, 9^{0}GF

	Starts	1st	2nd	3rd	Win & Pl
Career Total (Turf)	4	0	0	0	0

Going (Turf): Sf: 0-1 GS: 0-1 Gd: 0-0 GF: 0-2 Fm: 0-0
Distance: 5f/6f: 0-0 7f-8f: 0-1 9f-13f: 0-3 14f+: 0-0
Track : LH: 0-3 RH: 0-1 Tight: 0-1 Gall: 0-0
Aids: Bl: 0-0 Vi: 0-0 Tstrap: 0-0
Best Rating: 38 5/01 Bevl 7f100y gd-fm

Beading

110 **74**

4-y-o b f Polish Precedent (USA)-Silver Braid (USA) (Miswaki (USA))
J W Hills Wyck Hall Stud

Placings:0/00251430-035332200 **(5259)**

2001: 8^{0}GS, 8^{3}GF, 7^{5}S, 7^{3}GF, 8^{3}GS, 8^{2}F, 6^{2}GF, 8^{0}S, 7^{0}GS

	Starts	1st	2nd	3rd	Win & Pl
Career Total (Turf)	18	1	3	4	16008

67 8/00 NmkJ 1m D(0-80)H G-F £4836
Total win prize-money £4836

Going (Turf): Sf: 0-4 GS: 0-5 Gd: 0-1 **GF: 1-6** Fm: 0-2
Distance: 5f/6f: 0-0 **7f-8f: 1-16** 9f-13f: 0-2 14f+: 0-0
Track : LH: 0-2 RH: 0-4 Tight: 0-3 Gall: 0-0
Aids: Bl: 0-0 Vi: 0-0 **Tstrap: 1-15**
Best Rating: 74 9/01 Sals 6f212y gd-fm

Fairly useful handicapper who handles the soft, but is better on a sound surface. Running consistently without reward this term, she has shown her best form on tracks with an uphill finish.

Beady (IRE)

91 **77**

2-y-o b c Eagle Eyed (USA)-Tales Of Wisdom (Rousillon (USA))
B Smart Anglia Bloodstock 2000

Placings:0430 **(5368)**

2001: 7^{0}G, 8^{4}GF, 7^{3}G, 8^{0}GS

	Starts	1st	2nd	3rd	Win & Pl
Career Total (Turf)	4	0	0	1	743

Going (Turf): Sf: 0-0 GS: 0-1 Gd: 0-2 GF: 0-1 Fm: 0-0
Distance: 5f/6f: 0-0 7f-8f: 0-3 9f-13f: 0-1 14f+: 0-0
Track : LH: 0-0 RH: 0-2 Tight: 0-0 Gall: 0-0
Aids: Bl: 0-0 Vi: 0-0 Tstrap: 0-0
Best Rating: 77 9/01 Bevl 7f100y good

Beanboy

96(61) (16)**41**

3-y-o ch g Clantime-Lady Blues Singer (Chief Singer)
Mrs S Lamyman P Lamyman

Placings:600-0002040005 **(5601)**

2001: 5^{0}G, 7^{0}GF, 6^{0}SD, 6^{2}GF, 5^{0}G, 8^{4}GF, 6^{0}HY, 10^{0}F, 7^{0}HY, 8^{5}GS

	Starts	1st	2nd	3rd	Win & Pl
Career Total (Turf)	11	0	1	0	1344
Career Total (AW)	2	0	0	0	

Going (Turf): Sf: 0-4 GS: 0-1 Gd: 0-2 GF: 0-3 Fm: 0-1
Distance: 5f/6f: 0-7 7f-8f: 0-4 9f-13f: 0-2 14f+: 0-0
Track : LH: 0-5 RH: 0-1 Tight: 0-0 Gall: 0-0
Aids: Bl: 0-0 Vi: 0-1 Tstrap: 0-0
Best Rating: 41 9/01 Hayd 6f heavy

Beasley

77 **59**

2-y-o b c First Trump-Le Shuttle (Presidium)
Miss Gay Kelleway Martin Butler

Placings:O004 **(2702)**
2001: 5°GF, 6^{0}GF, 6^{0}GF, 6^{4}F

	Starts	1st	2nd	3rd	Win & Pl
Career Total (Turf)	4	0	0	0	0

Going (Turf): **Sf:** 0-0 **GS:** 0-0 **Gd:** 0-0 **GF:** 0-3 **Fm:** 0-1
Distance: 5f/6f: 0-2 7f-8f: 0-2 9f-13f: 0-0 14f+: 0-0
Track : LH: 0-1 RH: 0-0 Tight: 0-0 Gall: 0-0
Aids: Bl: 0-1 Vi: 0-0 Tstrap: 0-0
Best Rating: **59** 7/01 Brig 6f209y firm

Beat The Ring (IRE)

87(81) (41)**33**

3-y-o br g Tagula (IRE)-Pursue (Auction Ring (USA))
G Brown Mrs K W Sneath

Placings:000-00 **(3701)**
2001: 8^{0}SD, 6^{0}GF

	Starts	1st	2nd	3rd	Win & Pl
Career Total (Turf)	1	0	0	0	
Career Total (AW)	4	0	0	0	

Going (Turf): **Sf:** 0-0 **GS:** 0-0 **Gd:** 0-0 **GF:** 0-1 **Fm:** 0-0
Distance: 5f/6f: 0-2 7f-8f: 0-3 9f-13f: 0-0 14f+: 0-0
Track : LH: 0-5 RH: 0-0 Tight: 0-3 Gall: 0-0
Aids: Bl: 0-0 Vi: 0-0 Tstrap: 0-0
Best Rating: **33** 8/01 Brig 6f209y gd-fm

Beau Duchess (FR)

98 **37**

4-y-o ch f Bering-Turkish Coffee (FR) (Gay Mecene (USA))
P W Harris Derbyshire,Elliott,Merritt & Seagroat

Placings:060-02026 **(3846)**
2001: 13^{0}GF, 11^{2}GF, 12^{0}GF, 11^{2}GS, 14^{6}G

	Starts	1st	2nd	3rd	Win & Pl
Career Total (Turf)	8	0	2	0	1455

Going (Turf): **Sf:** 0-0 **GS:** 0-2 **Gd:** 0-1 **GF:** 0-5 **Fm:** 0-0
Distance: 5f/6f: 0-0 7f-8f: 0-0 9f-13f: 0-6 14f+: 0-2
Track : LH: 0-3 RH: 0-3 Tight: 0-3 Gall: 0-1
Aids: Bl: 0-0 Vi: 0-0 Tstrap: 0-0
Best Rating: **37** 7/01 Leic 1m3f183y gd-sft

Beau Roberto

33

7-y-o b g Robellino (USA)-Night Jar (Night Shift (USA))
J S Goldie J W Armstrong

Placings:3060/0033656000/**334**603043214413460/04 032600144313424052/00 **(1809)**
2001: 12^{0}GF, 12^{0}GF

	Starts	1st	2nd	3rd	Win & Pl
Career Total (Turf)	52	4	4	9	23291
Career Total (AW)	3	0	0	2	832

49	8/99	Haml	1m5f9y	E(0-70)H	G-F	£2835
45	7/99	Haml	1m5f9y	E(0-75)H	FRM	£3225
46	8/98	Haml	1m3f16y	F(0-70)H	SFT	£2808
40	7/98	Haml	1m3f16y	E(0-70)H	GD	£2671

Total win prize-money £11539

Going (Turf): **Sf: 1-11** GS: 0-6 **Gd: 1-12 GF: 1-20 Fm: 1-3**
Distance: 5f/6f: 0-1 7f-8f: 0-13 9f-13f: 2-34 14f+: 2-7
Track : LH: 0-22 **RH: 4-27 Tight: 4-28** Gall: 0-3
Aids: Bl: 0-2 Vi: 0-0 Tstrap: 0-0
Best Rating: **33** 5/01 Muss 1m4f gd-fm

Beau Sauvage

99(71) (26)**53**

3-y-o b g Wolfhound (USA)-Maestrale (Top Ville)
M W Easterby Guy Reed

Placings:005000-00066316046303 **(5375)**
2001: 6^{0}HY, 8^{0}HY, 8^{0}F, 6^{6}F, 8^{6}GF, 7^{3}G, 8^{1}GF, 8^{6}GF, 7^{0}GF, 8^{4}G, 8^{6}F, 6^{3}F, 9^{0}G, 7^{3}G

	Starts	1st	2nd	3rd	Win & Pl
Career Total (Turf)	19	1	0	3	3642
Career Total (AW)	1	0	0	0	

53	6/01	Rdcr	1m	G(0-70)H	G-F	£2023

Total win prize-money £2023

Going (Turf): Sf: 0-4 GS: 0-2 Gd: 0-4 **GF: 1-4** Fm: 0-5
Distance: 5f/6f: 0-7 **7f-8f: 1-10** 9f-13f: 0-3 14f+: 0-0
Track : LH: 0-6 RH: 0-3 Tight: 0-2 Gall: 0-2
Aids: Bl: 0-4 Vi: 0-0 Tstrap: 0-0
Best Rating: **53** 6/01 Rdcr 1m gd-fm

Made all when winning a ladies' race over a mile at Redcar. Best on fast ground, has worn blinkers in recent runs.

Beau Tudor (IRE)

87 **30**

7-y-o b g Aragon-Sunley Silks (Formidable (USA))
Miss L C Siddall Lynn Siddall Racing

Placings:006006/500000 **(5374)**
2001: 5^{5}F, 6^{0}GF, 5^{0}F, 5^{0}G, 7^{0}G, 6^{0}G

	Starts	1st	2nd	3rd	Win & Pl
Career Total (Turf)	12	0	0	0	0

Going (Turf): **Sf:** 0-0 **GS:** 0-2 **Gd:** 0-4 **GF:** 0-4 **Fm:** 0-2
Distance: 5f/6f: 0-8 7f-8f: 0-3 9f-13f: 0-1 14f+: 0-0
Track : LH: 0-2 RH: 0-0 Tight: 0-0 Gall: 0-0
Aids: Bl: 0-0 Vi: 0-0 Tstrap: 0-0
Best Rating: **30** 8/01 Newc 7f good

Beauchamp Magic

(100) (54)**33**

6-y-o b g Northern Park (USA)-Beauchamp Buzz (High Top)
M D I Usher The Magic And Dance Partnership

Placings:000/032650/060000**016**/**04054301116113-324** **(0105)**
2001: 16^{3}SD, 16^{2}SW, 16^{4}SW

	Starts	1st	2nd	3rd	Win & Pl
Career Total (Turf)	19	2	1	1	6498
Career Total (AW)	16	4	1	3	9713

46	12/00	Wolv	2m46y	F(0-65)H	STD	£2317
39	11/00	Ling	2m	F(0-65)H	STD	£1725
33	8/00	Thsk	2m	F(0-60)H	GD	£2957
37	8/00	Wolv	1m6f166y	G(0-60)H	STD	£1928
29	7/00	Brig	1m3f196y	F(0-60)H	FRM	£2299
34	12/99	Wolv	2m46y	F(0-65)H	STD	£2358

Total win prize-money £13588

Going (Turf): Sf: 0-3 GS: 0-1 **Gd: 1-4** GF: 0-9 **Fm: 1-2**
Distance: 5f/6f: 0-0 7f-8f: 0-3 9f-13f: 1-6 **14f+: 5-26**
Track : **LH: 6-29** RH: 0-4 **Tight: 5-22** Gall: 0-2
Aids: Bl: 0-1 Vi: 0-1 Tstrap: 0-5
Best Rating: **54** 1/01 Wolv 2m46y slow

Beauchamp Nyx

89(79) (24)**25**

5-y-o b m Northern Park (USA)-Beauchamp Image (Midyan (USA))
P A Pritchard P A Pritchard

Placings:0/006/000-0 **(1460)**
2001: 13^{0}G

	Starts	1st	2nd	3rd	Win & Pl
Career Total (Turf)	5	0	0	0	
Career Total (AW)	3	0	0	0	0

Going (Turf): **Sf:** 0-4 **GS:** 0-0 **Gd:** 0-1 **GF:** 0-0 **Fm:** 0-0
Distance: 5f/6f: 0-0 7f-8f: 0-1 9f-13f: 0-5 14f+: 0-2
Track : LH: 0-6 RH: 0-1 Tight: 0-3 Gall: 0-0
Aids: Bl: 0-0 Vi: 0-0 Tstrap: 0-0
Best Rating: **25** 5/01 Bath 1m5f22y good

Beauchamp Pilot

103(85) (32)**86+**

3-y-o ch g Inchinor-Beauchamp Image (Midyan (USA))
G A Butler E Penser

Placings:0-030111 **(5608)**
2001: 6^{0}GF, 5^{3}GF, 7^{0}G, 8^{1}G, 8^{1}S, 7^{1}GS

	Starts	1st	2nd	3rd	Win & Pl
Career Total (Turf)	6	3	0	1	17652
Career Total (AW)	1	0	0	0	

86	11/01	NmkR	7f	D(0-85)H	G-S	£5161
81	10/01	Rdcr	1m	E(0-75)H	SFT	£4273
73	9/01	Asct	1m	D(0-80)H	GD	£7540

Total win prize-money £16975

Going (Turf): **Sf: 1-1 GS: 1-1 Gd: 1-2** GF: 0-2 Fm: 0-0
Distance: 5f/6f: 0-2 **7f-8f: 3-4** 9f-13f: 0-1 14f+: 0-0
Track : LH: 0-1 RH: 0-0 Tight: 0-1 Gall: 0-0
Aids: Bl: 0-0 Vi: 0-0 Tstrap: 0-0
Best Rating: **86** 11/01 NmkR 7f gd-sft

Handicapped on the basis of disappointing performances over inadequate trips, he improved when stepped up to a mile at Ascot, and supplemented that at Redcar and Newmarket on easy ground. On the upgrade.

Beauchamp Quiz

(82) (39)**61**

2-y-o gr f Inchinor-Beauchamp Jade (Kalaglow)
G A Butler E Penser

Placings:00 **(5665)**
2001: 7^{0}GS, 6^{0}HY

	Starts	1st	2nd	3rd	Win & Pl
Career Total (Turf)	2	0	0	0	

Going (Turf): **Sf:** 0-1 **GS:** 0-1 **Gd:** 0-0 **GF:** 0-0 **Fm:** 0-0
Distance: 5f/6f: 0-1 7f-8f: 0-1 9f-13f: 0-0 14f+: 0-0
Track : LH: 0-0 RH: 0-0 Tight: 0-0 Gall: 0-0
Aids: Bl: 0-0 Vi: 0-0 Tstrap: 0-0
Best Rating: **61** 11/01 NmkR 7f gd-sft

Beaudacious (IRE)

77 **53**

2-y-o b c Indian Ridge-Marwell (Habitat)
N Tinkler Mrs D Wright

Placings:060 **(5250)**
2001: 6^{0}G, 7^{6}HY, 6^{0}S

	Starts	1st	2nd	3rd	Win & Pl
Career Total (Turf)	3	0	0	0	

Going (Turf): **Sf:** 0-2 **GS:** 0-0 **Gd:** 0-1 **GF:** 0-0 **Fm:** 0-0
Distance: 5f/6f: 0-2 7f-8f: 0-1 9f-13f: 0-0 14f+: 0-0
Track : LH: 0-1 RH: 0-0 Tight: 0-0 Gall: 0-0
Aids: Bl: 0-0 Vi: 0-0 Tstrap: 0-0
Best Rating: **53** 9/01 Hayd 7f30y heavy

Beaufort Lady (IRE)

94(86) (37)**75**

2-y-o b f Alhaarth (IRE)-Brentsville (USA) (Arctic Tern (USA))
M Johnston D Brennan

Placings:66256 **(5379)**
2001: 5^{6}GF, 6^{6}GS, 7^{2}G, 8^{5}SD, 7^{6}S

	Starts	1st	2nd	3rd	Win & Pl

	Starts	1st	2nd	3rd	Win & Pl
Career Total (Turf)	4	0	1	0	1072
Career Total (AW)	1	0	0	0	0

Going (Turf): Sf: 0-1 GS: 0-1 Gd: 0-1 GF: 0-1 Fm: 0-0
Distance: 5f/6f: 0-1 7f-8f: 0-3 9f-13f: 0-1 14f+: 0-0
Track : LH: 0-2 RH: 0-0 Tight: 0-2 Gall: 0-0
Aids: Bl: 0-0 Vi: 0-0 Tstrap: 0-0
Best Rating: 75 8/01 Rdcr 7f good

She showed improvement when stepped up to seven furlongs at Redcar on her third start, but did not take to sand when tried on it next time.

Beausejour (USA)

(94) (54)**45**
3-y-o ch f Diesis-Libeccio (NZ) (Danzatore (CAN))
J W Hills Wood Hall Stud Limited

Placings:0060462260 **(5398)**
2001: 7^{0}G, 7^{0}GF, 6^{6}GF, 10^{0}GF, 8^{4}SD, 10^{6}G, 9^{2}SW, 8^{2}SD, 9^{6}S, 8^{0}SD

	Starts	1st	2nd	3rd	Win & Pl
Career Total (Turf)	6	0	0	0	0
Career Total (AW)	4	0	2	0	1529

Going (Turf): Sf: 0-1 GS: 0-0 Gd: 0-2 GF: 0-3 Fm: 0-0
Distance: 5f/6f: 0-0 7f-8f: 0-3 9f-13f: 0-7 14f+: 0-0
Track : LH: 0-7 RH: 0-1 Tight: 0-5 Gall: 0-0
Aids: Bl: 0-0 Vi: 0-0 Tstrap: 0-5
Best Rating: 58 5/01 Gdwd 7f gd-fm

Maiden handicapper, stays ten furlongs, has shown most of her best form on the All-Weather.

Beauteous (IRE)

86 **80**
2-y-o ch c Tagula (IRE)-Beauty Appeal (USA) (Shadeed (USA))
A Berry Paul J Dixon

Placings:031600 **(5487)**
2001: 6^{0}GF, 5^{3}GF, 7^{1}GF, 7^{6}GS, 6^{0}G, 6^{0}HY

	Starts	1st	2nd	3rd	Win & Pl
Career Total (Turf)	6	1	0	1	3383

80 6/01 Muss 7f30y F G-F £2968
Total win prize-money £2968

Going (Turf): Sf: 0-1 GS: 0-1 Gd: 0-1 **GF: 1-3** Fm: 0-0
Distance: 5f/6f: 0-4 **7f-8f: 1-2** 9f-13f: 0-0 14f+: 0-0
Track : LH: 0-0 RH: 0-1 Tight: 0-0 Gall: 0-0
Aids: Bl: 0-0 Vi: 0-0 Tstrap: 0-0
Best Rating: 80 6/01 Muss 7f30y gd-fm

Relished the step up to seven furlongs when winning at Musselburgh.

Beautifultommorrow

(83) (47)**59**
2-y-o ch f Pursuit Of Love-Bella Domani (Cadeaux Genereux)
K R Burke Mrs Elaine M Burke

Placings:600 **(4797)**
2001: 5^{6}SD, 7^{0}G, 6^{0}G

	Starts	1st	2nd	3rd	Win & Pl
Career Total (Turf)	2	0	0	0	
Career Total (AW)	1	0	0	0	0

Going (Turf): Sf: 0-0 GS: 0-0 Gd: 0-2 GF: 0-0 Fm: 0-0
Distance: 5f/6f: 0-2 7f-8f: 0-1 9f-13f: 0-0 14f+: 0-0
Track : LH: 0-0 RH: 0-0 Tight: 0-0 Gall: 0-0
Aids: Bl: 0-0 Vi: 0-0 Tstrap: 0-0
Best Rating: 59 8/01 NmkJ 7f good

Beckett (IRE)

106 **116**
3-y-o b c Fairy King (USA)-Groom Order (Groom Dancer (USA))
A P O'Brien Mrs John Magnier & Mr M Tabor

Placings:131-210 **(5389)**
2001: 8^{2}GF, 8^{1}GS, 10^{0}GS

	Starts	1st	2nd	3rd	Win & Pl
Career Total (Turf)	6	3	1	1	152574

107 10/01 NmkR 1m A G-S £16124
116 9/00 Curr 7f YLD £114600
88 6/00 Leop 6f GD £6900
Total win prize-money £137624

Going (Turf): Sf: 0-0 **GS: 1-2 Gd: 1-2** GF: 0-1 Fm: 0-0
Distance: 5f/6f: 1-1 **7f-8f: 2-4** 9f-13f: 0-1 14f+: 0-0
Track : LH: 0-0 RH: 0-0 Tight: 0-0 Gall: 0-1
Aids: Bl: 0-0 Vi: 0-0 Tstrap: 0-0
Best Rating: 107 10/01 NmkR 1m gd-sft

His dam is out of a half-sister to the 2000 Guineas winner Entrepreneur, and he is bred to be a miler. He improved considerably to beat King's County easily in the National Stakes at the Curragh as a juvenile. Not seen again for a year, he was just touched off in a Listed event on his return, but made no mistake in a similar event at Newmarket. Retired after running unplaced in the Dubai Champion Stakes,

Beckon

99(99) (44)**38**
5-y-o ch m Beveled (USA)-Carolynchristensen (Sweet Revenge)
B R Johnson B A Whittaker

Placings:000/456300013/545015061040-00305210325 **(4377)**
2001: 12^{0}SD, 10^{0}SD, 9^{3}G, 9^{0}F, 11^{5}F, 11^{2}F, 10^{1}GF, 11^{0}GF, 11^{3}G, 10^{2}F, 11^{5}GF

	Starts	1st	2nd	3rd	Win & Pl
Career Total (Turf)	22	2	2	3	7075
Career Total (AW)	13	2	0	1	3791

34 7/01 Ling 1m2f G G-F £2075
39 8/00 Brig 1m1f209yF(0-65)H FRM £2705
52 6/00 Ling 1m2f G(0-60)H STD £2002
44 11/99 Ling 1m2f G STD £1532
Total win prize-money £8317

Going (Turf): Sf: 0-2 GS: 0-0 Gd: 0-4 **GF: 1-9 Fm: 1-7**
Distance: 5f/6f: 0-3 7f-8f: 0-5 **9f-13f: 4-27** 14f+: 0-0
Track : **LH: 4-29** RH: 0-1 **Tight: 3-20** Gall: 0-0
Aids: Bl: 0-0 Vi: 0-1 Tstrap: 0-0
Best Rating: 41 1/01 Ling 1m4f stand

Becky Simmons

(79) (34)**80d**
3-y-o b f Mujadil (USA)-Jolies Eaux (Shirley Heights)
A P Jarvis Mrs S Clifford

Placings:111500-140000 **(5352)**
2001: 6^{1}GF, 7^{4}G, 7^{0}GF, 7^{0}G, 5^{0}F, 6^{0}SD

	Starts	1st	2nd	3rd	Win & Pl
Career Total (Turf)	11	4	0	0	18484
Career Total (AW)	1	0	0	0	

77 6/01 Kemp 6f D(0-80) G-F £4251
84 8/00 Rdcr 6f C FRM £7605
77 7/00 Sals 6f F GD £2394
66 6/00 Haml 5f4y E GD £3510
Total win prize-money £17760

Going (Turf): Sf: 0-0 GS: 0-1 **Gd: 2-6** GF: 1-2 Fm: 1-2
Distance: **5f/6f: 4-6** 7f-8f: 0-6 9f-13f: 0-0 14f+: 0-0
Track : LH: 0-4 RH: 0-1 Tight: 0-2 Gall: 0-1
Aids: Bl: 0-0 Vi: 0-0 Tstrap: 0-0
Best Rating: 77 6/01 Kemp 6f gd-fm

She won her first three starts at two before losing her form. She made a winning reappearance at Kempton in June and obviously goes well fresh. Yet to prove she stays seven furlongs.

Bedevilled

97(103) (60d)**40**
6-y-o ch g Beveled (USA)-Putout (Dowsing (USA))
P D Evans Treble Chance Partnership

Placings:23/4450/00626010/2025100200160300006520550460 **(4897)**
2001: 6^{0}SD, 5^{6}SW, 6^{5}G, 5^{2}F, 5^{0}GF, 5^{5}G, 5^{5}GF, 5^{0}GF, 5^{4}G, 5^{6}GF, 5^{0}GS

	Starts	1st	2nd	3rd	Win & Pl
Career Total (Turf)	33	3	4	2	14648
Career Total (AW)	9	0	2	0	1916

57 8/00 Catt 5f F G-S £2268
74 3/00 Newc 5f D(0-85)H GD £3835
68 8/99 Bevl 5f D GD £3764
Total win prize-money £9867

Going (Turf): Sf: 0-4 GS: 1-6 **Gd: 2-11** GF: 0-10 Fm: 0-2
Distance: **5f/6f: 3-39** 7f-8f: 0-3 9f-13f: 0-0 14f+: 0-0
Track : LH: 0-16 RH: 0-2 Tight: 0-9 Gall: 0-4
Aids: Bl: 0-2 Vi: 0-3 Tstrap: 0-0
Best Rating: 50 5/01 Brig 5f213y firm

Inconsistent performer. Best with give in ground.

Bee Gee

(100) (38)**44**
4-y-o b f Beveled (USA)-Bunny Gee (Last Tycoon)
M Blanshard J M Beever

Placings:0000/014305004333-3236 **(0688)**
2001: 16^{3}SD, 11^{2}SD, 11^{3}SD, 11^{6}SD

	Starts	1st	2nd	3rd	Win & Pl
Career Total (Turf)	12	0	0	1	260
Career Total (AW)	8	1	1	5	4233

51 5/00 Ling 1m4f G STD £1834
Total win prize-money £1834

Going (Turf): Sf: 0-1 GS: 0-3 Gd: 0-2 GF: 0-4 Fm: 0-2
Distance: 5f/6f: 0-1 7f-8f: 0-2 **9f-13f: 1-14** 14f+: 0-3
Track : **LH: 1-14** RH: 0-2 **Tight: 1-5** Gall: 0-0
Aids: Bl: 0-0 Vi: 0-0 Tstrap: 0-0
Best Rating: 38 3/01 Sthl 1m3f stand

Bee J Gee

89(90) (62d)**47**
3-y-o b c Dilum (USA)-Sound Check (Formidable (USA))
Mrs Lydia Pearce B J Goldsmith

Placings:6004040-0000 **(3890)**
2001: 9^{0}GF, 11^{0}GF, 12^{0}SD, 7^{0}F

	Starts	1st	2nd	3rd	Win & Pl
Career Total (Turf)	8	0	0	0	0
Career Total (AW)	3	0	0	0	179

Going (Turf): Sf: 0-1 GS: 0-1 Gd: 0-1 GF: 0-4 Fm: 0-1
Distance: 5f/6f: 0-2 7f-8f: 0-6 9f-13f: 0-3 14f+: 0-0
Track : LH: 0-7 RH: 0-1 Tight: 0-2 Gall: 0-0
Aids: Bl: 0-0 Vi: 0-0 Tstrap: 0-0
Best Rating: 39 6/01 Wind 1m3f135y gd-fm

Beechy Bank (IRE)

(84) (29)**2**
3-y-o b f Shareef Dancer (USA)-Neptunalia (Slip Anchor)
R T Phillips (Mrs Mary Hambro 12/1) Cotswold Stud

Placings:006 **(5395)**
2001: 8^{0}SD, 10^{0}G, 7^{6}SD

	Starts	1st	2nd	3rd	Win & Pl
Career Total (Turf)	1	0	0	0	
Career Total (AW)	2	0	0	0	0

Going (Turf): Sf: 0-0 GS: 0-0 Gd: 0-1 GF: 0-0 Fm: 0-0

Distance: 5f/6f: 0-0 7f-8f: 0-2 9f-13f: 0-1 14f+: 0-0
Track : LH: 0-3 RH: 0-0 Tight: 0-2 Gall: 0-0
Aids: Bl: 0-1 Vi: 0-0 Tstrap: 0-0
Best Rating: 29 10/01 Wolv 7f stand

Beekeeper

115 **113**

3-y-o b c Rainbow Quest (USA)-Chief Bee (Chief's Crown (USA))
Sir Michael Stoute Sheikh Maktoum Bin Mohammed Al Maktoum

Placings:55-114 **(4114)**
2001: 12^{1}GF, 12^{1}GF, 11^{4}G

	Starts	1st	2nd	3rd	Win & Pl
Career Total (Turf)	5	2	0	0	56767

110	6/01	Asct	1m4f	B(0-105)H	G-F	£35750
67	5/01	Thsk	1m4f	D	G-F	£4348

Total win prize-money £40099

Going (Turf): Sf: 0-0 GS: 0-1 Gd: 0-1 **GF: 2-3** Fm: 0-0
Distance: 5f/6f: 0-0 7f-8f: 0-2 **9f-13f: 2-3** 14f+: 0-0
Track : LH: 1-2 RH: 1-1 Tight: 1-1 Gall: 1-2
Aids: Bl: 0-0 Vi: 0-0 Tstrap: 0-0
Best Rating: 113 8/01 York 1m3f195y good

Well-bred colt, dam won from nine to 14.5 furlongs and is a full-sister to the Racing Post Trophy winner Be My Chief (won Racing Post Trophy). Odds-on, made hard work of beating Arabie in maiden over 12 furlongs at Thirsk in May but showed improvement when defying top weight in the King George V handicap at the Royal meeting. A close fourth in the Great Voltigeur, he has reportedly been sold to race in Dubai.

Beenaboutabit

96 **60**

3-y-o b f Komaite (USA)-Tassagh Bridge (IRE) (Double Schwartz)
R Ingram The Banter Boyz

Placings:020-0005000 **(5626)**
2001: 7^{0}GF, 6^{0}GF, 6^{0}GF, 6^{5}GF, 5^{0}GF, 6^{0}G, 8^{0}GS

	Starts	1st	2nd	3rd	Win & Pl
Career Total (Turf)	10	0	1	0	895

Going (Turf): Sf: 0-0 GS: 0-3 Gd: 0-2 GF: 0-5 Fm: 0-0
Distance: 5f/6f: 0-7 7f-8f: 0-2 9f-13f: 0-1 14f+: 0-0
Track : LH: 0-2 RH: 0-2 Tight: 0-1 Gall: 0-1
Aids: Bl: 0-0 Vi: 0-4 Tstrap: 0-5
Best Rating: 60 8/01 Epsm 6f gd-fm

Still a maiden, although she has run some fair races, a drop to selling class may give her best opportunity.

Bel

106 **76+**

3-y-o b f Darshaan-Jezebel Monroe (USA) (Lyphard (USA))
R Charlton Lady Rothschild

Placings:331 **(5637)**
2001: 12^{3}GF, 11^{3}G, 11^{1}G

	Starts	1st	2nd	3rd	Win & Pl
Career Total (Turf)	3	1	0	2	4073

40	11/01	Catt	1m3f214yD		GD	£2982

Total win prize-money £2982

Going (Turf): Sf: 0-0 GS: 0-0 **Gd: 1-2** GF: 0-1 Fm: 0-0
Distance: 5f/6f: 0-0 7f-8f: 0-0 **9f-13f: 1-3** 14f+: 0-0
Track : **LH: 1-2** RH: 0-1 **Tight: 1-2** Gall: 0-0
Aids: Bl: 0-0 Vi: 0-0 Tstrap: 0-0
Best Rating: 76 10/01 Bath 1m3f144y good

A Darshaan filly out of a ten-furlong winner, she made a belated debut when a strong-finishing third in a Kempton maiden in September 2001, and ran the same sort of race at Bath before getting off the mark in a poor heat at Catterick.

Belinda

(105) (59)**46**

4-y-o ch f Mizoram (USA)-Mountain Dew (Pharly (FR))
K Bell North Farm Stud

Placings:040100300-0400232 **(5394)**
2001: 10^{0}GS, 10^{4}GF, 10^{0}GF, 10^{0}GF, 11^{2}SD, 12^{3}SD, 12^{2}SD

	Starts	1st	2nd	3rd	Win & Pl
Career Total (Turf)	7	0	0	0	
Career Total (AW)	9	1	2	2	5412

64	6/00	Sthl	1m	E	STD	£2737

Total win prize-money £2737

Going (Turf): Sf: 0-1 GS: 0-1 Gd: 0-1 GF: 0-4 Fm: 0-0
Distance: 5f/6f: 0-0 **7f-8f: 1-6** 9f-13f: 0-10 14f+: 0-0
Track : **LH: 1-14** RH: 0-0 Tight: 0-6 Gall: 0-1
Aids: Bl: 0-0 Vi: 0-0 Tstrap: 0-0
Best Rating: 59 10/01 Wolv 1m4f stand

Moderate filly, stays well and suited by Fibresand.

Bella Beguine

58 **8**

2-y-o b f Komaite (USA)-On The Record (Record Token)
A Bailey Granite By Design Ltd

Placings:0 **(0772)**
2001: 5^{0}S

	Starts	1st	2nd	3rd	Win & Pl
Career Total (Turf)	1	0	0	0	

Going (Turf): Sf: 0-1 GS: 0-0 Gd: 0-0 GF: 0-0 Fm: 0-0
Distance: 5f/6f: 0-1 7f-8f: 0-0 9f-13f: 0-0 14f+: 0-0
Track : LH: 0-0 RH: 0-0 Tight: 0-0 Gall: 0-0
Aids: Bl: 0-0 Vi: 0-0 Tstrap: 0-0
Best Rating: 8 4/01 Nott 5f13y soft

Bella Chica (IRE)

99 **97**

2-y-o b f Bigstone (IRE)-Just Like Annie (IRE) (Mujadil (USA))
J A Glover Carlton Partnership

Placings:1011456 **(5498)**
2001: 5^{1}F, 6^{0}GF, 5^{1}G, 6^{1}GY, 6^{4}GF, 6^{5}G, 6^{6}HY

	Starts	1st	2nd	3rd	Win & Pl
Career Total (Turf)	7	3	0	0	109314

90	8/01	Curr	6f		G-Y	£98000
80	6/01	Ripn	5f	E	GD	£3304
88	6/01	Nott	5f13y	F	FRM	£2348

Total win prize-money £103653

Going (Turf): Sf: 0-1 GS: 0-0 **Gd: 1-2** GF: 0-2 **Fm: 1-1**
Distance: **5f/6f: 3-7** 7f-8f: 0-0 9f-13f: 0-0 14f+: 0-0
Track : LH: 0-1 RH: 0-0 Tight: 0-1 Gall: 0-0
Aids: Bl: 0-0 Vi: 0-0 Tstrap: 0-0
Best Rating: 97 9/01 Ayr 6f gd-fm

She is a very speedy juvenile, winner of three of her first four starts including a valuable event at the Curragh and has continued to run well in some hot contests since. Goes well on a sound surface, but handles cut.

Bella Fregata

80 **52**

2-y-o ch f Dancing Spree (USA)-Bella Bambola (IRE) (Tate Gallery (USA))
J S Wainwright S Pedersen

Placings:00 **(5248)**
2001: 6^{0}GF, 7^{0}S

	Starts	1st	2nd	3rd	Win & Pl
Career Total (Turf)	2	0	0	0	

Going (Turf): **Sf: 0-1 GS: 0-0 Gd: 0-0 GF: 0-1 Fm: 0-0**
Distance: 5f/6f: 0-1 7f-8f: 0-1 9f-13f: 0-0 14f+: 0-0
Track : LH: 0-1 RH: 0-0 Tight: 0-0 Gall: 0-1
Aids: Bl: 0-0 Vi: 0-0 Tstrap: 0-0
Best Rating: 52 9/01 Rdcr 6f gd-fm

Bella Pavlina

97 **47**

3-y-o ch f Sure Blade (USA)-Pab's Choice (Telsmoss)
M Blanshard C Papaioannou

Placings:0065-45000 **(5041)**
2001: 8^{4}G, 10^{5}GF, 8^{0}GF, 7^{0}GF, 10^{0}G

	Starts	1st	2nd	3rd	Win & Pl
Career Total (Turf)	9	0	0	0	0

Going (Turf): **Sf: 0-2 GS: 0-0 Gd: 0-4 GF: 0-3 Fm: 0-0**
Distance: 5f/6f: 0-4 7f-8f: 0-2 9f-13f: 0-3 14f+: 0-0
Track : LH: 0-4 RH: 0-1 Tight: 0-2 Gall: 0-1
Aids: Bl: 0-0 Vi: 0-0 Tstrap: 0-0
Best Rating: 54 5/01 Bath 1m5y good

Bella Pupa

65

5-y-o ch m Theatrical Charmer-Louisa Anne (Mummy's Pet)
N M Babbage Colin Rashbrook

Placings:00/0 **(1938)**
2001: 11^{0}GF

	Starts	1st	2nd	3rd	Win & Pl
Career Total (Turf)	2	0	0	0	
Career Total (AW)	1	0	0	0	

Going (Turf): **Sf: 0-0 GS: 0-0 Gd: 0-0 GF: 0-2 Fm: 0-0**
Distance: 5f/6f: 0-0 7f-8f: 0-1 9f-13f: 0-2 14f+: 0-0
Track : LH: 0-2 RH: 0-0 Tight: 0-1 Gall: 0-0
Aids: Bl: 0-0 Vi: 0-2 Tstrap: 0-0

Bellas Gate Boy

88(83) (42)**43**

9-y-o b g Doulab (USA)-Celestial Air (Rheingold)
Mrs Lydia Pearce (J Pearce 26/2) Miss Ann Pauline Meadows

Placings:002243/000260/2000004/056124040026/014604/6110/000305-0000 **(1740)**
2001: 7^{0}SW, 8^{0}S, 7^{0}G, 10^{0}GF

	Starts	1st	2nd	3rd	Win & Pl
Career Total (Turf)	45	3	6	2	16234
Career Total (AW)	7	1	0	0	2099

42	6/99	Wolv	1m100y	F(0-70)H	STD	£2099
63	5/99	Wwck	7f164y	G(0-65)H	GD	£2407
52	5/98	Ling	7f	F(0-75)H	GD	£2679
51	5/97	Ling	7f	E(0-75)H	G-F	£3122

Total win prize-money £10308

Going (Turf): Sf: 0-2 GS: 0-5 **Gd: 2-16** GF: 1-18 Fm: 0-4
Distance: 5f/6f: 0-3 **7f-8f: 3-22** 9f-13f: 1-27 14f+: 0-0
Track : **LH: 2-28** RH: 0-10 **Tight: 1-21** Gall: 0-5
Aids: Bl: 0-1 Vi: 0-0 Tstrap: 0-0
Best Rating: 27 5/01 Ling 7f good

He is not inconvenienced by carrying big weights, and goes well for an amateur.

Bellbit

(67)

6-y-o b m Henbit (USA)-Bell Cord (Beldale Flutter (USA))
R Lee Dan Jones Partnership

Placings:0 **(1086)**

2001: 6^{0}SD

	Starts	1st	2nd	3rd	Win & Pl
Career Total (Turf)	0	0	0	0	
Career Total (AW)	1	0	0	0	

Going (Turf): Sf: 0-0 GS: 0-0 Gd: 0-0 GF: 0-0 Fm: 0-0
Distance: 5f/6f: 0-1 7f-8f: 0-0 9f-13f: 0-0 14f+: 0-0
Track : LH: 0-1 RH: 0-0 Tight: 0-1 Gall: 0-0
Aids: Bl: 0-0 Vi: 0-0 Tstrap: 0-0

Bellbottom

87 **65**
2-y-o b c Mtoto-Satin Bell (Midyan (USA))
J L Dunlop E S Tudor-Evans

Placings:65060 **(5467)**
2001: 6^{6}GF, 7^{5}GF, 7^{0}G, 7^{6}HY, 6^{0}S

	Starts	1st	2nd	3rd	Win & Pl
Career Total (Turf)	5	0	0	0	0

Going (Turf): Sf: 0-2 GS: 0-0 Gd: 0-1 GF: 0-2 Fm: 0-0
Distance: 5f/6f: 0-0 7f-8f: 0-5 9f-13f: 0-0 14f+: 0-0
Track : LH: 0-1 RH: 0-0 Tight: 0-0 Gall: 0-0
Aids: Bl: 0-0 Vi: 0-0 Tstrap: 0-0
Best Rating: 65 8/01 Folk 7f good

Belle D'Anjou (FR)

104 **73**
4-y-o b f Saint Cyrien (FR)-Epsibelle (IRE) (Darshaan)
M C Pipe Network Training

Placings:1-203011 **(4983)**
2001: 10^{2}GF, 10^{0}GF, 11^{3}GF, 10^{0}HY, 10^{1}F, 12^{1}G

	Starts	1st	2nd	3rd	Win & Pl
Career Total (Turf)	7	3	1	1	11566

73 9/01 Asct 1m4f E(0-85)H GD £5167
69 9/01 Chep 1m2f36y F(0-65)H FRM £2681
3/00 Lrch 1m2f165y SFT £1921
Total win prize-money £9770

Going (Turf): Sf: 0-1 GS: 0-0 **Gd: 1-1** GF: 0-3 **Fm: 1-1**
Distance: 5f/6f: 0-0 7f-8f: 0-0 **9f-13f: 2-6** 14f+: 0-0
Track : LH: 1-4 RH: 1-1 Tight: 0-2 **Gall: 1-1**
Aids: Bl: 0-0 Vi: 0-0 Tstrap: 0-0
Best Rating: 73 9/01 Asct 1m4f good

She hit form in the autumn Effective ten to 12 furlongs suited by good ground or faster.

Belle Of The Manor (IRE)

(99) (48)**64**
3-y-o b f Bluebird (USA)-Pharsala (FR) (Hello Gorgeous (USA))
G A Butler Eastwind Racing Ltd

Placings:033026022 **(5631)**
2001: 6^{0}G, 6^{3}GF, 6^{3}GF, 6^{0}GF, 9^{2}GF, 10^{6}S, 11^{0}GS, 10^{2}S, 10^{2}G

	Starts	1st	2nd	3rd	Win & Pl
Career Total (Turf)	9	0	3	2	3953

Going (Turf): Sf: 0-2 GS: 0-1 Gd: 0-2 GF: 0-4 Fm: 0-0
Distance: 5f/6f: 0-3 7f-8f: 0-1 9f-13f: 0-5 14f+: 0-0
Track : LH: 0-5 RH: 0-0 Tight: 0-3 Gall: 0-0
Aids: Bl: 0-2 Vi: 0-0 Tstrap: 0-0
Best Rating: 64 9/01 Nott 1m1f213y gd-fm

She has made the frame several times on turf and sand and just needs a change of luck.

Belle Rouge

101 **54**
3-y-o b f Celtic Swing-Gunner's Belle (Gunner B)
M Blanshard Mrs B Woodford

Placings:0-00504 **(4290)**
2001: 10^{0}G, 10^{0}F, 12^{5}G, 14^{0}GF, 16^{4}GF

	Starts	1st	2nd	3rd	Win & Pl
Career Total (Turf)	6	0	0	0	0

Going (Turf): Sf: 0-1 GS: 0-0 Gd: 0-2 GF: 0-2 Fm: 0-1
Distance: 5f/6f: 0-0 7f-8f: 0-1 9f-13f: 0-3 14f+: 0-2
Track : LH: 0-3 RH: 0-1 Tight: 0-2 Gall: 0-0
Aids: Bl: 0-0 Vi: 0-0 Tstrap: 0-0
Best Rating: 54 7/01 Chep 1m4f23y good

Bellino Empresario (IRE)

88(94) (46)**30**
3-y-o b g Robellino (USA)-The Last Empress (IRE) (Last Tycoon)
I A Wood Happy Days Partnership

Placings:0060-05200030 **(4290)**
2001: 10^{0}SD, 10^{5}SW, 10^{2}SW, 8^{0}SD, 9^{0}S, 11^{0}GF, 11^{3}GF, 16^{0}GF

	Starts	1st	2nd	3rd	Win & Pl
Career Total (Turf)	6	0	0	1	464
Career Total (AW)	6	0	1	0	834

Going (Turf): Sf: 0-2 GS: 0-0 Gd: 0-1 GF: 0-3 Fm: 0-0
Distance: 5f/6f: 0-0 7f-8f: 0-5 9f-13f: 0-6 14f+: 0-1
Track : LH: 0-11 RH: 0-1 Tight: 0-5 Gall: 0-1
Aids: Bl: 0-2 Vi: 0-1 Tstrap: 0-1
Best Rating: 46 2/01 Ling 1m2f slow

Bells Beach (IRE)

(101) (55)**56**
3-y-o b f General Monash (USA)-Clifton Beach (Auction Ring (USA))
A G Newcombe Alex Gorrie Combi (uk)

Placings:0330-41012300 **(5051)**
2001: 5^{4}SD, 6^{1}SD, 6^{0}SD, 5^{1}G, 6^{2}SD, 5^{3}G, 6^{0}GF, 6^{0}SD

	Starts	1st	2nd	3rd	Win & Pl
Career Total (Turf)	4	1	0	1	3244
Career Total (AW)	8	1	1	2	3641

54 5/01 Brig 5f59y E(0-70)H GD £2814
47 3/01 Wolv 6f F(0-60)H STD £2261
Total win prize-money £5075

Going (Turf): Sf: 0-1 GS: 0-0 **Gd: 1-2** GF: 0-1 Fm: 0-0
Distance: **5f/6f: 2-12** 7f-8f: 0-0 9f-13f: 0-0 14f+: 0-0
Track : **LH: 2-8** RH: 0-0 **Tight: 1-4** Gall: 0-0
Aids: Bl: 0-0 Vi: 0-0 Tstrap: 0-0
Best Rating: 56 8/01 Folk 5f good

A moderate mover, has won over six and five furlongs in modest company at Wolverhampton and Brighton respectively.

Bells Boy'S

81 **58**
2-y-o b g Mind Games-Millie's Lady (IRE) (Common Grounds)
A Dickman Mike Smallman

Placings:000 **(4777)**
2001: 5^{0}S, 6^{0}GF, 5^{0}G

	Starts	1st	2nd	3rd	Win & Pl
Career Total (Turf)	3	0	0	0	

Going (Turf): Sf: 0-1 GS: 0-0 Gd: 0-1 GF: 0-1 Fm: 0-0
Distance: 5f/6f: 0-3 7f-8f: 0-0 9f-13f: 0-0 14f+: 0-0
Track : LH: 0-0 RH: 0-0 Tight: 0-0 Gall: 0-0
Aids: Bl: 0-0 Vi: 0-0 Tstrap: 0-0
Best Rating: 58 9/01 Rdcr 6f gd-fm

Bells For Marlin (USA)

102 **89+**
2-y-o b f Marlin (USA)-Bells For Thee (USA) (Sette Bello (USA))
P F I Cole Brereton C Jones

Placings:210 **(4970a)**
2001: 6^{2}GF, 7^{1}GF, 8^{0}S

	Starts	1st	2nd	3rd	Win & Pl
Career Total (Turf)	3	1	1	0	6890

89 8/01 Folk 7f D G-F £4680
Total win prize-money £4680

Going (Turf): Sf: 0-1 GS: 0-0 Gd: 0-0 **GF: 1-2** Fm: 0-0
Distance: 5f/6f: 0-1 **7f-8f: 1-2** 9f-13f: 0-0 14f+: 0-0
Track : LH: 0-0 RH: 0-1 Tight: 0-0 Gall: 0-0
Aids: Bl: 0-0 Vi: 0-0 Tstrap: 0-0
Best Rating: 89 8/01 Folk 7f gd-fm

Showed plenty of promise on her debut at Goodwood. Appreciated the step up in trip at Folkestone in August 2001, but was unplaced in a french group Three on soft. She could be useful over middle distances next term.

Belstane Badger (IRE)

80 **31**
3-y-o b f Blues Traveller (IRE)-Brigadina (Brigadier Gerard)
I Semple Belstane Racing Partnership (two)

Placings:0-060 **(5173)**
2001: 8^{0}GF, 7^{6}GF, 8^{0}GS

	Starts	1st	2nd	3rd	Win & Pl
Career Total (Turf)	4	0	0	0	0

Going (Turf): Sf: 0-1 GS: 0-1 Gd: 0-0 GF: 0-2 Fm: 0-0
Distance: 5f/6f: 0-0 7f-8f: 0-3 9f-13f: 0-1 14f+: 0-0
Track : LH: 0-3 RH: 0-1 Tight: 0-2 Gall: 0-0
Aids: Bl: 0-0 Vi: 0-0 Tstrap: 0-0
Best Rating: 31 6/01 Ayr 7f gd-fm

Belstane Fox (IRE)

(85) (33)**44**
3-y-o ch f General Monash (USA)-Countess Kildare (Dominion)
I Semple Belstane Racing Partnership (one)

Placings:0-55000103000 **(5418)**
2001: 7^{5}GF, 6^{5}F, 7^{0}GF, 7^{0}G, 8^{0}F, 7^{1}GS, 7^{0}GF, 7^{3}GF, 8^{0}GF, 9^{0}HY, 7^{0}SD

	Starts	1st	2nd	3rd	Win & Pl
Career Total (Turf)	11	1	0	1	2960
Career Total (AW)	1	0	0	0	

44 7/01 Ayr 7f F G-S £2492
Total win prize-money £2492

Going (Turf): Sf: 0-2 **GS: 1-1** Gd: 0-1 GF: 0-5 Fm: 0-2
Distance: 5f/6f: 0-1 **7f-8f: 1-9** 9f-13f: 0-2 14f+: 0-0
Track : **LH: 1-4** RH: 0-4 Tight: 0-3 Gall: 0-1
Aids: Bl: 0-0 Vi: 0-0 Tstrap: 0-0
Best Rating: 59 5/01 Ayr 7f gd-fm

Beltane

95 **40**
3-y-o b c Magic Ring (IRE)-Sally's Trust (IRE) (Classic Secret (USA))
W De Best-Turner Mrs Gillian Swanton

Placings:00-000100 **(4521)**
2001: 10^{0}S, 8^{0}GF, 8^{0}GF, 6^{1}GF, 6^{0}GF, 7^{0}GF

	Starts	1st	2nd	3rd	Win & Pl
Career Total (Turf)	8	1	0	0	3147

40 8/01 Brig 6f209y F(0-60)H G-F £3146
Total win prize-money £3147

Going (Turf): Sf: 0-1 GS: 0-0 Gd: 0-1 **GF: 1-6** Fm: 0-0
Distance: 5f/6f: 0-1 **7f-8f: 1-5** 9f-13f: 0-2 14f+: 0-0
Track : **LH: 1-3** RH: 0-3 Tight: 0-1 Gall: 0-1
Aids: Bl: 0-0 Vi: 0-0 Tstrap: 0-0
Best Rating: 40 8/01 Brig 6f209y gd-fm

Modest performer who caused a surprise when winning a Brighton maiden handicap.

Beluga Bay

92 **80+**

2-y-o b g Millkom-Bellyphax (Bellypha)
J R Fanshawe Beluga Bay Partnership

Placings:1 **(5405)**
2001: 6^{1}S

	Starts	1st	2nd	3rd	Win & Pl
Career Total (Turf)	1	1	0	0	3575

80 10/01 Pont 6f F SFT £3575
Total win prize-money £3575

Going (Turf): Sf: 1-1 GS: 0-0 Gd: 0-0 GF: 0-0 Fm: 0-0
Distance: 5f/6f: 1-1 7f-8f: 0-0 9f-13f: 0-0 14f+: 0-0
Track : LH: 1-1 RH: 0-0 Tight: 0-0 Gall: 0-0
Aids: Bl: 0-0 Vi: 0-0 Tstrap: 0-0
Best Rating: 80 10/01 Pont 6f soft

Got off the mark on his debut over six furlongs on soft ground at Pontefract.

Ben Britten

54

2-y-o ch g Sabrehill (USA)-Golden Panda (Music Boy)
J S Wainwright J S Wainwright

Placings:00 **(5227)**
2001: 7^{0}GS, 6^{0}S

	Starts	1st	2nd	3rd	Win & Pl
Career Total (Turf)	2	0	0	0	

Going (Turf): Sf: 0-1 GS: 0-1 Gd: 0-0 GF: 0-0 Fm: 0-0
Distance: 5f/6f: 0-0 7f-8f: 0-2 9f-13f: 0-0 14f+: 0-0
Track : LH: 0-1 RH: 0-0 Tight: 0-0 Gall: 0-1
Aids: Bl: 0-0 Vi: 0-0 Tstrap: 0-0

Ben Eagle (IRE)

91 **69**

2-y-o ch c Eagle Eyed (USA)-Checkers (Habat)
B R Millman High Stool Partners

Placings:00406 **(3739)**
2001: 5^{0}GF, 6^{0}GF, 7^{4}GF, 7^{0}GS, 6^{6}S

	Starts	1st	2nd	3rd	Win & Pl
Career Total (Turf)	5	0	0	0	0

Going (Turf): Sf: 0-1 GS: 0-1 Gd: 0-0 GF: 0-3 Fm: 0-0
Distance: 5f/6f: 0-2 7f-8f: 0-3 9f-13f: 0-0 14f+: 0-0
Track : LH: 0-1 RH: 0-0 Tight: 0-0 Gall: 0-0
Aids: Bl: 0-0 Vi: 0-0 Tstrap: 0-0
Best Rating: 69 7/01 Wwck 7f26y gd-fm

Ben Kenobi

31

3-y-o ch g Accondy (IRE)-Nour El Sahar (USA) (Sagace (FR))
Mrs P Ford K Marritt

Placings:0 **(5281)**
2001: 7^{0}S

	Starts	1st	2nd	3rd	Win & Pl
Career Total (Turf)	1	0	0	0	

Going (Turf): Sf: 0-1 GS: 0-0 Gd: 0-0 GF: 0-0 Fm: 0-0
Distance: 5f/6f: 0-0 7f-8f: 0-1 9f-13f: 0-0 14f+: 0-0
Track : LH: 0-0 RH: 0-0 Tight: 0-0 Gall: 0-0
Aids: Bl: 0-0 Vi: 0-0 Tstrap: 0-0

Benbyas

109(97) (42)**73d**

4-y-o b g Rambo Dancer (CAN)-Light The Way (Nicholas Bill)
J L Eyre C H Stephenson & Partners

Placings:00400/061004305600-611322000 **(5151)**
2001: 8^{6}SD, 8^{1}S, 11^{1}S, 12^{3}G, 12^{2}GF, 10^{2}GF, 10^{0}GF, 14^{0}SD, 10^{0}G

	Starts	1st	2nd	3rd	Win & Pl
Career Total (Turf)	20	3	2	2	14419
Career Total (AW)	6	0	0	0	0

65 5/01 Rdcr 1m3f E(0-70)H SFT £3360
57 4/01 Pont 1m4y F(0-60) SFT £2859
58 6/00 Carl 5f207y F(0-60) SFT £2352
Total win prize-money £8572

Going (Turf): Sf: 3-6 GS: 0-1 Gd: 0-8 GF: 0-3 Fm: 0-2
Distance: 5f/6f: 1-5 7f-8f: 0-6 **9f-13f: 2-13** 14f+: 0-2
Track : LH: 2-14 RH: 1-7 Tight: 1-6 Gall: 1-2
Aids: Bl: 0-7 **Vi: 1-5** Tstrap: 0-0
Best Rating: 73 6/01 Ayr 1m2f gd-fm

He was consistent in the first half of 2001, winning over a mile at Pontefract and 11 furlongs at Redcar, but struggled after returning from a break. He acts on fast ground but his wins have been in the soft.

Bend Wavy (IRE)

84 **47**

9-y-o ch g Kefaah (USA)-Prosodie (FR) (Relko)
T H Caldwell A J McDonald

Placings:34/2310/00060/661610300/0 **(4572)**
2001: 10^{0}HY

	Starts	1st	2nd	3rd	Win & Pl
Career Total (Turf)	20	3	1	3	14901
Career Total (AW)	1	0	0	0	

76 6/98 Thsk 1m4f D(0-80)H SFT £3626
72 6/98 Hayd 1m2f120yG(0-70)H GD £2150
82 7/96 Bevl 1m100y D(0-85)H G-F £5824
Total win prize-money £11600

Going (Turf): Sf: 1-5 GS: 0-1 **Gd: 1-7 GF: 1-7** Fm: 0-0
Distance: 5f/6f: 0-0 7f-8f: 0-3 **9f-13f: 3-18** 14f+: 0-0
Track : LH: 2-13 RH: 1-5 **Tight: 1-4** Gall: 0-2
Aids: Bl: 0-0 Vi: 0-0 Tstrap: 0-1
Best Rating: 47 9/01 Hayd 1m2f120y heavy

Benedictine

102 **85**

3-y-o b c Primo Dominie-Benedicite (Lomond (USA))
R Hannon N Ahamad

Placings:2-522610 **(5097)**
2001: 6^{5}GS, 6^{2}GS, 7^{2}GS, 6^{6}G, 6^{1}GF, 6^{0}GS

	Starts	1st	2nd	3rd	Win & Pl
Career Total (Turf)	7	1	3	0	7364

76 7/01 Sals 6f D G-F £3757
Total win prize-money £3757

Going (Turf): Sf: 0-1 GS: 0-4 Gd: 0-1 **GF: 1-1** Fm: 0-0
Distance: 5f/6f: 1-6 7f-8f: 0-1 9f-13f: 0-0 14f+: 0-0
Track : LH: 0-1 RH: 0-0 Tight: 0-0 Gall: 0-0
Aids: Bl: 0-0 Vi: 0-0 Tstrap: 0-0
Best Rating: 76 7/01 Sals 6f gd-fm

Costly to follow before breaking his duck in a Salisbury maiden. Six furlongs looks his trip.

Benjambo

3-y-o b g Primo Dominie-Young Lady (Young Generation)
R M Flower Richard J Gurr

Placings:0 **(3032)**
2001: 8^{0}GF

	Starts	1st	2nd	3rd	Win & Pl
Career Total (Turf)	1	0	0	0	

Going (Turf): Sf: 0-0 GS: 0-0 Gd: 0-0 GF: 0-1 Fm: 0-0
Distance: 5f/6f: 0-0 7f-8f: 0-1 9f-13f: 0-0 14f+: 0-0
Track : LH: 0-0 RH: 0-0 Tight: 0-0 Gall: 0-0
Aids: Bl: 0-0 Vi: 0-0 Tstrap: 0-0

Bennochy

78(97) (38)**21**

4-y-o ch g Factual (USA)-Agreloui (Tower Walk)
A Berry Mrs Norma Peebles

Placings:066000/1050454600005-000 **(0820)**
2001: 5^{0}SD, 6^{0}SD, 5^{0}S

	Starts	1st	2nd	3rd	Win & Pl
Career Total (Turf)	19	1	0	0	2798
Career Total (AW)	3	0	0	0	0

61 3/00 Catt 5f F(0-60) GD £2254
Total win prize-money £2254

Going (Turf): Sf: 0-4 GS: 0-3 **Gd: 1-5** GF: 0-5 Fm: 0-2
Distance: 5f/6f: 1-21 7f-8f: 0-1 9f-13f: 0-0 14f+: 0-0
Track : LH: 0-3 RH: 0-1 Tight: 0-3 Gall: 0-1
Aids: Bl: 0-0 Vi: 0-0 Tstrap: 0-0
Best Rating: 17 3/01 Wolv 5f stand

Benny The Vice (USA)

102 **85**

2-y-o ch c Benny The Dip (USA)-Vice On Ice (USA) (Vice Regent (CAN))
M Johnston E Grayson

Placings:35200 **(5628)**
2001: 8^{3}F, 8^{5}GF, 7^{2}HY, 7^{0}S, 8^{0}G

	Starts	1st	2nd	3rd	Win & Pl
Career Total (Turf)	5	0	1	1	1703

Going (Turf): Sf: 0-2 GS: 0-0 Gd: 0-1 GF: 0-1 Fm: 0-1
Distance: 5f/6f: 0-0 7f-8f: 0-4 9f-13f: 0-1 14f+: 0-0
Track : LH: 0-3 RH: 0-1 Tight: 0-1 Gall: 0-1
Aids: Bl: 0-0 Vi: 0-0 Tstrap: 0-0
Best Rating: 85 9/01 Hayd 7f30y heavy

Bentyheath Lane

55(72) (10)**10**

4-y-o b g Puissance-Eye Sight (Roscoe Blake)
M Mullineaux The Hon Mrs S Pakenham

Placings:00/00-00 **(0506)**
2001: 12^{0}SD, 10^{0}S

	Starts	1st	2nd	3rd	Win & Pl
Career Total (Turf)	5	0	0	0	
Career Total (AW)	1	0	0	0	

Going (Turf): Sf: 0-4 GS: 0-1 Gd: 0-0 GF: 0-0 Fm: 0-0
Distance: 5f/6f: 0-0 7f-8f: 0-2 9f-13f: 0-3 14f+: 0-1
Track : LH: 0-3 RH: 0-0 Tight: 0-2 Gall: 0-1
Aids: Bl: 0-0 Vi: 0-0 Tstrap: 0-0
Best Rating: 10 2/01 Wolv 1m4f stand

Benzoe (IRE)

101 **55**

11-y-o b g Taufan (USA)-Saintly Guest (What A Guest)
K A Ryan Tony Fawcett

Placings:0333412/0400062100/00600000/0010206240 00/0000120332100000/0003310602135000/00041503 60022001530/00060001000000/506153046-003020 **(3847)**
2001: 5^{0}GF, 7^{0}GF, 5^{3}GS, 5^{0}G, 6^{2}F, 6^{0}G

	Starts	1st	2nd	3rd	Win & Pl
Career Total (Turf)	117	11	10	11	104734
Career Total (AW)	1	0	0	1	297

54 7/00 Hayd 5f D(0-80)H G-F £7507

61	7/99	Leic	5f218y	E(0-70)H	G-F	£3252
74	9/98	Rdcr	6f	E(0-80)H	G-F	£3582
73	5/98	Thsk	6f	C(0-95)H	G-F	£7200
77	7/97	Thsk	6f	D(0-80)H	GD	£3761
65	6/97	Thsk	5f	D(0-75)H	G-F	£3860
81	8/96	Thsk	6f	D(0-80)H	G-F	£3873
72	5/96	Thsk	6f	E(0-70)H	G-F	£4471
71	5/95	Thsk	6f	D(0-75)H	G-F	£4971
84	10/93	York	6f	C(0-100)H	HVY	£13500
79	9/92	Ayr	6f	F	SFT	£2710

Total win prize-money £58689

Going (Turf): Sf: 2-15 GS: 0-18 Gd: 1-34 **GF: 8-39** Fm: 0-11
Distance: **5f/6f: 11-107** 7f-8f: 0-11 9f-13f: 0-0 14f+: 0-0
Track : LH: 0-8 RH: 0-0 Tight: 0-2 Gall: 0-2
Aids: **Bl: 1-10** Vi: 0-1 Tstrap: 0-0
Best Rating: 49 8/01 Thsk 6f firm

Formerly with Lynda Ramsden, he is a useful performer if everything goes his way, although he is often slowly away. He excels at Thirsk, though he can win elsewhere.

Bergamo

106 **58**

5-y-o b g Robellino (USA)-Pretty Thing (Star Appeal)
B Ellison Ashley Young

Placings:553510/06015661344435/00050-03150263454 **(3043)**
2001: 12^{0}GS, 13^{3}S, 14^{1}GS, 16^{5}G, 13^{0}GF, 14^{2}GF, 12^{6}F, 12^{3}GF, 12^{4}G, 12^{5}GF, 14^{4}GF

	Starts	1st	2nd	3rd	Win & Pl
Career Total (Turf)	36	4	1	5	21082

58	4/01	Muss	1m6f	E(0-70)H	G-S	£3656
79	6/99	Yarm	1m6f17y	E(0-75)H	GD	£3377
73	5/99	Bevl	1m3f216y	E(0-70)H	GD	£3018
78	9/98	Bath	1m2f46y	D	G-S	£3257

Total win prize-money £13310

Going (Turf): Sf: 0-2 **GS: 2-7 Gd: 2-11** GF: 0-13 Fm: 0-3
Distance: 5f/6f: 0-0 7f-8f: 0-3 9f-13f: 2-19 14f+: 2-14
Track : LH: 2-14 RH: 2-19 **Tight: 4-14** Gall: 0-7
Aids: **Bl: 3-20** Vi: 0-4 Tstrap: 0-0
Best Rating: 58 5/01 Muss 1m6f gd-fm

Stays 14 furlongs. Had dropped in the ratings before scoring at Musselburgh. Acts on any ground.

Bergen (IRE)

103(96) (48)**57**

6-y-o b g Ballad Rock-Local Custom (IRE) (Be My Native (USA))
D Nicholls James E Greaves

Placings:15/00302/060020/0500-**06355502**4015133 **(3041)**
2001: 7^{0}SD, 7^{6}SD, 7^{3}SW, 7^{5}SD, 7^{5}SD, 7^{5}SD, 6^{0}SD, 6^{2}SD, 7^{4}S, 6^{0}G, 5^{1}F, 6^{5}F, 5^{1}GS, 6^{3}F, 6^{3}GF

	Starts	1st	2nd	3rd	Win & Pl
Career Total (Turf)	24	3	2	3	13249
Career Total (AW)	8	0	1	1	875

49	6/01	Haml	5f4y	F	G-S	£2674
52	5/01	Brig	5f213y	G	FRM	£1883
86	7/97	Pont	6f	D	G-F	£3485

Total win prize-money £8042

Going (Turf): Sf: 0-3 **GS: 1-5** Gd: 0-6 **GF: 1-7 Fm: 1-3**
Distance: **5f/6f: 3-8** 7f-8f: 0-17 9f-13f: 0-7 14f+: 0-0
Track : **LH: 2-23** RH: 0-1 Tight: 0-5 Gall: 0-2
Aids: Bl: 0-0 Vi: 0-0 **Tstrap: 2-11**
Best Rating: 57 6/01 Brig 6f209y firm

Berk The Jerk (IRE)

106 **94**

2-y-o b c Bahamian Bounty-Pocket Book (IRE)

(Reference Point)
P W D'Arcy (M H Tompkins 8/7) Mrs A Lovat

Placings:1031032 **(5256)**
2001: 5^{1}GS, 6^{0}GF, 5^{3}GF, 5^{1}G, 6^{0}GS, 5^{3}G, 5^{2}GS

	Starts	1st	2nd	3rd	Win & Pl
Career Total (Turf)	7	2	1	2	32913

92	7/01	Sand	5f6y	A	GD	£13650
78	4/01	Wind	5f10y	D	G-S	£3272

Total win prize-money £16923

Going (Turf): Sf: 0-0 **GS: 1-3 Gd: 1-2** GF: 0-2 Fm: 0-0
Distance: **5f/6f: 2-7** 7f-8f: 0-0 9f-13f: 0-0 14f+: 0-0
Track : LH: 0-0 **RH: 1-1** Tight: 0-0 **Gall: 1-1**
Aids: Bl: 0-0 Vi: 0-0 Tstrap: 0-0
Best Rating: 94 10/01 Asct 5f gd-sft

Out of a half-sister to top-class miler Indian Lodge, he finished strongly to win his debut at Windsor and added to that in a Listed event at Sandown. Out of his depth in the Coventry and Prix Morny when tried at six furlongs, but ran a cracker in the Flying Childers at Doncaster. Beaten favourite in the Cornwallis, but was up against a progressive filly. Suited by five furlongs and does not want the ground too fast. Sold to race in Hong Kong.

Berkeley Hall

101(81) (20)**48**

4-y-o b f Saddlers' Hall (IRE)-Serious Affair (Valiyar)
B Palling Glyn And Albert Yemm

Placings:003/0012600-00534222 **(4618)**
2001: 6^{0}G, 5^{0}F, 7^{5}F, 6^{3}GF, 6^{4}GF, 6^{2}G, 6^{2}GF, 6^{2}F

	Starts	1st	2nd	3rd	Win & Pl
Career Total (Turf)	16	1	4	2	6122
Career Total (AW)	2	0	0	0	

60	5/00	Nott	6f15y	G(0-70)H	G-F	£2198

Total win prize-money £2198

Going (Turf): Sf: 0-1 GS: 0-1 Gd: 0-6 **GF: 1-5** Fm: 0-3
Distance: 5f/6f: 0-9 **7f-8f: 1-7** 9f-13f: 0-2 14f+: 0-0
Track : LH: 0-8 RH: 0-0 Tight: 0-3 Gall: 0-0
Aids: **Bl: 1-8** Vi: 0-0 Tstrap: 0-0
Best Rating: 48 9/01 Newc 6f firm

Suited by six furlongs and fast ground. Goes well from the front and is best when equipped with blinkers. Unlucky to be beaten on more than one occasion in the summer of 2001.

Berkeleysquare Boy (IRE)

80 **67**

2-y-o b c Spectrum (IRE)-Galatrix (Be My Guest (USA))
W J Haggas Http Partnership Ltd

Placings:0 **(4873)**
2001: 7^{0}G

	Starts	1st	2nd	3rd	Win & Pl
Career Total (Turf)	1	0	0	0	

Going (Turf): Sf: 0-0 GS: 0-0 Gd: 0-1 GF: 0-0 Fm: 0-0
Distance: 5f/6f: 0-0 7f-8f: 0-1 9f-13f: 0-0 14f+: 0-0
Track : LH: 0-0 RH: 0-0 Tight: 0-0 Gall: 0-0
Aids: Bl: 0-0 Vi: 0-0 Tstrap: 0-0
Best Rating: 67 9/01 NmkR 7f good

Bernardo Bellotto (IRE)

69(92) (43)**42**

6-y-o b g High Estate-Naivity (IRE) (Auction Ring (USA))
G A Swinbank Alan Swinbank

Placings:224222103/00000/03000110/**00**0000213124-0 **(5539)**
2001: 8^{0}S

	Starts	1st	2nd	3rd	Win & Pl
Career Total (Turf)	27	3	5	2	14070

	Starts	1st	2nd	3rd	Win & Pl
Career Total (AW)	8	2	2	1	10024

	9/00	Mija	1m		GD	£1893
	8/00	Mija	1m		GD	£1893
59	6/99	Muss	7f30y	F	GD	£2416
56	5/99	Rdcr	7f	F	G-F	£2390
78	8/97	Epsm	6f	D	GD	£3468

Total win prize-money £12061

Going (Turf): Sf: 0-4 GS: 0-6 **Gd: 4-14** GF: 1-6 Fm: 0-2
Distance: 5f/6f: 1-11 **7f-8f: 4-21** 9f-13f: 0-3 14f+: 0-0
Track : LH: 1-14 RH: 1-7 **Tight: 2-10** Gall: 0-3
Aids: **Bl: 2-5** Vi: 0-0 Tstrap: 0-0
Best Rating: 78 8/97 Epsm 6f G

Berneen

56(53)

2-y-o b f Alzao (USA)-Chickamauga (USA) (Wild Again (USA))
C Smith The Brave Few

Placings:0000 **(4488)**
2001: 5^{0}SD, 7^{0}G, 5^{0}GF, 6^{0}S

	Starts	1st	2nd	3rd	Win & Pl
Career Total (Turf)	3	0	0	0	
Career Total (AW)	1	0	0	0	

Going (Turf): Sf: 0-1 GS: 0-0 Gd: 0-1 GF: 0-1 Fm: 0-0
Distance: 5f/6f: 0-2 7f-8f: 0-2 9f-13f: 0-0 14f+: 0-0
Track : LH: 0-0 RH: 0-0 Tight: 0-0 Gall: 0-0
Aids: Bl: 0-0 Vi: 0-1 Tstrap: 0-0

Berry Brook

8

2-y-o ch f Magic Ring (IRE)-Star Entry (In The Wings)
E A Wheeler J H Widdows

Placings:0 **(5665)**
2001: 6^{0}HY

	Starts	1st	2nd	3rd	Win & Pl
Career Total (Turf)	1	0	0	0	

Going (Turf): Sf: 0-1 GS: 0-0 Gd: 0-0 GF: 0-0 Fm: 0-0
Distance: 5f/6f: 0-1 7f-8f: 0-0 9f-13f: 0-0 14f+: 0-0
Track : LH: 0-0 RH: 0-0 Tight: 0-0 Gall: 0-0
Aids: Bl: 0-0 Vi: 0-0 Tstrap: 0-0
Best Rating: 8 11/01 Wind 6f heavy

Bersaglio

(88) (41)**47**

6-y-o ch h Rainbow Quest (USA)-Escrime (USA) (Sharpen Up)
K A Morgan J A Outwin

Placings:06434030/02005/**400** **(0984)**
2001: 12^{4}SD, 16^{0}SD, 12^{0}SD

	Starts	1st	2nd	3rd	Win & Pl
Career Total (Turf)	13	0	1	2	2693
Career Total (AW)	3	0	0	0	0

Going (Turf): Sf: 0-1 GS: 0-2 Gd: 0-4 GF: 0-6 Fm: 0-0
Distance: 5f/6f: 0-0 7f-8f: 0-0 9f-13f: 0-5 14f+: 0-11
Track : LH: 0-10 RH: 0-6 Tight: 0-4 Gall: 0-4
Aids: Bl: 0-0 Vi: 0-3 Tstrap: 0-3
Best Rating: 41 3/01 Sthl 1m4f stand

Bertolini (USA)

110(30) (113)**117**

5-y-o b h Danzig (USA)-Aquilegia (USA) (Alydar (USA))
Saeed Bin Suroor Godolphin

Placings:2512402/1033320/236200-345 **(2259)**
2001: 6^{3}FT, 6^{4}GF, 5^{5}G

	Starts	1st	2nd	3rd	Win & Pl
Career Total (Turf)	21	2	5	4	204574

	Starts	1st	2nd	3rd	Win & Pl				
Career Total (AW)	2	0	1	1	255284				
113	4/99	NmkJ	7f		H			GD	£17150
106	7/98	NmkJ	6f		A			G-F	£18260

Total win prize-money £35410

Going (Turf): Sf: 0-1 GS: 0-2 **Gd: 1-8 GF: 1-9** Fm: 0-0
Distance: 5f/6f: 1-18 7f-8f: 1-5 9f-13f: 0-0 14f+: 0-0
Track: LH: 0-1 RH: 0-1 Tight: 0-1 Gall: 0-0
Aids: Bl: 0-2 Vi: 0-12 Tstrap: 0-0
Best Rating: 111 3/01 Ndas 6f fast

A very able sprinter, he often runs well in the highest class, such as when chasing home Nuclear Debate in the Nunthorpe in 2000, but has not won a race since landing the Free Handicap on his reapperance at three. Best suited by six furlongs and a sound surface, and often visored. Retired to Overbury Stud.

Berzoud

101(91) (48)**54**
4-y-o b f Ezzoud (IRE)-Bertie's Girl (Another Realm)
J R Jenkins Miss I Leitendorfa

Placings:021-0500114563 **(4361)**
2001: 11^{0}SD, 12^{5}SW, 8^{0}GS, 8^{0}G, 9^{1}F, 11^{1}F, 11^{4}GF, 12^{5}G, 12^{6}GF, 11^{3}GF

	Starts	1st	2nd	3rd	Win & Pl
Career Total (Turf)	11	3	1	1	8977
Career Total (AW)	2	0	0	0	0

41	6/01	Ling	1m3f106yG		FRM	£2086
43	6/01	Brig	1m1f209yG		FRM	£1932
49	8/00	Rdcr	1m1f	E	FRM	£2964

Total win prize-money £6982

Going (Turf): Sf: 0-1 GS: 0-1 Gd: 0-2 GF: 0-4 **Fm: 3-3**
Distance: 5f/6f: 0-0 7f-8f: 0-0 **9f-13f: 3-13** 14f+: 0-0
Track: **LH: 3-9** RH: 0-3 **Tight: 2-8** Gall: 0-0
Aids: Bl: 0-0 Vi: 0-1 Tstrap: 0-0
Best Rating: 54 8/01 Brig 1m3f196y gd-fm

Best Bond

97(98) (51)**44**
4-y-o ch g Cadeaux Genereux-My Darlingdaughter (Night Shift (USA))
N P Littmoden Miss Vanessa Church

Placings:055/0300056063060-0234350250006 **(5287)**
2001: 6^{0}SW, 7^{2}SW, 5^{3}SW, 5^{4}SD, 5^{3}SD, 6^{5}SD, 5^{0}G, 6^{2}GF, 8^{5}GF, 6^{0}GF, 7^{0}GF, 6^{0}F, 6^{6}HY

	Starts	1st	2nd	3rd	Win & Pl
Career Total (Turf)	22	0	1	2	1920
Career Total (AW)	7	0	1	2	1302

Going (Turf): Sf: 0-4 GS: 0-1 Gd: 0-4 GF: 0-10 Fm: 0-3
Distance: 5f/6f: 0-20 7f-8f: 0-9 9f-13f: 0-0 14f+: 0-0
Track: LH: 0-8 RH: 0-5 Tight: 0-4 Gall: 0-3
Aids: Bl: 0-1 Vi: 0-18 Tstrap: 0-0
Best Rating: 52 6/01 Haml 6f5y gd-fm

Best Ever

92(84) (30)**50**
4-y-o ch g Rock City-Better Still (IRE) (Glenstal (USA))
M W Easterby Mrs Jean Turpin

Placings:0003252000/000250-0305 **(4481)**
2001: 6^{0}SD, 7^{3}F, 10^{0}G, 8^{5}F

	Starts	1st	2nd	3rd	Win & Pl
Career Total (Turf)	19	0	3	2	5839
Career Total (AW)	1	0	0	0	

Going (Turf): Sf: 0-4 GS: 0-2 Gd: 0-4 GF: 0-5 Fm: 0-4
Distance: 5f/6f: 0-4 7f-8f: 0-11 9f-13f: 0-5 14f+: 0-0
Track: LH: 0-8 RH: 0-4 Tight: 0-7 Gall: 0-2
Aids: Bl: 0-0 Vi: 0-0 Tstrap: 0-0
Best Rating: 43 9/01 Muss 1m firm

Still a maiden, he has nevertheless shown some ability over distances up to a mile. Has failed to stay when tried beyond eight furlongs.

Best Guest (IRE)

93 **25**
3-y-o b c Barathea (IRE)-Common Rumpus (IRE) (Common Grounds)
G G Margarson John Guest

Placings:000-000000 **(5383)**
2001: 8^{0}F, 8^{0}G, 9^{0}GF, 8^{0}G, 9^{0}GF, 13^{0}S

	Starts	1st	2nd	3rd	Win & Pl
Career Total (Turf)	9	0	0	0	

Going (Turf): Sf: 0-2 GS: 0-1 Gd: 0-3 GF: 0-2 Fm: 0-1
Distance: 5f/6f: 0-1 7f-8f: 0-2 9f-13f: 0-5 14f+: 0-1
Track: LH: 0-8 RH: 0-0 Tight: 0-3 Gall: 0-2
Aids: Bl: 0-0 Vi: 0-0 Tstrap: 0-0
Best Rating: 41 5/01 Newc 1m firm

Best Lead

96 **87**
2-y-o b c Distant Relative-Bestemor (Selkirk (USA))
G A Butler M Berger

Placings:3214160 **(5150)**
2001: 5^{3}GF, 5^{2}GF, 5^{1}GF, 5^{4}S, 5^{1}GF, 5^{6}G, 6^{0}G

	Starts	1st	2nd	3rd	Win & Pl
Career Total (Turf)	7	2	1	1	9490

86	8/01	Chep	5f16y	D H	G-F	£3471
80	8/01	Leic	5f2y	D	G-F	£3705

Total win prize-money £7176

Going (Turf): Sf: 0-1 GS: 0-0 Gd: 0-2 **GF: 2-4** Fm: 0-0
Distance: **5f/6f: 2-7** 7f-8f: 0-0 9f-13f: 0-0 14f+: 0-0
Track: LH: 0-0 RH: 0-1 Tight: 0-0 Gall: 0-1
Aids: Bl: 0-0 Vi: 0-0 Tstrap: 0-0
Best Rating: 87 9/01 Ayr 5f good

Twice a winner over five furlongs, he appreciates fast ground and did well to defy top weight in a Chepstow nursery. Not disgraced in a listed race next time.

Best Of The Bests (IRE)

106 (121)**120**
4-y-o ch h Machiavellian (USA)-Sueboog (IRE) (Darshaan)
Saeed Bin Suroor Godolphin

Placings:312/344133-100 **(5389)**
2001: 9^{1}FT, 10^{0}FT, 10^{0}GS

	Starts	1st	2nd	3rd	Win & Pl
Career Total (Turf)	10	2	1	4	237888
Career Total (AW)	2	1	0	0	38251

121	2/01	Ndas	1m1f		FST	£38251
115	8/00	Deau	1m2f		G-F	£28818
112	8/99	Sand	7f16y	A	GD	£16075

Total win prize-money £83144

Going (Turf): Sf: 0-1 GS: 0-2 **Gd: 1-4 GF: 1-2** Fm: 0-1
Distance: 5f/6f: 0-0 7f-8f: 1-4 **9f-13f: 2-8** 14f+: 0-0
Track: LH: 0-3 **RH: 2-5** Tight: 0-1 Gall: 0-3
Aids: Bl: 0-0 Vi: 0-0 Tstrap: 0-1
Best Rating: 121 2/01 Ndas 1m1f fast

Out of a mare that finished fourth in the Oaks, he sprang a 20-1 surprise when winning the Solario Stakes in 1999 when trained by Clive Brittain. Snapped up by Godolphin, he finished third in the 2000 Dante Stakes on his first run for them and fourth in the Derby over a trip too far for. Dropped back to ten furlongs to win a Group Two in France in August 2000 and finished third in both the Irish Champion Stakes and the QE II. Won on his dirt debut in Dubai at the start of this season, but ran too freely in the Dubai World Cup. Not seen again until disappointing in the Champion Stakes on easy ground. Suited by ten furlongs and a sound surface.

Best Port (IRE)

108(95) (34)**51**
5-y-o b g Be My Guest (USA)-Portree (Slip Anchor)
J Parkes W A Sellers

Placings:00/0006006/**003**4300212005-43131612 **(5033)**
2001: 12^{4}S, 14^{3}F, 14^{1}F, 12^{3}GF, 16^{1}GF, 16^{6}GF, 16^{1}GF, 16^{2}GF

	Starts	1st	2nd	3rd	Win & Pl
Career Total (Turf)	26	4	3	4	17211
Career Total (AW)	4	0	0	0	0

50	8/01	Rdcr	2m4y	E(0-75)H	G-F	£3234
44	7/01	Bevl	2m35y	E(0-70)H	G-F	£4602
40	6/01	Nott	1m6f15y	E(0-70)H	FRM	£3206
35	8/00	Bevl	2m35y	F(0-60)H	G-F	£2296

Total win prize-money £13338

Going (Turf): Sf: 0-4 GS: 0-4 Gd: 0-2 **GF: 3-11** Fm: 1-5
Distance: 5f/6f: 0-0 7f-8f: 0-3 9f-13f: 0-10 **14f+: 4-17**
Track: LH: 2-17 RH: 2-11 **Tight: 3-18** Gall: 0-1
Aids: Bl: 0-0 Vi: 0-0 Tstrap: 0-0
Best Rating: 51 9/01 Muss 2m gd-fm

He is quite an effective fast-ground staying handicapper at a modest level and won three times in the summer at Nottingham, Beverley and Redcar.

Bestam

101 **91+**
2-y-o b c Selkirk (USA)-Showery (Rainbow Quest (USA))
J L Dunlop Hamdan Al Maktoum

Placings:4113 **(5606)**
2001: 7^{4}GF, 8^{1}G, 8^{1}GS, 10^{3}GS

	Starts	1st	2nd	3rd	Win & Pl
Career Total (Turf)	4	2	0	1	11889

91	10/01	NmkR	1m	D(0-95)	G-S	£5122
84	8/01	NmkJ	1m	D	GD	£4104

Total win prize-money £9227

Going (Turf): Sf: 0-0 **GS: 1-2 Gd: 1-1** GF: 0-1 Fm: 0-0
Distance: 5f/6f: 0-0 **7f-8f: 2-3** 9f-13f: 0-1 14f+: 0-0
Track: LH: 0-0 RH: 0-1 Tight: 0-0 Gall: 0-1
Aids: Bl: 0-0 Vi: 0-0 Tstrap: 0-0
Best Rating: 91 10/01 NmkR 1m gd-sft

By Selkirk and bought for 200,000 guineas, he landed a fair maiden at Newmarket and added to that in a nursery on the Rowley Mile in October. Appeared not to stay in a ten-furlong Listed race at the back-end.

Bestmortgage Uk

46(63)
4-y-o b f Emperor Jones (USA)-Lady Lustre (On Your Mark)
T T Clement The Mortgage Shop

Placings:000 **(3381)**
2001: 8^{0}SW, 5^{0}SD, 8^{0}GF

	Starts	1st	2nd	3rd	Win & Pl
Career Total (Turf)	1	0	0	0	
Career Total (AW)	2	0	0	0	

Going (Turf): Sf: 0-0 GS: 0-0 Gd: 0-0 GF: 0-1 Fm: 0-0
Distance: 5f/6f: 0-1 7f-8f: 0-1 9f-13f: 0-1 14f+: 0-0
Track: LH: 0-1 RH: 0-1 Tight: 0-0 Gall: 0-0
Aids: Bl: 0-0 Vi: 0-0 Tstrap: 0-0

Bethania

99 **69**
3-y-o gr f Mark Of Esteem (IRE)-Anneli Rose (Superlative)
Mrs A J Perrett Usk Valley Stud

Placings:0-530365 (5670)
2001: 7^{5}GF, 7^{3}GF, 9^{0}GF, 8^{3}GF, 9^{6}GS, 8^{5}HY

	Starts	1st	2nd	3rd	Win & Pl
Career Total (Turf)	7	0	0	2	1281

Going (Turf): Sf: 0-2 GS: 0-1 Gd: 0-0 GF: 0-4 Fm: 0-0
Distance: 5f/6f: 0-1 7f-8f: 0-2 9f-13f: 0-4 14f+: 0-0
Track : LH: 0-1 RH: 0-5 Tight: 0-4 Gall: 0-0
Aids: Bl: 0-0 Vi: 0-0 Tstrap: 0-0
Best Rating: 70 5/01 Gdwd 7f gd-fm

Bethesda

104 **82**
4-y-o gr f Distant Relative-Anneli Rose (Superlative)
Mrs A J Perrett Usk Valley Stud

Placings:265/645-6110 (4780)
2001: 7^{6}GF, 6^{1}GF, 5^{1}F, 6^{0}G

	Starts	1st	2nd	3rd	Win & Pl
Career Total (Turf)	10	2	1	0	9302

82	9/01	Bath	5f161y	D(0-80)H	FRM	£4004
69	8/01	Sals	6f	E(0-70)H	G-F	£3500

Total win prize-money £7504

Going (Turf): Sf: 0-2 GS: 0-3 Gd: 0-2 **GF: 1-2 Fm: 1-1**
Distance: **5f/6f: 2-7** 7f-8f: 0-3 9f-13f: 0-0 14f+: 0-0
Track : **LH: 1-2** RH: 0-1 Tight: 0-0 **Gall: 1-2**
Aids: **Bl: 2-3** Vi: 0-0 Tstrap: 0-1
Best Rating: 82 9/01 Bath 5f161y firm

Betsmart Girl

(83) (52)**52**
2-y-o b f Danzig Connection (USA)-Mira Lady (Henbit (USA))
M Dods The Newcastle Racing C Lub

Placings:6006225500 (5049)
2001: 5^{6}GF, 6^{0}F, 6^{0}SD, 6^{6}G, 7^{2}SD, 7^{2}GF, 7^{5}GF, 7^{5}SD, 7^{0}HY, 7^{0}SD

	Starts	1st	2nd	3rd	Win & Pl
Career Total (Turf)	6	0	1	0	692
Career Total (AW)	4	0	1	0	538

Going (Turf): Sf: 0-1 GS: 0-0 Gd: 0-1 GF: 0-3 Fm: 0-1
Distance: 5f/6f: 0-4 7f-8f: 0-6 9f-13f: 0-0 14f+: 0-0
Track : LH: 0-5 RH: 0-1 Tight: 0-0 Gall: 0-0
Aids: Bl: 0-0 Vi: 0-0 Tstrap: 0-10
Best Rating: 52 7/01 Bevl 7f100y gd-fm

Better Moment (IRE)

94(95) (42)**47**
4-y-o b g Turtle Island (IRE)-Snoozeandyoulose (IRE) (Scenic)
John Berry (J G Fitzgerald 5/5) P M Harley

Placings:404-226 (3454)
2001: 10^{2}S, 12^{2}SD, 14^{6}GF

	Starts	1st	2nd	3rd	Win & Pl
Career Total (Turf)	5	0	1	0	1366
Career Total (AW)	1	0	1	0	550

Going (Turf): Sf: 0-1 GS: 0-0 Gd: 0-2 GF: 0-2 Fm: 0-0
Distance: 5f/6f: 0-0 7f-8f: 0-0 9f-13f: 0-5 14f+: 0-1
Track : LH: 0-4 RH: 0-2 Tight: 0-1 Gall: 0-0
Aids: Bl: 0-3 Vi: 0-0 Tstrap: 0-0
Best Rating: 42 7/01 Sthl 1m4f stand

Better Off

(103) (75)**50**
3-y-o ch g Bettergeton-Miami Pride (Miami Springs)
Mrs N Macauley Classic Glass & Dishwashing Systems Ltd

Placings:550131-2122432031350050 (5352)
2001: 6^{2}SD, 7^{1}SD, 7^{2}SD, 6^{2}SD, 7^{4}SD, 7^{3}SD, 7^{2}SD, 8^{0}SD, 7^{3}SD, 6^{1}SW, 6^{3}SD, 6^{5}S, 6^{0}SD, 7^{0}G, 7^{5}SD, 6^{0}SD

	Starts	1st	2nd	3rd	Win & Pl
Career Total (Turf)	2	0	0	0	0
Career Total (AW)	20	4	4	4	20199

75	4/01	Sthl	7f	D(0-80)H	SLW	£3825
71	1/01	Wolv	7f	D(0-85)H	STD	£3484
65	12/00	Sthl	6f	E(0-85)	STD	£2695
56	11/00	Sthl	6f	G	STD	£1869

Total win prize-money £11873

Going (Turf): Sf: 0-1 GS: 0-0 Gd: 0-1 GF: 0-0 Fm: 0-0
Distance: **5f/6f: 3-12** 7f-8f: 1-10 9f-13f: 0-0 14f+: 0-0
Track : **LH: 4-20** RH: 0-0 **Tight: 1-8** Gall: 0-0
Aids: Bl: 0-0 Vi: 0-0 Tstrap: 0-0
Best Rating: 75 4/01 Sthl 6f slow

Better Pal

89(70) (40)**71**
2-y-o ch c Prince Sabo-Rattle Along (Tap On Wood)
W Jarvis Miss E G Macgregor

Placings:505 (5689)
2001: 6^{5}G, 6^{0}SD, 6^{5}S

	Starts	1st	2nd	3rd	Win & Pl
Career Total (Turf)	2	0	0	0	0
Career Total (AW)	1	0	0	0	0

Going (Turf): Sf: 0-1 GS: 0-0 Gd: 0-1 GF: 0-0 Fm: 0-0
Distance: 5f/6f: 0-2 7f-8f: 0-1 9f-13f: 0-0 14f+: 0-0
Track : LH: 0-1 RH: 0-0 Tight: 0-1 Gall: 0-0
Aids: Bl: 0-0 Vi: 0-0 Tstrap: 0-0
Best Rating: 71 9/01 Nott 6f15y good

Has shown promise in all three starts in maidens so far, and can now run in handicaps.

Bettergetgone

(70) (15)**31**
2-y-o b f Bettergeton-Impromptu Melody (IRE) (Mac's Imp (USA))
Mrs N Macauley Derek Boulton

Placings:000000 (5345)
2001: 5^{0}SD, 6^{0}SD, 5^{0}F, 6^{0}GF, 6^{0}HY, 6^{0}SD

	Starts	1st	2nd	3rd	Win & Pl
Career Total (Turf)	3	0	0	0	
Career Total (AW)	3	0	0	0	

Going (Turf): Sf: 0-1 GS: 0-0 Gd: 0-0 GF: 0-1 Fm: 0-1
Distance: 5f/6f: 0-5 7f-8f: 0-1 9f-13f: 0-0 14f+: 0-0
Track : LH: 0-2 RH: 0-0 Tight: 0-0 Gall: 0-0
Aids: Bl: 0-0 Vi: 0-1 Tstrap: 0-0
Best Rating: 31 6/01 Nott 5f13y firm

Has shown little ability in all starts to date.

Betterthedeviluno

79 **62**
2-y-o b c Hector Protector (USA)-Aquaglow (Caerleon (USA))
E J O'Neill Mrs Melissa O'Neill

Placings:3 (2702)
2001: 6^{3}F

	Starts	1st	2nd	3rd	Win & Pl
Career Total (Turf)	1	0	0	1	320

Going (Turf): Sf: 0-0 GS: 0-0 Gd: 0-0 GF: 0-0 Fm: 0-1
Distance: 5f/6f: 0-0 7f-8f: 0-1 9f-13f: 0-0 14f+: 0-0
Track : LH: 0-1 RH: 0-0 Tight: 0-0 Gall: 0-0
Aids: Bl: 0-0 Vi: 0-0 Tstrap: 0-0
Best Rating: 62 7/01 Brig 6f209y firm

Bettina Blue (IRE)

(89) (36)**40**
4-y-o b/br f Paris House-Born To Fly (IRE) (Last Tycoon)
R Ingram Epsom Sporting Proposals Ltd

Placings:5065/660000604-0630 (0271)
2001: 6^{0}SD, 8^{6}SD, 7^{3}SW, 7^{0}SW

	Starts	1st	2nd	3rd	Win & Pl
Career Total (Turf)	11	0	0	0	0
Career Total (AW)	6	0	0	1	464

Going (Turf): Sf: 0-2 GS: 0-1 Gd: 0-2 GF: 0-5 Fm: 0-1
Distance: 5f/6f: 0-11 7f-8f: 0-5 9f-13f: 0-1 14f+: 0-0
Track : LH: 0-8 RH: 0-2 Tight: 0-8 Gall: 0-1
Aids: Bl: 0-0 Vi: 0-0 Tstrap: 0-0
Best Rating: 36 1/01 Ling 7f slow

Betty Bathwick (IRE)

99(84) (25)**52**
4-y-o b f Common Grounds-Tynaghmile (IRE) (Lyphard's Special (USA))
J Akehurst R P Tullett

Placings:0002/001000-6000 (2879)
2001: 5^{6}GS, 7^{0}G, 5^{0}G, 6^{0}GF

	Starts	1st	2nd	3rd	Win & Pl
Career Total (Turf)	12	1	1	0	2925
Career Total (AW)	2	0	0	0	

50	10/00	Catt	5f212y	F	SFT	£2310

Total win prize-money £2310

Going (Turf): Sf: 1-2 GS: 0-2 Gd: 0-5 GF: 0-2 Fm: 0-1
Distance: **5f/6f: 1-7** 7f-8f: 0-7 9f-13f: 0-0 14f+: 0-0
Track : **LH: 1-7** RH: 0-1 **Tight: 1-3** Gall: 0-2
Aids: Bl: 0-0 Vi: 0-0 Tstrap: 0-0
Best Rating: 47 5/01 Brig 5f213y gd-sft

She caused a 50/1 surprise in a soft-ground Catterick maiden at the end of last season, but her form otherwise has been mainly very moderate.

Bettys Pride

95 **84**
2-y-o b f Lion Cavern (USA)-Final Verdict (IRE) (Law Society (USA))
A Berry Betty's Brigade

Placings:052035 (5378)
2001: 5^{0}G, 5^{5}GS, 5^{2}GF, 6^{0}G, 5^{3}GF, 5^{5}S

	Starts	1st	2nd	3rd	Win & Pl
Career Total (Turf)	6	0	1	1	1629

Going (Turf): Sf: 0-1 GS: 0-1 Gd: 0-2 GF: 0-2 Fm: 0-0
Distance: 5f/6f: 0-6 7f-8f: 0-0 9f-13f: 0-0 14f+: 0-0
Track : LH: 0-0 RH: 0-0 Tight: 0-0 Gall: 0-0
Aids: Bl: 0-0 Vi: 0-0 Tstrap: 0-0
Best Rating: 84 9/01 Muss 5f gd-fm

Has shown varied ability in all starts to date, with her best effort coming in a Ripon maiden.

Bevel Blue

93 **41**
3-y-o b g Beveled (USA)-Blue Angel (Lord Gayle (USA))
G B Balding Rocaro Partnership

Placings:000-0000 (4677)
2001: 5^{0}GF, 5^{0}GF, 6^{0}S, 7^{0}G

	Starts	1st	2nd	3rd	Win & Pl
Career Total (Turf)	7	0	0	0	

Going (Turf): Sf: 0-2 GS: 0-0 Gd: 0-2 GF: 0-2 Fm: 0-0
Distance: 5f/6f: 0-4 7f-8f: 0-2 9f-13f: 0-0 14f+: 0-0
Track : LH: 0-0 RH: 0-0 Tight: 0-0 Gall: 0-0
Aids: Bl: 0-0 Vi: 0-0 Tstrap: 0-0
Best Rating: 41 7/01 Sand 5f6y gd-fm

Beveled Leggings

64 **17**

2-y-o b f Beveled (USA)-Nahla (Wassl)
Miss Jacqueline S Doyle The Safe Six

Placings:00 **(4072)**
2001: 5^0GF, 5^0G

	Starts	1st	2nd	3rd	Win & Pl
Career Total (Turf)	2	0	0	0	

Going (Turf): Sf: 0-0 GS: 0-0 Gd: 0-1 GF: 0-1 Fm: 0-0
Distance: 5f/6f: 0-2 7f-8f: 0-0 9f-13f: 0-0 14f+: 0-0
Track : LH: 0-2 RH: 0-0 Tight: 0-0 Gall: 0-2
Aids: Bl: 0-0 Vi: 0-0 Tstrap: 0-0
Best Rating: 17 8/01 Bath 5f11y good

Beverley Macca

(104) (67)**70**

3-y-o ch f Piccolo-Kangra Valley (Indian Ridge)
A Berry Mrs Margaret Forsyth

Placings:221140-**0021**203000 **(4785)**
2001: 5^0SW, 6^0SD, 5^2SD, 5^1SD, 5^2SD, 5^0S, 5^3F, 5^0G, 5^0G, 5^0G

	Starts	1st	2nd	3rd	Win & Pl
Career Total (Turf)	9	1	1	1	3771
Career Total (AW)	7	2	3	0	8297

67 3/01 Ling 5f D(0-85)H STD £3737
70 5/00 Rdcr 5f F G-F £2299
64 5/00 Wolv 5f F STD £2240
Total win prize-money £8278

Going (Turf): Sf: 0-2 GS: 0-1 Gd: 0-4 **GF: 1-1** Fm: 0-1
Distance: **5f/6f: 3-16** 7f-8f: 0-0 9f-13f: 0-0 14f+: 0-0
Track : **LH: 2-7** RH: 0-1 **Tight: 2-5** Gall: 0-2
Aids: Bl: 0-0 Vi: 0-0 Tstrap: 0-0
Best Rating: 70 5/01 Brig 5f59y firm

Out of a speedily-bred dam, shows her best form when either able to make the running, or race close to the pace. She is suited by five furlongs and seems best on sand.

Beyond Calculation (USA)

105(99) (58)**79**

7-y-o ch g Geiger Counter (USA)-Placer Queen (Habitat)
J M Bradley E A Hayward

Placings:4/4035**2**10/0634050000/00505621321110400 0/515016442000**06-004**31004200023106O **(5097)**
2001: 6^0SD, 6^0SD, 6^4SD, 5^3F, 5^1GF, 5^0GS, 5^0GF, 5^4GF, 5^2G, 5^0GS, 5^0GF, 5^0GF, 5^2G, 5^3GF, 6^1GF, 5^0G, 5^6G, 6^0GS

	Starts	1st	2nd	3rd	Win & Pl
Career Total (Turf)	62	9	5	5	53363
Career Total (AW)	6	0	1	0	976

79 9/01 Rdcr 6f D(0-85)H G-F £6851
70 6/01 Ches 5f16y D(0-85)H G-F £4465
68 6/00 Wind 6f D(0-80)H GD £4218
66 5/00 Nott 6f15y E(0-65) G-S £3164
73 8/99 Brig 5f213y C(0-90)H FRM £7002
64 7/99 Thsk 6f D(0-80)H FRM £4040
60 7/99 Bath 5f161y D(0-80)H FRM £3818
52 6/99 Wind 6f D(0-80)H G-F £3792
74 10/97 Rdcr 6f D G-F £3525
Total win prize-money £40880

Going (Turf): Sf: 0-3 GS: 1-12 Gd: 1-15 **GF: 4-25** Fm: 3-7
Distance: **5f/6f: 8-58** 7f-8f: 1-10 9f-13f: 0-0 14f+: 0-0
Track : **LH: 3-25** RH: 2-8 Tight: 1-7 **Gall: 3-17**
Aids: Bl: 0-0 Vi: 0-0 Tstrap: 0-0
Best Rating: 79 9/01 Rdcr 6f gd-fm

He has won over five furlongs, but looks better over six. Suited by fast ground and is another success story for the Bradley yard.

Beyond The Clouds (IRE)

109 (28)**84**

5-y-o b g Midhish-Tongabezi (IRE) (Shernazar)
J S Wainwright J S Wainwright

Placings:06**0**03065/00261414210-0113400045000 **(5685)**
2001: 5^0S, 5^1G, 5^1GF, 5^3GF, 5^4GS, 5^0GF, 8^0G, 5^0G, 5^4G, 5^5GS, 5^0S, 5^0HY, 5^0S

	Starts	1st	2nd	3rd	Win & Pl
Career Total (Turf)	31	5	2	2	54724
Career Total (AW)	1	0	0	0	

84 6/01 Wind 5f10y B(0-105)H G-F £29000
79 5/01 Bevl 5f E(0-70)H GD £6422
67 8/00 Bevl 5f E(0-75)H G-F £6344
60 7/00 Wind 5f10y E(0-70)H GD £2870
51 6/00 Haml 5f4y F(0-60)H GD £3818
Total win prize-money £48455

Going (Turf): Sf: 0-7 GS: 0-3 **Gd: 3-7** GF: 2-14 Fm: 0-0
Distance: **5f/6f: 5-28** 7f-8f: 0-4 9f-13f: 0-0 14f+: 0-0
Track : LH: 0-4 **RH: 2-7** Tight: 0-1 **Gall: 2-7**
Aids: Bl: 0-0 Vi: 0-5 Tstrap: 0-0
Best Rating: 84 6/01 Wind 5f10y gd-fm

Useful sprinter at the minimum trip and is suited by fast ground. He won at Beverley and Windsor in the spring, but has since found life tougher off a higher mark.

Bezwell Prince

79 **71**

2-y-o ch g Bluegrass Prince (IRE)-Money Supply (Brigadier Gerard)
N Tinkler Bezwell Fixings Limited

Placings:064 **(5088)**
2001: 7^0G, 7^6HY, 6^4GS

	Starts	1st	2nd	3rd	Win & Pl
Career Total (Turf)	3	0	0	0	0

Going (Turf): Sf: 0-1 GS: 0-1 Gd: 0-1 GF: 0-0 Fm: 0-0
Distance: 5f/6f: 0-1 7f-8f: 0-2 9f-13f: 0-0 14f+: 0-0
Track : LH: 0-2 RH: 0-0 Tight: 0-1 Gall: 0-0
Aids: Bl: 0-0 Vi: 0-0 Tstrap: 0-0
Best Rating: 71 10/01 Newc 6f gd-sft

Bezwell's Guest (IRE)

84 **57**

2-y-o ch c Be My Guest (USA)-Fine Project (IRE) (Project Manager)
R M Beckett Bezwell Fixings Limited

Placings:30 **(1634)**
2001: 5^3G, 5^0F

	Starts	1st	2nd	3rd	Win & Pl
Career Total (Turf)	2	0	0	1	470

Going (Turf): Sf: 0-0 GS: 0-0 Gd: 0-1 GF: 0-0 Fm: 0-1
Distance: 5f/6f: 0-2 7f-8f: 0-0 9f-13f: 0-0 14f+: 0-0
Track : LH: 0-0 RH: 0-0 Tight: 0-0 Gall: 0-0
Aids: Bl: 0-0 Vi: 0-0 Tstrap: 0-0
Best Rating: 57 5/01 Leic 5f2y firm

Bezza (IRE)

87 **52**

3-y-o ch f Dob Dack (USA)-Lady Lord (IRE) (Coquelin (USA))
M H Tompkins Mrs Beryl Lockey

Placings:00-6000 **(4483)**
2001: 9^6GF, 10^0GF, 10^0G, 14^0S

	Starts	1st	2nd	3rd	Win & Pl
Career Total (Turf)	6	0	0	0	0

Going (Turf): Sf: 0-3 GS: 0-0 Gd: 0-1 GF: 0-2 Fm: 0-0
Distance: 5f/6f: 0-0 7f-8f: 0-1 9f-13f: 0-4 14f+: 0-1
Track : LH: 0-2 RH: 0-2 Tight: 0-2 Gall: 0-1
Aids: Bl: 0-1 Vi: 0-0 Tstrap: 0-0
Best Rating: 45 5/01 Bevl 1m1f207y gd-fm

Bhutan (IRE)

104 **64**

6-y-o b g Polish Patriot (USA)-Bustinetta (Bustino)
Mrs M Reveley P D Savill

Placings:050000/0115361/33133300144/160012423-53P20504264 **(5152)**
2001: 14^5GS, 12^3GF, 14^PF, 16^2GF, 12^0GF, 12^5G, 12^0GF, 15^4GF, 12^2F, 15^6GF, 14^4G

	Starts	1st	2nd	3rd	Win & Pl
Career Total (Turf)	44	7	4	8	43893

68 8/00 Catt 1m5f175yE(0-70)H G-F £3656
68 5/00 Haml 1m5f9y E(0-70)H G-F £3818
59 10/99 Catt 1m5f175yF(0-60) GD £2213
67 7/99 Newc 1m4f93y E(0-70)H FRM £3230
71 10/98 Curr 1m (0-90)H SFT £8250
71 7/98 Klny 1m3f (0-75)H GD £3437
71 6/98 Cork 1m1f (0-60)H YLD £4110
Total win prize-money £28716

Going (Turf): Sf: 1-4 GS: 0-3 **Gd: 2-8 GF: 2-19** Fm: 1-5
Distance: 5f/6f: 0-3 7f-8f: 1-4 9f-13f: 3-23 14f+: 3-14
Track : **LH: 4-21** RH: 2-18 **Tight: 3-16** Gall: 2-5
Aids: Bl: 0-0 Vi: 0-1 Tstrap: 0-0
Best Rating: 73 6/01 Muss 1m4f good

Successful both over hurdles and on the Flat in recent seasons, is an effective sort in modest company over a marathon trip. Acts on fast ground.

Bianchi (USA)

100 **70**

3-y-o b f Gulch (USA)-Northern Trick (USA) (Northern Dancer)
P F I Cole Mrs Belinda Strudwick

Placings:4-4223445 **(4426)**
2001: 8^4G, 8^4G, 10^2GF, 12^3GF, 10^4GF, 11^4GF, 10^5GF

	Starts	1st	2nd	3rd	Win & Pl
Career Total (Turf)	8	0	2	1	5617

Going (Turf): Sf: 0-0 GS: 0-0 Gd: 0-2 GF: 0-6 Fm: 0-0
Distance: 5f/6f: 0-1 7f-8f: 0-0 9f-13f: 0-7 14f+: 0-0
Track : LH: 0-4 RH: 0-2 Tight: 0-4 Gall: 0-0
Aids: Bl: 0-0 Vi: 0-0 Tstrap: 0-0
Best Rating: 75 6/01 Ches 1m4f66y gd-fm

Bible Box (IRE)

103 **75**

3-y-o b f Bin Ajwaad (IRE)-Addie Pray (IRE) (Great Commotion (USA))
Mrs Lydia Pearce M Sinclair

Placings:0-2401340 **(5275)**
2001: 8^2GS, 8^4G, 8^0GF, 7^1GF, 7^3GS, 8^4GF, 8^0GS

	Starts	1st	2nd	3rd	Win & Pl
Career Total (Turf)	8	1	1	1	6856

75 7/01 Yarm 7f3y E(0-70)H G-F £4394
Total win prize-money £4394

Going (Turf): Sf: 0-0 GS: 0-3 Gd: 0-1 **GF: 1-4** Fm: 0-0
Distance: 5f/6f: 0-1 **7f-8f: 1-3** 9f-13f: 0-4 14f+: 0-0
Track : LH: 0-1 RH: 0-2 Tight: 0-1 Gall: 0-0
Aids: Bl: 0-0 Vi: 0-0 Tstrap: 0-0
Best Rating: 75 7/01 Yarm 7f3y gd-fm

Lightly-raced filly. Chased home the subsequent Irish Oaks winner Lailani on her seasonal debut, but had disappointed before landing a gamble when dropped back to seven furlongs at Yarmouth. Has won on a fast surface, handles easier ground.

Bid For Fame (USA)

106 **82**

4-y-o b/br c Quest For Fame-Shroud (USA) (Vaguely Noble)
T G Mills T G Mills

Placings:530130-00523205060 **(4983)**
2001: 12^{0}S, 14^{0}GF, 10^{5}GF, 12^{2}GF, 12^{3}GF, 12^{2}GF, 12^{0}GF, 13^{5}GF, 12^{0}G, 12^{6}G, 12^{0}G

	Starts	1st	2nd	3rd	Win & Pl
Career Total (Turf)	17	1	2	3	11838
82 6/00 Pont 1m4f8y D				G-F	£2860

Total win prize-money £2860

Going (Turf): Sf: 0-1 GS: 0-3 Gd: 0-4 **GF: 1-9** Fm: 0-0
Distance: 5f/6f: 0-0 7f-8f: 0-0 **9f-13f: 1-13** 14f+: 0-4
Track : **LH: 1-5** RH: 0-12 Tight: 0-4 Gall: 0-9
Aids: Bl: 0-1 Vi: 0-0 Tstrap: 0-0
Best Rating: 84 6/01 NmkJ 1m4f gd-fm

Running well in mile and a half handicaps in the summer, although he does not find a great deal in the finish.

Bid Me Welcome

99 **58**

5-y-o b g Alzao (USA)-Blushing Barada (USA) (Blushing Groom (FR))
Mrs J R Ramsden Mrs J R Ramsden

Placings:4/6015540332151/005231520630-00000600 **(3281)**
2001: 12^{0}GS, 12^{0}S, 13^{0}GF, 17^{0}F, 14^{0}F, 14^{8}GF, 16^{0}GF, 16^{0}F

	Starts	1st	2nd	3rd	Win & Pl
Career Total (Turf)	34	4	3	4	32411
82 7/00 Newb 2m D(0-85)H				G-F	£4342
81 10/99 NmkJ 1m6f175yC(0-95)H				GD	£7960
75 8/99 Nott 1m6f15y D(0-80)H				G-F	£7522
73 5/99 Wwck 1m4f115yD(0-80)H				GD	£4077

Total win prize-money £23903

Going (Turf): Sf: 0-2 GS: 0-5 **Gd: 2-9 GF: 2-14** Fm: 0-4
Distance: 5f/6f: 0-1 7f-8f: 0-0 9f-13f: 1-11 **14f+: 3-22**
Track : **LH: 3-20** RH: 1-12 Tight: 0-5 **Gall: 1-13**
Aids: Bl: 0-0 Vi: 0-1 Tstrap: 0-0
Best Rating: 64 5/01 York 1m5f194y gd-fm

Bid Spotter (IRE)

(81) (46)**74**

2-y-o b c Eagle Eyed (USA)-Bebe Auction (IRE) (Auction Ring (USA))
R Hannon Seth Melhado

Placings:600 **(5420)**
2001: 6^{6}GF, 6^{0}GF, 7^{0}SD

	Starts	1st	2nd	3rd	Win & Pl
Career Total (Turf)	2	0	0	0	0
Career Total (AW)	1	0	0	0	

Going (Turf): Sf: 0-0 GS: 0-0 Gd: 0-0 GF: 0-2 Fm: 0-0
Distance: 5f/6f: 0-2 7f-8f: 0-1 9f-13f: 0-0 14f+: 0-0
Track : LH: 0-1 RH: 0-0 Tight: 0-1 Gall: 0-0
Aids: Bl: 0-0 Vi: 0-0 Tstrap: 0-0
Best Rating: 74 6/01 Wind 6f gd-fm

Biddy

82 **36**

2-y-o b f Rock Hopper-Wanda (Taufan (USA))
M W Easterby E J Mangan

Placings:600 **(5684)**
2001: 7^{6}S, 7^{0}G, 8^{0}S

	Starts	1st	2nd	3rd	Win & Pl
Career Total (Turf)	3	0	0	0	0

Going (Turf): Sf: 0-2 GS: 0-0 Gd: 0-1 GF: 0-0 Fm: 0-0
Distance: 5f/6f: 0-0 7f-8f: 0-3 9f-13f: 0-0 14f+: 0-0
Track : LH: 0-1 RH: 0-0 Tight: 0-1 Gall: 0-0
Aids: Bl: 0-0 Vi: 0-0 Tstrap: 0-0
Best Rating: 36 11/01 Rdcr 7f good

Biff-Em (IRE)

94 **21**

7-y-o ch g Durgam (USA)-Flash The Gold (Ahonoora)
Miss L A Perratt Cree Lodge Racing Club

Placings:031/0060000/303003534140055000/432203000/50304260000506-50050500 **(5287)**
2001: 5^{5}F, 6^{0}GF, 6^{0}G, 5^{5}GF, 6^{0}G, 7^{5}GS, 5^{0}S, 6^{0}HY

	Starts	1st	2nd	3rd	Win & Pl
Career Total (Turf)	59	2	3	8	14194
45 7/98 Haml 6f5y E(0-75)H				FRM	£3647
61 6/96 Haml 5f4y E				GD	£3060

Total win prize-money £6708

Going (Turf): Sf: 0-23 GS: 0-9 **Gd: 1-12** GF: 0-9 **Fm: 1-6**
Distance: 5f/6f: 1-35 7f-8f: 1-21 9f-13f: 0-3 14f+: 0-0
Track : LH: 0-6 RH: 0-7 Tight: 0-7 Gall: 0-3
Aids: Bl: 0-0 Vi: 0-0 Tstrap: 0-0
Best Rating: 29 6/01 Haml 6f5y gd-fm

A very moderate sprint handicapper, he is currently on a very long losing run.

Big Bertha

97 **64**

3-y-o ch f Dancing Spree (USA)-Bertrade (Homeboy)
John Berry Miss Amanda J Rawding

Placings:300 **(5664)**
2001: 8^{3}HY, 6^{0}HY, 8^{0}HY

	Starts	1st	2nd	3rd	Win & Pl
Career Total (Turf)	3	0	0	1	708

Going (Turf): Sf: 0-3 GS: 0-0 Gd: 0-0 GF: 0-0 Fm: 0-0
Distance: 5f/6f: 0-1 7f-8f: 0-0 9f-13f: 0-2 14f+: 0-0
Track : LH: 0-1 RH: 0-1 Tight: 0-1 Gall: 0-0
Aids: Bl: 0-0 Vi: 0-0 Tstrap: 0-0
Best Rating: 64 10/01 Nott 1m54y heavy

Big Bopper (IRE)

93 **75**

2-y-o b c Danehill Dancer (IRE)-Apocalypse (Auction Ring (USA))
R Hannon Speedlith Group

Placings:6040 **(5289)**
2001: 6^{6}GF, 6^{0}GF, 7^{4}S, 7^{0}S

	Starts	1st	2nd	3rd	Win & Pl
Career Total (Turf)	4	0	0	0	350

Going (Turf): Sf: 0-2 GS: 0-0 Gd: 0-0 GF: 0-2 Fm: 0-0
Distance: 5f/6f: 0-2 7f-8f: 0-2 9f-13f: 0-0 14f+: 0-0
Track : LH: 0-1 RH: 0-0 Tight: 0-1 Gall: 0-0
Aids: Bl: 0-0 Vi: 0-0 Tstrap: 0-0
Best Rating: 75 9/01 Ches 7f2y soft

Unplaced in two starts on firm before a better effort on soft.

Big Future

107 **101**

4-y-o b c Bigstone (IRE)-Star Of The Future (USA) (El Gran Senor (USA))
Mrs A J Perrett K Abdulla

Placings:141533010-0230020 **(5142)**
2001: 7^{0}G, 8^{2}GF, 8^{3}G, 8^{0}G, 7^{0}G, 8^{2}GS, 9^{0}G

	Starts	1st	2nd	3rd	Win & Pl
Career Total (Turf)	16	3	2	3	57609
95 10/00 York 6f214y B(0-105)H				SFT	£10377
88 7/00 Ling 7f D(0-85)H				G-F	£4251
80 4/00 Kemp 7f D				SFT	£3913

Total win prize-money £18541

Going (Turf): Sf: 2-3 GS: 0-2 Gd: 0-7 GF: 1-4 Fm: 0-0
Distance: 5f/6f: 0-0 **7f-8f: 3-14** 9f-13f: 0-2 14f+: 0-0
Track : LH: 1-2 RH: 1-6 Tight: 0-0 **Gall: 2-3**
Aids: Bl: 0-0 Vi: 0-0 Tstrap: 0-0
Best Rating: 101 6/01 Asct 1m gd-fm

Useful handicapper who handles most ground. Far from disgraced in his outings this season, notably when second in the Hunt Cup, and well up to winning more decent handicaps. Stays a mile.

Big Issue

84(75) (32)**50**

4-y-o b g First Trump-Hollow Heart (Wolver Hollow)
A Bailey Willie McKay

Placings:0010/0-6 **(1079)**
2001: 7^{6}S

	Starts	1st	2nd	3rd	Win & Pl
Career Total (Turf)	5	1	0	0	2164
Career Total (AW)	1	0	0	0	
10/99 Bath 5f161y G				SFT	£2164

Total win prize-money £2164

Going (Turf): Sf: 1-3 GS: 0-1 Gd: 0-0 GF: 0-1 Fm: 0-0
Distance: **5f/6f: 1-2** 7f-8f: 0-4 9f-13f: 0-0 14f+: 0-0
Track : **LH: 1-3** RH: 0-0 Tight: 0-1 **Gall: 1-2**
Aids: Bl: 0-0 Vi: 0-0 Tstrap: 0-0
Best Rating: 25 5/01 Rdcr 7f soft

Big John (IRE)

97(84) (46)**60**

3-y-o ch c Cadeaux Genereux-India Atlanta (Ahonoora)
Miss S J Wilton (E A L Dunlop 6/6) John Pointon And Sons

Placings:40-0010600 **(3560)**
2001: 7^{0}SD, 6^{0}S, 6^{1}GF, 6^{0}GF, 6^{6}GF, 8^{0}GF, 6^{0}GF

	Starts	1st	2nd	3rd	Win & Pl
Career Total (Turf)	8	1	0	0	2066
Career Total (AW)	1	0	0	0	
60 5/01 Brig 6f209y F				G-F	£1799

Total win prize-money £1799

Going (Turf): Sf: 0-1 GS: 0-0 Gd: 0-0 **GF: 1-7** Fm: 0-0
Distance: 5f/6f: 0-5 **7f-8f: 1-4** 9f-13f: 0-0 14f+: 0-0
Track : **LH: 1-3** RH: 0-0 Tight: 0-2 Gall: 0-0
Aids: Bl: 0-0 Vi: 0-0 Tstrap: 0-0
Best Rating: 60 5/01 Hayd 6f gd-fm

A half-brother to five winners, most notably the smart 6f - 1m juvenile, Ventiquattrofogli, won one of his nine starts in a claimer at Brighton, for new connections. He is proven over six furlongs on a sound surface.

Big Moment

111 **100**

3-y-o ch c Be My Guest (USA)-Petralona (USA) (Alleged (USA))
B W Hills K Abdulla

Placings:2-42211430 **(5387)**
2001: 10^{4}GS, 10^{2}GF, 11^{2}GF, 12^{1}GF, 14^{1}G, 13^{4}G, 14^{3}GS, 18^{0}GS

	Starts	1st	2nd	3rd	Win & Pl
Career Total (Turf)	9	2	3	1	25055
92 8/01 Gdwd 1m6f C(0-95)H				GD	£9813
82 7/01 Donc 1m4f D				G-F	£4329

Total win prize-money £14143

Going (Turf): Sf: 0-0 GS: 0-3 **Gd: 1-3 GF: 1-3** Fm: 0-0
Distance: 5f/6f: 0-0 7f-8f: 0-1 9f-13f: 1-4 14f+: 1-4

Track : LH: 1-4 RH: 1-2 Tight: 1-2 Gall: 1-4
Aids: Bl: 0-0 Vi: 0-0 Tstrap: 0-0
Best Rating: 100 9/01 Donc 1m6f132y gd-sft

He had finished runner-up three times, and had not always looked too keen, before getting off the mark in a modest Doncaster maiden in July 2001 on his first try over 12 furlongs. Stepped up to 14 furlongs successfully at Glorious Goodwood and has lost little in defeat since. Acts on a sound surface.

Big Red

8-y-o ch g Left To Me-Backherorbust (Casino Boy)
Miss K M George Miss K George

Placings:0 **(2810)**
2001: 8^{0}GF

	Starts	1st	2nd	3rd	Win & Pl
Career Total (Turf)	1	0	0	0	

Going (Turf): Sf: 0-0 GS: 0-0 Gd: 0-0 GF: 0-1 Fm: 0-0
Distance: 5f/6f: 0-0 7f-8f: 0-0 9f-13f: 0-1 14f+: 0-0
Track : LH: 0-0 RH: 0-0 Tight: 0-0 Gall: 0-0
Aids: Bl: 0-0 Vi: 0-0 Tstrap: 0-0

Biggles (IRE)

25 **64d**
4-y-o b g Desert Style (IRE)-Excruciating (CAN) (Bold Forbes (USA))
Andrew Turnell Mrs Claire Hollowood

Placings:40-00 **(1082)**
2001: 8^{0}HY, 11^{0}S

	Starts	1st	2nd	3rd	Win & Pl
Career Total (Turf)	4	0	0	0	266

Going (Turf): Sf: 0-2 GS: 0-1 Gd: 0-0 GF: 0-1 Fm: 0-0
Distance: 5f/6f: 0-0 7f-8f: 0-1 9f-13f: 0-3 14f+: 0-0
Track : LH: 0-2 RH: 0-2 Tight: 0-2 Gall: 0-1
Aids: Bl: 0-1 Vi: 0-0 Tstrap: 0-1
Best Rating: 100 9/01 Donc 1m6f132y gd-sft

Bigwig (IRE)

(100) (45)**22**
8-y-o ch g Thatching-Sabaah (USA) (Nureyev (USA))
G L Moore Mrs Elizabeth Kiernan

Placings:0000/461145/5-2 **(0038)**
2001: 16^{2}SD

	Starts	1st	2nd	3rd	Win & Pl
Career Total (Turf)	2	0	0	0	
Career Total (AW)	10	2	1	0	6068

45	3/99	Ling	1m5f	E(0-70)H	STD	£2696
43	2/99	Ling	1m5f	E(0-70)H	STD	£2721

Total win prize-money £5419

Going (Turf): Sf: 0-0 GS: 0-0 Gd: 0-0 GF: 0-2 Fm: 0-0
Distance: 5f/6f: 0-0 7f-8f: 0-0 **9f-13f: 2-7** 14f+: 0-5
Track : **LH: 2-10** RH: 0-1 **Tight: 2-11** Gall: 0-0
Aids: **Bl: 2-8** Vi: 0-0 Tstrap: 0-0
Best Rating: 45 1/01 Ling 2m stand

Bijan (IRE)

103(95) (75d)**69d**
3-y-o b f Mukaddamah (USA)-Alkariyh (USA) (Alydar (USA))
R Hollinshead Geoff Lloyd

Placings:53104430-000006000 **(5593)**
2001: 7^{0}SD, 5^{0}GF, 7^{0}GF, 5^{0}G, 6^{0}G, 6^{6}GF, 6^{0}GS, 5^{0}G, 5^{0}GS

	Starts	1st	2nd	3rd	Win & Pl
Career Total (Turf)	13	1	0	1	4015
Career Total (AW)	4	0	0	1	386

68	6/00	Carl	5f	E	G-F	£2977

Total win prize-money £2977

Going (Turf): Sf: 0-0 GS: 0-3 Gd: 0-3 **GF: 1-6** Fm: 0-0
Distance: **5f/6f: 1-13** 7f-8f: 0-3 9f-13f: 0-1 14f+: 0-0
Track : LH: 0-7 **RH: 1-1** Tight: 0-3 **Gall: 1-2**
Aids: Bl: 0-0 Vi: 0-1 Tstrap: 0-0
Best Rating: 69 9/01 Kemp 6f gd-fm

She got off the mark in a fast-ground maiden at Carlisle on her third start as a juvenile and looks best suited by those conditions.

Bijou Belle

74 **30**
2-y-o b f Bijou D'Inde-Primitive Gift (Primitive Rising (USA))
Mrs A Duffield S Smith & T Shaw

Placings:500 **(5378)**
2001: 6^{5}GF, 5^{0}GF, 5^{0}S

	Starts	1st	2nd	3rd	Win & Pl
Career Total (Turf)	3	0	0	0	

Going (Turf): Sf: 0-1 GS: 0-0 Gd: 0-0 GF: 0-2 Fm: 0-0
Distance: 5f/6f: 0-3 7f-8f: 0-0 9f-13f: 0-0 14f+: 0-0
Track : LH: 0-2 RH: 0-0 Tight: 0-1 Gall: 0-0
Aids: Bl: 0-0 Vi: 0-0 Tstrap: 0-0
Best Rating: 30 9/01 Catt 5f212y gd-fm

Has shown little to date.

Bijou Bounty

48
2-y-o b f Bijou D'Inde-Kick The Boss (Robellino (USA))
A Smith Alfred Smith

Placings:00 **(2397)**
2001: 5^{0}S, 7^{0}GF

	Starts	1st	2nd	3rd	Win & Pl
Career Total (Turf)	2	0	0	0	

Going (Turf): Sf: 0-1 GS: 0-0 Gd: 0-0 GF: 0-1 Fm: 0-0
Distance: 5f/6f: 0-1 7f-8f: 0-1 9f-13f: 0-0 14f+: 0-0
Track : LH: 0-0 RH: 0-0 Tight: 0-0 Gall: 0-0
Aids: Bl: 0-1 Vi: 0-0 Tstrap: 0-0

Bijou Star

89 **71**
2-y-o b c Bijou D'Inde-Starisk (Risk Me (FR))
S Kirk Dan Dare Syndicate

Placings:6500 **(5127)**
2001: 6^{6}GF, 7^{5}GF, 7^{0}GF, 7^{0}HY

	Starts	1st	2nd	3rd	Win & Pl
Career Total (Turf)	4	0	0	0	0

Going (Turf): Sf: 0-1 GS: 0-0 Gd: 0-0 GF: 0-3 Fm: 0-0
Distance: 5f/6f: 0-0 7f-8f: 0-4 9f-13f: 0-0 14f+: 0-0
Track : LH: 0-3 RH: 0-0 Tight: 0-0 Gall: 0-1
Aids: Bl: 0-0 Vi: 0-0 Tstrap: 0-0
Best Rating: 71 8/01 Brig 6f209y gd-fm

Billaddie

105(100) (60)**55**
8-y-o b g Touch Of Groy Young Lady (Young Generation)
R M Flower Richard J Gurr

Placings:0061/34/66033/13330042130622212315/000/0-506300052651040 **(4274)**
2001: 12^{5}SD, 11^{0}SD, 12^{6}S, 10^{3}G, 10^{0}S, 10^{0}G, 12^{0}GF, 9^{5}GF, 10^{2}GF, 12^{6}GF, 11^{5}F, 12^{1}GS, 10^{0}GS, 12^{4}GF, 12^{0}G

	Starts	1st	2nd	3rd	Win & Pl
Career Total (Turf)	33	4	5	3	31105
Career Total (AW)	16	2	0	6	7090

55	8/01	NmkJ	1m4f	D(0-80)H	G-S	£4036
70	10/98	Newb	1m2f6y	C(0-90)H	HVY	£6222
61	9/98	Kemp	1m4f	D(0-75)H	G-S	£4070
58	6/98	NmkJ	1m4f	D(0-80)H	GD	£6004
61	1/98	Ling	1m2f	F(0-65)H	STD	£1892
53	1/96	Ling	1m	F(0-60)	STD	£2786

Total win prize-money £25013

Going (Turf): Sf: 1-7 **GS: 2-3** Gd: 1-10 GF: 0-11 Fm: 0-2
Distance: 5f/6f: 0-1 7f-8f: 1-6 **9f-13f: 5-41** 14f+: 0-1
Track : LH: 3-24 RH: 3-21 Tight: 2-23 **Gall: 3-11**
Aids: Bl: 0-1 Vi: 0-0 Tstrap: 0-0
Best Rating: 60 3/01 Sthl 1m4f stand

Won his first race since October 1998 when getting his head in front at Newmarket in early August 2001. Suited by cut in the ground, he stays a mile and a half well.

Billichang

(105) (40)**51**
5-y-o b h Chilibang-Swing O'The Kilt (Hotfoot)
P Howling Paul Howling Racing Syndicate

Placings:0040/44520240530301/2333344261004454200-6440 **(0577)**
2001: 10^{6}SD, 8^{4}SW, 8^{4}SW, 10^{0}SW

	Starts	1st	2nd	3rd	Win & Pl
Career Total (Turf)	7	0	0	0	240
Career Total (AW)	35	2	5	6	9863

55	3/00	Ling	1m2f	G	STD	£1886
44	12/99	Ling	1m2f	D	STD	£2741

Total win prize-money £4628

Going (Turf): Sf: 0-0 GS: 0-1 Gd: 0-2 GF: 0-3 Fm: 0-1
Distance: 5f/6f: 0-1 7f-8f: 0-9 **9f-13f: 2-32** 14f+: 0-0
Track : **LH: 2-37** RH: 0-2 **Tight: 2-32** Gall: 0-2
Aids: Bl: 0-7 Vi: 0-3 Tstrap: 0-0
Best Rating: 40 2/01 Ling 1m slow

Billie H

(97) (61)**47**
3-y-o ch f Cool Jazz-Rachels Eden (Ring Bidder)
C E Brittain C E Brittain

Placings:000610-0233220545010 **(5592)**
2001: 7^{0}SD, 8^{2}SD, 8^{3}SW, 7^{3}SD, 7^{2}SD, 6^{2}GF, 7^{0}F, 7^{5}G, 6^{4}G, 6^{5}GF, 7^{0}GF, 7^{1}SD, 6^{0}GS

	Starts	1st	2nd	3rd	Win & Pl
Career Total (Turf)	12	1	1	0	3290
Career Total (AW)	7	1	2	2	4328

48	10/01	Wolv	7f	G	STD	£1967
59	8/00	Brig	6f209y	E	FRM	£2775

Total win prize-money £4743

Going (Turf): Sf: 0-0 GS: 0-1 Gd: 0-5 GF: 0-4 **Fm: 1-2**
Distance: 5f/6f: 0-2 **7f-8f: 2-17** 9f-13f: 0-0 14f+: 0-0
Track : **LH: 2-13** RH: 0-1 **Tight: 1-4** Gall: 0-1
Aids: **Bl: 1-11** Vi: 0-0 Tstrap: 0-0
Best Rating: 61 3/01 Ling 7f stand

She has shown better form on sand than on turf so far.

Billie Holiday

89 **47**
3-y-o b f Fairy King (USA)-Raymouna (IRE) (High Top)
B J Meehan Lindy Regis & Geoff Howard-Spink

Placings:006600 **(3871)**
2001: 7^{0}G, 6^{0}G, 6^{6}GF, 8^{6}GS, 7^{0}GF, 6^{0}G

	Starts	1st	2nd	3rd	Win & Pl
Career Total (Turf)	6	0	0	0	0

Going (Turf): Sf: 0-0 GS: 0-1 Gd: 0-3 GF: 0-2 Fm: 0-0
Distance: 5f/6f: 0-2 7f-8f: 0-3 9f-13f: 0-1 14f+: 0-0
Track : LH: 0-1 RH: 0-0 Tight: 0-0 Gall: 0-0
Aids: Bl: 0-1 Vi: 0-0 Tstrap: 0-0

Best Rating: 55 5/01 NmkR 7f good

Billy Bathwick (IRE)

105(87) (56)**58**

4-y-o ch c Fayruz-Cut It Fine (USA) (Big Spruce (USA))
Dr J R J Naylor B C Mills

Placings:440406/555201000324450-0216000003 **(4899)**
2001: 7^{0}GS, 8^{2}G, 10^{1}GF, 10^{6}GF, 10^{0}GF, 9^{0}G, 9^{0}G, 8^{0}GF, 8^{0}GF, 8^{3}GS

	Starts	1st	2nd	3rd	Win & Pl
Career Total (Turf)	30	2	3	2	11910
Career Total (AW)	1	0	0	0	0

62 6/01 Wind 1m2f7y D(0-85)H G-F £4166
66 6/00 Carl 5f207y E G-F £2743
Total win prize-money £6910

Going (Turf): Sf: 0-7 GS: 0-4 Gd: 0-6 GF: 2-12 Fm: 0-1
Distance: 5f/6f: 1-6 7f-8f: 0-10 9f-13f: 1-15 14f+: 0-0
Track : LH: 0-13 RH: 1-5 Tight: 1-11 Gall: 1-3
Aids: Bl: 0-5 Vi: 0-0 Tstrap: 0-0
Best Rating: 65 7/01 Wind 1m2f7y gd-fm

Best suited to ten furlongs and acts on fast ground, but does not want to see daylight too soon in his races and was particularly well ridden when winning at Windsor in June.

Billyjo (IRE)

(85) (24)**32**

3-y-o b g Idris (IRE)-Village Countess (IRE) (Reasonable (FR))
Miss A Stokell Ms Caron Stokell

Placings:6644503-64000003000066 **(5412)**
2001: 8^{6}SW, 9^{4}SW, 8^{0}SD, 9^{0}SD, 9^{0}GF, 10^{0}GF, 7^{0}GF, 7^{3}SD, 8^{0}SD, 7^{0}GS, 12^{0}SD, 13^{0}GF, 5^{6}GS, 6^{6}SD

	Starts	1st	2nd	3rd	Win & Pl
Career Total (Turf)	9	0	0	0	0
Career Total (AW)	12	0	0	2	593

Going (Turf): Sf: 0-0 GS: 0-3 Gd: 0-0 GF: 0-6 Fm: 0-0
Distance: 5f/6f: 0-5 7f-8f: 0-6 9f-13f: 0-9 14f+: 0-1
Track : LH: 0-17 RH: 0-3 Tight: 0-12 Gall: 0-2
Aids: Bl: 0-2 Vi: 0-1 Tstrap: 0-0
Best Rating: 32 10/01 Catt 5f212y gd-sft

Still a maiden and no sign of any ability.

Binary File (USA)

104 **102+**

3-y-o b c Nureyev (USA)-Binary (Rainbow Quest (USA))
J H M Gosden K Abdulla

Placings:11 **(2384)**
2001: 6^{1}GF, 8^{1}GF

	Starts	1st	2nd	3rd	Win & Pl
Career Total (Turf)	2	2	0	0	12625

102 6/01 Asct 1m B(0-95) G-F £8984
84 6/01 Sals 6f212y D G-F £3640
Total win prize-money £12625

Going (Turf): Sf: 0-0 GS: 0-0 Gd: 0-0 GF: 2-2 Fm: 0-0
Distance: 5f/6f: 0-0 7f-8f: 2-2 9f-13f: 0-0 14f+: 0-0
Track : LH: 0-0 RH: 1-1 Tight: 0-0 Gall: 1-1
Aids: Bl: 0-0 Vi: 0-0 Tstrap: 0-0
Best Rating: 102 6/01 Asct 1m gd-fm

Progressive colt, winning his first two runs at Salisbury and Ascot. Deserves to step up to Listed class and should get a bit further than a mile in time.

Bint Habibi

(101) (67)**54**

4-y-o b f Bin Ajwaad (IRE)-High Stepping (IRE) (Taufan (USA))
Mrs Lydia Pearce (J Pearce 15/2) Mrs Linda Leech

Placings:4200/01663153030026250 5-1322 **(0428)**
2001: 9^{1}SW, 9^{3}SD, 9^{2}SD, 8^{2}SD

	Starts	1st	2nd	3rd	Win & Pl
Career Total (Turf)	16	2	1	3	6954
Career Total (AW)	10	1	4	1	5253

62 1/01 Wolv 1m1f79y F(0-65)H SLW £1715
50 7/00 Leic 1m8y G G-F £2023
54 6/00 Chep 7f16y F G-F £2446
Total win prize-money £6185

Going (Turf): Sf: 0-2 GS: 0-3 Gd: 0-2 GF: 2-7 Fm: 0-2
Distance: 5f/6f: 0-0 7f-8f: 1-12 9f-13f: 2-14 14f+: 0-0
Track : LH: 1-18 RH: 0-2 Tight: 1-12 Gall: 0-0
Aids: Bl: 0-0 Vi: 0-1 Tstrap: 0-0
Best Rating: 67 3/01 Wolv 1m100y stand

Bint Royal (IRE)

100(96) (42)**47**

3-y-o ch f Royal Abjar (USA)-Living Legend (USA) (Septieme Ciel (USA))
Miss V Haigh Tune Pack Produce Ltd

Placings:010-0000023400363304 **(4621)**
2001: 7^{0}SD, 6^{0}HY, 5^{0}GF, 5^{0}F, 5^{0}GF, 6^{2}GF, 6^{3}SD, 6^{4}GF, 5^{0}G, 6^{0}F, 5^{3}G, 6^{6}G, 6^{3}G, 5^{3}G, 5^{0}G, 6^{4}F

	Starts	1st	2nd	3rd	Win & Pl
Career Total (Turf)	17	1	1	3	5011
Career Total (AW)	2	0	0	1	337

62 10/00 Catt 5f D SFT £2730
Total win prize-money £2730

Going (Turf): Sf: 1-3 GS: 0-0 Gd: 0-6 GF: 0-5 Fm: 0-3
Distance: 5f/6f: 1-14 7f-8f: 0-5 9f-13f: 0-0 14f+: 0-0
Track : LH: 0-4 RH: 0-0 Tight: 0-1 Gall: 0-0
Aids: Bl: 0-11 Vi: 0-1 Tstrap: 0-0
Best Rating: 49 6/01 Wwck 6f21y gd-fm

Bint St James

81 (19)**19**

6-y-o b m Shareef Dancer (USA)-St James's Antigua (IRE) (Law Society (USA))
W Clay Dave Dutton

Placings:044340340304/0/000 **(4079)**
2001: 14^{0}GF, 12^{0}GS, 17^{0}GF

	Starts	1st	2nd	3rd	Win & Pl
Career Total (Turf)	8	0	0	1	1296
Career Total (AW)	8	0	0	2	1057

Going (Turf): Sf: 0-0 GS: 0-1 Gd: 0-3 GF: 0-4 Fm: 0-0
Distance: 5f/6f: 0-0 7f-8f: 0-2 9f-13f: 0-8 14f+: 0-6
Track : LH: 0-12 RH: 0-3 Tight: 0-5 Gall: 0-2
Aids: Bl: 0-0 Vi: 0-0 Tstrap: 0-0
Best Rating: 19 7/01 Nott 1m6f15y gd-fm

Bintalbawadi (IRE)

95 **72+**

3-y-o b f Diesis-Solar Star (USA) (Lear Fan (USA))
M P Tregoning Hamdan Al Maktoum

Placings:1 **(4381)**
2001: 8^{1}GF

	Starts	1st	2nd	3rd	Win & Pl
Career Total (Turf)	1	1	0	0	3660

72 8/01 Sals 1m D G-F £3659
Total win prize-money £3660

Going (Turf): Sf: 0-0 GS: 0-0 Gd: 0-0 GF: 1-1 Fm: 0-0
Distance: 5f/6f: 0-0 7f-8f: 1-1 9f-13f: 0-0 14f+: 0-0
Track : LH: 0-0 RH: 0-0 Tight: 0-0 Gall: 0-0
Aids: Bl: 0-0 Vi: 0-0 Tstrap: 0-0
Best Rating: 72 8/01 Sals 1m gd-fm

Bintang Timor (USA)

99(97) (70d)**58**

7-y-o ch g Mt. Livermore (USA)-Frisky Kitten (USA) (Isopach (USA))
W J Musson Goodey & Broughton

Placings:24/440/02420014026 0000/310223030000013/034625000001202 06-004420050000565 **(5688)**
2001: 8^{0}SD, 8^{0}SW, 6^{4}HY, 7^{4}S, 6^{2}GF, 6^{0}GF, 6^{0}GF, 6^{5}G, 7^{0}G, 7^{0}GF, 8^{0}G, 6^{0}G, 7^{5}S, 7^{6}GS, 7^{5}S

	Starts	1st	2nd	3rd	Win & Pl
Career Total (Turf)	61	4	9	5	40652
Career Total (AW)	6	0	1	0	660

66 10/00 Yarm 6f3y D(0-85)H HVY £3981
65 10/99 Yarm 7f3y E(0-75)H G-S £7532
68 5/99 NmkJ 7f E(0-75)H G-F £3368
70 7/98 Leic 5f218y E(0-70)H GD £3246
Total win prize-money £18128

Going (Turf): Sf: 1-14 GS: 1-5 Gd: 1-23 GF: 1-18 Fm: 0-1
Distance: 5f/6f: 1-18 7f-8f: 3-47 9f-13f: 0-2 14f+: 0-0
Track : LH: 0-12 RH: 0-11 Tight: 0-4 Gall: 0-10
Aids: Bl: 0-0 Vi: 0-0 Tstrap: 0-0
Best Rating: 68 5/01 Thsk 6f gd-fm

Modest form on sand during the winter, but has been running quite well back on turf, usually over inadequate trips, and he remains one to keep an eye on. Looks best over seven furlongs these days.

Birchwood Sun

99 **42**

11-y-o b g Bluebird (USA)-Shapely Test (USA) (Elocutionist (USA))
M Dods Mrs C E Dods

Placings:22001002160/066014040235006 56/04160322300000/305356101052353 6100/000000P/05100000420 0/22111063100000/01320003/334030-52023 **(3209)**
2001: 7^{5}S, 7^{2}S, 6^{0}GF, 6^{2}G, 6^{3}G

	Starts	1st	2nd	3rd	Win & Pl
Career Total (Turf)	111	13	13	14	53092
Career Total (AW)	2	0	0	0	

61 4/99 Pont 6f F SFT £2553
58 6/98 Carl 5f207y F G-S £2444
61 5/98 Newc 7f F G-S £2326
62 4/98 Rdcr 7f F SFT £2477
52 4/98 Carl 5f207y F(0-65)H G-S £2584
59 5/97 Carl 5f207y E(0-70)H G-S £2960
69 9/95 Newc 7f E(0-70)H GD £3209
60 6/95 Carl 5f207y E(0-70)H FRM £3152
50 5/94 Carl 5f207y E(0-70)H HVY £3131
66 5/93 Rdcr 6f F GD £2601
70 10/92 York 6f D G-S £7375
62 8/92 Hayd 5f F G-F £1590
Total win prize-money £36407

Going (Turf): Sf: 3-16 GS: 5-20 Gd: 2-27 GF: 1-37 Fm: 2-11
Distance: 5f/6f: 9-52 7f-8f: 4-58 9f-13f: 0-3 14f+: 0-0
Track : LH: 1-23 RH: 5-24 Tight: 0-7 Gall: 5-19
Aids: Bl: 6-60 Vi: 5-31 Tstrap: 0-0
Best Rating: 42 7/01 Haml 6f5y good

Birdie

101 **76**

2-y-o b f Alhaarth (IRE)-Fade (Persepolis (FR))
M L W Bell Lady Carolyn Warren

Placings:0422 **(5668)**
2001: 7^{0}GF, 7^{4}GS, 6^{2}S, 8^{2}HY

	Starts	1st	2nd	3rd	Win & Pl
Career Total (Turf)	4	0	2	0	3162

Going (Turf): Sf: 0-2 GS: 0-0 Gd: 0-1 GF: 0-1 Fm: 0-0
Distance: 5f/6f: 0-0 7f-8f: 0-3 9f-13f: 0-1 14f+: 0-0
Track : LH: 0-1 RH: 0-2 Tight: 0-1 Gall: 0-0
Aids: Bl: 0-0 Vi: 0-0 Tstrap: 0-0

Best Rating: 76 11/01 Wind 1m67y heavy

She has shown some form in maidens and a nursery, but has not looked too keen under pressure.

Birdlip Hill

(92) (68)**68**

2-y-o br f Prince Sabo-Be My Bird (Be My Chief (USA))

A Berry Tweenhills Racing (catsbury Syndicate)

Placings:034061**400** **(5396)**

2001: 7^{0}F, 7^{3}GS, 7^{4}GF, 8^{0}G, 7^{6}GF, **7**^{1}SD, **7**^{4}SD, **8**^{0}SD, **8**^{0}SD

	Starts	1st	2nd	3rd	Win & Pl
Career Total (Turf)	**5**	**0**	**0**	**1**	**413**
Career Total (AW)	**4**	**1**	**0**	**0**	**1994**

68	9/01	Wolv	7f	G	STD	£1993

Total win prize-money £1994

Going (Turf): Sf: 0-0 GS: 0-1 Gd: 0-1 GF: 0-2 Fm: 0-1
Distance: 5f/6f: 0-0 **7f-8f: 1-7** 9f-13f: 0-2 14f+: 0-0
Track : **LH: 1-6** RH: 0-0 **Tight: 1-4** Gall: 0-0
Aids: Bl: 0-0 Vi: 0-0 Tstrap: 0-0
Best Rating: 68 9/01 Wolv 7f stand

Plating class juvenile. Suited by seven furlongs on Fibresand.

Birdwatching

(55) (7)**49**

2-y-o b g Primo Dominie-Area Girl (Jareer (USA))

S C Williams Fenland Twitchers Racing Syndicate

Placings:00 **(5590)**

2001: 7^{0}G, 9^{0}GS

	Starts	1st	2nd	3rd	Win & Pl
Career Total (Turf)	**2**	**0**	**0**	**0**	

Going (Turf): Sf: 0-0 GS: 0-1 Gd: 0-1 GF: 0-0 Fm: 0-0
Distance: 5f/6f: 0-0 7f-8f: 0-1 9f-13f: 0-1 14f+: 0-0
Track : LH: 0-1 RH: 0-1 Tight: 0-0 Gall: 0-0
Aids: Bl: 0-0 Vi: 0-0 Tstrap: 0-0
Best Rating: 49 8/01 Bevl 7f100y good

Birth Of The Blues

98(88) (23)**45**

5-y-o ch g Efisio-Great Steps (Vaigly Great)

K O Cunningham-Brown (Mark Campion 13/1) Supreme Racing Limited

Placings:050/01000/00005000-**60**15515 **(3678)**

2001: 13^{0}SW, 16^{0}SD, 9^{1}GF, 9^{5}F, 11^{5}F, 12^{1}GF, 11^{5}G

	Starts	1st	2nd	3rd	Win & Pl
Career Total (Turf)	**21**	**3**	**0**	**0**	**8719**
Career Total (AW)	**2**	**0**	**0**	**0**	**0**

45	7/01	Sals	1m4f	E(0-75)H	G-F	£3220
40	5/01	Brig	1m1f209yG		G-F	£1925
73	4/99	Leic	1m8y	E(0-75)H	HVY	£3574

Total win prize-money £8719

Going (Turf): Sf: 1-4 GS: 0-4 Gd: 0-3 **GF: 2-6** Fm: 0-4
Distance: 5f/6f: 0-0 7f-8f: 0-5 **9f-13f: 3-17** 14f+: 0-1
Track : LH: 1-10 RH: 1-8 **Tight: 1-12** Gall: 0-1
Aids: Bl: 0-1 Vi: 0-3 Tstrap: 0-0
Best Rating: 45 7/01 Sals 1m4f gd-fm

Birthday Belle

80 **23**

5-y-o ch m Lycius (USA)-Dance Festival (Nureyev (USA))

P Monteith G M Cowan

Placings:3542/000000 **(2356)**

2001: 8^{0}GS, 7^{0}GF, 6^{0}F, 6^{0}GF, 7^{0}G, 8^{0}GF

	Starts	1st	2nd	3rd	Win & Pl
Career Total (Turf)	**10**	**0**	**1**	**1**	**1500**

Going (Turf): Sf: 0-1 GS: 0-1 Gd: 0-2 GF: 0-3 Fm: 0-1
Distance: 5f/6f: 0-1 7f-8f: 0-8 9f-13f: 0-1 14f+: 0-0
Track : LH: 0-1 RH: 0-3 Tight: 0-1 Gall: 0-1
Aids: Bl: 0-4 Vi: 0-2 Tstrap: 0-0
Best Rating: 23 6/01 Ayr 1m gd-fm

Bishop's Blade

100 **49**

4-y-o b g Sure Blade (USA)-Myrtilla (Beldale Flutter (USA))

J S King Robert Long

Placings:000-000 **(2965)**

2001: 11^{0}F, 14^{0}F, 16^{0}GF

	Starts	1st	2nd	3rd	Win & Pl
Career Total (Turf)	**6**	**0**	**0**	**0**	

Going (Turf): Sf: 0-0 GS: 0-1 Gd: 0-1 GF: 0-2 Fm: 0-2
Distance: 5f/6f: 0-0 7f-8f: 0-0 9f-13f: 0-4 14f+: 0-2
Track : LH: 0-5 RH: 0-1 Tight: 0-3 Gall: 0-1
Aids: Bl: 0-0 Vi: 0-0 Tstrap: 0-0
Best Rating: 49 5/01 Brig 1m3f196y firm

Bishop's Secret

79(90) (47d)**18**

3-y-o b g Bishop Of Cashel-Secret Rapture (USA) (Woodman (USA))

P T Dalton (Mrs N Macauley 17/8) Thringstone Racing Club

Placings:0005640-350000040000 **(4031)**

2001: 7^{3}SD, 7^{5}SW, 7^{0}SD, 8^{0}SD, 7^{0}SW, 5^{0}SD, 6^{0}G, 11^{4}SD, 9^{0}F, 8^{0}SD, 8^{0}GF, 10^{0}G

	Starts	1st	2nd	3rd	Win & Pl
Career Total (Turf)	**8**	**0**	**0**	**0**	**0**
Career Total (AW)	**11**	**0**	**0**	**1**	**344**

Going (Turf): Sf: 0-2 GS: 0-0 Gd: 0-3 GF: 0-2 Fm: 0-1
Distance: 5f/6f: 0-3 7f-8f: 0-12 9f-13f: 0-4 14f+: 0-0
Track : LH: 0-13 RH: 0-0 Tight: 0-1 Gall: 0-1
Aids: Bl: 0-3 Vi: 0-11 Tstrap: 0-0
Best Rating: 59 1/01 Sthl 7f stand

Bishop's Wing's

(88) (40)

3-y-o br f Bishop Of Cashel-Butterfly Rose (USA) (Iron Ruler (USA))

P R Chamings Mrs Ann Jenkins

Placings:40-60005 **(2168)**

2001: 8^{6}SD, 7^{0}SD, 6^{0}GF, 6^{0}S, 6^{5}SD

	Starts	1st	2nd	3rd	Win & Pl
Career Total (Turf)	**2**	**0**	**0**	**0**	
Career Total (AW)	**5**	**0**	**0**	**0**	**0**

Going (Turf): Sf: 0-1 GS: 0-0 Gd: 0-0 GF: 0-1 Fm: 0-0
Distance: 5f/6f: 0-1 7f-8f: 0-5 9f-13f: 0-1 14f+: 0-0
Track : LH: 0-6 RH: 0-0 Tight: 0-4 Gall: 0-0
Aids: Bl: 0-0 Vi: 0-0 Tstrap: 0-0
Best Rating: 13 3/01 Ling 7f stand

Bishop's Wood (IRE)

96 **82**

2-y-o b c Charnwood Forest (IRE)-Samnah (IRE) (Wassl)

M G Quinlan Mrs Joan Lay

Placings:31 **(2554)**

2001: 6^{3}GF, 6^{1}GF

	Starts	1st	2nd	3rd	Win & Pl
Career Total (Turf)	**2**	**1**	**0**	**1**	**2962**

82	6/01	Folk	6f189y	F	G-F	£2495

Total win prize-money £2496

Going (Turf): Sf: 0-0 GS: 0-0 Gd: 0-0 **GF: 1-2** Fm: 0-0
Distance: 5f/6f: 0-1 **7f-8f: 1-1** 9f-13f: 0-0 14f+: 0-0
Track : LH: 0-0 **RH: 1-1 Tight: 1-1** Gall: 0-0
Aids: Bl: 0-0 Vi: 0-0 Tstrap: 0-0
Best Rating: 82 6/01 Folk 6f189y gd-fm

This May foal, whose grandam was the useful 6-7f winner, Top Treat, ran out a clear-cut winner in an auction maiden at Folkestone. His owners have received offers from the United States.

Bishops Court

111 **112**

7-y-o ch g Clantime-Indigo (Primo Dominie)

Mrs J R Ramsden D R Brotherton

Placings:31/3313322424/0341022542311/051-3010430 **(4861)**

2001: 5^{3}S, 5^{0}GF, 5^{1}GF, 5^{0}Y, 5^{4}GF, 5^{3}G, 5^{0}GF

	Starts	1st	2nd	3rd	Win & Pl
Career Total (Turf)	**35**	**7**	**6**	**9**	**217848**

112	6/01	Epsm	5f	A(0-110)H	G-F	£58000
106	6/00	Sand	5f6y	C	G-F	£6148
115	10/98	Lonc	5f		HVY	£22222
116	10/98	NmkR	5f	A	GD	£10471
103	6/98	Epsm	5f	A(0-105)H	GD	£28276
88	5/97	Ches	6f18y	C(0-90)H	SFT	£11178
78	9/96	Haml	5f4y	E	GD	£3376

Total win prize-money £139672

Going (Turf): Sf: 2-5 GS: 0-4 **Gd: 3-12** GF: 2-12 Fm: 0-1
Distance: **5f/6f: 6-34** 7f-8f: 1-1 9f-13f: 0-0 14f+: 0-0
Track : **LH: 1-3** RH: 0-0 **Tight: 1-3** Gall: 0-0
Aids: Bl: 0-0 Vi: 0-0 **Tstrap: 1-3**
Best Rating: 112 8/01 York 5f good

He is a very useful sprinter who needs to be delivered just at the right time. A fast-run five furlongs is ideal, as he demonstrated at Epsom on Derby day, but he then seemed to lose his way until bouncing right back to form when third in the Nunthorpe. Injured his pelvis in September.

Bishopstone Belle

(39)

4-y-o b f Formidable (USA)-Relatively Easy (Relkino)

J A Moore (S Mellor 12/3) J A Moore

Placings:0 **(0209)**

2001: 9^{0}SD

	Starts	1st	2nd	3rd	Win & Pl
Career Total (Turf)	**0**	**0**	**0**	**0**	
Career Total (AW)	**1**	**0**	**0**	**0**	

Going (Turf): Sf: 0-0 GS: 0-0 Gd: 0-0 GF: 0-0 Fm: 0-0
Distance: 5f/6f: 0-0 7f-8f: 0-0 9f-13f: 0-1 14f+: 0-0
Track : LH: 0-1 RH: 0-0 Tight: 0-1 Gall: 0-0
Aids: Bl: 0-0 Vi: 0-0 Tstrap: 0-0

Bishopstone Man

98(98) (56)**61**

4-y-o b g Piccolo-Auntie Gladys (Great Nephew)

H Candy (S Mellor 24/6) The Bishopstone Ducks

Placings:00030/400351020035060-40026520424406200 **(5181)**

2001: **7**^{1}SW, **10**^{0}SW, **8**^{0}SD, **7**^{2}SD, 7^{0}SD, 7^{3}SD, 7^{2}SD, **8**^{0}SD, 8^{4}SD, 7^{2}GF, **7**^{4}SD, 7^{4}F, 7^{0}F, 6^{6}GF, 7^{2}G, 8^{0}GS, 6^{0}HY

	Starts	1st	2nd	3rd	Win & Pl
Career Total (Turf)	**27**	**1**	**3**	**3**	**7630**
Career Total (AW)	**10**	**0**	**2**	**0**	**1428**

67	7/00	Leic	1m8y	E(0-70)H	G-F	£3168

Total win prize-money £3169

Going (Turf): Sf: 0-5 GS: 0-4 Gd: 0-5 **GF: 1-11** Fm: 0-2
Distance: 5f/6f: 0-4 7f-8f: 0-25 **9f-13f: 1-8** 14f+: 0-0

Track : LH: 0-16 RH: 0-2 Tight: 0-8 Gall: 0-1
Aids: Bl: 0-0 Vi: 0-9 Tstrap: 0-0
Best Rating: 65 5/01 Ling 7f gd-fm

Bishr

97 **76**

2-y-o b c Royal Applause-Hawayah (IRE) (Shareef Dancer (USA))
M P Tregoning Hamdan Al Maktoum

Placings:552 (3516)
2001: 6^{5}GF, 6^{5}GF, 6^{2}GF

	Starts	1st	2nd	3rd	Win & Pl
Career Total (Turf)	3	0	1	0	3400

Going (Turf): Sf: 0-0 GS: 0-0 Gd: 0-0 GF: 0-3 Fm: 0-0
Distance: 5f/6f: 0-1 7f-8f: 0-2 9f-13f: 0-0 14f+: 0-0
Track : LH: 0-0 RH: 0-0 Tight: 0-0 Gall: 0-0
Aids: Bl: 0-0 Vi: 0-0 Tstrap: 0-1
Best Rating: 76 7/01 Gdwd 6f gd-fm

Bisque

90 **43**

3-y-o ch f Inchinor-Biscay (Unfuwain (USA))
R Charlton Lady Rothschild

Placings:0-20000 (4734)
2001: 8^{2}F, 8^{0}GS, 7^{0}GF, 7^{0}G, 8^{0}F

	Starts	1st	2nd	3rd	Win & Pl
Career Total (Turf)	6	0	1	0	697

Going (Turf): Sf: 0-1 GS: 0-1 Gd: 0-1 GF: 0-1 Fm: 0-2
Distance: 5f/6f: 0-0 7f-8f: 0-4 9f-13f: 0-2 14f+: 0-0
Track : LH: 0-1 RH: 0-0 Tight: 0-0 Gall: 0-0
Aids: Bl: 0-0 Vi: 0-0 Tstrap: 0-0
Best Rating: 67 5/01 Leic 1m9y firm

Bisquet-De-Bouche

100(78) **31**

7-y-o ch m Most Welcome-Larive (Blakeney)
A W Carroll Martin Brook

Placings:00/04360/00/0-010 (4079)
2001: 16^{0}SW, 18^{1}GF, 17^{0}GF

	Starts	1st	2nd	3rd	Win & Pl
Career Total (Turf)	12	1	0	1	3596
Career Total (AW)	1	0	0	0	

31 7/01 Chep 2m2f E(0-70)H G-F £2863
Total win prize-money £2863

Going (Turf): Sf: 0-3 GS: 0-0 Gd: 0-5 **GF: 1-4** Fm: 0-0
Distance: 5f/6f: 0-0 7f-8f: 0-2 9f-13f: 0-1 **14f+: 1-10**
Track : **LH: 1-8** RH: 0-3 Tight: 0-3 Gall: 0-1
Aids: Bl: 0-0 Vi: 0-0 Tstrap: 0-0
Best Rating: 31 7/01 Chep 2m2f gd-fm

He stays forever and is suited by fast ground.

Bit Of Luck

103 **94**

2-y-o ch c First Trump-Elle Reef (Shareef Dancer (USA))
M H Tompkins Mrs Beryl Lockey

Placings:52221225 (5401)
2001: 6^{5}G, 6^{2}GF, 7^{2}GF, 7^{2}G, 7^{1}GS, 8^{2}GF, 8^{2}GF, 8^{5}S

	Starts	1st	2nd	3rd	Win & Pl
Career Total (Turf)	8	1	5	0	18073

82 8/01 Bevl 7f100y D G-S £3838
Total win prize-money £3838

Going (Turf): Sf: 0-1 **GS: 1-1** Gd: 0-2 GF: 0-4 Fm: 0-0
Distance: 5f/6f: 0-1 **7f-8f: 1-5** 9f-13f: 0-2 14f+: 0-0
Track : LH: 0-3 **RH: 1-1** Tight: 0-0 Gall: 0-0
Aids: Bl: 0-0 Vi: 0-0 Tstrap: 0-0
Best Rating: 94 10/01 Pont 1m4y soft

Progressed with racing and got off the mark over seven at Beverley in August. He has continued to run well since and stays a mile.

Bitter Sweet

103(89) (23)**52**

5-y-o gr m Deploy-Julia Flyte (Drone (USA))
J L Spearing Masonaires

Placings:5554300/00020/0403540050660-066310123552530 (5026)
2001: 10^{0}G, 10^{6}GF, 8^{6}GF, 8^{3}GF, 9^{1}GF, 9^{0}G, 10^{1}G, 9^{2}GF, 9^{3}GF, 9^{5}GF, 10^{5}G, 10^{2}GF, 9^{5}GF, 10^{3}GF, 9^{0}S

	Starts	1st	2nd	3rd	Win & Pl
Career Total (Turf)	38	2	3	5	14005
Career Total (AW)	2	0	0	0	211

52 7/01 Epsm 1m2f18y E(0-75)H GD £3503
45 7/01 Folk 1m1f149yE(0-70)H G-F £3075
Total win prize-money £6580

Going (Turf): Sf: 0-5 GS: 0-5 **Gd: 1-9 GF: 1-15** Fm: 0-3
Distance: 5f/6f: 0-1 7f-8f: 0-5 **9f-13f: 2-32** 14f+: 0-1
Track : LH: 1-23 RH: 1-10 **Tight: 2-19** Gall: 0-3
Aids: Bl: 0-0 Vi: 0-2 Tstrap: 0-0
Best Rating: 52 9/01 York 1m2f85y gd-fm

A winner twice on the Flat at around ten furlongs, she acts on a sound surface.

Biya (IRE)

(87) (20)

9-y-o ch g Shadeed (USA)-Rosie Potts (Shareef Dancer (USA))
D McCain Champ Chicken Co Ltd

Placings:2160/531400/0060/00 (0483)
2001: 8^{0}SD, 10^{0}SD

	Starts	1st	2nd	3rd	Win & Pl
Career Total (Turf)	5	0	0	0	0
Career Total (AW)	11	2	1	1	7582

48 1/97 Ling 1m2f F(0-65)H STD £2518
56 1/95 Ling 1m D STD £3758
Total win prize-money £6276

Going (Turf): Sf: 0-1 GS: 0-0 Gd: 0-0 GF: 0-4 Fm: 0-0
Distance: 5f/6f: 0-0 7f-8f: 1-3 9f-13f: 1-12 14f+: 0-1
Track : **LH: 2-15** RH: 0-1 **Tight: 2-12** Gall: 0-0
Aids: Bl: 0-1 Vi: 0-0 Tstrap: 0-0
Best Rating: 20 3/01 Wolv 1m100y stand

Black Army

100(97) (63)

6-y-o b g Aragon-Morgannwg (IRE) (Simply Great (FR))
Andrew Reid (K A Ryan 7/5) A S Reid

Placings:040/4010053030/051560240-0001060 (2113)
2001: 5^{0}SD, 7^{0}SD, 5^{0}GS, 6^{1}G, 5^{0}GF, 5^{6}F, 6^{0}F

	Starts	1st	2nd	3rd	Win & Pl
Career Total (Turf)	20	3	0	0	9863
Career Total (AW)	9	0	1	2	1979

47 5/01 Donc 6f E GD £2990
39 7/00 Catt 5f212y G G-F £1911
72 5/99 Bevl 5f D(0-80)H GD £4744
Total win prize-money £9645

Going (Turf): Sf: 0-3 GS: 0-5 **Gd: 2-7** GF: 1-3 Fm: 0-2
Distance: **5f/6f: 3-23** 7f-8f: 0-6 9f-13f: 0-0 14f+: 0-0
Track : **LH: 1-9** RH: 0-1 **Tight: 1-4** Gall: 0-2
Aids: Bl: 0-3 Vi: 0-0 Tstrap: 0-0
Best Rating: 48 5/01 Bath 5f11y gd-fm

Modest sprinter on a decent surface.

Black Ice Boy (IRE)

89(96) (30)**19**

10-y-o b g Law Society (USA)-Hogan's Sister (USA) (Speak John)
R Bastiman Mrs Judith Marshall

Placings:0/000/0060/0116400/410333/60010P/5000004 06002300-060 (5683)
2001: 17^{0}HY, 21^{6}S, 14^{0}S

	Starts	1st	2nd	3rd	Win & Pl
Career Total (Turf)	37	4	1	4	16276
Career Total (AW)	8	0	0	0	0

48 10/99 Pont 2m1f22y E(0-70)H SFT £4045
42 4/98 Pont 2m5f122yE(0-70)H G-S £3210
37 7/97 Bevl 2m35y E(0-70)H HVY £3062
31 6/97 Carl 2m1f52y F(0-60)H G-F £2654
Total win prize-money £12971

Going (Turf): Sf: 2-14 GS: 1-8 Gd: 0-6 GF: 1-8 Fm: 0-1
Distance: 5f/6f: 0-0 7f-8f: 0-1 9f-13f: 0-2 **14f+: 4-42**
Track : LH: 2-37 RH: 2-7 Tight: 1-8 Gall: 1-8
Aids: **Bl: 3-13** Vi: 1-21 Tstrap: 0-0
Best Rating: 19 11/01 Donc 1m6f132y soft

Requires a real test of stamina.

Black Knight

108 **104**

3-y-o b/br c Contract Law (USA)-Another Move (Farm Walk)
S P C Woods W J P Jackson

Placings:3116632-334105 (2802)
2001: 8^{3}S, 10^{3}S, 10^{4}GF, 8^{1}GF, 10^{0}GF, 8^{5}GF

	Starts	1st	2nd	3rd	Win & Pl
Career Total (Turf)	13	3	1	4	29051

104 5/01 Thsk 1m B(0-95) G-F £10257
85 7/00 Bevl 7f100y D GD £4342
85 6/00 Folk 7f F FRM £2488
Total win prize-money £17088

Going (Turf): Sf: 0-4 GS: 0-0 **Gd: 1-1 GF: 1-7 Fm: 1-1**
Distance: 5f/6f: 0-0 **7f-8f: 3-8** 9f-13f: 0-5 14f+: 0-0
Track : LH: 1-3 RH: 1-6 **Tight: 1-3** Gall: 0-1
Aids: Bl: 0-0 Vi: 0-0 Tstrap: 0-0
Best Rating: 104 5/01 Thsk 1m gd-fm

A winner at Folkestone and Beverley in 2000, he looked fairly exposed, but he improvedlast year - running third in Derby trials. He stays ten furlongs, acts on good to firm and soft, and usually races prominently. Dropped back in trip when scoring at Thirsk in May. Has gone to Hong Kong.

Black Minnaloushe (USA)

(113)**121**

3-y-o b c Storm Cat (USA)-Coral Dance (FR) (Green Dancer (USA))
A P O'Brien Mrs John Magnier

Placings:11-256115340 (5580a)
2001: 7^{2}S, 7^{5}G, 8^{6}G, 8^{1}GY, 8^{1}G, 10^{5}GF, 8^{3}GF, 10^{4}G, 10^{0}FT

	Starts	1st	2nd	3rd	Win & Pl
Career Total (Turf)	10	4	1	1	385200
Career Total (AW)	1	0	0	0	

120 6/01 Asct 1m A GD £156600
121 5/01 Curr 1m G-Y £126675
102 9/00 Curr 6f YLD £26050
85 8/00 Cork 6f G-F £6900
Total win prize-money £316225

Going (Turf): Sf: 0-1 GS: 0-0 **Gd: 1-4 GF: 1-3** Fm: 0-0
Distance: 5f/6f: 2-2 7f-8f: 2-6 9f-13f: 0-3 14f+: 0-0
Track : LH: 0-2 **RH: 1-3** Tight: 0-0 **Gall: 1-2**
Aids: Bl: 0-0 Vi: 0-0 Tstrap: 0-0
Best Rating: 121 5/01 Curr 1m gd-yld

A half-brother to Dewhurst and 2000 Guineas winner Pennekamp, he put up a smart performance to win the Irish 2000 Guineas from Mozart. He had a troubled passage in the French equivalent, but enjoyed the run of the race in the Irish version at the Curragh, then follow up in the St James' Palace at Ascot. Ran a bit flat when fifth to Medicean in the Eclipse Stakes, and could not cope with

Noverre, whom he had beaten at Ascot, in the Sussex Stakes. Never really fired when fourth in the Juddmonte International at York, and did not appear to stay in the Breeders' Cup Classic. A high-class miler when the ground is not too fast.

Black Sam Bellamy (IRE)

96 **114**

2-y-o b c Sadler's Wells (USA)-Urban Sea (USA) (Miswaki (USA))
A P O'Brien Michael Tabor

Placings:36 **(5361)**
2001: 8^{3}S, 8^{6}GS

	Starts	1st	2nd	3rd	Win & Pl
Career Total (Turf)	2	0	0	1	872

Going (Turf): Sf: 0-1 GS: 0-1 Gd: 0-0 GF: 0-0 Fm: 0-0
Distance: 5f/6f: 0-0 7f-8f: 0-2 9f-13f: 0-0 14f+: 0-0
Track : LH: 0-0 RH: 0-0 Tight: 0-0 Gall: 0-0
Aids: Bl: 0-0 Vi: 0-0 Tstrap: 0-0
Best Rating: 91 10/01 NmkR 1m soft

A full-brother to Galileo, he was beaten in a three-way-photo on his debut at Newmarket but disappointed on a return trip two weeks later. Third in france in November, he looks immature and will win races over a longer trip next season.

Black Silver

(91) (67)**57**

2-y-o br f Dilum (USA)-Silver Charm (Dashing Blade)
J M P Eustace J C Smith

Placings:35025 **(5049)**
2001: 5^{3}S, 5^{5}G, 5^{0}G, 7^{2}SD, 7^{5}SD

	Starts	1st	2nd	3rd	Win & Pl
Career Total (Turf)	3	0	0	1	496
Career Total (AW)	2	0	1	0	570

Going (Turf): Sf: 0-1 GS: 0-0 Gd: 0-2 GF: 0-0 Fm: 0-0
Distance: 5f/6f: 0-3 7f-8f: 0-2 9f-13f: 0-0 14f+: 0-0
Track : LH: 0-3 RH: 0-0 Tight: 0-1 Gall: 0-0
Aids: Bl: 0-0 Vi: 0-0 Tstrap: 0-0
Best Rating: 67 9/01 Wolv 7f stand

Black Weasel (IRE)

102(102) (39)**37**

6-y-o br g Lahib (USA)-Glowlamp (IRE) (Glow (USA))
A Bailey S A Pritchard

Placings:3/00401000/**0000524**/056255542-53244300 **(3064)**
2001: 16^{5}SD, 16^{3}SD, 16^{2}SD, 17^{4}HY, 17^{4}GF, 16^{3}GF, 16^{0}F, 17^{0}G

	Starts	1st	2nd	3rd	Win & Pl
Career Total (Turf)	21	1	0	2	6214
Career Total (AW)	13	0	4	1	2602

61 7/98 Pont 1m2f6y E(0-70) G-F £2736
Total win prize-money £2736

Going (Turf): Sf: 0-5 GS: 0-2 Gd: 0-5 **GF: 1-8** Fm: 0-1
Distance: 5f/6f: 0-1 7f-8f: 0-3 **9f-13f: 1-11** 14f+: 0-19
Track : **LH: 1-27** RH: 0-7 Tight: 0-17 Gall: 0-2
Aids: **Bl: 1-8** Vi: 0-2 Tstrap: 0-1
Best Rating: 38 2/01 Wolv 2m46y stand

Stays forever but takes his time in doing so. Stays two miles. Acts on a sound surface. Handles heavy.

Blackheath (IRE)

106 **73**

5-y-o ch g Common Grounds-Queen Caroline (USA) (Chief's Crown (USA))
J A R Toller G H Toller

Placings:23100330/00000-233000000 **(5145)**
2001: 5^{2}GS, 6^{3}GF, 6^{3}GF, 6^{0}GF, 5^{0}GS, 6^{0}GF, 5^{0}F, 7^{0}G

	Starts	1st	2nd	3rd	Win & Pl
Career Total (Turf)	22	1	2	5	19408

79 6/99 Ling 6f D GD £3786
Total win prize-money £3787

Going (Turf): Sf: 0-1 GS: 0-2 **Gd: 1-8** GF: 0-10 Fm: 0-1
Distance: **5f/6f: 1-16** 7f-8f: 0-6 9f-13f: 0-0 14f+: 0-0
Track : LH: 0-2 RH: 0-0 Tight: 0-1 Gall: 0-1
Aids: Bl: 0-1 Vi: 0-0 Tstrap: 0-0
Best Rating: 86 5/01 Gdwd 6f gd-fm

He is a useful sprint-handicapper, but has only won once and his come-from-behind style means he sometimes runs into traffic problems. Suited by six furlongs and a strongly-run race.

Blacks Boy (IRE)

99 **82**

2-y-o b c Fayruz-Wolverstar (Wolverlife)
J J Quinn G McKee

Placings:10446 **(3862)**
2001: 5^{1}S, 5^{0}G, 5^{4}GF, 5^{4}GS, 6^{6}GF

	Starts	1st	2nd	3rd	Win & Pl
Career Total (Turf)	5	1	0	0	5359

62 4/01 Ripn 5f D SFT £4225
Total win prize-money £4225

Going (Turf): Sf: 1-1 GS: 0-1 Gd: 0-1 GF: 0-2 Fm: 0-0
Distance: **5f/6f: 1-5** 7f-8f: 0-0 9f-13f: 0-0 14f+: 0-0
Track : LH: 0-0 RH: 0-0 Tight: 0-0 Gall: 0-0
Aids: Bl: 0-0 Vi: 0-0 Tstrap: 0-0
Best Rating: 82 7/01 Leic 5f218y gd-sft

Won a Ripon maiden over five furlongs on his debut, despite running green. Prefers cut in the ground. Stays six furlongs well enough.

Blacksmith Lane

84 **49**

2-y-o b f Makbul-Dutch Auntie (Prince Sabo)
D R C Elsworth P W Taylor

Placings:004 **(5079)**
2001: 6^{0}GF, 6^{0}GF, 5^{4}S

	Starts	1st	2nd	3rd	Win & Pl
Career Total (Turf)	3	0	0	0	0

Going (Turf): Sf: 0-1 GS: 0-0 Gd: 0-0 GF: 0-2 Fm: 0-0
Distance: 5f/6f: 0-2 7f-8f: 0-1 9f-13f: 0-0 14f+: 0-0
Track : LH: 0-1 RH: 0-0 Tight: 0-0 Gall: 0-0
Aids: Bl: 0-0 Vi: 0-0 Tstrap: 0-0
Best Rating: 49 10/01 Brig 5f59y soft

Blackthorn

101 **88**

2-y-o ch c Deploy-Balliasta (USA) (Lyphard (USA))
Mrs A J Perrett K Abdulla

Placings:41603 **(5280)**
2001: 6^{4}GF, 8^{1}GS, 8^{6}GF, 8^{0}GS, 9^{3}S

	Starts	1st	2nd	3rd	Win & Pl
Career Total (Turf)	5	1	0	1	4505

88 8/01 NmkJ 1m E G-S £3396
Total win prize-money £3396

Going (Turf): Sf: 0-1 **GS: 1-2** Gd: 0-0 GF: 0-2 Fm: 0-0
Distance: 5f/6f: 0-0 **7f-8f: 1-4** 9f-13f: 0-1 14f+: 0-0
Track : LH: 0-0 RH: 0-3 Tight: 0-1 Gall: 0-0
Aids: Bl: 0-0 Vi: 0-0 Tstrap: 0-0
Best Rating: 88 8/01 NmkJ 1m gd-sft

Winner of a soft-ground maiden, he will probably be a middle distance horse in due course, being out of a half-sister to the Prix du Jockey-Club winner Sanglamore and the Ribblesdale Stakes winner Ballinderry.

Blagovest

99 **82**

2-y-o b c Singspiel (IRE)-Tass (Soviet Star (USA))
R Charlton Tarville Int Limited & C Coleridge-Cole

Placings:660 **(5604)**
2001: 6^{6}GS, 7^{6}S, 7^{0}GS

	Starts	1st	2nd	3rd	Win & Pl
Career Total (Turf)	3	0	0	0	0

Going (Turf): Sf: 0-1 GS: 0-2 Gd: 0-0 GF: 0-0 Fm: 0-0
Distance: 5f/6f: 0-0 7f-8f: 0-3 9f-13f: 0-0 14f+: 0-0
Track : LH: 0-0 RH: 0-0 Tight: 0-0 Gall: 0-0
Aids: Bl: 0-0 Vi: 0-0 Tstrap: 0-0
Best Rating: 82 11/01 NmkR 7f gd-sft

From the family of Nomrood and Dilshaan, made a promising debut in novice company at Salisbury but failed to build on that.

Blair (IRE)

98(78) (25)**40d**

4-y-o b g Persian Bold-Zara's Birthday (IRE) (Waajib)
G A Swinbank Leading Star Racing

Placings:0/004005050-001006 **(4901)**
2001: 13^{0}GF, 16^{0}F, 14^{1}GF, 16^{0}GS, 14^{0}GF, 11^{6}G

	Starts	1st	2nd	3rd	Win & Pl
Career Total (Turf)	14	1	0	0	2086
Career Total (AW)	2	0	0	0	

34 7/01 Nott 1m6f15y G(0-60)H G-F £2086
Total win prize-money £2086

Going (Turf): Sf: 0-1 GS: 0-2 Gd: 0-5 **GF: 1-5** Fm: 0-1
Distance: 5f/6f: 0-0 7f-8f: 0-4 9f-13f: 0-7 **14f+: 1-5**
Track : **LH: 1-10** RH: 0-6 Tight: 0-10 Gall: 0-0
Aids: Bl: 0-0 Vi: 0-0 Tstrap: 0-0
Best Rating: 34 7/01 Nott 1m6f15y gd-fm

Blakeset

(107) (98)**61**

6-y-o ch g Midyan (USA)-Penset (Red Sunset)
T D Barron Nigel Shields

Placings:31253/0005422/020500260**120/55**100006001 112-1 **(0076)**
2001: 6^{1}SW

	Starts	1st	2nd	3rd	Win & Pl
Career Total (Turf)	29	2	5	2	19713
Career Total (AW)	10	5	2	0	26918

98	1/01	Wolv	6f	C(0-100)H	SLW	£8151
94	11/00	Sthl	6f	C(0-95)H	STD	£7020
94	11/00	Sthl	6f	D(0-80)H	STD	£3266
60	9/00	Yarm	7f3y	G(0-75)H	G-F	£1935
79	3/00	Wolv	7f	F	STD	£2415
75	11/99	Ling	7f	E(0-75)H	STD	£2450
76	4/97	NmkR	5f	D	G-F	£4347

Total win prize-money £29585

Going (Turf): Sf: 0-2 GS: 0-3 Gd: 0-10 **GF: 2-14** Fm: 0-0
Distance: **5f/6f: 4-14** 7f-8f: 3-23 9f-13f: 0-2 14f+: 0-0
Track : **LH: 5-16** RH: 0-8 **Tight: 3-8** Gall: 0-4
Aids: **Bl: 6-16** Vi: 0-0 Tstrap: 0-1
Best Rating: 98 1/01 Wolv 6f slow

He was largely disappointing last term before rhitting form.

Blakeshall

85 **57**

2-y-o ch g Piccolo-Corniche Quest (IRE) (Salt Dome (USA))
M R Channon M Bishop

Placings:00661 **(2436)**
2001: 5^{0}S, 5^{0}S, 5^{6}F, 7^{6}GF, 5^{1}G

	Starts	1st	2nd	3rd	Win & Pl
Career Total (Turf)	5	1	0	0	1887

57 6/01 Yarm 5f43y G GD £1886
Total win prize-money £1887

Going (Turf): Sf: 0-2 GS: 0-0 **Gd: 1-1** GF: 0-1 Fm: 0-1
Distance: **5f/6f: 1-4** 7f-8f: 0-1 9f-13f: 0-0 14f+: 0-0
Track : LH: 0-0 RH: 0-0 Tight: 0-0 Gall: 0-0
Aids: Bl: 0-0 Vi: 0-0 Tstrap: 0-0
Best Rating: 57 6/01 Yarm 5f43y good

A late foal who is sprint bred, he got off the mark in a seller.

Blakeshall Boy

109 **79**
3-y-o b g Piccolo-Giggleswick Girl (Full Extent (USA))
M R Channon M Bishop

Placings:34140321353000-0023100010300045500 **(5258)**
2001: 6^{0}S, 6^{0}S, 5^{2}GF, 6^{3}S, 5^{1}G, 6^{0}GF, 6^{0}GF, 5^{0}GF, 5^{1}GF, 6^{0}GS, 5^{3}F, 5^{0}G, 5^{0}GF, 5^{0}G, 5^{4}GF, 5^{5}G, 5^{5}G, 5^{0}GS, 5^{0}GS

	Starts	1st	2nd	3rd	Win & Pl
Career Total (Turf)	33	4	2	6	28589

83 6/01 NmkJ 5f D(0-85)H G-F £4862
84 5/01 Wind 5f10y D(0-85)H GD £7787
78 8/00 Sand 5f6y D GD £4368
70 5/00 Brig 5f59y D G-F £2746
Total win prize-money £19763

Going (Turf): Sf: 0-6 GS: 0-4 **Gd: 2-12 GF: 2-10** Fm: 0-1
Distance: **5f/6f: 4-30** 7f-8f: 0-3 9f-13f: 0-0 14f+: 0-0
Track : LH: 1-4 RH: 1-1 Tight: 0-0 **Gall: 1-2**
Aids: Bl: 0-0 Vi: 0-0 Tstrap: 0-0
Best Rating: 84 7/01 Bath 5f11y firm

Fair sprinter who takes a lot of racing well. Five furlongs and good ground suits. Has won twice in 2001 and likes to come from well off the pace, which means he is sometimes unlucky in running.

Blakeshall Joe

(76) (27)
3-y-o ch g Fraam-Lorcanjo (Hallgate)
J G Given A Clarke

Placings:4-003 **(0140)**
2001: 7^{0}SD, 8^{0}SD, 9^{3}SW

	Starts	1st	2nd	3rd	Win & Pl
Career Total (Turf)	0	0	0	0	
Career Total (AW)	4	0	0	1	260

Going (Turf): Sf: 0-0 GS: 0-0 Gd: 0-0 GF: 0-0 Fm: 0-0
Distance: 5f/6f: 0-1 7f-8f: 0-2 9f-13f: 0-1 14f+: 0-0
Track : LH: 0-4 RH: 0-0 Tight: 0-2 Gall: 0-0
Aids: Bl: 0-3 Vi: 0-0 Tstrap: 0-0
Best Rating: 27 1/01 Wolv 1m1f79y slow

Blayney Dancer

80(94) (55)**3**
4-y-o b c Contract Law (USA)-Lady Poly (Dunbeath (USA))
Jamie Poulton Mrs M Liston

Placings:060/036500300-000 **(5471)**
2001: 12^{0}GF, 11^{0}S, 11^{0}S

	Starts	1st	2nd	3rd	Win & Pl
Career Total (Turf)	9	0	0	1	329
Career Total (AW)	6	0	0	1	418

Going (Turf): Sf: 0-4 GS: 0-1 Gd: 0-0 GF: 0-4 Fm: 0-0
Distance: 5f/6f: 0-2 7f-8f: 0-2 9f-13f: 0-8 14f+: 0-3
Track : LH: 0-11 RH: 0-2 Tight: 0-10 Gall: 0-0
Aids: Bl: 0-0 Vi: 0-0 Tstrap: 0-0
Best Rating: 3 10/01 Brig 1m3f196y soft

Blazing Billy

83(49) **11**
6-y-o ch g Anshan-Worthy Venture (Northfields (USA))
C A Dwyer R West

Placings:0/460000/0000/0-00 **(2113)**
2001: 5^{0}G, 6^{0}F

	Starts	1st	2nd	3rd	Win & Pl
Career Total (Turf)	11	0	0	0	
Career Total (AW)	3	0	0	0	0

Going (Turf): Sf: 0-0 GS: 0-1 Gd: 0-5 GF: 0-2 Fm: 0-3
Distance: 5f/6f: 0-8 7f-8f: 0-4 9f-13f: 0-2 14f+: 0-0
Track : LH: 0-5 RH: 0-0 Tight: 0-3 Gall: 0-0
Aids: Bl: 0-0 Vi: 0-1 Tstrap: 0-0
Best Rating: 11 5/01 Yarm 5f43y good

Blazing Saddles (IRE)

83 **72**
2-y-o b c Sadler's Wells (USA)-Dalawara (IRE) (Top Ville)
I A Balding Mike Charlton And Rodger Sargent

Placings:0 **(5367)**
2001: 8^{0}GS

	Starts	1st	2nd	3rd	Win & Pl
Career Total (Turf)	1	0	0	0	

Going (Turf): Sf: 0-0 GS: 0-1 Gd: 0-0 GF: 0-0 Fm: 0-0
Distance: 5f/6f: 0-0 7f-8f: 0-1 9f-13f: 0-0 14f+: 0-0
Track : LH: 0-0 RH: 0-0 Tight: 0-0 Gall: 0-0
Aids: Bl: 0-0 Vi: 0-0 Tstrap: 0-0
Best Rating: 72 10/01 NmkR 1m gd-sft

Blenheim Terrace

100 (42)**35**
8-y-o b g Rambo Dancer (CAN)-Boulevard Girl (Nicholas Bill)
W H Tinning W H Tinning

Placings:3000/044122220/200414/10-0002055 **(4901)**
2001: 12^{0}GF, 10^{0}GF, 10^{0}GF, 12^{2}G, 11^{0}GF, 14^{5}GF, 11^{5}G

	Starts	1st	2nd	3rd	Win & Pl
Career Total (Turf)	26	3	6	0	14948
Career Total (AW)	2	0	0	1	329

43 10/00 Rdcr 1m3f F SFT £2373
56 9/97 Muss 1m4f E(0-70)H G-F £3132
50 7/96 Muss 1m3f32y F GD £2577
Total win prize-money £8082

Going (Turf): Sf: 1-1 GS: 0-2 **Gd: 1-8 GF: 1-15** Fm: 0-0
Distance: 5f/6f: 0-1 7f-8f: 0-3 **9f-13f: 3-21** 14f+: 0-3
Track : LH: 1-16 **RH: 2-10 Tight: 3-16** Gall: 0-6
Aids: Bl: 0-0 Vi: 0-0 Tstrap: 0-0
Best Rating: 35 9/01 Rdcr 1m6f19y gd-fm

A winner of a claimer at Redcar in 2000 having not raced on the Flat for three years. Little show on fast ground in 2001. He needs holding up.

Bless

79(106) (48)**51**
4-y-o ch f Beveled (USA)-Ballystate (Ballacashtal (CAN))
M Madgwick Gail Gaisford And Friends

Placings:40006/0060033003-0100 **(0733)**
2001: 7^{0}SW, 12^{1}SW, 13^{0}SD, 11^{0}GS

	Starts	1st	2nd	3rd	Win & Pl
Career Total (Turf)	14	0	0	2	848
Career Total (AW)	5	1	0	1	3217

48 2/01 Ling 1m4f E(0-75)H SLW £2891
Total win prize-money £2891

Going (Turf): Sf: 0-2 GS: 0-3 Gd: 0-0 GF: 0-4 Fm: 0-5
Distance: 5f/6f: 0-4 7f-8f: 0-2 **9f-13f: 1-13** 14f+: 0-0
Track : **LH: 1-11** RH: 0-3 **Tight: 1-10** Gall: 0-1
Aids: Bl: 0-1 **Vi: 1-8** Tstrap: 0-0
Best Rating: 48 2/01 Ling 1m4f slow

Blessingindisguise

105 **67**
8-y-o b g Kala Shikari-Blowing Bubbles (Native Admiral (USA))
M W Easterby A G Black

Placings:01220/040400050/00022101211133U03/6011000/00000400010/5020620000-000410604405000 **(5685)**
2001: 5^{0}S, 5^{0}S, 5^{0}GS, 5^{4}GF, 5^{1}F, 5^{0}GF, 5^{6}G, 5^{0}GF, 6^{4}F, 5^{4}GF, 6^{0}GF, 5^{5}S, 5^{0}GS, 5^{0}S, 5^{0}S

	Starts	1st	2nd	3rd	Win & Pl
Career Total (Turf)	74	10	7	3	93725

71 6/01 Newc 5f E(0-70)H FRM £3815
76 9/99 Newc 5f C(0-100)H G-F £7165
100 7/98 Asct 5f B(0-100)H G-F £15854
97 7/98 York 5f C(0-100)H G-F £7115
94 7/97 Asct 5f B(0-100)H GD £15520
80 7/97 Ayr 5f C(0-90)H G-F £5121
71 7/97 Hayd 5f E(0-70)H GD £3078
67 6/97 Ripn 5f D(0-80)H GD £3501
61 5/97 Rdcr 5f C(0-90)H G-F £5328
58 5/95 Newc 5f F GD £2274
Total win prize-money £68774

Going (Turf): Sf: 0-7 GS: 0-6 Gd: 4-30 **GF: 5-24** Fm: 1-7
Distance: **5f/6f: 10-72** 7f-8f: 0-2 9f-13f: 0-0 14f+: 0-0
Track : LH: 0-4 RH: 0-0 Tight: 0-0 Gall: 0-0
Aids: **Bl: 9-58** Vi: 0-0 Tstrap: 0-0
Best Rating: 71 8/01 Thsk 6f firm

He had been in the doldrums for a while, but a steady drop in the handicap finally saw him return to winning form at Newcastle in June. He is a true five-furlong specialist with all of his career wins having come over that trip.

Blind Spot

103(87) (34)**60+**
3-y-o ch c Inchinor-High Tern (High Line)
E A L Dunlop Abdulla Buhaleeba

Placings:000-06100 **(3369)**
2001: 11^{0}SD, 8^{6}GF, 8^{1}GF, 8^{0}GF, 7^{0}GF

	Starts	1st	2nd	3rd	Win & Pl
Career Total (Turf)	7	1	0	0	3528
Career Total (AW)	1	0	0	0	

60 6/01 Nott 1m54y E(0-70)H G-F £3528
Total win prize-money £3528

Going (Turf): Sf: 0-1 GS: 0-1 Gd: 0-1 **GF: 1-4** Fm: 0-0
Distance: 5f/6f: 0-1 7f-8f: 0-3 **9f-13f: 1-4** 14f+: 0-0
Track : **LH: 1-2** RH: 0-1 Tight: 0-1 Gall: 0-0
Aids: Bl: 0-0 Vi: 0-0 Tstrap: 0-0
Best Rating: 60 6/01 Nott 1m54y gd-fm

Blixen (USA)

85 **80**
3-y-o b f Gone West (USA)-Danish (IRE) (Danehill (USA))
Saeed Bin Suroor Godolphin

Placings:13-4 **(1844)**
2001: 7^{4}GF

	Starts	1st	2nd	3rd	Win & Pl
Career Total (Turf)	3	1	0	1	9672

80 7/00 Curr 6f G-Y £6900
Total win prize-money £6900

Going (Turf): Sf: 0-0 GS: 0-0 Gd: 0-0 GF: 0-1 Fm: 0-0
Distance: **5f/6f: 1-1** 7f-8f: 0-1 9f-13f: 0-0 14f+: 0-0

Track : LH: 0-0 RH: 0-0 Tight: 0-0 Gall: 0-0
Aids: Bl: 0-0 Vi: 0-0 Tstrap: 0-0
Best Rating: 55 6/01 Leic 7f9y gd-fm

Blodwen (USA)

93 **50**

3-y-o b f Mister Baileys-Ma Biche (USA) (Key To The Kingdom (USA))
M L W Bell Usk Valley Stud

Placings:00000000 **(5601)**
2001: 7^{0}G, 6^{0}F, 6^{0}G, 8^{0}GS, 8^{0}GF, 12^{0}F, 9^{0}G, 8^{0}GS

	Starts	1st	2nd	3rd	Win & Pl
Career Total (Turf)	8	0	0	0	

Going (Turf): Sf: 0-0 GS: 0-2 Gd: 0-3 GF: 0-1 Fm: 0-2
Distance: 5f/6f: 0-2 7f-8f: 0-2 9f-13f: 0-4 14f+: 0-0
Track : LH: 0-3 RH: 0-1 Tight: 0-2 Gall: 0-0
Aids: Bl: 0-1 Vi: 0-0 Tstrap: 0-0
Best Rating: 63 5/01 NmkR 7f good

Blooming Lucky (IRE)

(68) (16)

2-y-o b f Lucky Guest-Persian Flower (Persian Heights)
J A Osborne Wetherby Racing Bureau 51

Placings:0 **(5614)**
2001: 6^{0}SD, 6^{0}SD

	Starts	1st	2nd	3rd	Win & Pl
Career Total (Turf)	0	0	0	0	
Career Total (AW)	1	0	0	0	

Going (Turf): Sf: 0-0 GS: 0-0 Gd: 0-0 GF: 0-0 Fm: 0-0
Distance: 5f/6f: 0-1 7f-8f: 0-0 9f-13f: 0-0 14f+: 0-0
Track : LH: 0-1 RH: 0-0 Tight: 0-1 Gall: 0-0
Aids: Bl: 0-0 Vi: 0-0 Tstrap: 0-0
Best Rating: 16 11/01 Wolv 6f stand

Blossom Whispers

(98) (57)**57**

4-y-o b f Ezzoud (IRE)-Springs Welcome (Blakeney)
C A Cyzer Mrs E A Cyzer

Placings:06432306-0220 **(5411)**
2001: 11^{0}GF, 10^{2}GF, 12^{2}SD, 14^{0}SD

	Starts	1st	2nd	3rd	Win & Pl
Career Total (Turf)	9	0	2	2	3252
Career Total (AW)	3	0	1	0	704

Going (Turf): Sf: 0-1 GS: 0-0 Gd: 0-2 GF: 0-6 Fm: 0-0
Distance: 5f/6f: 0-0 7f-8f: 0-0 9f-13f: 0-7 14f+: 0-5
Track : LH: 0-7 RH: 0-5 Tight: 0-5 Gall: 0-1
Aids: Bl: 0-0 Vi: 0-0 Tstrap: 0-0
Best Rating: 57 9/01 Wolv 1m4f stand

Blowing Away (IRE)

88(94) (19)**14**

7-y-o b/br m Last Tycoon-Taken By Force (Persian Bold)
Julian Poulton (J Pearce 25/1) Mrs M B Fernandez

Placings:0/335600010/432524033630/00/00050310440 5-6545060060 **(2047)**
2001: 16^{6}SD, 14^{5}SW, 12^{4}SD, 10^{5}SD, 12^{0}SW, 10^{6}SD, 15^{0}HY, 9^{0}GF, 11^{6}F, 11^{0}GF

	Starts	1st	2nd	3rd	Win & Pl
Career Total (Turf)	33	2	2	7	9351
Career Total (AW)	13	0	0	0	0

28 8/00 Brig 1m3f196yF(0-60)H G-F £2299
54 10/97 Leic 1m8y F GD £2868
Total win prize-money £5168

Going (Turf): Sf: 0-4 GS: 0-3 **Gd: 1-8 GF: 1-15** Fm: 0-3
Distance: 5f/6f: 0-0 7f-8f: 0-2 **9f-13f: 2-35** 14f+: 0-9
Track : **LH: 1-32** RH: 0-7 Tight: 0-21 Gall: 0-0
Aids: Bl: 0-0 Vi: 0-4 Tstrap: 0-0
Best Rating: 22 3/01 Ling 1m4f slow

Blue Away (IRE)

106(87) (39)**65**

3-y-o b/br g Blues Traveller (IRE)-Lomond Heights (IRE) (Lomond (USA))
C F Wall N Ahamad

Placings:0-0341152 **(5098)**
2001: 7^{0}SD, 11^{3}SD, 11^{4}G, 12^{1}GF, 16^{1}GF, 16^{5}GF, 14^{2}GS

	Starts	1st	2nd	3rd	Win & Pl
Career Total (Turf)	6	2	1	0	7389
Career Total (AW)	2	0	0	1	322

63 7/01 Yarm 2m E(0-70)H G-F £3526
59 6/01 Wwck 1m4f134yF(0-60)H G-F £2474
Total win prize-money £6001

Going (Turf): Sf: 0-1 GS: 0-1 Gd: 0-1 **GF: 2-3** Fm: 0-0
Distance: 5f/6f: 0-0 7f-8f: 0-2 9f-13f: 1-3 14f+: 1-3
Track : **LH: 2-4** RH: 0-3 **Tight: 1-3** Gall: 0-0
Aids: Bl: 0-0 Vi: 0-0 Tstrap: 0-0
Best Rating: 65 10/01 Sals 1m6f15y gd-sft

Has improved for a step up in distance, winning over an extended mile and a half before a cosy success over two miles at Yarmouth. Although he was disappointing at Ripon when reportedly returning with fibrillating heart, he showed no ill effects next time when second at Salisbury. Acts on most ground.

Blue Cascade (IRE)

73 **31**

2-y-o b c Royal Academy (USA)-Blaine (USA) (Lyphard's Wish (FR))
J D Bethell M J Dawson

Placings:00 **(5262)**
2001: 6^{0}GF, 7^{0}GS

	Starts	1st	2nd	3rd	Win & Pl
Career Total (Turf)	2	0	0	0	

Going (Turf): Sf: 0-0 GS: 0-1 Gd: 0-0 GF: 0-1 Fm: 0-0
Distance: 5f/6f: 0-0 7f-8f: 0-2 9f-13f: 0-0 14f+: 0-0
Track : LH: 0-2 RH: 0-0 Tight: 0-0 Gall: 0-2
Aids: Bl: 0-0 Vi: 0-0 Tstrap: 0-0
Best Rating: 31 9/01 York 6f214y gd-fm

Blue Eyes

(98) (47)**45**

3-y-o br g Imp Society (USA)-Morning Surprise (Tragic Role (USA))
S R Bowring (A P Jarvis 29/5) Roland M Wheatley

Placings:46-6100000 **(5349)**
2001: 6^{6}SD, 5^{1}SD, 5^{0}SD, 6^{0}SD, 5^{0}G, 5^{0}F, 5^{0}SD

	Starts	1st	2nd	3rd	Win & Pl
Career Total (Turf)	2	0	0	0	
Career Total (AW)	7	1	0	0	1813

62 3/01 Sthl 5f G STD £1813
Total win prize-money £1813

Going (Turf): Sf: 0-0 GS: 0-0 Gd: 0-1 GF: 0-0 Fm: 0-1
Distance: **5f/6f: 1-9** 7f-8f: 0-0 9f-13f: 0-0 14f+: 0-0
Track : LH: 0-3 RH: 0-0 Tight: 0-0 Gall: 0-0
Aids: Bl: 0-1 Vi: 0-0 Tstrap: 0-0
Best Rating: 62 3/01 Sthl 5f stand

Blue Forest (IRE)

(93) (81)**81**

3-y-o b c Charnwood Forest (IRE)-Vian (USA) (Far Out East (USA))
P C Haslam Alex Gorrie

Placings:1264-P **(0047)**
2001: 7^{P}SD

	Starts	1st	2nd	3rd	Win & Pl
Career Total (Turf)	2	1	1	0	4533
Career Total (AW)	3	0	0	0	0

70 3/00 Newc 5f D GD £3419
Total win prize-money £3419

Going (Turf): Sf: 0-1 GS: 0-0 **Gd: 1-1** GF: 0-0 Fm: 0-0
Distance: **5f/6f: 1-1** 7f-8f: 0-3 9f-13f: 0-1 14f+: 0-0
Track : LH: 0-3 RH: 0-0 Tight: 0-2 Gall: 0-0
Aids: Bl: 0-0 Vi: 0-0 Tstrap: 0-0
Best Rating: 70 3/00 Newc 5f G

Blue Gold

110 **106**

4-y-o b c Rainbow Quest (USA)-Relatively Special (Alzao (USA))
R Hannon Mohamed Suhail

Placings:5133/420120123-4615034 **(4847)**
2001: 9^{4}GF, 11^{6}G, 10^{1}GF, 12^{5}GF, 10^{0}GF, 10^{3}G, 10^{4}GF

	Starts	1st	2nd	3rd	Win & Pl
Career Total (Turf)	20	4	3	4	92483

106 6/01 Kemp 1m2f A G-F £15275
104 8/00 Gdwd 1m4f B(0-105)H G-F £45500
97 6/00 Sand 1m2f7y C(0-100)H G-F £10725
83 7/99 Sand 7f16y D G-F £3761
Total win prize-money £75261

Going (Turf): Sf: 0-1 GS: 0-0 Gd: 0-8 **GF: 4-11** Fm: 0-0
Distance: 5f/6f: 0-1 7f-8f: 1-2 **9f-13f: 3-17** 14f+: 0-0
Track : LH: 0-6 **RH: 4-11** Tight: 1-7 Gall: 1-5
Aids: Bl: 0-0 Vi: 0-0 Tstrap: 0-0
Best Rating: 107 5/01 Gdwd 1m1f192y gd-fm

A game performer, he landed a valuable handicap at Glorious Goodwood in 2000 and stepped up in class and distance when a good third to Lear Spear in 12-furlong Listed event at Doncaster on his last start at three. Landed a listed race at Kempton in 2001, but has not really fired otherwise. Acts on a sound surface and is usually held up.

Blue Hawaii (IRE)

(83) (2)**54**

4-y-o ch g Up And At 'Em-Astral Way (Hotfoot)
S R Bowring Simon Mapletoft

Placings:36000/2000000-0 **(0030)**
2001: 16^{0}SD

	Starts	1st	2nd	3rd	Win & Pl
Career Total (Turf)	7	0	1	1	1462
Career Total (AW)	6	0	0	0	

Going (Turf): Sf: 0-1 GS: 0-2 Gd: 0-3 GF: 0-1 Fm: 0-0
Distance:. 5f/6f: 0-2 7f-8f: 0-5 9f-13f: 0-4 14f+: 0-2
Track : LH: 0-7 RH: 0-2 Tight: 0-2 Gall: 0-1
Aids: Bl: 0-1 Vi: 0-0 Tstrap: 0-1
Best Rating: 2 1/01 Sthl 2m stand

Blue Hawk (IRE)

(99) (54)**49**

4-y-o ch g Prince Of Birds (USA)-Classic Queen (IRE) (Classic Secret (USA))
R Hollinshead Mrs Dianne E Edwards

Placings:050300/0060-2021020 **(5411)**
2001: 16^{2}GF, 14^{0}GF, 14^{2}SD, 15^{1}G, 15^{0}GF, 12^{2}SD, 14^{0}SD

	Starts	1st	2nd	3rd	Win & Pl
Career Total (Turf)	14	1	1	1	5186
Career Total (AW)	3	0	2	0	1542

49 8/01 Catt 1m7f177yE(0-70)H GD £3304
Total win prize-money £3304

Going (Turf): Sf: 0-1 GS: 0-1 **Gd: 1-4** GF: 0-8 Fm: 0-0
Distance: 5f/6f: 0-1 7f-8f: 0-6 9f-13f: 0-4 **14f+: 1-6**
Track : **LH: 1-10** RH: 0-3 **Tight: 1-8** Gall: 0-0
Aids: Bl: 0-0 Vi: 0-0 Tstrap: 0-0

Best Rating: 54 8/01 Wolv 1m6f166y stand

Blue Holly (IRE)

102(88) (40)**79**

4-y-o b f Blues Traveller (IRE)-Holly Bird (Runnett)

J S Moore (J M Bradley 18/7) Andrew Sim

Placings:000223123/5201000000-00040050216100210000 **(5381)**

2001: 5^{0}S, 5^{0}GS, 5^{0}G, 5^{4}F, 5^{0}GF, 5^{0}GF, 5^{5}GF, 6^{0}GF, 7^{2}GS, 6^{1}F, 5^{6}G, 5^{1}G, 5^{0}GF, 5^{0}G, 5^{2}GF, 5^{1}GF, 5^{0}GF, 5^{0}GS, 6^{0}GS, 5^{0}S

	Starts	1st	2nd	3rd	Win & Pl
Career Total (Turf)	38	5	6	2	24801
Career Total (AW)	1	0	0	0	

79	8/01	Folk	5f	E(0-75)H	G-F	£2821
78	8/01	Leic	5f2y	E(0-70)H	GD	£3094
68	7/01	Ling	6f	E(0-70)H	FRM	£3416
80	6/00	Chep	5f16y	D(0-85)H	GD	£3900
87	10/99	Ling	5f	F	G-F	£2594

Total win prize-money £15825

Going (Turf): Sf: 0-8 GS: 0-5 **Gd: 2-9 GF: 2-14** Fm: 1-2
Distance: **5f/6f: 5-38** 7f-8f: 0-1 9f-13f: 0-0 14f+: 0-0
Track : LH: 0-8 RH: 0-1 Tight: 0-2 Gall: 0-5
Aids: **Bl: 2-10** Vi: 0-1 Tstrap: 0-0
Best Rating: 79 8/01 Folk 5f gd-fm

Has been running well on fast ground this season. Likes fast ground and effective over five or six furlongs. Effective with or without blinkers, needs producing late.

Blue Jay Way

54

3-y-o b g Dr Devious (IRE)-Skuld (Kris)

J S Wainwright M J Sissons

Placings:00 **(2029)**

2001: 7^{0}GF, 9^{0}GF

	Starts	1st	2nd	3rd	Win & Pl
Career Total (Turf)	2	0	0	0	

Going (Turf): Sf: 0-0 GS: 0-0 Gd: 0-0 GF: 0-2 Fm: 0-0
Distance: 5f/6f: 0-0 7f-8f: 0-1 9f-13f: 0-1 14f+: 0-0
Track : LH: 0-0 RH: 0-2 Tight: 0-1 Gall: 0-0
Aids: Bl: 0-0 Vi: 0-0 Tstrap: 0-0

Blue Kite

(111) (49)**31**

6-y-o ch g Silver Kite (USA)-Gold And Blue (IRE) (Bluebird (USA))

M Mullineaux (N P Littmoden 13/6) T Clarke

Placings:222626105/545002204000050/504204000501 2233261/1660345100246000500-0030000314000U000 **(4603)**

2001: 6^{0}SD, 6^{0}SD, 7^{3}SD, 6^{0}SD, 7^{0}SD, 6^{0}SD, 7^{0}SD, 6^{3}SD, 6^{1}SD, 6^{4}GF, 6^{0}SD, 6^{0}GF, 6^{0}GF, 7^{U}GF, 7^{0}G, 6^{0}GS, 7^{0}SD

	Starts	1st	2nd	3rd	Win & Pl
Career Total (Turf)	32	0	4	0	5075
Career Total (AW)	47	6	7	5	33295

45	5/01	Wolv	6f	G	STD	£1372
84	3/00	Sthl	6f	D(0-80)H	STD	£4348
79	1/00	Wolv	6f	D(0-85)H	STD	£5291
71	12/99	Sthl	6f	E(0-75)H	SLW	£2374
66	9/99	Wolv	6f	E(0-70)H	STD	£2932
72	9/97	Wolv	5f	F	STD	£2277

Total win prize-money £18596

Going (Turf): Sf: 0-3 GS: 0-6 Gd: 0-11 GF: 0-11 Fm: 0-1
Distance: **5f/6f: 6-53** 7f-8f: 0-26 9f-13f: 0-0 14f+: 0-0
Track : **LH: 6-53** RH: 0-2 **Tight: 4-37** Gall: 0-2
Aids: Bl: 0-1 Vi: 0-4 Tstrap: 0-2
Best Rating: 67 3/01 Wolv 6f stand

He showed a useful level of form on both Fibresand and turf as a juvenile, but went on a long losing run after that. He has returned to something like his best this winter, winning some decent six-furlong handicaps on Fibresand. A strongly-run race suits him best.

Blue Knight (IRE)

87 **70**

2-y-o ch c Bluebird (USA)-Fer De Lance (IRE) (Diesis)

A P Jarvis Jarvis Associates

Placings:00 **(5343)**

2001: 6^{0}S, 6^{0}GS

	Starts	1st	2nd	3rd	Win & Pl
Career Total (Turf)	2	0	0	0	

Going (Turf): Sf: 0-1 GS: 0-1 Gd: 0-0 GF: 0-0 Fm: 0-0
Distance: 5f/6f: 0-2 7f-8f: 0-0 9f-13f: 0-0 14f+: 0-0
Track : LH: 0-0 RH: 0-0 Tight: 0-0 Gall: 0-0
Aids: Bl: 0-0 Vi: 0-0 Tstrap: 0-0
Best Rating: 70 10/01 NmkR 6f gd-sft

Blue Lady (IRE)

(96) (35)**27**

3-y-o b f College Chapel-Dancing Bluebell (IRE) (Bluebird (USA))

B P J Baugh Joe Singh

Placings:06506336126541-20060600000 **(5418)**

2001: 6^{2}SD, 6^{0}SW, 8^{0}SD, 8^{6}SW, 8^{0}HY, 8^{6}F, 8^{0}SD, 8^{0}GF, 7^{0}GF, 9^{0}GS, 7^{0}SD, 6^{0}SD

	Starts	1st	2nd	3rd	Win & Pl
Career Total (Turf)	10	0	0	0	0
Career Total (AW)	15	2	2	2	9247

58	12/00	Wolv	6f	F	STD	£2240
56	10/00	Wolv	6f	F	STD	£1736

Total win prize-money £3976

Going (Turf): Sf: 0-2 GS: 0-2 Gd: 0-1 GF: 0-4 Fm: 0-1
Distance: **5f/6f: 2-11** 7f-8f: 0-9 9f-13f: 0-5 14f+: 0-0
Track : **LH: 2-20** RH: 0-2 **Tight: 2-10** Gall: 0-2
Aids: Bl: 0-0 Vi: 0-0 Tstrap: 0-0
Best Rating: 55 1/01 Sthl 6f stand

Blue Lagoon

75 **33**

2-y-o gr g Lugana Beach-Aimee Jane (USA) (Our Native (USA))

N Tinkler Philip J Grundy

Placings:000 **(5627)**

2001: 5^{0}GF, 5^{0}GF, 7^{0}G

	Starts	1st	2nd	3rd	Win & Pl
Career Total (Turf)	3	0	0	0	

Going (Turf): Sf: 0-0 GS: 0-0 Gd: 0-1 GF: 0-2 Fm: 0-0
Distance: 5f/6f: 0-2 7f-8f: 0-1 9f-13f: 0-0 14f+: 0-0
Track : LH: 0-0 RH: 0-0 Tight: 0-0 Gall: 0-0
Aids: Bl: 0-0 Vi: 0-0 Tstrap: 0-0
Best Rating: 33 7/01 Bevl 5f gd-fm

Blue Legend (IRE)

90 (38)**18**

4-y-o b f Blues Traveller (IRE)-Swoon Along (Dunphy)

B Mactaggart Mrs Hilary Mactaggart

Placings:00216000/0456-040060 **(3951)**

2001: 8^{0}GF, 8^{4}G, 8^{0}GF, 8^{0}F, 12^{6}G, 13^{0}GS

	Starts	1st	2nd	3rd	Win & Pl
Career Total (Turf)	17	1	1	0	3868
Career Total (AW)	1	0	0	0	0

65	7/99	Brig	6f209y	F	FRM	£2571

Total win prize-money £2572

Going (Turf): Sf: 0-2 GS: 0-3 Gd: 0-5 GF: 0-3 **Fm: 1-4**
Distance: 5f/6f: 0-2 **7f-8f: 1-9** 9f-13f: 0-6 14f+: 0-1
Track : **LH: 1-6** RH: 0-8 Tight: 0-8 Gall: 0-1
Aids: Bl: 0-0 Vi: 0-0 Tstrap: 0-0
Best Rating: 18 8/01 Muss 1m4f good

Blue Line Angel

90 **26**

5-y-o b g Cyrano De Bergerac-Northern Line (Camden Town)

John Berry P M Harley

Placings:000/034404000/00 **(4624)**

2001: 5^{0}G, 8^{0}GF

	Starts	1st	2nd	3rd	Win & Pl
Career Total (Turf)	13	0	0	1	1074
Career Total (AW)	1	0	0	0	

Going (Turf): Sf: 0-2 GS: 0-1 Gd: 0-3 GF: 0-7 Fm: 0-0
Distance: 5f/6f: 0-4 7f-8f: 0-5 9f-13f: 0-5 14f+: 0-0
Track : LH: 0-3 RH: 0-4 Tight: 0-2 Gall: 0-0
Aids: Bl: 0-0 Vi: 0-0 Tstrap: 0-0
Best Rating: 26 9/01 Nott 1m54y gd-fm

Blue Line Lady (IRE)

(76) (1)**42**

4-y-o b f Common Grounds-Best Academy (USA) (Roberto (USA))

K A Ryan Peter Tingey

Placings:20206000/005000050-**00** **(0658)**

2001: 7^{0}SW, 7^{0}SD

	Starts	1st	2nd	3rd	Win & Pl
Career Total (Turf)	17	0	2	0	2872
Career Total (AW)	2	0	0	0	

Going (Turf): Sf: 0-2 GS: 0-1 Gd: 0-5 GF: 0-8 Fm: 0-1
Distance: 5f/6f: 0-11 7f-8f: 0-8 9f-13f: 0-0 14f+: 0-0
Track : LH: 0-6 RH: 0-2 Tight: 0-2 Gall: 0-0
Aids: Bl: 0-4 Vi: 0-0 Tstrap: 0-0
Best Rating: 1 4/01 Sthl 7f stand

Blue Mantle (IRE)

84 **55**

2-y-o ch f Barathea (IRE)-Blue Wedding (USA) (Irish River (FR))

Sir Mark Prescott Sir Edmund Loder

Placings:006 **(5282)**

2001: 8^{0}HY, 8^{0}HY, 8^{6}HY

	Starts	1st	2nd	3rd	Win & Pl
Career Total (Turf)	3	0	0	0	0

Going (Turf): Sf: 0-3 GS: 0-0 Gd: 0-0 GF: 0-0 Fm: 0-0
Distance: 5f/6f: 0-0 7f-8f: 0-1 9f-13f: 0-2 14f+: 0-0
Track : LH: 0-3 RH: 0-0 Tight: 0-0 Gall: 0-0
Aids: Bl: 0-0 Vi: 0-0 Tstrap: 0-0
Best Rating: 55 9/01 Hayd 1m30y heavy

By Barathea, and a half-sister to several winners, her best performance was in an Ayr maiden over a mile in heavy ground. Now qualified for handicaps, she may appreciate faster ground.

Blue Mountain

113 **102**

4-y-o ch h Elmaamul (USA)-Glenfinlass (Lomond (USA))

R F Johnson Houghton Mrs C J Hue Williams

Placings:235/52211020135-53605000200 **(4782)**

2001: 7^{5}G, 8^{3}G, 7^{6}GF, 8^{0}GF, 8^{5}GF, 8^{0}G, 7^{0}GF, 8^{0}G, 8^{2}G, 7^{0}GF, 7^{0}G

	Starts	1st	2nd	3rd	Win & Pl
Career Total (Turf)	25	3	5	3	53409

100	9/00	Gdwd	7f	C	GD	£6322
93	7/00	Gdwd	6f	C(0-90)H	GD	£14267
88	6/00	Kemp	6f	D(0-85)H	G-F	£4543

Total win prize-money £25134

Going (Turf): Sf: 0-0 GS: 0-3 **Gd: 2-12** GF: 1-10 Fm: 0-0
Distance: **5f/6f: 2-8** 7f-8f: 1-12 9f-13f: 0-5 14f+: 0-0
Track : LH: 0-4 **RH: 1-9** Tight: 0-4 Gall: 0-3
Aids: Bl: 0-0 Vi: 0-0 Tstrap: 0-0
Best Rating: 106 5/01 NmkR 7f good

A winner three times in 2000 at up to seven furlongs, he does just about get a mile but he is high in the handicap and does not look quite good enough for Pattern company. Acts on fast ground.

Blue Orleans

81(95) (54)**46**
3-y-o b g Dancing Spree (USA)-Blues Player (Jaazeiro (USA))
A G Newcombe Advanced Marketing Services Ltd

Placings:3000606-000 **(2522)**
2001: 9^{0}GS, 10^{0}GF, 10^{0}GF

	Starts	1st	2nd	3rd	Win & Pl
Career Total (Turf)	7	0	0	0	0
Career Total (AW)	3	0	0	1	320

Going (Turf): Sf: 0-0 GS: 0-1 Gd: 0-1 GF: 0-5 Fm: 0-0
Distance: 5f/6f: 0-3 7f-8f: 0-3 9f-13f: 0-4 14f+: 0-0
Track : LH: 0-6 RH: 0-0 Tight: 0-2 Gall: 0-2
Aids: Bl: 0-1 Vi: 0-0 Tstrap: 0-0
Best Rating: 16 6/01 Wwck 1m2f188y gd-fm

Blue Planet (IRE)

107 **85**
3-y-o b g Bluebird (USA)-Millie Musique (Miller's Mate)
Sir Mark Prescott Meg Dennis,Michael Blackburn,John Brown

Placings:135-20653 **(4963)**
2001: 8^{2}GF, 8^{0}GF, 8^{6}GF, 8^{5}GF, 10^{3}S

	Starts	1st	2nd	3rd	Win & Pl
Career Total (Turf)	8	1	1	2	8955
64 6/00 Haml 6f5y	D			G-F	£3789

Total win prize-money £3790

Going (Turf): Sf: 0-2 GS: 0-0 Gd: 0-1 **GF: 1-5** Fm: 0-0
Distance: 5f/6f: 0-0 **7f-8f: 1-6** 9f-13f: 0-2 14f+: 0-0
Track : LH: 0-3 RH: 0-1 Tight: 0-0 Gall: 0-0
Aids: Bl: 0-0 Vi: 0-0 Tstrap: 0-0
Best Rating: 85 5/01 Ayr 1m gd-fm

Won on his juvenile debut over six furlongs at Hamilton. Ran respectably on his reappearance in 2001 but failed to build on that.

Blue Pool

92 **36**
3-y-o b f Saddlers' Hall (IRE)-Blue Brocade (Reform)
J A R Toller Alan Gibson

Placings:00-0000 **(5106)**
2001: 6^{0}HY, 14^{0}GF, 11^{0}GF, 12^{0}GS

	Starts	1st	2nd	3rd	Win & Pl
Career Total (Turf)	6	0	0	0	

Going (Turf): Sf: 0-3 GS: 0-1 Gd: 0-0 GF: 0-2 Fm: 0-0
Distance: 5f/6f: 0-0 7f-8f: 0-3 9f-13f: 0-2 14f+: 0-1
Track : LH: 0-2 RH: 0-2 Tight: 0-3 Gall: 0-1
Aids: Bl: 0-0 Vi: 0-0 Tstrap: 0-0
Best Rating: 36 6/01 Yarm 1m6f17y gd-fm

Blue Reigns

104 **92+**
3-y-o b c Whittingham (IRE)-Gold And Blue (IRE) (Bluebird (USA))
N P Littmoden J R Salter

Placings:5112-2060 **(3857)**
2001: 6^{2}G, 7^{0}GF, 6^{6}GF, 5^{0}GS

	Starts	1st	2nd	3rd	Win & Pl
Career Total (Turf)	8	2	2	0	42823
86 9/00 Donc 6f	B			G-F	£27000
73 7/00 Sand 5f6y	E			G-F	£3558

Total win prize-money £30559

Going (Turf): Sf: 0-2 GS: 0-1 Gd: 0-1 **GF: 2-4** Fm: 0-0
Distance: **5f/6f: 2-7** 7f-8f: 0-1 9f-13f: 0-0 14f+: 0-0
Track : LH: 0-1 RH: 0-1 Tight: 0-0 Gall: 0-1
Aids: Bl: 0-0 Vi: 0-0 Tstrap: 0-0
Best Rating: 92 5/01 Ling 6f good

Twice a winner on fast ground as a juvenile in 2000, looked unlucky when touched off on his seasonal debut, then failed to settle on his first try at seven furlongs at Goodwood after which he was tubed. Well regarded, sprinting looks to be his forte.

Blue River (IRE)

(97) (40)**40**
7-y-o ch g River Falls-Royal Resident (Prince Regent (FR))
T G Mills M J Legg

Placings:541155/53250/20 **(0636)**
2001: 12^{2}SD, 13^{0}SD

	Starts	1st	2nd	3rd	Win & Pl
Career Total (Turf)	11	2	1	1	15518
Career Total (AW)	2	0	1	0	542
92 8/96 NmkJ 1m	C			G-S	£6056
86 8/96 NmkJ 7f	D			G-F	£4737

Total win prize-money £10793

Going (Turf): Sf: 0-1 **GS: 1-2** Gd: 0-3 **GF: 1-5** Fm: 0-0
Distance: 5f/6f: 0-0 **7f-8f: 2-6** 9f-13f: 0-7 14f+: 0-0
Track : LH: 0-3 RH: 0-7 Tight: 0-3 Gall: 0-3
Aids: Bl: 0-0 Vi: 0-0 Tstrap: 0-0
Best Rating: 40 3/01 Wolv 1m4f stand

Blue Safari (IRE)

82 **54**
2-y-o b/br f Blues Traveller (IRE)-Lady Montekin (Montekin)
R Hannon Peter M Crane

Placings:0056 **(4410)**
2001: 6^{0}GF, 7^{0}GF, 7^{5}GF, 7^{6}GS

	Starts	1st	2nd	3rd	Win & Pl
Career Total (Turf)	4	0	0	0	0

Going (Turf): Sf: 0-0 GS: 0-1 Gd: 0-0 GF: 0-3 Fm: 0-0
Distance: 5f/6f: 0-1 7f-8f: 0-3 9f-13f: 0-0 14f+: 0-0
Track : LH: 0-1 RH: 0-1 Tight: 0-1 Gall: 0-0
Aids: Bl: 0-0 Vi: 0-0 Tstrap: 0-0
Best Rating: 54 7/01 Folk 7f gd-fm

Blue Satin (IRE)

78 **63?**
4-y-o b f Bluebird (USA)-Cheviot Amble (IRE) (Pennine Walk)
K A Ryan Mrs J Ryan

Placings:4/0020-0 **(1578)**
2001: 10^{0}F

	Starts	1st	2nd	3rd	Win & Pl
Career Total (Turf)	6	0	1	0	1700

Going (Turf): Sf: 0-2 GS: 0-0 Gd: 0-0 GF: 0-1 Fm: 0-1
Distance: 5f/6f: 0-2 7f-8f: 0-1 9f-13f: 0-3 14f+: 0-0
Track : LH: 0-3 RH: 0-2 Tight: 0-0 Gall: 0-0
Aids: Bl: 0-2 Vi: 0-0 Tstrap: 0-0
Best Rating: 8 5/01 Pont 1m2f6y firm

Blue Song

45
3-y-o b f Shaamit (IRE)-November Song (Scorpio (FR))
N P Littmoden T Clarke

Placings:0 **(5631)**
2001: 10^{0}G

	Starts	1st	2nd	3rd	Win & Pl
Career Total (Turf)	1	0	0	0	

Going (Turf): Sf: 0-0 GS: 0-0 Gd: 0-1 GF: 0-0 Fm: 0-0
Distance: 5f/6f: 0-0 7f-8f: 0-0 9f-13f: 0-1 14f+: 0-0
Track : LH: 0-1 RH: 0-0 Tight: 0-1 Gall: 0-0
Aids: Bl: 0-0 Vi: 0-0 Tstrap: 0-0

Blue Streak (IRE)

101(88) (42)**54**
4-y-o ch g Bluebird (USA)-Fleet Amour (USA) (Afleet (CAN))
K Bell Mrs J A Hubbard

Placings:004460-00503500 **(5043)**
2001: 10^{0}G, 8^{0}GF, 10^{5}GF, 7^{0}GF, 8^{3}GF, 8^{5}GF, 9^{0}GF, 8^{0}G

	Starts	1st	2nd	3rd	Win & Pl
Career Total (Turf)	13	0	0	1	1689
Career Total (AW)	1	0	0	0	

Going (Turf): Sf: 0-0 GS: 0-2 Gd: 0-5 GF: 0-6 Fm: 0-0
Distance: 5f/6f: 0-0 7f-8f: 0-5 9f-13f: 0-9 14f+: 0-0
Track : LH: 0-7 RH: 0-4 Tight: 0-6 Gall: 0-2
Aids: Bl: 0-0 Vi: 0-1 Tstrap: 0-0
Best Rating: 54 8/01 Bath 1m5y gd-fm

Blue Street

108(92) (37)**49**
5-y-o b g Deploy-Kumzar (Hotfoot)
S C Williams Tyrnest Ltd

Placings:0060231600004-011000 **(5167)**
2001: 9^{0}GF, 12^{1}S, 14^{1}G, 16^{0}F, 16^{0}GS, 12^{0}GS

	Starts	1st	2nd	3rd	Win & Pl
Career Total (Turf)	16	3	1	1	10877
Career Total (AW)	3	0	0	0	0
49 8/01 Yarm 1m6f17y	E(0-75)H			GD	£3867
42 8/01 Chep 1m4f23y	F(0-65)H			SFT	£2527
53 8/00 Bevl 1m3f216yF(0-60)				G-F	£2310

Total win prize-money £8705

Going (Turf): Sf: 1-3 GS: 0-5 **Gd: 1-4 GF: 1-3** Fm: 0-1
Distance: 5f/6f: 0-0 7f-8f: 0-2 **9f-13f: 2-14** 14f+: 1-3
Track : **LH: 2-13** RH: 1-5 **Tight: 2-9** Gall: 0-2
Aids: Bl: 0-0 Vi: 0-1 Tstrap: 0-0
Best Rating: 49 8/01 Yarm 1m6f17y good

Tough handicapper, successful at Chepstow and Yarmouth in August.

Blue Style (IRE)

99(81) (36)**52**
5-y-o ch g Bluebird (USA)-Style For Life (IRF) (Law Society (USA))
Miss L A Perratt M Mason

Placings:00/612100000-0600 **(5447)**
2001: 13^{0}G, 10^{6}G, 12^{0}GF, 10^{0}HY

	Starts	1st	2nd	3rd	Win & Pl
Career Total (Turf)	13	2	1	0	12726
Career Total (AW)	2	0	0	0	0
65 5/00 Kemp 1m4f	C(0-90)H			G-S	£7182
66 4/00 Brig 1m3f196yF				G-S	£2228

Total win prize-money £9412

Going (Turf): Sf: 0-4 **GS: 2-2** Gd: 0-3 GF: 0-2 Fm: 0-0
Distance: 5f/6f: 0-0 7f-8f: 0-1 **9f-13f: 2-11** 14f+: 0-2
Track : LH: 1-9 RH: 1-5 Tight: 0-6 Gall: 0-2

Aids:	Bl: 0-2 Vi: 0-0 **Tstrap: 1-8**					
Best Rating: 52	9/01	Haml	1m4f17y	gd-fm		

A fair handicappe, has joined Linda Perratt in 2001, but has been lightly-raced.

Blue Sugar (USA)

105 **94**

4-y-o ch g Shuailaan (USA)-Chelsea My Love (USA) (Opening Verse (USA))

J R Fanshawe G Algranti

Placings:1/42221-62003210 **(5142)**

2001: 10^{6}G, 12^{2}F, 12^{0}G, 10^{0}G, 10^{3}GF, 10^{2}G, 10^{1}G, 9^{0}G

	Starts	1st	2nd	3rd	Win & Pl
Career Total (Turf)	14	3	5	1	38777

88	9/01	Epsm	1m2f18y	C(0-90)	GD	£6825
94	8/00	NmkJ	1m2f	C(0-95)H	G-F	£10770
88	8/99	Ling	7f140y	F	G-F	£2165

Total win prize-money £19762

Going (Turf): Sf: 0-1 GS: 0-1 Gd: 1-6 **GF: 2-5** Fm: 0-1
Distance: 5f/6f: 0-0 7f-8f: 1-4 **9f-13f: 2-10** 14f+: 0-0
Track : LH: 1-5 RH: 1-4 Tight: 1-3 Gall: 1-5
Aids: Bl: 0-0 Vi: 0-1 Tstrap: 0-1
Best Rating: 95 6/01 Thsk 1m4f firm

Ended a frustrating run of seconds when winning a rated stakes at Newmarket in August 2000 on his first attempt at ten furlongs. Has shown enough this term to suggest he retains his ability, including when winning at Epsom in September. Best at ten furlongs on a fast surface.

Blue Velvet

108 (65+)**89**

4-y-o gr f Formidable (USA)-Sweet Whisper (Petong)

K T Ivory K T Ivory

Placings:442342120061024/6000011650623063-243006000400 **(5403)**

2001: 5^{2}GS, 5^{4}GS, 5^{3}G, 6^{0}GF, 6^{0}GF, 6^{6}Y, 5^{0}GF, 5^{0}G, 6^{0}G, 5^{4}HY, 5^{0}HY, 5^{0}S

	Starts	1st	2nd	3rd	Win & Pl
Career Total (Turf)	41	3	6	4	59316
Career Total (AW)	2	1	0	0	2464

89	7/00	NmkJ	6f	B(0-100)H	G-S	£10092
86	7/00	Sand	5f6y	D(0-80)H	GD	£5073
81	9/99	NmkJ	5f	C(0-95)H	G-S	£8025
65	6/99	Sthl	5f	F	STD	£2253

Total win prize-money £25443

Going (Turf): Sf: 0-9 **GS: 2-6** Gd: 1-12 GF: 0-13 Fm: 0-0
Distance: **5f/6f: 4-37** 7f-8f: 0-6 9f-13f: 0-0 14f+: 0-0
Track : LH: 0-6 RH: 0-1 Tight: 0-1 Gall: 0-3
Aids: Bl: 0-0 Vi: 0-0 Tstrap: 0-0
Best Rating: 97 5/01 Bath 5f11y gd-sft

A useful sprint handicapper, she won two handicaps in July 2000 at Sandown and Newmarket, but she has found life tougher this season, being short of Pattern class and unable to give lumps of weight away in top handicap company.

Blueberry Rhyme

99 **76**

2-y-o b g Alhijaz-Irenic (Mummy's Pet)

P J Makin Mrs P J Makin

Placings:005204 **(5526)**

2001: 6^{0}GF, 6^{0}G, 5^{5}HY, 5^{2}GS, 6^{0}GS, 5^{4}S

	Starts	1st	2nd	3rd	Win & Pl
Career Total (Turf)	6	0	1	0	2433

Going (Turf): Sf: 0-2 GS: 0-2 Gd: 0-1 GF: 0-1 Fm: 0-0
Distance: 5f/6f: 0-4 7f-8f: 0-2 9f-13f: 0-0 14f+: 0-0
Track : LH: 0-0 RH: 0-0 Tight: 0-0 Gall: 0-0
Aids: Bl: 0-0 Vi: 0-2 Tstrap: 0-0
Best Rating: 76 10/01 NmkR 5f gd-sft

Signs of ability although improvement needed to win a race.

Bluegrass

56 **37**

2-y-o ch c Bluegrass Prince (IRE)-Seymour Ann (Krayyan)

M Madgwick Exors Of The Late J M T Gaisford

Placings:00 **(5177)**

2001: 7^{0}F, 6^{0}HY

	Starts	1st	2nd	3rd	Win & Pl
Career Total (Turf)	2	0	0	0	

Going (Turf): Sf: 0-1 GS: 0-0 Gd: 0-0 GF: 0-0 Fm: 0-1
Distance: 5f/6f: 0-1 7f-8f: 0-1 9f-13f: 0-0 14f+: 0-0
Track : LH: 0-0 RH: 0-0 Tight: 0-0 Gall: 0-0
Aids: Bl: 0-0 Vi: 0-0 Tstrap: 0-0
Best Rating: 37 10/01 Wind 6f heavy

Bluegrass Hopper

58 **1**

2-y-o b f Bluegrass Prince (IRE)-Heavenly State (Enchantment)

M Madgwick Mrs Gail Gaisford

Placings:050 **(3804)**

2001: 5^{0}GF, 6^{5}F, 6^{0}GF

	Starts	1st	2nd	3rd	Win & Pl
Career Total (Turf)	3	0	0	0	0

Going (Turf): Sf: 0-0 GS: 0-0 Gd: 0-0 GF: 0-2 Fm: 0-1
Distance: 5f/6f: 0-2 7f-8f: 0-1 9f-13f: 0-0 14f+: 0-0
Track : LH: 0-1 RH: 0-0 Tight: 0-0 Gall: 0-0
Aids: Bl: 0-0 Vi: 0-1 Tstrap: 0-0
Best Rating: 1 7/01 Brig 6f209y firm

Blues Band (IRE)

84 **32**

2-y-o b/br f Blues Traveller (IRE)-Davenport Goddess (IRE) (Classic Secret (USA))

R Hannon Speedlith Group

Placings:00 **(4287)**

2001: 7^{0}GF, 8^{0}GF

	Starts	1st	2nd	3rd	Win & Pl
Career Total (Turf)	2	0	0	0	

Going (Turf): Sf: 0-0 GS: 0-0 Gd: 0-0 GF: 0-2 Fm: 0-0
Distance: 5f/6f: 0-0 7f-8f: 0-1 9f-13f: 0-1 14f+: 0-0
Track : LH: 0-0 RH: 0-0 Tight: 0-0 Gall: 0-0
Aids: Bl: 0-0 Vi: 0-0 Tstrap: 0-0
Best Rating: 32 8/01 Chep 1m14y gd-fm

Bluewatch (IRE)

95 **64**

3-y-o b c Bluebird (USA)-Fire Of London (Shirley Heights)

G Wragg Mollers Racing

Placings:6066 **(5173)**

2001: 8^{6}GF, 7^{0}GF, 7^{6}GF, 8^{6}GS

	Starts	1st	2nd	3rd	Win & Pl
Career Total (Turf)	4	0	0	0	0

Going (Turf): Sf: 0-0 GS: 0-1 Gd: 0-0 GF: 0-3 Fm: 0-0
Distance: 5f/6f: 0-0 7f-8f: 0-3 9f-13f: 0-1 14f+: 0-0
Track : LH: 0-2 RH: 0-0 Tight: 0-1 Gall: 0-0
Aids: Bl: 0-0 Vi: 0-0 Tstrap: 0-0
Best Rating: 64 8/01 NmkJ 1m gd-fm

Blundell Lane (IRE)

(93) (56)**66**

6-y-o ch g Shalford (IRE)-Rathbawn Realm (Doulab (USA))

A P Jarvis Nick Coverdale

Placings:25015/301000000/0041036000000/100604004-0531340100 **(5051)**

2001: 6^{0}SD, 5^{5}F, 6^{3}GF, 6^{1}GF, 7^{3}GS, 6^{4}GF, 5^{0}GF, 6^{1}G, 6^{0}GF, 6^{0}SD

	Starts	1st	2nd	3rd	Win & Pl
Career Total (Turf)	39	6	1	3	33786
Career Total (AW)	7	0	0	1	1221

66	8/01	NmkJ	6f	D(0-80)H	GD	£5057
52	7/01	Haml	6f5y	F(0-60)	G-F	£2674
74	5/00	Brig	5f213y	D(0-80)H	G-F	£4160
74	5/99	Wwck	6f	E(0-70)	GD	£3052
86	5/98	Ches	6f18y	C(0-90)H	GD	£10866
76	10/97	Rdcr	6f	E(0-75)	G-F	£3171

Total win prize-money £28980

Going (Turf): Sf: 0-2 GS: 0-1 **Gd: 3-11 GF: 3-22** Fm: 0-3
Distance: **5f/6f: 4-36** 7f-8f: 2-10 9f-13f: 0-0 14f+: 0-0
Track : **LH: 3-20** RH: 0-0 **Tight: 1-8** Gall: 0-3
Aids: Bl: 0-1 Vi: 0-6 Tstrap: 0-0
Best Rating: 66 8/01 NmkJ 6f good

A pacey front runner suited by six furlongs, he was operated on for a wind problem and should find further success with that problem apparently having been solved.

Blushing Grenadier (IRE)

96(102) (46)**46**

9-y-o ch g Salt Dome (USA)-La Duse (Junius (USA))

S R Bowring S R Bowring

Placings:0060/0044103440540/0061000002/30200000/2133010234010310000/40062140123500340/33433016660210020002300-0000502400 **(5629)**

2001: 6^{0}SW, 6^{0}SD, 7^{0}S, 6^{0}G, 6^{5}SD, 5^{0}SD, 7^{2}SD, 6^{4}SD, 7^{0}SD, 5^{0}G

	Starts	1st	2nd	3rd	Win & Pl
Career Total (Turf)	58	8	3	2	30156
Career Total (AW)	46	2	7	11	10155

39	6/00	Catt	5f212y	F	GD	£1897
51	2/00	Sthl	6f	G(0-60)H	STD	£1534
57	6/99	Carl	5f207y	F	G-F	£2542
65	5/99	Rdcr	6f	F	SFT	£2512
62	10/98	Newc	6f	D(0-85)H	SFT	£7295
55	9/98	Hayd	6f	G(0-60)H	GD	£2402
47	6/98	Wwck	6f	F	GD	£2035
56	3/98	Wolv	6f	G	STD	£1738
57	7/96	Wind	5f217y	E(0-70)H	SFT	£2981
52	7/95	Donc	6f	E(0-70)H	GD	£3699

Total win prize-money £28636

Going (Turf): Sf: 3-15 GS: 0-10 **Gd: 4-21** GF: 1-11 Fm: 0-1
Distance: **5f/6f: 10-62** 7f-8f: 0-37 9f-13f: 0-5 14f+: 0-0
Track : **LH: 4-50** RH: 2-9 Tight: 2-28 Gall: 2-7
Aids: **Bl: 7-67** Vi: 3-15 Tstrap: 0-0
Best Rating: 46 6/01 Sthl 7f stand

An effective sprinter on turf and Fibresand, six furlongs is his trip.

Blushing Prince (IRE)

(105) (76)**68**

3-y-o b c Priolo (USA)-Eliade (IRE) (Flash Of Steel)

J Noseda Mrs D M Solomon

Placings:64-13002 **(5416)**

2001: 9^{1}SW, 10^{3}SW, 9^{0}G, 8^{0}G, 9^{2}SD

	Starts	1st	2nd	3rd	Win & Pl
Career Total (Turf)	3	0	0	0	0
Career Total (AW)	4	1	1	1	4739

66	1/01	Wolv	1m1f79y	D	SLW	£2905

Total win prize-money £2905

Going (Turf): Sf: 0-1 GS: 0-0 Gd: 0-2 GF: 0-0 Fm: 0-0
Distance: 5f/6f: 0-0 7f-8f: 0-2 **9f-13f: 1-5** 14f+: 0-0
Track : **LH: 1-4** RH: 0-1 **Tight: 1-4** Gall: 0-0
Aids: Bl: 0-0 Vi: 0-0 **Tstrap: 1-4**
Best Rating: 76 10/01 Wolv 1m1f79y stand

His best performances so far have come on the Wolverhampton Fibresand.

Blushing Queen (IRE)

(94) (72)**72**
2-y-o gr f Desert King (IRE)-Phazania (Tap On Wood)
J Noseda Mrs D M Solomon

Placings:0403 **(5420)**
2001: 6^0G, 7^4G, 8^0HY, 7^3SD

	Starts	1st	2nd	3rd	Win & Pl
Career Total (Turf)	3	0	0	0	320
Career Total (AW)	1	0	0	1	414

Going (Turf): Sf: 0-1 GS: 0-0 Gd: 0-2 GF: 0-0 Fm: 0-0
Distance: 5f/6f: 0-1 7f-8f: 0-2 9f-13f: 0-1 14f+: 0-0
Track : LH: 0-3 RH: 0-0 Tight: 0-2 Gall: 0-0
Aids: Bl: 0-0 Vi: 0-1 Tstrap: 0-0
Best Rating: 72 10/01 Wolv 7f stand

Did not take to the turf, but made a promising sand debut. There is a similar race in her over a longer trip.

Blushing Spur

(97) (67)**59**
3-y-o b g Flying Spur (AUS)-Bogus John (CAN) (Blushing John (USA))
D Shaw J C Fretwell

Placings:5025236-305650604 **(5051)**
2001: 7^3SD, 6^0GF, 7^5G, 6^6GF, 6^5SD, 6^0S, 8^6HY, 7^0G, 6^4SD

	Starts	1st	2nd	3rd	Win & Pl
Career Total (Turf)	11	0	1	1	1386
Career Total (AW)	5	0	1	1	1272

Going (Turf): Sf: 0-5 GS: 0-1 Gd: 0-3 GF: 0-2 Fm: 0-0
Distance: 5f/6f: 0-8 7f-8f: 0-7 9f-13f: 0-1 14f+: 0-0
Track : LH: 0-10 RH: 0-1 Tight: 0-3 Gall: 0-0
Aids: Bl: 0-0 Vi: 0-3 Tstrap: 0-0
Best Rating: 62 5/01 Wolv 7f stand

Blusienka (IRE)

(80) (29)**96d**
4-y-o b f Blues Traveller (IRE)-Pudgy Poppet (Danehill (USA))
G A Butler Mrs Renata Tanaka

Placings:1/435403-0 **(0424)**
2001: 7^0SD

	Starts	1st	2nd	3rd	Win & Pl
Career Total (Turf)	7	1	0	2	8474
Career Total (AW)	1	0	0	0	
80 11/99 Donc 1m	E			SFT	£3225

Total win prize-money £3225

Going (Turf): Sf: 1-3 GS: 0-1 Gd: 0-2 GF: 0-0 Fm: 0-1
Distance: 5f/6f: 0-0 **7f-8f: 1-5** 9f-13f: 0-3 14f+: 0-0
Track : LH: 0-2 RH: 0-3 Tight: 0-2 Gall: 0-1
Aids: Bl: 0-0 Vi: 0-0 Tstrap: 0-0
Best Rating: 29 3/01 Wolv 7f stand

Blythe Princess

(85) (47)
2-y-o b f Makbul-Miss Petella (Dunphy)
K A Ryan Wooster Partnership

Placings:5 **(0709)**
2001: 5^5SD

	Starts	1st	2nd	3rd	Win & Pl
Career Total (Turf)	0	0	0	0	
Career Total (AW)	1	0	0	0	0

Going (Turf): Sf: 0-0 GS: 0-0 Gd: 0-0 GF: 0-0 Fm: 0-0
Distance: 5f/6f: 0-1 7f-8f: 0-0 9f-13f: 0-0 14f+: 0-0
Track : LH: 0-0 RH: 0-0 Tight: 0-0 Gall: 0-0
Aids: Bl: 0-0 Vi: 0-0 Tstrap: 0-0
Best Rating: 47 4/01 Sthl 5f stand

Blythe Spirit

93 **81**
2-y-o b c Bahamian Bounty-Lithe Spirit (IRE) (Dancing Dissident (USA))
R A Fahey Mrs Janis Macpherson

Placings:200 **(4064)**
2001: 6^2F, 6^0G, 6^0G

	Starts	1st	2nd	3rd	Win & Pl
Career Total (Turf)	3	0	1	0	1200

Going (Turf): Sf: 0-0 GS: 0-0 Gd: 0-2 GF: 0-0 Fm: 0-1
Distance: 5f/6f: 0-3 7f-8f: 0-0 9f-13f: 0-0 14f+: 0-0
Track : LH: 0-0 RH: 0-0 Tight: 0-0 Gall: 0-0
Aids: Bl: 0-0 Vi: 0-0 Tstrap: 0-0
Best Rating: 81 6/01 Thsk 6f firm

Boadicea

81 **33**
3-y-o b f Celtic Swing-Another Legend (USA) (Lyphard's Wish (FR))
Mrs J R Ramsden P D Savill

Placings:61035-000 **(1721)**
2001: 7^0GS, 10^0GS, 8^0GF

	Starts	1st	2nd	3rd	Win & Pl
Career Total (Turf)	8	1	0	1	6100
9/00 Divo 1m110y				VS	£2882

Total win prize-money £2882

Going (Turf): Sf: 0-0 GS: 0-2 Gd: 0-0 GF: 0-1 Fm: 0-0
Distance: 5f/6f: 0-0 7f-8f: 0-2 **9f-13f: 1-2** 14f+: 0-0
Track : LH: 0-1 RH: 0-1 Tight: 0-1 Gall: 0-0
Aids: Bl: 0-0 Vi: 0-0 Tstrap: 0-0
Best Rating: 33 5/01 Pont 1m2f6y gd-sft

A winning ex-French juvenile, now with Lynda Ramsden.

Boadicea The Red (IRE)

105(102) (53)**59**
4-y-o gr f Inchinor-Kanika (Be My Chief (USA))
B S Rothwell Mrs D E Sharp

Placings:256203/500022-213360013300463 **(3736)**
2001: 7^2SD, 7^1SW, 8^3SD, 7^3SW, 7^6GF, 7^0SD, 7^0GF, 6^1F, 6^3GF, 6^3GF, 6^0GF, 7^0GF, 6^4F, 6^6GF, 5^3G

	Starts	1st	2nd	3rd	Win & Pl
Career Total (Turf)	18	1	2	3	8377
Career Total (AW)	9	1	3	3	5750
52 6/01 Donc 6f	D(0-80)H			FRM	£4504
49 1/01 Sthl 7f	F			SLW	£2233

Total win prize-money £6738

Going (Turf): Sf: 0-4 GS: 0-1 Gd: 0-4 GF: 0-7 **Fm: 1-2**
Distance: 5f/6f: 1-13 7f-8f: 1-14 9f-13f: 0-0 14f+: 0-0
Track : **LH: 1-12** RH: 0-0 Tight: 0-2 Gall: 0-0
Aids: Bl: 0-0 **Vi: 1-14** Tstrap: 0-0
Best Rating: 59 6/01 Donc 6f gd-fm

Boanerges (IRE)

107 **84**
4-y-o br g Caerleon (USA)-Sea Siren (Slip Anchor)
R Guest P A & D G Sakal

Placings:432/0001130604000-0310500200600 **(5403)**
2001: 5^0GS, 5^3GF, 5^1GF, 6^0GF, 5^5GF, 5^0GF, 5^0GF, 5^2GS, 5^0GF, 6^0G, 6^6G, 6^0GS, 5^0S

	Starts	1st	2nd	3rd	Win & Pl
Career Total (Turf)	29	3	2	3	32391
78 6/01 Muss 5f	C(0-95)H			G-F	£17400
79 6/00 NmkJ 5f	D(0-85)H			G-F	£4966
73 6/00 Gdwd 6f	D(0-80)H			G-F	£3900

Total win prize-money £26266

Going (Turf): Sf: 0-4 GS: 0-8 Gd: 0-6 **GF: 3-11** Fm: 0-0
Distance: **5f/6f: 3-23** 7f-8f: 0-5 9f-13f: 0-1 14f+: 0-0
Track : LH: 0-5 RH: 0-0 Tight: 0-1 Gall: 0-0
Aids: Bl: 0-0 Vi: 0-1 Tstrap: 0-0
Best Rating: 84 9/01 Ayr 6f good

Winning sprint handicapper over five and six furlongs. Suited by fast ground but also handles cut. Won at Musselburgh in June but has been held off his higher mark since. Goes well for Darryl Holland.

Boater

98 (75)**55**
7-y-o b g Batshoof-Velvet Beret (IRE) (Dominion)
R J Baker Christine And Aubrey Loze

Placings:003/14235/230340000/420/36-04 **(2246)**
2001: 8^0GF, 10^4GF

	Starts	1st	2nd	3rd	Win & Pl
Career Total (Turf)	22	1	3	4	10241
Career Total (AW)	2	0	0	1	445
71 4/97 Brig 7f214y	E(0-70)H			FRM	£3044

Total win prize-money £3044

Going (Turf): Sf: 0-3 GS: 0-3 Gd: 0-8 GF: 0-4 **Fm: 1-4**
Distance: 5f/6f: 0-0 **7f-8f: 1-11** 9f-13f: 0-13 14f+: 0-0
Track : **LH: 1-14** RH: 0-5 Tight: 0-8 Gall: 0-3
Aids: Bl: 0-1 Vi: 0-0 Tstrap: 0-0
Best Rating: 55 6/01 Wwck 1m2f188y gd-fm

Bobanvi

93(92) (45)**35**
3-y-o b f Timeless Times (USA)-Bobanlyn (IRE) (Dance Of Life (USA))
J S Wainwright S Pedersen

Placings:540036556-000000 **(4105)**
2001: 10^0F, 11^0GF, 12^0G, 12^0GS, 16^0GF, 12^0S

	Starts	1st	2nd	3rd	Win & Pl
Career Total (Turf)	13	0	0	0	0
Career Total (AW)	2	0	0	1	266

Going (Turf): Sf: 0-4 GS: 0-1 Gd: 0-3 GF: 0-3 Fm: 0-2
Distance: 5f/6f: 0-4 7f-8f: 0-4 9f-13f: 0-6 14f+: 0-1
Track : LH: 0-5 RH: 0-5 Tight: 0-4 Gall: 0-1
Aids: Bl: 0-1 Vi: 0-0 Tstrap: 0-0
Best Rating: 44 6/01 Bevl 1m3f216y gd-fm

Bobbydazzle

(103) (58)
6-y-o ch m Rock Hopper-Billie Blue (Ballad Rock)
C A Dwyer Ms Bobby Cohen

Placings:026410/0614000/55300003/244034040253-

2001:

	Starts	1st	2nd	3rd	Win & Pl
Career Total (Turf)	26	2	1	2	37471
Career Total (AW)	7	0	2	2	2912
79 6/98 Newc 1m3y	C(0-95)H			SFT	£5283
78 8/97 Newc 1m3y	C			GD	£28660

Total win prize-money £33944

Going (Turf): Sf: 1-6 GS: 0-2 **Gd: 1-14** GF: 0-3 Fm: 0-0
Distance: 5f/6f: 0-1 7f-8f: 0-13 **9f-13f: 2-18** 14f+: 0-0
Track : LH: 0-12 RH: 0-4 Tight: 0-7 Gall: 0-1
Aids: Bl: 0-5 Vi: 0-0 Tstrap: 0-0
Best Rating: 78 8/97 Newc 1m3y G

Bobona

(94) (30)

5-y-o b g Interrex (CAN)-Puella Bona (Handsome Sailor)

B J Llewellyn Miss Emily Jane Jones

Placings:0005003401/0265060-

2001:

	Starts	1st	2nd	3rd	Win & Pl
Career Total (Turf)	5	0	0	0	170
Career Total (AW)	12	1	1	1	2520

35	12/99	Sthl	1m3f	G(0-60)	STD	£1829

Total win prize-money £1829

Going (Turf): Sf: 0-2 GS: 0-0 Gd: 0-1 GF: 0-1 Fm: 0-1
Distance: 5f/6f: 0-2 7f-8f: 0-3 **9f-13f: 1-9** 14f+: 0-3
Track : **LH: 1-14** RH: 0-1 Tight: 0-7 Gall: 0-0
Aids: Bl: 0-1 Vi: 0-0 Tstrap: 0-0
Best Rating: 35 12/99 Sthl 1m3f SD

Bobsleigh

83 **55**

2-y-o b c Robellino (USA)-Do Run Run (Commanche Run)

Mrs A J Perrett A Ogilvy And Mrs F Ogilvy

Placings:006 **(4574)**

2001: 7^{0}GF, 7^{0}G, 8^{6}G

	Starts	1st	2nd	3rd	Win & Pl
Career Total (Turf)	3	0	0	0	0

Going (Turf): Sf: 0-0 GS: 0-0 Gd: 0-2 GF: 0-1 Fm: 0-0
Distance: 5f/6f: 0-0 7f-8f: 0-3 9f-13f: 0-0 14f+: 0-0
Track : LH: 0-0 RH: 0-1 Tight: 0-0 Gall: 0-0
Aids: Bl: 0-0 Vi: 0-0 Tstrap: 0-0
Best Rating: 55 9/01 Kemp 1m good

Bocelli (NZ)

108 **120**

5-y-o b g Lord Ballina (AUS)-Sweet Vienna (NZ) (Dahar (USA))

P Busuttin J Sprague, Dato Terry Lee & R Nobillo

Placings:13000/2111-111112403 **(5738a)**

2001: 7^{1}Y, 7^{1}G, 7^{1}G, 8^{1}G, 10^{1}GF, 9^{2}G, 7^{4}GF, 8^{0}S, 11^{3}G

	Starts	1st	2nd	3rd	Win & Pl
Career Total (Turf)	18	9	2	2	459847

120	6/01	Kran	1m2f		G-F	£168340
	6/01	Kran	1m		GD	£47186
	5/01	Kran	7f		GD	£59546
	4/01	Kran	7f	H	GD	£22973
	1/01	Kran	7f	H	YLD	£22973
	12/00	Kran	7f	H	GD	£22037
	10/00	Kran	7f	H	GD	£16528
	10/00	Kran	7f	H	GD	£12120
	9/99	Mwtu	6f		FRM	£1032

Total win prize-money £372735

Going (Turf): Sf: 0-1 GS: 0-0 **Gd: 6-9** GF: 1-2 Fm: 1-2
Distance: 5f/6f: 1-2 **7f-8f: 7-10** 9f-13f: 1-4 14f+: 0-0
Track : LH: 0-1 RH: 0-1 Tight: 0-0 Gall: 0-2
Aids: **Bl: 7-11** Vi: 0-0 Tstrap: 0-0
Best Rating: 120 6/01 Kran 1m2f gd-fm

Had one win from five runs before moving to Singapore. Only just beaten on his first start for new connections, he went on to win his next eight races. Holds the track record over seven furlongs at Kranji. Earlier in 2001 he won a Group Two and a Group Three and the ten-furlong Group One Emirates Singapore Derby. Ran a bit flat after the Derby when just beaten in the Group One Raffles International Cup. Showed ability in two runs in Britain in September over inadequate trips. Suited by a good pace and good ground.

Bodfari Anna

99(99) (28)**54**

5-y-o br m Casteddu-Lowrianna (IRE) (Cyrano De Bergerac)

J L Eyre The Haydock Badgeholders

Placings:05**52**4202162445**00**/000**4**3542410000/**305**450 1003143002004-**0**04010400006B **(4859)**

2001: 7^{0}SD, 6^{0}G, 7^{4}GF, 7^{0}GF, 7^{1}GF, 7^{0}GF, 7^{4}GF, 7^{0}GF, 7^{0}GF, 7^{0}GF, 8^{0}G, 8^{6}F, 7^{B}GF

	Starts	1st	2nd	3rd	Win & Pl
Career Total (Turf)	51	5	5	3	21171
Career Total (AW)	11	0	1	1	768

57	5/01	Sthl	7f	E(0-70)H	G-F	£2989
56	7/00	Ches	7f122y	E(0-70)H	G-S	£2951
52	5/00	Sthl	7f	E(0-70)H	HVY	£3115
46	9/99	Hayd	6f	G(0-60)H	G-F	£2458
64	8/98	Nott	6f15y	G	G-F	£2110

Total win prize-money £13623

Going (Turf): Sf: 1-7 GS: 1-5 Gd: 0-12 **GF: 3-22** Fm: 0-5
Distance: 5f/6f: 1-28 **7f-8f: 4-31** 9f-13f: 0-3 14f+: 0-0
Track : **LH: 3-27** RH: 0-8 **Tight: 1-15** Gall: 0-0
Aids: Bl: 1-19 **Vi: 4-40** Tstrap: 0-0
Best Rating: 57 5/01 Sthl 7f gd-fm

A modest handicapper, she needs to be covered up. Suited by seven furlongs and a sharp left-handed track.

Bodfari Komaite

106 **77**

5-y-o b g Komaite (USA)-Gypsy's Barn Rat (Balliol)

M W Easterby Bodfari Stud Ltd

Placings:06631000/0601414066/211340000-0302100100 **(5685)**

2001: 5^{0}S, 5^{3}GS, 5^{0}F, 5^{2}GF, 5^{1}GF, 5^{0}S, 5^{0}G, 5^{1}G, 5^{0}S, 5^{0}S

	Starts	1st	2nd	3rd	Win & Pl
Career Total (Turf)	37	7	2	3	45960

77	9/01	Ches	5f16y	D(0-85)H	GD	£6006
72	6/01	Ches	5f16y	C(0-95)H	G-F	£14300
69	6/00	Catt	5f	D(0-85)H	GD	£4329
62	5/00	Thsk	5f	D(0-80)H	GD	£4595
61	7/99	Donc	5f	E(0-70)H	G-F	£2970
58	6/99	Muss	5f	E(0-70)H	GD	£2762
68	9/98	Rdcr	5f	E(0-75)H	G-F	£3267

Total win prize-money £38230

Going (Turf): Sf: 0-14 GS: 0-4 **Gd: 4-9** GF: 3-8 Fm: 0-2
Distance: **5f/6f: 7-35** 7f-8f: 0-2 9f-13f: 0-0 14f+: 0-0
Track : **LH: 2-8** RH: 0-0 **Tight: 2-7** Gall: 0-0
Aids: **Bl: 2-6** Vi: 0-0 Tstrap: 0-0
Best Rating: 77 9/01 Ches 5f16y good

In fine form in the early part of 2000, he scored for the first time in a year when blinkered at Chester in June and confirmed his liking for that track when winning there again in September. Races prominently, acts on fast ground and five furlongs is his trip.

Bodfari Millennium

79(64) **54**

3-y-o b g Tragic Role (USA)-Petomania (Petong)

M W Easterby Bodfari Stud Ltd

Placings:0-0000 **(2518)**

2001: 8^{0}SD, 8^{0}GF, 14^{0}F, 16^{0}F

	Starts	1st	2nd	3rd	Win & Pl
Career Total (Turf)	4	0	0	0	
Career Total (AW)	1	0	0	0	

Going (Turf): Sf: 0-0 GS: 0-0 Gd: 0-1 GF: 0-1 Fm: 0-2
Distance: 5f/6f: 0-0 7f-8f: 0-3 9f-13f: 0-0 14f+: 0-2
Track : LH: 0-5 RH: 0-0 Tight: 0-4 Gall: 0-0
Aids: Bl: 0-1 Vi: 0-0 Tstrap: 0-0
Best Rating: 28 5/01 Thsk 1m gd-fm

Bodfari Pride (IRE)

107(99) (76)**82**

6-y-o b g Pips Pride-Renata's Ring (IRE) (Auction Ring (USA))

D Nicholls Bodfari Stud Ltd

Placings:30/5115203500/**0**0011620022-62**2**51**0**0600 **(4944)**

2001: 5^{6}S, 5^{2}GS, 6^{2}SD, 5^{5}GS, 5^{1}GS, 6^{0}SD, 5^{0}G, 5^{6}HY, 6^{0}G, 5^{0}S

	Starts	1st	2nd	3rd	Win & Pl
Career Total (Turf)	30	5	5	2	53412
Career Total (AW)	3	0	1	0	1210

82	5/01	Ling	5f	D(0-85)H	G-S	£8775
81	6/00	Ches	5f16y	D(0-85)H	G-S	£4407
68	6/00	Gdwd	6f	D(0-80)H	G-S	£4368
76	5/98	Ches	7f122y	C(0-100)H	GD	£18147
76	4/98	Rdcr	7f	E	SFT	£3078

Total win prize-money £38776

Going (Turf): Sf: 1-10 **GS: 3-11** Gd: 1-7 GF: 0-2 Fm: 0-0
Distance: **5f/6f: 3-25** 7f-8f: 2-8 9f-13f: 0-0 14f+: 0-0
Track : **LH: 2-16** RH: 0-1 **Tight: 2-12** Gall: 0-0
Aids: Bl: 0-0 Vi: 0-0 Tstrap: 0-0
Best Rating: 82 5/01 Ling 5f gd-sft

He was given a chance by the Handicapper in 2000 and took advantage with two victories. He has risen again since, but did manage a victory at Lingfield in May. Suited by five furlongs or an easy six and shows his best form with some cut in the ground.

Bodfari Signet

85 (22)**42**

5-y-o ch g King's Signet (USA)-Darakah (Doulab (USA))

Mrs S C Bradburne Strath Pack Partnership

Placings:000506502502/0000015W50/0000000600-350 **(4908)**

2001: 12^{3}GF, 12^{5}F, 9^{0}G

	Starts	1st	2nd	3rd	Win & Pl
Career Total (Turf)	33	1	2	1	5786
Career Total (AW)	2	0	0	0	

54	6/99	Haml	1m65y	F(0-65)H	GD	£3712

Total win prize-money £3713

Going (Turf): Sf: 0-5 GS: 0-4 **Gd: 1-6** GF: 0-14 Fm: 0-4
Distance: 5f/6f: 0-8 7f-8f: 0-9 **9f-13f: 1-18** 14f+: 0-0
Track : LH: 0-12 **RH: 1-12 Tight: 1-13** Gall: 0-1
Aids: **Bl: 1-21** Vi: 0-1 Tstrap: 0-1
Best Rating: 44 8/01 Muss 1m4f gd-fm

Bogus Ballet

82 **51**

2-y-o ch f Halling (USA)-Classic Ballet (FR) (Fabulous Dancer (USA))

M L W Bell Northmore Stud

Placings:0 **(3635)**

2001: 7^{0}GS

	Starts	1st	2nd	3rd	Win & Pl
Career Total (Turf)	1	0	0	0	

Going (Turf): Sf: 0-0 GS: 0-1 Gd: 0-0 GF: 0-0 Fm: 0-0
Distance: 5f/6f: 0-0 7f-8f: 0-1 9f-13f: 0-0 14f+: 0-0
Track : LH: 0-0 RH: 0-0 Tight: 0-0 Gall: 0-0
Aids: Bl: 0-0 Vi: 0-0 Tstrap: 0-0
Best Rating: 51 8/01 NmkJ 7f gd-sft

Bogus Dreams (IRE)

108 **106**

4-y-o ch c Lahib (USA)-Dreams Are Free (IRE) (Caerleon (USA))

S P C Woods Dwayne Woods

Placings:113/53-633112525 **(4949)**

2001: 10^{6}S, 10^{3}G, 10^{3}G, 10^{1}GF, 10^{1}GF, 10^{2}GF, 12^{5}G, 10^{2}G, 9^{5}G

	Starts	1st	2nd	3rd	Win & Pl
Career Total (Turf)	14	4	2	4	70529

56	7/01	Donc	1m2f60y	C	G-F	£7085
106	6/01	Epsm	1m2f18y	B H	G-F	£29000
98	9/99	Asct	7f	B	HVY	£12633
84	9/99	Thsk	7f	F	FRM	£3095

Total win prize-money £51813

Going (Turf): Sf: 1-3 GS: 0-0 Gd: 0-7 **GF: 2-3** Fm: 1-1
Distance: 5f/6f: 0-0 7f-8f: 2-3 9f-13f: 2-11 14f+: 0-0
Track : **LH: 3-5** RH: 0-6 **Tight: 2-7** Gall: 1-4
Aids: Bl: 0-0 Vi: 0-0 Tstrap: 0-0
Best Rating: **106** 7/01 Asct 1m2f gd-fm

Not quite up to Listed company in 2000. He shaped with promise in a couple of ten-furlong handicaps at Newmarket and Windsor, before winning a valuable handicap over the same trip at Epsom on Derby Day. Followed up in a non-event at Doncaster and ran well to finish runner-up in a valuable Ascot handicap. Handles fast ground and soft.

Bogus Penny (IRE)

104(98) (53)**79**

3-y-o b f Pennekamp (USA)-Dreams Are Free (IRE) (Caerleon (USA))
S P C Woods Northmore Stud

Placings:4220-3252 **(2110)**
2001: 8^{3}SW, 8^{2}S, 10^{5}GF, 9^{2}F

	Starts	1st	2nd	3rd	Win & Pl
Career Total (Turf)	7		4	0	5830
Career Total (AW)	1	0	0	1	397

Going (Turf): Sf: 0-1 GS: 0-1 Gd: 0-0 **GF: 0-4 Fm: 0-1**
Distance: 5f/6f: 0-1 7f-8f: 0-4 9f-13f: 0-3 14f+: 0-0
Track : LH: 0-5 RH: 0-0 Tight: 0-2 Gall: 0-0
Aids: Bl: 0-0 Vi: 0-0 Tstrap: 0-0
Best Rating: 78 6/01 Ling 1m1f firm

Bohemian Spirit (IRE)

(95) (53)**60**

3-y-o b g Eagle Eyed (USA)-Tuesday Morning (Sadler's Wells (USA))
P G Murphy Mrs Dianne Abel

Placings:540-500 **(5050)**
2001: 8^{5}SD, 9^{0}SW, 11^{0}SD

	Starts	1st	2nd	3rd	Win & Pl
Career Total (Turf)	3	0	0	0	0
Career Total (AW)	3	0	0	0	0

Going (Turf): Sf: 0-0 GS: 0-2 Gd: 0-1 GF: 0-0 Fm: 0-0
Distance: 5f/6f: 0-3 7f-8f: 0-0 9f-13f: 0-3 14f+: 0-0
Track : LH: 0-4 RH: 0-0 Tight: 0-2 Gall: 0-1
Aids: Bl: 0-0 Vi: 0-0 Tstrap: 0-0
Best Rating: 53 3/01 Wolv 1m100y stand

Boiling Point

(56)

5-y-o b m Beveled (USA)-A Little Hot (Petong)
E A Wheeler You'Re Having A Laugh Racing Club

Placings:0-0 **(0018)**
2001: 8^{0}SD

	Starts	1st	2nd	3rd	Win & Pl
Career Total (Turf)	1	0	0	0	
Career Total (AW)	1	0	0	0	

Going (Turf): Sf: 0-1 GS: 0-0 Gd: 0-0 GF: 0-0 Fm: 0-0
Distance: 5f/6f: 0-0 7f-8f: 0-2 9f-13f: 0-1 14f+: 0-0
Track : LH: 0-1 RH: 0-0 Tight: 0-1 Gall: 0-0
Aids: Bl: 0-0 Vi: 0-0 Tstrap: 0-0

Boira (USA)

107 **73**

3-y-o b f Diesis-Noblissima (IRE) (Sadler's Wells (USA))
D Morris Cuadra Africa

Placings:6-2240336 **(5528)**
2001: 7^{2}GF, 8^{2}GF, 8^{4}G, 9^{0}GF, 7^{3}GF, 8^{3}GS, 8^{6}HY

	Starts	1st	2nd	3rd	Win & Pl
Career Total (Turf)	8	0	2	2	4707

Going (Turf): Sf: 0-1 GS: 0-1 Gd: 0-2 GF: 0-4 Fm: 0-0
Distance: 5f/6f: 0-0 7f-8f: 0-4 9f-13f: 0-4 14f+: 0-0
Track : LH: 0-2 RH: 0-3 Tight: 0-0 Gall: 0-0
Aids: Bl: 0-0 Vi: 0-0 Tstrap: 0-0
Best Rating: **77** 5/01 Gdwd 7f gd-fm

She has finished runner-up to some decent fillies in maiden company.

Bois De Citron (USA)

102 **84**

3-y-o b f Woodman (USA)-Lemon Souffle (Salse (USA))
R Hannon Fieldspring Racing

Placings:34106-0500000 **(5694)**
2001: 5^{0}F, 5^{5}GF, 6^{0}GS, 6^{0}G, 5^{0}G, 6^{0}G, 6^{0}S

	Starts	1st	2nd	3rd	Win & Pl
Career Total (Turf)	12	1	0	1	5110

84	8/00	Leic	5f2y	D	G-F	£3601

Total win prize-money £3601

Going (Turf): Sf: 0-2 GS: 0-1 Gd: 0-3 **GF: 1-5** Fm: 0-1
Distance: **5f/6f: 1-12** 7f-8f: 0-0 9f-13f: 0-0 14f+: 0-0
Track : LH: 0-1 RH: 0-0 Tight: 0-0 Gall: 0-1
Aids: Bl: 0-0 Vi: 0-0 Tstrap: 0-0
Best Rating: **84** 6/01 Asct 5f gd-fm

Scored on her third outing at two, but found Listed company too hot on last two juvenile runs. Has won over five furlongs on good to firm, but has disappointed since then.

Boisdale (IRE)

(72) (18)**82d**

3-y-o b c Common Grounds-Alstomeria (Petoski)
J A R Toller Buckingham Thoroughbreds

Placings:0064011-00000 **(4605)**
2001: 7^{0}GS, 7^{0}G, 6^{0}G, 7^{0}GS, 7^{0}SD

	Starts	1st	2nd	3rd	Win & Pl
Career Total (Turf)	11	2	0	0	10038
Career Total (AW)	1	0	0	0	

81	9/00	Ling	7f	F(0-75)	SFT	£3342
73	9/00	Ches	7f2y	C(0-95)	SFT	£6695

Total win prize-money £10038

Going (Turf): Sf: 2-2 GS: 0-2 Gd: 0-3 GF: 0-3 Fm: 0-1
Distance: 5f/6f: 0-2 **7f-8f: 2-10** 9f-13f: 0-0 14f+: 0-0
Track : **LH: 1-3** RH: 0-0 **Tight: 1-2** Gall: 0-1
Aids: Bl: 0-0 Vi: 0-0 Tstrap: 0-1
Best Rating: **76** 4/01 NmkR 7f gd-sft

Appreciated the soft ground when winning two back end nurseries in 2000. Best suited by forcing tactics, he failed to fire this term.

Bold Amusement

104 **58**

11-y-o ch g Never So Bold-Hysterical (High Top)
W S Cunningham Mrs Ann Bell

Placings:1/42023/200100/00155000/002562005/0051/5 5112250/200166-0550210410 **(5632)**
2001: 10^{0}GF, 9^{5}GF, 9^{5}GF, 9^{0}GF, 10^{2}G, 10^{1}G, 11^{0}S, 10^{4}HY, 11^{1}S, 10^{0}G

	Starts	1st	2nd	3rd	Win & Pl
Career Total (Turf)	56	9	9	1	42135
Career Total (AW)	1	0	0	0	

44	10/01	Rdcr	1m3f	F	SFT	£2453
58	9/01	Ayr	1m2f192y	E(0-70)H	GD	£2800
63	7/00	Bevl	1m1f207y	E(0-75)H	GD	£3146
60	6/99	Newc	1m2f32y	E(0-75)H	GD	£3485
58	6/99	Newc	1m2f32y	D(0-85)H	G-F	£3533
60	11/98	Rdcr	1m2f	E(0-70)H	G-S	£3225
84	7/95	Bevl	1m100y	D(0-80)H	G-F	£4323
85	7/94	Donc	1m2f60y	D(0-85)H	G-F	£4581
53	8/92	Haml	6f5y	F	GD	£2654

Total win prize-money £30202

Going (Turf): Sf: 1-9 GS: 1-6 **Gd: 4-16** GF: 3-20 Fm: 0-5
Distance: 5f/6f: 0-0 7f-8f: 1-14 **9f-13f: 8-43** 14f+: 0-0
Track : **LH: 6-30** RH: 2-17 Tight: 2-18 **Gall: 3-19**
Aids: Bl: 0-3 Vi: 0-0 Tstrap: 0-0
Best Rating: **59** 6/01 Bevl 1m1f207y gd-fm

He is not getting any younger, but retains his enthusiasm. Ten furlongs is his trip and he seems best on good ground. Suited by waiting tactics.

Bold Aristocrat (IRE)

(92) (26)**24**

10-y-o b g Bold Arrangement-Wyn Mipet (Welsh Saint)
R Hollinshead Mrs J Hughes

Placings:3030/06665600000/0330004135055**6000/001 653105004203320**3/53250162453201364403534**5/3621 4112635005/40622113/004000000-00** **(0329)**
2001: 5^{0}SD, 6^{0}SD

	Starts	1st	2nd	3rd	Win & Pl
Career Total (Turf)	20	0	1	0	1610
Career Total (AW)	94	11	9	17	34920

65	2/99	Sthl	6f	G	STD	£1855
64	2/99	Sthl	6f	F	STD	£2347
61	3/98	Sthl	6f	G	STD	£1847
60	2/98	Sthl	6f	G	STD	£1738
56	2/98	Sthl	6f	G	STD	£1738
68	6/97	Sthl	6f	F(0-65)	STD	£2600
60	2/97	Sthl	6f	F(0-60)H	STD	£2083
46	2/96	Sthl	6f	F(0-60)H	STD	£2048
48	1/96	Sthl	6f	F	STD	£2398
47	7/95	Sthl	6f	F(0-60)H	STD	£2519
79	4/93	Sthl	5f	F	STD	£2444

Total win prize-money £23620

Going (Turf): Sf: 0-3 GS: 0-2 Gd: 0-8 GF: 0-6 Fm: 0-1
Distance: **5f/6f: 11-81** 7f-8f: 0-32 9f-13f: 0-1 14f+: 0-0
Track : **LH: 10-91** RH: 0-2 Tight: 0-24 Gall: 0-1
Aids: Bl: 0-1 Vi: 0-0 Tstrap: 0-0
Best Rating: 26 1/01 Sthl 5f stand

He pops up in modest company on Fibresand from time to time, though all of his recent victories have been over six furlongs at Southwell.

Bold Bird

99(93) (47)**45**

4-y-o b g Puissance-Plum Bold (Be My Guest (USA))
D J Coakley David F Wilson

Placings:0/3-300002 **(2991)**
2001: 8^{3}SD, 10^{0}SD, 9^{0}F, 8^{0}G, 8^{0}SD, 8^{2}G

	Starts	1st	2nd	3rd	Win & Pl
Career Total (Turf)	4	0	1	0	708
Career Total (AW)	4	0	0	2	806

Going (Turf): Sf: 0-0 GS: 0-1 Gd: 0-2 GF: 0-0 Fm: 0-1
Distance: 5f/6f: 0-1 7f-8f: 0-3 9f-13f: 0-4 14f+: 0-0
Track : LH: 0-5 RH: 0-1 Tight: 0-2 Gall: 0-1
Aids: Bl: 0-0 Vi: 0-1 Tstrap: 0-0
Best Rating: 47 1/01 Ling 1m stand

Bold Century

85(96) (47)**28**

4-y-o b g Casteddu-Bold Green (FR) (Green Dancer (USA))

T J Naughton The Millennium Partnership

Placings:235-160 **(1207)**
2001: 13^1SW, 16^6SW, 10^0GS

	Starts	1st	2nd	3rd	Win & Pl
Career Total (Turf)	1	0	0	0	
Career Total (AW)	5	1	1	1	3386

47 2/01 Ling 1m5f F SLW £2177
Total win prize-money £2177

Going (Turf): **Sf: 0-0 GS: 0-1 Gd: 0-0 GF: 0-0 Fm: 0-0**
Distance: 5f/6f: 0-0 7f-8f: 0-0 **9f-13f: 1-5** 14f+: 0-1
Track : **LH: 1-5** RH: 0-0 **Tight: 1-6** Gall: 0-0
Aids: Bl: 0-0 Vi: 0-0 Tstrap: 0-0
Best Rating: 47 2/01 Ling 1m5f slow

Bold Classic (IRE)

76 **27**

8-y-o b g Persian Bold-Bay Street (Grundy)
C Grant (J R Adam 23/6) Chris Grant

Placings:45/0421206/00 **(3866)**
2001: 16^0GF, 16^0GF

	Starts	1st	2nd	3rd	Win & Pl
Career Total (Turf)	11	1	2	0	6346

75 7/96 Yarm 1m6f17y D(0-75)H FRM £3960
Total win prize-money £3960

Going (Turf): Sf: 0-0 GS: 0-2 Gd: 0-2 GF: 0-3 **Fm: 1-2**
Distance: 5f/6f: 0-0 7f-8f: 0-0 9f-13f: 0-2 **14f+: 1-7**
Track : **LH: 1-9** RH: 0-0 **Tight: 1-6** Gall: 0-1
Aids: Bl: 0-0 Vi: 0-1 Tstrap: 0-0
Best Rating: 27 7/01 Donc 2m110y gd-fm

Bold Dance

(76) (37)**56**

2-y-o b f Marju (IRE)-Tropical Dance (USA) (Thorn Dance (USA))
K McAuliffe The Hare And Hounds Partnership

Placings:03450 **(5049)**
2001: 6^0GF, 7^3GF, 7^4G, 7^5HY, 7^0SD

	Starts	1st	2nd	3rd	Win & Pl
Career Total (Turf)	4	0	0	1	669
Career Total (AW)	1	0	0	0	

Going (Turf): **Sf: 0-1 GS: 0-0 Gd: 0-1 GF: 0-2 Fm: 0-0**
Distance: 5f/6f: 0-0 7f-8f: 0-5 9f-13f: 0-0 14f+: 0-0
Track : LH: 0-2 RH: 0-1 Tight: 0-0 Gall: 0-0
Aids: Bl: 0-0 Vi: 0-0 Tstrap: 0-0
Best Rating: 56 9/01 Sand 7f16y good

Bold Effort (FR)

105(99) (68d)**77**

9-y-o b g Bold Arrangement-Malham Tarn (Riverman (USA))
K O Cunningham-Brown A J Richards

Placings:024220/21310013210020050/0006001301001/262600010205040000/630316010005000/145006400 0/04001005210501000000-0000410000040 **(5097)**
2001: 6^0SD, 5^0SW, 6^0SD, 6^0G, 5^4G, 5^1F, 6^0GF, 5^0G, 5^0GF, 8^0S, 6^0G, 6^4SD, 6^0GS

	Starts	1st	2nd	3rd	Win & Pl
Career Total (Turf)	78	9	4	4	145949
Career Total (AW)	35	6	6	1	32673

78	6/01	Bath	5f161y	D(0-85)H		FRM	£3844
80	8/00	Bath	5f161y	C(0-90)H		GD	£6857
80	6/00	Sals	6f	C(0-90)H		G-F	£7735
77	3/00	Ling	5f	D(0-85)H		STD	£3705
97	2/99	Ling	6f	C(0-95)H		STD	£6097
95	7/98	Sand	5f6y	C(0-95)H		G-S	£5680
91	5/98	Kemp	6f	C(0-90)H		G-F	£14785
94	5/97	Wolv	6f	C(0-100)H		STD	£5352
89	12/96	Ling	6f	D(0-85)H		STD	£2801
80	9/96	MsnL	6f		H	VS	£22398
78	8/96	Claf	1m			SFT	£5929
94	6/95	York	6f	B(0-105)H		G-F	£38958
82	5/95	Sals	6f	B(0-100)H		G-F	£8030
74	2/95	Ling	6f	D(0-80)H		STD	£3723
64	1/95	Ling	6f	E		STD	£2966

Total win prize-money £138867

Going (Turf): Sf: 1-10 GS: 1-13 Gd: 1-30 **GF: 4-21** Fm: 1-2
Distance: **5f/6f: 14-88** 7f-8f: 1-23 9f-13f: 0-1 14f+: 0-0
Track : **LH: 8-44** RH: 1-2 **Tight: 6-35** Gall: 2-6
Aids: **Bl: 11-70** Vi: 0-8 Tstrap: 0-0
Best Rating: 78 6/01 Bath 5f161y firm

He is an inconsistent sprint handicapper, but capable of useful form on his day as when scoring at Bath in June. He acts on any ground and on sand.

Bold Ewar (IRE)

(108) (77)**71**

4-y-o ch c Persian Bold-Hot Curry (USA) (Sharpen Up)
C E Brittain A J Richards

Placings:0205300**41**/**5**32505201500**6**0-**6**23000100 **(3016)**
2001: 9^6SW, 8^2SW, 8^3SD, 8^0S, 8^0GS, 8^0GF, 6^1F, 7^0GF, 8^0SD

	Starts	1st	2nd	3rd	Win & Pl
Career Total (Turf)	24	2	3	1	14943
Career Total (AW)	8	1	1	2	6190

71 6/01 Brig 6f209y E(0-75)H FRM £2989
81 8/00 Brig 7f214y E(0-75)H G-F £3558
74 11/99 Sthl 1m E(0-75)H STD £2402
Total win prize-money £8950

Going (Turf): Sf: 0-3 GS: 0-3 Gd: 0-8 **GF: 1-8 Fm: 1-2**
Distance: 5f/6f: 0-0 **7f-8f: 3-22** 9f-13f: 0-10 14f+: 0-0
Track : **LH: 3-15** RH: 0-5 Tight: 0-7 Gall: 0-4
Aids: **Bl: 3-27** Vi: 0-0 Tstrap: 0-0
Best Rating: 77 3/01 Wolv 1m100y stand

Fairly useful if frustrating handicapper, effective from seven to nine furlongs. Does not win as often as he should but goes well at Brighton and got off the mark for the season there in June over seven furlongs. Best on a fast surface.

Bold King

(72+)**85**

6-y-o br g Anshan-Spanish Heart (King Of Spain)
J W Hills The Farleigh Court Racing Partnership

Placings:2220/1464530/23201524/103000164-260000040 **(5608)**
2001: 8^2GS, 8^6G, 8^0GF, 7^0G, 8^0G, 7^0G, 7^0S, 7^4S, 7^0GS

	Starts	1st	2nd	3rd	Win & Pl
Career Total (Turf)	36	3	7	3	76012
Career Total (AW)	1	1	0	0	2427

90 9/00 Gdwd 1m B(0-95) SFT £8775
97 5/00 Asct 7f B(0-110)H G-S £22750
87 8/99 Newb 7f C(0-95)H GD £13379
72 4/98 Sthl 1m F STD £2427
Total win prize-money £47331

Going (Turf): **Sf: 1-5 GS: 1-4 Gd: 1-19** GF: 0-7 Fm: 0-1
Distance: 5f/6f: 0-2 **7f-8f: 4-29** 9f-13f: 0-6 14f+: 0-0
Track : LH: 1-10 RH: 1-8 Tight: 0-3 Gall: 0-5
Aids: Bl: 0-0 Vi: 0-0 Tstrap: 0-0
Best Rating: 94 5/01 Kemp 1m gd-sft

A mile performer, he enjoyed a fine season in 2000, winning at Ascot on his first start and at Goodwood later on. Ran a cracking race behind a progressive sort on his reappearance, but has not performed as well since. Stays a mile.

Bold Lady

81 **46**

2-y-o b f Never So Bold-Perfect Lady (Petong)
John Berry Simon Stratford

Placings:300 **(3869)**
2001: 5^3G, 6^0GF, 5^0G

	Starts	1st	2nd	3rd	Win & Pl
Career Total (Turf)	3	0	0	1	270

Going (Turf): **Sf: 0-0 GS: 0-0 Gd: 0-2 GF: 0-1 Fm: 0-0**
Distance: 5f/6f: 0-3 7f-8f: 0-0 9f-13f: 0-0 14f+: 0-0
Track : LH: 0-0 RH: 0-0 Tight: 0-0 Gall: 0-0
Aids: Bl: 0-0 Vi: 0-0 Tstrap: 0-0
Best Rating: 46 6/01 Yarm 5f43y good

Bold Light

85 **74**

2-y-o b c Persian Bold-Kind Of Light (Primo Dominie)
T D Easterby Mrs Janis Macpherson

Placings:0500 **(4771)**
2001: 6^0GS, 7^5GS, 8^0G, 7^0G

	Starts	1st	2nd	3rd	Win & Pl
Career Total (Turf)	4	0	0	0	0

Going (Turf): **Sf: 0-0 GS: 0-2 Gd: 0-2 GF: 0-0 Fm: 0-0**
Distance: 5f/6f: 0-1 7f-8f: 0-2 9f-13f: 0-1 14f+: 0-0
Track : LH: 0-0 RH: 0-2 Tight: 0-0 Gall: 0-0
Aids: Bl: 0-1 Vi: 0-0 Tstrap: 0-0
Best Rating: 74 8/01 Bevl 7f100y gd-sft

Bold McLaughlan

94 **42**

3-y-o b g Mind Games-Stoneydale (Tickled Pink)
J S Goldie Martin Delaney & Frank Brady

Placings:0006540-00000 **(3075)**
2001: 6^0G, 6^0GF, 5^0G, 5^0F, 7^0GS

	Starts	1st	2nd	3rd	Win & Pl
Career Total (Turf)	12	0	0	0	234

Going (Turf): **Sf: 0-0 GS: 0-3 Gd: 0-3 GF: 0-5 Fm: 0-1**
Distance: 5f/6f: 0-11 7f-8f: 0-1 9f-13f: 0-0 14f+: 0-0
Track : LH: 0-1 RH: 0-0 Tight: 0-0 Gall: 0-0
Aids: Bl: 0-1 Vi: 0-0 Tstrap: 0-0
Best Rating: 40 5/01 Ripn 6f gd-fm

Moderate maiden sprinter.

Bold Precedent

104(96) (60)**60d**

4-y-o b g Polish Precedent (USA)-Shining Water (USA) (Riverman (USA))
P W Harris The Shining Examples

Placings:0/4340015-00040304050 **(5400)**
2001: 12^0SD, 9^0F, 9^0GF, 8^4GF, 8^0GF, 8^3GF, 10^0GF, 9^4GF, 10^0GF, 10^5F, 10^0S

	Starts	1st	2nd	3rd	Win & Pl
Career Total (Turf)	16	0	0	2	1698
Career Total (AW)	3	1	0	0	0

Going (Turf): **Sf: 0-2 GS: 0-1 Gd: 0-1 GF: 0-10 Fm: 0-2**
Distance: 5f/6f: 0-0 7f-8f: 0-2 **9f-13f: 1-17** 14f+: 0-0
Track : **LH: 1-11** RH: 0-5 **Tight: 1-9** Gall: 0-2
Aids: Bl: 0-0 Vi: 0-9 Tstrap: 0-0
Best Rating: 60 7/01 Pont 1m4y gd-fm

Bold Raider

107 **79**

4-y-o b g Rudimentary (USA)-Spanish Heart (King Of Spain)
I A Balding The Farleigh Court Racing Partnership

Placings:000/1234351-204142645022 **(5669)**

2001: 8^{2}S, 8^{0}GF, 7^{4}GF, 8^{1}G, 8^{4}GF, 8^{2}GS, 8^{6}G, 8^{4}G, 8^{5}HY, 8^{0}GS, 8^{2}HY, 10^{2}HY

	Starts	1st	2nd	3rd	Win & Pl
Career Total (Turf)	22	3	5	2	21404

73	6/01	Wind	1m67y	E(0-75)H	GD	£3248
57	10/00	Wind	1m67y	E(0-70)	G-S	£2786
63	4/00	Nott	1m54y	F(0-60)H	SFT	£2593

Total win prize-money £8628

Going (Turf): Sf: 1-8 GS: 1-5 Gd: 1-6 GF: 0-3 Fm: 0-0
Distance: 5f/6f: 0-0 7f-8f: 0-10 **9f-13f: 3-12** 14f+: 0-0
Track : LH: 1-11 **RH: 2-6 Tight: 2-7** Gall: 0-2
Aids: Bl: 0-0 Vi: 0-0 Tstrap: 0-0
Best Rating: 79 11/01 Wind 1m2f7y heavy

Best at a mile when the ground is on the easy side and suited by a flat track, he goes particularly well at Windsor and won his second race there in June.

Bold Saboteur

79(74) (1)**23**
4-y-o b g Prince Sabo-Latest Flame (IRE) (Last Tycoon)
K O Cunningham-Brown Woodhaven Racing Syndicate

Placings:000/0000-00P (2556)
2001: 7^{0}SD, 5^{0}F, 6^{P}GF

	Starts	1st	2nd	3rd	Win & Pl
Career Total (Turf)	9	0	0	0	
Career Total (AW)	1	0	0	0	

Going (Turf): Sf: 0-1 GS: 0-2 Gd: 0-2 GF: 0-3 Fm: 0-1
Distance: 5f/6f: 0-5 7f-8f: 0-5 9f-13f: 0-0 14f+: 0-0
Track : LH: 0-4 RH: 0-1 Tight: 0-0 Gall: 0-1
Aids: Bl: 0-0 Vi: 0-0 Tstrap: 0-0
Best Rating: 23 5/01 Brig 5f213y firm

Bold State

(99) (62)**65**
4-y-o b g Never So Bold-Multi-Sofft (Northern State (USA))
M H Tompkins The Toy Boy Partnership

Placings:2536252100/00011225-005240402 **(5413)**
2001: 7^{0}GF, 8^{0}GF, 8^{5}G, 8^{2}GF, 8^{4}GF, 8^{0}G, 9^{4}G, 8^{0}GF, 8^{2}SD

	Starts	1st	2nd	3rd	Win & Pl
Career Total (Turf)	26	3	6	1	20646
Career Total (AW)	1	0	1	0	648

66	6/00	Haml	1m65y	E(0-65)	G-F	£2716
66	6/00	Nott	1m54y	E(0-70)H	G-F	£3159
80	9/99	York	7f202y	E	G-F	£7278

Total win prize-money £13153

Going (Turf): Sf: 0-2 GS: 0-3 Gd: 0-9 **GF: 3-10** Fm: 0-2
Distance: 5f/6f: 0-2 7f-8f: 1-13 **9f-13f: 2-12** 14f+: 0-0
Track : **LH: 2-11** RH: 1-7 Tight: 1-5 Gall: 1-3
Aids: Bl: 0-7 Vi: 0-2 Tstrap: 0-0
Best Rating: 65 7/01 Bevl 1m100y gd-fm

Was in fine form in the summer of 2000, scoring back to back victories at Nottingham and Hamilton over a mile. Has run some decent races without winning this term including on his sand debut. Acts on fast ground.

Bold View

(72) (5)**43**
3-y-o b g Nalchik (USA)-Corvo Cutie (Rolfe (USA))
M Mullineaux J Hardman

Placings:6600 **(2650)**
2001: 8^{6}S, 10^{6}GF, 10^{0}GF, 8^{0}SD

	Starts	1st	2nd	3rd	Win & Pl
Career Total (Turf)	3	0	0	0	0
Career Total (AW)	1	0	0	0	

Going (Turf): Sf: 0-1 GS: 0-0 Gd: 0-0 GF: 0-2 Fm: 0-0

Distance: 5f/6f: 0-0 7f-8f: 0-2 9f-13f: 0-2 14f+: 0-0
Track : LH: 0-3 RH: 0-1 Tight: 0-2 Gall: 0-0
Aids: Bl: 0-0 Vi: 0-0 Tstrap: 0-0
Best Rating: 43 5/01 Ches 1m2f75y gd-fm

Bold Willy

79 **9**
4-y-o b g Never So Bold-Indian Star (Indian King (USA))
J E Long Terry Waters

Placings:060/00-000 **(1810)**
2001: 7^{0}GS, 7^{0}GF, 8^{0}GF

	Starts	1st	2nd	3rd	Win & Pl
Career Total (Turf)	8	0	0	0	0

Going (Turf): Sf: 0-2 GS: 0-3 Gd: 0-0 GF: 0-3 Fm: 0-0
Distance: 5f/6f: 0-2 7f-8f: 0-4 9f-13f: 0-2 14f+: 0-0
Track : LH: 0-1 RH: 0-1 Tight: 0-0 Gall: 0-0
Aids: Bl: 0-0 Vi: 0-0 Tstrap: 0-0
Best Rating: 9 6/01 NmkR 1m gd-fm

Bolder Alexander (IRE)

94 (37)**34**
4-y-o b g Persian Bold-Be Yourself (USA) (Noalcoholic (FR))
F Jordan M W Doyle

Placings:00616230030/0000F0-03000 **(3734)**
2001: 10^{0}F, 11^{3}F, 10^{0}GF, 14^{0}GF, 11^{0}G

	Starts	1st	2nd	3rd	Win & Pl
Career Total (Turf)	22	1	1	3	3373
Career Total (AW)	1	0	0	0	0

62	6/99	Brig	6f209y	G	GD	£1850

Total win prize-money £1851

Going (Turf): Sf: 0-2 GS: 0-2 **Gd: 1-6** GF: 0-8 Fm: 0-4
Distance: 5f/6f: 0-4 **7f-8f: 1-7** 9f-13f: 0-11 14f+: 0-1
Track : **LH: 1-13** RH: 0-4 Tight: 0-8 Gall: 0-0
Aids: **Bl: 1-7** Vi: 0-0 Tstrap: 0-0
Best Rating: 34 6/01 Ling 1m3f106y firm

Boldly Cliff (BEL)

(102) (65)**50**
7-y-o br h Never So Bold-Miami Beach (Miami Springs)
E C Denderland Ecurie Denderland

Placings:0/215323522/33120040240/**40**15215605**401/2** 062410024**2-60**000
2001: 5^{6}SD, 5^{0}SW, 5^{0}G, 5^{0}S, 5^{0}S

	Starts	1st	2nd	3rd	Win & Pl
Career Total (Turf)	41	5	9	4	29130
Career Total (AW)	9	1	2	0	3533

	7/00	Vich	5f	H	SFT	£5764
51	12/99	Ling	5f	F(0-60)H	STD	£2211
	6/99	Chan	5f	H	SFT	£5382
	4/99	Oste	5f	H	SFT	£700

Total win prize-money £16555

Going (Turf): Sf: 1-4 GS: 0-0 Gd: 0-1 GF: 0-1 Fm: 0-0
Distance: **5f/6f: 3-26** 7f-8f: 0-5 9f-13f: 1-1 14f+: 0-0
Track : **LH: 1-9** RH: 0-0 **Tight: 1-9** Gall: 0-0
Aids: **Bl: 1-12** Vi: 0-0 Tstrap: 0-0
Best Rating: 60 2/01 Ling 5f slow

Boldly Goes

(80) (87d)
5-y-o b g Bold Arrangement-Reine De Thebes (FR) (Darshaan)
C W Fairhurst G H & S Leggott

Placings:11101/63/006043100601400650-
2001:

	Starts	1st	2nd	3rd	Win & Pl
Career Total (Turf)	22	5	0	2	32559
Career Total (AW)	3	1	0	0	3080

87	8/00	Newc	7f	C(0-90)H	SFT	£6581
98	8/98	Ripn	6f	A	G-F	£13088
88	7/98	Thsk	7f	C	FRM	£4941
87	6/98	Wolv	6f	E	STD	£3080
62	4/98	Pont	5f	D	G-S	£3837

Total win prize-money £31529

Going (Turf): Sf: 1-5 GS: 1-3 Gd: 0-6 **GF: 2-6** Fm: 1-2
Distance: **5f/6f: 4-14** 7f-8f: 2-10 9f-13f: 0-1 14f+: 0-0
Track : **LH: 3-9** RH: 0-1 **Tight: 2-5** Gall: 0-1
Aids: **Bl: 2-12** Vi: 0-0 Tstrap: 0-0
Best Rating: 62 4/98 Pont 5f GS

Boleyn Castle (USA)

109 **90**
4-y-o ch g River Special (USA)-Dance Skirt (CAN) (Caucasus (USA))
T G Mills M A Shipman

Placings:165/05000-4100 **(5018)**
2001: 5^{4}GF, 5^{1}G, 5^{0}GF, 5^{0}S

	Starts	1st	2nd	3rd	Win & Pl
Career Total (Turf)	12	2	0	0	21778

90	8/01	Epsm	5f	B(0-105)H	GD	£17400
78	4/99	Wind	5f10y	D	G-S	£3485

Total win prize-money £20885

Going (Turf): Sf: 0-4 **GS: 1-1 Gd: 1-2** GF: 0-5 Fm: 0-0
Distance: **5f/6f: 2-12** 7f-8f: 0-0 9f-13f: 0-0 14f+: 0-0
Track : LH: 0-1 **RH: 1-1** Tight: 0-1 **Gall: 1-1**
Aids: Bl: 0-0 Vi: 0-0 Tstrap: 0-0
Best Rating: 90 8/01 Epsm 5f good

Suffered from a high handicap mark in 2000 as a result of his two-year-old exploits, but came back from ten months off with a promising effort at Newbury in August. Showed blistering speed to win an Epsom handicap, but there was controversy as not all the stalls opened at the same time.

Bolham Lady

(102) (52?)**24**
3-y-o b f Timeless Times (USA)-Stratford Lady (Touching Wood (USA))
J Balding J M Lacey

Placings:005-64160304 **(2168)**
2001: 7^{6}SD, 6^{4}SW, 5^{1}SW, 6^{6}SD, 5^{0}S, 5^{3}SD, 5^{0}GF, 6^{4}SD

	Starts	1st	2nd	3rd	Win & Pl
Career Total (Turf)	3	0	0	0	
Career Total (AW)	8	1	0	1	2292

52	2/01	Sthl	5f	G	SLW	£1890

Total win prize-money £1890

Going (Turf): Sf: 0-2 GS: 0-0 Gd: 0-0 GF: 0-1 Fm: 0-0
Distance: **5f/6f: 1-9** 7f-8f: 0-2 9f-13f: 0-0 14f+: 0-0
Track : LH: 0-6 RH: 0-0 Tight: 0-1 Gall: 0-0
Aids: **Bl: 1-8** Vi: 0-0 Tstrap: 0-0
Best Rating: 52 2/01 Sthl 5f slow

Bolingbroke Castle (IRE)

85 **22**
3-y-o ch g Goldmark (USA)-Ruby River (Red God)
Miss J A Camacho L A Bolingbroke

Placings:50-00000 **(5173)**
2001: 7^{0}GF, 6^{0}GF, 8^{0}G, 10^{0}G, 8^{0}GS

	Starts	1st	2nd	3rd	Win & Pl
Career Total (Turf)	7	0	0	0	0

Going (Turf): Sf: 0-1 GS: 0-2 Gd: 0-2 GF: 0-2 Fm: 0-0
Distance: 5f/6f: 0-3 7f-8f: 0-1 9f-13f: 0-3 14f+: 0-0
Track : LH: 0-4 RH: 0-0 Tight: 0-0 Gall: 0-0
Aids: Bl: 0-0 Vi: 0-1 Tstrap: 0-2
Best Rating: 33 5/01 Sthl 7f gd-fm

Bollin Edward

94 **78**

2-y-o b c Timeless Times (USA)-Bollin Harriet (Lochnager)

T D Easterby Sir Neil Westbrook

Placings:33 **(3256)**

2001: 5^{3}GF, 5^{3}GF

	Starts	1st	2nd	3rd	Win & Pl
Career Total (Turf)	2	0	0	2	1268

Going (Turf): Sf: 0-0 GS: 0-0 Gd: 0-0 GF: 0-2 Fm: 0-0

Distance: 5f/6f: 0-2 7f-8f: 0-0 9f-13f: 0-0 14f+: 0-0

Track : LH: 0-0 RH: 0-0 Tight: 0-0 Gall: 0-0

Aids: Bl: 0-0 Vi: 0-0 Tstrap: 0-0

Best Rating: 78 7/01 Ripn 5f gd-fm

Bollin Eric

102 **92+**

2-y-o b c Shaamit (IRE)-Bollin Zola (Alzao (USA))

T D Easterby Sir Neil Westbrook

Placings:3211 **(4678)**

2001: 6^{3}GF, 7^{2}G, 8^{1}GF, 8^{1}G

	Starts	1st	2nd	3rd	Win & Pl
Career Total (Turf)	4	2	1	1	24631

92	9/01	Donc	1m	B	GD	£18931
89	8/01	Bevl	1m100y	E	G-F	£3672

Total win prize-money £22604

Going (Turf): Sf: 0-0 GS: 0-0 **Gd: 1-2 GF: 1-2** Fm: 0-0

Distance: 5f/6f: 0-1 7f-8f: 1-2 9f-13f: 1-1 14f+: 0-0

Track : LH: 0-1 **RH: 1-1** Tight: 0-0 Gall: 0-0

Aids: Bl: 0-0 Vi: 0-0 Tstrap: 0-0

Best Rating: 92 9/01 Donc 1m good

By Shaamit, and half-brother to the notably high-class sprinter, Bollin Joanne, won his last two starts, one of which was a decent nursery at Doncaster. Highly-rated, he stays a mile and acts on good ground.

Bollin Nellie

108 **73**

4-y-o ch f Rock Hopper-Bollin Magdalene (Teenoso (USA))

T D Easterby Lady Westbrook

Placings:4354/45050216210-0160621631 **(5599)**

2001: 11^{0}F, 11^{1}GF, 12^{6}G, 12^{0}GF, 12^{6}GF, 10^{2}G, 10^{1}G, 9^{6}GF, 10^{3}G, 12^{1}GS

	Starts	1st	2nd	3rd	Win & Pl
Career Total (Turf)	25	5	3	2	28675

73	11/01	NmkR	1m4f	D(0-80)H	G-S	£6955
69	8/01	Ripn	1m2f	D(0-80)H	GD	£7020
63	6/01	Bevl	1m3f216y	E(0-70)H	G-F	£3867
62	10/00	Catt	1m3f214y	E(0-70)H	SFT	£3510
54	8/00	Hayd	1m3f200y	F(0-60)H	GD	£2740

Total win prize-money £24094

Going (Turf): Sf: 1-3 GS: 1-1 **Gd: 2-10** GF: 1-7 Fm: 0-4

Distance: 5f/6f: 0-0 7f-8f: 0-3 **9f-13f: 5-21** 14f+: 0-1

Track : LH: 2-14 **RH: 3-7 Tight: 3-11** Gall: 1-4

Aids: Bl: 0-0 Vi: 0-0 Tstrap: 0-0

Best Rating: 73 11/01 NmkR 1m4f gd-sft

A fair middle-distance handicapper, she has won three times this season. Best over 12 furlongs but is effective over shorter when there is plenty of pace. Acts on any ground.

Bollin Thomas

109 **67**

3-y-o b g Alhijaz-Bollin Magdalene (Teenoso (USA))

T D Easterby Sir Neil Westbrook

Placings:0000-00115252322 **(5373)**

2001: 11^{0}GF, 14^{0}F, 11^{1}GF, 11^{1}GF, 11^{5}F, 11^{2}GF, 11^{5}GS, 11^{2}GF, 11^{3}G, 11^{2}GS, 14^{2}G

	Starts	1st	2nd	3rd	Win & Pl
Career Total (Turf)	15	2	4	1	15369

57	7/01	Bevl	1m3f216y	E(0-70)H	G-F	£5434
54	6/01	Bevl	1m3f216y	E(0-75)H	G-F	£3864

Total win prize-money £9298

Going (Turf): Sf: 0-1 GS: 0-2 Gd: 0-3 **GF: 2-7** Fm: 0-2

Distance: 5f/6f: 0-1 7f-8f: 0-1 **9f-13f: 2-11** 14f+: 0-2

Track : LH: 0-8 **RH: 2-7 Tight: 2-11** Gall: 0-0

Aids: Bl: 0-0 Vi: 0-0 Tstrap: 0-0

Best Rating: 67 10/01 Rdcr 1m6f19y good

Lightly raced, he won twice this summer, on both occasions over 12 furlongs at Beverley on good to firm, and he has since been out of the frame on only two occasions. He got 14 furlongs well at Redcar in October.

Bolshoi Ballet

102 **56**

3-y-o b g Dancing Spree (USA)-Broom Isle (Damister (USA))

T D Barron C A Washbourn

Placings:033224-000006030 **(4905)**

2001: 8^{0}S, 8^{0}GF, 10^{0}GF, 12^{0}GF, 10^{0}GF, 9^{6}GF, 8^{0}GF, 8^{3}GS, 8^{0}G

	Starts	1st	2nd	3rd	Win & Pl
Career Total (Turf)	15	0	2	3	3799

Going (Turf): Sf: 0-2 GS: 0-2 Gd: 0-1 GF: 0-9 Fm: 0-1

Distance: 5f/6f: 0-1 7f-8f: 0-5 9f-13f: 0-9 14f+: 0-0

Track : LH: 0-7 RH: 0-5 Tight: 0-3 Gall: 0-3

Aids: Bl: 0-0 Vi: 0-0 Tstrap: 0-0

Best Rating: 56 7/01 Nott 1m1f213y gd-fm

Bolt From The Blue

(98) (30)**32**

5-y-o b g Grand Lodge (USA)-Lightning Legacy (USA) (Super Concorde (USA))

Don Enrico Incisa Don Enrico Incisa

Placings:0040/00306502240/005606000-30 **(0546)**

2001: 16^{3}SD, 11^{0}SD

	Starts	1st	2nd	3rd	Win & Pl
Career Total (Turf)	21	0	2	1	2142
Career Total (AW)	5	0	0	1	250

Going (Turf): Sf: 0-6 GS: 0-2 Gd: 0-7 GF: 0-4 Fm: 0-2

Distance: 5f/6f: 0-4 7f-8f: 0-2 9f-13f: 0-14 14f+: 0-6

Track : LH: 0-17 RH: 0-4 Tight: 0-9 Gall: 0-1

Aids: Bl: 0-1 Vi: 0-0 Tstrap: 0-0

Best Rating: 27 1/01 Sthl 2m stand

Boltoutoftheblue

91(63) (20)**63**

2-y-o ch g Bluegrass Prince (IRE)-Forget To Remindme (Forzando)

J S Moore W J S Ratcliffe

Placings:65000 **(5590)**

2001: 6^{6}GF, 6^{5}GF, 8^{0}SD, 6^{0}HY, 9^{0}GS

	Starts	1st	2nd	3rd	Win & Pl
Career Total (Turf)	4	0	0	0	0
Career Total (AW)	1	0	0	0	

Going (Turf): Sf: 0-1 GS: 0-1 Gd: 0-0 GF: 0-2 Fm: 0-0

Distance: 5f/6f: 0-1 7f-8f: 0-3 9f-13f: 0-1 14f+: 0-0

Track : LH: 0-3 RH: 0-0 Tight: 0-0 Gall: 0-0

Aids: Bl: 0-0 Vi: 0-0 Tstrap: 0-0

Best Rating: 63 9/01 Brig 6f209y gd-fm

Bolula

95(77) (37)**51**

2-y-o b f Tagula (IRE)-Bollin Dorothy (Rambo Dancer (CAN))

T D Easterby T H Bennett

Placings:63040 **(4714)**

2001: 5^{6}S, 5^{3}S, 6^{0}SD, 5^{4}G, 7^{0}G

	Starts	1st	2nd	3rd	Win & Pl
Career Total (Turf)	4	0	0	1	879
Career Total (AW)	1	0	0	0	

Going (Turf): Sf: 0-2 GS: 0-0 Gd: 0-2 GF: 0-0 Fm: 0-0

Distance: 5f/6f: 0-4 7f-8f: 0-1 9f-13f: 0-0 14f+: 0-0

Track : LH: 0-2 RH: 0-0 Tight: 0-0 Gall: 0-0

Aids: Bl: 0-0 Vi: 0-0 Tstrap: 0-0

Best Rating: 51 8/01 Bevl 5f good

Bomb Alaska

102 **100**

6-y-o br g Polar Falcon (USA)-So True (So Blessed)

G B Balding Miss B Swire

Placings:05/604226102/1131221/4434000600-0600 **(5142)**

2001: 8^{0}S, 7^{6}GF, 7^{0}G, 9^{0}G

	Starts	1st	2nd	3rd	Win & Pl
Career Total (Turf)	32	5	5	2	104707

109	10/99	NmkJ	1m	A	SFT	£13778
95	5/99	Gdwd	1m	C(0-100)H	GD	£7002
85	4/99	Newb	1m7y	B(0-105)H	G-F	£18643
79	3/99	Donc	1m	B H	G-S	£14135
81	9/98	Newb	1m	D	GD	£3766

Total win prize-money £57326

Going (Turf): Sf: 1-10 GS: 1-4 **Gd: 2-10** GF: 1-8 Fm: 0-0

Distance: 5f/6f: 0-0 **7f-8f: 4-22** 9f-13f: 1-10 14f+: 0-0

Track : LH: 1-6 RH: 1-8 Tight: 0-1 **Gall: 1-7**

Aids: Bl: 0-0 Vi: 0-0 Tstrap: 0-0

Best Rating: 100 7/01 Newb 7f64y gd-fm

He enjoyed a fantastic season in 1999, but was held by the handicapper in 2000 after beginning the campaign in Listed races. Reported to have undergone a wind operation during the winter, he failed to recapture his best this season. He is tough and genuine, is suited by easy ground, and has dropped to a reasonable mark.

Bon Ami (IRE)

106 **77**

5-y-o b g Paris House-Felin Special (Lyphard's Special (USA))

K T Ivory K T Ivory

Placings:134222321120/4000032422 0/0040000346024 00004-3200000000040 **(4891)**

2001: 7^{3}S, 6^{2}G, 7^{0}G, 6^{0}F, 6^{0}GF, 5^{0}GF, 6^{0}GF, 6^{0}G, 6^{0}G, 6^{0}G, 7^{0}GF, 7^{4}GF, 8^{0}GF

	Starts	1st	2nd	3rd	Win & Pl
Career Total (Turf)	54	3	10	5	76696

88	8/98	Ripn	6f	C	G-F	£4667
100	8/98	Newc	6f	D H	GD	£3517
77	4/98	Leic	5f2y	F	SFT	£2427

Total win prize-money £10613

Going (Turf): Sf: 1-10 GS: 0-4 **Gd: 1-21 GF: 1-14** Fm: 0-5

Distance: **5f/6f: 3-45** 7f-8f: 0-9 9f-13f: 0-0 14f+: 0-0

Track : LH: 0-5 RH: 0-3 Tight: 0-1 Gall: 0-1

Aids: Bl: 0-3 Vi: 0-2 Tstrap: 0-0

Best Rating: 86 5/01 NmkR 6f good

A useful sprint handicapper, he ran his best race when beating all except Tayseer in the 2000 Stewards' Cup, but that is the story with him. He can run superbly in the top sprint handicaps, but has not won since he was a two-year-old.

Bon Marche

98 **75**

2-y-o ch f Definite Article-Sabre Penny (IRE) (Sabrehill (USA))
A P Jarvis Christopher Shankland

Placings:220100 **(5496)**
2001: 7^{2}GF, 7^{2}GF, 6^{0}G, 7^{1}S, 8^{0}GS, 7^{0}HY

	Starts	1st	2nd	3rd	Win & Pl
Career Total (Turf)	6	1	2	0	22054

75	10/01	NmkR	7f	B	SFT	£19500

Total win prize-money £19500

Going (Turf): Sf: **1-2** GS: 0-1 Gd: 0-1 GF: 0-2 Fm: 0-0
Distance: 5f/6f: 0-1 **7f-8f: 1-5** 9f-13f: 0-0 14f+: 0-0
Track : LH: 0-1 RH: 0-0 Tight: 0-0 Gall: 0-0
Aids: Bl: 0-0 Vi: 0-0 Tstrap: 0-0
Best Rating: 82 7/01 Newb 7f gd-fm

A bargain buy at 800gns, she finished runner-up in her first two starts, both over seven furlongs, but was not helped by being dropped down to six for her third start. Returned to seven to win a valuable Newmarket nursery in October. Stays seven furlongs and seems to handle any ground.

Bonaguil (USA)

107(100) (75)**95**
4-y-o b g Septieme Ciel (USA)-Chateaubrook (USA) (Alleged (USA))
C F Wall Mrs R M S Neave

Placings:04/1113420231-0605550 **(4863)**
2001: 8^{0}S, 10^{6}GF, 12^{0}G, 11^{5}G, 10^{5}G, 12^{5}G, 10^{0}GF

	Starts	1st	2nd	3rd	Win & Pl
Career Total (Turf)	18	3	2	2	48670
Career Total (AW)	1	1	0	0	2247

95	10/00	Newb	1m2f6y	C(0-100)H	HVY	£7182
89	5/00	Kemp	1m1f	C(0-90)H	G-S	£7377
80	3/00	Sand	1m14y	C(0-90)H	GD	£7150
75	2/00	Ling	1m	F	STD	£2247

Total win prize-money £23958

Going (Turf): Sf: 1-3 GS: 1-1 Gd: 1-8 GF: 0-6 Fm: 0-0
Distance: 5f/6f: 0-0 **7f-8f: 1-3 9f-13f: 3-16** 14f+: 0-0
Track : LH: 2-9 RH: 2-7 Tight: 1-1 Gall: 1-9
Aids: Bl: 0-0 Vi: 0-0 Tstrap: 0-0
Best Rating: 95 5/01 York 1m2f85y gd-fm

A progressive middle-distance handicapper, he has hung left on more than one occasion but is genuine. Yet to prove he stays a mile and a half. Well held in handicaps all season. Has never won on ground faster than good.

Bond Boy

110 **79**
4-y-o b c Piccolo-Arabellajill (Aragon)
B Smart R C Bond

Placings:4362/4510003-36445201101 **(5685)**
2001: 5^{3}S, 5^{6}GS, 6^{4}GF, 6^{4}G, 6^{5}G, 6^{2}G, 6^{0}G, 5^{1}S, 5^{1}G, 5^{0}S, 5^{1}S

	Starts	1st	2nd	3rd	Win & Pl
Career Total (Turf)	22	4	2	3	32628

78	11/01	Donc	5f	D(0-80)H	SFT	£4582
62	10/01	Rdcr	5f	E(0-70)	GD	£3178
79	9/01	Pont	5f	E(0-70)H	SFT	£4030
42	7/00	Bevl	5f	D	GD	£3809

Total win prize-money £15600

Going (Turf): Sf: 2-8 GS: 0-2 **Gd: 2-10** GF: 0-2 Fm: 0-0
Distance: 5f/6f: 4-22 7f-8f: 0-0 9f-13f: 0-0 14f+: 0-0
Track : LH: 1-5 RH: 0-1 Tight: 0-0 Gall: 0-3
Aids: Bl: 0-0 Vi: 0-0 Tstrap: 0-0
Best Rating: 79 9/01 Pont 5f soft

He won a Beverley maiden in 2000 and he has run some fine races in handicap company since, culminating in three wins from his last four turf starts of the year. Effective over five or six furlongs, he acts well with cut in the ground.

Bond Diamond

102(103) (69d)**60**
4-y-o gr g Prince Sabo-Alsiba (Northfields (USA))
B Smart R C Bond

Placings:0054/1050000300-0123 **(5276)**
2001: 8^{0}GF, 8^{1}F, 8^{2}GF, 8^{3}GS

	Starts	1st	2nd	3rd	Win & Pl
Career Total (Turf)	15	1	1	2	4249
Career Total (AW)	3	1	0	0	2279

54	7/01	Rdcr	1m	G(0-60)H	FRM	£2121
69	1/00	Sthl	7f	F	STD	£2278

Total win prize-money £4400

Going (Turf): Sf: 0-1 GS: 0-3 Gd: 0-4 GF: 0-2 **Fm: 1-5**
Distance: 5f/6f: 0-2 **7f-8f: 2-10** 9f-13f: 0-6 14f+: 0-0
Track : LH: 1-11 RH: 0-2 Tight: 0-5 Gall: 0-1
Aids: Bl: 0-0 Vi: 0-0 Tstrap: 0-0
Best Rating: 60 10/01 Leic 1m9y gd-sft

Half-brother to the ten to 12-furlong winner, Smart Blade, has not achieved much beyond selling class. He has won on the All-Weather and on firm ground.

Bond Domingo

96 **78**
2-y-o b g Mind Games-Antonia's Folly (Music Boy)
B Smart R C Bond

Placings:24400100 **(5636)**
2001: 5^{2}S, 5^{4}S, 5^{4}F, 5^{0}GF, 6^{0}GF, 5^{1}G, 6^{0}GS, 5^{0}G

	Starts	1st	2nd	3rd	Win & Pl
Career Total (Turf)	8	1	1	0	4710

78	9/01	Haml	5f4y	E(0-75)	GD	£3640

Total win prize-money £3640

Going (Turf): Sf: 0-2 GS: 0-1 **Gd: 1-2** GF: 0-2 Fm: 0-1
Distance: 5f/6f: 1-7 7f-8f: 0-1 9f-13f: 0-0 14f+: 0-0
Track : LH: 0-1 RH: 0-0 Tight: 0-1 Gall: 0-0
Aids: Bl: 1-4 Vi: 0-0 Tstrap: 0-0
Best Rating: 78 9/01 Haml 5f4y good

Speedy type. Does not look an easy ride but won in blinkers over five furlongs in September on good ground.

Bond Jovi (IRE)

(87) (73)**73**
2-y-o b g Danehill Dancer (IRE)-Vieux Carre (Pas De Seul)
B Smart R C Bond

Placings:6540 **(5536)**
2001: 5^{6}G, 5^{6}GF, 6^{4}HY, 6^{0}S

	Starts	1st	2nd	3rd	Win & Pl
Career Total (Turf)	4	0	0	0	314

Going (Turf): Sf: 0-2 GS: 0-0 Gd: 0-1 GF: 0-1 Fm: 0-0
Distance: 5f/6f: 0-4 7f-8f: 0-0 9f-13f: 0-0 14f+: 0-0
Track : LH: 0-0 RH: 0-0 Tight: 0-0 Gall: 0-0
Aids: Bl: 0-0 Vi: 0-0 Tstrap: 0-0
Best Rating: 73 10/01 Wind 6f heavy

He has already been gelded and did well when switched to the All-Weather in November.

Bond Millennium

(105) (78)**76**
3-y-o ch g Piccolo-Farmer's Pet (Sharrood (USA))
B Smart R C Bond

Placings:00-210001510224006 **(5624)**
2001: 7^{2}SD, 8^{1}SW, 8^{0}GS, 8^{0}SD, 8^{0}GF, 8^{1}G, 8^{5}GF, 8^{1}GF, 8^{0}GF, 10^{2}G, 9^{2}S, 9^{4}GF, 10^{0}HY, 10^{0}S, 9^{6}GS,

	Starts	1st	2nd	3rd	Win & Pl
Career Total (Turf)	14	2	2	0	9961
Career Total (AW)	3	1	1	0	3042

67	7/01	Bevl	1m100y	F(0-65)H	G-F	£2604
64	6/01	Nott	1m54y	E(0-70)H	GD	£3514
71	2/01	Ling	1m	F	SLW	£2198

Total win prize-money £8316

Going (Turf): Sf: 0-4 GS: 0-2 **Gd: 1-2 GF: 1-6** Fm: 0-0
Distance: 5f/6f: 0-0 7f-8f: 1-5 **9f-13f: 2-12** 14f+: 0-0
Track : LH: 2-10 RH: 1-5 **Tight: 1-6** Gall: 0-1
Aids: Bl: 0-0 Vi: 0-0 Tstrap: 0-0
Best Rating: 76 8/01 Wind 1m2f7y good

Has scored four times over a mile, twice on the All-Weather. Acts on fast ground but handles soft.

Bond Mirage

79 **25**
3-y-o b g Primo Dominie-Arabellajill (Aragon)
B Smart R C Bond

Placings:000 **(4324)**
2001: 6^{0}GF, 7^{0}S, 7^{0}GF

	Starts	1st	2nd	3rd	Win & Pl
Career Total (Turf)	3	0	0	0	

Going (Turf): Sf: 0-1 GS: 0-0 Gd: 0-0 GF: 0-2 Fm: 0-0
Distance: 5f/6f: 0-1 7f-8f: 0-2 9f-13f: 0-0 14f+: 0-0
Track : LH: 0-1 RH: 0-0 Tight: 0-0 Gall: 0-0
Aids: Bl: 0-0 Vi: 0-0 Tstrap: 0-0
Best Rating: 25 8/01 Wwck 7f26y gd-fm

Bonds Gully (IRE)

97(99) (54)**43**
5-y-o b h Pips Pride-Classic Ring (IRE) (Auction Ring (USA))
Mrs Lydia Pearce M M Foulger

Placings:04000/3204404-004050 **(4908)**
2001: 11^{0}GF, 10^{0}G, 10^{4}GS, 10^{0}G, 9^{5}GS, 9^{0}G

	Starts	1st	2nd	3rd	Win & Pl
Career Total (Turf)	16	0	0	0	300
Career Total (AW)	2	0	1	1	902

Going (Turf): Sf: 0-2 GS: 0-2 Gd: 0-4 GF: 0-8 Fm: 0-0
Distance: 5f/6f: 0-0 7f-8f: 0-5 9f-13f: 0-12 14f+: 0-1
Track : LH: 0-11 RH: 0-4 Tight: 0-9 Gall: 0-2
Aids: Bl: 0-1 Vi: 0-1 Tstrap: 0-1
Best Rating: 50 8/01 Yarm 1m2f21y gd-sft

Bonecrusher

98 **81**
2-y-o b c Revoque (IRE)-Eurolink Mischief (Be My Chief (USA))
J L Dunlop Eurolink Group Plc

Placings:010 **(5099)**
2001: 7^{0}GF, 7^{1}HY, 6^{0}GS

	Starts	1st	2nd	3rd	Win & Pl
Career Total (Turf)	3	1	0	0	4024

81	9/01	Hayd	7f30y	D	HVY	£4023

Total win prize-money £4024

Going (Turf): Sf: 1-1 GS: 0-1 Gd: 0-0 GF: 0-1 Fm: 0-0
Distance: 5f/6f: 0-0 **7f-8f: 1-3** 9f-13f: 0-0 14f+: 0-0
Track : LH: 1-1 RH: 0-1 Tight: 0-0 Gall: 0-1
Aids: Bl: 0-0 Vi: 0-0 Tstrap: 0-0
Best Rating: 81 9/01 Hayd 7f30y heavy

Got off the mark at the second attempt in heavy ground, but was disappointing next time.

Bonella (IRE)

98 **49**
3-y-o gr f Eagle Eyed (USA)-Mettlesome (Lomond (USA))
Mrs Lydia Pearce Mrs Anne V Holman-Chappell

Placings:000-1002 **(5026)**

2001: 8^{1}GF, 10^{0}G, 8^{0}GF, 9^{2}S

	Starts	1st	2nd	3rd	Win & Pl
Career Total (Turf)	**7**	**1**	**1**	**0**	**4561**

49 8/01 Leic 1m9y E(0-70)H G-F £3241

Total win prize-money £3241

Going (Turf): Sf: 0-2 GS: 0-0 Gd: 0-2 **GF: 1-3** Fm: 0-0
Distance: 5f/6f: 0-2 7f-8f: 0-1 **9f-13f: 1-4** 14f+: 0-0
Track : LH: 0-2 RH: 0-1 Tight: 0-1 Gall: 0-0
Aids: Bl: 0-0 Vi: 0-0 Tstrap: 0-0
Best Rating: 49 9/01 Brig 1m1f209y soft

Moderate handicapper, usually held up, stays a mile, acts on any ground.

Bonnard (IRE)

106 **117**

3-y-o b c Nureyev (USA)-Utr (USA) (Mr Prospector (USA))
A P O'Brien Michael Tabor

Placings:132203-33255 **(4243)**

2001: 10^{3}GF, 9^{3}G, 10^{2}GF, 8^{5}GS, 8^{5}GF

	Starts	1st	2nd	3rd	Win & Pl
Career Total (Turf)	**11**	**1**	**3**	**4**	**113263**

80 5/00 Fair 6f G-Y £5865

Total win prize-money £5865

Going (Turf): Sf: 0-1 GS: 0-2 Gd: 0-2 GF: 0-4 Fm: 0-0
Distance: **5f/6f: 1-1** 7f-8f: 0-7 9f-13f: 0-3 14f+: 0-0
Track : LH: 0-1 **RH: 1-3** Tight: 0-0 Gall: 0-1
Aids: Bl: 0-1 Vi: 0-0 Tstrap: 0-0
Best Rating: 117 8/01 Deau 1m gd-sft

Third to Dilshaan and Tamburlaine in the Racing Post Trophy at two, he looks short of top class. Has run well at up to ten furlongs and needs to be held up for a late run.

Bonners Bar

(61) **26**

2-y-o b f Bluegrass Prince (IRE)-Another Batchworth (Beveled (USA))
E A Wheeler M V Kirby

Placings:0 **(4211)**

2001: 5^{0}GF

	Starts	1st	2nd	3rd	Win & Pl
Career Total (Turf)	**1**	**0**	**0**	**0**	

Going (Turf): Sf: 0-0 GS: 0-0 Gd: 0-0 GF: 0-1 Fm: 0-0
Distance: 5f/6f: 0-1 7f-8f: 0-0 9f-13f: 0-0 14f+: 0-0
Track : LH: 0-1 RH: 0-0 Tight: 0-0 Gall: 0-1
Aids: Bl: 0-0 Vi: 0-0 Tstrap: 0-0
Best Rating: 26 8/01 Bath 5f11y gd-fm

Bonnie Flora

102(52) **46**

5-y-o b m Then Again-My Minnie (Kind Of Hush)
K Bishop Mrs W J B Protheroe-Beynon

Placings:00/003U000-600210 **(4162)**

2001: 11^{6}GS, 12^{0}S, 12^{0}G, 10^{2}F, 9^{1}GF, 10^{0}GF

	Starts	1st	2nd	3rd	Win & Pl
Career Total (Turf)	**14**	**1**	**1**	**1**	**6637**
Career Total (AW)	**1**	**0**	**0**	**0**	

43 8/01 Brig 1m1f209yE(0-70)H G-F £5135

Total win prize-money £5135

Going (Turf): Sf: 0-1 GS: 0-1 Gd: 0-4 **GF: 1-7** Fm: 0-1
Distance: 5f/6f: 0-0 7f-8f: 0-1 **9f-13f: 1-14** 14f+: 0-0
Track : **LH: 1-8** RH: 0-6 Tight: 0-9 Gall: 0-1
Aids: Bl: 0-0 Vi: 0-0 Tstrap: 0-0
Best Rating: 46 5/01 Bath 1m3f144y gd-sft

Bonnie Lad (IRE)

88 **73**

2-y-o b c Tagula (IRE)-Sabonis (USA) (The Minstrel (CAN))
A Berry Owen Promotions Limited

Placings:650630 **(4695)**

2001: 5^{6}GF, 6^{5}GF, 5^{0}GF, 5^{6}GF, 5^{3}GF, 6^{0}GS

	Starts	1st	2nd	3rd	Win & Pl
Career Total (Turf)	**6**	**0**	**0**	**1**	**908**

Going (Turf): Sf: 0-0 GS: 0-1 Gd: 0-0 GF: 0-5 Fm: 0-0
Distance: 5f/6f: 0-6 7f-8f: 0-0 9f-13f: 0-0 14f+: 0-0
Track : LH: 0-4 RH: 0-0 Tight: 0-3 Gall: 0-0
Aids: Bl: 0-1 Vi: 0-0 Tstrap: 0-0
Best Rating: 73 8/01 Pont 5f gd-fm

Has only made the frame once and could be better suited to six furlongs.

Bonnie Maite

78 **56**

2-y-o ch f Komaite (USA)-Narbonne (Rousillon (USA))
P D Evans J Powell-Tuck

Placings:60 **(5037)**

2001: 5^{6}GF, 5^{0}G

	Starts	1st	2nd	3rd	Win & Pl
Career Total (Turf)	**2**	**0**	**0**	**0**	**0**

Going (Turf): Sf: 0-0 GS: 0-0 Gd: 0-1 GF: 0-1 Fm: 0-0
Distance: 5f/6f: 0-2 7f-8f: 0-0 9f-13f: 0-0 14f+: 0-0
Track : LH: 0-1 RH: 0-0 Tight: 0-0 Gall: 0-1
Aids: Bl: 0-0 Vi: 0-0 Tstrap: 0-0
Best Rating: 56 9/01 Nott 5f13y gd-fm

Bonny Ruan

97 **87**

2-y-o b f So Factual (USA)-Sans Diablo (IRE) (Mac's Imp (USA))
D Haydn Jones Mrs Judy Mihalop

Placings:115100 **(5364)**

2001: 5^{1}G, 5^{1}G, 5^{5}G, 5^{1}GF, 5^{0}GS, 6^{0}GS

	Starts	1st	2nd	3rd	Win & Pl
Career Total (Turf)	**6**	**3**	**0**	**0**	**12866**

87 9/01 Nott 5f13y D(0-85) G-F £3770
87 7/01 Chep 5f16y D GD £3987
64 6/01 Bath 5f11y E GD £2793

Total win prize-money £10551

Going (Turf): Sf: 0-0 GS: 0-2 **Gd: 2-3** GF: 1-1 Fm: 0-0
Distance: **5f/6f: 3-6** 7f-8f: 0-0 9f-13f: 0-0 14f+: 0-0
Track : **LH: 1-1** RH: 0-0 Tight: 0-0 **Gall: 1-1**
Aids: Bl: 0-0 Vi: 0-0 Tstrap: 0-0
Best Rating: 87 9/01 Nott 5f13y gd-fm

Decent sprint juvenile, winner three times over the minimum trip on good and good to firm. Unlucky in running on first try at six in the Tattersalls Autumn Auction Stakes.

Bonnyella

100(78) (35d)**25**

3-y-o b f Phountzi (USA)-Diavalezza (Connaught)
B Palling The Saturday Seven

Placings:500-000440500 **(4854)**

2001: 12^{0}SD, 9^{0}G, 8^{0}F, 9^{4}F, 10^{4}GF, 9^{0}GF, 16^{5}GF, 16^{0}GF, 13^{0}GF

	Starts	1st	2nd	3rd	Win & Pl
Career Total (Turf)	**10**	**0**	**0**	**0**	**0**
Career Total (AW)	**2**	**0**	**0**	**0**	

Going (Turf): Sf: 0-0 GS: 0-0 Gd: 0-1 GF: 0-7 Fm: 0-2
Distance: 5f/6f: 0-2 7f-8f: 0-1 9f-13f: 0-6 14f+: 0-3
Track : LH: 0-8 RH: 0-1 Tight: 0-2 Gall: 0-0
Aids: Bl: 0-3 Vi: 0-0 Tstrap: 0-0
Best Rating: 38 6/01 Nott 1m1f213y firm

Bontadini

77 **52**

2-y-o b c Emarati (USA)-Kintail (Kris)
D Morris Stag And Huntsman

Placings:0 **(3867)**

2001: 7^{0}G

	Starts	1st	2nd	3rd	Win & Pl
Career Total (Turf)	**1**	**0**	**0**	**0**	

Going (Turf): Sf: 0-0 GS: 0-0 Gd: 0-1 GF: 0-0 Fm: 0-0
Distance: 5f/6f: 0-0 7f-8f: 0-1 9f-13f: 0-0 14f+: 0-0
Track : LH: 0-0 RH: 0-0 Tight: 0-0 Gall: 0-0
Aids: Bl: 0-0 Vi: 0-0 Tstrap: 0-0
Best Rating: 52 8/01 Folk 7f good

Boo B Prize (USA)

89 **63**

2-y-o b g Prized (USA)-Sugar Hollow (USA) (Val De L'Orne (FR))
T D Barron Ian Armitage

Placings:625 **(5537)**

2001: 6^{6}GF, 7^{2}S, 7^{5}S

	Starts	1st	2nd	3rd	Win & Pl
Career Total (Turf)	**3**	**0**	**1**	**0**	**888**

Going (Turf): Sf: 0-2 GS: 0-0 Gd: 0-0 GF: 0-1 Fm: 0-0
Distance: 5f/6f: 0-1 7f-8f: 0-2 9f-13f: 0-0 14f+: 0-0
Track : LH: 0-1 RH: 0-0 Tight: 0-1 Gall: 0-0
Aids: Bl: 0-0 Vi: 0-0 Tstrap: 0-0
Best Rating: 63 10/01 Catt 7f soft

Boobala (IRE)

99 **84**

2-y-o b f General Monash (USA)-Best Swinger (IRE) (Ela-Mana-Mou)
D R C Elsworth W V M W & Mrs E S Robins

Placings:041060 **(4668)**

2001: 6^{0}GF, 6^{4}GF, 5^{1}S, 5^{0}GF, 5^{6}G, 6^{0}GF

	Starts	1st	2nd	3rd	Win & Pl
Career Total (Turf)	**6**	**1**	**0**	**0**	**3346**

84 8/01 Chep 5f16y E SFT £2793

Total win prize-money £2793

Going (Turf): Sf: 1-1 GS: 0-0 Gd: 0-1 GF: 0-4 Fm: 0-0
Distance: **5f/6f: 1-6** 7f-8f: 0-0 9f-13f: 0-0 14f+: 0-0
Track : LH: 0-0 RH: 0-0 Tight: 0-0 Gall: 0-0
Aids: Bl: 0-0 Vi: 0-0 Tstrap: 0-0
Best Rating: 84 8/01 Chep 5f16y soft

A half-sister to Scarteen Fox. Dropped to the minimum trip to score on third outing. Should stay six furlongs. Has won on soft ground.

Boogarbaroo (IRE)

89 **53**

3-y-o gr g Turtle Island (IRE)-Lingdale Lass (Petong)
Julian Poulton Mrs Elizabeth Reed

Placings:400 (5083)
2001: 6^4F, 8^0GF, 7^0S

	Starts	1st	2nd	3rd	Win & Pl
Career Total (Turf)	3	0	0	0	280

Going (Turf): Sf: 0-1 GS: 0-0 Gd: 0-0 GF: 0-1 Fm: 0-1
Distance: 5f/6f: 0-0 7f-8f: 0-2 9f-13f: 0-1 14f+: 0-0
Track : LH: 0-1 RH: 0-0 Tight: 0-0 Gall: 0-0
Aids: Bl: 0-0 Vi: 0-0 Tstrap: 0-0
Best Rating: 53 8/01 Sals 6f212y firm

Books Law

78 22
3-y-o b g Contract Law (USA)-In A Whirl (USA) (Island Whirl (USA))
J M Bradley Gwynne Phillips

Placings:000 (4324)
2001: 7^0G, 7^0S, 7^0GF

	Starts	1st	2nd	3rd	Win & Pl
Career Total (Turf)	3	0	0	0	

Going (Turf): Sf: 0-1 GS: 0-0 Gd: 0-1 GF: 0-1 Fm: 0-0
Distance: 5f/6f: 0-0 7f-8f: 0-3 9f-13f: 0-0 14f+: 0-0
Track : LH: 0-1 RH: 0-0 Tight: 0-0 Gall: 0-0
Aids: Bl: 0-0 Vi: 0-0 Tstrap: 0-0
Best Rating: 22 8/01 Wwck 7f26y gd-fm

Boom Or Bust (IRE)

91 64
2-y-o ch g Entrepreneur-Classic Affair (USA) (Trempolino (USA))
A Berry Gordon B Cunningham

Placings:504460 (5086)
2001: 5^5GF, 6^0Y, 7^4G, 7^4GF, 8^6G, 7^0GS

	Starts	1st	2nd	3rd	Win & Pl
Career Total (Turf)	6	0	0	0	0

Going (Turf): Sf: 0-0 GS: 0-1 Gd: 0-2 GF: 0-2 Fm: 0-0
Distance: 5f/6f: 0-1 7f-8f: 0-5 9f-13f: 0-0 14f+: 0-0
Track : LH: 0-2 RH: 0-0 Tight: 0-1 Gall: 0-0
Aids: Bl: 0-0 Vi: 0-0 Tstrap: 0-0
Best Rating: 64 9/01 Thsk 7f gd-fm

Boomshadow

94(84) (29)31
4-y-o ch g Imperial Frontier (USA)-Marie De Sologne (Lashkari)
J L Eyre Miss C King

Placings:00/600056-04 (5534)
2001: 11^0S, 11^4S

	Starts	1st	2nd	3rd	Win & Pl
Career Total (Turf)	8	0	0	0	0
Career Total (AW)	2	0	0	0	0

Going (Turf): Sf: 0-3 GS: 0-1 Gd: 0-3 GF: 0-1 Fm: 0-0
Distance: 5f/6f: 0-1 7f-8f: 0-4 9f-13f: 0-5 14f+: 0-0
Track : LH: 0-8 RH: 0-1 Tight: 0-7 Gall: 0-0
Aids: Bl: 0-0 Vi: 0-0 Tstrap: 0-3
Best Rating: 31 10/01 Rdcr 1m3f soft

Boon Companion

71 25
2-y-o b g Sure Blade (USA)-Pea Green (Try My Best (USA))
John Berry Miss Amanda J Rawding

Placings:0 (3869)
2001: 5^0G

	Starts	1st	2nd	3rd	Win & Pl
Career Total (Turf)	1	0	0	0	

Going (Turf): Sf: 0-0 GS: 0-0 Gd: 0-1 GF: 0-0 Fm: 0-0
Distance: 5f/6f: 0-1 7f-8f: 0-0 9f-13f: 0-0 14f+: 0-0
Track : LH: 0-0 RH: 0-0 Tight: 0-0 Gall: 0-0
Aids: Bl: 0-0 Vi: 0-0 Tstrap: 0-0
Best Rating: 25 8/01 Folk 5f good

Slowly away on Folkestone debut.

Bop

102(96) (37)51
4-y-o b/br f Darkwood Bay (USA)-Call Of The Night (IRE) (Night Shift (USA))
K R Burke Champagne Racing

Placings:000-5062000020 (2868)
2001: 8^5SW, 8^0SD, 8^6SW, 9^2GS, 8^0S, 10^0SD, 8^0GF, 8^0GF, 9^2G, 10^0GF

	Starts	1st	2nd	3rd	Win & Pl
Career Total (Turf)	8	0	2	0	1764
Career Total (AW)	5	0	0	0	0

Going (Turf): Sf: 0-2 GS: 0-2 Gd: 0-1 GF: 0-3 Fm: 0-0
Distance: 5f/6f: 0-0 7f-8f: 0-7 9f-13f: 0-6 14f+: 0-0
Track : LH: 0-8 RH: 0-4 Tight: 0-6 Gall: 0-1
Aids: Bl: 0-0 Vi: 0-1 Tstrap: 0-0
Best Rating: 51 4/01 Muss 1m1f gd-sft

Border Arrow

117 116
6-y-o ch g Selkirk (USA)-Nibbs Point (IRE) (Sure Blade (USA))
I A Balding R P B Michaelson & Wafic Said

Placings:1/1333/3/623062-121032 (5691)
2001: 10^1S, 10^2S, 10^1GF, 10^0GF, 10^3GS, 12^2S

	Starts	1st	2nd	3rd	Win & Pl		
Career Total (Turf)	18	4	4	6	322120		
116	5/01	Sand	1m2f7y	A		G-F	£24000
116	4/01	Kemp	1m2f	A		SFT	£15210
104	4/98	NmkR	1m1f	A		SFT	£11169
95	10/97	NmkR	1m	D		G-S	£8334

Total win prize-money £58713

Going (Turf): Sf: 2-5 GS: 1-5 Gd: 0-5 GF: 1-2 Fm: 0-0
Distance: 5f/6f: 0-0 7f-8f: 1-2 9f-13f: 3-15 14f+: 0-0
Track : LH: 0-4 RH: 2-8 Tight: 0-3 Gall: 1-5
Aids: Bl: 0-0 Vi: 1-3 Tstrap: 0-1
Best Rating: 116 5/01 Sand 1m2f7y gd-fm

Finished third in both the Guineas and Derby in 1998, but had his problems and it was not until this season's Brigadier Gerard Stakes that he gained his first Group victory. He has shown a liking for soft ground in the past, but it was fast when he won at Sandown and ten furlongs does look to be his best trip. He was well beaten behind Fantastic Light in June, and returned from a break to finish a distant third at Newmarket, before a well beaten second at Doncaster in Newmarket behind Boreas in November. Has worn a visor in recent races.

Border Artist

97 69
2-y-o ch c Selkirk (USA)-Aunt Tate (Tate Gallery (USA))
M Blanshard The Borderers

Placings:665100 (4668)
2001: 6^6S, 6^6GF, 7^5GF, 6^1GF, 6^0G, 6^0GF

	Starts	1st	2nd	3rd	Win & Pl		
Career Total (Turf)	6	1	0	0	4042		
69	7/01	Wind	6f	D		G-F	£3893

Total win prize-money £3894

Going (Turf): Sf: 0-1 GS: 0-0 Gd: 0-1 GF: 1-4 Fm: 0-0
Distance: 5f/6f: 1-4 7f-8f: 0-2 9f-13f: 0-0 14f+: 0-0
Track : LH: 0-0 RH: 0-0 Tight: 0-0 Gall: 0-0
Aids: Bl: 0-0 Vi: 0-0 Tstrap: 0-0
Best Rating: 69 7/01 Wind 6f gd-fm

By Selkirk, has run in decent company, winning a maiden over six furlongs on a sound surface.

Border Comet

102 92
3-y-o b c Selkirk (USA)-Starlet (Teenoso (USA))
Sir Michael Stoute The Queen

Placings:42-201650 (5057)
2001: 10^2GF, 12^0GF, 10^1GF, 9^6G, 13^5GF, 12^0S

	Starts	1st	2nd	3rd	Win & Pl		
Career Total (Turf)	8	1	2	0	10302		
92	7/01	Asct	1m2f	D		G-F	£6743

Total win prize-money £6744

Going (Turf): Sf: 0-1 GS: 0-0 Gd: 0-2 GF: 1-5 Fm: 0-0
Distance: 5f/6f: 0-0 7f-8f: 0-2 9f-13f: 1-5 14f+: 0-1
Track : LH: 0-1 RH: 1-5 Tight: 0-2 Gall: 1-4
Aids: Bl: 0-0 Vi: 0-0 Tstrap: 0-0
Best Rating: 92 7/01 Asct 1m2f gd-fm

He showed some decent form in maiden company before winning a weakly-contested event at Ascot in July. Not disgraced in a warm handicap at Glorious Goodwood, but disappointed afterwards. Stays ten furlongs and acts on fast ground.

Border Edge

96(95) (68)58
3-y-o b g Beveled (USA)-Seymour Ann (Krayyan)
K McAuliffe Allsorts

Placings:04050060-422021500 (5461)
2001: 9^4SW, 8^2SD, 9^2SD, 8^0S, 8^2SD, 8^1G, 8^5HY, 7^0HY, 8^0G

	Starts	1st	2nd	3rd	Win & Pl		
Career Total (Turf)	10	1	0	0	2548		
Career Total (AW)	7	0	3	0	2335		
58	5/01	Wwck	1m22y	F(0-65)H		GD	£2548

Total win prize-money £2548

Going (Turf): Sf: 0-5 GS: 0-2 Gd: 1-3 GF: 0-0 Fm: 0-0
Distance: 5f/6f: 0-2 7f-8f: 0-7 9f-13f: 1-8 14f+: 0-0
Track : LH: 0-12 RH: 0-0 Tight: 0-6 Gall: 0-0
Aids: Bl: 0-0 Vi: 1-10 Tstrap: 0-0
Best Rating: 68 4/01 Sthl 1m stand

A half-brother to five-furlong juvenile scorer Silver Lining, he is considerably better on Fibresand, despite a low-grade handicap win over a mile in May 2001.

Border Glen

(105) (61)44
5-y-o b g Selkirk (USA)-Sulitelma (USA) (The Minstrel (CAN))
J J Bridger Terry Thorn

Placings:00000/001100054334/3626005005306433605023-61U12400000000000 (5161)
2001: 7^6SD, 6^1SD, 5^USD, 6^1SW, 6^2SW, 6^4SD, 6^0SD, 6^0HY,

7^{0}G, 5^{0}G, 5^{0}GF, 6^{0}GF, 6^{0}GF, 6^{0}GF, 6^{0}F, 5^{0}G, 6^{0}SD

	Starts	1st	2nd	3rd	Win & Pl
Career Total (Turf)	32	1	0	3	4217
Career Total (AW)	24	3	3	4	11947

61	2/01	Ling	6f	F(0-70)H	SLW	£2205
58	1/01	Ling	6f	E(0-70)H	STD	£2919
55	6/99	Muss	1m	F(0-65)H	GD	£2766
56	6/99	Sthl	1m	F(0-60)H	STD	£2584

Total win prize-money £10474

Going (Turf): Sf: 0-7 GS: 0-4 **Gd: 1-4** GF: 0-15 Fm: 0-2
Distance: 5f/6f: 2-33 7f-8f: 2-16 9f-13f: 0-7 14f+: 0-0
Track : **LH: 3-28** RH: 1-5 **Tight: 3-25** Gall: 0-4
Aids: Bl: 1-24 **Vi: 2-19** Tstrap: 0-0
Best Rating: 61 2/01 Ling 6f slow

Border Marauder (IRE)

(91) (77)**35**

2-y-o b g Priolo (USA)-Irrestible Lady (IRE) (Mtoto)
J A Osborne Chris & Antonia Deuters

Placings:00 **(5610)**
2001: 8^{0}G, 8^{0}SD

	Starts	1st	2nd	3rd	Win & Pl
Career Total (Turf)	1	0	0	0	
Career Total (AW)	1	0	0	0	

Going (Turf): Sf: 0-0 GS: 0-0 Gd: 0-1 GF: 0-0 Fm: 0-0
Distance: 5f/6f: 0-0 7f-8f: 0-1 9f-13f: 0-1 14f+: 0-0
Track : LH: 0-1 RH: 0-0 Tight: 0-1 Gall: 0-0
Aids: Bl: 0-0 Vi: 0-0 Tstrap: 0-0
Best Rating: 43 11/01 Wolv 1m100y stand

Border Minstral (IRE)

83 **77**

2-y-o b/br f Sri Pekan (USA)-Persian Song (Persian Bold)
B J Meehan Mrs R D Peacock

Placings:001000 **(4894)**
2001: 5^{0}GF, 6^{0}GF, 6^{1}G, 5^{0}GF, 6^{0}GF, 5^{0}GS

	Starts	1st	2nd	3rd	Win & Pl
Career Total (Turf)	6	1	0	0	3699

77	8/01	Wind	6f	D	GD	£3698

Total win prize-money £3699

Going (Turf): Sf: 0-0 GS: 0-1 **Gd: 1-1** GF: 0-4 Fm: 0-0
Distance: **5f/6f: 1-6** 7f-8f: 0-0 9f-13f: 0-0 14f+: 0-0
Track : LH: 0-0 RH: 0-0 Tight: 0-0 Gall: 0-0
Aids: Bl: 0-0 Vi: 0-1 Tstrap: 0-0
Best Rating: 77 8/01 Wind 6f good

Got off the mark in good style in Windsor maiden fillies event where she broke well after some previous tardy starts. Stays six furlongs and acts on good ground.

Border Prince

(78) (14)**83**

5-y-o ch g Selkirk (USA)-Princess Oberon (IRE) (Fairy King (USA))
I A Wood Neardown Stables

Placings:06/22032/6 **(0313)**
2001: 8^{6}SW

	Starts	1st	2nd	3rd	Win & Pl
Career Total (Turf)	7	0	3	1	4161
Career Total (AW)	1	0	0	0	0

Going (Turf): Sf: 0-1 GS: 0-0 Gd: 0-3 GF: 0-3 Fm: 0-0
Distance: 5f/6f: 0-1 7f-8f: 0-6 9f-13f: 0-1 14f+: 0-0
Track : LH: 0-3 RH: 0-1 Tight: 0-2 Gall: 0-1

Aids: Bl: 0-0 Vi: 0-0 Tstrap: 0-0
Best Rating: 14 2/01 Ling 1m slow

Border Run

68(86) (31)**63d**

4-y-o b g Missed Flight-Edraianthus (Windjammer (USA))
M Mullineaux P T Hollins

Placings:056/50036030-0 **(0585)**
2001: 14^{0}HY

	Starts	1st	2nd	3rd	Win & Pl
Career Total (Turf)	10	0	0	2	1014
Career Total (AW)	2	0	0	0	0

Going (Turf): Sf: 0-3 GS: 0-1 Gd: 0-1 GF: 0-5 Fm: 0-0
Distance: 5f/6f: 0-0 7f-8f: 0-2 9f-13f: 0-9 14f+: 0-1
Track : LH: 0-4 RH: 0-4 Tight: 0-7 Gall: 0-1
Aids: Bl: 0-2 Vi: 0-0 Tstrap: 0-0
Best Rating: 2 3/01 Nott 1m6f15y heavy

Border Subject

113 **101**

4-y-o b c Selkirk (USA)-Topicality (USA) (Topsider (USA))
R Charlton K Abdulla

Placings:60110-106 **(2972)**
2001: 7^{1}G, 8^{0}GF, 7^{6}G

	Starts	1st	2nd	3rd	Win & Pl
Career Total (Turf)	8	3	0	0	21771

101	5/01	Ling	7f	B(0-105)H	GD	£11700
91	8/00	Wind	1m67y	C(0-90)H	GD	£6301
71	8/00	Chep	7f16y	D	G-F	£3770

Total win prize-money £21771

Going (Turf): Sf: 0-0 GS: 0-2 **Gd: 2-3** GF: 1-3 Fm: 0-0
Distance: 5f/6f: 0-0 **7f-8f: 2-7** 9f-13f: 1-1 14f+: 0-0
Track : LH: 0-0 **RH: 1-1 Tight: 1-1** Gall: 0-0
Aids: Bl: 0-0 Vi: 0-0 **Tstrap: 1-3**
Best Rating: 101 5/01 Ling 7f good

Smart handicapper on fast ground, he likes to dominate as when successful at Windsor last season and at Lingfield this term. Effective over seven furlongs or an easy mile.

Borderline

(101) (48)**66t**

4-y-o ch c Polish Precedent (USA)-Brecon Beacons (IRE) (Shirley Heights)
M Quinn Jalons Partnership 2

Placings:0000000450-6040 **(0160)**
2001: 12^{6}SD, 8^{0}SW, 10^{4}SD, 8^{0}SD

	Starts	1st	2nd	3rd	Win & Pl
Career Total (Turf)	5	0	0	0	
Career Total (AW)	9	0	0	0	0

Going (Turf): Sf: 0-1 GS: 0-1 Gd: 0-2 GF: 0-1 Fm: 0-0
Distance: 5f/6f: 0-0 7f-8f: 0-7 9f-13f: 0-7 14f+: 0-0
Track : LH: 0-11 RH: 0-1 Tight: 0-11 Gall: 0-1
Aids: Bl: 0-0 Vi: 0-1 Tstrap: 0-0
Best Rating: 39 1/01 Ling 1m2f stand

Borders

113 **110**

5-y-o b g Selkirk (USA)-Pretty Poppy (Song)
H Candy Mrs J E L Wright

Placings:00/2314212/13200 **(4683)**
2001: 5^{1}G, 5^{3}GF, 5^{2}S, 5^{0}GF, 5^{0}GS

	Starts	1st	2nd	3rd	Win & Pl
Career Total (Turf)	14	3	4	2	36000

94	5/01	Bevl	5f	C	GD	£6878
91	9/99	Bevl	5f	C	SFT	£6035
85	6/99	Donc	5f	D	GD	£4221

Total win prize-money £17136

Going (Turf): Sf: 1-4 GS: 0-1 **Gd: 2-5** GF: 0-4 Fm: 0-0
Distance: **5f/6f: 3-13** 7f-8f: 0-1 9f-13f: 0-0 14f+: 0-0
Track : LH: 0-1 RH: 0-0 Tight: 0-0 Gall: 0-0
Aids: Bl: 0-0 Vi: 0-0 Tstrap: 0-0
Best Rating: 110 6/01 Sand 5f6y soft

Started his career over six furlongs, but it was only when he was dropped to the minimum that he got off the mark, bolting home at Doncaster. He returned from a lengthy absence to win at Beverley from a good draw and clearly retains plenty of ability. Acts on any ground.

Borders Belle (IRE)

107 **81**

3-y-o b f Pursuit Of Love-Sheryl Lynn (Miller's Mate)
J D Bethell M J Dawson

Placings:4320601-536431200 **(5501)**
2001: 10^{5}S, 12^{3}GF, 12^{6}GF, 11^{4}S, 11^{3}GS, 11^{1}G, 11^{2}HY, 12^{0}S, 12^{0}HY

	Starts	1st	2nd	3rd	Win & Pl
Career Total (Turf)	16	2	2	3	31786

79	8/01	York	1m3f195yC(0-95)H		GD	£20218
74	10/00	Donc	1m	D(0-90)	GD	£5050

Total win prize-money £25269

Going (Turf): Sf: 0-6 GS: 0-2 **Gd: 2-3** GF: 0-4 Fm: 0-1
Distance: 5f/6f: 0-2 7f-8f: 1-4 9f-13f: 1-10 14f+: 0-0
Track : **LH: 2-10** RH: 0-2 Tight: 0-4 **Gall: 2-4**
Aids: Bl: 0-0 Vi: 0-0 Tstrap: 0-0
Best Rating: 84 5/01 Ches 1m4f66y gd-fm

Got off the mark on her final start at two over a mile on good ground. Stepped up to middle distances this season, she gained reward for some decent runs when landing the Knavesmire Handicap at the York Ebor meeting. Suited by 12 furlongs on good ground, but has run well on heavy.

Boreas

114 **115**

6-y-o b g In The Wings-Reamur (Top Ville)
L M Cumani Aston House Stud

Placings:55143/1231-63301 **(5691)**
2001: 12^{6}G, 12^{3}GS, 12^{3}S, 12^{0}HY, 12^{1}S

	Starts	1st	2nd	3rd	Win & Pl
Career Total (Turf)	14	4	1	4	95245

115	11/01	Donc	1m4f	A	SFT	£15229
115	11/00	Donc	1m4f	A	HVY	£14235
89	7/00	York	1m3f195yB(0-100)H		GD	£10869
84	8/98	Ripn	1m2f	D	G-F	£3517

Total win prize-money £43853

Going (Turf): Sf: 2-5 GS: 0-1 Gd: 1-5 GF: 1-3 Fm: 0-0
Distance: 5f/6f: 0-0 7f-8f: 0-0 **9f-13f: 4-13** 14f+: 0-1
Track : **LH: 3-7** RH: 1-7 Tight: 1-1 **Gall: 3-12**
Aids: Bl: 0-0 Vi: 0-0 Tstrap: 0-0
Best Rating: 115 11/01 Donc 1m4f soft

Interesting middle-distance performer. Runner-up to Give The Slip in the 2000 Ebor, followed up by running third in Group Three at Newbury and beating Zilarator by 13 lengths in Listed event over 12 furlongs at Doncaster. He seemed to find the step up in class too much in the Jockey Club Stakes on his reappearance, but ran better in the Cumberland Lodge before repeating his Listed Doncaster victory in similar runaway style. Handles heavy ground but has also won on firm.

Borehill Joker

72

5-y-o ch g Pure Melody (USA)-Queen Matilda (Castle Keep)

W G M Turner O J Stokes

Placings:25446/00/0 **(5330)**

2001: 16^{0}HY

	Starts	1st	2nd	3rd	Win & Pl
Career Total (Turf)	4	0	0	0	0
Career Total (AW)	4	0	1	0	515

Going (Turf): Sf: 0-2 GS: 0-0 Gd: 0-0 GF: 0-2 Fm: 0-0
Distance: 5f/6f: 0-4 7f-8f: 0-2 9f-13f: 0-1 14f+: 0-1
Track : LH: 0-5 RH: 0-0 Tight: 0-4 Gall: 0-0
Aids: Bl: 0-1 Vi: 0-2 Tstrap: 0-1

Born Special

83 **53**

2-y-o b g Bluebird (USA)-Dixie Eyes Blazing (USA) (Gone West (USA))

P C Haslam Les Buckley & S A B Dinsmore

Placings:000 **(4903)**

2001: 6^{0}G, 6^{0}G, 5^{0}G

	Starts	1st	2nd	3rd	Win & Pl
Career Total (Turf)	3	0	0	0	

Going (Turf): Sf: 0-0 GS: 0-0 Gd: 0-3 GF: 0-0 Fm: 0-0
Distance: 5f/6f: 0-3 7f-8f: 0-0 9f-13f: 0-0 14f+: 0-0
Track : LH: 0-0 RH: 0-0 Tight: 0-0 Gall: 0-0
Aids: Bl: 0-0 Vi: 0-0 Tstrap: 0-0
Best Rating: 53 9/01 Ayr 6f good

Born Wild (FR)

79 **28**

3-y-o b f Exit To Nowhere (USA)-Passerella (FR) (Brustolon)

K A Ryan Tony Fawcett

Placings:0-000 **(1660)**

2001: 7^{0}G, 8^{0}GF, 14^{0}F

	Starts	1st	2nd	3rd	Win & Pl
Career Total (Turf)	4	0	0	0	

Going (Turf): Sf: 0-0 GS: 0-0 Gd: 0-1 GF: 0-2 Fm: 0-1
Distance: 5f/6f: 0-0 7f-8f: 0-3 9f-13f: 0-0 14f+: 0-1
Track : LH: 0-3 RH: 0-1 Tight: 0-3 Gall: 0-0
Aids: Bl: 0-0 Vi: 0-0 Tstrap: 0-0
Best Rating: 28 5/01 Thsk 1m gd-fm

Borofan

78 **9**

5-y-o b g Mon Tresor-Musical Drive (Hotfoot)

M Dods A F Monk

Placings:0000 **(1168)**

2001: 12^{0}S, 5^{0}S, 7^{0}S, 7^{0}S

	Starts	1st	2nd	3rd	Win & Pl
Career Total (Turf)	4	0	0	0	

Going (Turf): Sf: 0-4 GS: 0-0 Gd: 0-0 GF: 0-0 Fm: 0-0
Distance: 5f/6f: 0-1 7f-8f: 0-2 9f-13f: 0-1 14f+: 0-0
Track : LH: 0-0 RH: 0-0 Tight: 0-0 Gall: 0-0
Aids: Bl: 0-1 Vi: 0-0 Tstrap: 0-1
Best Rating: 9 4/01 Ripn 5f soft

Bosham Mill

111 **111**

3-y-o ch c Nashwan (USA)-Mill On The Floss (Mill Reef (USA))

G Wragg John Pearce Racing Ltd

Placings:31164031 **(5676a)**

2001: 12^{3}GS, 12^{1}GS, 12^{1}S, 16^{6}GF, 14^{4}G, 16^{0}G, 18^{3}G, 15^{1}HO

	Starts	1st	2nd	3rd	Win & Pl
Career Total (Turf)	8	3	0	2	35080

107	11/01	MsnL	1m7f110y		HLD	£13579
94	5/01	Sals	1m4f	B(0-95)	SFT	£10096
89	5/01	Sals	1m4f	D	G-S	£3614

Total win prize-money £27290

Going (Turf): Sf: 1-1 GS: 1-2 Gd: 0-3 GF: 0-1 Fm: 0-0
Distance: 5f/6f: 0-0 7f-8f: 0-0 **9f-13f: 2-3** 14f+: 1-5
Track : LH: 0-1 **RH: 3-7 Tight: 2-3** Gall: 0-4
Aids: Bl: 0-0 Vi: 0-0 Tstrap: 0-0
Best Rating: 111 9/01 Donc 2m2f good

A 120,000 gns yearling by Nashwan out of a high-class middle-distance mare, he scored twice over 12 furlongs at Salisbury in May, but was held in Pattern company before winning a French Listed race on soft. Suited by an easy surface.

Bosra Badger

98(76) (43)**48**

3-y-o ch g Emarati (USA)-Mrs McBadger (Weldnaas (USA))

Mrs L C Jewell Godelpus

Placings:0000500-06060004500 **(5593)**

2001: 5^{0}GF, 5^{6}G, 6^{0}F, 5^{6}GF, 5^{0}G, 6^{0}GF, 5^{0}GF, 6^{4}GF, 5^{5}G, 5^{0}HY, 5^{0}GS

	Starts	1st	2nd	3rd	Win & Pl
Career Total (Turf)	17	0	0	0	0
Career Total (AW)	1	0	0	0	

Going (Turf): Sf: 0-2 GS: 0-1 Gd: 0-4 GF: 0-9 Fm: 0-1
Distance: 5f/6f: 0-18 7f-8f: 0-0 9f-13f: 0-0 14f+: 0-0
Track : LH: 0-6 RH: 0-1 Tight: 0-0 Gall: 0-1
Aids: Bl: 0-0 Vi: 0-5 Tstrap: 0-0
Best Rating: 48 9/01 Gdwd 5f good

Boss Tweed (IRE)

100(100) (62)**47**

4-y-o b g Persian Bold-Betty Kenwood (Dominion)

Ronald Thompson B Bruce

Placings:0650/1143105030006O-140505 **(3179)**

2001: 10^{1}SD, 12^{4}SD, 12^{0}SD, 10^{5}S, 11^{0}SD, 9^{5}GS

	Starts	1st	2nd	3rd	Win & Pl
Career Total (Turf)	10	1	0	1	3497
Career Total (AW)	14	3	0	1	6546

62	1/01	Ling	1m2f	F(0-60)	STD	£2184
65	4/00	Ripn	1m2f	E(0-70)H	SFT	£2980
62	1/00	Ling	1m	F(0-60)H	STD	£2236
60	1/00	Sthl	1m	G	STD	£1909

Total win prize-money £9311

Going (Turf): Sf: 1-6 GS: 0-2 Gd: 0-1 GF: 0-1 Fm: 0-0
Distance: 5f/6f: 0-3 7f-8f: 2-4 9f-13f: 2-16 14f+: 0-1
Track : **LH: 3-19** RH: 1-4 **Tight: 3-9** Gall: 0-1
Aids: Bl: 0-0 Vi: 0-0 Tstrap: 0-6
Best Rating: 62 1/01 Ling 1m2f stand

Bossarati Rock

23

3-y-o b f Emarati (USA)-La Bossette (IRE) (Cyrano De Bergerac)

A G Newcombe Black Rock Racing

Placings:0 **(4842)**

2001: 8^{0}G

	Starts	1st	2nd	3rd	Win & Pl
Career Total (Turf)	1	0	0	0	

Going (Turf): Sf: 0-0 GS: 0-0 Gd: 0-1 GF: 0-0 Fm: 0-0
Distance: 5f/6f: 0-0 7f-8f: 0-0 9f-13f: 0-1 14f+: 0-0
Track : LH: 0-1 RH: 0-0 Tight: 0-0 Gall: 0-0
Aids: Bl: 0-0 Vi: 0-0 Tstrap: 0-0

Bosscat

(54) **61**

4-y-o b g Presidium-Belltina (Belfort (FR))

K McAuliffe Boss Racing

Placings:0600/05000-00 **(3157)**

2001: 12^{0}SW, 10^{0}GS

	Starts	1st	2nd	3rd	Win & Pl
Career Total (Turf)	10	0	0	0	0
Career Total (AW)	1	0	0	0	

Going (Turf): Sf: 0-2 GS: 0-1 Gd: 0-2 GF: 0-4 Fm: 0-1
Distance: 5f/6f: 0-2 7f-8f: 0-3 9f-13f: 0-6 14f+: 0-0
Track : LH: 0-6 RH: 0-2 Tight: 0-2 Gall: 0-2
Aids: Bl: 0-3 Vi: 0-0 Tstrap: 0-0
Best Rating: 62 1/01 Ling 1m2f stand

Bossy Spice

92 **35**

4-y-o br f Emperor Jones (USA)-Million Heiress (Auction Ring (USA))

N M Babbage B & M Babbage & Co Ltd

Placings:6000/0000-060 **(2989)**

2001: 11^{0}GS, 11^{6}F, 12^{0}G

	Starts	1st	2nd	3rd	Win & Pl
Career Total (Turf)	10	0	0	0	0
Career Total (AW)	1	0	0	0	

Going (Turf): Sf: 0-1 GS: 0-3 Gd: 0-2 GF: 0-2 Fm: 0-2
Distance: 5f/6f: 0-2 7f-8f: 0-0 9f-13f: 0-7 14f+: 0-2
Track : LH: 0-9 RH: 0-1 Tight: 0-4 Gall: 0-1
Aids: Bl: 0-0 Vi: 0-1 Tstrap: 0-0
Best Rating: 35 5/01 Bath 1m3f144y gd-sft

Bottelino Joe (IRE)

(93) (20)**44**

4-y-o b/br g Bluebird (USA)-My-O-My (IRE) (Waajib)

M S Saunders Il Bottelino

Placings:0045/000000-500 **(0483)**

2001: 8^{5}SW, 7^{0}SW, 10^{0}SD

	Starts	1st	2nd	3rd	Win & Pl
Career Total (Turf)	8	0	0	0	268
Career Total (AW)	5	0	0	0	0

Going (Turf): Sf: 0-2 GS: 0-2 Gd: 0-4 GF: 0-0 Fm: 0-0
Distance: 5f/6f: 0-3 7f-8f: 0-8 9f-13f: 0-2 14f+: 0-0
Track : LH: 0-9 RH: 0-0 Tight: 0-4 Gall: 0-2
Aids: Bl: 0-1 Vi: 0-0 Tstrap: 0-0
Best Rating: 20 2/01 Ling 1m slow

Bouchra (IRE)

101(101) (66)**69**

3-y-o ch f Inchinor-My Darlingdaughter (Night Shift (USA))
I Semple Gordon McDowall

Placings:2203603-2501405200 **(5630)**
2001: 7^{2}SW, 5^{5}GS, 6^{0}GF, 6^{1}S, 6^{4}GS, 9^{0}S, 7^{5}HY, 6^{2}SD, 6^{0}HY, 6^{0}G

	Starts	1st	2nd	3rd	Win & Pl	
Career Total (Turf)	14	1	2	1	9489	
Career Total (AW)	3	0	2	1	1785	
66 7/01 Haml	6f5y	D			SFT	£3558

Total win prize-money £3559

Going (Turf): Sf: 1-6 GS: 0-3 Gd: 0-2 GF: 0-2 Fm: 0-1
Distance: 5f/6f: 0-8 **7f-8f: 1-8** 9f-13f: 0-1 14f+: 0-0
Track : LH: 0-5 RH: 0-1 Tight: 0-5 Gall: 0-0
Aids: Bl: 0-0 **Vi: 1-9** Tstrap: 0-0
Best Rating: 69 7/01 Haml 6f5y gd-sft

Fair sprinter, effective five to seven furlongs, goes well on soft ground and got off the mark under those conditions at Hamilton in July. Best served by racing up with the pace and has shown a bit of form on Fibresand.

Boulevard (IRE)

102(98) (77)**82**
5-y-o gr g Sadler's Wells (USA)-Ispahan (Rusticaro (FR))
M F Morris (S Kirk 30/7) Mrs Marie Jordan

Placings:52116/60200200036 **(5437a)**
2001: 12^{6}SW, 12^{0}S, 16^{2}GF, 13^{0}GF, 20^{0}GF, 16^{2}GF, 16^{0}GF, 16^{0}Y, 12^{0}G, 14^{3}GY, 12^{6}S

	Starts	1st	2nd	3rd	Win & Pl
Career Total (Turf)	15	2	3	1	28639
Career Total (AW)	1	0	0	0	0
7/99 Deau 1m2f				GD	£9688
5/99 Comp 1m2f				GD	£7535

Total win prize-money £17223

Going (Turf): Sf: 0-2 GS: 0-0 **Gd: 1-2** GF: 0-5 Fm: 0-0
Distance: 5f/6f: 0-0 7f-8f: 0-0 **9f-13f: 1-6** 14f+: 0-7
Track : LH: 0-5 RH: 0-3 Tight: 0-1 Gall: 0-3
Aids: Bl: 0-0 Vi: 0-0 Tstrap: 0-0
Best Rating: 82 6/01 Wwck 2m39y gd-fm

Bouncing Bowdler

106 **100**
3-y-o b c Mujadil (USA)-Prima Volta (Primo Dominie)
M Johnston Paul Doan

Placings:322122211-003001455000 **(5694)**
2001: 6^{0}GF, 6^{0}F, 6^{3}GF, 6^{0}G, 6^{0}GY, 7^{1}GS, 6^{4}G, 7^{5}GF, 6^{5}S, 6^{0}S, 6^{0}HY, 6^{0}S

	Starts	1st	2nd	3rd	Win & Pl	
Career Total (Turf)	21	4	5	2	101465	
104 8/01 Epsm	7f	A			G-S	£14950
107 9/00 Newb	6f8y	A			G-F	£30000
99 8/00 York	5f	A			GD	£18053
76 5/00 Ripn	5f	D			GD	£3471

Total win prize-money £66475

Going (Turf): Sf: 0-5 GS: 1-3 **Gd: 2-5** GF: 1-6 Fm: 0-1
Distance: 5f/6f: 2-16 7f-8f: 2-5 9f-13f: 0-0 14f+: 0-0
Track : **LH: 1-2** RH: 0-0 **Tight: 1-1** Gall: 0-1
Aids: Bl: 0-0 Vi: 0-0 Tstrap: 0-0
Best Rating: 107 9/01 Newb 7f64y gd-fm

Tough and speedy, he was very consistent in his first season and ended the campaign with two victories, the latter being in the Mill Reef Stakes. Badly hampered on his reappearance in the Cork and Orrery and was well beaten in a Group Three sprint at Newcastle, but caused something of a surprise when winning a Listed race over seven furlongs on soft ground at Epsom in August. Held since in similar company. Effective on most surfaces.

Bound

(107) (73+)**72**
3-y-o b c Kris-Tender Moment (IRE) (Caerleon (USA))
B W Hills Ray Richards

Placings:0003610-6 **(1485)**
2001: 10^{6}GF

	Starts	1st	2nd	3rd	Win & Pl
Career Total (Turf)	7	0	0	1	1068
Career Total (AW)	1	1	0	0	2737
73 10/00 Wolv 1m1f79y D				STD	£2737

Total win prize-money £2737

Going (Turf): Sf: 0-2 GS: 0-0 Gd: 0-2 GF: 0-3 Fm: 0-0
Distance: 5f/6f: 0-0 7f-8f: 0-5 **9f-13f: 1-3** 14f+: 0-0
Track : **LH: 1-4** RH: 0-3 **Tight: 1-3** Gall: 0-0
Aids: Bl: 0-0 Vi: 0-0 Tstrap: 0-1
Best Rating: 73 10/00 Wolv 1m1f79y SD

Bound By Law (IRE)

90 **76**
2-y-o b f Dolphin Street (FR)-Basovizza (Statoblest)
L M Cumani Allevamento Gialloblu

Placings:50503 **(5474a)**
2001: 7^{5}G, 8^{0}GF, 7^{5}G, 7^{0}GF, 7^{3}G, 7^{2}VS

	Starts	1st	2nd	3rd	Win & Pl
Career Total (Turf)	5	0	0	1	1577

Going (Turf): Sf: 0-0 GS: 0-0 Gd: 0-3 GF: 0-2 Fm: 0-0
Distance: 5f/6f: 0-0 7f-8f: 0-4 9f-13f: 0-1 14f+: 0-0
Track : LH: 0-1 RH: 0-2 Tight: 0-1 Gall: 0-1
Aids: Bl: 0-0 Vi: 0-0 Tstrap: 0-0
Best Rating: 76 10/01 Siro 7f good

Speedily bred, has shown some ability in maidens in Britain and Italy.

Bound For Pleasure (IRE)

101 **92**
5-y-o gr h Barathea (IRE)-Dazzlingly Radiant (Try My Best (USA))
J H M Gosden Action Bloodstock

Placings:021/0600/23110-00 **(5261)**
2001: 10^{0}GF, 10^{0}GS

	Starts	1st	2nd	3rd	Win & Pl		
Career Total (Turf)	14	3	2	1	33020		
92 9/00 Donc	1m2f60y	C(0-95)H				G-F	£19987
88 8/00 Gdwd	1m1f	E(0-85)H				GD	£3575
82 10/98 Ling	7f	D				HVY	£3525

Total win prize-money £27088

Going (Turf): Sf: 1-1 GS: 0-3 **Gd: 1-7 GF: 1-3** Fm: 0-0
Distance: 5f/6f: 0-0 7f-8f: 1-6 **9f-13f: 2-8** 14f+: 0-0
Track : LH: 1-2 RH: 1-5 Tight: 1-4 Gall: 1-3
Aids: Bl: 0-1 Vi: 0-0 **Tstrap: 2-7**
Best Rating: 86 6/01 Asct 1m2f gd-fm

He scored at Goodwood and Newmarket last season, showing a good turn of foot in both occasions. Lightly-raced this term.

Bound To Please

(104) (67)**56**
6-y-o b g Warrshan (USA)-Hong Kong Girl (Petong)
P J Makin Mrs P J Makin

Placings:502U440/6005013/110-3120403 **(5347)**
2001: 8^{3}SD, 8^{1}SD, 7^{2}SD, 7^{0}SD, 7^{4}HY, 8^{0}SD, 8^{3}SD

	Starts	1st	2nd	3rd	Win & Pl		
Career Total (Turf)	12	1	1	0	3367		
Career Total (AW)	12	3	1	3	9315		
63 2/01 Sthl	1m	E(0-75)H				STD	£3010
52 10/00 Wind	6f	F(0-60)H				G-S	£1869
63 1/00 Sthl	7f	E(0-70)H				STD	£2470
61 11/99 Sthl	7f	F(0-60)H				STD	£2018

Total win prize-money £9368

Going (Turf): Sf: 0-3 **GS: 1-3** Gd: 0-5 GF: 0-1 Fm: 0-0
Distance: 5f/6f: 1-11 **7f-8f: 3-13** 9f-13f: 0-0 14f+: 0-0
Track : **LH: 3-16** RH: 1-4 Tight: 0-2 **Gall: 1-6**
Aids: Bl: 0-0 Vi: 0-0 Tstrap: 0-0
Best Rating: 67 10/01 Sthl 1m stand

He won his first ever race on turf at Windsor last October, but has enjoyed more success on sand at Southwell. Best at around seven furlongs.

Bourgainville

107 **101**
3-y-o b c Pivotal-Petonica (IRE) (Petoski)
I A Balding Exors Of The Late Robert Hitchins

Placings:110-5222430 **(5142)**
2001: 9^{5}GS, 9^{2}GF, 8^{2}GF, 8^{2}GF, 9^{4}G, 8^{3}GF, 9^{0}G

	Starts	1st	2nd	3rd	Win & Pl	
Career Total (Turf)	10	2	3	1	29591	
87 9/00 Kemp	7f	C			GD	£6351
84 8/00 Sals	6f212y	E			G-F	£2925

Total win prize-money £9276

Going (Turf): Sf: 0-0 GS: 0-1 **Gd: 1-4 GF: 1-5** Fm: 0-0
Distance: 5f/6f: 0-0 **7f-8f: 2-6** 9f-13f: 0-4 14f+: 0-0
Track : LH: 0-0 **RH: 1-5** Tight: 0-3 **Gall: 1-2**
Aids: Bl: 0-0 Vi: 0-0 Tstrap: 0-0
Best Rating: 101 8/01 Gdwd 1m1f192y good

Won an ordinary race at Salisbury on his juvenile debut, but was very impressive when following up in a Kempton conditions event. He has not won since, but has run some fine races in defeat this season if looking vulnerable off his current mark. Suited by a mile and fast ground.

Bourgeois

103
4-y-o ch g Sanglamore (USA)-Bourbon Girl (Ile De Bourbon (USA))
T D Easterby C H Stevens

Placings:24123425-0 **(1004)**
2001: 12^{0}S

	Starts	1st	2nd	3rd	Win & Pl
Career Total (Turf)	9	1	3	1	27760
5/00 MsnL 1m5f				SFT	£7685

Total win prize-money £7685

Going (Turf): Sf: 0-2 GS: 0-0 Gd: 0-1 GF: 0-1 Fm: 0-0
Distance: 5f/6f: 0-0 7f-8f: 0-0 9f-13f: 0-4 14f+: 0-2
Track : LH: 0-0 RH: 0-4 Tight: 0-1 Gall: 0-0
Aids: Bl: 0-1 Vi: 0-0 Tstrap: 0-0
Best Rating: 5/00 MsnL 1m5f S

Bow Peep (IRE)

78 (46)**54**
6-y-o b/br m Shalford (IRE)-Gale Force Seven (Strong Gale)
M W Easterby Mrs Anne Jarvis

Placings:5444/0511040/000000/124000-0 **(0595)**
2001: 5^{0}S

	Starts	1st	2nd	3rd	Win & Pl

	Starts	1st	2nd	3rd	Win & Pl
Career Total (Turf)	23	3	1	0	11388
Career Total (AW)	1	0	0	0	0

48	3/00	Muss	5f	E(0-70)H	GD	£2847
63	7/98	Nott	5f13y	F(0-65)	G-F	£2448
63	7/98	Ripn	6f	D(0-80)H	GD	£4406

Total win prize-money £9701

Going (Turf): Sf: 0-3 GS: 0-1 **Gd: 2-9** GF: 1-9 Fm: 0-1
Distance: **5f/6f: 3-24** 7f-8f: 0-0 9f-13f: 0-0 14f+: 0-0
Track : LH: 0-3 RH: 0-1 Tight: 0-0 Gall: 0-1
Aids: **Bl: 1-9** Vi: 0-0 Tstrap: 0-0
Best Rating: 15 3/01 Muss 5f soft

Bow Strada

105 **71**

4-y-o ch g Rainbow Quest (USA)-La Strada (Niniski (USA))
P W Harris (P J Hobbs 24/2) Doolan, Haygarth, Rice & Strachan

Placings:11/500-00510 **(5693)**
2001: 13^{0}GF, 16^{0}GF, 16^{5}GS, 13^{1}GS, 12^{0}S

	Starts	1st	2nd	3rd	Win & Pl
Career Total (Turf)	10	3	0	0	17176

71	10/01	York	1m5f194y	D(0-85)H	G-S	£8401
86	10/99	Leic	1m1f218y	C	G-S	£5257
79	8/99	Yarm	1m3y	E	GD	£3517

Total win prize-money £17176

Going (Turf): Sf: 0-2 **GS: 2-3** Gd: 1-4 GF: 0-1 Fm: 0-0
Distance: 5f/6f: 0-0 7f-8f: 0-0 **9f-13f: 2-5** 14f+: 1-5
Track : LH: 1-4 RH: 1-4 Tight: 0-2 **Gall: 1-5**
Aids: Bl: 0-0 Vi: 0-0 Tstrap: 0-0
Best Rating: 71 10/01 York 1m5f194y gd-sft

Scored twice from first two runs as a two-year-old, but found life tougher off marks in the 80s and 70s afterwards. Came good over 14 furlongs at York in October on his second outing since being gelded, and may well be due for a jumping campaign. Enjoys some cut in the ground.

Bowcliffe

96(100) (68d)**41**

10-y-o b g Petoski-Gwiffina (Welsh Saint)
W Storey J P Hames

Placings:4/0501/0546/00100000/03315162366435/**142**00456020532100/0100000222060/**0436**022100100-00005000000 **(4662)**
2001: 8^{0}S, 8^{0}GS, 8^{0}G, 7^{0}F, 8^{5}GF, 8^{0}G, 8^{0}GF, 8^{0}F, 8^{0}F, 8^{0}GF, 10^{0}GF

	Starts	1st	2nd	3rd	Win & Pl
Career Total (Turf)	76	8	8	5	64238
Career Total (AW)	10	1	1	1	4374

44	8/00	Rdcr	1m	E(0-65)	FRM	£3042
60	6/00	Carl	7f214y	F(0-60)	G-F	£2383
66	4/99	Muss	1m16y	E(0-70)	G-F	£2626
68	9/98	Donc	1m	C(0-100)H	GD	£19412
62	1/98	Wolv	1m1f79y	E(0-70)H	STD	£2414
62	7/97	Carl	7f214y	F(0-60)H	GD	£3074
54	6/97	Pont	1m4y	E(0-70)H	G-F	£3353
50	5/96	Muss	1m16y	F(0-60)H	G-S	£2766
58	8/94	Ripn	1m2f	E(0-70)H	G-F	£4068

Total win prize-money £43141

Going (Turf): Sf: 0-4 GS: 1-10 Gd: 2-24 **GF: 4-30** Fm: 1-8
Distance: 5f/6f: 0-0 7f-8f: 4-34 **9f-13f: 5-50** 14f+: 0-2
Track : LH: 3-39 **RH: 5-34 Tight: 4-39** Gall: 1-13
Aids: Bl: 0-1 Vi: 0-2 Tstrap: 0-0
Best Rating: 48 6/01 Newc 1m gd-fm

Suited by a strongly-run mile.

Bowcliffe Grange (IRE)

(91) **27**

9-y-o b g Dominion Royale-Cala-Vadella (Mummy's Pet)
D W Chapman David W Chapman

Placings:0/00003/**0606**2613130113056/**44000**560300/023200504/**661**060304001**2000**/0030060050-000 **(499)**
2001: 5^{0}SD, 5^{0}SD, 5^{0}SD

	Starts	1st	2nd	3rd	Win & Pl
Career Total (Turf)	46	5	2	8	19478
Career Total (AW)	26	1	2	0	4453

36	9/99	Haml	5f4y	F(0-70)H	G-F	£2486
40	3/99	Ling	5f	E(0-70)H	STD	£2532
50	7/96	Donc	5f	E(0-70)H	G-F	£3160
50	7/96	Wind	5f10y	F(0-60)H	G-F	£3030
39	6/96	Ling	5f	E(0-70)H	FRM	£3152
25	6/96	Bevl	5f	G(0-75)H	G-F	£2133

Total win prize-money £16495

Going (Turf): Sf: 0-2 GS: 0-3 Gd: 0-9 **GF: 4-23** Fm: 1-9
Distance: **5f/6f: 6-69** 7f-8f: 0-1 9f-13f: 0-2 14f+: 0-0
Track : LH: 1-23 RH: 1-7 Tight: 1-20 Gall: 1-6
Aids: **Bl: 3-13** Vi: 0-0 Tstrap: 0-0
Best Rating: 25 6/96 Bevl 5f GF

Bowfell

83(72) (17)**27**

3-y-o b f Alflora (IRE)-April City (Lidhame)
C Smith Mr & Mrs T I Gourley

Placings:06010-0000 **(5292)**
2001: 6^{0}GF, 5^{0}G, 6^{0}GF, 7^{0}S

	Starts	1st	2nd	3rd	Win & Pl
Career Total (Turf)	8	1	0	0	2268
Career Total (AW)	1	0	0	0	

62	11/00	Muss	5f	F(0-65)	G-S	£2268

Total win prize-money £2268

Going (Turf): Sf: 0-2 **GS: 1-1** Gd: 0-1 GF: 0-4 Fm: 0-0
Distance: **5f/6f: 1-5** 7f-8f: 0-4 9f-13f: 0-0 14f+: 0-0
Track : LH: 0-2 RH: 0-0 Tight: 0-1 Gall: 0-0
Aids: Bl: 0-0 Vi: 0-2 Tstrap: 0-0
Best Rating: 27 6/01 Leic 5f218y good

Bowland Prince (USA)

88 **29**

3-y-o gr c Rubiano (USA)-Lake Champlain (King's Lake (USA))
E J Alston G Lowe

Placings:004 **(3860)**
2001: 10^{0}GF, 10^{0}S, 9^{4}GF

	Starts	1st	2nd	3rd	Win & Pl
Career Total (Turf)	3	0	0	0	0

Going (Turf): Sf: 0-1 GS: 0-0 Gd: 0-0 GF: 0-2 Fm: 0-0
Distance: 5f/6f: 0-0 7f-8f: 0-0 9f-13f: 0-3 14f+: 0-0
Track : LH: 0-3 RH: 0-0 Tight: 0-1 Gall: 0-0
Aids: Bl: 0-0 Vi: 0-0 Tstrap: 0-0
Best Rating: 29 8/01 Rdcr 1m1f gd-fm

Bowlers Boy

100 (37)**61**

8-y-o ch g Risk Me (FR)-Snow Wonder (Music Boy)
J J Quinn Bowlers Racing

Placings:00/30502310210/04050212030651220200/000613000406121/0005500000035/0241215403521-004020300 **(5685)**
2001: 5^{0}G, 5^{0}G, 5^{4}GF, 6^{0}G, 6^{2}HY, 5^{0}S, 5^{3}HY, 6^{0}G, 5^{0}S

	Starts	1st	2nd	3rd	Win & Pl
Career Total (Turf)	82	10	12	6	55213
Career Total (AW)	1	0	0	1	505

62	10/00	Newc	6f	E(0-70)H	HVY	£2905
56	6/00	Haml	6f5y	F(0-60)H	GD	£2898
56	6/00	Carl	5f	F(0-65)H	SFT	£2632
65	11/98	Rdcr	5f	D(0-75)	G-S	£3512
74	10/98	Pont	5f	D(0-85)H	SFT	£7555
70	6/98	Pont	6f	E(0-70)H	SFT	£3980
71	8/97	Ripn	6f	F(0-75)H	GD	£2608
68	7/97	Bevl	5f	D(0-80)H	HVY	£3730
69	9/96	Pont	5f	E(0-70)H	G-F	£3314
64	7/96	Pont	6f	F(0-65)	G-F	£2738

Total win prize-money £35873

Going (Turf): Sf: 5-20 GS: 1-15 Gd: 2-29 GF: 2-17 Fm: 0-1
Distance: **5f/6f: 9-73** 7f-8f: 1-10 9f-13f: 0-0 14f+: 0-0
Track : **LH: 4-33** RH: 1-2 Tight: 0-2 **Gall: 1-6**
Aids: Bl: 0-2 Vi: 0-0 Tstrap: 0-0
Best Rating: 61 10/01 Nott 6f15y heavy

He has won several races over the years and is a regular in northern sprint handicaps. Has won on fast ground, but is particularly effective with some give over either five or six furlongs.

Box Builder

104 **63**

4-y-o ch g Fraam-Ena Olley (Le Moss)
B G Powell M Hutchinson

Placings:33514400-020000 **(4212)**
2001: 14^{0}GS, 14^{2}GF, 13^{0}GF, 16^{0}GF, 13^{0}GF, 13^{0}GF

	Starts	1st	2nd	3rd	Win & Pl
Career Total (Turf)	14	1	1	2	8653

85	7/00	Sand	1m6f	D	GD	£4173

Total win prize-money £4173

Going (Turf): Sf: 0-3 GS: 0-1 **Gd: 1-3** GF: 0-7 Fm: 0-0
Distance: 5f/6f: 0-0 7f-8f: 0-0 9f-13f: 0-2 **14f+: 1-12**
Track : LH: 0-8 **RH: 1-6** Tight: 0-4 Gall: 0-6
Aids: Bl: 0-1 Vi: 0-0 Tstrap: 0-0
Best Rating: 82 5/01 Hayd 1m6f gd-fm

Winner of a 14-furlong Sandown maiden last term, he has mainly struggled in handicap company since with his best subsequent effort coming when beaten a head over the same trip at Haydock in May 2001.

Box Car (IRE)

95(93) (58)**51**

4-y-o b g Blues Traveller (IRE)-Racey Naskra (USA) (Star De Naskra (USA))
R Wilman (G L Moore 23/5) Mrs Joanna Hughes

Placings:000**6625**/322006000-006 **(3263)**
2001: 11^{0}F, 16^{0}GF, 12^{6}GS

	Starts	1st	2nd	3rd	Win & Pl
Career Total (Turf)	15	0	2	0	3056
Career Total (AW)	4	0	1	1	1190

Going (Turf): Sf: 0-2 GS: 0-2 Gd: 0-6 GF: 0-3 Fm: 0-2
Distance: 5f/6f: 0-0 7f-8f: 0-4 9f-13f: 0-14 14f+: 0-1
Track : LH: 0-8 RH: 0-4 Tight: 0-11 Gall: 0-1

Aids: Bl: 0-0 Vi: 0-0 Tstrap: 0-0
Best Rating: 26 7/01 Wwck 1m4f134y gd-sft

Box Hill Western

87 73

2-y-o b c Lugana Beach-Currer Bell (Belmez (USA))
R Hannon Paul Jubert

Placings:000 (3491)
2001: 6^{0}GF, 6^{0}GF, 5^{0}GF

	Starts	1st	2nd	3rd	Win & Pl
Career Total (Turf)	3	0	0	0	

Going (Turf): Sf: 0-0 GS: 0-0 Gd: 0-0 GF: 0-3 Fm: 0-0
Distance: 5f/6f: 0-1 7f-8f: 0-2 9f-13f: 0-0 14f+: 0-0
Track : LH: 0-0 RH: 0-2 Tight: 0-1 Gall: 0-1
Aids: Bl: 0-0 Vi: 0-0 Tstrap: 0-0
Best Rating: 73 7/01 Chep 6f16y gd-fm

Boxer Bill

99(94) (56)67

2-y-o b c Atraf-Paper Maze (Mazilier (USA))
W G M Turner Sigwells Racing Club 2000

Placings:6452422046 (4086)
2001: 5^{6}GS, 5^{4}SD, 5^{5}GS, 5^{2}GS, 5^{4}GF, 6^{2}F, 5^{2}GF, 5^{0}F, 5^{4}GS, 5^{6}S

	Starts	1st	2nd	3rd	Win & Pl
Career Total (Turf)	9	0	3	0	2441
Career Total (AW)	1	0	0	0	0

Going (Turf): Sf: 0-1 GS: 0-4 Gd: 0-0 GF: 0-2 Fm: 0-2
Distance: 5f/6f: 0-10 7f-8f: 0-0 9f-13f: 0-0 14f+: 0-0
Track : LH: 0-3 RH: 0-0 Tight: 0-1 Gall: 0-1
Aids: Bl: 0-0 Vi: 0-2 Tstrap: 0-0
Best Rating: 67 8/01 Sand 5f6y gd-sft

A fair juvenile, effective 5-6 furlongs.

Boy Band (IRE)

84 32

3-y-o b g Desert Style (IRE)-Arab Scimetar (IRE) (Sure Blade (USA))
J W Mullins (M R Channon 17/5) Trevor Mitchell

Placings:06-6050 (1383)
2001: 8^{0}S, 8^{0}S, 6^{5}GF, 6^{0}S

	Starts	1st	2nd	3rd	Win & Pl
Career Total (Turf)	6	0	0	0	0

Going (Turf): Sf: 0-4 GS: 0-1 Gd: 0-0 GF: 0-1 Fm: 0-0
Distance: 5f/6f: 0-0 7f-8f: 0-5 9f-13f: 0-1 14f+: 0-0
Track : LH: 0-2 RH: 0-0 Tight: 0-0 Gall: 0-0
Aids: Bl: 0-0 Vi: 0-0 Tstrap: 0-0
Best Rating: 50 3/01 Donc 1m soft

Brady Boys (USA)

97 48

4-y-o b g Cozzene (USA)-Elvia (USA) (Roberto (USA))
J G M O'Shea K W Bell & Son Ltd

Placings:02-003 (5664)
2001: 5^{0}G, 10^{0}GF, 8^{3}HY

	Starts	1st	2nd	3rd	Win & Pl
Career Total (Turf)	5	0	1	1	1508

Going (Turf): Sf: 0-3 GS: 0-0 Gd: 0-1 GF: 0-1 Fm: 0-0
Distance: 5f/6f: 0-1 7f-8f: 0-0 9f-13f: 0-4 14f+: 0-0
Track : LH: 0-2 RH: 0-3 Tight: 0-2 Gall: 0-0
Aids: Bl: 0-1 Vi: 0-0 Tstrap: 0-0
Best Rating: 48 11/01 Wind 1m67y heavy

Bragadino

103 103+

2-y-o b c Zilzal (USA)-Graecia Magna (USA) (Private Account (USA))
Sir Michael Stoute Athos Christodoulou

Placings:126 (5002)
2001: 7^{1}GF, 7^{2}GF, 8^{6}S

	Starts	1st	2nd	3rd	Win & Pl
Career Total (Turf)	3	1	1	0	18488

90	7/01	Sand	7f16y	D	G-F	£6987

Total win prize-money £6988

Going (Turf): Sf: 0-1 GS: 0-0 Gd: 0-0 GF: 1-2 Fm: 0-0
Distance: 5f/6f: 0-0 7f-8f: 1-3 9f-13f: 0-0 14f+: 0-0
Track : LH: 0-0 RH: 1-3 Tight: 0-0 Gall: 0-1
Aids: Bl: 0-0 Vi: 0-0 Tstrap: 0-0
Best Rating: 103 8/01 Gdwd 7f gd-fm

Looked a good prospect when winning his debut at Sandown in July. He is a half-brother to several winners who have been at least useful around ten furlongs, the miler Thourios and this year's three-year-old Demophilos. Found only Naheef too good in a Group Three at Goodwood, but did not handle the soft at ascot. Will appreciate further in time.

Braigo (IRE)

85 54

2-y-o ch f Woodborough (USA)-Golden Form (Formidable (USA))
H Morrison H Morrison

Placings:0 (5594)
2001: 6^{0}GS

	Starts	1st	2nd	3rd	Win & Pl
Career Total (Turf)	1	0	0	0	

Going (Turf): Sf: 0-0 GS: 0-1 Gd: 0-0 GF: 0-0 Fm: 0-0
Distance: 5f/6f: 0-1 7f-8f: 0-0 9f-13f: 0-0 14f+: 0-0
Track : LH: 0-0 RH: 0-0 Tight: 0-0 Gall: 0-0
Aids: Bl: 0-0 Vi: 0-0 Tstrap: 0-0
Best Rating: 54 11/01 NmkR 6f gd-sft

Brainwave

107 67

3-y-o b f Mind Games-Thorner Lane (Tina's Pet)
H Candy Henry Candy & Partners

Placings:4-4040151F (4543)
2001: 5^{4}S, 6^{0}GS, 6^{4}GF, 6^{0}GF, 5^{1}G, 5^{5}G, 5^{1}G, 5^{F}GF

	Starts	1st	2nd	3rd	Win & Pl
Career Total (Turf)	9	2	0	0	5915

67	8/01	Folk	5f	F(0-65)H	GD	£2646
64	7/01	Chep	5f16y	E(0-65)	GD	£2968

Total win prize-money £5614

Going (Turf): Sf: 0-2 GS: 0-1 Gd: 2-3 GF: 0-3 Fm: 0-0
Distance: 5f/6f: 2-8 7f-8f: 0-1 9f-13f: 0-0 14f+: 0-0
Track : LH: 0-0 RH: 0-0 Tight: 0-0 Gall: 0-0
Aids: Bl: 0-0 Vi: 0-1 Tstrap: 0-0
Best Rating: 67 8/01 Folk 5f good

Bram Stoker (IRE)

95 96

3-y-o ch c General Monash (USA)-Taniokey (Grundy)
O Pessi (R Hannon 18/5) Allevamento White Star

Placings:211233330-40600 (5357a)
2001: 7^{4}S, 8^{0}G, 6^{6}S, 5^{0}G, 8^{0}GS, 6^{0}VS

	Starts	1st	2nd	3rd	Win & Pl
Career Total (Turf)	14	2	2	4	40258

87	5/00	Nott	6f15y	D	G-S	£3380
93	4/00	Donc	5f	F	G-S	£2912

Total win prize-money £6292

Going (Turf): Sf: 0-2 GS: 2-4 Gd: 0-4 GF: 0-3 Fm: 0-0
Distance: 5f/6f: 1-7 7f-8f: 1-6 9f-13f: 0-0 14f+: 0-0
Track : LH: 0-1 RH: 0-1 Tight: 0-0 Gall: 0-0
Aids: Bl: 0-1 Vi: 0-0 Tstrap: 0-0
Best Rating: 96 4/01 NmkR 7f soft

Twice a winner on easy ground in the spring of 2000, he ran consistently on all sorts of ground, mainly at Group level, thereafter. Appeared not to train on in 2001.

Bramble

91 62

3-y-o ch g Polar Falcon (USA)-Sharpthorne (USA) (Sharpen Up)
Mrs L Stubbs (R Charlton 7/6) Des Thurlby

Placings:00100000 (4785)
2001: 6^{0}GS, 6^{0}G, 5^{1}GF, 5^{0}GF, 5^{0}GF, 5^{0}GS, 5^{0}G, 5^{0}G

	Starts	1st	2nd	3rd	Win & Pl
Career Total (Turf)	8	1	0	0	3484

71	5/01	Bath	5f11y	D	G-F	£3484

Total win prize-money £3484

Going (Turf): Sf: 0-0 GS: 0-2 Gd: 0-3 GF: 1-3 Fm: 0-0
Distance: 5f/6f: 1-7 7f-8f: 0-1 9f-13f: 0-0 14f+: 0-0
Track : LH: 1-1 RH: 0-0 Tight: 0-0 Gall: 1-1
Aids: Bl: 0-0 Vi: 0-0 Tstrap: 0-1
Best Rating: 71 5/01 Bath 5f11y gd-fm

By Polar Falcon, he won a fair maiden over five furlongs in May, but has failed to feature since.

Brand New Day (IRE)

95(83) (27)28

3-y-o b c Robellino (USA)-Nawaji (USA) (Trempolino (USA))
D W P Arbuthnot Philip Banfield

Placings:00-0000050 (4854)
2001: 8^{0}SD, 8^{0}SD, 7^{0}SD, 11^{0}SD, 9^{0}G, 9^{5}GF, 13^{0}GF

	Starts	1st	2nd	3rd	Win & Pl
Career Total (Turf)	5	0	0	0	0
Career Total (AW)	4	0	0	0	

Going (Turf): Sf: 0-2 GS: 0-0 Gd: 0-1 GF: 0-2 Fm: 0-0
Distance: 5f/6f: 0-0 7f-8f: 0-5 9f-13f: 0-3 14f+: 0-1
Track : LH: 0-7 RH: 0-0 Tight: 0-3 Gall: 0-0
Aids: Bl: 0-3 Vi: 0-1 Tstrap: 0-0
Best Rating: 28 8/01 Brig 1m1f209y gd-fm

Brandon Court (IRE)

93(89) (36)**59**

10-y-o b g Law Society (USA)-Dance Date (IRE) (Sadler's Wells (USA))

I A Balding Tunnel Vision

Placings:453/1421422043/55/4006201/000 **(1204)**

2001: 12^{0}SD, 11^{0}SD, 11^{0}GS

	Starts	1st	2nd	3rd	Win & Pl
Career Total (Turf)	23	3	4	2	25838
Career Total (AW)	2	0	0	0	

59 9/99 Ayr 1m2f192yE(0-70) G-S £2570
84 5/94 Sand 1m3f91y D(0-80)H GD £4279
75 4/94 Hayd 1m2f120yC(0-95)H SFT £5442

Total win prize-money £12293

Going (Turf): Sf: **1-3** GS: **1-6** Gd: **1-7** GF: 0-7 Fm: 0-0
Distance: 5f/6f: 0-0 7f-8f: 0-2 **9f-13f: 3-19** 14f+: 0-4
Track : **LH: 2-12** RH: 1-10 Tight: 0-7 Gall: 0-6
Aids: Bl: 0-0 Vi: 0-0 Tstrap: 0-0
Best Rating: 37 5/01 Wind 1m3f135y gd-sft

Brandon Rock

89(79) (20)**29**

4-y-o b g Robellino (USA)-The Kings Daughter (Indian King (USA))

Julian Poulton (N P Littmoden 15/2) There Goes The School Fees Partnership

Placings:0100/000-0000000 **(3381)**

2001: 7^{0}SD, 5^{0}SD, 5^{0}F, 5^{0}GF, 7^{0}F, 5^{0}GF, 8^{0}GF

	Starts	1st	2nd	3rd	Win & Pl
Career Total (Turf)	12	1	0	0	3778
Career Total (AW)	2	0	0	0	

82 9/99 Sand 5f6y E GD £3777

Total win prize-money £3778

Going (Turf): Sf: 0-1 GS: 0-2 **Gd: 1-3** GF: 0-4 Fm: 0-2
Distance: **5f/6f: 1-10** 7f-8f: 0-3 9f-13f: 0-1 14f+: 0-0
Track : LH: 0-3 RH: 0-2 Tight: 0-1 Gall: 0-2
Aids: Bl: 0-1 Vi: 0-0 Tstrap: 0-0
Best Rating: 29 6/01 Ling 7f firm

Brandy Cove

86(99) (65)**50**

4-y-o b c Lugana Beach-Tender Moment (IRE) (Caerleon (USA))

B Smart Miss N Jefford

Placings:021-030000 **(2092)**

2001: 8^{0}SD, 8^{3}SD, 8^{0}SD, 8^{0}HY, 7^{0}G, 7^{0}GF

	Starts	1st	2nd	3rd	Win & Pl
Career Total (Turf)	5	0	1	0	1420
Career Total (AW)	4	1	0	1	3181

53 11/00 Sthl 1m D STD £2751

Total win prize-money £2751

Going (Turf): Sf: 0-2 GS: 0-0 Gd: 0-2 GF: 0-1 Fm: 0-0
Distance: 5f/6f: 0-0 **7f-8f: 1-5** 9f-13f: 0-4 14f+: 0-0
Track : **LH: 1-7** RH: 0-1 Tight: 0-1 Gall: 0-1
Aids: Bl: 0-0 Vi: 0-0 Tstrap: 0-0
Best Rating: 65 2/01 Sthl 1m stand

Branston Gem

93(90) (56)**59**

3-y-o br f So Factual (USA)-Branston Jewel (IRE) (Prince Sabo)

M Johnston J David Abell

Placings:005024-5050 **(4802)**

2001: 5^{5}GF, 5^{0}SD, 7^{5}GF, 8^{0}F

	Starts	1st	2nd	3rd	Win & Pl
Career Total (Turf)	7	0	0	0	
Career Total (AW)	3	0	1	0	530

Going (Turf): Sf: 0-0 GS: 0-1 Gd: 0-1 GF: 0-3 Fm: 0-2
Distance: 5f/6f: 0-8 7f-8f: 0-1 9f-13f: 0-1 14f+: 0-0
Track : LH: 0-4 RH: 0-1 Tight: 0-2 Gall: 0-1
Aids: Bl: 0-0 Vi: 0-0 Tstrap: 0-0
Best Rating: 33 6/01 Muss 5f gd-fm

Branston Lucy

(98) (44)**58**

4-y-o b f Prince Sabo-Softly Spoken (Mummy's Pet)

J Pearce Mrs Jennifer Marsh

Placings:40531/000212243000000-0 **(0017)**

2001: 6^{0}SD

	Starts	1st	2nd	3rd	Win & Pl
Career Total (Turf)	13	2	3	2	8964
Career Total (AW)	8	0	0	0	0

56 7/00 Muss 5f F(0-60)H G-S £2576
62 9/99 Rdcr 5f E(0-75)H G-F £3183

Total win prize-money £5759

Going (Turf): Sf: 0-0 **GS: 1-3** Gd: 0-3 **GF: 1-5** Fm: 0-2
Distance: **5f/6f: 2-21** 7f-8f: 0-0 9f-13f: 0-0 14f+: 0-0
Track : LH: 0-6 RH: 0-1 Tight: 0-6 Gall: 0-1
Aids: Bl: 0-1 Vi: 0-0 Tstrap: 0-0
Best Rating: 28 1/01 Ling 6f stand

Branston Pickle

(106) (72)**40**

4-y-o ch g Piccolo-Indefinite Article (IRE) (Indian Ridge)

P D Evans Treble Chance Partnership

Placings:660361410 1/2000000012000631506 3-62352210533000030202215 00 **(5414)**

2001: 5^{6}SD, 5^{2}SD, 5^{3}SW, 5^{5}SW, 6^{2}SD, 5^{2}SW, 6^{1}SD, 5^{0}SD, 5^{5}SW, 6^{3}SD, 6^{3}SW, 5^{0}SD, 6^{0}SD, 5^{0}SD, 5^{0}S, 5^{0}GF, 5^{3}SD, 5^{0}GF, 5^{2}SD, 5^{0}SD, 6^{2}SD, 6^{2}SW, 6^{1}SD, 6^{5}SD, 5^{0}SD, 6^{0}SD

	Starts	1st	2nd	3rd	Win & Pl
Career Total (Turf)	22	2	1	0	8249
Career Total (AW)	34	5	7	7	20919

68 9/01 Wolv 6f E(0-70)H STD £3006
73 2/01 Wolv 6f F STD £2107
59 11/00 Sthl 5f F STD £2362
61 9/00 Haml 5f4y F(0-70)H SFT £2954
78 11/99 Wolv 6f F STD £2190
80 11/99 Catt 5f212y D(0-85)H SFT £3822
69 10/99 Wolv 5f G STD £1966

Total win prize-money £18410

Going (Turf): **Sf: 2-10** GS: 0-1 Gd: 0-6 GF: 0-4 Fm: 0-1
Distance: **5f/6f: 7-55** 7f-8f: 0-1 9f-13f: 0-0 14f+: 0-0
Track : **LH: 5-34** RH: 0-1 **Tight: 5-28** Gall: 0-1
Aids: Bl: 0-2 **Vi: 1-11** Tstrap: 0-2
Best Rating: 74 1/01 Sthl 5f stand

Branston Tiger

(97) (79)**76**

2-y-o b c Mark Of Esteem (IRE)-Tuxford Hideaway (Cawston's Clown)

M Johnston J David Abell

Placings:0223 **(4067)**

2001: 6^{0}GF, 7^{2}F, 7^{2}F, 7^{3}SD

	Starts	1st	2nd	3rd	Win & Pl
Career Total (Turf)	3	0	2	0	2331
Career Total (AW)	1	0	0	1	539

Going (Turf): Sf: 0-0 GS: 0-0 Gd: 0-0 GF: 0-1 Fm: 0-2
Distance: 5f/6f: 0-0 7f-8f: 0-4 9f-13f: 0-0 14f+: 0-0
Track : LH: 0-1 RH: 0-0 Tight: 0-1 Gall: 0-0
Aids: Bl: 0-0 Vi: 0-0 Tstrap: 0-0
Best Rating: 79 8/01 Wolv 7f stand

Brassika

100 **63**

2-y-o ch f Whittingham (IRE)-Tough Nell (IRE) (Archway (IRE))

S Dow (G L Moore 24/5) K K L M

Placings:400 **(5125)**

2001: 5^{4}GS, 6^{0}GF, 5^{0}HY

	Starts	1st	2nd	3rd	Win & Pl
Career Total (Turf)	3	0	0	0	0

Going (Turf): Sf: 0-1 GS: 0-1 Gd: 0-0 GF: 0-1 Fm: 0-0
Distance: 5f/6f: 0-3 7f-8f: 0-0 9f-13f: 0-0 14f+: 0-0
Track : LH: 0-1 RH: 0-0 Tight: 0-0 Gall: 0-0
Aids: Bl: 0-0 Vi: 0-0 Tstrap: 0-0
Best Rating: 63 5/01 Gdwd 6f gd-fm

Bratby (IRE)

(84) (19)

5-y-o b g Distinctly North (USA)-Aridje (Mummy's Pet)

M C Chapman W P Gaff

Placings:000/156054000/000-000000000 **(0539)**

2001: 7^{0}SD, 7^{0}SD, 6^{0}SW, 6^{0}SD, 7^{0}SW, 7^{0}SW, 5^{0}SD, 7^{0}SD, 16^{0}SD

	Starts	1st	2nd	3rd	Win & Pl
Career Total (Turf)	10	0	0	0	0
Career Total (AW)	14	1	0	0	1892

44 1/99 Ling 1m G(0-60)H STD £1891

Total win prize-money £1892

Going (Turf): Sf: 0-1 GS: 0-2 Gd: 0-4 GF: 0-2 Fm: 0-1
Distance: 5f/6f: 0-6 **7f-8f: 1-12** 9f-13f: 0-5 14f+: 0-1
Track : **LH: 1-18** RH: 0-0 **Tight: 1-3** Gall: 0-0
Aids: Bl: 0-0 Vi: 0-0 Tstrap: 0-5
Best Rating: 27 2/01 Sthl 7f slow

Brave Burt (IRE)

106 **89**

4-y-o ch c Pips Pride-Friendly Song (Song)

D Nicholls Lucayan Stud

Placings:1130/0300-0001200 **(5502)**

2001: 6^{0}S, 6^{0}G, 5^{0}GF, 5^{1}GS, 5^{2}GF, 5^{0}G, 5^{0}HY

	Starts	1st	2nd	3rd	Win & Pl
Career Total (Turf)	15	3	1	2	25947

87 7/01 NmkJ 5f D(0-85)H G-S £6890
92 5/99 Bath 5f11y D GD £3225
81 5/99 Carl 5f D FRM £3375

Total win prize-money £13491

Going (Turf): Sf: 0-3 **GS: 1-1 Gd: 1-6** GF: 0-4 **Fm: 1-1**
Distance: **5f/6f: 3-15** 7f-8f: 0-0 9f-13f: 0-0 14f+: 0-0
Track : LH: 1-2 RH: 1-1 Tight: 0-0 **Gall: 2-2**
Aids: Bl: 0-0 Vi: 0-0 Tstrap: 0-0
Best Rating: 89 7/01 Asct 5f gd-fm

Sprint-bred, he won his first two starts at two, but struggled afterwards in Pattern and handicap company and changed stables. Having plummeted in the weights, he showed promise at Newcastle in June and went on to win with a bit in hand at Newmarket. Heavily backed at Ascot, he did nothing wrong, but disappointed afterwards. Yet to prove he truly stays six furlongs.

Brave Edge

97 **87**

10-y-o b g Beveled (USA)-Daring Ditty (Daring March)
R Hannon Lady Whent And Friends

Placings:002312203/1040/211430030/5521600004342/30260043456601240/6420061006304/200360206000440/03302304230-000 **(1608)**
2001: 5^{0}GS, 6^{0}GF, 6^{0}GF

	Starts	1st	2nd	3rd	Win & Pl
Career Total (Turf)	94	7	13	13	153938

100	7/98	Newb	6f8y	B(0-105)H	GD	£12892
90	9/97	Haml	6f5y	C	GD	£5017
107	6/96	Kemp	5f	A	G-F	£10500
92	5/95	York	5f	B(0-105)H	GD	£15270
83	4/95	Sand	5f6y	C(0-90)H	GD	£5680
84	4/94	Wind	5f10y	C(0-95)H	GD	£4667
83	8/93	Sand	5f6y	D	G-F	£4240

Total win prize-money £58269

Going (Turf): Sf: 0-9 GS: 0-16 **Gd: 5-28** GF: 2-37 Fm: 0-3
Distance: **5f/6f: 5-78** 7f-8f: 2-16 9f-13f: 0-0 14f+: 0-0
Track : LH: 0-3 **RH: 1-5** Tight: 0-1 **Gall: 1-4**
Aids: Bl: 0-0 Vi: 0-0 Tstrap: 0-0
Best Rating: 73 5/01 Gdwd 6f gd-fm

Useful sprint handicapper in his prime but on a long losing run and difficult to win with. Effective on any ground, he has often gone well for Pat Eddery.

Brave Emir

(84) (41)**55**

2-y-o b c Emarati (USA)-Hearten (Hittite Glory)
J W Hills The Farleigh Court Racing Partnership

Placings:0400 **(5408)**
2001: 5^{0}GF, 5^{4}GF, 5^{0}G, 6^{0}SD

	Starts	1st	2nd	3rd	Win & Pl
Career Total (Turf)	3	0	0	0	283
Career Total (AW)	1	0	0	0	

Going (Turf): Sf: 0-0 GS: 0-0 Gd: 0-1 GF: 0-2 Fm: 0-0
Distance: 5f/6f: 0-4 7f-8f: 0-0 9f-13f: 0-0 14f+: 0-0
Track : LH: 0-1 RH: 0-1 Tight: 0-0 Gall: 0-1
Aids: Bl: 0-0 Vi: 0-0 Tstrap: 0-1
Best Rating: 55 7/01 Wind 5f10y gd-fm

Brave Giraffe

76 **58**

2-y-o b c Distant Relative-Prinia (Priolo (USA))
Miss D A McHale Havin A Giraffe Partnership

Placings:00 **(5367)**
2001: 6^{0}GF, 8^{0}GS

	Starts	1st	2nd	3rd	Win & Pl
Career Total (Turf)	2	0	0	0	

Going (Turf): Sf: 0-0 GS: 0-1 Gd: 0-0 GF: 0-1 Fm: 0-0
Distance: 5f/6f: 0-1 7f-8f: 0-1 9f-13f: 0-0 14f+: 0-0
Track : LH: 0-0 RH: 0-0 Tight: 0-0 Gall: 0-0
Aids: Bl: 0-0 Vi: 0-0 Tstrap: 0-0
Best Rating: 58 10/01 NmkR 1m gd-sft

Brave Knight

96 **34**

4-y-o b g Presidium-Agnes Jane (Sweet Monday)
N Bycroft P Casimir-Mrowczynsk

Placings:0/36-0006003300 **(4906)**
2001: 10^{0}F, 9^{0}GF, 10^{0}F, 10^{6}S, 9^{0}GF, 16^{0}GF, 8^{3}GF, 9^{3}GF, 10^{0}G, 9^{0}G

	Starts	1st	2nd	3rd	Win & Pl
Career Total (Turf)	13	0	0	3	2114

Going (Turf): Sf: 0-2 GS: 0-1 Gd: 0-2 GF: 0-6 Fm: 0-2
Distance: 5f/6f: 0-0 7f-8f: 0-2 9f-13f: 0-10 14f+: 0-1
Track : LH: 0-8 RH: 0-5 Tight: 0-1 Gall: 0-2
Aids: Bl: 0-0 Vi: 0-0 Tstrap: 0-0
Best Rating: 42 7/01 Hayd 1m2f120y soft

Brave Shaman (IRE)

2-y-o b c Common Grounds-Indiana Bride (IRE) (Indian Ridge)
K A Ryan Mrs Margaret Forsyth

Placings:P **(1464)**
2001: 5^{P}GF

	Starts	1st	2nd	3rd	Win & Pl
Career Total (Turf)	1	0	0	0	

Going (Turf): Sf: 0-0 GS: 0-0 Gd: 0-0 GF: 0-1 Fm: 0-0
Distance: 5f/6f: 0-1 7f-8f: 0-0 9f-13f: 0-0 14f+: 0-0
Track : LH: 0-0 RH: 0-0 Tight: 0-0 Gall: 0-0
Aids: Bl: 0-0 Vi: 0-0 Tstrap: 0-0
Best Rating: 42 7/01 Hayd 1m2f120y soft

Bravo

101(93) (57)**50**

3-y-o b/br g Efisio-Apache Squaw (Be My Guest (USA))
C W Thornton Guy Reed

Placings:0-0034636206 **(4776)**
2001: 7^{0}SD, 8^{0}SW, 8^{3}SD, 8^{4}S, 9^{6}SD, 12^{3}G, 12^{6}G, 12^{2}GF, 12^{0}G, 11^{6}G

	Starts	1st	2nd	3rd	Win & Pl
Career Total (Turf)	7	0	1	1	1933
Career Total (AW)	4	0	0	1	429

Going (Turf): Sf: 0-2 GS: 0-0 Gd: 0-4 GF: 0-1 Fm: 0-0
Distance: 5f/6f: 0-0 7f-8f: 0-5 9f-13f: 0-6 14f+: 0-0
Track : LH: 0-8 RH: 0-3 Tight: 0-4 Gall: 0-4
Aids: Bl: 0-0 Vi: 0-0 Tstrap: 0-0
Best Rating: 59 5/01 Newc 1m soft

Bravura

(99) (61)**53**

3-y-o ch g Never So Bold-Sylvan Song (Song)
G L Moore R Kiernan

Placings:0000-14000000 **(5406)**
2001: 7^{1}SD, 7^{4}SD, 6^{0}F, 7^{0}F, 7^{0}GF, 7^{0}GF, 6^{0}GF, 8^{0}SD

	Starts	1st	2nd	3rd	Win & Pl
Career Total (Turf)	9	0	0	0	
Career Total (AW)	3	1	0	0	2191

60	3/01	Ling	7f	F(0-60)H	STD	£2191

Total win prize-money £2191

Going (Turf): Sf: 0-1 GS: 0-0 Gd: 0-1 GF: 0-4 Fm: 0-2
Distance: 5f/6f: 0-3 **7f-8f: 1-8** 9f-13f: 0-0 14f+: 0-0
Track : **LH: 1-4** RH: 0-0 **Tight: 1-2** Gall: 0-0
Aids: Bl: 0-3 Vi: 0-0 Tstrap: 0-0
Best Rating: 61 3/01 Ling 7f stand

Only win came in March 2001, has disappointed since then. Best over seven furlongs.

Brazilian Mood (IRE)

42(86) (58)**70**

5-y-o b g Doyoun-Sea Mistress (Habitat)
C E Brittain C E Brittain

Placings:0210/50-00 **(0897)**
2001: 10^{0}SD, 9^{0}HY

	Starts	1st	2nd	3rd	Win & Pl
Career Total (Turf)	5	0	1	0	768
Career Total (AW)	3	1	0	0	2879

58	11/99	Ling	1m2f	D	STD	£2879

Total win prize-money £2879

Going (Turf): Sf: 0-1 GS: 0-1 Gd: 0-1 GF: 0-1 Fm: 0-1
Distance: 5f/6f: 0-0 7f-8f: 0-0 **9f-13f: 1-8** 14f+: 0-0
Track : **LH: 1-5** RH: 0-3 **Tight: 1-5** Gall: 0-1
Aids: Bl: 0-1 Vi: 0-0 Tstrap: 0-0
Best Rating: 27 4/01 Ling 1m2f stand

Break The Glass (USA)

(79) (13)**57**

4-y-o b/br g Dynaformer (USA)-Greek Wedding (USA) (Blushing Groom (FR))
R Ford Nick Shutts

Placings:44/3233-60 **(0287)**
2001: 9^{6}SW, 12^{0}SW

	Starts	1st	2nd	3rd	Win & Pl
Career Total (Turf)	6	0	1	3	3578
Career Total (AW)	2	0	0	0	0

Going (Turf): Sf: 0-1 GS: 0-3 Gd: 0-1 GF: 0-1 Fm: 0-0
Distance: 5f/6f: 0-0 7f-8f: 0-4 9f-13f: 0-4 14f+: 0-0
Track : LH: 0-5 RH: 0-1 Tight: 0-2 Gall: 0-0
Aids: Bl: 0-0 Vi: 0-0 Tstrap: 0-0
Best Rating: 13 1/01 Wolv 1m1f79y slow

Break The Rules

(84) (17)**39**

9-y-o b g Dominion-Surf Bird (Shareef Dancer (USA))
A G Juckes Whistlejacket Partnership

Placings:5140/42310/403221404231/1141600020604/40030631034/0/00-0 **(0538)**
2001: 12^{0}SD

	Starts	1st	2nd	3rd	Win & Pl
Career Total (Turf)	44	8	5	6	56924
Career Total (AW)	5	0	0	0	243

71	5/98	Ches	1m2f75y	C(0-95)H	GD	£10606
70	6/97	Ches	1m2f75y	D	SFT	£3493
83	5/97	Ches	1m2f75y	C(0-95)H	SFT	£10866
82	3/97	Donc	1m2f60y	G(0-80)H	GD	£2402
79	10/96	Donc	1m2f60y	D	GD	£4597
68	7/96	Ches	1m4f66y	D(0-70)	G-F	£3972

75	8/95	Rdcr	1m	D(0-85)H	G-F	£7457
70	4/94	Pont	5f	D	SFT	£3143

Total win prize-money £46539

Going (Turf): Sf: 3-8 GS: 0-10 **Gd: 3-12** GF: 2-11 Fm: 0-3
Distance: 5f/6f: 1-2 7f-8f: 1-6 **9f-13f: 6-40** 14f+: 0-1
Track : **LH: 7-32** RH: 0-12 **Tight: 4-25** Gall: 2-8
Aids: Bl: 0-1 Vi: 0-1 Tstrap: 0-0
Best Rating: 70 4/94 Pont 5f S

Breakfast Bay (IRE)

103 **74**

3-y-o b/br f Charnwood Forest (IRE)-Diavolina (USA) (Lear Fan (USA))
R Charlton F M Alger

Placings:310-0645050 **(4733)**
2001: 7^{0}G, 7^{6}GF, 8^{4}GF, 8^{5}GF, 8^{0}GF, 8^{5}GF, 7^{0}F

	Starts	1st	2nd	3rd	Win & Pl
Career Total (Turf)	10	1	0	1	5387

78	8/00	Folk	7f	D	G-F	£4407

Total win prize-money £4407

Going (Turf): Sf: 0-0 GS: 0-1 Gd: 0-2 **GF: 1-6** Fm: 0-1
Distance: 5f/6f: 0-0 **7f-8f: 1-9** 9f-13f: 0-1 14f+: 0-0
Track : LH: 0-2 RH: 0-2 Tight: 0-1 Gall: 0-1
Aids: Bl: 0-0 Vi: 0-0 Tstrap: 0-0
Best Rating: 74 7/01 Newb 1m gd-fm

Breathless Dreams (IRE)

99(93) (45)**53**

4-y-o ch g College Chapel-Foston Bridge (Relkino)
M Wigham (G Brown 29/9) Cable Media Consultancy Ltd

Placings:21/500-0020600 **(5292)**
2001: 7^{0}F, 5^{0}G, 7^{2}GF, 7^{0}GF, 5^{6}G, 5^{0}SD, 7^{0}S

	Starts	1st	2nd	3rd	Win & Pl
Career Total (Turf)	11	1	2	0	4247
Career Total (AW)	1	0	0	0	

75	6/99	Sals	6f212y	F	FRM	£2495

Total win prize-money £2495

Going (Turf): Sf: 0-2 GS: 0-1 Gd: 0-3 GF: 0-3 **Fm: 1-2**
Distance: 5f/6f: 0-4 **7f-8f: 1-6** 9f-13f: 0-2 14f+: 0-0
Track : LH: 0-3 RH: 0-3 Tight: 0-2 Gall: 0-3
Aids: Bl: 0-0 Vi: 0-2 Tstrap: 0-0
Best Rating: 53 7/01 Chep 5f16y good

Winner of a Salisbury maiden at two for Michael Bell, he has shown only bits of form since.

Brecongill Lad

105 **61**

9-y-o b g Clantime-Chikala (Pitskelly)
Mrs M Reveley (D Nicholls 23/6) P Davidson-Brown

Placings:34020/030313140/000005120640/03602233 030/2020306040/6060601112133/303220031202300-050040003006001 **(5639)**
2001: 6^{0}S, 5^{5}GF, 5^{0}GF, 5^{0}GF, 5^{4}GF, 6^{0}GF, 5^{0}GF, 6^{0}F, 5^{3}G, 5^{0}GF, 5^{0}GS, 5^{6}G, 5^{0}G, 5^{0}G, 5^{4}G

	Starts	1st	2nd	3rd	Win & Pl
Career Total (Turf)	91	8	11	16	83872

80	7/00	Newc	5f	C(0-90)H	G-F	£6906
74	9/99	Gdwd	6f	C(0-95)H	G-F	£14915
65	8/99	Yarm	5f43y	C(0-90)H	GD	£5920
59	8/99	Pont	5f	F(0-65)H	GD	£4630
53	8/99	Catt	5f	F(0-65)H	FRM	£2283
67	8/96	Bevl	5f	D(0-80)H	G-F	£4081
78	8/95	Thsk	5f	D(0-80)H	G-F	£3877
69	6/95	NmkJ	6f	D(0-80)H	GD	£6316

Total win prize-money £48930

Going (Turf): Sf: 0-6 GS: 0-12 Gd: 3-33 **GF: 4-37** Fm: 1-3
Distance: **5f/6f: 8-87** 7f-8f: 0-4 9f-13f: 0-0 14f+: 0-0
Track : **LH: 1-13** RH: 0-2 Tight: 0-4 Gall: 0-2
Aids: **Bl: 2-11** Vi: 0-4 Tstrap: 0-0
Best Rating: 79 6/01 Ripn 5f gd-fm

He has won over six, but probably needs fast ground and the minimum trip to show his best. Had a disappointing seasonin 2001, but is at least now back on a winning mark.

Bremridge (IRE)

(78) (34)**36**

4-y-o ch g Ridgewood Ben-Eimkar (Junius (USA))
G Brown Gary Brown

Placings:05002/500-30 **(0430)**
2001: 12^{3}SD, 8^{0}SD

	Starts	1st	2nd	3rd	Win & Pl
Career Total (Turf)	8	0	1	0	856
Career Total (AW)	2	0	0	1	417

Going (Turf): Sf: 0-1 GS: 0-1 Gd: 0-2 GF: 0-2 Fm: 0-2
Distance: 5f/6f: 0-0 7f-8f: 0-4 9f-13f: 0-6 14f+: 0-0
Track : LH: 0-4 RH: 0-2 Tight: 0-4 Gall: 0-0
Aids: Bl: 0-0 Vi: 0-0 Tstrap: 0-0
Best Rating: 34 2/01 Wolv 1m4f stand

Bressbee (USA)

(103) (71)**75**

3-y-o ch c Twining (USA)-Bressay (USA) (Nureyev (USA))
K R Burke Breakfast In America P'Ship

Placings:2432-2160000 **(5171)**
2001: 8^{2}SD, 7^{1}SD, 9^{6}S, 8^{0}G, 7^{0}GF, 8^{0}SD, 8^{0}GS

	Starts	1st	2nd	3rd	Win & Pl
Career Total (Turf)	8	0	2	1	4065
Career Total (AW)	3	1	1	0	3806

71	2/01	Sthl	7f	D	STD	£2954

Total win prize-money £2954

Going (Turf): Sf: 0-1 GS: 0-1 Gd: 0-2 GF: 0-2 Fm: 0-0
Distance: 5f/6f: 0-1 **7f-8f: 1-7** 9f-13f: 0-3 14f+: 0-0
Track : **LH: 1-6** RH: 0-3 Tight: 0-0 Gall: 0-0
Aids: Bl: 0-0 Vi: 0-0 Tstrap: 0-0
Best Rating: 75 4/01 Kemp 1m1f soft

Brest (IRE)

98 **74**

2-y-o b f General Monash (USA)-Armadillo (IRE) (Dominion)
G C Bravery The Tt Partnership

Placings:5100 **(5140)**
2001: 6^{5}GF, 5^{1}GF, 6^{0}GY, 6^{0}G

	Starts	1st	2nd	3rd	Win & Pl
Career Total (Turf)	4	1	0	0	3193

74	8/01	Bath	5f161y	E	G-F	£2961

Total win prize-money £2961

Going (Turf): Sf: 0-0 GS: 0-0 Gd: 0-1 **GF: 1-2** Fm: 0-0
Distance: **5f/6f: 1-4** 7f-8f: 0-0 9f-13f: 0-0 14f+: 0-0
Track : **LH: 1-1** RH: 0-0 Tight: 0-0 **Gall: 1-1**
Aids: Bl: 0-0 Vi: 0-0 Tstrap: 0-0
Best Rating: 74 8/01 Bath 5f161y gd-fm

She got off the mark in a Bath maiden auction event on her second start, but finished down the field in better company since.

Brevity

114(96) (51++)**102**

6-y-o b g Tenby-Rive (USA) (Riverman (USA))
J M Bradley E A Hayward

Placings:02/0000541225060/00002-0666360111211011003042 **(4849)**
2001: 5^{0}SW, 6^{6}SW, 5^{6}SD, 7^{6}SW, 5^{3}GS, 5^{6}S, 6^{0}HY, 6^{1}GF, 5^{1}F, 5^{1}F, 6^{1}F, 7^{2}GF, 6^{1}GF, 6^{1}GF, 6^{0}F, 6^{1}GF, 6^{1}GF, 6^{0}G, 6^{0}G, 5^{3}G, 6^{0}GF, 5^{4}GF, 6^{2}GF

	Starts	1st	2nd	3rd	Win & Pl
Career Total (Turf)	37	9	6	2	101946
Career Total (AW)	7	0	0	0	286

96	7/01	Asct	6f	C(0-95)H	G-F	£12632
90	7/01	Epsm	6f	C(0-90)H	G-F	£6792
84	6/01	Sals	6f	C(0-90)H	G-F	£7182
96	6/01	Epsm	6f	C(0-100)H	G-F	£23200
78	6/01	Brig	6f209y	D(0-80)H	FRM	£4056
86	5/01	Leic	5f218y	E(0-75)H	FRM	£4988
70	5/01	Brig	5f213y	F(0-65)H	FRM	£2723
56	5/01	Haml	6f5y	F(0-60)	G-F	£2828
57	8/99	Newb	6f8y	E(0-75)H	GD	£3727

Total win prize-money £68131

Going (Turf): Sf: 0-7 GS: 0-2 Gd: 1-9 **GF: 5-15** Fm: 3-4
Distance: **5f/6f: 6-27** 7f-8f: 3-13 9f-13f: 0-4 14f+: 0-0
Track : **LH: 4-12** RH: 0-6 **Tight: 2-9** Gall: 0-3
Aids: Bl: 0-0 Vi: 0-0 **Tstrap: 1-14**
Best Rating: 102 9/01 Ayr 6f gd-fm

He has enjoyed a fine season. The Milton Bradley magic has seen him gain eight victories in handicap company since May despite a huge hike in the handicap. All of those wins have been over six furlongs on fast ground, with his two victories at Epsom and one at Ascot standing out. Whatever he does from now on, he owes no-one anything.

Brew

89 **25**

5-y-o b g Primo Dominie-Boozy (Absalom)
A Berry Robert Heathcote

Placings:020/200060/060000-000 **(4601)**
2001: 5^{0}GF, 5^{0}GF, 5^{0}GF

	Starts	1st	2nd	3rd	Win & Pl
Career Total (Turf)	18	0	2	0	1902

Going (Turf): Sf: 0-3 GS: 0-1 Gd: 0-3 GF: 0-10 Fm: 0-1
Distance: 5f/6f: 0-14 7f-8f: 0-4 9f-13f: 0-0 14f+: 0-0
Track : LH: 0-3 RH: 0-0 Tight: 0-0 Gall: 0-2
Aids: Bl: 0-0 Vi: 0-0 Tstrap: 0-0
Best Rating: 21 9/01 Thsk 5f gd-fm

Brians Bay

89(59) (1)**37**

3-y-o b g River Falls-Petrina Bay (Clantime)
J Gallagher Horses Away Racing Club

Placings:050000000 (5524)
2001: 6^0GF, 7^5G, 6^0SD, 5^0GF, 6^0S, 8^0GS, 7^0S, 9^0GS, 10^0HY

	Starts	1st	2nd	3rd	Win & Pl
Career Total (Turf)	8	0	0	0	0
Career Total (AW)	1	0	0	0	

Going (Turf): Sf: 0-3 GS: 0-2 Gd: 0-1 GF: 0-2 Fm: 0-0
Distance: 5f/6f: 0-2 7f-8f: 0-4 9f-13f: 0-3 14f+: 0-0
Track : LH: 0-3 RH: 0-2 Tight: 0-2 Gall: 0-0
Aids: Bl: 0-0 Vi: 0-0 Tstrap: 0-0
Best Rating: 53 6/01 Thsk 7f good

Bride's Bounty

74 **36**

2-y-o b f Aragon-Bride's Reprisal (Dunbeath (USA))
E W Tuer E Tuer

Placings:000 (5635)
2001: 5^0GF, 7^0S, 7^0G

	Starts	1st	2nd	3rd	Win & Pl
Career Total (Turf)	3	0	0	0	

Going (Turf): Sf: 0-1 GS: 0-0 Gd: 0-1 GF: 0-1 Fm: 0-0
Distance: 5f/6f: 0-1 7f-8f: 0-2 9f-13f: 0-0 14f+: 0-0
Track : LH: 0-2 RH: 0-0 Tight: 0-2 Gall: 0-0
Aids: Bl: 0-0 Vi: 0-0 Tstrap: 0-0
Best Rating: 36 10/01 Catt 7f soft

Bridewell (USA)

83 **83**

2-y-o b c Woodman (USA)-La Alleged (USA) (Alleged (USA))
M R Channon Jumeirah Racing

Placings:0020 (5268)
2001: 6^0GF, 8^0GF, 7^2HY, 7^0HY

	Starts	1st	2nd	3rd	Win & Pl
Career Total (Turf)	4	0	1	0	1340

Going (Turf): Sf: 0-2 GS: 0-0 Gd: 0-0 GF: 0-2 Fm: 0-0
Distance: 5f/6f: 0-1 7f-8f: 0-3 9f-13f: 0-0 14f+: 0-0
Track : LH: 0-1 RH: 0-0 Tight: 0-0 Gall: 0-0
Aids: Bl: 0-0 Vi: 0-0 Tstrap: 0-0
Best Rating: 83 9/01 Hayd 7f30y heavy

Bridge Street Lad

67

3-y-o b g Puissance-Bridge Street Lady (Decoy Boy)
M R Bosley C R Marks (banbury)

Placings:000 (5522)
2001: 7^0GF, 6^0F, 6^0HY

	Starts	1st	2nd	3rd	Win & Pl
Career Total (Turf)	3	0	0	0	

Going (Turf): Sf: 0-1 GS: 0-0 Gd: 0-0 GF: 0-1 Fm: 0-1
Distance: 5f/6f: 0-2 7f-8f: 0-1 9f-13f: 0-0 14f+: 0-0
Track : LH: 0-1 RH: 0-0 Tight: 0-0 Gall: 0-0
Aids: Bl: 0-0 Vi: 0-0 Tstrap: 0-0

Bridie's Pride

86 (35)**29**

10-y-o b g Alleging (USA)-Miss Monte Carlo (Reform)
G A Ham K C White

Placings:00/65600/0356210/61220362/3200/2400-000 (0879)
2001: 16^0HY, 16^0S, 21^0S

	Starts	1st	2nd	3rd	Win & Pl
Career Total (Turf)	31	2	6	3	22313
Career Total (AW)	2	0	0	0	0

57 6/98 Asct 2m45y D(0-80)H GD £5940
50 7/97 Chep 2m2f F(0-65)H G-S £2635
Total win prize-money £8575

Going (Turf): Sf: 0-12 **GS: 1-6 Gd: 1-10** GF: 0-3 Fm: 0-0
Distance: 5f/6f: 0-0 7f-8f: 0-0 9f-13f: 0-7 **14f+: 2-26**
Track : LH: 1-20 RH: 1-13 Tight: 0-6 **Gall: 1-10**
Aids: Bl: 0-0 Vi: 0-0 Tstrap: 0-0
Best Rating: 29 4/01 Pont 2m5f122y soft

A decent staying handicapper a few seasons ago, he put up ran a couple of creditable efforts last season, but looks to be rather on the decline.

Brief Contact (IRE)

92 **37**

3-y-o b g Brief Truce (USA)-Incommunicado (IRE) (Sadler's Wells (USA))
Jamie Poulton George H Gibson

Placings:000-060600 (4380)
2001: 8^0HY, 10^6GF, 9^0GF, 11^6F, 10^0GF, 8^0GF

	Starts	1st	2nd	3rd	Win & Pl
Career Total (Turf)	9	0	0	0	0

Going (Turf): Sf: 0-4 GS: 0-0 Gd: 0-0 GF: 0-4 Fm: 0-1
Distance: 5f/6f: 0-1 7f-8f: 0-3 9f-13f: 0-5 14f+: 0-0
Track : LH: 0-5 RH: 0-1 Tight: 0-2 Gall: 0-0
Aids: Bl: 0-0 Vi: 0-0 Tstrap: 0-0
Best Rating: 48 6/01 Gdwd 1m1f192y gd-fm

Brief Key (IRE)

75(75) (28)**23**

3-y-o b f Brief Truce (USA)-Latch Key Lady (USA) (Tejano (USA))
Don Enrico Incisa (N Tinkler 12/1) Don Enrico Incisa

Placings:00-000 (1850)
2001: 7^0SD, 7^0GF, 6^0F

	Starts	1st	2nd	3rd	Win & Pl
Career Total (Turf)	3	0	0	0	
Career Total (AW)	2	0	0	0	

Going (Turf): Sf: 0-1 GS: 0-0 Gd: 0-0 GF: 0-1 Fm: 0-1
Distance: 5f/6f: 0-2 7f-8f: 0-3 9f-13f: 0-0 14f+: 0-0
Track : LH: 0-2 RH: 0-1 Tight: 0-0 Gall: 0-0
Aids: Bl: 0-0 Vi: 0-0 Tstrap: 0-1
Best Rating: 28 1/01 Sthl 7f stand

Briery (IRE)

98 **65**

3-y-o ch f Salse (USA)-Wedgewood (USA) (Woodman (USA))
W J Haggas Mr & Mrs G Middlebrook

Placings:013 (4525)
2001: 6^0G, 7^1G, 7^3GF

	Starts	1st	2nd	3rd	Win & Pl
Career Total (Turf)	3	1	0	1	3445

49 8/01 Newc 7f D GD £2989
Total win prize-money £2989

Going (Turf): Sf: 0-0 GS: 0-0 **Gd: 1-2** GF: 0-1 Fm: 0-0
Distance: 5f/6f: 0-1 **7f-8f: 1-2** 9f-13f: 0-0 14f+: 0-0
Track : LH: 0-0 RH: 0-0 Tight: 0-0 Gall: 0-0
Aids: Bl: 0-0 Vi: 0-0 Tstrap: 0-0
Best Rating: 65 8/01 NmkJ 6f good

Briery Mec

99(99) (50)**58**

6-y-o b g Ron's Victory (USA)-Briery Fille (Sayyaf)
H J Collingridge N H Gardner

Placings:00/000/000233/01503123-30303101400 (5055)
2001: 12^3SD, 9^0G, 9^3F, 10^0G, 10^3G, 10^1GF, 11^0F, 10^1G, 9^4GF, 10^0GF, 10^0S

	Starts	1st	2nd	3rd	Win & Pl
Career Total (Turf)	26	4	1	5	16622
Career Total (AW)	4	0	1	2	1118

58 8/01 Wind 1m2f7y E(0-80)H GD £2898
57 7/01 Pont 1m2f6y F(0-60)H G-F £3900
46 7/00 NmkJ 1m2f E(0-75)H GD £3893
45 5/00 Brig 1m1f209yF(0-65)H SFT £2509
Total win prize-money £13202

Going (Turf): Sf: 1-4 GS: 0-1 **Gd: 2-11** GF: 1-8 Fm: 0-2
Distance: 5f/6f: 0-1 7f-8f: 0-1 **9f-13f: 4-28** 14f+: 0-0
Track : **LH: 2-21** RH: 1-6 Tight: 1-12 Gall: 1-4
Aids: Bl: 0-0 Vi: 0-0 Tstrap: 0-0
Best Rating: 58 8/01 Wind 1m2f7y good

Brig O'Turk

88(90) (52)**51**

4-y-o ch g Inchinor-Sharmood (USA) (Sharpen Up)
C J Mann David & Stewart Yates

Placings:0/434-1000 (3301)
2001: 11^1GF, 10^0F, 10^0GF, 11^0GF

	Starts	1st	2nd	3rd	Win & Pl
Career Total (Turf)	7	1	0	1	3226
Career Total (AW)	1	0	0	0	0

45 6/01 Wind 1m3f135yF G-F £2569
Total win prize-money £2569

Going (Turf): Sf: 0-1 GS: 0-1 Gd: 0-0 **GF: 1-4** Fm: 0-1
Distance: 5f/6f: 0-0 7f-8f: 0-0 **9f-13f: 1-8** 14f+: 0-0
Track : LH: 0-5 RH: 0-0 **Tight: 1-7** Gall: 0-0
Aids: Bl: 0-0 Vi: 0-0 Tstrap: 0-0
Best Rating: 51 7/01 Wind 1m2f7y gd-fm

Brigadier Jones (IRE)

(94) (78+)**76**

2-y-o br g Emperor Jones (USA)-Fight Right (FR) (Crystal Glitters (USA))
H Akbary Charles Alan McKechnie

Placings:41 (5345)
2001: 7^4GS, 6^1SD

	Starts	1st	2nd	3rd	Win & Pl
Career Total (Turf)	1	0	0	0	0
Career Total (AW)	1	1	0	0	2982

78 10/01 Sthl 6f E STD £2982
Total win prize-money £2982

Going (Turf): Sf: 0-0 GS: 0-1 Gd: 0-0 GF: 0-0 Fm: 0-0
Distance: **5f/6f: 1-1** 7f-8f: 0-1 9f-13f: 0-0 14f+: 0-0

Track : **LH: 1-1** RH: 0-0 Tight: 0-0 Gall: 0-0
Aids: Bl: 0-0 Vi: 0-0 Tstrap: 0-0
Best Rating: 78 10/01 Sthl 6f stand

Dropped back a furlong from his debut when bolting up in a six-furlong maiden on the Southwell Fibresand. He should win more races on sand or turf.

Brigadore

101 **90**
2-y-o b c Magic Ring (IRE)-Music Mistress (IRE) (Classic Music (USA))
J R Weymes White Rose Poultry Ltd

Placings:6241125430 **(4659)**
2001: 5⁶S, 5²GS, 5⁴GS, 5¹S, 5¹F, 5²GF, 5⁵GF, 5⁴G, 5³GF, 6⁰GF

	Starts	1st	2nd	3rd	Win & Pl
Career Total (Turf)	10	2	2	1	16688

68 5/01 Newc 5f D FRM £3594
61 5/01 Newc 5f F SFT £2611
Total win prize-money £6206

Going (Turf): Sf: 1-2 GS: 0-2 Gd: 0-1 GF: 0-4 **Fm: 1-1**
Distance: **5f/6f: 2-10** 7f-8f: 0-0 9f-13f: 0-0 14f+: 0-0
Track : LH: 0-1 RH: 0-0 Tight: 0-1 Gall: 0-0
Aids: Bl: 0-0 Vi: 0-0 Tstrap: 0-0
Best Rating: 90 8/01 Gdwd 5f gd-fm

A workmanlike sort, he got off the mark on his fourth attempt on soft ground over the minimum trip at Newcastle and followed up at the same track on much faster ground. Not disgraced in much better company since, he is suited by forcing tactics.

Bright And Clear

104 **95**
2-y-o b f Danehill (USA)-Shining Water (Kalaglow)
B W Hills K Abdulla

Placings:2150 **(5390)**
2001: 7²G, 7¹G, 7⁵GY, 7⁰GS

	Starts	1st	2nd	3rd	Win & Pl
Career Total (Turf)	4	1	1	0	12289

84 8/01 NmkJ 7f D GD £4153
Total win prize-money £4154

Going (Turf): Sf: 0-0 GS: 0-1 **Gd: 1-2** GF: 0-0 Fm: 0-0
Distance: 5f/6f: 0-0 **7f-8f: 1-4** 9f-13f: 0-0 14f+: 0-0
Track : LH: 0-0 RH: 0-1 Tight: 0-0 Gall: 0-0
Aids: Bl: 0-0 Vi: 0-0 Tstrap: 0-0
Best Rating: 94 9/01 Curr 7f gd-yld

A half-sister to the high-class Tenby, made a promising debut at Goodwood, and made no mistake at Newmarket next time beating a field of well-bred newcomers. A close fifth in the Moyglare Stud Stakes, she struggled on soft next time, but looks capable of winning at Pattern level.

Bright Edge

92 **76**
2-y-o ch f Danehill Dancer (IRE)-Beveled Edge (Beveled (USA))
B Palling Christopher J Mason

Placings:21124 **(4276)**
2001: 5²F, 6¹GF, 6¹GF, 6²GF, 7⁴GS
Starts 1st 2nd 3rd Win & Pl

	Starts	1st	2nd	3rd	Win & Pl
Career Total (Turf)	5	2	2	0	14222

76 7/01 Wind 6f C G-F £5735
76 6/01 Nott 6f15y E G-F £3542
Total win prize-money £9277

Going (Turf): Sf: 0-0 GS: 0-1 Gd: 0-0 **GF: 2-3** Fm: 0-1
Distance: 5f/6f: 1-3 7f-8f: 1-2 9f-13f: 0-0 14f+: 0-0
Track : LH: 0-0 RH: 0-1 Tight: 0-0 Gall: 0-0
Aids: Bl: 0-0 Vi: 0-0 Tstrap: 0-0
Best Rating: 76 8/01 Gdwd 7f gd-sft

Came on from her debut to win a Nottingham maiden and Windsor conditions event. Clearly well suited by fast ground.

Bright Hope (IRE)

94 **73**
5-y-o b m Danehill (USA)-Crystal Cross (USA) (Roberto (USA))
P W Harris Mrs P W Harris

Placings:0/31/0-05 **(2575)**
2001: 11⁰GS, 10⁵GF

	Starts	1st	2nd	3rd	Win & Pl
Career Total (Turf)	6	1	0	1	4819

82 9/99 Pont 1m2f6y D G-F £3875
Total win prize-money £3875

Going (Turf): Sf: 0-1 GS: 0-1 Gd: 0-0 **GF: 1-4** Fm: 0-0
Distance: 5f/6f: 0-0 7f-8f: 0-1 **9f-13f: 1-5** 14f+: 0-0
Track : **LH: 1-3** RH: 0-3 Tight: 0-0 Gall: 0-5
Aids: Bl: 0-0 Vi: 0-0 Tstrap: 0-0
Best Rating: 73 6/01 NmkJ 1m2f gd-fm

Winner of a Pontefract maiden in 1999, she has been very lightly raced and must have had problems.

Bright Mist

59 **39**
2-y-o b f Anita's Prince-Out On Her Own (Superlative)
B Palling Mrs L Hedlund,Mr P Morgan,Mrs M Palling

Placings:0 **(5110)**
2001: 6⁰HY

	Starts	1st	2nd	3rd	Win & Pl
Career Total (Turf)	1	0	0	0	

Going (Turf): Sf: 0-1 GS: 0-0 Gd: 0-0 GF: 0-0 Fm: 0-0
Distance: 5f/6f: 0-0 7f-8f: 0-1 9f-13f: 0-0 14f+: 0-0
Track : LH: 0-0 RH: 0-0 Tight: 0-0 Gall: 0-0
Aids: Bl: 0-0 Vi: 0-0 Tstrap: 0-0
Best Rating: 39 10/01 Nott 6f15y heavy

Bright Smile (IRE)

(97) (73)**82**
3-y-o b f Caerleon (USA)-Never So Fair (Never So Bold)
J H M Gosden Mrs B V Sangster, R E Sangster

Placings:4210 **(5486)**
2001: 8⁴GS, 10²GF, 9¹GF, 10⁰HY

	Starts	1st	2nd	3rd	Win & Pl
Career Total (Turf)	4	1	1	0	5567

77 7/01 Nott 1m1f213yD G-F £4446
Total win prize-money £4446

Going (Turf): Sf: 0-1 GS: 0-1 Gd: 0-0 **GF: 1-2** Fm: 0-0
Distance: 5f/6f: 0-0 7f-8f: 0-1 **9f-13f: 1-3** 14f+: 0-0
Track : **LH: 1-3** RH: 0-0 Tight: 0-0 Gall: 0-1
Aids: Bl: 0-0 Vi: 0-0 Tstrap: 0-0
Best Rating: 82 7/01 Chep 1m2f36y gd-fm

Showed ability in two starts before getting off the mark in a Nottingham maiden over ten furlongs. Should stay a mile and a half. Acts on fast ground.

Bright Spangle (IRE)

94(80) (33)**81**
2-y-o ch f General Monash (USA)-No Shame (Formidable (USA))
B Palling Christopher J Cox

Placings:6020100 **(4714)**
2001: 5⁶G, 5⁰SD, 6²GF, 7⁰F, 6¹GF, 5⁰GS, 7⁰G

	Starts	1st	2nd	3rd	Win & Pl
Career Total (Turf)	6	1	1	0	4046
Career Total (AW)	1	0	0	0	

81 7/01 Chep 6f16y E G-F £2926
Total win prize-money £2926

Going (Turf): Sf: 0-0 GS: 0-1 Gd: 0-2 **GF: 1-2** Fm: 0-1
Distance: 5f/6f: 0-4 **7f-8f: 1-3** 9f-13f: 0-0 14f+: 0-0
Track : LH: 0-2 RH: 0-0 Tight: 0-0 Gall: 0-1
Aids: Bl: 0-0 Vi: 0-0 Tstrap: 0-0
Best Rating: 81 7/01 Chep 6f16y gd-fm

Bred for speed, a plating class filly who acts best of firm ground.

Bright Spark (IRE)

109 **74**
4-y-o b c Sri Pekan (USA)-Exciting (Mill Reef (USA))
G Wragg Mollers Racing

Placings:40101206 **(4592)**
2001: 8⁴HY, 9⁰GS, 6¹HY, 10⁰G, 8¹G, 7²GS, 7⁰G, 10⁶G

	Starts	1st	2nd	3rd	Win & Pl
Career Total (Turf)	8	2	1	0	8259

66 6/01 Muss 1m D GD £4173
62 4/01 Folk 6f189y D HVY £2562
Total win prize-money £6735

Going (Turf): Sf: 1-2 GS: 0-2 **Gd: 1-4** GF: 0-0 Fm: 0-0
Distance: 5f/6f: 0-0 **7f-8f: 2-4** 9f-13f: 0-4 14f+: 0-0
Track : LH: 0-2 **RH: 2-3 Tight: 2-3** Gall: 0-1
Aids: Bl: 0-0 Vi: 0-0 Tstrap: 0-0
Best Rating: 74 9/01 Kemp 1m2f good

Unraced at two, he has won a Folkestone maiden and a Musselburgh classified event this term but has struggled in proper handicaps. Suited by a mile and cut in the ground.

Brighter Future

88 **60**
2-y-o b f Night Shift (USA)-Welsh Mist (Damister (USA))
B W Hills R J C Upton

Placings:000 **(5665)**
2001: 5⁰G, 6⁰GS, 6⁰HY

	Starts	1st	2nd	3rd	Win & Pl
Career Total (Turf)	3	0	0	0	

Going (Turf): Sf: 0-1 GS: 0-1 Gd: 0-1 GF: 0-0 Fm: 0-0
Distance: 5f/6f: 0-3 7f-8f: 0-0 9f-13f: 0-0 14f+: 0-0
Track : LH: 0-0 RH: 0-1 Tight: 0-0 Gall: 0-1
Aids: Bl: 0-0 Vi: 0-0 Tstrap: 0-0

Best Rating: 60 11/01 NmkR 6f gd-sft

Brillano (FR)

84 **75**

2-y-o b f Desert King (IRE)-Voliere (USA) (Arctic Tern (USA))

Miss J A Camacho Brian Nordan

Placings:01 (5446)

2001: 7^0G, 7^1HY

	Starts	1st	2nd	3rd	Win & Pl
Career Total (Turf)	2	1	0	0	3038

75 10/01 Newc 7f D HVY £3038

Total win prize-money £3038

Going (Turf): **Sf: 1-1** GS: 0-0 Gd: 0-1 GF: 0-0 Fm: 0-0
Distance: 5f/6f: 0-0 **7f-8f: 1-2** 9f-13f: 0-0 14f+: 0-0
Track : LH: 0-0 RH: 0-0 Tight: 0-0 Gall: 0-0
Aids: Bl: 0-0 Vi: 0-0 Tstrap: 0-0
Best Rating: 75 10/01 Newc 7f heavy

A 41,000gns yearling, he improved from his debut to win a back-end Newcastle maiden on heavy ground. Has the scope to make a decent three-year-old for his new trainer.

Brilliant Red

108(101) (92)**98**

8-y-o b g Royal Academy (USA)-Red Comes Up (USA) (Blushing Groom (FR))

Mrs L Richards Mrs M J George

Placings:32135/650/23164063**4**/**3110**032100/02113000 21/000362000-00510460630 (5607)

2001: 10^0SD, 10^0S, 8^5S, 8^1GF, 8^0GF, 8^4G, 8^6G, 8^0G, 9^6GF, 8^3GS, 8^0GS

	Starts	1st	2nd	3rd	Win & Pl
Career Total (Turf)	49	6	5	8	152938
Career Total (AW)	8	3	1	1	18051

98	5/01	Gdwd	1m	C(0-100)H	G-F	£11602
92	11/99	Ling	1m2f	B	STD	£9103
99	7/99	Sand	1m14y	B(0-105)H	G-F	£12520
98	6/99	Asct	1m2f	B(0-105)H	G-F	£25800
95	9/98	Newb	1m2f6y	B(0-105)H	GD	£43000
92	2/98	Ling	1m2f	D(0-85)H	SLW	£3420
81	2/98	Ling	1m2f	D(0-80)H	SLW	£3517
83	7/97	Ling	7f140y	C(0-90)	G-F	£5447
90	8/95	Kemp	7f	D	G-F	£3826

Total win prize-money £118238

Going (Turf): Sf: 0-6 GS: 0-7 Gd: 1-14 **GF: 5-21** Fm: 0-1
Distance: 5f/6f: 0-1 7f-8f: 3-28 **9f-13f: 6-28** 14f+: 0-0
Track : LH: 4-18 RH: 4-25 Tight: 3-11 Gall: 3-18
Aids: Bl: 0-0 Vi: 1-3 **Tstrap: 4-25**
Best Rating: 98 5/01 Gdwd 1m gd-fm

A useful handicapper at around a mile to ten furlongs. He acts on fast ground and is normally equipped with a tongue-strap. Latest win came in tongue-strap and visor.

Brilliantrio

102 **66**

3-y-o ch f Selkirk (USA)-Loucoum (FR) (Iron Duke (FR))

Miss J A Camacho Brian Nordan

Placings:106-04553352 (4167)

2001: 8^0S, 8^4G, 9^5GF, 8^5GF, 8^3GF, 7^3GF, 7^5GF, 7^2GF

	Starts	1st	2nd	3rd	Win & Pl
Career Total (Turf)	11	1	1	2	10448

78 7/00 Newc 7f E G-F £6955

Total win prize-money £6955

Going (Turf): Sf: 0-1 GS: 0-1 Gd: 0-1 **GF: 1-8** Fm: 0-0
Distance: 5f/6f: 0-0 **7f-8f: 1-8** 9f-13f: 0-3 14f+: 0-0
Track : LH: 0-2 RH: 0-7 Tight: 0-2 Gall: 0-1
Aids: Bl: 0-0 Vi: 0-0 Tstrap: 0-0
Best Rating: 73 5/01 Ripn 1m good

Brillyant Dancer

93 **57**

3-y-o b f Environment Friend-Brillyant Glen (IRE) (Glenstal (USA))

Mrs A Duffield Clarks New Town

Placings:00-6000 (4481)

2001: 7^6GF, 8^0GF, 8^0GF, 8^0F

	Starts	1st	2nd	3rd	Win & Pl
Career Total (Turf)	6	0	0	0	0

Going (Turf): **Sf: 0-1 GS: 0-0 Gd: 0-0 GF: 0-4 Fm: 0-1**
Distance: 5f/6f: 0-1 7f-8f: 0-4 9f-13f: 0-1 14f+: 0-0
Track : LH: 0-2 RH: 0-2 Tight: 0-1 Gall: 0-1
Aids: Bl: 0-0 Vi: 0-0 Tstrap: 0-0
Best Rating: 57 5/01 Bevl 7f100y gd-fm

Brimstone (IRE)

100(95) (50)**45**

6-y-o ch g Ballad Rock-Blazing Glory (IRE) (Glow (USA))

Mrs D Haine Miss Linsey Knocker

Placings:0612/240/00**006**/**0**000-46062 (4621)

2001: 5^4G, 5^6GF, 5^0G, 5^6S, 6^2F

	Starts	1st	2nd	3rd	Win & Pl
Career Total (Turf)	17	1	3	0	6975
Career Total (AW)	4	0	0	0	0

78 7/97 Sand 5f6y D G-F £3485

Total win prize-money £3485

Going (Turf): Sf: 0-2 GS: 0-3 Gd: 0-6 **GF: 1-5** Fm: 0-1
Distance: **5f/6f: 1-16** 7f-8f: 0-4 9f-13f: 0-1 14f+: 0-0
Track : LH: 0-7 RH: 0-1 Tight: 0-4 Gall: 0-3
Aids: Bl: 0-0 Vi: 0-6 Tstrap: 0-0
Best Rating: 45 9/01 Newc 6f firm

Gained his only win as a two-year-old in 1997. Ran some decent races in 2001. Suited by fast ground.

Bring Sweets

106 **85**

5-y-o b g Sabrehill (USA)-Che Gambe (USA) (Lyphard (USA))

B Ellison Spring Cottage Syndicate

Placings:00112/330/0-3 (0522)

2001: 12^3S

	Starts	1st	2nd	3rd	Win & Pl
Career Total (Turf)	10	2	1	3	16646

87	11/98	Donc	1m	C	SFT	£5097
79	10/98	Rdcr	1m	E	HVY	£3120

Total win prize-money £8218

Going (Turf): **Sf: 2-6** GS: 0-0 Gd: 0-3 GF: 0-1 Fm: 0-0
Distance: 5f/6f: 0-0 **7f-8f: 2-6** 9f-13f: 0-4 14f+: 0-0
Track : LH: 0-4 RH: 0-2 Tight: 0-3 Gall: 0-2
Aids: Bl: 0-1 Vi: 0-0 Tstrap: 0-0
Best Rating: 85 3/01 Donc 1m4f soft

A smart hurdler on his day, he was lighlty raced on the Flat in recent years but ran well to finish third in a conditions event at Doncaster on Lincoln day. (DEAD)

Brioney (IRE)

(101) (61)**73**

4-y-o ch f Barathea (IRE)-La Vigie (King Of Clubs)

J A Glover (J H M Gosden 2/2) David Jenkins

Placings:00411-600 (2319)

2001: 12^6SD, 12^0SD, 12^0SD

	Starts	1st	2nd	3rd	Win & Pl
Career Total (Turf)	3	0	0	0	367
Career Total (AW)	5	2	0	0	3751

61 12/00 Wolv 1m4f D(0-75) STD £3750

Total win prize-money £3751

Going (Turf): Sf: 0-1 GS: 0-1 Gd: 0-0 GF: 0-1 Fm: 0-0
Distance: 5f/6f: 0-0 7f-8f: 0-0 **9f-13f: 2-8** 14f+: 0-0
Track : **LH: 2-6** RH: 0-2 **Tight: 2-6** Gall: 0-0
Aids: Bl: 0-1 Vi: 0-0 **Tstrap: 2-8**
Best Rating: 36 1/01 Wolv 1m4f stand

Brittany Girl

19

3-y-o b f Faustus (USA)-Kimble Princess (Kala Shikari)

J W Unett Mrs S Lee

Placings:000 (5617)

2001: 8^0GF, 8^0HY, 8^0SD

	Starts	1st	2nd	3rd	Win & Pl
Career Total (Turf)	2	0	0	0	
Career Total (AW)	1	0	0	0	

Going (Turf): Sf: 0-1 GS: 0-0 Gd: 0-0 GF: 0-1 Fm: 0-0
Distance: 5f/6f: 0-0 7f-8f: 0-0 9f-13f: 0-3 14f+: 0-0
Track : LH: 0-2 RH: 0-0 Tight: 0-1 Gall: 0-0
Aids: Bl: 0-0 Vi: 0-0 Tstrap: 0-0
Best Rating: 19 10/01 Nott 1m54y heavy

Broadway Banker (FR)

83 **59**

2-y-o b c Broadway Flyer (USA)-Hariti (IRE) (Flash Of Steel)

J W Hills Freddy Bienstock And Martin Boase

Placings:50 (5371)

2001: 8^5G, 8^0G

	Starts	1st	2nd	3rd	Win & Pl
Career Total (Turf)	2	0	0	0	0

Going (Turf): Sf: 0-0 GS: 0-0 Gd: 0-2 GF: 0-0 Fm: 0-0
Distance: 5f/6f: 0-0 7f-8f: 0-2 9f-13f: 0-0 14f+: 0-0
Track : LH: 0-0 RH: 0-1 Tight: 0-0 Gall: 0-0
Aids: Bl: 0-0 Vi: 0-0 Tstrap: 0-0
Best Rating: 59 9/01 Kemp 1m good

Broadway Legend (IRE)

96 **80**

4-y-o b f Caerleon (USA)-Tetradonna (IRE) (Teenoso (USA))

J W Hills Freddy Bienstock And Martin Boase

Placings:30/10020-000 (1948)

2001: 10^0G, 10^0GF, 10^0GF

	Starts	1st	2nd	3rd	Win & Pl
Career Total (Turf)	10	1	1	1	6674

85 5/00 Hayd 1m2f120yD GD £4004
Total win prize-money £4004

Going (Turf): Sf: 0-1 GS: 0-0 **Gd: 1-4** GF: 0-5 Fm: 0-0
Distance: 5f/6f: 0-0 7f-8f: 0-3 **9f-13f: 1-7** 14f+: 0-0
Track : **LH: 1-7** RH: 0-1 Tight: 0-0 Gall: 0-6
Aids: Bl: 0-0 Vi: 0-0 Tstrap: 0-0
Best Rating: 68 5/01 Donc 1m2f60y good

A 100,000 guineas half-sister to Alberich, she looks the part, but only has a Haydock maiden victory to her name and does not look at all an easy ride.

Broadway Score (USA)

106 **83**

3-y-o b c Theatrical-Brocaro (USA) (Mr Prospector (USA))
J W Hills Freddy Dienstock And Martin Boase

Placings:61 **(4447)**
2001: 8^6S, 9^1G

	Starts	1st	2nd	3rd	Win & Pl
Career Total (Turf)	2	1	0	0	4173

83 9/01 Sand 1m1f D GD £4173
Total win prize-money £4173

Going (Turf): Sf: 0-1 GS: 0-0 **Gd: 1-1** GF: 0-0 Fm: 0-0
Distance: 5f/6f: 0-0 7f-8f: 0-1 **9f-13f: 1-1** 14f+: 0-0
Track : LH: 0-0 **RH: 1-1** Tight: 0-0 Gall: 0-0
Aids: Bl: 0-0 Vi: 0-0 Tstrap: 0-0
Best Rating: 83 9/01 Sand 1m1f good

Got off the mark at the second time of asking in a Sandown maiden, after a promising run in the Wood Ditton. Suited by good ground and acts well over nine furlongs.

Broche (USA)

104(30) (113)**109**

4-y-o b c Summer Squall (USA)-Ribbonwood (USA) (Diesis)
Saeed Bin Suroor Godolphin

Placings:1/00150-**412062** **(4045)**
2001: 8^4FT, 12^1FT, 10^2FT, 10^0FT, 10^6GF, 11^2HY

	Starts	1st	2nd	3rd	Win & Pl
Career Total (Turf)	7	2	1	0	35523
Career Total (AW)	5	1	1	0	26867

1/01 Ndas 1m4f (90-110)H FST £10929
100 5/00 Donc 1m2f60y B G-S £9078
96 6/00 Curr 7f GD £6875
Total win prize-money £26882

Going (Turf): Sf: 0-1 **GS: 1-1 Gd: 1-3** GF: 0-1 Fm: 0-0
Distance: 5f/6f: 0-0 7f-8f: 1-3 **9f-13f: 2-9** 14f+: 0-0
Track : **LH: 1-4** RH: 0-2 Tight: 0-1 **Gall: 1-1**
Aids: Bl: 0-0 Vi: 0-2 **Tstrap: 1-1**
Best Rating: 113 3/01 Ndas 1m2f fast

A Godolphin inmate, he is a useful colt, but he has faced some stiff tasks and has been found wanting at the top level. Used as a pacemaker for more illustrious stable-mates.

Brocketeer

88 **45**

2-y-o b g Prince Sabo-Mistral's Dancer (Shareef Dancer (USA))
J A Osborne The Memory Lane Partnership

Placings:000 **(5126)**
2001: 6^0GF, 5^0G, 6^0HY

	Starts	1st	2nd	3rd	Win & Pl
Career Total (Turf)	3	0	0	0	

Going (Turf): Sf: 0-1 GS: 0-0 Gd: 0-1 GF: 0-1 Fm: 0-0
Distance: 5f/6f: 0-3 7f-8f: 0-0 9f-13f: 0-0 14f+: 0-0
Track : LH: 0-1 RH: 0-0 Tight: 0-0 Gall: 0-1
Aids: Bl: 0-0 Vi: 0-0 Tstrap: 0-0
Best Rating: 45 9/01 Ling 6f gd-fm

Broke Road (IRE)

(80) (19)**19**

5-y-o b g Deploy-Shamaka (Kris)
Mrs V C Ward Broke Road Partnerhsip

Placings:0/042034333614/0-40 **(2981)**
2001: 12^4GF, 16^0SD

	Starts	1st	2nd	3rd	Win & Pl
Career Total (Turf)	11	1	0	4	4875
Career Total (AW)	5	0	1	0	724

42 9/99 Haml 1m65y F(0-60)H SFT £2619
Total win prize-money £2619

Going (Turf): Sf: 1-3 GS: 0-0 Gd: 0-3 GF: 0-3 Fm: 0-2
Distance: 5f/6f: 0-0 7f-8f: 0-6 **9f-13f: 1-9** 14f+: 0-1
Track : LH: 0-10 **RH: 1-6 Tight: 1-7** Gall: 0-0
Aids: **Bl: 1-5** Vi: 0-0 Tstrap: 0-0
Best Rating: 32 7/01 Sthl 1m4f gd-fm

Broken Barricades (IRE)

94 **93d**

2-y-o gr c Common Grounds-Gratclo (Belfort (FR))
B W Hills C Wright & The Hon Mrs J M Corbett

Placings:31000 **(5340)**
2001: 6^3GF, 6^1GF, 6^0GF, 7^0S, 6^0GS

	Starts	1st	2nd	3rd	Win & Pl
Career Total (Turf)	5	1	0	1	5958

93 8/01 Sals 6f D G-F £4257
Total win prize-money £4258

Going (Turf): Sf: 0-1 GS: 0-1 Gd: 0-0 **GF: 1-3** Fm: 0-0
Distance: **5f/6f: 1-4** 7f-8f: 0-1 9f-13f: 0-0 14f+: 0-0
Track : LH: 0-1 RH: 0-0 Tight: 0-1 Gall: 0-0
Aids: Bl: 0-0 Vi: 0-0 Tstrap: 0-0
Best Rating: 93 8/01 Sals 6f gd-fm

A 50,000gns full-brother to Rich Ground, he showed the benefit of his Goodwood debut with an impressive all-the-way victory at Salisbury over six furlongs, but he was out of his depth in a valuable race at Doncaster. Did not appear to handle soft ground at Chester or Newmarket.

Bronx Bomber

92 **39**

3-y-o ch g Prince Sabo-Super Yankee (IRE) (Superlative)
Dr J D Scargill R A Dalton

Placings:4000 **(4988)**
2001: 6^4GF, 7^0GS, 6^0G, 8^0G

	Starts	1st	2nd	3rd	Win & Pl
Career Total (Turf)	4	0	0	0	0

Going (Turf): Sf: 0-0 GS: 0-1 Gd: 0-2 GF: 0-1 Fm: 0-0
Distance: 5f/6f: 0-1 7f-8f: 0-3 9f-13f: 0-0 14f+: 0-0
Track : LH: 0-0 RH: 0-1 Tight: 0-1 Gall: 0-0
Aids: Bl: 0-0 Vi: 0-0 Tstrap: 0-0
Best Rating: 39 6/01 Folk 6f189y gd-fm

Brooksby Whorlton (IRE)

74 **19**

7-y-o b g Commanche Run-Superlee (IRE) (Le Moss)
R Bastiman G L Mason

Placings:00 **(5683)**
2001: 14^0HY, 14^0S

	Starts	1st	2nd	3rd	Win & Pl
Career Total (Turf)	2	0	0	0	

Going (Turf): Sf: 0-2 GS: 0-0 Gd: 0-0 GF: 0-0 Fm: 0-0
Distance: 5f/6f: 0-0 7f-8f: 0-0 9f-13f: 0-0 14f+: 0-2
Track : LH: 0-2 RH: 0-0 Tight: 0-0 Gall: 0-1
Aids: Bl: 0-0 Vi: 0-0 Tstrap: 0-0
Best Rating: 19 4/01 Nott 1m6f15y heavy

Brother Joe (NZ)

108 **106+**

7-y-o ch g Hula Town (NZ)-Olivia Rose (NZ) (Travolta (FR))
P J Hobbs Sir Robert Ogden

Placings:32/4263 **(4172)**
2001: 8^4G, 16^2G, 16^6F, 13^3G

	Starts	1st	2nd	3rd	Win & Pl
Career Total (Turf)	6	0	2	2	30664

Going (Turf): Sf: 0-0 GS: 0-0 Gd: 0-3 GF: 0-0 Fm: 0-1
Distance: 5f/6f: 0-0 7f-8f: 0-0 9f-13f: 0-1 14f+: 0-3
Track : LH: 0-3 RH: 0-1 Tight: 0-1 Gall: 0-2
Aids: Bl: 0-0 Vi: 0-0 Tstrap: 0-0
Best Rating: 106 8/01 York 1m5f194y good

Better known as a hurdler, he is useful over staying distances. He finished a useful second over two miles at Haydock on his second start of this season and was a cracking third in the Ebor.

Broughton Knows

95 **51**

4-y-o b g Most Welcome-Broughtons Pet (IRE) (Cyrano De Bergerac)
W J Musson Droughton Thermal Insulation

Placings:00003 **(4908)**
2001: 8^0HY, 6^0HY, 7^0G, 8^0GF, 9^3G

	Starts	1st	2nd	3rd	Win & Pl
Career Total (Turf)	5	0	0	1	443

Going (Turf): Sf: 0-2 GS: 0-0 Gd: 0-2 GF: 0-1 Fm: 0-0
Distance: 5f/6f: 0-0 7f-8f: 0-2 9f-13f: 0-3 14f+: 0-0
Track : LH: 0-1 RH: 0-3 Tight: 0-2 Gall: 0-0
Aids: Bl: 0-0 Vi: 0-0 Tstrap: 0-0
Best Rating: 51 5/01 Donc 7f good

Broughton Magic (IRE)

(104) (43)**39**

6-y-o ch g Archway (IRE)-Magic Green (Magic Mirror)
W J Musson Broughton Thermal Insulation

Placings:000500/51000-0102 **(1455)**

2001: 8^{0}SD, 8^{1}SW, 9^{0}SD, 8^{2}SD

	Starts	1st	2nd	3rd	Win & Pl
Career Total (Turf)	5	0	0	0	
Career Total (AW)	10	2	1	0	4750

40	2/01	Sthl	1m	F(0-65)H	SLW	£1785
43	2/00	Sthl	1m	F(0-65)H	STD	£2326

Total win prize-money £4112

Going (Turf): Sf: 0-1 GS: 0-1 Gd: 0-2 GF: 0-1 Fm: 0-0
Distance: 5f/6f: 0-2 **7f-8f: 2-10** 9f-13f: 0-3 14f+: 0-0
Track : **LH: 2-10** RH: 0-0 Tight: 0-3 Gall: 0-0
Aids: Bl: 0-1 Vi: 0-0 Tstrap: 0-0
Best Rating: 43 5/01 Wolv 1m100y stand

Broughton Melody

83 **60**

2-y-o ch f Alhijaz-Broughton Singer (IRE) (Common Grounds)
W J Musson Broughton Thermal Insulation

Placings:00 **(5682)**
2001: 7^{0}GS, 7^{0}S

	Starts	1st	2nd	3rd	Win & Pl
Career Total (Turf)	2	0	0	0	

Going (Turf): Sf: 0-1 GS: 0-1 Gd: 0-0 GF: 0-0 Fm: 0-0
Distance: 5f/6f: 0-0 7f-8f: 0-2 9f-13f: 0-0 14f+: 0-0
Track : LH: 0-0 RH: 0-0 Tight: 0-0 Gall: 0-0
Aids: Bl: 0-0 Vi: 0-0 Tstrap: 0-0
Best Rating: 60 11/01 NmkR 7f gd-sft

Broughton Storm

87(79) (13)**17**

3-y-o ch g Chaddleworth (IRE)-Rainy Day Song (Persian Bold)
W J Musson Broughton Thermal Insulation

Placings:0060-00050000 **(1787)**
2001: 10^{0}SD, 8^{0}SD, 8^{0}SD, 8^{5}HY, 8^{0}S, 9^{0}GF, 11^{0}GF, 9^{0}F

	Starts	1st	2nd	3rd	Win & Pl
Career Total (Turf)	9	0	0	0	0
Career Total (AW)	3	0	0	0	

Going (Turf): Sf: 0-2 GS: 0-0 Gd: 0-3 GF: 0-3 Fm: 0-1
Distance: 5f/6f: 0-2 7f-8f: 0-4 9f-13f: 0-6 14f+: 0-0
Track : LH: 0-8 RH: 0-2 Tight: 0-3 Gall: 0-2
Aids: Bl: 0-2 Vi: 0-0 Tstrap: 0-3
Best Rating: 17 5/01 Ling 1m3f106y gd-fm

Broughton Zest

84 **66d**

2-y-o b f Colonel Collins (USA)-Broughtons Relish (Nomination)
W J Musson Broughton Thermal Insulation

Placings:0000 **(5342)**
2001: 6^{0}G, 7^{0}GF, 6^{0}HY, 7^{0}GS

	Starts	1st	2nd	3rd	Win & Pl
Career Total (Turf)	4	0	0	0	

Going (Turf): Sf: 0-1 GS: 0-1 Gd: 0-1 GF: 0-1 Fm: 0-0
Distance: 5f/6f: 0-2 7f-8f: 0-2 9f-13f: 0-0 14f+: 0-0
Track : LH: 0-0 RH: 0-1 Tight: 0-0 Gall: 0-1
Aids: Bl: 0-0 Vi: 0-0 Tstrap: 0-0
Best Rating: 66 9/01 Kemp 6f good

Broughtons Flush

(96) (41)**54**

3-y-o b g First Trump-Glowing Reference (Reference Point)
W J Musson Broughton Thermal Insulation

Placings:00-005032 **(3233)**
2001: 8^{0}SD, 9^{0}S, 12^{5}SD, 11^{0}G, 12^{3}SD, 12^{2}SD

	Starts	1st	2nd	3rd	Win & Pl
Career Total (Turf)	4	0	0	0	
Career Total (AW)	4	0	1	1	1023

Going (Turf): Sf: 0-2 GS: 0-0 Gd: 0-1 GF: 0-1 Fm: 0-0
Distance: 5f/6f: 0-0 7f-8f: 0-3 9f-13f: 0-5 14f+: 0-0
Track : LH: 0-6 RH: 0-0 Tight: 0-2 Gall: 0-0
Aids: Bl: 0-0 Vi: 0-0 Tstrap: 0-0
Best Rating: 41 7/01 Sthl 1m4f stand

Still a maiden, he has been running well on the All-Weather at around 12 furlongs, and may get further.

Broughtons Mill

83(85) (14)**43**

6-y-o gr g Ron's Victory (USA)-Sandra's Desire (Grey Desire)
W J Musson Windmill Racing

Placings:6/5003/00423606-00 **(1739)**
2001: 12^{0}SD, 11^{0}GF

	Starts	1st	2nd	3rd	Win & Pl
Career Total (Turf)	9	0	1	2	1377
Career Total (AW)	6	0	0	0	0

Going (Turf): Sf: 0-2 GS: 0-2 Gd: 0-4 GF: 0-1 Fm: 0-0
Distance: 5f/6f: 0-1 7f-8f: 0-3 9f-13f: 0-10 14f+: 0-1
Track : LH: 0-12 RH: 0-2 Tight: 0-5 Gall: 0-1
Aids: Bl: 0-1 Vi: 0-0 Tstrap: 0-0
Best Rating: 41 7/01 Sthl 1m4f stand

Broughtons Motto

(101) (63)**41**

3-y-o b f Mtoto-Ice Chocolate (USA) (Icecapade (USA))
W J Musson Broughton Thermal Insulation

Placings:0146-00022400 **(5601)**
2001: 9^{0}S, 8^{0}HY, 7^{0}S, 8^{2}SD, 8^{2}SD, 9^{4}SW, 8^{0}G, 8^{0}GS

	Starts	1st	2nd	3rd	Win & Pl
Career Total (Turf)	8	0	0	0	0
Career Total (AW)	4	1	2	0	4238

60	5/00	Sthl	5f	F	STD	£2233

Total win prize-money £2233

Going (Turf): Sf: 0-3 GS: 0-2 Gd: 0-3 GF: 0-0 Fm: 0-0
Distance: **5f/6f: 1-4** 7f-8f: 0-3 9f-13f: 0-5 14f+: 0-0
Track : LH: 0-5 RH: 0-1 Tight: 0-3 Gall: 0-1
Aids: Bl: 0-0 Vi: 0-0 Tstrap: 0-0
Best Rating: 63 8/01 Wolv 1m100y stand

Broughty Castle (IRE)

81 **48**

3-y-o b g Inzar (USA)-Heavenly Note (Chief Singer)
B J Meehan Mrs E A Lerpiniere

Placings:000 **(5024)**
2001: 9^{0}GF, 10^{0}G, 11^{0}S

	Starts	1st	2nd	3rd	Win & Pl
Career Total (Turf)	3	0	0	0	

Going (Turf): Sf: 0-1 GS: 0-0 Gd: 0-1 GF: 0-1 Fm: 0-0
Distance: 5f/6f: 0-0 7f-8f: 0-0 9f-13f: 0-3 14f+: 0-0
Track : LH: 0-2 RH: 0-1 Tight: 0-1 Gall: 0-0
Aids: Bl: 0-0 Vi: 0-0 Tstrap: 0-0
Best Rating: 48 9/01 Epsm 1m2f18y good

Brown Eyes

98 **98**

2-y-o b f Danehill (USA)-La Belle Otero (USA) (Nureyev (USA))
B W Hills Mrs Belinda Harvey

Placings:310 **(5144)**
2001: 6^{3}GF, 6^{1}GF, 7^{0}G

	Starts	1st	2nd	3rd	Win & Pl
Career Total (Turf)	3	1	0	1	5516

98	8/01	Sals	6f212y	D	G-F	£4680

Total win prize-money £4680

Going (Turf): Sf: 0-0 GS: 0-0 Gd: 0-1 **GF: 1-2** Fm: 0-0
Distance: 5f/6f: 0-1 **7f-8f: 1-2** 9f-13f: 0-0 14f+: 0-0
Track : LH: 0-0 RH: 0-0 Tight: 0-0 Gall: 0-0
Aids: Bl: 0-0 Vi: 0-0 Tstrap: 0-0
Best Rating: 98 8/01 Sals 6f212y gd-fm

By Danehill, made a good start to her career with a decent maiden win, only to be plunged in at the deep end in a Listed race at Newmarket next time out, which she found all too much.

Brown Holly

79(81) (39)**24**

3-y-o br c So Factual (USA)-Scarlett Holly (Red Sunset)
H E Haynes Miss Sally R Haynes

Placings:000-0 **(4610)**
2001: 5^{0}F

	Starts	1st	2nd	3rd	Win & Pl
Career Total (Turf)	3	0	0	0	
Career Total (AW)	1	0	0	0	

Going (Turf): Sf: 0-1 GS: 0-0 Gd: 0-0 GF: 0-1 Fm: 0-1
Distance: 5f/6f: 0-4 7f-8f: 0-0 9f-13f: 0-0 14f+: 0-0
Track : LH: 0-2 RH: 0-0 Tight: 0-1 Gall: 0-1
Aids: Bl: 0-0 Vi: 0-0 Tstrap: 0-0
Best Rating: 24 9/01 Bath 5f161y firm

Brown Madder (IRE)

85 **66**

2-y-o ch g Perugino (USA)-El Pina (Be My Guest (USA))
T D Easterby The Rumpole Partnership

Placings:4000 **(4827)**
2001: 5^{4}F, 5^{0}G, 5^{0}GF, 8^{0}G

	Starts	1st	2nd	3rd	Win & Pl
Career Total (Turf)	4	0	0	0	0

Going (Turf): Sf: 0-0 GS: 0-0 Gd: 0-2 GF: 0-1 Fm: 0-1
Distance: 5f/6f: 0-3 7f-8f: 0-1 9f-13f: 0-0 14f+: 0-0
Track : LH: 0-1 RH: 0-0 Tight: 0-0 Gall: 0-0
Aids: Bl: 0-0 Vi: 0-0 Tstrap: 0-0
Best Rating: 66 6/01 Newc 5f firm

Browning

105(106) (64)**80**

6-y-o b g Warrshan (USA)-Mossy Rose (King Of Spain)

M P Tregoning Stanley J Sharp

Placings:0045/**222**06414/002200/20**654-122113** **(4836)**

2001: 12^{1}SW, 12^{2}SD, 12^{2}GF, 14^{1}GF, 14^{1}GF, 16^{3}GF

	Starts	1st	2nd	3rd	Win & Pl
Career Total (Turf)	19	3	4	1	21223
Career Total (AW)	10	1	4	0	6689

74	7/01	Sand	1m6f	D(0-80)H	G-F	£4914
68	7/01	Kemp	1m6f92y	C(0-90)H	G-F	£7085
64	1/01	Ling	1m4f	E(0-75)H	SLW	£2947
60	8/98	Wind	1m3f135y	E(0-70)H	G-F	£3013

Total win prize-money £17960

Going (Turf): Sf: 0-0 GS: 0-2 Gd: 0-3 **GF: 3-14** Fm: 0-0
Distance: 5f/6f: 0-0 7f-8f: 0-7 9f-13f: 2-18 14f+: 2-4
Track : LH: 1-16 **RH: 2-9 Tight: 2-14** Gall: 0-0
Aids: Bl: 0-1 Vi: 0-0 Tstrap: 0-0
Best Rating: 77 9/01 Newb 2m gd-fm

Suited by 12-14 furlongs on fast ground. Has formed a good partnership with Alan Daly and was produced with a well-timed run to land spoils at Kempton and Sandown in July, both over 14 furlongs. Is a bit of a character but has the ability. Needs to come with a late challenge.

Browns Delight

91(87) (47)**40**

4-y-o b f Runnett-Fearless Princess (Tyrnavos)

M Tate B Staight

Placings:000**20**/0**44**00065000**2**41-00 **(4727)**

2001: 10^{0}GF, 10^{0}GF

	Starts	1st	2nd	3rd	Win & Pl
Career Total (Turf)	14	1	1	0	3091
Career Total (AW)	6	0	1	0	1374

40	8/00	Bath	1m3f144yF		FRM	£2289

Total win prize-money £2289

Going (Turf): Sf: 0-1 GS: 0-0 Gd: 0-4 GF: 0-5 **Fm: 1-3**
Distance: 5f/6f: 0-4 7f-8f: 0-6 **9f-13f: 1-9** 14f+: 0-0
Track : **LH: 1-14** RH: 0-1 **Tight: 1-8** Gall: 0-1
Aids: Bl: 0-0 Vi: 0-2 Tstrap: 0-0
Best Rating: 31 6/01 Wwck 1m2f188y gd-fm

Brunnhilde

93 **48**

3-y-o ch f Wolfhound (USA)-Vilanika (FR) (Top Ville)

John Berry H R Moszkowicz

Placings:005-000 **(2140)**

2001: 7^{0}S, 10^{0}GF, 10^{0}GF

	Starts	1st	2nd	3rd	Win & Pl
Career Total (Turf)	6	0	0	0	0

Going (Turf): Sf: 0-2 GS: 0-1 Gd: 0-0 GF: 0-3 Fm: 0-0
Distance: 5f/6f: 0-2 7f-8f: 0-1 9f-13f: 0-3 14f+: 0-0
Track : LH: 0-3 RH: 0-1 Tight: 0-1 Gall: 0-1
Aids: Bl: 0-0 Vi: 0-0 Tstrap: 0-0
Best Rating: 48 5/01 Ayr 1m2f192y gd-fm

Bryano De Bergerac

96 **80?**

2-y-o b c Cyrano De Bergerac-Cow Pastures (Homing)

M D I Usher Bryan Fry

Placings:0100 **(3581)**

2001: 5^{0}GS, 5^{1}F, 5^{0}G, 5^{0}GF

	Starts	1st	2nd	3rd	Win & Pl
Career Total (Turf)	4	1	0	0	2464

77	6/01	Ling	5f	F	FRM	£2464

Total win prize-money £2464

Going (Turf): Sf: 0-0 GS: 0-1 Gd: 0-1 GF: 0-1 **Fm: 1-1**
Distance: **5f/6f: 1-4** 7f-8f: 0-0 9f-13f: 0-0 14f+: 0-0
Track : LH: 0-1 RH: 0-1 Tight: 0-0 Gall: 0-2
Aids: Bl: 0-0 Vi: 0-0 Tstrap: 0-0
Best Rating: 80 8/01 Gdwd 5f gd-fm

He got off the mark on very fast ground at Lingfield on his second start but was very disappointing afterwards.

Bualadhbos (IRE)

93 **68**

2-y-o b g Royal Applause-Goodnight Girl (IRE) (Alzao (USA))

F Jordan Graham Brown

Placings:0056 **(4725)**

2001: 6^{0}GF, 6^{0}GF, 7^{5}GS, 7^{6}GF

	Starts	1st	2nd	3rd	Win & Pl
Career Total (Turf)	4	0	0	0	0

Going (Turf): Sf: 0-0 GS: 0-1 Gd: 0-0 GF: 0-3 Fm: 0-0
Distance: 5f/6f: 0-2 7f-8f: 0-2 9f-13f: 0-0 14f+: 0-0
Track : LH: 0-1 RH: 0-0 Tight: 0-0 Gall: 0-0
Aids: Bl: 0-0 Vi: 0-0 Tstrap: 0-0
Best Rating: 68 7/01 Wwck 7f26y gd-sft

Has yet to make the frame in three outings.

Buckenham Jem

75 **8**

3-y-o b f Wing Park-Walk That Walk (Hadeer)

Mrs Lydia Pearce M M Foulger

Placings:0 **(4226)**

2001: 7^{0}GF

	Starts	1st	2nd	3rd	Win & Pl
Career Total (Turf)	1	0	0	0	

Going (Turf): Sf: 0-0 GS: 0-0 Gd: 0-0 GF: 0-1 Fm: 0-0
Distance: 5f/6f: 0-0 7f-8f: 0-1 9f-13f: 0-0 14f+: 0-0
Track : LH: 0-0 RH: 0-0 Tight: 0-0 Gall: 0-0
Aids: Bl: 0-0 Vi: 0-0 Tstrap: 0-0
Best Rating: 8 8/01 NmkJ 7f gd-fm

Bucks

99 **79**

4-y-o b g Slip Anchor-Alligram (USA) (Alysheba (USA))

Mrs A J Perrett Michael H Watt

Placings:2340 **(5492)**

2001: 14^{2}GF, 12^{3}G, 14^{4}F, 16^{0}HY

	Starts	1st	2nd	3rd	Win & Pl
Career Total (Turf)	4	0	1	1	2280

Going (Turf): Sf: 0-1 GS: 0-0 Gd: 0-1 GF: 0-1 Fm: 0-1
Distance: 5f/6f: 0-0 7f-8f: 0-0 9f-13f: 0-1 14f+: 0-3
Track : LH: 0-2 RH: 0-2 Tight: 0-1 Gall: 0-1
Aids: Bl: 0-0 Vi: 0-0 Tstrap: 0-0
Best Rating: 79 8/01 NmkJ 1m4f good

Still a maiden, but ran well in each of his first three starts over trips ranging from 12 to 14 furlongs, although he has found himself on a stiff mark as a result.

Buddeliea

(105) (69)**73**

3-y-o b f Pivotal-Fernlea (USA) (Sir Ivor)

J S Moore Alljays Racing

Placings:52-1422010620604 **(5611)**

2001: 8^{1}SD, 10^{4}SW, 10^{2}SD, 11^{2}SD, 9^{0}GS, 8^{1}F, 8^{0}GF, 7^{6}GF, 8^{2}G, 7^{0}G, 8^{6}GF, 8^{0}SD, 8^{4}SD

	Starts	1st	2nd	3rd	Win & Pl
Career Total (Turf)	7	1	1	0	4973
Career Total (AW)	8	1	3	0	5530

73	5/01	Newc	1m	E(0-70)H	FRM	£3045
63	2/01	Sthl	1m	E	STD	£2632

Total win prize-money £5677

Going (Turf): Sf: 0-0 GS: 0-1 Gd: 0-2 GF: 0-3 **Fm: 1-1**
Distance: 5f/6f: 0-0 **7f-8f: 2-9** 9f-13f: 0-6 14f+: 0-0
Track : **LH: 2-10** RH: 0-2 Tight: 0-5 **Gall: 1-1**
Aids: Bl: 0-0 Vi: 0-0 Tstrap: 0-0
Best Rating: 73 5/01 Newc 1m firm

Has won twice this season, both over a mile, although she looks in the grasp of the handicapper at the moment. Suited by Fibresand and a sound surface on turf.

Bude

(85) (66)**61**

2-y-o gr g Environment Friend-Gay Da Cheen (IRE) (Tenby)

S A Brookshaw L Briggs

Placings:0 **(3969)**

2001: 7^{0}GS

	Starts	1st	2nd	3rd	Win & Pl
Career Total (Turf)	1	0	0	0	

Going (Turf): Sf: 0-0 GS: 0-1 Gd: 0-0 GF: 0-0 Fm: 0-0
Distance: 5f/6f: 0-0 7f-8f: 0-1 9f-13f: 0-0 14f+: 0-0
Track : LH: 0-0 RH: 0-1 Tight: 0-0 Gall: 0-0
Aids: Bl: 0-0 Vi: 0-0 Tstrap: 0-0
Best Rating: 61 8/01 Bevl 7f100y gd-sft

Budelli (IRE)

108 **81**

4-y-o b g Elbio-Eves Temptation (IRE) (Glenstal (USA))

M R Channon Mrs C Roper

Placings:5/362312502004-635050220626222221**0** **(5630)**

2001: 6^{6}S, 6^{3}F, 6^{5}GF, 6^{0}F, 6^{5}GF, 5^{0}GF, 6^{2}GF, 6^{2}GF, 6^{0}GF, 6^{6}GS, 6^{2}F, 5^{6}G, 6^{2}GF, 6^{2}GF, 6^{2}G, 6^{2}GS, 5^{2}GS, 5^{1}S, 6^{0}G

	Starts	1st	2nd	3rd	Win & Pl
Career Total (Turf)	32	2	11	3	30033

81	10/01	Pont	5f	D(0-85)H	SFT	£5460
77	5/00	Ling	6f	D	GD	£3298

Total win prize-money £8759

Going (Turf): Sf: 1-5 GS: 0-5 **Gd: 1-8** GF: 0-11 Fm: 0-3
Distance: **5f/6f: 2-28** 7f-8f: 0-4 9f-13f: 0-0 14f+: 0-0
Track : **LH: 1-7** RH: 0-2 Tight: 0-1 Gall: 0-2
Aids: Bl: 0-0 Vi: 0-1 Tstrap: 0-0
Best Rating: 81 10/01 Pont 5f soft

Considering his ability a record of just two wins is pretty poor, and he has finished runner-up this season more often than is desirable, though he appears to have done little wrong in recent efforts. Suited by six furlongs, seems to handle any ground.

Budoor (IRE)

90 **79**

2-y-o b f Darshaan-Haddeyah (USA) (Dayjur (USA))

J L Dunlop Khalil Alsayegh

Placings:31 **(5014)**
2001: 8^{3}GF, 8^{1}HY

	Starts	1st	2nd	3rd	Win & Pl
Career Total (Turf)	2	1	0	1	5235

79 9/01 Hayd 1m30y D HVY £4631
Total win prize-money £4631

Going (Turf): Sf: 1-1 GS: 0-0 Gd: 0-0 GF: 0-1 Fm: 0-0
Distance: 5f/6f: 0-0 7f-8f: 0-0 **9f-13f: 1-2** 14f+: 0-0
Track : **LH: 1-1** RH: 0-0 Tight: 0-0 Gall: 0-0
Aids: Bl: 0-0 Vi: 0-0 Tstrap: 0-0
Best Rating: 79 9/01 Hayd 1m30y heavy

Made an eyecatching debut in a Leicester maiden before scoring on heavy ground at Haydock.

Bueno Vida (IRE)

81 **58**
2-y-o b c Petardia-Pat Said No (IRE) (Last Tycoon)
D J S Cosgrove Winning Circle Racing Club Ltd

Placings:000 **(5364)**
2001: 6^{0}GF, 7^{0}GS, 6^{0}GS

	Starts	1st	2nd	3rd	Win & Pl
Career Total (Turf)	3	0	0	0	

Going (Turf): Sf: 0-0 GS: 0-2 Gd: 0-0 GF: 0-1 Fm: 0-0
Distance: 5f/6f: 0-2 7f-8f: 0-1 9f-13f: 0-0 14f+: 0-0
Track : LH: 0-0 RH: 0-0 Tight: 0-0 Gall: 0-0
Aids: Bl: 0-0 Vi: 0-0 Tstrap: 0-0
Best Rating: 58 10/01 NmkR 7f gd-sft

Buffoon

93(69) (31)**59**
2-y-o ch g Bijou D'Inde-Jelabna (Jalmood (USA))
I A Balding D H Caslon

Placings:04005 **(5404)**
2001: 6^{0}GF, 6^{4}GF, 8^{0}SW, 8^{0}G, 8^{5}S

	Starts	1st	2nd	3rd	Win & Pl
Career Total (Turf)	4	0	0	0	0
Career Total (AW)	1	0	0	0	

Going (Turf): Sf: 0-1 GS: 0-0 Gd: 0-1 GF: 0-2 Fm: 0-0
Distance: 5f/6f: 0-0 7f-8f: 0-3 9f-13f: 0-2 14f+: 0-0
Track : LH: 0-3 RH: 0-0 Tight: 0-1 Gall: 0-0
Aids: Bl: 0-0 Vi: 0-0 Tstrap: 0-0
Best Rating: 66 8/01 Sals 6f212y gd-fm

Still a maiden but showed enough promise at Pontefract on his fifth start to suggest he will win a race.

Bula Rose (IRE)

95 **50**
3-y-o ch f Alphabatim (USA)-Titled Dancer (IRE) (Where To Dance (USA))
E W Tuer E Tuer

Placings:5231400-00040 **(3712)**
2001: 8^{0}GF, 11^{0}GF, 11^{0}GF, 12^{4}GF, 14^{0}G

	Starts	1st	2nd	3rd	Win & Pl
Career Total (Turf)	12	1	1	1	2971

54 6/00 Rdcr 7f G FRM £1841
Total win prize-money £1841

Going (Turf): Sf: 0-2 GS: 0-0 Gd: 0-3 GF: 0-5 **Fm: 1-2**
Distance: 5f/6f: 0-2 **7f-8f: 1-6** 9f-13f: 0-3 14f+: 0-1
Track : LH: 0-2 RH: 0-4 Tight: 0-4 Gall: 0-1
Aids: Bl: 0-0 Vi: 0-0 Tstrap: 0-0
Best Rating: 50 7/01 Muss 1m4f gd-fm

Bulawayo

(99) (61)**54**
4-y-o b g Prince Sabo-Ra Ra Girl (Shack (USA))
B A McMahon D J Allen

Placings:06/1404650-004300006042 **(5392)**
2001: 6^{0}HY, 5^{0}F, 7^{4}F, 8^{3}G, 7^{0}GF, 7^{0}GF, 7^{0}GF, 8^{0}G, 8^{6}SD, 6^{0}SD, 6^{4}SD, 6^{2}SD

	Starts	1st	2nd	3rd	Win & Pl
Career Total (Turf)	13	0	0	1	1225
Career Total (AW)	8	1	1	0	4072

69 1/00 Wolv 7f D STD £2795
Total win prize-money £2795

Going (Turf): Sf: 0-2 GS: 0-0 Gd: 0-5 GF: 0-4 Fm: 0-2
Distance: 5f/6f: 0-9 **7f-8f: 1-9** 9f-13f: 0-3 14f+: 0-0
Track : **LH: 1-11** RH: 0-2 **Tight: 1-6** Gall: 0-0
Aids: Bl: 0-0 Vi: 0-0 Tstrap: 0-0
Best Rating: 61 10/01 Wolv 6f stand

Winner of a seven-furlong maiden at Wolverhampton in 2000, his best runs of late have been over six furlongs on the same track. Stays a mile and acts on good or faster ground on turf.

Bullet

89 (49)**37**
6-y-o b g Alhijaz-Beacon (High Top)
M C Pipe Mrs Rita Butler & Mrs Gabrielle McNeela

Placings:323/245612120/00 **(5294)**
2001: 12^{0}GS, 11^{0}S

	Starts	1st	2nd	3rd	Win & Pl
Career Total (Turf)	13	2	4	2	11979
Career Total (AW)	1	0	0	0	0

72 7/99 Carl 1m4f E(0-70) FRM £2892
65 6/99 Bevl 1m3f216yF G-F £2495
Total win prize-money £5387

Going (Turf): Sf: 0-3 GS: 0-1 Gd: 0-2 **GF: 1-6 Fm: 1-1**
Distance: 5f/6f: 0-0 7f-8f: 0-0 **9f-13f: 2-11** 14f+: 0-3
Track : LH: 0-6 **RH: 2-8 Tight: 1-7** Gall: 0-2
Aids: Bl: 0-0 Vi: 0-0 Tstrap: 0-0
Best Rating: 37 10/01 Leic 1m3f183y soft

Bullfighter

(90) (70)**70**
2-y-o b g Makbul-Bollin Victoria (Jalmood (USA))
N P Littmoden Paul J Dixon

Placings:0542053200050 **(5393)**
2001: 5^{0}GS, 5^{5}SD, 5^{4}GF, 5^{2}G, 5^{0}GF, 5^{5}F, 6^{3}GS, 5^{2}G, 5^{0}GF, 6^{0}GF, 5^{0}S, 5^{5}SD, 6^{0}SD

	Starts	1st	2nd	3rd	Win & Pl
Career Total (Turf)	10	0	2	1	3557
Career Total (AW)	3	0	0	0	0

Going (Turf): Sf: 0-1 GS: 0-2 Gd: 0-2 GF: 0-4 Fm: 0-1
Distance: 5f/6f: 0-12 7f-8f: 0-1 9f-13f: 0-0 14f+: 0-0
Track : LH: 0-6 RH: 0-0 Tight: 0-4 Gall: 0-0
Aids: Bl: 0-2 Vi: 0-0 Tstrap: 0-0
Best Rating: 70 10/01 Wolv 5f stand

Bullsefia (USA)

105 **78**
3-y-o gr c Holy Bull (USA)-Yousefia (USA) (Danzig (USA))
B W Hills Maktoum Al Maktoum

Placings:32-1500 **(3288)**
2001: 7^{1}GF, 7^{5}GF, 7^{0}G, 7^{0}GS

	Starts	1st	2nd	3rd	Win & Pl
Career Total (Turf)	6	1	1	1	5854

56 5/01 Wwck 7f26y D G-F £4013
Total win prize-money £4014

Going (Turf): Sf: 0-0 GS: 0-1 Gd: 0-1 **GF: 1-4** Fm: 0-0
Distance: 5f/6f: 0-1 **7f-8f: 1-5** 9f-13f: 0-0 14f+: 0-0
Track : **LH: 1-4** RH: 0-0 Tight: 0-0 Gall: 0-1
Aids: Bl: 0-0 Vi: 0-0 Tstrap: 0-0
Best Rating: 78 6/01 Ling 7f gd-fm

Showed ability at two and got off the mark with a narrow win at Warwick on his reappearance. Disappointing since, he needs to learn to settle.

Bundy

101 (44)**56**
5-y-o b g Ezzoud (IRE)-Sanctuary Cove (Habitat)
M Dods A J Henderson

Placings:63004131000/343644000/15311003006-60032005054 **(5287)**
2001: 6^{6}GF, 6^{0}GF, 6^{0}GF, 6^{3}GF, 5^{2}GS, 6^{0}GS, 7^{0}GF, 6^{5}G, 7^{0}G, 6^{5}HY, 6^{4}HY

	Starts	1st	2nd	3rd	Win & Pl
Career Total (Turf)	41	5	1	7	25103
Career Total (AW)	1	0	0	0	

64 7/00 Pont 6f D(0-80)H GD £7702
62 6/00 Pont 6f E(0-70)H G-F £3094
60 3/00 Nott 6f15y E(0-70)H GD £3255
71 8/98 Wwck 6f E H G-F £3262
68 7/98 Newc 6f F GD £2221
Total win prize-money £19536

Going (Turf): Sf: 0-5 GS: 0-8 **Gd: 3-12** GF: 2-15 Fm: 0-1
Distance: **5f/6f: 4-23** 7f-8f: 1-18 9f-13f: 0-1 14f+: 0-0
Track : **LH: 3-11** RH: 0-4 Tight: 0-2 Gall: 0-3
Aids: Bl: 0-1 Vi: 0-0 Tstrap: 0-0
Best Rating: 64 7/01 Leic 5f218y gd-sft

Bunkum

93(94) (60)**54d**
3-y-o b g Robellino (USA)-Spinning Mouse (Bustino)
M L W Bell Lord Hartington

Placings:000-1005 **(2754)**
2001: 12^{1}SD, 11^{0}F, 12^{0}GF, 14^{5}GF

	Starts	1st	2nd	3rd	Win & Pl
Career Total (Turf)	6	0	0	0	0
Career Total (AW)	1	1	0	0	2324

60 5/01 Wolv 1m4f F(0-65)H STD £2324
Total win prize-money £2324

Going (Turf): Sf: 0-2 GS: 0-0 Gd: 0-0 GF: 0-3 Fm: 0-1
Distance: 5f/6f: 0-1 7f-8f: 0-2 **9f-13f: 1-3** 14f+: 0-1
Track : **LH: 1-4** RH: 0-2 **Tight: 1-2** Gall: 0-0
Aids: Bl: 0-0 Vi: 0-1 Tstrap: 0-0
Best Rating: 60 5/01 Wolv 1m4f stand

Bunty

98(100) (35)**36**
5-y-o b m Presidium-Shirlstar Investor (Some Hand)
R C Spicer G D J Linder

Placings:43040460500/000600241600016/406040000400-023000500000 **(3412)**
2001: 8^{0}SD, 8^{2}SD, 9^{3}SW, 8^{0}SW, 8^{0}SW, 8^{0}HY, 6^{5}GS, 7^{0}GF, 5^{0}G, 7^{0}GF, 5^{0}GS, 7^{0}GF

	Starts	1st	2nd	3rd	Win & Pl
Career Total (Turf)	34	2	1	1	8579
Career Total (AW)	15	0	1	1	947

50 11/99 Nott 1m54y F(0-60)H SFT £3197
47 7/99 Epsm 1m114y E(0-70)H G-F £3598
Total win prize-money £6796

Going (Turf): Sf: 1-5 GS: 0-8 Gd: 0-6 **GF: 1-12** Fm: 0-3
Distance: 5f/6f: 0-14 7f-8f: 0-25 **9f-13f: 2-10** 14f+: 0-0
Track : **LH: 2-27** RH: 0-4 **Tight: 1-10** Gall: 0-3
Aids: Bl: 0-0 Vi: 0-0 Tstrap: 0-0
Best Rating: 36 6/01 Leic 5f218y good

Burgundy

104(111) (97)**78**
4-y-o b g Lycius (USA)-Decant (Rousillon (USA))
S Dow Mrs Mandy Hall

Placings:12-6002450550 (5607)
2001: 8^{6}SD, 10^{0}G, 8^{0}GF, 10^{2}GF, 10^{4}G, 10^{5}G, 10^{0}GF, 10^{5}G, 10^{5}S, 8^{0}GS

	Starts	1st	2nd	3rd	Win & Pl
Career Total (Turf)	10	1	1	0	6280
Career Total (AW)	2	0	1	0	1293

73	8/00	Sals	6f212y	D	G-F	£3497

Total win prize-money £3497

Going (Turf): Sf: 0-1 GS: 0-1 Gd: 0-4 **GF: 1-4** Fm: 0-0
Distance: 5f/6f: 0-0 **7f-8f: 1-4** 9f-13f: 0-8 14f+: 0-0
Track : LH: 0-2 RH: 0-6 Tight: 0-2 Gall: 0-4
Aids: Bl: 0-0 Vi: 0-0 Tstrap: 0-0
Best Rating: 87 6/01 NmkJ 1m2f gd-fm

Lightly raced, he won on his debut at Salisbury last season and ran well on his first start on sand when runner-up to Hail The Chief. Yet to win in 2001, but has run some decent races. Suited by ten furlongs and fast ground.

Burj Al Arab

96 **82**
2-y-o b c Alderbrook-Princess Moodyshoe (Jalmood (USA))
M C Pipe Mrs Alison C Farrant

Placings:553 (5094)
2001: 6^{5}GF, 8^{5}G, 8^{3}GS

	Starts	1st	2nd	3rd	Win & Pl
Career Total (Turf)	3	0	0	1	699

Going (Turf): Sf: 0-0 GS: 0-1 Gd: 0-1 GF: 0-1 Fm: 0-0
Distance: 5f/6f: 0-1 7f-8f: 0-1 9f-13f: 0-1 14f+: 0-0
Track : LH: 0-0 RH: 0-0 Tight: 0-0 Gall: 0-0
Aids: Bl: 0-0 Vi: 0-0 Tstrap: 0-0
Best Rating: 82 9/01 Chep 1m14y good

A half-brother to decent juvenile Misbehave, he was beaten in maidens on various surfaces in the second half of 2001. Suited by a mile.

Burn Baby Burn (IRE)

80 **47**
2-y-o b f King's Theatre (IRE)-Tropicaro (FR) (Caro)
R Hollinshead Geoff Lloyd

Placings:0 (5682)
2001: 7^{0}S

	Starts	1st	2nd	3rd	Win & Pl
Career Total (Turf)	1	0	0	0	

Going (Turf): Sf: 0-1 GS: 0-0 Gd: 0-0 GF: 0-0 Fm: 0-0
Distance: 5f/6f: 0-0 7f-8f: 0-1 9f-13f: 0-0 14f+: 0-0
Track : LH: 0-0 RH: 0-0 Tight: 0-0 Gall: 0-0
Aids: Bl: 0-0 Vi: 0-0 Tstrap: 0-0
Best Rating: 47 11/01 Donc 7f soft

Burning Cost

15
11-y-o br m Lochnager-Sophie Avenue (Guillaume Tell (USA))
R E Peacock R E Peacock

Placings:000/5540600/00/000/5000500/00/6 (3576)
2001: 8^{6}GF

	Starts	1st	2nd	3rd	Win & Pl
Career Total (Turf)	14	0	0	0	0
Career Total (AW)	11	0	0	0	0

Going (Turf): Sf: 0-0 GS: 0-2 Gd: 0-6 GF: 0-6 Fm: 0-0
Distance: 5f/6f: 0-1 7f-8f: 0-3 9f-13f: 0-17 14f+: 0-4
Track : LH: 0-17 RH: 0-3 Tight: 0-12 Gall: 0-0
Aids: Bl: 0-1 Vi: 0-0 Tstrap: 0-0
Best Rating: 15 8/01 Wwck 1m22y gd-fm

Burning Impulse

107 **86+**
3-y-o b c Cadeaux Genereux-Isle Of Flame (Shirley Heights)
J Noseda Mrs Seamus Burns

Placings:2101 (5366)
2001: 8^{2}GF, 8^{1}F, 7^{0}G, 8^{1}GS

	Starts	1st	2nd	3rd	Win & Pl
Career Total (Turf)	4	2	1	0	11753

86	10/01	NmkR	1m	C(0-100)H	G-S	£7328
62	9/01	Newc	1m	D	FRM	£2940

Total win prize-money £10269

Going (Turf): Sf: 0-0 **GS: 1-1** Gd: 0-1 GF: 0-1 **Fm: 1-1**
Distance: 5f/6f: 0-0 **7f-8f: 2-4** 9f-13f: 0-0 14f+: 0-0
Track : **LH: 1-1** RH: 0-0 Tight: 0-0 **Gall: 1-1**
Aids: Bl: 0-0 Vi: 0-0 Tstrap: 0-0
Best Rating: 86 10/01 NmkR 1m gd-sft

Easily landed the odds in a weak Newcastle maiden before showing an admirable attitude to take a decent mile handicap at Newmarket in October. Has plenty of scope and looks capable of improvement. Has joined Paul Webber to go hurdling.

Burning Sun (USA)

92 **75+**
2-y-o b c Danzig (USA)-Media Nox (Lycius (USA))
H R A Cecil K Abdulla

Placings:5 (5682)
2001: 7^{5}S

	Starts	1st	2nd	3rd	Win & Pl
Career Total (Turf)	1	0	0	0	0

Going (Turf): Sf: 0-1 GS: 0-0 Gd: 0-0 GF: 0-0 Fm: 0-0
Distance: 5f/6f: 0-0 7f-8f: 0-1 9f-13f: 0-0 14f+: 0-0
Track : LH: 0-0 RH: 0-0 Tight: 0-0 Gall: 0-0
Aids: Bl: 0-0 Vi: 0-0 Tstrap: 0-0
Best Rating: 75 11/01 Donc 7f soft

Burning Truth (USA)

(106) **(76)63**
7-y-o ch g Known Fact (USA)-Galega (Sure Blade (USA))
Mrs A Duffield Middleham Park Racing Iv

Placings:0/332232/0002205/033044/6020014110-4160005 (5347)
2001: 11^{4}SW, 12^{1}SD, 10^{6}G, 9^{0}GF, 8^{0}GF, 10^{0}GF, 8^{5}SD

	Starts	1st	2nd	3rd	Win & Pl
Career Total (Turf)	28	0	6	5	13754
Career Total (AW)	9	4	0	0	11064

64	3/01	Wolv	1m4f	D(0-75)	STD	£3191
76	12/00	Wolv	1m1f79y	E(0-70)H	STD	£2730
67	11/00	Ling	1m2f	E(0-70)H	STD	£2320
66	10/00	Wolv	1m100y	F(0-60)H	STD	£2534

Total win prize-money £10777

Going (Turf): Sf: 0-6 GS: 0-6 Gd: 0-4 GF: 0-12 Fm: 0-0
Distance: 5f/6f: 0-0 7f-8f: 0-11 **9f-13f: 4-26** 14f+: 0-0
Track : **LH: 4-20** RH: 0-9 **Tight: 4-14** Gall: 0-2
Aids: Bl: 0-0 Vi: 0-0 Tstrap: 0-0
Best Rating: 75 2/01 Sthl 1m3f slow

Despite finishing in the frame in varied company, he looks very one-paced and has had plenty of chances on turf. Much better on Fibresand and should continue to pay his way on that surface.

Burra Sahib

89(96) **(48)13**
5-y-o b g First Trump-Old Flower (Persian Bold)
J Akehurst Fraser Miller

Placings:600/5-50 (4523)
2001: 16^{5}SD, 16^{0}GF

	Starts	1st	2nd	3rd	Win & Pl
Career Total (Turf)	1	0	0	0	
Career Total (AW)	5	0	0	0	0

Going (Turf): Sf: 0-0 GS: 0-0 Gd: 0-0 GF: 0-1 Fm: 0-0
Distance: 5f/6f: 0-1 7f-8f: 0-2 9f-13f: 0-0 14f+: 0-3
Track : LH: 0-6 RH: 0-0 Tight: 0-4 Gall: 0-0
Aids: Bl: 0-0 Vi: 0-0 Tstrap: 0-0
Best Rating: 38 1/01 Ling 2m stand

Burry Brave

81 **73?**
2-y-o b g Presidium-Keep Mum (Mummy's Pet)
J S Goldie Patrick H Marron

Placings:06400 (4538)
2001: 6^{0}GS, 6^{6}GS, 6^{4}G, 7^{0}GF, 7^{0}GF

	Starts	1st	2nd	3rd	Win & Pl
Career Total (Turf)	5	0	0	0	0

Going (Turf): Sf: 0-0 GS: 0-2 Gd: 0-1 GF: 0-2 Fm: 0-0
Distance: 5f/6f: 0-3 7f-8f: 0-2 9f-13f: 0-0 14f+: 0-0
Track : LH: 0-0 RH: 0-0 Tight: 0-0 Gall: 0-0
Aids: Bl: 0-0 Vi: 0-0 Tstrap: 0-0
Best Rating: 73 8/01 Newc 6f good

Buscador (USA)

95 **70**
2-y-o ch c Crafty Prospector (USA)-Fairway Flag (USA) (Fairway Phantom (USA))
E L James Tantivy Racing Partnership

Placings:0660 (4577)
2001: 6^{0}GF, 6^{6}GF, 6^{6}F, 6^{0}G

	Starts	1st	2nd	3rd	Win & Pl
Career Total (Turf)	4	0	0	0	0

Going (Turf): Sf: 0-0 GS: 0-0 Gd: 0-1 GF: 0-2 Fm: 0-1
Distance: 5f/6f: 0-1 7f-8f: 0-3 9f-13f: 0-0 14f+: 0-0
Track : LH: 0-0 RH: 0-0 Tight: 0-0 Gall: 0-0
Aids: Bl: 0-0 Vi: 0-0 Tstrap: 0-0
Best Rating: 70 7/01 Chep 6f16y gd-fm

Bushie Bill

99 **73**
3-y-o ch g Captain Webster-Mistress Royal (Royalty)
P R Hedger Bill Broomfield

Placings:0304 (5463)
2001: 12^{0}G, 11^{3}G, 12^{0}GF, 11^{4}G

	Starts	1st	2nd	3rd	Win & Pl
Career Total (Turf)	4	0	0	1	843

Going (Turf): Sf: 0-0 GS: 0-0 Gd: 0-3 GF: 0-1 Fm: 0-0
Distance: 5f/6f: 0-0 7f-8f: 0-0 9f-13f: 0-4 14f+: 0-0
Track : LH: 0-2 RH: 0-2 Tight: 0-2 Gall: 0-0
Aids: Bl: 0-0 Vi: 0-0 Tstrap: 0-0
Best Rating: 73 9/01 Kemp 1m4f gd-fm

Bustle (USA)

95(78) **(11)48**
3-y-o ch f Chief Honcho (USA)-Parliament House (USA) (General Assembly (USA))
J A R Toller P C J Dalby

Placings:00-00350 (4858)
2001: 5^{0}SD, 8^{0}GF, 16^{3}GF, 14^{5}S, 15^{0}GF

	Starts	1st	2nd	3rd	Win & Pl
Career Total (Turf)	6	0	0	1	334
Career Total (AW)	1	0	0	0	

Going (Turf): Sf: 0-1 GS: 0-1 Gd: 0-0 GF: 0-4 Fm: 0-0
Distance: 5f/6f: 0-2 7f-8f: 0-1 9f-13f: 0-1 14f+: 0-3
Track : LH: 0-3 RH: 0-2 Tight: 0-4 Gall: 0-1
Aids: Bl: 0-0 Vi: 0-0 Tstrap: 0-0
Best Rating: 48 8/01 Folk 2m93y gd-fm

Bustling Rio (IRE)

(104) (73+)**74**
5-y-o b g Up And At 'Em-Une Venitienne (FR) (Green Dancer (USA))
P C Haslam Rio Stainless Engineering Limited

Placings:000/4314143421/15001115135-21 (0049)
2001: 16^{2}SD, 16^{1}SD

	Starts	1st	2nd	3rd	Win & Pl
Career Total (Turf)	11	5	0	1	23760
Career Total (AW)	15	4	2	2	14225

73	1/01	Wolv	2m46y	D(0-85)H	STD	£2877
72	8/00	Bevl	2m35y	D(0-80)H	G-F	£4342
64	7/00	Donc	2m110y	F(0-80)H	GD	£2247
65	7/00	Bevl	2m35y	E(0-70)H	GD	£4628
57	6/00	Pont	2m1f216y	D(0-80)H	G-F	£7345
66	1/00	Sthl	2m	E(0-70)H	STD	£3526
60	11/99	Sthl	2m	E(0-75)H	STD	£2691
56	5/99	Pont	1m4f8y	D(0-80)H	GD	£4175
55	2/99	Sthl	1m3f	F(0-60)H	STD	£2633

Total win prize-money £34465

Going (Turf): Sf: 0-0 GS: 0-1 **Gd: 3-4** GF: 2-5 Fm: 0-1
Distance: 5f/6f: 0-2 7f-8f: 0-2 9f-13f: 2-5 **14f+: 7-17**
Track : **LH: 7-21** RH: 2-3 **Tight: 3-9** Gall: 1-3
Aids: Bl: 0-0 Vi: 0-0 Tstrap: 0-0
Best Rating: 73 1/01 Wolv 2m46y stand

A winner on the All-Weather and turf, he stepped up successfully to two miles at Southwell during the winter.

Busy Busy Bee

88(100) (37)**18**
4-y-o gr f Batshoof-Rectitude (Runnymede)
N P Littmoden The Busy Bee Partnership

Placings:002/504646442-2615506 0000 (5534)
2001: 11^{2}SD, 12^{6}SD, 9^{1}SW, 9^{5}SD, 9^{5}SD, 8^{0}SD, 9^{6}SD, 9^{0}G, 12^{0}G, 9^{0}SW, 11^{0}S

	Starts	1st	2nd	3rd	Win & Pl
Career Total (Turf)	5	0	0	0	
Career Total (AW)	18	1	3	0	4961

47	1/01	Wolv	1m1f79y	D	SLW	£2597

Total win prize-money £2597

Going (Turf): Sf: 0-1 GS: 0-0 Gd: 0-2 GF: 0-2 Fm: 0-0
Distance: 5f/6f: 0-0 7f-8f: 0-3 **9f-13f: 1-20** 14f+: 0-0
Track : **LH: 1-21** RH: 0-2 **Tight: 1-19** Gall: 0-0
Aids: **Bl: 1-6** Vi: 0-3 Tstrap: 0-0
Best Rating: 48 2/01 Wolv 1m1f79y stand

Butrinto

99(101) (60)**61**
7-y-o ch g Anshan-Bay Bay (Bay Express)
B R Johnson Miss Julie Reeves

Placings:0366140/001005000625100/0250000000/506114023220540-014636025140 (5025)
2001: 7^{0}SW, 8^{1}SD, 8^{4}SD, 13^{6}SD, 8^{3}SD, 9^{6}GF, 7^{0}G, 7^{2}GF, 7^{5}G, 7^{1}GF, 7^{4}GF, 6^{0}S

	Starts	1st	2nd	3rd	Win & Pl
Career Total (Turf)	40	5	4	2	22460
Career Total (AW)	20	2	2	1	6590

49	8/01	Brig	7f214y	E	G-F	£2758
57	2/01	Wolv	1m100y	F(0-60)	STD	£2177
58	5/00	Brig	6f209y	F(0-60)H	FRM	£2194
50	5/00	Brig	6f209y	E(0-70)H	FRM	£2905
70	12/98	Ling	7f	E(0-75)H	STD	£2463
74	5/98	Newb	6f8y	D(0-80)H	GD	£3678
69	8/97	Sals	6f	D	G-F	£3678

Total win prize-money £19854

Going (Turf): Sf: 0-6 GS: 0-3 Gd: 1-12 **GF: 2-13 Fm: 2-6**
Distance: 5f/6f: 1-15 **7f-8f: 5-36** 9f-13f: 1-8 14f+: 0-1
Track : **LH: 5-30** RH: 0-3 **Tight: 2-16** Gall: 0-1
Aids: Bl: 0-3 Vi: 0-2 Tstrap: 0-0
Best Rating: 61 9/01 Ling 7f140y gd-fm

Fair handicapper who stays a mile but is possibly better at seven. Acts on All-Weather and fast ground on turf. Most recent wins have been in claimers.

Buttermans Bay

74 **35**
4-y-o b g Muhtarram (USA)-River Fantasy (USA) (Irish River (FR))
C F Wall Mrs J Harman

Placings:0 (0758)
2001: 7^{0}S

	Starts	1st	2nd	3rd	Win & Pl
Career Total (Turf)	1	0	0	0	

Going (Turf): Sf: 0-1 GS: 0-0 Gd: 0-0 GF: 0-0 Fm: 0-0
Distance: 5f/6f: 0-0 7f-8f: 0-1 9f-13f: 0-0 14f+: 0-0
Track : LH: 0-0 RH: 0-1 Tight: 0-0 Gall: 0-1
Aids: Bl: 0-0 Vi: 0-0 Tstrap: 0-0
Best Rating: 35 4/01 Kemp 7f soft

Butterwick Chief

52
4-y-o b g Be My Chief (USA)-Swift Return (Double Form)
R A Fahey P S Cresswell

Placings:0400-0 (5531)
2001: 16^{0}HY

	Starts	1st	2nd	3rd	Win & Pl
Career Total (Turf)	5	0	0	0	259

Going (Turf): Sf: 0-3 GS: 0-1 Gd: 0-0 GF: 0-1 Fm: 0-0
Distance: 5f/6f: 0-0 7f-8f: 0-1 9f-13f: 0-3 14f+: 0-1
Track : LH: 0-3 RH: 0-2 Tight: 0-2 Gall: 0-0
Aids: Bl: 0-1 Vi: 0-0 Tstrap: 0-0
Best Rating: 35 4/01 Kemp 7f soft

Buying A Dream (IRE)

104 **49**
4-y-o ch g Prince Of Birds (USA)-Cartagena Lady (IRE) (Prince Rupert (FR))
Andrew Turnell Mrs Claire Hollowood

Placings:0124/30-0006600240 (5167)
2001: 9^{0}HY, 10^{0}S, 8^{0}GF, 10^{0}F, 10^{6}F, 11^{6}S, 12^{0}G, 10^{0}G, 10^{2}G, 9^{4}GF, 12^{0}GS

	Starts	1st	2nd	3rd	Win & Pl
Career Total (Turf)	17	1	2	1	6915

56	6/99	Thsk	7f	F	G-F	£2526

Total win prize-money £2526

Going (Turf): Sf: 0-3 GS: 0-1 Gd: 0-6 **GF: 1-4** Fm: 0-3
Distance: 5f/6f: 0-2 **7f-8f: 1-2** 9f-13f: 0-13 14f+: 0-0
Track : **LH: 1-12** RH: 0-4 **Tight: 1-5** Gall: 0-1
Aids: Bl: 0-2 Vi: 0-0 Tstrap: 0-0
Best Rating: 50 6/01 Ling 1m2f firm

Buz Kiri (USA)

(94) (59)**57**
3-y-o b c Gulch (USA)-Whitecorners (USA) (Caro)
A W Carroll Serafino Agodino

Placings:065-35226000 (5348)
2001: 11^{3}G, 11^{5}F, 14^{2}GF, 16^{2}G, 15^{6}G, 14^{0}S, 16^{0}G, 12^{0}SD

	Starts	1st	2nd	3rd	Win & Pl
Career Total (Turf)	8	0	2	1	2738
Career Total (AW)	3	0	0	0	0

Going (Turf): **Sf: 0-2 GS: 0-0 Gd: 0-4 GF: 0-1 Fm: 0-1**
Distance: 5f/6f: 0-1 7f-8f: 0-2 9f-13f: 0-3 14f+: 0-5
Track : LH: 0-8 RH: 0-2 Tight: 0-5 Gall: 0-0
Aids: Bl: 0-0 Vi: 0-0 Tstrap: 0-0
Best Rating: 57 7/01 Chep 2m49y good

By Definition (IRE)

91 **52**
3-y-o br/gr f Definite Article-Miss Goodbody (Castle Keep)
P W Harris The Definite Dozen

Placings:00-00330 (2835)
2001: 7^{0}S, 8^{0}G, 7^{3}F, 8^{3}GF, 8^{0}GF

	Starts	1st	2nd	3rd	Win & Pl
Career Total (Turf)	7	0	0	2	635

Going (Turf): **Sf: 0-1 GS: 0-0 Gd: 0-1 GF: 0-4 Fm: 0-1**
Distance: 5f/6f: 0-1 7f-8f: 0-4 9f-13f: 0-2 14f+: 0-0
Track : LH: 0-1 RH: 0-1 Tight: 0-0 Gall: 0-1
Aids: Bl: 0-0 Vi: 0-0 Tstrap: 0-0
Best Rating: 52 5/01 Brig 7f214y firm

Bylaw (USA)

104 **93**
3-y-o b f Lear Fan (USA)-Byre Bird (USA) (Diesis)
J H M Gosden Sheikh Mohammed

Placings:203-402122633 (4803)
2001: 8^{4}GS, 9^{0}G, 13^{2}G, 12^{1}GS, 12^{2}GF, 13^{2}GF, 14^{6}G, 15^{3}S, 17^{3}F

	Starts	1st	2nd	3rd	Win & Pl
Career Total (Turf)	12	1	4	3	16938

83	6/01	Sals	1m4f	D(0-80)H	G-S	£4387

Total win prize-money £4388

Going (Turf): Sf: 0-3 **GS: 1-2** Gd: 0-3 GF: 0-3 Fm: 0-1
Distance: 5f/6f: 0-0 7f-8f: 0-2 **9f-13f: 1-5** 14f+: 0-5
Track : LH: 0-3 **RH: 1-5 Tight: 1-5** Gall: 0-1
Aids: **Bl: 1-6** Vi: 0-0 Tstrap: 0-0
Best Rating: 93 8/01 Deau 1m7f soft

Placed over seven furlongs and a mile as a juvenile, she came into her own when blinkered and stepped up to a middle distances this term. She scored at Salisbury in June and clearly enjoys front-running. Seems ideally suited by a bit of give.

Byo (IRE)

100(104) (82)**58**
3-y-o gr c Paris House-Navan Royal (IRE) (Dominion Royale)
G M McCourt (M Quinn 26/7) Jalons Partnership 2

Placings:01512435640-0543504000006000606500 (5671)
2001: 5^{0}SD, 5^{5}SD, 5^{4}SW, 5^{3}S, 5^{5}S, 5^{0}GF, 5^{4}F, 6^{0}GF, 5^{0}GF, 5^{0}GF, 5^{0}GF, 5^{0}G, 5^{6}G, 5^{0}F, 5^{0}GS, 5^{0}G, 5^{6}G, 5^{0}GS, 5^{6}HY, 6^{5}HY, 5^{0}GS, 6^{0}HY

	Starts	1st	2nd	3rd	Win & Pl
Career Total (Turf)	30	2	1	2	13414
Career Total (AW)	3	0	0	0	295

85	7/00	Bevl	5f	D	GD	£3412
67	6/00	Ripn	5f	E	G-F	£2765

Total win prize-money £6179

Going (Turf): Sf: 0-8 GS: 0-4 **Gd: 1-7 GF: 1-8** Fm: 0-2
Distance: **5f/6f: 2-32** 7f-8f: 0-0 9f-13f: 0-0 14f+: 0-0
Track : LH: 0-10 RH: 0-0 Tight: 0-7 Gall: 0-2
Aids: Bl: 0-0 Vi: 0-0 Tstrap: 0-0
Best Rating: 90 4/01 Nott 5f13y soft

Modest sprinter. Needs decent ground and is best at the minimum trip.

C'Est Fantastique (IRE)

100 **57**

4-y-o b f Hernando (FR)-Dolcezza (FR) (Lichine (USA))
E J O'Neill (P Rau 15/7) Mrs Melissa O'Neill

Placings:10410-000 **(5661)**
2001: 11^{0}S, 12^{0}GS, 16^{0}G

	Starts	1st	2nd	3rd	Win & Pl		
Career Total (Turf)	8	2	0	0	3483		
9/00	Gels	1m2f55y	H		SFT	£1613	
6/00	Hanv	1m1f110y			GD	£1677	

Total win prize-money £3290

Going (Turf): Sf: 1-3 GS: 0-1 **Gd: 1-2** GF: 0-0 Fm: 0-0
Distance: 5f/6f: 0-0 7f-8f: 0-0 **9f-13f: 2-7** 14f+: 0-1
Track : LH: 0-0 RH: 0-3 Tight: 0-1 Gall: 0-1
Aids: Bl: 0-0 Vi: 0-0 Tstrap: 0-0
Best Rating: 57 11/01 NmkR 1m4f gd-sft

Caballe (USA)

104(107) (70)**75**

4-y-o ch f Opening Verse (USA)-Attirance (FR) (Crowned Prince (USA))
S P C Woods B Allen/r Hine/r Dawson/a Duke

Placings:2/23322130-0442252 **(4461)**
2001: 10^{0}G, 8^{4}SD, 10^{4}GF, 12^{2}SD, 16^{2}GF, 16^{5}GS, 12^{2}GS

	Starts	1st	2nd	3rd	Win & Pl	
Career Total (Turf)	14	1	6	3	11230	
Career Total (AW)	2	0	1	0	1100	
41 8/00	Brig	1m1f209yE			G-F	£2717

Total win prize-money £2717

Going (Turf): Sf: 0-0 GS: 0-4 Gd: 0-5 **GF: 1-3** Fm: 0-2
Distance: 5f/6f: 0-0 7f-8f: 0-4 **9f-13f: 1-10** 14f+: 0-2
Track : **LH: 1-9** RH: 0-3 Tight: 0-6 Gall: 0-2
Aids: Bl: 0-0 Vi: 0-0 Tstrap: 0-0
Best Rating: 75 7/01 Sthl 2m gd-fm

Front-runner who handles fast ground, her only win came in a very poor maiden at Brighton in August 2000.

Caballo Nobile (USA)

84 **58**

2-y-o b f Kris S (USA)-Serene Nobility (USA) (His Majesty (USA))
B J Meehan Joe L Allbritton

Placings:00 **(5361)**
2001: 6^{0}GF, 8^{0}GS

	Starts	1st	2nd	3rd	Win & Pl
Career Total (Turf)	2	0	0	0	

Going (Turf): Sf: 0-0 GS: 0-1 Gd: 0-0 GF: 0-1 Fm: 0-0
Distance: 5f/6f: 0-1 7f-8f: 0-1 9f-13f: 0-0 14f+: 0-0
Track : LH: 0-0 RH: 0-0 Tight: 0-0 Gall: 0-0
Aids: Bl: 0-0 Vi: 0-0 Tstrap: 0-0
Best Rating: 58 10/01 NmkR 1m gd-sft

Cabaret Quest

103 **42**

5-y-o ch g Pursuit Of Love-Cabaret Artiste (Shareef Dancer (USA))
J M Bradley Miss S Howell

Placings:000/00136/0000603362-5600100 **(3932)**
2001: 9^{5}F, 8^{6}GF, 7^{0}GF, 8^{0}HD, 7^{1}GF, 8^{0}G, 8^{0}G

	Starts	1st	2nd	3rd	Win & Pl		
Career Total (Turf)	25	2	1	3	8602		
42 7/01	Bevl	7f100y	F(0-60)H		G-F	£3587	
57 5/99	Leic	1m8y	F		G-F	£2742	

Total win prize-money £6330

Going (Turf): Sf: 0-3 GS: 0-1 Gd: 0-6 **GF: 2-11** Fm: 0-4
Distance: 5f/6f: 0-1 7f-8f: 1-8 9f-13f: 1-16 14f+: 0-0
Track : LH: 0-10 **RH: 1-8** Tight: 0-9 Gall: 0-2

Aids: **Bl: 1-4** Vi: 0-0 Tstrap: 0-0
Best Rating: 42 7/01 Bevl 7f100y gd-fm

Cadeaux Cher

110 **78**

7-y-o ch g Cadeaux Genereux-Home Truth (Known Fact (USA))
B W Hills N N Browne

Placings:0224/146004/005500611001000/006000000 40/220001005055-10200000000 **(5138)**
2001: 6^{1}S, 6^{0}G, 6^{2}F, 6^{0}G, 6^{0}F, 6^{0}GF, 6^{0}G, 6^{0}G, 6^{0}G, 6^{0}G, 6^{0}G

	Starts	1st	2nd	3rd	Win & Pl		
Career Total (Turf)	60	7	5	0	92927		
84 3/01	Donc	6f	C(0-90)H		SFT	£7410	
82 7/00	Wwck	6f21y	D(0-85)H		G-F	£10790	
93 9/98	Donc	5f140y	B(0-110)H		GD	£24465	
86 8/98	Ripn	6f	B(0-105)H		G-F	£24125	
76 8/98	Leic	5f218y	F(0-65)		G-F	£2469	
78 7/98	Donc	6f	E(0-70)		G-F	£2872	
76 3/97	Donc	6f	D		G-F	£3525	

Total win prize-money £75656

Going (Turf): Sf: 1-5 GS: 0-5 Gd: 1-27 **GF: 5-20** Fm: 0-3
Distance: **5f/6f: 6-53** 7f-8f: 1-7 9f-13f: 0-0 14f+: 0-0
Track : **LH: 1-2** RH: 0-1 Tight: 0-0 Gall: 0-1
Aids: Bl: 0-5 Vi: 0-0 Tstrap: 0-0
Best Rating: 88 6/01 Pont 6f firm

A useful sprint handicapper over the years, he does not win very often these days, but decided to put his best foot forward in a soft ground six furlong Doncaster handicap at the start of this season. Needs to be produced late.

Caerdydd Fach

100(89) (14)**37**

5-y-o b m Bluebird (USA)-Waitingformargaret (Kris)
A B Mulholland Miss K Watson

Placings:03506000/56005044650/0400000000-06560360600 **(4450)**
2001: 9^{0}GS, 10^{6}GF, 8^{5}GF, 10^{6}GF, 8^{0}GF, 10^{3}GF, 8^{6}F, 9^{0}GS, 11^{6}GS, 9^{0}GF, 8^{0}GF

	Starts	1st	2nd	3rd	Win & Pl
Career Total (Turf)	30	0	0	2	630
Career Total (AW)	10	0	0	0	0

Going (Turf): Sf: 0-1 GS: 0-6 Gd: 0-9 GF: 0-12 Fm: 0-2
Distance: 5f/6f: 0-2 7f-8f: 0-11 9f-13f: 0-27 14f+: 0-0
Track : LH: 0-22 RH: 0-6 Tight: 0-18 Gall: 0-2
Aids: Bl: 0-0 Vi: 0-2 Tstrap: 0-0
Best Rating: 37 8/01 Haml 1m3f16y gd-sft

Caernomore

96 **74**

3-y-o b c Caerleon (USA)-Nuryana (Nureyev (USA))
J H M Gosden A E Oppenheimer

Placings:430 **(5464)**
2001: 9^{4}G, 9^{3}G, 11^{0}G

	Starts	1st	2nd	3rd	Win & Pl
Career Total (Turf)	3	0	0	1	1026

Going (Turf): Sf: 0-0 GS: 0-0 Gd: 0-3 GF: 0-0 Fm: 0-0
Distance: 5f/6f: 0-0 7f-8f: 0-0 9f-13f: 0-3 14f+: 0-0
Track : LH: 0-1 RH: 0-2 Tight: 0-2 Gall: 0-0
Aids: Bl: 0-0 Vi: 0-0 Tstrap: 0-0
Best Rating: 74 9/01 Gdwd 1m1f192y good

Caesarean Hunter (USA)

81 **54**

2-y-o ch c Jade Hunter (USA)-Grey Fay (USA) (Grey Dawn Ii)
S Kirk Frank Brady

Placings:000 **(5290)**
2001: 7^{0}GF, 8^{0}G, 7^{0}S

	Starts	1st	2nd	3rd	Win & Pl
Career Total (Turf)	3	0	0	0	

Going (Turf): Sf: 0-1 GS: 0-0 Gd: 0-1 GF: 0-1 Fm: 0-0
Distance: 5f/6f: 0-0 7f-8f: 0-3 9f-13f: 0-0 14f+: 0-0
Track : LH: 0-0 RH: 0-1 Tight: 0-0 Gall: 0-0
Aids: Bl: 0-0 Vi: 0-0 Tstrap: 0-0
Best Rating: 54 8/01 Newb 7f gd-fm

Cafe Grande (IRE)

104 **85+**

3-y-o b c Grand Lodge (USA)-Olean (Sadler's Wells (USA))
M A Jarvis Ivan Allan

Placings:2-21 **(4720)**
2001: 10^{2}S, 10^{1}G

	Starts	1st	2nd	3rd	Win & Pl		
Career Total (Turf)	3	1	2	0	8451		
78 9/01	Epsm	1m2f18y	D		GD	£4290	

Total win prize-money £4290

Going (Turf): Sf: 0-2 GS: 0-0 **Gd: 1-1** GF: 0-0 Fm: 0-0
Distance: 5f/6f: 0-0 7f-8f: 0-1 **9f-13f: 1-2** 14f+: 0-0
Track : **LH: 1-2** RH: 0-0 **Tight: 1-2** Gall: 0-0
Aids: Bl: 0-0 Vi: 0-0 Tstrap: 0-0
Best Rating: 85 8/01 Epsm 1m2f18y soft

Cafeteria Bay (USA)

100 **102**

3-y-o ch c Sky Classic (CAN)-Go On Zen (USA) (Zen (USA))
K R Burke Kenneth Lau

Placings:1315-040 **(1598)**
2001: 9^{0}S, 8^{4}GF, 8^{0}GF

	Starts	1st	2nd	3rd	Win & Pl		
Career Total (Turf)	7	2	0	1	9529		
89 9/00	Leic	7f9y	D		G-S	£4199	
79 8/00	Yarm	6f3y	D		G-F	£3461	

Total win prize-money £7660

Going (Turf): Sf: 0-2 **GS: 1-1** Gd: 0-1 **GF: 1-3** Fm: 0-0
Distance: 5f/6f: 0-0 **7f-8f: 2-5** 9f-13f: 0-2 14f+: 0-0
Track : LH: 0-2 RH: 0-0 Tight: 0-1 Gall: 0-0
Aids: Bl: 0-0 Vi: 0-0 Tstrap: 0-0
Best Rating: 99 5/01 Thsk 1m gd-fm

He progressed well as a juvenile, winning twice, but struggled against better company afterwards. Seems suited by a positive ride.

Cair Paravel (IRE)

100 **68**

4-y-o b/br c Dolphin Street (FR)-Queen's Ransom (IRE) (Last Tycoon)
R Hannon Mrs Caroline Parker

Placings:11/530001000-040030004 **(5503)**
2001: 8^{0}GS, 8^{4}F, 7^{0}GF, 8^{0}GF, 7^{3}G, 7^{0}HY, 7^{0}GS, 7^{0}G, 7^{4}HY

	Starts	1st	2nd	3rd	Win & Pl		
Career Total (Turf)	20	3	0	2	15796		
86 7/00	Sals	1m	D(0-85)H		GD	£5681	
71 6/99	Donc	6f	D		G-S	£4170	
78 6/99	Leic	5f2y	F		GD	£2763	

Total win prize-money £12614

Going (Turf): Sf: 0-3 GS: 1-3 **Gd: 2-6** GF: 0-7 Fm: 0-1
Distance: **5f/6f: 2-3** 7f-8f: 1-16 9f-13f: 0-1 14f+: 0-0
Track : LH: 0-5 RH: 0-3 Tight: 0-2 Gall: 0-1
Aids: Bl: 0-5 Vi: 0-1 Tstrap: 0-0
Best Rating: 83 5/01 Leic 1m9y firm

Winner of three races but struggled in handicaps in

2001. Acts on most types of ground, and is suited by a mile.

Caitland

92 **63?**

2-y-o b f Puissance-Lorlanne (Bustino)
D Moffatt David Doughty

Placings:50655 **(5282)**
2001: 5^{5}GS, 7^{0}G, 8^{6}S, 8^{5}G, 8^{5}HY

	Starts	1st	2nd	3rd	Win & Pl
Career Total (Turf)	5	0	0	0	0

Going (Turf): Sf: 0-2 GS: 0-1 Gd: 0-2 GF: 0-0 Fm: 0-0
Distance: 5f/6f: 0-1 7f-8f: 0-3 9f-13f: 0-1 14f+: 0-0
Track : LH: 0-3 RH: 0-1 Tight: 0-2 Gall: 0-0
Aids: Bl: 0-0 Vi: 0-0 Tstrap: 0-0
Best Rating: 63 10/01 Ayr 1m heavy

Has not cut much ice in moderate company.

Cal Mac

100 **94+**

2-y-o b g Botanic (USA)-Shifting Mist (Night Shift (USA))
H Morrison Adrian McAlpine & Partners

Placings:04 **(4830)**
2001: 6^{0}GF, 6^{4}GF

	Starts	1st	2nd	3rd	Win & Pl
Career Total (Turf)	2	0	0	0	440

Going (Turf): Sf: 0-0 GS: 0-0 Gd: 0-0 GF: 0-2 Fm: 0-0
Distance: 5f/6f: 0-1 7f-8f: 0-1 9f-13f: 0-0 14f+: 0-0
Track : LH: 0-0 RH: 0-0 Tight: 0-0 Gall: 0-0
Aids: Bl: 0-0 Vi: 0-0 Tstrap: 0-0
Best Rating: 94 9/01 Newb 6f8y gd-fm

Cala Di Volpe (USA)

102 **89+**

2-y-o ch c Mt. Livermore (USA)-Frenchman's Cove (IRE) (Caerleon (USA))
P F I Cole Christopher Wright

Placings:3325110 **(5021)**
2001: 5^{3}S, 5^{3}GS, 5^{2}GF, 6^{5}GF, 7^{1}GF, 7^{1}S, 7^{0}HY

	Starts	1st	2nd	3rd	Win & Pl
Career Total (Turf)	7	2	1	2	16660

89	8/01	Sand	7f16y	C	SFT	£6409
89	8/01	Newb	7f	D	G-F	£7475

Total win prize-money £13884

Going (Turf): Sf: 1-3 GS: 0-1 Gd: 0-0 **GF: 1-3** Fm: 0-0
Distance: 5f/6f: 0-4 **7f-8f: 2-3** 9f-13f: 0-0 14f+: 0-0
Track : LH: 0-0 **RH: 1-2** Tight: 0-0 Gall: 0-1
Aids: Bl: 0-0 Vi: 0-0 Tstrap: 0-0
Best Rating: 89 8/01 Sand 7f16y soft

Bred to stay a mile, he ran with promise over sprint trips, but came into his own when stepped up to seven furlongs at Newbury in August before adding to that at Sandown. Acts on any ground.

Calamint

91 **73**

2-y-o gr c Kaldoun (FR)-Coigach (Niniski (USA))
J R Fanshawe Dr Catherine Wills

Placings:002 **(5620)**
2001: 7^{0}GS, 7^{0}S, 8^{2}GS

	Starts	1st	2nd	3rd	Win & Pl
Career Total (Turf)	3	0	1	0	1145

Going (Turf): Sf: 0-1 GS: 0-2 Gd: 0-0 GF: 0-0 Fm: 0-0
Distance: 5f/6f: 0-0 7f-8f: 0-2 9f-13f: 0-1 14f+: 0-0
Track : LH: 0-1 RH: 0-0 Tight: 0-0 Gall: 0-0
Aids: Bl: 0-0 Vi: 0-0 Tstrap: 0-1
Best Rating: 73 11/01 Nott 1m54y gd-sft

A 30,000gns son of a Park Hill winner, he faced stiff tasks in his first two starts before finishing runner-up in a Nottingham maiden. He looks to need a test of stamina.

Calanda

96 **45**

3-y-o b f Aragon-Henceforth (Full Of Hope)
H Candy Henry Candy

Placings:6-000000 **(5083)**
2001: 7^{0}GF, 6^{0}GF, 7^{0}GF, 7^{0}GF, 6^{0}GF, 7^{0}S

	Starts	1st	2nd	3rd	Win & Pl
Career Total (Turf)	7	0	0	0	0

Going (Turf): Sf: 0-1 GS: 0-0 Gd: 0-0 GF: 0-5 Fm: 0-1
Distance: 5f/6f: 0-2 7f-8f: 0-5 9f-13f: 0-0 14f+: 0-0
Track : LH: 0-3 RH: 0-1 Tight: 0-0 Gall: 0-2
Aids: Bl: 0-0 Vi: 0-0 Tstrap: 0-0
Best Rating: 45 7/01 Kemp 7f gd-fm

Calatagan (IRE)

88 **66**

2-y-o ch g Danzig Connection (USA)-Calachuchi (Martinmas)
Miss J A Camacho Mrs S Camacho

Placings:60 **(5088)**
2001: 7^{6}G, 6^{0}GS

	Starts	1st	2nd	3rd	Win & Pl
Career Total (Turf)	2	0	0	0	0

Going (Turf): Sf: 0-0 GS: 0-1 Gd: 0-1 GF: 0-0 Fm: 0-0
Distance: 5f/6f: 0-1 7f-8f: 0-1 9f-13f: 0-0 14f+: 0-0
Track : LH: 0-0 RH: 0-0 Tight: 0-0 Gall: 0-0
Aids: Bl: 0-0 Vi: 0-0 Tstrap: 0-0
Best Rating: 66 8/01 Newc 7f good

Calcavella

105(90) (44)**62**

5-y-o b m Pursuit Of Love-Brightside (IRE) (Last Tycoon)
M Kettle Pillar To Post Racing Partnership (iii)

Placings:3022/000/40504250-53500 **(4675)**
2001: 8^{5}SD, 7^{3}GF, 7^{5}GF, 7^{0}F, 7^{0}G

	Starts	1st	2nd	3rd	Win & Pl
Career Total (Turf)	18	0	3	2	6238
Career Total (AW)	2	0	0	0	0

Going (Turf): Sf: 0-3 GS: 0-1 Gd: 0-5 GF: 0-8 Fm: 0-1
Distance: 5f/6f: 0-6 7f-8f: 0-13 9f-13f: 0-1 14f+: 0-0
Track : LH: 0-3 RH: 0-4 Tight: 0-1 Gall: 0-3
Aids: Bl: 0-0 Vi: 0-0 Tstrap: 0-0
Best Rating: 62 5/01 Donc 7f gd-fm

Calcutta

112 **99**

5-y-o b h Indian Ridge-Echoing (Formidable (USA))
B W Hills The Hon Mrs J M Corbett & Mr C Wright

Placings:331/3400122106/0006300-0421000055145 **(5366)**
2001: 8^{0}S, 7^{4}S, 8^{2}GF, 8^{1}G, 8^{0}GF, 8^{0}G, 8^{0}GF, 8^{0}G, 8^{5}G, 7^{5}G, 8^{1}G, 7^{4}G, 8^{5}GS

	Starts	1st	2nd	3rd	Win & Pl
Career Total (Turf)	33	5	3	4	91287

95	9/01	Donc	1m	B(0-105)H	GD	£15993
96	5/01	Sand	1m14y	B(0-105)H	GD	£15399
98	9/99	Donc	1m	B(0-105)H	G-F	£14174
86	7/99	NmkJ	1m	C(0-95)H	G-F	£8415
80	7/98	Ayr	6f	D	GD	£3571

Total win prize-money £57552

Going (Turf): Sf: 0-5 GS: 0-4 **Gd: 3-15** GF: 2-9 Fm: 0-0
Distance: 5f/6f: 1-3 **7f-8f: 3-25** 9f-13f: 1-5 14f+: 0-0
Track : LH: 0-5 **RH: 1-11** Tight: 0-1 Gall: 0-7
Aids: Bl: 0-1 Vi: 0-0 Tstrap: 0-0
Best Rating: 99 10/01 NmkR 1m gd-sft

A regular in classy, big-field handicaps, his appetite for a battle has often been questioned, but this come-from-behind performer was in good form in the first part of the season and was not hard pressed to get off the mark for the year at Sandown in May. Held afterwards, he dropped to a reasonable mark and won at Doncaster in September. Stays a mile and acts on fast ground.

Caldiz

(94) (31)**31**

4-y-o b g Warning-Segovia (Groom Dancer (USA))
Mrs A L M King Mrs A L M King

Placings:666400-6603065 **(0346)**
2001: 8^{6}SD, 12^{6}SD, 12^{0}SW, 12^{3}SD, 13^{0}SD, 12^{6}SW, 16^{5}SD

	Starts	1st	2nd	3rd	Win & Pl
Career Total (Turf)	6	0	0	0	0
Career Total (AW)	7	0	0	1	198

Going (Turf): Sf: 0-1 GS: 0-1 Gd: 0-1 GF: 0-2 Fm: 0-1
Distance: 5f/6f: 0-0 7f-8f: 0-1 9f-13f: 0-11 14f+: 0-1
Track : LH: 0-10 RH: 0-2 Tight: 0-7 Gall: 0-0
Aids: Bl: 0-0 Vi: 0-0 Tstrap: 0-13
Best Rating: 31 1/01 Sthl 1m4f slow

Calgarth (IRE)

(72) (52)**28**

2-y-o b f Efisio-Waypoint (Cadeaux Genereux)
W J Haggas Mr & Mrs G Middlebrook

Placings:006 **(5346)**
2001: 6^{0}S, 6^{0}HY, 6^{6}SD

	Starts	1st	2nd	3rd	Win & Pl
Career Total (Turf)	2	0	0	0	
Career Total (AW)	1	0	0	0	0

Going (Turf): Sf: 0-2 GS: 0-0 Gd: 0-0 GF: 0-0 Fm: 0-0
Distance: 5f/6f: 0-3 7f-8f: 0-0 9f-13f: 0-0 14f+: 0-0
Track : LH: 0-2 RH: 0-0 Tight: 0-0 Gall: 0-0
Aids: Bl: 0-0 Vi: 0-0 Tstrap: 0-0
Best Rating: 52 10/01 Sthl 6f stand

Has shown bits of form over six furlongs, but improvement needed in order to win a race.

Caliban (IRE)

(96) (50)**56**

3-y-o ch g Rainbows For Life (CAN)-Amour Toujours (IRE) (Law Society (USA))
Ian Williams (N P Littmoden 17/4) Jim Edmunds

Placings:050200-0214610 **(0797)**
2001: 8^{0}SD, 9^{2}SD, 11^{1}SD, 12^{4}SD, 9^{6}SD, 11^{1}SD, 12^{0}SD

	Starts	1st	2nd	3rd	Win & Pl
Career Total (Turf)	4	0	0	0	0
Career Total (AW)	9	2	2	0	4874

43	3/01	Sthl	1m3f	G	STD	£1799
50	2/01	Sthl	1m3f	F(0-60)H	STD	£1694

Total win prize-money £3493

Going (Turf): Sf: 0-1 GS: 0-0 Gd: 0-0 GF: 0-3 Fm: 0-0
Distance: 5f/6f: 0-0 7f-8f: 0-4 **9f-13f: 2-9** 14f+: 0-0
Track : **LH: 2-10** RH: 0-0 Tight: 0-4 Gall: 0-0
Aids: Bl: 0-0 **Vi: 2-6** Tstrap: 0-0
Best Rating: 50 2/01 Sthl 1m3f stand

Caliwag (IRE)

(94) (35)**46**

5-y-o b g Lahib (USA)-Mitsubishi Style (Try My Best

(USA))
Jamie Poulton Lottie Collins Partnership

Placings:4650/000-03000040 **(5178)**
2001: 7^{0}SD, 6^{3}HY, 8^{0}GS, 7^{0}GF, 9^{0}GF, 8^{0}G, 12^{4}GF, 11^{0}HY

	Starts	1st	2nd	3rd	Win & Pl
Career Total (Turf)	14	0	0	1	1198
Career Total (AW)	1	0	0	0	

Going (Turf): Sf: 0-3 GS: 0-1 Gd: 0-3 GF: 0-7 Fm: 0-0
Distance: 5f/6f: 0-2 7f-8f: 0-8 9f-13f: 0-5 14f+: 0-0
Track : LH: 0-2 RH: 0-6 Tight: 0-4 Gall: 0-2
Aids: Bl: 0-2 Vi: 0-0 Tstrap: 0-0
Best Rating: 46 9/01 Kemp 1m4f gd-fm

Calko

(98) (49) **32**
4-y-o ch g Timeless Times (USA)-Jeethgaya (USA) (Critique (USA))
Mrs H L Walton (S R Bowring 10/4) Mrs Joanna Hughes

Placings:03006315/3111000-2600000 **(1134)**
2001: 8^{2}SW, 8^{6}SD, 8^{0}SD, 8^{0}SD, 9^{0}HY, 7^{0}SD, 9^{0}GS

	Starts	1st	2nd	3rd	Win & Pl
Career Total (Turf)	10	0	0	2	814
Career Total (AW)	12	4	1	1	10925

67	2/00	Sthl	1m	E(0-70)H	STD	£4095
69	1/00	Sthl	1m	F(0-65)	STD	£2052
66	1/00	Sthl	7f	G	STD	£1918
60	11/99	Sthl	6f	G	STD	£1913

Total win prize-money £9979

Going (Turf): Sf: 0-2 GS: 0-2 Gd: 0-5 GF: 0-0 Fm: 0-1
Distance: 5f/6f: 1-9 **7f-8f: 3-8** 9f-13f: 0-5 14f+: 0-0
Track : **LH: 4-16** RH: 0-2 Tight: 0-5 Gall: 0-0
Aids: **Bl: 4-15** Vi: 0-1 Tstrap: 0-0
Best Rating: 51 1/01 Sthl 1m slow

Call My Guest (IRE)

(94) (21)
11-y-o b g Be My Guest (USA)-Overcall (Bustino)
R E Peacock Mr Derek D & Mrs Jean P Clee

Placings:54000/6445102210/0/5000/00000/46/06 **(0311)**
2001: 16^{0}SD, 16^{6}SD

	Starts	1st	2nd	3rd	Win & Pl
Career Total (Turf)	21	2	2	0	7160
Career Total (AW)	8	0	0	0	0

	8/93	Slig	1m4f	(0-75)H	HVY	£2760
	6/93	Clon	1m4f	(0-75)H	SFT	£2245

Total win prize-money £5005

Going (Turf): Sf: 0-0 GS: 0-2 Gd: 0-2 GF: 0-1 Fm: 0-1
Distance: 5f/6f: 0-0 7f-8f: 0-0 9f-13f: 0-6 14f+: 0-8
Track : LH: 0-13 RH: 0-1 Tight: 0-6 Gall: 0-1
Aids: Bl: 0-0 Vi: 0-0 Tstrap: 0-0
Best Rating: 21 2/01 Sthl 2m stand

Call The Mark (IRE)

83 **53**
2-y-o b c Goldmark (USA)-Shalerina (USA) (Shalford (IRE))
P Mitchell Crossbar Racing Partnership (jdrp)

Placings:50 **(5459)**
2001: 8^{5}G, 8^{0}G

	Starts	1st	2nd	3rd	Win & Pl
Career Total (Turf)	2	0	0	0	0

Going (Turf): Sf: 0-0 GS: 0-0 Gd: 0-2 GF: 0-0 Fm: 0-0
Distance: 5f/6f: 0-0 7f-8f: 0-1 9f-13f: 0-1 14f+: 0-0
Track : LH: 0-1 RH: 0-1 Tight: 0-1 Gall: 0-0
Aids: Bl: 0-0 Vi: 0-0 Tstrap: 0-1
Best Rating: 53 9/01 Gdwd 1m good

Calldat Seventeen

(107) (70) **80**
5-y-o b g Komaite (USA)-Westminster Waltz (Dance In Time (CAN))
P W D'Arcy Keith Harrison & Terry Miller

Placings:0/10100300163040/024606001L00-204 **(0361)**
2001: 16^{2}SD, 16^{0}SD, 14^{4}SW

	Starts	1st	2nd	3rd	Win & Pl
Career Total (Turf)	24	3	1	2	15206
Career Total (AW)	6	1	1	0	2821

73	9/00	Nott	1m1f213y	E(0-65)	SFT	£3315
80	8/99	Epsm	1m114y	E(0-75)H	GD	£3533
79	4/99	Epsm	1m114y	E(0-70)	SFT	£4338
70	2/99	Ling	1m	F	STD	£1999

Total win prize-money £13186

Going (Turf): Sf: 2-5 GS: 0-5 Gd: 1-7 GF: 0-5 Fm: 0-2
Distance: 5f/6f: 0-0 7f-8f: 1-7 **9f-13f: 3-20** 14f+: 0-3
Track : **LH: 4-18** RH: 0-7 **Tight: 3-9** Gall: 0-5
Aids: Bl: 0-0 Vi: 0-1 **Tstrap: 1-3**
Best Rating: 70 1/01 Wolv 2m46y stand

Has been tried over a variety of trips but seems best at around ten furlongs. Effective on sand and won on his first start for 262 days at Southwell in November.

Calling Dot Com (IRE)

90 **34**
3-y-o ch c Halling (USA)-Rawya (USA) (Woodman (USA))
Sir Michael Stoute Larry C K Yung

Placings:0-000 **(3317)**
2001: 6^{0}GS, 7^{0}GS, 7^{0}G

	Starts	1st	2nd	3rd	Win & Pl
Career Total (Turf)	4	0	0	0	

Going (Turf): Sf: 0-0 GS: 0-3 Gd: 0-1 GF: 0-0 Fm: 0-0
Distance: 5f/6f: 0-1 7f-8f: 0-3 9f-13f: 0-0 14f+: 0-0
Track : LH: 0-0 RH: 0-0 Tight: 0-0 Gall: 0-0
Aids: Bl: 0-0 Vi: 0-0 Tstrap: 0-0
Best Rating: 27 7/01 Yarm 7f3y good

Calling The Shots

(104) (70) **56**
4-y-o b g Democratic (USA)-Two Shots (Dom Racine (FR))
S R Bowring D H Bowring

Placings:000/000042405-513021134220045000 04 **(5612)**
2001: 8^{5}SD, 12^{1}SD, 11^{3}SW, 16^{0}SD, 8^{2}SD, 8^{1}SD, 7^{1}SD, 7^{3}SD, 8^{4}SD, 6^{2}SD, 7^{2}GF, 5^{0}GF, 6^{0}GF, 7^{1}F, 6^{6}GF, 7^{0}GF, 5^{0}G, 8^{0}GD, 6^{4}SD

	Starts	1st	2nd	3rd	Win & Pl
Career Total (Turf)	18	0	2	0	2872
Career Total (AW)	13	3	2	2	9984

70	3/01	Wolv	7f	E(0-70)H	STD	£2891
61	3/01	Sthl	1m	F(0-60)H	STD	£1827
55	1/01	Sthl	1m4f	F(0-60)H	STD	£1662

Total win prize-money £6381

Going (Turf): Sf: 0-3 GS: 0-0 Gd: 0-3 GF: 0-10 Fm: 0-2
Distance: 5f/6f: 0-8 **7f-8f: 2-18** 9f-13f: 1-4 14f+: 0-1
Track : **LH: 3-17** RH: 0-3 **Tight: 1-5** Gall: 0-1
Aids: Bl: 0-4 **Vi: 2-13** Tstrap: 0-6
Best Rating: 70 5/01 Sthl 6f stand

Won three races at the begining of the year from seven to 12 furlongs, all of which were on Fibresand, but he has been well held since then.

Callisto (IRE)

81 **56**

2-y-o br f Darshaan-Moon Parade (Welsh Pageant)
J L Dunlop Sir Nevil Macready (susan Abbott Racing)

Placings:00 **(5603)**
2001: 7^{0}GS, 7^{0}GS

	Starts	1st	2nd	3rd	Win & Pl
Career Total (Turf)	2	0	0	0	

Going (Turf): Sf: 0-0 GS: 0-2 Gd: 0-0 GF: 0-0 Fm: 0-0
Distance: 5f/6f: 0-0 7f-8f: 0-2 9f-13f: 0-0 14f+: 0-0
Track : LH: 0-0 RH: 0-0 Tight: 0-0 Gall: 0-0
Aids: Bl: 0-0 Vi: 0-0 Tstrap: 0-0
Best Rating: 56 10/01 Leic 7f9y gd-sft

Camaraderie

102 (44) **48**
5-y-o b g Most Welcome-Secret Valentine (Wollow)
Mrs M Reveley The Mary Reveley Racing Club

Placings:66500034/330-6140150 **(4218)**
2001: 9^{6}S, 8^{1}GF, 8^{4}GF, 10^{0}F, 8^{1}F, 8^{5}GF, 9^{0}G

	Starts	1st	2nd	3rd	Win & Pl
Career Total (Turf)	17	2	0	3	7165
Career Total (AW)	1	0	0	0	0

48	7/01	Rdcr	1m	G(0-60)H	FRM	£2121
48	6/01	Newc	1m	F(0-60)H	G-F	£3010

Total win prize-money £5131

Going (Turf): Sf: 0-3 GS: 0-2 Gd: 0-5 **GF: 1-5 Fm: 1-2**
Distance: 5f/6f: 0-1 **7f-8f: 2-8** 9f-13f: 0-9 14f+: 0-0
Track : **LH: 1-11** RH: 0-2 Tight: 0-4 **Gall: 1-5**
Aids: **Bl: 2-6** Vi: 0-0 Tstrap: 0-0
Best Rating: 48 7/01 Rdcr 1m firm

Moderate handicapper, suited by fast ground.

Camaret

96 **86**
2-y-o b f Danehill (USA)-Armorique (IRE) (Top Ville)
J H M Gosden Mrs Dare Wigan

Placings:3 **(5277)**
2001: 7^{3}GS

	Starts	1st	2nd	3rd	Win & Pl
Career Total (Turf)	1	0	0	1	626

Going (Turf): Sf: 0-0 GS: 0-1 Gd: 0-0 GF: 0-0 Fm: 0-0
Distance: 5f/6f: 0-0 7f-8f: 0-1 9f-13f: 0-0 14f+: 0-0
Track : LH: 0-0 RH: 0-0 Tight: 0-0 Gall: 0-0
Aids: Bl: 0-0 Vi: 0-0 Tstrap: 0-0
Best Rating: 86 10/01 Leic 7f9y gd-sft

She showed a lot of promise on her Leicester debut and looks a ready-made winner.

Camargue

96 **53**
3-y-o ch g Pivotal-Colonial Line (USA) (Plenty Old (USA))
E A Wheeler M V Kirby

Placings:006606 **(3978)**
2001: 10^{0}GS, 10^{0}GS, 7^{6}GS, 8^{6}F, 7^{0}GF, 6^{6}F

	Starts	1st	2nd	3rd	Win & Pl
Career Total (Turf)	6	0	0	0	0

Going (Turf): Sf: 0-0 GS: 0-3 Gd: 0-0 GF: 0-1 Fm: 0-2
Distance: 5f/6f: 0-1 7f-8f: 0-2 9f-13f: 0-3 14f+: 0-0
Track : LH: 0-1 RH: 0-0 Tight: 0-2 Gall: 0-0
Aids: Bl: 0-5 Vi: 0-0 Tstrap: 0-0
Best Rating: 53 5/01 Leic 1m9y firm

Camberley (IRE)

112 **90**

4-y-o b c Sri Pekan (USA)-Nsx (Roi Danzig (USA))
P F I Cole H R H Sultan Ahmad Shah

Placings:62/322106-050046054 (5137)
2001: 8^{0}GF, 7^{5}F, 7^{0}G, 7^{0}GF, 7^{4}G, 7^{6}GF, 7^{0}GS, 7^{5}G, 8^{4}G

	Starts	1st	2nd	3rd	Win & Pl
Career Total (Turf)	17	1	3	1	47406

97 5/00 Gdwd 7f B(0-110)H SFT £32500
Total win prize-money £32500

Going (Turf): Sf: 1-1 GS: 0-4 Gd: 0-8 GF: 0-3 Fm: 0-1
Distance: 5f/6f: 0-1 **7f-8f: 1-16** 9f-13f: 0-0 14f+: 0-0
Track : LH: 0-1 **RH: 1-5** Tight: 0-1 Gall: 0-3
Aids: Bl: 0-3 Vi: 0-0 Tstrap: 0-0
Best Rating: 96 6/01 Newc 7f firm

A good mover, he ran a couple of good races in competitive handicaps in2000 before getting his head in front at Goodwood. He made a belated reappearance this term and has shown signs of encouragement. Campaigned mainly around seven furlongs so far, he does not want the ground too fast.

Cambiado (IRE)

94 **60**
3-y-o ch g Ashkalani (IRE)-Changed Around (IRE) (Doulab (USA))
J R Fanshawe Mrs David Russell

Placings:03-30 (5375)
2001: 7^{3}HY, 7^{0}G

	Starts	1st	2nd	3rd	Win & Pl
Career Total (Turf)	4	0	0	2	1041

Going (Turf): Sf: 0-1 GS: 0-0 Gd: 0-2 GF: 0-1 Fm: 0-0
Distance: 5f/6f: 0-1 7f-8f: 0-3 9f-13f: 0-0 14f+: 0-0
Track : LH: 0-2 RH: 0-0 Tight: 0-0 Gall: 0-0
Aids: Bl: 0-0 Vi: 0-0 Tstrap: 0-0
Best Rating: 60 9/01 Hayd 7f30y heavy

Cambio (IRE)

(93) (40)**60**
3-y-o b g Turtle Island (IRE)-Motley (Rainbow Quest (USA))
B R Johnson (T D Easterby 29/5) Mrs Beryl Williams

Placings:5640 (5591)
2001: 7^{5}G, 10^{6}F, 7^{4}S, 9^{0}GS

	Starts	1st	2nd	3rd	Win & Pl
Career Total (Turf)	4	0	0	0	0

Going (Turf): Sf: 0-1 GS: 0-1 Gd: 0-1 GF: 0-0 Fm: 0-1
Distance: 5f/6f: 0-0 7f-8f: 0-2 9f-13f: 0-2 14f+: 0-0
Track : LH: 0-4 RH: 0-0 Tight: 0-2 Gall: 0-0
Aids: Bl: 0-0 Vi: 0-0 Tstrap: 0-0
Best Rating: 60 10/01 Brig 7f214y soft

Cameo Cooler

75 **41**
2-y-o ch c Inchinor-Mystique Smile (Music Boy)
Miss L A Perratt Ollard Westcombe (2000) Ltd

Placings:000 (5268)
2001: 6^{0}G, 5^{0}GF, 7^{0}HY

	Starts	1st	2nd	3rd	Win & Pl
Career Total (Turf)	3	0	0	0	

Going (Turf): Sf: 0-1 GS: 0-0 Gd: 0-1 GF: 0-1 Fm: 0-0
Distance: 5f/6f: 0-2 7f-8f: 0-1 9f-13f: 0-0 14f+: 0-0
Track : LH: 0-0 RH: 0-0 Tight: 0-0 Gall: 0-0
Aids: Bl: 0-0 Vi: 0-0 Tstrap: 0-0
Best Rating: 41 9/01 Ayr 6f good

Cammaeus

94 **59**
2-y-o ch f Greensmith-Pastelle (Tate Gallery (USA))
J Akehurst David S Morley

Placings:63356520 (5458)
2001: 5^{6}GF, 5^{3}GF, 5^{3}GF, 5^{5}GF, 5^{6}GF, 5^{5}S, 5^{2}HY, 5^{0}G

	Starts	1st	2nd	3rd	Win & Pl
Career Total (Turf)	8	0	1	2	1321

Going (Turf): Sf: 0-2 GS: 0-0 Gd: 0-1 GF: 0-5 Fm: 0-0
Distance: 5f/6f: 0-8 7f-8f: 0-0 9f-13f: 0-0 14f+: 0-0
Track : LH: 0-5 RH: 0-1 Tight: 0-0 Gall: 0-4
Aids: Bl: 0-0 Vi: 0-0 Tstrap: 0-0
Best Rating: 59 10/01 Ling 5f heavy

A plating-class filly, she may have been flattered by racing on the best ground when runner-up in a heavy-ground Lingfield seller in October.

Camp Commander (IRE)

(84) (61)**86**
2-y-o b c Pennekamp (USA)-Khalatara (IRE) (Kalaglow)
C E Brittain A J Richards & S A Richards

Placings:65050 (5498)
2001: 5^{6}G, 6^{5}GF, 6^{0}G, 7^{5}S, 6^{0}HY

	Starts	1st	2nd	3rd	Win & Pl
Career Total (Turf)	5	0	0	0	250

Going (Turf): Sf: 0-2 GS: 0-0 Gd: 0-2 GF: 0-1 Fm: 0-0
Distance: 5f/6f: 0-3 7f-8f: 0-2 9f-13f: 0-0 14f+: 0-0
Track : LH: 0-0 RH: 0-0 Tight: 0-0 Gall: 0-0
Aids: Bl: 0-0 Vi: 0-0 Tstrap: 0-1
Best Rating: 86 9/01 Newb 6f8y gd-fm

He showed some promise on his second start at Newbury, but ran too freely on soft ground when trying seven furlongs on his fourth start.

Camp David (USA)

99 **102**
2-y-o b c Deputy Minister (CAN)-Alamosa (Alydar (USA))
A P O'Brien Mrs John Magnier

Placings:125 (5500)
2001: 7^{1}GY, 8^{2}Y, 8^{5}HY

	Starts	1st	2nd	3rd	Win & Pl
Career Total (Turf)	3	1	1	0	21800

83 8/01 Naas 7f G-Y £10400
Total win prize-money £10400

Going (Turf): Sf: 0-1 GS: 0-0 Gd: 0-0 GF: 0-0 Fm: 0-0
Distance: 5f/6f: 0-0 **7f-8f: 1-3** 9f-13f: 0-0 14f+: 0-0
Track : LH: 0-0 RH: 0-0 Tight: 0-0 Gall: 0-1
Aids: Bl: 0-0 Vi: 0-0 Tstrap: 0-0
Best Rating: 102 10/01 Curr 1m yield

Out of an unraced half-sister to Swain, he was a comfortable winner of a Naas maiden on easy ground on his debut, but was well beaten by his stable companion Castle Gandolfo in a Curragh Group Three.

Camzo (USA)

98(96) (74)**68**
3-y-o ch c Diesis-Cary Grove (USA) (Theatrical)
P W Harris Mrs P W Harris

Placings:0-0205450 (4721)
2001: 8^{0}S, 8^{2}SD, 10^{0}S, 9^{5}GF, 8^{4}GF, 10^{5}GF, 12^{0}G

	Starts	1st	2nd	3rd	Win & Pl
Career Total (Turf)	7	0	0	0	347
Career Total (AW)	1	0	1	0	808

Going (Turf): Sf: 0-3 GS: 0-0 Gd: 0-1 GF: 0-3 Fm: 0-0
Distance: 5f/6f: 0-0 7f-8f: 0-2 9f-13f: 0-6 14f+: 0-0
Track : LH: 0-5 RH: 0-1 Tight: 0-3 Gall: 0-1
Aids: Bl: 0-0 Vi: 0-0 Tstrap: 0-0
Best Rating: 74 3/01 Ling 1m stand

Who had shown nothing in two previous outings, finished runner-up on his second start at three on the All-Weather over a mile.

Can Pau

74 **25**
2-y-o b f Tragic Role (USA)-Distant Isle (IRE) (Bluebird (USA))
K A Ryan Tony Fawcett

Placings:00 (1124)
2001: 5^{0}S, 5^{0}GS

	Starts	1st	2nd	3rd	Win & Pl
Career Total (Turf)	2	0	0	0	

Going (Turf): Sf: 0-1 GS: 0-1 Gd: 0-0 GF: 0-0 Fm: 0-0
Distance: 5f/6f: 0-2 7f-8f: 0-0 9f-13f: 0-0 14f+: 0-0
Track : LH: 0-1 RH: 0-0 Tight: 0-0 Gall: 0-0
Aids: Bl: 0-0 Vi: 0-0 Tstrap: 0-0
Best Rating: 25 5/01 Thsk 5f gd-sft

Half-sister to 6f juvenile/mile four-year-old winner Entropy. Outpaced on first two starts over 5f.

Canada

106 **98**
3-y-o b c Ezzoud (IRE)-Chancel (USA) (Al Nasr (FR))
B W Hills W J Gredley

Placings:422-501160032 (5135)
2001: 10^{5}G, 10^{0}F, 10^{1}GF, 10^{1}GS, 10^{6}GF, 9^{0}G, 10^{0}G, 11^{3}GF, 10^{2}G

	Starts	1st	2nd	3rd	Win & Pl
Career Total (Turf)	12	2	3	1	26250

98 6/01 York 1m2f85y B(0-100)H G-S £12261
65 6/01 Ayr 1m2f D G-F £3978
Total win prize-money £16239

Going (Turf): Sf: 0-1 **GS: 1-2** Gd: 0-5 **GF: 1-3** Fm: 0-1
Distance: 5f/6f: 0-0 7f-8f: 0-2 **9f-13f: 2-10** 14f+: 0-0
Track : **LH: 2-5** RH: 0-2 Tight: 0-1 **Gall: 1-4**
Aids: Bl: 0-0 Vi: 0-1 Tstrap: 0-0
Best Rating: 98 10/01 NmkR 1m2f good

He shaped well in Listed company at Newmarket on his seasonal bow and did not need to be at best to break his maiden. Followed up in a valuable handicap at York, but has been held since. Stays ten furlongs, effective on firm and soft.

Canadian Con (USA)

100 **79**
2-y-o b/br c Foxhound (USA)-Me And Molly (USA) (Slewpy (USA))
N P Littmoden Ivan Allan

Placings:6125 (4309)
2001: 6^{6}GF, 6^{1}GF, 7^{2}G, 8^{5}GF

	Starts	1st	2nd	3rd	Win & Pl
Career Total (Turf)	4	1	1	0	3373

69 7/01 Folk 6f189y F G-F £2527
Total win prize-money £2527

Going (Turf): Sf: 0-0 GS: 0-0 Gd: 0-1 **GF: 1-3** Fm: 0-0
Distance: 5f/6f: 0-0 **7f-8f: 1-3** 9f-13f: 0-1 14f+: 0-0
Track : LH: 0-0 **RH: 1-2 Tight: 1-2** Gall: 0-0
Aids: Bl: 0-1 Vi: 0-0 Tstrap: 0-0
Best Rating: 79 8/01 Newc 7f good

A half-brother to four winners in the US. Made a strong move a furlong and a half out when winning a seven-furlong maiden at Folkestone in July, and ran well under top weight in a nursery at Newcastle.

Cancun Caribe (IRE)

103(100) (56)69

4-y-o ch g Port Lucaya-Miss Tuko (Good Times (ITY))

K McAuliffe Michael H Keogh

Placings:04301-0P320 **(5225)**

2001: 9^{0}HY, 9^{P}SW, 10^{3}S, 9^{2}HY, 10^{0}S

	Starts	1st	2nd	3rd	Win & Pl
Career Total (Turf)	6	0	1	2	2235
Career Total (AW)	4	1	0	0	2702

50 12/00 Wolv 1m100y D STD £2702

Total win prize-money £2702

Going (Turf): Sf: 0-5 GS: 0-1 Gd: 0-0 GF: 0-0 Fm: 0-0

Distance: 5f/6f: 0-0 7f-8f: 0-1 9f-13f: 1-9 14f+: 0-0

Track : LH: 1-7 RH: 0-2 Tight: 1-6 Gall: 0-2

Aids: Bl: 1-4 Vi: 0-0 Tstrap: 0-0

Best Rating: 69 10/01 Nott 1m1f213y heavy

Scored in first-time blinkers on Wolverhampton's All-Weather surface in the winter of 2000. Lightly-raced in 2001, he reappeared in April but finished tailed-off and was not seen out again until September when he was pulled-up after going wrong behind. Put in a couple of improved performances in the autumn.

Candice (IRE)

105 101

3-y-o br f Caerleon (USA)-Criquette (Shirley Heights)

E A L Dunlop Maktoum Al Maktoum

Placings:3313-304250 **(5339)**

2001: 9^{3}GF, 12^{0}GF, 8^{4}G, 10^{2}GF, 10^{5}VS, 10^{0}GS

	Starts	1st	2nd	3rd	Win & Pl
Career Total (Turf)	10	1	1	4	19100

81 8/00 Chep 1m14y D G-F £3484

Total win prize-money £3484

Going (Turf): Sf: 0-0 GS: 0-1 Gd: 0-2 GF: 1-5 Fm: 0-1

Distance: 5f/6f: 0-0 7f-8f: 0-3 9f-13f: 1-7 14f+: 0-0

Track : LH: 0-3 RH: 0-3 Tight: 0-2 Gall: 0-2

Aids: Bl: 0-0 Vi: 0-0 Tstrap: 0-0

Best Rating: 101 5/01 Gdwd 1m1f192y gd-fm

She got off the mark as a juvenile when stepped up to a mile on her third start. Third in the Lupe Stakes on her reappearance in May 2001, she was outclassed in the Oaks at Epsom. She was suited by the return to ten furlongs when second to the Lupe winner Foodbroker Fancy at Newbury. Acts on fast ground.

Candid

89 74

2-y-o ch f Lion Cavern (USA)-Shady Deed (USA) (Shadeed (USA))

B J Meehan Wyck Hall Stud

Placings:346 **(4573)**

2001: 5^{3}S, 6^{4}GF, 6^{6}G

	Starts	1st	2nd	3rd	Win & Pl
Career Total (Turf)	3	0	0	1	953

Going (Turf): Sf: 0-1 GS: 0-0 Gd: 0-1 GF: 0-1 Fm: 0-0

Distance: 5f/6f: 0-3 7f-8f: 0-0 9f-13f: 0-0 14f+: 0-0

Track : LH: 0-0 RH: 0-0 Tight: 0-0 Gall: 0-0

Aids: Bl: 0-0 Vi: 0-0 Tstrap: 0-0

Best Rating: 74 9/01 Kemp 6f good

Candleriggs (IRE)

111 98

5-y-o ch g Indian Ridge-Ridge Pool (IRE) (Bluebird (USA))

E A L Dunlop The Right Angle Club

Placings:052/16205/120-203600060 **(5266)**

2001: 6^{2}GF, 6^{0}GF, 5^{3}GF, 5^{6}GF, 6^{0}G, 5^{0}GF, 6^{0}GF, 5^{6}GS, 6^{0}GS

	Starts	1st	2nd	3rd	Win & Pl
Career Total (Turf)	20	2	4	1	36501

87 9/00 Kemp 6f C(0-95)H GD £15730

81 4/99 Kemp 6f D(0-85)H GD £4318

Total win prize-money £20049

Going (Turf): Sf: 0-3 GS: 0-4 Gd: 2-6 GF: 0-7 Fm: 0-0

Distance: 5f/6f: 2-16 7f-8f: 0-4 9f-13f: 0-0 14f+: 0-0

Track : LH: 0-0 RH: 0-0 Tight: 0-0 Gall: 0-0

Aids: Bl: 0-0 Vi: 0-0 Tstrap: 0-0

Best Rating: 98 10/01 NmkR 5f gd-sft

A comparatively lightly-raced five-year-old. Best over six furlongs, he is an able sprint handicapper who goes very well fresh, but currently looks too high in the handicap. Usually held up and likes some give in the ground.

Candothat

87(95) (56)45

3-y-o b g Thatching-Yo-Cando (IRE) (Cyrano De Bergerac)

P W Harris The Thatchers

Placings:061515000-600000 **(5497)**

2001: 5^{6}SD, 6^{0}GF, 5^{0}GF, 5^{0}GF, 5^{0}G, 5^{0}HY

	Starts	1st	2nd	3rd	Win & Pl
Career Total (Turf)	14	2	0	0	7215
Career Total (AW)	1	0	0	0	0

77 8/00 Muss 5f E GD £4290

72 7/00 Pont 5f E GD £2925

Total win prize-money £7215

Going (Turf): Sf: 0-2 GS: 0-1 Gd: 2-6 GF: 0-5 Fm: 0-0

Distance: 5f/6f: 2-15 7f-8f: 0-0 9f-13f: 0-0 14f+: 0-0

Track : LH: 1-3 RH: 0-0 Tight: 0-1 Gall: 0-0

Aids: Bl: 0-0 Vi: 0-2 Tstrap: 0-5

Best Rating: 56 4/01 Ling 5f stand

Candour

77 43

2-y-o b f So Factual (USA)-Outward's Gal (Ashmore (FR))

Mrs D Haine G Haine

Placings:00 **(5603)**

2001: 6^{0}GS, 7^{0}GS

	Starts	1st	2nd	3rd	Win & Pl
Career Total (Turf)	2	0	0	0	

Going (Turf): Sf: 0-0 GS: 0-2 Gd: 0-0 GF: 0-0 Fm: 0-0

Distance: 5f/6f: 0-1 7f-8f: 0-1 9f-13f: 0-0 14f+: 0-0

Track : LH: 0-0 RH: 0-0 Tight: 0-0 Gall: 0-0

Aids: Bl: 0-0 Vi: 0-0 Tstrap: 0-0

Best Rating: 43 11/01 NmkR 7f gd-sft

Candy Anchor (FR)

77(66) (23)38

2-y-o b f Slip Anchor-Kandavu (Safawan)

J G Given Eric Clarke

Placings:5000 **(4772)**

2001: 7^{5}GF, 7^{0}SD, 7^{0}G, 7^{0}G

	Starts	1st	2nd	3rd	Win & Pl
Career Total (Turf)	3	0	0	0	0
Career Total (AW)	1	0	0	0	

Going (Turf): Sf: 0-0 GS: 0-0 Gd: 0-2 GF: 0-1 Fm: 0-0

Distance: 5f/6f: 0-0 7f-8f: 0-4 9f-13f: 0-0 14f+: 0-0

Track : LH: 0-1 RH: 0-2 Tight: 0-0 Gall: 0-0

Aids: Bl: 0-0 Vi: 0-0 Tstrap: 0-0

Best Rating: 38 8/01 Bevl 7f100y good

Canford (IRE)

106 90

4-y-o b g Caerleon (USA)-Veronica (Persian Bold)

W Jarvis Woodcote Stud Ltd

Placings:4/1355520-62060400 **(4709)**

2001: 10^{6}HY, 10^{2}GS, 12^{0}S, 10^{6}GF, 10^{0}G, 10^{4}G, 14^{0}HY, 12^{0}G

	Starts	1st	2nd	3rd	Win & Pl
Career Total (Turf)	16	1	2	1	13540

86 5/00 Sand 1m2f7y D HVY £4368

Total win prize-money £4368

Going (Turf): Sf: 1-7 GS: 0-2 Gd: 0-5 GF: 0-2 Fm: 0-0

Distance: 5f/6f: 0-0 7f-8f: 0-1 9f-13f: 1-13 14f+: 0-2

Track : LH: 0-10 RH: 1-5 Tight: 0-1 Gall: 0-10

Aids: Bl: 0-0 Vi: 0-3 Tstrap: 0-0

Best Rating: 90 8/01 York 1m2f85y good

Useful middle-distance handicapper. Came back to form with a fine second on good to soft ground at Newbury in April, but did not improve on that.

Canlis

71 39

2-y-o b c Halling (USA)-Fajjoura (IRE) (Fairy King (USA))

B W Hills J Hanson

Placings:0 **(5343)**

2001: 6^{0}GS

	Starts	1st	2nd	3rd	Win & Pl
Career Total (Turf)	1	0	0	0	

Going (Turf): Sf: 0-0 GS: 0-1 Gd: 0-0 GF: 0-0 Fm: 0-0

Distance: 5f/6f: 0-1 7f-8f: 0-0 9f-13f: 0-0 14f+: 0-0

Track : LH: 0-0 RH: 0-0 Tight: 0-0 Gall: 0-0

Aids: Bl: 0-0 Vi: 0-0 Tstrap: 0-0

Best Rating: 39 10/01 NmkR 6f gd-sft

Canny Hill

55(89) (62)43

4-y-o ch g Bold Arrangement-Jersey Maid (On Your Mark)

D Moffatt The Sheroot Partnership

Placings:064/300500-0 **(0592)**

2001: 9^{0}S

	Starts	1st	2nd	3rd	Win & Pl
Career Total (Turf)	8	0	0	0	0
Career Total (AW)	2	0	0	1	379

Going (Turf): Sf: 0-5 GS: 0-1 Gd: 0-2 GF: 0-0 Fm: 0-0

Distance: 5f/6f: 0-1 7f-8f: 0-4 9f-13f: 0-5 14f+: 0-0

Track : LH: 0-6 RH: 0-2 Tight: 0-3 Gall: 0-0

Aids: Bl: 0-0 Vi: 0-1 Tstrap: 0-0

Best Rating: 39 10/01 NmkR 6f gd-sft

Canopy

101 72

3-y-o b f Ezzoud (IRE)-Zenith (Shirley Heights)

R Hannon The Queen

Placings:50-003340 **(5026)**

2001: 10^{0}GF, 10^{0}GF, 8^{3}GS, 8^{3}GF, 9^{4}GF, 9^{0}S

	Starts	1st	2nd	3rd	Win & Pl
Career Total (Turf)	8	0	0	2	1567

Going (Turf): Sf: 0-1 GS: 0-1 Gd: 0-1 GF: 0-5 Fm: 0-0

Distance: 5f/6f: 0-1 7f-8f: 0-2 9f-13f: 0-5 14f+: 0-0

Track : LH: 0-2 RH: 0-1 Tight: 0-1 Gall: 0-1

Aids: Bl: 0-0 Vi: 0-0 Tstrap: 0-0

Best Rating: 72 7/01 Wwck 1m22y gd-sft

Canovas Heart

103 63

12-y-o b g Balidar-Worthy Venture (Northfields (USA))
Bob Jones D S Blake And Mr M J Osborne

Placings:355/0031/1424**12**45/135110061/100601**6**6/50 5100/406501/P-00010 **(4448)**
2001: 7^{0}GF, 6^{0}GF, 7^{0}G, 5^{1}G, 5^{0}G

	Starts	1st	2nd	3rd	Win & Pl
Career Total (Turf)	**43**	**11**	**1**	**2**	**71252**
Career Total (AW)	**7**	**1**	**1**	**1**	**3699**

63	8/01	Wind	5f10y	E(0-70)H	GD	£3038
81	10/99	York	6f214y	D(0-85)H	SFT	£12009
86	9/98	Nott	6f15y	B(0-105)H	G-F	£11283
86	10/97	York	5f	D(0-80)H	GD	£6680
84	5/97	Ripn	5f	C(0-90)H	G-S	£7100
73	9/96	Yarm	5f43y	C(0-90)H	GD	£5439
71	6/96	York	5f	C(0-100)H	GD	£7765
68	5/96	Folk	5f	E(0-70)H	GD	£3343
66	4/96	Wwck	5f	E(0-70)H	GD	£3397
53	6/95	Sthl	5f	F(0-65)H	STD	£2519
54	4/95	Wwck	5f	E(0-70)H	G-S	£3786
45	10/94	Wwck	5f	D(0-75)H	SFT	£4012

Total win prize-money £70376

Going (Turf): Sf: 2-7 GS: 2-6 **Gd: 6-19** GF: 1-11 Fm: 0-0
Distance: **5f/6f: 10-38** 7f-8f: 2-8 9f-13f: 0-4 14f+: 0-0
Track : **LH: 4-12** RH: 1-2 Tight: 0-3 **Gall: 5-8**
Aids: Bl: 0-0 Vi: 0-0 Tstrap: 0-0
Best Rating: 63 8/01 Wind 5f10y good

A veteran handicapper, he showed there is life in him yet when winning at Windsor in August.

Canovas Kingdom

100 **55**

3-y-o ch g Aragon-Joan's Venture (Beldale Flutter (USA))
Bob Jones The Canova's Kingdom Partnership

Placings:050-20043 **(5593)**
2001: 7^{2}G, 8^{0}G, 6^{0}GF, 6^{4}F, 5^{3}GS

	Starts	1st	2nd	3rd	Win & Pl
Career Total (Turf)	**8**	**0**	**1**	**1**	**1191**

Going (Turf): Sf: 0-2 GS: 0-2 Gd: 0-2 GF: 0-1 Fm: 0-1
Distance: 5f/6f: 0-3 7f-8f: 0-4 9f-13f: 0-1 14f+: 0-0
Track : LH: 0-6 RH: 0-0 Tight: 0-0 Gall: 0-1
Aids: Bl: 0-0 Vi: 0-0 Tstrap: 0-0
Best Rating: 54 11/01 Brig 5f213y gd-sft

Canterloupe (IRE)

106 **81+**

3-y-o b f Wolfhound (USA)-Missed Again (High Top)
P J Makin R A Ballin & The Billinomas

Placings:14-133 **(5258)**
2001: 5^{1}GF, 5^{3}GF, 5^{3}GS

	Starts	1st	2nd	3rd	Win & Pl
Career Total (Turf)	**5**	**2**	**0**	**2**	**10751**

80	6/01	Wind	5f10y	D(0-75)	G-F	£3883
72	9/00	Bath	5f161y	D	SFT	£2918

Total win prize-money £6803

Going (Turf): **Sf: 1-2** GS: 0-1 Gd: 0-0 **GF: 1-2** Fm: 0-0
Distance: **5f/6f: 2-4** 7f-8f: 0-1 9f-13f: 0-0 14f+: 0-0
Track : LH: 1-1 RH: 1-1 Tight: 0-0 **Gall: 2-2**
Aids: Bl: 0-0 Vi: 0-0 Tstrap: 0-0
Best Rating: 81 10/01 Asct 5f gd-sft

Lightly raced, she won first time out at two and three and ran a fine race in a valuable handicap at Ascot in October. She still has scope for improvement and obviously goes well fresh.

Cantgetyourbreath (IRE)

64(92) (13)**10**

5-y-o ch g College Chapel-Cathy Garcia (IRE) (Be My Guest (USA))
B P J Baugh C Harrison

Placings:0362**31462/40340000000051/000000000-00000** **(1843)**
2001: 7^{0}SW, 7^{0}SD, 6^{0}SD, 6^{0}GF, 8^{0}GF

	Starts	1st	2nd	3rd	Win & Pl
Career Total (Turf)	**10**	**0**	**1**	**1**	**1083**
Career Total (AW)	**28**	**2**	**1**	**2**	**5459**

48	12/99	Sthl	6f	G	STD	£1574
69	11/98	Sthl	6f	G	STD	£1966

Total win prize-money £3540

Going (Turf): Sf: 0-1 GS: 0-0 Gd: 0-1 GF: 0-8 Fm: 0-0
Distance: **5f/6f: 2-22** 7f-8f: 0-13 9f-13f: 0-3 14f+: 0-0
Track : **LH: 2-29** RH: 0-0 Tight: 0-18 Gall: 0-0
Aids: **Bl: 2-21** Vi: 0-10 Tstrap: 0-0
Best Rating: 13 5/01 Wolv 6f stand

His only victory to date came when he bolted home in a seller on the Southwell Fibresand at the end of 1999, but looks very moderate now.

Cantina

108(80) (68)**85**

7-y-o b m Tina's Pet-Real Claire (Dreams To Reality (USA))
A Bailey R Kinsey,Mrs M Kinsey & Miss B Roberts

Placings:3100/0001301300/6005613045**020/0**1431110 0-00001054000 **(4826)**
2001: 8^{0}G, 7^{0}GF, 7^{0}GF, 7^{0}S, 7^{1}GF, 7^{0}F, 7^{5}GF, 7^{4}GS, 7^{0}GF, 7^{0}G, 6^{0}G

	Starts	1st	2nd	3rd	Win & Pl
Career Total (Turf)	**43**	**9**	**0**	**4**	**56983**
Career Total (AW)	**4**	**0**	**1**	**1**	**1719**

89	6/01	Ayr	7f	C(0-90)H	G-F	£10952
95	8/00	Ches	7f2y	B(0-100)H	GD	£9387
90	8/00	Ches	7f122y	C(0-90)H	GD	£8892
83	8/00	Carl	6f206y	E(0-75)H	GD	£2795
70	5/00	Bevl	7f100y	E(0-70)H	G-F	£3146
68	7/99	Rdcr	7f	G(0-70)	FRM	£1940
77	8/98	Ling	7f140y	C(0-100)H	G-F	£7327
72	7/98	Ches	7f122y	E(0-70)H	G-F	£2897
62	9/97	Catt	7f	D	G-F	£3821

Total win prize-money £51159

Going (Turf): Sf: 0-3 GS: 0-7 Gd: 3-12 **GF: 5-19** Fm: 1-2
Distance: 5f/6f: 0-5 **7f-8f: 9-41** 9f-13f: 0-1 14f+: 0-0
Track : **LH: 5-28** RH: 2-5 **Tight: 4-24** Gall: 0-0
Aids: Bl: 0-0 Vi: 0-0 Tstrap: 0-0
Best Rating: 89 6/01 Ayr 7f gd-fm

Seven furlongs and fast ground suit her admirably and she is hard to peg back when on song. She had slipped back to a fair mark when getting back to winning ways at Ayr in June and has not run too badly in some non-handicaps since. Goes particularly well on a tight left-handed track.

Canton Venture

9-y-o ch g Arctic Tern (USA)-Ski Michaela (USA) (Devil's Bag (USA))
A W Carroll Miss E J Marley

Placings:0401**50100/211112161312**06/**15262660/35/60 0040/0** **(4323)**
2001: 16^{0}GF

	Starts	1st	2nd	3rd	Win & Pl
Career Total (Turf)	**27**	**6**	**4**	**1**	**28529**
Career Total (AW)	**13**	**4**	**1**	**1**	**12650**

79	5/97	Ling	1m4f	D(0-75)H	STD	£3720
73	8/96	Brig	1m3f196y	D(0-80)H	FRM	£3496
67	7/96	Brig	1m3f196y	D(0-85)H	FRM	£3529
63	6/96	Newc	1m4f93y	C(0-90)H	FRM	£6807
61	6/96	Thsk	1m4f	D(0-80)H	FRM	£3910
54	6/96	Wwck	1m4f115y	D(0-80)H	FRM	£3655
55	5/96	Folk	1m4f	F	GD	£2381
70	5/96	Sthl	1m3f	G(0-65)H	STD	£2070
67	9/95	Wolv	1m4f	E(0-70)H	STD	£2976
65	7/95	Wolv	1m4f	F(0-65)H	STD	£2381

Total win prize-money £34926

Going (Turf): Sf: 0-0 GS: 0-0 Gd: 1-5 GF: 0-14 **Fm: 5-8**
Distance: 5f/6f: 0-0 7f-8f: 0-0 **9f-13f: 10-32** 14f+: 0-8
Track : **LH: 9-37** RH: 1-3 **Tight: 5-26** Gall: 1-2
Aids: Bl: 0-2 Vi: 0-1 Tstrap: 0-0

Capa

90 **81**

4-y-o b g Salse (USA)-Pippas Song (Reference Point)
B W Hills R J McCreery & S P Tindall

Placings:22/452-000 **(1722)**
2001: 12^{0}S, 10^{0}G, 16^{0}GF

	Starts	1st	2nd	3rd	Win & Pl
Career Total (Turf)	**8**	**0**	**3**	**0**	**4226**

Going (Turf): Sf: 0-2 GS: 0-2 Gd: 0-1 GF: 0-3 Fm: 0-0
Distance: 5f/6f: 0-0 7f-8f: 0-2 9f-13f: 0-5 14f+: 0-1
Track : LH: 0-2 RH: 0-3 Tight: 0-1 Gall: 0-2
Aids: Bl: 0-1 Vi: 0-0 Tstrap: 0-0
Best Rating: 43 5/01 NmkR 1m2f good

Capacoostic

(96) (38)**38**

4-y-o ch f Savahra Sound-Cocked Hat Girl (Ballacashtal (CAN))
S R Bowring Mr J E Reed & Mr P M Sedgwick

Placings:00**0**/002**000000-0000**2655**003**550 **(5503)**
2001: 5^{0}SD, 6^{0}SD, 6^{0}SD, 7^{0}SD, 5^{2}SD, 5^{6}S, 7^{5}GF, 8^{5}GF, 5^{0}G, 8^{0}SD, 5^{3}SD, 5^{5}GS, 6^{5}F, 7^{0}HY

	Starts	1st	2nd	3rd	Win & Pl
Career Total (Turf)	**14**	**0**	**1**	**0**	**975**
Career Total (AW)	**12**	**0**	**1**	**1**	**851**

Going (Turf): Sf: 0-3 GS: 0-1 Gd: 0-3 GF: 0-6 Fm: 0-1
Distance: 5f/6f: 0-12 7f-8f: 0-8 9f-13f: 0-6 14f+: 0-0
Track : LH: 0-10 RH: 0-2 Tight: 0-2 Gall: 0-0
Aids: Bl: 0-9 Vi: 0-0 Tstrap: 0-0
Best Rating: 38 8/01 Thsk 6f firm

Modest handicapper. Has been tried over a variety of distances but best efforts so far have been over the minimum trip. Acts on most types of surfaces but seems to have a preference for easy ground.

Capal Garmon (IRE)

107 **110**

3-y-o b g Caerleon (USA)-Elevate (Ela-Mana-Mou)
J H M Gosden R E Sangster & A K Collins

Placings:4312-500221 **(5385)**
2001: 10^{5}GS, 16^{0}GF, 15^{0}G, 15^{2}GS, 15^{2}VS, 16^{1}GS

	Starts	1st	2nd	3rd	Win & Pl
Career Total (Turf)	**10**	**2**	**3**	**1**	**57670**

110	10/01	NmkR	2m	A	G-S	£29000
86	9/00	Bath	1m2f46y	D	SFT	£3415

Total win prize-money £32416

Going (Turf): **Sf: 1-2 GS: 1-3** Gd: 0-2 GF: 0-2 Fm: 0-0
Distance: 5f/6f: 0-0 7f-8f: 0-1 9f-13f: 1-4 14f+: 1-5
Track : LH: 1-3 RH: 1-5 Tight: 1-2 Gall: 1-4
Aids: Bl: 0-0 Vi: 0-0 Tstrap: 0-0
Best Rating: 110 10/01 NmkR 2m gd-sft

Stoutly-bred out of a half-sister to Sun Princess and Saddlers' Hall, he progressed steadily when facing a trip and easy ground in the autumn of 2000. Suited by staying distances and cut in the ground, he twice ran well at Longchamp in the autumn before landing the Jockey Club Cup at Newmarket where he finished distressed.

Capallin (IRE)

(95) (50)**44**

2-y-o gr f Desert Style (IRE)-Rustic Lawn (Rusticaro (FR))
M H Tompkins M H Tompkins

Placings:04 **(5410)**
2001: 6^{0}G, 7^{4}SD

	Starts	1st	2nd	3rd	Win & Pl
Career Total (Turf)	1	0	0	0	
Career Total (AW)	1	0	0	0	0

Going (Turf): Sf: 0-0 GS: 0-0 Gd: 0-1 GF: 0-0 Fm: 0-0
Distance: 5f/6f: 0-1 7f-8f: 0-1 9f-13f: 0-0 14f+: 0-0
Track : LH: 0-1 RH: 0-0 Tight: 0-0 Gall: 0-0
Aids: Bl: 0-0 Vi: 0-0 Tstrap: 0-0
Best Rating: 50 10/01 Sthl 7f stand

Cape Coast (IRE)

100(95) (56)**69**

4-y-o b g Common Grounds-Strike It Rich (FR) (Rheingold)
N P Littmoden Miss Vanessa Church

Placings:26/00163042112630**600-0606050** **(2746)**
2001: 7^{0}SD, 7^{6}SD, 7^{0}SW, 6^{6}S, 6^{0}F, 6^{5}GF, 7^{0}GF

	Starts	1st	2nd	3rd	Win & Pl
Career Total (Turf)	19	3	3	2	17355
Career Total (AW)	7	0	0	0	0

68	9/00	Epsm	7f	D(0-80)H	GD	£7410
62	8/00	Epsm	6f	E	GD	£3640
63	5/00	Nott	6f15y	G	G-S	£2002

Total win prize-money £13052

Going (Turf): Sf: 0-5 GS: 1-2 **Gd: 2-4** GF: 0-6 Fm: 0-2
Distance: 5f/6f: 1-9 **7f-8f: 2-17** 9f-13f: 0-0 14f+: 0-0
Track : **LH: 2-14** RH: 0-2 **Tight: 2-9** Gall: 0-1
Aids: Bl: 0-1 Vi: 0-0 Tstrap: 0-0
Best Rating: 65 5/01 Sals 6f212y soft

In good form in the autumn of 2000, he has not been at his best this year.

Cape Cod (IRE)

102 **61**

3-y-o b f Unfuwain (USA)-Haboobti (Habitat)
J W Hills C Wright, E Whitehouse, D Murrell

Placings:403-000 **(2717)**
2001: 7^{0}F, 7^{0}GF, 9^{0}GF

	Starts	1st	2nd	3rd	Win & Pl
Career Total (Turf)	6	0	0	1	789

Going (Turf): Sf: 0-0 GS: 0-1 Gd: 0-0 GF: 0-4 Fm: 0-1
Distance: 5f/6f: 0-0 7f-8f: 0-4 9f-13f: 0-2 14f+: 0-0
Track : LH: 0-1 RH: 0-2 Tight: 0-0 Gall: 0-1
Aids: Bl: 0-0 Vi: 0-0 Tstrap: 0-0
Best Rating: 58 7/01 Kemp 1m1f gd-fm

Cape Of Good Hope

104 **95**

3-y-o ch c Inchinor-Cape Merino (Clantime)
D R C Elsworth D R C Elsworth

Placings:514 **(4700)**
2001: 7^{5}S, 7^{1}GS, 8^{4}GS

	Starts	1st	2nd	3rd	Win & Pl
Career Total (Turf)	3	1	0	0	5453

88	5/01	NmkR	7f	D	G-S	£4953

Total win prize-money £4953

Going (Turf): Sf: 0-1 **GS: 1-2** Gd: 0-0 GF: 0-0 Fm: 0-0
Distance: 5f/6f: 0-0 **7f-8f: 1-3** 9f-13f: 0-0 14f+: 0-0
Track : LH: 0-1 RH: 0-0 Tight: 0-0 Gall: 0-1
Aids: Bl: 0-0 Vi: 0-0 Tstrap: 0-0
Best Rating: 95 9/01 Donc 1m gd-sft

Impressed when winning a maiden in May, but was absent until running well in a conditions event four months later.

Cape Society

91 **65**

3-y-o ch f Imp Society (USA)-La Noisette (Rock Hopper)
J G Smyth-Osbourne The Cape Society Partnership

Placings:0-400 **(2451)**
2001: 8^{4}G, 8^{0}G, 11^{0}F

	Starts	1st	2nd	3rd	Win & Pl
Career Total (Turf)	4	0	0	0	0

Going (Turf): Sf: 0-0 GS: 0-1 Gd: 0-2 GF: 0-0 Fm: 0-1
Distance: 5f/6f: 0-1 7f-8f: 0-0 9f-13f: 0-3 14f+: 0-0
Track : LH: 0-2 RH: 0-1 Tight: 0-2 Gall: 0-1
Aids: Bl: 0-0 Vi: 0-0 Tstrap: 0-0
Best Rating: 65 5/01 Wwck 1m22y good

Cape Town (IRE)

113 **117**

4-y-o gr h Desert Style (IRE)-Rossaldene (Mummy's Pet)
R Hannon S A Six

Placings:12/10302333-116 **(3551)**
2001: 7^{1}G, 8^{1}GF, 8^{6}GF

	Starts	1st	2nd	3rd	Win & Pl
Career Total (Turf)	13	4	2	4	126640

117	7/01	Asct	1m	A	G-F	£36400
109	7/01	Yarm	7f3y	C	GD	£6545
112	4/00	NmkR	7f	A H	G-S	£17400
85	10/99	Ling	7f	D	G-S	£3752

Total win prize-money £64098

Going (Turf): Sf: 0-0 **GS: 2-4** Gd: 1-3 GF: 1-5 Fm: 0-0
Distance: 5f/6f: 0-0 **7f-8f: 4-13** 9f-13f: 0-0 14f+: 0-0
Track : LH: 0-3 **RH: 1-4** Tight: 0-0 **Gall: 1-6**
Aids: Bl: 0-0 Vi: 0-0 Tstrap: 0-0
Best Rating: 117 7/01 Asct 1m gd-fm

He won the Free Handicap in 2000 and ran a string of good races in warm company. After suffering a back problem, he returned in good form this season and showed his well-being with comfortable success on reappearance at Yarmouth in conditions race before out-battling Swallow Flight in a three-runner Ascot Listed event. Effective at a mile, he has plenty of toe and acts on all bar extremes of going. Outclassed in Group One company at Goodwood.

Capital Access

92 **83**

2-y-o b c Efisio-Thilda (IRE) (Roi Danzig (USA))
B J Meehan Matham Investments

Placings:3630 **(5253)**
2001: 6^{3}HY, 6^{6}GF, 7^{3}G, 6^{0}S

	Starts	1st	2nd	3rd	Win & Pl
Career Total (Turf)	4	0	0	2	1359

Going (Turf): Sf: 0-2 GS: 0-0 Gd: 0-1 GF: 0-1 Fm: 0-0
Distance: 5f/6f: 0-3 7f-8f: 0-1 9f-13f: 0-0 14f+: 0-0
Track : LH: 0-1 RH: 0-0 Tight: 0-1 Gall: 0-0
Aids: Bl: 0-2 Vi: 0-0 Tstrap: 0-0
Best Rating: 83 9/01 Epsm 7f good

Showed promise in maidens. Does not want fast going.

Capital Breeze (IRE)

80 **34**

3-y-o b c Shareef Dancer (USA)-Crystal Land (Kris)
G L Moore (D R C Elsworth 19/5) Rdm Racing

Placings:00000 **(5524)**
2001: 8^{0}GS, 10^{0}S, 8^{0}G, 11^{0}S, 10^{0}HY

	Starts	1st	2nd	3rd	Win & Pl
Career Total (Turf)	5	0	0	0	

Going (Turf): Sf: 0-3 GS: 0-1 Gd: 0-1 GF: 0-0 Fm: 0-0
Distance: 5f/6f: 0-0 7f-8f: 0-1 9f-13f: 0-4 14f+: 0-0
Track : LH: 0-2 RH: 0-1 Tight: 0-2 Gall: 0-1
Aids: Bl: 0-0 Vi: 0-0 Tstrap: 0-1
Best Rating: 34 8/01 Wind 1m67y good

Capital Lad (IRE)

82(90) (42)**22**

3-y-o br g Charnwood Forest (IRE)-Casla (Lomond (USA))
G Brown Capital Accomodation Ltd

Placings:046-050000 **(5528)**
2001: 9^{0}HY, 11^{5}SD, 9^{0}F, 11^{0}F, 12^{0}GS, 8^{0}HY

	Starts	1st	2nd	3rd	Win & Pl
Career Total (Turf)	7	0	0	0	330
Career Total (AW)	2	0	0	0	0

Going (Turf): Sf: 0-2 GS: 0-1 Gd: 0-1 GF: 0-1 Fm: 0-2
Distance: 5f/6f: 0-1 7f-8f: 0-1 9f-13f: 0-7 14f+: 0-0
Track : LH: 0-8 RH: 0-0 Tight: 0-3 Gall: 0-0
Aids: Bl: 0-1 Vi: 0-0 Tstrap: 0-0
Best Rating: 42 4/01 Sthl 1m3f stand

Caposo (IRE)

94 **43**

3-y-o gr f Common Grounds-High Mare (FR) (Highest Honor (FR))
P W Harris The Mare High Club

Placings:00-500000 **(4601)**
2001: 6^{5}GF, 5^{0}GF, 6^{0}GF, 5^{0}GF, 6^{0}GF, 5^{0}GF

	Starts	1st	2nd	3rd	Win & Pl
Career Total (Turf)	8	0	0	0	0

Going (Turf): Sf: 0-1 GS: 0-1 Gd: 0-0 GF: 0-6 Fm: 0-0
Distance: 5f/6f: 0-6 7f-8f: 0-2 9f-13f: 0-0 14f+: 0-0
Track : LH: 0-0 RH: 0-1 Tight: 0-0 Gall: 0-1
Aids: Bl: 0-1 Vi: 0-0 Tstrap: 0-0
Best Rating: 48 6/01 Sals 6f212y gd-fm

Cappellina (IRE)

(99) (49)**56**

4-y-o b f College Chapel-Santa Ana Wind (Busted)
P G Murphy Mrs John Spielman

Placings:00/00420**00054-130** **(0351)**
2001: 7^{1}SD, 8^{3}SD, 7^{0}SD

	Starts	1st	2nd	3rd	Win & Pl
Career Total (Turf)	7	0	1	0	975
Career Total (AW)	8	1	0	1	2817

49	1/01	Wolv	7f	D	STD	£2625

Total win prize-money £2625

Going (Turf): Sf: 0-0 GS: 0-1 Gd: 0-1 GF: 0-5 Fm: 0-0
Distance: 5f/6f: 0-4 **7f-8f: 1-7** 9f-13f: 0-4 14f+: 0-0
Track : **LH: 1-10** RH: 0-1 **Tight: 1-9** Gall: 0-0
Aids: Bl: 0-0 Vi: 0-0 Tstrap: 0-0
Best Rating: 49 1/01 Wolv 7f stand

Capriccio (IRE)

66 **70**

4-y-o gr g Robellino (USA)-Yamamah (Siberian Express (USA))
C G Cox Axom

Placings:43525200-0 **(5492)**
2001: 16^{0}HY

	Starts	1st	2nd	3rd	Win & Pl
Career Total (Turf)	9	0	2	1	4305

Going (Turf): Sf: 0-4 GS: 0-2 Gd: 0-1 GF: 0-2 Fm: 0-0
Distance: 5f/6f: 0-0 7f-8f: 0-1 9f-13f: 0-7 14f+: 0-1
Track : LH: 0-5 RH: 0-3 Tight: 0-4 Gall: 0-2
Aids: Bl: 0-0 Vi: 0-0 Tstrap: 0-0
Best Rating: 1 10/01 Newb 2m heavy

He handles any ground, but his best efforts to date have come over ten furlongs with cut in the ground.

Capricho (IRE)

111 **92**

4-y-o gr g Lake Coniston (IRE)-Star Spectacle (Spectacular Bid (USA))
W J Haggas M Tabor

Placings:2112001-46260 **(5005)**
2001: 6^{4}GF, 6^{6}GF, 6^{2}G, 7^{6}GS, 7^{0}S

	Starts	1st	2nd	3rd	Win & Pl
Career Total (Turf)	12	3	3	0	35282

92	9/00	NmkR	7f	B(0-100)H	GD	£10407
92	7/00	NmkJ	7f	D(0-80)H	G-F	£4862
78	6/00	Ayr	7f	D	GD	£3867

Total win prize-money £19138

Going (Turf): Sf: 0-2 GS: 0-1 **Gd: 2-6** GF: 1-3 Fm: 0-0
Distance: 5f/6f: 0-4 **7f-8f: 3-8** 9f-13f: 0-0 14f+: 0-0
Track : **LH: 1-2** RH: 0-1 Tight: 0-0 Gall: 0-0
Aids: Bl: 0-0 Vi: 0-0 Tstrap: 0-0
Best Rating: 92 5/01 York 6f gd-fm

A very useful handicapper, he has done his winning over seven furlongs but is also effective over six when there is plenty of pace on. Best on top of the ground.

Capriolo (IRE)

101(93) (60)**70**

5-y-o ch g Priolo (USA)-Carroll's Canyon (IRE) (Hatim (USA))
R Hannon Taylor Homer Racing

Placings:3430/002312062001/6001631320-05050245630 **(5465)**
2001: 12^{0}S, 10^{5}G, 12^{0}GF, 12^{5}GF, 12^{0}GF, 9^{2}GF, 10^{4}G, 12^{5}G, 12^{6}GS, 9^{3}GS, 10^{0}G

	Starts	1st	2nd	3rd	Win & Pl
Career Total (Turf)	36	4	5	6	35698
Career Total (AW)	1	0	0	0	

74	8/00	York	1m3f195y	D(0-85)H	GD	£8079
57	7/00	Ches	1m4f66y	E(0-70)	SFT	£3961
72	10/99	Leic	1m1f218y	E(0-75)H	GD	£7912
67	6/99	Sals	1m1f198y	F(0-65)H	FRM	£2780

Total win prize-money £22735

Going (Turf): Sf: 1-5 GS: 0-3 **Gd: 2-15** GF: 0-11 Fm: 1-2
Distance: 5f/6f: 0-2 7f-8f: 0-2 **9f-13f: 4-33** 14f+: 0-0
Track : LH: 2-10 RH: 2-23 **Tight: 2-19** Gall: 1-7
Aids: **Bl: 4-23** Vi: 0-1 Tstrap: 0-0
Best Rating: 80 5/01 Sand 1m2f7y good

Front runner, best with some give. Sometimes carries his head awkwardly.

Captain Brady (IRE)

89 (59)**27**

6-y-o ch g Soviet Lad (USA)-Eight Mile Rock (Dominion)
J S Goldie Frank Brady

Placings:043000/3015230210030/136000-000 **(5657)**
2001: 10^{0}HY, 11^{0}S, 8^{0}G

	Starts	1st	2nd	3rd	Win & Pl
Career Total (Turf)	26	3	2	4	20616
Career Total (AW)	2	0	0	1	350

55	8/00	Haml	1m3f16y	D(0-80)H	SFT	£4192
55	8/99	Ripn	1m1f	D(0-80)H	GD	£7815
52	5/99	Haml	1m65y	E(0-70)H	SFT	£3566

Total win prize-money £15574

Going (Turf): Sf: 2-12 GS: 0-3 Gd: 1-7 GF: 0-3 Fm: 0-1
Distance: 5f/6f: 0-6 7f-8f: 0-1 **9f-13f: 3-21** 14f+: 0-0
Track : LH: 0-9 **RH: 3-14 Tight: 3-14** Gall: 0-2
Aids: Bl: 0-1 Vi: 0-0 Tstrap: 0-0
Best Rating: 27 10/01 Rdcr 1m3f soft

A useful front-running handicapper. Usually wins one in the summer months. Best at around ten furlongs on an easy surface. Last seen out on the level in October 2000.

Captain Crusoe

100 **80**

3-y-o b g Selkirk (USA)-Desert Girl (Green Desert (USA))
C A Horgan Mrs B Sumner

Placings:0-240 **(4275)**
2001: 8^{2}GF, 9^{4}GF, 9^{0}GS

	Starts	1st	2nd	3rd	Win & Pl
Career Total (Turf)	4	0	1	0	1881

Going (Turf): Sf: 0-1 GS: 0-1 Gd: 0-0 GF: 0-2 Fm: 0-0
Distance: 5f/6f: 0-0 7f-8f: 0-2 9f-13f: 0-2 14f+: 0-0
Track : LH: 0-1 RH: 0-2 Tight: 0-1 Gall: 0-1
Aids: Bl: 0-0 Vi: 0-0 Tstrap: 0-0
Best Rating: 80 6/01 Gdwd 1m gd-fm

A strong gelding. From the family of Park Hill Stakes winner Upend and disqualified Gold Cup winner (and Champion Hurdler) Royal Gait, he was never going to make a two-year-old. His outings this term suggest he will need middle distances to be seen at his best.

Captain Gibson

97 **69**

3-y-o b g Beveled (USA)-Little Egret (Carwhite)
D J S Ffrench Davis M Duthie

Placings:5006212-004000440030 **(5688)**
2001: 6^{0}S, 6^{0}GS, 6^{4}G, 6^{0}GF, 6^{0}G, 6^{0}GF, 7^{4}GS, 7^{4}GS, 7^{0}HY, 6^{0}HY, 6^{3}HY, 7^{0}S

	Starts	1st	2nd	3rd	Win & Pl
Career Total (Turf)	19	1	2	1	5193

72	10/00	Pont	6f	F	HVY	£1820

Total win prize-money £1820

Going (Turf): Sf: 1-8 GS: 0-3 Gd: 0-5 GF: 0-3 Fm: 0-0
Distance: **5f/6f: 1-13** 7f-8f: 0-6 9f-13f: 0-0 14f+: 0-0
Track : **LH: 1-3** RH: 0-2 Tight: 0-0 Gall: 0-2
Aids: Bl: 0-2 Vi: 0-7 Tstrap: 0-0
Best Rating: 78 5/01 Wind 6f good

Is not an easy ride and tends to hang in his races. Nevertheless, he has ability and managed to score on heavy ground over six furlongs at the back-end of 2000. Modest form in 2001 for the most part.

Captain Kozando

(104) (73d)**55**

3-y-o b g Komaite (USA)-Times Zando (Forzando)
P C Haslam Mrs B Hawkins

Placings:521-**1544**0000**0** **(5450)**
2001: 6^{1}SD, 7^{5}SD, 7^{4}SD, 7^{4}SD, 7^{0}GF, 6^{0}F, 8^{0}GF, 7^{0}SD, 8^{0}HY

	Starts	1st	2nd	3rd	Win & Pl
Career Total (Turf)	7	1	1	0	2510
Career Total (AW)	5	1	0	0	8772

73	1/01	Sthl	6f	C(0-90)H	STD	£8151
59	10/00	Pont	6f	F	HVY	£1820

Total win prize-money £9971

Going (Turf): Sf: 1-2 GS: 0-0 Gd: 0-1 GF: 0-3 Fm: 0-1
Distance: **5f/6f: 2-3** 7f-8f: 0-8 9f-13f: 0-1 14f+: 0-0
Track : **LH: 2-9** RH: 0-2 Tight: 0-3 Gall: 0-2
Aids: Bl: 0-0 Vi: 0-0 Tstrap: 0-0
Best Rating: 73 1/01 Sthl 6f stand

Got off the mark in a Pontefract maiden on his third start at two on heavy and followed up on the All-Weather. less effective on fast ground.

Captain McCloy (USA)

95(52) (33)**39**

6-y-o ch g Lively One (USA)-Fly Me First (USA) (Herbager)
N E Berry D W Smith

Placings:3660545/0003000/034441632640050/633301 0-00000 **(3171)**
2001: 9^{0}F, 10^{0}F, 10^{0}F, 8^{0}GF, 10^{0}G

	Starts	1st	2nd	3rd	Win & Pl
Career Total (Turf)	38	2	1	6	8064
Career Total (AW)	3	0	0	1	295

45	8/00	Wind	1m2f7y	E(0-80)H	GD	£2814
38	7/99	Wwck	1m2f110y	G(0-60)H	G-F	£2267

Total win prize-money £5082

Going (Turf): Sf: 0-5 GS: 0-2 **Gd: 1-9 GF: 1-15** Fm: 0-7
Distance: 5f/6f: 0-2 7f-8f: 0-6 **9f-13f: 2-33** 14f+: 0-0
Track : **LH: 1-20** RH: 0-12 **Tight: 1-15** Gall: 0-3
Aids: **Bl: 2-19** Vi: 0-2 Tstrap: 0-0
Best Rating: 39 7/01 Sals 1m gd-fm

Captain Miller

93 **83**

5-y-o b g Batshoof-Miller's Gait (Mill Reef (USA))
N J Henderson W H Ponsonby

Placings:065210656564/110210/1206-0 **(5226)**
2001: 11^{0}S

	Starts	1st	2nd	3rd	Win & Pl
Career Total (Turf)	23	5	3	0	29393

75	4/00	Kemp	2m	C(0-100)H	SFT	£10871
70	5/99	Ripn	1m	F	G-F	£2305
69	4/99	Haml	1m65y	E(0-65)	HVY	£2801
70	4/99	Leic	7f9y	C(0-90)H	G-S	£7158
82	6/98	Ling	7f	F	SFT	£2070

Total win prize-money £25206

Going (Turf): Sf: 3-9 GS: 1-2 Gd: 0-6 GF: 1-5 Fm: 0-1
Distance: 5f/6f: 0-5 **7f-8f: 3-9** 9f-13f: 1-7 14f+: 1-2
Track : LH: 0-8 **RH: 3-8 Tight: 2-6** Gall: 0-6
Aids: Bl: 0-0 Vi: 0-0 Tstrap: 0-0
Best Rating: 56 10/01 York 1m3f195y soft

Better known as a hurdler, he won the Queen's Prize in 2000, but ran just once on the Flat in 2001.

Captain Rio

101 **103**

2-y-o ch c Pivotal-Beloved Visitor (USA) (Miswaki (USA))
R M Whitaker D Samuel

Placings:013311 **(5571a)**
2001: 5^{0}G, 6^{1}GF, 6^{3}GF, 5^{3}G, 6^{1}G, 6^{1}HY

	Starts	1st	2nd	3rd	Win & Pl
Career Total (Turf)	6	3	0	2	210241

103	10/01	MsnL	6f		HVY	£67895
102	10/01	Rdcr	6f	B	GD	£105908
103	9/01	Ripn	6f	D	G-F	£3900

Total win prize-money £177703

Going (Turf): Sf: 1-1 GS: 0-0 **Gd: 1-3 GF: 1-2** Fm: 0-0
Distance: **5f/6f: 3-6** 7f-8f: 0-0 9f-13f: 0-0 14f+: 0-0
Track : LH: 0-0 RH: 0-0 Tight: 0-0 Gall: 0-0
Aids: Bl: 0-0 Vi: 0-0 Tstrap: 0-0
Best Rating: 103 10/01 MsnL 6f heavy

Won three times as a juvenile, including the very valuable Redcar Two-Year-Old Trophy and the Group Two Criterium de Maisons-Laffitte. Acts on fast ground and has the pace for five.

Captain Ron (IRE)

92 **53**

5-y-o b g Marju (IRE)-Callas Star (Chief Singer)
P D Evans N E Powell

Placings:00/600 **(2410)**
2001: 11^{6}F, 10^{0}G, 17^{0}GF

	Starts	1st	2nd	3rd	Win & Pl
Career Total (Turf)	5	0	0	0	0

Going (Turf): Sf: 0-1 GS: 0-0 Gd: 0-2 GF: 0-1 Fm: 0-1
Distance: 5f/6f: 0-0 7f-8f: 0-2 9f-13f: 0-2 14f+: 0-1
Track : LH: 0-3 RH: 0-0 Tight: 0-0 Gall: 0-0
Aids: Bl: 0-0 Vi: 0-0 Tstrap: 0-0
Best Rating: 53 5/01 Brig 1m3f196y firm

Captain Scott (IRE)

57 (94)**85**

7-y-o b g Polar Falcon (USA)-Camera Girl (Kalaglow)
G A Butler The Write State Partnership

Placings:13510/63326/12400/0P-0 **(0523)**
2001: 8^{0}S

			Starts	1st	2nd	3rd	Win & Pl
Career Total (Turf)			16	1	2	3	23596
Career Total (AW)			2	2	0	0	35841
94 3/99	Wolv	1m100y	B(0-105)H			STD	£32275
84 7/97	Ayr	1m2f	D(0-80)			G-F	£3403
70 3/97	Sthl	1m	D			STD	£3566

Total win prize-money £39245

Going (Turf): Sf: 0-3 GS: 0-3 Gd: 0-3 **GF: 1-6** Fm: 0-1
Distance: 5f/6f: 0-0 7f-8f: 1-9 **9f-13f: 2-9** 14f+: 0-0
Track : **LH: 3-13** RH: 0-0 **Tight: 1-5** Gall: 0-3
Aids: Bl: 0-0 Vi: 0-0 Tstrap: 0-2
Best Rating: 70 3/97 Sthl 1m SD

Ran just twice in 2000. Effective up to a mile and a quarter, he goes well on a sound surface and has shown his best form when ridden patiently in a fast run race. Lightly-raced in recent seasons.

Captain Scottland

81 **47**

2-y-o b g Beveled (USA)-Little Egret (Carwhite)
D J S Ffrench Davis Norcosse Partnership

Placings:000 **(5126)**
2001: 7^{0}G, 7^{0}GF, 6^{0}HY

	Starts	1st	2nd	3rd	Win & Pl
Career Total (Turf)	3	0	0	0	

Going (Turf): Sf: 0-1 GS: 0-0 Gd: 0-1 GF: 0-1 Fm: 0-0
Distance: 5f/6f: 0-1 7f-8f: 0-2 9f-13f: 0-0 14f+: 0-0
Track : LH: 0-0 RH: 0-1 Tight: 0-0 Gall: 0-0
Aids: Bl: 0-0 Vi: 0-0 Tstrap: 0-0
Best Rating: 47 9/01 Newb 7f gd-fm

Captain Venti

101 **88**

2-y-o br g Ventiquattrofogli (IRE)-Lady Liza (Air Trooper)
J J Quinn Mrs S Quinn

Placings:001130453 **(5487)**
2001: 5^{0}F, 5^{0}G, 6^{1}GF, 7^{1}GS, 7^{3}GF, 7^{0}HY, 7^{4}G, 7^{5}G, 6^{3}HY

			Starts	1st	2nd	3rd	Win & Pl
Career Total (Turf)			9	2	0	2	11496
77 7/01	Ayr	7f	E			G-S	£3132
64 7/01	Haml	6f5y	F			G-F	£2747

Total win prize-money £5881

Going (Turf): Sf: 0-2 **GS: 1-1** Gd: 0-3 **GF: 1-2** Fm: 0-1
Distance: 5f/6f: 0-3 **7f-8f: 2-6** 9f-13f: 0-0 14f+: 0-0
Track : **LH: 1-3** RH: 0-2 Tight: 0-0 Gall: 0-0
Aids: Bl: 0-0 Vi: 0-0 Tstrap: 0-0
Best Rating: 88 10/01 Donc 6f heavy

By Ventiquattrofogli, an improving sort who, since winning a nusery at Ayr in July, was jumped up in grade and looked to hande the company. He stays seven furlongs and acts on any ground.

Captain's Folly

68 **38**

3-y-o b f Mind Games-Miss Petella (Dunphy)
J S Wainwright Steve Dalton

Placings:00500-0 **(3279)**
2001: 5^{0}F

	Starts	1st	2nd	3rd	Win & Pl
Career Total (Turf)	6	0	0	0	

Going (Turf): Sf: 0-1 GS: 0-0 Gd: 0-1 GF: 0-3 Fm: 0-1
Distance: 5f/6f: 0-5 7f-8f: 0-1 9f-13f: 0-0 14f+: 0-0
Track : LH: 0-1 RH: 0-0 Tight: 0-1 Gall: 0-0
Aids: Bl: 0-0 Vi: 0-0 Tstrap: 0-0
Best Rating: 88 10/01 Donc 6f heavy

Captain's Log

105 **86**

6-y-o b g Slip Anchor-Cradle Of Love (USA) (Roberto (USA))
M L W Bell Christopher Wright

Placings:60105162400/45240660/42511415042-10431100000 **(5669)**
2001: 9^{1}G, 10^{0}G, 10^{4}GF, 11^{3}G, 10^{1}GF, 10^{1}GS, 10^{0}GF, 12^{0}G, 10^{0}S, 12^{0}GS, 10^{0}HY

			Starts	1st	2nd	3rd	Win & Pl
Career Total (Turf)			42	8	4	1	56585
86 8/01	Ayr	1m2f	D(0-80)			G-S	£3971
56 7/01	Newc	1m2f32y	D(0-80)			G-F	£5161
70 5/01	Nott	1m1f213y	D(0-80)			GD	£4095
82 7/00	Newc	1m4f93y	D(0-80)			G-F	£5018
80 6/00	York	1m3f195y	D(0-75)			GD	£5265
78 6/00	Wind	1m2f7y	D(0-85)H			GD	£4179
76 6/98	Newc	1m1f9y	D(0-75)H			G-S	£7457
74 5/98	Wwck	1m	D			GD	£3330

Total win prize-money £38479

Going (Turf): Sf: 0-7 GS: 2-8 **Gd: 4-14** GF: 2-13 Fm: 0-0
Distance: 5f/6f: 0-0 7f-8f: 1-3 **9f-13f: 7-39** 14f+: 0-0
Track : **LH: 7-21** RH: 0-16 Tight: 1-7 **Gall: 4-22**
Aids: Bl: 0-0 Vi: 0-0 Tstrap: 0-0
Best Rating: 86 8/01 Ayr 1m2f gd-sft

A game winner at Nottingham on his reappearance this season, he then scored twice in the summer over ten furlongs at Newcastle and Ayr, although he has looked held off higher marks of late. His come-from-behind style means he often finds trouble in running. Handles any ground.

Caqui D'Or (IRE)

108 **83+**

3-y-o b c Danehill (USA)-Ghaiya (USA) (Alleged (USA))
J L Dunlop Windflower Overseas Holdings Inc

Placings:000-612110 **(5143)**
2001: 10^{6}GS, 11^{1}GF, 12^{4}GF, 14^{1}G, 14^{1}HY, 14^{0}G

			Starts	1st	2nd	3rd	Win & Pl
Career Total (Turf)			9	3	1	0	30849
83 9/01	Hayd	1m6f	D(0-85)H			HVY	£21352
77 8/01	Nott	1m6f15y	D(0-80)H			GD	£4368
76 5/01	Bevl	1m3f216y	E(0-70)H			G-F	£3818

Total win prize-money £29540

Going (Turf): Sf: 1-2 GS: 0-1 **Gd: 1-3 GF: 1-3** Fm: 0-0
Distance: 5f/6f: 0-0 7f-8f: 0-3 9f-13f: 1-3 **14f+: 2-3**
Track : **LH: 2-3** RH: 1-3 **Tight: 1-2** Gall: 0-1
Aids: Bl: 0-0 Vi: 0-0 Tstrap: 0-0
Best Rating: 83 9/01 Hayd 1m6f heavy

He improved as he was stepped up in trip, winning over 12 furlongs at Beverley in May and excelled over the extra quarter-mile when winning at Nottingham in August and Haydock in September. Acts on any ground.

Carabosse

89 **66d**

2-y-o b f Salse (USA)-Ballet (Sharrood (USA))
M L W Bell Lady Carolyn Warren

Placings:0000 **(5127)**
2001: 6^{0}G, 7^{0}GF, 6^{0}G, 7^{0}HY

	Starts	1st	2nd	3rd	Win & Pl
Career Total (Turf)	4	0	0	0	

Going (Turf): Sf: 0-1 GS: 0-0 Gd: 0-2 GF: 0-1 Fm: 0-0
Distance: 5f/6f: 0-1 7f-8f: 0-3 9f-13f: 0-0 14f+: 0-0
Track : LH: 0-1 RH: 0-0 Tight: 0-0 Gall: 0-0
Aids: Bl: 0-0 Vi: 0-0 Tstrap: 0-0
Best Rating: 66 7/01 York 6f good

Caradaya

47

5-y-o b m Presidium-Caraniya (Darshaan)
W M Brisbourne Mrs E A Dawson

Placings:40 **(4803)**
2001: 12^{4}GS, 17^{0}F

	Starts	1st	2nd	3rd	Win & Pl
Career Total (Turf)	2	0	0	0	332

Going (Turf): Sf: 0-0 GS: 0-1 Gd: 0-0 GF: 0-0 Fm: 0-1
Distance: 5f/6f: 0-0 7f-8f: 0-0 9f-13f: 0-1 14f+: 0-1
Track : LH: 0-2 RH: 0-0 Tight: 0-1 Gall: 0-0
Aids: Bl: 0-0 Vi: 0-0 Tstrap: 0-0

Caradoc

47

6-y-o ch g Bustino-Hathaway (Connaught)
Mrs L C Jewell John D Hurd

Placings:000/004/0/0 **(0733)**
2001: 11^{0}GS

	Starts	1st	2nd	3rd	Win & Pl
Career Total (Turf)	7	0	0	0	0
Career Total (AW)	1	0	0	0	

Going (Turf): Sf: 0-2 GS: 0-1 Gd: 0-4 GF: 0-0 Fm: 0-0
Distance: 5f/6f: 0-0 7f-8f: 0-1 9f-13f: 0-5 14f+: 0-2
Track : LH: 0-6 RH: 0-1 Tight: 0-4 Gall: 0-1
Aids: Bl: 0-0 Vi: 0-0 Tstrap: 0-0

Carafe

85 **65+**

2-y-o b f Selkirk (USA)-Caramba (Belmez (USA))
Sir Michael Stoute Lord Carnarvon

Placings:4 **(3403)**
2001: 6^{4}GF

	Starts	1st	2nd	3rd	Win & Pl
Career Total (Turf)	1	0	0	0	620

Going (Turf): Sf: 0-0 GS: 0-0 Gd: 0-0 GF: 0-1 Fm: 0-0
Distance: 5f/6f: 0-1 7f-8f: 0-0 9f-13f: 0-0 14f+: 0-0
Track : LH: 0-0 RH: 0-0 Tight: 0-0 Gall: 0-0
Aids: Bl: 0-0 Vi: 0-0 Tstrap: 0-0
Best Rating: 65 7/01 Asct 6f gd-fm

Second foal of dam who won Nassau Stakes and Falmouth Stakes, she was green on her Ascot debut and should have learnt a lot from the experience.

Carbon Copy

101 **68**
3-y-o ch f Pivotal-Astolat (Rusticaro (FR))
W J Haggas Tprc Limited

Placings:35-3520210 **(4988)**
2001: 6^{3}G, 7^{5}G, 7^{2}GF, 7^{0}G, 7^{2}GF, 8^{1}GF, 8^{0}G

	Starts	1st	2nd	3rd	Win & Pl
Career Total (Turf)	9	1	2	2	5578

67 9/01 Wwck 1m22y F G-F £2611
Total win prize-money £2611

Going (Turf): Sf: 0-1 GS: 0-1 Gd: 0-4 **GF: 1-3** Fm: 0-0
Distance: 5f/6f: 0-2 7f-8f: 0-6 **9f-13f: 1-1** 14f+: 0-0
Track : LH: 0-1 RH: 0-1 Tight: 0-0 Gall: 0-0
Aids: **Bl: 1-4** Vi: 0-0 Tstrap: 0-0
Best Rating: 68 8/01 NmkJ 7f gd-fm

Card Games

95 **53**
4-y-o b f First Trump-Pericardia (Petong)
M W Easterby (S C Williams 3/6) Ladies Who Lunch

Placings:340131420/000120050200-000000 **(2016)**
2001: 6^{0}S, 7^{0}S, 6^{0}G, 7^{0}GF, 8^{0}G, 8^{0}GF

	Starts	1st	2nd	3rd	Win & Pl
Career Total (Turf)	27	3	3	2	30960

80 5/00 Rdcr 5f D(0-80)H G-S £4829
85 8/99 Pont 6f D H GD £3817
76 7/99 Sals 6f F G-F £2402
Total win prize-money £11050

Going (Turf): Sf: 0-11 **GS: 1-1 Gd: 1-6 GF: 1-8** Fm: 0-1
Distance: **5f/6f: 3-17** 7f-8f: 0-8 9f-13f: 0-2 14f+: 0-0
Track : **LH: 1-6** RH: 0-3 Tight: 0-2 Gall: 0-3
Aids: Bl: 0-0 Vi: 0-2 Tstrap: 0-0
Best Rating: 53 6/01 Hayd 1m30y gd-fm

Modest sprinter, basically inconsistent.

Cardinal Venture (IRE)

106 **85**
3-y-o b g Bishop Of Cashel-Phoenix Venture (IRE) (Thatching)
K A Ryan Tony Fawcett

Placings:04-42014340100 **(5391)**
2001: 8^{4}S, 8^{2}GF, 8^{0}GF, 7^{1}GF, 7^{4}GF, 8^{3}GF, 8^{4}GS, 7^{0}GF, 7^{1}GS, 6^{0}GS, 7^{0}GS

	Starts	1st	2nd	3rd	Win & Pl
Career Total (Turf)	13	2	1	1	17355

85 9/01 Donc 7f C(0-95)H G-S £8157
80 6/01 Rdcr 7f D(0-80)H G-F £5551
Total win prize-money £13709

Going (Turf): Sf: 0-2 **GS: 1-4** Gd: 0-0 **GF: 1-7** Fm: 0-0
Distance: 5f/6f: 0-1 **7f-8f: 2-11** 9f-13f: 0-1 14f+: 0-0
Track : LH: 0-5 RH: 0-0 Tight: 0-3 Gall: 0-1
Aids: Bl: 0-0 Vi: 0-0 Tstrap: 0-0
Best Rating: 85 9/01 Donc 7f gd-sft

He showed promise at two and got off the mark in a Redcar handicap in June. Added a handicap at Doncaster in September and is an effective sort over seven furlongs.

Carefully

(91) (54)**52**
3-y-o ch g Caerleon (USA)-Sabaah Elfull (Kris)
N A Graham David J Simpson

Placings:006-650 **(0507)**
2001: 7^{6}SW, 7^{5}SD, 6^{0}SD

	Starts	1st	2nd	3rd	Win & Pl
Career Total (Turf)	3	0	0	0	0
Career Total (AW)	3	0	0	0	0

Going (Turf): Sf: 0-0 GS: 0-0 Gd: 0-0 GF: 0-3 Fm: 0-0
Distance: 5f/6f: 0-3 7f-8f: 0-3 9f-13f: 0-0 14f+: 0-0
Track : LH: 0-3 RH: 0-0 Tight: 0-3 Gall: 0-0
Aids: Bl: 0-0 Vi: 0-0 Tstrap: 0-0
Best Rating: 54 2/01 Ling 7f slow

Carel

104 **79**
3-y-o b c Polish Precedent (USA)-Castle Peak (Darshaan)
M L W Bell Baron F C Oppenheim

Placings:0-235 **(4581)**
2001: 8^{2}HY, 8^{3}GF, 10^{5}HY

	Starts	1st	2nd	3rd	Win & Pl
Career Total (Turf)	4	0	1	1	2331

Going (Turf): Sf: 0-3 GS: 0-0 Gd: 0-0 GF: 0-1 Fm: 0-0
Distance: 5f/6f: 0-0 7f-8f: 0-1 9f-13f: 0-3 14f+: 0-0
Track : LH: 0-2 RH: 0-0 Tight: 0-0 Gall: 0-0
Aids: Bl: 0-0 Vi: 0-0 Tstrap: 0-0
Best Rating: 79 8/01 NmkJ 1m gd-fm

He was beaten by a 100/1 shot on his reappearance, but it was a long way back to the third. Returned from a five-month break to run well at Newmarket in August. Could be more suited to handicaps. Acts on fast gruond and heavy.

Carens Hero (IRE)

(91) (58)**64**
4-y-o ch g Petardia-Clearglade (Vitiges (FR))
R Brotherton (Mrs A J Perrett 25/7) Mrs S Arcourt-Rippingale

Placings:0/310460-0023245200 **(5406)**
2001: 7^{0}S, 10^{0}G, 8^{2}GF, 6^{3}GF, 8^{2}HD, 8^{4}GF, 8^{5}G, 8^{2}GF, 9^{0}G, 8^{0}SD

	Starts	1st	2nd	3rd	Win & Pl
Career Total (Turf)	16	1	3	2	6660
Career Total (AW)	1	0	0	0	

73 5/00 Bath 1m5y F G-F £1869
Total win prize-money £1869

Going (Turf): Sf: 0-3 GS: 0-1 Gd: 0-5 **GF: 1-5** Fm: 0-1
Distance: 5f/6f: 0-0 7f-8f: 0-6 **9f-13f: 1-10** 14f+: 0-0
Track : **LH: 1-9** RH: 0-3 **Tight: 1-6** Gall: 0-2
Aids: Bl: 0-1 Vi: 0-0 Tstrap: 0-0
Best Rating: 64 8/01 Epsm 1m114y gd-fm

He has been running well in modest company this season. Handles fast ground, and goes well at Bath.

Carequick

57(96) (30)**29**
5-y-o ch m Risk Me (FR)-Miss Serlby (Runnett)
W M Brisbourne Reds Bar Four Partnership

Placings:00050/0000053/356-0 **(5503)**
2001: 7^{0}HY

	Starts	1st	2nd	3rd	Win & Pl
Career Total (Turf)	9	0	0	0	0
Career Total (AW)	7	0	0	2	545

Going (Turf): Sf: 0-2 GS: 0-1 Gd: 0-1 GF: 0-4 Fm: 0-1
Distance: 5f/6f: 0-7 7f-8f: 0-7 9f-13f: 0-2 14f+: 0-0
Track : LH: 0-9 RH: 0-0 Tight: 0-7 Gall: 0-0
Aids: Bl: 0-1 Vi: 0-0 Tstrap: 0-0
Best Rating: 64 8/01 Epsm 1m114y gd-fm

Cargo

96(98) (60)**57**
2-y-o b g Emarati (USA)-Portvasco (Sharpo)
M W Easterby Guy Reed

Placings:000451540 **(5536)**
2001: 5^{0}S, 5^{0}F, 7^{0}F, 6^{4}G, 6^{5}G, 6^{1}SW, 6^{5}SD, 6^{4}S, 6^{0}S

	Starts	1st	2nd	3rd	Win & Pl
Career Total (Turf)	7	0	0	0	549
Career Total (AW)	2	1	0	0	2814

60 9/01 Wolv 6f E(0-75) SLW £2814
Total win prize-money £2814

Going (Turf): Sf: 0-3 GS: 0-0 Gd: 0-2 GF: 0-0 Fm: 0-2
Distance: **5f/6f: 1-8** 7f-8f: 0-1 9f-13f: 0-0 14f+: 0-0
Track : **LH: 1-4** RH: 0-0 **Tight: 1-3** Gall: 0-0
Aids: Bl: 0-0 Vi: 0-0 Tstrap: 0-0
Best Rating: 60 10/01 Wolv 6f stand

Bred for speed, gained his only win when making all on the All-Weather in a nursery. He is suited by six furlongs and front-running tactics.

Carib Lady (IRE)

79 **52**
2-y-o b f Sadler's Wells (USA)-Belle Passe (Be My Guest (USA))
H R A Cecil M P Burke

Placings:0 **(5484)**
2001: 8^{0}HY

	Starts	1st	2nd	3rd	Win & Pl
Career Total (Turf)	1	0	0	0	

Going (Turf): Sf: 0-1 GS: 0-0 Gd: 0-0 GF: 0-0 Fm: 0-0
Distance: 5f/6f: 0-0 7f-8f: 0-1 9f-13f: 0-0 14f+: 0-0
Track : LH: 0-1 RH: 0-0 Tight: 0-0 Gall: 0-1
Aids: Bl: 0-0 Vi: 0-0 Tstrap: 0-0
Best Rating: 52 10/01 Donc 1m heavy

Caribbean Coral

100 **89**
2-y-o ch c Brief Truce (USA)-Caribbean Star (Soviet Star (USA))
C F Wall The Boardroom Syndicate

Placings:01540 **(5264)**
2001: 6^{0}GF, 5^{1}F, 6^{5}GF, 6^{4}G, 6^{0}GS

	Starts	1st	2nd	3rd	Win & Pl
Career Total (Turf)	5	1	0	0	11122

84 7/01 Brig 5f213y E FRM £2919
Total win prize-money £2919

Going (Turf): Sf: 0-0 GS: 0-1 Gd: 0-1 GF: 0-2 **Fm: 1-1**
Distance: **5f/6f: 1-5** 7f-8f: 0-0 9f-13f: 0-0 14f+: 0-0
Track : **LH: 1-1** RH: 0-0 Tight: 0-0 Gall: 0-0
Aids: Bl: 0-0 Vi: 0-0 Tstrap: 0-0
Best Rating: 89 9/01 Donc 6f gd-fm

A half-brother to Caribbean Monarch, showed the benefit of his debut when scoring narrowly at Brighton despite running a little green. Good efforts in big fields afterwards and looks capable of winning more races.

Carina Too (IRE)

70 **34**
2-y-o b f Entrepreneur-Highly Respected (IRE) (High Estate)
M A Jarvis M P Burke

Placings:0 **(3584)**
2001: 7^{0}G

	Starts	1st	2nd	3rd	Win & Pl
Career Total (Turf)	1	0	0	0	

Going (Turf): Sf: 0-0 GS: 0-0 Gd: 0-1 GF: 0-0 Fm: 0-0
Distance: 5f/6f: 0-0 7f-8f: 0-1 9f-13f: 0-0 14f+: 0-0
Track : LH: 0-0 RH: 0-1 Tight: 0-0 Gall: 0-0
Aids: Bl: 0-0 Vi: 0-0 Tstrap: 0-0
Best Rating: 34 8/01 Gdwd 7f good

Carinae (USA)

102 **98**

2-y-o b f Nureyev (USA)-Turning Wheel (USA) (Seeking The Gold (USA))
Sir Michael Stoute Niarchos Family

Placings:162 **(5264)**
2001: 6^{1}GF, 6^{6}G, 6^{2}GS

	Starts	1st	2nd	3rd	Win & Pl
Career Total (Turf)	3	1	1	0	10191

88 7/01 NmkJ 6f D G-F £4075
Total win prize-money £4076

Going (Turf): Sf: 0-0 GS: 0-1 Gd: 0-1 **GF: 1-1** Fm: 0-0
Distance: **5f/6f: 1-3** 7f-8f: 0-0 9f-13f: 0-0 14f+: 0-0
Track : LH: 0-0 RH: 0-0 Tight: 0-0 Gall: 0-0
Aids: Bl: 0-0 Vi: 0-0 Tstrap: 0-0
Best Rating: 98 10/01 York 6f gd-sft

Won a four-runner event at Newmarket on her debut, but was then well beaten behind Queen's Logic in the Lowther. She may have lacked the experience for a race like that and still looks a decent prospect.

Carioca Dream (USA)

103 **71**
3-y-o b f Diesis-Highland Ceilidh (IRE) (Scottish Reel)
W J Haggas Cyril Humphris

Placings:2-015600 **(5622)**
2001: 8^{0}S, 12^{1}HY, 11^{5}G, 11^{6}HY, 12^{0}GS, 14^{0}GS

	Starts	1st	2nd	3rd	Win & Pl
Career Total (Turf)	7	1	1	0	4180

70 4/01 Folk 1m4f D HVY £2898
Total win prize-money £2898

Going (Turf): **Sf: 1-4** GS: 0-2 Gd: 0-1 GF: 0-0 Fm: 0-0
Distance: 5f/6f: 0-0 7f-8f: 0-1 **9f-13f: 1-5** 14f+: 0-1
Track : LH: 0-1 **RH: 1-5 Tight: 1-3** Gall: 0-1
Aids: Bl: 0-0 Vi: 0-0 Tstrap: 0-0
Best Rating: 71 5/01 Leic 1m3f183y good

She showed ability on her only start at two over a mile and duly scored when stepped up to a mile and a half on her second start at three, albeit dropping back to maiden company after being well beaten in Listed company. Suited by testing conditions.

Cark

108 **65**
3-y-o b g Farfelu-Precious Girl (Precious Metal)
M Todhunter P G Airey & R R Whitton

Placings:1450-0052524033230 **(5451)**
2001: 5^{0}GF, 5^{0}GF, 5^{5}GF, 5^{2}GF, 5^{5}GS, 5^{2}G, 5^{4}GF, 5^{0}G, 5^{3}S, 5^{3}G, 5^{2}HY, 5^{3}HY, 5^{0}HY

	Starts	1st	2nd	3rd	Win & Pl
Career Total (Turf)	17	1	3	3	11449

51 6/00 Carl 5f E SFT £2834
Total win prize-money £2834

Going (Turf): **Sf: 1-5** GS: 0-2 Gd: 0-3 GF: 0-6 Fm: 0-1
Distance: **5f/6f: 1-17** 7f-8f: 0-0 9f-13f: 0-0 14f+: 0-0
Track : LH: 0-0 **RH: 1-1** Tight: 0-0 **Gall: 1-1**
Aids: Bl: 0-0 Vi: 0-0 Tstrap: 0-0
Best Rating: 65 9/01 Hayd 5f heavy

Won moderate event on soft on juvenile debut, has failed to build on that since and is slipping down the handicap as a consequence.

Carlos Girl (IRE)

70 **41**
2-y-o b f Sri Pekan (USA)-Sliding (Formidable (USA))
B A McMahon Stefan Uppstrom

Placings:00 **(5110)**
2001: 5^{0}GF, 6^{0}HY

	Starts	1st	2nd	3rd	Win & Pl
Career Total (Turf)	2	0	0	0	

Going (Turf): Sf: 0-1 GS: 0-0 Gd: 0-0 GF: 0-1 Fm: 0-0
Distance: 5f/6f: 0-1 7f-8f: 0-1 9f-13f: 0-0 14f+: 0-0
Track : LH: 0-0 RH: 0-0 Tight: 0-0 Gall: 0-0
Aids: Bl: 0-0 Vi: 0-0 Tstrap: 0-0
Best Rating: 41 9/01 Nott 5f13y gd-fm

Carlton Rode

75 **4**
4-y-o b g Carlton (GER)-Alghabrah (Lomond (USA))
D R C Elsworth The Sunday Lunch Partnership

Placings:0 **(1184)**
2001: 9^{0}GF

	Starts	1st	2nd	3rd	Win & Pl
Career Total (Turf)	1	0	0	0	

Going (Turf): Sf: 0-0 GS: 0-0 Gd: 0-0 GF: 0-1 Fm: 0-0
Distance: 5f/6f: 0-0 7f-8f: 0-0 9f-13f: 0-1 14f+: 0-0
Track : LH: 0-1 RH: 0-0 Tight: 0-0 Gall: 0-0
Aids: Bl: 0-0 Vi: 0-0 Tstrap: 0-0
Best Rating: 4 5/01 Brig 1m1f209y gd-fm

Carlys Quest

110 (51)**90**
7-y-o ch g Primo Dominie-Tuppy (USA) (Sharpen Up)
J Neville Yorkeys Knob Racing Club

Placings:040P/3536450/1315022322/40033302/313004 0552-4320 **(2305)**
2001: 16^{4}GS, 16^{3}GF, 12^{2}GF, 20^{0}GF

	Starts	1st	2nd	3rd	Win & Pl
Career Total (Turf)	41	3	7	10	63344
Career Total (AW)	2	0	0	0	

87 5/00 Newb 1m4f5y C(0-90)H G-F £7748
79 5/98 Wwck 1m2f169yD(0-80)H G-F £3785
70 5/98 NmkR 1m2f D(0-85)H G-S £6888
Total win prize-money £18421

Going (Turf): Sf: 0-9 GS: 1-4 Gd: 0-6 **GF: 2-18** Fm: 0-4
Distance: 5f/6f: 0-0 7f-8f: 0-5 **9f-13f: 3-32** 14f+: 0-6
Track : **LH: 2-25** RH: 0-15 Tight: 0-7 **Gall: 1-22**
Aids: Bl: 0-5 **Vi: 3-27** Tstrap: 1-14
Best Rating: 90 5/01 Kemp 2m gd-fm

Scored his first success for two years in May 2000. His style of racing makes it difficult for him to win as he lacks early pace, and often find himself caught for a turn of foot when staying on towards the finish. Two miles is his limit. Best over a mile and a half. Acts on any going.

Carmosine (IRE)

89(57) **31**
3-y-o b g Tagula (IRE)-Adocentyn (USA) (Upper Nile (USA))
J L Eyre M Gleason

Placings:060 **(4600)**
2001: 8^{0}SW, 8^{6}GS, 6^{0}GF

	Starts	1st	2nd	3rd	Win & Pl
Career Total (Turf)	2	0	0	0	0
Career Total (AW)	1	0	0	0	

Going (Turf): Sf: 0-0 GS: 0-1 Gd: 0-0 GF: 0-1 Fm: 0-0
Distance: 5f/6f: 0-1 7f-8f: 0-2 9f-13f: 0-0 14f+: 0-0
Track : LH: 0-2 RH: 0-0 Tight: 0-0 Gall: 0-0
Aids: Bl: 0-0 Vi: 0-0 Tstrap: 0-3
Best Rating: 31 9/01 Thsk 6f gd-fm

Carnage (IRE)

98 **46**
4-y-o b g Catrail (USA)-Caranina (USA) (Caro)
Mrs P N Dutfield Mrs C A Clarke

Placings:000/00260-6033 **(3875)**
2001: 6^{6}HY, 7^{0}S, 8^{3}G, 8^{3}GS

	Starts	1st	2nd	3rd	Win & Pl
Career Total (Turf)	12	0	1	2	1752

Going (Turf): Sf: 0-4 GS: 0-3 Gd: 0-1 GF: 0-4 Fm: 0-0
Distance: 5f/6f: 0-5 7f-8f: 0-3 9f-13f: 0-4 14f+: 0-0
Track : LH: 0-3 RH: 0-3 Tight: 0-3 Gall: 0-3
Aids: Bl: 0-0 Vi: 0-0 Tstrap: 0-0
Best Rating: 44 8/01 Thsk 1m gd-sft

Carnival Dancer

110 **115**
3-y-o b c Sadler's Wells (USA)-Red Carnival (USA) (Mr Prospector (USA))
Sir Michael Stoute Cheveley Park Stud

Placings:4-1215 **(5389)**
2001: 7^{1}GS, 8^{2}GF, 10^{1}GS, 10^{5}GS

	Starts	1st	2nd	3rd	Win & Pl
Career Total (Turf)	5	2	1	0	41876

115 7/01 Ayr 1m2f A G-S £20300
91 6/01 York 7f202y D G-S £7020
Total win prize-money £27320

Going (Turf): Sf: 0-1 **GS: 2-3** Gd: 0-0 GF: 0-1 Fm: 0-0
Distance: 5f/6f: 0-0 7f-8f: 1-2 9f-13f: 1-3 14f+: 0-0
Track : **LH: 2-2** RH: 0-1 Tight: 0-0 **Gall: 1-1**
Aids: Bl: 0-0 Vi: 0-0 Tstrap: 0-0
Best Rating: 115 7/01 Ayr 1m2f gd-sft

Showed a nice turn of foot to score in impressive fashion at York, and took another step in the right direction when second to Vicious Knight over a mile at Sandown. He stayed on well there and appreciated the step up to ten furlongs and easy ground when a clear-cut winner of the Scottish Classic.Fair effort in the Champion Stakes.

Carnoustie (USA)

101 **77**
3-y-o gr f Ezzoud (IRE)-Sarba (USA) (Persepolis (FR))
M A Jarvis John Poynton

Placings:0222410 **(4828)**
2001: 10^{0}GS, 10^{2}G, 12^{2}GF, 11^{2}G, 12^{4}G, 9^{1}GF, 10^{0}G

	Starts	1st	2nd	3rd	Win & Pl
Career Total (Turf)	7	1	3	0	9356

30 8/01 Bevl 1m1f207yD G-F £4355
Total win prize-money £4355

Going (Turf): Sf: 0-0 GS: 0-1 Gd: 0-4 **GF: 1-2** Fm: 0-0
Distance: 5f/6f: 0-0 7f-8f: 0-0 **9f-13f: 1-7** 14f+: 0-0
Track : LH: 0-4 **RH: 1-2** Tight: 0-1 Gall: 0-3
Aids: Bl: 0-0 Vi: 0-0 Tstrap: 0-0
Best Rating: 77 7/01 York 1m3f195y good

Narrow winner of a Beverley maiden, effective 9-12 furlongs.

Carole's Dove

59 **35**
5-y-o b m Manhal-Nimble Dove (Starch Reduced)
C J Price Mrs C A Crawford

Placings:0/0000-0 **(5531)**
2001: 16^{0}HY

	Starts	1st	2nd	3rd	Win & Pl
Career Total (Turf)	6	0	0	0	

Going (Turf): Sf: 0-3 GS: 0-2 Gd: 0-1 GF: 0-0 Fm: 0-0
Distance: 5f/6f: 0-2 7f-8f: 0-2 9f-13f: 0-0 14f+: 0-2
Track : LH: 0-4 RH: 0-0 Tight: 0-0 Gall: 0-1
Aids: Bl: 0-0 Vi: 0-0 Tstrap: 0-0
Best Rating: 77 7/01 York 1m3f195y good

Carolina Silk (IRE)

91 **83**

2-y-o b c Barathea (IRE)-Bold Fashion (FR) (Nashwan (USA))

R Hannon Kenneth Kornfeld

Placings:062 **(5495)**

2001: 8^{0}G, 8^{6}GF, 8^{2}HY

	Starts	1st	2nd	3rd	Win & Pl
Career Total (Turf)	3	0	1	0	3110

Going (Turf): **Sf: 0-1 GS: 0-0 Gd: 0-1 GF: 0-1 Fm: 0-0**
Distance: 5f/6f: 0-0 7f-8f: 0-3 9f-13f: 0-0 14f+: 0-0
Track : LH: 0-0 RH: 0-1 Tight: 0-0 Gall: 0-0
Aids: Bl: 0-0 Vi: 0-0 Tstrap: 0-0
Best Rating: 83 10/01 Newb 1m heavy

He has shown some ability and there is a race in him.

Caroline Island (IRE)

97 **83+**

2-y-o b f Catrail (USA)-Pacific Grove (Persian Bold)

H Morrison C J Burley & Partners

Placings:651 **(3566)**

2001: 5^{6}GF, 7^{5}GF, 5^{1}GF

	Starts	1st	2nd	3rd	Win & Pl
Career Total (Turf)	3	1	0	0	3063

83 8/01 Leic 5f218y E G-F £3062
Total win prize-money £3063

Going (Turf): Sf: 0-0 GS: 0-0 Gd: 0-0 **GF: 1-3** Fm: 0-0
Distance: **5f/6f: 1-2** 7f-8f: 0-1 9f-13f: 0-0 14f+: 0-0
Track : LH: 0-0 RH: 0-1 Tight: 0-0 Gall: 0-1
Aids: Bl: 0-0 Vi: 0-0 Tstrap: 0-0
Best Rating: 83 8/01 Leic 5f218y gd-fm

Out of a useful two-year-old over 6-7f, she has clearly inherited some of this talent, as her impressive win at Leicester is testimony to. She is suited to six furlongs on a sound surface.

Carols Choice

(101) (53)**51**

4-y-o ch f Emarati (USA)-Lucky Song (Lucky Wednesday)

D Haydn Jones Monolithic Refractories Ltd

Placings:00536/420332356206-533506023402 **(4556)**

2001: 5^{5}SD, 6^{3}SD, 6^{3}SD, 5^{5}SD, 5^{0}GS, 6^{6}SD, 5^{0}SD, 5^{2}G, 5^{3}F, 5^{4}G, 5^{0}G, 5^{2}SW

	Starts	1st	2nd	3rd	Win & Pl
Career Total (Turf)	14	0	1	3	2705
Career Total (AW)	15	0	4	4	5334

Going (Turf): **Sf: 0-0 GS: 0-3 Gd: 0-8 GF: 0-2 Fm: 0-1**
Distance: 5f/6f: 0-26 7f-8f: 0-3 9f-13f: 0-0 14f+: 0-0
Track : LH: 0-15 RH: 0-3 Tight: 0-12 Gall: 0-6
Aids: Bl: 0-1 Vi: 0-3 Tstrap: 0-0
Best Rating: 61 1/01 Ling 5f stand

Carousing

101 **87**

4-y-o b g Selkirk (USA)-Moon Carnival (Be My Guest (USA))

A Bailey (R M Beckett 7/4) Willie McKay

Placings:611/15001040-000106130000 **(5693)**

2001: 12^{0}GS, 13^{0}S, 12^{0}S, 12^{1}GF, 10^{0}GF, 12^{6}GF, 16^{1}F, 16^{3}GF, 16^{0}G, 16^{0}F, 16^{0}G, 12^{0}S

	Starts	1st	2nd	3rd	Win & Pl
Career Total (Turf)	23	6	0	1	34061

86 5/01 Newc 2m19y D(0-80)H FRM £3903
84 5/01 Muss 1m4f D(0-80)H G-F £4251
70 9/00 Ayr 1m1f20y E SFT £3796
92 6/00 Pont 1m2f6y C(0-90) SFT £6792
86 7/99 Gdwd 7f C H FRM £10885
79 6/99 Ling 7f F GD £2502
Total win prize-money £32131

Going (Turf): Sf: 2-8 GS: 0-2 Gd: 1-4 GF: 1-6 **Fm: 2-3**
Distance: 5f/6f: 0-1 7f-8f: 2-2 **9f-13f: 3-15** 14f+: 1-5
Track : **LH: 3-12** RH: 1-8 Tight: 0-5 **Gall: 1-8**
Aids: **Bl: 1-3** Vi: 0-0 Tstrap: 0-0
Best Rating: 87 6/01 Muss 2m gd-fm

He is a decent stayer, if a little in and out. Successful at Musselburgh and Newcastle this season. Effective at a mile and a half to two miles, suited by a sound surface.

Carpet Lady (IRE)

46 **75**

3-y-o b f Night Shift (USA)-Lucky Fountain (IRE) (Lafontaine (USA))

Mrs P N Dutfield Axminster Carpets Ltd

Placings:3305-0 **(2232)**

2001: 8^{0}GS

	Starts	1st	2nd	3rd	Win & Pl
Career Total (Turf)	5	0	0	2	2023

Going (Turf): Sf: 0-1 GS: 0-1 Gd: 0-2 GF: 0-1 Fm: 0-0
Distance: 5f/6f: 0-4 7f-8f: 0-1 9f-13f: 0-0 14f+: 0-0
Track : LH: 0-0 RH: 0-0 Tight: 0-0 Gall: 0-1
Aids: Bl: 0-0 Vi: 0-0 Tstrap: 0-0
Best Rating: 87 6/01 Muss 2m gd-fm

Carpet Princess (IRE)

95 **53**

3-y-o gr/ro f Prince Of Birds (USA)-Krayyalei (IRE) (Krayyan)

Mrs P N Dutfield Axminster Carpets Ltd

Placings:40-40003 **(5043)**

2001: 7^{4}S, 10^{0}GF, 8^{0}G, 8^{0}GS, 8^{3}G

	Starts	1st	2nd	3rd	Win & Pl
Career Total (Turf)	7	0	0	1	804

Going (Turf): Sf: 0-1 GS: 0-1 Gd: 0-3 GF: 0-2 Fm: 0-0
Distance: 5f/6f: 0-2 7f-8f: 0-2 9f-13f: 0-3 14f+: 0-0
Track : LH: 0-2 RH: 0-3 Tight: 0-2 Gall: 0-2
Aids: Bl: 0-0 Vi: 0-0 Tstrap: 0-0
Best Rating: 56 5/01 Rdcr 7f soft

Carraca (IRE)

96

3-y-o b g Alzao (USA)-Honey Bun (Unfuwain (USA))

J D Bethell M J Dawson

Placings:004-30200P **(5190)**

2001: 8^{3}HY, 9^{0}GF, 10^{2}GF, 12^{0}GF, 10^{0}G, 11^{P}GS

	Starts	1st	2nd	3rd	Win & Pl
Career Total (Turf)	9	0	1	1	1445

Going (Turf): Sf: 0-2 GS: 0-2 Gd: 0-1 GF: 0-4 Fm: 0-0
Distance: 5f/6f: 0-1 7f-8f: 0-2 9f-13f: 0-6 14f+: 0-0
Track : LH: 0-5 RH: 0-2 Tight: 0-3 Gall: 0-1
Aids: Bl: 0-7 Vi: 0-0 Tstrap: 0-0
Best Rating: 62 6/01 Rdcr 1m2f gd-fm

Carradale

92 **78**

2-y-o ch f Pursuit Of Love-Rynavey (Rousillon (USA))

Denys Smith Evelyn Duchess Of Sutherland

Placings:133 **(3284)**

2001: 5^{1}G, 6^{3}GS, 6^{3}GS

	Starts	1st	2nd	3rd	Win & Pl
Career Total (Turf)	3	1	0	2	4159

78 6/01 Muss 5f E GD £2982
Total win prize-money £2982

Going (Turf): Sf: 0-0 GS: 0-2 **Gd: 1-1** GF: 0-0 Fm: 0-0
Distance: **5f/6f: 1-3** 7f-8f: 0-0 9f-13f: 0-0 14f+: 0-0
Track : LH: 0-0 RH: 0-0 Tight: 0-0 Gall: 0-0
Aids: Bl: 0-0 Vi: 0-0 Tstrap: 0-0
Best Rating: 78 7/01 Hayd 6f gd-sft

Lightly-raced, she has won over five furlongs, and her breeding suggests she will get a mile with normal improvement.

Carrick Lady (IRE)

98(94) (47)**44**

3-y-o ch f Fayruz-Mantlepiece (IRE) (Common Grounds)

G P Enright The Carrick Partnership

Placings:000053-3306050 **(5524)**

2001: 7^{3}SD, 8^{3}SD, 8^{0}SD, 6^{6}GF, 8^{0}G, 7^{5}GF, 10^{0}HY

	Starts	1st	2nd	3rd	Win & Pl
Career Total (Turf)	8	0	0	0	0
Career Total (AW)	5	0	0	3	824

Going (Turf): Sf: 0-3 GS: 0-0 Gd: 0-2 GF: 0-3 Fm: 0-0
Distance: 5f/6f: 0-4 7f-8f: 0-6 9f-13f: 0-3 14f+: 0-0
Track : LH: 0-8 RH: 0-1 Tight: 0-4 Gall: 0-1
Aids: Bl: 0-1 Vi: 0-0 Tstrap: 0-0
Best Rating: 47 1/01 Sthl 1m stand

Carrie Can Can

(101) (69)

4-y-o b f Green Tune (USA)-Maidenhair (IRE) (Darshaan)

J G Given A W Robinson & Ian Robinson

Placings:65305434110-0 **(0149)**

2001: 11^{0}SW

	Starts	1st	2nd	3rd	Win & Pl
Career Total (Turf)	6	0	0	1	1269
Career Total (AW)	6	2	0	1	5356

69 12/00 Wolv 1m1f79y E(0-70)H STD £2219
64 12/00 Wolv 1m1f79y E(0-75)H STD £2789
Total win prize-money £5009

Going (Turf): Sf: 0-3 GS: 0-0 Gd: 0-1 GF: 0-2 Fm: 0-0
Distance: 5f/6f: 0-0 7f-8f: 0-0 **9f-13f: 2-12** 14f+: 0-0
Track : **LH: 2-12** RH: 0-0 **Tight: 2-5** Gall: 0-2
Aids: Bl: 0-0 Vi: 0-0 Tstrap: 0-0
Best Rating: 51 1/01 Sthl 1m3f slow

Carrie Pooter

(110) (91+)

5-y-o b m Tragic Role (USA)-Ginny Binny (Ahonoora)

T D Barron Stephen Woodall

Placings:051404/**32212**332200010245/1600000111-412 **(0436)**

2001: 6^{4}SD, 6^{1}SD, 6^{2}SD

	Starts	1st	2nd	3rd	Win & Pl
Career Total (Turf)	24	5	2	2	29084
Career Total (AW)	12	3	5	1	20774

91 2/01 Wolv 6f C(0-100)H STD £6841
76 9/00 Haml 6f5y D(0-85)H SFT £7507
65 7/00 Pont 6f D(0-85)H GD £6955
70 3/00 Sthl 6f E(0-75)H STD £2408
65 7/99 Haml 6f5y D(0-85)H G-F £6970
62 3/99 Sthl 7f F(0-65)H SLW £2379
73 5/98 Rdcr 6f E G-F £2940
Total win prize-money £36002

Going (Turf): Sf: 1-5 GS: 0-3 Gd: 1-6 **GF: 2-7** Fm: 1-3
Distance: **5f/6f: 5-19** 7f-8f: 3-17 9f-13f: 0-0 14f+: 0-0
Track : **LH: 4-18** RH: 0-1 **Tight: 1-5** Gall: 0-2
Aids: **Bl: 6-20** Vi: 0-0 Tstrap: 0-0
Best Rating: 91 2/01 Wolv 6f stand

An effective sprinter on turf and Fibresand.

Carrington Dynasty

74 **30**

2-y-o b g Flockton's Own-Starlite Night (USA) (Star De Naskra (USA))
M Madgwick Carrington Network Services Ltd

Placings:000 **(4524)**
2001: 5^{0}GF, 6^{0}GF, 6^{0}GF

	Starts	1st	2nd	3rd	Win & Pl
Career Total (Turf)	3	0	0	0	

Going (Turf): Sf: 0-0 GS: 0-0 Gd: 0-0 GF: 0-3 Fm: 0-0
Distance: 5f/6f: 0-2 7f-8f: 0-1 9f-13f: 0-0 14f+: 0-0
Track : LH: 0-0 RH: 0-1 Tight: 0-0 Gall: 0-1
Aids: Bl: 0-0 Vi: 0-0 Tstrap: 0-0
Best Rating: 30 9/01 Ling 6f gd-fm

Carrozzina

92 **77**

2-y-o br f Vettori (IRE)-Doliouchka (Saumarez)
J G Given C G Rowles Nicholson

Placings:1 **(4723)**
2001: 7^{1}GF

	Starts	1st	2nd	3rd	Win & Pl
Career Total (Turf)	1	1	0	0	3949

77 9/01 Wwck 7f26y D G-F £3948
Total win prize-money £3949

Going (Turf): Sf: 0-0 GS: 0-0 Gd: 0-0 **GF: 1-1** Fm: 0-0
Distance: 5f/6f: 0-0 **7f-8f: 1-1** 9f-13f: 0-0 14f+: 0-0
Track : **LH: 1-1** RH: 0-0 Tight: 0-0 Gall: 0-0
Aids: Bl: 0-0 Vi: 0-0 Tstrap: 0-0
Best Rating: 77 9/01 Wwck 7f26y gd-fm

She made a winning debut in a Warwick maiden in September and should be able to win again.

Carson Dancer (USA)

83 **59**

3-y-o ch f Carson City (USA)-All Dance (USA) (Northern Dancer)
M L W Bell Mı Lee Amaltis

Placings:0600 **(4905)**
2001: 8^{0}G, 8^{6}F, 10^{0}GF, 8^{0}G

	Starts	1st	2nd	3rd	Win & Pl
Career Total (Turf)	4	0	0	0	0

Going (Turf): Sf: 0-0 GS: 0-0 Gd: 0-2 GF: 0-1 Fm: 0-1
Distance: 5f/6f: 0-0 7f-8f: 0-1 9f-13f: 0-3 14f+: 0-0
Track : LH: 0-1 RH: 0-3 Tight: 0-2 Gall: 0-1
Aids: Bl: 0-0 Vi: 0-0 Tstrap: 0-0
Best Rating: 59 5/01 Wind 1m67y good

Cartmel Park

99(106) (57)**57**

5-y-o b g Skyliner-Oh My Oh My (Ballacashtal (CAN))
J R Weymes (M Todhunter 6/6) P G Airey & R R Whitton

Placings:022212310/000321605001/050010300400020-010000 **(2865)**
2001: 5^{0}GF, 5^{1}GF, 5^{0}GF, 5^{0}GF, 5^{0}SD, 5^{0}GF

	Starts	1st	2nd	3rd	Win & Pl
Career Total (Turf)	36	5	5	3	25309
Career Total (AW)	6	1	1	0	4523

57 6/01 Newc 5f F G-F £2359
81 6/00 Wolv 5f D(0-80)H STD £3848
79 10/99 Catt 5f D(0-80)H GD £5312
77 7/99 Sand 5f6y D(0-80)H GD £3875
60 9/98 Newc 5f D GD £3436
69 7/98 Muss 5f E GD £2979
Total win prize-money £21811

Going (Turf): Sf: 0-5 GS: 0-6 **Gd: 4-10** GF: 1-12 Fm: 0-3
Distance: **5f/6f: 6-42** 7f-8f: 0-0 9f-13f: 0-0 14f+: 0-0
Track : **LH: 1-9** RH: 0-1 **Tight: 1-6** Gall: 0-4
Aids: Bl: 0-5 Vi: 1-6 Tstrap: 1-3
Best Rating: 57 6/01 Newc 5f gd-fm

Inconsistent, but showed his best when scoring at Newcastle in June. Seems happiest when able to dominate.

Cartouche

7-y-o gr g Terimon-Emblazon (Wolver Hollow)
Miss H M Irving Miss H M Irving

Placings:050/20210/0 **(0691)**
2001: 16^{0}SD

	Starts	1st	2nd	3rd	Win & Pl
Career Total (Turf)	6	1	0	0	2277
Career Total (AW)	3	0	2	0	1444

69 6/97 Ling 1m1f F SFT £2277
Total win prize-money £2277

Going (Turf): **Sf: 1-1** GS: 0-1 Gd: 0-1 GF: 0-2 Fm: 0-1
Distance: 5f/6f: 0-0 7f-8f: 0-6 **9f-13f: 1-2** 14f+: 0-1
Track : **LH: 1-7** RH: 0-1 **Tight: 1-2** Gall: 0-0
Aids: Bl: 0-0 Vi: 0-0 Tstrap: 0-0
Best Rating: 69 6/97 Ling 1m1f S

Caruso's

85(68) **26**

3-y-o b f Be My Guest (USA)-Courtisane (Persepolis (FR))
E J O'Neill The Ballybrit Partnership

Placings:00360-000000 **(4267)**
2001: 8^{0}SD, 8^{0}SD, 6^{0}GF, 10^{0}GF, 9^{0}GF, 7^{0}GF

	Starts	1st	2nd	3rd	Win & Pl
Career Total (Turf)	9	0	0	1	326
Career Total (AW)	2	0	0	0	

Going (Turf): Sf: 0-0 GS: 0-1 Gd: 0-1 GF: 0-5 Fm: 0-2
Distance: 5f/6f: 0-5 7f-8f: 0-4 9f-13f: 0-2 14f+: 0-0
Track : LH: 0-4 RH: 0-2 Tight: 0-3 Gall: 0-0
Aids: Bl: 0-0 Vi: 0-0 Tstrap: 0-0
Best Rating: 26 6/01 Wind 1m2f7y gd-fm

Carys Lyn

71

3-y-o b f Awesome-Reigning Royal (Tina's Pet)
D Burchell Lyn Phillips

Placings:00 **(4084)**
2001: 7^{0}GS, 8^{0}GF

	Starts	1st	2nd	3rd	Win & Pl
Career Total (Turf)	2	0	0	0	

Going (Turf): Sf: 0-0 GS: 0-1 Gd: 0-0 GF: 0-1 Fm: 0-0
Distance: 5f/6f: 0-0 7f-8f: 0-1 9f-13f: 0-1 14f+: 0-0
Track : LH: 0-1 RH: 0-0 Tight: 0-0 Gall: 0-0
Aids: Bl: 0-0 Vi: 0-0 Tstrap: 0-0

Casa Grande (IRE)

91 **52**

3-y-o b f Grand Lodge (USA)-Sodium's Niece (Northfields (USA))
R Guest J W Biswell

Placings:05020 **(5557)**
2001: 8^{0}G, 8^{5}S, 7^{0}S, 10^{2}HY, 14^{0}S

	Starts	1st	2nd	3rd	Win & Pl
Career Total (Turf)	5	0	1	0	868

Going (Turf): Sf: 0-4 GS: 0-0 Gd: 0-1 GF: 0-0 Fm: 0-0
Distance: 5f/6f: 0-0 7f-8f: 0-1 9f-13f: 0-3 14f+: 0-1
Track : LH: 0-3 RH: 0-2 Tight: 0-2 Gall: 0-0
Aids: Bl: 0-0 Vi: 0-0 Tstrap: 0-0
Best Rating: 52 8/01 Sand 1m14y soft

Modest form to date. Best effort came in a heavy ground claimer over ten and a half furlongs at Ayr in October.

Case Study (IRE)

92 **59**

2-y-o ch f Case Law-Look Nonchalant (IRE) (Fayruz)
Mrs P N Dutfield The Bright And Early Partnership

Placings:01 **(1574)**
2001: 5^{0}S, 5^{1}GF

	Starts	1st	2nd	3rd	Win & Pl
Career Total (Turf)	2	1	0	0	2758

59 5/01 Hayd 5f F G-F £2758
Total win prize-money £2758

Going (Turf): Sf: 0-1 GS: 0-0 Gd: 0-0 **GF: 1-1** Fm: 0-0
Distance: **5f/6f: 1-2** 7f-8f: 0-0 9f-13f: 0-0 14f+: 0-0
Track : LH: 0-0 RH: 0-0 Tight: 0-0 Gall: 0-0
Aids: Bl: 0-0 Vi: 0-0 Tstrap: 0-0
Best Rating: 59 5/01 Hayd 5f gd-fm

Whose dam is a sister to a two-year-old Italian Listed winner, Don Fayruz, responded to pressure to take a maiden over five furlongs on good-firm ground.

Cash

(97) (51)**35**

3-y-o b g Bishop Of Cashel-Ballad Island (Ballad Rock)
M Brittain Northgate Autumn

Placings:0-044015 **(5619)**
2001: 7^{0}GS, 6^{4}HY, 6^{4}SD, 6^{0}SD, 6^{1}SD, 6^{5}SD

	Starts	1st	2nd	3rd	Win & Pl
Career Total (Turf)	3	0	0	0	0
Career Total (AW)	4	1	0	0	2254

48 10/01 Sthl 6f F STD £2254
Total win prize-money £2254

Going (Turf): **Sf: 0-2** GS: 0-1 Gd: 0-0 GF: 0-0 Fm: 0-0
Distance: **5f/6f: 1-5** 7f-8f: 0-2 9f-13f: 0-0 14f+: 0-0
Track : **LH: 1-4** RH: 0-0 Tight: 0-2 Gall: 0-0
Aids: Bl: 0-0 Vi: 0-0 Tstrap: 0-0
Best Rating: 51 11/01 Wolv 6f stand

He showed a little ability before winning a maiden on the Southwell Fibresand in October at odds of 33/1.

Cashel Bay (USA)

98 **87**

3-y-o b c Nureyev (USA)-Madame Premier (USA) (Raja Baba (USA))
Luke Comer Luke Comer

Placings:2105-54600005000 **(3783a)**
2001: 8^{5}S, 8^{4}G, 14^{6}G, 8^{0}GY, 12^{0}GF, 8^{0}GF, 12^{0}Y, 9^{5}G, 12^{0}G, 12^{0}Y, 8^{0}GY, 10^{0}S

	Starts	1st	2nd	3rd	Win & Pl
Career Total (Turf)	15	1	1	0	9450

87 9/00 Gway 1m100y YLD £5865
Total win prize-money £5865

Going (Turf): Sf: 0-3 GS: 0-0 Gd: 0-4 GF: 0-2 Fm: 0-0
Distance: 5f/6f: 0-0 7f-8f: 0-5 **9f-13f: 1-8** 14f+: 0-1
Track : LH: 0-3 **RH: 1-1** Tight: 0-1 Gall: 0-0
Aids: Bl: 0-9 Vi: 0-0 Tstrap: 0-0
Best Rating: 99 6/01 Epsm 1m4f10y gd-fm

An Aidan O'Brien cast-off, won a Galway maiden on his second start at two, but has mainly been running in Listed company since. Has finished last in two Classics this term.

Cashel Dancer

(68) (28)**47**

2-y-o b f Bishop Of Cashel-Dancing Debut (Polar Falcon (USA))

S A Brookshaw Ken Edwards

Placings:0040 **(5168)**

2001: 6^{0}SD, 7^{0}GF, 7^{4}HY, 10^{0}GS

	Starts	1st	2nd	3rd	Win & Pl
Career Total (Turf)	3	0	0	0	0
Career Total (AW)	1	0	0	0	

Going (Turf): Sf: 0-1 GS: 0-1 Gd: 0-0 GF: 0-1 Fm: 0-0
Distance: 5f/6f: 0-1 7f-8f: 0-2 9f-13f: 0-1 14f+: 0-0
Track : LH: 0-4 RH: 0-0 Tight: 0-0 Gall: 0-0
Aids: Bl: 0-0 Vi: 0-0 Tstrap: 0-0
Best Rating: 47 9/01 Hayd 7f30y heavy

Cashmere

80 **70+**

2-y-o ch f Barathea (IRE)-Wanton (Kris)

J R Fanshawe Lady Halifax

Placings:0 **(5139)**

2001: 6^{0}G

	Starts	1st	2nd	3rd	Win & Pl
Career Total (Turf)	1	0	0	0	

Going (Turf): Sf: 0-0 GS: 0-0 Gd: 0-1 GF: 0-0 Fm: 0-0
Distance: 5f/6f: 0-1 7f-8f: 0-0 9f-13f: 0-0 14f+: 0-0
Track : LH: 0-0 RH: 0-0 Tight: 0-0 Gall: 0-0
Aids: Bl: 0-0 Vi: 0-0 Tstrap: 0-0
Best Rating: 70 10/01 NmkR 6f good

Cashmere Lady

105(91) (55)**59**

9-y-o b m Hubbly Bubbly (USA)-Choir (High Top)

J L Eyre Mrs Sybil Howe

Placings:2311/2514425234450/0004451120410000006/4110005022004544/00436100065/011020400005-1000 **(3228)**

2001: 9^{1}HY, 9^{0}G, 12^{0}GF, 12^{0}GF

	Starts	1st	2nd	3rd	Win & Pl
Career Total (Turf)	60	7	6	3	40104
Career Total (AW)	18	5	2	0	23863

59	5/01	Nott	1m1f213y	D(0-80)H	HVY	£4264
53	7/00	Hayd	1m3f200y	D(0-80)H	G-F	£3867
60	4/00	Ripn	1m4f60y	E(0-70)H	SFT	£2814
63	9/99	Hayd	1m2f120y	E(0-80)H	G-F	£2850
78	4/98	Thsk	1m	D(0-80)H	G-S	£3782
89	3/98	Sthl	1m4f	C(0-100)H	STD	£5368
78	8/97	Rdcr	1m	D(0-80)H	FRM	£3912
89	6/97	Wolv	1m100y	C(0-95)H	STD	£5257
70	6/97	Thsk	1m	D(0-80)H	GD	£3600
77	3/96	Wolv	1m100y	D(0-80)H	STD	£3485
66	12/95	Wolv	7f	F(0-65)H	STD	£2187
64	11/95	Wolv	1m100y	E	STD	£3081

Total win prize-money £44470

Going (Turf): Sf: 2-8 GS: 1-5 Gd: 1-17 **GF: 2-27** Fm: 1-3
Distance: 5f/6f: 0-0 7f-8f: 4-27 **9f-13f: 8-49** 14f+: 0-2
Track : LH: 10-59 RH: 1-10 **Tight: 7-32** Gall: 0-13
Aids: Bl: 0-0 Vi: 0-0 Tstrap: 0-0
Best Rating: 59 5/01 Nott 1m1f213y heavy

Fair middle-distance handicapper. Won on her Nottingham reappearance but did not repeat that form afterwards. Acts on any ground.

Cashneem (IRE)

104 **81**

3-y-o b g Case Law-Haanem (Mtoto)

P W Harris Law Abiding Citizens

Placings:4120-003010 **(3559)**

2001: 8^{0}GS, 7^{0}G, 7^{3}GF, 7^{0}GF, 6^{1}GF, 7^{0}GF

	Starts	1st	2nd	3rd	Win & Pl
Career Total (Turf)	10	2	1	1	12043

81	7/01	Newb	6f8y	C(0-95)H	G-F	£7442
72	8/00	Muss	7f30y	F	GD	£2604

Total win prize-money £10047

Going (Turf): Sf: 0-1 GS: 0-1 **Gd: 1-3 GF: 1-5** Fm: 0-0
Distance: 5f/6f: 0-0 **7f-8f: 2-10** 9f-13f: 0-0 14f+: 0-0
Track : LH: 0-0 **RH: 1-5 Tight: 1-1** Gall: 0-1
Aids: Bl: 0-0 Vi: 0-0 Tstrap: 0-0
Best Rating: 81 7/01 Newb 6f8y gd-fm

A good-looking individual, he struggled on his first two starts of the season but shaped better at Lingfield in June, and caused a surprise when scoring at Newbury the following month. Best suited by a sound surface.

Casing (IRE)

96 **41**

3-y-o gr f Case Law-Singhana (IRE) (Mouktar)

F Jordan The Fab Five

Placings:0500 **(5593)**

2001: 7^{0}GF, 6^{5}F, 7^{0}GF, 5^{0}GS

	Starts	1st	2nd	3rd	Win & Pl
Career Total (Turf)	4	0	0	0	0

Going (Turf): Sf: 0-0 GS: 0-1 Gd: 0-0 GF: 0-2 Fm: 0-1
Distance: 5f/6f: 0-2 7f-8f: 0-2 9f-13f: 0-0 14f+: 0-0
Track : LH: 0-2 RH: 0-0 Tight: 0-0 Gall: 0-0
Aids: Bl: 0-0 Vi: 0-0 Tstrap: 0-0
Best Rating: 41 9/01 Ling 7f gd-fm

Caspian Sea

72 **48**

2-y-o ch c Cadeaux Genereux-Zilayah (USA) (Zilzal (USA))

E A L Dunlop Saeed Suhail

Placings:0 **(2729)**

2001: 6^{0}GF

	Starts	1st	2nd	3rd	Win & Pl
Career Total (Turf)	1	0	0	0	

Going (Turf): Sf: 0-0 GS: 0-0 Gd: 0-0 GF: 0-1 Fm: 0-0
Distance: 5f/6f: 0-0 7f-8f: 0-1 9f-13f: 0-0 14f+: 0-0
Track : LH: 0-0 RH: 0-0 Tight: 0-0 Gall: 0-0
Aids: Bl: 0-0 Vi: 0-0 Tstrap: 0-0
Best Rating: 48 7/01 Yarm 6f3y gd-fm

Cassandra

101 **45**

5-y-o b m Catrail (USA)-Circo (High Top)

M Brittain Mel Brittain

Placings:640500/250200400-410000030 **(5225)**

2001: 9^{4}HY, 10^{1}G, 11^{0}GF, 9^{0}GF, 10^{0}G, 10^{0}G, 10^{0}G, 9^{3}G, 10^{0}S

	Starts	1st	2nd	3rd	Win & Pl
Career Total (Turf)	24	1	2	1	7127

49	5/01	Ripn	1m2f	D(0-80)H	GD	£4134

Total win prize-money £4134

Going (Turf): Sf: 0-4 GS: 0-1 **Gd: 1-9** GF: 0-9 Fm: 0-1
Distance: 5f/6f: 0-1 7f-8f: 0-3 **9f-13f: 1-20** 14f+: 0-0
Track : LH: 0-11 **RH: 1-9 Tight: 1-6** Gall: 0-4
Aids: Bl: 0-0 Vi: 0-0 Tstrap: 0-0
Best Rating: 49 5/01 Ripn 1m2f good

Got off the mark at the 17th attempt in a Ripon handicap. Suited by ten furlongs and good ground. Likes to make the running.

Cassandra Go (IRE)

119 **115**

5-y-o gr m Indian Ridge-Rahaam (USA) (Secreto (USA))

G Wragg Trevor C Stewart

Placings:0/1301460/12621-2112 **(2971)**

2001: 5^{2}G, 5^{1}GF, 5^{1}G, 6^{2}G

	Starts	1st	2nd	3rd	Win & Pl
Career Total (Turf)	17	6	4	1	244592

115	6/01	Asct	5f	A	GD	£81000
110	5/01	Sand	5f6y	A	G-F	£36000
109	8/00	Gdwd	5f	A	G-F	£30000
102	5/00	Bath	5f11y	A	G-S	£12818
94	6/99	NmkJ	6f	C	G-F	£5743
89	4/99	NmkJ	7f	D	GD	£4500

Total win prize-money £170061

Going (Turf): Sf: 0-0 GS: 1-2 Gd: 2-9 **GF: 3-5** Fm: 0-0
Distance: 5f/6f: 5-12 7f-8f: 1-5 9f-13f: 0-0 14f+: 0-0
Track : LH: 1-1 RH: 0-1 Tight: 0-0 **Gall: 1-3**
Aids: Bl: 0-0 Vi: 0-0 **Tstrap: 1-3**
Best Rating: 115 7/01 NmkJ 6f good

High-class sprinter, better than ever this term, winning the Temple Stakes despite her saddle slipping as she left the stalls, and following up in the King's Stand. She is in foal to Green Desert, and retired to stud after chasing home Mozart in the July Cup.

Casse-Noisette (IRE)

82 **35**

3-y-o b f Brief Truce (USA)-Highdrive (Ballymore)

Miss Gay Kelleway Mrs Andrea Wilkinson

Placings:000000 **(5557)**

2001: 6^{0}GF, 10^{0}GF, 7^{0}GS, 9^{0}G, 7^{0}HY, 14^{0}S

	Starts	1st	2nd	3rd	Win & Pl
Career Total (Turf)	6	0	0	0	

Going (Turf): Sf: 0-2 GS: 0-1 Gd: 0-1 GF: 0-2 Fm: 0-0
Distance: 5f/6f: 0-0 7f-8f: 0-3 9f-13f: 0-2 14f+: 0-1
Track : LH: 0-2 RH: 0-1 Tight: 0-1 Gall: 0-1
Aids: Bl: 0-3 Vi: 0-0 Tstrap: 0-0
Best Rating: 35 7/01 NmkJ 7f gd-sft

Lightly raced maiden. Has been tried from seven furlongs to ten without making the frame.

Cassirer (IRE)

100 **81**

2-y-o ch c Zafonic (USA)-Oriane (Nashwan (USA))

Sir Michael Stoute Lady Clague

Placings:321 **(5289)**

2001: 6^{3}GF, 6^{2}S, 7^{1}S

	Starts	1st	2nd	3rd	Win & Pl
Career Total (Turf)	3	1	1	1	6097

81	10/01	Leic	7f9y	D	SFT	£4108

Total win prize-money £4108

Going (Turf): Sf: 1-2 GS: 0-0 Gd: 0-0 GF: 0-1 Fm: 0-0
Distance: 5f/6f: 0-2 **7f-8f: 1-1** 9f-13f: 0-0 14f+: 0-0
Track : LH: 0-1 RH: 0-0 Tight: 0-0 Gall: 0-0
Aids: Bl: 0-0 Vi: 0-0 Tstrap: 0-0
Best Rating: 81 10/01 Leic 7f9y soft

He improved in each of his first three outings and got of the mark with an all-the-way win in a soft-ground Leicester maiden in October.

Cassius

89 **78d**

3-y-o b g Machiavellian (USA)-Chain Dance (Shareef Dancer (USA))

J R Fanshawe J M Greetham

Placings:50-000 **(2657)**

2001: 7^{0}GS, 10^{0}GF, 10^{0}GF

	Starts	1st	2nd	3rd	Win & Pl

	Starts	1st	2nd	3rd	Win & Pl
Career Total (Turf)	5	0	0	0	0

Going (Turf): Sf: 0-0 GS: 0-1 Gd: 0-2 GF: 0-2 Fm: 0-0
Distance: 5f/6f: 0-0 7f-8f: 0-3 9f-13f: 0-2 14f+: 0-0
Track : LH: 0-1 RH: 0-0 Tight: 0-2 Gall: 0-0
Aids: Bl: 0-0 Vi: 0-1 Tstrap: 0-0
Best Rating: 59 6/01 Ches 1m2f75y gd-fm

Cast Iron

83(84) (44)**42**
2-y-o b g Efisio-Misellina (FR) (Polish Precedent (USA))
R Guest E P Duggan

Placings:040 (5530)
2001: 6^{0}HY, 8^{4}SD, 8^{0}HY

	Starts	1st	2nd	3rd	Win & Pl
Career Total (Turf)	2	0	0	0	
Career Total (AW)	1	0	0	0	0

Going (Turf): Sf: 0-2 GS: 0-0 Gd: 0-0 GF: 0-0 Fm: 0-0
Distance: 5f/6f: 0-1 7f-8f: 0-1 9f-13f: 0-1 14f+: 0-0
Track : LH: 0-2 RH: 0-0 Tight: 0-0 Gall: 0-0
Aids: Bl: 0-0 Vi: 0-0 Tstrap: 0-0
Best Rating: 44 10/01 Sthl 1m stand

Casta Diva (IRE)

99 **73**
2-y-o ch f Case Law-Casting Vote (USA) (Monteverdi)
C F Wall David Allan

Placings:03016 (5052)
2001: 6^{0}G, 5^{3}G, 6^{0}GY, 7^{1}GF, 7^{6}S

	Starts	1st	2nd	3rd	Win & Pl
Career Total (Turf)	5	1	0	1	4116

73 9/01 Thsk 7f F G-F £3500
Total win prize-money £3500

Going (Turf): Sf: 0-1 GS: 0-0 Gd: 0-2 **GF: 1-1** Fm: 0-0
Distance: 5f/6f: 0-3 **7f-8f: 1-2** 9f-13f: 0-0 14f+: 0-0
Track : **LH: 1-1** RH: 0-0 **Tight: 1-1** Gall: 0-0
Aids: Bl: 0-0 Vi: 0-0 Tstrap: 0-0
Best Rating: 73 9/01 Thsk 7f gd-fm

She improved for the step up to seven furlongs when getting off the mark at Thirsk on her fourth start. Looks suited by seven furlongs and good ground or faster.

Castanet

90 **76**
2-y-o b f Pennekamp (USA)-Addaya (IRE) (Persian Bold)
Sir Michael Stoute Highclere Thoroughbred Racing Ltd

Placings:20 (3971)
2001: 6^{2}GS, 5^{0}GS

	Starts	1st	2nd	3rd	Win & Pl
Career Total (Turf)	2	0	1	0	1257

Going (Turf): Sf: 0-0 GS: 0-2 Gd: 0-0 GF: 0-0 Fm: 0-0
Distance: 5f/6f: 0-2 7f-8f: 0-0 9f-13f: 0-0 14f+: 0-0
Track : LH: 0-0 RH: 0-0 Tight: 0-0 Gall: 0-0
Aids: Bl: 0-0 Vi: 0-0 Tstrap: 0-0
Best Rating: 76 8/01 NmkJ 6f gd-sft

Castaway Queen (IRE)

89 **76**
2-y-o ch f Selkirk (USA)-Surfing (Grundy)
W R Muir M J Caddy

Placings:2060 (5052)
2001: 6^{2}G, 6^{0}GF, 6^{8}GF, 7^{0}S

	Starts	1st	2nd	3rd	Win & Pl
Career Total (Turf)	4	0	1	0	1138

Going (Turf): Sf: 0-1 GS: 0-0 Gd: 0-1 GF: 0-2 Fm: 0-0
Distance: 5f/6f: 0-1 7f-8f: 0-3 9f-13f: 0-0 14f+: 0-0
Track : LH: 0-0 RH: 0-0 Tight: 0-0 Gall: 0-0
Aids: Bl: 0-0 Vi: 0-0 Tstrap: 0-0
Best Rating: 76 8/01 Wind 6f good

She showed ability when runner-up on her Windsor debut, but has not shown the same sort of form on faster ground since and probably needs cut.

Castle Belle

83 **13**
5-y-o ch m King's Signet (USA)-Castle Maid (Castle Keep)
R J Hodges R T Sercombe

Placings:000/0 (3391)
2001: 5^{0}F

	Starts	1st	2nd	3rd	Win & Pl
Career Total (Turf)	4	0	0	0	

Going (Turf): Sf: 0-0 GS: 0-0 Gd: 0-0 GF: 0-2 Fm: 0-2
Distance: 5f/6f: 0-3 7f-8f: 0-1 9f-13f: 0-0 14f+: 0-0
Track : LH: 0-2 RH: 0-0 Tight: 0-0 Gall: 0-2
Aids: Bl: 0-0 Vi: 0-0 Tstrap: 0-0
Best Rating: 13 7/01 Bath 5f11y firm

Castle Gandolfo (USA)

108 **116**
2-y-o ch c Gone West (USA)-Golden Oriole (USA) (Northern Dancer)
A P O'Brien Mrs John Magnier

Placings:112 (5500)
2001: 6^{1}S, 8^{1}Y, 8^{2}HY

	Starts	1st	2nd	3rd	Win & Pl
Career Total (Turf)	3	2	1	0	93100

116 10/01 Curr 1m YLD £39000
88 4/01 Cork 6f SFT £10400
Total win prize-money £49400

Going (Turf): Sf: 1-2 GS: 0-0 Gd: 0-0 GF: 0-0 Fm: 0 0
Distance: 5f/6f: 1-1 7f-8f: 1-2 9f-13f: 0-0 14f+: 0-0
Track : LH: 0-0 RH: 0-0 Tight: 0-0 **Gall: 1-1**
Aids: Bl: 0-0 Vi: 0-0 Tstrap: 0-0
Best Rating: 116 10/01 Donc 1m heavy

Battled on well to win a maiden at Cork on his debut over six furlongs on soft ground before running away with a Curragh Group Three. Caught close home by his stable companion in the Racing Post Trophy, he suffered a similar fate in the Criterium de Saint-Cloud in November.

Castle Ring

83(80) (48)**63**
2-y-o b c Sri Pekan (USA)-Understudy (In The Wings)
R Hollinshead The C H F Partnership

Placings:050 (5684)
2001: 5^{0}GF, 6^{5}SD, 8^{0}S

	Starts	1st	2nd	3rd	Win & Pl
Career Total (Turf)	2	0	0	0	
Career Total (AW)	1	0	0	0	0

Going (Turf): Sf: 0-1 GS: 0-0 Gd: 0-0 GF: 0-1 Fm: 0-0
Distance: 5f/6f: 0-2 7f-8f: 0-1 9f-13f: 0-0 14f+: 0-0
Track : LH: 0-2 RH: 0-0 Tight: 0-2 Gall: 0-0
Aids: Bl: 0-0 Vi: 0-0 Tstrap: 0-0
Best Rating: 63 11/01 Donc 1m soft

Castle River (USA)

92(84) (62)**77**
2-y-o b c Irish River (FR)-Castellina (USA) (Danzig Connection (USA))
B W Hills D J Deer

Placings:640 (5665)
2001: 7^{6}G, 7^{4}SD, 6^{0}HY

	Starts	1st	2nd	3rd	Win & Pl
Career Total (Turf)	2	0	0	0	165
Career Total (AW)	1	0	0	0	0

Going (Turf): Sf: 0-1 GS: 0-0 Gd: 0-1 GF: 0-0 Fm: 0-0
Distance: 5f/6f: 0-1 7f-8f: 0-2 9f-13f: 0-0 14f+: 0-0
Track : LH: 0-1 RH: 0-1 Tight: 0-1 Gall: 0-1
Aids: Bl: 0-0 Vi: 0-0 Tstrap: 0-0
Best Rating: 77 9/01 Kemp 7f good

Castlebar

(94) (57d)**53**
4-y-o b g Formidable (USA)-Nineteenth Of May (Homing)
K R Burke Nigel Shields

Placings:1000-00 (5398)
2001: 8^{0}SD, 8^{0}SD

	Starts	1st	2nd	3rd	Win & Pl
Career Total (Turf)	3	0	0	0	
Career Total (AW)	3	1	0	0	2769

57 2/00 Sthl 6f D STD £2769
Total win prize-money £2769

Going (Turf): Sf: 0-3 GS: 0-0 Gd: 0-0 GF: 0-0 Fm: 0-0
Distance: **5f/6f: 1-2** 7f-8f: 0-2 9f-13f: 0-2 14f+: 0-0
Track : **LH: 1-5** RH: 0-0 Tight: 0-2 Gall: 0-0
Aids: Bl: 0-0 Vi: 0-0 Tstrap: 0-0
Best Rating: 30 10/01 Wolv 1m100y stand

Castlebridge

100(92) (12)**42**
4-y-o b g Batshoof-Super Sisters (AUS) (Call Report (USA))
M D I Usher P Sweeting

Placings:000/0116153045000000-0001400001 (5469)
2001: 9^{0}F, 10^{0}GF, 10^{0}F, 8^{1}G, 10^{4}G, 7^{0}GF, 9^{0}G, 12^{0}SD, 10^{0}GF, 9^{1}S

	Starts	1st	2nd	3rd	Win & Pl
Career Total (Turf)	17	3	0	1	8940
Career Total (AW)	11	2	0	0	3673

40 10/01 Brig 1m1f209yF(0-60)H SFT £2579
41 7/01 Chep 1m14y F(0-60)H GD £2478
74 4/00 Wwck 1m2f110yE(0-70)H HVY £2993
69 2/00 Wolv 1m1f79y G STD £1822
64 1/00 Wolv 1m100y G STD £1850
Total win prize-money £11724

Going (Turf): Sf: 2-5 GS: 0-0 Gd: 1-3 GF: 0-6 Fm: 0-3
Distance: 5f/6f: 0-0 7f-8f: 0-5 **9f-13f: 5-22** 14f+: 0-1
Track : **LH: 4-22** RH: 0-3 **Tight: 2-14** Gall: 0-1
Aids: Bl: 2-8 **Vi: 3-12** Tstrap: 0-0
Best Rating: 42 7/01 Epsm 1m2f18y good

Has won five times, twice on Fibresand and the others all on good ground or softer. Four of his wins have been around a mile, the other ten furlongs, although the latter looks to be as far as he wants to go.

Castleshane (IRE)

108 **79d**
4-y-o b g Kris-Ahbab (IRE) (Ajdal (USA))
S Gollings John King, Bill Hobson, Graham King

Placings:631401/636055430-00304063 (4983)
2001: 10^{0}G, 8^{0}GF, 10^{3}GF, 7^{0}GF, 10^{4}GF, 9^{0}GS, 12^{6}G, 12^{3}G

	Starts	1st	2nd	3rd	Win & Pl
Career Total (Turf)	23	2	0	5	18454

84 9/99 Gway 1m100y H SFT £5520
73 7/99 Leop 7f G-F £6556
Total win prize-money £12076

Going (Turf): **Sf: 1-3** GS: 0-1 Gd: 0-5 **GF: 1-6** Fm: 0-1
Distance: 5f/6f: 0-2 7f-8f: 1-5 9f-13f: 1-14 14f+: 0-0
Track : LH: 1-5 RH: 1-8 Tight: 0-1 Gall: 0-2
Aids: Bl: 0-2 Vi: 0-0 Tstrap: 0-0
Best Rating: 79 8/01 Donc 1m2f60y gd-fm

Useful on the Flat in Ireland, he was best at around a mile on a soft surface. Gradually dropped in the ratings this term and ran well at Ascot in September.

Castletown Count

(82) (6)**36**

9-y-o b g Then Again-Pepeke (Mummy's Pet)
M W Easterby Abbots Salford Caravan Park

Placings:00100/000000/24/0/6-0 **(0539)**
2001: 16^{0}SD

	Starts	1st	2nd	3rd	Win & Pl
Career Total (Turf)	15	1	1	0	3427
Career Total (AW)	1	0	0	0	

59 7/94 Rdcr 7f F G-F £2679
Total win prize-money £2679

Going (Turf): Sf: 0-0 GS: 0-2 Gd: 0-3 **GF: 1-8** Fm: 0-2
Distance: 5f/6f: 0-1 **7f-8f: 1-5** 9f-13f: 0-7 14f+: 0-3
Track : LH: 0-7 RH: 0-6 Tight: 0-8 Gall: 0-1
Aids: Bl: 0-1 Vi: 0-0 Tstrap: 0-0
Best Rating: 6 3/01 Sthl 2m stand

Castrato

68(63) **22**

5-y-o b g Rock City-Vocalist (Crooner)
B N Doran P N Exton

Placings:0000000-0 **(1041)**
2001: 14^{0}HY

	Starts	1st	2nd	3rd	Win & Pl
Career Total (Turf)	5	0	0	0	
Career Total (AW)	3	0	0	0	

Going (Turf): Sf: 0-2 GS: 0-0 Gd: 0-1 GF: 0-2 Fm: 0-0
Distance: 5f/6f: 0-0 7f-8f: 0-4 9f-13f: 0-3 14f+: 0-1
Track : LH: 0-4 RH: 0-0 Tight: 0-2 Gall: 0-0
Aids: Bl: 0-0 Vi: 0-0 Tstrap: 0-0
Best Rating: 6 3/01 Sthl 2m stand

Cat's Whiskers

94 **72**

2-y-o b g Catrail (USA)-Haut Volee (Top Ville)
M W Easterby J W Dolby

Placings:050130 **(5368)**
2001: 5^{0}GS, 5^{5}GF, 5^{0}GF, 7^{1}GF, 7^{3}G, 8^{0}GS

	Starts	1st	2nd	3rd	Win & Pl
Career Total (Turf)	6	1	0	1	4712

70 9/01 Rdcr 7f E(0-75) G-F £3472
Total win prize-money £3472

Going (Turf): Sf: 0-0 GS: 0-2 Gd: 0-1 **GF: 1-3** Fm: 0-0
Distance: 5f/6f: 0-3 **7f-8f: 1-3** 9f-13f: 0-0 14f+: 0-0
Track : LH: 0-1 RH: 0-0 Tight: 0-0 Gall: 0-0
Aids: Bl: 0-0 Vi: 0-0 Tstrap: 0-0
Best Rating: 72 9/01 Donc 7f good

Improved for the step up to seven furlongs when landing a Redcar nursery in September.

Catcando (IRE)

97 **70**

3-y-o ch c Catrail (USA)-Tongabezi (IRE) (Shernazar)
C N Allen Green Square Racing

Placings:0100 **(2330)**
2001: 8^{0}G, 8^{1}G, 8^{0}GF, 8^{0}GF

	Starts	1st	2nd	3rd	Win & Pl
Career Total (Turf)	4	1	0	0	2296

70 5/01 Bath 1m5y F GD £2296
Total win prize-money £2296

Going (Turf): Sf: 0-0 GS: 0-0 **Gd: 1-2** GF: 0-2 Fm: 0-0
Distance: 5f/6f: 0-0 7f-8f: 0-3 **9f-13f: 1-1** 14f+: 0-0
Track : **LH: 1-2** RH: 0-0 **Tight: 1-1** Gall: 0-1
Aids: Bl: 0-0 Vi: 0-0 **Tstrap: 1-3**
Best Rating: 70 5/01 Bath 1m5y good

Catch Fire (IRE)

90 **67**

2-y-o b f Entrepreneur-Lyric Theatre (USA) (Seeking The Gold (USA))
C R Egerton Austin Allison & Mrs R Lowe

Placings:00200 **(5370)**
2001: 6^{0}GF, 7^{0}GF, 7^{2}HY, 8^{0}S, 7^{0}G

	Starts	1st	2nd	3rd	Win & Pl
Career Total (Turf)	5	0	1	0	763

Going (Turf): Sf: 0-2 GS: 0-0 Gd: 0-1 GF: 0-2 Fm: 0-0
Distance: 5f/6f: 0-0 7f-8f: 0-4 9f-13f: 0-1 14f+: 0-0
Track : LH: 0-2 RH: 0-0 Tight: 0-0 Gall: 0-0
Aids: Bl: 0-3 Vi: 0-0 Tstrap: 0-0
Best Rating: 67 9/01 Hayd 7f30y heavy

Catch The Cat (IRE)

90 **56**

2-y-o b g Catrail (USA)-Tongabezi (IRE) (Shernazar)
J S Wainwright T W Heseltine

Placings:0230000 **(5253)**
2001: 5^{0}GS, 5^{2}S, 5^{3}GF, 5^{0}GF, 5^{0}G, 6^{0}GS, 6^{0}S

	Starts	1st	2nd	3rd	Win & Pl
Career Total (Turf)	7	0	1	1	2621

Going (Turf): Sf: 0-2 GS: 0-2 Gd: 0-1 GF: 0-2 Fm: 0-0
Distance: 5f/6f: 0-7 7f-8f: 0-0 9f-13f: 0-0 14f+: 0-0
Track : LH: 0-0 RH: 0-0 Tight: 0-0 Gall: 0-0
Aids: Bl: 0-0 Vi: 0-0 Tstrap: 0-0
Best Rating: 56 5/01 Muss 5f gd-fm

Well beaten in the Brocklesby after a slow start, he shaped much better on his next outing at Newmarket but has been disappointing since.

Catch The Chron

(56) **37**

3-y-o b f Clantime-Emerald Gulf (IRE) (Wassl)
N Tinkler The Oldham Chronicle Racing Club

Placings:20401620-030000 **(2342)**
2001: 5^{0}S, 5^{3}HY, 6^{0}S, 6^{0}GF, 6^{0}GF, 7^{0}SD

	Starts	1st	2nd	3rd	Win & Pl
Career Total (Turf)	13	1	2	1	4832
Career Total (AW)	1	0	0	0	

62 8/00 Haml 5f4y F SFT £2646
Total win prize-money £2646

Going (Turf): Sf: 1-7 GS: 0-1 Gd: 0-0 GF: 0-5 Fm: 0-0
Distance: **5f/6f: 1-12** 7f-8f: 0-2 9f-13f: 0-0 14f+: 0-0
Track : LH: 0-4 RH: 0-0 Tight: 0-1 Gall: 0-0
Aids: Bl: 0-0 Vi: 0-0 Tstrap: 0-0
Best Rating: 37 4/01 Nott 5f13y soft

Catchthebatch

99(101) (50)**45**

5-y-o b g Beveled (USA)-Batchworth Dancer (Ballacashtal (CAN))
E A Wheeler The Over The Bridge Partnership

Placings:004/4156500300/0050-0023030 **(4950)**
2001: 5^{0}G, 5^{0}HD, 5^{2}SD, 5^{3}G, 5^{0}GF, 5^{3}SW, 5^{0}G

	Starts	1st	2nd	3rd	Win & Pl
Career Total (Turf)	13	0	0	2	946
Career Total (AW)	11	1	1	1	3606

77 1/99 Ling 6f E STD £2583
Total win prize-money £2583

Going (Turf): Sf: 0-2 GS: 0-1 Gd: 0-6 GF: 0-3 Fm: 0-1
Distance: **5f/6f: 1-24** 7f-8f: 0-0 9f-13f: 0-0 14f+: 0-0
Track : **LH: 1-14** RH: 0-4 **Tight: 1-11** Gall: 0-6
Aids: Bl: 0-2 Vi: 0-0 Tstrap: 0-0
Best Rating: 50 9/01 Wolv 5f slow

Catchy Word

108 **100**

4-y-o ch c Cadeaux Genereux-Lora's Guest (Be My Guest (USA))
E A L Dunlop Abdulla Buhaleeba

Placings:1361/20540031-43100050 **(4710)**
2001: 10^{4}S, 10^{3}GF, 10^{1}G, 10^{0}GF, 10^{0}GF, 10^{0}GF, 10^{5}G, 8^{0}G

	Starts	1st	2nd	3rd	Win & Pl
Career Total (Turf)	20	4	1	3	41743

105 6/01 Wind 1m2f7y B(0-105)H GD £9303
99 9/00 NmkR 1m2f B(0-100) SFT £8850
105 10/99 Yarm 7f3y D G-F £3557
78 6/99 Hayd 6f D SFT £3501
Total win prize-money £25213

Going (Turf): Sf: 2-4 GS: 0-4 Gd: 1-4 GF: 1-8 Fm: 0-0
Distance: 5f/6f: 1-1 7f-8f: 1-10 **9f-13f: 2-9** 14f+: 0-0
Track : LH: 0-5 RH: 0-4 **Tight: 1-4** Gall: 0-4
Aids: Bl: 0-0 Vi: 0-2 Tstrap: 0-0
Best Rating: 105 6/01 Wind 1m2f7y good

A half-brother to Centre Stalls, he handles soft ground well and improved for a step up in trip at the end of 2000, including winning at Newmarket. He gradually found his form this season and won well at Windsor in June when given a much more positive ride, but has struggled off a higher mark since. Ten furlongs and forcing tactics seem to suit him.

Cateel Bay

100(83) (19)**48**

3-y-o ch f Most Welcome-Calachuchi (Martinmas)
Miss J A Camacho Stuart Postill

Placings:60-00010 **(5284)**
2001: 7^{0}SD, 8^{0}F, 11^{0}SD, 8^{1}GS, 9^{0}HY

	Starts	1st	2nd	3rd	Win & Pl
Career Total (Turf)	5	1	0	0	2632
Career Total (AW)	2	0	0	0	

48 8/01 Hayd 1m30y F G-S £2632
Total win prize-money £2632

Going (Turf): Sf: 0-2 **GS: 1-2** Gd: 0-0 GF: 0-0 Fm: 0-1
Distance: 5f/6f: 0-0 7f-8f: 0-4 **9f-13f: 1-3** 14f+: 0-0
Track : **LH: 1-5** RH: 0-0 Tight: 0-0 Gall: 0-2
Aids: Bl: 0-0 Vi: 0-0 Tstrap: 0-0
Best Rating: 48 8/01 Hayd 1m30y gd-sft

Caterham Common

88 **79**

2-y-o b c Common Grounds-Pennine Pink (IRE) (Pennine Walk)
D W Chapman (B J Meehan 11/10) David W Chapman

Placings:64100 **(5636)**
2001: 6^{6}G, 7^{4}G, 7^{1}F, 7^{0}S, 5^{0}G

	Starts	1st	2nd	3rd	Win & Pl
Career Total (Turf)	5	1	0	0	2513

79 9/01 Chep 7f16y F FRM £2366
Total win prize-money £2366

Going (Turf): Sf: 0-1 GS: 0-0 Gd: 0-3 GF: 0-0 **Fm: 1-1**
Distance: 5f/6f: 0-2 **7f-8f: 1-3** 9f-13f: 0-0 14f+: 0-0
Track : LH: 0-2 RH: 0-0 Tight: 0-1 Gall: 0-1
Aids: Bl: 0-0 Vi: 0-0 Tstrap: 0-0
Best Rating: 79 9/01 Chep 7f16y firm

A half-brother to Never Diss Miss. Appreciated fast ground when winning his maiden.

Catstreet (IRE)

75(97) (59)**40**

3-y-o b g Catrail (USA)-Catherinofaragon (USA) (Chief's Crown (USA))

P S McEntee (B W Hills 16/1) Travel Spot Ltd

Placings:000-11020000 **(2728)**

2001: 8^{1}SW, 8^{1}SD, 7^{0}SW, 8^{0}SW, 7^{2}SD, 7^{0}SD, 7^{0}F, 9^{0}SD, 7^{0}GF

	Starts	1st	2nd	3rd	Win & Pl
Career Total (Turf)	3	0	0	0	
Career Total (AW)	9	2	1	0	4294

57	1/01	Ling	1m	G(0-60)H	STD	£1820
57	1/01	Wolv	1m100y	G	SLW	£1848

Total win prize-money £3668

Going (Turf): Sf: 0-1 GS: 0-0 Gd: 0-0 GF: 0-1 Fm: 0-1
Distance: 5f/6f: 0-2 7f-8f: 1-8 9f-13f: 1-2 14f+: 0-0
Track : **LH: 2-9** RH: 0-0 **Tight: 2-7** Gall: 0-0
Aids: Bl: 0-0 Vi: 0-0 Tstrap: 0-3
Best Rating: 59 3/01 Ling 7f stand

Cauda Equina

101 **77**

7-y-o gr g Statoblest-Sea Fret (Habat)

M R Channon Michael A Foy

Placings:300/1104100600/05560005322535301621106223/65301206401004312000300/02056043020400465211305000-456553500040 **(4612)**

2001: 5^{4}S, 7^{5}G, 5^{6}G, 5^{5}F, 7^{5}F, 5^{3}G, 6^{5}G, 6^{0}GF, 6^{0}GF, 5^{0}GF, 5^{4}GF, 5^{0}F

	Starts	1st	2nd	3rd	Win & Pl
Career Total (Turf)	101	11	10	11	66818

55	8/00	Gdwd	7f	D(0-75)	GD	£4192
66	8/00	Bath	5f11y	D(0-80)	FRM	£3711
79	8/99	Ling	5f	D(0-80)	GD	£3770
81	6/99	Bath	5f11y	D(0-80)	GD	£3519
76	9/98	Bath	5f161y	D(0-80)H	GD	£3728
67	9/98	Sals	5f	D(0-80)H	GD	£3863
64	8/98	Bath	5f161y	E	GD	£2840
76	7/97	Ripn	6f	D(0-80)H	G-S	£4380
71	5/97	Bath	5f11y	D	G-S	£3351
63	4/97	Bath	5f11y	G	G-F	£2262

Total win prize-money £35621

Going (Turf): Sf: 0-16 GS: 2-10 **Gd: 7-38** GF: 1-32 Fm: 1-5
Distance: **5f/6f: 10-90** 7f-8f: 1-11 9f-13f: 0-0 14f+: 0 0
Track : **LH: 7-35** RH: 1-5 Tight: 0-10 **Gall: 7-26**
Aids: Bl: 0-0 Vi: 0-2 Tstrap: 0-0
Best Rating: 74 6/01 Bath 5f161y good

A genuine sprinter who is kept very busy, he appears to go on all types of ground and has a fine record at Bath. Probably best over six and seven these days.

Caughnawaga (FR)

111 **96**

3-y-o b c Indian Ridge-Wakria (IRE) (Sadler's Wells (USA))

H R A Cecil Lady Harrison

Placings:61-32524212 **(5271)**

2001: 7^{3}GS, 7^{2}G, 8^{5}G, 9^{2}G, 10^{4}GF, 8^{2}GS, 8^{1}G, 8^{2}HY

	Starts	1st	2nd	3rd	Win & Pl
Career Total (Turf)	10	2	4	1	21973

70	10/01	Bath	1m5y	C	GD	£6075
86	10/00	Yarm	1m3y	D	SFT	£3932

Total win prize-money £10008

Going (Turf): Sf: 1-3 GS: 0-2 **Gd: 1-4** GF: 0-1 Fm: 0-0
Distance: 5f/6f: 0-0 7f-8f: 0-6 **9f-13f: 2-4** 14f+: 0-0
Track : **LH: 1-3** RH: 0-2 **Tight: 1-1** Gall: 0-2
Aids: Bl: 0-0 Vi: 0-0 Tstrap: 0-0
Best Rating: 96 10/01 Ayr 1m heavy

Has ran quite well over seven during a lean spell for his stable, and made all at Bath in October. He looks to need some give in the ground. Proved difficult to settle on his step up to ten furlongs. Now with Philip Mitchell.

Caught In The Rain

98 **69**

3-y-o b f Spectrum (IRE)-Captive Heart (Conquistador Cielo (USA))

J L Dunlop James Barber (susan Abbott Racing)

Placings:02 **(4446)**

2001: 9^{0}GF, 9^{2}G

	Starts	1st	2nd	3rd	Win & Pl
Career Total (Turf)	2	0	1	0	1290

Going (Turf): Sf: 0-0 GS: 0-0 Gd: 0-1 GF: 0-1 Fm: 0-0
Distance: 5f/6f: 0-0 7f-8f: 0-0 9f-13f: 0-2 14f+: 0-0
Track : LH: 0-1 RH: 0-1 Tight: 0-0 Gall: 0-1
Aids: Bl: 0-0 Vi: 0-0 Tstrap: 0-0
Best Rating: 69 9/01 Sand 1m1f good

Caught Short (IRE)

66 **39**

2-y-o ch c Night Shift (USA)-Sharp Deposit (Sharpo)

J A R Toller P C J Dalby

Placings:000 **(5125)**

2001: 6^{0}GF, 5^{0}G, 5^{0}HY

	Starts	1st	2nd	3rd	Win & Pl
Career Total (Turf)	3	0	0	0	

Going (Turf): Sf: 0-1 GS: 0-0 Gd: 0-1 GF: 0-1 Fm: 0-0
Distance: 5f/6f: 0-3 7f-8f: 0-0 9f-13f: 0-0 14f+: 0-0
Track : LH: 0-0 RH: 0-0 Tight: 0-0 Gall: 0-0
Aids: Bl: 0-0 Vi: 0-0 Tstrap: 0-0
Best Rating: 39 9/01 Folk 5f good

Caused Confusion (USA)

(76) (8)

6-y-o ch g Miswaki (USA)-Reassert (USA) (Assert)

G Barnett J C Bradbury

Placings:65/00 **(5191)**

2001: 14^{0}HY, 12^{0}SD

	Starts	1st	2nd	3rd	Win & Pl
Career Total (Turf)	3	0	0	0	0
Career Total (AW)	1		0	0	0

Going (Turf): Sf: 0-1 GS: 0-1 Gd: 0-1 GF: 0-0 Fm: 0-0
Distance: 5f/6f: 0-0 7f-8f: 0-0 9f-13f: 0-3 14f+: 0-1
Track : LH: 0-3 RH: 0-1 Tight: 0-2 Gall: 0-0
Aids: Bl: 0-0 Vi: 0-0 Tstrap: 0-0
Best Rating: 8 10/01 Wolv 1m4f stand

Caution

103(98) (54)**56**

7-y-o b m Warning-Fairy Flax (IRE) (Dancing Brave (USA))

S Gollings Mr Ian & Mrs Irene Thomas

Placings:231/01143002000/0520406230001/0202305/606000422523334046-44061652004060 **(4773)**

2001: 7^{4}SD, 8^{4}SD, 9^{0}HY, 10^{6}F, 8^{1}GF, 8^{6}G, 8^{5}GF, 8^{2}GF, 7^{0}GF, 7^{0}GF, 8^{4}G, 7^{0}GF, 8^{6}GF, 8^{0}G

	Starts	1st	2nd	3rd	Win & Pl
Career Total (Turf)	61	5	10	7	35883
Career Total (AW)	5	0	0	0	533

56	6/01	Rdcr	1m	E(0-70)H	G-F	£4192
65	10/98	Rdcr	5f	E(0-70)	HVY	£2910
61	7/97	Bevl	7f100y	E	G-F	£3208
70	6/97	Ches	6f18y	D	G-F	£3551
79	9/96	Ayr	6f	E	G-F	£4240

Total win prize-money £18104

Going (Turf): Sf: 1-9 GS: 0-4 Gd: 0-22 **GF: 4-24** Fm: 0-2
Distance: 5f/6f: 2-32 **7f-8f: 3-25** 9f-13f: 0-9 14f+: 0-0
Track : LH: 1-29 RH: 1-6 **Tight: 1-11** Gall: 0-2
Aids: Bl: 0-1 Vi: 0-0 Tstrap: 0-0
Best Rating: 56 8/01 NmkJ 1m good

She tries hard, but has a poor winning record in recent seasons. Goes on fast ground, but handles heavy extremely well. Stays a mile and is habitually held up.

Cautious Joe

103(88) (70)**59**

4-y-o b f First Trump-Jomel Amou (IRE) (Ela-Mana-Mou)

R A Fahey Exors Of The Late T P Staunton

Placings:100/00035503011200-0230010450 **(5539)**

2001: 10^{0}S, 8^{2}S, 9^{3}GF, 8^{0}GF, 8^{0}GF, 8^{1}GS, 8^{0}G, 8^{4}GS, 10^{5}HY, 8^{0}S

	Starts	1st	2nd	3rd	Win & Pl
Career Total (Turf)	23	4	2	3	15835
Career Total (AW)	4	0	0	0	

58	7/01	Ayr	1m	D(0-80)H	G-S	£4205
69	10/00	Leic	1m8y	F(0-60)	HVY	£3194
54	9/00	Leic	1m8y	F(0-60)	G-S	£2466
64	5/99	Newc	5f	F	G-F	£2379

Total win prize-money £12247

Going (Turf): Sf: 1-6 **GS: 2-4** Gd: 0-6 GF: 1-6 Fm: 0-1
Distance: 5f/6f: 1-9 7f-8f: 1-5 **9f-13f: 2-13** 14f+: 0-0
Track : **LH: 1-14** RH: 0-3 Tight: 0-5 Gall: 0-5
Aids: Bl: 0-0 Vi: 0-1 Tstrap: 0-0
Best Rating: 59 10/01 Newc 1m3y gd-sft

Improved for a step up in trip at the end of last season, winning twice on soft ground. Her best form this term has been on easy ground, including when winning at Ayr in July. Less effective on a fast surface.

Cauvery

109 **108**

3-y-o ch c Exit To Nowhere (USA)-Triple Zee (USA) (Zilzal (USA))

S P C Woods W J P Jackson

Placings:210300-245235 **(3629)**

2001: 7^{2}GS, 8^{4}G, 7^{5}GF, 8^{2}GF, 8^{3}GF, 8^{5}G

	Starts	1st	2nd	3rd	Win & Pl
Career Total (Turf)	12	1	3	2	40077

86	6/00	Newc	7f	D	FRM	£3575

Total win prize-money £3575

Going (Turf): Sf: 0-1 GS: 0-1 Gd: 0-3 GF: 0-6 **Fm: 1-1**
Distance: 5f/6f: 0-1 **7f-8f: 1-10** 9f-13f: 0-1 14f+: 0-0
Track : LH: 0-2 RH: 0-5 Tight: 0-1 Gall: 0-2
Aids: Bl: 0-0 Vi: 0-0 Tstrap: 0-0
Best Rating: 108 6/01 Epsm 1m114y gd-fm

Useful as a juvenile if not quite Group class, he was runner-up in a Newmarket conditions event on his reappearance. Subsequently fourth in the Italian Guineas, and stepped up on that effort with a fine second in the Diomed Stakes at Epsom on Derby day. Best on fast ground. Has gone to race in Hong Kong.

Cavernara (IRE)

(95) (65)**50**

3-y-o b f Lion Cavern (USA)-Rainbow Ring (Rainbow Quest (USA))

T D Barron Nigel Shields

Placings:454-0 **(5611)**

2001: 8^{0}SD

	Starts	1st	2nd	3rd	Win & Pl
Career Total (Turf)	2	0	0	0	288

	Starts	1st	2nd	3rd	Win & Pl
Career Total (AW)	2	0	0	0	265

Going (Turf): Sf: 0-0 GS: 0-0 Gd: 0-1 GF: 0-1 Fm: 0-0
Distance: 5f/6f: 0-1 7f-8f: 0-2 9f-13f: 0-1 14f+: 0-0
Track : LH: 0-4 RH: 0-0 Tight: 0-3 Gall: 0-0
Aids: Bl: 0-0 Vi: 0-0 Tstrap: 0-0
Best Rating: 23 11/01 Wolv 1m100y stand

Caversfield

96(101) (55)**37**
6-y-o ch h Tina's Pet-Canoodle (Warpath)
J M Bradley S E Hall

Placings:200011/004036020300**336**/62443533000/000060300**412220-3416301500**000 **(1728)**
2001: 8^{3}SD, 7^{4}SD, 8^{1}SW, 7^{6}SD, 8^{3}SW, 8^{0}SW, 8^{1}SD, 7^{5}SD, 8^{0}SW, 7^{0}SD, 8^{0}GF, 8^{0}G, 7^{0}GF

			Starts	1st	2nd	3rd	Win & Pl
Career Total (Turf)			39	2	3	7	13141
Career Total (AW)			21	3	3	3	8308
46	3/01	Sthl	1m	F(0-60)		STD	£2135
55	1/01	Sthl	1m	F		SLW	£2254
42	11/00	Sthl	7f	G		STD	£1512
76	10/97	Leic	7f9y	E(0-85)		GD	£3353
76	8/97	Wind	5f217y	D		G-F	£3290

Total win prize-money £12544

Going (Turf): Sf: 0-8 GS: 0-3 **Gd: 1-7 GF: 1-14** Fm: 0-7
Distance: 5f/6f: 1-6 **7f-8f: 4-44** 9f-13f: 0-10 14f+: 0-0
Track : **LH: 3-36** RH: 1-9 Tight: 0-19 **Gall: 1-3**
Aids: Bl: 0-1 Vi: 0-1 Tstrap: 0-0
Best Rating: 55 1/01 Sthl 1m slow

Caxton Lad

84(68) (78)**60**
4-y-o b g Cyrano De Bergerac-Urania (Most Welcome)
P J Makin Four Seasons Racing Ltd

Placings:360161/000-0000 **(5497)**
2001: 5^{0}GS, 5^{0}HY, 5^{0}HY, 5^{0}HY

			Starts	1st	2nd	3rd	Win & Pl
Career Total (Turf)			12	1	0	1	4189
Career Total (AW)			1	1	0	0	2668
94	12/99	Sthl	5f	E(0-85)H		STD	£2668
78	10/99	Hayd	5f	D H		HVY	£3663

Total win prize-money £6332

Going (Turf): Sf: 1-8 GS: 0-3 Gd: 0-1 GF: 0-0 Fm: 0-0
Distance: **5f/6f: 2-13** 7f-8f: 0-0 9f-13f: 0-0 14f+: 0-0
Track : LH: 0-0 RH: 0-2 Tight: 0-0 Gall: 0-2
Aids: Bl: 0-0 Vi: 0-1 Tstrap: 0-0
Best Rating: 39 7/01 Ayr 5f gd-sft

Won two nurseries as a juvenile, but has clearly had training problems and has shown little of late.

Cayman Expresso (IRE)

98 **63**
3-y-o b f Fayruz-Cappuchino (IRE) (Roi Danzig (USA))
R Hannon The Cayman 'A' Team

Placings:6350-033064010 **(4785)**
2001: 5^{0}GS, 6^{3}G, 5^{3}GF, 6^{0}GF, 6^{6}GF, 5^{4}G, 5^{0}G, 5^{1}GF, 5^{0}G

			Starts	1st	2nd	3rd	Win & Pl
Career Total (Turf)			13	1	0	3	4580
61	8/01	Folk	5f	E		G-F	£2884

Total win prize-money £2884

Going (Turf): Sf: 0-0 GS: 0-1 Gd: 0-5 **GF: 1-7** Fm: 0-0
Distance: **5f/6f: 1-13** 7f-8f: 0-0 9f-13f: 0-0 14f+: 0-0
Track : LH: 0-1 RH: 0-1 Tight: 0-0 Gall: 0-2
Aids: Bl: 0-0 Vi: 0-0 Tstrap: 0-0
Best Rating: 82 5/01 Wind 6f good

Showed good two-year-old form but had been slightly disappointing before scoring at Folkestone in August 2001. Suited by five furlongs and fast ground.

Cayman Lodge (IRE)

93 **76**
2-y-o b f Grand Lodge (USA)-Damezao (Alzao (USA))
M W Easterby M P Burke

Placings:56030 **(5229)**
2001: 5^{5}G, 6^{6}G, 7^{0}G, 8^{3}HY, 7^{0}S

	Starts	1st	2nd	3rd	Win & Pl
Career Total (Turf)	5	0	0	1	713

Going (Turf): Sf: 0-2 GS: 0-0 Gd: 0-3 GF: 0-0 Fm: 0-0
Distance: 5f/6f: 0-1 7f-8f: 0-3 9f-13f: 0-1 14f+: 0-0
Track : LH: 0-3 RH: 0-0 Tight: 0-0 Gall: 0-2
Aids: Bl: 0-0 Vi: 0-0 Tstrap: 0-0
Best Rating: 76 9/01 Hayd 1m30y heavy

Cayman Sound

79 **35**
2-y-o b f Turtle Island (IRE)-Kukri (Kris)
C F Wall The Triple S Partnership

Placings:0 **(4960)**
2001: 6^{0}S

	Starts	1st	2nd	3rd	Win & Pl
Career Total (Turf)	1	0	0	0	

Going (Turf): Sf: 0-1 GS: 0-0 Gd: 0-0 GF: 0-0 Fm: 0-0
Distance: 5f/6f: 0-1 7f-8f: 0-0 9f-13f: 0-0 14f+: 0-0
Track : LH: 0-1 RH: 0-0 Tight: 0-0 Gall: 0-0
Aids: Bl: 0-0 Vi: 0-0 Tstrap: 0-0
Best Rating: 35 9/01 Pont 6f soft

Cayman Sunset (IRE)

106 **107**
4-y-o ch f Night Shift (USA)-Robinia (USA) (Roberto (USA))
E A L Dunlop M P Burke

Placings:16424-1464040300 **(5241a)**
2001: 9^{1}G, 10^{4}GF, 10^{6}G, 8^{4}GF, 8^{0}G, 9^{4}G, 9^{0}S, 9^{3}F, 10^{0}G, 8^{0}F

			Starts	1st	2nd	3rd	Win & Pl
Career Total (Turf)			15	2	1	1	46771
103	5/01	NmkR	1m1f	A		GD	£13572
81	7/00	Kemp	7f	D		G-S	£4134

Total win prize-money £17706

Going (Turf): Sf: 0-3 **GS: 1-1 Gd: 1-6** GF: 0-3 Fm: 0-2
Distance: 5f/6f: 0-0 7f-8f: 1-6 9f-13f: 1-9 14f+: 0-0
Track : LH: 0-4 **RH: 1-3** Tight: 0-2 **Gall: 1-2**
Aids: Bl: 0-0 Vi: 0-0 Tstrap: 0-0
Best Rating: 107 5/01 StCl 1m2f110y good

She looks an improved filly this season and ran out the clear-cut winner of a Newmarket Listed event on her return. She has continued to run with credit since and was unlucky not to finish closer in the Diomed Stakes at Epsom, and ran well in a Grade Two at Woodbine in September. Does not seem to quite get ten furlongs, swishes her tail under pressure, but looks genuine. Seems to handle most ground.

Cd Europe (IRE)

104 **108**
3-y-o ch c Royal Academy (USA)-Woodland Orchid (IRE) (Woodman (USA))
M R Channon Graeme Love

Placings:11240-406023 **(4700)**
2001: 8^{4}S, 8^{0}G, 8^{6}GF, 7^{0}G, 7^{2}GF, 8^{3}GS

			Starts	1st	2nd	3rd	Win & Pl
Career Total (Turf)			11	2	2	1	78326
104	6/00	Asct	6f	A		G-F	£36000
89	5/00	Gdwd	6f	D		SFT	£4426

Total win prize-money £40427

Going (Turf): Sf: 1-4 GS: 0-1 Gd: 0-2 **GF: 1-4** Fm: 0-0
Distance: **5f/6f: 2-2** 7f-8f: 0-9 9f-13f: 0-0 14f+: 0-0
Track : LH: 0-2 RH: 0-3 Tight: 0-0 Gall: 0-2
Aids: Bl: 0-0 Vi: 0-0 Tstrap: 0-0
Best Rating: 108 4/01 NmkR 1m soft

Landed the Coventry Stakes at Royal Ascot last year, then after a break put in decent efforts to finish runner-up in the Champagne Stakes and fourth in the Grand Criterium in France. He was running on at the finish when making his seasonal debut in the Craven and was badly drawn when disappointing in the Italian 2000 Guineas. Showed signs of a return to form in conditions events in the autumn.

Cd Flyer (IRE)

108 **76**
4-y-o ch g Grand Lodge (USA)-Pretext (Polish Precedent (USA))
M R Channon Graeme Love

Placings:6341340105/0644633003-55442042000 **(5688)**
2001: 6^{5}G, 5^{5}G, 6^{4}G, 6^{4}G, 6^{2}G, 7^{0}GF, 6^{4}S, 6^{2}HY, 5^{0}HY, 6^{0}G, 7^{0}S

			Starts	1st	2nd	3rd	Win & Pl
Career Total (Turf)			31	2	2	5	25454
80	10/99	NmkJ	6f	C(0-95)H		SFT	£6745
77	5/99	Thsk	5f	D		G-S	£3847

Total win prize-money £10592

Going (Turf): Sf: 1-8 GS: 1-3 Gd: 0-14 GF: 0-6 Fm: 0-0
Distance: **5f/6f: 2-23** 7f-8f: 0-8 9f-13f: 0-0 14f+: 0-0
Track : LH: 0-3 RH: 0-7 Tight: 0-1 Gall: 0-8
Aids: Bl: 0-0 Vi: 0-0 Tstrap: 0-0
Best Rating: 76 9/01 Kemp 6f good

Successful in a Thirsk maiden and a Newmarket nursery in 1999, he has failed to add to that since but has run consistently well. Suited by six furlongs and cut in the ground

Cead Mile Failte

101 **39?**
6-y-o ch g Most Welcome-Avionne (Derrylin)
B J Llewellyn B W Parren

Placings:65003005000/10 **(3745)**
2001: 11^{1}GS, 12^{0}S

			Starts	1st	2nd	3rd	Win & Pl
Career Total (Turf)			10	1	0	1	2954
Career Total (AW)			3	0	0	0	0
39	7/01	Leic	1m3f183yF			G-S	£2523

Total win prize-money £2524

Going (Turf): Sf: 0-1 **GS: 1-3** Gd: 0-1 GF: 0-2 Fm: 0-3
Distance: 5f/6f: 0-5 7f-8f: 0-5 **9f-13f: 1-3** 14f+: 0-0
Track : LH: 0-7 **RH: 1-3** Tight: 0-3 Gall: 0-2
Aids: Bl: 0-0 Vi: 0-0 Tstrap: 0-0
Best Rating: 39 7/01 Leic 1m3f183y gd-sft

Cearnach

100(94) (61)**46**
3-y-o b g Night Shift (USA)-High Matinee (Shirley Heights)
J M Bradley (B J Meehan 7/8) Leeway (wholesale) Meats Ltd

Placings:005430-0036546006006 **(5027)**
2001: 7^{0}SD, 7^{0}GS, 6^{3}SD, 7^{6}F, 5^{5}GF, 6^{4}GF, 6^{6}GF, 5^{0}F, 5^{0}GF, 6^{6}GF, 6^{0}GF, 6^{0}F, 5^{6}S

	Starts	1st	2nd	3rd	Win & Pl
Career Total (Turf)	17	0	0	1	1295
Career Total (AW)	2	0	0	1	429

Going (Turf): Sf: 0-3 GS: 0-2 Gd: 0-2 GF: 0-7 Fm: 0-3

Distance: 5f/6f: 0-10 7f-8f: 0-9 9f-13f: 0-0 14f+: 0-0
Track : LH: 0-8 RH: 0-1 Tight: 0-1 Gall: 0-3
Aids: Bl: 0-5 Vi: 0-0 Tstrap: 0-6
Best Rating: 61 4/01 Sthl 6f stand

Cedar Flag (IRE)

89(103) (35)**26**
7-y-o br g Jareer (USA)-Sasha Lea (Cawston's Clown)
M R Ewer-Hoad (R J O'Sullivan 19/1) Southdowns Partnership

Placings:060/32431004000-0000 **(4181)**
2001: 12^{0}SW, 10^{0}GF, 11^{0}G, 12^{0}GF

	Starts	1st	2nd	3rd	Win & Pl
Career Total (Turf)	7	0	0	0	0
Career Total (AW)	11	1	1	2	3451

44 3/00 Sthl 1m4f F(0-70)H STD £1799
Total win prize-money £1799

Going (Turf): Sf: 0-0 GS: 0-2 Gd: 0-1 GF: 0-3 Fm: 0-1
Distance: 5f/6f: 0-0 7f-8f: 0-1 **9f-13f: 1-13** 14f+: 0-4
Track : **LH: 1-17** RH: 0-1 Tight: 0-9 Gall: 0-0
Aids: Bl: 0-0 Vi: 0-0 Tstrap: 0-2
Best Rating: 15 1/01 Sthl 1m4f slow

Cedar Gold (IRE)

90 **54**
3-y-o ch c Rainbows For Life (CAN)-Miss Roberto (FR) (Don Roberto (USA))
R J O'Sullivan R O S Racing

Placings:5 **(2367)**
2001: 9^{5}GF

	Starts	1st	2nd	3rd	Win & Pl
Career Total (Turf)	1	0	0	0	0

Going (Turf): Sf: 0-0 GS: 0-0 Gd: 0-0 GF: 0-1 Fm: 0-0
Distance: 5f/6f: 0-0 7f-8f: 0-0 9f-13f: 0-1 14f+: 0-0
Track : LH: 0-0 RH: 0-1 Tight: 0-1 Gall: 0-0
Aids: Bl: 0-0 Vi: 0-0 Tstrap: 0-0
Best Rating: 54 6/01 Gdwd 1m1f gd-fm

Cedar Hoops

88 **54**
3-y-o b c Charnwood Forest (IRE)-Zagreb Flyer (Old Vic)
R J O'Sullivan R O S Racing

Placings:600 **(4641)**
2001: 7^{6}S, 6^{0}GF, 7^{0}GF

	Starts	1st	2nd	3rd	Win & Pl
Career Total (Turf)	3	0	0	0	0

Going (Turf): Sf: 0-1 GS: 0-0 Gd: 0-0 GF: 0-2 Fm: 0-0
Distance: 5f/6f: 0-1 7f-8f: 0-2 9f-13f: 0-0 14f+: 0-0
Track : LH: 0-0 RH: 0-0 Tight: 0-0 Gall: 0-0
Aids: Bl: 0-0 Vi: 0-0 Tstrap: 0-0
Best Rating: 54 8/01 Ling 6f gd-fm

Cedar Jeneva

(94) (34)**27**
3-y-o b f Muhtarram (USA)-Soba Up (Persian Heights)
R J O'Sullivan Robert Allen

Placings:0U0060-4504 **(0483)**
2001: 10^{4}SD, 12^{5}SD, 6^{0}SW, 10^{4}SD

	Starts	1st	2nd	3rd	Win & Pl
Career Total (Turf)	4	0	0	0	
Career Total (AW)	6	0	0	0	0

Going (Turf): Sf: 0-1 GS: 0-1 Gd: 0-0 GF: 0-2 Fm: 0-0
Distance: 5f/6f: 0-5 7f-8f: 0-2 9f-13f: 0-3 14f+: 0-0
Track : LH: 0-8 RH: 0-1 Tight: 0-6 Gall: 0-2
Aids: Bl: 0-3 Vi: 0-0 Tstrap: 0-0
Best Rating: 34 2/01 Ling 1m4f stand

Cedar Master (IRE)

101 **78**
4-y-o b g Soviet Lad (USA)-Samriah (IRE) (Wassl)
R J O'Sullivan Robert Allen

Placings:5310333024/0556032004-060 **(2105)**
2001: 8^{0}GF, 8^{6}GF, 9^{0}GF

	Starts	1st	2nd	3rd	Win & Pl
Career Total (Turf)	23	1	2	5	29625

83 5/99 Chep 6f16y E GD £2864
Total win prize-money £2864

Going (Turf): Sf: 0-3 GS: 0-2 **Gd: 1-3** GF: 0-14 Fm: 0-1
Distance: 5f/6f: 0-7 **7f-8f: 1-11** 9f-13f: 0-5 14f+: 0-0
Track : LH: 0-6 RH: 0-6 Tight: 0-1 Gall: 0-2
Aids: Bl: 0-10 Vi: 0-4 Tstrap: 0-0
Best Rating: 74 6/01 Kemp 1m gd-fm

Fair sprinter on a long losing run, goes well on sharp tracks.

Cedar Rangers (USA)

96 **52**
3-y-o b g Anabaa (USA)-Chelsea (USA) (Miswaki (USA))
R J O'Sullivan 'We Are Qpr' Racing Partnership

Placings:510-0000000 **(4415)**
2001: 6^{0}G, 6^{0}GF, 5^{0}GF, 5^{0}GF, 6^{0}GF, 7^{0}G, 7^{0}S

	Starts	1st	2nd	3rd	Win & Pl
Career Total (Turf)	10	1	0	0	4024

73 7/00 Ling 6f D GD £4023
Total win prize-money £4024

Going (Turf): Sf: 0-1 GS: 0-0 **Gd: 1-4** GF: 0-5 Fm: 0-0
Distance: **5f/6f: 1-8** 7f-8f: 0-2 9f-13f: 0-0 14f+: 0-0
Track : LH: 0-1 RH: 0-1 Tight: 0-1 Gall: 0-1
Aids: Bl: 0-0 Vi: 0-0 Tstrap: 0-0
Best Rating: 67 5/01 Gdwd 6f gd-fm

Winner of a Lingfield maiden in 2000, he has shown little in sprints this term. Dropping down the handicap.

Cedar Treble

91 **40**
3-y-o b c Emperor Jones (USA)-Tjakka (USA) (Little Missouri (USA))
R J O'Sullivan Mrs R J Doorgachurn

Placings:3-000005 **(4019)**
2001: 7^{0}S, 8^{0}GS, 9^{0}F, 7^{0}GF, 8^{0}G, 12^{5}G

	Starts	1st	2nd	3rd	Win & Pl
Career Total (Turf)	7	0	0	1	568

Going (Turf): Sf: 0-2 GS: 0-1 Gd: 0-2 GF: 0-1 Fm: 0-1
Distance: 5f/6f: 0-1 7f-8f: 0-3 9f-13f: 0-3 14f+: 0-0
Track : LH: 0-3 RH: 0-3 Tight: 0-1 Gall: 0-1
Aids: Bl: 0-0 Vi: 0-0 Tstrap: 0-0
Best Rating: 53 5/01 Kemp 1m gd-sft

Cedar Tsar (IRE)

70(100) (51)**27**
3-y-o b c Inzar (USA)-The Aspecto Girl (IRE) (Alzao (USA))
D W Chapman Michael Hill

Placings:62021333100006P0-0023456000 **(1728)**
2001: 7^{0}SD, 6^{0}SD, 6^{2}SW, 7^{3}SD, 6^{4}SD, 6^{5}SD, 6^{6}SD, 6^{0}SD, 6^{0}GF, 7^{0}GF

	Starts	1st	2nd	3rd	Win & Pl
Career Total (Turf)	11	0	2	3	2615
Career Total (AW)	15	2	1	1	5653

78 7/00 Sthl 6f E STD £2741
67 6/00 Sthl 7f G STD £1869
Total win prize-money £4610

Going (Turf): Sf: 0-0 GS: 0-1 Gd: 0-3 GF: 0-4 Fm: 0-3
Distance: 5f/6f: 1-18 7f-8f: 1-8 9f-13f: 0-0 14f+: 0-0
Track : **LH: 2-19** RH: 0-0 Tight: 0-7 Gall: 0-0
Aids: Bl: 0-3 Vi: 0-0 Tstrap: 0-0
Best Rating: 51 3/01 Sthl 6f stand

Ceepio (IRE)

103 **101**
3-y-o b c Pennekamp (USA)-Boranwood (IRE) (Exhibitioner)
T G Mills Mr C Stephens

Placings:3135-200050 **(4986)**
2001: 6^{2}S, 6^{0}GF, 6^{0}GF, 7^{0}GF, 7^{5}GF, 6^{0}G

	Starts	1st	2nd	3rd	Win & Pl
Career Total (Turf)	10	1	1	2	13626

93 6/00 Nott 6f15y D G-F £3575
Total win prize-money £3575

Going (Turf): Sf: 0-2 GS: 0-0 Gd: 0-2 **GF: 1-6** Fm: 0-0
Distance: 5f/6f: 0-5 **7f-8f: 1-5** 9f-13f: 0-0 14f+: 0-0
Track : LH: 0-0 RH: 0-0 Tight: 0-0 Gall: 0-0
Aids: Bl: 0-0 Vi: 0-0 Tstrap: 0-0
Best Rating: 101 5/01 Newb 6f8y soft

An attractive colt. Ran a good third in Richmond Stakes at Goodwood as a juvenile, after having impressed winning his maiden at Nottingham. He looked to have trained on when going down narrowly at Newbury on his reappearance but has disappointed all attempts since. Suited by anything from good to firm to soft.

Ceilidh Jig (IRE)

81(50) **39**
2-y-o b f General Monash (USA)-Ringawoody (Auction Ring (USA))
J J Quinn Mrs S Quinn

Placings:000000 **(5370)**
2001: 5^{0}GF, 5^{0}GF, 7^{0}SD, 6^{0}G, 8^{0}G, 7^{0}G

	Starts	1st	2nd	3rd	Win & Pl
Career Total (Turf)	5	0	0	0	
Career Total (AW)	1	0	0	0	

Going (Turf): Sf: 0-0 GS: 0-0 Gd: 0-3 GF: 0-2 Fm: 0-0
Distance: 5f/6f: 0-3 7f-8f: 0-3 9f-13f: 0-0 14f+: 0-0
Track : LH: 0-2 RH: 0-0 Tight: 0-0 Gall: 0-1
Aids: Bl: 0-0 Vi: 0-1 Tstrap: 0-0
Best Rating: 39 8/01 Newc 1m good

Ceinwen

67
6-y-o ch m Keen-Drudwen (Sayf El Arab (USA))
A W Carroll C F Basterfield

Placings:000-00 **(4526)**
2001: 10^{0}GF, 7^{0}GF

	Starts	1st	2nd	3rd	Win & Pl
Career Total (Turf)	4	0	0	0	
Career Total (AW)	1	0	0	0	

Going (Turf): Sf: 0-1 GS: 0-0 Gd: 0-0 GF: 0-2 Fm: 0-1
Distance: 5f/6f: 0-0 7f-8f: 0-3 9f-13f: 0-2 14f+: 0-0
Track : LH: 0-3 RH: 0-0 Tight: 0-1 Gall: 0-0
Aids: Bl: 0-0 Vi: 0-0 Tstrap: 0-0

Celebration Town (IRE)

106 **91d**
4-y-o b/br g Case Law-Battle Queen (Kind Of Hush)
D Morris Meadowcrest Limited

Placings:505/1016121-000205000 **(5608)**
2001: 7^{0}S, 6^{0}G, 8^{0}GF, 7^{2}G, 8^{0}G, 8^{5}GF, 9^{0}G, 8^{0}GS, 7^{0}GS

	Starts	1st	2nd	3rd	Win & Pl
Career Total (Turf)	19	4	2	0	33559

90	10/00	York	7f202y	B(0-100)H	SFT	£10655
85	8/00	NmkJ	7f	D(0-80)H	GD	£4621
78	5/00	Sand	7f16y	D(0-80)H	HVY	£5573
69	4/00	Sthl	7f	D(0-80)H	G-S	£4121

Total win prize-money £24973

Going (Turf): Sf: 2-4 GS: 1-5 Gd: 1-6 GF: 0-3 Fm: 0-1
Distance: 5f/6f: 0-4 **7f-8f: 4-14** 9f-13f: 0-1 14f+: 0-0
Track : **LH: 2-7** RH: 1-4 Tight: 0-0 **Gall: 1-4**
Aids: Bl: 0-0 Vi: 0-0 Tstrap: 0-0
Best Rating: 89 9/01 Ayr 1m gd-fm

A winner four times over in 2000, he has not recaptured his best in 2001. He acts on good but is suited by soft ground. Usually held up.

Celebre Blu

104(84) (41)**67**
4-y-o b g Suave Dancer (USA)-Taufan Blu (IRE) (Taufan (USA))
J Mackie Tim Kelly

Placings:6333000360-110 **(1599)**
2001: 10^{1}S, 12^{1}S, 14^{0}GF

	Starts	1st	2nd	3rd	Win & Pl
Career Total (Turf)	12	2	0	4	9038
Career Total (AW)	1	0	0	0	0

67	5/01	Newc	1m4f93y	E(0-70)H	SFT	£3059
58	4/01	Pont	1m2f6y	E(0-75)H	SFT	£4160

Total win prize-money £7219

Going (Turf): Sf: 2-3 GS: 0-2 Gd: 0-2 GF: 0-3 Fm: 0-2
Distance: 5f/6f: 0-1 7f-8f: 0-5 **9f-13f: 2-6** 14f+: 0-1
Track : **LH: 2-7** RH: 0-4 Tight: 0-3 **Gall: 1-1**
Aids: Bl: 0-0 Vi: 0-0 Tstrap: 0-0
Best Rating: 67 5/01 Newc 1m4f93y soft

Celerity (IRE)

92(95) (53)**37**
3-y-o b f Fairy King (USA)-Three Terns (USA) (Arctic Tern (USA))
M J Polglase Gen Sir G Howlett, M Doury & T Swift

Placings:06006505-540314000000460 **(5681)**
2001: 6^{5}SD, 7^{4}SD, 8^{0}SD, 8^{3}S, 8^{1}HY, 7^{4}SD, 8^{0}G, 10^{0}GF, 8^{0}SD, 9^{0}GF, 10^{0}S, 10^{0}HY, 7^{4}HY, 8^{6}GS, 8^{0}S, 8^{0}HY

	Starts	1st	2nd	3rd	Win & Pl
Career Total (Turf)	12	1	0	1	3344
Career Total (AW)	11	0	0	0	0

51	4/01	Wwck	1m22y	F(0-60)H	HVY	£3052

Total win prize-money £3052

Going (Turf): Sf: 1-6 GS: 0-1 Gd: 0-1 GF: 0-4 Fm: 0-0
Distance: 5f/6f: 0-4 7f-8f: 0-11 **9f-13f: 1-8** 14f+: 0-0
Track : LH: 0-15 RH: 0-1 Tight: 0-2 Gall: 0-2
Aids: Bl: 0-0 Vi: 0-0 Tstrap: 0-0
Best Rating: 53 2/01 Sthl 7f stand

Modest handicapper, her only win came in a small Warwick handicap on heavy ground. Stays a mile although has been tried over further.

Celestial Power

89 **42**
3-y-o b f Superpower-Heavenly Queen (Scottish Reel)
A Bailey Mrs V Farrington

Placings:00-5600 **(3643)**
2001: 7^{5}GF, 7^{6}G, 6^{0}GF, 6^{0}F

	Starts	1st	2nd	3rd	Win & Pl
Career Total (Turf)	6	0	0	0	0

Going (Turf): Sf: 0-0 GS: 0-1 Gd: 0-2 GF: 0-2 Fm: 0-1
Distance: 5f/6f: 0-3 7f-8f: 0-3 9f-13f: 0-0 14f+: 0-0
Track : LH: 0-2 RH: 0-1 Tight: 0-2 Gall: 0-0
Aids: Bl: 0-0 Vi: 0-0 Tstrap: 0-0
Best Rating: 42 6/01 Bevl 7f100y gd-fm

Celestien

96 **78**
2-y-o ch f Hurricane Sky (AUS)-Gate Of Heaven (Starry Night (USA))
I A Wood John Purcell

Placings:4210 **(3581)**
2001: 7^{4}F, 5^{2}G, 5^{1}G, 5^{0}GF

	Starts	1st	2nd	3rd	Win & Pl
Career Total (Turf)	4	1	1	0	6070

78	7/01	Donc	5f	D	GD	£4754

Total win prize-money £4755

Going (Turf): Sf: 0-0 GS: 0-0 **Gd: 1-2** GF: 0-1 Fm: 0-1
Distance: **5f/6f: 1-3** 7f-8f: 0-1 9f-13f: 0-0 14f+: 0-0
Track : LH: 0-0 RH: 0-0 Tight: 0-0 Gall: 0-0
Aids: Bl: 0-0 Vi: 0-0 Tstrap: 0-0
Best Rating: 78 7/01 Donc 5f good

She stepped up on her debut effort over seven furlongs when dropped back to five and has since won over that trip at Doncaster. She has plenty of speed.

Celler Wine

2-y-o b g Lugana Beach-Noble Canonire (Gunner B)
B Palling B A Evans

Placings:0 **(1474)**
2001: 6^{0}SD

	Starts	1st	2nd	3rd	Win & Pl
Career Total (Turf)	0	0	0	0	
Career Total (AW)	1	0	0	0	

Going (Turf): Sf: 0-0 GS: 0-0 Gd: 0-0 GF: 0-0 Fm: 0-0
Distance: 5f/6f: 0-1 7f-8f: 0-0 9f-13f: 0-0 14f+: 0-0
Track : LH: 0-1 RH: 0-0 Tight: 0-0 Gall: 0-0
Aids: Bl: 0-0 Vi: 0-0 Tstrap: 0-0
Best Rating: none

Cello Solo

96(82) (23)**48**
4-y-o b g Piccolo-Whirling Words (Sparkler)
P J Makin Mrs P J Makin

Placings:30-000 **(5292)**
2001: 7^{0}S, 5^{0}G, 7^{0}S

	Starts	1st	2nd	3rd	Win & Pl
Career Total (Turf)	4	0	0	1	394
Career Total (AW)	1	0	0	0	

Going (Turf): Sf: 0-3 GS: 0-0 Gd: 0-1 GF: 0-0 Fm: 0-0
Distance: 5f/6f: 0-1 7f-8f: 0-3 9f-13f: 0-1 14f+: 0-0
Track : LH: 0-1 RH: 0-1 Tight: 0-0 Gall: 0-1
Aids: Bl: 0-0 Vi: 0-0 Tstrap: 0-0
Best Rating: 48 6/01 Sand 5f6y good

Showed promise on his debut at the back-end of 2000 but has failed to build on that so far. Has yet to race on fast ground.

Celotti (IRE)

100(87) (61)**23**
3-y-o b f Celtic Swing-Zalotti (IRE) (Polish Patriot (USA))
R Hollinshead P D Savill

Placings:3510200-00005000000 **(5273)**
2001: 6^{0}G, 7^{0}G, 5^{0}GF, 5^{0}GF, 5^{5}GF, 5^{0}SD, 5^{0}F, 6^{0}G, 5^{0}GS, 6^{0}GS, 5^{0}HY

	Starts	1st	2nd	3rd	Win & Pl
Career Total (Turf)	16	0	1	1	1655
Career Total (AW)	2	1	0	0	2205

68	7/00	Sthl	5f	F	STD	£2205

Total win prize-money £2205

Going (Turf): Sf: 0-2 GS: 0-2 Gd: 0-5 GF: 0-6 Fm: 0-1
Distance: **5f/6f: 1-15** 7f-8f: 0-3 9f-13f: 0-0 14f+: 0-0
Track : LH: 0-1 RH: 0-1 Tight: 0-0 Gall: 0-0
Aids: Bl: 0-0 Vi: 0-0 Tstrap: 0-1
Best Rating: 55 7/01 Leic 5f218y gd-fm

Celtic Ballet

101 **83**
2-y-o b f Celtic Swing-Fairy Feet (Sadler's Wells (USA))
M A Jarvis P D Savill

Placings:2141 **(5379)**
2001: 7^{2}F, 7^{1}G, 6^{4}G, 7^{1}S

	Starts	1st	2nd	3rd	Win & Pl
Career Total (Turf)	4	2	1	0	21453

83	10/01	Catt	7f	D(0-85)	SFT	£4322
72	9/01	Bevl	7f100y	E	GD	£3220

Total win prize-money £7543

Going (Turf): Sf: 1-1 GS: 0-0 **Gd: 1-2** GF: 0-0 Fm: 0-1
Distance: 5f/6f: 0-0 **7f-8f: 2-4** 9f-13f: 0-0 14f+: 0-0
Track : LH: 1-1 RH: 1-1 **Tight: 1-1** Gall: 0-0
Aids: Bl: 0-0 Vi: 0-0 Tstrap: 0-0
Best Rating: 83 10/01 Catt 7f soft

Got off the mark at the second time of asking in a seven-furlong auction maiden on good and later took a nursery. Acts on any ground.

Celtic Exit (FR)

91 **52**
7-y-o b g Exit To Nowhere (USA)-Amour Celtique (Northfields (USA))
I A Balding Action Bloodstock

Placings:2353000/05100000020/010635060/50515-000000 **(5145)**
2001: 7^{0}S, 7^{0}G, 7^{0}GF, 7^{0}S, 7^{0}G, 7^{0}G

	Starts	1st	2nd	3rd	Win & Pl
Career Total (Turf)	38	3	2	3	43465

81	6/00	Gdwd	7f	C(0-90)H	GD	£11163
	4/99	Lonc	1m	H	VS	£13994
	4/98	Lonc	7f	H	HVY	£5051

Total win prize-money £30209

Going (Turf): Sf: 0-2 GS: 0-1 **Gd: 1-4** GF: 0-2 Fm: 0-0
Distance: 5f/6f: 0-0 **7f-8f: 1-9** 9f-13f: 0-0 14f+: 0-0
Track : LH: 0-0 **RH: 1-5** Tight: 0-0 Gall: 0-1
Aids: Bl: 0-0 Vi: 0-0 **Tstrap: 1-6**
Best Rating: 64 4/01 Kemp 7f soft

Ex-French, he landed a Goodwood handicap on his second start in this country in the summer of 2000, but has not gone on from there. Best over seven furlongs.

Celtic H'Alo

96(70) (13)**54**
3-y-o b f Celtic Swing-Alo Ez (Alzao (USA))
R Guest (Miss J A Camacho 12/5) T H Rossiter

Placings:000100 **(5601)**
2001: 7^{0}SD, 7^{0}S, 8^{0}GF, 8^{1}G, 8^{0}SD, 8^{0}GS

	Starts	1st	2nd	3rd	Win & Pl
Career Total (Turf)	4	1	0	0	2492
Career Total (AW)	2	0	0	0	

54	10/01	Bath	1m5y	F(0-60)H	GD	£2492

Total win prize-money £2492

Going (Turf): Sf: 0-1 GS: 0-1 **Gd: 1-1** GF: 0-1 Fm: 0-0
Distance: 5f/6f: 0-0 7f-8f: 0-4 **9f-13f: 1-2** 14f+: 0-0
Track : **LH: 1-4** RH: 0-0 **Tight: 1-3** Gall: 0-0
Aids: Bl: 0-0 Vi: 0-0 Tstrap: 0-0
Best Rating: 54 10/01 Bath 1m5y good

Showed nothing in three runs in the spring, but landed a Bath apprentice handicap in October.

Celtic Island

107 **89**

3-y-o b f Celtic Swing-Chief Island (Be My Chief (USA))
Mrs M Reveley (W G M Turner 9/7) Bill Brown

Placings:212201400-234542120 **(5501)**
2001: 8^{2}S, 10^{3}GS, 10^{4}GF, 9^{5}GF, 11^{4}GF, 12^{2}GF, 10^{1}GF, 11^{2}S, 12^{0}HY

	Starts	1st	2nd	3rd	Win & Pl
Career Total (Turf)	18	3	6	1	38567

72 9/01 Donc 1m2f60y C(0-85) G-F £7572
80 6/00 Sals 6f212y B G-F £10401
74 4/00 Pont 5f E HVY £3146
Total win prize-money £21121

Going (Turf): Sf: 1-4 GS: 0-2 Gd: 0-1 **GF: 2-11** Fm: 0-0
Distance: 5f/6f: 1-4 7f-8f: 1-6 9f-13f: 1-8 14f+: 0-0
Track : **LH: 2-7** RH: 0-3 Tight: 0-3 **Gall: 1-4**
Aids: Bl: 0-0 Vi: 0-0 Tstrap: 0-0
Best Rating: 95 5/01 Bath 1m2f46y gd-sft

Fairly useful juvenile in in the first half of 2000, winning on heavy and fast ground. She put in a string of creditable efforts this season, but did not manage to force her head in front until Doncaster in September. Stays 12 furlongs.

Celtic Maid

94 **67**

2-y-o b f Celtic Swing-Native Thatch (IRE) (Thatching)
Mrs M Reveley (W G M Turner 30/6) Bill Brown

Placings:51356 **(2589)**
2001: 5^{5}S, 5^{1}HY, 5^{3}GS, 5^{5}S, 5^{6}GF

	Starts	1st	2nd	3rd	Win & Pl
Career Total (Turf)	5	1	0	1	4817

4/01 Wwck 5f D HVY £3360
Total win prize-money £3360

Going (Turf): **Sf: 1-3** GS: 0-1 Gd: 0-0 GF: 0-1 Fm: 0-0
Distance: **5f/6f: 1-5** 7f-8f: 0-0 9f-13f: 0-0 14f+: 0-0
Track : **LH: 1-2** RH: 0-0 Tight: 0-1 **Gall: 1-1**
Aids: Bl: 0-0 Vi: 0-0 Tstrap: 0-0
Best Rating: 67 6/01 Ches 5f16y gd-fm

A mudlark, whose dam was the very smart two-year-old, she won a maiden in May over five furlongs, but was not seen after June.

Celtic Mill

107 **68**

3-y-o b g Celtic Swing-Madam Millie (Milford)
D W Barker P Asquith

Placings:05001206 **(5171)**
2001: 12^{0}GS, 12^{5}GF, 10^{0}GF, 10^{0}GF, 8^{1}G, 8^{2}GF, 8^{0}G, 8^{6}GS

	Starts	1st	2nd	3rd	Win & Pl
Career Total (Turf)	8	1	1	0	6281

65 8/01 Pont 1m4y F(0-65)H GD £3981
Total win prize-money £3981

Going (Turf): Sf: 0-0 GS: 0-2 **Gd: 1-2** GF: 0-4 Fm: 0-0
Distance: 5f/6f: 0-0 7f-8f: 0-1 **9f-13f: 1-7** 14f+: 0-0
Track : **LH: 1-7** RH: 0-1 Tight: 0-4 Gall: 0-0
Aids: Bl: 0-0 Vi: 0-0 Tstrap: 0-0
Best Rating: 68 8/01 Pont 1m4y gd-fm

Lightly raced. Made all when scoring at Pontefract, but was upped 10lb for that and has been held..

Celtic Miss

64 **70**

3-y-o b f Celtic Swing-Regent Miss (CAN) (Vice Regent (CAN))
J L Dunlop R Barnett

Placings:036-00 **(1326)**
2001: 11^{0}GS, 11^{0}G

	Starts	1st	2nd	3rd	Win & Pl
Career Total (Turf)	5	0	0	1	540

Going (Turf): Sf: 0-2 GS: 0-1 Gd: 0-1 GF: 0-1 Fm: 0-0
Distance: 5f/6f: 0-0 7f-8f: 0-3 9f-13f: 0-2 14f+: 0-0
Track : LH: 0-0 RH: 0-0 Tight: 0-2 Gall: 0-0
Aids: Bl: 0-0 Vi: 0-0 Tstrap: 0-0
Best Rating: 7 4/01 Wind 1m3f135y gd-sft

Celtic Mission (USA)

109(101) (78)**100**

3-y-o ch g Cozzene (USA)-Norfolk Lavender (CAN) (Ascot Knight (CAN))
M Johnston C H Racing Partnership

Placings:0531-46210430051222212016 **(5501)**
2001: 8^{4}SD, 12^{6}SD, 8^{2}S, 8^{1}GS, 8^{0}G, 7^{4}GF, 10^{3}GF, 10^{0}GF, 8^{0}GF, 10^{5}GF, 11^{1}S, 10^{2}GF, 11^{2}GS, 11^{2}G, 12^{2}GF, 10^{1}HY, 12^{2}S, 10^{0}S, 11^{1}YS, 12^{6}HY

	Starts	1st	2nd	3rd	Win & Pl
Career Total (Turf)	21	5	6	1	69400
Career Total (AW)	3	0	0	1	735

100 10/01 Naas 1m3f H Y-S £29250
93 9/01 Hayd 1m2f120yC(0-90)H HVY £8027
82 7/01 Hayd 1m3f200yC(0-95)H SFT £7182
83 4/01 Wind 1m67y D(0-85)H G-S £4303
84 11/00 Muss 1m D G-S £3526
Total win prize-money £52290

Going (Turf): **Sf: 2-6 GS: 2-3** Gd: 0-2 GF: 0-9 Fm: 0-0
Distance: 5f/6f: 0-0 7f-8f: 1-8 **9f-13f: 4-16** 14f+: 0-0
Track : **LH: 3-13** RH: 2-6 **Tight: 2-10** Gall: 0-5
Aids: Bl: 0-0 Vi: 0-0 Tstrap: 0-0
Best Rating: 100 10/01 Naas 1m3f yld-sft

Very useful handicapper, showed he had stamina when winning over 12 furlongs in soft ground at Haydock in July and has continued to run well off higher marks since including victories over ten furlongs at Haydock and in a valuable handicap at Naas. Best suited by give in the ground, although he acts on fast.

Celtic Romance

93(76) (39)**83**

2-y-o b f Celtic Swing-Southern Sky (Comedy Star (USA))
Mrs M Reveley (W G M Turner 2/7) Bill Brown

Placings:200120210 **(5052)**
2001: 5^{2}S, 5^{0}SD, 6^{0}F, 5^{1}GF, 6^{2}GF, 6^{0}GF, 7^{2}GF, 7^{1}G, 7^{0}S

	Starts	1st	2nd	3rd	Win & Pl
Career Total (Turf)	8	2	3	0	15505
Career Total (AW)	1	0	0	0	

83 9/01 Donc 7f D(0-85) GD £8060
55 6/01 Haml 5f4y E G-F £3010
Total win prize-money £11070

Going (Turf): Sf: 0-2 GS: 0-0 **Gd: 1-1 GF: 1-4** Fm: 0-1
Distance: 5f/6f: 1-6 7f-8f: 1-3 9f-13f: 0-0 14f+: 0-0
Track : LH: 0-0 RH: 0-0 Tight: 0-0 Gall: 0-0
Aids: Bl: 0-0 Vi: 0-0 Tstrap: 0-0
Best Rating: 83 9/01 Donc 7f good

She had a busy season, winning over the minimum trip at Hamilton in June and over seven furlongs at Doncaster in September. She looks as though she will stay a bit further.

Celtic Rover

84 **11**

3-y-o b g Celtic Swing-Lady Sabo (Prince Sabo)
R C Spicer Mrs J A Nichols

Placings:00000000 **(3730)**
2001: 5^{0}S, 7^{0}SD, 7^{0}G, 5^{0}GF, 5^{0}S, 5^{0}F, 10^{0}GF, 8^{0}GS

	Starts	1st	2nd	3rd	Win & Pl
Career Total (Turf)	7	0	0	0	
Career Total (AW)	1	0	0	0	

Going (Turf): **Sf: 0-2 GS: 0-1 Gd: 0-1 GF: 0-2 Fm: 0-1**
Distance: 5f/6f: 0-4 7f-8f: 0-2 9f-13f: 0-2 14f+: 0-0
Track : LH: 0-1 RH: 0-1 Tight: 0-0 Gall: 0-1
Aids: Bl: 0-1 Vi: 0-0 Tstrap: 0-0
Best Rating: 42 4/01 Nott 5f13y soft

Celtic Silence

110 (102)**115**

3-y-o b c Celtic Swing-Smart 'n Noble (USA) (Smarten (USA))
Saeed Bin Suroor Godolphin

Placings:11-42 **(1374)**
2001: 9^{4}FT, 10^{2}GF

	Starts	1st	2nd	3rd	Win & Pl
Career Total (Turf)	3	2	1	0	59200
Career Total (AW)	1	0	0	0	66667

101 6/00 Asct 7f A G-F £24375
85 6/00 Ayr 6f E G-F £2925
Total win prize-money £27300

Going (Turf): Sf: 0-0 GS: 0-0 Gd: 0-0 **GF: 2-3** Fm: 0-0
Distance: 5f/6f: 1-1 7f-8f: 1-1 9f-13f: 0-2 14f+: 0-0
Track : LH: 0-1 **RH:** 0-0 Tight: 0-0 Gall: 0-1
Aids: Bl: 0-0 Vi: 0-0 Tstrap: 0-0
Best Rating: 115 5/01 York 1m2f85y gd-fm

Snapped up by Godolphin after winning the Chesham Stakes at Royal Ascot for Mark Johnston, he ws a promising fourth in the UAE Derby in the spring. He put up a better performance when going down narrowly to Dilshaan in the Dante but was reported lame later that month and did not reappear.

Celtic Star (IRE)

96 **52**

3-y-o b g Celtic Swing-Recherchee (Rainbow Quest (USA))
Nick Williams (M R Channon 10/9) Mrs Jane Kelly

Placings:0040006 **(4609)**
2001: 8^{0}GS, 8^{0}S, 9^{4}F, 9^{0}GF, 8^{0}G, 8^{0}G, 8^{6}F

	Starts	1st	2nd	3rd	Win & Pl
Career Total (Turf)	7	0	0	0	

Going (Turf): **Sf: 0-1 GS: 0-1 Gd: 0-2 GF: 0-1 Fm: 0-2**
Distance: 5f/6f: 0-0 7f-8f: 0-2 9f-13f: 0-5 14f+: 0-0
Track : LH: 0-3 RH: 0-2 Tight: 0-2 Gall: 0-0
Aids: Bl: 0-0 Vi: 0-1 Tstrap: 0-0
Best Rating: 64 5/01 Wind 1m67y gd-sft

Celtic Style

98 **86**

2-y-o b c Celtic Swing-Stylish Rose (IRE) (Don't Forget Me)
M Johnston T McDonagh

Placings:421 **(5662)**
2001: 10^{4}GS, 8^{2}G, 8^{1}G

	Starts	1st	2nd	3rd	Win & Pl
Career Total (Turf)	3	1	1	0	5513

83 11/01 Muss 1m D GD £4348
Total win prize-money £4349

Going (Turf): Sf: 0-0 GS: 0-1 **Gd: 1-2** GF: 0-0 Fm: 0-0
Distance: 5f/6f: 0-0 **7f-8f: 1-1** 9f-13f: 0-2 14f+: 0-0
Track : LH: 0-2 **RH: 1-1 Tight: 1-2** Gall: 0-0
Aids: Bl: 0-0 Vi: 0-0 Tstrap: 0-0
Best Rating: 86 10/01 Bath 1m5y good

Made an encouraging debut at Pontefract in October. Still looked green when breaking his maiden at Musselburgh in November. Should make a nice three-year-old.

Celtic Thatcher

(104) (77)**64**
3-y-o b c Celtic Swing-Native Thatch (IRE) (Thatching)
N P Littmoden (W G M Turner 12/7) Nigel Shields

Placings:6600**136103** **(5416)**
2001: 7^{6}GS, 8^{6}G, 10^{0}F, 8^{0}HD, 9^{1}SD, 8^{3}SD, 9^{6}SD, 8^{1}SD, 8^{0}SD, 9^{3}SD

	Starts	1st	2nd	3rd	Win & Pl
Career Total (Turf)	4	0	0	0	0
Career Total (AW)	6	2	0	2	6365

77 10/01 Wolv 1m100y E(0-70)H STD £2975
64 7/01 Wolv 1m1f79y F STD £2296
Total win prize-money £5271

Going (Turf): Sf: 0-0 GS: 0-1 Gd: 0-1 GF: 0-0 Fm: 0-2
Distance: 5f/6f: 0-0 7f-8f: 0-2 **9f-13f: 2-8** 14f+: 0-0
Track : **LH: 2-9** RH: 0-0 **Tight: 2-8** Gall: 0-0
Aids: Bl: 0-0 **Vi: 1-3** Tstrap: 0-0
Best Rating: 77 10/01 Wolv 1m100y stand

Gained a nine-length victory in a claimer on the Wolverhampton Fibresand in July and landed a handicap in a first-time visor at the same track in October. Suited by forcing tactics.

Celtic Venture

106(98) (47)**55**
6-y-o ch g Risk Me (FR)-Celtic River (IRE) (Caerleon (USA))
K T Ivory (Miss Sheena West 5/6) Sapphire Racing

Placings:062/100**00**/661006-**3463441**013 **(2707)**
2001: 6^{3}SD, 6^{4}SD, 8^{6}SD, 6^{3}SW, 6^{4}SW, 6^{4}SD, 7^{1}F, 8^{0}GF, 7^{1}GF, 6^{3}F

	Starts	1st	2nd	3rd	Win & Pl
Career Total (Turf)	14	4	1	1	12274
Career Total (AW)	10	0	0	2	572

55 6/01 Gdwd 7f E(0-80)H G-F £3640
47 6/01 Ling 7f E FRM £2899
39 7/00 Brig 6f209y F FRM £2362
47 4/99 Brig 5f59y F G-F £2232
Total win prize-money £11134

Going (Turf): Sf: 0-0 GS: 0-0 Gd: 0-4 **GF: 2-5 Fm: 2-5**
Distance: 5f/6f: 1-16 **7f-8f: 3-7** 9f-13f: 0-1 14f+: 0-0
Track : **LH: 2-17** RH: 1-2 Tight: 0-10 Gall: 0-2
Aids: Bl: 0-0 Vi: 0-0 Tstrap: 0-0
Best Rating: 55 6/01 Gdwd 7f gd-fm

Moderate handicapper, well suited by fast ground and a sharp track. Likes to be ridden close to the pace.

Celts Dawn

90(83) (27)**33**
3-y-o b f Celtic Swing-Susie's Baby (Balidar)
M S Saunders (J G Smyth-Osbourne 11/5) W H Joyce

Placings:0-60000 **(4785)**
2001: 8^{6}SD, 6^{0}G, 6^{0}G, 6^{0}GF, 5^{0}G

	Starts	1st	2nd	3rd	Win & Pl
Career Total (Turf)	5	0	0	0	
Career Total (AW)	1	0	0	0	0

Going (Turf): Sf: 0-0 GS: 0-0 Gd: 0-3 GF: 0-2 Fm: 0-0
Distance: 5f/6f: 0-2 7f-8f: 0-4 9f-13f: 0-0 14f+: 0-0
Track : LH: 0-1 RH: 0-0 Tight: 0-0 Gall: 0-0
Aids: Bl: 0-0 Vi: 0-0 Tstrap: 0-0
Best Rating: 33 5/01 Nott 6f15y good

Centaur Spirit

82 **40**
4-y-o b g Distant Relative-Winnie Reckless (Local Suitor (USA))
A Streeter Centaur Racing Ltd

Placings:0/040010-00 **(4727)**
2001: 12^{0}GF, 10^{0}GF

	Starts	1st	2nd	3rd	Win & Pl
Career Total (Turf)	9	1	0	0	1974

40 10/00 Leic 1m1f218yG HVY £1974
Total win prize-money £1974

Going (Turf): Sf: 1-3 GS: 0-2 Gd: 0-0 GF: 0-4 Fm: 0-0
Distance: 5f/6f: 0-0 7f-8f: 0-1 **9f-13f: 1-8** 14f+: 0-0
Track : LH: 0-5 **RH: 1-3** Tight: 0-1 Gall: 0-0
Aids: Bl: 0-0 Vi: 0-0 Tstrap: 0-0
Best Rating: 17 7/01 Wwck 1m4f134y gd-fm

Centimetre

89 **44**
2-y-o ch g Inchinor-Matisse (Shareef Dancer (USA))
M W Easterby Guy Reed

Placings:0040000 **(5229)**
2001: 6^{0}GF, 5^{0}GF, 7^{4}F, 8^{0}GF, 8^{0}G, 6^{0}GS, 7^{0}S

	Starts	1st	2nd	3rd	Win & Pl
Career Total (Turf)	7	0	0	0	288

Going (Turf): Sf: 0-1 GS: 0-1 Gd: 0-1 GF: 0-3 Fm: 0-1
Distance: 5f/6f: 0-3 7f-8f: 0-3 9f-13f: 0-1 14f+: 0-0
Track : LH: 0-4 RH: 0-0 Tight: 0-1 Gall: 0-1
Aids: Bl: 0-2 Vi: 0-0 Tstrap: 0-0
Best Rating: 70 8/01 Thsk 7f firm

Century City (IRE)

104 **99+**
2-y-o b c Danzig (USA)-Alywow (CAN) (Alysheba (USA))
A P O'Brien Mrs John Magnier

Placings:31 **(5363)**
2001: 7^{3}GS, 7^{1}GS

	Starts	1st	2nd	3rd	Win & Pl
Career Total (Turf)	2	1	0	1	9020

99 10/01 NmkR 7f B G-S £8120
Total win prize-money £8120

Going (Turf): Sf: 0-0 **GS: 1-2** Gd: 0-0 GF: 0-0 Fm: 0-0
Distance: 5f/6f: 0-0 **7f-8f: 1-2** 9f-13f: 0-0 14f+: 0-0
Track : LH: 0-0 RH: 0-0 Tight: 0-0 Gall: 0-0
Aids: Bl: 0-0 Vi: 0-0 Tstrap: 0-0
Best Rating: 99 10/01 NmkR 7f gd-sft

A half-brother to a minor stakes winner in the USA by Storm Cat, his dam was champion three-year-old filly in Canada. Improved markedly upon a promising debut effort when taking a decent Newmarket event over seven in October, showing a willing attitude in the process. Looks well up to pattern class. Has only raced on good to soft. Sure to stay a mile plus.

Ceralbi (IRE)

105 **73**
3-y-o b c Goldmark (USA)-Siwana (IRE) (Dom Racine (FR))
R Hollinshead L & R Roadlines

Placings:622000-1210302 **(5486)**
2001: 9^{1}GF, 11^{2}F, 10^{1}GF, 12^{0}GF, 11^{3}G, 11^{0}GF, 10^{2}HY

	Starts	1st	2nd	3rd	Win & Pl
Career Total (Turf)	13	2	4	1	18120

73 6/01 Pont 1m2f6y D(0-80)H G-F £7377
70 5/01 Bevl 1m1f207yD(0-80)H G-F £4459
Total win prize-money £11837

Going (Turf): Sf: 0-3 GS: 0-0 Gd: 0-2 **GF: 2-6** Fm: 0-1
Distance: 5f/6f: 0-2 7f-8f: 0-3 **9f-13f: 2-7** 14f+: 0-0
Track : LH: 1-9 RH: 1-1 Tight: 0-5 Gall: 0-3
Aids: Bl: 0-0 Vi: 0-0 Tstrap: 0-0
Best Rating: 73 8/01 Rdcr 1m3f good

Fair middle-distance handicapper. Acts on good to firm ground.

Ceremonial

102(81) (44)**71**
3-y-o b f Lion Cavern (USA)-Blessed Event (King's Lake (USA))
Sir Mark Prescott Cheveley Park Stud

Placings:261 **(3615)**
2001: 7^{2}GF, 8^{6}SD, 8^{1}G

	Starts	1st	2nd	3rd	Win & Pl
Career Total (Turf)	2	1	1	0	4090
Career Total (AW)	1	0	0	0	0

64 8/01 Nott 1m54y E GD £3318
Total win prize-money £3318

Going (Turf): Sf: 0-0 GS: 0-0 **Gd: 1-1** GF: 0-1 Fm: 0-0
Distance: 5f/6f: 0-0 7f-8f: 0-2 **9f-13f: 1-1** 14f+: 0-0
Track : **LH: 1-2** RH: 0-0 Tight: 0-0 Gall: 0-0
Aids: Bl: 0-0 Vi: 0-0 Tstrap: 0-0
Best Rating: 71 6/01 Yarm 7f3y gd-fm

Cereus (USA)

101 **87+**
2-y-o ch c Gilded Time (USA)-Dayflower (USA) (Majestic Light (USA))
B W Hills Maktoum Al Maktoum

Placings:5210 **(4678)**
2001: 7^{5}GS, 7^{2}G, 7^{1}G, 8^{0}G

	Starts	1st	2nd	3rd	Win & Pl
Career Total (Turf)	4	1	1	0	5121

87 9/01 Ches 7f2y D GD £3688
Total win prize-money £3689

Going (Turf): Sf: 0-0 GS: 0-1 **Gd: 1-3** GF: 0-0 Fm: 0-0
Distance: 5f/6f: 0-0 **7f-8f: 1-4** 9f-13f: 0-0 14f+: 0-0
Track : **LH: 1-1** RH: 0-1 **Tight: 1-1** Gall: 0-0
Aids: Bl: 0-0 Vi: 0-0 Tstrap: 0-0
Best Rating: 87 9/01 Ches 7f2y good

From the family of the smart two-year-old Raise A Grand, came up against some decent sorts before he got off the mark in a decent maiden in September.

Certain Justice (USA)

104 **93**
3-y-o gr c Lit De Justice (USA)-Pure Misk (Rainbow Quest (USA))
P F I Cole The Blenheim Partnership

Placings:11-32250 **(5494)**
2001: 6^{3}GF, 6^{2}GF, 7^{2}G, 6^{5}S, 6^{0}HY

	Starts	1st	2nd	3rd	Win & Pl
Career Total (Turf)	7	2	2	1	18906

108 5/00 Wind 5f10y B G-F £7308
90 4/00 NmkR 5f D SFT £4914
Total win prize-money £12222

Going (Turf): Sf: 1-3 GS: 0-0 Gd: 0-1 **GF: 1-3** Fm: 0-0
Distance: **5f/6f: 2-2** 7f-8f: 0-5 9f-13f: 0-0 14f+: 0-0
Track : LH: 0-1 **RH: 1-1** Tight: 0-0 **Gall: 1-2**
Aids: Bl: 0-0 Vi: 0-0 Tstrap: 0-0
Best Rating: 99 6/01 Yarm 6f3y gd-fm

He showed plenty of speed to win twice in the spring of 2000 but was then off the track for over a year with a leg injury. He reappeared at Yarmouth in June and ran well in conditions events without winning.

Certainly So

91 **53**
3-y-o ch f So Factual (USA)-Indubitable (Sharpo)
G B Balding Miss B Swire

Placings:00-000 **(3081)**
2001: 8^{0}GS, 8^{0}GF, 8^{0}GF

	Starts	1st	2nd	3rd	Win & Pl
Career Total (Turf)	5	0	0	0	

Going (Turf): Sf: 0-1 GS: 0-1 Gd: 0-1 GF: 0-2 Fm: 0-0
Distance: 5f/6f: 0-1 7f-8f: 0-1 9f-13f: 0-3 14f+: 0-0
Track : LH: 0-0 RH: 0-5 Tight: 0-3 Gall: 0-2
Aids: Bl: 0-0 Vi: 0-0 Tstrap: 0-0
Best Rating: 48 7/01 Wind 1m67y gd-fm

Cerulean Rose

81 **43**

2-y-o ch f Bluegrass Prince (IRE)-Elegant Rose (Noalto)
A W Carroll Rob Willis

Placings:00 **(4454)**
2001: 5^{0}GF, 6^{0}GF

	Starts	1st	2nd	3rd	Win & Pl
Career Total (Turf)	2	0	0	0	

Going (Turf): Sf: 0-0 GS: 0-0 Gd: 0-0 GF: 0-2 Fm: 0-0
Distance: 5f/6f: 0-2 7f-8f: 0-0 9f-13f: 0-0 14f+: 0-0
Track : LH: 0-0 RH: 0-1 Tight: 0-0 Gall: 0-1
Aids: Bl: 0-0 Vi: 0-0 Tstrap: 0-0
Best Rating: 43 9/01 York 6f gd-fm

Cezzaro (IRE)

98 **57**

3-y-o ch g Ashkalani (IRE)-Sept Roses (USA) (Septieme Ciel (USA))
W R Muir (D Nicholls 24/7) Fayzad Thoroughbred Limited

Placings:50300-40004510 **(5624)**
2001: 6^{4}S, 7^{0}GF, 6^{0}G, 7^{0}GS, 7^{4}GF, 8^{5}GS, 10^{1}HY, 9^{0}GS

	Starts	1st	2nd	3rd	Win & Pl
Career Total (Turf)	13	1	0	1	2933

56 10/01 Wind 1m2f7y G HVY £2054
Total win prize-money £2055

Going (Turf): Sf: 1-2 GS: 0-5 Gd: 0-3 GF: 0-3 Fm: 0-0
Distance: 5f/6f: 0-3 7f-8f: 0-6 **9f-13f: 1-4** 14f+: 0-0
Track : LH: 0-5 RH: 0-0 **Tight: 1-3** Gall: 0-1
Aids: Bl: 0-0 Vi: 0-2 Tstrap: 0-0
Best Rating: 62 6/01 Ches 7f2y gd-fm

Moderate handicapper, handles any ground.

Chabibi

91 **66**

2-y-o br f Mark Of Esteem (IRE)-Nunsharpa (Sharpo)
T H Caldwell R S G Jones

Placings:0652300 **(4962)**
2001: 5^{0}GF, 5^{6}GF, 5^{5}GF, 6^{2}GS, 6^{3}F, 7^{0}G, 8^{0}S

	Starts	1st	2nd	3rd	Win & Pl
Career Total (Turf)	7	0	1	1	1775

Going (Turf): Sf: 0-1 GS: 0-1 Gd: 0-1 GF: 0-3 Fm: 0-1
Distance: 5f/6f: 0-5 7f-8f: 0-1 9f-13f: 0-1 14f+: 0-0
Track : LH: 0-3 RH: 0-0 Tight: 0-1 Gall: 0-0
Aids: Bl: 0-0 Vi: 0-0 Tstrap: 0-0
Best Rating: 81 7/01 Ayr 6f gd-sft

Chablis

(89) (29)**58**

3-y-o b f Kingmambo (USA)-Nicer (IRE) (Pennine Walk)
P F I Cole Lord Lloyd-Webber

Placings:60300 **(5461)**
2001: 7^{6}GS, 7^{0}G, 8^{3}HY, 8^{0}GS, 8^{0}G

	Starts	1st	2nd	3rd	Win & Pl
Career Total (Turf)	5	0	0	1	708

Going (Turf): Sf: 0-1 GS: 0-2 Gd: 0-2 GF: 0-0 Fm: 0-0
Distance: 5f/6f: 0-0 7f-8f: 0-2 9f-13f: 0-3 14f+: 0-0
Track : LH: 0-2 RH: 0-0 Tight: 0-1 Gall: 0-0

Aids: Bl: 0-0 Vi: 0-0 Tstrap: 0-0
Best Rating: 58 9/01 Hayd 1m30y heavy

Out of an Irish 1000 Guineas winner, but has looked ordinary.

Chabrol (CAN)

87 (8)**31**

8-y-o b g El Gran Senor (USA)-Off The Record (USA) (Chas Conerly (USA))
Ms A E Embiricos Ms A E Embiricos

Placings:654010000/533420250/20504/**3550**050/00040 0 **(3727)**
2001: 12^{0}GF, 10^{0}G, 13^{0}GF, 16^{4}GF, 14^{0}GF, 14^{0}GS

	Starts	1st	2nd	3rd	Win & Pl
Career Total (Turf)	31	1	2	2	6349
Career Total (AW)	5	0	1	1	1156

61 8/96 Yarm 1m2f21y F G-F £2945
Total win prize-money £2945

Going (Turf): Sf: 0-3 GS: 0-4 Gd: 0-10 **GF: 1-13** Fm: 0-1
Distance: 5f/6f: 0-0 7f-8f: 0-1 **9f-13f: 1-16** 14f+: 0-19
Track : **LH: 1-24** RH: 0-9 **Tight: 1-13** Gall: 0-11
Aids: Bl: 0-0 Vi: 0-0 Tstrap: 0-6
Best Rating: 31 7/01 Newb 1m5f61y gd-fm

Chafaya (IRE)

107 **84**

3-y-o ch f Mark Of Esteem (IRE)-Matila (IRE) (Persian Bold)
N A Graham Hamdan Al Maktoum

Placings:30-135100 **(5145)**
2001: 7^{1}G, 8^{3}GF, 7^{5}GF, 7^{1}G, 7^{0}GS, 7^{0}G

	Starts	1st	2nd	3rd	Win & Pl
Career Total (Turf)	8	2	0	2	9880

84 8/01 NmkJ 7f D(0-85)H GD £4953
70 5/01 Thsk 7f D GD £3695
Total win prize-money £8648

Going (Turf): Sf: 0-2 GS: 0-1 **Gd: 2-3** GF: 0-2 Fm: 0-0
Distance: 5f/6f: 0-0 **7f-8f: 2-8** 9f-13f: 0-0 14f+: 0-0
Track : **LH: 1-2** RH. 0-1 **Tight: 1-2** Gall. 0-1
Aids: Bl: 0-0 Vi: 0-0 Tstrap: 0-0
Best Rating: 84 8/01 NmkJ 7f good

Got off the mark at the third time of asking, but disappointed in her next two runs before coming good again at Newmarket. Was possibly not at home on the soft after that. Suited by seven furlongs.

Chagall

101 **109**

4-y-o ch c Fraam-Pooka (Dominion)
Bruce Hellier Stall Florian

Placings:121031/26612300-4632520 **(5386)**
2001: 6^{4}, 6^{0}G, 6^{3}S, 6^{2}G, 6^{5}G, 6^{2}S, 7^{0}GS

	Starts	1st	2nd	3rd	Win & Pl
Career Total (Turf)	21	4	5	3	107936

6/00 Badn 6f110y GD £17742
87 10/99 Donc 6f B G-S £17840
7/99 Duss 5f GD £20578
6/99 Badn 5f SFT £4332
Total win prize-money £60492

Going (Turf): Sf: 0-3 **GS: 1-2** Gd: 0-5 GF: 0-1 Fm: 0-0
Distance: **5f/6f: 1-7** 7f-8f: 0-5 9f-13f: 0-0 14f+: 0-0
Track : LH: 0-1 RH: 0-0 Tight: 0-0 Gall: 0-0
Aids: **Bl: 1-1** Vi: 0-0 Tstrap: 0-0
Best Rating: 109 7/01 Hopp 6f110y good

A useful German-trained sprinter, he has run well on his visits to Britain.

Chahaya Timor (IRE)

(96)

9-y-o b g Slip Anchor-Roxy Hart (High Top)
Miss S J Wilton John Pointon And Sons

Placings:0/663**412**/4116**4**/4/33-60 **(2323)**
2001: 14^{6}SD, 16^{0}SD

	Starts	1st	2nd	3rd	Win & Pl
Career Total (Turf)	4	0	0	1	572
Career Total (AW)	13	3	1	2	8903

59 2/98 Wolv 2m46y G STD £1738
62 1/98 Wolv 1m6f166yG STD £1738
67 8/95 Wolv 1m4f E(0-70)H STD £3502
Total win prize-money £6978

Going (Turf): Sf: 0-0 GS: 0-0 Gd: 0-1 GF: 0-3 Fm: 0-0
Distance: 5f/6f: 0-0 7f-8f: 0-1 9f-13f: 1-3 **14f+: 2-13**
Track : **LH: 3-14** RH: 0-2 **Tight: 3-11** Gall: 0-1
Aids: Bl: 0-0 Vi: 0-0 Tstrap: 0-0
Best Rating: 67 8/95 Wolv 1m4f SD

Plating-class All-Weather stayer.

Chai-Yo

(101) (51)

11-y-o b g Rakaposhi King-Ballysax Lass (Main Reef)
J A B Old Nick Viney

Placings:0/520/0/00-30 **(0219)**
2001: 12^{3}SD, 12^{0}SD

	Starts	1st	2nd	3rd	Win & Pl
Career Total (Turf)	6	0	1	0	1938
Career Total (AW)	3	0	0	1	425

Going (Turf): Sf: 0-4 GS: 0-1 Gd: 0-0 GF: 0-1 Fm: 0-0
Distance: 5f/6f: 0-0 7f-8f: 0-2 9f-13f: 0-7 14f+: 0-0
Track : LH: 0-5 RH: 0-1 Tight: 0-1 Gall: 0-2
Aids: Bl: 0-0 Vi: 0-0 Tstrap: 0-0
Best Rating: 51 1/01 Sthl 1m4f stand

Chairman Bobby

98(99) (68)**52**

3-y-o ch g Clantime-Formidable Liz (Formidable (USA))
Jedd O'Keeffe (T D Barron 27/6) John Johnson - Roland Roper

Placings:305-2020300600 **(4601)**
2001: 6^{2}SW, 6^{0}G, 5^{2}GF, 5^{0}G, 6^{3}F, 6^{0}GF, 5^{0}GF, 5^{6}GF, 5^{0}GF, 5^{0}GF

	Starts	1st	2nd	3rd	Win & Pl
Career Total (Turf)	11	0	1	2	1957
Career Total (AW)	2	0	1	0	1177

Going (Turf): Sf: 0-0 GS: 0-0 Gd: 0-4 GF: 0-6 Fm: 0-1
Distance: 5f/6f: 0-13 7f-8f: 0-0 9f-13f: 0-0 14f+: 0-0
Track : LH. 0-4 RH: 0-1 Tight: 0-1 Gall: 0-1
Aids: Bl: 0-0 Vi: 0-0 Tstrap: 0-0
Best Rating: 68 4/01 Sthl 6f slow

He has made the frame a few times but is yet to win. Has plenty of early pace and barely stays the minimum trip.

Chaka Zulu

100(78) (31)**65d**

4-y-o b g Muhtarram (USA)-African Dance (USA) (El Gran Senor (USA))
W J Haggas J D Ashenheim

Placings:000/13113120-00033200 **(4983)**
2001: 11^{0}GF, 12^{0}GF, 9^{0}GF, 11^{3}GF, 11^{3}G, 12^{2}GF, 12^{0}G, 12^{0}G

	Starts	1st	2nd	3rd	Win & Pl
Career Total (Turf)	18	4	2	4	15313
Career Total (AW)	1	0	0	0	

67 8/00 Newc 1m4f93y E(0-75)H FRM £2870
70 7/00 Newc 1m4f93y E(0-70)H GD £2756
60 7/00 Catt 1m3f214yE(0-70)H G-F £3672
44 7/00 Bath 1m2f46y F(0-60)H FRM £2436

Total win prize-money £11735

Going (Turf): Sf: 0-0 GS: 0-2 Gd: 0-4 GF: 1-9 **Fm: 2-2**
Distance: 5f/6f: 0-3 7f-8f: 0-0 **9f-13f: 3-15** 14f+: 0-0
Track : **LH: 3-9** RH: 0-7 **Tight: 2-8** Gall: 1-4
Aids: Bl: 0-0 Vi: 0-2 Tstrap: 0-1
Best Rating: 65 8/01 Ling 1m3f106y gd-fm

Chakra

105(101) (34)**48**
7-y-o gr g Mystiko (USA)-Maracuja (USA) (Riverman (USA))
M S Saunders B McFadzean

Placings:0/00000100/0300101600536/004230006403040/065061060000213021665500-002210005060 (5027)
2001: 6^{0}SW, 8^{0}SD, 5^{2}G, 5^{2}F, 6^{1}GF, 5^{0}G, 5^{0}GS, 6^{0}GF, 5^{5}F, 5^{0}G, 6^{6}GF, 5^{0}S

	Starts	1st	2nd	3rd	Win & Pl
Career Total (Turf)	63	6	5	5	23888
Career Total (AW)	11	1	0	0	1897

52	5/01	Gdwd	6f	D(0-80)H	G-F	£4582
48	8/00	Brig	5f213y	F(0-65)H	GD	£2599
38	6/00	Folk	6f	F	FRM	£1939
37	3/00	Ling	6f	F(0-60)H	STD	£1897
52	8/98	Wwck	5f	F(0-60)H	G-F	£2700
46	7/98	Wwck	5f	E(0-70)H	G-F	£3236
48	7/97	Brig	5f59y	F(0-60)H	FRM	£2277

Total win prize-money £19232

Going (Turf): Sf: 0-3 GS: 0-5 Gd: 1-27 **GF: 3-18** Fm: 2-10
Distance: **5f/6f: 7-66** 7f-8f: 0-8 9f-13f: 0-0 14f+: 0-0
Track : **LH: 5-37** RH: 0-3 Tight: 1-12 **Gall: 2-13**
Aids: Bl: 0-0 Vi: 0-0 Tstrap: 0-0
Best Rating: 52 5/01 Gdwd 6f gd-fm

Chalcedony

99(106) (67d)**46**
5-y-o ch g Highest Honor (FR)-Sweet Holland (USA) (Alydar (USA))
G L Moore Lancing Racing Syndicate

Placings:40034/11350/12404036210-00 (5098)
2001: 11^{0}GF, 14^{0}GS

	Starts	1st	2nd	3rd	Win & Pl
Career Total (Turf)	12	0	1	1	2121
Career Total (AW)	11	4	1	2	14608

51	9/00	Ling	1m4f	G(0-65)	STD	£2014
69	1/00	Sthl	1m3f	D(0-80)H	STD	£4134
63	4/99	Sthl	1m3f	F(0-65)H	STD	£2190
59	1/99	Ling	1m2f	E(0-75)H	STD	£2671

Total win prize-money £11010

Going (Turf): Sf: 0-1 GS: 0-4 Gd: 0-3 GF: 0-3 Fm: 0-1
Distance: 5f/6f: 0-3 7f-8f: 0-2 **9f-13f: 4-14** 14f+: 0-4
Track : **LH: 4-14** RH: 0-7 **Tight: 2-9** Gall: 0-3
Aids: Bl: 0-2 Vi: 0-0 Tstrap: 0-0
Best Rating: 38 10/01 Sals 1m6f15y gd-sft

Moderate middle-distance handicapper, he has gained all his wins on the All-Weather

Chalfont (IRE)

96 **73**
2-y-o b f Common Grounds-Pirie (USA) (Green Dancer (USA))
H Morrison Stonethorn Stud Farms Limited

Placings:03 (4456)
2001: 6^{0}F, 6^{3}G

	Starts	1st	2nd	3rd	Win & Pl
Career Total (Turf)	2	0	0	1	402

Going (Turf): Sf: 0-0 GS: 0-0 Gd: 0-1 GF: 0-0 Fm: 0-1
Distance: 5f/6f: 0-1 7f-8f: 0-1 9f-13f: 0-0 14f+: 0-0
Track : LH: 0-0 RH: 0-0 Tight: 0-0 Gall: 0-0
Aids: Bl: 0-0 Vi: 0-0 Tstrap: 0-0
Best Rating: 73 9/01 Folk 6f good

Challenger Two (IRE)

96(98) (58)**44**
6-y-o b g Petorius-Blue Elver (King's Lake (USA))
K A Ryan (Ferdy Murphy 28/4) Dubai Connection

Placings:025652001525/600010006006/3340304000/200-500000 (2784)
2001: 11^{5}SD, 11^{0}SD, 7^{0}SD, 7^{0}GF, 8^{0}G, 7^{0}GF

	Starts	1st	2nd	3rd	Win & Pl
Career Total (Turf)	40	2	4	3	13204
Career Total (AW)	3	0	0	0	0

75	7/98	Klny	1m100y	(0-75)H	G-F	£3437
85	9/97	Gowr	7f		G-Y	£4110

Total win prize-money £7548

Going (Turf): Sf: 0-5 GS: 0-0 Gd: 0-7 **GF: 1-10** Fm: 0-0
Distance: 5f/6f: 0-5 7f-8f: 1-27 9f-13f: 1-11 14f+: 0-0
Track : LH: 1-14 RH: 1-19 Tight: 0-1 Gall: 0-4
Aids: Bl: 0-10 Vi: 0-0 Tstrap: 0-1
Best Rating: 58 4/01 Sthl 1m3f stand

Challenor

(89) (47)**44**
3-y-o ch g Casteddu-Expletive (Shiny Tenth)
N P Littmoden Paul Sandy

Placings:600-0002021 (5617)
2001: 9^{0}GF, 8^{0}GF, 10^{0}G, 7^{2}GF, 7^{0}G, 7^{2}SD, 8^{1}SD

	Starts	1st	2nd	3rd	Win & Pl
Career Total (Turf)	8	0	1	0	935
Career Total (AW)	2	1	1	0	3902

47	11/01	Wolv	1m100y	D	STD	£3052

Total win prize-money £3052

Going (Turf): Sf: 0-1 GS: 0-1 Gd: 0-2 GF: 0-4 Fm: 0-0
Distance: 5f/6f: 0-1 7f-8f: 0-4 **9f-13f: 1-5** 14f+: 0-0
Track : **LH: 1-4** RH: 0-2 **Tight: 1-2** Gall: 0-2
Aids: Bl: 0-0 Vi: 0-0 Tstrap: 0-0
Best Rating: 47 11/01 Wolv 1m100y stand

Moderate form so far. Clear second-best in a median auction maiden stakes at Wolverhampton in October 2001 and went one better next time in a weak maiden over the extended mile.

Chalom (IRE)

103 **78**
3-y-o b g Mujadil (USA)-The Poachers Lady (IRE) (Salmon Leap (USA))
B J Meehan Maagar Uk Ltd

Placings:060-4613 (3743)
2001: 8^{4}GS, 10^{6}GF, 8^{1}G, 8^{3}S

	Starts	1st	2nd	3rd	Win & Pl
Career Total (Turf)	7	1	0	1	5498

78	7/01	Chep	1m14y	D(0-80)H	GD	£3825

Total win prize-money £3825

Going (Turf): Sf: 0-3 GS: 0-1 **Gd: 1-1** GF: 0-2 Fm: 0-0
Distance: 5f/6f: 0-0 7f-8f: 0-3 **9f-13f: 1-4** 14f+: 0-0
Track : LH: 0-0 RH: 0-1 Tight: 0-2 Gall: 0-0
Aids: Bl: 0-0 Vi: 0-0 Tstrap: 0-0
Best Rating: 78 7/01 Chep 1m14y good

Showed little at two. Stepped up to a mile at three and ran a decent race on reappearance at Windsor. Scored at Chepstow on good ground.

Chamlang

65(68) **16**
3-y-o b f Petong-Makalu (Godswalk (USA))
N A Graham Flying Colours Racing

Placings:00-0000 (5131)
2001: 6^{0}HY, 6^{0}GF, 6^{0}SD, 7^{0}HY

	Starts	1st	2nd	3rd	Win & Pl
Career Total (Turf)	5	0	0	0	
Career Total (AW)	1	0	0	0	

Going (Turf): Sf: 0-4 GS: 0-0 Gd: 0-0 GF: 0-1 Fm: 0-0
Distance: 5f/6f: 0-5 7f-8f: 0-1 9f-13f: 0-0 14f+: 0-0
Track : LH: 0-2 RH: 0-0 Tight: 0-0 Gall: 0-0
Aids: Bl: 0-0 Vi: 0-0 Tstrap: 0-2
Best Rating: 16 4/01 Pont 6f heavy

Champagne King

76 **62**
2-y-o b c Prince Sabo-Champagne Season (USA) (Vaguely Noble)
P W Harris Mrs P W Harris

Placings:000 (5684)
2001: 7^{0}S, 8^{0}G, 8^{0}S

	Starts	1st	2nd	3rd	Win & Pl
Career Total (Turf)	3	0	0	0	

Going (Turf): Sf: 0-2 GS: 0-0 Gd: 0-1 GF: 0-0 Fm: 0-0
Distance: 5f/6f: 0-0 7f-8f: 0-2 9f-13f: 0-1 14f+: 0-0
Track : LH: 0-2 RH: 0-0 Tight: 0-1 Gall: 0-1
Aids: Bl: 0-0 Vi: 0-0 Tstrap: 0-0
Best Rating: 62 10/01 Bath 1m5y good

Champagne Rider

111(110) (79)**80**
5-y-o b g Presidium-Petitesse (Petong)
K McAuliffe Highgrove Developments Limited

Placings:1310465/04050330500100/000006000402600-122060 (5265)
2001: 9^{1}SD, 8^{2}SD, 10^{2}S, 8^{0}GS, 9^{6}GF, 8^{0}GS

	Starts	1st	2nd	3rd	Win & Pl
Career Total (Turf)	38	3	2	3	39790
Career Total (AW)	4	1	1	0	7877

73	2/01	Wolv	1m1f79y	D(0-85)H	STD	£3747
89	8/99	Leic	5f218y	B(0-105)H	G-F	£9495
83	5/98	Kemp	6f	C	GD	£4518
74	4/98	Kemp	5f	D	HVY	£3452

Total win prize-money £21213

Going (Turf): Sf: 1-6 GS: 0-8 **Gd: 1-15 GF: 1-9** Fm: 0-0
Distance: **5f/6f: 3-20** 7f-8f: 0-15 9f-13f: 1-7 14f+: 0-0
Track : **LH: 1-11** RH: 0-5 **Tight: 1-7** Gall: 0-4
Aids: Bl: 0-1 Vi: 0-0 Tstrap: 0-0
Best Rating: 79 3/01 Wolv 1m100y stand

Busy through the winter on the All-Weather, he won after being gelded and relished the step up to nine furlongs. Good run on turf at Kempton in April 2001. Likes cut in the ground.

Champain Sands (IRE)

80 **68+**
2-y-o b c Green Desert (USA)-Grecian Bride (IRE) (Groom Dancer (USA))
P W Harris Board, Coppen, Day & Hatch

Placings:0 (5107)
2001: 7^{0}GS

	Starts	1st	2nd	3rd	Win & Pl
Career Total (Turf)	1	0	0	0	

Going (Turf): Sf: 0-0 GS: 0-1 Gd: 0-0 GF: 0-0 Fm: 0-0
Distance: 5f/6f: 0-0 7f-8f: 0-1 9f-13f: 0-0 14f+: 0-0
Track : LH: 0-0 RH: 0-0 Tight: 0-0 Gall: 0-0
Aids: Bl: 0-0 Vi: 0-0 Tstrap: 0-0
Best Rating: 68 10/01 NmkR 7f gd-sft

Champfis

(101) (53)**57**

4-y-o b g Efisio-Champ D'Avril (Northfields (USA))

W M Brisbourne Mrs L A Windsor

Placings:03/425202-0623300 **(5287)**

2001: 7^{0}GF, 7^{6}SD, 6^{2}SD, 7^{3}G, 6^{3}F, 9^{0}GS, 6^{0}HY

	Starts	1st	2nd	3rd	Win & Pl
Career Total (Turf)	11	0	2	3	3602
Career Total (AW)	4	0	2	0	1380

Going (Turf): Sf: 0-6 GS: 0-1 Gd: 0-1 GF: 0-1 Fm: 0-2
Distance: 5f/6f: 0-7 7f-8f: 0-7 9f-13f: 0-1 14f+: 0-0
Track : LH: 0-7 RH: 0-1 Tight: 0-4 Gall: 0-1
Aids: Bl: 0-0 Vi: 0-0 Tstrap: 0-0
Best Rating: 57 8/01 Thsk 6f firm

Champion Lodge (IRE)

105 **83**

4-y-o b c Sri Pekan (USA)-Legit (IRE) (Runnett)

J A R Toller P C J Dalby

Placings:211000-000030 **(5607)**

2001: 7^{0}G, 9^{0}G, 8^{0}GF, 9^{0}G, 8^{3}GS, 8^{0}GS

	Starts	1st	2nd	3rd	Win & Pl
Career Total (Turf)	12	2	1	1	17624

97 5/00 Thsk 1m B(0-95) GD £9717
96 5/00 NmkR 1m D GD £6006
Total win prize-money £15724

Going (Turf): Sf: 0-0 GS: 0-3 **Gd: 2-6** GF: 0-3 Fm: 0-0
Distance: 5f/6f: 0-0 **7f-8f: 2-8** 9f-13f: 0-4 14f+: 0-0
Track : **LH: 1-3** RH: 0-2 **Tight: 1-2** Gall: 0-1
Aids: Bl: 0-0 Vi: 0-4 Tstrap: 0-0
Best Rating: 83 10/01 NmkR 1m gd-sft

A dual winner at a mile in 2000, achieving useful form. Has found his form since being equipped with a visor this autumn and was unlucky not to score in a decent Newmarket handicap in October. Seems best on good-ish ground around a mile. Usually held up.

Chance Remark (IRE)

87(86) (32)**30**

3-y-o ch f Goldmark (USA)-Fair Chance (Young Emperor)

M Todhunter (A Berry 8/6) B Batey

Placings:00-066540 **(1961)**

2001: 8^{0}SW, 7^{6}SW, 7^{6}SD, 7^{5}S, 8^{4}F, 7^{0}GF

	Starts	1st	2nd	3rd	Win & Pl
Career Total (Turf)	4	0	0	0	0
Career Total (AW)	4	0	0	0	0

Going (Turf): Sf: 0-2 GS: 0-0 Gd: 0-0 GF: 0-1 Fm: 0-1
Distance: 5f/6f: 0-0 7f-8f: 0-6 9f-13f: 0-2 14f+: 0-0
Track : LH: 0-5 RH: 0-1 Tight: 0-0 Gall: 0-0
Aids: Bl: 0-0 Vi: 0-0 Tstrap: 0-0
Best Rating: 32 2/01 Sthl 7f slow

Chancellor (IRE)

110 **114**

3-y-o ch c Halling (USA)-Isticanna (USA) (Far North (CAN))

B W Hills W J Gredley

Placings:01-102520 **(5389)**

2001: 10^{1}HY, 12^{0}GF, 10^{2}S, 11^{5}GF, 9^{2}VS, 10^{0}GS

	Starts	1st	2nd	3rd	Win & Pl
Career Total (Turf)	8	2	2	0	63859

106 4/01 Sand 1m2f7y A HVY £36000
90 11/00 Donc 7f D HVY £3331
Total win prize-money £39331

Going (Turf): Sf: 2-3 GS: 0-1 Gd: 0-0 GF: 0-3 Fm: 0-0
Distance: 5f/6f: 0-0 7f-8f: 1-2 9f-13f: 1-6 14f+: 0-0
Track : LH: 0-2 **RH: 1-2** Tight: 0-1 Gall: 0-1
Aids: Bl: 0-0 Vi: 0-0 Tstrap: 0-0
Best Rating: 114 10/01 Lonc 1m1f165y v soft

A good-actioned colt, he started off the 2001 campaign with a narrow defeat of Asian Heights on testing ground in the Sandown Classic Trial, looking a top-class middle-distance prospect. Below par on fast ground in the Derby, but finished runner-up back on soft ground in a Group Two at Deauville, and on similar ground was just touched off in the Prix Dollar. Suited by ten furlongs, he has further improvement in him.

Chancit

(87) (52)**62**

2-y-o b f Piccolo-Polly Worth (Wolver Hollow)

Andrew Reid (M R Channon 4/6) A S Reid

Placings:02433F00260005 **(5396)**

2001: 5^{0}GS, 5^{2}G, 5^{4}F, 5^{3}GF, 6^{3}F, 6^{F}GF, 5^{0}F, 6^{0}GF, 7^{2}G, 7^{6}G, 6^{0}GF, 8^{0}G, 6^{0}GF, 8^{5}SD

	Starts	1st	2nd	3rd	Win & Pl
Career Total (Turf)	13	0	2	2	2214
Career Total (AW)	1	0	0	0	0

Going (Turf): Sf: 0-0 GS: 0-1 Gd: 0-4 GF: 0-5 Fm: 0-3
Distance: 5f/6f: 0-9 7f-8f: 0-3 9f-13f: 0-2 14f+: 0-0
Track : LH: 0-3 RH: 0-0 Tight: 0-1 Gall: 0-1
Aids: Bl: 0-0 Vi: 0-0 Tstrap: 0-0
Best Rating: 69 5/01 Ripn 5f good

Chandler's Secret

(95) (66)

2-y-o ch f So Factual (USA)-Sheila's Secret (IRE) (Bluebird (USA))

C N Allen Newmarketconnections.Com

Placings:2 **(5420)**

2001: 7^{2}SD

	Starts	1st	2nd	3rd	Win & Pl
Career Total (Turf)	0	0	0	0	
Career Total (AW)	1	0	1	0	828

Going (Turf): Sf: 0-0 GS: 0-0 Gd: 0-0 GF: 0-0 Fm: 0-0
Distance: 5f/6f: 0-0 7f-8f: 0-1 9f-13f: 0-1 14f+: 0-0
Track : LH: 0-1 RH: 0-0 Tight: 0-1 Gall: 0-0
Aids: Bl: 0-0 Vi: 0-0 Tstrap: 0-0
Best Rating: 66 10/01 Wolv 7f stand

Bred to sprint, did not disgrace on her debut at Wolverhampton. There is a race in her on the sand.

Chandris

83 **62**

2-y-o b c Son Pardo-Dash Cascade (Absalom)

J A Glover Mrs Andrea M Mallinson

Placings:5 **(4536)**

2001: 6^{5}GF

	Starts	1st	2nd	3rd	Win & Pl
Career Total (Turf)	1	0	0	0	0

Going (Turf): Sf: 0-0 GS: 0-0 Gd: 0-0 GF: 0-1 Fm: 0-0
Distance: 5f/6f: 0-1 7f-8f: 0-0 9f-13f: 0-0 14f+: 0-0
Track : LH: 0-0 RH: 0-0 Tight: 0-0 Gall: 0-0
Aids: Bl: 0-0 Vi: 0-0 Tstrap: 0-0
Best Rating: 62 9/01 Rdcr 6f gd-fm

Change Of Image

98(59) (13)**55+**

3-y-o b f Spectrum (IRE)-Reveuse Du Soir (Vision (USA))

H R A Cecil (J M P Eustace 30/5) J Shack

Placings:640-0001 **(4463)**

2001: 7^{0}S, 8^{0}GF, 10^{0}G, 9^{1}GS

	Starts	1st	2nd	3rd	Win & Pl
Career Total (Turf)	6	1	0	0	2594
Career Total (AW)	1	0	0	0	

55 9/01 Folk 1m1f149yF(0-60)H G-S £2394
Total win prize-money £2394

Going (Turf): Sf: 0-1 **GS: 1-2** Gd: 0-1 GF: 0-2 Fm: 0-0
Distance: 5f/6f: 0-3 7f-8f: 0-1 **9f-13f: 1-3** 14f+: 0-0
Track : LH: 0-1 **RH: 1-1 Tight: 1-2** Gall: 0-0
Aids: Bl: 0-0 Vi: 0-0 Tstrap: 0-0
Best Rating: 55 9/01 Folk 1m1f149y gd-sft

She changed stables in 2001, and landed an ordinary handicap at Folkestone.

Changing Guard (IRE)

(95) (65)**60**

2-y-o b g Royal Applause-Milne's Way (The Noble Player (USA))

B W Hills N N Browne

Placings:005 **(4585)**

2001: 5^{0}GS, 6^{0}S, 7^{5}HY

	Starts	1st	2nd	3rd	Win & Pl
Career Total (Turf)	3	0	0	0	0

Going (Turf): Sf: 0-2 GS: 0-1 Gd: 0-0 GF: 0-0 Fm: 0-0
Distance: 5f/6f: 0-1 7f-8f: 0-2 9f-13f: 0-0 14f+: 0-0
Track : LH: 0-1 RH: 0-0 Tight: 0-0 Gall: 0-0
Aids: Bl: 0-0 Vi: 0-0 Tstrap: 0-0
Best Rating: 60 9/01 Hayd 7f30y heavy

Chanson

64 **10**

2-y-o ch f Bijou D'Inde-Tiny Feet (Music Maestro)

J D Czerpak K C Payne

Placings:0 **(1175)**

2001: 5^{0}G

	Starts	1st	2nd	3rd	Win & Pl
Career Total (Turf)	1	0	0	0	

Going (Turf): Sf: 0-0 GS: 0-0 Gd: 0-1 GF: 0-0 Fm: 0-0
Distance: 5f/6f: 0-1 7f-8f: 0-0 9f-13f: 0-0 14f+: 0-0
Track : LH: 0-1 RH: 0-0 Tight: 0-0 Gall: 0-1
Aids: Bl: 0-0 Vi: 0-0 Tstrap: 0-0
Best Rating: 10 5/01 Wwck 5f good

Chantaigne (IRE)

99 **58**

3-y-o ch f General Monash (USA)-Blue Vista (IRE) (Pennine Walk)

A Bailey Ray Bailey

Placings:0530-3000 **(5447)**

2001: 7^{3}G, 7^{0}G, 6^{0}GF, 10^{0}HY

	Starts	1st	2nd	3rd	Win & Pl
Career Total (Turf)	8	0	0	2	1336

Going (Turf): Sf: 0-4 GS: 0-0 Gd: 0-3 GF: 0-1 Fm: 0-0
Distance: 5f/6f: 0-2 7f-8f: 0-4 9f-13f: 0-2 14f+: 0-0
Track : LH: 0-5 RH: 0-0 Tight: 0-2 Gall: 0-1
Aids: Bl: 0-0 Vi: 0-0 Tstrap: 0-0
Best Rating: 58 7/01 Ches 7f122y good

Chantessa Sioux

81 **32**

3-y-o b f Paley Prince (USA)-Legendary Lady (Reprimand)

M D I Usher I E Chant

Placings:00000 **(4993)**

2001: 6^{0}GS, 8^{0}GF, 6^{0}GF, 6^{0}GF, 7^{0}HY

	Starts	1st	2nd	3rd	Win & Pl
Career Total (Turf)	5	0	0	0	

Going (Turf): Sf: 0-1 GS: 0-1 Gd: 0-0 GF: 0-3 Fm: 0-0
Distance: 5f/6f: 0-3 7f-8f: 0-2 9f-13f: 0-0 14f+: 0-0
Track : LH: 0-1 RH: 0-1 Tight: 0-0 Gall: 0-0
Aids: Bl: 0-0 Vi: 0-0 Tstrap: 0-0
Best Rating: 32 7/01 Kemp 1m gd-fm

Chantilly Gold (USA)

85 **59d**

2-y-o ch f Mutakddim (USA)-Bouffant (USA) (Alydar (USA))
N P Littmoden Hanibel Racing Partnership

Placings:254000 **(4437)**
2001: 6^{2}GF, 6^{5}GF, 6^{4}GS, 6^{0}GS, 6^{0}GF, 5^{0}G

	Starts	1st	2nd	3rd	Win & Pl
Career Total (Turf)	6	0	1	0	1075

Going (Turf): Sf: 0-0 GS: 0-2 Gd: 0-1 GF: 0-3 Fm: 0-0
Distance: 5f/6f: 0-4 7f-8f: 0-2 9f-13f: 0-0 14f+: 0-0
Track : LH: 0-0 RH: 0-0 Tight: 0-0 Gall: 0-0
Aids: Bl: 0-0 Vi: 0-0 Tstrap: 0-0
Best Rating: 71 6/01 Haml 6f5y gd-fm

She has gone backwards since finishing runner-up at Hamilton on her debut.

Chantilly Myth

93 **68+**

2-y-o b f Sri Pekan (USA)-Charolles (Ajdal (USA))
T D Easterby T Herbert-Jackson

Placings:30410 **(4695)**
2001: 6^{3}F, 5^{0}GF, 6^{4}GF, 6^{1}F, 6^{0}GS

	Starts	1st	2nd	3rd	Win & Pl
Career Total (Turf)	5	1	0	1	5085

68 7/01 Thsk 6f D FRM £4020
Total win prize-money £4020

Going (Turf): Sf: 0-0 GS: 0-1 Gd: 0-0 GF: 0-2 **Fm: 1-2**
Distance: **5f/6f: 1-5** 7f-8f: 0-0 9f-13f: 0-0 14f+: 0-0
Track : LH: 0-0 RH: 0-0 Tight: 0-0 Gall: 0-0
Aids: Bl: 0-0 Vi: 0-0 Tstrap: 0-0
Best Rating: 68 7/01 Thsk 6f firm

Well regarded, she went some way to justifying some big race entries when comfortably winning a Thirsk maiden on his fourth start.

Chantress Lorelei

97 **66**

3-y-o b f So Factual (USA)-Sound Of The Sea (Windjammer (USA))
Mrs A J Perrett Mrs Z O'Brien,D Broad,A Ambler

Placings:05-04340 **(5082)**
2001: 6^{0}G, 6^{4}GF, 7^{3}G, 8^{4}GF, 7^{0}S

	Starts	1st	2nd	3rd	Win & Pl
Career Total (Turf)	7	0	0	1	416

Going (Turf): Sf: 0-3 GS: 0-0 Gd: 0-2 GF: 0-2 Fm: 0-0
Distance: 5f/6f: 0-3 7f-8f: 0-3 9f-13f: 0-1 14f+: 0-0
Track : LH: 0-1 RH: 0-0 Tight: 0-0 Gall: 0-0
Aids: Bl: 0-0 Vi: 0-0 Tstrap: 0-0
Best Rating: 66 8/01 Ling 6f gd-fm

Chaparro Amargoso (IRE)

8-y-o b g Ela-Mana-Mou-Champanera (Top Ville)
B Ellison E J Berry

Placings:5 **(2891)**
2001: 12^{5}GF

	Starts	1st	2nd	3rd	Win & Pl
Career Total (Turf)	1	0	0	0	0

Going (Turf): Sf: 0-0 GS: 0-0 Gd: 0-0 GF: 0-1 Fm: 0-0
Distance: 5f/6f: 0-0 7f-8f: 0-0 9f-13f: 0-1 14f+: 0-0
Track : LH: 0-1 RH: 0-0 Tight: 0-0 Gall: 0-0
Aids: Bl: 0-0 Vi: 0-0 Tstrap: 0-0

Chapeau

82 **58**

2-y-o ch f Zafonic (USA)-Barboukh (Night Shift (USA))
D R C Elsworth R J McCreery

Placings:0 **(5277)**
2001: 7^{0}GS

	Starts	1st	2nd	3rd	Win & Pl
Career Total (Turf)	1	0	0	0	

Going (Turf): Sf: 0-0 GS: 0-1 Gd: 0-0 GF: 0-0 Fm: 0-0
Distance: 5f/6f: 0-0 7f-8f: 0-1 9f-13f: 0-0 14f+: 0-0
Track : LH: 0-0 RH: 0-0 Tight: 0-0 Gall: 0-0
Aids: Bl: 0-0 Vi: 0-0 Tstrap: 0-0
Best Rating: 58 10/01 Leic 7f9y gd-sft

Chapel Orchid

87 **62**

2-y-o b f College Chapel-Royal Orchid (IRE) (Shalford (IRE))
T D Easterby W H Ponsonby

Placings:0 **(4454)**
2001: 6^{0}GF

	Starts	1st	2nd	3rd	Win & Pl
Career Total (Turf)	1	0	0	0	

Going (Turf): Sf: 0-0 GS: 0-0 Gd: 0-0 GF: 0-1 Fm: 0-0
Distance: 5f/6f: 0-1 7f-8f: 0-0 9f-13f: 0-0 14f+: 0-0
Track : LH: 0-0 RH: 0-0 Tight: 0-0 Gall: 0-0
Aids: Bl: 0-0 Vi: 0-0 Tstrap: 0-0
Best Rating: 62 9/01 York 6f gd-fm

Chapel Royale (IRE)

(82) (35)**68**

4-y-o gr c College Chapel-Merci Royale (Fairy King (USA))
D Nicholls Prospect Estates Ltd

Placings:001/5002031000330000-04450000 **(5413)**
2001: 8^{0}HY, 8^{4}G, 8^{4}G, 8^{5}GS, 8^{0}GF, 8^{0}G, 9^{0}GS, 8^{0}SD

	Starts	1st	2nd	3rd	Win & Pl
Career Total (Turf)	26	2	1	3	16574
Career Total (AW)	1	0	0	0	

85 7/00 NmkJ 1m C(0-95)H G-S £7709
87 9/99 Newc 7f F SFT £1819
Total win prize-money £9528

Going (Turf): Sf: 1-8 GS: 1-5 Gd: 0-9 GF: 0-4 Fm: 0-0
Distance: 5f/6f: 0-2 **7f-8f: 2-13** 9f-13f: 0-12 14f+: 0-0
Track : LH: 0-6 RH: 0-11 Tight: 0-9 Gall: 0-1
Aids: Bl: 0-0 Vi: 0-0 Tstrap: 0-5
Best Rating: 76 5/01 Bevl 1m100y good

Fairly useful 1m handicapper who goes particularly well in the mud. Showed first form for David Nicholls when fourth in the Thirsk Hunt Cup, but has not built on that.

Chaperone

77(95) (46)**3**

3-y-o b f Shaamit (IRE)-Loving Legacy (Caerleon (USA))
W J Haggas Les McLaughlin

Placings:5600 **(1737)**
2001: 8^{5}SW, 11^{6}SD, 12^{0}HY, 8^{0}GF

	Starts	1st	2nd	3rd	Win & Pl
Career Total (Turf)	2	0	0	0	
Career Total (AW)	2	0	0	0	0

Going (Turf): Sf: 0-1 GS: 0-0 Gd: 0-0 GF: 0-1 Fm: 0-0
Distance: 5f/6f: 0-0 7f-8f: 0-1 9f-13f: 0-3 14f+: 0-0
Track : LH: 0-2 RH: 0-1 Tight: 0-1 Gall: 0-0
Aids: Bl: 0-0 Vi: 0-1 Tstrap: 0-1
Best Rating: 46 2/01 Sthl 1m slow

Charango (USA)

105(101) (61)**81**

4-y-o br c Danzig (USA)-Nidd (USA) (Known Fact (USA))
G C Bravery The Iona Stud

Placings:3100 **(4868)**
2001: 5^{3}SD, 5^{1}G, 5^{0}GS, 5^{0}G

	Starts	1st	2nd	3rd	Win & Pl
Career Total (Turf)	3	1	0	0	3510
Career Total (AW)	1	0	0	1	420

70 8/01 Ripn 5f D GD £3510
Total win prize-money £3510

Going (Turf): Sf: 0-0 GS: 0-1 **Gd: 1-2** GF: 0-0 Fm: 0-0
Distance: **5f/6f: 1-4** 7f-8f: 0-0 9f-13f: 0-0 14f+: 0-0
Track : LH: 0-0 RH: 0-0 Tight: 0-0 Gall: 0-0
Aids: Bl: 0-0 Vi: 0-0 Tstrap: 0-0
Best Rating: 81 9/01 Donc 5f gd-sft

Got off the mark comfortably on his turf debut after an absence of 145 days. Has won over five furlongs on good ground and looks to have plenty of ability, but was up against it in better company afterwards.

Charente (USA)

(99) (66)**69**

3-y-o ch c Hennessy (USA)-Zalamalec (USA) (Septieme Ciel (USA))
P G Murphy The Golden Anorak Partnership

Placings:5003530-61400 **(5166)**
2001: 9^{6}SW, 10^{1}SW, 12^{4}SD, 10^{0}S, 9^{0}SD

	Starts	1st	2nd	3rd	Win & Pl
Career Total (Turf)	5	0	0	1	398
Career Total (AW)	7	1	0	1	3449

66 2/01 Ling 1m2f D SLW £2891
Total win prize-money £2891

Going (Turf): Sf: 0-1 GS: 0-1 Gd: 0-1 GF: 0-2 Fm: 0-0
Distance: 5f/6f: 0-1 7f-8f: 0-4 **9f-13f: 1-7** 14f+: 0-0
Track : **LH: 1-8** RH: 0-0 **Tight: 1-8** Gall: 0-0
Aids: Bl: 0-0 Vi: 0-1 Tstrap: 0-0
Best Rating: 66 2/01 Ling 1m2f slow

Bred to race on dirt, had not run particularly well in two efforts at Wolverhampton, but seemed to find the surface at Lingfield more to his liking. Suited by 1m2f.

Charge

89(105) (63)**61**

5-y-o gr g Petong-Madam Petoski (Petoski)
K R Burke Nigel Shields

Placings:343/043416/002215005000P0-6013001106 **(1105)**
2001: 6^{6}SD, 5^{0}SD, 6^{1}SW, 6^{3}SW, 6^{0}SW, 6^{0}SD, 6^{1}SD, 6^{1}SD, 5^{0}SD, 5^{6}GF

	Starts	1st	2nd	3rd	Win & Pl
Career Total (Turf)	12	0	0	3	2121
Career Total (AW)	22	5	2	1	14020

63 3/01 Ling 6f F STD £2233
63 3/01 Ling 6f F(0-65)H STD £1722
56 2/01 Ling 6f F(0-60) SLW £2135
78 3/00 Ling 6f F(0-65)H STD £2331

55	11/99	Ling	6f	D	STD	£3783

Total win prize-money £12205

Going (Turf): Sf: 0-1 GS: 0-1 Gd: 0-4 GF: 0-6 Fm: 0-0
Distance: **5f/6f: 5-33** 7f-8f: 0-1 9f-13f: 0-0 14f+: 0-0
Track : **LH: 5-25** RH: 0-2 **Tight: 5-20** Gall: 0-5
Aids: Bl: 0-2 Vi: 0-0 **Tstrap: 5-30**
Best Rating: 63 3/01 Ling 6f stand

Charitable (IRE)

(98) (82)
3-y-o b f Mujadil (USA)-Verusa (IRE) (Petorius)
J A Osborne L Queally

Placings:31-436 **(0207)**
2001: 6^{4}SD, 7^{3}SD, 6^{6}SW

	Starts	1st	2nd	3rd	Win & Pl
Career Total (Turf)	0	0	0	0	
Career Total (AW)	5	1	0	2	3786

82	12/00	Sthl	6f	F	STD	£2233

Total win prize-money £2233

Going (Turf): Sf: 0-0 GS: 0-0 Gd: 0-0 GF: 0-0 Fm: 0-0
Distance: **5f/6f: 1-4** 7f-8f: 0-1 9f-13f: 0-1 14f+: 0-0
Track : **LH: 1-5** RH: 0-0 Tight: 0-1 Gall: 0-0
Aids: Bl: 0-0 Vi: 0-0 Tstrap: 0-1
Best Rating: 76 1/01 Sthl 7f stand

Charlatan (IRE)

81 **34**
3-y-o b g Charnwood Forest (IRE)-Taajreh (IRE) (Mtoto)
Mrs C A Dunnett Mrs Christine Dunnett

Placings:0-00000 **(5557)**
2001: 8^{0}GF, 8^{0}GF, 10^{0}G, 9^{0}GS, 14^{0}S

	Starts	1st	2nd	3rd	Win & Pl
Career Total (Turf)	6	0	0	0	

Going (Turf): Sf: 0-1 GS: 0-2 Gd: 0-1 GF: 0-2 Fm: 0-0
Distance: 5f/6f: 0-0 7f-8f: 0-2 9f-13f: 0-3 14f+: 0-1
Track : LH: 0-2 RH: 0-2 Tight: 0-3 Gall: 0-0
Aids: Bl: 0-0 Vi: 0-0 Tstrap: 0-0
Best Rating: 34 7/01 Donc 1m gd-fm

Charlem

(93) (26)**20**
4-y-o br f Petardia-La Neva (FR) (Arctic Tern (USA))
D Shaw R A B Saville

Placings:00/66602000-00000 **(0356)**
2001: 8^{0}SD, 9^{0}SW, 8^{0}SW, 12^{0}SD, 8^{0}SW

	Starts	1st	2nd	3rd	Win & Pl
Career Total (Turf)	6	0	0	0	
Career Total (AW)	9	0	1	0	650

Going (Turf): Sf: 0-1 GS: 0-1 Gd: 0-1 GF: 0-2 Fm: 0-0
Distance: 5f/6f: 0-0 7f-8f: 0-6 9f-13f: 0-8 14f+: 0-0
Track : LH: 0-10 RH: 0-1 Tight: 0-6 Gall: 0-0
Aids: Bl: 0-4 Vi: 0-6 Tstrap: 0-0
Best Rating: 28 1/01 Sthl 1m slow

Charles Spencelayh (IRE)

103 **89**
5-y-o b g Tenby-Legit (IRE) (Runnett)
M C Pipe (Rune Haugen 4/10) Mick Fletcher

Placings:3116/4442315/04020-2442062 **(5106)**
2001: 11^{2}G, 12^{4}GS, 13^{4}S, 14^{2}G, 13^{0}G, 12^{6}S, 12^{2}GS

	Starts	1st	2nd	3rd	Win & Pl
Career Total (Turf)	20	2	4	1	35029
Career Total (AW)	3	1	1	1	5069

	9/99	Ovrl	1m6f		SFT	£7886
94	9/98	Sals	6f212y	D	HVY	£3428
83	8/98	Wolv	7f	D	STD	£3677

Total win prize-money £14991

Going (Turf): Sf: 2-5 GS: 0-2 Gd: 0-14 GF: 0-0 Fm: 0-0
Distance: 5f/6f: 0-1 **7f-8f: 2-5** 9f-13f: 0-14 14f+: 1-3
Track : **LH: 1-9** RH: 0-1 **Tight: 1-3** Gall: 0-1
Aids: Bl: 0-0 Vi: 0-0 Tstrap: 0-0
Best Rating: 89 9/01 Ches 1m5f89y good

Formerly with Paul Cole, he was trained in Norway for over two years where he has won over 14 furlongs on soft ground. He was claimed by Martin Pipe to continue his career over jumps.

Charley Bates (USA)

96 **84**
2-y-o b/br c Benny The Dip (USA)-Vouch (USA) (Halo (USA))
J H M Gosden Strawbridge,Knight,Stonerside,Hancock

Placings:224 **(5056)**
2001: 7^{2}GF, 8^{2}G, 8^{4}S

	Starts	1st	2nd	3rd	Win & Pl
Career Total (Turf)	3	0	2	0	3264

Going (Turf): Sf: 0-1 GS: 0-0 Gd: 0-1 GF: 0-1 Fm: 0-0
Distance: 5f/6f: 0-0 7f-8f: 0-3 9f-13f: 0-0 14f+: 0-0
Track : LH: 0-0 RH: 0-1 Tight: 0-0 Gall: 0-0
Aids: Bl: 0-0 Vi: 0-1 Tstrap: 0-0
Best Rating: 84 10/01 NmkR 1m soft

Showed ability in fair company as a juvenile.

Charley Farley

86 **66**
2-y-o ch c Bluegrass Prince (IRE)-Miss Copyforce (Aragon)
E A Wheeler Ifield Frozen Foods Limited

Placings:000 **(5588)**
2001: 6^{0}HY, 7^{0}S, 5^{0}GS

	Starts	1st	2nd	3rd	Win & Pl
Career Total (Turf)	3	0	0	0	

Going (Turf): Sf: 0-2 GS: 0-1 Gd: 0-0 GF: 0-0 Fm: 0-0
Distance: 5f/6f: 0-2 7f-8f: 0-1 9f-13f: 0-0 14f+: 0-0
Track : LH: 0-1 RH: 0-0 Tight: 0-0 Gall: 0-0
Aids: Bl: 0-0 Vi: 0-0 Tstrap: 0-0
Best Rating: 66 11/01 Brig 5f213y gd-sft

Charlie Chap (IRE)

98 **78**
2-y-o ch c College Chapel-Fable (Absalom)
Miss L A Perratt Miss L A Perratt

Placings:011243 **(4823)**
2001: 5^{0}GF, 5^{1}GF, 5^{1}G, 6^{2}S, 5^{4}G, 6^{3}G

	Starts	1st	2nd	3rd	Win & Pl
Career Total (Turf)	6	2	1	1	8867

78	7/01	Haml	5f4y	F	GD	£3493
76	6/01	Ayr	5f	E	G-F	£2870

Total win prize-money £6364

Going (Turf): Sf: 0-1 GS: 0-0 **Gd: 1-3 GF: 1-2** Fm: 0-0
Distance: **5f/6f: 2-5** 7f-8f: 0-1 9f-13f: 0-0 14f+: 0-0
Track : LH: 0-0 RH: 0-0 Tight: 0-0 Gall: 0-0
Aids: Bl: 0-0 Vi: 0-0 Tstrap: 0-0
Best Rating: 78 9/01 Ayr 6f good

Has won twice this season and put up a good show when third at Ayr. Suited by all types of ground and five to six furlongs.

Charlie Parkes

107 **96**
3-y-o ch c Pursuit Of Love-Lucky Parkes (Full Extent (USA))
A Berry Joseph Heler

Placings:222-16000026 **(5341)**
2001: 5^{1}G, 5^{6}GF, 5^{0}GF, 5^{0}GF, 6^{0}G, 5^{0}GF, 5^{2}G, 5^{6}GS

	Starts	1st	2nd	3rd	Win & Pl
Career Total (Turf)	11	1	4	0	12811

79	5/01	Bevl	5f	D	GD	£4780

Total win prize-money £4781

Going (Turf): Sf: 0-0 GS: 0-1 **Gd: 1-6** GF: 0-4 Fm: 0-0
Distance: **5f/6f: 1-11** 7f-8f: 0-0 9f-13f: 0-0 14f+: 0-0
Track : LH: 0-2 RH: 0-0 Tight: 0-2 Gall: 0-0
Aids: Bl: 0-0 Vi: 0-0 Tstrap: 0-0
Best Rating: 102 5/01 Kemp 5f gd-fm

A speedy colt, he was unlucky not to get off the mark as a two-year-old. Subsequently injured, he returned to the track after an absence of nearly a year and made no mistake from a good draw at Beverley in May 2001. Not disgraced behind Emerald Peace at Kempton, but has found life tough since. A fast-ground five furlongs is his trip.

Charlie Simmons (IRE)

101 **70**
3-y-o ch g Forest Wind (USA)-Ballinlee (IRE) (Skyliner)
A P Jarvis The Aston Partnership

Placings:042 **(2845)**
2001: 8^{0}S, 8^{4}GF, 8^{2}F

	Starts	1st	2nd	3rd	Win & Pl
Career Total (Turf)	3	0	1	0	1278

Going (Turf): Sf: 0-1 GS: 0-0 Gd: 0-0 GF: 0-1 Fm: 0-1
Distance: 5f/6f: 0-0 7f-8f: 0-3 9f-13f: 0-0 14f+: 0-0
Track : LH: 0-1 RH: 0-1 Tight: 0-0 Gall: 0-1
Aids: Bl: 0-0 Vi: 0-0 Tstrap: 0-0
Best Rating: 70 6/01 Gdwd 1m gd-fm

Charlie's Quest

95(88) (13)**28**
5-y-o b g Kylian (USA)-Pleasure Quest (Efisio)
D W P Arbuthnot Miss P E Decker

Placings:006/00 0504 **(1767)**
2001: 13^{0}SW, 16^{5}SD, 11^{0}F, 10^{4}F

	Starts	1st	2nd	3rd	Win & Pl
Career Total (Turf)	6	0	0	0	0
Career Total (AW)	3	0	0	0	0

Going (Turf): Sf: 0-2 GS: 0-1 Gd: 0-1 GF: 0-0 Fm: 0-2
Distance: 5f/6f: 0-0 7f-8f: 0-1 9f-13f: 0-7 14f+: 0-1
Track : LH: 0-6 RH: 0-2 Tight: 0-3 Gall: 0-1
Aids: Bl: 0-3 Vi: 0-1 Tstrap: 0-0
Best Rating: 28 6/01 Bath 1m2f46y firm

Charlottevalentina (IRE)

104 **69**
4-y-o ch f Perugino (USA)-The Top Diesis (USA) (Diesis)
R Ingram Ellangowan Racing Partners

Placings:460106/020005-0000 **(4718)**
2001: 6^{0}GF, 6^{0}GF, 5^{0}G, 5^{0}G

	Starts	1st	2nd	3rd	Win & Pl
Career Total (Turf)	16	1	1	0	7160

77	6/99	Catt	5f212y	D	G-F	£2770

Total win prize-money £2770

Going (Turf): Sf: 0-2 GS: 0-1 Gd: 0-5 **GF: 1-8** Fm: 0-0
Distance: **5f/6f: 1-13** 7f-8f: 0-3 9f-13f: 0-0 14f+: 0-0
Track : **LH: 1-8** RH: 0-2 **Tight: 1-6** Gall: 0-3
Aids: Bl: 0-0 Vi: 0-1 Tstrap: 0-0
Best Rating: 69 7/01 Epsm 6f gd-fm

Won a fairly modest maiden at Catterick over the minimum trip in 1999. Highly tried the following season, but has dropped in grade in 2001. Suited by six furlongs and a sound surface.

Charm Offensive

102 **51**

3-y-o b f Zieten (USA)-Shoag (USA) (Affirmed (USA))

K A Ryan (Mrs J R Ramsden 7/5) Mrs Margaret Forsyth

Placings:165405040 **(4905)**

2001: 7^{1}S, 6^{6}S, 7^{5}G, 8^{4}G, 10^{0}GY, 8^{5}G, 9^{0}G, 7^{4}GF, 8^{0}G

	Starts	1st	2nd	3rd	Win & Pl
Career Total (Turf)	9	1	0	0	2079

53 5/01 Newc 7f F SFT £2079

Total win prize-money £2079

Going (Turf): Sf: 1-2 GS: 0-0 Gd: 0-5 GF: 0-1 Fm: 0-0
Distance: 5f/6f: 0-0 **7f-8f: 1-4** 9f-13f: 0-5 14f+: 0-0
Track : LH: 0-3 RH: 0-3 Tight: 0-0 Gall: 0-0
Aids: Bl: 0-0 Vi: 0-0 Tstrap: 0-0
Best Rating: 53 5/01 Newc 7f soft

Unraced at two, she made a winning debut in soft ground at Newcastle in May, but has not enjoyed the best of luck in handicap company since.

Charmante Femme

100(71) (2)**52?**

3-y-o b f Bin Ajwaad (IRE)-Charmante Dame (FR) (Bellypha)

K McAuliffe G E Amey

Placings:0005000 **(4076)**

2001: 9^{0}SD, 11^{0}SD, 11^{0}GS, 10^{5}F, 10^{0}GF, 12^{0}S, 11^{0}G

	Starts	1st	2nd	3rd	Win & Pl
Career Total (Turf)	5	0	0	0	0
Career Total (AW)	2	0	0	0	

Going (Turf): Sf: 0-1 GS: 0-1 Gd: 0-1 GF: 0-1 Fm: 0-1
Distance: 5f/6f: 0-0 7f-8f: 0-0 9f-13f: 0-7 14f+: 0-0
Track : LH: 0-7 RH: 0-0 Tight: 0-3 Gall: 0-1
Aids: Bl: 0-0 Vi: 0-0 Tstrap: 0-0
Best Rating: 68 6/01 Bath 1m2f46y firm

Charmaway

87 **77**

3-y-o b g Charmer-Dismiss (Daring March)

C E Brittain Michael Clarke

Placings:00 **(1167)**

2001: 7^{0}GS, 8^{0}GS

	Starts	1st	2nd	3rd	Win & Pl
Career Total (Turf)	2	0	0	0	

Going (Turf): Sf: 0-0 GS: 0-2 Gd: 0-0 GF: 0-0 Fm: 0-0
Distance: 5f/6f: 0-0 7f-8f: 0-2 9f-13f: 0-0 14f+: 0-0
Track : LH: 0-0 RH: 0-1 Tight: 0-0 Gall: 0-0
Aids: Bl: 0-0 Vi: 0-0 Tstrap: 0-0
Best Rating: 77 4/01 Newb 7f gd-sft

Charmed

93(75) (8)**21**

3-y-o ch g Savahra Sound-Sweet And Lucky (Lucky Wednesday)

M J Gingell (N P Littmoden 29/1) Gentlemen Don't Work On Mondays

Placings:000-**0000**030000 **(2372)**

2001: 8^{0}SD, 6^{0}SD, 12^{0}SD, 8^{0}SD, 6^{0}GS, 6^{3}HY, 6^{0}GF, 6^{0}G, 5^{0}GF, 8^{0}GF

	Starts	1st	2nd	3rd	Win & Pl
Career Total (Turf)	9	0	0	1	284
Career Total (AW)	4	0	0	0	

Going (Turf): Sf: 0-1 GS: 0-1 Gd: 0-2 GF: 0-5 Fm: 0-0
Distance: 5f/6f: 0-5 7f-8f: 0-7 9f-13f: 0-1 14f+: 0-0
Track : LH: 0-7 RH: 0-0 Tight: 0-3 Gall: 0-0
Aids: Bl: 0-0 Vi: 0-6 Tstrap: 0-0
Best Rating: 36 5/01 Nott 6f15y heavy

Charmer Venture

98(98) (61+)**90**

3-y-o ch f Zilzal (USA)-City Of Angels (Woodman (USA))

S P C Woods S P C Woods

Placings:4-13064 **(3483)**

2001: 10^{1}SD, 11^{3}G, 12^{0}GF, 10^{6}GF, 9^{4}GF

	Starts	1st	2nd	3rd	Win & Pl
Career Total (Turf)	5	0	0	1	4278
Career Total (AW)	1	1	0	0	2744

61 4/01 Ling 1m2f E STD £2744

Total win prize-money £2744

Going (Turf): Sf: 0-0 GS: 0-0 Gd: 0-2 GF: 0-3 Fm: 0-0
Distance: 5f/6f: 0-0 7f-8f: 0-1 **9f-13f: 1-5** 14f+: 0-0
Track : **LH: 1-4** RH: 0-2 **Tight: 1-3** Gall: 0-3
Aids: Bl: 0-0 Vi: 0-0 Tstrap: 0-0
Best Rating: 90 5/01 Ling 1m3f106y good

Made an encouraging debut at two over a mile at Doncaster. Scored at Lingfield on the All-Weather when stepped up to ten furlongs but subsequently struggled. Acts on good ground and Equitrack.

Charming Admiral (IRE)

(88) (23)**55**

8-y-o b g Shareef Dancer (USA)-Lilac Charm (Bustino)

Mrs A Duffield The Old Spice Girls

Placings:0/050322/024/**3000**/423345/012003030-51 **(0879)**

2001: 17^{5}HY, 21^{1}S

	Starts	1st	2nd	3rd	Win & Pl
Career Total (Turf)	25	2	5	5	15858
Career Total (AW)	6	0	0	1	307

50 4/01 Pont 2m5f122yE(0-70)H SFT £3705
59 4/00 Pont 2m1f22y E(0-75)H G-S £3029

Total win prize-money £6734

Going (Turf): Sf: 1-8 GS: 1-4 Gd: 0-7 GF: 0-6 Fm: 0-0
Distance: 5f/6f: 0-0 7f-8f: 0-0 9f-13f: 0-5 **14f+: 2-26**
Track : **LH: 2-25** RH: 0-5 Tight: 0-8 Gall: 0-1
Aids: **Bl: 2-12** Vi: 0-1 Tstrap: 0-0
Best Rating: 50 4/01 Pont 2m5f122y soft

Better known as a hurdler/chaser these days, won a long distance handicap in the spring.

Charming Lotte

105(84) (27)**61**

4-y-o b f Nicolotte-Courtisane (Persepolis (FR))

Don Enrico Incisa (N Tinkler 21/5) Don Enrico Incisa

Placings:32000315/0005130350-6131363600040242 **(5638)**

2001: 6^{6}HY, 6^{1}HY, 6^{3}HY, 6^{1}HY, 6^{3}G, 6^{6}G, 6^{3}G, 6^{6}G, 6^{0}GF, 6^{0}GF, 6^{0}F, 6^{4}G, 6^{0}G, 6^{2}G, 6^{4}HY, 6^{2}HY, 7^{0}G

	Starts	1st	2nd	3rd	Win & Pl
Career Total (Turf)	34	4	3	7	19288
Career Total (AW)	1	0	0	0	

70 5/01 Nott 6f15y E(0-70)H HVY £3150
59 4/01 Pont 6f F HVY £2817
60 6/00 Ches 6f18y E G-S £3718
76 10/99 Ayr 6f D(0-85)H SFT £3730

Total win prize-money £13416

Going (Turf): Sf: 3-12 GS: 1-3 Gd: 0-12 GF: 0-5 Fm: 0-2
Distance: 5f/6f: 2-19 7f-8f: 2-16 9f-13f: 0-0 14f+: 0-0
Track : **LH: 2-6** RH: 0-0 **Tight: 1-3** Gall: 0-0
Aids: Bl: 0-0 **Vi: 4-29** Tstrap: 0-0
Best Rating: 70 5/01 Nott 6f15y heavy

A modest sprint handicapper, she was busy early on this season and managed to win a Pontefract seller and a Nottingham fillies' handicap. Six furlongs and soft ground are ideal for her.

Charnwood Boy

(94) (62)**50**

3-y-o b g Charnwood Forest (IRE)-Jeanne Avril (Music Boy)

W Jarvis The Charnwood Boy Partnership

Placings:002050 **(4876)**

2001: 6^{0}GS, 6^{0}GF, 6^{2}SD, 5^{0}GS, 6^{5}G, 6^{0}SD

	Starts	1st	2nd	3rd	Win & Pl
Career Total (Turf)	4	0	0	0	0
Career Total (AW)	2	0	1	0	796

Going (Turf): Sf: 0-0 GS: 0-2 Gd: 0-1 GF: 0-1 Fm: 0-0
Distance: 5f/6f: 0-6 7f-8f: 0-0 9f-13f: 0-0 14f+: 0-0
Track : LH: 0-3 RH: 0-0 Tight: 0-1 Gall: 0-0
Aids: Bl: 0-0 Vi: 0-1 Tstrap: 0-0
Best Rating: 62 6/01 Sthl 6f stand

Charnwood Princess (IRE)

(91) (61)**41**

3-y-o b f Charnwood Forest (IRE)-Desert Gift (Green Desert (USA))

E A Wheeler Mrs Julie Kelly

Placings:0000**663**-34040 **(1476)**

2001: 5^{3}SD, 5^{4}SD, 6^{0}SD, 6^{4}SW, 6^{0}G

	Starts	1st	2nd	3rd	Win & Pl
Career Total (Turf)	5	0	0	0	
Career Total (AW)	7	0	0	2	730

Going (Turf): Sf: 0-1 GS: 0-0 Gd: 0-1 GF: 0-1 Fm: 0-0
Distance: 5f/6f: 0-9 7f-8f: 0-3 9f-13f: 0-0 14f+: 0-0
Track : LH: 0-9 RH: 0-0 Tight: 0-6 Gall: 0-0
Aids: Bl: 0-4 Vi: 0-0 Tstrap: 0-0
Best Rating: 61 1/01 Ling 5f stand

Charnwood Street (IRE)

91(85) (64)**78?**

2-y-o b c Charnwood Forest (IRE)-La Vigie (King Of Clubs)

D Shaw Swann Racing Ltd

Placings:054600 **(5628)**

2001: 6^{0}SD, 7^{5}SD, 7^{4}GS, 7^{6}G, 8^{0}GF, 8^{0}G

	Starts	1st	2nd	3rd	Win & Pl
Career Total (Turf)	4	0	0	0	0
Career Total (AW)	2	0	0	0	0

Going (Turf): Sf: 0-0 GS: 0-1 Gd: 0-2 GF: 0-1 Fm: 0-0
Distance: 5f/6f: 0-1 7f-8f: 0-4 9f-13f: 0-1 14f+: 0-0
Track : LH: 0-2 RH: 0-0 Tight: 0-0 Gall: 0-0
Aids: Bl: 0-0 Vi: 0-1 Tstrap: 0-0
Best Rating: 78 7/01 Wwck 7f26y gd-sft

Signs of ability in ordinary maidens on turf and All-Weather.

Charter Flight

(101) (59)**45**

5-y-o b g Cosmonaut-Irene's Charter (Persian Bold)

K R Burke (A G Newcombe 9/2) Nigel Shields

Placings:02/301/0400006-10 **(0341)**

2001: 12^{1}SW, 12^{0}SW

	Starts	1st	2nd	3rd	Win & Pl
Career Total (Turf)	5	0	0	0	
Career Total (AW)	9	2	1	1	5758

59 2/01 Sthl 1m4f F SLW £2163
63 9/99 Wolv 1m100y F(0-65)H STD £2409

Total win prize-money £4572

Going (Turf): Sf: 0-2 GS: 0-0 Gd: 0-1 GF: 0-1 Fm: 0-1
Distance: 5f/6f: 0-0 7f-8f: 0-4 9f-13f: 2-10 14f+: 0-0
Track : LH: 2-11 RH: 0-1 Tight: 1-6 Gall: 0-0
Aids: Bl: 0-0 Vi: 0-0 Tstrap: 0-0
Best Rating: 59 2/01 Sthl 1m4f slow

He had shown some ability on Fibresand before getting off the mark in a maiden handicap at Wolverhampton in September.

Chartleys Princess

93(95) (57)**53**
3-y-o b f Prince Sabo-Ethel Knight (Thatch (USA))
K R Burke M Nelmes-Crocker

Placings:533500-03030000 **(3643)**
2001: 6^{0}SW, 6^{3}SD, 6^{0}GF, 6^{3}F, 6^{0}GF, 5^{0}GF, 5^{0}F, 6^{0}F

	Starts	1st	2nd	3rd	Win & Pl
Career Total (Turf)	12	0	0	3	1217
Career Total (AW)	2	0	0	1	394

Going (Turf): Sf: 0-1 GS: 0-1 Gd: 0-1 GF: 0-5 Fm: 0-4
Distance: 5f/6f: 0-13 7f-8f: 0-1 9f-13f: 0-0 14f+: 0-0
Track : LH: 0-2 RH: 0-0 Tight: 0-2 Gall: 0-0
Aids: Bl: 0-1 Vi: 0-3 Tstrap: 0-0
Best Rating: 57 4/01 Ling 6f stand

Chase The Blues (IRE)

(75) (16)**35**
4-y-o b g Blues Traveller (IRE)-Highdrive (Ballymore)
H Akbary Egerton Stud Farm Limited

Placings:650000-0 **(0263)**
2001: 8^{0}SW

	Starts	1st	2nd	3rd	Win & Pl
Career Total (Turf)	5	0	0	0	0
Career Total (AW)	2	0	0	0	

Going (Turf): Sf: 0-0 GS: 0-0 Gd: 0-2 GF: 0-3 Fm: 0-0
Distance: 5f/6f: 0-3 7f-8f: 0-4 9f-13f: 0-0 14f+: 0-0
Track : LH: 0-3 RH: 0-0 Tight: 0-1 Gall: 0-0
Aids: Bl: 0-0 Vi: 0-0 Tstrap: 0-0
Best Rating: 57 4/01 Ling 6f stand

Chase The Gold

(83) (51)**52**
2-y-o ch c Greensmith-Rainbow Chaser (IRE) (Rainbow Quest (USA))
J G Portman Madhatter Racing

Placings:00006 **(5618)**
2001: 7^{0}GS, 6^{0}G, 6^{0}GF, 8^{0}SD, 8^{6}SD

	Starts	1st	2nd	3rd	Win & Pl
Career Total (Turf)	3	0	0	0	
Career Total (AW)	2	0	0	0	0

Going (Turf): Sf: 0-0 GS: 0-1 Gd: 0-1 GF: 0-1 Fm: 0-0
Distance: 5f/6f: 0-1 7f-8f: 0-2 9f-13f: 0-2 14f+: 0-0
Track : LH: 0-3 RH: 0-0 Tight: 0-2 Gall: 0-0
Aids: Bl: 0-0 Vi: 0-0 Tstrap: 0-0
Best Rating: 52 8/01 Folk 6f good

Chateau Nicol

(98) (85)**58+**
2-y-o b g Distant Relative-Glensara (Petoski)
R Guest Basingstoke Commercials

Placings:011 **(4069)**
2001: 6^{0}GF, 6^{1}GF, 6^{1}SD

	Starts	1st	2nd	3rd	Win & Pl
Career Total (Turf)	2	1	0	0	2982
Career Total (AW)	1	1	0	0	19140
85	8/01	Wolv	6f	B	STD £19140
58	8/01	Wwck	6f21y	E	G-F £2982

Total win prize-money £22122

Going (Turf): Sf: 0-0 GS: 0-0 Gd: 0-0 GF: 1-2 Fm: 0-0
Distance: 5f/6f: 1-2 7f-8f: 1-1 9f-13f: 0-0 14f+: 0-0
Track : LH: 1-1 RH: 0-0 Tight: 1-1 Gall: 0-0
Aids: Bl: 0-0 Vi: 0-0 Tstrap: 0-0
Best Rating: 85 8/01 Wolv 6f stand

She got off the mark in a Warwick maiden on her second start and followed up in the Weatherbys Dash on the Wolverhampton Fibresand. She should be even better suited by seven furlongs.

Chater Flair

(103) (56)**53**
4-y-o b g Efisio-Native Flair (Be My Native (USA))
W R Muir Hong Kong Cricket Club

Placings:00/04100-211300000036 **(5615)**
2001: 14^{2}SD, 16^{1}SW, 16^{1}SD, 16^{3}SW, 16^{0}SD, 13^{0}GF, 14^{0}G, 16^{0}G, 16^{0}G, 14^{0}SD, 12^{3}SD, 12^{6}SD

	Starts	1st	2nd	3rd	Win & Pl
Career Total (Turf)	11	1	0	0	4427
Career Total (AW)	8	2	1	2	5567
65	1/01	Sthl	2m	E(0-70)H	STD £2422
63	1/01	Wolv	2m46y	F(0-65)H	SLW £1729
63	7/00	Epsm	1m4f10y	E(0-70)H	G-S £4426

Total win prize-money £8578

Going (Turf): Sf: 0-0 GS: 1-2 Gd: 0-4 GF: 0-4 Fm: 0-1
Distance: 5f/6f: 0-0 7f-8f: 0-2 9f-13f: 1-6 14f+: 2-11
Track : LH: 3-11 RH: 0-6 Tight: 2-4 Gall: 0-1
Aids: Bl: 0-2 Vi: 0-0 Tstrap: 0-0
Best Rating: 71 2/01 Sthl 2m slow

Won twice over two miles on Fibresand at the start of 2001 and looks very much an out-and-out stayer.

Chaweng Beach

93(91) (52)**55**
3-y-o ro f Chaddleworth (IRE)-Swallow Bay (Penmarric (USA))
S Kirk F Coen

Placings:01645110340-6000 **(5592)**
2001: 8^{6}GF, 7^{0}G, 9^{0}S, 6^{0}GS

	Starts	1st	2nd	3rd	Win & Pl
Career Total (Turf)	13	3	0	1	12723
Career Total (AW)	2	0	0	0	0
64	9/00	Ling	7f	E(0-75)	G-F £3010
69	8/00	Epsm	7f	C	GD £7085
47	5/00	Ling	6f	G	GD £1928

Total win prize-money £12024

Going (Turf): Sf: 0-3 GS: 0-1 Gd: 2-6 GF: 1-3 Fm: 0-0
Distance: 5f/6f: 1-5 7f-8f: 2-8 9f-13f: 0-2 14f+: 0-0
Track : LH: 1-7 RH: 0-3 Tight: 1-4 Gall: 0-2
Aids: Bl: 0-0 Vi: 0-0 Tstrap: 0-0
Best Rating: 55 8/01 Wind 1m67y gd-fm

Che Guevara

102(84) (40)**62**
3-y-o b c Machiavellian (USA)-Girl From Ipanema (Salse (USA))
J W Hills Christoper Wright & David Murrell

Placings:0003064000 **(5375)**
2001: 8^{0}S, 8^{0}G, 7^{0}GF, 9^{3}G, 10^{0}GF, 8^{6}G, 8^{4}GF, 8^{0}GF, 8^{0}SD, 7^{0}G

	Starts	1st	2nd	3rd	Win & Pl
Career Total (Turf)	9	0	0	1	544
Career Total (AW)	1	0	0	0	

Going (Turf): Sf: 0-1 GS: 0-0 Gd: 0-4 GF: 0-4 Fm: 0-0
Distance: 5f/6f: 0-0 7f-8f: 0-5 9f-13f: 0-5 14f+: 0-0
Track : LH: 0-4 RH: 0-1 Tight: 0-4 Gall: 0-0
Aids: Bl: 0-4 Vi: 0-0 Tstrap: 0-5

Best Rating: 68 5/01 NmkR 1m good

Some promise in modest handicaps at around ten furlongs.

Cheeney Basin (IRE)

61
3-y-o ch g King's Signet (USA)-Gratclo (Belfort (FR))
M Johnston N Cowes, R Holleyhead, P Proud

Placings:03100 **(5630)**
2001: 6^{0}G, 6^{3}GF, 5^{1}GS, 5^{0}S, 6^{0}G

	Starts	1st	2nd	3rd	Win & Pl
Career Total (Turf)	5	1	0	1	3063
61	10/01	Catt	5f212y	F	G-S £2306

Total win prize-money £2307

Going (Turf): Sf: 0-1 GS: 1-1 Gd: 0-2 GF: 0-1 Fm: 0-0
Distance: 5f/6f: 1-5 7f-8f: 0-0 9f-13f: 0-0 14f+: 0-0
Track : LH: 1-2 RH: 0-0 Tight: 1-1 Gall: 0-0
Aids: Bl: 0-0 Vi: 0-0 Tstrap: 0-0
Best Rating: 61 10/01 Catt 5f212y gd-sft

Ran well on his first two runs before getting off the mark over six furlongs on good to soft at Catterick.

Cheerful Groom (IRE)

(81) (11)**30**
10-y-o ch g Shy Groom (USA)-Carange (Known Fact (USA))
Mrs H L Walton (D Shaw 24/2) Bill Cahill

Placings:043002340/3610355000004/32304000060200 0/002605100/060400630/3446322626401041310/00000 05066000/00-0600000 **(1587)**
2001: 8^{0}SW, 8^{6}SW, 12^{0}SD, 8^{0}SD, 11^{0}SD, 11^{0}SD, 8^{0}SD

	Starts	1st	2nd	3rd	Win & Pl
Career Total (Turf)	34	2	1	4	9508
Career Total (AW)	62	3	6	6	14105
59	7/98	Wolv	1m100y	D(0-85)H	STD £3590
52	6/98	Wolv	1m100y	F(0-70)H	STD £2469
50	5/98	Wolv	1m100y	G(0-85)H	STD £1725
42	5/96	Donc	7f	D(0-75)H	G-F £4175
49	5/94	Carl	6f206y	E(0-70)H	FRM £3002

Total win prize-money £14961

Going (Turf): Sf: 0-4 GS: 0-5 Gd: 0-12 GF: 1-10 Fm: 1-3
Distance: 5f/6f: 0-26 7f-8f: 2-54 9f-13f: 3-16 14f+: 0-0
Track : LH: 3-62 RH: 1-8 Tight: 3-22 Gall: 0-2
Aids: Bl: 0-0 Vi: 0-1 Tstrap: 0-0
Best Rating: 11 2/01 Sthl 1m stand

He has enjoyed a fair amount of success at around a mile on Fibresand, especially over Wolverhampton's extended mile, but the signs are that time is catching up with him.

Chelsea Blue (ITY)

98 **65**
3-y-o ch f Barathea (IRE)-Indigo Blue (IRE) (Bluebird (USA))
J W Payne C Cotran

Placings:504630 **(3961)**
2001: 7^{5}G, 7^{0}GS, 6^{4}G, 6^{6}GF, 6^{3}GF, 6^{0}G

	Starts	1st	2nd	3rd	Win & Pl
Career Total (Turf)	6	0	0	1	1481

Going (Turf): Sf: 0-0 GS: 0-1 Gd: 0-3 GF: 0-2 Fm: 0-0
Distance: 5f/6f: 0-2 7f-8f: 0-4 9f-13f: 0-0 14f+: 0-0
Track : LH: 0-1 RH: 0-0 Tight: 0-1 Gall: 0-0
Aids: Bl: 0-0 Vi: 0-0 Tstrap: 0-0
Best Rating: 65 7/01 Ripn 6f gd-fm

Chem's Truce (IRE)

109 **87**

4-y-o b g Brief Truce (USA)-In The Rigging (USA) (Topsider (USA))
W R Muir The Parkside Partnership

Placings:521/30003454436-41304002003 **(5226)**
2001: 10^{4}G, 10^{1}GF, 10^{3}GF, 10^{0}G, 10^{4}GF, 10^{0}G, 10^{0}GF, 10^{2}GF, 10^{0}GF, 9^{0}G, 11^{3}S

	Starts	1st	2nd	3rd	Win & Pl
Career Total (Turf)	25	2	2	5	27443

89 5/01 Kemp 1m2f C(0-90)H G-F £8060
82 11/99 Catt 7f E SFT £2882
Total win prize-money £10942

Going (Turf): **Sf: 1-7** GS: 0-0 Gd: 0-9 **GF: 1-9** Fm: 0-0
Distance: 5f/6f: 0-2 7f-8f: 1-3 9f-13f: 1-20 14f+: 0-0
Track : LH: 1-11 RH: 1-10 Tight: 1-5 Gall: 1-15
Aids: Bl: 0-1 Vi: 0-0 Tstrap: 0-0
Best Rating: 94 6/01 Asct 1m2f gd-fm

He was well backed when returning to winning form over ten furlongs at Kempton in May and that looks to be his best trip, but as a result went up sharply in the handicap. Acts on fast ground and comes with a late run off a strong pace.

Chemicalattraction (IRE)

108 **70**

3-y-o b g Definite Article-Domino's Nurse (Dom Racine (FR))
R A Fahey George Murray

Placings:004000-53121P **(5661)**
2001: 8^{5}GF, 9^{3}G, 12^{1}G, 10^{2}HY, 11^{1}GS, 16^{P}G

	Starts	1st	2nd	3rd	Win & Pl
Career Total (Turf)	12	2	1	1	10214

70 10/01 Catt 1m3f214yE(0-70)H G-S £3696
62 9/01 Haml 1m4f17y F(0-60)H GD £3094
Total win prize-money £6790

Going (Turf): Sf: 0-2 **GS: 1-1 Gd: 1-5** GF: 0-4 Fm: 0-0
Distance: 5f/6f: 0-1 7f-8f: 0-5 **9f-13f: 2-5** 14f+: 0-1
Track : LH: 1-5 RH: 1-4 **Tight: 2-6** Gall: 0-0
Aids: Bl: 0-0 Vi: 0-0 Tstrap: 0-0
Best Rating: 70 10/01 Catt 1m3f214y gd-sft

He has improved with experience and longer trips this season. Won a small handicap at Hamilton in September when upped to 12 furlongs before scoring at Catterick in October.

Cherine (IRE)

79 **61**

2-y-o b f Robellino (USA)-Escrime (USA) (Sharpen Up)
M A Jarvis Ivan Allan

Placings:00 **(5602)**
2001: 6^{0}G, 7^{0}GS

	Starts	1st	2nd	3rd	Win & Pl
Career Total (Turf)	2	0	0	0	

Going (Turf): Sf: 0-0 GS: 0-1 Gd: 0-1 GF: 0-0 Fm: 0-0
Distance: 5f/6f: 0-1 7f-8f: 0-1 9f-13f: 0-0 14f+: 0-0
Track : LH: 0-0 RH: 0-0 Tight: 0-0 Gall: 0-0
Aids: Bl: 0-0 Vi: 0-0 Tstrap: 0-0
Best Rating: 61 10/01 NmkR 6f good

Cherished Number

86 **61**

2-y-o b g King's Signet (USA)-Pretty Average (Skyliner)
I Semple The Northreg Racing Partnership

Placings:06563 **(5270)**
2001: 5^{0}GF, 7^{6}G, 5^{5}GF, 6^{6}GS, 6^{3}HY

	Starts	1st	2nd	3rd	Win & Pl
Career Total (Turf)	5	0	0	1	568

Going (Turf): Sf: 0-1 GS: 0-1 Gd: 0-1 GF: 0-2 Fm: 0-0
Distance: 5f/6f: 0-4 7f-8f: 0-1 9f-13f: 0-0 14f+: 0-0
Track : LH: 0-2 RH: 0-0 Tight: 0-1 Gall: 0-0
Aids: Bl: 0-0 Vi: 0-0 Tstrap: 0-0
Best Rating: 61 10/01 Ayr 6f heavy

Moderate form to date but does not look totally devoid of ability. Placed form over six furlongs in heavy ground but has shaped as though a step up in trip would suit.

Cherry Hills (IRE)

80 **53**

2-y-o b f Anabaa (USA)-Fernanda (Be My Chief (USA))
P F I Cole John Poynton

Placings:5 **(1864)**
2001: 5^{5}GF

	Starts	1st	2nd	3rd	Win & Pl
Career Total (Turf)	1	0	0	0	0

Going (Turf): Sf: 0-0 GS: 0-0 Gd: 0-0 GF: 0-1 Fm: 0-0
Distance: 5f/6f: 0-1 7f-8f: 0-0 9f-13f: 0-0 14f+: 0-0
Track : LH: 0-0 RH: 0-1 Tight: 0-0 Gall: 0-1
Aids: Bl: 0-0 Vi: 0-0 Tstrap: 0-0
Best Rating: 53 6/01 Wind 5f10y gd-fm

Cherrycombe-Row

104 **78**

2-y-o gr f Classic Cliche (IRE)-Key In The Ring (Pyjama Hunt)
P R Hedger D S Rigby

Placings:00261 **(5496)**
2001: 6^{0}GF, 6^{0}GF, 7^{2}G, 8^{6}HY, 7^{1}HY

	Starts	1st	2nd	3rd	Win & Pl
Career Total (Turf)	5	1	1	0	8021

78 10/01 Newb 7f D(0-85) HVY £5447
Total win prize-money £5447

Going (Turf): Sf: 1-2 GS: 0-0 Gd: 0-1 GF: 0-2 Fm: 0-0
Distance: 5f/6f: 0-1 **7f-8f: 1-3** 9f-13f: 0-1 14f+: 0-0
Track : LH: 0-0 RH: 0-2 Tight: 0-1 Gall: 0-0
Aids: Bl: 0-0 Vi: 0-0 Tstrap: 0-0
Best Rating: 78 10/01 Newb 7f heavy

She showed much improved form when encountering softer ground and landed a nursery in desperate conditions at Newbury in October.

Chesnut Ripple

97 **67**

2-y-o ch f Cosmonaut-Shaft Of Sunlight (Sparkler)
R M Whitaker C W Jones & Miss Caroline Jones

Placings:0350043 **(5628)**
2001: 5^{0}GF, 7^{3}G, 7^{5}GF, 7^{0}GF, 8^{0}GF, 7^{4}S, 8^{3}G

	Starts	1st	2nd	3rd	Win & Pl
Career Total (Turf)	7	0	0	2	1116

Going (Turf): Sf: 0-1 GS: 0-0 Gd: 0-2 GF: 0-4 Fm: 0-0
Distance: 5f/6f: 0-1 7f-8f: 0-6 9f-13f: 0-0 14f+: 0-0
Track : LH: 0-1 RH: 0-2 Tight: 0-2 Gall: 0-0
Aids: Bl: 0-0 Vi: 0-0 Tstrap: 0-0
Best Rating: 67 11/01 Rdcr 1m good

She has run some fair races, but tends to find one or two too good.

Chestino

74 **57**

3-y-o ch c Bustino-Coir 'A' Ghaill (Jalmood (USA))
C E Brittain The Boaz Partnership

Placings:0 **(0791)**
2001: 10^{0}GS

	Starts	1st	2nd	3rd	Win & Pl
Career Total (Turf)	1	0	0	0	

Going (Turf): Sf: 0-0 GS: 0-1 Gd: 0-0 GF: 0-0 Fm: 0-0
Distance: 5f/6f: 0-0 7f-8f: 0-0 9f-13f: 0-1 14f+: 0-0
Track : LH: 0-0 RH: 0-0 Tight: 0-0 Gall: 0-0
Aids: Bl: 0-0 Vi: 0-0 Tstrap: 0-0
Best Rating: 57 4/01 NmkR 1m2f gd-sft

Chevening Lodge

(103) (66)**52**

3-y-o ch g Eagle Eyed (USA)-Meadmore Magic (Mansingh (USA))
K R Burke Nigel Shields

Placings:460035**131-563360**5602**000** **(5406)**
2001: 8^{5}SD, 10^{6}SW, 10^{3}SD, 7^{3}SD, 7^{6}SD, 8^{0}SD, 8^{5}GF, 11^{6}F, 8^{0}GF, 7^{2}GF, 9^{0}GS, 6^{0}SD, 8^{0}SD

	Starts	1st	2nd	3rd	Win & Pl
Career Total (Turf)	11	0	1	1	1698
Career Total (AW)	11	2	0	3	6938

67 12/00 Ling 1m E(0-80) STD £2726
57 11/00 Ling 1m E(0-85) STD £2842
Total win prize-money £5569

Going (Turf): Sf: 0-2 GS: 0-3 Gd: 0-0 GF: 0-5 Fm: 0-1
Distance: 5f/6f: 0-5 **7f-8f: 2-10** 9f-13f: 0-7 14f+: 0-0
Track : **LH: 2-14** RH: 0-2 **Tight: 2-11** Gall: 0-2
Aids: Bl: 0-1 Vi: 0-4 Tstrap: 0-0
Best Rating: 66 3/01 Ling 7f stand

Cheyenne Chief

(75) (29)

2-y-o b c Be My Chief (USA)-Cartuccia (IRE) (Doyoun)
G M Moore John Lishman

Placings:0 **(1472)**
2001: 5^{0}SD

	Starts	1st	2nd	3rd	Win & Pl
Career Total (Turf)	0	0	0	0	
Career Total (AW)	1	0	0	0	

Going (Turf): Sf: 0-0 GS: 0-0 Gd: 0-0 GF: 0-0 Fm: 0-0
Distance: 5f/6f: 0-1 7f-8f: 0-0 9f-13f: 0-0 14f+: 0-0
Track : LH: 0-0 RH: 0-0 Tight: 0-0 Gall: 0-0
Aids: Bl: 0-0 Vi: 0-0 Tstrap: 0-0
Best Rating: 29 5/01 Sthl 5f stand

Chez Bonito (IRE)

87(96) (40)**44**

4-y-o br f Persian Bold-Tycoon Aly (IRE) (Last Tycoon)
J M Bradley (R Wilman 5/1) Mrs J K Bradley

Placings:52054005410**000-005** **(2559)**
2001: 16^{0}SD, 8^{0}GF, 9^{5}GF

	Starts	1st	2nd	3rd	Win & Pl
Career Total (Turf)	13	1	1	0	3076
Career Total (AW)	4	0	0	0	

44 9/00 Yarm 1m3f101yF G-F £2324
Total win prize-money £2324

Going (Turf): Sf: 0-2 GS: 0-0 Gd: 0-2 **GF: 1-6** Fm: 0-3
Distance: 5f/6f: 0-0 7f-8f: 0-2 **9f-13f: 1-13** 14f+: 0-2
Track : **LH: 1-9** RH: 0-6 **Tight: 1-7** Gall: 0-0
Aids: Bl: 0-0 Vi: 0-0 Tstrap: 0-1
Best Rating: 19 6/01 Folk 1m1f149y gd-fm

Chez Foret (IRE)

80 **48**

2-y-o b c Charnwood Forest (IRE)-Ezilana (IRE) (Shardari)
E A L Dunlop Mrs Janice Quy

Placings:000 **(5361)**

2001: 7^{0}S, 8^{0}G, 8^{0}GS

	Starts	1st	2nd	3rd	Win & Pl
Career Total (Turf)	3	0	0	0	

Going (Turf): Sf: 0-1 GS: 0-1 Gd: 0-1 GF: 0-0 Fm: 0-0
Distance: 5f/6f: 0-0 7f-8f: 0-2 9f-13f: 0-1 14f+: 0-0
Track : LH: 0-1 RH: 0-0 Tight: 0-0 Gall: 0-0
Aids: Bl: 0-0 Vi: 0-0 Tstrap: 0-0
Best Rating: 48 9/01 Nott 1m54y good

Chianti (IRE)

109 **107**

3-y-o b c Danehill (USA)-Sabaah (USA) (Nureyev (USA))
J L Dunlop Wafic Said

Placings:11630-0021242 **(5597)**
2001: 8^{0}S, 7^{0}GF, 10^{2}GF, 10^{1}GF, 10^{2}G, 12^{4}GS, 10^{2}GS

	Starts	1st	2nd	3rd	Win & Pl
Career Total (Turf)	12	3	3	1	44640

106	7/01	Epsm	1m2f18y	C	G-F	£6426
98	7/00	York	6f214y	B	GD	£10602
87	6/00	York	6f	D	G-F	£5564

Total win prize-money £22593

Going (Turf): Sf: 0-1 GS: 0-3 Gd: 1-2 **GF: 2-6** Fm: 0-0
Distance: 5f/6f: 1-1 7f-8f: 1-6 9f-13f: 1-5 14f+: 0-0
Track : **LH: 2-4** RH: 0-3 Tight: 1-1 Gall: 1-3
Aids: Bl: 0-0 Vi: 0-0 **Tstrap: 1-6**
Best Rating: 107 11/01 NmkR 1m2f gd-sft

He looked smart when winning his first two starts at two, both at York, but just looked held in three subsequent starts in Group company. Well beaten twice in Listed company in 2001, he scored in a conditions stakes at Epsom in July and ran well to finish runner-up in a Group Three at Haydock. Ten furlongs looks his trip, and fast ground suits.

Chiaro

(76) **25**

4-y-o b f Safawan-Bold Dove (Never So Bold)
M P Muggeridge Shefford Valley Stud

Placings:00-00 **(0190)**
2001: 6^{0}SD, 7^{0}SD

	Starts	1st	2nd	3rd	Win & Pl
Career Total (Turf)	2	0	0	0	
Career Total (AW)	2	0	0	0	

Going (Turf): Sf: 0-0 GS: 0-0 Gd: 0-0 GF: 0-2 Fm: 0-0
Distance: 5f/6f: 0-1 7f-8f: 0-3 9f-13f: 0-0 14f+: 0-0
Track : LH: 0-2 RH: 0-0 Tight: 0-1 Gall: 0-0
Aids: Bl: 0-0 Vi: 0-0 Tstrap: 0-0

Chicago Blues (IRE)

(87) (24)

4-y-o b f Blues Traveller (IRE)-Flight Of Pleasure (USA) (Roberto (USA))
A G Newcombe A G Newcombe

Placings:0000050646/000 **(1992)**
2001: 12^{0}SD, 8^{0}SD, 14^{0}SD

	Starts	1st	2nd	3rd	Win & Pl
Career Total (Turf)	8	0	0	0	0
Career Total (AW)	5	0	0	0	0

Going (Turf): Sf: 0-3 GS: 0-1 Gd: 0-3 GF: 0-0 Fm: 0-1
Distance: 5f/6f: 0-4 7f-8f: 0-5 9f-13f: 0-3 14f+: 0-1
Track : LH: 0-8 RH: 0-0 Tight: 0-1 Gall: 0-3
Aids: Bl: 0-0 Vi: 0-0 Tstrap: 0-0
Best Rating: 24 3/01 Sthl 1m stand

Chicago Bulls (IRE)

97 **76d**

3-y-o b c Darshaan-Celestial Melody (USA) (The Minstrel (CAN))
A King (C F Wall 4/9) J A H West

Placings:45-4530 **(4483)**
2001: 12^{4}GS, 12^{5}GS, 11^{3}GS, 14^{0}S

	Starts	1st	2nd	3rd	Win & Pl
Career Total (Turf)	6	0	0	1	2314

Going (Turf): Sf: 0-2 GS: 0-4 Gd: 0-0 GF: 0-0 Fm: 0-0
Distance: 5f/6f: 0-0 7f-8f: 0-1 9f-13f: 0-4 14f+: 0-1
Track : LH: 0-2 RH: 0-3 Tight: 0-2 Gall: 0-1
Aids: Bl: 0-0 Vi: 0-0 Tstrap: 0-0
Best Rating: 76 4/01 NmkR 1m4f gd-sft

Chicago Sox (IRE)

94 **69**

3-y-o b c Grand Lodge (USA)-Elle Meme (Ela-Mana-Mou)
C F Wall Ettore Landi

Placings:3-00 **(2433)**
2001: 7^{0}GS, 8^{0}GF

	Starts	1st	2nd	3rd	Win & Pl
Career Total (Turf)	3	0	0	1	1562

Going (Turf): Sf: 0-0 GS: 0-2 Gd: 0-0 GF: 0-1 Fm: 0-0
Distance: 5f/6f: 0-0 7f-8f: 0-2 9f-13f: 0-1 14f+: 0-0
Track : LH: 0-0 RH: 0-2 Tight: 0-1 Gall: 0-0
Aids: Bl: 0-0 Vi: 0-0 Tstrap: 0-1
Best Rating: 69 5/01 NmkR 7f gd-sft

Chicane (IRE)

87 **68**

3-y-o ch c Mark Of Esteem (IRE)-Rapid Repeat (IRE) (Exactly Sharp (USA))
L M Cumani Lord Hartington

Placings:4-00 **(0894)**
2001: 7^{0}S, 6^{0}HY

	Starts	1st	2nd	3rd	Win & Pl
Career Total (Turf)	3	0	0	0	259

Going (Turf): Sf: 0-3 GS: 0-0 Gd: 0-0 GF: 0-0 Fm: 0-0
Distance: 5f/6f: 0-1 7f-8f: 0-2 9f-13f: 0-0 14f+: 0-0
Track : LH: 0-0 RH: 0-2 Tight: 0-1 Gall: 0-1
Aids: Bl: 0-0 Vi: 0-0 Tstrap: 0-0
Best Rating: 59 4/01 Kemp 7f soft

Chicanery (IRE)

(97) (45)**34**

4-y-o b g Irish River (FR)-Deceive (Machiavellian (USA))
Mrs L Stubbs F W Swain

Placings:600-4660003650 **(5503)**
2001: 8^{4}SW, 7^{6}SD, 8^{6}HY, 8^{0}SW, 9^{0}S, 8^{0}G, 7^{3}GS, 7^{6}GF, 8^{5}GS, 7^{0}HY

	Starts	1st	2nd	3rd	Win & Pl
Career Total (Turf)	10	0	0	1	352
Career Total (AW)	3	0	0	0	0

Going (Turf): Sf: 0-5 GS: 0-2 Gd: 0-1 GF: 0-2 Fm: 0-0
Distance: 5f/6f: 0-1 7f-8f: 0-9 9f-13f: 0-3 14f+: 0-0
Track : LH: 0-5 RH: 0-2 Tight: 0-3 Gall: 0-1
Aids: Bl: 0-0 Vi: 0-0 Tstrap: 0-0
Best Rating: 45 2/01 Sthl 1m slow

Chicara

86(90) (53)**25**

3-y-o ch f Beveled (USA)-Chili Lass (Chilibang)
John A Harris (J L Harris 5/1) Exors Of The Late J L Harris

Placings:3030-0500 **(4634)**
2001: 7^{0}SD, 7^{5}SD, 8^{0}G, 5^{0}GF

	Starts	1st	2nd	3rd	Win & Pl
Career Total (Turf)	4	0	0	1	595
Career Total (AW)	4	0	0	1	387

Going (Turf): Sf: 0-0 GS: 0-0 Gd: 0-2 GF: 0-2 Fm: 0-0
Distance: 5f/6f: 0-4 7f-8f: 0-3 9f-13f: 0-1 14f+: 0-0
Track : LH: 0-5 RH: 0-0 Tight: 0-0 Gall: 0-1
Aids: Bl: 0-0 Vi: 0-1 Tstrap: 0-0
Best Rating: 21 1/01 Sthl 7f stand

Chickasaw Trail

101(84) (43)**50**

3-y-o ch f Be My Chief (USA)-Maraschino (Lycius (USA))
R Hollinshead Anthony White

Placings:000045-440434542454400 **(4901)**
2001: 7^{4}SD, 9^{4}SW, 8^{0}SD, 9^{4}G, 8^{3}F, 8^{4}GF, 9^{5}GF, 12^{4}GF, 10^{2}GF, 8^{4}GF, 12^{5}F, 11^{4}G, 10^{4}G, 8^{0}GF, 11^{0}G

	Starts	1st	2nd	3rd	Win & Pl
Career Total (Turf)	15	0	1	1	1128
Career Total (AW)	6	0	0	0	0

Going (Turf): Sf: 0-0 GS: 0-0 Gd: 0-6 GF: 0-7 Fm: 0-2
Distance: 5f/6f: 0-0 7f-8f: 0-7 9f-13f: 0-14 14f+: 0-0
Track : LH: 0-11 RH: 0-7 Tight: 0-9 Gall: 0-0
Aids: Bl: 0-0 Vi: 0-0 Tstrap: 0-0
Best Rating: 50 8/01 Bevl 1m3f216y good

Chief Cashier

106 **74**

6-y-o b g Persian Bold-Kentfield (Busted)
G B Balding Surgical Spirits

Placings:6030/204164146/2140/5000146006-2641222000 **(5669)**
2001: 10^{2}S, 10^{6}GF, 10^{4}GF, 10^{1}GF, 10^{2}G, 10^{2}G, 9^{2}GF, 12^{0}GF, 10^{0}G, 10^{0}HY

	Starts	1st	2nd	3rd	Win & Pl
Career Total (Turf)	37	5	6	1	46176

87	6/01	Wind	1m2f7y	D(0-85)H	G-F	£4127
79	7/00	Bath	1m2f46y	D(0-80)H	G-S	£6938
83	4/99	Epsm	1m2f18y	B(0-105)H	SFT	£10552
75	9/98	Epsm	1m2f18y	D(0-85)H	SFT	£3550
72	7/98	Epsm	1m2f18y	E(0-70)H	G-F	£2819

Total win prize-money £27989

Going (Turf): Sf: 2-8 GS: 1-4 Gd: 0-7 **GF: 2-17** Fm: 0-1
Distance: 5f/6f: 0-0 7f-8f: 0-5 **9f-13f: 5-32** 14f+: 0-0
Track : **LH: 4-16** RH: 0-11 **Tight: 5-20** Gall: 0-5
Aids: Bl: 0-0 Vi: 0-0 Tstrap: 0-0
Best Rating: 89 7/01 Sand 1m2f7y good

A useful handicapper on his day, he picked up a Windsor handicap in June and has since gone close without winning in similar events. He has a fine record at Epsom and is best on easy ground, but has won on good to firm. Stays ten furlongs.

Chief Of Justice

(109) (72)**73**

4-y-o b c Be My Chief (USA)-Clare Court (Glint Of Gold)
D Shaw J C Fretwell

Placings:000/113000022034-0 **(0054)**
2001: 11^{0}SD

	Starts	1st	2nd	3rd	Win & Pl
Career Total (Turf)	6	0	0	1	402
Career Total (AW)	10	2	2	1	8136

74	3/00	Wolv	1m4f	E(0-75)H	STD	£2613
61	2/00	Sthl	1m3f	F(0-60)H	STD	£2251

Total win prize-money £4865

Going (Turf): Sf: 0-2 GS: 0-1 Gd: 0-2 GF: 0-1 Fm: 0-0
Distance: 5f/6f: 0-0 7f-8f: 0-3 9f-13f: 2-10 14f+: 0-3
Track: LH: 2-14 RH: 0-0 Tight: 1-6 Gall: 0-1
Aids: Bl: 0-0 Vi: 0-0 Tstrap: 0-0
Best Rating: 37 1/01 Sthl 1m3f stand

Chief Wallah

102(87) (45)**53**
5-y-o b g Be My Chief (USA)-Arusha (IRE) (Dance Of Life (USA))
N J Henderson Raymond Tooth

Placings:6/042600-600 **(2821)**
2001: 14^{6}GF, 16^{0}GF, 18^{0}GF

	Starts	1st	2nd	3rd	Win & Pl
Career Total (Turf)	9	0	1	0	1456
Career Total (AW)	1	0	0	0	0

Going (Turf): Sf: 0-2 GS: 0-0 Gd: 0-2 GF: 0-4 Fm: 0-1
Distance: 5f/6f: 0-0 7f-8f: 0-0 9f-13f: 0-3 14f+: 0-7
Track: LH: 0-7 RH: 0-3 Tight: 0-3 Gall: 0-0
Aids: Bl: 0-1 Vi: 0-0 Tstrap: 0-0
Best Rating: 54 6/01 Kemp 1m6f92y gd-fm

Modest staying maiden.

Chief Wardance

105 **61**
7-y-o ch g Profilic-Dolly Wardance (Warpath)
Mrs S Lamyman Mrs Jennifer Woodward

Placings:530-414005 **(1830)**
2001: 12^{4}GS, 10^{1}HY, 10^{4}S, 10^{0}G, 12^{0}F, 10^{5}F

	Starts	1st	2nd	3rd	Win & Pl
Career Total (Turf)	9	1	0	1	3554

61 4/01 Pont 1m2f6y F(0-70)H HVY £2600
Total win prize-money £2601

Going (Turf): Sf: 1-2 GS: 0-2 Gd: 0-1 GF: 0-2 Fm: 0-2
Distance: 5f/6f: 0-0 7f-8f: 0-0 9f-13f: 1-9 14f+: 0-0
Track: LH: 1-6 RH: 0-2 Tight: 0-0 Gall: 0-1
Aids: Bl: 0-0 Vi: 0-0 Tstrap: 0-0
Best Rating: 61 4/01 Pont 1m2f6y heavy

Fair middle-distance handicapper, suited by soft ground.

Chili Pepper

86(96) (44)**34**
4-y-o gr f Chilibang-Game Germaine (Mummy's Game)
A Smith Mrs R Auchterlounie

Placings:2044450/610300-000000 **(4233)**
2001: 6^{0}SD, 7^{0}SD, 7^{0}SD, 8^{0}SD, 10^{0}GF, 5^{0}G

	Starts	1st	2nd	3rd	Win & Pl
Career Total (Turf)	11	0	1	0	635
Career Total (AW)	8	1	0	1	2620

55 3/00 Wolv 6f F(0-60)H STD £2194
Total win prize-money £2195

Going (Turf): Sf: 0-3 GS: 0-1 Gd: 0-4 GF: 0-3 Fm: 0-0
Distance: 5f/6f: 1-10 7f-8f: 0-7 9f-13f: 0-2 14f+: 0-0
Track: LH: 1-10 RH: 0-2 Tight: 1-3 Gall: 0-0
Aids: Bl: 0-4 Vi: 0-0 Tstrap: 0-0
Best Rating: 44 3/01 Sthl 6f stand

Chilli

86(93) (52)**39**
4-y-o br g Most Welcome-So Saucy (Teenoso (USA))
K Bell Mrs L L Edwards

Placings:0040/33233035050-000 **(3730)**
2001: 10^{0}GF, 9^{0}G, 8^{0}GS

	Starts	1st	2nd	3rd	Win & Pl
Career Total (Turf)	13	0	0	2	1098
Career Total (AW)	5	0	1	3	1898

Going (Turf): Sf: 0-2 GS: 0-3 Gd: 0-6 GF: 0-2 Fm: 0-0
Distance: 5f/6f: 0-1 7f-8f: 0-4 9f-13f: 0-12 14f+: 0-1
Track: LH: 0-15 RH: 0-0 Tight: 0-8 Gall: 0-1
Aids: Bl: 0-0 Vi: 0-4 Tstrap: 0-1
Best Rating: 32 8/01 Nott 1m1f213y good

Chilli Boy

66(65) (1)**44**
3-y-o gr g Belfort (FR)-Con Carni (Blakeney)
J R Turner J R Turner

Placings:000-00 **(2041)**
2001: 6^{0}G, 8^{0}GF

	Starts	1st	2nd	3rd	Win & Pl
Career Total (Turf)	4	0	0	0	
Career Total (AW)	1	0	0	0	

Going (Turf): Sf: 0-0 GS: 0-1 Gd: 0-1 GF: 0-2 Fm: 0-0
Distance: 5f/6f: 0-3 7f-8f: 0-1 9f-13f: 0-1 14f+: 0-0
Track: LH: 0-2 RH: 0-0 Tight: 0-1 Gall: 0-0
Aids: Bl: 0-0 Vi: 0-0 Tstrap: 0-0
Best Rating: 8 6/01 Pont 1m4y gd-fm

Chiltern Bucks

74 **36**
2-y-o ch c Muhtarram (USA)-Lavender Della (IRE) (Shernazar)
J A R Toller Abigail Limited

Placings:00 **(5290)**
2001: 7^{0}GF, 7^{0}S

	Starts	1st	2nd	3rd	Win & Pl
Career Total (Turf)	2	0	0	0	

Going (Turf): Sf: 0-1 GS: 0-0 Gd: 0-0 GF: 0-1 Fm: 0-0
Distance: 5f/6f: 0-0 7f-8f: 0-2 9f-13f: 0-0 14f+: 0-0
Track: LH: 0-1 RH: 0-0 Tight: 0-0 Gall: 0-0
Aids: Bl: 0-0 Vi: 0-0 Tstrap: 0-0
Best Rating: 36 9/01 Wwck 7f26y gd-fm

Chilworth (IRE)

90(66) (27)**41**
4-y-o ch g Shalford (IRE)-Close The Till (Formidable (USA))
T M Jones John Crouch

Placings:064/00560420003000-040 **(2159)**
2001: 7^{0}GF, 7^{4}F, 7^{0}GF

	Starts	1st	2nd	3rd	Win & Pl
Career Total (Turf)	18	0	1	0	354
Career Total (AW)	2	0	0	0	

Going (Turf): Sf: 0-3 GS: 0-2 Gd: 0-3 GF: 0-9 Fm: 0-1
Distance: 5f/6f: 0-2 7f-8f: 0-15 9f-13f: 0-3 14f+: 0-0
Track: LH: 0-5 RH: 0-3 Tight: 0-3 Gall: 0-1
Aids: Bl: 0-3 Vi: 0-8 Tstrap: 0-0
Best Rating: 40 6/01 Gdwd 7f gd-fm

Chimes At Midnight (USA)

106 **104**
4-y-o b h Danzig (USA)-Surely Georgies (USA) (Alleged (USA))
Luke Comer Luke Comer

Placings:54131002362000-601500600 **(5647a)**
2001: 12^{6}GF, 20^{0}GF, 14^{1}Y, 14^{5}G, 12^{0}GF, 10^{0}G, 14^{6}GF, 12^{0}HO, 10^{0}Y

	Starts	1st	2nd	3rd	Win & Pl
Career Total (Turf)	23	3	2	2	115595

106 6/01 Curr 1m6f YLD £36000
82 7/00 Gway 1m4f (0-85)H GD £5865
86 7/00 Leop 1m2f G-F £4830
Total win prize-money £46695

Going (Turf): Sf: 0-1 GS: 0-0 Gd: 0-8 GF: 1-6 Fm: 0-1
Distance: 5f/6f: 0-0 7f-8f: 0-2 9f-13f: 1-10 14f+: 1-8
Track: LH: 1-9 RH: 0-8 Tight: 0-1 Gall: 0-4
Aids: Bl: 1-11 Vi: 0-0 Tstrap: 0-0
Best Rating: 106 6/01 Curr 1m6f yield

A winner twice last season, he ran some good races in top company including when third to Millenary in the St Leger. Well beaten in Group Ones over various trips, he showed what he was capable of when winning the Group Three Curragh Cup over 14 furlongs. Seems to handle and ground.

China

100 **69**
3-y-o b f Royal Academy (USA)-One Way Street (Habitat)
H R A Cecil Newgate Stud

Placings:03240 **(5039)**
2001: 10^{0}GS, 14^{3}G, 14^{2}F, 15^{4}G, 17^{0}G

	Starts	1st	2nd	3rd	Win & Pl
Career Total (Turf)	5	0	1	1	2039

Going (Turf): Sf: 0-0 GS: 0-1 Gd: 0-3 GF: 0-0 Fm: 0-1
Distance: 5f/6f: 0-0 7f-8f: 0-0 9f-13f: 0-1 14f+: 0-4
Track: LH: 0-5 RH: 0-0 Tight: 0-4 Gall: 0-1
Aids: Bl: 0-0 Vi: 0-0 Tstrap: 0-0
Best Rating: 74 6/01 Yarm 1m6f17y good

Out of a mare that has produced three Group winners, showed little in a 1m2f maiden at Newbury in April, but has improved since upped in trip.

China Castle

(111) (69)**51**
8-y-o b g Sayf El Arab (USA)-Honey Plum (Kind Of Hush)
P C Haslam Middleham Park Racing I & Others

Placings:0616000/1114413000330044/111243500000/2114324000/111131131005010254/06621-11422111 **(5615)**
2001: 12^{1}SW, 12^{1}SD, 11^{4}SD, 12^{2}SD, 14^{2}SD, 11^{1}SD, 11^{1}SD, 12^{1}SD

	Starts	1st	2nd	3rd	Win & Pl
Career Total (Turf)	13	1	0	1	3390
Career Total (AW)	63	23	7	6	110932

69	11/01	Wolv	1m4f	F	STD	£2352
42	7/01	Sthl	1m3f	G	STD	£1851
62	6/01	Sthl	1m3f	F	STD	£2450
59	3/01	Sthl	1m4f	F	STD	£2303
67	1/01	Wolv	1m4f	F	SLW	£2107
89	3/00	Ling	1m4f	C(0-100)H	STD	£10286
51	7/99	Haml	1m3f16y	F(0-65)H	FRM	£2905
103	3/99	Sthl	1m4f	C(0-100)H	STD	£6937
96	2/99	Wolv	1m4f	C(0-95)H	STD	£6068
94	2/99	Wolv	1m4f	C(0-100)H	STD	£6097
86	1/99	Wolv	1m4f	C(0-95)H	STD	£6970
93	1/99	Sthl	1m3f	D(0-80)H	STD	£6905
76	1/99	Sthl	1m4f	D(0-75)	STD	£3809
73	1/99	Sthl	1m3f	D(0-80)H	STD	£7132
75	1/98	Wolv	1m4f	D(0-85)H	STD	£3420
75	1/98	Sthl	1m4f	D(0-75)	STD	£3387
82	1/97	Sthl	1m4f	E(0-70)H	STD	£2801
87	1/97	Sthl	1m3f	E(0-70)H	STD	£2957
77	1/97	Sthl	1m3f	D(0-80)H	STD	£3533
67	2/96	Sthl	1m3f	F	STD	£2398
72	1/96	Wolv	1m100y	C(0-90)H	STD	£5582
64	1/96	Ling	1m2f	D(0-75)H	STD	£3761
72	1/96	Sthl	7f	F(0-65)H	STD	£2821
64	8/95	Sthl	7f	G	STD	£2780

Total win prize-money £101620

Going (Turf): Sf: 0-3 GS: 0-1 Gd: 0-2 GF: 0-6 Fm: 1-1
Distance: 5f/6f: 0-2 7f-8f: 2-10 9f-13f: 22-60 14f+: 0-

4

Track : **LH: 23-69** RH: 1-5 **Tight: 10-45** Gall: 0-1
Aids: Bl: 0-0 Vi: 0-0 Tstrap: 0-0
Best Rating: 69 11/01 Wolv 1m4f stand

Modest on the turf, he is a prolific winner on the All-Weather, being particularly effective on Fibresand. Best over a mile and a half these days, he needs plenty of driving but is genuine in a finish.

China Fain (IRE)

61(95) (47)

3-y-o b f Emarati (USA)-Oriental Air (IRE) (Taufan (USA))
K McAuliffe Mrs H Raw

Placings:6-30600 **(5186)**
2001: 6^{3}SD, 7^{0}SD, 5^{6}SD, 6^{0}SD, 5^{0}GS

	Starts	1st	2nd	3rd	Win & Pl
Career Total (Turf)	2	0	0	0	0
Career Total (AW)	4	0	0	1	420

Going (Turf): Sf: 0-0 GS: 0-1 Gd: 0-0 GF: 0-1 Fm: 0-0
Distance: 5f/6f: 0-4 7f-8f: 0-2 9f-13f: 0-0 14f+: 0-0
Track : LH: 0-4 RH: 0-0 Tight: 0-2 Gall: 0-0
Aids: Bl: 0-0 Vi: 0-5 Tstrap: 0-1
Best Rating: 47 2/01 Sthl 6f stand

China Red (USA)

110(100) (69)**48**

7-y-o br g Red Ransom (USA)-Akamare (FR) (Akarad (FR))
J J Quinn Mrs Marie Taylor

Placings:424/10500/**5**120162/0**1**3**1**00/**0**000100060**0**-**0500**42100000 **(5092)**
2001: 7^{0}SW, 8^{5}SW, 10^{0}SW, 8^{0}SD, 10^{4}S, 8^{2}HY, 8^{1}S, 8^{0}GF, 8^{0}G, 7^{0}G, 8^{0}HY, 8^{0}GS

	Starts	1st	2nd	3rd	Win & Pl
Career Total (Turf)	34	5	4	1	38345
Career Total (AW)	10	2	0	0	14044

70	4/01	Nott	1m54y	E(0-70)H	SFT	£3262
72	8/00	Epsm	1m114y	F	GD	£2834
95	5/99	Ling	1m	C(0-90)H	STD	£7058
89	5/99	Ling	1m	C(0-95)H	STD	£6985
85	7/98	Gdwd	1m	D(0-85)H	G-F	£9523
82	5/98	Gdwd	1m	C(0-100)H	G-F	£7440
85	4/97	Nott	1m54y	D	G-F	£4441

Total win prize-money £41546

Going (Turf): Sf: 1-6 GS: 0-4 Gd: 1-12 **GF: 3-13** Fm: 0-0
Distance: 5f/6f: 0-2 **7f-8f: 4-22** 9f-13f: 3-20 14f+: 0-0
Track : **LH: 5-25** RH: 2-10 **Tight: 3-14** Gall: 0-5
Aids: Bl: 0-0 Vi: 0-0 Tstrap: 0-0
Best Rating: 70 4/01 Nott 1m54y soft

He is a game front-runner and goes particularly well on turning tracks. Best on fast ground in the past, his best form this season has been on soft, including his win over a mile at Nottingham in April.

China Visit (USA)

116(30) (126)**121**

4-y-o b c Red Ransom (USA)-Furajet (USA) (The Minstrel (CAN))
Saeed Bin Suroor Godolphin

Placings:1/160-124212 **(5353a)**
2001: 8^{1}FT, 8^{2}FT, 8^{4}FT, 8^{2}G, 8^{1}VS, 7^{2}VS

	Starts	1st	2nd	3rd	Win & Pl
Career Total (Turf)	5	2	2	0	77084
Career Total (AW)	5	2	1	0	259757

119	10/01	Lonc	1m	VS	£38797
	1/01	Ndas	1m	FST	£38251
125	3/00	Ndas	1m1f	FST	£182927
	8/99	Deau	6f110y	VS	£9688

Total win prize-money £269663

Going (Turf): Sf: 0-0 GS: 0-0 Gd: 0-1 GF: 0-1 Fm: 0-0
Distance: 5f/6f: 0-0 **7f-8f: 2-7** 9f-13f: 1-2 14f+: 0-0
Track : LH: 1-3 RH: 1-3 Tight: 0-0 Gall: 0-2
Aids: Bl: 0-0 Vi: 0-0 Tstrap: 0-0
Best Rating: 126 3/01 Ndas 1m fast

Hugely impressive when slamming a big field in the 2000 UAE Derby, but could only finish sixth in the Kentucky Derby. He was then very disappointing at Ascot, where something looked amiss. He was not seen out again until making a winning reappearance January 2001 where he won at Nad Al Sheba. Most of his runs had been on dirt, but he showed he could act on turf when second to Tough Speed at Doncaster after nearly six months off, before making all to win the Prix du Rond-Point. He found Mount Abu too quick when trying to supplement that success in the Prix de la Foret. Well suited by soft ground on turf, he does not have many miles on the clock and may prove up to Group One level in 2002.

Chinese Cracker

3-y-o b g King's Signet (USA)-Heart Broken (Bustino)
N Tinkler Michael Ng

Placings:5 **(3677)**
2001: 10^{5}G

	Starts	1st	2nd	3rd	Win & Pl
Career Total (Turf)	1	0	0	0	0

Going (Turf): Sf: 0-0 GS: 0-0 Gd: 0-1 GF: 0-0 Fm: 0-0
Distance: 5f/6f: 0-0 7f-8f: 0-0 9f-13f: 0-1 14f+: 0-0
Track : LH: 0-0 RH: 0-1 Tight: 0-1 Gall: 0-0
Aids: Bl: 0-0 Vi: 0-0 Tstrap: 0-0

Chinon (IRE)

67 **43**

2-y-o b f Entrepreneur-Ivyanna (IRE) (Reference Point)
B J Meehan Fieldspring Racing

Placings:00 **(5520)**
2001: 6^{0}G, 8^{0}HY

	Starts	1st	2nd	3rd	Win & Pl
Career Total (Turf)	2	0	0	0	

Going (Turf): Sf: 0-1 GS: 0-0 Gd: 0-1 GF: 0-0 Fm: 0-0
Distance: 5f/6f: 0-1 7f-8f: 0-0 9f-13f: 0-1 14f+: 0-0
Track : LH: 0-0 RH: 0-1 Tight: 0-1 Gall: 0-0
Aids: Bl: 0-0 Vi: 0-0 Tstrap: 0-0
Best Rating: 43 10/01 NmkR 6f good

Chiomara (IRE)

84(60) **14**

3-y-o b f Namaqualand (USA)-Violet Crown (IRE) (Kefaah (USA))
F Jordan Tony Cocum

Placings:0001000-00000 **(3412)**
2001: 9^{0}S, 7^{0}SD, 5^{0}GF, 6^{0}GF, 7^{0}GF

	Starts	1st	2nd	3rd	Win & Pl
Career Total (Turf)	11	1	0	0	3450
Career Total (AW)	1	0	0	0	

72	8/00	Slig	6f110y	SFT	£3450

Total win prize-money £3450

Going (Turf): Sf: 1-3 GS: 0-0 Gd: 0-1 GF: 0-5 Fm: 0-0
Distance: 5f/6f: 0-3 **7f-8f: 1-8** 9f-13f: 0-1 14f+: 0-0
Track : LH: 0-4 **RH: 1-3** Tight: 0-1 Gall: 0-0
Aids: **Bl: 1-6** Vi: 0-0 Tstrap: 0-0
Best Rating: 14 6/01 Leic 5f218y gd-fm

Chispa

107(106) (88)**90**

3-y-o b f Imperial Frontier (USA)-Digamist Girl (IRE) (Digamist (USA))
M C Chapman Miss C T Hickford

Placings:000**503112**-**14142**0160000 **(5630)**
2001: 5^{1}SW, 5^{4}SW, 6^{1}SD, 6^{4}SD, 6^{2}SD, 5^{0}GS, 5^{1}S, 5^{6}GS, 5^{0}G, 5^{0}GF, 5^{0}GF, 6^{0}G

	Starts	1st	2nd	3rd	Win & Pl
Career Total (Turf)	10	1	0	0	8814
Career Total (AW)	11	4	2	1	18683

90	4/01	Epsm	5f	C(0-95)H	SFT	£8814
76	2/01	Sthl	6f	C	STD	£6075
88	1/01	Sthl	5f	D(0-80)H	SLW	£3835
82	12/00	Wolv	5f	E(0-85)	STD	£2681
63	11/00	Sthl	5f	E(0-75)	STD	£2709

Total win prize-money £24114

Going (Turf): Sf: 1-1 GS: 0-4 Gd: 0-2 GF: 0-3 Fm: 0-0
Distance: **5f/6f: 5-21** 7f-8f: 0-0 9f-13f: 0-0 14f+: 0-0
Track : **LH: 2-7** RH: 0-1 **Tight: 1-4** Gall: 0-1
Aids: Bl: 0-0 Vi: 0-0 Tstrap: 0-0
Best Rating: 90 4/01 Epsm 5f soft

She had a wonderful winter, winning four times on Fibresand, but showed she could act on turf too when bolting up at Epsom in April. Best suited by the minimum trip on easy ground..

Chiu Chow Kid

103(102) (78)**79**

3-y-o b g Wolfhound (USA)-Sakura Queen (IRE) (Woodman (USA))
S P C Woods Charles Lam Leung Seng

Placings:323010 **(2248)**
2001: 6^{3}SD, 7^{2}GS, 8^{3}GS, 8^{0}G, 7^{1}GF, 7^{0}GF

	Starts	1st	2nd	3rd	Win & Pl
Career Total (Turf)	5	1	1	1	4477
Career Total (AW)	1	0	0	1	540

76	6/01	Yarm	7f3y	F	G-F	£2702

Total win prize-money £2702

Going (Turf): Sf: 0-0 GS: 0-2 Gd: 0-1 **GF: 1-2** Fm: 0-0
Distance: 5f/6f: 0-1 **7f-8f: 1-3** 9f-13f: 0-2 14f+: 0-0
Track : LH: 0-3 RH: 0-1 Tight: 0-3 Gall: 0-0
Aids: Bl: 0-0 Vi: 0-0 Tstrap: 0-0
Best Rating: 79 4/01 Muss 7f30y gd-sft

Chivalry

87 **68+**

2-y-o b g Mark Of Esteem (IRE)-Gai Bulga (Kris)
Sir Mark Prescott W E Sturt - Osborne House Iv

Placings:506 **(5588)**
2001: 6^{5}S, 6^{0}HY, 5^{6}GS

	Starts	1st	2nd	3rd	Win & Pl
Career Total (Turf)	3	0	0	0	0

Going (Turf): Sf: 0-2 GS: 0-1 Gd: 0-0 GF: 0-0 Fm: 0-0
Distance: 5f/6f: 0-3 7f-8f: 0-0 9f-13f: 0-0 14f+: 0-0
Track : LH: 0-2 RH: 0-0 Tight: 0-0 Gall: 0-0
Aids: Bl: 0-0 Vi: 0-0 Tstrap: 0-0
Best Rating: 68 11/01 Brig 5f213y gd-sft

Chivite (IRE)

82 **66**

2-y-o b c Alhaarth (IRE)-Laura Margaret (Persian Bold)
Mrs A J Perrett Lady Harrison

Placings:0 **(4222)**
2001: 7^{0}GF

	Starts	1st	2nd	3rd	Win & Pl
Career Total (Turf)	1	0	0	0	

Going (Turf): Sf: 0-0 GS: 0-0 Gd: 0-0 GF: 0-1 Fm: 0-0
Distance: 5f/6f: 0-0 7f-8f: 0-1 9f-13f: 0-0 14f+: 0-0
Track : LH: 0-0 RH: 0-0 Tight: 0-0 Gall: 0-0

Aids: Bl: 0-0 Vi: 0-0 Tstrap: 0-0
Best Rating: 66 8/01 NmkJ 7f gd-fm

Chocolate Boy (IRE)

82 49

2-y-o b c Dolphin Street (FR)-Kawther (Tap On Wood)

T P McGovern Sigma Estates

Placings:000 (4639)

2001: 6^{0}GS, 6^{0}GF, 6^{0}GF

	Starts	1st	2nd	3rd	Win & Pl
Career Total (Turf)	3	0	0	0	

Going (Turf): Sf: 0-0 GS: 0-1 Gd: 0-0 GF: 0-2 Fm: 0-0
Distance: 5f/6f: 0-3 7f-8f: 0-0 9f-13f: 0-0 14f+: 0-0
Track : LH: 0-0 RH: 0-0 Tight: 0-0 Gall: 0-0
Aids: Bl: 0-0 Vi: 0-0 Tstrap: 0-0
Best Rating: 49 9/01 Ling 6f gd-fm

Chookie Heiton (IRE)

111 92

3-y-o br g Fumo Di Londra (IRE)-Royal Wolff (Prince Tenderfoot (USA))

I Semple Hamilton Park Members Syndicate

Placings:2-6314162 (5341)

2001: 5^{6}GS, 6^{3}GF, 6^{1}F, 5^{4}GF, 6^{1}G, 6^{6}G, 5^{2}GS

	Starts	1st	2nd	3rd	Win & Pl
Career Total (Turf)	8	2	2	1	12675

86	8/01	Newc	6f	D(0-80)	GD	£4104
73	5/01	Rdcr	6f	E	FRM	£2891

Total win prize-money £6996

Going (Turf): Sf: 0-0 GS: 0-2 Gd: 1-2 GF: 0-3 Fm: 1-1
Distance: 5f/6f: 2-8 7f-8f: 0-0 9f-13f: 0-0 14f+: 0-0
Track : LH: 0-0 RH: 0-0 Tight: 0-0 Gall: 0-0
Aids: Bl: 0-0 Vi: 0-0 Tstrap: 0-0
Best Rating: 92 10/01 NmkR 5f gd-sft

Got off the mark on his fourth start at Redcar, and followed up two runs later at Newcastle, before running well in a competitive Ascot handicap and a Newmarket rated stakes. Suited by six furlongs, he handles fast ground but has looked better recently with cut in the ground.

Chorist

74 30

2-y-o ch f Pivotal-Choir Mistress (Chief Singer)

W J Haggas Cheveley Park Stud

Placings:0 (5371)

2001: 8^{0}G

	Starts	1st	2nd	3rd	Win & Pl
Career Total (Turf)	1	0	0	0	

Going (Turf): Sf: 0-0 GS: 0-0 Gd: 0-1 GF: 0-0 Fm: 0-0
Distance: 5f/6f: 0-0 7f-8f: 0-1 9f-13f: 0-0 14f+: 0-0
Track : LH: 0-0 RH: 0-0 Tight: 0-0 Gall: 0-0
Aids: Bl: 0-0 Vi: 0-0 Tstrap: 0-0
Best Rating: 30 10/01 Rdcr 1m good

Chorus

95(92) (60)54

4-y-o b f Bandmaster (USA)-Name That Tune (Fayruz)

B R Millman In The Know

Placings:06244552544/20063232160100-000000206 (5497)

2001: 5^{0}HY, 5^{0}G, 5^{0}GF, 5^{0}S, 6^{0}GF, 7^{0}G, 5^{2}GS, 5^{0}G, 5^{6}HY

	Starts	1st	2nd	3rd	Win & Pl
Career Total (Turf)	34	2	6	1	14743
Career Total (AW)	1	0	0	1	403

70	10/00	Wind	5f10y	E(0-70)H	G-S	£2940
70	8/00	Sand	5f6y	D	GD	£4134

Total win prize-money £7074

Going (Turf): Sf: 0-8 GS: 1-9 Gd: 1-8 GF: 0-9 Fm: 0-0
Distance: 5f/6f: 2-33 7f-8f: 0-2 9f-13f: 0-0 14f+: 0-0
Track : LH: 0-7 RH: 1-6 Tight: 0-0 Gall: 1-11
Aids: Bl: 0-4 Vi: 1-4 Tstrap: 0-0
Best Rating: 54 8/01 Sals 6f212y gd-fm

Chorus Girl

(71) (15)43

3-y-o ch f Dancing Spree (USA)-Better Still (IRE) (Glenstal (USA))

S E Kettlewell W B Imison

Placings:543046500-00 (0140)

2001: 8^{0}SW, 9^{0}SW

	Starts	1st	2nd	3rd	Win & Pl
Career Total (Turf)	9	0	0	1	889
Career Total (AW)	2	0	0	0	

Going (Turf): Sf: 0-1 GS: 0-2 Gd: 0-4 GF: 0-1 Fm: 0-1
Distance: 5f/6f: 0-5 7f-8f: 0-4 9f-13f: 0-2 14f+: 0-0
Track : LH: 0-6 RH: 0-1 Tight: 0-6 Gall: 0-0
Aids: Bl: 0-0 Vi: 0-0 Tstrap: 0-0
Best Rating: 15 1/01 Wolv 1m100y slow

Choto Mate (IRE)

(93) (58)83

5-y-o ch g Brief Truce (USA)-Greatest Pleasure (Be My Guest (USA))

S Kirk Vernon Carl Matalon

Placings:310046/04100000-2600001101 (5592)

2001: 7^{2}GS, 8^{6}GF, 7^{0}G, 8^{0}GF, 6^{0}G, 7^{0}GF, 8^{1}G, 7^{1}GF, 6^{0}GS, 6^{1}GS

	Starts	1st	2nd	3rd	Win & Pl
Career Total (Turf)	24	5	1	1	33898

74	11/01	Brig	6f209y	F	G-S	£2429
83	9/01	Ling	7f	D(0-85)H	G-F	£4264
81	8/01	Bath	1m5y	D(0-80)H	GD	£4221
89	6/00	Sand	7f16y	C(0-100)H	G-F	£14218
85	5/98	Gdwd	5f	D	G-F	£4889

Total win prize-money £30024

Going (Turf): Sf: 0-4 GS: 1-4 Gd: 1-6 GF: 3-10 Fm: 0-0
Distance: 5f/6f: 1-8 7f-8f: 3-15 9f-13f: 1-1 14f+: 0-0
Track : LH: 2-5 RH: 1-6 Tight: 1-1 Gall: 0-4
Aids: Bl: 0-0 Vi: 0-0 Tstrap: 0-0
Best Rating: 83 9/01 Ling 7f gd-fm

Useful handicapper at seven furlongs to a mile, he dropped in the handicap during the season and hit form in August with a victory at Bath. Followed up at Lingfield, and took advantage of favourable terms to score in claiming company at Brighton in November.

Chris's Little Lad (IRE)

(65) 61d

4-y-o ch g Hamas (IRE)-Jeema (Thatch (USA))

W R Muir Hugh Smith

Placings:040/2000-0 (2649)

2001: 11^{0}SD

	Starts	1st	2nd	3rd	Win & Pl
Career Total (Turf)	6	0	1	0	536
Career Total (AW)	2	0	0	0	

Going (Turf): Sf: 0-0 GS: 0-1 Gd: 0-0 GF: 0-5 Fm: 0-0
Distance: 5f/6f: 0-1 7f-8f: 0-4 9f-13f: 0-3 14f+: 0-0
Track : LH: 0-5 RH: 0-0 Tight: 0-3 Gall: 0-0
Aids: Bl: 0-0 Vi: 0-0 Tstrap: 0-0

Christiansted (IRE)

81 47

6-y-o ch g Soviet Lad (USA)-How True (Known Fact (USA))

Ferdy Murphy (K A Ryan 21/9) John Duddy

Placings:33610/14152/610500-6600 (4829)

2001: 15^{6}GF, 16^{6}GF, 16^{0}GF, 17^{0}G

	Starts	1st	2nd	3rd	Win & Pl
Career Total (Turf)	20	4	1	2	23349

83	6/00	Muss	2m	D(0-85)H	FRM	£6347
75	6/99	Nott	1m6f15y	F(0-70)H	GD	£2721
69	4/99	Ripn	1m4f60y	E(0-70)H	G-F	£2957
90	5/98	Klny	1m4f		SFT	£3425

Total win prize-money £15450

Going (Turf): Sf: 1-2 GS: 0-1 Gd: 1-6 GF: 1-6 Fm: 1-2
Distance: 5f/6f: 0-0 7f-8f: 0-0 9f-13f: 2-7 14f+: 2-13
Track : LH: 2-10 RH: 2-10 Tight: 2-4 Gall: 0-5
Aids: Bl: 0-0 Vi: 0-0 Tstrap: 0-0
Best Rating: 47 7/01 Donc 2m110y gd-fm

Christmas Morning (IRE)

102 45

3-y-o b g Brief Truce (USA)-Maid O'Cannie (Efisio)

M W Easterby Lord & Lady Manton

Placings:00000-00060 (3085)

2001: 9^{0}F, 8^{0}GF, 9^{0}GF, 6^{6}GF, 8^{0}GF

	Starts	1st	2nd	3rd	Win & Pl
Career Total (Turf)	10	0	0	0	0

Going (Turf): Sf: 0-2 GS: 0-0 Gd: 0-2 GF: 0-5 Fm: 0-1
Distance: 5f/6f: 0-4 7f-8f: 0-2 9f-13f: 0-4 14f+: 0-0
Track : LH: 0-7 RH: 0-1 Tight: 0-3 Gall: 0-1
Aids: Bl: 0-2 Vi: 0-0 Tstrap: 0-0
Best Rating: 45 5/01 Rdcr 1m1f firm

Christmas Truce (IRE)

98 81

2-y-o b c Brief Truce (USA)-Superflash (Superlative)

M H Tompkins Flint Fairyhouse Partnership

Placings:0010 (5229)

2001: 7^{0}G, 8^{0}G, 7^{1}HY, 7^{0}S

	Starts	1st	2nd	3rd	Win & Pl
Career Total (Turf)	4	1	0	0	2681

81	9/01	Hayd	7f30y	F	HVY	£2681

Total win prize-money £2681

Going (Turf): Sf: 1-2 GS: 0-0 Gd: 0-2 GF: 0-0 Fm: 0-0
Distance: 5f/6f: 0-0 7f-8f: 1-3 9f-13f: 0-1 14f+: 0-0
Track : LH: 1-2 RH: 0-0 Tight: 0-0 Gall: 0-1
Aids: Bl: 0-0 Vi: 0-0 Tstrap: 0-0
Best Rating: 81 9/01 Hayd 7f30y heavy

Revelled in the heavy ground at Haydock to take a 7f-claimer. Bred to stay a mile.

Christopherssister

(97) (36)29

4-y-o br f Timeless Times (USA)-Petite Elite (Anfield)

N Bycroft Paul J Dixon

Placings:664520/10004000060-000000500 (5287)

2001: 5^{0}S, 5^{0}GF, 5^{0}F, 5^{0}SD, 5^{0}GF, 6^{0}F, 6^{5}G, 5^{0}G, 6^{0}HY

	Starts	1st	2nd	3rd	Win & Pl
Career Total (Turf)	19	0	0	0	286
Career Total (AW)	7	1	1	0	2734

59	1/00	Sthl	6f	F	STD	£2091

Total win prize-money £2092

Going (Turf): Sf: 0-4 GS: 0-0 Gd: 0-4 GF: 0-6 Fm: 0-5
Distance: 5f/6f: 1-24 7f-8f: 0-2 9f-13f: 0-0 14f+: 0-0
Track : LH: 1-3 RH: 0-3 Tight: 0-1 Gall: 0-2
Aids: Bl: 0-1 Vi: 0-0 Tstrap: 0-1
Best Rating: 35 5/01 Rdcr 5f soft

Chrysolite (IRE)

(92) (32)42

6-y-o ch g Kris-Alamiya (IRE) (Doyoun)
B W Hills Mrs B W Hills

Placings:043/01040/65000/00000-2044P **(1184)**
2001: 12^{0}SD, 12^{0}SD, 9^{4}SD, 10^{4}SW, 9^{P}GF

	Starts	1st	2nd	3rd	Win & Pl
Career Total (Turf)	15	1	0	1	6866
Career Total (AW)	8	0	1	0	422

78 5/98 Ling 1m1f C(0-100)H GD £5711
Total win prize-money £5711

Going (Turf): Sf: 0-3 GS: 0-1 **Gd: 1-5** GF: 0-4 Fm: 0-2
Distance: 5f/6f: 0-0 7f-8f: 0-6 **9f-13f: 1-17** 14f+: 0-0
Track : **LH: 1-15** RH: 0-4 **Tight: 1-11** Gall: 0-2
Aids: Bl: 0-2 Vi: 0-4 Tstrap: 0-1
Best Rating: 32 1/01 Wolv 1m4f stand

Church Farm Flyer (IRE)

(101) (57d)**57**
4-y-o b f College Chapel-Young Isabel (IRE) (Last Tycoon)
C N Allen Felix Snell

Placings:0066311/236324-000 **(0874)**
2001: 9^{0}SD, 7^{0}SD, 8^{0}S

	Starts	1st	2nd	3rd	Win & Pl
Career Total (Turf)	5	0	0	0	0
Career Total (AW)	11	2	2	3	9062

58 12/99 Wolv 7f D(0-85)H STD £3566
58 12/99 Ling 1m G STD £1891
Total win prize-money £5458

Going (Turf): Sf: 0-2 GS: 0-0 Gd: 0-2 GF: 0-0 Fm: 0-1
Distance: 5f/6f: 0-0 **7f-8f: 2-11** 9f-13f: 0-5 14f+: 0-0
Track : **LH: 2-12** RH: 0-0 **Tight: 2-8** Gall: 0-0
Aids: Bl: 0-0 Vi: 0-0 Tstrap: 0-0
Best Rating: 29 4/01 Sthl 7f stand

Church Mice (IRE)

101(91) (67)**75**
3-y-o br f Petardia-Negria (IRE) (Al Hareb (USA))
W H Tinning W H Tinning

Placings:24215364132-001525030 **(5630)**
2001: 7^{0}SD, 6^{0}S, 6^{1}GF, 6^{5}GF, 6^{2}GS, 7^{5}S, 6^{0}F, 7^{3}GS, 6^{0}G

	Starts	1st	2nd	3rd	Win & Pl
Career Total (Turf)	16	3	3	2	17444
Career Total (AW)	4	0	1	1	1036

82 6/01 Newc 6f D(0-85)H G-F £3981
68 9/00 Hayd 6f D(0-85) HVY £3835
67 5/00 Leic 5f2y F SFT £2488
Total win prize-money £10305

Going (Turf): Sf: 2-7 GS: 0-2 Gd: 0-3 GF: 1-3 Fm: 0-1
Distance: **5f/6f: 3-14** 7f-8f: 0-6 9f-13f: 0-0 14f+: 0-0
Track : LH: 0-5 RH: 0-1 Tight: 0-1 Gall: 0-1
Aids: Bl: 0-0 **Vi: 3-16** Tstrap: 0-0
Best Rating: 82 6/01 Newc 6f gd-fm

Won twice as a juvenile on soft ground, but caused a surprise when scoring at Newcastle in June 2001 on good to firm, and she has continued to run well in similar events. She seems to get seven furlongs, but has been known to miss the break on occasions. She goes well at Newcastle.

Churchill's Shadow (IRE)

(92) (37)**31**
7-y-o b g Polish Precedent (USA)-Shy Princess (USA) (Irish River (FR))
B A Pearce A Leg Each Partnership

Placings:5000020112/615000/540012453/5000-0 **(0579)**
2001: 8^{0}SW

	Starts	1st	2nd	3rd	Win & Pl
Career Total (Turf)	17	2	2	0	7633
Career Total (AW)	13	2	1	1	6094

47 7/99 Chep 1m14y F(0-60)H G-F £2612
49 5/98 Donc 7f F(0-70)H G-F £2547
53 11/97 Ling 7f E(0-70)H STD £2466
46 11/97 Ling 7f E(0-70)H STD £2479
Total win prize-money £10104

Going (Turf): Sf: 0-1 GS: 0-1 Gd: 0-6 **GF: 2-8** Fm: 0-1
Distance: 5f/6f: 0-3 **7f-8f: 3-24** 9f-13f: 1-3 14f+: 0-0
Track : **LH: 2-17** RH: 0-1 **Tight: 2-14** Gall: 0-2
Aids: Bl: 0-0 Vi: 0-0 Tstrap: 0-0
Best Rating: 5 3/01 Ling 1m slow

Churlish Charm

105 **106**
6-y-o b h Niniski (USA)-Blushing Storm (USA) (Blushing Groom (FR))
R Hannon Mohamed Suhail

Placings:0/215110/310/032361246-050636 **(2772a)**
2001: 12^{0}GS, 16^{5}G, 13^{0}GF, 16^{6}G, 15^{3}S, 15^{6}S

	Starts	1st	2nd	3rd	Win & Pl
Career Total (Turf)	25	5	3	4	157626

109 8/00 Sals 1m6f15y C G-F £6322
115 5/99 York 1m5f194yA SFT £71375
104 9/98 Newb 2m B(0-105)H GD £14005
95 6/98 Gdwd 1m4f C(0-90) GD £8236
81 5/98 NmkR 1m4f D G-F £4347
Total win prize-money £104286

Going (Turf): Sf: 1-5 GS: 0-4 **Gd: 2-8 GF: 2-6** Fm: 0-1
Distance: 5f/6f: 0-0 7f-8f: 0-1 9f-13f: 2-6 **14f+: 3-18**
Track : LH: 2-6 **RH: 3-16** Tight: 2-5 Gall: 2-11
Aids: Bl: 0-0 Vi: 0-3 Tstrap: 0-0
Best Rating: 106 5/01 Sand 2m78y good

Tough performer, probably best at a mile and three quarters although he stays further. He is a little below the best Cup horses. Prefers cut in the ground.

Cielito Lindo

102 **83d**
3-y-o b f Pursuit Of Love-Seal Indigo (IRE) (Glenstal (USA))
R Hannon Geoff Howard-Spink & Lindy Regis

Placings:20-13000 **(4804)**
2001: 6^{1}GF, 7^{3}GF, 6^{0}G, 6^{0}GF, 6^{0}F

	Starts	1st	2nd	3rd	Win & Pl
Career Total (Turf)	7	1	1	1	7179

77 7/01 Sals 6f D G-F £4329
Total win prize-money £4329

Going (Turf): Sf: 0-1 GS: 0-0 Gd: 0-2 **GF: 1-3** Fm: 0-1
Distance: **5f/6f: 1-4** 7f-8f: 0-3 9f-13f: 0-0 14f+: 0-0
Track : LH: 0-1 RH: 0-1 Tight: 0-0 Gall: 0-0
Aids: Bl: 0-0 Vi: 0-0 Tstrap: 0-0
Best Rating: 83 7/01 Sand 7f16y gd-fm

Made a belated seasonal debut when winning a six-furlong maiden at Salisbury in July, but has disappointed in handicap company since.

Cilantro

(96) (17)**14**
4-y-o b g Minshaanshu Amad (USA)-Laquette (Bairn (USA))
A G Newcombe Robert Beckett

Placings:50000/06600066 **(4552)**
2001: 8^{0}SD, 9^{6}SW, 11^{6}GS, 11^{0}SD, 14^{0}SD, 16^{0}F, 12^{6}SD, 14^{6}SW

	Starts	1st	2nd	3rd	Win & Pl
Career Total (Turf)	6	0	0	0	0
Career Total (AW)	7	0	0	0	0

Going (Turf): Sf: 0-1 GS: 0-1 Gd: 0-3 GF: 0-0 Fm: 0-1
Distance: 5f/6f: 0-2 7f-8f: 0-4 9f-13f: 0-4 14f+: 0-3

Track : LH: 0-10 RH: 0-0 Tight: 0-5 Gall: 0-0
Aids: Bl: 0-0 Vi: 0-0 Tstrap: 0-0
Best Rating: 23 2/01 Wolv 1m1f79y slow

Cindesti (IRE)

(76)
5-y-o b g Barathea (IRE)-Niamh Cinn Oir (IRE) (King Of Clubs)
J G Given J E Titley

Placings:00/40011/000000-00 **(0186)**
2001: 16^{0}SW, 16^{0}SD

	Starts	1st	2nd	3rd	Win & Pl
Career Total (Turf)	10	0	0	0	297
Career Total (AW)	5	2	0	0	4496

64 9/99 Wolv 1m6f166yF(0-60) STD £2171
58 9/99 Wolv 1m4f F(0-65)H STD £2325
Total win prize-money £4496

Going (Turf): Sf: 0-1 GS: 0-5 Gd: 0-2 GF: 0-2 Fm: 0-0
Distance: 5f/6f: 0-0 7f-8f: 0-1 9f-13f: 1-6 14f+: 1-8
Track : **LH: 2-12** RH: 0-2 **Tight: 2-6** Gall: 0-2
Aids: Bl: 0-3 Vi: 0-0 Tstrap: 0-0
Best Rating: 17 1/01 Wolv 2m46y slow

Cindrier (IRE)

(67) (26)**56**
2-y-o b c Alhaarth (IRE)-Fag End (IRE) (Treasure Kay)
G C Bravery The Tt Partnership

Placings:003500000 **(5193)**
2001: 5^{0}SD, 5^{0}GF, 5^{3}F, 7^{5}F, 5^{0}G, 6^{0}G, 6^{0}S, 7^{0}G, 6^{0}SD

	Starts	1st	2nd	3rd	Win & Pl
Career Total (Turf)	7	0	0	1	417
Career Total (AW)	2	0	0	0	

Going (Turf): Sf: 0-1 GS: 0-0 Gd: 0-3 GF: 0-1 Fm: 0-2
Distance: 5f/6f: 0-6 7f-8f: 0-3 9f-13f: 0-0 14f+: 0-0
Track : LH: 0-5 RH: 0-1 Tight: 0-3 Gall: 0-0
Aids: Bl: 0-0 Vi: 0-0 Tstrap: 0-2
Best Rating: 75 7/01 Brig 5f213y firm

Cinema Paradiso

89 **23**
7-y-o b g Polar Falcon (USA)-Epure (Bellypha)
N G Richards Edward Melville

Placings:120/35010000/0 **(2226)**
2001: 8^{0}G

	Starts	1st	2nd	3rd	Win & Pl
Career Total (Turf)	12	2	1	1	11607

91 6/97 Sals 1m C(0-100)H SFT £5507
94 7/96 Newb 6f8y D G-F £3649
Total win prize-money £9157

Going (Turf): Sf: 1-1 GS: 0-0 Gd: 0-6 **GF: 1-5** Fm: 0-0
Distance: 5f/6f: 0-0 **7f-8f: 2-5** 9f-13f: 0-7 14f+: 0-0
Track : LH: 0-5 RH: 0-4 Tight: 0-3 Gall: 0-4
Aids: Bl: 0-0 Vi: 0-0 Tstrap: 0-0
Best Rating: 23 6/01 Muss 1m good

Circle Of Light

101 **79**
4-y-o b f Anshan-Cockatoo Island (High Top)
P W D'Arcy Lord Derby

Placings:10/3233040-030 **(4984)**
2001: 7^{0}G, 10^{3}G, 12^{0}G

	Starts	1st	2nd	3rd	Win & Pl
Career Total (Turf)	12	1	1	4	14721

85 8/99 Ling 7f140y F G-F £2165
Total win prize-money £2166

Going (Turf): Sf: 0-0 GS: 0-1 Gd: 0-6 **GF: 1-5** Fm: 0-0
Distance: 5f/6f: 0-0 **7f-8f: 1-5** 9f-13f: 0-7 14f+: 0-0

Track : LH: 0-7 RH: 0-3 Tight: 0-3 Gall: 0-6
Aids: Bl: 0-0 Vi: 0-0 Tstrap: 0-0
Best Rating: 79 8/01 Yarm 1m2f21y good

Circle Of Wolves

83 **64**

3-y-o ch g Wolfhound (USA)-Misty Halo (High Top)
Bob Jones The Circle Of Wolves Partnership

Placings:00-50 **(1619)**
2001: 8^{5}S, 10^{0}GF

	Starts	1st	2nd	3rd	Win & Pl
Career Total (Turf)	4	0	0	0	0

Going (Turf): Sf: 0-1 GS: 0-0 Gd: 0-0 GF: 0-3 Fm: 0-0
Distance: 5f/6f: 0-1 7f-8f: 0-1 9f-13f: 0-2 14f+: 0-0
Track : LH: 0-2 RH: 0-0 Tight: 0-0 Gall: 0-0
Aids: Bl: 0-0 Vi: 0-0 Tstrap: 0-0
Best Rating: 35 5/01 Wwck 1m2f188y gd-fm

Circlet

104 **71**

3-y-o ch f Lion Cavern (USA)-Chiltern Court (USA) (Topsider (USA))
J W Hills Wyck Hall Stud

Placings:0-100 **(2380)**
2001: 8^{1}G, 7^{0}GF, 8^{0}GF

	Starts	1st	2nd	3rd	Win & Pl
Career Total (Turf)	4	1	0	0	2289

71 5/01 Bath 1m5y F GD £2289
Total win prize-money £2289

Going (Turf): Sf: 0-0 GS: 0-0 **Gd: 1-1** GF: 0-3 Fm: 0-0
Distance: 5f/6f: 0-1 7f-8f: 0-2 **9f-13f: 1-1** 14f+: 0-0
Track : **LH: 1-1** RH: 0-1 **Tight: 1-1** Gall: 0-1
Aids: Bl: 0-0 Vi: 0-0 Tstrap: 0-0
Best Rating: 71 5/01 Bath 1m5y good

She got off the mark in a Bath maiden on her second start, but was well beaten in better company subsequently.

Circuit Life (IRE)

97(84) (53)**36**

3-y-o ch g Rainbows For Life (CAN)-Alicedale (USA) (Trempolino (USA))
A Berry David Fish

Placings:053066623433-00060006 **(3461)**
2001: 8^{0}S, 8^{0}S, 5^{0}SD, 9^{6}GS, 9^{0}G, 10^{0}GF, 10^{0}GF, 11^{6}F

	Starts	1st	2nd	3rd	Win & Pl
Career Total (Turf)	18	0	1	4	2923
Career Total (AW)	2	0	0	0	0

Going (Turf): Sf: 0-3 GS: 0-4 Gd: 0-3 GF: 0-7 Fm: 0-1
Distance: 5f/6f: 0-8 7f-8f: 0-6 9f-13f: 0-6 14f+: 0-0
Track : LH: 0-7 RH: 0-5 Tight: 0-5 Gall: 0-0
Aids: Bl: 0-1 Vi: 0-1 Tstrap: 0-0
Best Rating: 36 5/01 Bevl 1m1f207y good

Circumstance

(43)

3-y-o ch f Beveled (USA)-Instant Pleasure (Bairn (USA))
Andrew Reid Rush Green Partnership

Placings:0 **(2578)**
2001: 6^{0}SD

	Starts	1st	2nd	3rd	Win & Pl
Career Total (Turf)	0	0	0	0	
Career Total (AW)	1	0	0	0	

Going (Turf): Sf: 0-0 GS: 0-0 Gd: 0-0 GF: 0-0 Fm: 0-0
Distance: 5f/6f: 0-1 7f-8f: 0-0 9f-13f: 0-0 14f+: 0-0
Track : LH: 0-1 RH: 0-0 Tight: 0-0 Gall: 0-0
Aids: Bl: 0-0 Vi: 0-0 Tstrap: 0-0

Citrine (IRE)

101 **67**

3-y-o ch f Selkirk (USA)-Classic Coral (USA) (Seattle Dancer (USA))
C F Wall Hintlesham Thoroughbreds

Placings:66400612 **(5622)**
2001: 8^{6}G, 10^{6}GF, 10^{4}GF, 10^{0}G, 14^{0}G, 14^{6}G, 16^{1}HY, 14^{2}GS

	Starts	1st	2nd	3rd	Win & Pl
Career Total (Turf)	8	1	1	0	3653

63 10/01 Ling 2m F(0-65)H HVY £2772
Total win prize-money £2772

Going (Turf): Sf: 1-1 GS: 0-1 Gd: 0-4 GF: 0-2 Fm: 0-0
Distance: 5f/6f: 0-0 7f-8f: 0-0 9f-13f: 0-4 **14f+: 1-4**
Track : **LH: 1-6** RH: 0-2 **Tight: 1-4** Gall: 0-1
Aids: Bl: 0-0 Vi: 0-1 Tstrap: 0-0
Best Rating: 67 11/01 Nott 1m6f15y gd-sft

Looked as though she would be suited by a test of stamina and got off the mark in a two-mile maiden handicap on bottomless ground at Lingfield in October.

Citrus Magic

97(100) (61)**55**

4-y-o b g Cosmonaut-Up All Night (Green Desert (USA))
K Bell Brian Footer

Placings:400023-062400 **(5263)**
2001: 11^{0}GS, 16^{6}SD, 14^{2}S, 16^{4}GS, 16^{0}G, 13^{0}GS

	Starts	1st	2nd	3rd	Win & Pl
Career Total (Turf)	9	0	1	0	1635
Career Total (AW)	3	0	1	1	1247

Going (Turf): Sf: 0-1 GS: 0-4 Gd: 0-1 GF: 0-2 Fm: 0-1
Distance: 5f/6f: 0-0 7f-8f: 0-0 9f-13f: 0-6 14f+: 0-6
Track : LH: 0-6 RH: 0-4 Tight: 0-7 Gall: 0-1
Aids: Bl: 0-0 Vi: 0-0 Tstrap: 0-0
Best Rating: 55 6/01 Sand 1m6f soft

Still a maiden, he is suited by test of stamina. Stays 14 furlongs and acts on an easy surface.

City Bank Dudley

74(80) **23**

4-y-o b g Noble Patriarch-Derry's Delight (Mufrij)
N Wilson J B Slatcher

Placings:036464005000-00 **(0703)**
2001: 8^{0}SD, 6^{0}HY

	Starts	1st	2nd	3rd	Win & Pl
Career Total (Turf)	11	0	0	1	623
Career Total (AW)	3	0	0	0	

Going (Turf): Sf: 0-3 GS: 0-0 Gd: 0-2 GF: 0-4 Fm: 0-2
Distance: 5f/6f: 0-3 7f-8f: 0-6 9f-13f: 0-5 14f+: 0-0
Track : LH: 0-7 RH: 0-6 Tight: 0-3 Gall: 0-2
Aids: Bl: 0-0 Vi: 0-0 Tstrap: 0-0
Best Rating: 5 4/01 Pont 6f heavy

City Faith

94 **84+**

2-y-o b f Glory Of Dancer-Broughtons Star (Belmez (USA))
G C Bravery J J May

Placings:140 **(5364)**
2001: 6^{1}GF, 6^{4}GS, 6^{0}GS

	Starts	1st	2nd	3rd	Win & Pl
Career Total (Turf)	3	1	0	0	3736

84 9/01 Ling 6f F G-F £3192
Total win prize-money £3192

Going (Turf): Sf: 0-0 GS: 0-2 Gd: 0-0 **GF: 1-1** Fm: 0-0
Distance: **5f/6f: 1-3** 7f-8f: 0-0 9f-13f: 0-0 14f+: 0-0
Track : LH: 0-0 RH: 0-0 Tight: 0-0 Gall: 0-0
Aids: Bl: 0-0 Vi: 0-0 Tstrap: 0-0
Best Rating: 84 9/01 Ling 6f gd-fm

Landed a monster gamble on her debut at Lingfield in September over six, but beaten in better events on soft ground subsequently.

City Flyer

96(90) (45)**46d**

4-y-o br g Night Shift (USA)-Al Guswa (Shernazar)
Miss J Feilden C Morris

Placings:04504/5000601000-40403000 **(4292)**
2001: 8^{4}SD, 9^{0}G, 7^{4}GF, 7^{0}SD, 10^{3}G, 10^{0}GF, 10^{0}G, 10^{0}GF

	Starts	1st	2nd	3rd	Win & Pl
Career Total (Turf)	20	1	0	1	3929
Career Total (AW)	3	0	0	0	0

55 8/00 Carl 7f214y F(0-60)H GD £3029
Total win prize-money £3030

Going (Turf): Sf: 0-1 GS: 0-1 **Gd: 1-8** GF: 0-10 Fm: 0-0
Distance: 5f/6f: 0-3 **7f-8f: 1-9** 9f-13f: 0-11 14f+: 0-0
Track : LH: 0-12 **RH: 1-7** Tight: 0-4 Gall: 0-4
Aids: Bl: 0-0 Vi: 0-2 Tstrap: 0-3
Best Rating: 46 7/01 Yarm 1m2f21y good

Moderate performer from seven to ten furlongs, appreciates good ground, likes to race prominently, goes well for an amateur.

City Of London (IRE)

105 **77**

3-y-o ch c Grand Lodge (USA)-Penny Fan (Nomination)
J W Payne C Cotran

Placings:6-0105 **(4486)**
2001: 6^{0}F, 6^{1}GF, 7^{0}GF, 7^{5}S

	Starts	1st	2nd	3rd	Win & Pl
Career Total (Turf)	5	1	0	0	3206

75 7/01 Folk 6f189y D G-F £3206
Total win prize-money £3206

Going (Turf): Sf: 0-1 GS: 0-1 Gd: 0-0 **GF: 1-2** Fm: 0-1
Distance: 5f/6f: 0-1 **7f-8f: 1-4** 9f-13f: 0-0 14f+: 0-0
Track : LH: 0-1 **RH: 1-2 Tight: 1-1** Gall: 0-1
Aids: Bl: 0-0 Vi: 0-0 Tstrap: 0-0
Best Rating: 77 8/01 Kemp 7f gd-fm

Won a seven-furlong maiden at Folkestone in July, but has found handicap company tougher since then. Best of fast ground.

City Player

(102) (81+)**46**

3-y-o ch c Komaite (USA)-Blink Naskra (USA) (Naskra (USA))
Sir Mark Prescott Ne'Er Do Wells Ii

Placings:0021-3 **(0041)**
2001: 6^{3}SD

	Starts	1st	2nd	3rd	Win & Pl
Career Total (Turf)	1	0	0	0	
Career Total (AW)	4	1	1	1	4318

81 12/00 Sthl 6f D STD £2744
Total win prize-money £2744

Going (Turf): Sf: 0-1 GS: 0-0 Gd: 0-0 GF: 0-0 Fm: 0-0
Distance: **5f/6f: 1-4** 7f-8f: 0-1 9f-13f: 0-0 14f+: 0-0
Track : **LH: 1-4** RH: 0-0 Tight: 0-3 Gall: 0-0
Aids: Bl: 0-0 Vi: 0-0 Tstrap: 0-0
Best Rating: 69 1/01 Ling 6f stand

City Reach

(102) (70)**48**

5-y-o b g Petong-Azola (IRE) (Alzao (USA))

P J Makin T W Wellard Partnership

Placings:2/006532/41305103311-00040 **(4052)**

2001: 6^{0}GF, 5^{0}G, 5^{0}F, 7^{4}SD, 6^{0}F

				Starts	1st	2nd	3rd	Win & Pl
Career Total (Turf)				12	1	1	1	3861
Career Total (AW)				11	3	1	3	9324
70	10/00	Wolv	6f	F(0-65)H		STD		£2534
63	9/00	Wolv	6f	F(0-65)H		STD		£2590
50	7/00	Brig	5f59y	F(0-60)		FRM		£2226
60	1/00	Sthl	7f	F		STD		£2215

Total win prize-money £9566

Going (Turf): Sf: 0-4 GS: 0-0 Gd: 0-2 GF: 0-2 **Fm: 1-4**
Distance: **5f/6f: 3-12** 7f-8f: 1-11 9f-13f: 0-0 14f+: 0-0
Track : **LH: 4-17** RH: 0-1 **Tight: 2-7** Gall: 0-2
Aids: Bl: 0-0 **Vi: 4-15** Tstrap: 0-0
Best Rating: 67 8/01 Wolv 7f stand

Claire's Dancer (IRE)

69

8-y-o b g Classic Music (USA)-Midnight Patrol (Ashmore (FR))

Andrew Turnell Mrs Claire Hollowood

Placings:0150600/0 **(2040)**

2001: 17^{0}GF

				Starts	1st	2nd	3rd	Win & Pl
Career Total (Turf)				8	1	0	0	2473
70	5/96	Ling	1m2f	F		GD		£2473

Total win prize-money £2473

Going (Turf): Sf: 0-0 GS: 0-1 **Gd: 1-2** GF: 0-4 Fm: 0-1
Distance: 5f/6f: 0-0 7f-8f: 0-1 **9f-13f: 1-6** 14f+: 0-1
Track : **LH: 1-5** RH: 0-2 **Tight: 1-2** Gall: 0-2
Aids: Bl: 0-0 Vi: 0-0 Tstrap: 0-0

Clan Chief

97 **60**

8-y-o b g Clantime-Mrs Meyrick (Owen Dudley)

M Blanshard Gathering Of The Clan

Placings:33224/52211121/45000/334204000/020050-160000 **(5462)**

2001: 5^{1}G, 5^{6}GF, 5^{0}G, 5^{0}HD, 5^{0}GS, 5^{0}G

				Starts	1st	2nd	3rd	Win & Pl
Career Total (Turf)				39	5	7	4	47118
64	5/01	Bath	5f161y	E(0-70)H		GD		£2884
81	9/96	Gdwd	6f	C(0-95)H		GD		£14915
75	8/96	Gdwd	5f	C(0-90)H		G-F		£7050
70	7/96	Sand	5f6y	D(0-80)H		G-F		£3680
60	7/96	Sand	5f6y	E(0-70)H		G-F		£3468

Total win prize-money £31998

Going (Turf): Sf: 0-1 GS: 0-4 Gd: 2-12 **GF: 3-19** Fm: 0-3
Distance: **5f/6f: 5-38** 7f-8f: 0-1 9f-13f: 0-0 14f+: 0-0
Track : **LH: 1-9** RH: 0-2 Tight: 0-2 **Gall: 1-8**
Aids: Bl: 0-1 Vi: 0-0 Tstrap: 0-0
Best Rating: 64 5/01 Bath 5f161y good

Showed his best form as a three-year-old, winning a handful of useful handicaps. He has failed to show much since then until a dramatic drop in grade saw him land a moderate handicap at Bath in October. He is best over five/six furlongs on a sound surface.

Clanbroad

(92) (68)**68**

3-y-o ch c Clantime-Under The Wing (Aragon)

K R Burke Sporty Mo P'Ship

Placings:4140143-0600461003000 **(5352)**

2001: 6^{0}SD, 6^{6}SD, 6^{0}SW, 6^{0}S, 6^{4}S, 6^{6}GF, 6^{1}GF, 6^{0}GF, 6^{0}GF, 6^{3}G, 6^{0}GF, 6^{0}GS, 6^{0}SD

				Starts	1st	2nd	3rd	Win & Pl
Career Total (Turf)				14	3	0	1	11874
Career Total (AW)				6	0	0	1	385
72	5/01	Ripn	6f	E(0-70)H		G-F		£3633
72	9/00	Ling	6f	F		SFT		£2660
71	8/00	Leic	5f218y	E(0-70)H		G-F		£3971

Total win prize-money £10265

Going (Turf): Sf: 1-3 GS: 0-1 Gd: 0-1 **GF: 2-7** Fm: 0-2
Distance: **5f/6f: 3-17** 7f-8f: 0-3 9f-13f: 0-0 14f+: 0-0
Track : LH: 0-8 RH: 0-0 Tight: 0-1 Gall: 0-2
Aids: Bl: 0-0 Vi: 0-1 Tstrap: 0-0
Best Rating: 72 5/01 Ripn 6f gd-fm

A small individual, he scored on his second outing at Leicester and handled a step up to six well. Has been kept busy during the winter on the All-Weather. Scored in spring of 2001 over six furlongs at Ripon. Has won on soft and good to firm.

Clandestine

59

5-y-o b m Saddlers' Hall (IRE)-Fleeting Affair (Hotfoot)

N J Henderson Brian & Gwen Griffiths

Placings:4160/0 **(3549)**

2001: 21^{0}GF

				Starts	1st	2nd	3rd	Win & Pl
Career Total (Turf)				5	1	0	0	4169
85	8/99	Hayd	1m3f200yD			SFT		£3915

Total win prize-money £3916

Going (Turf): **Sf: 1-1** GS: 0-0 Gd: 0-2 GF: 0-2 Fm: 0-0
Distance: 5f/6f: 0-0 7f-8f: 0-0 **9f-13f: 1-3** 14f+: 0-2
Track : **LH: 1-4** RH: 0-0 Tight: 0-0 Gall: 0-2
Aids: Bl: 0-1 Vi: 0-0 Tstrap: 0-0
Best Rating: 59 8/01 Gdwd 2m5f gd-fm

Highly tried after winning a maiden for John Gosden in '99, she is better known as a hurdler these days.

Clansinge

89(74) (28)**12**

3-y-o ch f Clantime-North Pine (Import)

H A McWilliams J K Brown & Partners

Placings:5313400602360-0000000 **(2514)**

2001: 6^{0}SD, 5^{0}GS, 6^{0}S, 5^{0}GF, 7^{0}F, 7^{0}F, 6^{0}F

				Starts	1st	2nd	3rd	Win & Pl
Career Total (Turf)				17	1	1	3	4922
Career Total (AW)				3	0	0	0	0
57	6/00	Bevl	5f	F		G-F		£2352

Total win prize-money £2352

Going (Turf): Sf: 0-4 GS: 0-3 Gd: 0-1 **GF: 1-4** Fm: 0-5
Distance: **5f/6f: 1-18** 7f-8f: 0-2 9f-13f: 0-0 14f+: 0-0
Track : LH: 0-4 **RH:** 0-0 Tight: 0-2 Gall: 0-0
Aids: Bl: 0-3 Vi: 0-0 Tstrap: 0-1
Best Rating: 36 5/01 Newc 6f soft

Clarendon (IRE)

104 **78**

5-y-o ch h Forest Wind (USA)-Sparkish (IRE) (Persian Bold)

P J Hobbs The Plus Fours

Placings:44606400/411300/006223030-04 **(1590)**

2001: 12^{0}S, 12^{4}GF

				Starts	1st	2nd	3rd	Win & Pl
Career Total (Turf)				25	2	2	3	19359
73	7/99	Asct	1m2f	C(0-90)H		G-F		£8559
65	6/99	Chep	1m2f36y	D(0-85)H		G-F		£3675

Total win prize-money £12234

Going (Turf): Sf: 0-4 GS: 0-4 Gd: 0-6 **GF: 2-10** Fm: 0-1
Distance: 5f/6f: 0-2 7f-8f: 0-4 **9f-13f: 2-17** 14f+: 0-2
Track : LH: 1-11 RH: 1-9 Tight: 0-4 **Gall: 1-11**
Aids: Bl: 0-1 Vi: 0-0 Tstrap: 0-0
Best Rating: 75 5/01 Donc 1m4f gd-fm

Claretelle (IRE)

91 **62+**

3-y-o ch f Ela-Mana-Mou-Kutaisi (IRE) (Soviet Star (USA))

D R C Elsworth Vrv Partnership & Mrs V Moeran

Placings:20 **(4784)**

2001: 8^{2}GF, 9^{0}G

	Starts	1st	2nd	3rd	Win & Pl
Career Total (Turf)	2	0	1	0	1126

Going (Turf): Sf: 0-0 GS: 0-0 Gd: 0-1 GF: 0-1 Fm: 0-0
Distance: 5f/6f: 0-0 7f-8f: 0-1 9f-13f: 0-1 14f+: 0-0
Track : LH: 0-0 RH: 0-1 Tight: 0-1 Gall: 0-0
Aids: Bl: 0-0 Vi: 0-0 Tstrap: 0-0
Best Rating: 62 8/01 Sals 1m gd-fm

Clarice Starling

95 **69**

3-y-o b f Saddlers' Hall (IRE)-Uncharted Waters (Celestial Storm (USA))

C A Cyzer Mrs E A Cyzer

Placings:44 **(2626)**

2001: 11^{4}GF, 12^{4}GF

	Starts	1st	2nd	3rd	Win & Pl
Career Total (Turf)	2	0	0	0	672

Going (Turf): Sf: 0-0 GS: 0-0 Gd: 0-0 GF: 0-2 Fm: 0-0
Distance: 5f/6f: 0-0 7f-8f: 0-0 9f-13f: 0-2 14f+: 0-0
Track : LH: 0-0 RH: 0-1 Tight: 0-1 Gall: 0-0
Aids: Bl: 0-0 Vi: 0-0 Tstrap: 0-0
Best Rating: 69 7/01 Gdwd 1m4f gd-fm

Clarinch Claymore

103(110) (70)**66**

5-y-o b g Sabrehill (USA)-Salu (Ardross)

J M Jefferson John Donald

Placings:0050/000341420/2300421114-120200 **(2242)**

2001: 14^{1}SD, 12^{2}SD, 14^{0}SW, 12^{4}S, 14^{0}G, 12^{0}G

				Starts	1st	2nd	3rd	Win & Pl
Career Total (Turf)				19	2	3	1	10264
Career Total (AW)				10	3	2	1	11719
67	1/01	Sthl	1m6f	F(0-65)H		STD		£2240
68	12/00	Sthl	1m4f	D(0-85)H		STD		£3740
60	11/00	Sthl	1m4f	F(0-60)H		STD		£2030
56	11/00	Muss	1m4f	E(0-70)H		G-S		£4238
55	8/99	Bevl	1m100y	E(0-75)		GD		£2979

Total win prize-money £15229

Going (Turf): Sf: 0-5 **GS: 1-2 Gd: 1-6** GF: 0-5 Fm: 0-1
Distance: 5f/6f: 0-0 7f-8f: 0-4 **9f-13f: 4-21** 14f+: 1-4
Track : **LH: 3-19** RH: 2-8 **Tight: 1-3** Gall: 0-2
Aids: Bl: 0-0 Vi: 0-0 Tstrap: 0-0
Best Rating: 70 2/01 Sthl 1m4f stand

Class Leader (USA)

99 **86**

2-y-o b c Honor Grades (USA)-Serena (SAF) (Jan Ekels)

D R Loder Sheikh Mohammed

Placings:12 **(2925)**

2001: 6^{1}GF, 7^{2}GF

				Starts	1st	2nd	3rd	Win & Pl
Career Total (Turf)				2	1	1	0	6910
80	6/01	NmkR	6f	D		G-F		£4810

Total win prize-money £4810

Going (Turf): Sf: 0-0 GS: 0-0 Gd: 0-0 **GF: 1-2** Fm: 0-0
Distance: **5f/6f: 1-1** 7f-8f: 0-1 9f-13f: 0-0 14f+: 0-0
Track : LH: 0-0 RH: 0-0 Tight: 0-0 Gall: 0-0
Aids: Bl: 0-0 Vi: 0-0 Tstrap: 0-0
Best Rating: 86 7/01 Donc 7f gd-fm

Needed all of the six furlong trip to stamp his authority when winning a Newmarket maiden on his debut and met one too good when stepped up to seven next time.

Class Wan

67 **9**

5-y-o ch m Safawan-Ayr Classic (Local Suitor (USA))
J S Goldie Frank Brady

Placings:005541610/00/00 **(0824)**
2001: 5^{0}S, 5^{0}S

	Starts	1st	2nd	3rd	Win & Pl
Career Total (Turf)	13	2	0	0	6830

76 10/98 Ayr 6f D(0-85)H G-S £3678
71 8/98 Muss 5f E G-F £2960
Total win prize-money £6638

Going (Turf): Sf: 0-4 **GS: 1-3** Gd: 0-4 **GF: 1-2** Fm: 0-0
Distance: **5f/6f: 2-12** 7f-8f: 0-1 9f-13f: 0-0 14f+: 0-0
Track : LH: 0-0 RH: 0-0 Tight: 0-0 Gall: 0-0
Aids: Bl: 0-0 Vi: 0-0 Tstrap: 0-0
Best Rating: 9 4/01 Ripn 5f soft

Classic Affair (FR)

77(49)

5-y-o b g Always Fair (USA)-Classic Storm (Belfort (FR))
Miss A Stokell Ms Caron Stokell

Placings:00000/0000 **(2518)**
2001: 8^{0}SD, 12^{0}SD, 8^{0}GF, 16^{0}F

	Starts	1st	2nd	3rd	Win & Pl
Career Total (Turf)	7	0	0	0	
Career Total (AW)	2	0	0	0	

Going (Turf): Sf: 0-2 GS: 0-0 Gd: 0-3 GF: 0-1 Fm: 0-1
Distance: 5f/6f: 0-1 7f-8f: 0-4 9f-13f: 0-3 14f+: 0-1
Track : LH: 0-4 RH: 0-1 Tight: 0-4 Gall: 0-0
Aids: Bl: 0-0 Vi: 0-0 Tstrap: 0-0

Classic Brief (IRE)

99 **76**

2-y-o b g Brief Truce (USA)-Shprinza (Vitiges (FR))
R M Beckett The Classic Strollers Partnership

Placings:321224 **(4611)**
2001: 6^{3}GF, 7^{2}GS, 6^{1}GF, 6^{2}G, 7^{2}G, 8^{4}F

	Starts	1st	2nd	3rd	Win & Pl
Career Total (Turf)	6	1	3	1	10554

78 8/01 Brig 6f209y E G-F £3031
Total win prize-money £3031

Going (Turf): Sf: 0-0 GS: 0-1 Gd: 0-2 **GF: 1-2** Fm: 0-1
Distance: 5f/6f: 0-1 **7f-8f: 1-4** 9f-13f: 0-1 14f+: 0-0
Track : **LH: 1-4** RH: 0-0 Tight: 0-2 Gall: 0-1
Aids: Bl: 0-0 Vi: 0-0 Tstrap: 0-0
Best Rating: 78 8/01 Brig 6f209y gd-fm

A half-brother to German nine-furlong Listed winner, Lucky Power, won a seven-furlong maiden auction in August. Suited by a sound surface.

Classic Calvados (FR)

86 **60**

2-y-o b/br c Thatching-Mountain Stage (IRE) (Pennine Walk)
T D Easterby D Hilton Cox

Placings:00 **(4307)**
2001: 7^{0}G, 7^{0}GF

	Starts	1st	2nd	3rd	Win & Pl
Career Total (Turf)	2	0	0	0	

Going (Turf): Sf: 0-0 GS: 0-0 Gd: 0-1 GF: 0-1 Fm: 0-0
Distance: 5f/6f: 0-0 7f-8f: 0-2 9f-13f: 0-0 14f+: 0-0
Track : LH: 0-0 RH: 0-0 Tight: 0-0 Gall: 0-0

Aids: Bl: 0-0 Vi: 0-0 Tstrap: 0-0
Best Rating: 60 8/01 Newc 7f gd-fm

Classic Colours (USA)

80 (32)**18**

8-y-o ch g Blushing John (USA)-All Agleam (USA) (Gleaming (USA))
G H Yardley Philip Jones

Placings:50/42253040/000/636500/46230000/0000-00 **(4844)**
2001: 11^{0}F, 9^{0}G

	Starts	1st	2nd	3rd	Win & Pl
Career Total (Turf)	29	0	3	3	5372
Career Total (AW)	4	0	0	0	0

Going (Turf): Sf: 0-3 GS: 0-5 Gd: 0-9 GF: 0-8 Fm: 0-4
Distance: 5f/6f: 0-0 7f-8f: 0-3 9f-13f: 0-29 14f+: 0-1
Track : LH: 0-27 RH: 0-4 Tight: 0-8 Gall: 0-1
Aids: Bl: 0-1 Vi: 0-0 Tstrap: 0-8
Best Rating: 18 7/01 Bath 1m3f144y firm

Classic Conkers (IRE)

98(81) (29)**53**

7-y-o b g Conquering Hero (USA)-Erck (Sun Prince)
Pat Mitchell Steven Rees

Placings:0500665120/00406005460/016024000-3152200 **(4983)**
2001: 12^{3}GF, 16^{1}GF, 16^{5}GF, 11^{2}G, 12^{2}GS, 12^{0}G, 12^{0}G

	Starts	1st	2nd	3rd	Win & Pl
Career Total (Turf)	35	3	4	1	12249
Career Total (AW)	2	0	0	0	

54 7/01 Donc 2m110y E(0-80)H G-F £3164
36 7/00 Wwck 1m4f56y E(0-75)H GD £2847
49 10/98 Yarm 1m3f101yG(0-60)H G-S £2005
Total win prize-money £8016

Going (Turf): Sf: 0-2 **GS: 1-4 Gd: 1-15 GF: 1-13** Fm: 0-1
Distance: 5f/6f: 0-1 7f-8f: 0-1 **9f-13f: 2-24** 14f+: 1-11
Track : **LH: 3-21** RH: 0-11 Tight: 1-19 Gall: 1-6
Aids: Bl: 0-0 Vi: 0-0 Tstrap: 0-0
Best Rating: 54 7/01 Donc 2m110y gd-fm

He tends to find his stride all too late, but unfortunately that stride is usually pretty slow. He did win a Doncaster amateur riders' event in July, but that victory was purely down to an enterprising ride.

Classic Defence (IRE)

80(78) (6)**40**

8-y-o b g Cyrano De Bergerac-My Alanna (Dalsaan)
B J Llewellyn The Welsh Valleys Syndicate

Placings:000/103120B/0/303500-0 **(1367)**
2001: 9^{0}G

	Starts	1st	2nd	3rd	Win & Pl
Career Total (Turf)	16	2	1	3	8907
Career Total (AW)	2	0	0	0	

74 6/96 Gdwd 1m2f D(0-85)H GD £3984
62 4/96 Muss 1m16y F GD £2576
Total win prize-money £6562

Going (Turf): Sf: 0-1 GS: 0-0 **Gd: 2-6** GF: 0-9 Fm: 0-0
Distance: 5f/6f: 0-1 7f-8f: 0-2 **9f-13f: 2-14** 14f+: 0-1
Track : LH: 0-9 **RH: 2-6 Tight: 2-9** Gall: 0-0
Aids: Bl: 0-0 Vi: 0-0 Tstrap: 0-0
Best Rating: 62 4/96 Muss 1m16y G

Classic Eagle

90(95) (37)**30**

8-y-o b g Unfuwain (USA)-La Lutine (My Swallow)
Pat Mitchell Steve Rees Racing Classic Eagle

Placings:1/0600640/00/004/000540050-600L **(3727)**
2001: 12^{6}GF, 12^{0}GF, 12^{0}GF, 14^{L}GS

	Starts	1st	2nd	3rd	Win & Pl
Career Total (Turf)	24	1	0	0	4722
Career Total (AW)	3	0	0	0	0

91 10/95 Chep 1m14y D SFT £3855
Total win prize-money £3855

Going (Turf): Sf: 1-1 GS: 0-3 Gd: 0-9 GF: 0-9 Fm: 0-2
Distance: 5f/6f: 0-0 7f-8f: 0-4 **9f-13f: 1-17** 14f+: 0-6
Track : LH: 0-16 RH: 0-7 Tight: 0-13 Gall: 0-1
Aids: Bl: 0-0 Vi: 0-3 Tstrap: 0-0
Best Rating: 30 6/01 Sals 1m4f gd-fm

Classic Manoeuvre (USA)

(80) (36)

6-y-o ch g Sky Classic (CAN)-Maid Of Honor (USA) (Blushing Groom (FR))
J M Bradley Paul Morgan

Placings:4420/43332003/0/00 **(0689)**
2001: 8^{0}SD, 11^{0}SD

	Starts	1st	2nd	3rd	Win & Pl
Career Total (Turf)	12	0	2	3	6898
Career Total (AW)	3	0	0	1	419

Going (Turf): Sf: 0-0 GS: 0-2 Gd: 0-7 GF: 0-3 Fm: 0-0
Distance: 5f/6f: 0-0 7f-8f: 0-5 9f-13f: 0-10 14f+: 0-0
Track : LH: 0-7 RH: 0-5 Tight: 0-7 Gall: 0-0
Aids: Bl: 0-0 Vi: 0-2 Tstrap: 0-0
Best Rating: 36 4/01 Ling 1m stand

Classic Millennium

98 **46**

3-y-o b f Midyan (USA)-Classic Colleen (IRE) (Sadler's Wells (USA))
Pat Mitchell Classic Bloodstock Plc

Placings:00000-0034300050535 **(5557)**
2001: 8^{0}GF, 11^{0}F, 8^{3}GF, 9^{4}GF, 10^{3}GF, 10^{0}G, 10^{0}G, 7^{0}GF, 9^{5}G, 8^{0}G, 9^{5}S, 11^{3}S, 14^{5}S

	Starts	1st	2nd	3rd	Win & Pl
Career Total (Turf)	18	0	0	3	1990

Going (Turf): Sf: 0-4 GS: 0-0 Gd: 0-5 GF: 0-8 Fm: 0-1
Distance: 5f/6f: 0-2 7f-8f: 0-5 9f-13f: 0-10 14f+: 0-1
Track : LH: 0-7 RH: 0-4 Tight: 0-3 Gall: 0-2
Aids: Bl: 0-0 Vi: 0-0 Tstrap: 0-0
Best Rating: 47 9/01 Nott 1m1f213y good

Classical Waltz (IRE)

94 **41**

3-y-o ch f In The Wings-Fascination Waltz (Shy Groom (USA))
J J Sheehan (M R Channon 13/7) Mrs Christina Dowling

Placings:4560506 **(5101)**
2001: 8^{4}F, 6^{5}GF, 9^{6}GF, 10^{0}GF, 11^{5}GF, 11^{0}G, 9^{6}GS

	Starts	1st	2nd	3rd	Win & Pl
Career Total (Turf)	7	0	0	0	529

Going (Turf): Sf: 0-0 GS: 0-1 Gd: 0-1 GF: 0-4 Fm: 0-1
Distance: 5f/6f: 0-0 7f-8f: 0-1 9f-13f: 0-6 14f+: 0-0
Track : LH: 0-3 RH: 0-2 Tight: 0-5 Gall: 0-0
Aids: Bl: 0-0 Vi: 0-0 Tstrap: 0-0
Best Rating: 46 6/01 Sals 6f212y gd-fm

Classy Act

99 **56**

3-y-o ch f Lycius (USA)-Stripanoora (Ahonoora)
A Berry C Shine, I Cunningham, J Lambert

Placings:2301610-005535060000 **(5626)**
2001: 7^{0}S, 7^{0}GF, 6^{5}GF, 7^{5}GF, 7^{3}GF, 6^{5}GF, 7^{0}GS, 6^{6}G, 7^{0}HY,

7^{0}G, 7^{0}HY, 8^{0}GS

	Starts	1st	2nd	3rd	Win & Pl
Career Total (Turf)	**19**	**2**	**1**	**2**	**8514**

70	10/00	Catt	7f	D(0-85)H	SFT	£5876

Total win prize-money £5876

Going (Turf): Sf: **2-7** GS: 0-3 Gd: 0-4 GF: 0-5 Fm: 0-0
Distance: 5f/6f: 0-5 **7f-8f: 2-13** 9f-13f: 0-1 14f+: 0-0
Track : **LH: 1-8** RH: 0-0 **Tight: 1-4** Gall: 0-0
Aids: Bl: 0-3 Vi: 0-0 Tstrap: 0-0
Best Rating: 68 7/01 Pont 6f gd-fm

Dual winner of ordinary nurseries on soft ground in the autumn as a juvenile. Has run some fair races on fast ground this season and now down to a fair mark.

Classy Clare

73 **15**

3-y-o b f Nicholas Bill-Clare's Choice (Pragmatic)
J M Bradley John Brookman

Placings:5000 **(4283)**
2001: 8^{5}F, 8^{0}GF, 7^{0}S, 7^{0}G

	Starts	1st	2nd	3rd	Win & Pl
Career Total (Turf)	**4**	**0**	**0**	**0**	**0**

Going (Turf): Sf: 0-1 GS: 0-0 Gd: 0-1 GF: 0-1 Fm: 0-1
Distance: 5f/6f: 0-0 7f-8f: 0-2 9f-13f: 0-2 14f+: 0-0
Track : LH: 0-1 RH: 0-1 Tight: 0-1 Gall: 0-0
Aids: Bl: 0-0 Vi: 0-0 Tstrap: 0-0
Best Rating: 15 8/01 Chep 7f16y soft

Classy Cleo (IRE)

92(107) (89)**62**

6-y-o b m Mujadil (USA)-Sybaris (Crowned Prince (USA))
P D Evans J E Abbey

Placings:23113025015321231**12/3520**04510001500022521**5/2434566**00502034300032050055523213**2/42300**00004640010030405**63504-3622**000000 **(1913)**
2001: 6^{3}SW, 6^{6}SD, 6^{2}SD, 6^{2}SD, 5^{0}HY, 6^{0}GF, 6^{0}SD, 6^{0}GF, 6^{0}F, 5^{0}GF

	Starts	1st	2nd	3rd	Win & Pl
Career Total (Turf)	**79**	**9**	**11**	**9**	**77632**
Career Total (AW)	**33**	**2**	**7**	**6**	**26490**

72	8/00	Ches	5f16y	D(0-85)H	GD	£5947
83	11/99	Rdcr	6f	C(0-90)H	G-S	£7652
93	11/98	Rdcr	6f	D(0-95)H	G-S	£7490
88	7/98	Ches	5f16y	C(0-95)H	G-F	£6417
87	5/98	Ches	5f16y	C(0-100)H	GD	£8367
105	11/97	Ling	5f	E	STD	£2765
86	11/97	Sthl	6f	E	STD	£2843
86	10/97	Yarm	5f43y	E(0-85)	FRM	£2961
68	9/97	Hayd	6f	F	G-S	£2885
79	4/97	Pont	5f	D	GD	£4013
79	4/97	Bevl	5f	F	G-F	£2742

Total win prize-money £54085

Going (Turf): Sf: 0-16 **GS: 3-9 Gd: 3-23** GF: 2-27 Fm: 1-4
Distance: **5f/6f: 11-93** 7f-8f: 0-19 9f-13f: 0-0 14f+: 0-0
Track : **LH: 6-58** RH: 0-4 **Tight: 4-44** Gall: 0-6
Aids: Bl: 0-0 Vi: 0-0 Tstrap: 0-0
Best Rating: 89 2/01 Wolv 6f stand

Vigorously campaigned - as are most of her stablemates - she is a tough sprint handicapper who acts on just about any surface, but does not win very often these days. A suitable mount for inexperienced riders, she often gets going too late.

Claudius Tertius

83(97) (40d)**17**

4-y-o b g Rudimentary (USA)-Sanctuary Cove (Habitat)
N B Mason (M E Sowersby 2/8) N B Mason

Placings:00000/000**34200-0000** **(3276)**
2001: 12^{0}SD, 8^{0}SD, 7^{0}GF, 8^{0}F

	Starts	1st	2nd	3rd	Win & Pl
Career Total (Turf)	**13**	**0**	**1**	**0**	**277**
Career Total (AW)	**4**	**0**	**0**	**1**	**318**

Going (Turf): Sf: 0-2 GS: 0-3 Gd: 0-3 GF: 0-4 Fm: 0-1
Distance: 5f/6f: 0-1 7f-8f: 0-10 9f-13f: 0-6 14f+: 0-0
Track : LH: 0-8 RH: 0-3 Tight: 0-4 Gall: 0-1
Aids: Bl: 0-2 Vi: 0-0 Tstrap: 0-0
Best Rating: 10 7/01 Bevl 7f100y gd-fm

Clear Crystal

(86) (15)**48**

4-y-o b f Zilzal (USA)-Shoot Clear (Bay Express)
R M H Cowell Bottisham Heath Stud

Placings:560/60066066005-00 **(0208)**
2001: 9^{0}SW, 5^{0}SD

	Starts	1st	2nd	3rd	Win & Pl
Career Total (Turf)	**11**	**0**	**0**	**0**	**0**
Career Total (AW)	**5**	**0**	**0**	**0**	**0**

Going (Turf): Sf: 0-1 GS: 0-2 Gd: 0-1 GF: 0-5 Fm: 0-1
Distance: 5f/6f: 0-2 7f-8f: 0-10 9f-13f: 0-3 14f+: 0-0
Track : LH: 0-9 RH: 0-0 Tight: 0-5 Gall: 0-1
Aids: Bl: 0-1 Vi: 0-2 Tstrap: 0-1
Best Rating: 10 7/01 Bevl 7f100y gd-fm

Clear Prospect (USA)

94 **44**

4-y-o b g Virginia Rapids (USA)-Cameo Performance (USA) (Be My Guest (USA))
M A Buckley C C Buckley

Placings:643/004040-000 **(2518)**
2001: 9^{0}G, 12^{0}F, 16^{0}F

	Starts	1st	2nd	3rd	Win & Pl
Career Total (Turf)	**12**	**0**	**0**	**1**	**1593**

Going (Turf): Sf: 0-0 GS: 0-2 Gd: 0-4 GF: 0-3 Fm: 0-3
Distance: 5f/6f: 0-0 7f-8f: 0-1 9f-13f: 0-10 14f+: 0-1
Track : LH: 0-11 RH: 0-1 Tight: 0-1 Gall: 0-5
Aids: Bl: 0-0 Vi: 0-0 Tstrap: 0-0
Best Rating: 44 5/01 Pont 1m4f8y firm

Clear Thought

69 **25**

2-y-o br f Mind Games-Awham (USA) (Lear Fan (USA))
A P Jarvis Jarvis Associates

Placings:00 **(5633)**
2001: 7^{0}S, 7^{0}G

	Starts	1st	2nd	3rd	Win & Pl
Career Total (Turf)	**2**	**0**	**0**	**0**	

Going (Turf): Sf: 0-1 GS: 0-0 Gd: 0-1 GF: 0-0 Fm: 0-0
Distance: 5f/6f: 0-0 7f-8f: 0-2 9f-13f: 0-0 14f+: 0-0
Track : LH: 0-2 RH: 0-0 Tight: 0-1 Gall: 0-1
Aids: Bl: 0-0 Vi: 0-0 Tstrap: 0-0
Best Rating: 25 11/01 Catt 7f good

Clearing

105 **118**

3-y-o b c Zafonic (USA)-Bright Spells (USA) (Alleged (USA))
J H M Gosden K Abdulla

Placings:2211-12 **(1401a)**
2001: 7^{1}S, 8^{2}G

	Starts	1st	2nd	3rd	Win & Pl
Career Total (Turf)	**6**	**3**	**3**	**0**	**83183**

115	4/01	NmkR	7f	A H	SFT	£17400
112	10/00	Newb	7f	A	SFT	£21000
89	9/00	Ches	7f2y	D	SFT	£3672

Total win prize-money £42073

Going (Turf): Sf: 3-3 GS: 0-1 Gd: 0-1 GF: 0-1 Fm: 0-0
Distance: 5f/6f: 0-0 **7f-8f: 3-6** 9f-13f: 0-0 14f+: 0-0
Track : **LH: 1-1** RH: 0-0 **Tight: 1-1** Gall: 0-0
Aids: Bl: 0-0 Vi: 0-0 Tstrap: 0-0
Best Rating: 118 5/01 Lonc 1m good

Improved with experience to win a Group Three on his final outing at two, and confirmed the promise when landing Listed handicap at Newmarket in April. Needed every yard of the seven furlongs to get on top and looked like a horse guaranteed to get a mile. Confirmed that with a good third to Noverre in the Poule d'Essai des Poulains at Longchamp. Put down due to an injury in the summer.

Cledlyn

41

3-y-o b g Awesome-Amany (IRE) (Waajib)
D Burchell Lyn Phillips

Placings:00 **(4085)**
2001: 7^{0}GS, 8^{0}GF

	Starts	1st	2nd	3rd	Win & Pl
Career Total (Turf)	**2**	**0**	**0**	**0**	

Going (Turf): Sf: 0-0 GS: 0-1 Gd: 0-0 GF: 0-1 Fm: 0-0
Distance: 5f/6f: 0-0 7f-8f: 0-1 9f-13f: 0-1 14f+: 0-0
Track : LH: 0-1 RH: 0-0 Tight: 0-0 Gall: 0-0
Aids: Bl: 0-0 Vi: 0-0 Tstrap: 0-0

Clever Girl (IRE)

105 **67**

4-y-o b f College Chapel-Damezao (Alzao (USA))
T D Easterby Peter C Bourke

Placings:653161215/4020004305000-0041105000100 **(5092)**
2001: 8^{0}G, 7^{0}GF, 8^{4}G, 8^{1}GF, 8^{1}GF, 8^{0}GF, 8^{5}GF, 8^{0}GF, 9^{0}G, 8^{0}G, 8^{1}F, 8^{0}G, 8^{0}GS

	Starts	1st	2nd	3rd	Win & Pl
Career Total (Turf)	**35**	**6**	**2**	**2**	**26850**

64	9/01	Muss	1m	F(0-60)H	FRM	£2555
66	6/01	Newc	1m	F(0-60)	G-F	£2702
67	6/01	Pont	1m4y	E(0-75)H	G-F	£4013
90	10/99	Ayr	1m	D(0-85)H	SFT	£3990
77	7/99	Ayr	7f	D H	GD	£3590
65	6/99	Pont	6f	E	GD	£3680

Total win prize-money £20532

Going (Turf): Sf: 1-10 GS: 0-3 **Gd: 2-10 GF: 2-10** Fm: 1-2
Distance: 5f/6f: 1-4 **7f-8f: 4-14** 9f-13f: 1-17 14f+: 0-0
Track : **LH: 5-17** RH: 1-9 Tight: 1-8 Gall: 1-4
Aids: Bl: 0-2 Vi: 0-0 Tstrap: 0-1
Best Rating: 67 6/01 Pont 1m4y gd-fm

She looked best on easy ground, but handled the faster surface well when scoring at Pontefract in June and followed up at Newcastle four days later. Out of form until winning a modest event at Musselburgh in September. Best over a mile.

Click-On (IRE)

101(101) (76)**82**

3-y-o b c Danehill (USA)-Bold Flawless (USA) (Bold Bidder)
J Noseda Ivan Allan

Placings:6-42 **(1129)**
2001: 6^{4}SD, 7^{2}G

	Starts	1st	2nd	3rd	Win & Pl
Career Total (Turf)	**2**	**0**	**1**	**0**	**1144**
Career Total (AW)	**1**	**0**	**0**	**0**	**270**

Going (Turf): Sf: 0-1 GS: 0-0 Gd: 0-1 GF: 0-0 Fm: 0-0
Distance: 5f/6f: 0-2 7f-8f: 0-1 9f-13f: 0-0 14f+: 0-0
Track : LH: 0-2 RH: 0-0 Tight: 0-2 Gall: 0-0
Aids: Bl: 0-0 Vi: 0-0 Tstrap: 0-0
Best Rating: 79 5/01 Thsk 7f good

Fair 6/7f maiden. Should win a race if kept to a realistic level.

Clifton Wood (IRE)

(76) (6)37
6-y-o b g Paris House-Millie's Lady (IRE) (Common Grounds)
J Gallagher Horses Away Racing Club

Placings:0/5600/600000-0 (0005)
2001: 8⁰SD

	Starts	1st	2nd	3rd	Win & Pl
Career Total (Turf)	9	0	0	0	0
Career Total (AW)	3	0	0	0	

Going (Turf): Sf: 0-0 GS: 0-1 Gd: 0-1 GF: 0-6 Fm: 0-1
Distance: 5f/6f: 0-2 7f-8f: 0-7 9f-13f: 0-3 14f+: 0-0
Track : LH: 0-7 RH: 0-1 Tight: 0-5 Gall: 0-0
Aids: Bl: 0-2 Vi: 0-0 Tstrap: 0-1

Climate (IRE)

96 74
2-y-o ch c Catrail (USA)-Burishki (Chilibang)
R Hannon Louis Stadler

Placings:23000 (5496)
2001: 6²GF, 6³GF, 6⁰GF, 6⁰G, 7⁰HY

	Starts	1st	2nd	3rd	Win & Pl
Career Total (Turf)	5	0	1	1	1981

Going (Turf): Sf: 0-1 GS: 0-0 Gd: 0-1 GF: 0-3 Fm: 0-0
Distance: 5f/6f: 0-3 7f-8f: 0-2 9f-13f: 0-0 14f+: 0-0
Track : LH: 0-0 RH: 0-0 Tight: 0-0 Gall: 0-0
Aids: Bl: 0-0 Vi: 0-0 Tstrap: 0-0
Best Rating: 74 6/01 Kemp 6f gd-fm

In the frame on his first two starts on fast ground.

Climate Control (USA)

89 64
2-y-o ch f Mt. Livermore (USA)-Descant (USA) (Nureyev (USA))
R Charlton K Abdulla

Placings:5 (2829)
2001: 6⁵GS

	Starts	1st	2nd	3rd	Win & Pl
Career Total (Turf)	1	0	0	0	0

Going (Turf): Sf: 0-0 GS: 0-1 Gd: 0-0 GF: 0-0 Fm: 0-0
Distance: 5f/6f: 0-1 7f-8f: 0-0 9f-13f: 0-0 14f+: 0-0
Track : LH: 0-0 RH: 0-0 Tight: 0-0 Gall: 0-0
Aids: Bl: 0-0 Vi: 0-0 Tstrap: 0-0
Best Rating: 64 7/01 Hayd 6f gd-sft

Climbing Rose (USA)

85 72
3-y-o b f Quest For Fame-Abeer (USA) (Dewan (USA))
A L T Moore (R Charlton 6/7) Mrs A L T Moore

Placings:53-0050 (5555a)
2001: 7⁰S, 6⁰GF, 6⁵GF, 7⁰SH

	Starts	1st	2nd	3rd	Win & Pl
Career Total (Turf)	6	0	0	1	496

Going (Turf): Sf: 0-2 GS: 0-0 Gd: 0-0 GF: 0-3 Fm: 0-0

Distance: 5f/6f: 0-2 7f-8f: 0-4 9f-13f: 0-0 14f+: 0-0
Track : LH: 0-0 RH: 0-1 Tight: 0-0 Gall: 0-1
Aids: Bl: 0-0 Vi: 0-0 Tstrap: 0-0
Best Rating: 46 6/01 Wind 6f gd-fm

Clipperton

86 63
2-y-o b c Mister Baileys-Theresita (GER) (Surumu (GER))
I A Balding Exors Of The Late Robert Hitchins

Placings:5 (2127)
2001: 6⁵GF

	Starts	1st	2nd	3rd	Win & Pl
Career Total (Turf)	1	0	0	0	245

Going (Turf): Sf: 0-0 GS: 0-0 Gd: 0-0 GF: 0-1 Fm: 0-0
Distance: 5f/6f: 0-0 7f-8f: 0-1 9f-13f: 0-0 14f+: 0-0
Track : LH: 0-0 RH: 0-0 Tight: 0-0 Gall: 0-0
Aids: Bl: 0-0 Vi: 0-0 Tstrap: 0-0
Best Rating: 63 6/01 Newb 6f8y gd-fm

Cliquey

(76) (41)
2-y-o b g Muhtarram (USA)-Meet Again (Lomond (USA))
J A Osborne Colin G R Booth

Placings:0 (5192)
2001: 8⁰SD

	Starts	1st	2nd	3rd	Win & Pl
Career Total (Turf)	0	0	0	0	
Career Total (AW)	1	0	0	0	

Going (Turf): Sf: 0-0 GS: 0-0 Gd: 0-0 GF: 0-0 Fm: 0-0
Distance: 5f/6f: 0-0 7f-8f: 0-0 9f-13f: 0-1 14f+: 0-0
Track : LH: 0-1 RH: 0-0 Tight: 0-1 Gall: 0-0
Aids: Bl: 0-0 Vi: 0-0 Tstrap: 0-0
Best Rating: 41 10/01 Wolv 1m100y stand

Cloondesh

(70) (5)43
3-y-o b g Forzando-Shalati (FR) (High Line)
R A Fahey Tommy Staunton

Placings:5000-00 (1010)
2001: 6⁰HY, 8⁰SD

	Starts	1st	2nd	3rd	Win & Pl
Career Total (Turf)	5	0	0	0	0
Career Total (AW)	1	0	0	0	

Going (Turf): Sf: 0-3 GS: 0-0 Gd: 0-1 GF: 0-1 Fm: 0-0
Distance: 5f/6f: 0-4 7f-8f: 0-2 9f-13f: 0-0 14f+: 0-0
Track : LH: 0-1 RH: 0-1 Tight: 0-0 Gall: 0-1
Aids: Bl: 0-0 Vi: 0-0 Tstrap: 0-0
Best Rating: 5 4/01 Sthl 1m stand

Cloone Express

68 52
2-y-o ch g Polar Falcon (USA)-Simple Logic (Aragon)
N A Callaghan Gallagher Equine Ltd

Placings:00 (5665)
2001: 6⁰GS, 6⁰HY

	Starts	1st	2nd	3rd	Win & Pl
Career Total (Turf)	2	0	0	0	

Going (Turf): Sf: 0-1 GS: 0-1 Gd: 0-0 GF: 0-0 Fm: 0-0
Distance: 5f/6f: 0-2 7f-8f: 0-0 9f-13f: 0-0 14f+: 0-0
Track : LH: 0-0 RH: 0-0 Tight: 0-0 Gall: 0-0
Aids: Bl: 0-0 Vi: 0-0 Tstrap: 0-0
Best Rating: 52 11/01 Wind 6f heavy

Clopton Green

96(98) (49)50
4-y-o b g Presidium-Silkstone Lady (Puissance)
J W Payne T W Morley

Placings:306/03335200645-1002000 (1185)
2001: 6¹SD, 6⁰SW, 7⁰SD, 6²SW, 6⁰SD, 6⁰SD, 6⁰GF

	Starts	1st	2nd	3rd	Win & Pl
Career Total (Turf)	3	0	0	0	
Career Total (AW)	18	1	2	4	4886

49 1/01 Sthl 6f E(0-70)H STD £2429
Total win prize-money £2429

Going (Turf): Sf: 0-1 GS: 0-0 Gd: 0-1 GF: 0-1 Fm: 0-0
Distance: 5f/6f: 1-19 7f-8f: 0-2 9f-13f: 0-0 14f+: 0-0
Track : LH: 1-17 RH: 0-0 Tight: 0-9 Gall: 0-0
Aids: Bl: 0-8 Vi: 0-0 Tstrap: 0-1
Best Rating: 49 2/01 Sthl 6f slow

Cloth Of Gold

97 69
4-y-o b g Barathea (IRE)-Bustinetta (Bustino)
Lady Herries Mrs H A Cameron-Rose

Placings:0/0-4 (5634)
2001: 11⁴G

	Starts	1st	2nd	3rd	Win & Pl
Career Total (Turf)	3	0	0	0	

Going (Turf): Sf: 0-2 GS: 0-0 Gd: 0-1 GF: 0-0 Fm: 0-0
Distance: 5f/6f: 0-0 7f-8f: 0-1 9f-13f: 0-2 14f+: 0-0
Track : LH: 0-1 RH: 0-1 Tight: 0-1 Gall: 0-0
Aids: Bl: 0-0 Vi: 0-0 Tstrap: 0-0
Best Rating: 53 11/01 Catt 1m3f214y good

Cloud Dancer

70
2-y-o b/br f Bishop Of Cashel-Summer Pageant (Chief's Crown (USA))
D J Coakley Cloud Dancer Racing

Placings:31 (4724)
2001: 6³F, 6¹GF

	Starts	1st	2nd	3rd	Win & Pl
Career Total (Turf)	2	1	0	1	3529

70 9/01 Wwck 6f21y E G-F £2954
Total win prize-money £2954

Going (Turf): Sf: 0-0 GS: 0-0 Gd: 0-0 GF: 1-1 Fm: 0-1
Distance: 5f/6f: 0-0 7f-8f: 1-2 9f-13f: 0-0 14f+: 0-0
Track : LH: 0-0 RH: 0-0 Tight: 0-0 Gall: 0-0
Aids: Bl: 0-0 Vi: 0-0 Tstrap: 0-0
Best Rating: 70 9/01 Wwck 6f21y gd-fm

Showed promise on her debut before getting off the mark in a six-furlong Warwick maiden. She should do even better over a longer trip.

Cloudy

69
3-y-o b f Ashkalani (IRE)-Shady Leaf (IRE) (Glint Of Gold)
Mrs Lydia Pearce (R F Johnson Houghton 5/7) James Furlong

Placings:560-00430 (4988)
2001: 10⁰GS, 8⁰G, 7⁴GF, 9³GF, 8⁰G

	Starts	1st	2nd	3rd	Win & Pl
Career Total (Turf)	8	0	0	1	645

Going (Turf): Sf: 0-0 GS: 0-1 Gd: 0-3 GF: 0-4 Fm: 0-0
Distance: 5f/6f: 0-2 7f-8f: 0-3 9f-13f: 0-3 14f+: 0-0
Track : LH: 0-3 RH: 0-1 Tight: 0-2 Gall: 0-0
Aids: Bl: 0-0 Vi: 0-0 Tstrap: 0-0

Best Rating: 69 6/01 Sand 1m14y good

Clownin Around

75(61) (3)**32**

2-y-o b f Mistertopogigo (IRE)-Pokey's Pet (Uncle Pokey)

M Mullineaux (B P J Baugh 24/3) D E Simpson

Placings:50 **(4797)**

2001: 5^{5}SD, 6^{0}G

	Starts	1st	2nd	3rd	Win & Pl
Career Total (Turf)	1	0	0	0	
Career Total (AW)	1	0	0	0	0

Going (Turf): Sf: 0-0 GS: 0-0 Gd: 0-1 GF: 0-0 Fm: 0-0
Distance: 5f/6f: 0-2 7f-8f: 0-0 9f-13f: 0-0 14f+: 0-0
Track : LH: 0-1 RH: 0-0 Tight: 0-1 Gall: 0-0
Aids: Bl: 0-0 Vi: 0-0 Tstrap: 0-0
Best Rating: 32 9/01 Ayr 6f good

Clytha Hill Lass

88 **63**

2-y-o ch f Bluegrass Prince (IRE)-Manhunt (Posse (USA))

J M Bradley Mrs Marion C Morgan

Placings:6005 **(3742)**

2001: 5^{6}G, 5^{0}HD, 6^{0}GF, 5^{5}S

	Starts	1st	2nd	3rd	Win & Pl
Career Total (Turf)	4	0	0	0	0

Going (Turf): Sf: 0-1 GS: 0-0 Gd: 0-1 GF: 0-1 Fm: 0-1
Distance: 5f/6f: 0-3 7f-8f: 0-1 9f-13f: 0-0 14f+: 0-0
Track : LH: 0-2 RH: 0-0 Tight: 0-0 Gall: 0-2
Aids: Bl: 0-0 Vi: 0-0 Tstrap: 0-0
Best Rating: 63 8/01 Chep 5f16y soft

Co Dot Uk

103(96) (54)**51**

3-y-o b g Distant Relative-Cubist (IRE) (Tale Gallery (USA))

T D Barron (K A Ryan 26/3) Nigel Shields

Placings:5301345020**236-03230**0202**0**660 **(3946)**

2001: 7^{0}SD, 7^{3}SW, 7^{2}SD, 7^{3}SD, 7^{0}SD, 8^{0}GF, 8^{2}GF, 8^{0}GF, 7^{2}G, 7^{0}GF, 7^{6}SD, 8^{6}GF, 9^{0}GS

	Starts	1st	2nd	3rd	Win & Pl
Career Total (Turf)	17	1	3	3	8011
Career Total (AW)	9	0	2	2	1626

66	5/00	Sthl	6f	D	HVY	£3523

Total win prize-money £3523

Going (Turf): Sf: 1-3 GS: 0-2 Gd: 0-5 GF: 0-5 Fm: 0-2
Distance: 5f/6f: 1-6 7f-8f: 0-16 9f-13f: 0-4 14f+: 0-0
Track : LH: 1-14 RH: 0-6 Tight: 0-7 Gall: 0-0
Aids: Bl: 0-13 Vi: 0-0 Tstrap: 0-0
Best Rating: 66 5/01 Muss 1m gd-fm

Co Vivante (IRE)

97 **77**

2-y-o b f Alzao (USA)-Springtime (IRE) (Generous (IRE))

R Hannon Fieldspring Racing

Placings:02400 **(5690)**

2001: 6^{0}GF, 5^{2}GF, 6^{4}GF, 6^{0}G, 7^{0}G

	Starts	1st	2nd	3rd	Win & Pl
Career Total (Turf)	5	0	1	0	1504

Going (Turf): Sf: 0-1 GS: 0-0 Gd: 0-1 GF: 0-3 Fm: 0-0
Distance: 5f/6f: 0-1 7f-8f: 0-4 9f-13f: 0-0 14f+: 0-0
Track : LH: 0-1 RH: 0-0 Tight: 0-0 Gall: 0-0
Aids: Bl: 0-0 Vi: 0-0 Tstrap: 0-0
Best Rating: 77 9/01 Sals 6f212y gd-fm

She ran with promise on her second start when finishing second of ten on good to firm, and again showed ability with a good fourth in a more competitive maiden. Appears suited by six furlongs on good to firm.

Coalition

82(85) (59)**47**

2-y-o b c Polish Precedent (USA)-Selection Board (Welsh Pageant)

Sir Mark Prescott Mrs F R Watts

Placings:000 **(5633)**

2001: 7^{0}S, 7^{0}SD, 7^{0}G

	Starts	1st	2nd	3rd	Win & Pl
Career Total (Turf)	2	0	0	0	
Career Total (AW)	1	0	0	0	

Going (Turf): Sf: 0-1 GS: 0-0 Gd: 0-1 GF: 0-0 Fm: 0-0
Distance: 5f/6f: 0-0 7f-8f: 0-3 9f-13f: 0-0 14f+: 0-0
Track : LH: 0-2 RH: 0-0 Tight: 0-2 Gall: 0-0
Aids: Bl: 0-0 Vi: 0-0 Tstrap: 0-0
Best Rating: 59 10/01 Wolv 7f stand

Coastal Bluff

109 **91**

9-y-o gr g Standaan (FR)-Combattente (Reform)

N P Littmoden Paul J Dixon

Placings:2/0154231/0111/51010/00/006000000/5021020404400-010000 **(3514)**

2001: 5^{0}GF, 5^{1}GF, 5^{0}GF, 5^{0}G, 5^{0}G, 5^{0}GF

	Starts	1st	2nd	3rd	Win & Pl
Career Total (Turf)	47	9	4	1	172864

91	5/01	Hayd	5f	B(0-105)H	G-F	£11258
80	6/00	Nott	5f13y	D(0-85)H	G-F	£3965
108	7/97	NmkJ	5f	C	GD	£5346
115	9/96	Ayr	6f	B H	G-F	£51630
101	8/96	Gdwd	6f	B H	G-F	£50687
91	7/96	York	5f	C(0-100)H	GD	£8285
88	10/95	Asct	5f	B(0-110)H	SFT	£15500
79	4/95	Nott	5f13y	F	G-F	£2888

Total win prize-money £149560

Going (Turf): Sf: 1-4 GS: 0-10 Gd: 3-13 **GF: 5-18** Fm: 0-2
Distance: 5f/6f: 9-47 7f-8f: 0-0 9f-13f: 0-0 14f+: 0-0
Track : LH: 0-1 RH: 0-1 Tight: 0-0 Gall: 0-2
Aids: Bl: 0-2 Vi: 0-0 Tstrap: 0-1
Best Rating: 91 5/01 Hayd 5f gd-fm

This fine stamp of a gelding dead-heated with Ya Malak in a sensational Nunthorpe in 1997, with rider Kevin Darley performing miracles after the bit broke early on. He then went through a quiet phase and joined Nick Littmoden, winning for him at Nottingham last season, but bounced back to something near his best with a fluent victory in a competitive handicap at Haydock in May. Best over five furlongs on fast ground.

Coccolona (IRE)

(106) (57)**50**

3-y-o b f Idris (IRE)-Fair Siobahn (Petingo)

D Haydn Jones Miss Gillian Byrne

Placings:4060-000**5016** **(5394)**

2001: 7^{0}GF, 6^{0}GF, 10^{0}GF, **8**^{5}SD, **12**^{0}SD, **11**^{1}SD, **12**^{6}SD

	Starts	1st	2nd	3rd	Win & Pl
Career Total (Turf)	7	0	0	0	232
Career Total (AW)	4	1	0	0	2345

57	10/01	Sthl	1m3f	F(0-60)	STD	£2345

Total win prize-money £2345

Going (Turf): Sf: 0-2 GS: 0-0 Gd: 0-2 GF: 0-3 Fm: 0-0
Distance: 5f/6f: 0-2 7f-8f: 0-4 **9f-13f: 1-5** 14f+: 0-0
Track : LH: 1-5 RH: 0-1 Tight: 0-3 Gall: 0-1
Aids: Bl: 0-0 Vi: 0-0 Tstrap: 0-0
Best Rating: 57 10/01 Sthl 1m3f stand

Got off the mark when dropped to claiming company on the All-Weather. Stays 11 furlongs.

Cockney Boss (IRE)

76 **32**

2-y-o b c General Monash (USA)-Cockney Ground (IRE) (Common Grounds)

B R Millman Rod Hamilton

Placings:00 **(4577)**

2001: 6^{0}F, 6^{0}G

	Starts	1st	2nd	3rd	Win & Pl
Career Total (Turf)	2	0	0	0	

Going (Turf): Sf: 0-0 GS: 0-0 Gd: 0-1 GF: 0-0 Fm: 0-1
Distance: 5f/6f: 0-1 7f-8f: 0-1 9f-13f: 0-0 14f+: 0-0
Track : LH: 0-0 RH: 0-0 Tight: 0-0 Gall: 0-0
Aids: Bl: 0-0 Vi: 0-0 Tstrap: 0-0
Best Rating: 32 8/01 Sals 6f212y firm

Coco De Mer

85(90) (44)**47**

4-y-o ch g Prince Sabo-Musica (Primo Dominie)

T Keddy (Miss D A McHale 31/1) Mrs Julie Mitchell

Placings:245210220/000000**0**60-500 **(4897)**

2001: 5^{5}SW, 5^{0}GF, 5^{0}GS

	Starts	1st	2nd	3rd	Win & Pl
Career Total (Turf)	18	1	4	0	11187
Career Total (AW)	3	0	0	0	0

70	7/99	Ches	5f16y	D	G-F	£4120

Total win prize-money £4120

Going (Turf): Sf: 0-2 GS: 0-3 Gd: 0-5 **GF: 1-8** Fm: 0-0
Distance: 5f/6f: 1-21 7f-8f: 0-0 9f-13f: 0-0 14f+: 0-0
Track : LH: 1-8 RH: 0-0 **Tight: 1-6** Gall: 0-0
Aids: Bl: 0-0 Vi: 0-0 Tstrap: 0-0
Best Rating: 40 1/01 Ling 5f slow

Coco Loco

112 **89**

4-y-o b f Bin Ajwaad (IRE)-Mainly Me (Huntingdale)

Mrs Lydia Pearce Mr & Mrs J Matthews

Placings:0/6006502111-2035 **(3810)**

2001: 16^{2}GS, 18^{0}GF, 14^{3}GF, 16^{5}G

	Starts	1st	2nd	3rd	Win & Pl
Career Total (Turf)	15	3	2	1	18268

87	11/00	Donc	2m110y	C(0-95)H	HVY	£8736
68	10/00	Yarm	1m6f17y	E(0-75)H	HVY	£2905
60	9/00	Catt	1m7f177y	F(0-65)H	SFT	£2572

Total win prize-money £14214

Going (Turf): Sf: 3-5 GS: 0-3 Gd: 0-2 GF: 0-5 Fm: 0-0
Distance: 5f/6f: 0-0 7f-8f: 0-2 9f-13f: 0-5 **14f+: 3-8**
Track : LH: 3-10 RH: 0-4 **Tight: 2-5** Gall: 1-3
Aids: Bl: 0-0 Vi: 0-0 Tstrap: 0-0
Best Rating: 89 4/01 Newb 2m gd-sft

A keen sort, she is a useful staying handicapper and scored a hat-trick in the autumn of 2000. She loves testing conditions and is best at up to two miles.

Coconut

84 **19**

5-y-o b g Shirley Heights-Magical Retreat (USA) (Sir Ivor)

W Clay M Braycotton

Placings:406/6P00 **(4079)**

2001: 9^{6}G, 12^{P}GF, 11^{0}G, 17^{0}GF

	Starts	1st	2nd	3rd	Win & Pl

Career Total (Turf) 7 0 0 0 257

Going (Turf): Sf: 0-0 GS: 0-0 Gd: 0-4 GF: 0-3 Fm: 0-0
Distance: 5f/6f: 0-0 7f-8f: 0-1 9f-13f: 0-5 14f+: 0-1
Track : LH: 0-4 RH: 0-2 Tight: 0-1 Gall: 0-0
Aids: Bl: 0-0 Vi: 0-0 Tstrap: 0-0
Best Rating: 19 8/01 Hayd 1m3f200y good

Cody

15

2-y-o ch c Zilzal (USA)-Ibtihaj (USA) (Raja Baba (USA))
R Hannon Exors Of The Late Earl Of Carnavon

Placings:00P (5417)
2001: 5⁰G, 6⁰HY, 7ᴾSD

	Starts	1st	2nd	3rd	Win & Pl
Career Total (Turf)	2	0	0	0	
Career Total (AW)	1	0	0	0	

Going (Turf): Sf: 0-1 GS: 0-0 Gd: 0-1 GF: 0-0 Fm: 0-0
Distance: 5f/6f: 0-2 7f-8f: 0-1 9f-13f: 0-0 14f+: 0-0
Track : LH: 0-1 RH: 0-0 Tight: 0-1 Gall: 0-0
Aids: Bl: 0-0 Vi: 0-0 Tstrap: 0-0
Best Rating: 15 5/01 Donc 5f good

Coffee Time (IRE)

82

2-y-o b f Efisio-Petula (Petong)
D J S Ffrench Davis Badgers Holt

Placings:5300245243 (5125)
2001: 5^0G, 5^3GF, 5^0GF, 5^0GF, 5^2S, 5^4GF, 5^5G, 5^2F, 5^4G, 5^3HY

	Starts	1st	2nd	3rd	Win & Pl
Career Total (Turf)	10	0	2	2	5635

Going (Turf): Sf: 0-2 GS: 0-0 Gd: 0-3 GF: 0-4 Fm: 0-1
Distance: 5f/6f: 0-10 7f-8f: 0-0 9f-13f: 0-0 14f+: 0-0
Track : LH: 0-3 RH: 0-0 Tight: 0-0 Gall: 0-3
Aids: Bl: 0-0 Vi: 0-0 Tstrap: 0-0
Best Rating: 82 10/01 Bath 5f161y good

A May foal, she came on a good deal for her debut, when running third in Listed event over the minimum trip at Beverley, but that was as good as it got and she became very disappointing.

Cold Climate

105 74+

6-y-o ch g Pursuit Of Love-Sharpthorne (USA) (Sharpen Up)
Bob Jones The Cold Climate Partnership

Placings:030000/0620502403130 0/5000405-12106 (3812)
2001: 6^1GF, 6^2G, 6^1GF, 6^0G, 6^6G

	Starts	1st	2nd	3rd	Win & Pl
Career Total (Turf)	32	3	3	3	27389

74	6/01	Rdcr	6f	C(0-90)H	G-F	£7442
58	5/01	Newb	6f8y	D(0-80)H	G-F	£7702
56	8/99	NmkJ	6f	D(0-85)H	GD	£4503

Total win prize-money £19649

Going (Turf): Sf: 0-5 GS: 0-5 Gd: 1-10 GF: 2-12 Fm: 0-0
Distance: 5f/6f: 2-24 7f-8f: 1-7 9f-13f: 0-1 14f+: 0-0
Track : LH: 0-6 RH: 0-7 Tight: 0-5 Gall: 0-5
Aids: Bl: 0-0 Vi: 0-6 Tstrap: 0-0
Best Rating: 74 6/01 Rdcr 6f gd-fm

Suited by six furlongs and fast ground, he returned from a nine-month break to win at Newbury in May and, despite a rise in the handicap,scored again at Redcar in June.

Coley

(92) (29)44

4-y-o ch f Pursuit Of Love-Cole Slaw (Absalom)
B A Pearce Miss J Webster

Placings:0100/35600000-00 (0067)
2001: 6^0SD, 6^0SD

	Starts	1st	2nd	3rd	Win & Pl
Career Total (Turf)	5	1	0	0	
Career Total (AW)	9	0	0	1	260

Going (Turf): Sf: 1-1 GS: 0-2 Gd: 0-2 GF: 0-0 Fm: 0-0
Distance: 5f/6f: 1-8 7f-8f: 0-5 9f-13f: 0-1 14f+: 0-0
Track : LH: 0-9 RH: 0-1 Tight: 0-8 Gall: 0-0
Aids: Bl: 0-6 Vi: 0-0 Tstrap: 0-0
Best Rating: 12 1/01 Ling 6f stand

Collard

102 78

3-y-o ch f Wolfhound (USA)-Collide (High Line)
H Candy Major M G Wyatt

Placings:6-126650 (5463)
2001: 8^1G, 8^2F, 9^6GF, 12^6GF, 10^5HY, 11^0G

	Starts	1st	2nd	3rd	Win & Pl
Career Total (Turf)	7	1	1	0	5680

67	5/01	Wind	1m67y	D	GD	£4361

Total win prize-money £4362

Going (Turf): Sf: 0-1 GS: 0-0 Gd: 1-3 GF: 0-2 Fm: 0-1
Distance: 5f/6f: 0-0 7f-8f: 0-1 9f-13f: 1-6 14f+: 0-0
Track : LH: 0-2 RH: 1-3 Tight: 1-4 Gall: 0-0
Aids: Bl: 0-0 Vi: 0-0 Tstrap: 0-0
Best Rating: 78 6/01 Nott 1m54y firm

Collectivity

94(92) (67)34

3-y-o b f Dr Devious (IRE)-Loch Quest (USA) (Lomond (USA))
J S Moore (B De Haan 3/8) Tidmarsh Racing Club

Placings:004-346000 (5084)
2001: 9^3SW, 12^4G, 16^6G, 7^0GF, 13^0F, 9^0S

	Starts	1st	2nd	3rd	Win & Pl
Career Total (Turf)	7	0	0	0	0
Career Total (AW)	2	0	0	1	596

Going (Turf): Sf: 0-2 GS: 0-0 Gd: 0-3 GF: 0-1 Fm: 0-1
Distance: 5f/6f: 0-1 7f-8f: 0-3 9f-13f: 0-3 14f+: 0-2
Track : LH: 0-7 RH: 0-0 Tight: 0-3 Gall: 0-0
Aids: Bl: 0-1 Vi: 0-0 Tstrap: 0-0
Best Rating: 55 7/01 Chep 1m4f23y good

College Blue (IRE)

90(103) (42)40

5-y-o b m College Chapel-Mitsubishi Centre (IRE) (Thatching)
Miss Sheena West Gerald West

Placings:220503/2/2001005-3000 (3151)
2001: 5^3F, 5^0GF, 10^0GF, 7^0GS

	Starts	1st	2nd	3rd	Win & Pl
Career Total (Turf)	7	0	2	1	2935
Career Total (AW)	11	1	2	1	4395

60	2/00	Ling	6f	F(0-60)	STD	£2081

Total win prize-money £2082

Going (Turf): Sf: 0-0 GS: 0-2 Gd: 0-0 GF: 0-4 Fm: 0-1
Distance: 5f/6f: 1-14 7f-8f: 0-3 9f-13f: 0-1 14f+: 0-0
Track : LH: 1-13 RH: 0-2 Tight: 1-12 Gall: 0-2
Aids: Bl: 0-1 Vi: 0-3 Tstrap: 0-0
Best Rating: 40 5/01 Brig 5f213y firm

College City (IRE)

79(65) (9)54

2-y-o b c College Chapel-Polish Crack (IRE) (Polish Patriot (USA))
T D Easterby The Riponians

Placings:00050 (4533)
2001: 5^0S, 5^0SD, 7^0F, 8^5G, 7^0GF

	Starts	1st	2nd	3rd	Win & Pl
Career Total (Turf)	4	0	0	0	0
Career Total (AW)	1	0	0	0	

Going (Turf): Sf: 0-1 GS: 0-0 Gd: 0-1 GF: 0-1 Fm: 0-1
Distance: 5f/6f: 0-2 7f-8f: 0-2 9f-13f: 0-1 14f+: 0-0
Track : LH: 0-1 RH: 0-0 Tight: 0-0 Gall: 0-1
Aids: Bl: 0-1 Vi: 0-0 Tstrap: 0-0
Best Rating: 54 8/01 Newc 1m3y good

College Dean (IRE)

93 (21)31

5-y-o ch g College Chapel-Phyllode (Pharly (FR))
P Monteith Burns Partnership

Placings:4630106/5000000000/60000-0000 (4108)
2001: 6^0G, 7^0GS, 9^0GS, 8^0S

	Starts	1st	2nd	3rd	Win & Pl
Career Total (Turf)	25	1	0	1	3918
Career Total (AW)	1	0	0	0	

70	8/98	Haml	6f5y	E H	SFT	£3192

Total win prize-money £3193

Going (Turf): Sf: 1-5 GS: 0-5 Gd: 0-9 GF: 0-6 Fm: 0-0
Distance: 5f/6f: 0-9 7f-8f: 1-10 9f-13f: 0-7 14f+: 0-0
Track : LH: 0-5 RH: 0-9 Tight: 0-7 Gall: 0-1
Aids: Bl: 0-0 Vi: 0-5 Tstrap: 0-2
Best Rating: 31 7/01 Haml 6f5y good

College Delinquent (IRE)

92 76

2-y-o br g College Chapel-St Cyr Aty (IRE) (Ela-Mana-Mou)
B J Meehan Martin Collins

Placings:00 (5290)
2001: 6^0GF, 7^0S

	Starts	1st	2nd	3rd	Win & Pl
Career Total (Turf)	2	0	0	0	

Going (Turf): Sf: 0-1 GS: 0-0 Gd: 0-0 GF: 0-1 Fm: 0-0
Distance: 5f/6f: 0-0 7f-8f: 0-2 9f-13f: 0-0 14f+: 0-0
Track : LH: 0-0 RH: 0-0 Tight: 0-0 Gall: 0-0
Aids: Bl: 0-0 Vi: 0-0 Tstrap: 0-0
Best Rating: 76 9/01 Newb 6f8y gd-fm

College Fact

45(59)

3-y-o b g So Factual (USA)-Starfida (Soviet Star (USA))
Mrs C A Dunnett Mrs Christine Dunnett

Placings:0-00000 (5278)
2001: 8^0SD, 6^0SD, 6^0GF, 5^0S, 9^0GS

	Starts	1st	2nd	3rd	Win & Pl
Career Total (Turf)	4	0	0	0	
Career Total (AW)	2	0	0	0	

Going (Turf): Sf: 0-1 GS: 0-1 Gd: 0-1 GF: 0-1 Fm: 0-0
Distance: 5f/6f: 0-2 7f-8f: 0-3 9f-13f: 0-1 14f+: 0-0
Track : LH: 0-3 RH: 0-1 Tight: 0-1 Gall: 0-0
Aids: Bl: 0-1 Vi: 0-1 Tstrap: 0-0

College Hippie

95(84) (40)**77?**
2-y-o b f Cosmonaut-Eccentric Dancer (Rambo Dancer (CAN))
J F Coupland J F Coupland

Placings:562325644 **(4777)**
2001: 5^{5}GF, 5^{6}SD, 5^{2}GF, 5^{3}G, 5^{2}GF, 5^{5}G, 5^{6}GF, 5^{4}GF, 5^{4}G

	Starts	1st	2nd	3rd	Win & Pl
Career Total (Turf)	8	0	2	1	4372
Career Total (AW)	1	0	0	0	0

Going (Turf): Sf: 0-0 GS: 0-0 Gd: 0-3 GF: 0-5 Fm: 0-0
Distance: 5f/6f: 0-9 7f-8f: 0-0 9f-13f: 0-0 14f+: 0-0
Track : LH: 0-1 RH: 0-0 Tight: 0-0 Gall: 0-0
Aids: Bl: 0-0 Vi: 0-0 Tstrap: 0-0
Best Rating: 77 7/01 Yarm 5f43y gd-fm

College King (IRE)

80 **26**
5-y-o b g College Chapel-Genetta (Green Desert (USA))
M Brittain Mel Brittain

Placings:045/00-0000 **(4031)**
2001: 8^{0}HY, 7^{0}S, 7^{0}GF, 10^{0}G

	Starts	1st	2nd	3rd	Win & Pl
Career Total (Turf)	9	0	0	0	261

Going (Turf): Sf: 0-2 GS: 0-1 Gd: 0-3 GF: 0-3 Fm: 0-0
Distance: 5f/6f: 0-0 7f-8f: 0-6 9f-13f: 0-3 14f+: 0-0
Track : LH: 0-5 RH: 0-2 Tight: 0-3 Gall: 0-1
Aids: Bl: 0-0 Vi: 0-0 Tstrap: 0-0
Best Rating: 26 6/01 Bevl 7f100y gd-fm

College Maid (IRE)

108 **72**
4-y-o b f College Chapel-Maid Of Mourne (Fairy King (USA))
J S Goldie S Bruce

Placings:04221234340056/2002112501005004002010-00030532003125030500030360 **(5535)**
2001: 7^{0}GS, 5^{0}S, 5^{0}S, 6^{3}G, 6^{0}GF, 7^{5}GF, 6^{3}GF, 6^{2}G, 7^{0}GF, 5^{0}GF, 6^{3}S, 5^{1}GS, 6^{2}GS, 5^{5}GF, 6^{0}GF, 6^{3}F, 5^{0}G, 6^{5}G, 5^{0}HY, 5^{0}G, 6^{0}G, 5^{3}GS, 5^{0}S, 6^{3}GS, 6^{6}HY, 7^{0}S

	Starts	1st	2nd	3rd	Win & Pl
Career Total (Turf)	62	6	9	8	50652

71	7/01	Ayr	5f	C(0-90)H	G-S	£6987
69	10/00	Newc	6f	C(0-95)H	HVY	£7117
71	6/00	Ayr	5f	D(0-85)H	GD	£7072
60	6/00	Catt	5f212y	E(0-70)H	GD	£3150
59	5/00	Ripn	6f	E(0-70)H	GD	£3354
61	5/99	Muss	5f	F	G-F	£2654

Total win prize-money £30336

Going (Turf): Sf: 1-19 GS: 1-13 **Gd: 3-12** GF: 1-12 Fm: 0-6
Distance: **5f/6f: 6-51** 7f-8f: 0-11 9f-13f: 0-0 14f+: 0-0
Track : **LH: 1-6** RH: 0-1 **Tight: 1-2** Gall: 0-2
Aids: Bl: 0-0 Vi: 0-0 Tstrap: 0-0
Best Rating: 77 8/01 Thsk 6f firm

Effective on all types of ground, she is a tough individual who tries hard. Suited by five or six furlongs, she has looked held by the Handicapper since winning at Ayr in July.

College Princess

94(93) (18)**28**
7-y-o b m Anshan-Tinkers Fairy (Myjinski (USA))
Mrs C A Dunnett Mrs Christine Dunnett

Placings:000/30042315300/30000/40540/40000-00006000 **(2730)**
2001: 5^{0}SD, 5^{0}SD, 6^{0}SW, 5^{0}SD, 6^{6}SD, 8^{0}GF, 5^{0}GF, 6^{0}GF

	Starts	1st	2nd	3rd	Win & Pl
Career Total (Turf)	26	1	1	3	4594
Career Total (AW)	11	0	0	1	285

46	7/97	Rdcr	5f	G(0-60)H	G-F	£2337

Total win prize-money £2338

Going (Turf): Sf: 0-1 GS: 0-3 Gd: 0-4 **GF: 1-14** Fm: 0-4
Distance: **5f/6f: 1-30** 7f-8f: 0-5 9f-13f: 0-2 14f+: 0-0
Track : LH: 0-17 RH: 0-1 Tight: 0-7 Gall: 0-4
Aids: Bl: 0-5 Vi: 0-0 Tstrap: 0-0
Best Rating: 23 6/01 Wwck 5f gd-fm

College Queen

(88) (61)**34**
3-y-o b f Lugana Beach-Eccentric Dancer (Rambo Dancer (CAN))
J G Given J F Coupland

Placings:044-50 **(0122)**
2001: 6^{5}SD, 6^{0}SW

	Starts	1st	2nd	3rd	Win & Pl
Career Total (Turf)	1	0	0	0	
Career Total (AW)	4	0	0	0	0

Going (Turf): Sf: 0-1 GS: 0-0 Gd: 0-0 GF: 0-0 Fm: 0-0
Distance: 5f/6f: 0-5 7f-8f: 0-0 9f-13f: 0-0 14f+: 0-0
Track : LH: 0-4 RH: 0-0 Tight: 0-1 Gall: 0-0
Aids: Bl: 0-0 Vi: 0-0 Tstrap: 0-0
Best Rating: 45 1/01 Sthl 6f stand

College Rock

103(98) (49d)**73**
4-y-o ch g Rock Hopper-Sea Aura (Roi Soleil)
R Brotherton Ms Gerardine P O'Reilly

Placings:00220033/0426306414613042430-002140003362004 **(5019)**
2001: 8^{0}SD, 8^{0}S, 7^{2}GS, 7^{1}G, 8^{4}GF, 8^{0}G, 8^{0}SD, 8^{0}SD, 8^{3}GF, 8^{3}GF, 10^{6}GF, 8^{2}G, 8^{0}GF, 8^{0}GF, 8^{4}S

	Starts	1st	2nd	3rd	Win & Pl
Career Total (Turf)	35	3	6	7	18102
Career Total (AW)	7	0	0	0	0

70	5/01	Brig	7f214y	E(0-75)H	GD	£2989
60	8/00	Leic	1m8y	F	G-F	£2520
60	7/00	Chep	1m14y	F	G-F	£2303

Total win prize-money £7812

Going (Turf): Sf: 0-5 GS: 0-5 Gd: 1-9 **GF: 2-12** Fm: 0-4
Distance: 5f/6f: 0-3 7f-8f: 1-14 **9f-13f: 2-25** 14f+: 0-0
Track : **LH: 1-24** RH: 0-5 Tight: 0-9 Gall: 0-0
Aids: Bl: 0-1 **Vi: 3-30** Tstrap: 0-0
Best Rating: 73 8/01 Bath 1m5y good

Has won three races at around a mile, the last of which was back in May 2001, has run well since then, but a drop in the weights is needed before he returns to winning ways. Suited by a mile on good and good to firm.

College Star

(87) (31)**32**
3-y-o b g Lugana Beach-Alis Princess (Sayf El Arab (USA))
J F Coupland J F Coupland

Placings:050-06500000 **(5173)**
2001: 7^{0}GF, 8^{6}SD, 9^{5}SD, 7^{0}GF, 8^{0}F, 10^{0}G, 7^{0}GF, 8^{0}GS

	Starts	1st	2nd	3rd	Win & Pl
Career Total (Turf)	8	0	0	0	0
Career Total (AW)	3	0	0	0	0

Going (Turf): Sf: 0-1 GS: 0-1 Gd: 0-1 GF: 0-4 Fm: 0-1
Distance: 5f/6f: 0-2 7f-8f: 0-6 9f-13f: 0-3 14f+: 0-0
Track : LH: 0-7 RH: 0-2 Tight: 0-3 Gall: 0-0
Aids: Bl: 0-0 Vi: 0-1 Tstrap: 0-0
Best Rating: 32 10/01 Pont 1m4y gd-sft

Colliers Treasure

(67) (4)
4-y-o b f Manhal-Indian Treasure (IRE) (Treasure Kay)
J S Moore Chasing Rainbows Partnership

Placings:0-0 **(0223)**
2001: 12^{0}SD

	Starts	1st	2nd	3rd	Win & Pl
Career Total (Turf)	1	0	0	0	
Career Total (AW)	1	0	0	0	

Going (Turf): Sf: 0-1 GS: 0-0 Gd: 0-0 GF: 0-0 Fm: 0-0
Distance: 5f/6f: 0-0 7f-8f: 0-0 9f-13f: 0-2 14f+: 0-0
Track : LH: 0-2 RH: 0-0 Tight: 0-2 Gall: 0-0
Aids: Bl: 0-0 Vi: 0-0 Tstrap: 0-0
Best Rating: 4 2/01 Ling 1m4f stand

Colline De Feu

(104) (55)**46d**
4-y-o ch f Sabrehill (USA)-Band Of Fire (USA) (Chief's Crown (USA))
Mrs P Sly David L Bayliss

Placings:040001-006600 **(1315)**
2001: 16^{0}SD, 16^{0}SW, 14^{6}SW, 14^{6}S, 14^{0}HY, 14^{0}SD

	Starts	1st	2nd	3rd	Win & Pl
Career Total (Turf)	6	0	0	0	307
Career Total (AW)	6	1	0	0	2751

55	11/00	Sthl	1m6f	E(0-75)H	STD	£2751

Total win prize-money £2751

Going (Turf): Sf: 0-3 GS: 0-1 Gd: 0-1 GF: 0-1 Fm: 0-0
Distance: 5f/6f: 0-0 7f-8f: 0-0 9f-13f: 0-4 **14f+: 1-8**
Track : **LH: 1-10** RH: 0-1 Tight: 0-2 Gall: 0-0
Aids: Bl: 0-0 Vi: 0-0 Tstrap: 0-0
Best Rating: 38 2/01 Sthl 1m6f slow

Colne Valley Amy

100 **65d**
4-y-o b f Mizoram (USA)-Panchellita (USA) (Pancho Villa (USA))
G L Moore (W J Musson 11/8) Colne Valley Golf (deluxeward Ltd)

Placings:000/2114325100-000005 **(4667)**
2001: 9^{0}GF, 9^{0}GF, 8^{0}GF, 10^{0}GS, 8^{0}G, 8^{5}GF

	Starts	1st	2nd	3rd	Win & Pl
Career Total (Turf)	19	3	2	1	15190

69	9/00	Sand	1m14y	D(0-85)H	G-F	£7410
61	7/00	Sals	1m	F(0-70)H	GD	£2793
54	6/00	Sals	1m	F(0-70)H	G-F	£2716

Total win prize-money £12919

Going (Turf): Sf: 0-3 GS: 0-1 Gd: 1-3 **GF: 2-10** Fm: 0-2
Distance: 5f/6f: 0-1 **7f-8f: 2-11** 9f-13f: 1-7 14f+: 0-0
Track : LH: 0-3 **RH: 1-7** Tight: 0-1 Gall: 0-1
Aids: Bl: 0-0 Vi: 0-0 Tstrap: 0-0
Best Rating: 52 7/01 Kemp 1m1f gd-fm

In fine form in 2000, winning three times over a mile. Acts on fast ground. Failed to find her form this term.

Colombe D'Or

(98) (52)**44d**
4-y-o gr g Petong-Deep Divide (Nashwan (USA))
M C Chapman Rasen Goes Racing

Placings:0006/2260003420-635411200030030400 **(5046)**
2001: 11^{6}SD, 7^{3}SD, 8^{5}SD, 8^{4}SW, 8^{1}SW, 8^{1}SD, 8^{2}SD, 10^{0}S, 11^{0}SD, 8^{0}SW, 8^{3}SD, 8^{0}GF, 8^{0}GF, 8^{3}SD, 8^{0}SD, 8^{4}GS, 10^{0}GF, 11^{0}SD

	Starts	1st	2nd	3rd	Win & Pl
Career Total (Turf)	12	0	0	1	602
Career Total (AW)	20	2	4	3	7146

50	3/01	Wolv	1m100y	G(0-60)H	STD	£1386
47	2/01	Sthl	1m	F(0-60)H	SLW	£2212

Total win prize-money £3598

Going (Turf): Sf: 0-1 GS: 0-3 Gd: 0-4 GF: 0-4 Fm: 0-0
Distance: 5f/6f: 0-2 7f-8f: 1-15 9f-13f: 1-14 14f+: 0-1
Track : **LH: 2-23** RH: 0-4 **Tight: 1-5** Gall: 0-3
Aids: Bl: 0-2 Vi: 0-0 Tstrap: 0-0
Best Rating: 55 2/01 Sthl 1m slow

Colonel Cotton (IRE)

99 **77**
2-y-o b c Royal Applause-Cutpurse Moll (Green Desert (USA))
N A Callaghan Jeremy Gompertz

Placings:046232 **(5689)**
2001: 6^0GS, 6^4G, 5^6GF, 6^2G, 7^3HY, 6^2S

	Starts	1st	2nd	3rd	Win & Pl
Career Total (Turf)	6	0	2	1	5293

Going (Turf): Sf: 0-2 GS: 0-1 Gd: 0-2 GF: 0-1 Fm: 0-0
Distance: 5f/6f: 0-3 7f-8f: 0-3 9f-13f: 0-0 14f+: 0-0
Track : LH: 0-1 RH: 0-0 Tight: 0-0 Gall: 0-0
Aids: Bl: 0-0 Vi: 0-0 Tstrap: 0-0
Best Rating: 87 8/01 Yarm 6f3y good

A half-brother to Inch Pincher. Still a maiden but has run some good races including in a competitive handicap at Ascot, and a maiden at Doncaster in November. Suited by cut in the ground.

Colonel Custer

(102) (53)**26**
6-y-o ch g Komaite (USA)-Mohican (Great Nephew)
R Brotherton Binding Matters Ltd

Placings:010/35250/5015605001/31005065040600002 3-111164002205045 **(5615)**
2001: 12^1SD, 12^1SD, 11^1SW, 9^1SD, 8^6SD, 12^4SD, 12^0SW, 10^0GF, 11^2SD, 11^2SD, 11^0GS, 9^5SW, 12^0SD, 11^4SD, 12^5SD

	Starts	1st	2nd	3rd	Win & Pl
Career Total (Turf)	10	0	0	0	0
Career Total (AW)	41	8	4	3	18613

57	1/01	Wolv	1m1f79y	G(0-65)H	STD	£1407
50	1/01	Sthl	1m3f	G	SLW	£1876
53	1/01	Sthl	1m4f	G	STD	£1876
34	1/01	Wolv	1m4f	G	STD	£1477
54	1/00	Wolv	1m4f	G(0-60)H	STD	£1545
48	12/99	Wolv	1m4f	G	STD	£1945
60	2/99	Sthl	1m3f	F(0-65)H	STD	£2431
61	7/97	Sthl	6f	F	STD	£2277

Total win prize-money £14836

Going (Turf): Sf: 0-2 GS: 0-4 Gd: 0-2 GF: 0-1 Fm: 0-1
Distance: 5f/6f: 1-4 7f-8f: 0-10 **9f-13f: 7-37** 14f+: 0-0
Track : **LH: 8-48** RH: 0-1 **Tight: 4-25** Gall: 0-1
Aids: Bl: 0-3 **Vi: 1-6** Tstrap: 0-0
Best Rating: 57 1/01 Wolv 1m1f79y stand

Plating-class handicapper, best on Fibresand, stays 12 furlongs.

Colonel Kozando

82 **57**
2-y-o b c Komaite (USA)-Times Zando (Forzando)
Mrs G S Rees Tom Murray

Placings:5500 **(5087)**
2001: 6^5GS, 7^5G, 7^0GF, 7^0GS

	Starts	1st	2nd	3rd	Win & Pl
Career Total (Turf)	4	0	0	0	0

Going (Turf): Sf: 0-0 GS: 0-2 Gd: 0-1 GF: 0-1 Fm: 0-0
Distance: 5f/6f: 0-0 7f-8f: 0-4 9f-13f: 0-0 14f+: 0-0
Track : LH: 0-1 RH: 0-0 Tight: 0-0 Gall: 0-1
Aids: Bl: 0-0 Vi: 0-0 Tstrap: 0-0
Best Rating: 57 8/01 Muss 7f30y good

Colonel Kurtz (USA)

93(63) (12)**35**
3-y-o b g Slip Anchor-Rustaka (USA) (Riverman (USA))
John Berry The 1997 Partnership

Placings:000-0000 **(3182)**
2001: 8^0F, 10^0GF, 12^0GF, 12^0GS

	Starts	1st	2nd	3rd	Win & Pl
Career Total (Turf)	6	0	0	0	
Career Total (AW)	1	0	0	0	

Going (Turf): Sf: 0-2 GS: 0-1 Gd: 0-0 GF: 0-2 Fm: 0-1
Distance: 5f/6f: 0-1 7f-8f: 0-3 9f-13f: 0-3 14f+: 0-0
Track : LH: 0-4 RH: 0-1 Tight: 0-2 Gall: 0-1
Aids: Bl: 0-0 Vi: 0-0 Tstrap: 0-0
Best Rating: 35 6/01 Rdcr 1m2f gd-fm

Colonel Mustard

(106) (62)**55**
5-y-o ch g Keen-Juliet Bravo (Glow (USA))
P G Murphy (J R Fanshawe 2/7) The Golden Anorak Partnership

Placings:6010/006100/003040051 **(5613)**
2001: 8^0GF, 10^0GF, 8^3GF, 8^0GF, 9^4GF, 10^0GF, 8^0GF, 8^5GS, 9^1SD

	Starts	1st	2nd	3rd	Win & Pl
Career Total (Turf)	18	2	0	1	6546
Career Total (AW)	1	1	0	0	2408

62	11/01	Wolv	1m1f79y	F(0-60)H	STD	£2408
75	6/99	Wind	1m2f7y	D(0-80)H	G-F	£3889
83	8/98	Ling	7f140y	F	FRM	£2077

Total win prize-money £8375

Going (Turf): Sf: 0-0 GS: 0-1 Gd: 0-4 **GF: 1-11 Fm: 1-2**
Distance: 5f/6f: 0-1 7f-8f: 1-7 **9f-13f: 2-11** 14f+: 0-0
Track : **LH: 1-5** RH: 0-6 **Tight: 2-5** Gall: 0-2
Aids: Bl: 0-0 Vi: 0-2 Tstrap: 0-0
Best Rating: 65 5/01 Gdwd 1m gd-fm

He had been mainly disappointing on turf, but his sire's progeny tend to perform significantly better on sand and he took to the surface on his All-Weather debut. Acts on fast ground. Has worn a visor.

Colonel Sam

98(99) (32)**34**
5-y-o b g Puissance-Indian Summer (Young Generation)
S R Bowring W I Derry

Placings:3550/506066002000/000050040L30004-000000505 **(3702)**
2001: 6^0SW, 5^0SD, 6^0SD, 5^0SD, 5^0SD, 6^0F, 5^5G, 6^0F, 5^5G

	Starts	1st	2nd	3rd	Win & Pl
Career Total (Turf)	27	0	1	2	2163
Career Total (AW)	14	0	0	0	0

Going (Turf): Sf: 0-0 GS: 0-3 Gd: 0-11 GF: 0-9 Fm: 0-4
Distance: 5f/6f: 0-33 7f-8f: 0-6 9f-13f: 0-2 14f+: 0-0
Track : LH: 0-13 RH: 0-2 Tight: 0-6 Gall: 0-1
Aids: Bl: 0-20 Vi: 0-1 Tstrap: 0-9
Best Rating: 34 7/01 Donc 5f good

Colonnade

77 **58**
2-y-o b f Blushing Flame (USA)-White Palace (Shirley Heights)
J R Fanshawe Cheveley Park Stud

Placings:6 **(5460)**
2001: 8^6G

	Starts	1st	2nd	3rd	Win & Pl
Career Total (Turf)	1	0	0	0	0

Going (Turf): Sf: 0-0 GS: 0-0 Gd: 0-1 GF: 0-0 Fm: 0-0
Distance: 5f/6f: 0-0 7f-8f: 0-0 9f-13f: 0-1 14f+: 0-0
Track : LH: 0-1 RH: 0-0 Tight: 0-1 Gall: 0-0
Aids: Bl: 0-0 Vi: 0-0 Tstrap: 0-0
Best Rating: 58 10/01 Bath 1m5y good

Colorado Falls (IRE)

102 **99**
3-y-o b c Nashwan (USA)-Ballet Shoes (IRE) (Ela-Mana-Mou)
H R A Cecil Mrs John Magnier & Mr M Tabor

Placings:31 **(1420)**
2001: 11^3GS, 12^1G

	Starts	1st	2nd	3rd	Win & Pl
Career Total (Turf)	2	1	0	1	5452

99	5/01	NmkR	1m4f	D	GD	£4667

Total win prize-money £4667

Going (Turf): Sf: 0-0 GS: 0-1 **Gd: 1-1** GF: 0-0 Fm: 0-0
Distance: 5f/6f: 0-0 7f-8f: 0-0 **9f-13f: 1-2** 14f+: 0-0
Track : LH: 0-1 **RH: 1-1** Tight: 0-0 **Gall: 1-2**
Aids: Bl: 0-0 Vi: 0-0 Tstrap: 0-0
Best Rating: 99 5/01 NmkR 1m4f good

180,000Irgns half-brother to the top-class Petrushka. Shaped well enough on his debut and won his maiden in May. Did not reappear.

Colour Purple

88 **49**
2-y-o b f Spectrum (IRE)-Awtaar (USA) (Lyphard (USA))
C E Brittain R Meredith

Placings:5000 **(5467)**
2001: 6^5GF, 7^0GF, 8^0GF, 6^0S

	Starts	1st	2nd	3rd	Win & Pl
Career Total (Turf)	4	0	0	0	264

Going (Turf): Sf: 0-1 GS: 0-0 Gd: 0-0 GF: 0-3 Fm: 0-0
Distance: 5f/6f: 0-1 7f-8f: 0-2 9f-13f: 0-1 14f+: 0-0
Track : LH: 0-1 RH: 0-1 Tight: 0-0 Gall: 0-0
Aids: Bl: 0-0 Vi: 0-0 Tstrap: 0-0
Best Rating: 49 9/01 Leic 1m9y gd-fm

Colour Sergeant (USA)

98(91) (55)**50**
3-y-o ch g Candy Stripes (USA)-Princess Afleet (USA) (Afleet (CAN))
Don Enrico Incisa (M L W Bell 4/7) Don Enrico Incisa

Placings:3-500044304540 **(5490)**
2001: 9^5SD, 5^0S, 8^0G, 7^0SD, 6^4F, 6^4GF, 7^3GF, 7^0GF, 8^4GS, 9^5GF, 8^4G, 7^0HY

	Starts	1st	2nd	3rd	Win & Pl
Career Total (Turf)	11	0	0	2	1261
Career Total (AW)	2	0	0	0	0

Going (Turf): Sf: 0-2 GS: 0-1 Gd: 0-3 GF: 0-4 Fm: 0-1
Distance: 5f/6f: 0-3 7f-8f: 0-7 9f-13f: 0-3 14f+: 0-0
Track : LH: 0-5 RH: 0-0 Tight: 0-2 Gall: 0-0
Aids: Bl: 0-0 Vi: 0-2 Tstrap: 0-0
Best Rating: 55 2/01 Wolv 1m1f79y stand

Columbine (IRE)

105(88) (66)**70**
3-y-o b f Pivotal-Heart Of India (IRE) (Try My Best (USA))
A Berry Miss Lilo Blum

Placings:133-0600504624060302 (5462)
2001: 6^{0}SD, 5^{6}GF, 5^{0}GF, 6^{0}G, 5^{5}GF, 5^{0}GF, 5^{4}GF, 5^{6}GF, 5^{2}GS, 6^{4}G, 5^{0}G, 6^{6}GF, 5^{0}GS, 6^{3}GS, 6^{0}SD, 5^{2}G

	Starts	1st	2nd	3rd	Win & Pl
Career Total (Turf)	16	1	2	2	8803
Career Total (AW)	3	0	0	1	524

66 7/00 Donc 5f D G-F £3510
Total win prize-money £3510

Going (Turf): Sf: 0-0 GS: 0-3 Gd: 0-5 **GF: 1-8** Fm: 0-0
Distance: **5f/6f: 1-17** 7f-8f: 0-2 9f-13f: 0-0 14f+: 0-0
Track : LH: 0-6 RH: 0-0 Tight: 0-3 Gall: 0-1
Aids: Bl: 0-1 Vi: 0-0 Tstrap: 0-0
Best Rating: 85 5/01 Thsk 5f gd-fm

Has not won since her debut but has run well on two or three occasions this term. Best at five furlongs, seems to appreciate a little cut in the ground. Has worn blinkers.

Columna

(78) (6)**56**
5-y-o gr m Deploy-Copper Trader (Faustus (USA))
M D I Usher The Ridgeway Partnership

Placings:0/0060/**0**-0 (0030)
2001: 16^{0}SD

	Starts	1st	2nd	3rd	Win & Pl
Career Total (Turf)	5	0	0	0	0
Career Total (AW)	2	0	0	0	

Going (Turf): Sf: 0-1 GS: 0-1 Gd: 0-1 GF: 0-2 Fm: 0-0
Distance: 5f/6f: 0-0 7f-8f: 0-1 9f-13f: 0-3 14f+: 0-3
Track : LH: 0-6 RH: 0-1 Tight: 0-3 Gall: 0-0
Aids: Bl: 0-1 Vi: 0-0 Tstrap: 0-0

Colway Ritz

106 **56**
7-y-o b g Rudimentary (USA)-Million Heiress (Auction Ring (USA))
W Storey Mrs M Tindale & Tom Park

Placings:552030360310/0562140325030/00301101345 036500/036112024500-00063466506 (4617)
2001: 8^{0}G, 11^{0}F, 10^{0}F, 10^{6}GF, 10^{3}G, 10^{4}GF, 12^{6}GF, 12^{6}G, 10^{5}GF, 12^{0}GF, 10^{6}F

	Starts	1st	2nd	3rd	Win & Pl
Career Total (Turf)	65	7	5	10	63811

78 6/00 Ripn 1m2f D(0-85)H G-F £4030
78 6/00 Ripn 1m2f D(0-85)H G-S £4901
82 6/99 Rdcr 1m2f C(0-90)H FRM £8656
78 5/99 Rdcr 1m2f B(0-105)H G-F £11452
75 5/99 Ripn 1m2f D(0-85)H G-S £5220
70 7/98 Bevl 1m100y D(0-85)H GD £4973
69 10/97 Donc 7f E(0-70)H GD £3642
Total win prize-money £42875

Going (Turf): Sf: 0-5 **GS: 2-8 Gd: 2-17 GF: 2-27** Fm: 1-8
Distance: 5f/6f: 0-5 7f-8f: 1-15 **9f-13f: 6-45** 14f+: 0-0
Track : LH: 2-34 **RH: 4-18 Tight: 5-25** Gall: 0-16
Aids: Bl: 0-3 Vi: 0-0 Tstrap: 0-0
Best Rating: 69 6/01 Newc 1m4f93y gd-fm

The winner of the 1999 Zetland Gold Cup, he scored twice over ten furlongs at Ripon last season, but went up in the handicap and struggled as a result. He has fallen in the weights now, but that has not been matched by improved performances.

Comanche Queen

102 **43**
4-y-o ch f Totem (USA)-Chess Mistress (USA) (Run The Gantlet (USA))
J S Wainwright Hurn Racing Club

Placings:0000/00000-032140406 (4478)
2001: 11^{0}GF, 16^{3}GF, 14^{2}GF, 12^{1}G, 13^{4}G, 11^{0}GS, 14^{4}GF, 11^{0}GF, 16^{6}F

	Starts	1st	2nd	3rd	Win & Pl
Career Total (Turf)	18	1	1	1	5249

30 8/01 Muss 1m4f F(0-60)H GD £3668
Total win prize-money £3668

Going (Turf): Sf: 0-0 GS: 0-3 **Gd: 1-5** GF: 0-9 Fm: 0-1
Distance: 5f/6f: 0-2 7f-8f: 0-1 **9f-13f: 1-9** 14f+: 0-6
Track : LH: 0-5 RH: 0-10 Tight: 0-12 Gall: 0-0
Aids: Bl: 0-1 Vi: 0-0 Tstrap: 0-0
Best Rating: 43 8/01 Muss 1m6f gd-fm

Come On Murgy

(97) (49)**42**
4-y-o b f Weldnaas (USA)-Forest Song (Forzando)
A Bailey Sandybrow Stables Ltd

Placings:0600000**6013**/**1444054300**6-**4242100103550** (4071)
2001: 7^{4}SD, 7^{2}SW, 9^{4}SW, 7^{2}SW, 8^{1}SD, 8^{0}SW, 9^{0}SD, 8^{1}SD, 8^{0}SD, 8^{3}SD, 8^{5}SD, 7^{5}GF, 8^{0}SD

	Starts	1st	2nd	3rd	Win & Pl
Career Total (Turf)	8	0	0	0	0
Career Total (AW)	26	4	2	3	8062

48 3/01 Wolv 1m100y G(0-60)H STD £1379
46 1/01 Wolv 1m100y G(0-70)H STD £1344
51 1/00 Sthl 7f G STD £1500
48 12/99 Wolv 7f G STD £1945
Total win prize-money £6169

Going (Turf): Sf: 0-1 GS: 0-1 Gd: 0-1 GF: 0-4 Fm: 0-1
Distance: 5f/6f: 0-13 7f-8f: 2-16 9f-13f: 2-5 14f+: 0-0
Track : **LH: 4-27** RH: 0-1 **Tight: 3-16** Gall: 0-1
Aids: Bl: 0-4 Vi: 0-0 Tstrap: 0-0
Best Rating: 49 4/01 Sthl 1m stand

Comeoutofthefog (IRE)

92(101) (30)**30**
6-y-o b g Mujadil (USA)-Local Belle (Ballymore)
R J Price (Miss S J Wilton 30/1) C Nenadich

Placings:605000**2**/**3421140025003**0**263345**/**040646103 02**/**5015006000**-060000 (5101)
2001: 9^{0}SD, 7^{6}SD, 6^{0}SD, 8^{0}HY, 8^{0}G, 9^{0}GS

	Starts	1st	2nd	3rd	Win & Pl
Career Total (Turf)	20	0	1	2	1283
Career Total (AW)	34	4	4	3	13954

52 2/00 Wolv 7f G STD £1922
59 6/99 Ling 7f G(0-60)H STD £2162
68 2/98 Ling 1m F SLW £2221
61 2/98 Ling 7f E SLW £2749
Total win prize-money £9057

Going (Turf): Sf: 0-3 GS: 0-3 Gd: 0-4 GF: 0-5 Fm: 0-1
Distance: 5f/6f: 0-5 **7f-8f: 4-35** 9f-13f: 0-14 14f+: 0-0
Track : **LH: 4-40** RH: 0-8 **Tight: 4-37** Gall: 0-1
Aids: Bl: 0-2 Vi: 0-0 Tstrap: 0-0
Best Rating: 30 9/01 Chep 1m14y good

He does not win that often, but when he does it is usually over seven furlongs on the All-Weather

Comeuppance (IRE)

98 **55**
3-y-o b g General Monash (USA)-Press Reception (Beldale Flutter (USA))
J G Given Alex Gorrie Combi (uk)

Placings:606-0200 (3617)
2001: 8^{0}G, 6^{2}F, 6^{0}GF, 6^{0}F

	Starts	1st	2nd	3rd	Win & Pl
Career Total (Turf)	7	0	1	0	980

Going (Turf): Sf: 0-0 GS: 0-0 Gd: 0-1 GF: 0-2 Fm: 0-4
Distance: 5f/6f: 0-4 7f-8f: 0-2 9f-13f: 0-1 14f+: 0-0
Track : LH: 0-3 RH: 0-2 Tight: 0-2 Gall: 0-1
Aids: Bl: 0-0 Vi: 0-0 Tstrap: 0-0
Best Rating: 48 6/01 Thsk 6f firm

Comex Flyer (IRE)

93(69) **48**
4-y-o ch g Prince Of Birds (USA)-Smashing Pet (Mummy's Pet)
P F Nicholls (D Nicholls 10/4) Neil Smith

Placings:0646/406001000-00 (0702)
2001: 8^{0}SD, 10^{0}HY

	Starts	1st	2nd	3rd	Win & Pl
Career Total (Turf)	14	1	0	0	2311
Career Total (AW)	1	0	0	0	

48 6/00 Catt 7f G(0-60) G-S £1855
Total win prize-money £1855

Going (Turf): Sf: 0-2 **GS: 1-3** Gd: 0-2 GF: 0-3 Fm: 0-4
Distance: 5f/6f: 0-5 **7f-8f: 1-8** 9f-13f: 0-2 14f+: 0-0
Track : **LH: 1-5** RH: 0-6 **Tight: 1-4** Gall: 0-2
Aids: Bl: 0-1 Vi: 0-0 Tstrap: 0-0
Best Rating: 35 4/01 Pont 1m2f6y heavy

Comfortable Call

104 **69**
3-y-o ch c Nashwan (USA)-High Standard (Kris)
E A L Dunlop Gainsborough Stud

Placings:0342340 (4483)
2001: 10^{0}GS, 10^{3}F, 14^{4}G, 14^{2}G, 14^{3}GF, 14^{4}GF, 14^{0}S

	Starts	1st	2nd	3rd	Win & Pl
Career Total (Turf)	7	0	1	2	2574

Going (Turf): Sf: 0-1 GS: 0-1 Gd: 0-2 GF: 0-2 Fm: 0-1
Distance: 5f/6f: 0-0 7f-8f: 0-0 9f-13f: 0-2 14f+: 0-5
Track : LH: 0-4 RH: 0-2 Tight: 0-6 Gall: 0-0
Aids: Bl: 0-0 Vi: 0-0 Tstrap: 0-0
Best Rating: 79 6/01 Yarm 1m6f17y good

Comfy (USA)

105 **105+**
2-y-o b c Lear Fan (USA)-Souplesse (USA) (Majestic Light (USA))
Sir Michael Stoute K Abdulla

Placings:315 (5388)
2001: 7^{3}GF, 6^{1}G, 7^{5}GS

	Starts	1st	2nd	3rd	Win & Pl
Career Total (Turf)	3	1	0	1	25277

105 8/01 York 6f214y A GD £19227
Total win prize-money £19227

Going (Turf): Sf: 0-0 GS: 0-1 **Gd: 1-1** GF: 0-1 Fm: 0-0
Distance: 5f/6f: 0-0 **7f-8f: 1-3** 9f-13f: 0-0 14f+: 0-0
Track : **LH: 1-1** RH: 0-0 Tight: 0-0 **Gall: 1-1**
Aids: Bl: 0-0 Vi: 0-0 Tstrap: 0-0
Best Rating: 105 8/01 York 6f214y good

Out of a half-sister to Eltish, he is quite a strong, medium-sized colt. He performed well on this debut at Ascot despite running green, but benefited from that to gain a clear-cut win over an extra furlong in the Acomb Stakes at York. Ran quite well in the Dewhurst, and should be capable of winning Pattern races.

Commanche Cup (IRE)

8-y-o b g Commanche Run-Royal Cup (Politico (USA))
A P James Jim Tew

Placings:0 (2323)
2001: 16^{0}SD

	Starts	1st	2nd	3rd	Win & Pl
Career Total (Turf)	0	0	0	0	
Career Total (AW)	1	0	0	0	

Going (Turf): Sf: 0-0 GS: 0-0 Gd: 0-0 GF: 0-0 Fm: 0-0
Distance: 5f/6f: 0-0 7f-8f: 0-0 9f-13f: 0-0 14f+: 0-1
Track : LH: 0-1 RH: 0-0 Tight: 0-1 Gall: 0-0
Aids: Bl: 0-0 Vi: 0-0 Tstrap: 0-0

Commanche Wind (IRE)

94 **35**

6-y-o b g Commanche Run-Delko (Decent Fellow)
E W Tuer G Tuer

Placings:2 **(2866)**
2001: 16^{2}GF

	Starts	1st	2nd	3rd	Win & Pl
Career Total (Turf)	1	0	1	0	852

Going (Turf): Sf: 0-0 GS: 0-0 Gd: 0-0 GF: 0-1 Fm: 0-0
Distance: 5f/6f: 0-0 7f-8f: 0-0 9f-13f: 0-0 14f+: 0-1
Track : LH: 0-0 RH: 0-1 Tight: 0-1 Gall: 0-0
Aids: Bl: 0-0 Vi: 0-0 Tstrap: 0-0
Best Rating: 35 7/01 Muss 2m gd-fm

Commander

77 **7**

5-y-o b g Puissance-Tarkhana (IRE) (Dancing Brave (USA))
D Morris Taylor Parker Associates

Placings:05/5030-00 **(5145)**
2001: 8^{0}GS, 7^{0}G

	Starts	1st	2nd	3rd	Win & Pl
Career Total (Turf)	8	0	0	1	399

Going (Turf): Sf: 0-1 GS: 0-1 Gd: 0-5 GF: 0-1 Fm: 0-0
Distance: 5f/6f: 0-0 7f-8f: 0-4 9f-13f: 0-4 14f+: 0-0
Track : LH: 0-3 RH: 0-3 Tight: 0-1 Gall: 0-2
Aids: Bl: 0-0 Vi: 0-1 Tstrap: 0-3
Best Rating: 7 10/01 NmkR 7f good

He has yet to win and has only shown glimpses of ability. His best effort to date came on soft ground.

Commanding

98 **80**

2-y-o ch c Pennekamp (USA)-Lady Joyce (FR) (Galetto (FR))
Mrs A J Perrett Cheveley Park Stud

Placings:415 **(4941)**
2001: 6^{4}GF, 6^{1}G, 7^{5}S

	Starts	1st	2nd	3rd	Win & Pl
Career Total (Turf)	3	1	0	0	3105
80 9/01 Folk 6f	D			GD	£2814

Total win prize-money £2814

Going (Turf): Sf: 0-1 GS: 0-0 **Gd: 1-1** GF: 0-1 Fm: 0-0
Distance: **5f/6f: 1-2** 7f-8f: 0-1 9f-13f: 0-0 14f+: 0-0
Track : LH: 0-1 RH: 0-0 Tight: 0-1 Gall: 0-0
Aids: Bl: 0-0 Vi: 0-0 Tstrap: 0-0
Best Rating: 80 9/01 Folk 6f good

A half-brother to Da Wolf, he landed a Folkestone maiden in September after a three month absence, and can be forgiven his subsequent defeat on soft ground.

Common Consent (IRE)

(94) (56)**61**

5-y-o b m Common Grounds-Santella Bell (Ballad Rock)
S Woodman Mrs Fiona Gordon & Mrs Jenny Carter

Placings:00/02400303/0610420600-4243500 **(4667)**
2001: 8^{4}GF, 9^{2}F, 9^{4}F, 9^{3}GF, 9^{5}GF, 9^{0}GF, 8^{0}GF

	Starts	1st	2nd	3rd	Win & Pl
Career Total (Turf)	27	1	3	3	13306
54 6/00 Folk 1m1f149yE(0-70)H				FRM	£2954

Total win prize-money £2954

Going (Turf): Sf: 0-1 GS: 0-4 Gd: 0-5 GF: 0-12 **Fm: 1-5**
Distance: 5f/6f: 0-1 7f-8f: 0-6 **9f-13f: 1-19** 14f+: 0-1
Track : LH: 0-11 **RH: 1-12 Tight: 1-15** Gall: 0-0
Aids: Bl: 0-0 Vi: 0-0 Tstrap: 0-0
Best Rating: 61 6/01 Ling 1m1f firm

A fair handicapper over a mile to nine furlongs. Needs a strong gallop. Has a poor wins to runs ratio. Acts on fast ground.

Common Thought (IRE)

91 **72**

2-y-o b c Common Grounds-Zuhal (Busted)
P W Harris The House Of Commons

Placings:01 **(3007)**
2001: 6^{0}GF, 7^{1}GF

	Starts	1st	2nd	3rd	Win & Pl
Career Total (Turf)	2	1	0	0	2716
72 7/01 Ling 7f	F			G-F	£2716

Total win prize-money £2716

Going (Turf): Sf: 0-0 GS: 0-0 Gd: 0-0 **GF: 1-2** Fm: 0-0
Distance: 5f/6f: 0-1 **7f-8f: 1-1** 9f-13f: 0-0 14f+: 0-0
Track : LH: 0-0 RH: 0-0 Tight: 0-0 Gall: 0-0
Aids: Bl: 0-0 Vi: 0-0 Tstrap: 0-0
Best Rating: 72 7/01 Ling 7f gd-fm

Bred to stay, appreciated a step up in trip and showed a good attitude to score his first victory on his second outing. Suited to seven furlongs ona sound surface.

Common World (USA)

101 **88+**

2-y-o ch c Spinning World (USA)-Spenderella (FR) (Common Grounds)
G A Butler Sheikh Khaled Duaij Al Sabah

Placings:61 **(5635)**
2001: 6^{6}GS, 7^{1}G

	Starts	1st	2nd	3rd	Win & Pl
Career Total (Turf)	2	1	0	0	2870
88 11/01 Catt 7f	E			GD	£2870

Total win prize-money £2870

Going (Turf): Sf: 0-0 GS: 0-1 **Gd: 1-1** GF: 0-0 Fm: 0-0
Distance: 5f/6f: 0-1 **7f-8f: 1-1** 9f-13f: 0-0 14f+: 0-0
Track : **LH: 1-1** RH: 0-0 **Tight: 1-1** Gall: 0-0
Aids: Bl: 0-0 Vi: 0-0 Tstrap: 0-0
Best Rating: 88 11/01 Catt 7f good

He appreciated the step up to seven furlongs when winning a maiden at Catterick with a little in hand. He is likely to improve further over a mile next season.

Communard (IRE)

98 **70**

2-y-o b c Sri Pekan (USA)-Broadway Rosie (Absalom)
R Hannon Michael Pescod

Placings:0551 **(4668)**
2001: 6^{0}GF, 7^{5}GF, 6^{5}GF, 6^{1}GF

	Starts	1st	2nd	3rd	Win & Pl
Career Total (Turf)	4	1	0	0	3900
70 9/01 Gdwd 6f	D(0-85)H			G-F	£3900

Total win prize-money £3900

Going (Turf): Sf: 0-0 GS: 0-0 Gd: 0-0 **GF: 1-4** Fm: 0-0
Distance: **5f/6f: 1-3** 7f-8f: 0-1 9f-13f: 0-0 14f+: 0-0
Track : LH: 0-1 RH: 0-0 Tight: 0-1 Gall: 0-0
Aids: Bl: 0-0 Vi: 0-0 Tstrap: 0-0
Best Rating: 70 9/01 Gdwd 6f gd-fm

Showed a little ability in maidens before making a successful nursery debut at Goodwood in September. Best over six furlongs.

Communicate (IRE)

(50) **42**

2-y-o b g Bigstone (IRE)-Sada (Mujtahid (USA))
T D Easterby Times Of Wigan

Placings:00 **(1995)**
2001: 5^{0}GF, 6^{0}SD

	Starts	1st	2nd	3rd	Win & Pl
Career Total (Turf)	1	0	0	0	
Career Total (AW)	1	0	0	0	

Going (Turf): Sf: 0-0 GS: 0-0 Gd: 0-0 GF: 0-1 Fm: 0-0
Distance: 5f/6f: 0-2 7f-8f: 0-0 9f-13f: 0-0 14f+: 0-0
Track : LH: 0-1 RH: 0-0 Tight: 0-0 Gall: 0-0
Aids: Bl: 0-0 Vi: 0-0 Tstrap: 0-0
Best Rating: 42 5/01 Hayd 5f gd-fm

Como (USA)

106 **88**

3-y-o b/br f Cozzene (USA)-Merida (Warning)
R Charlton K Abdulla

Placings:40-03113430 **(5258)**
2001: 8^{0}GS, 6^{3}GF, 6^{1}GF, 6^{1}GF, 5^{3}GS, 6^{4}G, 5^{3}G, 5^{0}GS

	Starts	1st	2nd	3rd	Win & Pl
Career Total (Turf)	10	2	0	3	16407
83 7/01 Kemp 6f	D(0-80)			G-F	£6773
60 7/01 Sthl 6f	D			G-F	£3024

Total win prize-money £9797

Going (Turf): Sf: 0-2 GS: 0-3 Gd: 0-2 **GF: 2-3** Fm: 0-0
Distance: **5f/6f: 2-7** 7f-8f: 0-2 9f-13f: 0-1 14f+: 0-0
Track : **LH: 1-1** RH: 0-1 Tight: 0-1 Gall: 0-0
Aids: Bl: 0-0 Vi: 0-0 Tstrap: 0-0
Best Rating: 88 9/01 NmkR 5f good

She was third to Ellens Academy in a classified stakes at Doncaster in May, and won a six-furlong Southwell maiden at long odds-on in July. Followed up in a classified event at Kempton, and has run well off her revised mark since. Suited by six furlongs and fast ground, likes to make the running.

Companion

(104) (86)**77d**

3-y-o b f Most Welcome-Benazir (High Top)
B A Pearce (W J Haggas 24/2) Custom Racing

Placings:464-352111000200060 **(3565)**
2001: 8^{3}SD, 7^{5}SD, 8^{2}SW, 7^{1}SD, 8^{1}SD, 8^{1}SD, 9^{0}S, 8^{0}G, 8^{0}GF, 8^{2}GF, 9^{0}F, 9^{0}GF, 7^{0}GF, 8^{6}GF, 8^{0}GF

	Starts	1st	2nd	3rd	Win & Pl
Career Total (Turf)	11	0	1	0	2657
Career Total (AW)	7	3	1	1	12182
86 4/01 Sthl 1m	D(0-80)H			STD	£3848
80 3/01 Sthl 1m	D(0-80)H			STD	£3874
76 3/01 Ling 7f	D			STD	£2926

Total win prize-money £10648

Going (Turf): Sf: 0-2 GS: 0-0 Gd: 0-1 GF: 0-7 Fm: 0-1
Distance: 5f/6f: 0-0 **7f-8f: 3-12** 9f-13f: 0-6 14f+: 0-0
Track : **LH: 3-9** RH: 0-6 **Tight: 1-4** Gall: 0-1
Aids: Bl: 0-0 Vi: 0-0 Tstrap: 0-0
Best Rating: 86 4/01 Sthl 1m stand

She looked a bit dodgy in her early starts, but moved to Brian Pearce and rattled up a hat-trick on sand in ever better company. She has not enjoyed the same success on turf, though she has run creditably on occasions.

Complete Class (USA)

71 **51**

3-y-o b c Dynaformer (USA)-Impertinent Lady (USA) (Sham (USA))

H R A Cecil The Thoroughbred Corporation

Placings:0 **(0791)**

2001: 10^{0}GS

	Starts	1st	2nd	3rd	Win & Pl
Career Total (Turf)	1	0	0	0	

Going (Turf): Sf: 0-0 GS: 0-1 Gd: 0-0 GF: 0-0 Fm: 0-0
Distance: 5f/6f: 0-0 7f-8f: 0-0 9f-13f: 0-1 14f+: 0-0
Track : LH: 0-0 RH: 0-0 Tight: 0-0 Gall: 0-0
Aids: Bl: 0-0 Vi: 0-0 Tstrap: 0-0
Best Rating: 51 4/01 NmkR 1m2f gd-sft

Compradore

106 **59**

6-y-o b m Mujtahid (USA)-Keswa (King's Lake (USA))

M Blanshard C McKenna

Placings:2100/00400040061/0435500264503 0/032110 3003030-0353002345000 **(5470)**

2001: 7^{0}S, 6^{3}GF, 6^{5}F, 7^{3}GF, 7^{0}GF, 8^{0}GS, 6^{2}G, 7^{3}G, 7^{4}G, 7^{5}G, 7^{0}G, 6^{0}HY, 7^{0}S

	Starts	1st	2nd	3rd	Win & Pl
Career Total (Turf)	55	4	4	9	26027

72 5/00 Brig 6f209y E(0-65) SFT £2791
68 5/00 Sals 6f212y D(0-80)H GD £4758
69 10/98 Folk 6f E(0-70) G-S £3209
82 5/97 Newb 5f34y D G-F £3610
Total win prize-money £14370

Going (Turf): Sf: 1-11 GS: 1-7 Gd: 1-17 GF: 1-18 Fm: 0-2
Distance: 5f/6f: 2-17 7f-8f: 2-36 9f-13f: 0-2 14f+: 0-0
Track : **LH: 1-12** RH: 0-9 Tight: 0-2 Gall: 0-7
Aids: Bl: 0-2 Vi: 0-0 Tstrap: 0-0
Best Rating: 67 8/01 Brig 6f209y good

Goes really well at Brighton. Ideally suited by seven furlongs and some cut in the ground.

Compton Admiral

101 **100**

5-y-o b h Suave Dancer (USA)-Sumoto (Mtoto)

G A Butler E Penser

Placings:2212/10015/3 **(1717)**

2001: 10^{3}GF

	Starts	1st	2nd	3rd	Win & Pl
Career Total (Turf)	10	3	3	1	222907

122 7/99 Sand 1m2f7y A G-F £174600
110 4/99 NmkJ 1m A GD £20000
96 7/98 Asct 7f D G-F £6872
Total win prize-money £201473

Going (Turf): Sf: 0-1 GS: 0-0 Gd: 1-4 **GF: 2-5** Fm: 0-0
Distance: 5f/6f: 0-1 **7f-8f: 2-5** 9f-13f: 1-4 14f+: 0-0
Track : LH: 0-3 **RH: 1-2** Tight: 0-1 Gall: 0-2
Aids: Bl: 0-0 Vi: 0-0 Tstrap: 0-0
Best Rating: 100 5/01 Newb 1m2f6y gd-fm

His finest hour came when causing a shock in the 1999 Eclipse. A respectable fifth in the York International subsequently, he picked up a knee injury there and only returned to action this May. He made a pleasing reappearance, but then suffered a further injury and retired to stud.

Compton Arrow (IRE)

107(101) (69)**63**

5-y-o b g Petardia-Impressive Lady (Mr Fluorocarbon)

G A Butler E Penser

Placings:510314/3600330/000005323-3352500 **(5391)**

2001: 7^{3}GF, 6^{3}GF, 7^{5}GF, 7^{2}GF, 5^{5}GS, 5^{0}S, 7^{0}GS

	Starts	1st	2nd	3rd	Win & Pl
Career Total (Turf)	27	2	1	7	19749
Career Total (AW)	3	0	1	1	1225

95 10/98 Asct 6f D SFT £7100
86 8/98 Hayd 6f E G-S £3352
Total win prize-money £10453

Going (Turf): Sf: 1-6 GS: 1-4 Gd: 0-9 GF: 0-8 Fm: 0-0
Distance: **5f/6f: 2-8** 7f-8f: 0-21 9f-13f: 0-1 14f+: 0-0
Track : LH: 0-9 RH: 0-7 Tight: 0-4 Gall: 0-5
Aids: Bl: 0-2 Vi: 0-0 Tstrap: 0-10
Best Rating: 73 7/01 Donc 6f gd-fm

Classy mile handicapper in his time, but not the force of old and keeps on finding one or two too good. Not getting any help from the Handicapper despite not winning.

Compton Aviator

102(102) (75)**72**

5-y-o ch g First Trump-Rifada (Ela-Mana-Mou)

A W Carroll Gary S Nichol

Placings:433/00012-40240000 **(4966)**

2001: 8^{4}GF, 16^{0}GF, 10^{2}GF, 9^{4}G, 10^{0}GF, 10^{0}G, 9^{0}GF, 10^{0}S

	Starts	1st	2nd	3rd	Win & Pl
Career Total (Turf)	14	0	1	2	4019
Career Total (AW)	2	1	1	0	2333

50 10/00 Ling 7f F STD £1785
Total win prize-money £1785

Going (Turf): Sf: 0-1 GS: 0-1 Gd: 0-3 GF: 0-9 Fm: 0-0
Distance: 5f/6f: 0-0 **7f-8f: 1-3** 9f-13f: 0-10 14f+: 0-3
Track : **LH: 1-9** RH: 0-6 **Tight: 1-5** Gall: 0-6
Aids: Bl: 0-0 Vi: 0-0 **Tstrap: 1-14**
Best Rating: 72 8/01 York 1m2f85y good

Has tried various trip from seven furlongs to two miles, but has just one win to his name on Equitrack over seven furlongs. Probably best suited to ten furlongs on a sound surface on turf.

Compton Banker (IRE)

107 **98**

4-y-o br c Distinctly North (USA)-Mary Hinge (Dowsing (USA))

G A Butler E Penser

Placings:605/051024410-006000 **(3029)**

2001: 5^{0}GS, 6^{0}GS, 6^{6}G, 5^{0}G, 5^{0}G, 5^{0}GF

	Starts	1st	2nd	3rd	Win & Pl
Career Total (Turf)	18	2	1	0	60396

98 9/00 Donc 5f140y B(0-110)H GD £22327
86 6/00 Asct 5f B(0-105)H G-F £17680
Total win prize-money £40008

Going (Turf): Sf: 0-0 GS: 0-5 **Gd: 1-9 GF: 1-4** Fm: 0-0
Distance: **5f/6f: 2-18** 7f-8f: 0-0 9f-13f: 0-0 14f+: 0-0
Track : LH: 0-0 RH: 0-1 Tight: 0-0 Gall: 0-1
Aids: Bl: 0-1 Vi: 0-0 Tstrap: 0-0
Best Rating: 97 6/01 Chan 5f good

Winner of last season's Portland Handicap at Doncaster, this useful sort needs a sound surface to be seen to best effect. Efforts at Group level subsequently suggest a drop to handicap company is required.

Compton Bolter (IRE)

114(113) (109)**113**

4-y-o b c Red Sunset-Milk And Honey (So Blessed)

G A Butler E Penser

Placings:32123/4050451041-3020441036 **(5016)**

2001: 10^{3}SD, 8^{0}FT, 10^{2}GF, 10^{0}GF, 12^{4}GF, 10^{4}GF, 12^{1}G, 10^{0}Y, 11^{3}GF, 12^{6}S

	Starts	1st	2nd	3rd	Win & Pl
Career Total (Turf)	20	3	3	3	92275
Career Total (AW)	5	1	0	1	31072

113 8/01 Gdwd 1m4f A(0-110)H GD £29000
107 11/00 Ling 1m2f A STD £17400
103 9/00 Newb 1m1f B G-F £9471
85 9/99 Chep 1m14y E GD £2808
Total win prize-money £58679

Going (Turf): Sf: 0-2 GS: 0-2 **Gd: 2-3** GF: 1-8 Fm: 0-1
Distance: 5f/6f: 0-0 7f-8f: 0-9 **9f-13f: 4-16** 14f+: 0-0
Track : **LH: 2-7** RH: 1-8 **Tight: 2-3** Gall: 1-6
Aids: Bl: 0-1 Vi: 0-0 **Tstrap: 2-5**
Best Rating: 113 8/01 Gdwd 1m4f good

A smart performer in 2000, he proved useful on the All-Weather during the winter and ran well back on turf at Sandown in May. Running in his first handicap, he returned to winning form in a valuable Listed event at Glorious Goodwood, over a mile and a half. He finished a remote second last in the Arlington Million in America when outclassed, and has since been well held back in England. Suited by most types of ground.

Compton Chick (IRE)

90(86) (45+)**54d**

3-y-o b f Dolphin Street (FR)-Cecina (Welsh Saint)

G A Butler E Penser

Placings:05-60200 **(4906)**

2001: 7^{6}SD, 7^{0}SD, 9^{2}S, 11^{0}F, 9^{0}G

	Starts	1st	2nd	3rd	Win & Pl
Career Total (Turf)	5	0	1	0	754
Career Total (AW)	2	0	0	0	0

Going (Turf): Sf: 0-2 GS: 0-1 Gd: 0-1 GF: 0-0 Fm: 0-1
Distance: 5f/6f: 0-0 7f-8f: 0-4 9f-13f: 0-3 14f+: 0-0
Track : LH: 0-4 RH: 0-2 Tight: 0-4 Gall: 0-0
Aids: Bl: 0-0 Vi: 0-0 Tstrap: 0-6
Best Rating: 54 4/01 Nott 1m1f213y soft

Compton Commander

110 **92**

3-y-o ch g Barathea (IRE)-Triodo (USA) (Sharpen Up)

G A Butler E Penser

Placings:031-201400020 **(5600)**

2001: 10^{2}GS, 10^{0}S, 12^{1}GF, 12^{4}GF, 11^{0}S, 14^{0}G, 13^{0}G, 14^{2}G, 16^{0}GS

	Starts	1st	2nd	3rd	Win & Pl
Career Total (Turf)	12	2	2	1	22079

95 5/01 Ches 1m4f66y C(0-95)H G-F £10286
80 10/00 Brig 1m1f209yD SFT £2873
Total win prize-money £13159

Going (Turf): Sf: 1-4 GS: 0-2 Gd: 0-3 **GF: 1-3** Fm: 0-0
Dictanoo: 5f/6f: 0-0 7f-8f: 0-1 **9f-13f: 2-7 14f+: 0-4**
Track : **LH: 2-6** RH: 0-4 **Tight: 1-3** Gall: 0-5
Aids: Bl: 0-0 Vi: 0-0 Tstrap: 0-0
Best Rating: 95 5/01 Ches 1m4f66y gd-fm

Showed potential as a two-year-old and put in a decent effort to finish second at Doncaster at the start of the season. Scored at Chester on his first run on fast ground since his debut and put in a sound effort at Royal Ascot. Lost his action when disappointing at Goodwood, and has mostly struggled since. Stays 14 furlongs and acts on any ground.

Compton Dictator

27

2-y-o b c Shareef Dancer (USA)-Princess Pati (Top Ville)

G A Butler E Penser

Placings:00 **(5666)**

2001: 6^{0}GS, 6^{0}HY

	Starts	1st	2nd	3rd	Win & Pl
Career Total (Turf)	2	0	0	0	

Going (Turf): Sf: 0-1 GS: 0-1 Gd: 0-0 GF: 0-0 Fm: 0-0
Distance: 5f/6f: 0-2 7f-8f: 0-0 9f-13f: 0-0 14f+: 0-0
Track: LH: 0-0 RH: 0-0 Tight: 0-0 Gall: 0-0
Aids: Bl: 0-0 Vi: 0-0 Tstrap: 0-0
Best Rating: 27 11/01 NmkR 6f gd-sft

Compton Dragon (USA)

66 **67+**

2-y-o ch c Woodman (USA)-Vilikaia (USA) (Nureyev (USA))
G A Butler E Penser

Placings:2 **(5369)**
2001: 7^{2}GS

	Starts	1st	2nd	3rd	Win & Pl
Career Total (Turf)	1	0	1	0	0

Going (Turf): Sf: 0-0 GS: 0-1 Gd: 0-0 GF: 0-0 Fm: 0-0
Distance: 5f/6f: 0-0 7f-8f: 0-1 9f-13f: 0-0 14f+: 0-0
Track: LH: 0-0 RH: 0-0 Tight: 0-0 Gall: 0-0
Aids: Bl: 0-0 Vi: 0-0 Tstrap: 0-0
Best Rating: 67 10/01 NmkR 7f gd-sft

Holds a Derby entry. He was not knocked about on this racecourse debut in the Newmarket Challenge Cup but still gave the winner a fright close home.

Compton Dynamo

93 **75**

2-y-o b c Wolfhound (USA)-Asteroid Field (USA) (Forli (ARG))
G A Butler E Penser

Placings:43 **(5658)**
2001: 6^{4}GS, 7^{3}G

	Starts	1st	2nd	3rd	Win & Pl
Career Total (Turf)	2	0	0	1	775

Going (Turf): Sf: 0-0 GS: 0-1 Gd: 0-1 GF: 0-0 Fm: 0-0
Distance: 5f/6f: 0-1 7f-8f: 0-1 9f-13f: 0-0 14f+: 0-0
Track: LH: 0-0 RH: 0-0 Tight: 0-0 Gall: 0-0
Aids: Bl: 0-0 Vi: 0-0 Tstrap: 0-0
Best Rating: 75 11/01 Muss 7f30y good

Ran with promise as a juvenile over six and seven furlongs. Should improve at three.

Comrade Chinnery (IRE)

87(84) (7)**13**

8-y-o ch g Jareer (USA)-Phar Lapa (Grundy)
J S Moore (B G Powell 20/3) Miss N Henton

Placings:0453500/60501133/25/00 **(2053)**
2001: 13^{0}SW, 16^{0}GF

	Starts	1st	2nd	3rd	Win & Pl
Career Total (Turf)	18	2	1	3	6253
Career Total (AW)	1	0	0	0	

40	8/96	Tram	1m4f	(0-50)H	GD	£2226
39	7/96	Wxfd	1m5f	(0-50)H	GD	£2568

Total win prize-money £4795

Going (Turf): Sf: 0-0 GS: 0-1 **Gd: 2-4** GF: 0-7 Fm: 0-3
Distance: 5f/6f: 0-1 7f-8f: 0-3 **9f-13f: 2-8** 14f+: 0-5
Track: LH: 0-5 **RH: 2-10** Tight: 0-2 Gall: 0-0
Aids: Bl: 0-4 Vi: 0-0 Tstrap: 0-0
Best Rating: 13 6/01 Rdcr 2m4y gd-fm

Comtesse Noire (CAN)

93 **71**

2-y-o b f Woodman (USA)-Faux Pas (IRE) (Sadler's Wells (USA))
I A Balding Holistic Racing Ltd

Placings:3306 **(4990)**
2001: 7^{3}GF, 6^{3}G, 8^{0}GF, 6^{6}HY

	Starts	1st	2nd	3rd	Win & Pl
Career Total (Turf)	4	0	0	2	1272

Going (Turf): Sf: 0-1 GS: 0-0 Gd: 0-1 GF: 0-2 Fm: 0-0
Distance: 5f/6f: 0-2 7f-8f: 0-2 9f-13f: 0-0 14f+: 0-0
Track: LH: 0-1 RH: 0-1 Tight: 0-0 Gall: 0-0
Aids: Bl: 0-0 Vi: 0-0 Tstrap: 0-0
Best Rating: 71 8/01 Pont 6f good

Concino (FR)

92(91) (40)**32**

4-y-o b g Zafonic (USA)-Petronella (USA) (Nureyev (USA))
Miss A Stokell T J Ford

Placings:000/03000060-00000300 **(4901)**
2001: 7^{0}GF, 7^{0}GF, 11^{0}GF, 16^{0}SD, 12^{0}GF, 15^{3}G, 16^{0}GS, 11^{0}G

	Starts	1st	2nd	3rd	Win & Pl
Career Total (Turf)	16	0	0	2	691
Career Total (AW)	3	0	0	0	0

Going (Turf): Sf: 0-1 GS: 0-1 Gd: 0-5 GF: 0-8 Fm: 0-1
Distance: 5f/6f: 0-1 7f-8f: 0-5 9f-13f: 0-6 14f+: 0-7
Track: LH: 0-10 RH: 0-6 Tight: 0-8 Gall: 0-2
Aids: Bl: 0-0 Vi: 0-1 Tstrap: 0-0
Best Rating: 44 6/01 Bevl 7f100y gd-fm

Conclude (USA)

112 **105**

3-y-o ch c Distant View (USA)-Private Line (USA) (Private Account (USA))
H R A Cecil K Abdulla

Placings:52154 **(3222)**
2001: 8^{5}G, 8^{2}S, 10^{1}GF, 10^{5}GF, 12^{4}GS

	Starts	1st	2nd	3rd	Win & Pl
Career Total (Turf)	5	1	1	0	7385

79	5/01	Ripn	1m2f	D	G-F	£4403

Total win prize-money £4404

Going (Turf): Sf: 0-1 GS: 0-1 Gd: 0-1 **GF: 1-2** Fm: 0-0
Distance: 5f/6f: 0-0 7f-8f: 0-2 **9f-13f: 1-3** 14f+: 0-0
Track: LH: 0-0 **RH: 1-2 Tight: 1-1** Gall: 0-1
Aids: Bl: 0-0 Vi: 0-0 Tstrap: 0-0
Best Rating: 105 7/01 NmkJ 1m4f gd-sft

Concubine (IRE)

96 **71**

2-y-o b f Danehill (USA)-Bye Bold Aileen (IRE) (Warning)
R Guest Ivan Allan

Placings:00430 **(4623)**
2001: 5^{0}GF, 6^{0}G, 5^{4}G, 5^{3}G, 5^{0}GF

	Starts	1st	2nd	3rd	Win & Pl
Career Total (Turf)	5	0	0	1	861

Going (Turf): Sf: 0-0 GS: 0-0 Gd: 0-3 GF: 0-2 Fm: 0-0
Distance: 5f/6f: 0-5 7f-8f: 0-0 9f-13f: 0-0 14f+: 0-0
Track: LH: 0-0 RH: 0-0 Tight: 0-0 Gall: 0-0
Aids: Bl: 0-0 Vi: 0-0 Tstrap: 0-0
Best Rating: 71 7/01 Yarm 5f43y good

Signs of ability so far but improvement needed to win a race.

Coney Kitty (IRE)

109 **103**

3-y-o ch f Lycius (USA)-Auntie Maureen (IRE) (Roi Danzig (USA))
D Hanley William J Betz

Placings:22416-040 **(4519a)**
2001: 8^{0}G, 7^{4}GF, 8^{0}GY

	Starts	1st	2nd	3rd	Win & Pl
Career Total (Turf)	8	1	2	0	35755

86	10/00	Cork	6f	YLD	£22750

Total win prize-money £22750

Going (Turf): Sf: 0-0 GS: 0-0 Gd: 0-2 GF: 0-1 Fm: 0-0
Distance: **5f/6f: 1-3** 7f-8f: 0-4 9f-13f: 0-0 14f+: 0-0
Track: LH: 0-0 RH: 0-0 Tight: 0-0 Gall: 0-0
Aids: Bl: 0-0 Vi: 0-0 Tstrap: 0-0
Best Rating: 103 6/01 Asct 7f gd-fm

Beat Keats by 3/4 length in Listed event at Cork in October 2000. She was beaten 11 lengths when tenth behind Imagine in the Irish 1000 Guineas on her seasonal debut. Fourth in the Jersey Stakes at Royal Ascot in a light campaign.

Congratulate

93 **65**

3-y-o ch g Mark Of Esteem (IRE)-Kiss (Habitat)
M P Tregoning Sheikh Mohammed

Placings:524 **(5182)**
2001: 9^{5}G, 12^{2}GF, 10^{4}HY

	Starts	1st	2nd	3rd	Win & Pl
Career Total (Turf)	3	0	1	0	868

Going (Turf): Sf: 0-1 GS: 0-0 Gd: 0-1 GF: 0-1 Fm: 0-0
Distance: 5f/6f: 0-0 7f-8f: 0-0 9f-13f: 0-3 14f+: 0-0
Track: LH: 0-0 RH: 0-1 Tight: 0-1 Gall: 0-0
Aids: Bl: 0-0 Vi: 0-0 Tstrap: 0-0
Best Rating: 65 9/01 Sand 1m1f good

Showed ability in 12 furlong maiden on fast ground, but well beaten on heavy next time.

Coniston Mill (IRE)

93(86) (38)**64**

4-y-o b f Lake Coniston (IRE)-Haiti Mill (Free State)
W R Muir Timothy N Chick

Placings:3450-064 **(3153)**
2001: 6^{0}G, 6^{6}GF, 7^{4}GS

	Starts	1st	2nd	3rd	Win & Pl
Career Total (Turf)	5	0	0	1	903
Career Total (AW)	2	0	0	0	0

Going (Turf): Sf: 0-2 GS: 0-1 Gd: 0-1 GF: 0-1 Fm: 0-0
Distance: 5f/6f: 0-1 7f-8f: 0-6 9f-13f: 0-0 14f+: 0-0
Track: LH: 0-3 RH: 0-0 Tight: 0-0 Gall: 0-0
Aids: Bl: 0-0 Vi: 0-0 Tstrap: 0-0
Best Rating: 30 7/01 Ling 7f gd-sft

Connect

106(99) (65)**82**

4-y-o b g Petong-Natchez Trace (Commanche Run)
M H Tompkins Www.Raceworld.Co.Uk

Placings:2136/000043056000-0104552610 **(4826)**
2001: 6^{0}GF, 5^{1}GF, 5^{0}GF, 5^{4}GF, 5^{5}GF, 5^{5}GF, 5^{2}G, 5^{6}GF, 5^{1}G, 6^{0}G

	Starts	1st	2nd	3rd	Win & Pl
Career Total (Turf)	24	3	2	2	22228
Career Total (AW)	2	0	0	0	

82	8/01	Yarm	5f43y	C(0-90)H	GD	£6438
75	6/01	Yarm	5f43y	D(0-85)H	G-F	£4329
79	9/99	Pont	5f	E	G-F	£2944

Total win prize-money £13711

Going (Turf): Sf: 0-0 GS: 0-3 Gd: 1-7 **GF: 2-13** Fm: 0-1
Distance: **5f/6f: 3-22** 7f-8f: 0-4 9f-13f: 0-0 14f+: 0-0
Track: **LH: 1-4** RH: 0-0 Tight: 0-2 Gall: 0-1

Aids: Bl: 0-2 Vi: 0-2 Tstrap: 0-0
Best Rating: 82 8/01 Yarm 5f43y good

Goes well at Yarmouth and has won twice over five furlongs there this season. He is sometimes slow into his stride. Has done most of his racing on fast ground but does handle an easier surface. Enjoys a battle.

Connor (IRE)

97 **85**

2-y-o ch c Alhaarth (IRE)-Ghayah (IRE) (Night Shift (USA))
R Hannon J T Thomas

Placings:10 **(4832)**
2001: 8^{1}G, 8^{0}GF

	Starts	1st	2nd	3rd	Win & Pl
Career Total (Turf)	2	1	0	0	4329

85	9/01	Kemp	1m	D	GD	£4329

Total win prize-money £4329

Going (Turf): Sf: 0-0 GS: 0-0 **Gd: 1-1** GF: 0-1 Fm: 0-0
Distance: 5f/6f: 0-0 **7f-8f: 1-2** 9f-13f: 0-0 14f+: 0-0
Track : LH: 0-0 **RH: 1-1** Tight: 0-0 Gall: 0-0
Aids: Bl: 0-0 Vi: 0-0 Tstrap: 0-0
Best Rating: 85 9/01 Kemp 1m good

Game winner on his Kempton debut, despite running free, but disappointed next time.

Conquering Love (IRE)

104 **63**

3-y-o b g Pursuit Of Love-Susquehanna Days (USA) (Chief's Crown (USA))
M L W Bell Nicholas R Hodges

Placings:000-45322125044 **(4776)**
2001: 11^{4}GS, 10^{5}GF, 10^{3}GF, 10^{2}GF, 10^{2}GF, 11^{1}G, 12^{2}GF, 12^{5}GS, 12^{0}G, 11^{4}GF, 11^{4}G

	Starts	1st	2nd	3rd	Win & Pl
Career Total (Turf)	14	1	3	1	7772

63	7/01	Brig	1m3f196yF(0-60)	GD	£2576

Total win prize-money £2576

Going (Turf): Sf: 0-1 GS: 0-2 **Gd: 1-4** GF: 0-7 Fm: 0-0
Distance: 5f/6f: 0-0 7f-8f: 0-3 **9f-13f: 1-11** 14f+: 0-0
Track : **LH: 1-7** RH: 0-4 Tight: 0-4 Gall: 0-3
Aids: Bl: 0-0 Vi: 0-0 Tstrap: 0-0
Best Rating: 63 7/01 Asct 1m4f gd-fm

He had been knocking at the door over shorter trips before scoring over just short of 12 furlongs at Brighton. Acts on fast ground and seems suited by being held up.

Conquestadora

107 **84+**

3-y-o b f Hernando (FR)-Seren Quest (Rainbow Quest (USA))
G A Butler The Fairy Story Partnership

Placings:30111031 **(5692)**
2001: 10^{3}S, 10^{0}G, 14^{1}GF, 13^{1}GS, 14^{1}HY, 13^{0}GS, 16^{3}G, 16^{1}S

	Starts	1st	2nd	3rd	Win & Pl
Career Total (Turf)	8	4	0	2	28827

84	11/01	Donc	2m110y	C(0-95)H	SFT	£11212
78	9/01	Hayd	1m6f	D(0-85)H	HVY	£8060
75	8/01	Haml	1m5f9y	E(0-70)H	G-S	£3290
42	7/01	Muss	1m6f	D	G-F	£2926

Total win prize-money £25489

Going (Turf): **Sf: 2-3** GS: 1-2 Gd: 0-2 GF: 1-1 Fm: 0-0
Distance: 5f/6f: 0-0 7f-8f: 0-0 9f-13f: 0-2 **14f+: 4-6**
Track : LH: 2-3 RH: 2-4 **Tight: 2-4** Gall: 1-2
Aids: Bl: 0-0 Vi: 0-0 Tstrap: 0-0
Best Rating: 84 11/01 Donc 2m110y soft

A half-sister to Saddler's Quest and Seren Hill, she made a promising debut at Sandown in April before appreciating the step up in trip to score at Musselburgh and Hamilton, She completed the hat-trick in heavy ground at Haydock, before disappointing after that at York, but showed that form to be wrong when gaining a fourth success at Doncaster in November. Stays well and is progressive.

Consensus (IRE)

102 **89**

2-y-o b f Common Grounds-Kilbride Lass (IRE) (Lahib (USA))
M Brittain Northgate Lodgers

Placings:422102131 **(5636)**
2001: 6^{4}G, 5^{2}GF, 6^{2}GS, 6^{1}G, 6^{0}GF, 6^{2}GF, 6^{1}G, 6^{3}S, 5^{1}G

	Starts	1st	2nd	3rd	Win & Pl
Career Total (Turf)	9	3	3	1	19045

89	11/01	Catt	5f212y	D(0-85)	GD	£3607
72	9/01	Ayr	6f	C(0-95)	GD	£7962
75	8/01	Ripn	6f	E	GD	£4030

Total win prize-money £15601

Going (Turf): Sf: 0-1 GS: 0-1 **Gd: 3-4** GF: 0-3 Fm: 0-0
Distance: **5f/6f: 3-9** 7f-8f: 0-0 9f-13f: 0-0 14f+: 0-0
Track : **LH: 1-1** RH: 0-0 **Tight: 1-1** Gall: 0-0
Aids: Bl: 0-0 Vi: 0-0 Tstrap: 0-0
Best Rating: 89 11/01 Catt 5f212y good

She got off the mark with a clear-cut win in a Ripon maiden auction event in August and added another victory in an Ayr nursery in September. Suited by six furlongs and being held up, she had her perfect conditions when showing a nice turn of foot to score at Catterick in November.

Consignia (IRE)

90 **68**

2-y-o ch f Definite Article-Coppelia (IRE) (Mac's Imp (USA))
G B Balding M Kerr Dineen, S Melhado & S Scott

Placings:0000 **(5340)**
2001: 6^{0}GF, 6^{0}GF, 6^{0}G, 6^{0}GS

	Starts	1st	2nd	3rd	Win & Pl
Career Total (Turf)	4	0	0	0	

Going (Turf): Sf: 0-0 GS: 0-1 Gd: 0-1 GF: 0-2 Fm: 0-0
Distance: 5f/6f: 0-3 7f-8f: 0-1 9f-13f: 0-0 14f+: 0-0
Track : LH: 0-0 RH: 0-0 Tight: 0-0 Gall: 0-0
Aids: Bl: 0-0 Vi: 0-0 Tstrap: 0-0
Best Rating: 68 10/01 NmkR 6f good

Veered left at the start on her debut and has yet to make the frame in subsequent outings. Has only raced on a sound surface.

Consort

98(90) (43)**43**

8-y-o b g Groom Dancer (USA)-Darnelle (Shirley Heights)
Mrs J R Ramsden Mrs C Stewart-Moore

Placings:213504/442301/060220020/00060446000030/0000000-040 **(5539)**
2001: 8^{0}GF, 8^{4}F, 8^{0}S

	Starts	1st	2nd	3rd	Win & Pl
Career Total (Turf)	40	2	5	2	70227
Career Total (AW)	5	0	0	1	556

89	11/97	NmkR	1m	C(0-100)H	G-F	£24234
74	8/96	Sals	6f212y	D	G-F	£3262

Total win prize-money £27496

Going (Turf): Sf: 0-5 GS: 0-4 Gd: 0-12 **GF: 2-18** Fm: 0-1
Distance: 5f/6f: 0-0 **7f-8f: 2-34** 9f-13f: 0-11 14f+: 0-0
Track : LH: 0-8 RH: 0-8 Tight: 0-10 Gall: 0-2
Aids: Bl: 0-0 Vi: 0-0 Tstrap: 0-1
Best Rating: 43 9/01 Pont 1m4y firm

Conspire (IRE)

99(90) (44)**62**

3-y-o b f Turtle Island (IRE)-Mild Intrigue (USA) (Sir Ivor)
G A Butler Anthony Rogers

Placings:34-232333230 **(4844)**
2001: 7^{2}SD, 10^{3}SD, 11^{2}GF, 9^{3}F, 7^{3}G, 9^{3}SD, 9^{2}F, 12^{3}GF, 9^{0}G

	Starts	1st	2nd	3rd	Win & Pl
Career Total (Turf)	8	0	2	4	4086
Career Total (AW)	3	0	1	2	1599

Going (Turf): Sf: 0-1 GS: 0-0 Gd: 0-2 GF: 0-3 Fm: 0-2
Distance: 5f/6f: 0-0 7f-8f: 0-2 9f-13f: 0-9 14f+: 0-0
Track : LH: 0-7 RH: 0-3 Tight: 0-5 Gall: 0-0
Aids: Bl: 0-1 Vi: 0-0 Tstrap: 0-4
Best Rating: 74 5/01 Haml 1m3f16y gd-fm

Constable

97 **86+**

2-y-o gr g Efisio-Tagiki (IRE) (Doyoun)
P F I Cole Richard Green (fine Paintings)

Placings:51 **(4853)**
2001: 6^{5}GF, 5^{1}GF

	Starts	1st	2nd	3rd	Win & Pl
Career Total (Turf)	2	1	0	0	3626

86	9/01	Catt	5f212y	D	G-F	£3626

Total win prize-money £3626

Going (Turf): Sf: 0-0 GS: 0-0 Gd: 0-0 **GF: 1-2** Fm: 0-0
Distance: **5f/6f: 1-2** 7f-8f: 0-0 9f-13f: 0-0 14f+: 0-0
Track : **LH: 1-1** RH: 0-0 **Tight: 1-1** Gall: 0-0
Aids: Bl: 0-0 Vi: 0-0 Tstrap: 0-0
Best Rating: 86 9/01 Catt 5f212y gd-fm

Half-brother to Peacock Alley and Barathiki, this tall, narrow type made an impressive start to his career winning a decent Catterick maiden over six furlongs on her second outing.

Constitute (USA)

74 **57**

2-y-o b f Gone West (USA)-Appointed One (USA) (Danzig (USA))
Sir Michael Stoute Cheveley Park Stud

Placings:0 **(5139)**
2001: 6^{0}G

	Starts	1st	2nd	3rd	Win & Pl
Career Total (Turf)	1	0	0	0	

Going (Turf): Sf: 0-0 GS: 0-0 Gd: 0-1 GF: 0-0 Fm: 0-0
Distance: 5f/6f: 0-1 7f-8f: 0-0 9f-13f: 0-0 14f+: 0-0
Track : LH: 0-0 RH: 0-0 Tight: 0-0 Gall: 0-0
Aids: Bl: 0-0 Vi: 0-0 Tstrap: 0-0
Best Rating: 57 10/01 NmkR 6f good

Contact (IRE)

80

4-y-o br g Grand Lodge (USA)-Pink Cashmere (IRE) (Polar Falcon (USA))
M Wigham D Hassan

Placings:3616/0006-0 **(5608)**
2001: 7^{0}GS

	Starts	1st	2nd	3rd	Win & Pl
Career Total (Turf)	9	1	0	1	7820

87	9/99	Leop	6f	Y-S	£6900

Total win prize-money £6900

Going (Turf): Sf: 0-1 GS: 0-1 Gd: 0-5 GF: 0-0 Fm: 0-0

Distance: 5f/6f: 1-5 7f-8f: 0-3 9f-13f: 0-1 14f+: 0-0
Track : LH: 0-1 RH: 0-2 Tight: 0-2 Gall: 0-0
Aids: Bl: 1-2 Vi: 0-0 Tstrap: 0-0
Best Rating: 41 11/01 NmkR 7f gd-sft

Contact Dancer (IRE)

76 **62**

2-y-o b c Sadler's Wells (USA)-Rain Queen (Rainbow Quest (USA))
J L Dunlop Michael H Watt

Placings:000 **(5527)**
2001: 8^{0}S, 8^{0}S, 8^{0}HY

	Starts	1st	2nd	3rd	Win & Pl
Career Total (Turf)	3	0	0	0	

Going (Turf): Sf: 0-3 GS: 0-0 Gd: 0-0 GF: 0-0 Fm: 0-0
Distance: 5f/6f: 0-0 7f-8f: 0-1 9f-13f: 0-2 14f+: 0-0
Track : LH: 0-1 RH: 0-0 Tight: 0-0 Gall: 0-0
Aids: Bl: 0-0 Vi: 0-0 Tstrap: 0-0
Best Rating: 62 10/01 Leic 1m9y soft

Continent

114 **101**

4-y-o ch g Lake Coniston (IRE)-Krisia (Kris)
D Nicholls Lucayan Stud

Placings:3/1542-0350013 **(5005)**
2001: 7^{0}S, 6^{3}F, 6^{5}F, 6^{0}GF, 6^{0}G, 6^{1}GF, 7^{3}S

				Starts	1st	2nd	3rd	Win & Pl
Career Total (Turf)				12	2	1	3	90977
99	9/01	Ayr	6f	BH			G-F	£65000
	5/00	Chan	5f110y				SFT	£8646

Total win prize-money £73646

Going (Turf): Sf: 0-3 GS: 0-1 Gd: 0-1 **GF: 1-2** Fm: 0-2
Distance: **5f/6f: 1-6** 7f-8f: 0-3 9f-13f: 0-0 14f+: 0-0
Track : LH: 0-1 RH: 0-0 Tight: 0-0 Gall: 0-0
Aids: Bl: 0-0 Vi: 0-0 Tstrap: 0-0
Best Rating: 101 9/01 Asct 7f soft

A winning ex-French performer now with Dandy Nicholls. He started favourite for a hot Ascot handicap in July, but got no sort of a run and again did not have the clearest of runs in the Stewards' Cup. He finally got his pay-day in the Ayr Gold Cup where he displayed a tremendous turn of foot. He looked all over the winner at Ascot in September but found little off the bridle. Handles fast ground well but his trainer believes he is better with cut.

Continuation (IRE)

105 **89**

3-y-o b c Sadler's Wells (USA)-Sequel (IRE) (Law Society (USA))
J H M Gosden Sheikh Mohammed

Placings:2-32330 **(2329)**
2001: 10^{3}GS, 12^{2}GS, 10^{3}S, 10^{3}GF, 12^{0}GF

	Starts	1st	2nd	3rd	Win & Pl
Career Total (Turf)	6	0	2	3	4566

Going (Turf): Sf: 0-2 GS: 0-2 Gd: 0-0 GF: 0-2 Fm: 0-0
Distance: 5f/6f: 0-0 7f-8f: 0-1 9f-13f: 0-5 14f+: 0-0
Track : LH: 0-2 RH: 0-2 Tight: 0-1 Gall: 0-2
Aids: Bl: 0-0 Vi: 0-2 Tstrap: 0-4
Best Rating: 89 5/01 Newb 1m2f6y soft

A lightly-made colt, has shown ability over middle distances. Best with cut

Continuously (USA)

105 **87**

2-y-o b c Diesis-Play On And On (USA) (Stop The Music (USA))
H R A Cecil S Khaled

Placings:216 **(4430)**
2001: 7^{2}GF, 7^{1}GF, 7^{6}G

				Starts	1st	2nd	3rd	Win & Pl
Career Total (Turf)				3	1	1	0	7077
87	7/01	NmkJ	7f	D			G-F	£4927

Total win prize-money £4927

Going (Turf): Sf: 0-0 GS: 0-0 Gd: 0-1 **GF: 1-2** Fm: 0-0
Distance: 5f/6f: 0-0 **7f-8f: 1-3** 9f-13f: 0-0 14f+: 0-0
Track : LH: 0-0 RH: 0-2 Tight: 0 0 Gall: 0-0
Aids: Bl: 0-0 Vi: 0-0 Tstrap: 0-0
Best Rating: 87 7/01 NmkJ 7f gd-fm

A half-brother to the quite useful Joyeux Player and winner Neverending, he got off the mark at Newmarket on his second run but took a long time to get on top. Out of his depth in the Solario next time.

Contraband

105 **89+**

3-y-o b g Red Ransom (USA)-Shortfall (Last Tycoon)
W J Haggas Highclere Thoroughbred Racing Ltd

Placings:0-25101 **(3471)**
2001: 8^{2}G, 8^{5}GF, 9^{1}G, 11^{0}S, 12^{1}GF

					Starts	1st	2nd	3rd	Win & Pl
Career Total (Turf)					6	2	1	0	12941
89	7/01	Asct	1m4f	D(0-85)H				G-F	£6792
67	6/01	Muss	1m1f	D				GD	£4173

Total win prize-money £10966

Going (Turf): Sf: 0-1 GS: 0-0 **Gd: 1-3 GF: 1-2** Fm: 0-0
Distance: 5f/6f: 0-0 7f-8f: 0-3 **9f-13f: 2-3** 14f+: 0-0
Track : LH: 0-1 **RH: 1-2** Tight: 0-0 **Gall: 1-1**
Aids: Bl: 0-0 Vi: 0-0 Tstrap: 0-0
Best Rating: 89 7/01 Asct 1m4f gd-fm

Ran well in defeat at Newmarket and Kempton before scoring an easy win over nine furlongs at Musselburgh. May not have handled the softer ground next time and returned to form with a very impressive win at Ascot. Stays 12 furlongs and needs a sound surface.

Contrary Mary

106(94) (58)**73**

6-y-o b m Mujadil (USA)-Love Street (Mummy's Pet)
N Hamilton (J Akehurst 11/8) The Grass Is Greener Partnership Ii

Placings:210540/00233010400/0100440345/00512201460-6303214122 **(5688)**
2001: 6^{6}GF, 6^{3}G, 7^{0}GF, 6^{3}GF, 6^{2}GF, 7^{1}G, 7^{4}F, 6^{1}HY, 6^{2}GS, 7^{2}S

					Starts	1st	2nd	3rd	Win & Pl
Career Total (Turf)					45	7	7	5	37902
Career Total (AW)					4	0	0	0	0
72	10/01	Wind	6f	E(0-75)H				HVY	£3514
66	8/01	NmkJ	7f	E				GD	£3562
65	9/00	Epsm	7f	E(0-70)H				GD	£4543
62	6/00	Sals	6f	E(0-70)H				G-F	£2977
66	4/99	Folk	7f	E(0-70)				SFT	£3052
71	8/98	Ling	7f	E(0-70)H				G-F	£3572
82	5/97	Ling	5f	E				G-F	£3148

Total win prize-money £24369

Going (Turf): Sf: 2-6 GS: 0-8 Gd: 2-15 **GF: 3-15** Fm: 0-1
Distance: 5f/6f: 3-25 **7f-8f: 4-24** 9f-13f: 0-0 14f+: 0-0
Track : **LH: 1-16** RH: 0-4 **Tight: 1-7** Gall: 0-6
Aids: Bl: 0-0 Vi: 0-0 Tstrap: 0-0
Best Rating: 73 11/01 Donc 7f soft

Fair handicapper, effective six to seven furlongs, seems to act on most surfaces.

Conundrum (IRE)

101 **71**

3-y-o ch g Dr Devious (IRE)-Wasabi (IRE) (Polar Falcon (USA))
P W Harris Mrs P W Harris

Placings:345 **(5631)**
2001: 8^{3}G, 10^{4}HY, 10^{5}G

	Starts	1st	2nd	3rd	Win & Pl
Career Total (Turf)	3	0	0	1	643

Going (Turf): Sf: 0-1 GS: 0-0 Gd: 0-2 GF: 0-0 Fm: 0-0
Distance: 5f/6f: 0-0 7f-8f: 0-0 9f-13f: 0-3 14f+: 0-0
Track : LH: 0-2 RH: 0-0 Tight: 0-2 Gall: 0-0
Aids: Bl: 0-0 Vi: 0-0 Tstrap: 0-0
Best Rating: 71 9/01 Nott 1m54y good

Has run well on all three starts so far, but pulled hard at Redcar in November.

Conwy Castle

105 **85**

4-y-o b c Sri Pekan (USA)-Dumayla (Shernazar)
Mrs S Lamyman (P R Webber 19/5) David Fravigar And Nigel Underwood

Placings:551-06530 **(4225)**
2001: 11^{0}GS, 12^{6}GF, 16^{5}G, 18^{3}G, 14^{0}GF

				Starts	1st	2nd	3rd	Win & Pl
Career Total (Turf)				8	1	0	1	5712
85	9/00	Brig	1m3f196yD				SFT	£2857

Total win prize-money £2857

Going (Turf): Sf: 1-1 GS: 0-1 Gd: 0-2 GF: 0-4 Fm: 0-0
Distance: 5f/6f: 0-0 7f-8f: 0-0 **9f-13f: 1-5** 14f+: 0-3
Track : **LH: 1-3** RH: 0-5 Tight: 0-1 Gall: 0-4
Aids: Bl: 0-0 Vi: 0-0 Tstrap: 0-0
Best Rating: 77 6/01 NmkJ 1m4f gd-fm

Winner of a soft-ground Brighton maiden on his third and final start of last season, he was then put over hurdles but returned to the level in the summer of 2001. Lightly raced over marathon trips, he stays well.

Cookie Crumble

94(106) (62)**46**

3-y-o b f Never So Bold-Well Tried (IRE) (Thatching)
R Hollinshead Mrs A D Williams

Placings:5-154406000 **(5292)**
2001: 6^{1}SD, 8^{5}SD, 6^{4}SD, 7^{4}G, 8^{0}GF, 7^{6}SD, 7^{0}GF, 7^{0}GS, 7^{0}S

				Starts	1st	2nd	3rd	Win & Pl
Career Total (Turf)				5	0	0	0	0
Career Total (AW)				5	1	0	0	3183
62	1/01	Wolv	6f	D			STD	£2891

Total win prize-money £2891

Going (Turf): Sf: 0-1 GS: 0-1 Gd: 0-1 GF: 0-2 Fm: 0-0
Distance: **5f/6f: 1-2** 7f-8f: 0-7 9f-13f: 0-1 14f+: 0-0
Track : **LH: 1-9** RH: 0-0 **Tight: 1-2** Gall: 0-0
Aids: Bl: 0-0 Vi: 0-0 Tstrap: 0-0
Best Rating: 62 1/01 Wolv 6f stand

Cool Bathwick (IRE)

86 **58**

2-y-o b c Entrepreneur-Tarafa (Akarad (FR))
E J O'Neill W Clifford

Placings:0 **(5606)**
2001: 10^{0}GS

	Starts	1st	2nd	3rd	Win & Pl
Career Total (Turf)	1	0	0	0	

Going (Turf): Sf: 0-0 GS: 0-1 Gd: 0-0 GF: 0-0 Fm: 0-0
Distance: 5f/6f: 0-0 7f-8f: 0-0 9f-13f: 0-1 14f+: 0-0
Track : LH: 0-0 RH: 0-0 Tight: 0-0 Gall: 0-0

Aids: Bl: 0-0 Vi: 0-0 Tstrap: 0-0
Best Rating: 58 11/01 NmkR 1m2f gd-sft

Cool Chron

83(79) (48)**37**
2-y-o b f Polar Falcon (USA)-Lough Graney (Sallust)
N Tinkler The Oldham Chronicle Racing Club

Placings:000300 **(4793)**
2001: 5^{0}GF, 6^{0}GF, 7^{0}GF, 7^{3}SD, 7^{0}HY, 8^{0}G

	Starts	1st	2nd	3rd	Win & Pl
Career Total (Turf)	5	0	0	0	
Career Total (AW)	1	0	0	1	271

Going (Turf): Sf: 0-1 GS: 0-0 Gd: 0-1 GF: 0-3 Fm: 0-0
Distance: 5f/6f: 0-2 7f-8f: 0-4 9f-13f: 0-0 14f+: 0-0
Track : LH: 0-4 RH: 0-0 Tight: 0-0 Gall: 0-0
Aids: Bl: 0-0 Vi: 0-0 Tstrap: 0-0
Best Rating: 48 7/01 Sthl 7f stand

Cool Investment (IRE)

101 **78**
4-y-o b g Prince Of Birds (USA)-Superb Investment (IRE) (Hatim (USA))
R M Stronge (M Johnston 20/10) A P Holland

Placings:1/20644135104-0005025 **(5622)**
2001: 12^{0}S, 10^{0}GF, 10^{0}G, 14^{5}G, 14^{0}HY, 11^{2}S, 14^{5}GS

	Starts	1st	2nd	3rd	Win & Pl
Career Total (Turf)	19	3	2	1	29494

95	9/00	Luce	1m7f	HVY	£9412
91	7/00	Wind	1m3f135yC(0-90)	SFT	£5562
48	9/99	Muss	1m E	G-F	£3436

Total win prize-money £18410

Going (Turf): Sf: 2-7 GS: 0-2 Gd: 0-5 GF: 1-4 Fm: 0-1
Distance: 5f/6f: 0-0 7f-8f: 1-2 9f-13f: 1-12 14f+: 1-5
Track : LH: 0-11 **RH: 1-6 Tight: 2-8** Gall: 0-5
Aids: Bl: 0-1 Vi: 0-0 Tstrap: 0-0
Best Rating: 82 4/01 Epsm 1m4f10y soft

Stays well, having won the Swiss St Leger in 2000. Appreciates easy ground and being ridden positively.

Cool Prospect

(98) (38)**53**
6-y-o b g Mon Tresor-I Ran Lovely (Persian Bold)
K A Ryan Mrs Candice Reilly

Placings:53200/024200**320**/**30**0006004100**000**/**050541**
04232200306-**060405** **(0458)**
2001: 6^{0}SW, 6^{0}SD, 7^{6}SW, 6^{0}SD, 6^{4}SD, 5^{0}SD, 8^{5}SD

	Starts	1st	2nd	3rd	Win & Pl
Career Total (Turf)	34	2	6	2	16435
Career Total (AW)	19	0	1	3	1917

51	5/00	Muss	5f	F(0-65)H	FRM	£2548
49	6/99	Rdcr	6f	G(0-60)H	FRM	£2360

Total win prize-money £4908

Going (Turf): Sf: 0-3 GS: 0-3 Gd: 0-8 GF: 0-15 **Fm: 2-5**
Distance: 5f/6f: 2-30 7f-8f: 0-15 9f-13f: 0-8 14f+: 0-0
Track : LH: 0-28 RH: 0-4 Tight: 0-18 Gall: 0-2
Aids: Bl: 2-18 Vi: 0-2 Tstrap: 0-0
Best Rating: 38 2/01 Sthl 6f stand

Cool Singer

(94) (50)
3-y-o b g Sea Raven (IRE)-Clean Singer (Chief Singer)
J G Given J Sheard & J Poole

Placings:04600 **(0753)**
2001: 8^{0}SD, 8^{4}SD, 8^{6}SW, 7^{0}SD, 7^{0}SW

	Starts	1st	2nd	3rd	Win & Pl
Career Total (Turf)	0	0	0	0	
Career Total (AW)	5	0	0	0	0

Going (Turf): Sf: 0-0 GS: 0-0 Gd: 0-0 GF: 0-0 Fm: 0-0
Distance: 5f/6f: 0-0 7f-8f: 0-5 9f-13f: 0-0 14f+: 0-0
Track : LH: 0-5 RH: 0-0 Tight: 0-0 Gall: 0-0
Aids: Bl: 0-0 Vi: 0-0 Tstrap: 0-0
Best Rating: 50 2/01 Sthl 1m slow

Cool Spice

102 **74**
4-y-o b f Karinga Bay-Cool Run (Deep Run)
B Palling Celtic Racing

Placings:046500-12221260165 **(4461)**
2001: 11^{1}GS, 11^{2}GS, 11^{2}G, 11^{2}GF, 12^{1}G, 11^{2}GF, 11^{6}GF, 11^{0}G, 13^{1}G, 13^{6}GF, 12^{5}GS

	Starts	1st	2nd	3rd	Win & Pl
Career Total (Turf)	17	3	4	0	10788

74	8/01	Bath	1m5f22y E(0-75)H	GD	£3073
65	7/01	Chep	1m4f23y F(0-70)H	GD	£2296
56	5/01	Brig	1m3f196yF(0-60)H	G-S	£1876

Total win prize-money £7245

Going (Turf): Sf: 0-1 GS: 1-5 **Gd: 2-5** GF: 0-5 Fm: 0-0
Distance: 5f/6f: 0-0 7f-8f: 0-2 **9f-13f: 2-12** 14f+: 1-2
Track : LH: 3-9 RH: 0-1 **Tight: 1-8** Gall: 0-0
Aids: Bl: 0-0 Vi: 0-0 Tstrap: 0-0
Best Rating: 74 8/01 Bath 1m5f22y good

Fair middle-distance handicapper, stays 13 furlongs appreciates give in the ground.

Cool Storm (IRE)

92 **60**
2-y-o b f Rainbow Quest (USA)-Classic Park (Robellino (USA))
P W Harris P A & D G Sakal

Placings:0 **(5112)**
2001: 8^{0}HY

	Starts	1st	2nd	3rd	Win & Pl
Career Total (Turf)	1	0	0	0	

Going (Turf): Sf: 0-1 GS: 0-0 Gd: 0-0 GF: 0-0 Fm: 0-0
Distance: 5f/6f: 0-0 7f-8f: 0-0 9f-13f: 0-1 14f+: 0-0
Track : LH: 0-1 RH: 0-0 Tight: 0-0 Gall: 0-0
Aids: Bl: 0-0 Vi: 0-0 Tstrap: 0-0
Best Rating: 60 10/01 Nott 1m54y heavy

Cool Temper

101(107) (77)**70**
5-y-o b g Magic Ring (IRE)-Ovideo (Domynsky)
J M P Eustace M J G Clubb

Placings:222222/555054400-**123**0302500 **(4452)**
2001: 8^{1}SD, 8^{2}SD, 10^{3}SD, 8^{0}G, 8^{3}G, 8^{0}GF, 8^{2}GF, 8^{5}SD, 7^{0}GF, 7^{0}GF

	Starts	1st	2nd	3rd	Win & Pl
Career Total (Turf)	20	0	7	1	9672
Career Total (AW)	5	1	1	1	3622

77	3/01	Wolv	1m100y E(0-70)H	STD	£2408

Total win prize-money £2408

Going (Turf): Sf: 0-3 GS: 0-2 Gd: 0-3 GF: 0-11 Fm: 0-1
Distance: 5f/6f: 0-4 7f-8f: 0-13 **9f-13f: 1-8** 14f+: 0-0
Track : LH: 1-10 RH: 0-2 **Tight: 1-4** Gall: 0-2
Aids: Bl: 0-0 Vi: 0-0 Tstrap: 0-6
Best Rating: 77 4/01 Ling 1m2f stand

Runner-up in six successive races as a juvenile, he eventually got off the mark on the Wolverhampton Fibresand in March 2001. He has also run a couple of creditable races on turf at Yarmouth this season.

Cool Tune

83 **79**
2-y-o b c Piccolo-Agony Aunt (Formidable (USA))
J R Fanshawe Ivan Allan

Placings:03 **(5088)**
2001: 6^{0}GS, 6^{3}GS

	Starts	1st	2nd	3rd	Win & Pl
Career Total (Turf)	2	0	0	1	433

Going (Turf): Sf: 0-0 GS: 0-2 Gd: 0-0 GF: 0-0 Fm: 0-0
Distance: 5f/6f: 0-2 7f-8f: 0-0 9f-13f: 0-0 14f+: 0-0
Track : LH: 0-0 RH: 0-0 Tight: 0-0 Gall: 0-0
Aids: Bl: 0-0 Vi: 0-0 Tstrap: 0-0
Best Rating: 79 10/01 Newc 6f gd-sft

Slowly away and hampered on Haydock debut, he was beaten at odds-on next time.

Coolers Quest

76 **46**
2-y-o b f Saddlers' Hall (IRE)-Lucidity (Vision (USA))
W G M Turner Mrs K A Davis

Placings:5 **(2502)**
2001: 7^{5}GF

	Starts	1st	2nd	3rd	Win & Pl
Career Total (Turf)	1	0	0	0	0

Going (Turf): Sf: 0-0 GS: 0-0 Gd: 0-0 GF: 0-1 Fm: 0-0
Distance: 5f/6f: 0-0 7f-8f: 0-1 9f-13f: 0-0 14f+: 0-0
Track : LH: 0-0 RH: 0-1 Tight: 0-0 Gall: 0-1
Aids: Bl: 0-0 Vi: 0-0 Tstrap: 0-0
Best Rating: 46 6/01 Kemp 7f gd-fm

Cooling Castle (FR)

85 **19**
5-y-o ch g Sanglamore (USA)-Syphaly (USA) (Lyphard (USA))
Ronald Thompson B Bruce

Placings:300/01056500/00 **(2375)**
2001: 12^{0}S, 10^{0}GF

	Starts	1st	2nd	3rd	Win & Pl
Career Total (Turf)	13	1	0	1	2838

59	4/99	Bevl	1m1f207yF	GD	£2364

Total win prize-money £2364

Going (Turf): Sf: 0-3 GS: 0-2 **Gd: 1-3** GF: 0-5 Fm: 0-0
Distance: 5f/6f: 0-1 7f-8f: 0-2 **9f-13f: 1-9** 14f+: 0-1
Track : LH: 0-5 **RH: 1-5** Tight: 0-5 Gall: 0-2
Aids: Bl: 0-0 Vi: 0-0 Tstrap: 0-0
Best Rating: 19 6/01 Rdcr 1m2f gd-fm

Cooling Off (IRE)

101(98) (55)**72**
4-y-o b f Brief Truce (USA)-Lovers' Parlour (Beldale Flutter (USA))
J R Jenkins Christopher Shankland

Placings:035042-42203550 **(4594)**
2001: 12^{4}SD, 12^{2}S, 12^{2}HY, 12^{0}GS, 13^{3}G, 14^{5}GF, 11^{5}GF, 14^{0}G

	Starts	1st	2nd	3rd	Win & Pl
Career Total (Turf)	13	0	3	2	5922
Career Total (AW)	1	0	0	0	0

Going (Turf): Sf: 0-4 GS: 0-1 Gd: 0-4 GF: 0-3 Fm: 0-0
Distance: 5f/6f: 0-0 7f-8f: 0-0 9f-13f: 0-10 14f+: 0-3
Track : LH: 0-4 RH: 0-9 Tight: 0-4 Gall: 0-2
Aids: Bl: 0-0 Vi: 0-0 Tstrap: 0-0
Best Rating: 76 4/01 Kemp 1m4f soft

Cop My Gator (IRE)

99 **73**

2-y-o b c Danehill Dancer (IRE)-Delta Blues (IRE) (Digamist (USA))
N A Callaghan Andy J Smith

Placings:454162 **(4041)**
2001: 5^{4}F, 5^{5}G, 6^{4}GF, 7^{1}G, 7^{6}GF, 5^{2}HY

				Starts	1st	2nd	3rd	Win & Pl
Career Total (Turf)				6	1	1	0	7183
73	7/01	NmkJ	7f	E			GD	£4862

Total win prize-money £4862

Going (Turf): Sf: 0-1 GS: 0-0 **Gd: 1-2** GF: 0-2 Fm: 0-1
Distance: 5f/6f: 0-4 **7f-8f: 1-2** 9f-13f: 0-0 14f+: 0-0
Track : LH: 0-1 RH: 0-1 Tight: 0-0 Gall: 0-1
Aids: Bl: 0-0 Vi: 0-0 Tstrap: 0-0
Best Rating: 73 8/01 Hayd 5f heavy

He got off the mark in a Newmarket seller at the fourth time of asking in July 2001. He was diappointing when subsequently upped in class, but ran well in testing ground in a Haydock nursery when dropped to five furlongs.

Copcourt Royale

(91) (45)**32**

3-y-o b f Rock City-Royal Meeting (Dara Monarch)
P L Clinton The Racing Court

Placings:6515-00000 **(5419)**
2001: 12^{0}SD, 10^{0}G, 10^{0}F, 12^{0}SD, 12^{0}SD

				Starts	1st	2nd	3rd	Win & Pl
Career Total (Turf)				2	0	0	0	
Career Total (AW)				7	1	0	0	1897
60	11/00	Wolv	1m100y	G			STD	£1897

Total win prize-money £1897

Going (Turf): Sf: 0-0 GS: 0-0 Gd: 0-1 GF: 0-0 Fm: 0-1
Distance: 5f/6f: 0-0 7f-8f: 0-1 **9f-13f: 1-8** 14f+: 0-0
Track : **LH: 1-8** RH: 0-1 **Tight: 1-6** Gall: 0-0
Aids: Bl: 0-0 Vi: 0-0 Tstrap: 0-0
Best Rating: 32 5/01 Ripn 1m2f good

Copeland

99 **102**

6-y-o b h Generous (IRE)-Whitehaven (Top Ville)
M C Pipe Dr D B A & Mrs Heather Silk

Placings:11222110523/4630142/00 **(2607)**
2001: 18^{0}GF, 16^{0}F

				Starts	1st	2nd	3rd	Win & Pl
Career Total (Turf)				20	5	5	2	97449
	6/99	Pari	1m4f				GD	£21529
111	8/98	Claf	1m4f				SFT	£14141
111	6/98	Frau	1m4f				GD	£19917
	3/98	Nant	1m4f				SFT	£4040
	3/98	Agtn	1m2f110y				HVY	£3535

Total win prize-money £63162

Going (Turf): Sf: 1-3 GS: 0-1 **Gd: 1-1** GF: 0-1 Fm: 0-1
Distance: 5f/6f: 0-0 7f-8f: 0-0 **9f-13f: 2-4** 14f+: 0-5
Track : LH: 0-4 **RH: 2-5** Tight: 0-1 Gall: 0-1
Aids: **Bl: 1-4** Vi: 0-2 Tstrap: 0-0
Best Rating: 101 5/01 Ches 2m2f147y gd-fm

A decent stayer on the level in France in 1998/1999, he is better known as a hurdler nowadays. Well beaten in Chester Cup on his first run on the level for nearly two years.

Copperfields Lass

51

2-y-o b f Millkom-Salvezza (IRE) (Superpower)
Mrs Lydia Pearce B J Goldsmith

Placings:6 **(5177)**
2001: 6^{6}HY

	Starts	1st	2nd	3rd	Win & Pl
Career Total (Turf)	1	0	0	0	0

Going (Turf): Sf: 0-1 GS: 0-0 Gd: 0-0 GF: 0-0 Fm: 0-0
Distance: 5f/6f: 0-1 7f-8f: 0-0 9f-13f: 0-0 14f+: 0-0
Track : LH: 0-0 RH: 0-0 Tight: 0-0 Gall: 0-0
Aids: Bl: 0-0 Vi: 0-0 Tstrap: 0-0
Best Rating: 51 10/01 Wind 6f heavy

Coppermalt (USA)

101 **74**

3-y-o b c Affirmed (USA)-Poppy Carew (IRE) (Danehill (USA))
P W Harris Mrs A M Palmer

Placings:0430 **(4851)**
2001: 8^{0}GS, 8^{4}GF, 8^{3}GF, 7^{0}GF

	Starts	1st	2nd	3rd	Win & Pl
Career Total (Turf)	4	0	0	1	998

Going (Turf): Sf: 0-0 GS: 0-1 Gd: 0-0 GF: 0-3 Fm: 0-0
Distance: 5f/6f: 0-0 7f-8f: 0-3 9f-13f: 0-1 14f+: 0-0
Track : LH: 0-0 RH: 0-2 Tight: 0-0 Gall: 0-0
Aids: Bl: 0-0 Vi: 0-0 Tstrap: 0-0
Best Rating: 74 7/01 Sand 1m14y gd-fm

Copplestone (IRE)

98(77) (73)**60**

5-y-o b g Second Set (IRE)-Queen Of The Brush (Averof)
P W Harris Mrs P W Harris

Placings:634343/4/02440432220-005400 **(5092)**
2001: 8^{0}SD, 8^{0}G, 8^{5}GF, 7^{4}GS, 8^{0}GF, 8^{0}GS

	Starts	1st	2nd	3rd	Win & Pl
Career Total (Turf)	22	0	4	3	13724
Career Total (AW)	2	0	0	1	465

Going (Turf): Sf: 0-1 GS: 0-3 Gd: 0-4 GF: 0-11 Fm: 0-3
Distance: 5f/6f: 0-1 7f-8f: 0-11 9f-13f: 0-12 14f+: 0-0
Track : LH: 0-11 RH: 0-6 Tight: 0-7 Gall: 0-2
Aids: Bl: 0-0 Vi: 0-2 Tstrap: 0-1
Best Rating: 66 7/01 Yarm 1m3y gd-fm

Copy-Cat

79 **59**

3-y-o b f Lion Cavern (USA)-Imperial Jade (Lochnager)
W R Muir Timothy N Chick

Placings:400-0 **(1615)**
2001: 5^{0}GF

	Starts	1st	2nd	3rd	Win & Pl
Career Total (Turf)	4	0	0	0	0

Going (Turf): Sf: 0-0 GS: 0-1 Gd: 0-1 GF: 0-2 Fm: 0-0
Distance: 5f/6f: 0-4 7f-8f: 0-0 9f-13f: 0-0 14f+: 0-0
Track : LH: 0-1 RH: 0-1 Tight: 0-0 Gall: 0-2
Aids: Bl: 0-0 Vi: 0-0 Tstrap: 0-0
Best Rating: 20 5/01 Ling 5f gd-fm

Copyforce Girl

98 (50)**59**

5-y-o b m Elmaamul (USA)-Sabaya (USA) (Seattle Dancer (USA))
Miss B Sanders Copy Xpress Ltd

Placings:0036/6020040/1322262-005300 **(5599)**
2001: 11^{0}F, 10^{0}F, 12^{5}GF, 14^{3}GF, 11^{0}S, 12^{0}GS

				Starts	1st	2nd	3rd	Win & Pl
Career Total (Turf)				22	1	5	3	10993
Career Total (AW)				2	0	0	0	0
55	6/00	Brig	1m3f196yE(0-65)				FRM	£2776

Total win prize-money £2776

Going (Turf): Sf: 0-1 GS: 0-5 Gd: 0-3 GF: 0-9 **Fm: 1-4**
Distance: 5f/6f: 0-1 7f-8f: 0-3 **9f-13f: 1-15** 14f+: 0-5
Track : **LH: 1-14** RH: 0-8 Tight: 0-11 Gall: 0-4
Aids: Bl: 0-0 Vi: 0-0 **Tstrap: 1-12**
Best Rating: 59 7/01 Epsm 1m4f10y gd-fm

She has made the frame several times, but only has one success to her name and the Handicapper seems to have her measure. Suited by 12 to 14 furlongs.

Coral Shells

(80) (2)**41**

4-y-o b f Formidable (USA)-Elle Reef (Shareef Dancer (USA))
R M Flower R M Flower

Placings:06025/0000060000-0 **(0065)**
2001: 8^{0}SD

	Starts	1st	2nd	3rd	Win & Pl
Career Total (Turf)	14	0	1	0	1416
Career Total (AW)	2	0	0	0	

Going (Turf): Sf: 0-4 GS: 0-0 Gd: 0-1 GF: 0-5 Fm: 0-3
Distance: 5f/6f: 0-0 7f-8f: 0-10 9f-13f: 0-5 14f+: 0-0
Track : LH: 0-9 RH: 0-2 Tight: 0-3 Gall: 0-0
Aids: Bl: 0-6 Vi: 0-0 Tstrap: 0-0

Corblets

73(99) (46)**57d**

4-y-o b f Timeless Times (USA)-Dear Glenda (Gold Song)
J J Quinn Mrs M Lingwood

Placings:4250/322500036306-0 **(0824)**
2001: 5^{0}S

	Starts	1st	2nd	3rd	Win & Pl
Career Total (Turf)	16	0	3	2	5858
Career Total (AW)	1	0	0	1	422

Going (Turf): Sf: 0-2 GS: 0-3 Gd: 0-4 GF: 0-7 Fm: 0-0
Distance: 5f/6f: 0-17 7f-8f: 0-0 9f-13f: 0-0 14f+: 0-0
Track : LH: 0-3 RH: 0-3 Tight: 0-1 Gall: 0-4
Aids: Bl: 0-0 Vi: 0-0 Tstrap: 0-0
Best Rating: 16 4/01 Ripn 5f soft

Cork Harbour (FR)

110(92) (72)**77**

5-y-o ch g Grand Lodge (USA)-Irish Sea (Irish River (FR))
Mrs N Smith Martin Ingram

Placings:63/105-506002220 **(5669)**
2001: 7^{5}GS, 10^{0}G, 10^{6}GF, 10^{0}GF, 12^{0}GF, 6^{2}S, 7^{2}GS, 7^{2}GS, 10^{0}HY

				Starts	1st	2nd	3rd	Win & Pl
Career Total (Turf)				13	1	3	1	9018
Career Total (AW)				1	0	0	0	0
71	9/00	Brig	7f214y	D			SFT	£3282

Total win prize-money £3283

Going (Turf): Sf: 1-5 GS: 0-4 Gd: 0-2 GF: 0-2 Fm: 0-0
Distance: 5f/6f: 0-0 **7f-8f: 1-5** 9f-13f: 0-9 14f+: 0-0
Track : **LH: 1-7** RH: 0-3 Tight: 0-5 Gall: 0-2
Aids: Bl: 0-6 Vi: 0-0 Tstrap: 0-0
Best Rating: 77 11/01 NmkR 7f gd-sft

Ran his best race of the season when dropped in trip at Brighton in September, and another good effort next time. Goes well in soft ground.

Cornelius

111 **106**

4-y-o b h Barathea (IRE)-Rainbow Mountain (Rainbow

Quest (USA))
P F I Cole Sir George Meyrick

Placings:136/2502040114-4551412 **(5678a)**
2001: 8^{4}GS, 8^{5}GS, 10^{5}GF, 8^{1}G, 9^{4}G, 7^{1}S, 8^{2}HO

	Starts	1st	2nd	3rd	Win & Pl
Career Total (Turf)	**20**	**5**	**3**	**1**	**68881**

106 10/01 York 7f202y B(0-105)H SFT £10219
99 7/01 Donc 1m C GD £7247
101 10/00 Newb 1m1f B(0-100)H HVY £9477
100 10/00 Ayr 1m C HVY £5834
81 5/99 York 6f D SFT £7700
Total win prize-money £40480

Going (Turf): Sf: 0-0 GS: 0-3 Gd: 1-6 GF: 0-4 Fm: 0-0
Distance: 5f/6f: 1-2 **7f-8f: 3-9** 9f-13f: 1-8 14f+: 0-0
Track : **LH: 3-7** RH: 0-5 Tight: 0-0 **Gall: 2-6**
Aids: Bl: 0-0 Vi: 0-0 Tstrap: 0-0
Best Rating: 106 11/01 StCl 1m holding

Imposing, very useful mile handicapper, bordering on Listed class. Took time to find his form in 2000, but won twice when the mud was flying in October (at Newbury and Ayr). Enjoys bowling along in front and got off the mark in a Doncaster conditions event, and had a difficult task at the weights next time. returned from a break to take a rated handicap at York in the autumn. Effective on a flat, left-handed track on easy ground.

Corridor Creeper (FR)

106 **89**
4-y-o ch g Polish Precedent (USA)-Sonia Rose (USA) (Superbity (USA))
P W Harris T Rattee & Mrs P W Harris

Placings:0221/03006300-01000 **(4718)**
2001: 6^{0}GF, 5^{1}GF, 5^{0}G, 5^{0}G, 5^{0}G

	Starts	1st	2nd	3rd	Win & Pl
Career Total (Turf)	**17**	**2**	**2**	**2**	**38789**

88 7/01 Asct 5f C(0-100)H G-F £24830
74 10/99 Brig 5f213y D G-S £3598
Total win prize-money £28429

Going (Turf): Sf: 0-0 **GS: 1-2** Gd: 0-6 **GF: 1-9** Fm: 0-0
Distance: **5f/6f: 2-15** 7f-8f: 0-2 9f-13f: 0-0 14f+: 0-0
Track : **LH: 1-1** RH: 0-0 Tight: 0-0 Gall: 0-0
Aids: Bl: 0-1 Vi: 0-0 Tstrap: 0-2
Best Rating: 88 7/01 Asct 5f gd-fm

A regular in good-class handicaps in 2000, he made a satisfactory reappearance at Goodwood, giving the impression that a return to five furlongs would suit him and confirmed that by going on to win a valuable Ascot handicap over that trip in July. The subsequent rise in the handicap seems to have found him out.

Corsican Sunset (USA)

105 **98**
3-y-o b f Thunder Gulch (USA)-Miss Evans (USA) (Nijinsky (CAN))
P F I Cole Christopher Wright

Placings:0212332045 **(5680a)**
2001: 10^{0}GS, 10^{2}S, 9^{1}GS, 12^{2}GF, 10^{3}G, 12^{3}G, 10^{2}G, 11^{0}G, 12^{4}S, 12^{5}S

	Starts	1st	2nd	3rd	Win & Pl
Career Total (Turf)	**10**	**1**	**3**	**2**	**33928**

77 5/01 Sals 1m1f198yD G-S £3055
Total win prize-money £3055

Going (Turf): Sf: 0-3 **GS: 1-2** Gd: 0-4 GF: 0-1 Fm: 0-0
Distance: 5f/6f: 0-0 7f-8f: 0-0 **9f-13f: 1-10** 14f+: 0-0
Track : LH: 0-4 **RH: 1-3 Tight: 1-1** Gall: 0-2
Aids: Bl: 0-0 Vi: 0-0 Tstrap: 0-0
Best Rating: 98 9/01 Chan 1m4f soft

Half-sister to smart French middle-distance performer Si Seductor. She won a ten-furlong maiden on easy ground, and has run creditably including in Pattern company since.

Corton (IRE)

100 **84**
2-y-o b c Definite Article-Limpopo (Green Desert (USA))
P F I Cole Mrs Belinda Harvey

Placings:534103 **(4678)**
2001: 7^{5}GF, 7^{3}GF, 8^{4}GS, 7^{1}G, 8^{0}GF, 8^{3}G

	Starts	1st	2nd	3rd	Win & Pl
Career Total (Turf)	**6**	**1**	**0**	**2**	**6777**

84 8/01 Folk 7f E GD £2961
Total win prize-money £2961

Going (Turf): Sf: 0-0 GS: 0-1 **Gd: 1-2** GF: 0-3 Fm: 0-0
Distance: 5f/6f: 0-0 **7f-8f: 1-5** 9f-13f: 0-1 14f+: 0-0
Track : LH: 0-0 RH: 0-1 Tight: 0-0 Gall: 0-1
Aids: Bl: 0-0 Vi: 0-0 Tstrap: 0-0
Best Rating: 84 9/01 Donc 1m good

Showed ability in ordinary maidens before taking a median auction event at Folkestone.

Corundum (USA)

92 **72**
2-y-o b/br c Benny The Dip (USA)-Santi Sana (Formidable (USA))
M H Tompkins Mrs A Lovat

Placings:02 **(2813)**
2001: 7^{0}S, 7^{2}GF

	Starts	1st	2nd	3rd	Win & Pl
Career Total (Turf)	**2**	**0**	**1**	**0**	**1372**

Going (Turf): Sf: 0-1 GS: 0-0 Gd: 0-0 GF: 0-1 Fm: 0-0
Distance: 5f/6f: 0-0 7f-8f: 0-2 9f-13f: 0-0 14f+: 0-0
Track : LH: 0-0 RH: 0-2 Tight: 0-0 Gall: 0-0
Aids: Bl: 0-0 Vi: 0-0 Tstrap: 0-0
Best Rating: 72 7/01 Bevl 7f100y gd-fm

Corunna

105 **79**
4-y-o b g Puissance-Kind Of Shy (Kind Of Hush)
A Berry Chris & Antonia Deuters

Placings:0222362406/331316600-00021410000 **(4684)**
2001: 5^{0}GF, 6^{0}GF, 7^{0}GF, 7^{2}GF, 7^{1}F, 7^{4}GF, 7^{1}GF, 7^{0}GF, 8^{0}GF, 7^{0}G, 7^{0}GS

	Starts	1st	2nd	3rd	Win & Pl
Career Total (Turf)	**30**	**4**	**5**	**4**	**26521**

73 7/01 Leic 7f9y E(0-70) G-F £3627
57 6/01 Ling 7f140y E(0-70) FRM £3136
80 6/00 Ling 6f D(0-85)H G-F £7540
69 6/00 Muss 5f D FRM £2795
Total win prize-money £17098

Going (Turf): Sf: 0-1 GS: 0-2 Gd: 0-5 **GF: 2-19 Fm: 2-3**
Distance: 5f/6f: 2-20 7f-8f: 2-10 9f-13f: 0-0 14f+: 0-0
Track : LH: 0-8 RH: 0-3 Tight: 0-5 Gall: 0-4
Aids: Bl: 0-0 Vi: 0-0 Tstrap: 0-0
Best Rating: 79 7/01 Ches 7f2y gd-fm

Fair handicapper, suited by seven furlongs and fast ground and had conditions in his favour when winning at Lingfield and Leicester this term.

Coshocton (USA)

105 **96**
2-y-o ch c Silver Hawk (USA)-Tribulation (USA) (Danzig (USA))
M A Jarvis John W Phillips

Placings:12 **(5255)**
2001: 6^{1}GF, 8^{2}GS

	Starts	1st	2nd	3rd	Win & Pl
Career Total (Turf)	**2**	**1**	**1**	**0**	**10841**

92 9/01 York 6f214y D G-F £6610
Total win prize-money £6611

Going (Turf): Sf: 0-0 GS: 0-1 Gd: 0-0 **GF: 1-1** Fm: 0-0
Distance: 5f/6f: 0-0 **7f-8f: 1-2** 9f-13f: 0-0 14f+: 0-0
Track : **LH: 1-1** RH: 0-1 Tight: 0-0 **Gall: 1-2**
Aids: Bl: 0-0 Vi: 0-0 Tstrap: 0-0
Best Rating: 96 10/01 Asct 1m gd-sft

Made a winning debut over seven furlongs at York, form that has worked out well, but was beaten a long way by Fight Your Corner in an Ascot Listed event next time. Should make up into a useful three-year-old.

Cosimworthit

80 **8**
5-y-o b m Imp Society (USA)-Sasha Lea (Cawston's Clown)
M R Ewer-Hoad Mrs J A Ewer

Placings:000000 **(3151)**
2001: 12^{0}SD, 9^{0}GF, 6^{0}G, 6^{0}F, 9^{0}GF, 7^{0}GS

	Starts	1st	2nd	3rd	Win & Pl
Career Total (Turf)	**5**	**0**	**0**	**0**	
Career Total (AW)	**1**	**0**	**0**	**0**	

Going (Turf): Sf: 0-0 GS: 0-1 Gd: 0-1 GF: 0-2 Fm: 0-1
Distance: 5f/6f: 0-1 7f-8f: 0-2 9f-13f: 0-3 14f+: 0-0
Track : LH: 0-3 RH: 0-1 Tight: 0-2 Gall: 0-0
Aids: Bl: 0-0 Vi: 0-0 Tstrap: 0-0
Best Rating: 8 5/01 Wind 6f good

Cosmic Case

108 **57**
6-y-o b m Casteddu-La Fontainova (IRE) (Lafontaine (USA))
J S Goldie The Cosmic Cases

Placings:66636403300/6031530004/005000/504004211345-0405221110323200034300 **(5033)**
2001: 12^{0}GS, 16^{1}S, 14^{0}GS, 13^{5}G, 13^{2}GF, 13^{2}G, 12^{1}F, 12^{1}GF, 12^{1}GF, 12^{0}G, 15^{3}GF, 12^{2}GF, 12^{3}GF, 14^{2}GF, 15^{0}GF, 16^{0}GF, 14^{3}G, 13^{4}GS, 14^{3}GF, 12^{0}GF, 16^{0}GF

	Starts	1st	2nd	3rd	Win & Pl
Career Total (Turf)	**60**	**6**	**5**	**10**	**38449**

58 6/01 Haml 1m4f17y E(0-75)H G-F £7202
55 6/01 Muss 1m4f E(0-70)H G-F £3484
50 5/01 Pont 1m4f8y E(0-70)H FRM £3851
39 7/00 Haml 1m4f17y E(0-70)H G-F £2658
39 7/00 Muss 2m F(0-60)H FRM £2194
64 5/98 Muss 1m F(0-65)H G-F £2981
Total win prize-money £22372

Going (Turf): Sf: 0-2 GS: 0-8 Gd: 0-17 **GF: 4-26** Fm: 2-7
Distance: 5f/6f: 0-8 7f-8f: 1-11 **9f-13f: 4-24** 14f+: 1-17
Track : LH: 1-13 **RH: 4-34 Tight: 4-35** Gall: 0-5
Aids: Bl: 0-0 Vi: 0-5 Tstrap: 0-0
Best Rating: 62 7/01 Hayd 1m6f gd-fm

Mixes Flat and Jumps and scored twice in 2000 on the level on consecutive days. She ran up a hat-trick of wins on fast ground in summer of 2001 before the Handicapper got stuck in, though she continued to run well. Stays two miles and likes to hear her feet rattle.

Cosmic Millennium (IRE)

100 **82**
3-y-o b c In The Wings-Windmill Princess (Gorytus (USA))
R Guest Cosmic Greyhound Racing Partnership Iii

Placings:61-04000 **(4161)**
2001: 8^{0}GS, 9^{4}GF, 6^{0}GS, 7^{0}GF, 7^{0}GF

	Starts	1st	2nd	3rd	Win & Pl

	Starts	1st	2nd	3rd	Win & Pl
Career Total (Turf)	7	1	0	0	6075

78 8/00 Ches 7f2y D GD £3575
Total win prize-money £3575

Going (Turf): Sf: 0-0 GS: 0-2 **Gd: 1-2** GF: 0-3 Fm: 0-0
Distance: 5f/6f: 0-1 **7f-8f: 1-4** 9f-13f: 0-2 14f+: 0-0
Track : **LH: 1-1** RH: 0-3 **Tight: 1-3** Gall: 0-0
Aids: Bl: 0-0 Vi: 0-0 Tstrap: 0-0
Best Rating: 82 5/01 Gdwd 1m1f gd-fm

Lightly raced. Scored over seven furlongs on his second start at two. He showed a marked improvement on his seasonal debut to finish fourth in a very valuable handicap at Goodwood in May when stepped up to nine furlongs, but has not performed so well over shorter trips since.

Cosmic Ranger

(92) (37)**49**
3-y-o b g Magic Ring (IRE)-Lismore (Relkino)
N P Littmoden Wetherby Racing Bureau 44

Placings:0506-0000005 **(3233)**
2001: 7^{0}SD, 8^{0}G, 10^{0}GF, 11^{0}GF, 16^{0}F, 12^{0}GF, 12^{5}SD

	Starts	1st	2nd	3rd	Win & Pl
Career Total (Turf)	9	0	0	0	0
Career Total (AW)	2	0	0	0	0

Going (Turf): Sf: 0-0 GS: 0-1 Gd: 0-2 GF: 0-5 Fm: 0-1
Distance: 5f/6f: 0-3 7f-8f: 0-3 9f-13f: 0-4 14f+: 0-1
Track : LH: 0-5 RH: 0-2 Tight: 0-4 Gall: 0-0
Aids: Bl: 0-0 Vi: 0-1 Tstrap: 0-0
Best Rating: 49 6/01 Bevl 1m3f216y gd-fm

Cosmic Song

106(83) (51)**34**
4-y-o b f Cosmonaut-Hotaria (Sizzling Melody)
R M Whitaker Country Lane Partnership

Placings:005/563514460500-0150000300 **(4482)**
2001: 11^{0}S, 9^{1}F, 10^{5}GF, 9^{0}GF, 8^{0}GF, 8^{0}F, 8^{0}G, 8^{3}GF, 8^{0}GF, 8^{0}F

	Starts	1st	2nd	3rd	Win & Pl
Career Total (Turf)	22	2	0	2	7299
Career Total (AW)	3	0	0	0	0

39 5/01 Rdcr 1m1f E(0-70)H FRM £3178
46 6/00 Carl 1m1f61y E(0-70)H SFT £2977
Total win prize-money £6155

Going (Turf): Sf: 1-5 GS: 0-0 Gd: 0-6 GF: 0-7 **Fm: 1-4**
Distance: 5f/6f: 0-2 7f-8f: 0-9 **9f-13f: 2-14** 14f+: 0-0
Track : LH: 1-12 RH: 1-9 **Tight: 1-10** Gall: 0-3
Aids: Bl: 0-0 Vi: 0-0 Tstrap: 0-0
Best Rating: 39 5/01 Rdcr 1m1f firm

Cosmocrat

(89) (46)**76d**
3-y-o b g Cosmonaut-Bella Coola (Northern State (USA))
M Meade Ladyswood Stud

Placings:02-0601000 **(5416)**
2001: 7^{0}GF, 10^{6}GF, 11^{0}GF, 8^{1}S, 8^{0}G, 8^{0}HY, 9^{0}SD

	Starts	1st	2nd	3rd	Win & Pl
Career Total (Turf)	8	1	1	0	3570
Career Total (AW)	1	0	0	0	

76 8/01 Chep 1m14y E(0-70)H SFT £2856
Total win prize-money £2856

Going (Turf): Sf: 1-2 GS: 0-1 Gd: 0-1 GF: 0-4 Fm: 0-0
Distance: 5f/6f: 0-0 7f-8f: 0-2 **9f-13f: 1-7** 14f+: 0-0
Track : LH: 0-5 RH: 0-0 Tight: 0-4 Gall: 0-0
Aids: Bl: 0-0 Vi: 0-0 Tstrap: 0-0
Best Rating: 76 8/01 Chep 1m14y soft

Cost Auditing

(89) (16)**50d**
4-y-o ch f Bluebird (USA)-Elabella (Ela-Mana-Mou)
Andrew Reid A S Reid

Placings:6442000/5000000-0000 **(0367)**
2001: 16^{0}SD, 8^{0}SW, 5^{0}SD, 10^{0}SW

	Starts	1st	2nd	3rd	Win & Pl
Career Total (Turf)	8	0	0	0	453
Career Total (AW)	10	0	1	0	785

Going (Turf): Sf: 0-1 GS: 0-1 Gd: 0-0 GF: 0-5 Fm: 0-1
Distance: 5f/6f: 0-10 7f-8f: 0-2 9f-13f: 0-5 14f+: 0-1
Track : LH: 0-10 RH: 0-1 Tight: 0-8 Gall: 0-1
Aids: Bl: 0-2 Vi: 0-0 Tstrap: 0-0
Best Rating: 16 2/01 Wolv 5f stand

Cote Soleil

102 **62**
4-y-o ch g Inchinor-Sunshine Coast (Posse (USA))
M L W Bell Mrs Evelyn Hankinson

Placings:12046404/330005000-000150464 **(5276)**
2001: 7^{0}GS, 7^{0}HY, 7^{0}F, 9^{1}F, 9^{5}G, 9^{0}G, 10^{4}G, 8^{6}G, 8^{4}GS

	Starts	1st	2nd	3rd	Win & Pl
Career Total (Turf)	26	2	1	2	12682

57 7/01 Muss 1m1f E(0-65) FRM £3080
66 4/99 Nott 5f13y D G-S £2723
Total win prize-money £5803

Going (Turf): Sf: 0-5 **GS: 1-3** Gd: 0-7 GF: 0-8 **Fm: 1-3**
Distance: 5f/6f: 1-5 7f-8f: 0-12 9f-13f: 1-9 14f+: 0-0
Track : LH: 0-9 RH: 0-7 Tight: 0-4 Gall: 0-1
Aids: Bl: 0-1 Vi: 0-2 Tstrap: 0-0
Best Rating: 62 7/01 Kemp 1m1f good

A debutant winner at two, he ended his first season rated 95, but has disappointed since and been dropped considerably in class. He won a moderate classified stakes over nine furlongs at Musselburgh in July. Suited by most types of ground and nine furlongs.

Cotebrook

90 **63**
2-y-o ch c First Trump-Chantelys (Ballacashtal (CAN))
A Bailey Willie McKay

Placings:56405 **(4106)**
2001: 6^{5}GS, 7^{6}GF, 7^{4}GS, 7^{0}GS, 8^{5}S

	Starts	1st	2nd	3rd	Win & Pl
Career Total (Turf)	5	0	0	0	271

Going (Turf): Sf: 0-1 GS: 0-3 Gd: 0-0 GF: 0-1 Fm: 0-0
Distance: 5f/6f: 0-0 7f-8f: 0-4 9f-13f: 0-1 14f+: 0-0
Track : LH: 0-2 RH: 0-2 Tight: 0-1 Gall: 0-0
Aids: Bl: 0-0 Vi: 0-0 Tstrap: 0-0
Best Rating: 63 7/01 Ayr 7f gd-sft

Cottam Lilly

99 **36**
4-y-o b f Sabrehill (USA)-Karminski (Pitskelly)
J S Wainwright Peter Easterby

Placings:0/000-50000 **(3086)**
2001: 9^{5}HY, 10^{0}G, 14^{0}F, 11^{0}GF, 16^{0}GF

	Starts	1st	2nd	3rd	Win & Pl
Career Total (Turf)	9	0	0	0	0

Going (Turf): Sf: 0-2 GS: 0-0 Gd: 0-3 GF: 0-3 Fm: 0-1
Distance: 5f/6f: 0-3 7f-8f: 0-0 9f-13f: 0-4 14f+: 0-2
Track : LH: 0-3 RH: 0-3 Tight: 0-5 Gall: 0-0
Aids: Bl: 0-0 Vi: 0-0 Tstrap: 0-0
Best Rating: 36 6/01 Bevl 1m3f216y gd-fm

Cotton House (IRE)

116 **101**
4-y-o b f Mujadil (USA)-Romanovna (Mummy's Pet)
M R Channon Michael A Foy

Placings:124/15156-02054400455 **(4081)**
2001: 6^{0}S, 5^{2}HY, 6^{0}GS, 5^{5}GS, 5^{4}GF, 6^{4}GF, 6^{0}GF, 5^{0}Y, 6^{4}G, 6^{5}G, 6^{5}GF

	Starts	1st	2nd	3rd	Win & Pl
Career Total (Turf)	19	3	2	0	64278

99 6/00 York 6f B(0-105)H G-F £38532
97 5/00 Leic 5f218y C(0-90) G-S £6500
88 4/99 Wwck 5f E GD £2880
Total win prize-money £47913

Going (Turf): Sf: 0-2 **GS: 1-4 Gd: 1-6 GF: 1-6** Fm: 0-0
Distance: **5f/6f: 3-19** 7f-8f: 0-0 9f-13f: 0-0 14f+: 0-0
Track : **LH: 1-3** RH: 0-0 Tight: 0-0 **Gall: 1-2**
Aids: Bl: 0-0 Vi: 0-0 Tstrap: 0-0
Best Rating: 104 5/01 Sand 5f6y gd-fm

Fractured her pelvis as a juvenile, but proved a useful sprinter in 2000. Handles most ground and likes to race prominently. She ran fourth to Cassandra Go in the Temple Stakes at Sandown in May but failed to build on that. Seems as effective at six furlongs as at five.

Cotton Kid (IRE)

91 **65**
2-y-o b c Lake Coniston (IRE)-La Suquet (Puissance)
W J Haggas Tprc Limited

Placings:046010 **(5340)**
2001: 5^{0}G, 5^{4}GF, 5^{6}GF, 7^{0}GF, 6^{1}GS, 6^{0}GS

	Starts	1st	2nd	3rd	Win & Pl
Career Total (Turf)	6	1	0	0	4396

65 10/01 Pont 6f E(0-75) G-S £4111
Total win prize-money £4111

Going (Turf): Sf: 0-0 **GS: 1-2** Gd: 0-1 GF: 0-3 Fm: 0-0
Distance: **5f/6f: 1-5** 7f-8f: 0-1 9f-13f: 0-0 14f+: 0-0
Track : **LH: 1-2** RH: 0-0 Tight: 0-1 Gall: 0-0
Aids: **Bl: 1-3** Vi: 0-0 Tstrap: 0-0
Best Rating: 65 10/01 Pont 6f gd-sft

A half-brother to Castle Sempill. Won his first race when encountering easy ground for the first time over six furlongs in blinkers.

Cottontail

70 **47**
3-y-o b g Alzao (USA)-Height Of Passion (Shirley Heights)
N Tinkler Mrs D Wright

Placings:006-0 **(1660)**
2001: 14^{0}F

	Starts	1st	2nd	3rd	Win & Pl
Career Total (Turf)	4	0	0	0	0

Going (Turf): Sf: 0-1 GS: 0-0 Gd: 0-1 GF: 0-1 Fm: 0-1
Distance: 5f/6f: 0-1 7f-8f: 0-2 9f-13f: 0-0 14f+: 0-1
Track : LH: 0-3 RH: 0-0 Tight: 0-1 Gall: 0-2
Aids: Bl: 0-0 Vi: 0-0 Tstrap: 0-0
Best Rating: 7 5/01 Rdcr 1m6f19y firm

Coual Crystal

82 **61**
2-y-o b f Cool Jazz-Indian Crystal (Petong)
J R Norton Miss A J Hurst

Placings:06500 **(5370)**
2001: 7^{0}G, 7^{6}HY, 7^{5}G, 7^{0}GS, 7^{0}G

	Starts	1st	2nd	3rd	Win & Pl
Career Total (Turf)	5	0	0	0	0

Going (Turf): Sf: 0-1 GS: 0-1 Gd: 0-3 GF: 0-0 Fm: 0-0
Distance: 5f/6f: 0-0 7f-8f: 0-5 9f-13f: 0-0 14f+: 0-0
Track : LH: 0-2 RH: 0-1 Tight: 0-1 Gall: 0-0
Aids: Bl: 0-0 Vi: 0-4 Tstrap: 0-0
Best Rating: 61 9/01 Bevl 7f100y good

Coughlan's Gift

99(101) (57)**57**
5-y-o ch m Alnasr Alwasheek-Superfrost (Tickled Pink)
J C Fox Mrs J A Cleary

Placings:063/0002052000125/000U050116-65000 **(5100)**
2001: 9^{6}HY, 10^{5}S, 10^{0}GF, 9^{0}GF, 9^{0}GS

	Starts	1st	2nd	3rd	Win & Pl
Career Total (Turf)	28	3	3	1	10664
Career Total (AW)	3	0	0	0	0

63 10/00 Nott 1m1f213yF(0-60) SFT £2903
57 9/00 Sals 1m1f198yF(0-70)H SFT £2103
58 10/99 Bath 1m5y F(0-60)H SFT £2640
Total win prize-money £7648

Going (Turf): Sf: 3-12 GS: 0-3 Gd: 0-9 GF: 0-4 Fm: 0-0
Distance: 5f/6f: 0-3 7f-8f: 0-12 9f-13f: 3-16 14f+: 0-0
Track : LH: 2-12 RH: 1-8 Tight: 2-8 Gall: 0-1
Aids: Bl: 0-0 Vi: 0-0 Tstrap: 0-0
Best Rating: 57 6/01 Wwck 1m2f188y gd-fm

Counsel's Opinion (IRE)

107(111) (71)**83**
4-y-o ch g Rudimentary (USA)-Fairy Fortune (Rainbow Quest (USA))
S P C Woods Mrs J Roberts

Placings:114001036 **(5669)**
2001: 12^{1}SD, 12^{1}SW, 12^{4}GS, 12^{0}GF, 10^{0}GF, 9^{1}G, 12^{0}S, 10^{3}S, 10^{6}HY

	Starts	1st	2nd	3rd	Win & Pl
Career Total (Turf)	7	1	0	1	11365
Career Total (AW)	2	2	0	0	7125

81 9/01 Sand 1m1f C(0-90)H GD £9750
71 4/01 Sthl 1m4f D SLW £3835
54 3/01 Ling 1m4f D STD £3290
Total win prize-money £16875

Going (Turf): Sf: 0-3 GS: 0-1 Gd: 1-1 GF: 0-2 Fm: 0-0
Distance: 5f/6f: 0-0 7f-8f: 0-0 9f-13f: 3-9 14f+: 0-0
Track : LH: 2-4 RH: 1-4 Tight: 1-3 Gall: 0-3
Aids: Bl: 0-0 Vi: 0-0 Tstrap: 0-0
Best Rating: 83 10/01 Yarm 1m2f21y soft

Showed a nice turn of foot to score on belated debut on Equitrack and followed up on the Southwell Fibresand, but suffered sore shins when raced on fast turf. Showed his potential when taking a competitive Sandown handicap on good ground. Suited by 12 furlongs on sand, but looks better at shorter on grass.

Count Calypso

97(101) (80)**67**
3-y-o ch g King's Signet (USA)-Atlantic Air (Air Trooper)
D J Coakley Count Calypso Racing

Placings:0003032-31104000 **(4632)**
2001: 6^{3}SW, 6^{1}SD, 6^{1}SD, 6^{0}S, 6^{4}GF, 6^{0}GF, 6^{0}GF, 7^{0}GF

	Starts	1st	2nd	3rd	Win & Pl
Career Total (Turf)	9	0	0	0	338
Career Total (AW)	6	2	1	3	8440

80 3/01 Sthl 6f D(0-85)H STD £3776
79 2/01 Wolv 6f E(0-75)H STD £2919
Total win prize-money £6696

Going (Turf): Sf: 0-1 GS: 0-0 Gd: 0-0 GF: 0-8 Fm: 0-0
Distance: 5f/6f: 2-13 7f-8f: 0-2 9f-13f: 0-0 14f+: 0-0
Track : LH: 2-5 RH: 0-0 Tight: 1-2 Gall: 0-1
Aids: Bl: 0-0 Vi: 0-0 Tstrap: 0-0
Best Rating: 80 3/01 Sthl 6f stand

Goes well on sand, having won two at six furlongs. Generally held up off the pace.

Count Frederick

92(86) (22)**29**
5-y-o b/br g Anshan-Minteen (Teenoso (USA))
J R Jenkins Mrs Stella Peirce

Placings:0/0304360220/006-0000 **(2809)**
2001: 11^{0}SD, 8^{0}SD, 10^{0}GF, 10^{0}GF

	Starts	1st	2nd	3rd	Win & Pl
Career Total (Turf)	15	0	2	2	2860
Career Total (AW)	3	0	0	0	0

Going (Turf): Sf: 0-5 GS: 0-1 Gd: 0-3 GF: 0-6 Fm: 0-0
Distance: 5f/6f: 0-0 7f-8f: 0-4 9f-13f: 0-14 14f+: 0-0
Track : LH: 0-9 RH: 0-5 Tight: 0-6 Gall: 0-2
Aids: Bl: 0-0 Vi: 0-1 Tstrap: 0-0
Best Rating: 29 5/01 Yarm 1m2f21y gd-fm

Count On Thunder (USA)

66(96) (29)**2**
4-y-o ch g Thunder Gulch (USA)-Count On A Change (USA) (Time For A Change (USA))
J Hetherton C D Barber-Lomax

Placings:000/565060006-6660 **(1136)**
2001: 8^{6}SD, 8^{6}SD, 8^{6}S, 11^{0}G

	Starts	1st	2nd	3rd	Win & Pl
Career Total (Turf)	11	0	0	0	0
Career Total (AW)	5	0	0	0	0

Going (Turf): Sf: 0-4 GS: 0-4 Gd: 0-2 GF: 0-1 Fm: 0-0
Distance: 5f/6f: 0-0 7f-8f: 0-4 9f-13f: 0-12 14f+: 0-0
Track : LH: 0-9 RH: 0-4 Tight: 0-8 Gall: 0-0
Aids: Bl: 0-0 Vi: 0-1 Tstrap: 0-0
Best Rating: 27 3/01 Sthl 1m stand

Count Tirol (IRE)

(89) (37)**25**
4-y-o b g Tirol-Bid High (IRE) (High Estate)
J R Payne (C G Cox 24/3) J R Payne

Placings:003/000-30 **(0538)**
2001: 9^{3}SW, 12^{0}SD

	Starts	1st	2nd	3rd	Win & Pl
Career Total (Turf)	6	0	0	1	336
Career Total (AW)	2	0	0	1	191

Going (Turf): Sf: 0-0 GS: 0-1 Gd: 0-1 GF: 0-2 Fm: 0-2
Distance: 5f/6f: 0-3 7f-8f: 0-1 9f-13f: 0-4 14f+: 0-0
Track : LH: 0-6 RH: 0-0 Tight: 0-2 Gall: 0-2
Aids: Bl: 0-0 Vi: 0-0 Tstrap: 0-0
Best Rating: 37 1/01 Wolv 1m1f79y slow

Count Tony

96 **41**
7-y-o ch g Keen-Turtle Dove (Gyr (USA))
P Bowen Brian Collett

Placings:400/1540201/0-54 **(2815)**
2001: 14^{5}GF, 16^{4}GF

	Starts	1st	2nd	3rd	Win & Pl
Career Total (Turf)	11	2	0	0	6137
Career Total (AW)	2	0	1	0	1165

65 8/97 Yarm 1m2f21y F(0-65) G-F £2469
69 3/97 Wwck 1m2f169yE(0-70)H G-F £3122
Total win prize-money £5591

Going (Turf): Sf: 0-0 GS: 0-2 Gd: 0-2 GF: 2-6 Fm: 0-1
Distance: 5f/6f: 0-0 7f-8f: 0-2 9f-13f: 2-8 14f+: 0-3
Track : LH: 2-8 RH: 0-4 Tight: 1-6 Gall: 0-2
Aids: Bl: 0-0 Vi: 0-2 Tstrap: 0-0
Best Rating: 41 7/01 Bevl 2m35y gd-fm

Countess Coldunell

(84) (28)**53**
4-y-o b f Bin Ajwaad (IRE)-Beau's Delight (USA) (Lypheor)
J W Payne John Dunsdon

Placings:600-00 **(0181)**
2001: 11^{0}SD, 16^{0}SD

	Starts	1st	2nd	3rd	Win & Pl
Career Total (Turf)	2	0	0	0	0
Career Total (AW)	3	0	0	0	

Going (Turf): Sf: 0-2 GS: 0-0 Gd: 0-0 GF: 0-0 Fm: 0-0
Distance: 5f/6f: 0-0 7f-8f: 0-2 9f-13f: 0-2 14f+: 0-1
Track : LH: 0-4 RH: 0-0 Tight: 0-1 Gall: 0-1
Aids: Bl: 0-1 Vi: 0-0 Tstrap: 0-0
Best Rating: 28 1/01 Sthl 1m3f stand

Countess Parker

90 **20**
5-y-o ch m First Trump-Hoist (IRE) (Bluebird (USA))
B Mactaggart B Mactaggart

Placings:204/000000-0000 **(3946)**
2001: 8^{0}G, 6^{0}G, 7^{0}GS, 9^{0}GS

	Starts	1st	2nd	3rd	Win & Pl
Career Total (Turf)	13	0	1	0	1407

Going (Turf): Sf: 0-1 GS: 0-3 Gd: 0-4 GF: 0-3 Fm: 0-2
Distance: 5f/6f: 0-2 7f-8f: 0-5 9f-13f: 0-6 14f+: 0-0
Track : LH: 0-3 RH: 0-4 Tight: 0-4 Gall: 0-0
Aids: Bl: 0-0 Vi: 0-0 Tstrap: 0-0
Best Rating: 20 7/01 Haml 6f5y good

Country Bumpkin

(80) (3)
5-y-o ch g Village Star (FR)-Malham Tarn (Riverman (USA))
H E Haynes Lainey Hilder & Vyv Attwood

Placings:00/0-00 **(0719)**
2001: 12^{0}SD, 10^{0}SD

	Starts	1st	2nd	3rd	Win & Pl
Career Total (Turf)	3	0	0	0	
Career Total (AW)	2	0	0	0	

Going (Turf): Sf: 0-0 GS: 0-0 Gd: 0-0 GF: 0-3 Fm: 0-0
Distance: 5f/6f: 0-0 7f-8f: 0-0 9f-13f: 0-5 14f+: 0-0
Track : LH: 0-4 RH: 0-1 Tight: 0-4 Gall: 0-0
Aids: Bl: 0-0 Vi: 0-0 Tstrap: 0-0
Best Rating: 3 4/01 Ling 1m2f stand

Countrywide Girl (IRE)

93(79) (31)**77**
2-y-o ch f Catrail (USA)-Polish Saga (Polish Patriot (USA))
A Berry Alan Berry

Placings:00520205110 **(5660)**
2001: 5^{0}SD, 5^{0}GF, 6^{5}F, 7^{2}GF, 6^{0}G, 6^{2}GF, 6^{0}SD, 6^{5}GF, 6^{1}HY, 5^{1}HY, 5^{0}G

	Starts	1st	2nd	3rd	Win & Pl
Career Total (Turf)	9	2	2	0	6500
Career Total (AW)	2	0	0	0	

77 10/01 Ling 5f G HVY £2240
57 10/01 Ling 6f F HVY £2982
Total win prize-money £5222

Going (Turf): Sf: 2-2 GS: 0-0 Gd: 0-2 GF: 0-4 Fm: 0-1

Distance: 5f/6f: **2-10** 7f-8f: 0-1 9f-13f: 0-0 14f+: 0-0
Track : LH: 0-1 RH: 0-0 Tight: 0-0 Gall: 0-0
Aids: Bl: 0-0 Vi: 0-0 Tstrap: 0-0
Best Rating: 77 10/01 Ling 5f heavy

Tends to sometimes hang badly in her races, but that did not stop her winning a claimer in very soft ground at Lingfield in October 2001 and followed up in a seller under similar conditions on the same track. Suited by five or six furlongs.

Countrywide Pride (IRE)

89(98) (69)**65**

3-y-o ch g Eagle Eyed (USA)-Lady's Dream (Mazilier (USA))
K R Burke Mrs Elaine M Burke

Placings:043046053-6340 **(1922)**
2001: 10^{6}SW, 10^{3}SW, 10^{4}GF, 8^{0}GF

	Starts	1st	2nd	3rd	Win & Pl
Career Total (Turf)	9	0	0	1	1183
Career Total (AW)	4	0	0	2	821

Going (Turf): Sf: 0-1 GS: 0-1 Gd: 0-2 GF: 0-5 Fm: 0-0
Distance: 5f/6f: 0-1 7f-8f: 0-7 9f-13f: 0-5 14f+: 0-0
Track : LH: 0-8 RH: 0-0 Tight: 0-5 Gall: 0-1
Aids: Bl: 0-0 Vi: 0-1 Tstrap: 0-0
Best Rating: 62 2/01 Ling 1m2f slow

Consistently in the frame on the All-Weather and the turf, but is host to a steadily decreasing handicap mark.

Countrywide Star (IRE)

(99) (65)**66**

3-y-o ch g Common Grounds-Silver Slipper (Indian Ridge)
K R Burke Countrywide Steel & Tubes Ltd

Placings:006601000 **(5601)**
2001: 8^{0}SD, 6^{0}GS, 6^{6}HY, 6^{6}F, 7^{0}G, 7^{1}HY, 7^{0}HY, 7^{0}HY, 8^{0}GS

	Starts	1st	2nd	3rd	Win & Pl
Career Total (Turf)	8	1	0	0	4524
Career Total (AW)	1	0	0	0	
66 9/01 Hayd 7f30y	D			HVY	£4524

Total win prize-money £4524

Going (Turf): Sf: 1-4 GS: 0-2 Gd: 0-1 GF: 0-0 Fm: 0-1
Distance: 5f/6f: 0-2 **7f-8f: 1-7** 9f-13f: 0-0 14f+: 0-0
Track : **LH: 1-4** RH: 0-0 Tight: 0-0 Gall: 0-0
Aids: Bl: 0-0 Vi: 0-0 Tstrap: 0-0
Best Rating: 66 9/01 Hayd 7f30y heavy

Got off the mark at the sixth attempt in heavy ground at Haydock in September after showing little in both maidens and handicaps, but has not done as well since then. Suited by cut in the ground.

Course Doctor (IRE)

100 **54**

9-y-o ch g Roselier (FR)-Faultless Girl (Crash Course)
A Dickman Mike Smallman

Placings:335500 **(3879)**
2001: 12^{3}GF, 12^{3}GF, 10^{5}S, 16^{5}F, 21^{0}GF, 16^{0}GS

	Starts	1st	2nd	3rd	Win & Pl
Career Total (Turf)	6	0	0	2	1209

Going (Turf): Sf: 0-1 GS: 0-1 Gd: 0-0 GF: 0-3 Fm: 0-1
Distance: 5f/6f: 0-0 7f-8f: 0-0 9f-13f: 0-3 14f+: 0-3
Track : LH: 0-5 RH: 0-0 Tight: 0-2 Gall: 0-1
Aids: Bl: 0-0 Vi: 0-0 Tstrap: 0-0
Best Rating: 54 7/01 Donc 1m4f gd-fm

He has not been disgraced on the Flat in 2001. Stays two miles and acts on a sound surface

Court Express

106 (32)**82**

7-y-o b g Then Again-Moon Risk (Risk Me (FR))
G A Swinbank Tim Hawkins

Placings:505/0011200/00400340005/001213111500/16 20530440-1P **(1490)**
2001: 8^{1}G, 8^{P}GF

					Starts	1st	2nd	3rd	Win & Pl
Career Total (Turf)					44	9	3	3	67540
Career Total (AW)					1	0	0	0	
82	5/01	Thsk	1m	C(0-95)H				GD	£11960
79	5/00	Bevl	1m100y	D(0-85)H				G-F	£3900
74	8/99	Rdcr	1m	D(0-85)H				FRM	£5540
69	7/99	Bevl	1m1f207y	D(0-85)H				G-F	£4549
66	7/99	Haml	1m1f36y	B H				FRM	£10650
59	6/99	Carl	7f214y	E(0-75)H				GD	£3680
51	5/99	Haml	1m65y	E(0-70)H				GD	£3615
68	6/97	Carl	5f207y	E(0-70)H				G-F	£3063
61	6/97	Carl	5f207y	F				FRM	£2612

Total win prize-money £49570

Going (Turf): Sf: 0-0 GS: 0-3 **Gd: 3-15 GF: 3-21** Fm: 3-5
Distance: 5f/6f: 2-7 7f-8f: 3-19 **9f-13f: 4-19** 14f+: 0-0
Track : LH: 1-13 **RH: 7-22 Tight: 3-11** Gall: 2-10
Aids: Bl: 0-1 Vi: 0-0 Tstrap: 0-0
Best Rating: 82 5/01 Thsk 1m good

Determined handicapper at around a mile. Best when the ground rode on the fast side and went particularly well fresh. (DEAD)

Court Music (IRE)

101 **75**

2-y-o b/br f Revoque (IRE)-Lute And Lyre (IRE) (The Noble Player (USA))
T D Easterby I Bray

Placings:004415 **(4990)**
2001: 6^{0}GF, 5^{0}GF, 6^{4}G, 6^{4}GF, 6^{1}G, 6^{5}HY

					Starts	1st	2nd	3rd	Win & Pl
Career Total (Turf)					6	1	0	0	5169
75	9/01	Nott	6f15y	E(0-75)				GD	£4208

Total win prize-money £4209

Going (Turf): Sf: 0-1 GS: 0-0 **Gd: 1-2** GF: 0-3 Fm: 0-0
Distance: 5f/6f: 0-5 **7f-8f: 1-1** 9f-13f: 0-0 14f+: 0-0
Track : LH: 0-0 RH: 0-0 Tight: 0-0 Gall: 0-0
Aids: Bl: 0-2 Vi: 0-0 Tstrap: 0-0
Best Rating: 75 9/01 Nott 6f15y good

Bred for sprinting, she came good in a Nottingham nursery in September 2001 over six furlongs without the blinkers, but struggled with the testing ground in a more competitive event at Haydock next time.

Court Of Appeal

107 **68**

4-y-o ch g Bering-Hiawatha's Song (USA) (Chief's Crown (USA))
G M McCourt Court Roof Tiling Ltd

Placings:0/01004-0045223000 **(4825)**
2001: 10^{0}GS, 10^{0}G, 10^{4}S, 11^{5}GF, 12^{2}GF, 11^{2}G, 10^{3}GF, 12^{0}G, 10^{0}G, 9^{0}G

					Starts	1st	2nd	3rd	Win & Pl
Career Total (Turf)					16	1	2	1	10777
89	5/00	Kemp	1m	D				SFT	£4524

Total win prize-money £4524

Going (Turf): Sf: 1-4 GS: 0-2 Gd: 0-6 GF: 0-4 Fm: 0-0
Distance: 5f/6f: 0-0 **7f-8f: 1-2** 9f-13f: 0-14 14f+: 0-0
Track : LH: 0-5 **RH: 1-6** Tight: 0-3 **Gall: 1-6**
Aids: Bl: 0-0 Vi: 0-0 Tstrap: 0-0
Best Rating: 74 7/01 Sand 1m2f7y gd-fm

Has shown improved form this season when stepped up to 11 furlongs plus. Can make the running and seems to prefer good ground.

Court One

91 **34**

3-y-o b g Shareef Dancer (USA)-Fairfields Cone (Celtic Cone)
R J Price Derek & Cheryl Holder

Placings:000-600 **(2858)**
2001: 11^{6}GF, 11^{0}GF, 11^{0}GF

	Starts	1st	2nd	3rd	Win & Pl
Career Total (Turf)	6	0	0	0	0

Going (Turf): Sf: 0-0 GS: 0-0 Gd: 0-1 GF: 0-5 Fm: 0-0
Distance: 5f/6f: 0-1 7f-8f: 0-2 9f-13f: 0-3 14f+: 0-0
Track : LH: 0-1 RH: 0-3 Tight: 0-3 Gall: 0-2
Aids: Bl: 0-0 Vi: 0-0 Tstrap: 0-0
Best Rating: 29 6/01 Wind 1m3f135y gd-fm

Court Shareef

109 **85**

6-y-o b g Shareef Dancer (USA)-Fairfields Cone (Celtic Cone)
R J Price Derek & Cheryl Holder

Placings:0/46113350/4504405/1311020-350410205000 **(4869)**
2001: 12^{3}G, 11^{5}F, 11^{0}GF, 12^{4}GF, 14^{1}GF, 11^{0}GS, 16^{2}G, 14^{0}GF, 16^{5}G, 13^{0}G, 13^{0}GF, 14^{0}G

					Starts	1st	2nd	3rd	Win & Pl
Career Total (Turf)					35	6	2	4	57121
82	6/01	Gdwd	1m6f	C(0-90)H				G-F	£10286
79	6/00	Carl	1m4f	D(0-80)H				G-F	£14820
72	6/00	Gdwd	1m4f	C(0-95)H				G-F	£10578
64	6/00	Wind	1m3f135y	F(0-60)H				GD	£2758
75	5/98	Leic	1m3f183y	E(0-70)H				GD	£3015
62	5/98	Wind	1m3f135y	E(0-70)H				G-F	£3095

Total win prize-money £44553

Going (Turf): Sf: 0-4 GS: 0-3 Gd: 2-10 **GF: 4-17** Fm: 0-1
Distance: 5f/6f: 0-0 7f-8f: 0-1 **9f-13f: 5-20** 14f+: 1-14
Track : LH: 0-11 **RH: 4-19 Tight: 4-12** Gall: 0-10
Aids: Bl: 0-0 Vi: 0-0 Tstrap: 0-0
Best Rating: 85 7/01 NmkJ 2m24y good

Appeared too high in the handicap before a step up in trip saw him back to winning form over 14 furlongs at Goodwood in June. Has since gone close in a competitive event Newmarket, but appears to be well held by the Handicapper on recent showings. Likes top of the ground.

Courteous

111 **112**

6-y-o b h Generous (IRE)-Dayanata (Shirley Heights)
P F I Cole Newgate Stud

Placings:41/10620/130/642306 **(4991)**
2001: 11^{6}G, 11^{4}G, 12^{2}GF, 14^{3}HO, 13^{0}G, 14^{6}HY

					Starts	1st	2nd	3rd	Win & Pl
Career Total (Turf)					16	3	2	2	178869
117	8/99	Deau	1m4f110y					GD	£53821
107	4/98	Sand	1m2f7y	A				SFT	£40706
84	10/97	Sals	1m	D				GD	£3980

Total win prize-money £98509

Going (Turf): Sf: 1-3 GS: 0-2 **Gd: 2-8** GF: 0-2 Fm: 0-0
Distance: 5f/6f: 0-0 7f-8f: 1-1 **9f-13f: 2-12** 14f+: 0-3
Track : LH: 0-6 **RH: 2-6** Tight: 0-2 Gall: 0-3
Aids: Bl: 0-1 Vi: 0-0 Tstrap: 0-0
Best Rating: 112 7/01 MsnL 1m6f holding

High-class middle distance performer at three and four,

he won the Grand Prix de Deauville and finished runner-up in the Canadian International before running seventh to Daylami in the Breeders' Cup Turf. He struggled after a season off, and his third in a Group Two in France was his best performance of the season so far.

Courtesy (USA)

86 **73**

2-y-o b f Diesis-Muscadel (Nashwan (USA))
Sir Michael Stoute Sheikh Mohammed

Placings:4 **(4485)**
2001: 8^{4}S

	Starts	1st	2nd	3rd	Win & Pl
Career Total (Turf)	1	0	0	0	298

Going (Turf): Sf: 0-1 GS: 0-0 Gd: 0-0 GF: 0-0 Fm: 0-0
Distance: 5f/6f: 0-0 7f-8f: 0-0 9f-13f: 0-1 14f+: 0-0
Track : LH: 0-0 RH: 0-0 Tight: 0-0 Gall: 0-0
Aids: Bl: 0-0 Vi: 0-0 Tstrap: 0-0
Best Rating: 73 9/01 Yarm 1m3y soft

Covent Garden

105 **86**

3-y-o b c Sadler's Wells (USA)-Temple Row (Ardross)
Sir Michael Stoute Mrs John Magnier & Lord Hartington

Placings:0-10 **(4987)**
2001: 12^{1}GF, 10^{0}G

	Starts	1st	2nd	3rd	Win & Pl
Career Total (Turf)	3	1	0	0	4232
78 7/01 Donc 1m4f D				G-F	£4231

Total win prize-money £4232

Going (Turf): Sf: 0-1 GS: 0-0 Gd: 0-1 **GF: 1-1** Fm: 0-0
Distance: 5f/6f: 0-0 7f-8f: 0-1 **9f-13f: 1-2** 14f+: 0-0
Track : **LH: 1-1** RH: 0-1 Tight: 0-0 **Gall: 1-2**
Aids: Bl: 0-0 Vi: 0-0 Tstrap: 0-0
Best Rating: 86 9/01 Asct 1m2f good

Lightly-raced colt. Stays a mile and a half. Acts on fast ground.

Cover Up (IRE)

109 **106**

4-y-o b g Machiavellian (USA)-Sought Out (IRE) (Rainbow Quest (USA))
Sir Michael Stoute Lord Weinstock

Placings:32/1030010-412460 **(5387)**
2001: 18^{4}GF, 20^{1}GF, 16^{2}F, 13^{4}G, 18^{6}G, 18^{0}GS

	Starts	1st	2nd	3rd	Win & Pl
Career Total (Turf)	15	3	2	2	91909
98 6/01 Asct 2m4f C(0-95)H				G-F	£29900
94 9/00 Muss 2m C(0-90)H				G-S	£8502
90 4/00 Wind 1m2f7y D				GD	£3055

Total win prize-money £41457

Going (Turf): Sf: 0-2 **GS: 1-3 Gd: 1-5 GF: 1-4** Fm: 0-1
Distance: 5f/6f: 0-0 7f-8f: 0-1 9f-13f: 1-3 **14f+: 2-11**
Track : LH: 0-7 **RH: 2-6 Tight: 2-4** Gall: 1-9
Aids: Bl: 0-0 Vi: 0-1 Tstrap: 0-0
Best Rating: 106 9/01 Donc 2m2f good

Bred to stay, he has scored three times over ten furlongs, two miles and two and a half. Game winner of the Ascot Stakes in 2001, he has since finished in the frame in the Northumberland Plate and the Ebor and run well upped in class at Doncaster. Best on good and good to soft ground when up with the pace.

Cowboys And Angels

103(93) (63)**68**

4-y-o b g Bin Ajwaad (IRE)-Halimah (Be My Guest (USA))
W G M Turner Mascalls Stud

Placings:320/**3**36010241206-0000251 **(5503)**
2001: 7^{0}SD, 6^{0}S, 7^{0}G, 7^{0}GF, 7^{2}F, 8^{5}G, 7^{1}HY

	Starts	1st	2nd	3rd	Win & Pl
Career Total (Turf)	19	3	4	1	15232
Career Total (AW)	3	0	0	2	756
62 10/01 Donc 7f E				HVY	£4758
74 7/00 Ayr 7f E(0-70)H				G-F	£2973
74 5/00 Sals 6f212y F				GD	£2548

Total win prize-money £10280

Going (Turf): Sf: 1-4 GS: 0-3 **Gd: 1-3 GF: 1-8** Fm: 0-1
Distance: 5f/6f: 0-3 **7f-8f: 3-14** 9f-13f: 0-5 14f+: 0-0
Track : **LH: 1-7** RH: 0-3 Tight: 0-4 Gall: 0-1
Aids: Bl: 0-0 Vi: 0-0 Tstrap: 0-0
Best Rating: 68 9/01 Chep 7f16y firm

Fair handicapper. Suited by good to firm and seven furlongs.

Coyote

107 **92**

3-y-o b f Indian Ridge-Caramba (Belmez (USA))
Sir Michael Stoute Lady Carolyn Warren

Placings:4-204135 **(4429)**
2001: 7^{2}GF, 9^{0}GF, 8^{4}GF, 8^{1}GS, 8^{3}G, 8^{5}G

	Starts	1st	2nd	3rd	Win & Pl
Career Total (Turf)	7	1	1	1	9414
92 8/01 Ayr 1m D				G-S	£3526

Total win prize-money £3526

Going (Turf): Sf: 0-1 **GS: 1-1** Gd: 0-2 GF: 0-3 Fm: 0-0
Distance: 5f/6f: 0-0 **7f-8f: 1-4** 9f-13f: 0-3 14f+: 0-0
Track : **LH: 1-2** RH: 0-4 Tight: 0-3 Gall: 0-1
Aids: Bl: 0-0 **Vi: 1-3** Tstrap: 0-0
Best Rating: 92 8/01 Asct 1m good

Had shown a degree of promise in maidens before getting off the mark at Ayr after being fitted with a visor. Made all on the soft ground to win unchallenged. Found the step up to Listed class on next two outings beyond her. Stays a mile.

Cozette (IRE)

90 **57**

2-y-o b f Danehill Dancer (IRE)-Great Splendour (Pharly (FR))
E J O'Neill The Ballybrit Partnership

Placings:054 **(4215)**
2001: 5^{0}GF, 7^{5}G, 8^{4}G

	Starts	1st	2nd	3rd	Win & Pl
Career Total (Turf)	3	0	0	0	0

Going (Turf): Sf: 0-0 GS: 0-0 Gd: 0-2 GF: 0-1 Fm: 0-0
Distance: 5f/6f: 0-1 7f-8f: 0-2 9f-13f: 0-0 14f+: 0-0
Track : LH: 0-3 RH: 0-0 Tight: 0-1 Gall: 0-2
Aids: Bl: 0-0 Vi: 0-0 Tstrap: 0-0
Best Rating: 57 8/01 Newc 1m good

Cozy Maria (USA)

99 **91**

2-y-o gr/ro f Cozzene (USA)-Mariamme (USA) (Verbatim (USA))
J H M Gosden Mrs A E Oppenheimer

Placings:336 **(5390)**
2001: 7^{3}G, 7^{3}GF, 7^{6}GS

	Starts	1st	2nd	3rd	Win & Pl
Career Total (Turf)	3	0	0	2	3224

Going (Turf): Sf: 0-0 GS: 0-1 Gd: 0-1 GF: 0-1 Fm: 0-0
Distance: 5f/6f: 0-0 7f-8f: 0-3 9f-13f: 0-0 14f+: 0-0
Track : LH: 0-0 RH: 0-0 Tight: 0-0 Gall: 0-0
Aids: Bl: 0-0 Vi: 0-0 Tstrap: 0-0
Best Rating: 91 9/01 Newb 7f gd-fm

A $300,000 yearling out of a half-sister to Miss Alleged, she has shown promise on both her runs in decent company. Will appreciate further and should have no trouble winning races.

Cozzie

(98) (57d)**57**

3-y-o ch f Cosmonaut-Royal Deed (USA) (Shadeed (USA))
J G Given D Bass

Placings:3051166146-015603 **(0489)**
2001: 5^{0}SD, 6^{1}SW, 5^{5}SW, 6^{6}SW, 5^{0}SD, 5^{3}SD

	Starts	1st	2nd	3rd	Win & Pl
Career Total (Turf)	8	2	0	0	6742
Career Total (AW)	8	2	0	2	4213
58 1/01 Ling 6f G				SLW	£1848
55 8/00 Bevl 5f D				G-F	£3591
57 6/00 Ling 5f G				STD	£1844
52 6/00 Muss 5f F				FRM	£2590

Total win prize-money £9874

Going (Turf): Sf: 0-1 GS: 0-1 Gd: 0-2 **GF: 1-2 Fm: 1-2**
Distance: **5f/6f: 4-16** 7f-8f: 0-0 9f-13f: 0-0 14f+: 0-0
Track : **LH: 2-7** RH: 0-0 **Tight: 2-7** Gall: 0-0
Aids: Bl: 0-0 Vi: 0-0 Tstrap: 0-0
Best Rating: 58 1/01 Ling 6f slow

Progressed to achieve back-to-back wins in sellers at Musselburgh and Lingfield in the summer of 2000, and a Beverley nursery two months later. Her best form on sand has been on the Equitrack. She is suited to five furlongs on a sound surface on turf.

Cracow (IRE)

110 **90**

4-y-o b c Polish Precedent (USA)-Height Of Secrecy (Shirley Heights)
J W Hills N N Browne

Placings:052/431052100-032030000 **(5057)**
2001: 10^{0}S, 11^{3}F, 12^{2}GF, 12^{0}G, 11^{3}GS, 14^{0}GF, 12^{0}G, 10^{0}GF, 12^{0}S

	Starts	1st	2nd	3rd	Win & Pl
Career Total (Turf)	21	2	3	3	42260
92 8/00 York 1m3f195yB(0-105)H				GD	£13705
75 5/00 Brig 1m3f196y				SFT	£3770

Total win prize-money £17475

Going (Turf): Sf: 1-4 GS: 0-4 **Gd: 1-5** GF: 0-7 Fm: 0-1
Distance: 5f/6f: 0-0 7f-8f: 0-3 **9f-13f: 2-16** 14f+: 0-2
Track : **LH: 2-10** RH: 0-7 Tight: 0-5 **Gall: 1-10**
Aids: Bl: 0-0 Vi: 0-0 Tstrap: 0-0
Best Rating: 94 7/01 Hayd 1m3f200y gd-sft

He was outclassed in the 2000 Derby, but put up some decent efforts in handicaps afterwards including making all to win at York in August. Very unlucky in running at Epsom on Derby Day 2001 on his third outing of the this season but disappointed in similar events. Acts on fast ground.

Crafty

2-y-o b f Mistertopogigo (IRE)-Tinkers Fairy (Myjinski (USA))
J R Norton John Richard Norton

Placings:0 **(2750)**
2001: 6^{0}GF

	Starts	1st	2nd	3rd	Win & Pl
Career Total (Turf)	1	0	0	0	

Going (Turf): Sf: 0-0 GS: 0-0 Gd: 0-0 GF: 0-1 Fm: 0-0

Distance: 5f/6f: 0-1 7f-8f: 0-0 9f-13f: 0-0 14f+: 0-0
Track : LH: 0-0 RH: 0-0 Tight: 0-0 Gall: 0-0
Aids: Bl: 0-0 Vi: 0-0 Tstrap: 0-0

Craigary

98 **17**

10-y-o b g Dunbeath (USA)-Velvet Pearl (Record Token)
D A Nolan James A Cringan

Placings:656304/00050/55303/004432100/**0**/056/0501-0000600 **(4440)**
2001: 13^{0}G, 12^{0}GF, 13^{0}GF, 14^{0}G, 13^{6}G, 12^{0}S, 11^{0}G

	Starts	1st	2nd	3rd	Win & Pl
Career Total (Turf)	39	2	1	4	7007
Career Total (AW)	1	0	0	0	

26	10/00	Muss	1m5f	F(0-60)H	SFT	£2310
41	9/97	Haml	1m4f17y	G(0-60)H	G-S	£2444

Total win prize-money £4754

Going (Turf): Sf: 1-5 GS: 1-3 Gd: 0-10 GF: 0-7 Fm: 0-1
Distance: 5f/6f: 0-0 7f-8f: 0-0 **9f-13f: 2-20** 14f+: 0-9
Track : LH: 0-6 **RH: 2-22 Tight: 2-19** Gall: 0-0
Aids: Bl: 0-7 Vi: 0-1 Tstrap: 0-0
Best Rating: 24 5/01 Haml 1m5f9y good

Craiova (IRE)

93 **81**

2-y-o b c Turtle Island (IRE)-Velvet Appeal (IRE) (Petorius)
B W Hills Ahmed Buhaleeba

Placings:4 **(5343)**
2001: 6^{4}GS

	Starts	1st	2nd	3rd	Win & Pl
Career Total (Turf)	1	0	0	0	446

Going (Turf): Sf: 0-0 GS: 0-1 Gd: 0-0 GF: 0-0 Fm: 0-0
Distance: 5f/6f: 0-1 7f-8f: 0-0 9f-13f: 0-0 14f+: 0-0
Track : LH: 0-0 RH: 0-0 Tight: 0-0 Gall: 0-0
Aids: Bl: 0-0 Vi: 0-0 Tstrap: 0-0
Best Rating: 81 10/01 NmkR 6f gd-sft

A 130,000gns son of Turtle Island, showed promise on his debut and looks capable of winning races.

Crandium

(71)

5-y-o br m Presidium-Crammond Brig (New Brig)
R D E Woodhouse W H Jackson

Placings:0 **(0220)**
2001: 11^{0}SD

	Starts	1st	2nd	3rd	Win & Pl
Career Total (Turf)	0	0	0	0	
Career Total (AW)	1	0	0	0	

Going (Turf): Sf: 0-0 GS: 0-0 Gd: 0-0 GF: 0-0 Fm: 0-0
Distance: 5f/6f: 0-0 7f-8f: 0-0 9f-13f: 0-1 14f+: 0-0
Track : LH: 0-1 RH: 0-0 Tight: 0-0 Gall: 0-0
Aids: Bl: 0-0 Vi: 0-0 Tstrap: 0-0

Crazy Larrys (USA)

95 **94**

3-y-o ch c Mutakddim (USA)-No Fear Of Flying (USA) (Super Concorde (USA))
J Noseda Crazy Radio Ltd

Placings:121-5 **(1143)**
2001: 7^{5}G

	Starts	1st	2nd	3rd	Win & Pl
Career Total (Turf)	4	2	1	0	13340

94	8/00	Kemp	7f	C	G-F	£5703
78	7/00	Newc	7f	D	G-F	£5239

Total win prize-money £10942

Going (Turf): Sf: 0-0 GS: 0-0 Gd: 0-2 **GF: 2-2** Fm: 0-0
Distance: 5f/6f: 0-0 **7f-8f: 2-4** 9f-13f: 0-0 14f+: 0-0
Track : LH: 0-0 **RH: 1-1** Tight: 0-0 **Gall: 1-1**
Aids: Bl: 0-0 Vi: 0-0 Tstrap: 0-0
Best Rating: 78 5/01 NmkR 7f good

A winner of a Newcastle maiden and a Kempton conditions event at two, but seen just once in 2001.

Cream Crackered

67 **2**

2-y-o ch f Dancing Spree (USA)-Badger Bay (IRE) (Salt Dome (USA))
C A Dwyer M E Hall

Placings:00 **(2111)**
2001: 5^{0}GF, 5^{0}F

	Starts	1st	2nd	3rd	Win & Pl
Career Total (Turf)	2	0	0	0	

Going (Turf): Sf: 0-0 GS: 0-0 Gd: 0-0 GF: 0-1 Fm: 0-1
Distance: 5f/6f: 0-2 7f-8f: 0-0 9f-13f: 0-0 14f+: 0-0
Track : LH: 0-0 RH: 0-0 Tight: 0-0 Gall: 0-0
Aids: Bl: 0-0 Vi: 0-0 Tstrap: 0-0
Best Rating: 2 5/01 Thsk 5f gd-fm

Cream Tease

108 **98?**

4-y-o b f Pursuit Of Love-Contralto (Busted)
D J S Ffrench Davis Badgers Holt

Placings:41600/00001-050 **(2014)**
2001: 7^{0}G, 7^{5}G, 7^{0}GF

	Starts	1st	2nd	3rd	Win & Pl
Career Total (Turf)	13	2	0	0	16841

78	8/00	Sals	6f212y	C(0-95)H	G-F	£12057
80	8/99	Sals	6f212y	D	GD	£3746

Total win prize-money £15805

Going (Turf): Sf: 0-1 GS: 0-0 **Gd: 1-4 GF: 1-8** Fm: 0-0
Distance: 5f/6f: 0-0 **7f-8f: 2-11** 9f-13f: 0-2 14f+: 0-0
Track : LH: 0-6 RH: 0-1 Tight: 0-1 Gall: 0-4
Aids: Bl: 0-1 Vi: 0-0 Tstrap: 0-0
Best Rating: 98 5/01 Ling 7f good

Narrow winner of a Salisbury maiden on her second start in 1999, she was totally outclassed in Group company afterwards, and reverted to handicaps, causing a surprise at Salisbury in August 2000. Acts on fast ground, and likes to race prominently. One to watch for on the Wiltshire track.

Credenza Moment

97(82) (47)**34**

3-y-o b c Pyramus (USA)-Mystoski (Petoski)
M Madgwick (R Hannon 9/8) W V Roker

Placings:00063-40200026 **(5524)**
2001: 9^{4}GS, 11^{0}GS, 11^{2}GF, 9^{0}F, 11^{0}GF, 12^{0}GF, 11^{2}G, 10^{6}HY

	Starts	1st	2nd	3rd	Win & Pl
Career Total (Turf)	11	0	2	0	1089
Career Total (AW)	2	0	0	1	270

Going (Turf): Sf: 0-3 GS: 0-2 Gd: 0-1 GF: 0-4 Fm: 0-1
Distance: 5f/6f: 0-0 7f-8f: 0-4 9f-13f: 0-9 14f+: 0-0
Track : LH: 0-7 RH: 0-0 Tight: 0-6 Gall: 0-0
Aids: Bl: 0-2 Vi: 0-0 Tstrap: 0-0
Best Rating: 41 5/01 Ling 1m3f106y gd-fm

Moderate maiden.

Credibility

93(87) (41)**64d**

3-y-o ch f Komaite (USA)-Integrity (Reform)
M Wigham T R Pearson

Placings:3-60304 **(3733)**
2001: 7^{6}SD, 9^{0}SD, 5^{3}SW, 5^{0}F, 5^{4}G

	Starts	1st	2nd	3rd	Win & Pl
Career Total (Turf)	3	0	0	1	430
Career Total (AW)	3	0	0	1	412

Going (Turf): Sf: 0-0 GS: 0-0 Gd: 0-2 GF: 0-0 Fm: 0-1
Distance: 5f/6f: 0-4 7f-8f: 0-1 9f-13f: 0-1 14f+: 0-0
Track : LH: 0-4 RH: 0-0 Tight: 0-2 Gall: 0-0
Aids: Bl: 0-0 Vi: 0-0 Tstrap: 0-0
Best Rating: 50 7/01 Ling 5f firm

Credible (USA)

99 **82**

2-y-o ch c Dixieland Band (USA)-Alleged Thoughts (USA) (Alleged (USA))
J H M Gosden Sheikh Mohammed

Placings:06 **(5604)**
2001: 7^{0}S, 7^{6}GS

	Starts	1st	2nd	3rd	Win & Pl
Career Total (Turf)	2	0	0	0	0

Going (Turf): Sf: 0-1 GS: 0-1 Gd: 0-0 GF: 0-0 Fm: 0-0
Distance: 5f/6f: 0-0 7f-8f: 0-2 9f-13f: 0-0 14f+: 0-0
Track : LH: 0-0 RH: 0-0 Tight: 0-0 Gall: 0-0
Aids: Bl: 0-0 Vi: 0-0 Tstrap: 0-0
Best Rating: 82 11/01 NmkR 7f gd-sft

Creg Willys Hill (IRE)

(83) (56)**25**

2-y-o b c Distinctly North (USA)-Need You Badly (Robellino (USA))
R Ford R Burgess

Placings:00400 **(5614)**
2001: 7^{0}G, 6^{0}GF, 5^{4}SD, 5^{0}G, 6^{0}SD

	Starts	1st	2nd	3rd	Win & Pl
Career Total (Turf)	3	0	0	0	
Career Total (AW)	2	0	0	0	0

Going (Turf): Sf: 0-0 GS: 0-0 Gd: 0-2 GF: 0-1 Fm: 0-0
Distance: 5f/6f: 0-3 7f-8f: 0-2 9f-13f: 0-0 14f+: 0-0
Track : LH: 0-4 RH: 0-0 Tight: 0-3 Gall: 0-1
Aids: Bl: 0-0 Vi: 0-0 Tstrap: 0-0
Best Rating: 56 10/01 Wolv 5f stand

Crepusculaire (FR)

100 **74**

4-y-o ch f Hernando (FR)-Guest Performer (Be My Guest (USA))
N A Callaghan Andy J Smith

Placings:2411016-0420 **(5471)**
2001: 9^{0}HY, 9^{4}GS, 10^{2}S, 11^{0}S

	Starts	1st	2nd	3rd	Win & Pl
Career Total (Turf)	11	3	2	0	11531

Total win prize-money £8932

Going (Turf): Sf: 0-4 GS: 0-1 Gd: 0-0 GF: 0-0 Fm: 0-0
Distance: 5f/6f: 0-0 7f-8f: 0-0 **9f-13f: 3-11** 14f+: 0-0
Track : LH: 0-3 RH: 0-1 Tight: 0-1 Gall: 0-0
Aids: Bl: 0-0 Vi: 0-0 Tstrap: 0-0
Best Rating: 74 10/01 Pont 1m2f6y soft

Good form in France, she was disappointing on her first start in Britain but registered two much improved effort at Salisbury and Pontefract. She looks her best over 11-12 furlongs, and needs ground on the soft side of good.

Creskeld (IRE)

97 **72**

2-y-o b c Sri Pekan (USA)-Pizzazz (Unfuwain (USA))

J L Eyre Creskeld Racing

Placings:52015050 **(5690)**

2001: 5^{5}S, 5^{2}S, 6^{0}GF, 5^{1}GF, 5^{5}G, 7^{0}S, 7^{5}S, 7^{0}S

	Starts	1st	2nd	3rd	Win & Pl
Career Total (Turf)	8	1	1	0	4383

68	5/01	Ripn	5f	D	G-F	£3471

Total win prize-money £3471

Going (Turf): Sf: 0-5 GS: 0-0 Gd: 0-1 **GF: 1-2** Fm: 0-0
Distance: **5f/6f: 1-5** 7f-8f: 0-3 9f-13f: 0-0 14f+: 0-0
Track : LH: 0-2 RH: 0-0 Tight: 0-2 Gall: 0-0
Aids: Bl: 0-0 Vi: 0-0 Tstrap: 0-0
Best Rating: 72 11/01 Donc 7f soft

Cresset

67(103) (30)

5-y-o ch g Arazi (USA)-Mixed Applause (USA) (Nijinsky (CAN))

D W Chapman Michael Hill

Placings:0006/02121220000-54000500 **(1408)**

2001: 12^{5}SD, 11^{4}SW, 11^{0}SD, 16^{0}SD, 16^{0}SD, 12^{5}SD, 16^{0}GF, 11^{0}G

	Starts	1st	2nd	3rd	Win & Pl
Career Total (Turf)	8	0	0	0	
Career Total (AW)	16	2	4	0	7873

61	2/00	Sthl	1m4f	E(0-75)H	STD	£2795
61	1/00	Wolv	1m4f	G(0-60)H	STD	£1545

Total win prize-money £4341

Going (Turf): Sf: 0-1 GS: 0-0 Gd: 0-1 GF: 0-3 Fm: 0-3
Distance: 5f/6f: 0-0 7f-8f: 0-1 **9f-13f: 2-14** 14f+: 0-9
Track : **LH: 2-19** RH: 0-5 **Tight: 1-8** Gall: 0-1
Aids: **Bl: 2-17** Vi: 0-0 Tstrap: 0-0
Best Rating: 30 2/01 Sthl 1m3f stand

Crest Wing (USA)

62

8-y-o b g Storm Bird (CAN)-Purify (USA) (Fappiano (USA))

Miss Z C Davison The Secret Circle (1)

Placings:004/0/0 **(1620)**

2001: 16^{0}GF

	Starts	1st	2nd	3rd	Win & Pl
Career Total (Turf)	5	0	0	0	248

Going (Turf): Sf: 0-1 GS: 0-0 Gd: 0-1 GF: 0-3 Fm: 0-0
Distance: 5f/6f: 0-0 7f-8f: 0-0 9f-13f: 0-4 14f+: 0-1
Track : LH: 0-4 RH: 0-0 Tight: 0-2 Gall: 0-1
Aids: Bl: 0-0 Vi: 0-0 Tstrap: 0-0

Cretan Gift

106(106) (106)**99**

10-y-o ch g Cadeaux Genereux-Caro's Niece (USA) (Caro)

N P Littmoden T Clarke

Placings:000/545365/2100421150024/3422201620221463664051100015/120220601544100536/122652042060030/54200220610051204030/0351465002344550004-530004040040 **(4117)**

2001: 7^{5}SD, 6^{3}SD, 6^{0}S, 6^{0}GS, 6^{0}G, 6^{4}GF, 6^{0}F, 6^{4}GF, 7^{0}G, 5^{0}GF, 6^{4}GS, 6^{0}G

	Starts	1st	2nd	3rd	Win & Pl
Career Total (Turf)	105	8	15	6	168243
Career Total (AW)	28	7	6	3	36498

111	4/00	NmkR	6f	A	G-S	£13711
100	8/99	Yarm	6f3y	C	GD	£6024
102	7/99	Asct	6f	C(0-95)H	FRM	£9468
103	3/98	Wolv	5f	C(0-100)H	STD	£5576
102	8/97	Leop	6f		GD	£19500
96	6/97	Newc	6f	C(0-95)	HVY	£13615
97	2/97	Sthl	6f	C(0-95)H	STD	£5246
81	11/96	Rdcr	6f	C(0-95)H	G-F	£6784
70	9/96	Ayr	6f	B H	G-F	£12427
69	9/96	Nott	5f13y	E(0-70)H	FRM	£3698
86	6/96	Wolv	6f	D(0-85)H	STD	£3993
82	4/96	Wolv	5f	F	STD	£2381
70	10/95	Wolv	6f	E(0-70)H	STD	£3080
64	9/95	Wolv	6f	F(0-65)H	STD	£2174
56	4/95	Sthl	6f	F(0-65)H	STD	£2846

Total win prize-money £110529

Going (Turf): Sf: 1-14 GS: 1-15 **Gd: 2-38 GF: 2-34** Fm: 2-4
Distance: **5f/6f: 14-91** 7f-8f: 1-42 9f-13f: 0-0 14f+: 0-0
Track : **LH: 7-37** RH: 0-2 **Tight: 5-23** Gall: 0-1
Aids: **Bl: 8-51** Vi: 6-61 Tstrap: 0-0
Best Rating: 106 3/01 Wolv 6f stand

He is as hard as nails and stands his racing well, but he is just finding Pattern company too hot these days. Invariably fitted with blinkers or a visor, he stays seven furlongs, acts on any ground and is best when coming late off a fast pace.

Cricketers Club

(90) (44)**41**

3-y-o b g Dancing Spree (USA)-Alacrity (Alzao (USA))

R Ingram Cricketers Club Owners Group (2000)

Placings:0006-63505 **(5593)**

2001: 8^{6}SD, 8^{3}SD, 10^{5}SW, 10^{0}G, 5^{5}GS

	Starts	1st	2nd	3rd	Win & Pl
Career Total (Turf)	5	0	0	0	0
Career Total (AW)	4	0	0	1	260

Going (Turf): Sf: 0-0 GS: 0-2 Gd: 0-1 GF: 0-2 Fm: 0-0
Distance: 5f/6f: 0-3 7f-8f: 0-4 9f-13f: 0-2 14f+: 0-0
Track : LH: 0-6 RH: 0-0 Tight: 0-5 Gall: 0-0
Aids: Bl: 0-0 Vi: 0-0 Tstrap: 0-0
Best Rating: 51 1/01 Ling 1m stand

Crimson Ridge

93 **59**

3-y-o b f King's Signet (USA)-Cloudy Reef (Cragador)

R Hollinshead M Johnson

Placings:3642-5000 **(4601)**

2001: 6^{5}F, 5^{0}G, 5^{0}G, 5^{0}GF

	Starts	1st	2nd	3rd	Win & Pl
Career Total (Turf)	8	0	1	1	1568

Going (Turf): Sf: 0-0 GS: 0-0 Gd: 0-3 GF: 0-4 Fm: 0-1
Distance: 5f/6f: 0-8 7f-8f: 0-0 9f-13f: 0-0 14f+: 0-0
Track : LH: 0-0 RH: 0-0 Tight: 0-0 Gall: 0-0
Aids: Bl: 0-0 Vi: 0-0 Tstrap: 0-0
Best Rating: 40 7/01 Leic 5f2y good

Crimson Tide (IRE)

115(113) (99)**103**

7-y-o b h Sadler's Wells (USA)-Sharata (IRE) (Darshaan)

J W Hills C Wright & Partners

Placings:21/30332111/6633150/35000211-400 **(2304)**

2001: 7^{4}GF, 10^{0}GF, 8^{0}GF

	Starts	1st	2nd	3rd	Win & Pl
Career Total (Turf)	25	5	2	6	127559
Career Total (AW)	3	2	1	0	13945

99	12/00	Ling	1m	D	STD	£3682
90	12/00	Ling	1m2f	D	STD	£3662
102	9/98	Epsm	1m4f10y	A	SFT	£18570
114	11/97	Capa	1m		HVY	£50721
109	10/97	Duss	1m110y		SFT	£30303
100	9/97	Bath	1m5y	C	G-F	£4817
92	10/96	NmkR	7f	B	GD	£6164

Total win prize-money £117920

Going (Turf): Sf: 3-5 GS: 0-2 Gd: 1-8 GF: 1-9 Fm: 0-1
Distance: 5f/6f: 0-0 7f-8f: 3-11 **9f-13f: 4-17** 14f+: 0-0
Track : **LH: 4-12** RH: 2-7 **Tight: 4-9** Gall: 0-4
Aids: Bl: 0-0 Vi: 0-0 Tstrap: 0-0
Best Rating: 101 5/01 York 7f202y gd-fm

A dual Group Two winner on the continent in his younger days, he developed into a useful horse on the All-Weather last winter. An encouraging reappearance in Listed company at York this season confirmed that he ideally needs further than a mile these days. Acts on a sound surface.

Cripsey Brook

99 **71**

3-y-o ch g Lycius (USA)-Duwon (IRE) (Polish Precedent (USA))

B R Millman (M Wigham 18/6) Normandy Developments (london)

Placings:450-504100 **(4988)**

2001: 8^{5}G, 9^{0}GF, 8^{4}GF, 6^{1}GF, 8^{0}F, 8^{0}G

	Starts	1st	2nd	3rd	Win & Pl
Career Total (Turf)	9	1	0	0	3849

69	6/01	Brig	6f209y	E(0-70)H	G-F	£2975

Total win prize-money £2975

Going (Turf): Sf: 0-1 GS: 0-0 Gd: 0-3 **GF: 1-4** Fm: 0-1
Distance: 5f/6f: 0-2 **7f-8f: 1-5** 9f-13f: 0-2 14f+: 0-0
Track : **LH: 1-1** RH: 0-2 Tight: 0-1 Gall: 0-1
Aids: Bl: 0-0 Vi: 0-0 Tstrap: 0-0
Best Rating: 71 5/01 NmkR 1m good

First win came in a Brighton maiden, but struggled in handicaps. Suited by seven furlongs and good to firm ground.

Cristoforo (IRE)

88(89) (49d)**15**

4-y-o b g Perugino (USA)-Red Barons Lady (IRE) (Electric)

B J Curley P Byrne

Placings:055-0000 **(4052)**

2001: 7^{0}SD, 7^{0}SD, 7^{0}SD, 6^{0}F

	Starts	1st	2nd	3rd	Win & Pl
Career Total (Turf)	1	0	0	0	
Career Total (AW)	6	0	0	0	0

Going (Turf): Sf: 0-0 GS: 0-0 Gd: 0-0 GF: 0-0 Fm: 0-1
Distance: 5f/6f: 0-1 7f-8f: 0-5 9f-13f: 0-1 14f+: 0-0
Track : LH: 0-6 RH: 0-0 Tight: 0-3 Gall: 0-0
Aids: Bl: 0-0 Vi: 0-0 Tstrap: 0-0
Best Rating: 30 2/01 Wolv 7f stand

Cristophe

97(94) (42)**41**

3-y-o b c Kris-Our Shirley (Shirley Heights)

S P C Woods S P C Woods

Placings:000003023 **(4377)**

2001: 12^{0}GS, 11^{0}SD, 12^{0}GS, 16^{0}GF, 14^{0}GF, 12^{3}SD, 16^{0}GF, 12^{2}G, 11^{3}GF

	Starts	1st	2nd	3rd	Win & Pl
Career Total (Turf)	7	0	1	1	825
Career Total (AW)	2	0	0	1	275

Going (Turf): Sf: 0-0 GS: 0-2 Gd: 0-1 GF: 0-4 Fm: 0-0
Distance: 5f/6f: 0-0 7f-8f: 0-0 9f-13f: 0-6 14f+: 0-3
Track : LH: 0-4 RH: 0-4 Tight: 0-5 Gall: 0-1

Aids: Bl: 0-0 Vi: 0-0 Tstrap: 0-0
Best Rating: 69 5/01 Sals 1m4f gd-sft

Critical Stage (IRE)

34

2-y-o b c King's Theatre (IRE)-Zandaka (FR) (Doyoun)
John Berry The 1997 Partnership

Placings:60 (5635)
2001: 6^{6}S, 7^{0}G

	Starts	1st	2nd	3rd	Win & Pl
Career Total (Turf)	2	0	0	0	0

Going (Turf): Sf: 0-1 GS: 0-0 Gd: 0-1 GF: 0-0 Fm: 0-0
Distance: 5f/6f: 0-1 7f-8f: 0-1 9f-13f: 0-0 14f+: 0-0
Track : LH: 0-2 RH: 0-0 Tight: 0-1 Gall: 0-0
Aids: Bl: 0-0 Vi: 0-0 Tstrap: 0-0
Best Rating: 34 11/01 Catt 7f good

Out of a half-sister to the French 1000 guineas winner, Zalaiyka.

Croeso Croeso

102 **62d**

3-y-o b f Most Welcome-Croeso-I-Cymru (Welsh Captain)
J L Spearing Mrs Richard Evans

Placings:0-0331000 (5027)
2001: 5^{0}F, 6^{3}F, 5^{3}G, 5^{1}G, 5^{0}G, 6^{0}F, 5^{0}S

	Starts	1st	2nd	3rd	Win & Pl
Career Total (Turf)	8	1	0	2	4181
62 8/01 Brig 5f59y F(0-60)				GD	£3265

Total win prize-money £3266

Going (Turf): Sf: 0-1 GS: 0-1 **Gd: 1-3** GF: 0-0 Fm: 0-3
Distance: **5f/6f: 1-7** 7f-8f: 0-1 9f-13f: 0-0 14f+: 0-0
Track : **LH: 1-2** RH: 0-0 Tight: 0-0 Gall: 0-0
Aids: Bl: 0-0 Vi: 0-0 Tstrap: 0-0
Best Rating: 62 8/01 Brig 5f59y good

Progressed steadily to get off the mark in a classified stakes at Brighton. Effective at five furlongs but stays six. Acts on good to firm and good ground, and suited by waiting tactics.

Crop Circle

81 **56**

2-y-o b g Magic Ring (IRE)-Surprise Surprise (Robellino (USA))
I A Balding Park House Partnership

Placings:040 (3387)
2001: 5^{0}GF, 5^{4}GF, 5^{0}F

	Starts	1st	2nd	3rd	Win & Pl
Career Total (Turf)	3	0	0	0	263

Going (Turf): Sf: 0-0 GS: 0-0 Gd: 0-0 GF: 0-2 Fm: 0-1
Distance: 5f/6f: 0-3 7f-8f: 0-0 9f-13f: 0-0 14f+: 0-0
Track : LH: 0-2 RH: 0-0 Tight: 0-0 Gall: 0-2
Aids: Bl: 0-0 Vi: 0-0 Tstrap: 0-0
Best Rating: 56 7/01 Bath 5f11y gd-fm

Crosby Dancer

83 **51**

2-y-o b c Glory Of Dancer-Mary Macblain (Damister (USA))
John A Harris (J L Harris 17/6) D Jackson

Placings:0040 (5628)
2001: 5^{0}GF, 6^{0}S, 7^{4}S, 8^{0}G

	Starts	1st	2nd	3rd	Win & Pl
Career Total (Turf)	4	0	0	0	0

Going (Turf): Sf: 0-2 GS: 0-0 Gd: 0-1 GF: 0-1 Fm: 0-0
Distance: 5f/6f: 0-1 7f-8f: 0-3 9f-13f: 0-0 14f+: 0-0
Track : LH: 0-3 RH: 0-0 Tight: 0-2 Gall: 0-1
Aids: Bl: 0-0 Vi: 0-0 Tstrap: 0-0
Best Rating: 51 10/01 Catt 7f soft

Crosby Donjohn

107(86) (45)**47**

4-y-o ch g Magic Ring (IRE)-Ovideo (Domynsky)
J R Weymes Don Raper

Placings:5450500**2**/60-00004021603**0** (5272)
2001: 9^{0}S, 7^{0}F, 6^{0}GF, 7^{0}F, 8^{4}GF, 8^{0}GF, 10^{2}G, 8^{1}GS, 9^{6}G, 10^{0}G, 8^{3}GF, 10^{0}HY

	Starts	1st	2nd	3rd	Win & Pl
Career Total (Turf)	18	1	1	1	5410
Career Total (AW)	4	0	1	0	1080
47 8/01 Haml 1m65y E(0-70)H				G-S	£3304

Total win prize-money £3304

Going (Turf): Sf: 0-2 **GS: 1-2** Gd: 0-4 GF: 0-7 Fm: 0-3
Distance: 5f/6f: 0-2 7f-8f: 0-12 **9f-13f: 1-8** 14f+: 0-0
Track : LH: 0-14 **RH: 1-4 Tight: 1-12** Gall: 0-1
Aids: **Bl: 1-15** Vi: 0-0 Tstrap: 0-0
Best Rating: 47 8/01 Newc 1m1f9y good

Moderate handicapper, effective from eight to ten furlongs, suited by cut in the ground. Scored his first success at Hamilton in summer of 2001.

Crosby Rocker

78 **26**

3-y-o b f Rock Hopper-Mary Macblain (Damister (USA))
John A Harris D Jackson

Placings:00 (4455)
2001: 8^{0}GF, 10^{0}GF

	Starts	1st	2nd	3rd	Win & Pl
Career Total (Turf)	2	0	0	0	

Going (Turf): Sf: 0-0 GS: 0-0 Gd: 0-0 GF: 0-2 Fm: 0-0
Distance: 5f/6f: 0-0 7f-8f: 0-0 9f-13f: 0-2 14f+: 0-0
Track : LH: 0-2 RH: 0-0 Tight: 0-0 Gall: 0-1
Aids: Bl: 0-0 Vi: 0-0 Tstrap: 0-0
Best Rating: 26 9/01 York 1m2f85y gd-fm

Crossbreeze (USA)

92 **74**

2-y-o b f Red Ransom (USA)-Crystal Crossing (IRE) (Royal Academy (USA))
J H M Gosden Mrs B V Sangster, R E Sangster

Placings:306 (4887)
2001: 6^{3}G, 6^{0}G, 7^{6}GF

	Starts	1st	2nd	3rd	Win & Pl
Career Total (Turf)	3	0	0	1	826

Going (Turf): Sf: 0-0 GS: 0-0 Gd: 0-2 GF: 0-1 Fm: 0-0
Distance: 5f/6f: 0-2 7f-8f: 0-1 9f-13f: 0-0 14f+: 0-0
Track : LH: 0-0 RH: 0-1 Tight: 0-0 Gall: 0-1
Aids: Bl: 0-0 Vi: 0-0 Tstrap: 0-0
Best Rating: 74 9/01 Kemp 7f gd-fm

Crossways

99(96) (51)**69**

3-y-o b g Mister Baileys-Miami Dancer (USA) (Seattle Dancer (USA))
C F Wall N Ahamad

Placings:00-3216134 (4030)
2001: 10^{3}SW, 11^{2}GF, 11^{1}F, 14^{6}G, 12^{1}GF, 12^{3}GS, 12^{4}G

	Starts	1st	2nd	3rd	Win & Pl
Career Total (Turf)	8	2	1	1	7586
Career Total (AW)	1	0	0	1	412
66 7/01 Folk 1m4f E(0-70)H				G-F	£3038
67 6/01 Ling 1m3f106yF(0-60)H				FRM	£2600

Total win prize-money £5639

Going (Turf): Sf: 0-1 GS: 0-1 Gd: 0-2 **GF: 1-3 Fm: 1-1**
Distance: 5f/6f: 0-0 7f-8f: 0-1 **9f-13f: 2-7** 14f+: 0-1
Track : **LH: 1-4 RH: 1-3 Tight: 2-5** Gall: 0-2
Aids: Bl: 0-0 Vi: 0-0 Tstrap: 0-0
Best Rating: 69 8/01 NmkJ 1m4f gd-sft

Won at Lingfield in June and Folkestone in July 2001, came from off the pace to lead close home at the latter course. Stays a mile and a half well, though reportedly found trip beyond him when tried over 14 furlongs.

Crow Wood

92(99) (81)**63**

2-y-o b c Halling (USA)-Play With Me (IRE) (Alzao (USA))
Sir Mark Prescott Tessona Racing Limited

Placings:55100 (4587)
2001: 6^{5}GF, 7^{5}GF, 7^{1}SD, 8^{0}GF, 7^{0}HY

	Starts	1st	2nd	3rd	Win & Pl
Career Total (Turf)	4	0	0	0	0
Career Total (AW)	1	1	0	0	3500
81 8/01 Wolv 7f D				STD	£3500

Total win prize-money £3500

Going (Turf): Sf: 0-1 GS: 0-0 Gd: 0-0 GF: 0-3 Fm: 0-0
Distance: 5f/6f: 0-1 **7f-8f: 1-3** 9f-13f: 0-1 14f+: 0-0
Track : **LH: 1-3** RH: 0-0 **Tight: 1-2** Gall: 0-0
Aids: Bl: 0-0 Vi: 0-0 Tstrap: 0-0
Best Rating: 81 8/01 Wolv 7f stand

Showed ability in two starts on turf and got off the mark in a maiden on the Wolverhampton Fibresand in August. He should be suited by a mile.

Crownfield

92 **74**

2-y-o b g Blushing Flame (USA)-Chief Island (Be My Chief (USA))
W G M Turner Bill Brown

Placings:402 (2702)
2001: 6^{4}GF, 6^{0}GF, 6^{2}F

	Starts	1st	2nd	3rd	Win & Pl
Career Total (Turf)	3	0	1	0	990

Going (Turf): Sf: 0-0 GS: 0-0 Gd: 0-0 GF: 0-2 Fm: 0-1
Distance: 5f/6f: 0-2 7f-8f: 0-1 9f-13f: 0-0 14f+: 0-0
Track : LH: 0-1 RH: 0-0 Tight: 0-0 Gall: 0-0
Aids: Bl: 0-0 Vi: 0-0 Tstrap: 0-0
Best Rating: 74 6/01 Ayr 6f gd-fm

Has shown ability on fast ground.

Cruagh Express (IRE)

107(101) (55)**54**

5-y-o b g Unblest-Cry In The Dark (Godswalk (USA))
G L Moore E Farncombe

Placings:6600503355/5600**1**163633-02503202040 (4951)
2001: 8^{0}SD, 8^{2}SD, 7^{5}GS, 7^{0}G, 8^{3}GF, 6^{2}GF, 7^{0}GS, 8^{2}G, 7^{0}G, 7^{4}S, 8^{0}G

	Starts	1st	2nd	3rd	Win & Pl
Career Total (Turf)	24	1	2	3	6454
Career Total (AW)	8	1	1	3	3305
54 9/00 Gdwd 1m E(0-65)H				HVY	£3250
46 9/00 Ling 1m2f G(0-60)H				STD	£2012

Total win prize-money £5263

Going (Turf): **Sf: 1-3** GS: 0-3 Gd: 0-6 GF: 0-8 Fm: 0-1

Distance: 5f/6f: 0-4 7f-8f: 1-20 9f-13f: 1-8 14f+: 0-0
Track : LH: 1-16 RH: 1-9 **Tight: 1-11** Gall: 0-0
Aids: **Bl: 2-16** Vi: 0-0 Tstrap: 0-3
Best Rating: 54 8/01 Wind 1m67y good

Cruise

81(86) (33)**50d**
4-y-o ch g Prince Sabo-Mistral's Dancer (Shareef Dancer (USA))
R M Flower K & D Computers Ltd

Placings:51/0500100-**0000000** **(2113)**
2001: 8^{0}SD, 8^{0}SD, 12^{0}SW, 10^{0}SD, 7^{0}G, 7^{0}GF, 6^{0}F

	Starts	1st	2nd	3rd	Win & Pl
Career Total (Turf)	10	1	0	0	2477
Career Total (AW)	6	1	0	0	2096

62 8/00 Brig 6f209y F(0-60) FRM £2476
61 12/99 Ling 6f F STD £2095
Total win prize-money £4573

Going (Turf): Sf: 0-1 GS: 0-1 Gd: 0-2 GF: 0-2 **Fm: 1-4**
Distance: 5f/6f: 1-3 7f-8f: 1-11 9f-13f: 0-2 14f+: 0-0
Track : **LH: 2-10** RH: 0-0 **Tight: 1-7** Gall: 0-0
Aids: Bl: 0-2 Vi: 0-0 Tstrap: 0-0
Best Rating: 33 1/01 Ling 1m stand

Crunchy (IRE)

97 **51**
3-y-o ch g Common Grounds-Credit Crunch (IRE) (Caerleon (USA))
J A R Toller The Half Moon Club

Placings:00406001 **(5084)**
2001: 7^{0}GS, 7^{0}GF, 6^{4}F, 8^{0}G, 9^{6}GF, 12^{0}G, 10^{0}S, 9^{1}S

	Starts	1st	2nd	3rd	Win & Pl
Career Total (Turf)	8	1	0	0	2649

51 10/01 Brig 1m1f209yF(0-60)H SFT £2366
Total win prize-money £2366

Going (Turf): **Sf: 1-2** GS: 0-1 Gd: 0-2 GF: 0-2 Fm: 0-1
Distance: 5f/6f: 0-1 7f-8f: 0-2 **9f-13f: 1-5** 14f+: 0-0
Track : **LH: 1-3** RH: 0-2 Tight: 0-4 Gall: 0-0
Aids: Bl: 0-0 Vi: 0-0 **Tstrap: 1-5**
Best Rating: 52 6/01 Ling 6f firm

Modest form before getting off the mark in a Brighton maiden in October, but the form may not mean a lot.

Crusading Times

69(75) (33)**24**
2-y-o b g Timeless Times (USA)-Marie's Crusader (IRE) (Last Tycoon)
M W Easterby B Bargh T Swain J Walsh & P Bown

Placings:066 **(0771)**
2001: 5^{0}S, 5^{6}SD, 5^{6}S

	Starts	1st	2nd	3rd	Win & Pl
Career Total (Turf)	2	0	0	0	0
Career Total (AW)	1	0	0	0	0

Going (Turf): Sf: 0-2 GS: 0-0 Gd: 0-0 GF: 0-0 Fm: 0-0
Distance: 5f/6f: 0-3 7f-8f: 0-0 9f-13f: 0-0 14f+: 0-0
Track : LH: 0-0 RH: 0-0 Tight: 0-0 Gall: 0-0
Aids: Bl: 0-0 Vi: 0-0 Tstrap: 0-0
Best Rating: 33 4/01 Sthl 5f stand

Crusty Lily

101 (24)**33**
5-y-o gr m Whittingham (IRE)-Miss Crusty (Belfort (FR))
N P Littmoden L H Ballinger

Placings:0/60025100/04200663056-0550030306 **(4385)**
2001: 5^{0}F, 5^{5}F, 6^{5}GF, 6^{0}GF, 7^{0}GF, 5^{3}GF, 5^{0}GF, 6^{3}G, 6^{0}F, 6^{6}GF

	Starts	1st	2nd	3rd	Win & Pl
Career Total (Turf)	28	1	2	3	6267

	Starts	1st	2nd	3rd	Win & Pl
Career Total (AW)	2	0	0	0	0

42 8/99 Yarm 6f3y E(0-70)H GD £3132
Total win prize-money £3132

Going (Turf): Sf: 0-1 GS: 0-1 **Gd: 1-5** GF: 0-15 Fm: 0-6
Distance: 5f/6f: 0-15 **7f-8f: 1-14** 9f-13f: 0-1 14f+: 0-0
Track : LH: 0-10 RH: 0-1 Tight: 0-2 Gall: 0-2
Aids: Bl: 0-0 Vi: 0-0 Tstrap: 0-0
Best Rating: 36 6/01 Nott 6f15y gd-fm

Cruz Santa

80 (40)**33**
8-y-o b m Lord Bud-Linpac Mapleleaf (Dominion)
Mrs M Reveley The Mary Reveley Racing Club

Placings:26000/04**60000**/**10004**630000/0P4/2-0 **(5383)**
2001: 13^{0}S

	Starts	1st	2nd	3rd	Win & Pl
Career Total (Turf)	17	0	2	1	2571
Career Total (AW)	11	1	0	0	2085

40 1/98 Sthl 1m3f F STD £2085
Total win prize-money £2085

Going (Turf): Sf: 0-2 GS: 0-1 Gd: 0-5 GF: 0-6 Fm: 0-3
Distance: 5f/6f: 0-2 7f-8f: 0-7 **9f-13f: 1-13** 14f+: 0-6
Track : **LH: 1-22** RH: 0-2 Tight: 0-10 Gall: 0-0
Aids: Bl: 0-0 Vi: 0-0 Tstrap: 0-0
Best Rating: 33 10/01 Catt 1m5f175y soft

Cryfield

104(102) (63)**68**
4-y-o b g Efisio-Ciboure (Norwick (USA))
N Tinkler Mr & Mrs G Middlebrook

Placings:050**2013100**62420-003444141555000 **(5681)**
2001: 7^{0}GF, 8^{0}F, 10^{3}GF, 10^{4}G, 7^{4}G, 9^{4}GF, 8^{1}SD, 8^{4}G, 7^{1}GF, 7^{5}G, 7^{5}GF, 7^{5}GF, 8^{0}G, 8^{0}SD, 8^{0}S

	Starts	1st	2nd	3rd	Win & Pl
Career Total (Turf)	26	3	2	2	19813
Career Total (AW)	4	1	1	0	2823

68 7/01 Asct 7f C(0-90)H G-F £8677
63 6/01 Sthl 1m G(0-70)H STD £1960
62 6/00 Carl 5f207y E(0-70)H G-F £3656
55 5/00 Rdcr 6f G(0-60)H G-S £2044
Total win prize-money £16338

Going (Turf): Sf: 0-5 GS: 1-4 Gd: 0-8 **GF: 2-8** Fm: 0-1
Distance: 5f/6f: 2-10 7f-8f: 2-15 9f-13f: 0-5 14f+: 0-0
Track : LH: 1-13 RH: 1-1 Tight: 0-3 **Gall: 1-2**
Aids: Bl: 0-0 **Vi: 1-12** Tstrap: 0-0
Best Rating: 68 7/01 Asct 7f gd-fm

He won twice over six furlongs last season and made no mistake in an amateur riders' event on the Southwell Fibresand in June. Landed a valuable ladies' race at Ascot in July and goes very well for Carol Williams. Versatile with regards to ground, he is at his best coming off a strong pace.

Crystal Canyon

99(95) (46)**46**
4-y-o ch f Efisio-Manor Adventure (Smackover)
B Smart Mrs Julie Martin

Placings:60/0-000400434440 **(5629)**
2001: 6^{0}SD, 6^{0}SD, 5^{0}G, 5^{4}GF, 5^{0}GF, 5^{0}SD, 5^{4}SD, 5^{3}GF, 5^{4}GF, 5^{4}S, 5^{4}G, 5^{0}G

	Starts	1st	2nd	3rd	Win & Pl
Career Total (Turf)	11	0	0	1	940
Career Total (AW)	4	0	0	0	0

Going (Turf): Sf: 0-1 GS: 0-1 Gd: 0-5 GF: 0-4 Fm: 0-0
Distance: 5f/6f: 0-14 7f-8f: 0-1 9f-13f: 0-0 14f+: 0-0
Track : LH: 0-3 RH: 0-0 Tight: 0-0 Gall: 0-1
Aids: Bl: 0-0 Vi: 0-0 Tstrap: 0-0
Best Rating: 48 6/01 Bevl 5f gd-fm

Crystal Creek (IRE)

99(64) **53**
5-y-o b g River Falls-Dazzling Maid (IRE) (Tate Gallery (USA))
D Nicholls Middleham Park Racing Xxv

Placings:00/100133250/06000-0050242600 **(5230)**
2001: 7^{0}SD, 10^{0}F, 8^{5}GF, 10^{0}GF, 10^{2}GF, 10^{4}GF, 11^{2}S, 12^{6}G, 9^{0}GS, 11^{0}S

	Starts	1st	2nd	3rd	Win & Pl
Career Total (Turf)	25	2	3	2	16606
Career Total (AW)	1	0	0	0	

85 6/99 Bath 1m5y C(0-90)H FRM £6243
80 5/99 Kemp 1m D GD £3883
Total win prize-money £10127

Going (Turf): Sf: 0-5 GS: 0-2 **Gd: 1-6** GF: 0-9 **Fm: 1-3**
Distance: 5f/6f: 0-0 7f-8f: 1-11 9f-13f: 1-15 14f+: 0-0
Track : LH: 1-12 RH: 1-9 Tight: 1-7 Gall: 1-5
Aids: Bl: 0-0 Vi: 0-0 Tstrap: 0-0
Best Rating: 56 7/01 Hayd 1m2f120y gd-fm

Winner of a Kempton maiden and a Bath handicap in 1999 but has not added to that since. Handles most surfaces, but may not stay 12 furlongs.

Crystal Flite (IRE)

106(90) (47)**71**
4-y-o b f Darshaan-Crystal City (Kris)
W R Muir The Wheet Partnership

Placings:05063/002605**500**-**1013** **(3364)**
2001: 11^{1}GF, 12^{0}GS, 11^{1}GF, 11^{3}G

	Starts	1st	2nd	3rd	Win & Pl
Career Total (Turf)	16	2	1	2	12739
Career Total (AW)	2	0	0	0	

63 7/01 Leic 1m3f183yD(0-85)H G-F £6942
54 6/01 Leic 1m3f183yE(0-70)H G-F £2978
Total win prize-money £9921

Going (Turf): Sf: 0-3 GS: 0-4 Gd: 0-2 **GF: 2-6** Fm: 0-0
Distance: 5f/6f: 0-0 7f-8f: 0-5 **9f-13f: 2-10** 14f+: 0-2
Track : LH: 0-6 **RH: 2-8** Tight: 0-6 Gall: 0-2
Aids: Bl: 0-0 Vi: 0-0 Tstrap: 0-0
Best Rating: 71 7/01 Leic 1m3f183y good

Fair handicapper, stays 12 furlongs, acts on fast ground.

Crystal Girl

65 **27**
2-y-o b f Presidium-Balgownie (Prince Tenderfoot (USA))
M Dods Magteam

Placings:0 **(5147)**
2001: 7^{0}G

	Starts	1st	2nd	3rd	Win & Pl
Career Total (Turf)	1	0	0	0	

Going (Turf): Sf: 0-0 GS: 0-0 Gd: 0-1 GF: 0-0 Fm: 0-0
Distance: 5f/6f: 0-0 7f-8f: 0-1 9f-13f: 0-0 14f+: 0-0
Track : LH: 0-0 RH: 0-0 Tight: 0-0 Gall: 0-0
Aids: Bl: 0-0 Vi: 0-0 Tstrap: 0-0
Best Rating: 27 10/01 Rdcr 7f good

Crystal Lass

(101) (69)**50**
5-y-o b m Ardkinglass-That's Rich (Hot Spark)
R Brotherton (J Balding 8/9) Binding Matters Ltd

Placings:550203344/25010404/05005050400-0600013131364030 **(5611)**
2001: 7^{0}SD, 8^{6}SD, 7^{0}SD, 8^{0}SD, 8^{0}SD, 7^{1}SD, 8^{3}SD, 7^{1}SD, 8^{3}SD, 8^{1}SD, 7^{3}SD, 7^{6}SD, 8^{4}GS, 9^{0}GS, 7^{3}SD, 8^{0}SD

	Starts	1st	2nd	3rd	Win & Pl
Career Total (Turf)	**14**	**0**	**0**	**0**	**250**
Career Total (AW)	**30**	**4**	**2**	**6**	**13872**

57	7/01	Sthl	1m	F	STD	£2310
53	7/01	Sthl	7f	F(0-65)H	STD	£2401
47	6/01	Sthl	7f	G(0-60)H	STD	£1890
73	6/99	Sthl	1m	E(0-75)H	STD	£2814

Total win prize-money £9415

Going (Turf): Sf: **0-1** GS: **0-3** Gd: **0-4** GF: **0-4** Fm: **0-2**
Distance: 5f/6f: 0-12 **7f-8f: 4-27** 9f-13f: 0-5 14f+: 0-0
Track : **LH: 4-29** RH: 0-1 Tight: 0-13 Gall: 0-0
Aids: Bl: 0-11 **Vi: 3-11** Tstrap: 0-0
Best Rating: 73 8/01 Wolv 7f stand

Winner of four races from seven furlongs to a mile, all of which have been at Southwell.

Crystal Music (USA)

111 **116**

3-y-o b f Nureyev (USA)-Crystal Spray (Beldale Flutter (USA))
J H M Gosden Lord Lloyd-Webber

Placings:111-42260 **(5577a)**
2001: 8^{4}G, 8^{2}G, 8^{2}GF, 10^{6}HO, 10^{0}F

	Starts	1st	2nd	3rd	Win & Pl
Career Total (Turf)	**8**	**3**	**2**	**0**	**243976**

113	9/00	Asct	1m	A	G-S	£116000
91	8/00	Sand	1m14y	C	G-F	£5886
94	7/00	NmkJ	7f	D	G-F	£4264

Total win prize-money £126151

Going (Turf): Sf: 0-0 GS: 1-1 Gd: 0-2 **GF: 2-3** Fm: 0-1
Distance: 5f/6f: 0-0 **7f-8f: 2-5** 9f-13f: 1-3 14f+: 0-0
Track : LH: 0-1 **RH: 2-4** Tight: 0-0 **Gall: 1-2**
Aids: Bl: 0-0 Vi: 0-0 Tstrap: 0-0
Best Rating: 116 6/01 Asct 1m gd-fm

Unbeaten as a juvenile, including running out a good winner of the Ascot Fillies' Mile. Fourth in the 1000 Guineas, she improved two places in the Irish equivalent, where the dead ground was not to her liking, and filled the same position in the Coronation Stakes. Possibly found ten furlongs on heavy ground against her in the Prix de l'Opera after a break and was running a good race in the Breeders' Cup Filly and Mare Turf when squeezed out a furlong from home.

Crystal Soldier

87 **44**

3-y-o ch f Infantry-Bottle Basher (Le Soleil)
D Burchell Three Acres Racing

Placings:0R0 **(1772)**
2001: 6^{0}GF, 9^{R}F, 10^{0}F

	Starts	1st	2nd	3rd	Win & Pl
Career Total (Turf)	**3**	**0**	**0**	**0**	

Going (Turf): Sf: 0-0 GS: 0-0 Gd: 0-0 GF: 0-1 Fm: 0-2
Distance: 5f/6f: 0-0 7f-8f: 0-1 9f-13f: 0-2 14f+: 0-0
Track : LH: 0-3 RH: 0-0 Tight: 0-1 Gall: 0-0
Aids: Bl: 0-0 Vi: 0-0 Tstrap: 0-0
Best Rating: 44 6/01 Bath 1m2f46y firm

Crystal Springs (IRE)

88 **76**

7-y-o b m Kahyasi-Aqua Lily (Kalaglow)
Patrick Martin Mrs Nuala Brennan

Placings:0551653/65312524200/1213440/5350130-0010 **(4653a)**
2001: 20^{0}GF, 16^{0}YS, 16^{1}G, 16^{0}G, 16^{0}S

	Starts	1st	2nd	3rd	Win & Pl
Career Total (Turf)	**36**	**6**	**4**	**5**	**49624**

76	8/01	Tram	2m	(0-82)H	GD	£9315
73	7/00	Curr	2m	(0-80)H	G-F	£9750
69	6/99	Curr	2m	(0-80)H	GD	£9712
69	5/99	Cork	1m6f	(0-75)H	Y-S	£4125
66	5/98	Wxfd	2m	(0-60)	GD	£2226
68	8/97	Tram	1m4f		GD	£2740

Total win prize-money £37869

Going (Turf): Sf: 0-8 GS: 0-0 **Gd: 4-10** GF: 1-5 Fm: 0-0
Distance: 5f/6f: 0-0 7f-8f: 0-0 9f-13f: 1-8 **14f+: 5-28**
Track : LH: 0-7 **RH: 5-27** Tight: 0-0 Gall: 0-1
Aids: Bl: 0-0 Vi: 0-0 Tstrap: 0-0
Best Rating: 76 8/01 Tram 2m good

Crystal Valkyrie (IRE)

79

2-y-o b f Danehill (USA)-Crystal Cross (USA) (Roberto (USA))
B W Hills Major Christopher Hanbury

Placings:64 **(4839)**
2001: 6^{6}GF, 6^{4}G

	Starts	1st	2nd	3rd	Win & Pl
Career Total (Turf)	**2**	**0**	**0**	**0**	**288**

Going (Turf): Sf: 0-0 GS: 0-0 Gd: 0-1 GF: 0-1 Fm: 0-0
Distance: 5f/6f: 0-0 7f-8f: 0-2 9f-13f: 0-0 14f+: 0-0
Track : LH: 0-0 RH: 0-0 Tight: 0-0 Gall: 0-0
Aids: Bl: 0-0 Vi: 0-0 Tstrap: 0-0
Best Rating: 79 8/01 Newb 6f8y gd-fm

Showed ability in a couple of turf maidens before winning a weak six-furlong maiden on the sand at Southwell in November. Should do better over further.

Cuba Gold (USA)

76 **43**

2-y-o b f Red Ransom (USA)-Recoleta (USA) (Wild Again (USA))
J L Dunlop J Higgins

Placings:0 **(1477)**
2001: 5^{0}G

	Starts	1st	2nd	3rd	Win & Pl
Career Total (Turf)	**1**	**0**	**0**	**0**	

Going (Turf): Sf: 0-0 GS: 0-0 Gd: 0-1 GF: 0-0 Fm: 0-0
Distance: 5f/6f: 0-1 7f-8f: 0-0 9f-13f: 0-0 14f+: 0-0
Track : LH: 0-0 RH: 0-1 Tight: 0-0 Gall: 0-1
Aids: Bl: 0-0 Vi: 0-0 Tstrap: 0-0
Best Rating: 43 5/01 Wind 5f10y good

Cubism (USA)

106 **92**

5-y-o b h Miswaki (USA)-Seattle Kat (USA) (Seattle Song (USA))
J W Hills K Y Lim

Placings:14105/012166064/035300-50300030 **(4870)**
2001: 6^{5}GF, 6^{0}GF, 6^{3}GF, 6^{0}G, 7^{0}GF, 6^{0}GF, 7^{3}G, 7^{0}G

	Starts	1st	2nd	3rd	Win & Pl
Career Total (Turf)	**28**	**4**	**1**	**4**	**58866**

98	5/99	Hayd	6f	A(0-110)H	GD	£12776
91	5/99	Sals	6f	B(0-100)H	G-F	£8854
89	8/98	Wind	6f	D H	G-F	£7197
77	7/98	Yarm	6f3y	D	GD	£3346

Total win prize-money £32174

Going (Turf): Sf: 0-1 GS: 0-0 **Gd: 2-12 GF: 2-14** Fm: 0-1
Distance: **5f/6f: 3-19** 7f-8f: 1-9 9f-13f: 0-0 14f+: 0-0
Track : LH: 0-0 **RH: 1-3** Tight: 0-0 **Gall: 1-1**
Aids: Bl: 0-0 Vi: 0-1 Tstrap: 0-8
Best Rating: 95 7/01 Newb 6f8y gd-fm

Probably a little below Listed class, he is a useful six-furlong handicapper though he has not won since May 1999.

Cuddles (FR)

71

2-y-o b f Anabaa (USA)-Palomelle (FR) (Moulin)
C E Brittain A J Richards

Placings:656144 **(5504)**
2001: 7^{6}G, 7^{5}GF, 8^{6}GF, 8^{1}S, 9^{4}S, 7^{4}HY

	Starts	1st	2nd	3rd	Win & Pl
Career Total (Turf)	**6**	**1**	**0**	**0**	**4959**

71	9/01	Pont	1m4y	E(0-85)	SFT	£3948

Total win prize-money £3949

Going (Turf): **Sf: 1-3** GS: 0-0 Gd: 0-1 GF: 0-2 Fm: 0-0
Distance: 5f/6f: 0-0 7f-8f: 0-3 **9f-13f: 1-3** 14f+: 0-0
Track : **LH: 1-1** RH: 0-1 Tight: 0-0 Gall: 0-0
Aids: Bl: 0-0 Vi: 0-0 Tstrap: 0-0
Best Rating: 71 10/01 Leic 1m1f218y soft

Out of a Group Three winner in France, did not disgrace herself when stepped up in class after winning a nursery at Pontefract and has since landed a very valuable nursery on the Lingfield Polytrack. Suited by a mile or a fast-run seven.

Cuigiu (IRE)

91(89) (46)**36**

4-y-o b g Persian Bold-Homosassa (Burslem)
A B Mulholland (T D Easterby 10/1) Toon Partners

Placings:00502540/0542054002300-0006000 **(3946)**
2001: 9^{0}GF, 8^{0}G, 11^{0}GF, 8^{6}F, 9^{0}GS, 10^{0}G, 9^{0}GS

	Starts	1st	2nd	3rd	Win & Pl
Career Total (Turf)	**22**	**0**	**3**	**1**	**2840**
Career Total (AW)	**6**	**0**	**0**	**0**	**202**

Going (Turf): Sf: 0-1 GS: 0-5 Gd: 0-5 GF: 0-8 Fm: 0-2
Distance: 5f/6f: 0-5 7f-8f: 0-9 9f-13f: 0-14 14f+: 0-0
Track : LH: 0-12 RH: 0-7 Tight: 0-9 Gall: 0-1
Aids: Bl: 0-3 Vi: 0-0 Tstrap: 0-7
Best Rating: 36 7/01 Rdcr 1m firm

Culminate

94(76) (6)**29**

4-y-o ch g Afzal-Straw Blade (Final Straw)
J E Long J King

Placings:00000-0030000 **(5182)**
2001: 12^{0}GF, 11^{0}F, 11^{3}F, 10^{0}GF, 9^{0}GF, 11^{0}G, 10^{0}HY

	Starts	1st	2nd	3rd	Win & Pl
Career Total (Turf)	**11**	**0**	**0**	**1**	**280**
Career Total (AW)	**1**	**0**	**0**	**0**	

Going (Turf): Sf: 0-2 GS: 0-0 Gd: 0-1 GF: 0-5 Fm: 0-2
Distance: 5f/6f: 0-0 7f-8f: 0-1 9f-13f: 0-9 14f+: 0-1
Track : LH: 0-5 RH: 0-3 Tight: 0-7 Gall: 0-2
Aids: Bl: 0-0 Vi: 0-0 Tstrap: 0-0
Best Rating: 29 8/01 Wind 1m3f135y good

Cultra (IRE)

92 **73**

2-y-o ch c Spectrum (IRE)-Ziggy Belle (USA) (Danzig (USA))
R Hannon Stonethorn Stud Farms Limited

Placings:00 **(5666)**
2001: 6^{0}GS, 6^{0}HY

	Starts	1st	2nd	3rd	Win & Pl
Career Total (Turf)	**2**	**0**	**0**	**0**	

Going (Turf): Sf: 0-1 GS: 0-1 Gd: 0-0 GF: 0-0 Fm: 0-0
Distance: 5f/6f: 0-2 7f-8f: 0-0 9f-13f: 0-0 14f+: 0-0

Track : LH: 0-0 RH: 0-0 Tight: 0-0 Gall: 0-0
Aids: Bl: 0-0 Vi: 0-0 Tstrap: 0-0
Best Rating: 73 11/01 NmkR 6f gd-sft

Culzean (IRE)

108(112) (91)87

5-y-o b g Machiavellian (USA)-Eileen Jenny (IRE) (Kris)
R Hannon Stonethorn Stud Farms Limited

Placings:10/2000455303/5360041203620051-20003433160 (4863)
2001: 8²SD, 10⁰SW, 8⁰S, 10⁰G, 10³GF, 10⁴G, 10³G, 10³G, 10¹G, 10⁶GF, 10⁰GF

	Starts	1st	2nd	3rd	Win & Pl
Career Total (Turf)	36	3	3	7	35946
Career Total (AW)	3	1	1	0	8939

85	7/01	Kemp	1m2f	C(0-90)H	GD	£8892
90	12/00	Wolv	1m1f79y	C(0-95)H	STD	£6418
84	6/00	NmkJ	1m2f	C(0-90)H	G-F	£6356
80	9/98	Leic	7f9y	D	G-S	£3427

Total win prize-money £25096

Going (Turf): Sf: 0-4 **GS: 1-4 Gd: 1-12 GF: 1-16** Fm: 0-0
Distance: 5f/6f: 0-0 7f-8f: 1-6 **9f-13f: 3-33** 14f+: 0-0
Track : LH: 1-20 **RH: 2-13** Tight: 1-10 **Gall: 2-13**
Aids: Bl: 0-2 Vi: 0-0 Tstrap: 0-0
Best Rating: 91 1/01 Sthl 1m stand

He is able on his day but is hard to place. Won at Kempton in July having dropped to a previous winning mark, but rose sharply in the weights because of that and predictably struggled. Ten furlongs is his trip and he is usually held up, but was ridden more positively at the Sunbury track.

Cumbrian Carleton

87 60

2-y-o b c Polar Falcon (USA)-Fly Dont Run (USA) (Lear Fan (USA))
T D Easterby Cumbrian Industrials Ltd

Placings:34 (2003)
2001: 5³F, 6⁴F

	Starts	1st	2nd	3rd	Win & Pl
Career Total (Turf)	2	0	0	1	806

Going (Turf): Sf: 0-0 GS: 0-0 Gd: 0-0 GF: 0-0 Fm: 0-2
Distance: 5f/6f: 0-2 7f-8f: 0-0 9f-13f: 0-0 14f+: 0-0
Track : LH: 0-0 RH: 0-0 Tight: 0-0 Gall: 0-0
Aids: Bl: 0-0 Vi: 0-0 Tstrap: 0-0
Best Rating: 60 6/01 Donc 6f firm

Cumbrian Crystal

100 72

2-y-o b f Mind Games-Crystal Sand (GER) (Forzando)
T D Easterby Cumbrian Industrials Ltd

Placings:43 (4565)
2001: 5⁴GF, 5³HY

	Starts	1st	2nd	3rd	Win & Pl
Career Total (Turf)	2	0	0	1	770

Going (Turf): Sf: 0-1 GS: 0-0 Gd: 0-0 GF: 0-1 Fm: 0-0
Distance: 5f/6f: 0-2 7f-8f: 0-0 9f-13f: 0-0 14f+: 0-0
Track : LH: 0-0 RH: 0-0 Tight: 0-0 Gall: 0-0
Aids: Bl: 0-0 Vi: 0-0 Tstrap: 0-0
Best Rating: 72 9/01 Hayd 5f heavy

Cumbrian Harmony (IRE)

107 67

3-y-o b f Distinctly North (USA)-Sawaki (Song)
T D Easterby Cumbrian Industrials Ltd

Placings:0230552100-002010000423120 (5638)
2001: 6⁰G, 6⁰GF, 6²GF, 6⁰GF, 6¹F, 7⁰GF, 6⁰GF, 6⁰F, 6⁰GF, 7⁴G, 7²GF, 8³GF, 7¹GF, 7²G, 7⁰G

	Starts	1st	2nd	3rd	Win & Pl
Career Total (Turf)	25	3	5	2	15348

64	9/01	Catt	7f	F(0-60)H	G-F	£2954
73	6/01	Thsk	6f	E(0-70)H	FRM	£3430
68	7/00	Newc	6f	E	GD	£3445

Total win prize-money £9829

Going (Turf): Sf: 0-1 GS: 0-1 Gd: 0-7 **GF: 1-11 Fm: 1-4**
Distance: 5f/6f: 1-15 7f-8f: 1-9 9f-13f: 0-0 14f+: 0-0
Track : **LH: 1-4** RH: 0-3 **Tight: 1-3** Gall: 0-2
Aids: Bl: 0-0 Vi: 0-0 Tstrap: 0-0
Best Rating: 73 6/01 Thsk 6f firm

Fair handicapper, effective 6-7 furlongs. Acts on most surfaces, but is best on a sound surface.

Cumbrian Princess

103 52

4-y-o gr f Mtoto-Cumbrian Melody (Petong)
M Blanshard David Sykes

Placings:60010/0006050-003324 (5254)
2001: 8⁰HY, 5⁰G, 6³GF, 6³S, 5²S, 6⁴S

	Starts	1st	2nd	3rd	Win & Pl
Career Total (Turf)	18	1	1	2	5982

60	10/99	Pont	6f	E(0-75)H	SFT	£3366

Total win prize-money £3366

Going (Turf): Sf: 1-6 GS: 0-4 Gd: 0-2 GF: 0-5 Fm: 0-1
Distance: **5f/6f: 1-7** 7f-8f: 0-7 9f-13f: 0-4 14f+: 0-0
Track : **LH: 1-8** RH: 0-2 Tight: 0-2 Gall: 0-3
Aids: Bl: 0-0 Vi: 0-0 Tstrap: 0-0
Best Rating: 69 9/01 Ches 6f18y soft

Moderate sprinter. Showed improved form in the autumn of 2001. Goes well on a soft surface, but handles faster.

Cumwhitton

77 27

2-y-o b f Jumbo Hirt (USA)-Dominanoo (Dominion)
P C Haslam J Roundtree

Placings:056 (4598)
2001: 6⁰GF, 7⁵GF, 8⁶GF

	Starts	1st	2nd	3rd	Win & Pl
Career Total (Turf)	3	0	0	0	0

Going (Turf): Sf: 0-0 GS: 0-0 Gd: 0-0 GF: 0-3 Fm: 0-0
Distance: 5f/6f: 0-1 7f-8f: 0-2 9f-13f: 0-0 14f+: 0-0
Track : LH: 0-1 RH: 0-1 Tight: 0-1 Gall: 0-0
Aids: Bl: 0-0 Vi: 0-0 Tstrap: 0-0
Best Rating: 27 9/01 Thsk 1m gd-fm

Cupids Charm

106 70

4-y-o b f Cadeaux Genereux-Chapka (IRE) (Green Desert (USA))
R Guest I Allan, Ming Yi Chen & Hung Chao-Hong

Placings:4/0010160043-000501 (4528)
2001: 6⁰G, 6⁰GF, 7⁰GF, 7⁵GF, 7⁰GF, 7¹GF

	Starts	1st	2nd	3rd	Win & Pl
Career Total (Turf)	17	3	0	1	12911

70	9/01	Ling	7f	D(0-85)H	G-F	£4264
75	6/00	Carl	5f	E(0-75)H	G-F	£3721
70	5/00	Brig	5f59y	E(0-70)H	FRM	£2829

Total win prize-money £10814

Going (Turf): Sf: 0-1 GS: 0-1 Gd: 0-2 **GF: 2-10** Fm: 1-2
Distance: **5f/6f: 2-11** 7f-8f: 1-5 9f-13f: 0-0 14f+: 0-0
Track : LH: 1-5 RH: 1-3 Tight: 0-1 **Gall: 1-2**
Aids: Bl: 0-0 Vi: 0-0 Tstrap: 0-0
Best Rating: 70 9/01 Ling 7f gd-fm

Lost her way in 2001, but was given a chance by the handicapper and bounced back to winning ways at Lingfield in September.

Curate (USA)

87 57

2-y-o ch c Unfuwain (USA)-Carniola (Rainbow Quest (USA))
M P Tregoning Sheikh Mohammed

Placings:60 (5604)
2001: 7⁶HY, 7⁰GS

	Starts	1st	2nd	3rd	Win & Pl
Career Total (Turf)	2	0	0	0	0

Going (Turf): Sf: 0-1 GS: 0-1 Gd: 0-0 GF: 0-0 Fm: 0-0
Distance: 5f/6f: 0-0 7f-8f: 0-2 9f-13f: 0-0 14f+: 0-0
Track : LH: 0-0 RH: 0-0 Tight: 0-0 Gall: 0-0
Aids: Bl: 0-0 Vi: 0-0 Tstrap: 0-0
Best Rating: 57 11/01 NmkR 7f gd-sft

Curfew

93 77

2-y-o b f Marju (IRE)-Twilight Patrol (Robellino (USA))
J R Fanshawe Patrick Veitch (bloodstock A/c)

Placings:16 (4276)
2001: 7¹GF, 7⁶GS

	Starts	1st	2nd	3rd	Win & Pl
Career Total (Turf)	2	1	0	0	3164

77	7/01	Yarm	7f3y	E	G-F	£3164

Total win prize-money £3164

Going (Turf): Sf: 0-0 GS: 0-1 Gd: 0-0 **GF: 1-1** Fm: 0-0
Distance: 5f/6f: 0-0 **7f-8f: 1-2** 9f-13f: 0-0 14f+: 0-0
Track : LH: 0-0 RH: 0-1 Tight: 0-0 Gall: 0-0
Aids: Bl: 0-0 Vi: 0-0 Tstrap: 0-0
Best Rating: 77 7/01 Yarm 7f3y gd-fm

She picked up nicely when asked to assert on her debut. Her dam was an useful winner over six and seven furlongs at two, and comes from the family of Nashwan, did not handle soft next time.

Currency

106(67) 76+

4-y-o b g Sri Pekan (USA)-On Tiptoes (Shareef Dancer (USA))
J M Bradley Robert Bailey

Placings:600-0001111212 (2753)
2001: 5⁰S, 5⁰GF, 5⁰GF, 6¹F, 6¹GF, 6¹GF, 6¹GF, 6²GF, 6¹GF, 6²GF

	Starts	1st	2nd	3rd	Win & Pl
Career Total (Turf)	12	5	2	0	20090
Career Total (AW)	1	0	0	0	

73	7/01	Wind	6f	D(0-80)H	G-F	£4303
74	6/01	Nott	6f15y	F(0-60)H	G-F	£2590
65	6/01	Gdwd	6f	E(0-70)H	G-F	£3835
59	6/01	Pont	6f	E(0-70)H	G-F	£3486
48	5/01	Rdcr	6f	G(0-60)H	FRM	£2044

Total win prize-money £16258

Going (Turf): Sf: 0-2 GS: 0-0 Gd: 0-1 **GF: 4-8** Fm: 1-1
Distance: **5f/6f: 4-11** 7f-8f: 1-1 9f-13f: 0-1 14f+: 0-0
Track : **LH: 1-4** RH: 0-1 Tight: 0-1 Gall: 0-2
Aids: Bl: 0-0 Vi: 0-0 Tstrap: 0-0
Best Rating: 76 6/01 Donc 6f gd-fm

A decent handicapper with a useful turn of foot, he is suited by six furlongs and fast ground. He scored five times this term and is yet another testament to his trainer's extraordinary skill with sprint handicappers.

Curtain Time (IRE)

99 **105**

3-y-o b c Sadler's Wells (USA)-Alidiva (Chief Singer)
H R A Cecil Greenbay Stables Ltd

Placings:165 **(1498)**
2001: 10^{1}GS, 12^{6}G, 11^{5}GF

	Starts	1st	2nd	3rd	Win & Pl
Career Total (Turf)	**3**	**1**	**0**	**0**	**5173**

94 4/01 NmkR 1m2f D G-S £5018
Total win prize-money £5018

Going (Turf): Sf: 0-0 **GS: 1-1** Gd: 0-1 GF: 0-1 Fm: 0-0
Distance: 5f/6f: 0-0 7f-8f: 0-0 **9f-13f: 1-3** 14f+: 0-0
Track : LH: 0-0 RH: 0-1 Tight: 0-0 Gall: 0-1
Aids: Bl: 0-0 Vi: 0-0 Tstrap: 0-0
Best Rating: 105 5/01 Gdwd 1m3f gd-fm

This half-brother to three Group One winners, Sleepytime, Ali-Royal and Taipan. He made a good impression when winning a maiden at Newmarket first time out. The form of that race has not worked out too well, and he disappointed subsequently. Stable out of form at the time, however, and stamina question remians unanswered.

Curtsey

95 **62**

3-y-o b f Mark Of Esteem (IRE)-Tabyan (USA) (Topsider (USA))
R Charlton Mountgrange Stud

Placings:0-0500 **(2837)**
2001: 6^{0}GS, 6^{5}GS, 5^{0}F, 5^{0}GF

	Starts	1st	2nd	3rd	Win & Pl
Career Total (Turf)	**5**	**0**	**0**	**0**	**0**

Going (Turf): Sf: 0-1 GS: 0-2 Gd: 0-0 GF: 0-1 Fm: 0-1
Distance: 5f/6f: 0-5 7f-8f: 0-0 9f-13f: 0-0 14f+: 0-0
Track : LH: 0-2 RH: 0-0 Tight: 0-0 Gall: 0-1
Aids: Bl: 0-0 Vi: 0-0 Tstrap: 0-0
Best Rating: 62 5/01 Sals 6f gd-sft

Curzon Ridge (IRE)

91 **80**

2-y-o b f Indian Ridge-Curzon Street (Night Shift (USA))
E Stanners George Ward

Placings:260 **(5588)**
2001: 5^{2}GS, 7^{6}GS, 5^{0}GS

	Starts	1st	2nd	3rd	Win & Pl
Career Total (Turf)	**3**	**0**	**1**	**0**	**1248**

Going (Turf): Sf: 0-0 GS: 0-3 Gd: 0-0 GF: 0-0 Fm: 0-0
Distance: 5f/6f: 0-2 7f-8f: 0-1 9f-13f: 0-0 14f+: 0-0
Track : LH: 0-1 RH: 0-0 Tight: 0-0 Gall: 0-0
Aids: Bl: 0-0 Vi: 0-0 Tstrap: 0-0
Best Rating: 80 10/01 Leic 7f9y gd-sft

Cusin

102(80) (23)**59**

5-y-o ch g Arazi (USA)-Fairy Tern (Mill Reef (USA))
M E Sowersby (D Nicholls 12/1) M E Sowersby

Placings:220/0400100/003050005205-000524026 **(4231)**
2001: 7^{0}SD, 8^{0}SD, 7^{0}F, 10^{5}GF, 10^{2}GF, 9^{4}GF, 8^{0}GF, 8^{2}GF, 8^{6}G

	Starts	1st	2nd	3rd	Win & Pl
Career Total (Turf)	**29**	**1**	**5**	**1**	**12339**
Career Total (AW)	**2**	**0**	**0**	**0**	

74 9/99 Sals 1m E(0-70)H G-F £3956
Total win prize-money £3956

Going (Turf): Sf: 0-3 GS: 0-1 Gd: 0-8 **GF: 1-15** Fm: 0-2
Distance: 5f/6f: 0-1 **7f-8f: 1-23** 9f-13f: 0-7 14f+: 0-0
Track : LH: 0-11 RH: 0-7 Tight: 0-5 Gall: 0-4
Aids: Bl: 0-1 Vi: 0-0 Tstrap: 0-7
Best Rating: 59 8/01 Thsk 1m good

Winner of a mile handicap at Salisbury in 1999, but on a long losing run since. Best suited by good to firm ground.

Custom Made

51

2-y-o ch c Zafonic (USA)-Asterita (Rainbow Quest (USA))
G A Butler The Thoroughbred Corporation

Placings:4 **(4107)**
2001: 6^{4}S

	Starts	1st	2nd	3rd	Win & Pl
Career Total (Turf)	**1**	**0**	**0**	**0**	**320**

Going (Turf): Sf: 0-1 GS: 0-0 Gd: 0-0 GF: 0-0 Fm: 0-0
Distance: 5f/6f: 0-0 7f-8f: 0-1 9f-13f: 0-0 14f+: 0-0
Track : LH: 0-0 RH: 0-0 Tight: 0-0 Gall: 0-0
Aids: Bl: 0-0 Vi: 0-0 Tstrap: 0-0
Best Rating: 51 8/01 Haml 6f5y soft

Customeyes

62 **16**

2-y-o b f Komaite (USA)-Mizog (Selkirk (USA))
B A Pearce Custom Racing

Placings:000 **(3697)**
2001: 6^{0}GF, 6^{0}GF, 6^{0}GF

	Starts	1st	2nd	3rd	Win & Pl
Career Total (Turf)	**3**	**0**	**0**	**0**	

Going (Turf): Sf: 0-0 GS: 0-0 Gd: 0-0 GF: 0-3 Fm: 0-0
Distance: 5f/6f: 0-2 7f-8f: 0-1 9f-13f: 0-0 14f+: 0-0
Track : LH: 0-1 RH: 0-0 Tight: 0-0 Gall: 0-0
Aids: Bl: 0-0 Vi: 0-0 Tstrap: 0-0
Best Rating: 16 7/01 Ling 6f gd-fm

Cut Rate (USA)

98 **65**

3-y-o ch c Diesis-Itsamazing (USA) (The Minstrel (CAN))
Mrs A J Perrett K Abdulla

Placings:0-30 **(1669)**
2001: 10^{3}GS, 10^{0}GF

	Starts	1st	2nd	3rd	Win & Pl
Career Total (Turf)	**3**	**0**	**0**	**1**	**436**

Going (Turf): Sf: 0-0 GS: 0-1 Gd: 0-1 GF: 0-1 Fm: 0-0
Distance: 5f/6f: 0-0 7f-8f: 0-1 9f-13f: 0-2 14f+: 0-0
Track : LH: 0-1 RH: 0-1 Tight: 0-1 Gall: 0-0
Aids: Bl: 0-0 Vi: 0-0 Tstrap: 0-1
Best Rating: 65 5/01 Bath 1m2f46y gd-sft

Cute Caroline

(88) (27)**52**

5-y-o ch m First Trump-Hissma (Midyan (USA))
J K Magee (A Berry 19/1) Cathal M McGovern

Placings:0/0300/35062300040-060 **(0124)**
2001: 8^{0}SD, 7^{6}SD, 8^{0}SW

	Starts	1st	2nd	3rd	Win & Pl
Career Total (Turf)	**13**	**0**	**1**	**3**	**2054**
Career Total (AW)	**6**	**0**	**0**	**0**	**0**

Going (Turf): Sf: 0-1 GS: 0-0 Gd: 0-4 GF: 0-5 Fm: 0-3
Distance: 5f/6f: 0-0 7f-8f: 0-13 9f-13f: 0-6 14f+: 0-0
Track : LH: 0-9 RH: 0-9 Tight: 0-9 Gall: 0-0
Aids: Bl: 0-3 Vi: 0-5 Tstrap: 0-0
Best Rating: 27 1/01 Sthl 7f stand

Cyber Babe (IRE)

94(100) (53)**34**

4-y-o ch f Persian Bold-Ervedya (IRE) (Doyoun)
A G Newcombe Advanced Marketing Services Ltd

Placings:564220000000/02100213100-000060 **(4361)**
2001: 8^{0}SD, 11^{0}GS, 11^{0}G, 12^{0}G, 12^{6}GF, 11^{0}GF

	Starts	1st	2nd	3rd	Win & Pl
Career Total (Turf)	**18**	**2**	**3**	**1**	**9895**
Career Total (AW)	**11**	**1**	**1**	**0**	**2455**

59 8/00 Sals 1m4f D(0-80)H GD £3861
53 7/00 Brig 1m1f209yF(0-60)H FRM £3861
53 5/00 Wolv 1m1f79y G STD £1813
Total win prize-money £9535

Going (Turf): Sf: 0-1 GS: 0-4 **Gd: 1-6** GF: 0-4 **Fm: 1-3**
Distance: 5f/6f: 0-4 7f-8f: 0-7 **9f-13f: 3-18** 14f+: 0-0
Track : **LH: 2-21** RH: 1-2 **Tight: 2-12** Gall: 0-1
Aids: Bl: 0-0 Vi: 0-7 Tstrap: 0-0
Best Rating: 50 5/01 Bath 1m3f144y gd-sft

Cyber Santa

47

3-y-o b g Celtic Swing-Qualitair Ridge (Indian Ridge)
J Hetherton Qualitair Holdings Limited

Placings:500-0100 **(4371)**
2001: 10^{0}GF, 12^{1}G, 12^{0}GS, 11^{0}GF

	Starts	1st	2nd	3rd	Win & Pl
Career Total (Turf)	**7**	**1**	**0**	**0**	**3673**

47 7/01 Newc 1m4f93y E(0-70)H GD £3672
Total win prize-money £3673

Going (Turf): Sf: 0-2 GS: 0-1 **Gd: 1-1** GF: 0-3 Fm: 0-0
Distance: 5f/6f: 0-0 7f-8f: 0-3 **9f-13f: 1-4** 14f+: 0-0
Track : **LH: 1-4** RH: 0-3 Tight: 0-2 **Gall: 1-3**
Aids: Bl: 0-0 Vi: 0-0 Tstrap: 0-0
Best Rating: 47 7/01 Newc 1m4f93y good

Bred to stay, duly scored when stepped up to a mile and a half in handicap company at Newcastle on his second start at three, but was well beaten afterwards until bouncing back on the Lingfield Polytrack in November.

Cybertechnology

82 **36**

7-y-o b g Environment Friend-Verchinina (Star Appeal)
M Dods P J Carr

Placings:012/42501404/010562500200/000632105000/00003161060-000060 **(3932)**
2001: 8^{0}S, 9^{0}GF, 9^{0}GF, 8^{0}GF, 9^{6}GS, 8^{0}G

	Starts	1st	2nd	3rd	Win & Pl
Career Total (Turf)	**52**	**6**	**5**	**2**	**39303**

62 8/00 Ayr 1m1f20y E(0-70)H G-F £3006
57 6/00 Bevl 1m1f207yD(0-80)H G-F £5564
68 7/99 Donc 1m D(0-85)H G-F £4143
82 7/98 Rdcr 7f D(0-85)H G-S £3704
80 8/97 NmkJ 7f C(0-90)H G-F £6116
84 10/96 York 7f202y E GD £6628
Total win prize-money £29161

Going (Turf): Sf: 0-7 GS: 1-5 Gd: 1-18 **GF: 4-22** Fm: 0-0
Distance: 5f/6f: 0-0 **7f-8f: 4-25** 9f-13f: 2-27 14f+: 0-0
Track : **LH: 3-22** RH: 1-14 Tight: 0-6 **Gall: 2-10**
Aids: Bl: 0-1 Vi: 0-1 Tstrap: 0-0
Best Rating: 48 5/01 Ayr 1m1f20y gd-fm

Modest handicapper, stays ten furlongs, suited by fast ground.

Cyclone Connie

107 **93?**

3-y-o ch f Dr Devious (IRE)-Cutpurse Moll (Green Desert (USA))

C A Cyzer Mrs E A Cyzer

Placings:23-5 **(5105)**

2001: 5^{5}GS

	Starts	1st	2nd	3rd	Win & Pl
Career Total (Turf)	3	0	1	1	2920

Going (Turf): Sf: 0-0 GS: 0-1 Gd: 0-0 GF: 0-2 Fm: 0-0
Distance: 5f/6f: 0-3 7f-8f: 0-0 9f-13f: 0-0 14f+: 0-0
Track : LH: 0-0 RH: 0-0 Tight: 0-0 Gall: 0-0
Aids: Bl: 0-0 Vi: 0-0 Tstrap: 0-0
Best Rating: 93 10/01 NmkR 5f gd-sft

A strong type, he is lightly raced but has ability.

Cyclonic Storm

91 **54**

2-y-o b f Catrail (USA)-Wheeler's Wonder (IRE) (Sure Blade (USA))

R A Fahey Galaxy Racing

Placings:0060 **(4772)**

2001: 6^{0}GF, 5^{0}GF, 7^{6}GF, 7^{0}G

	Starts	1st	2nd	3rd	Win & Pl
Career Total (Turf)	4	0	0	0	0

Going (Turf): Sf: 0-0 GS: 0-0 Gd: 0-1 GF: 0-3 Fm: 0-0
Distance: 5f/6f: 0-2 7f-8f: 0-2 9f-13f: 0-0 14f+: 0-0
Track : LH: 0-1 RH: 0-1 Tight: 0-1 Gall: 0-0
Aids: Bl: 0-0 Vi: 0-0 Tstrap: 0-0
Best Rating: 54 8/01 Catt 7f gd-fm

Cymru-Am-Byth

70 **21**

4-y-o ch g Primo Dominie-Croeso-I-Cymru (Welsh Captain)

J L Spearing Mrs Richard Evans

Placings:0000 **(1630)**

2001: 6^{0}HY, 6^{0}GS, 9^{0}G, 9^{0}F

	Starts	1st	2nd	3rd	Win & Pl
Career Total (Turf)	4	0	0	0	

Going (Turf): Sf: 0-1 GS: 0-1 Gd: 0-1 GF: 0-0 Fm: 0-1
Distance: 5f/6f: 0-1 7f-8f: 0-1 9f-13f: 0-2 14f+: 0-0
Track : LH: 0-1 RH: 0-2 Tight: 0-1 Gall: 0-0
Aids: Bl: 0-0 Vi: 0-0 Tstrap: 0-0
Best Rating: 21 5/01 Sals 6f gd-sft

Cynara

100 **50**

3-y-o b f Imp Society (USA)-Reina (Homeboy)

G M Moore W C Bircham

Placings:05215510-053266000 **(5448)**

2001: 10^{0}G, 8^{5}F, 10^{3}GF, 8^{2}GS, 9^{6}GF, 8^{6}GF, 8^{0}HY, 11^{0}G, 10^{0}HY

	Starts	1st	2nd	3rd	Win & Pl
Career Total (Turf)	17	2	2	1	7561

64	9/00	Pont	1m4y	E(0-85)	G-S	£3068
58	8/00	Newc	7f	E	GD	£2782

Total win prize-money £5850

Going (Turf): Sf: 0-2 **GS: 1-2 Gd: 1-5** GF: 0-7 Fm: 0-1
Distance: 5f/6f: 0-2 7f-8f: 1-7 9f-13f: 1-8 14f+: 0-0
Track : **LH: 1-8** RH: 0-5 Tight: 0-5 Gall: 0-5
Aids: Bl: 0-0 Vi: 0-0 Tstrap: 0-0

Best Rating: 63 6/01 Rdcr 1m2f gd-fm

Cynosure

83(82) (13)**21**

4-y-o b g Runnett-Polly Two (Reesh)

J R Weymes B B Pratt

Placings:000000 **(2337)**

2001: 8^{0}SW, 11^{0}SD, 7^{0}SD, 7^{0}S, 7^{0}F, 10^{0}GF

	Starts	1st	2nd	3rd	Win & Pl
Career Total (Turf)	3	0	0	0	
Career Total (AW)	3	0	0	0	

Going (Turf): Sf: 0-1 GS: 0-0 Gd: 0-0 GF: 0-1 Fm: 0-1
Distance: 5f/6f: 0-0 7f-8f: 0-4 9f-13f: 0-2 14f+: 0-0
Track : LH: 0-3 RH: 0-1 Tight: 0-2 Gall: 0-0
Aids: Bl: 0-0 Vi: 0-0 Tstrap: 0-0
Best Rating: 21 5/01 Rdcr 7f firm

Cypress Avenue (IRE)

(87) (23)**23**

9-y-o b g Law Society (USA)-Flying Diva (Chief Singer)

Mrs V C Ward Kgb Partnership

Placings:5324355/0006400/5000 **(3433)**

2001: 16^{5}SD, 16^{0}GF, 16^{0}SD, 16^{0}SD

	Starts	1st	2nd	3rd	Win & Pl
Career Total (Turf)	15	0	1	2	4697
Career Total (AW)	3	0	0	0	0

Going (Turf): Sf: 0-0 GS: 0-1 Gd: 0-5 GF: 0-8 Fm: 0-1
Distance: 5f/6f: 0-0 7f-8f: 0-0 9f-13f: 0-2 14f+: 0-16
Track : LH: 0-11 RH: 0-7 Tight: 0-8 Gall: 0-4
Aids: Bl: 0-1 Vi: 0-0 Tstrap: 0-0
Best Rating: 23 6/01 Wolv 2m46y stand

Cyrazy

59

3-y-o b f Cyrano De Bergerac-Hazy Kay (IRE) (Treasure Kay)

J G Given Mrs R E Digby

Placings:304-R **(0902)**

2001: 5^{R}GS

	Starts	1st	2nd	3rd	Win & Pl
Career Total (Turf)	4	0	0	1	651

Going (Turf): Sf: 0-1 GS: 0-1 Gd: 0-0 GF: 0-2 Fm: 0-0
Distance: 5f/6f: 0-4 7f-8f: 0-0 9f-13f: 0-0 14f+: 0-0
Track : LH: 0-0 RH: 0-0 Tight: 0-0 Gall: 0-0
Aids: Bl: 0-1 Vi: 0-0 Tstrap: 0-0

Cyrian (IRE)

89 **55**

7-y-o b g Persian Bold-Regina St Cyr (IRE) (Doulab (USA))

M C Pipe Lord Donoughmore

Placings:121006/340104/0 **(5387)**

2001: 18^{0}GS

	Starts	1st	2nd	3rd	Win & Pl
Career Total (Turf)	12	2	1	1	84473
Career Total (AW)	1	1	0	0	3420

89	6/98	Newc	2m19y	B H	SFT	£68950
85	5/97	Newb	1m4f5y	C(0-95)	SFT	£9365
66	3/97	Wolv	1m100y	D	STD	£3420

Total win prize-money £81736

Going (Turf): Sf: 2-3 GS: 0-2 Gd: 0-5 GF: 0-2 Fm: 0-0
Distance: 5f/6f: 0-0 7f-8f: 0-0 **9f-13f: 2-6** 14f+: 1-7
Track : **LH: 3-10** RH: 0-3 Tight: 1-4 **Gall: 2-6**

Aids: Bl: 0-0 Vi: 0-0 Tstrap: 0-0
Best Rating: 55 10/01 NmkR 2m2f gd-sft

Formerly useful stayer who won the Northumberland Plate. Likes soft ground and is suited by two miles.

Czar Wars

(110) (82)**70**

6-y-o b g Warrshan (USA)-Dutch Czarina (Prince Sabo)

J Balding Men Behaving Badly

Placings:54100/000240400200/05455000000035044/00034613002111-65130104100 **(4701)**

2001: 6^{6}SD, 6^{5}SD, 6^{1}SW, 6^{3}SD, 6^{0}SD, 6^{1}SD, 6^{0}G, 6^{4}SD, 6^{1}GF, 6^{0}GS, 5^{0}GS

	Starts	1st	2nd	3rd	Win & Pl
Career Total (Turf)	35	3	2	2	16688
Career Total (AW)	25	5	1	2	15498

64	7/01	Hayd	6f	D(0-80)H	G-F	£8027
78	4/01	Sthl	6f	D(0-80)H	STD	£3932
77	1/01	Sthl	6f	D(0-80)H	SLW	£3874
66	12/00	Wolv	6f	E(0-70)H	STD	£2310
58	12/00	Sthl	6f	F(0-60)H	STD	£1890
53	11/00	Wolv	6f	F(0-65)H	STD	£1778
41	8/00	Hayd	6f	F	GD	£2425
70	8/97	Wwck	7f	F	G-S	£2319

Total win prize-money £26559

Going (Turf): Sf: 0-6 **GS: 1-7 Gd: 1-13 GF: 1-9** Fm: 0-0
Distance: **5f/6f: 7-30** 7f-8f: 1-22 9f-13f: 0-8 14f+: 0-0
Track : **LH: 6-38** RH: 0-1 **Tight: 2-10** Gall: 0-0
Aids: **Bl: 7-35** Vi: 0-0 Tstrap: 0-1
Best Rating: 82 5/01 Sthl 6f stand

Enjoyed a good winter campaign on the All-Weather and scored at Haydock in July. Suited by six furlongs.

Czarina

82 **44**

3-y-o b f Emperor Jones (USA)-Topwinder (USA) (Topsider (USA))

J Gallagher Mrs H Corr

Placings:0000 **(2249)**

2001: 6^{0}GS, 8^{0}G, 6^{0}GF, 6^{0}GF

	Starts	1st	2nd	3rd	Win & Pl
Career Total (Turf)	4	0	0	0	

Going (Turf): Sf: 0-0 GS: 0-1 Gd: 0-1 GF: 0-2 Fm: 0-0
Distance: 5f/6f: 0-1 7f-8f: 0-2 9f-13f: 0-1 14f+: 0-0
Track : LH: 0-0 RH: 0-0 Tight: 0-0 Gall: 0-0
Aids: Bl: 0-0 Vi: 0-0 Tstrap: 0-0
Best Rating: 44 4/01 NmkR 6f gd-sft

Czarina Waltz

92 **73**

2-y-o b f Emperor Jones (USA)-Ballerina Bay (Myjinski (USA))

C F Wall Acorn Racing

Placings:00 **(5603)**

2001: 7^{0}GS, 7^{0}GS

	Starts	1st	2nd	3rd	Win & Pl
Career Total (Turf)	2	0	0	0	

Going (Turf): Sf: 0-0 GS: 0-2 Gd: 0-0 GF: 0-0 Fm: 0-0
Distance: 5f/6f: 0-0 7f-8f: 0-2 9f-13f: 0-0 14f+: 0-0
Track : LH: 0-0 RH: 0-0 Tight: 0-0 Gall: 0-0
Aids: Bl: 0-0 Vi: 0-0 Tstrap: 0-0
Best Rating: 73 11/01 NmkR 7f gd-sft

D J Supreme (IRE)

80 **58**

2-y-o b c Blues Traveller (IRE)-Musical Gem (USA) (The Minstrel (CAN))

G M McCourt (M Quinn 11/7) David Richardson

Placings:00000 **(5530)**

2001: 5^0GF, 6^0GF, 7^0G, 6^0HY, 8^0HY

	Starts	1st	2nd	3rd	Win & Pl
Career Total (Turf)	5	0	0	0	

Going (Turf): Sf: 0-2 GS: 0-0 Gd: 0-1 GF: 0-2 Fm: 0-0
Distance: 5f/6f: 0-3 7f-8f: 0-1 9f-13f: 0-1 14f+: 0-0
Track : LH: 0-2 RH: 0-0 Tight: 0-0 Gall: 0-0
Aids: Bl: 0-1 Vi: 0-0 Tstrap: 0-0
Best Rating: 58 9/01 Chep 7f16y good

D'Accord

106(98) (87)**77**

4-y-o ch g Beveled (USA)-National Time (USA) (Lord Avie (USA))

S Kirk (M Kettle 10/9) Dagfell Properties Limited

Placings:044311/53506424-0000660 **(5671)**

2001: 6^0G, 6^0GF, 6^0G, 6^0G, 6^0HY, 5^6HY, 6^0HY

	Starts	1st	2nd	3rd	Win & Pl
Career Total (Turf)	17	0	1	1	3085
Career Total (AW)	4	2	0	1	5876

80	12/99	Ling	5f	E(0-75)H	STD	£2590
80	12/99	Ling	6f	D	STD	£2703

Total win prize-money £5294

Going (Turf): Sf: 0-6 GS: 0-0 Gd: 0-6 GF: 0-5 Fm: 0-0
Distance: 5f/6f: 2-21 7f-8f: 0-0 9f-13f: 0-0 14f+: 0-0
Track : LH: 2-4 RH: 0-2 **Tight: 2-4** Gall: 0-2
Aids: Bl: 0-0 Vi: 0-1 Tstrap: 0-0
Best Rating: 77 7/01 Gdwd 6f gd-fm

Little show in 2001 season.

Da Vinci (IRE)

89(82) (48)**79d**

3-y-o b g Inzar (USA)-Tuft Hill (Grundy)

J A Osborne Andy Miller

Placings:10016-000 **(4898)**

2001: 6^0SW, 5^0GS, 5^0GS

	Starts	1st	2nd	3rd	Win & Pl
Career Total (Turf)	7	2	0	0	6893
Career Total (AW)	1	0	0	0	

79	9/00	Haml	5f4y	E(0-75)H	SFT	£3757
69	6/00	Pont	5f	F	SFT	£3136

Total win prize-money £6893

Going (Turf): Sf: 2-3 GS: 0-2 Gd: 0-0 GF: 0-2 Fm: 0-0
Distance: 5f/6f: 2-8 7f-8f: 0-0 9f-13f: 0-0 14f+: 0-0
Track : LH: 1-3 RH: 0-1 Tight: 0-0 Gall: 0-2
Aids: Bl: 0-0 Vi: 0-0 Tstrap: 0-0
Best Rating: 48 4/01 Sthl 6f slow

Da Wolf (IRE)

96 **37**

3-y-o ch g Wolfhound (USA)-Lady Joyce (FR) (Galetto (FR))

W R Muir R Haim

Placings:60-001404000 **(4628)**

2001: 8^0S, 6^0F, 5^1GF, 6^4F, 7^0G, 5^4GF, 7^0G, 6^0GF, 8^0GF

	Starts	1st	2nd	3rd	Win & Pl
Career Total (Turf)	11	1	0	0	2282

52	6/01	Brig	5f213y	F(0-65)H	G-F	£2282

Total win prize-money £2282

Going (Turf): Sf: 0-2 GS: 0-1 Gd: 0-2 **GF: 1-4** Fm: 0-2
Distance: 5f/6f: 1-5 7f-8f: 0-4 9f-13f: 0-2 14f+: 0-0
Track : LH: 1-6 RH: 0-0 Tight: 0-2 Gall: 0-0
Aids: Bl: 1-6 Vi: 0-0 Tstrap: 0-0
Best Rating: 52 6/01 Brig 5f213y gd-fm

Winner of a Brighton handicap on fast ground in first-time blinkers during the summer, he has run well on the same track since.

Daana

90 **72**

2-y-o b f Green Desert (USA)-Shining Water (USA) (Riverman (USA))

J L Dunlop Kuwait Racing Syndicate Iii

Placings:05 **(5485)**

2001: 6^0G, 7^5HY

	Starts	1st	2nd	3rd	Win & Pl
Career Total (Turf)	2	0	0	0	0

Going (Turf): Sf: 0-1 GS: 0-0 Gd: 0-1 GF: 0-0 Fm: 0-0
Distance: 5f/6f: 0-1 7f-8f: 0-1 9f-13f: 0-0 14f+: 0-0
Track : LH: 0-0 RH: 0-0 Tight: 0-0 Gall: 0-0
Aids: Bl: 0-0 Vi: 0-0 Tstrap: 0-0
Best Rating: 72 10/01 Donc 7f heavy

Dadeland (IRE)

96 **77**

2-y-o b f Desert King (IRE)-Bubbling Heights (FR) (Darshaan)

M W Easterby M P Burke

Placings:250313 **(5229)**

2001: 6^2F, 7^5G, 6^0G, 8^3G, 9^1HY, 7^3S

	Starts	1st	2nd	3rd	Win & Pl
Career Total (Turf)	6	1	1	2	6820

77	10/01	Nott	1m1f213yE(0-75)		HVY	£3276

Total win prize-money £3276

Going (Turf): Sf: 1-2 GS: 0-0 Gd: 0-3 GF: 0-0 Fm: 0-1
Distance: 5f/6f: 0-2 7f-8f: 0-3 **9f-13f: 1-1** 14f+: 0-0
Track : LH: 1-3 RH: 0-0 Tight: 0-0 Gall: 0-1
Aids: Bl: 0-0 Vi: 0-0 Tstrap: 0-0
Best Rating: 77 10/01 Nott 1m1f213y heavy

Progressive form at the back-endof 2001. Bred to stay middle-distances..

Daffodil Girl

92 **65**

2-y-o ch f Vettori (IRE)-Top Treat (USA) (Topsider (USA))

B Palling Mr Derek D & Mrs Jean P Clee

Placings:004 **(5633)**

2001: 8^0GF, 7^0GF, 7^4G

	Starts	1st	2nd	3rd	Win & Pl
Career Total (Turf)	3	0	0	0	0

Going (Turf): Sf: 0-0 GS: 0-0 Gd: 0-1 GF: 0-2 Fm: 0-0
Distance: 5f/6f: 0-0 7f-8f: 0-2 9f-13f: 0-1 14f+: 0-0
Track : LH: 0-1 RH: 0-1 Tight: 0-1 Gall: 0-1
Aids: Bl: 0-0 Vi: 0-0 Tstrap: 0-0
Best Rating: 65 9/01 Kemp 7f gd-fm

Daffs

90 **43**

3-y-o b f Alhijaz-Magnolia (Petong)

P J Makin T G Warner

Placings:0500 **(4292)**

2001: 8^0GS, 7^5G, 7^0S, 10^0GF

	Starts	1st	2nd	3rd	Win & Pl
Career Total (Turf)	4	0	0	0	0

Going (Turf): Sf: 0-1 GS: 0-1 Gd: 0-1 GF: 0-1 Fm: 0-0
Distance: 5f/6f: 0-0 7f-8f: 0-3 9f-13f: 0-1 14f+: 0-0
Track : LH: 0-1 RH: 0-0 Tight: 0-0 Gall: 0-0
Aids: Bl: 0-0 Vi: 0-0 Tstrap: 0-0
Best Rating: 43 7/01 Chep 7f16y good

Dafne

80 **52**

2-y-o ch f Nashwan (USA)-El Opera (IRE) (Sadler's Wells (USA))

Sir Mark Prescott Faisal Salman

Placings:060 **(4177)**

2001: 8^0GS, 7^6G, 7^0GF

	Starts	1st	2nd	3rd	Win & Pl
Career Total (Turf)	3	0	0	0	0

Going (Turf): Sf: 0-0 GS: 0-1 Gd: 0-1 GF: 0-1 Fm: 0-0
Distance: 5f/6f: 0-0 7f-8f: 0-3 9f-13f: 0-0 14f+: 0-0
Track : LH: 0-0 RH: 0-1 Tight: 0-0 Gall: 0-0
Aids: Bl: 0-0 Vi: 0-0 Tstrap: 0-0
Best Rating: 52 8/01 Folk 7f gd-fm

Dahlidya

(104) (63)**49**

6-y-o b m Midyan (USA)-Dahlawise (IRE) (Caerleon (USA))

M J Polglase The Lovatt Partnership

Placings:064/04103050000041/34436402000005310/3461101503133000000022365-124003230322503000 00 **(5051)**

2001: 6^1SD, 6^2SD, 6^4SD, 7^0SW, 6^0SW, 6^3SD, 6^2SD, 6^3SD, 5^0SD, 6^3SD, 6^2SD, 6^2SD, 7^5SD, 6^0SD, 5^3G, 6^0SD, 5^0F, 6^0G, 6^0SW, 6^0SD

	Starts	1st	2nd	3rd	Win & Pl
Career Total (Turf)	16	0	0	2	1267
Career Total (AW)	64	8	7	11	33526

67	1/01	Sthl	6f	E(0-70)H	STD	£2436
63	3/00	Sthl	6f	E(0-75)H	STD	£2408
60	2/00	Sthl	6f	F	STD	£2320
61	2/00	Sthl	6f	G	STD	£1867
49	2/00	Wolv	6f	G	STD	£1941
59	12/99	Sthl	6f	D(0-85)H	STD	£5017
56	12/98	Sthl	6f	E(0-75)H	STD	£2899
52	2/98	Wolv	5f	D(0-80)H	STD	£3387

Total win prize-money £22278

Going (Turf): Sf: 0-1 GS: 0-2 Gd: 0-6 GF: 0-5 Fm: 0-2
Distance: 5f/6f: 8-53 7f-8f: 0-25 9f-13f: 0-2 14f+: 0-0
Track : LH: 8-68 RH: 0-1 **Tight: 2-22** Gall: 0-1
Aids: Bl: 0-2 Vi: 0-0 Tstrap: 0-0
Best Rating: 67 1/01 Sthl 6f stand

Daily Sport (USA)

(90) (78)**94**

2-y-o b c Forest Wildcat (USA)-French Lake (USA) (Lac Ouimet (USA))

B J Meehan Roldvale Limited

Placings:53104 **(5194)**

2001: 5^5GF, 6^3G, 5^1F, 6^0GF, 5^4SD

	Starts	1st	2nd	3rd	Win & Pl
Career Total (Turf)	4	1	0	1	5304
Career Total (AW)	1	0	0	0	271

94	7/01	Bath	5f11y	D	FRM	£3386

Total win prize-money £3387

Going (Turf): Sf: 0-0 GS: 0-0 Gd: 0-1 GF: 0-2 **Fm: 1-1**
Distance: 5f/6f: 1-5 7f-8f: 0-0 9f-13f: 0-0 14f+: 0-0
Track : LH: 1-2 RH: 0-0 Tight: 0-1 **Gall: 1-1**
Aids: Bl: 0-1 Vi: 0-0 Tstrap: 0-0
Best Rating: 94 7/01 Bath 5f11y firm

Made a promising debut in the Windsor Castle at Royal Ascot. Scored in a four-runner race at Bath on his third start Disappointed when stepped up in class after that and did not sparkle when tried on sand.

Daimajin (IRE)

93 **70**

2-y-o b g Dr Devious (IRE)-Arrow Field (USA) (Sunshine Forever (USA))

B J Meehan H Date

Placings:4 (4895)

2001: 7^{4}GS

	Starts	1st	2nd	3rd	Win & Pl
Career Total (Turf)	1	0	0	0	358

Going (Turf): Sf: 0-0 GS: 0-1 Gd: 0-0 GF: 0-0 Fm: 0-0
Distance: 5f/6f: 0-0 7f-8f: 0-1 9f-13f: 0-0 14f+: 0-0
Track : LH: 0-0 RH: 0-0 Tight: 0-0 Gall: 0-0
Aids: Bl: 0-0 Vi: 0-0 Tstrap: 0-0
Best Rating: 70 9/01 Leic 7f9y gd-sft

Daisy Buttons (IRE)

93 **60**

2-y-o b f Bluebird (USA)-Centella (IRE) (Thatching)

T D Easterby Mrs Jean P Connew

Placings:45056056 (5404)

2001: 5^{4}GF, 6^{5}GF, 5^{0}GF, 5^{5}GF, 6^{6}G, 5^{0}GS, 7^{5}G, 8^{6}S

	Starts	1st	2nd	3rd	Win & Pl
Career Total (Turf)	8	0	0	0	267

Going (Turf): Sf: 0-1 GS: 0-1 Gd: 0-2 GF: 0-4 Fm: 0-0
Distance: 5f/6f: 0-5 7f-8f: 0-2 9f-13f: 0-1 14f+: 0-0
Track : LH: 0-1 RH: 0-0 Tight: 0-0 Gall: 0-0
Aids: Bl: 0-3 Vi: 0-0 Tstrap: 0-0
Best Rating: 60 10/01 Rdcr 7f good

Dajam Vu

91 **26**

4-y-o ch f Lyphento (USA)-Dancing Diamond (IRE) (Alzao (USA))

J S King Dajam Ltd

Placings:0000-000 (2821)

2001: 17^{0}GF, 16^{0}GF, 18^{0}GF

	Starts	1st	2nd	3rd	Win & Pl
Career Total (Turf)	7	0	0	0	

Going (Turf): Sf: 0-0 GS: 0-1 Gd: 0-2 GF: 0-4 Fm: 0-0
Distance: 5f/6f: 0-0 7f-8f: 0-0 9f-13f: 0-4 14f+: 0-3
Track : LH: 0-6 RH: 0-1 Tight: 0-4 Gall: 0-0
Aids: Bl: 0-1 Vi: 0-0 Tstrap: 0-0
Best Rating: 26 5/01 Bath 2m1f34y gd-fm

Dakhira

93 **54d**

3-y-o b f Emperor Jones (USA)-Fakhira (IRE) (Jareer (USA))

D R C Elsworth Teviot Stud,Ann Coles, J Richmond Watson

Placings:6-04000 (4386)

2001: 8^{0}GF, 6^{4}GF, 10^{0}GF, 6^{0}F, 6^{0}GF

	Starts	1st	2nd	3rd	Win & Pl
Career Total (Turf)	6	0	0	0	280

Going (Turf): Sf: 0-0 GS: 0-1 Gd: 0-0 GF: 0-4 Fm: 0-1
Distance: 5f/6f: 0-0 7f-8f: 0-5 9f-13f: 0-1 14f+: 0-0
Track : LH: 0-0 RH: 0-1 Tight: 0-1 Gall: 0-0
Aids: Bl: 0-0 Vi: 0-0 Tstrap: 0-0
Best Rating: 69 6/01 Gdwd 1m gd-fm

Dakota Sioux (IRE)

107 **73**

4-y-o ch f College Chapel-Batilde (IRE) (Victory Piper (USA))

R A Fahey Mrs Una Towell

Placings:3/36011010-00120016 (5529)

2001: 6^{0}GF, 6^{0}GF, 8^{1}G, 8^{2}GF, 10^{0}S, 8^{0}S, 7^{1}S, 8^{6}HY

	Starts	1st	2nd	3rd	Win & Pl
Career Total (Turf)	17	5	1	2	36471

71	10/01	Catt	7f	E(0-70)H	SFT	£3808
72	6/01	Thsk	1m	C(0-90)H	GD	£6987
73	9/00	Hayd	7f30y	C(0-95)H	HVY	£14300
58	8/00	Hayd	7f30y	E(0-70)H	G-S	£3122
60	7/00	Newc	7f	F(0-65)H	GD	£2709

Total win prize-money £30927

Going (Turf): Sf: 2-7 GS: 1-1 Gd: 1-3 GF: 0-4 Fm: 0-1
Distance: 5f/6f: 0-4 **7f-8f: 4-9** 9f-13f: 0-3 14f+: 0-0
Track : **LH: 4-10** RH: 0-2 **Tight: 2-3** Gall: 0-2
Aids: **Bl: 2-3** Vi: 1-5 Tstrap: 0-0
Best Rating: 72 7/01 Gdwd 1m gd-fm

Ridden positively when gaining her three wins last season, but was ridden much more patiently when winning at Thirsk in June 2001. Suited by seven furlongs or a mile. Acts on easy ground and handles fast ground.

Dalal

89 **73+**

2-y-o b f Cadeaux Genereux-Proudfoot (IRE) (Shareef Dancer (USA))

E A L Dunlop Mohammed Jaber

Placings:0 (5602)

2001: 7^{0}GS

	Starts	1st	2nd	3rd	Win & Pl
Career Total (Turf)	1	0	0	0	

Going (Turf): Sf: 0-0 GS: 0-1 Gd: 0-0 GF: 0-0 Fm: 0-0
Distance: 5f/6f: 0-0 7f-8f: 0-1 9f-13f: 0-0 14f+: 0-0
Track : LH: 0-0 RH: 0-0 Tight: 0-0 Gall: 0-0
Aids: Bl: 0-0 Vi: 0-0 Tstrap: 0-0
Best Rating: 73 11/01 NmkR 7f gd-sft

Dalampour (IRE)

109 **109**

4-y-o b h Shernazar-Dalara (IRE) (Doyoun)

Sir Michael Stoute H H Aga Khan

Placings:01135-34040 (4696)

2001: 12^{3}GS, 13^{4}GF, 10^{0}GF, 13^{4}GF, 10^{0}GS

	Starts	1st	2nd	3rd	Win & Pl
Career Total (Turf)	10	2	0	2	70858

103	6/00	Asct	2m45y	A	G-F	£36000
90	6/00	NmkR	1m4f	D	G-F	£4758

Total win prize-money £40758

Going (Turf): Sf: 0-0 GS: 0-2 Gd: 0-1 **GF: 2-7** Fm: 0-0
Distance: 5f/6f: 0-0 7f-8f: 0-0 9f-13f: 1-6 14f+: 1-4
Track : LH: 0-8 **RH: 2-2** Tight: 0-0 **Gall: 2-10**
Aids: Bl: 0-0 Vi: 0-0 Tstrap: 0-0
Best Rating: 109 8/01 Newb 1m5f61y gd-fm

He was a decent stayer at three, winner of Ascot's Queen's Vase, but he has proved vey difficult to settle this year and is not getting home. Best form on good or faster. Sold for 100,000 gns in the autumn.

Dalblair (IRE)

87 **66**

2-y-o b c Lake Coniston (IRE)-Cartagena Lady (IRE) (Prince Rupert (FR))

J A Glover Mrs Janis Macpherson

Placings:400 (4454)

2001: 6^{4}GF, 6^{0}G, 6^{0}GF

	Starts	1st	2nd	3rd	Win & Pl
Career Total (Turf)	3	0	0	0	344

Going (Turf): Sf: 0-0 GS: 0-0 Gd: 0-1 GF: 0-2 Fm: 0-0
Distance: 5f/6f: 0-3 7f-8f: 0-0 9f-13f: 0-0 14f+: 0-0
Track : LH: 0-0 RH: 0-0 Tight: 0-0 Gall: 0-0
Aids: Bl: 0-0 Vi: 0-0 Tstrap: 0-0
Best Rating: 66 9/01 York 6f gd-fm

Dalby Of York

(30)**58**

5-y-o ch g Polar Falcon (USA)-Miller's Creek (USA) (Star De Naskra (USA))

M E Sowersby M E Sowersby

Placings:00040/131523000/6-0 (1283)

2001: 16^{0}G

	Starts	1st	2nd	3rd	Win & Pl
Career Total (Turf)	15	2	1	2	7357
Career Total (AW)	1	0	0	0	

70	5/99	Muss	1m6f	F(0-60)	G-F	£2542
60	4/99	Wind	1m3f135y	E(0-70)H	G-F	£2808

Total win prize-money £5350

Going (Turf): Sf: 0-1 GS: 0-4 Gd: 0-2 **GF: 2-7** Fm: 0-1
Distance: 5f/6f: 0-3 7f-8f: 0-1 9f-13f: 1-6 14f+: 1-6
Track : LH: 0-6 **RH: 1-4 Tight: 2-11** Gall: 0-1
Aids: Bl: 0-1 Vi: 0-0 Tstrap: 0-0

Dalyan (IRE)

(72) **52**

4-y-o b g Turtle Island (IRE)-Salette (Sallust)

A J Lockwood A J Lockwood

Placings:0445/0040500-040 (3433)

2001: 8^{0}GF, 16^{4}F, 16^{0}SD

	Starts	1st	2nd	3rd	Win & Pl
Career Total (Turf)	13	0	0	0	676
Career Total (AW)	1	0	0	0	

Going (Turf): Sf: 0-2 GS: 0-2 Gd: 0-4 GF: 0-3 Fm: 0-2
Distance: 5f/6f: 0-0 7f-8f: 0-6 9f-13f: 0-6 14f+: 0-2
Track : LH: 0-7 RH: 0-6 Tight: 0-6 Gall: 0-1
Aids: Bl: 0-0 Vi: 0-0 Tstrap: 0-0
Best Rating: 44 6/01 Thsk 2m firm

Damages

52(82) (21)**10**

3-y-o b f Contract Law (USA)-Treasure Time (IRE) (Treasure Kay)

D J Wintle Red & Black Racing

Placings:000-00 (3741)

2001: 8^{0}G, 10^{0}S

	Starts	1st	2nd	3rd	Win & Pl
Career Total (Turf)	3	0	0	0	
Career Total (AW)	2	0	0	0	

Going (Turf): Sf: 0-1 GS: 0-1 Gd: 0-1 GF: 0-0 Fm: 0-0
Distance: 5f/6f: 0-3 7f-8f: 0-0 9f-13f: 0-2 14f+: 0-0
Track : LH: 0-3 RH: 0-1 Tight: 0-1 Gall: 0-1
Aids: Bl: 0-0 Vi: 0-0 Tstrap: 0-0
Best Rating: 10 7/01 Leic 1m9y good

Damalis (IRE)

107 **102**

5-y-o b m Mukaddamah (USA)-Art Age (Artaius (USA))

E J Alston Liam & Tony Ferguson

Placings:321434166/314646440/461001003550-061030326062 (5136)

2001: 6^{0}S, 5^{6}GS, 5^{1}GF, 5^{0}GF, 6^{3}GF, 6^{0}Y, 5^{3}GF, 6^{2}G, 6^{6}G, 6^{0}GF, 5^{6}S, 6^{2}G

	Starts	1st	2nd	3rd	Win & Pl
Career Total (Turf)	42	6	3	6	87157

99	5/01	Ches	5f16y	B(0-100)H	G-F	£12351
95	6/00	Ches	5f16y	C(0-95)H	G-F	£11017

93	5/00	Ches	5f16y	B(0-100)H	GD	£9451
93	4/99	Sand	5f6y	B(0-100)H	SFT	£7275
86	9/98	Ripn	5f	C	SFT	£4513
86	5/98	Ches	5f16y	D	G-F	£7262

Total win prize-money £51874

Going (Turf): Sf: 2-9 GS: 0-5 Gd: 1-11 **GF: 3-15** Fm: 0-1
Distance: **5f/6f: 6-38** 7f-8f: 0-4 9f-13f: 0-0 14f+: 0-0
Track : **LH: 4-15** RH: 0-1 **Tight: 4-9** Gall: 0-3
Aids: Bl: 0-0 Vi: 0-0 Tstrap: 0-0
Best Rating: 102 7/01 Ches 5f16y gd-fm

A fair sprinter, she goes particularly well at Chester. She has won on soft, but seems more effective on faster going these days.

Damask Rose (IRE)

110 **94**

3-y-o ch f Dr Devious (IRE)-Solac (FR) (Gay Lussac (ITY))
L M Cumani Mrs Belinda Strudwick

Placings:41600436 **(5693)**
2001: 9^{4}GS, 14^{1}GF, 12^{6}GS, 14^{0}G, 13^{0}G, 14^{4}G, 14^{3}G, 12^{6}S

	Starts	1st	2nd	3rd	Win & Pl
Career Total (Turf)	8	1	0	1	7488

79 6/01 Rdcr 1m6f19y D G-F £3430

Total win prize-money £3430

Going (Turf): Sf: 0-1 GS: 0-2 Gd: 0-4 **GF: 1-1** Fm: 0-0
Distance: 5f/6f: 0-0 7f-8f: 0-0 9f-13f: 0-3 **14f+: 1-5**
Track : **LH: 1-3** RH: 0-4 **Tight: 1-3** Gall: 0-4
Aids: Bl: 0-0 Vi: 0-0 Tstrap: 0-0
Best Rating: 94 9/01 NmkR 1m6f good

Half-sister to top stayers Double Trigger and Double Eclipse, she took an extended 14 furlong maiden on her second attempt. Has found life tougher since. Acts on good ground or faster and is open to further improvement.

Damasquiner

103(95) (42) **47**

4-y-o b f Casteddu-Hymn Book (IRE) (Darshaan)
T E Powell Miss P I Westbrook

Placings:000066/4163563-03043060 **(4052)**
2001: 6^{0}SD, 7^{3}SD, 6^{0}SW, 7^{4}SW, 5^{3}GF, 6^{0}GF, 5^{6}F, 6^{0}F

	Starts	1st	2nd	3rd	Win & Pl
Career Total (Turf)	9	0	0	1	412
Career Total (AW)	12	1	0	3	3181

62 2/00 Ling 7f F(0-60) STD £2289

Total win prize-money £2289

Going (Turf): Sf: 0-0 GS: 0-1 Gd: 0-3 GF: 0-3 Fm: 0-2
Distance: 5f/6f: 0-13 **7f-8f: 1-8** 9f-13f: 0-0 14f+: 0-0
Track : **LH: 1-13** RH: 0-1 **Tight: 1-12** Gall: 0-1
Aids: Bl: 0-0 Vi: 0-0 Tstrap: 0-0
Best Rating: 47 6/01 Ling 5f gd-fm

Dame Fonteyn

(72) (4) **61**

4-y-o b f Suave Dancer (USA)-Her Honour (Teenoso (USA))
C Tizzard (M C Pipe 18/5) Miss Sarah Tizzard

Placings:000/P2261300-0 **(0484)**
2001: 13^{0}SD

	Starts	1st	2nd	3rd	Win & Pl
Career Total (Turf)	11	1	2	1	4630
Career Total (AW)	1	0	0	0	

61 5/00 Rdcr 1m6f19y F(0-60)H G-S £2404

Total win prize-money £2405

Going (Turf): Sf: 0-7 **GS: 1-2** Gd: 0-1 GF: 0-1 Fm: 0-0
Distance: 5f/6f: 0-0 7f-8f: 0-1 9f-13f: 0-7 **14f+: 1-4**
Track : **LH: 1-10** RH: 0-2 **Tight: 1-6** Gall: 0-2
Aids: Bl: 0-0 Vi: 0-0 Tstrap: 0-0
Best Rating: 4 3/01 Ling 1m5f stand

Dame Sharp

(76) (36) **53**

2-y-o b f Sabrehill (USA)-Dame Helene (USA) (Sir Ivor)
E J Alston M Graham

Placings:0500 **(5415)**
2001: 6^{0}GS, 7^{5}G, 7^{0}GF, 6^{0}SD

	Starts	1st	2nd	3rd	Win & Pl
Career Total (Turf)	3	0	0	0	0
Career Total (AW)	1	0	0	0	

Going (Turf): Sf: 0-0 GS: 0-1 Gd: 0-1 GF: 0-1 Fm: 0-0
Distance: 5f/6f: 0-1 7f-8f: 0-3 9f-13f: 0-0 14f+: 0-0
Track : LH: 0-2 RH: 0-1 Tight: 0-2 Gall: 0-0
Aids: Bl: 0-0 Vi: 0-0 Tstrap: 0-0
Best Rating: 53 8/01 Bevl 7f100y gd-fm

Damien's Law

42(64) (4)

4-y-o b g Contract Law (USA)-Cinderella Derek (Hittite Glory)
A D Smith Pertemps Group Limited

Placings:0/000 **(0730)**
2001: 12^{0}SD, 9^{0}SD, 6^{0}GS

	Starts	1st	2nd	3rd	Win & Pl
Career Total (Turf)	2	0	0	0	
Career Total (AW)	2	0	0	0	

Going (Turf): Sf: 0-0 GS: 0-2 Gd: 0-0 GF: 0-0 Fm: 0-0
Distance: 5f/6f: 0-0 7f-8f: 0-2 9f-13f: 0-2 14f+: 0-0
Track : LH: 0-3 RH: 0-0 Tight: 0-2 Gall: 0-0
Aids: Bl: 0-0 Vi: 0-0 Tstrap: 0-0
Best Rating: 4 2/01 Ling 1m4f stand

Dan De Lion

58 **14**

2-y-o b c Danzig Connection (USA)-Fiorini (Formidable (USA))
Jedd O'Keeffe Wetherby Racing Bureau 49

Placings:000 **(5537)**
2001: 5^{0}F, 7^{0}S, 7^{0}S

	Starts	1st	2nd	3rd	Win & Pl
Career Total (Turf)	3	0	0	0	

Going (Turf): Sf: 0-2 GS: 0-0 Gd: 0-0 GF: 0-0 Fm: 0-1
Distance: 5f/6f: 0-1 7f-8f: 0-2 9f-13f: 0-0 14f+: 0-0
Track : LH: 0-2 RH: 0-0 Tight: 0-1 Gall: 0-0
Aids: Bl: 0-0 Vi: 0-0 Tstrap: 0-0
Best Rating: 14 9/01 Pont 5f firm

Danakil

(104) (64) **66**

6-y-o b g Warning-Danilova (USA) (Lyphard (USA))
S Dow The Danakilists

Placings:33/5010036/5663516l206-50000035234 **(5230)**
2001: 8^{5}SW, 8^{0}SD, 8^{0}S, 8^{0}G, 7^{0}GF, 7^{0}G, 8^{3}GF, 9^{5}G, 10^{2}G, 12^{3}G, 11^{4}S

	Starts	1st	2nd	3rd	Win & Pl
Career Total (Turf)	18	1	2	5	12823
Career Total (AW)	13	2	0	1	7039

66	5/00	Wind	1m67y	E(0-70)H	GD	£3136
66	3/00	Wolv	1m1f79y	D(0-85)H	STD	£3926
68	3/99	Wolv	1m1f79y	D	STD	£2736

Total win prize-money £9798

Going (Turf): Sf: 0-4 GS: 0-0 **Gd: 1-9** GF: 0-3 Fm: 0-0
Distance: 5f/6f: 0-2 7f-8f: 0-7 **9f-13f: 3-21** 14f+: 0-0
Track : **LH: 2-19** RH: 1-10 **Tight: 3-21** Gall: 0-4
Aids: Bl: 0-0 Vi: 0-1 Tstrap: 0-0
Best Rating: 66 9/01 Epsm 1m4f10y good

Won a Wolverhampton maiden in March and a Windsor handicap in May, but often found one or two too good since then.

Danakim

102(84) (37) **55**

4-y-o b g Emarati (USA)-Kangra Valley (Indian Ridge)
J R Weymes John Weymes Racing Club

Placings:642040/00024050000-653032326600015350004000 **(5189)**
2001: 7^{6}GS, 5^{5}GS, 5^{3}GF, 5^{0}GF, 6^{3}F, 5^{2}F, 5^{3}GF, 5^{2}F, 5^{6}GF, 5^{6}GF, 5^{0}F, 5^{0}GS, 5^{0}G, 6^{1}GF, 5^{5}GF, 5^{3}G, 6^{5}G, 5^{0}GF, 6^{0}GF, 5^{0}GF, 5^{4}GF, 5^{0}G, 7^{0}GS, 5^{0}GS

	Starts	1st	2nd	3rd	Win & Pl
Career Total (Turf)	37	1	4	4	9680
Career Total (AW)	4	0	0	0	

55 7/01 Ripn 6f E(0-70)H G-F £3250

Total win prize-money £3250

Going (Turf): Sf: 0-3 GS: 0-6 Gd: 0-7 **GF: 1-16** Fm: 0-5
Distance: **5f/6f: 1-37** 7f-8f: 0-3 9f-13f: 0-1 14f+: 0-0
Track : LH: 0-11 RH: 0-2 Tight: 0-7 Gall: 0-2
Aids: Bl: 0-3 Vi: 0-0 Tstrap: 0-0
Best Rating: 60 7/01 Bevl 5f gd-fm

Dananeyev (FR)

98 **112**

5-y-o b h Goldneyev (USA)-Danagroom (USA) (Groom Dancer (USA))
C Laffon-Parias Wertheimer Brothers

Placings:31345/13100/1565540-31511000 **(5244a)**
2001: 7^{3}G, 5^{1}HY, 5^{5}HY, 5^{1}G, 5^{1}G, 5^{0}G, 6^{0}VS, 5^{0}HO

	Starts	1st	2nd	3rd	Win & Pl
Career Total (Turf)	25	7	0	4	122582

112	6/01	Chan	5f		GD	£29098
108	5/01	Lonc	5f		GD	£21339
	4/01	Lonc	5f		HVY	£13579
105	4/00	MsnL	5f110y		HVY	£13449
	6/99	Chan	5f110y		SFT	£10764
	5/99	Chan	6f	H	GD	£8073
	7/98	Vich	7f		SFT	£8080

Total win prize-money £104383

Going (Turf): Sf: 3-5 GS: 0-1 Gd: 2-9 GF: 0-0 Fm: 0-0
Distance: **5f/6f: 4-16** 7f-8f: 1-4 9f-13f: 0-0 14f+: 0-0
Track : LH: 0-0 RH: 0-1 Tight: 0-0 Gall: 0-0
Aids: Bl: 0-0 Vi: 0-0 Tstrap: 0-0
Best Rating: 112 6/01 Chan 5f good

Decent French sprinter who gained his best result so far at Chantilly this season when winner of the Prix du Gros-Chene. Acts on good ground and soft.

Dance Alive

92 **71**

3-y-o b c Rainbow Quest (USA)-Tashinsky (USA) (Nijinsky (CAN))
G A Butler T D Holland-Martin

Placings:50 **(1434)**
2001: 11^{5}GS, 10^{0}S

	Starts	1st	2nd	3rd	Win & Pl
Career Total (Turf)	2	0	0	0	0

Going (Turf): Sf: 0-1 GS: 0-1 Gd: 0-0 GF: 0-0 Fm: 0-0
Distance: 5f/6f: 0-0 7f-8f: 0-0 9f-13f: 0-2 14f+: 0-0
Track : LH: 0-2 RH: 0-0 Tight: 0-0 Gall: 0-2
Aids: Bl: 0-0 Vi: 0-0 Tstrap: 0-0
Best Rating: 71 5/01 Newb 1m2f6y soft

Dance All Night

(75) (40)**63**
2-y-o b c Suave Dancer (USA)-Lyndseylee (Swing Easy (USA))
A Berry G Syvret

Placings:0000 **(5194)**
2001: 6^{0}S, 6^{0}G, 5^{0}HY, 5^{0}SD

	Starts	1st	2nd	3rd	Win & Pl
Career Total (Turf)	3	0	0	0	
Career Total (AW)	1	0	0	0	

Going (Turf): Sf: 0-2 GS: 0-0 Gd: 0-1 GF: 0-0 Fm: 0-0
Distance: 5f/6f: 0-4 7f-8f: 0-0 9f-13f: 0-0 14f+: 0-0
Track : LH: 0-2 RH: 0-0 Tight: 0-1 Gall: 0-0
Aids: Bl: 0-0 Vi: 0-0 Tstrap: 0-0
Best Rating: 63 8/01 Pont 6f good

Dance Director (IRE)

101 **86**
4-y-o b c Sadler's Wells (USA)-Memories (USA) (Hail The Pirates (USA))
C R Egerton Dr G Madan Mohan

Placings:421-0 **(1541)**
2001: 14^{0}GF

	Starts	1st	2nd	3rd	Win & Pl
Career Total (Turf)	4	1	1	0	6438

84 9/00 Kemp 1m4f D SFT £4062
Total win prize-money £4063

Going (Turf): Sf: 1-1 GS: 0-1 Gd: 0-1 GF: 0-1 Fm: 0-0
Distance: 5f/6f: 0-0 7f-8f: 0-0 **9f-13f: 1-3** 14f+: 0-1
Track : LH: 0-2 **RH: 1-2** Tight: 0-1 Gall: 0-1
Aids: Bl: 0-0 Vi: 0-0 Tstrap: 0-0
Best Rating: 86 5/01 Gdwd 1m6f gd-fm

A half-brother to Group Three winner Russian Revival, he won over a mile and a half at three. Runs under both codes, acts on good and soft.

Dance In The Day (IRE)

110 **72**
3-y-o b c Caerleon (USA)-One To One (Shirley Heights)
E A L Dunlop Khalid Ali

Placings:00-0221310 **(4855)**
2001: 8^{0}GS, 10^{2}GF, 11^{2}F, 11^{1}GF, 13^{3}GS, 11^{1}GF, 11^{0}GF

	Starts	1st	2nd	3rd	Win & Pl
Career Total (Turf)	9	2	2	1	10930

72 8/01 Bevl 1m3f216yE(0-75)H G-F £4878
67 7/01 Ling 1m3f106yE(0-70)H G-F £3248
Total win prize-money £8126

Going (Turf): Sf: 0-1 GS: 0-2 Gd: 0-0 **GF: 2-5** Fm: 0-1
Distance: 5f/6f: 0-0 7f-8f: 0-1 **9f-13f: 2-7** 14f+: 0-1
Track : LH: 1-5 RH: 1-2 **Tight: 2-4** Gall: 0-0
Aids: Bl: 0-0 Vi: 0-0 Tstrap: 0-0
Best Rating: 72 8/01 Bevl 1m3f216y gd-fm

Fair handicapper at a mile and a half, acts on fast ground.

Dance Lesson

79 **48**
2-y-o b f In The Wings-Be Discreet (Junius (USA))
S Kirk N Hayes

Placings:00 **(5520)**
2001: 8^{0}HY, 8^{0}HY

	Starts	1st	2nd	3rd	Win & Pl
Career Total (Turf)	2	0	0	0	

Going (Turf): Sf: 0-2 GS: 0-0 Gd: 0-0 GF: 0-0 Fm: 0-0
Distance: 5f/6f: 0-0 7f-8f: 0-0 9f-13f: 0-2 14f+: 0-0
Track : LH: 0-1 RH: 0-1 Tight: 0-1 Gall: 0-0
Aids: Bl: 0-0 Vi: 0-0 Tstrap: 0-0
Best Rating: 48 10/01 Wind 1m67y heavy

Dance Little Lady (IRE)

78(55) (56)**28**
4-y-o b f Common Grounds-Kentucky Tears (USA) (Cougar (CHI))
M Todhunter G B Stuart

Placings:0060064/01600-000 **(3161)**
2001: 6^{0}GF, 5^{0}GF, 6^{0}G

	Starts	1st	2nd	3rd	Win & Pl
Career Total (Turf)	12	1	0	0	3315
Career Total (AW)	3	0	0	0	0

53 6/00 Rdcr 6f E(0-70)H GD £3315
Total win prize-money £3315

Going (Turf): Sf: 0-2 GS: 0-1 **Gd: 1-3** GF: 0-5 Fm: 0-1
Distance: **5f/6f: 1-14** 7f-8f: 0-1 9f-13f: 0-0 14f+: 0-0
Track : LH: 0-3 RH: 0-2 Tight: 0-2 Gall: 0-2
Aids: Bl: 0-1 Vi: 0-0 Tstrap: 0-0
Best Rating: 18 7/01 Muss 5f gd-fm

Dance Master (IRE)

92 **58**
3-y-o b c Nureyev (USA)-Bay Queen (Damister (USA))
M L W Bell B J Warren

Placings:000110600 **(4952)**
2001: 8^{0}GS, 8^{0}GF, 8^{0}F, 11^{1}GF, 11^{1}F, 12^{0}GF, 10^{6}GS, 12^{0}GF, 11^{0}G

	Starts	1st	2nd	3rd	Win & Pl
Career Total (Turf)	9	2	0	0	5961

71 6/01 Ling 1m3f106yE(0-75)H FRM £2880
63 6/01 Rdcr 1m3f F(0-65) G-F £3080
Total win prize-money £5961

Going (Turf): Sf: 0-0 GS: 0-2 Gd: 0-1 **GF: 1-4 Fm: 1-2**
Distance: 5f/6f: 0-0 7f-8f: 0-1 **9f-13f: 2-8** 14f+: 0-0
Track : **LH: 2-5** RH: 0-3 **Tight: 2-4** Gall: 0-1
Aids: Bl: 0-0 Vi: 0-0 Tstrap: 0-0
Best Rating: 71 6/01 Ling 1m3f106y firm

He needed the step up to a mile and three furlongs to achieve back-to-back wins in modest company in June on fast ground, but subsequently went off the boil.

Dance On The Top

109 **90**
3-y-o ch c Caerleon (USA)-Fern (Shirley Heights)
E A L Dunlop Khalifa Sultan

Placings:61200-136 **(2329)**
2001: 8^{1}G, 9^{3}GF, 12^{6}GF

	Starts	1st	2nd	3rd	Win & Pl
Career Total (Turf)	8	2	1	1	27594

90 5/01 NmkR 1m C(0-90)H GD £14560
80 7/00 Kemp 7f D G-F £4533
Total win prize-money £19094

Going (Turf): Sf: 0-0 GS: 0-3 **Gd: 1-2 GF: 1-3** Fm: 0-0
Distance: 5f/6f: 0-1 **7f-8f: 2-4** 9f-13f: 0-3 14f+: 0-0
Track : LH: 0-0 **RH: 1-4** Tight: 0-1 **Gall: 1-2**
Aids: Bl: 0-0 Vi: 0-0 Tstrap: 0-0
Best Rating: 90 5/01 NmkR 1m good

Useful fast ground handicapper.

Dance Theatre (IRE)

90 **80d**
3-y-o b g Sadler's Wells (USA)-Noora Abu (Ahonoora)
J R Jenkins (J S Bolger 17/6) Miss I Leitendorfa

Placings:24450 **(4893)**
2001: 12^{2}S, 10^{4}SH, 10^{4}GF, 10^{5}G, 12^{0}GF

	Starts	1st	2nd	3rd	Win & Pl
Career Total (Turf)	5	0	1	0	2440

Going (Turf): Sf: 0-1 GS: 0-0 Gd: 0-1 GF: 0-2 Fm: 0-0
Distance: 5f/6f: 0-0 7f-8f: 0-0 9f-13f: 0-5 14f+: 0-0
Track : LH: 0-0 RH: 0-1 Tight: 0-0 Gall: 0-0
Aids: Bl: 0-2 Vi: 0-0 Tstrap: 0-0
Best Rating: 92 4/01 Leop 1m4f soft

Danceabout

104 **109**
4-y-o b f Shareef Dancer (USA)-Putupon (Mummy's Pet)
G Wragg Bloomsbury Stud

Placings:153121-446300 **(5141)**
2001: 8^{4}S, 8^{4}G, 9^{6}G, 8^{3}GY, 8^{0}GS, 8^{0}G

	Starts	1st	2nd	3rd	Win & Pl
Career Total (Turf)	12	3	1	2	96318

109 9/00 NmkR 1m A GD £34800
104 8/00 Gdwd 7f A GD £22750
78 5/00 Gdwd 7f D SFT £5622
Total win prize-money £63173

Going (Turf): Sf: 1-2 GS: 0-1 **Gd: 2-6** GF: 0-2 Fm: 0-0
Distance: 5f/6f: 0-0 **7f-8f: 3-11** 9f-13f: 0-1 14f+: 0-0
Track : LH: 0-0 **RH: 2-4** Tight: 0-1 Gall: 0-1
Aids: Bl: 0-0 Vi: 0-1 Tstrap: 0-0
Best Rating: 109 7/01 NmkJ 1m good

A very useful filly at a mile who ended 2000 on a high note when beating Alshakr by a neck in the Sun Chariot Stakes. Some good efforts in 2001, fourth in the Lockinge. Has been retired.

Dancehall Darcy

68 **25**
2-y-o ch f Bahamian Bounty-Dancing Chimes (London Bells (CAN))
K O Cunningham-Brown Alan Barrington

Placings:0 **(2507)**
2001: 5^{0}GF

	Starts	1st	2nd	3rd	Win & Pl
Career Total (Turf)	1	0	0	0	

Going (Turf): Sf: 0-0 GS: 0-0 Gd: 0-0 GF: 0-1 Fm: 0-0
Distance: 5f/6f: 0-1 7f-8f: 0-0 9f-13f: 0-0 14f+: 0-0
Track : LH: 0-0 RH: 0-0 Tight: 0-0 Gall: 0-0
Aids: Bl: 0-0 Vi: 0-0 Tstrap: 0-0
Best Rating: 25 6/01 Sals 5f gd-fm

Dancemma

79(91) (39)**24**
4-y-o ch f Emarati (USA)-Hanglands (Bustino)
H J Collingridge D T Thom

Placings:40032602/000250004000-P00 **(5374)**
2001: 10^{P}HY, 8^{0}SD, 6^{0}G

	Starts	1st	2nd	3rd	Win & Pl
Career Total (Turf)	21	0	3	1	4330
Career Total (AW)	2	0	0	0	

Going (Turf): Sf: 0-4 GS: 0-5 Gd: 0-7 GF: 0-5 Fm: 0-0
Distance: 5f/6f: 0-16 7f-8f: 0-5 9f-13f: 0-2 14f+: 0-0
Track : LH: 0-5 RH: 0-4 Tight: 0-1 Gall: 0-5
Aids: Bl: 0-0 Vi: 0-0 Tstrap: 0-0
Best Rating: 21 10/01 Rdcr 6f good

Dancing Al

102(87) (33)**36**
6-y-o br g Alnasr Alwasheek-Lyne Dancer (Be My Native (USA))
J S Moore Miss L D Martin

Placings:0005/600/0-3250 **(5085)**
2001: 14^{3}HY, 11^{2}GS, 14^{5}S, 11^{0}S

	Starts	1st	2nd	3rd	Win & Pl
Career Total (Turf)	11	0	1	1	1128

Career Total (AW)	1	0	0	0

Going (Turf): Sf: 0-4 GS: 0-1 Gd: 0-2 GF: 0-3 Fm: 0-1
Distance: 5f/6f: 0-1 7f-8f: 0-4 9f-13f: 0-4 14f+: 0-3
Track : LH: 0-7 RH: 0-1 Tight: 0-0 Gall: 0-0
Aids: Bl: 0-0 Vi: 0-0 Tstrap: 0-0
Best Rating: 36 3/01 Nott 1m6f15y heavy

Dancing Bay

111 **85**

4-y-o b g Suave Dancer (USA)-Kabayil (Dancing Brave (USA))
Miss J A Camacho Elite Racing Club

Placings:50/11041-00066010 **(5693)**
2001: 12^{0}S, 11^{0}F, 13^{0}G, 11^{6}G, 14^{6}HY, 14^{0}HY, 13^{1}HY, 12^{0}S

	Starts	1st	2nd	3rd	Win & Pl
Career Total (Turf)	15	4	0	0	26437

85 10/01 Ayr 1m5f13y C(0-95)H HVY £7215
93 10/00 Ayr 1m5f13y C(0-95)H HVY £7247
89 5/00 Pont 1m2f6y D(0-85)H SFT £7280
86 3/00 Newc 7f D GD £3848
Total win prize-money £25591

Going (Turf): Sf: 3-7 GS: 0-1 **Gd: 1-4** GF: 0-2 Fm: 0-1
Distance: 5f/6f: 0-0 7f-8f: 1-3 9f-13f: 1-7 **14f+: 2-5**
Track : **LH: 3-13** RH: 0-0 Tight: 0-2 Gall: 0-5
Aids: Bl: 0-0 Vi: 0-0 Tstrap: 0-1
Best Rating: 86 5/01 York 1m3f195y firm

Lightly-raced fair handicapper with a high knee-action. Tends to run well at Ayr in October. Stays 13 furlongs, loves the mud.

Dancing Dervish

(86) (16) **44**

6-y-o b g Shareef Dancer (USA)-Taj Victory (Final Straw)
D Burchell Vivian Guy

Placings:64/2000205310/00/00-**0056** **(1086)**
2001: 16^{0}SW, 9^{0}SD, 12^{5}SD, 6^{6}SD

	Starts	1st	2nd	3rd	Win & Pl
Career Total (Turf)	16	1	2	1	5123
Career Total (AW)	4	0	0	0	0

59 8/98 Brig 7f214y E(0-70)H G-F £2913
Total win prize-money £2913

Going (Turf): Sf: 0-3 GS: 0-3 Gd: 0-3 **GF: 1-6** Fm: 0-1
Distance: 5f/6f: 0-2 **7f-8f: 1-6** 9f-13f: 0-11 14f+: 0-1
Track : **LH: 1-12** RH: 0-4 Tight: 0-8 Gall: 0-0
Aids: Bl: 0-1 **Vi: 1-10** Tstrap: 0-0
Best Rating: 33 3/01 Wolv 1m4f stand

Dancing Dolphin (IRE)

79 **51**

2-y-o b f Dolphin Street (FR)-Dance Model (Unfuwain (USA))
J E Long (M D I Usher 21/9) Wilwyn Executive Racing Wwwwilwyncom

Placings:00 **(5367)**
2001: 6^{0}GF, 8^{0}GS

	Starts	1st	2nd	3rd	Win & Pl
Career Total (Turf)	2	0	0	0	

Going (Turf): Sf: 0-0 GS: 0-1 Gd: 0-0 GF: 0-1 Fm: 0-0
Distance: 5f/6f: 0-0 7f-8f: 0-2 9f-13f: 0-0 14f+: 0-0
Track : LH: 0-0 RH: 0-0 Tight: 0-0 Gall: 0-0
Aids: Bl: 0-0 Vi: 0-0 Tstrap: 0-0
Best Rating: 51 9/01 Newb 6f8y gd-fm

Dancing Free

(80) (38) **52**

2-y-o b f Dancing Spree (USA)-Keep Quiet (Reprimand)

K R Burke Mrs Elaine M Burke

Placings:552656 **(5410)**
2001: 6^{5}G, 7^{5}G, 7^{2}GF, 5^{6}G, 7^{5}G, 7^{6}SD

	Starts	1st	2nd	3rd	Win & Pl
Career Total (Turf)	5	0	1	0	526
Career Total (AW)	1	0	0	0	0

Going (Turf): Sf: 0-0 GS: 0-0 Gd: 0-4 GF: 0-1 Fm: 0-0
Distance: 5f/6f: 0-2 7f-8f: 0-4 9f-13f: 0-0 14f+: 0-0
Track : LH: 0-1 RH: 0-0 Tight: 0-0 Gall: 0-0
Aids: Bl: 0-0 Vi: 0-0 Tstrap: 0-0
Best Rating: 52 7/01 Muss 7f30y gd-fm

Dancing Hill

92(93) (52)**62**

2-y-o b f Piccolo-Ryewater Dream (Touching Wood (USA))
W G M Turner (M Blanshard 27/6) Mrs E A Loftus

Placings:0560314006 **(5079)**
2001: 5^{0}GS, 6^{5}GF, 5^{6}GF, 5^{0}HD, 5^{3}SD, 5^{1}GS, 6^{4}S, 7^{0}GF, 7^{0}SD, 5^{6}S

	Starts	1st	2nd	3rd	Win & Pl
Career Total (Turf)	8	1	0	0	2167
Career Total (AW)	2	0	0	1	267

62 7/01 Leic 5f2y G G-S £1897
Total win prize-money £1897

Going (Turf): Sf: 0-2 **GS: 1-2** Gd: 0-0 GF: 0-3 Fm: 0-1
Distance: **5f/6f: 1-7** 7f-8f: 0-3 9f-13f: 0-0 14f+: 0-0
Track : LH: 0-5 RH: 0-0 Tight: 0-2 Gall: 0-2
Aids: Bl: 0-0 Vi: 0-0 Tstrap: 0-0
Best Rating: 62 7/01 Leic 5f2y gd-sft

A plating-class half-sister to seven furlong two-year-old winner Buzz.

Dancing Jack

94(95) (32)**23**

8-y-o ch g Clantime-Sun Follower (Relkino)
J J Bridger Mrs J M Stamp

Placings:035645640133/24252400060000/000000/00605060266/625655000400003000006/5000006201-00R00000000 **(3010)**
2001: 6^{0}SD, 5^{0}SD, 5^{R}SW, 5^{0}SW, 6^{0}SD, 5^{0}SD, 5^{0}G, 5^{0}GF, 6^{0}GF, 6^{0}F, 5^{0}GF

	Starts	1st	2nd	3rd	Win & Pl
Career Total (Turf)	40	0	0	2	1676
Career Total (AW)	45	2	6	2	10521

42 12/00 Ling 5f E(0-70)H STD £2772
53 11/95 Ling 5f E STD £2211
Total win prize-money £4983

Going (Turf): Sf: 0-2 GS: 0-3 Gd: 0-8 GF: 0-23 Fm: 0-4
Distance: **5f/6f: 2-75** 7f-8f: 0-9 9f-13f: 0-1 14f+: 0-0
Track : **LH: 2-51** RH: 0-8 **Tight: 2-45** Gall: 0-11
Aids: Bl: 0-2 Vi: 0-0 Tstrap: 0-0
Best Rating: 36 5/01 Bath 5f11y good

Dancing King (IRE)

101(72) **40?**

5-y-o b g Fairy King (USA)-Zariysha (IRE) (Darshaan)
P W Hiatt P W Hiatt

Placings:0/0/**0000**-0400040 **(4672)**
2001: 14^{0}SW, 8^{4}GS, 8^{0}GF, 8^{0}G, 7^{0}GF, 8^{4}GF, 8^{0}G

	Starts	1st	2nd	3rd	Win & Pl
Career Total (Turf)	9	0	0	0	608
Career Total (AW)	4	0	0	0	

Going (Turf): Sf: 0-1 GS: 0-2 Gd: 0-2 GF: 0-4 Fm: 0-0
Distance: 5f/6f: 0-1 7f-8f: 0-5 9f-13f: 0-6 14f+: 0-1
Track : LH: 0-7 RH: 0-1 Tight: 0-6 Gall: 0-0
Aids: Bl: 0-0 Vi: 0-0 Tstrap: 0-0
Best Rating: 40 9/01 Thsk 1m gd-fm

Dancing Kris

101 **39**

8-y-o b g Kris-Liska's Dance (USA) (Riverman (USA))
Ian Williams Paul Robson

Placings:65144/401/132310/00-00340000 **(5376)**
2001: 10^{0}GS, 9^{0}G, 10^{3}G, 9^{4}GF, 8^{0}GS, 9^{0}GS, 9^{0}G, 9^{0}G

	Starts	1st	2nd	3rd	Win & Pl
Career Total (Turf)	24	4	1	3	75675

97 8/99 Deau 1m H VS £18299
4/99 Lonc 1m1f165y SFT £8611
5/98 Lonc 1m110y GD £12121
9/97 Lonc 7f H GD £8979
Total win prize-money £48010

Going (Turf): Sf: 0-1 GS: 0-3 Gd: 0-5 GF: 0-3 Fm: 0-0
Distance: 5f/6f: 0-0 **7f-8f: 1-5** 9f-13f: 0-11 14f+: 0-0
Track : LH: 0-8 **RH: 1-6** Tight: 0-3 Gall: 0-3
Aids: Bl: 0-1 Vi: 0-0 Tstrap: 0-0
Best Rating: 68 6/01 Gdwd 1m1f gd-fm

A winner on the Flat in France, he was bought to go jumping. Modest form on the level to date.

Dancing Lily

90(96) (36)**27**

4-y-o ch f Clantime-Sun Follower (Relkino)
J J Bridger Mrs J M Stamp

Placings:0005000/000020500**003-4630000000** **(5101)**
2001: 10^{4}SD, 6^{6}SD, 7^{3}SW, 7^{0}SW, 6^{0}GS, 7^{0}GF, 6^{0}GF, 8^{0}GF, 7^{0}GF, 7^{0}GF, 9^{0}GS

	Starts	1st	2nd	3rd	Win & Pl
Career Total (Turf)	23	0	1	0	538
Career Total (AW)	7	0	0	2	567

Going (Turf): Sf: 0-1 GS: 0-4 Gd: 0-4 GF: 0-13 Fm: 0-1
Distance: 5f/6f: 0-15 7f-8f: 0-12 9f-13f: 0-3 14f+: 0-0
Track : LH: 0-8 RH: 0-5 Tight: 0-8 Gall: 0-3
Aids: Bl: 0-0 Vi: 0-0 Tstrap: 0-0
Best Rating: 36 1/01 Ling 6f stand

Dancing Marmy

71 **1**

3-y-o b f Dancing Spree (USA)-Marmy (Midyan (USA))
K McAuliffe Arrow Mushroom And Pea Partnership

Placings:00000 **(3932)**
2001: 8^{0}S, 6^{0}G, 9^{0}F, 10^{0}S, 8^{0}G

	Starts	1st	2nd	3rd	Win & Pl
Career Total (Turf)	5	0	0	0	

Going (Turf): Sf: 0-2 GS: 0-0 Gd: 0-2 GF: 0-0 Fm: 0-1
Distance: 5f/6f: 0-1 7f-8f: 0-1 9f-13f: 0-3 14f+: 0-0
Track : LH: 0-2 RH: 0-1 Tight: 0-1 Gall: 0-0
Aids: Bl: 0-1 Vi: 0-0 Tstrap: 0-0
Best Rating: 1 6/01 Ling 1m1f firm

Dancing Mary

82(97) (40)**51**

4-y-o gr f Sri Pekan (USA)-Fontenoy (USA) (Lyphard's Wish (FR))
J S Wainwright (B Smart 8/3) R C Bond

Placings:5550/3035043**6**06054-02200 **(3228)**
2001: 16^{0}SD, 12^{2}SW, 12^{2}SW, 12^{0}SD, 12^{0}GF

	Starts	1st	2nd	3rd	Win & Pl
Career Total (Turf)	10	0	0	1	345
Career Total (AW)	12	0	2	2	2526

Going (Turf): Sf: 0-1 GS: 0-0 Gd: 0-5 GF: 0-4 Fm: 0-0
Distance: 5f/6f: 0-0 7f-8f: 0-3 9f-13f: 0-13 14f+: 0-6
Track : LH: 0-19 RH: 0-3 Tight: 0-7 Gall: 0-0

Aids: Bl: 0-1 Vi: 0-3 Tstrap: 0-0
Best Rating: 36 2/01 Sthl 1m4f slow

Dancing Milly

(76) (1)**22**
3-y-o ch f Dancing Spree (USA)-Maid Welcome (Mummy's Pet)
P J Makin Mrs Anna L Sanders

Placings:U60-000 **(3820)**
2001: 6^{0}G, 8^{0}GF, 6^{0}SD

	Starts	1st	2nd	3rd	Win & Pl
Career Total (Turf)	5	0	0	0	0
Career Total (AW)	1	0	0	0	

Going (Turf): Sf: 0-0 GS: 0-1 Gd: 0-1 GF: 0-2 Fm: 0-1
Distance: 5f/6f: 0-5 7f-8f: 0-0 9f-13f: 0-1 14f+: 0-0
Track : LH: 0-4 RH: 0-0 Tight: 0-1 Gall: 0-3
Aids: Bl: 0-1 Vi: 0-0 Tstrap: 0-0
Best Rating: 22 6/01 Wind 6f good

Dancing Mystery

110(111) (94+)**103**
7-y-o b g Beveled (USA)-Batchworth Dancer (Ballacashtal (CAN))
E A Wheeler Austin Stroud & Co Ltd

Placings:04/0000522500011/60063210004321**3**/63123 **1**051354224001**0**/0033510301401121 1-**4**505000030002142 **(5584a)**
2001: 5^{4}SD, 5^{5}GS, 5^{0}GF, 5^{5}GF, 5^{0}GF, 5^{0}G, 5^{0}GF, 5^{0}GS, 5^{3}G, 5^{0}G, 6^{0}GF, 5^{0}G, 5^{2}S, 5^{1}GS, 5^{4}GS, 5^{2}HY

	Starts	1st	2nd	3rd	Win & Pl
Career Total (Turf)	73	12	9	8	133562
Career Total (AW)	9	3	1	2	10099

100	10/01	Asct	5f	B(0-110)H	G-S	£21515
106	10/00	Donc	5f	B(0-100)H	SFT	£9657
104	10/00	NmkR	5f	B(0-105)H	SFT	£9458
91	9/00	NmkR	5f	C(0-95)H	SFT	£15236
90	9/00	Yarm	5f43y	C(0-90)H	G-F	£7572
82	8/00	Asct	5f	D(0-80)H	G-F	£6906
78	6/00	Sals	5f	D(0-85)H	G-F	£7150
68	11/99	Rdcr	5f	D(0-75)	G-S	£3703
67	7/99	Wwck	5f	E(0-70)H	G-F	£3088
78	6/99	Sthl	5f	E(0-75)H	STD	£2814
59	5/99	Ling	5f	E(0-70)H	G-F	£3125
56	9/98	Gdwd	5f	E(0-70)H	G-F	£4060
50	7/98	Wind	5f10y	E(0-70)H	GD	£2950
67	11/97	Ling	5f	E(0-70)H	STD	£2440
63	10/97	Sthl	6f	F	STD	£2277

Total win prize-money £102045

Going (Turf): Sf: 3-10 GS: 2-11 Gd: 1-22 **GF: 6-27** Fm: 0-3
Distance: **5f/6f: 15-82** 7f-8f: 0-0 9f-13f: 0-0 14f+: 0-0
Track : **LH: 3-21** RH: 1-11 Tight: 1-7 **Gall: 2-18**
Aids: **Bl: 2-13** Vi: 0-0 Tstrap: 0-0
Best Rating: 103 10/01 Lonc 5f heavy

Scored six times in 2000. He had struggled against the Handicapper this term but, shown some leniency, won a valuable handicap at Ascot next time. Equally effective over the minimum trip on turf and Fibresand, he handles fast ground but prefers some cut.

Dancing Penney (IRE)

(91) (53d)**29**
3-y-o b f General Monash (USA)-Penultimate Cress (IRE) (My Generation)
R M Flower (K A Ryan 3/2) K & D Computers Ltd

Placings:5001**2**21660**3430-41420**6656403060060 **(4603)**
2001: 7^{4}SD, 8^{1}SD, 8^{4}SW, 8^{2}SW, 7^{0}SD, 10^{6}SW, 6^{6}GF, 6^{5}S, 10^{6}GF, 7^{4}F, 5^{0}GF, 8^{3}GF, 8^{0}GF, 9^{6}F, 7^{0}GS, 5^{0}GF, 6^{6}F, 7^{0}SD

	Starts	1st	2nd	3rd	Win & Pl
Career Total (Turf)	20	2	1	1	5287
Career Total (AW)	12	1	2	2	3686

54	1/01	Sthl	1m	G	STD	£1974
58	8/00	Rdcr	6f	F	FRM	£2310
49	7/00	Catt	5f	G	G-F	£1890

Total win prize-money £6174

Going (Turf): Sf: 0-2 GS: 0-2 Gd: 0-3 **GF: 1-9 Fm: 1-4**
Distance: **5f/6f: 2-14** 7f-8f: 1-14 9f-13f: 0-4 14f+: 0-0
Track : **LH: 1-19** RH: 0-0 Tight: 0-9 Gall: 0-2
Aids: **Bl: 1-4** Vi: 0-0 Tstrap: 0-0
Best Rating: 54 1/01 Sthl 1m stand

A bad mover, she got off the mark on the back of a six-week lay-off in a five-furlong seller at Catterick and duly followed this up with a repeat performance in similar company at Redcar a month later. She has been fitted with blinkers and is suited to fast ground.

Dancing Phantom

109 **97**
6-y-o b g Darshaan-Dancing Prize (IRE) (Sadler's Wells (USA))
M W Easterby Bernard Bargh & John Walsh

Placings:2/210/004002001/020 **(5501)**
2001: 11^{0}G, 13^{2}HY, 12^{0}HY

	Starts	1st	2nd	3rd	Win & Pl
Career Total (Turf)	16	2	4	0	22739

97	10/99	Donc	1m4f	C(0-100)H	SFT	£10991
91	5/98	Sand	1m2f7y	D	G-S	£3696

Total win prize-money £14687

Going (Turf): **Sf: 1-5 GS: 1-3** Gd: 0-6 GF: 0-2 Fm: 0-0
Distance: 5f/6f: 0-0 7f-8f: 0-2 **9f-13f: 2-13** 14f+: 0-1
Track : LH: 1-11 RH: 1-4 Tight: 0-3 **Gall: 1-8**
Aids: Bl: 0-0 Vi: 0-0 Tstrap: 0-0
Best Rating: 97 10/01 Ayr 1m5f13y heavy

An in-and-out performer, he was given a fine tactical ride by Ray Cochrane when winning on soft ground at Doncaster in October 1999. He won over hurdles afterwards and has been lightly raced since, but he ran a cracker in heavy ground at Ayr in October.

Dancing Ridge (IRE)

108(99) (46)**46**
4-y-o b g Ridgewood Ben-May We Dance (IRE) (Dance Of Life (USA))
A Senior Michael Duffy

Placings:662060/000-00663053403 **(3821)**
2001: 8^{0}S, 7^{0}GF, 6^{0}GF, 5^{6}F, 5^{3}SD, 5^{0}GF, 5^{5}SD, 5^{3}S, 6^{4}SD, 6^{0}F, 5^{3}SD

	Starts	1st	2nd	3rd	Win & Pl
Career Total (Turf)	16	0	1	1	2386
Career Total (AW)	4	0	0	2	917

Going (Turf): **Sf: 0-5 GS: 0-2 Gd: 0-1 GF: 0-5 Fm: 0-3**
Distance: 5f/6f: 0-17 7f-8f: 0-2 9f-13f: 0-1 14f+: 0-0
Track : LH: 0-8 RH: 0-1 Tight: 0-3 Gall: 0-2
Aids: Bl: 0-0 Vi: 0-0 Tstrap: 0-0
Best Rating: 46 8/01 Wolv 5f stand

Dancing Tilly

69 **22**
3-y-o b f Dancing Spree (USA)-L'Ancressaan (Dalsaan)
W M Brisbourne The 'We Believe In Miracles' Partnership

Placings:000 **(2017)**
2001: 8^{0}GS, 11^{0}GF, 8^{0}GF

	Starts	1st	2nd	3rd	Win & Pl
Career Total (Turf)	3	0	0	0	

Going (Turf): **Sf: 0-0 GS: 0-1 Gd: 0-0 GF: 0-2 Fm: 0-0**
Distance: 5f/6f: 0-0 7f-8f: 0-1 9f-13f: 0-2 14f+: 0-0
Track : LH: 0-2 RH: 0-0 Tight: 0-0 Gall: 0-0
Aids: Bl: 0-0 Vi: 0-0 Tstrap: 0-0
Best Rating: 22 6/01 Hayd 1m30y gd-fm

Dancing Tsar

104(103) (75)**72**
3-y-o b c Salse (USA)-Lunda (IRE) (Soviet Star (USA))
G A Butler R J Styles

Placings:6-140401205 **(5416)**
2001: 8^{1}SD, 8^{4}SD, 11^{0}GF, 8^{4}GF, 7^{0}G, 9^{1}G, 9^{2}GF, 10^{0}G, 9^{5}SD

	Starts	1st	2nd	3rd	Win & Pl
Career Total (Turf)	7	1	1	0	6420
Career Total (AW)	3	1	0	0	2842

72	8/01	Leic	1m1f218y	E(0-70)H	GD	£4647
64	3/01	Ling	1m	D	STD	£2842

Total win prize-money £7490

Going (Turf): Sf: 0-1 GS: 0-0 **Gd: 1-3** GF: 0-3 Fm: 0-0
Distance: 5f/6f: 0-1 7f-8f: 1-3 9f-13f: 1-6 14f+: 0-0
Track : LH: 1-5 RH: 1-3 **Tight: 1-3** Gall: 0-1
Aids: Bl: 0-0 Vi: 0-0 Tstrap: 0-0
Best Rating: 75 4/01 Sthl 1m stand

Fair handicapper. Has won at a mile on Equitrack, but stays ten furlongs on turf.

Dancing Water

104 **91**
2-y-o gr c Halling (USA)-Gleaming Water (Kalaglow)
R F Johnson Houghton R Crutchley

Placings:40 **(5367)**
2001: 7^{4}GF, 8^{0}GS

	Starts	1st	2nd	3rd	Win & Pl
Career Total (Turf)	2	0	0	0	444

Going (Turf): **Sf: 0-0 GS: 0-1 Gd: 0-0 GF: 0-1 Fm: 0-0**
Distance: 5f/6f: 0-0 7f-8f: 0-2 9f-13f: 0-0 14f+: 0-0
Track : LH: 0-0 RH: 0-0 Tight: 0-0 Gall: 0-0
Aids: Bl: 0-0 Vi: 0-0 Tstrap: 0-0
Best Rating: 91 9/01 Newb 7f gd-fm

A half-brother to Paradise Waters, Faraway Waters and Prince Of Denial showed ability on his Newbury debut and will be suited by further next term.

Dandilum

95 **45**
4-y-o b g Dilum (USA)-Renira (Relkino)
J M Bradley The Dilum Partnership

Placings:23022/40200-000000000 **(3881)**
2001: 7^{0}G, 6^{0}S, 7^{0}GF, 8^{0}HD, 7^{0}GF, 6^{0}GF, 7^{0}GS, 7^{0}GF, 10^{0}G

	Starts	1st	2nd	3rd	Win & Pl
Career Total (Turf)	19	0	4	1	4574

Going (Turf): **Sf: 0-4 GS: 0-3 Gd: 0-4 GF: 0-6 Fm: 0-2**
Distance: 5f/6f: 0-4 7f-8f: 0-11 9f-13f: 0-4 14f+: 0-0
Track : LH: 0-4 RH: 0-2 Tight: 0-3 Gall: 0-1
Aids: Bl: 0-4 Vi: 0-0 Tstrap: 0-0
Best Rating: 55 5/01 Thsk 7f good

Moderate handicapper.

Dandoona

41
2-y-o b f Zafonic (USA)-Speedybird (IRE) (Danehill (USA))
J D Czerpak Z Kulaib

Placings:00 **(5603)**
2001: 5^{0}S, 7^{0}GS

	Starts	1st	2nd	3rd	Win & Pl
Career Total (Turf)	2	0	0	0	

Going (Turf): Sf: 0-1 GS: 0-1 Gd: 0-0 GF: 0-0 Fm: 0-0
Distance: 5f/6f: 0-1 7f-8f: 0-1 9f-13f: 0-0 14f+: 0-0
Track : LH: 0-0 RH: 0-0 Tight: 0-0 Gall: 0-0
Aids: Bl: 0-0 Vi: 0-0 Tstrap: 0-0
Best Rating: 41 10/01 Catt 5f soft

Dandoun

115 **111**

3-y-o b c Halling (USA)-Moneefa (Darshaan)
J L Dunlop H R H Prince Fahd Salman

Placings:11105 **(4197a)**
2001: 8^1S, 8^1G, 8^1GF, 8^0G, 10^5S

	Starts	1st	2nd	3rd	Win & Pl
Career Total (Turf)	5	3	0	0	35108

111	5/01	Kemp	1m	A	G-F	£17468
109	5/01	Donc	1m	B	GD	£9657
90	4/01	NmkR	1m	D	SFT	£6041

Total win prize-money £33168

Going (Turf): Sf: 1-2 GS: 0-0 **Gd: 1-2 GF: 1-1** Fm: 0-0
Distance: 5f/6f: 0-0 **7f-8f: 3-4** 9f-13f: 0-1 14f+: 0-0
Track : LH: 1-1 RH: 1-2 Tight: 0-0 **Gall: 1-2**
Aids: Bl: 0-0 Vi: 0-0 Tstrap: 0-0
Best Rating: 111 8/01 Deau 1m2f soft

The form of his Wood Ditton win is working out well and he put up an improved performance at Doncaster where he got the better of Aldebaran. He impressed even more when beaten the same rival again at Kempton, where he quickened significantly before coming off a true line, and won easily. Ran too freely in the St. James's Palace Stakes. Did not quite get home over ten furlongs on soft ground in August.

Dandy Regent

(79) (30)**42**

7-y-o b g Green Desert (USA)-Tahilla (Moorestyle)
John A Harris (J L Harris 17/6) Mrs A E Harris

Placings:0/00542/**2**13006000**005/6000**254450/10100400 350-00040 **(5681)**
2001: 7^0GF, 8^0G, 5^0GS, 8^4HY, 8^0S

	Starts	1st	2nd	3rd	Win & Pl
Career Total (Turf)	34	3	2	2	12629
Career Total (AW)	9	0	1	0	570

63	5/00	Thsk	7f	G	GD	£3045
49	3/00	Leic	7f9y	G	GD	£2033
73	4/98	Brig	6f209y	D(0-85)H	GD	£3582

Total win prize-money £8662

Going (Turf): Sf: 0-6 GS: 0-3 **Gd: 3-14** GF: 0-10 Fm: 0-1
Distance: 5f/6f: 0-10 **7f-8f: 3-32** 9f-13f: 0-1 14f+: 0-0
Track : **LH: 2-22** RH: 0-4 **Tight: 1-10** Gall: 0-3
Aids: Bl: 0-0 Vi: 0-0 Tstrap: 0-0
Best Rating: 42 10/01 Newc 1m heavy

Dane Dancing (IRE)

(95) (63)

3-y-o b f Danehill (USA)-My Ballerina (USA) (Sir Ivor)
A Berry T G Holdcroft

Placings:500030**050-4**1340 **(0262)**
2001: 7^4SD, 9^1SW, 8^3SD, 8^4SD, 8^0SD

	Starts	1st	2nd	3rd	Win & Pl
Career Total (Turf)	6	0	0	1	708
Career Total (AW)	8	1	0	1	3229

55	1/01	Wolv	1m1f79y	D	SLW	£2912

Total win prize-money £2912

Going (Turf): Sf: 0-3 GS: 0-0 Gd: 0-1 GF: 0-2 Fm: 0-0
Distance: 5f/6f: 0-3 7f-8f: 0-8 **9f-13f: 1-3** 14f+: 0-0
Track : **LH: 1-8** RH: 0-0 **Tight: 1-5** Gall: 0-0
Aids: **Bl: 1-6** Vi: 0-0 Tstrap: 0-0
Best Rating: 63 2/01 Sthl 1m stand

Dane Flyer (IRE)

99 **66**

3-y-o b c Danehill (USA)-Old Domesday Book (High Top)
M R Channon John Carey

Placings:000-0534500000 **(4736)**
2001: 6^0GF, 5^5GF, 6^3GF, 6^4F, 5^5GF, 7^0GF, 5^0G, 6^0GF, 7^0G, 6^0F

	Starts	1st	2nd	3rd	Win & Pl
Career Total (Turf)	13	0	0	1	1006

Going (Turf): Sf: 0-1 GS: 0-0 Gd: 0-3 GF: 0-7 Fm: 0-2
Distance: 5f/6f: 0-9 7f-8f: 0-4 9f-13f: 0-0 14f+: 0-0
Track : LH: 0-1 RH: 0-0 Tight: 0-0 Gall: 0-1
Aids: Bl: 0-0 Vi: 0-0 Tstrap: 0-1
Best Rating: 66 6/01 Gdwd 6f gd-fm

Modest handicapper on fast ground.

Danegold (IRE)

106 (61)**64**

9-y-o b g Danehill (USA)-Cistus (Sun Prince)
R T Phillips Graeme Love

Placings:03036/3**35**102212104001000/06250053000/3 000060/03410411160/10630513206000/04540004630 0-52353122104 **(4020)**
2001: 17^5GF, 16^2GF, 17^3GF, 17^5GF, 16^3GF, 18^1GF, 16^2GF, 17^2G, 16^1GF, 16^0GF, 16^4G

	Starts	1st	2nd	3rd	Win & Pl
Career Total (Turf)	87	12	8	10	81630
Career Total (AW)	3	0	0	2	1034

61	7/01	Newb	2m	D(0-85)H	G-F	£4498
55	7/01	Chep	2m2f	E(0-70)H	G-F	£2877
66	7/99	Asct	2m45y	D(0-85)H	G-F	£11235
68	3/99	Donc	2m2f	C(0-90)H	G-S	£6970
65	10/98	Asct	2m45y	C(0-90)H	SFT	£9145
58	10/98	Catt	1m7f177y	F(0-60)H	GD	£3408
58	9/98	Gdwd	2m	E(0-70)H	G-F	£3712
52	7/98	Yarm	2m	E(0-70)H	G-F	£3002
81	9/95	Sand	1m14y	D(0-80)H	G-S	£4591
81	6/95	Gdwd	1m2f	D(0-85)H	G-F	£3520
66	6/95	Bath	1m5y	E(0-70)H	GD	£3441
64	4/95	Ripn	1m	E(0-70)	G-F	£3046

Total win prize-money £59449

Going (Turf): Sf: 1-11 GS: 2-9 Gd: 2-29 **GF: 7-33** Fm: 0-5
Distance: 5f/6f: 0-0 7f-8f: 1-9 9f-13f: 3-34 **14f+: 8-47**
Track : LH: 6-52 RH: 6-31 **Tight: 6-29** Gall: 3-20
Aids: Bl: 0-0 **Vi: 4-34** Tstrap: 0-0
Best Rating: 63 7/01 Bath 2m1f34y good

A prolific scorer in modest staying handicaps over the years, he likes to come late and he has been running consistently well during this summer including wins at Chepstow and Newbury, but his style of racing means that he sometimes finds trouble when trying to get a run. He has won on easy ground but looks much better on fast.

Danehurst

114(108) (104+)**114+**

3-y-o b f Danehill (USA)-Miswaki Belle (USA) (Miswaki (USA))
Sir Mark Prescott Cheveley Park Stud

Placings:111-001011 **(5694)**
2001: 5^0G, 5^0Y, 5^1GF, 5^0HO, 6^1GS, 6^1S

	Starts	1st	2nd	3rd	Win & Pl
Career Total (Turf)	8	5	0	0	72199
Career Total (AW)	1	1	0	0	3406

103	11/01	Donc	6f	A	SFT	£15730
114	10/01	NmkR	6f	A	G-S	£16008
114	7/01	Ches	5f16y	A	G-F	£20300
109	10/00	Newb	5f34y	A	SFT	£16950
104	10/00	Wolv	5f	D	STD	£3406
72	6/00	Wwck	5f	D	G-F	£3211

Total win prize-money £75605

Going (Turf): Sf: 2-2 GS: 1-1 Gd: 0-1 **GF: 2-2** Fm: 0-0
Distance: **5f/6f: 6-9** 7f-8f: 0-0 9f-13f: 0-0 14f+: 0-0
Track : **LH: 3-3** RH: 0-0 **Tight: 2-2** Gall: 1-1
Aids: Bl: 0-0 Vi: 0-0 Tstrap: 0-0
Best Rating: 114 10/01 NmkR 6f gd-sft

She broke the two-year-old course record at Wolverhampton on her second start in 2000, before winning the Cornwallis Stakes in impressive style. Had excuses for her first two reverses of 2001 before winning Listed sprints at Chester in July, Newmarket in October and Doncaster in November. Effective on good to firm but goes well with cut in the ground.

Danelor (IRE)

102 **86**

3-y-o b c Danehill (USA)-Formulate (Reform)
E A L Dunlop Littleton Manor Racing

Placings:6413 **(3252)**
2001: 8^6G, 8^4GF, 7^1GF, 8^3GS

	Starts	1st	2nd	3rd	Win & Pl
Career Total (Turf)	4	1	0	1	8101

86	7/01	Hayd	7f30y	D	G-F	£4335

Total win prize-money £4336

Going (Turf): Sf: 0-0 GS: 0-0 Gd: 0-1 **GF: 1-2** Fm: 0-0
Distance: 5f/6f: 0-0 **7f-8f: 1-4** 9f-13f: 0-0 14f+: 0-0
Track : **LH: 1-1** RH: 0-1 Tight: 0-0 Gall: 0-0
Aids: Bl: 0-0 Vi: 0-0 Tstrap: 0-0
Best Rating: 86 7/01 Hayd 7f30y gd-fm

Showed his effectiveness on fast ground in three maidens, the last of which he won at Haydock in July 2001, before a good effort in a decent Newmarket handicap. Seems equally happy over seven furlongs and a mile.

Danemere (IRE)

78 **79**

2-y-o b f Danehill (USA)-Kentmere (FR) (Galetto (FR))
J W Hills Wyck Hall Stud

Placings:41 **(5175)**
2001: 5^4GF, 6^1HY

	Starts	1st	2nd	3rd	Win & Pl
Career Total (Turf)	2	1	0	0	4404

79	10/01	Wind	6f	D	HVY	£4078

Total win prize-money £4079

Going (Turf): Sf: 1-1 GS: 0-0 Gd: 0-0 GF: 0-1 Fm: 0-0
Distance: **5f/6f: 1-2** 7f-8f: 0-0 9f-13f: 0-0 14f+: 0-0
Track : LH: 0-0 RH: 0-0 Tight: 0-0 Gall: 0-0
Aids: Bl: 0-0 Vi: 0-0 Tstrap: 0-0
Best Rating: 79 10/01 Wind 6f heavy

A half-sister to middle-distance three-year-old winner Love Bitten. Bred to stay and appreciated the step up to six when scoring at Windsor. Has won on heavy ground.

Daneswood

89 **64**

2-y-o b g Be My Chief (USA)-Floria Tosca (Petong)
B R Millman J A Pickford

Placings:000240 **(5130)**
2001: 7^0F, 7^0GF, 5^0F, 6^2GF, 7^4GF, 7^0HY

	Starts	1st	2nd	3rd	Win & Pl
Career Total (Turf)	6	0	1	0	872

Going (Turf): Sf: 0-1 GS: 0-0 Gd: 0-0 GF: 0-3 Fm: 0-2
Distance: 5f/6f: 0-1 7f-8f: 0-5 9f-13f: 0-0 14f+: 0-0
Track : LH: 0-1 RH: 0-0 Tight: 0-0 Gall: 0-1
Aids: Bl: 0-2 Vi: 0-3 Tstrap: 0-0
Best Rating: 64 8/01 Ling 7f gd-fm

Dangerous Liaison

102(73) (40)**78**

2-y-o b g Great Commotion (USA)-Courtisane (Persepolis (FR))

C A Dwyer (B J Meehan 7/8) S B Components (international) Ltd

Placings:3314030011204002 **(5660)**

2001: 5^{3}S, 5^{3}GS, 5^{1}S, 5^{4}GF, 5^{0}GF, 5^{3}GF, 6^{0}GF, 5^{0}GF, 5^{1}GF, 5^{1}GF, 5^{2}F, 5^{0}G, 5^{4}GF, 5^{0}GS, 6^{0}SD, 5^{2}G

	Starts	1st	2nd	3rd	Win & Pl
Career Total (Turf)	15	3	2	3	13136
Career Total (AW)	1	0	0	0	

78	8/01	Bath	5f11y	F	G-F	£2296
78	7/01	Folk	5f	F	G-F	£2527
71	4/01	Nott	5f13y	E	SFT	£3094

Total win prize-money £7917

Going (Turf): Sf: 1-2 GS: 0-2 Gd: 0-2 **GF: 2-8** Fm: 0-1
Distance: **5f/6f: 3-16** 7f-8f: 0-0 9f-13f: 0-0 14f+: 0-0
Track : **LH: 1-4** RH: 0-1 Tight: 0-2 **Gall: 1-2**
Aids: **Bl: 2-5** Vi: 0-4 Tstrap: 0-0
Best Rating: 78 9/01 Nott 5f13y gd-fm

Plating-class sprinter, has won in blinkers.

Dangerously Good

92 **69**

3-y-o b c Shareef Dancer (USA)-Ecologically Kind (Alleged (USA))

D Morris W J Gredley

Placings:4 **(2207)**

2001: 7^{4}GS

	Starts	1st	2nd	3rd	Win & Pl
Career Total (Turf)	1	0	0	0	540

Going (Turf): Sf: 0-0 GS: 0-1 Gd: 0-0 GF: 0-0 Fm: 0-0
Distance: 5f/6f: 0-0 7f-8f: 0-1 9f-13f: 0-0 14f+: 0-0
Track : LH: 0-1 RH: 0-0 Tight: 0-0 Gall: 0-1
Aids: Bl: 0-0 Vi: 0-0 Tstrap: 0-0
Best Rating: 69 6/01 York 7f202y gd-sft

Daniavi (IRE)

99 **76**

3-y-o ch g Kris-Danishara (IRE) (Slew O'Gold (USA))

J A Glover (Sir Michael Stoute 27/6) P B A (skegness) Ltd

Placings:0-0400 **(5557)**

2001: 10^{0}GS, 11^{4}HD, 9^{0}S, 14^{0}S

	Starts	1st	2nd	3rd	Win & Pl
Career Total (Turf)	5	0	0	0	264

Going (Turf): Sf: 0-2 GS: 0-1 Gd: 0-1 GF: 0-0 Fm: 0-1
Distance: 5f/6f: 0-0 7f-8f: 0-1 9f-13f: 0-3 14f+: 0-1
Track : LH: 0-3 RH: 0-1 Tight: 0-2 Gall: 0-0
Aids: Bl: 0-1 Vi: 0-0 Tstrap: 0-0
Best Rating: 76 6/01 Bath 1m3f144y hard

Daniella Ridge (IRE)

92(96) (49)**33**

5-y-o b m Indian Ridge-Daniella Drive (USA) (Shelter Half (USA))

B G Powell A F Harrington

Placings:35/36330/000254040-46006 **(2234)**

2001: 7^{4}SW, 9^{6}F, 11^{0}GF, 12^{0}GF, 7^{6}GF

	Starts	1st	2nd	3rd	Win & Pl
Career Total (Turf)	17	0	1	4	3925
Career Total (AW)	4	0	0	0	0

Going (Turf): Sf: 0-0 GS: 0-4 Gd: 0-2 GF: 0-8 Fm: 0-3
Distance: 5f/6f: 0-2 7f-8f: 0-6 9f-13f: 0-13 14f+: 0-0
Track : LH: 0-9 RH: 0-5 Tight: 0-6 Gall: 0-4
Aids: Bl: 0-2 Vi: 0-0 Tstrap: 0-0
Best Rating: 37 1/01 Ling 7f slow

Danielle's Lad

109(72) (73)**85**

5-y-o b g Emarati (USA)-Cactus Road (FR) (Iron Duke (FR))

B Palling Mrs P K Chick

Placings:4310310/02036002500/040110406060-50400300105030004 **(5608)**

2001: 5^{5}S, 5^{0}GS, 6^{4}HY, 6^{0}G, 6^{0}GF, 6^{3}GF, 6^{0}GF, 5^{0}GF, 6^{1}G, 6^{0}G, 5^{5}GF, 6^{0}G, 7^{3}GF, 6^{0}G, 6^{0}GS, 6^{0}GS, 7^{4}GS

	Starts	1st	2nd	3rd	Win & Pl
Career Total (Turf)	45	5	2	5	40712
Career Total (AW)	2	0	0	0	

93	7/01	Chep	6f16y	C(0-90)	GD	£7458
95	5/00	Kemp	6f	C(0-90)H	SFT	£7637
91	5/00	Gdwd	6f	C(0-95)H	SFT	£7913
84	11/98	Donc	5f	D(0-85)H	SFT	£3751
77	8/98	Gdwd	5f	E	G-F	£3465

Total win prize-money £30227

Going (Turf): Sf: 3-13 GS: 0-4 Gd: 1-13 GF: 1-15 Fm: 0-0
Distance: **5f/6f: 4-42** 7f-8f: 1-5 9f-13f: 0-0 14f+: 0-0
Track : LH: 0-1 RH: 0-3 Tight: 0-1 Gall: 0-3
Aids: **Bl: 1-7** Vi: 0-0 Tstrap: 0-0
Best Rating: 93 7/01 Chep 6f16y good

Fairly useful sprint handicapper. Best when given an easy lead over six furlongs, he has come down the weights and took advantage to win at Chepstow in July. Best form on an easy surface but effective on faster.

Danish Decorum (IRE)

92 **74**

2-y-o ch c Danehill Dancer (IRE)-Dignified Air (FR) (Wolver Hollow)

M A Jarvis Peter J Stevenson

Placings:410 **(5368)**

2001: 6^{4}GF, 6^{1}GF, 8^{0}GS

	Starts	1st	2nd	3rd	Win & Pl
Career Total (Turf)	3	1	0	0	4621

74	7/01	Sals	6f212y	D	G-F	£4251

Total win prize-money £4251

Going (Turf): Sf: 0-0 GS: 0-1 Gd: 0-0 **GF: 1-2** Fm: 0-0
Distance: 5f/6f: 0-1 **7f-8f: 1-2** 9f-13f: 0-0 14f+: 0-0
Track : LH: 0-0 RH: 0-0 Tight: 0-0 Gall: 0-0
Aids: Bl: 0 0 Vi: 0 0 Tstrap: 0 0
Best Rating: 74 7/01 Sals 6f212y gd-fm

Justified his market support in ground that was plenty fast enough for him at Salisbury in July, but was disappointing when stepped up to a mile in a Newmarket nursery in October.

Danity Fair

81(89) (25)**25**

3-y-o b f Cool Jazz-Flute Royale (Horage)

R Bastiman J M Darraclough

Placings:400-000000 **(5374)**

2001: 6^{0}SD, 6^{0}SD, 6^{0}SW, 5^{0}SD, 5^{0}GS, 6^{0}G

	Starts	1st	2nd	3rd	Win & Pl
Career Total (Turf)	3	0	0	0	
Career Total (AW)	6	0	0	0	0

Going (Turf): Sf: 0-0 GS: 0-1 Gd: 0-1 GF: 0-1 Fm: 0-0
Distance: 5f/6f: 0-9 7f-8f: 0-0 9f-13f: 0-0 14f+: 0-0
Track : LH: 0-4 RH: 0-0 Tight: 0-0 Gall: 0-0
Aids: Bl: 0-0 Vi: 0-0 Tstrap: 0-0
Best Rating: 25 10/01 Rdcr 6f good

Danka

(88) (26?)

7-y-o gr g Petong-Angel Drummer (Dance In Time (CAN))

J C Fox S J V Construction

Placings:0604/0644/030003/0100004005/00-00005 **(4552)**

2001: 12^{0}SD, 12^{0}SD, 14^{0}HY, 12^{0}GF, 14^{5}SW

	Starts	1st	2nd	3rd	Win & Pl
Career Total (Turf)	11	0	0	0	260
Career Total (AW)	20	1	0	2	2777

47	3/99	Sthl	1m3f	G	STD	£1813

Total win prize-money £1814

Going (Turf): Sf: 0-3 GS: 0-1 Gd: 0-4 GF: 0-2 Fm: 0-1
Distance: 5f/6f: 0-1 7f-8f: 0-5 **9f-13f: 1-16** 14f+: 0-9
Track : **LH: 1-25** RH: 0-2 Tight: 0-17 Gall: 0-1
Aids: Bl: 0-0 Vi: 0-11 Tstrap: 0-0
Best Rating: 26 9/01 Wolv 1m6f166y slow

Danny Bell (IRE)

8-y-o b g Be My Native (USA)-Rhein Valley (IRE) (King's Lake (USA))

J G M O'Shea K W Bell

Placings:0 **(0617)**

2001: 12^{0}SD

	Starts	1st	2nd	3rd	Win & Pl
Career Total (Turf)	0	0	0	0	
Career Total (AW)	1	0	0	0	

Going (Turf): Sf: 0-0 GS: 0-0 Gd: 0-0 GF: 0-0 Fm: 0-0
Distance: 5f/6f: 0-0 7f-8f: 0-0 9f-13f: 0-1 14f+: 0-0
Track : LH: 0-1 RH: 0-0 Tight: 0-1 Gall: 0-0
Aids: Bl: 0-0 Vi: 0-0 Tstrap: 0-0

Danton (IRE)

99 **79**

3-y-o ch g Cadeaux Genereux-Royal Circle (Sadler's Wells (USA))

M Johnston The Bearbarians, Middleham

Placings:1300 **(5146)**

2001: 9^{1}G, 8^{3}GF, 11^{0}GF, 8^{0}G

	Starts	1st	2nd	3rd	Win & Pl
Career Total (Turf)	4	1	0	1	3537

74	8/01	Newc	1m1f9y	D	GD	£2884

Total win prize-money £2884

Going (Turf): Sf: 0-0 GS: 0-0 **Gd: 1-2** GF: 0-2 Fm: 0-0
Distance: 5f/6f: 0-0 7f-8f: 0-1 **9f-13f: 1-3** 14f+: 0-0
Track : **LH: 1-2** RH: 0-1 Tight: 0-0 **Gall: 1-2**
Aids: Bl: 0-0 Vi: 0-0 Tstrap: 0-0
Best Rating: 79 8/01 Bevl 1m100y gd-fm

Made a winning debut at Newcastle over nine furlongs. Bred to stay middle distances.

Danza Montana (USA)

82 **68**

3-y-o ch f Diesis-Valsora (IRE) (Tate Gallery (USA))

L M Cumani Mrs Belinda Strudwick

Placings:00-60 **(1466)**

2001: 8^{6}GS, 7^{0}GF

	Starts	1st	2nd	3rd	Win & Pl
Career Total (Turf)	4	0	0	0	0

Going (Turf): Sf: 0-0 GS: 0-1 Gd: 0-0 GF: 0-3 Fm: 0-0
Distance: 5f/6f: 0-2 7f-8f: 0-1 9f-13f: 0-1 14f+: 0-0
Track : LH: 0-0 RH: 0-1 Tight: 0-1 Gall: 0-0
Aids: Bl: 0-0 Vi: 0-0 Tstrap: 0-0
Best Rating: 45 4/01 Wind 1m67y gd-sft

Danzas

100(94) (41)**32**

7-y-o b g Polish Precedent (USA)-Dancing Rocks (Green Dancer (USA))

J M Bradley Martyn James, Pete Smith, Neil Jenkins

Placings:33300/0000400/00401262000004025/**606460 6**10326250466506-00100600000 **(5023)**

2001: 7^{0}F, 7^{0}GF, 6^{1}GF, 7^{0}GF, 5^{0}G, 7^{6}GS, 7^{0}G, 7^{0}GF, 7^{0}GF, 6^{0}GF, 7^{0}S

	Starts	1st	2nd	3rd	Win & Pl
Career Total (Turf)	54	3	5	4	12590
Career Total (AW)	9	0	0	0	0

42	6/01	Folk	6f	F	G-F	£2380
47	4/00	Brig	6f209y	F(0-70)H	G-S	£2256
44	5/99	Nott	1m54y	G(0-75)H	FRM	£1971

Total win prize-money £6608

Going (Turf): Sf: 0-9 **GS: 1-8** Gd: 0-10 **GF: 1-16 Fm: 1-11**
Distance: 5f/6f: 1-2 7f-8f: 1-36 9f-13f: 1-25 14f+: 0-0
Track : **LH: 2-41** RH: 0-7 Tight: 0-24 Gall: 0-2
Aids: **Bl: 2-40** Vi: 0-0 Tstrap: 0-0
Best Rating: 42 6/01 Folk 6f gd-fm

Danzig Flyer (IRE)

6-y-o b g Roi Danzig (USA)-Fenland Express (IRE) (Reasonable (FR))

M Mullineaux Mrs Renee Farrington-Kirkham

Placings:4243000/00000000/0000/00-0 **(4825)**

2001: 9^{0}G

	Starts	1st	2nd	3rd	Win & Pl
Career Total (Turf)	16	0	0	1	738
Career Total (AW)	6	0	1	0	627

Going (Turf): Sf: 0-1 GS: 0-3 Gd: 0-7 GF: 0-4 Fm: 0-1
Distance: 5f/6f: 0-0 7f-8f: 0-7 9f-13f: 0-14 14f+: 0-1
Track : LH: 0-16 RH: 0-2 Tight: 0-11 Gall: 0-0
Aids: Bl: 0-2 Vi: 0-1 Tstrap: 0-0

Danzigeuse (IRE)

89(50) **18**

4-y-o b f Zieten (USA)-Baliana (Midyan (USA))

C B B Booth A Kay

Placings:500/004000-00000 **(4060)**

2001: 7^{0}S, 8^{0}GF, 8^{0}GF, 7^{0}G, 5^{0}G

	Starts	1st	2nd	3rd	Win & Pl
Career Total (Turf)	13	0	0	0	278
Career Total (AW)	1	0	0	0	

Going (Turf): Sf: 0-1 GS: 0-1 Gd: 0-6 GF: 0-5 Fm: 0-0
Distance: 5f/6f: 0-5 7f-8f: 0-9 9f-13f: 0-0 14f+: 0-0
Track : LH: 0-4 RH: 0-3 Tight: 0-0 Gall: 0-5
Aids: Bl: 0-0 Vi: 0-0 Tstrap: 0-0
Best Rating: 18 8/01 Ripn 5f good

Daphne Odora

92 **50**

3-y-o b f Elmaamul (USA)-Heavenly Goddess (Soviet Star (USA))

B G Powell W G R Wightman

Placings:036005 **(5664)**

2001: 8^{0}GF, 9^{3}F, 9^{6}GF, 10^{0}GF, 8^{0}G, 8^{5}HY

	Starts	1st	2nd	3rd	Win & Pl
Career Total (Turf)	6	0	0	1	391

Going (Turf): Sf: 0-1 GS: 0-0 Gd: 0-1 GF: 0-3 Fm: 0-1
Distance: 5f/6f: 0-0 7f-8f: 0-0 9f-13f: 0-6 14f+: 0-0
Track : LH: 0-3 RH: 0-3 Tight: 0-4 Gall: 0-0
Aids: Bl: 0-0 Vi: 0-0 Tstrap: 0-0
Best Rating: 50 8/01 Folk 1m1f149y gd-fm

Daphne's Doll (IRE)

102(95) (38)**43**

6-y-o b m Polish Patriot (USA)-Helietta (Tyrnavos)

Dr J R J Naylor Mrs S P Elphick

Placings:4503**41/0**0403200**41/000**0030-**5030**050010 **(4624)**

2001: 12^{5}SW, **8**^{0}SD, **8**^{3}SD, **7**^{0}SD, 10^{0}GS, 8^{5}GF, 8^{0}GF, 7^{0}G, 7^{1}GF, 8^{0}GF

	Starts	1st	2nd	3rd	Win & Pl
Career Total (Turf)	21	1	1	3	4993
Career Total (AW)	12	2	0	1	5092

43	8/01	Ling	7f	F(0-65)H	G-F	£2534
50	12/99	Ling	1m2f	F(0-60)H	STD	£1882
65	12/98	Ling	7f	D	STD	£2697

Total win prize-money £7113

Going (Turf): Sf: 0-2 GS: 0-2 Gd: 0-7 **GF: 1-10** Fm: 0-0
Distance: 5f/6f: 0-2 **7f-8f: 2-18** 9f-13f: 1-13 14f+: 0-0
Track : **LH: 2-17** RH: 0-4 **Tight: 2-16** Gall: 0-2
Aids: Bl: 0-0 Vi: 0-0 Tstrap: 0-0
Best Rating: 43 8/01 Ling 7f gd-fm

Modest handicapper, likes Lingfield.

Dara Mac

80 **53**

2-y-o b c Presidium-Nishara (Nishapour (FR))

N Bycroft N Bycroft

Placings:600 **(4271)**

2001: 7^{6}F, 6^{0}G, 8^{0}GF

	Starts	1st	2nd	3rd	Win & Pl
Career Total (Turf)	3	0	0	0	0

Going (Turf): Sf: 0-0 GS: 0-0 Gd: 0-1 GF: 0-1 Fm: 0-1
Distance: 5f/6f: 0-1 7f-8f: 0-1 9f-13f: 0-1 14f+: 0-0
Track : LH: 0-0 RH: 0-1 Tight: 0-0 Gall: 0-0
Aids: Bl: 0-0 Vi: 0-0 Tstrap: 0-0
Best Rating: 53 8/01 Bevl 1m100y gd-fm

Daramsan (IRE)

86 **69**

4-y-o br g Doyoun-Daralaka (IRE) (The Minstrel (CAN))

Denys Smith B Batey

Placings:4P **(2604)**

2001: 12^{4}G, 8^{P}F

	Starts	1st	2nd	3rd	Win & Pl
Career Total (Turf)	2	0	0	0	336

Going (Turf): Sf: 0-0 GS: 0-0 Gd: 0-1 GF: 0-0 Fm: 0-1
Distance: 5f/6f: 0-0 7f-8f: 0-1 9f-13f: 0-1 14f+: 0-0
Track : LH: 0-1 RH: 0-1 Tight: 0-1 Gall: 0-1
Aids: Bl: 0-0 Vi: 0-0 Tstrap: 0-0
Best Rating: 69 6/01 Ripn 1m4f60y good

Darandala (IRE)

113 **104**

3-y-o b f Ashkalani (IRE)-Daralinsha (USA) (Empery (USA))

Sir Michael Stoute H H Aga Khan

Placings:15304 **(5691)**

2001: 10^{1}GF, 10^{5}GF, 12^{3}GF, 11^{0}G, 12^{4}S

	Starts	1st	2nd	3rd	Win & Pl
Career Total (Turf)	5	1	0	1	8306

78	7/01	Pont	1m2f6y	D	G-F	£3591

Total win prize-money £3591

Going (Turf): Sf: 0-1 GS: 0-0 Gd: 0-1 **GF: 1-3** Fm: 0-0
Distance: 5f/6f: 0-0 7f-8f: 0-0 **9f-13f: 1-5** 14f+: 0-0
Track : **LH: 1-5** RH: 0-0 Tight: 0-0 Gall: 0-3
Aids: Bl: 0-0 Vi: 0-0 Tstrap: 0-0
Best Rating: 104 8/01 Newb 1m4f5y gd-fm

Winner of a ten-furlong maiden at Pontefract on her debut, has run well in small Pattern events since. Stays 12 furlongs.

Darara Star (USA)

86 **78**

2-y-o b c Dariyoun (USA)-Tuviah (USA) (Eastern Echo (USA))

J Noseda Syd Belzberg

Placings:000 **(5056)**

2001: 8^{0}GF, 7^{0}G, 8^{0}S

	Starts	1st	2nd	3rd	Win & Pl
Career Total (Turf)	3	0	0	0	

Going (Turf): Sf: 0-1 GS: 0-0 Gd: 0-1 GF: 0-1 Fm: 0-0
Distance: 5f/6f: 0-0 7f-8f: 0-3 9f-13f: 0-0 14f+: 0-0
Track : LH: 0-0 RH: 0-0 Tight: 0-0 Gall: 0-0
Aids: Bl: 0-0 Vi: 0-0 Tstrap: 0-0
Best Rating: 78 9/01 NmkR 7f good

Darasim (IRE)

106 **103**

3-y-o b c Kahyasi-Dararita (IRE) (Halo (USA))

M Johnston (John M Oxx 24/6) Markus Graff

Placings:3101415 **(4978a)**

2001: 10^{3}HY, 13^{1}YS, 12^{0}G, 14^{1}GF, 13^{4}G, 14^{1}GS, 12^{5}HY

	Starts	1st	2nd	3rd	Win & Pl
Career Total (Turf)	7	3	0	1	41364

103	9/01	Donc	1m6f132y	B(0-105)H	G-S	£21645
88	6/01	Gowr	1m6f	(0-95)H	G-F	£10400
80	5/01	Wxfd	1m5f		Y-S	£4830

Total win prize-money £36875

Going (Turf): Sf: 0-2 **GS: 1-1** Gd: 0-2 **GF: 1-1** Fm: 0-0
Distance: 5f/6f: 0-0 7f-8f: 0-0 9f-13f: 1-4 **14f+: 2-3**
Track : **LH: 1-2** RH: 0-0 Tight: 0-1 **Gall: 1-1**
Aids: **Bl: 2-4** Vi: 0-0 Tstrap: 0-0
Best Rating: 103 9/01 Donc 1m6f132y gd-sft

Unraced as a juvenile, has won a maiden and a handicap from four runs in Ireland in 2001. Handles fast and easy ground. Now with Mark Johnston, he won a decent handicap at the backend. Needs blinkers.

Darcy Dancer

42

4-y-o b g Be My Chief (USA)-Little White Star (Mill Reef (USA))

D J S Cosgrove J P Racing

Placings:350/0000-0 **(0893)**

2001: 15^{0}HY

	Starts	1st	2nd	3rd	Win & Pl
Career Total (Turf)	8	0	0	1	543

Going (Turf): Sf: 0-2 GS: 0-0 Gd: 0-2 GF: 0-4 Fm: 0-0
Distance: 5f/6f: 0-0 7f-8f: 0-1 9f-13f: 0-5 14f+: 0-2
Track : LH: 0-4 RH: 0-1 Tight: 0-3 Gall: 0-0
Aids: Bl: 0-1 Vi: 0-0 Tstrap: 0-0

Dardanus

106(98) (74)**77d**

3-y-o ch g Komaite (USA)-Dance On A Cloud (USA) (Capote (USA))

R J White (E A L Dunlop 3/8) Littleton Manor Racing

Placings:4043-**13**010245000 **(4946)**

2001: 12^{1}SW, **12**^{3}SD, 10^{0}GS, 12^{1}GS, 11^{0}G, 12^{2}GF, 12^{4}G, 12^{5}GS, 10^{0}G, 10^{0}G, 12^{0}G

	Starts	1st	2nd	3rd	Win & Pl

Career Total (Turf)	13	1	1	1	7078
Career Total (AW)	2	1	0	1	3495

78 5/01 Pont 1m4f8y D(0-80)H G-S £4290
55 2/01 Sthl 1m4f D SLW £2912
Total win prize-money £7202

Going (Turf): Sf: 0-2 **GS: 1-4** Gd: 0-6 GF: 0-1 Fm: 0-0
Distance: 5f/6f: 0-0 7f-8f: 0-2 **9f-13f: 2-13** 14f+: 0-0
Track : **LH: 2-6** RH: 0-5 Tight: 0-4 Gall: 0-5
Aids: Bl: 0-0 **Vi: 1-4** Tstrap: 0-0
Best Rating: 78 5/01 Pont 1m4f8y gd-sft

A useful handicapper over a mile and a half. Not that consistent. Has won on good to soft ground.

Dare

109(107) (60)**60**
6-y-o b g Beveled (USA)-Run Amber Run (Run The Gantlet (USA))
P D Evans P D Evans

Placings:6/040000/000011115301000/3220003500304600050-101 **(5624)**
2001: 12[1]SD, 9[0]SD, 9[1]GS

	Starts	1st	2nd	3rd	Win & Pl
Career Total (Turf)	22	4	0	1	18426
Career Total (AW)	22	3	2	3	11194

60 11/01 Nott 1m1f213yE(0-70)H G-S £3304
58 10/01 Sthl 1m4f F(0-60) STD £2415
61 11/99 Sthl 1m G(0-60)H STD £1626
55 10/99 Leic 1m8y E(0-75)H SFT £8386
51 10/99 Sthl 1m G(0-75)H STD £2018
46 9/99 Sals 1m1f198yF(0-70)H HVY £2708
44 9/99 Haml 1m65y F(0-60)H SFT £2619
Total win prize-money £23080

Going (Turf): Sf: 3-5 GS: 1-5 Gd: 0-6 GF: 0-3 Fm: 0-3
Distance: 5f/6f: 0-1 7f-8f: 2-11 **9f-13f: 5-32** 14f+: 0-0
Track : **LH: 4-32** RH: 2-7 **Tight: 2-25** Gall: 0-0
Aids: Bl: 0-6 **Vi: 3-19** Tstrap: 0-0
Best Rating: 60 11/01 Nott 1m1f213y gd-sft

He enjoyed a purple patch both on the turf and on sand towards the end of 1999 before embarking on a long losing run. Successfully returned from injury to win over 12 furlongs on the Southwell Fibresand in October 2001, and supplemented that at Nottingham. Effective ten to 12 furlongs, suited by cut on turf.

Dargo

99(90) (64d)**47**
7-y-o b g Formidable (USA)-Mountain Memory (High Top)
D G Bridgwater The Rule Racing Syndicate

Placings:25/0/000204002342/13/6-3 **(2053)**
2001: 16[3]GF

	Starts	1st	2nd	3rd	Win & Pl
Career Total (Turf)	12	0	2	2	2718
Career Total (AW)	7	1	2	1	3837

77 2/99 Wolv 2m46y F(0-65)H STD £2284
Total win prize-money £2285

Going (Turf): Sf: 0-5 GS: 0-2 Gd: 0-3 GF: 0-2 Fm: 0-0
Distance: 5f/6f: 0-0 7f-8f: 0-4 9f-13f: 0-10 **14f+: 1-5**
Track : **LH: 1-12** RH: 0-6 **Tight: 1-12** Gall: 0-1
Aids: Bl: 0-0 Vi: 0-0 Tstrap: 0-0
Best Rating: 46 6/01 Rdcr 2m4y gd-fm

Fair staying handicapper, managed to win a two-mile handicap at Wolverhampton by a distance, though the opposition was modest, and he was unable to cope with a better field at the same track next time.

Daring Dancer

44
2-y-o ch f Bold Arrangement-Glenrock Dancer (IRE) (Glenstal (USA))
A Berry The 4 Man Trio

Placings:00 **(3842)**
2001: 6[0]GF, 6[0]G

	Starts	1st	2nd	3rd	Win & Pl
Career Total (Turf)	2	0	0	0	

Going (Turf): Sf: 0-0 GS: 0-0 Gd: 0-1 GF: 0-1 Fm: 0-0
Distance: 5f/6f: 0-2 7f-8f: 0-0 9f-13f: 0-0 14f+: 0-0
Track : LH: 0-0 RH: 0-0 Tight: 0-0 Gall: 0-0
Aids: Bl: 0-0 Vi: 0-0 Tstrap: 0-0

Daring Gamble

(92) (39)
4-y-o b f Barrys Gamble-Rachel Sharp (Daring March)
R A Fahey R A Fahey

Placings:560 **(0427)**
2001: 6[5]SD, 5[6]SD, 5[0]SD

	Starts	1st	2nd	3rd	Win & Pl
Career Total (Turf)	0	0	0	0	
Career Total (AW)	3	0	0	0	0

Going (Turf): Sf: 0-0 GS: 0-0 Gd: 0-0 GF: 0-0 Fm: 0-0
Distance: 5f/6f: 0-3 7f-8f: 0-0 9f-13f: 0-0 14f+: 0-0
Track : LH: 0-3 RH: 0-0 Tight: 0-3 Gall: 0-0
Aids: Bl: 0-0 Vi: 0-0 Tstrap: 0-0
Best Rating: 39 1/01 Wolv 6f stand

Darjingle

86 **60**
2-y-o b f Darshaan-Delightful Chime (IRE) (Alzao (USA))
T D Easterby Burton Agnes Bloodstock

Placings:060 **(3843)**
2001: 6[0]G, 7[6]GF, 7[0]G

	Starts	1st	2nd	3rd	Win & Pl
Career Total (Turf)	3	0	0	0	0

Going (Turf): Sf: 0-0 GS: 0-0 Gd: 0-2 GF: 0-1 Fm: 0-0
Distance: 5f/6f: 0 0 7f-8f: 0 3 9f-13f: 0-0 14f+: 0-0
Track : LH: 0-1 RH: 0-1 Tight: 0-0 Gall: 0-1
Aids: Bl: 0-0 Vi: 0-0 Tstrap: 0-0
Best Rating: 60 7/01 Bevl 7f100y gd-fm

Dark Before Dawn (USA)

96(87) (32)**44**
4-y-o ch g Sheikh Albadou-Garza (Kris)
A Berry A K Collins

Placings:006004003 **(5450)**
2001: 6[0]SD, 6[0]GS, 6[6]GF, 6[0]GF, 5[0]S, 6[4]G, 8[0]G, 9[0]HY, 8[3]HY

	Starts	1st	2nd	3rd	Win & Pl
Career Total (Turf)	8	0	0	1	410
Career Total (AW)	1	0	0	0	

Going (Turf): Sf: 0-3 GS: 0-1 Gd: 0-2 GF: 0-2 Fm: 0-0
Distance: 5f/6f: 0-6 7f-8f: 0-1 9f-13f: 0-2 14f+: 0-0
Track : LH: 0-3 RH: 0-1 Tight: 0-0 Gall: 0-1
Aids: Bl: 0-3 Vi: 0-0 Tstrap: 0-7
Best Rating: 51 5/01 Thsk 6f gd-fm

Dark Dolores

94(64) (14)**41**
3-y-o b f Inchinor-Pingin (Corvaro (USA))
C Weedon J D Knight & Mrs V A Knight

Placings:0000-020 **(4385)**
2001: 9[0]GF, 6[2]GF, 6[0]GF

	Starts	1st	2nd	3rd	Win & Pl
Career Total (Turf)	6	0	1	0	899
Career Total (AW)	1	0	0	0	

Going (Turf): Sf: 0-2 GS: 0-0 Gd: 0-0 GF: 0-4 Fm: 0-0
Distance: 5f/6f: 0-2 7f-8f: 0-3 9f-13f: 0-2 14f+: 0-0
Track : LH: 0-4 RH: 0-1 Tight: 0-2 Gall: 0-0
Aids: Bl: 0-0 Vi: 0-0 Tstrap: 0-0
Best Rating: 41 8/01 Brig 6f209y gd-fm

Dark Fairy

98(87) (45)**60**
3-y-o br f Tragic Role (USA)-Sharp Fairy (Sharpo)
M C Pipe (P W D'Arcy 24/9) D A Johnson

Placings:404061 **(4896)**
2001: 7[4]GF, 8[0]G, 8[4]G, 7[0]GF, 8[6]SD, 9[1]GS

	Starts	1st	2nd	3rd	Win & Pl
Career Total (Turf)	5	1	0	0	2044
Career Total (AW)	1	0	0	0	0

55 9/01 Leic 1m1f218yG G-S £2044
Total win prize-money £2044

Going (Turf): Sf: 0-0 **GS: 1-1** Gd: 0-2 GF: 0-2 Fm: 0-0
Distance: 5f/6f: 0-0 7f-8f: 0-2 **9f-13f: 1-4** 14f+: 0-0
Track : LH: 0-3 **RH: 1-1** Tight: 0-1 Gall: 0-0
Aids: Bl: 0-0 Vi: 0-0 Tstrap: 0-0
Best Rating: 60 8/01 Nott 1m54y good

Plating-class filly.

Dark Finish (IRE)

98 **58**
3-y-o b f Night Shift (USA)-Varnish (Final Straw)
W M Brisbourne Mrs C P Lees-Jones

Placings:4-550 **(4840)**
2001: 7[5]G, 7[5]F, 6[0]G

	Starts	1st	2nd	3rd	Win & Pl
Career Total (Turf)	4	0	0	0	357

Going (Turf): Sf: 0-1 GS: 0-0 Gd: 0-2 GF: 0-0 Fm: 0-1
Distance: 5f/6f: 0-1 7f-8f: 0-3 9f-13f: 0-0 14f+: 0-0
Track : LH: 0-2 RH: 0-0 Tight: 0-2 Gall: 0-0
Aids: Bl: 0-0 Vi: 0-0 Tstrap: 0-1
Best Rating: 56 7/01 Ches 7f122y good

Dark Flower (IRE)

94 **83**
2-y-o b f Sadler's Wells (USA)-Marino Casino (USA) (Alleged (USA))
B W Hills C Wright,Mrs Corbett,R A N Bonnycastle

Placings:344 **(5484)**
2001: 8[3]GF, 6[4]GS, 8[4]HY

	Starts	1st	2nd	3rd	Win & Pl
Career Total (Turf)	3	0	0	1	1860

Going (Turf): Sf: 0-1 GS: 0-1 Gd: 0-0 GF: 0-1 Fm: 0-0
Distance: 5f/6f: 0-0 7f-8f: 0-3 9f-13f: 0-0 14f+: 0-0
Track : LH: 0-1 RH: 0-0 Tight: 0-0 Gall: 0-1
Aids: Bl: 0-0 Vi: 0-0 Tstrap: 0-0
Best Rating: 83 9/01 Donc 1m gd-fm

Dark Shadows

98 **58**
6-y-o b g Machiavellian (USA)-Instant Desire (USA) (Northern Dancer)
W Storey D O Cremin

Placings:536310-00200 **(5663)**
2001: 12[0]S, 12[0]GF, 14[2]G, 13[0]S, 12[0]G

	Starts	1st	2nd	3rd	Win & Pl
Career Total (Turf)	11	1	1	2	5724

62 8/00 Ripn 1m4f60y E(0-70)H GD £2941
Total win prize-money £2941

Going (Turf): Sf: 0-4 GS: 0-1 **Gd: 1-3** GF: 0-3 Fm: 0-0

Distance: 5f/6f: 0-0 7f-8f: 0-0 9f-13f: 1-8 14f+: 0-3
Track : LH: 0-7 RH: 1-3 Tight: 1-7 Gall: 0-3
Aids: Bl: 0-0 Vi: 0-0 Tstrap: 0-0
Best Rating: 58 10/01 Rdcr 1m6f19y good

Fair handicapper. Acts on good ground.

Dark Society

96 60

3-y-o b g Imp Society (USA)-No Candles Tonight (Star Appeal)
P W Harris Skeltools Ltd

Placings:400-0000 (4735)
2001: 9^{0}G, 9^{0}G, 10^{0}GF, 10^{0}F

	Starts	1st	2nd	3rd	Win & Pl
Career Total (Turf)	7	0	0	0	258

Going (Turf): Sf: 0-2 GS: 0-1 Gd: 0-2 GF: 0-1 Fm: 0-1
Distance: 5f/6f: 0-2 7f-8f: 0-1 9f-13f: 0-4 14f+: 0-0
Track : LH: 0-4 RH: 0-1 Tight: 0-1 Gall: 0-0
Aids: Bl: 0-0 Vi: 0-2 Tstrap: 0-0
Best Rating: 68 8/01 Leic 1m1f218y good

Dark Sorcerer

100 89

2-y-o b c So Factual (USA)-Pipistrelle (Shareef Dancer (USA))
A P Jarvis The Aston Partnership

Placings:32016305 (5227)
2001: 5^{3}GF, 6^{2}GF, 6^{0}GF, 6^{1}G, 6^{6}GF, 7^{3}G, 6^{0}G, 6^{5}S

	Starts	1st	2nd	3rd	Win & Pl
Career Total (Turf)	8	1	1	2	20232

89	7/01	York	6f	E	GD	£8255

Total win prize-money £8255

Going (Turf): Sf: 0-1 GS: 0-0 Gd: 1-3 GF: 0-4 Fm: 0-0
Distance: 5f/6f: 1-6 7f-8f: 0-2 9f-13f: 0-0 14f+: 0-0
Track : LH: 0-2 RH: 0-0 Tight: 0-1 Gall: 0-1
Aids: Bl: 0-0 Vi: 0-0 Tstrap: 0-0
Best Rating: 89 9/01 Ayr 7f50y good

Highly tried on his second and third starts before winning a York maiden in workmanlike style. Suited by six furlongs, again proved he was not up to Group class at Goodwood, but has run with credit in some decent events since. Sold to race in America.

Dark Storm

(69) (26)

2-y-o gr g Terimon-Norstock (Norwick (USA))
J White The Norstock Partnership

Placings:0 (5665)
2001: 6^{0}HY

	Starts	1st	2nd	3rd	Win & Pl
Career Total (Turf)	1	0	0	0	

Going (Turf): Sf: 0-1 GS: 0-0 Gd: 0-0 GF: 0-0 Fm: 0-0
Distance: 5f/6f: 0-1 7f-8f: 0-0 9f-13f: 0-0 14f+: 0-0
Track : LH: 0-0 RH: 0-0 Tight: 0-0 Gall: 0-0
Aids: Bl: 0-0 Vi: 0-0 Tstrap: 0-0

Dark Trojan (IRE)

95 96

5-y-o b h Darshaan-Trojan Miss (Troy)
P Hughes Exors Of The Late D McKey

Placings:223225/3-305 (5434a)
2001: 14^{3}GY, 20^{0}GF, 16^{5}S

	Starts	1st	2nd	3rd	Win & Pl
Career Total (Turf)	10	0	4	3	11696

Going (Turf): Sf: 0-4 GS: 0-1 Gd: 0-1 GF: 0-2 Fm: 0-0
Distance: 5f/6f: 0-0 7f-8f: 0-0 9f-13f: 0-6 14f+: 0-3
Track : LH: 0-4 RH: 0-3 Tight: 0-0 Gall: 0-4
Aids: Bl: 0-0 Vi: 0-0 Tstrap: 0-0
Best Rating: 79 6/01 Asct 2m4f gd-fm

Useful form when with Sir Michael Stoute, he has shown fair form in staying handicaps since joining his current yard.

Dark Victor (IRE)

102(102) (72+)67

5-y-o b g Cadeaux Genereux-Dimmer (Kalaglow)
D Shaw J C Fretwell

Placings:40501066233110-04060110652 (5640)
2001: 8^{0}SD, 8^{4}S, 8^{0}GS, 8^{6}SD, 9^{0}G, 9^{1}G, 8^{1}GS, 10^{0}G, 8^{6}GS, 10^{5}S, 13^{2}G

	Starts	1st	2nd	3rd	Win & Pl
Career Total (Turf)	16	3	2	1	12630
Career Total (AW)	9	2	0	1	4704

67	10/01	Newc	1m3y	E(0-70)H	G-S	£3171
58	9/01	Bevl	1m1f207y	F(0-60)H	GD	£3097
72	12/00	Sthl	1m	G(0-60)	STD	£1932
57	12/00	Wolv	1m100y	F(0-60)H	STD	£2282
53	4/00	Donc	1m2f60y	E(0-70)H	G-S	£3926

Total win prize-money £14409

Going (Turf): Sf: 0-7 GS: 2-4 Gd: 1-4 GF: 0-1 Fm: 0-0
Distance: 5f/6f: 0-1 7f-8f: 1-5 9f-13f: 4-18 14f+: 0-1
Track : LH: 3-18 RH: 1-4 Tight: 1-10 Gall: 1-3
Aids: Bl: 2-9 Vi: 2-5 Tstrap: 0-0
Best Rating: 67 10/01 Newc 1m3y gd-sft

Found his form in the autumn of 2001 with back-to-back wins at Beverley and Newcastle, but was disappointing after that. Effective at a mile or ten furlongs, but appeared suited by the step up to 14 furlongs at Catterick in November. He likes soft ground and acts well on Fibresand.

Darwell's Folly (USA)

68(102) (38)20

6-y-o ch g Blushing John (USA)-Hispanolia (FR) (Kris)
P Monteith (M Johnston 16/3) G M Cowan

Placings:160/11000/01020010/3000000-00200 (4440)
2001: 9^{0}SW, 8^{0}SD, 11^{2}SD, 12^{0}SD, 11^{0}G

	Starts	1st	2nd	3rd	Win & Pl
Career Total (Turf)	18	2	1	1	8402
Career Total (AW)	10	3	1	0	9504

56	10/99	Wolv	7f	F	STD	£1989
66	9/99	Leic	7f9y	E(0-70)H	FRM	£3756
87	3/98	Wolv	7f	D(0-85)H	STD	£3623
82	2/98	Wolv	6f	D(0-85)H	STD	£3387
79	7/97	Newc	6f	E	G-F	£3230

Total win prize-money £15986

Going (Turf): Sf: 0-5 GS: 0-2 Gd: 0-7 GF: 1-3 Fm: 1-1
Distance: 5f/6f: 2-2 7f-8f: 3-14 9f-13f: 0-12 14f+: 0-0
Track : LH: 3-16 RH: 0-2 Tight: 3-8 Gall: 0-4
Aids: Bl: 1-2 Vi: 1-12 Tstrap: 2-13
Best Rating: 38 2/01 Sthl 1m3f stand

Moderate handicapper on sand.

Darwin (IRE)

101 98

3-y-o b c Danehill (USA)-Armorique (IRE) (Top Ville)
A P O'Brien M Tabor & Mrs John Magnier

Placings:164-0150000 (4113)
2001: 8^{0}G, 7^{1}GF, 7^{5}G, 8^{0}G, 10^{0}GF, 8^{0}GF, 10^{0}G

	Starts	1st	2nd	3rd	Win & Pl
Career Total (Turf)	10	2	0	0	28875

93	5/01	Tipp	7f		G-F	£9750
100	5/00	Curr	6f		G-Y	£6900

Total win prize-money £16650

Going (Turf): Sf: 0-1 GS: 0-0 Gd: 0-4 GF: 1-3 Fm: 0-0
Distance: 5f/6f: 1-1 7f-8f: 1-7 9f-13f: 0-2 14f+: 0-0
Track : LH: 0-2 RH: 0-3 Tight: 0-0 Gall: 0-3
Aids: Bl: 0-0 Vi: 0-0 Tstrap: 0-0
Best Rating: 98 5/01 NmkR 1m good

Very impressive on his debut in 2000, he reportedly finished lame when odds-on in the Group One National Stakes at the Curragh nearly four months later, and did too much too early on heavy ground when well beaten fourth to Dilshaan in a Group One at Doncaster in October. Disappointing this term but did land a minor event at Tipperary.

Darwin Tower

91(78) (28)44

3-y-o gr g Bin Ajwaad (IRE)-Floria Tosca (Petong)
B W Murray B Murray

Placings:000000220-00300000 (5254)
2001: 8^{0}S, 8^{0}S, 7^{3}G, 7^{0}GF, 7^{0}GF, 7^{0}GF, 7^{0}GS, 6^{0}S

	Starts	1st	2nd	3rd	Win & Pl
Career Total (Turf)	16	0	2	1	1890
Career Total (AW)	1	0	0	0	

Going (Turf): Sf: 0-6 GS: 0-2 Gd: 0-3 GF: 0-4 Fm: 0-1
Distance: 5f/6f: 0-7 7f-8f: 0-9 9f-13f: 0-1 14f+: 0-0
Track : LH: 0-7 RH: 0-1 Tight: 0-4 Gall: 0-0
Aids: Bl: 0-3 Vi: 0-1 Tstrap: 0-0
Best Rating: 49 6/01 Hayd 7f30y good

Daryabad (IRE)

100(97) (69)59

9-y-o b g Thatching-Dayanata (Shirley Heights)
N A Graham The Three Amigos

Placings:01/10341/000051000/50/00012346042/000116/00301313360-426100 (5145)
2001: 7^{4}G, 8^{2}GF, 7^{6}F, 8^{1}G, 8^{0}G, 7^{0}G

	Starts	1st	2nd	3rd	Win & Pl
Career Total (Turf)	42	8	2	6	38250
Career Total (AW)	11	2	1	0	6173

59	6/01	Leic	1m9y	F(0-65)H	GD	£3835
55	8/00	Yarm	7f3y	D(0-80)H	G-F	£5265
46	7/00	Yarm	7f3y	E(0-70)H	GD	£3984
69	11/99	Ling	7f	E(0-75)H	STD	£2528
59	10/99	Ling	7f	E(0-65)	STD	£2889
64	7/98	Catt	7f	F(0-65)	GD	£2318
73	8/96	Rdcr	7f	D(0-80)H	G-F	£3810
	10/95	Leop	1m	(0-105)H	GD	£6850
	10/94	Naas	6f		Y-S	£3767

Total win prize-money £35248

Going (Turf): Sf: 0-3 GS: 0-3 Gd: 2-14 GF: 2-13 Fm: 0-1
Distance: 5f/6f: 0-0 7f-8f: 5-36 9f-13f: 1-10 14f+: 0-0
Track : LH: 3-16 RH: 0-6 Tight: 3-11 Gall: 0-5
Aids: Bl: 6-27 Vi: 0-0 Tstrap: 0-0
Best Rating: 59 6/01 Leic 1m9y good

He was in good heart earlier this term and won a moderate race at Leicester off a mark of 57 in June, but below par after suffering an injury.

Dash For Glory

81 58

2-y-o ch c Bluegrass Prince (IRE)-Rekindled Flame (IRE) (King's Lake (USA))
M Kettle Good Connection Ii

Placings:00 (5175)
2001: 6^{0}GF, 6^{0}HY

	Starts	1st	2nd	3rd	Win & Pl
Career Total (Turf)	2	0	0	0	

Going (Turf): Sf: 0-1 GS: 0-0 Gd: 0-0 GF: 0-1 Fm: 0-0

Distance: 5f/6f: 0-2 7f-8f: 0-0 9f-13f: 0-0 14f+: 0-0
Track : LH: 0-0 RH: 0-0 Tight: 0-0 Gall: 0-0
Aids: Bl: 0-0 Vi: 0-0 Tstrap: 0-0
Best Rating: 58 9/01 Ling 6f gd-fm

Dash For Gold

88 **79**
2-y-o br f Highest Honor (FR)-Dashing Water (Dashing Blade)
D R C Elsworth J C Smith

Placings:055 (5468)
2001: 6^{0}GF, 8^{5}GS, 7^{5}S

	Starts	1st	2nd	3rd	Win & Pl
Career Total (Turf)	3	0	0	0	0

Going (Turf): Sf: 0-1 GS: 0-1 Gd: 0-0 GF: 0-1 Fm: 0-0
Distance: 5f/6f: 0-0 7f-8f: 0-3 9f-13f: 0-0 14f+: 0-0
Track : LH: 0-1 RH: 0-0 Tight: 0-0 Gall: 0-0
Aids: Bl: 0-0 Vi: 0-0 Tstrap: 0-0
Best Rating: 79 9/01 Sals 6f212y gd-fm

Dash Of Magic

93 **50+**
3-y-o b f Magic Ring (IRE)-Praglia (IRE) (Darshaan)
J G Given 21st Century Racing

Placings:6-3020 (2192)
2001: 7^{3}GS, 8^{0}G, 7^{2}GF, 9^{0}G

	Starts	1st	2nd	3rd	Win & Pl
Career Total (Turf)	5	0	1	1	1083

Going (Turf): Sf: 0-1 GS: 0-1 Gd: 0-2 GF: 0-1 Fm: 0-0
Distance: 5f/6f: 0-0 7f-8f: 0-3 9f-13f: 0-2 14f+: 0-0
Track : LH: 0-2 RH: 0-1 Tight: 0-0 Gall: 0-0
Aids: Bl: 0-0 Vi: 0-0 Tstrap: 0-0
Best Rating: 50 6/01 Bevl 7f100y gd-fm

Dasharan (IRE)

78 **5**
8-y-o b g Shahrastani (USA)-Delsy (FR) (Abdos)
Ian Williams Mr & Mrs John Poynton

Placings:160/365302/0/0 (2040)
2001: 17^{0}GF

	Starts	1st	2nd	3rd	Win & Pl
Career Total (Turf)	11	1	1	2	1465

Going (Turf): Sf: 0-0 GS: 0-0 Gd: 0-5 GF: 0-1 Fm: 0-0
Distance: 5f/6f: 0-0 7f-8f: 0-0 **9f-13f: 1-5** 14f+: 0-6
Track : LH: 0-7 **RH: 1-4** Tight: 0-0 Gall: 0-0
Aids: Bl: 0-0 Vi: 0-0 Tstrap: 0-0
Best Rating: 5 6/01 Pont 2m1f22y gd-fm

Dashing Beau (USA)

81 **66**
2-y-o b g Beau Genius (CAN)-Fullocherries (USA) (Full Out (USA))
T D Barron J Falvey & G Williamson

Placings:500 (4423)
2001: 6^{5}GS, 6^{0}G, 6^{0}GF

	Starts	1st	2nd	3rd	Win & Pl
Career Total (Turf)	3	0	0	0	0

Going (Turf): Sf: 0-0 GS: 0-1 Gd: 0-1 GF: 0-1 Fm: 0-0
Distance: 5f/6f: 0-3 7f-8f: 0-0 9f-13f: 0-0 14f+: 0-0
Track : LH: 0-0 RH: 0-0 Tight: 0-0 Gall: 0-0
Aids: Bl: 0-0 Vi: 0-0 Tstrap: 0-0
Best Rating: 66 7/01 Ayr 6f gd-sft

Dashing Blue

93 **64**
8-y-o ch g Dashing Blade-Blubella (Balidar)
I A Balding Mrs Duncan Allen

Placings:242141/13064032/02052133121/5040305330 3/02134353600/060000-000 (4718)
2001: 5^{0}G, 5^{0}HY, 5^{0}G

	Starts	1st	2nd	3rd	Win & Pl
Career Total (Turf)	56	7	7	11	151603

103	6/99	Sand	5f6y	C	GD	£6108
108	10/97	NmkR	5f	A	GD	£10471
111	9/97	Donc	5f140y	B(0-110)H	G-F	£18128
103	7/97	York	5f	C(0-100)H	GD	£7895
94	4/96	Sand	5f6y	B(0-100)H	GD	£7565
91	10/95	York	6f	C	GD	£6472
85	8/95	Ripn	6f	D	G-F	£4416

Total win prize-money £61056

Going (Turf): Sf: 0-1 GS: 0-8 **Gd: 5-26** GF: 2-19 Fm: 0-2
Distance: **5f/6f: 7-54** 7f-8f: 0-2 9f-13f: 0-0 14f+: 0-0
Track : LH: 0-3 RH: 0-0 Tight: 0-2 Gall: 0-1
Aids: Bl: 0-1 Vi: 0-0 Tstrap: 0-0
Best Rating: 59 9/01 Epsm 5f good

Difficult-to-win-with handicapper over sprint distances. Keeps decent company. Acts on a sound surface.

Dashoski (IRE)

78 **47**
4-y-o b f Petoski-Dashing March (Daring March)
M S Saunders M S Saunders

Placings:000 (5041)
2001: 8^{0}G, 11^{0}HD, 10^{0}G

	Starts	1st	2nd	3rd	Win & Pl
Career Total (Turf)	3	0	0	0	

Going (Turf): Sf: 0-0 GS: 0-0 Gd: 0-2 GF: 0-0 Fm: 0-1
Distance: 5f/6f: 0-0 7f-8f: 0-0 9f-13f: 0-3 14f+: 0-0
Track : LH: 0-2 RH: 0-0 Tight: 0-2 Gall: 0-0
Aids: Bl: 0-0 Vi: 0-0 Tstrap: 0-0
Best Rating: 47 5/01 Wwck 1m22y good

Datin Star

86(95) (36)**48d**
3-y-o ch f Inchinor-Halimah (Be My Guest (USA))
D J Coakley David F Wilson

Placings:60640020-05630006 (2169)
2001: 6^{0}SD, 6^{5}SW, 8^{6}SD, 5^{3}SD, 6^{0}SD, 5^{0}G, 6^{0}F, 6^{8}SD

	Starts	1st	2nd	3rd	Win & Pl
Career Total (Turf)	8	0	0	0	214
Career Total (AW)	8	0	1	1	895

Going (Turf): Sf: 0-1 GS: 0-0 Gd: 0-2 GF: 0-3 Fm: 0-2
Distance: 5f/6f: 0-9 7f-8f: 0-7 9f-13f: 0-0 14f+: 0-0
Track : LH: 0-14 RH: 0-0 Tight: 0-5 Gall: 0-1
Aids: Bl: 0-0 Vi: 0-0 Tstrap: 0-0
Best Rating: 36 3/01 Wolv 5f stand

Daunted (IRE)

82(105) (57)**36**
5-y-o b g Priolo (USA)-Dauntess (Formidable (USA))
G L Moore David Allen

Placings:0000213211/2235030345064000/02054-1434440350 (3263)
2001: 10^{1}SD, 9^{4}SD, 10^{3}SD, 12^{4}SW, 12^{4}SD, 10^{4}SD, 11^{0}GS, 11^{3}GF, 11^{5}SD, 12^{0}GS

	Starts	1st	2nd	3rd	Win & Pl
Career Total (Turf)	17	0	1	1	1534
Career Total (AW)	24	4	4	5	18949

52	1/01	Ling	1m2f	E	STD	£2723
83	1/99	Ling	1m	E	STD	£2608
84	12/98	Ling	1m	D	STD	£2736
80	11/98	Ling	1m	D	STD	£3236

Total win prize-money £11303

Going (Turf): Sf: 0-4 GS: 0-5 Gd: 0-3 GF: 0-5 Fm: 0-0
Distance: 5f/6f: 0-2 **7f-8f: 3-11** 9f-13f: 1-28 14f+: 0-0
Track : **LH: 4-29** RH: 0-4 **Tight: 4-29** Gall: 0-0
Aids: **Bl: 4-37** Vi: 0-0 Tstrap: 0-0
Best Rating: 57 3/01 Ling 1m4f stand

Very much suited by a mile on Equitrack, his turf form has been a bit disappointing.

Davey's Panacea (IRE)

(100) (45)**52**
4-y-o ch f Paris House-Pampoushka (Pampabird)
R D Wylie Daveys Chemists (Ipool) Ltd

Placings:2533300060-035 (0301)
2001: 5^{0}SD, 5^{3}SD, 5^{5}SD

	Starts	1st	2nd	3rd	Win & Pl
Career Total (Turf)	7	0	1	3	2315
Career Total (AW)	6	0	0	1	351

Going (Turf): Sf: 0-0 GS: 0-0 Gd: 0-1 GF: 0-6 Fm: 0-0
Distance: 5f/6f: 0-12 7f-8f: 0-1 9f-13f: 0-0 14f+: 0-0
Track : LH: 0-4 RH: 0-1 Tight: 0-4 Gall: 0-1
Aids: Bl: 0-4 Vi: 0-0 Tstrap: 0-0
Best Rating: 45 1/01 Sthl 5f stand

Daveysfire

84 **32**
3-y-o b f Gildoran-Doubtfire (Jalmood (USA))
A R Dicken J A Davidson

Placings:630-000 (3948)
2001: 6^{0}F, 6^{0}GF, 6^{0}GS

	Starts	1st	2nd	3rd	Win & Pl
Career Total (Turf)	6	0	0	1	309

Going (Turf): Sf: 0-1 GS: 0-1 Gd: 0-1 GF: 0-2 Fm: 0-1
Distance: 5f/6f: 0-3 7f-8f: 0-3 9f-13f: 0-0 14f+: 0-0
Track : LH: 0-1 RH: 0-0 Tight: 0-0 Gall: 0-0
Aids: Bl: 0-0 Vi: 0-0 Tstrap: 0-0
Best Rating: 32 6/01 Newc 6f firm

David Wynne

94(100) (59)**40**
3-y-o b c Dolphin Street (FR)-Statuette (Statoblest)
D Shaw Swann Racing Ltd

Placings:000-050000000 (3752)
2001: 5^{0}SD, 5^{5}SD, 5^{0}SD, 5^{0}SD, 5^{0}G, 5^{0}GF, 5^{0}G, 7^{0}F, 7^{0}GS

	Starts	1st	2nd	3rd	Win & Pl
Career Total (Turf)	6	0	0	0	
Career Total (AW)	6	0	0	0	0

Going (Turf): Sf: 0-0 GS: 0-1 Gd: 0-3 GF: 0-1 Fm: 0-1
Distance: 5f/6f: 0-9 7f-8f: 0-3 9f-13f: 0-0 14f+: 0-0
Track : LH: 0-6 RH: 0-0 Tight: 0-4 Gall: 0-0
Aids: Bl: 0-1 Vi: 0-0 Tstrap: 0-0
Best Rating: 59 3/01 Sthl 5f stand

Davide D'Donatello

(85) (23)**63**
4-y-o b h Robellino (USA)-Thimblerigger (Sharpen Up)
John J Foley (J W Mullins 10/1) Robert M Foley

Placings:20050/00000000-500 (3124a)
2001: 10^{5}SD, 12^{0}GF, 13^{0}GY

	Starts	1st	2nd	3rd	Win & Pl
Career Total (Turf)	14	0	1	0	960
Career Total (AW)	2	0	0	0	0

Going (Turf): Sf: 0-3 GS: 0-0 Gd: 0-2 GF: 0-1 Fm: 0-0

Distance: 5f/6f: 0-0 7f-8f: 0-3 9f-13f: 0-12 14f+: 0-1
Track : LH: 0-5 RH: 0-7 Tight: 0-2 Gall: 0-1
Aids: Bl: 0-2 Vi: 0-1 Tstrap: 0-0
Best Rating: 23 1/01 Ling 1m2f stand

Davis Rock

95(105) (60)**51**
7-y-o ch m Rock City-Sunny Davis (USA) (Alydar (USA))
W R Muir Gordon B Cunningham

Placings:2221560/62032240412353/13322200000010/0 262035155/110166264000-31600 **(0982)**
2001: 10^{3}SD, 8^{1}SD, 8^{6}SW, 8^{0}SW, 8^{0}SD

	Starts	1st	2nd	3rd	Win & Pl
Career Total (Turf)	26	2	9	1	13513
Career Total (AW)	35	7	4	6	24547

60	1/01	Sthl	1m	E(0-75)H	STD	£2912
66	2/00	Sthl	1m	D(0-85)H	STD	£4153
65	1/00	Sthl	7f	F(0-60)	STD	£2160
59	1/00	Sthl	7f	F(0-60)	STD	£1732
51	11/99	Nott	1m54y	F(0-60)H	SFT	£3197
64	11/98	Wolv	7f	G	STD	£1563
67	1/98	Ling	7f	D(0-75)H	STD	£3387
52	10/97	Folk	6f189y	F	G-S	£2277
69	10/96	Wolv	6f	F	STD	£2519

Total win prize-money £23904

Going (Turf): Sf: 1-6 GS: 1-4 Gd: 0-7 GF: 0-9 Fm: 0-0
Distance: 5f/6f: 1-9 **7f-8f: 7-45** 9f-13f: 1-7 14f+: 0-0
Track : **LH: 8-43** RH: 1-4 **Tight: 4-24** Gall: 0-1
Aids: **Bl: 1-5** Vi: 0-0 Tstrap: 0-0
Best Rating: 60 1/01 Sthl 1m stand

Fair handicapper at around amile on turf or sand.

Dawari (IRE)

105 **101**
3-y-o b c In The Wings-Dawala (IRE) (Lashkari)
Sir Michael Stoute H H Aga Khan

Placings:034-14 **(1192)**
2001: 10^{1}GS, 12^{4}GF

	Starts	1st	2nd	3rd	Win & Pl
Career Total (Turf)	5	1	0	1	9023

69	4/01	Wind	1m2f7y	D	G-S	£4244

Total win prize-money £4245

Going (Turf): Sf: 0-1 **GS: 1-2** Gd: 0-1 GF: 0-1 Fm: 0-0
Distance: 5f/6f: 0-0 7f-8f: 0-3 **9f-13f: 1-2** 14f+: 0-0
Track : LH: 0-1 RH: 0-0 **Tight: 1-2** Gall: 0-0
Aids: Bl: 0-0 Vi: 0-0 Tstrap: 0-0
Best Rating: 101 5/01 Ches 1m4f66y gd-fm

A half-brother to Daliapour, he looked a useful prospect when running away with a Windsor maiden first time out but was found wanting in the Chester Vase. The track and faster ground seemed against him there, and he missed the rest of the campaign.

Dawn

79 **60**
4-y-o b f Owington-Realisatrice (USA) (Raja Baba (USA))
J S Wainwright Matthew Sharkey

Placings:634/360360-0 **(2419)**
2001: 5^{0}GF

	Starts	1st	2nd	3rd	Win & Pl
Career Total (Turf)	10	0	0	3	2056

Going (Turf): Sf: 0-1 GS: 0-2 Gd: 0-3 GF: 0-4 Fm: 0-0
Distance: 5f/6f: 0-10 7f-8f: 0-0 9f-13f: 0-0 14f+: 0-0
Track : LH: 0-2 RH: 0-0 Tight: 0-1 Gall: 0-1
Aids: Bl: 0-0 Vi: 0-0 Tstrap: 0-0
Best Rating: 22 6/01 Muss 5f gd-fm

Dawn Invasion (IRE)

92 **89+**
2-y-o b c Common Grounds-Princess Of Zurich (IRE) (Law Society (USA))
Mrs A J Perrett K Abdulla

Placings:21 **(5095)**
2001: 7^{2}G, 8^{1}GS

	Starts	1st	2nd	3rd	Win & Pl
Career Total (Turf)	2	1	1	0	5844

89	10/01	Sals	1m	D	G-S	£4524

Total win prize-money £4524

Going (Turf): Sf: 0-0 **GS: 1-1** Gd: 0-1 GF: 0-0 Fm: 0-0
Distance: 5f/6f: 0-0 **7f-8f: 1-2** 9f-13f: 0-0 14f+: 0-0
Track : LH: 0-0 RH: 0-1 Tight: 0-0 Gall: 0-0
Aids: Bl: 0-0 Vi: 0-0 Tstrap: 0-0
Best Rating: 89 10/01 Sals 1m gd-sft

A 210,000gns half-brother to Princely Dream, made a promising debut at Sandown and got off the mark cosily at Salisbury next time. Stays a mile handles good and easy ground.

Dawn Traveller (IRE)

67 **37**
4-y-o b f Blues Traveller (IRE)-All Alright (Alzao (USA))
H J Collingridge D Burke

Placings:00500-0 **(2313)**
2001: 8^{0}G

	Starts	1st	2nd	3rd	Win & Pl
Career Total (Turf)	6	0	0	0	0

Going (Turf): Sf: 0-0 GS: 0-2 Gd: 0-1 GF: 0-3 Fm: 0-0
Distance: 5f/6f: 0-0 7f-8f: 0-3 9f-13f: 0-3 14f+: 0-0
Track : LH: 0-2 RH: 0-2 Tight: 0-1 Gall: 0-0
Aids: Bl: 0-0 Vi: 0-0 Tstrap: 0-0

Dawn's Sharp Shot (IRE)

68
2-y-o b/br f Son Of Sharp Shot (IRE)-Dawn Star (High Line)
J L Dunlop Windflower Overseas Holdings Inc

Placings:5 **(4629)**
2001: 8^{5}GF

	Starts	1st	2nd	3rd	Win & Pl
Career Total (Turf)	1	0	0	0	0

Going (Turf): Sf: 0-0 GS: 0-0 Gd: 0-0 GF: 0-1 Fm: 0-0
Distance: 5f/6f: 0-0 7f-8f: 0-0 9f-13f: 0-1 14f+: 0-0
Track : LH: 0-0 RH: 0-0 Tight: 0-0 Gall: 0-0
Aids: Bl: 0-0 Vi: 0-0 Tstrap: 0-0
Best Rating: 68 9/01 Leic 1m9y gd-fm

Day-Boy

91(100) (66)**67d**
5-y-o b g Prince Sabo-Lady Day (FR) (Lightning (FR))
Denys Smith J A Bianchi

Placings:140/040430/304440053-000 **(1110)**
2001: 8^{0}SD, 8^{0}S, 7^{0}GF

	Starts	1st	2nd	3rd	Win & Pl
Career Total (Turf)	18	1	0	2	6252
Career Total (AW)	3	0	0	1	583

70	5/98	Ayr	6f	E	GD	£2804

Total win prize-money £2804

Going (Turf): Sf: 0-5 GS: 0-5 **Gd: 1-2** GF: 0-5 Fm: 0-1
Distance: **5f/6f: 1-6** 7f-8f: 0-15 9f-13f: 0-0 14f+: 0-0
Track : LH: 0-10 RH: 0-5 Tight: 0-8 Gall: 0-0
Aids: Bl: 0-0 Vi: 0-0 Tstrap: 0-0
Best Rating: 45 5/01 Muss 7f30y gd-fm

Dayglow Dancer

108 **87**
3-y-o b c Fraam-Fading (Pharly (FR))
M R Channon Surrey Laminators Ltd

Placings:1324252262-163500560 **(5607)**
2001: 8^{1}S, 8^{6}S, 8^{3}G, 8^{5}GF, 7^{0}GF, 8^{0}GF, 7^{5}G, 7^{6}S, 8^{0}GS

	Starts	1st	2nd	3rd	Win & Pl
Career Total (Turf)	19	2	5	2	33180

98	3/01	Donc	1m	C	SFT	£6955
63	4/00	Nott	5f13y	D	SFT	£2842

Total win prize-money £9797

Going (Turf): Sf: 2-7 GS: 0-1 Gd: 0-6 GF: 0-5 Fm: 0-0
Distance: 5f/6f: 1-3 7f-8f: 1-15 9f-13f: 0-1 14f+: 0-0
Track : LH: 0-6 RH: 0-5 Tight: 0-2 Gall: 0-3
Aids: Bl: 0-0 Vi: 0-0 Tstrap: 0-0
Best Rating: 98 5/01 Donc 1m good

Consistent juvenile who won only once, but was placed in Group company later in the season. He made a winning reappearance at Doncaster but has been well held since. He goes well fresh and is suited by soft ground.

Daylily (IRE)

(96) (43)**47**
4-y-o ch f Pips Pride-Leaping Water (Sure Blade (USA))
T D Easterby M H Easterby

Placings:006033235036-00240600 **(3014)**
2001: 5^{0}GS, 8^{0}S, 6^{2}SD, 6^{4}F, 7^{0}SD, 6^{6}SD, 5^{0}GS, 5^{0}SD

	Starts	1st	2nd	3rd	Win & Pl
Career Total (Turf)	16	0	1	4	3537
Career Total (AW)	4	0	1	0	674

Going (Turf): Sf: 0-5 GS: 0-4 Gd: 0-3 GF: 0-2 Fm: 0-2
Distance: 5f/6f: 0-16 7f-8f: 0-2 9f-13f: 0-2 14f+: 0-0
Track : LH: 0-8 RH: 0-0 Tight: 0-1 Gall: 0-0
Aids: Bl: 0-0 Vi: 0-0 Tstrap: 0-0
Best Rating: 47 5/01 Rdcr 6f firm

Days Of Grace

106(104) (64)**66**
6-y-o gr m Wolfhound (USA)-Inshirah (USA) (Caro)
L Montague Hall Omni Colour Presentations Ltd

Placings:544164363/0540/30034034131242/12313220 053114206550-0633505521350 **(5462)**
2001: 7^{0}SD, 5^{6}SW, 6^{3}SD, 6^{3}SD, 7^{5}SW, 6^{0}GF, 5^{5}GF, 6^{5}G, 5^{2}S, 5^{1}G, 6^{3}SW, 5^{5}G, 5^{0}G

	Starts	1st	2nd	3rd	Win & Pl
Career Total (Turf)	39	4	2	7	21548
Career Total (AW)	21	4	5	5	17609

66	9/01	Sand	5f6y	E(0-75)H	GD	£4719
62	8/00	Ling	6f	F(0-65)H	G-F	£2656
56	8/00	Sals	6f	E(0-70)H	G-F	£3136
61	2/00	Wolv	6f	E(0-70)H	STD	£3493
64	1/00	Sthl	6f	E(0-75)H	STD	£2769
60	10/99	Wolv	6f	F(0-60)H	STD	£2553
52	9/99	Sthl	6f	F(0-60)H	STD	£2024
69	5/97	Rdcr	5f	E	FRM	£2898

Total win prize-money £24250

Going (Turf): Sf: 0-6 GS: 0-2 Gd: 1-11 **GF: 2-16** Fm: 1-4
Distance: **5f/6f: 8-49** 7f-8f: 0-11 9f-13f: 0-0 14f+: 0-0
Track : **LH: 4-24** RH: 0-3 **Tight: 2-16** Gall: 0-5
Aids: Bl: 0-0 Vi: 0-0 Tstrap: 0-0
Best Rating: 66 9/01 Gdwd 5f good

She does not win very often these days, but a good draw helped her gain a battling victory over the minimum trip at Sandown in September. Suited by five to six furlongs and most ground.

Dazzling Daisy

84(89) (18)**32d**
4-y-o b f Shareef Dancer (USA)-Mariette (Blushing Scribe (USA))

N A Graham (Pat Mitchell 11/9) Miss H M A Omersa

Placings:440606-40000 **(5471)**
2001: 12^{4}SW, 9^{0}GF, 11^{0}GF, 11^{0}S, 11^{0}S

	Starts	1st	2nd	3rd	Win & Pl
Career Total (Turf)	9	0	0	0	444
Career Total (AW)	2	0	0	0	0

Going (Turf): Sf: 0-3 GS: 0-0 Gd: 0-0 GF: 0-6 Fm: 0-0
Distance: 5f/6f: 0-0 7f-8f: 0-1 9f-13f: 0-10 14f+: 0-0
Track : LH: 0-9 RH: 0-0 Tight: 0-3 Gall: 0-0
Aids: Bl: 0-0 Vi: 0-0 Tstrap: 0-0
Best Rating: 35 9/01 Ling 1m3f106y gd-fm

Dazzling Quintet

100(95) (21)**44**
5-y-o ch m Superlative-Miss Display (Touch Paper)
C Smith Roman Bath V

Placings:000413435/0000020/6021000000-0330002050 **(3372)**
2001: 5^{0}SD, 5^{3}SD, 5^{3}SD, 5^{0}SD, 5^{0}SD, 5^{0}G, 5^{2}GF, 5^{0}GF, 5^{5}GF, 5^{0}F

	Starts	1st	2nd	3rd	Win & Pl
Career Total (Turf)	29	2	3	2	9139
Career Total (AW)	7	0	0	2	506

47 6/00 Bevl 5f E(0-70)H G-F £3107
78 7/98 Bevl 5f F G-F £2477
Total win prize-money £5585

Going (Turf): Sf: 0-6 GS: 0-0 Gd: 0-4 **GF: 2-16** Fm: 0-3
Distance: **5f/6f: 2-34** 7f-8f: 0-2 9f-13f: 0-0 14f+: 0-0
Track : LH: 0-8 RH: 0-1 Tight: 0-4 Gall: 0-1
Aids: Bl: 0-0 Vi: 0-8 Tstrap: 0-0
Best Rating: 44 6/01 Bevl 5f gd-fm

Dazzling Rio (IRE)

87(88) (46)**61**
2-y-o b g Ashkalani (IRE)-Dazzling Fire (IRE) (Bluebird (USA))
P C Haslam Rio Stainless Engineering Limited

Placings:04040 **(5404)**
2001: 6^{0}GF, 6^{4}G, 6^{0}GS, 6^{4}G, 8^{0}S

	Starts	1st	2nd	3rd	Win & Pl
Career Total (Turf)	5	0	0	0	649

Going (Turf): Sf: 0-1 GS: 0-1 Gd: 0-2 GF: 0-1 Fm: 0-0
Distance: 5f/6f: 0-3 7f-8f: 0-1 9f-13f: 0-1 14f+: 0-0
Track : LH: 0-1 RH: 0-0 Tight: 0-0 Gall: 0-0
Aids: Bl: 0-0 Vi: 0-0 Tstrap: 0-0
Best Rating: 61 8/01 Hayd 6f gd-sft

De Haute Lutte (USA)

103 **68**
5-y-o b m Alleged (USA)-Baranciaga (USA) (Bering)
E Danel (N A Gaselee 15/7) Lord Wolverton

Placings:031231/020023542-0202431
2001: 16^{0}GS, 17^{2}GF, 16^{0}GF, 11^{2}S, 16^{4}GS, 15^{3}G, 12^{1}HO

	Starts	1st	2nd	3rd	Win & Pl
Career Total (Turf)	22	3	6	4	44094

10/01 Lonc 1m4f H HLD £7759
11/99 StCl 1m6f H HVY £6459
9/99 NrSE 1m4f110y VS £3014
Total win prize-money £17232

Going (Turf): Sf: 0-1 GS: 0-2 Gd: 0-2 GF: 0-2 Fm: 0-0
Distance: 5f/6f: 0-0 7f-8f: 0-0 **9f-13f: 2-7** 14f+: 0-8
Track : LH: 0-2 **RH: 1-3** Tight: 0-1 Gall: 0-1
Aids: **Bl: 2-9** Vi: 0-0 Tstrap: 0-0
Best Rating: 68 5/01 Bath 2m1f34y gd-fm

De Tramuntana

92

4-y-o b f Alzao (USA)-Glamour Game (Nashwan (USA))
P R Hedger P R Hedger

Placings:00/242505-00 **(4594)**
2001: 11^{0}GS, 14^{0}G

	Starts	1st	2nd	3rd	Win & Pl
Career Total (Turf)	10	0	2	0	4151

Going (Turf): Sf: 0-2 GS: 0-4 Gd: 0-2 GF: 0-2 Fm: 0-0
Distance: 5f/6f: 0-0 7f-8f: 0-1 9f-13f: 0-8 14f+: 0-1
Track : LH: 0-4 RH: 0-5 Tight: 0-5 Gall: 0-0
Aids: Bl: 0-0 Vi: 0-0 Tstrap: 0-2
Best Rating: 55 5/01 Bath 1m3f144y gd-sft

Deal In Facts

92(78) (21)**67**
2-y-o ch f So Factual (USA)-Timely Raise (USA) (Raise A Man (USA))
R Hannon J C Smith

Placings:0620040 **(5079)**
2001: 7^{0}GF, 7^{6}GF, 5^{2}GF, 6^{0}S, 7^{0}GF, 6^{4}GF, 5^{0}S

	Starts	1st	2nd	3rd	Win & Pl
Career Total (Turf)	7	0	1	0	722

Going (Turf): Sf: 0-2 GS: 0-0 Gd: 0-0 GF: 0-5 Fm: 0-0
Distance: 5f/6f: 0-3 7f-8f: 0-4 9f-13f: 0-0 14f+: 0-0
Track : LH: 0-2 RH: 0-2 Tight: 0-0 Gall: 0-1
Aids: Bl: 0-0 Vi: 0-0 Tstrap: 0-0
Best Rating: 67 7/01 Brig 5f59y gd-fm

Deano's Beeno

96 **63**
9-y-o b g Far North (CAN)-Sans Dot (Busted)
M C Pipe Axom

Placings:231/320504/603330206032/3 **(0516)**
2001: 18^{3}S

	Starts	1st	2nd	3rd	Win & Pl
Career Total (Turf)	22	1	4	7	13247

73 10/94 Nott 1m1f213yF G-F £2837
Total win prize-money £2838

Going (Turf): Sf: 0-3 GS: 0-2 Gd: 0-7 **GF: 1-9** Fm: 0-1
Distance: 5f/6f: 0-0 7f-8f: 0-1 **9f-13f: 1-12** 14f+: 0-9
Track : **LH: 1-17** RH: 0-5 Tight: 0-6 Gall: 0-9
Aids: Bl: 0-0 Vi: 0-0 Tstrap: 0-0
Best Rating: 63 3/01 Donc 2m2f soft

Formerly useful staying handicapper, likes to dominate.

Dear Bridie (IRE)

84 **69**
2-y-o ch f Entrepreneur-Shebasis (USA) (General Holme (USA))
B W Hills John C Grant

Placings:04 **(5491)**
2001: 6^{0}GF, 6^{4}HY

	Starts	1st	2nd	3rd	Win & Pl
Career Total (Turf)	2	0	0	0	422

Going (Turf): Sf: 0-1 GS: 0-0 Gd: 0-0 GF: 0-1 Fm: 0-0
Distance: 5f/6f: 0-0 7f-8f: 0-2 9f-13f: 0-0 14f+: 0-0
Track : LH: 0-0 RH: 0-0 Tight: 0-0 Gall: 0-0
Aids: Bl: 0-0 Vi: 0-0 Tstrap: 0-0
Best Rating: 69 10/01 Newb 6f8y heavy

Dear Daughter

107 **106**
3-y-o ch f Polish Precedent (USA)-Darayna (IRE) (Shernazar)
Sir Michael Stoute Philip Newton

Placings:34-12554 **(4865)**
2001: 8^{1}F, 8^{2}GF, 8^{5}G, 9^{5}G, 10^{4}GF

	Starts	1st	2nd	3rd	Win & Pl
Career Total (Turf)	7	1	1	1	19739

89 6/01 Bath 1m5y D FRM £6873
Total win prize-money £6874

Going (Turf): Sf: 0-1 GS: 0-0 Gd: 0-2 GF: 0-3 **Fm: 1-1**
Distance: 5f/6f: 0-0 7f-8f: 0-3 **9f-13f: 1-4** 14f+: 0-0
Track : **LH: 1-2** RH: 0-1 **Tight: 1-2** Gall: 0-1
Aids: Bl: 0-0 Vi: 0-0 Tstrap: 0-0
Best Rating: 106 6/01 Asct 1m gd-fm

She beat quite a useful maiden filly when getting off the mark at Bath on her third start and ran well to finish runner-up in an Ascot Listed handicap next time. Not disgraced in the Group Two Falmouth Stakes. Bred to stay beyond a mile.

Dear Girl (IRE)

(97) (47)**101**
4-y-o b f Fairy King (USA)-Alidiva (Chief Singer)
D Sepulchre Charles H Wacker Iii

Placings:34-544
2001: 10^{5}GS, 10^{4}GS, 10^{4}G

	Starts	1st	2nd	3rd	Win & Pl
Career Total (Turf)	4	0	0	1	16548
Career Total (AW)	1	0	0	0	180

Going (Turf): Sf: 0-0 GS: 0-2 Gd: 0-1 GF: 0-1 Fm: 0-0
Distance: 5f/6f: 0-0 7f-8f: 0-0 9f-13f: 0-5 14f+: 0-0
Track : LH: 0-1 RH: 0-2 Tight: 0-1 Gall: 0-0
Aids: Bl: 0-0 Vi: 0-0 Tstrap: 0-0
Best Rating: 101 8/01 Deau 1m2f gd-sft

Dearest Daisy

99 **86**
2-y-o ch f Forzando-Sylhall (Sharpo)
J Noseda Lucayan Stud

Placings:03120 **(4659)**
2001: 5^{0}GF, 6^{3}GF, 5^{1}GF, 5^{2}GF, 6^{0}GF

	Starts	1st	2nd	3rd	Win & Pl
Career Total (Turf)	5	1	1	1	5182

77 8/01 Muss 5f F G-F £2548
Total win prize-money £2548

Going (Turf): Sf: 0-0 GS: 0-0 Gd: 0-0 **GF: 1-5** Fm: 0-0
Distance: **5f/6f: 1-5** 7f-8f: 0-0 9f-13f: 0-0 14f+: 0-0
Track : LH: 0-1 RH: 0-1 Tight: 0-1 Gall: 0-1
Aids: Bl: 0-0 Vi: 0-0 Tstrap: 0-0
Best Rating: 86 8/01 Ripn 5f gd-fm

Whose dam is an unraced half-sister to several useful eight to 12 furlong handicappers, including Tell No Lies and The Wild Widow, showed promise on her debut. Scored over five furlongs in August.

Deb's Son

80 **37**
4-y-o b g Minster Son-Deb's Ball (Glenstal (USA))
D Moffatt Mr & Mrs A G Milligan

Placings:454/6660-00 **(4014)**
2001: 14^{0}GF, 15^{0}G

	Starts	1st	2nd	3rd	Win & Pl
Career Total (Turf)	9	0	0	0	269

Going (Turf): Sf: 0-2 GS: 0-2 Gd: 0-2 GF: 0-2 Fm: 0-1
Distance: 5f/6f: 0-0 7f-8f: 0-0 9f-13f: 0-5 14f+: 0-4
Track : LH: 0-5 RH: 0-3 Tight: 0-5 Gall: 0-0
Aids: Bl: 0-0 Vi: 0-0 Tstrap: 0-0
Best Rating: 9 6/01 Rdcr 1m6f19y gd-fm

Debbie's Hope

99 36

5-y-o ch m Be My Chief (USA)-Appleton Heights (Shirley Heights)

Mrs A M Naughton John E Lund

Placings:053/2303330000/004000 **(5284)**

2001: 10^{0}GS, 9^{0}GS, 8^{4}GS, 8^{0}GF, 8^{0}G, 9^{0}HY

	Starts	1st	2nd	3rd	Win & Pl
Career Total (Turf)	17	0	1	4	2571
Career Total (AW)	2	0	0	1	285

Going (Turf): Sf: 0-3 GS: 0-5 Gd: 0-3 GF: 0-2 Fm: 0-4
Distance: 5f/6f: 0-4 7f-8f: 0-12 9f-13f: 0-3 14f+: 0-0
Track : LH: 0-9 RH: 0-1 Tight: 0-5 Gall: 0-0
Aids: Bl: 0-0 Vi: 0-0 Tstrap: 0-4
Best Rating: 39 8/01 Thsk 1m gd-sft

Far from reliable plater. Best over a mile.

Debbie's Warning

103(97) (83)78

5-y-o b h Warning-Lomond Blossom (Lomond (USA))

K A Ryan Mrs N L Spence

Placings:230150530/064006005000-3300040 **(5254)**

2001: 7^{3}F, 6^{3}G, 6^{0}F, 5^{0}GF, 6^{0}GF, 6^{4}G, 6^{0}S

	Starts	1st	2nd	3rd	Win & Pl
Career Total (Turf)	27	1	1	4	14368
Career Total (AW)	1	0	0	0	

80	5/99	Kemp	1m	D	G-F	£3907

Total win prize-money £3908

Going (Turf): Sf: 0-4 GS: 0-3 Gd: 0-10 **GF: 1-8** Fm: 0-2
Distance: 5f/6f: 0-9 **7f-8f: 1-16** 9f-13f: 0-3 14f+: 0-0
Track : LH: 0-7 **RH: 1-7** Tight: 0-4 **Gall: 1-5**
Aids: Bl: 0-0 Vi: 0-0 Tstrap: 0-5
Best Rating: 78 9/01 Ayr 6f good

Unraced at two, he looked Group-class early on at three, but lost his way after being set a series of impossible tasks. His sights have been lowered since..

Debbies Treasure (IRE)

(57) (6)23

2-y-o b g Idris (IRE)-Treasure Ring (IRE) (Treasure Kay)

Mrs N Macauley (P D Evans 29/6) R J Hayward

Placings:0000 **(5197)**

2001: 6^{0}G, 6^{0}G, 7^{0}SD, 8^{0}SD

	Starts	1st	2nd	3rd	Win & Pl
Career Total (Turf)	2	0	0	0	
Career Total (AW)	2	0	0	0	

Going (Turf): Sf: 0-0 GS: 0-0 Gd: 0-2 GF: 0-0 Fm: 0-0
Distance: 5f/6f: 0-2 7f-8f: 0-1 9f-13f: 0-1 14f+: 0-0
Track : LH: 0-2 RH: 0-0 Tight: 0-1 Gall: 0-0
Aids: Bl: 0-0 Vi: 0-0 Tstrap: 0-0
Best Rating: 23 6/01 Wind 6f good

Deceitful

103(102) (72)81

3-y-o ch g Most Welcome-Sure Care (Caerleon (USA))

P D Evans (Andrew Reid 14/8) Waterline Racing Club

Placings:134-**0161530**0051416000440051 1 **(5688)**

2001: 10^{0}SD, 6^{1}SW, 6^{6}SD, 7^{1}SW, 6^{5}SD, 6^{3}SW, 6^{0}SD, 6^{0}GF, 6^{0}G, 7^{5}G, 6^{1}F, 5^{4}G, 7^{1}GF, 6^{6}GF, 6^{0}GF, 5^{0}GS, 5^{0}G, 7^{4}GF, 7^{4}HY, 8^{0}S, 7^{0}S, 6^{5}G, 7^{1}G, 7^{1}S

	Starts	1st	2nd	3rd	Win & Pl
Career Total (Turf)	20	5	0	1	23669
Career Total (AW)	7	2	0	1	7239

81	11/01	Donc	7f	E(0-90)H	SFT	£3948
72	11/01	Catt	7f	D(0-80)H	GD	£7475
76	8/01	Catt	7f	D(0-85)H	G-F	£4212
62	8/01	Brig	6f209y	F	FRM	£2352
72	3/01	Ling	7f	E(0-70)H	SLW	£2884
69	1/01	Ling	6f	D(0-85)H	SLW	£3766
55	6/00	Brig	5f59y	F	FRM	£2278

Total win prize-money £26918

Going (Turf): Sf: 1-4 GS: 0-1 Gd: 1-6 GF: 1-6 **Fm: 2-3**
Distance: 5f/6f: 2-12 **7f-8f: 5-14** 9f-13f: 0-1 14f+: 0-0
Track : **LH: 6-15** RH: 0-0 **Tight: 4-9** Gall: 0-1
Aids: Bl: 0-0 Vi: 0-0 Tstrap: 0-0
Best Rating: 81 11/01 Donc 7f soft

A winner twice on Equitrack and four times on turf this season, most of his wins have come on a sharp left-handed track. Acts well on most types of ground ground.

Deceives The Eye

(83) (36)14

3-y-o b g Dancing Spree (USA)-Lycius Touch (Lycius (USA))

A G Newcombe Mrs Trude Cutler

Placings:244016-060 **(0309)**

2001: 7^{0}SD, 7^{6}SD, 8^{0}SD

	Starts	1st	2nd	3rd	Win & Pl
Career Total (Turf)	2	0	0	0	0
Career Total (AW)	7	1	1	0	2340

53	6/00	Wolv	6f	G	STD	£1813

Total win prize-money £1813

Going (Turf): Sf: 0-1 GS: 0-1 Gd: 0-0 GF: 0-0 Fm: 0-0
Distance: **5f/6f: 1-5** 7f-8f: 0-4 9f-13f: 0-0 14f+: 0-0
Track : **LH: 1-8** RH: 0-0 **Tight: 1-4** Gall: 0-0
Aids: Bl: 0-1 Vi: 0-0 Tstrap: 0-0
Best Rating: 23 2/01 Wolv 7f stand

Deceptor (USA)

99 87

2-y-o b c Machiavellian (USA)-Satin Flower (USA) (Shadeed (USA))

D R Loder Sheikh Mohammed

Placings:15 **(3217)**

2001: 5^{1}GF, 6^{5}GF

	Starts	1st	2nd	3rd	Win & Pl
Career Total (Turf)	2	1	0	0	7246

86	6/01	Donc	5f	C	G-F	£6760

Total win prize-money £6760

Going (Turf): Sf: 0-0 GS: 0-0 Gd: 0-0 **GF: 1-2** Fm: 0-0
Distance: **5f/6f: 1-1** 7f-8f: 0-1 9f-13f: 0-0 14f+: 0-0
Track : LH: 0-0 RH: 0-0 Tight: 0-0 Gall: 0-0
Aids: Bl: 0-0 Vi: 0-0 Tstrap: 0-0
Best Rating: 87 7/01 Newb 6f8y gd-fm

A well-bred individual who is closely related to Middle Park winner Lujain, she won a decent five-furlong conditions race on her racecourse debut at Doncaster and showed enthusiasm when stepped up into Listed company at Newbury a month later.

Dechtire (IRE)

82 46

2-y-o b f Thatching-Derena (FR) (Crystal Palace (FR))

R Hannon E K Cleveland

Placings:0 **(4637)**

2001: 7^{0}GF

	Starts	1st	2nd	3rd	Win & Pl
Career Total (Turf)	1	0	0	0	

Going (Turf): Sf: 0-0 GS: 0-0 Gd: 0-0 GF: 0-1 Fm: 0-0
Distance: 5f/6f: 0-0 7f-8f: 0-1 9f-13f: 0-0 14f+: 0-0
Track : LH: 0-0 RH: 0-0 Tight: 0-0 Gall: 0-0
Aids: Bl: 0-0 Vi: 0-0 Tstrap: 0-0
Best Rating: 46 9/01 Ling 7f gd-fm

Decima

91(98) (73)71

2-y-o b f Puissance-Kaleidophone (Kalaglow)

Mrs N Macauley (P D Evans 18/8) R J Hayward

Placings:2220431304020 **(5408)**

2001: 5^{2}SD, 5^{2}SD, 5^{2}GS, 5^{0}GS, 5^{4}GF, 6^{3}G, 6^{1}GF, 5^{3}G, 5^{0}GF, 6^{4}SD, 6^{0}GF, 5^{2}SD, 6^{0}SD

	Starts	1st	2nd	3rd	Win & Pl
Career Total (Turf)	8	1	1	2	5753
Career Total (AW)	5	0	3	0	3895

71	6/01	Wind	6f	E	G-F	£3262

Total win prize-money £3262

Going (Turf): Sf: 0-0 GS: 0-2 Gd: 0-2 **GF: 1-4** Fm: 0-0
Distance: **5f/6f: 1-13** 7f-8f: 0-0 9f-13f: 0-0 14f+: 0-0
Track : LH: 0-6 RH: 0-1 Tight: 0-3 Gall: 0-2
Aids: Bl: 0-0 Vi: 0-0 Tstrap: 0-0
Best Rating: 73 10/01 Wolv 5f stand

From a good family, she performed consistently in the six races prior to her first victory where she made all in a Windsor maiden in June 2001. She begins her winter campaign on the sand with new trainer, Norma Macauley.

Decoy

83 44

2-y-o b f Double Eclipse (IRE)-Kilcoy (USA) (Secreto (USA))

M Johnston The Middleham Partnership

Placings:65 **(5371)**

2001: 10^{6}GS, 8^{5}G

	Starts	1st	2nd	3rd	Win & Pl
Career Total (Turf)	2	0	0	0	0

Going (Turf): Sf: 0-0 GS: 0-1 Gd: 0-1 GF: 0-0 Fm: 0-0
Distance: 5f/6f: 0-0 7f-8f: 0-1 9f-13f: 0-1 14f+: 0-0
Track : LH: 0-1 RH: 0-0 Tight: 0-0 Gall: 0-0
Aids: Bl: 0-0 Vi: 0-0 Tstrap: 0-0
Best Rating: 44 10/01 Rdcr 1m good

Dee Pee Tee Cee (IRE)

97 57

7-y-o b g Tidaro (USA)-Silver Glimpse (Petingo)

M W Easterby Mrs M E Curtis

Placings:16655066/00101111340/000/611116100/0000 0-00040 **(5632)**

2001: 8^{0}GF, 11^{0}GF, 11^{0}S, 8^{4}S, 10^{0}G

	Starts	1st	2nd	3rd	Win & Pl
Career Total (Turf)	41	11	0	1	67931

86	8/99	York	1m3f195y	C(0-95)H	GD	£21687
82	6/99	Haml	1m1f36y	E(0-75)H	GD	£3485
78	6/99	York	1m205y	C(0-100)H	G-S	£15045
74	6/99	Pont	1m2f6y	F(0-70)H	SFT	£2193
66	6/99	Ches	1m2f75y	D(0-80)H	SFT	£4143
74	7/97	Muss	1m	F(0-65)H	GD	£3030
74	7/97	Bevl	1m100y	D(0-85)H	HVY	£5082
65	6/97	Carl	7f214y	F	GD	£2598
58	6/97	Rdcr	1m1f	E(0-70)H	GD	£2898
54	6/97	Bevl	7f100y	E(0-70)H	G-F	£3834
59	6/96	Rdcr	7f	G	G-F	£2267

Total win prize-money £66264

Going (Turf): Sf: 3-13 GS: 1-1 **Gd: 5-13** GF: 2-11 Fm: 0-3
Distance: 5f/6f: 0-3 7f-8f: 4-19 **9f-13f: 7-19** 14f+: 0-0
Track : LH: 5-23 RH: 5-10 **Tight: 4-10** Gall: 2-13
Aids: Bl: 0-0 Vi: 0-0 Tstrap: 0-0
Best Rating: 57 10/01 Rdcr 1m soft

A credit to connections, he won five races in the summer of 1999. Has failed to recapture his best Flat form in the last couple of seasons despite dropping in the weights.

Deekazz (IRE)

85 56

2-y-o b f Definite Article-Lyric Junction (IRE) (Classic Secret (USA))
A Berry C Hignett & G Flitcroft

Placings:4500 **(4962)**
2001: 7^{4}GF, 7^{5}F, 7^{0}G, 8^{0}S

	Starts	1st	2nd	3rd	Win & Pl
Career Total (Turf)	4	0	0	0	320

Going (Turf): Sf: 0-1 GS: 0-0 Gd: 0-1 GF: 0-1 Fm: 0-1
Distance: 5f/6f: 0-0 7f-8f: 0-3 9f-13f: 0-1 14f+: 0-0
Track : LH: 0-1 RH: 0-0 Tight: 0-0 Gall: 0-0
Aids: Bl: 0-0 Vi: 0-0 Tstrap: 0-0
Best Rating: 56 8/01 Newc 7f good

Deep Blue

103(99) (69)**70**
4-y-o b c Lake Coniston (IRE)-Billie Blue (Ballad Rock)
Dr J D Scargill R A Dalton

Placings:53220/1-**0**010000000 **(5391)**
2001: 6^{0}SW, 6^{0}SD, 7^{1}G, 7^{0}S, 7^{0}GS, 7^{0}G, 7^{0}GF, 8^{0}G, 7^{0}S, 7^{0}GS

	Starts	1st	2nd	3rd	Win & Pl
Career Total (Turf)	14	2	2	1	10013
Career Total (AW)	2	0	0	0	
80 5/01 Leic	7f9y	D(0-80)H		GD	£4017
47 10/00 Wind	6f	D		HVY	£3006

Total win prize-money £7023

Going (Turf): **Sf: 1-4** GS: 0-2 **Gd: 1-6** GF: 0-2 Fm: 0-0
Distance: 5f/6f: 1-8 7f-8f: 1-7 9f-13f: 0-1 14f+: 0-0
Track : LH: 0-4 **RH: 1-2** Tight: 0-3 **Gall: 1-2**
Aids: Bl: 0-0 Vi: 0-2 Tstrap: 0-0
Best Rating: 80 5/01 Leic 7f9y good

Best over seven furlongs, he has shown his best form when fresh, on ground with some cut in it. Has shown little since successful at Leicester in May, but has ability on Fibresand and may well be of interest when sent back onto that surface.

Deep Dale

87 **51**
5-y-o b g Pharly (FR)-L'Oraz (Ile De Bourbon (USA))
Mrs S Lamyman P Lamyman

Placings:00500 **(3879)**
2001: 14^{0}G, 12^{0}GF, 12^{5}GF, 16^{0}GF, 16^{0}GS

	Starts	1st	2nd	3rd	Win & Pl
Career Total (Turf)	5	0	0	0	0

Going (Turf): Sf: 0-0 GS: 0-1 Gd: 0-1 GF: 0-3 Fm: 0-0
Distance: 5f/6f: 0-0 7f-8f: 0-0 9f-13f: 0-2 14f+: 0-3
Track : LH: 0-4 RH: 0-1 Tight: 0-2 Gall: 0-1
Aids: Bl: 0-0 Vi: 0-0 Tstrap: 0-2
Best Rating: 51 6/01 Wwck 1m4f134y gd-fm

Deep Ravine (USA)

(90) (41+)**35**
3-y-o ch f Gulch (USA)-Summertown (USA) (Diesis)
J A Osborne T Hyde

Placings:0-3301 **(0797)**
2001: 12^{3}SD, 12^{3}SD, 11^{0}SD, 12^{1}SD

	Starts	1st	2nd	3rd	Win & Pl
Career Total (Turf)	1	0	0	0	
Career Total (AW)	4	1	0	2	3170
41 4/01 Sthl	1m4f	F(0-60)H		STD	£2345

Total win prize-money £2345

Going (Turf): Sf: 0-0 GS: 0-0 Gd: 0-0 GF: 0-0 Fm: 0-0
Distance: 5f/6f: 0-0 7f-8f: 0-0 **9f-13f: 1-4** 14f+: 0-0
Track : **LH: 1-4** RH: 0-0 Tight: 0-2 Gall: 0-0
Aids: Bl: 0-1 Vi: 0-0 Tstrap: 0-0
Best Rating: 41 4/01 Sthl 1m4f stand

Deep Space (IRE)

107 **102**
6-y-o br g Green Desert (USA)-Dream Season (USA) (Mr Prospector (USA))
E A L Dunlop Maktoum Al Maktoum

Placings:40/240141600/0162100120/63543013-063040 **(3631)**
2001: 6^{0}G, 6^{6}GF, 5^{3}GF, 6^{0}GF, 7^{4}GF, 6^{0}G

	Starts	1st	2nd	3rd	Win & Pl
Career Total (Turf)	35	6	3	4	119626
105 8/00 Yarm	6f3y	C		G-F	£5945
106 8/99 Nott	6f15y	C		G-F	£5978
97 6/99 Asct	6f	B(0-110)H		G-F	£57330
88 5/99 Ling	7f	B(0-105)H		G-F	£10950
85 8/98 NmkJ	6f	D(0-85)H		FRM	£4971
79 7/98 Sand	5f6y	D(0-85)H		GD	£3403

Total win prize-money £88579

Going (Turf): Sf: 0-2 GS: 0-4 Gd: 1-9 **GF: 4-18** Fm: 1-2
Distance: 5f/6f: 3-24 7f-8f: 3-11 9f-13f: 0-0 14f+: 0-0
Track : LH: 0-1 RH: 0-1 Tight: 0-1 Gall: 0-0
Aids: Bl: 0-0 Vi: 0-2 Tstrap: 0-0
Best Rating: 102 6/01 Epsm 5f gd-fm

A useful sprinter whowon the Wokingham in 1999, best over six furlongs on a fast surface, he tended to find trouble in running as he needed to be brought with a late challenge. Has been retired.

Deeper In Debt

96(82) (53+)**50**
3-y-o ch c Piccolo-Harold's Girl (FR) (Northfields (USA))
J A Osborne J Palmer-Brown

Placings:06400 **(5461)**
2001: 6^{0}GS, 6^{6}G, 6^{4}SD, 8^{0}G, 8^{0}G

	Starts	1st	2nd	3rd	Win & Pl
Career Total (Turf)	4	0	0	0	0
Career Total (AW)	1	0	0	0	0

Going (Turf): Sf: 0-0 GS: 0-1 Gd: 0-3 GF: 0-0 Fm: 0-0
Distance: 5f/6f: 0-2 7f-8f: 0-1 9f-13f: 0-2 14f+: 0-0
Track : LH: 0-2 RH: 0-1 Tight: 0-1 Gall: 0-0
Aids: Bl: 0-1 Vi: 0-0 Tstrap: 0-0
Best Rating: 53 6/01 Sthl 6f stand

Deferlant (FR)

94 **77**
4-y-o ch c Bering-Sail Storm (USA) (Topsider (USA))
M C Pipe Mrs G McNeela

Placings:25022010040/031443522321-5 **(4669)**
2001: 16^{5}GF

	Starts	1st	2nd	3rd	Win & Pl
Career Total (Turf)	23	3	6	3	43203
Career Total (AW)	1	0	0	0	
5/00 StCl	1m4f			HLD	£6724
3/00 StCl	1m2f110y			HVY	£5764
9/99 MsnL	7f			SFT	£6459

Total win prize-money £18947

Going (Turf): Sf: 0-0 GS: 0-0 Gd: 0-1 GF: 0-1 Fm: 0-0
Distance: 5f/6f: 0-0 7f-8f: 0-3 9f-13f: 0-4 14f+: 0-1
Track : LH: 0-0 RH: 0-1 Tight: 0-1 Gall: 0-0
Aids: Bl: 0-0 Vi: 0-1 Tstrap: 0-0
Best Rating: 77 9/01 Gdwd 2m gd-fm

Defiance

98(85) (10)**41**
6-y-o b g Warning-Princess Athena (Ahonoora)
A P James Anne & Mahendra Ramkaran

Placings:633/0/0000050/**0**000000000-03402500 **(5148)**
2001: 5^{0}GF, 5^{3}G, 5^{4}GF, 5^{0}G, 5^{2}GF, 6^{5}GF, 6^{0}G, 5^{0}G

	Starts	1st	2nd	3rd	Win & Pl
Career Total (Turf)	26	0	1	3	2057
Career Total (AW)	4	0	0	0	

Going (Turf): Sf: 0-2 GS: 0-2 Gd: 0-9 GF: 0-12 Fm: 0-1
Distance: 5f/6f: 0-16 7f-8f: 0-8 9f-13f: 0-6 14f+: 0-0
Track : LH: 0-18 RH: 0-0 Tight: 0-5 Gall: 0-4
Aids: Bl: 0-12 Vi: 0-0 Tstrap: 0-0
Best Rating: 47 7/01 Chep 5f16y good

Defining

77 **52**
2-y-o b g Definite Article-Gooseberry Pie (Green Desert (USA))
J R Fanshawe Mrs V Shelton

Placings:6 **(5459)**
2001: 8^{6}G

	Starts	1st	2nd	3rd	Win & Pl
Career Total (Turf)	1	0	0	0	0

Going (Turf): Sf: 0-0 GS: 0-0 Gd: 0-1 GF: 0-0 Fm: 0-0
Distance: 5f/6f: 0-0 7f-8f: 0-0 9f-13f: 0-1 14f+: 0-0
Track : LH: 0-1 RH: 0-0 Tight: 0-1 Gall: 0-0
Aids: Bl: 0-0 Vi: 0-0 Tstrap: 0-0
Best Rating: 52 10/01 Bath 1m5y good

Definite Flash (IRE)

91 **46**
3-y-o b f Definite Article-Superflash (Superlative)
G C Bravery Mrs F E Bravery

Placings:0606 **(5085)**
2001: 8^{0}GF, 8^{6}GF, 11^{0}GF, 11^{6}S

	Starts	1st	2nd	3rd	Win & Pl
Career Total (Turf)	4	0	0	0	0

Going (Turf): Sf: 0-1 GS: 0-0 Gd: 0-0 GF: 0-3 Fm: 0-0
Distance: 5f/6f: 0-0 7f-8f: 0-2 9f-13f: 0-2 14f+: 0-0
Track : LH: 0-2 RH: 0-0 Tight: 0-1 Gall: 0-0
Aids: Bl: 0-0 Vi: 0-0 Tstrap: 0-0
Best Rating: 46 9/01 Ling 1m3f106y gd-fm

Definite Guest (IRE)

102 **79**
3-y-o gr g Definite Article-Nicea (IRE) (Dominion)
G G Margarson John Guest

Placings:6040-053010553130 **(4959)**
2001: 8^{0}GS, 7^{5}F, 6^{3}GF, 8^{0}GF, 7^{1}GF, 7^{0}GS, 7^{5}GS, 6^{5}G, 7^{3}GF, 7^{1}G, 7^{3}GF, 7^{0}GS

	Starts	1st	2nd	3rd	Win & Pl
Career Total (Turf)	16	2	0	3	7850
77 9/01 Folk	7f	E(0-70)H		GD	£2912
67 7/01 Ling	7f	F(0-65)H		G-F	£3248

Total win prize-money £6160

Going (Turf): Sf: 0-2 GS: 0-4 **Gd: 1-2 GF: 1-7** Fm: 0-1
Distance: 5f/6f: 0-2 **7f-8f: 2-14** 9f-13f: 0-0 14f+: 0-0
Track : LH: 0-2 RH: 0-1 Tight: 0-1 Gall: 0-0
Aids: Bl: 0-1 Vi: 0-0 Tstrap: 0-0
Best Rating: 79 9/01 Leic 7f9y gd-fm

Winner of ordinary handicaps at Lingfield and Folkestone in 2001. Appears to be slightly quirky and acts on fast ground.

Definite Return (IRE)

89(81) (33)**64**
3-y-o ch f Definite Article-Keen Note (Sharpo)
B Palling B A Evans

Placings:040-00 **(4733)**
2001: 11^{0}GF, 7^{0}F

	Starts	1st	2nd	3rd	Win & Pl
Career Total (Turf)	4	0	0	0	
Career Total (AW)	1	0	0	0	0

Going (Turf): Sf: 0-0 GS: 0-1 Gd: 0-1 GF: 0-1 Fm: 0-1
Distance: 5f/6f: 0-1 7f-8f: 0-1 9f-13f: 0-3 14f+: 0-0
Track : LH: 0-3 RH: 0-0 Tight: 0-3 Gall: 0-0
Aids: Bl: 0-0 Vi: 0-0 Tstrap: 0-0
Best Rating: 30 9/01 Chep 7f16y firm

Definitely Special (IRE)

80 **46**

3-y-o b f Definite Article-Legit (IRE) (Runnett)
D R C Elsworth R Fabrizius

Placings:0 **(2854)**
2001: 10^{0}G

	Starts	1st	2nd	3rd	Win & Pl
Career Total (Turf)	1	0	0	0	

Going (Turf): Sf: 0-0 GS: 0-0 Gd: 0-1 GF: 0-0 Fm: 0-0
Distance: 5f/6f: 0-0 7f-8f: 0-0 9f-13f: 0-1 14f+: 0-0
Track : LH: 0-0 RH: 0-1 Tight: 0-0 Gall: 0-0
Aids: Bl: 0-0 Vi: 0-0 Tstrap: 0-0
Best Rating: 46 7/01 Sand 1m2f7y good

Degree Of Power

65(69) (6)**28**

3-y-o b f Sure Blade (USA)-One Degree (Crooner)
Mrs L Richards (Miss D A McHale 7/5) Manor Boys

Placings:4000-000 **(5469)**
2001: 8^{0}G, 9^{0}S, 9^{0}S

	Starts	1st	2nd	3rd	Win & Pl
Career Total (Turf)	6	0	0	0	274
Career Total (AW)	1	0	0	0	

Going (Turf): Sf: 0-3 GS: 0-0 Gd: 0-1 GF: 0-2 Fm: 0-0
Distance: 5f/6f: 0-1 7f-8f: 0-2 9f-13f: 0-4 14f+: 0-0
Track : LH: 0-5 RH: 0-0 Tight: 0-1 Gall: 0-1
Aids: Bl: 0-0 Vi: 0-0 Tstrap: 0-0
Best Rating: 28 5/01 Wwck 1m22y good

Deidamia (USA)

86 **37**

3-y-o b f Dayjur (USA)-Home Again (USA) (Forty Niner (USA))
P W Harris Mrs A Palmer & Mrs S Harris

Placings:4040-000 **(3153)**
2001: 8^{0}GS, 8^{0}GF, 7^{0}GS

	Starts	1st	2nd	3rd	Win & Pl
Career Total (Turf)	7	0	0	0	601

Going (Turf): Sf: 0-1 GS: 0-2 Gd: 0-0 GF: 0-4 Fm: 0-0
Distance: 5f/6f: 0-4 7f-8f: 0-3 9f-13f: 0-0 14f+: 0-0
Track : LH: 0-1 RH: 0-0 Tight: 0-0 Gall: 0-0
Aids: Bl: 0-0 Vi: 0-1 Tstrap: 0-0
Best Rating: 24 6/01 Sals 1m gd-sft

Del Mar Sunset

86 **66**

2-y-o b c Unfuwain (USA)-City Of Angels (Woodman (USA))
S P C Woods R A Dawson

Placings:0 **(5559)**
2001: 8^{0}S

	Starts	1st	2nd	3rd	Win & Pl
Career Total (Turf)	1	0	0	0	

Going (Turf): Sf: 0-1 GS: 0-0 Gd: 0-0 GF: 0-0 Fm: 0-0

Distance: 5f/6f: 0-0 7f-8f: 0-0 9f-13f: 0-1 14f+: 0-0
Track : LH: 0-0 RH: 0-0 Tight: 0-0 Gall: 0-0
Aids: Bl: 0-0 Vi: 0-0 Tstrap: 0-0
Best Rating: 66 10/01 Yarm 1m3y soft

Improved on his debut to run third in a maiden on Polytrack at Lingfield in November 2001.

Delaware Bay

89(75) (37)**60**

2-y-o ch g Karinga Bay-Galacia (IRE) (Gallic League)
W G M Turner A P Hedditch

Placings:220000 **(5590)**
2001: 5^{2}S, 5^{2}HY, 5^{0}GF, 8^{0}SD, 8^{0}G, 9^{0}GS

	Starts	1st	2nd	3rd	Win & Pl
Career Total (Turf)	5	0	2	0	1501
Career Total (AW)	1	0	0	0	

Going (Turf): Sf: 0-2 GS: 0-1 Gd: 0-1 GF: 0-1 Fm: 0-0
Distance: 5f/6f: 0-3 7f-8f: 0-0 9f-13f: 0-3 14f+: 0-0
Track : LH: 0-3 RH: 0-0 Tight: 0-2 Gall: 0-0
Aids: Bl: 0-0 Vi: 0-0 Tstrap: 0-1
Best Rating: 60 5/01 Nott 5f13y heavy

Delaware Trail

47

2-y-o b g Catrail (USA)-Dilwara (IRE) (Lashkari)
J S Wainwright Barry J Ross

Placings:0 **(5483)**
2001: 7^{0}HY

	Starts	1st	2nd	3rd	Win & Pl
Career Total (Turf)	1	0	0	0	

Going (Turf): Sf: 0-1 GS: 0-0 Gd: 0-0 GF: 0-0 Fm: 0-0
Distance: 5f/6f: 0-0 7f-8f: 0-1 9f-13f: 0-0 14f+: 0-0
Track : LH: 0-0 RH: 0-0 Tight: 0-0 Gall: 0-0
Aids: Bl: 0-0 Vi: 0-0 Tstrap: 0-0

Delegate

105(98) (74)**78**

8-y-o ch g Polish Precedent (USA)-Dangora (USA) (Sovereign Dancer (USA))
N A Callaghan Mrs P Reditt

Placings:1/240/5/4/43630/0642020056**6**-0004454360051020031 **(5629)**
2001: 6^{0}G, 5^{0}GF, 6^{0}GF, 6^{4}GF, 6^{4}G, 6^{5}GF, 5^{4}GF, 5^{3}GS, 5^{6}GF, 5^{0}GS, 6^{0}GS, 6^{5}G, 5^{1}GF, 5^{0}G, 5^{2}GS, 5^{0}G, 6^{0}G, 5^{3}HY, 5^{1}G

	Starts	1st	2nd	3rd	Win & Pl
Career Total (Turf)	39	3	4	4	52436
Career Total (AW)	1	0	0	0	0

61 11/01 Rdcr 5f D(0-75) GD £4264
73 8/01 NmkJ 5f D(0-85)H G-F £4104
7/95 Chan 6f GD £10180
Total win prize-money £18549

Going (Turf): Sf: 0-6 GS: 0-7 **Gd: 1-12 GF: 1-10** Fm: 0-1
Distance: **5f/6f: 2-30** 7f-8f: 0-7 9f-13f: 0-0 14f+: 0-0
Track : LH: 0-2 RH: 0-2 Tight: 0-2 Gall: 0-1
Aids: Bl: 0-0 Vi: 0-0 Tstrap: 0-0
Best Rating: 78 9/01 Donc 5f gd-sft

Runner-up in the Prix Djebel at Evry as a three-year-old for Andre Fabre, has obviously had his training problems and was sold for 14,000 guineas. He went six years without winning until finally scoring at Newmarket in August 2001, having dropped a mile down the handicap, he then continued to run well before scoring again at Redcar in November.

Delgado

97 **89**

2-y-o b g Alhaarth (IRE)-Nur (USA) (Diesis)
B J Meehan Kennet Valley Thoroughbreds Iii

Placings:323041300 **(5140)**
2001: 5^{3}GS, 5^{2}GS, 6^{3}GF, 5^{0}GF, 5^{4}GF, 5^{1}G, 5^{3}G, 5^{0}G, 6^{0}G

	Starts	1st	2nd	3rd	Win & Pl
Career Total (Turf)	9	1	1	3	7281

8/01 Folk 5f D GD £3471
Total win prize-money £3471

Going (Turf): Sf: 0-0 GS: 0-2 **Gd: 1-4** GF: 0-3 Fm: 0-0
Distance: **5f/6f: 1-9** 7f-8f: 0-0 9f-13f: 0-0 14f+: 0-0
Track : LH: 0-1 RH: 0-0 Tight: 0-0 Gall: 0-0
Aids: Bl: 0-1 Vi: 0-0 Tstrap: 0-1
Best Rating: 89 9/01 Sand 5f6y good

A half-brother to four winners, he had become disappointing but eventually got off the mark at Folkestone. Not disgraced since.

Delius (USA)

113 **107**

4-y-o b h A.P. Indy (USA)-Hot Novel (USA) (Mari's Book (USA))
Sir Michael Stoute M Tabor & Mrs John Magnier

Placings:1/433133 **(4847)**
2001: 11^{4}G, 10^{3}GF, 12^{3}G, 11^{1}GF, 12^{3}G, 10^{3}GF

	Starts	1st	2nd	3rd	Win & Pl
Career Total (Turf)	7	2	0	4	26872

94 8/01 Wind 1m3f135yC G-F £6104
90 10/99 Leic 1m8y D SFT £4630
Total win prize-money £10734

Going (Turf): Sf: 1-1 GS: 0-0 Gd: 0-3 **GF: 1-3** Fm: 0-0
Distance: 5f/6f: 0-0 7f-8f: 0-0 **9f-13f: 2-7** 14f+: 0-0
Track : LH: 0-1 RH: 0-2 **Tight: 1-3** Gall: 0-0
Aids: Bl: 0-0 Vi: 0-0 Tstrap: 0-0
Best Rating: 107 9/01 Kemp 1m4f good

A half-brother to the top-class American dirt performer Behrens, he won a soft-ground maiden on his debut in 1999 but was subsequently injured and missed the following season. He returned to winning form over an extended 11 furlongs at Windsor on his fourth start of 2001. Stays a mile and a half. Has occasionally got himself into a state at the start.

Della Francesca (USA)

104 **104**

2-y-o b c Danzig (USA)-La Affirmed (USA) (Affirmed (USA))
A P O'Brien Mr Tabor,Mrs Magnier & Mrs Maxwell Moran

Placings:312 **(5134)**
2001: 6^{3}G, 6^{1}G, 7^{2}G

	Starts	1st	2nd	3rd	Win & Pl
Career Total (Turf)	3	1	1	1	23441

88 9/01 Leop 6f GD £13000
Total win prize-money £13000

Going (Turf): Sf: 0-0 GS: 0-0 **Gd: 1-3** GF: 0-0 Fm: 0-0
Distance: **5f/6f: 1-2** 7f-8f: 0-1 9f-13f: 0-0 14f+: 0-0
Track : LH: 0-0 RH: 0-0 Tight: 0-0 Gall: 0-0
Aids: Bl: 0-0 Vi: 0-0 Tstrap: 0-0
Best Rating: 104 10/01 NmkR 7f good

Struggled to go the early pace on his debut over 6f at York in 2001 when finishing a staying on third, but had enough class to overcome that problem when winning at Leopardstown. Appreciated the extra furlong when a staying-on second in a Newmarket Group Three in October.

Delmo

76

6-y-o ch g Democratic (USA)-Charlotte Piaf (Morston (FR))

J White Mrs P A White

Placings:06/U0/0 (4048)
2001: 10^{0}F

	Starts	1st	2nd	3rd	Win & Pl
Career Total (Turf)	3	0	0	0	0
Career Total (AW)	2	0	0	0	

Going (Turf): Sf: 0-0 GS: 0-1 Gd: 0-0 GF: 0-1 Fm: 0-1
Distance: 5f/6f: 0-0 7f-8f: 0-1 9f-13f: 0-3 14f+: 0-1
Track: LH: 0-5 RH: 0-0 Tight: 0-3 Gall: 0-0
Aids: Bl: 0-0 Vi: 0-0 Tstrap: 0-0

Delphyllia

91 25
3-y-o b f Mind Games-Euphyllia (Superpower)
G G Margarson The Del Boys

Placings:000000-0006000 (4360)
2001: 5^{0}G, 5^{0}F, 6^{0}F, 5^{6}F, 5^{0}F, 7^{0}G, 9^{0}GF

	Starts	1st	2nd	3rd	Win & Pl
Career Total (Turf)	13	0	0	0	0

Going (Turf): Sf: 0-1 GS: 0-2 Gd: 0-5 GF: 0-1 Fm: 0-4
Distance: 5f/6f: 0-11 7f-8f: 0-1 9f-13f: 0-1 14f+: 0-0
Track: LH: 0-5 RH: 0-1 Tight: 0-0 Gall: 0-4
Aids: Bl: 0-5 Vi: 0-1 Tstrap: 0-0
Best Rating: 25 7/01 Muss 5f firm

Delta Georgia

(90) (31)49
5-y-o ch m Tina's Pet-Bacolet (Dominion)
A Bailey David English

Placings:5502/000-6 (0483)
2001: 10^{6}SD

	Starts	1st	2nd	3rd	Win & Pl
Career Total (Turf)	5	0	1	0	656
Career Total (AW)	3	0	0	0	0

Going (Turf): Sf: 0-1 GS: 0-2 Gd: 0-1 GF: 0-1 Fm: 0-0
Distance: 5f/6f: 0-2 7f-8f: 0-3 9f-13f: 0-3 14f+: 0-0
Track: LH: 0-6 RH: 0-0 Tight: 0-2 Gall: 0-0
Aids: Bl: 0-0 Vi: 0-0 Tstrap: 0-0
Best Rating: 16 3/01 Ling 1m2f stand

Demi Beau

103 75
3-y-o b c Dr Devious (IRE)-Charming Life (NZ) (Sir Tristram)
W Jarvis Plantation Stud

Placings:4331 (3935)
2001: 10^{4}G, 10^{3}GF, 12^{3}GF, 11^{1}G

	Starts	1st	2nd	3rd	Win & Pl
Career Total (Turf)	4	1	0	2	4960
68 8/01 Bevl 1m3f216yD				GD	£3150

Total win prize-money £3150

Going (Turf): Sf: 0-0 GS: 0-0 **Gd: 1-2** GF: 0-2 Fm: 0-0
Distance: 5f/6f: 0-0 7f-8f: 0-0 **9f-13f: 1-4** 14f+: 0-0
Track: LH: 0-1 **RH: 1-3 Tight: 1-1** Gall: 0-2
Aids: Bl: 0-0 Vi: 0-0 Tstrap: 0-0
Best Rating: 75 7/01 Kemp 1m4f gd-fm

A half-brother to the high-class smart middle-distance performers Wellbeing and Kingfisher Mill, he was reported to have made a noise in the paddock on his first appearance, but it did not hinder him in his progression to win a Beverley maiden in the late summer of 2001. The result was testimony to the fact that he had looked to need this 12-furlong trip prior to this run.

Demo Boys (IRE)

(100) (50?)26t
5-y-o b g De My Guest (USA)-Karine (Habitat)
C N Allen Shadowfax Racing.Com

Placings:0/443-0 (0060)
2001: 12^{0}SW

	Starts	1st	2nd	3rd	Win & Pl
Career Total (Turf)	1	0	0	0	
Career Total (AW)	4	0	0	1	565

Going (Turf): Sf: 0-0 GS: 0-0 Gd: 0-0 GF: 0-1 Fm: 0-0
Distance: 5f/6f: 0-1 7f-8f: 0-0 9f-13f: 0-3 14f+: 0-1
Track: LH: 0-4 RH: 0-0 Tight: 0-2 Gall: 0-0
Aids: Bl: 0-0 Vi: 0-0 Tstrap: 0-0

Democracy (IRE)

103(104) (52)53
5-y-o ch g Common Grounds-Inonder (Belfort (FR))
P G Murphy The Golden Anorak Partnership

Placings:3/636323342210/0053000000005340400-12105460 (3873)
2001: 6^{1}G, 7^{2}F, 9^{1}GF, 8^{0}GF, 9^{5}GF, 10^{4}GF, 9^{6}GF, 9^{0}G

	Starts	1st	2nd	3rd	Win & Pl
Career Total (Turf)	31	3	4	6	17399
Career Total (AW)	7	0	0	1	335
53 6/01 Gdwd 1m1f E(0-70)H				G-F	£3948
48 5/01 Brig 6f209y F(0-60)H				GD	£2429
78 9/99 Bath 5f161y D				G-F	£3779

Total win prize-money £10157

Going (Turf): Sf: 0-2 GS: 0-2 Gd: 1-8 **GF: 2-12** Fm: 0-7
Distance: 5f/6f: 1-5 7f-8f: 1-19 9f-13f: 1-14 14f+: 0-0
Track: **LH: 2-22** RH: 1-5 Tight: 1-14 Gall: 1-2
Aids: **Bl: 1-12** Vi: 0-3 Tstrap: 0-0
Best Rating: 53 6/01 Gdwd 1m1f gd-fm

He has been called some rude names in the past, but has been running well this season under inexperienced riders. Suited by a mile to nine furlongs and fast ground.

Demonstrate (USA)

67 - 17
3-y-o ch c Storm Bird (CAN)-Substance (USA) (Diesis)
J H M Gosden K Abdulla

Placings:0 (1751)
2001: 7^{0}GF

	Starts	1st	2nd	3rd	Win & Pl
Career Total (Turf)	1	0	0	0	

Going (Turf): Sf: 0-0 GS: 0-0 Gd: 0-0 GF: 0-1 Fm: 0-0
Distance: 5f/6f: 0-0 7f-8f: 0-1 9f-13f: 0-0 14f+: 0-0
Track: LH: 0-0 RH: 0-1 Tight: 0-0 Gall: 0-0
Aids: Bl: 0-0 Vi: 0-0 Tstrap: 0-0
Best Rating: 17 5/01 Gdwd 7f gd-fm

Demophilos

113 117
3-y-o b c Dr Devious (IRE)-Graecia Magna (USA) (Private Account (USA))
Mrs A J Perrett Athos Christodoulou

Placings:1-0303232 (4711)
2001: 11^{0}GF, 10^{3}GF, 10^{0}GF, 10^{3}G, 12^{2}GF, 11^{3}G, 14^{2}G

	Starts	1st	2nd	3rd	Win & Pl
Career Total (Turf)	8	1	2	3	124596
90 9/00 NmkR 7f D				GD	£5102

Total win prize-money £5103

Going (Turf): Sf: 0-0 GS: 0-0 **Gd: 1-4** GF: 0-4 Fm: 0-0
Distance: 5f/6f: 0-0 **7f-8f: 1-1** 9f-13f: 0-6 14f+: 0-1
Track: LH: 0-2 RH: 0-3 Tight: 0-1 Gall: 0-4
Aids: Bl: 0-0 Vi: 0-0 Tstrap: 0-0
Best Rating: 117 9/01 Donc 1m6f132y good

Showed promise when winning his only outing at two at Newmarket in 2000. He was found wanting in Listed races early in 2001, but appreciated the step up to 12 furlongs and waiting tactics when runner-up in the Gordon Stakes and third in the Great Voltigeur, but finished further behind the Voltigeur winner Milan in the St Leger. Acts on sound surface and has worn a net muzzle.

Demosthenes (IRE)

93 67
2-y-o b c Lycius (USA)-Fantasy Girl (IRE) (Marju (IRE))
J L Dunlop Windflower Overseas Holdings Inc

Placings:066 (3008)
2001: 6^{0}GF, 6^{6}GF, 6^{6}GF

	Starts	1st	2nd	3rd	Win & Pl
Career Total (Turf)	3	0	0	0	0

Going (Turf): Sf: 0-0 GS: 0-0 Gd: 0-0 GF: 0-3 Fm: 0-0
Distance: 5f/6f: 0-2 7f-8f: 0-1 9f-13f: 0-0 14f+: 0-0
Track: LH: 0-0 RH: 0-0 Tight: 0-0 Gall: 0-0
Aids: Bl: 0-0 Vi: 0-0 Tstrap: 0-0
Best Rating: 67 6/01 Nott 6f15y gd-fm

Den's-Joy

109(97) (62)80
5-y-o b m Archway (IRE)-Bonvin (Taufan (USA))
Miss D A McHale N T Davis & M Watmore

Placings:35/3001001200540200-0040031111060 (5019)
2001: 8^{0}GS, 8^{0}G, 9^{4}GF, 8^{0}GF, 9^{0}GF, 10^{3}GF, 8^{1}G, 8^{1}G, 8^{1}GF, 8^{1}GF, 9^{0}GF, 8^{6}S, 8^{0}S

	Starts	1st	2nd	3rd	Win & Pl
Career Total (Turf)	28	6	2	2	31675
Career Total (AW)	3	0	0	1	436
80 9/01 Thsk 1m C(0-90)H				G-F	£7475
80 8/01 Wind 1m67y D(0-85)H				G-F	£4111
68 8/01 Wind 1m67y D(0-80)H				GD	£4244
62 8/01 Wind 1m67y E(0-70)H				GD	£3164
60 6/00 Ling 1m1f D(0-85)H				FRM	£3848
60 5/00 Wind 1m67y D(0-85)H				G-S	£3965

Total win prize-money £26808

Going (Turf): Sf: 0-2 GS: 1-5 **Gd: 2-5 GF: 2-15** Fm: 1-1
Distance: 5f/6f: 0-0 7f-8f: 1-10 **9f-13f: 5-21** 14f+: 0-0
Track: LH: 2-5 **RH: 4-15 Tight: 6-15** Gall: 0-0
Aids: Bl: 0-0 Vi: 0-1 Tstrap: 0-0
Best Rating: 80 9/01 Thsk 1m gd-fm

A real Windsor specialist, she completed a four-timer in the summer of 2001, but has not surprisingly gone up in the weights as a result. Likes to come from behind off a fast pace, acts well on most goings and is suited by trips of around a mile.

Denarius Secundus

82 43
4-y-o ch g Barathea (IRE)-Penny Drops (Sharpo)
E A Wheeler The Guinness & Oyster Partnership

Placings:0000-000 (2250)
2001: 10^{0}GS, 11^{0}GF, 16^{0}GF

	Starts	1st	2nd	3rd	Win & Pl
Career Total (Turf)	7	0	0	0	

Going (Turf): Sf: 0-1 GS: 0-1 Gd: 0-1 GF: 0-4 Fm: 0-0
Distance: 5f/6f: 0-0 7f-8f: 0-3 9f-13f: 0-3 14f+: 0-1
Track: LH: 0-2 RH: 0-1 Tight: 0-3 Gall: 0-0
Aids: Bl: 0-2 Vi: 0-0 Tstrap: 0-0
Best Rating: 14 5/01 Wind 1m2f7y gd-sft

Denbrae (IRE)

93(97) (51)40

9-y-o b g Sure Blade (USA)-Fencing (Viking (USA))
Mrs Lydia Pearce (J Pearce 26/2) Mrs P O'Shea

Placings:3424/11246005/4033424410050/300354410/3 45050403600560/3120120300/0-2220005 **(5027)**
2001: 8^{2}SD, 7^{2}SW, 8^{2}SD, 8^{0}SD, 7^{0}GF, 8^{0}SD, 5^{5}S

	Starts	1st	2nd	3rd	Win & Pl
Career Total (Turf)	49	4	3	7	22711
Career Total (AW)	18	2	5	2	7795

51	5/99	Haml	6f5y	F(0-65)H	SFT	£2948
49	3/99	Sthl	7f	G(0-75)H	STD	£1522
68	8/97	Leic	7f9y	F(0-65)	GD	£2847
69	6/96	Chep	6f16y	D(0-75)H	G-F	£3621
64	4/95	Nott	6f15y	E(0-70)H	GD	£3473
57	2/95	Sthl	6f	F	STD	£2789

Total win prize-money £17201

Going (Turf): Sf: 1-5 GS: 0-8 Gd: 2-18 GF: 1-17 Fm: 0-1
Distance: 5f/6f: 1-30 7f-8f: 5-33 9f-13f: 0-4 14f+: 0-0
Track : LH: 2-22 RH: 0-4 Tight: 0-8 Gall: 0-3
Aids: Bl: 0-0 Vi: 0-0 Tstrap: 0-0
Best Rating: 51 3/01 Wolv 1m100y stand

Moderate handicapper at 6-7 furlongs, acts on any ground on turf and Fibresand.

Denise Best (IRE)

87(63) **44**
3-y-o ch f Goldmark (USA)-Titchwell Lass (Lead On Time (USA))
A Berry Alan Berry

Placings:02405-06505000500 **(5625)**
2001: 8^{0}G, 10^{6}G, 10^{5}GF, 7^{0}F, 8^{5}GF, 8^{0}GF, 8^{0}G, 9^{0}GF, 8^{5}HY, 8^{0}HY, 8^{0}GS

	Starts	1st	2nd	3rd	Win & Pl
Career Total (Turf)	15	0	1	0	3888
Career Total (AW)	1	0	0	0	

Going (Turf): Sf: 0-5 GS: 0-1 Gd: 0-3 GF: 0-5 Fm: 0-1
Distance: 5f/6f: 0-0 7f-8f: 0-10 9f-13f: 0-6 14f+: 0-0
Track : LH: 0-10 RH: 0-4 Tight: 0-8 Gall: 0-2
Aids: Bl: 0-0 Vi: 0-0 Tstrap: 0-0
Best Rating: 60 5/01 Donc 1m2f60y gd-fm

Denise Margaret (IRE)

107 **87**
3-y-o b f Flying Spur (AUS)-Rachel Pringle (IRE) (Doulab (USA))
J Noseda Martin O'Connor & Kurt Stern

Placings:300-21016600 **(5135)**
2001: 8^{2}GS, 9^{1}F, 12^{0}GF, 10^{1}GF, 10^{6}G, 9^{6}GF, 10^{0}GF, 10^{0}G

	Starts	1st	2nd	3rd	Win & Pl
Career Total (Turf)	11	2	1	1	12184

87	7/01	Sand	1m2f7y	D(0-85)H	G-F	£7410
80	5/01	Brig	1m1f209yF		FRM	£2884

Total win prize-money £10294

Going (Turf): Sf: 0-0 GS: 0-1 Gd: 0-3 GF: 1-4 Fm: 1-2
Distance: 5f/6f: 0-0 7f-8f: 0-3 9f-13f: 2-8 14f+: 0-0
Track : LH: 1-4 RH: 1-5 Tight: 0-2 Gall: 0-3
Aids: Bl: 0-0 Vi: 0-0 Tstrap: 0-0
Best Rating: 87 7/01 York 1m2f85y good

Formerly trained in Ireland, she landed a Brighton maiden in May on her second start in this country and ran with credit in the King George V Handicap at Royal Ascot. Returned to winning form over ten furlongs at Sandown in July and ran a blinder in the John Smith's Cup considering she had the worst draw. Disappointing towards the back-end of the season.

Denmark (IRE)

99 **84**
2-y-o b c Danehill (USA)-Shamarra (FR) (Zayyani)
Sir Mark Prescott Graham Rock - Osborne House

Placings:1 **(5445)**
2001: 6^{1}HY

	Starts	1st	2nd	3rd	Win & Pl
Career Total (Turf)	1	1	0	0	2982

84	10/01	Newc	6f	D	HVY	£2982

Total win prize-money £2982

Going (Turf): Sf: 1-1 GS: 0-0 Gd: 0-0 GF: 0-0 Fm: 0-0
Distance: 5f/6f: 1-1 7f-8f: 0-0 9f-13f: 0-0 14f+: 0-0
Track : LH: 0-0 RH: 0-0 Tight: 0-0 Gall: 0-0
Aids: Bl: 0-0 Vi: 0-0 Tstrap: 0-0
Best Rating: 84 10/01 Newc 6f heavy

An IR100,000gns half-brother to Shantaroun, he won a back-end maiden at Newcastle on heavy ground on his sole start of 2001.

Dennis Bergkamp (IRE)

83(80) (13)**30**
4-y-o b g Night Shift (USA)-Indian Express (Indian Ridge)
W Clay Dave Dutton

Placings:000300/00000-000050050600 **(4940)**
2001: 5^{0}SD, 7^{0}SD, 12^{0}S, 8^{0}F, 10^{5}F, 9^{0}GF, 6^{0}GF, 8^{5}GS, 8^{0}GF, 7^{6}GS, 8^{0}GF, 6^{0}S

	Starts	1st	2nd	3rd	Win & Pl
Career Total (Turf)	18	0	0	1	595
Career Total (AW)	5	0	0	0	

Going (Turf): Sf: 0-4 GS: 0-3 Gd: 0-0 GF: 0-9 Fm: 0-2
Distance: 5f/6f: 0-5 7f-8f: 0-7 9f-13f: 0-9 14f+: 0-2
Track : LH: 0-12 RH: 0-2 Tight: 0-4 Gall: 0-4
Aids: Bl: 0-0 Vi: 0-3 Tstrap: 0-7
Best Rating: 30 8/01 Pont 1m4y gd-fm

Dennis El Menace

109(84) (58)**78**
3-y-o b g College Chapel-Spanish Craft (IRE) (Jareer (USA))
W R Muir Brian & Helen Moss

Placings:04643203-0300222623621200 **(5669)**
2001: 7^{0}GS, 8^{3}HY, 7^{0}G, 8^{0}G, 8^{2}GF, 8^{2}GF, 9^{2}F, 8^{6}G, 7^{2}GF, 8^{3}GF, 8^{6}G, 8^{2}G, 9^{1}G, 8^{2}GF, 8^{0}S, 10^{0}HY

	Starts	1st	2nd	3rd	Win & Pl
Career Total (Turf)	22	1	7	4	16991
Career Total (AW)	2	0	0	0	214

72	9/01	Haml	1m1f36y	E(0-70)	GD	£2968

Total win prize-money £2968

Going (Turf): Sf: 0-3 GS: 0-2 Gd: 1-10 GF: 0-6 Fm: 0-1
Distance: 5f/6f: 0-3 7f-8f: 0-14 9f-13f: 1-7 14f+: 0-0
Track : LH: 0-5 RH: 1-2 Tight: 1-4 Gall: 0-0
Aids: Bl: 1-10 Vi: 0-3 Tstrap: 0-0
Best Rating: 78 9/01 Newb 1m gd-fm

Seems best suited by fast ground has been running well in blinkers in 2001, finally getting off the mark over nine furlongs on good ground after a number of placed efforts. Suited by most goings and acts well at seven furlongs to a mile.

Dennis Our Menace

107(97) (62)**72**
3-y-o b g Piccolo-Free On Board (Free State)
S Dow The Champagne Quartet

Placings:0330-34050422000 **(4988)**
2001: 9^{3}SW, 10^{4}SD, 10^{0}S, 9^{5}GS, 9^{0}GF, 9^{4}S, 8^{2}GF, 8^{2}GF, 8^{0}GF, 8^{0}G, 8^{0}G

	Starts	1st	2nd	3rd	Win & Pl
Career Total (Turf)	13	0	2	2	3818
Career Total (AW)	2	0	0	1	702

Going (Turf): Sf: 0-3 GS: 0-1 Gd: 0-2 GF: 0-7 Fm: 0-0
Distance: 5f/6f: 0-0 7f-8f: 0-8 9f-13f: 0-7 14f+: 0-0
Track : LH: 0-3 RH: 0-4 Tight: 0-3 Gall: 0-0
Aids: Bl: 0-0 Vi: 0-0 Tstrap: 0-0
Best Rating: 75 6/01 Sals 1m gd-fm

A useful two-year-old, he ran his best races at around seven furlongs on a sound surface. Has yet to recapture that form at three but has ran some of his better races this season on the All-Weather. Has run well over nine furlongs.

Dennis's Bismarck

80 **42**
2-y-o b f Pyramus (USA)-Lady Antoinette (Pharly (FR))
S Dow Barry Dennis

Placings:50 **(4470)**
2001: 5^{5}G, 6^{0}GF

	Starts	1st	2nd	3rd	Win & Pl
Career Total (Turf)	2	0	0	0	0

Going (Turf): Sf: 0-0 GS: 0-0 Gd: 0-1 GF: 0-1 Fm: 0-0
Distance: 5f/6f: 0-1 7f-8f: 0-1 9f-13f: 0-0 14f+: 0-0
Track : LH: 0-2 RH: 0-0 Tight: 0-0 Gall: 0-0
Aids: Bl: 0-0 Vi: 0-0 Tstrap: 0-0
Best Rating: 42 8/01 Brig 5f213y good

Densim Blue (IRE)

(94) (53)**62**
3-y-o b c Lake Coniston (IRE)-Surprise Visitor (IRE) (Be My Guest (USA))
N E Berry The Square Milers

Placings:024145240-0061400566000500 **(5418)**
2001: 6^{0}GS, 6^{0}G, 6^{6}G, 7^{1}F, 7^{4}GF, 7^{0}G, 7^{0}GF, 7^{5}GF, 7^{6}G, 7^{6}GF, 6^{0}GF, 6^{0}GF, 7^{0}SD, 7^{5}G, 5^{0}GS, 7^{0}SD

	Starts	1st	2nd	3rd	Win & Pl
Career Total (Turf)	23	2	2	0	8413
Career Total (AW)	2	0	0	0	

70	6/01	Ling	7f	E(0-65)	FRM	£3126
72	5/00	Brig	5f59y	E	G-S	£2832

Total win prize-money £5959

Going (Turf): Sf: 0-0 GS: 1-3 Gd: 0-8 GF: 0-10 Fm: 1-2
Distance: 5f/6f: 1-13 7f-8f: 1-12 9f-13f: 0-0 14f+: 0-0
Track : LH: 1-9 RH: 0-2 Tight: 0-4 Gall: 0-2
Aids: Bl: 0-0 Vi: 0-0 Tstrap: 0-0
Best Rating: 70 6/01 Ling 7f firm

Dere Lyn

91(79) (33)**50**
3-y-o b g Awesome-Our Resolution (Caerleon (USA))
D Burchell Lyn Phillips

Placings:30600 **(2216)**
2001: 6^{3}HY, 9^{0}SD, 7^{6}F, 9^{0}GF, 7^{0}G

	Starts	1st	2nd	3rd	Win & Pl
Career Total (Turf)	4	0	0	1	532
Career Total (AW)	1	0	0	0	

Going (Turf): Sf: 0-1 GS: 0-0 Gd: 0-1 GF: 0-1 Fm: 0-1
Distance: 5f/6f: 0-0 7f-8f: 0-3 9f-13f: 0-2 14f+: 0-0
Track : LH: 0-1 RH: 0-2 Tight: 0-3 Gall: 0-0
Aids: Bl: 0-0 Vi: 0-0 Tstrap: 0-0
Best Rating: 50 5/01 Leic 7f9y firm

Derek's Pride (IRE)

91(60) **27**
3-y-o b f General Monash (USA)-Likeness (Young Generation)
J Parkes P J Sweeney

Placings:0-0000000 **(5186)**
2001: 8^{0}S, 7^{0}S, 5^{0}GF, 8^{0}F, 9^{0}GF, 5^{0}G, 5^{0}GS

	Starts	1st	2nd	3rd	Win & Pl
Career Total (Turf)	7	0	0	0	
Career Total (AW)	1	0	0	0	

Going (Turf): Sf: 0-2 GS: 0-1 Gd: 0-1 GF: 0-2 Fm: 0-1
Distance: 5f/6f: 0-3 7f-8f: 0-4 9f-13f: 0-1 14f+: 0-0
Track : LH: 0-2 RH: 0-2 Tight: 0-2 Gall: 0-0
Aids: Bl: 0-1 Vi: 0-0 Tstrap: 0-0
Best Rating: 32 4/01 Ripn 1m soft

Dericou (IRE)

91 **46**

3-y-o b g Sri Pekan (USA)-Cartagena Lady (IRE) (Prince Rupert (FR))
J Noseda John Breslin

Placings:05600 **(5043)**
2001: 8^{0}G, 7^{5}GF, 7^{6}GF, 10^{0}G, 8^{0}G

	Starts	1st	2nd	3rd	Win & Pl
Career Total (Turf)	5	0	0	0	0

Going (Turf): Sf: 0-0 GS: 0-0 Gd: 0-3 GF: 0-2 Fm: 0-0
Distance: 5f/6f: 0-0 7f-8f: 0-3 9f-13f: 0-2 14f+: 0-0
Track : LH: 0-2 RH: 0-2 Tight: 0-2 Gall: 0-0
Aids: Bl: 0-0 Vi: 0-1 Tstrap: 0-0
Best Rating: 65 5/01 NmkR 1m good

Derryquin

101 **70**

6-y-o b g Lion Cavern (USA)-Top Berry (High Top)
P L Gilligan Lady Bland

Placings:011/405000/056400/0102040110-0006065 **(3865)**
2001: 8^{0}GS, 7^{0}GF, 8^{0}GF, 7^{6}F, 8^{0}GS, 5^{6}GF, 8^{5}GF

	Starts	1st	2nd	3rd	Win & Pl
Career Total (Turf)	32	5	1	0	24981

70	8/00	Rdcr	1m	D(0-80)H	FRM	£5369
66	8/00	Leic	1m8y	D(0-85)H	G-F	£7442
55	5/00	Rdcr	1m	F(0-65)H	G-F	£3211
95	11/97	Donc	1m	C	GD	£4428
81	10/97	Ling	7f	D	GD	£3143

Total win prize-money £23594

Going (Turf): Sf: 0-3 GS: 0-5 **Gd: 2-8 GF: 2-14** Fm: 1-2
Distance: 5f/6f: 0-6 **7f-8f: 4-22** 9f-13f: 1-4 14f+: 0-0
Track : LH: 0-5 RH: 0-5 Tight: 0-1 Gall: 0-4
Aids: **Bl: 3-19** Vi: 0-1 Tstrap: 0-0
Best Rating: 70 6/01 Kemp 1m gd-fm

Useful performer in his time, enjoyed something of a revival in 2000 winning back-to-back handicaps in August. Moderate efforts since, likes to dominate.

Derwent (USA)

94 **94**

2-y-o b/br c Distant View (USA)-Nothing Sweeter (USA) (Darby Creek Road (USA))
L M Cumani M J Dawson

Placings:03 **(5367)**
2001: 8^{0}S, 8^{3}GS

	Starts	1st	2nd	3rd	Win & Pl
Career Total (Turf)	2	0	0	1	870

Going (Turf): Sf: 0-1 GS: 0-1 Gd: 0-0 GF: 0-0 Fm: 0-0
Distance: 5f/6f: 0-0 7f-8f: 0-2 9f-13f: 0-0 14f+: 0-0
Track : LH: 0-0 RH: 0-0 Tight: 0-0 Gall: 0-0
Aids: Bl: 0-0 Vi: 0-0 Tstrap: 0-0
Best Rating: 94 10/01 NmkR 1m gd-sft

A half-brother to several winners abroad, he improved on his debut effort to finish third in a Newmarket maiden over a mile in October.

Desaru (USA)

106 **63**

5-y-o br g Chief's Crown (USA)-Team Colors (USA) (Mr Prospector (USA))
D Nicholls J E Swiers

Placings:213/00/000-000005002046 **(4424)**
2001: 8^{0}S, 7^{0}S, 6^{0}G, 8^{0}F, 6^{0}G, 10^{5}GF, 10^{0}GF, 9^{0}GS, 9^{2}GF, 8^{0}GF, 11^{4}GF, 12^{6}GF

	Starts	1st	2nd	3rd	Win & Pl
Career Total (Turf)	20	1	2	1	21202

99	9/98	Donc	7f	C	GD	£5552

Total win prize-money £5553

Going (Turf): Sf: 0-3 GS: 0-2 **Gd: 1-4** GF: 0-10 Fm: 0-1
Distance: 5f/6f: 0-2 **7f-8f: 1-10** 9f-13f: 0-8 14f+: 0-0
Track : LH: 0-3 RH: 0-5 Tight: 0-3 Gall: 0-1
Aids: Bl: 0-0 Vi: 0-1 Tstrap: 0-0
Best Rating: 63 7/01 Bevl 1m1f207y gd-fm

Has kept useful company over the last couple of years, but had his sights lowered in 2001 and remains hard to win with.

Desert Air (JPN)

90 **75**

2-y-o ch c Desert King (IRE)-Greek Air (IRE) (Ela-Mana-Mou)
P F I Cole Mrs Belinda Harvey

Placings:024 **(4307)**
2001: 7^{0}G, 7^{2}GS, 7^{4}GF

	Starts	1st	2nd	3rd	Win & Pl
Career Total (Turf)	3	0	1	0	1592

Going (Turf): Sf: 0-0 GS: 0-1 Gd: 0-1 GF: 0-1 Fm: 0-0
Distance: 5f/6f: 0-0 7f-8f: 0-3 9f-13f: 0-0 14f+: 0-0
Track : LH: 0-0 RH: 0-1 Tight: 0-0 Gall: 0-0
Aids: Bl: 0-0 Vi: 0-0 Tstrap: 0-0
Best Rating: 75 8/01 Gdwd 7f good

Desert Alchemy (IRE)

96 **89**

2-y-o b f Green Desert (USA)-Waffle On (Chief Singer)
Mrs A J Perrett R Grossman And S Tullah

Placings:4 **(5274)**
2001: 7^{4}GS

	Starts	1st	2nd	3rd	Win & Pl
Career Total (Turf)	1	0	0	0	313

Going (Turf): Sf: 0-0 GS: 0-1 Gd: 0-0 GF: 0-0 Fm: 0-0
Distance: 5f/6f: 0-0 7f-8f: 0-1 9f-13f: 0-0 14f+: 0-0
Track : LH: 0-0 RH: 0-0 Tight: 0-0 Gall: 0-0
Aids: Bl: 0-0 Vi: 0-0 Tstrap: 0-0
Best Rating: 89 10/01 Leic 7f9y gd-sft

Desert Charm

(64)

4-y-o b f Desert Style (IRE)-Autumn Fall (USA) (Sanglamore (USA))
H J Manners H J Manners

Placings:000/00-0 **(0376)**
2001: 12^{0}SD

	Starts	1st	2nd	3rd	Win & Pl
Career Total (Turf)	4	0	0	0	
Career Total (AW)	2	0	0	0	

Going (Turf): Sf: 0-1 GS: 0-1 Gd: 0-1 GF: 0-1 Fm: 0-0
Distance: 5f/6f: 0-0 7f-8f: 0-3 9f-13f: 0-3 14f+: 0-0
Track : LH: 0-3 RH: 0-1 Tight: 0-3 Gall: 0-0
Aids: Bl: 0-1 Vi: 0-0 Tstrap: 0-0

Desert City

98 **70**

2-y-o b g Darnay-Oasis (Valiyar)
R Hannon Park Walk Racing

Placings:345433 **(4954)**
2001: 5^{3}GF, 6^{4}GF, 5^{5}GF, 7^{4}GS, 7^{3}GF, 8^{3}GS

	Starts	1st	2nd	3rd	Win & Pl
Career Total (Turf)	6	0	0	3	2455

Going (Turf): Sf: 0-0 GS: 0-2 Gd: 0-0 GF: 0-4 Fm: 0-0
Distance: 5f/6f: 0-3 7f-8f: 0-3 9f-13f: 0-0 14f+: 0-0
Track : LH: 0-1 RH: 0-2 Tight: 0-0 Gall: 0-0
Aids: Bl: 0-0 Vi: 0-0 Tstrap: 0-0
Best Rating: 70 9/01 Gdwd 1m gd-sft

A half-brother to four winners from the family of Magic Ring, has run fair races in maidens and nurseries. Stays a mile, acts on fast and good to soft ground.

Desert Deer

108 **104+**

3-y-o ch c Cadeaux Genereux-Tuxford Hideaway (Cawston's Clown)
M Johnston Jaber Abdullah

Placings:2111 **(2853)**
2001: 8^{2}S, 9^{1}F, 8^{1}F, 8^{1}G

	Starts	1st	2nd	3rd	Win & Pl
Career Total (Turf)	4	3	1	0	35345

104	7/01	Sand	1m14y	B(0-105)H	GD	£26100
90	5/01	Pont	1m4y	D(0-85)H	FRM	£4894
74	5/01	Haml	1m1f36y	D	FRM	£3542

Total win prize-money £34538

Going (Turf): Sf: 0-1 GS: 0-0 Gd: 1-1 GF: 0-0 **Fm: 2-2**
Distance: 5f/6f: 0-0 7f-8f: 0-1 **9f-13f: 3-3** 14f+: 0-0
Track : LH: 1-1 **RH: 2-3 Tight: 1-2** Gall: 0-0
Aids: Bl: 0-0 Vi: 0-0 Tstrap: 0-0
Best Rating: 104 7/01 Sand 1m14y good

A half-brother to multiple winner Branston Abby, was installed a red-hot favourite on his racecourse bow in April 2001 but met an experienced, race-fit rival who was in no mood for defeat. Scored next time out over nine furlongs and followed up with two successes over a mile, taking a handicap at Sandown on his last start of 2001. Acts on fast ground.

Desert Fighter

99 (77?)**63d**

10-y-o b g Green Desert (USA)-Jungle Rose (Shirley Heights)
Mrs M Reveley A Frame

Placings:0342151160/0/0003/3114/032032544/311114/0010212-515 **(3710)**
2001: 12^{5}F, 12^{1}G, 12^{5}G

	Starts	1st	2nd	3rd	Win & Pl
Career Total (Turf)	43	12	4	6	55130
Career Total (AW)	1	0	1	0	986

47	7/01	Newc	1m4f93y	F	GD	£2474
58	7/00	Catt	1m3f214y	F	G-F	£2268
51	5/00	Thsk	1m4f	E	GD	£3038
65	7/99	Catt	1m3f214y	F	FRM	£2241
55	7/99	Haml	1m3f16y	F(0-65)	FRM	£3436
68	7/99	Hayd	1m3f200y	E(0-70)	G-S	£2668
50	5/99	Thsk	1m4f	E	G-S	£2883
75	5/97	Newc	1m4f93y	D(0-80)H	G-F	£4065
76	4/97	Thsk	1m4f	E	G-F	£2880
89	8/94	Hayd	1m2f120y	D(0-85)H	GD	£3610
82	7/94	Wind	1m2f7y	D(0-80)H	G-F	£4347
70	6/94	Rdcr	1m	D	G-F	£3342

Total win prize-money £37255

Going (Turf): Sf: 0-2 GS: 2-10 Gd: 3-11 **GF: 5-15** Fm: 2-5
Distance: 5f/6f: 0-0 7f-8f: 1-5 **9f-13f: 11-38** 14f+: 0-1

Track : LH: 9-37 RH: 1-2 **Tight: 7-22** Gall: 2-10
Aids: Bl: 0-0 Vi: 0-0 Tstrap: 0-0
Best Rating: 47 7/01 Newc 1m4f93y good

He is a fair middle-distance performer, but all his recent victories have been in claimers. Not nearly so effective in handicaps. Winning hurdler.

Desert Fury

110 **79**

4-y-o b g Warning-Number One Spot (Reference Point)
B Hanbury J A Thompson

Placings:13/30006046540-0223615200 **(5366)**
2001: 10^{0}G, 8^{2}GS, 8^{2}GF, 7^{3}GF, 7^{6}GF, 7^{1}GS, 8^{5}G, 7^{2}GF, 8^{0}G, 8^{0}GS

	Starts	1st	2nd	3rd	Win & Pl
Career Total (Turf)	23	2	3	3	23198

56	7/01	Ayr	7f	D(0-80)	G-S	£3991
82	5/99	Ches	5f16y	D	G-F	£7067

Total win prize-money £11058

Going (Turf): Sf: 0-3 **GS: 1-4** Gd: 0-5 **GF: 1-11** Fm: 0-0
Distance: 5f/6f: 1-6 7f-8f: 1-13 9f-13f: 0-4 14f+: 0-0
Track : **LH: 2-5** RH: 0-5 **Tight: 1-3** Gall: 0-4
Aids: Bl: 0-0 Vi: 0-0 Tstrap: 0-0
Best Rating: 81 5/01 NmkR 1m gd-sft

He gradually returned to form in 2001 and scored for the first time since his racecourse debut at Ayr in July. He has won on fast ground, but acts on easier.

Desert Island Disc

94(66) **52**

4-y-o b f Turtle Island (IRE)-Distant Music (Darshaan)
J J Bridger (Ms A E Embiricos 12/1) W Wood

Placings:050/65100-0000000 **(5592)**
2001: 9^{0}GS, 8^{0}GF, 8^{0}GF, 8^{0}G, 9^{0}GS, 7^{0}S, 6^{0}GS

	Starts	1st	2nd	3rd	Win & Pl
Career Total (Turf)	13	1	0	0	4030
Career Total (AW)	2	0	0	0	0

71	5/00	Wwck	1m2f110yD(0-80)H	HVY	£4030

Total win prize-money £4030

Going (Turf): Sf: 1-4 GS: 0-5 Gd: 0-2 GF: 0-2 Fm: 0-0
Distance: 5f/6f: 0-0 7f-8f: 0-9 **9f-13f: 1-5** 14f+: 0-1
Track : **LH: 1-7** RH: 0-4 Tight: 0-3 Gall: 0-1
Aids: Bl: 0-0 Vi: 0-0 Tstrap: 0-0
Best Rating: 52 10/01 Brig 7f214y soft

Desert Knight

96 **93**

5-y-o b h Green Desert (USA)-Green Leaf (USA) (Alydar (USA))
J Noseda Sheikh Khaled Duaij Al Sabah

Placings:12/315-560 **(1297)**
2001: 8^{5}GS, 6^{0}HY, 7^{0}G

	Starts	1st	2nd	3rd	Win & Pl
Career Total (Turf)	8	2	1	1	14657

91	4/00	Wwck	6f168y	C	HVY	£5927
92	8/99	Pont	1m4y	D	GD	£4513

Total win prize-money £10442

Going (Turf): Sf: 1-2 GS: 0-1 **Gd: 1-3** GF: 0-2 Fm: 0-0
Distance: 5f/6f: 0-0 7f-8f: 1-7 9f-13f: 1-1 14f+: 0-0
Track : **LH: 2-6** RH: 0-0 Tight: 0-0 Gall: 0-3
Aids: Bl: 0-0 Vi: 0-0 Tstrap: 0-0
Best Rating: 68 5/01 Ling 7f good

Lightly-raced. Has shown useful form in Listed events but disappointed this term. Wears bandages.

Desert Music

98 **31**

5-y-o b m Ardkinglass-Musical Princess (Cavo Doro)
J R Weymes Mrs N Napier

Placings:055500-50500 **(5382)**
2001: 12^{5}GF, 11^{0}GF, 16^{5}GF, 16^{0}F, 11^{0}S

	Starts	1st	2nd	3rd	Win & Pl
Career Total (Turf)	11	0	0	0	0

Going (Turf): Sf: 0-1 GS: 0-0 Gd: 0-3 GF: 0-4 Fm: 0-2
Distance: 5f/6f: 0-0 7f-8f: 0-0 9f-13f: 0-7 14f+: 0-3
Track : LH: 0-6 RH: 0-4 Tight: 0-7 Gall: 0-1
Aids: Bl: 0-0 Vi: 0-0 Tstrap: 0-0
Best Rating: 37 7/01 Pont 1m4f8y gd-fm

Desert Royal (IRE)

95 **71**

2-y-o ch c Ali-Royal (IRE)-Hajat (Mujtahid (USA))
R Hannon The Waney Racing Group Inc

Placings:5260631465 **(5342)**
2001: 5^{5}GS, 5^{2}F, 5^{6}F, 6^{0}GF, 5^{6}GF, 7^{3}G, 6^{1}GF, 8^{4}GS, 9^{6}HY, 7^{5}GS

	Starts	1st	2nd	3rd	Win & Pl
Career Total (Turf)	10	1	1	1	4759

71	8/01	Sals	6f212y	F	G-F	£3052

Total win prize-money £3052

Going (Turf): Sf: 0-1 GS: 0-3 Gd: 0-1 **GF: 1-3** Fm: 0-2
Distance: 5f/6f: 0-5 **7f-8f: 1-4** 9f-13f: 0-1 14f+: 0-0
Track : LH: 0-2 RH: 0-2 Tight: 0-0 Gall: 0-1
Aids: Bl: 0-0 Vi: 0-0 Tstrap: 0-0
Best Rating: 71 10/01 NmkR 7f gd-sft

Plating-class colt. Stays a mile.

Desert Spa (USA)

(105) (61)**39d**

6-y-o b g Sheikh Albadou-Healing Waters (USA) (Temperence Hill (USA))
P J Makin D M Ahier

Placings:546/306000103/02/1101020-10 **(5191)**
2001: 12^{1}SD, 12^{0}SD

	Starts	1st	2nd	3rd	Win & Pl
Career Total (Turf)	12	0	0	1	768
Career Total (AW)	11	5	2	1	13005

61	6/01	Sthl	1m4f	F	STD	£2310
58	5/00	Wolv	1m4f	F(0-60)	STD	£2219
58	2/00	Wolv	1m4f	F(0-60)H	STD	£2425
54	1/00	Wolv	1m4f	F(0-60)H	STD	£1928
55	9/98	Wolv	1m4f	F(0-60)H	STD	£2402

Total win prize-money £11286

Going (Turf): Sf: 0-3 GS: 0-2 Gd: 0-2 GF: 0-3 Fm: 0-2
Distance: 5f/6f: 0-0 7f-8f: 0-2 **9f-13f: 5-21** 14f+: 0-0
Track : **LH: 5-17** RH: 0-2 **Tight: 4-13** Gall: 0-0
Aids: Bl: 0-2 Vi: 0-0 Tstrap: 0-0
Best Rating: 61 6/01 Sthl 1m4f stand

One-paced on turf, suited by 12 furlongs on Fibresand.

Desert Valentine

102 **53**

6-y-o b g Midyan (USA)-Mo Ceri (Kampala)
L G Cottrell Mrs Lucy Halloran

Placings:00/060160/0050/0251P-0002656 **(4983)**
2001: 10^{0}S, 10^{0}F, 12^{0}GF, 12^{2}GF, 12^{6}GF, 12^{5}G, 12^{6}G

	Starts	1st	2nd	3rd	Win & Pl
Career Total (Turf)	24	2	2	0	8901

49	9/00	Gdwd	1m4f	E(0-80)H	GD	£3705
60	9/98	Gdwd	1m	E(0-70)H	G-S	£3465

Total win prize-money £7170

Going (Turf): Sf: 0-5 **GS: 1-3 Gd: 1-6** GF: 0-8 Fm: 0-2
Distance: 5f/6f: 0-1 7f-8f: 1-6 9f-13f: 1-15 14f+: 0-2
Track : LH: 0-8 **RH: 2-9 Tight: 1-10** Gall: 0-2
Aids: Bl: 0-0 Vi: 0-0 Tstrap: 0-0
Best Rating: 53 7/01 Wwck 1m4f134y gd-fm

Desert Warning

100 **96**

2-y-o b c Mark Of Esteem (IRE)-Warning Belle (Warning)
D R Loder Sheikh Mohammed

Placings:143 **(5053)**
2001: 7^{1}GF, 7^{4}G, 7^{3}S

	Starts	1st	2nd	3rd	Win & Pl
Career Total (Turf)	3	1	0	1	44938

77	8/01	Epsm	7f	D	G-F	£4387

Total win prize-money £4388

Going (Turf): Sf: 0-1 GS: 0-0 Gd: 0-1 **GF: 1-1** Fm: 0-0
Distance: 5f/6f: 0-0 **7f-8f: 1-3** 9f-13f: 0-0 14f+: 0-0
Track : **LH: 1-1** RH: 0-1 **Tight: 1-1** Gall: 0-1
Aids: Bl: 0-0 Vi: 0-0 Tstrap: 0-0
Best Rating: 96 10/01 NmkR 7f soft

Out of a half-sister to Stagecraft, made a winning debut at Epsom in August, but well held in better class next time. Handled soft ground when running well from the front in a Newmarket sales race. Bred to stay a little further.

Desilu

(57)

4-y-o b f Skyliner-Munequita (Marching On)
G A Swinbank Coal Trade Partnership

Placings:05/0 **(0713)**
2001: 7^{0}SD

	Starts	1st	2nd	3rd	Win & Pl
Career Total (Turf)	2	0	0	0	0
Career Total (AW)	1	0	0	0	

Going (Turf): Sf: 0-0 GS: 0-0 Gd: 0-0 GF: 0-2 Fm: 0-0
Distance: 5f/6f: 0-2 7f-8f: 0-1 9f-13f: 0-0 14f+: 0-0
Track : LH: 0-2 RH: 0-0 Tight: 0-1 Gall: 0-0
Aids: Bl: 0-0 Vi: 0-0 Tstrap: 0-1

Desire Me

(85) (21)**37**

3-y-o b f Silca Blanka (IRE)-Dazzle Me (Kalaglow)
A D Smith Duckhaven Stud

Placings:505-06000050300 **(5395)**
2001: 7^{0}SD, 7^{6}SD, 9^{0}GS, 8^{0}S, 8^{0}G, 7^{0}F, 6^{5}F, 6^{9}G, 6^{3}GF, 9^{0}G, 7^{0}SD

	Starts	1st	2nd	3rd	Win & Pl
Career Total (Turf)	11	0	0	1	450
Career Total (AW)	3	0	0	0	0

Going (Turf): Sf: 0-1 GS: 0-1 Gd: 0-3 GF: 0-3 Fm: 0-2
Distance: 5f/6f: 0-2 7f-8f: 0-7 9f-13f: 0-4 14f+: 0-0
Track : LH: 0-11 RH: 0-0 Tight: 0-4 Gall: 0-1
Aids: Bl: 0-0 Vi: 0-0 Tstrap: 0-0
Best Rating: 37 8/01 Brig 6f209y gd-fm

Desraya (IRE)

103 **75d**

4-y-o b g Desert Style (IRE)-Madaraya (USA) (Shahrastani (USA))
K A Ryan Pendle Inn Partnership

Placings:04000/0602311100-0560060500 **(4451)**
2001: 5^{0}GS, 6^{5}G, 6^{6}GF, 5^{0}GF, 6^{0}GF, 6^{6}GF, 6^{0}GS, 6^{5}F, 7^{0}G, 6^{0}GF

	Starts	1st	2nd	3rd	Win & Pl
Career Total (Turf)	25	3	1	1	15290

75	7/00	Ripn	6f	D(0-80)H	G-F	£4875
61	7/00	Haml	6f5y	E(0-70)H	G-F	£2938
57	7/00	Ripn	6f	D(0-80)H	G-S	£5723

Total win prize-money £13536

Going (Turf): Sf: 0-2 GS: 1-6 Gd: 0-6 **GF: 2-9** Fm: 0-2
Distance: **5f/6f: 2-19** 7f-8f: 1-5 9f-13f: 0-1 14f+: 0-0
Track : LH: 0-5 RH: 0-2 Tight: 0-3 Gall: 0-3
Aids: **Bl: 3-13** Vi: 0-1 Tstrap: 0-0
Best Rating: 75 5/01 Donc 6f good

Sprint handicapper who looked exposed in 2001. Has worn blinkers.

Destination

(100) (68)**56**
4-y-o ch g Deploy-Veuve (Tirol)
C A Cyzer Mrs E A Cyzer

Placings:0/52445322-00001 **(5044)**
2001: 16^{0}HY, 16^{0}S, 14^{0}GS, 13^{0}GF, 14^{1}SD

	Starts	1st	2nd	3rd	Win & Pl
Career Total (Turf)	10	0	2	0	3986
Career Total (AW)	4	1	1	1	3137

65 10/01 Sthl 1m6f G(0-65)H STD £2016
Total win prize-money £2016

Going (Turf): Sf: 0-5 GS: 0-3 Gd: 0-1 GF: 0-1 Fm: 0-0
Distance: 5f/6f: 0-0 7f-8f: 0-0 9f-13f: 0-7 **14f+: 1-7**
Track : **LH: 1-9** RH: 0-3 Tight: 0-9 Gall: 0-2
Aids: Bl: 0-0 Vi: 0-1 Tstrap: 0-0
Best Rating: 65 10/01 Sthl 1m6f stand

He has shown bits and pieces of form, but did not win until landing an amateur riders' handicap on the Southwell Fibresand in October 2001.

Destiny Bound

78 **51**
2-y-o ch c Bluegrass Prince (IRE)-Eastbury Rose (Beveled (USA))
E A Wheeler Four Of A Kind Racing

Placings:00 **(5666)**
2001: 7^{0}S, 6^{0}HY

	Starts	1st	2nd	3rd	Win & Pl
Career Total (Turf)	2	0	0	0	

Going (Turf): **Sf: 0-2 GS: 0-0 Gd: 0-0 GF: 0-0 Fm: 0-0**
Distance: 5f/6f: 0-1 7f-8f: 0-1 9f-13f: 0-0 14f+: 0-0
Track : LH: 0-0 RH: 0-0 Tight: 0-0 Gall: 0-0
Aids: Bl: 0-0 Vi: 0-0 Tstrap: 0-0
Best Rating: 51 11/01 Wind 6f heavy

Destructive (USA)

96 **45**
3-y-o b/br c Dehere (USA)-Respectability (USA) (His Majesty (USA))
W J Haggas B Haggas

Placings:50064200 **(5330)**
2001: 7^{5}GF, 8^{0}GF, 10^{0}GF, 8^{6}GF, 14^{4}G, 14^{2}GF, 14^{0}S, 16^{0}HY

	Starts	1st	2nd	3rd	Win & Pl
Career Total (Turf)	8	0	1	0	788

Going (Turf): **Sf: 0-2 GS: 0-0 Gd: 0-1 GF: 0-5 Fm: 0-0**
Distance: 5f/6f: 0-0 7f-8f: 0-2 9f-13f: 0-2 14f+: 0-4
Track : LH: 0-4 RH: 0-2 Tight: 0-4 Gall: 0-1
Aids: Bl: 0-0 Vi: 0-0 Tstrap: 0-0
Best Rating: 55 6/01 NmkR 1m gd-fm

Detaching (IRE)

63(79) (19)**47**
3-y-o b f Thatching-David's Star (Welsh Saint)
I A Balding D H Caslon

Placings:00-00 **(1914)**
2001: 8^{0}SD, 9^{0}GF

	Starts	1st	2nd	3rd	Win & Pl
Career Total (Turf)	3	0	0	0	
Career Total (AW)	1	0	0	0	

Going (Turf): **Sf: 0-2 GS: 0-0 Gd: 0-0 GF: 0-1 Fm: 0-0**
Distance: 5f/6f: 0-0 7f-8f: 0-3 9f-13f: 0-1 14f+: 0-0
Track : LH: 0-2 RH: 0-1 Tight: 0-0 Gall: 0-0
Aids: Bl: 0-0 Vi: 0-0 Tstrap: 0-0
Best Rating: 19 4/01 Sthl 1m stand

Detachment (USA)

83
8-y-o b g Night Shift (USA)-Mumble Peg (General Assembly (USA))
Miss Z C Davison The Secret Circle (1)

Placings:223/550504/0000/06 **(4892)**
2001: 6^{0}GS, 12^{6}GF

	Starts	1st	2nd	3rd	Win & Pl
Career Total (Turf)	15	0	2	1	5012

Going (Turf): **Sf: 0-0 GS: 0-4 Gd: 0-3 GF: 0-5 Fm: 0-3**
Distance: 5f/6f: 0-2 7f-8f: 0-9 9f-13f: 0-4 14f+: 0-0
Track : LH: 0-7 RH: 0-4 Tight: 0-2 Gall: 0-0
Aids: Bl: 0-1 Vi: 0-1 Tstrap: 0-0
Best Rating: 30 9/01 Kemp 1m4f gd-fm

Detective

73(95) (46)**54**
5-y-o ch g Wolfhound (USA)-Ivoronica (Targowice (USA))
Dr J D Scargill Mrs Susan Scargill

Placings:0/005200/5000-450 **(1629)**
2001: 6^{4}SD, 6^{5}SW, 5^{0}F

	Starts	1st	2nd	3rd	Win & Pl
Career Total (Turf)	12	0	1	0	806
Career Total (AW)	2	0	0	0	0

Going (Turf): **Sf: 0-0 GS: 0-1 Gd: 0-6 GF: 0-3 Fm: 0-2**
Distance: 5f/6f: 0-9 7f-8f: 0-5 9f-13f: 0-0 14f+: 0-0
Track : LH: 0-5 RH: 0-2 Tight: 0-3 Gall: 0-2
Aids: Bl: 0-4 Vi: 0-0 Tstrap: 0-0
Best Rating: 46 1/01 Wolv 6f stand

Detention

89 **74**
2-y-o b c Reprimand-June Fayre (Sagaro)
W J Musson Mrs Rita Brown

Placings:034 **(5666)**
2001: 6^{0}HY, 6^{3}S, 6^{4}HY

	Starts	1st	2nd	3rd	Win & Pl
Career Total (Turf)	3	0	0	1	841

Going (Turf): **Sf: 0-3 GS: 0-0 Gd: 0-0 GF: 0-0 Fm: 0-0**
Distance: 5f/6f: 0-3 7f-8f: 0-0 9f-13f: 0-0 14f+: 0-0
Track : LH: 0-1 RH: 0-0 Tight: 0-0 Gall: 0-0
Aids: Bl: 0-0 Vi: 0-0 Tstrap: 0-0
Best Rating: 74 11/01 Wind 6f heavy

Showed promise in six-furlong maidens at the back-end of 2001.

Devise (IRE)

99 **70**
2-y-o b c Hamas (IRE)-Soreze (IRE) (Gallic League)
M S Saunders D Naylor

Placings:410 **(2326)**
2001: 5^{4}GS, 5^{1}G, 5^{0}GF

	Starts	1st	2nd	3rd	Win & Pl
Career Total (Turf)	3	1	0	0	4225

70 5/01 Wwck 5f D GD £3835
Total win prize-money £3835

Going (Turf): Sf: 0-0 GS: 0-1 **Gd: 1-1** GF: 0-1 Fm: 0-0
Distance: **5f/6f: 1-3** 7f-8f: 0-0 9f-13f: 0-0 14f+: 0-0
Track : **LH: 1-1** RH: 0-0 Tight: 0-0 **Gall: 1-1**
Aids: Bl: 0-0 Vi: 0-0 Tstrap: 0-0
Best Rating: 70 5/01 Wwck 5f good

53,000Irgns half-brother to decent six/seven furlong handicapper Strahan. Ran with credit on his Newbury debut and scored next time out at Warwick over the minimum trip. Acts on good ground.

Devolution (IRE)

92(112) (71)**66**
3-y-o b g Distinctly North (USA)-Election Special (Chief Singer)
J M P Eustace The Macdougall Partnership

Placings:523R00 **(4988)**
2001: 5^{5}GF, 6^{2}G, 8^{3}SD, 7^{R}GF, 7^{0}GF, 8^{0}G

	Starts	1st	2nd	3rd	Win & Pl
Career Total (Turf)	5	0	1	0	1342
Career Total (AW)	1	0	0	1	423

Going (Turf): **Sf: 0-0 GS: 0-0 Gd: 0-2 GF: 0-3 Fm: 0-0**
Distance: 5f/6f: 0-2 7f-8f: 0-4 9f-13f: 0-0 14f+: 0-0
Track : LH: 0-2 RH: 0-0 Tight: 0-0 Gall: 0-0
Aids: Bl: 0-0 Vi: 0-0 Tstrap: 0-0
Best Rating: 66 9/01 Asct 1m good

A half-brother to two-mile winner First Ballot, he refused to race on one occasion in 2001, but always looked to have some ability and won the very first race on the Lingfield Polytrack in fine style in November.

Devon Dream (IRE)

101 **53d**
5-y-o b g Paris House-Share The Vision (Vision (USA))
J M Bradley (M J Weeden 27/7) Dr Ian R Shenkin

Placings:000/013633040/000330 **(4675)**
2001: 5^{0}F, 5^{0}G, 8^{0}HD, 6^{3}G, 7^{3}GF, 7^{0}G

	Starts	1st	2nd	3rd	Win & Pl
Career Total (Turf)	18	1	0	5	4995

57 5/99 Brig 5f59y E(0-70)H FRM £2924
Total win prize-money £2925

Going (Turf): Sf: 0-1 GS: 0-0 Gd: 0-6 GF: 0-6 **Fm: 1-5**
Distance: **5f/6f: 1-12** 7f-8f: 0-5 9f-13f: 0-1 14f+: 0-0
Track : **LH: 1-11** RH: 0-1 Tight: 0-1 Gall: 0-3
Aids: Bl: 0-0 Vi: 0-0 Tstrap: 0-0
Best Rating: 40 7/01 Chep 7f16y gd-fm

Devote

83 **50**
3-y-o b c Pennekamp (USA)-Radiant Bride (USA) (Blushing Groom (FR))
B J Llewellyn The Welsh Valleys Syndicate

Placings:6 **(4076)**
2001: 11^{6}G

	Starts	1st	2nd	3rd	Win & Pl
Career Total (Turf)	1	0	0	0	0

Going (Turf): **Sf: 0-0 GS: 0-0 Gd: 0-1 GF: 0-0 Fm: 0-0**
Distance: 5f/6f: 0-0 7f-8f: 0-0 9f-13f: 0-1 14f+: 0-0
Track : LH: 0-1 RH: 0-0 Tight: 0-1 Gall: 0-0
Aids: Bl: 0-0 Vi: 0-0 Tstrap: 0-0
Best Rating: 50 8/01 Bath 1m3f144y good

Dextrous

102 **49**
4-y-o gr c Machiavellian (USA)-Heavenly Cause (USA) (Grey Dawn Ii)

N Tinkler Mike Gosse

Placings:33-0060600400 (5167)
2001: 9^0GS, 10^0S, 9^6F, 7^0F, 8^6GF, 8^0GF, 11^0G, 10^4F, 10^0G, 12^0GS

	Starts	1st	2nd	3rd	Win & Pl
Career Total (Turf)	12	0	0	2	1908

Going (Turf): Sf: 0-2 GS: 0-2 Gd: 0-2 GF: 0-3 Fm: 0-3
Distance: 5f/6f: 0-0 7f-8f: 0-2 9f-13f: 0-10 14f+: 0-0
Track : LH: 0-8 RH: 0-2 Tight: 0-3 Gall: 0-2
Aids: Bl: 0-0 Vi: 0-0 Tstrap: 0-4
Best Rating: 61 5/01 Rdcr 1m1f firm

Dhuhook (USA)

110 **83**
3-y-o b f Dixieland Band (USA)-Basma (USA) (Grey Dawn Ii)
B Hanbury Hamdan Al Maktoum

Placings:5122560 (5366)
2001: 8^5GF, 9^1F, 8^2GF, 10^2GF, 9^5GF, 10^6G, 8^0GS

	Starts	1st	2nd	3rd	Win & Pl
Career Total (Turf)	7	1	2	0	8791

61 6/01 Ling 1m1f D FRM £3835
Total win prize-money £3835

Going (Turf): Sf: 0-0 GS: 0-1 Gd: 0-1 GF: 0-4 **Fm: 1-1**
Distance: 5f/6f: 0-0 7f-8f: 0-3 **9f-13f: 1-4** 14f+: 0-0
Track : **LH: 1-2** RH: 0-1 **Tight: 1-2** Gall: 0-1
Aids: Bl: 0-0 Vi: 0-0 Tstrap: 0-0
Best Rating: 99 7/01 Donc 1m2f60y gd-fm

A daughter of Cheveley Park third Basma, ran with promise on her racecourse bow at Newmarket in June. Got off the mark on her second outing when stepped up to nine furlongs. Some fair efforts since. Acts on fast ground.

Di Canio

89(88) (43)**45**
3-y-o ch g Piccolo-Conquista (Aragon)
D Nicholls W McKay & P Di Canio

Placings:0-5055 (1874)
2001: 6^5SD, 7^0S, 5^5SD, 6^5F

	Starts	1st	2nd	3rd	Win & Pl
Career Total (Turf)	3	0	0	0	0
Career Total (AW)	2	0	0	0	0

Going (Turf): Sf: 0-1 GS: 0-0 Gd: 0-0 GF: 0-1 Fm: 0-1
Distance: 5f/6f: 0-4 7f-8f: 0-1 9f-13f: 0-0 14f+: 0-0
Track : LH: 0-2 RH: 0-0 Tight: 0-1 Gall: 0-0
Aids: Bl: 0-0 Vi: 0-0 Tstrap: 0-0
Best Rating: 45 6/01 Ling 6f firm

Diablo Dancer (IRE)

91 **56**
5-y-o b g Deploy-Scharade (Lombard (GER))
A C Whillans (C J Mann 10/1) I Campbell

Placings:1332145435/426P0000/0510-000 (5033)
2001: 10^0S, 10^0G, 16^0GF

	Starts	1st	2nd	3rd	Win & Pl
Career Total (Turf)	25	3	2	3	18859

69 5/00 Wwck 1m2f110yF(0-65)H SFT £2635
82 7/98 Ling 7f D G-F £3850
75 4/98 Nott 5f13y F SFT £2574
Total win prize-money £9060

Going (Turf): Sf: 2-7 GS: 0-4 Gd: 0-6 GF: 1-6 Fm: 0-2
Distance: 5f/6f: 1-3 7f-8f: 1-4 9f-13f: 1-14 14f+: 0-4
Track : **LH: 1-12** RH: 0-7 Tight: 0-6 Gall: 0-3
Aids: Bl: 0-1 **Vi: 1-4** Tstrap: 0-0
Best Rating: 44 4/01 Pont 1m2f6y soft

Formerly useful juvenile, has dropped to ordinary handicap level since.

Diabolo (IRE)

91 **50**
3-y-o b g Magic Ring (IRE)-First Play (Primo Dominie)
M W Easterby Guy Reed

Placings:000-0020000 (2763)
2001: 6^0F, 5^0F, 7^2G, 6^0GF, 6^0G, 6^0F, 6^0GF

	Starts	1st	2nd	3rd	Win & Pl
Career Total (Turf)	10	0	1	0	940

Going (Turf): Sf: 0-2 GS: 0-1 Gd: 0-2 GF: 0-2 Fm: 0-3
Distance: 5f/6f: 0-9 7f-8f: 0-1 9f-13f: 0-0 14f+: 0-0
Track : LH: 0-3 RH: 0-0 Tight: 0-0 Gall: 0-0
Aids: Bl: 0-5 Vi: 0-0 Tstrap: 0-0
Best Rating: 50 6/01 Hayd 7f30y good

Diaghilev (IRE)

94 **97**
2-y-o b c Sadler's Wells (USA)-Darara (Top Ville)
A P O'Brien Michael Tabor

Placings:245 (5677a)
2001: 8^2YS, 8^4GS, 8^5HO

	Starts	1st	2nd	3rd	Win & Pl
Career Total (Turf)	3	0	1	0	7735

Going (Turf): Sf: 0-0 GS: 0-1 Gd: 0-0 GF: 0-0 Fm: 0-0
Distance: 5f/6f: 0-0 7f-8f: 0-3 9f-13f: 0-0 14f+: 0-0
Track : LH: 0-1 RH: 0-0 Tight: 0-0 Gall: 0-0
Aids: Bl: 0-0 Vi: 0-0 Tstrap: 0-0
Best Rating: 97 11/01 StCl 1m holding

A weak favourite when beaten into second on his Leopardstown debut back in August, but did not get the clearest of runs in a Newmarket maiden in October. Does not look an easy ride.

Diamond Beach

96 **31**
8-y-o b g Lugana Beach-Cannon Boy (USA) (Canonero (USA))
B J Llewellyn (M J M Evans 10/5) Miss Emily Jane Jones

Placings:0520/3252450/0/64000/46 (4019)
2001: 12^4GS, 12^6G

	Starts	1st	2nd	3rd	Win & Pl
Career Total (Turf)	19	0	3	1	5684

Going (Turf): Sf: 0-1 GS: 0-3 Gd: 0-6 GF: 0-7 Fm: 0-2
Distance: 5f/6f: 0-2 7f-8f: 0-9 9f-13f: 0-7 14f+: 0-1
Track : LH: 0-6 RH: 0-4 Tight: 0-3 Gall: 0-4
Aids: Bl: 0-0 Vi: 0-0 Tstrap: 0-0
Best Rating: 31 8/01 Folk 1m4f good

Diamond Crown (IRE)

99(90) (12)**37**
10-y-o ch g Kris-State Treasure (USA) (Secretariat (USA))
Denys Smith Mr B R Bradbury

Placings:44/06200310/002306123004/3004350353410 6/20531050605055/0330210103356206/043201425400 0/02004-0320 (3879)
2001: 14^0SD, 12^3G, 15^2GS, 16^0GS

	Starts	1st	2nd	3rd	Win & Pl
Career Total (Turf)	86	7	10	14	31262
Career Total (AW)	2	0	0	0	0

42 7/99 Haml 1m5f9y F(0-65)H FRM £2853
47 8/98 Newc 1m4f93y G GD £1819
47 7/98 Ayr 1m2f192yF GD £2276
45 6/97 Nott 1m1f213yG(0-60)H GD £1984
44 10/96 Newc 1m F(0-60)H G-F £2983
56 8/95 Bevl 1m3f216yF G-F £2693
49 8/94 Nott 1m1f213yG(0-60)H G-F £2174
Total win prize-money £16783

Going (Turf): Sf: 0-3 GS: 0-9 **Gd: 3-22 GF: 3-37** Fm: 1-15
Distance: 5f/6f: 0-0 7f-8f: 1-13 **9f-13f: 5-50** 14f+: 1-25
Track : **LH: 5-50** RH: 2-36 Tight: 2-46 Gall: 2-6
Aids: Bl: 0-0 Vi: 0-1 Tstrap: 0-0
Best Rating: 37 7/01 Newc 1m4f93y good

Diamond Darren (IRE)

94(77) (44)**53**
2-y-o ch c Dolphin Street (FR)-Deerussa (IRE) (Jareer (USA))
P D Evans Diamond Racing Ltd

Placings:000622320 (4313)
2001: 5^0S, 5^0GF, 6^0SD, 6^6SD, 5^2F, 6^2G, 7^3G, 5^2G, 6^0G

	Starts	1st	2nd	3rd	Win & Pl
Career Total (Turf)	7	0	3	1	2015
Career Total (AW)	2	0	0	0	0

Going (Turf): Sf: 0-1 GS: 0-0 Gd: 0-4 GF: 0-1 Fm: 0-1
Distance: 5f/6f: 0-8 7f-8f: 0-1 9f-13f: 0-0 14f+: 0-0
Track : LH: 0-4 RH: 0-0 Tight: 0-1 Gall: 0-0
Aids: Bl: 0-1 Vi: 0-6 Tstrap: 0-0
Best Rating: 53 8/01 Leic 5f218y good

Diamond Decorum (IRE)

96(94) (39)**62**
5-y-o ch g Fayruz-Astra Adastra (Mount Hagen (FR))
Andrew Turnell (J Hetherton 18/6) Diamond Racing Ltd

Placings:0041654/005051024**0**040000/61060000-06604001260 (3643)
2001: 7^0SD, 7^6SW, 7^6SD, 7^0SD, 7^4SW, 7^0S, 7^0F, 7^1G, 6^2GF, 6^6F, 6^0F

	Starts	1st	2nd	3rd	Win & Pl
Career Total (Turf)	35	4	2	0	29841
Career Total (AW)	7	0	0	0	0

45 6/01 Muss 7f30y F GD £2443
68 5/00 Thsk 6f E(0-75)H GD £8489
77 6/99 Ling 6f D(0-85)H G-F £7400
77 8/98 Thsk 5f E G-F £3324
Total win prize-money £21656

Going (Turf): Sf: 0-6 GS: 0-5 **Gd: 2-8 GF: 2-11** Fm: 0-5
Distance: **5f/6f: 3-17** 7f-8f: 1-25 9f-13f: 0-0 14f+: 0-0
Track : LH: 0-13 RH: 0-3 Tight: 0-5 Gall: 0-3
Aids: Bl: 0-0 Vi: 0-1 Tstrap: 0-2
Best Rating: 62 7/01 Yarm 6f3y gd-fm

A winner over the minimum trip at two, he started off this season running over seven furlongs, but was inclined to pull too hard and not getting home. Dropping back to Lingfield's sharp six did the trick in June. Ironically, his best performance since then was over seven furlongs at Glorious Goodwood behind Petrus, and he now seems to find six too sharp.

Diamond Discovery (USA)

82(69) (23)**46**
3-y-o b c Weather Break-Ali's Diamond (USA) (Caracolero (USA))
Andrew Lee (Ian Williams 7/7) Lisselan Farms Ltd

Placings:00000 (5310a)
2001: 6^0GS, 10^0GF, 8^0SD, 8^0GF, 7^0G

	Starts	1st	2nd	3rd	Win & Pl
Career Total (Turf)	4	0	0	0	
Career Total (AW)	1	0	0	0	

Going (Turf): Sf: 0-0 GS: 0-1 Gd: 0-1 GF: 0-2 Fm: 0-0
Distance: 5f/6f: 0-1 7f-8f: 0-2 9f-13f: 0-2 14f+: 0-0
Track : LH: 0-1 RH: 0-0 Tight: 0-1 Gall: 0-0
Aids: Bl: 0-0 Vi: 0-0 Tstrap: 0-0
Best Rating: 46 6/01 Wind 1m2f7y gd-fm

Diamond Falls

89 **67**

2-y-o b f River Falls-Compton Lady (USA) (Sovereign Dancer (USA))
Mrs A J Perrett K J Buchanan

Placings:56 **(5468)**
2001: 7^{5}GF, 7^{6}S

	Starts	1st	2nd	3rd	Win & Pl
Career Total (Turf)	2	0	0	0	0

Going (Turf): Sf: 0-1 GS: 0-0 Gd: 0-0 GF: 0-1 Fm: 0-0
Distance: 5f/6f: 0-0 7f-8f: 0-2 9f-13f: 0-0 14f+: 0-0
Track : LH: 0-1 RH: 0-1 Tight: 0-0 Gall: 0-0
Aids: Bl: 0-0 Vi: 0-0 Tstrap: 0-0
Best Rating: 67 6/01 Gdwd 7f gd-fm

Diamond Geezer (IRE)

104(110) (78)**63**

5-y-o br g Tenby-Unaria (Prince Tenderfoot (USA))
J J Quinn (R Hannon 28/6) A Page, L Pickering, J Taylor, J Ward

Placings:0060105**0000/5125**04230115025**02123/5**0244 3061422400041**031**-**00**40022000005 **(5012)**
2001: 5^{0}SD, 6^{0}SD, 5^{4}GS, 5^{0}GS, 5^{0}GF, 5^{2}G, 5^{2}GF, 5^{0}GF, 5^{0}G, 5^{0}GF, 6^{0}GF, 5^{0}G, 5^{5}HY

	Starts	1st	2nd	3rd	Win & Pl
Career Total (Turf)	45	4	5	2	21697
Career Total (AW)	20	4	5	2	16978

54	12/00	Ling	6f	E	STD	£2744
71	11/00	Wolv	5f	E(0-75)H	STD	£2898
64	7/00	Wind	6f	D(0-80)H	GD	£4140
62	11/99	Ling	6f	D(0-80)H	STD	£3947
65	7/99	Wind	6f	E(0-75)H	G-F	£2808
62	7/99	Wind	6f	E(0-70)H	GD	£2976
57	1/99	Ling	6f	F(0-65)H	STD	£2028
62	9/98	Sand	5f6y	E	G-S	£2996

Total win prize-money £24539

Going (Turf): Sf: 0-4 GS: 1-9 **Gd: 2-14** GF: 1-17 Fm: 0-1
Distance: 5f/6f: 8-55 7f-8f: 0-10 9f-13f: 0-0 14f+: 0-0
Track : LH: 4-26 RH: 3-12 **Tight: 4-19** Gall: 3-17
Aids: Bl: 0-1 Vi: 0-0 Tstrap: 0-0
Best Rating: 78 6/01 Wind 5f10y gd-fm

Equally effective in modest handicap company on sand and turf and probably better suited by six furlongs than five.

Diamond Green (ARG)

99 **65**

3-y-o ch f Roy (USA)-Diamond Ring (ARG) (El Basco (USA))
B R Millman Lau Po Man, James & Woo Wai See,

Placings:040 **(5182)**
2001: 8^{0}GF, 9^{4}GS, 10^{0}HY

	Starts	1st	2nd	3rd	Win & Pl
Career Total (Turf)	3	0	0	0	370

Going (Turf): Sf: 0-1 GS: 0-1 Gd: 0-0 GF: 0-1 Fm: 0-0
Distance: 5f/6f: 0-0 7f-8f: 0-1 9f-13f: 0-2 14f+: 0-0
Track : LH: 0-0 RH: 0-1 Tight: 0-2 Gall: 0-0
Aids: Bl: 0-0 Vi: 0-0 Tstrap: 0-0
Best Rating: 65 9/01 Gdwd 1m1f192y gd-sft

Diamond Jayne (IRE)

85 **19**

3-y-o ch f Royal Abjar (USA)-Valiant Friend (USA) (Shahrastani (USA))
J Hetherton Diamond Racing Ltd

Placings:000-000 **(2054)**
2001: 8^{0}S, 7^{0}GF, 10^{0}GF

	Starts	1st	2nd	3rd	Win & Pl
Career Total (Turf)	6	0	0	0	0

Going (Turf): Sf: 0-3 GS: 0-0 Gd: 0-0 GF: 0-3 Fm: 0-0
Distance: 5f/6f: 0-2 7f-8f: 0-2 9f-13f: 0-2 14f+: 0-0
Track : LH: 0-3 RH: 0-0 Tight: 0-2 Gall: 0-0
Aids: Bl: 0-0 Vi: 0-0 Tstrap: 0-0
Best Rating: 19 6/01 Rdcr 1m2f gd-fm

Diamond Jobe (IRE)

89 **51**

2-y-o ch g College Chapel-Dazzling Maid (IRE) (Tate Gallery (USA))
A Berry Diamond Racing Ltd

Placings:3500 **(4841)**
2001: 5^{3}G, 5^{5}F, 7^{0}G, 6^{0}G

	Starts	1st	2nd	3rd	Win & Pl
Career Total (Turf)	4	0	0	1	590

Going (Turf): Sf: 0-0 GS: 0-0 Gd: 0-3 GF: 0-0 Fm: 0-1
Distance: 5f/6f: 0-2 7f-8f: 0-2 9f-13f: 0-0 14f+: 0-0
Track : LH: 0-3 RH: 0-0 Tight: 0-1 Gall: 0-1
Aids: Bl: 0-0 Vi: 0-0 Tstrap: 0-0
Best Rating: 51 5/01 Wwck 5f good

Diamond Joshua (IRE)

104 **46**

3-y-o b g Mujadil (USA)-Elminya (IRE) (Sure Blade (USA))
John Berry Diamond Racing Ltd

Placings:000000260 **(4858)**
2001: 5^{0}G, 6^{0}G, 6^{0}GF, 7^{0}G, 10^{0}GF, 12^{0}G, 16^{2}GF, 14^{6}G, 15^{0}GF

	Starts	1st	2nd	3rd	Win & Pl
Career Total (Turf)	9	0	1	0	684

Going (Turf): Sf: 0-2 GS: 0-0 Gd: 0-3 GF: 0-4 Fm: 0-0
Distance: 5f/6f: 0-2 7f-8f: 0-2 9f-13f: 0-2 14f+: 0-3
Track : LH: 0-5 RH: 0-2 Tight: 0-4 Gall: 0-1
Aids: Bl: 0-1 Vi: 0-0 Tstrap: 0-0
Best Rating: 46 8/01 Chep 2m49y gd-fm

Diamond Lover (IRE)

99 **86**

2-y-o ch c Alhaarth (IRE)-Silent Love (USA) (Hansel (USA))
N A Graham J Kok

Placings:31 **(5089)**
2001: 7^{3}G, 8^{1}GS

	Starts	1st	2nd	3rd	Win & Pl
Career Total (Turf)	2	1	0	1	3522

86	10/01	Newc	1m	D	G-S	£3059

Total win prize-money £3059

Going (Turf): Sf: 0-0 **GS: 1-1** Gd: 0-1 GF: 0-0 Fm: 0-0
Distance: 5f/6f: 0-0 **7f-8f: 1-2** 9f-13f: 0-0 14f+: 0-0
Track : LH: 1-1 RH: 0-1 Tight: 0-0 **Gall: 1-1**
Aids: Bl: 0-0 Vi: 0-0 Tstrap: 0-0
Best Rating: 86 10/01 Newc 1m gd-sft

Styed on well to land a Newcastle maiden on his second start.

Diamond Lydia (IRE)

80 **45**

3-y-o gr f Petong-Nagida (Skyliner)
John Berry Diamond Racing Ltd

Placings:600 **(4600)**
2001: 5^{6}GF, 5^{0}GF, 6^{0}GF

	Starts	1st	2nd	3rd	Win & Pl
Career Total (Turf)	3	0	0	0	0

Going (Turf): Sf: 0-0 GS: 0-0 Gd: 0-0 GF: 0-3 Fm: 0-0
Distance: 5f/6f: 0-3 7f-8f: 0-0 9f-13f: 0-0 14f+: 0-0
Track : LH: 0-0 RH: 0-0 Tight: 0-0 Gall: 0-0
Aids: Bl: 0-0 Vi: 0-0 Tstrap: 0-0
Best Rating: 45 6/01 Folk 5f gd-fm

Diamond Max (IRE)

107(103) (83)**100**

3-y-o b c Nicolotte-Kawther (Tap On Wood)
P D Evans Diamond Racing Ltd

Placings:04145513-**1**4302101 **(5354a)**
2001: 7^{1}SD, 8^{4}SD, 7^{3}GS, 8^{0}G, 7^{2}GS, 8^{1}S, 8^{0}S, 8^{1}VS, 8^{0}HY

	Starts	1st	2nd	3rd	Win & Pl
Career Total (Turf)	14	4	1	2	29907
Career Total (AW)	2	1	0	0	4193

100	10/01	Lonc	1m		VS	£13579
90	8/01	Chep	1m14y	C(0-90)H	SFT	£6695
83	1/01	Sthl	7f	D(0-85)H	STD	£3903
75	10/00	Rdcr	6f	E(0-75)	SFT	£2925
64	4/00	Nott	5f13y	G	SFT	£1926

Total win prize-money £29028

Going (Turf): Sf: 3-6 GS: 0-3 Gd: 0-2 GF: 0-2 Fm: 0-0
Distance: 5f/6f: 2-6 7f-8f: 2-8 9f-13f: 1-2 14f+: 0-0
Track : LH: 1-4 RH: 1-2 Tight: 0-2 Gall: 0-1
Aids: Bl: 0-0 Vi: 0-0 Tstrap: 0-0
Best Rating: 100 10/01 Lonc 1m v soft

A real mud-lover, he proved equally adept on the All-Weather surface at Southwell where he scored in January 2001. Running well on turf this term, he took a handicap at Chepstow in August, and exceeded expectations by taking a Longchamp Listed event in October. Suited by seven furlongs to a mile and soft ground.

Diamond Mill (IRE)

83 **49**

2-y-o ch f Desert King (IRE)-Euromill (Shirley Heights)
R Hannon Stonethorn Stud Farms Limited

Placings:504 **(2502)**
2001: 5^{5}G, 5^{0}GF, 7^{4}GF

	Starts	1st	2nd	3rd	Win & Pl
Career Total (Turf)	3	0	0	0	321

Going (Turf): Sf: 0-0 GS: 0-0 Gd: 0-1 GF: 0-2 Fm: 0-0
Distance: 5f/6f: 0-2 7f-8f: 0-1 9f-13f: 0-0 14f+: 0-0
Track : LH: 0-1 RH: 0-1 Tight: 0-0 Gall: 0-2
Aids: Bl: 0-0 Vi: 0-0 Tstrap: 0-0
Best Rating: 49 6/01 Kemp 7f gd-fm

Diamond Olivia

86(86) (38)**60**

4-y-o b f Beveled (USA)-Queen Of The Quorn (Governor General)
John Berry Diamond Racing Ltd

Placings:3640/340625013500-04 **(1168)**
2001: 8^{0}S, 7^{4}S

	Starts	1st	2nd	3rd	Win & Pl
Career Total (Turf)	12	1	1	2	5265
Career Total (AW)	6	0	0	1	310

59	9/00	Ling	7f	E(0-70)H	SFT	£3640

Total win prize-money £3640

Going (Turf): Sf: 1-6 GS: 0-0 Gd: 0-2 GF: 0-2 Fm: 0-1

Distance: 5f/6f: 0-4 **7f-8f: 1-11** 9f-13f: 0-2 14f+: 0-0
Track : LH: 0-12 RH: 0-0 Tight: 0-6 Gall: 0-0
Aids: Bl: 0-0 Vi: 0-0 Tstrap: 0-0
Best Rating: 29 4/01 Nott 1m54y soft

Diamond Promise (IRE)

94(91) (42)**61**

4-y-o b f Fayruz-Cupid Miss (Anita's Prince)
P D Evans J E Potter

Placings:25121206021235/2041000000-0 **(0044)**
2001: 5^{0}SD

	Starts	1st	2nd	3rd	Win & Pl
Career Total (Turf)	17	4	4	1	11341
Career Total (AW)	8	0	2	0	1062

61 6/00 Bath 5f11y F G-S £2275
69 5/99 Leic 5f2y F GD £2280
69 4/99 Thsk 5f E GD £2818
Total win prize-money £7374

Going (Turf): Sf: 1-2 GS: 1-8 **Gd: 2-4** GF: 0-2 Fm: 0-1
Distance: **5f/6f: 4-24** 7f-8f: 0-1 9f-13f: 0-0 14f+: 0-0
Track : **LH: 1-12** RH: 0-1 Tight: 0-7 **Gall: 1-4**
Aids: Bl: 0-1 Vi: 0-0 Tstrap: 0-0
Best Rating: 9 1/01 Wolv 5f stand

Nippy sort, effective in claimers.

Diamond Rachael (IRE)

102(101) (56)**64**

4-y-o b f Shalford (IRE)-Brown Foam (Horage)
J Hetherton (Mrs N Macauley 5/7) Diamond Racing Ltd

Placings:034/01236601200156-05440000 **(4603)**
2001: 7^{0}SD, 7^{5}SD, 7^{4}SD, 6^{4}SD, 7^{0}SD, 7^{0}GF, 7^{0}GF, 7^{0}SD

	Starts	1st	2nd	3rd	Win & Pl
Career Total (Turf)	8	1	1	0	5489
Career Total (AW)	17	2	1	2	7846

68 10/00 Wolv 7f E(0-70)H STD £2957
58 7/00 Leic 7f9y D(0-80)H G-F £4121
68 2/00 Wolv 6f D STD £2834
Total win prize-money £9913

Going (Turf): Sf: 0-1 GS: 0-1 Gd: 0-0 **GF: 1-6** Fm: 0-0
Distance: 5f/6f: 1-9 **7f-8f: 2-16** 9f-13f: 0-0 14f+: 0-0
Track : **LH: 2-16** RH: 0-0 **Tight: 2-9** Gall: 0-1
Aids: Bl: 0-0 **Vi: 3-23** Tstrap: 0-0
Best Rating: 64 1/01 Ling 7f stand

Diamond Ring

95 **85**

2-y-o b f Magic Ring (IRE)-Reticent Bride (IRE) (Shy Groom (USA))
J L Dunlop Mrs P G M Jamison

Placings:312 **(3143)**
2001: 5^{3}GF, 5^{1}GF, 5^{2}G

	Starts	1st	2nd	3rd	Win & Pl
Career Total (Turf)	3	1	1	1	6393

70 6/01 Sals 5f D G-F £4387
Total win prize-money £4388

Going (Turf): Sf: 0-0 GS: 0-0 Gd: 0-1 **GF: 1-2** Fm: 0-0
Distance: **5f/6f: 1-3** 7f-8f: 0-0 9f-13f: 0-0 14f+: 0-0
Track : LH: 0-0 RH: 0-0 Tight: 0-0 Gall: 0-0
Aids: Bl: 0-0 Vi: 0-0 Tstrap: 0-0
Best Rating: 85 7/01 Donc 5f good

A five-furlong fast ground performer. She got off the mark on her second start at Salisbury in June 2001.

Diamond Road (IRE)

100 **60**

4-y-o gr g Dolphin Street (FR)-Tiffany's Case (IRE) (Thatching)
C A Horgan Winterfields Farm Ltd

Placings:0/332600-0650 **(4891)**
2001: 9^{0}GF, 8^{6}GF, 9^{5}GF, 8^{0}GF

	Starts	1st	2nd	3rd	Win & Pl
Career Total (Turf)	11	0	1	2	2514

Going (Turf): Sf: 0-0 GS: 0-1 Gd: 0-1 GF: 0-9 Fm: 0-0
Distance: 5f/6f: 0-0 7f-8f: 0-4 9f-13f: 0-7 14f+: 0-0
Track : LH: 0-0 RH: 0-10 Tight: 0-5 Gall: 0-1
Aids: Bl: 0-0 Vi: 0-0 Tstrap: 0-0
Best Rating: 60 7/01 Gdwd 1m1f gd-fm

Diamond Sinead (IRE)

78 **47**

2-y-o b f Fayruz-Pink Eyes (IRE) (Vision (USA))
T Keddy (P D Evans 16/4) S R Partnership

Placings:52 **(0771)**
2001: 5^{5}S, 5^{2}S

	Starts	1st	2nd	3rd	Win & Pl
Career Total (Turf)	2	0	1	0	529

Going (Turf): Sf: 0-2 GS: 0-0 Gd: 0-0 GF: 0-0 Fm: 0-0
Distance: 5f/6f: 0-2 7f-8f: 0-0 9f-13f: 0-0 14f+: 0-0
Track : LH: 0-0 RH: 0-0 Tight: 0-0 Gall: 0-0
Aids: Bl: 0-0 Vi: 0-0 Tstrap: 0-0
Best Rating: 47 4/01 Nott 5f13y soft

Showed ability in two starts in 2001.

Diamond Zoe

92(83) (21)**37**

3-y-o b f Whittingham (IRE)-Sharp Gazelle (Beveled (USA))
J L Eyre Diamond Racing Ltd

Placings:440-0005000 **(3668)**
2001: 5^{0}GS, 6^{0}SD, 6^{0}F, 6^{5}G, 6^{0}GS, 7^{0}GS, 6^{0}S

	Starts	1st	2nd	3rd	Win & Pl
Career Total (Turf)	9	0	0	0	210
Career Total (AW)	1	0	0	0	

Going (Turf): Sf: 0-4 GS: 0-3 Gd: 0-1 GF: 0-0 Fm: 0-1
Distance: 5f/6f: 0-6 7f-8f: 0-4 9f-13f: 0-0 14f+: 0-0
Track : LH: 0-2 RH: 0-0 Tight: 0-0 Gall: 0-0
Aids: Bl: 0-1 Vi: 0-0 Tstrap: 0-0
Best Rating: 37 6/01 Thsk 6f good

Diana Panagaea

96 **72**

2-y-o ch f Polar Falcon (USA)-Pandrop (Sharrood (USA))
A C Stewart Paterson, Costain & Woodward

Placings:10 **(4985)**
2001: 6^{1}GF, 6^{0}G

	Starts	1st	2nd	3rd	Win & Pl
Career Total (Turf)	2	1	0	0	3575

72 8/01 Ling 6f E G-F £3575
Total win prize-money £3575

Going (Turf): Sf: 0-0 GS: 0-0 Gd: 0-1 **GF: 1-1** Fm: 0-0
Distance: **5f/6f: 1-1** 7f-8f: 0-1 9f-13f: 0-0 14f+: 0-0
Track : LH: 0-0 RH: 0-0 Tight: 0-0 Gall: 0-0
Aids: Bl: 0-0 Vi: 0-0 Tstrap: 0-0
Best Rating: 72 8/01 Ling 6f gd-fm

Got off the mark at the first time of asking when taking an auction maiden at Lingfield on good to firm over six furlongs.

Diaphanous

59

3-y-o b f Beveled (USA)-Sharp Venita (Sharp Edge)
N E Berry The Purple People Racing Partnership

Placings:000 **(5670)**
2001: 7^{0}S, 6^{0}HY, 8^{0}HY

	Starts	1st	2nd	3rd	Win & Pl
Career Total (Turf)	3	0	0	0	

Going (Turf): Sf: 0-3 GS: 0-0 Gd: 0-0 GF: 0-0 Fm: 0-0
Distance: 5f/6f: 0-1 7f-8f: 0-1 9f-13f: 0-1 14f+: 0-0
Track : LH: 0-0 RH: 0-1 Tight: 0-1 Gall: 0-0
Aids: Bl: 0-0 Vi: 0-0 Tstrap: 0-0

Dick Whittingham

60(52) **11**

2-y-o ch g Whittingham (IRE)-Comme Une Fleur (FR) (Sharpo)
D Shaw Moneyleague Ltd

Placings:00 **(3262)**
2001: 6^{0}SD, 7^{0}GS

	Starts	1st	2nd	3rd	Win & Pl
Career Total (Turf)	1	0	0	0	
Career Total (AW)	1	0	0	0	

Going (Turf): Sf: 0-0 GS: 0-1 Gd: 0-0 GF: 0-0 Fm: 0-0
Distance: 5f/6f: 0-1 7f-8f: 0-1 9f-13f: 0-0 14f+: 0-0
Track : LH: 0-1 RH: 0-0 Tight: 0-0 Gall: 0-0
Aids: Bl: 0-0 Vi: 0-0 Tstrap: 0-0
Best Rating: 11 7/01 Wwck 7f26y gd-sft

Dick'n Mick

91 **36**

4-y-o b g Secret Appeal-Gilboa (Shirley Heights)
J G Smyth-Osbourne (Lady Connell 19/5) Sir Michael Connell

Placings:500 **(3255)**
2001: 6^{5}GF, 8^{0}GF, 8^{0}GF

	Starts	1st	2nd	3rd	Win & Pl
Career Total (Turf)	3	0	0	0	0

Going (Turf): Sf: 0-0 GS: 0-0 Gd: 0-0 GF: 0-3 Fm: 0-0
Distance: 5f/6f: 0-0 7f-8f: 0-2 9f-13f: 0-1 14f+: 0-0
Track : LH: 0-0 RH: 0-1 Tight: 0-1 Gall: 0-0
Aids: Bl: 0-0 Vi: 0-2 Tstrap: 0-0
Best Rating: 36 6/01 Folk 6f189y gd-fm

Did You Miss Me (IRE)

85 **20**

4-y-o ch f Indian Ridge-Upward Trend (Salmon Leap (USA))
P Monteith Brandkey Limited

Placings:05-0000 **(4439)**
2001: 5^{0}GS, 8^{0}GS, 8^{0}GF, 6^{0}G

	Starts	1st	2nd	3rd	Win & Pl
Career Total (Turf)	6	0	0	0	0

Going (Turf): Sf: 0-0 GS: 0-2 Gd: 0-3 GF: 0-1 Fm: 0-0
Distance: 5f/6f: 0-2 7f-8f: 0-3 9f-13f: 0-1 14f+: 0-0
Track : LH: 0-2 RH: 0-1 Tight: 0-1 Gall: 0-0
Aids: Bl: 0-0 Vi: 0-0 Tstrap: 0-0
Best Rating: 20 6/01 Ayr 1m gd-fm

Diddymu (IRE)

93 **74**

2-y-o b f Revoque (IRE)-Family At War (USA) (Explodent (USA))
M R Channon Mr Derek D & Mrs Jean P Clee

Placings:050 **(5112)**
2001: 6^{0}GF, 7^{5}GF, 8^{0}HY

	Starts	1st	2nd	3rd	Win & Pl
Career Total (Turf)	3	0	0	0	0

Going (Turf): Sf: 0-1 GS: 0-0 Gd: 0-0 GF: 0-2 Fm: 0-0
Distance: 5f/6f: 0-0 7f-8f: 0-2 9f-13f: 0-1 14f+: 0-0
Track : LH: 0-2 RH: 0-0 Tight: 0-0 Gall: 0-0
Aids: Bl: 0-0 Vi: 0-0 Tstrap: 0-0
Best Rating: 74 9/01 Wwck 7f26y gd-fm

Didnt Tell My Wife

83(90) (65)**56**

2-y-o ch g Aragon-Bee Dee Dancer (Ballacashtal (CAN))
S C Williams R P Stubbings

Placings:002 **(5614)**
2001: 6^{0}HY, 7^{0}GS, 6^{2}SD

	Starts	1st	2nd	3rd	Win & Pl
Career Total (Turf)	2	0	0	0	
Career Total (AW)	1	0	1	0	848

Going (Turf): Sf: 0-1 GS: 0-1 Gd: 0-0 GF: 0-0 Fm: 0-0
Distance: 5f/6f: 0-2 7f-8f: 0-1 9f-13f: 0-0 14f+: 0-0
Track : LH: 0-1 RH: 0-0 Tight: 0-1 Gall: 0-0
Aids: Bl: 0-0 Vi: 0-0 Tstrap: 0-0
Best Rating: 65 11/01 Wolv 6f stand

Plating class. Flattered to finish five lengths second to Pious over six at Wolverhampton.

Diesan (USA)

60

10-y-o b g Diesis-Bold Courtesan (USA) (Bold Bidder)
S Woodman Ron Atkins

Placings:5123121/6300321/5545/05101/00 **(1750)**
2001: 8^{0}GF, 8^{0}GF

	Starts	1st	2nd	3rd	Win & Pl
Career Total (Turf)	25	6	3	3	41946

	6/96	Dort	7f	H	GD	£4505
	5/96	Gels	7f	H	GD	£4054
102	8/94	Gdwd	7f	B(0-105)H	GD	£10046
106	10/93	Donc	7f	C	GD	£4480
100	9/93	Gdwd	7f	D H	G-S	£4045
83	7/93	NmkJ	6f	D	G-S	£3850

Total win prize-money £30980

Going (Turf): Sf: 0-2 GS: 2-4 **Gd: 4-12** GF: 0-5 Fm: 0-0
Distance: 5f/6f: 1-3 **7f-8f: 5-20** 9f-13f: 0-0 14f+: 0-0
Track : LH: 0-4 **RH: 2-5** Tight: 0-0 Gall: 0-3
Aids: Bl: 0-0 Vi: 0-0 Tstrap: 0-0

Dietrich (USA)

107 **102+**

3-y-o br f Storm Cat (USA)-Piquetnol (USA) (Private Account (USA))
A P O'Brien Michael Tabor

Placings:24100-1010 **(5244a)**
2001: 5^{1}GY, 5^{0}G, 5^{1}GF, 5^{0}HO

	Starts	1st	2nd	3rd	Win & Pl
Career Total (Turf)	9	3	1	0	77140

101	7/01	Gdwd	5f	A	G-F	£30000
102	6/01	Leop	5f		G-Y	£35750
85	7/00	Tipp	5f		G-F	£8280

Total win prize-money £74030

Going (Turf): Sf: 0-1 GS: 0-1 Gd: 0-1 **GF: 2-3** Fm: 0-0
Distance: **5f/6f: 3-9** 7f-8f: 0-0 9f-13f: 0-0 14f+: 0-0
Track : LH: 0-0 RH: 0-0 Tight: 0-0 Gall: 0-0
Aids: Bl: 0-0 Vi: 0-0 Tstrap: 0-0
Best Rating: 102 6/01 Leop 5f gd-yld

On her reappearance this season she scored impressively from Final Exam, coming from last to first with a well-timed run. Did not get the best of runs in the King's Stand, and gained compensation in the King George Stakes at Goodwood. She is open to plenty of improvement at the minimum trip.

Differential (USA)

110 **86**

4-y-o b/br c Known Fact (USA)-Talk About Home (USA) (Elocutionist (USA))
B Smart Smart Movers

Placings:1340/554-4000 **(5138)**
2001: 6^{4}GF, 6^{0}G, 6^{0}G, 6^{0}G

	Starts	1st	2nd	3rd	Win & Pl
Career Total (Turf)	11	1	0	1	7894

82	7/99	Wind	5f10y	D	G-F	£3647

Total win prize-money £3648

Going (Turf): Sf: 0-0 GS: 0-0 Gd: 0-4 **GF: 1-7** Fm: 0-0
Distance: **5f/6f: 1-11** 7f-8f: 0-0 9f-13f: 0-0 14f+: 0-0
Track : LH: 0-0 **RH: 1-1** Tight: 0-0 **Gall: 1-1**
Aids: Bl: 0-0 Vi: 0-0 Tstrap: 0-0
Best Rating: 86 7/01 Asct 6f gd-fm

A winner on his debut at Windsor at two, he has been lightly raced since and has faced some very stiff tasks. Ran really well on his return to action at Ascot in July, but broke a blood-vesel next time and showed little afterwards.

Dig For Gold

90

8-y-o ch g Digamist (USA)-Formidable Task (Formidable (USA))
R D E Woodhouse R D E Woodhouse

Placings:0/000/050 **(3086)**
2001: 16^{0}F, 16^{5}GF, 16^{0}GF

	Starts	1st	2nd	3rd	Win & Pl
Career Total (Turf)	7	0	0	0	0

Going (Turf): Sf: 0-0 GS: 0-2 Gd: 0-0 GF: 0-3 Fm: 0-2
Distance: 5f/6f: 0-0 7f-8f: 0-0 9f-13f: 0-3 14f+: 0-4
Track : LH: 0-5 RH: 0-2 Tight: 0-4 Gall: 0-0
Aids: Bl: 0-0 Vi: 0-0 Tstrap: 0-4
Best Rating: 40 7/01 Sthl 2m gd-fm

Digger (IRE)

84 **70**

2-y-o ch g Danzig Connection (USA)-Baliana (Midyan (USA))
G B Balding Peter Richardson

Placings:000 **(5037)**
2001: 5^{0}G, 6^{0}GF, 5^{0}G

	Starts	1st	2nd	3rd	Win & Pl
Career Total (Turf)	3	0	0	0	

Going (Turf): Sf: 0-0 GS: 0-0 Gd: 0-2 GF: 0-1 Fm: 0-0
Distance: 5f/6f: 0-2 7f-8f: 0-1 9f-13f: 0-0 14f+: 0-0
Track : LH: 0-1 RH: 0-0 Tight: 0-0 Gall: 0-1
Aids: Bl: 0-0 Vi: 0-0 Tstrap: 0-3
Best Rating: 70 10/01 Bath 5f161y good

Digital

105 **87**

4-y-o ch g Safawan-Heavenly Goddess (Soviet Star (USA))
M R Channon W G R Wightman

Placings:423021-2020031000 **(5142)**
2001: 8^{2}S, 10^{0}S, 8^{2}G, 8^{0}GF, 8^{0}GF, 8^{3}GF, 6^{1}G, 8^{0}G, 7^{0}S, 9^{0}G

	Starts	1st	2nd	3rd	Win & Pl
Career Total (Turf)	16	2	4	2	25585

87	7/01	York	6f214y	C(0-90)H	GD	£9880
84	10/00	Nott	1m54y	E(0-75)H	SFT	£3172

Total win prize-money £13052

Going (Turf): Sf: 1-5 GS: 0-0 **Gd: 1-4** GF: 0-6 Fm: 0-0
Distance: 5f/6f: 0-0 7f-8f: 1-10 9f-13f: 1-5 14f+: 0-0
Track : **LH: 2-6** RH: 0-3 Tight: 0-2 **Gall: 1-3**
Aids: Bl: 0-0 Vi: 0-0 Tstrap: 0-0
Best Rating: 87 7/01 York 6f214y good

Mile handicapper who excels on an easy surface. Took advantage of a good draw to score at York in July.

Digital Image

(86) (36)**50**

4-y-o b h Presidium-Sally Tadpole (Jester)
S Donohoe (R Hannon 13/1) Thomas Kelly

Placings:1060/6000**000**-0600 **(4126a)**
2001: 7^{0}SD, 8^{6}GF, 7^{0}GY, 7^{0}G

	Starts	1st	2nd	3rd	Win & Pl
Career Total (Turf)	11	1	0	0	7602
Career Total (AW)	4	0	0	0	

92	5/99	Ches	5f16y	B	G-F	£7422

Total win prize-money £7422

Going (Turf): Sf: 0-0 GS: 0-2 Gd: 0-4 **GF: 1-4** Fm: 0-0
Distance: **5f/6f: 1-5** 7f-8f: 0-9 9f-13f: 0-1 14f+: 0-0
Track : **LH: 1-7** RH: 0-0 **Tight: 1-7** Gall: 0-0
Aids: Bl: 0-1 Vi: 0-0 Tstrap: 0-3
Best Rating: 46 7/01 Bell 1m gd-fm

Made a winning debut at Chester, though was found out in hotter company subsequently.

Digon Da

88(84) (21)**58**

5-y-o ch g Sparky Lad-Fleur Power (IRE) (The Noble Player (USA))
R Brotherton Davies And Bridgeman

Placings:030400/00-0000 **(4471)**
2001: 8^{0}G, 12^{0}SD, 7^{0}GF, 6^{0}GF

	Starts	1st	2nd	3rd	Win & Pl
Career Total (Turf)	11	0	0	1	934
Career Total (AW)	1	0	0	0	

Going (Turf): Sf: 0-0 GS: 0-1 Gd: 0-4 GF: 0-6 Fm: 0-0
Distance: 5f/6f: 0-0 7f-8f: 0-4 9f-13f: 0-8 14f+: 0-0
Track : LH: 0-5 RH: 0-4 Tight: 0-8 Gall: 0-0
Aids: Bl: 0-0 Vi: 0-1 Tstrap: 0-0
Best Rating: 29 9/01 Brig 6f209y gd-fm

Dihatjum

106 **53**

4-y-o b g Mujtahid (USA)-Rosie Potts (Shareef Dancer (USA))
R M Flower M Lickert

Placings:003305026/3240123300-0052000025250 **(4721)**
2001: 7^{0}GS, 6^{0}GF, 9^{5}F, 8^{2}GF, 10^{0}GF, 9^{0}G, 8^{0}GF, 9^{0}GF, 9^{2}G, 12^{5}GF, 9^{2}GS, 9^{5}GF, 12^{0}G

	Starts	1st	2nd	3rd	Win & Pl
Career Total (Turf)	32	1	6	5	10610

62	8/00	Carl	6f206y	F	FRM	£2299

Total win prize-money £2300

Going (Turf): Sf: 0-1 GS: 0-3 Gd: 0-6 GF: 0-18 **Fm: 1-4**
Distance: 5f/6f: 0-4 **7f-8f: 1-16** 9f-13f: 0-12 14f+: 0-0
Track : LH: 0-10 **RH: 1-14** Tight: 0-7 Gall: 0-1
Aids: Bl: 0-3 Vi: 0-3 Tstrap: 0-0
Best Rating: 53 9/01 Folk 1m1f149y gd-sft

Dil

67(107) (68)**58**

6-y-o b g Primo Dominie-Swellegant (Midyan (USA))
Andrew Reid (Mrs N Macauley 20/1) A S Reid

Placings:0264/30414100010/1001000000**0503/010000 000020-0100000** **(1586)**
2001: **5**^{0}SD, **5**^{1}SW, **5**^{0}SD, **6**^{0}SD, **5**^{0}SD, 6^{0}GF, **6**^{0}SD

	Starts	1st	2nd	3rd	Win & Pl
Career Total (Turf)	27	3	1	1	14092
Career Total (AW)	21	4	1	1	21126

60	1/01	Wolv	5f	F	SLW	£2107
91	1/00	Wolv	5f	C(0-95)H	STD	£6630
95	4/99	Wolv	5f	C(0-90)H	STD	£7002
85	3/99	Sthl	5f	D(0-85)H	SLW	£3701
82	9/98	Leic	5f2y	D(0-80)H	G-F	£4402
76	7/98	Donc	6f	D(0-85)H	G-F	£3882
74	5/98	Donc	5f	E	G-F	£3132

Total win prize-money £30859

Going (Turf): Sf: 0-2 GS: 0-5 Gd: 0-8 **GF: 3-12** Fm: 0-0
Distance: **5f/6f: 7-41** 7f-8f: 0-6 9f-13f: 0-1 14f+: 0-0
Track : **LH: 3-21** RH: 0-1 **Tight: 3-15** Gall: 0-1
Aids: Bl: 0-0 Vi: 0-6 Tstrap: 0-0
Best Rating: 69 1/01 Sthl 5f stand

Reserves his best for Fibresand sprints these days, especially the minimum trip at Wolverhampton.

Dileer (IRE)

94 **89**
2-y-o b c Barathea (IRE)-Stay Sharpe (USA) (Sharpen Up)
M R Channon Sheikh Mohammed Obaid Al Maktoum

Placings:3 **(2128)**
2001: 6^{3}GF

	Starts	1st	2nd	3rd	Win & Pl
Career Total (Turf)	1	0	0	1	720

Going (Turf): Sf: 0-0 GS: 0-0 Gd: 0-0 GF: 0-1 Fm: 0-0
Distance: 5f/6f: 0-0 7f-8f: 0-1 9f-13f: 0-0 14f+: 0-0
Track : LH: 0-0 RH: 0-0 Tight: 0-0 Gall: 0-0
Aids: Bl: 0-0 Vi: 0-0 Tstrap: 0-0
Best Rating: 89 6/01 Newb 6f8y gd-fm

Diliza

88 **47**
2-y-o b f Dilum (USA)-Little White Lies (Runnett)
G B Balding Redenham Racing Group

Placings:00450 **(4638)**
2001: 5^{0}GF, 6^{0}GF, 6^{4}GF, 6^{5}GF, 7^{0}GF

	Starts	1st	2nd	3rd	Win & Pl
Career Total (Turf)	5	0	0	0	0

Going (Turf): Sf: 0-0 GS: 0-0 Gd: 0-0 GF: 0-5 Fm: 0-0
Distance: 5f/6f: 0-3 7f-8f: 0-2 9f-13f: 0-0 14f+: 0-0
Track : LH: 0-1 RH: 0-0 Tight: 0-0 Gall: 0-1
Aids: Bl: 0-0 Vi: 0-0 Tstrap: 0-0
Best Rating: 47 8/01 Kemp 6f gd-fm

Dilkusha (IRE)

100(93) (70)**77d**
6-y-o b g Indian Ridge-Crimson Glen (Glenstal (USA))
B A Pearce Trevor Painting

Placings:66/04056361520/101503066/0043540-000300 **(1631)**
2001: 7^{0}SD, 7^{0}SW, 5^{0}GS, 7^{3}G, 8^{0}GF, 8^{0}F

	Starts	1st	2nd	3rd	Win & Pl
Career Total (Turf)	33	3	1	4	17153
Career Total (AW)	3	0	0	0	0

76	7/99	Newb	7f	D(0-85)H	G-F	£4211
75	6/99	Kemp	7f	D(0-85)H	G-F	£4201
72	8/98	Brig	6f209y	E(0-70)H	FRM	£2924

Total win prize-money £11338

Going (Turf): Sf: 0-1 GS: 0-5 Gd: 0-7 **GF: 2-16** Fm: 1-3
Distance: 5f/6f: 0-3 **7f-8f: 3-28** 9f-13f: 0-4 14f+: 0-0
Track : LH: 1-9 RH: 1-12 Tight: 0-6 **Gall: 1-5**
Aids: Bl: 0-2 Vi: 0-0 Tstrap: 0-0
Best Rating: 69 5/01 Brig 7f214y good

Fair handicapper at around seven furlongs on fast ground.

Dilly

97(89) (58)**73**
3-y-o br f Dilum (USA)-Princess Rosananti (IRE) (Shareef Dancer (USA))
P R Chamings Mrs J E L Wright

Placings:2431-00054 **(2968)**
2001: 7^{0}G, 7^{0}GF, 8^{0}GF, 9^{5}GF, 9^{4}GF

	Starts	1st	2nd	3rd	Win & Pl
Career Total (Turf)	9	1	1	1	5943

73	9/00	Yarm	7f3y	D(0-85)	G-F	£4543

Total win prize-money £4544

Going (Turf): Sf: 0-0 GS: 0-0 Gd: 0-2 **GF: 1-7** Fm: 0-0
Distance: 5f/6f: 0-0 **7f-8f: 1-6** 9f-13f: 0-3 14f+: 0-0
Track : LH: 0-4 RH: 0-2 Tight: 0-1 Gall: 0-1
Aids: Bl: 0-0 Vi: 0-0 Tstrap: 0-0
Best Rating: 69 7/01 Folk 1m1f149y gd-fm

Dilsaa

101(99) (60)**48**
4-y-o ch g Night Shift (USA)-Llia (Shirley Heights)
K A Ryan (P W Harris 30/1) Yorkshire Racing Club V

Placings:5525/50006460236-600600310 **(4541)**
2001: 12^{6}SD, 5^{0}G, 6^{0}F, 7^{6}GF, 8^{0}G, 8^{0}GF, 11^{3}GF, 14^{1}GF, 14^{0}GF

	Starts	1st	2nd	3rd	Win & Pl
Career Total (Turf)	19	1	1	1	5908
Career Total (AW)	5	0	1	1	1098

48	7/01	Nott	1m6f15y	E(0-75)H	G-F	£3556

Total win prize-money £3556

Going (Turf): Sf: 0-1 GS: 0-1 Gd: 0-6 **GF: 1-10** Fm: 0-1
Distance: 5f/6f: 0-2 7f-8f: 0-11 9f-13f: 0-9 **14f+: 1-2**
Track : **LH: 1-11** RH: 0-3 Tight: 0-8 Gall: 0-0
Aids: Bl: 0-2 Vi: 0-0 Tstrap: 0-0
Best Rating: 50 1/01 Wolv 1m4f stand

Modest staying handicapper on a sound surface.

Dilshaan

111 **116+**
3-y-o b c Darshaan-Avila (Ajdal (USA))
Sir Michael Stoute Saeed Suhail

Placings:21-10 **(2008)**
2001: 10^{1}GF, 12^{0}GF

	Starts	1st	2nd	3rd	Win & Pl
Career Total (Turf)	4	2	1	0	190612

116	5/01	York	1m2f85y	A	G-F	£84100
116	10/00	Donc	1m	A	SFT	£105000

Total win prize-money £189100

Going (Turf): Sf: 1-1 GS: 0-0 Gd: 0-0 **GF: 1-3** Fm: 0-0
Distance: 5f/6f: 0-0 7f-8f: 1-2 9f-13f: 1-2 14f+: 0-0
Track : **LH: 2-3** RH: 0-1 Tight: 0-1 **Gall: 2-2**
Aids: Bl: 0-0 Vi: 0-0 Tstrap: 0-0
Best Rating: 116 5/01 York 1m2f85y gd-fm

Put up a fine performance for one with so little experience when running out an authoritative winner over Tamburlaine in the Racing Post Trophy in October 2000. Made a fine reappearance when gaining a brave victory over Celtic Silence in the Dante Stakes at York. Unsuited by the steady early pace in the Derby, he later injured a joint and was not seen again. Stays in training.

Dilys

91 **74**
2-y-o b f Efisio-Ramajana (USA) (Shadeed (USA))
W S Kittow Mrs Jenny Hopkins

Placings:3401 **(5665)**
2001: 5^{3}GF, 5^{4}G, 6^{0}GS, 6^{1}HY

	Starts	1st	2nd	3rd	Win & Pl
Career Total (Turf)	4	1	0	1	4614

74	11/01	Wind	6f	D	HVY	£3753

Total win prize-money £3754

Going (Turf): Sf: 1-1 GS: 0-1 Gd: 0-1 GF: 0-1 Fm: 0-0
Distance: **5f/6f: 1-4** 7f-8f: 0-0 9f-13f: 0-0 14f+: 0-0
Track : LH: 0-1 RH: 0-0 Tight: 0-0 Gall: 0-1
Aids: Bl: 0-0 Vi: 0-0 Tstrap: 0-0
Best Rating: 74 11/01 Wind 6f heavy

Made an encouraging debut at Sandown over the minimum trip, and again showed ability when fourth over five and a half furlongs at Bath, before facing a very stiff task at Newmarket in a sales race. Ended the season with a win on heavy at Windsor. Acts well with cut in the ground.

Dim Byd

2-y-o ch c So Factual (USA)-Time Clash (Timeless Times (USA))
Mrs Merrita Jones Mrs D J Hughes

Placings:0 **(3493)**
2001: 6^{0}GF

	Starts	1st	2nd	3rd	Win & Pl
Career Total (Turf)	1	0	0	0	

Going (Turf): Sf: 0-0 GS: 0-0 Gd: 0-0 GF: 0-1 Fm: 0-0
Distance: 5f/6f: 0-1 7f-8f: 0-0 9f-13f: 0-0 14f+: 0-0
Track : LH: 0-0 RH: 0-0 Tight: 0-0 Gall: 0-0
Aids: Bl: 0-0 Vi: 0-0 Tstrap: 0-0

Dimple Chad

92 **69**
2-y-o b c Sadler's Wells (USA)-Fern (Shirley Heights)
L M Cumani Fittocks Stud

Placings:0 **(5604)**
2001: 7^{0}GS

	Starts	1st	2nd	3rd	Win & Pl
Career Total (Turf)	1	0	0	0	

Going (Turf): Sf: 0-0 GS: 0-1 Gd: 0-0 GF: 0-0 Fm: 0-0
Distance: 5f/6f: 0-0 7f-8f: 0-1 9f-13f: 0-0 14f+: 0-0
Track : LH: 0-0 RH: 0-0 Tight: 0-0 Gall: 0-0
Aids: Bl: 0-0 Vi: 0-0 Tstrap: 0-0
Best Rating: 69 11/01 NmkR 7f gd-sft

Dinami

67 **24**
3-y-o b g Young Ern-Born To Be (Never So Bold)
S Dow J A Redmond

Placings:000 **(2553)**
2001: 6^{0}G, 6^{0}GF, 6^{0}GF

	Starts	1st	2nd	3rd	Win & Pl
Career Total (Turf)	3	0	0	0	

Going (Turf): Sf: 0-0 GS: 0-0 Gd: 0-1 GF: 0-2 Fm: 0-0
Distance: 5f/6f: 0-2 7f-8f: 0-1 9f-13f: 0-0 14f+: 0-0
Track : LH: 0-0 RH: 0-0 Tight: 0-0 Gall: 0-0
Aids: Bl: 0-0 Vi: 0-0 Tstrap: 0-0
Best Rating: 24 6/01 Sals 6f212y gd-fm

Dinar (USA)

103(87) (45)**59**
6-y-o b h Dixieland Band (USA)-Bold Jessie (Never So Bold)
B J Llewellyn (R Brotherton 11/5) J Rees

Placings:0003041200/30202011-06005524440 **(4635)**
2001: 8^{0}HY, 8^{6}SD, 8^{0}S, 9^{0}G, 12^{5}GF, 8^{5}GF, 10^{2}GF, 9^{4}GF, 11^{4}GF, 11^{4}GF, 9^{0}GF

	Starts	1st	2nd	3rd	Win & Pl
Career Total (Turf)	28	3	4	2	13686
Career Total (AW)	1	0	0	0	0

62 7/00 Wind 1m67y E(0-70)H SFT £3307
50 7/00 Wind 1m67y E(0-70)H GD £3045
42 9/99 Kemp 1m4f E(0-75)H G-F £3139
Total win prize-money £9492

Going (Turf): Sf: 1-8 GS: 0-1 **Gd: 1-8 GF: 1-11** Fm: 0-0
Distance: 5f/6f: 0-1 7f-8f: 0-4 **9f-13f: 3-23** 14f+: 0-1
Track : LH: 0-16 **RH: 3-9 Tight: 2-8** Gall: 0-2
Aids: Bl: 0-0 Vi: 0-0 Tstrap: 0-0
Best Rating: 59 7/01 Wind 1m3f135y gd-fm

Fair handicapper at around a mile, goes well at Windsor. Handles most ground.

Dinky

(77) (4)**28**
4-y-o ch f Floose-Marinsky (USA) (Diesis)
M J Ryan M J Ryan

Placings:00000/00000000-00 **(0710)**
2001: 12^{0}SD, 11^{0}SD

	Starts	1st	2nd	3rd	Win & Pl
Career Total (Turf)	10	0	0	0	
Career Total (AW)	5	0	0	0	

Going (Turf): Sf: 0-1 GS: 0-1 Gd: 0-4 GF: 0-4 Fm: 0-0
Distance: 5f/6f: 0-3 7f-8f: 0-2 9f-13f: 0-10 14f+: 0-0
Track : LH: 0-10 RH: 0-3 Tight: 0-6 Gall: 0-1
Aids: Bl: 0-0 Vi: 0-0 Tstrap: 0-0
Best Rating: 4 4/01 Sthl 1m3f stand

Dinofelis

98(83) (33)**45**
3-y-o b g Rainbow Quest (USA)-Revonda (IRE) (Sadler's Wells (USA))
K A Ryan (P W Harris 1/8) The Gloria Darley Racing Partnership

Placings:050-06634006 **(5269)**
2001: 10^{0}GS, 14^{6}GF, 14^{6}F, 12^{3}GS, 12^{1}G, 10^{0}GS, 11^{0}SD, 10^{6}HY

	Starts	1st	2nd	3rd	Win & Pl
Career Total (Turf)	10	0	0	1	288
Career Total (AW)	1	0	0	0	

Going (Turf): Sf: 0-3 GS: 0-3 Gd: 0-2 GF: 0-1 Fm: 0-1
Distance: 5f/6f: 0-0 7f-8f: 0-3 9f-13f: 0-5 14f+: 0-3
Track : LH: 0-5 RH: 0-2 Tight: 0-4 Gall: 0-1
Aids: Bl: 0-0 Vi: 0-0 Tstrap: 0-0
Best Rating: 54 6/01 Yarm 1m6f17y gd-fm

Dion Dee

97(99) (42)**48d**
5-y-o ch m Anshan-Jade Mistress (Damister (USA))
Dr J R J Naylor B C Mills

Placings:300/0/00300361025640-650143 **(2230)**
2001: 16^{6}SW, 12^{5}SD, 14^{0}S, 11^{1}GS, 11^{4}GF, 12^{3}GS

	Starts	1st	2nd	3rd	Win & Pl
Career Total (Turf)	18	2	1	3	7541
Career Total (AW)	6	0	0	1	428

48 5/01 Brig 1m3f196yF(0-60)H G-S £1883
42 6/00 Nott 1m1f213yE(0-70)H G-F £2968
Total win prize-money £4851

Going (Turf): Sf: 0-2 **GS: 1-4** Gd: 0-5 **GF: 1-5** Fm: 0-1
Distance: 5f/6f: 0-0 7f-8f: 0-2 **9f-13f: 2-19** 14f+: 0-2
Track : **LH: 2-14** RH: 0-7 Tight: 0-13 Gall: 0-2
Aids: Bl: 0-0 Vi: 0-0 Tstrap: 0-0
Best Rating: 48 5/01 Brig 1m3f196y gd-sft

Direct Deal

105 **50**
5-y-o b g Rainbow Quest (USA)-Al Najah (USA) (Topsider (USA))
G M McCourt Admin Of The Late Mrs B N Taylor

Placings:3/000413/00000010-01 **(3263)**
2001: 10^{0}GF, 12^{1}GS

	Starts	1st	2nd	3rd	Win & Pl
Career Total (Turf)	17	3	0	2	9710

50 7/01 Wwck 1m4f134yG(0-60)H G-S £2018
50 7/00 Wind 1m3f135yG GD £1907
72 7/99 Bath 1m2f46y D G-F £4091
Total win prize-money £8018

Going (Turf): Sf: 0-1 **GS: 1-3 Gd: 1-4 GF: 1-7** Fm: 0-1
Distance: 5f/6f: 0-0 7f-8f: 0-2 **9f-13f: 3-14** 14f+: 0-0
Track : **LH: 1-4** RH: 0-7 **Tight: 2-6** Gall: 0-1
Aids: Bl: 0-1 Vi: 0-0 **Tstrap: 2-8**
Best Rating: 50 7/01 Wwck 1m4f134y gd-sft

Plating-class, stays a mile and a half, likes to dominate.

Direct Descendant (IRE)

83 **66**
2-y-o ch c Be My Guest (USA)-Prague Spring (Salse (USA))
S P C Woods Dwayne Woods

Placings:000 **(5056)**
2001: 8^{0}G, 8^{0}G, 8^{0}S

	Starts	1st	2nd	3rd	Win & Pl
Career Total (Turf)	3	0	0	0	

Going (Turf): Sf: 0-1 GS: 0-0 Gd: 0-2 GF: 0-0 Fm: 0-0
Distance: 5f/6f: 0-0 7f-8f: 0-2 9f-13f: 0-1 14f+: 0-0
Track : LH: 0-1 RH: 0-1 Tight: 0-0 Gall: 0-0
Aids: Bl: 0-0 Vi: 0-0 Tstrap: 0-0
Best Rating: 66 9/01 Kemp 1m good

Direct Play

96 **82**
2-y-o b c Muhtarram (USA)-Direct Fortune (USA) (Java Gold (USA))
B W Hills The Anglo Irish Choral Society

Placings:315015135 **(5340)**
2001: 5^{3}GS, 6^{1}GF, 6^{5}GF, 5^{0}GS, 6^{1}GF, 7^{5}G, 6^{1}GF, 7^{3}GF, 6^{5}GS

	Starts	1st	2nd	3rd	Win & Pl
Career Total (Turf)	9	3	0	2	11913

82 8/01 Wwck 6f21y E G-F £2075
81 8/01 Kemp 6f D G-F £4231
80 6/01 Folk 6f E G-F £2814
Total win prize-money £10021

Going (Turf): Sf: 0-0 GS: 0-3 Gd: 0-1 **GF: 3-5** Fm: 0-0
Distance: **5f/6f: 2-6** 7f-8f: 1-3 9f-13f: 0-0 14f+: 0-0
Track : LH: 0-2 RH: 0-0 Tight: 0-0 Gall: 0-1
Aids: Bl: 0-0 Vi: 0-0 Tstrap: 0-0
Best Rating: 82 9/01 Wwck 7f26y gd-fm

Has won three races this season all of which were on good to firm over six furlongs.

Discerning

108 **92**
3-y-o b f Darshaan-Tromond (Lomond (USA))
J R Fanshawe Cheveley Park Stud

Placings:510366 **(5600)**
2001: 10^{5}GF, 11^{1}G, 12^{0}GS, 12^{3}GS, 13^{6}G, 16^{6}GS

	Starts	1st	2nd	3rd	Win & Pl
Career Total (Turf)	6	1	0	1	5518

91 7/01 Yarm 1m3f101yD GD £3659
Total win prize-money £3660

Going (Turf): Sf: 0-0 GS: 0-3 **Gd: 1-2** GF: 0-1 Fm: 0-0
Distance: 5f/6f: 0-0 7f-8f: 0-0 **9f-13f: 1-4** 14f+: 0-2
Track : **LH: 1-2** RH: 0-2 **Tight: 1-2** Gall: 0-2
Aids: Bl: 0-0 Vi: 0-0 Tstrap: 0-0
Best Rating: 92 9/01 Ches 1m5f89y good

A half-sister to Group Three winner over 12 furlongs Nowhere to Exit, she made an encouraging debut at Newmarket over ten furlongs. Stepped up to 11 furlongs to score on second run. Has failed in better company since. Does not want toe ground too fast.

Disco Volante

96 **89**
2-y-o b f Sadler's Wells (USA)-Divine Danse (FR) (Kris)
J H M Gosden Hugo Morris

Placings:5 **(5274)**
2001: 7^{5}GS

	Starts	1st	2nd	3rd	Win & Pl
Career Total (Turf)	1	0	0	0	0

Going (Turf): Sf: 0-0 GS: 0-1 Gd: 0-0 GF: 0-0 Fm: 0-0
Distance: 5f/6f: 0-0 7f-8f: 0-1 9f-13f: 0-0 14f+: 0-0
Track : LH: 0-0 RH: 0-0 Tight: 0-0 Gall: 0-0
Aids: Bl: 0-0 Vi: 0-0 Tstrap: 0-0
Best Rating: 89 10/01 Leic 7f9y gd-sft

Half-sister to three winners including the very useful Valentino.

Disglair

82(65) **6**
3-y-o b f River Falls-Bold Dove (Never So Bold)
D Burchell Mrs S Geen

Placings:000-00 **(2739)**
2001: 7^{0}GF, 8^{0}GF

	Starts	1st	2nd	3rd	Win & Pl
Career Total (Turf)	4	0	0	0	
Career Total (AW)	1	0	0	0	

Going (Turf): Sf: 0-0 GS: 0-0 Gd: 0-1 GF: 0-3 Fm: 0-0
Distance: 5f/6f: 0-3 7f-8f: 0-1 9f-13f: 0-1 14f+: 0-0
Track : LH: 0-1 RH: 0-0 Tight: 0-0 Gall: 0-0
Aids: Bl: 0-0 Vi: 0-0 Tstrap: 0-0
Best Rating: 6 6/01 Brig 7f214y gd-fm

Dispol Chieftan

94(88) (38)**38**
3-y-o b c Clantime-Ski Baby (Petoski)
Mrs A Duffield W B Imison

Placings:0550304-030000 **(2240)**
2001: 5^{0}SD, 5^{3}S, 6^{0}S, 6^{0}GF, 7^{0}GF, 7^{0}G

	Starts	1st	2nd	3rd	Win & Pl
Career Total (Turf)	12	0	0	2	745
Career Total (AW)	1	0	0	0	

Going (Turf): Sf: 0-3 GS: 0-3 Gd: 0-3 GF: 0-3 Fm: 0-0
Distance: 5f/6f: 0-11 7f-8f: 0-2 9f-13f: 0-0 14f+: 0-0
Track : LH: 0-0 RH: 0-1 Tight: 0-0 Gall: 0-0
Aids: Bl: 0-1 Vi: 0-0 Tstrap: 0-2
Best Rating: 53 4/01 Nott 5f13y soft

Dispol Evita

89(89) (46)**60**
2-y-o ch f Presidium-She's A Breeze (Crofthall)
Andrew Reid (S E Kettlewell 4/7) A S Reid

Placings:063R11454230 **(4793)**
2001: 5^{0}S, 5^{6}S, 6^{3}F, 6^{R}F, 7^{1}GF, 6^{1}F, 7^{4}G, 6^{5}GF, 6^{4}GF, 6^{2}GF, 8^{3}SD, 8^{0}G

	Starts	1st	2nd	3rd	Win & Pl
Career Total (Turf)	11	2	1	1	5695
Career Total (AW)	1	0	0	1	403

60 7/01 Brig 6f209y F FRM £2240

48 6/01 Rdcr 7f G G-F £1841

Total win prize-money £4081

Going (Turf): Sf: 0-2 GS: 0-0 Gd: 0-2 **GF: 1-4 Fm: 1-3**
Distance: 5f/6f: 0-4 **7f-8f: 2-7** 9f-13f: 0-1 14f+: 0-0
Track : **LH: 1-6** RH: 0-0 Tight: 0-1 Gall: 0-0
Aids: Bl: 0-0 Vi: 0-0 Tstrap: 0-0
Best Rating: 60 8/01 Sals 6f212y gd-fm

She looked to be going the right way when she surprised connections by refusing to race at Thirsk in the summer of 2001. Fortunately, she proved this was not going to be a habit with back-to-back wins at Redcar and Brighton on fast ground over seven furlongs.

Dispol Foxtrot

102(96) (51)**50d**

3-y-o ch f Alhijaz-Foxtrot Pie (Shernazar)
S E Kettlewell W B Imison

Placings:0463-01204363011500 **(4438)**
2001: 9^{0}SW, 8^{1}SW, 10^{2}SW, 11^{0}SW, 9^{4}S, 12^{3}S, 9^{6}G, 9^{3}F, 10^{0}GF, 9^{1}S, 9^{1}G, 10^{5}GF, 10^{0}G, 9^{0}G

	Starts	1st	2nd	3rd	Win & Pl
Career Total (Turf)	13	2	0	2	7194
Career Total (AW)	5	1	1	1	2897

50 7/01 Haml 1m1f36y E(0-75)H GD £3688
48 7/01 Haml 1m1f36y F(0-60) SFT £2576
49 2/01 Sthl 1m G SLW £1890

Total win prize-money £8155

Going (Turf): **Sf: 1-5** GS: 0-0 **Gd: 1-5** GF: 0-2 Fm: 0-1
Distance: 5f/6f: 0-1 7f-8f: 1-2 **9f-13f: 2-15** 14f+: 0-0
Track : LH: 1-11 **RH: 2-6 Tight: 2-9** Gall: 0-1
Aids: Bl: 0-0 Vi: 0-0 Tstrap: 0-0
Best Rating: 50 7/01 Haml 1m1f36y good

Dispol Jazz

(76) (3)**62d**

4-y-o ch f Alhijaz-Foxtrot Pie (Shernazar)
D Broad (S E Kettlewell 20/1) P Travers

Placings:013321652410/30000-00 **(4928a)**
2001: 7^{0}SD, 7^{0}F

	Starts	1st	2nd	3rd	Win & Pl
Career Total (Turf)	18	3	2	3	14503
Career Total (AW)	1	0	0	0	

74 10/99 Catt 7f D(0-85)H SFT £4703
70 7/99 Carl 5f207y F GD £2521
64 5/99 Thsk 6f E G-F £2851

Total win prize-money £10075

Going (Turf): **Sf: 1-3** GS: 0-2 **Gd: 1-4 GF: 1-5** Fm: 0-4
Distance: **5f/6f: 2-8** 7f-8f: 1-10 9f-13f: 0-1 14f+: 0-0
Track : LH: 1-5 RH: 1-5 Tight: 1-8 Gall: 1-1
Aids: Bl: 0-0 Vi: 0-0 Tstrap: 0-0
Best Rating: 38 9/01 DRoy 7f firm

Dispol Laird

89 **45**

3-y-o ch g Clantime-She's A Breeze (Crofthall)
S E Kettlewell W B Imison

Placings:500-60 **(1637)**
2001: 5^{6}GF, 7^{0}F

	Starts	1st	2nd	3rd	Win & Pl
Career Total (Turf)	5	0	0	0	0

Going (Turf): **Sf: 0-0 GS: 0-1 Gd: 0-1 GF: 0-2 Fm: 0-1**
Distance: 5f/6f: 0-3 7f-8f: 0-2 9f-13f: 0-0 14f+: 0-0
Track : LH: 0-0 RH: 0-0 Tight: 0-0 Gall: 0-0
Aids: Bl: 0-0 Vi: 0-0 Tstrap: 0-0
Best Rating: 26 5/01 Muss 5f gd-fm

Dispol Rock (IRE)

106 **58**

5-y-o b g Ballad Rock-Havana Moon (Ela-Mana-Mou)
T D Barron W B Imison

Placings:301/00322160/0000-200322200 **(4541)**
2001: 9^{2}F, 9^{0}GF, 12^{0}GF, 10^{3}F, 10^{2}GS, 12^{2}G, 11^{2}G, 10^{0}G, 14^{0}GF

	Starts	1st	2nd	3rd	Win & Pl
Career Total (Turf)	24	2	6	3	14389

71 8/99 Ripn 1m2f E(0-70)H G-F £3470
66 9/98 Newc 7f F GD £1903

Total win prize-money £5373

Going (Turf): Sf: 0-2 GS: 0-4 **Gd: 1-7 GF: 1-9** Fm: 0-2
Distance: 5f/6f: 0-0 7f-8f: 1-4 9f-13f: 1-19 14f+: 0-1
Track : LH: 0-14 **RH: 1-6 Tight: 1-9** Gall: 0-8
Aids: Bl: 0-0 Vi: 0-0 Tstrap: 0-0
Best Rating: 59 5/01 Rdcr 1m1f firm

Fair handicapper at ten furlongs on good ground.

Distant Cheers (USA)

(98) (65)**54**

3-y-o ch f Distant View (USA)-With Cheer (CAN) (With Approval (CAN))
T G Mills Goodfellows Racing

Placings:306000010 **(5166)**
2001: 8^{3}SD, 8^{0}GS, 8^{6}G, 9^{0}F, 8^{0}GS, 8^{0}GF, 8^{0}SD, 8^{1}SD, 9^{0}SD

	Starts	1st	2nd	3rd	Win & Pl
Career Total (Turf)	5	0	0	0	0
Career Total (AW)	4	1	0	1	2900

65 9/01 Wolv 1m100y F(0-65)H STD £2495

Total win prize-money £2496

Going (Turf): **Sf: 0-0 GS: 0-2 Gd: 0-1 GF: 0-1 Fm: 0-1**
Distance: 5f/6f: 0-0 7f-8f: 0-3 **9f-13f: 1-6** 14f+: 0-0
Track : **LH: 1-5** RH: 0-1 **Tight: 1-5** Gall: 0-0
Aids: Bl: 0-0 Vi: 0-0 Tstrap: 0-0
Best Rating: 65 9/01 Wolv 1m100y stand

From the same family as the top-class Distant Music, she was disappointing until winning a maiden over an extended mile on the All-Weather under newly-adopted front-running tactics.

Distant Cousin

101(105) (80)**50**

4-y-o b g Distant Relative-Tinaca (USA) (Manila (USA))
M A Buckley C C Buckley

Placings:2310-00000030 **(5640)**
2001: 13^{0}GF, 12^{0}F, 12^{0}G, 14^{0}GF, 15^{0}GS, 15^{0}GS, 11^{3}S, 13^{0}G

	Starts	1st	2nd	3rd	Win & Pl
Career Total (Turf)	11	0	1	2	1885
Career Total (AW)	1	1	0	0	2974

80 9/00 Ling 1m5f D STD £2973

Total win prize-money £2974

Going (Turf): **Sf: 0-3 GS: 0-2 Gd: 0-2 GF: 0-3 Fm: 0-1**
Distance: 5f/6f: 0-0 7f-8f: 0-0 **9f-13f: 1-6** 14f+: 0-6
Track : **LH: 1-10** RH: 0-1 **Tight: 1-6** Gall: 0-2
Aids: Bl: 0-0 Vi: 0-2 Tstrap: 0-0
Best Rating: 57 6/01 Thsk 1m4f good

Moderate handicapper at around a mile and a half.

Distant Dawn

(80) (35)**48**

3-y-o b f Petong-Turbo Rose (Taufan (USA))
K T Ivory Dean Ivory

Placings:4026004-0460 **(0281)**
2001: 5^{0}SD, 7^{4}SD, 9^{6}SD, 8^{0}SW

	Starts	1st	2nd	3rd	Win & Pl
Career Total (Turf)	7	0	1	0	627
Career Total (AW)	4	0	0	0	0

Going (Turf): **Sf: 0-2 GS: 0-0 Gd: 0-2 GF: 0-2 Fm: 0-1**
Distance: 5f/6f: 0-4 7f-8f: 0-6 9f-13f: 0-1 14f+: 0-0
Track : LH: 0-7 RH: 0-0 Tight: 0-2 Gall: 0-2
Aids: Bl: 0-4 Vi: 0-3 Tstrap: 0-0
Best Rating: 35 1/01 Sthl 7f stand

Distant Decree (USA)

78 **12**

3-y-o ch f Distant View (USA)-Nobile Decretum (USA) (Noble Decree (USA))
J A Osborne Wood Hall Stud Limited

Placings:0-00000 **(3577)**
2001: 8^{0}G, 8^{0}G, 9^{0}GF, 9^{0}GF, 8^{0}GF

	Starts	1st	2nd	3rd	Win & Pl
Career Total (Turf)	6	0	0	0	

Going (Turf): **Sf: 0-0 GS: 0-0 Gd: 0-3 GF: 0-3 Fm: 0-0**
Distance: 5f/6f: 0-0 7f-8f: 0-1 9f-13f: 0-5 14f+: 0-0
Track : LH: 0-3 RH: 0-1 Tight: 0-0 Gall: 0-1
Aids: Bl: 0-1 Vi: 0-0 Tstrap: 0-0
Best Rating: 25 5/01 Wwck 1m22y good

Distant Diva

96 **89**

2-y-o b f Distant Relative-Miss Poll Flinders (Swing Easy (USA))
N A Callaghan Norcroft Park Stud

Placings:5214130 **(5256)**
2001: 6^{5}GF, 5^{2}GF, 5^{1}GS, 6^{4}GF, 5^{1}G, 5^{3}GS, 5^{0}GS

	Starts	1st	2nd	3rd	Win & Pl
Career Total (Turf)	7	2	1	1	12774

89 9/01 Sand 5f6y D(0-85) GD £5278
82 8/01 Bevl 5f D G-S £3701

Total win prize-money £8980

Going (Turf): Sf: 0-0 **GS: 1-3 Gd: 1-1** GF: 0-3 Fm: 0-0
Distance: **5f/6f: 2-6** 7f-8f: 0-1 9f-13f: 0-0 14f+: 0-0
Track : LH: 0-0 RH: 0-0 Tight: 0-0 Gall: 0-0
Aids: Bl: 0-0 Vi: 0-0 Tstrap: 0-0
Best Rating: 89 9/01 Sand 5f6y good

Showed ability before getting off the mark in a Beverley maiden over the minimum trip, and again scored over that distance in a Sandown nursery. Has won on good to soft, and good. Acts on faster ground.

Distant Mist (USA)

86(101) (69)**66**

2-y-o ch c Distant View (USA)-Sage Mist (USA) (Capote (USA))
J Noseda Swan Horse Racing

Placings:1500 **(5690)**
2001: 5^{1}SD, 5^{5}G, 7^{0}GS, 7^{0}S

	Starts	1st	2nd	3rd	Win & Pl
Career Total (Turf)	3	0	0	0	0
Career Total (AW)	1	1	0	0	2940

69 3/01 Ling 5f D STD £2940

Total win prize-money £2940

Going (Turf): **Sf: 0-1 GS: 0-1 Gd: 0-1 GF: 0-0 Fm: 0-0**
Distance: **5f/6f: 1-2** 7f-8f: 0-2 9f-13f: 0-0 14f+: 0-0
Track : **LH: 1-1** RH: 0-0 **Tight: 1-1** Gall: 0-0
Aids: Bl: 0-0 Vi: 0-0 Tstrap: 0-0
Best Rating: 69 3/01 Ling 5f stand

Won on his debut on the Equitrack surface at Lingfield but was off the track for almost six months before returning at Beverley and has been disappointing since.

Distant Music (USA)

111 **116**

4-y-o b h Distant View (USA)-Musicanti (USA) (Nijinsky (CAN))

B W Hills K Abdulla

Placings:111/20130-415566 **(5389)**
2001: 9^{4}S, 9^{1}G, 8^{5}GF, 10^{5}G, 8^{6}G, 10^{6}GS

	Starts	1st	2nd	3rd	Win & Pl
Career Total (Turf)	**14**	**5**	**1**	**1**	**349615**

119 7/01 Curr 1m1f GD £69000
119 9/00 Donc 1m A G-F £21000
114 10/99 NmkJ 7f A GD £117600
119 9/99 Donc 7f A G-F £60840
95 7/99 Donc 7f D G-F £3680
Total win prize-money £272120

Going (Turf): Sf: 0-1 GS: 0-3 Gd: 2-5 **GF: 3-4** Fm: 0-1
Distance: 5f/6f: 0-0 **7f-8f: 4-9** 9f-13f: 1-5 14f+: 0-0
Track : **LH: 1-4** RH: 0-1 Tight: 0-1 **Gall: 1-3**
Aids: Bl: 0-0 Vi: 0-0 Tstrap: 0-0
Best Rating: 119 7/01 Curr 1m1f good

Winner of the Champagne Stakes at Doncaster and the Dewhurst Stakes as a juvenile, he struggled early in 2000 including when disappointing in the 2000 Guineas. Came back from three months off to take a Group Three at Doncaster before running third in the Champion Stakes. Found little on his return this term at Newmarket, but was gifted a Curragh Group Two. Comfortably held since, he was best on a fast surface and suited by being held up for a late run. Retired.

Distant Prospect (IRE)

107 **91**
4-y-o b g Namaqualand (USA)-Ukraine's Affair (USA) (The Minstrel (CAN))
I A Balding The Rae Smiths And Pauline Gale

Placings:0030/2354111-005514 **(5600)**
2001: 18^{0}GF, 14^{0}GF, 16^{5}F, 14^{5}G, 18^{1}GS, 16^{4}GS

	Starts	1st	2nd	3rd	Win & Pl
Career Total (Turf)	**17**	**4**	**1**	**2**	**104035**

91 10/01 NmkR 2m2f B H G-S £78000
84 10/00 Newb 2m C(0-90)H SFT £7280
81 10/00 York 1m5f194yD(0-85)H HVY £8329
74 9/00 Bath 1m5f22y E(0-70)H GD £2834
Total win prize-money £96444

Going (Turf): Sf: 2-3 GS: 1-5 Gd: 1-3 GF: 0-5 Fm: 0-1
Distance: 5f/6f: 0-1 7f-8f: 0-3 9f-13f: 0-4 **14f+: 4-9**
Track : **LH: 3-8** RH: 1-7 Tight: 1-6 **Gall: 2-7**
Aids: Bl: 0-0 Vi: 0-0 Tstrap: 0-0
Best Rating: 91 10/01 NmkR 2m2f gd-sft

A useful staying handicapper in 2000. Held in handicaps this term before landing the Cesarewitch, the first time this season that he had suitable conditions. Best on soft and heavy ground, he can also act on good. Stays two miles.

Distant Scene (USA)

97 **66**
3-y-o b c Distant View (USA)-Dangora (USA) (Sovereign Dancer (USA))
B W Hills K Abdulla

Placings:02545 **(4857)**
2001: 8^{0}GF, 7^{2}G, 7^{5}GS, 5^{4}F, 7^{5}GF

	Starts	1st	2nd	3rd	Win & Pl
Career Total (Turf)	**5**	**0**	**1**	**0**	**1571**

Going (Turf): Sf: 0-0 GS: 0-1 Gd: 0-1 GF: 0-2 Fm: 0-1
Distance: 5f/6f: 0-1 7f-8f: 0-4 9f-13f: 0-0 14f+: 0-0
Track : LH: 0-3 RH: 0-0 Tight: 0-2 Gall: 0-1
Aids: Bl: 0-0 Vi: 0-0 Tstrap: 0-0
Best Rating: 67 6/01 Thsk 7f good

Distant Sky (USA)

102(92) (49)**58**
4-y-o ch c Distant View (USA)-Nijinsky Star (USA) (Nijinsky (CAN))
P Mitchell Richard J Cohen

Placings:03300000 **(5463)**
2001: 11^{0}SD, 8^{3}S, 10^{3}G, 10^{0}G, 12^{0}GF, 12^{0}G, 13^{0}GS, 11^{0}G,

	Starts	1st	2nd	3rd	Win & Pl
Career Total (Turf)	**7**	**0**	**0**	**2**	**1283**
Career Total (AW)	**1**	**0**	**0**	**0**	

Going (Turf): Sf: 0-1 GS: 0-1 Gd: 0-4 GF: 0-1 Fm: 0-0
Distance: 5f/6f: 0-0 7f-8f: 0-0 9f-13f: 0-7 14f+: 0-1
Track : LH: 0-6 RH: 0-2 Tight: 0-4 Gall: 0-2
Aids: Bl: 0-2 Vi: 0-0 Tstrap: 0-0
Best Rating: 76 5/01 Sand 1m2f7y good

Distant Storm

99(71) (36)**44**
8-y-o ch g Pharly (FR)-Candle In The Wind (Thatching)
B J Llewellyn D H Driscoll

Placings:01060/52/**0/3235**23/**0**222/400-**0**3400O **(3411)**
2001: 16^{0}SD, 17^{3}HY, 21^{4}S, 16^{0}GF, 17^{0}GF, 16^{0}GF

	Starts	1st	2nd	3rd	Win & Pl
Career Total (Turf)	**20**	**1**	**5**	**2**	**9153**
Career Total (AW)	**7**	**0**	**1**	**2**	**1829**

66 7/95 Brig 6f209y G FRM £2243
Total win prize-money £2243

Going (Turf): Sf: 0-5 GS: 0-0 Gd: 0-4 GF: 0-8 **Fm: 1-3**
Distance: 5f/6f: 0-0 **7f-8f: 1-5** 9f-13f: 0-1 14f+: 0-21
Track : **LH: 1-25** RH: 0-1 Tight: 0-10 Gall: 0-2
Aids: **Bl: 1-22** Vi: 0-2 Tstrap: 0-5
Best Rating: 45 4/01 Pont 2m1f22y heavy

Distant Valley

110 **100**
2-y-o b f Distant Relative-Down The Valley (Kampala)
R Hannon J R Shannon

Placings:1121 **(5390)**
2001: 6^{1}G, 7^{1}G, 7^{2}GF, 7^{1}GS

	Starts	1st	2nd	3rd	Win & Pl
Career Total (Turf)	**4**	**3**	**1**	**0**	**44477**

100 10/01 NmkR 7f A G-S £29000
89 9/01 Kemp 7f C GD £6438
83 8/01 Asct 6f D GD £5369
Total win prize-money £40807

Going (Turf): Sf: 0-0 GS: 1-1 **Gd: 2-2** GF: 0-1 Fm: 0-0
Distance: 5f/6f: 1-1 **7f-8f: 2-3** 9f-13f: 0-0 14f+: 0-0
Track : LH: 0-0 **RH: 1-1** Tight: 0-0 **Gall: 1-1**
Aids: Bl: 0-0 Vi: 0-0 Tstrap: 0-0
Best Rating: 100 10/01 NmkR 7f gd-sft

A half-sister to Mayaro Bay, she made a winning debut at Ascot in August and followed up in a Kempton conditions event. Only went down by a short-head at Newbury next time before returning to winning ways in the Rockfel at Newmarket. Genuine sort.

Distinctive Dream (IRE)

106(105) (47)**63**
7-y-o b g Distinctly North (USA)-Green Side (USA) (Green Dancer (USA))
A Bailey A Thomson

Placings:0000/40**50**5402111**1**1126012602/0220000/662140/**6215341036**02600040500**2**00**0005-23023053**0623135501**20** **(2627)**
2001: 7^{2}SD, 8^{3}SW, 7^{0}SW, 7^{2}SW, 7^{3}SD, 7^{0}SD, 7^{5}SW, 7^{3}SD, 8^{0}SD, 8^{6}GS, 6^{2}GF, 5^{3}G, 7^{1}GF, 5^{3}GF, 6^{5}GF, 5^{5}GF, 6^{0}GF, 6^{1}GS, 6^{2}G, 6^{0}GF

	Starts	1st	2nd	3rd	Win & Pl
Career Total (Turf)	**61**	**8**	**10**	**2**	**45520**
Career Total (AW)	**26**	**3**	**4**	**5**	**11620**

61 6/01 Haml 6f5y D(0-80)H G-S £4348
57 5/01 Donc 7f E(0-70)H G-F £3374
65 2/00 Sthl 7f G(0-75)H STD £1526
57 2/00 Wolv 7f G STD £1932
73 7/99 Hayd 7f30y D(0-75) FRM £3954
79 9/97 Kemp 6f D(0-85)H G-F £3533
70 8/97 Wind 5f10y E(0-70)H GD £2851
66 7/97 Sthl 5f D(0-75)H STD £3677
61 7/97 Wind 5f217y E(0-70)H G-F £3160
53 7/97 Sals 6f F(0-60)H G-F £3120
50 7/97 Wind 5f217y E(0-70)H GD £3046
Total win prize-money £34524

Going (Turf): Sf: 0-5 GS: 1-10 Gd: 2-20 **GF: 4-22** Fm: 1-4
Distance: **5f/6f: 6-36** 7f-8f: 5-46 9f-13f: 0-5 14f+: 0-0
Track : LH: 3-35 RH: 3-7 Tight: 1-18 **Gall: 3-5**
Aids: **Bl: 8-38** Vi: 1-5 Tstrap: 0-0
Best Rating: 63 7/01 Gdwd 6f gd-fm

Formerly a multiple winner on turf, he has run well at distances between five furlongs and a mile. In good form in the 2001 season. A bit of a character, he acts on all bar extremes of going.

Distinctly East (IRE)

(101) (37)**57**
4-y-o b g Distinctly North (USA)-Raggy (Smoggy)
Miss S J Wilton John Pointon And Sons

Placings:1456020/04056**1-06400450** **(2342)**
2001: 7^{0}SD, 7^{6}SW, 8^{4}SW, 8^{0}SD, 8^{0}SD, 7^{4}SD, 8^{5}SD, 7^{0}SD

	Starts	1st	2nd	3rd	Win & Pl
Career Total (Turf)	**12**	**1**	**1**	**0**	**6315**
Career Total (AW)	**9**	**1**	**0**	**0**	**1757**

44 11/00 Wolv 7f F STD £1757
74 4/99 Ripn 5f D G-F £3146
Total win prize-money £4903

Going (Turf): Sf: 0-2 GS: 0-0 Gd: 0-4 **GF: 1-5** Fm: 0-1
Distance: 5f/6f: 1-4 7f-8f: 1-10 9f-13f: 0-7 14f+: 0-0
Track : **LH: 1-12** RH: 0-0 **Tight: 1-8** Gall: 0-0
Aids: Bl: 0-1 Vi: 0-2 Tstrap: 0-0
Best Rating: 38 1/01 Wolv 7f slow

Distinctly Well (IRE)

104(81) (24)**52**
4-y-o b g Distinctly North (USA)-Brandywell (Skyliner)
B A McMahon The Bears Syndicate

Placings:22**2**0444655160000/23026-**0000**0003230 **(4906)**
2001: 9^{0}SW, 9^{0}SD, 8^{0}SW, 11^{0}SW, 8^{0}S, 8^{0}F, 8^{0}G, 8^{0}G, 10^{3}GF, 10^{2}GF, 11^{3}G, 9^{0}G

	Starts	1st	2nd	3rd	Win & Pl
Career Total (Turf)	**29**	**1**	**5**	**3**	**13219**
Career Total (AW)	**5**	**0**	**1**	**0**	**848**

77 8/99 Ches 7f2y C H G-S £6092
Total win prize-money £6093

Going (Turf): Sf: 0-6 **GS: 1-3** Gd: 0-11 GF: 0-8 Fm: 0-1
Distance: 5f/6f: 0-10 **7f-8f: 1-7** 9f-13f: 0-17 14f+: 0-0
Track : **LH: 1-20** RH: 0-2 **Tight: 1-19** Gall: 0-2
Aids: Bl: 0-1 Vi: 0-1 Tstrap: 0-0
Best Rating: 52 7/01 Wind 1m2f7y gd-fm

Diva La Vida (IRE)

85 **56**
2-y-o ch f Perugino (USA)-First Nadia (Auction Ring (USA))
J S Wainwright J S Wainwright

Placings:000600 **(5370)**
2001: 5^{0}GF, 6^{0}G, 5^{0}GF, 8^{6}GF, 7^{0}G, 7^{0}G

	Starts	1st	2nd	3rd	Win & Pl
Career Total (Turf)	**6**	**0**	**0**	**0**	**0**

Going (Turf): Sf: 0-0 GS: 0-0 Gd: 0-3 GF: 0-3 Fm: 0-0
Distance: 5f/6f: 0-3 7f-8f: 0-2 9f-13f: 0-1 14f+: 0-0

Track : LH: 0-0 RH: 0-2 Tight: 0-0 Gall: 0-0
Aids: Bl: 0-0 Vi: 0-0 Tstrap: 0-0
Best Rating: 56 8/01 Bevl 1m100y gd-fm

Diva's Robe (IRE)

94(80) (7)**58d**

3-y-o b f Robellino (USA)-High Note (Shirley Heights)
N A Graham Paul G Jacobs

Placings:66-0060 **(2648)**
2001: 6^{0}GS, 8^{0}G, 9^{6}G, 12^{0}SD

	Starts	1st	2nd	3rd	Win & Pl
Career Total (Turf)	5	0	0	0	0
Career Total (AW)	1	0	0	0	

Going (Turf): Sf: 0-0 GS: 0-1 Gd: 0-2 GF: 0-2 Fm: 0-0
Distance: 5f/6f: 0-1 7f-8f: 0-2 9f-13f: 0-3 14f+: 0-0
Track : LH: 0-2 RH: 0-1 Tight: 0-0 Gall: 0-1
Aids: Bl: 0-0 Vi: 0-0 Tstrap: 0-0
Best Rating: 48 6/01 Nott 1m1f213y good

Divine Grace (IRE)

71 **32**

2-y-o b f Definite Article-Grey Patience (IRE) (Common Grounds)
Mrs P N Dutfield M Bevan

Placings:00 **(4158)**
2001: 6^{0}GF, 7^{0}GF

	Starts	1st	2nd	3rd	Win & Pl
Career Total (Turf)	2	0	0	0	

Going (Turf): Sf: 0-0 GS: 0-0 Gd: 0-0 GF: 0-2 Fm: 0-0
Distance: 5f/6f: 0-1 7f-8f: 0-1 9f-13f: 0-0 14f+: 0-0
Track : LH: 0-0 RH: 0-0 Tight: 0-0 Gall: 0-0
Aids: Bl: 0-0 Vi: 0-0 Tstrap: 0-0
Best Rating: 32 8/01 Ling 7f140y gd-fm

Divine Task (USA)

105 **99**

3-y-o ch c Irish River (FR)-Set In Motion (USA) (Mr Prospector (USA))
Saeed Bin Suroor Godolphin

Placings:010 **(5103)**
2001: 8^{0}G, 7^{1}GF, 8^{0}GS

	Starts	1st	2nd	3rd	Win & Pl
Career Total (Turf)	3	1	0	0	4388

90 9/01 Ling 7f D G-F £4387
Total win prize-money £4388

Going (Turf): Sf: 0-0 GS: 0-1 Gd: 0-1 **GF: 1-1** Fm: 0-0
Distance: 5f/6f: 0-0 **7f-8f: 1-3** 9f-13f: 0-0 14f+: 0-0
Track : LH: 0-0 RH: 0-0 Tight: 0-0 Gall: 0-0
Aids: Bl: 0-0 Vi: 0-0 Tstrap: 0-0
Best Rating: 99 10/01 NmkR 1m gd-sft

He ran in his first proper race in the 2000 Guineas and was nowhere near good enough there, but had little difficulty in winning a Lingfield maiden in September.

Divine Wind

101(100) (62)**60**

3-y-o ch f Clantime-Breezy Day (Day Is Done)
B A McMahon Mrs J McMahon

Placings:14033400002005-5024264263 **(3702)**
2001: 7^{5}SD, 7^{0}G, 6^{2}GF, 6^{4}GF, 6^{2}SD, 7^{6}GF, 5^{4}GF, 6^{2}SD, 6^{6}GF, 5^{3}G

	Starts	1st	2nd	3rd	Win & Pl
Career Total (Turf)	21	1	2	3	8631
Career Total (AW)	3	0	2	0	1472

67 3/00 Donc 5f E GD £3705
Total win prize-money £3705

Going (Turf): Sf: 0-3 GS: 0-4 **Gd: 1-5** GF: 0-9 Fm: 0-0
Distance: **5f/6f: 1-15** 7f-8f: 0-9 9f-13f: 0-0 14f+: 0-0
Track : LH: 0-6 RH: 0-0 Tight: 0-1 Gall: 0-0
Aids: Bl: 0-0 Vi: 0-0 Tstrap: 0-0
Best Rating: 62 7/01 Sthl 6f stand

Divorce Action (IRE)

97(81) (33)

5-y-o b g Common Grounds-Overdue Reaction (Be My Guest (USA))
R M Stronge Kevin Elliott

Placings:5300/550150/0250051-00350 **(2625)**
2001: 10^{0}G, 10^{0}S, 10^{3}GF, 10^{5}G, 9^{0}GF

	Starts	1st	2nd	3rd	Win & Pl
Career Total (Turf)	21	2	1	2	6642
Career Total (AW)	1	0	0	0	

54 8/00 Wwck 1m2f188yG GD £2060
67 8/99 Kemp 1m1f E G-F £2788
Total win prize-money £4849

Going (Turf): Sf: 0-2 GS: 0-3 **Gd: 1-5 GF: 1-10** Fm: 0-1
Distance: 5f/6f: 0-1 7f-8f: 0-4 **9f-13f: 2-17** 14f+: 0-0
Track : LH: 1-10 RH: 1-7 Tight: 0-8 Gall: 0-2
Aids: Bl: 0-0 Vi: 0-0 Tstrap: 0-0
Best Rating: 57 5/01 Sthl 1m2f gd-fm

Dixie Dancing

77 **50**

2-y-o ch f Greensmith-Daylight Dreams (Indian Ridge)
C A Cyzer Mrs E A Cyzer

Placings:0 **(5274)**
2001: 7^{0}GS

	Starts	1st	2nd	3rd	Win & Pl
Career Total (Turf)	1	0	0	0	

Going (Turf): Sf: 0-0 GS: 0-1 Gd: 0-0 GF: 0-0 Fm: 0-0
Distance: 5f/6f: 0-0 7f-8f: 0-1 9f-13f: 0-0 14f+: 0-0
Track : LH: 0-0 RH: 0-0 Tight: 0-0 Gall: 0-0
Aids: Bl: 0-0 Vi: 0-0 Tstrap: 0-0
Best Rating: 50 10/01 Leic 7f9y gd-sft

Dixie Island (USA)

103(109) (73)**75**

4-y-o b g Dixieland Band (USA)-Cranberry Island (USA) (Private Account (USA))
B J Meehan (A T Murphy 31/1) E H Jones (paints) Ltd

Placings:1262-56540300 **(1414)**
2001: 16^{5}SD, 9^{6}SW, 10^{5}SW, 7^{4}GS, 8^{0}GS, 10^{3}GF, 10^{0}G, 10^{0}S

	Starts	1st	2nd	3rd	Win & Pl
Career Total (Turf)	9	1	2	1	9700
Career Total (AW)	3	0	0	0	0

4/00 Chol 1m1f55y HLD £2881
Total win prize-money £2882

Going (Turf): Sf: 0-1 GS: 0-3 Gd: 0-1 GF: 0-1 Fm: 0-0
Distance: 5f/6f: 0-0 7f-8f: 0-3 **9f-13f: 1-7** 14f+: 0-1
Track : LH: 0-6 RH: 0-0 Tight: 0-5 Gall: 0-1
Aids: Bl: 0-1 Vi: 0-1 Tstrap: 0-0
Best Rating: 75 5/01 Ches 1m2f75y gd-fm

Dixie's Darts

100 **65**

3-y-o b g Mistertopogigo (IRE)-Maestrette (Manado)
M H Tompkins Yours For A Day Limited

Placings:00-5055465 **(5490)**
2001: 6^{5}GS, 7^{0}GF, 6^{5}GF, 6^{5}GS, 6^{4}G, 6^{6}GF, 7^{5}HY

	Starts	1st	2nd	3rd	Win & Pl
Career Total (Turf)	9	0	0	0	271

Going (Turf): Sf: 0-2 GS: 0-2 Gd: 0-1 GF: 0-4 Fm: 0-0
Distance: 5f/6f: 0-6 7f-8f: 0-3 9f-13f: 0-0 14f+: 0-0

Track : LH: 0-3 RH: 0-1 Tight: 0-1 Gall: 0-0
Aids: Bl: 0-0 Vi: 0-0 Tstrap: 0-0
Best Rating: 65 8/01 Pont 6f good

Dizzy In The Head

94(48) **76**

2-y-o b c Mind Games-Giddy (Polar Falcon (USA))
D W P Arbuthnot Noel Cronin

Placings:01200500004 **(5521)**
2001: 5^{0}GS, 5^{1}GS, 5^{2}G, 5^{0}GF, 6^{0}GF, 5^{5}GF, 5^{0}S, 6^{0}GS, 5^{0}GS, 6^{0}SD, 6^{4}HY

	Starts	1st	2nd	3rd	Win & Pl
Career Total (Turf)	10	1	1	0	8352
Career Total (AW)	1	0	0	0	

69 5/01 Wind 5f10y D G-S £3815
Total win prize-money £3815

Going (Turf): Sf: 0-2 **GS: 1-4** Gd: 0-1 GF: 0-3 Fm: 0-0
Distance: **5f/6f: 1-11** 7f-8f: 0-0 9f-13f: 0-0 14f+: 0-0
Track : LH: 0-1 **RH: 1-3** Tight: 0-0 **Gall: 1-3**
Aids: Bl: 0-0 Vi: 0-3 Tstrap: 0-0
Best Rating: 84 6/01 Asct 5f gd-fm

Got off the mark on second outing at two in a Windsor maiden over the minimum trip, but has disappointed since. Tried in a visor to little effect.

Dizzy Knight

90(98) (59)**61**

4-y-o b f Distant Relative-Top Treat (USA) (Topsider (USA))
B Palling Mr Derek D & Mrs Jean P Clee

Placings:0/400**160**-000 **(2042)**
2001: 5^{0}SD, 5^{0}SD, 6^{0}GF

	Starts	1st	2nd	3rd	Win & Pl
Career Total (Turf)	5	0	0	0	313
Career Total (AW)	5	1	0	0	1768

59 12/00 Ling 6f F(0-65)H STD £1767
Total win prize-money £1768

Going (Turf): Sf: 0-2 GS: 0-0 Gd: 0-0 GF: 0-3 Fm: 0-0
Distance: **5f/6f: 1-7** 7f-8f: 0-2 9f-13f: 0-1 14f+: 0-0
Track : **LH: 1-6** RH: 0-0 **Tight: 1-4** Gall: 0-0
Aids: Bl: 0-1 Vi: 0-0 Tstrap: 0-0
Best Rating: 45 1/01 Sthl 5f stand

Dizzy Tart (IRE)

90 **65**

2-y-o b f Definite Article-Tizzy (Formidable (USA))
Mrs P N Dutfield Darren C Mercer

Placings:5035 **(3878)**
2001: 5^{5}GF, 5^{0}GF, 6^{3}GF, 7^{5}GS

	Starts	1st	2nd	3rd	Win & Pl
Career Total (Turf)	4	0	0	1	654

Going (Turf): Sf: 0-0 GS: 0-1 Gd: 0-0 GF: 0-3 Fm: 0-0
Distance: 5f/6f: 0-2 7f-8f: 0-2 9f-13f: 0-0 14f+: 0-0
Track : LH: 0-1 RH: 0-0 Tight: 0-1 Gall: 0-0
Aids: Bl: 0-0 Vi: 0-0 Tstrap: 0-0
Best Rating: 65 7/01 Sals 6f212y gd-fm

Dizzy Tilly

(100) (34)**56**

7-y-o b m Anshan-Nadema (Artaius (USA))
A J Martin L R Gotch

Placings:64300/3151420050/0300005506/0055124536 230/000433010600**000260**-5134 **(3107a)**
2001: 12^{5}F, 13^{1}GY, 14^{3}F, 12^{4}F

	Starts	1st	2nd	3rd	Win & Pl
Career Total (Turf)	52	5	3	6	23158
Career Total (AW)	8	0	1	2	1331

56 6/01 Wxfd 1m5f (0-50)H G-Y £4830

50	7/00	Wind	1m3f135yE(0-75)H		GD	£2842
46	6/99	Wind	1m3f135yE(0-75)H		G-F	£2752
66	6/97	Wind	1m2f7y	F(0-65)	G-S	£2612
64	6/97	Wind	1m3f135yF(0-60)H		G-F	£2836

Total win prize-money £15872

Going (Turf): Sf: 0-7 GS: 1-2 Gd: 1-17 **GF: 2-19** Fm: 0-5
Distance: 5f/6f: 0-2 7f-8f: 0-3 **9f-13f: 5-46** 14f+: 0-8
Track : LH: 0-19 RH: 0-15 **Tight: 4-32** Gall: 0-3
Aids: Bl: 0-1 Vi: 0-0 Tstrap: 0-0
Best Rating: 56 7/01 Dund 1m4f firm

Djais (FR)

(101) (13)**30**
12-y-o ch g Vacarme (USA)-Dame De Carreau (FR) (Targowice (USA))
J R Jenkins Christopher Shankland

Placings:1330/021460/2506/54/360/6/**1**200-00 **(0161)**
2001: 16^{0}SD, 16^{0}SD

	Starts	1st	2nd	3rd	Win & Pl
Career Total (Turf)	21	2	2	3	94211
Career Total (AW)	5	1	1	0	2815

60	6/00	Sthl	2m	F	STD	£2191
	7/93	LE L	1m7f		GD	£35842
105	6/92	Lonc	1m7f		SFT	£20555

Total win prize-money £58588

Going (Turf): **Sf: 1-8** GS: 0-0 Gd: 0-4 GF: 0-4 Fm: 0-0
Distance: 5f/6f: 0-0 7f-8f: 0-0 9f-13f: 0-6 **14f+: 2-15**
Track : LH: 1-11 RH: 1-9 Tight: 0-3 Gall: 0-4
Aids: Bl: 0-0 **Vi: 1-5** Tstrap: 0-0
Best Rating: 13 1/01 Sthl 2m stand

Doberman (IRE)

103(100) (46)**54**
6-y-o br g Dilum (USA)-Switch Blade (IRE) (Robellino (USA))
W M Brisbourne Mrs I M Folkes

Placings:2254**4**00/520**6**6000**4**20240036**404**/40350310022200**4**22**4**23-235202334003 **(5681)**
2001: 9^{2}SD, 8^{3}SD, 12^{5}SD, 8^{2}GS, 9^{0}G, 8^{2}S, 8^{3}S, 8^{3}GF, 8^{4}G, 8^{0}GF, 8^{0}GF, 8^{3}S

	Starts	1st	2nd	3rd	Win & Pl
Career Total (Turf)	26	0	8	4	9476
Career Total (AW)	32	1	6	4	6447

47	2/00	Wolv	1m100y	F(0-60)	STD	£2166

Total win prize-money £2167

Going (Turf): **Sf: 0-5 GS: 0-2 Gd: 0-7 GF: 0-9 Fm: 0-3**
Distance: 6f/6f: 0-4 7f-8f: 0-17 **9f-13f: 1-37** 14f+: 0-0
Track : **LH: 1-44** RH: 0-3 **Tight: 1-32** Gall: 0-1
Aids: **Bl: 1-20** Vi: 0-22 Tstrap: 0-1
Best Rating: 54 11/01 Donc 1m soft

Moderate handicapper, often in the frame but has won only once. Usually wears a visor, and front runs

Doc Holiday (IRE)

103 **102**
2-y-o ch c Dr Devious (IRE)-Easter Heroine (IRE) (Exactly Sharp (USA))
B J Meehan Racegoers Club Owners Group

Placings:1641530 **(5571a)**
2001: 5^{1}S, 7^{6}GF, 6^{4}G, 6^{1}G, 7^{5}G, 6^{3}GS, 6^{0}HY

	Starts	1st	2nd	3rd	Win & Pl
Career Total (Turf)	7	2	0	1	28505

102	8/01	Hayd	6f	C	GD	£6235
89	5/01	Sals	5f	D	SFT	£3770

Total win prize-money £10005

Going (Turf): **Sf: 1-2** GS: 0-1 **Gd: 1-3** GF: 0-1 Fm: 0-0
Distance: **5f/6f: 2-5** 7f-8f: 0-2 9f-13f: 0-0 14f+: 0-0
Track : LH: 0-0 RH: 0-1 Tight: 0-0 Gall: 0-0
Aids: Bl: 0-0 Vi: 0-0 Tstrap: 0-0
Best Rating: 102 10/01 NmkR 6f gd-sft

Looked useful when making virtually all over five furlongs at Salisbury in May on his racecourse debut. Far from disgraced in the Chesham Stakes at Royal Ascot and the July Stakes at Newmarket. He went on to win at Haydock, but appeared to struggle with the step up to seven furlongs when finishing a one-paced fifth in the Solario. Performed well back over six in the Middle Park. Acts on soft ground. Has been sold to the USA.

Dock Leaf (USA)

82 **61**
2-y-o ch f Woodman (USA)-Dokki (USA) (Northern Dancer)
J H M Gosden K Abdulla

Placings:0 **(2931)**
2001: 7^{0}GF

	Starts	1st	2nd	3rd	Win & Pl
Career Total (Turf)	1	0	0	0	

Going (Turf): Sf: 0-0 GS: 0-0 Gd: 0-0 GF: 0-1 Fm: 0-0
Distance: 5f/6f: 0-0 7f-8f: 0-1 9f-13f: 0-0 14f+: 0-0
Track : LH: 0-0 RH: 0-1 Tight: 0-0 Gall: 0-1
Aids: Bl: 0-0 Vi: 0-0 Tstrap: 0-0
Best Rating: 61 7/01 Kemp 7f gd-fm

Docklands Limo

90 **70**
8-y-o b h Most Welcome-Bugle Sound (Bustino)
N A Twiston-Davies John Marks

Placings:5/14162/00303100/0330/0 **(2305)**
2001: 20^{0}GF

	Starts	1st	2nd	3rd	Win & Pl
Career Total (Turf)	17	2	1	4	41835
Career Total (AW)	2	1	0	0	2529

78	7/97	DRoy	1m4f68y		G-F	£30000
74	4/96	Nott	1m1f213yE(0-70)		G-F	£3206
59	2/96	Ling	1m	F	STD	£2528

Total win prize-money £35736

Going (Turf): Sf: 0-2 GS: 0-3 Gd: 0-3 **GF: 2-9** Fm: 0-0
Distance: 5f/6f: 0-0 7f-8f: 1-2 **9f-13f: 2-15** 14f+: 0-2
Track : **LH: 2-8** RH: 1-11 **Tight: 1-4** Gall: 0-11
Aids: Bl: 0-0 Vi: 0-0 Tstrap: 0-0
Best Rating: 70 6/01 Asct 2m4f gd-fm

Useful stayer on the level, lightly-raced these days.

Doctor Dennis (IRE)

106(105) (74)**68**
4-y-o b g Last Tycoon-Noble Lustre (USA) (Lyphard's Wish (FR))
Mrs Lydia Pearce (Andrew Reid 29/6) The Exclusive Two Partnership

Placings:0506002/00021201224420**1**26-000**1**01603300 **(5612)**
2001: 6^{0}HY, 6^{0}SD, 6^{0}G, 6^{1}SD, 6^{0}GF, 6^{1}F, 6^{6}G, 6^{0}GF, 6^{3}GF, 5^{3}S, 6^{0}HY, 6^{0}SD

	Starts	1st	2nd	3rd	Win & Pl
Career Total (Turf)	29	3	5	2	13248
Career Total (AW)	7	2	2	0	7515

68	6/01	Ling	6f	F	FRM	£2485
74	5/01	Sthl	6f	D(0-85)H	STD	£3893
60	11/00	Sthl	6f	F	STD	£1764
57	7/00	Wind	6f	E(0-70)H	SFT	£3237
48	5/00	Brig	5f213y	G	SFT	£1901

Total win prize-money £13282

Going (Turf): Sf: 2-8 GS: 0-4 Gd: 0-5 GF: 0-10 Fm: 1-2
Distance: **5f/6f: 5-24** 7f-8f: 0-9 9f-13f: 0-3 14f+: 0-0
Track : **LH: 3-16** RH: 1-8 Tight: 0-6 **Gall: 1-5**
Aids: **Bl: 2-13** Vi: 0-1 Tstrap: 0-0
Best Rating: 74 5/01 Sthl 6f stand

Doctor John

92(87) (53d)**22**
4-y-o ch g Handsome Sailor-Bollin Sophie (Efisio)
Andrew Turnell Dr John Hollowood

Placings:0044-0000 **(2040)**
2001: 14^{0}S, 12^{0}S, 11^{0}F, 17^{0}GF

	Starts	1st	2nd	3rd	Win & Pl
Career Total (Turf)	7	0	0	0	220
Career Total (AW)	1	0	0	0	0

Going (Turf): Sf: 0-2 GS: 0-1 Gd: 0-1 GF: 0-2 Fm: 0-1
Distance: 5f/6f: 0-0 7f-8f: 0-0 9f-13f: 0-6 14f+: 0-2
Track : LH: 0-7 RH: 0-1 Tight: 0-1 Gall: 0-2
Aids: Bl: 0-0 Vi: 0-0 Tstrap: 0-0
Best Rating: 22 5/01 Leic 1m3f183y firm

Doctor No No (IRE)

101 **60**
3-y-o b g Dr Devious (IRE)-Silver Echo (Caerleon (USA))
J A Osborne Martin Myers

Placings:552500 **(5179)**
2001: 10^{5}GF, 10^{5}S, 10^{2}GF, 10^{5}GF, 10^{0}G, 10^{0}HY

	Starts	1st	2nd	3rd	Win & Pl
Career Total (Turf)	6	0	1	0	836

Going (Turf): Sf: 0-2 GS: 0-0 Gd: 0-1 GF: 0-3 Fm: 0-0
Distance: 5f/6f: 0-0 7f-8f: 0-0 9f-13f: 0-6 14f+: 0-0
Track : LH: 0-2 RH: 0-3 Tight: 0-2 Gall: 0-1
Aids: Bl: 0-1 Vi: 0-0 Tstrap: 0-0
Best Rating: 79 7/01 Bath 1m2f46y gd-fm

Doctor Spin (IRE)

111 **104**
5-y-o b h Namaqualand (USA)-Madam Loving (Vaigly Great)
R F Johnson Houghton Anthony Pye-Jeary

Placings:511/406340/1502-00054600 **(4062)**
2001: 6^{0}G, 6^{0}GF, 5^{0}GF, 6^{5}GF, 6^{4}F, 6^{6}GF, 7^{0}GF, 6^{0}G

	Starts	1st	2nd	3rd	Win & Pl
Career Total (Turf)	21	3	1	1	32252

103	5/00	NmkR	6f	B(0-110)H	GD	£9439
93	5/98	Ling	5f	E	GD	£3235
82	5/98	Wind	5f10y	D	G-F	£3225

Total win prize-money £15900

Going (Turf): Sf: 0-2 GS: 0-0 **Gd: 2-7** GF: 1-10 Fm: 0-2
Distance: **5f/6f: 3-16** 7f-8f: 0-5 9f-13f: 0-0 14f+: 0-0
Track : LH: 0-1 **RH: 1-3** Tight: 0-0 **Gall: 1-3**
Aids: Bl: 0-0 Vi: 0-0 Tstrap: 0-0
Best Rating: 104 6/01 Newc 6f firm

Overcame a long layoff to win first time out at Newmarket in 2000, but failed in his attempt to do the same thing this season. Decent fifth in the Wokingham when racing down the unfavoured middle of the course and fourth to Volata in a Group Three over six furlongs at Newcastle in July. Best over six furlong on a sound surface and needs to be covered up.

Dodona

101 **56**
3-y-o b/br f Lahib (USA)-Dukrame (Top Ville)
T D McCarthy A D Spence

Placings:400400-0005541215035 **(5525)**
2001: 8^{0}S, 11^{0}G, 9^{0}GF, 11^{5}F, 12^{5}GF, 8^{4}GF, 9^{1}G, 9^{2}G, 10^{1}S, 10^{5}G, 11^{0}G, 9^{3}S, 11^{5}HY

	Starts	1st	2nd	3rd	Win & Pl
Career Total (Turf)	19	2	1	1	10815

55	8/01	Epsm	1m2f18y	E(0-70)H	SFT	£6136
50	8/01	Brig	1m1f209yF(0-65)H		GD	£3073

Total win prize-money £9209

Going (Turf): Sf: 1-7 GS: 0-1 Gd: 1-5 GF: 0-5 Fm: 0-1
Distance: 5f/6f: 0-0 7f-8f: 0-6 9f-13f: 2-13 14f+: 0-0
Track : LH: 2-8 RH: 0-3 Tight: 1-5 Gall: 0-2
Aids: Bl: 0-0 Vi: 0-0 Tstrap: 0-0
Best Rating: 56 10/01 Brig 1m1f209y soft

Hit form in August with wins at Brighton and Epsom, but may not be totally suited by undulating tracks as she hung badly on the second occasion. Attacked by a bull terrier and ran loose before finishing third at the former track in October, but was well beaten in a better race after that at Windsor. Best over ten furlongs and appreciates cut in the ground.

Dolfinesse (IRE)

102(98) (45)**44**
4-y-o ch f Dolphin Street (FR)-Gortadoo (USA) (Sharpen Up)
M Brittain Steven J Box

Placings:605050/05234062060-21330005100 **(4450)**
2001: 9^{2}S, 8^{1}GS, 7^{3}GF, 8^{3}SD, 8^{0}SD, 7^{0}GF, 8^{0}G, 8^{5}SD, 7^{1}GS, 9^{0}G, 8^{0}GF

	Starts	1st	2nd	3rd	Win & Pl
Career Total (Turf)	25	2	3	2	8634
Career Total (AW)	3	0	0	1	415

44 8/01 Leic 7f9y G G-S £2380
45 4/01 Muss 1m F(0-60)H G-S £2814
Total win prize-money £5194

Going (Turf): Sf: 0-1 **GS: 2-4** Gd: 0-7 GF: 0-11 Fm: 0-2
Distance: 5f/6f: 0-2 **7f-8f: 2-17** 9f-13f: 0-9 14f+: 0-0
Track : LH: 0-11 **RH: 1-9 Tight: 1-4** Gall: 0-2
Aids: Bl: 0-0 **Vi: 2-19** Tstrap: 0-0
Best Rating: 45 5/01 Sthl 1m stand

Dollar King (IRE)

96 **74**
3-y-o b c Ela-Mana-Mou-Summerhill (Habitat)
J Noseda Epona Partnership

Placings:054621003 **(4988)**
2001: 8^{0}S, 8^{5}GF, 7^{4}GF, 7^{6}GS, 8^{2}G, 9^{1}GF, 9^{0}GS, 8^{0}F, 8^{3}G

	Starts	1st	2nd	3rd	Win & Pl
Career Total (Turf)	9	1	1	1	5508

53 8/01 Rdcr 1m1f E G-F £3066
Total win prize-money £3066

Going (Turf): Sf: 0-1 GS: 0-2 Gd: 0-2 **GF: 1-3** Fm: 0-1
Distance: 5f/6f: 0-0 7f-8f: 0-5 **9f-13f: 1-4** 14f+: 0-0
Track : **LH: 1-4** RH: 0-1 **Tight: 1-3** Gall: 0-0
Aids: Bl: 0-0 Vi: 0-1 Tstrap: 0-0
Best Rating: 74 9/01 Asct 1m good

He just prevailed in a weak contest at Redcar, where getting first run made all the difference. Needs a decent pace and a sound surface. Needs a decent pace. Best at around a mile.

Dollar Law

99(83) (39)**57**
5-y-o ch g Selkirk (USA)-Western Heights (Shirley Heights)
R J Price (W M Brisbourne 21/6) The Cleobury Partnership

Placings:241/0000/500030002 **(5626)**
2001: 8^{5}S, 8^{0}F, 8^{0}G, 8^{0}SD, 7^{3}G, 6^{0}S, 6^{0}HY, 8^{0}SD, 8^{2}GS

	Starts	1st	2nd	3rd	Win & Pl
Career Total (Turf)	14	1	2	1	6452
Career Total (AW)	2	0	0	0	

81 10/98 Leic 1m8y D G-S £4042
Total win prize-money £4042

Going (Turf): Sf: 0-3 **GS: 1-5** Gd: 0-3 GF: 0-2 Fm: 0-1
Distance: 5f/6f: 0-1 7f-8f: 0-6 **9f-13f: 1-9** 14f+: 0-0
Track : LH: 0-7 RH: 0-3 Tight: 0-2 Gall: 0-3

Aids: Bl: 0-0 Vi: 0-0 Tstrap: 0-0
Best Rating: 70 4/01 Kemp 1m soft

A half-brother to mile and a quarter winner Pinchincha, he won his maiden over a mile at Leicester on easy ground, but has been lightly raced and disappointing since. He missed the whole of the 2000 season, but put up a couple of decent efforts in2001 in modest handicaps, and is on a fair mark.

Dolly Dimple

77 **45**
2-y-o b f Son Pardo-Anne's Bank (IRE) (Burslem)
G L Moore Mrs L B Jones

Placings:0000 **(5130)**
2001: 6^{0}G, 6^{0}G, 6^{0}F, 7^{0}HY

	Starts	1st	2nd	3rd	Win & Pl
Career Total (Turf)	4	0	0	0	

Going (Turf): Sf: 0-1 GS: 0-0 Gd: 0-2 GF: 0-0 Fm: 0-1
Distance: 5f/6f: 0-2 7f-8f: 0-2 9f-13f: 0-0 14f+: 0-0
Track : LH: 0-1 RH: 0-0 Tight: 0-0 Gall: 0-0
Aids: Bl: 0-0 Vi: 0-0 Tstrap: 0-0
Best Rating: 58 7/01 Kemp 6f good

Dolores

95 **90+**
2-y-o b f Danehill (USA)-Agnus (IRE) (In The Wings)
Mrs A J Perrett Normandie Stud Ltd

Placings:2 **(5367)**
2001: 8^{2}GS

	Starts	1st	2nd	3rd	Win & Pl
Career Total (Turf)	1	0	1	0	1740

Going (Turf): Sf: 0-0 GS: 0-1 Gd: 0-0 GF: 0-0 Fm: 0-0
Distance: 5f/6f: 0-0 7f-8f: 0-1 9f-13f: 0-0 14f+: 0-0
Track : LH: 0-0 RH: 0-0 Tight: 0-0 Gall: 0-0
Aids: Bl: 0-0 Vi: 0-0 Tstrap: 0-0
Best Rating: 90 10/01 NmkR 1m gd-sft

A well regarded filly, she finished runner-up on her Newmarket debut over a mile.

Dolphin Dancer

88 **44**
3-y-o b f Dolphin Street (FR)-Hot Lavender (CAN) (Shadeed (USA))
Miss J F Craze D G Clayton

Placings:00000 **(2267)**
2001: 7^{0}GS, 5^{0}G, 6^{0}F, 5^{0}GF, 6^{0}G

	Starts	1st	2nd	3rd	Win & Pl
Career Total (Turf)	5	0	0	0	

Going (Turf): Sf: 0-0 GS: 0-1 Gd: 0-2 GF: 0-1 Fm: 0-1
Distance: 5f/6f: 0-4 7f-8f: 0-1 9f-13f: 0-0 14f+: 0-0
Track : LH: 0-1 RH: 0-0 Tight: 0-0 Gall: 0-0
Aids: Bl: 0-0 Vi: 0-0 Tstrap: 0-1
Best Rating: 44 6/01 Bevl 5f gd-fm

Dolphinelle (IRE)

99(102) (35)**38**
5-y-o b g Dolphin Street (FR)-Mamie's Joy (Prince Tenderfoot (USA))
Jamie Poulton Mrs G M Temmerman

Placings:6000340/50301020025404654/104544303403403
160000600-003050650040600 **(5592)**
2001: 8^{0}SD, 8^{0}SD, 7^{3}SD, 7^{0}SW, 8^{5}SD, 7^{0}GS, 7^{6}G, 8^{5}GF, 7^{0}GF, 6^{0}GF, 7^{4}GF, 7^{0}GF, 7^{6}G, 7^{0}GF, 6^{0}GS

	Starts	1st	2nd	3rd	Win & Pl
Career Total (Turf)	38	2	2	3	13107
Career Total (AW)	22	1	0	3	2795

66 5/00 Newb 7f D(0-85)H G-S £5434
55 1/00 Ling 6f F(0-70)H STD £1855
71 6/99 Brig 5f213y E(0-75)H G-F £3972
Total win prize-money £11262

Going (Turf): Sf: 0-7 **GS: 1-6** Gd: 0-5 **GF: 1-18** Fm: 0-2
Distance: **5f/6f: 2-21** 7f-8f: 1-37 9f-13f: 0-2 14f+: 0-0
Track : **LH: 2-32** RH: 0-3 **Tight: 1-21** Gall: 0-1
Aids: Bl: 0-18 Vi: 0-1 Tstrap: 0-0
Best Rating: 49 5/01 Gdwd 1m gd-fm

Dome

99 **59d**
3-y-o b/br g Be My Chief (USA)-Round Tower (High Top)
S Dow (R Charlton 9/7) Troubleshooters

Placings:00020000 **(3874)**
2001: 8^{0}GS, 8^{0}GS, 8^{0}G, 12^{2}GF, 11^{0}GF, 14^{0}G, 16^{0}G, 12^{0}G

	Starts	1st	2nd	3rd	Win & Pl
Career Total (Turf)	8	0	1	0	707

Going (Turf): Sf: 0-0 GS: 0-2 Gd: 0-4 GF: 0-2 Fm: 0-0
Distance: 5f/6f: 0-0 7f-8f: 0-1 9f-13f: 0-5 14f+: 0-2
Track : LH: 0-5 RH: 0-2 Tight: 0-5 Gall: 0-0
Aids: Bl: 0-0 Vi: 0-3 Tstrap: 0-0
Best Rating: 59 6/01 Wwck 1m4f134y gd-fm

Dominic

87 **74**
2-y-o b c Primo Dominie-Pleasant Memories (Danehill (USA))
G C Bravery M I L Racing

Placings:43000 **(5368)**
2001: 6^{4}GF, 6^{3}GS, 6^{0}G, 7^{0}GF, 8^{0}GS

	Starts	1st	2nd	3rd	Win & Pl
Career Total (Turf)	5	0	0	1	512

Going (Turf): Sf: 0-0 GS: 0-2 Gd: 0-1 GF: 0-2 Fm: 0-0
Distance: 5f/6f: 0-3 7f-8f: 0-2 9f-13f: 0-0 14f+: 0-0
Track : LH: 0-0 RH: 0-0 Tight: 0-0 Gall: 0-0
Aids: Bl: 0-0 Vi: 0-0 Tstrap: 0-0
Best Rating: 74 8/01 Hayd 6f gd-sft

Dominica

105 **95**
2-y-o ch f Alhaarth (IRE)-Dominio (IRE) (Dominion)
M P Tregoning Major & Mrs R B Kennard

Placings:3311 **(5256)**
2001: 5^{3}G, 6^{3}GF, 5^{1}GF, 5^{1}GS

	Starts	1st	2nd	3rd	Win & Pl
Career Total (Turf)	4	2	0	2	29328

95 10/01 Asct 5f A G-S £24000
93 9/01 Muss 5f D G-F £4192
Total win prize-money £28193

Going (Turf): Sf: 0-0 **GS: 1-1** Gd: 0-1 **GF: 1-2** Fm: 0-0
Distance: **5f/6f: 2-4** 7f-8f: 0-0 9f-13f: 0-0 14f+: 0-0
Track : LH: 0-0 RH: 0-0 Tight: 0-0 Gall: 0-0
Aids: Bl: 0-0 Vi: 0-0 Tstrap: 0-0
Best Rating: 95 10/01 Asct 5f gd-sft

Ran two good races before getting off the mark in a Musselburgh maiden over five furlongs. Improved considerably to make all in the Cornwallis at Ascot.

Dominion Prince

(66) (4)**58**
3-y-o b c First Trump-Lammastide (Martinmas)
R Hannon Major A M Everett

Placings:00000-00 **(0362)**
2001: 8^{0}SD, 8^{0}SW

	Starts	1st	2nd	3rd	Win & Pl
Career Total (Turf)	5	0	0	0	
Career Total (AW)	2	0	0	0	

Going (Turf): Sf: 0-1 GS: 0-0 Gd: 0-4 GF: 0-0 Fm: 0-0
Distance: 5f/6f: 0-2 7f-8f: 0-4 9f-13f: 0-1 14f+: 0-0
Track : LH: 0-2 RH: 0-2 Tight: 0-2 Gall: 0-1
Aids: Bl: 0-0 Vi: 0-0 Tstrap: 0-0
Best Rating: 4 2/01 Ling 1m slow

Dominique

77 **15**
3-y-o ch f Primo Dominie-Tender Loving Care (Final Straw)
R Hannon Park Walk Racing

Placings:03-05 **(2739)**
2001: 6⁰GS, 8⁵GF

	Starts	1st	2nd	3rd	Win & Pl
Career Total (Turf)	4	0	0	1	404

Going (Turf): Sf: 0-0 GS: 0-2 Gd: 0-0 GF: 0-2 Fm: 0-0
Distance: 5f/6f: 0-3 7f-8f: 0-0 9f-13f: 0-1 14f+: 0-0
Track : LH: 0-2 RH: 0-0 Tight: 0-0 Gall: 0-2
Aids: Bl: 0-0 Vi: 0-0 Tstrap: 0-0
Best Rating: 15 5/01 Sals 6f gd-sft

Domquista D'Or

93(91) (51)**35**
4-y-o b g Superpower-Gild The Lily (Ile De Bourbon (USA))
G A Ham Colin B Taylor

Placings:0-223400605 **(3744)**
2001: 8²SW, 9²SW, 9³SD, 9⁴SD, 8⁰GF, 9⁰G, 10⁶GF, 7⁰GS, 7⁵S

	Starts	1st	2nd	3rd	Win & Pl
Career Total (Turf)	5	0	0	0	0
Career Total (AW)	5	0	2	1	1998

Going (Turf): Sf: 0-1 GS: 0-1 Gd: 0-1 GF: 0-2 Fm: 0-0
Distance: 5f/6f: 0-0 7f-8f: 0-2 9f-13f: 0-8 14f+: 0-0
Track : LH: 0-7 RH: 0-0 Tight: 0-5 Gall: 0-0
Aids: Bl: 0-2 Vi: 0-1 Tstrap: 0-0
Best Rating: 51 1/01 Wolv 1m1f79y slow

Don Alfred (IRE)

(92) (66)**77**
3-y-o b g Mark Of Esteem (IRE)-Jezyah (USA) (Chief's Crown (USA))
P F I Cole Alessandro Gaucci

Placings:50330-244 **(1650)**
2001: 9²SD, 8⁴SD, 8⁴F

	Starts	1st	2nd	3rd	Win & Pl
Career Total (Turf)	6	0	0	2	1195
Career Total (AW)	2	0	1	0	826

Going (Turf): Sf: 0-2 GS: 0-1 Gd: 0-1 GF: 0-1 Fm: 0-1
Distance: 5f/6f: 0-0 7f-8f: 0-4 9f-13f: 0-4 14f+: 0-0
Track : LH: 0-4 RH: 0-0 Tight: 0-3 Gall: 0-0
Aids: Bl: 0-2 Vi: 0-0 Tstrap: 0-0
Best Rating: 66 3/01 Ling 1m stand

Don Bosco (IRE)

94(100) (50)**55**
5-y-o ch g Grand Lodge (USA)-Suyayeb (USA) (The Minstrel (CAN))
E Stanners Mrs Patricia E Cunningham

Placings:00/610/000030010254-50464 **(5397)**
2001: 8⁵SD, 7⁰G, 7⁴GF, 7⁶G, 8⁴SD

	Starts	1st	2nd	3rd	Win & Pl
Career Total (Turf)	16	2	0	1	9563
Career Total (AW)	6	0	1	0	836
45 8/00 Ling 1m2f	G			G-F	£2002
72 6/99 Ripn 6f	C(0 95)H			G-F	£7132

Total win prize-money £9135

Going (Turf): Sf: 0-0 GS: 0-2 Gd: 0-3 **GF: 2-8** Fm: 0-2
Distance: 5f/6f: 1-3 7f-8f: 0-13 9f-13f: 1-5 14f+: 0-0
Track : **LH: 1-11** RH: 0-0 **Tight: 1-8** Gall: 0-0
Aids: Bl: 0-2 Vi: 0-2 Tstrap: 0-4
Best Rating: 48 9/01 NmkR 7f good

A fair handicapper on the All-Weather and on turf. Best at distances in excess seven furlongs these days.

Don Fayruz (IRE)

106(86) (35)**53**
9-y-o b g Fayruz-Gobolino (Don)
Mrs A J Bowlby J A Danahar

Placings:41/0/0504412 **(2876)**
2001: 11⁰SD, 8⁵S, 8⁰SD, 9⁴F, 8⁴G, 8¹HD, 8²GF

	Starts	1st	2nd	3rd	Win & Pl
Career Total (Turf)	7	2	1	0	25649
Career Total (AW)	3	0	0	0	
51 6/01 Bath 1m5y	E(0-70)H			HRD	£3150
90 7/94 Siro 7f110y				FRM	£17766

Total win prize-money £20916

Going (Turf): Sf: 0-2 GS: 0-0 Gd: 0-1 GF: 0-1 **Fm: 2-3**
Distance: 5f/6f: 0-1 7f-8f: 1-2 9f-13f: 1-7 14f+: 0-0
Track : LH: 1-5 RH: 1-4 **Tight: 1-3** Gall: 0-0
Aids: Bl: 0-0 Vi: 0-0 Tstrap: 0-0
Best Rating: 53 7/01 Wind 1m67y gd-fm

Don Fernando

94 **88**
2-y-o b c Zilzal (USA)-Teulada (USA) (Riverman (USA))
S P C Woods Lucayan Stud

Placings:130 **(5401)**
2001: 7¹G, 8³GF, 8⁰S

	Starts	1st	2nd	3rd	Win & Pl
Career Total (Turf)	3	1	0	1	6094
78 9/01 Sand 7f16y	D			GD	£4290

Total win prize-money £4290

Going (Turf): Sf: 0-1 GS: 0-0 **Gd: 1-1** GF: 0-1 Fm: 0-0
Distance: 5f/6f: 0-0 **7f-8f: 1-2** 9f-13f: 0-1 14f+: 0-0
Track : LH: 0-1 **RH: 1-1** Tight: 0-0 Gall: 0-0
Aids: Bl: 0-0 Vi: 0-0 Tstrap: 0-0
Best Rating: 88 9/01 Newb 1m gd-fm

Won nicely on his Sandown debut, despite looking short of peak fitness, but was held in better company subsequently.

Don Quixote (IRE)

88(101) (42)**34**
5-y-o b g Waajib-Maimiti (Goldhill)
Miss B Sanders Mrs Monica Caine

Placings:0/0030/060000045-3410060 **(2748)**
2001: 10³SD, 8⁴SD, 7¹SD, 7⁰SD, 6⁰F, 7⁶F, 8⁰GF

	Starts	1st	2nd	3rd	Win & Pl
Career Total (Turf)	14	0	0	1	428
Career Total (AW)	7	1	0	1	2648
42 1/01 Ling 7f	F			STD	£2233

Total win prize-money £2233

Going (Turf): **Sf: 0-1 GS: 0-4 Gd: 0-1 GF: 0-5 Fm: 0-3**
Distance: 5f/6f: 0-7 **7f-8f: 1-11** 9f-13f: 0-3 14f+: 0-0
Track : **LH: 1-12** RH: 0-1 **Tight: 1-10** Gall: 0-1
Aids: Bl: 0-2 Vi: 0-0 **Tstrap: 1-7**
Best Rating: 42 1/01 Ling 7f stand

Don Rubini

(88) (32)**27**
3-y-o b c Emarati (USA)-Emerald Ring (Auction Ring (USA))
B Smart The Tenors 2000

Placings:000-6 **(0156)**
2001: 6⁶SW

	Starts	1st	2nd	3rd	Win & Pl
Career Total (Turf)	1	0	0	0	
Career Total (AW)	3	0	0	0	0

Going (Turf): Sf: 0-1 GS: 0-0 Gd: 0-0 GF: 0-0 Fm: 0-0
Distance: 5f/6f: 0-1 7f-8f: 0-3 9f-13f: 0-0 14f+: 0-0
Track : LH: 0-4 RH: 0-0 Tight: 0-2 Gall: 0-0
Aids: Bl: 0-0 Vi: 0-0 Tstrap: 0-0
Best Rating: 22 1/01 Wolv 6f slow

Don't Sioux Me (IRE)

110 **97**
3-y-o b c Sadler's Wells (USA)-Commanche Belle (Shirley Heights)
H R A Cecil Wafic Said

Placings:1240 **(5693)**
2001: 12¹GF, 12²GS, 14⁴GF, 12⁰S

	Starts	1st	2nd	3rd	Win & Pl
Career Total (Turf)	4	1	1	0	6631
80 7/01 Newb 1m4f5y	D			G-F	£4049

Total win prize-money £4050

Going (Turf): Sf: 0-1 GS: 0-1 Gd: 0-0 **GF: 1-2** Fm: 0-0
Distance: 5f/6f: 0-0 7f-8f: 0-0 **9f-13f: 1-3** 14f+: 0-1
Track : **LH: 1-2** RH: 0-2 Tight: 0-1 **Gall: 1-3**
Aids: Bl: 0-0 Vi: 0-0 Tstrap: 0-0
Best Rating: 97 9/01 Sals 1m6f15y gd-fm

Unraced at two, he won a 12-furlong maiden at Newbury in July despite pulling hard and running green. He has run with credit in a couple of decent conditions events since.

Don't Tell Dad

80 **44**
2-y-o ch c King's Signet (USA)-Princess Tallulah (Chief Singer)
W G M Turner Mrs Tracy Turner

Placings:006 **(2135)**
2001: 5⁰S, 5⁰GF, 7⁶GF

	Starts	1st	2nd	3rd	Win & Pl
Career Total (Turf)	3	0	0	0	0

Going (Turf): Sf: 0-1 GS: 0-0 Gd: 0-0 GF: 0-2 Fm: 0-0
Distance: 5f/6f: 0-2 7f-8f: 0-1 9f-13f: 0-0 14f+: 0-0
Track : LH: 0-0 RH: 0-0 Tight: 0-0 Gall: 0-0
Aids: Bl: 0-0 Vi: 0-0 Tstrap: 0-2
Best Rating: 44 6/01 Muss 5f gd-fm

Donatello Primo (IRE)

96 **74**
2-y-o ch c Entrepreneur-Mystical River (USA) (Riverman (USA))
G L Moore Pietro Addis & Sons Ltd

Placings:40445 **(5521)**
2001: 5⁴GF, 6⁰GF, 5⁴GF, 6⁴GF, 6⁵HY

	Starts	1st	2nd	3rd	Win & Pl
Career Total (Turf)	5	0	0	0	593

Going (Turf): Sf: 0-1 GS: 0-0 Gd: 0-0 GF: 0-4 Fm: 0-0
Distance: 5f/6f: 0-4 7f-8f: 0-1 9f-13f: 0-0 14f+: 0-0
Track : LH: 0-2 RH: 0-0 Tight: 0-0 Gall: 0-1
Aids: Bl: 0-0 Vi: 0-0 Tstrap: 0-0
Best Rating: 74 9/01 Gdwd 6f gd-fm

Has shown promise over five and six furlongs.

Donatus (IRE)

99(98) (72)61
5-y-o b g Royal Academy (USA)-La Dame Du Lac (USA) (Round Table)
S Dow Michael A J Hall & Miss M Shields

Placings:305/0200260/20-0636540 **(4296)**
2001: 13⁰GF, 12⁶GF, 12³GF, 10⁶G, 12⁵GF, 12⁴GF, 12⁰G

	Starts	1st	2nd	3rd	Win & Pl
Career Total (Turf)	18	0	2	2	7736
Career Total (AW)	1	0	1	0	852

Going (Turf): Sf: 0-3 GS: 0-1 Gd: 0-5 GF: 0-8 Fm: 0-1
Distance: 5f/6f: 0-2 7f-8f: 0-2 9f-13f: 0-13 14f+: 0-2
Track : LH: 0-9 RH: 0-5 Tight: 0-9 Gall: 0-2
Aids: Bl: 0-0 Vi: 0-0 Tstrap: 0-0
Best Rating: 61 7/01 Epsm 1m4f10y gd-fm

Done And Dusted (IRE)

(101) (45)54
5-y-o ch m Up And At 'Em-Florentink (USA) (The Minstrel (CAN))
R Brotherton Binding Matters Ltd

Placings:503260**434114**/**6143315000601**/**0631560**-04060 **(0456)**
2001: 7⁰SW, 6⁴SD, 6⁰SD, 6⁶SD, 6⁰SD

	Starts	1st	2nd	3rd	Win & Pl
Career Total (Turf)	11	1	1	1	8718
Career Total (AW)	27	5	0	4	11940

65	2/00	Wolv	7f	F(0-65)H	STD	£1939
63	12/99	Wolv	6f	F(0-65)H	STD	£1892
68	4/99	Wind	6f	D(0-80)H	GD	£7652
70	2/99	Ling	7f	E(0-70)H	STD	£2658
67	12/98	Ling	7f	F	STD	£2085
54	11/98	Sthl	7f	G	STD	£1892

Total win prize-money £18122

Going (Turf): Sf: 0-1 GS: 0-1 **Gd: 1-4** GF: 0-4 Fm: 0-1
Distance: 5f/6f: 2-22 **7f-8f: 4-15** 9f-13f: 0-1 14f+: 0-0
Track : **LH: 5-29** RH: 1-2 **Tight: 4-24** Gall: 1-2
Aids: Bl: 0-0 Vi: 0-0 Tstrap: 0-0
Best Rating: 45 3/01 Wolv 6f stand

Inconsistent handicapper.

Donegal Shore (IRE)

108 99
2-y-o b c Mujadil (USA)-Distant Shore (IRE) (Jareer (USA))
B W Hills John C Grant

Placings:1022 **(5598)**
2001: 5¹G, 6⁰GF, 6²HY, 6²GS

	Starts	1st	2nd	3rd	Win & Pl
Career Total (Turf)	4	1	2	0	17179
99 9/01 Folk 5f		D			GD £2891

Total win prize-money £2891

Going (Turf): Sf: 0-1 GS: 0-1 **Gd: 1-1** GF: 0-1 Fm: 0-0
Distance: **5f/6f: 1-4** 7f-8f: 0-0 9f-13f: 0-0 14f+: 0-0
Track : LH: 0-0 RH: 0-0 Tight: 0-0 Gall: 0-0
Aids: Bl: 0-0 Vi: 0-0 Tstrap: 0-0
Best Rating: 99 9/01 Folk 5f good

Who cost 35,000 gns as a yearling, made a winning debut at Folkestone in September over five furlongs on good ground, and good efforts in decent company subsequently.

Donna's Double

107 (47)70
6-y-o ch g Weldnaas (USA)-Shadha (Shirley Heights)
D Eddy James R Adams

Placings:0006/303342401130/**00**260426022060110/05 6352103402400-602104010000 **(5535)**
2001: 8⁶GF, 8⁰GF, 8²GF, 10¹GF, 7⁰G, 10⁴GF, 9⁰G, 10¹F, 8⁰GF, 8⁰GS, 6⁰HY, 7⁰S

	Starts	1st	2nd	3rd	Win & Pl
Career Total (Turf)	58	7	8	6	58180
Career Total (AW)	2	0	0	0	

70	9/01	Newc	1m2f32y	D(0-80)H	FRM	£4059
68	6/01	Ripn	1m2f	D(0-85)H	G-F	£5928
66	7/00	York	6f214y	C(0-90)H	GD	£9724
65	10/99	Rdcr	1m	E(0-75)H	SFT	£7685
62	10/99	Catt	7f	E(0-70)H	GD	£4458
54	9/98	Haml	1m65y	F(0-60)H	SFT	£2108
54	9/98	Muss	7f30y	F(0-60)H	G-S	£2425

Total win prize-money £36387

Going (Turf): Sf: 2-16 GS: 1-8 **Gd: 2-14** GF: 1-15 Fm: 1-5
Distance: 5f/6f: 0-3 **7f-8f: 4-28** 9f-13f: 3-29 14f+: 0-0
Track : LH: 3-26 RH: 3-20 **Tight: 4-22** Gall: 2-11
Aids: Bl: 0-0 Vi: 0-0 Tstrap: 0-0
Best Rating: 70 9/01 Newc 1m2f32y firm

Useful handicapper. Suited by ten furlongs, fast ground and a good gallop.

Donnini (IRE)

84 48
4-y-o ch g Kris-La Luna (USA) (Lyphard (USA))
P W Harris Mrs P W Harris

Placings:0-0 **(2251)**
2001: 12⁰GF

	Starts	1st	2nd	3rd	Win & Pl
Career Total (Turf)	2	0	0	0	

Going (Turf): Sf: 0-1 GS: 0-0 Gd: 0-0 GF: 0-1 Fm: 0-0
Distance: 5f/6f: 0-0 7f-8f: 0-0 9f-13f: 0-2 14f+: 0-0
Track : LH: 0-2 RH: 0-0 Tight: 0-0 Gall: 0-0
Aids: Bl: 0-0 Vi: 0-0 Tstrap: 0-0
Best Rating: 48 6/01 Wwck 1m4f134y gd-fm

Dont Worry Bout Me (IRE)

102(100) (50d)53
4-y-o b g Brief Truce (USA)-Coggle (Kind Of Hush)
T G Mills Thorpe Vernon

Placings:3263000/0162620006-501040 **(4735)**
2001: 10⁵SD, 12⁰SW, 9¹F, 9⁰GF, 9⁴GS, 10⁰F

	Starts	1st	2nd	3rd	Win & Pl
Career Total (Turf)	13	1	2	1	5113
Career Total (AW)	10	1	1	1	4128

53	5/01	Brig	1m1f209y	F(0-65)H	FRM	£2632
67	2/00	Ling	1m4f	D	STD	£2808

Total win prize-money £5440

Going (Turf): Sf: 0-0 GS: 0-3 Gd: 0-4 GF: 0-3 **Fm: 1-3**
Distance: 5f/6f: 0-5 7f-8f: 0-2 **9f-13f: 2-16** 14f+: 0-0
Track : **LH: 2-17** RH: 0-2 **Tight: 1-13** Gall: 0-0
Aids: Bl: 0-0 **Vi: 2-14** Tstrap: 0-0
Best Rating: 53 9/01 Folk 1m1f149y gd-sft

Dontbesobold (IRE)

(100) (41)57
4-y-o b g River Falls-Jarmar Moon (Unfuwain (USA))
B S Rothwell J Eddings

Placings:4060040/**043662440502060-00** **(0150)**
2001: 8⁰SD, 7⁰SW

	Starts	1st	2nd	3rd	Win & Pl
Career Total (Turf)	15	0	1	0	1194
Career Total (AW)	9	0	1	1	1391

Going (Turf): Sf: 0-4 GS: 0-3 Gd: 0-5 GF: 0-2 Fm: 0-1
Distance: 5f/6f: 0-3 7f-8f: 0-11 9f-13f: 0-10 14f+: 0-0
Track : LH: 0-18 RH: 0-1 Tight: 0-8 Gall: 0-0
Aids: Bl: 0-0 Vi: 0-9 Tstrap: 0-0
Best Rating: 5 1/01 Wolv 7f slow

Doodle Bug

70(90) (24)72
4-y-o b f Missed Flight-Kaiserlinde (GER) (Frontal)
Miss K Marks (Jedd O'Keeffe 16/4) Nick Shutts

Placings:30/35364-00 **(0585)**
2001: 16⁰SD, 14⁰HY

	Starts	1st	2nd	3rd	Win & Pl
Career Total (Turf)	7	0	0	3	1561
Career Total (AW)	2	0	0	0	0

Going (Turf): Sf: 0-2 GS: 0-1 Gd: 0-3 GF: 0-1 Fm: 0-0
Distance: 5f/6f: 0-0 7f-8f: 0-1 9f-13f: 0-4 14f+: 0-4
Track : LH: 0-7 RH: 0-0 Tight: 0-1 Gall: 0-2
Aids: Bl: 0-0 Vi: 0-0 Tstrap: 0-0
Best Rating: 12 3/01 Nott 1m6f15y heavy

Dora Carrington (IRE)

95 108
3-y-o b f Sri Pekan (USA)-Dorothea Brooke (IRE) (Dancing Brave (USA))
P W Harris Mrs P W Harris

Placings:113-0 **(1142)**
2001: 8⁰G

	Starts	1st	2nd	3rd	Win & Pl
Career Total (Turf)	4	2	0	1	50242

108	7/00	NmkJ	6f	A	G-S	£29000
79	6/00	Pont	6f	D	G-F	£5141

Total win prize-money £34142

Going (Turf): Sf: 0-0 **GS: 1-1** Gd: 0-2 **GF: 1-1** Fm: 0-0
Distance: **5f/6f: 2-3** 7f-8f: 0-1 9f-13f: 0-0 14f+: 0-0
Track : **LH: 1-1** RH: 0-0 Tight: 0-0 Gall: 0-0
Aids: Bl: 0-0 Vi: 0-0 Tstrap: 0-0
Best Rating: 88 5/01 NmkR 1m good

She has plenty of speed and after making a winning debut at Pontefract in 2000, hit the big time with a clear-cut victory in the Cherry Hinton. She had a few traffic problems in the Heinz 57 Phoenix Stakes, but still finished a creditable third. Lost a shoe in the 1000 Guineas on her only run of 2001.

Dorans Pride (IRE)

104 81
12-y-o ch g Orchestra-Marians Pride (Pry)
Michael Hourigan T J Doran

Placings:5/14/151-60320 **(5321a)**
2001: 14⁶G, 20⁰GF, 22³GF, 16²GF, 16⁰Y

	Starts	1st	2nd	3rd	Win & Pl
Career Total (Turf)	11	3	1	1	29363

74	11/00	Leop	2m	H	SFT	£19500
73	3/99	Curr	2m		SFT	£4812

Total win prize-money £24313

Going (Turf): Sf: 2-4 GS: 0-0 Gd: 0-1 GF: 0-3 Fm: 0-0
Distance: 5f/6f: 0-0 7f-8f: 0-0 9f-13f: 0-0 **14f+: 2-9**
Track : LH: 1-1 RH: 1-6 Tight: 0-0 Gall: 0-2
Aids: Bl: 0-0 Vi: 0-0 Tstrap: 0-0
Best Rating: 81 6/01 Asct 2m6f34y gd-fm

Dorchester

109 (79)62
4-y-o b g Primo Dominie-Penthouse Lady (Last Tycoon)
W J Musson The Square Table

Placings:001112304/000530-00600000503 **(5685)**
2001: 6⁰GF, 5⁰G, 5⁶GS, 5⁰GS, 6⁰GS, 5⁰S, 5⁰G, 5⁰G, 6⁵G, 5⁰HY, 5³S

Starts 1st 2nd 3rd Win & Pl

	Starts	1st	2nd	3rd	Win & Pl
Career Total (Turf)	26	2	1	3	16462
Career Total (AW)	1	1	0	0	2668

86 7/99 Donc 5f D G-F £3371
79 7/99 Sthl 5f E H STD £2668
80 7/99 Nott 5f13y F G-F £2722
Total win prize-money £8762

Going (Turf): Sf: 0-3 GS: 0-3 Gd: 0-9 **GF: 2-11** Fm: 0-0
Distance: **5f/6f: 3-26** 7f-8f: 0-1 9f-13f: 0-0 14f+: 0-0
Track : LH: 0-0 RH: 0-3 Tight: 0-0 Gall: 0-2
Aids: Bl: 0-1 Vi: 0-0 Tstrap: 0-0
Best Rating: 77 7/01 NmkJ 5f gd-sft

He was a very speedy two-year-old, winning three times, including once on Fibresand. He has struggled since then in varied company.

Dorothea Sharp (IRE)

(86) (38)**21**
4-y-o b/br f Foxhound (USA)-Captain's Niece (Vitiges (FR))
Mrs A Duffield Turf 2000 Limited

Placings:000/050000-40 **(1587)**
2001: 7^{4}S, 8^{0}SD

	Starts	1st	2nd	3rd	Win & Pl
Career Total (Turf)	7	0	0	0	0
Career Total (AW)	4	0	0	0	0

Going (Turf): Sf: 0-2 GS: 0-1 Gd: 0-0 GF: 0-4 Fm: 0-0
Distance: 5f/6f: 0-2 7f-8f: 0-4 9f-13f: 0-5 14f+: 0-0
Track : LH: 0-8 RH: 0-0 Tight: 0-3 Gall: 0-0
Aids: Bl: 0-0 Vi: 0-2 Tstrap: 0-0
Best Rating: 21 5/01 Newc 7f soft

Dottie Digger (IRE)

60
2-y-o b f Catrail (USA)-Hint-Of-Romance (IRE) (Treasure Kay)
I Semple Joseph Leckie & Sons Ltd

Placings:00 **(5268)**
2001: 7^{0}G, 7^{0}HY

	Starts	1st	2nd	3rd	Win & Pl
Career Total (Turf)	2	0	0	0	0

Going (Turf): Sf: 0-1 GS: 0-0 Gd: 0-1 GF: 0-0 Fm: 0-0
Distance: 5f/6f: 0-0 7f-8f: 0-2 9f-13f: 0-0 14f+: 0-0
Track : LH: 0-0 RH: 0-0 Tight: 0-0 Gall: 0-0
Aids: Bl: 0-0 Vi: 0-0 Tstrap: 0-0
Best Rating: 60 9/01 Ayr 7f50y good

Double Baileys

96 **30**
5-y-o b g Robellino (USA)-Thimblerigger (Sharpen Up)
C P Morlock The Trogs

Placings:3/52023050/000000 **(4523)**
2001: 13^{0}GF, 18^{0}GF, 17^{0}G, 14^{0}GF, 16^{0}G, 16^{0}GF

	Starts	1st	2nd	3rd	Win & Pl
Career Total (Turf)	14	0	2	2	3477
Career Total (AW)	1	0	0	0	0

Going (Turf): Sf: 0-0 GS: 0-1 Gd: 0-5 GF: 0-7 Fm: 0-1
Distance: 5f/6f: 0-0 7f-8f: 0-0 9f-13f: 0-5 14f+: 0-10
Track : LH: 0-9 RH: 0-6 Tight: 0-9 Gall: 0-4
Aids: Bl: 0-4 Vi: 0-3 Tstrap: 0-0
Best Rating: 44 7/01 Bath 2m1f34y good

Fair staying handicapper.

Double Blade

102 **60**
6-y-o b g Kris-Sesame (Derrylin)

Mrs M Reveley The Mary Reveley Racing Club

Placings:52/32303056/040/2011-2420000 **(5534)**
2001: 10^{2}GF, 10^{4}GF, 9^{2}F, 10^{0}GF, 11^{0}GF, 8^{0}GF, 11^{0}S

	Starts	1st	2nd	3rd	Win & Pl
Career Total (Turf)	24	2	5	3	17785

66 8/00 Rdcr 1m3f E(0-70)H FRM £4030
61 7/00 Donc 1m4f D(0-80)H G-F £4270
Total win prize-money £8301

Going (Turf): Sf: 0-3 GS: 0-1 Gd: 0-6 **GF: 1-11 Fm: 1-3**
Distance: 5f/6f: 0-0 7f-8f: 0-1 **9f-13f: 2-15** 14f+: 0-8
Track : **LH: 2-19** RH: 0-4 Tight: 1-11 Gall: 1-8
Aids: Bl: 0-1 Vi: 0-0 Tstrap: 0-0
Best Rating: 69 6/01 Rdcr 1m2f gd-fm

Double Brew

102 **75**
3-y-o ch c Primo Dominie-Boozy (Absalom)
R Hannon Robert Heathcote

Placings:3422546-3400406 **(5108)**
2001: 6^{3}GF, 5^{4}GF, 5^{0}GF, 5^{0}F, 6^{4}G, 6^{0}G, 5^{6}GS

	Starts	1st	2nd	3rd	Win & Pl
Career Total (Turf)	14	0	2	2	8113

Going (Turf): Sf: 0-1 GS: 0-1 Gd: 0-5 GF: 0-6 Fm: 0-1
Distance: 5f/6f: 0-13 7f-8f: 0-1 9f-13f: 0-0 14f+: 0-0
Track : LH: 0-1 RH: 0-0 Tight: 0-0 Gall: 0-1
Aids: Bl: 0-0 Vi: 0-0 Tstrap: 0-0
Best Rating: 81 6/01 NmkJ 5f gd-fm

Consistent if exposed handicapper. Tends to race close to the pace and seems best suited by a fastish surface. Six furlongs looks his best trip.

Double Crossed

104 **102**
3-y-o b f Caerleon (USA)-Quandary (USA) (Blushing Groom (FR))
H R A Cecil K Abdulla

Placings:4-116 **(5691)**
2001: 10^{1}S, 11^{1}G, 12^{6}S

	Starts	1st	2nd	3rd	Win & Pl
Career Total (Turf)	4	2	0	0	24633

102 5/01 Ling 1m3f106yA GD £20100
82 4/01 Sand 1m2f7y D SFT £4212
Total win prize-money £24312

Going (Turf): Sf: 1-3 GS: 0-0 **Gd: 1-1** GF: 0-0 Fm: 0-0
Distance: 5f/6f: 0-0 7f-8f: 0-0 **9f-13f: 2-4** 14f+: 0-0
Track : LH: 1-2 RH: 1-2 **Tight: 1-2** Gall: 0-1
Aids: Bl: 0-0 Vi: 0-0 Tstrap: 0-0
Best Rating: 102 5/01 Ling 1m3f106y good

Smart filly at around a mile and a half, taking the Lingfield Oaks Trial in May, although she was initially disqualified. Absent until well beaten on the last day of the 2001 season in a Listed race. Handles soft ground.

Double Destiny

98(91) (34)**51**
5-y-o b g Anshan-Double Gift (Cragador)
K T Ivory Mrs P Scott-Dunn

Placings:600/0000300-33030650 **(3679)**
2001: 7^{3}GS, 7^{3}GF, 7^{0}F, 7^{3}GF, 7^{0}GF, 7^{6}G, 7^{5}GF, 8^{0}G

	Starts	1st	2nd	3rd	Win & Pl
Career Total (Turf)	17	0	0	4	2513
Career Total (AW)	1	0	0	0	

Going (Turf): Sf: 0-0 GS: 0-2 Gd: 0-4 GF: 0-9 Fm: 0-2
Distance: 5f/6f: 0-2 7f-8f: 0-13 9f-13f: 0-3 14f+: 0-0
Track : LH: 0-2 RH: 0-4 Tight: 0-1 Gall: 0-3
Aids: Bl: 0-7 Vi: 0-1 Tstrap: 0-0
Best Rating: 58 5/01 Ling 7f gd-sft

Double Digit

85 **19**
3-y-o b f Timeless Times (USA)-Kagram Queen (Prince Ragusa)
D W Barker Robert E Cook

Placings:0000-000 **(4013)**
2001: 11^{0}F, 8^{0}S, 5^{0}G

	Starts	1st	2nd	3rd	Win & Pl
Career Total (Turf)	7	0	0	0	

Going (Turf): Sf: 0-1 GS: 0-2 Gd: 0-2 GF: 0-1 Fm: 0-1
Distance: 5f/6f: 0-4 7f-8f: 0-1 9f-13f: 0-2 14f+: 0-0
Track : LH: 0-3 RH: 0-0 Tight: 0-2 Gall: 0-0
Aids: Bl: 0-0 Vi: 0-0 Tstrap: 0-0
Best Rating: 19 8/01 Catt 5f good

Double Em

89(79) (30)**61**
2-y-o b g Balnibarbi-Something Speedy (IRE) (Sayf El Arab (USA))
C W Fairhurst David Bartlett

Placings:6000300 **(5115)**
2001: 5^{6}S, 5^{0}SD, 7^{0}GF, 7^{0}GF, 8^{3}G, 8^{0}GF, 9^{0}HY

	Starts	1st	2nd	3rd	Win & Pl
Career Total (Turf)	6	0	0	1	352
Career Total (AW)	1	0	0	0	

Going (Turf): Sf: 0-2 GS: 0-0 Gd: 0-1 GF: 0-3 Fm: 0-0
Distance: 5f/6f: 0-2 7f-8f: 0-4 9f-13f: 0-1 14f+: 0-0
Track : LH: 0-3 RH: 0-1 Tight: 0-2 Gall: 0-1
Aids: Bl: 0-0 Vi: 0-0 Tstrap: 0-0
Best Rating: 61 8/01 Newc 1m good

Best efforts so far in claimers at around a mile.

Double Fantasy

105(70) (23)**70**
3-y-o b f Mind Games-Song's Best (Never So Bold)
D Nicholls Harry Redknapp

Placings:06104-005060003 **(2927)**
2001: 6^{0}SW, 6^{0}S, 6^{5}S, 6^{0}GF, 5^{6}F, 6^{0}GF, 6^{0}G, 5^{0}GF, 6^{3}GF

	Starts	1st	2nd	3rd	Win & Pl
Career Total (Turf)	13	1	0	1	4579
Career Total (AW)	2	0	0	0	

79 8/00 Bath 5f11y D FRM £3503
Total win prize-money £3504

Going (Turf): Sf: 0-3 GS: 0-0 Gd: 0-3 GF: 0-5 **Fm: 1-2**
Distance: **5f/6f: 1-13** 7f-8f: 0-1 9f-13f: 0-0 14f+: 0-0
Track : **LH: 1-4** RH: 0-0 Tight: 0-1 **Gall: 1-1**
Aids: Bl: 0-0 Vi: 0-0 Tstrap: 0-0
Best Rating: 66 5/01 Brig 5f59y firm

A daughter of Mind Games, she got off the mark in fine style over the minimum trip on fast ground last summer. Has found life tougher since, but looked to be on the way back given a chance by the Handicapper at Doncaster in July.

Double Fare

98 **72**
3-y-o b f Mtoto-Double Flutter (Beldale Flutter (USA))
M R Channon P Trant

Placings:553553 **(3872)**
2001: 8^{5}G, 9^{5}GF, 10^{3}GF, 8^{5}GF, 7^{5}G, 9^{3}G

	Starts	1st	2nd	3rd	Win & Pl
Career Total (Turf)	6	0	0	2	1574

Going (Turf): Sf: 0-0 GS: 0-0 Gd: 0-3 GF: 0-3 Fm: 0-0
Distance: 5f/6f: 0-0 7f-8f: 0-2 9f-13f: 0-4 14f+: 0-0
Track : LH: 0-3 RH: 0-2 Tight: 0-2 Gall: 0-1
Aids: Bl: 0-0 Vi: 0-0 Tstrap: 0-0
Best Rating: 72 5/01 Gdwd 1m1f gd-fm

Double Fault (IRE)

(83) (27)**52**
4-y-o br f Zieten (USA)-Kashapour (Nishapour (FR))
J A Gilbert Terry Connors

Placings:002040/50033000045500-00 (0083)
2001: 8^{0}SD, 16^{0}SD

	Starts	1st	2nd	3rd	Win & Pl
Career Total (Turf)	17	0	1	2	2120
Career Total (AW)	5	0	0	0	

Going (Turf): Sf: 0-4 GS: 0-2 Gd: 0-4 GF: 0-5 Fm: 0-2
Distance: 5f/6f: 0-4 7f-8f: 0-11 9f-13f: 0-6 14f+: 0-1
Track : LH: 0-11 RH: 0-2 Tight: 0-6 Gall: 0-1
Aids: Bl: 0-11 Vi: 0-0 Tstrap: 0-0
Best Rating: 21 1/01 Sthl 1m stand

Double Gamble

101 **78**
3-y-o b f Ela-Mana-Mou-Helen's Gamble (IRE) (Spectacular Bid (USA))
M Johnston R W Huggins

Placings:423610 (5359a)
2001: 12^{4}GF, 12^{2}G, 11^{3}GF, 11^{6}GF, 12^{1}GF, 14^{0}G

	Starts	1st	2nd	3rd	Win & Pl
Career Total (Turf)	6	1	1	1	5124

46	9/01	Muss	1m4f	D	G-F	£3038

Total win prize-money £3038

Going (Turf): Sf: 0-0 GS: 0-0 Gd: 0-2 **GF: 1-4** Fm: 0-0
Distance: 5f/6f: 0-0 7f-8f: 0-0 **9f-13f: 1-5** 14f+: 0-1
Track : LH: 0-3 RH: 0-2 Tight: 0-3 Gall: 0-1
Aids: Bl: 0-0 Vi: 0-0 Tstrap: 0-0
Best Rating: 78 8/01 Ripn 1m4f60y good

Got off the mark over 12 furlongs at Musselburgh in September 2001. Bred to stay further.

Double Honour (FR)

113 **117**
3-y-o gr c Highest Honor (FR)-Silver Cobra (USA) (Silver Hawk (USA))
M Johnston The 4th Middleham Partnership

Placings:241-21152001 (5683)
2001: 10^{2}S, 12^{1}GF, 11^{1}GF, 16^{5}GF, 16^{2}G, 18^{0}G, 15^{0}HY, 14^{1}S

	Starts	1st	2nd	3rd	Win & Pl
Career Total (Turf)	11	4	3	0	49867

80	11/01	Donc	1m6f132yC		SFT	£6857
99	6/01	Hayd	1m3f200yB(0-100)H		G-F	£9146
98	5/01	Gdwd	1m4f	C(0-95)H	G-F	£6968
82	9/00	Haml	1m65y	D	SFT	£3461

Total win prize-money £26434

Going (Turf): Sf: 2-4 GS: 0-0 Gd: 0-2 **GF: 2-4** Fm: 0-1
Distance: 5f/6f: 0-0 7f-8f: 0-2 **9f-13f: 3-4** 14f+: 1-5
Track : LH: 2-3 RH: 2-6 **Tight: 2-3** Gall: 1-3
Aids: Bl: 0-0 Vi: 0-0 Tstrap: 0-0
Best Rating: 117 8/01 Gdwd 2m good

The winner of a soft-ground Hamilton maiden at two, he has looked a very progressive sort this season in winning handicaps at Goodwood and Haydock and ran well in the Queen's Vase and Goodwood Cup. Acts on fast and soft ground and stays two miles.

Double Kay (IRE)

81 **44**
3-y-o gr g Treasure Kay-Heart To Heart (IRE) (Double Schwartz)
J A Glover Boston R S

Placings:05-00 (2426)
2001: 6^{0}HY, 8^{0}GF

	Starts	1st	2nd	3rd	Win & Pl
Career Total (Turf)	4	0	0	0	0

Going (Turf): Sf: 0-1 GS: 0-0 Gd: 0-1 GF: 0-1 Fm: 0-1
Distance: 5f/6f: 0-2 7f-8f: 0-1 9f-13f: 0-1 14f+: 0-0
Track : LH: 0-1 RH: 0-0 Tight: 0-0 Gall: 0-0
Aids: Bl: 0-0 Vi: 0-0 Tstrap: 0-0
Best Rating: 36 6/01 Nott 1m54y gd-fm

Double M

99(99) (56)**54**
4-y-o ch c First Trump-Girton Degree (Balliol)
Mrs L Richards Mrs Lydia Richards

Placings:6241404/06000100-3200004060 (4950)
2001: 5^{3}SW, 6^{2}SW, 6^{0}SW, 5^{0}SD, 5^{0}F, 5^{0}G, 5^{4}G, 5^{0}F, 5^{6}F, 5^{0}G

	Starts	1st	2nd	3rd	Win & Pl
Career Total (Turf)	14	1	0	0	4821
Career Total (AW)	11	1	2	1	3292

42	11/00	Ling	5f	G	STD	£1865
83	7/99	Nott	5f13y	D	G-F	£3655

Total win prize-money £5521

Going (Turf): Sf: 0-0 GS: 0-0 Gd: 0-5 **GF: 1-5** Fm: 0-4
Distance: **5f/6f: 2-24** 7f-8f: 0-1 9f-13f: 0-0 14f+: 0-0
Track : **LH: 1-14** RH: 0-2 **Tight: 1-10** Gall: 0-4
Aids: Bl: 0-6 **Vi: 2-16** Tstrap: 0-0
Best Rating: 56 1/01 Ling 5f slow

Double March

100 (57)**50**
8-y-o b g Weldnaas (USA)-Double Gift (Cragador)
H Morrison Mrs P Scott-Dunn

Placings:20000045/650030/10314324401/0050040/050 0-446000 (4677)
2001: 6^{4}GF, 6^{4}GF, 6^{6}GF, 6^{0}GF, 6^{0}GF, 7^{0}G

	Starts	1st	2nd	3rd	Win & Pl
Career Total (Turf)	37	3	2	3	18837
Career Total (AW)	5	0	0	0	226

68	10/98	Nott	6f15y	D(0-80)H	SFT	£4175
58	6/98	Wind	6f	D(0-75)H	SFT	£5823
53	5/98	Nott	6f15y	G(0-70)H	G-F	£2425

Total win prize-money £12423

Going (Turf): Sf: 2-6 GS: 0-4 Gd: 0-13 GF: 1-11 Fm: 0-3
Distance: 5f/6f: 1-20 **7f-8f: 2-17** 9f-13f: 0-5 14f+: 0-0
Track : LH: 0-6 **RH: 1-6** Tight: 0-6 **Gall: 1-5**
Aids: Bl: 0-1 Vi: 0-0 Tstrap: 0-0
Best Rating: 50 7/01 Wind 6f gd-fm

Moderate handicapper.

Double Oscar (IRE)

104(109) (81)**68**
8-y-o ch g Royal Academy (USA)-Broadway Rosie (Absalom)
D Nicholls Trilby Racing

Placings:134054/0432330460/602044301240432152110016030/1223031400561130000/0020601240200040 00/00056321000-0600060004022000 (4466)
2001: 5^{0}SD, 5^{6}SD, 6^{0}SD, 5^{0}S, 5^{0}G, 5^{6}F, 6^{0}GF, 5^{0}GF, 5^{0}G, 5^{4}GF, 5^{0}G, 6^{2}GF, 5^{2}GF, 6^{0}G, 5^{0}G, 5^{0}G

	Starts	1st	2nd	3rd	Win & Pl
Career Total (Turf)	91	10	10	8	68451
Career Total (AW)	18	2	3	3	14928

73	7/00	Newc	5f	E(0-70)H	FRM	£3640
78	6/99	Ayr	5f	D(0-80)H	GD	£3658
84	8/98	Asct	5f	D(0-80)H	G-F	£7457
80	7/98	Gdwd	5f	D(0-80)H	G-S	£7790
88	4/98	Wolv	5f	C(0-100)H	STD	£7067
75	1/98	Ling	6f	E	STD	£2778
80	8/97	Carl	5f	D(0-80)H	FRM	£3647
76	8/97	Pont	5f	E(0-70)H	G-F	£3980
69	8/97	Catt	5f	F(0-65)H	G-F	£2973
61	7/97	Folk	6f	F(0-65)H	G-F	£2277
53	4/97	Nott	5f13y	F	G-F	£2854
68	6/95	Ayr	6f	D(0-70)	G-F	£4143

Total win prize-money £52270

Going (Turf): Sf: 0-6 GS: 1-8 Gd: 1-30 **GF: 6-37** Fm: 2-10
Distance: **5f/6f: 12-94** 7f-8f: 0-15 9f-13f: 0-0 14f+: 0-0
Track : **LH: 3-32** RH: 1-6 **Tight: 2-22** Gall: 1-2
Aids: **Bl: 10-70** Vi: 0-2 Tstrap: 0-0
Best Rating: 81 1/01 Sthl 5f stand

Not at his best in recent seasons, but is certainly on a winning mark and ran his best race for a while at Pontefract in July 2001. Has won on a softish surface but is much better suited by fast ground.

Double Ping

79 **34**
3-y-o gr f Petong-Paircullis (Tower Walk)
M W Easterby Andrew Scott

Placings:050-00 (1281)
2001: 9^{0}S, 9^{0}G

	Starts	1st	2nd	3rd	Win & Pl
Career Total (Turf)	5	0	0	0	0

Going (Turf): Sf: 0-1 GS: 0-1 Gd: 0-3 GF: 0-0 Fm: 0-0
Distance: 5f/6f: 0-3 7f-8f: 0-0 9f-13f: 0-2 14f+: 0-0
Track : LH: 0-2 RH: 0-1 Tight: 0-1 Gall: 0-0
Aids: Bl: 0-0 Vi: 0-0 Tstrap: 0-0
Best Rating: 27 5/01 Rdcr 1m1f soft

Double Play (IRE)

104 **82**
2-y-o b c Mujadil (USA)-Skinity (Rarity)
J Noseda B E Nielsen

Placings:21210 (4659)
2001: 5^{2}GS, 5^{1}GS, 5^{2}GS, 5^{1}GF, 6^{0}GF

	Starts	1st	2nd	3rd	Win & Pl
Career Total (Turf)	5	2	2	0	9198

82	8/01	Rdcr	5f	E	G-F	£2940
75	4/01	Brig	5f59y	D	G-S	£2898

Total win prize-money £5838

Going (Turf): Sf: 0-0 **GS: 1-3** Gd: 0-0 **GF: 1-2** Fm: 0-0
Distance: **5f/6f: 2-5** 7f-8f: 0-0 9f-13f: 0-0 14f+: 0-0
Track : **LH: 1-1** RH: 0-0 Tight: 0-0 Gall: 0-0
Aids: Bl: 0-0 Vi: 0-0 Tstrap: 0-0
Best Rating: 82 8/01 Rdcr 5f gd-fm

A half-brother to three winners out of a mare who won in Belgium, finished runner-up in the Brocklesby before scrambling home at Brighton. Ran well when conceding weight all round at Newbury. Had to work hard for Redcar success.

Double Ransom

94(69) (30)**74**
2-y-o b g Bahamian Bounty-Secrets Of Honour (Belmez (USA))
C A Dwyer Tyme Partnership

Placings:05000 (5589)
2001: 8^{0}GS, 8^{5}G, 8^{0}SW, 7^{0}S, 7^{0}GS

	Starts	1st	2nd	3rd	Win & Pl
Career Total (Turf)	4	0	0	0	0
Career Total (AW)	1	0	0	0	

Going (Turf): Sf: 0-1 GS: 0-2 Gd: 0-1 GF: 0-0 Fm: 0-0
Distance: 5f/6f: 0-0 7f-8f: 0-3 9f-13f: 0-2 14f+: 0-0
Track : LH: 0-3 RH: 0-0 Tight: 0-1 Gall: 0-1
Aids: Bl: 0-0 Vi: 0-0 Tstrap: 0-0
Best Rating: 74 8/01 Yarm 1m3y good

Double Spey

89(68) (31)**61**

2-y-o b g Atraf-Yankee Special (Bold Lad (IRE))
P C Haslam Mrs B M Hawkins & A Dixon

Placings:0003 **(5169)**
2001: 6^{0}G, 7^{0}SD, 5^{0}G, 6^{3}GS

	Starts	1st	2nd	3rd	Win & Pl
Career Total (Turf)	3	0	0	1	633
Career Total (AW)	1	0	0	0	

Going (Turf): Sf: 0-0 GS: 0-1 Gd: 0-2 GF: 0-0 Fm: 0-0
Distance: 5f/6f: 0-3 7f-8f: 0-1 9f-13f: 0-0 14f+: 0-0
Track : LH: 0-2 RH: 0-0 Tight: 0-0 Gall: 0-0
Aids: Bl: 0-0 Vi: 0-0 Tstrap: 0-0
Best Rating: 61 10/01 Pont 6f gd-sft

Double Spice

98 **50**

3-y-o b f Saddlers' Hall (IRE)-Island Lake (Kalaglow)
M Johnston R W Huggins

Placings:43 **(5634)**
2001: 10^{4}HY, 11^{3}G

	Starts	1st	2nd	3rd	Win & Pl
Career Total (Turf)	2	0	0	1	742

Going (Turf): Sf: 0-1 GS: 0-0 Gd: 0-1 GF: 0-0 Fm: 0-0
Distance: 5f/6f: 0-0 7f-8f: 0-0 9f-13f: 0-2 14f+: 0-0
Track : LH: 0-2 RH: 0-0 Tight: 0-1 Gall: 0-0
Aids: Bl: 0-0 Vi: 0-0 Tstrap: 0-0
Best Rating: 50 11/01 Catt 1m3f214y good

She appears to lack gears and is bred to stay a trip.

Double Splendour (IRE)

104(99) (69)**70**

11-y-o b g Double Schwartz-Princess Pamela (Dragonara Palace (USA))
P S Felgate M Heywood, E Rollinson

Placings:000021/1301411/1452212342/540003002/145 24000000/00231650000/000620**250-2**0552061 **(4227)**
2001: 6^{2}SD, 7^{0}SD, 6^{5}G, 7^{5}GF, 6^{2}GF, 6^{0}GS, 6^{0}G, 6^{1}GF

	Starts	1st	2nd	3rd	Win & Pl
Career Total (Turf)	64	9	10	4	80200
Career Total (AW)	8	1	2	0	4168

70	8/01	NmkJ	6f	E(0-80)H	G-F	£3562
86	7/99	NmkJ	6f	C(0-90)H	G-F	£6608
100	5/98	NmkR	6f	B(0-110)H	GD	£7538
87	7/96	York	6f	C(0-90)H	GD	£6732
83	4/96	Nott	6f15y	E(0-70)H	G-F	£3598
70	10/95	Newc	6f	E(0-70)H	G-F	£3467
64	10/95	Hayd	6f	D(0-80)H	G-S	£4240
61	9/95	Yarm	6f3y	E(0-70)H	GD	£3931
46	4/95	Nott	6f15y	E(0-70)H	G-F	£3340
39	12/94	Ling	6f	F(0-60)H	STD	£2612

Total win prize-money £45630

Going (Turf): Sf: 0-3 GS: 1-11 Gd: 3-25 **GF: 5-23** Fm: 0-2
Distance: **5f/6f: 7-49** 7f-8f: 3-23 9f-13f: 0-0 14f+: 0-0
Track : **LH: 1-12** RH: 0-0 **Tight: 1-5** Gall: 0-2
Aids: Bl: 0-0 Vi: 0-0 Tstrap: 0-0
Best Rating: 70 8/01 NmkJ 6f gd-fm

He has proved he is no back number this summer, running well in some hot sprints without quite managing to get himself into the frame. Suited by a strong pace.

Doublet

101 **57**

6-y-o ch g Bustino-Pas De Deux (Nijinsky (CAN))
B R Millman Pine Crest Racing

Placings:563/050630 **(3984)**
2001: 14^{0}S, 18^{5}GF, 16^{0}GF, 15^{6}GF, 11^{3}G, 14^{0}F

	Starts	1st	2nd	3rd	Win & Pl
Career Total (Turf)	9	0	0	2	1004

Going (Turf): Sf: 0-2 GS: 0-0 Gd: 0-2 GF: 0-3 Fm: 0-2
Distance: 5f/6f: 0-0 7f-8f: 0-0 9f-13f: 0-4 14f+: 0-5
Track : LH: 0-3 RH: 0-4 Tight: 0-4 Gall: 0-2
Aids: Bl: 0-0 Vi: 0-0 Tstrap: 0-0
Best Rating: 57 7/01 Chep 2m2f gd-fm

Doubtless Risk

92 **27**

4-y-o b g Risk Me (FR)-Doubtfire (Jalmood (USA))
A R Dicken (Miss L A Perratt 14/2) J A Davidson

Placings:6540000/000-006 **(2604)**
2001: 8^{0}GF, 8^{0}GF, 8^{6}F

	Starts	1st	2nd	3rd	Win & Pl
Career Total (Turf)	13	0	0	0	226

Going (Turf): Sf: 0-3 GS: 0-2 Gd: 0-4 GF: 0-2 Fm: 0-2
Distance: 5f/6f: 0-3 7f-8f: 0-9 9f-13f: 0-1 14f+: 0-0
Track : LH: 0-5 RH: 0-5 Tight: 0-4 Gall: 0-2
Aids: Bl: 0-2 Vi: 0-0 Tstrap: 0-0
Best Rating: 27 6/01 Newc 1m firm

Dove From Above

67 **5**

8-y-o b g Henbit (USA)-Sally's Dove (Celtic Cone)
R J Price Mrs Chris Davies

Placings:0 **(0641)**
2001: 14^{0}HY

	Starts	1st	2nd	3rd	Win & Pl
Career Total (Turf)	1	0	0	0	

Going (Turf): Sf: 0-1 GS: 0-0 Gd: 0-0 GF: 0-0 Fm: 0-0
Distance: 5f/6f: 0-0 7f-8f: 0-0 9f-13f: 0-0 14f+: 0-1
Track : LH: 0-1 RH: 0-0 Tight: 0-0 Gall: 0-0
Aids: Bl: 0-0 Vi: 0-0 Tstrap: 0-0
Best Rating: 5 4/01 Nott 1m6f15y heavy

Dove's Dominion

86(74) (7)**18**

4-y-o b g Primo Dominie-Dame Helene (USA) (Sir Ivor)
A J Chamberlain (D N Carey 10/6) D N Carey

Placings:000/50005500-**00000** **(3579)**
2001: 12^{0}SD, 12^{0}SW, 8^{0}GF, 11^{0}GF, 14^{0}GF

	Starts	1st	2nd	3rd	Win & Pl
Career Total (Turf)	13	0	0	0	269
Career Total (AW)	3	0	0	0	

Going (Turf): Sf: 0-1 GS: 0-5 Gd: 0-0 GF: 0-7 Fm: 0-0
Distance: 5f/6f: 0-2 7f-8f: 0-4 9f-13f: 0-9 14f+: 0-1
Track : LH: 0-6 RH: 0-3 Tight: 0-3 Gall: 0-4
Aids: Bl: 0-0 Vi: 0-6 Tstrap: 0-0
Best Rating: 18 7/01 Wind 1m3f135y gd-fm

Dovebrace

102 (60?)**52**

8-y-o b g Dowsing (USA)-Naufrage (Main Reef)
A Bailey Dovebrace Ltd Air-Conditioning-Projects

Placings:1153155/500000/00005/**66**00205000060/030 603006/321216662300-00520502200 **(4907)**
2001: 7^{0}GF, 7^{0}GF, 8^{5}GF, 7^{2}G, 8^{0}GS, 8^{5}G, 8^{0}GF, 8^{2}F, 8^{2}GF, 8^{0}F, 7^{0}G

	Starts	1st	2nd	3rd	Win & Pl
Career Total (Turf)	60	5	7	5	35068
Career Total (AW)	4	0	0	0	0

55	7/00	Catt	7f	D(0-80)H	G-F	£4192
47	6/00	Ayr	1m	G(0-60)H	GD	£2107
95	8/95	Ches	6f18y	C	G-F	£6677
92	5/95	York	6f	B	GD	£6898
98	5/95	Hayd	5f	D	G-F	£4065

Total win prize-money £23941

Going (Turf): Sf: 0-3 GS: 0-9 Gd: 2-15 **GF: 3-24** Fm: 0-9
Distance: 5f/6f: 2-11 **7f-8f: 3-46** 9f-13f: 0-7 14f+: 0-0
Track : **LH: 3-33** RH: 0-12 **Tight: 2-22** Gall: 0-2
Aids: Bl: 0-2 Vi: 0-1 Tstrap: 0-0
Best Rating: 52 9/01 Nott 1m54y gd-fm

Dovedon Supreme

85 **40**

3-y-o b f Emperor Jones (USA)-Secreto Bold (Never So Bold)
H Akbary Michael C Whatley

Placings:0-50 **(2973)**
2001: 8^{5}GF, 10^{0}G

	Starts	1st	2nd	3rd	Win & Pl
Career Total (Turf)	3	0	0	0	0

Going (Turf): Sf: 0-1 GS: 0-0 Gd: 0-1 GF: 0-1 Fm: 0-0
Distance: 5f/6f: 0-1 7f-8f: 0-0 9f-13f: 0-2 14f+: 0-0
Track : LH: 0-0 RH: 0-2 Tight: 0-0 Gall: 0-1
Aids: Bl: 0-0 Vi: 0-0 Tstrap: 0-0
Best Rating: 40 6/01 Bevl 1m100y gd-fm

Dower House

108 **91**

6-y-o ch g Groom Dancer (USA)-Rose Noble (USA) (Vaguely Noble)
M W Easterby Mrs Claire Hollowood

Placings:52414/23130/U450/04 **(1391)**
2001: 10^{0}S, 10^{4}GF

	Starts	1st	2nd	3rd	Win & Pl
Career Total (Turf)	16	2	2	2	49098

97	6/98	Epsm	1m2f18y	C(0-100)H	GD	£17993
84	9/97	Yarm	1m3y	D	FRM	£3512

Total win prize-money £21506

Going (Turf): Sf: 0-3 GS: 0-0 **Gd: 1-6** GF: 0-4 **Fm: 1-3**
Distance: 5f/6f: 0-1 7f-8f: 0-4 **9f-13f: 2-11** 14f+: 0-0
Track : **LH: 1-7** RH: 0-5 **Tight: 1-4** Gall: 0-6
Aids: Bl: 0-0 Vi: 0-0 Tstrap: 0-2
Best Rating: 91 5/01 York 1m2f85y gd-fm

Tough and genuine at his best, he stays a mile and a half and goes well on fast ground.

Dowhatjen

101 **79**

2-y-o b f Desert Style (IRE)-Cupid Miss (Anita's Prince)
M R Channon Phil Jen Racing

Placings:41000130 **(5253)**
2001: 5^{4}HD, 5^{1}G, 7^{0}GF, 6^{0}G, 5^{0}G, 7^{1}G, 7^{3}S, 6^{0}S

	Starts	1st	2nd	3rd	Win & Pl
Career Total (Turf)	8	2	0	1	15558

79	9/01	Epsm	7f	C	GD	£9009
78	7/01	Bath	5f161y	E	GD	£3549

Total win prize-money £12558

Going (Turf): Sf: 0-2 GS: 0-0 **Gd: 2-4** GF: 0-1 Fm: 0-1
Distance: 5f/6f: 1-5 7f-8f: 1-3 9f-13f: 0-0 14f+: 0-0
Track : **LH: 2-3** RH: 0-0 Tight: 1-1 Gall: 1-2
Aids: Bl: 0-0 Vi: 0-0 Tstrap: 0-0
Best Rating: 79 10/01 NmkR 7f soft

A sharply-bred sort from a good yard, showed plenty of speed on her debut and won decisively at Bath on her second start. Held in better company subsequently, but she had dropped back to a fair mark when coming good at Epsom in September despite not appearing to handle the track, and ran well on soft ground at Newmarket afterwards.

Down To The Woods (USA)

105 **102**

3-y-o ch c Woodman (USA)-Riviera Wonder (USA) (Batonnier (USA))
M Johnston Miller/richards Partnership

Placings:15142-00235035 **(3981)**
2001: 7^{0}S, 6^{0}GF, 10^{2}F, 10^{3}GF, 10^{5}GF, 9^{0}G, 10^{3}G, 8^{5}F

	Starts	1st	2nd	3rd	Win & Pl
Career Total (Turf)	**13**	**2**	**2**	**2**	**31966**

102	9/00	Donc	6f	C	G-F	£7247
95	6/00	Donc	6f	E	G-F	£3120

Total win prize-money £10368

Going (Turf): Sf: 0-2 GS: 0-0 Gd: 0-3 **GF: 2-5** Fm: 0-2
Distance: **5f/6f: 2-4** 7f-8f: 0-4 9f-13f: 0-5 14f+: 0-0
Track : LH: 0-2 RH: 0-3 Tight: 0-1 Gall: 0-3
Aids: Bl: 0-1 Vi: 0-0 Tstrap: 0-7
Best Rating: 102 7/01 Asct 1m2f gd-fm

Won twice at Doncaster as a juvenile and was just beaten on soft ground there on his final start of 2000. Decent efforts over further in 2001. A front-runner, he seems best on a quicker surface.

Downland (IRE)

115 **86**

5-y-o b g Common Grounds-Boldabsa (Persian Bold)
R M Beckett (T D Barron 24/10) The Hon W E Beckett

Placings:0/210620/060220-0000300001001 **(5449)**
2001: 7^{0}S, 6^{0}S, 6^{0}GF, 7^{0}GF, 8^{3}GF, 8^{0}GF, 8^{0}GF, 8^{0}GF, 7^{0}HY, 7^{1}S, 6^{0}G, 6^{0}GS, 6^{1}HY

	Starts	1st	2nd	3rd	Win & Pl
Career Total (Turf)	**26**	**3**	**4**	**1**	**61997**

86	10/01	Newc	6f	C(0-95)H	HVY	£7182
78	9/01	Asct	7f	B H	SFT	£43500
78	7/99	Ling	6f	E	G-F	£3622

Total win prize-money £54306

Going (Turf): Sf: 2-9 GS: 0-3 Gd: 0-5 GF: 1-9 Fm: 0-0
Distance: **5f/6f: 2-13** 7f-8f: 1-10 9f-13f: 0-3 14f+: 0-0
Track : LH: 0-8 RH: 0-2 Tight: 0-2 Gall: 0-4
Aids: Bl: 0-3 Vi: 0-0 Tstrap: 0-0
Best Rating: 86 10/01 Newc 6f heavy

He struggled to find his form for his new connections this season but dropped down to a good mark in the meantime. Sprang a 40/1 surprise on soft ground in a valuable handicap over seven furlongs. He has won on fast ground, but is especially suited by cut.

Downpour (USA)

97(104) (87)**69**

3-y-o b g Torrential (USA)-Juliac (USA) (Accipiter (USA))
Sir Mark Prescott W E Sturt - Osborne House Iii

Placings:005-4101223 **(5230)**
2001: 13^{4}GF, 12^{1}SD, 12^{0}G, 11^{1}SD, 10^{2}GS, 12^{2}SD, 11^{3}S

	Starts	1st	2nd	3rd	Win & Pl
Career Total (Turf)	**7**	**0**	**1**	**1**	**2115**
Career Total (AW)	**3**	**2**	**1**	**0**	**6621**

86	7/01	Sthl	1m3f	E(0-70)H	STD	£3010
67	6/01	Sthl	1m4f	F(0-65)H	STD	£2345

Total win prize-money £5355

Going (Turf): Sf: 0-4 GS: 0-1 Gd: 0-1 GF: 0-1 Fm: 0-0
Distance: 5f/6f: 0-1 7f-8f: 0-2 **9f-13f: 2-6** 14f+: 0-1
Track : **LH: 2-8** RH: 0-0 Tight: 0-2 Gall: 0-2
Aids: Bl: 0-0 Vi: 0-0 Tstrap: 0-0
Best Rating: 87 10/01 Wolv 1m4f stand

A dual winner on the All-Weather, he has yet to prove he is as good on turf.

Doyle (USA)

95(84) (34)**49**

3-y-o b g Odyle (USA)-Miss Riverton (USA) (Fred Astaire (USA))
T D Easterby Times Of Wigan

Placings:066506 **(4032)**
2001: 8^{0}S, 7^{6}SD, 8^{6}SD, 12^{5}S, 9^{0}GF, 10^{6}G

	Starts	1st	2nd	3rd	Win & Pl
Career Total (Turf)	**4**	**0**	**0**	**0**	**0**
Career Total (AW)	**2**	**0**	**0**	**0**	**0**

Going (Turf): Sf: 0-2 GS: 0-0 Gd: 0-1 GF: 0-1 Fm: 0-0
Distance: 5f/6f: 0-0 7f-8f: 0-3 9f-13f: 0-3 14f+: 0-0
Track : LH: 0-3 RH: 0-2 Tight: 0-1 Gall: 0-1
Aids: Bl: 0-0 Vi: 0-0 Tstrap: 0-0
Best Rating: 49 3/01 Donc 1m soft

A half-brother to useful handicapper River Times, he has shown modest form so far in handicap company.

Dr Booby (IRE)

84 **47**

3-y-o b f Bluebird (USA)-Chellita (Habitat)
N A Callaghan M Tabor

Placings:0000 **(3318)**
2001: 10^{0}GS, 9^{0}GF, 8^{0}GF, 14^{0}G

	Starts	1st	2nd	3rd	Win & Pl
Career Total (Turf)	**4**	**0**	**0**	**0**	

Going (Turf): Sf: 0-0 GS: 0-1 Gd: 0-1 GF: 0-2 Fm: 0-0
Distance: 5f/6f: 0-0 7f-8f: 0-1 9f-13f: 0-2 14f+: 0-1
Track : LH: 0-1 RH: 0-1 Tight: 0-2 Gall: 0-0
Aids: Bl: 0-0 Vi: 0-0 Tstrap: 0-0
Best Rating: 47 5/01 Gdwd 1m1f gd-fm

Dr Charlie

94 **68**

3-y-o ch c Dr Devious (IRE)-Miss Toot (Ardross)
R Charlton Mountgrange Stud

Placings:2 **(0857)**
2001: 8^{2}GS

	Starts	1st	2nd	3rd	Win & Pl
Career Total (Turf)	**1**	**0**	**1**	**0**	**1420**

Going (Turf): Sf: 0-0 GS: 0-1 Gd: 0-0 GF: 0-0 Fm: 0-0
Distance: 5f/6f: 0-0 7f-8f: 0-1 9f-13f: 0-0 14f+: 0-0
Track : LH: 0-0 RH: 0-0 Tight: 0-0 Gall: 0-0
Aids: Bl: 0-0 Vi: 0-0 Tstrap: 0-0
Best Rating: 68 4/01 Newb 1m gd-sft

Dr Comfort (USA)

84 **55**

2-y-o ch g Spinning World (USA)-Hot Thong (BRZ) (Jarraar (USA))
B J Meehan Miss K Rausing

Placings:4 **(4947)**
2001: 8^{4}G

	Starts	1st	2nd	3rd	Win & Pl
Career Total (Turf)	**1**	**0**	**0**	**0**	**331**

Going (Turf): Sf: 0-0 GS: 0-0 Gd: 0-1 GF: 0-0 Fm: 0-0
Distance: 5f/6f: 0-0 7f-8f: 0-1 9f-13f: 0-0 14f+: 0-0
Track : LH: 0-0 RH: 0-1 Tight: 0-0 Gall: 0-0
Aids: Bl: 0-0 Vi: 0-0 Tstrap: 0-0
Best Rating: 55 9/01 Gdwd 1m good

Dr Cool

105(58) (60)**69**

4-y-o b g Ezzoud (IRE)-Vayavaig (Damister (USA))
J Akehurst Canisbay Bloodstock Ltd

Placings:03/054000-214301140 **(5230)**
2001: 11^{2}GS, 11^{1}GF, 12^{4}GF, 12^{3}G, 11^{0}G, 12^{1}G, 12^{1}G, 12^{4}G, 11^{0}S

	Starts	1st	2nd	3rd	Win & Pl
Career Total (Turf)	**16**	**3**	**1**	**1**	**14304**
Career Total (AW)	**1**	**0**	**0**	**1**	**428**

69	9/01	Gdwd	1m4f	E(0-80)H	GD	£3591
63	9/01	Epsm	1m4f10y	E(0-75)H	GD	£5778
54	6/01	Wind	1m3f135y	F(0-60)H	G-F	£2884

Total win prize-money £12254

Going (Turf): Sf: 0-4 GS: 0-2 **Gd: 2-8** GF: 1-2 Fm: 0-0
Distance: 5f/6f: 0-0 7f-8f: 0-3 **9f-13f: 3-13** 14f+: 0-1
Track : LH: 1-8 RH: 1-5 **Tight: 3-7** Gall: 0-4
Aids: Bl: 0-2 Vi: 0-1 Tstrap: 0-0
Best Rating: 69 9/01 Gdwd 1m4f good

A fair handicapper at around twelve furlongs, scoring at Epsom and Goodwood in the space of four days in September.

Dr Gordon (IRE)

99 **86?**

3-y-o b c Definite Article-Bristle (Thatch (USA))
C E Brittain Alessandro Gaucci

Placings:0-0500 **(2376)**
2001: 9^{0}S, 9^{5}GS, 11^{0}G, 14^{0}GF

	Starts	1st	2nd	3rd	Win & Pl
Career Total (Turf)	**5**	**0**	**0**	**0**	**0**

Going (Turf): Sf: 0-1 GS: 0-1 Gd: 0-2 GF: 0-1 Fm: 0-0
Distance: 5f/6f: 0-0 7f-8f: 0-1 9f-13f: 0-3 14f+: 0-1
Track : LH: 0-3 RH: 0-1 Tight: 0-2 Gall: 0-1
Aids: Bl: 0-0 Vi: 0-0 Tstrap: 0-0
Best Rating: 86 5/01 Ling 1m3f106y good

Well held in Listed company and decent maidens in 2001.

Dr Greenfield (IRE)

(102) (87+)**109**

3-y-o ch c Dr Devious (IRE)-Memory Green (USA) (Green Forest (USA))
G A Butler Team Valor

Placings:01-110 **(2144a)**
2001: 10^{1}S, 10^{1}GF, 12^{0}FT

	Starts	1st	2nd	3rd	Win & Pl
Career Total (Turf)	**3**	**2**	**0**	**0**	**41178**
Career Total (AW)	**2**	**1**	**0**	**0**	**2327**

109	5/01	Ches	1m2f75y	A	G-F	£34450
104	4/01	Kemp	1m2f	C(0-90)	SFT	£6727
87	11/00	Ling	1m	D	STD	£2327

Total win prize-money £43505

Going (Turf): Sf: 1-2 GS: 0-0 Gd: 0-0 **GF: 1-1** Fm: 0-0

Distance: 5f/6f: 0-0 7f-8f: 1-2 **9f-13f: 2-3** 14f+: 0-0

Track : **LH: 2-2** RH: 1-1 **Tight: 2-2** Gall: 1-1

Aids: Bl: 0-0 Vi: 0-0 Tstrap: 0-0

Best Rating: 109 5/01 Ches 1m2f75y gd-fm

Got off the mark in good style on Equitrack, and started his three-year-old career with an impressive soft-ground victory at Kempton. Followed up in good style in the Dee Stakes at Chester, but bled and finished last in the Belmont Stakes. He continues his career in the US.

Dr Strangelove (IRE)

94 **70**

3-y-o ch c Dr Devious (IRE)-Renzola (Dragonara Palace (USA))

B W Hills Wafic Said

Placings:56-50330 **(4414)**

2001: 10^{5}G, 9^{0}F, 10^{3}G, 9^{3}G, 10^{0}S

	Starts	1st	2nd	3rd	Win & Pl
Career Total (Turf)	7	0	0	2	1165

Going (Turf): Sf: 0-1 GS: 0-0 Gd: 0-4 GF: 0-1 Fm: 0-1

Distance: 5f/6f: 0-0 7f-8f: 0-2 9f-13f: 0-5 14f+: 0-0

Track : LH: 0-4 RH: 0-2 Tight: 0-4 Gall: 0-1

Aids: Bl: 0-0 Vi: 0-1 Tstrap: 0-0

Best Rating: 70 8/01 Sand 1m1f good

Dragnet (IRE)

99 **78**

3-y-o ch f Rainbow Quest (USA)-River Dancer (Irish River (FR))

Sir Michael Stoute Lord Weinstock

Placings:65-1 **(4784)**

2001: 9^{1}G

	Starts	1st	2nd	3rd	Win & Pl
Career Total (Turf)	3	1	0	0	4573
73 9/01 Gdwd 1m1f192yD				GD	£4572

Total win prize-money £4573

Going (Turf): Sf: 0-1 GS: 0-0 **Gd: 1-2** GF: 0-0 Fm: 0-0

Distance: 5f/6f: 0-0 7f-8f: 0-1 **9f-13f: 1-2** 14f+: 0-0

Track : LH: 0-0 **RH: 1-1 Tight: 1-1** Gall: 0-0

Aids: Bl: 0-0 Vi: 0-0 Tstrap: 0-0

Best Rating: 73 9/01 Gdwd 1m1f192y good

Dragon Flyer (IRE)

99 **90+**

2-y-o b f Tagula (IRE)-Noble Rocket (Reprimand)

G M McCourt (M Quinn 26/6) Miss A Jones

Placings:411 **(5562)**

2001: 5^{4}F, 5^{1}HY, 5^{1}S

	Starts	1st	2nd	3rd	Win & Pl
Career Total (Turf)	3	2	0	0	8791
90 10/01 Yarm 5f43y D(0-85)				SFT	£4251
73 10/01 Ling 5f D				HVY	£4251

Total win prize-money £8502

Going (Turf): Sf: 2-2 GS: 0-0 Gd: 0-0 GF: 0-0 Fm: 0-1

Distance: 5f/6f: 2-3 7f-8f: 0-0 9f-13f: 0-0 14f+: 0-0

Track : LH: 0-0 RH: 0-0 Tight: 0-0 Gall: 0-0

Aids: Bl: 0-0 Vi: 0-0 Tstrap: 0-0

Best Rating: 90 10/01 Yarm 5f43y soft

Came good at the second attempt in a maiden at Lingfield and followed up under top weight in a Yarmouth nursery .Suited by soft ground.

Drama King

100 (35)**44**

9-y-o b g Tragic Role (USA)-Consistent Queen (Queens Hussar)

B J Llewellyn Alan J Williams

Placings:05/00/40126005/0265/040220/10 **(0879)**

2001: 17^{1}HY, 21^{0}S

	Starts	1st	2nd	3rd	Win & Pl
Career Total (Turf)	7	1	1	0	3846
Career Total (AW)	17	1	3	0	4649
44 4/01 Pont 2m1f22y E(0-75)H				HVY	£3094
35 8/96 Wolv 1m4f F(0-65)H				STD	£2484

Total win prize-money £5578

Going (Turf): Sf: 1-2 GS: 0-1 Gd: 0-2 GF: 0-2 Fm: 0-0

Distance: 5f/6f: 0-0 7f-8f: 0-2 9f-13f: 1-6 14f+: 1-16

Track : **LH: 2-23** RH: 0-1 **Tight: 1-11** Gall: 0-0

Aids: **Bl: 2-17** Vi: 0-0 Tstrap: 0-0

Best Rating: 44 4/01 Pont 2m1f22y heavy

Drama Of Life (USA)

74 **56**

2-y-o ch f Royal Academy (USA)-Hot Princess (Hot Spark)

J H M Gosden R E Sangster

Placings:6 **(5561)**

2001: 7^{6}S

	Starts	1st	2nd	3rd	Win & Pl
Career Total (Turf)	1	0	0	0	0

Going (Turf): Sf: 0-1 GS: 0-0 Gd: 0-0 GF: 0-0 Fm: 0-0

Distance: 5f/6f: 0-0 7f-8f: 0-1 9f-13f: 0-0 14f+: 0-0

Track : LH: 0-0 RH: 0-0 Tight: 0-0 Gall: 0-0

Aids: Bl: 0-0 Vi: 0-0 Tstrap: 0-0

Best Rating: 56 10/01 Yarm 7f3y soft

Drama Premiere

100(85) (51)**71**

3-y-o br f Emarati (USA)-Dramatic Mood (Jalmood (USA))

I A Balding Ann Plummer & Friends

Placings:006-0214500 **(4988)**

2001: 7^{0}F, 0^{2}G, 0^{1}GS, 0^{4}GF, 0^{5}G, 0^{0}G, 8^{0}G

	Starts	1st	2nd	3rd	Win & Pl
Career Total (Turf)	9	1	1	0	7342
Career Total (AW)	1	0	0	0	0
71 7/01 Hayd 1m30y D(0-80)H				G-S	£4602

Total win prize-money £4602

Going (Turf): Sf: 0-1 **GS: 1-1** Gd: 0-5 GF: 0-1 Fm: 0-1

Distance: 5f/6f: 0-3 **7f-8f: 0-3 9f-13f: 1-4** 14f+: 0-0

Track : **LH: 1-2** RH: 0-4 Tight: 0-1 Gall: 0-0

Aids: Bl: 0-0 Vi: 0-0 Tstrap: 0-0

Best Rating: 71 7/01 Wind 1m67y gd-fm

Dramatic Quest

113 **107**

4-y-o b g Zafonic (USA)-Ultra Finesse (USA) (Rahy (USA))

M Johnston Maktoum Al Maktoum

Placings:0115/5-163 **(5132)**

2001: 10^{1}GF, 12^{6}GS, 12^{3}G

	Starts	1st	2nd	3rd	Win & Pl
Career Total (Turf)	8	3	0	1	21037
104 5/01 Newb 1m2f6y C				G-F	£6409
105 7/99 Asct 7f D				G-F	£5498
84 5/99 Pont 6f C				G-F	£6127

Total win prize-money £18034

Going (Turf): Sf: 0-1 GS: 0-1 Gd: 0-1 **GF: 3-5** Fm: 0-0

Distance: 5f/6f: 1-2 7f-8f: 1-3 9f-13f: 1-3 14f+: 0-0

Track : **LH: 2-4** RH: 0-1 Tight: 0-0 **Gall: 1-4**

Aids: Bl: 0-0 Vi: 0-0 Tstrap: 0-0

Best Rating: 107 10/01 NmkR 1m4f good

A tough and able juvenile, he proved no match for Distant Music and company in the Champagne Stakes at Doncaster in 1999. He ran only once in 2000, finishing fifth in a hot conditions stakes over a mile at Doncaster, but came back to gamely win a similar event at Newbury in 2001. Has since finished third in a listed race. Stays twelve furlongs and acts on fast ground.

Dramatic Ring

88 **52**

2-y-o b c Magic Ring (IRE)-Dramatic Mood (Jalmood (USA))

I A Balding Mrs Richard Plummer & Partners

Placings:6000000 **(5175)**

2001: 6^{6}GF, 6^{0}GF, 5^{0}F, 7^{0}G, 6^{0}GF, 5^{0}G, 6^{0}HY

	Starts	1st	2nd	3rd	Win & Pl
Career Total (Turf)	7	0	0	0	249

Going (Turf): Sf: 0-1 GS: 0-0 Gd: 0-2 GF: 0-3 Fm: 0-1

Distance: 5f/6f: 0-6 7f-8f: 0-1 9f-13f: 0-0 14f+: 0-0

Track : LH: 0-2 RH: 0-0 Tight: 0-0 Gall: 0-2

Aids: Bl: 0-2 Vi: 0-0 Tstrap: 0-0

Best Rating: 52 10/01 Wind 6f heavy

Dream A Dream

69 **33**

2-y-o b f Emperor Jones (USA)-Thornbury (IRE) (Tender King)

P S McEntee Mrs Susan Mountain

Placings:00 **(5466)**

2001: 7^{0}GS, 6^{0}S

	Starts	1st	2nd	3rd	Win & Pl
Career Total (Turf)	2	0	0	0	

Going (Turf): Sf: 0-1 GS: 0-1 Gd: 0-0 GF: 0-0 Fm: 0-0

Distance: 5f/6f: 0-0 7f-8f: 0-2 9f-13f: 0-0 14f+: 0-0

Track : LH: 0-1 RH: 0-0 Tight: 0-0 Gall: 0-0

Aids: Bl: 0-0 Vi: 0-0 Tstrap: 0-0

Best Rating: 33 10/01 Leic 7f9y gd-sft

Dream Bird

80(65) **37**

3-y-o b f Prince Of Birds (USA)-Baliana (Midyan (USA))

N A Graham Second Millennium Racing

Placings:0060 **(1943)**

2001: 7^{0}SD, 6^{0}HY, 7^{6}G, 7^{0}G

	Starts	1st	2nd	3rd	Win & Pl
Career Total (Turf)	3	0	0	0	0
Career Total (AW)	1	0	0	0	

Going (Turf): Sf: 0-1 GS: 0-0 Gd: 0-2 GF: 0-0 Fm: 0-0

Distance: 5f/6f: 0-0 7f-8f: 0-4 9f-13f: 0-0 14f+: 0-0

Track : LH: 0-2 RH: 0-1 Tight: 0-1 Gall: 0-0

Aids: Bl: 0-0 Vi: 0-0 Tstrap: 0-0

Best Rating: 37 5/01 Leic 7f9y good

Dream Carrier (IRE)

76(83) (13)**9**

13-y-o b g Doulab (USA)-Dream Trader (Auction Ring (USA))

R E Peacock R E Peacock

Placings:055004400/226012152130050/000020210440 0/613005303650000012012/213524400140160532/5134 546665050604/03453000/053342401344 5300/460000/0 5506/000000-000000 **(3859)**

2001: 8^{0}SD, 10^{0}SW, 7^{0}SD, 7^{0}GF, 8^{0}GF, 9^{0}GS

	Starts	1st	2nd	3rd	Win & Pl
Career Total (Turf)	57	4	6	2	28218

Career Total (AW)	81	8	6	11		34380
45	6/97	Sthl	7f	G(0-65)H	STD	£1984
69	1/95	Sthl	7f	F	STD	£2537
67	10/94	Wolv	7f	E(0-70)H	STD	£3677
56	9/94	Wolv	7f	F	STD	£2387
68	1/94	Sthl	7f	F	STD	£2243
71	12/93	Wolv	7f	C(0-90)H	STD	£4498
69	11/93	Sthl	7f	C(0-90)H	STD	£5047
67	2/93	Sthl	7f	F(0-70)H	STD	£2364
59	7/92	Sand	7f16y	E(0-100)H	GD	£3171
76	7/91	Ches	7f122y	D(0-100)H	GD	£7096
75	6/91	Folk	7f	F(0-70)H	FRM	£2856
65	5/91	Sand	7f	D(0-90)H	GD	£4458

Total win prize-money £42320

Going (Turf): Sf: 0-6 GS: 0-6 **Gd: 3-25** GF: 0-15 Fm: 1-5
Distance: 5f/6f: 0-10 **7f-8f: 12-107** 9f-13f: 0-21 14f+: 0-0
Track : **LH: 9-102** RH: 3-17 **Tight: 5-55** Gall: 0-7
Aids: Bl: 0-14 Vi: 0-1 Tstrap: 0-0
Best Rating: 13 2/01 Wolv 1m100y stand

Dream Experience

82(82) (51)**43**

2-y-o b/br f Reprimand-Dependable (Formidable (USA))
J S Moore Chris Bradbury

Placings:41250 **(2049)**
2001: 5^{4}S, 5^{1}SD, 5^{2}SD, 5^{5}S, 7^{0}GF

	Starts	1st	2nd	3rd	Win & Pl
Career Total (Turf)	3	0	0	0	0
Career Total (AW)	2	1	1	0	2454
44 3/01 Wolv 5f G				STD	£1806

Total win prize-money £1806

Going (Turf): Sf: 0-2 GS: 0-0 Gd: 0-0 GF: 0-1 Fm: 0-0
Distance: **5f/6f: 1-4** 7f-8f: 0-1 9f-13f: 0-0 14f+: 0-0
Track : **LH: 1-2** RH: 0-0 **Tight: 1-2** Gall: 0-0
Aids: Bl: 0-0 Vi: 0-0 Tstrap: 0-0
Best Rating: 51 4/01 Ling 5f stand

A March foal, has shown ability at a modest level on sand and turf.

Dream Magic

105 **76**

3-y-o b g Magic Ring (IRE)-Pip's Dream (Glint Of Gold)
M J Ryan P E Axon

Placings:0640-000302124 **(5135)**
2001: 8^{0}G, 8^{0}F, 8^{0}G, 8^{3}GF, 9^{0}GF, 8^{2}HY, 8^{1}GF, 8^{2}G, 10^{4}G

	Starts	1st	2nd	3rd	Win & Pl
Career Total (Turf)	13	1	2	1	10765
72 9/01 Gdwd 1m E(0-70)H				G-F	£6142

Total win prize-money £6143

Going (Turf): Sf: 0-4 GS: 0-0 Gd: 0-4 **GF: 1-4** Fm: 0-1
Distance: 5f/6f: 0-1 **7f-8f: 1-6** 9f-13f: 0-6 14f+: 0-0
Track : LH: 0-4 **RH: 1-2** Tight: 0-0 Gall: 0-0
Aids: Bl: 0-0 Vi: 0-0 Tstrap: 0-0
Best Rating: 76 9/01 Asct 1m good

Useful handicapper at around a mile.

Dream On Me

86(90) (19)**20**

5-y-o b m Prince Sabo-Helens Dreamgirl (Caerleon (USA))
H J Manners H J Manners

Placings:3224011/65225001304350/160-040000 (3388)
2001: 13^{0}SD, 11^{4}F, 11^{0}F, 11^{0}F, 12^{0}GF, 11^{0}F

	Starts	1st	2nd	3rd	Win & Pl
Career Total (Turf)	14	1	2	2	3669
Career Total (AW)	16	3	2	1	8273
37 1/00 Wolv 1m4f G				STD	£1512
50 7/99 Leic 1m8y G				G-F	£2024
62 1/99 Ling 7f D(0-80)H				STD	£3517
58 12/98 Ling 1m G				STD	£1737

Total win prize-money £8791

Going (Turf): Sf: 0-2 GS: 0-0 Gd: 0-2 **GF: 1-5** Fm: 0-5
Distance: 5f/6f: 0-3 7f-8f: 2-12 9f-13f: 2-15 14f+: 0-0
Track : **LH: 3-22** RH: 0-3 **Tight: 3-20** Gall: 0-1
Aids: Bl: 0-0 Vi: 0-0 Tstrap: 0-1
Best Rating: 20 7/01 Sals 1m4f gd-fm

Dream Time

94 **73**

3-y-o b f Rainbow Quest (USA)-Grey Angel (Kenmare (FR))
Sir Michael Stoute The Queen

Placings:0-30 **(4047)**
2001: 11^{3}GF, 14^{0}F

	Starts	1st	2nd	3rd	Win & Pl
Career Total (Turf)	3	0	0	1	571

Going (Turf): Sf: 0-0 GS: 0-0 Gd: 0-1 GF: 0-1 Fm: 0-1
Distance: 5f/6f: 0-0 7f-8f: 0-1 9f-13f: 0-1 14f+: 0-1
Track : LH: 0-3 RH: 0-0 Tight: 0-1 Gall: 0-1
Aids: Bl: 0-0 Vi: 0-2 Tstrap: 0-0
Best Rating: 73 8/01 Brig 1m3f196y gd-fm

Lightly-raced filly with her own ideas about the game.

Dream With Me (FR)

106 **96**

4-y-o b g Johann Quatz (FR)-Midnight Ride (FR) (Fast Topaze (USA))
C R Egerton Dr G Madan Mohan

Placings:6121312-620 **(5693)**
2001: 12^{6}G, 12^{2}HY, 12^{0}S

	Starts	1st	2nd	3rd	Win & Pl
Career Total (Turf)	10	3	3	1	41623
8/00 Deau 1m2f H				GD	£9606
6/00 Comp 1m4f				G-S	£4803
4/00 Comp 1m4f				HLD	£3842

Total win prize-money £18251

Going (Turf): Sf: 0-2 **GS: 1-1** Gd: 0-1 GF: 0-0 Fm: 0-0
Distance: 5f/6f: 0-0 7f-8f: 0-0 **9f-13f: 2-5** 14f+: 0-0
Track : LH: 0-2 RH: 0-1 Tight: 0-0 Gall: 0-3
Aids: Bl: 0-0 Vi: 0-0 Tstrap: 0-0
Best Rating: 96 11/01 Donc 1m4f soft

Smart French stayer, he improved throughout last season, winning three times, twice over 12 furlongs and once over ten. Untried on ground faster than good. Now with Charlie Egerton, for whom he ran a promising race at Doncaster in September after almost a year off, he confirmed the impression at Ascot next time. Stays a mile and a half.

Dreamie Battle

(94) (35)**48**

3-y-o br f Makbul-Highland Rossie (Pablond)
R Hollinshead Tim Leadbeater

Placings:33505-0656546B0 **(5375)**
2001: 6^{0}GF, 7^{6}GF, 8^{5}GS, 8^{6}F, 7^{5}F, 5^{4}GF, 8^{6}F, 7^{B}GF, 7^{0}G,

	Starts	1st	2nd	3rd	Win & Pl
Career Total (Turf)	14	0	0	2	1303

Going (Turf): Sf: 0-1 GS: 0-1 Gd: 0-2 GF: 0-6 Fm: 0-4
Distance: 5f/6f: 0-1 7f-8f: 0-10 9f-13f: 0-3 14f+: 0-0
Track : LH: 0-8 RH: 0-1 Tight: 0-6 Gall: 0-0
Aids: Bl: 0-0 Vi: 0-0 Tstrap: 0-0
Best Rating: 55 6/01 Wwck 6f21y gd-fm

Dreaming Diva

98 **72**

2-y-o ch f Whittingham (IRE)-Any Dream (IRE) (Shernazar)
J C Fox (R Hannon 18/6) Dr Thomas Wade

Placings:311 **(4277)**
2001: 6^{3}G, 7^{1}G, 7^{1}GS

	Starts	1st	2nd	3rd	Win & Pl
Career Total (Turf)	3	2	0	1	11033
72 8/01 Gdwd 7f C H				G-S	£7280
66 8/01 NmkJ 7f E				GD	£3474

Total win prize-money £10754

Going (Turf): Sf: 0-0 **GS: 1-1 Gd: 1-2** GF: 0-0 Fm: 0-0
Distance: 5f/6f: 0-1 **7f-8f: 2-2** 9f-13f: 0-0 14f+: 0-0
Track : LH: 0-0 **RH: 1-1** Tight: 0-0 Gall: 0-0
Aids: Bl: 0-0 Vi: 0-0 Tstrap: 0-0
Best Rating: 72 8/01 Gdwd 7f gd-sft

Looked better than a plater when winning a seller on his debut and followed up in a Goodwod nursery.

Dreams Desire

104 **46**

3-y-o b f Mind Games-Champenoise (Forzando)
J A Glover Sports Mania

Placings:110-000500600 **(4539)**
2001: 5^{0}S, 5^{0}GF, 6^{0}G, 6^{5}GF, 6^{0}G, 6^{0}F, 7^{6}G, 5^{0}GF, 6^{0}GF

	Starts	1st	2nd	3rd	Win & Pl
Career Total (Turf)	12	2	0	0	7550
82 5/00 Thsk 5f D				GD	£4153
71 5/00 Donc 5f E				G-S	£3396

Total win prize-money £7550

Going (Turf): Sf: 0-1 **GS: 1-1 Gd: 1-4** GF: 0-5 Fm: 0-1
Distance: **5f/6f: 2-10** 7f-8f: 0-2 9f-13f: 0-0 14f+: 0-0
Track : LH: 0-0 RH: 0-0 Tight: 0-0 Gall: 0-0
Aids: Bl: 0-1 Vi: 0-0 Tstrap: 0-0
Best Rating: 74 7/01 Donc 6f gd-fm

Twice a juvenile winner before running unplaced in the Queen Mary, she did not reappear until April this year. She has taken time to find her form and has slipped to a decent mark as a result.

Dress Rehearsal

102 **87**

3-y-o b c Machiavellian (USA)-Dance To The Top (Sadler's Wells (USA))
Sir Michael Stoute Cheveley Park Stud

Placings:0-021002 **(4370)**
2001: 10^{0}S, 8^{2}GF, 8^{1}GF, 8^{0}GS, 7^{0}GF, 7^{2}GF

	Starts	1st	2nd	3rd	Win & Pl
Career Total (Turf)	7	1	2	0	6195
70 7/01 Ripn 1m D				G-F	£3575

Total win prize-money £3575

Going (Turf): Sf: 0-1 GS: 0-1 Gd: 0-0 **GF: 1-5** Fm: 0-0
Distance: 5f/6f: 0-0 **7f-8f: 1-5** 9f-13f: 0-2 14f+: 0-0
Track : LH: 0-2 **RH: 1-2 Tight: 1-3** Gall: 0-1
Aids: Bl: 0-0 Vi: 0-0 Tstrap: 0-0
Best Rating: 87 8/01 Catt 7f gd-fm

Out of a dam who was placed at Group level. Ran well over a mile at Windsor then won a modest maiden over a mile at Ripon next time. Fair form in Handicaps. Killed by a car in September. (DEAD)

Drift

101 **52**

7-y-o b g Slip Anchor-Norgabie (Northfields (USA))

J M Bradley (B J Llewellyn 26/5) Miss S Howell

Placings:000/500203/03240P/P20 **(1620)**
2001: 16^{P}HY, 15^{2}HY, 16^{0}GF

	Starts	1st	2nd	3rd	Win & Pl
Career Total (Turf)	16	0	3	2	3791
Career Total (AW)	2	0	0	0	

Going (Turf): Sf: 0-5 GS: 0-1 Gd: 0-3 GF: 0-6 Fm: 0-1
Distance: 5f/6f: 0-0 7f-8f: 0-3 9f-13f: 0-5 14f+: 0-10
Track : LH: 0-11 RH: 0-4 Tight: 0-8 Gall: 0-0
Aids: Bl: 0-3 Vi: 0-0 Tstrap: 0-2
Best Rating: 52 4/01 Folk 1m7f92y heavy

Drinkin Time

100 **72**

2-y-o ch f Timeless Times (USA)-Mashin Time (Palm Track)
T D Easterby P Baillie

Placings:54 **(4565)**
2001: 5^{5}GF, 5^{4}HY

	Starts	1st	2nd	3rd	Win & Pl
Career Total (Turf)	2	0	0	0	385

Going (Turf): Sf: 0-1 GS: 0-0 Gd: 0-0 GF: 0-1 Fm: 0-0
Distance: 5f/6f: 0-2 7f-8f: 0-0 9f-13f: 0-0 14f+: 0-0
Track : LH: 0-1 RH: 0-0 Tight: 0-0 Gall: 0-0
Aids: Bl: 0-0 Vi: 0-0 Tstrap: 0-0
Best Rating: 72 9/01 Hayd 5f heavy

Dripping In Gold (IRE)

(73) (25)**26**

3-y-o ch f Alhijaz-Fanny's Choice (IRE) (Fairy King (USA))
J J Bridger J J Bridger

Placings:3000000-6 **(0040)**
2001: 5^{6}SD

	Starts	1st	2nd	3rd	Win & Pl
Career Total (Turf)	4	0	0	1	318
Career Total (AW)	4	0	0	0	0

Going (Turf): Sf: 0-1 GS: 0-2 Gd: 0-1 GF: 0-0 Fm: 0-0
Distance: 5f/6f: 0-6 7f-8f: 0-2 9f-13f: 0-0 14f+: 0-0
Track : LH: 0-5 RH: 0-0 Tight: 0-3 Gall: 0-1
Aids: Bl: 0-0 Vi: 0-0 Tstrap: 0-1
Best Rating: 25 1/01 Ling 5f stand

Drowned In Bubbly

(77) **30**

5-y-o b g Tragic Role (USA)-Champenoise (Forzando)
J G Given Lovely Bubbly Racing

Placings:00/000400000/2213-0 **(0540)**
2001: 16^{0}SD

	Starts	1st	2nd	3rd	Win & Pl
Career Total (Turf)	14	1	2	1	1550
Career Total (AW)	2	0	0	0	

Total win prize-money £1050

Going (Turf): Sf: 0-2 GS: 0-1 Gd: 0-4 GF: 0-5 Fm: 0-1
Distance: 5f/6f: 0-2 7f-8f: 0-3 9f-13f: 0-1 **14f+: 1-10**
Track : LH: 0-7 RH: 0-3 Tight: 0-7 Gall: 0-0
Aids: Bl: 0-1 Vi: 0-0 Tstrap: 0-1

Druridge Bay (IRE)

88(68) **20**

5-y-o b g Turtle Island (IRE)-Lady Of Shalott (King's Lake (USA))
D G Bridgwater Mrs Mary Bridgwater

Placings:4504060002062240/06600/000000-000060 **(3889)**
2001: 7^{0}SD, 9^{0}SW, 7^{0}GF, 6^{0}GF, 6^{6}GF, 6^{0}F

	Starts	1st	2nd	3rd	Win & Pl
Career Total (Turf)	25	0	1	0	1106
Career Total (AW)	8	0	2	0	942

Going (Turf): Sf: 0-5 GS: 0-2 Gd: 0-6 GF: 0-9 Fm: 0-3
Distance: 5f/6f: 0-6 7f-8f: 0-15 9f-13f: 0-12 14f+: 0-0
Track : LH: 0-20 RH: 0-0 Tight: 0-8 Gall: 0-0
Aids: Bl: 0-1 Vi: 0-1 Tstrap: 0-0
Best Rating: 20 7/01 Brig 6f209y gd-fm

Dry Martini

103 **79**

3-y-o b c Darshaan-Drei (USA) (Lyphard (USA))
J W Hills Jampot Partners, E Whitehouse & T Milson

Placings:54356 **(4784)**
2001: 10^{5}G, 10^{4}GF, 8^{3}HY, 11^{5}GF, 9^{6}G

	Starts	1st	2nd	3rd	Win & Pl
Career Total (Turf)	5	0	0	1	947

Going (Turf): Sf: 0-1 GS: 0-0 Gd: 0-2 GF: 0-2 Fm: 0-0
Distance: 5f/6f: 0-0 7f-8f: 0-0 9f-13f: 0-5 14f+: 0-0
Track : LH: 0-2 RH: 0-3 Tight: 0-2 Gall: 0-1
Aids: Bl: 0-0 Vi: 0-0 Tstrap: 0-0
Best Rating: 79 9/01 Ling 1m3f106y gd-fm

Has shown ability in maiden company at around ten furlongs.

Dryad

(93) (53)

6-y-o ch g Risk Me (FR)-Lizzy Cantle (Homing)
N P Littmoden Miss Vanessa Church

Placings:4/643002052022/415223051453/54 **(0605)**
2001: 6^{5}SD, 6^{4}SD

	Starts	1st	2nd	3rd	Win & Pl
Career Total (Turf)	6	0	0	1	261
Career Total (AW)	21	2	6	2	10878

57 6/99 Sthl 6f F(0-60) STD £2253
67 1/99 Wolv 6f D STD £2788
Total win prize-money £5041

Going (Turf): Sf: 0-1 GS: 0-2 Gd: 0-1 GF: 0-2 Fm: 0-0
Distance: 5f/6f: 2-21 7f-8f: 0-6 9f-13f: 0-0 14f+: 0-0
Track : LH: 2-21 RH: 0-2 **Tight: 1-18** Gall: 0-2
Aids: Bl: 2-11 Vi: 0-1 Tstrap: 0-0
Best Rating: 53 3/01 Sthl 6f stand

Dryden House (IRE)

96 **84+**

2-y-o b f Cadeaux Genereux-For Example (USA) (Northern Baby (CAN))
M A Jarvis M P Burke

Placings:04 **(5372)**
2001: 7^{0}GF, 6^{4}G

	Starts	1st	2nd	3rd	Win & Pl
Career Total (Turf)	2	0	0	0	0

Going (Turf): Sf: 0-0 GS: 0-0 Gd: 0-1 GF: 0-1 Fm: 0-0
Distance: 5f/6f: 0-1 7f-8f: 0-1 9f-13f: 0-0 14f+: 0-0
Track : LH: 0-0 RH: 0-1 Tight: 0-0 Gall: 0-1
Aids: Bl: 0-0 Vi: 0-0 Tstrap: 0-0
Best Rating: 84 10/01 Rdcr 6f good

Has shown ability in maiden company.

Dubai Belle (USA)

89 **78**

2-y-o b f Mr Prospector (USA)-Flagbird (USA) (Nureyev (USA))
D R Loder Sheikh Mohammed

Placings:2 **(5014)**
2001: 8^{2}HY

	Starts	1st	2nd	3rd	Win & Pl
Career Total (Turf)	1	0	1	0	1425

Going (Turf): Sf: 0-1 GS: 0-0 Gd: 0-0 GF: 0-0 Fm: 0-0
Distance: 5f/6f: 0-0 7f-8f: 0-0 9f-13f: 0-1 14f+: 0-0
Track : LH: 0-1 RH: 0-0 Tight: 0-0 Gall: 0-0
Aids: Bl: 0-0 Vi: 0-0 Tstrap: 0-0
Best Rating: 78 9/01 Hayd 1m30y heavy

Dubai Destination (USA)

108 **112+**

2-y-o b c Kingmambo (USA)-Mysterial (USA) (Alleged (USA))
D R Loder Sheikh Mohammed

Placings:211 **(4698)**
2001: 6^{2}GF, 7^{1}GS, 7^{1}GS

	Starts	1st	2nd	3rd	Win & Pl
Career Total (Turf)	3	2	1	0	66926

112 9/01 Donc 7f A G-S £60000
102 7/01 NmkJ 7f D G-S £5486
Total win prize-money £65486

Going (Turf): Sf: 0-0 **GS: 2-2** Gd: 0-0 GF: 0-1 Fm: 0-0
Distance: 5f/6f: 0-0 **7f-8f: 2-3** 9f-13f: 0-0 14f+: 0-0
Track : LH: 0-0 RH: 0-0 Tight: 0-0 Gall: 0-0
Aids: Bl: 0-0 Vi: 0-0 Tstrap: 0-0
Best Rating: 112 9/01 Donc 7f gd-sft

A $1.5 million yearling out of a half-sister to Agnes World, his name was changed from Copernican when he began to show talent at home. He found one too good on his Newbury debut, but made amends at Newmarket in a traditionally hot maiden. Was most impressive in beating Rock Of Gibraltar in the Champagne Stakes at Doncaster, but the fast pace did play into his hands. Had a setback and missed the Dewhurst.

Dubai Excellence

95 **86+**

2-y-o br c Highest Honor (FR)-Colorado Dancer (Shareef Dancer (USA))
D R Loder Sheikh Mohammed

Placings:1 **(4670)**
2001: 7^{1}G

	Starts	1st	2nd	3rd	Win & Pl
Career Total (Turf)	1	1	0	0	3562

86 9/01 Chep 7f16y D GD £3562
Total win prize-money £3562

Going (Turf): Sf: 0-0 GS: 0-0 **Gd: 1-1** GF: 0-0 Fm: 0-0
Distance: 5f/6f: 0-0 **7f-8f: 1-1** 9f-13f: 0-0 14f+: 0-0
Track : LH: 0-0 RH: 0-0 Tight: 0-0 Gall: 0-0
Aids: Bl: 0-0 Vi: 0-0 Tstrap: 0-0
Best Rating: 86 9/01 Chep 7f16y good

A half-brother to Dubai Millennium, he ran green before going on to win on his racecourse debut. Bred to stay middle distances and is a bright prospect.

Dubai Midnight (USA)

93 **79**

2-y-o ch c Saint Ballado (CAN)-Lituya Bay (USA) (Empery (USA))
J H M Gosden Sheikh Rashid Bin Mohammed Al Maktoum

Placings:6 **(4056)**

2001: 7^{6}GF

	Starts	1st	2nd	3rd	Win & Pl
Career Total (Turf)	1	0	0	0	0

Going (Turf): Sf: 0-0 GS: 0-0 Gd: 0-0 GF: 0-1 Fm: 0-0
Distance: 5f/6f: 0-0 7f-8f: 0-1 9f-13f: 0-0 14f+: 0-0
Track : LH: 0-0 RH: 0-0 Tight: 0-0 Gall: 0-0
Aids: Bl: 0-0 Vi: 0-0 Tstrap: 0-0
Best Rating: 79 8/01 Newb 7f gd-fm

Looked in need of the experience on his Newbury debut and should improve.

Dubai Nurse

101(82) (19)**34**
7-y-o ch m Handsome Sailor-Lady Eccentric (IRE) (Magical Wonder (USA))
A R Dicken Tony Curson

Placings:00020620020002/00/046000-3504000 (3695)
2001: 5^{3}GS, 5^{5}GF, 5^{0}GF, 5^{4}G, 5^{0}F, 6^{0}G, 5^{0}G

	Starts	1st	2nd	3rd	Win & Pl
Career Total (Turf)	26	0	4	1	4152
Career Total (AW)	3	0	0	0	

Going (Turf): Sf: 0-4 GS: 0-8 Gd: 0-8 GF: 0-4 Fm: 0-2
Distance: 5f/6f: 0-25 7f-8f: 0-4 9f-13f: 0-0 14f+: 0-0
Track : LH: 0-3 RH: 0-1 Tight: 0-0 Gall: 0-1
Aids: Bl: 0-2 Vi: 0-1 Tstrap: 0-0
Best Rating: 34 6/01 Newc 5f firm

Dubai Prince (IRE)

91 **66**
2-y-o b g Anita's Prince-Balqis (USA) (Advocator)
D Nicholls D Nicholls

Placings:3424 (4228)
2001: 5^{3}GF, 6^{4}GS, 5^{2}G, 6^{4}G

	Starts	1st	2nd	3rd	Win & Pl
Career Total (Turf)	4	0	1	1	2341

Going (Turf): Sf: 0-0 GS: 0-1 Gd: 0-2 GF: 0-1 Fm: 0-0
Distance: 5f/6f: 0-4 7f-8f: 0-0 9f-13f: 0-0 14f+: 0-0
Track : LH: 0-0 RH: 0-0 Tight: 0-0 Gall: 0-0
Aids: Bl: 0-0 Vi: 0-0 Tstrap: 0-0
Best Rating: 66 8/01 Thsk 6f good

Dubai Seven Stars

102 **69**
3-y-o ch f Suave Dancer (USA)-Her Honour (Teenoso (USA))
M C Pipe Mrs Alison C Farrant

Placings:45225-422360 (5463)
2001: 10^{4}GF, 9^{2}S, 10^{2}F, 12^{3}GF, 14^{6}G, 11^{0}G

	Starts	1st	2nd	3rd	Win & Pl
Career Total (Turf)	11	0	4	1	4561

Going (Turf): Sf: 0-2 GS: 0-2 Gd: 0-2 GF: 0-4 Fm: 0-1
Distance: 5f/6f: 0-1 7f-8f: 0-3 9f-13f: 0-6 14f+: 0-1
Track : LH: 0-5 RH: 0-2 Tight: 0-5 Gall: 0-1
Aids: Bl: 0-0 Vi: 0-0 Tstrap: 0-0
Best Rating: 73 6/01 Bath 1m2f46y firm

Dubai Status (USA)

99 **89**
2-y-o b c Seeking The Gold (USA)-Possibly Perfect (USA) (Northern Baby (CAN))
D R Loder Sheikh Mohammed

Placings:16 (4656)

2001: 7^{1}GF, 7^{6}GF

	Starts	1st	2nd	3rd	Win & Pl
Career Total (Turf)	2	1	0	0	4823
80 6/01 NmkJ 7f	D			G-F	£4823

Total win prize-money £4823

Going (Turf): Sf: 0-0 GS: 0-0 Gd: 0-0 GF: 1-2 Fm: 0-0
Distance: 5f/6f: 0-0 **7f-8f: 1-2** 9f-13f: 0-0 14f+: 0-0
Track : LH: 0-0 RH: 0-0 Tight: 0-0 Gall: 0-0
Aids: Bl: 0-0 Vi: 0-0 Tstrap: 0-0
Best Rating: 89 9/01 Donc 7f gd-fm

Cost $700,000 as a yearling and made no mistake in a Newmarket maiden on his debut in June.

Dubai Visit (USA)

(93)**97**
3-y-o b f Quiet American (USA)-Furajet (USA) (The Minstrel (CAN))
Saeed Bin Suroor Godolphin

Placings:2106-4312 (5673a)
2001: 8^{4}FT, 9^{3}FT, 8^{1}S, 8^{2}HY

	Starts	1st	2nd	3rd	Win & Pl
Career Total (Turf)	4	1	1	0	10775
Career Total (AW)	4	1	1	1	28007
76 10/01 Leic 1m9y C				SFT	£6119
9/00 Baym 1m				FST	£9390

Total win prize-money £15509

Going (Turf): Sf: 1-2 GS: 0-0 Gd: 0-0 GF: 0-0 Fm: 0-1
Distance: 5f/6f: 0-1 7f-8f: 1-4 9f-13f: 1-2 14f+: 0-0
Track : LH: 0-0 RH: 0-0 Tight: 0-0 Gall: 0-0
Aids: Bl: 1-2 Vi: 0-0 Tstrap: 1-2
Best Rating: 97 10/01 MsnL 1m heavy

A half-sister to China Visit, she was in the frame in two good events in Dubai in the spring and scraped home in a backend conditions event on her first run in this country. Just beaten in a french Listed event after.

Dubaian Gift

94 **83**
2-y-o b c Bahamian Bounty-Hot Lavender (CAN) (Shadeed (USA))
I A Balding Dubai Thoroughbred Racing

Placings:406 (5038)
2001: 6^{4}GF, 6^{0}GF, 5^{6}G

	Starts	1st	2nd	3rd	Win & Pl
Career Total (Turf)	3	0	0	0	0

Going (Turf): Sf: 0-0 GS: 0-0 Gd: 0-1 GF: 0-2 Fm: 0-0
Distance: 5f/6f: 0-2 7f-8f: 0-1 9f-13f: 0-0 14f+: 0-0
Track : LH: 0-1 RH: 0-0 Tight: 0-0 Gall: 0-1
Aids: Bl: 0-0 Vi: 0-0 Tstrap: 0-0
Best Rating: 83 9/01 Newb 6f8y gd-fm

Dubianstar (USA)

71 **24**
3-y-o b f Shadeed (USA)-Dubian (High Line)
B W Hills Mohamed Obaida

Placings:0 (0810)
2001: 7^{0}S

	Starts	1st	2nd	3rd	Win & Pl
Career Total (Turf)	1	0	0	0	

Going (Turf): Sf: 0-1 GS: 0-0 Gd: 0-0 GF: 0-0 Fm: 0-0
Distance: 5f/6f: 0-0 7f-8f: 0-1 9f-13f: 0-0 14f+: 0-0
Track : LH: 0-0 RH: 0-0 Tight: 0-0 Gall: 0-0
Aids: Bl: 0-0 Vi: 0-0 Tstrap: 0-0
Best Rating: 24 4/01 NmkR 7f soft

Duc's Dream

99(96) (66)**69**
3-y-o b g Bay Tern (USA)-Kala's Image (Kala Shikari)
D Morris Mrs Susan I Parry

Placings:451-40511330 (5486)
2001: 9^{4}SW, 10^{0}GS, 8^{5}G, 10^{1}GF, 9^{1}GF, 10^{3}GF, 12^{3}SD, 10^{0}H

	Starts	1st	2nd	3rd	Win & Pl
Career Total (Turf)	8	2	0	1	8192
Career Total (AW)	3	1	0	1	2738
69 6/01 Gdwd 1m1f192yD(0-80)H				G-F	£4465
64 5/01 Ling 1m2f F(0-65)H				G-F	£2632
60 12/00 Sthl 1m D				STD	£2191

Total win prize-money £9289

Going (Turf): Sf: 0-2 GS: 0-1 Gd: 0-2 **GF: 2-3** Fm: 0-0
Distance: 5f/6f: 0-0 7f-8f: 1-2 **9f-13f: 2-9** 14f+: 0-0
Track : **LH: 2-7** RH: 1-1 **Tight: 2-3** Gall: 0-2
Aids: Bl: 0-0 Vi: 0-0 Tstrap: 0-0
Best Rating: 69 6/01 Pont 1m2f6y gd-fm

He got off the mark in a maiden on the Southwell Fibresand at the end of last year, but did not show much until winning a modest handicap on fast ground at Lingfield in June and followed up with a game victory in a better race at Goodwood. His good form continued with good thirds at Pontefract and Southwell. Suited by ten furlongs and fast ground.

Duchamp (USA)

93 **75**
4-y-o b g Pine Bluff (USA)-Higher Learning (USA) (Fappiano (USA))
I A Balding Exors Of The Late Robert Hitchins

Placings:66221/54021500-0 (2305)
2001: 20^{0}GF

	Starts	1st	2nd	3rd	Win & Pl
Career Total (Turf)	14	2	3	0	21266
87 7/00 Newb 1m5f61y C(0-90)H				G-F	£7052
85 10/99 York 7f202y C H				G-S	£7590

Total win prize-money £14643

Going (Turf): Sf: 0-0 **GS: 1-3** Gd: 0-3 **GF: 1-8** Fm: 0-0
Distance: 5f/6f: 0-0 7f-8f: 1-2 9f-13f: 0-7 14f+: 1-5
Track : **LH: 2-8** RH: 0-5 Tight: 0-4 **Gall: 2-7**
Aids: Bl: 0-0 Vi: 0-1 Tstrap: 0-0
Best Rating: 75 6/01 Asct 2m4f gd-fm

A progressive handicapper on the level, he slightly lost his way after winning the Ladbroke Handicap at Newbury in July 2000. He stays a mile five furlongs.

Duchcov

100 **99**
3-y-o ch f Caerleon (USA)-Amandine (IRE) (Darshaan)
L M Cumani Raimon Bloodstock & Geoff Howard-Spink

Placings:3-12 (2129)
2001: 9^{1}GF, 10^{2}GF

	Starts	1st	2nd	3rd	Win & Pl
Career Total (Turf)	3	1	1	1	10044
76 5/01 Bevl 1m1f207yD				G-F	£4231

Total win prize-money £4232

Going (Turf): Sf: 0-0 GS: 0-0 Gd: 0-0 **GF: 1-3** Fm: 0-0
Distance: 5f/6f: 0-0 7f-8f: 0-1 **9f-13f: 1-2** 14f+: 0-0
Track : LH: 0-1 **RH: 1-1** Tight: 0-0 Gall: 0-1
Aids: Bl: 0-0 Vi: 0-0 Tstrap: 0-0
Best Rating: 99 6/01 Newb 1m2f6y gd-fm

She got off the mark in a Beverley maiden on her reappearance and was not disgraced in a Newbury Listed event next time.

Duck Row (USA)

109 **111**

6-y-o ch g Diesis-Sunny Moment (USA) (Roberto (USA))
J A R Toller Duke Of Devonshire

Placings:16/63303/0160/12232034-45201535 **(5362)**
2001: 8^4G, 8^5GF, 8^2G, 8^0GF, 8^1G, 8^5G, 9^3G, 9^5GS

	Starts	1st	2nd	3rd	Win & Pl
Career Total (Turf)	**27**	**4**	**4**	**6**	**118807**

89	8/01	Bath	1m5y	C	GD	£7221
106	5/00	Hayd	1m30y	C	G-S	£6069
109	4/99	Asct	1m	C	GD	£6257
100	9/97	Newb	1m	B	SFT	£9416

Total win prize-money £28963

Going (Turf): Sf: 1-5 GS: 1-4 **Gd: 2-15** GF: 0-3 Fm: 0-0
Distance: 5f/6f: 0-0 7f-8f: 2-14 9f-13f: 2-13 14f+: 0-0
Track : **LH: 2-6** RH: 1-7 Tight: 1-3 Gall: 1-7
Aids: Bl: 0-0 Vi: 0-0 Tstrap: 0-0
Best Rating: 111 10/01 NmkR 1m1f good

Useful miler whose penchant for pulling hard early on in his races often results in him meeting trouble in running. Given his ability, he does not have a great win record and has spent most of his racing career competing in conditions races. Looked as good as ever when getting a less-than-clear passage in the Diomed Stakes at Epsom, and has been campaigned in France and Germany in 2001. Best with some give in the ground. Won a conditions race at Bath in August, but again disappointed when stepped up in class.

Dudleys Delight

100 **84**

2-y-o b f Makbul-Steadfast Elite (IRE) (Glenstal (USA))
A Berry W R Milner & D G Jones

Placings:110442 **(5487)**
2001: 5^1S, 5^1G, 5^0GF, 5^4GF, 5^4GF, 6^2HY

	Starts	1st	2nd	3rd	Win & Pl
Career Total (Turf)	**6**	**2**	**1**	**0**	**16007**

83	5/01	Nott	5f13y	F	GD	£2408
83	4/01	NmkR	5f	D	SFT	£4745

Total win prize-money £7153

Going (Turf): Sf: 1-2 GS: 0-0 **Gd: 1-1** GF: 0-3 Fm: 0-0
Distance: **5f/6f: 2-6** 7f-8f: 0-0 9f-13f: 0-0 14f+: 0-0
Track : LH: 0-0 RH: 0-0 Tight: 0-0 Gall: 0-0
Aids: Bl: 0-0 Vi: 0-0 Tstrap: 0-0
Best Rating: 84 10/01 Donc 6f heavy

A sister to a six furlong juvenile winner, she showed ability on easy ground over 5-6 furlongs, but broke a blood-vessel at Ripon in August.

Duds (IRE)

90 **73**

2-y-o ch g Definite Article-Domino's Nurse (Dom Racine (FR))
P F I Cole W J Smith And M D Dudley

Placings:3000 **(5342)**
2001: 5^3GF, 7^0S, 7^0S, 7^0GS

	Starts	1st	2nd	3rd	Win & Pl
Career Total (Turf)	**4**	**0**	**0**	**1**	**518**

Going (Turf): Sf: 0-2 GS: 0-1 Gd: 0-0 GF: 0-1 Fm: 0-0
Distance: 5f/6f: 0-1 7f-8f: 0-3 9f-13f: 0-0 14f+: 0-0
Track : LH: 0-3 RH: 0-0 Tight: 0-1 Gall: 0-1
Aids: Bl: 0-1 Vi: 0-0 Tstrap: 0-0
Best Rating: 73 9/01 Catt 5f212y gd-fm

Due West

84 **33**

3-y-o b f Inchinor-Western Sal (Salse (USA))
Mrs J R Ramsden Mrs J R Ramsden

Placings:400 **(1721)**
2001: 6^4HY, 7^0G, 8^0GF

	Starts	1st	2nd	3rd	Win & Pl
Career Total (Turf)	**3**	**0**	**0**	**0**	**289**

Going (Turf): Sf: 0-1 GS: 0-0 Gd: 0-1 GF: 0-1 Fm: 0-0
Distance: 5f/6f: 0-1 7f-8f: 0-2 9f-13f: 0-0 14f+: 0-0
Track : LH: 0-2 RH: 0-1 Tight: 0-2 Gall: 0-0
Aids: Bl: 0-0 Vi: 0-1 Tstrap: 0-0
Best Rating: 33 5/01 Thsk 7f good

Duel Island

(72) **46**

6-y-o b g Jupiter Island-Duellist (Town Crier)
A G Hobbs C J Hitchings

Placings:24400/00/00 **(0346)**
2001: 9^0SW, 16^0SD

	Starts	1st	2nd	3rd	Win & Pl
Career Total (Turf)	**7**	**0**	**1**	**0**	**1354**
Career Total (AW)	**2**	**0**	**0**	**0**	

Going (Turf): Sf: 0-0 GS: 0-2 Gd: 0-3 GF: 0-2 Fm: 0-0
Distance: 5f/6f: 0-0 7f-8f: 0-0 9f-13f: 0-8 14f+: 0-1
Track : LH: 0-6 RH: 0-2 Tight: 0-6 Gall: 0-0
Aids: Bl: 0-1 Vi: 0-0 Tstrap: 0-2

Duello

(98) (65) **73**

10-y-o b g Sure Blade (USA)-Royal Loft (Homing)
M C Pipe M C Pipe

Placings:53466/00600030602/2**35**260054031200/2001 33264413020/**4**004564524000020/00040435202166/02 05050521/33311-1121652**3** **(5615)**
2001: 10^1G, 0^1GF, 10^2GF, 12^1GF, 11^6G, 12^5GS, 12^2G, **12**^{3}GD

	Starts	1st	2nd	3rd	Win & Pl
Career Total (Turf)	**95**	**10**	**15**	**10**	**60013**
Career Total (AW)	**4**	**0**	**0**	**2**	**1146**

68	7/01	Wwck	1m4f134y	E(0-75)H	G-F	£3066
56	6/01	Brig	1m1f209y	F(0-60)	G-F	£2338
64	6/01	Hayd	1m2f120y	G(0-70)H	GD	£2296
44	8/00	Folk	1m4f	G	G-F	£1897
38	7/00	Bath	1m3f144y	F	FRM	£2317
53	10/99	Leic	1m3f183y	F	GD	£2784
59	9/98	Nott	1m6f15y	E(0-70)H	G-F	£3951
66	9/96	Newb	7f64y	C(0-95)H	G-F	£6193
62	5/96	Newb	7f64y	D(0-85)H	SFT	£5410
62	9/95	Epsm	1m114y	D(0-75)H	SFT	£4650

Total win prize-money £34902

Going (Turf): Sf: 2-17 GS: 0-11 Gd: 2-26 **GF: 5-38** Fm: 1-3
Distance: 5f/6f: 0-3 7f-8f: 2-45 **9f-13f: 7-44** 14f+: 1-7
Track : **LH: 8-35** RH: 2-30 **Tight: 3-25** Gall: 2-11
Aids: Bl: 0-1 **Vi: 5-11** Tstrap: 0-0
Best Rating: 73 6/01 Newc 1m2f32y gd-fm

Best when being held up for a late run, he had a productive summer over middle distances, and is at his best on fast ground.

Duke Of Earl (IRE)

101 **84+**

2-y-o ch c Ali-Royal (IRE)-Faye (Monsanto (FR))
S Kirk Speedlith Group

Placings:0030024110 **(5401)**
2001: 5^0S, 5^0GS, 6^3GF, 7^0G, 7^0G, 7^2GS, 7^4GF, 7^1S, 8^1HY, 8^0S

	Starts	1st	2nd	3rd	Win & Pl
Career Total (Turf)	**10**	**2**	**1**	**1**	**8621**

84	10/01	Wind	1m67y	E(0-75)	HVY	£3332
82	9/01	Brig	7f214y	F	SFT	£2688

Total win prize-money £6020

Going (Turf): Sf: 2-4 GS: 0-2 Gd: 0-2 GF: 0-2 Fm: 0-0
Distance: 5f/6f: 0-2 7f-8f: 1-6 9f-13f: 1-2 14f+: 0-0
Track : LH: 1-2 RH: 1-5 **Tight: 1-2** Gall: 0-1
Aids: Bl: 0-0 Vi: 0-0 Tstrap: 0-0
Best Rating: 84 10/01 Wind 1m67y heavy

Modest form in maiden and nursery company, getting off the mark in a weak race in soft ground at Brighton and following up in a Windsor nursery on heavy ground.

Duke Of Modena

113 **104**

4-y-o ch g Salse (USA)-Palace Street (USA) (Secreto (USA))
G B Balding Miss B Swire

Placings:603/115144614-6200003000 **(5607)**
2001: 7^6G, 8^2G, 8^0GF, 7^0G, 7^0GF, 7^0G, 7^3G, 7^0S, 7^0S, 8^0GS

	Starts	1st	2nd	3rd	Win & Pl
Career Total (Turf)	**22**	**4**	**1**	**2**	**94757**

101	9/00	Asct	7f	B H	G-S	£43500
96	6/00	Newb	7f	B(0-105)H	G-F	£13044
91	5/00	Sals	6f	B(0-100)H	G-F	£9106
85	4/00	Kemp	6f	D(0-85)H	SFT	£5414

Total win prize-money £71066

Going (Turf): Sf: 1-6 GS: 1-3 Gd: 0-7 **GF: 2-6** Fm: 0-0
Distance: 5f/6f: 2-3 7f-8f: 2-18 9f-13f: 0-1 14f+: 0-0
Track : LH: 0-2 RH: 0-4 Tight: 0-0 Gall: 0-3
Aids: Bl: 0-0 Vi: 0-0 Tstrap: 0-0
Best Rating: 104 8/01 York 7f202y good

Classy handicapper at around seven furlongs who is versatile with regard to underfoot conditions. Running well this year and capable of winning another decent handicap.

Dulcet Spear

101 **96+**

2-y-o b c Vettori (IRE)-Honeyspike (IRE) (Chief's Crown (USA))
D R Loder Sheikh Mohammed

Placings:110 **(4430)**
2001: 7^1GF, 7^1GF, 7^0G

	Starts	1st	2nd	3rd	Win & Pl
Career Total (Turf)	**3**	**2**	**0**	**0**	**14601**

96	7/01	Newb	7f	B	G-F	£11170
85	7/01	Sthl	7f	E	G-F	£3430

Total win prize-money £14601

Going (Turf): Sf: 0-0 GS: 0-0 Gd: 0-1 **GF: 2-2** Fm: 0-0
Distance: 5f/6f: 0-0 **7f-8f: 2-3** 9f-13f: 0-0 14f+: 0-0
Track : **LH: 1-1** RH: 0-1 Tight: 0-0 Gall: 0-0
Aids: Bl: 0-0 Vi: 0-0 Tstrap: 0-0
Best Rating: 96 7/01 Newb 7f gd-fm

Bred to get a mile, he is a half-brother to the juvenile winners Unicamp and Via Camp. Made a winning debut in four runner maiden over seven furlongs at Southwell in July and followed up in better class at Newbury before disappointing when favourite for the Solario at Sandown.

Dulcification

98 **64**

3-y-o b c So Factual (USA)-Dunloe (IRE) (Shaadi (USA))
J R Weymes Mrs R L Heaton

Placings:04-224504300 **(5375)**

2001: 6^{2}GF, 5^{2}GF, 5^{4}GF, 6^{5}GF, 8^{0}GS, 7^{4}GF, 8^{3}GF, 8^{0}G, 7^{0}G

	Starts	1st	2nd	3rd	Win & Pl
Career Total (Turf)	11	0	2	1	3116

Going (Turf): Sf: 0-0 GS: 0-2 Gd: 0-2 GF: 0-6 Fm: 0-1
Distance: 5f/6f: 0-6 7f-8f: 0-3 9f-13f: 0-2 14f+: 0-0
Track : LH: 0-1 RH: 0-1 Tight: 0-1 Gall: 0-0
Aids: Bl: 0-1 Vi: 0-0 Tstrap: 0-0
Best Rating: 69 5/01 Thsk 6f gd-fm

Dulzie

(98) (38) **32**

4-y-o b f Safawan-Dulzura (Daring March)
A P Jarvis Mrs D B Brazier

Placings:60/246550040-6110630000 **(4606)**
2001: 9^{6}SD, 11^{1}SD, 12^{1}SD, 11^{0}GS, 9^{6}G, 11^{3}GF, 16^{0}GF, 11^{0}GS, 11^{0}GF, 12^{0}SD

	Starts	1st	2nd	3rd	Win & Pl
Career Total (Turf)	12	0	0	1	426
Career Total (AW)	9	2	1	0	4437

37 4/01 Sthl 1m4f G STD £1830
38 3/01 Sthl 1m3f G STD £1869
Total win prize-money £3700

Going (Turf): Sf: 0-0 GS: 0-4 Gd: 0-3 GF: 0-5 Fm: 0-0
Distance: 5f/6f: 0-0 7f-8f: 0-5 **9f-13f: 2-15** 14f+: 0-1
Track : **LH: 2-15** RH: 0-4 Tight: 0-6 Gall: 0-0
Aids: Bl: 0-0 Vi: 0-0 Tstrap: 0-0
Best Rating: 38 3/01 Sthl 1m3f stand

Dumaran (IRE)

105 **82**
3-y-o b c Be My Chief (USA)-Pine Needle (Kris)
I A Balding Exors Of The Late Robert Hitchins

Placings:0-151006 **(5267)**
2001: 7^{1}G, 8^{5}S, 9^{1}GS, 9^{0}G, 10^{0}HY, 6^{6}GS

	Starts	1st	2nd	3rd	Win & Pl
Career Total (Turf)	7	2	0	0	18600

82 8/01 Gdwd 1m1f C(0-95)H G-S £14560
76 7/01 Chep 7f16y D GD £4040
Total win prize-money £18600

Going (Turf): Sf: 0-2 **GS: 1-2 Gd: 1-2** GF: 0-1 Fm: 0-0
Distance: 5f/6f: 0-0 7f-8f: 1-3 9f-13f: 1-4 14f+: 0-0
Track : LH: 0-2 **RH: 1-2 Tight: 1-1** Gall: 0-1
Aids: Bl: 0-0 Vi: 0-0 Tstrap: 0-0
Best Rating: 82 10/01 York 6f214y gd-sft

Out of a mare who won at up to 14 furlongs, he scored at Chepstow in July in the style of one who really needs further. He ran too keen on his first try on soft ground next time, but bounced back at Goodwood before a rise in the handicap appeared to find him out. Stays nine furlongs and acts on an easy surface.

Dun Distinctly (IRE)

(100) (49) **49**
4-y-o b g Distinctly North (USA)-Dunbally (Dunphy)
P C Haslam Lady Kitson

Placings:40000/42656-41 **(0094)**
2001: 12^{4}SD, 12^{1}SD

	Starts	1st	2nd	3rd	Win & Pl
Career Total (Turf)	6	0	0	0	405
Career Total (AW)	6	1	1	0	2526

49 1/01 Sthl 1m4f F(0-60)H STD £1666
Total win prize-money £1666

Going (Turf): Sf: 0-2 GS: 0-1 Gd: 0-3 GF: 0-0 Fm: 0-0
Distance: 5f/6f: 0-4 7f-8f: 0-2 **9f-13f: 1-6** 14f+: 0-0
Track : **LH: 1-9** RH: 0-0 Tight: 0-3 Gall: 0-0
Aids: Bl: 0-0 Vi: 0-1 Tstrap: 0-0
Best Rating: 49 1/01 Sthl 1m4f stand

Dunbrody River (IRE)

53(78) **37**
4-y-o b f River Falls-Caria (IRE) (Sure Blade (USA))
J J Quinn Mrs H A Letzerich

Placings:640000/0040504-00 **(1000)**
2001: 7^{0}SW, 10^{0}S

	Starts	1st	2nd	3rd	Win & Pl
Career Total (Turf)	14	0	0	0	580
Career Total (AW)	1	0	0	0	

Going (Turf): Sf: 0-1 GS: 0-0 Gd: 0-3 GF: 0-2 Fm: 0-0
Distance: 5f/6f: 0-0 7f-8f: 0-8 9f-13f: 0-6 14f+: 0-0
Track : LH: 0-3 RH: 0-11 Tight: 0-1 Gall: 0-0
Aids: Bl: 0-0 Vi: 0-0 Tstrap: 0-3
Best Rating: 49 1/01 Sthl 1m4f stand

Dundonald

36
2-y-o ch g Magic Ring (IRE)-Cal Norma's Lady (IRE) (Lyphard's Special (USA))
K A Ryan Kenneth Macpherson

Placings:5 **(5268)**
2001: 7^{5}HY

	Starts	1st	2nd	3rd	Win & Pl
Career Total (Turf)	1	0	0	0	0

Going (Turf): Sf: 0-1 GS: 0-0 Gd: 0-0 GF: 0-0 Fm: 0-0
Distance: 5f/6f: 0-0 7f-8f: 0-1 9f-13f: 0-0 14f+: 0-0
Track : LH: 0-0 RH: 0-0 Tight: 0-0 Gall: 0-0
Aids: Bl: 0-0 Vi: 0-0 Tstrap: 0-0
Best Rating: 36 10/01 Ayr 7f50y heavy

Dune

89 **69**
2-y-o b c Desert King (IRE)-Flamands (IRE) (Sadler's Wells (USA))
R Charlton Mountgrange Stud

Placings:00 **(5682)**
2001: 7^{0}GS, 7^{0}S

	Starts	1st	2nd	3rd	Win & Pl
Career Total (Turf)	2	0	0	0	

Going (Turf): Sf: 0-1 GS: 0-1 Gd: 0-0 GF: 0-0 Fm: 0-0
Distance: 5f/6f: 0-0 7f-8f: 0-2 9f-13f: 0-0 14f+: 0-0
Track : LH: 0-0 RH: 0-0 Tight: 0-0 Gall: 0-0
Aids: Bl: 0-0 Vi: 0-0 Tstrap: 0-0
Best Rating: 69 11/01 Donc 7f soft

Dunedin Rascal

(106) (75+) **69**
4-y-o b g Piccolo-Thorner Lane (Tina's Pet)
E A Wheeler (T Stack 22/2) Halewood International Ltd

Placings:54/33042310-0103642000006000 **(5462)**
2001: 5^{0}SD, 5^{1}SW, 6^{0}SD, 6^{3}SD, 5^{6}S, 5^{4}GS, 5^{2}GF, 6^{0}GF, 5^{0}GF, 5^{0}F, 5^{0}GF, 5^{0}GF, 5^{6}GF, 5^{0}G, 5^{0}F, 5^{0}G

	Starts	1st	2nd	3rd	Win & Pl
Career Total (Turf)	22	1	2	3	12275
Career Total (AW)	4	1	0	1	4435

75 3/01 Ling 5f D(0-85)H SLW £3835
89 9/00 Fair 6f G-F £4140
Total win prize-money £7975

Going (Turf): Sf: 0-2 GS: 0-1 Gd: 0-3 **GF: 1-8** Fm: 0-3
Distance: **5f/6f: 2-26** 7f-8f: 0-0 9f-13f: 0-0 14f+: 0-0

Track : LH: 1-9 RH: 1-2 **Tight: 1-4** Gall: 0-3
Aids: Bl: 0-1 Vi: 0-0 Tstrap: 0-0
Best Rating: 81 5/01 Ches 5f16y gd-fm

Fair sprint handicapper, goes well on a tight left-handed track and looks best suited by fast ground.

Dunkeld Champ

60 **12**
4-y-o br g Be My Chief (USA)-Callipoli (USA) (Green Dancer (USA))
P Monteith J W D Campbell

Placings:00/000-06 **(0687)**
2001: 9^{0}S, 8^{6}S

	Starts	1st	2nd	3rd	Win & Pl
Career Total (Turf)	7	0	0	0	0

Going (Turf): Sf: 0-2 GS: 0-1 Gd: 0-2 GF: 0-1 Fm: 0-1
Distance: 5f/6f: 0-1 7f-8f: 0-4 9f-13f: 0-2 14f+: 0-0
Track : LH: 0-0 RH: 0-4 Tight: 0-4 Gall: 0-0
Aids: Bl: 0-0 Vi: 0-0 Tstrap: 0-0
Best Rating: 3 4/01 Muss 1m soft

Dunkerron

99 **78**
4-y-o b g Pursuit Of Love-Top Berry (High Top)
P L Gilligan Lady Bland

Placings:34300 **(5293)**
2001: 10^{3}GF, 11^{4}G, 8^{3}GS, 8^{0}GF, 9^{0}S

	Starts	1st	2nd	3rd	Win & Pl
Career Total (Turf)	5	0	0	2	1512

Going (Turf): Sf: 0-1 GS: 0-1 Gd: 0-1 GF: 0-2 Fm: 0-0
Distance: 5f/6f: 0-0 7f-8f: 0-2 9f-13f: 0-3 14f+: 0-0
Track : LH: 0-3 RH: 0-2 Tight: 0-1 Gall: 0-1
Aids: Bl: 0-0 Vi: 0-2 Tstrap: 0-0
Best Rating: 85 6/01 Donc 1m2f60y gd-fm

Dunkineely Boy (IRE)

(90) (37) **65**
3-y-o b c Hamas (IRE)-Eimkar (Junius (USA))
R Hannon The South-Western Partnership Ii

Placings:560204325630 **(5416)**
2001: 8^{5}GS, 9^{6}GS, 8^{0}S, 8^{2}F, 8^{0}GF, 10^{4}GF, 9^{3}GF, 8^{2}G, 9^{5}GF, 10^{6}S, 7^{3}S, 9^{0}SD

	Starts	1st	2nd	3rd	Win & Pl
Career Total (Turf)	11	0	2	2	3131
Career Total (AW)	1	0	0	0	

Going (Turf): Sf: 0-3 GS: 0-2 Gd: 0-1 GF: 0-4 Fm: 0-1
Distance: 5f/6f: 0-0 7f-8f: 0-3 9f-13f: 0-9 14f+: 0-0
Track : LH: 0-6 RH: 0-3 Tight: 0-7 Gall: 0-0
Aids: Bl: 0-0 Vi: 0-0 Tstrap: 0-0
Best Rating: 65 10/01 Brig 7f214y soft

A massive horse, he has run well in handicap company and handles undulating courses well for a horse of his size.

Dunkirk Spirit

91(85) (32) **38**
3-y-o b c Whittingham (IRE)-Ruda (FR) (Free Round (USA))
Mrs Lydia Pearce B & G Racing

Placings:0000-0000 **(3720)**
2001: 8^{0}G, 8^{0}GF, 12^{0}SD, 8^{0}G

	Starts	1st	2nd	3rd	Win & Pl
Career Total (Turf)	7	0	0	0	

Career Total (AW) 1 0 0 0

Going (Turf): Sf: 0-3 GS: 0-0 Gd: 0-2 GF: 0-2 Fm: 0-0
Distance: 5f/6f: 0-2 7f-8f: 0-2 9f-13f: 0-4 14f+: 0-0
Track : LH: 0-3 RH: 0-1 Tight: 0-1 Gall: 0-1
Aids: Bl: 0-0 Vi: 0-0 Tstrap: 0-0
Best Rating: 38 5/01 Wwck 1m22y good

Dunnes River (USA)

97 **75+**
3-y-o b f Danzig (USA)-Elizabeth Bay (USA) (Mr Prospector (USA))
Saeed Bin Suroor Godolphin

Placings:1 **(1984)**
2001: 8^{1}GF

	Starts	1st	2nd	3rd	Win & Pl
Career Total (Turf)	1	1	0	0	4524

75	6/01	Gdwd	1m	D	G-F	£4524

Total win prize-money £4524

Going (Turf): Sf: 0-0 GS: 0-0 Gd: 0-0 **GF: 1-1** Fm: 0-0
Distance: 5f/6f: 0-0 **7f-8f: 1-1** 9f-13f: 0-0 14f+: 0-0
Track : LH: 0-0 **RH: 1-1** Tight: 0-0 Gall: 0-0
Aids: Bl: 0-0 Vi: 0-0 Tstrap: 0-0
Best Rating: 75 6/01 Gdwd 1m gd-fm

Showed some ability in one of the Godolphin trials and made a winning debut in a proper race at Goodwood in June.

Dunston Durgam (IRE)

(69)
7-y-o b g Durgam (USA)-Blazing Sunset (Blazing Saddles (AUS))
R Hollinshead Mrs H J Bannister

Placings:36F500000005000/0/6 **(0104)**
2001: 12^{6}SW

	Starts	1st	2nd	3rd	Win & Pl
Career Total (Turf)	3	0	0	0	
Career Total (AW)	14	0	0	1	285

Going (Turf): Sf: 0-0 GS: 0-0 Gd: 0-2 GF: 0-1 Fm: 0-0
Distance: 5f/6f: 0-0 7f-8f: 0-1 9f-13f: 0-11 14f+: 0-5
Track : LH: 0-16 RH: 0-0 Tight: 0-4 Gall: 0-0
Aids: Bl: 0-0 Vi: 0-0 Tstrap: 0-0

Dupont

103 **94**
2-y-o b c Zafonic (USA)-June Moon (IRE) (Sadler's Wells (USA))
W J Haggas Wentworth Racing (pty) Ltd

Placings:21106 **(5053)**
2001: 6^{2}G, 6^{1}F, 7^{1}GF, 7^{0}G, 7^{6}S

	Starts	1st	2nd	3rd	Win & Pl
Career Total (Turf)	5	2	1	0	14890

94	8/01	Ling	7f	D	G-F	£3679
93	6/01	Donc	6f	E	FRM	£3802

Total win prize-money £7482

Going (Turf): Sf: 0-1 GS: 0-0 Gd: 0-2 **GF: 1-1 Fm: 1-1**
Distance: 5f/6f: 1-1 7f-8f: 1-4 9f-13f: 0-0 14f+: 0-0
Track : LH: 0-0 RH: 0-1 Tight: 0-0 Gall: 0-0
Aids: Bl: 0-0 Vi: 0-0 Tstrap: 0-0
Best Rating: 94 8/01 Ling 7f gd-fm

A brother to the miler Pacino, he stepped up on his debut to win a maiden at Doncaster in good style. Given a short break, he came back to win a novice event at Lingfield, but may have hurt himself leaving the stalls when unplaced in a Longchamp Group Three next time.

Stays seven furlongs, suited by fast ground.

Duraid (IRE)

105(78) (36)**82**
9-y-o ch g Irish River (FR)-Fateful Princess (USA) (Vaguely Noble)
Denys Smith A Suddes

Placings:40504102440410/004650500/62106010401/42141656440-00035330504 **(5638)**
2001: 8^{0}G, 10^{0}GF, 8^{0}GF, 7^{3}G, 8^{5}F, 8^{3}G, 7^{3}GF, 7^{0}GS, 8^{5}F, 8^{0}GS, 7^{4}G

	Starts	1st	2nd	3rd	Win & Pl
Career Total (Turf)	55	7	3	3	68843
Career Total (AW)	1	0	0	0	

83	7/00	York	7f202y	B(0-100)H	GD	£9483
79	6/00	Catt	7f	D(0-85)H	SFT	£4673
75	11/99	Catt	7f	D(0-80)H	SFT	£7360
68	8/99	Ripn	1m	C(0-100)H	G-F	£7165
65	7/99	Bevl	1m100y	D(0-85)H	G-F	£7025
82	9/97	Hayd	1m30y	D(0-85)H	GD	£3891
73	6/97	Newc	1m	D(0-85)H	GD	£7360

Total win prize-money £46958

Going (Turf): Sf: 2-6 GS: 0-2 **Gd: 3-22** GF: 2-22 Fm: 0-3
Distance: 5f/6f: 0-0 **7f-8f: 5-41** 9f-13f: 2-15 14f+: 0-0
Track : **LH: 5-35** RH: 2-13 **Tight: 3-18** Gall: 2-17
Aids: Bl: 0-0 Vi: 0-1 Tstrap: 0-0
Best Rating: 83 7/01 York 7f202y good

Come-from-behind 7f/1m handicapper who needs a fast pace to shine. Versatile as regards ground, and usually pops up once or twice a year.

Durandana (FR)

87 **63**
2-y-o b f Selkirk (USA)-Damanka (IRE) (Slip Anchor)
J R Fanshawe Mme R G Ehrnrooth

Placings:44 **(4625)**
2001: 7^{4}GS, 8^{4}GF

	Starts	1st	2nd	3rd	Win & Pl
Career Total (Turf)	2	0	0	0	0

Going (Turf): Sf: 0-0 GS: 0-1 Gd: 0-0 GF: 0-1 Fm: 0-0
Distance: 5f/6f: 0-0 7f-8f: 0-1 9f-13f: 0-1 14f+: 0-0
Track : LH: 0-2 RH: 0-0 Tight: 0-1 Gall: 0-0
Aids: Bl: 0-0 Vi: 0-0 Tstrap: 0-0
Best Rating: 63 9/01 Nott 1m54y gd-fm

Durham

(80) (35)
10-y-o ch g Caerleon (USA)-Sanctuary (Welsh Pageant)
J Neville Shark Racing

Placings:0/5244/**3**/**042**03351**2**234121103/00056422152065/36213043/20541632200/01503-05050600 **(4552)**
2001: 17^{0}GF, 17^{5}G, 18^{0}GF, 14^{5}GF, 14^{0}GF, 17^{6}GF, 14^{0}G, 14^{0}SW

	Starts	1st	2nd	3rd	Win & Pl
Career Total (Turf)	61	8	10	8	43823
Career Total (AW)	9	0	2	2	1968

60	6/00	Nott	1m6f15y	G(0-60)H	G-F	£2018
62	6/99	Gdwd	1m6f	D(0-85)H	G-F	£3881
64	7/98	Sand	1m6f	D(0-80)H	G-F	£4357
64	8/97	Yarm	1m6f17y	D(0-80)H	G-F	£3677
68	9/96	Ayr	1m5f13y	C(0-90)H	G-F	£6264
61	9/96	Kemp	1m6f92y	E(0-70)H	GD	£3176
55	8/96	Ling	1m6f	F	G-F	£2588
56	6/96	Nott	1m6f15y	F(0-70)H	G-F	£2742

Total win prize-money £28705

Going (Turf): Sf: 0-7 GS: 0-2 Gd: 1-17 **GF: 7-33** Fm: 0-2
Distance: 5f/6f: 0-0 7f-8f: 0-2 9f-13f: 0-11 **14f+: 8-57**
Track : **LH: 5-41** RH: 3-28 **Tight: 3-32** Gall: 0-10
Aids: **Bl: 8-51** Vi: 0-7 Tstrap: 0-8
Best Rating: 45 7/01 Nott 1m6f15y gd-fm

Something of a character, he was a fair sort in modest staying handicaps, but needed fast ground. (DEAD)

Durkar Star (IRE)

86 **38**
3-y-o b g Bin Ajwaad (IRE)-Faith Alone (Safawan)
M C Chapman Eric Knowles

Placings:0000 **(3366)**
2001: 7^{0}G, 5^{0}G, 7^{0}GF, 5^{0}G

	Starts	1st	2nd	3rd	Win & Pl
Career Total (Turf)	4	0	0	0	

Going (Turf): Sf: 0-0 GS: 0-0 Gd: 0-3 GF: 0-1 Fm: 0-0
Distance: 5f/6f: 0-2 7f-8f: 0-2 9f-13f: 0-0 14f+: 0-0
Track : LH: 0-1 RH: 0-1 Tight: 0-1 Gall: 0-0
Aids: Bl: 0-0 Vi: 0-0 Tstrap: 0-0
Best Rating: 38 5/01 Bevl 5f good

Dusky Blue (IRE)

86 **52**
2-y-o b c Bluebird (USA)-Massada (Most Welcome)
J J O'Neill Mrs G Smith

Placings:600 **(4565)**
2001: 5^{6}GF, 5^{0}GF, 5^{0}HY

	Starts	1st	2nd	3rd	Win & Pl
Career Total (Turf)	3	0	0	0	0

Going (Turf): Sf: 0-1 GS: 0-0 Gd: 0-0 GF: 0-2 Fm: 0-0
Distance: 5f/6f: 0-3 7f-8f: 0-0 9f-13f: 0-0 14f+: 0-0
Track : LH: 0-1 RH: 0-0 Tight: 0-0 Gall: 0-0
Aids: Bl: 0-0 Vi: 0-0 Tstrap: 0-0
Best Rating: 52 8/01 Pont 5f gd-fm

Dusky Virgin

100 **60**
4-y-o b f Missed Flight-Rosy Sunset (IRE) (Red Sunset)
S Woodman Mrs W Edgar

Placings:00651/0040212320-35 **(2366)**
2001: 7^{3}F, 7^{5}GF

	Starts	1st	2nd	3rd	Win & Pl
Career Total (Turf)	17	2	3	2	10844

58	8/00	Epsm	1m114y	E(0-75)H	GD	£4270
59	8/99	Brig	6f209y	F	FRM	£2211

Total win prize-money £6482

Going (Turf): Sf: 0-0 GS: 0-0 **Gd: 1-6** GF: 0-5 **Fm: 1-6**
Distance: 5f/6f: 0-5 7f-8f: 1-8 9f-13f: 1-4 14f+: 0-0
Track : **LH: 2-11** RH: 0-2 **Tight: 1-2** Gall: 0-1
Aids: Bl: 0-0 Vi: 0-0 Tstrap: 0-0
Best Rating: 58 5/01 Brig 7f214y firm

Dusky Warbler

102 **101**
2-y-o br g Ezzoud (IRE)-Bronzewing (Beldale Flutter (USA))
M L W Bell Sir Thomas Pilkington

Placings:12 **(5606)**
2001: 7^{1}G, 10^{2}GS

	Starts	1st	2nd	3rd	Win & Pl
Career Total (Turf)	2	1	1	0	10506

101	9/01	NmkR	7f	D	GD	£5824

Total win prize-money £5824

Going (Turf): Sf: 0-0 GS: 0-1 **Gd: 1-1** GF: 0-0 Fm: 0-0

Distance: 5f/6f: 0-0 **7f-8f: 1-1** 9f-13f: 0-1 14f+: 0-0
Track : LH: 0-0 RH: 0-0 Tight: 0-0 Gall: 0-0
Aids: Bl: 0-0 Vi: 0-0 Tstrap: 0-0
Best Rating: 101 9/01 NmkR 7f good

A half-brother to Merry Merlin, he was awarded a Newmarket maiden on his debut over seven furlongs. Placed in Listed company subsequently. Acts on good ground.

Dust Flicker

88 **74**

2-y-o ch f Suave Dancer (USA)-Galaxie Dust (USA) (Blushing Groom (FR))
J L Dunlop Hesmonds Stud

Placings:0 **(5274)**
2001: 7^{0}GS

	Starts	1st	2nd	3rd	Win & Pl
Career Total (Turf)	1	0	0	0	

Going (Turf): Sf: 0-0 GS: 0-1 Gd: 0-0 GF: 0-0 Fm: 0-0
Distance: 5f/6f: 0-0 7f-8f: 0-1 9f-13f: 0-0 14f+: 0-0
Track : LH: 0-0 RH: 0-0 Tight: 0-0 Gall: 0-0
Aids: Bl: 0-0 Vi: 0-0 Tstrap: 0-0
Best Rating: 74 10/01 Leic 7f9y gd-sft

Dust To Dust (IRE)

(92) (69)**55**

2-y-o ch g College Chapel-Poscimur (IRE) (Prince Rupert (FR))
A Crook (W G M Turner 15/6) Jay Dee Bloodstock Limited

Placings:061000 **(5408)**
2001: 5^{0}GS, 6^{0}GS, 5^{1}SD, 6^{0}G, 5^{0}SD, 6^{0}SD

	Starts	1st	2nd	3rd	Win & Pl
Career Total (Turf)	3	0	0	0	0
Career Total (AW)	3	1	0	0	2282

69 5/01 Sthl 5f F STD £2282
Total win prize-money £2282

Going (Turf): Sf: 0-0 GS: 0-2 Gd: 0-1 GF: 0-0 Fm: 0-0
Distance: 5f/6f: 1-6 7f-8f: 0-0 9f-13f: 0-0 14f+: 0-0
Track : LH: 0-3 RH: 0-1 Tight: 0-1 Gall: 0-1
Aids: Bl: 0-0 Vi: 0-0 Tstrap: 0-0
Best Rating: 69 5/01 Sthl 5f stand

He did not take to easy ground on the turf and needed the relatively fast sand at Southwell to clock up a win in claiming company in May 2001. He has failed to trouble the judges since.

Dusty Answer

100 **76**

2-y-o b f Zafonic (USA)-Dust Dancer (Suave Dancer (USA))
J L Dunlop Hesmonds Stud

Placings:21 **(3557)**
2001: 7^{2}GF, 7^{1}GF

	Starts	1st	2nd	3rd	Win & Pl
Career Total (Turf)	2	1	1	0	5652

76 8/01 Kemp 7f D G-F £4368
Total win prize-money £4368

Going (Turf): Sf: 0-0 GS: 0-0 Gd: 0-0 **GF: 1-2** Fm: 0-0
Distance: 5f/6f: 0-0 **7f-8f: 1-2** 9f-13f: 0-0 14f+: 0-0
Track : LH: 0-0 **RH: 1-2** Tight: 0-0 **Gall: 1-2**
Aids: Bl: 0-0 Vi: 0-0 Tstrap: 0-0
Best Rating: 76 8/01 Kemp 7f gd-fm

A 120,000gns first foal of a high-class ten-furlong winner, she ran with plenty of promise on her Kempton debut and scored nicely on her only other run at the same track. Has only raced at seven furlongs on fast ground.

Dusty Bankes

(90) (50)**64**

2-y-o ch f Greensmith-Heather Honey (Insan (USA))
W G M Turner T Lightbowne

Placings:32313120212060 **(5195)**
2001: 5^{3}SD, 5^{2}SD, 5^{3}S, 5^{1}SD, 5^{3}F, 5^{1}GF, 6^{2}GF, 5^{0}G, 5^{2}GF, 6^{1}GF, 7^{2}F, 6^{0}GF, 7^{6}HY, 6^{0}SD

	Starts	1st	2nd	3rd	Win & Pl
Career Total (Turf)	10	2	3	2	7625
Career Total (AW)	4	1	1	1	2607

64 7/01 Newc 6f F G-F £2310
72 6/01 Muss 5f G G-F £2194
50 4/01 Sthl 5f G STD £1827
Total win prize-money £6332

Going (Turf): Sf: 0-2 GS: 0-0 Gd: 0-1 **GF: 2-5** Fm: 0-2
Distance: 5f/6f: 3-10 7f-8f: 0-4 9f-13f: 0-0 14f+: 0-0
Track : LH: 0-6 RH: 0-0 Tight: 0-4 Gall: 0-0
Aids: Bl: 0-0 Vi: 0-0 Tstrap: 0-0
Best Rating: 72 6/01 Muss 5f gd-fm

A plating-class filly, she is suited to sprinting on a fast surface.

Dusty Carpet

106(101) (79)**82**

3-y-o ch g Pivotal-Euridice (IRE) (Woodman (USA))
C A Dwyer Mrs C M Goode

Placings:6464303021-35233220 **(5279)**
2001: 7^{3}G, 8^{5}GF, 7^{2}GF, 10^{3}G, 10^{3}GS, 10^{2}GS, 10^{2}S, 11^{0}S

	Starts	1st	2nd	3rd	Win & Pl
Career Total (Turf)	16	0	3	5	11771
Career Total (AW)	2	1	1	0	3681

78 12/00 Wolv 1m100y D STD £2716
Total win prize-money £2716

Going (Turf): Sf: 0-3 GS: 0-2 Gd: 0-7 GF: 0-4 Fm: 0-0
Distance: 5f/6f: 0-2 7f-8f: 0-9 **9f-13f: 1-7** 14f+: 0-0
Track : LH: 1-9 RH: 0-1 **Tight: 1-6** Gall: 0-2
Aids: Bl: 0-0 Vi: 0-0 Tstrap: 0-0
Best Rating: 82 9/01 Pont 1m2f6y soft

Dusty Democrat

(82) (40)**12**

3-y-o b g Democratic (USA)-Two Shots (Dom Racine (FR))
W G M Turner Tocs Ltd

Placings:000045-0 **(0107)**
2001: 8^{0}SW

	Starts	1st	2nd	3rd	Win & Pl
Career Total (Turf)	2	0	0	0	
Career Total (AW)	6	0	0	0	0

Going (Turf): Sf: 0-1 GS: 0-0 Gd: 0-0 GF: 0-1 Fm: 0-0
Distance: 5f/6f: 0-2 7f-8f: 0-5 9f-13f: 0-1 14f+: 0-0
Track : LH: 0-6 RH: 0-1 Tight: 0-6 Gall: 0-0
Aids: Bl: 0-0 Vi: 0-1 Tstrap: 0-0
Best Rating: 25 1/01 Wolv 1m100y slow

Dusty Star

(44)

2-y-o b f Danzig Connection (USA)-Sindos (Busted)
W G M Turner Tocs Ltd

Placings:00 **(5396)**
2001: 8^{0}GF, 8^{0}SD

	Starts	1st	2nd	3rd	Win & Pl
Career Total (Turf)	1	0	0	0	
Career Total (AW)	1	0	0	0	

Going (Turf): Sf: 0-0 GS: 0-0 Gd: 0-0 GF: 0-1 Fm: 0-0
Distance: 5f/6f: 0-0 7f-8f: 0-0 9f-13f: 0-2 14f+: 0-0
Track : LH: 0-1 RH: 0-1 Tight: 0-1 Gall: 0-0
Aids: Bl: 0-0 Vi: 0-0 Tstrap: 0-0

Dusty Wugg (IRE)

100 **70**

2-y-o b f General Monash (USA)-Welsh Berry (USA) (Sir Ivor)
T D Easterby Mrs Jennifer Houghton

Placings:6444420 **(5504)**
2001: 5^{6}GF, 5^{4}GF, 5^{4}GF, 6^{4}G, 6^{4}GS, 7^{2}S, 7^{0}HY

	Starts	1st	2nd	3rd	Win & Pl
Career Total (Turf)	7	0	1	0	2278

Going (Turf): Sf: 0-2 GS: 0-1 Gd: 0-1 GF: 0-3 Fm: 0-0
Distance: 5f/6f: 0-5 7f-8f: 0-2 9f-13f: 0-0 14f+: 0-0
Track : LH: 0-2 RH: 0-0 Tight: 0-1 Gall: 0-0
Aids: Bl: 0-2 Vi: 0-0 Tstrap: 0-0
Best Rating: 70 10/01 Catt 7f soft

Dutch Dyane

94(93) (35)**46**

8-y-o b m Midyan (USA)-Double Dutch (Nicholas Bill)
G P Enright L Fuller, Miss P Ross, Neil Kenworthy

Placings:00/6062/0032/03/5300-00004 **(2965)**
2001: 16^{0}S, 14^{0}SD, 16^{0}SD, 16^{0}GF, 16^{4}GF

	Starts	1st	2nd	3rd	Win & Pl
Career Total (Turf)	14	0	2	3	2791
Career Total (AW)	7	0	0	0	0

Going (Turf): Sf: 0-8 GS: 0-1 Gd: 0-1 GF: 0-4 Fm: 0-0
Distance: 5f/6f: 0-0 7f-8f: 0-0 9f-13f: 0-5 14f+: 0-16
Track : LH: 0-14 RH: 0-7 Tight: 0-9 Gall: 0-2
Aids: Bl: 0-0 Vi: 0-0 Tstrap: 0-0
Best Rating: 46 4/01 Kemp 2m soft

Moderate staying handicapper..

Dutch Nightingale

(46) **41**

7-y-o b m Warrshan (USA)-Double Dutch (Nicholas Bill)
G P Enright The Aedean Partnership

Placings:00/60600/0 **(0224)**
2001: 13^{0}SD

	Starts	1st	2nd	3rd	Win & Pl
Career Total (Turf)	7	0	0	0	0
Career Total (AW)	1	0	0	0	

Going (Turf): Sf: 0-3 GS: 0-2 Gd: 0-0 GF: 0-2 Fm: 0-0
Distance: 5f/6f: 0-0 7f-8f: 0-0 9f-13f: 0-8 14f+: 0-0
Track : LH: 0-3 RH: 0-4 Tight: 0-5 Gall: 0-0
Aids: Bl: 0-0 Vi: 0-0 Tstrap: 0-0

Dynamic Times

76 **26**

2-y-o ch g Timeless Times (USA)-Naufrage (Main Reef)
M W Easterby B Bargh,P Berry,K Wreglesworth & R Tyson

Placings:00 **(2266)**
2001: 5^{0}GF, 6^{0}G

	Starts	1st	2nd	3rd	Win & Pl
Career Total (Turf)	2	0	0	0	

Going (Turf): Sf: 0-0 GS: 0-0 Gd: 0-1 GF: 0-1 Fm: 0-0
Distance: 5f/6f: 0-2 7f-8f: 0-0 9f-13f: 0-0 14f+: 0-0
Track : LH: 0-0 RH: 0-0 Tight: 0-0 Gall: 0-0
Aids: Bl: 0-0 Vi: 0-0 Tstrap: 0-0
Best Rating: 26 6/01 Bevl 5f gd-fm

E Minor (IRE)

88 **66**

2-y-o b f Blushing Flame (USA)-Watch The Clock (Mtoto)

G A Butler Thyroidea Ab Ecurie Adiel

Placings:0050 **(5467)**

2001: 5^{0}G, 6^{0}HY, 5^{5}GS, 6^{0}S

	Starts	1st	2nd	3rd	Win & Pl
Career Total (Turf)	4	0	0	0	0

Going (Turf): Sf: 0-2 GS: 0-1 Gd: 0-1 GF: 0-0 Fm: 0-0
Distance: 5f/6f: 0-2 7f-8f: 0-2 9f-13f: 0-0 14f+: 0-0
Track : LH: 0-2 RH: 0-0 Tight: 0-0 Gall: 0-1
Aids: Bl: 0-0 Vi: 0-0 Tstrap: 0-0
Best Rating: 66 10/01 Nott 6f15y heavy

Has shown little ability so far, should do better with age.

Eachy Peachy (IRE)

92(87) (56)**59**

2-y-o ch f Perugino (USA)-Miss Big John (IRE) (Martin John)

J R Best Damian Walker

Placings:053004420 **(5342)**

2001: 5^{0}SD, 5^{5}GS, 5^{3}SD, 5^{0}SD, 7^{0}SD, 6^{4}GF, 8^{4}GF, 7^{2}G, 7^{0}GS

	Starts	1st	2nd	3rd	Win & Pl
Career Total (Turf)	5	0	1	0	752
Career Total (AW)	4	0	0	1	340

Going (Turf): Sf: 0-0 GS: 0-2 Gd: 0-1 GF: 0-2 Fm: 0-0
Distance: 5f/6f: 0-5 7f-8f: 0-3 9f-13f: 0-1 14f+: 0-0
Track : LH: 0-2 RH: 0-1 Tight: 0-1 Gall: 0-0
Aids: Bl: 0-0 Vi: 0-0 Tstrap: 0-0
Best Rating: 59 9/01 Bevl 7f100y good

Eager Angel (IRE)

88(81) (36)**25**

3-y-o b f Up And At 'Em-Seanee Squaw (Indian Ridge)

J L Eyre C I S Racing

Placings:500-000040 **(3672)**

2001: 6^{0}G, 6^{0}F, 5^{0}F, 7^{0}GF, 6^{4}SD, 5^{0}G

	Starts	1st	2nd	3rd	Win & Pl
Career Total (Turf)	8	0	0	0	0
Career Total (AW)	1	0	0	0	0

Going (Turf): Sf: 0-0 GS: 0-0 Gd: 0-3 GF: 0-3 Fm: 0-2
Distance: 5f/6f: 0-7 7f-8f: 0-2 9f-13f: 0-0 14f+: 0-0
Track : LH: 0-2 RH: 0-1 Tight: 0-0 Gall: 0-0
Aids: Bl: 0-2 Vi: 0-0 Tstrap: 0-0
Best Rating: 36 7/01 Sthl 6f stand

Eagle Park (IRE)

99 **70**

2-y-o ch g Eagle Eyed (USA)-Avidal Park (Horage)

J L Eyre Billy Parker

Placings:00340434 **(5031)**

2001: 5^{0}GF, 7^{0}G, 7^{3}G, 7^{4}GS, 8^{0}GF, 8^{4}GF, 8^{3}GF, 8^{4}GF

	Starts	1st	2nd	3rd	Win & Pl
Career Total (Turf)	8	0	0	2	1966

Going (Turf): Sf: 0-0 GS: 0-1 Gd: 0-2 GF: 0-5 Fm: 0-0
Distance: 5f/6f: 0-1 7f-8f: 0-5 9f-13f: 0-2 14f+: 0-0
Track : LH: 0-1 RH: 0-4 Tight: 0-4 Gall: 0-0
Aids: Bl: 0-0 Vi: 0-0 Tstrap: 0-0
Best Rating: 70 9/01 Muss 1m gd-fm

Has shown signs of ability in small races in the north. Usually ridden from behind.

Eagle's Landing

87(104) (68+)**52**

3-y-o b f Eagle Eyed (USA)-Anchorage (IRE) (Slip Anchor)

N A Graham Paul G Jacobs

Placings:02-23310 **(1326)**

2001: 8^{2}SD, 8^{3}SD, 9^{3}SD, 11^{1}SD, 11^{0}G

	Starts	1st	2nd	3rd	Win & Pl
Career Total (Turf)	1	0	0	0	
Career Total (AW)	6	1	2	2	5073

68 3/01 Sthl 1m3f E(0-70)H STD £2786
Total win prize-money £2786

Going (Turf): Sf: 0-0 GS: 0-0 Gd: 0-1 GF: 0-0 Fm: 0-0
Distance: 5f/6f: 0-0 7f-8f: 0-4 **9f-13f: 1-3** 14f+: 0-0
Track : **LH: 1-6** RH: 0-0 Tight: 0-3 Gall: 0-0
Aids: Bl: 0-0 Vi: 0-0 Tstrap: 0-0
Best Rating: 68 3/01 Sthl 1m3f stand

Eaglerider (IRE)

91 **38**

3-y-o b g Eagle Eyed (USA)-What A Summer (USA) (What Luck (USA))

J G Given Mr & Mrs G Calder

Placings:36-600 **(5626)**

2001: 5^{6}F, 8^{0}GS, 8^{0}GS

	Starts	1st	2nd	3rd	Win & Pl
Career Total (Turf)	5	0	0	1	344

Going (Turf): Sf: 0-2 GS: 0-2 Gd: 0-0 GF: 0-0 Fm: 0-1
Distance: 5f/6f: 0-3 7f-8f: 0-0 9f-13f: 0-2 14f+: 0-0
Track : LH: 0-1 RH: 0-0 Tight: 0-0 Gall: 0-0
Aids: Bl: 0-1 Vi: 0-0 Tstrap: 0-0
Best Rating: 38 10/01 Leic 1m9y gd-sft

Eagles Fortune (IRE)

90(83) (39)**37**

3-y-o ch f Eagle Eyed (USA)-Black Orchid (IRE) (Persian Bold)

I A Wood Jenko Partnership

Placings:0005003 **(5409)**

2001: 7^{0}SD, 5^{0}S, 6^{0}GS, 5^{5}G, 6^{0}F, 6^{0}F, 6^{3}SD

	Starts	1st	2nd	3rd	Win & Pl
Career Total (Turf)	5	0	0	0	0
Career Total (AW)	2	0	0	1	322

Going (Turf): Sf: 0-1 GS: 0-1 Gd: 0-1 GF: 0-0 Fm: 0-2
Distance: 5f/6f: 0-6 7f-8f: 0-1 9f-13f: 0-0 14f+: 0-0
Track : LH: 0-3 RH: 0-0 Tight: 0-0 Gall: 0-0
Aids: Bl: 0-0 Vi: 0-0 Tstrap: 0-0
Best Rating: 39 10/01 Sthl 6f stand

Eagles High (IRE)

96 **69**

2-y-o ch g Eagle Eyed (USA)-Bint Al Balad (IRE) (Ahonoora)

R Hannon T A Daniels

Placings:305403 **(5496)**

2001: 5^{3}GF, 5^{0}S, 5^{5}F, 6^{4}GF, 8^{0}GS, 7^{3}HY

	Starts	1st	2nd	3rd	Win & Pl
Career Total (Turf)	6	0	0	2	2270

Going (Turf): Sf: 0-2 GS: 0-1 Gd: 0-0 GF: 0-2 Fm: 0-1
Distance: 5f/6f: 0-4 7f-8f: 0-2 9f-13f: 0-0 14f+: 0-0
Track : LH: 0-2 RH: 0-0 Tight: 0-2 Gall: 0-0
Aids: Bl: 0-0 Vi: 0-0 Tstrap: 0-0
Best Rating: 69 10/01 Newb 7f heavy

Eaglet (IRE)

84(85) (40)**47**

3-y-o b g Eagle Eyed (USA)-Justice System (USA) (Criminal Type (USA))

A Scott Andy Scott

Placings:000545500-060000 **(5451)**

2001: 8^{0}SD, 8^{6}S, 8^{0}S, 5^{0}S, 6^{0}S, 5^{0}HY

	Starts	1st	2nd	3rd	Win & Pl
Career Total (Turf)	14	0	0	0	251
Career Total (AW)	1	0	0	0	

Going (Turf): Sf: 0-5 GS: 0-1 Gd: 0-3 GF: 0-2 Fm: 0-3
Distance: 5f/6f: 0-7 7f-8f: 0-7 9f-13f: 0-1 14f+: 0-0
Track : LH: 0-4 RH: 0-1 Tight: 0-2 Gall: 0-0
Aids: Bl: 0-1 Vi: 0-0 Tstrap: 0-0
Best Rating: 47 4/01 Nott 5f13y soft

Very moderate maiden.

Earl Of Dunton (IRE)

69 **21**

2-y-o b c Dr Devious (IRE)-Jade Vine (IRE) (Alzao (USA))

S C Williams Alan W Ansell

Placings:600 **(3368)**

2001: 5^{6}F, 6^{0}GF, 7^{0}GF

	Starts	1st	2nd	3rd	Win & Pl
Career Total (Turf)	3	0	0	0	0

Going (Turf): Sf: 0-0 GS: 0-0 Gd: 0-0 GF: 0-2 Fm: 0-1
Distance: 5f/6f: 0-2 7f-8f: 0-1 9f-13f: 0-0 14f+: 0-0
Track : LH: 0-1 RH: 0-0 Tight: 0-0 Gall: 0-0
Aids: Bl: 0-0 Vi: 0-0 Tstrap: 0-0
Best Rating: 21 7/01 Ling 7f gd-fm

Earl Sigurd (IRE)

94 **62**

3-y-o ch g High Kicker (USA)-My Kind (Mon Tresor)

L Lungo William Jardine

Placings:5545 **(4468)**

2001: 10^{5}GF, 7^{5}GS, 8^{4}F, 9^{5}G

	Starts	1st	2nd	3rd	Win & Pl
Career Total (Turf)	4	0	0	0	521

Going (Turf): Sf: 0-0 GS: 0-1 Gd: 0-1 GF: 0-1 Fm: 0-1
Distance: 5f/6f: 0-0 7f-8f: 0-2 9f-13f: 0-2 14f+: 0-0
Track : LH: 0-3 RH: 0-1 Tight: 0-1 Gall: 0-2
Aids: Bl: 0-0 Vi: 0-0 Tstrap: 0-0
Best Rating: 62 6/01 Newc 1m firm

Earldom

88 **63**

2-y-o b c Distant Relative-Noble Story (Last Tycoon)

P F I Cole The Fairy Story Partnership

Placings:6 **(4719)**

2001: 8^{6}G

	Starts	1st	2nd	3rd	Win & Pl
Career Total (Turf)	1	0	0	0	0

Going (Turf): Sf: 0-0 GS: 0-0 Gd: 0-1 GF: 0-0 Fm: 0-0
Distance: 5f/6f: 0-0 7f-8f: 0-0 9f-13f: 0-1 14f+: 0-0
Track : LH: 0-1 RH: 0-0 Tight: 0-1 Gall: 0-0
Aids: Bl: 0-0 Vi: 0-0 Tstrap: 0-0
Best Rating: 63 9/01 Epsm 1m114y good

Moderate ability shown in maidens so far.

Early Morning Mist (IRE)

105 **85**

3-y-o b f Alzao (USA)-Welsh Mist (Damister (USA))
M Johnston Alan Lillingston

Placings:31-33300530602 **(5470)**
2001: 7^{3}G, 10^{3}GF, 10^{3}GS, 8^{0}GF, 8^{0}GF, 9^{5}GF, 10^{3}G, 8^{0}GF, 10^{6}GF, 8^{0}GF, 7^{2}S

	Starts	1st	2nd	3rd	Win & Pl
Career Total (Turf)	13	1	1	5	16192

82 8/00 Asct 6f D G-F £6760
Total win prize-money £6760

Going (Turf): Sf: 0-1 GS: 0-1 Gd: 0-2 **GF: 1-9** Fm: 0-0
Distance: **5f/6f: 1-2** 7f-8f: 0-5 9f-13f: 0-6 14f+: 0-0
Track : LH: 0-6 RH: 0-2 Tight: 0-3 Gall: 0-3
Aids: Bl: 0-2 Vi: 0-0 Tstrap: 0-0
Best Rating: 94 6/01 Epsm 1m2f18y gd-fm

She ran well in a very hot handicap at Epsom on her second start of 2001, but has been somewhat disappointing since then. She has the ability to win a big handicap if she can find her best form again. Stays ten furlongs and best suited by a sound surface.

Early Wish (USA)

96(87) (58)**70**
3-y-o ch f Rahy (USA)-Heaven's Nook (USA) (Great Above (USA))
B Hanbury Abdulla Buhaleeba

Placings:63306-600146 **(4439)**
2001: 7^{6}GF, 7^{0}GF, 10^{0}GF, 6^{1}GF, 7^{4}G, 6^{6}G

	Starts	1st	2nd	3rd	Win & Pl
Career Total (Turf)	10	1	0	2	5675
Career Total (AW)	1	0	0	0	0

70 7/01 Ling 6f E(0-70)H G-F £3883
Total win prize-money £3884

Going (Turf): Sf: 0-1 GS: 0-2 Gd: 0-2 **GF: 1-5** Fm: 0-0
Distance: **5f/6f: 1-3** 7f-8f: 0-6 9f-13f: 0-2 14f+: 0-0
Track : LH: 0-2 RH: 0-3 Tight: 0-2 Gall: 0-2
Aids: **Bl: 1-3** Vi: 0-0 Tstrap: 0-0
Best Rating: 70 7/01 Leic 7f9y good

A half-sister to four winners in the US, notably the Grade 3 sprinter Frisco View, she had a drop in trip, first-time blinkers and a good draw to get her off the mark on the turf at Lingfield in the summer of 2001, but has not looked like continuining this form of late.

Earth Spirit

93(81) (37)**46**
3-y-o b g Ezzoud (IRE)-Ideal Candidate (Celestial Storm (USA))
C A Cyzer Mrs E A Cyzer

Placings:306600 **(5622)**
2001: 10^{3}GS, 12^{0}GS, 9^{6}SD, 11^{6}S, 11^{0}HY, 14^{0}GS

	Starts	1st	2nd	3rd	Win & Pl
Career Total (Turf)	5	0	0	1	653
Career Total (AW)	1	0	0	0	0

Going (Turf): Sf: 0-2 GS: 0-3 Gd: 0-0 GF: 0-0 Fm: 0-0
Distance: 5f/6f: 0-0 7f-8f: 0-0 9f-13f: 0-5 14f+: 0-1
Track : LH: 0-2 RH: 0-2 Tight: 0-4 Gall: 0-0
Aids: Bl: 0-1 Vi: 0-0 Tstrap: 0-0
Best Rating: 49 4/01 Wind 1m2f7y gd-sft

Easaar

101 (120)**105**
5-y-o b h Machiavellian (USA)-Matila (IRE) (Persian Bold)
M P Tregoning Hamdan Al Maktoum

Placings:21/0/1200-22 **(1571)**
2001: 8^{2}GS, 8^{2}GF

	Starts	1st	2nd	3rd	Win & Pl
Career Total (Turf)	9	2	4	0	264006

2/00 Ndas 1m110y GD £5824
91 10/98 NmkR 7f D GD £8217
Total win prize-money £14041

Going (Turf): Sf: 0-1 GS: 0-2 **Gd: 1-2** GF: 0-3 Fm: 0-0
Distance: 5f/6f: 0-0 **7f-8f: 1-5** 9f-13f: 0-3 14f+: 0-0
Track : LH: 0-2 RH: 0-2 Tight: 0-0 Gall: 0-0
Aids: Bl: 0-0 Vi: 0-0 Tstrap: 0-0
Best Rating: 101 5/01 Kemp 1m gd-sft

East Cape

95(78) (20)**51**
4-y-o b g Bering-Reine De Danse (USA) (Nureyev (USA))
Don Enrico Incisa (N Tinkler 13/8) Don Enrico Incisa

Placings:54210-00000000022 **(5448)**
2001: 8^{0}HY, 10^{0}GS, 11^{0}SD, 8^{0}G, 8^{0}GF, 10^{0}G, 7^{0}G, 8^{0}GS, 8^{0}GF, 9^{2}HY, 10^{2}HY

	Starts	1st	2nd	3rd	Win & Pl
Career Total (Turf)	15	1	3	0	7349
Career Total (AW)	1	0	0	0	

76 6/00 Wind 1m67y D G-F £4179
Total win prize-money £4180

Going (Turf): Sf: 0-4 GS: 0-3 Gd: 0-4 **GF: 1-3** Fm: 0-1
Distance: 5f/6f: 0-0 7f-8f: 0-3 **9f-13f: 1-13** 14f+: 0-0
Track : LH: 0-8 **RH: 1-4 Tight: 1-4** Gall: 0-3
Aids: Bl: 0-0 Vi: 0-1 Tstrap: 0-0
Best Rating: 51 10/01 Ayr 1m1f20y heavy

Given too stiff a mark after his win in a maiden at Windsor in the summer of 2000, he has shown poor form since and now runs off a plating mark.

East Of Java

99 **70**
3-y-o b g Greensmith-Krakatoa (Shirley Heights)
P J Makin Snowdrop 2000 Partnership

Placings:0300-43000 **(4527)**
2001: 6^{4}GF, 6^{3}GF, 5^{0}GS, 7^{0}GF, 6^{0}GF

	Starts	1st	2nd	3rd	Win & Pl
Career Total (Turf)	9	0	0	2	1313

Going (Turf): Sf: 0-1 GS: 0-3 Gd: 0-0 GF: 0-5 Fm: 0-0
Distance: 5f/6f: 0-7 7f-8f: 0-2 9f-13f: 0-0 14f+: 0-0
Track : LH: 0-1 RH: 0-0 Tight: 0-0 Gall: 0-1
Aids: Bl: 0-0 Vi: 0-0 Tstrap: 0-0
Best Rating: 71 6/01 Gdwd 6f gd-fm

Lightly-raced maiden, suited by a fast surface and six furlongs.

Eastborough (IRE)

96(101) (77)**66**
2-y-o b g Woodborough (USA)-Easter Girl (Efisio)
A P Jarvis Christopher Shankland

Placings:61505200 **(5636)**
2001: 6^{6}GF, 7^{1}GS, 7^{5}G, 6^{0}G, 6^{5}GS, 8^{2}SD, 8^{0}HY, 5^{0}G

	Starts	1st	2nd	3rd	Win & Pl
Career Total (Turf)	7	1	0	0	2891
Career Total (AW)	1	0	1	0	805

82 7/01 Wwck 7f26y E G-S £2891
Total win prize-money £2891

Going (Turf): Sf: 0-1 **GS: 1-2** Gd: 0-3 GF: 0-1 Fm: 0-0
Distance: 5f/6f: 0-3 **7f-8f: 1-3** 9f-13f: 0-2 14f+: 0-0
Track : LH: 0-5 RH: 0-2 Tight: 0-5 Gall: 0-1
Aids: Bl: 0-0 Vi: 0-0 Tstrap: 0-0
Best Rating: 82 7/01 Wwck 7f26y gd-sft

Tailed off on his Epsom debut, he was suited by the easier ground when causing a 33/1 surprise at Warwick next time and showed encouragement on Fibresand.

Easter Bonnet

3-y-o ch f My Generation-Flower Othe Forest (Indian Forest (USA))
N M Babbage B Babbage

Placings:0-5 **(0334)**
2001: 12^{5}SD

	Starts	1st	2nd	3rd	Win & Pl
Career Total (Turf)	1	0	0	0	
Career Total (AW)	1	0	0	0	0

Going (Turf): Sf: 0-0 GS: 0-1 Gd: 0-0 GF: 0-0 Fm: 0-0
Distance: 5f/6f: 0-1 7f-8f: 0-0 9f-13f: 0-1 14f+: 0-0
Track : LH: 0-1 RH: 0-0 Tight: 0-1 Gall: 0-0
Aids: Bl: 0-0 Vi: 0-0 Tstrap: 0-0

Easter Ogil (IRE)

104(91) (52)**65**
6-y-o ch g Pips Pride-Piney Pass (Persian Bold)
I A Balding Westenders

Placings:02/1002442310/0306006230415000/5006412 50004000-**0650**U00400 **(4386)**
2001: 7^{0}SW, 7^{6}SD, 7^{5}SD, 7^{0}S, 5^{U}GS, 7^{0}G, 5^{0}G, 7^{4}G, 7^{0}GF, 6^{0}GF

	Starts	1st	2nd	3rd	Win & Pl
Career Total (Turf)	50	4	5	3	31700
Career Total (AW)	3	0	0	0	0

80 5/00 Donc 6f D(0-80) G-S £5668
85 9/99 Bath 5f161y D(0-80)H G-F £4533
83 9/98 Sand 7f16y D(0-80) GD £3517
83 4/98 Bevl 5f D G-S £3574
Total win prize-money £17293

Going (Turf): Sf: 0-8 **GS: 2-10** Gd: 1-12 GF: 1-19 Fm: 0-1
Distance: **5f/6f: 3-29** 7f-8f: 1-23 9f-13f: 0-1 14f+: 0-0
Track : LH: 1-19 RH: 1-7 Tight: 0-4 **Gall: 1-12**
Aids: Bl: 0-0 **Vi: 3-32** Tstrap: 0-0
Best Rating: 65 5/01 Bath 5f11y gd-sft

He won a Doncaster classified stakes early on last season, but his form went downhill from there and a few tries on sand did not make much difference.

Eastern Blue (IRE)

96 **69**
2-y-o ch f Be My Guest (USA)-Stifen (Burslem)
K A Ryan T C Chiang

Placings:4401330 **(5140)**
2001: 5^{4}GF, 6^{4}F, 5^{0}GS, 6^{1}G, 6^{3}G, 6^{3}G, 6^{0}G

	Starts	1st	2nd	3rd	Win & Pl
Career Total (Turf)	7	1	0	2	5306

69 8/01 Nott 6f15y E GD £3688
Total win prize-money £3689

Going (Turf): Sf: 0-0 GS: 0-1 **Gd: 1-4** GF: 0-1 Fm: 0-1
Distance: 5f/6f: 0-4 **7f-8f: 1-3** 9f-13f: 0-0 14f+: 0-0
Track : LH: 0-0 RH: 0-0 Tight: 0-0 Gall: 0-0
Aids: Bl: 0-0 Vi: 0-0 Tstrap: 0-0
Best Rating: 69 9/01 Nott 6f15y good

Fair runs in nurseries after winning a Nottingham maiden. Should stay seven.

Eastern Breeze (IRE)

106 **86+**
3-y-o b g Sri Pekan (USA)-Elegant Bloom (IRE) (Be My Guest (USA))
P W Harris Brosnan, Cage, Coppen & Lupson

Placings:303-545 **(3231)**
2001: 9^{5}S, 10^{4}GF, 10^{5}GF

	Starts	1st	2nd	3rd	Win & Pl

	Starts	1st	2nd	3rd	Win & Pl
Career Total (Turf)	6	0	0	2	1619

Going (Turf): Sf: 0-3 GS: 0-0 Gd: 0-1 GF: 0-2 Fm: 0-0
Distance: 5f/6f: 0-1 7f-8f: 0-2 9f-13f: 0-3 14f+: 0-0
Track : LH: 0-1 RH: 0-2 Tight: 0-0 Gall: 0-0
Aids: Bl: 0-0 Vi: 0-0 Tstrap: 0-0
Best Rating: 86 7/01 Sand 1m2f7y gd-fm

Eastern Hope (IRE)

95 **86**

2-y-o b g Danehill Dancer (IRE)-Hope And Glory (USA) (Well Decorated (USA))
K A Ryan T C Chiang

Placings:5330 **(3468)**
2001: 6^{5}GF, 6^{3}GF, 7^{3}G, 7^{0}GF

	Starts	1st	2nd	3rd	Win & Pl
Career Total (Turf)	4	0	0	2	920

Going (Turf): Sf: 0-0 GS: 0-0 Gd: 0-1 GF: 0-3 Fm: 0-0
Distance: 5f/6f: 0-2 7f-8f: 0-2 9f-13f: 0-0 14f+: 0-0
Track : LH: 0-1 RH: 0-0 Tight: 0-1 Gall: 0-0
Aids: Bl: 0-0 Vi: 0-0 Tstrap: 0-0
Best Rating: 86 5/01 York 6f gd-fm

Having made a promising debut at York, he has been held in maiden company since.

Eastern Image (USA)

98 **88**

2-y-o ch c Gone West (USA)-My True Lady (USA) (Seattle Slew (USA))
J L Dunlop The Thoroughbred Corporation

Placings:4411 **(5537)**
2001: 6^{4}GF, 7^{4}HY, 6^{1}S, 7^{1}S

	Starts	1st	2nd	3rd	Win & Pl
Career Total (Turf)	4	2	0	0	8055

88	10/01	Rdcr	7f	D	SFT	£3388
73	9/01	Pont	6f	D	SFT	£4030

Total win prize-money £7418

Going (Turf): Sf: 2-3 GS: 0-0 Gd: 0-0 GF: 0-1 Fm: 0-0
Distance: 5f/6f: 1-2 7f-8f: 1-2 9f-13f: 0-0 14f+: 0-0
Track : **LH: 1-2** RH: 0-0 Tight: 0-0 Gall: 0-0
Aids: Bl: 0-0 Vi: 0-0 Tstrap: 0-0
Best Rating: 88 10/01 Rdcr 7f soft

He had shown promise in maidens before beating a field of newcomers over six at Pontefract in September and augmented this with a similar win at Redcar over an extra furlong next time. He should appreciate longer trips in time.

Eastern Jewel

101 **35**

3-y-o b f Anshan-China's Pearl (Shirley Heights)
Mrs A J Perrett C Duncan

Placings:00-5000035200 **(5469)**
2001: 12^{5}HY, 11^{0}G, 11^{0}F, 14^{0}GF, 11^{0}F, 9^{3}GF, 9^{5}GF, 9^{2}GF, 9^{0}GS, 9^{0}S

	Starts	1st	2nd	3rd	Win & Pl
Career Total (Turf)	12	0	1	1	1068

Going (Turf): Sf: 0-3 GS: 0-1 Gd: 0-2 GF: 0-4 Fm: 0-2
Distance: 5f/6f: 0-0 7f-8f: 0-2 9f-13f: 0-9 14f+: 0-1
Track : LH: 0-5 RH: 0-5 Tight: 0-4 Gall: 0-1
Aids: Bl: 0-3 Vi: 0-5 Tstrap: 0-0
Best Rating: 48 5/01 Wind 1m3f135y good

Eastern Project (IRE)

66 **1**

7-y-o b g Project Manager-Diandra (Shardari)
A Crook (M D Hammond 20/4) Steve Semple

Placings:35046420/0/0 **(3797)**
2001: 11^{0}G

	Starts	1st	2nd	3rd	Win & Pl
Career Total (Turf)	10	0	1	1	1248

Going (Turf): Sf: 0-0 GS: 0-1 Gd: 0-4 GF: 0-1 Fm: 0-1
Distance: 5f/6f: 0-0 7f-8f: 0-1 9f-13f: 0-9 14f+: 0-0
Track : LH: 0-5 RH: 0-5 Tight: 0-0 Gall: 0-1
Aids: Bl: 0-1 Vi: 0-0 Tstrap: 0-0
Best Rating: 1 8/01 Hayd 1m3f200y good

Eastern Promise

96 **47**

3-y-o gr f Factual (USA)-Indian Crystal (Petong)
J G Given Mrs B A Matthews

Placings:24140-400605400 **(4618)**
2001: 6^{4}GF, 7^{0}G, 6^{0}F, 8^{6}GF, 7^{0}GF, 10^{5}F, 7^{4}GS, 9^{0}GF, 6^{0}F

	Starts	1st	2nd	3rd	Win & Pl
Career Total (Turf)	14	1	1	0	4299

63	6/00	Muss	5f	E	FRM	£2795

Total win prize-money £2795

Going (Turf): Sf: 0-1 GS: 0-2 Gd: 0-2 GF: 0-5 **Fm: 1-4**
Distance: **5f/6f: 1-8** 7f-8f: 0-4 9f-13f: 0-2 14f+: 0-0
Track : LH: 0-1 RH: 0-1 Tight: 0-1 Gall: 0-0
Aids: Bl: 0-0 Vi: 0-1 Tstrap: 0-0
Best Rating: 63 6/01 Newc 6f gd-fm

A winner on fast ground at Musselburgh at two, but she has not build on her promising seasonal reappearance.

Eastern Prophets

90(94) (52)**29**

8-y-o b g Emarati (USA)-Four Love (Pas De Seul)
M Dods Graham And Barbara Spencer

Placings:51121002205/5300000505/1340000002**6524**/3336061450304042200**6**/40100002022303200/3000044010**006**-0000050 **(3592)**
2001: 8^{0}GF, 7^{0}GF, 5^{0}GF, 6^{0}F, 6^{0}GF, 6^{5}G, 7^{0}GS

	Starts	1st	2nd	3rd	Win & Pl
Career Total (Turf)	78	7	9	6	49699
Career Total (AW)	14	0	2	3	2907

52	8/00	Newc	6f	F(0-65)H	G-F	£2548
58	5/99	Nott	6f15y	G(0-70)H	FRM	£2102
70	5/98	Donc	6f	E	G-F	£2976
82	3/97	Kemp	6f	D(0-85)H	G-F	£3550
86	6/95	Bevl	5f	B	G-S	£7918
76	5/95	Bath	5f11y	C	G-F	£4677
64	5/95	Donc	5f	E	G-F	£3582

Total win prize-money £27354

Going (Turf): Sf: 0-6 GS: 1-6 Gd: 0-22 **GF: 5-34** Fm: 1-10
Distance: **5f/6f: 6-74** 7f-8f: 1-18 9f-13f: 0-0 14f+: 0-0
Track : **LH: 1-29** RH: 0-5 Tight: 0-20 **Gall: 1-7**
Aids: Bl: 1-25 **Vi: 2-20** Tstrap: 0-0
Best Rating: 39 6/01 Newc 5f gd-fm

Eastern Purple (IRE)

115 **109**

6-y-o b g Petorius-Broadway Rosie (Absalom)
K A Ryan T C Chiang

Placings:01544/0100535060/201553000/03005621062 0-0040403235242 **(5694)**
2001: 5^{0}G, 6^{0}GF, 6^{4}GY, 6^{0}GF, 5^{4}GF, 5^{0}GF, 5^{3}GF, 5^{2}G, 6^{3}GF, 5^{5}GF, 5^{2}GF, 5^{4}HO, 6^{2}S

	Starts	1st	2nd	3rd	Win & Pl
Career Total (Turf)	49	4	6	5	141669

112	8/00	Leop	6f		GD	£22750
111	5/99	Curr	6f		GD	£27625
106	5/98	Hayd	6f	A(0-110)H	G-F	£12486
71	8/97	Newc	6f	F	G-F	£2620

Total win prize-money £65482

Going (Turf): Sf: 0-6 GS: 0-5 **Gd: 2-14 GF: 2-20** Fm: 0-1
Distance: **5f/6f: 4-45** 7f-8f: 0-4 9f-13f: 0-0 14f+: 0-0
Track : LH: 0-5 RH: 0-0 Tight: 0-2 Gall: 0-2
Aids: Bl: 0-14 Vi: 0-1 Tstrap: 0-0
Best Rating: 109 9/01 Newb 5f34y gd-fm

He is a few pounds below the leading sprinters but was in good heart in the summer of 2000 and deserved his Group Three success at Leopardstown. He has run some decent races this season, but keeps finding one or two too good. Produced his best performance in group company when fourth in the Prix de l'Abbaye in October. Effective over five and six furlongs. Acts on any ground.

Eastern Red

71(88) (39)**46**

3-y-o b f Contract Law (USA)-Gagajulu (Al Hareb (USA))
Miss M Bragg (Ronald Thompson 25/6) Miss M Bragg

Placings:05620546233-60050 **(2426)**
2001: 6^{6}SD, 7^{0}SD, 8^{0}SD, 10^{5}F, 8^{0}GF

	Starts	1st	2nd	3rd	Win & Pl
Career Total (Turf)	11	0	2	1	1436
Career Total (AW)	5	0	0	1	242

Going (Turf): Sf: 0-2 GS: 0-0 Gd: 0-2 GF: 0-4 Fm: 0-3
Distance: 5f/6f: 0-8 7f-8f: 0-4 9f-13f: 0-4 14f+: 0-0
Track : LH: 0-8 RH: 0-1 Tight: 0-1 Gall: 0-0
Aids: Bl: 0-1 Vi: 0-0 Tstrap: 0-0
Best Rating: 19 6/01 Nott 1m54y gd-fm

Eastern Royal

81 **60**

2-y-o b g Royal Applause-Kentfield (Busted)
K A Ryan T C Chiang

Placings:60 **(3468)**
2001: 6^{6}GF, 7^{0}GF

	Starts	1st	2nd	3rd	Win & Pl
Career Total (Turf)	2	0	0	0	0

Going (Turf): Sf: 0-0 GS: 0-0 Gd: 0-0 GF: 0-2 Fm: 0-0
Distance: 5f/6f: 0-1 7f-8f: 0-1 9f-13f: 0-0 14f+: 0-0
Track : LH: 0-0 RH: 0-0 Tight: 0-0 Gall: 0-0
Aids: Bl: 0-0 Vi: 0-0 Tstrap: 0-0
Best Rating: 60 7/01 Donc 6f gd-fm

Eastern Trumpeter

106(111) (85)**89**

5-y-o b h First Trump-Oriental Air (IRE) (Taufan (USA))
J M Bradley R G G Racing

Placings:52/5104310530000330**5**/**141**000**2111130**2103004**004531**-0110030315002400 **(5258)**
2001: 6^{0}SD, 5^{1}SW, 5^{1}SW, 5^{0}SD, 5^{0}GF, 5^{3}F, 5^{0}GF, 5^{3}GF, 5^{1}G, 5^{5}GS, 5^{0}GF, 5^{0}GF, 5^{2}G, 5^{4}GF, 5^{0}GF, 5^{0}GS

	Starts	1st	2nd	3rd	Win & Pl
Career Total (Turf)	46	8	3	7	60993
Career Total (AW)	15	5	1	2	30687

86	6/01	York	5f	C(0-100)H	GD	£7280
85	2/01	Ling	5f	C(0-90)H	SLW	£8014
82	1/01	Wolv	5f	C(0-95)H	SLW	£8014
78	12/00	Wolv	5f	D(0-85)H	STD	£4026
79	7/00	York	5f	C(0-95)H	GD	£9061
73	6/00	Ripn	5f	C(0-90)H	G-S	£7150
69	5/00	Rdcr	5f	C(0-90)H	G-S	£7475
66	5/00	Ling	5f	D(0-85)H	GD	£4075
68	5/00	Carl	5f	F(0-60)	FRM	£2562
69	3/00	Wolv	5f	D(0-85)H	STD	£3750
66	2/00	Wolv	5f	D(0-85)H	STD	£3848
62	6/99	Ayr	5f	D(0-85)H	SFT	£7103
70	4/99	Folk	5f	F	HVY	£2219

Total win prize-money £74582

Going (Turf): Sf: 2-13 GS: 2-6 **Gd: 3-9** GF: 0-15 Fm: 1-3
Distance: **5f/6f: 13-61** 7f-8f: 0-0 9f-13f: 0-0 14f+: 0-0
Track : **LH: 5-22** RH: 1-5 **Tight: 5-18** Gall: 1-8
Aids: Bl: 0-0 Vi: 0-0 Tstrap: 0-0
Best Rating: 89 8/01 Newb 5f34y gd-fm

He is an effective sort in handicaps over the minimum trip on both turf and Fibresand. Acts on a sound surface but prefers a bit of give in the ground. Likes a fast pace, goes well at York.

Eastern Venture

96 **54**

4-y-o b c Last Tycoon-Imperial Jade (Lochnager)
W R Muir D J Deer

Placings:00/40000 **(3220)**
2001: 7^{4}GS, 6^{0}GF, 6^{0}GF, 6^{0}GF, 7^{0}GF

	Starts	1st	2nd	3rd	Win & Pl
Career Total (Turf)	7	0	0	0	321

Going (Turf): Sf: 0-1 GS: 0-2 Gd: 0-0 GF: 0-4 Fm: 0-0
Distance: 5f/6f: 0-3 7f-8f: 0-3 9f-13f: 0-1 14f+: 0-0
Track : LH: 0-0 RH: 0-1 Tight: 0-0 Gall: 0-1
Aids: Bl: 0-0 Vi: 0-0 Tstrap: 0-2
Best Rating: 57 5/01 Ling 7f gd-sft

Easternking

80 **48**

2-y-o ch f Sabrehill (USA)-Kshessinskaya (Hadeer)
J S Wainwright Peter Easterby

Placings:000 **(5371)**
2001: 7^{0}GS, 7^{0}S, 8^{0}G

	Starts	1st	2nd	3rd	Win & Pl
Career Total (Turf)	3	0	0	0	

Going (Turf): Sf: 0-1 GS: 0-1 Gd: 0-1 GF: 0-0 Fm: 0-0
Distance: 5f/6f: 0-0 7f-8f: 0-3 9f-13f: 0-0 14f+: 0-0
Track : LH: 0-1 RH: 0-0 Tight: 0-0 Gall: 0-1
Aids: Bl: 0-0 Vi: 0-0 Tstrap: 0-0
Best Rating: 48 10/01 York 7f202y soft

Eastwell Hall

103 **80**

6-y-o b g Saddlers' Hall (IRE)-Kinchenjunga (Darshaan)
T P McGovern Eastwell Manor Racing

Placings:00000/11122603/054/515205-0050 **(2305)**
2001: 12^{0}S, 14^{0}GS, 16^{5}GF, 20^{0}GF

	Starts	1st	2nd	3rd	Win & Pl
Career Total (Turf)	26	4	3	1	25376

84	6/00	Chep	2m2f	D(0-85)H	GD	£3874
68	5/98	Wwck	1m4f115y	D(0-80)H	GD	£3817
70	4/98	Bath	1m2f46y	D(0-80)H	SFT	£3647
52	4/98	Folk	1m1f149y	E(0-70)H	GD	£3054

Total win prize-money £14394

Going (Turf): Sf: 1-4 GS: 0-4 **Gd: 3-9** GF: 0-9 Fm: 0-0
Distance: 5f/6f: 0-3 7f-8f: 0-0 **9f-13f: 3-9** 14f+: 1-14
Track : **LH: 3-10** RH: 1-14 **Tight: 2-11** Gall: 0-6
Aids: Bl: 0-1 Vi: 0-0 Tstrap: 0-0
Best Rating: 77 6/01 Folk 2m93y gd-fm

An out-and-out stayer, he scored just once at Chepstow in 2000. Handles most surfaces, but seen more often over hurdles these days.

Eastwell Manor

92(78) (13)**50**

3-y-o b g Dancing Spree (USA)-Kinchenjunga (Darshaan)
T P McGovern Eastwell Manor Racing

Placings:00-6500060 **(4159)**
2001: 10^{6}SW, 6^{5}HY, 6^{0}GS, 10^{0}GF, 10^{0}F, 12^{6}GF, 6^{0}GF

	Starts	1st	2nd	3rd	Win & Pl
Career Total (Turf)	8	0	0	0	0
Career Total (AW)	1	0	0	0	0

Going (Turf): **Sf: 0-1 GS: 0-1 Gd: 0-2 GF: 0-3 Fm: 0-1**
Distance: 5f/6f: 0-1 7f-8f: 0-4 9f-13f: 0-4 14f+: 0-0
Track : LH: 0-4 RH: 0-4 Tight: 0-5 Gall: 0-1
Aids: Bl: 0-2 Vi: 0-0 Tstrap: 0-0
Best Rating: 50 5/01 Brig 6f209y gd-sft

Easy Dollar

101 **61**

9-y-o ch g Gabitat-Burglars Girl (Burglar)
B Gubby Brian Gubby Ltd

Placings:430/53450421153500/24203200/22306/00/56 005554602106/6000550050-0040323 **(4715)**
2001: 7^{0}GF, 6^{0}GF, 5^{4}G, 5^{0}G, 6^{3}G, 6^{2}GF, 6^{3}G

	Starts	1st	2nd	3rd	Win & Pl
Career Total (Turf)	63	3	8	7	80225

88	9/99	Nott	6f15y	B(0-105)H	GD	£14980
89	7/95	Gdwd	7f	C(0-100)H	GD	£19820
83	7/95	NmkJ	6f	D	GD	£4659

Total win prize-money £39459

Going (Turf): Sf: 0-6 GS: 0-4 **Gd: 3-26** GF: 0-24 Fm: 0-3
Distance: 5f/6f: 1-38 **7f-8f: 2-24** 9f-13f: 0-1 14f+: 0-0
Track : LH: 0-9 **RH: 1-9** Tight: 0-3 Gall: 0-7
Aids: **Bl: 3-40** Vi: 0-17 Tstrap: 0-0
Best Rating: 70 8/01 Asct 5f good

A fine servant although he rarely won, a drop in the handicap saw him run a bit better during the summer. Fatally injured in September. (DEAD).

Easy Enigma (IRE)

86(87) (40)**70**

3-y-o ch c Selkirk (USA)-Moonlight Saunter (USA) (Woodman (USA))
B W Hills Maktoum Al Maktoum

Placings:05-30 **(3978)**
2001: 8^{3}SD, 6^{0}F

	Starts	1st	2nd	3rd	Win & Pl
Career Total (Turf)	3	0	0	0	0
Career Total (AW)	1	0	0	1	428

Going (Turf): **Sf: 0-0 GS: 0-0 Gd: 0-1 GF: 0-1 Fm: 0-1**
Distance: 5f/6f: 0-1 7f-8f: 0-2 9f-13f: 0-1 14f+: 0-0
Track : LH: 0-2 RH: 0-0 Tight: 0-2 Gall: 0-0
Aids: Bl: 0-0 Vi: 0-0 Tstrap: 0-0
Best Rating: 45 8/01 Sals 6f firm

Eau Rouge

106 **67**

3-y-o ch f Grand Lodge (USA)-Tarsa (Ballad Rock)
M A Jarvis Miss D F Fleming

Placings:022-44312 **(3040)**
2001: 7^{4}GS, 5^{4}GF, 5^{3}GF, 5^{1}GF, 5^{2}GF

	Starts	1st	2nd	3rd	Win & Pl
Career Total (Turf)	8	1	3	1	7003

57	6/01	Muss	5f	D	G-F	£2996

Total win prize-money £2996

Going (Turf): Sf: 0-1 GS: 0-1 Gd: 0-0 **GF: 1-6** Fm: 0-0
Distance: **5f/6f: 1-7** 7f-8f: 0-1 9f-13f: 0-0 14f+: 0-0
Track : LH: 0-1 RH: 0-1 Tight: 0-0 Gall: 0-1
Aids: Bl: 0-0 Vi: 0-0 Tstrap: 0-0
Best Rating: 67 7/01 Nott 5f13y gd-fm

She took advantage of a drop in class to get off the mark at Musselburgh in June, but she did not win anywhere near as comfortably as her best form suggested she ought to. She is bred to stay further than five furlongs.

Ebinzayd (IRE)

96 **79**

5-y-o b g Tenby-Sharakawa (IRE) (Darshaan)
L Lungo Miss S Blumberg

Placings:4010/35345/0 **(1548)**
2001: 16^{0}F

	Starts	1st	2nd	3rd	Win & Pl
Career Total (Turf)	10	1	0	2	7171

83	9/98	Newc	1m3y	D	GD	£3371

Total win prize-money £3371

Going (Turf): Sf: 0-0 GS: 0-2 **Gd: 1-5** GF: 0-2 Fm: 0-1
Distance: 5f/6f: 0-0 7f-8f: 0-1 **9f-13f: 1-8** 14f+: 0-1
Track : LH: 0-7 RH: 0-2 Tight: 0-2 Gall: 0-4
Aids: Bl: 0-0 Vi: 0-0 Tstrap: 0-0
Best Rating: 79 5/01 Newc 2m19y firm

Ebony Bound (USA)

91 **69d**

3-y-o b c Woodman (USA)-Truly Bound (USA) (In Reality)
M L W Bell Wafic Said

Placings:005360 **(4844)**
2001: 8^{0}S, 12^{0}GF, 10^{5}F, 12^{3}F, 14^{6}G, 9^{0}G

	Starts	1st	2nd	3rd	Win & Pl
Career Total (Turf)	6	0	0	1	669

Going (Turf): **Sf: 0-1 GS: 0-0 Gd: 0-2 GF: 0-1 Fm: 0-2**
Distance: 5f/6f: 0-0 7f-8f: 0-1 9f-13f: 0-4 14f+: 0-1
Track : LH: 0-4 RH: 0-1 Tight: 0-2 Gall: 0-0
Aids: Bl: 0-0 Vi: 0-0 Tstrap: 0-0
Best Rating: 71 6/01 Ling 1m2f firm

Ec Lady

98(95) (26)**86?**

2-y-o ch f Dilum (USA)-Pooka (Dominion)
J L Spearing The Square Milers

Placings:431034116454 **(5487)**
2001: 5^{4}SD, 5^{3}SD, 6^{1}GF, 6^{0}GF, 6^{3}GF, 6^{4}GF, 5^{1}G, 6^{1}G, 6^{6}G, 6^{4}GF, 6^{5}G, 6^{4}HY

	Starts	1st	2nd	3rd	Win & Pl
Career Total (Turf)	10	3	0	1	12511
Career Total (AW)	2	0	0	1	249

88	8/01	Wind	6f	D	GD	£3640
70	8/01	Leic	5f218y	G	GD	£1876
58	5/01	Gdwd	6f	E	G-F	£3493

Total win prize-money £9010

Going (Turf): Sf: 0-1 GS: 0-0 **Gd: 2-4** GF: 1-5 Fm: 0-0
Distance: **5f/6f: 3-9** 7f-8f: 0-3 9f-13f: 0-0 14f+: 0-0
Track : LH: 0-1 RH: 0-0 Tight: 0-0 Gall: 0-0
Aids: Bl: 0-0 Vi: 0-0 Tstrap: 0-0
Best Rating: 88 8/01 Wind 6f good

A front-runner, she progressed with her racing and scored at Leicester and Windsor in August. Suited by six furlongs and good ground or faster.

Ecclesiastical

111 **102+**

3-y-o b c Bishop Of Cashel-Rachael Tennessee (USA) (Matsadoon (USA))
J R Fanshawe Cheveley Park Stud

Placings:02-112 **(2330)**
2001: 7^{1}G, 8^{1}GF, 8^{2}GF

	Starts	1st	2nd	3rd	Win & Pl
Career Total (Turf)	5	2	2	0	58970

97	5/01	Hayd	1m30y	B(0-110)H	G-F	£43290
87	5/01	Leic	7f9y	D	GD	£3965

Total win prize-money £47255

Going (Turf): Sf: 0-0 GS: 0-1 **Gd: 1-1 GF: 1-2** Fm: 0-0
Distance: 5f/6f: 0-0 **7f-8f: 1-3 9f-13f: 1-1** 14f+: 0-0
Track: **LH: 1-1** RH: 0-1 Tight: 0-1 Gall: 0-0
Aids: Bl: 0-0 Vi: 0-0 Tstrap: 0-0
Best Rating: 102 6/01 Asct 1m gd-fm

A very nice colt, he shaped like a future black type contender when winning a mile handicap at Haydock in May, where he was travelling like a winner some way out and beat Lord Protector easily by two lengths. Finished second in the Britannia. Stays a mile. Best on an easy surface but acts on good to firm.

Echo River (USA)

104 **98**

2-y-o ch f Irish River (FR)-Monaassabaat (USA) (Zilzal (USA))
D R Loder Maktoum Al Maktoum

Placings:14125 **(5390)**
2001: 6^{1}GF, 6^{4}G, 7^{1}GF, 8^{2}G, 7^{5}GS

	Starts	1st	2nd	3rd	Win & Pl
Career Total (Turf)	5	2	1	0	34289

86 7/01 Sand 7f16y A G-F £13975
78 6/01 Wind 6f C G-F £6130
Total win prize-money £20106

Going (Turf): Sf: 0-0 GS: 0-1 Gd: 0-2 **GF: 2-2** Fm: 0-0
Distance: 5f/6f: 1-2 7f-8f: 1-3 9f-13f: 0-0 14f+: 0-0
Track: LH: 0-1 **RH: 1-1** Tight: 0-0 Gall: 0-1
Aids: Bl: 0-0 Vi: 0-0 Tstrap: 0-0
Best Rating: 98 9/01 Donc 1m good

Made an impressive debut at Windsor over six furlongs. Disappointed in a Group Three in Italy the following month, but resumed winning ways in a Listed race over seven furlongs at Sandown in July before a good second in the May Hill. Has won on fast ground but connections feel she will be better on soft.

Ecstasy

105 **71**

4-y-o b f Pursuit Of Love-Gong (Bustino)
R M Beckett A D G Oldrey

Placings:6214030/01300-300004 **(4844)**
2001: 10^{3}G, 11^{0}GF, 10^{0}GF, 9^{0}GF, 9^{0}GF, 9^{4}G

	Starts	1st	2nd	3rd	Win & Pl
Career Total (Turf)	18	2	1	3	13659

79 5/00 Bath 1m2f46y D(0-80) G-F £3701
78 7/99 Wwck 6f168y E G-F £3214
Total win prize-money £6917

Going (Turf): Sf: 0-1 GS: 0-2 Gd: 0-5 **GF: 2-9** Fm: 0-1
Distance: 5f/6f: 0-3 7f-8f: 1-4 9f-13f: 1-11 14f+: 0-0
Track: **LH: 2-5** RH: 0-4 **Tight: 1-5** Gall: 0-2
Aids: Bl: 0-0 Vi: 0-0 Tstrap: 0-0
Best Rating: 71 5/01 Wind 1m2f7y good

Ten furlongs and fast ground seem her ideal conditions.

Ecstatic

110 **88**

3-y-o ch f Nashwan (USA)-Divine Quest (Kris)
R Hannon Plantation Stud

Placings:24331-402252360 **(5259)**
2001: 7^{4}GF, 9^{0}GF, 9^{2}S, 9^{2}GF, 8^{5}GS, 8^{2}GF, 8^{3}GF, 9^{6}GF, 7^{0}GS

	Starts	1st	2nd	3rd	Win & Pl
Career Total (Turf)	14	1	4	3	17532

64 10/00 Brig 5f213y D SFT £3693
Total win prize-money £3693

Going (Turf): **Sf: 1-3** GS: 0-3 Gd: 0-1 GF: 0-7 Fm: 0-0
Distance: **5f/6f: 1-4** 7f-8f: 0-6 9f-13f: 0-4 14f+: 0-0
Track: **LH: 1-4** RH: 0-3 Tight: 0-3 Gall: 0-1
Aids: Bl: 0-0 Vi: 0-0 Tstrap: 0-0

Best Rating: 89 9/01 Thsk 1m gd-fm

Has run reasonable races this season without altogether convincing with her attitude. Best with give underfoot. Stays nine furlongs.

Eddie Royale (IRE)

95(83) (57)**42**

3-y-o b g Elbio-Persian Royale (Persian Bold)
D Nicholls Mike Browne

Placings:050-5000 **(4601)**
2001: 7^{5}SD, 7^{0}GS, 7^{0}GF, 5^{0}GF

	Starts	1st	2nd	3rd	Win & Pl
Career Total (Turf)	5	0	0	0	
Career Total (AW)	2	0	0	0	0

Going (Turf): **Sf: 0-0 GS: 0-2 Gd: 0-0 GF: 0-2 Fm: 0-1**
Distance: 5f/6f: 0-4 7f-8f: 0-3 9f-13f: 0-0 14f+: 0-0
Track: LH: 0-2 RH: 0-0 Tight: 0-0 Gall: 0-0
Aids: Bl: 0-0 Vi: 0-0 Tstrap: 0-0
Best Rating: 42 7/01 Ayr 7f gd-sft

Eddu

102 **82**

3-y-o ch g Casteddu-Cabra (Red Sunset)
W M Brisbourne Michael F Blackham

Placings:620103 **(2630)**
2001: 11^{6}S, 10^{2}GF, 10^{0}GF, 10^{1}GF, 12^{0}GF, 9^{3}GF

	Starts	1st	2nd	3rd	Win & Pl
Career Total (Turf)	6	1	1	1	9298

82 6/01 Ches 1m2f75y D(0-75) G-F £6405
Total win prize-money £6406

Going (Turf): Sf: 0-1 GS: 0-0 Gd: 0-0 **GF: 1-5** Fm: 0-0
Distance: 5f/6f: 0-0 7f-8f: 0-0 **9f-13f: 1-6** 14f+: 0-0
Track: **LH: 1-3** RH: 0-3 **Tight: 1-3** Gall: 0-0
Aids: Bl: 0-0 Vi: 0-0 Tstrap: 0-0
Best Rating: 82 6/01 Ches 1m2f75y gd-fm

Eddys Lad

99(88) (47)**57**

3-y-o br g Lahib (USA)-Glamour Model (Last Tycoon)
J Balding (R M H Cowell 16/10) Mrs Jo Hardy

Placings:23-2000046430 **(5560)**
2001: 7^{2}S, 7^{0}G, 7^{0}SD, 7^{0}F, 7^{0}GS, 8^{4}SD, 6^{6}S, 7^{4}HY, 7^{3}S, 7^{0}S

	Starts	1st	2nd	3rd	Win & Pl
Career Total (Turf)	10	0	2	2	2641
Career Total (AW)	2	0	0	0	0

Going (Turf): **Sf: 0-5 GS: 0-1 Gd: 0-1 GF: 0-2 Fm: 0-1**
Distance: 5f/6f: 0-0 7f-8f: 0-11 9f-13f: 0-1 14f+: 0-0
Track: LH: 0-5 RH: 0-1 Tight: 0-3 Gall: 0-0
Aids: Bl: 0-0 Vi: 0-2 Tstrap: 0-3
Best Rating: 66 5/01 Rdcr 7f soft

He appeared to improve for being gelded and ran very well on heavy ground at Lingfield in October. Should be capable of winning a small handicap under similar conditions.

Edel's Joy (IRE)

80

3-y-o b f General Monash (USA)-Belle-Cote (Coquelin (USA))
J Parkes P J Sweeney

Placings:000 **(5534)**
2001: 10^{0}GF, 11^{0}G, 11^{0}S

	Starts	1st	2nd	3rd	Win & Pl
Career Total (Turf)	3	0	0	0	

Going (Turf): **Sf: 0-1 GS: 0-0 Gd: 0-1 GF: 0-1 Fm: 0-0**
Distance: 5f/6f: 0-0 7f-8f: 0-0 9f-13f: 0-3 14f+: 0-0
Track: LH: 0-1 RH: 0-2 Tight: 0-3 Gall: 0-0
Aids: Bl: 0-0 Vi: 0-0 Tstrap: 0-0

Edifice (JPN)

100(74) (23)**45**

5-y-o ch g Carroll House-Moon Tosho (JPN) (Steel Heart)
B Ellison Keith Middleton

Placings:0/050400/560000-0000440404240 **(4858)**
2001: 10^{0}HY, 8^{0}S, 8^{0}GS, 9^{0}F, 8^{4}GF, 8^{4}GF, 10^{0}GF, 10^{4}F, 9^{0}CF, 10^{4}G, 11^{2}GF, 14^{4}GF, 15^{0}GF

	Starts	1st	2nd	3rd	Win & Pl
Career Total (Turf)	25	0	1	0	1953
Career Total (AW)	1	0	0	0	

Going (Turf): **Sf: 0-5 GS: 0-2 Gd: 0-5 GF: 0-9 Fm: 0-4**
Distance: 5f/6f: 0-0 7f-8f: 0-4 9f-13f: 0-20 14f+: 0-2
Track: LH: 0-14 RH: 0-8 Tight: 0-11 Gall: 0-5
Aids: Bl: 0-1 Vi: 0-0 Tstrap: 0-0
Best Rating: 45 8/01 Rdcr 1m3f gd-fm

Editor In Chief (USA)

94 **83**

2-y-o b c Kingmambo (USA)-Cymbala (FR) (Assert)
J L Dunlop The Thoroughbred Corporation

Placings:312 **(5280)**
2001: 7^{3}GF, 8^{1}GF, 9^{2}S

	Starts	1st	2nd	3rd	Win & Pl
Career Total (Turf)	3	1	1	1	6757

80 8/01 Chep 1m14y D G-F £3464
Total win prize-money £3465

Going (Turf): Sf: 0-1 GS: 0-0 Gd: 0-0 **GF: 1-2** Fm: 0-0
Distance: 5f/6f: 0-0 7f-8f: 0-1 **9f-13f: 1-2** 14f+: 0-0
Track: LH: 0-0 RH: 0-2 Tight: 0-0 Gall: 0-0
Aids: Bl: 0-0 Vi: 0-0 Tstrap: 0-0
Best Rating: 83 10/01 Leic 1m1f218y soft

Out of a Grade Three-winning mare and bought for 140,000 guineas, this colt has made a promising start to his career with a decent win in a maiden at Chepstow, followed up by a creditable second in a Class C Conditions Stakes at Leicester.

Edmo Lift (IRE)

90 **64**

2-y-o b f Alhaarth (IRE)-Pollyfidra (USA) (In Fijar (USA))
T D Easterby Edmolift Uk Ltd

Placings:626256005600 **(5370)**
2001: 6^{6}GF, 5^{2}F, 6^{6}GF, 5^{2}GF, 5^{5}GF, 5^{6}G, 7^{0}GS, 5^{0}GF, 5^{5}GF, 5^{6}GF, 6^{0}GS, 7^{0}G

	Starts	1st	2nd	3rd	Win & Pl
Career Total (Turf)	12	0	2	0	2215

Going (Turf): **Sf: 0-0 GS: 0-2 Gd: 0-2 GF: 0-7 Fm: 0-1**
Distance: 5f/6f: 0-10 7f-8f: 0-2 9f-13f: 0-0 14f+: 0-0
Track: LH: 0-4 RH: 0-1 Tight: 0-1 Gall: 0-0
Aids: Bl: 0-1 Vi: 0-0 Tstrap: 0-0
Best Rating: 71 7/01 Pont 5f gd-fm

Effervesce (IRE)

101 **73**

3-y-o b f Sri Pekan (USA)-Arctic Winter (CAN) (Briartic (CAN))
M A Buckley C C Buckley

Placings:4601200-0520330000 **(5254)**
2001: 7^{0}GS, 6^{5}G, 5^{2}GF, 5^{0}GS, 5^{3}G, 5^{3}GS, 5^{0}G, 6^{0}G, 5^{0}GS, 6^{0}S

	Starts	1st	2nd	3rd	Win & Pl
Career Total (Turf)	17	1	2	2	7518

71	8/00	Hayd	5f	E	G-S	£3108

Total win prize-money £3108

Going (Turf): Sf: 0-3 **GS: 1-6** Gd: 0-5 GF: 0-3 Fm: 0-0
Distance: **5f/6f: 1-16** 7f-8f: 0-1 9f-13f: 0-0 14f+: 0-0
Track : LH: 0-1 RH: 0-0 Tight: 0-0 Gall: 0-0
Aids: Bl: 0-0 Vi: 0-0 Tstrap: 0-0
Best Rating: 78 6/01 NmkJ 5f gd-fm

Needs an easy surface to be seen to best effect. She has tried seven furlongs but failed to settle.

Effervescent

101(111) (88)**72**

4-y-o b f Efisio-Sharp Chief (Chief Singer)
A G Newcombe Mr A Newby

Placings:02341300**002-1221405**0345500 **(5671)**
2001: 6^{1}SD, 6^{2}SW, 6^{2}SW, 6^{1}SD, 7^{4}SD, 6^{0}G, 6^{5}SD, 6^{0}G, 7^{3}GF, 5^{4}G, 7^{5}GF, 7^{5}GY, 7^{0}GF, 6^{0}HY

	Starts	1st	2nd	3rd	Win & Pl
Career Total (Turf)	16	1	1	3	6177
Career Total (AW)	9	2	3	0	15972

80	1/01	Wolv	6f	C(0-90)H	STD	£8151
75	1/01	Sthl	6f	E(0-75)H	STD	£2933
49	7/00	Catt	5f212y	D	G-F	£2730

Total win prize-money £13814

Going (Turf): Sf: 0-3 GS: 0-0 Gd: 0-4 **GF: 1-8** Fm: 0-0
Distance: **5f/6f: 3-17** 7f-8f: 0-8 9f-13f: 0-0 14f+: 0-0
Track : **LH: 3-12** RH: 0-2 **Tight: 2-5** Gall: 0-2
Aids: Bl: 0-0 Vi: 0-0 Tstrap: 0-0
Best Rating: 88 1/01 Sthl 6f slow

Has won on turf at Catterick in 2000 and twice on the Fibresand at the start of the year, but has been held since then. Seems best over six furlongs.

Effervescing

96(89) (66)**75**

2-y-o ch g Efisio-Superspring (Superlative)
C R Egerton Charles Egerton

Placings:62305002 **(5562)**
2001: 6^{6}SD, 6^{2}GF, 5^{3}GF, 5^{0}GF, 6^{5}SW, 7^{0}S, 6^{0}GS, 5^{2}S

	Starts	1st	2nd	3rd	Win & Pl
Career Total (Turf)	6	0	2	1	3078
Career Total (AW)	2	0	0	0	0

Going (Turf): Sf: 0-2 GS: 0-1 Gd: 0-0 GF: 0-3 Fm: 0-0
Distance: 5f/6f: 0-7 7f-8f: 0-1 9f-13f: 0-0 14f+: 0-0
Track : LH: 0-4 RH: 0-0 Tight: 0-2 Gall: 0-0
Aids: Bl: 0-0 Vi: 0-0 Tstrap: 0-0
Best Rating: 82 7/01 Pont 5f gd-fm

Yet to win but has made the frame in maiden and nursery company. Possibly best suited by fast ground.

Effie Gray

90 **82**

2-y-o b f Sri Pekan (USA)-Rose Bouquet (General Assembly (USA))
P W Harris The Achab Partnership

Placings:660 **(4702)**
2001: 6^{6}F, 6^{6}GF, 7^{0}G

	Starts	1st	2nd	3rd	Win & Pl
Career Total (Turf)	3	0	0	0	0

Going (Turf): Sf: 0-0 GS: 0-0 Gd: 0-1 GF: 0-1 Fm: 0-1
Distance: 5f/6f: 0-0 7f-8f: 0-3 9f-13f: 0-0 14f+: 0-0
Track : LH: 0-2 RH: 0-0 Tight: 0-1 Gall: 0-0
Aids: Bl: 0-0 Vi: 0-0 Tstrap: 0-0
Best Rating: 82 8/01 Sals 6f212y gd-fm

Efharisto

91 **29**

12-y-o b g Dominion-Excellent Alibi (USA) (Exceller (USA))
J White Mrs P A White

Placings:046/021120/00536050050/550/06/06 **(2941)**
2001: 8^{0}GF, 10^{6}GF

	Starts	1st	2nd	3rd	Win & Pl
Career Total (Turf)	26	2	2	1	43454
Career Total (AW)	1	0	0	0	

84	6/92	Asct	1m	B(0-110)H	G-F	£18656
78	6/92	Epsm	7f	D(0-90)H	GD	£3692

Total win prize-money £22349

Going (Turf): Sf: 0-2 GS: 0-7 **Gd: 1-7 GF: 1-10** Fm: 0-0
Distance: 5f/6f: 0-0 **7f-8f: 2-15** 9f-13f: 0-11 14f+: 0-1
Track : **LH: 1-9** RH: 0-8 **Tight: 1-7** Gall: 0-5
Aids: Bl: 0-3 Vi: 0-4 Tstrap: 0-0
Best Rating: 29 7/01 Ling 1m2f gd-fm

Efidium

104(97) (67d)**48**

3-y-o b g Presidium-Efipetite (Efisio)
N Bycroft Hambleton Racing Partnership

Placings:5000010-600000200005100 **(5375)**
2001: 5^{6}SW, 6^{0}SW, 5^{0}SD, 6^{0}S, 6^{0}GF, 5^{0}GF, 6^{2}GF, 6^{0}G, 6^{0}F, 8^{0}F, 8^{0}F, 6^{5}F, 6^{1}GF, 6^{0}F, 7^{0}G

	Starts	1st	2nd	3rd	Win & Pl
Career Total (Turf)	15	1	1	0	3662
Career Total (AW)	7	1	0	0	2170

48	8/01	Rdcr	6f	F(0-60)	G-F	£2590
67	12/00	Sthl	5f	F	STD	£2170

Total win prize-money £4760

Going (Turf): Sf: 0-2 GS: 0-0 Gd: 0-4 **GF: 1-4** Fm: 0-5
Distance: **5f/6f: 2-18** 7f-8f: 0-4 9f-13f: 0-0 14f+: 0-0
Track : LH: 0-7 RH: 0-1 Tight: 0-2 Gall: 0-2
Aids: **Bl: 1-3** Vi: 0-0 Tstrap: 0-0
Best Rating: 52 6/01 Rdcr 6f gd-fm

Egypt

104(102) (77+)**74**

3-y-o b c Green Desert (USA)-Just You Wait (Nonoalco (USA))
Sir Mark Prescott Newgate Stud

Placings:000-14122224 **(5529)**
2001: 8^{1}SD, 6^{4}GF, 7^{1}SD, 8^{2}SD, 7^{2}S, 8^{2}GS, 7^{2}HY, 8^{4}HY

	Starts	1st	2nd	3rd	Win & Pl
Career Total (Turf)	8	0	3	0	4786
Career Total (AW)	3	2	1	0	5281

71	6/01	Sthl	7f	G(0-65)H	STD	£1932
68	6/01	Sthl	1m	F(0-60)H	STD	£2485

Total win prize-money £4417

Going (Turf): Sf: 0-5 GS: 0-2 Gd: 0-0 GF: 0-1 Fm: 0-0
Distance: 5f/6f: 0-3 **7f-8f: 2-6** 9f-13f: 0-2 14f+: 0-0
Track : **LH: 2-8** RH: 0-0 Tight: 0-0 Gall: 0-0
Aids: Bl: 0-1 Vi: 0-0 Tstrap: 0-0
Best Rating: 77 6/01 Sthl 1m stand

He has shown better form on Fibresand than turf so far, winning twice at Southwell in June. Suited by a mile.

Ehtefaal (USA)

99 (38)**47**

10-y-o b g Alysheba (USA)-Bolt From The Blue (USA) (Blue Times (USA))
J S King Mrs Marygold O'Kelly

Placings:3/6313/4/6/200 **(3579)**
2001: 16^{2}GF, 18^{0}GF, 14^{0}GF

	Starts	1st	2nd	3rd	Win & Pl
Career Total (Turf)	9	1	1	3	6148
Career Total (AW)	1	0	0	0	

67	6/94	Hayd	1m6f	D	GD	£3538

Total win prize-money £3538

Going (Turf): Sf: 0-0 GS: 0-2 **Gd: 1-2** GF: 0-4 Fm: 0-1
Distance: 5f/6f: 0-0 7f-8f: 0-1 9f-13f: 0-2 **14f+: 1-7**
Track : **LH: 1-6** RH: 0-3 Tight: 0-3 Gall: 0-1
Aids: Bl: 0-1 **Vi: 1-2** Tstrap: 0-0
Best Rating: 45 7/01 Chep 2m2f gd-fm

Eibh'n Abbie

89(93) (62)**73**

2-y-o b g Forzando-Brookhead Lady (Petong)
P D Evans J E Abbey

Placings:5020400063024 **(5393)**
2001: 5^{5}G, 6^{0}GF, 5^{2}GF, 6^{0}GF, 5^{4}G, 6^{0}GF, 5^{0}GS, 5^{0}GF, 6^{6}SD, 5^{3}GF, 6^{0}S, 6^{2}SD, 6^{4}SD, 5^{4}SD

	Starts	1st	2nd	3rd	Win & Pl
Career Total (Turf)	10	0	1	1	1428
Career Total (AW)	3	0	1	0	1157

Going (Turf): Sf: 0-1 GS: 0-1 Gd: 0-2 GF: 0-6 Fm: 0-0
Distance: 5f/6f: 0-12 7f-8f: 0-1 9f-13f: 0-0 14f+: 0-0
Track : LH: 0-3 RH: 0-1 Tight: 0-3 Gall: 0-1
Aids: Bl: 0-5 Vi: 0-4 Tstrap: 0-0
Best Rating: 73 8/01 Wind 5f10y gd-fm

Eight (IRE)

101(81) (27)**57**

5-y-o ch g Thatching-Up To You (Sallust)
C G Cox Charles Curtis

Placings:0/63300/035403000-613006 **(5373)**
2001: 9^{6}GF, 12^{1}GF, 14^{3}GS, 12^{0}G, 14^{0}SD, 14^{6}G

	Starts	1st	2nd	3rd	Win & Pl
Career Total (Turf)	19	1	0	5	5433
Career Total (AW)	2	0	0	0	

54	7/01	Chep	1m4f23y	F(0-70)H	G-F	£2520

Total win prize-money £2520

Going (Turf): Sf: 0-1 GS: 0-1 Gd: 0-9 **GF: 1-7** Fm: 0-1
Distance: 5f/6f: 0-1 7f-8f: 0-4 **9f-13f: 1-13** 14f+: 0-3
Track : **LH: 1-11** RH: 0-7 Tight: 0-10 Gall: 0-3
Aids: Bl: 0-1 Vi: 0-5 Tstrap: 0-0
Best Rating: 57 8/01 Yarm 1m6f17y gd-sft

His only win came at Chepstow over 12 furlongs in July of 2001, and although back down to a mark similar to that of the one he won off, he is struggling to find that same level of form.

Eighty Two (USA)

105(107) (85)**76**

5-y-o b/br h Theatrical-Heaven Knows Why (USA) (Star De Naskra (USA))
S P C Woods P K L Chu

Placings:12250/00**415-1354154**000 **(5249)**
2001: 12^{1}SD, 12^{3}GS, 12^{5}F, 12^{4}G, 10^{1}GF, 10^{5}GF, 10^{4}GS, 10^{0}G, 10^{0}G, 10^{0}S

	Starts	1st	2nd	3rd	Win & Pl
Career Total (Turf)	16	2	2	1	21835
Career Total (AW)	4	2	0	0	7686

80	7/01	Ches	1m2f75y	D(0-80)H	G-F	£5798
85	3/01	Ling	1m4f	D(0-85)H	STD	£3883
79	11/00	Ling	1m2f	D(0-85)H	STD	£3802
	3/99	Toul	1m2f		VS	£4090

Total win prize-money £17575

Going (Turf): Sf: 0-2 GS: 0-3 Gd: 0-3 **GF: 1-2** Fm: 0-1
Distance: 5f/6f: 0-0 7f-8f: 0-0 **9f-13f: 3-14** 14f+: 0-1
Track : **LH: 3-10** RH: 0-4 **Tight: 3-7** Gall: 0-5
Aids: Bl: 0-0 Vi: 0-0 Tstrap: 0-0
Best Rating: 85 3/01 Ling 1m4f stand

A French import, he is suited by a tight left-handed track as he has shown with two victories on the Lingfield Equitrack and one at Chester. He has won over 12 furlongs, but looks better over shorter.

Eiraardia (IRE)

73(68) (23)**26**

2-y-o br f Petardia-Eiras Mood (Jalmood (USA))

P D Evans Miss D L Wisbey

Placings:6000 **(2583)**

2001: 5^{6}S, 5^{0}SD, 7^{0}GF, 7^{0}SD

	Starts	1st	2nd	3rd	Win & Pl
Career Total (Turf)	2	0	0	0	0
Career Total (AW)	2	0	0	0	

Going (Turf): Sf: 0-1 GS: 0-0 Gd: 0-0 GF: 0-1 Fm: 0-0

Distance: 5f/6f: 0-2 7f-8f: 0-2 9f-13f: 0-0 14f+: 0-0

Track : LH: 0-1 RH: 0-0 Tight: 0-0 Gall: 0-0

Aids: Bl: 0-0 Vi: 0-0 Tstrap: 0-0

Best Rating: 26 3/01 Donc 5f soft

Ekraar (USA)

116 (112)**118**

4-y-o b h Red Ransom (USA)-Sacahuista (USA) (Raja Baba (USA))

Saeed Bin Suroor Godolphin

Placings:2143/34111-403451 **(4699)**

2001: 10^{4}FT, 10^{0}FT, 9^{3}G, 12^{4}GF, 12^{5}GS, 12^{1}GS

	Starts	1st	2nd	3rd	Win & Pl
Career Total (Turf)	13	5	1	3	162488
Career Total (AW)	2	0	0	0	3188

112	9/01	Donc	1m4f	A	G-S	£17956
120	9/00	Gdwd	1m1f192yA		GD	£24000
114	8/00	Hayd	1m2f120yA		GD	£23200
113	7/00	Newb	1m2f6y	C	G-F	£6235
113	7/99	Gdwd	7f	A	G-F	£26600

Total win prize-money £97991

Going (Turf): Sf: 0-1 GS: 1-3 **Gd: 2-4 GF: 2-4** Fm: 0-0

Distance: 5f/6f: 0-0 7f-8f: 1-6 **9f-13f: 4-9** 14f+: 0-0

Track : **LH: 3-5** RH: 2-4 Tight: 1-2 **Gall: 2-4**

Aids: Bl: 0-4 Vi: 1-2 Tstrap: 1-3

Best Rating: 118 6/01 Epsm 1m4f10y gd-fm

A useful two-year-old, he was held in top company at the start of 2000, but went on to complete a hat-trick with wins at Newbury, Haydock and Goodwood. He has again been taking on some of the best this season and was being comfortably held until taking a Listed event at Doncaster. Suited by ten to 12 furlongs and fast ground, but handles cut.

El Dolor (IRE)

105(103) (60)**59**

4-y-o br g Elbio-Payne's Grey (Godswalk (USA))

R A Fahey Mrs M W Kenyon

Placings:2500/**0135330**13 **(3077)**

2001: 7^{0}SW, **5^{1}**SD, **6^{3}**SD, 5^{5}GF, **5^{3}**SD, 5^{3}GF, 5^{0}GF, **5^{1}**SD, 5^{3}GS

	Starts	1st	2nd	3rd	Win & Pl
Career Total (Turf)	8	0	1	2	2790
Career Total (AW)	5	2	0	2	5787

60	7/01	Sthl	5f	E(0-75)H	STD	£3458
42	4/01	Sthl	5f	F	STD	£1792

Total win prize-money £5250

Going (Turf): Sf: 0-1 GS: 0-2 Gd: 0-1 GF: 0-4 Fm: 0-0

Distance: **5f/6f: 2-12** 7f-8f: 0-1 9f-13f: 0-0 14f+: 0-0

Track : LH: 0-3 RH: 0-0 Tight: 0-1 Gall: 0-0

Aids: Bl: 1-3 Vi: 1-4 Tstrap: 0-0

Best Rating: 60 7/01 Sthl 5f stand

A winner of a maiden and a handicap at Southwell, both over five furlongs on the All-Weather, he is effective both racing near and off the pace, but is not a consistent sort.

El Emel (USA)

76(87) (55)**31**

4-y-o b g Green Dancer (USA)-Moivouloirtoi (USA) (Bering)

I A Balding Rodger Sargent

Placings:2/123540-500 **(0463)**

2001: 8^{5}SD, 8^{0}SW, 9^{0}SD

	Starts	1st	2nd	3rd	Win & Pl
Career Total (Turf)	7	1	2	1	8343
Career Total (AW)	3	0	0	0	266

3/00	Kref	1m110y	HVY	£1774

Total win prize-money £1774

Going (Turf): Sf: 0-1 GS: 0-0 Gd: 0-1 GF: 0-0 Fm: 0-0

Distance: 5f/6f: 0-0 7f-8f: 0-0 9f-13f: 0-5 14f+: 0-0

Track : LH: 0-4 RH: 0-0 Tight: 0-3 Gall: 0-1

Aids: Bl: 0-1 Vi: 0-0 Tstrap: 0-0

Best Rating: 55 2/01 Wolv 1m100y stand

El Fuerte

88(74) **4**

6-y-o b g Perpendicular-Sleekit (Blakeney)

W Clay Lee Heath

Placings:00500/00/00000 **(1137)**

2001: 12^{0}SD, 12^{0}SW, 9^{0}SW, 14^{0}S, 11^{0}G

	Starts	1st	2nd	3rd	Win & Pl
Career Total (Turf)	7	0	0	0	0
Career Total (AW)	5	0	0	0	

Going (Turf): Sf: 0-2 GS: 0-1 Gd: 0-1 GF: 0-3 Fm: 0-0

Distance: 5f/6f: 0-0 7f-8f: 0-0 9f-13f: 0-9 14f+: 0-3

Track : LH: 0-8 RH: 0-2 Tight: 0-5 Gall: 0-0

Aids: Bl: 0-0 Vi: 0-3 Tstrap: 0-2

Best Rating: 4 4/01 Nott 1m6f15y soft

El Giza (USA)

97 **50**

3-y-o ch c Cozzene (USA)-Gazayil (USA) (Irish River (FR))

H R A Cecil Raymond Tooth

Placings:0-500 **(5098)**

2001: 11^{5}G, 12^{0}G, 14^{0}GS

	Starts	1st	2nd	3rd	Win & Pl
Career Total (Turf)	4	0	0	0	0

Going (Turf): Sf: 0-1 GS: 0-1 Gd: 0-2 GF: 0-0 Fm: 0-0

Distance: 5f/6f: 0-1 7f-8f: 0-0 9f-13f: 0-2 14f+: 0-1

Track : LH: 0-1 RH: 0-2 Tight: 0-2 Gall: 0-0

Aids: Bl: 0-0 Vi: 0-0 Tstrap: 0-0

Best Rating: 50 8/01 Bevl 1m3f216y good

El Gran Hombre (USA)

87(82) (19)87

5-y-o ch g El Gran Senor (USA)-Conquistress (USA) (Conquistador Cielo (USA))

D Nicholls (C J Mann 27/4) Richard Longley

Placings:460/1/0060 **(3875)**

2001: 12^{0}SD, 12^{0}G, 8^{6}SD, 8^{0}GS

	Starts	1st	2nd	3rd	Win & Pl
Career Total (Turf)	6	1	0	0	2747
Career Total (AW)	2	0	0	0	0

73	8/99	Wxfd	1m5f	GD	£2484

Total win prize-money £2484

Going (Turf): Sf: 0-1 GS: 0-1 **Gd: 1-2** GF: 0-0 Fm: 0-0

Distance: 5f/6f: 0-0 7f-8f: 0-5 **9f-13f: 1-3** 14f+: 0-0

Track : LH: 0-4 **RH: 1-4** Tight: 0-1 Gall: 0-3

Aids: Bl: 0-0 Vi: 0-0 Tstrap: 0-3

Best Rating: 27 8/01 Thsk 1m gd-sft

El Hakma

107 **84**

3-y-o b f Shareef Dancer (USA)-Clare Court (Glint Of Gold)

C E Brittain Saeed Manana

Placings:4104 **(4991)**

2001: 9^{4}G, 12^{1}GS, 14^{0}GF, 14^{4}HY

	Starts	1st	2nd	3rd	Win & Pl
Career Total (Turf)	4	1	0	0	4867

76	8/01	Ches	1m4f66y	D	G-S £4309

Total win prize-money £4310

Going (Turf): Sf: 0-1 **GS: 1-1** Gd: 0-1 GF: 0-1 Fm: 0-0

Distance: 5f/6f: 0-0 7f-8f: 0-0 **9f-13f: 1-2** 14f+: 0-2

Track : **LH: 1-3** RH: 0-1 **Tight: 1-2** Gall: 0-1

Aids: Bl: 0-0 Vi: 0-0 Tstrap: 0-0

Best Rating: 84 9/01 Donc 1m6f132y gd-fm

Bred to stay, showed the benefit of her debut when taking a small 12-furlong maiden at Chester. Has won on good to soft ground.

El Hamra (IRE)

96(98) (71+)**64**

3-y-o gr c Royal Abjar (USA)-Cherlinoa (FR) (Crystal Palace (FR))

B A McMahon R Thornhill

Placings:503335231-600635 **(3457)**

2001: 7^{6}S, 10^{0}S, 8^{0}F, 8^{6}GF, 8^{3}GF, 8^{5}GF

	Starts	1st	2nd	3rd	Win & Pl
Career Total (Turf)	10	0	0	3	1422
Career Total (AW)	5	1	1	2	3299

71	10/00	Wolv	1m100y	F	STD	£1694

Total win prize-money £1694

Going (Turf): Sf: 0-2 GS: 0-0 Gd: 0-2 GF: 0-5 Fm: 0-1

Distance: 5f/6f: 0-2 7f-8f: 0-6 **9f-13f: 1-7** 14f+: 0-0

Track : **LH: 1-8** RH: 0-1 **Tight: 1-5** Gall: 0-0

Aids: Bl: 0-0 Vi: 0-0 Tstrap: 0-0

Best Rating: 64 4/01 NmkR 1m2f soft

El Karim (USA)

82(66) 30

5-y-o ch h Storm Cat (USA)-Gmaasha (IRE) (Kris)

R Ford R Burgess

Placings:03/00/05-00000 **(2342)**

2001: 9^{0}G, 6^{0}F, 6^{0}GF, 6^{0}GF, 7^{0}SD

	Starts	1st	2nd	3rd	Win & Pl
Career Total (Turf)	10	0	0	1	808
Career Total (AW)	1	0	0	0	

Going (Turf): Sf: 0-0 GS: 0-1 Gd: 0-1 GF: 0-6 Fm: 0-2

Distance: 5f/6f: 0-2 7f-8f: 0-7 9f-13f: 0-2 14f+: 0-0

Track : LH: 0-1 RH: 0-3 Tight: 0-0 Gall: 0-0

Aids: Bl: 0-0 Vi: 0-0 Tstrap: 0-7

Best Rating: 30 6/01 Haml 6f5y gd-fm

El Maximo (IRE)

90 **65**

3-y-o b g First Trump-Kentucky Starlet (USA) (Cox's Ridge (USA))

M G Quinlan Mario Lanfranchi

Placings:6326152400-0001 **(4967a)**

2001: 7^{0}G, 8^{0}GF, 7^{0}F, 7^{1}G

	Starts	1st	2nd	3rd	Win & Pl
Career Total (Turf)	14	2	2	1	6590

65	9/01	Turi	7f		GD	£1971
73	7/00	Folk	7f	F	GD	£1778

Total win prize-money £3749

Going (Turf): Sf: 0-2 GS: 0-1 **Gd: 2-6** GF: 0-4 Fm: 0-1

Distance: 5f/6f: 0-5 **7f-8f: 2-9** 9f-13f: 0-0 14f+: 0-0

Track : LH: 0-2 RH: 0-1 Tight: 0-0 Gall: 0-1

Aids: Bl: 0-7 Vi: 0-0 Tstrap: 0-7

Best Rating: 65 9/01 Turi 7f good

El Misti

95(80) (48)61

2-y-o b f Elmaamul (USA)-Sherrington (Thatching)

M D I Usher B H Simpson

Placings:005002530 **(5458)**

2001: 5^{0}SD, 6^{0}GF, 5^{5}F, 7^{0}SD, 6^{0}GF, 6^{2}S, 6^{5}SD, 5^{3}HY, 5^{0}G

	Starts	1st	2nd	3rd	Win & Pl
Career Total (Turf)	6	0	1	1	995
Career Total (AW)	3	0	0	0	0

Going (Turf): Sf: 0-2 GS: 0-0 Gd: 0-1 GF: 0-2 Fm: 0-1
Distance: 5f/6f: 0-7 7f-8f: 0-2 9f-13f: 0-0 14f+: 0-0
Track : LH: 0-4 RH: 0-0 Tight: 0-1 Gall: 0-1
Aids: Bl: 0-0 Vi: 0-0 Tstrap: 0-0
Best Rating: 61 9/01 Yarm 6f3y soft

El Raymondo

66 43

2-y-o b g Night Shift (USA)-Alaraby (IRE) (Caerleon (USA))

M Blanshard Mrs P Buckley

Placings:00 **(5094)**

2001: 7^{0}G, 8^{0}GS

	Starts	1st	2nd	3rd	Win & Pl
Career Total (Turf)	2	0	0	0	

Going (Turf): Sf: 0-0 GS: 0-1 Gd: 0-1 GF: 0-0 Fm: 0-0
Distance: 5f/6f: 0-0 7f-8f: 0-2 9f-13f: 0-0 14f+: 0-0
Track : LH: 0-0 RH: 0-0 Tight: 0-0 Gall: 0-0
Aids: Bl: 0-0 Vi: 0-0 Tstrap: 0-0
Best Rating: 43 10/01 Sals 1m gd-sft

El Talgo (IRE)

89(60) (6)56

2-y-o b c Common Grounds-Lovely Me (IRE) (Vision (USA))

N Tinkler Mike Gosse

Placings:000000 **(4777)**

2001: 5^{0}GF, 5^{0}SD, 5^{0}GS, 5^{0}GF, 5^{0}HY, 5^{0}G

	Starts	1st	2nd	3rd	Win & Pl
Career Total (Turf)	5	0	0	0	
Career Total (AW)	1	0	0	0	

Going (Turf): Sf: 0-1 GS: 0-1 Gd: 0-1 GF: 0-2 Fm: 0-0
Distance: 5f/6f: 0-6 7f-8f: 0-0 9f-13f: 0-0 14f+: 0-0
Track : LH: 0-1 RH: 0-0 Tight: 0-0 Gall: 0-0
Aids: Bl: 0-0 Vi: 0-0 Tstrap: 0-4
Best Rating: 56 9/01 Hayd 5f heavy

El Uno (IRE)

101(82) (48)47

3-y-o ch c Elmaamul (USA)-Fawaakeh (USA) (Lyphard (USA))

J L Eyre E Richmond

Placings:00650046-003425000 **(4422)**

2001: 7^{0}GF, 7^{0}GF, 11^{3}GF, 10^{4}GF, 9^{2}S, 8^{5}G, 8^{0}F, 9^{0}G, 10^{0}GF

	Starts	1st	2nd	3rd	Win & Pl
Career Total (Turf)	14	0	1	1	1176
Career Total (AW)	3	0	0	0	0

Going (Turf): Sf: 0-3 GS: 0-0 Gd: 0-3 GF: 0-7 Fm: 0-1
Distance: 5f/6f: 0-3 7f-8f: 0-6 9f-13f: 0-8 14f+: 0-0
Track : LH: 0-8 RH: 0-7 Tight: 0-9 Gall: 0-0
Aids: Bl: 0-1 Vi: 0-0 Tstrap: 0-0
Best Rating: 49 6/01 Rdcr 1m3f gd-fm

El Zito (IRE)

(89) (67)89

4-y-o b g Mukaddamah (USA)-Samite (FR) (Tennyson (FR))

M G Quinlan Mario Lanfranchi

Placings:23/021103300-0 **(0426)**

2001: 12^{0}SD

	Starts	1st	2nd	3rd	Win & Pl
Career Total (Turf)	10	2	2	2	16422
Career Total (AW)	2	0	0	1	315

85 6/00 Bevl 1m3f216yE(0-75)H G-F £3841
84 6/00 Ches 1m2f75y D(0-75) G-S £6272
Total win prize-money £10115

Going (Turf): Sf: 0-2 **GS: 1-2** Gd: 0-1 **GF: 1-3** Fm: 0-0
Distance: 5f/6f: 0-0 7f-8f: 0-1 **9f-13f: 2-10** 14f+: 0-0
Track : LH: 1-7 RH: 1-3 **Tight: 2-6** Gall: 0-1
Aids: Bl: 0-0 Vi: 0-0 Tstrap: 0-1
Best Rating: 60 3/01 Wolv 1m4f stand

Ela Athena

113 119

5-y-o gr m Ezzoud (IRE)-Crodelle (IRE) (Formidable (USA))

M A Jarvis Gary A Tanaka

Placings:1212/041252342-2263 **(4686a)**

2001: 11^{2}G, 12^{2}G, 12^{6}G, 11^{3}F

	Starts	1st	2nd	3rd	Win & Pl
Career Total (Turf)	17	3	7	2	736763

109 7/00 Hayd 1m3f200yA G-F £24000
107 7/99 Chep 1m2f36y A G-F £12718
79 4/99 Newb 1m2f6y D G-F £4727
Total win prize-money £41446

Going (Turf): Sf: 0-0 GS: 0-0 Gd: 0-7 **GF: 3-5** Fm: 0-4
Distance: 5f/6f: 0-0 7f-8f: 0-0 **9f-13f: 3-17** 14f+: 0-0
Track : **LH: 3-9** RH: 0-5 Tight: 0-2 **Gall: 1-5**
Aids: Bl: 0-0 Vi: 0-0 Tstrap: 0-0
Best Rating: 116 6/01 Wind 1m3f135y good

A high-class mare, she won the Lancashire Oaks in 2000 before embarking on a world tour, running a series of fine races at the top level. Retired to stud.

Ela D'Argent (IRE)

91 72d

2-y-o b f Ela-Mana-Mou-Petite-D-Argent (Noalto)

M Johnston D Couper,G Hosie, D Ward & Co

Placings:441000 **(5690)**

2001: 5^{4}S, 5^{4}G, 8^{1}G, 8^{0}G, 8^{0}S, 7^{0}S

	Starts	1st	2nd	3rd	Win & Pl
Career Total (Turf)	6	1	0	0	2401

72 8/01 Newc 1m3y F GD £2401
Total win prize-money £2401

Going (Turf): Sf: 0-3 GS: 0-0 **Gd: 1-3** GF: 0-0 Fm: 0-0
Distance: 5f/6f: 0-2 7f-8f: 0-2 **9f-13f: 1-2** 14f+: 0-0
Track : LH: 0-2 RH: 0-0 Tight: 0-0 Gall: 0-0
Aids: Bl: 0-0 Vi: 0-0 Tstrap: 0-1
Best Rating: 72 8/01 Newc 1m3y good

A full-sister to the stable's useful staying handicapper Mana d'Argent, she relished the step up to a mile on rain-softened ground when scoring in maiden company at Newcastle in August. Held in handicaps since, including back down to seven furlongs.

Ela Jay

88

2-y-o b f Double Eclipse (IRE)-Papirusa (IRE) (Pennine Walk)

G A Butler J & L Wetherald - M & M Glover

Placings:0 **(5038)**

2001: 5^{0}G

	Starts	1st	2nd	3rd	Win & Pl
Career Total (Turf)	1	0	0	0	

Going (Turf): Sf: 0-0 GS: 0-0 Gd: 0-1 GF: 0-0 Fm: 0-0
Distance: 5f/6f: 0-1 7f-8f: 0-0 9f-13f: 0-0 14f+: 0-0
Track : LH: 0-1 RH: 0-0 Tight: 0-0 Gall: 0-1
Aids: Bl: 0-0 Vi: 0-0 Tstrap: 0-0

Ela Marathona (IRE)

89 91

2-y-o b c Doyoun-Peace Melody (IRE) (Classic Music (USA))

L M Cumani Andreas Michael

Placings:25 **(5658)**

2001: 7^{2}S, 7^{5}G

	Starts	1st	2nd	3rd	Win & Pl
Career Total (Turf)	2	0	1	0	1398

Going (Turf): Sf: 0-1 GS: 0-0 Gd: 0-1 GF: 0-0 Fm: 0-0
Distance: 5f/6f: 0-0 7f-8f: 0-2 9f-13f: 0-0 14f+: 0-0
Track : LH: 0-0 RH: 0-0 Tight: 0-0 Gall: 0-0
Aids: Bl: 0-0 Vi: 0-0 Tstrap: 0-0
Best Rating: 91 10/01 Yarm 7f3y soft

He showed plenty of promise on his Yarmouth debut and should have little difficulty getting off the mark.

Ela-Darlin-Mou

80 57d

3-y-o gr f Mtoto-Ancestry (Persepolis (FR))

K T Ivory Mrs Andry Muinos

Placings:000-0000 **(2426)**

2001: 8^{0}GF, 6^{0}GF, 6^{0}GF, 8^{0}GF

	Starts	1st	2nd	3rd	Win & Pl
Career Total (Turf)	7	0	0	0	

Going (Turf): Sf: 0-0 GS: 0-0 Gd: 0-0 GF: 0-7 Fm: 0-0
Distance: 5f/6f: 0-0 7f-8f: 0-6 9f-13f: 0-1 14f+: 0-0
Track : LH: 0-1 RH: 0-1 Tight: 0-0 Gall: 0-0
Aids: Bl: 0-2 Vi: 0-0 Tstrap: 0-0
Best Rating: 45 5/01 Gdwd 1m gd-fm

Elayoon (USA)

86 75

2-y-o b f Danzig (USA)-Ajfan (USA) (Woodman (USA))

M P Tregoning Hamdan Al Maktoum

Placings:2 **(4458)**

2001: 6^{2}G

	Starts	1st	2nd	3rd	Win & Pl
Career Total (Turf)	1	0	1	0	804

Going (Turf): Sf: 0-0 GS: 0-0 Gd: 0-1 GF: 0-0 Fm: 0-0
Distance: 5f/6f: 0-1 7f-8f: 0-0 9f-13f: 0-0 14f+: 0-0
Track : LH: 0-0 RH: 0-0 Tight: 0-0 Gall: 0-0
Aids: Bl: 0-0 Vi: 0-0 Tstrap: 0-0
Best Rating: 75 9/01 Folk 6f good

Elder Princess (IRE)

74 27

2-y-o b f Houmayoun (FR)-Lanesra (IRE) (Taufan (USA))

T P McGovern Richard Matthews

Placings:00 **(5590)**

2001: 6^{0}S, 9^{0}GS

	Starts	1st	2nd	3rd	Win & Pl
Career Total (Turf)	2	0	0	0	

Going (Turf): Sf: 0-1 GS: 0-1 Gd: 0-0 GF: 0-0 Fm: 0-0
Distance: 5f/6f: 0-0 7f-8f: 0-1 9f-13f: 0-1 14f+: 0-0
Track : LH: 0-2 RH: 0-0 Tight: 0-0 Gall: 0-0
Aids: Bl: 0-0 Vi: 0-0 Tstrap: 0-0
Best Rating: 27 10/01 Brig 6f209y soft

Electrum (IRE)

81 **77**

5-y-o b g Up And At 'Em-Short Stay (Be My Guest (USA))
Eddie Creighton (J C Hayden 9/6) Mrs C Creighton

Placings:434302403150/03-**21010** **(3974)**
2001: 8^{2}SD, 9^{1}SD, 8^{0}SD, 6^{1}SW, 7^{0}GF

	Starts	1st	2nd	3rd	Win & Pl
Career Total (Turf)	15	1	1	4	10991
Career Total (AW)	4	2	1	0	3862

6/01 Mija 6f SLW £1625
5/01 Mija 1m1f STD £1625
88 9/99 Curr 5f SFT £6900
Total win prize-money £10150

Going (Turf): Sf: 1-7 GS: 0-2 Gd: 0-1 GF: 0-4 Fm: 0-0
Distance: **5f/6f: 2-14** 7f-8f: 0-4 9f-13f: 1-1 14f+: 0-0
Track : LH: 0-3 RH: 0-1 Tight: 0-1 Gall: 0-0
Aids: **Bl: 1-5** Vi: 0-1 Tstrap: 0-0
Best Rating: 31 8/01 Epsm 7f gd-fm

Elegant Escort (USA)

88(88) (11)**60**

4-y-o b c Take Me Out (USA)-Get With It (USA) (King Pellinore (USA))
Mrs G S Rees Times Of Wigan

Placings:31/6000-000 **(0338)**
2001: 8^{0}SD, 8^{0}SD, 9^{0}SD

	Starts	1st	2nd	3rd	Win & Pl
Career Total (Turf)	2	0	0	0	0
Career Total (AW)	7	1	0	1	3103

74 12/99 Sthl 1m D STD £2794
Total win prize-money £2794

Going (Turf): Sf: 0-0 GS: 0-1 Gd: 0-1 GF: 0-0 Fm: 0-0
Distance: 5f/6f: 0-1 **7f-8f: 1-4** 9f-13f: 0-4 14f+: 0-0
Track : **LH: 1-8** RH: 0-1 Tight: 0-5 Gall: 0-0
Aids: Bl: 0-0 Vi: 0-0 Tstrap: 0-0
Best Rating: 11 1/01 Sthl 1m stand

Elgria (IRE)

101 **78**

3-y-o b/br c Distinctly North (USA)-Perfect Swinger (Shernazar)
R Hannon Mrs Betty Valentine

Placings:3-030661000 **(5267)**
2001: 8^{0}GF, 6^{3}GF, 10^{0}GF, 8^{6}GF, 8^{6}G, 8^{1}GF, 9^{0}GS, 8^{0}G, 6^{0}GS

	Starts	1st	2nd	3rd	Win & Pl
Career Total (Turf)	10	1	0	2	5336

78 8/01 Epsm 1m114y D G-F £4095
Total win prize-money £4095

Going (Turf): Sf: 0-1 GS: 0-2 Gd: 0-2 **GF: 1-5** Fm: 0-0
Distance: 5f/6f: 0-1 7f-8f: 0-5 **9f-13f: 1-4** 14f+: 0-0
Track : **LH: 1-2** RH: 0-6 **Tight: 1-3** Gall: 0-1
Aids: Bl: 0-0 Vi: 0-0 Tstrap: 0-0
Best Rating: 78 8/01 Epsm 1m114y gd-fm

He looked pretty much exposed before landing a modest four-runner maiden at Epsom in August and has shown little since then.

Elheba (IRE)

93(91) (59)**62**

2-y-o b/br g Elbio-Fireheba (ITY) (Fire Of Life (USA))
J S Moore Ernie Houghton

Placings:600324 **(5667)**
2001: 5^{6}S, 5^{0}GS, 8^{0}G, 8^{3}SD, 8^{2}HY, 8^{4}HY

	Starts	1st	2nd	3rd	Win & Pl
Career Total (Turf)	5	0	1	0	562
Career Total (AW)	1	0	0	1	528

Going (Turf): Sf: 0-3 GS: 0-1 Gd: 0-1 GF: 0-0 Fm: 0-0
Distance: 5f/6f: 0-2 7f-8f: 0-2 9f-13f: 0-2 14f+: 0-0
Track : LH: 0-4 RH: 0-1 Tight: 0-1 Gall: 0-1
Aids: Bl: 0-0 Vi: 0-0 Tstrap: 0-0
Best Rating: 62 10/01 Nott 1m54y heavy

He is only modest, but looks as though he is going to need a real test of stamina.

Eliipop

101 **69**

3-y-o b g First Trump-Hasty Key (USA) (Key To The Mint (USA))
J R Fanshawe Mrs Hannele Morgan

Placings:43320 **(3957)**
2001: 8^{4}G, 7^{3}GF, 9^{3}F, 10^{2}GF, 9^{0}GF

	Starts	1st	2nd	3rd	Win & Pl
Career Total (Turf)	5	0	1	2	3089

Going (Turf): Sf: 0-0 GS: 0-0 Gd: 0-1 GF: 0-3 Fm: 0-1
Distance: 5f/6f: 0-0 7f-8f: 0-1 9f-13f: 0-4 14f+: 0-0
Track : LH: 0-2 RH: 0-3 Tight: 0-3 Gall: 0-1
Aids: Bl: 0-0 Vi: 0-0 Tstrap: 0-0
Best Rating: 69 6/01 Bevl 7f100y gd-fm

Eljohar (IRE)

111 **90**

4-y-o ch c Nashwan (USA)-Mehthaaf (USA) (Nureyev (USA))
J H M Gosden Hamdan Al Maktoum

Placings:3-22 **(2257)**
2001: 10^{2}GF, 10^{2}G

	Starts	1st	2nd	3rd	Win & Pl
Career Total (Turf)	3	0	2	1	3196

Going (Turf): Sf: 0-0 GS: 0-0 Gd: 0-2 GF: 0-1 Fm: 0-0
Distance: 5f/6f: 0-0 7f-8f: 0-1 9f-13f: 0-2 14f+: 0-0
Track : LH: 0-0 RH: 0-1 Tight: 0-1 Gall: 0-0
Aids: Bl: 0-0 Vi: 0-0 Tstrap: 0-1
Best Rating: 90 5/01 Sand 1m2f7y gd-fm

Eljutan (IRE)

105 **54**

3-y-o b g Namaqualand (USA)-Camarat (Ahonoora)
R J O'Sullivan Jack Joseph

Placings:0000450 **(5330)**
2001: 8^{0}GF, 9^{0}F, 8^{0}GF, 12^{0}G, 12^{4}GF, 16^{5}GF, 16^{0}HY

	Starts	1st	2nd	3rd	Win & Pl
Career Total (Turf)	7	0	0	0	389

Going (Turf): Sf: 0-1 GS: 0-0 Gd: 0-1 GF: 0-4 Fm: 0-1
Distance: 5f/6f: 0-0 7f-8f: 0-1 9f-13f: 0-4 14f+: 0-2
Track : LH: 0-5 RH: 0-1 Tight: 0-5 Gall: 0-0
Aids: Bl: 0-0 Vi: 0-0 Tstrap: 0-0
Best Rating: 58 5/01 Kemp 1m gd-fm

Ella Carisa

88 **57**

2-y-o b f Elmaamul (USA)-Salty Girl (IRE) (Scenic)
K O Cunningham-Brown Lenan Pipco Limited

Placings:0600 **(5459)**
2001: 7^{0}GF, 8^{6}G, 7^{0}S, 8^{0}G

	Starts	1st	2nd	3rd	Win & Pl
Career Total (Turf)	4	0	0	0	0

Going (Turf): Sf: 0-1 GS: 0-0 Gd: 0-2 GF: 0-1 Fm: 0-0
Distance: 5f/6f: 0-0 7f-8f: 0-2 9f-13f: 0-2 14f+: 0-0
Track : LH: 0-3 RH: 0-0 Tight: 0-1 Gall: 0-1
Aids: Bl: 0-0 Vi: 0-0 Tstrap: 0-0
Best Rating: 57 9/01 Nott 1m54y good

Ella Falls (IRE)

99 **47**

6-y-o b m Dancing Dissident (USA)-Over Swing (FR) (Saint Cyrien (FR))
Mrs H Dalton Ray Bailey, Andrew Dalton

Placings:4060/340P60650000055/116320 **(4728)**
2001: 16^{1}F, 16^{1}GF, 14^{6}GF, 16^{3}GF, 16^{2}F, 16^{0}GF

	Starts	1st	2nd	3rd	Win & Pl
Career Total (Turf)	19	2	1	1	6876
Career Total (AW)	6	0	0	1	238

41 7/01 Folk 2m93y F(0-60)H G-F £2464
35 7/01 Muss 2m F(0-60)H FRM £2786
Total win prize-money £5250

Going (Turf): Sf: 0-0 GS: 0-1 Gd: 0-6 **GF: 1-9 Fm: 1-3**
Distance: 5f/6f: 0-5 7f-8f: 0-7 9f-13f: 0-7 **14f+: 2-6**
Track : LH: 0-11 **RH: 2-6 Tight: 2-4** Gall: 0-0
Aids: Bl: 0-1 Vi: 0-0 Tstrap: 0-0
Best Rating: 47 9/01 Muss 2m firm

A winning hurdler/pointer, she broke her maiden on the Flat when stepped up to two miles in an apprentice handicap at Musselburgh in July. She was held up that day, but raced prominently when following up over an extended two miles at Folkestone ten days later.

Ella Pee-Elle

80 **24**

6-y-o b m Elmaamul (USA)-Alipampa (IRE) (Glenstal (USA))
R J Price Rock Racing Club

Placings:0-00 **(5041)**
2001: 9^{0}GF, 10^{0}G

	Starts	1st	2nd	3rd	Win & Pl
Career Total (Turf)	2	0	0		
Career Total (AW)	1	0	0	0	

Going (Turf): Sf: 0-0 GS: 0-0 Gd: 0-1 GF: 0-1 Fm: 0-0
Distance: 5f/6f: 0-0 7f-8f: 0-0 9f-13f: 0-3 14f+: 0-0
Track : LH: 0-2 RH: 0-1 Tight: 0-2 Gall: 0-0
Aids: Bl. 0-0 Vi. 0-0 Tstrap. 0-0
Best Rating: 6 9/01 Leic 1m1f218y gd-fm

Ella-Tino

69 **61d**

3-y-o b f Reprimand-Tino-Ella (Bustino)
J A Glover B H Farr

Placings:654-600 **(2042)**
2001: 6^{6}HY, 6^{0}HY, 6^{0}GF

	Starts	1st	2nd	3rd	Win & Pl
Career Total (Turf)	6	0	0	0	255

Going (Turf): Sf: 0-4 GS: 0-1 Gd: 0-0 GF: 0-1 Fm: 0-0
Distance: 5f/6f: 0-2 7f-8f: 0-3 9f-13f: 0-1 14f+: 0-0
Track : LH: 0-3 RH: 0-0 Tight: 0-0 Gall: 0-0
Aids: Bl: 0-0 Vi: 0-1 Tstrap: 0-0
Best Rating: 23 4/01 Pont 6f heavy

Ellamine

102(99) (32)**30**

7-y-o b m Warrshan (USA)-Anhaar (Ela-Mana-Mou)
M C Pipe (J Neville 20/10) Mrs Jayne Lewis

Placings:0016/605/03524 **(3816)**

2001: 12^{0}SD, 13^{3}SD, 12^{5}SD, 16^{2}GF, 14^{4}SD

	Starts	1st	2nd	3rd	Win & Pl
Career Total (Turf)	1	0	1	0	684
Career Total (AW)	11	1	0	1	2070

40 12/97 Wolv 1m6f166yG STD £1738
Total win prize-money £1738

Going (Turf): Sf: 0-0 GS: 0-0 Gd: 0-0 GF: 0-1 Fm: 0-0
Distance: 5f/6f: 0-0 7f-8f: 0-1 9f-13f: 0-6 **14f+: 1-5**
Track : **LH: 1-12** RH: 0-0 **Tight: 1-10** Gall: 0-0
Aids: Bl: 0-2 Vi: 0-0 Tstrap: 0-0
Best Rating: 32 4/01 Ling 1m4f stand

Elle Royal (IRE)

95 **79**
2-y-o br f Ali-Royal (IRE)-Silvretta (IRE) (Tirol)
T P McGovern The Green And Gold Partnership

Placings:063 **(5520)**
2001: 7^{0}GF, 6^{6}HY, 8^{3}HY

	Starts	1st	2nd	3rd	Win & Pl
Career Total (Turf)	3	0	0	1	603

Going (Turf): Sf: 0-2 GS: 0-0 Gd: 0-0 GF: 0-1 Fm: 0-0
Distance: 5f/6f: 0-1 7f-8f: 0-1 9f-13f: 0-1 14f+: 0-0
Track : LH: 0-0 RH: 0-1 Tight: 0-1 Gall: 0-0
Aids: Bl: 0-0 Vi: 0-0 Tstrap: 0-0
Best Rating: 79 10/01 Wind 1m67y heavy

Ellen Mooney

106 **77**
2-y-o ch f Efisio-Budby (Rock City)
B Smart E A Draper, J K Walker & G Edmondson

Placings:32210210 **(5379)**
2001: 5^{3}HY, 6^{2}GF, 7^{2}GF, 7^{1}GS, 6^{0}GS, 7^{2}S, 7^{1}HY, 7^{0}S

	Starts	1st	2nd	3rd	Win & Pl
Career Total (Turf)	8	2	3	1	10870

77 10/01 Ling 7f E(0-75) HVY £3290
77 8/01 Bevl 7f100y E G-S £3136
Total win prize-money £6426

Going (Turf): Sf: 1-4 GS: 1-2 Gd: 0-0 GF: 0-2 Fm: 0-0
Distance: 5f/6f: 0-2 **7f-8f: 2-6** 9f-13f: 0-0 14f+: 0-0
Track : LH: 0-3 **RH: 1-2** Tight: 0-2 Gall: 0-1
Aids: Bl: 0-0 Vi: 0-0 Tstrap: 0-0
Best Rating: 77 10/01 Ling 7f heavy

Got off the mark in a maiden auction at the fourth attempt. Suited by seven furlongs, seems to handle fast, but at her best with cut. Defied top weight in a nursery at Lingfield in October.

Ellendune Girl

105 **67**
3-y-o b f Mistertopogigo (IRE)-Perfidy (FR) (Persian Bold)
D J S Ffrench Davis Wroughton Racing Partnership

Placings:050400-22005000041205 **(5671)**
2001: 5^{2}GS, 5^{2}G, 5^{0}GF, 6^{0}GF, 6^{5}GF, 6^{0}GF, 6^{0}G, 5^{0}G, 5^{0}GF, 6^{4}G, 6^{1}G, 5^{2}HY, 5^{0}GS, 6^{5}HY

	Starts	1st	2nd	3rd	Win & Pl
Career Total (Turf)	20	1	3	0	6601

65 9/01 Nott 6f15y E(0-70)H GD £3340
Total win prize-money £3340

Going (Turf): Sf: 0-3 GS: 0-3 **Gd: 1-8** GF: 0-6 Fm: 0-0
Distance: 5f/6f: 0-17 **7f-8f: 1-3** 9f-13f: 0-0 14f+: 0-0
Track : LH: 0-6 RH: 0-1 Tight: 0-1 Gall: 0-3
Aids: Bl: 0-0 Vi: 0-0 Tstrap: 0-0
Best Rating: 67 10/01 Newb 5f34y heavy

She got off the mark at the 17th attempt at Nottingham in September and ran very well in a big field of handicappers at Newbury next time. She is suited to soft ground.

Ellens Academy (IRE)

115(105) (85)**104**
6-y-o b g Royal Academy (USA)-Lady Ellen (Horage)
E J Alston K Lee And Mr I Davies

Placings:43020/421041000/043030400-01512023305 **(5018)**
2001: 6^{0}S, 6^{1}SD, 6^{5}GF, 6^{1}GF, 6^{2}GF, 6^{0}F, 5^{2}GF, 6^{3}GF, 6^{3}GF, 6^{0}GF, 5^{5}S

	Starts	1st	2nd	3rd	Win & Pl
Career Total (Turf)	33	3	4	5	73352
Career Total (AW)	1	1	0	0	3978

91 5/01 Donc 6f D(0-80) G-F £7637
85 4/01 Sthl 6f D(0-85)H STD £3978
78 7/99 NmkJ 6f C(0-90)H G-F £6764
71 5/99 Newb 6f8y D(0-80)H G-F £7425
Total win prize-money £25806

Going (Turf): Sf: 0-5 GS: 0-3 Gd: 0-4 **GF: 3-18** Fm: 0-3
Distance: **5f/6f: 3-23** 7f-8f: 1-8 9f-13f: 0-3 14f+: 0-0
Track : **LH: 1-5** RH: 0-4 Tight: 0-0 Gall: 0-4
Aids: Bl: 0-7 Vi: 0-0 Tstrap: 0-0
Best Rating: 104 9/01 York 6f gd-fm

A useful sprint handicapper, he has been in good form this season. Suited by coming from behind on a decent surface. Best over six furlongs. A fine second in the Wokingham, he found the step up to Group Three company beyond him at Newcastle.

Ellens Lad (IRE)

115 **107d**
7-y-o b g Polish Patriot (USA)-Lady Ellen (Horage)
W J Musson Mrs Rita Brown

Placings:0003151/256046/4601660063/006362300011412/050150110501-100006520000 **(5341)**
2001: 5^{1}S, 5^{0}GF, 5^{0}G, 5^{0}Y, 5^{0}GF, 5^{6}GF, 5^{5}G, 6^{2}GF, 5^{0}GF, 5^{0}S, 5^{0}GS, 5^{0}GS

	Starts	1st	2nd	3rd	Win & Pl
Career Total (Turf)	62	11	4	4	134213

107 4/01 Nott 5f13y C SFT £6583
107 9/00 Asct 5f B(0-105)H SFT £15648
103 7/00 Asct 5f C(0-100)H GD £24700
98 7/00 Donc 5f B(0-100)H GD £10764
96 5/00 York 5f B(0-110)H FRM £19058
94 10/99 NmkJ 5f B(0-105)H GD £9471
86 9/99 Hayd 5f C(0-95)H G-F £6905
81 8/99 Newb 5f34y C(0-95)H GD £6927
86 7/98 NmkJ 5f D(0-85)H G-F £6420
86 11/96 NmkR 5f D GD £3655
76 9/96 Folk 5f D(0-85) G-F £3468
Total win prize-money £113601

Going (Turf): Sf: 2-10 GS: 0-5 **Gd: 5-21** GF: 3-24 Fm: 1-1
Distance: **5f/6f: 11-59** 7f-8f: 0-3 9f-13f: 0-0 14f+: 0-0
Track : LH: 0-1 RH: 0-2 Tight: 0-0 Gall: 0-3
Aids: Bl: 0-1 Vi: 0-0 Tstrap: 0-0
Best Rating: 107 9/01 York 6f gd-fm

He enjoyed a fine season in handicaps in 2000 and returned with a bang to claim a clear-cut success at Nottingham on his reappearance in 2001. He did not look up to Pattern company, but has run well back in handicap company. Best at five furlongs though he just about gets six, he is often held up. Has won on soft ground and firm.

Ellieberry (IRE)

80 **11**
3-y-o ch f Lucky Guest-Persian Flower (Persian Heights)
I W McInnes (B Ellison 4/8) Ian McInnes

Placings:0-66 **(3646)**
2001: 7^{6}F, 7^{6}F

	Starts	1st	2nd	3rd	Win & Pl
Career Total (Turf)	3	0	0	0	0

Going (Turf): Sf: 0-1 GS: 0-0 Gd: 0-0 GF: 0-0 Fm: 0-2
Distance: 5f/6f: 0-1 7f-8f: 0-2 9f-13f: 0-0 14f+: 0-0
Track : LH: 0-2 RH: 0-0 Tight: 0-2 Gall: 0-0
Aids: Bl: 0-0 Vi: 0-0 Tstrap: 0-1
Best Rating: 11 8/01 Thsk 7f firm

Ellway Heights

103(89) (32)**52**
4-y-o b g Shirley Heights-Amina (Brigadier Gerard)
I A Balding Ellway Racing

Placings:0645-330003 **(4727)**
2001: 11^{3}GF, 11^{3}F, 12^{0}G, 12^{0}GF, 12^{0}SD, 10^{3}GF

	Starts	1st	2nd	3rd	Win & Pl
Career Total (Turf)	9	0	0	3	1693
Career Total (AW)	1	0	0	0	

Going (Turf): Sf: 0-0 GS: 0-0 Gd: 0-2 GF: 0-6 Fm: 0-1
Distance: 5f/6f: 0-0 7f-8f: 0-0 9f-13f: 0-10 14f+: 0-0
Track : LH: 0-7 RH: 0-2 Tight: 0-6 Gall: 0-1
Aids: Bl: 0-0 Vi: 0-0 Tstrap: 0-0
Best Rating: 57 6/01 Wind 1m3f135y gd-fm

Ellway Prince

(112) (53d)**53**
6-y-o b g Prince Sabo-Star Arrangement (Star Appeal)
Mrs N Macauley Stephen Roots

Placings:44/0600424212232/50602050606000040/02262501143240000-562000 **(1266)**
2001: 12^{5}SD, 9^{6}SD, 10^{2}SW, 10^{0}SD, 10^{0}SD, 8^{0}SD

	Starts	1st	2nd	3rd	Win & Pl
Career Total (Turf)	21	0	2	1	3770
Career Total (AW)	35	3	9	1	16443

62 4/00 Ling 1m2f E(0-70)H STD £2870
62 3/00 Ling 1m F(0-60)H STD £2362
61 11/98 Ling 6f D STD £2741
Total win prize-money £7974

Going (Turf): Sf: 0-2 GS: 0-1 Gd: 0-8 GF: 0-9 Fm: 0-1
Distance: 5f/6f: 1-23 7f-8f: 1-22 9f-13f: 1-11 14f+: 0-0
Track : **LH: 3-37** RH: 0-3 **Tight: 3-29** Gall: 0-1
Aids: Bl: 0-2 **Vi: 1-31** Tstrap: 0-2
Best Rating: 53 3/01 Ling 1m4f stand

Ellway Queen (USA)

83 **38**
4-y-o b f Bahri (USA)-Queen Linear (USA) (Polish Navy (USA))
G A Butler Ellway Racing

Placings:0610-00 **(5116)**
2001: 7^{0}F, 9^{0}HY

	Starts	1st	2nd	3rd	Win & Pl
Career Total (Turf)	6	1	0	0	3055

75 8/00 Nott 1m54y E G-F £3055
Total win prize-money £3055

Going (Turf): Sf: 0-1 GS: 0-1 Gd: 0-0 **GF: 1-3** Fm: 0-1
Distance: 5f/6f: 0-0 7f-8f: 0-3 **9f-13f: 1-3** 14f+: 0-0
Track : **LH: 1-2** RH: 0-1 Tight: 0-0 Gall: 0-1
Aids: Bl: 0-0 Vi: 0-0 Tstrap: 0-0
Best Rating: 38 9/01 Chep 7f16y firm

Elmhurst Boy

106(104) (82)**88**
5-y-o b h Merdon Melody-Young Whip (Bold Owl)
S Dow R E Anderson

Placings:30/2324532310021/545660103045200155 0-0100045000 **(5607)**
2001: 10^{0}SD, 8^{1}S, 10^{0}GF, 12^{0}GF, 10^{0}GF, 10^{4}G, 9^{5}G, 9^{0}G, 10^{0}GS, 8^{0}GS

Starts 1st 2nd 3rd Win & Pl

Career Total (Turf) 38 4 4 5 40483
Career Total (AW) 6 1 1 0 5788
86 4/01 Sand 1m14y C(0-95)H SFT £12458
86 9/00 Kemp 1m2f D(0-85)H GD £5596
77 6/00 Brig 6f209y D(0-80)H G-F £3835
82 12/99 Ling 7f D(0-80)H STD £3892
77 8/99 Epsm 7f D GD £3728
Total win prize-money £29512

Going (Turf): Sf: 1-9 GS: 0-4 **Gd: 2-10** GF: 1-14 Fm: 0-1
Distance: 5f/6f: 0-7 **7f-8f: 3-24** 9f-13f: 2-13 14f+: 0-0
Track : **LH: 3-15** RH: 2-15 **Tight: 2-14** Gall: 1-5
Aids: Bl: 0-1 **Vi: 2-14** Tstrap: 0-0
Best Rating: 88 10/01 NmkR 1m1f good

He confirmed his versatility when coping well with soft ground to land a mile handicap at Sandown in April 2001, but has struggled in handicap company since. Not always the best of battlers, he sometimes carries his head high. Usually held up.

Elmonjed (USA)

105 **94**
3-y-o b c Gulch (USA)-Aqaarid (USA) (Nashwan (USA))
J L Dunlop Hamdan Al Maktoum

Placings:00215-3205 **(2877)**
2001: 8^{3}S, 10^{2}GF, 12^{0}GF, 11^{5}GF
Starts 1st 2nd 3rd Win & Pl
Career Total (Turf) 9 1 2 1 9338
81 9/00 Gdwd 1m D GD £4280
Total win prize-money £4280

Going (Turf): Sf: 0-1 GS: 0-0 **Gd: 1-3** GF: 0-5 Fm: 0-0
Distance: 5f/6f: 0-0 **7f-8f: 1-6** 9f-13f: 0-3 14f+: 0-0
Track : LH: 0-2 **RH: 1-5** Tight: 0-2 Gall: 0-2
Aids: Bl: 0-0 Vi: 0-0 Tstrap: 0-0
Best Rating: 94 5/01 Hayd 1m2f120y gd-fm

Appreciated the step up to a mile when taking a Goodwood nursery on a sound surface as a juvenile, but has only shown moderate form to date.

Elmutabaki

100 **35**
5-y-o b g Unfuwain (USA)-Bawaeth (USA) (Blushing Groom (FR))
D Nicholls Eugene O'Connell

Placings:5/4221150/5060-P000 **(5225)**
2001: 8^{P}GF, 10^{0}GF, 13^{0}GF, 10^{0}S
Starts 1st 2nd 3rd Win & Pl
Career Total (Turf) 16 2 2 0 54820
102 7/99 Hayd 1m3f200yA G-S £13810
100 6/99 Asct 1m4f B(0-105)H G-F £35505
Total win prize-money £49315

Going (Turf): Sf: 0-3 **GS: 1-1** Gd: 0-4 **GF: 1-8** Fm: 0-0
Distance: 5f/6f: 0-0 7f-8f: 0-2 **9f-13f: 2-11** 14f+: 0-3
Track : LH: 1-11 RH: 1-3 Tight: 0-3 **Gall: 1-7**
Aids: Bl: 0-1 Vi: 0-0 Tstrap: 0-0
Best Rating: 59 9/01 Donc 1m2f60y gd-fm

He was a useful three-year-old, bolting up in Ascot's King George V Handicap before following up in a listed race. Missed a season and changed stables, and pulled up lame in a seller on his reappearance, but ran a much better race at Doncaster.

Elnahaar (USA)

99 **102**
3-y-o b c Silver Hawk (USA)-Futuh (USA) (Diesis)
E A L Dunlop Hamdan Al Maktoum

Placings:11-3 **(0813)**
2001: 9^{3}S
Starts 1st 2nd 3rd Win & Pl
Career Total (Turf) 3 2 0 1 11993
92 9/00 Ches 7f122y C SFT £5539
79 7/00 Sals 6f212y D GD £3913
Total win prize-money £9452

Going (Turf): Sf: 1-2 GS: 0-0 **Gd: 1-1** GF: 0-0 Fm: 0-0
Distance: 5f/6f: 0-0 **7f-8f: 2-2** 9f-13f: 0-1 14f+: 0-0
Track : **LH: 1-1** RH: 0-0 **Tight: 1-1** Gall: 0-0
Aids: Bl: 0-0 Vi: 0-0 Tstrap: 0-0
Best Rating: 102 4/01 NmkR 1m1f soft

He won both his starts as a juvenile, but after finishing third in the Feilden Stakes he broke a leg on the gallops. (DEAD).

Elrehaan

100 **96**
3-y-o b f Sadler's Wells (USA)-Moss (USA) (Woodman (USA))
J L Dunlop Hamdan Al Maktoum

Placings:2106-310 **(4984)**
2001: 11^{3}GF, 12^{1}GF, 12^{0}G
Starts 1st 2nd 3rd Win & Pl
Career Total (Turf) 7 2 1 1 16425
95 5/01 Wwck 1m4f134yC G-F £6634
86 8/00 Rdcr 7f D FRM £2834
Total win prize-money £9468

Going (Turf): Sf: 0-1 GS: 0-0 Gd: 0-1 **GF: 1-4 Fm: 1-1**
Distance: 5f/6f: 0-0 7f-8f: 1-4 9f-13f: 1-3 14f+: 0-0
Track : **LH: 1-3** RH: 0-1 Tight: 0-1 Gall: 0-2
Aids: Bl: 0-0 Vi: 0-0 Tstrap: 0-0
Best Rating: 96 5/01 Ches 1m3f79y gd-fm

Successful on her second start at two over seven furlongs, she failed to cope with a step up to Group and Listed class over a mile subsequently, but found step up to middle distences to her liking when making all in a four runner conditions event at Warwick. Acts on a firm surface.

Elsaamri (USA)

107 **94**
3-y-o b/br c Silver Hawk (USA)-Muhbubh (USA) (Blushing Groom (FR))
M P Tregoning Hamdan Al Maktoum

Placings:43-5114015 **(5057)**
2001: 11^{5}GF, 12^{1}GF, 11^{1}G, 12^{4}GF, 10^{0}G, 12^{1}GF, 12^{5}S
Starts 1st 2nd 3rd Win & Pl
Career Total (Turf) 9 3 0 1 19793
61 9/01 Kemp 1m4f C(0-90) G-F £7062
90 7/01 Bath 1m3f144yD(0-80) GD £3757
80 7/01 Kemp 1m4f D G-F £4231
Total win prize-money £15042

Going (Turf): Sf: 0-2 GS: 0-1 Gd: 1-2 **GF: 2-4** Fm: 0-0
Distance: 5f/6f: 0-0 7f-8f: 0-2 **9f-13f: 3-7** 14f+: 0-0
Track : LH: 1-2 **RH: 2-5 Tight: 1-2** Gall: 0-2
Aids: Bl: 0-0 Vi: 0-0 Tstrap: 0-0
Best Rating: 94 10/01 NmkR 1m4f soft

Got off the mark in a 12-furlong Kempton maiden in July 2001 and followed up narrowly at Bath. Stiff tasks afterwards, but managed to find a simple classified event at Kempton in September.

Elsie Plunkett

104 **88**
3-y-o b f Mind Games-Snow Eagle (IRE) (Polar Falcon (USA))
R Hannon The C J Partnership

Placings:5111324430-2000500050 **(5391)**
2001: 5^{2}S, 5^{0}GS, 6^{0}GF, 6^{0}GF, 6^{5}GF, 6^{0}G, 6^{0}HY, 6^{0}G, 6^{5}G, 7^{0}GS
Starts 1st 2nd 3rd Win & Pl
Career Total (Turf) 20 3 2 2 64997
86 5/00 Newb 5f34y C G-F £5597
81 5/00 Nott 5f13y F G-F £2299
78 4/00 Sand 5f6y E SFT £3542
Total win prize-money £11440

Going (Turf): Sf: 1-7 GS: 0-2 Gd: 0-5 **GF: 2-6** Fm: 0-0
Distance: **5f/6f: 3-19** 7f-8f: 0-1 9f-13f: 0-0 14f+: 0-0
Track : LH: 0-1 RH: 0-0 Tight: 0-0 Gall: 0-1
Aids: Bl: 0-1 Vi: 0-0 Tstrap: 0-0
Best Rating: 92 4/01 Sand 5f6y soft

A fast juvenile in 2000, in the frame in a couple of valuable sales races, she has struggled to find her level so far this season. Seems to act on any ground, and likes to race prominently.

Elsundus (USA)

98 **85+**
3-y-o b c Gone West (USA)-Aljawza (USA) (Riverman (USA))
J H M Gosden Hamdan Al Maktoum

Placings:1 **(4380)**
2001: 8^{1}GF
Starts 1st 2nd 3rd Win & Pl
Career Total (Turf) 1 1 0 0 3660
85 8/01 Sals 1m D G-F £3659
Total win prize-money £3660

Going (Turf): Sf: 0-0 GS: 0-0 Gd: 0-0 **GF: 1-1** Fm: 0-0
Distance: 5f/6f: 0-0 **7f-8f: 1-1** 9f-13f: 0-0 14f+: 0-0
Track : LH: 0-0 RH: 0-0 Tight: 0-0 Gall: 0-0
Aids: Bl: 0-0 Vi: 0-0 Tstrap: 0-0
Best Rating: 85 8/01 Sals 1m gd-fm

Elucidate

98 **62**
2-y-o ch f Elmaamul (USA)-Speed To Lead (IRE) (Darshaan)
I A Wood John Purcell

Placings:04601600 **(5589)**
2001: 7^{0}F, 5^{4}GF, 5^{6}G, 6^{0}GF, 7^{1}GF, 8^{6}GF, 6^{0}GS, 7^{0}GS
Starts 1st 2nd 3rd Win & Pl
Career Total (Turf) 8 1 0 0 3650
64 9/01 Catt 7f E(0-75) G-F £3318
Total win prize-money £3318

Going (Turf): Sf: 0-0 GS: 0-2 Gd: 0-1 **GF: 1-4** Fm: 0-1
Distance: 5f/6f: 0-4 **7f-8f: 1-4** 9f-13f: 0-0 14f+: 0-0
Track : **LH: 1-3** RH: 0-1 **Tight: 1-2** Gall: 0-1
Aids: Bl: 0-0 Vi: 0-0 Tstrap: 0-0
Best Rating: 64 9/01 Catt 7f gd-fm

Had shown little in all starts prior to winning a Catterick nursery at 40-1, but since ran too free over a mile at Musselburgh.

Elusive Treasure (IRE)

91 **66**
2-y-o b f Entrepreneur-Hidden Crest (USA) (Gold Crest (USA))
R M Beckett Tweenhills Racing (treasure Seekers)

Placings:55350 **(3684)**
2001: 5^{5}GF, 6^{5}GF, 7^{3}GF, 6^{5}GS, 5^{0}GF
Starts 1st 2nd 3rd Win & Pl
Career Total (Turf) 5 0 0 1 418

Going (Turf): Sf: 0-0 GS: 0-1 Gd: 0-0 GF: 0-4 Fm: 0-0
Distance: 5f/6f: 0-4 7f-8f: 0-1 9f-13f: 0-0 14f+: 0-0
Track : LH: 0-2 RH: 0-0 Tight: 0-0 Gall: 0-1
Aids: Bl: 0-0 Vi: 0-1 Tstrap: 0-0
Best Rating: 66 6/01 Sals 6f gd-fm

Elvington Boy

105 **74**
4-y-o ch g Emarati (USA)-Catherines Well (Junius (USA))
M W Easterby Mr K Hodgson & Mrs J Hodgson

Placings:22100/003262200-00200010 **(3937)**
2001: 5^{0}GS, 6^{0}GF, 5^{2}GF, 5^{0}G, 5^{0}GF, 5^{0}G, 5^{1}GF, 5^{0}G

	Starts	1st	2nd	3rd	Win & Pl
Career Total (Turf)	24	2	6	1	21578

74	7/01	Muss	5f	D(0-85)H	G-F	£4407
73	8/99	Ripn	5f	F	GD	£2970

Total win prize-money £7377

Going (Turf): Sf: 0-2 GS: 0-4 **Gd: 1-10 GF: 1-7** Fm: 0-1
Distance: **5f/6f: 2-24** 7f-8f: 0-0 9f-13f: 0-0 14f+: 0-0
Track : LH: 0-1 RH: 0-2 Tight: 0-0 Gall: 0-2
Aids: Bl: 0-0 Vi: 0-2 Tstrap: 0-1
Best Rating: 74 7/01 Muss 5f gd-fm

A fair sprint handicapper who goes best on a sound surface, he won at Ripon as a two-year-old but has not managed to score since despite having plenty of chances. Bits and pieces of form earlier this season, but got back to winning ways at Musselburgh in July. Not easy to predict.

Elwood Blues (IRE)

2-y-o b g Blues Traveller (IRE)-Tolomena (Tolomeo)
S C Williams The Blues Brothers

Placings:0 **(5107)**
2001: 7^{0}GS

	Starts	1st	2nd	3rd	Win & Pl
Career Total (Turf)	1	0	0	0	

Going (Turf): Sf: 0-0 GS: 0-1 Gd: 0-0 GF: 0-0 Fm: 0-0
Distance: 5f/6f: 0-0 7f-8f: 0-1 9f-13f: 0-0 14f+: 0-0
Track : LH: 0-0 RH: 0-0 Tight: 0-0 Gall: 0-0
Aids: Bl: 0-0 Vi: 0-0 Tstrap: 0-0

Emali

97(75) **41**
4-y-o b g Emarati (USA)-Princess Poquito (Hard Fought)
J S Moore The Country Life Partnership

Placings:06/22043032500-00000 **(2808)**
2001: 8^{0}SW, 10^{0}SD, 9^{0}GF, 11^{0}F, 8^{0}GF

	Starts	1st	2nd	3rd	Win & Pl
Career Total (Turf)	15	0	3	2	3497
Career Total (AW)	3	0	0	0	

Going (Turf): Sf: 0-1 GS: 0-2 Gd: 0-4 GF: 0-6 Fm: 0-2
Distance: 5f/6f: 0-0 7f-8f: 0-3 9f-13f: 0-15 14f+: 0-0
Track : LH: 0-10 RH: 0-5 Tight: 0-7 Gall: 0-1
Aids: Bl: 0-0 Vi: 0-4 Tstrap: 0-2
Best Rating: 41 6/01 Gdwd 1m1f gd-fm

Emarati's Image

66 **31**
3-y-o b g Emarati (USA)-Choir's Image (Lochnager)
W S Cunningham A Skelton

Placings:030 **(3861)**
2001: 10^{0}F, 9^{3}G, 9^{0}GF

	Starts	1st	2nd	3rd	Win & Pl
Career Total (Turf)	3	0	0	1	412

Going (Turf): Sf: 0-0 GS: 0-0 Gd: 0-1 GF: 0-1 Fm: 0-1
Distance: 5f/6f: 0-0 7f-8f: 0-0 9f-13f: 0-3 14f+: 0-0
Track : LH: 0-3 RH: 0-0 Tight: 0-1 Gall: 0-2
Aids: Bl: 0-0 Vi: 0-0 Tstrap: 0-0
Best Rating: 31 8/01 Newc 1m1f9y good

Ember Days

91(82) (43)**71**
2-y-o gr f Reprimand-Evening Falls (Beveled (USA))
G C H Chung Mrs Carol J Welch

Placings:020 **(5610)**
2001: 7^{0}GF, 7^{2}S, 8^{0}SD

	Starts	1st	2nd	3rd	Win & Pl
Career Total (Turf)	2	0	1	0	888
Career Total (AW)	1	0	0	0	

Going (Turf): Sf: 0-1 GS: 0-0 Gd: 0-0 GF: 0-1 Fm: 0-0
Distance: 5f/6f: 0-0 7f-8f: 0-2 9f-13f: 0-1 14f+: 0-0
Track : LH: 0-2 RH: 0-1 Tight: 0-2 Gall: 0-1
Aids: Bl: 0-0 Vi: 0-0 Tstrap: 0-0
Best Rating: 71 10/01 Catt 7f soft

Emerald Fire

99 **74**
2-y-o b f Pivotal-Four-Legged Friend (Aragon)
I A Balding T M Mason

Placings:5201 **(5340)**
2001: 5^{5}GS, 5^{2}G, 5^{0}GF, 6^{1}GS

	Starts	1st	2nd	3rd	Win & Pl
Career Total (Turf)	4	1	1	0	8512

74	10/01	NmkR	6f	C(0-95)	G-S	£7150

Total win prize-money £7150

Going (Turf): Sf: 0-0 **GS: 1-2** Gd: 0-1 GF: 0-1 Fm: 0-0
Distance: **5f/6f: 1-4** 7f-8f: 0-0 9f-13f: 0-0 14f+: 0-0
Track : LH: 0-1 RH: 0-0 Tight: 0-0 Gall: 0-1
Aids: Bl: 0-0 Vi: 0-0 Tstrap: 0-0
Best Rating: 74 10/01 NmkR 6f gd-sft

A half-sister to multiple eight and ten-furlong winner Herr Trigger and dual five-furlong scorer Quite Happy. She showed ability in maidens before taking a Newmarket nursery in October. Suited by cut in the ground.

Emerald Hunter (USA)

6-y-o b/br g Quest For Fame-In Jubilation (USA) (Isgala)
K O Cunningham-Brown Miss C Berry

Placings:55/000100/0 **(1315)**
2001: 14^{0}SD

	Starts	1st	2nd	3rd	Win & Pl
Career Total (Turf)	6	0	0	0	0
Career Total (AW)	3	1	0	0	1819

40	5/99	Wolv	1m6f166yG	STD	£1819

Total win prize-money £1819

Going (Turf): Sf: 0-1 GS: 0-0 Gd: 0-2 GF: 0-3 Fm: 0-0
Distance: 5f/6f: 0-0 7f-8f: 0-0 9f-13f: 0-5 **14f+: 1-4**
Track : **LH: 1-3** RH: 0-5 **Tight: 1-4** Gall: 0-1
Aids: Bl: 0-1 Vi: 0-0 Tstrap: 0-0

Emerald Imp (IRE)

77(69) (10)**4**
4-y-o ch f Mac's Imp (USA)-Lady Montekin (Montekin)
M S Saunders Chris Scott

Placings:04/600-000 **(4609)**
2001: 10^{0}GF, 7^{0}GF, 8^{0}F

	Starts	1st	2nd	3rd	Win & Pl
Career Total (Turf)	7	0	0	0	244
Career Total (AW)	1	0	0	0	0

Going (Turf): Sf: 0-2 GS: 0-0 Gd: 0-0 GF: 0-3 Fm: 0-2
Distance: 5f/6f: 0-2 7f-8f: 0-3 9f-13f: 0-3 14f+: 0-0
Track : LH: 0-5 RH: 0-0 Tight: 0-3 Gall: 0-0
Aids: Bl: 0-0 Vi: 0-0 Tstrap: 0-0
Best Rating: 4 9/01 Bath 1m5y firm

Emerald Lake (USA)

88 **65**
3-y-o b c Green Dancer (USA)-Dame Avie (USA) (Lord Gaylord (USA))
J H M Gosden George Strawbridge

Placings:606 **(1990)**
2001: 10^{6}GS, 10^{0}S, 14^{6}G

	Starts	1st	2nd	3rd	Win & Pl
Career Total (Turf)	3	0	0	0	0

Going (Turf): Sf: 0-1 GS: 0-1 Gd: 0-1 GF: 0-0 Fm: 0-0
Distance: 5f/6f: 0-0 7f-8f: 0-0 9f-13f: 0-2 14f+: 0-1
Track : LH: 0-2 RH: 0-0 Tight: 0-1 Gall: 0-1
Aids: Bl: 0-0 Vi: 0-0 Tstrap: 0-0
Best Rating: 65 6/01 Hayd 1m6f good

Emerald Mist (IRE)

79 **35**
2-y-o b f Sacrament-Jade's Gem (Sulaafah (USA))
G B Balding The Roman Legion

Placings:00000 **(5667)**
2001: 7^{0}GF, 6^{0}GF, 7^{0}GF, 8^{0}HY, 8^{0}HY

	Starts	1st	2nd	3rd	Win & Pl
Career Total (Turf)	5	0	0	0	

Going (Turf): Sf: 0-2 GS: 0-0 Gd: 0-0 GF: 0-3 Fm: 0-0
Distance: 5f/6f: 0-0 7f-8f: 0-3 9f-13f: 0-2 14f+: 0-0
Track : LH: 0-0 RH: 0-2 Tight: 0-2 Gall: 0-0
Aids: Bl: 0-0 Vi: 0-0 Tstrap: 0-0
Best Rating: 35 8/01 Folk 7f gd-fm

Emerald Palm

93(84) (37)**62**
3-y-o b f Green Desert (USA)-Opus One (Slip Anchor)
P J Hobbs (J Noseda 13/6) Sir Robert Ogden

Placings:66-5300 **(2110)**
2001: 8^{5}SD, 8^{3}GS, 7^{0}GF, 9^{0}F

	Starts	1st	2nd	3rd	Win & Pl
Career Total (Turf)	5	0	0	1	530
Career Total (AW)	1	0	0	0	0

Going (Turf): Sf: 0-1 GS: 0-1 Gd: 0-1 GF: 0-1 Fm: 0-1
Distance: 5f/6f: 0-1 7f-8f: 0-3 9f-13f: 0-2 14f+: 0-0
Track : LH: 0-3 RH: 0-1 Tight: 0-3 Gall: 0-0
Aids: Bl: 0-0 Vi: 0-0 Tstrap: 0-0
Best Rating: 62 4/01 Wind 1m67y gd-sft

Emerald Peace (IRE)

111 **104**
4-y-o b f Green Desert (USA)-Puck's Castle (Shirley Heights)
M A Jarvis M P Burke

Placings:52112/00164-4165 **(2605)**
2001: 5^{4}G, 5^{1}GF, 5^{6}G, 6^{5}F

	Starts	1st	2nd	3rd	Win & Pl
Career Total (Turf)	14	4	2	0	45589

104	5/01	Kemp	5f	A	G-F	£15795
95	9/00	Leic	5f2y	C	G-F	£5805
87	8/99	Ling	5f	C	G-F	£5639
87	8/99	Ling	5f	D	GD	£3785

Total win prize-money £31026

Going (Turf): Sf: 0-0 GS: 0-0 Gd: 1-6 **GF: 3-7** Fm: 0-1
Distance: **5f/6f: 4-14** 7f-8f: 0-0 9f-13f: 0-0 14f+: 0-0
Track : LH: 0-1 RH: 0-0 Tight: 0-0 Gall: 0-1
Aids: Bl: 0-0 Vi: 0-0 Tstrap: 0-0
Best Rating: 104 5/01 Kemp 5f gd-fm

Progressive at two, she was well held in Group company last term but won well in lesser company at Leicester.

She looked as if five furlongs might be a bit sharp for her when fourth on her reappearance at Beverley, but she posted a career-best effort when getting up late in the day over that trip at Kempton.

Emily Dee

86 **72**
2-y-o b f Classic Cliche (IRE)-Alpi Dora (Valiyar)
J M Bradley K C Trotman

Placings:64050 **(5405)**
2001: 7^{6}GS, 7^{4}GF, 6^{0}GF, 6^{5}HY, 6^{0}S

	Starts	1st	2nd	3rd	Win & Pl
Career Total (Turf)	5	0	0	0	327

Going (Turf): Sf: 0-2 GS: 0-1 Gd: 0-0 GF: 0-2 Fm: 0-0
Distance: 5f/6f: 0-1 7f-8f: 0-4 9f-13f: 0-0 14f+: 0-0
Track : LH: 0-1 RH: 0-0 Tight: 0-0 Gall: 0-0
Aids: Bl: 0-0 Vi: 0-0 Tstrap: 0-0
Best Rating: 72 10/01 Nott 6f15y heavy

Eminently

82 **69**
2-y-o b g Deploy-Lady Clementine (He Loves Me)
R M Beckett Maybejustmaybe Partnership

Placings:0050 **(5176)**
2001: 7^{0}GF, 7^{0}GF, 7^{5}F, 8^{0}HY

	Starts	1st	2nd	3rd	Win & Pl
Career Total (Turf)	4	0	0	0	0

Going (Turf): Sf: 0-1 GS: 0-0 Gd: 0-0 GF: 0-2 Fm: 0-1
Distance: 5f/6f: 0-0 7f-8f: 0-3 9f-13f: 0-1 14f+: 0-0
Track : LH: 0-0 RH: 0-1 Tight: 0-1 Gall: 0-0
Aids: Bl: 0-0 Vi: 0-0 Tstrap: 0-0
Best Rating: 69 9/01 Chep 7f16y firm

Emissary

95(88) (32)**46**
3-y-o gr g Primo Dominie-Misty Goddess (IRE) (Godswalk (USA))
N P Littmoden Turf 2000 Limited

Placings:664024500-66000 **(2426)**
2001: 11^{6}SD, 8^{6}GF, 9^{0}GF, 6^{0}GF, 8^{0}GF

	Starts	1st	2nd	3rd	Win & Pl
Career Total (Turf)	12	0	1	0	1337
Career Total (AW)	2	0	0	0	0

Going (Turf): Sf: 0-3 GS: 0-2 Gd: 0-2 GF: 0-4 Fm: 0-1
Distance: 5f/6f: 0-7 7f-8f: 0-4 9f-13f: 0-3 14f+: 0-0
Track : LH: 0-7 RH: 0-2 Tight: 0-2 Gall: 0-0
Aids: Bl: 0-1 Vi: 0-0 Tstrap: 0-0
Best Rating: 46 5/01 Muss 1m gd-fm

Emma Clare (IRE)

93(88) (38)**34**
3-y-o b f Namaqualand (USA)-Medicosma (USA) (The Minstrel (CAN))
J A Osborne The Woolfie And Tom Partnership

Placings:0002410063-6400300 **(3669)**
2001: 8^{6}SD, 9^{4}SD, 11^{0}SD, 9^{0}SD, 10^{3}GF, 9^{0}GF, 14^{0}S

	Starts	1st	2nd	3rd	Win & Pl
Career Total (Turf)	11	1	1	1	4429
Career Total (AW)	6	0	0	1	264

46 8/00 Muss 1m E G-F £3428
Total win prize-money £3429

Going (Turf): Sf: 0-1 GS: 0-3 Gd: 0-1 **GF: 1-6** Fm: 0-0
Distance: 5f/6f: 0-2 **7f-8f: 1-5** 9f-13f: 0-9 14f+: 0-1
Track : LH: 0-10 **RH: 1-2 Tight: 1-7** Gall: 0-0
Aids: Bl: 0-5 Vi: 0-0 Tstrap: 0-0
Best Rating: 38 1/01 Sthl 1m stand

Emma Thomas

94(82) (2)**23**
3-y-o b f Puissance-Clan Scotia (Clantime)
A Berry Alan Berry

Placings:0000300-0000000000000 **(4902)**
2001: 6^{0}SD, 5^{0}SW, 6^{0}SD, 5^{0}S, 6^{0}G, 5^{0}G, 5^{0}F, 6^{0}GF, 6^{0}GF, 5^{0}S, 5^{0}G, 6^{0}HY, 5^{0}GF, 5^{0}G

	Starts	1st	2nd	3rd	Win & Pl
Career Total (Turf)	16	0	0	0	
Career Total (AW)	5	0	0	1	282

Going (Turf): Sf: 0-3 GS: 0-2 Gd: 0-6 GF: 0-4 Fm: 0-1
Distance: 5f/6f: 0-18 7f-8f: 0-3 9f-13f: 0-0 14f+: 0-0
Track : LH: 0-4 RH: 0-1 Tight: 0-3 Gall: 0-0
Aids: Bl: 0-0 Vi: 0-0 Tstrap: 0-0
Best Rating: 26 4/01 Nott 5f13y soft

Emma-Lyne

84(63) **34**
5-y-o b m Emarati (USA)-Moreton's Martha (Derrylin)
G Brown K Powell

Placings:223/0666650/000-0 **(0694)**
2001: 8^{0}SD

	Starts	1st	2nd	3rd	Win & Pl
Career Total (Turf)	12	0	2	1	2104
Career Total (AW)	2	0	0	0	

Going (Turf): Sf: 0-0 GS: 0-3 Gd: 0-2 GF: 0-6 Fm: 0-1
Distance: 5f/6f: 0-3 7f-8f: 0-8 9f-13f: 0-3 14f+: 0-0
Track : LH: 0-8 RH: 0-1 Tight: 0-2 Gall: 0-0
Aids: Bl: 0-0 Vi: 0-2 Tstrap: 0-0

Emmas Hope

(76) **10**
4-y-o b f Emarati (USA)-Ray Of Hope (Rainbow Quest (USA))
B P J Baugh Mrs Joan M Chrimes

Placings:040000050/000-00600050 **(4553)**
2001: 8^{0}SD, 12^{0}SD, 11^{6}G, 11^{0}F, 14^{0}GF, 10^{0}GF, 12^{5}G, 14^{0}SW

	Starts	1st	2nd	3rd	Win & Pl
Career Total (Turf)	14	0	0	0	0
Career Total (AW)	6	0	0	0	0

Going (Turf): Sf: 0-1 GS: 0-0 Gd: 0-7 GF: 0-5 Fm: 0-1
Distance: 5f/6f: 0-8 7f-8f: 0-1 9f-13f: 0-9 14f+: 0-2
Track : LH: 0-14 RH: 0-2 Tight: 0-8 Gall: 0-0
Aids: Bl: 0-2 Vi: 0-3 Tstrap: 0-0
Best Rating: 10 5/01 Haml 1m3f16y good

Emmeranne

101 **61**
4-y-o b f Warning-Empress Matilda (IRE) (Sadler's Wells (USA))
E J O'Neill Mrs Patrick O'Neill

Placings:4420004 **(4168)**
2001: 7^{4}GF, 7^{4}F, 7^{2}G, 6^{0}GF, 8^{0}GF, 7^{0}GF, 8^{4}GF

	Starts	1st	2nd	3rd	Win & Pl
Career Total (Turf)	7	0	1	0	1612

Going (Turf): Sf: 0-0 GS: 0-0 Gd: 0-1 GF: 0-5 Fm: 0-1
Distance: 5f/6f: 0-0 7f-8f: 0-6 9f-13f: 0-1 14f+: 0-0
Track : LH: 0-3 RH: 0-2 Tight: 0-3 Gall: 0-0
Aids: Bl: 0-1 Vi: 0-0 Tstrap: 0-0
Best Rating: 61 7/01 Sals 6f212y gd-fm

Lightly-raced, has shown ability in maidens and handicaps

Emmervale

89 **68**
2-y-o b f Emarati (USA)-Raintree Venture (Good Times (ITY))
J G Portman Miss D Birkbeck

Placings:420450 **(5364)**
2001: 5^{4}GF, 6^{2}GF, 6^{0}GF, 5^{4}F, 5^{5}GS, 6^{0}GS

	Starts	1st	2nd	3rd	Win & Pl
Career Total (Turf)	6	0	1	0	1186

Going (Turf): Sf: 0-0 GS: 0-2 Gd: 0-0 GF: 0-3 Fm: 0-1
Distance: 5f/6f: 0-6 7f-8f: 0-0 9f-13f: 0-0 14f+: 0-0
Track : LH: 0-1 RH: 0-0 Tight: 0-0 Gall: 0-1
Aids: Bl: 0-0 Vi: 0-0 Tstrap: 0-0
Best Rating: 68 9/01 Bath 5f11y firm

Emms (USA)

100 **93**
3-y-o gr c Fastness (IRE)-Carnation (FR) (Carwhite)
P F I Cole Sir George Meyrick

Placings:23120-000 **(3273)**
2001: 8^{0}GF, 8^{0}G, 8^{0}GF

	Starts	1st	2nd	3rd	Win & Pl
Career Total (Turf)	8	1	2	1	15365

82 8/00 NmkJ 7f D G-F £4163
Total win prize-money £4163

Going (Turf): Sf: 0-2 GS: 0-1 Gd: 0-2 **GF: 1-3** Fm: 0-0
Distance: 5f/6f: 0-1 **7f-8f: 1-6** 9f-13f: 0-1 14f+: 0-0
Track : LH: 0-1 RH: 0-2 Tight: 0-0 Gall: 0-2
Aids: Bl: 0-0 Vi: 0-0 Tstrap: 0-0
Best Rating: 93 6/01 Asct 1m gd-fm

A tall weak type as a juvenile, he scored once at two over seven furlongs. Ran well in the Britannia on his return but did not progress.

Emperor Of Dreams

85 **61**
2-y-o b c Emperor Jones (USA)-Girl Of My Dreams (IRE) (Marju (IRE))
R Hannon Mrs Caroline Parker

Placings:00005 **(5405)**
2001: 6^{0}GF, 6^{0}GF, 6^{0}G, 7^{0}S, 6^{5}S

	Starts	1st	2nd	3rd	Win & Pl
Career Total (Turf)	5	0	0	0	0

Going (Turf): Sf: 0-2 GS: 0-0 Gd: 0-1 GF: 0-2 Fm: 0-0
Distance: 5f/6f: 0-3 7f-8f: 0-2 9f-13f: 0-0 14f+: 0-0
Track : LH: 0-2 RH: 0-0 Tight: 0-0 Gall: 0-0
Aids: Bl: 0-0 Vi: 0-0 Tstrap: 0-0
Best Rating: 61 10/01 Pont 6f soft

Emperor's Castle

83 **42**
2-y-o b g Emperor Jones (USA)-Riyoom (USA) (Vaguely Noble)
P C Haslam Northern Lights Racing

Placings:000 **(4229)**
2001: 6^{0}GF, 7^{0}G, 7^{0}G

	Starts	1st	2nd	3rd	Win & Pl
Career Total (Turf)	3	0	0	0	

Going (Turf): Sf: 0-0 GS: 0-0 Gd: 0-2 GF: 0-1 Fm: 0-0
Distance: 5f/6f: 0-1 7f-8f: 0-2 9f-13f: 0-0 14f+: 0-0
Track : LH: 0-2 RH: 0-0 Tight: 0-2 Gall: 0-0
Aids: Bl: 0-0 Vi: 0-0 Tstrap: 0-0
Best Rating: 42 8/01 Catt 7f good

Emperor's Well

87 **65**

2-y-o ch c First Trump-Catherines Well (Junius (USA))
M W Easterby Mr K Hodgson & Mrs J Hodgson

Placings:5535000 **(4269)**
2001: 5^{5}S, 5^{5}GF, 5^{3}F, 5^{5}GF, 5^{0}G, 5^{0}F, 5^{0}GF

	Starts	1st	2nd	3rd	Win & Pl
Career Total (Turf)	7	0	0	1	0

Going (Turf): Sf: 0-1 GS: 0-0 Gd: 0-1 GF: 0-3 Fm: 0-2
Distance: 5f/6f: 0-7 7f-8f: 0-0 9f-13f: 0-0 14f+: 0-0
Track : LH: 0-0 RH: 0-0 Tight: 0-0 Gall: 0-0
Aids: Bl: 0-0 Vi: 0-0 Tstrap: 0-0
Best Rating: 65 5/01 Rdcr 5f firm

Emperors Folly

80 **36**

3-y-o b g Emperor Jones (USA)-Highest Bid (FR) (Highest Honor (FR))
C A Dwyer Roalco Limited

Placings:0-00 **(2109)**
2001: 7^{0}GF, 9^{0}F

	Starts	1st	2nd	3rd	Win & Pl
Career Total (Turf)	3	0	0	0	

Going (Turf): Sf: 0-0 GS: 0-1 Gd: 0-0 GF: 0-1 Fm: 0-1
Distance: 5f/6f: 0-0 7f-8f: 0-2 9f-13f: 0-1 14f+: 0-0
Track : LH: 0-2 RH: 0-0 Tight: 0-1 Gall: 0-0
Aids: Bl: 0-0 Vi: 0-0 Tstrap: 0-0
Best Rating: 36 5/01 Yarm 7f3y gd-fm

Emporio

98 **64**

3-y-o b g Emperor Jones (USA)-Lykoa (Shirley Heights)
L M Cumani Mrs V Shelton

Placings:040-20456 **(2864)**
2001: 7^{2}GS, 7^{0}G, 9^{4}GF, 10^{5}G, 9^{6}GF

	Starts	1st	2nd	3rd	Win & Pl
Career Total (Turf)	8	0	1	0	1180

Going (Turf): Sf: 0-2 GS: 0-1 Gd: 0-3 GF: 0-2 Fm: 0-0
Distance: 5f/6f: 0-0 7f-8f: 0-5 9f-13f: 0-3 14f+: 0-0
Track : LH: 0-3 RH: 0-1 Tight: 0-1 Gall: 0-0
Aids: Bl: 0-0 Vi: 0-0 Tstrap: 0-0
Best Rating: 69 4/01 Brig 7f214y gd-sft

Empress Alice

65

4-y-o b f Petoski-Blue Empress (Blue Cashmere)
R E Peacock Three Of A Kind Racing

Placings:0-00 **(4631)**
2001: 7^{0}GF, 9^{0}GF

	Starts	1st	2nd	3rd	Win & Pl
Career Total (Turf)	2	0	0	0	
Career Total (AW)	1	0	0	0	

Going (Turf): Sf: 0-0 GS: 0-0 Gd: 0-0 GF: 0-2 Fm: 0-0
Distance: 5f/6f: 0-0 7f-8f: 0-1 9f-13f: 0-2 14f+: 0-0
Track : LH: 0-2 RH: 0-1 Tight: 0-1 Gall: 0-0
Aids: Bl: 0-0 Vi: 0-0 Tstrap: 0-0

Empress Emmilline

79

5-y-o ch m My Generation-Over The Mill (Milford)
M Mullineaux E H E Garth Ormond

Placings:00000 **(3228)**
2001: 8^{0}GF, 12^{0}G, 10^{0}F, 8^{0}GF, 12^{0}GF

	Starts	1st	2nd	3rd	Win & Pl
Career Total (Turf)	5	0	0	0	

Going (Turf): Sf: 0-0 GS: 0-0 Gd: 0-1 GF: 0-3 Fm: 0-1
Distance: 5f/6f: 0-0 7f-8f: 0-1 9f-13f: 0-4 14f+: 0-0
Track : LH: 0-4 RH: 0-1 Tight: 0-3 Gall: 0-0
Aids: Bl: 0-0 Vi: 0-0 Tstrap: 0-0
Best Rating: 29 5/01 Thsk 1m gd-fm

Emteyaz

95 **55**

3-y-o b c Mark Of Esteem (IRE)-Najmat Alshemaal (IRE) (Dancing Brave (USA))
A C Stewart Sheikh Ahmed Al Maktoum

Placings:0600140 **(4483)**
2001: 10^{0}GF, 11^{6}GF, 10^{0}GF, 12^{0}GS, 12^{1}G, 16^{4}HY, 14^{0}S

	Starts	1st	2nd	3rd	Win & Pl
Career Total (Turf)	7	1	0	0	3465

55 8/01 Folk 1m4f F(0-60)H GD £3465
Total win prize-money £3465

Going (Turf): Sf: 0-2 GS: 0-1 **Gd: 1-1** GF: 0-3 Fm: 0-0
Distance: 5f/6f: 0-0 7f-8f: 0-0 **9f-13f: 1-5** 14f+: 0-2
Track : LH: 0-4 **RH: 1-3 Tight: 1-4** Gall: 0-2
Aids: Bl: 0-0 Vi: 0-0 Tstrap: 0-0
Best Rating: 55 8/01 Folk 1m4f good

Enchanted

96 **84**

2-y-o b f Magic Ring (IRE)-Snugfit Annie (Midyan (USA))
N A Callaghan Norcroft Park Stud

Placings:51154 **(3638)**
2001: 6^{5}GF, 5^{1}GF, 6^{1}GF, 6^{5}GF, 6^{4}GS

	Starts	1st	2nd	3rd	Win & Pl
Career Total (Turf)	5	2	0	0	7996

84 7/01 Sals 6f212y E G-F £3066
84 6/01 Wwck 5f D G-F £3430
Total win prize-money £6496

Going (Turf): Sf: 0-0 GS: 0-1 Gd: 0-0 **GF: 2-4** Fm: 0-0
Distance: 5f/6f: 1-4 7f-8f: 1-1 9f-13f: 0-0 14f+: 0-0
Track : **LH: 1-1** RH: 0-0 Tight: 0-0 **Gall: 1-1**
Aids: Bl: 0-0 Vi: 0-0 Tstrap: 0-0
Best Rating: 84 7/01 Sals 6f212y gd-fm

A May foal, fifth to Silent Honor in a hot maiden at Newmarket, before winning five-furlong maiden at Warwick and a seven-furlong nursery at Salisbury. May have been coming into season next time.

Enchanted Ocean (USA)

80 **68+**

2-y-o b f Royal Academy (USA)-Ocean Jewel (USA) (Alleged (USA))
M Johnston Miller/richards Partnership

Placings:40 **(5484)**
2001: 7^{4}G, 8^{0}HY

	Starts	1st	2nd	3rd	Win & Pl
Career Total (Turf)	2	0	0	0	350

Going (Turf): Sf: 0-1 GS: 0-0 Gd: 0-1 GF: 0-0 Fm: 0-0
Distance: 5f/6f: 0-0 7f-8f: 0-2 9f-13f: 0-0 14f+: 0-0
Track : LH: 0-1 RH: 0-0 Tight: 0-0 Gall: 0-1
Aids: Bl: 0-0 Vi: 0-0 Tstrap: 0-0
Best Rating: 68 9/01 Ayr 7f50y good

Enchanting (IRE)

83 **37**

3-y-o b f Bigstone (IRE)-Spire (Shirley Heights)
B J Meehan Fieldspring Racing

Placings:0-4000 **(1718)**
2001: 6^{4}HY, 6^{0}GF, 6^{0}S, 10^{0}GF

	Starts	1st	2nd	3rd	Win & Pl
Career Total (Turf)	5	0	0	0	0

Going (Turf): Sf: 0-2 GS: 0-1 Gd: 0-0 GF: 0-2 Fm: 0-0
Distance: 5f/6f: 0-0 7f-8f: 0-4 9f-13f: 0-1 14f+: 0-0
Track : LH: 0-2 RH: 0-1 Tight: 0-1 Gall: 0-1
Aids: Bl: 0-1 Vi: 0-0 Tstrap: 0-0
Best Rating: 31 5/01 Brig 6f209y gd-fm

Encore Du Cristal (USA)

103 **77**

4-y-o b f Quiet American (USA)-Elegant Champagne (USA) (Alleged (USA))
J H M Gosden Thomas P Tatham

Placings:0-41030 **(4592)**
2001: 10^{4}G, 9^{1}GF, 9^{0}GF, 12^{3}GF, 10^{0}G

	Starts	1st	2nd	3rd	Win & Pl
Career Total (Turf)	6	1	0	1	4235

64 6/01 Sals 1m1f198yD G-F £3575
Total win prize-money £3575

Going (Turf): Sf: 0-0 GS: 0-1 Gd: 0-2 **GF: 1-3** Fm: 0-0
Distance: 5f/6f: 0-0 7f-8f: 0-1 **9f-13f: 1-5** 14f+: 0-0
Track : LH: 0-0 **RH: 1-4 Tight: 1-4** Gall: 0-1
Aids: Bl: 0-0 Vi: 0-0 Tstrap: 0-0
Best Rating: 77 8/01 Sals 1m4f gd-fm

Lightly-raced filly, but showed she has ability when winning a moderate Salisbury maiden in June. Suited by fast ground.

Encore Ma Fille

98 **71**

2-y-o b f Royal Applause-Collide (High Line)
R M Whitaker Country Lane Partnership

Placings:051560 **(4823)**
2001: 6^{0}GF, 6^{5}GF, 5^{1}GF, 5^{5}G, 6^{6}GF, 6^{0}G

	Starts	1st	2nd	3rd	Win & Pl
Career Total (Turf)	6	1	0	0	3381

71 7/01 Ripn 5f F G-F £3381
Total win prize-money £3381

Going (Turf): Sf: 0-0 GS: 0-0 Gd: 0-2 **GF: 1-4** Fm: 0-0
Distance: **5f/6f: 1-5** 7f-8f: 0-1 9f-13f: 0-0 14f+: 0-0
Track : LH: 0-0 RH: 0-0 Tight: 0-0 Gall: 0-0
Aids: Bl: 0-0 Vi: 0-0 Tstrap: 0-0
Best Rating: 71 9/01 Donc 6f gd-fm

She managed to win a maiden auction event at Ripon on her third start, but it was not a great race and her other form is moderate.

Encore My Love

88 **65**

2-y-o b f Royal Applause-Lady Be Mine (USA) (Sir Ivor)
J L Dunlop Mrs Mark Burrell

Placings:2 **(2156)**
2001: 6^{2}GF

	Starts	1st	2nd	3rd	Win & Pl
Career Total (Turf)	1	0	1	0	1353

Going (Turf): Sf: 0-0 GS: 0-0 Gd: 0-0 GF: 0-1 Fm: 0-0
Distance: 5f/6f: 0-1 7f-8f: 0-0 9f-13f: 0-0 14f+: 0-0
Track : LH: 0-0 RH: 0-0 Tight: 0-0 Gall: 0-0
Aids: Bl: 0-0 Vi: 0-0 Tstrap: 0-0
Best Rating: 65 6/01 Gdwd 6f gd-fm

Encounter

107 (29)**54**

5-y-o br g Primo Dominie-Dancing Spirit (IRE) (Ahonoora)

J Hetherton Qualitair Holdings Limited

Placings:0300060/526000003041126000000/400400052 11016054502-005060120446106106000000 **(5681)**
2001: 7^{0}GF, 6^{0}GF, 7^{5}GF, 8^{0}GF, 7^{6}GF, 7^{0}GF, 7^{1}GF, 7^{2}GF, 7^{0}GF, 7^{4}GS, 7^{4}GF, 8^{6}GS, 7^{1}G, 7^{0}GF, 7^{6}G, 7^{1}S, 10^{0}GF, 8^{6}G, 7^{0}GF, 8^{0}G, 6^{0}HY, 7^{0}S, 7^{0}GS, 8^{0}S

	Starts	1st	2nd	3rd	Win & Pl
Career Total (Turf)	67	8	5	2	33988
Career Total (AW)	4	0	0	0	0

59	8/01	Epsm	7f	E(0-70)H	SFT	£4699
57	8/01	Catt	7f	F(0-60)H	GD	£2943
51	6/01	NmkJ	7f	E(0-70)H	G-F	£4260
52	8/00	Thsk	6f	F(0-60)H	G-F	£3602
47	7/00	Catt	7f	F(0-65)H	G-F	£2233
47	7/00	Haml	6f5y	E(0-70)H	G-F	£2899
53	8/99	Haml	6f5y	E(0-70)H	G-F	£3826
45	8/99	Ayr	7f	F	G-F	£2290

Total win prize-money £26845

Going (Turf): Sf: 1-13 GS: 0-7 Gd: 1-11 **GF: 6-28** Fm: 0-8
Distance: 5f/6f: 1-16 **7f-8f: 7-50** 9f-13f: 0-5 14f+: 0-0
Track : **LH: 4-22** RH: 0-16 **Tight: 3-16** Gall: 0-4
Aids: Bl: 0-0 Vi: 0-0 Tstrap: 0-0
Best Rating: 59 8/01 Epsm 7f soft

He has won three times over seven furlongs this season, at Newmarket, Catterick and Epsom. Handles all types of ground, although he has looked high enough in the handicap since.

Encyclopedia

98 **55**

3-y-o b f So Factual (USA)-Wakayi (Persian Bold)
T D Easterby Lady Halifax

Placings:505-3002 **(4219)**
2001: 6^{3}GF, 7^{0}GF, 6^{0}GF, 7^{2}G

	Starts	1st	2nd	3rd	Win & Pl
Career Total (Turf)	7	0	1	1	1296

Going (Turf): Sf: 0-1 GS: 0-0 Gd: 0-1 GF: 0-5 Fm: 0-0
Distance: 5f/6f: 0-5 7f-8f: 0-2 9f-13f: 0-0 14f+: 0-0
Track : LH: 0-0 RH: 0-0 Tight: 0-0 Gall: 0-0
Aids: Bl: 0-0 Vi: 0-0 Tstrap: 0-0
Best Rating: 55 7/01 Donc 7f gd-fm

End Of An Error

88(76) (25)**59**

2-y-o b f Charmer-Needwood Poppy (Rolfe (USA))
M C Chapman (B A McMahon 11/9) David Fravigar,Alan Mann,David Marshall

Placings:0063100 **(5280)**
2001: 6^{0}G, 5^{0}SD, 7^{6}SD, 7^{3}G, 8^{1}GF, 7^{0}GS, 9^{0}S

	Starts	1st	2nd	3rd	Win & Pl
Career Total (Turf)	5	1	0	1	2415
Career Total (AW)	2	0	0	0	0

59 9/01 Leic 1m9y G(0-65) G-F £1967
Total win prize-money £1967

Going (Turf): Sf: 0-1 GS: 0-1 Gd: 0-2 **GF: 1-1** Fm: 0-0
Distance: 5f/6f: 0-2 7f-8f: 0-3 **9f-13f: 1-2** 14f+: 0-0
Track : LH: 0-3 RH: 0-1 Tight: 0-2 Gall: 0-0
Aids: Bl: 0-0 Vi: 0-0 Tstrap: 0-0
Best Rating: 59 9/01 Leic 1m9y gd-fm

Improved with racing to win a Leicester seller in September, but was let go for just 2,500gns.

Endless Hall

117 **125**

5-y-o b h Saddlers' Hall (IRE)-Endless Joy (Law Society (USA))
L M Cumani Il Paralupo

Placings:1321/250131/5011-41604 **(4687a)**
2001: 12^{4}G, 10^{1}F, 10^{6}GF, 10^{0}GF, 12^{4}G

	Starts	1st	2nd	3rd	Win & Pl
Career Total (Turf)	19	7	2	2	965389

125	5/01	Kran	1m2f		FRM	£694981
125	7/00	Ayr	1m2f	A	G-F	£20300
122	6/00	Siro	1m4f		G-F	£100685
98	10/99	Siro	1m4f		YLD	£10935
97	7/99	Siro	1m2f		G-F	£21870
	11/98	Capa	1m1f		SFT	£8596
	7/98	Siro	7f		HVY	£5157

Total win prize-money £862524

Going (Turf): Sf: 0-2 GS: 0-1 Gd: 0-3 **GF: 3-6** Fm: 1-1
Distance: 5f/6f: 0-0 7f-8f: 0-3 **9f-13f: 5-11** 14f+: 0-0
Track : LH: 1-1 **RH: 3-11** Tight: 0-0 Gall: 0-1
Aids: Bl: 0-0 Vi: 0-0 Tstrap: 0-0
Best Rating: 125 5/01 Kran 1m2f firm

Suited by the top of the ground, he ran a cracker in Dubai on his reappearance and beat the smart international performer Jim And Tonic in a very valuable race in Singapore. Put up a respectable effort at Royal Ascot, his first run in England, but ran unaccountably badly in the Eclipse before being beaten at long-odds on in Turkey. A game front-runner, if connections persevere with him he can pick up further good races next season.

Endless Q

82 **42**

2-y-o ch f Timeless Times (USA)-Off Camera (Efisio)
T D Easterby D B Lamplough

Placings:0 **(2869)**
2001: 5^{0}GF

	Starts	1st	2nd	3rd	Win & Pl
Career Total (Turf)	1	0	0	0	

Going (Turf): Sf: 0-0 GS: 0-0 Gd: 0-0 GF: 0-1 Fm: 0-0
Distance: 5f/6f: 0-1 7f-8f: 0-0 9f-13f: 0-0 14f+: 0-0
Track : LH: 0-0 RH: 0-0 Tight: 0-0 Gall: 0-0
Aids: Bl: 0-0 Vi: 0-0 Tstrap: 0-0
Best Rating: 42 7/01 Ripn 5f gd-fm

Endymion (IRE)

95 **40**

4-y-o ch f Paris House-Vaguely Jade (Corvaro (USA))
Mrs P N Dutfield Matt Tompkins

Placings:0543U030/000304600-00000 **(4159)**
2001: 5^{0}F, 6^{0}F, 7^{0}GF, 6^{0}G, 6^{0}GF

	Starts	1st	2nd	3rd	Win & Pl
Career Total (Turf)	22	0	0	3	2096

Going (Turf): Sf: 0-1 GS: 0-1 Gd: 0-6 GF: 0-11 Fm: 0-2
Distance: 5f/6f: 0-19 7f-8f: 0-3 9f-13f: 0-0 14f+: 0-0
Track : LH: 0-4 RH: 0-4 Tight: 0-0 Gall: 0-7
Aids: Bl: 0-0 Vi: 0-0 Tstrap: 0-0
Best Rating: 37 7/01 Newb 7f gd-fm

English Harbour

96 **75**

3-y-o ch f Sabrehill (USA)-Water Woo (USA) (Tom Rolfe)
B W Hills W J Gredley

Placings:004222-13 **(0875)**
2001: 9^{1}GS, 9^{3}S

	Starts	1st	2nd	3rd	Win & Pl
Career Total (Turf)	8	1	3	1	7184

75 4/01 Brig 1m1f209yD G-S £3292
Total win prize-money £3293

Going (Turf): Sf: 0-4 **GS: 1-2** Gd: 0-1 GF: 0-1 Fm: 0-0
Distance: 5f/6f: 0-0 7f-8f: 0-3 **9f-13f: 1-5** 14f+: 0-0
Track : **LH: 1-6** RH: 0-1 Tight: 0-0 Gall: 0-0
Aids: Bl: 0-0 Vi: 0-0 Tstrap: 0-0
Best Rating: 75 4/01 Brig 1m1f209y gd-sft

Engstrum (IRE)

97(89) (30)**41**

3-y-o ch g Grand Lodge (USA)-Gentle Guest (IRE) (Be My Guest (USA))
H Morrison Lady Margadale

Placings:06623106 **(5114)**
2001: 14^{0}G, **11**^{6}SD, **12**^{6}SD, 16^{2}GF, 16^{3}G, 16^{1}GF, 16^{0}GF, 16^{6}HY

	Starts	1st	2nd	3rd	Win & Pl
Career Total (Turf)	6	1	1	1	3594
Career Total (AW)	2	0	0	0	0

41 8/01 Muss 2m F(0-60)H G-F £2394
Total win prize-money £2394

Going (Turf): Sf: 0-1 GS: 0-0 Gd: 0-2 **GF: 1-3** Fm: 0-0
Distance: 5f/6f: 0-0 7f-8f: 0-0 9f-13f: 0-2 **14f+: 1-6**
Track : LH: 0-6 **RH: 1-2 Tight: 1-2** Gall: 0-0
Aids: Bl: 0-0 **Vi: 1-2** Tstrap: 0-0
Best Rating: 41 8/01 Muss 2m gd-fm

Enigmatic Spirit (IRE)

79 **41**

2-y-o b f Petorius-Bakema (IRE) (King Of Clubs)
A B Mulholland Miss K Watson

Placings:000000 **(5633)**
2001: 6^{0}GF, 5^{0}GF, 7^{0}GS, 9^{0}S, 8^{0}HY, 7^{0}G

	Starts	1st	2nd	3rd	Win & Pl
Career Total (Turf)	6	0	0	0	

Going (Turf): Sf: 0-2 GS: 0-1 Gd: 0-1 GF: 0-2 Fm: 0-0
Distance: 5f/6f: 0-2 7f-8f: 0-2 9f-13f: 0-2 14f+: 0-0
Track : LH: 0-3 RH: 0-1 Tight: 0-1 Gall: 0-0
Aids: Bl: 0-0 Vi: 0-2 Tstrap: 0-0
Best Rating: 41 11/01 Catt 7f good

Enjoy The Buzz

87 **61**

2-y-o b c Prince Of Birds (USA)-Abaklea (IRE) (Doyoun)
E J Alston Miss F Fenley

Placings:0050 **(5487)**
2001: 6^{0}GF, 6^{0}GF, 6^{5}S, 6^{0}HY

	Starts	1st	2nd	3rd	Win & Pl
Career Total (Turf)	4	0	0	0	0

Going (Turf): Sf: 0-2 GS: 0-0 Gd: 0-0 GF: 0-2 Fm: 0-0
Distance: 5f/6f: 0-3 7f-8f: 0-1 9f-13f: 0-0 14f+: 0-0
Track : LH: 0-1 RH: 0-0 Tight: 0-0 Gall: 0-0
Aids: Bl: 0-0 Vi: 0-0 Tstrap: 0-0
Best Rating: 61 9/01 York 6f gd-fm

Ennoblement (IRE)

108 **104**

3-y-o ch c Halling (USA)-Royal Touch (Tap On Wood)
M P Tregoning Sheikh Mohammed

Placings:1203 **(4949)**
2001: 10^{1}G, 10^{2}GF, 10^{0}GS, 9^{3}G

	Starts	1st	2nd	3rd	Win & Pl
Career Total (Turf)	4	1	1	1	10304

70 5/01 Ling 1m2f D GD £4030
Total win prize-money £4030

Going (Turf): Sf: 0-0 GS: 0-1 **Gd: 1-2** GF: 0-1 Fm: 0-0
Distance: 5f/6f: 0-0 7f-8f: 0-0 **9f-13f: 1-4** 14f+: 0-0
Track : **LH: 1-3** RH: 0-1 **Tight: 1-2** Gall: 0-2
Aids: Bl: 0-0 Vi: 0-0 Tstrap: 0-0
Best Rating: 104 9/01 Gdwd 1m1f192y good

Won an ordinary Lingfield maiden on his debut, and was

only touched off by a more experienced opponent next time. Handles fastish ground, and looks open to more improvement. Stays ten furlongs.

Enrich (USA)

100 (80)**95**

3-y-o b f Dynaformer (USA)-Eternal Reve (USA) (Diesis)
Saeed Bin Suroor Godolphin

Placings:13-50 **(1972)**
2001: 8^{5}FT, 8^{0}GF

	Starts	1st	2nd	3rd	Win & Pl
Career Total (Turf)	3	1	0	1	11400
Career Total (AW)	1	0	0	0	5000

85 9/00 Cork 6f G-F £6900
Total win prize-money £6900

Going (Turf): Sf: 0-0 GS: 0-0 Gd: 0-0 **GF: 1-2** Fm: 0-0
Distance: **5f/6f: 1-1** 7f-8f: 0-2 9f-13f: 0-1 14f+: 0-0
Track : LH: 0-1 RH: 0-0 Tight: 0-1 Gall: 0-0
Aids: Bl: 0-0 Vi: 0-0 Tstrap: 0-0
Best Rating: 91 6/01 Epsm 1m114y gd-fm

She won a weak Cork maiden over six furlongs as a juvenile when trained by John Oxx, then ran well over seven furlongs on only other start. Now with Godolphin, she was fifth in the UAE 1000 Guineas. Has won on a sound surface.

Entail (USA)

109(85) (38)**90**

4-y-o b/br f Riverman (USA)-Estala (Be My Guest (USA))
W Jarvis Plantation Stud

Placings:3/5343-01110 **(2972)**
2001: 8^{0}SD, 7^{1}GF, 7^{1}S, 8^{1}GF, 7^{0}G

	Starts	1st	2nd	3rd	Win & Pl
Career Total (Turf)	9	3	0	3	30972
Career Total (AW)	1	0	0	0	

90 6/01 NmkJ 1m C(0-90)H G-F £6743
82 6/01 Sand 7f16y C(0-100)H SFT £14316
71 6/01 Bevl 7f100y E(0-70)H G-F £7670
Total win prize-money £28730

Going (Turf): Sf: 1-2 GS: 0-1 Gd: 0-2 **GF: 2-3** Fm: 0-0
Distance: 5f/6f: 0-0 **7f-8f: 3-9** 9f-13f: 0-0 14f+: 0-0
Track : LH: 0-3 **RH: 2-2** Tight: 0-0 Gall: 0-1
Aids: Bl: 0-0 Vi: 0-0 Tstrap: 0-0
Best Rating: 90 6/01 NmkJ 1m gd-fm

Showed fair form for John Gosden last season without winning, but being in foal has worked the oracle for her as she completed a hat-trick in June with wins at Beverley, Sandown and Newmarket. Effective at seven furlongs or a mile.

Enthused (USA)

108 **110**

3-y-o b f Seeking The Gold (USA)-Magic Of Life (USA) (Seattle Slew (USA))
Sir Michael Stoute Niarchos Family

Placings:12116-500 **(2971)**
2001: 8^{5}G, 8^{0}GF, 6^{0}G

	Starts	1st	2nd	3rd	Win & Pl
Career Total (Turf)	8	3	1	0	95764

110 8/00 York 6f A GD £46400
113 7/00 Asct 6f A G-F £24000
80 6/00 NmkJ 6f D G-F £4914
Total win prize-money £75314

Going (Turf): Sf: 0-0 GS: 0-2 Gd: 1-3 **GF: 2-3** Fm: 0-0
Distance: **5f/6f: 3-6** 7f-8f: 0-2 9f-13f: 0-0 14f+: 0-0
Track : LH: 0-0 RH: 0-1 Tight: 0-0 Gall: 0-1
Aids: Bl: 0-0 Vi: 0-0 Tstrap: 0-0
Best Rating: 110 6/01 Asct 1m gd-fm

She showed high-class form at two, winning the Princess Margaret and Lowther in good style, but did not train on. Retired to stud.

Entity

104 **81**

4-y-o ch g Rudimentary (USA)-Desert Ditty (Green Desert (USA))
T D Barron Mrs J Hazell

Placings:05440/0003L0050012110-0001100 **(4109)**
2001: 9^{0}S, 10^{0}G, 8^{0}G, 8^{1}GF, 9^{1}GS, 9^{0}GF, 9^{0}S

	Starts	1st	2nd	3rd	Win & Pl
Career Total (Turf)	27	5	1	1	22199

81 6/01 Haml 1m1f36y E(0-75)H G-S £3721
74 6/01 Bevl 1m100y D(0-80)H G-F £4377
74 9/00 Bevl 1m100y E(0-70)H HVY £3360
61 9/00 Haml 1m1f36y E(0-75)H SFT £4628
56 8/00 Haml 1m65y F(0-65)H SFT £3055
Total win prize-money £19143

Going (Turf): **Sf: 3-8** GS: 1-4 Gd: 0-6 GF: 1-6 Fm: 0-3
Distance: 5f/6f: 0-4 7f-8f: 0-9 **9f-13f: 5-14** 14f+: 0-0
Track : LH: 0-8 **RH: 5-13 Tight: 3-12** Gall: 0-4
Aids: Bl: 0-2 Vi: 0-0 Tstrap: 0-0
Best Rating: 81 6/01 Haml 1m1f36y gd-sft

Something of a character, but he has plenty of ability and scored twice in June. Likes cut in the ground.

Entrap (USA)

101 **94**

2-y-o b f Phone Trick (USA)-Mystic Lure (Green Desert (USA))
W J Haggas Cheveley Park Stud

Placings:1430 **(5144)**
2001: 6^{1}G, 6^{4}GF, 6^{3}GF, 7^{0}G

	Starts	1st	2nd	3rd	Win & Pl
Career Total (Turf)	4	1	0	1	8979

94 7/01 Kemp 6f E GD £4368
Total win prize-money £4368

Going (Turf): Sf: 0-0 GS: 0-0 **Gd: 1-2** GF: 0-2 Fm: 0-0
Distance: **5f/6f: 1-3** 7f-8f: 0-1 9f-13f: 0-0 14f+: 0-0
Track : LH: 0-0 RH: 0-0 Tight: 0-0 Gall: 0-0
Aids: Bl: 0-0 Vi: 0-0 Tstrap: 0-0
Best Rating: 94 7/01 Kemp 6f good

Won on her Kempton debut despite running green, before finishing a good fourth in an Ascot Group Three.

Entropy

99(91) (36)**52d**

5-y-o b m Brief Truce (USA)-Distant Isle (IRE) (Bluebird (USA))
B A Pearce T M J Keep

Placings:32335160/0005000050/00230510360-0500 **(2342)**
2001: 7^{0}SD, 6^{5}G, 7^{0}F, 7^{0}SD

	Starts	1st	2nd	3rd	Win & Pl
Career Total (Turf)	27	2	2	4	10038
Career Total (AW)	7	0	0	1	343

47 7/00 Bath 1m5y E(0-70)H FRM £2919
73 8/98 Bath 5f161y E H FRM £2723
Total win prize-money £5642

Going (Turf): Sf: 0-1 GS: 0-4 Gd: 0-7 GF: 0-9 **Fm: 2-6**
Distance: 5f/6f: 1-12 7f-8f: 0-17 9f-13f: 1-5 14f+: 0-0
Track : **LH: 2-20** RH: 0-2 Tight: 1-12 Gall: 1-1
Aids: Bl: 0-0 Vi: 0-0 Tstrap: 0-0
Best Rating: 39 5/01 Brig 6f209y good

Envious

96 **67**

2-y-o ch g Hernando (FR)-Prima Verde (Leading Counsel (USA))
Sir Mark Prescott The Four Speculators

Placings:06 **(5466)**
2001: 8^{0}G, 6^{6}S

	Starts	1st	2nd	3rd	Win & Pl
Career Total (Turf)	2	0	0	0	0

Going (Turf): Sf: 0-1 GS: 0-0 Gd: 0-1 GF: 0-0 Fm: 0-0
Distance: 5f/6f: 0-0 7f-8f: 0-2 9f-13f: 0-0 14f+: 0-0
Track : LH: 0-1 RH: 0-0 Tight: 0-0 Gall: 0-0
Aids: Bl: 0-0 Vi: 0-0 Tstrap: 0-0
Best Rating: 67 10/01 Brig 6f209y soft

Environment Audit

97 **74**

2-y-o ch c Kris-Bold And Beautiful (Bold Lad (IRE))
B W Hills W J Gredley

Placings:03 **(5689)**
2001: 7^{0}GS, 6^{3}S

	Starts	1st	2nd	3rd	Win & Pl
Career Total (Turf)	2	0	0	1	741

Going (Turf): Sf: 0-1 GS: 0-1 Gd: 0-0 GF: 0-0 Fm: 0-0
Distance: 5f/6f: 0-1 7f-8f: 0-1 9f-13f: 0-0 14f+: 0-0
Track : LH: 0-0 RH: 0-0 Tight: 0-0 Gall: 0-0
Aids: Bl: 0-0 Vi: 0-0 Tstrap: 0-0
Best Rating: 74 11/01 Donc 6f soft

Good form in competitive maidens.

Epicentre (USA)

93 **80**

2-y-o b c Kris S (USA)-Carya (USA) (Northern Dancer)
J H M Gosden K Abdulla

Placings:65 **(4832)**
2001: 8^{6}G, 8^{5}GF

	Starts	1st	2nd	3rd	Win & Pl
Career Total (Turf)	2	0	0	0	410

Going (Turf): Sf: 0-0 GS: 0-0 Gd: 0-1 GF: 0-1 Fm: 0-0
Distance: 5f/6f: 0-0 7f-8f: 0-2 9f-13f: 0-0 14f+: 0-0
Track : LH: 0-0 RH: 0-1 Tight: 0-0 Gall: 0-0
Aids: Bl: 0-0 Vi: 0-0 Tstrap: 0-0
Best Rating: 80 9/01 Newb 1m gd-fm

Epping

99(102) (64++)**57**

3-y-o b f Charnwood Forest (IRE)-Dansara (Dancing Brave (USA))
B W Hills K Abdulla

Placings:031 **(5395)**
2001: 8^{0}GS, 8^{3}GS, 7^{1}SD

	Starts	1st	2nd	3rd	Win & Pl
Career Total (Turf)	2	0	0	1	558
Career Total (AW)	1	1	0	0	2975

64 10/01 Wolv 7f F STD £2975
Total win prize-money £2975

Going (Turf): Sf: 0-0 GS: 0-2 Gd: 0-0 GF: 0-0 Fm: 0-0
Distance: 5f/6f: 0-0 **7f-8f: 1-2** 9f-13f: 0-1 14f+: 0-0
Track : **LH: 1-2** RH: 0-0 **Tight: 1-1** Gall: 0-0
Aids: Bl: 0-0 Vi: 0-0 Tstrap: 0-0
Best Rating: 64 10/01 Wolv 7f stand

Caught for second, as her rider looked over the wrong shoulder, on her second start at Pontefract. Made up for that when scoring on her All-Weather debut at Wolverhampton in October over seven furlongs.

Erebus (IRE)

106(91) (45)**59**

4-y-o b g Desert Style (IRE)-Almost A Lady (IRE) (Entitled)
J A Glover Mrs Janis Macpherson

Placings:06340-0050030 **(5450)**
2001: 9^0F, 7^0F, 8^5GF, 8^0GF, 8^0GS, 8^3SD, 8^0HY

	Starts	1st	2nd	3rd	Win & Pl
Career Total (Turf)	11	0	0	1	267
Career Total (AW)	1	0	0	1	357

Going (Turf): **Sf: 0-2 GS: 0-2 Gd: 0-1 GF: 0-3 Fm: 0-3**
Distance: 5f/6f: 0-0 7f-8f: 0-6 9f-13f: 0-6 14f+: 0-0
Track : LH: 0-9 RH: 0-1 Tight: 0-6 Gall: 0-1
Aids: Bl: 0-0 Vi: 0-5 Tstrap: 0-0
Best Rating: 59 7/01 Ripn 1m gd-fm

Eric Le Beau (IRE)

89 **84**

2-y-o ch c Great Commotion (USA)-Mirmande (Kris)
G C Bravery M I L Racing

Placings:0 **(5367)**
2001: 8^0GS

	Starts	1st	2nd	3rd	Win & Pl
Career Total (Turf)	1	0	0	0	

Going (Turf): **Sf: 0-0 GS: 0-1 Gd: 0-0 GF: 0-0 Fm: 0-0**
Distance: 5f/6f: 0-0 7f-8f: 0-1 9f-13f: 0-0 14f+: 0-0
Track : LH: 0-0 RH: 0-0 Tight: 0-0 Gall: 0-0
Aids: Bl: 0-0 Vi: 0-0 Tstrap: 0-0
Best Rating: 84 10/01 NmkR 1m gd-sft

With stamina in his pedigree, was doing all his best work late on in a Newmarket maiden over a mile in October.

Erracht

104(91) (42)**75d**

3-y-o gr f Emarati (USA)-Port Na Blath (On Your Mark)
P C Haslam Mrs B Hawkins

Placings:2162-040116 **(4898)**
2001: 5^0SW, 6^4SD, 8^0SD, 6^1F, 6^1G, 5^6GS

	Starts	1st	2nd	3rd	Win & Pl
Career Total (Turf)	6	3	1	0	9165
Career Total (AW)	4	0	1	0	494

49	7/01	Haml	6f5y	E	GD	£3234
38	6/01	Thsk	6f	F	FRM	£2555
77	8/00	Bevl	5f	F	GD	£2408

Total win prize-money £8197

Going (Turf): Sf: 0-1 GS: 0-2 **Gd: 2-2** GF: 0-0 Fm: 1-1
Distance: **5f/6f: 2-8** 7f-8f: 1-2 9f-13f: 0-0 14f+: 0-0
Track : LH: 0-5 RH: 0-0 Tight: 0-2 Gall: 0-0
Aids: Bl: 0-0 Vi: 0-0 Tstrap: 0-0
Best Rating: 49 7/01 Haml 6f5y good

Not the best mover, she has been lightly raced due to sore shins, but she came away from an unsuccessful stint on the All-Weather to achieve back-to-back wins on a Scottish raid, albeit in moderate company. She is suited to six furlongs on a sound surface.

Erro Codigo

103(92) (49)**62**

6-y-o b g Formidable (USA)-Home Wrecker (DEN) (Affiliation Order (USA))
F P Murtagh Mrs Anna Kenny

Placings:4520322/6136500342355/0000410034/6-2000 **(1242)**
2001: 6^2HY, 5^0S, 8^0S, 6^0G

	Starts	1st	2nd	3rd	Win & Pl
Career Total (Turf)	27	1	5	3	11180
Career Total (AW)	9	1	0	2	4681

52	10/99	Ling	6f	E(0-70)H	G-F	£3643
62	2/98	Sthl	6f	D	STD	£3550

Total win prize-money £7193

Going (Turf): Sf: 0-4 GS: 0-3 Gd: 0-11 **GF: 1-8** Fm: 0-1
Distance: **5f/6f: 2-25** 7f-8f: 0-10 9f-13f: 0-1 14f+: 0-0
Track : **LH: 1-18** RH: 0-3 Tight: 0-10 Gall: 0-1
Aids: Bl: 0-0 Vi: 0-1 Tstrap: 0-0
Best Rating: 62 4/01 Pont 6f heavy

Ertlon

99(92) (24)**45**

11-y-o b g Shareef Dancer (USA)-Sharpina (Sharpen Up)
C E Brittain C E Brittain

Placings:35/45340002051000 2/60044500511/2223010006450/00030503040000 5645/224123230006206/304/33536/0000603551200-040 **(0272)**
2001: 8^0SW, 7^4SD, 8^0SW

	Starts	1st	2nd	3rd	Win & Pl
Career Total (Turf)	66	4	4	7	44795
Career Total (AW)	32	2	7	5	19543

43	8/00	Brig	7f214y	E	FRM	£2301
76	3/97	Ling	7f	E	STD	£2869
86	4/95	Brig	6f209y	C(0-90)H	G-F	£6264
82	11/94	Ling	1m	D(0-75)H	STD	£3288
68	10/94	Yarm	7f3y	E(0-70)H	GD	£4240
80	9/93	York	7f202y	D(0-80)H	G-F	£5253

Total win prize-money £24217

Going (Turf): Sf: 0-5 GS: 0-6 Gd: 1-20 **GF: 2-26** Fm: 1-9
Distance: 5f/6f: 0-0 **7f-8f: 6-81** 9f-13f: 0-17 14f+: 0-0
Track : **LH: 5-57** RH: 0-6 **Tight: 2-36** Gall: 1-7
Aids: Bl: 0-1 Vi: 0-0 Tstrap: 0-0
Best Rating: 24 1/01 Ling 7f stand

Usually there or thereabouts both on turf and sand, he deserves more successes on his consistency alone. The handicapper has relented a little.

Erupt

99(100) (38)**41**

8-y-o b g Beveled (USA)-Sparklingsovereign (Sparkler)
M Brittain Northgate Lodge Racing Club

Placings:204653012/4000/655526600/0010500060/2000006440021000 6/20421130000400 0-000026060 **(5539)**
2001: 7^0GF, 8^0GF, 7^0GF, 8^0G, 8^2GS, 8^6GF, 8^0GS, 8^6HY, 8^0S

	Starts	1st	2nd	3rd	Win & Pl
Career Total (Turf)	59	5	6	2	22138
Career Total (AW)	14	0	2	0	1339

55	5/00	Sthl	7f	F(0-60)	HVY	£1918
52	5/00	Muss	7f30y	E(0-70)H	FRM	£3003
50	9/99	Newc	1m3y	E(0-70)H	SFT	£3228
62	5/98	Muss	7f30y	F(0-65)H	GD	£2981
73	10/95	Chep	6f16y	E(0-75)H	SFT	£3415

Total win prize-money £14545

Going (Turf): **Sf: 3-9** GS: 0-8 Gd: 1-18 GF: 0-22 Fm: 1-2
Distance: 5f/6f: 0-18 **7f-8f: 4-46** 9f-13f: 1-9 14f+: 0-0
Track : LH: 1-31 **RH: 2-10 Tight: 2-17** Gall: 0-6
Aids: Bl: 0-1 **Vi: 1-9** Tstrap: 0-1
Best Rating: 46 8/01 Thsk 1m gd-sft

Esatto

93(88) (60)**65**

2-y-o b c Puissance-Stoneydale (Tickled Pink)
R Hollinshead (M J Polglase 4/8) D S Lovatt

Placings:02445345005 **(5660)**
2001: 5^0SD, 5^2F, 5^4G, 5^4GF, 5^5GF, 5^3SD, 5^4F, 5^5GS, 6^0S, 5^0GS, 5^5G

	Starts	1st	2nd	3rd	Win & Pl
Career Total (Turf)	9	0	1	0	1983
Career Total (AW)	2	0	0	1	320

Going (Turf): **Sf: 0-1 GS: 0-2 Gd: 0-2 GF: 0-2 Fm: 0-2**
Distance: 5f/6f: 0-11 7f-8f: 0-0 9f-13f: 0-0 14f+: 0-0
Track : LH: 0-1 RH: 0-0 Tight: 0-0 Gall: 0-0
Aids: Bl: 0-0 Vi: 0-0 Tstrap: 0-0
Best Rating: 76 6/01 York 5f good

Still a maiden but has shown enough in maidens and nurseries to suggest he can win a race.

Escalade

111 **73**

4-y-o b g Green Desert (USA)-Sans Escale (USA) (Diesis)
W M Brisbourne William D Day

Placings:00630/0-053420111140 **(5529)**
2001: 6^0F, 8^5GF, 8^3HD, 8^4F, 8^2GS, 8^0GF, 8^1GF, 8^1G, 8^1GS, 8^1HY, 8^4GS, 8^0HY

	Starts	1st	2nd	3rd	Win & Pl
Career Total (Turf)	18	4	1	2	18258

68	9/01	Hayd	1m30y	D(0-85)H	HVY	£5050
71	9/01	Leic	1m9y	F(0-60)	G-S	£3178
58	9/01	Bevl	1m100y	F(0-65)H	GD	£3622
55	9/01	Nott	1m54y	E(0-75)H	G-F	£3381

Total win prize-money £15233

Going (Turf): **Sf: 1-2 GS: 1-4 Gd: 1-1 GF: 1-8** Fm: 0-3
Distance: 5f/6f: 0-2 7f-8f: 0-5 **9f-13f: 4-11** 14f+: 0-0
Track : **LH: 2-9** RH: 1-5 Tight: 0-6 Gall: 0-2
Aids: Bl: 0-0 Vi: 0-0 Tstrap: 0-0
Best Rating: 73 10/01 York 1m205y gd-sft

A lightly-raced gelding. Has improved steadily throughout this term and notched up four wins in a row in September over a mile, before looking in the Handicappers grasp.

Escenica (IRE)

91 **79**

2-y-o b f Charnwood Forest (IRE)-Scenic Spirit (IRE) (Scenic)
C F Wall F Hinojosa

Placings:54 **(5147)**
2001: 7^5GF, 7^4G

	Starts	1st	2nd	3rd	Win & Pl
Career Total (Turf)	2	0	0	0	0

Going (Turf): **Sf: 0-0 GS: 0-0 Gd: 0-1 GF: 0-1 Fm: 0-0**
Distance: 5f/6f: 0-0 7f-8f: 0-2 9f-13f: 0-0 14f+: 0-0
Track : LH: 0-0 RH: 0-0 Tight: 0-0 Gall: 0-0
Aids: Bl: 0-0 Vi: 0-0 Tstrap: 0-0
Best Rating: 79 10/01 Rdcr 7f good

Showed Improvement on her debut running when fourth at Redcar.

Escort

82 **34**

5-y-o b g Most Welcome-Benazir (High Top)
W Clay The Escort Partnership

Placings:001/44006/00 **(0708)**
2001: 14^0HY, 17^0HY

	Starts	1st	2nd	3rd	Win & Pl
Career Total (Turf)	10	1	0	0	4400

74	11/98	Donc	1m	E	SFT	£3427

Total win prize-money £3428

Going (Turf): **Sf: 1-5** GS: 0-1 Gd: 0-2 GF: 0-2 Fm: 0-0
Distance: 5f/6f: 0-2 **7f-8f: 1-1** 9f-13f: 0-5 14f+: 0-2
Track : LH: 0-3 RH: 0-1 Tight: 0-2 Gall: 0-0
Aids: Bl: 0-0 Vi: 0-0 Tstrap: 0-0
Best Rating: 34 3/01 Nott 1m6f15y heavy

Esenin

94 **88**

2-y-o b c Danehill (USA)-Boojum (Mujtahid (USA))
N A Callaghan M Tabor

Placings:156 **(4373)**
2001: 6^{1}G, 6^{5}GF, 7^{6}GF

	Starts	1st	2nd	3rd	Win & Pl
Career Total (Turf)	3	1	0	0	8651

88 7/01 NmkJ 6f D GD £6776
Total win prize-money £6776

Going (Turf): Sf: 0-0 GS: 0-0 **Gd: 1-1** GF: 0-2 Fm: 0-0
Distance: **5f/6f: 1-2** 7f-8f: 0-1 9f-13f: 0-0 14f+: 0-0
Track : LH: 0-0 RH: 0-0 Tight: 0-0 Gall: 0-0
Aids: Bl: 0-0 Vi: 0-0 Tstrap: 0-0
Best Rating: 88 7/01 NmkJ 6f good

His dam won over six and seven furlongs at two and he comes from the family of the Preakness winner Red Bullet. Bolted up in a six-furlong novice stakes at Newmarket on his debut in July, but found the step up to Group Two company in the Richmond Stakes too much for him. He is still a useful prospect.

Esher Common (IRE)

104 **93**
3-y-o b g Common Grounds-Alsahah (IRE) (Unfuwain (USA))
T G Mills David J Archer

Placings:51-540004 **(4383)**
2001: 8^{5}S, 8^{4}S, 7^{0}G, 8^{0}GF, 7^{0}GF, 8^{4}GF

	Starts	1st	2nd	3rd	Win & Pl
Career Total (Turf)	8	1	0	0	5791

84 9/00 Hayd 7f30y D HVY £3991
Total win prize-money £3991

Going (Turf): Sf: 1-3 GS: 0-0 Gd: 0-1 GF: 0-4 Fm: 0-0
Distance: 5f/6f: 0-0 **7f-8f: 1-7** 9f-13f: 0-1 14f+: 0-0
Track : LH: 1-2 RH: 0-1 Tight: 0-0 Gall: 0-0
Aids: Bl: 0-0 Vi: 0-0 Tstrap: 0-0
Best Rating: 93 5/01 NmkR 7f good

He got off the mark on heavy ground at Haydock on his second and final start at two, but was well beaten on his Doncaster reappearance at three when stepped up to a mile. Has given the impression that he save a bit for himself. Acts on a soft surface.

Eshraag

97(89) (71+)**81**
2-y-o ch c Lion Cavern (USA)-Val D'Erica (Ashmore (FR))
P W D'Arcy M Al Salem

Placings:02010 **(5368)**
2001: 7^{0}GS, 8^{2}GS, 6^{0}G, 8^{1}SD, 8^{0}GS

	Starts	1st	2nd	3rd	Win & Pl
Career Total (Turf)	4	0	1	0	1045
Career Total (AW)	1	1	0	0	3445

71 10/01 Sthl 1m E STD £3445
Total win prize-money £3445

Going (Turf): Sf: 0-0 GS: 0-3 Gd: 0-1 GF: 0-0 Fm: 0-0
Distance: 5f/6f: 0-0 **7f-8f: 1-5** 9f-13f: 0-0 14f+: 0-0
Track : LH: 1-2 RH: 0-0 Tight: 0-0 Gall: 0-1
Aids: Bl: 0-0 Vi: 0-0 Tstrap: 0-0
Best Rating: 81 8/01 NmkJ 1m gd-sft

A half-brother to middle-distance winner Verardi, he improved from his debut to finish runner-up in a Newmarket maiden next time. Well beaten in a York Listed event, but got off the mark with a workmanlike victory in a maiden on the Southwell Fibresand.

Esligier (IRE)

106(90) (60)**96**
2-y-o ch f Sabrehill (USA)-Norbella (Nordico (USA))
B A McMahon Philip G Harvey

Placings:21215 **(4683)**
2001: 5^{2}SD, 5^{1}G, 5^{2}G, 5^{1}GF, 5^{5}GS

	Starts	1st	2nd	3rd	Win & Pl
Career Total (Turf)	4	2	1	0	10250
Career Total (AW)	1	0	1	0	640

89 8/01 Ripn 5f C G-F £5475
75 8/01 Nott 5f13y D GD £3607
Total win prize-money £9083

Going (Turf): Sf: 0-0 GS: 0-1 **Gd: 1-2 GF: 1-1** Fm: 0-0
Distance: **5f/6f: 2-5** 7f-8f: 0-0 9f-13f: 0-0 14f+: 0-0
Track : LH: 0-0 RH: 0-0 Tight: 0-0 Gall: 0-0
Aids: Bl: 0-0 Vi: 0-0 Tstrap: 0-0
Best Rating: 96 9/01 Donc 5f gd-sft

Has won twice over five furlongs on good and good to firm. Ran well in Listed company at Doncaster in September.

Esloob (USA)

105 **100**
2-y-o b f Diesis-Roseate Tern (Blakeney)
M P Tregoning Hamdan Al Maktoum

Placings:13 **(5003)**
2001: 7^{1}GF, 8^{3}S

	Starts	1st	2nd	3rd	Win & Pl
Career Total (Turf)	2	1	0	1	26966

87 8/01 NmkJ 7f D G-F £4966
Total win prize-money £4966

Going (Turf): Sf: 0-1 GS: 0-0 Gd: 0-0 **GF: 1-1** Fm: 0-0
Distance: 5f/6f: 0-0 **7f-8f: 1-2** 9f-13f: 0-0 14f+: 0-0
Track : LH: 0-0 RH: 0-1 Tight: 0-0 Gall: 0-1
Aids: Bl: 0-0 Vi: 0-0 Tstrap: 0-0
Best Rating: 100 9/01 Asct 1m soft

A half-sister to Listed Stakes winner Siyadah out of the top class Roseate Tern, she beat several subsequent winners in a Newmarket maiden on her debut, and improved to run third in the Fillies' Mile on ground plenty soft enough. She should make up into a smart performer over ten to 12 furlongs next term.

Espada (IRE)

104 **77**
5-y-o b g Mukaddamah (USA)-Folk Song (CAN) (The Minstrel (CAN))
J A Glover Mrs Janis Macpherson

Placings:54221/51502150/62100000-000350 **(3834)**
2001: 8^{0}S, 8^{0}GS, 7^{0}GF, 7^{3}S, 7^{5}GS, 8^{0}G

	Starts	1st	2nd	3rd	Win & Pl
Career Total (Turf)	27	4	4	1	58615

93 5/00 Kemp 1m B(0-110)H G-S £29000
84 9/99 Ayr 7f C(0-90)H G-S £7922
80 5/99 Thsk 7f D(0-80) G-F £3821
79 8/98 Ripn 6f E G-F £4299
Total win prize-money £45042

Going (Turf): Sf: 0-6 **GS: 2-6** Gd: 0-8 **GF: 2-7** Fm: 0-0
Distance: 5f/6f: 1-5 **7f-8f: 3-20** 9f-13f: 0-2 14f+: 0-0
Track : LH: 2-8 RH: 1-6 Tight: 1-3 Gall: 1-4
Aids: Bl: 0-0 Vi: 0-1 Tstrap: 0-0
Best Rating: 77 6/01 Sand 7f16y soft

A decent performer in handicaps over a mile who goes very well at Kempton, he has struggled in decent contests this term

Espana

99(99) (70+)**68**
3-y-o gr f Hernando (FR)-Pamela Peach (Habitat)
B W Hills The Hon Mrs J M Corbett & Mr C Wright

Placings:030520-2145254 **(2587)**
2001: 9^{2}SW, 12^{1}SD, 10^{4}GS, 10^{5}GS, 10^{2}GF, 11^{5}GF, 12^{4}GF

	Starts	1st	2nd	3rd	Win & Pl
Career Total (Turf)	11	0	2	1	3588
Career Total (AW)	2	1	1	0	3749

70 2/01 Wolv 1m4f D STD £2919
Total win prize-money £2919

Going (Turf): Sf: 0-1 GS: 0-3 Gd: 0-0 GF: 0-7 Fm: 0-0
Distance: 5f/6f: 0-3 7f-8f: 0-1 **9f-13f: 1-9** 14f+: 0-0
Track : LH: 1-8 RH: 0-2 **Tight: 1-5** Gall: 0-2
Aids: Bl: 0-0 Vi: 0-0 Tstrap: 0-0
Best Rating: 70 2/01 Wolv 1m4f stand

Espere D'Or

-5(77) (35d)**18**
4-y-o b g Golden Heights-Drummer's Dream (IRE) (Drumalis)
A Streeter Snax Catering Services

Placings:0/0005000600000-0 **(5503)**
2001: 7^{0}HY

	Starts	1st	2nd	3rd	Win & Pl
Career Total (Turf)	9	0	0	0	0
Career Total (AW)	6	0	0	0	0

Going (Turf): Sf: 0-2 GS: 0-1 Gd: 0-0 GF: 0-4 Fm: 0-1
Distance: 5f/6f: 0-2 7f-8f: 0-4 9f-13f: 0-7 14f+: 0-1
Track : LH: 0-11 RH: 0-0 Tight: 0-6 Gall: 0-1
Aids: Bl: 0-0 Vi: 0-0 Tstrap: 0-0
Best Rating: 70 2/01 Wolv 1m4f stand

Esprit D'Artiste (IRE)

84 **59**
2-y-o ch c Selkirk (USA)-Fracci (Raise A Cup (USA))
C E Brittain Abdullah Saeed Belhab

Placings:000 **(5620)**
2001: 7^{0}S, 8^{0}HY, 8^{0}GS

	Starts	1st	2nd	3rd	Win & Pl
Career Total (Turf)	3	0	0	0	

Going (Turf): Sf: 0-2 GS: 0-1 Gd: 0-0 GF: 0-0 Fm: 0-0
Distance: 5f/6f: 0-0 7f-8f: 0-1 9f-13f: 0-2 14f+: 0-0
Track : LH: 0-2 RH: 0-0 Tight: 0-0 Gall: 0-0
Aids: Bl: 0-0 Vi: 0-0 Tstrap: 0-0
Best Rating: 59 11/01 Nott 1m54y gd-sft

Essie

(30)**48**
4-y-o b f Ezzoud (IRE)-Safari Park (Absalom)
Miss D A McHale Ms D A Stevens

Placings:00520/0-0 **(0776)**
2001: 14^{0}S

	Starts	1st	2nd	3rd	Win & Pl
Career Total (Turf)	6	0	1	0	575
Career Total (AW)	1	0	0	0	

Going (Turf): Sf: 0-1 GS: 0-1 Gd: 0-2 GF: 0-2 Fm: 0-0
Distance: 5f/6f: 0-3 7f-8f: 0-2 9f-13f: 0-1 14f+: 0-1
Track : LH: 0-3 RH: 0-0 Tight: 0-1 Gall: 0-0
Aids: Bl: 0-4 Vi: 0-0 Tstrap: 0-0

Estabella (IRE)

96(101) (40)**28**
4-y-o ch f Mujtahid (USA)-Lady In Green (Shareef Dancer (USA))
B R Johnson (R T Phillips 4/5) Mrs P J Sheen

Placings:0005/2130555401-050000 **(5622)**
2001: 16^{0}GF, 13^{5}GF, 12^{0}GF, 16^{0}G, 9^{0}GF, 14^{0}GS

	Starts	1st	2nd	3rd	Win & Pl
Career Total (Turf)	16	1	1	0	3589
Career Total (AW)	4	1	0	1	3172

62 9/00 Ling 2m E(0-70)H STD £2852
64 4/00 Bevl 1m3f216yE(0-70)H HVY £2852
Total win prize-money £5706

Going (Turf): Sf: 1-1 GS: 0-2 Gd: 0-5 GF: 0-7 Fm: 0-1
Distance: 5f/6f: 0-1 7f-8f: 0-3 9f-13f: 1-11 14f+: 1-5
Track : LH: 1-12 RH: 1-5 **Tight: 2-11** Gall: 0-1
Aids: Bl: 0-1 Vi: 0-3 Tstrap: 0-0
Best Rating: 46 7/01 Newb 1m5f61y gd-fm

Established

107(94) (30)**42**
4-y-o b g Not In Doubt (USA)-Copper Trader (Faustus (USA))
J R Best Teapot Lane Partnership

Placings:6000000/05035501313-00664635062604O **(5531)**
2001: 16^{0}HY, 17^{0}HY, 16^{6}GF, 16^{6}GF, 16^{4}GF, 18^{6}GF, 16^{3}GF, 15^{5}GF, 16^{0}GS, 16^{6}G, 16^{2}GF, 16^{8}GF, 16^{0}G, 15^{4}GS, 16^{0}HY

	Starts	1st	2nd	3rd	Win & Pl
Career Total (Turf)	31	2	1	4	8193
Career Total (AW)	2	0	0	0	

49 8/00 Ling 2m E(0-70)H G-F £3052
44 8/00 Nott 2m9y F(0-65)H G-F £2815
Total win prize-money £5867

Going (Turf): Sf: 0-6 GS: 0-3 Gd: 0-2 **GF: 2-16** Fm: 0-4
Distance: 5f/6f: 0-2 7f-8f: 0-3 9f-13f: 0-8 **14f+: 2-20**
Track : **LH: 2-20** RH: 0-7 **Tight: 1-14** Gall: 0-0
Aids: Bl: 0-3 Vi: 0-0 Tstrap: 0-0
Best Rating: 47 6/01 Folk 2m93y gd-fm

A fair staying handicapper. Won two handicaps in the summer of 2000 but has not found his form this term. Acts on fast ground.

Establishment

107(105) (75)**76**
4-y-o b g Muhtarram (USA)-Uncharted Waters (Celestial Storm (USA))
C A Cyzer Mrs E A Cyzer

Placings:600/6402156666-221036246 **(5692)**
2001: 11^{2}F, 10^{2}GF, 12^{1}GF, 12^{0}GF, 13^{3}GF, 13^{6}GF, 16^{2}S, 18^{4}GS, 16^{8}S

	Starts	1st	2nd	3rd	Win & Pl
Career Total (Turf)	19	2	3	1	30240
Career Total (AW)	2	0	1	0	645

66 7/01 Asct 1m4f C(0-90)H G-F £13942
68 6/00 Brig 1m3f196yE(0-70)H FRM £2927
Total win prize-money £16870

Going (Turf): Sf: 0-2 GS: 0-3 Gd: 0-1 **GF: 1-10 Fm: 1-3**
Distance: 5f/6f: 0-0 7f-8f: 0-3 **9f-13f: 2-13** 14f+: 0-5
Track : LH: 1-13 RH: 1-6 Tight: 0-8 **Gall: 1-7**
Aids: Bl: 0-1 Vi: 0-0 Tstrap: 0-0
Best Rating: 76 10/01 NmkR 2m2f gd-sft

A winner at Brighton in June 2000, he looked soft in a finish in his first two starts of this season, but was resolute enough when winning at Ascot in July off a favourable mark. A keen sort, he improved for the step up to two miles in September and ran a blinder to be fourth in the Cesarewitch from 10lb out of the handicap.

Estacado (IRE)

92(97) (40)**42**
5-y-o b m Dolphin Street (FR)-Raubritter (Levmoss)
J W Mullins Woodford Valley Racing

Placings:0006/00/50-40 **(0181)**
2001: 16^{4}SD, 16^{0}SD

	Starts	1st	2nd	3rd	Win & Pl
Career Total (Turf)	8	0	0	0	75
Career Total (AW)	2	0	0	0	0

Going (Turf): Sf: 0-2 GS: 0-1 Gd: 0-3 GF: 0-2 Fm: 0-0
Distance: 5f/6f: 0-2 7f-8f: 0-2 9f-13f: 0-2 14f+: 0-4
Track : LH: 0-3 RH: 0-3 Tight: 0-5 Gall: 0-0
Aids: Bl: 0-0 Vi: 0-5 Tstrap: 0-0

Best Rating: 40 1/01 Ling 2m stand

Esteemed Master (USA)

102 **90**
2-y-o b c Mark Of Esteem (IRE)-Jasminola (FR) (Seattle Dancer (USA))
G A Butler Trik Bas Mal

Placings:4324212 **(5687)**
2001: 7^{4}GF, 7^{3}G, 6^{2}F, 8^{4}GF, 10^{2}G, 9^{1}GS, 8^{2}S

	Starts	1st	2nd	3rd	Win & Pl
Career Total (Turf)	7	1	3	1	10374

87 11/01 Brig 1m1f209yD G-S £3041
Total win prize-money £3042

Going (Turf): Sf: 0-1 **GS: 1-1** Gd: 0-2 GF: 0-2 Fm: 0-1
Distance: 5f/6f: 0-0 7f-8f: 0-4 **9f-13f: 1-3** 14f+: 0-0
Track : **LH: 1-2** RH: 0-1 Tight: 0-1 Gall: 0-0
Aids: **Bl: 1-2** Vi: 0-0 Tstrap: 0-0
Best Rating: 90 8/01 Sals 6f212y firm

He ran some fine races in competitive events before losing his maiden tag at Brighton in November. He seems suited by easier ground and looks a stayer.

Estihan (USA)

100(94) (53)**58**
3-y-o b f Silver Hawk (USA)-Dance Image (IRE) (Sadler's Wells (USA))
C E Brittain Saeed Manana

Placings:6-45034544 **(5637)**
2001: 11^{4}F, 10^{5}GF, 11^{0}GF, 10^{3}G, 14^{4}S, 16^{5}GS, 12^{4}SD, 11^{4}G

	Starts	1st	2nd	3rd	Win & Pl
Career Total (Turf)	8	0	0	1	1308
Career Total (AW)	1	0	0	0	267

Going (Turf): Sf: 0-1 GS: 0-1 Gd: 0-2 GF: 0-3 Fm: 0-1
Distance: 5f/6f: 0-0 7f-8f: 0-1 9f-13f: 0-6 14f+: 0-2
Track : LH: 0-8 RH: 0-0 Tight: 0-4 Gall: 0-1
Aids: Bl: 0-0 Vi: 0-0 Tstrap: 0-0
Best Rating: 67 7/01 Chep 1m2f36y gd-fm

Middle-distance maiden, suited by ten to 12 furlongs and good or faster ground on turf.

Estomaque

62 **31**
2-y-o br g Mark Of Esteem (IRE)-Allespagne (USA) (Trempolino (USA))
S C Williams Alasdair Simpson

Placings:0 **(5367)**
2001: 8^{0}GS

	Starts	1st	2nd	3rd	Win & Pl
Career Total (Turf)	1	0	0	0	

Going (Turf): Sf: 0-0 GS: 0-1 Gd: 0-0 GF: 0-0 Fm: 0-0
Distance: 5f/6f: 0-0 7f-8f: 0-1 9f-13f: 0-0 14f+: 0-0
Track : LH: 0-0 RH: 0-0 Tight: 0-0 Gall: 0-0
Aids: Bl: 0-0 Vi: 0-0 Tstrap: 0-0
Best Rating: 31 10/01 NmkR 1m gd-sft

Estuary (USA)

94(102) (65)**52**
6-y-o ch g Riverman (USA)-Ocean Ballad (Grundy)
Ms A E Embiricos D W Haggie

Placings:2300-22132060 **(3415)**
2001: 13^{2}SD, 12^{2}SW, 12^{1}SW, 12^{3}SD, 8^{2}GF, 8^{0}G, 12^{6}GF, 10^{0}GF

	Starts	1st	2nd	3rd	Win & Pl
Career Total (Turf)	6	0	1	0	1588
Career Total (AW)	6	1	3	2	6042

44 2/01 Wolv 1m4f D SLW £2898
Total win prize-money £2898

Going (Turf): Sf: 0-0 GS: 0-1 Gd: 0-1 GF: 0-4 Fm: 0-0
Distance: 5f/6f: 0-0 7f-8f: 0-2 **9f-13f: 1-10** 14f+: 0-0
Track : **LH: 1-8** RH: 0-1 **Tight: 1-6** Gall: 0-1
Aids: Bl: 0-0 Vi: 0-0 Tstrap: 0-1
Best Rating: 64 1/01 Ling 1m5f stand

Fair handicapper over 12 furlongs on the All-Weather, he has shown form at shorter trips on turf.

Esyoueffcee (IRE)

108 **99**
3-y-o b f Alzao (USA)-Familiar (USA) (Diesis)
M W Easterby M P Burke

Placings:2102-3201 **(5339)**
2001: 10^{3}GF, 10^{2}GF, 8^{0}G, 10^{1}GS, 10^{4}S

	Starts	1st	2nd	3rd	Win & Pl
Career Total (Turf)	8	2	3	1	32164

99 10/01 NmkR 1m2f A G-S £14384
82 8/00 Bevl 7f100y D G-F £3705
Total win prize-money £18089

Going (Turf): Sf: 0-1 **GS: 1-1** Gd: 0-1 **GF: 1-5** Fm: 0-0
Distance: 5f/6f: 0-0 7f-8f: 1-5 9f-13f: 1-3 14f+: 0-0
Track : LH: 0-3 **RH: 1-2** Tight: 0-0 Gall: 0-2
Aids: Bl: 0-0 Vi: 0-0 Tstrap: 0-0
Best Rating: 99 10/01 NmkR 1m2f gd-sft

Well beaten in a Group Three after winning her maiden in good style in 2000, she ran with credit in Listed company before scoring at that level at Newmarket in October 2001. A rather keen sort who tends to hang and is not an easy ride, she stays ten furlongs, and seems to handle any ground.

Eternal Spring (IRE)

111 **103**
4-y-o b g Persian Bold-Emerald Waters (King's Lake (USA))
J R Fanshawe Paul & Jenny Green

Placings:2132/15-2360 **(4601)**
2001: 12^{2}S, 13^{3}GF, 13^{6}G, 18^{0}G

	Starts	1st	2nd	3rd	Win & Pl
Career Total (Turf)	10	2	3	2	38848

103 4/00 Epsm 1m2f18y B HVY £12480
80 8/99 Bevl 7f100y D GD £4107
Total win prize-money £16587

Going (Turf): Sf: 1-2 GS. 0-2 **Gd: 1-4** GF: 0-2 Fm: 0-0
Distance: 5f/6f: 0-0 7f-8f: 1-4 9f-13f: 1-3 14f+: 0-3
Track : LH: 1-6 **RH: 1-2 Tight: 1-3** Gall: 0-3
Aids: Bl: 0-0 Vi: 0-0 Tstrap: 0-0
Best Rating: 103 5/01 York 1m5f194y gd-fm

Reappeared in 2001 to finish second after a spell of hurdling and ran a blinder to finish third in the Group Two Yorkshire Cup. Stays 14 furlongs and though he acts on fast ground, has won on heavy. Fairly versatile.

Eternelle

81 **56**
2-y-o b f Green Desert (USA)-Eversince (USA) (Foolish Pleasure (USA))
Sir Michael Stoute Miss K Rausing

Placings:0 **(5602)**
2001: 7^{0}GS

	Starts	1st	2nd	3rd	Win & Pl
Career Total (Turf)	1	0	0	0	

Going (Turf): Sf: 0-0 GS: 0-1 Gd: 0-0 GF: 0-0 Fm: 0-0
Distance: 5f/6f: 0-0 7f-8f: 0-1 9f-13f: 0-0 14f+: 0-0
Track : LH: 0-0 RH: 0-0 Tight: 0-0 Gall: 0-0
Aids: Bl: 0-0 Vi: 0-0 Tstrap: 0-0

Best Rating: 56 11/01 NmkR 7f gd-sft

Etisalat (IRE)

95(100) (51)**37**

6-y-o b h Lahib (USA)-Sweet Repose (High Top)

Mrs Lydia Pearce (J Pearce 3/2) Mrs E M Clarke

Placings:050/0021006001**0/31263111300006003**-**423060006060** **(5023)**

2001: 9^{4}SW, 9^{2}SD, 10^{3}SD, 8^{0}SD, 10^{6}SD, 8^{0}SD, 8^{0}GF, 9^{0}GF, 9^{6}G, 9^{0}G, 10^{6}GF, 7^{0}S

	Starts	1st	2nd	3rd	Win & Pl
Career Total (Turf)	26	4	1	1	13322
Career Total (AW)	17	2	2	4	5548

58	5/00	Carl	1m1f61y	E(0-70)H	FRM	£3302
62	5/00	Haml	1m65y	E(0-70)H	G-F	£3770
48	5/00	Muss	7f30y	F(0-65)H	FRM	£2842
56	1/00	Wolv	1m1f79y	G(0-65)H	STD	£1627
49	11/99	Ling	1m2f	F(0-60)H	STD	£1861
50	6/99	Yarm	1m3y	G(0-60)H	G-F	£2285

Total win prize-money £15688

Going (Turf): Sf: 0-3 GS: 0-3 Gd: 0-6 **GF: 2-12 Fm: 2-2**
Distance: 5f/6f: 0-0 7f-8f: 1-13 **9f-13f: 5-30** 14f+: 0-0
Track : LH: 2-24 **RH: 3-7 Tight: 4-22** Gall: 0-1
Aids: Bl: 0-0 Vi: 0-0 Tstrap: 0-0
Best Rating: 53 1/01 Wolv 1m1f79y stand

Eton (GER)

97 **66**

5-y-o ch g Suave Dancer (USA)-Ermione (Surumu (GER))

D Nicholls (Miss Venetia Williams 4/5) V Greaves

Placings:120/44153410/5000 **(5230)**

2001: 8^{5}G, 11^{0}GF, 11^{0}GF, 11^{0}S

	Starts	1st	2nd	3rd	Win & Pl
Career Total (Turf)	15	3	1	1	19124

10/99	Dort	1m165y	SFT	£3610
5/99	Kref	1m2f65y	GD	£2527
8/98	Hanv	7f	GD	£2027

Total win prize-money £8164

Going (Turf): Sf: 1-5 GS: 0-0 **Gd: 2-3** GF: 0-2 Fm: 0-0
Distance: 5f/6f: 0-0 7f-8f: 1-5 **9f-13f: 2-9** 14f+: 0-0
Track : LH: 0-5 RH: 0-4 Tight: 0-2 Gall: 0-2
Aids: **Bl: 1-1** Vi: 0-0 Tstrap: 0-0
Best Rating: 73 8/01 Thsk 1m good

Ettrick Water

95 **77**

2-y-o ch c Selkirk (USA)-Sadly Sober (IRE) (Roi Danzig (USA))

L M Cumani Mrs E H Vestey

Placings:0332 **(5662)**

2001: 7^{0}GF, 7^{3}HY, 7^{3}S, 8^{2}G

	Starts	1st	2nd	3rd	Win & Pl
Career Total (Turf)	4	0	1	2	2587

Going (Turf): Sf: 0-2 GS: 0-0 Gd: 0-1 GF: 0-1 Fm: 0-0
Distance: 5f/6f: 0-0 7f-8f: 0-4 9f-13f: 0-0 14f+: 0-0
Track : LH: 0-1 RH: 0-1 Tight: 0-1 Gall: 0-0
Aids: Bl: 0-0 Vi: 0-0 Tstrap: 0-0
Best Rating: 77 11/01 Muss 1m good

He looks a potential stayer and has shown enough to suggest he could be of interest if tried in handicaps.

Eucalyptus (IRE)

87(84) (32)**59**

4-y-o ch g Mujtahid (USA)-Imprecise (Polish Precedent (USA))

S Dow T G Parker

Placings:0-50050 **(5181)**

2001: 7^{5}SD, 7^{0}S, 7^{0}G, 7^{5}GF, 6^{0}HY

	Starts	1st	2nd	3rd	Win & Pl
Career Total (Turf)	5	0	0	0	0
Career Total (AW)	1	0	0	0	0

Going (Turf): Sf: 0-2 GS: 0-1 Gd: 0-1 GF: 0-1 Fm: 0-0
Distance: 5f/6f: 0-1 7f-8f: 0-5 9f-13f: 0-0 14f+: 0-0
Track : LH: 0-1 RH: 0-1 Tight: 0-1 Gall: 0-1
Aids: Bl: 0-0 Vi: 0-0 Tstrap: 0-0
Best Rating: 59 4/01 Kemp 7f soft

Euro Venture

106(95) (69)**74**

6-y-o b g Prince Sabo-Brave Advance (USA) (Bold Laddie (USA))

Mrs H L Walton (D Nicholls 6/9) R Rayner

Placings:3564/**10040/4215**212120**3/0000600161440**0-**5466050051050034** **(5616)**

2001: 5^{5}SD, 6^{4}SD, 6^{6}SD, 6^{6}SD, 6^{0}GF, 5^{5}F, 7^{0}G, 7^{0}GF, 6^{5}GF, 6^{1}F, 6^{0}G, 5^{5}GF, 7^{0}GF, 6^{0}S, 6^{3}SD, 7^{4}SD

	Starts	1st	2nd	3rd	Win & Pl
Career Total (Turf)	37	5	3	2	41007
Career Total (AW)	13	2	1	1	9879

74	8/01	Thsk	6f	D(0-80)H	FRM	£4598
72	7/00	Bevl	5f	D(0-80)H	GD	£6110
70	6/00	Rdcr	6f	C(0-90)H	FRM	£7182
70	6/99	Carl	6f206y	D(0-80)H	G-F	£3983
67	5/99	Thsk	6f	E(0-75)H	SFT	£8234
72	2/99	Sthl	6f	E(0-75)H	STD	£2463
75	1/98	Wolv	6f	D	STD	£3485

Total win prize-money £36058

Going (Turf): Sf: 1-2 GS: 0-3 Gd: 1-13 GF: 1-14 **Fm: 2-5**
Distance: **5f/6f: 6-43** 7f-8f: 1-7 9f-13f: 0-0 14f+: 0-0
Track : **LH: 2-17** RH: 1-2 **Tight: 1-8** Gall: 0-1
Aids: Bl: 0-0 Vi: 0-0 Tstrap: 0-0
Best Rating: 74 8/01 Thsk 6f firm

Another Dandy Nicholls success story, he appeared to lose his form and changed stables in the autumn. Acts on turf and Fibresand and six furlongs looks his best trip now.

Eurolink Artemis

102(86) (55)**72**

4-y-o b f Common Grounds-Taiga (Northfields (USA))

M Johnston Eurolink Group Plc

Placings:435140-0121500 **(5249)**

2001: 8^{0}GF, 10^{1}GF, 9^{2}F, 10^{1}GF, 9^{5}GF, 10^{0}S, 10^{0}S

	Starts	1st	2nd	3rd	Win & Pl
Career Total (Turf)	13	3	1	1	16686

72	6/01	Rdcr	1m2f	C(0-90)H	G-F	£8697
70	6/01	Newc	1m2f32y	E(0-75)H	G-F	£3045
74	7/00	Leic	1m1f218yF		G-F	£2520

Total win prize-money £14262

Going (Turf): Sf: 0-6 GS: 0-0 Gd: 0-0 **GF: 3-6** Fm: 0-1
Distance: 5f/6f: 0-0 7f-8f: 0-1 **9f-13f: 3-12** 14f+: 0-0
Track : **LH: 2-6** RH: 1-6 Tight: 1-5 Gall: 1-2
Aids: Bl: 0-0 Vi: 0-0 Tstrap: 0-0
Best Rating: 72 6/01 Rdcr 1m2f gd-fm

Fair handicapper over ten furlongs on fast ground. Has scored twice this term at Newcastle and Redcar.

Eurolink Rooster

79(91) (45)**77**

3-y-o b g Turtle Island (IRE)-Eurolink Virago (Charmer)

M Johnston (G A Butler 3/5) Eurolink Group Plc

Placings:435316000 **(5413)**

2001: 7^{4}SD, 8^{3}GS, 7^{5}S, 10^{3}GS, 9^{1}GF, 9^{6}S, 7^{0}GF, 8^{0}GS, 8^{0}SD

	Starts	1st	2nd	3rd	Win & Pl
Career Total (Turf)	7	1	0	2	4551
Career Total (AW)	2	0	0	0	0

43	8/01	Rdcr	1m1f	E	G-F	£3066

Total win prize-money £3066

Going (Turf): Sf: 0-2 GS: 0-3 Gd: 0-0 **GF: 1-2** Fm: 0-0
Distance: 5f/6f: 0-0 7f-8f: 0-5 **9f-13f: 1-4** 14f+: 0-0
Track : **LH: 1-6** RH: 0-1 **Tight: 1-3** Gall: 0-1
Aids: Bl: 0-0 Vi: 0-0 Tstrap: 0-0
Best Rating: 77 4/01 Newb 1m gd-sft

Showed promise before scoring in a weak race at Redcar in August. An edgy sort, he has struggled in stronger company since. Stays nine furlongs and acts on fast ground.

Eurolink Sundance

104 **80**

3-y-o ch f Night Shift (USA)-Eurolink Mischief (Be My Chief (USA))

J L Dunlop Eurolink Group Plc

Placings:01343-0601600 **(5685)**

2001: 7^{0}S, 7^{6}GF, 6^{0}GF, 6^{1}GS, 6^{6}GF, 6^{0}G, 5^{0}S

	Starts	1st	2nd	3rd	Win & Pl
Career Total (Turf)	12	2	0	2	10442

80	7/01	NmkJ	6f	D(0-80)H	G-S	£4095
69	7/00	Gdwd	6f	D	GD	£4407

Total win prize-money £8502

Going (Turf): Sf: 0-2 **GS: 1-1 Gd: 1-5** GF: 0-4 Fm: 0-0
Distance: **5f/6f: 2-10** 7f-8f: 0-2 9f-13f: 0-0 14f+: 0-0
Track : LH: 0-1 RH: 0-0 Tight: 0-1 Gall: 0-0
Aids: Bl: 0-0 Vi: 0-0 Tstrap: 0-0
Best Rating: 80 7/01 NmkJ 6f gd-sft

She bounced back to from, having lost her way since winning a Goodwood maiden on her second outing, with victory in a similar event at Newmarket over six furlongs. She likes to get her toe in.

Eurolink Zante (IRE)

103 **72**

5-y-o b g Turtle Island (IRE)-Lady Eurolink (Kala Shikari)

T D McCarthy Eurolink Group Plc

Placings:50-24460 **(5535)**

2001: 6^{2}GS, 7^{4}G, 8^{4}G, 7^{6}HY, 7^{0}S

	Starts	1st	2nd	3rd	Win & Pl
Career Total (Turf)	7	0	1	0	1217

Going (Turf): Sf: 0-3 GS: 0-1 Gd: 0-3 GF: 0-0 Fm: 0-0
Distance: 5f/6f: 0-1 7f-8f: 0-4 9f-13f: 0-2 14f+: 0-0
Track : LH: 0-1 RH: 0-2 Tight: 0-1 Gall: 0-0
Aids: Bl: 0-0 Vi: 0-0 Tstrap: 0-0
Best Rating: 72 9/01 Hayd 7f30y heavy

Still a maiden, but he has shown enough to suggest he can win a race. Needs the ground good or softer.

Europrime Games

90 **51**

3-y-o b c Mind Games-Flower Princess (Slip Anchor)

John A Harris (R J Smith 25/7) Robin Hood Racing

Placings:0-005040 **(3373)**

2001: 7^{0}S, 7^{0}S, 7^{5}GF, 6^{0}GF, 8^{4}GF, 11^{0}F

	Starts	1st	2nd	3rd	Win & Pl
Career Total (Turf)	7	0	0	0	0

Going (Turf): Sf: 0-3 GS: 0-0 Gd: 0-0 GF: 0-3 Fm: 0-1
Distance: 5f/6f: 0-2 7f-8f: 0-3 9f-13f: 0-2 14f+: 0-0
Track : LH: 0-3 RH: 0-0 Tight: 0-1 Gall: 0-0
Aids: Bl: 0-0 Vi: 0-0 Tstrap: 0-0
Best Rating: 53 4/01 NmkR 7f soft

Eurotwist

(75)
12-y-o b g Viking (USA)-Orange Bowl (General Assembly (USA))
Dr P Pritchard Dominic Ryan

Placings:055536000/311216000240/3000540/0410/60/100/00/0 **(0719)**
2001: 10^{0}SD

	Starts	1st	2nd	3rd	Win & Pl
Career Total (Turf)	31	5	2	2	19924
Career Total (AW)	9	0	0	1	309

46 4/96 Haml 1m4f17y F(0-60)H G-S £2962
48 10/94 York 1m3f195yE(0-70)H G-S £6888
73 7/92 Bevl 1m3f216yF(0-80)H G-S £2726
65 5/92 Haml 1m4f17y F H SFT £2574
65 4/92 Carl 1m4f F(0-70)H GD £2402
Total win prize-money £17553

Going (Turf): Sf: 1-5 **GS: 3-9** Gd: 1-8 GF: 0-7 Fm: 0-2
Distance: 5f/6f: 0-3 7f-8f: 0-7 **9f-13f: 5-26** 14f+: 0-4
Track : LH: 1-21 **RH: 4-14 Tight: 3-19** Gall: 1-5
Aids: Bl: 0-1 Vi: 0-0 Tstrap: 0-0

Evening Chase (IRE)

95(101) (56+)**54**
3-y-o b g Pursuit Of Love-Late Evening (USA) (Riverman (USA))
J L Eyre (H Morrison 13/7) Mrs Angela C Seed

Placings:000310000 **(5375)**
2001: 6^{0}GS, 5^{0}GF, 5^{0}F, 6^{3}SD, 7^{1}SD, 6^{0}G, 6^{0}G, 8^{0}G, 7^{0}G

	Starts	1st	2nd	3rd	Win & Pl
Career Total (Turf)	7	0	0	0	
Career Total (AW)	2	1	0	1	2607

56 7/01 Sthl 7f F STD £2282
Total win prize-money £2282

Going (Turf): Sf: 0-0 GS: 0-1 Gd: 0-4 GF: 0-1 Fm: 0-1
Distance: 5f/6f: 0-6 **7f-8f: 1-2** 9f-13f: 0-1 14f+: 0-0
Track : **LH: 1-4** RH: 0-1 Tight: 0-0 Gall: 0-2
Aids: Bl: 0-0 Vi: 0-0 Tstrap: 0-1
Best Rating: 62 5/01 Bath 5f11y gd-fm

Evening Press

81 **49**
2-y-o b f River Falls-Shiny Kay (Star Appeal)
T J Etherington The Evening Press Partnership

Placings:000 **(5627)**
2001: 6^{0}F, 6^{0}G, 7^{0}G

	Starts	1st	2nd	3rd	Win & Pl
Career Total (Turf)	3	0	0	0	

Going (Turf): Sf: 0-0 GS: 0-0 Gd: 0-2 GF: 0-0 Fm: 0-1
Distance: 5f/6f: 0-2 7f-8f: 0-1 9f-13f: 0-0 14f+: 0-0
Track : LH: 0-0 RH: 0-0 Tight: 0-0 Gall: 0-0
Aids: Bl: 0-0 Vi: 0-0 Tstrap: 0-0
Best Rating: 49 10/01 Rdcr 6f good

Evening Scent

102(85) (36)**65**
5-y-o b m Ardkinglass-Fresh Line (High Line)
J Hetherton N Hetherton

Placings:0040130/6032016411560-0 **(0037)**
2001: 16^{0}SD

	Starts	1st	2nd	3rd	Win & Pl
Career Total (Turf)	15	4	1	2	22101
Career Total (AW)	6	0	0	0	0

65 10/00 York 1m3f195yE(0-75)H SFT £7283
56 9/00 Hayd 1m6f D(0-85)H HVY £7605
48 6/00 Haml 1m5f9y F(0-60)H GD £3003
46 9/99 Catt 1m5f175yG G-F £1982
Total win prize-money £19873

Going (Turf): Sf: 2-7 GS: 0-2 Gd: 1-3 GF: 1-1 Fm: 0-2

Distance: 5f/6f: 0-0 7f-8f: 0-1 9f-13f: 1-9 **14f+: 3-11**
Track : **LH: 3-17** RH: 1-4 **Tight: 2-11** Gall: 1-2
Aids: Bl: 0-0 Vi: 0-0 Tstrap: 0-0
Best Rating: 17 1/01 Sthl 2m stand

Evening Serenade (IRE)

92 **76**
2-y-o b f Night Shift (USA)-Flying Diva (Chief Singer)
M L W Bell Deln Ltd

Placings:621600 **(5052)**
2001: 6^{6}GF, 7^{2}GF, 7^{1}GF, 7^{6}G, 7^{0}GF, 7^{0}S

	Starts	1st	2nd	3rd	Win & Pl
Career Total (Turf)	6	1	1	0	5583

76 7/01 Folk 7f D G-F £4251
Total win prize-money £4251

Going (Turf): Sf: 0-1 GS: 0-0 Gd: 0-1 **GF: 1-4** Fm: 0-0
Distance: 5f/6f: 0-1 **7f-8f: 1-5** 9f-13f: 0-0 14f+: 0-0
Track : LH: 0-2 RH: 0-1 Tight: 0-1 Gall: 0-1
Aids: Bl: 0-0 Vi: 0-0 Tstrap: 0-0
Best Rating: 76 7/01 Folk 7f gd-fm

A half-sister to Prix Robert Papin winner Black Amber and prolific scorer White Plains, she was second to Muklah on her second outing at Kempton and went on to win a seven-furlong maiden at Folkestone in July. Held in nurseries since.

Eventuality

97(99) (66)**56**
5-y-o b m Petoski-Queen's Tickle (Tickled Pink)
R F Johnson Houghton Anthony Harrison

Placings:34/60014146/50012000205-500 **(2510)**
2001: 5^{5}F, 6^{0}GF, 6^{0}GF

	Starts	1st	2nd	3rd	Win & Pl
Career Total (Turf)	21	3	1	1	16006
Career Total (AW)	3	0	1	0	740

63 7/00 Ling 6f E(0-70)H GD £3097
68 9/99 Epsm 7f E(0-70)H GD £3810
63 7/99 Sals 6f212y D(0-80)H FRM £4169
Total win prize-money £11077

Going (Turf): Sf: 0-5 GS: 0-0 **Gd: 2-3** GF: 0-10 Fm: 1-3
Distance: 5f/6f: 1-8 **7f-8f: 2-13** 9f-13f: 0-3 14f+: 0-0
Track : **LH: 1-9** RH: 0-1 **Tight: 1-7** Gall: 0-1
Aids: Bl: 0-0 Vi: 0-0 Tstrap: 0-0
Best Rating: 54 5/01 Leic 5f218y firm

Ever Revie (IRE)

55(81) (20)**54d**
4-y-o b f Hamas (IRE)-Lucy Limelight (Hot Spark)
Miss S J Wilton John Pointon And Sons

Placings:60100/0014000-00 **(1064)**
2001: 8^{0}S, 8^{0}GS

	Starts	1st	2nd	3rd	Win & Pl
Career Total (Turf)	12	2	0	0	4400
Career Total (AW)	2	0	0	0	

54 5/00 Sthl 7f F(0-60) HVY £1918
59 7/99 Bevl 7f100y F SFT £2372
Total win prize-money £4291

Going (Turf): Sf: 2-5 GS: 0-2 Gd: 0-3 GF: 0-2 Fm: 0-0
Distance: 5f/6f: 0-2 **7f-8f: 2-7** 9f-13f: 0-5 14f+: 0-0
Track : LH: 1-11 RH: 1-3 Tight: 0-2 Gall: 0-0
Aids: **Bl: 2-7** Vi: 0-0 Tstrap: 0-1
Best Rating: 59 7/99 Bevl 7f100y S

Everbold

82(58) **21**
4-y-o b f Never So Bold-Out Of Hours (Lochnager)
D McCain Mrs D McCain

Placings:0000-00 **(2514)**

2001: 9^{0}SD, 6^{0}F

	Starts	1st	2nd	3rd	Win & Pl
Career Total (Turf)	4	0	0	0	
Career Total (AW)	2	0	0	0	

Going (Turf): Sf: 0-0 GS: 0-1 Gd: 0-0 GF: 0-2 Fm: 0-1
Distance: 5f/6f: 0-2 7f-8f: 0-3 9f-13f: 0-1 14f+: 0-0
Track : LH: 0-2 RH: 0-0 Tight: 0-2 Gall: 0-0
Aids: Bl: 0-1 Vi: 0-0 Tstrap: 0-0
Best Rating: 9 6/01 Thsk 6f firm

Everest (IRE)

99 **74**
4-y-o ch g Indian Ridge-Reine D'Beaute (Caerleon (USA))
B Ellison I S Sandhu And Partners

Placings:2/23211150-0000060 **(5344)**
2001: 8^{0}S, 7^{0}GF, 8^{0}GF, 7^{0}GF, 8^{0}GF, 10^{6}S, 8^{0}GS

	Starts	1st	2nd	3rd	Win & Pl
Career Total (Turf)	16	3	3	1	34418

89 8/00 Gdwd 1m1f C(0-95)H GD £15210
87 8/00 Pont 1m4y C(0-90)H G-F £6955
84 5/00 Thsk 1m D GD £4439
Total win prize-money £26605

Going (Turf): Sf: 0-5 GS: 0-2 **Gd: 2-3** GF: 1-6 Fm: 0-0
Distance: 5f/6f: 0-0 7f-8f: 1-8 **9f-13f: 2-8** 14f+: 0-0
Track : **LH: 2-6** RH: 1-5 **Tight: 2-3** Gall: 0-1
Aids: Bl: 0-0 Vi: 0-0 Tstrap: 0-0
Best Rating: 74 9/01 Ayr 1m gd-fm

He was in fine form in 2000, but has not shown much this year. Effective at around a mile.

Everlasting Love

106 **95**
4-y-o b f Pursuit Of Love-Now And Forever (IRE) (Kris)
M L W Bell Dgh Partnership

Placings:04120/5560-03560 **(4865)**
2001: 9^{0}G, 10^{3}GF, 12^{5}G, 10^{6}GF, 10^{0}GF

	Starts	1st	2nd	3rd	Win & Pl
Career Total (Turf)	14	1	1	1	17893

82 8/99 Rdcr 7f E GD £4232
Total win prize-money £4232

Going (Turf): Sf: 0-1 GS: 0-1 **Gd: 1-5** GF: 0-7 Fm: 0-0
Distance: 5f/6f: 0-0 **7f-8f: 1-6** 9f-13f: 0-8 14f+: 0-0
Track : LH: 0-6 RH: 0-0 Tight: 0-1 Gall: 0-5
Aids: Bl: 0-0 Vi: 0-0 Tstrap: 0-0
Best Rating: 95 6/01 Siro 1m4f good

She got off the mark in a four-runner event at Redcar on her third start at two, but has looked held in Pattern company since then. She is probably best at around ten furlongs. Acts on fast ground.

Every Right (IRE)

82(90) (30)**2**
3-y-o b g Common Grounds-Incendio (Siberian Express (USA))
D W Chapman David W Chapman

Placings:0-6000000000 **(3643)**
2001: 5^{6}SD, 7^{0}SD, 5^{0}SD, 5^{0}GF, 6^{0}GF, 6^{0}GF, 6^{0}SD, 6^{0}GS, 5^{0}F, 6^{0}F

	Starts	1st	2nd	3rd	Win & Pl
Career Total (Turf)	7	0	0	0	
Career Total (AW)	4	0	0	0	0

Going (Turf): Sf: 0-0 GS: 0-1 Gd: 0-0 GF: 0-4 Fm: 0-2
Distance: 5f/6f: 0-9 7f-8f: 0-2 9f-13f: 0-0 14f+: 0-0
Track : LH: 0-4 RH: 0-0 Tight: 0-1 Gall: 0-0
Aids: Bl: 0-5 Vi: 0-0 Tstrap: 0-0
Best Rating: 30 3/01 Sthl 5f stand

Evezio Rufo

(108) (43)**44**

9-y-o b g Blakeney-Empress Corina (Free State)

N P Littmoden O A Gunter

Placings:3210/00/00500040/66001304406/0321163225221645034356045336625/34361006160455/4651314511510003-3423464003500 **(5615)**

2001: 14^{3}SD, 11^{4}SD, 11^{2}SW, 12^{3}SD, 16^{4}SD, 12^{6}SD, 16^{4}SD, 12^{0}SD, 16^{0}SD, 14^{3}SD, 12^{5}SD, 16^{0}SD, 12^{0}SD

	Starts	1st	2nd	3rd	Win & Pl
Career Total (Turf)	22	2	1	1	9219
Career Total (AW)	77	10	7	14	33053

44	5/00	Brig	1m3f196y	F(0-60)H	G-F	£2394
59	3/00	Wolv	1m4f	F(0-65)H	STD	£2299
52	3/00	Sthl	1m4f	F(0-70)H	STD	£1795
52	2/00	Wolv	1m4f	F(0-80)H	STD	£2149
50	2/00	Wolv	1m4f	E(0-70)H	STD	£2651
44	3/99	Wolv	1m4f	F(0-65)H	STD	£2304
45	1/99	Wolv	1m6f166y	G	STD	£1861
57	4/98	Wolv	1m4f	D(0-85)H	STD	£3525
61	2/98	Sthl	1m4f	E(0-70)H	STD	£2840
47	1/98	Ling	1m5f	G(0-60)H	STD	£1822
50	5/97	Sthl	1m3f	G(0-65)H	STD	£1984
82	11/94	Folk	1m1f149y	E	SFT	£3162

Total win prize-money £28791

Going (Turf): Sf: 1-3 GS: 0-3 Gd: 0-9 **GF: 1-4** Fm: 0-1
Distance: 5f/6f: 0-0 7f-8f: 0-0 **9f-13f: 11-69** 14f+: 1-29
Track : **LH: 11-90** RH: 1-7 **Tight: 8-50** Gall: 0-4
Aids: **Bl: 7-44** Vi: 4-41 Tstrap: 0-0
Best Rating: 55 1/01 Sthl 1m6f stand

A real Fibresand regular, he remains capable of winning modest middle-distance events on that surface, but does not seem to like being crowded by other horses. He is therefore probably not suited by large fields.

Evidence

97 **63**

3-y-o ch f Machiavellian (USA)-Beyond Doubt (Belmez (USA))

R Charlton The Queen

Placings:4-005 **(3149)**

2001: 9^{0}GS, 12^{0}GF, 12^{5}G

	Starts	1st	2nd	3rd	Win & Pl
Career Total (Turf)	4	0	0	0	864

Going (Turf): Sf: 0-0 GS: 0-1 Gd: 0-1 GF: 0-1 Fm: 0-0
Distance: 5f/6f: 0-0 7f-8f: 0-0 9f-13f: 0-4 14f+: 0-0
Track : LH: 0-1 RH: 0-2 Tight: 0-1 Gall: 0-1
Aids: Bl: 0-0 Vi: 0-0 Tstrap: 0-0
Best Rating: 63 7/01 Newb 1m4f5y gd-fm

Eviyrn (IRE)

90(84) (37)**35**

5-y-o b g In The Wings-Evrana (USA) (Nureyev (USA))

J R Jenkins Home Counties Finance Limited

Placings:04/060-640 **(5531)**

2001: 12^{6}GF, 18^{4}GF, 16^{0}HY

	Starts	1st	2nd	3rd	Win & Pl
Career Total (Turf)	7	0	0	0	200
Career Total (AW)	1	0	0	0	

Going (Turf): Sf: 0-2 GS: 0-0 Gd: 0-1 GF: 0-2 Fm: 0-0
Distance: 5f/6f: 0-0 7f-8f: 0-1 9f-13f: 0-5 14f+: 0-2
Track : LH: 0-7 RH: 0-1 Tight: 0-2 Gall: 0-0
Aids: Bl: 0-0 Vi: 0-1 Tstrap: 0-0
Best Rating: 35 7/01 Chep 2m2f gd-fm

Ewar Bold

38

8-y-o b g Bold Arrangement-Monaneigue Lady (Julio Mariner)

K G Wingrove Mrs H Noonan

Placings:5636606000000/5/0 **(5622)**

2001: 14^{0}GS

	Starts	1st	2nd	3rd	Win & Pl
Career Total (Turf)	14	0	0	1	416
Career Total (AW)	1	0	0	0	

Going (Turf): Sf: 0-3 GS: 0-3 Gd: 0-4 GF: 0-2 Fm: 0-2
Distance: 5f/6f: 0-0 7f-8f: 0-1 9f-13f: 0-9 14f+: 0-5
Track : LH: 0-6 RH: 0-8 Tight: 0-7 Gall: 0-2
Aids: Bl: 0-6 Vi: 0-0 Tstrap: 0-0
Best Rating: 35 7/01 Chep 2m2f gd-fm

Ewar Victoria (FR)

88(72) (25)**64**

2-y-o b f Valanour (IRE)-Ewar Empress (IRE) (Persian Bold)

K O Cunningham-Brown A J Richards

Placings:0600000

2001: 5^{0}S, 7^{6}GF, 6^{0}GF, 8^{0}G, 8^{0}SD, 8^{0}GS, 8^{0}HO

	Starts	1st	2nd	3rd	Win & Pl
Career Total (Turf)	6	0	0	0	0
Career Total (AW)	1	0	0	0	

Going (Turf): Sf: 0-1 GS: 0-1 Gd: 0-1 GF: 0-2 Fm: 0-0
Distance: 5f/6f: 0-1 7f-8f: 0-5 9f-13f: 0-1 14f+: 0-0
Track : LH: 0-1 RH: 0-3 Tight: 0-1 Gall: 0-0
Aids: Bl: 0-0 Vi: 0-0 Tstrap: 0-0
Best Rating: 64 6/01 Gdwd 7f gd-fm

Exalted (IRE)

106 (65)**64**

8-y-o b g High Estate-Heavenward (USA) (Conquistador Cielo (USA))

T A K Cuthbert Mrs Elva Maxwell & Roy Thorburn

Placings:1336/0025530000/0/40/15650-22261300 **(4883)**

2001: 13^{2}G, 12^{2}F, 13^{2}GF, 11^{6}GS, 13^{1}G, 13^{3}S, 10^{0}G, 12^{0}GF

	Starts	1st	2nd	3rd	Win & Pl
Career Total (Turf)	29	3	4	4	26912
Career Total (AW)	1	0	0	0	

62	6/01	Haml	1m5f9y	F(0-75)H	GD	£2996
64	4/00	Haml	1m5f9y	D(0-85)H	GD	£10676
67	7/95	Thsk	7f	D	GD	£3940

Total win prize-money £17612

Going (Turf): Sf: 0-6 GS: 0-3 **Gd: 3-10** GF: 0-9 Fm: 0-1
Distance: 5f/6f: 0-0 7f-8f: 1-3 9f-13f: 0-16 **14f+: 2-11**
Track : LH: 1-18 **RH: 2-10 Tight: 3-13** Gall: 0-8
Aids: Bl: 0-0 Vi: 0-0 Tstrap: 0-0
Best Rating: 64 7/01 Haml 1m5f9y soft

He does not have a great winning record on the Flat, but tries his best in modest handicaps at around 12 furlongs. Best on fast ground.

Exceptional Paddy (IRE)

(82) (58)**96**

3-y-o b c Common Grounds-Itkan (IRE) (Marju (IRE))

M Halford Mrs Beatrice Durkan

Placings:364-034011440 **(5549a)**

2001: 8^{0}S, 6^{3}G, 7^{4}G, 7^{0}G, 6^{1}S, 7^{1}G, 8^{4}GY, 6^{4}S, 6^{0}YS

	Starts	1st	2nd	3rd	Win & Pl
Career Total (Turf)	11	2	0	2	31953
Career Total (AW)	1	0	0	0	0

81	8/01	Curr	7f	(0-95)H	GD	£14625
75	8/01	Curr	6f	(60-92)H	SFT	£13000

Total win prize-money £27625

Going (Turf): Sf: 1-4 GS: 0-1 **Gd: 1-4** GF: 0-0 Fm: 0-0
Distance: 5f/6f: 1-7 7f-8f: 1-5 9f-13f: 0-0 14f+: 0-0
Track : LH: 0-2 RH: 0-0 Tight: 0-0 Gall: 0-0
Aids: Bl: 0-0 Vi: 0-0 Tstrap: 0-0
Best Rating: 96 10/01 Curr 6f soft

Exclusive Air (USA)

84 **62**

2-y-o ch c Affirmed (USA)-Lac Dessert (USA) (Lac Ouimet (USA))

T D Barron Carequick Ltd-(air Conditioning)

Placings:506 **(5537)**

2001: 7^{5}G, 8^{0}GS, 7^{6}S

	Starts	1st	2nd	3rd	Win & Pl
Career Total (Turf)	3	0	0	0	278

Going (Turf): Sf: 0-1 GS: 0-1 Gd: 0-1 GF: 0-0 Fm: 0-0
Distance: 5f/6f: 0-0 7f-8f: 0-3 9f-13f: 0-0 14f+: 0-0
Track : LH: 0-0 RH: 0-0 Tight: 0-0 Gall: 0-0
Aids: Bl: 0-0 Vi: 0-0 Tstrap: 0-0
Best Rating: 62 10/01 NmkR 1m gd-sft

Exeat (USA)

108 **61**

5-y-o b/br g Dayjur (USA)-By Your Leave (USA) (Private Account (USA))

J S Goldie (D Nicholls 21/9) W M Johnstone

Placings:2124/2002353/20062-0310100 **(5607)**

2001: 8^{0}S, 7^{3}G, 8^{1}GF, 7^{0}GS, 9^{1}G, 6^{0}GS, 8^{0}GS

	Starts	1st	2nd	3rd	Win & Pl
Career Total (Turf)	23	3	6	3	72264

61	9/01	Ayr	1m1f20y	E	GD	£4166
56	5/01	Gdwd	1m	C(0-85)	G-F	£6351
84	7/98	Hayd	6f	D	G-F	£3631

Total win prize-money £14149

Going (Turf): Sf: 0-4 GS: 0-6 Gd: 1-7 **GF: 2-6** Fm: 0-0
Distance: 5f/6f: 1-4 7f-8f: 1-16 9f-13f: 1-3 14f+: 0-0
Track : LH: 0-3 **RH: 1-5** Tight: 0-1 Gall: 0-2
Aids: Bl: 0-0 Vi: 0-3 Tstrap: 0-0
Best Rating: 91 5/01 Thsk 7f good

Group-class performer in his prime, he has slipped down to a very favourable rating but is not the most straightforward of characters. Still capable in more modest grade and has won a Goodwood classified event and an Ayr claimer this season.

Executive Choice (IRE)

73 **32**

7-y-o b g Don't Forget Me-Shadia (USA) (Naskra (USA))

B Ellison The Couriers Syndicate

Placings:560000/000364040/0500/0 **(3967)**

2001: 8^{0}GS

	Starts	1st	2nd	3rd	Win & Pl
Career Total (Turf)	20	0	0	1	219

Going (Turf): Sf: 0-3 GS: 0-3 Gd: 0-5 GF: 0-2 Fm: 0-1
Distance: 5f/6f: 0-0 7f-8f: 0-7 9f-13f: 0-13 14f+: 0-0
Track : LH: 0-8 RH: 0-11 Tight: 0-5 Gall: 0-0
Aids: Bl: 0-3 Vi: 0-0 Tstrap: 0-1
Best Rating: 27 8/01 Bevl 1m100y gd-sft

Executive Network

88(79) (24)**45**

3-y-o b g Silca Blanka (IRE)-Scene Stealer (Scenic)

A D Smith The Purple Partnership Limited

Placings:004 **(5524)**

2001: 11^{0}S, 7^{0}SD, 10^{4}HY

	Starts	1st	2nd	3rd	Win & Pl
Career Total (Turf)	2	0	0	0	0

	Starts	1st	2nd	3rd	Win & Pl
Career Total (AW)	1	0	0	0	

Going (Turf): Sf: 0-2 GS: 0-0 Gd: 0-0 GF: 0-0 Fm: 0-0
Distance: 5f/6f: 0-0 7f-8f: 0-1 9f-13f: 0-2 14f+: 0-0
Track : LH: 0-2 RH: 0-0 Tight: 0-2 Gall: 0-0
Aids: Bl: 0-0 Vi: 0-0 Tstrap: 0-0
Best Rating: 45 10/01 Wind 1m2f7y heavy

Exellent Adventure

76(66) (26)**16**
3-y-o ch g Gold Dust-Freedom Weekend (USA) (Shahrastani (USA))
D Burchell Mrs D L Smith-Hopper

Placings:565-00000 **(2739)**
2001: 10^{0}GS, 6^{0}GS, 8^{0}F, 5^{0}GF, 8^{0}GF

	Starts	1st	2nd	3rd	Win & Pl
Career Total (Turf)	6	0	0	0	0
Career Total (AW)	2	0	0	0	0

Going (Turf): Sf: 0-0 GS: 0-3 Gd: 0-0 GF: 0-2 Fm: 0-1
Distance: 5f/6f: 0-5 7f-8f: 0-0 9f-13f: 0-3 14f+: 0-0
Track : LH: 0-2 RH: 0-0 Tight: 0-1 Gall: 0-0
Aids: Bl: 0-0 Vi: 0-0 Tstrap: 0-0
Best Rating: 16 5/01 Sals 6f gd-sft

Exhibit (IRE)

100 **60**
3-y-o b c Royal Academy (USA)-Juno Madonna (IRE) (Sadler's Wells (USA))
Sir Michael Stoute Highclere Thoroughbred Racing Ltd

Placings:0400 **(4624)**
2001: 10^{0}G, 8^{4}GF, 8^{0}G, 8^{0}GF

	Starts	1st	2nd	3rd	Win & Pl
Career Total (Turf)	4	0	0	0	333

Going (Turf): Sf: 0-0 GS: 0-0 Gd: 0-2 GF: 0-2 Fm: 0-0
Distance: 5f/6f: 0-0 7f-8f: 0-0 9f-13f: 0-4 14f+: 0-0
Track : LH: 0-1 RH: 0-3 Tight: 0-2 Gall: 0-1
Aids: Bl: 0-0 Vi: 0-0 Tstrap: 0-0
Best Rating: 60 7/01 Wind 1m67y gd-fm

Exhibition Girl (IRE)

(82) (7)**36**
4-y-o ch f Perugino (USA)-Shy Jinks (Shy Groom (USA))
Andrew Turnell Mrs Kate Dalton

Placings:500-00050 **(3433)**
2001: 9^{0}G, 9^{0}F, 8^{0}GF, 11^{5}GF, 16^{0}SD

	Starts	1st	2nd	3rd	Win & Pl
Career Total (Turf)	7	0	0	0	0
Career Total (AW)	1	0	0	0	

Going (Turf): Sf: 0-1 GS: 0-2 Gd: 0-1 GF: 0-2 Fm: 0-1
Distance: 5f/6f: 0-0 7f-8f: 0-1 9f-13f: 0-6 14f+: 0-1
Track : LH: 0-3 RH: 0-4 Tight: 0-3 Gall: 0-1
Aids: Bl: 0-0 Vi: 0-0 Tstrap: 0-0
Best Rating: 36 5/01 Leic 1m1f218y firm

Exhibitor (USA)

82 **62**
2-y-o b f Royal Academy (USA)-Akadya (FR) (Akarad (FR))
J R Fanshawe Cheveley Park Stud

Placings:0 **(5274)**
2001: 7^{0}GS

	Starts	1st	2nd	3rd	Win & Pl
Career Total (Turf)	1	0	0	0	

Going (Turf): Sf: 0-0 GS: 0-1 Gd: 0-0 GF: 0-0 Fm: 0-0
Distance: 5f/6f: 0-0 7f-8f: 0-1 9f-13f: 0-0 14f+: 0-0
Track : LH: 0-0 RH: 0-0 Tight: 0-0 Gall: 0-0
Aids: Bl: 0-0 Vi: 0-0 Tstrap: 0-0
Best Rating: 62 10/01 Leic 7f9y gd-sft

Exile

104 **76**
4-y-o b g Emperor Jones (USA)-Silver Venture (USA) (Silver Hawk (USA))
R T Phillips Ellangowan Racing Partners

Placings:4460400/25212-010 **(2855)**
2001: 13^{0}GF, 12^{1}GF, 11^{0}G

	Starts	1st	2nd	3rd	Win & Pl
Career Total (Turf)	15	2	3	0	12307

76 6/01 Kemp 1m4f E(0-75)H G-F £4387
71 8/00 Kemp 1m4f E(0-75)H G-F £3415
Total win prize-money £7804

Going (Turf): Sf: 0-1 GS: 0-0 Gd: 0-5 **GF: 2-9** Fm: 0-0
Distance: 5f/6f: 0-4 7f-8f: 0-3 **9f-13f: 2-7** 14f+: 0-1
Track : LH: 0-4 **RH: 2-6** Tight: 0-3 Gall: 0-2
Aids: Bl: 0-2 Vi: 0-0 Tstrap: 0-0
Best Rating: 76 6/01 Kemp 1m4f gd-fm

Exjaysix

63
3-y-o b g Chocolat De Meguro (USA)-Secret Chant (Silly Prices)
M A Barnes M Barnes

Placings:3 **(3078)**
2001: 10^{3}GS

	Starts	1st	2nd	3rd	Win & Pl
Career Total (Turf)	1	0	0	1	617

Going (Turf): Sf: 0-0 GS: 0-1 Gd: 0-0 GF: 0-0 Fm: 0-0
Distance: 5f/6f: 0-0 7f-8f: 0-0 9f-13f: 0-1 14f+: 0-0
Track : LH: 0-1 RH: 0-0 Tight: 0-0 Gall: 0-0
Aids: Bl: 0-0 Vi: 0-0 Tstrap: 0-0

Exotic Fan (USA)

(103) (97)
3-y-o b/br f Lear Fan (USA)-Green Moon (FR) (Shirley Heights)
R Guest S Lury

Placings:4020-061111550 **(5591)**
2001: 7^{0}GF, 13^{6}GF, 8^{1}SD, 10^{1}GS, 12^{1}SD, 8^{1}SD, 9^{5}GS, 10^{5}HY, 9^{0}GS, 10^{0}SD

	Starts	1st	2nd	3rd	Win & Pl
Career Total (Turf)	10	1	1	0	4574
Career Total (AW)	3	3	0	0	8588

97 8/01 Wolv 1m100y D(0-85)H STD £3883
81 7/01 Sthl 1m4f F(0-65)H STD £2408
75 7/01 Ling 1m2f E(0-65) G-S £3220
74 7/01 Wolv 1m100y F(0-65)H STD £2296
Total win prize-money £11808

Going (Turf): Sf: 0-2 **GS: 1-4** Gd: 0-0 GF: 0-3 Fm: 0-1
Distance: 5f/6f: 0-0 7f-8f: 0-3 **9f-13f: 4-9** 14f+: 0-1
Track : **LH: 4-7** RH: 0-2 **Tight: 3-5** Gall: 0-0
Aids: Bl: 0-0 Vi: 0-0 Tstrap: 0-0
Best Rating: 97 8/01 Wolv 1m100y stand

She finally got off the mark when bolting up in a maiden on the Wolverhampton Fibresand in July 2001. Followed up in equally emphatic style on turf at Lingfield and back on Fibresand at Southwell just 48 hours later. Completed the four-timer with another easy win at Wolverhampton. Effective from eight to 12 furlongs and handles testing conditions well.

Expected Bonus (USA)

99 **92**
2-y-o b/br c Kris S (USA)-Nidd (USA) (Known Fact (USA))
B W Hills K Abdulla

Placings:215 **(5363)**
2001: 6^{2}G, 7^{1}G, 7^{5}GS

	Starts	1st	2nd	3rd	Win & Pl
Career Total (Turf)	3	1	1	0	12211

89 9/01 Kemp 7f C GD £6380
Total win prize-money £6380

Going (Turf): Sf: 0-0 GS: 0-1 **Gd: 1-2** GF: 0-0 Fm: 0-0
Distance: 5f/6f: 0-1 **7f-8f: 1-2** 9f-13f: 0-0 14f+: 0-0
Track : LH: 0-0 **RH: 1-1** Tight: 0-0 **Gall: 1-1**
Aids: Bl: 0-0 Vi: 0-0 Tstrap: 0-0
Best Rating: 92 10/01 NmkR 7f gd-sft

Got off the mark in a decent event at Kempton on his second run before disappointing in the Houghton Stakes at Newmarket. Has won over seven furlongs on a sound surface. The type to do well in decent handicaps as a three-year-old.

Expectedtofli (IRE)

34
3-y-o b f Mujadil (USA)-Zurarah (Siberian Express (USA))
C N Allen H H N C Partnership

Placings:00040 **(5608)**
2001: 6^{0}G, 8^{0}GF, 6^{0}GF, 5^{4}GS, 7^{0}GS

	Starts	1st	2nd	3rd	Win & Pl
Career Total (Turf)	5	0	0	0	0

Going (Turf): Sf: 0-0 GS: 0-2 Gd: 0-1 GF: 0-2 Fm: 0-0
Distance: 5f/6f: 0-3 7f-8f: 0-2 9f-13f: 0-0 14f+: 0-0
Track : LH: 0-1 RH: 0-0 Tight: 0-1 Gall: 0-0
Aids: Bl: 0-0 Vi: 0-0 Tstrap: 0-3
Best Rating: 34 10/01 Catt 5f212y gd-sft

Explode

87 **104**
4-y-o b c Zafonic (USA)-Didicoy (USA) (Danzig (USA))
R Charlton K Abdulla

Placings:3113-0 **(1123)**
2001: 10^{0}G

	Starts	1st	2nd	3rd	Win & Pl
Career Total (Turf)	5	2	0	2	13359

95 7/00 Epsm 1m2f18y C G-S £6572
84 6/00 Sals 1m1f198yD G-F £3688
Total win prize-money £10261

Going (Turf): Sf: 0-1 **GS: 1-1** Gd: 0-2 **GF: 1-1** Fm: 0-0
Distance: 5f/6f: 0-0 7f-8f: 0-0 **9f-13f: 2-5** 14f+: 0-0
Track : LH: 1-2 RH: 1-1 **Tight: 2-2** Gall: 0-0
Aids: Bl: 0-0 Vi: 0-0 Tstrap: 0-0
Best Rating: 85 5/01 NmkR 1m2f good

Exploring (IRE)

92 **70**
2-y-o br c Charnwood Forest (IRE)-Caribbean Quest (Rainbow Quest (USA))
R F Johnson Houghton Anthony Pye-Jeary And Michael Smith

Placings:550 **(5095)**
2001: 7^{5}GF, 8^{5}G, 8^{0}GS

	Starts	1st	2nd	3rd	Win & Pl
Career Total (Turf)	3	0	0	0	0

Going (Turf): Sf: 0-0 GS: 0-1 Gd: 0-1 GF: 0-1 Fm: 0-0
Distance: 5f/6f: 0-0 7f-8f: 0-3 9f-13f: 0-0 14f+: 0-0
Track : LH: 0-0 RH: 0-2 Tight: 0-0 Gall: 0-1
Aids: Bl: 0-0 Vi: 0-0 Tstrap: 0-0
Best Rating: 70 9/01 Kemp 1m good

Still a maiden, although he has run well in all starts to date, but does appear on a stiff mark for what he has achieved.

Explosive

88(88) **57d**

3-yo b g Saddlers' Hall (IRE)-Pursuit Of Glory (Shirley Heights)

C A Cyzer Mrs E A Cyzer

Placings:00-40500U (5050)

2001: 10^{4}SD, 14^{0}GF, 9^{5}G, 12^{0}GF, 14^{0}SW, 11^{U}SD

	Starts	1st	2nd	3rd	Win & Pl
Career Total (Turf)	5	0	0	0	0
Career Total (AW)	3	0	0	0	0

Going (Turf): Sf: 0-0 GS: 0-0 Gd: 0-2 GF: 0-3 Fm: 0-0
Distance: 5f/6f: 0-0 7f-8f: 0-2 9f-13f: 0-4 14f+: 0-2
Track : LH: 0-3 RH: 0-3 Tight: 0-4 Gall: 0-0
Aids: Bl: 0-1 Vi: 0-0 Tstrap: 0-0
Best Rating: 50 8/01 Folk 1m1f149y good

Extra Guest

92 **73**

3-yo b f Fraam-Gibaltarik (IRE) (Jareer (USA))

N Tinkler Mr James Marshall & Mrs Susan Marshall

Placings:4326222422233445-04 (1307)

2001: 7^{0}GS, 6^{4}GF

	Starts	1st	2nd	3rd	Win & Pl
Career Total (Turf)	18	0	7	3	15591

Going (Turf): Sf: 0-6 GS: 0-1 Gd: 0-4 GF: 0-6 Fm: 0-1
Distance: 5f/6f: 0-14 7f-8f: 0-4 9f-13f: 0-0 14f+: 0-0
Track : LH: 0-3 RH: 0-1 Tight: 0-0 Gall: 0-2
Aids: Bl: 0-0 Vi: 0-0 Tstrap: 0-0
Best Rating: 51 5/01 Thsk 6f gd-fm

Only out of the frame in two of her 16 races as a juvenile, but she failed to win. Seems to act on most ground, but is short of a turn of foot.

Extremist (USA)

92 **72**

2-y-o b c Dynaformer (USA)-Strumming (IRE) (Ballad Rock)

R Hannon Highclere Thoroughbred Racing Ltd

Placings:046 (5040)

2001: 7^{0}GF, 8^{4}G, 10^{6}G

	Starts	1st	2nd	3rd	Win & Pl
Career Total (Turf)	3	0	0	0	335

Going (Turf): Sf: 0-0 GS: 0-0 Gd: 0-2 GF: 0-1 Fm: 0-0
Distance: 5f/6f: 0-0 7f-8f: 0-1 9f-13f: 0-2 14f+: 0-0
Track : LH: 0-2 RH: 0-0 Tight: 0-2 Gall: 0-0
Aids: Bl: 0-0 Vi: 0-0 Tstrap: 0-0
Best Rating: 72 10/01 Bath 1m2f46y good

Exuberant

93 **50**

3-y-o ch g Exit To Nowhere (USA)-Pitcroy (Unfuwain (USA))

J R Fanshawe Dr Catherine Wills

Placings:00500 (4951)

2001: 10^{0}G, 10^{0}G, 9^{5}F, 9^{0}GF, 8^{0}G

	Starts	1st	2nd	3rd	Win & Pl
Career Total (Turf)	5	0	0	0	0

Going (Turf): Sf: 0-0 GS: 0-0 Gd: 0-3 GF: 0-1 Fm: 0-1
Distance: 5f/6f: 0-0 7f-8f: 0-1 9f-13f: 0-4 14f+: 0-0
Track : LH: 0-2 RH: 0-1 Tight: 0-3 Gall: 0-0
Aids: Bl: 0-0 Vi: 0-0 Tstrap: 0-0

Best Rating: 61 5/01 Wind 1m2f7y good

Eye Of Gold

89(87) (44)**74**

3-y-o b f Wolfhound (USA)-Blade Of Grass (Kris)

J R Fanshawe The Snailwell Stud Company Limited

Placings:5-04 (2578)

2001: 5^{0}GF, 6^{4}SD

	Starts	1st	2nd	3rd	Win & Pl
Career Total (Turf)	2	0	0	0	0
Career Total (AW)	1	0	0	0	0

Going (Turf): Sf: 0-0 GS: 0-0 Gd: 0-1 GF: 0-1 Fm: 0-0
Distance: 5f/6f: 0-3 7f-8f: 0-0 9f-13f: 0-0 14f+: 0-0
Track : LH: 0-1 RH: 0-0 Tight: 0-0 Gall: 0-0
Aids: Bl: 0-0 Vi: 0-0 Tstrap: 0-0
Best Rating: 44 6/01 Sthl 6f stand

Eyelets Echo

102 **55**

4-y-o b g Inchinor-Kinkajoo (Precocious)

D Morris Mrs G M Peel

Placings:6/000150600-00065400 (5632)

2001: 7^{0}GF, 9^{0}GF, 10^{0}G, 11^{6}F, 11^{5}G, 14^{4}G, 14^{0}GS, 10^{0}G

	Starts	1st	2nd	3rd	Win & Pl
Career Total (Turf)	18	1	0	0	3905

68 6/00 Newc 1m1f9y E(0-75)H FRM £3607
Total win prize-money £3608

Going (Turf): Sf: 0-2 GS: 0-3 Gd: 0-8 GF: 0-3 **Fm: 1-2**
Distance: 5f/6f: 0-0 7f-8f: 0-4 **9f-13f: 1-12** 14f+: 0-2
Track : **LH: 1-10** RH: 0-4 Tight: 0-7 **Gall: 1-4**
Aids: Bl: 0-2 Vi: 0-3 Tstrap: 0-0
Best Rating: 57 6/01 Kemp 1m1f gd-fm

Eyes Dont Lie (IRE)

75 **22**

3-y-o b g Namaqualand (USA)-Avidal Park (Horage)

D A Nolan (I Semple 21/9) Mrs J McFadyen-Murray

Placings:0400060-20060 (5663)

2001: 9^{2}GF, 8^{0}F, 9^{0}G, 8^{6}HY, 12^{0}G

	Starts	1st	2nd	3rd	Win & Pl
Career Total (Turf)	12	0	1	0	1272

Going (Turf): Sf: 0-2 GS: 0-0 Gd: 0-4 GF: 0-4 Fm: 0-2
Distance: 5f/6f: 0-3 7f-8f: 0-6 9f-13f: 0-3 14f+: 0-0
Track : LH: 0-3 RH: 0-2 Tight: 0-2 Gall: 0-0
Aids: Bl: 0-2 Vi: 0-3 Tstrap: 0-1
Best Rating: 45 8/01 Muss 1m1f gd-fm

Eyes To The Right (IRE)

94(83) (66)**66**

2-y-o ch g Eagle Eyed (USA)-Capable Kate (IRE) (Alzao (USA))

P S McEntee (Mrs J R Ramsden 11/9) N C Brown & Miss S Walcott

Placings:0300105540 (5404)

2001: 5^{0}GF, 7^{3}G, 6^{0}GF, 6^{0}GF, 7^{1}G, 8^{0}GF, 8^{5}GF, 7^{5}S, 8^{4}SD, 8^{0}S

	Starts	1st	2nd	3rd	Win & Pl
Career Total (Turf)	9	1	0	1	3948
Career Total (AW)	1	0	0	0	265

63 8/01 Newc 7f E GD £2961
Total win prize-money £2961

Going (Turf): Sf: 0-2 GS: 0-0 **Gd: 1-2** GF: 0-5 Fm: 0-0
Distance: 5f/6f: 0-3 **7f-8f: 1-5** 9f-13f: 0-2 14f+: 0-0
Track : LH: 0-5 RH: 0-1 Tight: 0-2 Gall: 0-0
Aids: Bl: 0-0 Vi: 0-0 Tstrap: 0-0
Best Rating: 66 10/01 Sthl 1m stand

His best effort to date was winning a Newcastle nursery over seven furlongs in the late summer.

Eyes Wide Open

87 **44**

3-y-o b f Fraam-Dreamtime Quest (Blakeney)

P F I Cole Mrs Stephanie Smith

Placings:00 (5113)

2001: 7^{0}HY, 8^{0}HY

	Starts	1st	2nd	3rd	Win & Pl
Career Total (Turf)	2	0	0	0	

Going (Turf): Sf: 0-2 GS: 0-0 Gd: 0-0 GF: 0-0 Fm: 0-0
Distance: 5f/6f: 0-0 7f-8f: 0-1 9f-13f: 0-1 14f+: 0-0
Track : LH: 0-2 RH: 0-0 Tight: 0-0 Gall: 0-0
Aids: Bl: 0-0 Vi: 0-0 Tstrap: 0-0
Best Rating: 44 10/01 Nott 1m54y heavy

Eyes Wide Shut

79(38) **45**

4-y-o b g Beveled (USA)-Dreamtime Quest (Blakeney)

D W P Arbuthnot Mrs Adrian Ireland

Placings:0000 (5046)

2001: 7^{0}GS, 10^{0}GF, 11^{0}GF, 11^{0}SD

	Starts	1st	2nd	3rd	Win & Pl
Career Total (Turf)	3	0	0	0	
Career Total (AW)	1	0	0	0	

Going (Turf): Sf: 0-0 GS: 0-1 Gd: 0-0 GF: 0-2 Fm: 0-0
Distance: 5f/6f: 0-0 7f-8f: 0-1 9f-13f: 0-3 14f+: 0-0
Track : LH: 0-2 RH: 0-1 Tight: 0-1 Gall: 0-0
Aids: Bl: 0-0 Vi: 0-0 Tstrap: 0-4
Best Rating: 45 9/01 Ling 1m3f106y gd-fm

Ezz Elkheil

98 **85+**

2-y-o b c Bering-Numidie (FR) (Baillamont (USA))

J W Payne C Cotran

Placings:2 (4888)

2001: 8^{2}GF

	Starts	1st	2nd	3rd	Win & Pl
Career Total (Turf)	1	0	1	0	1374

Going (Turf): Sf: 0-0 GS: 0-0 Gd: 0-0 GF: 0-1 Fm: 0-0
Distance: 5f/6f: 0-0 7f-8f: 0-1 9f-13f: 0-0 14f+: 0-0
Track : LH: 0-0 RH: 0-1 Tight: 0-0 Gall: 0-0
Aids: Bl: 0-0 Vi: 0-0 Tstrap: 0-0
Best Rating: 85 9/01 Kemp 1m gd-fm

Runner-up on his Kempton debut, he should improve for the experience.

F-Zero

90(101) (62)**49**

4-y-o b g Bin Ajwaad (IRE)-Saluti Tutti (Trojan Fen)

C F Wall S Fustok

Placings:020/10-00 (5400)

2001: 10^{0}S, 10^{0}S

	Starts	1st	2nd	3rd	Win & Pl
Career Total (Turf)	6	0	1	0	860
Career Total (AW)	1	1	0	0	2717

62 3/00 Ling 1m D STD £2717
Total win prize-money £2717

Going (Turf): Sf: 0-2 GS: 0-0 Gd: 0-0 GF: 0-4 Fm: 0-0
Distance: 5f/6f: 0-0 **7f-8f: 1-4** 9f-13f: 0-3 14f+: 0-0
Track : **LH: 1-6** RH: 0-1 **Tight: 1-1** Gall: 0-1
Aids: Bl: 0-0 Vi: 0-0 Tstrap: 0-0
Best Rating: 52 10/01 Pont 1m2f6y soft

Fabrezan (FR)

79 **51**

2-y-o b g Nikos-Fabulous Secret (FR) (Fabulous Dancer (USA))

Nick Williams Mrs Jane Kelly

Placings:000 **(5459)**

2001: 5^{0}S, 7^{0}GS, 8^{0}G

	Starts	1st	2nd	3rd	Win & Pl
Career Total (Turf)	3	0	0	0	

Going (Turf): Sf: 0-1 GS: 0-1 Gd: 0-1 GF: 0-0 Fm: 0-0
Distance: 5f/6f: 0-1 7f-8f: 0-1 9f-13f: 0-1 14f+: 0-0
Track : LH: 0-1 RH: 0-0 Tight: 0-1 Gall: 0-0
Aids: Bl: 0-0 Vi: 0-0 Tstrap: 0-0
Best Rating: 51 8/01 Chep 5f16y soft

Face D Facts

104 **76**

3-y-o b f So Factual (USA)-Water Well (Sadler's Wells (USA))

C F Wall The Boardroom Syndicate

Placings:5130243-02453050 **(5490)**

2001: 6^{0}S, 7^{2}S, 7^{4}GF, 7^{5}GF, 7^{3}G, 7^{0}GF, 6^{5}S, 7^{0}HY

	Starts	1st	2nd	3rd	Win & Pl
Career Total (Turf)	15	1	2	3	7985

68 6/00 Ling 5f E G-F £3640

Total win prize-money £3640

Going (Turf): Sf: 0-6 GS: 0-0 Gd: 0-5 GF: 1-4 Fm: 0-0
Distance: 5f/6f: 1-9 7f-8f: 0-6 9f-13f: 0-0 14f+: 0-0
Track : LH: 0-0 RH: 0-3 Tight: 0-0 Gall: 0-2
Aids: Bl: 0-0 Vi: 0-1 Tstrap: 0-0
Best Rating: 77 5/01 Newb 7f soft

Face The Judge (USA)

91(82) (44)**65**

2-y-o b f Benny The Dip (USA)-Lyrebird (USA) (Storm Bird (CAN))

A Berry Robert Aird

Placings:26600 **(5628)**

2001: 8^{2}F, 7^{6}G, 8^{6}SD, 8^{0}HY, 8^{0}G

	Starts	1st	2nd	3rd	Win & Pl
Career Total (Turf)	4	0	1	0	736
Career Total (AW)	1	0	0	0	0

Going (Turf): Sf: 0-1 GS: 0-0 Gd: 0-2 GF: 0-0 Fm: 0-1
Distance: 5f/6f: 0-0 7f-8f: 0-4 9f-13f: 0-1 14f+: 0-0
Track : LH: 0-2 RH: 0-1 Tight: 0-2 Gall: 0-0
Aids: Bl: 0-0 Vi: 0-0 Tstrap: 0-0
Best Rating: 65 9/01 Muss 1m firm

Face The Limelight (IRE)

95(89) (62)**69**

2-y-o b c Quest For Fame-Miss Boniface (Tap On Wood)

J G Smyth-Osbourne Mrs E T Smyth-Osbourne & Partners

Placings:0644405021 **(5690)**

2001: 6^{0}GF, 6^{6}GF, 7^{4}GF, 7^{4}GF, 7^{4}SD, 8^{0}GF, 7^{5}GF, 9^{0}HY, 7^{2}GS, 7^{1}S

	Starts	1st	2nd	3rd	Win & Pl
Career Total (Turf)	9	1	1	0	6048
Career Total (AW)	1	0	0	0	0

69 11/01 Donc 7f D(0-85) SFT £4563

Total win prize-money £4563

Going (Turf): Sf: 1-2 GS: 0-1 Gd: 0-0 GF: 0-6 Fm: 0-0
Distance: 5f/6f: 0-2 7f-8f: 1-7 9f-13f: 0-1 14f+: 0-0
Track : LH: 0-4 RH: 0-0 Tight: 0-1 Gall: 0-0
Aids: Bl: 0-0 Vi: 0-0 Tstrap: 0-0
Best Rating: 69 11/01 Donc 7f soft

Has shown ability in small events, but is bred to stay and looks to need a distance of ground already. Put up improved display when adopting front-running tactics at Brighton when he was second, before going one better at Doncaster in November.

Facile Tigre

82(96) (33)**49**

6-y-o gr g Efisio-Dancing Diana (Raga Navarro (ITY))

R Hollinshead Miss Sarah Hollinshead

Placings:004004/042214600006001**0/5**000005000200**4 466/06000**050605503000230003**565-0040**0 **(5028)**

2001: 6^{0}SD, 6^{0}SD, 6^{4}SW, 6^{0}SD, 5^{0}S

	Starts	1st	2nd	3rd	Win & Pl
Career Total (Turf)	51	2	4	2	10642
Career Total (AW)	19	0	0	1	513

68 11/98 Brig 5f213y F(0-65)H SFT £1966
74 6/98 Brig 5f59y E(0-70)H FRM £2684

Total win prize-money £4650

Going (Turf): Sf: 1-12 GS: 0-7 Gd: 0-6 GF: 0-19 Fm: 1-7
Distance: 5f/6f: 2-66 7f-8f: 0-4 9f-13f: 0-0 14f+: 0-0
Track : LH: 2-31 RH: 0-3 Tight: 0-12 Gall: 0-4
Aids: Bl: 0-0 Vi: 0-0 Tstrap: 0-0
Best Rating: 33 1/01 Wolv 6f stand

He looks best suited by a sharp downhill track, and both of his wins in 1998 came at Brighton. He has a poor strike rate though, and failed to show any worthwhile form this season.

Fact O' The Matter

94 **75**

2-y-o b g So Factual (USA)-Edgeaway (Ajdal (USA))

M Blanshard Holt Farms Ltd

Placings:30365024 **(5496)**

2001: 5^{3}G, 6^{0}GF, 6^{3}GF, 7^{6}G, 5^{5}GF, 6^{0}G, 7^{2}HY, 7^{4}HY

	Starts	1st	2nd	3rd	Win & Pl
Career Total (Turf)	8	0	1	2	2531

Going (Turf): Sf: 0-2 GS: 0-0 Gd: 0-3 GF: 0-3 Fm: 0-0
Distance: 5f/6f: 0-3 7f-8f: 0-5 9f-13f: 0-0 14f+: 0-0
Track : LH: 0-1 RH: 0-0 Tight: 0-0 Gall: 0-0
Aids: Bl: 0-1 Vi: 0-0 Tstrap: 0-0
Best Rating: 75 10/01 Ling 7f heavy

Factual Lad

106 **77**

3-y-o b g So Factual (USA)-Surprise Surprise (Robellino (USA))

B R Millman Tarka Racing

Placings:2332310600-46403005 **(4959)**

2001: 8^{4}GS, 8^{6}GF, 7^{4}GF, 8^{0}GF, 8^{3}GF, 8^{0}G, 8^{0}G, 7^{5}GS

	Starts	1st	2nd	3rd	Win & Pl
Career Total (Turf)	18	1	2	4	17559

81 7/00 Chep 6f16y E G-F £2788

Total win prize-money £2789

Going (Turf): Sf: 0-2 GS: 0-2 Gd: 0-7 GF: 1-7 Fm: 0-0
Distance: 5f/6f: 0-6 7f-8f: 1-10 9f-13f: 0-2 14f+: 0-0
Track : LH: 0-4 RH: 0-4 Tight: 0-1 Gall: 0-2
Aids: Bl: 0-1 Vi: 0-0 Tstrap: 0-0
Best Rating: 85 7/01 Nott 1m54y gd-fm

Running respectably in handicaps this term, he seems best at around seven furlongs and a mile on good ground or faster.

Faddad (USA)

90 **61**

5-y-o b g Irish River (FR)-Miss Mistletoes (IRE) (The Minstrel (CAN))

D C O'Brien J S Court

Placings:14/655/00 **(2001)**

2001: 10^{0}G, 12^{0}F

	Starts	1st	2nd	3rd	Win & Pl
Career Total (Turf)	7	1	0	0	5363

73 8/98 Tral 1m GD £4812

Total win prize-money £4813

Going (Turf): Sf: 0-1 GS: 0-0 Gd: 1-3 GF: 0-1 Fm: 0-1
Distance: 5f/6f: 0-0 7f-8f: 1-1 9f-13f: 0-6 14f+: 0-0
Track : LH: 1-5 RH: 0-2 Tight: 0-0 Gall: 0-1
Aids: Bl: 0-1 Vi: 0-0 Tstrap: 0-0
Best Rating: 61 5/01 Ling 1m2f7y good

A winner over a mile at Tralee as a two-year-old, he has shown no form since joining his present trainer.

Fadhel (USA)

86 **31**

5-y-o b g Zilzal (USA)-Nice Life (USA) (Sportin' Life (USA))

E W Tuer E Tuer

Placings:0/02550/000 **(2518)**

2001: 12^{0}GF, 9^{0}GF, 16^{0}F

	Starts	1st	2nd	3rd	Win & Pl
Career Total (Turf)	9	0	1	0	788

Going (Turf): Sf: 0-0 GS: 0-1 Gd: 0-3 GF: 0-4 Fm: 0-1
Distance: 5f/6f: 0-0 7f-8f: 0-3 9f-13f: 0-5 14f+: 0-1
Track : LH: 0-3 RH: 0-4 Tight: 0-3 Gall: 0-0
Aids: Bl: 0-2 Vi: 0-0 Tstrap: 0-0
Best Rating: 31 6/01 Bevl 1m1f207y gd-fm

Faerie Realm (IRE)

100 **75**

3-y-o b f Fairy King (USA)-Marie Noelle (FR) (Brigadier Gerard)

Sir Michael Stoute Mrs Belinda Strudwick

Placings:5-22 **(3149)**

2001: 10^{2}S, 12^{2}G

	Starts	1st	2nd	3rd	Win & Pl
Career Total (Turf)	3	0	2	0	2706

Going (Turf): Sf: 0-2 GS: 0-0 Gd: 0-1 GF: 0-0 Fm: 0-0
Distance: 5f/6f: 0-0 7f-8f: 0-1 9f-13f: 0-2 14f+: 0-0
Track : LH: 0-0 RH: 0-2 Tight: 0-0 Gall: 0-0
Aids: Bl: 0-0 Vi: 0-0 Tstrap: 0-0
Best Rating: 75 6/01 Sand 1m2f7y soft

Fahs (USA)

96(102) (82d)**77d**

9-y-o b/br g Riverman (USA)-Tanwi (Vision (USA))

N Hamilton Epsom Downs Racing Club

Placings:03310/43632020063/01300636010/33363544 030024**1**/053412236**031/25**01211500**3304-000** **(2106)**

2001: 14^{0}SD, 12^{0}SD, 12^{0}GF

	Starts	1st	2nd	3rd	Win & Pl
Career Total (Turf)	60	7	6	14	59163
Career Total (AW)	11	2	1	3	6532

85 8/00 Leic 1m3f183yD(0-75) G-F £3796
79 8/00 NmkJ 1m4f D(0-80)H GD £4368
73 7/00 Yarm 1m3f101yE(0-70)H GD £2842
72 12/99 Ling 1m5f G(0-80)H STD £1776
71 6/99 Yarm 1m2f21y E(0-75)H G-F £2807
75 11/98 Ling 1m4f G(0-80)H STD £1737
79 10/97 Yarm 1m2f21y D(0-85)H GD £3995
80 5/97 Sand 1m2f7y D(0-80)H G-F £3663
5/95 Tram 1m4f GD £2226

Total win prize-money £27213

Going (Turf): Sf: 0-7 GS: 0-3 Gd: 3-16 GF: 3-29 Fm: 0-0

Distance: 5f/6f: 0-0 7f-8f: 0-2 **9f-13f: 8-61** 14f+: 0-3
Track : **LH: 5-41** RH: 3-20 **Tight: 5-33** Gall: 1-15
Aids: Bl: 0-0 Vi: 0-0 Tstrap: 0-0
Best Rating: 60 6/01 Kemp 1m4f gd-fm

No world beater, but is a consistent sort in modest middle-distance handicaps on sand and turf. Best when held up for a late run.

Failed To Hit

(107) (67)**40**
8-y-o b g Warrshan (USA)-Missed Again (High Top)
N P Littmoden M C S D Racing Ltd

Placings:241006/006500202304300/431411041343041 05413/10526003515224/232016343652631515313-141163042 **(5615)**
2001: 12^{1}SW, 12^{4}SD, 12^{1}SD, 12^{1}SD, 12^{6}SD, 14^{3}SW, 12^{0}SD, 12^{4}SD, 12^{2}SD

	Starts	1st	2nd	3rd	Win & Pl
Career Total (Turf)	11	1	1	0	3091
Career Total (AW)	74	15	9	14	52567

59	2/01	Wolv	1m4f	F	STD	£2114
69	2/01	Wolv	1m4f	G(0-70)H	STD	£1365
61	1/01	Wolv	1m4f	F	SLW	£2156
67	11/00	Wolv	1m4f	G(0-70)H	STD	£1904
71	10/00	Wolv	1m4f	F	STD	£2240
61	10/00	Wolv	1m4f	E(0-75)H	STD	£2758
59	2/00	Wolv	1m4f	F	STD	£2062
60	11/99	Ling	1m4f	F	STD	£2158
71	1/99	Wolv	1m4f	D(0-85)H	STD	£3582
65	12/98	Wolv	1m1f79y	C(0-90)H	STD	£5439
60	10/98	Ling	1m4f	G(0-65)	STD	£1725
66	3/98	Wolv	1m1f79y	E(0-70)H	STD	£2587
62	2/98	Ling	1m2f	F	SLW	£1850
65	2/98	Wolv	1m100y	F(0-55)	STD	£2085
51	2/98	Ling	1m	E(0-70)H	STD	£2872
67	8/96	Folk	6f	F	G-F	£2381

Total win prize-money £39283

Going (Turf): Sf: 0-1 GS: 0-2 Gd: 0-2 **GF: 1-5** Fm: 0-1
Distance: 5f/6f: 1-2 7f-8f: 1-10 **9f-13f: 14-67** 14f+: 0-6
Track : **LH: 15-78** RH: 0-3 **Tight: 15-69** Gall: 0-0
Aids: Bl: 4-23 **Vi: 11-57** Tstrap: 0-0
Best Rating: 69 2/01 Wolv 1m4f stand

An effective and game front runner on both types of artificial surface on his day, he has notched up eleven wins at Wolverhampton, the last eight over a mile and a half.

Fair Finnish (IRE)

90 (16)**43**
7-y-o b g Commanche Run-Karelia (USA) (Sir Ivor)
W Clay W Clay

Placings:5/0-00 **(1283)**
2001: 12^{0}S, 16^{0}G

	Starts	1st	2nd	3rd	Win & Pl
Career Total (Turf)	3	0	0	0	
Career Total (AW)	1	0	0	0	0

Going (Turf): Sf: 0-1 GS: 0-0 Gd: 0-1 GF: 0-1 Fm: 0-0
Distance: 5f/6f: 0-0 7f-8f: 0-0 9f-13f: 0-2 14f+: 0-2
Track : LH: 0-2 RH: 0-2 Tight: 0-3 Gall: 0-0
Aids: Bl: 0-0 Vi: 0-2 Tstrap: 0-0
Best Rating: 5 5/01 Bevl 2m35y good

Fair Prince

85(55) **54**
3-y-o ch g Rakaposhi King-Lady Llanfair (Prince Tenderfoot (USA))
B J Meehan N G Anderson

Placings:0000 **(2343)**
2001: 7^{0}S, 8^{0}GS, 7^{0}SD, 12^{0}SD

	Starts	1st	2nd	3rd	Win & Pl
Career Total (Turf)	2	0	0	0	
Career Total (AW)	2	0	0	0	

Going (Turf): Sf: 0-1 GS: 0-1 Gd: 0-0 GF: 0-0 Fm: 0-0
Distance: 5f/6f: 0-0 7f-8f: 0-3 9f-13f: 0-1 14f+: 0-0
Track : LH: 0-2 RH: 0-1 Tight: 0-0 Gall: 0-1
Aids: Bl: 0-0 Vi: 0-0 Tstrap: 0-0
Best Rating: 54 4/01 Kemp 7f soft

Fair Princess

97 **80**
3-y-o b f Efisio-Fair Attempt (IRE) (Try My Best (USA))
B W Hills Stephen Crown

Placings:22062220-1005 **(4314)**
2001: 6^{1}G, 6^{0}S, 6^{0}GF, 6^{5}G

	Starts	1st	2nd	3rd	Win & Pl
Career Total (Turf)	12	1	5	0	20103

60	5/01	Ripn	6f	D	GD	£3510

Total win prize-money £3510

Going (Turf): Sf: 0-4 GS: 0-0 **Gd: 1-2** GF: 0-5 Fm: 0-1
Distance: **5f/6f: 1-10** 7f-8f: 0-2 9f-13f: 0-1 14f+: 0-0
Track : LH: 0-1 RH: 0-1 Tight: 0-0 Gall: 0-2
Aids: Bl: 0-1 Vi: 0-0 Tstrap: 0-0
Best Rating: 70 8/01 Ripn 6f good

Has been running well but is still a maiden and has finished runner-up on far too many occasions.

Fair Question (IRE)

111 **111**
3-y-o b c Rainbow Quest (USA)-Fair Of The Furze (Ela-Mana-Mou)
J L Dunlop Tessona Racing Limited

Placings:14-202610 **(5585a)**
2001: 10^{2}G, 11^{0}GF, 14^{2}G, 14^{6}GF, 14^{1}S, 15^{0}HY

	Starts	1st	2nd	3rd	Win & Pl
Career Total (Turf)	8	2	2	0	56878

111	9/01	Dort	1m6f		SFT	£39088
86	8/00	NmkJ	7f	D	G-F	£4862

Total win prize-money £43950

Going (Turf): Sf: 1-2 GS: 0-0 Gd: 0-2 **GF: 1-4** Fm: 0-0
Distance: 5f/6f: 0-0 7f-8f: 1-2 9f-13f: 0-2 14f+: 1-4
Track : LH: 0-0 **RH: 1-4** Tight: 0-1 Gall: 0-1
Aids: Bl: 0-0 Vi: 0-0 Tstrap: 0-0
Best Rating: 111 9/01 Dort 1m6f soft

This half-brother to White Muzzle showed a nice turn of foot to score on his debut at two before going on to finish fourth behind Nayef at Newbury. Good effort to go down narrowly to his stable companion Rosi's Boy on his return at Newmarket. Showed he stays well when runner-up over an extended 14 furlongs at Newmarket, and gained his first win of the season when taking the German St Leger.

Fair Step

99 **50**
3-y-o ch f King's Signet (USA)-Miss Hocroft (Dominion)
G A Swinbank David C Young

Placings:2305-50232 **(3279)**
2001: 5^{5}F, 5^{0}GF, 5^{2}GS, 5^{3}F, 5^{2}F

	Starts	1st	2nd	3rd	Win & Pl
Career Total (Turf)	9	0	3	2	2688

Going (Turf): Sf: 0-0 GS: 0-1 Gd: 0-1 GF: 0-4 Fm: 0-3
Distance: 5f/6f: 0-9 7f-8f: 0-0 9f-13f: 0-0 14f+: 0-0
Track : LH: 0-1 RH: 0-0 Tight: 0-0 Gall: 0-1
Aids: Bl: 0-0 Vi: 0-0 Tstrap: 0-0
Best Rating: 50 7/01 Rdcr 5f firm

Fair Time (USA)

85 **81**
2-y-o b f Woodman (USA)-Anakid (USA) (Danzig (USA))
E A L Dunlop Abdulla Buhaleeba

Placings:000 **(5559)**
2001: 8^{0}G, 8^{0}GS, 8^{0}S

	Starts	1st	2nd	3rd	Win & Pl
Career Total (Turf)	3	0	0	0	

Going (Turf): Sf: 0-1 GS: 0-1 Gd: 0-1 GF: 0-0 Fm: 0-0
Distance: 5f/6f: 0-0 7f-8f: 0-2 9f-13f: 0-1 14f+: 0-0
Track : LH: 0-0 RH: 0-0 Tight: 0-0 Gall: 0-0
Aids: Bl: 0-0 Vi: 0-0 Tstrap: 0-0
Best Rating: 81 9/01 NmkR 1m good

Fairgame Man

101 **87**
3-y-o ch g Clantime-Thalya (Crofthall)
A Berry Sir Robert Ogden

Placings:31130-00255000 **(5630)**
2001: 6^{0}GF, 6^{0}G, 5^{2}G, 5^{5}F, 5^{5}G, 5^{0}HY, 5^{0}HY, 6^{0}G

	Starts	1st	2nd	3rd	Win & Pl
Career Total (Turf)	13	2	1	2	10606

85	8/00	Ches	6f18y	D	GD	£3640
77	7/00	Carl	5f	E	FRM	£2795

Total win prize-money £6435

Going (Turf): Sf: 0-3 GS: 0-0 **Gd: 1-6** GF: 0-2 **Fm: 1-2**
Distance: 5f/6f: 1-11 7f-8f: 1-2 9f-13f: 0-0 14f+: 0-0
Track : LH: 1-5 RH: 1-1 Tight: 1-3 Gall: 1-2
Aids: Bl: 0-0 Vi: 0-0 Tstrap: 0-0
Best Rating: 87 7/01 Ches 5f16y good

Fairmead Princess

52 **42**
3-y-o b f Rudimentary (USA)-Lessons Lass (IRE) (Doyoun)
C F Wall C N & Mrs A V Roberts

Placings:00 **(5182)**
2001: 8^{0}GF, 10^{0}HY

	Starts	1st	2nd	3rd	Win & Pl
Career Total (Turf)	2	0	0	0	

Going (Turf): Sf: 0-1 GS: 0-0 Gd: 0-0 GF: 0-1 Fm: 0-0
Distance: 5f/6f: 0-0 7f-8f: 0-0 9f-13f: 0-2 14f+: 0-0
Track : LH: 0-0 RH: 0-0 Tight: 0-1 Gall: 0-0
Aids: Bl: 0-0 Vi: 0-0 Tstrap: 0-0
Best Rating: 42 9/01 Wwck 1m22y gd-fm

Fairtoto

93 (40)**49**
5-y-o b g Mtoto-Fairy Feet (Sadler's Wells (USA))
D J Wintle Mrs Joan L Egan

Placings:000/003/30-152 **(5188)**
2001: 16^{1}GF, 16^{5}GF, 15^{2}GS

	Starts	1st	2nd	3rd	Win & Pl
Career Total (Turf)	9	1	1	1	3911
Career Total (AW)	2	0	0	1	314

46	6/01	Wwck	2m39y	F(0-65)H	G-F	£2684

Total win prize-money £2685

Going (Turf): Sf: 0-3 GS: 0-1 Gd: 0-3 **GF: 1-2** Fm: 0-0
Distance: 5f/6f: 0-0 7f-8f: 0-2 9f-13f: 0-3 **14f+: 1-6**
Track : **LH: 1-8** RH: 0-2 Tight: 0-6 Gall: 0-0
Aids: Bl: 0-0 Vi: 0-0 **Tstrap: 1-3**
Best Rating: 49 10/01 Catt 1m7f177y gd-sft

Won a weak event over two miles at Warwick in June, and has continued to run well including a good second to a well handicapped type at Catterick in October after pulling hard. Acts on a sound surface but is best with cut in the ground.

Fairy Loch

61

2-y-o b f Sure Blade (USA)-Tremloch (Tremblant)

W G M Turner Mrs K A Davis

Placings:0 **(1858)**

2001: 6^{0}F

	Starts	1st	2nd	3rd	Win & Pl
Career Total (Turf)	1	0	0	0	

Going (Turf): Sf: 0-0 GS: 0-0 Gd: 0-0 GF: 0-0 Fm: 0-1
Distance: 5f/6f: 0-1 7f-8f: 0-0 9f-13f: 0-0 14f+: 0-0
Track : LH: 0-0 RH: 0-0 Tight: 0-0 Gall: 0-0
Aids: Bl: 0-0 Vi: 0-0 Tstrap: 0-0

Fairy Monarch (IRE)

100 **83**

2-y-o b c Ali-Royal (IRE)-Cookawara (IRE) (Fairy King (USA))

B J Meehan Merlyn Ii

Placings:343521100635 **(5280)**

2001: 5^{3}S, 5^{4}GS, 6^{3}GF, 6^{5}GF, 7^{2}GF, 6^{1}GF, 7^{1}GF, 7^{0}G, 6^{0}G, 8^{6}G, 7^{3}S, 9^{5}S

	Starts	1st	2nd	3rd	Win & Pl
Career Total (Turf)	12	2	1	3	14202

90	7/01	NmkJ	7f	D	G-F	£4953
77	7/01	Epsm	6f	E	G-F	£4114

Total win prize-money £9068

Going (Turf): Sf: 0-3 GS: 0-1 Gd: 0-3 **GF: 2-5** Fm: 0-0
Distance: 5f/6f: 1-6 7f-8f: 1-5 9f-13f: 0-1 14f+: 0-0
Track : **LH: 1-5** RH: 0-2 **Tight: 1-4** Gall: 0-0
Aids: **Bl: 2-7** Vi: 0-0 Tstrap: 0-0
Best Rating: 90 7/01 NmkJ 7f gd-fm

A March foal, he is a close-coupled individual. Got off the mark when dropping in class and trip at Epsom in July and followed up over seven in a Newmarket nursery despite charting a wayward course. Mixed form since. Acts on a sound surface, but handles softer.

Fairy Prince (IRE)

107 (17)**62**

8-y-o b g Fairy King (USA)-Danger Ahead (Mill Reef (USA))

Mrs A L M King All The Kings Horses

Placings:50/003124623/00241110500/020501204620/000552226200/04510044300-00240001330 **(4235)**

2001: 6^{0}G, 5^{0}F, 6^{2}GF, 6^{4}GF, 6^{0}GF, 6^{6}GF, 5^{6}GF, 6^{1}GF, 6^{3}GS, 6^{3}F, 5^{0}GF

	Starts	1st	2nd	3rd	Win & Pl
Career Total (Turf)	71	7	12	5	44808
Career Total (AW)	1	0	0	0	

60	7/01	NmkJ	6f	C(0-90)H	G-F	£7150
62	6/00	Nott	6f15y	F(0-60)H	G-F	£2593
67	7/98	Bevl	5f	E(0-70)	G-F	£2889
72	7/97	Donc	6f	E(0-70)	GD	£3102
65	7/97	Nott	5f13y	F(0-65)	G-F	£2508
67	7/97	Pont	6f	F	G-F	£2801
54	6/96	Carl	5f207y	E(0-70)H	FRM	£3036

Total win prize-money £24082

Going (Turf): Sf: 0-1 GS: 0-6 Gd: 1-17 **GF: 5-37** Fm: 1-10
Distance: **5f/6f: 6-56** 7f-8f: 1-16 9f-13f: 0-0 14f+: 0-0
Track : LH: 1-20 RH: 1-12 Tight: 0-1 **Gall: 1-18**
Aids: **Bl: 1-12** Vi: 0-1 Tstrap: 0-0
Best Rating: 62 8/01 Ling 6f firm

He is an effective sprint handicapper who wins in his turn. Suited by six furlongs and fast ground.

Fairy Star

102 **77**

3-y-o b f Fairy King (USA)-Gold Rose (FR) (Noblequest (FR))

D R C Elsworth Lordship Stud

Placings:63421 **(5664)**

2001: 10^{6}G, 8^{3}G, 10^{4}G, 10^{2}HY, 8^{1}HY

	Starts	1st	2nd	3rd	Win & Pl
Career Total (Turf)	5	1	1	1	4066

52	11/01	Wind	1m67y	D	HVY	£3136

Total win prize-money £3136

Going (Turf): Sf: 1-2 GS: 0-0 Gd: 0-3 GF: 0-0 Fm: 0-0
Distance: 5f/6f: 0-0 7f-8f: 0-0 **9f-13f: 1-5** 14f+: 0-0
Track : LH: 0-1 **RH: 1-3 Tight: 1-3** Gall: 0-1
Aids: Bl: 0-0 Vi: 0-0 Tstrap: 0-0
Best Rating: 77 9/01 Sand 1m14y good

A half-sister to Group One Grand Criterium winner Goldmark. Has shown ability and got off the mark on her fifth attempt, a career at stud now beckons.

Faith Again (IRE)

92(100) (35)**47**

5-y-o b m Namaqualand (USA)-Intricacy (Formidable (USA))

A Streeter Racing For You Limited

Placings:5560/002534/00-155 **(0247)**

2001: 16^{1}SW, 16^{5}SD, 16^{5}SD

	Starts	1st	2nd	3rd	Win & Pl
Career Total (Turf)	12	0	1	1	1612
Career Total (AW)	3	1	0	0	1729

35	1/01	Wolv	2m46y	F(0-65)H	SLW	£1729

Total win prize-money £1729

Going (Turf): Sf: 0-1 GS: 0-1 Gd: 0-3 GF: 0-4 Fm: 0-3
Distance: 5f/6f: 0-2 7f-8f: 0-3 9f-13f: 0-5 **14f+: 1-5**
Track : **LH: 1-9** RH: 0-3 **Tight: 1-3** Gall: 0-0
Aids: Bl: 0-4 Vi: 0-0 Tstrap: 0-0
Best Rating: 35 1/01 Wolv 2m46y slow

Faithful Warrior (USA)

108 **92**

3-y-o ch c Diesis-Dabaweyaa (Shareef Dancer (USA))

B W Hills Mohamed Obaida

Placings:454-010110 **(5142)**

2001: 7^{0}GF, 8^{1}G, 8^{0}GF, 8^{1}GF, 7^{1}G, 9^{0}G

	Starts	1st	2nd	3rd	Win & Pl
Career Total (Turf)	9	3	0	0	31229

92	9/01	Ches	7f122y	C(0-100)H	GD	£15080
83	8/01	Pont	1m4y	C(0-90)H	G-F	£7475
82	6/01	Sand	1m14y	D(0-80)H	GD	£7897

Total win prize-money £30453

Going (Turf): Sf: 0-1 GS: 0-0 **Gd: 2-3** GF: 1-4 Fm: 0-0
Distance: 5f/6f: 0-0 7f-8f: 1-5 **9f-13f: 2-3** 14f+: 0-0
Track : **LH: 2-3** RH: 1-2 **Tight: 1-1** Gall: 0-1
Aids: Bl: 0-0 Vi: 0-0 Tstrap: 0-0
Best Rating: 92 9/01 Ches 7f122y good

Improving as he matures and got off the mark in a Sandown handicap in June despite not getting the clearest of runs. Added to that win at Pontefract and Chester. Acts on fast ground and suited by a mile, but should stay further and there may be more to come from him.

Faiza

91 **73**

2-y-o b f Efisio-Nanouche (Dayjur (USA))

R Hannon The Sussex Stud Limited

Placings:45 **(2850)**

2001: 5^{4}GF, 5^{5}G

	Starts	1st	2nd	3rd	Win & Pl
Career Total (Turf)	2	0	0	0	323

Going (Turf): Sf: 0-0 GS: 0-0 Gd: 0-1 GF: 0-1 Fm: 0-0
Distance: 5f/6f: 0-2 7f-8f: 0-0 9f-13f: 0-0 14f+: 0-0
Track : LH: 0-0 HH: 0-0 Tight: 0-0 Gall: 0-0
Aids: Bl: 0-0 Vi: 0-0 Tstrap: 0-0
Best Rating: 73 7/01 Sand 5f6y good

Fajara Boy

64 **23**

2-y-o b g Cool Jazz-Prudent Pet (Distant Relative)

C W Fairhurst J G Brearley

Placings:0 **(5533)**

2001: 5^{0}S

	Starts	1st	2nd	3rd	Win & Pl
Career Total (Turf)	1	0	0	0	

Going (Turf): Sf: 0-1 GS: 0-0 Gd: 0-0 GF: 0-0 Fm: 0-0
Distance: 5f/6f: 0-1 7f-8f: 0-0 9f-13f: 0-0 14f+: 0-0
Track : LH: 0-0 RH: 0-0 Tight: 0-0 Gall: 0-0
Aids: Bl: 0-0 Vi: 0-0 Tstrap: 0-0
Best Rating: 23 10/01 Rdcr 5f soft

Falcon Georgie

69 **29**

2-y-o b f Sri Pekan (USA)-Georgia Stephens (USA) (The Minstrel (CAN))

N Tinkler J M Quinn

Placings:300 **(4839)**

2001: 6^{3}G, 6^{0}G, 6^{0}G

	Starts	1st	2nd	3rd	Win & Pl
Career Total (Turf)	3	0	0	1	625

Going (Turf): Sf: 0-0 GS: 0-0 Gd: 0-3 GF: 0-0 Fm: 0-0
Distance: 5f/6f: 0-2 7f-8f: 0-1 9f-13f: 0-0 14f+: 0-0
Track : LH: 0-0 RH: 0-0 Tight: 0-0 Gall: 0-0
Aids: Bl: 0-0 Vi: 0-0 Tstrap: 0-0
Best Rating: 29 8/01 Hayd 6f good

Falcon Goa (IRE)

109(102) (71)**67**

3-y-o b f Sri Pekan (USA)-Minden (IRE) (Bluebird (USA))

N Tinkler Racingclubcouk

Placings:04162-00005411000 **(5685)**

2001: 5^{0}GS, 5^{0}GS, 6^{0}GF, 7^{0}F, 6^{5}GF, 6^{4}G, 6^{1}GF, 5^{1}G, 6^{0}GF, 5^{0}S, 5^{0}S

	Starts	1st	2nd	3rd	Win & Pl
Career Total (Turf)	15	3	0	0	13525
Career Total (AW)	1	0	1	0	7260

67	7/01	Newc	5f	E(0-75)H	GD	£4030
63	7/01	Donc	6f	D(0-85)H	G-F	£5255
66	6/00	Pont	5f	F	SFT	£3152

Total win prize-money £12438

Going (Turf): Sf: 1-3 GS: 0-4 **Gd: 1-2 GF: 1-5** Fm: 0-1
Distance: **5f/6f: 3-15** 7f-8f: 0-1 9f-13f: 0-0 14f+: 0-0
Track : **LH: 1-2** RH: 0-0 Tight: 0-1 Gall: 0-0
Aids: Bl: 0-0 **Vi: 2-6** Tstrap: 0-0
Best Rating: 67 7/01 Newc 5f good

Winner over five on soft as a juvenile, had been tried over further in 2001, and slipped down the weights. Has won twice on the bounce this summer over five and six furlongs.

Falcon Hill

103 **100**

2-y-o b c Polar Falcon (USA)-Branston Jewel (IRE) (Prince Sabo)

M Johnston Tweenhills Racing (may Hill Syndicate)

Placings:520110321061 **(5498)**

2001: 5^{5}GS, 5^{2}GF, 5^{0}GF, 5^{1}GF, 6^{1}GF, 5^{0}GF, 6^{3}GS, 6^{2}G, 6^{1}GF, 6^{0}G, 6^{6}GS, 6^{1}HY

	Starts	1st	2nd	3rd	Win & Pl

	Starts	1st	2nd	3rd	Win & Pl
Career Total (Turf)	12	4	2	1	52857

100	10/01	Donc	6f	A	HVY	£14170
96	8/01	NmkJ	6f	B	G-F	£17966
82	7/01	Asct	6f	C	G-F	£6987
89	7/01	Pont	5f	E	G-F	£3770

Total win prize-money £42894

Going (Turf): Sf: 1-1 GS: 0-3 Gd: 0-2 **GF: 3-6** Fm: 0-0
Distance: **5f/6f: 4-12** 7f-8f: 0-0 9f-13f: 0-0 14f+: 0-0
Track : **LH: 1-1** RH: 0-0 Tight: 0-0 Gall: 0-0
Aids: Bl: 0-0 Vi: 0-0 Tstrap: 0-0
Best Rating: 100 10/01 Donc 6f heavy

Made all at Pontefract on his fourth start, and followed up winning a good nursery over six furlongs at Ascot. Won a competitive nursery at Newmarket. Ran his heart out when sixth in the Tattersalls Autumn Auction Stakes and ended the season by winning a Doncaster Listed event. A tough individual, he acts on fast ground and handles good to soft.

Falcon Spirit

93(98) (52)**49**

5-y-o b g Polar Falcon (USA)-Amina (Brigadier Gerard)
John G Carr (Mrs M Reveley 2/8) A-One Syndicate

Placings:03255**32**0/0040**505**-00 **(1657)**
2001: 11^{0}G, 9^{0}F

	Starts	1st	2nd	3rd	Win & Pl
Career Total (Turf)	12	0	1	1	2012
Career Total (AW)	5	0	1	1	978

Going (Turf): Sf: 0-1 GS: 0-0 Gd: 0-4 GF: 0-4 Fm: 0-3
Distance: 5f/6f: 0-0 7f-8f: 0-2 9f-13f: 0-15 14f+: 0-0
Track : LH: 0-9 RH: 0-6 Tight: 0-12 Gall: 0-2
Aids: Bl: 0-7 Vi: 0-4 Tstrap: 0-0
Best Rating: 21 5/01 Rdcr 1m1f firm

Falconidae

105 **85+**

4-y-o ch g Polar Falcon (USA)-Barbary Court (Grundy)
P J Makin A W Schiff

Placings:64/05120U0-4 **(2046)**
2001: 8^{4}GF

	Starts	1st	2nd	3rd	Win & Pl
Career Total (Turf)	10	1	1	0	9771

85	7/00	Bath	1m5y	C(0-90)H	FRM	£6987

Total win prize-money £6988

Going (Turf): Sf: 0-2 GS: 0-1 Gd: 0-0 GF: 0-6 **Fm: 1-1**
Distance: 5f/6f: 0-1 7f-8f: 0-4 **9f-13f: 1-5** 14f+: 0-0
Track : **LH: 1-2** RH: 0-4 **Tight: 1-2** Gall: 0-2
Aids: Bl: 0-0 Vi: 0-0 Tstrap: 0-0
Best Rating: 72 6/01 Wind 1m67y gd-fm

Fallachan (USA)

104(106) (73)**80d**

5-y-o ch g Diesis-Afaff (USA) (Nijinsky (CAN))
M A Jarvis Mrs Gay Jarvis

Placings:004/11250220/0440300000**50-1010005 (3819)**
2001: 8^{1}SD, 8^{0}SD, 8^{1}SD, 8^{0}G, 8^{0}G, 8^{0}SD, 7^{5}SD

	Starts	1st	2nd	3rd	Win & Pl
Career Total (Turf)	21	2	3	1	18343
Career Total (AW)	8	2	0	0	4785

73	3/01	Wolv	1m100y	E(0-75)H	STD	£2772
65	1/01	Sthl	1m	F(0-65)H	STD	£1813
78	4/99	Nott	1m54y	E(0-70)H	G-S	£3162
68	4/99	Muss	1m	E(0-70)H	GD	£2905

Total win prize-money £10652

Going (Turf): Sf: 0-5 **GS: 1-3 Gd: 1-7** GF: 0-6 Fm: 0-0
Distance: 5f/6f: 0-0 7f-8f: 2-21 9f-13f: 2-8 14f+: 0-0
Track : **LH: 3-13** RH: 1-6 **Tight: 2-10** Gall: 0-1
Aids: Bl: 0-0 Vi: 0-0 Tstrap: 0-0
Best Rating: 75 6/01 Wind 1m67y good

Won twice on Fibresand this year and goes well for a girl.

Fallen Star

106 **100+**

3-y-o b f Brief Truce (USA)-Rise And Fall (Mill Reef (USA))
J L Dunlop Nicholas Cooper

Placings:2112 **(5007)**
2001: 7^{2}GS, 6^{1}F, 7^{1}S, 8^{2}S

	Starts	1st	2nd	3rd	Win & Pl
Career Total (Turf)	4	2	2	0	18449

96	9/01	Yarm	7f3y	C	SFT	£6119
67	8/01	Sals	6f212y	D	FRM	£3640

Total win prize-money £9759

Going (Turf): Sf: 1-2 GS: 0-1 Gd: 0-0 GF: 0-0 **Fm: 1-1**
Distance: 5f/6f: 0-0 **7f-8f: 2-4** 9f-13f: 0-0 14f+: 0-0
Track : LH: 0-0 RH: 0-0 Tight: 0-0 Gall: 0-0
Aids: Bl: 0-0 Vi: 0-0 Tstrap: 0-0
Best Rating: 100 9/01 Asct 1m soft

A 140,000gns half-sister to the smart miler Fly To The Stars, she made a winning reappearance on firm ground at Salisbury in August 2001. Showed her versatility with a plucky win on soft ground at Yarmouth, and ran well in defeat at Ascot. Looks to have bags of improvement in her.

Falls O'Moness (IRE)

102(94) (36)**41**

7-y-o b m River Falls-Sevens Are Wild (Petorius)
E J Alston Piquet Opera House Partnership

Placings:2203200/034500566431046O/**000**400035613 545130/300644010043050/20020000206-500343300 00 **(5539)**
2001: 7^{5}S, 8^{0}G, 8^{0}GF, 8^{3}GF, 9^{4}GF, 8^{3}GF, 7^{3}GF, 7^{0}G, 8^{0}GF, 7^{0}GF, 8^{0}S

	Starts	1st	2nd	3rd	Win & Pl
Career Total (Turf)	76	4	6	11	30712
Career Total (AW)	4	0	0	0	0

50	8/99	Thsk	1m	F(0-60)H	SFT	£3134
50	9/98	Haml	1m65y	F(0-60)H	SFT	£2122
48	8/98	Thsk	1m	F(0-60)H	G-F	£3078
65	9/97	Ayr	1m1f	D	G-S	£3766

Total win prize-money £12100

Going (Turf): Sf: 2-16 GS: 1-16 Gd: 0-13 GF: 1-25 Fm: 0-5
Distance: 5f/6f: 0-7 7f-8f: 2-36 9f-13f: 2-37 14f+: 0-0
Track : **LH: 3-44** RH: 1-22 **Tight: 3-29** Gall: 0-7
Aids: Bl: 0-2 Vi: 0-1 Tstrap: 0-0
Best Rating: 42 7/01 Pont 1m4y gd-fm

False Promise

75 **61d**

3-y-o b g Bluebird (USA)-Funoon (IRE) (Kris)
E A L Dunlop Khalifa Sultan

Placings:000-0 **(0775)**
2001: 9^{0}S

	Starts	1st	2nd	3rd	Win & Pl
Career Total (Turf)	4	0	0	0	

Going (Turf): Sf: 0-3 GS: 0-0 Gd: 0-0 GF: 0-1 Fm: 0-0
Distance: 5f/6f: 0-0 7f-8f: 0-2 9f-13f: 0-2 14f+: 0-0
Track : LH: 0-2 RH: 0-0 Tight: 0-0 Gall: 0-0
Aids: Bl: 0-0 Vi: 0-0 Tstrap: 0-0
Best Rating: 23 4/01 Nott 1m1f213y soft

Famous (FR)

87(93) (19)**33**

8-y-o b g Tropular-Famous Horse (FR) (Labus (FR))
J J Bridger J J Bridger

Placings:3/401000/006400506302062**00**/**0206**6400000 51201004**502**/**00**050000000**600**-**0505**600000 **(2649)**
2001: 12^{0}SD, 16^{5}SD, 13^{0}SD, 12^{5}SD, 12^{6}SW, 11^{0}GS, 8^{0}S, 8^{0}GF, 12^{0}GF, 11^{0}SD

	Starts	1st	2nd	3rd	Win & Pl
Career Total (Turf)	49	3	2	2	12794
Career Total (AW)	22	0	3	0	1757

48	10/99	Sand	1m2f7y	E(0-70)H	SFT	£2728
39	8/99	Brig	1m1f209y	F(0-60)H	G-S	£2864
	5/97	StCl	1m2f110y		HLD	£4489

Total win prize-money £10081

Going (Turf): Sf: 1-9 GS: 1-9 Gd: 0-9 GF: 0-14 Fm: 0-1
Distance: 5f/6f: 0-0 7f-8f: 0-13 **9f-13f: 2-49** 14f+: 0-2
Track : LH: 1-33 RH: 1-24 Tight: 0-39 Gall: 0-1
Aids: Bl: 0-21 Vi: 0-2 Tstrap: 0-0
Best Rating: 51 4/01 Kemp 1m soft

Moderate middle-distance handicapper. (DEAD)

Fanaar

110 **110**

4-y-o ch h Unfuwain (USA)-Catalonda (African Sky)
J Noseda Saleh Al Homeizi

Placings:1013-360 **(2258)**
2001: 9^{3}S, 8^{6}S, 8^{0}G

	Starts	1st	2nd	3rd	Win & Pl
Career Total (Turf)	7	2	0	2	19735

110	7/00	Sand	1m14y	C	GD	£6380
98	4/00	NmkR	1m	D	G-S	£6175

Total win prize-money £12555

Going (Turf): Sf: 0-2 **GS: 1-1 Gd: 1-3** GF: 0-1 Fm: 0-0
Distance: 5f/6f: 0-0 7f-8f: 1-3 9f-13f: 1-4 14f+: 0-0
Track : LH: 0-1 **RH: 1-3** Tight: 0-0 Gall: 0-2
Aids: Bl: 0-0 Vi: 0-0 Tstrap: 0-0
Best Rating: 110 4/01 NmkR 1m1f soft

Ran a race full of promise first time out, when third to Right Wing in the Earl Of Sefton Stakes at Newmarket, but has been highly-tried since. Listed company his more his level.

Fandango Dream (IRE)

94 **37**

5-y-o ch g Magical Wonder (USA)-Fandikos (IRE) (Taufan (USA))
M D I Usher Midweek Racing

Placings:0/004600400000/04504413550-05103 **(3556)**
2001: 12^{0}GF, 12^{5}GF, 12^{1}G, 12^{0}GF, 12^{3}GF

	Starts	1st	2nd	3rd	Win & Pl
Career Total (Turf)	29	2	0	2	9356

37	7/01	Epsm	1m4f10y	E(0-70)H	GD	£5050
31	7/00	Chep	1m4f23y	F(0-70)H	G-F	£2268

Total win prize-money £7319

Going (Turf): Sf: 0-4 GS: 0-5 **Gd: 1-4 GF: 1-14** Fm: 0-2
Distance: 5f/6f: 0-1 7f-8f: 0-3 **9f-13f: 2-21** 14f+: 0-4
Track : **LH: 2-14** RH: 0-9 **Tight: 1-10** Gall: 0-2
Aids: Bl: 0-1 Vi: 0-2 Tstrap: 0-0
Best Rating: 37 7/01 Epsm 1m4f10y good

Fair handicapper, stays 12 furlongs, suited by good or faster ground and waiting tactics. Both wins have been in July.

Fandanita (IRE)

91 **60**

2-y-o b f Anita's Prince-Fandangerina (USA) (Grey Dawn Ii)
N P Littmoden Joy And Valentine Feerick

Placings:302406 **(4092)**
2001: 5^{3}GF, 5^{0}G, 6^{2}F, 5^{4}S, 5^{0}G, 5^{6}G

	Starts	1st	2nd	3rd	Win & Pl

	Starts	1st	2nd	3rd	Win & Pl
Career Total (Turf)	6	0	1	1	1161

Going (Turf): Sf: 0-1 GS: 0-0 Gd: 0-3 GF: 0-1 Fm: 0-1
Distance: 5f/6f: 0-6 7f-8f: 0-0 9f-13f: 0-0 14f+: 0-0
Track : LH: 0-2 RH: 0-0 Tight: 0-0 Gall: 0-0
Aids: Bl: 0-0 Vi: 0-0 Tstrap: 0-0
Best Rating: 60 7/01 Rdcr 6f firm

Fangio's Quest

89 **86**

2-y-o ch c Piccolo-Periscope (Legend Of France (USA))
T D Easterby Roland Hope And Mervyn Sanderson

Placings:014 (5536)
2001: 5^{0}G, 6^{1}GS, 6^{4}S

	Starts	1st	2nd	3rd	Win & Pl
Career Total (Turf)	3	1	0	0	3031
86 10/01 Newc 6f D G-S					£3031
					Total win prize-money £3031

Going (Turf): Sf: 0-1 **GS: 1-1** Gd: 0-1 GF: 0-0 Fm: 0-0
Distance: **5f/6f: 1-3** 7f-8f: 0-0 9f-13f: 0-0 14f+: 0-0
Track : LH: 0-0 RH: 0-0 Tight: 0-0 Gall: 0-0
Aids: Bl: 0-0 Vi: 0-0 Tstrap: 0-0
Best Rating: 86 10/01 Newc 6f gd-sft

Stepped up on his debut to land a small race at Newcastle.

Fanny Bay (IRE)

99 **75**

2-y-o b f Key Of Luck (USA)-Disregard That (IRE) (Don't Forget Me)
Mrs P N Dutfield Colin Coxon

Placings:22 (1431)
2001: 5^{2}GS, 6^{2}S

	Starts	1st	2nd	3rd	Win & Pl
Career Total (Turf)	2	0	2	0	2176

Going (Turf): Sf: 0-1 GS: 0-1 Gd: 0-0 GF: 0-0 Fm: 0-0
Distance: 5f/6f: 0-1 7f-8f: 0-1 9f-13f: 0-0 14f+: 0-0
Track : LH: 0-1 RH: 0-0 Tight: 0-0 Gall: 0-1
Aids: Bl: 0-0 Vi: 0-0 Tstrap: 0-0
Best Rating: 75 5/01 Newb 6f8y soft

Fantastic Champion (IRE)

83 **44**

2-y-o b c Entrepreneur-Reine Mathilde (USA) (Vaguely Noble)
Sir Michael Stoute Saeed Suhail

Placings:5 (3473)
2001: 7^{5}GF

	Starts	1st	2nd	3rd	Win & Pl
Career Total (Turf)	1	0	0	0	0

Going (Turf): Sf: 0-0 GS: 0-0 Gd: 0-0 GF: 0-1 Fm: 0-0
Distance: 5f/6f: 0-0 7f-8f: 0-1 9f-13f: 0-0 14f+: 0-0
Track : LH: 0-0 RH: 0-0 Tight: 0-0 Gall: 0-0
Aids: Bl: 0-0 Vi: 0-0 Tstrap: 0-0
Best Rating: 44 7/01 NmkJ 7f gd-fm

Fantastic Light (USA)

124 **132**

5-y-o b h Rahy (USA)-Jood (USA) (Nijinsky (CAN))
Saeed Bin Suroor Godolphin

Placings:113/1423110/125214531-211211 (5579a)
2001: 12^{2}G, 10^{1}G, 10^{1}GF, 12^{2}GF, 10^{1}G, 12^{1}F

	Starts	1st	2nd	3rd	Win & Pl
Career Total (Turf)	25	12	5	3	4323304
127 10/01 Belm 1m4f					FRM£741867
132 9/01 Loop 1m2f					GD £476750
131 6/01 Asct 1m2f A					G-F £145000
120 5/01 Curr 1m2f110y					GD £124000
126 12/00 ShTn 1m2f					G-F £628930
120 9/00 Belm 1m3f					FRM£182927
125 3/00 Ndas 1m4f					GD £731707
125 9/99 Newb 1m3f5y A					G-S £28750
121 8/99 York 1m3f195yA					GD £57000
108 4/99 Sand 1m2f7y A					SFT £39870
93 8/98 Sand 1m14y C					G-F £4278
82 8/98 Sand 7f16y D					GD £4104
					Total win prize-money £3165185

Going (Turf): Sf: 1-2 GS: 1-3 **Gd: 5-7** GF: 3-8 Fm: 2-5
Distance: 5f/6f: 0-0 7f-8f: 1-2 **9f-13f: 11-23** 14f+: 0-0
Track : **LH: 6-11** RH: 4-11 Tight: 0-2 **Gall: 3-6**
Aids: Bl: 0-0 Vi: 0-0 **Tstrap: 3-4**
Best Rating: 132 9/01 Leop 1m2f good

High-class, globe-trotting horse, winner of the Thresher Classic Trial, Dubai Arc Trial and Great Voltigeur as a three-year-old, he improved throughout his career, winning the Sheema Classic in Dubai, the Man O'War at Belmont and the Hong Kong Cup at Sha Tin in 2000. Having run a close second in Dubai on his return, he had a fitness advantage when taking the Tattersalls Gold Cup in May and gave a superb display in the Prince of Wales's Stakes at Royal Ascot. He went down narrowly to Galileo in the King George, but exacted revenge over a shorter trip at Leopardstown and had the fast ground he loves when winning the Breeders' Cup Turf. Has won on soft, but was at his best when his hooves were rattling. He retires to Dalham Hall Stud as a sound, top-class international competitor.

Fantasy Adventurer

80(84) (23)**21**

4-y-o b g Magic Ring (IRE)-Delicious (Dominion)
J Cullinan (J J Quinn 21/7) The Fantasy Fellowship

Placings:040/00040400000-U000 (5617)
2001: 6^{U}G, 7^{0}SD, 6^{0}GF, 8^{0}SD

	Starts	1st	2nd	3rd	Win & Pl
Career Total (Turf)	15	0	0	0	905
Career Total (AW)	3	0	0	0	

Going (Turf): Sf: 0-1 GS: 0-2 Gd: 0-5 GF: 0-6 Fm: 0-1
Distance: 5f/6f: 0-9 7f-8f: 0-7 9f-13f: 0-2 14f+: 0-0
Track : LH: 0-4 RH: 0-3 Tight: 0-3 Gall: 0-1
Aids: Bl: 0-0 Vi: 0-1 Tstrap: 0-0
Best Rating: 16 11/01 Wolv 1m100y stand

Fantasy Believer

114 **94**

3-y-o b g Sure Blade (USA)-Delicious (Dominion)
J J Quinn The Fantasy Fellowship

Placings:3242216020-045U0142013150101 (5502)
2001: 6^{0}S, 6^{4}S, 6^{5}S, 6^{U}GF, 5^{0}G, 6^{1}GF, 6^{4}G, 6^{2}GF, 5^{0}S, 6^{1}GS, 6^{3}G, 6^{1}G, 6^{5}G, 6^{0}GF, 6^{1}G, 6^{0}GS, 5^{1}HY

	Starts	1st	2nd	3rd	Win & Pl
Career Total (Turf)	27	6	5	2	58158
94 10/01 Donc 5f B(0-100)H					HVY £10734
92 9/01 Asct 6f B(0-105)H					GD £21320
86 8/01 Ripn 6f D(0-80)H					GD £5349
79 7/01 Ling 6f D(0-80)H					G-S £4543
79 6/01 Kemp 6f D(0-85)H					G-F £4387
73 7/00 Muss 5f E					G-S £2808
					Total win prize-money £49145

Going (Turf): Sf: 1-7 **GS: 2-4 Gd: 2-8** GF: 1-8 Fm: 0-0
Distance: **5f/6f: 6-26** 7f-8f: 0-1 9f-13f: 0-0 14f+: 0-0
Track : LH: 0-0 RH: 0-2 Tight: 0-0 Gall: 0-2
Aids: Bl: 0-0 Vi: 0-0 Tstrap: 0-0
Best Rating: 94 10/01 Donc 5f heavy

An improving sprinter, he has scored four times over six furlongs so far this season and has a smart turn of foot. Should stay seven furlongs. Suited by anything from good to firm to soft.

Fantasy Crusader

99 **47**

2-y-o ch c Beveled (USA)-Cranfield Charger (Northern State (USA))
Mrs Lydia Pearce The Fantasy Fellowship

Placings:010600 (4882)
2001: 5^{0}F, 7^{1}F, 7^{0}GF, 7^{6}GS, 5^{0}G, 6^{0}GF

	Starts	1st	2nd	3rd	Win & Pl
Career Total (Turf)	6	1	0	0	3203
84 6/01 Ling 7f E FRM					£3202
					Total win prize-money £3203

Going (Turf): Sf: 0-0 GS: 0-1 Gd: 0-1 GF: 0-2 **Fm: 1-2**
Distance: 5f/6f: 0-2 **7f-8f: 1-4** 9f-13f: 0-0 14f+: 0-0
Track : LH: 0-1 RH: 0-1 Tight: 0-0 Gall: 0-0
Aids: Bl: 0-0 Vi: 0-0 Tstrap: 0-0
Best Rating: 84 6/01 Ling 7f firm

By Beveled, he has regressed since winning a Lingfield maiden auction in the summer on firm ground.

Fantasy Flight

75 **12**

7-y-o b m Forzando-Ryewater Dream (Touching Wood (USA))
N Tinkler Michael Ng

Placings:0/050/0000/00 (1965)
2001: 8^{0}GF, 7^{0}GF

	Starts	1st	2nd	3rd	Win & Pl
Career Total (Turf)	9	0	0	0	
Career Total (AW)	1	0	0	0	

Going (Turf): Sf: 0-1 GS: 0-0 Gd: 0-2 GF: 0-6 Fm: 0-0
Distance: 5f/6f: 0-2 7f-8f: 0-5 9f-13f: 0-3 14f+: 0-0
Track : LH: 0-6 RH: 0-3 Tight: 0-4 Gall: 0-2
Aids: Bl: 0-2 Vi: 0-0 Tstrap: 0-0
Best Rating: 12 6/01 Bevl 7f100y gd-fm

Fantasy Park

96 **75**

4-y-o b g Sanglamore (USA)-Fantasy Flyer (USA) (Lear Fan (USA))
G M McCourt Elizabeth Lewis & McCourt Fine Meats Ltd

Placings:1-400 (4721)
2001: 12^{4}GF, 15^{0}G, 12^{0}G

	Starts	1st	2nd	3rd	Win & Pl
Career Total (Turf)	4	1	0	0	4464
85 5/00 Bath 1m2f46y D G-S					£3945
					Total win prize-money £3946

Going (Turf): Sf: 0-0 **GS: 1-1** Gd: 0-2 GF: 0-1 Fm: 0-0
Distance: 5f/6f: 0-0 7f-8f: 0-0 **9f-13f: 1-3** 14f+: 0-1
Track : **LH: 1-3** RH: 0-1 **Tight: 1-3** Gall: 0-1
Aids: Bl: 0-0 Vi: 0-0 Tstrap: 0-0
Best Rating: 75 6/01 NmkR 1m4f gd-fm

Fantasy Ridge

105 **90**

3-y-o ch f Indian Ridge-Footlight Fantasy (USA) (Nureyev (USA))
M R Channon Helena Springfield Ltd

Placings:150-200003 (4383)
2001: 7^{2}GF, 8^{0}GF, 6^{0}G, 7^{0}GF, 8^{0}G, 8^{3}GF

	Starts	1st	2nd	3rd	Win & Pl
Career Total (Turf)	9	1	1	1	7496
85 8/00 Sals 6f212y D G-F					£3815
					Total win prize-money £3816

Going (Turf): Sf: 0-0 GS: 0-1 Gd: 0-3 **GF: 1-5** Fm: 0-0
Distance: 5f/6f: 0-1 **7f-8f: 1-8** 9f-13f: 0-0 14f+: 0-0
Track : LH: 0-0 RH: 0-3 Tight: 0-0 Gall: 0-1
Aids: Bl: 0-0 Vi: 0-0 Tstrap: 0-0
Best Rating: 93 8/01 Gdwd 7f gd-fm

She won by eight lengths on her racecourse debut at Salisbury last season, but her bubble has been well and truly burst in Pattern company since.

Far Lane (USA)

86 **77**

2-y-o b c Lear Fan (USA)-Pattimech (USA) (Nureyev (USA))
B W Hills K Abdulla

Placings:0 **(4708)**
2001: 6^{0}G

	Starts	1st	2nd	3rd	Win & Pl
Career Total (Turf)	1	0	0	0	

Going (Turf): Sf: 0-0 GS: 0-0 Gd: 0-1 GF: 0-0 Fm: 0-0
Distance: 5f/6f: 0-1 7f-8f: 0-0 9f-13f: 0-0 14f+: 0-0
Track : LH: 0-0 RH: 0-0 Tight: 0-0 Gall: 0-0
Aids: Bl: 0-0 Vi: 0-0 Tstrap: 0-0
Best Rating: 77 9/01 Donc 6f good

Far Note (USA)

101 **82**

3-y-o ch c Distant View (USA)-Descant (USA) (Nureyev (USA))
B W Hills K Abdulla

Placings:33222 **(5281)**
2001: 8^{3}S, 7^{3}G, 7^{2}GF, 8^{2}G, 7^{2}S

	Starts	1st	2nd	3rd	Win & Pl
Career Total (Turf)	5	0	3	2	5170

Going (Turf): Sf: 0-2 GS: 0-0 Gd: 0-2 GF: 0-1 Fm: 0-0
Distance: 5f/6f: 0-0 7f-8f: 0-4 9f-13f: 0-1 14f+: 0-0
Track : LH: 0-1 RH: 0-0 Tight: 0-0 Gall: 0-0
Aids: Bl: 0-0 Vi: 0-0 Tstrap: 0-0
Best Rating: 84 4/01 NmkR 1m soft

Regularly in the frame and deserves a change of luck.

Far Pavilions

85 **80t**

2-y-o b c Halling (USA)-Flambera (FR) (Akarad (FR))
M Johnston J David Abell

Placings:15 **(4088)**
2001: 6^{1}GF, 7^{5}S

	Starts	1st	2nd	3rd	Win & Pl
Career Total (Turf)	2	1	0	0	6988

80 7/01 Asct 6f D G-F £6711
Total win prize-money £6711

Going (Turf): Sf: 0-1 GS: 0-0 Gd: 0-0 **GF: 1-1** Fm: 0-0
Distance: **5f/6f: 1-1** 7f-8f: 0-1 9f-13f: 0-0 14f+: 0-0
Track : LH: 0-0 RH: 0-1 Tight: 0-0 Gall: 0-0
Aids: Bl: 0-0 Vi: 0-0 Tstrap: 0-0
Best Rating: 80 7/01 Asct 6f gd-fm

Rallied close home to land a newcomers' race at Ascot on his debut. His dam was a ten-furlong winner at three in France, and he looks to need seven already.

Far South Trader

93 **70**

3-y-o gr g Blushing Flame (USA)-Podrida (Persepolis (FR))
R J O'Sullivan Isle Of Wight Bloodstock And Racing

Placings:04-5 **(1565)**
2001: 11^{5}F

	Starts	1st	2nd	3rd	Win & Pl
Career Total (Turf)	3	0	0	0	222

Going (Turf): Sf: 0-2 GS: 0-0 Gd: 0-0 GF: 0-0 Fm: 0-1
Distance: 5f/6f: 0-1 7f-8f: 0-1 9f-13f: 0-1 14f+: 0-0
Track : LH: 0-2 RH: 0-0 Tight: 0-0 Gall: 0-0
Aids: Bl: 0-0 Vi: 0-0 Tstrap: 0-0
Best Rating: 54 5/01 Brig 1m3f196y firm

Faraude

93(73) (6)**50**

3-y-o b f Farfelu-Pennine Star (IRE) (Pennine Walk)
W R Muir John O'Mulloy

Placings:0400-0314234 **(4026)**
2001: 11^{0}SD, 8^{3}GF, 8^{1}GF, 8^{4}G, 8^{2}GF, 9^{3}G, 8^{4}GF

	Starts	1st	2nd	3rd	Win & Pl
Career Total (Turf)	9	1	1	2	4921
Career Total (AW)	2	0	0	0	

43 7/01 Chep 1m14y F G-F £2296
Total win prize-money £2296

Going (Turf): Sf: 0-3 GS: 0-0 Gd: 0-2 **GF: 1-4** Fm: 0-0
Distance: 5f/6f: 0-1 7f-8f: 0-3 **9f-13f: 1-7** 14f+: 0-0
Track : LH: 0-5 RH: 0-0 Tight: 0-0 Gall: 0-0
Aids: Bl: 0-0 Vi: 0-0 Tstrap: 0-0
Best Rating: 50 8/01 Newb 1m gd-fm

Faraway John (IRE)

97(85) (44)**58**

3-y-o b g Farhaan-Indiana Dancer (Hallgate)
G P Enright Neil Kenworthy

Placings:P60-42160 **(5081)**
2001: 11^{4}SW, 9^{2}GS, 11^{1}GS, 11^{6}GS, 9^{0}S

	Starts	1st	2nd	3rd	Win & Pl
Career Total (Turf)	5	1	1	0	3936
Career Total (AW)	3	0	0	0	0

58 4/01 Wind 1m3f135yE(0-70)H G-S £3080
Total win prize-money £3080

Going (Turf): Sf: 0-1 **GS: 1-3** Gd: 0-1 GF: 0-0 Fm: 0-0
Distance: 5f/6f: 0-1 7f-8f: 0-2 **9f-13f: 1-5** 14f+: 0-0
Track : LH: 0-5 RH: 0-0 **Tight: 1-4** Gall: 0-0
Aids: Bl: 0-0 Vi: 0-0 Tstrap: 0-0
Best Rating: 58 4/01 Wind 1m3f135y gd-sft

Faraway Look (USA)

107(100) (88+)**87**

4-y-o br g Distant View (USA)-Summer Trip (USA) (L'Emigrant (USA))
J R Fanshawe Cheveley Park Stud

Placings:42011-2000 **(5366)**
2001: 10^{2}G, 10^{0}GF, 10^{0}GF, 8^{0}GS

	Starts	1st	2nd	3rd	Win & Pl
Career Total (Turf)	7	0	2	0	3767
Career Total (AW)	2	2	0	0	5140

88 10/00 Wolv 1m1f79y E(0-75)H STD £2843
69 10/00 Wolv 1m1f79y F(0-65)H STD £2296
Total win prize-money £5140

Going (Turf): Sf: 0-1 GS: 0-1 Gd: 0-3 GF: 0-2 Fm: 0-0
Distance: 5f/6f: 0-0 7f-8f: 0-2 **9f-13f: 2-7** 14f+: 0-0
Track : **LH: 2-5** RH: 0-3 **Tight: 2-3** Gall: 0-1
Aids: Bl: 0-0 Vi: 0-0 Tstrap: 0-0
Best Rating: 87 6/01 Hayd 1m2f120y good

Made a promising return to action at Haydock in June. Not so good since but at least he is on a winning mark.

Farha (USA)

101 **81**

3-y-o b f Nureyev (USA)-Arutua (USA) (Riverman (USA))
B Hanbury Hamdan Al Maktoum

Placings:321-061 **(3945)**
2001: 5^{0}G, 7^{6}G, 6^{1}GF

	Starts	1st	2nd	3rd	Win & Pl
Career Total (Turf)	6	2	1	1	10780

83 8/01 Epsm 6f D(0-80)H G-F £4959
81 9/00 Nott 6f15y D G-S £3217
Total win prize-money £8178

Going (Turf): Sf: 0-0 **GS: 1-1** Gd: 0-2 **GF: 1-3** Fm: 0-0
Distance: 5f/6f: 1-4 7f-8f: 1-2 9f-13f: 0-0 14f+: 0-0
Track : **LH: 1-1** RH: 0-0 **Tight: 1-1** Gall: 0-0
Aids: Bl: 0-0 Vi: 0-0 Tstrap: 0-0
Best Rating: 83 8/01 Epsm 6f gd-fm

A well-bred filly out of a daughter of All Along. She won once as a juvenile, but had looked not to have trained on until winning at Epsom in August. Reportedly retired to stud after that victory.

Farqad (USA)

105 **103+**

2-y-o b c Danzig (USA)-Futuh (USA) (Diesis)
D R Loder Hamdan Al Maktoum

Placings:14 **(5104)**
2001: 6^{1}GF, 6^{4}GS

	Starts	1st	2nd	3rd	Win & Pl
Career Total (Turf)	2	1	0	0	13220

103 9/01 Newb 6f8y D G-F £5720
Total win prize-money £5720

Going (Turf): Sf: 0-0 GS: 0-1 Gd: 0-0 **GF: 1-1** Fm: 0-0
Distance: 5f/6f: 0-1 **7f-8f: 1-1** 9f-13f: 0-0 14f+: 0-0
Track : LH: 0-0 RH: 0-0 Tight: 0-0 Gall: 0-0
Aids: Bl: 0-0 Vi: 0-0 Tstrap: 0-0
Best Rating: 103 9/01 Newb 6f8y gd-fm

A half-brother to Hayil, he made a winning debut against a big field of maidens over six furlongs at Newbury in September and looks sure to go on to better things.

Farrier's Gamble

76 **40**

5-y-o ch m Belmez (USA)-Chrisanthy (So Blessed)
R M Flower D Leadbetter & J M Gamble

Placings:0/50050-0 **(1189)**
2001: 5^{0}GF

	Starts	1st	2nd	3rd	Win & Pl
Career Total (Turf)	7	0	0	0	0

Going (Turf): Sf: 0-1 GS: 0-1 Gd: 0-0 GF: 0-4 Fm: 0-1
Distance: 5f/6f: 0-3 7f-8f: 0-3 9f-13f: 0-1 14f+: 0-0
Track : LH: 0-1 RH: 0-1 Tight: 0-1 Gall: 0-0
Aids: Bl: 0-1 Vi: 0-0 Tstrap: 0-0
Best Rating: 103 9/01 Newb 6f8y gd-fm

Fas

68(88) (26)**25**

5-y-o ch g Weldnaas (USA)-Polly's Teahouse (Shack (USA))
J D Bethell F & T Walton

Placings:50600000/605040000004-00 **(1637)**
2001: 7^{0}S, 7^{0}F

	Starts	1st	2nd	3rd	Win & Pl
Career Total (Turf)	17	0	0	0	509
Career Total (AW)	5	0	0	0	0

Going (Turf): Sf: 0-2 GS: 0-1 Gd: 0-2 GF: 0-9 Fm: 0-3
Distance: 5f/6f: 0-6 7f-8f: 0-12 9f-13f: 0-4 14f+: 0-0
Track : LH: 0-10 RH: 0-4 Tight: 0-6 Gall: 0-0
Aids: Bl: 0-8 Vi: 0-6 Tstrap: 0-0
Best Rating: 2 5/01 Rdcr 7f firm

Fashionable Man (USA)

98 **86**

2-y-o ch c Unbridled (USA)-Too Chic (USA) (Blushing Groom (FR))
M Johnston Ali Saeed

Placings:4312 **(4827)**
2001: 7^{4}GF, 7^{3}G, 7^{1}GF, 8^{2}G

	Starts	1st	2nd	3rd	Win & Pl
Career Total (Turf)	4	1	1	1	6513

83 8/01 Newc 7f D G-F £3532
Total win prize-money £3533

Going (Turf): Sf: 0-0 GS: 0-0 Gd: 0-2 **GF: 1-2** Fm: 0-0
Distance: 5f/6f: 0-0 **7f-8f: 1-4** 9f-13f: 0-0 14f+: 0-0
Track : LH: 0-2 RH: 0-1 Tight: 0-0 Gall: 0-0
Aids: Bl: 0-0 Vi: 0-0 Tstrap: 0-0
Best Rating: 86 9/01 Ayr 1m good

Gradually improved with his racing and got off the mark with a last-gasp victory at Newcastle on his third start. He will be suited by a mile.

Fast And Furious (IRE)

(98) (54++)**74**

4-y-o b g Brief Truce (USA)-Zing Ping (IRE) (Thatching)
T Stack M A Begley

Placings:0263245300-14406134000 **(5074a)**
2001: 9^{1}SD, 10^{4}S, 10^{4}HY, 8^{0}GF, 9^{6}GF, 8^{1}G, 7^{3}GY, 8^{4}GY, 8^{0}G, 9^{0}G, 8^{0}GF

	Starts	1st	2nd	3rd	Win & Pl
Career Total (Turf)	20	1	2	3	11700
Career Total (AW)	1	1	0	0	2919

74 7/01 Klny 1m100y (0-75)H GD £5865
54 2/01 Wolv 1m1f79y D STD £2919
Total win prize-money £8784

Going (Turf): Sf: 0-5 GS: 0-0 **Gd: 1-6** GF: 0-4 Fm: 0-0
Distance: 5f/6f: 0-0 7f-8f: 0-12 **9f-13f: 2-9** 14f+: 0-0
Track : **LH: 1-6** RH: 0-5 **Tight: 1-1** Gall: 0-1
Aids: Bl: 0-0 Vi: 0-0 **Tstrap: 2-16**
Best Rating: 74 8/01 Cway 1m100y gd-yld

Fast As Luck

90(68) (12)**21**

3-y-o b g Pursuit Of Love-Dominio (IRE) (Dominion)
K McAuliffe The Dish Dash Partnership

Placings:0005000 **(4019)**
2001: 8^{0}SD, 8^{0}SD, 11^{0}GS, 9^{5}F, 10^{0}HD, 11^{0}SD, 12^{0}G

	Starts	1st	2nd	3rd	Win & Pl
Career Total (Turf)	4	0	0	0	0
Career Total (AW)	3	0	0	0	

Going (Turf): Sf: 0-0 GS: 0-1 Gd: 0-1 GF: 0-0 Fm: 0-2
Distance: 5f/6f: 0-0 7f-8f: 0-1 9f-13f: 0-6 14f+: 0-0
Track : LH: 0-6 RH: 0-1 Tight: 0-4 Gall: 0-1
Aids: Bl: 0-0 Vi: 0-0 Tstrap: 0-0
Best Rating: 46 6/01 Ling 1m1f firm

Fast Cindy (USA)

93 **67**

2-y-o b f Fastness (IRE)-Forever Cindy (ARG) (Forever Sparkle (USA))
P F I Cole Andy J Smith, Fields & Elliot

Placings:0004 **(5589)**
2001: 6^{0}GF, 6^{0}GF, 6^{0}GF, 7^{4}GS

	Starts	1st	2nd	3rd	Win & Pl
Career Total (Turf)	4	0	0	0	276

Going (Turf): Sf: 0-0 GS: 0-1 Gd: 0-0 GF: 0-3 Fm: 0-0
Distance: 5f/6f: 0-2 7f-8f: 0-2 9f-13f: 0-0 14f+: 0-0
Track : LH: 0-1 RH: 0-0 Tight: 0-0 Gall: 0-0
Aids: Bl: 0-0 Vi: 0-0 Tstrap: 0-0
Best Rating: 74 8/01 Newb 6f8y gd-fm

Fast Foil (IRE)

101 **64**

3-y-o b f Lahib (USA)-Fast Chick (Henbit (USA))
M R Channon The Savoyards

Placings:32630-6160550 **(4293)**
2001: 8^{6}S, 6^{1}GS, 8^{6}G, 11^{0}GF, 8^{5}GF, 7^{5}F, 10^{0}GF

	Starts	1st	2nd	3rd	Win & Pl
Career Total (Turf)	12	1	1	2	6573

76 5/01 Brig 6f209y D(0-75) G-S £3903
Total win prize-money £3903

Going (Turf): Sf: 0-2 **GS: 1-1** Gd: 0-2 GF: 0-5 Fm: 0-2
Distance: 5f/6f: 0-4 **7f-8f: 1-6** 9f-13f: 0-2 14f+: 0-0
Track : **LH: 1-5** RH: 0-2 Tight: 0-2 Gall: 0-2
Aids: Bl: 0-0 Vi: 0-0 Tstrap: 0-0
Best Rating: 76 5/01 Brig 6f209y gd-sft

She won over seven furlongs at Brighton in May but is bred to get further. Suited by some give in the ground.

Fast Fortune

91(84) (23)**38**

3-y-o ch f Forzando-High Cut (Dashing Blade)
M Quinn M Quinn

Placings:006-40060600 **(3063)**
2001: 10^{4}SD, 8^{0}SD, 10^{0}SD, 7^{6}SD, 8^{0}F, 6^{6}SD, 9^{0}SD, 5^{0}G

	Starts	1st	2nd	3rd	Win & Pl
Career Total (Turf)	3	0	0	0	
Career Total (AW)	8	0	0	0	0

Going (Turf): Sf: 0-1 GS: 0-0 Gd: 0-1 GF: 0-0 Fm: 0-1
Distance: 5f/6f: 0-4 7f-8f: 0-3 9f-13f: 0-4 14f+: 0-0
Track : LH: 0-9 RH: 0-0 Tight: 0-7 Gall: 0-1
Aids: Bl: 0-0 Vi: 0-0 Tstrap: 0-0
Best Rating: 34 7/01 Bath 5f161y good

Fast Forward Fred

103 **54**

10-y-o gr g Sharrood (USA)-Sun Street (Ile De Bourbon (USA))
L Montague Hall Freddie And The Dreamers

Placings:05/000/20055/5212110/0/003524-4 **(3481)**
2001: 15^{4}GF

	Starts	1st	2nd	3rd	Win & Pl
Career Total (Turf)	24	3	4	1	13655
Career Total (AW)	1	0	0	0	0

57 8/98 Sand 2m78y E(0-70)H G-F £3696
52 8/98 Bath 2m1f34y D(0-75)H FRM £3452
49 7/98 Chep 2m2f F(0-65)H GD £2549
Total win prize-money £9698

Going (Turf): Sf: 0-0 GS: 0-2 **Gd: 1-7 GF: 1-11 Fm: 1-3**
Distance: 5f/6f: 0-0 7f-8f: 0-0 9f-13f: 0-6 **14f+: 3-18**
Track : **LH: 2-10** **RH: 1-14** **Tight: 1-13** Gall: 0-0
Aids: Bl: 0-0 Vi: 0-0 Tstrap: 0-0
Best Rating: 43 7/01 Folk 1m7f92y gd-fm

Fast Track (IRE)

109 **65**

4-y-o b/br c Doyoun-Manntika (Kalamoun)
G M McCourt Mccourt Fine Meats,D J Rushen,E Lewis

Placings:1/36-002400 **(5465)**
2001: 8^{0}GS, 10^{0}G, 8^{2}F, 7^{4}GF, 8^{0}GF, 10^{0}G

	Starts	1st	2nd	3rd	Win & Pl
Career Total (Turf)	9	1	1	1	8386

87 10/99 Yarm 7f3y D G-S £3330
Total win prize-money £3330

Going (Turf): Sf: 0-0 **GS: 1-2** Gd: 0-2 GF: 0-3 Fm: 0-2
Distance: 5f/6f: 0 0 **7f-8f: 1-4** 9f-13f: 0-5 14f+: 0-0
Track : LH: 0-3 RH: 0-2 Tight: 0-1 Gall: 0-1
Aids: Bl: 0-0 Vi: 0-0 Tstrap: 0-0
Best Rating: 65 6/01 Gdwd 7f gd-fm

Fastina (DEN)

106 **71**

3-y-o b f Dunphy-Farandole (DEN) (Gay Baron)
R Guest Bo Ejler Rasmussen & Jan Hansen

Placings:430345-0301002 **(5524)**
2001: 8^{0}GS, 9^{3}GF, 9^{0}GF, 10^{1}GF, 10^{0}GF, 10^{0}S, 10^{2}HY

	Starts	1st	2nd	3rd	Win & Pl
Career Total (Turf)	13	1	1	3	7445

71 7/01 Wind 1m2f7y D(0-80)H G-F £4504
Total win prize-money £4505

Going (Turf): Sf: 0-2 GS: 0-3 Gd: 0-0 **GF: 1-7** Fm: 0-1
Distance: 5f/6f: 0-1 7f-8f: 0-3 **9f-13f: 1-9** 14f+: 0-0
Track : LH: 0-3 RH: 0-4 **Tight: 1-5** Gall: 0-1
Aids: Bl: 0-0 Vi: 0-0 Tstrap: 0-0
Best Rating: 72 5/01 Bevl 1m1f207y gd-fm

She won at Windsor in July over ten furlongs, on good to firm, but was well held after that until going close back at Windsor in October.

Fastrack Time

94(98) (39)**41**

4-y-o ch g Clantime-Bitch (Risk Me (FR))
S Mellor S P Tindall

Placings:00000/000000-042000 **(1086)**
2001: 8^{0}SD, 6^{4}SD, 6^{2}SW, 6^{0}SD, 5^{0}SD, 6^{0}SD

	Starts	1st	2nd	3rd	Win & Pl
Career Total (Turf)	10	0	0	0	
Career Total (AW)	7	0	1	0	630

Going (Turf): Sf: 0-1 GS: 0-0 Gd: 0-4 GF: 0-5 Fm: 0-0
Distance: 5f/6f: 0-13 7f-8f: 0-4 9f-13f: 0-0 14f+: 0-0
Track : LH: 0-8 RH: 0-0 Tight: 0-5 Gall: 0-1
Aids: Bl: 0-0 Vi: 0-1 Tstrap: 0-0
Best Rating: 39 2/01 Ling 6f slow

Fatehalkhair (IRE)

98(95) (50)**65**

9-y-o ch g Kris-Midway Lady (USA) (Alleged (USA))
B Ellison R Wagner

Placings:400/002500/053/42/21013124130/40231504-530 **(5640)**
2001: 11^{5}SD, 11^{3}GF, 13^{0}G

	Starts	1st	2nd	3rd	Win & Pl
Career Total (Turf)	30	5	3	5	32840
Career Total (AW)	6	0	2	0	1739

68 6/00 Thsk 1m4f D(0-80)H FRM £3971
61 9/99 Thsk 1m4f D(0-85)H FRM £7327
52 6/99 Catt 1m3f214yE(0-75)H G-F £3571
47 6/99 Catt 1m3f214yE(0-70)H GD £4354
42 4/99 Rdcr 1m3f E(0-70)H G-S £3611
Total win prize-money £22837

Going (Turf): Sf: 0-1 GS: 1-4 Gd: 1-9 GF: 1-12 **Fm: 2-4**
Distance: 5f/6f: 0-0 7f-8f: 0-5 **9f-13f: 5-28** 14f+: 0-3
Track : **LH: 5-27** RH: 0-8 **Tight: 5-21** Gall: 0-7
Aids: Bl: 0-0 Vi: 0 1 Tstrap: 0-0
Best Rating: 65 9/01 Catt 1m3f214y gd-fm

An useful hurdler and chaser, he has ability on the Flat too and ran well on his two turf starts this term at Catterick. He has sometimes not appeared to relish being put under pressure. Must have a left-handed track

Fath (USA)

114 **114**

4-y-o b h Danzig (USA)-Desirable (Lord Gayle (USA))
M P Tregoning Hamdan Al Maktoum

Placings:12/0614-255201102 **(5386)**
2001: 6^{2}GS, 5^{5}G, 5^{5}GF, 7^{2}GF, 6^{0}GF, 7^{1}GF, 7^{1}G, 8^{0}G, 7^{2}GS

	Starts	1st	2nd	3rd	Win & Pl
Career Total (Turf)	15	4	4	0	121946

Rating	Date	Course	Dist	Class	Going	Prize
112	8/01	Gdwd	7f	A	GD	£30000
101	7/01	Ches	7f2y	B	G-F	£9613
105	8/00	Donc	6f	C	G-F	£7540
96	8/99	York	6f	D	GD	£14490

Total win prize-money £61643

Going (Turf): Sf: 0-0 GS: 0-3 **Gd: 2-5 GF: 2-7** Fm: 0-0
Distance: 5f/6f: 2-8 7f-8f: 2-7 9f-13f: 0-0 14f+: 0-0
Track : LH: 1-3 RH: 1-1 **Tight: 1-1** Gall: 0-1
Aids: Bl: 0-0 Vi: 0-0 **Tstrap: 1-2**
Best Rating: 114 10/01 NmkR 7f gd-sft

He has gone from Marcus Tregoning to Godolphin and back again in his short career. He initially failed to come up to expectations and was held in Group company, but comfortably won a conditions event at Chester in July and followed up with a fine win in a Group Three at Glorious Goodwood. Something seemed amiss when he was well held at Doncaster, but he ran well in a Newmarket Group Two. Seven furlongs is his best trip now.

Father Juninho (IRE)

109 **96**

4-y-o b g Distinctly North (USA)-Shane's Girl (IRE) (Marktingo)
A P Jarvis Haleray Ltd

Placings:0021012/06523354045-010400 **(3600)**
2001: 12^{0}S, 11^{1}F, 14^{0}GF, 12^{4}GF, 12^{0}G, 12^{0}G

	Starts	1st	2nd	3rd	Win & Pl
Career Total (Turf)	24	3	3	2	41585

Rating	Date	Course	Dist	Class	Going	Prize
93	5/01	York	1m3f195yC(0-95)H		FRM	£11310
84	9/99	Donc	7f	D(0-85)H	G-F	£4455
84	7/99	Rdcr	7f	D H	FRM	£5182

Total win prize-money £20948

Going (Turf): Sf: 0-2 GS: 0-2 Gd: 0-8 GF: 1-10 **Fm: 2-2**
Distance: 5f/6f: 0-1 **7f-8f: 2-4** 9f-13f: 1-17 14f+: 0-2
Track : **LH: 1-8** RH: 0-11 Tight: 0-8 **Gall: 1-10**
Aids: Bl: 0-0 Vi: 0-1 Tstrap: 0-0
Best Rating: 96 6/01 Epsm 1m4f10y gd-fm

Progressed throughout his juvenile season and continued to run well in 2000, but found it hard to put his head in front. Showed a good turn of foot when scoring in a York handicap in 2001, but was unlucky in running when fourth in an Epsom handicap on Derby Day. Best over a mile and a half and suited by fast ground, but did not seem suited by a visor. His style of running invites trouble.

Father Seamus

85(79) (17)**21**

3-y-o b g Bin Ajwaad (IRE)-Merry Rous (Rousillon (USA))
P Butler P Butler

Placings:00030000-0000665000 **(5470)**
2001: 7^{0}GS, 6^{0}GS, 6^{0}GS, 7^{0}GS, 8^{6}GF, 8^{6}GS, 11^{5}F, 11^{0}S, 11^{0}HY, 7^{0}S

	Starts	1st	2nd	3rd	Win & Pl
Career Total (Turf)	18	0	0	1	478
Career Total (AW)	1	0	0	0	

Going (Turf): Sf: 0-6 GS: 0-6 Gd: 0-2 **GF: 0-3 Fm: 0-1**
Distance: 5f/6f: 0-3 7f-8f: 0-12 9f-13f: 0-4 14f+: 0-0
Track : LH: 0-7 RH: 0-4 Tight: 0-3 Gall: 0-1
Aids: Bl: 0-0 Vi: 0-0 Tstrap: 0-0
Best Rating: 54 5/01 Ling 7f140y gd-sft

Father Thames

108 **109**

3-y-o b c Bishop Of Cashel-Mistress Thames (Sharpo)
J R Fanshawe Mrs Denis Haynes

Placings:31-20140 **(5386)**
2001: 7^{2}G, 7^{0}G, 7^{1}G, 8^{4}GS, 7^{0}GS

	Starts	1st	2nd	3rd	Win & Pl
Career Total (Turf)	7	2	1	1	17363

Rating	Date	Course	Dist	Class	Going	Prize
107	9/01	Gdwd	7f	B(0-105)H	GD	£9465
88	10/00	Brig	6f209y	E	SFT	£3157

Total win prize-money £12623

Going (Turf): Sf: 1-2 GS: 0-2 **Gd: 1-3** GF: 0-0 Fm: 0-0
Distance: 5f/6f: 0-1 **7f-8f: 2-6** 9f-13f: 0-0 14f+: 0-0
Track : LH: 1-2 RH: 1-1 Tight: 0-0 Gall: 0-1
Aids: Bl: 0-0 Vi: 0-0 Tstrap: 0-0
Best Rating: 109 5/01 NmkR 7f good

Lightly-raced winner of a soft ground maiden at Brighton as a juvenile, he showed plenty of promise when chasing home Shibboleth on his debut in 2001. Reappeared three months later at York, running a race full of promise, and made no mistake at Goodwood in September. Decent effort in Listed company next time. Possibly unsuited by fast ground.

Fathers Footsteps

90(54) **28**

3-y-o ch g Clantime-Cousin Jenny (Midyan (USA))
C Smith A E Needham

Placings:00000-05000 **(4610)**
2001: 5^{0}F, 5^{5}F, 5^{0}F, 5^{0}GF, 5^{0}F

	Starts	1st	2nd	3rd	Win & Pl
Career Total (Turf)	9	0	0	0	0
Career Total (AW)	1	0	0	0	

Going (Turf): Sf: 0-2 GS: 0-0 Gd: 0-0 GF: 0-3 Fm: 0-4
Distance: 5f/6f: 0-10 7f-8f: 0-0 9f-13f: 0-0 14f+: 0-0
Track : LH: 0-3 RH: 0-0 Tight: 0-0 Gall: 0-1
Aids: Bl: 0-1 Vi: 0-0 Tstrap: 0-0
Best Rating: 34 7/01 Muss 5f firm

Fatwa (IRE)

109 **97**

3-y-o ch f Lahib (USA)-Mayaasa (USA) (Lyphard (USA))
B Hanbury Hamdan Al Maktoum

Placings:126 **(1300)**
2001: 6^{1}HY, 7^{2}GS, 7^{6}G

	Starts	1st	2nd	3rd	Win & Pl
Career Total (Turf)	3	1	1	0	12933

Rating	Date	Course	Dist	Class	Going	Prize
81	4/01	Pont	6f	D	HVY	£3753

Total win prize-money £3754

Going (Turf): Sf: 1-1 GS: 0-1 Gd: 0-1 GF: 0-0 Fm: 0-0
Distance: **5f/6f: 1-1** 7f-8f: 0-2 9f-13f: 0-0 14f+: 0-0
Track : **LH: 1-1** RH: 0-0 Tight: 0-0 Gall: 0-0
Aids: Bl: 0-0 Vi: 0-0 Tstrap: 0-0
Best Rating: 97 4/01 Newb 7f gd-sft

Unraced as a juvenile, she ran away with a Pontefract maiden on heavy ground on her debut and finished a good second on similar ground in the Fred Darling. She did not look so well suited by the faster ground in a Lingfield Listed event on her third start.

Faute De Mieux

97(89) (45)**68**

6-y-o ch g Beveled (USA)-Supreme Rose (Frimley Park)
M Kettle Dagfell Properties Limited

Placings:522006/40102200000/60103320-00500 **(2799)**
2001: 5^{0}S, 5^{0}GS, 5^{5}GF, 6^{0}GF, 5^{0}GF

Starts 1st 2nd 3rd Win & Pl

	Starts	1st	2nd	3rd	Win & Pl
Career Total (Turf)	28	2	5	2	15027
Career Total (AW)	2	0	0	0	0

Rating	Date	Course	Dist	Class	Going	Prize
71	4/00	Folk	5f	E(0-70)	SFT	£2817
71	6/99	Wind	5f10y	E(0-70)	SFT	£2626

Total win prize-money £5444

Going (Turf): Sf: 2-6 GS: 0-3 Gd: 0-8 GF: 0-10 Fm: 0-1
Distance: **5f/6f: 2-29** 7f-8f: 0-1 9f-13f: 0-0 14f+: 0-0
Track : LH: 0-5 **RH: 1-4** Tight: 0-1 **Gall: 1-7**
Aids: Bl: 0-1 Vi: 0-0 Tstrap: 0-2
Best Rating: 68 6/01 Wind 5f10y gd-fm

Favorisio

102(103) (68)**60**

4-y-o br g Efisio-Dixie Favor (USA) (Dixieland Band (USA))
Miss J A Camacho Elite Racing Club

Placings:00/11600000-0554130 **(5152)**
2001: 8^{0}SD, 11^{5}SW, 11^{5}SD, 12^{4}SD, 11^{1}G, 14^{3}GF, 14^{0}G

	Starts	1st	2nd	3rd	Win & Pl
Career Total (Turf)	9	1	0	1	3180
Career Total (AW)	8	2	0	0	5894

Rating	Date	Course	Dist	Class	Going	Prize
55	8/01	Bevl	1m3f216yF(0-60)		GD	£2394
77	3/00	Wolv	1m1f79y	E(0-75)H	STD	£2782
74	2/00	Wolv	1m1f79y	D	STD	£2795

Total win prize-money £7971

Going (Turf): Sf: 0-3 GS: 0-0 **Gd: 1-4** GF: 0-2 Fm: 0-0
Distance: 5f/6f: 0-2 7f-8f: 0-3 **9f-13f: 3-10** 14f+: 0-2
Track : **LH: 2-13** RH: 1-1 **Tight: 3-5** Gall: 0-2
Aids: Bl: 0-0 **Vi: 1-3** Tstrap: 0-0
Best Rating: 67 6/01 Sthl 1m4f stand

His first two wins came on Fibresand at the start of last year, but did not win on turf until landing a Beverley classified event in August of this year. Twelve furlongs looks his best trip now.

Fax To Sooty

92 **68**

2-y-o b g Factual (USA)-Saltina (Bustino)
J S Moore A D Crook

Placings:64600330 **(4374)**
2001: 6^{6}F, 6^{4}G, 6^{6}GF, 6^{0}GF, 5^{0}GS, 6^{3}GF, 6^{3}GF, 7^{0}GF

	Starts	1st	2nd	3rd	Win & Pl
Career Total (Turf)	8	0	0	2	705

Going (Turf): Sf: 0-0 GS: 0-1 Gd: 0-1 GF: 0-5 Fm: 0-1
Distance: 5f/6f: 0-4 7f-8f: 0-4 9f-13f: 0-0 14f+: 0-0
Track : LH: 0-1 RH: 0-0 Tight: 0-0 Gall: 0-0
Aids: Bl: 0-1 Vi: 0-1 Tstrap: 0-0
Best Rating: 70 5/01 Yarm 6f3y good

Faydah (USA)

94 **82**

2-y-o b f Bahri (USA)-Lady Cutlass (USA) (Cutlass (USA))
J L Dunlop Hamdan Al Maktoum

Placings:05 **(5602)**
2001: 7^{0}G, 7^{5}GS

	Starts	1st	2nd	3rd	Win & Pl
Career Total (Turf)	2	0	0	0	

Going (Turf): Sf: 0-0 GS: 0-1 Gd: 0-1 GF: 0-0 Fm: 0-0
Distance: 5f/6f: 0-0 7f-8f: 0-2 9f-13f: 0-0 14f+: 0-0
Track : LH: 0-0 RH: 0-1 Tight: 0-0 Gall: 0-1
Aids: Bl: 0-0 Vi: 0-0 Tstrap: 0-0
Best Rating: 82 11/01 NmkR 7f gd-sft

Faye Ellen

90(87) (51)**72**

2-y-o ch f Elmaamul (USA)-Iradah (USA) (Topsider

(USA))
D J Coakley I E And Mrs K E D'Arcy

Placings:32040 **(5364)**
2001: 5^{3}SD, 6^{2}GF, 5^{0}F, 6^{4}G, 6^{0}GS

	Starts	1st	2nd	3rd	Win & Pl
Career Total (Turf)	4	0	1	0	1128
Career Total (AW)	1	0	0	1	417

Going (Turf): **Sf: 0-0 GS: 0-1 Gd: 0-1 GF: 0-1 Fm: 0-1**
Distance: 5f/6f: 0-5 7f-8f: 0-1 9f-13f: 0-0 14f+: 0-0
Track : LH: 0-1 RH: 0-0 Tight: 0-0 Gall: 0-1
Aids: Bl: 0-0 Vi: 0-0 Tstrap: 0-0
Best Rating: 72 7/01 Ling 6f gd-fm

Has shown ability in a handful of starts. Best effort over six at Lingfield on her second start.

Faymist (IRE)

90 **70d**
2-y-o ch g Fayruz-Grave Error (Northern Treat (USA))
J L Eyre Billy Parker

Placings:4050 **(4538)**
2001: 5^{4}GF, 6^{0}G, 5^{5}GF, 7^{0}GF

	Starts	1st	2nd	3rd	Win & Pl
Career Total (Turf)	4	0	0	0	309

Going (Turf): Sf: 0-0 GS: 0-0 Gd: 0-1 GF: 0-3 Fm: 0-0
Distance: 5f/6f: 0-3 7f-8f: 0-1 9f-13f: 0-0 14f+: 0-0
Track : LH: 0-0 RH: 0-0 Tight: 0-0 Gall: 0-0
Aids: Bl: 0-0 Vi: 0-0 Tstrap: 0-2
Best Rating: 70 7/01 Bevl 5f gd-fm

Fayr Jag (IRE)

94 **70**
2-y-o b c Fayruz-Lominda (IRE) (Lomond (USA))
T D Easterby T E F Freight (scarborough) Ltd

Placings:21206 **(5378)**
2001: 5^{2}GS, 5^{1}F, 6^{2}G, 6^{0}GF, 5^{6}S

	Starts	1st	2nd	3rd	Win & Pl
Career Total (Turf)	5	1	2	0	7651

67 8/01 Thsk 5f D FRM £4400
Total win prize-money £4401

Going (Turf): Sf: 0-1 GS: 0-1 Gd: 0-1 GF: 0-1 **Fm: 1-1**
Distance: 5f/6f: 1-4 7f-8f: 0-1 9f-13f: 0-0 14f+: 0-0
Track : LH: 0-1 RH: 0-0 Tight: 0-1 Gall: 0-0
Aids: Bl: 0-0 Vi: 0-0 Tstrap: 0-0
Best Rating: 70 9/01 Donc 6f gd-fm

He shaped well on debut, but was absent for three months with a blood disorder before making a winning reappearance at Thirsk in August. Beaten by a useful sort on his third start. Acts on firm ground.

Fazenda

38(87) (42)
3-y-o b f Piccolo-Petra's Star (Rock City)
K McAuliffe Miss J Hall

Placings:0-0 **(4896)**
2001: 9^{0}GS

	Starts	1st	2nd	3rd	Win & Pl
Career Total (Turf)	1	0	0	0	
Career Total (AW)	1	0	0	0	

Going (Turf): Sf: 0-0 GS: 0-1 Gd: 0-0 GF: 0-0 Fm: 0-0
Distance: 5f/6f: 0-1 7f-8f: 0-0 9f-13f: 0-1 14f+: 0-0
Track : LH: 0-1 RH: 0-1 Tight: 0-1 Gall: 0-0
Aids: Bl: 0-0 Vi: 0-0 Tstrap: 0-0

Fazzani (IRE)

98(91) (40)**56**
3-y-o b f Shareef Dancer (USA)-Taj Victory (Final Straw)
M W Easterby Chris Brasher

Placings:044430121220-00000000 **(5394)**
2001: 8^{0}S, 10^{0}GS, 11^{0}GF, 8^{0}GF, 8^{0}GF, 8^{0}GF, 10^{0}G, 12^{0}SD

	Starts	1st	2nd	3rd	Win & Pl
Career Total (Turf)	19	2	3	1	12744
Career Total (AW)	1	0	0	0	

66 8/00 Newc 1m E SFT £2744
58 8/00 Thsk 7f E GD £2388
Total win prize-money £5133

Going (Turf): Sf: 1-6 GS: 0-2 **Gd: 1-3** GF: 0-7 Fm: 0-1
Distance: 5f/6f: 0-3 **7f-8f: 2-13** 9f-13f: 0-4 14f+: 0-0
Track : LH: 2-8 RH: 0-5 Tight: 1-6 Gall: 1-4
Aids: Bl: 0-2 Vi: 0-0 Tstrap: 0-0
Best Rating: 56 5/01 Pont 1m2f6y gd-sft

A winner twice in August last season at seven furlongs and a mile, she has shown little this term and looks to need the ground on the soft side.

Fearby Cross (IRE)

108 **79**
5-y-o b g Unblest-Two Magpies (Doulab (USA))
W J Musson Mrs Rita Brown

Placings:3105/00400006/134100000-400023106 **(5138)**
2001: 6^{4}S, 6^{0}G, 6^{0}G, 6^{0}GS, 6^{2}G, 6^{3}GF, 5^{1}GS, 5^{0}G, 6^{6}G

	Starts	1st	2nd	3rd	Win & Pl
Career Total (Turf)	30	4	1	3	29240

79 9/01 Donc 5f D(0-80)H G-S £6500
79 5/00 Newb 6f8y D(0-80)H G-S £7832
76 3/00 Sand 5f6y D(0-80)H G-F £4309
91 9/98 Ayr 6f E G-S £3824
Total win prize-money £22468

Going (Turf): Sf: 0-6 **GS: 3-10** Gd: 0-11 GF: 1-2 Fm: 0-1
Distance: 5f/6f: 3-25 7f-8f: 1-5 9f-13f: 0-0 14f+: 0-0
Track : LH: 0-3 RH: 0-2 Tight: 0-0 Gall: 0-2
Aids: Bl: 0-1 Vi: 0-0 Tstrap: 0-0
Best Rating: 79 9/01 Donc 5f gd-sft

Winner over five furlongs at Doncaster in September, he is also effective over six. Acts on fast ground, but best on as easy surface, although he has never won on ground worse than good to soft. Needs to be held up and produced with a late run.

Feast Of Romance

90(108) (75)**55**
4-y-o b g Pursuit Of Love-June Fayre (Sagaro)
N P Littmoden K & W Racing Partnership

Placings:00513/16560603004000-02441160500 **(1544)**
2001: 7^{0}SW, 6^{2}SD, 6^{4}SW, 6^{4}SD, 6^{1}SD, 6^{1}SD, 7^{6}SD, 6^{0}SD, 5^{5}SD, 6^{0}GF, 5^{0}GF

	Starts	1st	2nd	3rd	Win & Pl
Career Total (Turf)	15	0	0	1	1160
Career Total (AW)	15	4	1	1	15478

75 3/01 Wolv 6f E(0-70) STD £2415
72 3/01 Wolv 6f D(0-80)H STD £3181
75 1/00 Wolv 6f C(0-90)H STD £6662
74 11/99 Sthl 6f F STD £2253
Total win prize-money £14513

Going (Turf): Sf: 0-4 GS: 0-0 Gd: 0-3 GF: 0-7 Fm: 0-1
Distance: 5f/6f: 4-21 7f-8f: 0-9 9f-13f: 0-0 14f+: 0-0
Track : LH: 4-17 RH: 0-2 **Tight: 3-11** Gall: 0-2
Aids: Bl: 0-3 Vi: 0-0 Tstrap: 0-0
Best Rating: 75 3/01 Wolv 6f stand

Feathers Flying (IRE)

101 **88?**
2-y-o b f Royal Applause-Dancing Feather (Suave Dancer (USA))
D J S Cosgrove Keith Wills

Placings:144606 **(5606)**
2001: 7^{1}F, 7^{4}GF, 7^{4}G, 8^{6}G, 7^{0}GS, 10^{6}GS

	Starts	1st	2nd	3rd	Win & Pl
Career Total (Turf)	6	1	0	0	5637

79 6/01 Ling 7f E FRM £3202
Total win prize-money £3203

Going (Turf): Sf: 0-0 GS: 0-2 Gd: 0-2 GF: 0-1 **Fm: 1-1**
Distance: 5f/6f: 0-0 **7f-8f: 1-5** 9f-13f: 0-1 14f+: 0-0
Track : LH: 0-1 RH: 0-1 Tight: 0-0 Gall: 0-1
Aids: Bl: 0-0 Vi: 0-0 Tstrap: 0-0
Best Rating: 88 9/01 Donc 1m good

Comfortable winner from a favourable draw on her debut, she has run creditably in Pattern company since. Suited by fast ground.

Featherstone Lane

84(104) (44)**35**
10-y-o b g Siberian Express (USA)-Try Gloria (Try My Best (USA))
Miss L C Siddall Miss L C Siddall

Placings:3/33212056034644000506030300/0033662042002423501423006 4/23212331541100305 60/0605600632060460450/44252223163363435020 6456-340000 **(4033)**
2001: 7^{3}SD, 7^{4}SD, 6^{0}SD, 6^{0}SD, 7^{0}GF, 6^{0}G

	Starts	1st	2nd	3rd	Win & Pl
Career Total (Turf)	62	1	4	7	12118
Career Total (AW)	100	7	18	20	36343

52 5/00 Wolv 7f E(0-70)H STD £2785
67 4/98 Wolv 5f F STD £2206
65 4/98 Wolv 5f F STD £1952
60 3/98 Wolv 5f G STD £1855
51 1/98 Wolv 5f E(0-70)H STD £2710
44 8/97 Wolv 5f G STD £1984
65 2/96 Wolv 5f D(0-80)H STD £3517
72 8/93 Newc 5f G G-F £2490
Total win prize-money £19503

Going (Turf): Sf: 0-0 GS: 0-5 Gd: 0-17 **GF: 1-30** Fm: 0-10
Distance: 5f/6f: 7-150 7f-8f: 1-12 9f-13f: 0-0 14f+: 0-0
Track : LH: 7-98 RH: 0-6 **Tight: 7-79** Gall: 0-6
Aids: Bl: 0-0 **Vi: 1-65** Tstrap: 0-0
Best Rating: 42 6/01 Sthl 7f stand

Feathertime

98 (27)**50**
5-y-o b m Puissance-Midnight Owl (FR) (Ardross)
Mrs G S Rees Mrs G S Rees

Placings:0/50036414/533-4030 **(5632)**
2001: 10^{4}S, 12^{0}GS, 10^{3}S, 10^{0}G

	Starts	1st	2nd	3rd	Win & Pl
Career Total (Turf)	14	1	0	4	5034
Career Total (AW)	2	0	0	0	

52 10/99 Newc 1m F(0-60)H G-S £2410
Total win prize-money £2411

Going (Turf): Sf: 0-3 **GS: 1-5** Gd: 0-3 GF: 0-3 Fm: 0-0
Distance: 5f/6f: 0-2 **7f-8f: 1-5** 9f-13f: 0-9 14f+: 0-0
Track : LH: 1-13 RH: 0-2 Tight: 0-6 **Gall: 1-3**
Aids: Bl: 0-0 Vi: 0-0 Tstrap: 0-0
Best Rating: 50 10/01 Pont 1m2f6y soft

February Mountain (IRE)

91(87) (47)**24**
4-y-o b f Symboli Heights (FR)-Mountain Sue (Lyphard's Special (USA))
B A McMahon M O'Toole

Placings:00/53640043-640000 **(0876)**
2001: 9^{6}SD, 12^{4}SW, 12^{0}SD, 12^{0}GS, 14^{0}S, 14^{0}S

	Starts	1st	2nd	3rd	Win & Pl

	Starts	1st	2nd	3rd	Win & Pl
Career Total (Turf)	13	0	0	2	1450
Career Total (AW)	3	0	0	0	0

Going (Turf): Sf: 0-5 GS: 0-1 Gd: 0-1 GF: 0-1 Fm: 0-0
Distance: 5f/6f: 0-0 7f-8f: 0-2 9f-13f: 0-10 14f+: 0-2
Track : LH: 0-10 RH: 0-3 Tight: 0-1 Gall: 0-1
Aids: Bl: 0-1 Vi: 0-0 Tstrap: 0-0
Best Rating: 47 2/01 Sthl 1m4f slow

Feet So Fast

104 **96**

2-y-o ch g Pivotal-Splice (Sharpo)
W J Musson Invoshire Ltd

Placings:01 **(5594)**
2001: 6^{0}HY, 6^{1}GS

	Starts	1st	2nd	3rd	Win & Pl
Career Total (Turf)	2	1	0	0	4329

96	11/01	NmkR	6f	D	G-S	£4329

Total win prize-money £4329

Going (Turf): Sf: 0-1 **GS: 1-1** Gd: 0-0 GF: 0-0 Fm: 0-0
Distance: **5f/6f: 1-2** 7f-8f: 0-0 9f-13f: 0-0 14f+: 0-0
Track : LH: 0-0 RH: 0-0 Tight: 0-0 Gall: 0-0
Aids: Bl: 0-0 Vi: 0-0 Tstrap: 0-0
Best Rating: 96 11/01 NmkR 6f gd-sft

Won a Newmarket maiden at 50/1 on his second start.

Fenwicks Pride (IRE)

97 **74**

3-y-o b g Imperial Frontier (USA)-Stunt Girl (IRE) (Thatching)
B S Rothwell J H Tattersall

Placings:5332661051-0000500046 **(5671)**
2001: 6^{0}S, 6^{0}G, 5^{0}GF, 6^{0}G, 6^{5}GF, 6^{0}G, 6^{0}G, 6^{0}S, 5^{4}HY, 6^{6}HY

	Starts	1st	2nd	3rd	Win & Pl
Career Total (Turf)	20	2	1	2	12866

78	10/00	York	6f	C	SFT	£6581
72	8/00	Ripn	5f	F	GD	£3081

Total win prize-money £9662

Going (Turf): Sf: 1-6 GS: 0-3 **Gd: 1-7** GF: 0-4 Fm: 0-0
Distance: **5f/6f: 2-19** 7f-8f: 0-1 9f-13f: 0-0 14f+: 0-0
Track : LH: 0-0 RH: 0-0 Tight: 0-0 Gall: 0-0
Aids: Bl: 0-0 **Vi: 1-11** Tstrap: 0-0
Best Rating: 74 7/01 Hayd 6f gd-fm

Little show in his early starts this season, but a drop in the handicap saw him put in a much better effort at Haydock in July.

Ferny Hill (IRE)

78(100) (52)**31**

7-y-o b g Danehill (USA)-Miss Allowed (USA) (Alleged (USA))
R Brotherton (W R Muir 2/2) Ms Gerardine P O'Reilly

Placings:424/21311/20130/060**0/20640124040 (5626)**
2001: 11^{2}SD, 12^{0}SW, 9^{6}SD, 12^{4}SD, 16^{0}SD, 12^{1}SD, 11^{2}SD, 11^{4}SD, 11^{0}GF, 14^{8}SD, 8^{0}GS

	Starts	1st	2nd	3rd	Win & Pl
Career Total (Turf)	17	4	2	2	28048
Career Total (AW)	11	1	3	0	3772

43	3/01	Wolv	1m4f	G	STD	£1897
80	8/98	Wind	1m3f135y	C	G-F	£5087
89	9/97	Rdcr	1m6f19y	C(0-95)H	FRM	£4528
90	9/97	Kemp	1m4f	D(0-85)	G-F	£3468
84	8/97	Newc	1m4f93y	D(0-80)	G-F	£5509

Total win prize-money £20491

Going (Turf): Sf: 0-1 GS: 0-2 Gd: 0-4 **GF: 3-9** Fm: 1-1
Distance: 5f/6f: 0-0 7f-8f: 0-2 **9f-13f: 4-21** 14f+: 1-5
Track : **LH: 3-21** RH: 1-5 **Tight: 3-9** Gall: 1-7
Aids: Bl: 0-0 Vi: 0-0 Tstrap: 0-0
Best Rating: 52 4/01 Sthl 1m3f stand

Ferzao (IRE)

110(101) (94)**92**

4-y-o b c Alzao (USA)-Fer De Lance (IRE) (Diesis)
Mrs A J Perrett Clive Batt & Mrs Elaine Batt

Placings:01/315004**020-12005040 (4170)**
2001: 10^{1}GF, 10^{2}G, 10^{0}G, 10^{0}GF, 8^{5}GF, 8^{0}G, 8^{4}G, 10^{0}G

	Starts	1st	2nd	3rd	Win & Pl
Career Total (Turf)	17	3	1	1	28613
Career Total (AW)	2	0	1	0	1127

94	5/01	York	1m2f85y	B(0-105)H	G-F	£9691
94	5/00	Wind	1m2f7y	C(0-90)	GD	£6695
84	10/99	Leic	7f9y	D	GD	£3687

Total win prize-money £20075

Going (Turf): Sf: 0-1 GS: 0-1 **Gd: 2-11** GF: 1-4 Fm: 0-0
Distance: 5f/6f: 0-0 7f-8f: 1-8 **9f-13f: 2-11** 14f+: 0-0
Track : **LH: 1-4** RH: 0-8 Tight: 1-6 Gall: 1-4
Aids: Bl: 0-0 Vi: 0-0 **Tstrap: 1-12**
Best Rating: 94 6/01 Wind 1m2f7y good

He reappeared in top form this term, winning well at York on his reappearance and running well next time, but has been held since. Suited by ten furlongs and fast ground, he wears a tongue strap.

Festive Affair

99(98) (63)**68**

3-y-o b g Mujadil (USA)-Christmas Kiss (Taufan (USA))
B Smart B Smart

Placings:00-03126005046 **(5619)**
2001: 6^{0}SD, 6^{3}SW, 6^{1}SD, 6^{2}HY, 6^{6}SW, 5^{0}GS, 5^{0}G, 6^{5}SD, 6^{0}HY, 6^{4}SD, 6^{6}SD

	Starts	1st	2nd	3rd	Win & Pl
Career Total (Turf)	6	0	1	0	884
Career Total (AW)	7	1	0	1	3262

58	2/01	Sthl	6f	D	STD	£2940

Total win prize-money £2940

Going (Turf): Sf: 0-3 GS: 0-1 Gd: 0-2 GF: 0-0 Fm: 0-0
Distance: **5f/6f: 1-11** 7f-8f: 0-2 9f-13f: 0-0 14f+: 0-0
Track : **LH: 1-8** RH: 0-1 Tight: 0-3 Gall: 0-2
Aids: Bl: 0-0 Vi: 0-0 Tstrap: 0-0
Best Rating: 68 3/01 Nott 6f15y heavy

Fair sprinter, improved with experience to win on the All-Weather, and only just beaten on his return to turf, but struggled off higher marks since.

Feuer

95 **89**

3-y-o b c Emperor Jones (USA)-Strapless (Bustino)
Bruno Nilsson Ab Capriole

Placings:1-1220 **(2382)**
2001: 8^{1}G, 10^{2}G, 12^{2}G, 10^{0}GF

	Starts	1st	2nd	3rd	Win & Pl
Career Total (Turf)	3	1	1	0	8907
Career Total (AW)	2	1	1	0	2325

	5/01	Taby	1m		GD	£1431
	7/00	Taby	7f110y		GD	£1754

Total win prize-money £3185

Going (Turf): Sf: 0-0 GS: 0-0 **Gd: 2-4** GF: 0-1 Fm: 0-0
Distance: 5f/6f: 0-0 **7f-8f: 2-2** 9f-13f: 0-3 14f+: 0-0
Track : LH: 0-0 RH: 0-1 Tight: 0-0 Gall: 0-1
Aids: Bl: 0-0 Vi: 0-0 Tstrap: 0-1
Best Rating: 89 6/01 Asct 1m2f gd-fm

Swedish-trained colt, winner at a mile and placed at 12 furlongs in his home country.

Ffal Forest

72 **31**

2-y-o b f Charnwood Forest (IRE)-Manarah (Marju (IRE))
M Dods P J Carr

Placings:000 **(4216)**
2001: 6^{0}GF, 7^{0}GS, 8^{0}G

	Starts	1st	2nd	3rd	Win & Pl
Career Total (Turf)	3	0	0	0	

Going (Turf): Sf: 0-0 GS: 0-1 Gd: 0-1 GF: 0-1 Fm: 0-0
Distance: 5f/6f: 0-1 7f-8f: 0-1 9f-13f: 0-1 14f+: 0-0
Track : LH: 0-2 RH: 0-0 Tight: 0-1 Gall: 0-0
Aids: Bl: 0-0 Vi: 0-0 Tstrap: 0-0
Best Rating: 31 8/01 Thsk 7f gd-sft

Ffiffiffer (IRE)

93 **38**

3-y-o b c Definite Article-Merry Twinkle (Martinmas)
A Dickman Mike Smallman

Placings:40-560053 **(5187)**
2001: 7^{5}G, 7^{6}F, 10^{0}G, 8^{0}GF, 6^{5}GF, 5^{3}GS

	Starts	1st	2nd	3rd	Win & Pl
Career Total (Turf)	8	0	0	1	330

Going (Turf): Sf: 0-0 GS: 0-1 Gd: 0-3 GF: 0-3 Fm: 0-1
Distance: 5f/6f: 0-2 7f-8f: 0-4 9f-13f: 0-2 14f+: 0-0
Track : LH: 0-4 RH: 0-1 Tight: 0-4 Gall: 0-1
Aids: Bl: 0-0 Vi: 0-1 Tstrap: 0-0
Best Rating: 46 6/01 Thsk 7f good

Ffynnon Gold

105(87) (51)**57**

4-y-o b f Beveled (USA)-Sparklingsovereign (Sparkler)
J G Portman R L Cox

Placings:00000**6044-15203150200 (4840)**
2001: 7^{1}GF, 6^{5}GF, 6^{2}F, 5^{0}G, 6^{3}GF, 6^{1}GF, 6^{5}GF, 6^{0}GF, 6^{2}F, 5^{0}F, 6^{0}G

	Starts	1st	2nd	3rd	Win & Pl
Career Total (Turf)	19	2	2	1	8172
Career Total (AW)	1	0	0	0	0

55	7/01	Wind	6f	E(0-70)H	G-F	£3325
52	5/01	Sthl	7f	F(0-60)	G-F	£2373

Total win prize-money £5698

Going (Turf): Sf: 0-3 GS: 0-1 Gd: 0-3 **GF: 2-9** Fm: 0-3
Distance: 5f/6f: 1-11 7f-8f: 1-6 9f-13f: 0-3 14f+: 0-0
Track : **LH: 1-5** RH: 0-5 Tight: 0-2 Gall: 0-3
Aids: Bl: 0-0 Vi: 0-0 Tstrap: 0-0
Best Rating: 57 8/01 Ling 6f firm

Winner of seven-furlong claiming stakes at Southwell in May and six-furlong handicap at Windsor in July. Acts on any ground on turf, and on Fibresand.

Fiaba (USA)

86 **49**

3-y-o b f St Jovite (USA)-Florie (FR) (Gay Mecene (USA))
J L Dunlop V Schirone

Placings:00 **(1613)**
2001: 9^{0}GF, 10^{0}GF

	Starts	1st	2nd	3rd	Win & Pl
Career Total (Turf)	2	0	0	0	

Going (Turf): Sf: 0-0 GS: 0-0 Gd: 0-0 GF: 0-2 Fm: 0-0
Distance: 5f/6f: 0-0 7f-8f: 0-0 9f-13f: 0-2 14f+: 0-0
Track : LH: 0-1 RH: 0-0 Tight: 0-1 Gall: 0-0
Aids: Bl: 0-0 Vi: 0-0 Tstrap: 0-0
Best Rating: 49 5/01 Ling 1m2f gd-fm

Fiamma Royale (IRE)

103 **58**

3-y-o b f Fumo Di Londra (IRE)-Ariadne (Bustino)

Mrs P N Dutfield The Foundry House Partnership

Placings:322524201-00505306000 **(5376)**
2001: 6^{0}S, 5^{0}GS, 5^{5}F, 5^{0}GF, 5^{5}GF, 5^{3}G, 5^{0}GS, 5^{6}G, 5^{0}GF, 5^{0}G, 7^{0}G

	Starts	1st	2nd	3rd	Win & Pl
Career Total (Turf)	20	1	4	2	8028

72 9/00 Sand 5f6y E G-F £3688
Total win prize-money £3689

Going (Turf): Sf: 0-3 GS: 0-2 Gd: 0-6 **GF: 1-7** Fm: 0-1
Distance: **5f/6f: 1-19** 7f-8f: 0-1 9f-13f: 0-0 14f+: 0-0
Track : LH: 0-6 RH: 0-2 Tight: 0-1 Gall: 0-6
Aids: Bl: 0-0 Vi: 0-0 Tstrap: 0-0
Best Rating: 64 7/01 Sand 5f6y gd-fm

A consistent individual, she was knocking at the door prior to scoring on her final start of 2000, but she has been well held since then, although she is well below the mark she won off last year. Best at the minimum distance on a sound surface.

Fiche And Chips

79(58) (3)**39**
2-y-o b c Distant Relative-Moorefield Girl (IRE) (Gorytus (USA))
A Dickman Mike Smallman

Placings:000 **(4875)**
2001: 5^{0}S, 7^{0}GF, 8^{0}SD

	Starts	1st	2nd	3rd	Win & Pl
Career Total (Turf)	2	0	0	0	
Career Total (AW)	1	0	0	0	

Going (Turf): Sf: 0-1 GS: 0-0 Gd: 0-0 GF: 0-1 Fm: 0-0
Distance: 5f/6f: 0-1 7f-8f: 0-1 9f-13f: 0-1 14f+: 0-0
Track : LH: 0-2 RH: 0-0 Tight: 0-2 Gall: 0-0
Aids: Bl: 0-0 Vi: 0-0 Tstrap: 0-0
Best Rating: 39 9/01 Thsk 7f gd-fm

Fiddler's Moll (IRE)

91(69) (14)**58d**
3-y-o b f Dr Devious (IRE)-Belle Bleue (Blazing Saddles (AUS))
B J Meehan Miss Gloria Abbey

Placings:40-00003 **(5461)**
2001: 10^{0}GS, 10^{0}GF, 9^{0}SD, 10^{0}GF, 8^{3}G

	Starts	1st	2nd	3rd	Win & Pl
Career Total (Turf)	6	0	0	1	581
Career Total (AW)	1	0	0	0	

Going (Turf): Sf: 0-2 GS: 0-1 Gd: 0-1 GF: 0-2 Fm: 0-0
Distance: 5f/6f: 0-0 7f-8f: 0-2 9f-13f: 0-5 14f+: 0-0
Track : LH: 0-3 RH: 0-1 Tight: 0-4 Gall: 0-1
Aids: Bl: 0-2 Vi: 0-0 Tstrap: 0-0
Best Rating: 52 10/01 Bath 1m5y good

Showed moderate form at start of her three-year-old career but performed better after a break at Bath in October. Stays a mile.

Fiddlesticks

91 **52**
3-y-o b f Missed Flight-Fiddling (Music Boy)
Mrs J R Ramsden Manor Farm Stud (rutland)

Placings:04033000 **(4601)**
2001: 6^{0}HY, 6^{4}G, 6^{0}F, 5^{3}GF, 6^{3}GF, 6^{0}F, 5^{0}GF, 5^{0}GF

	Starts	1st	2nd	3rd	Win & Pl
Career Total (Turf)	8	0	0	2	841

Going (Turf): Sf: 0-1 GS: 0-0 Gd: 0-1 GF: 0-4 Fm: 0-2
Distance: 5f/6f: 0-6 7f-8f: 0-2 9f-13f: 0-0 14f+: 0-0
Track : LH: 0-2 RH: 0-0 Tight: 0-0 Gall: 0-0
Aids: Bl: 0-0 Vi: 0-0 Tstrap: 0-0
Best Rating: 56 6/01 Bevl 5f gd-fm

Field Master (IRE)

97(104) (45)**54**
4-y-o ch g Foxhound (USA)-Bold Avril (IRE) (Persian Bold)
C J Gray (S Dow 19/3) A P Smith

Placings:04440/0322100050000-00250 **(0484)**
2001: 10^{0}SD, 10^{0}SD, 9^{2}SW, 9^{5}SD, 13^{0}SD

	Starts	1st	2nd	3rd	Win & Pl
Career Total (Turf)	16	0	1	1	3791
Career Total (AW)	7	1	2	0	5246

62 3/00 Ling 1m2f D STD £2717
Total win prize-money £2717

Going (Turf): Sf: 0-3 GS: 0-2 Gd: 0-5 GF: 0-5 Fm: 0-1
Distance: 5f/6f: 0-2 7f-8f: 0-4 **9f-13f: 1-17** 14f+: 0-0
Track : **LH: 1-14** RH: 0-4 **Tight: 1-12** Gall: 0-1
Aids: Bl: 0-0 Vi: 0-0 Tstrap: 0-0
Best Rating: 57 1/01 Ling 1m2f stand

Field Of Vision (IRE)

106 (49)**37**
11-y-o b g Vision (USA)-Bold Meadows (Persian Bold)
Mrs A Duffield Mrs L J Tounsend

Placings:4506210543/14211022254365**2**/0643**203**/**011**
4605134**240**3234/5**0**/**463024**1**14**505/40/0243214522241
5-3503325224 **(4469)**
2001: 13^{3}G, 11^{5}G, 12^{0}GF, 13^{3}GF, 11^{3}GF, 12^{2}F, 12^{5}G, 11^{2}G, 12^{2}S, 12^{4}G

	Starts	1st	2nd	3rd	Win & Pl
Career Total (Turf)	67	9	14	10	52348
Career Total (AW)	22	2	4	2	14742

40 9/00 Bevl 1m3f216yG HVY £2054
45 6/00 Carl 1m4f F SFT £2268
74 5/98 Bevl 1m3f216yD(0-80)H G-F £3712
66 5/98 Haml 1m5f9y E(0-70)H G-S £3582
64 4/96 Haml 1m1f36y F G-S £2675
72 1/96 Wolv 1m1f79y C(0-90)H STD £5329
65 1/96 Wolv 1m1f79y D(0-80)H STD £3813
71 7/93 Sand 7f16y C(0-95)H G-F £7425
59 6/93 Rdcr 7f D(0-80)H G-F £3494
57 5/93 Ling 7f E(0-80)H G-F £3288
61 6/92 Haml 5f4y F FRM £1492
Total win prize-money £39137

Going (Turf): Sf: 2-12 GS: 2-7 Gd: 0-17 **GF: 4-21** Fm: 1-10
Distance: 5f/6f: 1-10 7f-8f: 3-23 **9f-13f: 6-44** 14f+: 1-12
Track : LH: 2-40 **RH: 6-29 Tight: 6-46** Gall: 0-5
Aids: **Bl: 1-12** Vi: 0-0 Tstrap: 0-0
Best Rating: 40 5/01 Haml 1m5f9y good

A veteran, plating-class gelding. Suited by easy ground and a right-handed track on turf, although has won over hurdles and on the All-Weather in his time.

Fiella (IRE)

74 **50**
2-y-o b c Petorius-Creggan Vale Lass (Simply Great (FR))
B R Millman Mrs Tina Ann Dormer

Placings:000 **(5037)**
2001: 5^{0}G, 6^{0}GF, 5^{0}G

	Starts	1st	2nd	3rd	Win & Pl
Career Total (Turf)	3	0	0	0	

Going (Turf): Sf: 0-1 GS: 0-0 Gd: 0-1 GF: 0-1 Fm: 0-0
Distance: 5f/6f: 0-3 7f-8f: 0-0 9f-13f: 0-0 14f+: 0-0
Track : LH: 0-1 RH: 0-0 Tight: 0-0 Gall: 0-1
Aids: Bl: 0-0 Vi: 0-0 Tstrap: 0-0
Best Rating: 50 10/01 Bath 5f161y good

Fiennes (USA)

87(105) (53)**57**
3-y-o b/br g Dayjur (USA)-Artic Strech (USA) (Arctic Tern (USA))
Mrs N Macauley (M L W Bell 3/2) Mrs N Macauley

Placings:506360-**5521425000524000** **(5349)**
2001: 5^{5}SD, 7^{5}SD, 5^{2}SW, 5^{1}SD, 6^{4}SD, 5^{2}SD, 6^{5}SW, 6^{0}SD, 5^{0}G, 5^{0}SD, 5^{5}SD, 6^{2}SD, 6^{4}SD, 6^{0}SD, 6^{0}SD, 5^{0}SD

	Starts	1st	2nd	3rd	Win & Pl
Career Total (Turf)	6	0	0	1	595
Career Total (AW)	16	1	3	0	3878

47 3/01 Wolv 5f G STD £1834
Total win prize-money £1834

Going (Turf): Sf: 0-1 GS: 0-0 Gd: 0-4 GF: 0-1 Fm: 0-0
Distance: **5f/6f: 1-20** 7f-8f: 0-2 9f-13f: 0-0 14f+: 0-0
Track : **LH: 1-12** RH: 0-2 **Tight: 1-7** Gall: 0-2
Aids: Bl: 0-0 **Vi: 1-15** Tstrap: 0-2
Best Rating: 56 4/01 Sthl 5f stand

He proved equally uneffective on sand and turf until a change of stable kicked him into touch with a selling-class win at Wolverhampton in March 2001.

Fiery Waters

94(101) (60)**50**
5-y-o b g Rudimentary (USA)-Idle Waters (Mill Reef (USA))
D W P Arbuthnot R Crutchley

Placings:03000/006000**211-602** **(1315)**
2001: 14^{6}SD, 12^{0}SD, 14^{2}SD

	Starts	1st	2nd	3rd	Win & Pl
Career Total (Turf)	11	0	0	1	354
Career Total (AW)	6	2	2	0	4829

60 12/00 Sthl 1m6f F(0-65)H STD £1799
51 12/00 Sthl 1m6f F(0-65)H STD £1764
Total win prize-money £3563

Going (Turf): Sf: 0-2 GS: 0-1 Gd: 0-4 GF: 0-4 Fm: 0-0
Distance: 5f/6f: 0-0 7f-8f: 0-0 9f-13f: 0-11 **14f+: 2-6**
Track : **LH: 2-9** RH: 0-6 Tight: 0-4 Gall: 0-1
Aids: **Bl: 2-7** Vi: 0-0 Tstrap: 0-0
Best Rating: 56 5/01 Sthl 1m6f stand

Fiesta

86 **39**
3-y-o ch f Most Welcome-Taza (Persian Bold)
C W Thornton Guy Reed

Placings:0040 **(3935)**
2001: 7^{0}S, 7^{0}GF, 8^{4}G, 11^{0}G

	Starts	1st	2nd	3rd	Win & Pl
Career Total (Turf)	4	0	0	0	321

Going (Turf): Sf: 0-1 GS: 0-0 Gd: 0-2 GF: 0-1 Fm: 0-0
Distance: 5f/6f: 0-0 7f-8f: 0-3 9f-13f: 0-1 14f+: 0-0
Track : LH: 0-0 RH: 0-3 Tight: 0-2 Gall: 0-0
Aids: Bl: 0-0 Vi: 0-0 Tstrap: 0-0
Best Rating: 39 6/01 Bevl 7f100y gd-fm

Fife And Drum (USA)

101(102) (69)**63**
4-y-o b/br g Rahy (USA)-Fife (IRE) (Lomond (USA))
J Akehurst Last Order's Partnership

Placings:000/00010010**510**-0003152 **(4735)**
2001: 10^{0}SW, 10^{0}GF, 10^{0}G, 9^{3}GF, 9^{1}G, 10^{5}G, 10^{2}F

	Starts	1st	2nd	3rd	Win & Pl
Career Total (Turf)	15	2	1	1	7940
Career Total (AW)	6	2	0	0	6771

61 8/01 Nott 1m1f213yE(0-75)H GD £3416
69 12/00 Ling 1m2f E(0-75)H STD £3887
64 10/00 Ling 1m4f E(0-70)H STD £2884

53	6/00	Nott	1m1f213yE(0-70)H		G-F	£2968

Total win prize-money £13155

Going (Turf): Sf: 0-3 GS: 0-2 **Gd: 1-4 GF: 1-4** Fm: 0-2
Distance: 5f/6f: 0-0 7f-8f: 0-3 **9f-13f: 4-18** 14f+: 0-0
Track : **LH: 4-13** RH: 0-5 **Tight: 2-12** Gall: 0-1
Aids: **Bl: 1-2** Vi: 0-0 Tstrap: 0-0
Best Rating: 63 9/01 Chep 1m2f36y firm

Equally effective on turf and Equitack, he is suited by ten to 12 furlongs and should make a fair hurdler.

Fifteen Reds

88(102) (45)**32**
6-y-o b g Jumbo Hirt (USA)-Dominance (Dominion)
F S Storey (P C Haslam 5/1) F S Storey

Placings:050000/260-0 **(0037)**
2001: 16^{0}SD

	Starts	1st	2nd	3rd	Win & Pl
Career Total (Turf)	4	0	0	0	
Career Total (AW)	6	0	1	0	860

Going (Turf): Sf: 0-0 GS: 0-1 Gd: 0-3 GF: 0-0 Fm: 0-0
Distance: 5f/6f: 0-0 7f-8f: 0-0 9f-13f: 0-4 14f+: 0-6
Track : LH: 0-8 RH: 0-2 Tight: 0-3 Gall: 0-1
Aids: Bl: 0-0 Vi: 0-4 Tstrap: 0-0
Best Rating: 16 1/01 Sthl 2m stand

Fifth Edition

94(78) (15)**33**
5-y-o b m Rock Hopper-Glossary (Reference Point)
R Guest Miss L Thompson

Placings:00405/0000-0406456 **(5471)**
2001: 12^{0}GF, 12^{4}GF, 18^{0}GF, 14^{6}G, 16^{4}GF, 11^{5}S, 11^{6}S

	Starts	1st	2nd	3rd	Win & Pl
Career Total (Turf)	15	0	0	0	280
Career Total (AW)	1	0	0	0	

Going (Turf): Sf: 0-3 GS: 0-1 Gd: 0-3 GF: 0-7 Fm: 0-0
Distance: 5f/6f: 0-0 7f-8f: 0-2 9f-13f: 0-10 14f+: 0-3
Track : LH: 0-6 RH: 0-6 Tight: 0-7 Gall: 0-0
Aids: Bl: 0-0 Vi: 0-0 Tstrap: 0-0
Best Rating: 36 6/01 Wwck 1m4f134y gd-fm

Fig Leaf (FR)

97 **72**
2-y-o b f Distant Relative-Shady Leaf (IRE) (Glint Of Gold)
R F Johnson Houghton Lady Rothschild

Placings:420 **(4384)**
2001: 6^{4}G, 7^{2}GF, 6^{0}GF

	Starts	1st	2nd	3rd	Win & Pl
Career Total (Turf)	3	0	1	0	1413

Going (Turf): Sf: 0-0 GS: 0-0 Gd: 0-1 GF: 0-2 Fm: 0-0
Distance: 5f/6f: 0-1 7f-8f: 0-2 9f-13f: 0-0 14f+: 0-0
Track : LH: 0-0 RH: 0-0 Tight: 0-0 Gall: 0-0
Aids: Bl: 0-0 Vi: 0-0 Tstrap: 0-0
Best Rating: 72 7/01 Ling 7f gd-fm

Figawin

(70) (38)**46**
6-y-o b g Rudimentary (USA)-Dear Person (Rainbow Quest (USA))
Mrs H L Walton A E Walton

Placings:54144530054/253640000400/0/0 **(0236)**
2001: 16^{0}SD

	Starts	1st	2nd	3rd	Win & Pl
Career Total (Turf)	11	0	0	1	389
Career Total (AW)	14	1	1	1	2953

59	6/97	Sthl	6f	F	STD	£1984

Total win prize-money £1985

Going (Turf): Sf: 0-4 GS: 0-1 Gd: 0-2 GF: 0-3 Fm: 0-1
Distance: **5f/6f: 1-7** 7f-8f: 0-13 9f-13f: 0-4 14f+: 0-1
Track : **LH: 1-20** RH: 0-0 Tight: 0-9 Gall: 0-0
Aids: Bl: 0-3 Vi: 0-0 Tstrap: 0-0

Fight Your Corner

110 **106+**
2-y-o b c Muhtarram (USA)-Dame Ashfield (Grundy)
M Johnston Greenland Park Ltd

Placings:13511 **(5255)**
2001: 6^{1}G, 6^{3}G, 7^{5}GF, 8^{1}GF, 8^{1}GS

	Starts	1st	2nd	3rd	Win & Pl
Career Total (Turf)	5	3	0	1	27030

106	10/01	Asct	1m	A	G-S	£13747
94	9/01	Newb	1m	B	G-F	£9512
94	8/01	Newc	6f	F	GD	£2688

Total win prize-money £25948

Going (Turf): Sf: 0-0 **GS: 1-1 Gd: 1-2 GF: 1-2** Fm: 0-0
Distance: 5f/6f: 1-2 **7f-8f: 2-3** 9f-13f: 0-0 14f+: 0-0
Track : LH: 0-0 **RH: 1-1** Tight: 0-0 **Gall: 1-1**
Aids: Bl: 0-0 Vi: 0-0 Tstrap: 0-0
Best Rating: 106 10/01 Asct 1m gd-sft

A scopey half-brother to six minor winners, he made an impressive winning debut at Newcastle over six furlongs, but looked as though he needed further in his next two starts and relished the step up to a mile to win the Haynes, Hanson And Clark at Newbury in September. Followed up in very impressive fashion in an Ascot Listed event and looks a smart prospect.

Figura

100 **74**
3-y-o b f Rudimentary (USA)-Dream Baby (Master Willie)
C G Cox (K McAuliffe 16/7) R J Broadbent

Placings:61640-0000 **(4988)**
2001: 8^{0}GF, 7^{0}GF, 11^{0}GF, 8^{0}G

	Starts	1st	2nd	3rd	Win & Pl
Career Total (Turf)	9	1	0	0	2893

74	7/00	Folk	7f	F	GD	£1778

Total win prize-money £1778

Going (Turf): Sf: 0-0 GS: 0-0 **Gd: 1-3** GF: 0-5 Fm: 0-1
Distance: 5f/6f: 0-0 **7f-8f: 1-8** 9f-13f: 0-1 14f+: 0-0
Track : LH: 0-0 RH: 0-1 Tight: 0-1 Gall: 0-0
Aids: Bl: 0-0 Vi: 0-0 Tstrap: 0-0
Best Rating: 72 6/01 Ling 7f gd-fm

She landed a Folkestone maiden on her second start at two, but was highly tried afterwards and was not up to it.

Figurehead

91(98) (78)**78**
2-y-o b c Entrepreneur-Noble Dane (IRE) (Danehill (USA))
Sir Michael Stoute Sheikh Mohammed

Placings:3332 **(4875)**
2001: 7^{3}GF, 7^{3}G, 8^{3}G, 8^{2}SD

	Starts	1st	2nd	3rd	Win & Pl
Career Total (Turf)	3	0	0	3	1904
Career Total (AW)	1	0	1	0	1135

Going (Turf): Sf: 0-0 GS: 0-0 Gd: 0-2 GF: 0-1 Fm: 0-0
Distance: 5f/6f: 0-0 7f-8f: 0-2 9f-13f: 0-2 14f+: 0-0
Track : LH: 0-1 RH: 0-3 Tight: 0-2 Gall: 0-0
Aids: Bl: 0-0 Vi: 0-1 Tstrap: 0-0
Best Rating: 78 9/01 Wolv 1m100y stand

Filial (IRE)

94(85)
8-y-o b g Danehill (USA)-Sephira (Luthier)
Mrs A Duffield Mrs Ann Swinbank

Placings:3100561/0000025120/2231210431204210/00 35/0-004026 **(4105)**
2001: 11^{0}SD, 12^{0}SD, 12^{4}F, 14^{0}GF, 12^{2}G, 12^{6}S

	Starts	1st	2nd	3rd	Win & Pl
Career Total (Turf)	31	4	5	3	17273
Career Total (AW)	13	3	3	1	8969

70	10/98	Rdcr	1m3f	F	SFT	£2206
73	5/98	Haml	1m5f9y	E(0-70)H	GD	£2749
66	4/98	Ripn	1m4f60y	E(0-70)H	SFT	£2815
61	3/98	Sthl	1m4f	F	STD	£2305
72	11/97	Wolv	1m4f	F	STD	£1932
86	12/96	Ling	1m4f	G(0-80)H	STD	£2221
75	8/96	Sand	1m2f7y	D	G-F	£3615

Total win prize-money £17845

Going (Turf): Sf: 2-7 GS: 0-2 Gd: 1-13 GF: 1-7 Fm: 0-2
Distance: 5f/6f: 0-0 7f-8f: 0-1 **9f-13f: 6-37** 14f+: 1-6
Track : **LH: 4-26** RH: 3-18 **Tight: 5-21** Gall: 0-7
Aids: Bl: 0-1 Vi: 0-0 Tstrap: 0-0
Best Rating: 30 8/01 Newc 1m4f93y good

He was in fair form on sand during the winter, and has shown mixed form back on turf, including winning a couple of times in modest company. He goes particularly well for Kieren Fallon.

Fille D'Argent (IRE)

91 **72**
2-y-o gr f Desert Style (IRE)-Talina (General Assembly (USA))
Mrs P N Dutfield Chris Scott

Placings:204003 **(5370)**
2001: 5^{2}GF, 6^{0}GF, 5^{4}G, 6^{0}GY, 8^{0}HY, 7^{3}G

	Starts	1st	2nd	3rd	Win & Pl
Career Total (Turf)	6	0	1	1	1991

Going (Turf): Sf: 0-1 GS: 0-0 Gd: 0-2 GF: 0-2 Fm: 0-0
Distance: 5f/6f: 0-4 7f-8f: 0-1 9f-13f: 0-1 14f+: 0-0
Track : LH: 0-0 RH: 0-1 Tight: 0-1 Gall: 0-0
Aids: Bl: 0-0 Vi: 0-1 Tstrap: 0-0
Best Rating: 72 7/01 Chep 5f16y good

Still a maiden, but has run some fair races. Seems suited by most types of ground, and has been tested from five furlongs to a mile.

Fille De Bucheron (USA)

94 **80**
3-y-o b f Woodman (USA)-Special Secreto (USA) (Secreto (USA))
H R A Cecil Clark Industrial Services Partnership

Placings:2-323 **(2445)**
2001: 8^{3}F, 7^{2}GF, 8^{3}GF

	Starts	1st	2nd	3rd	Win & Pl
Career Total (Turf)	4	0	2	2	3228

Going (Turf): Sf: 0-0 GS: 0-0 Gd: 0-0 GF: 0-3 Fm: 0-1
Distance: 5f/6f: 0-0 7f-8f: 0-2 9f-13f: 0-2 14f+: 0-0
Track : LH: 0-1 RH: 0-1 Tight: 0-0 Gall: 0-0
Aids: Bl: 0-0 Vi: 0-0 Tstrap: 0-0
Best Rating: 80 6/01 Yarm 7f3y gd-fm

Fille De Dauphin (IRE)

85(60) **20**
3-y-o b f Dolphin Street (FR)-Asturiana (Julio Mariner)
N Bycroft N Bycroft

Placings:0000-0 **(0306)**
2001: 11^{0}SD

Starts	1st	2nd	3rd	Win & Pl

Career Total (Turf)	3	0	0	0
Career Total (AW)	2	0	0	0

Going (Turf): Sf: 0-1 GS: 0-0 Gd: 0-0 GF: 0-1 Fm: 0-1
Distance: 5f/6f: 0-2 7f-8f: 0-2 9f-13f: 0-1 14f+: 0-0
Track : LH: 0-2 RH: 0-1 Tight: 0-0 Gall: 0-0
Aids: Bl: 0-0 Vi: 0-0 Tstrap: 0-0

Fille De Joie (IRE)

98 **59**

3-y-o b f Royal Academy (USA)-Courtesane (USA) (Majestic Light (USA))
R F Johnson Houghton Bob Lanigan

Placings:20265 **(5173)**
2001: 8^{2}GF, 9^{0}GF, 6^{2}G, 8^{6}GF, 8^{5}GS

	Starts	1st	2nd	3rd	Win & Pl
Career Total (Turf)	5	0	2	0	2184

Going (Turf): Sf: 0-0 GS: 0-1 Gd: 0-1 GF: 0-3 Fm: 0-0
Distance: 5f/6f: 0-0 7f-8f: 0-3 9f-13f: 0-2 14f+: 0-0
Track : LH: 0-3 RH: 0-1 Tight: 0-0 Gall: 0-1
Aids: Bl: 0-0 Vi: 0-0 Tstrap: 0-0
Best Rating: 70 7/01 Kemp 1m gd-fm

A half-sister to the smart middle-distance stayer Delilah, she looked to need further when second on her debut over a mile. Has looked a bit keen since and ran better when dropped back to seven furlongs. Finished lame after her Salisbury run in August. Acts on a sound surface.

Fille Genereux

101 **44**

3-y-o ch f Cadeaux Genereux-Mohican Girl (Dancing Brave (USA))
R M H Cowell T J Le Blanc-Smith And Partners

Placings:033300 **(5601)**
2001: 7^{0}G, 8^{3}G, 6^{3}GF, 8^{3}G, 8^{0}GF, 8^{0}GS

	Starts	1st	2nd	3rd	Win & Pl
Career Total (Turf)	6	0	0	3	1684

Going (Turf): Sf: 0-0 GS: 0-1 Gd: 0-3 GF: 0-2 Fm: 0-0
Distance: 5f/6f: 0-0 7f-8f: 0-4 9f-13f: 0-2 14f+: 0-0
Track : LH: 0-2 RH: 0-2 Tight: 0-4 Gall: 0-0
Aids: Bl: 0-0 Vi: 0-0 Tstrap: 0-0
Best Rating: 44 7/01 Epsm 1m114y good

Filum Terminale (IRE)

94 **71**

2-y-o b c Mujadil (USA)-Millie's Return (IRE) (Ballad Rock)
M R Channon Ridgeway Downs Racing

Placings:0244 **(1960)**
2001: 5^{0}S, 5^{2}GF, 5^{4}F, 5^{4}GF

	Starts	1st	2nd	3rd	Win & Pl
Career Total (Turf)	4	0	1	0	1117

Going (Turf): Sf: 0-1 GS: 0-0 Gd: 0-0 GF: 0-2 Fm: 0-1
Distance: 5f/6f: 0-4 7f-8f: 0-0 9f-13f: 0-0 14f+: 0-0
Track : LH: 0-1 RH: 0-0 Tight: 0-0 Gall: 0-1
Aids: Bl: 0-0 Vi: 0-0 Tstrap: 0-0
Best Rating: 71 6/01 Ling 5f firm

Final Dividend (IRE)

100(102) (72)**60**

5-y-o b g Second Set (IRE)-Prime Interest (IRE) (King's Lake (USA))
J M P Eustace Charles Curtis

Placings:053050/4310066100/45000154-1025020 **(2756)**
2001: 12^{1}SD, 10^{0}S, 12^{2}SW, 8^{5}S, 9^{0}G, 12^{2}GF, 13^{0}GF

					Starts	1st	2nd	3rd	Win & Pl
Career Total (Turf)					25	2	1	2	8596
Career Total (AW)					6	2	1	0	5502
72	1/01	Ling	1m4f	F(0-70)H			STD		£2282
62	11/00	Ling	1m4f	G(0-80)H			STD		£1883
70	9/99	Bevl	1m100y	E(0-70)H			SFT		£3311
70	5/99	Sals	1m	E(0-70)H			G-F		£3074

Total win prize-money £10550

Going (Turf): Sf: 1-8 GS: 0-1 Gd: 0-5 **GF: 1-9** Fm: 0-2
Distance: 5f/6f: 0-5 7f-8f: 1-12 **9f-13f: 3-13** 14f+: 0-1
Track : **LH: 2-16** RH: 1-6 **Tight: 2-8** Gall: 0-8
Aids: Bl: 0-0 Vi: 0-0 Tstrap: 0-0
Best Rating: 72 1/01 Ling 1m4f stand

He was successful twice on sand during the winter of 2000/2001 under amateur Joanna Rees and looks best suited by 12 furlongs now.

Final Faze

83 **67**

2-y-o ch f Chaddleworth (IRE)-Fine Fettle (Final Straw)
J G Given The Fine Line Racing Partnership

Placings:0 **(4873)**
2001: 7^{0}G

	Starts	1st	2nd	3rd	Win & Pl
Career Total (Turf)	1	0	0	0	

Going (Turf): Sf: 0-0 GS: 0-0 Gd: 0-1 GF: 0-0 Fm: 0-0
Distance: 5f/6f: 0-0 7f-8f: 0-1 9f-13f: 0-0 14f+: 0-0
Track : LH: 0-0 RH: 0-0 Tight: 0-0 Gall: 0-0
Aids: Bl: 0-0 Vi: 0-0 Tstrap: 0-0
Best Rating: 67 9/01 NmkR 7f good

Final Lap

89(80) (48)**53**

5-y-o b g Batshoof-Lap Of Honour (Final Straw)
Simon T Lewis (G M McCourt 5/8) Simon T Lewis

Placings:04245/00000100-000 **(2807)**
2001: 16^{0}SW, 11^{0}GF, 14^{0}GF

					Starts	1st	2nd	3rd	Win & Pl
Career Total (Turf)					13	1	1	0	6737
Career Total (AW)					3	0	0	0	0
53	9/00	NmkR	1m4f	E			GD		£5021

Total win prize-money £5021

Going (Turf): Sf: 0-3 GS: 0-2 **Gd: 1-4** GF: 0-3 Fm: 0-1
Distance: 5f/6f: 0-0 7f-8f: 0-3 **9f-13f: 1-10** 14f+: 0-3
Track : LH: 0-8 **RH: 1-3** Tight: 0-9 **Gall: 1-2**
Aids: Bl: 0-1 Vi: 0-0 Tstrap: 0-0
Best Rating: 30 6/01 Wind 1m3f135y gd-fm

Final Pursuit

101 **92**

3-y-o b f Pursuit Of Love-Final Shot (Dalsaan)
D Haydn Jones Jack Brown (bookmaker) Ltd

Placings:01000-0300500 **(3597)**
2001: 7^{0}GS, 6^{3}S, 6^{0}GF, 8^{0}GF, 7^{5}GS, 8^{0}GF, 7^{0}G

					Starts	1st	2nd	3rd	Win & Pl
Career Total (Turf)					12	1	0	1	5770
92	6/00	Bath	5f161y	D			G-S		£3562

Total win prize-money £3562

Going (Turf): Sf: 0-1 **GS: 1-4** Gd: 0-2 GF: 0-5 Fm: 0-0
Distance: **5f/6f: 1-6** 7f-8f: 0-6 9f-13f: 0-0 14f+: 0-0
Track : **LH: 1-1** RH: 0-1 Tight: 0-0 **Gall: 1-1**
Aids: Bl: 0-0 Vi: 0-1 Tstrap: 0-0
Best Rating: 92 7/01 NmkJ 7f gd-sft

A half-sister to the useful juvenile Sir Nicholas, she won her maiden at Bath in 2000, but looked out of her depth when upped in class. Much the same story this season.

Final Settlement (IRE)

109 **65**

6-y-o b g Soviet Lad (USA)-Tender Time (Tender King)
J R Jenkins T H Ounsley

Placings:000/311/0433/16534140-0340515506 **(4953)**
2001: 16^{0}GF, 14^{3}GF, 14^{4}S, 14^{0}GF, 14^{5}GF, 14^{1}GF, 14^{5}G, 14^{5}GF, 16^{0}GF, 16^{6}GS

					Starts	1st	2nd	3rd	Win & Pl
Career Total (Turf)					28	5	0	5	31997
65	7/01	NmkJ	1m6f175yD(0-85)H				G-F		£6792
68	7/00	NmkJ	1m6f175yD(0-85)H				G-F		£7085
64	3/00	Kemp	1m6f92y	D(0-85)H			GD		£7085
64	7/98	Ling	1m3f106yE(0-70)H				G-F		£2924
60	6/98	Wind	1m67y	E(0-70)H			GD		£3317

Total win prize-money £27206

Going (Turf): Sf: 0-5 GS: 0-1 Gd: 2-5 **GF: 3-17** Fm: 0-0
Distance: 5f/6f: 0-1 7f-8f: 0-2 9f-13f: 2-10 **14f+: 3-15**
Track : LH: 1-9 **RH: 4-19** Tight: 2-7 Gall: 2-8
Aids: Bl: 0-0 Vi: 0-0 Tstrap: 0-0
Best Rating: 65 8/01 Sand 1m6f good

A fair staying handicapper, he acted well on fast ground. Stayed 14 furlongs and went well at Kempton. Scored a game win at Newmarket in July over 15 furlongs, but died after breaking down in a hurdle at Huntingdon in October 2001.

Find The King (IRE)

105 **82**

3-y-o b c King's Theatre (IRE)-Undiscovered (Tap On Wood)
D W P Arbuthnot J S Gutkin

Placings:40-503142200 **(4582)**
2001: 8^{5}GS, 9^{0}GS, 11^{3}GF, 12^{1}GF, 12^{4}GF, 14^{2}GF, 14^{2}G, 13^{0}G, 14^{0}HY

					Starts	1st	2nd	3rd	Win & Pl
Career Total (Turf)					11	1	2	1	11905
78	6/01	Newb	1m4f5y	D(0-85)H			G-F		£4316

Total win prize-money £4316

Going (Turf): Sf: 0-3 GS: 0-2 Gd: 0-2 **GF: 1-4** Fm: 0-0
Distance: 5f/6f: 0-0 7f-8f: 0-3 **9f-13f: 1-4** 14f+: 0-4
Track : **LH: 1-4** RH: 0-4 Tight: 0-2 **Gall: 1-3**
Aids: Bl: 0-0 Vi: 0-0 Tstrap: 0-0
Best Rating: 82 8/01 Gdwd 1m6f good

Useful staying handicapper. Improved for step up to a mile and a half when winning at Newbury in June 2001. Acts on fast ground.

Finished Article (IRE)

111 **82**

4-y-o b c Indian Ridge-Summer Fashion (Moorestyle)
D R C Elsworth The Caledonian Racing Society

Placings:50/46352100-05326612040 **(5607)**
2001: 6^{0}S, 8^{5}G, 9^{3}GF, 8^{2}HD, 8^{6}GF, 9^{6}G, 9^{1}GS, 9^{2}GF, 8^{0}S, 8^{4}GS, 8^{0}GS

					Starts	1st	2nd	3rd	Win & Pl
Career Total (Turf)					21	2	3	2	16399
78	8/01	Gdwd	1m1f192yE(0-80)H				G-S		£4641
81	8/00	Epsm	1m114y	D			G-F		£4095

Total win prize-money £8736

Going (Turf): Sf: 0-6 **GS: 1-3** Gd: 0-4 **GF: 1-7** Fm: 0-1
Distance: 5f/6f: 0-0 7f-8f: 0-9 **9f-13f: 2-12** 14f+: 0-0
Track : LH: 1-4 RH: 1-10 **Tight: 2-10** Gall: 0-3
Aids: Bl: 0-0 Vi: 0-0 Tstrap: 0-0
Best Rating: 82 10/01 NmkR 1m gd-sft

A full-brother to Definite Article and a half-brother to Dante winner Salford Express, he requires exaggerated waiting tactics.He scored under a cheeky ride from Richard Hughes at Goodwood in August, and followed up with a good second in a more competitive event. Stays ten furlongs and acts on most surfaces.

Finmar

101 **68**

3-yo b g Efisio-Patiala (IRE) (Nashwan (USA))

Miss L A Perratt T P Finch

Placings:5004-05352442005 **(5659)**

2001: 5^{0}GS, 6^{5}S, 8^{3}F, 7^{5}F, 7^{2}G, 7^{4}GF, 8^{4}GF, 8^{2}G, 10^{0}GS, 7^{0}S, 8^{5}G

	Starts	1st	2nd	3rd	Win & Pl
Career Total (Turf)	15	0	2	1	5049

Going (Turf): **Sf: 0-3 GS: 0-2 Gd: 0-3 GF: 0-5 Fm: 0-2**
Distance: 5f/6f: 0-5 7f-8f: 0-6 9f-13f: 0-4 14f+: 0-0
Track : LH: 0-4 RH: 0-4 Tight: 0-5 Gall: 0-0
Aids: Bl: 0-0 Vi: 0-0 Tstrap: 0-0
Best Rating: 68 6/01 Rdcr 7f gd-fm

Regularly in the frame, but lacks the pace to get his head in front.

Finn McCool (IRE)

100(93) (56)**52**

3-yo b g Blues Traveller (IRE)-Schonbein (IRE) (Persian Heights)

R A Fahey Yorkshire Racing Club Owners Group 1990

Placings:610205-001004 **(5448)**

2001: 10^{0}GF, 12^{0}SD, 10^{1}G, 10^{0}G, 10^{0}F, 10^{4}HY

	Starts	1st	2nd	3rd	Win & Pl
Career Total (Turf)	7	1	0	0	3045
Career Total (AW)	5	1	1	0	2499

52 8/01 Newc 1m2f32y E(0-70)H GD £3045
55 9/00 Wolv 7f G STD £1970
Total win prize-money £5016

Going (Turf): Sf: 0-2 GS: 0-0 **Gd: 1-2** GF: 0-2 Fm: 0-1
Distance: 5f/6f: 0-0 7f-8f: 1-5 9f-13f: 1-7 14f+: 0-0
Track : **LH: 2-10** RH: 0-1 Tight: 1-4 Gall: 1-2
Aids: Bl: 0-0 Vi: 0-0 Tstrap: 0-0
Best Rating: 52 8/01 Newc 1m2f32y good

Fiori

105(101) (81)**85**

5-yo b g Anshan-Fen Princess (IRE) (Trojan Fen)

P C Haslam Wilson Imports I

Placings:632422233/01311550/**62**0064413220-50362440 **(4883)**

2001: 14^{5}SD, 16^{0}S, 13^{3}GF, 16^{6}F, 14^{2}G, 13^{4}G, 15^{4}GF, 12^{0}GF

	Starts	1st	2nd	3rd	Win & Pl
Career Total (Turf)	32	4	6	5	45864
Career Total (AW)	5	0	2	1	2123

80 6/00 Ayr 1m7f C(0-90)H GD £6825
88 6/99 York 1m2f85y B(0-100)H G-S £9338
85 6/99 Bevl 1m3f216yD(0-85)H SFT £4412
64 5/99 Haml 1m1f36y E G-F £2570
Total win prize-money £23146

Going (Turf): **Sf: 1-5 GS: 1-4 Gd: 1-10 GF: 1-11** Fm: 0-2
Distance: 5f/6f: 0-3 7f-8f: 0-7 **9f-13f: 3-13** 14f+: 1-14
Track : LH: 2-24 RH: 2-9 **Tight: 2-11** Gall: 1-15
Aids: Bl: 0-0 Vi: 0-0 Tstrap: 0-0
Best Rating: 85 6/01 Hayd 1m6f good

A fair staying handicapper, he scored just once at Ayr last term, but has run some decent races in defeat in recent seasons. Suited by two miles on a sound surface.

Fire Dome (IRE)

107(91) (87)**78**

9-yo ch g Salt Dome (USA)-Penny Habit (Habitat)

Andrew Reid A S Reid

Placings:1315/3200002265/152/**66**010051000/3056023101004/**0**3311110013040-**0**2016563031200060 **(5688)**

2001: 7^{0}SW, 6^{2}S, 6^{0}GS, 6^{1}HY, 6^{6}S, 6^{5}GF, 6^{6}GF, 6^{3}G, 6^{0}GF, 6^{3}GF, 6^{1}G, 6^{2}HY, 6^{0}GF, 6^{0}GS, 6^{0}GS, 6^{6}HY, 7^{0}S

	Starts	1st	2nd	3rd	Win & Pl
Career Total (Turf)	67	14	7	9	146070
Career Total (AW)	5	0	0	0	0

66 8/01 Hayd 6f F GD £2723
69 4/01 Wwck 6f21y C HVY £6351
89 9/00 Sals 6f C(0-95)H SFT £9877
87 6/00 Epsm 6f C(0-100)H GD £32500
79 6/00 Ling 6f D(0-85)H G-S £4082
66 5/00 Wind 6f F G-S £2509
65 5/00 Rdcr 6f F G-F £2488
68 10/99 Rdcr 6f F GD £2880
82 10/99 Sand 5f6y E HVY £2970
109 7/98 Sand 5f6y A G-S £13940
106 4/98 Thsk 6f C G-S £6184
107 3/96 Donc 6f A G-S £12648
95 9/94 Asct 5f B GD £9507
74 7/94 Yarm 5f43y D GD £4161
Total win prize-money £112823

Going (Turf): Sf: 3-19 **GS: 5-12 Gd: 5-22** GF: 1-13 Fm: 0-1
Distance: **5f/6f: 13-59** 7f-8f: 1-13 9f-13f: 0-0 14f+: 0-0
Track : LH: 1-8 RH: 1-1 Tight: 1-4 Gall: 1-1
Aids: Bl: 0-2 Vi: 0-1 Tstrap: 0-0
Best Rating: 104 6/01 Wind 6f gd-fm

Eight-length winner of conditions stakes over six furlongs on heavy ground at Warwick in April and scored at Haydock in August, but has since looked in the grasp of the handicapper. He occasionally misses the break, but is best suited by being held up. Is considered to be at his best when the ground is so bad that the meeting is on the verge of being abandoned.

Fire In Ice

83(78) (34)**50**

2-yo b f Missed Flight-Boulabas (IRE) (Nashamaa)

B P J Baugh C Harrison

Placings:000000 **(5614)**

2001: 5^{0}GF, 5^{0}GF, 7^{0}GS, 7^{0}HY, 6^{0}SD, 6^{0}SD

	Starts	1st	2nd	3rd	Win & Pl
Career Total (Turf)	4	0	0	0	
Career Total (AW)	2	0	0	0	

Going (Turf): **Sf: 0-1 GS: 0-1 Gd: 0-0 GF: 0-2 Fm: 0-0**
Distance: 5f/6f: 0-4 7f-8f: 0-2 9f-13f: 0-0 14f+: 0-0
Track : LH: 0-5 RH: 0-0 Tight: 0-3 Gall: 0-0
Aids: Bl: 0-0 Vi: 0-0 Tstrap: 0-0
Best Rating: 50 7/01 Wwck 7f26y gd-sft

Fire Moon (IRE)

95 **57**

2-yo b c Royal Applause-Welwyn (Welsh Saint)

M R Channon Salem Suhail

Placings:6046 **(4427)**

2001: 5^{6}G, 7^{0}GF, 6^{4}GF, 8^{6}GF

	Starts	1st	2nd	3rd	Win & Pl
Career Total (Turf)	4	0	0	0	340

Going (Turf): **Sf: 0-0 GS: 0-0 Gd: 0-1 GF: 0-3 Fm: 0-0**
Distance: 5f/6f: 0-1 7f-8f: 0-3 9f-13f: 0-0 14f+: 0-0
Track : LH: 0-1 RH: 0-1 Tight: 0-1 Gall: 0-1
Aids: Bl: 0-0 Vi: 0-0 Tstrap: 0-0
Best Rating: 57 9/01 Ripn 1m gd-fm

Firebreak

106 **103**

2-yo b c Charnwood Forest (IRE)-Breakaway (Song)

I A Balding Kennet Valley Thoroughbreds I

Placings:112141 **(4833)**

2001: 5^{1}GF, 5^{1}GF, 6^{2}GF, 6^{1}S, 6^{4}GS, 6^{1}GF

	Starts	1st	2nd	3rd	Win & Pl
Career Total (Turf)	6	4	1	0	85982

103 9/01 Newb 6f8y A G-F £29000
103 8/01 Deau 6f SFT £21339
86 6/01 Bevl 5f B G-F £9891
68 5/01 Gdwd 5f D G-F £4192
Total win prize-money £64424

Going (Turf): Sf: 1-1 GS: 0-1 Gd: 0-0 **GF: 3-4** Fm: 0-0
Distance: **5f/6f: 3-5** 7f-8f: 1-1 9f-13f: 0-0 14f+: 0-0
Track : LH: 0-0 RH: 0-0 Tight: 0-0 Gall: 0-0
Aids: Bl: 0-0 Vi: 0-0 Tstrap: 0-0
Best Rating: 103 9/01 Newb 6f8y gd-fm

Successful at Goodwood and Beverley, he was only beaten a neck in the Coventry Stakes at Royal Ascot on his first attempt at six furlongs. Showed his versatility at Deauville when scoring in soft ground, but was only fourth behind Johannesburg in the Prix Morny. Back to winning ways in the Mill Reef Stakes at Newbury, he was then sold for a record 525,000 gns to race in Dubai.

Fireside Legend (IRE)

92(89) (63)**66**

2-yo b g College Chapel-Miss Sandman (Manacle)

W G M Turner Sigwells Racing Club 2000

Placings:0150043320 **(5667)**

2001: 6^{0}GF, 6^{1}SD, 7^{5}GF, 7^{0}G, 5^{0}G, 8^{4}SD, 8^{3}SD, 8^{3}HY, 8^{2}SD, 8^{0}HY

	Starts	1st	2nd	3rd	Win & Pl
Career Total (Turf)	6	0	0	1	281
Career Total (AW)	4	1	1	1	2745

63 6/01 Sthl 6f G STD £1911
Total win prize-money £1911

Going (Turf): **Sf: 0-2 GS: 0-0 Gd: 0-2 GF: 0-2 Fm: 0-0**
Distance: **5f/6f: 1-3** 7f-8f: 0-3 9f-13f: 0-4 14f+: 0-0
Track : **LH: 1-5** RH: 0-1 Tight: 0-3 Gall: 0-0
Aids: Bl: 0-0 Vi: 0-0 Tstrap: 0-0
Best Rating: 66 10/01 Nott 1m54y heavy

A plater who stays a mile, he managed to win a modest seller on the Southwell Fibresand in June 2001.

Firestone (GER)

99 **73**

4-yo b g Dictator's Song (USA)-Fatinizza (IRE) (Niniski (USA))

A W Carroll K Marshall

Placings:0325316/30105654-500 **(4891)**

2001: 9^{5}GF, 8^{0}G, 8^{0}GF

	Starts	1st	2nd	3rd	Win & Pl
Career Total (Turf)	18	2	1	3	12231

7/00 Hanv 1m H GD £3774
9/99 Duss 1m GD £2527
Total win prize-money £6301

Going (Turf): Sf: 0-2 GS: 0-0 **Gd: 2-5** GF: 0-2 Fm: 0-0
Distance: 5f/6f: 0-0 **7f-8f: 2-7** 9f-13f: 0-7 14f+: 0-0
Track : LH: 0-1 RH: 0-3 Tight: 0-2 Gall: 0-0
Aids: Bl: 0-2 Vi: 0-0 Tstrap: 0-0
Best Rating: 73 6/01 Gdwd 1m1f gd-fm

Firewire

103 **71**

3-yo b g Blushing Flame (USA)-Bay Risk (Risk Me (FR))

N Hamilton Miss Jennie Wisher

Placings:00-00124 **(3705)**

2001: 10^{0}GS, 10^{0}GF, 9^{1}G, 9^{2}GF, 9^{4}G

Starts	1st	2nd	3rd	Win & Pl

	Starts	1st	2nd	3rd	Win & Pl
Career Total (Turf)	7	1	1	0	4820

67 6/01 Nott 1m1f213yE(0-70)H GD £3808

Total win prize-money £3808

Going (Turf): Sf: 0-2 GS: 0-1 **Gd: 1-2** GF: 0-2 Fm: 0-0
Distance: 5f/6f: 0-0 7f-8f: 0-2 **9f-13f: 1-5** 14f+: 0-0
Track : **LH: 1-3** RH: 0-1 Tight: 0-2 Gall: 0-0
Aids: Bl: 0-0 Vi: 0-0 Tstrap: 0-0
Best Rating: 71 8/01 Leic 1m1f218y good

Firework

108(85) (61)**72**

3-y-o b c Primo Dominie-Prancing (Prince Sabo)
R Guest M Sakal

Placings:2230-000036343643 **(5522)**
2001: 6^{0}S, 6^{0}G, 6^{0}GF, 5^{0}GF, 6^{3}GF, 6^{6}G, 6^{3}GF, 5^{4}F, 7^{3}GS, 7^{6}HY, 6^{4}G, 6^{3}HY

	Starts	1st	2nd	3rd	Win & Pl
Career Total (Turf)	15	0	2	5	7341
Career Total (AW)	1	0	0	0	

Going (Turf): Sf: 0-4 GS: 0-1 Gd: 0-4 GF: 0-4 Fm: 0-2
Distance: 5f/6f: 0-14 7f-8f: 0-2 9f-13f: 0-0 14f+: 0-0
Track : LH: 0-1 RH: 0-1 Tight: 0-1 Gall: 0-0
Aids: Bl: 0-3 Vi: 0-1 Tstrap: 0-0
Best Rating: 80 6/01 NmkR 6f gd-fm

Placed a number of times, he has yet to prove conclusively he gets seven furlongs, but has only raced on easy ground over that trip. Wears blinkers, acts on any ground.

Firozi

92 **62**

2-y-o b f Forzando-Lambast (Relkino)
C G Cox Galaxy Racing li

Placings:0340000 **(5496)**
2001: 5^{0}F, 6^{3}GF, 5^{4}G, 7^{0}GF, 5^{0}GS, 7^{0}HY, 7^{0}HY

	Starts	1st	2nd	3rd	Win & Pl
Career Total (Turf)	7	0	0	1	950

Going (Turf): Sf: 0-2 GS: 0-1 Gd: 0-1 GF: 0-2 Fm: 0-1
Distance: 5f/6f: 0-4 7f-8f: 0-3 9f-13f: 0-0 14f+: 0-0
Track : LH: 0-2 RH: 0-0 Tight: 0-0 Gall: 0-2
Aids: Bl: 0-3 Vi: 0-0 Tstrap: 0-0
Best Rating: 72 7/01 Bath 5f161y good

First Alert

100 **76**

2-y-o ch f Miswaki (USA)-First Amendment (IRE) (Caerleon (USA))
W J Haggas Cheveley Park Stud

Placings:4312610 **(5052)**
2001: 5^{4}S, 6^{3}F, 5^{1}GF, 6^{2}G, 7^{6}GF, 7^{1}HY, 7^{0}S

	Starts	1st	2nd	3rd	Win & Pl
Career Total (Turf)	7	2	1	1	7229

76 9/01 Hayd 7f30y F HVY £2670
74 7/01 Bevl 5f F G-F £2576

Total win prize-money £5247

Going (Turf): Sf: 1-3 GS: 0-0 Gd: 0-1 **GF: 1-2** Fm: 0-1
Distance: 5f/6f: 1-3 7f-8f: 1-4 9f-13f: 0-0 14f+: 0-0
Track : **LH: 1-2** RH: 0-0 Tight: 0-1 Gall: 0-0
Aids: Bl: 0-0 Vi: 0-0 Tstrap: 0-0
Best Rating: 76 9/01 Hayd 7f30y heavy

She looked an awkward ride when getting off the mark on fast ground at Beverley on her third start and did not look to be enjoying the heavy going when winning a Haydock claimer in September. Stays seven furlongs and would probably get further.

First Back (IRE)

100 **39**

4-y-o b g Fourstars Allstar (USA)-Par Un Nez (IRF) (Cyrano De Bergerac)
C W Fairhurst Twinacre Nurseries Ltd

Placings:006/400301-06000500 **(4825)**
2001: 9^{0}F, 9^{6}GF, 12^{0}GF, 9^{0}GF, 8^{0}GF, 10^{5}G, 11^{0}GF, 9^{0}G

	Starts	1st	2nd	3rd	Win & Pl
Career Total (Turf)	17	1	0	1	4767

48 8/00 Bevl 1m1f207yD G-F £4095

Total win prize-money £4095

Going (Turf): Sf: 0-1 GS: 0-2 Gd: 0-4 **GF: 1-9** Fm: 0-1
Distance: 5f/6f: 0-0 7f-8f: 0-1 **9f-13f: 1-15** 14f+: 0-1
Track : LH: 0-11 **RH: 1-5** Tight: 0-5 Gall: 0-3
Aids: Bl: 0-2 Vi: 0-1 Tstrap: 0-0
Best Rating: 50 6/01 Bevl 1m1f207y gd-fm

First Ballot (IRE)

109 **101**

5-y-o b g Perugino (USA)-Election Special (Chief Singer)
D R C Elsworth J C Smith

Placings:0/41610/000363-1223120 **(4172)**
2001: 14^{1}GS, 14^{2}GF, 20^{2}GF, 16^{3}GF, 14^{1}GF, 16^{2}G, 13^{0}G

	Starts	1st	2nd	3rd	Win & Pl
Career Total (Turf)	19	4	3	3	90752

101 7/01 Gdwd 1m6f B(0-105)H G-F £32500
92 5/01 Sals 1m6f15y C(0-90)H G-S £7488
89 8/99 Asct 2m45y C(0-90)H GD £12008
83 7/99 Newb 1m4f5y D G-F £4788

Total win prize-money £56784

Going (Turf): Sf: 0-2 GS: 1-1 Gd: 1-7 **GF: 2-8** Fm: 0-1
Distance: 5f/6f: 0-0 7f-8f: 0-1 9f-13f: 1-5 **14f+: 3-13**
Track : LH: 1-5 **RH: 3-13** Tight: 2-6 Gall: 2-8
Aids: Bl: 0-0 Vi: 0-0 Tstrap: 0-0
Best Rating: 101 8/01 Asct 2m45y good

Won over hurdles in February, and made all to land staying handicap at Salisbury in May, coasting home by seven lengths. Ran good races after, including when runner-up at Ascot, before landing a competitive Goodwood handicap in game fashion. He is apparently not the best of travellers and all his victories have come in the south. Acts on any ground and stays two and a half miles.

First Base

87 **47**

2-y-o ch g First Trump-Rose Music (Luthier)
Mrs J R Ramsden Mrs J R Ramsden

Placings:0000 **(4793)**
2001: 5^{0}GF, 6^{0}GF, 6^{0}G, 8^{0}G

	Starts	1st	2nd	3rd	Win & Pl
Career Total (Turf)	4	0	0	0	

Going (Turf): Sf: 0-0 GS: 0-0 Gd: 0-2 GF: 0-2 Fm: 0-0
Distance: 5f/6f: 0-3 7f-8f: 0-1 9f-13f: 0-0 14f+: 0-0
Track : LH: 0-1 RH: 0-0 Tight: 0-0 Gall: 0-0
Aids: Bl: 0-0 Vi: 0-1 Tstrap: 0-0
Best Rating: 47 9/01 Ayr 1m good

First Charter

97 **90**

2-y-o b c Polish Precedent (USA)-By Charter (Shirley Heights)
Sir Michael Stoute Saeed Suhail

Placings:02 **(5596)**
2001: 8^{0}G, 8^{2}GS

	Starts	1st	2nd	3rd	Win & Pl
Career Total (Turf)	2	0	1	0	2057

Going (Turf): Sf: 0-0 GS: 0-1 Gd: 0-1 GF: 0-0 Fm: 0-0
Distance: 5f/6f: 0-0 7f-8f: 0-2 9f-13f: 0-0 14f+: 0-0
Track : LH: 0-0 RH: 0-0 Tight: 0-0 Gall: 0-0
Aids: Bl: 0-0 Vi: 0-0 Tstrap: 0-0
Best Rating: 90 11/01 NmkR 1m gd-sft

First Degree

82 **48**

3-y-o br f Sabrehill (USA)-Degree (Warning)
S C Williams D A Shekells

Placings:0005-00 **(3618)**
2001: 9^{0}S, 12^{0}F

	Starts	1st	2nd	3rd	Win & Pl
Career Total (Turf)	6	0	0	0	0

Going (Turf): Sf: 0-3 GS: 0-0 Gd: 0-2 GF: 0-0 Fm: 0-1
Distance: 5f/6f: 0-3 7f-8f: 0-1 9f-13f: 0-2 14f+: 0-0
Track : LH: 0-3 RH: 0-2 Tight: 0-1 Gall: 0-2
Aids: Bl: 0-0 Vi: 0-0 Tstrap: 0-0
Best Rating: 30 8/01 Thsk 1m4f firm

First Eagle

83(88) (49)**60**

2-y-o b g Hector Protector (USA)-Merlin's Fancy (Caerleon (USA))
M R Channon The Fore Eagles

Placings:000 **(5177)**
2001: 6^{0}GF, 6^{0}S, 6^{0}HY

	Starts	1st	2nd	3rd	Win & Pl
Career Total (Turf)	3	0	0	0	

Going (Turf): Sf: 0-2 GS: 0-0 Gd: 0-0 GF: 0-1 Fm: 0-0
Distance: 5f/6f: 0-1 7f-8f: 0-2 9f-13f: 0-0 14f+: 0-0
Track : LH: 0-1 RH: 0-0 Tight: 0-0 Gall: 0-0
Aids: Bl: 0-0 Vi: 0-0 Tstrap: 0-0
Best Rating: 60 9/01 Newb 6f8y gd-fm

First Impression

103 **72**

6-y-o b g Saddlers' Hall (IRE)-First Sapphire (Simply Great (FR))
Mrs A J Perrett Ms E Reffo & B Cooper

Placings:600/245/20206-3330210 **(5463)**
2001: 9^{3}HY, 12^{3}S, 13^{3}GF, 14^{0}GF, 13^{2}GF, 11^{1}HY, 11^{0}G

	Starts	1st	2nd	3rd	Win & Pl
Career Total (Turf)	18	1	4	3	10594

72 10/01 Wind 1m3f135yD(0-75) HVY £4205

Total win prize-money £4206

Going (Turf): Sf: 1-6 GS: 0-0 Gd: 0-4 GF: 0-8 Fm: 0-0
Distance: 5f/6f: 0-0 7f-8f: 0-2 **9f-13f: 1-11** 14f+: 0-5
Track : LH: 0-9 RH: 0-6 **Tight: 1-8** Gall: 0-4
Aids: Bl: 0-0 Vi: 0-0 Tstrap: 0-0
Best Rating: 72 10/01 Wind 1m3f135y heavy

Not without ability but took 17 runs to lose his maiden tag. Stays middle distances. Acts on fast ground but more effective on heavy as it slows the others down. Does not have much in the way of a turn of foot.

First Maite

104(111) (88)**70**

8-y-o b g Komaite (USA)-Marina Plata (Julio Mariner)
S R Bowring S R Bowring

Placings:00100/25116220540/0516145600620/332623 3421235140010044/010001000210001540/4003244650 0340000000-602006400650023201 **(5681)**
2001: 7^{6}G, 5^{0}G, 6^{2}GF, 6^{0}F, 6^{0}G, 6^{6}GF, 6^{4}GF, 6^{0}G, 7^{0}GS, 5^{6}GF, 6^{5}GF, 5^{0}G, 5^{0}HY, 8^{2}G, 9^{3}G, 7^{2}S, 7^{0}GS, 8^{1}S

	Starts	1st	2nd	3rd	Win & Pl
Career Total (Turf)	75	8	8	4	109640
Career Total (AW)	32	5	5	4	30918

70	11/01	Donc	1m	E(0-80)H	SFT	£4699
88	11/99	Sthl	7f	D(0-85)H	STD	£3746
103	9/99	Asct	5f	B(0-105)H	HVY	£15317
101	8/99	Hayd	5f	C(0-100)H	SFT	£14395
97	5/99	York	6f	B(0-105)H	SFT	£13859
93	10/98	Asct	5f	B(0-110)H	SFT	£18156
83	7/98	Sthl	7f	D(0-85)H	STD	£3557
84	5/98	Ripn	5f	C(0-90)H	G-F	£7262
75	5/97	Bevl	5f	D(0-80)H	GD	£4614
67	4/97	Wolv	5f	F	STD	£2277
77	2/96	Sthl	6f	D(0-75)H	STD	£3517
78	2/96	Sthl	6f	E(0-70)H	STD	£2818
70	9/95	Bevl	5f	D	GD	£3678

Total win prize-money £97900

Going (Turf): Sf: 5-16 GS: 0-12 Gd: 2-28 GF: 1-18 Fm: 0-1
Distance: **5f/6f: 10-77** 7f-8f: 3-29 9f-13f: 0-1 14f+: 0-0
Track : **LH: 5-44** RH: 0-0 **Tight: 1-15** Gall: 0-1
Aids: **Bl: 12-88** Vi: 0-6 Tstrap: 1-5
Best Rating: 72 5/01 Donc 6f gd-fm

He has been around for a while now and tries hard, and he ended a long losing run when scoring at Doncaster in November. Effective between five furlongs and a mile. Goes well with cut in the ground. Acts on the All-Weather.

First Meeting

72 **52**
3-y-o b f Contract Law (USA)-Sunday News'N'Echo (USA) (Trempolino (USA))
M Dods D C Batey

Placings:2504-00 **(1469)**
2001: 6^{0}HY, 8^{0}GF

	Starts	1st	2nd	3rd	Win & Pl
Career Total (Turf)	6	0	1	0	1046

Going (Turf): Sf: 0-3 GS: 0-0 Gd: 0-1 GF: 0-2 Fm: 0-0
Distance: 5f/6f: 0-1 7f-8f: 0-5 9f-13f: 0-0 14f+: 0-0
Track : LH: 0-2 RH: 0-3 Tight: 0-3 Gall: 0-1
Aids: Bl: 0-0 Vi: 0-0 Tstrap: 0-0
Best Rating: 72 5/01 Donc 6f gd-fm

First Of Many

92 **91+**
2-y-o b f Darshaan-Star Profile (IRE) (Sadler's Wells (USA))
Sir Michael Stoute Maktoum Al Maktoum

Placings:5 **(4545)**
2001: 6^{5}GF

	Starts	1st	2nd	3rd	Win & Pl
Career Total (Turf)	1	0	0	0	0

Going (Turf): Sf: 0-0 GS: 0-0 Gd: 0-0 GF: 0-1 Fm: 0-0
Distance: 5f/6f: 0-0 7f-8f: 0-1 9f-13f: 0-0 14f+: 0-0
Track : LH: 0-0 RH: 0-0 Tight: 0-0 Gall: 0-0
Aids: Bl: 0-0 Vi: 0-0 Tstrap: 0-0
Best Rating: 91 9/01 Sals 6f212y gd-fm

First Ordained (IRE)

97(85) (66)**74**
2-y-o b c Mujadil (USA)-Ordinate (Nashwan (USA))
R Hannon T R Smith

Placings:6034234220052 **(5628)**
2001: 5^{6}GS, 6^{0}GF, 6^{3}G, 6^{4}GF, 7^{2}G, 7^{3}GF, 7^{4}G, 8^{2}GF, 6^{2}GF, 8^{0}G, 8^{0}G, 7^{5}S, 8^{2}G

	Starts	1st	2nd	3rd	Win & Pl
Career Total (Turf)	13	0	4	2	7036

Going (Turf): Sf: 0-1 GS: 0-1 Gd: 0-6 GF: 0-5 Fm: 0-0
Distance: 5f/6f: 0-3 7f-8f: 0-10 9f-13f: 0-0 14f+: 0-0
Track : LH: 0-3 RH: 0-0 Tight: 0-0 Gall: 0-0
Aids: Bl: 0-0 Vi: 0-0 Tstrap: 0-0
Best Rating: 77 9/01 Brig 6f209y gd-fm

First Steps (IRE)

102(103) (71)**61**
3-y-o b f Brief Truce (USA)-Wilsonic (Damister (USA))
B Smart B Smart

Placings:604-**0221**60424314**3**414 **(5416)**
2001: 8^{0}SD, 8^{2}SD, 8^{2}SW, 9^{1}SD, 8^{6}SD, 10^{0}GS, 9^{4}G, 9^{2}SD, 11^{4}GF, 10^{3}GF, 10^{1}GF, 9^{4}G, 10^{3}G, 9^{4}S, 9^{1}SD, 9^{4}SD

	Starts	1st	2nd	3rd	Win & Pl
Career Total (Turf)	10	1	0	2	9492
Career Total (AW)	9	2	3	0	7643

68	10/01	Wolv	1m1f79y	F(0-65)H	STD	£2394
60	8/01	Newb	1m2f6y	D(0-85)H	G-F	£7377
62	2/01	Wolv	1m1f79y	D	STD	£2961

Total win prize-money £12733

Going (Turf): Sf: 0-3 GS: 0-1 Gd: 0-3 **GF: 1-3** Fm: 0-0
Distance: 5f/6f: 0-1 7f-8f: 0-5 **9f-13f: 3-13** 14f+: 0-0
Track : **LH: 3-14** RH: 0-2 **Tight: 2-9** Gall: 1-3
Aids: **Bl: 2-9** Vi: 0-0 Tstrap: 0-0
Best Rating: 71 10/01 Wolv 1m1f79y stand

She got off the mark in a maiden on the Wolverhampton Fibresand in February and ran well on turf during the summer, including a victory in a fillies' handicap at Newbury in August. Returned to winning form back at Wolverhampton in October. Suited by nine to ten furlongs and likes to come off a strong pace.

First To Go

86 **52**
2-y-o ch f First Trump-Port Na Blath (On Your Mark)
M Dods Harry Whitton

Placings:0000 **(5086)**
2001: 6^{0}GF, 6^{0}GS, 7^{0}G, 7^{0}GS

	Starts	1st	2nd	3rd	Win & Pl
Career Total (Turf)	4	0	0	0	

Going (Turf): Sf: 0-0 GS: 0-2 Gd: 0-1 GF: 0-1 Fm: 0-0
Distance: 5f/6f: 0-2 7f-8f: 0-2 9f-13f: 0-0 14f+: 0-0
Track : LH: 0-2 RH: 0-0 Tight: 0-1 Gall: 0-0
Aids: Bl: 0-0 Vi: 0-0 Tstrap: 0-0
Best Rating: 52 8/01 Hayd 6f gd-sft

First Toast

73 **35**
3-y-o ch g First Trump-Toast (IRE) (Be My Guest (USA))
Miss Gay Kelleway Millennium 15

Placings:000 **(1870)**
2001: 8^{0}G, 7^{0}GF, 7^{0}F

	Starts	1st	2nd	3rd	Win & Pl
Career Total (Turf)	3	0	0	0	

Going (Turf): Sf: 0-0 GS: 0-0 Gd: 0-1 GF: 0-1 Fm: 0-1
Distance: 5f/6f: 0-0 7f-8f: 0-3 9f-13f: 0-0 14f+: 0-0
Track : LH: 0-1 RH: 0-0 Tight: 0-0 Gall: 0-0
Aids: Bl: 0-0 Vi: 0-0 Tstrap: 0-0
Best Rating: 35 5/01 NmkR 1m good

First Truth

91 **54**
4-y-o b g Rudimentary (USA)-Pursuit Of Truth (USA) (Irish River (FR))
Mrs H Dalton Ray Bailey

Placings:040215/6420465-000 **(5632)**
2001: 10^{0}S, 8^{0}GS, 10^{0}G

	Starts	1st	2nd	3rd	Win & Pl
Career Total (Turf)	16	1	2	0	11446

81	9/99	Pont	1m4y	D	GD	£4005

Total win prize-money £4005

Going (Turf): Sf: 0-5 GS: 0-2 **Gd: 1-7** GF: 0-2 Fm: 0-0
Distance: 5f/6f: 0-3 7f-8f: 0-3 **9f-13f: 1-9** 14f+: 0-1
Track : **LH: 1-13** RH: 0-0 Tight: 0-4 Gall: 0-1
Aids: Bl: 0-0 Vi: 0-0 Tstrap: 0-0
Best Rating: 54 11/01 Rdcr 1m2f good

Only success came in a Pontefract maiden over a mile at two. Now trained by Heather Dalton. Has gradually slipped down the weights. Acts on soft ground.

First Venture

105(103) (74d)**62**
4-y-o b g Formidable (USA)-Diamond Wedding (USA) (Diamond Shoal)
C N Allen Pelicas Partnership

Placings:002235/2230044200215045-3240404236401600003 **(4475)**
2001: 6^{3}SD, 7^{2}SD, 6^{4}SD, 7^{0}SW, 6^{4}SD, 6^{0}SD, 7^{4}SD, 6^{2}GF, 6^{3}G, 5^{6}F, 5^{4}GF, 5^{0}F, 5^{1}GF, 5^{6}GF, 5^{0}GF, 5^{0}G, 5^{0}G, 7^{0}S, 5^{3}GF

	Starts	1st	2nd	3rd	Win & Pl
Career Total (Turf)	23	1	3	3	8153
Career Total (AW)	18	1	5	2	8351

62	6/01	Ling	5f	E(0-75)H	G-F	£2884
66	11/00	Sthl	7f	D	STD	£2716

Total win prize-money £5600

Going (Turf): Sf: 0-4 GS: 0-0 Gd: 0-9 **GF: 1-8** Fm: 0-2
Distance: 5f/6f: 1-24 7f-8f: 1-17 9f-13f: 0-0 14f+: 0-0
Track : **LH: 1-27** RH: 0-2 Tight: 0-10 Gall: 0-2
Aids: Bl: 1-11 Vi: 1-14 Tstrap: 0-0
Best Rating: 74 1/01 Sthl 7f stand

Fisher Island (IRE)

103(103) (52)**42**
4-y-o b/br f Sri Pekan (USA)-Liberty Song (IRE) (Last Tycoon)
R Hollinshead The C H F Partnership

Placings:45053450/**6344**0401053**343445**-02423533265 **(4800)**
2001: 8^{0}HY, 9^{2}HY, 12^{4}F, 11^{2}GF, 12^{3}SD, 11^{5}GF, 9^{3}GF, 9^{3}GF, 9^{2}GF, 14^{6}GF, 10^{5}F

	Starts	1st	2nd	3rd	Win & Pl
Career Total (Turf)	24	1	3	3	9676
Career Total (AW)	12	0	0	5	2168

52	7/00	Nott	1m1f213yE(0-70)H		G-F	£3005

Total win prize-money £3006

Going (Turf): Sf: 0-6 GS: 0-4 Gd: 0-3 **GF: 1-8** Fm: 0-3
Distance: 5f/6f: 0-3 7f-8f: 0-6 **9f-13f: 1-24** 14f+: 0-3
Track : **LH: 1-24** RH: 0-7 Tight: 0-11 Gall: 0-0
Aids: Bl: 0-0 Vi: 0-0 Tstrap: 0-0
Best Rating: 43 5/01 Nott 1m1f213y heavy

Fittonia (FR)

86 **70**
2-y-o ch f Ashkalani (IRE)-Fly For Fame (Shaadi (USA))
J D Bethell Mrs John Moore

Placings:5 **(5147)**
2001: 7^{5}G

	Starts	1st	2nd	3rd	Win & Pl
Career Total (Turf)	1	0	0	0	0

Going (Turf): Sf: 0-0 GS: 0-0 Gd: 0-1 GF: 0-0 Fm: 0-0
Distance: 5f/6f: 0-0 7f-8f: 0-1 9f-13f: 0-0 14f+: 0-0
Track : LH: 0-0 RH: 0-0 Tight: 0-0 Gall: 0-0
Aids: Bl: 0-0 Vi: 0-0 Tstrap: 0-0
Best Rating: 70 10/01 Rdcr 7f good

Made a promising debut at Redcar.

Five Stars

99 **89+**

2-y-o ch f Bahamian Bounty-Star Ridge (USA) (Storm Bird (CAN))
H R A Cecil Buckram Oak Holdings

Placings:1 **(5623)**
2001: 8^{1}GS

	Starts	1st	2nd	3rd	Win & Pl
Career Total (Turf)	1	1	0	0	3705

89 11/01 Nott 1m54y D G-S £3705
Total win prize-money £3705

Going (Turf): Sf: 0-0 **GS: 1-1** Gd: 0-0 GF: 0-0 Fm: 0-0
Distance: 5f/6f: 0-0 7f-8f: 0-0 **9f-13f: 1-1** 14f+: 0-0
Track : **LH: 1-1** RH: 0-0 Tight: 0-0 Gall: 0-0
Aids: Bl: 0-0 Vi: 0-0 Tstrap: 0-0
Best Rating: 89 11/01 Nott 1m54y gd-sft

She made a winning debut at Nottingham in November and should progress.

Fiveeightsarf

79 **50**

2-y-o b c Forzando-Fair Eleanor (Saritamer (USA))
B R Millman David Morgan (essex)

Placings:0000 **(5128)**
2001: 5^{0}GF, 6^{0}GF, 6^{0}G, 6^{0}HY

	Starts	1st	2nd	3rd	Win & Pl
Career Total (Turf)	4	0	0	0	

Going (Turf): Sf: 0-1 GS: 0-0 Gd: 0-1 GF: 0-2 Fm: 0-0
Distance: 5f/6f: 0-3 7f-8f: 0-1 9f-13f: 0-0 14f+: 0-0
Track : LH: 0-0 RH: 0-1 Tight: 0-0 Gall: 0-1
Aids: Bl: 0-0 Vi: 0-0 Tstrap: 0-0
Best Rating: 50 8/01 Sals 6f212y gd-fm

Fiza (IRE)

79 **46**

2-y-o b c Revoque (IRE)-Double Eight (IRE) (Common Grounds)
M L W Bell Richard I Morris Jr

Placings:000 **(5184)**
2001: 5^{0}G, 6^{0}GF, 5^{0}GS

	Starts	1st	2nd	3rd	Win & Pl
Career Total (Turf)	3	0	0	0	

Going (Turf): Sf: 0-0 GS: 0-1 Gd: 0-1 GF: 0-1 Fm: 0-0
Distance: 5f/6f: 0-3 7f-8f: 0-0 9f-13f: 0-0 14f+: 0-0
Track : LH: 0-0 RH: 0-0 Tight: 0-0 Gall: 0-0
Aids: Bl: 0-0 Vi: 0-0 Tstrap: 0-0
Best Rating: 46 7/01 Donc 6f gd-fm

Fizzy Treat

103 **61**

3-y-o b f Efisio-Special Guest (Be My Guest (USA))
R Guest S Lury

Placings:203 **(5528)**
2001: 8^{2}HY, 7^{0}S, 8^{3}HY

	Starts	1st	2nd	3rd	Win & Pl
Career Total (Turf)	3	0	1	1	2072

Going (Turf): Sf: 0-3 GS: 0-0 Gd: 0-0 GF: 0-0 Fm: 0-0
Distance: 5f/6f: 0-0 7f-8f: 0-1 9f-13f: 0-2 14f+: 0-0
Track : LH: 0-2 RH: 0-0 Tight: 0-0 Gall: 0-0
Aids: Bl: 0-0 Vi: 0-0 Tstrap: 0-0
Best Rating: 61 9/01 Hayd 1m30y heavy

Flag Fen (USA)

103 (32?)**48**

10-y-o b/br g Riverman (USA)-Damascus Flag (USA) (Damascus (USA))
H J Collingridge Mrs Carol Dolan

Placings:223/112/000/30040005422000/**250106/500**15 4100/00331005/0620600-33606 **(2669)**
2001: 10^{3}S, 10^{3}S, 11^{6}GF, 12^{0}GF, 10^{6}G

	Starts	1st	2nd	3rd	Win & Pl
Career Total (Turf)	53	6	6	6	42061
Career Total (AW)	5	0	1	0	937

68 7/99 Yarm 1m2f21y F(0-75)H GD £2469
60 9/98 NmkR 1m2f E(0-85)H GD £5425
60 7/98 NmkJ 1m2f E(0-70)H GD £4110
65 5/97 Ripn 1m F G-S £2866
8/94 Curr 1m2f (0-110)H SFT £12900
8/94 Rosc 1m2f GD £2226
Total win prize-money £29996

Going (Turf): Sf: 0-5 GS: 1-5 **Gd: 3-17** GF: 0-17 Fm: 0-3
Distance: 5f/6f: 0-1 7f-8f: 1-15 **9f-13f: 3-36** 14f+: 0-0
Track : LH: 1-24 **RH: 2-19 Tight: 2-12** Gall: 1-15
Aids: Bl: 0-1 Vi: 0-0 Tstrap: 0-0
Best Rating: 48 5/01 Yarm 1m3f101y gd-fm

Flag Of Democracy (USA)

101(103) (65)**69**

3-y-o ch c Distant View (USA)-Capital Hill (USA) (Temperence Hill (USA))
J Noseda The Socrates Partnership

Placings:106203 **(5131)**
2001: 8^{1}SW, 8^{0}G, 8^{6}SD, 8^{2}G, 8^{0}G, 7^{3}HY

	Starts	1st	2nd	3rd	Win & Pl
Career Total (Turf)	4	0	1	1	1627
Career Total (AW)	2	1	0	0	2884

62 2/01 Ling 1m D SLW £2884
Total win prize-money £2884

Going (Turf): Sf: 0-1 GS: 0-0 Gd: 0-3 GF: 0-0 Fm: 0-0
Distance: 5f/6f: 0-0 **7f-8f: 1-5** 9f-13f: 0-1 14f+: 0-0
Track : **LH: 1-4** RH: 0-1 **Tight: 1-2** Gall: 0-0
Aids: Bl: 0-0 Vi: 0-3 Tstrap: 0-0
Best Rating: 69 8/01 Hayd 1m30y good

Scored on his racecourse debut on sand over a mile in spring of 2001. Lightly raced and hung badly in a first-time visor at Haydock in August.

Flak Jacket

111 **74**

6-y-o b g Magic Ring (IRE)-Vaula (Henbit (USA))
D Nicholls The Knavesmire Alliance

Placings:00311/00002600/00002111300000-03002412410000 **(5381)**
2001: 5^{0}S, 5^{3}S, 7^{0}GF, 7^{0}GF, 6^{2}GF, 5^{4}GS, 5^{1}S, 5^{2}GF, 5^{4}GF, 6^{1}G, 6^{0}G, 5^{0}GS, 5^{0}GS, 5^{0}S

	Starts	1st	2nd	3rd	Win & Pl
Career Total (Turf)	41	7	4	3	79971

74 8/01 Gdwd 6f B H GD £17485
70 7/01 Hayd 5f D(0-80)H SFT £11277
71 8/00 Gdwd 6f B H GD £17290
72 7/00 Catt 5f D(0-85)H G-F £3984
69 7/00 Pont 6f E(0-65) G-F £3198
83 7/98 Hayd 6f C(0-100)H G-F £5569
79 6/98 Kemp 6f D(0-80)H HVY £3566
Total win prize-money £62372

Going (Turf): Sf: 2-11 GS: 0-7 Gd: 2-10 **GF: 3-13** Fm: 0-0
Distance: **5f/6f: 7-35** 7f-8f: 0-6 9f-13f: 0-0 14f+: 0-0
Track : **LH: 1-4** RH: 0-0 Tight: 0-2 Gall: 0-0
Aids: Bl: 0-1 Vi: 0-0 **Tstrap: 5-18**
Best Rating: 74 8/01 Gdwd 6f good

Fair sprinter, though disappointing on occasions. He has shown his best form in midsummer and that has been the case again this term, including victories at Haydock in July and the same race at Glorious Goodwood that he won last season. Likes five or six furlongs and fast ground, although he has won on much softer.

Flambe

108(98) (75)**73**

3-y-o b g Whittingham (IRE)-Uaeflame (IRE) (Polish Precedent (USA))
P C Haslam Mrs B M Hawkins & Marquess Of Downshire

Placings:030111-5300110000 **(5406)**
2001: 6^{5}SD, 9^{3}SW, 6^{0}S, 8^{0}S, 8^{1}F, 8^{1}GF, 8^{0}G, 7^{0}GF, 8^{0}GS, 8^{0}SD

	Starts	1st	2nd	3rd	Win & Pl
Career Total (Turf)	9	2	0	1	7337
Career Total (AW)	7	3	0	1	8832

73 6/01 Newc 1m D(0-85)H G-F £3952
67 5/01 Newc 1m E(0-70)H FRM £3045
73 11/00 Sthl 1m E(0-75) STD £2842
75 11/00 Sthl 7f E(0-85) STD £2772
61 11/00 Sthl 6f E(0-75) STD £2793
Total win prize-money £15404

Going (Turf): Sf: 0-2 GS: 0-1 Gd: 0-1 **GF: 1-4 Fm: 1-1**
Distance: 5f/6f: 1-6 **7f-8f: 4-7** 9f-13f: 0-3 14f+: 0-0
Track : **LH: 5-11** RH: 0-0 Tight: 0-2 **Gall: 2-3**
Aids: Bl: 0-0 Vi: 0-0 Tstrap: 0-0
Best Rating: 73 6/01 Newc 1m gd-fm

A gelding with an unusually high knee action, he completed a Southwell hat-trick in November 2000 in nurseries up to a mile. His form floundered before he found his feet on the grass with back-to-back wins at Newcastle the following summer, but he has since lost his way again. He goes best on a sound surface.

Flamebird (IRE)

92(87) (31)**31**

4-y-o b f Mukaddamah (USA)-Flamenco (USA) (Dance Spell (USA))
Mrs A L M King Mrs L R Lovell

Placings:0050-06004 **(3621)**
2001: 8^{0}SD, 10^{6}SD, 10^{0}GF, 5^{0}GS, 7^{4}F

	Starts	1st	2nd	3rd	Win & Pl
Career Total (Turf)	7	0	0	0	273
Career Total (AW)	2	0	0	0	0

Going (Turf): Sf: 0-0 GS: 0-2 Gd: 0-1 GF: 0-3 Fm: 0-1
Distance: 5f/6f: 0-1 7f-8f: 0-5 9f-13f: 0-3 14f+: 0-0
Track : LH: 0-6 RH: 0-0 Tight: 0-3 Gall: 0-0
Aids: Bl: 0-2 Vi: 0-0 Tstrap: 0-0
Best Rating: 31 4/01 Ling 1m stand

Flamenca (USA)

80 **46**

2-y-o b f Diesis-Highland Ceilidh (IRE) (Scottish Reel)
Sir Mark Prescott Cyril Humphris

Placings:60 **(5168)**
2001: 7^{6}HY, 10^{0}GS

	Starts	1st	2nd	3rd	Win & Pl
Career Total (Turf)	2	0	0	0	0

Going (Turf): Sf: 0-1 GS: 0-1 Gd: 0-0 GF: 0-0 Fm: 0-0
Distance: 5f/6f: 0-0 7f-8f: 0-1 9f-13f: 0-1 14f+: 0-0
Track : LH: 0-2 RH: 0-0 Tight: 0-0 Gall: 0-0
Aids: Bl: 0-0 Vi: 0-0 Tstrap: 0-0
Best Rating: 46 9/01 Hayd 7f30y heavy

Flaming Spirt

51

2-y-o b f Blushing Flame (USA)-Fair Test (Fair Season)
J S Moore W J Wyatt

Placings:5 **(5665)**

2001: 6^{5}HY

	Starts	1st	2nd	3rd	Win & Pl
Career Total (Turf)	1	0	0	0	0

Going (Turf): Sf: 0-1 GS: 0-0 Gd: 0-0 GF: 0-0 Fm: 0-0
Distance: 5f/6f: 0-1 7f-8f: 0-0 9f-13f: 0-0 14f+: 0-0
Track : LH: 0-0 RH: 0-0 Tight: 0-0 Gall: 0-0
Aids: Bl: 0-0 Vi: 0-0 Tstrap: 0-0
Best Rating: 51 11/01 Wind 6f heavy

Flamme De La Vie

84(91) (53)**34**
3-y-o b g Blushing Flame (USA)-La Belle Vie (Indian King (USA))
J K Price (G A Butler 5/7) J K Price

Placings:400-2005 **(2767)**
2001: 11^{2}SD, 10^{0}GF, 9^{0}G, 16^{5}GF

	Starts	1st	2nd	3rd	Win & Pl
Career Total (Turf)	5	0	0	0	179
Career Total (AW)	2	0	1	0	644

Going (Turf): Sf: 0-1 GS: 0-1 Gd: 0-1 GF: 0-2 Fm: 0-0
Distance: 5f/6f: 0-0 7f-8f: 0-2 9f-13f: 0-4 14f+: 0-1
Track : LH: 0-6 RH: 0-0 Tight: 0-2 Gall: 0-0
Aids: Bl: 0-0 Vi: 0-0 Tstrap: 0-1
Best Rating: 46 4/01 Sthl 1m3f stand

Flapdoodle

97(106) (56)**49**
3-y-o b f Superpower-My Concordia (Belfort (FR))
A W Carroll John Halsey

Placings:0031-250534005 **(1569)**
2001: 5^{2}SD, 5^{5}SW, 5^{0}SD, 5^{5}SD, 5^{3}SD, 5^{4}SD, 5^{0}SD, 5^{0}GS, 5^{5}F

	Starts	1st	2nd	3rd	Win & Pl
Career Total (Turf)	4	0	0	0	0
Career Total (AW)	9	1	1	2	3118

57 11/00 Wolv 5f G STD £1834
Total win prize-money £1834

Going (Turf): Sf: 0-1 GS: 0-1 Gd: 0-1 GF: 0-0 Fm: 0-1
Distance: 5f/6f: 1-13 7f-8f: 0-0 9f-13f: 0-0 14f+: 0-0
Track : LH: 1-9 RH: 0-2 **Tight: 1-7** Gall: 0-3
Aids: Bl: 0-0 Vi: 0-0 Tstrap: 0-0
Best Rating: 56 1/01 Wolv 5f stand

Flash Of Light (IRE)

89(71) (20)**35**
3-y-o b f Brief Truce (USA)-Dancing Light (Dancer's Image (USA))
P D Evans P D Evans

Placings:000-000 **(2101)**
2001: 8^{0}GF, 10^{0}GF, 11^{0}GF

	Starts	1st	2nd	3rd	Win & Pl
Career Total (Turf)	5	0	0	0	
Career Total (AW)	1	0	0	0	

Going (Turf): Sf: 0-0 GS: 0-0 Gd: 0-0 GF: 0-5 Fm: 0-0
Distance: 5f/6f: 0-0 7f-8f: 0-4 9f-13f: 0-2 14f+: 0-0
Track : LH: 0-2 RH: 0-2 Tight: 0-4 Gall: 0-0
Aids: Bl: 0-0 Vi: 0-2 Tstrap: 0-1
Best Rating: 35 5/01 Ripn 1m gd-fm

Flashfeet

99(98) (22)**5**
11-y-o b g Rousillon (USA)-Miellita (King Emperor (USA))
P D Purdy P D Purdy

Placings:2/23646003**056**/323043500/**0**2431350/**6056**/0/00/000000/0000046004060000-000 **(5100)**
2001: 7^{0}GF, 8^{0}GF, 9^{0}GS,

	Starts	1st	2nd	3rd	Win & Pl
Career Total (Turf)	26	0	3	2	4492
Career Total (AW)	35	1	1	5	5636

47 6/95 Wolv 7f F(0-65)H STD £2519
Total win prize-money £2519

Going (Turf): Sf: 0-5 GS: 0-4 Gd: 0-5 GF: 0-12 Fm: 0-0
Distance: 5f/6f: 0-0 **7f-8f: 1-45** 9f-13f: 0-16 14f+: 0-0
Track : LH: 1-39 RH: 0-10 **Tight: 1-22** Gall: 0-6
Aids: Bl: 0-2 Vi: 0-0 Tstrap: 0-0
Best Rating: 5 6/01 NmkJ 7f gd-fm

Flashtalkin' Flood

63(91) (34)**39**
7-y-o ch g Then Again-Linguistic (Porto Bello)
C A Dwyer M O Golam Rassoude

Placings:60035100**0**/310000/004020**0-050600 (0643)**
2001: 12^{0}SW, 8^{5}SD, 8^{0}SW, 8^{6}SD, 12^{0}SW, 9^{0}HY

	Starts	1st	2nd	3rd	Win & Pl
Career Total (Turf)	20	2	1	2	7758
Career Total (AW)	8	0	0	0	0

63 5/98 Haml 1m65y E(0-70)H G-S £3533
70 6/97 Nott 1m54y G(0-60)H SFT £2513
Total win prize-money £6048

Going (Turf): Sf: 1-5 GS: 1-4 Gd: 0-4 GF: 0-6 Fm: 0-1
Distance: 5f/6f: 0-0 7f-8f: 0-7 **9f-13f: 2-21** 14f+: 0-0
Track : LH: 1-19 RH: 1-7 **Tight: 1-14** Gall: 0-2
Aids: Bl: 0-0 Vi: 0-0 Tstrap: 0-0
Best Rating: 36 2/01 Sthl 1m stand

Flat Spin

98 **95**
2-y-o b c Spinning World (USA)-Trois Graces (USA) (Alysheba (USA))
J L Dunlop Wafic Said

Placings:140 **(5134)**
2001: 7^{1}GF, 7^{4}GF, 7^{0}G

	Starts	1st	2nd	3rd	Win & Pl
Career Total (Turf)	3	1	0	0	6259

88 8/01 Newb 7f D G-F £5694
Total win prize-money £5694

Going (Turf): Sf: 0-0 GS: 0-0 Gd: 0-1 **GF: 1-2** Fm: 0-0
Distance: 5f/6f: 0-0 **7f-8f: 1-3** 9f-13f: 0-0 14f+: 0-0
Track : LH: 0-0 RH: 0-0 Tight: 0-0 Gall: 0-0
Aids: Bl: 0-0 Vi: 0-0 Tstrap: 0-0
Best Rating: 95 9/01 Donc 7f gd-fm

Won a Newbury maiden in good style but was soundly beaten in a Doncaster conditions event. Suited by seven furlongs, and has only raced on good to firm ground.

Flat Stanley

79 **46**
2-y-o b c Celtic Swing-Cool Grey (Absalom)
T D Easterby John Endersby

Placings:000 **(5371)**
2001: 7^{0}G, 7^{0}GS, 8^{0}G

	Starts	1st	2nd	3rd	Win & Pl
Career Total (Turf)	3	0	0	0	

Going (Turf): Sf: 0-0 GS: 0-1 Gd: 0-2 GF: 0-0 Fm: 0-0
Distance: 5f/6f: 0-0 7f-8f: 0-3 9f-13f: 0-0 14f+: 0-0
Track : LH: 0-0 RH: 0-1 Tight: 0-0 Gall: 0-0
Aids: Bl: 0-0 Vi: 0-0 Tstrap: 0-0
Best Rating: 46 10/01 Newc 7f gd-sft

Flaxen Pride (IRE)

101 **34**
6-y-o ch m Pips Pride-Fair Chance (Young Emperor)
Mrs M Reveley A Evans, M Bailey, D Playforth, J Snaith

Placings:200/000004/000156/000-005350 **(4272)**
2001: 11^{0}S, 10^{0}GF, 10^{5}GF, 12^{3}F, 9^{5}F, 9^{0}GF

	Starts	1st	2nd	3rd	Win & Pl
Career Total (Turf)	24	1	1	1	4572

41 8/99 Leic 1m8y E(0-70)H G-F £3096
Total win prize-money £3097

Going (Turf): Sf: 0-3 GS: 0-0 Gd: 0-6 **GF: 1-11** Fm: 0-4
Distance: 5f/6f: 0-3 7f-8f: 0-11 **9f-13f: 1-10** 14f+: 0-0
Track : LH: 0-5 RH: 0-6 Tight: 0-5 Gall: 0-3
Aids: Bl: 0-0 Vi: 0-0 Tstrap: 0-0
Best Rating: 34 7/01 Rdcr 1m1f firm

Fledge

80 **50**
2-y-o b f Botanic (USA)-Kitty Kitty Cancan (Warrshan (USA))
D R C Elsworth The Fledglings

Placings:00 **(5491)**
2001: 6^{0}GS, 6^{0}HY

	Starts	1st	2nd	3rd	Win & Pl
Career Total (Turf)	2	0	0	0	

Going (Turf): Sf: 0-1 GS: 0-1 Gd: 0-0 GF: 0-0 Fm: 0-0
Distance: 5f/6f: 0-1 7f-8f: 0-1 9f-13f: 0-0 14f+: 0-0
Track : LH: 0-0 RH: 0-0 Tight: 0-0 Gall: 0-0
Aids: Bl: 0-0 Vi: 0-0 Tstrap: 0-0
Best Rating: 50 10/01 NmkR 6f gd-sft

Fleeting Fancy

90(80) (9)**33**
4-y-o b f Thatching-Fleetwood Fancy (Taufan (USA))
G M McCourt (S Dow 11/4) M Israr Ahmad

Placings:00/030050400-**00050**000 **(3734)**
2001: 7^{0}SD, 7^{0}SW, 9^{0}SW, 7^{5}SW, 10^{0}SD, 10^{0}GF, 11^{0}GF, 11^{0}G

	Starts	1st	2nd	3rd	Win & Pl
Career Total (Turf)	14	0	0	1	693
Career Total (AW)	5	0	0	0	0

Going (Turf): Sf: 0-1 GS: 0-1 Gd: 0-3 GF: 0-7 Fm: 0-2
Distance: 5f/6f: 0-8 7f-8f: 0-6 9f-13f: 0-5 14f+: 0-0
Track : LH: 0-7 RH: 0-3 Tight: 0-7 Gall: 0-3
Aids: Bl: 0-0 Vi: 0-3 Tstrap: 0-0
Best Rating: 27 7/01 Wind 1m2f7y gd-fm

Fletcher

104(34) (31)**68**
7-y-o b g Salse (USA)-Ballet Classique (USA) (Sadler's Wells (USA))
H Morrison Lady Margadale

Placings:1044020/0336506000/4032526521**0**/0602300 0/0000223211510200**0**-35451331640020 **(5492)**
2001: 11^{3}GS, 14^{5}GS, 12^{4}S, 13^{5}GF, 12^{1}GF, 14^{3}S, 16^{3}GF, 13^{1}GF, 12^{6}GF, 14^{0}GF, 14^{0}GF, 14^{0}GS, 16^{2}GS, 16^{0}HY

	Starts	1st	2nd	3rd	Win & Pl
Career Total (Turf)	66	7	10	8	48265
Career Total (AW)	1	0	0	0	

67 7/01 Newb 1m5f61y E(0-80)H G-F £3568
62 6/01 NmkR 1m4f F(0-60)H G-F £4514
67 8/00 Sals 1m6f15y E(0-70)H G-F £2892
61 7/00 Sand 1m6f D(0-80)H G-F £4192
58 7/00 Sals 1m4f F(0-75)H GD £2590
78 10/98 Asct 1m4f E(0-90)H SFT £4713
83 4/96 NmkR 5f D G-F £4230
Total win prize-money £26702

Going (Turf): Sf: 1-13 GS: 0-10 Gd: 1-10 **GF: 5-31** Fm: 0-2
Distance: 5f/6f: 1-4 7f-8f: 0-3 9f-13f: 3-26 14f+: 3-34
Track : LH: 1-23 **RH: 5-37** Tight: 2-22 **Gall: 3-20**
Aids: Bl: 0-0 Vi: 0-1 Tstrap: 0-0
Best Rating: 67 7/01 Newb 1m5f61y gd-fm

He is not the most straightforward of rides, but goes well for Sarah Bosley who has won twice on him this season. Suited by 12 to 14 furlongs, he handles soft ground but is better on fast.

Flight Of Dreams (IRE)

99(98) (40)52

4-y-o b f College Chapel-Lady Portobello (Porto Bello)
M Wigham Cable Media Consultancy Ltd

Placings:000/006134-0220125500 **(3730)**
2001: 8^{0}SW, 8^{2}SW, 8^{2}SD, 7^{0}G, 7^{1}F, 8^{2}G, 7^{5}GF, 9^{5}GF, 8^{0}GF, 8^{0}GS

	Starts	1st	2nd	3rd	Win & Pl
Career Total (Turf)	16	2	1	1	6774
Career Total (AW)	3	0	2	0	1223

45	5/01	Brig	7f214y	E(0-70)H	FRM	£3010
41	8/00	Brig	6f209y	F(0-60)H	GD	£2467

Total win prize-money £5478

Going (Turf): Sf: 0-2 GS: 0-2 **Gd: 1-6** GF: 0-4 **Fm: 1-2**
Distance: 5f/6f: 0-3 **7f-8f: 2-10** 9f-13f: 0-6 14f+: 0-0
Track : **LH: 2-13** RH: 0-0 Tight: 0-2 Gall: 0-2
Aids: Bl: 0-1 Vi: 0-0 Tstrap: 0-0
Best Rating: 52 5/01 Yarm 1m3y good

Flight Of Eagles (IRE)

88 73

2-y-o gr c Paris House-Wisdom To Know (Bay Express)
A Berry Chris & Antonia Deuters

Placings:6360 **(3242)**
2001: 5^{6}GF, 5^{3}F, 5^{6}G, 5^{0}GF

	Starts	1st	2nd	3rd	Win & Pl
Career Total (Turf)	4	0	0	1	578

Going (Turf): Sf: 0-0 GS: 0-0 Gd: 0-1 GF: 0-2 Fm: 0-1
Distance: 5f/6f: 0-4 7f-8f: 0-0 9f-13f: 0-0 14f+: 0-0
Track : LH: 0-1 RH: 0-0 Tight: 0-1 Gall: 0-0
Aids: Bl: 0-0 Vi: 0-0 Tstrap: 0-1
Best Rating: 73 6/01 Ling 5f firm

A half-brother to Selhurstpark Flyer, and bred for speed, he was a promising third at Lingfiled on his second start but failed to build on that effort.

Flight Of Fancy

109 112+

3-y-o b f Sadler's Wells (USA)-Phantom Gold (Machiavellian (USA))
Sir Michael Stoute The Queen

Placings:21-42 **(1975)**
2001: 10^{4}F, 12^{2}GF

	Starts	1st	2nd	3rd	Win & Pl
Career Total (Turf)	4	1	2	0	89433

89	8/00	Sals	6f212y	D	G-F	£5044

Total win prize-money £5044

Going (Turf): Sf: 0-0 GS: 0-0 Gd: 0-1 **GF: 1-2** Fm: 0-1
Distance: 5f/6f: 0-0 **7f-8f: 1-2** 9f-13f: 0-2 14f+: 0-0
Track : LH: 0-2 RH: 0-0 Tight: 0-1 Gall: 0-1
Aids: Bl: 0-0 Vi: 0-0 Tstrap: 0-0
Best Rating: 112 6/01 Epsm 1m4f10y gd-fm

She was not given a hard race in the Musidora at York, despite not getting the best of runs, and was beaten fair and square by Imagine in the Oaks. Not seen again and retired to the paddocks.

Flight Refund

4-y-o ch g Missed Flight-Settlement (USA) (Irish River (FR))
R Hollinshead Mrs A L Wood

Placings:000/006-P **(0287)**
2001: 12^{P}SW

	Starts	1st	2nd	3rd	Win & Pl
Career Total (Turf)	5	0	0	0	0
Career Total (AW)	2	0	0	0	

Going (Turf): Sf: 0-2 GS: 0-1 Gd: 0-1 GF: 0-1 Fm: 0-0
Distance: 5f/6f: 0-0 7f-8f: 0-3 9f-13f: 0-4 14f+: 0-0
Track : LH: 0-5 RH: 0-0 Tight: 0-1 Gall: 0-0
Aids: Bl: 0-0 Vi: 0-0 Tstrap: 0-0

Flight Sequence

108 76

5-y-o b m Polar Falcon (USA)-Doubles (Damister (USA))
Lady Herries Tony Perkins

Placings:2424/602016-13 **(2045)**
2001: 10^{1}G, 10^{3}GF

	Starts	1st	2nd	3rd	Win & Pl
Career Total (Turf)	12	2	3	1	13059

76	5/01	Wind	1m2f7y	D(0-75)	GD	£4166
75	8/00	Epsm	1m2f18y	D(0-75)	GD	£4173

Total win prize-money £8340

Going (Turf): Sf: 0-1 GS: 0-1 **Gd: 2-6** GF: 0-4 Fm: 0-0
Distance: 5f/6f: 0-0 7f-8f: 0-3 **9f-13f: 2-9** 14f+: 0-0
Track : **LH: 1-3** RH: 0-6 **Tight: 2-6** Gall: 0-1
Aids: Bl: 0-0 **Vi: 1-2** Tstrap: 0-0
Best Rating: 76 5/01 Wind 1m2f7y good

Flight To Tuscany

87(66) 33

3-y-o b f Bonny Scot (IRE)-Tuscan Butterfly (Beldale Flutter (USA))
J M Bradley A C Jones

Placings:00060 **(2821)**
2001: 8^{0}SW, 10^{0}GS, 9^{0}S, 14^{6}F, 18^{0}GF

	Starts	1st	2nd	3rd	Win & Pl
Career Total (Turf)	4	0	0	0	0
Career Total (AW)	1	0	0	0	

Going (Turf): Sf: 0-1 GS: 0-1 Gd: 0-0 GF: 0-1 Fm: 0-1
Distance: 5f/6f: 0-0 7f-8f: 0-1 9f-13f: 0-2 14f+: 0-2
Track : LH: 0-4 RH: 0-1 Tight: 0-3 Gall: 0-0
Aids: Bl: 0-0 Vi: 0-0 Tstrap: 0-0
Best Rating: 33 5/01 Sals 1m1f198y soft

Flint River

101 80

3-y-o b c Red Ransom (USA)-She's All Class (USA) (Rahy (USA))
R F Johnson Houghton Mrs C J Hue Williams

Placings:220210-060004400 **(5391)**
2001: 6^{0}G, 6^{6}GF, 7^{0}GF, 7^{0}GF, 6^{0}GF, 6^{4}GF, 7^{4}G, 7^{0}GF, 7^{0}GS

	Starts	1st	2nd	3rd	Win & Pl
Career Total (Turf)	15	1	3	0	7981

78	9/00	Wwck	6f21y	E	G-F	£2415

Total win prize-money £2415

Going (Turf): Sf: 0-0 GS: 0-1 Gd: 0-5 **GF: 1-9** Fm: 0-0
Distance: 5f/6f: 0-9 **7f-8f: 1-6** 9f-13f: 0-0 14f+: 0-0
Track : **LH: 1-3** RH: 0-2 Tight: 0-1 Gall: 0-1
Aids: Bl: 0-1 Vi: 0-0 Tstrap: 0-0
Best Rating: 82 6/01 NmkR 6f gd-fm

He got off the mark at the fifth time of asking at two and has run well in some hot handicaps since, but he may need some more help from the Handicapper. Best at six furlongs and acts on fast ground.

Flipside (IRE)

85(73) (4)25

3-y-o b c Dolphin Street (FR)-Trinity Hall (Hallgate)
J W Hills The Dan Abbott Racing Partnership

Placings:00-000 **(2522)**
2001: 8^{0}SW, 8^{0}F, 10^{0}GF

	Starts	1st	2nd	3rd	Win & Pl
Career Total (Turf)	4	0	0	0	
Career Total (AW)	1	0	0	0	

Going (Turf): Sf: 0-0 GS: 0-1 Gd: 0-0 GF: 0-2 Fm: 0-1
Distance: 5f/6f: 0-0 7f-8f: 0-2 9f-13f: 0-3 14f+: 0-0
Track : LH: 0-3 RH: 0-0 Tight: 0-2 Gall: 0-0
Aids: Bl: 0-0 Vi: 0-0 Tstrap: 0-0
Best Rating: 23 6/01 Wwck 1m2f188y gd-fm

Fliquet Bay (IRE)

85 57

4-y-o b g Namaqualand (USA)-Thatcherite (Final Straw)
G M McCourt A J Ballantyne

Placings:600/420303-0 **(1869)**
2001: 11^{0}GF

	Starts	1st	2nd	3rd	Win & Pl
Career Total (Turf)	10	0	1	2	1865

Going (Turf): Sf: 0-2 GS: 0-2 Gd: 0-1 GF: 0-5 Fm: 0-0
Distance: 5f/6f: 0-0 7f-8f: 0-3 9f-13f: 0-5 14f+: 0-2
Track : LH: 0-2 RH: 0-1 Tight: 0-4 Gall: 0-1
Aids: Bl: 0-5 Vi: 0-0 Tstrap: 0-0
Best Rating: 21 6/01 Wind 1m3f135y gd-fm

Flite Of Araby

101(84) (21)43

4-y-o b g Green Desert (USA)-Allegedly Blue (USA) (Alleged (USA))
W R Muir The Wheet Partnership

Placings:000/346-00360040 **(5640)**
2001: 11^{0}SD, 12^{0}S, 12^{3}GF, 12^{6}GF, 14^{0}GF, 11^{0}F, 11^{4}S, 13^{0}G

	Starts	1st	2nd	3rd	Win & Pl
Career Total (Turf)	13	0	0	2	1394
Career Total (AW)	1	0	0	0	

Going (Turf): Sf: 0-2 GS: 0-2 Gd: 0-2 GF: 0-6 Fm: 0-1
Distance: 5f/6f: 0-0 7f-8f: 0-2 9f-13f: 0-10 14f+: 0-2
Track : LH: 0-8 RH: 0-4 Tight: 0-6 Gall: 0-1
Aids: Bl: 0-0 Vi: 0-0 Tstrap: 0-0
Best Rating: 49 6/01 Kemp 1m4f gd-fm

Floating Charge

102(115) (85)82

7-y-o b g Sharpo-Poyle Fizz (Damister (USA))
J R Fanshawe The Leonard Curtis Partnership

Placings:02/5051060/10024361/2U00114-0300 **(3605)**
2001: 7^{0}GS, 7^{3}G, 8^{0}GF, 8^{0}GS

	Starts	1st	2nd	3rd	Win & Pl
Career Total (Turf)	26	5	2	2	35935
Career Total (AW)	2	0	1	0	2060

82	9/00	Newb	7f64y	C(0-95)H	G-F	£7930
78	9/00	Kemp	7f	D(0-80)H	GD	£7767
76	9/99	Kemp	1m	D(0-80)H	HVY	£7522
69	4/99	Wind	1m67y	E(0-70)H	GD	£2878
62	7/98	Rdcr	1m1f	E(0-70)	G-F	£2884

Total win prize-money £28983

Going (Turf): Sf: 1-4 GS: 0-5 **Gd: 2-9 GF: 2-8** Fm: 0-0
Distance: 5f/6f: 0-1 **7f-8f: 3-17** 9f-13f: 2-10 14f+: 0-0
Track : LH: 2-11 **RH: 3-10** Tight: 2-9 Gall: 2-5
Aids: Bl: 0-1 Vi: 0-1 Tstrap: 0-0
Best Rating: 71 4/01 Brig 7f214y gd-sft

Floating Ember

92(56) 36

4-y-o b f Rambo Dancer (CAN)-Spark (IRE) (Flash Of Steel)

Miss L A Perratt (J L Eyre 3/2) Martin West

Placings:00600/00103-**00000** **(2360)**
2001: 12^{0}SD, 14^{0}SD, 13^{0}GF, 11^{0}G, 10^{0}GF

	Starts	1st	2nd	3rd	Win & Pl
Career Total (Turf)	13	1	0	1	3918
Career Total (AW)	2	0	0	0	

44 6/00 Pont 1m2f6y E SFT £3591
Total win prize-money £3591

Going (Turf): Sf: 1-2 GS: 0-2 Gd: 0-5 GF: 0-3 Fm: 0-1
Distance: 5f/6f: 0-3 7f-8f: 0-3 **9f-13f: 1-7** 14f+: 0-2
Track : **LH: 1-8** RH: 0-3 Tight: 0-5 Gall: 0-0
Aids: Bl: 0-0 Vi: 0-0 Tstrap: 0-0
Best Rating: 20 5/01 Ayr 1m5f13y gd-fm

Floodgate

(70) (15)
4-y-o b g Bin Ajwaad (IRE)-Miss Haversham (Salse (USA))
C A Cyzer Mrs E A Cyzer

Placings:0 **(1450)**
2001: 9^{0}SD

	Starts	1st	2nd	3rd	Win & Pl
Career Total (Turf)	0	0	0	0	
Career Total (AW)	1	0	0	0	

Going (Turf): Sf: 0-0 GS: 0-0 Gd: 0-0 GF: 0-0 Fm: 0-0
Distance: 5f/6f: 0-0 7f-8f: 0-0 9f-13f: 0-1 14f+: 0-0
Track : LH: 0-1 RH: 0-0 Tight: 0-1 Gall: 0-0
Aids: Bl: 0-0 Vi: 0-0 Tstrap: 0-0
Best Rating: 15 5/01 Wolv 1m1f79y stand

Floot

99 **67**
3-y-o b c Piccolo-Midnight Owl (FR) (Ardross)
J L Dunlop Mrs Patrick Darling(susan Abbott Racing)

Placings:0003-13305030 **(4988)**
2001: 8^{1}HY, 7^{3}G, 8^{3}F, 10^{0}G, 10^{5}GS, 9^{0}G, 7^{3}GF, 8^{0}G

	Starts	1st	2nd	3rd	Win & Pl
Career Total (Turf)	12	1	0	4	5624

79 5/01 Nott 1m54y E(0-70)H HVY £3360
Total win prize-money £3360

Going (Turf): Sf: 1-3 GS: 0-1 Gd: 0-4 GF: 0-3 Fm: 0-1
Distance: 5f/6f: 0-1 7f-8f: 0-6 **9f-13f: 1-5** 14f+: 0-0
Track : **LH: 1-3** RH: 0-1 Tight: 0-2 Gall: 0-0
Aids: Bl: 0-0 Vi: 0-0 Tstrap: 0-0
Best Rating: 79 5/01 Nott 1m54y heavy

He relished the heavy going when stepped up to a mile in a Nottingham handicap in May, but has not had the suitable ground to race on since then.

Florentine Flutter

89 **70**
2-y-o b c Machiavellian (USA)-Party Doll (Be My Guest (USA))
J H M Gosden Wafic Said And Lord Lloyd Webber

Placings:00 **(5594)**
2001: 7^{0}GS, 6^{0}GS

	Starts	1st	2nd	3rd	Win & Pl
Career Total (Turf)	2	0	0	0	

Going (Turf): Sf: 0-0 GS: 0-2 Gd: 0-0 GF: 0-0 Fm: 0-0
Distance: 5f/6f: 0-1 7f-8f: 0-1 9f-13f: 0-0 14f+: 0-0
Track : LH: 0-0 RH: 0-0 Tight: 0-0 Gall: 0-0
Aids: Bl: 0-0 Vi: 0-0 Tstrap: 0-0
Best Rating: 70 10/01 NmkR 7f gd-sft

Florenzar (IRE)

31
3-y-o b f Inzar (USA)-Nurse Tyra (USA) (Dr Blum (USA))
Miss Sheena West Miss Elaine Parry

Placings:0 **(5670)**
2001: 8^{0}HY

	Starts	1st	2nd	3rd	Win & Pl
Career Total (Turf)	1	0	0	0	

Going (Turf): Sf: 0-1 GS: 0-0 Gd: 0-0 GF: 0-0 Fm: 0-0
Distance: 5f/6f: 0-0 7f-8f: 0-0 9f-13f: 0-1 14f+: 0-0
Track : LH: 0-0 RH: 0-1 Tight: 0-1 Gall: 0-0
Aids: Bl: 0-0 Vi: 0-0 Tstrap: 0-0

Florhill (IRE)

94 **75**
2-y-o ch c Danehill Dancer (IRE)-Florissa (FR) (Persepolis (FR))
N P Littmoden Joy And Valentine Feerick

Placings:04113 **(2813)**
2001: 5^{0}G, 5^{4}GF, 5^{1}F, 6^{1}GF, 7^{3}GF

	Starts	1st	2nd	3rd	Win & Pl
Career Total (Turf)	5	2	0	1	5194

74 7/01 Chep 6f16y F G-F £2282
64 6/01 Brig 5f213y F FRM £2226
Total win prize-money £4508

Going (Turf): Sf: 0-0 GS: 0-0 Gd: 0-1 **GF: 1-3 Fm: 1-1**
Distance: 5f/6f: 1-3 7f-8f: 1-2 9f-13f: 0-0 14f+: 0-0
Track : **LH: 1-1** RH: 0-1 Tight: 0-0 Gall: 0-0
Aids: Bl: 0-0 Vi: 0-0 Tstrap: 0-0
Best Rating: 75 7/01 Bevl 7f100y gd-fm

By Danehill Dancer, this lightly-made colt progressed to score a double over six furlongs iin the summer on firm ground, but the step up in class at Beverley two days later may have come too soon for him.

Florian

81(95) (45)**42**
3-y-o b g Young Ern-Murmuring (Kind Of Hush)
P Mitchell J A Redmond

Placings:005 **(2744)**
2001: 7^{0}GS, 7^{0}GF, 10^{5}GF

	Starts	1st	2nd	3rd	Win & Pl
Career Total (Turf)	3	0	0	0	0

Going (Turf): Sf: 0-0 GS: 0-1 Gd: 0-0 GF: 0-2 Fm: 0-0
Distance: 5f/6f: 0-0 7f-8f: 0-2 9f-13f: 0-1 14f+: 0-0
Track : LH: 0-1 RH: 0-1 Tight: 0-1 Gall: 0-0
Aids: Bl: 0-0 Vi: 0-0 Tstrap: 0-0
Best Rating: 42 5/01 Gdwd 7f gd-fm

Florida (IRE)

94(94) (40)**39**
3-y-o b f Sri Pekan (USA)-Florinda (CAN) (Vice Regent (CAN))
I A Wood Neardown Stables

Placings:0000-306624036300 **(4854)**
2001: 6^{3}SW, 6^{0}SW, 7^{6}SW, 9^{6}S, 11^{2}SD, 11^{4}F, 12^{0}SD, 12^{3}GF, 12^{6}SD, 16^{3}HY, 16^{0}GF, 13^{0}GF

	Starts	1st	2nd	3rd	Win & Pl
Career Total (Turf)	9	0	0	2	837
Career Total (AW)	7	0	1	1	828

Going (Turf): Sf: 0-3 GS: 0-0 Gd: 0-0 GF: 0-5 Fm: 0-1
Distance: 5f/6f: 0-3 7f-8f: 0-4 9f-13f: 0-6 14f+: 0-3
Track : LH: 0-13 RH: 0-1 Tight: 0-2 Gall: 0-1
Aids: Bl: 0-0 Vi: 0-0 Tstrap: 0-0
Best Rating: 41 6/01 Brig 1m3f196y firm

Florie Nightingale

93(85) (51)**60**
2-y-o b f Tragic Role (USA)-Florentynna Bay (Aragon)
K A Ryan T G Holdcroft

Placings:046226130 **(4856)**
2001: 6^{0}F, 5^{4}GF, 6^{6}GF, 7^{2}GF, 7^{2}G, 7^{6}SD, 7^{1}G, 7^{3}GF, 7^{0}GF

	Starts	1st	2nd	3rd	Win & Pl
Career Total (Turf)	8	1	2	1	5727
Career Total (AW)	1	0	0	0	0

60 8/01 Thsk 7f F GD £3132
Total win prize-money £3133

Going (Turf): Sf: 0-0 GS: 0-0 **Gd: 1-2** GF: 0-5 Fm: 0-1
Distance: 5f/6f: 0-3 **7f-8f: 1-6** 9f-13f: 0-0 14f+: 0-0
Track : **LH: 1-3** RH: 0-0 **Tight: 1-3** Gall: 0-0
Aids: Bl: 0-0 Vi: 0-0 Tstrap: 0-0
Best Rating: 60 9/01 Rdcr 7f gd-fm

From a good family, she is bred to get further than the seven furlongs she won over in a seller at Thirsk at the end of the summer.

Flossy

109 (49)**101**
5-y-o b m Efisio-Sirene Bleu Marine (USA) (Secreto (USA))
C W Thornton Guy Reed

Placings:54501112211621/044102331205-3550540001005000 **(5693)**
2001: 9^{3}G, 10^{5}GF, 11^{5}G, 11^{0}G, 10^{5}GS, 12^{4}GS, 12^{0}G, 12^{0}G, 11^{0}G, 13^{1}G, 14^{0}GF, 12^{0}G, 12^{5}S, 12^{0}GS, 10^{0}HO, 12^{0}S

	Starts	1st	2nd	3rd	Win & Pl
Career Total (Turf)	39	9	5	3	111688
Career Total (AW)	3	0	0	0	201

101	9/01	Ches	1m5f89y	A(0-110)H	GD	£18722
95	9/00	NmkR	1m4f	B(0-100)H	G-S	£9625
87	8/00	Ches	1m4f66y	C(0-90)H	GD	£7117
86	11/99	Donc	1m4f	B H	SFT	£23250
81	9/99	Hayd	1m3f200y	D(0-80)H	G-F	£7685
70	8/99	Newc	1m4f93y	E(0-75)H	GD	£2944
59	7/99	Newb	1m2f6y	D(0-80)H	G-F	£4484
57	7/99	Muss	1m4f	F(0-65)H	G-S	£2766
47	7/99	Bevl	1m1f207y	E(0-70)H	G-F	£3077

Total win prize-money £79672

Going (Turf): Sf: 1-9 GS: 2-6 **Gd: 3-14 GF: 3-8** Fm: 0-1
Distance: 5f/6f: 0-0 7f-8f: 0-2 **9f-13f: 8-35** 14f+: 1-5
Track : **LH: 6-23** RH: 3-16 Tight: 3-7 **Gall: 4-22**
Aids: Bl: 0-0 Vi: 0-0 Tstrap: 0-0
Best Rating: 102 7/01 Ayr 1m2f gd-sft

Suited by 12 to 13 furlongs, she usually hit form in the second half of the season. Has generally had to race in Pattern company and won a Listed handicap at Chester in September. Not ideally suited by fast ground and needed a strongly-run race. Retired.

Flounce

100 **75**
3-y-o b/br f Unfuwain (USA)-Flo Russell (USA) (Round Table)
Mrs A J Perrett Sir Eric Parker

Placings:622440 **(5279)**
2001: 11^{6}GF, 12^{2}GF, 12^{2}GF, 11^{4}GF, 12^{4}GF, 11^{0}S

	Starts	1st	2nd	3rd	Win & Pl
Career Total (Turf)	6	0	2	0	3224

Going (Turf): Sf: 0-1 GS: 0-0 Gd: 0-0 GF: 0-5 Fm: 0-0
Distance: 5f/6f: 0-0 7f-8f: 0-0 9f-13f: 0-6 14f+: 0-0
Track : LH: 0-1 RH: 0-4 Tight: 0-2 Gall: 0-1
Aids: Bl: 0-0 Vi: 0-0 Tstrap: 0-0
Best Rating: 75 9/01 Ling 1m3f106y gd-fm

She has shown ability in fast-ground maidens over a mile and a half but seems short of pace.

Flow Beau

93(90) (6)**25**

4-y-o b f Mtoto-Radiance (FR) (Blakeney)
J O'Reilly Burntwood Sports Ltd

Placings:40600000-00060060 **(4877)**
2001: 12^{0}SD, 8^{0}SD, 8^{0}GF, 12^{6}GF, 16^{0}GF, 13^{0}G, 16^{6}GS, 14^{0}SD

	Starts	1st	2nd	3rd	Win & Pl
Career Total (Turf)	10	0	0	0	192
Career Total (AW)	6	0	0	0	

Going (Turf): Sf: 0-0 GS: 0-3 Gd: 0-3 GF: 0-4 Fm: 0-0
Distance: 5f/6f: 0-0 7f-8f: 0-4 9f-13f: 0-6 14f+: 0-6
Track : LH: 0-7 RH: 0-5 Tight: 0-8 Gall: 0-0
Aids: Bl: 0-5 Vi: 0-5 Tstrap: 0-0
Best Rating: 25 7/01 Bevl 2m35y gd-fm

Flowing Rio

96(86) (57)**71**

3-y-o b f First Trump-Deanta In Eirinn (Red Sunset)
P C Haslam Rio Stainless Engineering Limited

Placings:0153302-00 **(0474)**
2001: 7^{0}SD, 7^{0}SD

	Starts	1st	2nd	3rd	Win & Pl
Career Total (Turf)	6	1	0	2	4601
Career Total (AW)	3	0	1	0	496

71 6/00 Haml 6f5y E GD £3526
Total win prize-money £3526

Going (Turf): Sf: 0-0 GS: 0-0 **Gd: 1-5** GF: 0-1 Fm: 0-0
Distance: 5f/6f: 0-3 **7f-8f: 1-6** 9f-13f: 0-0 14f+: 0-0
Track : LH: 0-5 RH: 0-0 Tight: 0-2 Gall: 0-0
Aids: Bl: 0-0 Vi: 0-0 Tstrap: 0-0
Best Rating: 32 1/01 Sthl 7f stand

Flowline River

78(80) (12)**24**

3-y-o b f Awesome-Gymcrak Dancer (Pennine Walk)
D Burchell Mrs J A Davies

Placings:000-060060 **(2185)**
2001: 6^{0}GS, 9^{6}SD, 6^{0}S, 7^{0}SD, 7^{6}GF, 5^{0}G

	Starts	1st	2nd	3rd	Win & Pl
Career Total (Turf)	6	0	0	0	156
Career Total (AW)	3	0	0	0	0

Going (Turf): Sf: 0-1 GS: 0-1 Gd: 0-1 GF: 0-3 Fm: 0-0
Distance: 5f/6f: 0-4 7f-8f: 0-4 9f-13f: 0-1 14f+: 0-0
Track : LH: 0-5 RH: 0-0 Tight: 0-1 Gall: 0-2
Aids: Bl: 0-0 Vi: 0-0 Tstrap: 0-0
Best Rating: 28 6/01 Leic 7f9y gd-fm

Flownaway

94 **75**

2-y-o b c Polar Falcon (USA)-No More Rosies (Warpath)
W Jarvis Sales Race 2001 Syndicate

Placings:64130 **(4714)**
2001: 6^{6}GF, 7^{4}GF, 7^{1}GS, 8^{3}GF, 7^{0}G

	Starts	1st	2nd	3rd	Win & Pl
Career Total (Turf)	5	1	0	1	8228

75 8/01 Thsk 7f E G-S £3727
Total win prize-money £3728

Going (Turf): Sf: 0-0 **GS: 1-1** Gd: 0-1 GF: 0-3 Fm: 0-0
Distance: 5f/6f: 0-1 **7f-8f: 1-3** 9f-13f: 0-1 14f+: 0-0
Track : **LH: 1-1** RH: 0-0 **Tight: 1-1** Gall: 0-0
Aids: Bl: 0-0 Vi: 0-0 Tstrap: 0-0
Best Rating: 75 8/01 Newc 1m3y gd-fm

Seemed suited by cut in the ground when scoring over seven furlongs at Thirsk on his third outing. Ran well when third over a mile next time on fast ground.

Fluent

83 **60**

2-y-o b f Polar Falcon (USA)-Lady Barrister (Law Society (USA))
M L W Bell Cheveley Park Stud

Placings:03 **(5665)**
2001: 7^{0}GS, 6^{3}HY

	Starts	1st	2nd	3rd	Win & Pl
Career Total (Turf)	2	0	0	1	578

Going (Turf): Sf: 0-1 GS: 0-1 Gd: 0-0 GF: 0-0 Fm: 0-0
Distance: 5f/6f: 0-1 7f-8f: 0-1 9f-13f: 0-0 14f+: 0-0
Track : LH: 0-0 RH: 0-0 Tight: 0-0 Gall: 0-0
Aids: Bl: 0-0 Vi: 0-0 Tstrap: 0-0
Best Rating: 60 10/01 Leic 7f9y gd-sft

Maiden who has shown enough promise to suggest she can win races.

Flur Na H Alba

94 **88**

2-y-o b c Atraf-Tyrian Belle (Enchantment)
Miss L A Perratt The Mathieson Partnership

Placings:6140 **(4795)**
2001: 6^{6}GS, 5^{1}GF, 6^{4}G, 5^{0}G

	Starts	1st	2nd	3rd	Win & Pl
Career Total (Turf)	4	1	0	0	4116

73 7/01 Muss 5f D G-F £3623
Total win prize-money £3624

Going (Turf): Sf: 0-0 GS: 0-1 Gd: 0-2 **GF: 1-1** Fm: 0-0
Distance: **5f/6f: 1-4** 7f-8f: 0-0 9f-13f: 0-0 14f+: 0-0
Track : LH: 0-0 RH: 0-0 Tight: 0-0 Gall: 0-0
Aids: Bl: 0-0 Vi: 0-0 Tstrap: 0-0
Best Rating: 88 8/01 Ripn 6f good

A good-looking individual. He won a Musselburgh maiden over the minimum trip in July 2001. An improving sort. Acts on fast ground.

Fly Back

69 **29**

2-y-o ch g Fraam-The Fernhill Flyer (IRE) (Red Sunset)
Mrs J R Ramsden Bernard Hathaway

Placings:0 **(4961)**
2001: 6^{0}S

	Starts	1st	2nd	3rd	Win & Pl
Career Total (Turf)	1	0	0	0	

Going (Turf): Sf: 0-1 GS: 0-0 Gd: 0-0 GF: 0-0 Fm: 0-0
Distance: 5f/6f: 0-1 7f-8f: 0-0 9f-13f: 0-0 14f+: 0-0
Track : LH: 0-1 RH: 0-0 Tight: 0-0 Gall: 0-0
Aids: Bl: 0-0 Vi: 0-0 Tstrap: 0-0
Best Rating: 29 9/01 Pont 6f soft

Fly Boy Fly (USA)

(95) (67)**71**

3-y-o b g Chief's Crown (USA)-Gillingham (USA) (Hatchet Man (USA))
M Johnston M J Pilkington

Placings:4644-46430 **(2525)**
2001: 8^{4}SD, 10^{6}SW, 9^{4}SD, 9^{3}SD, 8^{0}GF

	Starts	1st	2nd	3rd	Win & Pl
Career Total (Turf)	4	0	0	0	530
Career Total (AW)	5	0	0	1	337

Going (Turf): Sf: 0-1 GS: 0-1 Gd: 0-1 GF: 0-1 Fm: 0-0
Distance: 5f/6f: 0-3 7f-8f: 0-2 9f-13f: 0-4 14f+: 0-0
Track : LH: 0-7 RH: 0-0 Tight: 0-6 Gall: 0-0
Aids: Bl: 0-0 Vi: 0-0 Tstrap: 0-0
Best Rating: 65 6/01 Wolv 1m1f79y stand

Fly Gold Air (USA)

101 **88**

2-y-o ch f Tactical Advantage (USA)-Festive Mood (USA) (Bering)
B J Meehan Gold Group International Ltd

Placings:3623103 **(5340)**
2001: 5^{3}F, 6^{6}GF, 5^{2}G, 6^{3}GF, 6^{1}GF, 7^{0}G, 6^{3}GS

	Starts	1st	2nd	3rd	Win & Pl
Career Total (Turf)	7	1	1	3	25100

83 9/01 Donc 6f B H G-F £21937
Total win prize-money £21938

Going (Turf): Sf: 0-0 GS: 0-1 Gd: 0-2 **GF: 1-3** Fm: 0-1
Distance: **5f/6f: 1-5** 7f-8f: 0-2 9f-13f: 0-0 14f+: 0-0
Track : LH: 0-0 RH: 0-0 Tight: 0-0 Gall: 0-0
Aids: Bl: 0-0 Vi: 0-0 Tstrap: 0-0
Best Rating: 88 10/01 NmkR 6f gd-sft

Out of a half-sister to Racing Post Trophy winner Peter Davies, she ran well to make the frame in maiden and nursery company and got off the mark in a six-furlong handicap at Doncaster in September. A free-running filly who is suited by a sound surface, has also shown she handles cut in the ground.

Fly Kicker

(90) (28)

4-y-o ch g High Kicker (USA)-Double Birthday (Cavo Doro)
E J Alston M D Townson

Placings:0-04 **(0061)**
2001: 12^{0}SD, 8^{4}SW

	Starts	1st	2nd	3rd	Win & Pl
Career Total (Turf)	0	0	0	0	
Career Total (AW)	3	0	0	0	0

Going (Turf): Sf: 0-0 GS: 0-0 Gd: 0-0 GF: 0-0 Fm: 0-0
Distance: 5f/6f: 0-0 7f-8f: 0-0 9f-13f: 0-3 14f+: 0-0
Track : LH: 0-3 RH: 0-0 Tight: 0-2 Gall. 0-0
Aids: Bl: 0-0 Vi: 0-0 Tstrap: 0-0
Best Rating: 28 1/01 Wolv 1m100y slow

Fly More

103 **76**

4-y-o ch g Lycius (USA)-Double River (USA) (Irish River (FR))
J M Bradley E A Hayward

Placings:455155-004030011140026 **(5381)**
2001: 5^{0}HY, 6^{0}GF, 6^{4}GF, 5^{0}GF, 6^{3}GF, 6^{0}GF, 5^{0}GF, 5^{1}GF, 5^{1}GF, 5^{1}GF, 5^{4}G, 5^{0}F, 6^{0}HY, 5^{2}S, 5^{6}S

	Starts	1st	2nd	3rd	Win & Pl
Career Total (Turf)	21	4	1	1	15373

75 7/01 Wind 5f10y E(0-70)H G-F £2968
68 7/01 Folk 5f E(0-70)H G-F £3262
70 7/01 Bath 5f11y F(0-65)H G-F £2254
70 7/00 Ripn 6f E(0-70)H G-F £3250
Total win prize-money £11734

Going (Turf): Sf: 0-5 GS: 0-0 Gd: 0-3 **GF: 4-12** Fm: 0-1
Distance: **5f/6f: 4-19** 7f-8f: 0-2 9f-13f: 0-0 14f+: 0-0
Track : LH: 1-5 RH: 1-1 Tight: 0-0 **Gall: 2-3**
Aids: Bl: 0-0 Vi: 0-0 Tstrap: 0-0
Best Rating: 76 10/01 York 5f soft

Completed a hat-trick in the space of seven days in July 2001 at Bath, Folkestone and Windsor. Suited by the minimum trip and fast ground.

Fly With Me

105(102) (56)**95**

3-y-o b c Pharly (FR)-Nelly Do Da (Derring Do)

T G Mills John Humphreys (turf Accountants) Ltd

Placings:60-22133120 (4194)
2001: 10^{2}SW, 12^{2}SD, 11^{1}GF, 12^{3}GF, 12^{3}GF, 11^{1}GF, 12^{2}GF, 13^{0}G

	Starts	1st	2nd	3rd	Win & Pl
Career Total (Turf)	8	2	1	2	24515
Career Total (AW)	2	0	2	0	1764

92 7/01 Wind 1m3f135yD(0-85)H G-F £4127
80 5/01 Gdwd 1m3f D(0-85)H G-F £4660
Total win prize-money £8789

Going (Turf): Sf: 0-1 GS: 0-0 Gd: 0-1 **GF: 2-6** Fm: 0-0
Distance: 5f/6f: 0-0 7f-8f: 0-1 **9f-13f: 2-8** 14f+: 0-1
Track : LH: 0-3 RH: 0-3 **Tight: 1-6** Gall: 0-1
Aids: Bl: 0-0 Vi: 0-0 Tstrap: 0-0
Best Rating: 95 8/01 Gdwd 1m4f gd-fm

He has become a useful middle-distance handicapper and has won at Goodwood and Windsor this season. Very consistent, he loves fast ground and is a very effective sort when able to dominate.

Flying Faisal (USA)

(97) (54)**49**
3-y-o b c Alydeed (CAN)-Peaceful Silence (USA) (Proper Reality (USA))
B A McMahon (J A Osborne 7/7) Syed Pervez Hussain

Placings:0630-61660000000260 (5619)
2001: 6^{6}SD, 7^{1}SD, 8^{6}SD, 7^{6}SD, 7^{0}SD, 7^{0}F, 8^{0}GF, 9^{0}GF, 8^{0}G, 8^{0}SD, 6^{0}GF, 6^{2}GS, 6^{6}SD, 6^{0}SD

	Starts	1st	2nd	3rd	Win & Pl
Career Total (Turf)	7	0	1	0	976
Career Total (AW)	11	1	0	1	3242

69 2/01 Wolv 7f E(0-70)H STD £2919
Total win prize-money £2919

Going (Turf): Sf: 0-0 GS: 0-2 Gd: 0-1 GF: 0-3 Fm: 0-1
Distance: 5f/6f: 0-6 **7f-8f: 1-7** 9f-13f: 0-5 14f+: 0-0
Track : **LH: 1-13** RH: 0-1 **Tight: 1-8** Gall: 0-0
Aids: **Bl: 1-8** Vi: 0-0 Tstrap: 0-1
Best Rating: 69 2/01 Wolv 7f stand

Flying Flip

103 **45**
7-y-o b m Rolfe (USA)-Needwood Sprite (Joshua)
R Hollinshead Tim Leadbeater

Placings:0040400/15234450/51514000/0330 (4330)
2001: 16^{0}G, 10^{3}F, 13^{3}G, 16^{0}GF

	Starts	1st	2nd	3rd	Win & Pl
Career Total (Turf)	26	3	1	3	12364
Career Total (AW)	1	0	0	0	240

60 5/99 Haml 1m5f9y F(0-60)H SFT £2416
54 4/99 Nott 1m6f15y E(0-70)H HVY £3223
56 4/98 Nott 1m1f213yD(0-80)H SFT £4077
Total win prize-money £9718

Going (Turf): Sf: 3-7 GS: 0-4 Gd: 0-8 GF: 0-5 Fm: 0-2
Distance: 5f/6f: 0-0 7f-8f: 0-1 9f-13f: 1-13 **14f+: 2-13**
Track : **LH: 2-17** RH: 1-10 **Tight: 1-10** Gall: 0-4
Aids: Bl: 0-0 Vi: 0-0 **Tstrap: 2-11**
Best Rating: 45 8/01 Ripn 2m gd-fm

Flying Fulmar

95 **76**
2-y-o ch f Bahamian Bounty-West Humble (Pharly (FR))
M L W Bell Sir Thomas Pilkington

Placings:21130 (4252)
2001: 6^{2}F, 5^{1}GF, 6^{1}GF, 6^{3}S, 6^{0}GF

	Starts	1st	2nd	3rd	Win & Pl
Career Total (Turf)	5	2	1	1	8465

76 7/01 Ling 6f D G-F £4251
67 6/01 Nott 5f13y F G-F £2705
Total win prize-money £6957

Going (Turf): Sf: 0-1 GS: 0-0 Gd: 0-0 **GF: 2-3** Fm: 0-1
Distance: **5f/6f: 2-4** 7f-8f: 0-1 9f-13f: 0-0 14f+: 0-0
Track : LH: 0-0 RH: 0-0 Tight: 0-0 Gall: 0-0
Aids: Bl: 0-0 Vi: 0-0 Tstrap: 0-0
Best Rating: 76 8/01 Chep 6f16y soft

A February foal who cost 42,000 gns as a yearling. Got off the mark on second start at Nottingham over five then followed up over six at Lingfield. Acts on fast ground.

Flying Gem

88 **57**
2-y-o ch g Wing Park-Manhattan Diamond (Primo Dominie)
A Bailey Dawson/kettles

Placings:405000 (5079)
2001: 5^{4}GF, 6^{0}GS, 6^{5}HY, 5^{0}F, 6^{0}G, 5^{0}S

	Starts	1st	2nd	3rd	Win & Pl
Career Total (Turf)	6	0	0	0	269

Going (Turf): Sf: 0-2 GS: 0-1 Gd: 0-1 GF: 0-1 Fm: 0-1
Distance: 5f/6f: 0-5 7f-8f: 0-1 9f-13f: 0-0 14f+: 0-0
Track : LH: 0-2 RH: 0-0 Tight: 0-1 Gall: 0-0
Aids: Bl: 0-1 Vi: 0-0 Tstrap: 0-0
Best Rating: 57 8/01 Hayd 6f heavy

Flying Lyric (IRE)

108 **85**
3-y-o b c Definite Article-Lyric Junction (IRE) (Classic Secret (USA))
S P C Woods Mrs Marian Borsberry

Placings:41-25200550 (5143)
2001: 10^{2}S, 12^{5}GF, 12^{2}S, 12^{0}GF, 14^{0}GF, 14^{5}HY, 16^{5}S, 14^{0}G

	Starts	1st	2nd	3rd	Win & Pl
Career Total (Turf)	10	1	2	0	8052

89 10/00 Bath 1m5y E G-S £2320
Total win prize-money £2321

Going (Turf): Sf: 0-4 **GS: 1-1** Gd: 0-1 GF: 0-4 Fm: 0-0
Distance: 5f/6f: 0-0 7f-8f: 0-0 **9f-13f: 1-6** 14f+: 0-4
Track : **LH: 1-4** RH: 0-5 **Tight: 1-2** Gall: 0-6
Aids: Bl: 0-0 Vi: 0-0 Tstrap: 0-0
Best Rating: 96 5/01 Newb 1m4f5y soft

Looked a likely stayer in two outings as a juvenile, and has shaped quite well this season without getting his head in front. Stays 14 furlongs. Suited by cut.

Flying Millie (IRE)

108 **94**
3-y-o b f Flying Spur (AUS)-Sweet Pleasure (Sweet Revenge)
R M Beckett John E Guest

Placings:160-501310 (4986)
2001: 6^{5}S, 5^{0}GF, 6^{1}GS, 6^{3}G, 6^{1}G, 6^{0}G

	Starts	1st	2nd	3rd	Win & Pl
Career Total (Turf)	9	3	0	1	40299

94 8/01 Asct 6f B(0-105)H GD £25000
89 7/01 NmkJ 6f B(0-100)H G-S £9251
82 5/00 Wind 5f10y D G-S £4504
Total win prize-money £38756

Going (Turf): Sf: 0-1 **GS: 2-2** Gd: 1-3 GF: 0-3 Fm: 0-0
Distance: **5f/6f: 3-7** 7f-8f: 0-2 9f-13f: 0-0 14f+: 0-0
Track : LH: 0-0 **RH: 1-1** Tight: 0-0 **Gall: 1-1**
Aids: Bl: 0-0 Vi: 0-0 Tstrap: 0-0
Best Rating: 94 8/01 Asct 6f good

A lightly-raced filly with ability, she beat Starbeck by a neck in a rated stakes over six furlongs at Newmarket in July and won a valuable race on Shergar Cup day at Ascot. Suited by six furlongs and likes the ground no faster than good.

Flying Pennant (IRE)

96(93) (39)**37**
8-y-o gr g Waajib-Flying Beckee (IRE) (Godswalk (USA))
J M Bradley E A Hayward

Placings:0/001423200/00460050/26313006300/000440050350/553061036305656-05005 (4362)
2001: 8^{0}HD, 7^{5}GF, 7^{0}G, 7^{0}GF, 7^{5}GF

	Starts	1st	2nd	3rd	Win & Pl
Career Total (Turf)	58	3	3	8	19011
Career Total (AW)	3	0	0	0	0

38 7/00 Brig 6f209y E(0-70)H SFT £5255
54 6/98 Chep 7f16y D(0-80)H G-S £3582
63 5/96 Sals 6f212y F G-F £2784
Total win prize-money £11622

Going (Turf): Sf: 1-4 GS: 1-9 Gd: 0-13 **GF: 1-22** Fm: 0-10
Distance: 5f/6f: 0-0 **7f-8f: 3-54** 9f-13f: 0-7 14f+: 0-0
Track : **LH: 1-26** RH: 0-9 Tight: 0-13 Gall: 0-1
Aids: **Bl: 2-37** Vi: 0-8 Tstrap: 0-0
Best Rating: 37 8/01 Brig 7f214y gd-fm

Scored over seven furlongs at Chepstow last season, but is on a long losing run.

Flying Petrel (USA)

91 **65**
3-y-o b f Storm Bird (CAN)-Olatha (USA) (Miswaki (USA))
M Johnston M J Pilkington

Placings:04-000 (1725)
2001: 5^{0}GS, 6^{0}S, 6^{0}GF

	Starts	1st	2nd	3rd	Win & Pl
Career Total (Turf)	5	0	0	0	351

Going (Turf): Sf: 0-1 GS: 0-2 Gd: 0-0 GF: 0-2 Fm: 0-0
Distance: 5f/6f: 0-5 7f-8f: 0-0 9f-13f: 0-0 14f+: 0-0
Track : LH: 0-0 RH: 0-0 Tight: 0-0 Gall: 0-0
Aids: Bl: 0-0 Vi: 0-0 Tstrap: 0-0
Best Rating: 50 5/01 Ripn 6f gd-fm

Flying Romance (IRE)

101(94) (53)**50**
3-y-o b f Flying Spur (AUS)-State Romance (Free State)
P D Evans (D W Barker 13/6) Swift Racing

Placings:0553040-02303004413355500 (5663)
2001: 6^{0}SD, 8^{2}HY, 8^{3}S, 8^{0}F, 8^{3}SD, 8^{0}GF, 8^{0}HD, 10^{4}GF, 9^{4}GF, 11^{1}GF, 10^{3}GS, 14^{3}SD, 11^{5}GF, 10^{5}G, 12^{5}SD, 12^{0}SD, 12^{0}G

	Starts	1st	2nd	3rd	Win & Pl
Career Total (Turf)	19	1	1	3	4536
Career Total (AW)	5	0	0	2	631

48 7/01 Bevl 1m3f216yF(0-60)H G-F £2534
Total win prize-money £2534

Going (Turf): Sf: 0-4 GS: 0-1 Gd: 0-4 **GF: 1-7** Fm: 0-3
Distance: 5f/6f: 0-5 7f-8f: 0-5 **9f-13f: 1-13** 14f+: 0-1
Track : LH: 0-16 **RH: 1-4 Tight: 1-11** Gall: 0-2
Aids: Bl: 0-0 Vi: 0-0 Tstrap: 0-0
Best Rating: 53 8/01 Wolv 1m6f166y stand

A half-sister to five winners including the Stewards Cup winner Very Adjacent, she took a while to find her trip but did so at the 17th attempt in a seller at Beverley over 12 furlongs on fast ground in July. He may be even better over a longer trip.

Flying Run (IRE)

98(87) (30)**39**
4-y-o b f Lake Coniston (IRE)-Kaskazi (Dancing Brave (USA))
J G Portman A H Robinson

Placings:4500/0000003006-034500000 (4159)
2001: 10^{0}GF, 8^{3}GF, 9^{4}F, 8^{5}GF, 8^{0}G, 8^{0}SD, 8^{0}GS, 7^{0}F, 6^{0}GF

	Starts	1st	2nd	3rd	Win & Pl

	Starts	1st	2nd	3rd	Win & Pl
Career Total (Turf)	19	0	0	2	980
Career Total (AW)	4	0	0	0	0

Going (Turf): Sf: 0-1 GS: 0-2 Gd: 0-6 GF: 0-7 Fm: 0-3
Distance: 5f/6f: 0-4 7f-8f: 0-7 9f-13f: 0-12 14f+: 0-0
Track : LH: 0-12 RH: 0-2 Tight: 0-5 Gall: 0-1
Aids: Bl: 0-4 Vi: 0-0 Tstrap: 0-0
Best Rating: 42 6/01 Leic 1m9y gd-fm

Flying Spirit (IRE)

92 **76**
2-y-o b c Flying Spur (AUS)-All Laughter (Vision (USA))
M H Tompkins Mrs Nicola Guest

Placings:6 **(2370)**
2001: 6^{6}GF

	Starts	1st	2nd	3rd	Win & Pl
Career Total (Turf)	1	0	0	0	0

Going (Turf): Sf: 0-0 GS: 0-0 Gd: 0-0 GF: 0-1 Fm: 0-0
Distance: 5f/6f: 0-1 7f-8f: 0-0 9f-13f: 0-0 14f+: 0-0
Track : LH: 0-0 RH: 0-0 Tight: 0-0 Gall: 0-0
Aids: Bl: 0-0 Vi: 0-0 Tstrap: 0-0
Best Rating: 76 6/01 NmkJ 6f gd-fm

Flying Tackle

108 **59**
3-y-o ch c First Trump-Frighten The Life (King's Lake (USA))
J S Wainwright Neil Harrison

Placings:000-004323210 **(5490)**
2001: 7^{0}F, 8^{0}GF, 6^{4}G, 6^{3}GS, 5^{2}G, 5^{3}G, 5^{2}HY, 6^{1}G, 7^{0}HY

	Starts	1st	2nd	3rd	Win & Pl
Career Total (Turf)	12	1	2	2	6927
59 10/01 Rdcr 6f	D			GD	£3864
				Total win prize-money	£3864

Going (Turf): Sf: 0-2 GS: 0-1 **Gd: 1-6** GF: 0-2 Fm: 0-1
Distance: **5f/6f: 1-8** 7f-8f: 0-3 9f-13f: 0-1 14f+: 0-0
Track : LH: 0-1 RH: 0-0 Tight: 0-0 Gall: 0-0
Aids: Bl: 0-0 **Vi: 1-6** Tstrap: 0-0
Best Rating: 59 10/01 Rdcr 6f good

Had run some good races before getting off the mark at Redcar in October over six furlongs. He has run his best races with cut in the ground, and is effective over sprint distances.

Flying Trapeze (USA)

105(82) (56)**72**
3-y-o ch c Trempolino (USA)-Loen (USA) (Accipiter (USA))
J Noseda W L Armitage

Placings:0-001114600 **(5198)**
2001: 8^{0}S, 7^{0}S, 10^{1}GF, 10^{1}HD, 10^{1}GF, 11^{4}F, 9^{6}GF, 10^{0}GF, 9^{0}SD

	Starts	1st	2nd	3rd	Win & Pl
Career Total (Turf)	9	3	0	0	9206
Career Total (AW)	1	0	0	0	
70 7/01 Hayd 1m2f120y	E(0-75)H			G-F	£3318
60 6/01 Bath 1m2f46y	E(0-70)H			HRD	£2877
50 6/01 Rdcr 1m2f	F(0-65)H			G-F	£2453
				Total win prize-money	£8649

Going (Turf): Sf: 0-3 GS: 0-0 Gd: 0-0 **GF: 2-4** Fm: 1-2
Distance: 5f/6f: 0-1 7f-8f: 0-2 **9f-13f: 3-7** 14f+: 0-0
Track : **LH: 3-7** RH: 0-1 **Tight: 2-5** Gall: 0-1
Aids: Bl: 0-0 Vi: 0-0 Tstrap: 0-0
Best Rating: 72 7/01 Rdcr 1m3f firm

He took advantage of a lenient mark to complete a hat-trick during the summer of 2001 at Redcar, Bath and Haydock. Raised a stone in the handicap after, which has seemed to find him out since. Suited by ten furlongs and fast ground.

Flying Treaty (USA)

80(104) (79)**75**
4-y-o br c You And I (USA)-Cherie's Hope (USA) (Flying Paster (USA))
Miss A Stokell R J Buxton

Placings:5230212-0222121003142 **(3819)**
2001: 8^{0}SD, 8^{2}SW, 9^{2}SD, 9^{2}SD, 8^{1}SD, 12^{2}SD, 12^{1}SW, 12^{0}SD, 12^{0}G, 12^{3}SD, 8^{1}SD, 8^{4}SD, 7^{2}SD

	Starts	1st	2nd	3rd	Win & Pl
Career Total (Turf)	5	0	1	1	2334
Career Total (AW)	15	4	7	1	20936
79 6/01 Sthl 1m	E(0-70)H			STD	£3024
69 3/01 Ling 1m4f	E(0-70)			SLW	£2898
70 2/01 Wolv 1m100y	D(0-85)H			STD	£3406
57 11/00 Wolv 1m100y	D			STD	£2730
				Total win prize-money	£12058

Going (Turf): Sf: 0-0 GS: 0-0 Gd: 0-2 GF: 0-2 Fm: 0-1
Distance: 5f/6f: 0-0 7f-8f: 1-5 **9f-13f: 3-15** 14f+: 0-0
Track : **LH: 4-17** RH: 0-2 **Tight: 3-14** Gall: 0-1
Aids: Bl: 0-0 Vi: 0-0 Tstrap: 0-0
Best Rating: 79 6/01 Sthl 1m stand

Flying Turk (IRE)

87(66) (14)**62**
3-y-o ch g Flying Spur (AUS)-Empress Wu (High Line)
J A Osborne Syed Pervez Hussain

Placings:3044660-000 **(2187)**
2001: 7^{0}GS, 8^{0}SD, 8^{0}GF

	Starts	1st	2nd	3rd	Win & Pl
Career Total (Turf)	9	0	0	1	2372
Career Total (AW)	1	0	0	0	

Going (Turf): Sf: 0-3 GS: 0-2 Gd: 0-0 GF: 0-4 Fm: 0-0
Distance: 5f/6f: 0-6 7f-8f: 0-3 9f-13f: 0-1 14f+: 0-0
Track : LH: 0-5 RH: 0-0 Tight: 0-0 Gall: 0-1
Aids: Bl: 0-0 Vi: 0-0 Tstrap: 0-2
Best Rating: 62 4/01 Brig 7f214y gd-sft

Flyover

94 **42**
4-y-o b f Presidium-Flash-By (Ilium)
B R Millman R J Tory

Placings:2013000/0051614-06005 **(4319)**
2001: 11^{0}G, 12^{6}GS, 12^{0}G, 12^{0}GF, 10^{5}GF

	Starts	1st	2nd	3rd	Win & Pl
Career Total (Turf)	19	3	1	1	12498
63 9/00 Epsm 1m2f18y	E(0-70)H			GD	£5928
54 8/00 Bath 1m3f144y	E(0-75)H			G-F	£2749
74 6/99 Sals 6f	F			GD	£2607
				Total win prize-money	£11286

Going (Turf): Sf: 0-2 GS: 0-4 **Gd: 2-4** GF: 1-6 Fm: 0-3
Distance: 5f/6f: 1-5 7f-8f: 0-4 **9f-13f: 2-10** 14f+: 0-0
Track : **LH: 2-7** RH: 0-5 **Tight: 2-5** Gall: 0-1
Aids: Bl: 0-1 Vi: 0-1 Tstrap: 0-0
Best Rating: 42 7/01 Chep 1m4f23y good

Focused Attraction (IRE)

95(109) (92+)**78**
3-y-o b g Eagle Eyed (USA)-Seattle Siren (USA) (Seattle Slew (USA))
R Hannon Mrs T M Moriarty

Placings:65400-11400 **(1916)**
2001: 6^{1}SW, 6^{1}SW, 7^{4}S, 6^{0}GS, 6^{0}GF

	Starts	1st	2nd	3rd	Win & Pl
Career Total (Turf)	7	0	0	0	810
Career Total (AW)	3	2	0	0	8289
92 2/01 Ling 6f	D(0-80)H			SLW	£5356
91 1/01 Wolv 6f	E(0-70)H			SLW	£2933
				Total win prize-money	£8289

Going (Turf): Sf: 0-1 GS: 0-1 Gd: 0-2 GF: 0-3 Fm: 0-0
Distance: **5f/6f: 2-9** 7f-8f: 0-1 9f-13f: 0-0 14f+: 0-0
Track : **LH: 2-3** RH: 0-2 **Tight: 2-3** Gall: 0-2
Aids: Bl: 0-0 Vi: 0-0 Tstrap: 0-0
Best Rating: 92 2/01 Ling 6f slow

Won twice on the All-Weather early in the season, but hung on soft ground when returning to turf.

Folaann (IRE)

93(98) (64)**82**
3-y-o ch c Pennekamp (USA)-Chaturanga (Night Shift (USA))
M A Jarvis Sheikh Ahmed Al Maktoum

Placings:0-30221 **(3817)**
2001: 8^{3}G, 10^{0}GF, 8^{2}GF, 8^{2}GS, 9^{1}SD

	Starts	1st	2nd	3rd	Win & Pl
Career Total (Turf)	5	0	2	1	3450
Career Total (AW)	1	1	0	0	3059
64 8/01 Wolv 1m1f79y	D			STD	£3059
				Total win prize-money	£3059

Going (Turf): Sf: 0-1 GS: 0-1 Gd: 0-1 GF: 0-2 Fm: 0-0
Distance: 5f/6f: 0-0 7f-8f: 0-3 **9f-13f: 1-3** 14f+: 0-0
Track : **LH: 1-1** RH: 0-1 **Tight: 1-3** Gall: 0-0
Aids: Bl: 0-0 Vi: 0-0 Tstrap: 0-0
Best Rating: 82 5/01 NmkR 1m good

Showed fair form on turf before getting off the mark at long odds-on in a maiden on the Wolverhampton Fibresand in Augsut, but had to fight very hard to do so.

Foley Millennium (IRE)

92 **52**
3-y-o ch c Tagula (IRE)-Inshirah (USA) (Caro)
M Quinn Mrs S G Davies

Placings:551341350-00000 **(2574)**
2001: 6^{0}GS, 5^{0}G, 7^{0}GF, 5^{0}HD, 5^{0}GF

	Starts	1st	2nd	3rd	Win & Pl
Career Total (Turf)	14	2	0	2	7976
80 8/00 Newb 5f34y	D			G-F	£3718
71 7/00 Hayd 6f	F			G-F	£2464
				Total win prize-money	£6182

Going (Turf): Sf: 0-1 GS: 0-1 Gd: 0-5 **GF: 2-4** Fm: 0-3
Distance: **5f/6f: 2-13** 7f-8f: 0-1 9f-13f: 0-0 14f+: 0-0
Track : LH: 0-6 RH: 0-0 Tight: 0-1 Gall: 0-3
Aids: Bl: 0-0 Vi: 0-0 Tstrap: 0-0
Best Rating: 52 6/01 NmkJ 5f gd-fm

Folie De Grandeur (USA)

89 **74**
2-y-o ch f Hennessy (USA)-Shameem (USA) (Nureyev (USA))
J L Dunlop Robin F Scully

Placings:00350 **(4638)**
2001: 6^{0}GF, 6^{0}GF, 6^{3}GF, 7^{5}G, 7^{0}GF

	Starts	1st	2nd	3rd	Win & Pl
Career Total (Turf)	5	0	0	1	568

Going (Turf): Sf: 0-0 GS: 0-0 Gd: 0-1 GF: 0-4 Fm: 0-0
Distance: 5f/6f: 0-3 7f-8f: 0-2 9f-13f: 0-0 14f+: 0-0
Track : LH: 0-0 RH: 0-0 Tight: 0-0 Gall: 0-0
Aids: Bl: 0-0 Vi: 0-0 Tstrap: 0-1
Best Rating: 74 7/01 Wind 6f gd-fm

Follow A Dream (USA)

105 **86**
3-y-o b f Gone West (USA)-Dance A Dream (Sadler's Wells (USA))
Sir Michael Stoute Cheveley Park Stud

Placings:632-222 (3306)
2001: 8^{2}GF, 8^{2}GF, 8^{2}GF

	Starts	1st	2nd	3rd	Win & Pl
Career Total (Turf)	6	0	4	1	5428

Going (Turf): Sf: 0-2 GS: 0-0 Gd: 0-0 GF: 0-4 Fm: 0-0
Distance: 5f/6f: 0-0 7f-8f: 0-4 9f-13f: 0-2 14f+: 0-0
Track : LH: 0-0 RH: 0-4 Tight: 0-2 Gall: 0-2
Aids: Bl: 0-0 Vi: 0-0 Tstrap: 0-0
Best Rating: 86 7/01 Wind 1m67y gd-fm

Follow Freddy

100 **62d**
3-y-o ch g Factual (USA)-Forgiving (Jellaby)
M Johnston Mrs S J Brookhouse

Placings:000-006 (3938)
2001: 8^{0}G, 12^{0}GS, 11^{6}G

	Starts	1st	2nd	3rd	Win & Pl
Career Total (Turf)	6	0	0	0	0

Going (Turf): Sf: 0-1 GS: 0-2 Gd: 0-3 GF: 0-0 Fm: 0-0
Distance: 5f/6f: 0-3 7f-8f: 0-0 9f-13f: 0-3 14f+: 0-0
Track : LH: 0-2 RH: 0-2 Tight: 0-2 Gall: 0-1
Aids: Bl: 0-0 Vi: 0-0 Tstrap: 0-0
Best Rating: 54 8/01 NmkJ 1m4f gd-sft

Follow Lammtarra (IRE)

104 **75d**
4-y-o ch g Lammtarra (USA)-Felawnah (USA) (Mr Prospector (USA))
M R Channon Sheikh Ahmed Al Maktoum

Placings:3616-4040035032 (5492)
2001: 12^{4}S, 16^{0}S, 16^{4}S, 13^{0}GF, 17^{0}F, 14^{3}GF, 15^{5}GF, 17^{0}G, 13^{3}GS, 16^{2}HY

	Starts	1st	2nd	3rd	Win & Pl
Career Total (Turf)	14	1	1	3	11299
74 6/00 Hayd 1m6f D				G-S	£4192

Total win prize-money £4193

Going (Turf): Sf: 0-5 **GS: 1-3** Gd: 0-2 GF: 0-3 Fm: 0-1
Distance: 5f/6f: 0-0 7f-8f: 0-0 9f-13f: 0-2 **14f+: 1-12**
Track : **LH: 1-11** RH: 0-3 Tight: 0-4 Gall: 0-4
Aids: Bl: 0-0 Vi: 0-1 Tstrap: 0-0
Best Rating: 83 4/01 Ripn 2m soft

Unraced at two, he looked a potentially useful stayer when winning a Haydock maiden in fine style in June 2000, but he has failed to build on that promise despite some fair efforts in staying handicaps this season. Suited by ease in the ground.

Follow Your Star

98 **78**
3-y-o ch g Pursuit Of Love-Possessive Artiste (Shareef Dancer (USA))
P W Harris Mrs P W Harris

Placings:66000-03 (2859)
2001: 9^{0}GS, 10^{3}GF

	Starts	1st	2nd	3rd	Win & Pl
Career Total (Turf)	7	0	0	1	1053

Going (Turf): Sf: 0-1 GS: 0-1 Gd: 0-3 GF: 0-2 Fm: 0-0
Distance: 5f/6f: 0-2 7f-8f: 0-3 9f-13f: 0-2 14f+: 0-0
Track : LH: 0-3 RH: 0-1 Tight: 0-2 Gall: 0-0
Aids: Bl: 0-0 Vi: 0-1 Tstrap: 0-0
Best Rating: 69 7/01 Bath 1m2f46y gd-fm

Foodbroker Fancy (IRE)

110 **111**
3-y-o ch f Halling (USA)-Red Rita (IRE) (Kefaah (USA))
D R C Elsworth Food Brokers Ltd

Placings:24102-26106612 (5141)
2001: 8^{2}S, 10^{6}F, 9^{1}GF, 12^{0}GF, 10^{6}G, 8^{6}G, 10^{1}GF, 8^{2}G

	Starts	1st	2nd	3rd	Win & Pl
Career Total (Turf)	13	3	4	0	64259
102 9/01 Newb 1m2f6y A				G-F	£13942
103 5/01 Gdwd 1m1f192yA				G-F	£19500
81 7/00 NmkJ 6f D				G-F	£4290

Total win prize-money £37733

Going (Turf): Sf: 0-1 GS: 0-0 Gd: 0-5 **GF: 3-6** Fm: 0-1
Distance: 5f/6f: 1-4 7f-8f: 0-3 **9f-13f: 2-6** 14f+: 0-0
Track : LH: 1-4 RH: 1-4 Tight: 1-2 Gall: 1-3
Aids: Bl: 0-0 Vi: 0-0 Tstrap: 0-0
Best Rating: 111 10/01 NmkR 1m good

She ran well to finish runner-up in the Masaka on her return, but had no luck in running in the Musidora. She gained a last-gasp victory in the Lupe next time, but then either faced impossible tasks or raced over the wrong trip until winning another Listed event at Newbury in September. Ran well when dropped to a mile in the Sun Chariot. Suited by ten furlongs and fast ground.

Fool On The Hill

103 **75**
4-y-o b g Reprimand-Stock Hill Lass (Air Trooper)
L G Cottrell E Gadsden

Placings:06/420-50062215 (5669)
2001: 7^{5}GS, 7^{0}GF, 8^{0}GF, 8^{6}GF, 11^{2}G, 9^{2}GS, 10^{1}G, 10^{5}HY

	Starts	1st	2nd	3rd	Win & Pl
Career Total (Turf)	13	1	3	0	6513
68 10/01 Bath 1m2f46y E(0-70)H				GD	£3066

Total win prize-money £3066

Going (Turf): Sf: 0-3 GS: 0-4 **Gd: 1-2** GF: 0-4 Fm: 0-0
Distance: 5f/6f: 0-1 7f-8f: 0-7 **9f-13f: 1-5** 14f+: 0-0
Track : **LH: 1-1** RH: 0-5 **Tight: 1-5** Gall: 0-2
Aids: Bl: 0-0 **Vi: 1-5** Tstrap: 0-0
Best Rating: 68 11/01 Wind 1m2f7y heavy

Fair handicapper who goes well for an apprentice and appeared to be improving in the second half of 2001. Stays 11½ furlongs, acts on any ground.

Foolish Whisper

54
2-y-o b f Makbul-Whisper Low (IRE) (Shalford (IRE))
R Hollinshead D Lowe

Placings:0 (5689)
2001: 6^{0}S

	Starts	1st	2nd	3rd	Win & Pl
Career Total (Turf)	1	0	0	0	

Going (Turf): Sf: 0-1 GS: 0-0 Gd: 0-0 GF: 0-0 Fm: 0-0
Distance: 5f/6f: 0-1 7f-8f: 0-0 9f-13f: 0-0 14f+: 0-0
Track : LH: 0-0 RH: 0-0 Tight: 0-0 Gall: 0-0
Aids: Bl: 0-0 Vi: 0-0 Tstrap: 0-0

Fools Rush In (IRE)

96 **86**
2-y-o b c Entrepreneur-Blinding (IRE) (High Top)
T G Mills T G Mills

Placings:425 (5053)
2001: 7^{4}GF, 7^{2}HY, 7^{5}S

	Starts	1st	2nd	3rd	Win & Pl
Career Total (Turf)	3	0	1	0	9676

Going (Turf): Sf: 0-2 GS: 0-0 Gd: 0-0 GF: 0-1 Fm: 0-0
Distance: 5f/6f: 0-0 7f-8f: 0-3 9f-13f: 0-0 14f+: 0-0
Track : LH: 0-1 RH: 0-0 Tight: 0-0 Gall: 0-0
Aids: Bl: 0-0 Vi: 0-0 Tstrap: 0-0
Best Rating: 86 10/01 NmkR 7f soft

A 200,000gns half-brother to two winners out of a half-sister to Hadeer, he showed definite promise on his Newbury debut, but may have been unsuited by the testing conditions when beaten favourite at Haydock next time, but performed well on soft in a Newmarket sales event. Well regarded by his trainer, he should have no trouble winning races.

Football Crazy (IRE)

99 **75**
2-y-o b c Mujadil (USA)-Schonbein (IRE) (Persian Heights)
N A Callaghan John Livock

Placings:0030026010 (5368)
2001: 6^{0}GF, 6^{0}GF, 6^{3}GF, 7^{0}GF, 7^{0}GF, 7^{2}GF, 7^{6}G, 7^{0}HY, 7^{1}S, 8^{0}GS

	Starts	1st	2nd	3rd	Win & Pl
Career Total (Turf)	10	1	1	1	8995
75 10/01 York 7f202y C H				SFT	£7488

Total win prize-money £7488

Going (Turf): Sf: 1-2 GS: 0-1 Gd: 0-1 GF: 0-6 Fm: 0-0
Distance: 5f/6f: 0-3 **7f-8f: 1-7** 9f-13f: 0-0 14f+: 0-0
Track : **LH: 1-2** RH: 0-0 Tight: 0-1 **Gall: 1-1**
Aids: Bl: 0-0 Vi: 0-0 Tstrap: 0-0
Best Rating: 79 6/01 Wind 6f gd-fm

Showed some ability in maiden and nursery company before winning a York nursery in October.

Footprints (IRE)

93 **50**
4-y-o b f College Chapel-Near Miracle (Be My Guest (USA))
W R Muir Mrs P A Garner

Placings:021/100201600-030000000 (5292)
2001: 5^{0}G, 6^{3}GF, 6^{0}GS, 6^{0}F, 7^{0}GF, 7^{0}GF, 6^{0}G, 8^{0}GS, 7^{0}S

	Starts	1st	2nd	3rd	Win & Pl
Career Total (Turf)	21	3	2	1	11164
67 8/00 Leic 7f9y F				G-F	£2478
79 4/00 Wwck 6f D(0-75)				HVY	£4084
75 10/99 Rdcr 5f F				SFT	£2407

Total win prize-money £8971

Going (Turf): Sf: 2-6 GS: 0-4 Gd: 0-4 GF: 1-6 Fm: 0-1
Distance: **5f/6f: 2-9** 7f-8f: 1-9 9f-13f: 0-3 14f+: 0-0
Track : **LH: 1-5** RH: 0-1 Tight: 0-0 Gall: 0-0
Aids: Bl: 0-1 Vi: 0-1 Tstrap: 0-2
Best Rating: 66 7/01 Sals 6f gd-fm

For Evva Silca

88 **51**
2-y-o ch f Piccolo-Silca-Cisa (Hallgate)
M R Channon Aldrigde Racing & McDowell Racing

Placings:400 (1848)
2001: 5^{4}S, 6^{0}GF, 5^{0}GF

	Starts	1st	2nd	3rd	Win & Pl
Career Total (Turf)	3	0	0	0	538

Going (Turf): Sf: 0-1 GS: 0-0 Gd: 0-0 GF: 0-2 Fm: 0-0
Distance: 5f/6f: 0-3 7f-8f: 0-0 9f-13f: 0-0 14f+: 0-0
Track : LH: 0-0 RH: 0-0 Tight: 0-0 Gall: 0-0
Aids: Bl: 0-0 Vi: 0-0 Tstrap: 0-0
Best Rating: 51 6/01 Leic 5f2y gd-fm

For Heavens Sake

94(98) (55)**48**
4-y-o b g Rambo Dancer (CAN)-Angel Fire (Nashwan (USA))
B S Rothwell (C W Thornton 14/2) Mrs C M Tinkler

Placings:0466/43260232356205-0305600 (3967)
2001: 8^{0}GF, 10^{3}GF, 12^{0}GF, 16^{5}GF, 9^{6}G, 10^{0}G, 8^{0}GS

	Starts	1st	2nd	3rd	Win & Pl
Career Total (Turf)	14	0	2	3	3136
Career Total (AW)	11	0	2	1	1744

Going (Turf): Sf: 0-2 GS: 0-2 Gd: 0-3 GF: 0-7 Fm: 0-0
Distance: 5f/6f: 0-3 7f-8f: 0-9 9f-13f: 0-12 14f+: 0-1
Track : LH: 0-16 RH: 0-6 Tight: 0-12 Gall: 0-2
Aids: Bl: 0-2 Vi: 0-1 Tstrap: 0-0
Best Rating: 60 6/01 Newc 1m2f32y gd-fm

For Your Eyes Only

(96) (57)**81**
7-y-o b g Pursuit Of Love-Rivers Rhapsody (Dominion)
C E Brittain C E Brittain

Placings:311066400/000306230022/32101106/403150 06/00-060 (0436)
2001: 10^{0}SW, 9^{6}SD, 6^{0}SD

	Starts	1st	2nd	3rd	Win & Pl
Career Total (Turf)	34	5	4	4	132250
Career Total (AW)	8	1	0	1	11947

3/99 Jebl 1m (0-95)H FST £4501
108 7/98 Gdwd 1m B H G-S £64350
103 7/98 Sand 1m14y B(0-105)H GD £12590
102 5/98 Sand 1m14y B(0-105)H GD £15520
91 6/96 Bevl 5f B G-F £7468
78 5/96 Ripn 6f D GD £3712
Total win prize-money £108142

Going (Turf): Sf: 0-3 GS: 1-5 **Gd: 3-13** GF: 1-13 Fm: 0-0
Distance: 5f/6f: 2-10 7f-8f: 1-18 9f-13f: 2-9 14f+: 0-0
Track : LH: 0-14 **RH: 3-5** Tight: 0-5 Gall: 0-7
Aids: **Bl: 3-19** Vi: 0-0 Tstrap: 0-0
Best Rating: 57 3/01 Wolv 6f stand

Force Four (USA)

(97) (49)**37**
3-y-o b g Gulch (USA)-Lantana Lady (CAN) (Vice Regent (CAN))
D Morris S L A M M Partners

Placings:5500 (5330)
2001: 10^{5}G, 9^{5}GF, 12^{0}GS, 16^{0}HY

	Starts	1st	2nd	3rd	Win & Pl
Career Total (Turf)	4	0	0	0	0

Going (Turf): Sf: 0-1 GS: 0-1 Gd: 0-1 GF: 0-1 Fm: 0-0
Distance: 5f/6f: 0-0 7f-8f: 0-0 9f-13f: 0-3 14f+: 0-1
Track : LH: 0-2 RH: 0-2 Tight: 0-2 Gall: 0-1
Aids: Bl: 0-0 Vi: 0-0 Tstrap: 0-0
Best Rating: 37 9/01 Leic 1m1f218y gd-fm

Force Of Destiny

92 **54**
3-y-o b g Polar Falcon (USA)-Springs Welcome (Blakeney)
C A Cyzer Mrs E A Cyzer

Placings:0P (2413)
2001: 10^{0}GF, 12^{P}GF

	Starts	1st	2nd	3rd	Win & Pl
Career Total (Turf)	2	0	0	0	

Going (Turf): Sf: 0-0 GS: 0-0 Gd: 0-0 GF: 0-2 Fm: 0-0
Distance: 5f/6f: 0-0 7f-8f: 0-0 9f-13f: 0-2 14f+: 0-0
Track : LH: 0-1 RH: 0-1 Tight: 0-0 Gall: 0-0
Aids: Bl: 0-0 Vi: 0-0 Tstrap: 0-0
Best Rating: 54 5/01 Sand 1m2f7y gd-fm

Foreign Accent

105 **83+**
2-y-o b c Machiavellian (USA)-Rappa Tap Tap (FR) (Tap On Wood)
J H M Gosden Manton Racing Partnership

Placings:1 (5483)
2001: 7^{1}HY

	Starts	1st	2nd	3rd	Win & Pl
Career Total (Turf)	1	1	0	0	4349

83 10/01 Donc 7f D HVY £4348
Total win prize-money £4349

Going (Turf): Sf: 1-1 GS: 0-0 Gd: 0-0 GF: 0-0 Fm: 0-0
Distance: 5f/6f: 0-0 **7f-8f: 1-1** 9f-13f: 0-0 14f+: 0-0
Track : LH: 0-0 RH: 0-0 Tight: 0-0 Gall: 0-0
Aids: Bl: 0-0 Vi: 0-0 Tstrap: 0-0
Best Rating: 83 10/01 Donc 7f heavy

A 270,000gns half-brother to Killer Instinct out of a half-sister to the dam of Kayf Tara and Opera House, he ran away with a Doncaster maiden on heavy ground on his only start in October 2001. Looks potentially useful.

Foreign Affairs

115(107) (90++)**111**
3-y-o ch c Hernando (FR)-Entente Cordiale (USA) (Affirmed (USA))
Sir Mark Prescott The Speculators

Placings:21-211120 (5247a)
2001: 10^{2}GF, 9^{1}GF, 9^{1}GF, 10^{1}G, 13^{2}G, 12^{0}HO

	Starts	1st	2nd	3rd	Win & Pl
Career Total (Turf)	6	3	2	0	148653
Career Total (AW)	2	1	1	0	2370

104 7/01 York 1m2f85y B(0-110)H GD £87750
96 6/01 Gdwd 1m1f192yC(0-90)H G-F £10595
93 6/01 Sals 1m1f198yC(0-85) G-F £7308
90 11/00 Wolv 7f F STD £1736
Total win prize-money £107389

Going (Turf): Sf: 0-0 GS: 0-0 Gd: 1-2 **GF: 2-3** Fm: 0-0
Distance: 5f/6f: 0-0 7f-8f: 1-2 **9f-13f: 3-5** 14f+: 0-1
Track : LH: 2-5 RH: 2-3 **Tight: 3-5** Gall: 1-2
Aids: Bl: 0-0 Vi: 0-0 Tstrap: 0-0
Best Rating: 111 8/01 York 1m5f194y good

Started off on the All-Weather last year and got off the mark on his second ever outing at Wolverhampton. Ran a fine race behind Lailani at Epsom on his reappearance in 2001 and quickly went on to win handicaps at Salisbury and Goodwood over ten furlongs and the John Smiths' Cup. Outstayed in the Ebor, he then put up a creditable effort in the Arc on an unsuitable surface. Lightly raced, he acts on fast ground and stays a mile and a half.

Foreign Editor

98(109) (70)**67**
5-y-o ch g Magic Ring (IRE)-True Precision (Presidium)
J J Quinn (K A Ryan 19/6) Pride Of Yorkshire Racing Club

Placings:305/00665411/01133200000210-656650005066 (5616)
2001: 7^{6}SW, 6^{5}SD, 7^{6}SD, 7^{6}SD, 6^{5}SD, 7^{0}GF, 6^{0}GF, 7^{0}G, 7^{5}G, 7^{0}G, 7^{6}SD, 7^{6}SD

	Starts	1st	2nd	3rd	Win & Pl
Career Total (Turf)	17	0	1	1	1812
Career Total (AW)	21	5	1	2	24408

84 12/00 Wolv 7f C(0-95)H STD £6418
75 1/00 Ling 7f C(0-100)H STD £7020
77 1/00 Wolv 7f D(0-80)H STD £3848
72 12/99 Wolv 6f F(0-65)H STD £1892
53 12/99 Wolv 7f F(0-60)H STD £1934
Total win prize-money £21115

Going (Turf): Sf: 0-3 GS: 0-2 Gd: 0-7 GF: 0-4 Fm: 0-1
Distance: 5f/6f: 1-17 **7f-8f: 4-19** 9f-13f: 0-2 14f+: 0-0
Track : **LH: 5-29** RH: 0-2 **Tight: 5-15** Gall: 0-2
Aids: Bl: 0-2 Vi: 0-0 Tstrap: 0-0
Best Rating: 75 1/01 Wolv 6f stand

Forest Bride (USA)

(98) (37)
4-y-o ch f Woodman (USA)-Lady In White (Shareef Dancer (USA))
J A Osborne The Woolfie And Tom Partnership

Placings:5/003360-00 (0297)
2001: 12^{0}SD, 9^{0}SD

	Starts	1st	2nd	3rd	Win & Pl
Career Total (Turf)	3	0	0	0	969
Career Total (AW)	6	0	0	2	774

Going (Turf): Sf: 0-0 GS: 0-0 Gd: 0-0 GF: 0-0 Fm: 0-0
Distance: 5f/6f: 0-0 7f-8f: 0-2 9f-13f: 0-5 14f+: 0-0
Track : LH: 0-7 RH: 0-0 Tight: 0-6 Gall: 0-0
Aids: Bl: 0-1 Vi: 0-0 Tstrap: 0-1

Forest Dancer (IRE)

107(97) (94+)**88**
3-y-o b/br c Charnwood Forest (IRE)-Forest Berries (IRE) (Thatching)
R Hannon Nicholas R Hodges

Placings:35001-03044010500 (5344)
2001: 8^{0}GS, 8^{3}G, 7^{0}GF, 7^{4}GF, 8^{4}F, 8^{0}GF, 8^{1}GF, 8^{0}GF, 7^{5}GF, 8^{0}S, 8^{0}GS

	Starts	1st	2nd	3rd	Win & Pl
Career Total (Turf)	15	1	0	2	10589
Career Total (AW)	1	1	0	0	2807

88 7/01 Newb 1m D(0-85)H G-F £4914
94 11/00 Wolv 6f D STD £2807
Total win prize-money £7721

Going (Turf): Sf: 0-4 GS: 0-2 Gd: 0-2 **GF: 1-6** Fm: 0-1
Distance: 5f/6f: 1-5 7f-8f: 1-10 9f-13f: 0-1 14f+: 0-0
Track : **LH: 1-4** RH: 0-2 **Tight: 1-1** Gall: 0-3
Aids: Bl: 0-0 Vi: 0-0 Tstrap: 0-0
Best Rating: 88 7/01 Newb 1m gd-fm

He came good in a mile handicap at Newbury in July, but has struggled since. Stays a mile. Acts on fast ground.

Forest Dream

102(100) (12)**49**
6-y-o b m Warrshan (USA)-Sirenivo (USA) (Sir Ivor)
L A Dace Eddie Davess

Placings:5036004/562010022240/000000230020400-60030 (4523)
2001: 16^{6}GS, 12^{0}GF, 16^{0}G, 14^{3}G, 16^{0}GF

	Starts	1st	2nd	3rd	Win & Pl
Career Total (Turf)	29	1	4	3	7933
Career Total (AW)	10	0	2	0	1523

56 8/99 Ling 1m2f E(0-70)H G-F £3088
Total win prize-money £3089

Going (Turf): Sf: 0-2 GS: 0-2 Gd: 0-9 **GF: 1-12** Fm: 0-4
Distance: 5f/6f: 0-0 7f-8f: 0-4 **9f-13f: 1-30** 14f+: 0-5
Track : **LH: 1-29** RH: 0-6 **Tight: 1-24** Gall: 0-1
Aids: Bl: 0-0 Vi: 0-0 Tstrap: 0-1
Best Rating: 49 8/01 Yarm 1m6f17y good

Forest Heath (IRE)

108 **81**
4-y-o gr g Common Grounds-Caroline Lady (JPN) (Caro)
H J Collingridge Forest Heath Partnership

Placings:00/21220-00553250 (5344)
2001: 10^{0}G, 10^{0}GF, 10^{5}G, 12^{5}GF, 10^{3}S, 9^{2}GS, 9^{5}GS, 8^{0}GS

	Starts	1st	2nd	3rd	Win & Pl
Career Total (Turf)	15	1	4	1	12006

73 6/00 Gdwd 1m1f192yE G-F £4114
Total win prize-money £4115

Going (Turf): Sf: 0-3 GS: 0-5 Gd: 0-3 **GF: 1-4** Fm: 0-0
Distance: 5f/6f: 0-1 7f-8f: 0-2 **9f-13f: 1-12** 14f+: 0-0

Track : LH: 0-4 **RH: 1-6 Tight: 1-2** Gall: 0-4
Aids: Bl: 0-0 Vi: 0-3 Tstrap: 0-0
Best Rating: 81 8/01 Leic 1m1f218y gd-sft

Gradually fell in the handicap this term and began to recapture some form. Ten furlongs looks his best trip. Best on as easy surface, he is usually held up.

Forest Leaf (IRE)

95 **78**
3-y-o b g Charnwood Forest (IRE)-Besito (Wassl)
Patrick Carey (M A Jarvis 11/5) Raymond Yeung

Placings:1560 **(4654a)**
2001: 8^{1}GS, 7^{5}GS, 8^{6}GF, 9^{0}G

	Starts	1st	2nd	3rd	Win & Pl
Career Total (Turf)	4	1	0	0	4615

69 4/01 Newb 1m D G-S £4615
Total win prize-money £4615

Going (Turf): Sf: 0-0 **GS: 1-2** Gd: 0-1 GF: 0-1 Fm: 0-0
Distance: 5f/6f: 0-0 **7f-8f: 1-3** 9f-13f: 0-0 14f+: 0-0
Track : LH: 0-1 RH: 0-0 Tight: 0-0 Gall: 0-0
Aids: Bl: 0-0 Vi: 0-0 Tstrap: 0-0
Best Rating: 78 5/01 Ling 7f140y gd-sft

Forest Light (IRE)

102 **66**
3-y-o gr f Rainbow Quest (USA)-Woodland Garden (Godswalk (USA))
R F Johnson Houghton Bob Lanigan

Placings:00-001030 **(4541)**
2001: 10^{0}GF, 12^{0}GF, 12^{1}GF, 11^{0}GF, 12^{3}GF, 14^{0}GF

	Starts	1st	2nd	3rd	Win & Pl
Career Total (Turf)	8	1	0	1	2948

66 6/01 Wwck 1m4f134yF(0-60)H G-F £2485
Total win prize-money £2485

Going (Turf): Sf: 0-0 GS: 0-1 Gd: 0-0 **GF: 1-7** Fm: 0-0
Distance: 5f/6f: 0-0 7f-8f: 0-2 **9f-13f: 1-5** 14f+: 0-1
Track : **LH: 1-5** RH: 0-1 Tight: 0-3 Gall: 0-1
Aids: Bl: 0-0 Vi: 0-0 Tstrap: 0-0
Best Rating: 66 6/01 Wwck 1m4f134y gd-fm

Won a maiden handicap at Warwick in June, but struggled afterwards.

Forest Moon

99(98) (53)**38**
3-y-o b f Charnwood Forest (IRE)-Moon Watch (Night Shift (USA))
Andrew Reid A S Reid

Placings:66010034-35363400000 **(4609)**
2001: 6^{3}SD, 7^{5}SD, 6^{3}SW, 6^{6}SW, 5^{3}GF, 6^{4}GF, 5^{0}G, 6^{0}GF, 6^{0}G, 6^{0}GF, 8^{0}F

	Starts	1st	2nd	3rd	Win & Pl
Career Total (Turf)	12	1	0	1	1866
Career Total (AW)	7	0	0	3	1210

45 6/00 Wind 6f G G-F £1865
Total win prize-money £1866

Going (Turf): Sf: 0-2 GS: 0-2 Gd: 0-2 **GF: 1-5** Fm: 0-1
Distance: **5f/6f: 1-14** 7f-8f: 0-4 9f-13f: 0-1 14f+: 0-0
Track : LH: 0-10 **RH: 1-3** Tight: 0-8 **Gall: 1-5**
Aids: Bl: 0-0 Vi: 0-0 Tstrap: 0-0
Best Rating: 53 6/01 Yarm 6f3y gd-fm

Forest Prize

95 **77**
2-y-o b f Charnwood Forest (IRE)-Midnight's Reward (Night Shift (USA))
T D Easterby April Fools

Placings:50110000 **(5185)**
2001: 6^{5}F, 6^{0}GF, 6^{1}GF, 6^{1}G, 6^{0}G, 6^{0}GF, 7^{0}S, 7^{0}GS

	Starts	1st	2nd	3rd	Win & Pl
Career Total (Turf)	8	2	0	0	7658

65 8/01 Hayd 6f D GD £4062
72 7/01 Hayd 6f E G-F £3332
Total win prize-money £7395

Going (Turf): Sf: 0-1 GS: 0-1 **Gd: 1-2 GF: 1-3** Fm: 0-1
Distance: **5f/6f: 2-5** 7f-8f: 0-3 9f-13f: 0-0 14f+: 0-0
Track : LH: 0-4 RH: 0-0 Tight: 0-2 Gall: 0-1
Aids: Bl: 0-0 Vi: 0-0 Tstrap: 0-0
Best Rating: 77 9/01 Donc 6f gd-fm

She has won twice over six furlongs at Haydock, but had fortune on her side on both occasions and did not run so well when tried over seven at York.

Forest Queen

94 **26**
4-y-o b f Risk Me (FR)-Grey Cree (Creetown)
J S Wainwright P W Cooper

Placings:042003050/0000060-00000000 **(4778)**
2001: 5^{0}GF, 8^{0}GF, 7^{0}GF, 8^{0}GF, 5^{0}GF, 6^{0}F, 5^{0}GF, 5^{0}G

	Starts	1st	2nd	3rd	Win & Pl
Career Total (Turf)	25	0	1	1	2197

Going (Turf): Sf: 0-3 GS: 0-3 Gd: 0-7 GF: 0-10 Fm: 0-1
Distance: 5f/6f: 0-15 7f-8f: 0-5 9f-13f: 0-4 14f+: 0-0
Track : LH: 0-2 RH: 0-4 Tight: 0-2 Gall: 0-1
Aids: Bl: 0-0 Vi: 0-0 Tstrap: 0-0
Best Rating: 26 8/01 Thsk 6f firm

Forest Ridge

73 **56**
2-y-o b/br g Charnwood Forest (IRE)-Away To Me (Exit To Nowhere (USA))
Mrs A J Perrett The Waywood Partnership

Placings:0 **(5460)**
2001: 8^{0}G

	Starts	1st	2nd	3rd	Win & Pl
Career Total (Turf)	1	0	0	0	

Going (Turf): Sf: 0-0 GS: 0-0 Gd: 0-1 GF: 0-0 Fm: 0-0
Distance: 5f/6f: 0-0 7f-8f: 0-0 9f-13f: 0-1 14f+: 0-0
Track : LH: 0-1 RH: 0-0 Tight: 0-1 Gall: 0-0
Aids: Bl: 0-0 Vi: 0-0 Tstrap: 0-0
Best Rating: 56 10/01 Bath 1m5y good

Forest Tune (IRE)

97 **68**
3-y-o b c Charnwood Forest (IRE)-Swift Chorus (Music Boy)
B Hanbury The Acorn Partnership

Placings:1506000640 **(5490)**
2001: 10^{1}HY, 10^{5}GS, 8^{0}G, 8^{6}GF, 8^{0}GS, 8^{0}G, 8^{0}G, 10^{6}HY, 8^{4}GS, 7^{0}HY

	Starts	1st	2nd	3rd	Win & Pl
Career Total (Turf)	10	1	0	0	4043

73 4/01 Pont 1m2f6y E HVY £3038
Total win prize-money £3038

Going (Turf): Sf: 1-3 GS: 0-3 Gd: 0-3 GF: 0-1 Fm: 0-0
Distance: 5f/6f: 0-0 7f-8f: 0-4 **9f-13f: 1-6** 14f+: 0-0
Track : **LH: 1-4** RH: 0-2 Tight: 0-0 Gall: 0-1
Aids: Bl: 0-1 Vi: 0-0 Tstrap: 0-1
Best Rating: 84 5/01 NmkR 1m good

A half-brother to four winners, he won a Pontefract maiden on his debut over ten furlongs on heavy ground in the spring of 2001, but has been found wanting in handicaps since. Seems best on an easy surface.

Forever Loved

94 **82**
2-y-o ch f Deploy-Truly Madly Deeply (Most Welcome)
D Haydn Jones The Preseli Partnership

Placings:00260 **(5368)**
2001: 6^{0}GF, 7^{0}GF, 7^{2}G, 7^{6}G, 8^{0}GS

	Starts	1st	2nd	3rd	Win & Pl
Career Total (Turf)	5	0	1	0	929

Going (Turf): Sf: 0-0 GS: 0-1 Gd: 0-2 GF: 0-2 Fm: 0-0
Distance: 5f/6f: 0-1 7f-8f: 0-4 9f-13f: 0-0 14f+: 0-0
Track : LH: 0-1 RH: 0-0 Tight: 0-0 Gall: 0-0
Aids: Bl: 0-0 Vi: 0-0 Tstrap: 0-0
Best Rating: 82 7/01 Leic 7f9y good

Ran well on her third start, but failed to build on that after. Suited by seven furlongs on good ground.

Forever My Lord

102 **54**
3-y-o b g Be My Chief (USA)-In Love Again (IRE) (Prince Rupert (FR))
R F Johnson Houghton W H Ponsonby

Placings:60111000-40066600 **(4667)**
2001: 6^{4}GS, 7^{0}GF, 7^{0}GF, 7^{6}GF, 10^{6}GF, 9^{6}G, 9^{0}GF, 8^{0}GF

	Starts	1st	2nd	3rd	Win & Pl
Career Total (Turf)	16	3	0	0	21971

79 8/00 Gdwd 7f C H GD £11375
73 7/00 NmkJ 7f D GD £5200
72 7/00 NmkJ 7f E GD £5096
Total win prize-money £21671

Going (Turf): Sf: 0-2 GS: 0-2 **Gd: 3-5** GF: 0-7 Fm: 0-0
Distance: 5f/6f: 0-2 **7f-8f: 3-10** 9f-13f: 0-4 14f+: 0-0
Track : LH: 0-5 **RH: 1-2** Tight: 0-1 Gall: 0-2
Aids: Bl: 0-2 Vi: 0-0 Tstrap: 0-4
Best Rating: 76 5/01 Brig 6f209y gd-sft

Forever Times

109(71) (27)**84**
3-y-o b f So Factual (USA)-Simply Times (USA) (Dodge (USA))
T D Easterby Times Of Wigan

Placings:36221033004-00012166220014 **(5598)**
2001: 7^{0}SD, 6^{0}S, 7^{0}GF, 7^{1}F, 7^{2}GF, 7^{1}GF, 7^{6}GF, 7^{6}G, 7^{2}GF, 7^{2}GS, 7^{0}GS, 6^{0}G, 5^{1}GS, 6^{4}GS

	Starts	1st	2nd	3rd	Win & Pl
Career Total (Turf)	24	4	5	3	38905
Career Total (AW)	1	0	0	0	

78 10/01 Catt 5f212y F(0-85) G-S £2401
82 6/01 Ches 7f2y D(0-80)H G-F £7637
51 5/01 Rdcr 7f E(0-70) FRM £3486
65 8/00 Thsk 5f E GD £3038
Total win prize-money £16564

Going (Turf): Sf: 0-4 **GS: 1-5 Gd: 1-5 GF: 1-8 Fm: 1-2**
Distance: 5f/6f: 2-11 7f-8f: 2-14 9f-13f: 0-0 14f+: 0-0
Track : **LH: 2-7** RH: 0-2 **Tight: 2-5** Gall: 0-0
Aids: Bl: 0-0 Vi: 0-0 Tstrap: 0-0
Best Rating: 93 8/01 NmkJ 7f gd-fm

In fine heart this term, winning seven-furlong handicaps at Redcar, Chester and a six furlong event at Catterick. Well suited by fast ground, and sprint distances.

Forge Valley Lady

91 **64**
2-y-o ch f Hamas (IRE)-Salul (Soviet Star (USA))
J L Eyre Wetherby Racing Bureau 53

Placings:443000 **(5169)**
2001: 5^{4}GF, 5^{4}GS, 6^{3}GF, 7^{0}G, 7^{0}GF, 6^{0}GS

	Starts	1st	2nd	3rd	Win & Pl
Career Total (Turf)	6	0	0	1	1300

Going (Turf): Sf: 0-0 GS: 0-2 Gd: 0-1 GF: 0-3 Fm: 0-0
Distance: 5f/6f: 0-4 7f-8f: 0-2 9f-13f: 0-0 14f+: 0-0
Track : LH: 0-2 RH: 0-0 Tight: 0-1 Gall: 0-0
Aids: Bl: 0-0 Vi: 0-0 Tstrap: 0-0
Best Rating: 64 9/01 York 6f gd-fm

She has shown plenty of ability in maidens and should make her mark.

Forgotten Invite

3-y-o ch f Forzando-Uninvited (Be My Guest (USA))
D A Nolan Mrs J McFadyen-Murray

Placings:00 **(4084)**
2001: 9^{0}GF, 8^{0}GF

	Starts	1st	2nd	3rd	Win & Pl
Career Total (Turf)	2	0	0	0	

Going (Turf): Sf: 0-0 GS: 0-0 Gd: 0-0 GF: 0-2 Fm: 0-0
Distance: 5f/6f: 0-0 7f-8f: 0-0 9f-13f: 0-2 14f+: 0-0
Track : LH: 0-2 RH: 0-0 Tight: 0-1 Gall: 0-0
Aids: Bl: 0-0 Vi: 0-0 Tstrap: 0-0

Forgotten Times (USA)

106 (71)**70**
7-y-o ch m Nabeel Dancer (USA)-Etoile D'Amore (USA) (The Minstrel (CAN))
K T Ivory John Crook

Placings:64**433/21221**0005060/**500105**00000005/0401 15514011401060/206221206003100-00052000666012 **(4950)**
2001: 5^{0}GS, 5^{0}F, 5^{0}GF, 5^{5}GF, 5^{2}GF, 5^{0}GF, 5^{0}GF, 5^{0}G, 5^{6}G, 5^{6}G, 5^{6}GF, 5^{0}F, 5^{1}G, 5^{2}G

	Starts	1st	2nd	3rd	Win & Pl
Career Total (Turf)	65	9	6	1	47128
Career Total (AW)	14	3	3	2	12978

68	9/01	Epsm	5f	C(0-90)H	GD	£10968
74	9/00	Epsm	5f	D(0-80)H	GD	£5005
73	6/00	Ling	5f	E(0-70)H	G-F	£3721
61	9/99	Gdwd	5f	E(0-70)H	HVY	£3829
59	8/99	Brig	5f59y	E(0-75)H	G-F	£3452
64	8/99	Wind	5f10y	F(0-70)H	SFT	£2105
50	7/99	Sals	5f	E(0-70)H	G-S	£2664
45	5/99	Folk	5f	E(0-70)H	G-F	£2856
51	5/99	Gdwd	5f	E(0-70)H	GD	£3615
71	2/98	Ling	6f	E(0-70)H	SLW	£2832
71	2/97	Ling	6f	E(0-70)H	STD	£2739
59	1/97	Ling	6f	D	STD	£3338

Total win prize-money £47128

Going (Turf): Sf: 2-8 GS: 1-7 **Gd: 3-16 GF: 3-29** Fm: 0-5
Distance: **5f/6f: 12-72** 7f-8f: 0-7 9f-13f: 0-0 14f+: 0-0
Track : **LH: 4-30** RH: 1-8 **Tight: 3-14** Gall: 1-14
Aids: Bl: 0-1 **Vi: 10-52** Tstrap: 0-0
Best Rating: 70 9/01 Gdwd 5f good

In cracking form in 1999, winning six times, climbed up the handicap as a result and found life a whole lot tougher. Has since dropped to a more realistic mark in 2001. Suited by the minimum trip on a sharp track, she acts on fast ground and Equitrack as well. Runs in a visor.

Formal Party

92 **32**
3-y-o ch f Formidable (USA)-Tea Colony (USA) (Pleasant Colony (USA))
T D McCarthy A D Spence

Placings:66300-000000 **(4385)**
2001: 8^{0}S, 6^{0}GF, 6^{0}F, 6^{0}GF, 6^{0}GF, 6^{0}GF

	Starts	1st	2nd	3rd	Win & Pl
Career Total (Turf)	11	0	0	1	397

Going (Turf): Sf: 0-2 GS: 0-1 Gd: 0-1 GF: 0-6 Fm: 0-1
Distance: 5f/6f: 0-6 7f-8f: 0-4 9f-13f: 0-1 14f+: 0-0
Track : LH: 0-3 RH: 0-0 Tight: 0-1 Gall: 0-0
Aids: Bl: 0-0 Vi: 0-0 Tstrap: 0-0
Best Rating: 32 7/01 Ling 6f gd-fm

Formeric

91 (12)**54**
5-y-o ch g Formidable (USA)-Irish Limerick (Try My Best (USA))
Miss L C Siddall Mrs Ann Morgan

Placings:00/000 **(2955)**
2001: 7^{0}G, 7^{0}F, 7^{0}GF

	Starts	1st	2nd	3rd	Win & Pl
Career Total (Turf)	4	0	0	0	
Career Total (AW)	1	0	0	0	

Going (Turf): Sf: 0-1 GS: 0-0 Gd: 0-1 GF: 0-1 Fm: 0-1
Distance: 5f/6f: 0-2 7f-8f: 0-3 9f-13f: 0-0 14f+: 0-0
Track : LH: 0-1 RH: 0-1 Tight: 0-0 Gall: 0-1
Aids: Bl: 0-0 Vi: 0-0 Tstrap: 0-0
Best Rating: 54 5/01 Donc 7f good

Very little cause for encouragement so far.

Foronlymo

93(94) (86)**75d**
2-y-o b g Forzando-Polish Descent (IRE) (Danehill (USA))
K R Burke Maurice Charge

Placings:22604106 **(5408)**
2001: 5^{2}S, 6^{2}GF, 6^{6}GF, 6^{0}GF, 6^{4}HY, 6^{1}SD, 6^{0}GS, 6^{6}SD

	Starts	1st	2nd	3rd	Win & Pl
Career Total (Turf)	6	0	2	0	1905
Career Total (AW)	2	1	0	0	2324

86	10/01	Wolv	6f	F	STD	£2324

Total win prize-money £2324

Going (Turf): Sf: 0-2 GS: 0-1 Gd: 0-0 GF: 0-3 Fm: 0-0
Distance: **5f/6f: 1-7** 7f-8f: 0-1 9f-13f: 0-0 14f+: 0-0
Track : **LH: 1-3** RH: 0-0 **Tight: 1-2** Gall: 0-0
Aids: Bl: 0-0 **Vi: 1-3** Tstrap: 0-0
Best Rating: 86 10/01 Wolv 6f stand

Showed some fair form on turf, but was a revelation on his first attempt on sand when bolting up in a claimer in a first-time visor at Wolverhampton in October. Suited by six furlongs.

Fort Sumter (USA)

93(102) (61)**60**
5-y-o b g Sea Hero (USA)-Gray And Red (USA) (Wolf Power (SAF))
P R Hedger E Whelan

Placings:022/606300/620**260-31**600 **(1384)**
2001: 12^{3}SD, 11^{1}SD, 11^{6}SD, 11^{0}GS, 12^{0}S

	Starts	1st	2nd	3rd	Win & Pl
Career Total (Turf)	13	0	3	1	3117
Career Total (AW)	7	1	1	1	3335

61	2/01	Sthl	1m3f	E(0-70)H	STD	£2443

Total win prize-money £2443

Going (Turf): Sf: 0-4 GS: 0-5 Gd: 0-2 GF: 0-2 Fm: 0-0
Distance: 5f/6f: 0-0 7f-8f: 0-2 **9f-13f: 1-16** 14f+: 0-2
Track : **LH: 1-11** RH: 0-7 **Tight: 0-12** Gall: 0-0
Aids: Bl: 0-0 Vi: 0-2 Tstrap: 0-0
Best Rating: 61 2/01 Sthl 1m3f stand

Forthechop

(95) (10)
4-y-o b g Minshaanshu Amad (USA)-Cousin Jenny (Midyan (USA))
Mrs H L Walton A E Walton

Placings:6006/454300-505000600 **(2323)**
2001: 8^{5}SD, 9^{0}SD, 8^{5}SD, 8^{0}SW, 9^{0}SD, 12^{0}SD, 11^{6}SD, 17^{0}F, 16^{0}SD

	Starts	1st	2nd	3rd	Win & Pl
Career Total (Turf)	3	0	0	0	
Career Total (AW)	16	0	0	1	338

Going (Turf): Sf: 0-1 GS: 0-0 Gd: 0-0 GF: 0-0 Fm: 0-2
Distance: 5f/6f: 0-0 7f-8f: 0-9 9f-13f: 0-8 14f+: 0-2
Track : LH: 0-18 RH: 0-1 Tight: 0-5 Gall: 0-0
Aids: Bl: 0-1 Vi: 0-0 Tstrap: 0-0
Best Rating: 28 1/01 Sthl 1m stand

Fortune Found (IRE)

(68) (1)
3-y-o b f Fumo Di Londra (IRE)-Trillick (IRE) (Treasure Kay)
C G Cox Mrs T L Cox

Placings:0-0 **(0978)**
2001: 7^{0}SD

	Starts	1st	2nd	3rd	Win & Pl
Career Total (Turf)	1	0	0	0	
Career Total (AW)	1	0	0	0	

Going (Turf): Sf: 0-1 GS: 0-0 Gd: 0-0 GF: 0-0 Fm: 0-0
Distance: 5f/6f: 0-0 7f-8f: 0-2 9f-13f: 0-0 14f+: 0-0
Track : LH: 0-1 RH: 0-0 Tight: 0-0 Gall: 0-0
Aids: Bl: 0-0 Vi: 0-0 Tstrap: 0-2
Best Rating: 1 4/01 Sthl 7f stand

Fortune Island (IRE)

94 **75**
2-y-o b c Turtle Island (IRE)-Blue Kestrel (IRE) (Bluebird (USA))
S P C Woods P K L Chu

Placings:044 **(5684)**
2001: 8^{0}S, 8^{4}G, 8^{4}S

	Starts	1st	2nd	3rd	Win & Pl
Career Total (Turf)	3	0	0	0	360

Going (Turf): Sf: 0-2 GS: 0-0 Gd: 0-1 GF: 0-0 Fm: 0-0
Distance: 5f/6f: 0-0 7f-8f: 0-3 9f-13f: 0-0 14f+: 0-0
Track : LH: 0-0 RH: 0-0 Tight: 0-0 Gall: 0-0
Aids: Bl: 0-0 Vi: 0-0 Tstrap: 0-0
Best Rating: 75 11/01 Donc 1m soft

Fortune Point (IRE)

95 **62**
3-y-o ch c Cadeaux Genereux-Mountains Of Mist (IRE) (Shirley Heights)
J Noseda Lucayan Stud

Placings:42-023 **(5374)**
2001: 7^{0}GF, 7^{2}HY, 6^{3}G

	Starts	1st	2nd	3rd	Win & Pl
Career Total (Turf)	5	0	2	1	3486

Going (Turf): Sf: 0-3 GS: 0-0 Gd: 0-1 GF: 0-1 Fm: 0-0
Distance: 5f/6f: 0-1 7f-8f: 0-4 9f-13f: 0-0 14f+: 0-0
Track : LH: 0-3 RH: 0-0 Tight: 0-0 Gall: 0-0
Aids: Bl: 0-0 Vi: 0-2 Tstrap: 0-0
Best Rating: 62 9/01 Hayd 7f30y heavy

Still a maiden, although he has run some good races, and it should not be long before he gets off the mark, although it has been said that he is not the toughest of battlers. Acts well with cut in the ground, and is suited by six and seven furlongs.

Fortune's Fool

87 **64**
2-y-o b c Zilzal (USA)-Peryllys (Warning)
B Smart Pinstripe Partners

Placings:3600 **(5169)**
2001: 6^{3}GF, 7^{6}F, 7^{0}GF, 6^{0}GS

	Starts	1st	2nd	3rd	Win & Pl
Career Total (Turf)	4	0	0	1	402

Going (Turf): Sf: 0-0 GS: 0-1 Gd: 0-0 GF: 0-2 Fm: 0-1
Distance: 5f/6f: 0-2 7f-8f: 0-2 9f-13f: 0-0 14f+: 0-0
Track : LH: 0-2 RH: 0-0 Tight: 0-0 Gall: 0-0
Aids: Bl: 0-0 Vi: 0-0 Tstrap: 0-0
Best Rating: 64 6/01 Folk 6f gd-fm

Forty Forte

103(105) (68)**74**
5-y-o b g Pursuit Of Love-Cominna (Dominion)
Miss S J Wilton (K R Burke 20/7) John Pointon And Sons

Placings:22312100001**3205/616244**1530**003-**2600**142**3**4**0100 **(5463)**
2001: 8^{2}SD, 10^{6}SD, 8^{0}SD, 9^{0}GF, 8^{1}SD, 8^{4}SD, 8^{2}SD, 9^{3}G, 9^{4}SD, 8^{0}GF, 10^{1}S, 9^{0}HY, 11^{0}G

	Starts	1st	2nd	3rd	Win & Pl
Career Total (Turf)	17	4	1	2	24552
Career Total (AW)	24	3	6	3	18432

74	9/01	Ches	1m2f75y	E(0-70)H	SFT	£4719
63	7/01	Sthl	1m	E(0-75)H	STD	£3115
78	3/00	Nott	1m1f213y	D(0-85)H	GD	£7410
73	1/00	Ling	1m2f	D(0-80)H	STD	£5239
69	11/99	Ling	1m2f	G(0-75)H	STD	£1542
76	4/99	Bevl	7f100y	C(0-90)H	GD	£6090
76	3/99	Nott	1m54y	G	G-S	£1952

Total win prize-money £30069

Going (Turf): Sf: 1-5 GS: 1-1 **Gd: 2-7** GF: 0-4 Fm: 0-0
Distance: 5f/6f: 0-1 7f-8f: 2-15 **9f-13f: 5-25** 14f+: 0-0
Track : **LH: 6-35** RH: 1-5 **Tight: 3-28** Gall: 0-1
Aids: Bl: 0-0 Vi: 0-0 Tstrap: 0-0
Best Rating: 74 9/01 Ches 1m2f75y soft

Acts well on the All-Weather, but has won four times on turf. Stays ten furlongs and suited by cut on turf. Likes to dominate and difficult to catch when given some rope.

Forty On Line

80 **46**
2-y-o ch f Pharly (FR)-Charming Bride (Charmer)
S C Williams Stuart C Williams

Placings:4 **(3476)**
2001: 6^{4}GF

	Starts	1st	2nd	3rd	Win & Pl
Career Total (Turf)	1	0	0	0	320

Going (Turf): Sf: 0-0 GS: 0-0 Gd: 0-0 GF: 0-1 Fm: 0-0
Distance: 5f/6f: 0-1 7f-8f: 0-0 9f-13f: 0-0 14f+: 0-0
Track : LH: 0-0 RH: 0-0 Tight: 0-0 Gall: 0-0
Aids: Bl: 0-0 Vi: 0-0 Tstrap: 0-0
Best Rating: 46 7/01 NmkJ 6f gd-fm

Forum Finale (USA)

104(103) (69)**70**
3-y-o b f Silver Hawk (USA)-Silk Masque (USA) (Woodman (USA))
M Johnston Mrs Jacqueline Conroy

Placings:25001-**2205**2**02316** **(3618)**
2001: 9^{2}SW, 8^{2}SD, 10^{0}SW, 10^{5}SW, 12^{2}SD, 11^{0}GS, 12^{2}F, 12^{3}GF, 11^{1}GF, 12^{6}F

	Starts	1st	2nd	3rd	Win & Pl
Career Total (Turf)	9	1	2	1	6974
Career Total (AW)	6	1	3	0	5624

66	7/01	Hayd	1m3f200y	D(0-80)H	G-F	£4062
66	10/00	Wolv	1m100y	E(0-75)	STD	£2772

Total win prize-money £6835

Going (Turf): Sf: 0-2 GS: 0-2 Gd: 0-0 **GF: 1-3** Fm: 0-2
Distance: 5f/6f: 0-2 7f-8f: 0-2 **9f-13f: 2-11** 14f+: 0-0
Track : **LH: 2-11** RH: 0-2 **Tight: 1-9** Gall: 0-0
Aids: Bl: 0-0 Vi: 0-0 **Tstrap: 1-4**
Best Rating: 70 8/01 Thsk 1m4f firm

A front-runner, she ironically gained her first turf success after missing the break and coming from behind. Acts on fast ground.

Forwood (IRE)

107 **104**
3-y-o b c Charnwood Forest (IRE)-Silver Hut (USA) (Silver Hawk (USA))
M A Jarvis Mr & Mrs Raymond Anderson Green

Placings:1144-64 **(1156)**
2001: 8^{6}S, 8^{4}G

	Starts	1st	2nd	3rd	Win & Pl
Career Total (Turf)	6	2	0	0	17931

92	7/00	Asct	7f	D	GD	£6646
94	6/00	Newb	6f8y	D	G-F	£4602

Total win prize-money £11248

Going (Turf): Sf: 0-1 GS: 0-0 **Gd: 1-3 GF: 1-2** Fm: 0-0
Distance: 5f/6f: 0-0 **7f-8f: 2-6** 9f-13f: 0-0 14f+: 0-0
Track : LH: 0-1 RH: 0-1 Tight: 0-0 Gall: 0-2
Aids: Bl: 0-0 Vi: 0-0 Tstrap: 0-0
Best Rating: 98 5/01 Donc 1m good

He looked a useful juvenile when winning his first two starts at Newbury and Ascot but looked held in two starts this season.

Forza Figlio

106(91) (56)**64**
8-y-o b g Warning-Wish You Well (Sadler's Wells (USA))
M Kettle Taylor Parker Associates

Placings:24135/025302040/03344000**04**-3031600203 **(5624)**
2001: 9^{3}G, 10^{0}G, 10^{3}GF, 10^{1}GF, 10^{6}GF, 10^{0}G, 9^{0}G, 9^{2}GS, 10^{0}G, 9^{3}GS

	Starts	1st	2nd	3rd	Win & Pl
Career Total (Turf)	31	2	4	7	23202
Career Total (AW)	2	0	0	0	0

62	7/01	Wind	1m2f7y	E(0-70)H	G-F	£3500
76	5/96	Gdwd	1m	D	GD	£4793

Total win prize-money £8294

Going (Turf): Sf: 0-2 GS: 0-3 **Gd: 1-13 GF: 1-13** Fm: 0-0
Distance: 5f/6f: 0-0 7f-8f: 1-6 9f-13f: 1-27 14f+: 0-0
Track : LH: 0-13 **RH: 1-12 Tight: 1-11** Gall: 0-7
Aids: Bl: 0-2 Vi: 0-0 Tstrap: 0-0
Best Rating: 64 10/01 Sals 1m1f198y gd-sft

Hit winning form in a ten-furlong handicap at Windsor in July, when staying on to beat Dinar on the nod. He had been placed twice earlier on, but this was his first win since 1996. Stays ten furlongs. Acts on fast ground, but handles some cut.

Forza Glory

70 **66**
2-y-o ch f Forzando-Glory Isle (Hittite Glory)
Miss B Sanders Mrs J Laycock & A C Verdie

Placings:006 **(5666)**
2001: 6^{0}GF, 6^{0}HY, 6^{6}HY

	Starts	1st	2nd	3rd	Win & Pl
Career Total (Turf)	3	0	0	0	0

Going (Turf): Sf: 0-2 GS: 0-0 Gd: 0-0 GF: 0-1 Fm: 0-0
Distance: 5f/6f: 0-3 7f-8f: 0-0 9f-13f: 0-0 14f+: 0-0
Track : LH: 0-0 RH: 0-0 Tight: 0-0 Gall: 0-0
Aids: Bl: 0-0 Vi: 0-0 Tstrap: 0-0
Best Rating: 66 11/01 Wind 6f heavy

Forza Vitale

69 **30**
2-y-o b f Forzando-Meeson Times (Enchantment)
G B Balding The Roman Legion

Placings:0 **(1477)**
2001: 5^{0}G

	Starts	1st	2nd	3rd	Win & Pl
Career Total (Turf)	1	0	0	0	

Going (Turf): Sf: 0-0 GS: 0-0 Gd: 0-1 GF: 0-0 Fm: 0-0
Distance: 5f/6f: 0-1 7f-8f: 0-0 9f-13f: 0-0 14f+: 0-0
Track : LH: 0-0 RH: 0-1 Tight: 0-0 Gall: 0-1
Aids: Bl: 0-0 Vi: 0-0 Tstrap: 0-0
Best Rating: 30 5/01 Wind 5f10y good

Forzacurity

100 **69**
2-y-o ch g Forzando-Nice Lady (Connaught)
R M Beckett The Forzacurity Partnership

Placings:652123 **(5283)**
2001: 6^{6}GF, 6^{5}GF, 7^{2}HY, 7^{1}G, 8^{2}GF, 8^{3}HY

	Starts	1st	2nd	3rd	Win & Pl
Career Total (Turf)	6	1	2	1	5678

69	9/01	Bevl	7f100y	F(0-65)	GD	£2632

Total win prize-money £2632

Going (Turf): Sf: 0-2 GS: 0-0 **Gd: 1-1** GF: 0-3 Fm: 0-0
Distance: 5f/6f: 0-1 **7f-8f: 1-5** 9f-13f: 0-0 14f+: 0-0
Track : LH: 0-2 **RH: 1-2** Tight: 0-1 Gall: 0-0
Aids: Bl: 0-0 Vi: 0-1 Tstrap: 0-0
Best Rating: 69 9/01 Muss 1m gd-fm

Beaten in a seller and a claimer before getting off the mark in a nursery, and came close to following that up with a good second in similar company next time.

Foston Fox

98(57) (32)**35**
4-y-o b f Foxhound (USA)-Enaam (Shirley Heights)
C B B Booth The Foston Partnership

Placings:000**64**/05006005040-00000350 **(4672)**
2001: 6^{0}G, 7^{0}F, 5^{0}G, 6^{0}G, 7^{0}GS, 7^{3}GS, 6^{5}GF, 8^{0}G

	Starts	1st	2nd	3rd	Win & Pl
Career Total (Turf)	21	0	0	1	340
Career Total (AW)	3	0	0	0	200

Going (Turf): Sf: 0-3 GS: 0-4 Gd: 0-8 GF: 0-5 Fm: 0-1
Distance: 5f/6f: 0-6 7f-8f: 0-12 9f-13f: 0-6 14f+: 0-0
Track : LH: 0-8 RH: 0-2 Tight: 0-4 Gall: 0-0
Aids: Bl: 0-14 Vi: 0-0 Tstrap: 0-0
Best Rating: 37 6/01 Leic 5f218y good

Foston Second (IRE)

90 **28**
4-y-o ch f Lycius (USA)-Gentle Guest (IRE) (Be My Guest (USA))
C Weedon Atlantic Foods Ltd

Placings:00/42430-00 **(2519)**
2001: 11^{0}GF, 12^{0}GF

	Starts	1st	2nd	3rd	Win & Pl
Career Total (Turf)	9	0	1	1	1252

Going (Turf): Sf: 0-3 GS: 0-0 Gd: 0-2 GF: 0-3 Fm: 0-1
Distance: 5f/6f: 0-1 7f-8f: 0-1 9f-13f: 0-5 14f+: 0-2
Track : LH: 0-6 RH: 0-1 Tight: 0-5 Gall: 0-1
Aids: Bl: 0-0 Vi: 0-0 Tstrap: 0-0

Best Rating: 28 6/01 Wind 1m3f135y gd-fm

Fouette

93 **60**

3-y-o b f Saddlers' Hall (IRE)-Tight Spin (High Top)

N A Graham Matthews Breeding And Racing

Placings:0-004506 **(5525)**

2001: 10^{0}GF, 10^{0}G, 14^{4}G, 16^{5}GS, 14^{0}S, 11^{6}HY

	Starts	1st	2nd	3rd	Win & Pl
Career Total (Turf)	7	0	0	0	0

Going (Turf): Sf: 0-3 GS: 0-1 Gd: 0-2 GF: 0-1 Fm: 0-0
Distance: 5f/6f: 0-0 7f-8f: 0 1 9f-13f: 0-3 14f+: 0-3
Track : LH: 0-3 RH: 0-0 Tight: 0-6 Gall: 0-0
Aids: Bl: 0-0 Vi: 0-0 Tstrap: 0-0
Best Rating: 60 7/01 Yarm 1m6f17y good

Foundry Lane

106

10-y-o b g Mtoto-Eider (Niniski (USA))

Mrs M Reveley Mrs T E Sharratt

Placings:032133021/2061345/006/054/10/53440/42133-034462 **(4620)**

2001: 14^{0}GF, 16^{3}G, 14^{4}GF, 16^{4}GF, 16^{6}GF, 16^{2}F

	Starts	1st	2nd	3rd	Win & Pl
Career Total (Turf)	40	5	5	8	59921

74	7/00	Hayd	1m6f	D(0-85)H	G-F	£3828
75	10/98	York	1m5f194y	D(0-85)H	GD	£8870
82	8/95	Hayd	1m6f	D(0-85)H	G-F	£3951
80	9/94	Hayd	1m3f200y	C(0-90)H	G-S	£5771
62	5/94	Ayr	1m5f13y	D	FRM	£3017

Total win prize-money £25438

Going (Turf): Sf: 0-5 GS: 1-4 Gd: 1-10 **GF: 2-17** Fm: 1-4
Distance: 5f/6f: 0-0 7f-8f: 0-0 9f-13f: 1-10 **14f+: 4-30**
Track : **LH: 5-34** RH: 0-6 Tight: 0-6 **Gall: 1-19**
Aids: Bl: 0-0 Vi: 0-0 Tstrap: 0-0
Best Rating: 70 6/01 Hayd 2m45y good

Has been running on the Flat, over hurdles and over fences in the last couple of years, but remains a decent staying-handicapper on the level. He is on a reasonable mark on his old form.

Four Eagles (USA)

104 **84**

3-y-o b g Lear Fan (USA)-Bloomingly (ARG) (Candy Stripes (USA))

D R C Elsworth Mcdowell Racing

Placings:5-63554 **(3247)**

2001: 8^{6}S, 8^{3}GF, 9^{5}GF, 8^{5}GF, 10^{4}GS

	Starts	1st	2nd	3rd	Win & Pl
Career Total (Turf)	6	0	0	1	1397

Going (Turf): Sf: 0-2 GS: 0-1 Gd: 0-0 GF: 0-3 Fm: 0-0
Distance: 5f/6f: 0-0 7f-8f: 0-4 9f-13f: 0-2 14f+: 0-0
Track : LH: 0-0 RH: 0-1 Tight: 0-1 Gall: 0-0
Aids: Bl: 0-1 Vi: 0-0 Tstrap: 0-0
Best Rating: 84 6/01 Sals 1m1f198y gd-fm

Four Legs Good (IRE)

89 **38**

3-y-o b f Be My Guest (USA)-Karine (Habitat)

G C Bravery G C Bravery

Placings:0000-000 **(5129)**

2001: 8^{0}GF, 7^{0}G, 7^{0}HY

	Starts	1st	2nd	3rd	Win & Pl
Career Total (Turf)	7	0	0	0	

Going (Turf): Sf: 0-2 GS: 0-1 Gd: 0-1 GF: 0-3 Fm: 0-0
Distance: 5f/6f: 0-1 7f-8f: 0-4 9f-13f: 0-2 14f+: 0-0
Track : LH: 0-2 RH: 0-2 Tight: 0-1 Gall: 0-0
Aids: Bl: 0-0 Vi: 0-0 Tstrap: 0-0
Best Rating: 38 5/01 Yarm 1m3y gd-fm

Four Men (IRE)

92(90) (30)**20**

4-y-o b g Nicolotte-Sound Pet (Runnett)

A Berry Alan Berry

Placings:0040/00006606565302060600-506000000000600200000000000050000000 **(5625)**

2001: 8^{5}SW, 9^{0}SD, 12^{6}SD, 9^{0}HY, 10^{0}HY, 12^{0}SW, 12^{0}S, 9^{0}G, 8^{0}GF, 7^{0}F, 8^{0}GF, 7^{6}F, 7^{0}G, 8^{0}GF, 8^{2}F, 8^{0}GF, 7^{0}GF, 6^{0}GF, 7^{0}S, 8^{0}G, 8^{0}F, 7^{0}GS, 8^{0}GF, 10^{0}GS, 8^{0}GF, 8^{0}GF, 8^{0}G, 10^{5}G, 7^{0}G, 9^{0}G, 8^{0}F, 6^{0}GF, 7^{0}GS, 7^{0}G, 8^{0}GS

	Starts	1st	2nd	3rd	Win & Pl
Career Total (Turf)	52	0	2	1	5768
Career Total (AW)	7	0	0	0	262

Going (Turf): Sf: 0-7 GS: 0-5 Gd: 0-11 GF: 0-21 Fm: 0-8
Distance: 5f/6f: 0-3 7f-8f: 0-30 9f-13f: 0-26 14f+: 0-0
Track : LH: 0-33 RH: 0-11 Tight: 0-20 Gall: 0-1
Aids: Bl: 0-0 Vi: 0-0 Tstrap: 0-0
Best Rating: 33 6/01 Hayd 7f30y good

Fourdaned (IRE)

75 **34d**

8-y-o b g Danehill (USA)-Pro Patria (Petingo)

Mrs L C Jewell The Lively Lads

Placings:44/26500/500042300000/06020004/65000504 00005/000-0 **(4019)**

2001: 12^{0}G

	Starts	1st	2nd	3rd	Win & Pl
Career Total (Turf)	33	0	3	1	3432
Career Total (AW)	11	0	0	0	0

Going (Turf): Sf: 0-4 GS: 0-2 Gd: 0-9 GF: 0-18 Fm: 0-0
Distance: 5f/6f: 0-0 7f-8f: 0-7 9f-13f: 0-33 14f+: 0-4
Track : LH: 0-25 RH: 0-14 Tight: 0-25 Gall: 0 6
Aids: Bl: 0-3 Vi: 0-0 Tstrap: 0-0
Best Rating: 33 6/01 Hayd 7f30y good

Fourloch (IRE)

95 **41**

3-y-o b f Fourstars Allstar (USA)-Loch Wee (IRE) (Colmore Row)

N G Richards Mrs Linda Bott

Placings:40540 **(5657)**

2001: 10^{4}GF, 7^{0}GF, 7^{5}GF, 10^{4}GF, 8^{0}G

	Starts	1st	2nd	3rd	Win & Pl
Career Total (Turf)	5	0	0	0	306

Going (Turf): Sf: 0-0 GS: 0-0 Gd: 0-1 GF: 0-4 Fm: 0-0
Distance: 5f/6f: 0-0 7f-8f: 0-3 9f-13f: 0-2 14f+: 0-0
Track : LH: 0-3 RH: 0-2 Tight: 0-1 Gall: 0-1
Aids: Bl: 0-0 Vi: 0-0 Tstrap: 0-0
Best Rating: 41 7/01 Newc 1m2f32y gd-fm

Foursome

91 **84**

2-y-o b f Makbul-Ra Ra (Lord Gayle (USA))

H Candy The Foursome Partnership

Placings:3510 **(5364)**

2001: 5^{3}GF, 6^{5}GF, 6^{1}HY, 6^{0}GS

	Starts	1st	2nd	3rd	Win & Pl
Career Total (Turf)	4	1	0	1	4260

84	10/01	Nott	6f15y	D	HVY	£3916

Total win prize-money £3916

Going (Turf): Sf: 1-1 GS: 0-1 Gd: 0-0 GF: 0-2 Fm: 0-0
Distance: 5f/6f: 0-2 **7f-8f: 1-2** 9f-13f: 0-0 14f+: 0-0
Track : LH: 0-0 RH: 0-0 Tight: 0-0 Gall: 0-0
Aids: Bl: 0-0 Vi: 0-0 Tstrap: 0-0
Best Rating: 84 10/01 Nott 6f15y heavy

Landed an ordinary maiden in heavy ground at Nottingham.

Fourth Dimension (IRE)

84 **60**

2-y-o b c Entrepreneur-Isle Of Spice (USA) (Diesis)

A C Stewart Ms E A Whelton

Placings:400 **(5295)**

2001: 8^{4}G, 8^{0}GF, 8^{0}S

	Starts	1st	2nd	3rd	Win & Pl
Career Total (Turf)	3	0	0	0	333

Going (Turf): Sf: 0-1 GS: 0-0 Gd: 0-1 GF: 0-1 Fm: 0-0
Distance: 5f/6f: 0-0 7f-8f: 0-2 9f-13f: 0-1 14f+: 0-0
Track : LH: 0-0 RH: 0-2 Tight: 0-0 Gall: 0-0
Aids: Bl: 0-0 Vi: 0-0 Tstrap: 0-0
Best Rating: 60 9/01 Kemp 1m good

Fourth Time Lucky

94(83) (24)**10**

5-y-o b g Timeless Times (USA)-Wych Willow (Hard Fought)

B W Murray B Murray

Placings:40000000/55200W060/0060-00000000 **(2398)**

2001: 8^{0}SW, 6^{0}SD, 5^{0}S, 6^{0}HY, 8^{0}GF, 7^{0}F, 8^{0}GF, 7^{0}GF

	Starts	1st	2nd	3rd	Win & Pl
Career Total (Turf)	18	0	0	0	222
Career Total (AW)	11	0	1	0	526

Going (Turf): Sf: 0-3 GS: 0-2 Gd: 0-2 GF: 0-7 Fm: 0-4
Distance: 5f/6f: 0-9 7f-8f: 0-17 9f-13f: 0-3 14f+: 0-0
Track : LH: 0-15 RH: 0-5 Tight: 0-7 Gall: 0-0
Aids: Bl: 0-1 Vi: 0-0 Tstrap: 0-0
Best Rating: 55 4/01 Nott 5f13y soft

Fox Cottage (IRE)

41

3-y-o ch f So Factual (USA)-Ever So Artful (Never So Bold)

D W P Arbuthnot Miss Samantha Dare

Placings:000-00 **(4376)**

2001: 7^{0}F, 7^{0}GF

	Starts	1st	2nd	3rd	Win & Pl
Career Total (Turf)	5	0	0	0	

Going (Turf): Sf: 0-0 GS: 0-1 Gd: 0-1 GF: 0-2 Fm: 0-1
Distance: 5f/6f: 0-3 7f-8f: 0-2 9f-13f: 0-0 14f+: 0-0
Track : LH: 0-1 RH: 0-1 Tight: 0-0 Gall: 0-1
Aids: Bl: 0-0 Vi: 0-0 Tstrap: 0-0
Best Rating: 55 4/01 Nott 5f13y soft

Foxcote

95 **80**

2-y-o ch c Lycius (USA)-Birdlip (USA) (Sanglamore (USA))

B W Hills K Abdulla

Placings:13330 **(4725)**

2001: 6^{1}GF, 6^{3}GF, 5^{3}G, 7^{3}GS, 7^{0}GF

	Starts	1st	2nd	3rd	Win & Pl
Career Total (Turf)	5	1	0	3	5773

76	7/01	Wind	6f	D	G-F	£3640

Total win prize-money £3640

Going (Turf): Sf: 0-0 GS: 0-1 Gd: 0-1 **GF: 1-3** Fm: 0-0

Distance: **5f/6f: 1-3** 7f-8f: 0-2 9f-13f: 0-0 14f+: 0-0
Track : LH: 0-2 RH: 0-0 Tight: 0-1 Gall: 0-0
Aids: Bl: 0-0 Vi: 0-0 Tstrap: 0-0
Best Rating: 89 7/01 NmkJ 6f gd-fm

Well bred January foal, who made good debut winning a six-furlong maiden at Windsor in July, but was unable to add to that.

Foxes Lair (IRE)

97(90) (48)55d
3-y-o b g Muhtarram (USA)-Forest Lair (Habitat)
M Dods D C Batey

Placings:54-40050000 (5190)
2001: 7^{4}SD, 8^{0}S, 8^{0}F, 10^{5}GF, 7^{0}GS, 6^{0}G, 10^{0}GF, 11^{0}GS

	Starts	1st	2nd	3rd	Win & Pl
Career Total (Turf)	9	0	0	0	0
Career Total (AW)	1	0	0	0	0

Going (Turf): Sf: 0-3 GS: 0-2 Gd: 0-1 GF: 0-2 Fm: 0-1
Distance: 5f/6f: 0-1 7f-8f: 0-6 9f-13f: 0-3 14f+: 0-0
Track : LH: 0-8 RH: 0-1 Tight: 0-4 Gall: 0-3
Aids: Bl: 0-0 Vi: 0-0 Tstrap: 0-4
Best Rating: 59 5/01 Newc 1m firm

Foxy Princess (IRE)

84(60) (6)56
2-y-o b f College Chapel-Love Dove (IRE) (Last Tycoon)
R Hannon Nicholas R Hodges

Placings:0400 (5345)
2001: 5^{0}GF, 6^{4}GF, 6^{0}G, 6^{0}SD

	Starts	1st	2nd	3rd	Win & Pl
Career Total (Turf)	3	0	0	0	338
Career Total (AW)	1	0	0	0	

Going (Turf): Sf: 0-0 GS: 0-0 Gd: 0-1 GF: 0-2 Fm: 0-0
Distance: 5f/6f: 0-4 7f-8f: 0-0 9f-13f: 0-0 14f+: 0-0
Track : LH: 0-1 RH: 0-0 Tight: 0-0 Gall: 0-0
Aids: Bl: 0-0 Vi: 0-0 Tstrap: 0-0
Best Rating: 56 6/01 Gdwd 6f gd-fm

Foxy Rockette

36
2-y-o ch f Rock City-Absolutley Foxed (Absalom)
C N Kellett Annwell Inn Syndicate

Placings:0 (3854)
2001: 7^{0}GS

	Starts	1st	2nd	3rd	Win & Pl
Career Total (Turf)	1	0	0	0	

Going (Turf): Sf: 0-0 GS: 0-1 Gd: 0-0 GF: 0-0 Fm: 0-0
Distance: 5f/6f: 0-0 7f-8f: 0-1 9f-13f: 0-0 14f+: 0-0
Track : LH: 0-0 RH: 0-0 Tight: 0-0 Gall: 0-0
Aids: Bl: 0-0 Vi: 0-0 Tstrap: 0-0

Foys (FR)

94 80+
2-y-o b c Danehill Dancer (IRE)-Ack's Secret (USA) (Ack Ack (USA))
R Charlton Mrs M E Slade

Placings:2 (3387)
2001: 5^{2}F

	Starts	1st	2nd	3rd	Win & Pl
Career Total (Turf)	1	0	1	0	810

Going (Turf): Sf: 0-0 GS: 0-0 Gd: 0-0 GF: 0-0 Fm: 0-1
Distance: 5f/6f: 0-1 7f-8f: 0-0 9f-13f: 0-0 14f+: 0-0
Track : LH: 0-1 RH: 0-0 Tight: 0-0 Gall: 0-1
Aids: Bl: 0-0 Vi: 0-0 Tstrap: 0-0

Best Rating: 80 7/01 Bath 5f161y firm

Fraamtastic

96(60) 27
4-y-o b f Fraam-Fading (Pharly (FR))
B A Pearce Richard J Gray

Placings:0030000 (5470)
2001: 13^{0}SW, 10^{0}G, 6^{3}F, 6^{0}GF, 7^{0}GF, 5^{0}S, 7^{0}S

	Starts	1st	2nd	3rd	Win & Pl
Career Total (Turf)	6	0	0	1	565
Career Total (AW)	1	0	0	0	

Going (Turf): Sf: 0-2 GS: 0-0 Gd: 0-1 GF: 0-2 Fm: 0-1
Distance: 5f/6f: 0-3 7f-8f: 0-2 9f-13f: 0-2 14f+: 0-0
Track : LH: 0-4 RH: 0-0 Tight: 0-2 Gall: 0-0
Aids: Bl: 0-0 Vi: 0-1 Tstrap: 0-0
Best Rating: 44 6/01 Ling 6f firm

Fragaria Girl

65 13
2-y-o b f Fraam-Chaconia Girl (Bay Express)
M A Allen John T Robson

Placings:000 (5590)
2001: 6^{0}GF, 7^{0}GF, 9^{0}GS

	Starts	1st	2nd	3rd	Win & Pl
Career Total (Turf)	3	0	0	0	

Going (Turf): Sf: 0-0 GS: 0-1 Gd: 0-0 GF: 0-2 Fm: 0-0
Distance: 5f/6f: 0-1 7f-8f: 0-1 9f-13f: 0-1 14f+: 0-0
Track : LH: 0-2 RH: 0-0 Tight: 0-0 Gall: 0-0
Aids: Bl: 0-0 Vi: 0-0 Tstrap: 0-0
Best Rating: 13 7/01 Wwck 7f26y gd-fm

Fragrant Cloud

82 29
3-y-o b f Zilzal (USA)-Stardyn (Star Appeal)
E A Wheeler M F Kentish

Placings:006 (3983)
2001: 8^{0}GF, 7^{0}S, 6^{6}F

	Starts	1st	2nd	3rd	Win & Pl
Career Total (Turf)	3	0	0	0	0

Going (Turf): Sf: 0-1 GS: 0-0 Gd: 0-0 GF: 0-1 Fm: 0-1
Distance: 5f/6f: 0-0 7f-8f: 0-3 9f-13f: 0-0 14f+: 0-0
Track : LH: 0-0 RH: 0-1 Tight: 0-0 Gall: 0-0
Aids: Bl: 0-0 Vi: 0-0 Tstrap: 0-0
Best Rating: 29 8/01 Sals 6f212y firm

Fragrant Storm (USA)

91 76
2-y-o b f Storm Bird (CAN)-Subtle Fragrance (USA) (Crafty Prospector (USA))
M Johnston J D Cotterill

Placings:421300 (4098)
2001: 5^{4}S, 5^{2}GF, 5^{1}F, 5^{3}G, 5^{0}G, 6^{0}G

	Starts	1st	2nd	3rd	Win & Pl
Career Total (Turf)	6	1	1	1	6276

60 6/01 Nott 5f13y D FRM £3640
Total win prize-money £3640

Going (Turf): Sf: 0-1 GS: 0-0 Gd: 0-3 GF: 0-1 **Fm: 1-1**
Distance: **5f/6f: 1-5** 7f-8f: 0-1 9f-13f: 0-0 14f+: 0-0
Track : LH: 0-0 RH: 0-0 Tight: 0-0 Gall: 0-0
Aids: Bl: 0-0 Vi: 0-0 Tstrap: 0-0
Best Rating: 76 7/01 York 5f good

Not very big, made all to win a Nottingham maiden and was not beaten far in a York nursery next time.

Fragrant View (USA)

96 86
2-y-o ch f Distant View (USA)-Musicanti (USA) (Nijinsky (CAN))
B W Hills K Abdulla

Placings:2 (5277)
2001: 7^{2}GS

	Starts	1st	2nd	3rd	Win & Pl
Career Total (Turf)	1	0	1	0	1252

Going (Turf): Sf: 0-0 GS: 0-1 Gd: 0-0 GF: 0-0 Fm: 0-0
Distance: 5f/6f: 0-0 7f-8f: 0-1 9f-13f: 0-0 14f+: 0-0
Track : LH: 0-0 RH: 0-0 Tight: 0-0 Gall: 0-0
Aids: Bl: 0-0 Vi: 0-0 Tstrap: 0-0
Best Rating: 86 10/01 Leic 7f9y gd-sft

She showed a lot of promise on her Leicester debut and looks a ready-made winner.

Frampant

89(99) (14)37
4-y-o ch f Fraam-Potent (IRE) (Posen (USA))
M Quinn The Frampant Fellows

Placings:0001404402/43000443060010300-000000 (3237)
2001: 6^{0}SD, 5^{0}S, 5^{0}HY, 5^{0}GS, 5^{0}G, 6^{0}SD

	Starts	1st	2nd	3rd	Win & Pl
Career Total (Turf)	25	2	1	1	9720
Career Total (AW)	8	0	0	2	1387

50 10/00 Newb 5f34y F(0-65)H SFT £3458
69 8/99 Wind 5f10y E SFT £3501
Total win prize-money £6959

Going (Turf): **Sf: 2-11** GS: 0-3 Gd: 0-2 GF: 0-8 Fm: 0-1
Distance: **5f/6f: 2-21** 7f-8f: 0-12 9f-13f: 0-0 14f+: 0-0
Track : LH: 0-14 **RH: 1-5** Tight: 0-6 **Gall: 1-7**
Aids: Bl: 0-0 Vi: 0-1 Tstrap: 0-0
Best Rating: 37 4/01 Nott 5f13y soft

Francis Flute

91 35
3-y-o b g Polar Falcon (USA)-Darshay (FR) (Darshaan)
B Mactaggart J Stephenson

Placings:46 (1762)
2001: 11^{4}G, 10^{6}GF

	Starts	1st	2nd	3rd	Win & Pl
Career Total (Turf)	2	0	0	0	276

Going (Turf): Sf: 0-0 GS: 0-0 Gd: 0-1 GF: 0-1 Fm: 0-0
Distance: 5f/6f: 0-0 7f-8f: 0-0 9f-13f: 0-2 14f+: 0-0
Track : LH: 0-1 RH: 0-1 Tight: 0-1 Gall: 0-0
Aids: Bl: 0-0 Vi: 0-0 Tstrap: 0-0
Best Rating: 35 6/01 Ayr 1m2f gd-fm

Francken (ITY)

73 34
2-y-o ro g Petit Loup (USA)-Filicaia (Sallust)
N Tinkler Razza Dormello Olgiata

Placings:00 (4838)
2001: 6^{0}F, 6^{0}G

	Starts	1st	2nd	3rd	Win & Pl
Career Total (Turf)	2	0	0	0	

Going (Turf): Sf: 0-0 GS: 0-0 Gd: 0-1 GF: 0-0 Fm: 0-1
Distance: 5f/6f: 0-1 7f-8f: 0-1 9f-13f: 0-0 14f+: 0-0
Track : LH: 0-0 RH: 0-0 Tight: 0-0 Gall: 0-0
Aids: Bl: 0-0 Vi: 0-0 Tstrap: 0-0
Best Rating: 34 9/01 Nott 6f15y good

Francport

103(93) (58)**76**

5-y-o b g Efisio-Elkie Brooks (Relkino)

K A Ryan Mr & Mrs Julian And Rosie Richer

Placings:510200/51000306000-31200063004**0** **(5612)**

2001: 6^{3}HY, 5^{1}S, 6^{2}G, 5^{0}GF, 6^{0}GF, 5^{0}GF, 6^{6}G, 5^{3}G, 6^{0}G, 5^{0}HY, 5^{4}S, 6^{0}SD

	Starts	1st	2nd	3rd	Win & Pl
Career Total (Turf)	28	3	2	3	22093
Career Total (AW)	1	0	0	0	

72	4/01	Ripn	5f	E(0-70)H	SFT	£3528
78	4/00	Ripn	6f	C(0-95)H	SFT	£6818
70	5/99	Bevl	5f	D	GD	£3991

Total win prize-money £14339

Going (Turf): Sf: 2-8 GS: 0-2 **Gd: 1-11** GF: 0-4 Fm: 0-3
Distance: **5f/6f: 3-26** 7f-8f: 0-3 9f-13f: 0-0 14f+: 0-0
Track : LH: 0-3 RH: 0-0 Tight: 0-1 Gall: 0-1
Aids: Bl: 0-0 Vi: 0-0 Tstrap: 0-0
Best Rating: 76 5/01 Haml 6f5y good

Effective over five furlongs with cut in the ground, but he is better over six and ran very well at Ayr on consecutive days at the Great Western meeting. Goes well at Ripon.

Frandaneil

89(73) (32)**53**

2-y-o b f Emarati (USA)-Luminary (Kalaglow)

J J Quinn Derrick Bloy

Placings:4004400 **(5370)**

2001: 5^{4}S, 5^{0}GF, 6^{0}G, 7^{4}G, 6^{4}S, 7^{0}SD, 7^{0}G

	Starts	1st	2nd	3rd	Win & Pl
Career Total (Turf)	6	0	0	0	0
Career Total (AW)	1	0	0	0	

Going (Turf): Sf: 0-2 GS: 0-0 Gd: 0-3 GF: 0-1 Fm: 0-0
Distance: 5f/6f: 0-3 7f-8f: 0-4 9f-13f: 0-0 14f+: 0-0
Track : LH: 0-2 RH: 0-0 Tight: 0-1 Gall: 0-0
Aids: Bl: 0-0 Vi: 0-0 Tstrap: 0-0
Best Rating: 53 9/01 Yarm 6f3y soft

Frank Mor (IRE)

93(90) (54)**76**

2-y-o ch g Common Grounds-Drowsy Maggie (Tumble Wind (USA))

K A Ryan Hokey Cokey Partnership

Placings:30402620 **(5379)**

2001: 5^{3}SD, 5^{0}SD, 6^{4}GF, 6^{0}Y, 6^{2}G, 6^{6}GF, 7^{2}GS, 7^{0}S

	Starts	1st	2nd	3rd	Win & Pl
Career Total (Turf)	6	0	2	0	1980
Career Total (AW)	2	0	0	1	250

Going (Turf): Sf: 0-1 GS: 0-1 Gd: 0-1 GF: 0-2 Fm: 0-0
Distance: 5f/6f: 0-4 7f-8f: 0-4 9f-13f: 0-0 14f+: 0-0
Track : LH: 0-1 RH: 0-0 Tight: 0-1 Gall: 0-0
Aids: Bl: 0-0 Vi: 0-0 Tstrap: 0-0
Best Rating: 76 10/01 Newc 7f gd-sft

Frank Murphy

79(76) **50**

2-y-o ch g Dr Devious (IRE)-Bacinella (USA) (El Gran Senor (USA))

M W Easterby The Shooting Syndicate

Placings:00030 **(4772)**

2001: 5^{0}S, 5^{0}SD, 6^{0}G, 7^{3}GF, 7^{0}G

	Starts	1st	2nd	3rd	Win & Pl
Career Total (Turf)	4	0	0	1	346
Career Total (AW)	1	0	0	0	

Going (Turf): Sf: 0-1 GS: 0-0 Gd: 0-2 GF: 0-1 Fm: 0-0
Distance: 5f/6f: 0-3 7f-8f: 0-2 9f-13f: 0-0 14f+: 0-0
Track : LH: 0-0 RH: 0-2 Tight: 0-0 Gall: 0-0
Aids: Bl: 0-0 Vi: 0-0 Tstrap: 0-0
Best Rating: 50 7/01 Bevl 7f100y gd-fm

Frankies Dream (IRE)

95 **95**

2-y-o b c Grand Lodge (USA)-Galyph (USA) (Lyphard (USA))

T G Mills J J Devaney

Placings:43 **(4873)**

2001: 7^{4}GF, 7^{3}G

	Starts	1st	2nd	3rd	Win & Pl
Career Total (Turf)	2	0	0	1	1217

Going (Turf): Sf: 0-0 GS: 0-0 Gd: 0-1 GF: 0-1 Fm: 0-0
Distance: 5f/6f: 0-0 7f-8f: 0-2 9f-13f: 0-0 14f+: 0-0
Track : LH: 0-0 RH: 0-0 Tight: 0-0 Gall: 0-0
Aids: Bl: 0-0 Vi: 0-0 Tstrap: 0-0
Best Rating: 95 9/01 NmkR 7f good

Franklin Lakes

76(95) (32)**31**

6-y-o ch g Sanglamore (USA)-Eclipsing (IRE) (Baillamont (USA))

M R Bosley M R Bosley

Placings:04/500040/00550600505**00**/**3053**600200-00 **(4303)**

2001: 5^{0}G, 7^{0}GF

	Starts	1st	2nd	3rd	Win & Pl
Career Total (Turf)	25	0	1	0	1064
Career Total (AW)	8	0	0	2	507

Going (Turf): Sf: 0-0 GS: 0-3 Gd: 0-7 GF: 0-13 Fm: 0-2
Distance: 5f/6f: 0-4 7f-8f: 0-20 9f-13f: 0-7 14f+: 0-2
Track : LH: 0-14 RH: 0-4 Tight: 0-8 Gall: 0-0
Aids: Bl: 0-18 Vi: 0-5 Tstrap: 0-4
Best Rating: 18 8/01 Folk 7f gd-fm

Franklin-D

92(101) (43)**26**

5-y-o ch g Democratic (USA)-English Mint (Jalmood (USA))

J R Jenkins Mrs Stella Peirce

Placings:500/000**3/2340500-5000**50 **(4097)**

2001: 7^{5}SW, 8^{0}SD, 7^{0}GF, 7^{0}SD, 6^{5}G, 7^{0}G

	Starts	1st	2nd	3rd	Win & Pl
Career Total (Turf)	10	0	0	0	0
Career Total (AW)	10	0	1	2	1327

Going (Turf): Sf: 0-0 GS: 0-1 Gd: 0-5 GF: 0-3 Fm: 0-1
Distance: 5f/6f: 0-6 7f-8f: 0-13 9f-13f: 0-1 14f+: 0-0
Track : LH: 0-13 RH: 0-2 Tight: 0-7 Gall: 0-2
Aids: Bl: 0-0 Vi: 0-2 Tstrap: 0-0
Best Rating: 27 6/01 Sthl 7f stand

Frankskips

97 **90**

2-y-o b g Bishop Of Cashel-Kevins Lady (Alzao (USA))

B R Johnson Peter Crate

Placings:4 **(5361)**

2001: 8^{4}GS

	Starts	1st	2nd	3rd	Win & Pl
Career Total (Turf)	1	0	0	0	436

Going (Turf): Sf: 0-0 GS: 0-1 Gd: 0-0 GF: 0-0 Fm: 0-0
Distance: 5f/6f: 0-0 7f-8f: 0-1 9f-13f: 0-0 14f+: 0-0
Track : LH: 0-0 RH: 0-0 Tight: 0-0 Gall: 0-0
Aids: Bl: 0-0 Vi: 0-0 Tstrap: 0-0
Best Rating: 90 10/01 NmkR 1m gd-sft

A big, strong sort from a small stable. He was making good late headway on his Newmarket debut and looks to have potential.

Fraternity

94(105) (63)**72**

4-y-o b g Grand Lodge (USA)-Catawba (Mill Reef (USA))

W Jarvis Exors Of The Late Lord Howard De Walden

Placings:02/4003-1 **(0020)**

2001: 12^{1}SD

	Starts	1st	2nd	3rd	Win & Pl
Career Total (Turf)	4	0	1	0	1273
Career Total (AW)	3	1	0	1	3341

63	1/01	Ling	1m4f	D	STD	£2905

Total win prize-money £2905

Going (Turf): Sf: 0-1 GS: 0-2 Gd: 0-0 GF: 0-1 Fm: 0-0
Distance: 5f/6f: 0-0 7f-8f: 0-1 **9f-13f: 1-6** 14f+: 0-0
Track : **LH: 1-4** RH: 0-0 **Tight: 1-4** Gall: 0-1
Aids: Bl: 0-0 Vi: 0-0 Tstrap: 0-0
Best Rating: 63 1/01 Ling 1m4f stand

Fraternize

98 **73**

3-y-o ch c Spectrum (IRE)-Proud Titania (IRE) (Fairy King (USA))

Sir Michael Stoute Lord Hartington

Placings:2225 **(4306)**

2001: 8^{2}GF, 10^{2}S, 9^{2}G, 9^{5}GF

	Starts	1st	2nd	3rd	Win & Pl
Career Total (Turf)	4	0	3	0	3253

Going (Turf): Sf: 0-1 GS: 0-0 Gd: 0-1 GF: 0-2 Fm: 0-0
Distance: 5f/6f: 0-0 7f-8f: 0-0 9f-13f: 0-4 14f+: 0-0
Track : LH: 0-3 RH: 0-1 Tight: 0-1 Gall: 0-1
Aids: Bl: 0-0 Vi: 0-0 Tstrap: 0-0
Best Rating: 73 8/01 Newc 1m1f9y good

Unraced at two, he wears a net muzzle and managed to finish runner-up in his first three starts, including when sent off at odds of 1/6 for a three-runner race at Newcastle.

Fraulein

104 **98**

2-y-o b f Acatenango (GER)-Francfurter (Legend Of France (USA))

E A L Dunlop Cliveden Stud

Placings:5115 (5003)
2001: 7^5G, 8^1S, 7^1GF, 8^5S

	Starts	1st	2nd	3rd	Win & Pl
Career Total (Turf)	4	2	0	0	18542

98 9/01 Newb 7f B G-F £9674
85 9/01 Yarm 1m3y D SFT £3867
Total win prize-money £13542

Going (Turf): Sf: 1-2 GS: 0-0 Gd: 0-1 GF: 1-1 Fm: 0-0
Distance: 5f/6f: 0-0 7f-8f: 1-3 9f-13f: 1-1 14f+: 0-0
Track : LH: 0-0 RH: 0-2 Tight: 0-0 Gall: 0-1
Aids: Bl: 0-0 Vi: 0-0 Tstrap: 0-0
Best Rating: 98 9/01 Asct 1m soft

She got off the mark over a mile on soft ground at Yarmouth on her second start and just managed to follow up over a furlong shorter and on much faster ground at Newbury.

Frazer's Lad

102(99) (52)44
4-y-o b g Whittingham (IRE)-Loch Tain (Lochnager)
A Bailey Gerald S Williams

Placings:5360-065024030 (4108)
2001: 9^0G, 8^6G, 8^5G, 8^0GF, 9^2GS, 10^4GS, 8^0S, 12^3SD, 8^0S

	Starts	1st	2nd	3rd	Win & Pl
Career Total (Turf)	9	0	1	0	780
Career Total (AW)	4	0	0	2	706

Going (Turf): Sf: 0-3 GS: 0-2 Gd: 0-3 GF: 0-1 Fm: 0-0
Distance: 5f/6f: 0-0 7f-8f: 0-3 9f-13f: 0-10 14f+: 0-0
Track : LH: 0-6 RH: 0-4 Tight: 0-6 Gall: 0-0
Aids: Bl: 0-1 Vi: 0-0 Tstrap: 0-0
Best Rating: 48 8/01 Wolv 1m4f stand

Frazzled

89 68
2-y-o b g Greensmith-Time For Tea (IRE) (Imperial Frontier (USA))
C A Cyzer Mrs E A Cyzer

Placings:043 (5126)
2001: 5^0GF, 6^4GF, 6^3HY

	Starts	1st	2nd	3rd	Win & Pl
Career Total (Turf)	3	0	0	1	763

Going (Turf): Sf: 0-1 GS: 0-0 Gd: 0-0 GF: 0-2 Fm: 0-0
Distance: 5f/6f: 0-3 7f-8f: 0-0 9f-13f: 0-0 14f+: 0-0
Track : LH: 0-1 RH: 0-0 Tight: 0-0 Gall: 0-0
Aids: Bl: 0-0 Vi: 0-0 Tstrap: 0-0
Best Rating: 68 10/01 Ling 6f heavy

Fred's Dream

91 64
2-y-o ch f Cadeaux Genereux-Vaguar (USA) (Vaguely Noble)
R Guest C J Murfitt

Placings:04 (5635)
2001: 6^0GS, 7^4G

	Starts	1st	2nd	3rd	Win & Pl
Career Total (Turf)	2	0	0	0	0

Going (Turf): Sf: 0-0 GS: 0-1 Gd: 0-1 GF: 0-0 Fm: 0-0
Distance: 5f/6f: 0-1 7f-8f: 0-1 9f-13f: 0-0 14f+: 0-0
Track : LH: 0-1 RH: 0-0 Tight: 0-1 Gall: 0-0
Aids: Bl: 0-0 Vi: 0-0 Tstrap: 0-0
Best Rating: 64 10/01 NmkR 6f gd-sft

Freddie Mercury (IRE)

91 65
2-y-o ch g Eagle Eyed (USA)-So Far Away (Robellino (USA))
D W P Arbuthnot M J Peters

Placings:55205 (5078)
2001: 5^5G, 5^5F, 5^2GF, 5^0F, 5^5S

	Starts	1st	2nd	3rd	Win & Pl
Career Total (Turf)	5	0	1	0	656

Going (Turf): Sf: 0-1 GS: 0-0 Gd: 0-1 GF: 0-1 Fm: 0-2
Distance: 5f/6f: 0-5 7f-8f: 0-0 9f-13f: 0-0 14f+: 0-0
Track : LH: 0-3 RH: 0-0 Tight: 0-0 Gall: 0-2
Aids: Bl: 0-0 Vi: 0-0 Tstrap: 0-0
Best Rating: 71 7/01 Chep 5f16y good

Freddy Flintstone

102 51
4-y-o b g Bigstone (IRE)-Daring Ditty (Daring March)
O Sherwood (R Hannon 30/8) Lady Whent And Friends

Placings:05/0400234302-000000000 (4386)
2001: 8^0S, 8^0GS, 8^0GF, 7^0GF, 9^0F, 9^0GF, 10^0GF, 8^0G, 6^0GF

	Starts	1st	2nd	3rd	Win & Pl
Career Total (Turf)	21	0	2	2	6203

Going (Turf): Sf: 0-4 GS: 0-3 Gd: 0-4 GF: 0-9 Fm: 0-1
Distance: 5f/6f: 0-0 7f-8f: 0-12 9f-13f: 0-9 14f+: 0-0
Track : LH: 0-4 RH: 0-5 Tight: 0-4 Gall: 0-3
Aids: Bl: 0-0 Vi: 0-5 Tstrap: 0-0
Best Rating: 73 5/01 Gdwd 1m gd-fm

Frederick James

80(99) (54?)45
7-y-o b g Efisio-Rare Roberta (USA) (Roberto (USA))
H E Haynes Miss Sally R Haynes

Placings:0/236000/44/53334103420240300/460000034 00-04000 (1176)
2001: 6^0SD, 6^4SD, 7^0SD, 7^0SD, 7^0G

	Starts	1st	2nd	3rd	Win & Pl
Career Total (Turf)	24	1	3	3	11431
Career Total (AW)	18	0	0	4	1772

65 3/99 Nott 6f15y E(0-70)H G-S £3272
Total win prize-money £3273

Going (Turf): Sf: 0-3 GS: 1-3 Gd: 0-12 GF: 0-5 Fm: 0-1
Distance: 5f/6f: 0-23 7f-8f: 1-18 9f-13f: 0-1 14f+: 0-0
Track : LH: 0-25 RH: 0-1 Tight: 0-17 Gall: 0-2
Aids: Bl: 0-3 Vi: 0-0 Tstrap: 0-0
Best Rating: 54 1/01 Ling 6f stand

Frederick Luigi

90 88
2-y-o b g Bal Harbour-Scented Message (Ivotino (USA))

H Candy The Shotts Farm Partnership

Placings:303 (5460)
2001: 8^3GF, 8^0G, 8^3G

	Starts	1st	2nd	3rd	Win & Pl
Career Total (Turf)	3	0	0	2	961

Going (Turf): Sf: 0-0 GS: 0-0 Gd: 0-2 GF: 0-1 Fm: 0-0
Distance: 5f/6f: 0-0 7f-8f: 0-0 9f-13f: 0-3 14f+: 0-0
Track : LH: 0-2 RH: 0-0 Tight: 0-1 Gall: 0-0
Aids: Bl: 0-0 Vi: 0-0 Tstrap: 0-0
Best Rating: 88 10/01 Bath 1m5y good

Encouraging form in three outings to date over a mile. Acts on good to firm and good to soft.

Free

91(98) (59)60
6-y-o ch g Gone West (USA)-Bemissed (USA) (Nijinsky (CAN))
Mrs M Reveley P D Savill

Placings:000/56400/635231223/0010-250 (2815)
2001: 16^2SD, 16^5GF, 16^0GF

	Starts	1st	2nd	3rd	Win & Pl
Career Total (Turf)	22	2	3	3	10575
Career Total (AW)	2	0	1	0	516

54 8/00 Newc 1m6f97y F(0-65)H GD £2730
54 8/99 Newc 2m19y E(0-70)H FRM £2815
Total win prize-money £5545

Going (Turf): Sf: 0-1 GS: 0-3 Gd: 1-3 GF: 0-12 Fm: 1-3
Distance: 5f/6f: 0-0 7f-8f: 0-2 9f-13f: 0-5 14f+: 2-17
Track : LH: 2-12 RH: 0-11 Tight: 0-14 Gall: 2-5
Aids: Bl: 0-0 Vi: 0-0 Tstrap: 0-0
Best Rating: 60 6/01 Muss 2m gd-fm

Free Kevin

94 25
5-y-o b g Midyan (USA)-Island Desert (IRE) (Green Desert (USA))
Dr J R J Naylor Miss J A Challen

Placings:3000-00060600 (5100)
2001: 7^0GF, 10^0GF, 10^0GF, 10^6S, 12^0G, 10^6GF, 11^0GF, 9^0GS

	Starts	1st	2nd	3rd	Win & Pl
Career Total (Turf)	12	0	0	1	580

Going (Turf): Sf: 0-2 GS: 0-2 Gd: 0-3 GF: 0-5 Fm: 0-0
Distance: 5f/6f: 0-0 7f-8f: 0-1 9f-13f: 0-11 14f+: 0-0
Track : LH: 0-7 RH: 0-3 Tight: 0-6 Gall: 0-2
Aids: Bl: 0-3 Vi: 0-0 Tstrap: 0-0
Best Rating: 25 8/01 Wwck 1m2f188y gd-fm

Free Option (IRE)

96 (57)95
6-y-o ch g Indian Ridge-Saneena (Kris)
B Hanbury Mrs G E M Brown

Placings:02023/4340123512/05100010610/303103600-00 (3241)
2001: 7^0G, 8^0GF

	Starts	1st	2nd	3rd	Win & Pl
Career Total (Turf)	36	6	4	5	76177
Career Total (AW)	1	0	0	1	535

95	7/00	Kemp	1m	C(0-95)H	G-F	£9382
93	10/99	NmkJ	1m	B(0-105)H	GD	£19250
85	7/99	Ches	7f2y	B	G F	£9519
92	5/99	Kemp	1m	B(0-100)H	G-F	£8805
94	9/98	Newb	7f64y	C(0-95)H	GD	£7652
72	7/98	Ling	7f140y	D	G-F	£3687

Total win prize-money £58297

Going (Turf): Sf: 0-2 GS: 0-1 Gd: 2-15 **GF: 4-16** Fm: 0-2
Distance: 5f/6f: 0-1 **7f-8f: 6-29** 9f-13f: 0-7 14f+: 0-0
Track : LH: 2-10 RH: 2-10 Tight: 1-6 Gall: 1-4
Aids: Bl: 0-0 Vi: 0-0 Tstrap: 0-0
Best Rating: 73 7/01 Newb 1m gd-fm

Free Rider

112 **102**

4-y-o b g Inchinor-Forever Roses (Forzando)
I A Balding J C Smith

Placings:221/20030-63405354210 **(5251)**
2001: 6⁶S, 7³S, 7⁴S, 7⁰G, 10⁵GF, 8³G, 7⁵GF, 7⁴G, 7²GS, 7¹G, 7⁰S

	Starts	1st	2nd	3rd	Win & Pl
Career Total (Turf)	19	2	4	3	38632

102	10/01	NmkR	7f	B(0-100)H	GD	£9680
85	11/99	Wind	6f	D	G-S	£3160

Total win prize-money £12840

Going (Turf): Sf: 0-6 **GS: 1-3 Gd: 1-6** GF: 0-4 Fm: 0-0
Distance: 5f/6f: 1-3 7f-8f: 1-15 9f-13f: 0-1 14f+: 0-0
Track : LH: 0-3 **RH: 1-5** Tight: 0-0 **Gall: 1-4**
Aids: Bl: 0-0 Vi: 0-1 Tstrap: 0-0
Best Rating: 106 4/01 NmkR 7f soft

He had not been getting home over seven furlongs this season, so it was a surprise to see him tackle a mile and a quarter at Newbury in May. Ran well over a mile next time, having been gelded and has put in some good efforts since then dropped back to seven furlongs, winning at Newmarket in October. He usually races prominently and acts on soft ground.

Free Will

104 **69+**

4-y-o ch g Indian Ridge-Free Guest (Be My Guest (USA))
A Scott A & J Scott Ltd

Placings:5634-0323002100 **(5249)**
2001: 12⁰S, 9³GS, 10²S, 8³G, 8⁰F, 8⁰GF, 10²F, 10¹F, 10⁰G, 10⁰S

	Starts	1st	2nd	3rd	Win & Pl
Career Total (Turf)	14	1	2	3	8101

69	9/01	Pont	1m2f6y	D	FRM	£3916

Total win prize-money £3916

Going (Turf): Sf: 0-3 GS: 0-3 Gd: 0-2 GF: 0-3 **Fm: 1-3**
Distance: 5f/6f: 0-0 7f-8f: 0-1 **9f-13f: 1-13** 14f+: 0-0
Track : **LH: 1-9** RH: 0-2 Tight: 0-4 Gall: 0-4
Aids: Bl: 0-0 Vi: 0-0 Tstrap: 0-0
Best Rating: 69 9/01 Pont 1m2f6y firm

Freecom Net (IRE)

92(92) (66)**55**

3-y-o b g Zieten (USA)-Radiance (IRE) (Thatching)
A P Jarvis A L R Morton

Placings:U0-013005 **(4521)**
2001: 8⁰SW, 7¹SD, 8³SD, 7⁰GF, 7⁰GF, 7⁵GF

	Starts	1st	2nd	3rd	Win & Pl
Career Total (Turf)	5	0	0	0	0
Career Total (AW)	3	1	0	1	3455

58	3/01	Wolv	7f	D	STD	£2863

Total win prize-money £2863

Going (Turf): Sf: 0-0 GS: 0-0 Gd: 0-1 GF: 0-4 Fm: 0-0
Distance: 5f/6f: 0-0 **7f-8f: 1-8** 9f-13f: 0-0 14f+: 0-0
Track : **LH: 1-4** RH: 0-0 **Tight: 1-1** Gall: 0-1
Aids: Bl: 0-0 Vi: 0-0 Tstrap: 0-0
Best Rating: 66 4/01 Sthl 1m stand

Unproven on the turf, his best effort was winning a seven-furlong maiden on the All-Weather in the spring.

Freedom Now (IRE)

99 **84**

3-y-o b c Sadler's Wells (USA)-Free At Last (Shirley Heights)
L M Cumani Gerald W Leigh - Cancer Bacup

Placings:0-26165 **(4409)**
2001: 12²G, 12⁶GF, 10¹GF, 12⁶GS, 10⁵GS

	Starts	1st	2nd	3rd	Win & Pl
Career Total (Turf)	6	1	1	0	5326

84	7/01	Wind	1m2f7y	D	G-F	£3981

Total win prize-money £3981

Going (Turf): Sf: 0-0 GS: 0-2 Gd: 0-2 **GF: 1-2** Fm: 0-0
Distance: 5f/6f: 0-0 7f-8f: 0-1 **9f-13f: 1-5** 14f+: 0-0
Track : LH: 0-2 RH: 0-2 **Tight: 1-3** Gall: 0-2
Aids: Bl: 0-0 Vi: 0-0 Tstrap: 0-0
Best Rating: 84 7/01 Wind 1m2f7y gd-fm

He won his maiden over ten furlongs at Windsor, but his good run against subsequent French Derby seventh Sydenham as a two-year old earned him a BHB rating of 87, and he might not be easy to place off that sort of mark.

Freefourinternet (USA)

103 **103**

3-y-o b c Tabasco Cat (USA)-Dixie Chimes (USA) (Dixieland Band (USA))
B J Meehan Roldvale Limited

Placings:352-116 **(4263)**
2001: 8¹F, 10¹GF, 10⁶GF

	Starts	1st	2nd	3rd	Win & Pl
Career Total (Turf)	6	2	1	1	28714

103	6/01	Asct	1m2f	A	G-F	£21547
76	6/01	Nott	1m54y	D	FRM	£3737

Total win prize-money £25286

Going (Turf): Sf: 0-0 GS: 0-0 Gd: 0-1 **GF: 1-4 Fm: 1-1**
Distance: 5f/6f: 0-1 7f-8f: 0-2 **9f-13f: 2-3** 14f+: 0-0
Track : LH: 1-1 RH: 1-1 Tight: 0-1 **Gall: 1-1**
Aids: Bl: 0-0 Vi: 0-0 Tstrap: 0-0
Best Rating: 103 6/01 Asct 1m2f gd-fm

Had been taking on some decent sorts prior to getting off the mark when stepped up to a mile at Nottingham in June. He followed up in Listed company at Ascot and appeared to appreciate the step up to ten furlongs, but was found out when tried in Group company. Acts well on fast ground.

French Bramble (IRE)

97(91) (47)**43**

3-y-o ch f General Monash (USA)-La Mazya (IRE) (Mazaad)
J Balding Tykes And Terriers Racing Club

Placings:600064400-50060510 **(4233)**
2001: 5⁵S, 6⁰SW, 5⁰GF, 6⁶F, 6⁰F, 5⁵F, 5¹GF, 5⁰G

	Starts	1st	2nd	3rd	Win & Pl
Career Total (Turf)	12	1	0	0	4563
Career Total (AW)	5	0	0	0	0

43	8/01	Donc	5f	E(0-70)H	G-F	£4563

Total win prize-money £4563

Going (Turf): Sf: 0-1 GS: 0-0 Gd: 0-3 **GF: 1-4** Fm: 0-4
Distance: **5f/6f: 1-17** 7f-8f: 0-0 9f-13f: 0-0 14f+: 0-0
Track : LH: 0-4 RH: 0-0 Tight: 0-1 Gall: 0-0
Aids: Bl: 0-7 **Vi: 1-3** Tstrap: 0-0
Best Rating: 43 8/01 Donc 5f gd-fm

She had gone 15 races without even being placed, but then popped up at 20/1 in a handicap at Doncaster in August. Suited by the minimum trip.

French Connection

95(99) (51)**28**

6-y-o b g Tirol-Heaven-Liegh-Grey (Grey Desire)
B D Leavy S H Riley

Placings:022/1124500/000044556505/**62000**-400 **(4046)**
2001: 9⁴HY, 12⁰GF, 10⁰HY

	Starts	1st	2nd	3rd	Win & Pl
Career Total (Turf)	26	2	3	0	31143
Career Total (AW)	4	0	1	0	617

81	5/98	Hayd	1m30y	B(0-110)H	G-F	£21690
79	5/98	Haml	1m1f36y	E	SFT	£2801

Total win prize-money £24491

Going (Turf): Sf: 1-9 GS: 0-3 Gd: 0-8 **GF: 1-6** Fm: 0-0
Distance: 5f/6f: 0-0 7f-8f: 0-13 **9f-13f: 2-17** 14f+: 0-0
Track : LH: 1-19 RH: 1-8 **Tight: 1-8** Gall: 0-5
Aids: Bl: 0-8 Vi: 0-1 Tstrap: 0-0
Best Rating: 53 4/01 Nott 1m1f213y heavy

Moderate handicapper, better known as a hurdler these days. Stays 12 furlongs, acts on any ground.

French Fancy (IRE)

51(94) (31)**31**

4-y-o gr f Paris House-Clipping (Kris)
B A Pearce J Salter

Placings:0304043040504/**0453042400410005000400-550015050400** **(2448)**
2001: 8⁵SD, 9⁵SW, 8⁰SD, 6⁰SW, 8¹SW, 7⁵SW, 9⁰SD, 7⁵SD, 8⁰SW, 8⁴SD, 8⁰SD, 7⁰F

	Starts	1st	2nd	3rd	Win & Pl
Career Total (Turf)	22	0	0	2	716
Career Total (AW)	25	2	1	1	5544

40	2/01	Ling	1m	G	SLW	£1869
47	6/00	Ling	6f	F(0-60)H	STD	£2320

Total win prize-money £4190

Going (Turf): Sf: 0-5 GS: 0-3 Gd: 0-6 GF: 0-5 Fm: 0-3
Distance: 5f/6f: 1-19 7f-8f: 1-25 9f-13f: 0-3 14f+: 0-0
Track : **LH: 2-28** RH: 0-1 **Tight: 2-24** Gall: 0-0

Aids: **Bl: 1-19** Vi: 0-2 Tstrap: 0-0
Best Rating: 40 2/01 Ling 7f slow

French Guest

79 **54**

2-y-o ch c Most Welcome-Laleston (Junius (USA))

M A Jarvis Yusof Sepiuddin

Placings:00 **(5483)**

2001: 8^{0}GS, 7^{0}HY

	Starts	1st	2nd	3rd	Win & Pl
Career Total (Turf)	2	0	0	0	

Going (Turf): **Sf: 0-1 GS: 0-1 Gd: 0-0 GF: 0-0 Fm: 0-0**
Distance: 5f/6f: 0-0 7f-8f: 0-2 9f-13f: 0-0 14f+: 0-0
Track : LH: 0-0 RH: 0-0 Tight: 0-0 Gall: 0-0
Aids: Bl: 0-0 Vi: 0-0 Tstrap: 0-0
Best Rating: 54 10/01 NmkR 1m gd-sft

French Lieutenant

105 **89**

4-y-o b g Cadeaux Genereux-Madame Crecy (USA) (Al Nasr (FR))

G A Butler Mrs T Stopford-Sackville

Placings:032/620-614 **(4662)**

2001: 10^{6}G, 9^{1}GF, 10^{4}GF

	Starts	1st	2nd	3rd	Win & Pl
Career Total (Turf)	9	1	2	1	10640
46 8/01 Bevl 1m1f207yD				G-F	£4377

Total win prize-money £4378

Going (Turf): Sf: 0-1 GS: 0-0 Gd: 0-5 **GF: 1-3** Fm: 0-0
Distance: 5f/6f: 0-0 7f-8f: 0-6 **9f-13f: 1-3** 14f+: 0-0
Track : LH: 0-1 **RH: 1-2** Tight: 0-1 Gall: 0-1
Aids: Bl: 0-0 Vi: 0-0 Tstrap: 0-0
Best Rating: 75 9/01 Donc 1m2f60y gd-fm

He managed to win a very bad maiden at odds of 1/8 at Beverley in August having previously looked held in handicap company.

French Mannequin (IRE)

90 **62**

2-y-o gr f Key Of Luck (USA)-Paris Model (IRE) (Thatching)

R M Beckett The Millennium Madness Partnership

Placings:00016 **(5690)**

2001: 5^{0}G, 6^{0}G, 7^{0}G, 6^{1}HY, 7^{6}S

	Starts	1st	2nd	3rd	Win & Pl
Career Total (Turf)	5	1	0	0	3689
60 10/01 Ayr 6f D(0-85)				HVY	£3688

Total win prize-money £3689

Going (Turf): **Sf: 1-2** GS: 0-0 Gd: 0-3 GF: 0-0 Fm: 0-0
Distance: **5f/6f: 1-2** 7f-8f: 0-3 9f-13f: 0-0 14f+: 0-0
Track : LH: 0-1 RH: 0-0 Tight: 0-1 Gall: 0-0
Aids: Bl: 0-0 **Vi: 1-2** Tstrap: 0-0
Best Rating: 62 11/01 Donc 7f soft

Has plenty of speed in her pedigree. Got off the mark at Ayr over six furlongs on heavy ground after failing to make the frame in three previous starts, although he was well beaten at Doncaster in November.

French Master (IRE)

98(93) (25) **23**

4-y-o b g Petardia-Reasonably French (Reasonable (FR))

Jedd O'Keeffe (J L Eyre 25/1) Wetherby Racing Bureau 48

Placings:0463364/33310332000600-660000500 **(4450)**

2001: 11^{6}SD, 12^{6}SD, 8^{0}GF, 10^{0}GF, 12^{0}GF, 10^{0}GF, 11^{5}G, 16^{0}GS, 8^{0}GF

	Starts	1st	2nd	3rd	Win & Pl
Career Total (Turf)	24	1	1	4	4955
Career Total (AW)	6	0	0	3	888
64 3/00 Sthl 1m2f G				GD	£1968

Total win prize-money £1968

Going (Turf): Sf: 0-4 GS: 0-1 **Gd: 1-7** GF: 0-10 Fm: 0-2
Distance: 5f/6f: 0-3 7f-8f: 0-8 **9f-13f: 1-18** 14f+: 0-1
Track : LH: 0-18 RH: 0-7 Tight: 0-11 Gall: 0-4
Aids: Bl: 0-4 **Vi: 1-13** Tstrap: 0-0
Best Rating: 25 1/01 Sthl 1m3f stand

Frenchmans Bay (FR)

111 **119+**

3-y-o br c Polar Falcon (USA)-River Fantasy (USA) (Irish River (FR))

R Charlton Michael Pescod

Placings:3-23 **(1119)**

2001: 7^{2}GS, 8^{3}G

	Starts	1st	2nd	3rd	Win & Pl
Career Total (Turf)	3	0	1	2	45825

Going (Turf): **Sf: 0-1 GS: 0-1 Gd: 0-1 GF: 0-0 Fm: 0-0**
Distance: 5f/6f: 0-0 7f-8f: 0-3 9f-13f: 0-0 14f+: 0-0
Track : LH: 0-0 RH: 0-0 Tight: 0-0 Gall: 0-0
Aids: Bl: 0-0 Vi: 0-0 Tstrap: 0-0
Best Rating: 119 5/01 NmkR 1m good

Imposing colt with plenty of scope. He ran a promising race on his debut behind Clearing in a Group Three as a juvenile, and ran second in the Greenham on his reappearanceFinished a fine third in the 200 Guineas, but chipped a bone in a knee and was not seen again.

Freud (USA)

112 **110**

3-y-o b c Storm Cat (USA)-Mariah's Storm (USA) (Rahy (USA))

A P O'Brien Michael Tabor

Placings:255-210306600 **(5218a)**

2001: 6^{2}S, 8^{1}G, 8^{0}GY, 6^{3}GF, 6^{0}G, 6^{6}Y, 6^{6}GS, 6^{0}S, 7^{0}S

	Starts	1st	2nd	3rd	Win & Pl
Career Total (Turf)	12	1	2	1	33850
90 5/01 Curr 1m				GD	£10400

Total win prize-money £10400

Going (Turf): Sf: 0-4 GS: 0-2 **Gd: 1-2** GF: 0-1 Fm: 0-0
Distance: 5f/6f: 0-7 **7f-8f: 1-5** 9f-13f: 0-0 14f+: 0-0
Track : LH: 0-2 RH: 0-0 Tight: 0-0 Gall: 0-1
Aids: Bl: 1-2 Vi: 0-0 Tstrap: 1-4
Best Rating: 110 6/01 Asct 6f gd-fm

A half-brother to Giant's Causeway showed ability in good company as a juvenile. Fitted with blinkers, he won a maiden at the Curragh in May, before finishing seventh to Black Minnaloushe in the Irish 2000 Guineas. Stayed on after getting tapped for toe in the Cork and Orrery and finished in front on the wrong side in the July Cup. He would be suited to American tracks.

Freya Alex

91 **60**

2-y-o b f Makbul-Crissem (IRE) (Thatching)

R Hollinshead Mrs Christine Johnson

Placings:05 **(5635)**

2001: 5^{0}GF, 7^{5}G

	Starts	1st	2nd	3rd	Win & Pl
Career Total (Turf)	2	0	0	0	0

Going (Turf): **Sf: 0-0 GS: 0-0 Gd: 0-1 GF: 0-1 Fm: 0-0**
Distance: 5f/6f: 0-1 7f-8f: 0-1 9f-13f: 0-0 14f+: 0-0
Track : LH: 0-1 RH: 0-0 Tight: 0-1 Gall: 0-0
Aids: Bl: 0-0 Vi: 0-0 Tstrap: 0-0
Best Rating: 60 11/01 Catt 7f good

Freya's Dream (IRE)

92 **71**

2-y-o b f Danehill Dancer (IRE)-Ruwy (Soviet Star (USA))

T D Easterby Sue Tindall And Hazel Lowrey

Placings:066540 **(4856)**

2001: 5^{0}S, 6^{6}GF, 6^{6}F, 5^{5}GF, 5^{4}GS, 7^{0}GF

	Starts	1st	2nd	3rd	Win & Pl
Career Total (Turf)	6	0	0	0	285

Going (Turf): **Sf: 0-1 GS: 0-1 Gd: 0-0 GF: 0-3 Fm: 0-1**
Distance: 5f/6f: 0-5 7f-8f: 0-1 9f-13f: 0-0 14f+: 0-0
Track : LH: 0-1 RH: 0-0 Tight: 0-1 Gall: 0-0
Aids: Bl: 0-0 Vi: 0-0 Tstrap: 0-0
Best Rating: 71 6/01 Newc 6f firm

Friar Tuck

104 **78d**

6-y-o ch g Inchinor-Jay Gee Ell (Vaigly Great)

Miss L A Perratt Cree Lodge Racing Club

Placings:413340/201030/000002450000/0210301130 00-260005000020 **(5449)**

2001: 6^{2}F, 5^{6}GF, 6^{0}GF, 6^{0}F, 6^{0}G, 6^{5}GS, 6^{0}GF, 6^{0}G, 5^{0}GF, 6^{0}GF, 6^{2}HY, 6^{0}HY

	Starts	1st	2nd	3rd	Win & Pl
Career Total (Turf)	49	5	5	5	68930
76 7/00 Ayr 6f C(0-90)H				FRM	£7182
57 7/00 Carl 5f E(0-70)				FRM	£2756
100 6/98 York 6f B(0-105)H				SFT	£37450
81 7/97 Ayr 6f D				G-F	£3517

Total win prize-money £50907

Going (Turf): Sf: 1-11 GS: 0-5 Gd: 0-14 **GF: 2-14 Fm: 2-5**
Distance: **5f/6f: 5-40** 7f-8f: 0-8 9f-13f: 0-1 14f+: 0-0
Track : LH: 0-5 **RH: 1-3** Tight: 0-5 **Gall: 1-1**
Aids: Bl: 0-0 Vi: 0-0 Tstrap: 0-0
Best Rating: 82 5/01 Haml 6f5y firm

Winner three times in the summer of 2000, he has been largely below par this season. Best over six furlongs on fast ground, but has won on soft. Now down to a reasonable mark, he is the type to pop up at a big price.

Friday's Takings

80 **52**

2-y-o ch c Beveled (USA)-Pretty Pollyanna (General Assembly (USA))
B Smart Paul Darling

Placings:0 **(2483)**
2001: 5^{0}HD

	Starts	1st	2nd	3rd	Win & Pl
Career Total (Turf)	1	0	0	0	

Going (Turf): Sf: 0-0 GS: 0-0 Gd: 0-0 GF: 0-0 Fm: 0-1
Distance: 5f/6f: 0-1 7f-8f: 0-0 9f-13f: 0-0 14f+: 0-0
Track : LH: 0-1 RH: 0-0 Tight: 0-0 Gall: 0-1
Aids: Bl: 0-0 Vi: 0-0 Tstrap: 0-0
Best Rating: 52 6/01 Bath 5f161y hard

Friendly Alliance

(103) (52)**43**

5-y-o b g Shareef Dancer (USA)-Snow Huntress (Shirley Heights)
R M Flower The Secret Circle Ii

Placings:P00/0026/**0301-64** **(0181)**
2001: 13^{6}SD, 16^{4}SD

	Starts	1st	2nd	3rd	Win & Pl
Career Total (Turf)	7	0	1	0	804
Career Total (AW)	6	1	0	1	3160

52	12/00	Ling	2m	E(0-75)H	STD	£2800

Total win prize-money £2800

Going (Turf): Sf: 0-1 GS: 0-1 Gd: 0-3 GF: 0-2 Fm: 0-0
Distance: 5f/6f: 0-0 7f-8f: 0-5 9f-13f: 0-5 **14f+: 1-3**
Track : **LH: 1-9** RH: 0-1 **Tight: 1-6** Gall: 0-0
Aids: Bl: 0-0 Vi: 0-0 Tstrap: 0-0
Best Rating: 49 1/01 Ling 2m stand

Frilly Front

(108) (66)**54**

5-y-o ch m Aragon-So So (Then Again)
T D Barron M Dalby

Placings:13434030/0003004000436230**3410/P11016**00 0500**4**2**001-03046** **(0460)**
2001: 5^{0}SD, **5^{3}**SD, **5^{0}**SW, **5^{4}**SD, **5^{6}**SD

	Starts	1st	2nd	3rd	Win & Pl
Career Total (Turf)	33	1	1	7	10110
Career Total (AW)	17	5	1	1	19039

66	12/00	Wolv	5f	F	STD	£2205
77	3/00	Ling	5f	D(0-80)H	STD	£3768
66	2/00	Ling	5f	C(0-90)H	STD	£6922
60	1/00	Ling	5f	E(0-75)H	STD	£2769
55	11/99	Wolv	5f	F(0-60)H	STD	£2316
84	6/98	Muss	5f	F	SFT	£2770

Total win prize-money £20751

Going (Turf): Sf: 1-9 GS: 0-6 Gd: 0-8 GF: 0-8 Fm: 0-2
Distance: **5f/6f: 6-49** 7f-8f: 0-1 9f-13f: 0-0 14f+: 0-0
Track : **LH: 5-20** RH: 0-1 **Tight: 5-17** Gall: 0-1
Aids: Bl: 0-1 Vi: 0-0 Tstrap: 0-0
Best Rating: 66 2/01 Wolv 5f stand

Frink (USA)

77 **45**

2-y-o ch f Royal Academy (USA)-Crafty Buzz (USA) (Crafty Prospector (USA))
M L W Bell Lord Hartington

Placings:0 **(5361)**
2001: 8^{0}GS

	Starts	1st	2nd	3rd	Win & Pl
Career Total (Turf)	1	0	0	0	

Going (Turf): Sf: 0-0 GS: 0-1 Gd: 0-0 GF: 0-0 Fm: 0-0
Distance: 5f/6f: 0-0 7f-8f: 0-1 9f-13f: 0-0 14f+: 0-0
Track : LH: 0-0 RH: 0-0 Tight: 0-0 Gall: 0-0
Aids: Bl: 0-0 Vi: 0-0 Tstrap: 0-0
Best Rating: 45 10/01 NmkR 1m gd-sft

Frisco Bay

85 **40**

3-y-o b g Efisio-Kabayil (Dancing Brave (USA))
T D Easterby Elite Racing Club

Placings:5-0 **(4857)**
2001: 7^{0}GF

	Starts	1st	2nd	3rd	Win & Pl
Career Total (Turf)	2	0	0	0	0

Going (Turf): Sf: 0-1 GS: 0-0 Gd: 0-0 GF: 0-1 Fm: 0-0
Distance: 5f/6f: 0-1 7f-8f: 0-1 9f-13f: 0-0 14f+: 0-0
Track : LH: 0-2 RH: 0-0 Tight: 0-1 Gall: 0-0
Aids: Bl: 0-0 Vi: 0-0 Tstrap: 0-0
Best Rating: 38 9/01 Catt 7f gd-fm

Frodo

94 **71**

2-y-o b c Magic Ring (IRE)-Prompt (Old Vic)
R Charlton Lady Rothschild

Placings:0030130 **(5253)**
2001: 6^{0}S, 5^{0}GF, 6^{3}GS, 6^{0}GF, 6^{1}G, 6^{3}HY, 6^{0}S

	Starts	1st	2nd	3rd	Win & Pl
Career Total (Turf)	7	1	0	2	4530

71	8/01	Nott	6f15y	E	GD	£3304

Total win prize-money £3304

Going (Turf): Sf: 0-3 GS: 0-1 **Gd: 1-1** GF: 0-2 Fm: 0-0
Distance: 5f/6f: 0-5 **7f-8f: 1-2** 9f-13f: 0-0 14f+: 0-0
Track : LH: 0-0 RH: 0-1 Tight: 0-0 Gall: 0-1
Aids: Bl: 0-0 Vi: 0-0 Tstrap: 0-0
Best Rating: 71 9/01 Hayd 6f heavy

His only win came in a six-furlong nursery at Nottingham at the end of the summer on good ground.

Froglet

(83) (46)**47**

2-y-o b f Shaamit (IRE)-Frog (Akarad (FR))
Sir Mark Prescott B Haggas

Placings:00 **(5665)**
2001: 6^{0}SD, 6^{0}HY

	Starts	1st	2nd	3rd	Win & Pl
Career Total (Turf)	1	0	0	0	
Career Total (AW)	1	0	0	0	

Going (Turf): Sf: 0-1 GS: 0-0 Gd: 0-0 GF: 0-0 Fm: 0-0
Distance: 5f/6f: 0-2 7f-8f: 0-0 9f-13f: 0-0 14f+: 0-0
Track : LH: 0-1 RH: 0-0 Tight: 0-1 Gall: 0-0
Aids: Bl: 0-0 Vi: 0-0 Tstrap: 0-0
Best Rating: 47 11/01 Wind 6f heavy

Fair form in maidens, and should be seen to better effect over middle distances in handicaps.

Frolicking

(70) (36)**37**

6-y-o b m Mujtahid (USA)-Perfect Desire (USA) (Green Forest (USA))
B S Rothwell Brian Rothwell

Placings:05404050/**00400300/0** **(0057)**
2001: 7^{0}SD

	Starts	1st	2nd	3rd	Win & Pl
Career Total (Turf)	10	0	0	1	1006
Career Total (AW)	7	0	0	0	0

Going (Turf): Sf: 0-1 GS: 0-3 Gd: 0-4 GF: 0-2 Fm: 0-0
Distance: 5f/6f: 0-4 7f-8f: 0-9 9f-13f: 0-4 14f+: 0-0
Track : LH: 0-11 RH: 0-1 Tight: 0-6 Gall: 0-2
Aids: Bl: 0-3 Vi: 0-1 Tstrap: 0-0

Fromsong (IRE)

108 **108**

3-y-o b c Fayruz-Lindas Delight (Batshoof)
B R Millman Mrs E Nelson, Mr Gary Dormer

Placings:512-140 **(1819)**
2001: 5^{1}S, 5^{4}GF, 6^{0}GF

	Starts	1st	2nd	3rd	Win & Pl
Career Total (Turf)	6	2	1	0	17771

108	4/01	Nott	5f13y	C	SFT	£7150
101	9/00	Bath	5f161y	D	SFT	£2908

Total win prize-money £10059

Going (Turf): Sf: 2-3 GS: 0-0 Gd: 0-1 GF: 0-2 Fm: 0-0
Distance: **5f/6f: 2-6** 7f-8f: 0-0 9f-13f: 0-0 14f+: 0-0
Track : **LH: 1-1** RH: 0-0 Tight: 0-0 **Gall: 1-1**
Aids: Bl: 0-0 Vi: 0-0 Tstrap: 0-0
Best Rating: 108 4/01 Nott 5f13y soft

Progressive at two, he finished runner-up in the Cornwallis on his final start and won well from a poor draw on his reappearance. Struggled in Listed company on fast ground. He has plenty of speed but needs soft ground.

Frontier Flight (USA)

79(79) (19)**14**

11-y-o b g Flying Paster (USA)-Sly Charmer (USA) (Valdez (USA))
P W Hiatt S F Holder

Placings:1/40004/0/000/00560/000-4 **(2628)**
2001: 8^{4}GF

	Starts	1st	2nd	3rd	Win & Pl
Career Total (Turf)	13	1	0	0	4354
Career Total (AW)	6	0	0	0	0

74	9/92	Wolv	7f	F	GD	£2553

Total win prize-money £2553

Going (Turf): Sf: 0-4 GS: 0-0 **Gd: 1-4** GF: 0-3 Fm: 0-1
Distance: 5f/6f: 0-0 **7f-8f: 1-3** 9f-13f: 0-8 14f+: 0-7
Track : **LH: 1-15** RH: 0-3 Tight: 0-6 Gall: 0-3
Aids: Bl: 0-0 Vi: 0-0 Tstrap: 0-1
Best Rating: 10 7/01 Gdwd 1m gd-fm

Frosty Welcome (USA)

95 **81**

2-y-o gr/ro f With Approval (CAN)-Light Ice (USA) (Arctic Tern (USA))
G Wragg Miss K Rausing

Placings:65 **(5372)**
2001: 6^{6}S, 6^{5}G

	Starts	1st	2nd	3rd	Win & Pl
Career Total (Turf)	2	0	0	0	0

Going (Turf): Sf: 0-1 GS: 0-0 Gd: 0-1 GF: 0-0 Fm: 0-0
Distance: 5f/6f: 0-2 7f-8f: 0-0 9f-13f: 0-0 14f+: 0-0
Track : LH: 0-1 RH: 0-0 Tight: 0-0 Gall: 0-0
Aids: Bl: 0-0 Vi: 0-0 Tstrap: 0-0
Best Rating: 81 10/01 Rdcr 6f good

Ran well on her first two starts. Has run only over six furlongs.

Frottola

98 **51**

3-y-o b f Muhtarram (USA)-For My Love (Kahyasi)
L M Cumani Scuderia Giocri

Placings:20504 **(5626)**
2001: 9^{2}GF, 10^{0}G, 8^{5}HY, 10^{0}HY, 8^{4}GS

	Starts	1st	2nd	3rd	Win & Pl
Career Total (Turf)	5	0	1	0	2891

Going (Turf): Sf: 0-2 GS: 0-1 Gd: 0-1 GF: 0-1 Fm: 0-0
Distance: 5f/6f: 0-0 7f-8f: 0-0 9f-13f: 0-5 14f+: 0-0
Track : LH: 0-3 RH: 0-0 Tight: 0-1 Gall: 0-0
Aids: Bl: 0-0 Vi: 0-0 Tstrap: 0-0
Best Rating: 51 9/01 Hayd 1m30y heavy

Narrowly beaten on her debut in Italy, has been lightly raced and has struggled since. Looks basically moderate at this stage.

Fruhling Feuer (FR)

107 **73**

3-y-o ch f Green Tune (USA)-Reef Squaw (Darshaan)
J L Dunlop Mrs Maria Mai Goransson

Placings:014350 **(5591)**
2001: 7^{0}S, 8^{1}G, 9^{4}GF, 10^{3}G, 10^{5}HY, 9^{0}GS

	Starts	1st	2nd	3rd	Win & Pl
Career Total (Turf)	6	1	0	1	5207

61 5/01 Nott 1m54y D GD £4240
Total win prize-money £4241

Going (Turf): Sf: 0-2 GS: 0-1 **Gd: 1-2** GF: 0-1 Fm: 0-0
Distance: 5f/6f: 0-0 7f-8f: 0-1 **9f-13f: 1-5** 14f+: 0-0
Track : **LH: 1-4** RH: 0-1 Tight: 0-0 Gall: 0-0
Aids: Bl: 0-0 Vi: 0-0 Tstrap: 0-0
Best Rating: 73 7/01 Kemp 1m1f gd-fm

She won a mile maiden at Nottingham in the spring and has run well over longer trips in handicap company since.

Fruit Of Glory

102 **82**

2-y-o b f Glory Of Dancer-Fresh Fruit Daily (Reprimand)
M R Channon Buy And Sell Partnership

Placings:52212 **(5021)**
2001: 6^{5}G, 6^{2}G, 6^{2}GS, 7^{1}G, 7^{2}HY

	Starts	1st	2nd	3rd	Win & Pl
Career Total (Turf)	5	1	3	0	10775

82 9/01 Epsm 7f E GD £4329
Total win prize-money £4329

Going (Turf): Sf: 0-1 GS: 0-1 **Gd: 1-3** GF: 0-0 Fm: 0-0
Distance: 5f/6f: 0-3 **7f-8f: 1-2** 9f-13f: 0-0 14f+: 0-0
Track : **LH: 1-1** RH: 0-0 **Tight: 1-1** Gall: 0-0
Aids: Bl: 0-0 Vi: 0-0 Tstrap: 0-0
Best Rating: 82 9/01 Asct 7f heavy

Appreciated the step up to seven furlongs when getting her head in front at Epsom on her fourth start despite not handling the track and was just caught in the dying strides in a decent nursery at Ascot next time.

Fruit Punch (IRE)

106 **70**

3-y-o b f Barathea (IRE)-Friendly Finance (Auction Ring (USA))
T D Easterby M P Burke

Placings:5500-24632400203 **(5286)**
2001: 10^{2}GS, 10^{4}G, 11^{6}GF, 9^{3}G, 9^{2}GF, 9^{4}GF, 9^{0}G, 10^{0}G, 10^{2}GF, 10^{0}S, 10^{3}HY

	Starts	1st	2nd	3rd	Win & Pl
Career Total (Turf)	15	0	3	2	6436

Going (Turf): Sf: 0-2 GS: 0-1 Gd: 0-7 GF: 0-5 Fm: 0-0
Distance: 5f/6f: 0-1 7f-8f: 0-3 9f-13f: 0-11 14f+: 0-0
Track : LH: 0-5 RH: 0-6 Tight: 0-4 Gall: 0-0
Aids: Bl: 0-7 Vi: 0-0 Tstrap: 0-0
Best Rating: 73 5/01 Pont 1m2f6y gd-sft

Fudge Brownie

107 **56**

5-y-o b g Deploy-Carte Blanche (Cadeaux Genereux)
G A Swinbank (D Eddy 30/5) Mr S V Rutter

Placings:00/32250 **(4773)**
2001: 8^{3}S, 8^{2}GS, 8^{2}G, 8^{5}GF, 8^{0}G

	Starts	1st	2nd	3rd	Win & Pl
Career Total (Turf)	7	0	2	1	2408

Going (Turf): Sf: 0-1 GS: 0-1 Gd: 0-3 GF: 0-2 Fm: 0-0
Distance: 5f/6f: 0-0 7f-8f: 0-4 9f-13f: 0-3 14f+: 0-0
Track : LH: 0-0 RH: 0-6 Tight: 0-5 Gall: 0-1
Aids: Bl: 0-0 Vi: 0-0 Tstrap: 0-0
Best Rating: 56 5/01 Haml 1m65y good

Fuegian

90(96) (36)**33**

6-y-o ch g Arazi (USA)-Well Beyond (IRE) (Don't Forget Me)
M Madgwick W V Roker

Placings:00004/00550212660/2010P000-600000 **(3492)**
2001: 8^{0}SD, 7^{0}GF, 9^{0}GF, 7^{0}GF, 7^{0}GS, 10^{0}GF

	Starts	1st	2nd	3rd	Win & Pl
Career Total (Turf)	26	2	3	0	8231
Career Total (AW)	4	0	0	0	189

57 6/00 Wind 1m67y E(0-75)H G-F £3010
56 7/99 Wind 1m67y E(0-70)H GD £2934
Total win prize-money £5944

Going (Turf): Sf: 0-2 GS: 0-3 **Gd: 1-8 GF: 1-12** Fm: 0-1
Distance: 5f/6f: 0-0 7f-8f: 0-15 **9f-13f: 2-15** 14f+: 0-0
Track : LH: 0-6 **RH: 2-16 Tight: 2-15** Gall: 0-0
Aids: Bl: 0-0 **Vi: 1-12** Tstrap: 0-0
Best Rating: 41 5/01 Ling 7f gd-fm

Fuero Real (FR)

75(93) (35)**42**

6-y-o b g Highest Honor (FR)-Highest Pleasure (USA) (Foolish Pleasure (USA))
R J Hodges Grandstand Jockeys

Placings:010/0602240/5310-00 **(1367)**
2001: 9^{0}GF, 9^{0}G

	Starts	1st	2nd	3rd	Win & Pl
Career Total (Turf)	14	2	2	1	7642
Career Total (AW)	2	0	0	0	0

42 5/00 Brig 1m3f196yG(0-60)H SFT £1968
6/98 Toul 1m4f H FRM £4040
Total win prize-money £6008

Going (Turf): **Sf: 1-2** GS: 0-2 Gd: 0-2 GF: 0-4 Fm: 0-1
Distance: 5f/6f: 0-0 7f-8f: 0-0 **9f-13f: 1-13** 14f+: 0-0
Track : **LH: 1-11** RH: 0-1 Tight: 0-7 Gall: 0-0
Aids: Bl: 0-0 Vi: 0-0 Tstrap: 0-0
Best Rating: 1 5/01 Brig 1m1f209y gd-fm

Full Ahead (IRE)

95(104) (79)**87d**

4-y-o b c Slip Anchor-Foulard (IRE) (Sadler's Wells (USA))
A King Nigel Bunter

Placings:45/33221600-50 **(0856)**
2001: 11^{5}SW, 16^{0}GS

	Starts	1st	2nd	3rd	Win & Pl
Career Total (Turf)	11	1	2	2	6807
Career Total (AW)	1	0	0	0	0

75 6/00 Rdcr 1m6f19y D FRM £2730
Total win prize-money £2730

Going (Turf): Sf: 0-0 GS: 0-3 Gd: 0-5 GF: 0-2 **Fm: 1-1**
Distance: 5f/6f: 0-0 7f-8f: 0-1 9f-13f: 0-6 **14f+: 1-5**
Track : **LH: 1-6** RH: 0-4 **Tight: 1-3** Gall: 0-4
Aids: Bl: 0-0 Vi: 0-0 Tstrap: 0-0
Best Rating: 79 2/01 Sthl 1m3f slow

Full Egalite

81(100) (47d)**23**

5-y-o gr g Ezzoud (IRE)-Milva (Jellaby)
B R Johnson Mrs P J Sheen

Placings:061/406000/0001200235030-3660400 **(3411)**
2001: 12^{3}SD, 12^{6}SD, 12^{6}SD, 15^{0}HY, 11^{4}F, 12^{0}GF, 16^{0}GF

	Starts	1st	2nd	3rd	Win & Pl

Career Total (Turf)	20	1	1	1	4107
Career Total (AW)	9	1	1	2	3066

42 6/00 Ling 1m4f G STD £1981
72 11/98 Brig 5f213y D SFT £2965
Total win prize-money £4946

Going (Turf): Sf: 1-5 GS: 0-1 Gd: 0-6 GF: 0-7 Fm: 0-1
Distance: 5f/6f: 1-2 7f-8f: 0-3 9f-13f: 1-21 14f+: 0-3
Track : **LH: 2-23** RH: 0-5 **Tight: 1-15** Gall: 0-3
Aids: **Bl: 1-9** Vi: 0-6 Tstrap: 0-0
Best Rating: 47 2/01 Wolv 1m4f stand

Full House (IRE)

99 **79+**

2-y-o br c King's Theatre (IRE)-Nirvavita (FR) (Highest Honor (FR))
P F I Cole The Blandford Partnership

Placings:31 **(4880)**
2001: 8^{3}HY, 8^{1}GF

	Starts	1st	2nd	3rd	Win & Pl
Career Total (Turf)	2	1	0	1	3951

79 9/01 Haml 1m65y E G-F £3461
Total win prize-money £3461

Going (Turf): Sf: 0-1 GS: 0-0 Gd: 0-0 **GF: 1-1** Fm: 0-0
Distance: 5f/6f: 0-0 7f-8f: 0-0 **9f-13f: 1-2** 14f+: 0-0
Track : LH: 0-1 **RH: 1-1 Tight: 1-1** Gall: 0-0
Aids: Bl: 0-0 Vi: 0-0 Tstrap: 0-0
Best Rating: 79 9/01 Haml 1m65y gd-fm

Followed up a promising Haydock debut on heavy ground with a comfortable victory on fast ground at Hamilton. Looks likely to progress from that.

Full Spate

103 **73**

6-y-o ch h Unfuwain (USA)-Double River (USA) (Irish River (FR))
J M Bradley E A Hayward

Placings:234/531500600000/360354103040-04030010030201560 **(5025)**
2001: 5^{0}HY, 6^{4}GF, 6^{0}GF, 6^{3}GF, 6^{0}G, 6^{0}G, 6^{1}GF, 6^{0}GF, 6^{0}GF, 6^{3}GF, 7^{0}GF, 7^{2}GF, 7^{0}GF, 7^{1}GF, 7^{5}GF, 7^{6}GF, 6^{0}S

	Starts	1st	2nd	3rd	Win & Pl
Career Total (Turf)	44	4	2	7	32156

73 8/01 Folk 7f E(0-70) G-F £2870
70 6/01 Wind 6f D(0-80)H G-F £4147
67 7/00 Hayd 6f D(0-80)H G-F £7962
76 5/99 Thsk 7f C(0-90)H GD £6775
Total win prize-money £21755

Going (Turf): Sf: 0-5 GS: 0-3 Gd: 1-12 **GF: 3-23** Fm: 0-1
Distance: 5f/6f: 2-21 7f-8f: 2-22 9f-13f: 0-1 14f+: 0-0
Track : **LH: 1-8** RH: 0-7 **Tight: 1-4** Gall: 0-5
Aids: Bl: 0-0 Vi: 0-0 Tstrap: 0-0
Best Rating: 73 8/01 Folk 7f gd-fm

Full Stop (IRE)

(88) (30)

4-y-o b f Zieten (USA)-Scherzo Impromptu (Music Boy)
B J Curley Catherine Allen & Rachael D S Hood

Placings:0 **(0721)**
2001: 5^{0}SD

	Starts	1st	2nd	3rd	Win & Pl
Career Total (Turf)	0	0	0	0	
Career Total (AW)	1	0	0	0	

Going (Turf): Sf: 0-0 GS: 0-0 Gd: 0-0 GF: 0-0 Fm: 0-0
Distance: 5f/6f: 0-1 7f-8f: 0-0 9f-13f: 0-0 14f+: 0-0
Track : LH: 0-1 RH: 0-0 Tight: 0-1 Gall: 0-0
Aids: Bl: 0-0 Vi: 0-0 Tstrap: 0-0
Best Rating: 30 4/01 Ling 5f stand

Full Time (IRE)

63(86) (51)

2-y-o b g Bigstone (IRE)-Oiche Mhaith (Night Shift (USA))
G A Swinbank Alan Swinbank

Placings:06 **(1472)**
2001: 5^{0}S, 5^{6}SD

	Starts	1st	2nd	3rd	Win & Pl
Career Total (Turf)	1	0	0	0	
Career Total (AW)	1	0	0	0	0

Going (Turf): Sf: 0-1 GS: 0-0 Gd: 0-0 GF: 0-0 Fm: 0-0
Distance: 5f/6f: 0-2 7f-8f: 0-0 9f-13f: 0-0 14f+: 0-0
Track : LH: 0-0 RH: 0-0 Tight: 0-0 Gall: 0-0
Aids: Bl: 0-0 Vi: 0-0 Tstrap: 0-0
Best Rating: 51 5/01 Sthl 5f stand

Fullopep

100 **62**

7-y-o b g Dunbeath (USA)-Suggia (Alzao (USA))
Mrs M Reveley Mr & Mrs W J Williams

Placings:020/00010440/634/2/0-200 **(5152)**
2001: 14^{2}GF, 14^{0}GF, 14^{0}G

	Starts	1st	2nd	3rd	Win & Pl
Career Total (Turf)	19	1	3	1	6043

57 5/97 Catt 1m3f214yF G-F £2617
Total win prize-money £2618

Going (Turf): Sf: 0-2 GS: 0-0 Gd: 0-7 **GF: 1-10** Fm: 0-0
Distance: 5f/6f: 0-2 7f-8f: 0-3 **9f-13f: 1-6** 14f+: 0-8
Track : **LH: 1-13** RH: 0-4 **Tight: 1-12** Gall: 0-2
Aids: Bl: 0-0 Vi: 0-0 Tstrap: 0-0
Best Rating: 62 6/01 Rdcr 1m6f19y gd-fm

Fully Invested (USA)

105 **102**

3-y-o b f Irish River (FR)-Shirley Valentine (Shirley Heights)
H R A Cecil K Abdulla

Placings:1-0366 **(5339)**
2001: 10^{0}G, 10^{3}S, 8^{6}G, 10^{6}GS

	Starts	1st	2nd	3rd	Win & Pl
Career Total (Turf)	5	1	0	1	7145

79 10/00 Ling 7f D SFT £3542
Total win prize-money £3543

Going (Turf): Sf: 1-2 GS: 0-1 Gd: 0-2 GF: 0-0 Fm: 0-0
Distance: 5f/6f: 0-0 **7f-8f: 1-2** 9f-13f: 0-3 14f+: 0-0
Track : LH: 0-1 RH: 0-0 Tight: 0-0 Gall: 0-1
Aids: Bl: 0-0 Vi: 0-0 Tstrap: 0-0
Best Rating: 102 10/01 NmkR 1m good

Did not run badly after a five-month absence in the Sun Chariot, but appeared not to stay back at ten furlongs two weeks later. Suited by give in the ground.

Fundamental

74 **42**

2-y-o ch g Rudimentary (USA)-I'Ll Try (Try My Best (USA))
T P Tate T P Tate

Placings:000 **(5371)**
2001: 8^{0}HY, 8^{0}GS, 8^{0}G

	Starts	1st	2nd	3rd	Win & Pl
Career Total (Turf)	3	0	0	0	

Going (Turf): Sf: 0-1 GS: 0-1 Gd: 0-1 GF: 0-0 Fm: 0-0
Distance: 5f/6f: 0-0 7f-8f: 0-2 9f-13f: 0-1 14f+: 0-0
Track : LH: 0-2 RH: 0-0 Tight: 0-0 Gall: 0-1
Aids: Bl: 0-0 Vi: 0-0 Tstrap: 0-0
Best Rating: 42 9/01 Hayd 1m30y heavy

Funfair Wane

102 **102**

2-y-o b c Unfuwain (USA)-Ivory Bride (Domynsky)
M R Channon Mrs Jean Keegan

Placings:211550 **(5256)**
2001: 6^{2}GF, 6^{1}G, 7^{1}GF, 6^{5}G, 7^{5}GF, 5^{0}GS

	Starts	1st	2nd	3rd	Win & Pl
Career Total (Turf)	6	2	1	0	27895

102 8/01 Newb 7f A G-F £11941
78 6/01 York 6f D GD £7020
Total win prize-money £18961

Going (Turf): Sf: 0-0 GS: 0-1 **Gd: 1-2 GF: 1-3** Fm: 0-0
Distance: 5f/6f: 1-4 7f-8f: 1-2 9f-13f: 0-0 14f+: 0-0
Track : LH: 0-0 RH: 0-0 Tight: 0-0 Gall: 0-0
Aids: Bl: 0-0 Vi: 0-0 Tstrap: 0-0
Best Rating: 102 8/01 Newb 7f gd-fm

Confirmed the promise of his debut when hacking up at York in June. Followed up in a Newbury Listed race in August after having suffered a rapped joint and was not disgraced in Group One company in Germany and Ireland. Acts on a sound surface.

Funksoulborough (IRE)

101 **80**

2-y-o b c Woodborough (USA)-White Paper (IRE) (Marignan (USA))
W Jarvis Rams Racing Club

Placings:21353040 **(5150)**
2001: 5^{2}F, 6^{1}GF, 6^{3}GF, 7^{5}GF, 6^{3}G, 7^{0}GF, 7^{4}S, 6^{0}G

	Starts	1st	2nd	3rd	Win & Pl
Career Total (Turf)	8	1	1	2	5722

80 6/01 Rdcr 6f E G-F £2912
Total win prize-money £2912

Going (Turf): Sf: 0-1 GS: 0-0 Gd: 0-2 **GF: 1-4** Fm: 0-1
Distance: **5f/6f: 1-4** 7f-8f: 0-4 9f-13f: 0-0 14f+: 0-0
Track : LH: 0-1 RH: 0-0 Tight: 0-1 Gall: 0-0
Aids: Bl: 0-0 Vi: 0-1 Tstrap: 0-0
Best Rating: 80 8/01 Nott 6f15y good

Made a promising debut and appreciated the step up to six when successful on his second start.

Funny Girl (IRE)

98 **68**

4-y-o b f Darshaan-Just For Fun (FR) (Lead On Time (USA))

W R Muir Vicki & David Fleet

Placings:45/56256-306 **(2366)**

2001: 8^{3}G, 7^{0}G, 7^{6}GF

	Starts	1st	2nd	3rd	Win & Pl
Career Total (Turf)	10	0	1	1	2035

Going (Turf): Sf: 0-0 GS: 0-2 Gd: 0-4 GF: 0-4 Fm: 0-0
Distance: 5f/6f: 0-0 7f-8f: 0-4 9f-13f: 0-6 14f+: 0-0
Track : LH: 0-3 RH: 0-5 Tight: 0-1 Gall: 0-3
Aids: Bl: 0-0 Vi: 0-0 Tstrap: 0-0
Best Rating: 65 5/01 Wwck 1m22y good

Frustrating filly who has ran well in Listed class but remains a maiden. Best form a round a mile on a fast surface.

Funny Valentine (IRE)

111(105) (83)**111**

3-y-o ch c Cadeaux Genereux-Aunt Hester (IRE) (Caerleon (USA))

T G Mills John Humphreys (turf Accountants) Ltd

Placings:25-141320 **(2839)**

2001: 6^{1}SD, 5^{4}S, 5^{1}G, 5^{3}G, 5^{2}GF, 5^{0}GF

	Starts	1st	2nd	3rd	Win & Pl
Career Total (Turf)	7	1	2	1	27319
Career Total (AW)	1	1	0	0	3510

81	5/01	Bath	5f11y	D(0-80)	GD	£3844
83	4/01	Ling	6f	D	STD	£3510

Total win prize-money £7355

Going (Turf): Sf: 0-3 GS: 0-0 **Gd: 1-2** GF: 0-2 Fm: 0-0
Distance: 5f/6f: 2-7 7f-8f: 0-1 9f-13f: 0-0 14f+: 0-0
Track : LH: 2-2 RH: 0-0 **Tight: 1-1 Gall: 1-1**
Aids: Bl: 0-0 Vi: 0-0 Tstrap: 0-0
Best Rating: 111 6/01 Asct 5f good

He got off the mark in a maiden on the sand at Lingfield and stepped up on that effort when fourth in a competitive little handicap at Sandown. He was ridden with a little more restraint when winning at Bath, and stepped up on previous form in the King's Stand. Although beaten in a handicap shortly afterwards, he is clearly going the right way. Injured in July, however.

Furness

(99) (62)**58**

4-y-o b g Emarati (USA)-Thelma (Blakeney)

P Haley (A Dickman 29/1) Mike Smallman

Placings:000/252510-33

2001: 16^{3}SD, 12^{3}S

	Starts	1st	2nd	3rd	Win & Pl
Career Total (Turf)	5	0	1	0	800
Career Total (AW)	6	1	1	2	5277

62	10/00	Sthl	1m6f	E(0-70)H	STD	£2373

Total win prize-money £2373

Going (Turf): Sf: 0-3 GS: 0-2 Gd: 0-1 GF: 0-0 Fm: 0-0
Distance: 5f/6f: 0-0 7f-8f: 0-2 9f-13f: 0-4 **14f+: 1-5**
Track : LH: 1-7 RH: 0-1 Tight: 0-1 Gall: 0-2
Aids: Bl: 0-0 Vi: 0-0 Tstrap: 0-0
Best Rating: 52 1/01 Sthl 2m stand

Further Outlook (USA)

111 **73**

7-y-o gr g Zilzal (USA)-Future Bright (USA) (Lyphard's Wish (FR))

D Nicholls Mark A Leatham

Placings:21314/560/0003002/0012101060/0000532536 4030031325-44205000000040 **(5266)**

2001: 5^{4}GS, 6^{4}S, 5^{2}S, 6^{0}GS, 5^{5}GS, 6^{0}G, 6^{0}GF, 5^{0}GF, 6^{0}GF, 6^{0}GF, 5^{0}GF, 7^{0}GF, 5^{4}GS, 6^{0}GS

	Starts	1st	2nd	3rd	Win & Pl
Career Total (Turf)	59	6	6	7	124481

102	10/00	York	6f	C(0-100)H	HVY	£25642
98	6/99	Donc	5f	B(0-100)H	G-F	£9007
94	6/99	Epsm	6f	C(0-100)H	GD	£25305
82	4/99	Pont	6f	D(0-80)H	G-S	£7522
96	9/96	Haml	1m65y	C	GD	£4664
85	8/96	Bevl	7f100y	D	G-F	£3847

Total win prize-money £75990

Going (Turf): Sf: 1-12 GS: 1-8 **Gd: 2-20 GF: 2-17** Fm: 0-2
Distance: 5f/6f: 4-39 7f-8f: 1-13 9f-13f: 1-7 14f+: 0-0
Track : LH: 2-10 RH: 2-8 **Tight: 2-8** Gall: 0-3
Aids: Bl: 0-0 Vi: 0-0 Tstrap: 0-0
Best Rating: 102 3/01 Donc 5f gd-sft

Front-running sprinter that handles most surfaces and is effective between five and seven furlongs. Not at his best of late and is hard to win with these days.

Fusul (USA)

(107) (60)**53d**

5-y-o ch g Miswaki (USA)-Silent Turn (USA) (Silent Cal (USA))

G L Moore Dave Allen,Barry Prichard,Wayne Russell

Placings:50/4000000**4**/11302502514-6106 **(0625)**

2001: 12^{6}SD, 13^{1}SW, 13^{0}SD, 12^{6}SD

	Starts	1st	2nd	3rd	Win & Pl
Career Total (Turf)	8	0	0	0	232
Career Total (AW)	16	4	2	1	13278

53	2/01	Ling	1m5f	F	SLW	£2205
60	11/00	Ling	1m4f	F	STD	£2289
61	2/00	Ling	1m4f	D(0-85)H	STD	£3768
50	1/00	Ling	1m4f	D	STD	£2795

Total win prize-money £11057

Going (Turf): Sf: 0-0 GS: 0-0 Gd: 0-4 GF: 0-4 Fm: 0-0
Distance: 5f/6f: 0-1 7f-8f: 0-7 **9f-13f: 4-15** 14f+: 0-1
Track : LH: 4-22 RH: 0-0 **Tight: 4-21** Gall: 0-0
Aids: Bl: 2-6 Vi: 0-0 Tstrap: 2-11
Best Rating: 54 1/01 Ling 1m4f stand

Futuna (IRE)

62 **16**

3-y-o b f Tagula (IRE)-Pleasant Outlook (USA) (El Gran Senor (USA))

I A Balding Robert Hitchins

Placings:0 **(0841)**

2001: 7^{0}GS

	Starts	1st	2nd	3rd	Win & Pl
Career Total (Turf)	1	0	0	0	

Going (Turf): Sf: 0-0 GS: 0-1 Gd: 0-0 GF: 0-0 Fm: 0-0
Distance: 5f/6f: 0-0 7f-8f: 0-1 9f-13f: 0-0 14f+: 0-0
Track : LH: 0-0 RH: 0-0 Tight: 0-0 Gall: 0-0
Aids: Bl: 0-0 Vi: 0-0 Tstrap: 0-0
Best Rating: 16 4/01 Newb 7f gd-sft

Future Flight

101 **84**

3-y-o b f Polar Falcon (USA)-My Branch (Distant Relative)

B W Hills Wafic Said

Placings:2-1400 **(5011)**

2001: 6^{1}HY, 7^{4}GS, 7^{0}G, 7^{0}HY

	Starts	1st	2nd	3rd	Win & Pl
Career Total (Turf)	5	1	1	0	4515

58	4/01	Folk	6f189y	D	HVY	£2548

Total win prize-money £2548

Going (Turf): Sf: 1-3 GS: 0-1 Gd: 0-1 GF: 0-0 Fm: 0-0
Distance: 5f/6f: 0-1 **7f-8f: 1-4** 9f-13f: 0-0 14f+: 0-0
Track : LH: 0-1 **RH: 1-2 Tight: 1-1** Gall: 0-0
Aids: Bl: 0-0 Vi: 0-0 Tstrap: 0-0
Best Rating: 78 5/01 Ling 7f140y gd-sft

A beaten favourite on her Newmarket debut, she made no mistake on her three-year-old bow in heavy ground at Folkestone, but has failed to progress since. Acts well with cut in the ground.

Future Prospect (IRE)

105 (52)**58**

7-y-o b g Marju (IRE)-Phazania (Tap On Wood)

M A Buckley Mrs N W Buckley & Mr G N Buckley

Placings:21056/100241003000/40526101004040**2000**/255000-1066362 **(4908)**

2001: 7^{1}GF, 7^{0}GF, 8^{6}GF, 8^{6}G, 8^{3}GF, 10^{6}GF, 9^{2}G

	Starts	1st	2nd	3rd	Win & Pl
Career Total (Turf)	40	5	5	2	26934
Career Total (AW)	8	1	1	0	2551

56	6/01	Bevl	7f100y	E(0-70)H	G-F	£4514
64	6/99	Rdcr	1m1f	E(0-70)H	FRM	£3113
60	5/99	Haml	1m65y	E(0-70)H	G-F	£3631
70	7/98	Wolv	1m100y	F	STD	£1996
73	5/98	Pont	1m4y	F	G-F	£2406
81	6/96	Hayd	5f	D	G-S	£3415

Total win prize-money £19075

Going (Turf): Sf: 0-4 GS: 1-3 Gd: 0-9 **GF: 3-21** Fm: 1-3
Distance: 5f/6f: 1-5 7f-8f: 1-15 **9f-13f: 4-28** 14f+: 0-0
Track : LH: 3-20 RH: 2-21 **Tight: 3-18** Gall: 0-4
Aids: Bl: 0-1 Vi: 0-0 Tstrap: 0-0
Best Rating: 58 9/01 Bevl 1m1f207y good

he goes well fresh and made a winning reappearance at beverley in June, where he usually runs well.

Gabby Hayes (IRE)

78 **57**

5-y-o b g Tirol-All Laughter (Vision (USA))

Ferdy Murphy (B G Powell 26/9) Access Computer Consulting Plc

Placings:603503/56441000/60-00 **(4077)**

2001: 16^{0}SD, 13^{0}G

	Starts	1st	2nd	3rd	Win & Pl
Career Total (Turf)	17	1	0	2	4461
Career Total (AW)	1	0	0	0	

80 6/99 Gowr 1m1f100y GD £3437

Total win prize-money £3438

Going (Turf): Sf: 0-2 GS: 0-0 **Gd: 1-6** GF: 0-3 Fm: 0-0
Distance: 5f/6f: 0-0 7f-8f: 0-5 **9f-13f: 1-10** 14f+: 0-3
Track : LH: 0-5 **RH: 1-11** Tight: 0-2 Gall: 0-3
Aids: **Bl: 1-11** Vi: 0-0 Tstrap: 0-0
Best Rating: 25 8/01 Bath 1m5f22y good

Gabi (IRE)

93 **42**

3-y-o ch f Gabitat-Gabibti (IRE) (Dara Monarch)

B Gubby Brian Gubby Ltd

Placings:0-0056 **(3809)**

2001: 8^{0}GF, 8^{0}GF, 6^{5}GF, 7^{6}GF

	Starts	1st	2nd	3rd	Win & Pl
Career Total (Turf)	5	0	0	0	0

Going (Turf): Sf: 0-1 GS: 0-0 Gd: 0-0 GF: 0-4 Fm: 0-0
Distance: 5f/6f: 0-1 7f-8f: 0-3 9f-13f: 0-1 14f+: 0-0
Track : LH: 0-0 RH: 0-2 Tight: 0-1 Gall: 0-0
Aids: Bl: 0-0 Vi: 0-0 Tstrap: 0-0
Best Rating: 41 8/01 Kemp 6f gd-fm

Gablesea

104(101) (15)**42**

7-y-o b g Beveled (USA)-Me Spede (Valiyar)

B P J Baugh Messrs Chrimes, Winn & Wilson

Placings:0200/6050001**0016044/630**355231100**232/02**
333060600000**/0246**1020500046**000-000**2600600 **(4046)**

2001: 8^{0}SD, 9^{0}SD, 8^{0}S, 8^{2}GF, 7^{6}F, 10^{0}GF, 7^{0}GF, 10^{6}GS, 10^{0}G, 10^{0}HY

	Starts	1st	2nd	3rd	Win & Pl
Career Total (Turf)	50	3	6	5	17201
Career Total (AW)	24	2	2	2	7034

53 4/00 Wwck 1m2f110yF(0-60)H HVY £2467
52 8/98 Hayd 1m30y E(0-70)H GD £3212
48 7/98 Chep 7f16y E(0-70)H GD £3022
56 11/97 Sthl 7f F(0-65)H STD £1944
47 9/97 Wolv 1m100y E(0-70)H STD £3154

Total win prize-money £13801

Going (Turf): Sf: 1-9 GS: 0-10 **Gd: 2-11** GF: 0-16 Fm: 0-4
Distance: 5f/6f: 0-4 7f-8f: 2-37 **9f-13f: 3-33** 14f+: 0-0
Track : **LH: 4-53** RH: 0-7 **Tight: 1-30** Gall: 0-2
Aids: Bl: 0-1 Vi: 0-9 Tstrap: 0-0
Best Rating: 42 5/01 Haml 1m65y gd-fm

Gabor

95 **77**

2-y-o b c Danzig Connection (USA)-Kiomi (Niniski (USA))

S P C Woods Leydens Farm Stud

Placings:03320 **(5590)**

2001: 7^{0}GS, 8^{3}GS, 8^{3}GF, 8^{2}F, 9^{0}GS

	Starts	1st	2nd	3rd	Win & Pl
Career Total (Turf)	5	0	1	2	3218

Going (Turf): Sf: 0-0 GS: 0-3 Gd: 0-0 GF: 0-1 Fm: 0-1
Distance: 5f/6f: 0-0 7f-8f: 0-2 9f-13f: 0-3 14f+: 0-0
Track : LH: 0-2 RH: 0-1 Tight: 0-1 Gall: 0-0
Aids: Bl: 0-0 Vi: 0-0 Tstrap: 0-0
Best Rating: 77 9/01 Bath 1m5y firm

Gad Yakoun

98(77) **29**

8-y-o ch g Cadeaux Genereux-Summer Impressions (USA) (Lyphard (USA))

Mrs G S Rees Capt James Wilson

Placings:365**100/50/00/0/0000000000-06**000 **(3672)**

2001: 5^{0}SW, 6^{6}SD, 5^{0}GS, 5^{0}G, 5^{0}G

	Starts	1st	2nd	3rd	Win & Pl
Career Total (Turf)	14	0	0	1	570
Career Total (AW)	13	1	0	0	3566

69 11/96 Ling 7f D STD £3566

Total win prize-money £3566

Going (Turf): Sf: 0-3 GS: 0-1 Gd: 0-4 GF: 0-6 Fm: 0-0
Distance: 5f/6f: 0-19 **7f-8f: 1-7** 9f-13f: 0-1 14f+: 0-0
Track : **LH: 1-15** RH: 0-1 **Tight: 1-11** Gall: 0-2
Aids: Bl: 0-0 Vi: 0-3 Tstrap: 0-9
Best Rating: 29 7/01 Hayd 5f gd-sft

Gadge

(94) (34)**44**

10-y-o br g Nomination-Queenstyle (Moorestyle)

A Bailey Sandybrow Stables Ltd

Placings:03410/06240030510/36355060000/06050056
0/640313312031111535200004**00/2024**0000240001004
0/23440000603**400/0030**004-05 **(0212)**

2001: 7^{0}SD, 7^{5}SD

	Starts	1st	2nd	3rd	Win & Pl
Career Total (Turf)	67	8	4	6	83177
Career Total (AW)	36	1	3	6	5340

68 10/98 Brig 6f209y F(0-65) GD £2389
80 5/97 Ayr 6f D(0-85)H G-F £3730
72 5/97 Gdwd 7f C(0-90)H GD £9552
66 5/97 Bath 1m5y C(0-95)H G-S £7067
63 5/97 Thsk 1m C(0-90)H G-F £12622
59 3/97 Newc 1m3y G(0-60)H G-F £2116
44 2/97 Ling 1m F(0-60)H STD £1784
71 9/94 Newb 1m7y C(0-100)H SFT £18910
68 10/93 NmkR 6f C G-S £11647

Total win prize-money £69821

Going (Turf): Sf: 1-10 GS: 2-13 Gd: 2-22 **GF: 3-21** Fm: 0-1
Distance: 5f/6f: 2-30 **7f-8f: 4-53** 9f-13f: 3-20 14f+: 0-0
Track : **LH: 5-53** RH: 1-16 **Tight: 3-35** Gall: 1-8
Aids: Bl: 0-1 Vi: 0-3 Tstrap: 0-0
Best Rating: 34 2/01 Wolv 7f stand

He was in brilliant form during the spring of '97, winning races ranging from sellers to valuable handicaps, but shot up the weights as a result and has not had much success since apart from the odd victory. Acts on Fibresand as well as turf.

Gaelic Foray (IRE)

(107) (62)**14**

5-y-o b m Unblest-Rich Heiress (IRE) (Last Tycoon)

M R Ewer-Hoad The Phoenix Partnership (lewes)

Placings:0/0035300511-30 **(0184)**

2001: 7^{3}SD, 7^{0}SD

	Starts	1st	2nd	3rd	Win & Pl
Career Total (Turf)	3	0	0	0	
Career Total (AW)	10	2	0	3	4673

62 12/00 Ling 7f F STD £2331
42 12/00 Ling 7f G STD £1344

Total win prize-money £3675

Going (Turf): Sf: 0-0 GS: 0-0 Gd: 0-0 GF: 0-2 Fm: 0-1
Distance: 5f/6f: 0-1 **7f-8f: 2-9** 9f-13f: 0-3 14f+: 0-0
Track : **LH: 2-11** RH: 0-0 **Tight: 2-10** Gall: 0-0
Aids: Bl: 0-0 Vi: 0-0 Tstrap: 0-0
Best Rating: 59 1/01 Ling 7f stand

Gaelic Storm

92 (88?)**86**

7-y-o b g Shavian-Shannon Princess (Connaught)

M Johnston H C Racing Club

Placings:34163/6011510060/0311020001136/2356126
0011**3400126/065**04641540121130-000 **(5494)**

2001: 7^{0}G, 7^{0}G, 6^{0}HY

	Starts	1st	2nd	3rd	Win & Pl
Career Total (Turf)	64	16	5	6	250407
Career Total (AW)	2	0	0	1	2669

116 10/00 Leop 6f H HVY £19500
111 10/00 Newb 6f8y B(0-110)H SFT £9709
60 9/00 Rdcr 7f C SFT £6351
93 8/00 Klam 6f GD £2538
108 10/99 NmkJ 6f A GD £15170
104 7/99 Ovrl 6f165y GD £39432
97 7/99 Ovrl 6f SFT £9858
111 5/99 Gdwd 6f C GD £6203
109 10/98 Newb 6f8y B(0-110)H HVY £8263
105 10/98 York 6f214y B(0-105)H GD £11281
98 6/98 Newc 6f C(0-95)H SFT £14590
94 6/98 York 6f B(0-100)H G-S £9402
76 9/97 Catt 5f212y G(0-85) GD £2238
83 8/97 Epsm 5f C(0-95)H GD £10357
78 8/97 Thsk 5f D(0-80)H G-F £4370
84 9/96 Sand 5f6y D G-F £3403

Total win prize-money £172670

Going (Turf): Sf: 5-17 GS: 1-9 **Gd: 7-23** GF: 2-12 Fm: 0-1
Distance: **5f/6f: 10-41** 7f-8f: 5-24 9f-13f: 0-0 14f+: 0-0
Track : **LH: 2-11** RH: 0-2 Tight: 1-4 Gall: 1-2
Aids: Bl: 0-0 Vi: 0-0 Tstrap: 0-0
Best Rating: 63 10/01 Newb 6f8y heavy

Almost unrideable before being gelded, this tough customer has gone from strength-to-strength. Best when coming from behind a fast pace on soft ground, he tends to hit form in the closing weeks of the season, though he has been lightly raced and did not do so this term. He is as equally effective over seven furlongs as he is over six.

Gainful

89 **70d**

2-y-o ch f Elmaamul (USA)-Regain (Relko)

B Smart Mrs P A Clark

Placings:4000 **(5628)**

2001: 7^{4}GF, 7^{0}GF, 6^{0}G, 8^{0}G

	Starts	1st	2nd	3rd	Win & Pl
Career Total (Turf)	4	0	0	0	0

Going (Turf): Sf: 0-0 GS: 0-0 Gd: 0-2 GF: 0-2 Fm: 0-0
Distance: 5f/6f: 0-0 7f-8f: 0-4 9f-13f: 0-0 14f+: 0-0
Track : LH: 0-2 RH: 0-0 Tight: 0-0 Gall: 0-0
Aids: Bl: 0-0 Vi: 0-0 Tstrap: 0-0
Best Rating: 70 9/01 Wwck 7f26y gd-fm

Gala Affair

78 **60**

2-y-o ch f Zilzal (USA)-Sally Slade (Dowsing (USA))

C A Cyzer Mrs E A Cyzer

Placings:06 **(4644)**

2001: 6^{0}G, 6^{6}GF

	Starts	1st	2nd	3rd	Win & Pl
Career Total (Turf)	2	0	0	0	0

Going (Turf): Sf: 0-0 GS: 0-0 Gd: 0-1 GF: 0-1 Fm: 0-0
Distance: 5f/6f: 0-2 7f-8f: 0-0 9f-13f: 0-0 14f+: 0-0

Track : LH: 0-0 RH: 0-0 Tight: 0-0 Gall: 0-0
Aids: Bl: 0-0 Vi: 0-0 Tstrap: 0-0
Best Rating: 60 9/01 Ling 6f gd-fm

Gala Gold

89 **50**

2-y-o b f Green Desert (USA)-Melting Gold (USA) (Cadeaux Genereux)
M Johnston Maktoum Al Maktoum

Placings:05 **(5627)**
2001: 6^{0}G, 7^{5}G

	Starts	1st	2nd	3rd	Win & Pl
Career Total (Turf)	2	0	0	0	

Going (Turf): Sf: 0-0 GS: 0-0 Gd: 0-2 GF: 0-0 Fm: 0-0
Distance: 5f/6f: 0-1 7f-8f: 0-1 9f-13f: 0-0 14f+: 0-0
Track : LH: 0-0 RH: 0-0 Tight: 0-0 Gall: 0-0
Aids: Bl: 0-0 Vi: 0-0 Tstrap: 0-0
Best Rating: 50 11/01 Rdcr 7f good

Came on for debut effort when fifth at Redcar in November.

Galant Eye (IRE)

90 **55**

2-y-o ch g Eagle Eyed (USA)-Galandria (Sharpo)
F Jordan Graham Brown

Placings:0000 **(5130)**
2001: 5^{0}GF, 6^{0}GF, 6^{0}GF, 7^{0}HY

	Starts	1st	2nd	3rd	Win & Pl
Career Total (Turf)	4	0	0	0	

Going (Turf): Sf: 0-1 GS: 0-0 Gd: 0-0 GF: 0-3 Fm: 0-0
Distance: 5f/6f: 0-2 7f-8f: 0-2 9f-13f: 0-0 14f+: 0-0
Track : LH: 0-1 RH: 0-0 Tight: 0-0 Gall: 0-1
Aids: Bl: 0-0 Vi: 0-0 Tstrap: 0-0
Best Rating: 55 7/01 Chep 6f16y gd-fm

Galapagos Girl (IRE)

99 (97) (77)**81**

3-y-o b f Turtle Island (IRE)-Shabby Doll (Northfields (USA))
B W Hills Mrs Simon Polito

Placings:120-3503 **(4605)**
2001: 8^{3}G, 7^{5}GF, 8^{0}G, 7^{3}SD

	Starts	1st	2nd	3rd	Win & Pl
Career Total (Turf)	6	1	1	1	14805
Career Total (AW)	1	0	0	1	633

73 7/00 Wind 6f D G-F £3688
Total win prize-money £3689

Going (Turf): Sf: 0-0 GS: 0-0 Gd: 0-4 **GF: 1-2** Fm: 0-0
Distance: 5f/6f: 1-3 7f-8f: 0-4 9f-13f: 0-0 14f+: 0-0
Track : LH: 0-3 **RH: 1-1** Tight: 0-3 **Gall: 1-1**
Aids: Bl: 0-0 Vi: 0-0 Tstrap: 0-0
Best Rating: 81 6/01 Thsk 1m good

Lightly-raced, she won a Windsor maiden on her debut in 2000, and has run reasonably since. Stays a mile, acts on fast ground.

Galapino

94 (63)**36**

8-y-o b g Charmer-Carousella (Rousillon (USA))
Jamie Poulton Glendale Partnership Ltd

Placings:43460000/**4311**2055605604/**2121**42001220202/**3**0004400010202**0**/0603313400/54060520004-406000 **(4020)**
2001: 15^{4}HY, 14^{0}S, 16^{8}GF, 16^{0}GF, 17^{0}G, 16^{0}G

	Starts	1st	2nd	3rd	Win & Pl
Career Total (Turf)	69	4	8	4	33410
Career Total (AW)	11	3	3	2	15647

59	8/99	Sand	2m78y	E(0-70)H		G-S	£3631
64	8/98	Gdwd	1m1f192yE(0-70)H			G-F	£4193
58	6/97	Wwck	1m4f115yD(0-80)H			G-F	£3518
53	3/97	Donc	1m4f	F(0-80)H		G-F	£2878
66	1/97	Wolv	1m4f	E		STD	£2843
76	2/96	Wolv	1m1f79y	D(0-80)H		STD	£3468
69	2/96	Ling	1m2f	C(0-90)H		STD	£5132

Total win prize-money £25664

Going (Turf): Sf: 0-15 GS: 1-8 Gd: 0-15 **GF: 3-29** Fm: 0-2
Distance: 5f/6f: 0-3 7f-8f: 0-7 **9f-13f: 6-32** 14f+: 1-38
Track : LH: 5-36 RH: 2-34 **Tight: 4-33** Gall: 1-14
Aids: Bl: 0-10 Vi: 0-4 Tstrap: 0-0
Best Rating: 36 7/01 Bath 2m1f34y good

Galaxy Drive (IRE)

86(71) (26)**45**

2-y-o b f Perugino (USA)-Madaraka (USA) (Arctic Tern (USA))
A Berry Michael Taylor (cheshire)

Placings:0540 **(5165)**
2001: 5^{0}GF, 6^{5}F, 5^{4}GF, 5^{0}SD

	Starts	1st	2nd	3rd	Win & Pl
Career Total (Turf)	3	0	0	0	0
Career Total (AW)	1	0	0	0	

Going (Turf): Sf: 0-0 GS: 0-0 Gd: 0-0 GF: 0-2 Fm: 0-1
Distance: 5f/6f: 0-4 7f-8f: 0-0 9f-13f: 0-0 14f+: 0-0
Track : LH: 0-1 RH: 0-0 Tight: 0-1 Gall: 0-0
Aids: Bl: 0-0 Vi: 0-0 Tstrap: 0-0
Best Rating: 45 7/01 Rdcr 6f firm

Galaxy Fallon

88 **30**

3-y-o b f Dancing Spree (USA)-No Comebacks (Last Tycoon)
A Berry Mrs Stella Barclay

Placings:00600 **(3503)**
2001: 7^{0}GF, 9^{0}GF, 12^{6}GF, 12^{0}G, 11^{0}GF

	Starts	1st	2nd	3rd	Win & Pl
Career Total (Turf)	5	0	0	0	0

Going (Turf): Sf: 0-0 GS: 0-0 Gd: 0-1 GF: 0-4 Fm: 0-0
Distance: 5f/6f: 0-0 7f-8f: 0-1 9f-13f: 0-4 14f+: 0-0
Track : LH: 0-2 RH: 0-3 Tight: 0-2 Gall: 0-1
Aids: Bl: 0-0 Vi: 0-0 Tstrap: 0-0
Best Rating: 31 5/01 Bevl 7f100y gd-fm

Galaxy Jewel

94(94) (56)**66**

2-y-o ch f Bijou D'Inde-Give Me A Day (Lucky Wednesday)
A Berry The Gazetters

Placings:02002414055 **(5165)**
2001: 5^{0}S, 5^{2}SD, 5^{0}SD, 6^{0}GF, 5^{2}GF, 5^{4}SD, 5^{1}GF, 5^{4}GS, 5^{0}GF, 5^{5}G, 5^{5}SD

	Starts	1st	2nd	3rd	Win & Pl
Career Total (Turf)	7	1	1	0	3035
Career Total (AW)	4	0	1	0	666

66 7/01 Bevl 5f F G-F £2408
Total win prize-money £2408

Going (Turf): Sf: 0-1 GS: 0-1 Gd: 0-1 **GF: 1-4** Fm: 0-0
Distance: 5f/6f: 1-10 7f-8f: 0-1 9f-13f: 0-0 14f+: 0-0
Track : LH: 0-4 RH: 0-0 Tight: 0-3 Gall: 0-0
Aids: Bl: 0-1 Vi: 0-0 Tstrap: 0-0
Best Rating: 66 7/01 Bevl 5f gd-fm

Plating class filly, who used her early speed to get to the rail when scoring at Beverley in July.

Galaxy Pasha (IRE)

72 **10**

2-y-o ch c Hector Protector (USA)-Blade Of Grass (Kris)
A Berry S Munir

Placings:0 **(3152)**
2001: 6^{0}GS

	Starts	1st	2nd	3rd	Win & Pl
Career Total (Turf)	1	0	0	0	

Going (Turf): Sf: 0-0 GS: 0-1 Gd: 0-0 GF: 0-0 Fm: 0-0
Distance: 5f/6f: 0-1 7f-8f: 0-0 9f-13f: 0-0 14f+: 0-0
Track : LH: 0-0 RH: 0-0 Tight: 0-0 Gall: 0-0
Aids: Bl: 0-0 Vi: 0-0 Tstrap: 0-0
Best Rating: 10 7/01 Ling 6f gd-sft

Galaxy Returns

101 **34**

3-y-o ch g Alhijaz-Naulakha (Bustino)
A Berry Ian A Bolland

Placings:0261000-0004400000 **(4898)**
2001: 7^{0}G, 6^{0}F, 7^{0}GF, 8^{4}F, 7^{4}GF, 7^{0}GF, 8^{0}GF, 7^{0}GF, 8^{0}GF, 5^{0}GS

	Starts	1st	2nd	3rd	Win & Pl
Career Total (Turf)	17	1	1	0	4652

62 8/00 Carl 5f207y E FRM £3233
Total win prize-money £3234

Going (Turf): Sf: 0-0 GS: 0-3 Gd: 0-2 GF: 0-8 **Fm: 1-4**
Distance: 5f/6f: 1-6 7f-8f: 0-9 9f-13f: 0-2 14f+: 0-0
Track : LH: 0-6 **RH: 1-4** Tight: 0-2 **Gall: 1-3**
Aids: Bl: 0-1 Vi: 0-0 Tstrap: 0-0
Best Rating: 51 7/01 Newc 1m firm

Galaxy Role

64(60) (8)**14**

2-y-o b c Tragic Role (USA)-Wasblest (Statoblest)
A Berry Galaxy Moss Side Racing Clubs Limited

Placings:003 **(5687)**
2001: 6^{0}S, 6^{0}SD, 8^{3}S

	Starts	1st	2nd	3rd	Win & Pl
Career Total (Turf)	2	0	0	1	927
Career Total (AW)	1	0	0	0	

Going (Turf): Sf: 0-2 GS: 0-0 Gd: 0-0 GF: 0-0 Fm: 0-0
Distance: 5f/6f: 0-1 7f-8f: 0-2 9f-13f: 0-0 14f+: 0-0
Track : LH: 0-2 RH: 0-0 Tight: 0-1 Gall: 0-1
Aids: Bl: 0-0 Vi: 0-0 Tstrap: 0-0
Best Rating: 14 10/01 York 6f214y soft

Galaxy Sam (USA)

88 **63+**

2-y-o ch c Royal Academy (USA)-Istiska (FR) (Irish River (FR))
A Berry S Munir

Placings:0350 **(5668)**
2001: 5^{0}GF, 7^{3}G, 8^{5}G, 8^{0}HY

	Starts	1st	2nd	3rd	Win & Pl
Career Total (Turf)	4	0	0	1	660

Going (Turf): Sf: 0-1 GS: 0-0 Gd: 0-2 GF: 0-1 Fm: 0-0
Distance: 5f/6f: 0-1 7f-8f: 0-1 9f-13f: 0-2 14f+: 0-0
Track : LH: 0-1 RH: 0-2 Tight: 0-1 Gall: 0-0
Aids: Bl: 0-0 Vi: 0-0 Tstrap: 0-0
Best Rating: 63 9/01 Nott 1m54y good

Galaxy Tee (IRE)

87(67) (23)**56**

2-y-o ch f Goldmark (USA)-Shepherd's Delight (Prince Sabo)

A Berry Michael Taylor (cheshire)

Placings:040000 (5536)
2001: 6^{0}GF, 5^{4}GF, 5^{0}GF, 6^{0}SD, 7^{0}G, 6^{0}S

	Starts	1st	2nd	3rd	Win & Pl
Career Total (Turf)	5	0	0	0	0
Career Total (AW)	1	0	0	0	

Going (Turf): Sf: 0-1 GS: 0-0 Gd: 0-1 GF: 0-3 Fm: 0-0
Distance: 5f/6f: 0-5 7f-8f: 0-1 9f-13f: 0-0 14f+: 0-0
Track : LH: 0-2 RH: 0-0 Tight: 0-2 Gall: 0-0
Aids: Bl: 0-0 Vi: 0-0 Tstrap: 0-0
Best Rating: 56 9/01 Catt 5f212y gd-fm

Galaxy Thunderbird

85 60
2-y-o ch c Bahamian Bounty-Milva (Jellaby)
A Berry S Munir

Placings:0365 (5526)
2001: 6^{0}GF, 6^{3}F, 6^{6}G, 5^{5}S

	Starts	1st	2nd	3rd	Win & Pl
Career Total (Turf)	4	0	0	1	574

Going (Turf): Sf: 0-1 GS: 0-0 Gd: 0-1 GF: 0-1 Fm: 0-1
Distance: 5f/6f: 0-3 7f-8f: 0-1 9f-13f: 0-0 14f+: 0-0
Track : LH: 0-0 RH: 0-0 Tight: 0-0 Gall: 0-0
Aids: Bl: 0-0 Vi: 0-0 Tstrap: 0-0
Best Rating: 60 10/01 Nott 5f13y soft

Galaxy Times

89(88) (57)58
2-y-o ch f Presidium-Oubeck (Mummy's Game)
A Berry Miss Lilo Blum

Placings:025220 (2924)
2001: 5^{0}SD, 5^{2}SD, 5^{5}GF, 5^{2}GF, 5^{2}SD, 5^{0}GF

	Starts	1st	2nd	3rd	Win & Pl
Career Total (Turf)	3	0	1	0	1656
Career Total (AW)	3	0	2	0	1328

Going (Turf): Sf: 0-0 GS: 0-0 Gd: 0-0 GF: 0-3 Fm: 0-0
Distance: 5f/6f: 0-6 7f-8f: 0-0 9f-13f: 0-0 14f+: 0-0
Track : LH: 0-1 RH: 0-0 Tight: 0-1 Gall: 0-0
Aids: Bl: 0-0 Vi: 0-0 Tstrap: 0-0
Best Rating: 58 6/01 Muss 5f gd-fm

Galey River (USA)

81 70
2-y-o ch c Irish River (FR)-Carefree Kate (USA) (Lyphard (USA))
J J Sheehan D J Dowling

Placings:30 (5290)
2001: 6^{3}G, 7^{0}S

	Starts	1st	2nd	3rd	Win & Pl
Career Total (Turf)	2	0	0	1	402

Going (Turf): Sf: 0-1 GS: 0-0 Gd: 0-1 GF: 0-0 Fm: 0-0
Distance: 5f/6f: 0-1 7f-8f: 0-1 9f-13f: 0-0 14f+: 0-0
Track : LH: 0-0 RH: 0-0 Tight: 0-0 Gall: 0-0
Aids: Bl: 0-0 Vi: 0-0 Tstrap: 0-0
Best Rating: 70 9/01 Folk 6f good

Gali

93 33
5-y-o gr g Petong-Wasimah (Caerleon (USA))
C A Horgan R Del Rosario

Placings:04/3000/0000-050 (4366)
2001: 8^{0}GF, 7^{5}F, 9^{0}GF

	Starts	1st	2nd	3rd	Win & Pl
Career Total (Turf)	13	0	0	1	501

Going (Turf): Sf: 0-2 GS: 0-0 Gd: 0-3 GF: 0-5 Fm: 0-2
Distance: 5f/6f: 0-3 7f-8f: 0-3 9f-13f: 0-6 14f+: 0-0
Track : LH: 0-3 RH: 0-6 Tight: 0-3 Gall: 0-1
Aids: Bl: 0-0 Vi: 0-0 Tstrap: 0-0
Best Rating: 33 8/01 Brig 7f214y firm

Galileo (IRE)

120 (118)132
3-y-o b c Sadler's Wells (USA)-Urban Sea (USA) (Miswaki (USA))
A P O'Brien Mrs John Magnier & Mr M Tabor

Placings:1-1111126 (5580a)
2001: 10^{1}S, 10^{1}G, 12^{1}GF, 12^{1}Y, 12^{1}GF, 10^{2}G, 10^{6}FT

	Starts	1st	2nd	3rd	Win & Pl
Career Total (Turf)	7	6	1	0	1766665
Career Total (AW)	1	0	0	0	

131 7/01 Asct 1m4f A G-F £435000
129 7/01 Curr 1m4f YLD £510865
125 6/01 Epsm 1m4f10y A G-F £580000
114 5/01 Leop 1m2f GD £48750
113 4/01 Leop 1m2f SFT £26000
112 10/00 Leop 1m HVY £11050
Total win prize-money £1611665

Going (Turf): Sf: 1-1 GS: 0-0 Gd: 1-2 GF: 2-2 Fm: 0-0
Distance: 5f/6f: 0-0 7f-8f: 0-0 9f-13f: 5-7 14f+: 0-0
Track : LH: 1-3 RH: 1-1 Tight: 1-1 Gall: 1-1
Aids: Bl: 0-0 Vi: 0-0 Tstrap: 0-0
Best Rating: 132 9/01 Leop 1m2f good

A beautifully-bred son of Sadler's Wells and the Arc winner Urban Sea, he was the winner of his only start at two and landed his first two starts this season before running out a very impressive winner of the Vodafone Derby at Epsom. He beat the 2000 Guineas winner Golan by three and a half lengths that day and more than doubled that margin in the Irish equivalent. Came through his biggest test when seeing off Fantastic Light in the King George, but was just beaten by the same rival in the Irish Champion Stakes back over ten furlongs. He did not appear to handle the surface in the Breeders' Cup Classic. He retires to stud with his image only slightly tarnished, and he should be remembered as a well-above-average dual Derby winner with a superb action who handled any ground, and whose finest moment was at Ascot in July.

Galla Placidia (IRE)

86(98) (63)74
3-y-o b f Royal Abjar (USA)-Merrie Moment (IRE) (Taufan (USA))
R Ingram Alex Fraser

Placings:65-03 (2448)
2001: 7^{0}GS, 7^{3}F

	Starts	1st	2nd	3rd	Win & Pl
Career Total (Turf)	3	0	0	1	448
Career Total (AW)	1	0	0	0	0

Going (Turf): Sf: 0-0 GS: 0-1 Gd: 0-1 GF: 0-0 Fm: 0-1
Distance: 5f/6f: 0-0 7f-8f: 0-3 9f-13f: 0-1 14f+: 0-0
Track : LH: 0-1 RH: 0-1 Tight: 0-1 Gall: 0-1
Aids: Bl: 0-0 Vi: 0-0 Tstrap: 0-0
Best Rating: 43 6/01 Ling 7f140y firm

Gallant

105 85
4-y-o b c Rainbow Quest (USA)-Gay Gallanta (USA) (Woodman (USA))
M Meade Ladyswood Stud

Placings:0/340-6132 (3849)
2001: 8^{6}G, 9^{1}GF, 8^{3}GF, 10^{2}G

	Starts	1st	2nd	3rd	Win & Pl
Career Total (Turf)	8	1	1	2	13925

80 0/01 Gdwd 1m1f C(0-90)H G-F £8658
Total win prize-money £8658

Going (Turf): Sf: 0-3 GS: 0-1 Gd: 0-2 GF: 1-2 Fm: 0-0
Distance: 5f/6f: 0-1 7f-8f: 0-3 9f-13f: 1-4 14f+: 0-0
Track : LH: 0-2 RH: 1-4 Tight: 1-2 Gall: 0-2
Aids: Bl: 0-0 Vi: 0-0 Tstrap: 0-0
Best Rating: 85 8/01 Asct 1m2f good

Lightly-raced colt with a Group-race pedigree. Having changed stables, won a fair handicap at Goodwood in June. Stays nine furlongs. Acts on fast ground, but handles soft.

Gallant Boy (IRE)

91 83
2-y-o ch c Grand Lodge (USA)-Damerela (IRE) (Alzao (USA))
Sir Michael Stoute Saeed Suhail

Placings:32 (4633)
2001: 7^{3}GF, 7^{2}GF

	Starts	1st	2nd	3rd	Win & Pl
Career Total (Turf)	2	0	1	1	2032

Going (Turf): Sf: 0-0 GS: 0-0 Gd: 0-0 GF: 0-2 Fm: 0-0
Distance: 5f/6f: 0-0 7f-8f: 0-2 9f-13f: 0-0 14f+: 0-0
Track : LH: 0-0 RH: 0-0 Tight: 0-0 Gall: 0-0
Aids: Bl: 0-0 Vi: 0-0 Tstrap: 0-0
Best Rating: 83 9/01 Leic 7f9y gd-fm

Galleon Beach

104 75
4-y-o b g Shirley Heights-Music In My Life (IRE) (Law Society (USA))
J W Hills Christopher Wright

Placings:3132/30P-0506200 (5387)
2001: 11^{0}GF, 16^{5}GF, 15^{0}G, 16^{6}GF, 17^{2}F, 12^{0}GS, 18^{0}GS

	Starts	1st	2nd	3rd	Win & Pl
Career Total (Turf)	14	1	2	3	13875

78 9/99 Haml 1m65y D G-F £3468
Total win prize-money £3469

Going (Turf): Sf: 0-3 GS: 0-2 Gd: 0-3 GF: 1-5 Fm: 0-1
Distance: 5f/6f: 0-0 7f-8f: 0-1 9f-13f: 1-8 14f+: 0-5
Track : LH: 0-6 RH: 1-7 Tight: 1-5 Gall: 0-4
Aids: Bl: 0-3 Vi: 0-0 Tstrap: 0-3
Best Rating: 85 7/01 Sand 2m78y gd-fm

Without a win since his two-yer-old days, he was runner-up at Pontefract in September when equipped with blinkers and a tongue strap.

Galleons Point

5-y-o b g Sabrehill (USA)-Rainbow Ring (Rainbow Quest (USA))
H A McWilliams Keith Jackson

Placings:0 (1661)
2001: 10^{0}F

	Starts	1st	2nd	3rd	Win & Pl
Career Total (Turf)	1	0	0	0	

Going (Turf): Sf: 0-0 GS: 0-0 Gd: 0-0 GF: 0-0 Fm: 0-1
Distance: 5f/6f: 0-0 7f-8f: 0-0 9f-13f: 0-1 14f+: 0-0
Track : LH: 0-1 RH: 0-0 Tight: 0-1 Gall: 0-0
Aids: Bl: 0-0 Vi: 0-0 Tstrap: 0-0

Gallery Breeze

88(66) (19)66
2-y-o b f Zamindar (USA)-Wantage Park (Pas De Seul)
T D Easterby J F Watson

Placings:042040 (5345)
2001: 6^{0}GF, 5^{4}G, 5^{2}GS, 6^{0}GF, 5^{4}GS, 6^{0}SD

	Starts	1st	2nd	3rd	Win & Pl
Career Total (Turf)	5	0	1	0	1417
Career Total (AW)	1	0	0	0	

Going (Turf): Sf: 0-0 GS: 0-2 Gd: 0-1 GF: 0-2 Fm: 0-0
Distance: 5f/6f: 0-5 7f-8f: 0-1 9f-13f: 0-0 14f+: 0-0
Track : LH: 0-1 RH: 0-0 Tight: 0-0 Gall: 0-0
Aids: Bl: 0-4 Vi: 0-0 Tstrap: 0-0
Best Rating: 66 8/01 Bevl 5f gd-sft

She has demonstrated some ability in maiden company, but has also suggested that she is not giving everything she has.

Gallery God (FR)

111 **108**
5-y-o ch g In The Wings-El Fabulous (FR) (Fabulous Dancer (USA))
G Wragg Takashi Watanabe

Placings:04/0330316/063122-13341 (5734a)
2001: 12^{1}F, 12^{3}G, 14^{3}GF, 14^{4}GF, 12^{1}VS

	Starts	1st	2nd	3rd	Win & Pl
Career Total (Turf)	20	4	2	6	68586

108	11/01	Nant	1m4f		VS	£19399
95	6/01	Thsk	1m4f	C(0-100)H	FRM	£6955
88	6/00	Thsk	1m4f	C(0-100)H	SFT	£7052
82	9/99	Newc	1m4f93y	D(0-80)	G-F	£5181

Total win prize-money £38588

Going (Turf): Sf: 1-4 GS: 0-3 Gd: 0-5 **GF: 1-6 Fm: 1-1**
Distance: 5f/6f: 0-1 7f-8f: 0-1 **9f-13f: 4-15** 14f+: 0-3
Track : **LH: 4-7** RH: 0-11 **Tight: 2-6** Gall: 1-7
Aids: Bl: 0-0 Vi: 0-0 Tstrap: 0-0
Best Rating: 108 11/01 Nant 1m4f v soft

Winner at Thirsk on his reappearance in 2001, staying on strongly, before finishing placed in Ascot's Duke of Edinburgh Handicap for the second year running. Ended the season with a Listed race victory in the French provinces.

Galloway Boy (IRE)

105 **88**
4-y-o ch g Mujtahid (USA)-Supportive (IRE) (Nashamaa)
D Nicholls C P Byrne

Placings:1461040/0300-00200300003000 (5258)
2001: 5^{0}GS, 6^{0}S, 5^{2}S, 6^{0}G, 5^{0}GF, 5^{3}GF, 6^{0}GF, 5^{0}GF, 6^{0}GF, 5^{0}GF, 5^{3}G, 6^{0}G, 5^{0}HY, 5^{0}GS

	Starts	1st	2nd	3rd	Win & Pl
Career Total (Turf)	25	2	1	3	25112

88	7/99	Tipp	5f	G-F	£4125
84	5/99	Navn	5f	Y-S	£4125

Total win prize-money £8250

Going (Turf): Sf: 0-4 GS: 0-2 Gd: 0-4 **GF: 1-9** Fm: 0-1
Distance: **5f/6f: 2-24** 7f-8f: 0-1 9f-13f: 0-0 14f+: 0-0
Track : **LH: 1-2** RH: 0-2 Tight: 0-1 Gall: 0-1
Aids: Bl: 0-2 Vi: 0-1 Tstrap: 0-16
Best Rating: 92 5/01 York 5f gd-fm

An ex-Irish colt and a winner twice over the minimum trip on soft ground. He is now with Dandy Nicholls and has gradually dropped in the weights. Worth watching out for when the ground turns in his favour. Regularly tongue tied.

Galy Bay

91 **46**
3-y-o b f Bin Ajwaad (IRE)-Sylhall (Sharpo)
A Bailey J A Bianchi

Placings:333260-20010 (5539)
2001: 8^{2}HY, 8^{0}G, 6^{0}G, 9^{1}HY, 8^{0}S

	Starts	1st	2nd	3rd	Win & Pl
Career Total (Turf)	11	1	2	3	7077

46	10/01	Ayr	1m1f20y	F	HVY	£2621

Total win prize-money £2622

Going (Turf): Sf: 1-7 GS: 0-1 Gd: 0-3 GF: 0-0 Fm: 0-0
Distance: 5f/6f: 0-3 7f-8f: 0-6 **9f-13f: 1-2** 14f+: 0-0
Track : LH: 0-5 RH: 0-0 Tight: 0-0 Gall: 0-0
Aids: Bl: 0-2 Vi: 0-0 Tstrap: 0-0
Best Rating: 46 10/01 Ayr 1m1f20y heavy

Only career win to date is a seller at Ayr in October. Stays nine furlongs, suited by heavy ground

Game Guru

89(98) (73)**65**
2-y-o b g First Trump-Scarlett Holly (Red Sunset)
T D Barron Mrs J Hazell

Placings:0455630 (5379)
2001: 5^{0}S, 5^{4}SW, 5^{5}SD, 5^{5}GS, 5^{6}HY, 6^{3}SD, 7^{0}S

	Starts	1st	2nd	3rd	Win & Pl
Career Total (Turf)	4	0	0	0	0
Career Total (AW)	3	0	0	1	331

Going (Turf): Sf: 0-3 GS: 0-1 Gd: 0-0 GF: 0-0 Fm: 0-0
Distance: 5f/6f: 0-6 7f-8f: 0-1 9f-13f: 0-0 14f+: 0-0
Track : LH: 0-2 RH: 0-0 Tight: 0-2 Gall: 0-0
Aids: Bl: 0-1 Vi: 0-0 Tstrap: 0-0
Best Rating: 66 4/01 Sthl 5f slow

Game Leader (IRE)

95 **68**
2-y-o b f Mukaddamah (USA)-Fauna (IRE) (Taufan (USA))
D Haydn Jones Kevan R Kynaston

Placings:0221050 (4695)
2001: 5^{0}GS, 5^{2}G, 5^{2}GF, 5^{1}F, 5^{0}GF, 5^{5}GF, 6^{0}GS

	Starts	1st	2nd	3rd	Win & Pl
Career Total (Turf)	7	1	2	0	5143

66	6/01	Bath	5f161y	D	FRM	£3464

Total win prize-money £3465

Going (Turf): Sf: 0-0 GS: 0-2 Gd: 0-1 GF: 0-3 **Fm: 1-1**
Distance: **5f/6f: 1-7** 7f-8f: 0-0 9f-13f: 0-0 14f+: 0-0
Track : **LH: 1-4** RH: 0-0 Tight: 0-0 **Gall: 1-4**
Aids: Bl: 0-0 Vi: 0-0 Tstrap: 0-0
Best Rating: 68 6/01 Asct 5f gd-fm

A rather fortunate winner of a maiden at Bath in early June, where she kicked for home early and just held on by a short head from Torrecilla. Unplaced in the Queen Mary, she finished last after a two-month break on her next run and followed that up with another last place at Doncaster. Suited by five and half furlongs on firm.

Game N Gifted

93 **56**
3-y-o b g Mind Games-Margaret's Gift (Beveled (USA))
B J Meehan Margaret's Partnership

Placings:2150-40000 (5138)
2001: 5^{4}S, 6^{0}S, 7^{0}G, 6^{0}G, 6^{0}G

	Starts	1st	2nd	3rd	Win & Pl
Career Total (Turf)	9	1	1	0	6982

68	6/00	Nott	5f13y	F	G-F	£2488

Total win prize-money £2489

Going (Turf): Sf: 0-2 GS: 0-1 Gd: 0-5 **GF: 1-1** Fm: 0-0
Distance: **5f/6f: 1-7** 7f-8f: 0-2 9f-13f: 0-0 14f+: 0-0
Track : LH: 0-0 RH: 0-1 Tight: 0-0 Gall: 0-0
Aids: Bl: 0-2 Vi: 0-0 Tstrap: 0-1
Best Rating: 79 4/01 Nott 5f13y soft

He got off the mark in a modest Nottingham maiden on his second start at two, but has been running in races he could not possibly win since due to a high handicap mark and needs to drop quite a bit. Acts on fast ground.

Game Pie

54
3-y-o ch f Selkirk (USA)-Pigeon Hole (Green Desert (USA))
R Hannon Lord Carnarvon

Placings:0P (3205)
2001: 6^{0}GF, 7^{P}G

	Starts	1st	2nd	3rd	Win & Pl
Career Total (Turf)	2	0	0	0	

Going (Turf): Sf: 0-0 GS: 0-0 Gd: 0-1 GF: 0-1 Fm: 0-0
Distance: 5f/6f: 0-0 7f-8f: 0-2 9f-13f: 0-0 14f+: 0-0
Track : LH: 0-0 RH: 0-0 Tight: 0-0 Gall: 0-0
Aids: Bl: 0-0 Vi: 0-0 Tstrap: 0-0

Game Time

91(90) (65)**61**
2-y-o b f Atraf-Real Popcorn (IRE) (Jareer (USA))
R Brotherton (A P Jarvis 1/10) Ms Gerardine P O'Reilly

Placings:063441 (5618)
2001: 5^{0}GF, 6^{6}GF, 7^{3}SD, 8^{4}SD, 8^{4}SD, 8^{1}SD

	Starts	1st	2nd	3rd	Win & Pl
Career Total (Turf)	2	0	0	0	0
Career Total (AW)	4	1	0	1	2210

65	11/01	Wolv	1m100y	G(0-65)	STD	£1932

Total win prize-money £1932

Going (Turf): Sf: 0-0 GS: 0-0 Gd: 0-0 GF: 0-2 Fm: 0-0
Distance: 5f/6f: 0-2 7f-8f: 0-1 **9f-13f: 1-3** 14f+: 0-0
Track : **LH: 1-5** RH: 0-0 **Tight: 1-4** Gall: 0-0
Aids: Bl: 0-0 Vi: 0-0 Tstrap: 0-0
Best Rating: 65 11/01 Wolv 1m100y stand

She improved for the step up to a mile and broke her maiden tag in a selling nursery at Wolverhampton.

Game Tufty

91(102) (39)**43**
5-y-o b g Sirgame-Melancolia (Legend Of France (USA))
P Howling Mrs J C Lewis

Placings:0305/054200030310/P0062250532-54100000 (3301)
2001: 12^{5}SW, 12^{4}SD, 11^{1}SD, 11^{0}SD, 9^{0}F, 12^{0}GF, 11^{0}F, 11^{0}GF

	Starts	1st	2nd	3rd	Win & Pl
Career Total (Turf)	25	1	3	3	5937
Career Total (AW)	10	1	1	1	2185

34	2/01	Sthl	1m3f	G	STD	£1372
51	10/99	Wind	1m2f7y	G	SFT	£1913

Total win prize-money £3286

Going (Turf): Sf: 1-5 GS: 0-3 Gd: 0-5 GF: 0-7 Fm: 0-5
Distance: 5f/6f: 0-0 7f-8f: 0-6 **9f-13f: 2-29** 14f+: 0-0
Track : **LH: 1-23** RH: 0-3 **Tight: 1-14** Gall: 0-1
Aids: Bl: 0-0 Vi: 0-0 Tstrap: 0-0
Best Rating: 43 5/01 Leic 1m1f218y firm

Games Mistress

91(78) (39)**54**
2-y-o b f Mind Games-Annaceramic (Horage)
T D Easterby Mrs Susie Dicker

Placings:50000 (3842)
2001: 5^{5}GF, 5^{0}SD, 5^{0}GF, 6^{0}GF, 6^{0}G

	Starts	1st	2nd	3rd	Win & Pl
Career Total (Turf)	4	0	0	0	0
Career Total (AW)	1	0	0	0	

Going (Turf): Sf: 0-0 GS: 0-0 Gd: 0-1 GF: 0-3 Fm: 0-0

Distance: 5f/6f: 0-5 7f-8f: 0-0 9f-13f: 0-0 14f+: 0-0
Track : LH: 0-0 RH: 0-0 Tight: 0-0 Gall: 0-0
Aids: Bl: 0-0 Vi: 0 0 Tstrap: 0-0
Best Rating: 54 5/01 Hayd 5f gd-fm

Gamitas

95(98) (63)**53**
3-y-o b f Dolphin Street (FR)-Driftholme (Safawan)
A P Jarvis St Davids Racing Syndicate 1

Placings:030-33006 **(3565)**
2001: 8^{3}SW, 11^{3}SD, 7^{0}G, 8^{0}GF, 8^{6}GF

	Starts	1st	2nd	3rd	Win & Pl
Career Total (Turf)	4	0	0	0	0
Career Total (AW)	4	0	0	3	1146

Going (Turf): Sf: 0-0 GS: 0-0 Gd: 0-1 GF: 0-3 Fm: 0-0
Distance: 5f/6f: 0-0 7f-8f: 0-4 9f-13f: 0-4 14f+: 0-0
Track : LH: 0-5 RH: 0-0 Tight: 0-2 Gall: 0-0
Aids: Bl: 0-0 Vi: 0-0 Tstrap: 0-0
Best Rating: 57 3/01 Sthl 1m3f stand

Gamut (IRE)

100 **84+**
2-y-o b c Spectrum (IRE)-Greektown (Ela-Mana-Mou)
Sir Michael Stoute Lord Weinstock

Placings:2 **(5604)**
2001: 7^{2}GS

	Starts	1st	2nd	3rd	Win & Pl
Career Total (Turf)	1	0	1	0	1347

Going (Turf): Sf: 0-0 GS: 0-1 Gd: 0-0 GF: 0-0 Fm: 0-0
Distance: 5f/6f: 0-0 7f-8f: 0-1 9f-13f: 0-0 14f+: 0-0
Track : LH: 0-0 RH: 0-0 Tight: 0-0 Gall: 0-0
Aids: Bl: 0-0 Vi: 0-0 Tstrap: 0-0
Best Rating: 84 11/01 NmkR 7f gd-sft

Gandon

99(98) (49)**42**
4-y-o ch g Hernando (FR)-Severine (USA) (Trempolino (USA))
P G Murphy On The Move

Placings:233-10000404130 **(5044)**
2001: 12^{1}SD, 13^{0}SD, 12^{0}SD, 10^{0}GF, 10^{0}GF, 8^{4}SD, 10^{0}GF, 12^{4}GF, 14^{1}SD, 16^{3}GF, 14^{0}SD

	Starts	1st	2nd	3rd	Win & Pl
Career Total (Turf)	8	0	1	3	1998
Career Total (AW)	6	2	0	0	4830

45	8/01	Wolv	1m6f166y	G(0-60)H	STD	£1932
49	3/01	Wolv	1m4f	D	STD	£2898

Total win prize-money £4830

Going (Turf): Sf: 0-0 GS: 0-0 Gd: 0-0 GF: 0-5 Fm: 0-1
Distance: 5f/6f: 0-0 7f-8f: 0-1 9f-13f: 1-8 14f+: 1-4
Track : **LH: 2-11** RH: 0-0 **Tight: 2-6** Gall: 0-0
Aids: Bl: 0-0 Vi: 0-0 Tstrap: 0-0
Best Rating: 49 3/01 Wolv 1m4f stand

Has gained both of his wins so far on the Wolverhampton Fibresand and looks very much a stayer.

Ganesha

87 **54d**
2-y-o b f Magic Ring (IRE)-Breed Reference (Reference Point)
J G Given Mr & Mrs G Calder

Placings:300000 **(4985)**
2001: 6^{3}GF, 5^{0}GF, 6^{0}GS, 6^{0}GF, 5^{0}GS, 6^{0}G

	Starts	1st	2nd	3rd	Win & Pl
Career Total (Turf)	6	0	0	1	506

Going (Turf): Sf: 0-0 GS: 0-2 Gd: 0-1 GF: 0-3 Fm: 0-0
Distance: 5f/6f: 0-3 7f-8f: 0-3 9f-13f: 0-0 14f+: 0-0
Track : LH. 0-0 RH: 0-0 Tight: 0-0 Gall: 0-0
Aids: Bl: 0-0 Vi: 0-0 Tstrap: 0-0
Best Rating: 65 6/01 Nott 6f15y gd-fm

Made a promising debut but has been disappointing since.

Garden Of Eden

95(107) (76+)**64**
3-y-o b f Green Desert (USA)-All The Time (Dancing Brave (USA))
Sir Michael Stoute Capt J Macdonald-Buchanan

Placings:6-201 **(5416)**
2001: 10^{2}GF, 10^{0}G, 9^{1}SD

	Starts	1st	2nd	3rd	Win & Pl
Career Total (Turf)	3	0	1	0	1355
Career Total (AW)	1	1	0	0	3476

76	10/01	Wolv	1m1f79y	E(0-75)H	STD	£3475

Total win prize-money £3476

Going (Turf): Sf: 0-1 GS: 0-0 Gd: 0-1 GF: 0-1 Fm: 0-0
Distance: 5f/6f: 0-0 7f-8f: 0-1 **9f-13f: 1-3** 14f+: 0-0
Track : **LH: 1-2** RH: 0-1 **Tight: 1-3** Gall: 0-0
Aids: Bl: 0-0 Vi: 0-0 Tstrap: 0-0
Best Rating: 76 10/01 Wolv 1m1f79y stand

Ran three times in maiden company on turf before getting off the mark in a handicap on the Wolverhampton Fibresand in October.

Garden Society (IRE)

106 **99**
4-y-o ch c Caerleon (USA)-Eurobird (Ela-Mana-Mou)
J A R Toller Lady Celina Carter

Placings:1336-6300 **(5600)**
2001: 12^{6}GS, 13^{3}G, 18^{0}GS, 16^{0}GS

	Starts	1st	2nd	3rd	Win & Pl
Career Total (Turf)	8	1	0	3	11304

74	5/00	Thsk	1m4f	D	GD	£4257

Total win prize-money £4258

Going (Turf): Sf: 0-0 GS: 0-3 **Gd: 1-2** GF: 0-3 Fm: 0-0
Distance: 5f/6f: 0-0 7f-8f: 0-0 **9f-13f: 1-4** 14f+: 0-4
Track : **LH: 1-5** RH: 0-3 **Tight: 1-2** Gall: 0-6
Aids: Bl: 0-0 Vi: 0-0 Tstrap: 0-0
Best Rating: 99 4/01 Newb 1m4f5y gd-sft

Overfaced at three in conditions events but has progressed physically since then. Ran right up to his best form on seasonal bow, when sixth to Lucido in Group Three at Newbury, and followed that run with a good effort over a mile and five furlongs in a Listed handicap at Chester. Suited by good ground.

Gardor (FR)

92 **57**
3-y-o b g Kendor (FR)-Garboesque (Priolo (USA))
J G Fitzgerald Halewood International Ltd

Placings:44426-0506 **(3939)**
2001: 10^{0}GF, 9^{5}GF, 7^{0}GF, 9^{6}G

	Starts	1st	2nd	3rd	Win & Pl
Career Total (Turf)	9	0	1	0	1979

Going (Turf): Sf: 0-1 GS: 0-0 Gd: 0-3 GF: 0-5 Fm: 0-0
Distance: 5f/6f: 0-1 7f-8f: 0-5 9f-13f: 0-3 14f+: 0-0
Track : LH: 0-3 RH: 0-2 Tight: 0-2 Gall: 0-0
Aids: Bl: 0-0 Vi: 0-0 Tstrap: 0-0
Best Rating: 57 7/01 Muss 1m1f gd-fm

Gardrum (IRE)

102 **51**
3-y-o ch g Lycius (USA)-Kafayef (USA) (Secreto (USA))
Miss L A Perratt David R Sutherland

Placings:L-050016405620000 **(5659)**
2001: 7^{0}S, 8^{5}S, 9^{0}GS, 8^{0}F, 6^{1}F, 7^{6}G, 6^{4}GF, 6^{0}F, 6^{5}GF, 7^{6}GS, 6^{2}GS, 7^{0}GF, 7^{0}GF, 6^{0}HY, 8^{0}G

	Starts	1st	2nd	3rd	Win & Pl
Career Total (Turf)	16	1	1	0	3618

51	6/01	Newc	6f	F(0-60)	FRM	£2478

Total win prize-money £2478

Going (Turf): Sf: 0-4 GS: 0-3 Gd: 0-2 GF: 0-4 **Fm: 1-3**
Distance: **5f/6f: 1-6** 7f-8f: 0-8 9f-13f: 0-2 14f+: 0-0
Track : LH: 0-2 RH: 0-3 Tight: 0-3 Gall: 0-0
Aids: **Bl: 1-10** Vi: 0-0 Tstrap: 0-0
Best Rating: 51 7/01 Haml 6f5y gd-sft

Caused a surprise when scoring in a poor fast ground maiden, but is something of a quirky sort.

Gargoyle Girl

54 **40**
4-y-o b f Be My Chief (USA)-May Hills Legacy (IRE) (Be My Guest (USA))
J S Goldie J S Morrison

Placings:0563000/0644555443-00 **(5663)**
2001: 10^{0}HY, 12^{0}G

	Starts	1st	2nd	3rd	Win & Pl
Career Total (Turf)	19	0	0	2	1543

Going (Turf): Sf: 0-3 GS: 0-3 Gd: 0-6 GF: 0-5 Fm: 0-2
Distance: 5f/6f: 0-2 7f-8f: 0-6 9f-13f: 0-10 14f+: 0-1
Track : LH: 0-12 RH: 0-2 Tight: 0-4 Gall: 0-1
Aids: Bl: 0-0 Vi: 0-0 Tstrap: 0-0
Best Rating: 51 7/01 Haml 6f5y gd-sft

Garnock Valley

96(107) (45)**62**
11-y-o b g Dowsing (USA)-Sunley Sinner (Try My Best (USA))
A Berry Robert Aird

Placings:35230/11003006/330044022066/40000/31610 1500001003/00424050000060/1306020020343/421120 10000021152/164003625201304310-014534466005 40 **(3309)**
2001: 6^{0}SD, 6^{1}SW, 7^{4}SD, 7^{5}SW, 6^{3}SD, 5^{4}S, 6^{4}HY, 6^{6}SD, 6^{6}SD, 6^{0}SD, 7^{0}SD, 7^{5}SD, 8^{4}SD, 8^{0}GS

	Starts	1st	2nd	3rd	Win & Pl
Career Total (Turf)	88	9	9	9	51054
Career Total (AW)	33	7	3	5	20743

60	1/01	Sthl	6f	G	SLW	£1344
62	10/00	Muss	5f	E(0-75)H	SFT	£2779
67	7/00	Sthl	6f	G	STD	£1869
74	1/00	Sthl	6f	E(0-70)H	STD	£3815
66	11/99	Sthl	6f	D(0-85)H	STD	£3343
49	10/99	Newb	5f34y	F(0-65)H	SFT	£4097
62	4/99	Sthl	7f	F(0-60)	STD	£2305
60	2/99	Ling	7f	F(0-60)	STD	£2038
60	2/99	Wolv	6f	F(0-60)	STD	£1678
64	4/98	Muss	5f	E(0-70)H	G-S	£3038
88	10/96	Hayd	6f	C(0-90)H	SFT	£6031
74	6/96	Ayr	5f	D(0-80)H	G-F	£3517
70	5/96	Muss	5f	D(0-75)H	G-S	£4086
62	4/96	Muss	5f	F(0-65)	GD	£2552
87	4/93	Kemp	6f	C(0-90)H	SFT	£4667
81	3/93	Donc	6f	D	G-F	£3348

Total win prize-money £50514

Going (Turf): **Sf: 4-24** GS: 2-14 Gd: 1-19 GF: 2-28 Fm: 0-3
Distance: **5f/6f: 14-90** 7f-8f: 2-31 9f-13f: 0 0 14f+: 0-0
Track : **LH: 7-41** RH: 0-5 **Tight: 2-13** Gall: 0-3
Aids: **Bl: 3-30** Vi: 0-1 Tstrap: 0-0
Best Rating: 60 1/01 Sthl 6f slow

Effective on turf and sand at a modest level, he has won over an easy seven furlongs, but looks suited by shorter.

Garrison (IRE)

98(91) (39)48

3-y-o b f College Chapel-Milain (IRE) (Unfuwain (USA))

Miss L A Perratt Mrs K T McCloskey

Placings:0406305-20500000 **(5273)**

2001: 6^{2}S, 6^{0}GF, 6^{5}F, 6^{0}GF, 6^{0}G, 5^{0}GF, 7^{0}F, 5^{0}HY

	Starts	1st	2nd	3rd	Win & Pl
Career Total (Turf)	13	0	1	1	1432
Career Total (AW)	2	0	0	0	0

Going (Turf): Sf: 0-5 GS: 0-1 Gd: 0-1 GF: 0-3 Fm: 0-3
Distance: 5f/6f: 0-14 7f-8f: 0-1 9f-13f: 0-0 14f+: 0-0
Track : LH: 0-2 RH: 0-1 Tight: 0-2 Gall: 0-1
Aids: Bl: 0-0 Vi: 0-0 Tstrap: 0-0
Best Rating: 54 5/01 Newc 6f soft

Moderate maiden sprinter, ran well on soft ground first time out, and may be best given those conditions.

Garw Valley

90 69

2-y-o b f Mtoto-Morgannwg (IRE) (Simply Great (FR))

A C Stewart Mr K J Mercer & Mrs S Mercer

Placings:0 **(5603)**

2001: 7^{0}GS

	Starts	1st	2nd	3rd	Win & Pl
Career Total (Turf)	1	0	0	0	

Going (Turf): Sf: 0-0 GS: 0-1 Gd: 0-0 GF: 0-0 Fm: 0-0
Distance: 5f/6f: 0-0 7f-8f: 0-1 9f-13f: 0-0 14f+: 0-0
Track : LH: 0-0 RH: 0-0 Tight: 0-0 Gall: 0-0
Aids: Bl: 0-0 Vi: 0-0 Tstrap: 0-0
Best Rating: 69 11/01 NmkR 7f gd-sft

Gascon

101(79) (13)63

5-y-o b g Beveled (USA)-Lady Roxanne (Cyrano De Bergerac)

D J Coakley I E And Mrs K E D'Arcy

Placings:024000-00212610 **(3418)**

2001: 6^{0}SW, 6^{0}HY, 6^{2}G, 5^{1}GF, 6^{2}GF, 6^{6}GF, 6^{1}GF, 6^{0}GF

	Starts	1st	2nd	3rd	Win & Pl
Career Total (Turf)	12	2	3	0	9070
Career Total (AW)	2	0	0	0	

63	7/01	Sals	6f	E(0-70)H	G-F	£3500
56	6/01	Leic	5f218y	G	G-F	£2058

Total win prize-money £5558

Going (Turf): Sf: 0-2 GS: 0-0 Gd: 0-3 **GF: 2-7** Fm: 0-0
Distance: **5f/6f: 2-13** 7f-8f: 0-1 9f-13f: 0-0 14f+: 0-0
Track : LH: 0-4 RH: 0-0 Tight: 0-0 Gall: 0-1
Aids: Bl: 0-0 Vi: 0-0 Tstrap: 0-0
Best Rating: 63 7/01 Sals 6f gd-fm

Gaudi Parc

54

3-y-o ch g King's Signet (USA)-Witch (Risk Me (FR))

J Hetherton Mrs S Watkinson

Placings:00 **(4806)**

2001: 10^{0}GF, 10^{0}F

	Starts	1st	2nd	3rd	Win & Pl
Career Total (Turf)	2	0	0	0	

Going (Turf): Sf: 0-0 GS: 0-0 Gd: 0-0 GF: 0-1 Fm: 0-1
Distance: 5f/6f: 0-0 7f-8f: 0-0 9f-13f: 0-2 14f+: 0-0
Track : LH: 0-2 RH: 0-0 Tight: 0-0 Gall: 0-1
Aids: Bl: 0-0 Vi: 0-0 Tstrap: 0-0

Gavrilov (IRE)

98(88) (60+)73

2-y-o b c Danehill Dancer (IRE)-Elminya (IRE) (Sure Blade (USA))

N A Callaghan M Tabor

Placings:00360 **(4839)**

2001: 6^{0}GF, 6^{0}F, 6^{3}GF, 7^{6}F, 6^{0}G

	Starts	1st	2nd	3rd	Win & Pl
Career Total (Turf)	5	0	0	1	633

Going (Turf): Sf: 0-0 GS: 0-0 Gd: 0-1 GF: 0-2 Fm: 0-2
Distance: 5f/6f: 0-2 7f-8f: 0-3 9f-13f: 0-0 14f+: 0-0
Track : LH: 0-1 RH: 0-0 Tight: 0-1 Gall: 0-0
Aids: Bl: 0-0 Vi: 0-0 Tstrap: 0-0
Best Rating: 73 7/01 Rdcr 7f firm

Cost IR£85,000 as a yearling. Has shown some form in maiden company but should do better next season over further.

Gay Breeze

102(96) (63)68

8-y-o b g Dominion-Judy's Dowry (Dragonara Palace (USA))

P S Felgate E Rollinson

Placings:000/03222115/11122005/63030522445/30350 06000221-**0**60**1**000**0**045000022 **(5671)**

2001: 5^{0}SD, 6^{6}SW, 6^{0}SD, 5^{0}SD, 6^{1}HY, 6^{0}G, 5^{0}F, 7^{0}SD, 6^{0}SD, 6^{0}GF, 6^{4}F, 5^{5}GF, 5^{0}G, 6^{0}GF, 6^{0}SD, 5^{0}HY, 6^{2}G, 6^{2}HY

	Starts	1st	2nd	3rd	Win & Pl
Career Total (Turf)	53	7	10	5	46566
Career Total (AW)	8	0	1	0	740

75	3/01	Nott	6f15y	E(0-70)H	HVY	£3080
64	10/00	Muss	7f30y	E(0-70)H	SFT	£2257
70	6/98	Hayd	5f	D(0-80)H	GD	£3598
60	5/98	Donc	6f	D(0-85)H	G-F	£5127
56	4/98	Nott	6f15y	E(0-70)H	SFT	£3659
48	9/97	Yarm	6f3y	F(0-60)H	FRM	£3249
42	8/97	Leic	5f2y	E(0-70)H	GD	£3275

Total win prize-money £24247

Going (Turf): **Sf: 3-8** GS: 0-8 Gd: 2-15 GF: 1-18 Fm: 1-4
Distance: 5f/6f: 3-51 **7f-8f: 4-9** 9f-13f: 0-1 14f+: 0-0
Track : LH: 0-9 **RH: 1-1 Tight: 1-4** Gall: 0-1
Aids: Bl: 0-0 Vi: 0-0 Tstrap: 0-0
Best Rating: 75 3/01 Nott 6f15y heavy

Won at Nottingham in March, but has looked held since then. Acts on most types of ground and is suited by forcing tactics and sprint trips.

Gay Challenger

88(78) (24)36

3-y-o b g Young Ern-Ship Of Gold (Glint Of Gold)

N A Callaghan N A Callaghan

Placings:5040000-56000006000 **(2726)**

2001: 10^{5}SD, 10^{6}S, 7^{0}GS, 6^{0}GS, 6^{0}G, 6^{0}GF, 7^{0}G, 5^{6}F, 8^{0}GF, 8^{0}GF, 8^{0}GF

	Starts	1st	2nd	3rd	Win & Pl
Career Total (Turf)	16	0	0	0	318
Career Total (AW)	2	0	0	0	0

Going (Turf): Sf: 0-2 GS: 0-3 Gd: 0-5 GF: 0-5 Fm: 0-1
Distance: 5f/6f: 0-3 7f-8f: 0-11 9f-13f: 0-4 14f+: 0-0
Track : LH: 0-5 RH: 0-2 Tight: 0-3 Gall: 0-1
Aids: Bl: 0-2 Vi: 0-0 Tstrap: 0-0
Best Rating: 48 5/01 Gdwd 6f gd-fm

Gay Heroine

108 92d

3-y-o b f Caerleon (USA)-Gay Gallanta (USA) (Woodman (USA))

Sir Michael Stoute Cheveley Park Stud

Placings:2-260223 **(4408)**

2001: 11^{2}GF, 12^{6}GF, 12^{0}GF, 10^{2}GF, 12^{2}GF, 12^{3}GS

	Starts	1st	2nd	3rd	Win & Pl
Career Total (Turf)	7	0	4	1	20742

Going (Turf): Sf: 0-0 GS: 0-1 Gd: 0-0 GF: 0-6 Fm: 0-0
Distance: 5f/6f: 0-0 7f-8f: 0-0 9f-13f: 0-7 14f+: 0-0
Track : LH: 0-4 RH: 0-3 Tight: 0-3 Gall: 0-2
Aids: Bl: 0-0 Vi: 0-1 Tstrap: 0-0
Best Rating: 105 6/01 Epsm 1m4f10y gd-fm

A filly whose dam won the Queen Mary and Cheveley Park, looked to have grown into a nice filly when runner-up to Rockerlong on her reappearance at Chester. Ran sixth in the Oaks at Epsom, but was unplaced in the Ribblesdale and failed to take advantage of easier opportunities afterwards. An under-achiever.

Gay Lover

71 21

4-y-o gr f Environment Friend-Gay Ming (Gay Meadow)

Dr J R J Naylor Mrs S Clifford

Placings:00-0 **(4643)**

2001: 11^{0}GF

	Starts	1st	2nd	3rd	Win & Pl
Career Total (Turf)	3	0	0	0	

Going (Turf): Sf: 0-1 GS: 0-1 Gd: 0-0 GF: 0-1 Fm: 0-0
Distance: 5f/6f: 0-0 7f-8f: 0-0 9f-13f: 0-3 14f+: 0-0
Track : LH: 0-2 RH: 0-1 Tight: 0-3 Gall: 0-0
Aids: Bl: 0-0 Vi: 0-0 Tstrap: 0-0
Best Rating: 10 9/01 Ling 1m3f106y gd-fm

Gaye Latino

65 37

2-y-o ch f Wing Park-Lombard Ships (Orchestra)

P S McEntee M D Queripel

Placings:00 **(3884)**

2001: 6^{0}G, 6^{0}G

	Starts	1st	2nd	3rd	Win & Pl
Career Total (Turf)	2	0	0	0	

Going (Turf): Sf: 0-0 GS: 0-0 Gd: 0-2 GF: 0-0 Fm: 0-0
Distance: 5f/6f: 0-1 7f-8f: 0-1 9f-13f: 0-0 14f+: 0-0
Track : LH: 0-0 RH: 0-0 Tight: 0-0 Gall: 0-0
Aids: Bl: 0-0 Vi: 0-0 Tstrap: 0-0
Best Rating: 37 7/01 Yarm 6f3y good

Gazeila

75 40

2-y-o b f Makbul-Liberatrice (FR) (Assert)

J J Bridger C J Butler

Placings:000 **(5331)**

2001: 6^{0}GF, 8^{0}GS, 5^{0}HY

	Starts	1st	2nd	3rd	Win & Pl
Career Total (Turf)	3	0	0	0	

Going (Turf): Sf: 0-1 GS: 0-1 Gd: 0-0 GF: 0-1 Fm: 0-0
Distance: 5f/6f: 0-2 7f-8f: 0-1 9f-13f: 0-0 14f+: 0-0
Track : LH: 0-0 RH: 0-0 Tight: 0-0 Gall: 0-0
Aids: Bl: 0-0 Vi: 0-0 Tstrap: 0-0
Best Rating: 40 10/01 Ling 5f heavy

Gazette It Tonight

100(91) (47)49

3-y-o b f Merdon Melody-Balidilemma (Balidar)

A Berry Triumph Racing International

Placings:556331331400-0504604100236603 **(5418)**

2001: 7^{0}SD, 9^{5}SD, 8^{0}F, 8^{4}GF, 7^{6}GF, 7^{0}G, 8^{4}GF, 7^{1}GF, 7^{0}GF, 8^{0}GF, 8^{2}F, 7^{3}G, 8^{6}GF, 8^{6}GF, 7^{0}S, 7^{3}SD

	Starts	1st	2nd	3rd	Win & Pl
Career Total (Turf)	23	3	1	4	9557
Career Total (AW)	6	0	0	2	541

47	7/01	Yarm	7f3y	G		G-F	£2023
56	8/00	Thsk	7f	F		G-F	£2975
52	7/00	Catt	7f	G		G-F	£1890

Total win prize-money £6888

Going (Turf): Sf: 0-3 GS: 0-2 Gd: 0-4 **GF: 3-12** Fm: 0-2
Distance: 5f/6f: 0-5 **7f-8f: 3-19** 9f-13f: 0-4 14f+: 0-0
Track : **LH: 2-14** RH: 0-5 **Tight: 2-14** Gall: 0-0
Aids: Bl: 0-0 Vi: 0-0 Tstrap: 0-0
Best Rating: 52 5/01 Haml 1m65y firm

Plating-class filly, best at seven furlongs on fast ground, suited by a sharp track.

Gdansk (IRE)

110 **81**

4-y-o b g Pips Pride-Merry Twinkle (Martinmas)
A Berry Chris & Antonia Deuters

Placings:055/40210040021O-11006005200520106O **(5523)**
2001: 5^{1}HY, 5^{1}GS, 5^{0}GF, 5^{0}GF, 5^{6}GF, 5^{0}G, 5^{0}GF, 6^{5}GF, 6^{2}S, 5^{0}GF, 6^{0}GS, 5^{5}G, 5^{2}HY, 5^{0}G, 5^{1}HY, 5^{0}GS, 5^{6}S, 5^{0}HY

	Starts	1st	2nd	3rd	Win & Pl
Career Total (Turf)	33	5	4	0	36222

81	9/01	Hayd	5f	C(0-90)H		HVY	£9733
74	5/01	Thsk	5f	D(0-85)H		G-S	£4862
59	4/01	Folk	5f	E(0-70)		HVY	£3080
57	9/00	Rdcr	5f	E(0-70)		SFT	£3029
66	6/00	Wwck	5f	D		G-S	£3965

Total win prize-money £24670

Going (Turf): Sf: 3-11 GS: 2-6 Gd: 0-9 GF: 0-7 Fm: 0-0
Distance: **5f/6f: 5-29** 7f-8f: 0-4 9f-13f: 0-0 14f+: 0-0
Track : **LH: 1-10** RH: 0-2 Tight: 0-4 **Gall: 1-3**
Aids: Bl: 0-0 Vi: 0-0 Tstrap: 0-0
Best Rating: 81 9/01 Hayd 5f heavy

Fairly useful sprint handicapper who needs good ground or softer to shine. In great heart earlier this term, landing back-to-back wins at Folkestone and Thirsk in the spring. Regained winning ways at Haydock in the autumn, appreciating the heavy ground.

Gee Bee Boy

91(76)

7-y-o ch g Beveled (USA)-Blue And White (Busted)
G M McCourt Daltagh Construction Ltd

Placings:0/55155540/2023602/**0406**/063-0 **(2035)**
2001: 14^{0}F

	Starts	1st	2nd	3rd	Win & Pl
Career Total (Turf)	19	1	3	2	5974
Career Total (AW)	5	0	0	0	0

68	6/97	Rdcr	1m3f	F(0-65)		GD	£2448

Total win prize-money £2448

Going (Turf): Sf: 0-1 GS: 0-1 **Gd: 1-9** GF: 0-6 Fm: 0-2
Distance: 5f/6f: 0-0 7f-8f: 0-1 **9f-13f: 1-19** 14f+: 0-4
Track : **LH: 1-16** RH: 0-4 **Tight: 1-15** Gall: 0-1
Aids: Bl: 0-0 Vi: 0-0 Tstrap: 0-0
Best Rating: 18 6/01 Nott 1m6f15y firm

Geegee Emmarr

93(81) **45?**

8-y-o b m Rakaposhi King-Fair Sara (Mcindoe)
A Berry Ian & Arthur Bolland

Placings:00503/0**4**0050000/000-0006500 **(1854)**
2001: 12^{0}SW, 6^{0}HY, 6^{0}S, 8^{6}SD, 8^{5}GF, 7^{0}F, 8^{0}GF

	Starts	1st	2nd	3rd	Win & Pl
Career Total (Turf)	16	0	0	1	1536
Career Total (AW)	8	0	0	0	0

Going (Turf): Sf: 0-3 GS: 0-1 Gd: 0-3 GF: 0-7 Fm: 0-2
Distance: 5f/6f: 0-3 7f-8f: 0-12 9f-13f: 0-7 14f+: 0-2
Track : LH: 0-10 RH: 0-6 Tight: 0-3 Gall: 0-3
Aids: Bl: 0-0 Vi: 0-0 Tstrap: 0-0
Best Rating: 45 5/01 Hayd 6f soft

Geespot

84 **44**

2-y-o b f Pursuit Of Love-My Discovery (IRE) (Imperial Frontier (USA))
D J S Ffrench Davis Whataracket Ii Patrick Gallagher

Placings:00500 **(5621)**
2001: 6^{0}GF, 6^{0}GF, 5^{5}HY, 5^{0}G, 5^{0}GS

	Starts	1st	2nd	3rd	Win & Pl
Career Total (Turf)	5	0	0	0	0

Going (Turf): Sf: 0-1 GS: 0-1 Gd: 0-1 GF: 0-2 Fm: 0-0
Distance: 5f/6f: 0-4 7f-8f: 0-1 9f-13f: 0-0 14f+: 0-0
Track : LH: 0-1 RH: 0-0 Tight: 0-0 Gall: 0-1
Aids: Bl: 0-0 Vi: 0-0 Tstrap: 0-0
Best Rating: 44 7/01 Wind 6f gd-fm

Geetee Eightyfive

3-y-o b g Magic Ring (IRE)-Versaillesprincess (Legend Of France (USA))
J J Bridger J J Bridger

Placings:00-0 **(5670)**
2001: 8^{0}HY

	Starts	1st	2nd	3rd	Win & Pl
Career Total (Turf)	3	0	0	0	

Going (Turf): Sf: 0-1 GS: 0-1 Gd: 0-0 GF: 0-1 Fm: 0-0
Distance: 5f/6f: 0-2 7f-8f: 0-0 9f-13f: 0-1 14f+: 0-0
Track : LH: 0-0 RH: 0-1 Tight: 0-1 Gall: 0-0
Aids: Bl: 0-0 Vi: 0-0 Tstrap: 0-0

Gem Bien (USA)

105 **78**

3-y-o b c Bien Bien (USA)-Eastern Gem (USA) (Jade Hunter (USA))
Andrew Turnell Mrs Claire Hollowood

Placings:501-23005100 **(4328)**
2001: 8^{2}GS, 8^{3}S, 7^{0}GF, 8^{0}GF, 8^{5}GF, 8^{1}GF, 8^{0}GS, 10^{0}GF

	Starts	1st	2nd	3rd	Win & Pl
Career Total (Turf)	11	2	1	1	11952

78	7/01	Nott	1m54y	D(0-85)H		G-F	£7182
71	10/00	Muss	7f30y	E		SFT	£2842

Total win prize-money £10025

Going (Turf): Sf: 1-3 GS: 0-3 Gd: 0-0 **GF: 1-5** Fm: 0-0
Distance: 5f/6f: 0-2 7f-8f: 1-5 9f-13f: 1-4 14f+: 0-0
Track : LH: 1-5 RH: 1-3 **Tight: 1-4** Gall: 0-2
Aids: Bl: 0-0 Vi: 0-0 Tstrap: 0-1
Best Rating: 81 5/01 Newc 1m soft

Has shown signs of temperament in the past, but won a Nottingham handicap in July. A mile is as far as he wants.

Gemtastic

101(100) (69)**55**

3-y-o b f Tagula (IRE)-It's So Easy (Shaadi (USA))
P D Evans Www.Gem Carpets.Co.Uk

Placings:603320**2251222**-0004**6**04334101000 **(3627)**
2001: 6^{0}SD, 6^{0}SW, 6^{0}SW, 6^{4}SD, 6^{6}SD, 5^{0}F, 5^{4}F, 6^{3}GF, 6^{3}F, 5^{4}G, 6^{1}GF, 7^{0}GF, 6^{1}GF, 5^{0}G, 6^{0}GF, 5^{0}GF

	Starts	1st	2nd	3rd	Win & Pl
Career Total (Turf)	17	2	1	4	8337
Career Total (AW)	12	1	5	0	6201

55	7/01	Sthl	6f	E(0-70)H		G-F	£3542
54	6/01	Wwck	6f21y	F(0-65)H		G-F	£2506
60	11/00	Ling	5f	D		STD	£2717

Total win prize-money £8765

Going (Turf): Sf: 0-1 GS: 0-2 Gd: 0-3 **GF: 2-8** Fm: 0-3
Distance: **5f/6f: 2-26** 7f-8f: 1-3 9f-13f: 0-0 14f+: 0-0
Track : **LH: 2-21** RH: 0-1 **Tight: 1-15** Gall: 0-4
Aids: Bl: 0-0 Vi: 0-0 Tstrap: 0-0
Best Rating: 59 4/01 Ling 6f stand

Ran well at two but only managed to score once on the All-Weather over five furlongs. Acts on fast ground. Winner of two six furlong handicaps in June and July of 2001. Six furlongs looks her trip now.

General

98 **66**

4-y-o b g Cadeaux Genereux-Bareilly (USA) (Lyphard (USA))
Mrs N Smith Tony Hayward

Placings:0642 **(5083)**
2001: 10^{0}GF, 10^{6}G, 10^{4}GF, 7^{2}S

	Starts	1st	2nd	3rd	Win & Pl
Career Total (Turf)	4	0	1	0	1192

Going (Turf): Sf: 0-1 GS: 0-0 Gd: 0-1 GF: 0-2 Fm: 0-0
Distance: 5f/6f: 0-0 7f-8f: 0-1 9f-13f: 0-3 14f+: 0-0
Track : LH: 0-2 RH: 0-1 Tight: 0-2 Gall: 0-0
Aids: Bl: 0-0 Vi: 0-0 Tstrap: 0-0
Best Rating: 66 10/01 Brig 7f214y soft

Started life in bumpers, he showed signs of ability in his few flat races.

General Amnesty (IRE)

93(86) (65)**49**

2-y-o b c General Monash (USA)-Beautyofthepeace (IRE) (Exactly Sharp (USA))
D Shaw G E Griffiths

Placings:050000 **(5628)**
2001: 6^{0}GF, 6^{5}SD, 6^{0}SD, 6^{0}GS, 8^{0}S, 8^{0}G

	Starts	1st	2nd	3rd	Win & Pl
Career Total (Turf)	4	0	0	0	
Career Total (AW)	2	0	0	0	0

Going (Turf): Sf: 0-1 GS: 0-1 Gd: 0-1 GF: 0-1 Fm: 0-0
Distance: 5f/6f: 0-4 7f-8f: 0-1 9f-13f: 0-1 14f+: 0-0
Track : LH: 0-5 RH: 0-0 Tight: 0-1 Gall: 0-0
Aids: Bl: 0-0 Vi: 0-0 Tstrap: 0-0
Best Rating: 65 6/01 Wolv 6f stand

General Dominion

55

4-y-o b g Governor General-Innocent Princess (NZ) (Full On Aces (AUS))
F P Murtagh T Mattinson

Placings:006400-U **(3692)**
2001: 7^{U}G

	Starts	1st	2nd	3rd	Win & Pl
Career Total (Turf)	7	0	0	0	0

Going (Turf): Sf: 0-1 GS: 0-2 Gd: 0-2 GF: 0-2 Fm: 0-0
Distance: 5f/6f: 0-3 7f-8f: 0-2 9f-13f: 0-2 14f+: 0-0
Track : LH: 0-3 RH: 0-2 Tight: 0-4 Gall: 0-1
Aids: Bl: 0-0 Vi: 0-0 Tstrap: 0-0

General Haven

95 **25**

8-y-o ch g Hadeer-Verchinina (Star Appeal)
J S Wainwright T W Heseltine

Placings:00/32313435514402 2/214024030060/000000

006 (4440)
2001: 14^{0}F, 11^{0}GF, 10^{0}GF, 10^{0}GF, 12^{0}GS, 10^{0}GF, 16^{0}GS, 17^{0}GF, 11^{6}G

	Starts	1st	2nd	3rd	Win & Pl
Career Total (Turf)	23	1	1	2	6345
Career Total (AW)	15	2	4	3	10484

79 1/97 Ling 1m4f E(0-70)H STD £2869
69 7/96 Wind 1m67y E(0-70)H GD £3273
56 3/96 Ling 7f F STD £2540
Total win prize-money £8684

Going (Turf): Sf: 0-0 GS: 0-4 **Gd: 1-5** GF: 0-11 Fm: 0-3
Distance: 5f/6f: 0-4 7f-8f: 1-5 **9f-13f: 2-25** 14f+: 0-4
Track : **LH: 2-26** RH: 1-10 **Tight: 3-21** Gall: 0-3
Aids: Bl: 0-3 Vi: 0-1 Tstrap: 0-0
Best Rating: 29 6/01 Newc 1m2f32y gd-fm

General Hawk (IRE)

108(96) (58)**60**
3-y-o b g Distinctly North (USA)-Sabev (USA) (Saber Thrust (CAN))
R A Fahey J E M Hawkins Ltd

Placings:3-0000512440 **(5375)**
2001: 7^{0}SD, 5^{0}GS, 6^{0}F, 6^{0}GF, 6^{5}GF, 7^{1}GF, 7^{2}GF, 8^{4}GF, 7^{4}SD, 7^{0}G

	Starts	1st	2nd	3rd	Win & Pl
Career Total (Turf)	9	1	1	1	5161
Career Total (AW)	2	0	0	0	316

56 7/01 Newc 7f F(0-65)H G-F £2751
Total win prize-money £2751

Going (Turf): Sf: 0-0 GS: 0-1 Gd: 0-2 **GF: 1-5** Fm: 0-1
Distance: 5f/6f: 0-5 **7f-8f: 1-6** 9f-13f: 0-0 14f+: 0-0
Track : LH: 0-2 RH: 0-0 Tight: 0-1 Gall: 0-0
Aids: Bl: 0-0 Vi: 0-0 Tstrap: 0-0
Best Rating: 60 8/01 Rdcr 1m gd-fm

He got off the mark in a seven-furlong handicap on fast ground at Newcastle in July, and has continued to run well in competitive handicaps since then, although finding a few too good in the process.

General Jackson

101 **55**
4-y-o ch g Cadeaux Genereux-Moidart (Electric)
Jane Southcombe Vivant & V R V Partnership

Placings:04300-0042020 **(4843)**
2001: 10^{0}G, 11^{0}F, 17^{4}G, 18^{2}GF, 21^{0}GF, 16^{2}G, 16^{0}G

	Starts	1st	2nd	3rd	Win & Pl
Career Total (Turf)	12	0	2	1	3305

Going (Turf): Sf: 0-2 GS: 0-1 Gd: 0-4 GF: 0-4 Fm: 0-1
Distance: 5f/6f: 0-0 7f-8f: 0-2 9f-13f: 0-5 14f+: 0-5
Track : LH: 0-4 RH: 0-5 Tight: 0-3 Gall: 0-0
Aids: Bl: 0-0 Vi: 0-0 Tstrap: 0-0
Best Rating: 55 9/01 Kemp 2m good

General Jane

76 **14**
3-y-o ch f Be My Chief (USA)-Brave Advance (USA) (Bold Laddie (USA))
B R Millman Miss Jane Collier

Placings:30-06 **(2739)**
2001: 6^{0}GF, 8^{6}GF

	Starts	1st	2nd	3rd	Win & Pl
Career Total (Turf)	4	0	0	1	547

Going (Turf): Sf: 0-1 GS: 0-1 Gd: 0-0 GF: 0-2 Fm: 0-0
Distance: 5f/6f: 0-2 7f-8f: 0-1 9f-13f: 0-1 14f+: 0-0
Track : LH: 0-1 RH: 0-0 Tight: 0-0 Gall: 0-1
Aids: Bl: 0-0 Vi: 0-0 Tstrap: 0-0
Best Rating: 14 6/01 Sals 6f212y gd-fm

General Smith

(87) (59)
2-y-o b c Greensmith-Second Call (Kind Of Hush)
J M Bradley D Holmes

Placings:03 **(5614)**
2001: 6^{0}SD, 6^{3}SD

	Starts	1st	2nd	3rd	Win & Pl
Career Total (Turf)	0	0	0	0	
Career Total (AW)	2	0	0	1	424

Going (Turf): Sf: 0-0 GS: 0-0 Gd: 0-0 GF: 0-0 Fm: 0-0
Distance: 5f/6f: 0-2 7f-8f: 0-0 9f-13f: 0-0 14f+: 0-0
Track : LH: 0-2 RH: 0-0 Tight: 0-1 Gall: 0-0
Aids: Bl: 0-0 Vi: 0-0 Tstrap: 0-0
Best Rating: 59 11/01 Wolv 6f stand

Generate

(107) (53)**59**
5-y-o b m Generous (IRE)-Ivorine (USA) (Blushing Groom (FR))
M J Polglase Dominic Racing

Placings:5000/**1**63**1**02**1**5-000 **(0754)**
2001: 11^{0}SD, 13^{0}S, 12^{0}SW

	Starts	1st	2nd	3rd	Win & Pl
Career Total (Turf)	9	1	1	1	5622
Career Total (AW)	6	2	0	0	5019

59 6/00 Pont 1m2f6y F(0-70)H SFT £3360
53 5/00 Sthl 1m3f F(0-65)H STD £2289
41 2/00 Wolv 1m1f79y D STD £2730
Total win prize-money £8380

Going (Turf): Sf: 1-4 GS: 0-0 Gd: 0-0 GF: 0-1 Fm: 0-0
Distance: 5f/6f: 0-0 7f-8f: 0-1 **9f-13f: 3-10** 14f+: 0-0
Track : **LH: 3-8** RH: 0-3 **Tight: 1-3** Gall: 0-1
Aids: Bl: 0-0 Vi: 0-0 Tstrap: 0-0
Best Rating: 33 3/01 Sthl 1m3f stand

Generous Diana

104 **83**
5-y-o ch m Generous (IRE)-Lypharitissima (FR) (Lightning (FR))
C G Cox Elite Racing Club

Placings:4221/2110-0030 **(5693)**
2001: 10^{0}HY, 10^{0}GS, 12^{3}GS, 12^{0}S

	Starts	1st	2nd	3rd	Win & Pl
Career Total (Turf)	12	3	3	1	23253

70 11/00 Donc 1m2f60y C HVY £7020
78 10/00 Yarm 1m2f21y C(0-85) SFT £6597
63 10/99 Ling 1m1f D SFT £3708
Total win prize-money £17327

Going (Turf): Sf: 3-7 GS: 0-2 Gd: 0-1 GF: 0-2 Fm: 0-0
Distance: 5f/6f: 0-0 7f-8f: 0-3 **9f-13f: 3-9** 14f+: 0-0
Track : **LH: 3-9** RH: 0-1 **Tight: 2-5** Gall: 1-3
Aids: Bl: 0-0 Vi: 0-0 Tstrap: 0-2
Best Rating: 83 11/01 NmkR 1m4f gd-sft

Unraced at two, she gradually improved last season when with Henry Cecil and ended the campaign with victories in soft-ground events at Yarmouth and Doncaster, but was well beaten when tried in Listed company. Now with Clive Cox and only lightly-raced in 2001. Best over ten furlongs.

Generous Ways

104(101) (62)**57**
6-y-o ch g Generous (IRE)-Clara Bow (USA) (Coastal (USA))
E J Alston Honest Traders

Placings:0535130/00350103550/405401022632-020 **(2764)**
2001: 13^{0}GF, 16^{2}GF, 16^{0}GF

	Starts	1st	2nd	3rd	Win & Pl
Career Total (Turf)	30	3	3	4	24638
Career Total (AW)	3	0	1	1	1365

59 6/00 Asct 2m45y D(0-80)H G-F £7085
62 6/99 Asct 2m45y D(0-80)H G-F £5888
70 8/98 Rdcr 1m6f19y E(0-70)H G-F £3120
Total win prize-money £16093

Going (Turf): Sf: 0-1 GS: 0-3 Gd: 0-7 **GF: 3-17** Fm: 0-2
Distance: 5f/6f: 0-0 7f-8f: 0-0 9f-13f: 0-7 **14f+: 3-26**
Track : LH: 1-16 **RH: 2-15** Tight: 1-12 **Gall: 2-11**
Aids: Bl: 0-1 Vi: 0-0 Tstrap: 0-0
Best Rating: 57 6/01 Asct 2m45y gd-fm

Rather inconsistent, but capable on his day. His only wins since 1998 came in the same race over two miles at Ascot in 1999 and 2000 and he finished runner-up this season. Suited by fast ground

Genial Genie

105(103) (71)**70**
5-y-o b g Sizzling Melody-Needwood Sprite (Joshua)
R Hollinshead Tim Leadbeater

Placings:33640600302141012302**4** **(5688)**
2001: 7^{3}SD, 9^{3}SD, 7^{6}SD, 7^{4}SD, 8^{0}SW, 8^{6}SD, 8^{0}GF, 9^{0}G, 7^{3}F, 8^{0}GF, 6^{2}GF, 6^{1}F, 6^{4}G, 5^{1}GF, 6^{0}GF, 7^{1}G, 7^{2}G, 7^{3}S, 7^{0}S, 7^{2}G, 7^{4}S

	Starts	1st	2nd	3rd	Win & Pl
Career Total (Turf)	15	3	3	2	17401
Career Total (AW)	6	0	0	2	840

61 9/01 Chep 7f16y F(0-65)H GD £2492
60 8/01 Pont 5f F(0-65)H G-F £4699
53 8/01 Thsk 6f E(0-70)H FRM £4364
Total win prize-money £11557

Going (Turf): Sf: 0-3 GS: 0-0 **Gd: 1-5 GF: 1-5 Fm: 1-2**
Distance: **5f/6f: 2-5** 7f-8f: 1-13 9f-13f: 0-3 14f+: 0-0
Track : **LH: 1-11** RH: 0-3 Tight: 0-8 Gall: 0-0
Aids: Bl: 0-0 Vi: 0-0 **Tstrap: 3-21**
Best Rating: 70 11/01 Catt 7f good

He took his time in getting off the mark, but had shown ability before winning a maiden handicap over six furlongs at Thirsk in August. Has since added victories at Pontefract and Chepstow, although he has looked in the grasp of the handicapper since then. Is effective from a stiff five to seven furlongs. Suited by fast ground. Gained his first victory on sand at Southwell in November.

Genie

20
3-y-o ch f Cool Jazz-Spice And Sugar (Chilibang)
J S Moore Miss Sally Thomas

Placings:6 **(5664)**
2001: 8^{6}HY

	Starts	1st	2nd	3rd	Win & Pl
Career Total (Turf)	1	0	0	0	0

Going (Turf): Sf: 0-1 GS: 0-0 Gd: 0-0 GF: 0-0 Fm: 0-0
Distance: 5f/6f: 0-0 7f-8f: 0-0 9f-13f: 0-1 14f+: 0-0
Track : LH: 0-0 RH: 0-1 Tight: 0-1 Gall: 0-0
Aids: Bl: 0-0 Vi: 0-0 Tstrap: 0-0
Best Rating: 20 11/01 Wind 1m67y heavy

Genius (IRE)

(94) (39)**30**
6-y-o b g Lycius (USA)-Once In My Life (IRE) (Lomond (USA))
A G Juckes A C W Price

Placings:600040/21104053005600003/00160000000 40/220040500-0 **(0048)**
2001: 12^{0}SD

	Starts	1st	2nd	3rd	Win & Pl
Career Total (Turf)	19	0	0	1	458
Career Total (AW)	29	3	3	1	10681

68 2/99 Ling 1m F(0-65)H STD £1717
73 2/98 Ling 1m D(0-80)H SLW £3420
66 2/98 Ling 1m E(0-70)H SLW £2818
Total win prize-money £7957

Going (Turf): Sf: 0-3 **GS: 0-3** Gd: 0-7 GF: 0-6 Fm: 0-0
Distance: 5f/6f: 0-2 **7f-8f: 3-31** 9f-13f: 0-15 14f+: 0-0
Track : **LH: 3-37** RH: 0-5 **Tight: 3-25** Gall: 0-2
Aids: Bl: 0-1 Vi: 0-0 Tstrap: 0-0
Best Rating: 66 2/98 Ling 1m SW

Genscher

93 **27**
5-y-o b g Cadeaux Genereux-Marienbad (FR) (Darshaan)
R Allan Robert Miller-Bakewell

Placings:00/341460/0-000 **(4440)**
2001: 12^{0}GF, 13^{0}GS, 11^{0}G

	Starts	1st	2nd	3rd	Win & Pl
Career Total (Turf)	12	1	0	1	5249

53 9/99 Haml 1m4f17y F(0-60)H G-F £4005
Total win prize-money £4005

Going (Turf): Sf: 0-3 GS: 0-2 Gd: 0-3 **GF: 1-4** Fm: 0-0
Distance: 5f/6f: 0-0 7f-8f: 0-2 **9f-13f: 1-9** 14f+: 0-1
Track : LH: 0-3 **RH: 1-7 Tight: 1-8** Gall: 0-1
Aids: Bl: 0-0 Vi: 0-1 Tstrap: 0-0
Best Rating: 27 6/01 Haml 1m4f17y gd-fm

Gentle Magic

84 **50**
3-y-o b f Magic Ring (IRE)-Gentle Stream (Sandy Creek)
H Akbary & Mrs Kit Dudley

Placings:0-000 **(4677)**
2001: 9^{0}GF, 7^{0}GF, 7^{0}G

	Starts	1st	2nd	3rd	Win & Pl
Career Total (Turf)	4	0	0	0	

Going (Turf): Sf: 0-1 GS: 0-0 Gd: 0-1 GF: 0-2 Fm: 0-0
Distance: 5f/6f: 0-1 7f-8f: 0-2 9f-13f: 0-1 14f+: 0-0
Track : LH: 0-0 RH: 0-1 Tight: 0-1 Gall: 0-0
Aids: Bl: 0-0 Vi: 0-0 Tstrap: 0-0
Best Rating: 50 5/01 Gdwd 1m1f gd-fm

Gentleman Venture

113 **90**
5-y-o b g Polar Falcon (USA)-Our Shirley (Shirley Heights)
J Akehurst Canisbay Bloodstock Ltd

Placings:310340000/36425513062-136 **(2010)**
2001: 10^{1}S, 10^{3}S, 12^{6}GF

	Starts	1st	2nd	3rd	Win & Pl
Career Total (Turf)	23	3	2	5	56450

89 4/01 Kemp 1m2f B(0-105)H SFT £23200
85 8/00 Epsm 1m4f10y D(0-85)H GD £7052
73 5/99 Rdcr 1m2f D SFT £3015
Total win prize-money £33268

Going (Turf): Sf: 2-6 GS: 0-4 Gd: 1-6 GF: 0-7 Fm: 0-0
Distance: 5f/6f: 0-0 7f-8f: 0-1 **9f-13f: 3-22** 14f+: 0-0
Track : **LH: 2-13** RH: 1-9 **Tight: 2-9** Gall: 1-11
Aids: Bl: 0-0 Vi: 0-0 Tstrap: 0-0
Best Rating: 90 6/01 Epsm 1m4f10y gd-fm

Effective at ten to 12 furlongs, appreciates cut in the ground. Difficult to pass when in front, he was a game winner of the Rosebery at Kempton this season and ran well under his penalty to finish third in the City And Suburban.

Genuine John (IRE)

94(101) (37)**32**
8-y-o b g High Estate-Fiscal Folly (USA) (Foolish Pleasure (USA))
J Parkes Mrs G M Z Spink

Placings:0565006/36002033065023**0/03522**143000350 0000**0050/33234**1155**2**015**0**350**5**0/**00**410050003**0063/3** **2**4505300000**0-14245**4 **(4901)**
2001: 11^{1}SD, 11^{4}SW, 11^{2}SD, 16^{4}SD, 16^{5}SD, 11^{4}G

	Starts	1st	2nd	3rd	Win & Pl
Career Total (Turf)	62	4	2	8	15448
Career Total (AW)	35	2	6	7	10904

37 1/01 Sthl 1m3f G(0-65)H STD £1456
52 4/99 Bevl 1m100y G G-F £2164
59 7/98 Ripn 1m E G-F £2600
50 5/98 Haml 1m65y E(0-70)H GD £3501
48 5/98 Muss 1m F(0-60)H GD £3096
64 3/97 Sthl 7f D(0-80)H STD £3371
Total win prize-money £16189

Going (Turf): Sf: 0-5 GS: 0-5 **Gd: 2-12 GF: 2-22** Fm: 0-6
Distance: 5f/6f: 0-2 7f-8f: 3-41 9f-13f: 3-45 14f+: 0-2
Track : LH: 2-49 **RH: 4-33 Tight: 3-30** Gall: 0-7
Aids: Bl: 0-15 Vi: 0-0 **Tstrap: 1-9**
Best Rating: 37 2/01 Sthl 2m stand

He has more ability on sand than on turf, but does not win very often despite being kept very busy

George Romney (USA)

94 **70**
2-y-o b c Distant View (USA)-Polish Socialite (USA) (Polish Navy (USA))
P F I Cole Richard Green (fine Paintings)

Placings:63 **(5289)**
2001: 7^{6}HY, 7^{3}S

	Starts	1st	2nd	3rd	Win & Pl
Career Total (Turf)	2	0	0	1	632

Going (Turf): Sf: 0-2 GS: 0-0 Gd: 0-0 GF: 0-0 Fm: 0-0
Distance: 5f/6f: 0-0 7f-8f: 0-2 9f-13f: 0-0 14f+: 0-0
Track : LH: 0-1 RH: 0-0 Tight: 0-0 Gall: 0-0
Aids: Bl: 0-0 Vi: 0-0 Tstrap: 0-0
Best Rating: 70 10/01 Leic 7f9y soft

Improved from his debut to make the frame at Leicester on his second start and again on Polytrack at Lingfield in November. Looks to need at least a mile.

George Street (IRE)

94 **57**
3-y-o b c Danehill (USA)-Sweet Justice (Law Society (USA))
J H M Gosden P G & J M Maher

Placings:000620 **(5330)**
2001: 8^{0}GF, 7^{0}GF, 8^{0}GF, 10^{6}G, 11^{2}G, 16^{0}HY

	Starts	1st	2nd	3rd	Win & Pl
Career Total (Turf)	6	0	1	0	1480

Going (Turf): Sf: 0-1 GS: 0-0 Gd: 0-2 GF: 0-3 Fm: 0-0
Distance: 5f/6f: 0-0 7f-8f: 0-2 9f-13f: 0-3 14f+: 0-1
Track : LH: 0-2 RH: 0-4 Tight: 0-4 Gall: 0-0
Aids: Bl: 0-3 Vi: 0-2 Tstrap: 0-0
Best Rating: 61 6/01 Gdwd 1m gd-fm

George Stubbs (USA)

102(102) (64)**83**
3-y-o b/br g Affirmed (USA)-Mia Duchessa (USA) (Nijinsky (CAN))
P F I Cole Richard Green (fine Paintings)

Placings:4-**31**3140 (5366)
2001: 7^{3}SD, 8^{1}SW, 9^{3}G, 10^{1}G, 9^{4}GF, 8^{0}GS

	Starts	1st	2nd	3rd	Win & Pl
Career Total (Turf)	5	1	0	1	5618
Career Total (AW)	2	1	0	1	3131

82 5/01 Bath 1m2f46y D(0-80) GD £3766
64 4/01 Sthl 1m D SLW £2779
Total win prize-money £6546

Going (Turf): Sf: 0-1 GS: 0-1 **Gd: 1-2** GF: 0-1 Fm: 0-0
Distance: 5f/6f: 0-0 7f-8f: 1-4 9f-13f: 1-3 14f+: 0-0
Track : **LH: 2-3** RH: 0-2 **Tight: 1-2** Gall: 0-0
Aids: Bl: 0-0 Vi: 0-0 Tstrap: 0-0
Best Rating: 83 7/01 Gdwd 1m1f192y gd-fm

A winner on the Southwell Fibresand in April and on turf at Bath in May, he has won his races by dominating from the front. Suited by ten furlongs.

Geri Roulette

92 **39**
3-y-o b f Perpendicular-Clashfern (Smackover)
E J Alston Ellison Racing

Placings:06406 **(5269)**
2001: 6^{0}GF, 7^{6}G, 10^{4}G, 10^{0}GF, 10^{6}HY

	Starts	1st	2nd	3rd	Win & Pl
Career Total (Turf)	5	0	0	0	266

Going (Turf): Sf: 0-1 GS: 0-0 Gd: 0-2 GF: 0-2 Fm: 0-0
Distance: 5f/6f: 0-1 7f-8f: 0-1 9f-13f: 0-3 14f+: 0-0
Track : LH: 0-3 RH: 0-1 Tight: 0-3 Gall: 0-0
Aids: Bl: 0-0 Vi: 0-0 Tstrap: 0-0
Best Rating: 41 7/01 Ches 7f122y good

Geronimo

101(100) (47)**53**
4-y-o b g Efisio-Apache Squaw (Be My Guest (USA))
M Wigham Michael Wigham

Placings:0/216**660B0-0002061**240 **(5560)**
2001: 7^{0}SD, 10^{0}SD, 6^{0}SD, 8^{2}SW, 8^{0}SD, 7^{6}SD, 6^{1}G, 6^{2}G, 6^{4}G, 7^{0}S

	Starts	1st	2nd	3rd	Win & Pl
Career Total (Turf)	5	1	1	0	4486
Career Total (AW)	14	1	2	0	4103

49 8/01 Rdcr 6f F(0-60)H GD £3710
71 7/00 Wolv 6f D STD £2765
Total win prize-money £6476

Going (Turf): Sf: 0-1 GS: 0-0 **Gd: 1-4** GF: 0-0 Fm: 0-0
Distance: **5f/6f: 2-7** 7f-8f: 0-7 9f-13f: 0-5 14f+: 0-0
Track : **LH: 1-14** RH: 0-1 **Tight: 1-12** Gall: 0-0
Aids: Bl: 0-1 Vi: 0-0 Tstrap: 0-0
Best Rating: 53 8/01 Newc 6f good

He returned from a four-month break to win at Redcar in August, only his second-ever outing on turf, and has continued to run well since. Suited by six furlongs and has done most of his racing until recently on sand.

Get Stuck In (IRE)

111 **89**
5-y-o b g Up And At 'Em-Shoka (FR) (Kaldoun (FR))
Miss L A Perratt David R Sutherland

Placings:52325022222/3004412651200140/060544000 230031-244002520000 **(5258)**
2001: 5^{2}GS, 5^{4}S, 6^{4}G, 5^{0}GF, 5^{0}GF, 5^{2}GF, 6^{5}S, 5^{2}GS, 5^{0}GF, 6^{0}GF, 5^{0}S, 5^{0}GS

	Starts	1st	2nd	3rd	Win & Pl
Career Total (Turf)	54	4	13	4	72178

83 11/00 Donc 5f D(0-80)H HVY £4485
85 10/99 York 6f C(0-100)H SFT £23150
75 8/99 Ripn 6f D(0-80)H GD £4185
68 6/99 Haml 6f5y E(0-70) GD £3485
Total win prize-money £35305

Going (Turf): Sf: 2-14 GS: 0-6 **Gd: 2-18** GF: 0-12 Fm: 0-4
Distance: **5f/6f: 3-50** 7f-8f: 1-4 9f-13f: 0-0 14f+: 0-0

Track : LH: 0-4 RH: 0-1 Tight: 0-3 Gall: 0-1
Aids: Bl: 0-1 Vi: 0-0 Tstrap: 0-0
Best Rating: 89 7/01 Ayr 5f gd-sft

A very capable front-running sprint handicapper, he is equally effective over five and six furlongs. Must have cut in the ground to show his best, but is a shade high in the handicap at present.

Getatem (IRE)

97 **70d**
2-y-o b c Up And At 'Em-Fiaba (Precocious)
Miss L A Perratt David R Sutherland

Placings:32555420000 **(5660)**
2001: 5^{3}GF, 5^{2}GF, 5^{5}GF, 5^{5}F, 5^{5}GS, 5^{4}GF, 5^{2}GF, 6^{0}GF, 6^{0}HY, 6^{0}S, 5^{0}G

	Starts	1st	2nd	3rd	Win & Pl
Career Total (Turf)	11	0	2	1	3605

Going (Turf): Sf: 0-2 GS: 0-1 Gd: 0-1 GF: 0-6 Fm: 0-1
Distance: 5f/6f: 0-11 7f-8f: 0-0 9f-13f: 0-0 14f+: 0-0
Track : LH: 0-0 RH: 0-0 Tight: 0-0 Gall: 0-0
Aids: Bl: 0-0 Vi: 0-0 Tstrap: 0-0
Best Rating: 70 8/01 Bevl 5f gd-fm

Has been running with credit over five furlongs on fast ground without managing to get his head in front. Below form on only attempt on easy ground.

Geyserville

80(74) (24)**54**
3-y-o ch g Mujtahid (USA)-Pennsylvania (USA) (Northjet)
Brendan W Duke (P W D'Arcy 11/6) Brendan W Duke Racing

Placings:0000 **(5617)**
2001: 8^{0}GF, 8^{0}GF, 8^{0}HY, 8^{0}SD

	Starts	1st	2nd	3rd	Win & Pl
Career Total (Turf)	3	0	0	0	
Career Total (AW)	1	0	0	0	

Going (Turf): Sf: 0-1 GS: 0-0 Gd: 0-0 GF: 0-2 Fm: 0-0
Distance: 5f/6f: 0-0 7f-8f: 0-1 9f-13f: 0-3 14f+: 0-0
Track : LH: 0-3 RH: 0-0 Tight: 0-1 Gall: 0-0
Aids: Bl: 0-0 Vi: 0-0 Tstrap: 0-0
Best Rating: 54 6/01 NmkR 1m gd-fm

Gezkat

79 **45**
2-y-o b f Petong-Petite Louie (Chilibang)
S C Williams Chris Wright

Placings:006 **(5363)**
2001: 6^{0}GF, 6^{0}G, 7^{6}GS

	Starts	1st	2nd	3rd	Win & Pl
Career Total (Turf)	3	0	0	0	210

Going (Turf): Sf: 0-0 GS: 0-1 Gd: 0-1 GF: 0-1 Fm: 0-0
Distance: 5f/6f: 0-1 7f-8f: 0-2 9f-13f: 0-0 14f+: 0-0
Track : LH: 0-0 RH: 0-0 Tight: 0-0 Gall: 0-0
Aids: Bl: 0-0 Vi: 0-0 Tstrap: 0-0
Best Rating: 45 10/01 NmkR 7f gd-sft

Ghannam (USA)

101 **91**
2-y-o b c Langfuhr (CAN)-Katerina Key (USA) (Key To The Mint (USA))
M P Tregoning Hamdan Al Maktoum

Placings:423 **(5594)**
2001: 8^{4}GF, 6^{2}GS, 6^{3}GS

	Starts	1st	2nd	3rd	Win & Pl
Career Total (Turf)	3	0	1	1	3270

Going (Turf): Sf: 0-0 GS: 0-2 Gd: 0-0 GF: 0-1 Fm: 0-0
Distance: 5f/6f: 0-2 7f-8f: 0-1 9f-13f: 0-0 14f+: 0-0
Track : LH: 0-0 RH: 0-0 Tight: 0-0 Gall: 0-0
Aids: Bl: 0-0 Vi: 0-0 Tstrap: 0-0
Best Rating: 91 11/01 NmkR 6f gd-sft

Half-brother to several winners in America, has shown ability in maidens and should win races.

Ghayth

92 **106**
3-y-o b c Sadler's Wells (USA)-Myself (Nashwan (USA))
Sir Michael Stoute Hamdan Al Maktoum

Placings:6130-05 **(2792)**
2001: 7^{0}S, 6^{5}GF

	Starts	1st	2nd	3rd	Win & Pl
Career Total (Turf)	6	1	0	1	15035
104 8/00 York 6f	D			GD	£14755

Total win prize-money £14755

Going (Turf): Sf: 0-1 GS: 0-0 **Gd: 1-2** GF: 0-3 Fm: 0-0
Distance: **5f/6f: 1-4** 7f-8f: 0-2 9f-13f: 0-0 14f+: 0-0
Track : LH: 0-0 RH: 0-0 Tight: 0-0 Gall: 0-0
Aids: Bl: 0-0 Vi: 0-0 Tstrap: 0-0
Best Rating: 86 4/01 NmkR 7f soft

A useful juvenile, but did not train on.

Ghazal (USA)

107 **100**
3-y-o b f Gone West (USA)-Touch Of Greatness (USA) (Hero's Honor (USA))
Sir Michael Stoute Hamdan Al Maktoum

Placings:21-0210 **(4849)**
2001: 7^{0}GS, 6^{2}G, 6^{1}G, 6^{0}GF

	Starts	1st	2nd	3rd	Win & Pl
Career Total (Turf)	6	2	2	0	21761
100 8/01 Yarm 6f3y	C			GD	£6206
92 9/00 NmkR 6f	D			GD	£5638

Total win prize-money £11845

Going (Turf): Sf: 0-0 GS: 0-1 **Gd: 2-4** GF: 0-1 Fm: 0-0
Distance: 5f/6f: 1-4 7f-8f: 1-2 9f-13f: 0-0 14f+: 0-0
Track : LH: 0-0 RH: 0-0 Tight: 0-0 Gall: 0-0
Aids: Bl: 0-0 Vi: 0-0 Tstrap: 0-0
Best Rating: 100 8/01 Yarm 6f3y good

A $575,000 yearling who is a half-sister to four winners, she is a useful filly who had just the two outings at two. Disappointed in the Nell Gwyn, but has returned in good heart after a break, winning a conditions event at Yarmouth in good style.

Ghost Of A Chance (IRE)

91 **33**
3-y-o b g Indian Ridge-Ma N'leme Biche (USA) (Key To The Kingdom (USA))
M H Tompkins Mrs Jane Bailey

Placings:000-43065 **(2728)**
2001: 6^{4}GF, 8^{3}F, 7^{0}GF, 8^{6}GF, 7^{5}GF

	Starts	1st	2nd	3rd	Win & Pl
Career Total (Turf)	8	0	0	1	356

Going (Turf): Sf: 0-2 GS: 0-0 Gd: 0-1 GF: 0-4 Fm: 0-1
Distance: 5f/6f: 0-2 7f-8f: 0-5 9f-13f: 0-1 14f+: 0-0
Track : LH: 0-1 RH: 0-1 Tight: 0-0 Gall: 0-0
Aids: Bl: 0-2 Vi: 0-0 Tstrap: 0-0
Best Rating: 33 5/01 Brig 6f209y gd-fm

Ghutah

94(75) (1)**28**
7-y-o ch g Lycius (USA)-Barada (USA) (Damascus (USA))
Mrs A M Thorpe (G A Swinbank 7/9) Three A's Caravan

Placings:0/00/050400/000-6 **(2053)**
2001: 16^{6}GF

	Starts	1st	2nd	3rd	Win & Pl
Career Total (Turf)	10	0	0	0	0
Career Total (AW)	3	0	0	0	

Going (Turf): Sf: 0-2 GS: 0-1 Gd: 0-2 GF: 0-2 Fm: 0-1
Distance: 5f/6f: 0-1 7f-8f: 0-3 9f-13f: 0-4 14f+: 0-2
Track : LH: 0-6 RH: 0-4 Tight: 0-2 Gall: 0-2
Aids: Bl: 0-3 Vi: 0-0 Tstrap: 0-0
Best Rating: 28 6/01 Rdcr 2m4y gd-fm

Gift Fountain

102 **68**
2-y-o b f Greensmith-Bright Fountain (IRE) (Cadeaux Genereux)
H Candy Mrs C M Poland

Placings:3 **(4287)**
2001: 8^{3}GF

	Starts	1st	2nd	3rd	Win & Pl
Career Total (Turf)	1	0	0	1	533

Going (Turf): Sf: 0-0 GS: 0-0 Gd: 0-0 GF: 0-1 Fm: 0-0
Distance: 5f/6f: 0-0 7f-8f: 0-0 9f-13f: 0-1 14f+: 0-0
Track : LH: 0-0 RH: 0-0 Tight: 0-0 Gall: 0-0
Aids: Bl: 0-0 Vi: 0-0 Tstrap: 0-0
Best Rating: 68 8/01 Chep 1m14y gd-fm

Gift Of Gold

103(104) (70)**80**
6-y-o ch g Statoblest-Ellebanna (Tina's Pet)
A Bailey Classic Gold

Placings:0042506**1**/2034013504**6**/**6**002015003040/450 013005006040**123**-4002 **(4401)**
2001: 7^{4}GS, 8^{0}G, 6^{0}G, 7^{2}G

	Starts	1st	2nd	3rd	Win & Pl
Career Total (Turf)	43	4	4	4	54114
Career Total (AW)	11	1	1	1	4847

64	11/00	Wolv	7f	E(0-75)H	STD	£2786
84	5/00	Gdwd	7f	C(0-90)H	SFT	£11635
83	6/99	Gdwd	7f	C(0-90)H	G-S	£7302
80	7/98	Ling	7f	C(0-90)H	G-F	£5911
73	11/97	Muss	7f30y	E	G-S	£3551

Total win prize-money £31187

Going (Turf): Sf: 1-10 **GS: 2-11** Gd: 0-15 GF: 1-7 Fm: 0-0
Distance: 5f/6f: 0-7 **7f-8f: 5-41** 9f-13f: 0-6 14f+: 0-0
Track : LH: 1-21 **RH: 3-8 Tight: 2-17** Gall: 0-2
Aids: Bl: 0-2 Vi: 0-0 Tstrap: 0-0
Best Rating: 78 7/01 Ayr 7f gd-sft

Fair seven-furlong handicapper, acts on Fibresand and easy ground on turf.

Gifted Flame

95 **75**
2-y-o b c Revoque (IRE)-Littleladyleah (USA) (Shareef Dancer (USA))
P G Murphy Raymond Miquel

Placings:00300 **(5496)**
2001: 7^{0}GF, 7^{0}GS, 7^{3}GF, 8^{0}GS, 7^{0}HY

	Starts	1st	2nd	3rd	Win & Pl
Career Total (Turf)	5	0	0	1	605

Going (Turf): Sf: 0-1 GS: 0-2 Gd: 0-0 GF: 0-2 Fm: 0-0

Distance: 5f/6f: 0-0 7f-8f: 0-5 9f-13f: 0-0 14f+: 0-0
Track : LH: 0-2 RH: 0-0 Tight: 0-1 Gall: 0-0
Aids: Bl: 0-0 Vi: 0-0 Tstrap: 0-0
Best Rating: 75 9/01 Wwck 7f26y gd-fm

Giko

103 (57)**48**
7-y-o b g Arazi (USA)-Gayane (Nureyev (USA))
Jane Southcombe V R V Partnership

Placings:2003301**3**600**40**/346131042/000/0006560000 30-00034410300 **(4946)**
2001: 8^{0}S, 8^{0}GF, 9^{0}F, 10^{3}F, 10^{4}GF, 12^{4}GF, 11^{1}GF, 12^{0}S, 13^{3}G, 12^{0}G, 12^{0}G

	Starts	1st	2nd	3rd	Win & Pl
Career Total (Turf)	45	4	2	8	33862
Career Total (AW)	3	0	0	0	0

48 7/01 Wind 1m3f135yE(0-70)H G-F £3276
69 7/98 Sand 1m14y D(0-85)H GD £3582
60 6/98 Gdwd 1m1f D(0-80)H G-F £5970
71 8/97 Chep 7f16y D G-S £3387
Total win prize-money £16217

Going (Turf): Sf: 0-7 GS: 1-7 Gd: 1-14 **GF: 2-14** Fm: 0-2
Distance: 5f/6f: 0-0 7f-8f: 1-24 **9f-13f: 3-22** 14f+: 0-1
Track : LH: 0-15 **RH: 2-13 Tight: 2-14** Gall: 0-4
Aids: Bl: 0-5 Vi: 0-0 Tstrap: 0-1
Best Rating: 48 9/01 Gdwd 1m4f good

He was winning his first race since July 1998 when taking a handicap at Windsor over the extended 11 furlongs in July. Needs fast ground.

Gilda (IRE)

(102) (77)**60**
3-y-o b f Goldmark (USA)-Pretty Precedent (Polish Precedent (USA))
R M H Cowell Mrs J M Penney

Placings:0512-25 **(0276)**
2001: 10^{2}SD, 10^{5}SW

	Starts	1st	2nd	3rd	Win & Pl
Career Total (Turf)	2	0	0	0	0
Career Total (AW)	4	1	2	0	5378

73 11/00 Ling 1m D STD £2327
Total win prize-money £2327

Going (Turf): Sf: 0-1 GS: 0-1 Gd: 0-0 GF: 0-0 Fm: 0-0
Distance: 5f/6f: 0-0 **7f-8f: 1-4** 9f-13f: 0-2 14f+: 0-0
Track : **LH: 1-4** RH: 0-1 **Tight: 1-5** Gall: 0-0
Aids: Bl: 0-0 Vi: 0-0 Tstrap: 0-0
Best Rating: 77 1/01 Ling 1m2f stand

Gilded Dancer

108 **87**
3-y-o b c Bishop Of Cashel-La Piaf (FR) (Fabulous Dancer (USA))
W R Muir Persipacious Punters Racing Club

Placings:3630-23 **(1598)**
2001: 8^{2}G, 8^{3}GF

	Starts	1st	2nd	3rd	Win & Pl
Career Total (Turf)	6	0	1	3	12153

Going (Turf): Sf: 0-0 GS: 0-2 Gd: 0-3 GF: 0-1 Fm: 0-0
Distance: 5f/6f: 0-1 7f-8f: 0-3 9f-13f: 0-2 14f+: 0-0
Track : LH: 0-3 RH: 0-1 Tight: 0-1 Gall: 0-0
Aids: Bl: 0-0 Vi: 0-0 Tstrap: 0-0
Best Rating: 87 5/01 Hayd 1m30y gd-fm

Gilden Magic

96 **56**
3-y-o b g Magic Ring (IRE)-Have Form (Haveroid)
M Blanshard Mrs Jane Gillett

Placings:020000 **(3206)**
2001: 7^{0}S, 6^{2}HY, 7^{0}GS, 8^{0}GS, 11^{0}GF, 10^{0}G

	Starts	1st	2nd	3rd	Win & Pl
Career Total (Turf)	6	0	1	0	732

Going (Turf): Sf: 0-2 GS: 0-2 Gd: 0-1 GF: 0-1 Fm: 0-0
Distance: 5f/6f: 0-0 7f-8f: 0-4 9f-13f: 0-2 14f+: 0-0
Track : LH: 0-1 RH: 0-2 Tight: 0-2 Gall: 0-1
Aids: Bl: 0-0 Vi: 0-0 Tstrap: 0-0
Best Rating: 56 4/01 Folk 6f189y heavy

Gill The Till (IRE)

88(68) (34)**62**
2-y-o ch f Anshan-Bilander (High Line)
M R Channon M Channon

Placings:060606 **(5667)**
2001: 6^{0}GF, 8^{6}GF, 8^{0}G, 8^{6}SD, 5^{0}G, 8^{6}HY

	Starts	1st	2nd	3rd	Win & Pl
Career Total (Turf)	5	0	0	0	0
Career Total (AW)	1	0	0	0	0

Going (Turf): Sf: 0-1 GS: 0-0 Gd: 0-2 GF: 0-2 Fm: 0-0
Distance: 5f/6f: 0-1 7f-8f: 0-2 9f-13f: 0-3 14f+: 0-0
Track : LH: 0-4 RH: 0-1 Tight: 0-2 Gall: 0-1
Aids: Bl: 0-0 Vi: 0-0 Tstrap: 0-0
Best Rating: 62 9/01 Nott 1m54y gd-fm

Gill's Diamond (IRE)

(96) (47)**34**
3-y-o ch f College Chapel-Yafford (Warrshan (USA))
N Tinkler Its A Little Bit Of Fun

Placings:3500**3**042-400004 **(5412)**
2001: 6^{4}SD, 5^{0}GF, 5^{0}GF, 5^{0}G, 6^{0}G, 6^{4}SD

	Starts	1st	2nd	3rd	Win & Pl
Career Total (Turf)	8	0	0	1	687
Career Total (AW)	6	0	1	1	806

Going (Turf): Sf: 0-0 GS: 0-1 Gd: 0-4 GF: 0-3 Fm: 0-0
Distance: 5f/6f: 0-14 7f-8f: 0-0 9f-13f: 0-0 14f+: 0-0
Track : LH: 0-5 RH: 0-1 Tight: 0-2 Gall: 0-1
Aids: Bl: 0-0 Vi: 0-0 Tstrap: 0-2
Best Rating: 47 1/01 Sthl 6f stand

Gilt Trip (IRE)

75(93) (41)**36**
3-y-o b g Goldmark (USA)-Opening Day (Day Is Done)
M J Polglase (N P Littmoden 14/3) Paul J Dixon

Placings:000-015604006 **(3691)**
2001: 8^{0}SD, 9^{1}SD, 11^{5}SD, 11^{6}SW, 12^{0}SD, 9^{4}SD, 12^{0}SD, 11^{0}GF, 15^{6}G

	Starts	1st	2nd	3rd	Win & Pl
Career Total (Turf)	4	0	0	0	0
Career Total (AW)	8	1	0	0	1883

51 2/01 Wolv 1m1f79y G STD £1883
Total win prize-money £1883

Going (Turf): Sf: 0-1 GS: 0-0 Gd: 0-1 GF: 0-2 Fm: 0-0
Distance: 5f/6f: 0-3 7f-8f: 0-1 **9f-13f: 1-7** 14f+: 0-1
Track : **LH: 1-10** RH: 0-0 **Tight: 1-6** Gall: 0-1
Aids: **Bl: 1-7** Vi: 0-0 Tstrap: 0-0
Best Rating: 51 2/01 Wolv 1m1f79y stand

Gin Palace (IRE)

109 **84**
3-y-o gr c King's Theatre (IRE)-Ikala (Lashkari)
G L Moore Mrs Patricia Gilmore

Placings:6-416305 **(5143)**
2001: 9^{4}GS, 9^{1}GS, 11^{6}GF, 14^{3}G, 13^{0}G, 14^{5}G

	Starts	1st	2nd	3rd	Win & Pl
Career Total (Turf)	7	1	0	1	8815

77 5/01 Brig 1m1f209yD G-S £6792
Total win prize-money £6793

Going (Turf): Sf: 0-1 **GS: 1-2** Gd: 0-3 GF: 0-1 Fm: 0-0
Distance: 5f/6f: 0-0 7f-8f: 0-1 **9f-13f: 1-3** 14f+: 0-3
Track : **LH: 1-3** RH: 0-3 Tight: 0-1 Gall: 0-2
Aids: Bl: 0-0 Vi: 0-0 Tstrap: 0-0
Best Rating: 84 8/01 Gdwd 1m6f good

Won a Brighton maiden in May and has run some fair races although held since. Suited by cut in the ground, stays 14 furlongs and may get further

Gina (IRE)

(80) (40)
3-y-o b f Lahib (USA)-Relankina (IRE) (Broken Hearted)
J A Glover Countrywide Classics Limited

Placings:06-0 **(2581)**
2001: 6^{0}SD

	Starts	1st	2nd	3rd	Win & Pl
Career Total (Turf)	1	0	0	0	
Career Total (AW)	2	0	0	0	0

Going (Turf): Sf: 0-1 GS: 0-0 Gd: 0-0 GF: 0-0 Fm: 0-0
Distance: 5f/6f: 0-3 7f-8f: 0-0 9f-13f: 0-0 14f+: 0-0
Track : LH: 0-1 RH: 0-0 Tight: 0-0 Gall: 0-0
Aids: Bl: 0-0 Vi: 0-0 Tstrap: 0-0

Ginanmix (IRE)

3-y-o gr f Linamix (FR)-Mill Rainbow (FR) (Rainbow Quest (USA))
S Kirk Fieldspring Racing

Placings:0 **(5522)**
2001: 6^{0}HY

	Starts	1st	2nd	3rd	Win & Pl
Career Total (Turf)	1	0	0	0	

Going (Turf): Sf: 0-1 GS: 0-0 Gd: 0-0 GF: 0-0 Fm: 0-0
Distance: 5f/6f: 0-1 7f-8f: 0-0 9f-13f: 0-0 14f+: 0-0
Track : LH: 0-0 RH: 0-0 Tight: 0-0 Gall: 0-0
Aids: Bl: 0-0 Vi: 0-0 Tstrap: 0-0

Ginger Rogers

(72) **53**
7-y-o ch m Gildoran-Axe Valley (Royben)
R E Peacock P Ponting

Placings:000/05211134/40430/0 **(1470)**
2001: 16^{0}SD

	Starts	1st	2nd	3rd	Win & Pl
Career Total (Turf)	15	3	1	2	10488
Career Total (AW)	2	0	0	0	

63 8/97 Bath 2m1f34y E(0-70)H GD £2917
63 7/97 Nott 2m9y F(0-65)H G-F £2277
48 6/97 Yarm 1m6f17y E(0-70)H GD £3044
Total win prize-money £8239

Going (Turf): Sf: 0-3 GS: 0-1 **Gd: 2-4** GF: 1-6 Fm: 0-1
Distance: 5f/6f: 0-0 7f-8f: 0-3 9f-13f: 0-2 **14f+: 3-12**
Track : **LH: 3-12** RH: 0-3 **Tight: 2-5** Gall: 0-2
Aids: Bl: 0-0 Vi: 0-0 Tstrap: 0-0
Best Rating: 48 6/97 Yarm 1m6f17y G

Gingko

107(104) (68)**68**
4-y-o b g Pursuit Of Love-Arboretum (IRE) (Green Desert (USA))
J G Smyth-Osbourne Highfields Partnership I

Placings:44460-224051050010 **(5465)**
2001: 7^{2}SD, 7^{2}SW, 8^{4}SD, 7^{0}SD, 10^{5}G, 10^{1}G, 10^{0}GF, 10^{5}GF, 10^{0}S, 9^{0}HY, 8^{1}SD, 10^{0}G

	Starts	1st	2nd	3rd	Win & Pl

	Starts	1st	2nd	3rd	Win & Pl
Career Total (Turf)	11	1	0	0	8267
Career Total (AW)	6	1	2	0	3694

68	10/01	Sthl	1m	G(0-75)H	STD	£2268
68	5/01	Donc	1m2f60y	C(0-90)H	GD	£7702

Total win prize-money £9971

Going (Turf): Sf: 0-2 GS: 0-1 **Gd: 1-4** GF: 0-4 Fm: 0-0
Distance: 5f/6f: 0-1 7f-8f: 1-8 9f-13f: 1-8 14f+: 0-0
Track : **LH: 2-11** RH: 0-1 Tight: 0-3 **Gall: 1-3**
Aids: Bl: 0-0 Vi: 0-0 Tstrap: 0-0
Best Rating: 68 10/01 Sthl 1m stand

Took his time in getting off the mark and finally did so in a Doncaster handicap over ten furlongs in May. Bits and pieces of form on sand before winning comfortably at Southwell in October.

Ginner Morris

101(68) (37)**48**

6-y-o b g Emarati (USA)-Just Run (IRE) (Runnett)
J Hetherton Formulated Polymer Products Ltd

Placings:0/000000424420/0045/00410-001 **(5450)**
2001: 11^{0}SD, 9^{0}HY, 8^{1}HY

	Starts	1st	2nd	3rd	Win & Pl
Career Total (Turf)	19	2	1	0	6459
Career Total (AW)	6	0	1	0	485

47	10/01	Newc	1m	F(0-60)H	HVY	£2870
48	10/00	Newc	1m	F(0-60)H	HVY	£2922

Total win prize-money £5793

Going (Turf): Sf: 2-8 GS: 0-5 Gd: 0-4 GF: 0-1 Fm: 0-1
Distance: 5f/6f: 0-2 **7f-8f: 2-12** 9f-13f: 0-11 14f+: 0-0
Track : **LH: 2-17** RH: 0-2 Tight: 0-5 **Gall: 2-4**
Aids: **Bl: 2-4** Vi: 0-0 Tstrap: 0-0
Best Rating: 47 10/01 Newc 1m heavy

Girl Friday

92(85) (42)**42**

3-y-o ch f Ajraas (USA)-Miss Nonnie (High Kicker (USA))
Mrs N Macauley G M Pugh

Placings:0-0602 **(5409)**
2001: 8^{0}G, 7^{6}GF, 7^{0}S, 6^{2}SD

	Starts	1st	2nd	3rd	Win & Pl
Career Total (Turf)	4	0	0	0	0
Career Total (AW)	1	0	1	0	644

Going (Turf): Sf: 0-2 GS: 0-0 Gd: 0-1 GF: 0-1 Fm: 0-0
Distance: 5f/6f: 0-2 7f-8f: 0-2 9f-13f: 0-1 14f+: 0-0
Track : LH: 0-3 RH: 0-1 Tight: 0-1 Gall: 0-0
Aids: Bl: 0-0 Vi: 0-0 Tstrap: 0-0
Best Rating: 42 10/01 Sthl 6f stand

Just beaten in a maiden on the Southwell Fibresand in October, but it was an awful race.

Girl Of Pleasure (IRE)

90 **73**

2-y-o b f Namaqualand (USA)-Shrewd Girl (USA) (Sagace (FR))
Mrs P N Dutfield Darren C Mercer

Placings:03600 **(4678)**
2001: 6^{0}GF, 7^{3}GF, 7^{6}GF, 6^{0}G, 8^{0}G

	Starts	1st	2nd	3rd	Win & Pl
Career Total (Turf)	5	0	0	1	666

Going (Turf): Sf: 0-0 GS: 0-0 Gd: 0-2 GF: 0-3 Fm: 0-0
Distance: 5f/6f: 0-1 7f-8f: 0-4 9f-13f: 0-0 14f+: 0-0
Track : LH: 0-1 RH: 0-1 Tight: 0-0 Gall: 0-2
Aids: Bl: 0-0 Vi: 0-0 Tstrap: 0-0
Best Rating: 73 7/01 Newb 7f gd-fm

Girl's Best Friend

(104) (61)**65?**

4-y-o b f Nicolotte-Diamond Princess (Horage)
D W P Arbuthnot (N J Henderson 20/3) Stephen Crown

Placings:021040/0560000-600 **(5362)**
2001: 7^{6}SD, 8^{0}GS, 9^{0}GS

	Starts	1st	2nd	3rd	Win & Pl
Career Total (Turf)	13	1	0	0	4258
Career Total (AW)	3	0	1	0	614

87	10/99	Ling	6f	D	HVY	£3460

Total win prize-money £3460

Going (Turf): Sf: 1-6 GS: 0-3 Gd: 0-3 GF: 0-1 Fm: 0-0
Distance: **5f/6f: 1-2** 7f-8f: 0-9 9f-13f: 0-5 14f+: 0-0
Track : LH: 0-8 RH: 0-2 Tight: 0-1 Gall: 0-3
Aids: Bl: 0-1 Vi: 0-0 Tstrap: 0-4
Best Rating: 65 10/01 NmkR 1m1f gd-sft

Was Listed class before sustaining an injury, and does not look anywhere near as good as she was. Her only win came at two over six furlongs in heavy ground.

Give An Inch (IRE)

90 **70**

6-y-o b m Inchinor-Top Heights (High Top)
W Storey Black Type Racing

Placings:650003012102100/44231410/000001100-00 **(1283)**
2001: 16^{0}S, 16^{0}G

	Starts	1st	2nd	3rd	Win & Pl
Career Total (Turf)	34	7	3	2	30875

70	9/00	Ayr	2m1f105y	D(0-80)H	SFT	£4940
70	9/99	Ayr	2m1f105y	D(0-80)H	G-S	£5377
65	6/99	Pont	2m1f216y	E(0-70)H	GD	£4854
61	9/98	Ayr	2m1f105y	D(0-80)H	G-S	£5215
53	8/98	Ayr	1m7f	E(0-70)H	G-S	£2901
45	7/98	Rdcr	1m3f	G	G-F	£1982

Total win prize-money £25271

Going (Turf): Sf: 2-7 **GS: 3-11** Gd: 1-12 GF: 1-4 Fm: 0-0
Distance: 5f/6f: 0-1 7f-8f: 0-5 9f-13f: 1-3 **14f+: 6-25**
Track : **LH: 7-24** RH: 0-9 **Tight: 1-13** Gall: 0-7
Aids: Bl: 0-0 Vi: 0-0 Tstrap: 0-0
Best Rating: 30 5/01 Bevl 2m35y good

Give Back Calais (IRE)

110 **92**

3-y-o b g Brief Truce (USA)-Nichodoula (Doulab (USA))
P J Makin Peter Melotti

Placings:3235-10400 **(4250)**
2001: 6^{1}GF, 5^{0}GF, 7^{4}GF, 7^{0}G, 10^{0}GF

	Starts	1st	2nd	3rd	Win & Pl
Career Total (Turf)	9	1	1	2	17526

89	6/01	Newb	6f8y	D	G-F	£5044

Total win prize-money £5044

Going (Turf): Sf: 0-0 GS: 0-0 Gd: 0-3 **GF: 1-6** Fm: 0-0
Distance: 5f/6f: 0-4 **7f-8f: 1-4** 9f-13f: 0-1 14f+: 0-0
Track : LH: 0-0 RH: 0-3 Tight: 0-0 Gall: 0-1
Aids: Bl: 0-1 Vi: 0-0 Tstrap: 0-0
Best Rating: 94 7/01 Sand 7f16y gd-fm

Ran well as a juvenile without getting his head in front. Got off the mark on his reappearance over six furlongs at Newbury and ran well on his first attempt over seven furlongs at Sandown. He was tried over ten furlongs but was never in the race. Acts on a fast surface.

Give Me A Ring (IRE)

107(69) **80**

8-y-o b g Be My Guest (USA)-Annsfield Lady (Red Sunset)
C W Thornton B Harrison-Burcombe

Placings:045/64211130/216/00020250/0111030 **(2535)**
2001: 11^{0}SD, 12^{1}F, 12^{1}GF, 12^{1}GF, 12^{0}F, 12^{3}G, 12^{0}GF

	Starts	1st	2nd	3rd	Win & Pl
Career Total (Turf)	27	7	3	2	55780
Career Total (AW)	2	0	1	0	949

75	5/01	Donc	1m4f	D(0-85)H	G-F	£4387
71	5/01	Muss	1m4f	F(0-65)H	G-F	£5300
49	5/01	Haml	1m4f17y	E(0-65)	FRM	£3346
94	5/97	York	1m2f85y	B(0-105)	GD	£9024
80	8/96	Ripn	1m1f	C(0-90)H	G-F	£5679
76	7/96	York	7f202y	C(0-90)H	GD	£7895
70	7/96	Bevl	1m100y	D(0-85)H	G-F	£3814

Total win prize-money £39449

Going (Turf): Sf: 0-0 GS: 0-1 Gd: 2-11 **GF: 4-13** Fm: 1-2
Distance: 5f/6f: 0-3 7f-8f: 1-3 **9f-13f: 6-23** 14f+: 0-0
Track : LH: 3-13 RH: 3-10 Tight: 2-6 **Gall: 3-10**
Aids: Bl: 0-1 Vi: 0-0 Tstrap: 0-0
Best Rating: 77 6/01 Muss 1m4f good

He was disappointed in 2000, but was back to form earlier this season, completing a hat trick in May, all over 12 furlongs on fast ground.

Give Notice

111 **97**

4-y-o b g Warning-Princess Genista (Ile De Bourbon (USA))
J L Dunlop I H Stewart-Brown

Placings:60/0611100-245031331 **(5600)**
2001: 12^{2}S, 14^{4}GF, 13^{5}G, 16^{0}F, 16^{3}G, 14^{1}GF, 14^{3}G, 18^{3}GS, 16^{1}GS

	Starts	1st	2nd	3rd	Win & Pl
Career Total (Turf)	18	5	1	3	59457

97	11/01	NmkR	2m	A(0-105)H	G-S	£13583
94	8/01	NmkJ	1m6f175y	C(0-95)H	G-F	£7020
88	7/00	Kemp	1m6f92y	C(0-90)H	G-S	£6922
95	7/00	Hayd	1m6f	D(0-80)H	G-F	£4199
77	6/00	Yarm	1m6f17y	E(0-70)H	G-F	£2899

Total win prize-money £34625

Going (Turf): Sf: 0-1 GS: 2-4 Gd: 0-6 **GF: 3-6** Fm: 0-1
Distance: 5f/6f: 0-0 7f-8f: 0-2 9f-13f: 0-3 **14f+: 5-13**
Track : LH: 2-6 **RH: 3-9** Tight: 1-4 **Gall: 2-9**
Aids: Bl: 0-0 Vi: 0-0 Tstrap: 0-0
Best Rating: 97 11/01 NmkR 2m gd-sft

Useful staying handicapper who notched up a hat-trick in the summer of 2000 over 14 furlongs. Suited by fast ground. He had looked weighted up to the hilt, but he showed plenty of resolution to score off his highest mark at Newmarket in August. Creditable third in the Cesarewitch and scored on the Rowley Mile in November.

Give The Slip

118 **119**

4-y-o b h Slip Anchor-Falafil (FR) (Fabulous Dancer (USA))
Saeed Bin Suroor Godolphin

Placings:34/312141-1545042 **(5735a)**
2001: 12^{1}G, 12^{5}G, 10^{4}G, 10^{5}GF, 12^{0}GF, 10^{4}G, 16^{2}GS

	Starts	1st	2nd	3rd	Win & Pl
Career Total (Turf)	15	4	2	2	528817

115	2/01	Ndas	1m4f		GD	£38251
109	8/00	York	1m5f194y	B H	GD	£113750
109	6/00	Asct	1m4f	B(0-105)H	G-F	£35750
87	5/00	Wind	1m2f7y	E	G-F	£3255

Total win prize-money £191006

Going (Turf): Sf: 0-0 GS: 0-3 **Gd: 2-7 GF: 2-5** Fm: 0-0
Distance: 5f/6f: 0-0 7f-8f: 0-2 **9f-13f: 3-11** 14f+: 1-2
Track : LH: 1-3 RH: 1-6 Tight: 1-4 **Gall: 2-4**
Aids: Bl: 0-0 Vi: 0-0 Tstrap: 0-0
Best Rating: 119 11/01 Flem 2m gd-sft

Took the King George V Handicap and the Ebor as a three-year-old when with Amanda Perrett. Made a winning debut for Godolphin at Nad Al Sheba in February 2001 and did a good job as pacemaker for Fantastic

Light after. All but won the Melbourne Cup on his final start. Best on a sound surface.

Givemethemoonlight

79 **59**

2-y-o ch f Woodborough (USA)-Rockin' Rosie (Song)
L G Cottrell P A & M J Reditt

Placings:64 **(5665)**
2001: 6^{6}HY, 6^{4}HY

	Starts	1st	2nd	3rd	Win & Pl
Career Total (Turf)	2	0	0	0	289

Going (Turf): Sf: 0-2 GS: 0-0 Gd: 0-0 GF: 0-0 Fm: 0-0
Distance: 5f/6f: 0-1 7f-8f: 0-1 9f-13f: 0-0 14f+: 0-0
Track : LH: 0-0 RH: 0-0 Tight: 0-0 Gall: 0-0
Aids: Bl: 0-0 Vi: 0-0 Tstrap: 0-0
Best Rating: 59 10/01 Newb 6f8y heavy

Fair efforts in maiden events so far.

Givre (IRE)

92 **60**

3-y-o b g Houmayoun (FR)-Interj (Salmon Leap (USA))
R A Fahey (J E Mulhern 27/5) P D Smith Holdings Ltd

Placings:0200-0000 **(4570)**
2001: 8^{0}S, 8^{0}G, 8^{0}G, 11^{0}HY

	Starts	1st	2nd	3rd	Win & Pl
Career Total (Turf)	8	0	1	0	1360

Going (Turf): Sf: 0-2 GS: 0-0 Gd: 0-2 GF: 0-0 Fm: 0-0
Distance: 5f/6f: 0-1 7f-8f: 0-3 9f-13f: 0-3 14f+: 0-0
Track : LH: 0-1 RH: 0-2 Tight: 0-0 Gall: 0-0
Aids: Bl: 0-0 Vi: 0-0 Tstrap: 0-0
Best Rating: 51 5/01 Curr 1m good

Glade Runner (USA)

72

2-y-o br f Woodman (USA)-Maid Of Camelot (Caerleon (USA))
R Charlton A E Oppenheimer

Placings:4 **(3680)**
2001: 6^{4}G

	Starts	1st	2nd	3rd	Win & Pl
Career Total (Turf)	1	0	0	0	285

Going (Turf): Sf: 0-0 GS: 0-0 Gd: 0-1 GF: 0-0 Fm: 0-0
Distance: 5f/6f: 0-1 7f-8f: 0-0 9f-13f: 0-0 14f+: 0-0
Track : LH: 0-0 RH: 0-0 Tight: 0-0 Gall: 0-0
Aids: Bl: 0-0 Vi: 0-0 Tstrap: 0-0
Best Rating: 72 8/01 Wind 6f good

Gleaming Blade (USA)

106 **98d**

3-y-o ch c Diesis-Gleam Of Light (IRE) (Danehill (USA))
Mrs A J Perrett K Abdulla

Placings:214-544220 **(5366)**
2001: 7^{5}GF, 6^{4}G, 8^{4}GF, 7^{2}G, 8^{2}G, 8^{0}GS

	Starts	1st	2nd	3rd	Win & Pl
Career Total (Turf)	9	1	3	0	12777

85 8/00 Leic 7f9y D G-F £3851
Total win prize-money £3851

Going (Turf): Sf: 0-0 GS: 0-1 Gd: 0-3 **GF: 1-5** Fm: 0-0
Distance: 5f/6f: 0-0 **7f-8f: 1-8** 9f-13f: 0-1 14f+: 0-0
Track : LH: 0-2 RH: 0-2 Tight: 0-2 Gall: 0-1
Aids: Bl: 0-0 Vi: 0-0 Tstrap: 0-0
Best Rating: 98 6/01 Epsm 7f gd-fm

Got of the mark at the second time of asking at two, but has struggled since at both Listed level and in handicaps at a variety of trips. Better effort at Newmarket in September. Suited by good to firm ground.

Glebe (USA)

70 **27**

2-y-o b c Meadowlake (USA)-Careful Approach (USA) (Relaunch (USA))
M R Channon Jumeirah Racing

Placings:00 **(5468)**
2001: 7^{0}GS, 7^{0}S

	Starts	1st	2nd	3rd	Win & Pl
Career Total (Turf)	2	0	0	0	

Going (Turf): Sf: 0-1 GS: 0-1 Gd: 0-0 GF: 0-0 Fm: 0-0
Distance: 5f/6f: 0-0 7f-8f: 0-2 9f-13f: 0-0 14f+: 0-0
Track : LH: 0-2 RH: 0-0 Tight: 0-0 Gall: 0-1
Aids: Bl: 0-0 Vi: 0-0 Tstrap: 0-0
Best Rating: 27 10/01 York 7f202y gd-sft

Glen Vale Walk (IRE)

101 **44**

4-y-o ch g Balla Cove-Winter Harvest (Grundy)
Mrs G S Rees D C Brady

Placings:003/00004022000-0310460004 **(5663)**
2001: 9^{0}F, 10^{3}GF, 10^{1}GF, 11^{0}S, 9^{4}GF, 11^{6}G, 10^{0}G, 10^{0}F, 12^{0}GS, 12^{4}G

	Starts	1st	2nd	3rd	Win & Pl
Career Total (Turf)	24	1	2	2	6083

48 7/01 Wwck 1m2f188yF(0-65)H G-F £3010
Total win prize-money £3010

Going (Turf): Sf: 0-4 GS: 0-3 Gd: 0-7 **GF: 1-5** Fm: 0-5
Distance: 5f/6f: 0-0 7f-8f: 0-7 **9f-13f: 1-17** 14f+: 0-0
Track : **LH: 1-15** RH: 0-7 Tight: 0-5 Gall: 0-3
Aids: Bl: 0-1 Vi: 0-0 Tstrap: 0-0
Best Rating: 50 8/01 Hayd 1m3f200y good

Glenburn (IRE)

92 **67**

3-y-o br g Dr Devious (IRE)-Edwina (IRE) (Caerleon (USA))
A C Stewart Robin Paterson

Placings:045 **(3715)**
2001: 8^{0}GF, 8^{4}GF, 8^{5}G

	Starts	1st	2nd	3rd	Win & Pl
Career Total (Turf)	3	0	0	0	329

Going (Turf): Sf: 0-0 GS: 0-0 Gd: 0-1 GF: 0-2 Fm: 0-0
Distance: 5f/6f: 0-0 7f-8f: 0-0 9f-13f: 0-3 14f+: 0-0
Track : LH: 0-1 RH: 0-2 Tight: 0-1 Gall: 0-0
Aids: Bl: 0-0 Vi: 0-0 Tstrap: 0-0
Best Rating: 67 7/01 Sand 1m14y gd-fm

Glendale Ridge (IRE)

(90) (25)**51**

6-y-o b g Indian Ridge-English Lily (Runnett)
Jamie Poulton Glendale Partnership Ltd

Placings:4440000400-0 **(0238)**
2001: 8^{0}SD

	Starts	1st	2nd	3rd	Win & Pl
Career Total (Turf)	9	0	0	0	1163
Career Total (AW)	2	0	0	0	

Going (Turf): Sf: 0-3 GS: 0-2 Gd: 0-1 GF: 0-3 Fm: 0-0
Distance: 5f/6f: 0-1 7f-8f: 0-6 9f-13f: 0-4 14f+: 0-0
Track : LH: 0-3 RH: 0-6 Tight: 0-3 Gall: 0-2
Aids: Bl: 0-0 Vi: 0-0 Tstrap: 0-0

Glendamah (IRE)

96 **43**

4-y-o b g Mukaddamah (USA)-Sea Glen (IRE) (Glenstal (USA))
J R Weymes Mrs A Birkett

Placings:53401302033/00000-50004000 **(4599)**
2001: 7^{5}GF, 7^{0}GF, 8^{0}GF, 10^{0}GF, 6^{4}G, 8^{0}GF, 8^{0}S, 8^{0}GF

	Starts	1st	2nd	3rd	Win & Pl
Career Total (Turf)	24	1	1	4	6525

74 8/99 Newc 6f F FRM £2452
Total win prize-money £2453

Going (Turf): Sf: 0-7 GS: 0-0 Gd: 0-6 GF: 0-8 **Fm: 1-3**
Distance: **5f/6f: 1-8** 7f-8f: 0-10 9f-13f: 0-6 14f+: 0-0
Track : LH: 0-6 RH: 0-6 Tight: 0-3 Gall: 0-2
Aids: Bl: 0-5 Vi: 0-3 Tstrap: 0-0
Best Rating: 47 5/01 Muss 7f30y gd-fm

Glenhurich (IRE)

97 **49**

4-y-o b f Sri Pekan (USA)-Forli's Treat (USA) (Forli (ARG))
J S Goldie J S Morrison & R A Dalglish

Placings:45-0500 **(4859)**
2001: 8^{0}GF, 8^{5}G, 8^{0}GS, 7^{0}GF

	Starts	1st	2nd	3rd	Win & Pl
Career Total (Turf)	6	0	0	0	350

Going (Turf): Sf: 0-0 GS: 0-1 Gd: 0-1 GF: 0-4 Fm: 0-0
Distance: 5f/6f: 0-0 7f-8f: 0-3 9f-13f: 0-3 14f+: 0-0
Track : LH: 0-3 RH: 0-2 Tight: 0-3 Gall: 0-0
Aids: Bl: 0-0 Vi: 0-0 Tstrap: 0-0
Best Rating: 49 8/01 Hayd 1m30y good

Glenmorangie

98 **94d**

2-y-o br/gr g Danzig Connection (USA)-In The Highlands (Petong)
R Hannon Major A M Everett

Placings:311000 **(5340)**
2001: 5^{3}S, 6^{1}GF, 5^{1}GF, 7^{0}GF, 6^{0}G, 6^{0}GS

	Starts	1st	2nd	3rd	Win & Pl
Career Total (Turf)	6	2	0	1	9258

94 6/01 Wind 5f10y D G-F £4134
82 5/01 Gdwd 6f D G-F £4543
Total win prize-money £8678

Going (Turf): Sf: 0-1 GS: 0-1 Gd: 0-1 **GF: 2-3** Fm: 0-0
Distance: **5f/6f: 2-5** 7f-8f: 0-1 9f-13f: 0-0 14f+: 0-0
Track : LH: 0-0 **RH: 1-1** Tight: 0-0 **Gall: 1-1**
Aids: Bl: 0-0 Vi: 0-0 Tstrap: 0-0
Best Rating: 94 6/01 Wind 5f10y gd-fm

Improved from his debut to win in good style at both Goodwood and Windsor but has failed to build on that. Acts on a fast surface. Has won over five and six furlongs.

Glenrock

108 **83**

4-y-o ch g Muhtarram (USA)-Elkie Brooks (Relkino)
A Berry Pisani Limited

Placings:220431103/065020060-33040324663104 **(5449)**
2001: 6^{3}S, 7^{3}GF, 6^{0}F, 7^{4}G, 7^{0}F, 7^{3}GF, 7^{2}G, 7^{4}GS, 7^{6}GF, 6^{6}G, 7^{3}GS, 6^{1}S, 6^{0}GS, 6^{4}HY

	Starts	1st	2nd	3rd	Win & Pl
Career Total (Turf)	32	3	4	6	29028

75 9/01 Ches 6f18y D(0-80) SFT £4368
89 8/99 Ches 6f18y C G-S £5468
75 8/99 Ling 6f F GD £2119
Total win prize-money £11955

Going (Turf): Sf: 1-6 GS: 1-5 Gd: 1-6 GF: 0-13 Fm: 0-2
Distance: 5f/6f: 1-19 **7f-8f: 2-13** 9f-13f: 0-0 14f+: 0-0

Track : LH: 2-14 RH: 0-3 Tight: 2-9 Gall: 0-2
Aids: Bl: 0-0 Vi: 0-0 Tstrap: 0-0
Best Rating: 86 7/01 Hayd 7f30y gd-fm

He has run some good races in the last couple of seasons, but has been too high in the handicap and gained his reward in a Chester classified event. Effective at six to seven furlongs, suited by cut and forcing tactics. Goes well around the Roodeye.

Glitter And Glory

71 **35**
2-y-o b g Classic Cliche (IRE)-Veuve (Tirol)
C A Cyzer Mrs E A Cyzer

Placings:0 **(5468)**
2001: 7^{0}S

	Starts	1st	2nd	3rd	Win & Pl
Career Total (Turf)	1	0	0	0	

Going (Turf): Sf: 0-1 GS: 0-0 Gd: 0-0 GF: 0-0 Fm: 0-0
Distance: 5f/6f: 0-0 7f-8f: 0-1 9f-13f: 0-0 14f+: 0-0
Track : LH: 0-1 RH: 0-0 Tight: 0-0 Gall: 0-0
Aids: Bl: 0-0 Vi: 0-0 Tstrap: 0-0
Best Rating: 35 10/01 Brig 7f214y soft

Gloaming

97 **72?**
3-y-o b f Celtic Swing-Kandavu (Safawan)
J Gallagher Mrs H Corr

Placings:03000 **(2062)**
2001: 7^{0}S, 6^{3}GS, 10^{0}F, 7^{0}GF, 6^{0}GF

	Starts	1st	2nd	3rd	Win & Pl
Career Total (Turf)	5	0	0	1	476

Going (Turf): Sf: 0-1 GS: 0-1 Gd: 0-0 GF: 0-2 Fm: 0-1
Distance: 5f/6f: 0-1 7f-8f: 0-3 9f-13f: 0-1 14f+: 0-0
Track : LH: 0-1 RH: 0-1 Tight: 0-0 Gall: 0-1
Aids: Bl: 0-0 Vi: 0-0 Tstrap: 0-0
Best Rating: 82 5/01 York 1m2f85y firm

Unraced at two, she was completely out of her depth in the Musidora, but had previously hinted at ability and should find a race in more realistic company.

Global Power (IRE)

86 **74**
2-y-o ch c Spinning World (USA)-Petroleuse (Habitat)
W R Muir M J Caddy

Placings:64 **(4670)**
2001: 7^{6}GF, 7^{4}G

	Starts	1st	2nd	3rd	Win & Pl
Career Total (Turf)	2	0	0	0	274

Going (Turf): Sf: 0-0 GS: 0-0 Gd: 0-1 GF: 0-1 Fm: 0-0
Distance: 5f/6f: 0-0 7f-8f: 0-2 9f-13f: 0-0 14f+: 0-0
Track : LH: 0-0 RH: 0-0 Tight: 0-0 Gall: 0-0
Aids: Bl: 0-0 Vi: 0-0 Tstrap: 0-0
Best Rating: 74 8/01 NmkJ 7f gd-fm

Global Princess (IRE)

98 **83**
2-y-o b f Dashing Blade-Brandon Princess (Waajib)
I A Balding W Aeberhard

Placings:321300 **(4795)**
2001: 5^{3}HD, 6^{2}GF, 5^{1}GF, 5^{3}F, 5^{0}GF, 5^{0}G

	Starts	1st	2nd	3rd	Win & Pl
Career Total (Turf)	6	1	1	2	4989

79 7/01 Brig 5f59y F G-F £2527
Total win prize-money £2527

Going (Turf): Sf: 0-0 GS: 0-0 Gd: 0-1 **GF: 1-3** Fm: 0-2
Distance: **5f/6f: 1-6** 7f-8f: 0-0 9f-13f: 0-0 14f+: 0-0
Track : **LH: 1-2** RH: 0-0 Tight: 0-0 Gall: 0-1
Aids: Bl: 0-0 Vi: 0-0 Tstrap: 0-0
Best Rating: 83 8/01 Thsk 5f firm

Apparently not an easy horse to train, she showed plenty of promise before scoring at Brighton in July over five furlongs. Not an easy ride.

Gloria Di Modena

88 **45**
3-y-o b f Glory Of Dancer-Star Of Modena (IRE) (Waajib)
H Akbary G P Bernacchi

Placings:0040 **(3318)**
2001: 10^{0}S, 10^{0}G, 8^{4}GF, 14^{0}G

	Starts	1st	2nd	3rd	Win & Pl
Career Total (Turf)	4	0	0	0	312

Going (Turf): Sf: 0-1 GS: 0-0 Gd: 0-2 GF: 0-1 Fm: 0-0
Distance: 5f/6f: 0-0 7f-8f: 0-0 9f-13f: 0-3 14f+: 0-1
Track : LH: 0-2 RH: 0-1 Tight: 0-2 Gall: 0-1
Aids: Bl: 0-0 Vi: 0-1 Tstrap: 0-0
Best Rating: 45 6/01 Bevl 1m100y gd-fm

Glorious Quest (IRE)

97(84) (35)**70**
3-y-o ch c Lake Coniston (IRE)-Lassalia (Sallust)
M A Jarvis & Mrs Nicholas Baker

Placings:30-026045 **(5395)**
2001: 6^{0}G, 6^{2}F, 7^{6}GS, 7^{0}GF, 7^{4}S, 7^{5}SD

	Starts	1st	2nd	3rd	Win & Pl
Career Total (Turf)	7	0	1	1	1974
Career Total (AW)	1	0	0	0	

Going (Turf): Sf: 0-2 GS: 0-1 Gd: 0-1 GF: 0-2 Fm: 0-1
Distance: 5f/6f: 0-2 7f-8f: 0-6 9f-13f: 0-0 14f+: 0-0
Track : LH: 0-1 RH: 0-0 Tight: 0-1 Gall: 0-0
Aids: Bl: 0-0 Vi: 0-0 Tstrap: 0-0
Best Rating: 70 8/01 NmkJ 7f gd-sft

Lightly-raced but yet to win despite decent efforts and has failed to reproduce his two-year-old form. Best effort came on fast ground over six furlongs.

Glorious Welcome

81 **40**
3-y-o b g Past Glories-Rest And Welcome (Town And Country)
Jane Southcombe Mrs V H Nicholas

Placings:0000 **(3274)**
2001: 8^{0}GS, 12^{0}GS, 9^{0}GF, 8^{0}GF

	Starts	1st	2nd	3rd	Win & Pl
Career Total (Turf)	4	0	0	0	

Going (Turf): Sf: 0-0 GS: 0-2 Gd: 0-0 GF: 0-2 Fm: 0-0
Distance: 5f/6f: 0-0 7f-8f: 0-2 9f-13f: 0-2 14f+: 0-0
Track : LH: 0-0 RH: 0-3 Tight: 0-2 Gall: 0-0
Aids: Bl: 0-1 Vi: 0-0 Tstrap: 0-1
Best Rating: 40 7/01 Kemp 1m gd-fm

Glory Days (IRE)

98 **60**
3-y-o ch c Lahib (USA)-Gloire (Thatching)
R Hannon A F Merritt

Placings:1-0660000 **(5131)**
2001: 6^{0}GF, 6^{6}GF, 6^{6}G, 5^{0}GF, 8^{0}G, 7^{0}GF, 7^{0}HY

	Starts	1st	2nd	3rd	Win & Pl
Career Total (Turf)	8	1	0	0	3891

82 5/00 Kemp 5f D G-S £3542
Total win prize-money £3543

Going (Turf): Sf: 0-1 **GS: 1-1** Gd: 0-2 GF: 0-4 Fm: 0-0
Distance: **5f/6f: 1-3** 7f-8f: 0-4 9f-13f: 0-1 14f+: 0-0
Track : LH: 0-0 RH: 0-1 Tight: 0-0 Gall: 0-0
Aids: Bl: 0-2 Vi: 0-0 Tstrap: 0-0
Best Rating: 80 5/01 Gdwd 6f gd-fm

Chipped a bone in his knee after winning on softish ground at Kempton as a juvenile, but was then off for over a year. Has shown limited signs of ability since his return.

Glory Of Love

86(69) **32**
6-y-o b g Belmez (USA)-Princess Lieven (Royal Palace)
Mrs A M Naughton Miss Lorna Preston

Placings:550/0650/0-0 **(0879)**
2001: 21^{0}S

	Starts	1st	2nd	3rd	Win & Pl
Career Total (Turf)	8	0	0	0	0
Career Total (AW)	1	0	0	0	

Going (Turf): Sf: 0-1 GS: 0-1 Gd: 0-2 GF: 0-2 Fm: 0-2
Distance: 5f/6f: 0-0 7f-8f: 0-3 9f-13f: 0-2 14f+: 0-4
Track : LH: 0-6 RH: 0-1 Tight: 0-4 Gall: 0-0
Aids: Bl: 0-0 Vi: 0-2 Tstrap: 0-0
Best Rating: 1 4/01 Pont 2m5f122y soft

Glory Quest (USA)

102(101) (78)**68**
4-y-o b c Quest For Fame-Sonseri (Prince Tenderfoot (USA))
Miss Gay Kelleway Quest To Win Partnership

Placings:33/2234221-0063540 **(5669)**
2001: 8^{0}GS, 7^{0}GS, 9^{6}GS, 9^{3}SD, 9^{5}S, 7^{4}S, 10^{0}HY

	Starts	1st	2nd	3rd	Win & Pl
Career Total (Turf)	15	1	4	3	10974
Career Total (AW)	1	0	0	1	590

77 10/00 Ling 7f140y D SFT £2561
Total win prize-money £2561

Going (Turf): **Sf: 1-6** GS: 0-4 Gd: 0-3 GF: 0-2 Fm: 0-0
Distance: 5f/6f: 0-2 **7f-8f: 1-8** 9f-13f: 0-6 14f+: 0-0
Track : LH: 0-3 RH: 0-5 Tight: 0-4 Gall: 0-1
Aids: Bl: 0-0 Vi: 0-1 Tstrap: 0-0
Best Rating: 78 8/01 Wolv 1m1f79y stand

Has won once, and that came last year on the soft ground at Lingfield, but has looked held since then. Acts well at around seven furlongs.

Glossy Eyed (IRE)

61 **8**
2-y-o ch g Eagle Eyed (USA)-Hi-Gloss (IRE) (Be My Guest (USA))
A Berry B Batey

Placings:000 **(4536)**
2001: 6^{0}GF, 7^{0}G, 6^{0}GF

	Starts	1st	2nd	3rd	Win & Pl
Career Total (Turf)	3	0	0	0	

Going (Turf): Sf: 0-0 GS: 0-0 Gd: 0-1 GF: 0-2 Fm: 0-0
Distance: 5f/6f: 0-2 7f-8f: 0-1 9f-13f: 0-0 14f+: 0-0
Track : LH: 0-1 RH: 0-0 Tight: 0-1 Gall: 0-0
Aids: Bl: 0-0 Vi: 0-0 Tstrap: 0-0
Best Rating: 8 9/01 Rdcr 6f gd-fm

Glowing

110 **87**
6-y-o ro m Chilibang-Juliet Bravo (Glow (USA))
J R Fanshawe Peters Friends

Placings:0324321/440110/2024150-201006 **(4780)**
2001: 5^{2}G, 6^{0}GF, 6^{1}GF, 6^{0}GF, 6^{0}GF, 6^{0}G

				Starts	1st	2nd	3rd	Win & Pl
Career Total (Turf)				**26**	**5**	**5**	**2**	**39951**
87	7/01	Gdwd	6f	C(0-90)H			G-F	£14755
79	7/00	NmkJ	6f	D(0-80)H			G-F	£4348
73	9/99	Donc	5f	D(0-80)H			G-F	£3870
68	8/99	Nott	6f15y	D(0-85)H			GD	£4597
67	8/98	Folk	6f	F			G-F	£2070

Total win prize-money £29642

Going (Turf): Sf: 0-1 GS: 0-1 Gd: 1-9 **GF: 4-15** Fm: 0-0
Distance: **5f/6f: 4-22** 7f-8f: 1-4 9f-13f: 0-0 14f+: 0-0
Track : LH: 0-2 RH: 0-2 Tight: 0-1 Gall: 0-3
Aids: Bl: 0-0 Vi: 0-0 Tstrap: 0-4
Best Rating: 87 7/01 Gdwd 6f gd-fm

Suited by six furlongs and fast ground, she seems at her best in the summer and bounced back to form with a last-gasp victory at Goodwood in July. Needs to be covered up.

Glowing Lake (IRE)

94(87) (45)**59**
2-y-o b f Lake Coniston (IRE)-Glowing Lines (IRE) (Glow (USA))
J S Wainwright Holme Lea Racing

Placings:03420060243000 **(5404)**
2001: 5^{0}S, 5^{3}S, 5^{4}GS, 5^{2}SD, 5^{0}SD, 6^{0}G, 7^{6}GF, 6^{0}G, 7^{2}G, 7^{4}GF, 8^{3}GF, 7^{0}S, 7^{0}GS, 8^{0}S

	Starts	1st	2nd	3rd	Win & Pl
Career Total (Turf)	**12**	**0**	**1**	**2**	**2164**
Career Total (AW)	**2**	**0**	**1**	**0**	**522**

Going (Turf): Sf: 0-4 GS: 0-2 Gd: 0-3 GF: 0-3 Fm: 0-0
Distance: 5f/6f: 0-7 7f-8f: 0-5 9f-13f: 0-2 14f+: 0-0
Track : LH: 0-5 RH: 0-1 Tight: 0-1 Gall: 0-3
Aids: Bl: 0-5 Vi: 0-3 Tstrap: 0-0
Best Rating: 59 9/01 Leic 1m9y gd-fm

Go Ahead Jo

(56) **18**
2-y-o b f Classic Cliche (IRE)-It's So Easy (Shaadi (USA))
A P James Joe Ryan

Placings:000 **(5197)**
2001: 6^{0}GF, 8^{0}HY, 8^{0}SD

	Starts	1st	2nd	3rd	Win & Pl
Career Total (Turf)	**2**	**0**	**0**	**0**	
Career Total (AW)	**1**	**0**	**0**	**0**	

Going (Turf): Sf: 0-1 GS: 0-0 Gd: 0-0 GF: 0-1 Fm: 0-0
Distance: 5f/6f: 0-0 7f-8f: 0-1 9f-13f: 0-2 14f+: 0-0
Track : LH: 0-2 RH: 0-0 Tight: 0-1 Gall: 0-0
Aids: Bl: 0-0 Vi: 0-0 Tstrap: 0-0
Best Rating: 18 7/01 Chep 6f16y gd-fm

Go For It Sweetie (IRE)

21
8-y-o b m Brush Aside (USA)-Arctic Mistress (Quayside)
B D Leavy Barry Leavy

Placings:0-0 **(0083)**
2001: 16^{0}SD

	Starts	1st	2nd	3rd	Win & Pl
Career Total (Turf)	**1**	**0**	**0**	**0**	
Career Total (AW)	**1**	**0**	**0**	**0**	

Going (Turf): Sf: 0-0 GS: 0-0 Gd: 0-0 GF: 0-0 Fm: 0-1
Distance: 5f/6f: 0-0 7f-8f: 0-0 9f-13f: 0-0 14f+: 0-2
Track : LH: 0-2 RH: 0-0 Tight: 0-1 Gall: 0-0
Aids: Bl: 0-0 Vi: 0-0 Tstrap: 0-2

Go Gabana

91(58) (1)**62**
2-y-o b c First Trump-Have Form (Haveroid)
N P Littmoden The Bouch And Feerick Families

Placings:6000600 **(5130)**
2001: 5^{6}F, 6^{0}GF, 5^{0}G, 7^{0}SD, 6^{6}G, 6^{0}GF, 7^{0}HY

	Starts	1st	2nd	3rd	Win & Pl
Career Total (Turf)	**6**	**0**	**0**	**0**	**1250**
Career Total (AW)	**1**	**0**	**0**	**0**	

Going (Turf): Sf: 0-1 GS: 0-0 Gd: 0-2 GF: 0-2 Fm: 0-1
Distance: 5f/6f: 0-4 7f-8f: 0-3 9f-13f: 0-0 14f+: 0-0
Track : LH: 0-2 RH: 0-0 Tight: 0-1 Gall: 0-0
Aids: Bl: 0-3 Vi: 0-0 Tstrap: 0-0
Best Rating: 62 9/01 Kemp 6f good

Go Thunder (IRE)

97 **27**
7-y-o b g Nordico (USA)-Moving Off (Henbit (USA))
D A Nolan Miss G Joughin

Placings:60521360/0435400/60030/000/000531403-00660450604000 **(5284)**
2001: 8^{0}GF, 6^{0}GF, 9^{6}GS, 9^{6}G, 8^{0}F, 8^{4}GS, 9^{5}G, 8^{0}F, 7^{6}GS, 9^{0}GS, 8^{4}S, 9^{0}G, 8^{0}F, 9^{0}HY

				Starts	1st	2nd	3rd	Win & Pl
Career Total (Turf)				**46**	**2**	**1**	**5**	**18674**
35	9/00	Haml	1m1f36y	F			SFT	£2380
90	8/96	Tral	1m	(0-100)			SFT	£13100

Total win prize-money £15480

Going (Turf): Sf: 2-11 GS: 0-5 Gd: 0-12 GF: 0-5 Fm: 0-5
Distance: 5f/6f: 0-0 7f-8f: 1-16 9f-13f: 1-27 14f+: 0-3
Track : LH: 1-12 RH: 1-30 **Tight: 1-17** Gall: 0-0
Aids: Bl: 0-0 Vi: 0-0 **Tstrap: 1-26**
Best Rating: 36 7/01 Ayr 7f gd-sft

Go With The Wind

95(70) (43d)**34**
8-y-o b g Unfuwain (USA)-Cominna (Dominion)
R A Fahey Alf Chadwick

Placings:00/443202260414/34/340/00612203/03206-0240 **(2632)**
2001: 11^{0}G, 13^{2}GF, 11^{4}GF, 16^{0}F

				Starts	1st	2nd	3rd	Win & Pl
Career Total (Turf)				**31**	**2**	**7**	**5**	**18809**
Career Total (AW)				**2**	**0**	**0**	**0**	**240**
48	7/99	Bevl	1m3f216y	E(0-70)H			G-F	£3904
67	9/96	Nott	2m9y	E(0-70)H			G-F	£3343

Total win prize-money £7247

Going (Turf): Sf: 0-2 GS: 0-3 Gd: 0-8 **GF: 2-15** Fm: 0-6
Distance: 5f/6f: 0-0 7f-8f: 0-3 9f-13f: 1-13 14f+: 1-20
Track : LH: 1-20 RH: 1-14 **Tight: 1-23** Gall: 0-3
Aids: Bl: 0-1 Vi: 0-1 Tstrap: 0-0
Best Rating: 34 6/01 Bevl 1m3f216y gd-fm

Goblet Of Fire (USA)

93 **82**
2-y-o b c Green Desert (USA)-Laurentine (USA) (Private Account (USA))
B J Meehan Mrs Susan Roy

Placings:04 **(5596)**
2001: 7^{0}S, 8^{4}GS

	Starts	1st	2nd	3rd	Win & Pl
Career Total (Turf)	**2**	**0**	**0**	**0**	**468**

Going (Turf): Sf: 0-1 GS: 0-1 Gd: 0-0 GF: 0-0 Fm: 0-0
Distance: 5f/6f: 0-0 7f-8f: 0-2 9f-13f: 0-0 14f+: 0-0
Track : LH: 0-0 RH: 0-0 Tight: 0-0 Gall: 0-0
Aids: Bl: 0-0 Vi: 0-0 Tstrap: 0-0

Best Rating: 82 11/01 NmkR 1m gd-sft

An 82,000gns son of a half-sister to Love Divine, he has ability and should do better at three.

Godmersham Park

(104) (35)
9-y-o b g Warrshan (USA)-Brown Velvet (Mansingh (USA))
P S Felgate P S Felgate

Placings:0/32220/6300/04205505**0611/1113100000000**
4400/2044006500433460305/23441400140500-405
(0285)
2001: 8^{4}SD, 8^{0}SD, 9^{5}SW

				Starts	1st	2nd	3rd	Win & Pl
Career Total (Turf)				**26**	**1**	**4**	**2**	**7604**
Career Total (AW)				**50**	**7**	**2**	**6**	**21113**
41	6/00	Ripn	1m	E			G-S	£2873
48	3/00	Sthl	1m	E(0-70)H			STD	£2509
73	2/98	Wolv	1m100y	D(0-85)H			STD	£3371
65	1/98	Sthl	1m	F(0-65)H			STD	£1735
63	1/98	Sthl	1m	E(0-70)H			STD	£2944
59	1/98	Sthl	7f	E(0-70)H			STD	£2476
54	12/97	Sthl	7f	F(0-60)H			STD	£1944
51	11/97	Sthl	1m	F(0-60)H			STD	£1944

Total win prize-money £19796

Going (Turf): Sf: 0-2 **GS: 1-6** Gd: 0-6 GF: 0-8 Fm: 0-4
Distance: 5f/6f: 0-1 **7f-8f: 7-52** 9f-13f: 1-22 14f+: 0-0
Track : **LH: 7-61** RH: 1-5 **Tight: 2-30** Gall: 0-1
Aids: Bl: 0-1 Vi: 0-1 Tstrap: 0-0
Best Rating: 35 2/01 Wolv 1m1f79y slow

Gog's Gift

82 **24**
3-y-o b g So Factual (USA)-Premium Gift (Most Welcome)
C B B Booth Ashley Carr

Placings:050-00 **(5374)**
2001: 6^{0}G, 6^{0}G

	Starts	1st	2nd	3rd	Win & Pl
Career Total (Turf)	**5**	**0**	**0**	**0**	**0**

Going (Turf): Sf: 0-2 GS: 0-0 Gd: 0-2 GF: 0-1 Fm: 0-0
Distance: 5f/6f: 0-5 7f-8f: 0-0 9f-13f: 0-0 14f+: 0-0
Track : LH: 0-0 RH: 0-0 Tight: 0-0 Gall: 0-0
Aids: Bl: 0-1 Vi: 0-0 Tstrap: 0-0
Best Rating: 24 10/01 Rdcr 6f good

Goggles (IRE)

110 **103**
3-y-o b c Eagle Eyed (USA)-Rock On (IRE) (Ballad Rock)
H Candy Mrs J K Powell

Placings:411-554021 **(3629)**
2001: 8^{5}GS, 6^{5}F, 7^{4}GF, 7^{0}GF, 8^{2}G, 8^{1}G

				Starts	1st	2nd	3rd	Win & Pl
Career Total (Turf)				**9**	**3**	**1**	**0**	**183965**
103	8/01	Gdwd	1m	A			GD	£16631
97	9/00	Donc	6f	B			GD	£155950
86	8/00	Gdwd	6f	D			G-F	£7182

Total win prize-money £179764

Going (Turf): Sf: 0-0 GS: 0-1 **Gd: 2-3** GF: 1-4 Fm: 0-1
Distance: **5f/6f: 2-2** 7f-8f: 1-7 9f-13f: 0-0 14f+: 0-0
Track : LH: 0-1 **RH: 1-1** Tight: 0-0 Gall: 0-1
Aids: Bl: 0-0 Vi: 0-0 Tstrap: 0-0
Best Rating: 103 8/01 Gdwd 1m good

Picked up a huge prize by winning the St Leger Yearling Stakes at Doncaster as a juvenile. Ran well when stepped up in trip early in the season and scored over a mile at Goodwood in August. Sold to Hong Kong.

Going Global (IRE)

93 **82**

4-y-o ch g Bob Back (USA)-Ukraine Girl (Targowice (USA))

G L Moore Mike Charlton And Rodger Sargent

Placings:31/132060405-000 **(5261)**

2001: 10^{0}S, 12^{0}S, 10^{0}GS

	Starts	1st	2nd	3rd	Win & Pl
Career Total (Turf)	**14**	**2**	**1**	**2**	**32778**

90	4/00	Ripn	1m1f	C(0-90)	SFT	£6331
77	9/99	Gdwd	1m	D	SFT	£3670

Total win prize-money £10001

Going (Turf): Sf: 2-5 GS: 0-2 Gd: 0-3 GF: 0-4 Fm: 0-0
Distance: 5f/6f: 0-0 7f-8f: 1-2 9f-13f: 1-10 14f+: 0-2
Track : LH: 0-4 **RH: 2-9 Tight: 1-6** Gall: 0-5
Aids: Bl: 0-0 Vi: 0-1 Tstrap: 0-1
Best Rating: 82 10/01 Asct 1m2f gd-sft

He took on the best at three and, after going the wrong way on the Flat, had an unsuccessful stint over hurdles. Well beaten when returned to the Flat.

Golan (IRE)

113 **122**

3-y-o b c Spectrum (IRE)-Highland Gift (IRE) (Generous (IRE))

Sir Michael Stoute Lord Weinstock

Placings:1-12314 **(5247a)**

2001: 8^{1}G, 12^{2}GF, 12^{3}Y, 12^{1}G, 12^{4}HO

	Starts	1st	2nd	3rd	Win & Pl
Career Total (Turf)	**6**	**3**	**1**	**1**	**579235**

122	9/01	Lonc	1m4f		GD	£38797
122	5/01	NmkR	1m	A	GD	£174000
95	9/00	Chep	7f16y	D	G-S	£3877

Total win prize-money £216674

Going (Turf): Sf: 0-0 GS: 1-1 **Gd: 2-2** GF: 0-1 Fm: 0-0
Distance: 5f/6f: 0-0 **7f-8f: 2-2** 9f-13f: 1-4 14f+: 0-0
Track : LH: 0-1 **RH: 1-2** Tight: 0-1 Gall: 0-0
Aids: Bl: 0-0 Vi: 0-0 Tstrap: 0-0
Best Rating: 122 9/01 Lonc 1m4f good

He ran in the 2000 Guineas as a prep race for the Derby, but came from near last to first to beat Tamburlaine in very good style. He confirmed his class, and stamina, when second to Galileo in the Derby, but was disappointing when third behind the same colt in the Irish version. Came back to win the Prix Niel for the Prix du Jockey-Club winner, and ran well to be fourth in the Arc. Suited by 12 furlongs and give in the ground.

Golconda (IRE)

107(107) (91)**91**

5-y-o br m Lahib (USA)-David's Star (Welsh Saint)

Lady Herries D K R & Mrs J B C Oliver

Placings:30/212112360/300001603-6436 **(3413)**

2001: 10^{6}G, 10^{4}GF, 10^{3}G, 10^{6}GF

	Starts	1st	2nd	3rd	Win & Pl
Career Total (Turf)	**21**	**3**	**2**	**4**	**51520**
Career Total (AW)	**3**	**1**	**1**	**1**	**6612**

85	7/00	Folk	1m1f149y	C(0-85)	G-F	£6027
75	5/99	Ling	1m2f	C(0-100)H	G-F	£7115
72	5/99	Kemp	1m1f	C(0-90)H	GD	£7327
63	2/99	Wolv	7f	D	STD	£2759

Total win prize-money £23229

Going (Turf): Sf: 0-1 GS: 0-1 **Gd: 1-9 GF: 1-8** Fm: 0-1
Distance: 5f/6f: 0-1 7f-8f: 1-3 **9f-13f: 2-19** 14f+: 0-0
Track : **LH: 2-14** RH: 1-5 **Tight: 2-7** Gall: 0-7
Aids: Bl: 0-0 Vi: 0-1 Tstrap: 0-0
Best Rating: 91 6/01 Kemp 1m2f gd-fm

Thoroughly genuine, she developed into a smart handicapper in 1999, but has rather struggled off her handicap mark since. Suited by ten furlongs and fast ground.

Gold Academy (IRE)

105 **98**

5-y-o b h Royal Academy (USA)-Soha (USA) (Dancing Brave (USA))

R Hannon George E K Teo

Placings:435/225130134/666240-35402060 **(4710)**

2001: 10^{3}GF, 9^{5}GF, 10^{4}GF, 10^{0}GF, 10^{2}GF, 9^{0}GF, 10^{6}G, 8^{0}G

	Starts	1st	2nd	3rd	Win & Pl
Career Total (Turf)	**26**	**2**	**4**	**4**	**127138**

113	9/99	York	1m205y	A	G-F	£19900
98	5/99	Chep	1m14y	D	GD	£3909

Total win prize-money £23809

Going (Turf): Sf: 0-2 GS: 0-2 **Gd: 1-11 GF: 1-11** Fm: 0-0
Distance: 5f/6f: 0-1 7f-8f: 0-8 **9f-13f: 2-17** 14f+: 0-0
Track : **LH: 1-6** RH: 0-12 Tight: 0-6 **Gall: 1-8**
Aids: Bl: 0-0 Vi: 0-0 Tstrap: 0-0
Best Rating: 105 5/01 Ches 1m2f75y gd-fm

High-class in '99, when he was fourth in the Champion Stakes, he has proved hard to place since and has been found wanting in the face of some stiff tasks. Needs to drop a bit more in the ratings.

Gold Ace (USA)

85 **77**

2-y-o ch c Gulch (USA)-Najecam (USA) (Trempolino (USA))

J Noseda K Y Lim

Placings:200 **(4939)**

2001: 6^{2}S, 6^{0}GF, 7^{0}S

	Starts	1st	2nd	3rd	Win & Pl
Career Total (Turf)	**3**	**0**	**1**	**0**	**1260**

Going (Turf): Sf: 0-2 GS: 0-0 Gd: 0-0 GF: 0-1 Fm: 0-0
Distance: 5f/6f: 0-2 7f-8f: 0-1 9f-13f: 0-0 14f+: 0-0
Track : LH: 0-1 RH: 0-0 Tight: 0-1 Gall: 0-0
Aids: Bl: 0-0 Vi: 0-0 Tstrap: 0-0
Best Rating: 77 7/01 Hayd 6f soft

Gold Blade

90(94) (39)**30**

12-y-o ch g Rousillon (USA)-Sharp Girl (FR) (Sharpman)

Mrs Lydia Pearce (J Pearce 27/2) Arthur Old

Placings:0/630242044/21212006145365/033546464/2102013230/21612431111100065/400P42200/00/33001125/40054610-03006500 **(3505)**

2001: 12^{0}SD, 12^{3}SD, 12^{0}SD, 12^{0}GF, 11^{6}F, 13^{5}G, 10^{0}GF, 9^{0}GF

	Starts	1st	2nd	3rd	Win & Pl
Career Total (Turf)	**61**	**11**	**7**	**4**	**41672**
Career Total (AW)	**35**	**4**	**6**	**6**	**17496**

41	8/00	Bevl	1m1f207y	E(0-75)H	GD	£3500
44	7/99	Pont	1m2f6y	F(0-60)H	G-S	£3444
38	6/99	Ling	1m3f106y	F(0-70)H	G-F	£2521
58	8/96	Catt	1m3f214y	G(0-70)H	G-F	£2343
68	7/96	Bevl	1m1f207y	E(0-80)H	G-F	£3208
61	7/96	Ayr	1m5f13y	E(0-70)H	G-F	£3176
60	7/96	Haml	1m1f36y	F(0-65)H	G-F	£2766
61	7/96	Pont	1m2f6y	F(0-60)H	G-F	£3132
48	4/96	Nott	1m1f213y	F(0-75)H	G-F	£2381
67	1/96	Sthl	1m4f	F(0-60)H	STD	£2222
49	7/95	Haml	1m3f16y	F(0-75)H	FRM	£2749
63	1/95	Wolv	1m4f	F(0-60)H	STD	£2537
53	9/93	Leic	1m1f218y	E(0-70)H	G-F	£4137
70	3/93	Ling	1m2f	E(0-70)H	STD	£2684
47	2/93	Ling	1m2f	F	STD	£2208

Total win prize-money £43012

Going (Turf): Sf: 0-6 GS: 1-7 Gd: 1-15 **GF: 8-25** Fm: 1-8
Distance: 5f/6f: 0-0 7f-8f: 0-7 **9f-13f: 14-84** 14f+: 1-5
Track : **LH: 10-67** RH: 5-25 **Tight: 7-44** Gall: 0-10
Aids: Bl: 0-3 Vi: 0-0 Tstrap: 0-0
Best Rating: 39 2/01 Wolv 1m4f stand

Gold Fervour (IRE)

90(72) (34)**56**

2-y-o b g Mon Tresor-Fervent Fan (IRE) (Soviet Lad (USA))

W M Brisbourne Major W R Paton-Smith

Placings:055340 **(5165)**

2001: 6^{0}S, 6^{5}G, 7^{5}G, 7^{3}HY, 7^{4}G, 5^{0}SD

	Starts	1st	2nd	3rd	Win & Pl
Career Total (Turf)	**5**	**0**	**0**	**1**	**383**
Career Total (AW)	**1**	**0**	**0**	**0**	

Going (Turf): Sf: 0-2 GS: 0-0 Gd: 0-3 GF: 0-0 Fm: 0-0
Distance: 5f/6f: 0-3 7f-8f: 0-3 9f-13f: 0-0 14f+: 0-0
Track : LH: 0-3 RH: 0-1 Tight: 0-2 Gall: 0-0
Aids: Bl: 0-0 Vi: 0-0 Tstrap: 0-0
Best Rating: 56 9/01 Hayd 7f30y heavy

Gold Guest

103 **87**

2-y-o ch c Vettori (IRE)-Cassilis (IRE) (Persian Bold)

M R Channon John Guest

Placings:616022503 **(4204a)**

2001: 5^{6}S, 5^{1}GS, 6^{6}F, 5^{0}GF, 6^{2}G, 6^{2}GF, 7^{5}GF, 7^{0}G, 7^{3}GS

	Starts	1st	2nd	3rd	Win & Pl
Career Total (Turf)	**9**	**1**	**2**	**1**	**10084**

67	5/01	Brig	5f59y	D	G-S	£2989

Total win prize-money £2989

Going (Turf): Sf: 0-1 **GS: 1-2** Gd: 0-2 GF: 0-3 Fm: 0-1
Distance: **5f/6f: 1-5** 7f-8f: 0-4 9f-13f: 0-0 14f+: 0-0
Track : **LH: 1-2** RH: 0-0 Tight: 0-0 Gall: 0-0
Aids: Bl: 0-0 Vi: 0-0 Tstrap: 0-0
Best Rating: 87 7/01 Asct 7f gd-fm

A winner over five at Brighton in May, he has since run well without winning.

Gold Kriek

76 (49)**34**

4-y-o b g High Kicker (USA)-Ship Of Gold (Glint Of Gold)

M E Sowersby The Southwold Set

Placings:000/000-00 **(2442)**

2001: 10^{0}HY, 11^{0}GF

	Starts	1st	2nd	3rd	Win & Pl
Career Total (Turf)	**6**	**0**	**0**	**0**	
Career Total (AW)	**2**	**0**	**0**	**0**	

Going (Turf): Sf: 0-2 GS: 0-0 Gd: 0-2 GF: 0-1 Fm: 0-1
Distance: 5f/6f: 0-0 7f-8f: 0-3 9f-13f: 0-5 14f+: 0-0
Track : LH: 0-4 RH: 0-3 Tight: 0-5 Gall: 0-0
Aids: Bl: 0-0 Vi: 0-0 Tstrap: 0-0
Best Rating: 32 4/01 Pont 1m2f6y heavy

Gold Point (IRE)

93 **79**

2-y-o b g Goldmark (USA)-Flashing Raven (IRE) (Maelstrom Lake)

A P Jarvis Jarvis Associates

Placings:21 **(3448)**

2001: 6^{2}G, 7^{1}GF

	Starts	1st	2nd	3rd	Win & Pl
Career Total (Turf)	**2**	**1**	**1**	**0**	**7100**

79	7/01	Newc	7f	E	G-F	£4940

Total win prize-money £4940

Going (Turf): Sf: 0-0 GS: 0-0 Gd: 0-1 **GF: 1-1** Fm: 0-0
Distance: 5f/6f: 0-1 **7f-8f: 1-1** 9f-13f: 0-0 14f+: 0-0
Track : LH: 0-0 RH: 0-0 Tight: 0-0 Gall: 0-0
Aids: Bl: 0-0 Vi: 0-0 Tstrap: 0-0
Best Rating: 79 7/01 Newc 7f gd-fm

From a useful family, he won a maiden auction at Newcastle having been gelded after his racecourse debut at York a month earlier. He stayed seven furlongs without trouble and will easily get a mile as a three-year-old.

Gold Rider (IRE)

50(70)

4-y-o b g Common Grounds-Baydon Belle (USA) (Al Nasr (FR))

Mrs C A Dunnett (J Pearce 16/2) E W Watts

Placings:0000005-0000 **(5557)**

2001: 12^{0}SD, 10^{0}G, 10^{0}S, 14^{0}S

	Starts	1st	2nd	3rd	Win & Pl
Career Total (Turf)	9	0	0	0	
Career Total (AW)	2	0	0	0	0

Going (Turf): Sf: 0-3 GS: 0-1 Gd: 0-1 GF: 0-2 Fm: 0-2
Distance: 5f/6f: 0-2 7f-8f: 0-3 9f-13f: 0-4 14f+: 0-2
Track : LH: 0-8 RH: 0-1 Tight: 0-4 Gall: 0-2
Aids: Bl: 0-1 Vi: 0-0 Tstrap: 0-1

Gold Standard (IRE)

106 **77**

3-y-o ch g Goldmark (USA)-Miss Audimar (USA) (Mr. Leader (USA))

D R C Elsworth R Black, J Stott, L Ferraris, D Watson

Placings:0-0630331220 **(5143)**

2001: 10^{0}G, 10^{6}F, 11^{3}G, 11^{0}GF, 11^{3}GF, 14^{3}GF, 14^{1}F, 12^{2}GF, 16^{2}GF, 14^{0}G

	Starts	1st	2nd	3rd	Win & Pl
Career Total (Turf)	11	1	2	3	8198

70 8/01 Sals 1m6f15y E(0-70)H FRM £3388
Total win prize-money £3388

Going (Turf): Sf: 0-0 GS: 0-1 Gd: 0-3 GF: 0-5 **Fm: 1-2**
Distance: 5f/6f: 0-0 7f-8f: 0-0 9f-13f: 0-7 **14f+: 1-4**
Track : LH: 0-4 **RH: 1-5 Tight: 1-8** Gall: 0-1
Aids: Bl: 0-0 Vi: 0-0 Tstrap: 0-0
Best Rating: 77 9/01 Newb 2m gd-fm

Made all at Salisbury in August and has run well since. Stays two miles.

Gold Statuette (IRE)

103 **83**

3-y-o ch c Caerleon (USA)-Nawara (Welsh Pageant)

J W Hills F Bienstock, M Boase, M Kerr-Dineen

Placings:0640-31024 **(4296)**

2001: 8^{3}G, 10^{1}GF, 12^{0}GF, 12^{2}GF, 12^{4}G

	Starts	1st	2nd	3rd	Win & Pl
Career Total (Turf)	9	1	1	1	8261

82 5/01 Wwck 1m2f188yD(0-80)H G-F £3967
Total win prize-money £3968

Going (Turf): Sf: 0-0 GS: 0-1 Gd: 0-4 **GF: 1-4** Fm: 0-0
Distance: 5f/6f: 0-0 7f-8f: 0-4 **9f-13f: 1-5** 14f+: 0-0
Track : **LH: 1-4** RH: 0-3 Tight: 0-4 Gall: 0-1
Aids: Bl: 0-0 Vi: 0-0 Tstrap: 0-0
Best Rating: 83 8/01 Epsm 1m4f10y good

He got off the mark in a Warwick handicap in May on his first attempt over ten furlongs. May not truly stay a mile and a half judged on his subsequent starts. Suited by a sound surface.

Goldbrook

91 **44**

3-y-o b g Alderbrook-Miss Marigold (Norwick (USA))

R J Hodges S J Norman

Placings:0000 **(2488)**

2001: 10^{0}GS, 10^{0}GF, 10^{0}GF, 10^{0}HD

	Starts	1st	2nd	3rd	Win & Pl
Career Total (Turf)	4	0	0	0	

Going (Turf): Sf: 0-0 GS: 0-1 Gd: 0-0 GF: 0-2 Fm: 0-1
Distance: 5f/6f: 0-0 7f-8f: 0-0 9f-13f: 0-4 14f+: 0-0
Track : LH: 0-3 RH: 0-0 Tight: 0-4 Gall: 0-0
Aids: Bl: 0-0 Vi: 0-0 Tstrap: 0-0
Best Rating: 44 6/01 Wind 1m2f7y gd-fm

Golden Boot

100 **87**

2-y-o ch g Unfuwain (USA)-Sports Delight (Star Appeal)

A Bailey (R M Beckett 11/10) Willie McKay

Placings:451006 **(5668)**

2001: 7^{4}GF, 6^{5}F, 8^{1}HY, 8^{0}G, 7^{0}S, 8^{6}HY

	Starts	1st	2nd	3rd	Win & Pl
Career Total (Turf)	6	1	0	0	3430

87 9/01 Hayd 1m30y E HVY £3430
Total win prize-money £3430

Going (Turf): Sf: 1-3 GS: 0-0 Gd: 0-1 GF: 0-1 Fm: 0-1
Distance: 5f/6f: 0-0 7f-8f: 0-4 **9f-13f: 1-2** 14f+: 0-0
Track : **LH: 1-3** RH: 0-1 Tight: 0-1 Gall: 0-1
Aids: Bl: 0-0 Vi: 0-0 Tstrap: 0-0
Best Rating: 87 9/01 Hayd 1m30y heavy

From the same family as the top-class two-year-old miler, Turtle Island, he has struggled in handicaps since winning a Haydock maiden in September in the mud.

Golden Bounty

98 **92+**

2-y-o b c Bahamian Bounty-Cumbrian Melody (Petong)

R Hannon George E K Teo

Placings:43315 **(5256)**

2001: 6^{4}GF, 6^{3}GF, 6^{3}G, 5^{1}F, 5^{5}GS

	Starts	1st	2nd	3rd	Win & Pl
Career Total (Turf)	5	1	0	2	6228

92 9/01 Pont 5f E FRM £4046
Total win prize-money £4046

Going (Turf): Sf: 0-0 GS: 0-1 Gd: 0-1 GF: 0-2 **Fm: 1-1**
Distance: **5f/6f: 1-5** 7f-8f: 0-0 9f-13f: 0-0 14f+: 0-0
Track : **LH: 1-1** RH: 0-0 Tight: 0-0 Gall: 0-0
Aids: Bl: 0-0 Vi: 0-0 Tstrap: 0-0
Best Rating: 92 9/01 Pont 5f firm

In the frame over six furlongs on his first three starts, he was dropped back to the minimum at Pontefract and won very easily. Should hold his own in better company.

Golden Brief (IRE)

101(90) (62d)**46**

3-y-o ch g Brief Truce (USA)-Tiffany's Case (IRE) (Thatching)

K R Burke John Kelsey-Fry

Placings:003-050044300 **(5413)**

2001: 7^{0}SW, 7^{5}SD, 7^{0}G, 6^{0}G, 7^{4}G, 9^{4}GF, 8^{3}GF, 8^{0}F, 8^{0}SD

	Starts	1st	2nd	3rd	Win & Pl
Career Total (Turf)	8	0	0	1	483
Career Total (AW)	4	0	0	1	358

Going (Turf): Sf: 0-2 GS: 0-0 Gd: 0-3 GF: 0-2 Fm: 0-1
Distance: 5f/6f: 0-0 7f-8f: 0-9 9f-13f: 0-3 14f+: 0-0
Track : LH: 0-8 RH: 0-0 Tight: 0-2 Gall: 0-0
Aids: Bl: 0-0 Vi: 0-1 Tstrap: 0-6
Best Rating: 48 5/01 Wolv 7f stand

Golden Chance (IRE)

100 **67**

4-y-o b g Unfuwain (USA)-Golden Digger (USA) (Mr Prospector (USA))

M W Easterby The Shooting Syndicate

Placings:322130426-00031020250 **(5263)**

2001: 8^{0}G, 8^{0}G, 8^{0}GF, 11^{3}GS, 12^{1}GF, 12^{0}GF, 9^{2}GF, 11^{0}G, 12^{2}GF, 10^{5}G, 13^{0}GS

	Starts	1st	2nd	3rd	Win & Pl
Career Total (Turf)	20	2	5	3	16276

70 6/01 Ripn 1m4f60y E(0-70)H G-F £3556
86 6/00 Rdcr 1m D FRM £2769
Total win prize-money £6325

Going (Turf): Sf: 0-1 GS: 0-3 Gd: 0-5 **GF: 1-9 Fm: 1-2**
Distance: 5f/6f: 0-0 7f-8f: 1-7 9f-13f: 1-12 14f+: 0-1
Track : LH: 0-11 **RH: 1-7 Tight: 1-6** Gall: 0-5
Aids: Bl: 0-0 Vi: 0-0 Tstrap: 0 0
Best Rating: 70 6/01 Ripn 1m4f60y gd-fm

He changed stables before this season and showed dramatic improvement when stepped up to middle distances. Seems to go well for his lady rider in amateur events, although does look in need of a bit of ease in the handicap.

Golden Chimes (USA)

101(79) (32)**62**

6-y-o ch g Woodman (USA)-Russian Ballet (USA) (Nijinsky (CAN))

E W Tuer G Tuer

Placings:05/15/0060030/16060-620 **(2394)**

2001: 17^{6}F, 14^{2}G, 14^{0}GF

	Starts	1st	2nd	3rd	Win & Pl
Career Total (Turf)	18	2	1	1	10910
Career Total (AW)	1	0	0	0	

65 6/00 Carl 1m6f32y D(0-80)H FRM £4153
87 9/98 List 1m2f G-Y £4468
Total win prize-money £8623

Going (Turf): Sf: 0-2 GS: 0-1 Gd: 0-4 GF: 0-5 **Fm: 1-3**
Distance: 5f/6f: 0-0 7f-8f: 0-2 9f-13f: 1-9 14f+: 1-8
Track : LH: 1-11 RH: 1-7 Tight: 0-3 Gall: 0-2
Aids: Bl: 0-2 Vi: 0-0 Tstrap: 0-1
Best Rating: 59 6/01 Muss 1m6f good

Golden Dragon

109 **89**

3-y-o ch g Piccolo-Aunt Judy (Great Nephew)

M A Jarvis N S Yong

Placings:62110250 **(5133)**

2001: 7^{6}S, 7^{2}G, 6^{1}GF, 7^{1}GF, 8^{0}GF, 7^{2}GF, 7^{5}GS, 7^{0}G

	Starts	1st	2nd	3rd	Win & Pl
Career Total (Turf)	8	2	2	0	12877

86 6/01 Ches 7f122y D(0-80) G-F £4192
49 5/01 Sthl 6f D G-F £3893
Total win prize-money £8087

Going (Turf): Sf: 0-1 GS: 0-1 Gd: 0-2 **GF: 2-4** Fm: 0-0
Distance: 5f/6f: 1-1 7f-8f: 1-7 9f-13f: 0-0 14f+: 0-0
Track : **LH: 2-3** RH: 0-0 **Tight: 1-2** Gall: 0-0
Aids: Bl: 0-0 Vi: 0-0 Tstrap: 0-0
Best Rating: 89 8/01 Newb 7f gd-fm

Progressed well to win a maiden on turf at Southwell in May and followed up in a Chester Handicap. He did not seem to get the mile at Newmarket next time, but ran better at Newbury over seven furlongs, which looks his best trip.

Golden Dragonfly (IRE)

96(89) (51)**36**

3-y-o ch g Eagle Eyed (USA)-Shanna (BEL) (River Smile (USA))

D Nicholls T S Palin & Barbara Cunningham

Placings:0060-0206464454 **(4422)**

2001: 7^{0}SD, 8^{2}SD, 7^{0}SW, 8^{6}SW, 7^{4}SW, 8^{6}GF, 10^{4}GF, 11^{4}F, 11^{5}GF, 10^{4}GF

	Starts	1st	2nd	3rd	Win & Pl
Career Total (Turf)	9	0	0	0	267
Career Total (AW)	5	0	1	0	0

Going (Turf): Sf: 0-2 GS: 0-0 Gd: 0-0 GF: 0-6 Fm: 0-1
Distance: 5f/6f: 0-3 7f-8f: 0-5 9f-13f: 0-6 14f+: 0-0
Track : LH: 0-8 RH: 0-3 Tight: 0-4 Gall: 0-1
Aids: Bl: 0-0 Vi: 0-0 Tstrap: 0-1
Best Rating: 51 1/01 Sthl 1m stand

Golden Fortuna

97(96) (52)**70**
3-y-o b f Turtle Island (IRE)-Shady Bank (USA) (Alleged (USA))
J W Hills George Tong

Placings:0-340 **(2935)**
2001: 8^{3}SD, 8^{4}GF, 9^{0}GF

	Starts	1st	2nd	3rd	Win & Pl
Career Total (Turf)	3	0	0	0	331
Career Total (AW)	1	0	0	1	427

Going (Turf): Sf: 0-0 GS: 0-0 Gd: 0-0 GF: 0-3 Fm: 0-0
Distance: 5f/6f: 0-0 7f-8f: 0-2 9f-13f: 0-2 14f+: 0-0
Track : LH: 0-1 RH: 0-2 Tight: 0-1 Gall: 0-0
Aids: Bl: 0-0 Vi: 0-0 Tstrap: 0-0
Best Rating: 70 6/01 Wind 1m67y gd-fm

Golden Hind (USA)

(102) (82)**50**
3-y-o ch f Seeking The Gold (USA)-Min Elreeh (USA) (Danzig (USA))
Sir Mark Prescott Sir Edmund Loder

Placings:515-253 **(0262)**
2001: 7^{2}SD, 7^{5}SD, 8^{3}SD

	Starts	1st	2nd	3rd	Win & Pl	
Career Total (Turf)	1	0	0	0	0	
Career Total (AW)	5	1	1	1	4382	
79	11/00	Sthl	5f	D	STD	£2730

Total win prize-money £2730

Going (Turf): Sf: 0-1 GS: 0-0 Gd: 0-0 GF: 0-0 Fm: 0-0
Distance: **5f/6f: 1-3** 7f-8f: 0-2 9f-13f: 0-1 14f+: 0-0
Track : LH: 0-3 RH: 0-0 Tight: 0-2 Gall: 0-0
Aids: Bl: 0-0 Vi: 0-0 Tstrap: 0-0
Best Rating: 82 2/01 Wolv 1m100y stand

Golden Legend (IRE)

101(76) (22)**62**
4-y-o b g Last Tycoon-Adjalisa (IRE) (Darshaan)
R J Price (A B Coogan 6/7) E G Bevan

Placings:00/4000-000230400120 **(3062)**
2001: 9^{0}SD, 6^{0}G, 7^{0}GF, 6^{2}F, 8^{3}GF, 7^{0}GF, 6^{4}GF, 7^{0}SD, 6^{0}GF, 9^{1}GF, 8^{2}GF, 8^{0}G

	Starts	1st	2nd	3rd	Win & Pl	
Career Total (Turf)	15	1	2	1	6160	
Career Total (AW)	3	0	0	0	0	
60	7/01	Kemp	1m1f	E(0-75)H	G-F	£3802

Total win prize-money £3803

Going (Turf): Sf: 0-0 GS: 0-2 Gd: 0-3 **GF: 1-9** Fm: 0-1
Distance: 5f/6f: 0-4 7f-8f: 0-10 **9f-13f: 1-4** 14f+: 0-0
Track : LH: 0-4 **RH: 1-2** Tight: 0-3 Gall: 0-0
Aids: Bl: 0-0 Vi: 0-0 Tstrap: 0-2
Best Rating: 62 7/01 Wwck 1m22y gd-fm

A half-brother to Access All Areas, has had spells over hurdles and the All-Weather. Goes well for amateur jockeys and scored his first success at Kempton in July.

Golden Locket

99(96) (58)**67**
4-y-o ch f Beveled (USA)-Rekindled Flame (IRE) (King's Lake (USA))
M Kettle Benham Racing

Placings:500/400323-5560060 **(5619)**
2001: 7^{5}G, 7^{5}GF, 7^{6}F, 7^{0}SD, 8^{0}GS, 8^{6}SD, 6^{0}SD

	Starts	1st	2nd	3rd	Win & Pl
Career Total (Turf)	10	0	0	0	305
Career Total (AW)	6	0	1	2	1561

Going (Turf): Sf: 0-2 GS: 0-2 Gd: 0-3 GF: 0-2 Fm: 0-1
Distance: 5f/6f: 0-1 7f-8f: 0-12 9f-13f: 0-3 14f+: 0-0
Track : LH: 0-6 RH: 0-2 Tight: 0-3 Gall: 0-1
Aids: Bl: 0-0 Vi: 0-0 Tstrap: 0-0
Best Rating: 67 9/01 Leic 7f9y gd-fm

Golden Needle (IRE)

(93) (60)
3-y-o b f Prince Of Birds (USA)-Royal Thimble (IRE) (Prince Rupert (FR))
Noel T Chance Family Tree Syndicate

Placings:44-3 **(0023)**
2001: 7^{3}SD

	Starts	1st	2nd	3rd	Win & Pl
Career Total (Turf)	0	0	0	0	
Career Total (AW)	3	0	0	1	633

Going (Turf): Sf: 0-0 GS: 0-0 Gd: 0-0 GF: 0-0 Fm: 0-0
Distance: 5f/6f: 0-0 7f-8f: 0-3 9f-13f: 0-0 14f+: 0-0
Track : LH: 0-3 RH: 0-0 Tight: 0-1 Gall: 0-0
Aids: Bl: 0-0 Vi: 0-0 Tstrap: 0-0
Best Rating: 41 1/01 Sthl 7f stand

Golden Oscar

91 **26**
4-y-o ch g Primo Dominie-Noble Destiny (Dancing Brave (USA))
Andrew Turnell Dr John Hollowood

Placings:0030-000400 **(4326)**
2001: 8^{0}HY, 7^{0}GF, 8^{0}GF, 7^{4}GF, 7^{0}F, 8^{0}GF

	Starts	1st	2nd	3rd	Win & Pl
Career Total (Turf)	10	0	0	1	643

Going (Turf): Sf: 0-2 GS: 0-1 Gd: 0-1 GF: 0-5 Fm: 0-1
Distance: 5f/6f: 0-0 7f-8f: 0-8 9f-13f: 0-2 14f+: 0-0
Track : LH: 0-5 RH: 0-4 Tight: 0-6 Gall: 0-0
Aids: Bl: 0-0 Vi: 0-0 Tstrap: 0-0
Best Rating: 30 6/01 Bevl 7f100y gd-fm

Golden Rod

102(109) (64)**47**
4-y-o ch g Rainbows For Life (CAN)-Noble Form (Double Form)
P W Harris Neil Rodway

Placings:400/00346000310-10601034412 **(5419)**
2001: 11^{1}SD, 12^{0}SD, 11^{6}SD, 10^{0}GS, 11^{1}F, 10^{0}GF, 14^{3}GF, 12^{4}G, 12^{4}GF, 12^{1}SD, 12^{2}SD

	Starts	1st	2nd	3rd	Win & Pl	
Career Total (Turf)	17	1	0	3	4524	
Career Total (AW)	8	3	1	0	7430	
60	9/01	Wolv	1m4f	F(0-60)H	STD	£2464
46	5/01	Leic	1m3f183y	F(0-65)H	FRM	£2723
64	3/01	Sthl	1m3f	E(0-70)H	STD	£2310
47	11/00	Wolv	1m1f79y	F(0-65)H	STD	£1960

Total win prize-money £9457

Going (Turf): Sf: 0-3 GS: 0-1 Gd: 0-2 GF: 0-10 **Fm: 1-1**
Distance: 5f/6f: 0-0 7f-8f: 0-3 **9f-13f: 4-18** 14f+: 0-4
Track : **LH: 3-15** RH: 1-4 **Tight: 2-13** Gall: 0-1
Aids: Bl: 0-0 Vi: 0-0 Tstrap: 0-0
Best Rating: 64 3/01 Sthl 1m3f stand

He won on turf at Leicester in May, but is a better horse on Fibresand and won his third race on that surface in September. Best over 12 furlongs.

Golden Shell

67 **26**
2-y-o ch f Hatim (USA)-Sonnenelle (Sonnen Gold)
A C Whillans Mrs L M Whillans

Placings:0 **(5029)**
2001: 5^{0}GF

	Starts	1st	2nd	3rd	Win & Pl
Career Total (Turf)	1	0	0	0	

Going (Turf): Sf: 0-0 GS: 0-0 Gd: 0-0 GF: 0-1 Fm: 0-0
Distance: 5f/6f: 0-1 7f-8f: 0-0 9f-13f: 0-0 14f+: 0-0
Track : LH: 0-0 RH: 0-0 Tight: 0-0 Gall: 0-0
Aids: Bl: 0-0 Vi: 0-0 Tstrap: 0-0
Best Rating: 26 9/01 Muss 5f gd-fm

Golden Silca

102 (92)**115**
5-y-o ch m Inchinor-Silca-Cisa (Hallgate)
M R Channon Aldridge Racing Limited

Placings:121163110/2022/0410541050-24020 **(3551)**
2001: 8^{2}G, 8^{4}G, 8^{0}G, 8^{2}G, 8^{0}GF

	Starts	1st	2nd	3rd	Win & Pl	
Career Total (Turf)	28	7	6	1	370427	
112	8/00	Curr	1m		GD	£29670
111	6/00	Epsm	1m114y	A	G-S	£22750
106	9/98	Newb	6f8y	A	GD	£32560
97	9/98	Badn	6f		SFT	£33784
97	7/98	Newb	6f8y	A	G-F	£9579
84	5/98	Newb	5f34y	C	GD	£4967
84	4/98	Newb	5f34y	E	HVY	£3525

Total win prize-money £136835

Going (Turf): Sf: 2-4 GS: 1-3 **Gd: 3-12** GF: 1-9 Fm: 0-0
Distance: 5f/6f: 3-7 7f-8f: 3-17 9f-13f: 1-4 14f+: 0-0
Track : **LH: 1-3** RH: 0-6 Tight: 1-2 Gall: 1-4
Aids: Bl: 0-0 Vi: 0-0 Tstrap: 0-0
Best Rating: 115 3/01 Ndas 1m195y good

Ran two cracking races in Dubai in the spring, but appeared to blow up after a three-month break at Royal Ascot. Her best chance of winning again is probably on the continent.

Golden Snake (USA)

110 **120**
5-y-o b h Danzig (USA)-Dubian (High Line)
J L Dunlop The National Stud

Placings:51/12160/45110-126 **(3444)**
2001: 10^{1}HO, 10^{2}G, 12^{6}GF

	Starts	1st	2nd	3rd	Win & Pl	
Career Total (Turf)	15	6	2	0	393364	
	4/01	Lonc	1m2f		HLD	£48497
120	10/00	Siro	1m4f		HVY	£106053
120	9/00	Colo	1m4f		SFT	£96774
117	6/99	Chan	1m1f		SFT	£43057
108	4/99	NmkJ	1m110y	A	GD	£12668
85	9/98	Donc	1m	D	GD	£3840

Total win prize-money £310889

Going (Turf): **Sf: 3-4** GS: 0-0 Gd: 2-7 GF: 0-1 Fm: 0-1
Distance: 5f/6f: 0-0 7f-8f: 1-2 **9f-13f: 5-13** 14f+: 0-0
Track : LH: 0-3 **RH: 3-6** Tight: 0-0 Gall: 0-4
Aids: Bl: 0-0 Vi: 0-0 Tstrap: 0-0
Best Rating: 120 5/01 Curr 1m2f110y good

He has established himself as a true Group One performer in the last couple of seasons and was winning for the fourth time in the top grade when taking the Prix Ganay in April. Split Fantastic Light and Kalanisi in the Tattersalls Gold Cup at the Curragh next time. Injured in the King George and retired to the National Stud.

Golden Sonata (USA)

82 **69**

2-y-o b/br f Mr Prospector (USA)-Elissa Beethoven (Royal Academy (USA))

J Noseda James C Spence

Placings:0 **(2974)**

2001: 6^{0}G

	Starts	1st	2nd	3rd	Win & Pl
Career Total (Turf)	1	0	0	0	

Going (Turf): Sf: 0-0 GS: 0-0 Gd: 0-1 GF: 0-0 Fm: 0-0
Distance: 5f/6f: 0-1 7f-8f: 0-0 9f-13f: 0-0 14f+: 0-0
Track: LH: 0-0 RH: 0-0 Tight: 0-0 Gall: 0-0
Aids: Bl: 0-0 Vi: 0-0 Tstrap: 0-0
Best Rating: 69 7/01 NmkJ 6f good

Golden Sparrow

104 **101**

3-y-o ch f Elmaamul (USA)-Moon Spin (Night Shift (USA))

J L Dunlop J L Dunlop

Placings:21-1 **(0812)**

2001: 10^{1}S

	Starts	1st	2nd	3rd	Win & Pl
Career Total (Turf)	3	2	1	0	12280

101 4/01 NmkR 1m2f C(0-95)H SFT £7202
87 11/00 Donc 1m E HVY £3997
Total win prize-money £11200

Going (Turf): Sf: 2-3 GS: 0-0 Gd: 0-0 GF: 0-0 Fm: 0-0
Distance: 5f/6f: 0-0 **7f-8f: 1-2 9f-13f: 1-1** 14f+: 0-0
Track: LH: 0-0 RH: 0-0 Tight: 0-0 Gall: 0-0
Aids: Bl: 0-0 Vi: 0-0 Tstrap: 0-0
Best Rating: 101 4/01 NmkR 1m2f soft

A gutsy individual he only had the two outings at two and won a Newmarket handicap on her return, but was not seen again.

Golden Spectrum (IRE)

97 **87**

2-y-o b c Spectrum (IRE)-Plessaya (USA) (Nureyev (USA))

R Hannon George E K Teo

Placings:22 **(4056)**

2001: 7^{2}G, 7^{2}GF

	Starts	1st	2nd	3rd	Win & Pl
Career Total (Turf)	2	0	2	0	3992

Going (Turf): Sf: 0-0 GS: 0-0 Gd: 0-1 GF: 0-1 Fm: 0-0
Distance: 5f/6f: 0-0 7f-8f: 0-2 9f-13f: 0-0 14f+: 0-0
Track: LH: 0-0 RH: 0-1 Tight: 0-0 Gall: 0-0
Aids: Bl: 0-0 Vi: 0-0 Tstrap: 0-0
Best Rating: 87 8/01 Newb 7f gd-fm

Made a promising debut at Goodwood then ran well at Newbury and ought to win races.

Golden Symbol

99(93) (43)**38**

4-y-o ch f Wolfhound (USA)-Nuriva (USA) (Woodman (USA))

J G Given (T Keddy 19/7) Mrs Julie Mitchell

Placings:0600006-5460000050 **(4481)**

2001: 6^{5}SD, 7^{4}SD, 6^{6}GF, 8^{0}GF, 10^{0}GF, 8^{0}G, 8^{0}GF, 5^{0}GS, 7^{5}GF, 8^{0}F

	Starts	1st	2nd	3rd	Win & Pl
Career Total (Turf)	13	0	0	0	0
Career Total (AW)	4	0	0	0	0

Going (Turf): Sf: 0-0 GS: 0-1 Gd: 0-1 GF: 0-5 Fm: 0-1
Distance: 5f/6f: 0-2 7f-8f: 0-7 9f-13f: 0-4 14f+: 0-0
Track: LH: 0-8 RH: 0-1 Tight: 0-3 Gall: 0-1
Aids: Bl: 0-5 Vi: 0-0 Tstrap: 0-0
Best Rating: 50 5/01 Brig 6f209y gd-fm

Golden Wells (IRE)

105 **107**

3-y-o b c Sadler's Wells (USA)-Golden Bloom (Main Reef)

M Johnston Dr Fuk To Chang

Placings:113056163 **(5693)**

2001: 9^{1}GS, 10^{1}GS, 12^{3}GF, 12^{0}GF, 11^{5}S, 12^{6}GF, 10^{1}GS, 10^{6}Y, 12^{3}S

	Starts	1st	2nd	3rd	Win & Pl
Career Total (Turf)	9	3	0	2	35099

103 10/01 Asct 1m2f B(0-105)H G-S £12209
100 4/01 Newb 1m2f6y B G-S £9282
76 4/01 Muss 1m1f D G-S £3108
Total win prize-money £24599

Going (Turf): Sf: 0-2 **GS: 3-3** Gd: 0-0 GF: 0-3 Fm: 0-0
Distance: 5f/6f: 0-0 7f-8f: 0-0 **9f-13f: 3-9** 14f+: 0-0
Track: LH: 1-5 RH: 1-3 Tight: 0-1 **Gall: 2-4**
Aids: Bl: 0-1 Vi: 0-0 Tstrap: 0-0
Best Rating: 107 11/01 Donc 1m4f soft

A 44,000gns son of Sadler's Wells, he did not race at two but won his maiden with the minimum of fuss at Musselburgh on his racecourse debut and followed up in better company at Newbury. He finished third to Mr Combustible in the Chester Vase, but disappointed in Pattern company afterwards and was successfully returned to handicap company at Ascot in October. Suited by give in the ground.

Golden Whisper (IRE)

86(75) (32)**40**

3-y-o b f Priolo (USA)-Gold Wind (IRE) (Marju (IRE))

P Howling Paul Howling

Placings:4030600-0056000 **(5131)**

2001: 8^{0}SD, 9^{0}G, 8^{5}F, 8^{6}GF, 8^{0}GF, 7^{0}G, 7^{0}HY

	Starts	1st	2nd	3rd	Win & Pl
Career Total (Turf)	11	0	0	1	744
Career Total (AW)	3	0	0	0	

Going (Turf): Sf: 0-2 GS: 0-1 Gd: 0-4 GF: 0-3 Fm: 0-1
Distance: 5f/6f: 0-5 7f-8f: 0-5 9f-13f: 0-4 14f+: 0-0
Track: LH: 0-6 RH: 0-2 Tight: 0-0 Gall: 0-1
Aids: Bl: 0-0 Vi: 0-0 Tstrap: 0-0
Best Rating: 40 6/01 Nott 1m54y gd-fm

Golden Wind

78(80) (9)**31**

5-y-o ch m Blaze O'Gold (USA)-Cool Wind (Windjammer (USA))

C J Price Golden Wind Syndicate

Placings:000500 **(1616)**

2001: 9^{0}SW, 9^{0}SD, 6^{0}SD, 8^{5}G, 5^{0}G, 8^{0}GF

	Starts	1st	2nd	3rd	Win & Pl
Career Total (Turf)	3	0	0	0	0
Career Total (AW)	3	0	0	0	

Going (Turf): Sf: 0-0 GS: 0-0 Gd: 0-2 GF: 0-1 Fm: 0-0
Distance: 5f/6f: 0-2 7f-8f: 0-0 9f-13f: 0-4 14f+: 0-0
Track: LH: 0-4 RH: 0-0 Tight: 0-2 Gall: 0-1
Aids: Bl: 0-0 Vi: 0-0 Tstrap: 0-0
Best Rating: 49 5/01 Wwck 1m22y good

Goldeva

104 **90?**

2-y-o gr f Makbul-Gold Belt (IRE) (Bellypha)

R Hollinshead M Pyle & Miss T Baulcombe

Placings:1222502 **(4903)**

2001: 5^{1}GF, 5^{2}G, 6^{2}GF, 6^{2}G, 6^{5}GS, 5^{0}GS, 5^{2}G

	Starts	1st	2nd	3rd	Win & Pl
Career Total (Turf)	7	1	4	0	14440

83 5/01 Ches 5f16y D G-F £7215
Total win prize-money £7215

Going (Turf): Sf: 0-0 GS: 0-2 Gd: 0-3 **GF: 1-2** Fm: 0-0
Distance: 5f/6f: 1-6 7f-8f: 0-1 9f-13f: 0-0 14f+: 0-0
Track: LH: 1-3 RH: 0-0 **Tight: 1-2** Gall: 0-0
Aids: Bl: 0-0 Vi: 0-0 Tstrap: 0-0
Best Rating: 90 9/01 Donc 5f gd-sft

From a smart family, she won a Chester maiden on her debut before notching up a run of seconds. She did not finish a mile behind Astonished in a Doncaster Listed event, but the higher up she goes in grade the further she finishes from the spoils and she looks most at home in more moderate company.

Goldie

104 **72**

3-y-o b f Celtic Swing-Hotel California (IRE) (Last Tycoon)

D J Coakley Chris Van Hoorn

Placings:123-0564140 **(4433)**

2001: 8^{0}G, 7^{5}G, 9^{6}GF, 8^{4}GF, 7^{1}GF, 7^{4}G, 7^{0}G

	Starts	1st	2nd	3rd	Win & Pl
Career Total (Turf)	10	2	1	1	17512

72 8/01 Wwck 7f26y E(0-75)H G-F £3052
72 8/00 Bath 5f161y E G-F £2762
Total win prize-money £5815

Going (Turf): Sf: 0-1 GS: 0-0 Gd: 0-4 **GF: 2-4** Fm: 0-1
Distance: 5f/6f: 1-3 7f-8f: 1-5 9f-13f: 0-2 14f+: 0-0
Track: LH: 2-3 RH: 0-4 Tight: 0-1 **Gall: 1-2**
Aids: Bl: 0-0 Vi: 0-0 Tstrap: 0-0
Best Rating: 72 8/01 NmkJ 7f good

She showed decent form at two, but struggled this season and her only win came in a modest fillies' handicp at Warwick.

Goldon Friendship (IRE)

84 **52**

2-y-o b f College Chapel-Claire's Thatch (Thatch (USA))

J R Weymes Don Raper

Placings:05000 **(4852)**

2001: 5^{0}S, 5^{5}GF, 6^{0}GF, 5^{0}GF, 5^{0}GF

	Starts	1st	2nd	3rd	Win & Pl
Career Total (Turf)	5	0	0	0	0

Going (Turf): Sf: 0-1 GS: 0-0 Gd: 0-0 GF: 0-4 Fm: 0-0
Distance: 5f/6f: 0-4 7f-8f: 0-1 9f-13f: 0-0 14f+: 0-0
Track: LH: 0-1 RH: 0-0 Tight: 0-1 Gall: 0-0
Aids: Bl: 0-0 Vi: 0-0 Tstrap: 0-0
Best Rating: 52 6/01 Bevl 5f gd-fm

Goldthroat (IRE)

96 **77**

2-y-o b f Zafonic (USA)-Winger (In The Wings)

J L Dunlop Sir Thomas Pilkington

Placings:0100 **(4954)**

2001: 7^{0}GS, 7^{1}G, 8^{0}GF, 8^{0}GS

	Starts	1st	2nd	3rd	Win & Pl
Career Total (Turf)	4	1	0	0	3752

77 8/01 Rdcr 7f D GD £3752
Total win prize-money £3752

Going (Turf): Sf: 0-0 GS: 0-2 **Gd: 1-1** GF: 0-1 Fm: 0-0
Distance: 5f/6f: 0-0 **7f-8f: 1-4** 9f-13f: 0-0 14f+: 0-0

Track : LH: 0-0 RH: 0-1 Tight: 0-0 Gall: 0-0
Aids: Bl: 0-0 Vi: 0-0 Tstrap: 0-0
Best Rating: 77 8/01 Rdcr 7f good

She has been disappointing in nurseries since winning an ordinary maiden at Redcar at the end of the summer.

Gompas Pal

97(83) (45)**51d**
3-y-o b g Petong-Impala Lass (Kampala)
K R Burke Mr I & Mrs A Russell

Placings:0050-53030300 **(4471)**
2001: 8^{5}HY, 7^{3}F, 9^{0}GF, 8^{3}GF, 8^{0}GF, 6^{3}G, 7^{0}G, 6^{0}GF

	Starts	1st	2nd	3rd	Win & Pl
Career Total (Turf)	9	0	0	3	1194
Career Total (AW)	3	0	0	0	0

Going (Turf): Sf: 0-2 GS: 0-0 Gd: 0-2 GF: 0-4 Fm: 0-1
Distance: 5f/6f: 0-1 7f-8f: 0-7 9f-13f: 0-4 14f+: 0-0
Track : LH: 0-8 RH: 0-1 Tight: 0-3 Gall: 0-0
Aids: Bl: 0-0 Vi: 0-6 Tstrap: 0-0
Best Rating: 51 7/01 Brig 6f209y good

Goncharova (USA)

104 **104**
3-y-o b f Gone West (USA)-Pure Grain (Polish Precedent (USA))
Sir Michael Stoute Mrs John Magnier & Mr M Tabor

Placings:10-0103 **(5339)**
2001: 7^{0}GS, 10^{1}GS, 11^{0}G, 10^{3}GS, 10^{1}S

	Starts	1st	2nd	3rd	Win & Pl
Career Total (Turf)	6	2	0	1	13200

91 8/01 Hayd 1m2f120yC(0-95)H G-S £7247
79 10/00 Leic 7f9y D HVY £3224
Total win prize-money £10472

Going (Turf): Sf: 1-2 GS: 1-3 Gd: 0-1 GF: 0-0 Fm: 0-0
Distance: 5f/6f: 0-0 7f-8f: 1-3 9f-13f: 1-3 14f+: 0-0
Track : LH: 1-2 RH: 0-0 Tight: 0-0 Gall: 0-1
Aids: Bl: 0-0 Vi: 0-0 Tstrap: 0-0
Best Rating: 98 10/01 NmkR 1m2f gd-sft

Stepped up to ten furlongs to take a handicap at Haydock on her second start at three and ran well in Listed company at Newmarket in October. Goes well on soft ground, and may get further than ten furlongs.

Gone Too Far

99 **57**
3-y-o b g Reprimand-Blue Nile (IRE) (Bluebird (USA))
M Dods P J Carr

Placings:02160-060346433 **(4478)**
2001: 8^{0}S, 8^{6}F, 10^{0}GF, 8^{3}GF, 8^{4}GF, 8^{6}GF, 10^{4}GS, 12^{3}G, 16^{3}F

	Starts	1st	2nd	3rd	Win & Pl
Career Total (Turf)	14	1	1	3	5873

74 9/00 Thsk 7f F GD £2925
Total win prize-money £2925

Going (Turf): Sf: 0-2 GS: 0-1 **Gd: 1-4** GF: 0-5 Fm: 0-2
Distance: 5f/6f: 0-3 **7f-8f: 1-6** 9f-13f: 0-4 14f+: 0-1
Track : LH: 1-9 RH: 0-2 **Tight: 1-3** Gall: 0-5
Aids: Bl: 0-0 Vi: 0-0 Tstrap: 0-0
Best Rating: 63 5/01 Newc 1m firm

Gone'N'Dunnett (IRE)

90(63) (11)**67**
2-y-o b c Petardia-Skerries Bell (Taufan (USA))
Mrs C A Dunnett College Farm Thoroughbreds

Placings:0056500 **(5130)**
2001: 5^{0}F, 6^{0}F, 6^{5}GF, 5^{6}GF, 6^{5}GF, 8^{0}SD, 7^{0}HY

	Starts	1st	2nd	3rd	Win & Pl
Career Total (Turf)	6	0	0	0	0
Career Total (AW)	1	0	0	0	

Going (Turf): Sf: 0-1 GS: 0-0 Gd: 0-0 GF: 0-3 Fm: 0-2
Distance: 5f/6f: 0-4 7f-8f: 0-3 9f-13f: 0-0 14f+: 0-0
Track : LH: 0-1 RH: 0-0 Tight: 0-0 Gall: 0-0
Aids: Bl: 0-1 Vi: 0-1 Tstrap: 0-0
Best Rating: 67 6/01 Yarm 6f3y gd-fm

Good Friday (IRE)

85 **60**
4-y-o b f Tenby-Sign Of Peace (IRE) (Posen (USA))
Mrs P N Dutfield Aidan Walsh

Placings:66530/656U60-0 **(1620)**
2001: 16^{0}GF

	Starts	1st	2nd	3rd	Win & Pl
Career Total (Turf)	12	0	0	1	490

Going (Turf): Sf: 0-1 GS: 0-2 Gd: 0-1 GF: 0-7 Fm: 0-1
Distance: 5f/6f: 0-1 7f-8f: 0-5 9f-13f: 0-4 14f+: 0-2
Track : LH: 0-4 RH: 0-3 Tight: 0-2 Gall: 0-2
Aids: Bl: 0-0 Vi: 0-0 Tstrap: 0-0
Best Rating: 40 5/01 Wwck 2m39y gd-fm

Good Girl (IRE)

110(84) (54)**102**
2-y-o b f College Chapel-Indian Honey (Indian King (USA))
T D Easterby Peter C Bourke

Placings:211514623 **(5054)**
2001: 5^{2}SD, 5^{1}G, 5^{1}GF, 5^{5}GF, 5^{1}GF, 6^{4}G, 5^{6}G, 6^{2}GF, 6^{3}S

	Starts	1st	2nd	3rd	Win & Pl
Career Total (Turf)	8	3	1	1	117888
Career Total (AW)	1	0	1	0	845

94 7/01 Newb 5f34y B G-F £78300
86 6/01 Bevl 5f A G-F £11020
82 5/01 Ripn 5f E GD £2996
Total win prize-money £92316

Going (Turf): Sf: 0-1 GS: 0-0 Gd: 1-3 **GF: 2-4** Fm: 0-0
Distance: 5f/6f: 3-9 7f-8f: 0-0 9f-13f: 0-0 14f+: 0-0
Track : LH: 0-0 RH: 0-0 Tight: 0-0 Gall: 0-0
Aids: Bl: 0-0 Vi: 0-0 Tstrap: 0-0
Best Rating: 102 9/01 Ayr 6f gd-fm

A very useful filly, she was favoured by the draw and the weights when taking a Listed event at Beverley in June before taking a valuable sales race at Newbury. Ran fifth to Queen's Logic in Queen Mary Stakes and fourth to the same filly in the Lowther. In-season when disappointing in the Flying Childers, she ran much better in a Listed event at Ayr, and was third behind Queen's Logic in the Cheveley Park. Suited by five to six furlongs and fast ground, although appears to handle an easier surface.

Good Standing (USA)

107 **86**
3-y-o b f Distant View (USA)-Storm Dove (USA) (Storm Bird (CAN))
B W Hills K Abdulla

Placings:1-034540 **(5607)**
2001: 7^{0}GS, 8^{3}GF, 8^{4}GF, 9^{5}GS, 6^{4}GF, 8^{0}GS

	Starts	1st	2nd	3rd	Win & Pl
Career Total (Turf)	7	1	0	1	7847

82 10/00 NmkR 7f D SFT £4862
Total win prize-money £4862

Going (Turf): Sf: 1-1 GS: 0-3 Gd: 0-0 GF: 0-3 Fm: 0-0
Distance: 5f/6f: 0-0 **7f-8f: 1-6** 9f-13f: 0-1 14f+: 0-0
Track : LH: 0-1 RH: 0-2 Tight: 0-2 Gall: 0-0
Aids: Bl: 0-0 Vi: 0-0 Tstrap: 0-0
Best Rating: 86 6/01 Ripn 1m gd-fm

An unfurnished daughter of a useful six to seven furlong winner, she won her only outing at two in good style on soft ground, but did not really fire this season.

Good Timing

102(84) (39)**57**
3-y-o bl g Timeless Times (USA)-Fort Vally (Belfort (FR))
J J Quinn Mrs M Lingwood

Placings:63-463562024 **(4905)**
2001: 7^{4}SD, 8^{6}F, 8^{3}G, 10^{5}GF, 8^{6}F, 7^{2}GF, 7^{0}GS, 7^{2}F, 8^{4}G

	Starts	1st	2nd	3rd	Win & Pl
Career Total (Turf)	10	0	2	2	2331
Career Total (AW)	1	0	0	0	0

Going (Turf): Sf: 0-1 GS: 0-1 Gd: 0-2 GF: 0-3 Fm: 0-3
Distance: 5f/6f: 0-2 7f-8f: 0-6 9f-13f: 0-3 14f+: 0-0
Track : LH: 0-8 RH: 0-1 Tight: 0-0 Gall: 0-2
Aids: Bl: 0-0 Vi: 0-0 Tstrap: 0-0
Best Rating: 57 7/01 Newc 7f gd-fm

Goodbye Goldstone

65(69) (49)**70**
5-y-o b g Mtoto-Shareehan (Dancing Brave (USA))
Miss J A Camacho Ashley Carr Racing 2

Placings:3/3061420/050600-0 **(0882)**
2001: 10^{0}S

	Starts	1st	2nd	3rd	Win & Pl
Career Total (Turf)	11	1	1	1	10318
Career Total (AW)	4	0	0	1	393

69 4/99 Folk 1m1f149yF(0-65)H SFT £2483
Total win prize-money £2484

Going (Turf): Sf: 1-3 GS: 0-3 Gd: 0-2 GF: 0-3 Fm: 0-0
Distance: 5f/6f: 0-0 7f-8f: 0-2 **9f-13f: 1-13** 14f+: 0-0
Track : LH: 0-11 **RH: 1-2 Tight: 1-10** Gall: 0-1
Aids: Bl: 0-0 Vi: 0-0 Tstrap: 0-0
Best Rating: 69 4/99 Folk 1m1f149y S

Goodenough Mover

104 **70d**
5-y-o ch g Beveled (USA)-Rekindled Flame (IRE) (King's Lake (USA))
J S King D Goodenough Removals & Transport

Placings:60600/011114200-4042320000 **(5465)**
2001: 6^{4}S, 6^{0}GF, 8^{4}GF, 8^{2}G, 7^{3}GS, 8^{2}GF, 6^{0}GF, 7^{0}GF, 8^{0}GF, 10^{0}G

	Starts	1st	2nd	3rd	Win & Pl
Career Total (Turf)	24	4	3	1	22424

80 7/00 Sals 6f E(0-70)H GD £3198
71 7/00 Chep 1m14y D(0-85)H G-F £4114
68 6/00 Chep 7f16y D(0-80)H G-F £3916
57 6/00 Chep 7f16y E(0-70)H GD £2908
Total win prize-money £14138

Going (Turf): Sf: 0-3 GS: 0-2 **Gd: 2-7 GF: 2-11** Fm: 0-0
Distance: 5f/6f: 1-2 **7f-8f: 2-15** 9f-13f: 1-6 14f+: 0-0
Track : LH: 0-4 RH: 0-5 Tight: 0-4 Gall: 0-2
Aids: Bl: 0-0 Vi: 0-0 Tstrap: 0-0
Best Rating: 77 7/01 Bath 1m5y good

Goodgollymissmolly

86 **42**
3-y-o b f Factual (USA)-Chardonnay Girl (Hubbly Bubbly (USA))
M A Allen John T Robson

Placings:00-P000 **(3809)**
2001: 9^{P}GF, 6^{0}GF, 9^{0}GF, 7^{0}GF

	Starts	1st	2nd	3rd	Win & Pl
Career Total (Turf)	6	0	0	0	

Going (Turf): Sf: 0-0 GS: 0-1 Gd: 0-0 GF: 0-5 Fm: 0-0

Distance: 5f/6f: 0-1 7f-8f: 0-3 9f-13f: 0-2 14f+: 0-0
Track : LH: 0-2 RH: 0-2 Tight: 0-2 Gall: 0-0
Aids: Bl: 0-0 Vi: 0-0 Tstrap: 0-0
Best Rating: 32 7/01 Folk 6f189y gd-fm

Goodie Twosues

104 **91d**

3-y-o b f Fraam-Aliuska (IRE) (Fijar Tango (FR))
R Hannon Lady Davis

Placings:134561-0640000 **(5391)**
2001: 7^{0}G, 8^{6}GF, 8^{4}GF, 7^{0}GF, 7^{0}GS, 8^{0}G, 7^{0}GS

	Starts	1st	2nd	3rd	Win & Pl
Career Total (Turf)	13	2	0	1	60070

79	10/00	NmkR	6f	B	SFT	£50825
77	5/00	Gdwd	6f	D	SFT	£4397

Total win prize-money £55222

Going (Turf): Sf: 2-2 GS: 0-3 Gd: 0-8 GF: 0-6 Fm: 0-0
Distance: 5f/6f: 2-4 7f-8f: 0-8 9f-13f: 0-1 14f+: 0-0
Track : LH: 0-2 RH: 0-2 Tight: 0-2 Gall: 0-1
Aids: Bl: 0-0 Vi: 0-0 Tstrap: 0-0
Best Rating: 93 6/01 Epsm 1m114y gd-fm

Found Group company a bit too much as a juvenile and lost her way a bit, but bounced back to form to win a valuable maiden at Newmarket in October 2000. Has not appeared to stay a mile at three and remains poorly handicapped. Has won on soft ground.

Goodwood Promise

85 **60**

2-y-o b c Primo Dominie-Noble Destiny (Dancing Brave (USA))
J L Dunlop Goodwood Racehorse Owners Group(six) Ltd

Placings:000 **(5290)**
2001: 6^{0}GF, 6^{0}GF, 7^{0}S

	Starts	1st	2nd	3rd	Win & Pl
Career Total (Turf)	3	0	0	0	

Going (Turf): Sf: 0-1 GS: 0-0 Gd: 0-0 GF: 0-2 Fm: 0-0
Distance: 5f/6f: 0-1 7f-8f: 0-2 9f-13f: 0-0 14f+: 0-0
Track : LH: 0-0 RH: 0-0 Tight: 0-0 Gall: 0-0
Aids: Bl: 0-0 Vi: 0-0 Tstrap: 0-0
Best Rating: 60 9/01 Newb 6f8y gd-fm

Googoosh (IRE)

102 **77**

2-y-o b f Danehill (USA)-Literary (Woodman (USA))
E A L Dunlop Mohammed Jaber

Placings:33225 **(4962)**
2001: 6^{3}GS, 7^{3}G, 6^{2}GF, 7^{2}GF, 8^{5}S

	Starts	1st	2nd	3rd	Win & Pl
Career Total (Turf)	5	0	2	2	3960

Going (Turf): Sf: 0-1 GS: 0-1 Gd: 0-1 GF: 0-2 Fm: 0-0
Distance: 5f/6f: 0-1 7f-8f: 0-3 9f-13f: 0-1 14f+: 0-0
Track : LH: 0-1 RH: 0-1 Tight: 0-0 Gall: 0-0
Aids: Bl: 0-2 Vi: 0-0 Tstrap: 0-0
Best Rating: 77 9/01 Pont 1m4y soft

Looks to be improving with experience.

Gordons Friend

103(74) (25)**47**

3-y-o ch g Clantime-Auntie Fay (IRE) (Fayruz)
B S Rothwell S P Hudson

Placings:6000-00135230 **(4185)**
2001: 8^{0}F, 8^{0}GF, 7^{1}G, 6^{3}G, 6^{5}F, 7^{2}GS, 8^{3}G, 7^{0}GF

	Starts	1st	2nd	3rd	Win & Pl
Career Total (Turf)	11	1	1	2	5505
Career Total (AW)	1	0	0	0	

47	6/01	Hayd	7f30y	E(0-70)H	GD	£3290

Total win prize-money £3290

Going (Turf): Sf: 0-0 GS: 0-2 **Gd: 1-5** GF: 0-2 Fm: 0-2
Distance: 5f/6f: 0-4 **7f-8f: 1-7** 9f-13f: 0-1 14f+: 0-0
Track : LH: 1-6 RH: 0-1 Tight: 0-2 Gall: 0-1
Aids: Bl: 0-0 Vi: 0-1 Tstrap: 0-0
Best Rating: 49 7/01 Ayr 7f gd-sft

Goretski (IRE)

109(103) (61)**65**

8-y-o ro g Polish Patriot (USA)-Celestial Path (Godswalk (USA))
N Tinkler P D Savill

Placings:0014500/2014222600000/400121111210000/000001051121050000З/00000105113000020/00000060
0601-0022032420045300021606012 **(5685)**
2001: 6^{0}SD, 6^{0}SD, 6^{2}SD, 5^{2}SD, 5^{0}SD, 5^{3}SD, 5^{2}SD, 5^{4}SD, 6^{2}SD, 5^{0}F, 5^{0}GF, 5^{4}G, 5^{5}F, 5^{3}F, 5^{0}GF, 5^{0}S, 6^{0}GF, 5^{2}GF, 5^{1}S, 5^{6}GF, 5^{0}GF, 6^{6}F, 5^{0}GS, 5^{1}HY

	Starts	1st	2nd	3rd	Win & Pl
Career Total (Turf)	91	13	10	3	66637
Career Total (AW)	17	5	4	1	16129

61	10/01	Newb	5f34y	F(0-65)H	HVY	£3444
61	8/01	Haml	5f4y	F(0-60)H	SFT	£3066
38	12/00	Sthl	6f	G	STD	£1932
73	8/99	Bevl	5f	D(0-80)H	GD	£7415
71	8/99	Pont	5f	E(0-70)H	G-F	£4815
66	6/99	Haml	5f4y	F(0-60)H	GD	£3761
74	8/98	Bevl	5f	D(0-80)H	G-F	£7805
80	7/98	Sthl	5f	D(0-75)H	STD	£3590
74	7/98	Sthl	5f	E(0-70)H	STD	£2885
66	6/98	Pont	5f	F(0-65)	SFT	£2221
78	8/97	Bevl	5f	D(0-80)H	G-S	£4263
63	7/97	Catt	5f	D(0-75)H	G-F	£3691
65	7/97	Bath	5f11y	G(0-65)H	GD	£2175
67	6/97	Sthl	5f	E(0-70)H	STD	£2940
63	6/97	Sthl	5f	F(0-65)H	STD	£2277
59	5/97	Haml	5f4y	F(0-70)H	G-S	£2511
57	4/96	Catt	5f	D(0-80)H	GD	£3850
66	8/95	Rdcr	6f	F	FRM	£2798

Total win prize-money £65443

Going (Turf): Sf: 3-19 GS: 2-14 **Gd: 4-27** GF: 3-25 Fm: 1-6
Distance: 5f/6f: 18-104 7f-8f: 0-4 9f-13f: 0-0 14f+: 0-0
Track : LH: 4-20 RH: 0-3 Tight: 0-6 **Gall: 1-5**
Aids: Bl: 1-12 Vi: 0-0 Tstrap: 0-0
Best Rating: 65 11/01 Donc 5f soft

He was a very decent sprint handicapper a few seasons ago, but is not the horse he was and has been beaten in All-Weather sellers this term, but he has plummeted down the handicap in the last couple of seasons and bolted up in a modest handicap at Hamilton in August, and also scored at Newbury in October. Goes well in soft ground.

Gormire

77 (19)**10**

8-y-o ro m Superlative-Lady Of The Lodge (Absalom)
B W Murray P Barron

Placings:2040000/000000/00/0/0000 **(3672)**
2001: 6^{0}GF, 8^{0}G, 8^{0}F, 5^{0}G

	Starts	1st	2nd	3rd	Win & Pl
Career Total (Turf)	14	0	1		1410
Career Total (AW)	6	0	0	0	

Going (Turf): Sf: 0-1 GS: 0-1 Gd: 0-3 GF: 0-8 Fm: 0-1
Distance: 5f/6f: 0-15 7f-8f: 0-5 9f-13f: 0-0 14f+: 0-0
Track : LH: 0-6 RH: 0-1 Tight: 0-3 Gall: 0-0
Aids: Bl: 0-3 Vi: 0-0 Tstrap: 0-0
Best Rating: 10 7/01 Donc 6f gd-fm

Gorse

102 **115**

6-y-o b h Sharpo-Pervenche (Latest Model)
H Candy Girsonfield Ltd

Placings:124011/331125/36213-0110 **(2971)**
2001: 6^{0}GS, 6^{1}G, 6^{1}S, 6^{0}G

	Starts	1st	2nd	3rd	Win & Pl
Career Total (Turf)	21	8	3	4	226145

115	7/01	Hamb	6f		SFT	£39088
115	5/01	Badn	6f		GD	£24430
114	7/00	Deau	6f		VS	£21134
103	8/99	Leop	6f		Y-S	£22770
106	7/99	Hamb	6f		GD	£43321
111	11/98	Donc	6f	A	SFT	£12170
98	10/98	NmkR	6f	C	SFT	£5199
100	5/98	Sals	6f	D	G-S	£3127

Total win prize-money £171241

Going (Turf): Sf: 3-6 GS: 1-3 Gd: 2-9 GF: 0-0 Fm: 0-0
Distance: 5f/6f: 8-19 7f-8f: 0-2 9f-13f: 0-0 14f+: 0-0
Track : LH: 0-0 **RH: 1-2** Tight: 0-0 Gall: 0-0
Aids: Bl: 0-0 Vi: 0-0 Tstrap: 0-0
Best Rating: 115 7/01 Hamb 6f soft

A useful sprinter, he won on heavy ground at Deauville in July 2000 and has never been out of the frame on all his visits to Germany, but he seemed to find domestic Group company a bit too much for him. Needed soft ground and six furlongs. Retired.

Goshin's Lad (USA)

81 **56**

2-y-o b c Nicholas (USA)-Maratha (USA) (Devil's Bag (USA))
G A Butler Beetle N Wedge Partnership

Placings:06 **(5633)**
2001: 7^{0}S, 7^{6}G,

	Starts	1st	2nd	3rd	Win & Pl
Career Total (Turf)	2	0	0	0	0

Going (Turf): Sf: 0-1 GS: 0-0 Gd: 0-1 GF: 0-0 Fm: 0-0
Distance: 5f/6f: 0-0 7f-8f: 0-2 9f-13f: 0-0 14f+: 0-0
Track : LH: 0-2 RH: 0-0 Tight: 0-1 Gall: 0-1
Aids: Bl: 0-0 Vi: 0-0 Tstrap: 0-0
Best Rating: 56 11/01 Catt 7f good

Gossamer

109 **108+**

2-y-o b f Sadler's Wells (USA)-Brocade (Habitat)
L M Cumani Gerald W Leigh - Cancer Bacup

Placings:111 **(5003)**
2001: 6^{1}G, 7^{1}GS, 8^{1}S

	Starts	1st	2nd	3rd	Win & Pl
Career Total (Turf)	3	3	0	0	145577

108	9/01	Asct	1m	A	SFT	£116000
105	8/01	Gdwd	7f	A	G-S	£24000
95	7/01	NmkJ	6f	D	GD	£5577

Total win prize-money £145577

Going (Turf): Sf: 1-1 GS: 1-1 Gd: 1-1 GF: 0-0 Fm: 0-0
Distance: 5f/6f: 1-1 **7f-8f: 2-2** 9f-13f: 0-0 14f+: 0-0
Track : LH: 0-0 **RH: 2-2** Tight: 0-0 **Gall: 1-1**
Aids: Bl: 0-0 Vi: 0-0 Tstrap: 0-0
Best Rating: 108 9/01 Asct 1m soft

A full-sister to Barathea, she is an exciting prospect, making a winning debut at Newmarket before following up in the Group Three Prestige Stakes at Goodwood. An impressive winner of the Fillies' Mile on her final start, she once again produced a sparkling turn of foot to seal matters. She heads into the winter as a leading fancy for the 1000 Guineas.

Got Alot On (USA)

(79) (29)**56**

3-y-o b/br g Charnwood Forest (IRE)-Fleety Belle (GER) (Assert)
Mrs J R Ramsden Mrs J R Ramsden

Placings:0006-00 **(1010)**
2001: 9^{0}S, 8^{0}SD

	Starts	1st	2nd	3rd	Win & Pl
Career Total (Turf)	5	0	0	0	0
Career Total (AW)	1	0	0	0	

Going (Turf): Sf: 0-2 GS: 0-1 Gd: 0-0 GF: 0-2 Fm: 0-0
Distance: 5f/6f: 0-3 7f-8f: 0-2 9f-13f: 0-1 14f+: 0-0
Track : LH: 0-2 RH: 0-0 Tight: 0-0 Gall: 0-0
Aids: Bl: 0-0 Vi: 0-0 Tstrap: 0-0
Best Rating: 29 4/01 Sthl 1m stand

Got To Be Cash

90(89) (52)**71**

2-y-o ch f Lake Coniston (IRE)-Rasayel (USA) (Bering)
B A McMahon Roy Penton

Placings:4004026 **(4554)**
2001: 5^{4}S, 5^{0}GF, 5^{0}GF, 6^{4}GS, 7^{0}G, 6^{2}HY, 6^{6}SW

	Starts	1st	2nd	3rd	Win & Pl
Career Total (Turf)	6	0	1	0	1681
Career Total (AW)	1	0	0	0	0

Going (Turf): Sf: 0-2 GS: 0-1 Gd: 0-1 GF: 0-2 Fm: 0-0
Distance: 5f/6f: 0-6 7f-8f: 0-1 9f-13f: 0-0 14f+: 0-0
Track : LH: 0-2 RH: 0-1 Tight: 0-2 Gall: 0-0
Aids: Bl: 0-0 Vi: 0-0 Tstrap: 0-0
Best Rating: 71 7/01 Hayd 6f gd-sft

Got To Go

108 **99?**

3-y-o b f Shareef Dancer (USA)-Ghost Tree (IRE) (Caerleon (USA))
B W Hills Mrs H Theodorou

Placings:100-5026400 **(5499)**
2001: 10^{5}G, 9^{0}GF, 8^{2}G, 7^{6}G, 8^{4}GS, 8^{0}G, 7^{0}HY

	Starts	1st	2nd	3rd	Win & Pl
Career Total (Turf)	10	1	1	0	10531

81 10/00 Wind 6f D G-S £2918
Total win prize-money £2919

Going (Turf): Sf: 0-2 **GS: 1-3** Gd: 0-4 GF: 0-1 Fm: 0-0
Distance: **5f/6f: 1-1** 7f-8f: 0-7 9f-13f: 0-2 14f+: 0-0
Track : LH: 0-0 **RH: 1-4** Tight: 0-1 **Gall: 1-2**
Aids: Bl: 0-0 Vi: 0-0 Tstrap: 0-2
Best Rating: 99 10/01 NmkR 1m good

Ran perhaps her best race in Listed events this term when runner-up at Ascot in August. Stays ten furlongs and appears to need cut in the ground.

Graceful Emperor

96(82) (23)**36**

3-y-o b g Emperor Jones (USA)-Juvenka (Shirley Heights)
D Eddy Kevin Elliott

Placings:00-0550 **(2028)**
2001: 10^{0}S, 12^{5}SD, 11^{5}G, 12^{0}GF

	Starts	1st	2nd	3rd	Win & Pl
Career Total (Turf)	5	0	0	0	0
Career Total (AW)	1	0	0	0	0

Going (Turf): Sf: 0-2 GS: 0-0 Gd: 0-1 GF: 0-2 Fm: 0-0
Distance: 5f/6f: 0-1 7f-8f: 0-1 9f-13f: 0-4 14f+: 0-0
Track : LH: 0-3 RH: 0-2 Tight: 0-2 Gall: 0-1
Aids: Bl: 0-0 Vi: 0-0 Tstrap: 0-0
Best Rating: 36 6/01 Ripn 1m4f60y gd-fm

Gracia

78 **48**

2-y-o gr f Linamix (FR)-Francia (Legend Of France (USA))
S C Williams D A Shekells

Placings:0 **(5623)**
2001: 8^{0}GS

	Starts	1st	2nd	3rd	Win & Pl
Career Total (Turf)	1	0	0	0	

Going (Turf): Sf: 0-0 GS: 0-1 Gd: 0-0 GF: 0-0 Fm: 0-0
Distance: 5f/6f: 0-0 7f-8f: 0-0 9f-13f: 0-1 14f+: 0-0
Track : LH: 0-1 RH: 0-0 Tight: 0-0 Gall: 0-0
Aids: Bl: 0-0 Vi: 0-0 Tstrap: 0-0
Best Rating: 48 11/01 Nott 1m54y gd-sft

Gracilis (IRE)

108(101) (52+)**80**

4-y-o b g Caerleon (USA)-Grace Note (FR) (Top Ville)
G A Swinbank Michael H Watt

Placings:40053-211112 **(3549)**
2001: 14^{2}S, 16^{1}SD, 17^{1}GF, 17^{1}GF, 16^{1}GF, 21^{2}GF

	Starts	1st	2nd	3rd	Win & Pl
Career Total (Turf)	10	3	2	1	35031
Career Total (AW)	1	1	0	0	2380

76 7/01 Sand 2m78y C(0-90)H G-F £14430
74 6/01 Pont 2m1f216yD(0-80)H G-F £7215
63 6/01 Pont 2m1f22y E(0-70)H G-F £3721
52 5/01 Sthl 2m F(0-65)H STD £2380
Total win prize-money £27746

Going (Turf): Sf: 0-3 GS: 0-0 Gd: 0-0 **GF: 3-7** Fm: 0-0
Distance: 5f/6f: 0-0 7f-8f: 0-0 9f-13f: 0-4 **14f+: 4-7**
Track : **LH: 3-7** RH: 1-2 Tight: 0-2 Gall: 0-0
Aids: Bl: 0-0 Vi: 0-0 Tstrap: 0-0
Best Rating: 80 8/01 Gdwd 2m5f gd-fm

An out-and-out stayer, he has been in fine form this summer, winning on the Southwell Fibresand, twice at Pontefract and once at Sandown. Suited by a real test of stamina and is still improving.

Gracious Air (USA)

95 **48**

3-y-o b f Bahri (USA)-Simply Bell (USA) (Simply Majestic (USA))
J R Weymes T A Scothern

Placings:0-0504005630 **(5663)**
2001: 7^{0}GF, 7^{5}GF, 8^{0}G, 12^{4}F, 14^{0}G, 9^{0}GF, 9^{5}GF, 10^{6}G, 11^{3}G, 12^{0}G

	Starts	1st	2nd	3rd	Win & Pl
Career Total (Turf)	11	0	0	1	761

Going (Turf): Sf: 0-1 GS: 0-0 Gd: 0-5 GF: 0-4 Fm: 0-1
Distance: 5f/6f: 0-0 7f-8f: 0-3 9f-13f: 0-7 14f+: 0-1
Track : LH: 0-8 RH: 0-2 Tight: 0-5 Gall: 0-1
Aids: Bl: 0-0 Vi: 0-0 Tstrap: 0-0
Best Rating: 50 7/01 Thsk 1m4f firm

Moderate maiden, she has tried various trips and seems to prefer fast ground.

Gracious King

101 **50**

3-y-o ro c King's Signet (USA)-Gracious Gretclo (Common Grounds)
R J Hodges R J Hodges

Placings:03000 **(3391)**
2001: 6^{0}S, 5^{3}F, 6^{0}GF, 6^{0}GF, 5^{0}F

	Starts	1st	2nd	3rd	Win & Pl
Career Total (Turf)	5	0	0	1	328

Going (Turf): Sf: 0-1 GS: 0-0 Gd: 0-0 GF: 0-2 Fm: 0-2
Distance: 5f/6f: 0-2 7f-8f: 0-3 9f-13f: 0-0 14f+: 0-0
Track : LH: 0-2 RH: 0-0 Tight: 0-0 Gall: 0-2
Aids: Bl: 0-0 Vi: 0-0 Tstrap: 0-0
Best Rating: 50 6/01 Sals 6f212y gd-fm

Grady

85 **72**

2-y-o ch c Bluegrass Prince (IRE)-Lady Sabina (Bairn (USA))
Miss Jacqueline S Doyle Blc Partnership

Placings:6 **(5037)**
2001: 5^{6}G

	Starts	1st	2nd	3rd	Win & Pl
Career Total (Turf)	1	0	0	0	0

Going (Turf): Sf: 0-0 GS: 0-0 Gd: 0-1 GF: 0-0 Fm: 0-0
Distance: 5f/6f: 0-1 7f-8f: 0-0 9f-13f: 0-0 14f+: 0-0
Track : LH: 0-1 RH: 0-0 Tight: 0-0 Gall: 0-1
Aids: Bl: 0-0 Vi: 0-0 Tstrap: 0-0
Best Rating: 72 10/01 Bath 5f161y good

Graft

85 **76**

2-y-o b c Entrepreneur-Mariakova (USA) (The Minstrel (CAN))
B W Hills Mrs Corbett,C Wright,R A N Bonnycastle

Placings:03 **(3958)**
2001: 7^{0}GS, 6^{3}GF

	Starts	1st	2nd	3rd	Win & Pl
Career Total (Turf)	2	0	0	1	660

Going (Turf): Sf: 0-0 GS: 0-1 Gd: 0-0 GF: 0-1 Fm: 0-0
Distance: 5f/6f: 0-0 7f-8f: 0-2 9f-13f: 0-0 14f+: 0-0
Track : LH: 0-0 RH: 0-0 Tight: 0-0 Gall: 0-0
Aids: Bl: 0-0 Vi: 0-0 Tstrap: 0-0
Best Rating: 76 8/01 Sals 6f212y gd-fm

Graig Park

61 **34**

3-y-o b g Mind Games-Flicker Toa Flame (USA) (Empery (USA))
A Berry D J Goddard

Placings:00-0 **(1637)**
2001: 7^{0}F

	Starts	1st	2nd	3rd	Win & Pl
Career Total (Turf)	3	0	0	0	

Going (Turf): Sf: 0-0 GS: 0-1 Gd: 0-1 GF: 0-0 Fm: 0-1
Distance: 5f/6f: 0-1 7f-8f: 0-2 9f-13f: 0-0 14f+: 0-0
Track : LH: 0-1 RH: 0-0 Tight: 0-0 Gall: 0-0
Aids: Bl: 0-0 Vi: 0-0 Tstrap: 0-0

Grain Of Gold

83 **70**

2-y-o b f Mr Prospector (USA)-Pure Grain (Polish Precedent (USA))
Sir Michael Stoute R Barnett

Placings:0 **(4384)**
2001: 6^{0}GF

	Starts	1st	2nd	3rd	Win & Pl
Career Total (Turf)	1	0	0	0	

Going (Turf): Sf: 0-0 GS: 0-0 Gd: 0-0 GF: 0-1 Fm: 0-0
Distance: 5f/6f: 0-0 7f-8f: 0-1 9f-13f: 0-0 14f+: 0-0
Track : LH: 0-0 RH: 0-0 Tight: 0-0 Gall: 0-0
Aids: Bl: 0-0 Vi: 0-0 Tstrap: 0-0

Best Rating: 70 8/01 Sals 6f212y gd-fm

Grain Storm (IRE)

92 **50**

3-y-o b f Marju (IRE)-Zuhal (Busted)

P C Haslam T S Palin

Placings:0050-0601500 **(3706)**

2001: 9^0G, 8^6GF, 8^0GF, 8^1GF, 9^5S, 8^0F, 7^0G

	Starts	1st	2nd	3rd	Win & Pl
Career Total (Turf)	10	1	0	0	2145
Career Total (AW)	1	0	0	0	

50 6/01 Nott 1m54y G(0-60)H G-F £2144

Total win prize-money £2145

Going (Turf): Sf: 0-1 GS: 0-1 Gd: 0-2 **GF: 1-5** Fm: 0-1
Distance: 5f/6f: 0-1 7f-8f: 0-6 **9f-13f: 1-4** 14f+: 0-0
Track : **LH: 1-5** RH: 0-3 Tight: 0-4 Gall: 0-0
Aids: Bl: 0-0 Vi: 0-0 Tstrap: 0-0
Best Rating: 50 6/01 Nott 1m54y gd-fm

Gralmano (IRE)

107(107) (91)**71**

6-y-o b g Scenic-Llangollen (IRE) (Caerleon (USA))

K A Ryan Coleorton Moor Racing

Placings:030020211/1320430535/44400066241120/14 5251641106-3055005060000 **(5151)**

2001: 8^3SD, 8^0SD, 12^5S, 8^5G, 10^0GF, 10^0F, 10^5G, 10^0GF, 10^6G, 10^0GF, 12^0GF, 10^0G, 10^0G

	Starts	1st	2nd	3rd	Win & Pl
Career Total (Turf)	41	5	3	2	48640
Career Total (AW)	17	4	3	3	21352

85 8/00 Donc 1m2f60y D(0-85)H G-F £15080
78 7/00 Ripn 1m1f D(0-80)H G-F £7637
80 6/00 Rdcr 1m2f C(0-90)H FRM £8697
87 2/00 Wolv 1m100y D(0-85)H STD £3477
68 8/99 Pont 1m4y C(0-90)H GD £7685
67 8/99 Rdcr 1m E(0-65) GD £2866
91 2/98 Ling 1m D SLW £3371
94 12/97 Wolv 7f D STD £2697
69 11/97 Wolv 1m100y D STD £2788

Total win prize-money £54300

Going (Turf): Sf: 0-2 GS: 0-4 **Gd: 2-15 GF: 2-16** Fm: 1-4
Distance: 5f/6f: 0-2 7f-8f: 3-11 **9f-13f: 6-44** 14f+: 0-1
Track : **LH: 7-39** RH: 1-15 **Tight: 6-34** Gall: 1-10
Aids: Bl: 0-10 Vi: 0-2 Tstrap: 0-0
Best Rating: 91 2/01 Wolv 1m100y stand

He is a tough handicapper, effective from a mile to ten furlongs on both turf and Fibresand, but struggled this term.

Grampas (USA)

107 **100**

4-y-o b/br c El Gran Senor (USA)-Let There Be Light (USA) (Sunny's Halo (CAN))

J H M Gosden Thomas P Tatham

Placings:2164-1 **(2383)**

2001: 10^1GF

	Starts	1st	2nd	3rd	Win & Pl
Career Total (Turf)	5	2	1	0	32748

100 6/01 Asct 1m2f B(0-105)H G-F £26000
88 8/00 Newb 1m1f D G-F £4387

Total win prize-money £30388

Going (Turf): Sf: 0-1 GS: 0-0 Gd: 0-1 **GF: 2-3** Fm: 0-0
Distance: 5f/6f: 0-0 7f-8f: 0-1 **9f-13f: 2-4** 14f+: 0-0
Track : LH: 1-2 RH: 1-1 Tight: 0-1 **Gall: 2-2**
Aids: Bl: 0-0 Vi: 0-0 Tstrap: 0-0
Best Rating: 100 6/01 Asct 1m2f gd-fm

Lightly raced, he landed a valuable Ascot handicap on his reappearance, but was not seen again. Ten furlongs looks his trip. Acts on fast ground.

Grampian

98 **88**

2-y-o b c Selkirk (USA)-Gryada (Shirley Heights)

L M Cumani M J Dawson

Placings:410 **(4656)**

2001: 7^4GS, 7^1G, 7^0GF

	Starts	1st	2nd	3rd	Win & Pl
Career Total (Turf)	3	1	0	0	4644

88 8/01 NmkJ 7f D GD £4221

Total win prize-money £4222

Going (Turf): Sf: 0-0 GS: 0-1 **Gd: 1-1** GF: 0-1 Fm: 0-0
Distance: 5f/6f: 0-0 **7f-8f: 1-3** 9f-13f: 0-0 14f+: 0-0
Track : LH: 0-0 RH: 0-0 Tight: 0-0 Gall: 0-0
Aids: Bl: 0-0 Vi: 0-0 Tstrap: 0-0
Best Rating: 88 9/01 Donc 7f gd-fm

A well-related son of Selkirk, he won a weak Newmarket maiden over seven furlongs in August. His pedigree suggests he will get further next year.

Gran Clicquot

97 **49**

6-y-o gr m Gran Alba (USA)-Tina's Beauty (Tina's Pet)

G P Enright Frederick Gray

Placings:10 **(4525)**

2001: 7^1F, 7^0GF

	Starts	1st	2nd	3rd	Win & Pl
Career Total (Turf)	2	1	0	0	1883

40 8/01 Brig 7f214y G FRM £1883

Total win prize-money £1883

Going (Turf): Sf: 0-0 GS: 0-0 Gd: 0-0 GF: 0-1 **Fm: 1-1**
Distance: 5f/6f: 0-0 **7f-8f: 1-2** 9f-13f: 0-0 14f+: 0-0
Track : **LH: 1-1** RH: 0-0 Tight: 0-0 Gall: 0-0
Aids: Bl: 0-0 Vi: 0-0 Tstrap: 0-0
Best Rating: 49 9/01 Ling 7f140y gd-fm

She had been pulled up in a soft-ground Fontwell bumper in her only start before springing a 100/1 surprise in a fast-ground Brighton seller in August.

Grand Aunt Dee (IRE)

78 **65**

2-y-o b f Distant Relative-Willow Dale (IRE) (Danehill (USA))

D R C Elsworth Miss D M Stafford

Placings:0 **(5139)**

2001: 6^0G

	Starts	1st	2nd	3rd	Win & Pl
Career Total (Turf)	1	0	0	0	

Going (Turf): Sf: 0-0 GS: 0-0 Gd: 0-1 GF: 0-0 Fm: 0-0
Distance: 5f/6f: 0-1 7f-8f: 0-0 9f-13f: 0-0 14f+: 0-0
Track : LH: 0-0 RH: 0-0 Tight: 0-0 Gall: 0-0
Aids: Bl: 0-0 Vi: 0-0 Tstrap: 0-0
Best Rating: 65 10/01 NmkR 6f good

Grand Bahamian (USA)

75(89) (45)**53**

4-y-o gr g Distant View (USA)-Flora Scent (USA) (Fluorescent Light (USA))

Miss J Feilden Hoofbeats Racing Club

Placings:010P04-000 **(5111)**

2001: 8^0GS, 7^0GF, 6^0HY

	Starts	1st	2nd	3rd	Win & Pl
Career Total (Turf)	8	1	0	0	2698
Career Total (AW)	1	0	0	0	0

83 4/00 Ling 7f D G-S £2697

Total win prize-money £2698

Going (Turf): Sf: 0-2 **GS: 1-3** Gd: 0-1 GF: 0-2 Fm: 0-0
Distance: 5f/6f: 0-0 **7f-8f: 1-8** 9f-13f: 0-1 14f+: 0-0
Track : LH: 0-2 RH: 0-0 Tight: 0-1 Gall: 0-0
Aids: Bl: 0-2 Vi: 0-0 Tstrap: 0-0
Best Rating: 26 7/01 Yarm 7f3y gd-fm

Grand Bankes

66

2-y-o b c Mistertopogigo (IRE)-Mayday Kitty (Interrex (CAN))

W G M Turner T Lightbowne

Placings:0 **(2111)**

2001: 5^0F

	Starts	1st	2nd	3rd	Win & Pl
Career Total (Turf)	1	0	0	0	

Going (Turf): Sf: 0-0 GS: 0-0 Gd: 0-0 GF: 0-0 Fm: 0-1
Distance: 5f/6f: 0-1 7f-8f: 0-0 9f-13f: 0-0 14f+: 0-0
Track : LH: 0-0 RH: 0-0 Tight: 0-0 Gall: 0-0
Aids: Bl: 0-0 Vi: 0-0 Tstrap: 0-0

Grand Cru

82(103) (31)**33**

10-y-o ch g Kabour-Hydrangea (Warpath)

J Cullinan Turf 2000 Limited

Placings:113130600/0004040/00000341/42300014600 00524-000 **(0585)**

2001: 16^0SD, 14^0SD, 14^0HY

	Starts	1st	2nd	3rd	Win & Pl
Career Total (Turf)	21	2	0	2	11028
Career Total (AW)	22	3	2	2	8623

43 4/00 Wwck 1m6f135yD(0-80)H HVY £4102
54 11/99 Sthl 1m6f G(0-65) STD £1934
67 5/97 Newb 2m C(0-90)H SFT £5524
67 4/97 Sthl 1m4f G STD £2095
39 2/97 Sthl 1m6f E STD £2788

Total win prize-money £16445

Going (Turf): Sf: 2-8 GS: 0-5 Gd: 0-7 GF: 0-1 Fm: 0-0
Distance: 5f/6f: 0-0 7f-8f: 0-0 9f-13f: 1-10 **14f+: 4-33**
Track : **LH: 5-33** RH: 0-10 Tight: 0-4 Gall: 0-3
Aids: Bl: 1-5 Vi: 1-17 Tstrap: 0-0
Best Rating: 31 2/01 Sthl 2m stand

Grand Estate

102(98) (43)**54**

6-y-o b g Prince Sabo-Ultimate Dream (Kafu)

D W Chapman J M Chapman

Placings:0443415/253060/02500110405/40000300545 235034000 0450620 **(4621)**

2001: 6^0GF, 5^4GF, 6^5G, 6^0GF, 6^6F, 5^2G, 6^0F

	Starts	1st	2nd	3rd	Win & Pl
Career Total (Turf)	41	3	3	4	16735
Career Total (AW)	10	0	1	1	780

63 7/99 Haml 6f5y E(0-70)H FRM £3143
55 6/99 Haml 6f5y F(0-60) GD £2262
75 8/97 Thsk 6f D G-F £3782

Total win prize-money £9188

Going (Turf): Sf: 0-3 GS: 0-4 **Gd: 1-11 GF: 1-17** Fm: 1-5
Distance: 5f/6f: 1-39 **7f-8f: 2-11** 9f-13f: 0-0 14f+: 0-0
Track : LH: 0-14 RH: 0-0 Tight: 0-6 Gall: 0-0
Aids: Bl: 0-3 Vi: 0-0 Tstrap: 0-0
Best Rating: 54 8/01 Ripn 5f good

Grand Fromage (IRE)

103 **67**

3-y-o ch g Grand Lodge (USA)-My First Paige (IRE) (Runnett)

H Candy Mrs J K Powell

Placings:60052410 **(4942)**

2001: 10^6GS, 10^0S, 10^0GF, 12^5GF, 14^2GF, 14^4G, 16^1G, 15^0S

	Starts	1st	2nd	3rd	Win & Pl
Career Total (Turf)	8	1	1	0	5350

67	9/01	Kemp	2m	E(0-70)H	GD	£3883

Total win prize-money £3884

Going (Turf): Sf: 0-2 GS: 0-1 **Gd: 1-2** GF: 0-3 Fm: 0-0
Distance: 5f/6f: 0-0 7f-8f: 0-0 9f-13f: 0-4 **14f+: 1-4**
Track : LH: 0-4 **RH: 1-3** Tight: 0-5 Gall: 0-1
Aids: Bl: 0-0 Vi: 0-0 Tstrap: 0-0
Best Rating: 67 9/01 Kemp 2m good

Lightly-raced stayer. Improving with experience and appreciated two miles and good gallop when scoring at Kempton. Has time on his side and can make up into a useful long-distance handicapper.

Grand Harbour (IRE)

92 **71**

2-y-o b c Grand Lodge (USA)-Port Isaac (USA) (Seattle Song (USA))
R Hannon J A Lazzari

Placings:30 **(5094)**
2001: 8^{3}G, 8^{0}GS

	Starts	1st	2nd	3rd	Win & Pl
Career Total (Turf)	2	0	0	1	686

Going (Turf): Sf: 0-0 GS: 0-1 Gd: 0-1 GF: 0-0 Fm: 0-0
Distance: 5f/6f: 0-0 7f-8f: 0-2 9f-13f: 0-0 14f+: 0-0
Track : LH: 0-0 RH: 0-1 Tight: 0-0 Gall: 0-0
Aids: Bl: 0-0 Vi: 0-0 Tstrap: 0-0
Best Rating: 71 9/01 Gdwd 1m good

Ran encouragingly on his Goodwood debut, but well beaten on soft ground next time.

Grand Illusion (IRE)

81 **50**

2-y-o b c Mukaddamah (USA)-Saint Cynthia (Welsh Saint)
P Mitchell Richard J Cohen

Placings:046 **(4458)**
2001: 5^{0}GF, 5^{4}GF, 6^{6}G

	Starts	1st	2nd	3rd	Win & Pl
Career Total (Turf)	3	0	0	0	335

Going (Turf): Sf: 0-0 GS: 0-0 Gd: 0-1 GF: 0-2 Fm: 0-0
Distance: 5f/6f: 0-3 7f-8f: 0-0 9f-13f: 0-0 14f+: 0-0
Track : LH: 0-0 RH: 0-0 Tight: 0-0 Gall: 0-0
Aids: Bl: 0-0 Vi: 0-0 Tstrap: 0-0
Best Rating: 50 9/01 Folk 6f good

Grand View

100(104) (44)**47**

5-y-o ch g Grand Lodge (USA)-Hemline (Sharpo)
H A McWilliams (D Nicholls 6/6) Sporting Occasions

Placings:506/240010300/613040-30015200110000 **(5629)**
2001: 6^{3}SD, 6^{0}SD, 6^{0}SD, 5^{1}GF, 5^{5}GF, 5^{2}GF, 5^{0}G, 6^{0}F, 6^{1}GF, 5^{1}GF, 6^{0}F, 6^{0}G, 5^{0}G, 5^{0}G

	Starts	1st	2nd	3rd	Win & Pl
Career Total (Turf)	25	4	2	1	12320
Career Total (AW)	7	1	0	2	2501

47	7/01	Muss	5f	F	G-F	£2369
49	7/01	Nott	6f15y	G	G-F	£2086
47	5/01	Muss	5f	F	G-F	£2646
59	3/00	Ling	6f	G	STD	£1850
67	7/99	Sals	6f	E(0-70)H	G-F	£3013

Total win prize-money £11967

Going (Turf): Sf: 0-2 GS: 0-3 Gd: 0-7 **GF: 4-11** Fm: 0-2
Distance: **5f/6f: 4-26** 7f-8f: 1-6 9f-13f: 0-0 14f+: 0-0
Track : **LH: 1-7** RH: 0-2 **Tight: 1-4** Gall: 0-2
Aids: Bl: 0-3 Vi: 0-0 Tstrap: 0-0
Best Rating: 49 7/01 Nott 6f15y gd-fm

He has won three times this season on fast ground over five and six furlongs, but is not all that consistent.

Grande Dame (IRE)

87 **70**

2-y-o b f Grand Lodge (USA)-Royal Hostess (IRE) (Be My Guest (USA))
I A Balding M E Wates

Placings:00 **(4887)**
2001: 6^{0}GF, 7^{0}GF

	Starts	1st	2nd	3rd	Win & Pl
Career Total (Turf)	2	0	0	0	

Going (Turf): Sf: 0-0 GS: 0-0 Gd: 0-0 GF: 0-2 Fm: 0-0
Distance: 5f/6f: 0-0 7f-8f: 0-2 9f-13f: 0-0 14f+: 0-0
Track : LH: 0-0 RH: 0-1 Tight: 0-0 Gall: 0-1
Aids: Bl: 0-0 Vi: 0-0 Tstrap: 0-0
Best Rating: 70 9/01 Kemp 7f gd-fm

Grandera (IRE)

118 **120**

3-y-o ch c Grand Lodge (USA)-Bordighera (USA) (Alysheba (USA))
J R Fanshawe Lael Stable & Mrs V Shelton

Placings:5120-23221 **(4862)**
2001: 10^{2}GF, 12^{3}G, 10^{2}GF, 10^{2}G, 11^{1}GF

	Starts	1st	2nd	3rd	Win & Pl
Career Total (Turf)	9	2	4	1	304380

117	9/01	Newb	1m3f5y	A	G-F	£29750
87	9/00	Wwck	7f26y	D	G-F	£3835

Total win prize-money £33585

Going (Turf): Sf: 0-1 GS: 0-0 Gd: 0-4 **GF: 2-4** Fm: 0-0
Distance: 5f/6f: 0-1 7f-8f: 1-3 9f-13f: 1-5 14f+: 0-0
Track : **LH: 2-5** RH: 0-1 Tight: 0-1 **Gall: 1-3**
Aids: Bl: 0-0 Vi: 0-0 Tstrap: 0-0
Best Rating: 120 8/01 York 1m2f85y good

A very smart middle-distance colt, he finished strongly and looked an unlucky loser when third in the Prix du Jockey-Club at Chantilly in June. He was then beaten only half a length by Medicean in the Eclipse and was again second behind the runaway winner Sakhee in the Juddmonte International at York. He gained a deserved win in the Listed Arc Trial at Newbury, but was far from impressive and is much better than that. Has joined Godolphin and should do well in 2002.

Grandma Griffiths

66 **34**

3-y-o b f Eagle Eyed (USA)-Buck Comtess (USA) (Spend A Buck (USA))
Mrs L Stubbs Doug Kirk,Darren Kirk,Winton Bloodstock

Placings:000-00 **(1734)**
2001: 9^{0}GS, 16^{0}GF

	Starts	1st	2nd	3rd	Win & Pl
Career Total (Turf)	5	0	0	0	

Going (Turf): Sf: 0-2 GS: 0-1 Gd: 0-0 GF: 0-2 Fm: 0-0
Distance: 5f/6f: 0-1 7f-8f: 0-0 9f-13f: 0-3 14f+: 0-1
Track : LH: 0-2 RH: 0-0 Tight: 0-1 Gall: 0-0
Aids: Bl: 0-0 Vi: 0-0 Tstrap: 0-0

Grandma Lily (IRE)

83(104) (84)**33**

3-y-o b f Bigstone (IRE)-Mrs Fisher (IRE) (Salmon Leap (USA))
Sir Mark Prescott G D Waters

Placings:05112 **(4068)**
2001: 8^{0}SD, 10^{5}GF, 6^{1}SD, 7^{1}SD, 9^{2}SD

	Starts	1st	2nd	3rd	Win & Pl
Career Total (Turf)	1	0	0	0	0
Career Total (AW)	4	2	1	0	8050

80	8/01	Wolv	7f	D(0-75)	STD	£3922
70	7/01	Wolv	6f	D	STD	£2947

Total win prize-money £6870

Going (Turf): Sf: 0-0 GS: 0-0 Gd: 0-0 GF: 0-1 Fm: 0-0
Distance: 5f/6f: 1-1 7f-8f: 1-2 9f-13f: 0-2 14f+: 0-0
Track : **LH: 2-4** RH: 0-1 **Tight: 2-4** Gall: 0-0
Aids: Bl: 0-0 Vi: 0-0 Tstrap: 0-0
Best Rating: 84 8/01 Wolv 1m1f79y stand

Showed little in her first two starts, but benefited from a drop in distance to win a maiden and a nursery on the Wolverhampton Fibresand. Seven furlongs looks her best trip.

Grange Clare (IRE)

83(89) (63)**63**

2-y-o b/br f Bijou D'Inde-Scarlet Slipper (Gay Mecene (USA))
P D Evans Ms Ann Cully

Placings:13 **(1825)**
2001: 5^{1}SD, 6^{3}GF

	Starts	1st	2nd	3rd	Win & Pl
Career Total (Turf)	1	0	0	1	538
Career Total (AW)	1	1	0	0	2380

63	5/01	Sthl	5f	E	STD	£2380

Total win prize-money £2380

Going (Turf): Sf: 0-0 GS: 0-0 Gd: 0-0 GF: 0-1 Fm: 0-0
Distance: **5f/6f: 1-2** 7f-8f: 0-0 9f-13f: 0-0 14f+: 0-0
Track : LH: 0-1 RH: 0-0 Tight: 0-0 Gall: 0-0
Aids: Bl: 0-0 Vi: 0-0 Tstrap: 0-0
Best Rating: 63 6/01 Pont 6f gd-fm

A well-bred filly, she ran green when landing her race-course debut on the All-Weather, but showed promise for the future. She is bred to stay a mile.

Grange Prince (IRE)

(78) (29)**50**

2-y-o b g Mujadil (USA)-Cashel Princess (IRE) (Fayruz)
P D Evans Ms Ann Cully

Placings:00 **(5079)**
2001: 6^{0}GF, 5^{0}S

	Starts	1st	2nd	3rd	Win & Pl
Career Total (Turf)	2	0	0	0	

Going (Turf): Sf: 0-1 GS: 0-0 Gd: 0-0 GF: 0-1 Fm: 0-0
Distance: 5f/6f: 0-2 7f-8f: 0-0 9f-13f: 0-0 14f+: 0-0
Track : LH: 0-1 RH: 0-0 Tight: 0-0 Gall: 0-0
Aids: Bl: 0-0 Vi: 0-0 Tstrap: 0-0
Best Rating: 50 9/01 Ling 6f gd-fm

Granite City

103 **44**

4-y-o ro g Clantime-Alhargah (Be My Guest (USA))
J S Goldie Aberdeenshire Racing Club

Placings:450350560/00000302166-0005001650333 **(5659)**
2001: 8^{0}GS, 7^{0}GF, 8^{0}GF, 7^{5}G, 8^{0}F, 8^{0}GF, 9^{1}G, 9^{6}G, 8^{5}F, 8^{0}GF, 6^{3}HY, 8^{3}S, 8^{3}G

	Starts	1st	2nd	3rd	Win & Pl
Career Total (Turf)	33	2	1	5	8911

44	8/01	Muss	1m1f	F(0-65)H	GD	£2733
48	8/00	Muss	7f30y	F(0-60)H	GD	£2562

Total win prize-money £5296

Going (Turf): Sf: 0-3 GS: 0-2 **Gd: 2-9** GF: 0-12 Fm: 0-7
Distance: 5f/6f: 0-12 7f-8f: 1-18 9f-13f: 1-3 14f+: 0-0
Track : LH: 0-5 **RH: 1-13 Tight: 1-14** Gall: 0-1
Aids: Bl: 0-0 Vi: 0-0 Tstrap: 0-0
Best Rating: 44 8/01 Muss 1m1f good

Moderate handicapper around a mile who goes particularly well at Musselburgh.

Granny's Pet

108 **103**

7-y-o ch g Selkirk (USA)-Patsy Western (Precocious)
P F I Cole Exors Of The Late Mrs D M Arbib

Placings:2210434/2534040/0651020/2002113121/3160532-443451246 **(5499)**
2001: 7^{4}G, 7^{4}F, 7^{3}GF, 7^{4}GF, 7^{5}G, 7^{1}GF, 7^{2}GF, 6^{4}S, 7^{6}HY

	Starts	1st	2nd	3rd	Win & Pl
Career Total (Turf)	47	8	9	6	119625

102	8/01	Gdwd	7f	B(0-105)H	G-F	£9546
105	5/00	Leic	7f9y	C	G-S	£6834
101	10/99	Donc	7f	B	SFT	£10796
103	9/99	Gdwd	7f	B(0-105)H	G-F	£9207
99	8/99	Gdwd	7f	B(0-105)H	GD	£9655
98	8/99	Ches	7f2y	B(0-100)H	G-S	£8738
99	9/98	Hayd	7f30y	C(0-90)H	GD	£6092
84	6/96	Epsm	5f	B	GD	£8929

Total win prize-money £69802

Going (Turf): Sf: 1-6 GS: 2-9 **Gd: 3-19** GF: 2-11 Fm: 0-2
Distance: 5f/6f: 1-10 **7f-8f: 7-36** 9f-13f: 0-1 14f+: 0-0
Track : LH: 2-11 **RH: 3-10 Tight: 1-2** Gall: 0-6
Aids: Bl: 0-3 Vi: 0-0 Tstrap: 0-0
Best Rating: 103 9/01 Gdwd 7f gd-fm

He won four times over his optimum distance of seven furlongs in 1999 and once in 2000 and once in the current season. Seemingly effective on all types of ground although particularly suited by some cut, he is best held up and goes particularly well for Jimmy Fortune.

Grantley

99(99) (54)**41**

4-y-o b g Deploy-Matisse (Shareef Dancer (USA))
J D Bethell Mrs James Bethell

Placings:00/000064223-64043 **(0903)**
2001: 8^{6}SD, 8^{4}SD, 9^{0}SD, 9^{4}S, 8^{3}GS

	Starts	1st	2nd	3rd	Win & Pl
Career Total (Turf)	9	0	0	1	402
Career Total (AW)	7	0	2	1	2183

Going (Turf): Sf: 0-2 GS: 0-4 Gd: 0-1 GF: 0-1 Fm: 0-1
Distance: 5f/6f: 0-2 7f-8f: 0-4 9f-13f: 0-9 14f+: 0-1
Track : LH: 0-8 RH: 0-5 Tight: 0-8 Gall: 0-0
Aids: Bl: 0-7 Vi: 0-3 Tstrap: 0-0
Best Rating: 48 1/01 Sthl 1m stand

Grasslandik

(97) (42)**31**

5-y-o b g Ardkinglass-Sophisticated Baby (Bairn (USA))
Miss A Stokell (A G Newcombe 9/2) M F Barraclough

Placings:1/3250042000502/35350045602-00600 **(5629)**
2001: 7^{0}SD, 8^{0}SD, 8^{6}SW, 7^{0}G, 5^{0}G

	Starts	1st	2nd	3rd	Win & Pl
Career Total (Turf)	10	0	1	0	721
Career Total (AW)	20	1	3	3	4934

53	12/98	Sthl	5f	G	STD	£1934

Total win prize-money £1935

Going (Turf): Sf: 0-0 GS: 0-2 Gd: 0-7 GF: 0-1 Fm: 0-0
Distance: **5f/6f: 1-23** 7f-8f: 0-6 9f-13f: 0-1 14f+: 0-0
Track : LH: 0-24 RH: 0-1 Tight: 0-12 Gall: 0-4
Aids: Bl: 0-2 Vi: 0-0 Tstrap: 0-0
Best Rating: 31 2/01 Sthl 1m slow

Fair handicapper at around a mile. Runs well on the All-Weather at Southwell.

Great As Gold (IRE)

(85) (50)**61**

2-y-o b g Goldmark (USA)-Great Land (USA) (Friend's Choice (USA))
Miss V Haigh Mrs Andrea M Mallinson

Placings:505603300005 **(5618)**
2001: 5^{5}F, 6^{0}SD, 7^{5}SD, 5^{6}G, 6^{0}G, 8^{3}G, 7^{3}GF, 6^{0}G, 7^{0}GF, 9^{0}HY, 7^{0}S, 8^{5}SD

	Starts	1st	2nd	3rd	Win & Pl
Career Total (Turf)	9	0	0	2	1583
Career Total (AW)	3	0	0	0	0

Going (Turf): Sf: 0-2 GS: 0-0 Gd: 0-4 GF: 0-2 Fm: 0-1
Distance: 5f/6f: 0-5 7f-8f: 0-4 9f-13f: 0-3 14f+: 0-0
Track : LH: 0-7 RH: 0-0 Tight: 0-2 Gall: 0-2
Aids: Bl: 0-5 Vi: 0-0 Tstrap: 0-0
Best Rating: 61 9/01 York 7f202y gd-fm

Great Hopper

75(78) **19**

6-y-o b m Rock Hopper-Spun Gold (Thatch (USA))
F Watson F Watson

Placings:000/00-04006 **(4477)**
2001: 8^{0}SW, 12^{4}SW, 13^{0}GF, 12^{0}GF, 12^{6}F

	Starts	1st	2nd	3rd	Win & Pl
Career Total (Turf)	8	0	0	0	0
Career Total (AW)	2	0	0	0	0

Going (Turf): Sf: 0-2 GS: 0-1 Gd: 0-2 GF: 0-2 Fm: 0-1
Distance: 5f/6f: 0-0 7f-8f: 0-1 9f-13f: 0-7 14f+: 0-2
Track : LH: 0-6 RH: 0-2 Tight: 0-4 Gall: 0-0
Aids: Bl: 0-0 Vi: 0-1 Tstrap: 0-0
Best Rating: 19 6/01 Ayr 1m5f13y gd-fm

Great News

(89) (54)**85**

6-y-o b g Elmaamul (USA)-Amina (Brigadier Gerard)
W J Haggas Executive Network (pertemps Group)

Placings:322321/2130130/000000111200-600100 **(5267)**
2001: 8^{6}GF, 6^{0}F, 6^{0}G, 8^{1}GF, 7^{0}S, 6^{0}GS

	Starts	1st	2nd	3rd	Win & Pl
Career Total (Turf)	30	7	5	4	96154
Career Total (AW)	1	0	0	0	

85	9/01	Ayr	1m	C(0-100)H	G-F	£19877
85	9/00	Ling	7f	E(0-70)H	GD	£3255
82	9/00	Ayr	1m	C(0-100)H	SFT	£19526
77	9/00	Ayr	7f	C(0-90)H	SFT	£7540
83	8/99	Wind	1m67y	C(0-90)H	GD	£5989
81	4/99	Asct	7f	B(0-110)H	GD	£22600
73	10/98	Ling	7f	E(0-70)H	SFT	£3701

Total win prize-money £82490

Going (Turf): Sf: 3-8 GS: 0-7 **Gd: 3-8** GF: 1-6 Fm: 0-1
Distance: 5f/6f: 0-2 **7f-8f: 6-23** 9f-13f: 1-6 14f+: 0-0
Track : **LH: 3-13** RH: 1-4 **Tight: 1-2** Gall: 0-5
Aids: Bl: 0-0 Vi: 0-0 Tstrap: 0-0
Best Rating: 85 9/01 Ayr 1m gd-fm

Found his form late in 2000 when completing a brilliant hat-trick within seven days, including two wins at Ayr. He returned to winning ways this season back at the same venue in September in a race he won the previous year. Has won over seven furlongs and a mile. Best on good ground or softer, although has won on fast.

Great Oration (IRE)

97 **45**

12-y-o b/br g Simply Great (FR)-Spun Gold (Thatch (USA))
F Watson F Watson

Placings:60/6/060240030/011223400/6321406/043031315333/153036410/05350/00/0040 **(4620)**
2001: 16^{0}GF, 17^{0}GF, 16^{4}GF, 16^{0}F

	Starts	1st	2nd	3rd	Win & Pl
Career Total (Turf)	56	7	3	12	36938
Career Total (AW)	4	0	1	0	839

66	8/97	Pont	2m1f22y	F(0-65)H	G-F	£3615
58	4/97	Pont	2m1f22y	D(0-80)H	G-F	£3687
56	7/96	Ches	1m7f195y	D(0-80)H	G-F	£6092
50	6/96	Pont	2m1f216y	E(0-70)H	G-F	£3785
46	8/95	Pont	2m1f22y	F(0-65)H	G-F	£2829
42	6/94	Catt	1m7f177y	E(0-70)H	FRM	£2976
34	6/94	Muss	1m7f16y	F(0-60)H	FRM	£2575

Total win prize-money £25562

Going (Turf): Sf: 0-1 GS: 0-1 Gd: 0-18 **GF: 5-30** Fm: 2-6
Distance: 5f/6f: 0-0 7f-8f: 0-2 9f-13f: 0-8 **14f+: 7-50**
Track : **LH: 6-38** RH: 1-20 **Tight: 3-33** Gall: 0-7
Aids: Bl: 0-0 Vi: 0-7 Tstrap: 0-0
Best Rating: 45 8/01 Ripn 2m gd-fm

Great View (IRE)

107 **91**

2-y-o b c Great Commotion (USA)-Tara View (IRE) (Wassl)
B J Meehan Mrs Susan McCarthy

Placings:6212400 **(4948)**
2001: 5^{6}G, 6^{2}GF, 6^{1}GF, 6^{2}S, 6^{4}G, 7^{0}GS, 7^{0}G

	Starts	1st	2nd	3rd	Win & Pl
Career Total (Turf)	7	1	2	0	6973

91	7/01	Chep	6f16y	E	G-F	£2940

Total win prize-money £2940

Going (Turf): Sf: 0-1 GS: 0-1 Gd: 0-3 **GF: 1-2** Fm: 0-0
Distance: 5f/6f: 0-2 **7f-8f: 1-5** 9f-13f: 0-0 14f+: 0-0
Track : LH: 0-1 RH: 0-2 Tight: 0-0 Gall: 0-2
Aids: Bl: 0-0 Vi: 0-0 Tstrap: 0-0
Best Rating: 91 8/01 York 6f214y good

A half-brother to juvenile winner Wind In Winnipeg, he made all to win his maiden at Chepstow on his third start and has run well in the face of stiff tasks since. Acts on fast ground and soft.

Greatdream (IRE)

(89) (60)

2-y-o ch c Hamas (IRE)-Simply A Dream (IRE) (Simply Great (FR))
E J O'Neill Mrs Patrick O'Neill

Placings:45 **(5614)**
2001: 6^{4}SD, 6^{5}SD

	Starts	1st	2nd	3rd	Win & Pl
Career Total (Turf)	0	0	0	0	
Career Total (AW)	2	0	0	0	0

Going (Turf): Sf: 0-0 GS: 0-0 Gd: 0-0 GF: 0-0 Fm: 0-0
Distance: 5f/6f: 0-2 7f-8f: 0-0 9f-13f: 0-0 14f+: 0-0
Track : LH: 0-2 RH: 0-0 Tight: 0-1 Gall: 0-0
Aids: Bl: 0-0 Vi: 0-0 Tstrap: 0-0
Best Rating: 60 7/01 Sthl 6f stand

Grecian Halo (USA)

(94) (57)**52**

3-y-o b f Southern Halo (USA)-Modern Grecian (USA) (Mr. Leader (USA))
M L W Bell D M Littlejohn & W J P Jackson

Placings:600-1400 **(2324)**
2001: 8^{1}SD, 10^{4}SW, 7^{0}F, 9^{0}SD

	Starts	1st	2nd	3rd	Win & Pl
Career Total (Turf)	4	0	0	0	0
Career Total (AW)	3	1	0	0	2219

56	1/01	Ling	1m	F(0-60)H	STD	£2219

Total win prize-money £2219

Going (Turf): Sf: 0-0 GS: 0-1 Gd: 0-0 GF: 0-1 Fm: 0-1
Distance: 5f/6f: 0-1 **7f-8f: 1-3** 9f-13f: 0-2 14f+: 0-0
Track : **LH: 1-4** RH: 0-1 **Tight: 1-3** Gall: 0-1

Aids: Bl: 0-0 Vi: 0-0 Tstrap: 0-0
Best Rating: 57 2/01 Ling 1m2f slow

Greek Dream (USA)

104 **72**

3-y-o ch f Distant View (USA)-Wandesta (Nashwan (USA))
B W Hills K Abdulla

Placings:6-3210 **(4370)**
2001: 7^{3}F, 7^{2}F, 7^{1}F, 7^{0}GF

	Starts	1st	2nd	3rd	Win & Pl
Career Total (Turf)	5	1	1	1	5989

59 8/01 Thsk 7f D FRM £4244
Total win prize-money £4245

Going (Turf): Sf: 0-0 GS: 0-1 Gd: 0-0 GF: 0-1 **Fm: 1-3**
Distance: 5f/6f: 0-1 **7f-8f: 1-4** 9f-13f: 0-0 14f+: 0-0
Track : **LH: 1-5** RH: 0-0 **Tight: 1-3** Gall: 0-1
Aids: Bl: 0-0 Vi: 0-0 Tstrap: 0-0
Best Rating: 72 7/01 Thsk 7f firm

The first foal of a smart middle-distance performer, she only had the one run in 2000, and did not look the most comfortable on the racecourse the following season, despite a modest win at Thirsk at the end of the summer. She has won over seven furlongs on firm ground but should get further as a four-year-old.

Green Bopper (USA)

102(109) (72)**62**

8-y-o b g Green Dancer (USA)-Wayage (USA) (Mr Prospector (USA))
J L Eyre Wetherby Racing Bureau 39

Placings:0/3100040/00/**21110546/551214**013620/**5234 2105500-01000166** **(5663)**
2001: 12^{0}SD, 12^{1}G, 12^{0}GF, 10^{0}S, 10^{0}G, 12^{1}GS, 10^{6}HY, 12^{6}G

	Starts	1st	2nd	3rd	Win & Pl
Career Total (Turf)	29	4	1	2	21191
Career Total (AW)	20	6	4	1	27041

62 8/01 Ches 1m4f66y E(0-80)H G-S £3535
62 6/01 Muss 1m4f E(0-75)H GD £8736
72 3/00 Sthl 1m4f C(0-100)H STD £6467
62 7/99 Hayd 1m2f120yE(0-75)H G-S £2864
68 3/99 Sthl 1m3f D(0-85)H STD £3584
61 2/99 Sthl 1m3f D(0-85)H STD £3718
64 4/98 Wolv 1m100y F(0-60) STD £2322
62 3/98 Wolv 1m100y F(0-65)H STD £2511
56 3/98 Sthl 1m E(0-70)H STD £2489
80 4/96 Newc 1m D GD £3566
Total win prize-money £39795

Going (Turf): Sf: 0-4 **GS: 2-7 Gd: 2-9** GF: 0-9 Fm: 0-0
Distance: 5f/6f: 0-0 7f-8f: 2-12 **9f-13f: 8-37** 14f+: 0-0
Track : **LH: 9-37** RH: 0-5 **Tight: 3-13** Gall: 1-7
Aids: Bl: 0-0 Vi: 0-1 Tstrap: 0-0
Best Rating: 62 8/01 Ches 1m4f66y gd-sft

He is a useful middle-distance handicapper on Fibresand. Won twice on turf in summer of 2001 over a mile and a half, for the first time for a couple of years. Acts on good ground, seems suited of late by making the running.

Green Card (USA)

97 **89**

7-y-o br h Green Dancer (USA)-Dunkellin (USA) (Irish River (FR))
S P C Woods P Pottinger/n Thomas/n Yardy

Placings:0/1034235/5012153446/3555433/4630416-0 **(1604)**
2001: 16^{0}GF

	Starts	1st	2nd	3rd	Win & Pl
Career Total (Turf)	33	4	2	7	53389

89 9/00 Donc 1m2f60y C(0-85) G-F £7377
110 7/98 Donc 1m C G-F £5645
98 6/98 Nott 1m54y C G-S £5170
81 4/97 Ripn 1m D G-F £3647
Total win prize-money £21841

Going (Turf): Sf: 0-5 GS: 1-4 Gd: 0-12 **GF: 3-11** Fm: 0-1
Distance: 5f/6f: 0-0 7f-8f: 2-19 9f-13f: 2-13 14f+: 0-1
Track : **LH: 2-10** RH: 1-12 Tight: 1-6 Gall: 1-6
Aids: Bl: 0-1 Vi: 0-2 Tstrap: 0-0
Best Rating: 83 5/01 Kemp 2m gd-fm

Green Casket (IRE)

106(96) (62)**76**

4-y-o b g Green Desert (USA)-Grecian Urn (Ela-Mana-Mou)
J A Glover David Jenkins

Placings:6/6-**04001120003** **(5106)**
2001: 7^{0}SD, 8^{4}SW, 9^{0}SD, 9^{0}GF, 9^{1}GF, 9^{1}GF, 9^{2}GF, 9^{0}GS, 10^{0}GF, 9^{0}GF, 12^{3}GS

	Starts	1st	2nd	3rd	Win & Pl
Career Total (Turf)	10	2	1	1	9359
Career Total (AW)	3	0	0	0	0

76 7/01 Bevl 1m1f207yE(0-70)H G-F £7254
Total win prize-money £7254

Going (Turf): Sf: 0-0 GS: 0-4 Gd: 0-0 **GF: 2-6** Fm: 0-0
Distance: 5f/6f: 0-0 7f-8f: 0-3 **9f-13f: 2-10** 14f+: 0-0
Track : LH: 0-3 **RH: 2-9** Tight: 0-3 Gall: 0-2
Aids: Bl: 0-0 Vi: 0-0 Tstrap: 0-3
Best Rating: 76 7/01 Bevl 1m1f207y gd-fm

He won twice over ten furlongs on fast ground at Beverley in the summer, but the resulting rise in the handicap seems to have found him out.

Green Crystal

84 **64**

2-y-o b f Green Dancer (USA)-Dunkellin (USA) (Irish River (FR))
S P C Woods Arashan Ali

Placings:600 **(4221)**
2001: 7^{6}GS, 7^{0}G, 7^{0}GF

	Starts	1st	2nd	3rd	Win & Pl
Career Total (Turf)	3	0	0	0	0

Going (Turf): Sf: 0-0 GS: 0-1 Gd: 0-1 GF: 0-1 Fm: 0-0
Distance: 5f/6f: 0-0 7f-8f: 0-3 9f-13f: 0-0 14f+: 0-0
Track : LH: 0-0 RH: 0-0 Tight: 0-0 Gall: 0-0
Aids: Bl: 0-0 Vi: 0-0 Tstrap: 0-0
Best Rating: 64 8/01 NmkJ 7f gd-fm

Green Eyed Lady

97(99) (60)**74+**

2-y-o b f Greensmith-Dark Eyed Lady (IRE) (Exhibitioner)
B J Meehan J S Gutkin

Placings:3121 **(1633)**
2001: 5^{3}SD, 5^{1}SD, 5^{2}SD, 5^{1}F

	Starts	1st	2nd	3rd	Win & Pl
Career Total (Turf)	1	1	0	0	2513
Career Total (AW)	3	1	1	1	3340

74 5/01 Leic 5f2y F FRM £2513
60 4/01 Ling 5f F STD £2268
Total win prize-money £4781

Going (Turf): Sf: 0-0 GS: 0-0 Gd: 0-0 GF: 0-0 **Fm: 1-1**
Distance: **5f/6f: 2-4** 7f-8f: 0-0 9f-13f: 0-0 14f+: 0-0
Track : **LH: 1-2** RH: 0-0 **Tight: 1-2** Gall: 0-0
Aids: Bl: 0-0 Vi: 0-0 Tstrap: 0-0
Best Rating: 74 5/01 Leic 5f2y firm

A winner of claimers on sand and turf, she has early pace and looks the type who will always need a sound surface. She was not seen out after May.

Green Ginger

98(89) (34)**42**

5-y-o ch g Ardkinglass-Bella Maggio (Rakaposhi King)
A Streeter Mrs D F Garrett

Placings:004/4443100/00000**0-00035** **(4628)**
2001: 7^{0}SD, 9^{0}GF, 9^{0}G, 8^{3}GF, 8^{5}GF

	Starts	1st	2nd	3rd	Win & Pl
Career Total (Turf)	19	1	0	2	4516
Career Total (AW)	2	0	0	0	

80 8/99 Nott 6f15y F G-F £2417
Total win prize-money £2418

Going (Turf): Sf: 0-0 GS: 0-1 Gd: 0-2 **GF: 1-12** Fm: 0-4
Distance: 5f/6f: 0-9 **7f-8f: 1-9** 9f-13f: 0-3 14f+: 0-0
Track : LH: 0-8 RH: 0-1 Tight: 0-1 Gall: 0-0
Aids: Bl: 0-0 Vi: 0-4 Tstrap: 0-0
Best Rating: 42 8/01 Ripn 1m gd-fm

Green Green Grass

96(88) (27)**27**

3-y-o b f Green Desert (USA)-Hulm (IRE) (Mujtahid (USA))
N P Littmoden Mrs Linda Francis

Placings:535-000060 **(4872)**
2001: 6^{0}GF, 5^{0}GF, 6^{0}SD, 6^{0}G, 7^{6}GF, 7^{0}G

	Starts	1st	2nd	3rd	Win & Pl
Career Total (Turf)	5	0	0	0	0
Career Total (AW)	4	0	0	1	476

Going (Turf): Sf: 0-0 GS: 0-0 Gd: 0-2 GF: 0-3 Fm: 0-0
Distance: 5f/6f: 0-6 7f-8f: 0-3 9f-13f: 0-0 14f+: 0-0
Track : LH: 0-2 RH: 0-1 Tight: 0-2 Gall: 0-0
Aids: Bl: 0-0 Vi: 0-0 Tstrap: 0-0
Best Rating: 27 8/01 Bevl 7f100y gd-fm

Green Ideal

109 **90**

3-y-o b c Mark Of Esteem (IRE)-Emerald (USA) (El Gran Senor (USA))
Mrs A J Perrett K Abdulla

Placings:15 **(4262)**
2001: 10^{1}GF, 11^{5}GF

	Starts	1st	2nd	3rd	Win & Pl
Career Total (Turf)	2	1	0	0	4592

90 7/01 Sand 1m2f7y D G-F £4329
Total win prize-money £4329

Going (Turf): Sf: 0-0 GS: 0-0 Gd: 0-0 **GF: 1-2** Fm: 0-0
Distance: 5f/6f: 0-0 7f-8f: 0-0 **9f-13f: 1-2** 14f+: 0-0
Track : LH: 0-0 **RH: 1-1** Tight: 0-1 Gall: 0-0
Aids: Bl: 0-0 Vi: 0-0 Tstrap: 0-0
Best Rating: 90 7/01 Sand 1m2f7y gd-fm

A tall, attractive colt from the family of Danehill, showed good battling qualities to score on his belated debut at Sandown, and is trainer believes he will be better on easier ground.

Green Magical (IRE)

(96) (30)**30**

5-y-o ch m Magical Strike (USA)-Green Legend (IRE) (Montekin)
T Hogan (J Cullinan 1/7) John M Carroll

Placings:00600/420304/00-**0063** **(2323)**
2001: 12^{0}SW, 11^{0}SD, 14^{6}SD, 16^{3}SD

	Starts	1st	2nd	3rd	Win & Pl
Career Total (Turf)	13	0	1	1	1402
Career Total (AW)	4	0	0	1	273

Going (Turf): Sf: 0-3 GS: 0-0 Gd: 0-3 GF: 0-5 Fm: 0-0

Distance: 5f/6f: 0-2 7f-8f: 0-4 9f-13f: 0-9 14f+: 0-2
Track : LH: 0-6 RH: 0-9 Tight: 0-3 Gall: 0-0
Aids: Bl: 0 3 Vi: 0 0 Tstrap: 0-0
Best Rating: 30 6/01 Wolv 2m46y stand

Green Missile

85 **44**

6-y-o b g Green Ruby (USA)-Amber Missile Vii (Damsire Unregistered)

G B Balding Mrs P D Gulliver

Placings:0 **(2355)**

2001: 22^{0}GF

	Starts	1st	2nd	3rd	Win & Pl
Career Total (Turf)	1	0	0	0	

Going (Turf): Sf: 0-0 GS: 0-0 Gd: 0-0 GF: 0-1 Fm: 0-0
Distance: 5f/6f: 0-0 7f-8f: 0-0 9f-13f: 0-0 14f+: 0-1
Track : LH: 0-0 RH: 0-1 Tight: 0-0 Gall: 0-1
Aids: Bl: 0-0 Vi: 0-0 Tstrap: 0-0
Best Rating: 44 6/01 Asct 2m6f34y gd-fm

Green Pursuit

95(97) (51)**40**

5-y-o b g Green Desert (USA)-Vayavaig (Damister (USA))

J G M O'Shea (J A Osborne 14/8) Gary Roberts

Placings:305/43106/0020-502440 **(4672)**

2001: 7^{5}GF, 8^{0}GF, 8^{2}SD, 8^{4}SD, 7^{4}F, 8^{0}G

	Starts	1st	2nd	3rd	Win & Pl
Career Total (Turf)	14	1	1	2	5866
Career Total (AW)	4	0	1	0	674

74 6/99 Cork 6f G-F £4296
Total win prize-money £4297

Going (Turf): Sf: 0-1 GS: 0-0 Gd: 0-3 **GF: 1-6** Fm: 0-2
Distance: **5f/6f: 1-8** 7f-8f: 0-9 9f-13f: 0-1 14f+: 0-0
Track : LH: 0-8 RH: 0-1 Tight: 0-1 Gall: 0-1
Aids: Bl: 0-2 Vi: 0-0 Tstrap: 0-0
Best Rating: 51 7/01 Sthl 1m stand

Green Ransom (USA)

84 **63**

3-y-o b c Red Ransom (USA)-Arjunand (USA) (Diesis)

H R A Cecil The Thoroughbred Corporation

Placings:0 **(0811)**

2001: 8^{0}S

	Starts	1st	2nd	3rd	Win & Pl
Career Total (Turf)	1	0	0	0	

Going (Turf): Sf: 0-1 GS: 0-0 Gd: 0-0 GF: 0-0 Fm: 0-0
Distance: 5f/6f: 0-0 7f-8f: 0-1 9f-13f: 0-0 14f+: 0-0
Track : LH: 0-0 RH: 0-0 Tight: 0-0 Gall: 0-0
Aids: Bl: 0-0 Vi: 0-0 Tstrap: 0-0
Best Rating: 63 4/01 NmkR 1m soft

Green Tambourine

99 **87**

3-y-o b f Green Desert (USA)-Maid For The Hills (Indian Ridge)

R Charlton Mountgrange Stud

Placings:16-00 **(4890)**

2001: 7^{0}G, 6^{0}GF

	Starts	1st	2nd	3rd	Win & Pl
Career Total (Turf)	4	1	0	0	3842

80 7/00 Hayd 6f D G-F £3841
Total win prize-money £3842

Going (Turf): Sf: 0-0 GS: 0-0 Gd: 0-1 **GF: 1-3** Fm: 0-0
Distance: **5f/6f: 1-3** 7f-8f: 0-1 9f-13f: 0-0 14f+: 0-0
Track : LH: 0-0 RH: 0-0 Tight: 0-0 Gall: 0-0
Aids: Bl: 0-0 Vi: 0-0 Tstrap: 0-0

Best Rating: 81 9/01 Kemp 6f gd-fm

Greenaway Bay (USA)

108(100) (65)**79**

7-y-o ch g Green Dancer (USA)-Raise 'n Dance (USA) (Raise A Native)

K R Burke Asterlane Ltd

Placings:16000/4030304043/50016463/51112-06000000214 **(5669)**

2001: 8^{0}SD, 8^{6}S, 8^{0}G, 8^{0}GF, 8^{0}GF, 10^{0}G, 7^{0}GF, 8^{0}G, 9^{2}G, 8^{1}HY, 10^{4}HY

	Starts	1st	2nd	3rd	Win & Pl
Career Total (Turf)	37	6	2	4	66957
Career Total (AW)	2	0	0	0	236

71 10/01 Nott 1m54y C(0-90)H HVY £7507
80 10/00 NmkR 1m C(0-100)H SFT £23200
72 10/00 Nott 1m54y C(0-90)H SFT £7442
66 10/00 York 1m205y D(0-80)H HVY £13689
56 8/99 Brig 7f214y E(0-70)H G-F £4151
80 3/97 Kemp 7f D G-F £2965
Total win prize-money £58956

Going (Turf): Sf: 4-10 GS: 0-2 Gd: 0-10 GF: 2-14 Fm: 0-1
Distance: 5f/6f: 0-0 7f-8f: 3-12 9f-13f: 3-27 14f+: 0-0
Track : **LH: 4-20** RH: 1-9 Tight: 0-14 **Gall: 2-11**
Aids: Bl: 0-0 Vi: 0-0 Tstrap: 0-0
Best Rating: 71 10/01 Nott 1m54y heavy

Enjoyed a good 2000 season, completing a handicap hat-trick in October 2000, winning at York, Nottingham and Newmarket. He had not sparkled this year but dropped in the weights as a result and he took advantage of that with a close second at Redcar, before getting off the mark for the year at Nottingham at the end of October. Loves the mud and comes with a late run.

Greenborough (IRE)

(93) (74)**38**

3-y-o b c Dr Devious (IRE)-Port Isaac (USA) (Seattle Song (USA))

P F I Cole Anthony Speelman

Placings:024-000 **(3233)**

2001: 9^{0}GF, 8^{0}G, 12^{0}SD

	Starts	1st	2nd	3rd	Win & Pl
Career Total (Turf)	3	0	0	0	
Career Total (AW)	3	0	1	0	720

Going (Turf): Sf: 0-1 GS: 0-0 Gd: 0-1 GF: 0-1 Fm: 0-0
Distance: 5f/6f: 0-0 7f-8f: 0-2 9f-13f: 0-4 14f+: 0-0
Track : LH: 0-4 RH: 0-2 Tight: 0-3 Gall: 0-0
Aids: Bl: 0-0 Vi: 0-0 Tstrap: 0-0
Best Rating: 38 6/01 Wind 1m67y good

Greenhills

99 **95?**

2-y-o br c Greensmith-Free As A Bird (Robellino (USA))

M Blanshard Tweenhills Racing (catsbury Syndicate)

Placings:2100324000 **(5364)**

2001: 6^{2}GF, 6^{1}GF, 5^{0}GF, 5^{0}S, 6^{3}GF, 6^{2}GF, 6^{4}G, 7^{0}S, 6^{0}G, 6^{0}GS

	Starts	1st	2nd	3rd	Win & Pl
Career Total (Turf)	10	1	2	1	8833

79 7/01 Ling 6f D G-F £3753
Total win prize-money £3754

Going (Turf): Sf: 0-2 GS: 0-1 Gd: 0-2 **GF: 1-5** Fm: 0-0
Distance: **5f/6f: 1-9** 7f-8f: 0-1 9f-13f: 0-0 14f+: 0-0
Track : LH: 0-1 RH: 0-0 Tight: 0-1 Gall: 0-0
Aids: Bl: 0-0 Vi: 0-0 Tstrap: 0-0
Best Rating: 95 9/01 Donc 6f good

Confirmed the promise shown on his Kempton debut with a cosy win over six furlongs at Lingfield. Some decent efforts since. Acts on fast ground and worth another try at seven.

Greenhope (IRE)

110(98) (65)**83**

3-y-o b g Definite Article-Unbidden Melody (USA) (Chieftain Ii)

N J Henderson (J A Osborne 16/8) Lynn Wilson

Placings:05-20422314 **(3975)**

2001: 8^{2}SD, 8^{0}SD, 11^{4}GF, 12^{2}GF, 12^{2}GF, 12^{3}GF, 11^{1}F, 10^{4}GF

	Starts	1st	2nd	3rd	Win & Pl
Career Total (Turf)	8	1	2	1	13624
Career Total (AW)	2	0	1	0	842

81 7/01 Rdcr 1m3f D(0-80)H FRM £7247
Total win prize-money £7248

Going (Turf): Sf: 0-1 GS: 0-1 Gd: 0-0 GF: 0-5 **Fm: 1-1**
Distance: 5f/6f: 0-0 7f-8f: 0-2 **9f-13f: 1-8** 14f+: 0-0
Track : **LH: 1-7** RH: 0-2 **Tight: 1-5** Gall: 0-1
Aids: Bl: 0-0 Vi: 0-0 Tstrap: 0-0
Best Rating: 83 5/01 Gdwd 1m4f gd-fm

Got off the mark at Redcar at the ninth attempt in July after some decent efforts previously. Stays 12 furlongs and acts well on fast ground.

Greenlees

54(64)

3-y-o b f Greensmith-Scawsby Lees (Stanford)

W G M Turner Hawks And Doves Racing Syndicate

Placings:00-600 **(1383)**

2001: 12^{6}S, 9^{0}SD, 6^{0}S

	Starts	1st	2nd	3rd	Win & Pl
Career Total (Turf)	3	0	0	0	0
Career Total (AW)	2	0	0	0	

Going (Turf): Sf: 0-2 GS: 0-1 Gd: 0-0 GF: 0-0 Fm: 0-0
Distance: 5f/6f: 0-0 7f-8f: 0-2 9f-13f: 0-3 14f+: 0-0
Track : LH: 0-3 RH: 0-0 Tight: 0-1 Gall: 0-0
Aids: Bl: 0-0 Vi: 0-0 Tstrap: 0-0

Greenslades

90 **86**

2-y-o ch c Perugino (USA)-Woodfield Rose (Scottish Reel)

P J Makin Four Seasons Racing Ltd

Placings:6 **(5367)**

2001: 8^{6}GS

	Starts	1st	2nd	3rd	Win & Pl
Career Total (Turf)	1	0	0	0	0

Going (Turf): Sf: 0-0 GS: 0-1 Gd: 0-0 GF: 0-0 Fm: 0-0
Distance: 5f/6f: 0-0 7f-8f: 0-1 9f-13f: 0-0 14f+: 0-0
Track : LH: 0-0 RH: 0-0 Tight: 0-0 Gall: 0-0
Aids: Bl: 0-0 Vi: 0-0 Tstrap: 0-0
Best Rating: 86 10/01 NmkR 1m gd-sft

Was too keen for his own good when sixth of 20 on his Newmarket debut over a mile.

Greenwood

107 **89**

3-y-o ch c Emarati (USA)-Charnwood Queen (Cadeaux Genereux)

J M P Eustace J C Smith

Placings:120-002005 **(5258)**

2001: 6^{0}G, 6^{0}GF, 6^{2}G, 5^{0}G, 6^{0}GS, 5^{5}GS

	Starts	1st	2nd	3rd	Win & Pl
Career Total (Turf)	9	1	2	0	8477

71 7/00 Wind 6f D G-F £4049
Total win prize-money £4050

Going (Turf): Sf: 0-1 GS: 0-2 Gd: 0-3 GF: 0-2 Fm: 0-0
Distance: 5f/6f: 0-6 7f-8f: 0-2 9f-13f: 0-0 14f+: 0-0
Track : LH: 0-0 RH: 0-0 Tight: 0-0 Gall: 0-0
Aids: Bl: 0-2 Vi: 0-0 Tstrap: 0-0
Best Rating: 89 7/01 Yarm 6f3y good

Found life difficult this term until dropped in class to finish runner-up at Yarmouth in July. Appreciates fast ground and races prominently.

Gremlin One

83(76) (1)**20**
4-y-o ch g Democratic (USA)-Calcutta Queen (Night Shift (USA))
W Storey Gremlin Racing

Placings:060-000600 **(4326)**
2001: 5^{0}GF, 7^{0}F, 6^{0}F, 7^{6}G, 8^{0}F, 8^{0}GF

	Starts	1st	2nd	3rd	Win & Pl
Career Total (Turf)	8	0	0	0	
Career Total (AW)	1	0	0	0	

Going (Turf): Sf: 0-0 GS: 0-0 Gd: 0-1 GF: 0-2 Fm: 0-5
Distance: 5f/6f: 0-4 7f-8f: 0-5 9f-13f: 0-0 14f+: 0-0
Track : LH: 0-1 RH: 0-3 Tight: 0-1 Gall: 0-1
Aids: Bl: 0-1 Vi: 0-4 Tstrap: 0-0
Best Rating: 20 6/01 Muss 7f30y good

Grenadier (IRE)

103 **65**
4-y-o b g Sadler's Wells (USA)-Sandhurst Goddess (Sandhurst Prince)
W R Muir Song And Dance Partnership

Placings:4/540-0340553000 **(4667)**
2001: 7^{0}G, 8^{3}GF, 9^{4}F, 9^{0}GF, 10^{5}GF, 8^{5}GF, 8^{3}GS, 8^{0}GF, 7^{0}GF, 8^{0}GF

	Starts	1st	2nd	3rd	Win & Pl
Career Total (Turf)	14	0	0	2	3476

Going (Turf): Sf: 0-4 GS: 0-1 Gd: 0-1 GF: 0-7 Fm: 0-1
Distance: 5f/6f: 0-0 7f-8f: 0-6 9f-13f: 0-8 14f+: 0-0
Track : LH: 0-5 RH: 0-5 Tight: 0-5 Gall: 0-1
Aids: Bl: 0-3 Vi: 0-0 Tstrap: 0-0
Best Rating: 69 5/01 Gdwd 1m gd-fm

Grey Cossack

105 **67**
4-y-o gr g Kasakov-Royal Rebeka (Grey Desire)
M Brittain Robert E Cook

Placings:4/63410-00400541003002 **(5254)**
2001: 7^{0}G, 6^{0}GF, 5^{4}GF, 6^{0}G, 5^{0}GF, 6^{5}G, 6^{4}GF, 6^{1}GS, 6^{0}G, 5^{0}G, 6^{3}G, 5^{0}HY, 5^{0}GS, 6^{2}S

	Starts	1st	2nd	3rd	Win & Pl		
Career Total (Turf)	20	2	1	2	12396		
67	7/01	Ayr	6f	D(0-80)H		G-S	£5232
63	5/00	Rdcr	6f	E		G-S	£2800

Total win prize-money £8033

Going (Turf): Sf: 0-4 **GS: 2-3** Gd: 0-9 GF: 0-4 Fm: 0-0
Distance: **5f/6f: 2-19** 7f-8f: 0-1 9f-13f: 0-0 14f+: 0-0
Track : LH: 0-4 RH: 0-0 Tight: 0-1 Gall: 0-0
Aids: Bl: 0-0 Vi: 0-1 Tstrap: 0-0
Best Rating: 67 8/01 Newc 6f good

He does not have a particularly good win record, but both his victories to date have come over six furlongs with give in the ground.

Grey Eminence (FR)

104 **98**
4-y-o gr c Indian Ridge-Rahaam (USA) (Secreto (USA))
R Hannon Jeffen Racing

Placings:5/22212021-00 **(1297)**
2001: 6^{0}GS, 7^{0}G

	Starts	1st	2nd	3rd	Win & Pl		
Career Total (Turf)	11	2	5	0	22977		
96	10/00	NmkR	6f	C		SFT	£6356
79	8/00	Asct	7f	D		G-F	£6695

Total win prize-money £13052

Going (Turf): Sf: 1-4 GS: 0-2 Gd: 0-3 **GF: 1-2** Fm: 0-0
Distance: 5f/6f: 1-3 7f-8f: 1-6 9f-13f: 0-2 14f+: 0-0
Track : LH: 0-1 RH: 0-1 Tight: 0-0 Gall: 0-0
Aids: Bl: 0-0 Vi: 0-0 Tstrap: 0-0
Best Rating: 98 4/01 NmkR 6f gd-sft

Grey Expectations

84(73) **26**
6-y-o gr g Terimon-Flammable (IRE) (Prince Rupert (FR))
A Crook (M D Hammond 3/4) Paul Sellars

Placings:00 **(2172)**
2001: 10^{0}GF, 11^{0}SD

	Starts	1st	2nd	3rd	Win & Pl
Career Total (Turf)	1	0	0	0	
Career Total (AW)	1	0	0	0	

Going (Turf): Sf: 0-0 GS: 0-0 Gd: 0-0 GF: 0-1 Fm: 0-0
Distance: 5f/6f: 0-0 7f-8f: 0-0 9f-13f: 0-2 14f+: 0-0
Track : LH: 0-2 RH: 0-0 Tight: 0-0 Gall: 0-0
Aids: Bl: 0-1 Vi: 0-0 Tstrap: 0-0
Best Rating: 26 6/01 Pont 1m2f6y gd-fm

Grey Flyer

87(103) (56)**28**
4-y-o gr g Factual (USA)-Faraway Grey (Absalom)
L R James (Mrs L Stubbs 7/2) Nelson Unit Ltd

Placings:6106421/205030104-550000000 **(4013)**
2001: 6^{5}SD, 5^{5}SD, 6^{0}SW, 5^{0}GF, 7^{0}GF, 5^{0}G, 5^{0}G, 5^{0}GF, 5^{0}G

	Starts	1st	2nd	3rd	Win & Pl		
Career Total (Turf)	13	2	0	1	5036		
Career Total (AW)	12	1	2	0	4147		
55	7/00	Muss	5f	F(0-60)H		FRM	£2310
56	1/00	Ling	6f	F(0-60)H		STD	£2730
63	9/99	Muss	5f	F		G-F	£2276

Total win prize-money £7316

Going (Turf): Sf: 0-1 GS: 0-0 Gd: 0-5 **GF: 1-4 Fm: 1-3**
Distance: **5f/6f: 3-24** 7f-8f: 0-1 9f-13f: 0-0 14f+: 0-0
Track : **LH: 1-14** RH: 0-0 **Tight: 1-13** Gall: 0-0
Aids: Bl: 0-0 Vi: 0-0 Tstrap: 0-0
Best Rating: 38 1/01 Ling 5f stand

Grey Imperial (IRE)

93 **64**
3-y-o gr g Imperial Frontier (USA)-Petrel (Petong)
P W Harris The Border Team

Placings:00-4 **(3973)**
2001: 8^{4}GF

	Starts	1st	2nd	3rd	Win & Pl
Career Total (Turf)	3	0	0	0	315

Going (Turf): Sf: 0-0 GS: 0-0 Gd: 0-0 GF: 0-3 Fm: 0-0
Distance: 5f/6f: 0-0 7f-8f: 0-2 9f-13f: 0-1 14f+: 0-0
Track : LH: 0-2 RH: 0-0 Tight: 0-2 Gall: 0-0
Aids: Bl: 0-0 Vi: 0-0 Tstrap: 0-0
Best Rating: 63 8/01 Epsm 1m114y gd-fm

Grey Pearl

94 **62**
2-y-o gr f Ali-Royal (IRE)-River's Rising (FR) (Mendez (FR))
Miss Gay Kelleway Miss Gay Kelleway

Placings:04 **(5689)**
2001: 7^{0}GS, 6^{4}S

	Starts	1st	2nd	3rd	Win & Pl
Career Total (Turf)	2	0	0	0	371

Going (Turf): Sf: 0-1 GS: 0-1 Gd: 0-0 GF: 0-0 Fm: 0-0
Distance: 5f/6f: 0-1 7f-8f: 0-1 9f-13f: 0-0 14f+: 0-0
Track : LH: 0-0 RH: 0-0 Tight: 0-0 Gall: 0-0
Aids: Bl: 0-0 Vi: 0-0 Tstrap: 0-0
Best Rating: 62 11/01 Donc 6f soft

Well beaten on her debut, she improved to be a good fourth at Doncaster in November.

Grey Son

66(67) (19)**22**
2-y-o gr g Son Pardo-Faraway Grey (Absalom)
Mrs L Stubbs Des Thurlby

Placings:0005 **(2832)**
2001: 5^{0}GS, 5^{0}SD, 7^{0}F, 5^{5}GF

	Starts	1st	2nd	3rd	Win & Pl
Career Total (Turf)	3	0	0	0	0
Career Total (AW)	1	0	0	0	

Going (Turf): Sf: 0-0 GS: 0-1 Gd: 0-0 GF: 0-1 Fm: 0-1
Distance: 5f/6f: 0-3 7f-8f: 0-1 9f-13f: 0-0 14f+: 0-0
Track : LH: 0-0 RH: 0-0 Tight: 0-0 Gall: 0-0
Aids: Bl: 0-0 Vi: 0-0 Tstrap: 0-0
Best Rating: 22 7/01 Leic 5f2y gd-fm

Greycoat

92(79) (43)**47**
3-y-o ch g Lion Cavern (USA)-It's Academic (Royal Academy (USA))
Jean-Rene Auvray (Mrs J R Ramsden 7/5) Lambourn Racing Limited

Placings:000-05050 **(3855)**
2001: 6^{0}S, 8^{5}GF, 6^{0}G, 8^{5}GF, 7^{0}GS

	Starts	1st	2nd	3rd	Win & Pl
Career Total (Turf)	7	0	0	0	379
Career Total (AW)	1	0	0	0	

Going (Turf): Sf: 0-2 GS: 0-2 Gd: 0-1 GF: 0-2 Fm: 0-0
Distance: 5f/6f: 0-4 7f-8f: 0-3 9f-13f: 0-1 14f+: 0-0
Track : LH: 0-2 RH: 0-0 Tight: 0-0 Gall: 0-0
Aids: Bl: 0-0 Vi: 0-0 Tstrap: 0-0
Best Rating: 47 7/01 Sals 1m gd-fm

Greyfield (IRE)

107 **72**
5-y-o b g Persian Bold-Noble Dust (USA) (Dust Commander (USA))
K Bishop Slabs And Lucan

Placings:0005404/222321123013306/4504544012-0400 **(4635)**
2001: 9^{0}GF, 9^{4}GS, 12^{0}G, 9^{0}GF

	Starts	1st	2nd	3rd	Win & Pl		
Career Total (Turf)	36	4	6	4	26472		
72	10/00	Bath	1m2f46y	E(0-70)H		G-S	£2970
75	8/99	Ches	1m2f75y	C(0-95)H		G-S	£7220
67	7/99	Folk	1m1f149y	E(0-65)		G-F	£2912

Total win prize-money £13103

Going (Turf): Sf: 0-2 **GS: 2-7** Gd: 0-12 **GF: 2-15** Fm: 0-0
Distance: 5f/6f: 0-0 7f-8f: 0-5 **9f-13f: 4-28** 14f+: 0-3
Track : LH: 2-17 RH: 2-15 **Tight: 3-14** Gall: 0-8
Aids: Bl: 0-0 Vi: 0-0 Tstrap: 0-0
Best Rating: 64 8/01 Leic 1m1f218y gd-sft

Grizedale (IRE)

95 **88**
2-y-o ch c Lake Coniston (IRE)-Zabeta (Diesis)
E A L Dunlop Byculla Thoroughbreds

Placings:23103 (5504)
2001: 5^2G, 6^3GF, 6^1GF, 6^0G, 7^3HY

	Starts	1st	2nd	3rd	Win & Pl
Career Total (Turf)	5	1	1	2	6933

76 7/01 NmkJ 6f E G-F £4163
Total win prize-money £4163

Going (Turf): Sf: 0-1 GS: 0-0 Gd: 0-2 **GF: 1-2** Fm: 0-0
Distance: **5f/6f: 1-4** 7f-8f: 0-1 9f-13f: 0-0 14f+: 0-0
Track : LH: 0-0 RH: 0-0 Tight: 0-0 Gall: 0-0
Aids: Bl: 0-0 Vi: 0-0 Tstrap: 0-0
Best Rating: 88 10/01 Rdcr 6f good

A January foal, he is bred to get seven furlongs in time. Disqualified from first place on his debut, he found the six furlongs on fast ground at Lingfield an insufficient test. Scored next time out at Newmarket over six on ground plenty fast enough.

Grizel

97(98) (83)**70**
2-y-o b f Lion Cavern (USA)-Polska (USA) (Danzig (USA))
B J Meehan F C T Wilson

Placings:003050150001 (5393)
2001: 5^0S, 6^0GF, 5^3GF, 5^0GF, 6^5GF, 6^0G, 6^1SD, 5^5G, 5^0G, 5^0F, 6^0HY, 6^1SD

	Starts	1st	2nd	3rd	Win & Pl
Career Total (Turf)	10	0	0	1	536
Career Total (AW)	2	2	0	0	5163

83 10/01 Wolv 6f F STD £2394
77 7/01 Sthl 6f E STD £2769
Total win prize-money £5163

Going (Turf): **Sf: 0-2 GS: 0-0 Gd: 0-3 GF: 0-4 Fm: 0-1**
Distance: **5f/6f: 2-12** 7f-8f: 0-0 9f-13f: 0-0 14f+: 0-0
Track : **LH: 2-2** RH: 0-0 **Tight: 1-1** Gall: 0-0
Aids: **Bl: 2-6** Vi: 0-0 Tstrap: 0-0
Best Rating: 83 10/01 Wolv 6f stand

Won a Southwell nursery in July after some good efforts in maiden company on turf, although well held after. Suited by six furlongs, he kept his unbeaten record on sand when scoring at Wolverhampton in October.

Groesfaen Lad

89(108) (33)**31**
4-y-o b g Casteddu-Curious Feeling (Nishapour (FR))
P S McEntee John Harris And Mrs Sian Harris

Placings:4255422000/040063531000-0235000404605 (3388)
2001: 9^0SD, 8^2SD, 8^3SD, 8^5SW, 8^0SD, 7^0GF, 8^0GF, 10^4GF, 9^0F, 16^4SD, 11^6SD, 16^0SD, 11^5F

	Starts	1st	2nd	3rd	Win & Pl
Career Total (Turf)	19	0	3	0	3440
Career Total (AW)	16	1	1	3	3636

65 10/00 Wolv 1m100y F(0-60)H STD £1792
Total win prize-money £1792

Going (Turf): **Sf: 0-2 GS: 0-2 Gd: 0-5 GF: 0-7 Fm: 0-3**
Distance: 5f/6f: 0-7 7f-8f: 0-9 **9f-13f: 1-16** 14f+: 0-2
Track : **LH: 1-26** RH: 0-1 **Tight: 1-16** Gall: 0-2
Aids: Bl: 0-7 **Vi: 1-5** Tstrap: 0-0
Best Rating: 59 3/01 Wolv 1m1f79y stand

Grooms Gold (IRE)

(102) (16)**25**
9-y-o ch g Groom Dancer (USA)-Gortynia (FR) (My Swallow)
J Pearce Jeff Pearce

Placings:55/001000/0/0322/20320660/4350400663433
0/0422000204066-03 (0261)
2001: 13^0SD, 16^3SD

	Starts	1st	2nd	3rd	Win & Pl
Career Total (Turf)	26	1	2	1	5489
Career Total (AW)	24	0	5	6	4118

67 7/95 Rdcr 1m2f E(0-70)H FRM £3280
Total win prize-money £3280

Going (Turf): Sf: 0-2 GS: 0-1 Gd: 0-9 GF: 0-10 **Fm: 1-4**
Distance: 5f/6f: 0-1 7f-8f: 0-8 **9f-13f: 1-33** 14f+: 0-8
Track : **LH: 1-39** RH: 0-5 **Tight: 1-24** Gall: 0-2
Aids: Bl: 0-3 Vi: 0-10 Tstrap: 0-0
Best Rating: 16 2/01 Wolv 2m46y stand

He has finished runner-up often enough, but winning seems to be beyond him nowadays.

Groovejet

74 **33**
2-y-o b g Emperor Jones (USA)-Sir Hollow (USA) (Sir Ivor)
J R Jenkins Mrs C M Hopkinson

Placings:6 (5291)
2001: 7^6S

	Starts	1st	2nd	3rd	Win & Pl
Career Total (Turf)	1	0	0	0	150

Going (Turf): **Sf: 0-1 GS: 0-0 Gd: 0-0 GF: 0-0 Fm: 0-0**
Distance: 5f/6f: 0-0 7f-8f: 0-1 9f-13f: 0-0 14f+: 0-0
Track : LH: 0-0 RH: 0-0 Tight: 0-0 Gall: 0-0
Aids: Bl: 0-0 Vi: 0-0 Tstrap: 0-0
Best Rating: 33 10/01 Leic 7f9y soft

Groundsfordivorce (IRE)

86(101) (65)**57**
3-y-o ch g Common Grounds-Nikki's Groom (Shy Groom (USA))
M Blanshard The Breeze-In Partnership

Placings:02350500 (5671)
2001: 8^0SD, 9^2SD, 8^3SD, 9^5SD, 7^0SD, 8^5HY, 6^0HY

	Starts	1st	2nd	3rd	Win & Pl
Career Total (Turf)	3	0	0	0	0
Career Total (AW)	5	0	1	1	1276

Going (Turf): **Sf: 0-3 GS: 0-0 Gd: 0-0 GF: 0-0 Fm: 0-0**
Distance: 5f/6f: 0-1 7f-8f: 0-2 9f-13f: 0-5 14f+: 0-0
Track : LH: 0-7 RH: 0-0 Tight: 0-3 Gall: 0-0
Aids: Bl: 0-0 Vi: 0-0 Tstrap: 0-0
Best Rating: 65 3/01 Wolv 1m100y stand

Groundswell (IRE)

101(92) (48)**55**
5-y-o b g Common Grounds-Fuchsia Belle (Vision (USA))
C W Thornton Miss J V Morgan

Placings:040/60011031/435 (5152)
2001: 14^4GF, 14^3SD, 14^5G

	Starts	1st	2nd	3rd	Win & Pl
Career Total (Turf)	13	3	0	1	12014
Career Total (AW)	1	0	0	1	331

69 10/99 DRoy 1m4f68y Y-S £3450
70 7/99 Klny 1m3f GD £3609
70 6/99 Gowr 1m1f100y (0-80)H GD £4125
Total win prize-money £11184

Going (Turf): Sf: 0-3 GS: 0-0 **Gd: 2-4** GF: 0-2 Fm: 0-0
Distance: 5f/6f: 0-0 7f-8f: 0-3 **9f-13f: 3-8** 14f+: 0-3
Track : LH: 1-6 **RH: 2-7** Tight: 0-2 Gall: 0-1
Aids: Bl: 0-0 Vi: 0-0 Tstrap: 0-0
Best Rating: 55 10/01 Rdcr 1m6f19y good

A winner three times in his native Ireland at up to a mile and a half. Now with Chris Thornton. Probably needed his debut run in this country, his first for fifteen months, but has still continued to look well held. Has won on good and easier ground.

Grove Dancer

102 **60**
3-y-o b f Reprimand-Brisighella (IRE) (Al Hareb (USA))
B G Powell P H Betts

Placings:1340000-23004 (4474)
2001: 8^2GF, 10^3GF, 8^0GF, 9^0G, 7^4GF

	Starts	1st	2nd	3rd	Win & Pl
Career Total (Turf)	12	1	1	2	5536

60 5/00 Yarm 6f3y D GD £3282
Total win prize-money £3283

Going (Turf): Sf: 0-2 GS: 0-0 **Gd: 1-2** GF: 0-8 Fm: 0-0
Distance: 5f/6f: 0-0 **7f-8f: 1-7** 9f-13f: 0-5 14f+: 0-0
Track : LH: 0-3 RH: 0-0 Tight: 0-1 Gall: 0-0
Aids: Bl: 0-1 Vi: 0-0 Tstrap: 0-0
Best Rating: 60 5/01 Yarm 1m3y gd-fm

Grub Street

85(84) (25)**54+**
5-y-o b h Barathea (IRE)-Broadmara (IRE) (Thatching)
M Brittain Mel Brittain

Placings:50/01-000 (1907)
2001: 8^0SD, 8^0SW, 8^0GF

	Starts	1st	2nd	3rd	Win & Pl
Career Total (Turf)	5	1	0	0	3426
Career Total (AW)	2	0	0	0	

54 6/00 Thsk 1m E(0-70)H SFT £3425
Total win prize-money £3426

Going (Turf): **Sf: 1-1** GS: 0-0 Gd: 0-3 GF: 0-1 Fm: 0-0
Distance: 5f/6f: 0-0 **7f-8f: 1-5** 9f-13f: 0-2 14f+: 0-0
Track : **LH: 1-5** RH: 0-1 **Tight: 1-1** Gall: 0-1
Aids: Bl: 0-0 Vi: 0-0 Tstrap: 0-0
Best Rating: 35 6/01 Bevl 1m100y gd-fm

Gruff

91 **66**
2-y-o ch g Presidium-Kagram Queen (Prince Ragusa)
D W Barker Robert E Cook

Placings:633026040 (5364)
2001: 6^6GF, 5^3GF, 5^3S, 5^0GS, 5^2GF, 6^6GF, 6^0G, 5^4GS, 6^0GS

	Starts	1st	2nd	3rd	Win & Pl
Career Total (Turf)	9	0	1	2	1638

Going (Turf): **Sf: 0-1 GS: 0-3 Gd: 0-1 GF: 0-4 Fm: 0-0**
Distance: 5f/6f: 0-9 7f-8f: 0-0 9f-13f: 0-0 14f+: 0-0
Track : LH: 0-0 RH: 0-0 Tight: 0-0 Gall: 0-0
Aids: Bl: 0-0 Vi: 0-0 Tstrap: 0-0
Best Rating: 66 10/01 Catt 5f gd-sft

Has shown some promise in ordinary maidens and enough to suggest he can win a race. Tested only between six and seven furlongs. Should stay further in time.

Gruinart (IRE)

99 **48**
4-y-o br g Elbio-Doppio Filo (Vision (USA))
H Morrison The Gruinart Partnership

Placings:0/00431400040-00001060 (5106)
2001: 7^0GS, 9^0F, 8^0GF, 10^0GF, 11^1GF, 11^0GF, 12^6GF, 12^0GS

	Starts	1st	2nd	3rd	Win & Pl
Career Total (Turf)	20	2	0	1	6332

43 7/01 Wind 1m3f135yG G-F £2054
76 6/00 Sals 1m E(0-70)H G-F £2884
Total win prize-money £4939

Going (Turf): Sf: 0-3 GS: 0-3 Gd: 0-6 **GF: 2-7** Fm: 0-1
Distance: 5f/6f: 0-1 7f-8f: 1-7 9f-13f: 1-12 14f+: 0-0

Track : LH: 0-3 RH: 0-7 **Tight: 1-7** Gall: 0-1
Aids: Bl: 0-0 Vi: 0-0 Tstrap: 0-0
Best Rating: 59 5/01 Brig 1m1f209y firm

He became disappointing after winning an apprentice handicap at Salisbury last season and had to be dropped into a seller at Windsor to regain winning ways. Best on fast ground.

Gryffindor

107 **101**

3-y-o b c Marju (IRE)-Hard Task (Formidable (USA))
B J Meehan Mrs Susan Roy

Placings:302-12304051 **(4866)**
2001: 8^{1}S, 8^{2}S, 10^{3}HY, 11^{0}GF, 10^{4}G, 12^{0}GF, 8^{5}GS, 9^{1}GF

	Starts	1st	2nd	3rd	Win & Pl
Career Total (Turf)	11	2	2	2	31504

100	9/01	Newb	1m1f	B	G-F	£9309
93	3/01	Donc	1m	D	SFT	£4465

Total win prize-money £13775

Going (Turf): Sf: 1-3 GS: 0-2 Gd: 0-1 **GF: 1-5** Fm: 0-0
Distance: 5f/6f: 0-0 7f-8f: 1-6 9f-13f: 1-5 14f+: 0-0
Track : LH: 1-2 RH: 0-3 Tight: 0-0 **Gall: 1-3**
Aids: Bl: 1-3 Vi: 0-0 Tstrap: 0-0
Best Rating: 103 5/01 Gdwd 1m3f gd-fm

He got off the mark at Doncaster reappearance, but just missed out when tried in Listed company and was not good enough in Group races. Returned to winning from in a conditions event at Newbury in September and those races look his best option, though he could enjoy more success abroad. Suited by trips of around a mile.

Guaranda

107 **95**

3-y-o b f Acatenango (GER)-Gryada (Shirley Heights)
W Jarvis Plantation Stud

Placings:52-1010300 **(5135)**
2001: 10^{1}G, 11^{0}S, 12^{1}GF, 12^{0}GS, 9^{3}GF, 10^{0}GF, 10^{0}G

	Starts	1st	2nd	3rd	Win & Pl
Career Total (Turf)	9	2	1	1	15592

95	6/01	Ches	1m4f66y	D(0-85)H	G-F	£6955
68	5/01	Ling	1m2f	D	GD	£4030

Total win prize-money £10985

Going (Turf): Sf: 0-2 GS: 0-1 **Gd: 1-2 GF: 1-4** Fm: 0-0
Distance: 5f/6f: 0-0 7f-8f: 0-2 **9f-13f: 2-7** 14f+: 0-0
Track : LH: 2-3 RH: 0-1 **Tight: 2-3** Gall: 0-1
Aids: Bl: 0-0 Vi: 0-0 Tstrap: 0-0
Best Rating: 95 8/01 Sals 1m1f198y gd-fm

Broke her maiden at Lingfield, although she did not achieve a great deal on the book. Out of her depth in the German Oaks next time, but the ground was unsuitably soft. She returned to take a fillies' handicap at Chester, but has just been found wanting in Listed company since.

Guard Duty

107 **84**

4-y-o b g Deploy-Hymne D'Amour (USA) (Dixieland Band (USA))
M C Pipe Neil Edwards And Malcolm Jones

Placings:33/62453-10645 **(5387)**
2001: 16^{1}S, 18^{0}GF, 20^{6}GF, 16^{4}GF, 18^{5}GS

	Starts	1st	2nd	3rd	Win & Pl
Career Total (Turf)	12	1	1	3	15074

79	4/01	Kemp	2m	C(0-100)H	SFT	£10871

Total win prize-money £10871

Going (Turf): Sf: 1-5 GS: 0-1 Gd: 0-2 GF: 0-4 Fm: 0-0
Distance: 5f/6f: 0-0 7f-8f: 0-1 9f-13f: 0-4 **14f+: 1-7**
Track : LH: 0-5 **RH: 1-5** Tight: 0-4 Gall: 0-3
Aids: Bl: 0-1 Vi: 0-0 **Tstrap: 1-6**
Best Rating: 84 5/01 Ches 2m2f147y gd-fm

He got off the mark on the level in the Queen's Prize at Kempton over Easter. Has won on soft, acts on good ground. Has looked quirky in the past. Regularly equipped with a tongue strap. Better known as a hurdler.

Guarded Secret

103(99) (69)**74**

4-y-o ro g Mystiko (USA)-Fen Dance (IRE) (Trojan Fen)
P J Makin D M Ahier

Placings:3/0221020-6502 **(5293)**
2001: 10^{6}GS, 10^{5}G, 11^{0}GF, 9^{2}S

	Starts	1st	2nd	3rd	Win & Pl
Career Total (Turf)	10	1	3	1	6352
Career Total (AW)	2	0	1	0	782

74	8/00	Sals	1m1f198y	E(0-70)H	GD	£3058

Total win prize-money £3058

Going (Turf): Sf: 0-2 GS: 0-2 **Gd: 1-2** GF: 0-4 Fm: 0-0
Distance: 5f/6f: 0-0 7f-8f: 0-2 **9f-13f: 1-10** 14f+: 0-0
Track : LH: 0-7 **RH: 1-2 Tight: 1-5** Gall: 0-1
Aids: Bl: 0-0 Vi: 0-0 Tstrap: 0-0
Best Rating: 72 10/01 Leic 1m1f218y soft

A winner at Salisbury last season, he has run a couple of promising races this season without winning. Possibly needs 12 furlongs now.

Guardia

87 **73**

3-y-o ch f Grand Lodge (USA)-Gisarne (USA) (Diesis)
J L Dunlop Plantation Stud

Placings:02-60 **(1501)**
2001: 10^{6}GS, 11^{0}GF

	Starts	1st	2nd	3rd	Win & Pl
Career Total (Turf)	4	0	1	0	1196

Going (Turf): Sf: 0-0 GS: 0-1 Gd: 0-0 GF: 0-3 Fm: 0-0
Distance: 5f/6f: 0-1 7f-8f: 0-0 9f-13f: 0-3 14f+: 0-0
Track : LH: 0-1 RH: 0-0 Tight: 0-0 Gall: 0-0
Aids: Bl: 0-0 Vi: 0-0 Tstrap: 0-0
Best Rating: 51 5/01 Gdwd 1m3f gd-fm

Gudlage (USA)

105 **82**

5-y-o b g Gulch (USA)-Triple Kiss (Shareef Dancer (USA))
M W Easterby Lord Daresbury & The Hon Mrs E Greenall

Placings:215/035/00-3060 **(3056)**
2001: 8^{3}G, 10^{0}F, 10^{6}GF, 10^{0}G

	Starts	1st	2nd	3rd	Win & Pl
Career Total (Turf)	12	1	1	2	12478

81	7/98	NmkJ	7f	D	GD	£4659

Total win prize-money £4659

Going (Turf): Sf: 0-1 GS: 0-1 **Gd: 1-5** GF: 0-4 Fm: 0-1
Distance: 5f/6f: 0-0 **7f-8f: 1-6** 9f-13f: 0-6 14f+: 0-0
Track : LH: 0-6 RH: 0-2 Tight: 0-4 Gall: 0-3
Aids: Bl: 0-1 Vi: 0-0 Tstrap: 0-4
Best Rating: 82 5/01 Thsk 1m good

Useful 1m/1m2f handicapper but has not stood much racing. Returned to form with a good effort at Thirsk in May after a run a brief spell of pointing.

Guest Envoy (IRE)

103(106) (52)**48**

6-y-o b m Paris House-Peace Mission (Dunbeath (USA))
C N Allen Shadowfax Racing.Com

Placings:0/500600021000005/00040**443104050/03121 44112605550546005-60512603505**3200 **(3962)**
2001: 7^{6}SW, 6^{0}SD, 7^{5}SW, 7^{1}SD, 7^{2}SD, 7^{6}SD, 7^{0}SD, 7^{3}SD, 8^{5}SD, 7^{0}GF, 7^{5}G, 7^{3}GF, 7^{2}GS, 8^{0}G, 7^{0}G

	Starts	1st	2nd	3rd	Win & Pl
Career Total (Turf)	36	2	2	1	10202
Career Total (AW)	31	5	3	3	17673

50	3/01	Wolv	7f	E(0-70)H	STD	£2394
51	4/00	Hayd	7f30y	E(0-75)H	GD	£2912
52	3/00	Sthl	7f	D(0-80)H	STD	£3789
48	2/00	Sthl	6f	E(0-75)H	STD	£3461
42	2/00	Sthl	7f	G	STD	£1909
50	8/99	Wolv	1m100y	E(0-70)H	STD	£2836
46	8/98	Haml	6f5y	E(0-70)H	SFT	£3745

Total win prize-money £21048

Going (Turf): Sf: 1-8 GS: 0-4 **Gd: 1-11** GF: 0-12 Fm: 0-1
Distance: 5f/6f: 1-14 **7f-8f: 5-46** 9f-13f: 1-7 14f+: 0-0
Track : LH: 6-37 RH: 0-4 **Tight: 2-14** Gall: 0-1
Aids: Bl: 0-0 Vi: 0-6 Tstrap: 0-5
Best Rating: 52 3/01 Wolv 7f stand

Best known as an All-Weather specialist, she has won on easy ground on turf as well. Stays a mile, but the majority of her wins have been at seven furlongs.

Guest Line (FR)

87 **59**

2-y-o ch g Ashkalani (IRE)-Double Line (FR) (What A Guest)
B J Meehan Matham Investments

Placings:66 **(2716)**
2001: 5^{6}GF, 6^{6}GF

	Starts	1st	2nd	3rd	Win & Pl
Career Total (Turf)	2	0	0	0	0

Going (Turf): Sf: 0-0 GS: 0-0 Gd: 0-0 GF: 0-2 Fm: 0-0
Distance: 5f/6f: 0-2 7f-8f: 0-0 9f-13f: 0-0 14f+: 0-0
Track : LH: 0-0 RH: 0-0 Tight: 0-0 Gall: 0-0
Aids: Bl: 0-0 Vi: 0-0 Tstrap: 0-0
Best Rating: 59 7/01 Kemp 6f gd-fm

Guild's Delight (IRE)

99 **74**

2-y-o b g College Chapel-Tamburello (IRE) (Roi Danzig (USA))
W S Kittow Racing Guild 2000

Placings:630036 **(5496)**
2001: 5^{6}GF, 6^{3}GF, 6^{0}G, 7^{0}G, 7^{3}F, 7^{6}HY

	Starts	1st	2nd	3rd	Win & Pl
Career Total (Turf)	6	0	0	2	758

Going (Turf): Sf: 0-1 GS: 0-0 Gd: 0-2 GF: 0-2 Fm: 0-1
Distance: 5f/6f: 0-1 7f-8f: 0-5 9f-13f: 0-0 14f+: 0-0
Track : LH: 0-0 RH: 0-1 Tight: 0-0 Gall: 0-0
Aids: Bl: 0-0 Vi: 0-0 Tstrap: 0-0
Best Rating: 77 7/01 Chep 6f16y gd-fm

Guilded Flyer

82 **59**

2-y-o b c Emarati (USA)-Mo Ceri (Kampala)
W S Kittow Racing Guild 2000

Placings:000 **(4830)**
2001: 6^{0}GF, 7^{0}GF, 6^{0}GF

	Starts	1st	2nd	3rd	Win & Pl
Career Total (Turf)	3	0	0	0	

Going (Turf): Sf: 0-0 GS: 0-0 Gd: 0-0 GF: 0-3 Fm: 0-0
Distance: 5f/6f: 0-1 7f-8f: 0-2 9f-13f: 0-0 14f+: 0-0
Track : LH: 0-0 RH: 0-0 Tight: 0-0 Gall: 0-0
Aids: Bl: 0-0 Vi: 0-0 Tstrap: 0-0
Best Rating: 59 9/01 Newb 6f8y gd-fm

Guilsborough

(106) (85)**68**

6-y-o br g Northern Score (USA)-Super Sisters (AUS) (Call Report (USA))

J G Smyth-Osbourne P A Mason

Placings:05/600540/221626**060**/**111023**-**4052**51021012 **(4628)**

2001: 8^{4}SD, 7^{0}SW, 7^{5}SD, 8^{2}SW, 8^{5}G, 8^{1}GF, 8^{0}F, 8^{2}G, 8^{1}GF, 8^{0}GS, 8^{1}GF, 8^{2}GF, 8^{2}SD

	Starts	1st	2nd	3rd	Win & Pl
Career Total (Turf)	21	3	3	0	15097
Career Total (AW)	14	4	4	1	15410

65	8/01	Bath	1m5y	E(0-70)H	G-F	£3101
60	8/01	Bath	1m5y	D(0-80)H	G-F	£6873
58	5/01	Wwck	1m22y	G(0-65)H	G-F	£2220
82	7/00	Sthl	1m	E(0-75)H	STD	£2873
76	6/00	Sthl	1m	G(0-70)H	STD	£1918
69	6/00	Sthl	1m	E(0-70)H	STD	£2863
67	6/99	Sthl	7f	G(0-65)H	STD	£1987

Total win prize-money £21836

Going (Turf): Sf: 0-1 GS: 0-6 Gd: 0-6 **GF: 3-7** Fm: 0-1
Distance: 5f/6f: 0-2 **7f-8f: 4-23** 9f-13f: 3-10 14f+: 0-0
Track : **LH: 6-19** RH: 0-0 **Tight: 2-5** Gall: 0-0
Aids: Bl: 0-0 Vi: 0-1 Tstrap: 0-0
Best Rating: 80 2/01 Sthl 1m slow

Goes well at Bath and won twice there and once at Warwick this season. Stays a mile and likes to come late off a strong pace. Acts on fast ground and Fibresand and goes very well at Southwell.

Guinea Hunter (IRE)

115 **110**

5-y-o b g Pips Pride-Preponderance (IRE) (Cyrano De Bergerac)

T D Easterby M P Burke

Placings:212/516003/0100100503500-20300130624 **(5365)**

2001: 6^{2}HY, 6^{0}GF, 5^{3}GF, 6^{0}GF, 5^{0}GF, 6^{1}G, 5^{3}GF, 6^{0}GF, 5^{6}S, 5^{2}GS, 6^{4}GS

	Starts	1st	2nd	3rd	Win & Pl
Career Total (Turf)	33	5	4	4	112308

103	8/01	Gdwd	6f	B H	GD	£55250
97	7/00	NmkJ	5f	C(0-100)H	G-F	£7358
95	5/00	Hayd	6f	C	GD	£6039
101	5/99	Hayd	6f	C	GD	£5462
80	6/98	Carl	5f207y	D	G-S	£3582

Total win prize-money £77692

Going (Turf): Sf: 0-8 GS: 1-5 **Gd: 3-10** GF: 1-10 Fm: 0-0
Distance: **5f/6f: 5-31** 7f-8f: 0-2 9f-13f: 0-0 14f+: 0-0
Track : LH: 0-1 **RH: 1-1** Tight: 0-1 **Gall: 1-1**
Aids: Bl: 0-6 Vi: 0-0 Tstrap: 0-0
Best Rating: 110 10/01 NmkR 6f gd-sft

A very able sprint handicapper, he finally won a big handicap when coming good in the 2001 Stewards' Cup and was a good third in the Portland. A fine fourth in Listed company at Newmarket in October, he has been sold to race in Malaysia.

Gulf Shaadi

(103) (47)**49**

9-y-o b g Shaadi (USA)-Ela Meem (USA) (Kris)

A G Newcombe Wetherby Racing Bureau 40

Placings:54650**613**/**11331166**2**1**0440000/00000034/41 **104345621**42460401**20141**/**6100**20200406000000/003 4232000**6000**/**04054053602516**-**026522235603 (5050)**

2001: 12^{0}SD, 12^{2}SW, 12^{6}SW, 10^{5}S, 11^{2}SD, 11^{2}SD, 12^{2}SD, 11^{3}SD, 10^{5}G, 10^{6}G, 9^{0}SW, 11^{3}SD

	Starts	1st	2nd	3rd	Win & Pl
Career Total (Turf)	67	4	7	3	106044
Career Total (AW)	49	10	6	7	39693

70	12/00	Sthl	1m3f	G(0-70)H	STD	£1400
90	3/98	Wolv	1m1f79y	C(0-100)H	STD	£6807
90	10/97	NmkR	1m	B H	GD	£37612
81	9/97	Asct	1m	B H	G-F	£29570
71	8/97	Sand	7f16y	D(0-85)H	G-F	£4357
62	4/97	Bevl	7f100y	E(0-70)H	G-F	£3286
67	1/97	Sthl	1m	F(0-65)H	STD	£1944
60	1/97	Sthl	1m	E(0-70)H	STD	£3289
81	5/95	Wolv	1m100y	F	STD	£2243
75	3/95	Ling	7f	E	STD	£3052
73	3/95	Ling	1m	F	STD	£2700
79	1/95	Wolv	7f	D(0-80)H	STD	£3487
68	1/95	Ling	7f	E	STD	£3009
71	12/94	Ling	7f	D	STD	£3243

Total win prize-money £106008

Going (Turf): Sf: 0-10 GS: 0-4 Gd: 1-19 **GF: 3-28** Fm: 0-5
Distance: 5f/6f: 0-3 **7f-8f: 11-69** 9f-13f: 3-44 14f+: 0-0
Track : **LH: 10-78** RH: 2-10 **Tight: 7-47** Gall: 0-8
Aids: Bl: 0-0 Vi: 0-1 Tstrap: 0-0
Best Rating: 70 2/01 Ling 1m4f slow

Veteran handicapper who has won just once since March 1998. Stays 12 furlongs and best on Fibresand these days.

Gulzaar

82 **54**

2-y-o b f Kris-Kilma (USA) (Silver Hawk (USA))

M P Tregoning Sheikh Ahmed Al Maktoum

Placings:60 **(5460)**

2001: 8^{6}GS, 8^{0}G

	Starts	1st	2nd	3rd	Win & Pl
Career Total (Turf)	2	0	0	0	0

Going (Turf): Sf: 0-0 GS: 0-1 Gd: 0-1 GF: 0-0 Fm: 0-0
Distance: 5f/6f: 0-0 7f-8f: 0-1 9f-13f: 0-1 14f+: 0-0
Track : LH: 0-2 RH: 0-0 Tight: 0-1 Gall: 0-1
Aids: Bl: 0-0 Vi: 0-0 Tstrap: 0-0
Best Rating: 54 10/01 Bath 1m5y good

Gumlayloy

59 **12**

2-y-o ch c Indian Ridge-Candide (USA) (Miswaki (USA))

Miss L A Perratt Capt Alasdair & Mrs Eliza Ross

Placings:0000 **(4823)**

2001: 6^{0}GS, 6^{0}F, 6^{0}F, 6^{0}G

	Starts	1st	2nd	3rd	Win & Pl
Career Total (Turf)	4	0	0	0	

Going (Turf): Sf: 0-0 GS: 0-1 Gd: 0-1 GF: 0-0 Fm: 0-2
Distance: 5f/6f: 0-3 7f-8f: 0-1 9f-13f: 0-0 14f+: 0-0
Track : LH: 0-0 RH: 0-0 Tight: 0-0 Gall: 0-0
Aids: Bl: 0-0 Vi: 0-0 Tstrap: 0-0
Best Rating: 12 6/01 Thsk 6f firm

He has finished last on all four starts to date.

Gumption

104 **76**

3-y-o b g Muhtarram (USA)-Dancing Spirit (IRE) (Ahonoora)

J L Dunlop The Hon Sir David Sieff

Placings:4-5504240 **(5692)**

2001: 8^{5}GS, 10^{5}GF, 14^{0}G, 11^{4}HY, 14^{2}HY, 14^{4}G, 16^{0}S

	Starts	1st	2nd	3rd	Win & Pl
Career Total (Turf)	8	0	1	0	3604

Going (Turf): Sf: 0-4 GS: 0-1 Gd: 0-2 GF: 0-1 Fm: 0-0
Distance: 5f/6f: 0-0 7f-8f: 0-2 9f-13f: 0-2 14f+: 0-4
Track : LH: 0-4 RH: 0-3 Tight: 0-3 Gall: 0-1
Aids: Bl: 0-0 Vi: 0-0 Tstrap: 0-0
Best Rating: 76 10/01 Rdcr 1m6f19y good

Still a maiden, but he has run some fair races, the best of which came over 14 furlongs. He acts with cut in the ground.

Gun Hill (IRE)

79(91) (33)**6**

4-y-o b g Ridgewood Ben-Lils Fairy (Fairy King (USA))

Mrs S J Smith (M C Chapman 4/6) Reg Racing

Placings:000000 **(1845)**

2001: 7^{0}SW, 6^{0}SD, 8^{0}SW, 5^{0}SD, 6^{0}HY, 5^{0}GF

	Starts	1st	2nd	3rd	Win & Pl
Career Total (Turf)	2	0	0	0	
Career Total (AW)	4	0	0	0	

Going (Turf): Sf: 0-1 GS: 0-0 Gd: 0-0 GF: 0-1 Fm: 0-0
Distance: 5f/6f: 0-4 7f-8f: 0-2 9f-13f: 0-0 14f+: 0-0
Track : LH: 0-4 RH: 0-0 Tight: 0-0 Gall: 0-0
Aids: Bl: 0-0 Vi: 0-0 Tstrap: 0-0
Best Rating: 33 2/01 Sthl 6f stand

Gunna B Nuts

13

3-y-o ch g Gunner B-Absolutely Nuts (Absalom)

B P J Baugh Seven Wise Owls

Placings:0 **(1632)**

2001: 8^{0}F

	Starts	1st	2nd	3rd	Win & Pl
Career Total (Turf)	1	0	0	0	

Going (Turf): Sf: 0-0 GS: 0-0 Gd: 0-0 GF: 0-0 Fm: 0-1
Distance: 5f/6f: 0-0 7f-8f: 0-0 9f-13f: 0-1 14f+: 0-0
Track : LH: 0-0 RH: 0-0 Tight: 0-0 Gall: 0-0
Aids: Bl: 0-0 Vi: 0-0 Tstrap: 0-0
Best Rating: 13 5/01 Leic 1m9y firm

Guns Blazing

96 **82**

2-y-o b c Puissance-Queen Of Aragon (Aragon)

B A McMahon J C Fretwell

Placings:14320 **(3884)**

2001: 5^{1}GS, 5^{4}G, 5^{3}GF, 5^{2}G, 6^{0}G

	Starts	1st	2nd	3rd	Win & Pl
Career Total (Turf)	5	1	1	1	5192

69	5/01	Bath	5f11y	E	G-S	£2429

Total win prize-money £2429

Going (Turf): Sf: 0-0 **GS: 1-1** Gd: 0-3 GF: 0-1 Fm: 0-0
Distance: **5f/6f: 1-5** 7f-8f: 0-0 9f-13f: 0-0 14f+: 0-0
Track : **LH: 1-2** RH: 0-1 Tight: 0-0 **Gall: 1-3**
Aids: Bl: 0-0 Vi: 0-0 Tstrap: 0-0
Best Rating: 82 6/01 Wind 5f10y good

Winner of a maiden on his debut, ran his best race since in a conditions event at Windsor in June. Seems to act on any ground.

Guru

102(75) (17)**70**

3-y-o b g Slip Anchor-Ower (IRE) (Lomond (USA))

I A Balding Dr J A E Hobby

Placings:0-3050030 **(5330)**

2001: 12^{3}GS, 10^{0}F, 11^{5}G, 11^{0}GF, 9^{0}SW, 11^{3}HY, 16^{0}HY

	Starts	1st	2nd	3rd	Win & Pl
Career Total (Turf)	7	0	0	2	1203
Career Total (AW)	1	0	0	0	

Going (Turf): Sf: 0-2 GS: 0-1 Gd: 0-2 GF: 0-1 Fm: 0-1
Distance: 5f/6f: 0-0 7f-8f: 0-1 9f-13f: 0-6 14f+: 0-1
Track : LH: 0-5 RH: 0-1 Tight: 0-7 Gall: 0-0
Aids: Bl: 0-0 Vi: 0-0 Tstrap: 0-0

Best Rating: 78 5/01 Sals 1m4f gd-sft

A half-brother to mile winner Borani. Stays a mile and a half. Acts on soft ground.

Guys And Dolls

97 **108**

2-y-o ch c Efisio-Dime Bag (High Line)
P F I Cole Anthony Speelman

Placings:1213 **(5677a)**
2001: 6[1]GS, 6[2]G, 7[1]G, 8[3]HO

	Starts	1st	2nd	3rd	Win & Pl		
Career Total (Turf)	4	2	1	1	43108		
105 9/01 Lonc 7f						GD	£21339
94 8/01 NmkJ 6f	D					G-S	£4085

Total win prize-money £25424

Going (Turf): Sf: 0-0 **GS: 1-1 Gd: 1-2** GF: 0-0 Fm: 0-0
Distance: 5f/6f: 1-2 7f-8f: 1-2 9f-13f: 0-0 14f+: 0-0
Track : LH: 0-1 **RH: 1-1** Tight: 0-0 Gall: 0-0
Aids: Bl: 0-0 Vi: 0-0 Tstrap: 0-0
Best Rating: 108 11/01 StCl 1m holding

Despite running green on his debut, he still won and ran on strongly at the finish. Looked likely to stay further when chasing home Pepperoni at Ripon and won a Group Three over seven furlongs at Longchamp in September.

Gwener Dda

70 **6**

3-y-o b g Mistertopogigo (IRE)-Good Holidays (Good Times (ITY))
J M Bradley Caleb Davies

Placings:00 **(4610)**
2001: 7[0]GF, 5[0]F

	Starts	1st	2nd	3rd	Win & Pl
Career Total (Turf)	2	0	0	0	

Going (Turf): Sf: 0-0 GS: 0-0 Gd: 0-0 GF: 0-1 Fm: 0-1
Distance: 5f/6f: 0-1 7f-8f: 0-1 9f-13f: 0-0 14f+: 0-0
Track : LH: 0-2 RH: 0-0 Tight: 0-0 Gall: 0-1
Aids: Bl: 0-0 Vi: 0-0 Tstrap: 0-0
Best Rating: 6 8/01 Wwck 7f26y gd-fm

Gwenllian Lyn

(79) (15)**31**

3-y-o b/br f Awesome-Regency Brighton (Royal Palace)
D Burchell Lyn Phillips

Placings:0600 **(1584)**
2001: 8[0]SW, 12[6]HY, 12[0]GS, 11[0]SD

	Starts	1st	2nd	3rd	Win & Pl
Career Total (Turf)	2	0	0	0	0
Career Total (AW)	2	0	0	0	

Going (Turf): Sf: 0-1 GS: 0-1 Gd: 0-0 GF: 0-0 Fm: 0-0
Distance: 5f/6f: 0-0 7f-8f: 0-1 9f-13f: 0-3 14f+: 0-0
Track : LH: 0-2 RH: 0-2 Tight: 0-2 Gall: 0-0
Aids: Bl: 0-0 Vi: 0-0 Tstrap: 0-0
Best Rating: 31 5/01 Sals 1m4f gd-sft

Gypsy (IRE)

100(103) (50)**68**

5-y-o b g Distinctly North (USA)-Winscarlet North (Garland Knight)
P R Chamings Twenty Twenty Research

Placings:03541056/21456/**3544**3056-**00**36360 **(1322)**
2001: 8[0]SD, 12[0]SD, 9[3]SW, 9[6]SD, 8[3]S, 7[6]GS, 10[0]G

	Starts	1st	2nd	3rd	Win & Pl		
Career Total (Turf)	20	2	1	3	12897		
Career Total (AW)	8	0	0	2	1118		
72 5/99 Ling 1m1f	C(0-100)H					G-F	£6696
68 7/98 Yarm 7f3y	E					G-F	£3002

Total win prize-money £9698

Going (Turf): Sf: 0-1 GS: 0-7 Gd: 0-6 **GF: 2-6** Fm: 0-0
Distance: 5f/6f: 0-1 7f-8f: 1-7 9f-13f: 1-20 14f+: 0-0
Track : **LH: 1-19** RH: 0-2 **Tight: 1-11** Gall: 0-2
Aids: Bl: 0-1 Vi: 0-0 Tstrap: 0-0
Best Rating: 68 4/01 Epsm 1m114y soft

Haafel (USA)

103 **50**

4-y-o ch g Diesis-Dish Dash (Bustino)
G L Moore Mrs J Moore

Placings:0-51 **(5557)**
2001: 10[5]HY, 14[1]S

	Starts	1st	2nd	3rd	Win & Pl		
Career Total (Turf)	3	1	0	0	2450		
50 10/01 Yarm 1m6f17y	F					SFT	£2450

Total win prize-money £2450

Going (Turf): Sf: 1-2 GS: 0-0 Gd: 0-1 GF: 0-0 Fm: 0-0
Distance: 5f/6f: 0-0 7f-8f: 0-0 9f-13f: 0-2 **14f+: 1-1**
Track : **LH: 1-2** RH: 0-0 **Tight: 1-3** Gall: 0-0
Aids: Bl: 0-0 Vi: 0-0 Tstrap: 0-0
Best Rating: 50 10/01 Yarm 1m6f17y soft

He got off the mark in a 14-furlong Yarmouth claimer in October and looks a staying hurdler in the making.

Haalim

41

3-y-o b/br c Lahib (USA)-Cancan Madame (USA) (Mr Prospector (USA))
C P Morlock (Kevin Prendergast 6/7) The Sporting Connection

Placings:050000 **(4879)**
2001: 10[0]S, 7[5]GF, 12[0]GF, 8[0]G, 7[0]GF, 12[0]SD

	Starts	1st	2nd	3rd	Win & Pl
Career Total (Turf)	5	0	0	0	
Career Total (AW)	1	0	0	0	

Going (Turf): Sf: 0-1 GS: 0-0 Gd: 0-1 GF: 0-3 Fm: 0-0
Distance: 5f/6f: 0-0 7f-8f: 0-2 9f-13f: 0-4 14f+: 0-0
Track : LH: 0-1 RH: 0-1 Tight: 0-2 Gall: 0-0
Aids: Bl: 0-0 Vi: 0-0 Tstrap: 0-0
Best Rating: 57 6/01 Gowr 7f gd-fm

Haasil (IRE)

103 **85**

3-y-o b c Machiavellian (USA)-Mahasin (USA) (Danzig (USA))
J L Dunlop Hamdan Al Maktoum

Placings:34-210000 **(5344)**
2001: 8[2]S, 8[1]S, 8[0]G, 8[0]G, 8[0]G, 8[0]GS

	Starts	1st	2nd	3rd	Win & Pl		
Career Total (Turf)	8	1	1	1	5772		
85 4/01 Ripn 1m	D					SFT	£3558

Total win prize-money £3559

Going (Turf): Sf: 1-3 GS: 0-1 Gd: 0-4 GF: 0-0 Fm: 0-0
Distance: 5f/6f: 0-0 **7f-8f: 1-8** 9f-13f: 0-0 14f+: 0-0
Track : LH: 0-0 **RH: 1-1 Tight: 1-1** Gall: 0-0
Aids: Bl: 0-0 Vi: 0-0 Tstrap: 0-0
Best Rating: 85 4/01 Ripn 1m soft

A lightly raced colt, he was second on his seasonal bow at Doncaster and duly scored at Ripon next time out. Held in warm handicaps since, he acts on soft ground.

Hadaani

93 **51**

3-y-o b f Mtoto-Trude (GER) (Windwurf (GER))
W J Haggas Khalifa Dasmal

Placings:55446 **(3977)**
2001: 8[5]F, 8[5]GF, 9[4]F, 12[4]F, 12[6]GF

	Starts	1st	2nd	3rd	Win & Pl
Career Total (Turf)	5	0	0	0	0

Going (Turf): Sf: 0-0 GS: 0-0 Gd: 0-0 GF: 0-2 Fm: 0-3
Distance: 5f/6f: 0-0 7f-8f: 0-0 9f-13f: 0-5 14f+: 0-0
Track : LH: 0-4 RH: 0-0 Tight: 0-3 Gall: 0-0
Aids: Bl: 0-0 Vi: 0-0 Tstrap: 0-0
Best Rating: 51 8/01 Thsk 1m4f firm

Haddice (USA)

84 **69**

2-y-o b c Dixieland Band (USA)-Bevel (USA) (Mr Prospector (USA))
C E Brittain Sheikh Marwan Al Maktoum

Placings:0 **(5056)**
2001: 8[0]S

	Starts	1st	2nd	3rd	Win & Pl
Career Total (Turf)	1	0	0	0	

Going (Turf): Sf: 0-1 GS: 0-0 Gd: 0-0 GF: 0-0 Fm: 0-0
Distance: 5f/6f: 0-0 7f-8f: 0-1 9f-13f: 0-0 14f+: 0-0
Track : LH: 0-0 RH: 0-0 Tight: 0-0 Gall: 0-0
Aids: Bl: 0-0 Vi: 0-0 Tstrap: 0-0
Best Rating: 69 10/01 NmkR 1m soft

Hadeqa

(83) (41)**27**

5-y-o ch g Hadeer-Heavenly Queen (Scottish Reel)
F Jordan The French Connection

Placings:55026130253005/51654061100/00000-**00** **(0290)**
2001: 12[0]SD, 12[0]SW

	Starts	1st	2nd	3rd	Win & Pl		
Career Total (Turf)	29	4	2	2	16806		
Career Total (AW)	3	0	0	0			
59 7/99 Carl 6f206y	E					GD	£2864
63 6/99 Pont 1m4y	F					GD	£2595
74 4/99 Catt 7f	E(0-70)H					SFT	£2915
63 8/98 Rdcr 6f	C					FRM	£4996

Total win prize-money £13370

Going (Turf): Sf: 1-7 GS: 0-5 **Gd: 2-10** GF: 0-5 Fm: 1-2
Distance: 5f/6f: 1-9 **7f-8f: 2-12** 9f-13f: 1-11 14f+: 0-0
Track : **LH: 2-16** RH: 1-3 **Tight: 1-13** Gall: 0-0
Aids: **Bl: 3-14** Vi: 1-11 Tstrap: 0-0
Best Rating: 16 2/01 Wolv 1m4f stand

Hadleigh (IRE)

108(103) (58)**59**

5-y-o b h Perugino (USA)-Risacca (ITY) (Sir Gaylord)
H J Collingridge C G Donovan

Placings:53104/00050/0000200**0601-615**053034340 **(4773)**
2001: 8[6]SD, 8[1]SD, 10[5]SW, 8[0]SD, 7[5]F, 8[3]GF, 9[0]G, 8[3]G, 8[4]G, 8[3]GF, 8[4]GF, 8[0]G

	Starts	1st	2nd	3rd	Win & Pl		
Career Total (Turf)	25	1	1	4	8667		
Career Total (AW)	8	2	0	0	4389		
58 1/01 Ling 1m	E(0-70)H					STD	£2961
50 12/00 Ling 1m	G					STD	£1428
83 8/98 Kemp 6f	E					G-F	£3728

Total win prize-money £8118

Going (Turf): Sf: 0-3 GS: 0-2 Gd: 0-10 **GF: 1-9** Fm: 0-1
Distance: 5f/6f: 1-4 **7f-8f: 2-19** 9f-13f: 0-10 14f+: 0-0
Track : **LH: 2-12** RH: 0-8 **Tight: 2-10** Gall: 0-2
Aids: Bl: 0-0 **Vi: 2-19** Tstrap: 0-0
Best Rating: 59 7/01 Donc 1m gd-fm

Best known as an All-Weather performer, stays a mile,

wears blinkers, and went well on the Equitrack at Lingfield.

Hagley Park

(99) (66)**56**

2-y-o b f Petong-Gi La High (Rich Charlie)
M Quinn Astaire & Partners (holdings) Ltd

Placings:1660**316** **(3431)**
2001: **5**^{1}SD, 5^{6}GS, 5^{6}F, 5^{0}GF, **5**^{3}SD, **5**^{1}SD, **6**^{6}SD

	Starts	1st	2nd	3rd	Win & Pl
Career Total (Turf)	3	0	0	0	162
Career Total (AW)	4	2	0	1	3892

66 7/01 Wolv 5f G STD £1869
66 4/01 Sthl 5f F STD £1750
Total win prize-money £3619

Going (Turf): Sf: 0-0 GS: 0-1 Gd: 0-0 GF: 0-1 Fm: 0-1
Distance: **5f/6f: 2-7** 7f-8f: 0-0 9f-13f: 0-0 14f+: 0-0
Track : **LH: 1-2** RH: 0-0 **Tight: 1-1** Gall: 0-0
Aids: Bl: 0-0 Vi: 0-0 Tstrap: 0-0
Best Rating: 66 7/01 Wolv 5f stand

His two plating-class wins have been over the minimum trip on sand, making all each time.

Hail Sheeva

88 **38**

4-y-o ch f Democratic (USA)-Sun Storm (Sunyboy)
Miss K M George R J Matthews

Placings:0/0-30 **(4844)**
2001: 10^{3}S, 9^{0}G

	Starts	1st	2nd	3rd	Win & Pl
Career Total (Turf)	4	0	0	1	342

Going (Turf): Sf: 0-1 GS: 0-0 Gd: 0-2 GF: 0-1 Fm: 0-0
Distance: 5f/6f: 0-1 7f-8f: 0-0 9f-13f: 0-3 14f+: 0-0
Track : LH: 0-3 RH: 0-0 Tight: 0-1 Gall: 0-0
Aids: Bl: 0-0 Vi: 0-0 Tstrap: 0-0
Best Rating: 38 8/01 Chep 1m2f36y soft

Hail The Chief

107(116) (108)**80**

4-y-o b c Be My Chief (USA)-Jade Pet (Petong)
R Hannon Peter M Crane

Placings:0/42601126**21111-1220**004000010 **(5142)**
2001: **8**^{1}SW, **8**^{2}SD, **10**^{2}SW, **10**^{0}SD, 8^{0}S, 8^{0}G, 8^{4}GF, 8^{0}GS, 9^{0}G, 9^{0}G, 8^{0}G, 8^{1}S, 9^{0}G

	Starts	1st	2nd	3rd	Win & Pl
Career Total (Turf)	18	3	2	0	43544
Career Total (AW)	9	5	3	0	33888

80 9/01 Asct 1m B H SFT £29000
83 1/01 Wolv 1m100y C SLW £6075
108 12/00 Wolv 1m1f79y C(0-100)H STD £6743
98 11/00 Wolv 1m100y C(0-100)H STD £6808
86 11/00 Wolv 1m100y D(0-80) STD £3770
81 11/00 Ling 1m E(0-75)H STD £2925
70 8/00 Brig 6f209y E(0-70) G-F £2804
72 7/00 Folk 7f D(0-80)H G-F £7124
Total win prize-money £65251

Going (Turf): Sf: 1-4 GS: 0-1 Gd: 0-6 **GF: 1-4** Fm: 0-2
Distance: 5f/6f: 0-0 7f-8f: 3-13 **9f-13f: 4-13** 14f+: 0-0
Track : **LH: 6-14** RH: 0-6 **Tight: 5-15** Gall: 0-0
Aids: Bl: 0-0 Vi: 0-0 Tstrap: 0-0
Best Rating: 103 2/01 Wolv 1m100y stand

He developed into a leading All-Weather performer and was nicely handicapped on turf if he could translate that improvement. He managed to do just that at Ascot in September when winning the Mail On Sunday Final at 33/1. Needs to be ridden near the front on sand as he does not like kickback.

Hailwood (USA)

89 **76**

2-y-o b c Twining (USA)-Beat (USA) (Nijinsky (CAN))
T D Easterby M J Dawson

Placings:416 **(4407)**
2001: 6^{4}G, 7^{1}F, 7^{6}GS

	Starts	1st	2nd	3rd	Win & Pl
Career Total (Turf)	3	1	0	0	4320

76 7/01 Rdcr 7f D FRM £3780
Total win prize-money £3780

Going (Turf): Sf: 0-0 GS: 0-1 Gd: 0-1 GF: 0-0 **Fm: 1-1**
Distance: 5f/6f: 0-1 **7f-8f: 1-2** 9f-13f: 0-0 14f+: 0-0
Track : LH: 0-1 RH: 0-0 Tight: 0-1 Gall: 0-0
Aids: Bl: 0-0 Vi: 0-0 Tstrap: 0-0
Best Rating: 76 7/01 Rdcr 7f firm

Improved on his debut effort to win at Redcar. That was over seven furlongs and he should stay further.

Hairy Night (IRE)

101 **71**

2-y-o b f Night Shift (USA)-Snowcap (IRE) (Snow Chief (USA))
M R Channon Lewis Caterers

Placings:222522224000400 **(5496)**
2001: 5^{2}S, 5^{2}GF, 6^{2}GF, 6^{5}GF, 6^{2}GF, 6^{2}GF, 6^{2}GF, 7^{2}GF, 6^{4}GF, 6^{0}G, 6^{0}G, 6^{0}GS, 6^{4}G, 6^{0}HY, 7^{0}HY

	Starts	1st	2nd	3rd	Win & Pl
Career Total (Turf)	15	0	7	0	15626

Going (Turf): Sf: 0-3 GS: 0-1 Gd: 0-3 GF: 0-8 Fm: 0-0
Distance: 5f/6f: 0-8 7f-8f: 0-7 9f-13f: 0-0 14f+: 0-0
Track : LH: 0-1 RH: 0-0 Tight: 0-0 Gall: 0-0
Aids: Bl: 0-0 Vi: 0-0 Tstrap: 0-0
Best Rating: 78 7/01 Sals 6f212y gd-fm

She managed to finish runner-up in seven of her first eight starts but has struggled since. Handles any ground and is effective over five to seven furlongs.

Haithem (IRE)

(101) (57d)**57**

4-y-o b g Mtoto-Wukk (IRE) (Glow (USA))
D Shaw Century Racing

Placings:420/060**0011-00**004000 **(5613)**
2001: **8**^{0}SD, **8**^{0}SD, 8^{0}S, **8**^{0}SD, 7^{4}GF, 7^{0}GF, 8^{0}G, **9**^{0}SD

	Starts	1st	2nd	3rd	Win & Pl
Career Total (Turf)	10	0	1	0	1393
Career Total (AW)	8	2	0	0	3787

57 12/00 Wolv 1m100y F(0-60)H STD £1841
51 12/00 Sthl 1m F(0-60)H STD £1946
Total win prize-money £3787

Going (Turf): Sf: 0-2 GS: 0-1 Gd: 0-1 GF: 0-6 Fm: 0-0
Distance: 5f/6f: 0-1 7f-8f: 1-9 9f-13f: 1-8 14f+: 0-0
Track : **LH: 2-13** RH: 0-1 **Tight: 1-4** Gall: 0-1
Aids: Bl: 0-0 Vi: 0-0 Tstrap: 0-0
Best Rating: 50 5/01 Donc 7f gd-fm

Haiyfoona

48

2-y-o b f Zafonic (USA)-Itqan (IRE) (Sadler's Wells (USA))
J D Czerpak Z Kulaib

Placings:0 **(5623)**
2001: 8^{0}GS

	Starts	1st	2nd	3rd	Win & Pl
Career Total (Turf)	1	0	0	0	

Going (Turf): Sf: 0-0 GS: 0-1 Gd: 0-0 GF: 0-0 Fm: 0-0
Distance: 5f/6f: 0-0 7f-8f: 0-0 9f-13f: 0-1 14f+: 0-0
Track : LH: 0-1 RH: 0-0 Tight: 0-0 Gall: 0-0
Aids: Bl: 0-0 Vi: 0-0 Tstrap: 0-0

Hajeer (IRE)

61

3-y-o b g Darshaan-Simouna (Ela-Mana-Mou)
P W Hiatt (A C Stewart 3/7) Phil Kelly

Placings:560 **(5637)**
2001: 12^{5}GF, 11^{6}G, 11^{0}G

	Starts	1st	2nd	3rd	Win & Pl
Career Total (Turf)	3	0	0	0	0

Going (Turf): Sf: 0-0 GS: 0-0 Gd: 0-2 GF: 0-1 Fm: 0-0
Distance: 5f/6f: 0-0 7f-8f: 0-0 9f-13f: 0-3 14f+: 0-0
Track : LH: 0-3 RH: 0-0 Tight: 0-2 Gall: 0-0
Aids: Bl: 0-0 Vi: 0-0 Tstrap: 0-0
Best Rating: 61 7/01 Yarm 1m3f101y good

Hakeem (IRE)

102 (42)**45**

6-y-o ch g Kefaah (USA)-Masarrah (Formidable (USA))
M Brittain Mel Brittain

Placings:314/0000000/**000**010020/022033000-500000 **(4899)**
2001: 7^{5}G, 8^{0}F, 7^{0}G, 7^{0}G, 6^{0}G, 8^{0}GS

	Starts	1st	2nd	3rd	Win & Pl
Career Total (Turf)	32	2	3	3	13339
Career Total (AW)	2	0	0	0	

56 5/99 Thsk 1m E(0-70)H G-F £3267
78 9/97 Folk 6f F GD £2389
Total win prize-money £5656

Going (Turf): Sf: 0-2 GS: 0-3 **Gd: 1-18 GF: 1-6** Fm: 0-3
Distance: 5f/6f: 1-7 7f-8f: 1-25 9f-13f: 0-2 14f+: 0-0
Track : **LH: 1-15** RH: 0-6 **Tight: 1-9** Gall: 0-6
Aids: Bl: 0-1 Vi: 0-0 Tstrap: 0-0
Best Rating: 57 6/01 Thsk 7f good

Hakeyma (USA)

94 **84**

3-y-o ch f Gone West (USA)-United Kingdom (USA) (Danzig (USA))
M R Channon Sheikh Ahmed Al Maktoum

Placings:4144 **(1828)**
2001: 7^{4}GS, 8^{1}GS, 10^{4}S, 10^{4}F

	Starts	1st	2nd	3rd	Win & Pl
Career Total (Turf)	4	1	0	0	9102

82 5/01 Kemp 1m C G-S £7001
Total win prize-money £7002

Going (Turf): Sf: 0-1 **GS: 1-2** Gd: 0-0 GF: 0-0 Fm: 0-1
Distance: 5f/6f: 0-0 **7f-8f: 1-2** 9f-13f: 0-2 14f+: 0-0
Track : LH: 0-2 **RH: 1-1** Tight: 0-0 Gall: 0-1
Aids: Bl: 0-0 Vi: 0-0 Tstrap: 0-0
Best Rating: 84 5/01 Newb 1m2f6y soft

Unraced at two, she is a grand-daughter of an Oaks winner, finished clear of the remainder in a good maiden on her debut at three. Followed up with an easy success at Kempton over a mile. Has only run and won on good to soft ground.

Hal Hoo Yaroom

94 (60)**59**

8-y-o b g Belmez (USA)-Princess Nawaal (USA) (Seattle Slew (USA))
J R Jenkins The East India Dock Partnership

Placings:000/01103/0000/**223630**/451145/32-0 **(4281)**
2001: 14^{0}G

	Starts	1st	2nd	3rd	Win & Pl
Career Total (Turf)	22	4	1	3	17607
Career Total (AW)	5	0	2	1	1880

59	7/96	Wwck	1m7f181yE(0-70)H	G-F	£3189
51	6/99	Bath	2m1f34y D(0-80)H	GD	£3714
82	7/96	Folk	1m7f92y E(0-70)H	GD	£3206
67	6/96	Yarm	1m6f17y D	FRM	£3628

Total win prize-money £13740

Going (Turf): Sf: 0-1 GS: 0-2 **Gd: 2-7** GF: 1-10 Fm: 1-2
Distance: 5f/6f: 0-0 7f-8f: 0-2 9f-13f: 0-4 **14f+: 4-21**
Track : **LH: 3-18** RH: 1-7 **Tight: 3-17** Gall: 0-3
Aids: Bl: 0-0 Vi: 0-0 Tstrap: 0-0
Best Rating: 43 8/01 Yarm 1m6f17y good

Halawan (IRE)

98 **96**

3-y-o b c Muhtarram (USA)-Haladiya (IRE) (Darshaan)
Sir Michael Stoute H H Aga Khan

Placings:2-105 **(4866)**
2001: 9^{1}G, 11^{0}G, 9^{5}GF

	Starts	1st	2nd	3rd	Win & Pl
Career Total (Turf)	4	1	1	0	6182

89	8/01	Sand	1m1f	D	GD £4114

Total win prize-money £4115

Going (Turf): Sf: 0-0 GS: 0-0 **Gd: 1-2** GF: 0-2 Fm: 0-0
Distance: 5f/6f: 0-0 7f-8f: 0-1 **9f-13f: 1-3** 14f+: 0-0
Track : LH: 0-2 **RH: 1-1** Tight: 0-0 Gall: 0-2
Aids: Bl: 0-0 Vi: 0-0 Tstrap: 0-0
Best Rating: 96 9/01 Newb 1m1f gd-fm

Won his maiden on his Sandown reappearancewith ease, displaying a fine turn of foot, but did not improve on that.

Halawellfin Hala

95 **85**

2-y-o ch c Kris-Tegwen (USA) (Nijinsky (CAN))
C E Brittain Abdullah Saeed Belhab

Placings:26 **(5677a)**
2001: 7^{2}GS, 8^{6}HO

	Starts	1st	2nd	3rd	Win & Pl
Career Total (Turf)	2	0	1	0	2270

Going (Turf): Sf: 0-0 GS: 0-1 Gd: 0-0 **GF: 0-0 Fm: 0-0**
Distance: 5f/6f: 0-0 7f-8f: 0-2 9f-13f: 0-0 14f+: 0-0
Track : LH: 0-2 RH: 0-0 Tight: 0-0 Gall: 0-1
Aids: Bl: 0-0 Vi: 0-0 Tstrap: 0-0
Best Rating: 85 11/01 StCl 1m holding

A half-brother to Teggiano, showed plenty of promise in an easy-ground York maiden. Should have no trouble winning races if not aimed too high.

Halcyon Daze

102 **83**

3-y-o ch f Halling (USA)-Ardisia (USA) (Affirmed (USA))
L M Cumani Christopher Wright

Placings:042-410026 **(5599)**
2001: 8^{4}HY, 11^{1}G, 12^{0}GF, 11^{0}HY, 11^{2}HY, 12^{6}GS

	Starts	1st	2nd	3rd	Win & Pl
Career Total (Turf)	9	1	2	0	7031

83	7/01	Yarm	1m3f101yD	GD	£4179

Total win prize-money £4180

Going (Turf): Sf: 0-5 GS: 0-1 **Gd: 1-1** GF: 0-2 Fm: 0-0
Distance: 5f/6f: 0-0 7f-8f: 0-3 **9f-13f: 1-6** 14f+: 0-0
Track : **LH: 1-2** RH: 0-2 **Tight: 1-3** Gall: 0-1
Aids: Bl: 0-0 Vi: 0-0 Tstrap: 0-0
Best Rating: 83 7/01 Yarm 1m3f101y good

A stoutly-bred filly, she won her maiden at Yarmouth when stepped up to middle distances but has not really progressed. Has heavy ground form but her win came on a sound surface.

Halcyon Magic

99(83) (49)**57**

3-y-o b g Magic Ring (IRE)-Consistent Queen (Queens Hussar)
Pat Mitchell The Magic Partnership

Placings:0045526220-600500300 **(5598)**
2001: 6^{6}S, 7^{0}SD, 6^{0}GF, 6^{5}GF, 6^{0}F, 6^{0}GF, 6^{3}GF, 7^{0}HY, 6^{0}GS

	Starts	1st	2nd	3rd	Win & Pl
Career Total (Turf)	17	0	3	1	3950
Career Total (AW)	2	0	0	0	0

Going (Turf): Sf: 0-3 GS: 0-1 Gd: 0-3 GF: 0-9 Fm: 0-1
Distance: 5f/6f: 0-15 7f-8f: 0-4 9f-13f: 0-0 14f+: 0-0
Track : LH: 0-3 RH: 0-0 Tight: 0-0 Gall: 0-0
Aids: Bl: 0-0 Vi: 0-0 Tstrap: 0-0
Best Rating: 65 4/01 NmkR 6f soft

Half Glance

104 **100+**

2-y-o b f Danehill (USA)-Fleeting Glimpse (Rainbow Quest (USA))
H R A Cecil K Abdulla

Placings:114 **(5003)**
2001: 7^{1}GS, 8^{1}G, 8^{4}S

	Starts	1st	2nd	3rd	Win & Pl
Career Total (Turf)	3	2	0	0	38134

100	9/01	Donc	1m	A	GD	£24000
76	8/01	NmkJ	7f	D	G-S	£4134

Total win prize-money £28134

Going (Turf): Sf: 0-1 **GS: 1-1 Gd: 1-1** GF: 0-0 Fm: 0-0
Distance: 5f/6f: 0-0 **7f-8f: 2-3** 9f-13f: 0-0 14f+: 0-0
Track : **LH: 1-1** RH: 0-1 Tight: 0-0 **Gall: 1-2**
Aids: Bl: 0-0 Vi: 0-0 Tstrap: 0-0
Best Rating: 100 9/01 Asct 1m soft

Comes from the same family as 1000 Guineas heroine Wince. She showed a nice turn of foot to win her maiden debut over seven furlongs on good to soft ground. Followed up in good style in a Doncaster Group Three, but was well held in the Fillies' Mile at Ascot when the soft ground may not have suited. She still possesses plenty of potential.

Half Moon Bay

97(97) (58)**56**

4-y-o b g Cyrano De Bergerac-Tarnside Rosal (Mummy's Game)
T D Barron Mrs Ann Lockhart

Placings:15511/6000-**000**6000 **(4080)**
2001: 5^{0}SD, 5^{0}S, 5^{0}SD, 5^{6}F, 5^{0}GS, 5^{0}GF, 5^{0}GF

	Starts	1st	2nd	3rd	Win & Pl
Career Total (Turf)	14	3	0	0	10468
Career Total (AW)	2	0	0	0	

88	7/99	Thsk	5f	D H	FRM	£3601
86	7/99	Donc	5f	D H	G-F	£3452
80	5/99	Thsk	5f	E	GD	£3413

Total win prize-money £10468

Going (Turf): Sf: 0-3 GS: 0-2 **Gd: 1-3 GF: 1-4 Fm: 1-2**
Distance: **5f/6f: 3-16** 7f-8f: 0-0 9f-13f: 0-0 14f+: 0-0
Track : LH: 0-3 RH: 0-0 Tight: 0-2 Gall: 0-0
Aids: Bl: 0-0 Vi: 0-0 Tstrap: 0-0
Best Rating: 58 3/01 Wolv 5f stand

Half Tide

(98) (44)**50**

7-y-o ch g Nashwan (USA)-Double River (USA) (Irish River (FR))
P Mitchell The Fruit Cake Partnership

Placings:0600**622/21330**/621050501**0-24P0** **(1315)**
2001: 16^{2}SD, 12^{4}SD, 15^{P}HY, 14^{0}SD

	Starts	1st	2nd	3rd	Win & Pl
Career Total (Turf)	13	1	1	0	4788
Career Total (AW)	13	2	4	2	8333

44	10/00	Sthl	1m6f	E(0-70)H	STD	£2362
47	7/00	Epsm	1m4f10y	E(0-75)H	G-S	£3425
48	2/99	Ling	1m4f	E(0-70)H	STD	£2621

Total win prize-money £8410

Going (Turf): Sf: 0-2 **GS: 1-3** Gd: 0-4 GF: 0-4 Fm: 0-0
Distance: 5f/6f: 0-1 7f-8f: 0-2 **9f-13f: 2-18** 14f+: 1-5
Track : **LH: 3-19** RH: 0-4 **Tight: 2-20** Gall: 0-0
Aids: Bl: 0-0 Vi: 0-0 Tstrap: 0-0
Best Rating: 44 3/01 Ling 2m stand

Halland

108 **100**

3-y-o ch c Halling (USA)-Northshiel (Northfields (USA))
G Wragg Mollers Racing

Placings:661-0212 **(5142)**
2001: 7^{0}GF, 8^{2}GF, 10^{1}GF, 9^{2}GF

	Starts	1st	2nd	3rd	Win & Pl
Career Total (Turf)	7	2	2	0	41229

95	8/01	Newb	1m2f6y	C(0-100)H	G-F	£7397
85	10/00	Yarm	7f3y	D	SFT	£4160

Total win prize-money £11557

Going (Turf): Sf: 1-1 GS: 0-0 Gd: 0-1 **GF: 1-5** Fm: 0-0
Distance: 5f/6f: 0-0 7f-8f: 1-5 9f-13f: 1-2 14f+: 0-0
Track : **LH: 1-1** RH: 0-1 Tight: 0-0 **Gall: 1-1**
Aids: Bl: 0-0 Vi: 0-0 Tstrap: 0-0
Best Rating: 100 10/01 NmkR 1m1f good

Game winner of a Yarmouth maiden on the last of three starts as a juvenile. Handles fast ground, but better on easier, as when winning over ten furlongs at Newbury in August.

Halland Park Lad (IRE)

96(92) (72)**80**

2-y-o ch c Danehill Dancer (IRE)-Lassalia (Sallust)
S Kirk Mrs B Burchett

Placings:00630110 **(5668)**
2001: 6^{0}GF, 6^{0}GF, 7^{6}GF, 6^{3}GF, 6^{0}HY, 8^{1}SD, 7^{1}GS, 8^{0}HY

	Starts	1st	2nd	3rd	Win & Pl
Career Total (Turf)	7	1	0	1	3986
Career Total (AW)	1	1	0	0	2905

80	11/01	Brig	7f214y	D(0-85)	G-S	£3588
72	10/01	Wolv	1m100y	F	STD	£2905

Total win prize-money £6493

Going (Turf): Sf: 0-2 **GS: 1-1** Gd: 0-0 GF: 0-4 Fm: 0-0
Distance: 5f/6f: 0-2 7f-8f: 1-4 9f-13f: 1-2 14f+: 0-0
Track : **LH: 2-4** RH: 0-1 **Tight: 1-2** Gall: 0-0
Aids: Bl: 0-0 Vi: 0-0 Tstrap: 0-0
Best Rating: 80 11/01 Brig 7f214y gd-sft

Slowly progressing on turf and got off the mark in a maiden over the extended mile on the Wolverhampton Fibresand in October and followed up in a nursery at Brighton.

Halland Park Lass (IRE)

65 **33**

2-y-o ch f Spectrum (IRE)-Palacegate Episode (IRE) (Drumalis)
S Kirk Mrs B Burchett

Placings:00 **(4457)**
2001: 5^{0}S, 5^{0}G

	Starts	1st	2nd	3rd	Win & Pl
Career Total (Turf)	2	0	0	0	

Going (Turf): Sf: 0-1 GS: 0-0 Gd: 0-1 GF: 0-0 Fm: 0-0
Distance: 5f/6f: 0-2 7f-8f: 0-0 9f-13f: 0-0 14f+: 0-0
Track : LH: 0-0 RH: 0-0 Tight: 0-0 Gall: 0-0

Aids: Bl: 0-0 Vi: 0-0 Tstrap: 0-0
Best Rating: 33 9/01 Folk 5f good

Hallivien (IRE)

91 **39**

3-y-o ch f Halling (USA)-Blasted Heath (Thatching)
W G M Turner J Ellis

Placings:00000 **(4094)**
2001: 10^{0}GS, 9^{0}GF, 6^{0}GF, 6^{0}GF, 9^{0}G

	Starts	1st	2nd	3rd	Win & Pl
Career Total (Turf)	5	0	0	0	

Going (Turf): Sf: 0-0 GS: 0-1 Gd: 0 1 GF: 0-3 Fm: 0-0
Distance: 5f/6f: 0-0 7f-8f: 0-2 9f-13f: 0-3 14f+: 0-0
Track : LH: 0-3 RH: 0-1 Tight: 0-1 Gall: 0-0
Aids: Bl: 0-0 Vi: 0-1 Tstrap: 0-0
Best Rating: 47 5/01 Bath 1m2f46y gd-sft

Halmahera (IRE)

114(24) **92**

6-y-o b g Petardia-Champagne Girl (Robellino (USA))
I A Balding Exors Of The Late Robert Hitchins

Placings:42113211/504455050/222212406/520556040 3-6200003206030 **(5258)**
2001: 5^{6}GS, 6^{2}S, 6^{0}GF, 5^{0}GF, 6^{0}GF, 7^{0}F, 6^{3}GF, 6^{2}G, 6^{0}G, 6^{6}GF, 6^{0}GF, 6^{3}GS, 5^{0}GS

	Starts	1st	2nd	3rd	Win & Pl
Career Total (Turf)	48	5	10	4	145783
Career Total (AW)	1	0	0	0	1096

110 6/99 Newc 6f A GD £12834
111 10/97 Asct 5f A HVY £23239
96 9/97 Ayr 5f A G-S £9992
89 7/97 Gdwd 6f C H G-F £7570
71 7/97 Chep 6f16y F G-S £3037
Total win prize-money £56674

Going (Turf): Sf: 1-10 **GS: 2-9** Gd: 1-12 GF: 1-17 Fm: 0-1
Distance: **5f/6f: 4-45** 7f-8f: 1-4 9f-13f: 0-0 14f+: 0-0
Track : LH: 0-0 RH: 0-2 Tight: 0-0 Gall: 0-2
Aids: Bl: 0-0 Vi: 0-3 Tstrap: 0-0
Best Rating: 92 10/01 Sals 6f gd-sft

Frustrating but useful sprint handicapper who often runs well but is very hard to win with. Best at six furlongs, suited by a stiff track and handles any ground. Runner-up in the Stewards' Cup in August 2001.

Hamadeenah

106 **82**

3-y-o ch f Alhijaz-Mahbob Dancer (FR) (Groom Dancer (USA))
K A Ryan Mrs N L Spence

Placings:150-060640 **(5145)**
2001: 6^{0}F, 6^{6}GF, 6^{0}GS, 7^{6}GF, 6^{4}G, 7^{0}G

	Starts	1st	2nd	3rd	Win & Pl
Career Total (Turf)	9	1	0	0	5639

72 8/00 NmkJ 6f D G-F £4810
Total win prize-money £4810

Going (Turf): Sf: 0-0 GS: 0-2 Gd: 0-2 **GF: 1-4** Fm: 0-1
Distance: **5f/6f: 1-4** 7f-8f: 0-5 9f-13f: 0-0 14f+: 0-0
Track : LH: 0-1 RH: 0-1 Tight: 0-0 Gall: 0-1
Aids: Bl: 0-0 Vi: 0-0 Tstrap: 0-0
Best Rating: 87 5/01 York 6f214y firm

Caused a bit of a surprise when making a winning debut at Newmarket last season. She has not won since and has changed stables, but has offered encouragement that a handicap can be found, possibly over seven furlongs. Suited by fast ground.

Hamasking (IRE)

83 **31**

3-y-o b f Hamas (IRE)-Sialia (IRE) (Bluebird (USA))
T D Easterby Ryedale Partners No 3

Placings:6610-0050 **(1728)**
2001: 8^{0}S, 8^{0}HY, 6^{5}HY, 7^{0}GF

	Starts	1st	2nd	3rd	Win & Pl
Career Total (Turf)	8	1	0	0	2300

51 6/00 Catt 5f212y F SFT £2299
Total win prize-money £2300

Going (Turf): Sf: 1-5 GS: 0-0 Gd: 0-1 GF: 0-2 Fm: 0-0
Distance: **5f/6f: 1-4** 7f-8f: 0-2 9f-13f: 0-2 14f+: 0-0
Track : **LH: 1-5** RH: 0-0 **Tight: 1-1** Gall: 0-0
Aids: Bl: 0-2 Vi: 0-0 Tstrap: 0-0
Best Rating: 25 5/01 Nott 6f15y heavy

Hamatara (IRE)

78(103) (80+)**73**

3-y-o ch g Tagula (IRE)-Arctic Poppy (USA) (Arctic Tern (USA))
I A Balding Exors Of The Late Robert Hitchins

Placings:404126-**02010** **(4898)**
2001: 6^{0}SD, 6^{2}SW, 6^{0}SD, 7^{1}SD, 5^{0}GS

	Starts	1st	2nd	3rd	Win & Pl
Career Total (Turf)	7	1	1	0	5941
Career Total (AW)	4	1	1	0	4615

80 2/01 Wolv 7f D(0-80)H STD £3776
67 7/00 Leic 5f2y E G-F £2925
Total win prize-money £6702

Going (Turf): Sf: 0-2 GS: 0-2 Gd: 0-2 **GF: 1-1** Fm: 0-0
Distance: 5f/6f: 1-9 7f-8f: 1-2 9f-13f: 0-0 14f+: 0-0
Track : **LH: 1-5** RH: 0-0 **Tight: 1-4** Gall: 0-0
Aids: Bl: 0-0 Vi: 0-0 **Tstrap: 2-9**
Best Rating: 80 2/01 Wolv 7f stand

It took him some adjusting on the sand before he clocked up a win at Wolverhampton in February over seven furlongs, after which he had a 221-day lay-off. He runs in a tongue-tie.

Hambleden

109(107) (78+)**93**

4-y-o b g Vettori (IRE)-Dalu (IRE) (Dancing Brave (USA))
M A Jarvis Stag And Huntsman

Placings:00/0310320104-21653525 **(4836)**
2001: 12^{2}GS, 14^{1}GF, 13^{6}G, 11^{5}GS, 12^{3}GF, 12^{5}G, 13^{2}GF, 16^{5}GF

	Starts	1st	2nd	3rd	Win & Pl
Career Total (Turf)	19	2	3	3	23414
Career Total (AW)	1	1	0	0	2212

90 5/01 Sand 1m6f D(0-85)H G-F £4485
83 9/00 Sand 1m6f D(0-80)H G-F £4641
78 5/00 Wolv 1m4f F(0-65)H STD £2212
Total win prize-money £11338

Going (Turf): Sf: 0-1 GS: 0-3 Gd: 0-7 **GF: 2-8** Fm: 0-0
Distance: 5f/6f: 0-1 7f-8f: 0-1 9f-13f: 1-8 **14f+: 2-10**
Track : LH: 1-9 **RH: 2-9 Tight: 1-2** Gall: 0-7
Aids: Bl: 0-0 Vi: 0-0 Tstrap: 0-0
Best Rating: 93 9/01 York 1m5f194y gd-fm

Returned to winning form in May over 14 furlongs at Sandown. Suited by fast ground and acts on Fibresand.

Hambleton Highlite (IRE)

92(89) (46)**29**

3-y-o ch g Paris House-Sempreverde (USA) (Lear Fan (USA))
K A Ryan Mrs C M Barlow

Placings:1304403-050000300 **(4422)**
2001: 5^{0}SW, 5^{5}SD, 7^{0}SD, 6^{0}GF, 6^{0}GF, 6^{0}SD, 9^{3}SD, 8^{0}GF, 10^{0}GF

	Starts	1st	2nd	3rd	Win & Pl
Career Total (Turf)	10	1	0	1	4249
Career Total (AW)	6	0	0	2	576

77 5/00 Haml 5f4y E FRM £2821
Total win prize-money £2821

Going (Turf): Sf: 0-0 GS: 0-1 Gd: 0-3 GF: 0-5 **Fm: 1-1**
Distance: **5f/6f: 1-11** 7f-8f: 0-2 9f-13f: 0-3 14f+: 0-0
Track : LH: 0-5 RH: 0-2 Tight: 0-4 Gall: 0-0
Aids: Bl: 0-4 Vi: 0-1 Tstrap: 0-0
Best Rating: 50 6/01 Newc 6f gd-fm

Hameeda

97 **79**

2-y-o b f Hector Protector (USA)-Habibti (Habitat)
R Hannon The Sussex Stud Limited

Placings:5302 **(5078)**
2001: 6^{5}GF, 7^{3}GS, 6^{0}GF, 5^{2}S

	Starts	1st	2nd	3rd	Win & Pl
Career Total (Turf)	4	0	1	1	1752

Going (Turf): Sf: 0-1 GS: 0-1 Gd: 0-0 GF: 0-2 Fm: 0-0
Distance: 5f/6f: 0-2 7f-8f: 0-2 9f-13f: 0-0 14f+: 0-0
Track : LH: 0-1 RH: 0-0 Tight: 0-0 Gall: 0-0
Aids: Bl: 0-0 Vi: 0-0 Tstrap: 0-0
Best Rating: 79 10/01 Brig 5f213y soft

Out of the champion sprinter Habibti, she has shown some ability and appears suited by cut in the ground.

Hamlyn (IRE)

103(99) (60)**67**

4-y-o gr g Lure (USA)-Passamaquoddy (USA) (Drone)
D R C Elsworth M Tabor

Placings:50/646400-24005 **(3944)**
2001: 7^{2}SD, 7^{4}GF, 8^{0}GF, 7^{0}S, 8^{5}GF

	Starts	1st	2nd	3rd	Win & Pl
Career Total (Turf)	12	0	0	0	1595
Career Total (AW)	1	0	1	0	860

Going (Turf): Sf: 0-3 GS: 0-2 Gd: 0-1 GF: 0-6 Fm: 0-0
Distance: 5f/6f: 0-1 7f-8f: 0-9 9f-13f: 0-3 14f+: 0-0
Track : LH: 0-2 RH: 0-3 Tight: 0-2 Gall: 0-0
Aids: Bl: 0-2 Vi: 0-0 Tstrap: 0-0
Best Rating: 67 5/01 Newb 7f gd-fm

Hammer And Sickle (IRE)

107 **63**

4-y-o b g Soviet Lad (USA)-Preponderance (IRE) (Cyrano De Bergerac)
M Johnston The 4th Middleham Partnership

Placings:10210/000-0000530300 **(4033)**
2001: 5^{0}S, 6^{0}F, 5^{0}GF, 8^{0}GF, 7^{5}F, 6^{3}GF, 6^{0}GF, 5^{3}GF, 5^{0}GF, 6^{0}G

	Starts	1st	2nd	3rd	Win & Pl
Career Total (Turf)	18	2	1	2	8420

78 5/99 Rdcr 5f E G-F £2940
82 4/99 Ripn 5f D GD £3103
Total win prize-money £6044

Going (Turf): Sf: 0-4 GS: 0-0 **Gd: 1-3 GF: 1-9** Fm: 0-2
Distance: **5f/6f: 2-15** 7f-8f: 0-3 9f-13f: 0-0 14f+: 0-0
Track : LH: 0-2 RH: 0-1 Tight: 0-3 Gall: 0-0
Aids: Bl: 0-5 Vi: 0-0 Tstrap: 0-1
Best Rating: 63 7/01 Epsm 6f gd-fm

Hammer And Tongs (IRE)

(54)

5-y-o ch g Hamas (IRE)-Bag Lady (Be My Guest (USA))
Miss V Haigh Tune Pack Produce Ltd

Placings:030/0 **(0163)**

2001: 9^{0}SD

	Starts	1st	2nd	3rd	Win & Pl
Career Total (Turf)	2	0	0	0	
Career Total (AW)	2	0	0	1	320

Going (Turf): Sf: 0-0 GS: 0-0 Gd: 0-0 GF: 0-2 Fm: 0-0
Distance: 5f/6f: 0-0 7f-8f: 0-3 9f-13f: 0-1 14f+: 0-0
Track : LH: 0-2 RH: 0-0 Tight: 0-2 Gall: 0-0
Aids: Bl: 0-0 Vi: 0-0 Tstrap: 0-0

Hammock (IRE)

83(76) (42)**54d**

3-y-o b/br g Hamas (IRE)-Sure Victory (IRE) (Stalker)
P S McEntee & Mrs Paul McEntee

Placings:0550000-06 **(1734)**
2001: 7^{0}G, 16^{6}GF

	Starts	1st	2nd	3rd	Win & Pl
Career Total (Turf)	6	0	0	0	0
Career Total (AW)	3	0	0	0	

Going (Turf): Sf: 0-1 GS: 0-0 Gd: 0-3 GF: 0-2 Fm: 0-0
Distance: 5f/6f: 0-1 7f-8f: 0-4 9f-13f: 0-3 14f+: 0-1
Track : LH: 0-5 RH: 0-1 Tight: 0-5 Gall: 0-1
Aids: Bl: 0-2 Vi: 0-1 Tstrap: 0-0
Best Rating: 24 5/01 Yarm 2m gd-fm

Hampton Lucy (IRE)

75 **42**

2-y-o b f Anabaa (USA)-Riveryev (USA) (Irish River (FR))
M A Buckley C C Buckley

Placings:0 **(4078)**
2001: 5^{0}GF

	Starts	1st	2nd	3rd	Win & Pl
Career Total (Turf)	1	0	0	0	

Going (Turf): Sf: 0-0 GS: 0-0 Gd: 0-0 GF: 0-1 Fm: 0-0
Distance: 5f/6f: 0-1 7f-8f: 0-0 9f-13f: 0-0 14f+: 0-0
Track : LH: 0-1 RH: 0-0 Tight: 0-0 Gall: 0-0
Aids: Bl: 0-0 Vi: 0-0 Tstrap: 0-0
Best Rating: 42 8/01 Pont 5f gd-fm

Hamunaptra

75 **44**

2-y-o ch c Alhijaz-Princess Dancer (Alzao (USA))
P L Gilligan Top Mark Partnership

Placings:00000 **(5342)**
2001: 5^{0}GF, 7^{0}G, 7^{0}G, 6^{0}S, 7^{0}GS

	Starts	1st	2nd	3rd	Win & Pl
Career Total (Turf)	5	0	0	0	

Going (Turf): Sf: 0-1 GS: 0-1 Gd: 0-2 GF: 0-1 Fm: 0-0
Distance: 5f/6f: 0-1 7f-8f: 0-4 9f-13f: 0-0 14f+: 0-0
Track : LH: 0-1 RH: 0-0 Tight: 0-0 Gall: 0-0
Aids: Bl: 0-1 Vi: 0-0 Tstrap: 0-0
Best Rating: 44 7/01 Leic 7f9y good

Hand Chime

110(105) (86)**90**

4-y-o ch g Clantime-Warning Bell (Bustino)
W J Haggas Mrs M M Haggas

Placings:01123111-030223100 **(5266)**
2001: 7^{0}G, 7^{3}G, 7^{0}GF, 7^{2}GF, 7^{2}G, 7^{3}G, 6^{1}HY, 7^{0}S, 6^{0}GS

	Starts	1st	2nd	3rd	Win & Pl
Career Total (Turf)	16	5	3	3	43341
Career Total (AW)	1	1	0	0	4102

79	9/01	Hayd	6f	C(0-90)	HVY	£7145
86	9/00	Wolv	7f	D(0-85)H	STD	£4101
84	8/00	Pont	6f	E(0-70)	G-F	£2860
83	8/00	Kemp	7f	D(0-85)H	G-F	£7605
67	6/00	Carl	7f214y	E(0-70)H	G-F	£3705
59	6/00	Catt	7f	F	SFT	£2646

Total win prize-money £28064

Going (Turf): Sf: 2-3 GS: 0-2 Gd: 0-5 **GF: 3-6** Fm: 0-0
Distance: 5f/6f: 2-4 **7f-8f: 4-12** 9f-13f: 0-1 14f+: 0-0
Track : **LH: 3-6** RH: 2-3 **Tight: 2-3** Gall: 1-1
Aids: Bl: 0-0 Vi: 0-0 Tstrap: 0-0
Best Rating: 90 8/01 NmkJ 7f good

He was a progressive handicapper last season, as he showed with five victories on widely varying ground of which one was on Fibresand. Not surprisingly went up the handicap as a result, but that has not stopped him, as his latest win over six at Haydock demonstrated. Effective from six furlongs to a mile.

Handa Island (USA)

97 **88**

2-y-o b c Pleasant Colony (USA)-Remote (USA) (Seattle Slew (USA))
H R A Cecil K Abdulla

Placings:55 **(5361)**
2001: 8^{5}GF, 8^{5}GS

	Starts	1st	2nd	3rd	Win & Pl
Career Total (Turf)	2	0	0	0	0

Going (Turf): Sf: 0-0 GS: 0-1 Gd: 0-0 GF: 0-1 Fm: 0-0
Distance: 5f/6f: 0-0 7f-8f: 0-2 9f-13f: 0-0 14f+: 0-0
Track : LH: 0-0 RH: 0-0 Tight: 0-0 Gall: 0-0
Aids: Bl: 0-0 Vi: 0-0 Tstrap: 0-0
Best Rating: 88 10/01 NmkR 1m gd-sft

Handful (IRE)

91 **73**

2-y-o b g Woodborough (USA)-Volkova (Green Desert (USA))
W J Haggas Mrs M M Haggas

Placings:3 **(1871)**
2001: 5^{3}F

	Starts	1st	2nd	3rd	Win & Pl
Career Total (Turf)	1	0	0	1	352

Going (Turf): Sf: 0-0 GS: 0-0 Gd: 0-0 GF: 0-0 Fm: 0-1
Distance: 5f/6f: 0-1 7f-8f: 0-0 9f-13f: 0-0 14f+: 0-0
Track : LH: 0-0 RH: 0-0 Tight: 0-0 Gall: 0-0
Aids: Bl: 0-0 Vi: 0-0 Tstrap: 0-0
Best Rating: 73 6/01 Ling 5f firm

Handsome Badsha (IRE)

(85) (63)**38**

3-y-o b c Petardia-Cape Shirley (Head For Heights)
J A Osborne Aziz Rahman, Sue Matthews, Tom Eales

Placings:6460-0 **(0047)**
2001: 7^{0}SD

	Starts	1st	2nd	3rd	Win & Pl
Career Total (Turf)	1	0	0	0	284
Career Total (AW)	4	0	0	0	0

Going (Turf): Sf: 0-1 GS: 0-0 Gd: 0-0 GF: 0-0 Fm: 0-0
Distance: 5f/6f: 0-3 7f-8f: 0-2 9f-13f: 0-0 14f+: 0-0
Track : LH: 0-5 RH: 0-0 Tight: 0-2 Gall: 0-0
Aids: Bl: 0-0 Vi: 0-0 Tstrap: 0-3
Best Rating: 10 1/01 Wolv 7f stand

Hangover Square (IRE)

95(24) (87)**68**

7-y-o ch h Jareer (USA)-Dancing Line (High Line)
L Reuterskiold Castle Stables

Placings:542505225/**41111412/2**1531**1**202/**11**121065/1 31341205-103100 **(3443)**
2001: 8^{1}G, 8^{0}FT, 9^{3}G, 9^{1}GS, 10^{0}G, 7^{0}GF

	Starts	1st	2nd	3rd	Win & Pl
Career Total (Turf)	31	9	7	2	124254
Career Total (AW)	18	8	2	2	31593

	6/01	Klam	1m1f	G-S	£8525
	4/01	Taby	1m	GD	£3577
	8/00	Klam	1m	GD	£6345
	6/00	Taby	1m1f165y	GD	£16813
	4/00	Jage	1m	GD	£3655
	7/99	Taby	1m	GD	£11119
87	6/99	Taby	1m1f165y	FRM	£26686
	5/99	Taby	1m2f	GD	£3706
	5/99	Taby	1m	GD	£3706
	7/98	Taby	1m	GD	£11477
	7/98	Taby	1m	VS	£3826
	5/98	Taby	1m1f165y	GD	£3826
	9/97	Klam	1m1f	GD	£1490
	8/97	Jage	1m143y	GD	£1110
	7/97	Jage	1m3f110y	GD	£1110
	6/97	Jage	1m143y	GD	£1110
	4/97	Jage	1m143y	GD	£1110

Total win prize-money £109191

Going (Turf): Sf: 0-1 GS: 1-3 **Gd: 14-26** GF: 0-5 Fm: 1-1
Distance: 5f/6f: 0-11 7f-8f: 7-13 **9f-13f: 10-25** 14f+: 0-0
Track : **LH: 1-5** RH: 0-0 Tight: 0-0 Gall: 0-0
Aids: Bl: 0-0 Vi: 0-0 Tstrap: 0-0
Best Rating: 100 7/01 Frnk 1m2f good

A fair sort when running in maiden company in this country, he is now trained in Sweden and has run with credit in Group races in Germany.

Hannah Park (IRE)

100 **47**

5-y-o b m Lycius (USA)-Wassl This Then (IRE) (Wassl)
P Monteith The Dregs Of Humanity

Placings:0/44204400236/111336-054566356 **(3951)**
2001: 16^{0}S, 12^{5}GS, 9^{4}GS, 12^{5}GF, 13^{6}GF, 13^{6}GF, 14^{3}G, 14^{5}F, 13^{6}GS

	Starts	1st	2nd	3rd	Win & Pl
Career Total (Turf)	27	3	2	4	9896

9/00	Herx	1m1f	H	GD	£1387
6/00	Hamb	1m3f		SFT	£3226
4/00	Zwei	1m1f110y		SFT	£806

Total win prize-money £5419

Going (Turf): **Sf: 2-7** GS: 0-4 Gd: 1-4 GF: 0-10 Fm: 0-2
Distance: 5f/6f: 0-0 7f-8f: 0-3 **9f-13f: 3-18** 14f+: 0-6
Track : LH: 0-9 RH: 0-8 Tight: 0-11 Gall: 0-0
Aids: Bl: 0-3 Vi: 0-2 Tstrap: 0-0
Best Rating: 47 6/01 Muss 1m6f good

Hannavee

65 **20**

2-y-o br g Hamas (IRE)-Secret Rapture (USA) (Woodman (USA))
S C Williams Spgs Pony Club

Placings:0 **(5527)**
2001: 8^{0}HY

	Starts	1st	2nd	3rd	Win & Pl
Career Total (Turf)	1	0	0	0	

Going (Turf): Sf: 0-1 GS: 0-0 Gd: 0-0 GF: 0-0 Fm: 0-0
Distance: 5f/6f: 0-0 7f-8f: 0-0 9f-13f: 0-1 14f+: 0-0
Track : LH: 0-1 RH: 0-0 Tight: 0-0 Gall: 0-0
Aids: Bl: 0-0 Vi: 0-0 Tstrap: 0-0
Best Rating: 20 10/01 Nott 1m54y heavy

Hannibal Lad

112(112) (85)**93**

5-y-o ch g Rock City-Appealing (Star Appeal)

W M Brisbourne John Pugh

Placings:51350/100**42/15231135**0421144135565**2-331203**4114660001 **(5020)**
2001: 9^{3}SW, **12**^{3}SD, **12**^{1}SD, **12**^{2}SW, **10**^{0}SW, **12**^{3}SW, 12^{4}F, 12^{1}GF, 11^{1}GS, 11^{4}G, 12^{6}G, 12^{6}G, 13^{0}G, 12^{0}G, 12^{0}G, 12^{1}HY

	Starts	1st	2nd	3rd	Win & Pl
Career Total (Turf)	**28**	**6**	**1**	**2**	**121952**
Career Total (AW)	**20**	**6**	**4**	**5**	**41436**

93	9/01	Asct	1m4f	B H	HVY	£40600
89	7/01	Hayd	1m3f200y	B(0-110)H	G-S	£36562
85	6/01	Gdwd	1m4f	C(0-95)H	G-F	£8697
84	1/01	Ling	1m4f	C(0-95)H	STD	£10738
81	7/00	Asct	1m4f	C(0-90)H	GD	£13682
73	6/00	Donc	1m4f	C(0-90)H	G-F	£7182
67	5/00	Sthl	1m4f	D(0-80)H	HVY	£3770
78	2/00	Sthl	1m3f	D(0-85)H	STD	£4114
72	2/00	Sthl	1m3f	D(0-85)H	STD	£4056
66	1/00	Wolv	1m1f79y	C(0-90)H	STD	£6857
64	4/99	Wolv	1m1f79y	G	STD	£1798
68	9/98	Sthl	7f	G	STD	£2302

Total win prize-money £140364

Going (Turf): Sf: 2-6 GS: 1-2 Gd: 1-11 **GF: 2-8** Fm: 0-1
Distance: 5f/6f: 0-1 7f-8f: 1-4 **9f-13f: 11-40** 14f+: 0-3
Track : **LH: 9-38** RH: 3-7 **Tight: 4-21** Gall: 3-12
Aids: Bl: 0-0 Vi: 0-0 Tstrap: 0-0
Best Rating: 93 9/01 Asct 1m4f heavy

After looking to be a Fibresand plater, he has developed into a useful middle distance handicapper on both turf and sand. Ran well after a break of four months at Doncaster in June and showed the benefit of that by going on to win a good handicap at Goodwood and the Old Newton Cup at Haydock. He was well held afterwards, but bounced back to win a very valuable handicap on soft ground at Ascot in September.

Hannon (FR)

80 **67**

2-y-o br c Exit To Nowhere (USA)-Delphania (FR) (Fabulous Dancer (USA))
R Hannon Capt C M Ryan

Placings:5 **(5095)**
2001: 8^{5}GS

	Starts	1st	2nd	3rd	Win & Pl
Career Total (Turf)	1	0	0	0	0

Going (Turf): Sf: 0-0 GS: 0-1 Gd: 0-0 GF: 0-0 Fm: 0-0
Distance: 5f/6f: 0-0 7f-8f: 0-1 9f-13f: 0-0 14f+: 0-0
Track : LH: 0-0 RH: 0-0 Tight: 0-0 Gall: 0-0
Aids: Bl: 0-0 Vi: 0-0 Tstrap: 0-0
Best Rating: 67 10/01 Sals 1m gd-sft

Hanworth (IRE)

77(74) (21)**34**

2-y-o b f Prince Of Birds (USA)-Regal Fanfare (IRE) (Taufan (USA))
M H Tompkins M H Tompkins

Placings:60040 **(4261)**
2001: 5^{6}SD, 7^{0}G, 7^{0}G, 6^{4}GF, 5^{0}GF

	Starts	1st	2nd	3rd	Win & Pl
Career Total (Turf)	4	0	0	0	0
Career Total (AW)	1	0	0	0	0

Going (Turf): Sf: 0-0 GS: 0-0 Gd: 0-2 GF: 0-2 Fm: 0-0
Distance: 5f/6f: 0-2 7f-8f: 0-3 9f-13f: 0-0 14f+: 0-0
Track : LH: 0-0 RH: 0-1 Tight: 0-0 Gall: 0-1
Aids: Bl: 0-0 Vi: 0-0 Tstrap: 0-3
Best Rating: 34 7/01 Yarm 6f3y gd-fm

Happy Are They

53

2-y-o b f Makbul-Safe Bid (Sure Blade (USA))
R M Flower Mrs Alyson Flower

Placings:00 **(5094)**
2001: 6^{0}GF, 8^{0}GS

	Starts	1st	2nd	3rd	Win & Pl
Career Total (Turf)	2	0	0	0	

Going (Turf): Sf: 0-0 GS: 0-1 Gd: 0-0 GF: 0-1 Fm: 0-0
Distance: 5f/6f: 0-1 7f-8f: 0-1 9f-13f: 0-0 14f+: 0-0
Track : LH: 0-0 RH: 0-0 Tight: 0-0 Gall: 0-0
Aids: Bl: 0-0 Vi: 0-0 Tstrap: 0-0

Happy Change (GER)

89(93) (64)**110**

7-y-o ch g Surumu (GER)-Happy Gini (USA) (Ginistrelli (USA))
M Johnston The Winning Line

Placings:260336/0615/21/3015326-050 **(3222)**
2001: 10^{0}SW, 10^{5}GF, 12^{0}GS

	Starts	1st	2nd	3rd	Win & Pl
Career Total (Turf)	**21**	**3**	**3**	**4**	**114060**
Career Total (AW)	**1**	**0**	**0**	**0**	

110	8/00	Wind	1m3f135y	C	GD	£5962
110	8/99	Epsm	1m2f18y	C	GD	£6522
108	8/98	Badn	1m2f		SFT	£25338

Total win prize-money £37822

Going (Turf): Sf: 1-5 GS: 0-3 **Gd: 2-11** GF: 0-1 Fm: 0-0
Distance: 5f/6f: 0-0 7f-8f: 0-2 **9f-13f: 3-20** 14f+: 0-0
Track : **LH: 2-6** RH: 0-13 **Tight: 2-4** Gall: 0-4
Aids: Bl: 0-0 Vi: 0-0 Tstrap: 0-0
Best Rating: 66 6/01 Kemp 1m2f gd-fm

A Group 3 winner in Germany, he has proved to be short of Pattern class since moving to England. He never figured from a poor draw on his sand debut. Stays a mile and a half. Acts on a sound surface.

Happy Clapper

86 **71**

2-y-o b f Royal Applause-Coir 'A' Ghaill (Jalmood (USA))
J G Portman Mrs H Murat

Placings:060 **(5520)**
2001: 6^{0}GF, 6^{6}G, 8^{0}HY

	Starts	1st	2nd	3rd	Win & Pl
Career Total (Turf)	3	0	0	0	0

Going (Turf): Sf: 0-1 GS: 0-0 Gd: 0-1 GF: 0-1 Fm: 0-0
Distance: 5f/6f: 0-1 7f-8f: 0-1 9f-13f: 0-1 14f+: 0-0
Track : LH: 0-0 RH: 0-1 Tight: 0-1 Gall: 0-0
Aids: Bl: 0-0 Vi: 0-0 Tstrap: 0-0
Best Rating: 71 10/01 NmkR 6f good

Happy Days

87(84) (9)**23**

6-y-o b g Primitive Rising (USA)-Miami Dolphin (Derrylin)
D Moffatt J W Barrett

Placings:24230260/00044600/051000/**0**00426252440**0**-00 **(4541)**
2001: 13^{0}GS, 14^{0}GF

	Starts	1st	2nd	3rd	Win & Pl
Career Total (Turf)	**36**	**1**	**6**	**1**	**11742**
Career Total (AW)	**1**	**0**	**0**	**0**	

44	5/99	Ripn	2m	E(0-75)H	G-F	£3663

Total win prize-money £3664

Going (Turf): Sf: 0-7 GS: 0-7 Gd: 0-9 **GF: 1-13** Fm: 0-0
Distance: 5f/6f: 0-9 7f-8f: 0-3 9f-13f: 0-6 **14f+: 1-19**
Track : LH: 0-11 **RH: 1-16 Tight: 1-17** Gall: 0-1
Aids: Bl: 0-1 Vi: 0-0 Tstrap: 0-0
Best Rating: 11 8/01 Haml 1m5f9y gd-sft

Happy Go Lucky

93 **44**

7-y-o ch m Toamster-Meritsu (IRE) (Lyphard's Special (USA))
M J Weeden M J Weeden

Placings:0310/401500040/3332001/06230-0500 **(3745)**
2001: 11^{0}GS, 13^{5}G, 12^{0}GS, 12^{0}S

	Starts	1st	2nd	3rd	Win & Pl
Career Total (Turf)	**29**	**3**	**2**	**5**	**17637**

68	9/98	Folk	1m4f	E(0-70)	G-F	£3209
78	6/97	Wwck	1m2f169y	D	FRM	£3454
78	8/96	Sand	1m14y	D	G-S	£3485

Total win prize-money £10150

Going (Turf): Sf: 0-4 **GS: 1-6** Gd: 0-6 **GF: 1-11 Fm: 1-2**
Distance: 5f/6f: 0-1 7f-8f: 0-2 **9f-13f: 3-22** 14f+: 0-4
Track : LH: 1-15 **RH: 2-13 Tight: 1-14** Gall: 0-6
Aids: Bl: 0-0 Vi: 0-0 Tstrap: 0-0
Best Rating: 44 5/01 Bath 1m5f22y good

Happy Guest (IRE)

97 **83**

2-y-o b c Be My Guest (USA)-Happy Lucy (IRE) (Alzao (USA))
E Stanners George Ward

Placings:5242020 **(5150)**
2001: 5^{5}G, 5^{2}GF, 6^{4}GF, 6^{2}G, 7^{0}GF, 6^{2}GF, 6^{0}G

	Starts	1st	2nd	3rd	Win & Pl
Career Total (Turf)	7	0	3	0	6439

Going (Turf): Sf: 0-0 GS: 0-0 Gd: 0-3 GF: 0-4 Fm: 0-0
Distance: 5f/6f: 0-6 7f-8f: 0-1 9f-13f: 0-0 14f+: 0-0
Track : LH: 0-0 RH: 0-2 Tight: 0-0 Gall: 0-2
Aids: Bl: 0-0 Vi: 0-0 Tstrap: 0-7
Best Rating: 83 9/01 Gdwd 6f gd-fm

Seems best at six furlongs and has run well in defeat. Looks up to winning a maiden.

Happy Union

95 **61**

2-y-o b c First Trump-Heights Of Love (Persian Heights)
K R Burke Mrs Elaine M Burke

Placings:0260640 **(5270)**
2001: 6^{0}GF, 5^{2}GF, 6^{6}S, 6^{0}GS, 6^{6}GF, 6^{4}HY, 6^{0}HY

	Starts	1st	2nd	3rd	Win & Pl
Career Total (Turf)	7	0	1	0	1660

Going (Turf): Sf: 0-3 GS: 0-1 Gd: 0-0 GF: 0-3 Fm: 0-0
Distance: 5f/6f: 0-6 7f-8f: 0-1 9f-13f: 0-0 14f+: 0-0
Track : LH: 0-0 RH: 0-0 Tight: 0-0 Gall: 0-0
Aids: Bl: 0-0 Vi: 0-0 Tstrap: 0-0
Best Rating: 81 7/01 Donc 5f140y gd-fm

He ran a blinder for a 50/1 shot when just beaten at Doncaster on his second start, but his other form is modest. Suited by a sound surface. Best over six at present.

Harbour Bell

93 **65**

2-y-o b c Bal Harbour-Bellara (Thowra (FR))
B R Millman Gary Leigh & Glyn Thayer

Placings:040 **(4320)**
2001: 7^{0}GS, 6^{4}F, 7^{0}GF

	Starts	1st	2nd	3rd	Win & Pl
Career Total (Turf)	3	0	0	0	288

Going (Turf): Sf: 0-0 GS: 0-1 Gd: 0-0 GF: 0-1 Fm: 0-1
Distance: 5f/6f: 0-0 7f-8f: 0-3 9f-13f: 0-0 14f+: 0-0
Track : LH: 0-1 RH: 0-0 Tight: 0-0 Gall: 0-0
Aids: Bl: 0-0 Vi: 0-0 Tstrap: 0-0
Best Rating: 65 8/01 Sals 6f212y firm

Harbour House

87 **76**

2-y-o b g Distant Relative-Double Flutter (Beldale Flutter (USA))

M R Channon P Trant

Placings:01 **(5658)**

2001: 7⁰GS, 7¹G

	Starts	1st	2nd	3rd	Win & Pl
Career Total (Turf)	2	1	0	0	3094
76 11/01 Muss 7f30y	E		GD		£3094

Total win prize-money £3094

Going (Turf): Sf: 0-0 GS: 0-1 **Gd: 1-1** GF: 0-0 Fm: 0-0
Distance: 5f/6f: 0-0 **7f-8f: 1-2** 9f-13f: 0-0 14f+: 0-0
Track : LH: 0-0 RH: 0-0 Tight: 0-0 Gall: 0-0
Aids: Bl: 0-0 Vi: 0-0 Tstrap: 0-0
Best Rating: 76 11/01 Muss 7f30y good

Scored on his second juvenile start in a muddling seven furlong conditions event at Musselburgh. Should stay beyond a mile.

Harbour Island

81 **24**

9-y-o b g Rainbow Quest (USA)-Quay Line (High Line)

B J Llewellyn (M C Pipe 11/2) Miss Emily Jane Jones

Placings:012/663040/0 **(1483)**

2001: 17⁰GF

	Starts	1st	2nd	3rd	Win & Pl
Career Total (Turf)	10	1	1	1	8239
75 9/95 Ling 1m6f	D		SFT		£4137

Total win prize-money £4138

Going (Turf): Sf: 1-1 GS: 0-0 Gd: 0-4 GF: 0-5 Fm: 0-0
Distance: 5f/6f: 0-0 7f-8f: 0-0 9f-13f: 0-2 **14f+: 1-8**
Track : **LH: 1-6** RH: 0-4 **Tight: 1-4** Gall: 0-6
Aids: **Bl: 1-8** Vi: 0-1 Tstrap: 0-0
Best Rating: 24 5/01 Bath 2m1f34y gd-fm

Harcelante (FR)

(83) (16)**34**

4-y-o br f Balleroy (USA)-Hekabe (GER) (Surumu (GER))

P W Hiatt S F Holder

Placings:5/000166001432125230200-0000 **(4603)**

2001: 8⁰S, 10⁰G, 11⁰GF, 7⁰SD

	Starts	1st	2nd	3rd	Win & Pl
Career Total (Turf)	24	3	4	2	21033
Career Total (AW)	2	0	0	0	
7/00 Bord 6f			G-S		£2882
6/00 Chan 1m			G-S		£5764
3/00 StCl 7f110y			HLD		£4803

Total win prize-money £13449

Going (Turf): Sf: 0-3 **GS: 1-2** Gd: 0-3 GF: 0-1 Fm: 0-0
Distance: **5f/6f: 1-2** 7f-8f: 0-8 9f-13f: 0-8 14f+: 0-0
Track : LH: 0-3 RH: 0-0 Tight: 0-5 Gall: 0-0
Aids: Bl: 0-0 Vi: 0-0 Tstrap: 0-0
Best Rating: 34 5/01 Wind 1m2f7y good

Hard Days Night (IRE)

104(70) **27**

4-y-o b g Mujtahid (USA)-Oiche Mhaith (Night Shift (USA))

M Blanshard David Sykes

Placings:0500060/00064620240-0636402600500 **(4942)**

2001: 14⁰HY, 11⁶GF, 17³GF, 14⁶G, 16⁴GF, 17⁰G, 12²GF, 11⁶F, 12⁰G, 14⁰GF, 16⁵G, 16⁰GF, 15⁰S

	Starts	1st	2nd	3rd	Win & Pl
Career Total (Turf)	30	0	3	1	2389
Career Total (AW)	1	0	0	0	

Going (Turf): Sf: 0-3 GS: 0-4 Gd: 0-6 GF: 0-14 Fm: 0-3
Distance: 5f/6f: 0-4 7f-8f: 0-2 9f-13f: 0-10 14f+: 0-15
Track : LH: 0-20 RH: 0-8 Tight: 0-19 Gall: 0-0
Aids: Bl: 0-2 Vi: 0-1 Tstrap: 0-0
Best Rating: 49 6/01 Folk 2m93y gd-fm

Hard Lines (USA)

(88) (28)**59**

5-y-o b g Silver Hawk (USA)-Arctic Eclipse (USA) (Northern Dancer)

A Crook (M D Hammond 10/3) Intercity Partnership

Placings:1/0/00004133-06151 **(4031)**

2001: 8⁰SD, 8⁶GF, 10¹GF, 9⁵GF, 10¹G

	Starts	1st	2nd	3rd	Win & Pl
Career Total (Turf)	13	4	0	2	11871
Career Total (AW)	2	0	0	0	0
48 8/01 Newc 1m2f32y	G		GD		£1918
38 7/01 Ripn 1m2f	F		G-F		£2695
60 9/00 Bath 1m5y	F(0-60)H		GD		£2345
83 5/98 Newb 6f8y	D		G-F		£4042

Total win prize-money £11000

Going (Turf): Sf: 0-2 GS: 0-2 **Gd: 2-3 GF: 2-6** Fm: 0-0
Distance: 5f/6f: 0-0 7f-8f: 1-6 **9f-13f: 3-9** 14f+: 0-0
Track : **LH: 2-6** RH: 1-3 **Tight: 2-5** Gall: 1-2
Aids: Bl: 0-0 Vi: 0-0 Tstrap: 0-0
Best Rating: 55 7/01 Bevl 1m1f207y gd-fm

A dual winner of sellers on the Flat in 2001, has also won over hurdles. Suited by ten furlongs and fast ground.

Hard To Catch (IRE)

101(99) (72)**73**

3-y-o b g Namaqualand (USA)-Brook's Dilemma (Known Fact (USA))

K T Ivory E H Maloney

Placings:5346010060653-043220115606 **(3945)**

2001: 6⁰SD, 7⁴SW, 7³SD, 7²SD, 6²SD, 6⁰GS, 5¹F, 6¹GF, 6⁵F, 6⁶GS, 5⁰GF, 6⁶GF

	Starts	1st	2nd	3rd	Win & Pl
Career Total (Turf)	15	3	0	1	11616
Career Total (AW)	10	0	2	2	2384
73 6/01 Gdwd 6f	D(0-80)H		G-F		£4543
71 6/01 Brig 5f213y	E(0-70)		FRM		£2905
71 8/00 Ling 5f	D		G-F		£3640

Total win prize-money £11089

Going (Turf): Sf: 0-2 GS: 0-2 Gd: 0-5 **GF: 2-4** Fm: 1-2
Distance: **5f/6f: 3-19** 7f-8f: 0-6 9f-13f: 0-0 14f+: 0-0
Track : **LH: 1-13** RH: 0-0 Tight: 0-9 Gall: 0-0
Aids: **Bl: 3-15** Vi: 0-0 Tstrap: 0-0
Best Rating: 73 6/01 Gdwd 6f gd-fm

He won a Lingfield maiden on grass in first-time blinkers in August 2000 but never found quite enough in handicaps on the All-Weather. He appreciated a return to turf with back-to-back wins in August at Goodwood and Brighton, but has gone off the boil since then. He is suited to six furlongs on a sound surface.

Hard To Lay (IRE)

93(78) (26)**56**

3-y-o br f Dolphin Street (FR)-Yavarro (Raga Navarro (ITY))

D J S Cosgrove Liam Mulryan

Placings:250023-0320 **(1961)**

2001: 8⁰SD, 6³GF, 8²F, 7⁰GF

	Starts	1st	2nd	3rd	Win & Pl
Career Total (Turf)	9	0	3	2	2902
Career Total (AW)	1	0	0	0	

Going (Turf): Sf: 0-1 GS: 0-0 Gd: 0-2 GF: 0-5 Fm: 0-1
Distance: 5f/6f: 0-3 7f-8f: 0-6 9f-13f: 0-1 14f+: 0-0
Track : LH: 0-7 RH: 0-1 Tight: 0-0 Gall: 0-0
Aids: Bl: 0-0 Vi: 0-0 Tstrap: 0-0
Best Rating: 56 5/01 Brig 6f209y gd-fm

Harewood End

(105) (75)**71**

3-y-o b g Bin Ajwaad (IRE)-Tasseled (USA) (Tate Gallery (USA))

S P C Woods G A Roberts

Placings:013300606 **(5486)**

2001: 8⁰S, 8¹SD, 10³GF, 10³G, 8⁰GF, 10⁰G, 8⁶G, 10⁰G, 10⁶HY

	Starts	1st	2nd	3rd	Win & Pl
Career Total (Turf)	8	0	0	2	2103
Career Total (AW)	1	1	0	0	2989
75 4/01 Sthl 1m	E		STD		£2989

Total win prize-money £2989

Going (Turf): Sf: 0-2 GS: 0-0 Gd: 0-4 GF: 0-2 Fm: 0-0
Distance: 5f/6f: 0-0 **7f-8f: 1-3** 9f-13f: 0-6 14f+: 0-0
Track : **LH: 1-4** RH: 0-2 Tight: 0-2 Gall: 0-2
Aids: Bl: 0-1 Vi: 0-0 Tstrap: 0-0
Best Rating: 87 5/01 Yarm 1m2f21y good

Ninth in the Wood Ditton, he scored next time out on Southwell's All-Weather track, and he has since been well held in handicap company. Acts on fast ground, and is suited by Fibresand.

Harik

87(105) (78)**48**

7-y-o ch g Persian Bold-Yaqut (USA) (Northern Dancer)

G L Moore The Best Beech Partnership

Placings:0/121006/3412200/31120-0614206 **(2807)**

2001: 12⁰SD, 16⁶SW, 16¹SW, 16⁴SD, 13²SD, 16⁰GF, 14⁶GF

	Starts	1st	2nd	3rd	Win & Pl
Career Total (Turf)	7	0	0	0	0
Career Total (AW)	19	6	5	2	26430
75 2/01 Ling 2m	D(0-85)H		SLW		£5291
80 2/00 Ling 2m	D(0-85)H		STD		£3768
75 1/00 Ling 2m	E(0-75)H		STD		£2651
70 2/99 Ling 2m	E(0-70)H		STD		£2633
73 3/98 Ling 1m5f	E(0-70)H		SLW		£2938
65 2/98 Ling 1m4f	D		SLW		£3452

Total win prize-money £20737

Going (Turf): Sf: 0-1 GS: 0-2 Gd: 0-2 GF: 0-2 Fm: 0-0
Distance: 5f/6f: 0-0 7f-8f: 0-1 9f-13f: 2-11 **14f+: 4-14**
Track : **LH: 6-21** RH: 0-2 **Tight: 6-20** Gall: 0-1
Aids: Bl: 0-0 Vi: 0-0 **Tstrap: 1-4**
Best Rating: 75 3/01 Wolv 2m46y stand

He seemed to show his best form in staying events on Equitrack and has also been successful over fences.

Harlequin

105 **98+**

3-y-o b c Halling (USA)-Russian Grace (IRE) (Soviet Star (USA))

Sir Michael Stoute Highclere Thoroughbred Racing Ltd

Placings:066-021150 **(5338)**

2001: 9⁰GS, 10²G, 11¹G, 12¹GF, 12⁵HY, 12⁰GS

	Starts	1st	2nd	3rd	Win & Pl
Career Total (Turf)	9	2	1	0	10924
98 6/01 Ripn 1m4f60y	D(0-80)H		G-F		£4257
86 6/01 Bath 1m3f144y	D(0-80)		GD		£3757

Total win prize-money £8015

Going (Turf): Sf: 0-3 GS: 0-2 **Gd: 1-3 GF: 1-1** Fm: 0-0
Distance: 5f/6f: 0-0 7f-8f: 0-3 **9f-13f: 2-6** 14f+: 0-0
Track : LH: 1-2 RH: 1-4 **Tight: 2-3** Gall: 0-2
Aids: Bl: 0-0 Vi: 0-0 Tstrap: 0-0
Best Rating: 98 6/01 Ripn 1m4f60y gd-fm

Has won twice this season at Bath and Ripon. He is suited by 12 furlongs and good to good to firm going, and has struggled since in better company on an easy surface.

Harlequin Dancer

96 **46**

5-y-o b g Distant Relative-Proudfoot (IRE) (Shareef Dancer (USA))

N A Callaghan Miss Charlotte Mooney

Placings:45413500/00000-03000 **(4366)**

2001: 9^{0}G, 7^{3}GF, 10^{0}GF, 8^{0}S, 9^{0}GF

	Starts	1st	2nd	3rd	Win & Pl
Career Total (Turf)	18	1	0	2	8689

83 5/99 Leic 1m8y F GD £2448

Total win prize-money £2448

Going (Turf): Sf: 0-3 GS: 0-0 **Gd: 1-7** GF: 0-8 Fm: 0-0
Distance: 5f/6f: 0-0 7f-8f: 0-6 **9f-13f: 1-12** 14f+: 0-0
Track : LH: 0-7 RH: 0-4 Tight: 0-1 Gall: 0-4
Aids: Bl: 0-0 Vi: 0-5 Tstrap: 0-0
Best Rating: 46 5/01 Yarm 7f3y gd-fm

Harlestone Bay

70 **32**

2-y-o b g Shaamit (IRE)-Harlestone Lake (Riboboy (USA))

J L Dunlop J L Dunlop

Placings:0 **(5682)**

2001: 7^{0}S

	Starts	1st	2nd	3rd	Win & Pl
Career Total (Turf)	1	0	0	0	

Going (Turf): Sf: 0-1 GS: 0-0 Gd: 0-0 GF: 0-0 Fm: 0-0
Distance: 5f/6f: 0-0 7f-8f: 0-1 9f-13f: 0-0 14f+: 0-0
Track : LH: 0-0 RH: 0-0 Tight: 0-0 Gall: 0-0
Aids: Bl: 0-0 Vi: 0-0 Tstrap: 0-0
Best Rating: 32 11/01 Donc 7f soft

Harlestone Grey

105 **94**

3-y-o gr g Shaamit (IRE)-Harlestone Lake (Riboboy (USA))

J L Dunlop J L Dunlop

Placings:016430 **(4697)**

2001: 12^{0}GF, 11^{1}HD, 12^{6}GS, 14^{4}G, 13^{3}G, 14^{0}GS

	Starts	1st	2nd	3rd	Win & Pl
Career Total (Turf)	6	1	0	1	8971

88 6/01 Bath 1m3f144yD HRD £3425

Total win prize-money £3426

Going (Turf): Sf: 0-0 GS: 0-2 Gd: 0-2 GF: 0-1 **Fm: 1-1**
Distance: 5f/6f: 0-0 7f-8f: 0-0 **9f-13f: 1-3** 14f+: 0-3
Track : **LH: 1-3** RH: 0-3 **Tight: 1-2** Gall: 0-3
Aids: Bl: 0-0 Vi: 0-0 Tstrap: 0-0
Best Rating: 94 8/01 York 1m5f194y good

Scored on his second start at three over a mile and a half at Bath, and has run some decent races since. Stays fourteen furlongs. Acts on fast ground. Will be more the finished article next year.

Harmonic (USA)

103 **65**

4-y-o b f Shadeed (USA)-Running Melody (Rheingold)

D R C Elsworth Mrs P J Sheen

Placings:6624/602220242-400500440 **(5465)**

2001: 8^{4}GS, 8^{0}GF, 8^{0}GF, 6^{5}GF, 6^{0}GF, 8^{0}GF, 8^{4}G, 8^{4}GS, 10^{0}G

	Starts	1st	2nd	3rd	Win & Pl
Career Total (Turf)	22	0	6	0	8727

Going (Turf): Sf: 0-2 GS: 0-3 Gd: 0-5 GF: 0-11 Fm: 0-1
Distance: 5f/6f: 0-5 7f-8f: 0-12 9f-13f: 0-5 14f+: 0-0
Track : LH: 0-3 RH: 0-6 Tight: 0-3 Gall: 0-1
Aids: Bl: 0 0 Vi: 0-0 Tstrap: 0-0
Best Rating: 71 5/01 Wind 1m67y gd-sft

Has yet to win a race but has gone close on a number of occasions. Suited by seven furlongs and good to firm.

Harmonic Way

116 **117**

6-y-o ch h Lion Cavern (USA)-Pineapple (Superlative)

R Charlton Mrs Alexandra J Chandris

Placings:145/62435043/02435212200/642162046040110000 **(5004)**

2001: 6^{4}G, 6^{0}GF, 6^{1}GF, 6^{1}GF, 6^{0}G, 5^{0}G, 6^{0}HY, 6^{0}S

	Starts	1st	2nd	3rd	Win & Pl
Career Total (Turf)	40	5	7	3	261348

117 6/01 Asct 6f A G-F £72000
113 6/01 Wind 6f A G-F £20358
113 6/00 Asct 6f B(0-110)H G-F £58000
99 7/99 Gdwd 6f B H G-F £51500
80 8/97 Sals 6f D G-F £3194

Total win prize-money £205052

Going (Turf): Sf: 0-8 GS: 0-2 Gd: 0-12 **GF: 5-15** Fm: 0-3
Distance: **5f/6f: 5-31** 7f-8f: 0-9 9f-13f: 0-0 14f+: 0-0
Track : LH: 0-1 RH: 0-1 Tight: 0-1 Gall: 0-0
Aids: Bl: 0-0 Vi: 0-0 **Tstrap: 1-5**
Best Rating: 117 6/01 Asct 6f gd-fm

Fast ground and a fast pace are essential for him to be able to execute his favoured come-from-behind tactics successfully. He had those conditions at Windsor this season and in the Cork and Orrery at Royal Ascot. He finds five furlongs too sharp and does not handle soft.

Harmony Hall

108 **61**

7-y-o ch g Music Boy-Fleeting Affair (Hotfoot)

J M Bradley E A Hayward

Placings:0660/0042300/2451536/00202256053040/4422200300-560001325423 **(4904)**

2001: 8^{5}G, 8^{6}F, 7^{0}GF, 8^{0}HD, 8^{0}GF, 8^{1}GF, 7^{3}G, 8^{2}GF, 8^{5}GF, 8^{4}GF, 8^{2}G, 7^{3}G

	Starts	1st	2nd	3rd	Win & Pl
Career Total (Turf)	55	2	11	6	33937

51 7/01 Wind 1m67y E(0-70)H G-F £3447
69 7/98 Nott 1m1f213yE(0-70)H G-F £5247

Total win prize-money £8696

Going (Turf): Sf: 0-4 GS: 0-3 Gd: 0-20 **GF: 2-23** Fm: 0-5
Distance: 5f/6f: 0-1 7f-8f: 0-17 **9f-13f: 2-35** 14f+: 0-2
Track : LH: 1-23 RH: 1-21 **Tight: 1-17** Gall: 0-7
Aids: Bl: 0-0 Vi: 0-1 Tstrap: 0-0
Best Rating: 61 7/01 Pont 1m4y gd-fm

He does not win that often, but came good in a mile handicap at Windsor in July. He has run some fine races in handicap company in the last couple of seasons. Effective from between a mile and ten furlongs, he needs fast ground

Harmony Row

89 **89**

3-y-o ch c Barathea (IRE)-Little Change (Grundy)

E A L Dunlop The Right Angle Club

Placings:31-4 **(5271)**

2001: 8^{4}HY

	Starts	1st	2nd	3rd	Win & Pl
Career Total (Turf)	3	1	0	1	4774

89 10/00 Donc 7f D GD £3477

Total win prize-money £3478

Going (Turf): Sf: 0-1 GS: 0-0 **Gd: 1-2** GF: 0-0 Fm: 0-0
Distance: 5f/6f: 0-0 **7f-8f: 1-3** 9f-13f: 0-0 14f+: 0-0
Track : LH: 0-1 RH: 0-0 Tight: 0-0 Gall: 0-0
Aids: Bl: 0-0 Vi: 0-0 Tstrap: 0-0
Best Rating: 58 10/01 Ayr 1m heavy

Harnour

101 **85**

2-y-o ch c Desert King (IRE)-Irish Light (USA) (Irish River (FR))

M R Channon Sheikh Ahmed Al Maktoum

Placings:325231105 **(5606)**

2001: 5^{3}GF, 6^{2}GF, 6^{5}G, 7^{2}GF, 8^{3}S, 8^{1}G, 8^{1}G, 8^{0}S, 10^{5}GS

	Starts	1st	2nd	3rd	Win & Pl
Career Total (Turf)	9	2	2	2	15603

85 9/01 Ayr 1m C(0-95) GD £7507
82 9/01 Haml 1m65y D GD £4225

Total win prize-money £11733

Going (Turf): Sf: 0-2 GS: 0-1 **Gd: 2-3** GF: 0-3 Fm: 0-0
Distance: 5f/6f: 0-1 7f-8f: 1-4 9f-13f: 1-4 14f+: 0-0
Track : LH: 1-3 RH: 1-3 **Tight: 1-2** Gall: 0-1
Aids: Bl: 0-0 Vi: 0-0 Tstrap: 0-0
Best Rating: 85 11/01 NmkR 1m2f gd-sft

He had looked exposed, but put up a fine front-running performance to win a Hamilton maiden over a mile in September. Followed up in an Ayr nursery. Stays a mile, suited by good ground.

Harry Bennett

97(84) (33)**57**

3-y-o b g Mind Games-Edraianthus (Windjammer (USA))

R A Fahey Mrs Janis Macpherson

Placings:4000660 **(3939)**

2001: 7^{4}SD, 7^{0}GS, 8^{0}GF, 7^{0}F, 8^{6}GS, 7^{6}G, 9^{0}G

	Starts	1st	2nd	3rd	Win & Pl
Career Total (Turf)	6	0	0	0	0
Career Total (AW)	1	0	0	0	0

Going (Turf): Sf: 0-0 GS: 0-2 Gd: 0-2 GF: 0-1 Fm: 0-1
Distance: 5f/6f: 0-0 7f-8f: 0-5 9f-13f: 0-2 14f+: 0-0
Track : LH. 0-2 RH: 0-2 Tight: 0-2 Gall: 0-0
Aids: Bl: 0-0 Vi: 0-0 Tstrap: 0-0
Best Rating: 57 6/01 Haml 1m65y gd-sft

Harry Horse

84(76) (19)**25**

3-y-o b g Cosmonaut-Bonny Melody (Sizzling Melody)

R J Hodges Mrs Anna L Sanders

Placings:000000 **(5278)**

2001: 6^{0}SD, 6^{0}GF, 6^{0}F, 6^{0}GF, 5^{0}G, 9^{0}GS

	Starts	1st	2nd	3rd	Win & Pl
Career Total (Turf)	5	0	0	0	
Career Total (AW)	1	0	0	0	

Going (Turf): Sf: 0-0 GS: 0-1 Gd: 0-1 GF: 0-2 Fm: 0-1
Distance: 5f/6f: 0-4 7f-8f: 0-1 9f-13f: 0-1 14f+: 0-0
Track : LH: 0-1 RH: 0-1 Tight: 0-1 Gall: 0-0
Aids: Bl: 0-0 Vi: 0-0 Tstrap: 0-0
Best Rating: 41 7/01 Sals 6f gd-fm

Harry Jake

105 **87+**

2-y-o b c Royal Applause-Flora Wood (IRE) (Bob Back (USA))

J-P Gallorini (H R A Cecil 20/8) M House

Placings:316

2001: 7^{3}GF, 6^{1}G, 7^{6}HO

	Starts	1st	2nd	3rd	Win & Pl
Career Total (Turf)	3	1	0	1	4394

87 8/01 Nott 6f15y E GD £3688

Total win prize-money £3689

Going (Turf): Sf: 0-0 GS: 0-0 **Gd: 1-1** GF: 0-1 Fm: 0-0
Distance: 5f/6f: 0-0 **7f-8f: 1-3** 9f-13f: 0-0 14f+: 0-0
Track : LH: 0-0 RH: 0-0 Tight: 0-0 Gall: 0-0
Aids: Bl: 0-0 Vi: 0-0 Tstrap: 0-0
Best Rating: 87 8/01 Nott 6f15y good

Finished third in a decent Doncaster maiden on his debut and saw off a modest field with ease at Nottingham next time.

Harry Junior

89(71) (14)**23**
3-y-o b g River Falls-Badger Bay (IRE) (Salt Dome (USA))
B W Murray (C A Dwyer 29/1) B Murray

Placings:605200-**00**000000000 **(5629)**
2001: 6^{0}SD, 8^{0}SD, 7^{0}GF, 8^{0}F, 7^{0}S, 5^{0}F, 7^{0}GF, 8^{0}GF, 6^{0}HY, 8^{0}F, 5^{0}G, 5^{0}G

	Starts	1st	2nd	3rd	Win & Pl
Career Total (Turf)	16	0	1	0	524
Career Total (AW)	2	0	0	0	

Going (Turf): Sf: 0-2 GS: 0-0 Gd: 0-4 GF: 0-6 Fm: 0-4
Distance: 5f/6f: 0-9 7f-8f: 0-7 9f-13f: 0-2 14f+: 0-0
Track : LH: 0-6 RH: 0-1 Tight: 0-1 Gall: 0-1
Aids: Bl: 0-0 Vi: 0-3 Tstrap: 0-1
Best Rating: 31 7/01 Newc 1m firm

Harry M

(66) (16)
3-y-o ch g River Falls-Sylvan Rime (Weldnaas (USA))
J A Glover Exors Of The Late E Morrell

Placings:00 **(0269)**
2001: 7^{0}SD, 7^{0}SW

	Starts	1st	2nd	3rd	Win & Pl
Career Total (Turf)	0	0	0	0	
Career Total (AW)	2	0	0	0	

Going (Turf): Sf: 0-0 GS: 0-0 Gd: 0-0 GF: 0-0 Fm: 0-0
Distance: 5f/6f: 0-0 7f-8f: 0-2 9f-13f: 0-0 14f+: 0-0
Track : LH: 0-2 RH: 0-0 Tight: 0-0 Gall: 0-0
Aids: Bl: 0-1 Vi: 0-0 Tstrap: 0-0
Best Rating: 16 1/01 Sthl 7f stand

Harry The Beaver (IRE)

86 **48**
2-y-o b c Bigstone (IRE)-Moon River (FR) (Groom Dancer (USA))
M H Tompkins Mrs C Gilliar

Placings:000 **(4533)**
2001: 7^{0}GF, 7^{0}GS, 7^{0}GF

	Starts	1st	2nd	3rd	Win & Pl
Career Total (Turf)	3	0	0	0	

Going (Turf): Sf: 0-0 GS: 0-1 Gd: 0-0 GF: 0-2 Fm: 0-0
Distance: 5f/6f: 0-0 7f-8f: 0-3 9f-13f: 0-0 14f+: 0-0
Track : LH: 0-1 RH: 0-0 Tight: 0-0 Gall: 0-1
Aids: Bl: 0-0 Vi: 0-0 Tstrap: 0-0
Best Rating: 48 9/01 York 7f202y gd-fm

Harryana

(71) (27)**79**
4-y-o b f Efisio-Allyana (IRE) (Thatching)
M Johnston S Kimberley

Placings:2151000**4**2/00-00 **(0234)**
2001: 5^{0}SD, 9^{0}SD

	Starts	1st	2nd	3rd	Win & Pl
Career Total (Turf)	11	2	2	0	12847
Career Total (AW)	2	0	0	0	

79	8/99	Rdcr	5f	E	GD	£2826
79	5/99	Ches	5f16y	D	G-F	£6970

Total win prize-money £9796

Going (Turf): Sf: 0-4 GS: 0-1 **Gd: 1-4 GF: 1-2** Fm: 0-0
Distance: 5f/6f: 2-12 7f-8f: 0-0 9f-13f: 0-1 14f+: 0-0
Track : LH: 1-3 RH: 0-0 **Tight: 1-3** Gall: 0-0
Aids: Bl: 0-0 Vi: 0-0 Tstrap: 0-0
Best Rating: 27 1/01 Ling 5f stand

Harvard (USA)

77 **31**
3-y-o b/br g Zafonic (USA)-Bright Generation (IRE) (Rainbow Quest (USA))
L M Cumani H R H Prince Fahd Salman

Placings:0 **(0816)**
2001: 7^{0}S

	Starts	1st	2nd	3rd	Win & Pl
Career Total (Turf)	1	0	0	0	

Going (Turf): Sf: 0-1 GS: 0-0 Gd: 0-0 GF: 0-0 Fm: 0-0
Distance: 5f/6f: 0-0 7f-8f: 0-1 9f-13f: 0-0 14f+: 0-0
Track : LH: 0-0 RH: 0-0 Tight: 0-0 Gall: 0-0
Aids: Bl: 0-0 Vi: 0-0 Tstrap: 0-0
Best Rating: 31 4/01 NmkR 7f soft

Harvey Leader

(106) (74d)**45**
6-y-o b g Prince Sabo-Mrs Leader (USA) (Mr. Leader (USA))
Miss J Feilden C Muirhead

Placings:30015-104060006 **(5413)**
2001: 8^{1}SD, 8^{0}SW, 7^{4}SW, 8^{0}SD, 8^{6}SD, 8^{0}SD, 8^{0}GS, 6^{0}GF, 8^{6}SD

	Starts	1st	2nd	3rd	Win & Pl
Career Total (Turf)	4	0	0	0	
Career Total (AW)	10	2	0	1	4352

74	1/01	Sthl	1m	E(0-70)H	STD	£2457
65	11/00	Sthl	1m	G(0-60)H	STD	£1522

Total win prize-money £3980

Going (Turf): Sf: 0-1 GS: 0-1 Gd: 0-1 GF: 0-1 Fm: 0-0
Distance: 5f/6f: 0-1 **7f-8f: 2-9** 9f-13f: 0-4 14f+: 0-0
Track : LH: 2-10 RH: 0-0 Tight: 0-4 Gall: 0-0
Aids: Bl: 0-0 Vi: 0-0 Tstrap: 0-0
Best Rating: 74 1/01 Sthl 1m stand

Harvey's Future

84(103) (51)**45**
7-y-o b g Never So Bold-Orba Gold (USA) (Gold Crest (USA))
P L Gilligan Treasure Seekers Partnership

Placings:6/6400/20**5**042463/**1**020/320620**1**42-0350 **(3840)**
2001: 7^{0}SD, 7^{3}SD, 8^{5}SD, 7^{0}G

	Starts	1st	2nd	3rd	Win & Pl
Career Total (Turf)	21	1	4	2	7219
Career Total (AW)	10	1	2	1	5142

46	11/00	Ling	7f	E(0-75)	STD	£2405
42	4/99	Bath	5f11y	E(0-70)H	SFT	£2920

Total win prize-money £5325

Going (Turf): Sf: 1-6 GS: 0-3 Gd: 0-11 GF: 0-1 Fm: 0-0
Distance: 5f/6f: 1-22 7f-8f: 1-9 9f-13f: 0-0 14f+: 0-0
Track : LH: 2-10 RH: 0-2 Tight: 1-5 Gall: 1-5
Aids: Bl: 0-1 Vi: 0-0 Tstrap: 0-0
Best Rating: 46 1/01 Ling 7f stand

Hasikiya (IRE)

94 **56**
3-y-o b f Green Desert (USA)-Hasainiya (IRE) (Top Ville)
Sir Michael Stoute H H Aga Khan

Placings:0 **(3683)**
2001: 8^{0}G

	Starts	1st	2nd	3rd	Win & Pl
Career Total (Turf)	1	0	0	0	

Going (Turf): Sf: 0-0 GS: 0-0 Gd: 0-1 GF: 0-0 Fm: 0-0
Distance: 5f/6f: 0-0 7f-8f: 0-0 9f-13f: 0-1 14f+: 0-0
Track : LH: 0-0 RH: 0-1 Tight: 0-1 Gall: 0-0
Aids: Bl: 0-0 Vi: 0-0 Tstrap: 0-0
Best Rating: 56 8/01 Wind 1m67y good

Hasta La Vista

104(98) (38)**43**
11-y-o b g Superlative-Falcon Berry (FR) (Bustino)
M W Easterby Mr K Hodgson & Mrs J Hodgson

Placings:2000044/006012165/1103304206066/500310 3530/414654000/4423421212155136102000/50411013 33005/00005664220/102143500030-362013303 **(5663)**
2001: 14^{3}GS, 13^{6}G, 12^{2}GF, 13^{0}GF, 12^{1}GS, 16^{3}SD, 12^{3}S, 15^{0}GF, 12^{3}G

	Starts	1st	2nd	3rd	Win & Pl
Career Total (Turf)	97	14	12	15	70168
Career Total (AW)	18	3	0	1	10200

43	7/01	Haml	1m4f17y	F(0-60)H	G-S	£3374
50	6/00	Catt	1m3f214y	E(0-70)H	G-S	£4046
47	4/00	Muss	1m6f	E(0-70)H	G-S	£3526
55	7/98	Bevl	1m3f216y	E(0-70)H	G-F	£3057
51	5/98	Catt	1m5f175y	E(0-70)H	G-S	£2973
47	5/98	Muss	1m4f	F(0-65)H	G-F	£2948
60	8/97	Ripn	1m4f60y	D(0-80)H	GD	£3840
55	8/97	Catt	1m5f175y	E(0-70)H	G-F	£3226
55	7/97	Catt	1m7f177y	E(0-70)H	SFT	£2940
54	6/97	Haml	1m5f9y	E(0-70)H	G-S	£3046
53	5/97	Muss	2m	F(0-60)H	G-F	£2687
54	4/96	Catt	1m3f214y	D(0-85)H	GD	£3752
48	8/95	Ripn	1m4f60y	D(0-80)H	G-F	£4250
61	2/94	Sthl	2m	D(0-80)H	STD	£3377
61	2/94	Sthl	1m4f	D(0-75)H	STD	£3655
56	7/93	Sthl	1m4f	E(0-70)H	STD	£2898
43	6/93	Catt	1m4f44y	E(0-70)H	G-F	£2950

Total win prize-money £56549

Going (Turf): Sf: 1-10 GS: 5-16 Gd: 2-25 **GF: 6-42** Fm: 0-4
Distance: 5f/6f: 0-4 7f-8f: 0-2 **9f-13f: 10-59** 14f+: 7-50
Track : LH: 9-76 RH: 8-35 **Tight: 14-74** Gall: 0-10
Aids: Bl: 14-82 Vi: 3-21 Tstrap: 0-0
Best Rating: 43 8/01 Haml 1m4f17y soft

Veteran staying handicapper, goes well on a sharp track. Most effective when making the running.

Hasty Prince

103 **94**
3-y-o ch c Halling (USA)-Sister Sophie (USA) (Effervescing (USA))
B Hanbury Ahmed Buhaleeba

Placings:6-4**1**0546 **(4863)**
2001: 8^{4}F, 10^{1}GF, 10^{0}G, 12^{5}GF, 10^{4}HY, 10^{6}GF

	Starts	1st	2nd	3rd	Win & Pl
Career Total (Turf)	7	1	0	0	6432

94	6/01	Donc	1m2f60y	D	G-F	£4212

Total win prize-money £4212

Going (Turf): Sf: 0-1 GS: 0-0 Gd: 0-1 **GF: 1-4** Fm: 0-1
Distance: 5f/6f: 0-0 7f-8f: 0-1 **9f-13f: 1-6** 14f+: 0-0
Track : LH: 1-4 RH: 0-2 Tight: 0-1 **Gall: 1-3**
Aids: Bl: 0-0 Vi: 0-0 Tstrap: 0-0
Best Rating: 94 6/01 Donc 1m2f60y gd-fm

Bred to stay middle distances, he scored on his second outing at three when stepped up to ten furlongs at Doncaster, but was very disappointing afterwards.

Hata (IRE)

109 **91**

3-y-o ch f Hamas (IRE)-Fnaya (Caerleon (USA))
N A Graham Hamdan Al Maktoum

Placings:4-212400 **(5259)**
2001: 6^{2}HY, 6^{1}HY, 6^{2}GS, 6^{4}HY, 5^{0}HY, 7^{0}GS

	Starts	1st	2nd	3rd	Win & Pl
Career Total (Turf)	7	1	2	0	9449

73 4/01 Wwck 6f21y D HVY £3835
Total win prize-money £3835

Going (Turf): Sf: 1-4 GS: 0-2 Gd: 0-0 GF: 0-1 Fm: 0-0
Distance: 5f/6f: 0-4 **7f-8f: 1-3** 9f-13f: 0-0 14f+: 0-0
Track : LH: 0-1 RH: 0-0 Tight: 0-0 Gall: 0-0
Aids: Bl: 0-0 Vi: 0-0 Tstrap: 0-0
Best Rating: 91 5/01 Sals 6f gd-sft

She got off the mark in a heavy-ground maiden at Warwick in April and has run well in some decent events since. Likes soft ground and still has some scope.

Hatalan

58

2-y-o ch f Mark Of Esteem (IRE)-Elbaaha (Arazi (USA))
M R Channon Sheikh Ahmed Al Maktoum

Placings:02 **(5627)**
2001: 7^{0}GF, 7^{2}G

	Starts	1st	2nd	3rd	Win & Pl
Career Total (Turf)	2	0	1	0	1072

Going (Turf): Sf: 0-0 GS: 0-0 Gd: 0-1 GF: 0-1 Fm: 0-0
Distance: 5f/6f: 0-0 7f-8f: 0-2 9f-13f: 0-0 14f+: 0-0
Track : LH: 0-0 RH: 0-1 Tight: 0-0 Gall: 0-1
Aids: Bl: 0-0 Vi: 0-0 Tstrap: 0-0
Best Rating: 58 11/01 Rdcr 7f good

Hatha Anna (IRE)

114 **111+**

4-y-o b h Sadler's Wells (USA)-Moon Cactus (Kris)
Saeed Bin Suroor Godolphin

Placings:560-241121 **(5737a)**
2001: 12^{2}GF, 12^{4}G, 10^{1}S, 14^{1}GF, 12^{2}G, 12^{1}G

	Starts	1st	2nd	3rd	Win & Pl
Career Total (Turf)	9	3	2	0	89595

111 11/01 Flem 1m4f110y GD £50191
104 9/01 Sals 1m6f15y C G-F £6217
60 7/01 Hayd 1m2f120yD SFT £4270
Total win prize-money £60680

Going (Turf): Sf: 1-1 GS: 0-0 **Gd: 1-4 GF: 1-3** Fm: 0-1
Distance: 5f/6f: 0-0 7f-8f: 0-0 **9f-13f: 2-8** 14f+: 1-1
Track : LH: 1-3 RH: 1-5 **Tight: 1-3** Gall: 0-4
Aids: **Bl: 1-1** Vi: 0-1 Tstrap: 0-0
Best Rating: 111 11/01 Flem 1m4f110y good

He took a while in getting off the mark having run well in very decent company, but did so with the minimum of fuss at Haydock in July. Followed up in a conditions event over 14 furlongs at Salisbury and was not disgraced in defeat at Newmarket. Ended the season with victory in a Grade Two at Flemington.

Hathaal (IRE)

96 **92**

2-y-o b c Alzao (USA)-Ballet Shoes (IRE) (Ela-Mana-Mou)
Sir Michael Stoute Hamdan Al Maktoum

Placings:21 **(5056)**
2001: 8^{2}G, 8^{1}S

	Starts	1st	2nd	3rd	Win & Pl
Career Total (Turf)	2	1	1	0	7000

92 10/01 NmkR 1m D SFT £5668
Total win prize-money £5668

Going (Turf): Sf: 1-1 GS: 0-0 Gd: 0-1 GF: 0-0 Fm: 0-0
Distance: 5f/6f: 0-0 **7f-8f: 1-2** 9f-13f: 0-0 14f+: 0-0
Track : LH: 0-0 RH: 0-1 Tight: 0-0 Gall: 0-0
Aids: Bl: 0-0 Vi: 0-0 Tstrap: 0-0
Best Rating: 92 10/01 NmkR 1m soft

A half-brother to Petrushka, he ran really well on his Kempton debut and put the experience to good use to just prevail in a decent Newmarket maiden next time.

Hatter's Lad (IRE)

(94) (77+)**63**

2-y-o b c Alzao (USA)-Shamsana (USA) (Nijinsky (CAN))
J A Osborne Mrs Leonard Hatton

Placings:41 **(5197)**
2001: 7^{4}G, 8^{1}SD

	Starts	1st	2nd	3rd	Win & Pl
Career Total (Turf)	1	0	0	0	0
Career Total (AW)	1	1	0	0	2898

77 10/01 Wolv 1m100y F STD £2898
Total win prize-money £2898

Going (Turf): Sf: 0-0 GS: 0-0 Gd: 0-1 GF: 0-0 Fm: 0-0
Distance: 5f/6f: 0-0 7f-8f: 0-1 **9f-13f: 1-1** 14f+: 0-0
Track : **LH: 1-1** RH: 0-1 **Tight: 1-1** Gall: 0-0
Aids: Bl: 0-0 Vi: 0-0 Tstrap: 0-0
Best Rating: 77 10/01 Wolv 1m100y stand

Showed ability on his Beverley debut and bolted up in a maiden on the Wolverhampton Fibresand next time. Looks a nice prospect.

Hattington

93 **53**

3-y-o b c Polish Precedent (USA)-Ruffle (FR) (High Line)
M R Channon Matthew Norman & Mrs Rebecca Philipps

Placings:500 **(5631)**
2001: 11^{5}S, 11^{0}G, 10^{0}G

	Starts	1st	2nd	3rd	Win & Pl
Career Total (Turf)	3	0	0	0	0

Going (Turf): Sf: 0-1 GS: 0-0 Gd: 0-2 GF: 0-0 Fm: 0-0
Distance: 5f/6f: 0-0 7f-8f: 0-0 9f-13f: 0-3 14f+: 0-0
Track : LH: 0-3 RH: 0-0 Tight: 0-2 Gall: 0-0
Aids: Bl: 0-0 Vi: 0-0 Tstrap: 0-0
Best Rating: 53 10/01 Bath 1m3f144y good

Haulage Man

101 **57**

3-y-o ch g Komaite (USA)-Texita (Young Generation)
D Eddy James R Adams

Placings:66-5010 **(4851)**
2001: 8^{5}F, 7^{0}GF, 6^{1}F, 7^{0}GF

	Starts	1st	2nd	3rd	Win & Pl
Career Total (Turf)	6	1	0	0	2443

52 9/01 Newc 6f F(0-65)H FRM £2443
Total win prize-money £2443

Going (Turf): Sf: 0-0 GS: 0-1 Gd: 0-0 GF: 0-2 **Fm: 1-3**
Distance: **5f/6f: 1-3** 7f-8f: 0-3 9f-13f: 0-1 14f+: 0-0
Track : LH: 0-1 RH: 0-0 Tight: 0-0 Gall: 0-1
Aids: Bl: 0-0 Vi: 0-0 Tstrap: 0-0
Best Rating: 57 9/01 Ayr 7f50y gd-fm

Caused a surprise when coming late to win a Newcastle handicap in September. Suited by fast ground and waiting tactics, he is lightly-raced and may have improvement in him.

Haunt The Zoo

(103) (64)**34**

6-y-o b m Komaite (USA)-Merryhill Maid (IRE) (M Double M (USA))
John A Harris (J L Harris 26/3) R Atkinson

Placings:046/3040546110/3000001030320250-551000400313150 **(5413)**
2001: 6^{5}SD, 7^{5}SD, 8^{1}SW, 8^{0}SD, 6^{0}SD, 8^{0}SW, 7^{4}SW, 7^{0}SD, 7^{0}SD, 8^{3}SD, 8^{1}SD, 8^{3}SD, 9^{1}SW, 9^{5}SD, 8^{0}SD

	Starts	1st	2nd	3rd	Win & Pl
Career Total (Turf)	14	0	0	2	1286
Career Total (AW)	30	6	2	4	17542

64 9/01 Wolv 1m1f79y F(0-65)H SLW £2338
54 7/01 Sthl 1m F STD £2310
64 1/01 Sthl 1m E(0-70)H SLW £2667
58 5/00 Sthl 7f F(0-65)H STD £2289
54 12/99 Ling 6f F(0-60)H STD £1840
45 11/99 Sthl 6f E(0-70)H STD £2814
Total win prize-money £14258

Going (Turf): Sf: 0-1 GS: 0-2 Gd: 0-4 GF: 0-6 Fm: 0-1
Distance: 5f/6f: 2-13 **7f-8f: 3-27** 9f-13f: 1-4 14f+: 0-0
Track : **LH: 6-31** RH: 0-2 **Tight: 2-7** Gall: 0-0
Aids: Bl: 0-0 Vi: 0-0 Tstrap: 0-0
Best Rating: 64 9/01 Wolv 1m1f79y slow

Fair handicapper, suited by a mile to ten furlongs on Fibresand.

Havana (IRE)

97 **42**

5-y-o b m Dolphin Street (FR)-Royaltess (Royal And Regal (USA))
R Ford Gary Williams

Placings:33/4233004-0020000 **(5170)**
2001: 9^{0}G, 16^{0}F, 16^{2}GF, 16^{0}GF, 16^{0}GS, 16^{0}GF, 17^{0}GS

	Starts	1st	2nd	3rd	Win & Pl
Career Total (Turf)	16	0	2	4	5231

Going (Turf): Sf: 0-1 GS: 0-4 Gd: 0-4 GF: 0-5 Fm: 0-2
Distance: 5f/6f: 0-0 7f-8f: 0-1 9f-13f: 0-8 14f+: 0-7
Track : LH: 0-11 RH: 0-5 Tight: 0-10 Gall: 0-0
Aids: Bl: 0-1 Vi: 0-0 Tstrap: 0-7
Best Rating: 46 7/01 Bevl 2m35y gd-fm

Havoc

94 **81+**

2-y-o b c Hurricane Sky (AUS)-Padelia (Thatching)
E A L Dunlop Dragon's Stud

Placings:02 **(5559)**
2001: 7^{0}S, 8^{2}S

	Starts	1st	2nd	3rd	Win & Pl
Career Total (Turf)	2	0	1	0	1392

Going (Turf): Sf: 0-2 GS: 0-0 Gd: 0-0 GF: 0-0 Fm: 0-0
Distance: 5f/6f: 0-0 7f-8f: 0-1 9f-13f: 0-1 14f+: 0-0
Track : LH: 0-0 RH: 0-0 Tight: 0-0 Gall: 0-0
Aids: Bl: 0-0 Vi: 0-0 Tstrap: 0-0
Best Rating: 81 10/01 Yarm 1m3y soft

Improved from his debut to finish runner-up in a Yarmouth maiden in October and should find a race over middle distances at three.

Hawayil (USA)

92 **66**

2-y-o b f Halling (USA)-Avice Caro (USA) (Caro)
C E Brittain Saeed Manana

Placings:450 **(5112)**
2001: 6^{4}GF, 7^{5}GF, 8^{0}HY

	Starts	1st	2nd	3rd	Win & Pl
Career Total (Turf)	3	0	0	0	313

Going (Turf): Sf: 0-1 GS: 0-0 Gd: 0-0 GF: 0-2 Fm: 0-0
Distance: 5f/6f: 0-0 7f-8f: 0-2 9f-13f: 0-1 14f+: 0-0
Track : LH: 0-1 RH: 0-0 Tight: 0-0 Gall: 0-0
Aids: Bl: 0-0 Vi: 0-0 Tstrap: 0-0
Best Rating: 66 9/01 Ling 7f gd-fm

Hawk

103 **72**

3-y-o b c A P Jet (USA)-Miss Enjoleur (USA) (L'Enjoleur (CAN))
R Hannon Highclere Thoroughbred Racing Ltd

Placings:333-325310 **(5108)**
2001: 5[3]GF, 5[2]GF, 6[5]G, 5[3]G, 5[1]F, 5[0]GS

	Starts	1st	2nd	3rd	Win & Pl
Career Total (Turf)	9	1	1	5	10196
72 9/01 Bath 5f161y D				FRM	£3545

Total win prize-money £3546

Going (Turf): Sf: 0-0 GS: 0-2 Gd: 0-3 GF: 0-2 **Fm: 1-1**
Distance: **5f/6f: 1-8** 7f-8f: 0-0 9f-13f: 0-0 14f+: 0-0
Track : **LH: 1-1** RH: 0-0 Tight: 0-0 **Gall: 1-1**
Aids: Bl: 0-0 Vi: 0-0 Tstrap: 0-0
Best Rating: 88 6/01 Asct 5f gd-fm

Ran well in good maidens in a light campaign as a juvenile. Took an age to get off the mark at three, but finally did so at Bath in September. Has plenty of speed but is not a battler.

Hawkes Run

102(94) (71)**84**

3-y-o b g Hernando (FR)-Wise Speculation (USA) (Mr Prospector (USA))
C J Mann (B J Meehan 17/6) The Baron Rouge Partnership

Placings:66452-2234 **(2228)**
2001: 9[2]S, 12[2]GS, 10[3]GF, 14[4]GS

	Starts	1st	2nd	3rd	Win & Pl
Career Total (Turf)	8	0	2	1	3793
Career Total (AW)	1	0	1	0	484

Going (Turf): Sf: 0-3 GS: 0-2 Gd: 0-2 GF: 0-1 Fm: 0-0
Distance: 5f/6f: 0-1 7f-8f: 0-3 9f-13f: 0-4 14f+: 0-1
Track : LH: 0-4 RH: 0-4 Tight: 0-2 Gall: 0-0
Aids: Bl: 0-1 Vi: 0-0 Tstrap: 0-0
Best Rating: 84 5/01 Pont 1m4f8y gd-sft

Half-brother to five winners including high-class middle-distance winner, Always Friendly, he had several near-misses, and seemed unable to find his exact trip.

Hawkeye (IRE)

116 **115**

3-y-o b c Danehill (USA)-Tea House (Sassafras (FR))
A P O'Brien Mrs John Magnier & Mr M Tabor

Placings:3-4111334 **(5389)**
2001: 8[4]S, 8[1]Y, 8[1]GF, 8[1]S, 8[3]GS, 8[3]S, 10[4]GS

	Starts	1st	2nd	3rd	Win & Pl
Career Total (Turf)	8	3	0	3	135894
109 8/01 Curr 1m				SFT	£39000
100 7/01 Curr 1m				G-F	£10400
90 6/01 Curr 1m				YLD	£9750

Total win prize-money £59150

Going (Turf): Sf: 1-3 GS: 0-2 Gd: 0-0 **GF: 1-1** Fm: 0-0
Distance: 5f/6f: 0-0 **7f-8f: 3-7** 9f-13f: 0-1 14f+: 0-0
Track : LH: 0-0 RH: 0-3 Tight: 0-0 Gall: 0-1
Aids: Bl: 0-0 Vi: 0-0 Tstrap: 0-0
Best Rating: 115 10/01 NmkR 1m2f gd-sft

Steadily improving having progressed to win a Curragh Group Three, he improved on that when third in both the Prix du Moulin and Queen Elizabeth II Stakes. He is suited by a mile but may well get ten furlongs. Acts on most surfaces. Sold to join the Michael Jarvis stable.

Hawkley

80 **53**

2-y-o ch c Arctic Tern (USA)-Last Ambition (IRE) (Cadeaux Genereux)
N P Littmoden Julian Smith

Placings:0000 **(4730)**
2001: 7[0]G, 5[0]GF, 6[0]GF, 5[0]F

	Starts	1st	2nd	3rd	Win & Pl
Career Total (Turf)	4	0	0	0	

Going (Turf): Sf: 0-0 GS: 0-0 Gd: 0-1 GF: 0-2 Fm: 0-1
Distance: 5f/6f: 0-3 7f-8f: 0-1 9f-13f: 0-0 14f+: 0-0
Track : LH: 0-0 RH: 0-1 Tight: 0-0 Gall: 0-0
Aids: Bl: 0-0 Vi: 0-0 Tstrap: 0-0
Best Rating: 53 8/01 Ling 6f gd-fm

Hawkwind (USA)

85 **70**

2-y-o gr/ro c El Prado (IRE)-Pleasantly Quick (USA) (Roanoke (USA))
J H M Gosden Manton Racing Partnership

Placings:00 **(5559)**
2001: 8[0]S, 8[0]S

	Starts	1st	2nd	3rd	Win & Pl
Career Total (Turf)	2	0	0	0	

Going (Turf): Sf: 0-2 GS: 0-0 Gd: 0-0 GF: 0-0 Fm: 0-0
Distance: 5f/6f: 0-0 7f-8f: 0-1 9f-13f: 0-1 14f+: 0-0
Track : LH: 0-0 RH: 0-0 Tight: 0-0 Gall: 0-0
Aids: Bl: 0-0 Vi: 0-0 Tstrap: 0-0
Best Rating: 70 10/01 NmkR 1m soft

Haydn Bowen

2-y-o ch c Most Welcome-Hi-Li (High Top)
R M Flower K & D Computers Ltd

Placings:P **(5095)**
2001: 8[P]GS

	Starts	1st	2nd	3rd	Win & Pl
Career Total (Turf)	1	0	0	0	

Going (Turf): Sf: 0-0 GS: 0-1 Gd: 0-0 GF: 0-0 Fm: 0-0
Distance: 5f/6f: 0-0 7f-8f: 0-1 9f-13f: 0-0 14f+: 0-0
Track : LH: 0-0 RH: 0-0 Tight: 0-0 Gall: 0-0
Aids: Bl: 0-0 Vi: 0-0 Tstrap: 0-0

Hayley's Affair (IRE)

88 **56**

3-y-o b f Night Shift (USA)-Sea Mistress (Habitat)
P W Harris Graham & Lynn Knight

Placings:5-00060 **(5461)**
2001: 7[0]S, 6[0]HY, 7[0]GF, 8[6]GS, 8[0]G

	Starts	1st	2nd	3rd	Win & Pl
Career Total (Turf)	6	0	0	0	0

Going (Turf): Sf: 0-3 GS: 0-1 Gd: 0-1 GF: 0-1 Fm: 0-0
Distance: 5f/6f: 0-0 7f-8f: 0-4 9f-13f: 0-2 14f+: 0-0
Track : LH: 0-1 RH: 0-2 Tight: 0-2 Gall: 0-1
Aids: Bl: 0-0 Vi: 0-0 Tstrap: 0-3
Best Rating: 56 4/01 Kemp 7f soft

Haymaker (IRE)

103(103) (66)**48**

5-y-o b g Thatching-Susie Sunshine (IRE) (Waajib)
R Craggs (G A Swinbank 6/9) Ray Craggs

Placings:0/3006320**2313**/030**622**345040 **(5376)**
2001: 8[0]GS, 8[3]S, 7[0]HY, 6[6]SD, 7[2]SD, 7[2]SD, 8[3]SD, 9[4]GS, 10[5]G, 10[0]HY, 9[4]SW, 9[0]G

	Starts	1st	2nd	3rd	Win & Pl
Career Total (Turf)	16	0	2	3	6309
Career Total (AW)	8	1	2	3	5262
60 11/99 Sthl 7f D				STD	£2853

Total win prize-money £2853

Going (Turf): Sf: 0-7 GS: 0-4 Gd: 0-4 GF: 0-1 Fm: 0-0
Distance: 5f/6f: 0-2 **7f-8f: 1-13** 9f-13f: 0-9 14f+: 0-0
Track : **LH: 1-16** RH: 0-2 Tight: 0-7 Gall: 0-0
Aids: Bl: 0-0 Vi: 0-0 Tstrap: 0-0
Best Rating: 66 7/01 Sthl 1m stand

A moderate performer at trips around a mile, although he has yet to achieve results of any note. Best efforts on the All-Weather. An habitual slow-starter.

Haystacks (IRE)

100 **54**

5-y-o b g Contract Law (USA)-Florissa (FR) (Persepolis (FR))
D Moffatt Mr & Mrs A G Milligan

Placings:36004052/63362056/0425-06331 **(4620)**
2001: 16[0]S, 12[6]GF, 15[3]GS, 14[3]G, 16[1]F

	Starts	1st	2nd	3rd	Win & Pl
Career Total (Turf)	27	1	3	5	8573
54 9/01 Newc 2m19y E(0-75)H				FRM	£3562

Total win prize-money £3562

Going (Turf): Sf: 0-5 GS: 0-3 Gd: 0-10 GF: 0-7 **Fm: 1-1**
Distance: 5f/6f: 0-7 7f-8f: 0-3 9f-13f: 0-11 **14f+: 1-5**
Track : **LH: 1-10** RH: 0-10 Tight: 0-10 **Gall: 1-5**
Aids: Bl: 0-0 Vi: 0-13 Tstrap: 0-0
Best Rating: 54 9/01 Newc 2m19y firm

A dual hurdles winner, got off the mark on the Flat at the 27th attempt at Newcastle in September. Handles any ground, stays two miles and suited by a good gallop.

Hazimah (USA)

93 **81**

2-y-o b f Gone West (USA)-Elrafa Ah (USA) (Storm Cat (USA))
M P Tregoning Hamdan Al Maktoum

Placings:34 **(5089)**
2001: 7[3]GF, 8[4]GS

	Starts	1st	2nd	3rd	Win & Pl
Career Total (Turf)	2	0	0	1	720

Going (Turf): Sf: 0-0 GS: 0-1 Gd: 0-0 GF: 0-1 Fm: 0-0
Distance: 5f/6f: 0-0 7f-8f: 0-2 9f-13f: 0-0 14f+: 0-0
Track : LH: 0-1 RH: 0-0 Tight: 0-0 Gall: 0-1
Aids: Bl: 0-0 Vi: 0-0 Tstrap: 0-0
Best Rating: 81 8/01 Folk 7f gd-fm

Haziraan (IRE)

(98) (36)**30**

4-y-o b g Primo Dominie-Hazaradjat (IRE) (Darshaan)
R A Fahey Exors Of The Late D A Read

Placings:03000-00405600 **(2173)**
2001: 7[0]SD, 6[0]SD, 6[4]SD, 6[0]SD, 7[5]SD, 7[6]GF, 8[0]F, 7[0]SD

	Starts	1st	2nd	3rd	Win & Pl
Career Total (Turf)	6	0	0	1	518
Career Total (AW)	7	0	0	0	0

Going (Turf): Sf: 0-1 GS: 0-2 Gd: 0-0 GF: 0-2 Fm: 0-1
Distance: 5f/6f: 0-3 7f-8f: 0-6 9f-13f: 0-4 14f+: 0-0
Track : LH: 0-10 RH: 0-1 Tight: 0-6 Gall: 0-0
Aids: Bl: 0-0 Vi: 0-0 Tstrap: 0-0
Best Rating: 44 3/01 Wolv 6f stand

Hazy Morn

(63) (2)**46**

2-y-o gr f Cyrano De Bergerac-Hazy Kay (IRE) (Treasure Kay)

N J Hawke R J Hart

Placings:00040466000 (5195)

2001: 5^{0}GS, 5^{0}G, 5^{0}GF, 5^{4}GF, 5^{0}F, 5^{4}G, 5^{6}GF, 5^{6}GS, 6^{0}GF, 5^{0}F, 6^{0}SD

	Starts	1st	2nd	3rd	Win & Pl
Career Total (Turf)	10	0	0	0	0
Career Total (AW)	1	0	0	0	

Going (Turf): Sf: 0-0 GS: 0-2 Gd: 0-2 GF: 0-4 Fm: 0-2
Distance: 5f/6f: 0-10 7f-8f: 0-1 9f-13f: 0-0 14f+: 0-0
Track : LH: 0-4 RH: 0-1 Tight: 0-1 Gall: 0-4
Aids: Bl: 0-1 Vi: 0-0 Tstrap: 0-0
Best Rating: 67 6/01 Wwck 5f gd-fm

He Who Dares (IRE)

100 **74**

3-y-o b c Distinctly North (USA)-Sea Clover (IRE) (Ela-Mana-Mou)

I A Balding Roger Clarke And Gwen Daffey

Placings:402 (5113)

2001: 7^{4}S, 7^{0}S, 8^{2}HY

	Starts	1st	2nd	3rd	Win & Pl
Career Total (Turf)	3	0	1	0	1754

Going (Turf): Sf: 0-3 GS: 0-0 Gd: 0-0 GF: 0-0 Fm: 0-0
Distance: 5f/6f: 0-0 7f-8f: 0-2 9f-13f: 0-1 14f+: 0-0
Track : LH: 0-1 RH: 0-1 Tight: 0-0 Gall: 0-1
Aids: Bl: 0-0 Vi: 0-0 Tstrap: 0-0
Best Rating: 74 10/01 Nott 1m54y heavy

Showed promise in the spring, and finished second in a backend maiden after a lengthy absence. Has only encountered testing ground so far.

He's A Rascal (IRE)

97(70) (6)**13**

3-y-o b g Fumo Di Londra (IRE)-Lovely Ali (IRE) (Dunbeath (USA))

H Morrison Entertainments Committee

Placings:0560000 (5524)

2001: 8^{0}G, 11^{5}G, 12^{6}G, 12^{0}SD, 14^{0}GS, 11^{0}S, 10^{0}HY

	Starts	1st	2nd	3rd	Win & Pl
Career Total (Turf)	6	0	0	0	0
Career Total (AW)	1	0	0	0	

Going (Turf): Sf: 0-2 GS: 0-1 Gd: 0-3 GF: 0-0 Fm: 0-0
Distance: 5f/6f: 0-0 7f-8f: 0-0 9f-13f: 0-6 14f+: 0-1
Track : LH: 0-4 RH: 0-2 Tight: 0-5 Gall: 0-0
Aids: Bl: 0-1 Vi: 0-1 Tstrap: 0-0
Best Rating: 63 9/01 Chep 1m4f23y good

Head In The Clouds (IRE)

121 **114**

3-y-o b f Rainbow Quest (USA)-Ballerina (IRE) (Dancing Brave (USA))

J L Dunlop L Neil Jones

Placings:53-4612012 (5595)

2001: 10^{4}G, 12^{6}GF, 11^{1}G, 13^{2}S, 11^{0}G, 12^{1}GS, 12^{2}GS

	Starts	1st	2nd	3rd	Win & Pl
Career Total (Turf)	9	2	2	1	59000

114 10/01 Asct 1m4f A G-S £30000
85 7/01 York 1m3f195yD GD £8632
Total win prize-money £38632

Going (Turf): Sf: 0-1 **GS: 1-3 Gd: 1-3** GF: 0-2 Fm: 0-0
Distance: 5f/6f: 0-0 7f-8f: 0-2 **9f-13f: 2-6** 14f+: 0-1
Track : LH: 1-2 RH: 1-3 Tight: 0-0 **Gall: 2-5**
Aids: Bl: 0-0 Vi: 0-0 Tstrap: 0-0
Best Rating: 114 10/01 Asct 1m4f gd-sft

Improved on her juvenile form when fourth to Mot Juste in Pretty Polly Stakes at Newmarket in May and settled better when scoring at York. Only just beaten at Deauville at beginning of August, she was well beaten in the Yorkshire Oaks, but had the ground in her favour when making all in the Princess Royal Stakes at Ascot. Has won on good ground, but is best on soft.

Head Scratcher

(89) (61)**56**

3-y-o ch g Alhijaz-Sabrata (IRE) (Zino)

A Bailey Sandybrow Stables Ltd

Placings:306-105 (0166)

2001: 7^{1}SD, 9^{0}SW, 8^{5}SD

	Starts	1st	2nd	3rd	Win & Pl
Career Total (Turf)	2	0	0	1	388
Career Total (AW)	4	1	0	0	1932

61 1/01 Sthl 7f G STD £1932
Total win prize-money £1932

Going (Turf): Sf: 0-1 GS: 0-0 Gd: 0-0 GF: 0-1 Fm: 0-0
Distance: 5f/6f: 0-3 **7f-8f: 1-1** 9f-13f: 0-2 14f+: 0-0
Track : **LH: 1-4** RH: 0-0 Tight: 0-3 Gall: 0-0
Aids: Bl: 0-0 Vi: 0-0 Tstrap: 0-0
Best Rating: 61 1/01 Sthl 7f stand

Headfort Rose (IRE)

(83) (37)**67**

4-y-o b f Desert Style (IRE)-Tamarsiya (USA) (Shahrastani (USA))

M Meade (Michael Cunningham 15/8) Ladyswood Stud

Placings:336626/006010000-00000200000 (5397)

2001: 8^{0}S, 9^{0}F, 8^{0}GF, 7^{0}F, 8^{0}GF, 7^{2}F, 7^{0}G, 9^{0}G, 8^{0}G, 8^{0}SD, 8^{0}SD

	Starts	1st	2nd	3rd	Win & Pl
Career Total (Turf)	24	1	2	2	6815
Career Total (AW)	2	0	0	0	

64 7/00 Bell 1m (50-87)H G-F £4312
Total win prize-money £4313

Going (Turf): Sf: 0-5 GS: 0-0 Gd: 0-6 **GF: 1-5** Fm: 0-4
Distance: 5f/6f: 0-4 **7f-8f: 1-16** 9f-13f: 0-5 14f+: 0-0
Track : **LH: 1-10** RH: 0-4 Tight: 0-2 Gall: 0-0
Aids: **Bl: 1-10** Vi: 0-0 Tstrap: 0-0
Best Rating: 67 7/01 Dund 7f166y firm

Headland (USA)

(104) (86)**82**

3-y-o b/br c Distant View (USA)-Fijar Echo (USA) (In Fijar (USA))

J M P Eustace The Macdougall Partnership

Placings:4-220201010 (5011)

2001: 5^{2}SD, 6^{2}HY, 6^{0}G, 6^{2}G, 5^{0}GF, 6^{1}SD, 5^{0}GS, 7^{1}SD, 7^{0}HY

	Starts	1st	2nd	3rd	Win & Pl
Career Total (Turf)	7	0	2	0	3753
Career Total (AW)	3	2	1	0	7898

86 9/01 Wolv 7f D(0-85)H STD £4111
82 7/01 Wolv 6f D STD £2947
Total win prize-money £7058

Going (Turf): Sf: 0-3 GS: 0-1 Gd: 0-2 GF: 0-1 Fm: 0-0
Distance: 5f/6f: 1-6 7f-8f: 1-4 9f-13f: 0-0 14f+: 0-0
Track : **LH: 2-3** RH: 0-0 **Tight: 2-2** Gall: 0-0
Aids: Bl: 0-0 Vi: 0-0 Tstrap: 0-0
Best Rating: 86 9/01 Wolv 7f stand

Somewhat inconsistent, but looks a much better horse on Fibresand and both his wins to date have come at Wolverhampton.

Healey (IRE)

92 **65**

3-y-o ch g Dr Devious (IRE) Bean Siamsa (Solinus)

J D Bethell Wwwclarendon Racingcom

Placings:1143-000300 (5151)

2001: 7^{0}S, 7^{0}GF, 8^{0}GF, 10^{3}F, 10^{0}GS, 10^{0}G

	Starts	1st	2nd	3rd	Win & Pl
Career Total (Turf)	10	2	0	2	13399

92 8/00 Ripn 6f C G-F £5783
67 8/00 Ripn 6f D GD £3484
Total win prize-money £9267

Going (Turf): Sf: 0-2 GS: 0-1 **Gd: 1-3 GF: 1-3** Fm: 0-1
Distance: **5f/6f: 2-3** 7f-8f: 0-3 9f-13f: 0-4 14f+: 0-0
Track : LH: 0-5 RH: 0-0 Tight: 0 2 Gall: 0-1
Aids: Bl: 0-0 Vi: 0-0 Tstrap: 0-1
Best Rating: 68 2/01 Cagn 7f110y soft

Won his first two starts as a juvenile over six furlongs but was not up to Listed company and started this season on a high handicap mark. Way below form over varying trips.

Heather Mix

98 **70d**

3-y-o gr f Linamix (FR)-Craigmill (Slip Anchor)

J L Dunlop P D Player

Placings:14P (4992)

2001: 10^{1}S, 11^{4}GF, 10^{P}HY

	Starts	1st	2nd	3rd	Win & Pl
Career Total (Turf)	3	1	0	0	4494

70 5/01 Hayd 1m2f120yD SFT £3965
Total win prize-money £3965

Going (Turf): Sf: 1-2 GS: 0-0 Gd: 0-0 GF: 0-1 Fm: 0-0
Distance: 5f/6f: 0-0 7f-8f: 0-0 **9f-13f: 1-3** 14f+: 0-0
Track : **LH: 1-2** RH: 0-0 Tight: 0-1 Gall: 0-0
Aids: Bl: 0-0 Vi: 0-0 Tstrap: 0-0
Best Rating: 70 5/01 Hayd 1m2f120y soft

From a good staying family, she won a soft-ground maiden on her debut, but seemed unsuited by the faster surface next time. Pulled up on her final start.

Heather Valley

91(89) (30)**35**

5-y-o ch m Clantime-Sannavally (Sagaro)

J Akehurst Miss Vivian Pratt

Placings:000/05540-000 (5028)

2001: 7^{0}GF, 5^{0}G, 5^{0}S

	Starts	1st	2nd	3rd	Win & Pl
Career Total (Turf)	9	0	0	0	217
Career Total (AW)	2	0	0	0	0

Going (Turf): Sf: 0-1 GS: 0-1 Gd: 0-3 GF: 0-3 Fm: 0-1
Distance: 5f/6f: 0-4 7f-8f: 0-6 9f-13f: 0-1 14f+: 0-0
Track : LH: 0-6 RH: 0-0 Tight: 0-2 Gall: 0-0
Aids: Bl: 0-0 Vi: 0-0 Tstrap: 0-0
Best Rating: 23 9/01 Ling 7f gd-fm

Heathman (IRE)

66 **6**

5-y-o b g Common Grounds-Dul Dul (USA) (Shadeed (USA))

R J Baker S M McCausland

Placings:0/000 (3744)

2001: 6^{0}GF, 11^{0}F, 7^{0}S

	Starts	1st	2nd	3rd	Win & Pl
Career Total (Turf)	4	0	0	0	

Going (Turf): Sf: 0-2 GS: 0-0 Gd: 0-0 GF: 0-1 Fm: 0-1
Distance: 5f/6f: 0-0 7f-8f: 0-3 9f-13f: 0-1 14f+: 0-0
Track : LH: 0-1 RH: 0-0 Tight: 0-1 Gall: 0-0

Aids: Bl: 0-0 Vi: 0-0 Tstrap: 0-0
Best Rating: 6 8/01 Chep 7f16y soft

Heathyards Friend

79 **42**

2-y-o b g Forest Wind (USA)-Heathyards Lady (USA) (Mining (USA))
R Hollinshead L A Morgan

Placings:00 **(5168)**
2001: 7^{0}GF, 10^{0}GS

	Starts	1st	2nd	3rd	Win & Pl
Career Total (Turf)	2	0	0	0	

Going (Turf): Sf: 0-0 GS: 0-1 Gd: 0-0 GF: 0-1 Fm: 0-0
Distance: 5f/6f: 0-0 7f-8f: 0-1 9f-13f: 0-1 14f+: 0-0
Track : LH: 0-2 RH: 0-0 Tight: 0-0 Gall: 0-0
Aids: Bl: 0-0 Vi: 0-0 Tstrap: 0-0
Best Rating: 42 10/01 Pont 1m2f6y gd-sft

Heathyards Guest (IRE)

96(83) (50)**51**

3-y-o ch g Be My Guest (USA)-Noble Nadia (Thatching)
R Hollinshead L A Morgan

Placings:02466-2050340000 **(5269)**
2001: 9^{2}SW, 9^{0}S, 10^{5}GF, 9^{0}GF, 8^{3}GF, 9^{4}GF, 9^{0}G, 10^{0}S, 11^{0}GS, 10^{0}HY

	Starts	1st	2nd	3rd	Win & Pl
Career Total (Turf)	13	0	1	1	1791
Career Total (AW)	2	0	1	0	832

Going (Turf): Sf: 0-5 GS: 0-1 Gd: 0-1 GF: 0-6 Fm: 0-0
Distance: 5f/6f: 0-0 7f-8f: 0-4 9f-13f: 0-11 14f+: 0-0
Track : LH: 0-9 RH: 0-3 Tight: 0-4 Gall: 0-0
Aids: Bl: 0-0 Vi: 0-2 Tstrap: 0-0
Best Rating: 65 6/01 Nott 1m54y gd-fm

Heathyards Lad (IRE)

91(89) (59)**34**

4-y-o b g Petardia-Maiden's Dance (Hotfoot)
M Wigham Norwester Racing Club

Placings:034546354454164/540632565500345040-000 **(4403)**
2001: 8^{0}G, 7^{0}G, 6^{0}G

	Starts	1st	2nd	3rd	Win & Pl
Career Total (Turf)	28	0	1	4	4416
Career Total (AW)	8	1	0	0	2396

62 9/99 Wolv 1m100y F STD £2199
Total win prize-money £2199

Going (Turf): Sf: 0-5 GS: 0-7 Gd: 0-9 GF: 0-5 Fm: 0-1
Distance: 5f/6f: 0-11 7f-8f: 0-11 **9f-13f: 1-13** 14f+: 0-0
Track : **LH: 1-20** RH: 0-4 **Tight: 1-11** Gall: 0-1
Aids: Bl: 0-1 Vi: 0-1 Tstrap: 0-0
Best Rating: 30 8/01 Brig 7f214y good

Heathyards Signet

93(97) (50)**36**

3-y-o b g King's Signet (USA)-Heathyards Gem (Governor General)
D McCain L A Morgan

Placings:560-5010530000 **(4944)**
2001: 6^{5}G, 6^{0}F, 6^{1}GF, 5^{0}GF, 6^{5}GF, 6^{3}SD, 7^{0}GS, 5^{0}G, 5^{0}SW, 5^{0}S

	Starts	1st	2nd	3rd	Win & Pl
Career Total (Turf)	11	1	0	0	3608
Career Total (AW)	2	0	0	1	427

49 6/01 Ches 6f18y E G-F £3607
Total win prize-money £3608

Going (Turf): Sf: 0-1 GS: 0-2 Gd: 0-3 **GF: 1-4** Fm: 0-1
Distance: 5f/6f: 0-10 **7f-8f: 1-3** 9f-13f: 0-0 14f+: 0-0
Track : **LH: 1-8** RH: 0-0 **Tight: 1-5** Gall: 0-0
Aids: Bl: 0-0 Vi: 0-0 Tstrap: 0-0
Best Rating: 50 7/01 Wolv 6f stand

He has had one break in a career of poor performances, but that was only in a Chester claimer over six furlongs on fast ground.

Heathyards Swing

97(91) (51)**78**

3-y-o b c Celtic Swing-Butsova (Formidable (USA))
R Hollinshead L A Morgan

Placings:0226100000 **(5416)**
2001: 8^{0}S, 7^{2}G, 10^{2}GF, 8^{6}GF, 10^{1}GF, 10^{0}GF, 10^{0}GS, 11^{0}HY, 11^{0}S, 9^{0}SD

	Starts	1st	2nd	3rd	Win & Pl
Career Total (Turf)	9	1	2	0	5426
Career Total (AW)	1	0	0	0	

66 6/01 Ripn 1m2f E G-F £2989
Total win prize-money £2989

Going (Turf): Sf: 0-3 GS: 0-1 Gd: 0-1 **GF: 1-4** Fm: 0-0
Distance: 5f/6f: 0-0 7f-8f: 0-2 **9f-13f: 1-8** 14f+: 0-0
Track : LH: 0-7 **RH: 1-2 Tight: 1-3** Gall: 0-1
Aids: Bl: 0-0 Vi: 0-0 Tstrap: 0-0
Best Rating: 78 8/01 Hayd 1m2f120y gd-sft

Heathyardsblessing (IRE)

105 **85**

4-y-o b g Unblest-Noble Nadia (Thatching)
R Hollinshead L A Morgan

Placings:0143210521/0-0030 **(5266)**
2001: 5^{0}G, 5^{0}GF, 5^{3}G, 6^{0}GS

	Starts	1st	2nd	3rd	Win & Pl
Career Total (Turf)	15	3	2	2	52060

103 10/99 Nott 6f15y F FRM £2742
83 7/99 Ches 5f16y H G-F £3452
75 5/99 Hayd 5f E GD £2752
Total win prize-money £8947

Going (Turf): Sf: 0-0 GS: 0-1 **Gd: 1-5 GF: 1-7 Fm: 1-1**
Distance: **5f/6f: 2-13** 7f-8f: 1-2 9f-13f: 0-0 14f+: 0-0
Track : **LH: 1-4** RH: 0-0 **Tight: 1-4** Gall: 0-0
Aids: Bl: 0-0 Vi: 0-0 Tstrap: 0-0
Best Rating: 85 8/01 Nott 5f13y good

Best effort in 2001 was when third from a good draw at Beverley. Seems suited by good ground.

Heaven Forbid

92(85) (27)**51**

3-y-o b g Beveled (USA)-Fayre Holly (IRE) (Fayruz)
J G Portman A S B Portman

Placings:500000 **(5497)**
2001: 6^{5}F, 6^{0}SD, 5^{0}GS, 5^{0}G, 5^{0}SD, 5^{0}HY

	Starts	1st	2nd	3rd	Win & Pl
Career Total (Turf)	4	0	0	0	0
Career Total (AW)	2	0	0	0	

Going (Turf): Sf: 0-1 GS: 0-1 Gd: 0-1 GF: 0-0 Fm: 0-1
Distance: 5f/6f: 0-6 7f-8f: 0-0 9f-13f: 0-0 14f+: 0-0
Track : LH: 0-1 RH: 0-0 Tight: 0-1 Gall: 0-0
Aids: Bl: 0-0 Vi: 0-0 Tstrap: 0-0
Best Rating: 51 6/01 Ling 6f firm

Heavenly Whisper (IRE)

109 **108**

3-y-o b f Halling (USA)-Rock The Boat (Slip Anchor)
M L W Bell Dgh Partnership

Placings:010-136200 **(5141)**
2001: 8^{1}S, 10^{3}F, 10^{6}Y, 8^{2}G, 8^{0}S, 8^{0}G

	Starts	1st	2nd	3rd	Win & Pl
Career Total (Turf)	9	2	1	1	38534

100 4/01 Kemp 1m A SFT £15600
84 10/00 Yarm 1m3y D HVY £3233
Total win prize-money £18834

Going (Turf): Sf: 2-3 GS: 0-1 Gd: 0-2 GF: 0-0 Fm: 0-1
Distance: 5f/6f: 0-0 7f-8f: 1-5 9f-13f: 1-3 14f+: 0-0
Track : LH: 0-1 **RH: 1-1** Tight: 0-0 Gall: 0-1
Aids: Bl: 0-0 Vi: 0-0 Tstrap: 0-0
Best Rating: 108 7/01 NmkJ 1m good

Battled home well in the Masaka Stakes at Kempton on her reappearance and finished a fine third on much faster ground in the Musidora at York. Best run since was when second in Newmarket's Child Stakes. Has won over a mile. Should stay a mile and a half. Acts on soft ground, handles firm.

Hefin

98 **45**

4-y-o ch g Red Rainbow-Summer Impressions (USA) (Lyphard (USA))
S C Williams Tyrnest Ltd

Placings:0004-03 **(5632)**
2001: 10^{0}HY, 10^{3}G

	Starts	1st	2nd	3rd	Win & Pl
Career Total (Turf)	6	0	0	1	780

Going (Turf): Sf: 0-2 GS: 0-0 Gd: 0-2 GF: 0-1 Fm: 0-1
Distance: 5f/6f: 0-0 7f-8f: 0-1 9f-13f: 0-5 14f+: 0-0
Track : LH: 0-3 RH: 0-2 Tight: 0-3 Gall: 0-2
Aids: Bl: 0-0 Vi: 0-0 Tstrap: 0-0
Best Rating: 45 11/01 Rdcr 1m2f good

Maiden, who has shown ability, and should pick up a handicap.

Heir To Be

81 **58**

2-y-o b c Elmaamul (USA)-Princess Genista (Ile De Bourbon (USA))
J L Dunlop I H Stewart-Brown

Placings:00 **(5684)**
2001: 7^{0}S, 8^{0}S

	Starts	1st	2nd	3rd	Win & Pl
Career Total (Turf)	2	0	0	0	

Going (Turf): Sf: 0-2 GS: 0-0 Gd: 0-0 GF: 0-0 Fm: 0-0
Distance: 5f/6f: 0-0 7f-8f: 0-2 9f-13f: 0-0 14f+: 0-0
Track : LH: 0-0 RH: 0-0 Tight: 0-0 Gall: 0-0
Aids: Bl: 0-0 Vi: 0-0 Tstrap: 0-0
Best Rating: 58 11/01 Donc 1m soft

Hejaziah (USA)

87 **90**

3-y-o b f Gone West (USA)-Toptrestle (USA) (Nijinsky (CAN))
P F I Cole H R H Prince Fahd Salman

Placings:2311-6 **(0746)**
2001: 8^{6}S

	Starts	1st	2nd	3rd	Win & Pl
Career Total (Turf)	5	2	1	1	32628

90 7/00 Siro 7f110y G-F £22772
86 6/00 Asct 6f D G-F £6841
Total win prize-money £29613

Going (Turf): Sf: 0-2 GS: 0-1 Gd: 0-0 **GF: 2-2** Fm: 0-0
Distance: 5f/6f: 1-3 7f-8f: 1-2 9f-13f: 0-0 14f+: 0-0
Track : LH: 0-0 **RH: 1-2** Tight: 0-0 Gall: 0-0
Aids: Bl: 0-0 Vi: 0-0 Tstrap: 0-0
Best Rating: 77 4/01 Kemp 1m soft

She improved steadily at two, ending the season with victories in an Ascot novice stakes and a San Siro Listed event, but was not seen after running poorly on her reappearance.

Helali Manor

86(46) **15**

3-y-o b f Muhtarram (USA)-Royal Mazi (King's Lake (USA))

G P Kelly A M McArdle

Placings:060-0000000000060000 **(5686)**

2001: 6^{0}G, 5^{0}G, 8^{0}GF, 8^{0}GF, 7^{0}F, 10^{0}GF, 11^{0}S, 8^{0}SD, 9^{0}GF, 6^{0}HY, 8^{0}GS, 6^{0}GF, 5^{0}G, 7^{0}GS, 5^{0}G, 10^{0}S

	Starts	1st	2nd	3rd	Win & Pl
Career Total (Turf)	18	0	0	0	171
Career Total (AW)	1	0	0	0	

Going (Turf): Sf: 0-4 GS: 0-2 Gd: 0-6 GF: 0-5 Fm: 0-1
Distance: 5f/6f: 0-7 7f-8f: 0-7 9f-13f: 0-5 14f+: 0-0
Track : LH: 0-7 RH: 0-2 Tight: 0-2 Gall: 0-2
Aids: Bl: 0-0 Vi: 0-0 Tstrap: 0-0
Best Rating: 33 5/01 Ayr 1m gd-fm

Helen Albadou (USA)

(97) (62)**70**

4-y-o b f Sheikh Albadou-Sister Troy (USA) (Far North (CAN))

K R Burke Lifestyle Bloodstock (uk) Ltd No 1

Placings:3/10-4050 **(3239)**

2001: 6^{4}SD, 7^{0}GF, 5^{5}SD, 6^{0}SD

	Starts	1st	2nd	3rd	Win & Pl
Career Total (Turf)	4	1	0	1	2784
Career Total (AW)	3	0	0	0	0

67 4/00 Nott 5f13y F SFT £2352
Total win prize-money £2352

Going (Turf): Sf: 1-1 GS: 0-0 Gd: 0-1 GF: 0-2 Fm: 0-0
Distance: 5f/6f: 1-6 7f-8f: 0-1 9f-13f: 0-0 14f+: 0-0
Track : LH: 0-2 RH: 0-2 Tight: 0-1 Gall: 0-2
Aids: Bl: 0-0 Vi: 0-0 Tstrap: 0-0
Best Rating: 62 5/01 Wolv 6f stand

Helen Bradley (IRE)

95 **81**

2-y-o ch f Indian Ridge-Touraya (Tap On Wood)

N P Littmoden Richard Green (fine Paintings)

Placings:10 **(5144)**

2001: 6^{1}G, 7^{0}G

	Starts	1st	2nd	3rd	Win & Pl
Career Total (Turf)	2	1	0	0	3738

81 9/01 Nott 6f15y D GD £3737
Total win prize-money £3738

Going (Turf): Sf: 0-0 GS: 0-0 **Gd: 1-2** GF: 0-0 Fm: 0-0
Distance: 5f/6f: 0-0 **7f-8f: 1-2** 9f-13f: 0-0 14f+: 0-0
Track : LH: 0-0 RH: 0-0 Tight: 0-0 Gall: 0-0
Aids: Bl: 0-0 Vi: 0-0 Tstrap: 0-0
Best Rating: 81 9/01 Nott 6f15y good

A half-sister to Group Three winner Tarwiya, who finished third in the Irish 1000 Guineas, she won over six furlongs on her racecourse debut at Nottingham, but was found out when jumped up in class to the Oh So Sharp Stakes at Newmarket next time.

Helical Girl

93(85) (36)**37**

3-y-o b f Presidium-Oubeck (Mummy's Game)

R M H Cowell Glyn Lewis

Placings:4045 **(5617)**

2001: 7^{4}F, 8^{0}S, 7^{4}SD, 8^{5}SD

	Starts	1st	2nd	3rd	Win & Pl
Career Total (Turf)	2	0	0	0	327
Career Total (AW)	2	0	0	0	0

Going (Turf): Sf: 0-1 GS: 0-0 Gd: 0-0 GF: 0-0 Fm: 0-1
Distance: 5f/6f: 0-0 7f-8f: 0-2 9f-13f: 0-2 14f+: 0-0
Track : LH: 0-3 RH: 0-1 Tight: 0-3 Gall: 0-0
Aids: Bl: 0-2 Vi: 0-2 Tstrap: 0-0
Best Rating: 37 8/01 Thsk 7f firm

Hello Holly

104 **49**

4-y-o b f Lake Coniston (IRE)-Amandine (IRE) (Darshaan)

Mrs A L M King Aiden Murphy

Placings:000/60300-00222435310 **(4953)**

2001: 9^{0}F, 9^{0}G, 10^{2}G, 10^{2}G, 11^{2}GF, 10^{4}GF, 12^{3}GS, 12^{5}GF, 9^{3}GF, 13^{1}F, 16^{0}GS

	Starts	1st	2nd	3rd	Win & Pl
Career Total (Turf)	19	1	3	3	7425

49 9/01 Bath 1m5f22y E(0-70)H FRM £3045
Total win prize-money £3045

Going (Turf): Sf: 0-2 GS: 0-3 Gd: 0-5 GF: 0-7 **Fm: 1-2**
Distance: 5f/6f: 0-0 7f-8f: 0-5 9f-13f: 0-12 **14f+: 1-2**
Track : LH: 1-9 RH: 0-7 **Tight: 1-6** Gall: 0-2
Aids: Bl: 0-0 Vi: 0-0 Tstrap: 0-0
Best Rating: 49 9/01 Bath 1m5f22y firm

Hello Schatzi

(68) (12)

5-y-o b g Ardkinglass-Hotaria (Sizzling Melody)

Miss A Stokell M F Barraclough

Placings:0 **(1450)**

2001: 9^{0}SD

	Starts	1st	2nd	3rd	Win & Pl
Career Total (Turf)	0	0	0	0	
Career Total (AW)	1	0	0	0	

Going (Turf): Sf: 0-0 GS: 0-0 Gd: 0-0 GF: 0-0 Fm: 0-0
Distance: 5f/6f: 0-0 7f-8f: 0-0 9f-13f: 0-1 14f+: 0-0
Track : LH: 0-1 RH: 0-0 Tight: 0-1 Gall: 0-0
Aids: Bl: 0-0 Vi: 0-0 Tstrap: 0-0
Best Rating: 12 5/01 Wolv 1m1f79y stand

Hello Sweety

108(81) (34)**77**

3-y-o br f Shaamit (IRF)-Madam Brady (USA) (Lomond (USA))

G C Bravery Khalifa Dasmal

Placings:5-15 **(3247)**

2001: 10^{1}GF, 10^{5}GS

	Starts	1st	2nd	3rd	Win & Pl
Career Total (Turf)	2	1	0	0	4466
Career Total (AW)	1	0	0	0	0

77 6/01 Kemp 1m2f D G-F £4465
Total win prize-money £4466

Going (Turf): Sf: 0-0 GS: 0-1 Gd: 0-0 **GF: 1-1** Fm: 0-0
Distance: 5f/6f: 0-0 7f-8f: 0-1 **9f-13f: 1-2** 14f+: 0-0
Track : LH: 0-1 **RH: 1-1** Tight: 0-0 **Gall: 1-1**
Aids: Bl: 0-0 Vi: 0-0 Tstrap: 0-0
Best Rating: 77 6/01 Kemp 1m2f gd-fm

Hello Vegas

91(76) (17)**13**

4-y-o b g First Trump-Meet Again (Lomond (USA))

Mrs Lydia Pearce (J Pearce 13/2) Roberto Favarulo

Placings:6/04P-000000 **(5557)**

2001: 7^{0}SD, 12^{0}SW, 11^{0}SD, 10^{0}S, 11^{0}S, 14^{0}S

	Starts	1st	2nd	3rd	Win & Pl
Career Total (Turf)	7	0	0	0	307
Career Total (AW)	3	0	0	0	

Going (Turf): Sf: 0-3 GS: 0-1 Gd: 0-1 GF: 0-2 Fm: 0-0
Distance: 5f/6f: 0-0 7f-8f: 0-2 9f-13f: 0-7 14f+: 0-1
Track : LH: 0-6 RH: 0-3 Tight: 0-4 Gall: 0-0
Aids: Bl: 0-0 Vi: 0-2 Tstrap: 0-0
Best Rating: 17 2/01 Sthl 7f stand

Hellofabundle

88 **32**

3-y-o b g Phountzi (USA)-Helleborus (King Of Spain)

T D McCarthy Ken Butler

Placings:030-00000 **(5278)**

2001: 11^{0}GF, 8^{0}GF, 8^{0}G, 9^{0}S, 9^{0}GS

	Starts	1st	2nd	3rd	Win & Pl
Career Total (Turf)	8	0	0	1	596

Going (Turf): Sf: 0-1 GS: 0-1 Gd: 0-1 GF: 0-4 Fm: 0-1
Distance: 5f/6f: 0-1 7f-8f: 0-2 9f-13f: 0-5 14f+: 0-0
Track : LH: 0-5 RH: 0-1 Tight: 0-3 Gall: 0-0
Aids: Bl: 0-1 Vi: 0-0 Tstrap: 0-0
Best Rating: 32 6/01 Nott 1m54y gd-fm

Helloimustbegoing (USA)

101 **78**

2-y-o b f Red Ransom (USA)-Arsaan (USA) (Nureyev (USA))

E A L Dunlop Maktoum Al Maktoum

Placings:2 **(4038)**

2001: 7^{2}G

	Starts	1st	2nd	3rd	Win & Pl
Career Total (Turf)	1	0	1	0	1278

Going (Turf): Sf: 0-0 GS: 0-0 Gd: 0-1 GF: 0-0 Fm: 0-0
Distance: 5f/6f: 0-0 7f-8f: 0-1 9f-13f: 0-0 14f+: 0-0
Track : LH: 0-0 RH: 0-0 Tight: 0-0 Gall: 0-0
Aids: Bl: 0-0 Vi: 0-0 Tstrap: 0-0
Best Rating: 78 8/01 NmkJ 7f good

Helvetius

98(92) (48)**73**

5-y-o b g In The Wings-Hejraan (USA) (Alydar (USA))

P C Ritchens John Pearl

Placings:2/435133560/546-0460 **(1719)**

2001: 14^{0}SD, 11^{4}GF, 12^{6}S, 13^{0}GF

	Starts	1st	2nd	3rd	Win & Pl
Career Total (Turf)	16	1	1	3	13703
Career Total (AW)	1	0	0	0	

55 5/99 Brig 1m3f196yD FRM £4380
Total win prize-money £4380

Going (Turf): Sf: 0-3 GS: 0-2 Gd: 0-4 GF: 0-6 **Fm: 1-1**
Distance: 5f/6f: 0-0 7f-8f: 0-1 **9f-13f: 1-13** 14f+: 0-3
Track : LH: 1-9 RH: 0-8 Tight: 0-4 Gall: 0-6
Aids: Bl: 0-1 Vi: 0-0 Tstrap: 0-0
Best Rating: 66 5/01 Brig 1m3f196y gd-fm

Henri Lebasque (IRE)

108 **101**

2-y-o b c Sri Pekan (USA)-Almost A Lady (IRE) (Entitled)

P F I Cole Richard Green (fine Paintings)

Placings:131 **(4781)**

2001: 6^{1}GF, 7^{3}GF, 8^{1}G

	Starts	1st	2nd	3rd	Win & Pl
Career Total (Turf)	3	2	0	1	21634

101 9/01 Gdwd 1m A GD £13516
89 6/01 Gdwd 6f D G-F £6987
Total win prize-money £20505

Going (Turf): Sf: 0-0 GS: 0-0 **Gd: 1-1 GF: 1-2** Fm: 0-0

Distance: 5f/6f: 1-1 7f-8f: 1-2 9f-13f: 0-0 14f+: 0-0
Track : LH: 0-0 **RH: 1-1** Tight: 0-0 Gall: 0-0
Aids: Bl: 0-0 Vi: 0-0 Tstrap: 0-0
Best Rating: 101 9/01 Gdwd 1m good

Looked smart when beating subsequent Group Two winner Mister Cosmi on his debut at Goodwood over six furlongs. Staying-on third next time out over seven at Doncaster. Stayed the mile well enough, but took time to get into gear, when winning a Listed event back at Goodwood in September.

Henry Hall (IRE)

110 **94**

5-y-o b h Common Grounds-Sovereign Grace (IRE) (Standaan (FR))
N Tinkler Mr James Marshall & Mrs Susan Marshall

Placings:12311540/202026000200/606003110000-54200400510 **(5341)**
2001: 5^5GF, 5^4GF, 5^2GF, 5^0GF, 5^0GF, 5^4GF, 5^0GF, 5^0G, 5^5G, 5^1G, 5^0GS

	Starts	1st	2nd	3rd	Win & Pl
Career Total (Turf)	44	6	6	2	79869

94	9/01	NmkR	5f	C(0-95)H	GD	£14137
98	6/00	Newc	5f	B(0-105)H	FRM	£17875
93	6/00	York	5f	C(0-100)H	GD	£7507
90	7/98	Donc	5f	D	G-F	£3492
90	7/98	Bevl	5f	D	GD	£3210
79	5/98	Thsk	5f	F	G-F	£2722

Total win prize-money £48947

Going (Turf): Sf: 0-4 GS: 0-5 **Gd: 3-13** GF: 2-20 Fm: 1-2
Distance: **5f/6f: 6-43** 7f-8f: 0-1 9f-13f: 0-0 14f+: 0-0
Track : LH: 0-1 RH: 0-1 Tight: 0-1 Gall: 0-1
Aids: Bl: 0-0 Vi: 0-1 Tstrap: 0-0
Best Rating: 94 9/01 NmkR 5f good

A five-furlong specialist, he won twice in June of last year and has run several creditable races in top-class sprint handicaps since. Ran well to finish runner-up in a very valuable handicap at Windsor in June, and again from a good draw at Ascot in July. Beat a big field at Newmarket in September. Effective when held up or ridden positively, he is game. Acts on good or fast ground.

Henry Harber (IRE)

78(61) (8)**30**

3-y-o b g Dilum (USA)-Marguerite Bay (IRE) (Darshaan)
T E Powell Lawrence Pratt

Placings:0600 **(4641)**
2001: 8^0SD, 9^6F, 8^0GF, 7^0GF

	Starts	1st	2nd	3rd	Win & Pl
Career Total (Turf)	3	0	0	0	0
Career Total (AW)	1	0	0	0	

Going (Turf): Sf: 0-0 GS: 0-0 Gd: 0-0 GF: 0-2 Fm: 0-1
Distance: 5f/6f: 0-0 7f-8f: 0-2 9f-13f: 0-2 14f+: 0-0
Track : LH: 0-2 RH: 0-1 Tight: 0-2 Gall: 0-0
Aids: Bl: 0-0 Vi: 0-0 Tstrap: 0-0
Best Rating: 30 6/01 Ling 1m1f firm

Henry Island (IRE)

105(100) (75)**68**

8-y-o ch g Sharp Victor (USA)-Monterana (Sallust)
Mrs A J Bowlby J G Hickford

Placings:4/321050241/010004/300/0-612040014 **(5692)**
2001: 16^6SD, 12^1SW, 12^2SW, 16^0GF, 11^4G, 11^0G, 14^0G, 12^1G, 16^4S

	Starts	1st	2nd	3rd	Win & Pl
Career Total (Turf)	24	4	2	2	35757
Career Total (AW)	5	1	1	0	3752

62	11/01	Muss	1m4f	E(0-70)H	GD	£3262
75	2/01	Sthl	1m4f	E(0-65)	SLW	£2912
93	5/98	Gdwd	1m6f	B(0-105)H	G-F	£9228
93	10/96	Donc	1m4f	C(0-100)H	GD	£12232
73	5/96	Leic	1m8y	F	G-S	£3003

Total win prize-money £30639

Going (Turf): Sf: 0-4 GS: 1-3 **Gd: 2-9** GF: 1-8 Fm: 0-0
Distance: 5f/6f: 0-0 7f-8f: 0-2 **9f-13f: 4-17** 14f+: 1-10
Track : **LH: 2-15** RH: 1-11 Tight: 1-6 Gall: 1-10
Aids: Bl: 0-0 Vi: 0-0 Tstrap: 0-0
Best Rating: 75 2/01 Sthl 1m4f slow

Described as a 'quirky character' by his trainer, he needs things to fall just right for him. He is nowhere near as good as he was, but got his head in front over a mile and a half twice in 2001, including in November at Musselburgh. Effective on the All-weather and on any going on turf.

Henry Pearson (USA)

100 **54d**

3-y-o ch c Distant View (USA)-Lady Ellen (USA) (Explosive Bid (USA))
T H Caldwell Hogarth Racing

Placings:050-000006400 **(4570)**
2001: 7^0GS, 6^0S, 8^0GF, 10^0GF, 10^0GF, 10^6G, 10^4G, 10^0HY, 11^0HY

	Starts	1st	2nd	3rd	Win & Pl
Career Total (Turf)	12	0	0	0	0

Going (Turf): Sf: 0-3 GS: 0-4 Gd: 0-2 GF: 0-3 Fm: 0-0
Distance: 5f/6f: 0-4 7f-8f: 0-1 9f-13f: 0-7 14f+: 0-0
Track : LH: 0-7 RH: 0-0 Tight: 0-1 Gall: 0-0
Aids: Bl: 0-0 Vi: 0-2 Tstrap: 0-0
Best Rating: 63 5/01 Hayd 6f soft

Henry Tun

98(106) (54)**50**

3-y-o b g Chaddleworth (IRE)-B Grade (Lucky Wednesday)
Miss J F Craze Mrs O Tunstall

Placings:600-3615600255060 **(5639)**
2001: 6^3SD, 6^6SW, 5^1SD, 5^5GS, 5^6GF, 5^0SD, 5^0SD, 6^2SD, 6^5S, 5^5GF, 5^0SW, 5^6SD, 5^0G

	Starts	1st	2nd	3rd	Win & Pl
Career Total (Turf)	7	0	0	0	0
Career Total (AW)	9	1	1	1	3989

53	4/01	Sthl	5f	E(0-70)H	STD	£2814

Total win prize-money £2814

Going (Turf): Sf: 0-1 GS: 0-1 Gd: 0-1 GF: 0-3 Fm: 0-1
Distance: **5f/6f: 1-15** 7f-8f: 0-1 9f-13f: 0-0 14f+: 0-0
Track : LH: 0-5 RH: 0-1 Tight: 0-2 Gall: 0-1
Aids: Bl: 0-0 Vi: 0-1 **Tstrap: 1-11**
Best Rating: 54 7/01 Wolv 6f stand

A half-brother to the useful handicapper Tom Tun, he has become disappointing on both grass and sand and does not always show the right attitude.

Henry's Hero

92 **68**

2-y-o b c Pyramus (USA)-Casbatina (Castle Keep)
C A Dwyer (G Brown 17/7) Mrs K W Sneath

Placings:051 **(5079)**
2001: 5^0GS, 5^5F, 5^1S

	Starts	1st	2nd	3rd	Win & Pl
Career Total (Turf)	3	1	0	0	1946

68	10/01	Brig	5f59y	G	SFT	£1946

Total win prize-money £1946

Going (Turf): Sf: 1-1 GS: 0-1 Gd: 0-0 GF: 0-0 Fm: 0-1
Distance: **5f/6f: 1-3** 7f-8f: 0-0 9f-13f: 0-0 14f+: 0-0
Track : **LH: 1-2** RH: 0-0 Tight: 0-0 Gall: 0-0
Aids: Bl: 0-0 Vi: 0-0 Tstrap: 0-0
Best Rating: 68 10/01 Brig 5f59y soft

He landed a gamble in a Brighton seller on his third start, but may struggle against better company.

Her Own Way (USA)

101 **81**

4-y-o b f Danzig (USA)-Formidable Lady (USA) (Silver Hawk (USA))
J H M Gosden George Strawbridge

Placings:4/3-00 **(4984)**
2001: 8^0G, 12^0G

	Starts	1st	2nd	3rd	Win & Pl
Career Total (Turf)	4	0	0	1	1338

Going (Turf): Sf: 0-1 GS: 0-0 Gd: 0-3 GF: 0-0 Fm: 0-0
Distance: 5f/6f: 0-0 7f-8f: 0-2 9f-13f: 0-2 14f+: 0-0
Track : LH: 0-0 RH: 0-2 Tight: 0-0 Gall: 0-1
Aids: Bl: 0-1 Vi: 0-0 Tstrap: 0-0
Best Rating: 81 9/01 Asct 1m4f good

Lightly raced, she looked outclassed when well beaten in a Listed race at four. Stays a mile.

Heracles

70 **72**

5-y-o b g Unfuwain (USA)-La Masse (High Top)
B G Powell Mrs D A La Trobe

Placings:634100624-0 **(1187)**
2001: 11^0GF

	Starts	1st	2nd	3rd	Win & Pl
Career Total (Turf)	10	1	1	1	6809

72	7/00	Catt	1m5f175yD		G-F	£2769

Total win prize-money £2769

Going (Turf): Sf: 0-3 GS: 0-1 Gd: 0-2 **GF: 1-4** Fm: 0-0
Distance: 5f/6f: 0-0 7f-8f: 0-0 9f-13f: 0-6 **14f+: 1-4**
Track : **LH: 1-7** RH: 0-3 **Tight: 1-6** Gall: 0-0
Aids: Bl: 0-0 Vi: 0-0 Tstrap: 0-0
Best Rating: 25 5/01 Brig 1m3f196y gd-fm

Herbie's Move

3-y-o b g Contract Law (USA)-Megan's Move (Move Off)
W Storey H S Hutchinson

Placings:0 **(5634)**
2001: 11^0G

	Starts	1st	2nd	3rd	Win & Pl
Career Total (Turf)	1	0	0	0	

Going (Turf): Sf: 0-0 GS: 0-0 Gd: 0-1 GF: 0-0 Fm: 0-0
Distance: 5f/6f: 0-0 7f-8f: 0-0 9f-13f: 0-1 14f+: 0-0
Track : LH: 0-1 RH: 0-0 Tight: 0-1 Gall: 0-0
Aids: Bl: 0-0 Vi: 0-0 Tstrap: 0-0

Here Comes Tom

47 **2**

3-y-o b g Puissance-Young Holly (Risk Me (FR))
Jamie Poulton Mrs S T Larner

Placings:00 **(5522)**
2001: 7^0S, 6^0HY

	Starts	1st	2nd	3rd	Win & Pl
Career Total (Turf)	2	0	0	0	

Going (Turf): Sf: 0-2 GS: 0-0 Gd: 0-0 GF: 0-0 Fm: 0-0
Distance: 5f/6f: 0-1 7f-8f: 0-1 9f-13f: 0-0 14f+: 0-0
Track : LH: 0-0 RH: 0-0 Tight: 0-0 Gall: 0-0
Aids: Bl: 0-0 Vi: 0-0 Tstrap: 0-0
Best Rating: 2 10/01 Wind 6f heavy

Heretic

107 **92+**

3-y-o b c Bishop Of Cashel-Barford Lady (Stanford)
J R Fanshawe Barford Bloodstock

Placings:61-100 **(2371)**
2001: 8^{1}S, 8^{0}G, 7^{0}GF

	Starts	1st	2nd	3rd	Win & Pl
Career Total (Turf)	5	2	0	0	11252

92 4/01 Kemp 1m C SFT £6662
89 10/00 NmkR 6f D SFT £4589
Total win prize-money £11252

Going (Turf): Sf: 2-3 GS: 0-0 Gd: 0-1 GF: 0-1 Fm: 0-0
Distance: 5f/6f: 1-1 7f-8f: 1-4 9f-13f: 0-0 14f+: 0-0
Track : LH: 0-0 **RH: 1-1** Tight: 0-0 Gall: 0-0
Aids: Bl: 0-0 Vi: 0-0 Tstrap: 0-0
Best Rating: 92 4/01 Kemp 1m soft

Reappeared to win a classified stakes over a mile at Kempton in April, but was out of his depth in the Guineas and did not show much on one more start in handicap company.

Hermit's Hideaway

95(77) (32)**46**

4-y-o b g Rock City-Adriya (Vayrann)
T D Barron B Elsworth

Placings:533-0000 **(5288)**
2001: 7^{0}SW, 5^{0}GF, 5^{0}G, 6^{0}HY

	Starts	1st	2nd	3rd	Win & Pl
Career Total (Turf)	6	0	0	2	1129
Career Total (AW)	1	0	0	0	

Going (Turf): Sf: 0-1 GS: 0-0 Gd: 0-1 GF: 0-3 Fm: 0-1
Distance: 5f/6f: 0-4 7f-8f: 0-3 9f-13f: 0-0 14f+: 0-0
Track : LH: 0-3 RH: 0-0 Tight: 0-3 Gall: 0-0
Aids: Bl: 0-0 Vi: 0-0 Tstrap: 0-0
Best Rating: 40 9/01 Thsk 5f gd-fm

Hernandita

105 **75**

3-y-o b f Hernando (FR)-Dara Dee (Dara Monarch)
J L Dunlop R N Khan

Placings:02-31002 **(5463)**
2001: 8^{3}HY, 9^{1}S, 10^{0}G, 10^{0}HY, 11^{2}G

	Starts	1st	2nd	3rd	Win & Pl
Career Total (Turf)	7	1	2	1	6951

75 4/01 Nott 1m1f213yD SFT £4134
Total win prize-money £4134

Going (Turf): Sf: 1-4 GS: 0-0 Gd: 0-2 GF: 0-1 Fm: 0-0
Distance: 5f/6f: 0-0 7f-8f: 0-2 **9f-13f: 1-5** 14f+: 0-0
Track : **LH: 1-3** RH: 0-0 Tight: 0-2 Gall: 0-0
Aids: Bl: 0-0 Vi: 0-0 Tstrap: 0-0
Best Rating: 75 10/01 Bath 1m3f144y good

She got off the mark in a slowly-run classified event at Nottingham in April and ran well when tried at an extended 11 furlongs at Bath in October. Looks much better on easy ground.

Hero's Son (FR)

74 **37**

5-y-o ch g Hero's Honor (USA)-Happy Waki (USA) (Miswaki (USA))
J J O'Neill Darren C Mercer

Placings:0/14004001/0 **(1226)**
2001: 18^{0}GF

	Starts	1st	2nd	3rd	Win & Pl
Career Total (Turf)	10	2	0	0	16793

10/99 Pari 1m3f VS £4306
3/99 StCl 1m HLD £8611

Total win prize-money £12917

Going (Turf): Sf: 0-0 GS: 0-0 Gd: 0-0 GF: 0-1 Fm: 0-0
Distance: 5f/6f: 0-0 7f-8f: 0-0 9f-13f: 0-0 14f+: 0-1
Track : LH: 0-1 RH: 0-0 Tight: 0-1 Gall: 0-0
Aids: Bl: 0-0 Vi: 0-0 Tstrap: 0-0
Best Rating: 36 5/01 Ches 2m2f147y gd-fm

Herodotus

108 **100**

3-y-o b c Zafonic (USA)-Thalestria (FR) (Mill Reef (USA))
C E Brittain A J Richards

Placings:15005400 **(5228)**
2001: 8^{1}S, 10^{5}HY, 11^{0}GF, 12^{0}GF, 10^{5}GS, 9^{4}GF, 12^{0}S, 6^{0}S

	Starts	1st	2nd	3rd	Win & Pl
Career Total (Turf)	8	1	0	0	17953

99 4/01 Kemp 1m A SFT £15210
Total win prize-money £15210

Going (Turf): Sf: 1-4 GS: 0-1 Gd: 0-0 GF: 0-3 Fm: 0-0
Distance: 5f/6f: 0-0 **7f-8f: 1-2** 9f-13f: 0-6 14f+: 0-0
Track : LH: 0-2 **RH: 1-4** Tight: 0-0 Gall: 0-4
Aids: Bl: 0-1 Vi: 0-0 Tstrap: 0-1
Best Rating: 104 5/01 Gdwd 1m3f gd-fm

He looked a promising colt when coming late to beat Gryffindor in the Easter Stakes on his debut, but floundered in heavy ground in the Classic Trial at Sandown and has not progressed back on a sound surface.

Heros Fatal (FR)

108 **96**

7-y-o ch g Hero's Honor (USA)-Femme Fatale (FR) (Garde Royale)
M C Pipe Frank A Farrant

Placings:0/00121/5453/301-340 **(5387)**
2001: 16^{3}F, 16^{4}G, 18^{0}GS

	Starts	1st	2nd	3rd	Win & Pl
Career Total (Turf)	16	3	1	3	147610

91 10/00 NmkR 2m2f BH G-S £78000
9/98 Toul 1m4f G-S £20202
8/98 Deau 1m4f110y H GD £10101
Total win prize-money £108303

Going (Turf): Sf: 0-0 **GS: 2-3** Gd: 0-2 GF: 0-3 Fm: 0-3
Distance: 5f/6f: 0-0 7f-8f: 0-2 9f-13f: 1-3 14f+: 1-7
Track : LH: 0-3 **RH: 2-7** Tight: 0-0 **Gall: 1-9**
Aids: Bl: 0-0 Vi: 0-0 Tstrap: 0-0
Best Rating: 96 8/01 Asct 2m45y good

The 2000 Cesarewitch winner, he fell over fences in February and was having his first run since when third in the Northumberland Plate. He has great reserves of stamina and acts on most types of ground.

Herr Trigger

90(87) (61d)**41**

10-y-o gr g Sharrood (USA)-Four-Legged Friend (Aragon)
Dr J D Scargill The Inn Crowd

Placings:450010/**1123U4/221114/2/0633/3135**04600/00 6513405/000-00 **(2669)**
2001: 12^{0}GF, 10^{0}G

	Starts	1st	2nd	3rd	Win & Pl
Career Total (Turf)	25	3	0	3	21315
Career Total (AW)	21	5	4	3	22571

68 5/99 Ling 1m2f E(0-70) STD £2758
81 3/98 Ling 1m2f D(0-80)H SLW £3501
68 6/95 NmkJ 1m2f C(0-90)H G-F £7245
61 6/95 Ripn 1m2f D(0-80)H FRM £3776
60 5/95 NmkR 1m2f D(0-80)H G-F £5832
71 2/94 Ling 1m E(0-70)H STD £2769
57 1/94 Ling 1m G STD £2322
77 9/93 Ling 1m G STD £2532

Total win prize-money £30736

Going (Turf): Sf: 0-0 GS: 0-1 Gd: 0-11 **GF: 2-10** Fm: 1-3
Distance: 5f/6f: 0-2 7f-8f: 3-7 **9f-13f: 5-37** 14f+: 0-0
Track : **LH: 5-26** RH: 2-13 **Tight: 6-28** Gall: 1-8
Aids: **Bl: 8-40** Vi: 0-2 Tstrap: 0-0
Best Rating: 32 6/01 NmkR 1m4f gd-fm

Herring Green

85 **28**

4-y-o b g Greensmith-Jane Herring (Nishapour (FR))
E A Wheeler Four Of A Kind Racing

Placings:00000-00 **(1872)**
2001: 6^{0}F, 7^{0}F

	Starts	1st	2nd	3rd	Win & Pl
Career Total (Turf)	7	0	0	0	

Going (Turf): Sf: 0-1 GS: 0-1 Gd: 0-0 GF: 0-3 Fm: 0-2
Distance: 5f/6f: 0-1 7f-8f: 0-3 9f-13f: 0-3 14f+: 0-0
Track : LH: 0-2 RH: 0-2 Tight: 0-1 Gall: 0-1
Aids: Bl: 0-0 Vi: 0-0 Tstrap: 0-0
Best Rating: 28 5/01 Brig 6f209y firm

Hesperus (IRE)

73 **47**

2-y-o ch c Catrail (USA)-Sweet Pleasure (Sweet Revenge)
R M Beckett John E Guest

Placings:000 **(5037)**
2001: 6^{0}GS, 5^{0}F, 5^{0}G

	Starts	1st	2nd	3rd	Win & Pl
Career Total (Turf)	3	0	0	0	

Going (Turf): Sf: 0-0 GS: 0-1 Gd: 0-1 GF: 0-0 Fm: 0-1
Distance: 5f/6f: 0-3 7f-8f: 0-0 9f-13f: 0-0 14f+: 0-0
Track : LH: 0-2 RH: 0-0 Tight: 0-0 Gall: 0-1
Aids: Bl: 0-0 Vi: 0-0 Tstrap: 0-0
Best Rating: 47 8/01 NmkJ 6f gd-sft

Hetra Hawk

74(77)

5-y-o ch g Be My Guest (USA)-Silver Ore (FR) (Silver Hawk (USA))
W J Musson K L West

Placings:00/00/0-0 **(5106)**
2001: 12^{0}GS

	Starts	1st	2nd	3rd	Win & Pl
Career Total (Turf)	4	0	0	0	
Career Total (AW)	2	0	0	0	

Going (Turf): Sf: 0-1 GS: 0-2 Gd: 0-1 GF: 0-0 Fm: 0-0
Distance: 5f/6f: 0-0 7f-8f: 0-3 9f-13f: 0-3 14f+: 0-0
Track : LH: 0-2 RH: 0-2 Tight: 0-1 Gall: 0-2
Aids: Bl: 0-0 Vi: 0-0 Tstrap: 0-0

Hetra Reef

84(70) **34d**

3-y-o b g First Trump-Cuban Reef (Dowsing (USA))
W J Musson K L West

Placings:000-0000 **(4422)**
2001: 8^{0}S, 8^{0}SD, 8^{0}GF, 10^{0}GF

	Starts	1st	2nd	3rd	Win & Pl
Career Total (Turf)	6	0	0	0	
Career Total (AW)	1	0	0	0	

Going (Turf): Sf: 0-2 GS: 0-0 Gd: 0-0 GF: 0-4 Fm: 0-0
Distance: 5f/6f: 0-0 7f-8f: 0-4 9f-13f: 0-3 14f+: 0-0
Track : LH: 0-5 RH: 0-1 Tight: 0-1 Gall: 0-0
Aids: Bl: 0-0 Vi: 0-0 Tstrap: 0-0

Best Rating: 11 9/01 Ripn 1m2f gd-fm

Hever Golf Glory

(100) (47)**30**

7-y-o b g Efisio-Zaius (Artaius (USA))

C N Kellett D H & Mrs R E Muir

Placings:4231640/4506020000640000/06105600010060 04000/0450303005600033505050-563 (0546)

2001: 11^{5}SD, 8^{6}SD, 11^{3}SD

	Starts	1st	2nd	3rd	Win & Pl
Career Total (Turf)	35	1	2	3	30360
Career Total (AW)	31	2	0	3	6842

72	5/99	Wolv	1m100y	G(0-80)H	STD	£1987
68	2/99	Wolv	1m100y	D(0-85)H	STD	£3420
81	6/97	Taby	1m		GD	£21990

Total win prize-money £27397

Going (Turf): Sf: 0-4 GS: 0-3 **Gd: 1-15** GF: 0-10 Fm: 0-2
Distance: 5f/6f: 0-0 7f-8f: 1-28 **9f-13f: 2-38** 14f+: 0-0
Track : **LH: 3-44** RH: 0-14 **Tight: 2-27** Gall: 0-3
Aids: Bl: 0-1 Vi: 0-3 Tstrap: 0-0
Best Rating: 35 1/01 Sthl 1m3f stand

Hi Buddy

65 (47)**60d**

4-y-o br g High Kicker (USA)-Star Thyme (Point North)

J Mackie R M Mitchell

Placings:6030420/00 (5383)

2001: 9^{0}HY, 13^{0}S

	Starts	1st	2nd	3rd	Win & Pl
Career Total (Turf)	8	0	1	1	1483
Career Total (AW)	1	0	0	0	

Going (Turf): Sf: 0-3 GS: 0-2 Gd: 0-1 GF: 0-2 Fm: 0-0
Distance: 5f/6f: 0-0 7f-8f: 0-6 9f-13f: 0-2 14f+: 0-1
Track : LH: 0-4 RH: 0-4 Tight: 0-5 Gall: 0-0
Aids: Bl: 0-3 Vi: 0-1 Tstrap: 0-0

Hi Ho Silca

90 **63**

2-y-o b f Atraf-You Make Me Real (USA) (Give Me Strength (USA))

M R Channon Aldridge Racing Limited

Placings:62 (4092)

2001: 6^{6}GF, 5^{2}G

	Starts	1st	2nd	3rd	Win & Pl
Career Total (Turf)	2	0	1	0	644

Going (Turf): Sf: 0-0 GS: 0-0 Gd: 0-1 GF: 0-1 Fm: 0-0
Distance: 5f/6f: 0-1 7f-8f: 0-1 9f-13f: 0-0 14f+: 0-0
Track : LH: 0-1 RH: 0-0 Tight: 0-0 Gall: 0-0
Aids: Bl: 0-0 Vi: 0-0 Tstrap: 0-0
Best Rating: 63 8/01 Brig 5f213y good

She has hinted at ability and should win a race as long as her sights are not set too high.

Hi Mujtahid (IRE)

74(101) (40)**21**

7-y-o ch g Mujtahid (USA)-High Tern (High Line)

J M Bradley J M Bradley

Placings:50006632123220/0000000000000001/60005030 00/000200044020100-00000 (5101)

2001: 9^{0}SW, 8^{0}SD, 8^{0}SD, 7^{0}F, 9^{0}GS

	Starts	1st	2nd	3rd	Win & Pl
Career Total (Turf)	34	1	5	2	8184
Career Total (AW)	24	2	1	1	5061

50	12/00	Ling	1m	E(0-75)H	STD	£2327
41	12/98	Wolv	1m100y	F(0-60)H	STD	£1945
50	7/97	Ayr	7f	F(0-60)H	G-F	£2883

Total win prize-money £7156

Going (Turf): Sf: 0-5 GS: 0-5 Gd: 0-7 **GF: 1-13** Fm: 0-4
Distance: 5f/6f: 0-11 **7f-8f: 2-29** 9f-13f: 1-18 14f+: 0-0
Track : **LH: 3-38** RH: 0-9 **Tight: 2-28** Gall: 0-4
Aids: Bl: 0-7 Vi: 0-0 Tstrap: 0-0
Best Rating: 50 7/97 Ayr 7f GF

Hi Nicky

68 **43**

5-y-o ch m High Kicker (USA)-Sharp Top (Sharpo)

D Eddy Dr P And Mrs D M Johnson

Placings:1/46030/00000040-0 (5450)

2001: 8^{0}HY

	Starts	1st	2nd	3rd	Win & Pl
Career Total (Turf)	15	1	0	1	5791

60	5/98	NmkR	6f	D	G-F	£4503

Total win prize-money £4503

Going (Turf): Sf: 0-2 GS: 0-3 Gd: 0-3 **GF: 1-5** Fm: 0-2
Distance: **5f/6f: 1-3** 7f-8f: 0-11 9f-13f: 0-1 14f+: 0-0
Track : LH: 0-6 RH: 0-5 Tight: 0-4 Gall: 0-4
Aids: Bl: 0-0 Vi: 0-0 Tstrap: 0-0
Best Rating: 60 5/98 NmkR 6f GF

Hi Red

94 **74**

2-y-o ch f Atraf-Red River Rose (IRE) (Red Sunset)

J G Portman Christopher Shankland

Placings:24004551260 (4962)

2001: 5^{2}S, 5^{4}GS, 6^{0}F, 6^{0}GF, 7^{4}F, 7^{5}GF, 7^{5}GF, 6^{1}GF, 8^{2}G, 8^{6}F, 8^{0}S

	Starts	1st	2nd	3rd	Win & Pl
Career Total (Turf)	11	1	2	0	5184

74	8/01	Sals	6f212y	F	G-F	£3038

Total win prize-money £3038

Going (Turf): Sf: 0-2 GS: 0-1 Gd: 0-1 **GF: 1-4** Fm: 0-3
Distance: 5f/6f: 0-4 **7f-8f: 1-4** 9f-13f: 0-3 14f+: 0-0
Track : LH: 0-3 RH: 0-0 Tight: 0-1 Gall: 0-1
Aids: **Bl: 1-3** Vi: 0-0 Tstrap: 0-0
Best Rating: 75 4/01 NmkR 5f soft

Overcame a difficult passage to get off the mark at Salisbury, when dropped in class and equipped with blinkers. Stays seven furlongs, acts on fast ground.

Hi-Falutin

70(70) **11**

5-y-o b m Lugana Beach-Hitravelscene (Mansingh (USA))

W M Brisbourne Clayfields Racing

Placings:0/000-000 (3276)

2001: 10^{0}GF, 10^{0}GF, 8^{0}F

	Starts	1st	2nd	3rd	Win & Pl
Career Total (Turf)	4	0	0	0	
Career Total (AW)	3	0	0	0	

Going (Turf): Sf: 0-1 GS: 0-0 Gd: 0-0 GF: 0-2 Fm: 0-1
Distance: 5f/6f: 0-0 7f-8f: 0-2 9f-13f: 0-4 14f+: 0-1
Track : LH: 0-4 RH: 0-1 Tight: 0-5 Gall: 0-0
Aids: Bl: 0-0 Vi: 0-0 Tstrap: 0-0

Hibaat

(84) (14)**34**

5-y-o ch g Zafonic (USA)-Realisatrice (USA) (Raja Baba (USA))

M C Chapman Barry Brown

Placings:0/0500/00000400P0-0 (0008)

2001: 16^{0}SD

	Starts	1st	2nd	3rd	Win & Pl
Career Total (Turf)	6	0	0	0	0
Career Total (AW)	10	0	0	0	0

Going (Turf): Sf: 0-1 GS: 0-1 Gd: 0-2 GF: 0-2 Fm: 0-0
Distance: 5f/6f: 0-1 7f-8f: 0-7 9f-13f: 0-4 14f+: 0-4
Track : LH: 0-13 RH: 0-1 Tight: 0-0 Gall: 0-1
Aids: Bl: 0-0 Vi: 0-0 Tstrap: 0-0

Hibernate (IRE)

102(88) (53)**71**

7-y-o ch g Lahib (USA)-Ministra (USA) (Deputy Minister (CAN))

K R Burke Nigel Shields

Placings:3/2155222110140240/000000420S00000-2104013446 (5382)

2001: 12^{2}GF, 11^{1}GS, 12^{0}GF, 8^{4}GF, 15^{0}GF, 12^{1}GF, 12^{3}G, 10^{4}GF, 10^{4}S, 11^{6}S

	Starts	1st	2nd	3rd	Win & Pl
Career Total (Turf)	37	5	6	2	63537
Career Total (AW)	5	1	1	0	4092

52	8/01	Muss	1m4f	F	G-F	£2376
63	6/01	York	1m3f195y	C(0-95)H	G-S	£11407
83	7/99	Brig	1m3f196y	D(0-85)H	FRM	£6905
76	6/99	Carl	1m4f	D(0-80)H	G-F	£14590
73	6/99	Muss	1m4f	E(0-75)H	GD	£8520
68	2/99	Ling	1m4f	D	STD	£3021

Total win prize-money £46822

Going (Turf): Sf: 0-4 GS: 1-5 Gd: 1-12 **GF: 2-14** Fm: 1-2
Distance: 5f/6f: 0-0 7f-8f: 0-1 **9f-13f: 6-39** 14f+: 0-2
Track : **LH: 3-31** RH: 2-10 **Tight: 2-19** Gall: 1-10
Aids: Bl: 0-0 Vi: 0-2 Tstrap: 0-0
Best Rating: 64 8/01 Epsm 1m4f10y good

He enjoyed quite a bit of success on both turf and sand a couple of years ago, but found things tougher last season Scored for the first time in two years at York in June and added a victory at Musselburgh in August. He shows his best when able to dominate.

Hickleton Dream

100 **36**

4-y-o b f Rambo Dancer (CAN)-Elegant Approach (Prince Ragusa)

G A Swinbank (A B Mulholland 22/6) D Leech

Placings:056-060230 (4858)

2001: 10^{0}GF, 12^{6}G, 12^{0}G, 14^{2}G, 14^{3}GF, 15^{0}GF

	Starts	1st	2nd	3rd	Win & Pl
Career Total (Turf)	9	0	1	1	1438

Going (Turf): Sf: 0-1 GS: 0-0 Gd: 0-3 GF: 0-5 Fm: 0-0
Distance: 5f/6f: 0-0 7f-8f: 0-0 9f-13f: 0-6 14f+: 0-3
Track : LH: 0-7 RH: 0-1 Tight: 0-4 Gall: 0-1
Aids: Bl: 0-0 Vi: 0-0 Tstrap: 0-0
Best Rating: 36 9/01 Rdcr 1m6f19y gd-fm

Hidden Enemy

84 **28**

5-y-o b g Meqdaam (USA)-Orchard Bay (Formidable (USA))

R Hollinshead J Holcombe

Placings:046/00-0 (5626)

2001: 8^{0}GS

	Starts	1st	2nd	3rd	Win & Pl
Career Total (Turf)	5	0	0	0	177
Career Total (AW)	1	0	0	0	0

Going (Turf): Sf: 0-1 GS: 0-3 Gd: 0-1 GF: 0-0 Fm: 0-0
Distance: 5f/6f: 0-0 7f-8f: 0-1 9f-13f: 0-5 14f+: 0-0
Track : LH: 0-5 RH: 0-1 Tight: 0-1 Gall: 0-1
Aids: Bl: 0-0 Vi: 0-0 Tstrap: 0-0
Best Rating: 28 11/01 Nott 1m54y gd-sft

Hidden Fort

94 **66**

4-y-o ch g Mujtahid (USA)-Temple Fortune (USA) (Ziggy's Boy (USA))
Mrs A J Perrett Mrs Amanda Perrett

Placings:510600/0-00 (3702)
2001: 7^{0}GF, 5^{0}G

	Starts	1st	2nd	3rd	Win & Pl
Career Total (Turf)	9	1	0	0	5154
85 6/99 Wind 5f10y	C			G-F	£5154

Total win prize-money £5154

Going (Turf): Sf: 0-2 GS: 0-1 Gd: 0-2 **GF: 1-4** Fm: 0-0
Distance: **5f/6f: 1-6** 7f-8f: 0-3 9f-13f: 0-0 14f+: 0-0
Track : LH: 0-0 **RH: 1-1** Tight: 0-0 **Gall: 1-1**
Aids: Bl: 0-0 Vi: 0-0 Tstrap: 0-0
Best Rating: 66 7/01 Asct 7f gd-fm

Hidden Lake (IRE)

94(85) (40)**41**

3-y-o b g Lake Coniston (IRE)-Valmarana (USA) (Danzig Connection (USA))
Mrs A J Bowlby Mrs Amanda Bowlby

Placings:506-0400060 (3289)
2001: 8^{0}SD, 11^{4}SD, 12^{0}SD, 11^{0}F, 12^{0}GF, 16^{6}G, 16^{0}GF

	Starts	1st	2nd	3rd	Win & Pl
Career Total (Turf)	7	0	0	0	0
Career Total (AW)	3	0	0	0	0

Going (Turf): Sf: 0-1 GS: 0-0 Gd: 0-2 GF: 0-3 Fm: 0-1
Distance: 5f/6f: 0-3 7f-8f: 0-1 9f-13f: 0-4 14f+: 0-2
Track : LH: 0-7 RH: 0-2 Tight: 0-2 Gall: 0-1
Aids: Bl: 0-0 Vi: 0-0 Tstrap: 0-0
Best Rating: 41 7/01 Chep 2m49y good

Hidden Meaning

92 **65**

3-y-o ch f Cadeaux Genereux-Cubby Hole (Town And Country)
R Hannon Lord Carnarvon

Placings:30-60 (1647)
2001: 6^{0}GS, 7^{0}G

	Starts	1st	2nd	3rd	Win & Pl
Career Total (Turf)	4	0	0	1	645

Going (Turf): Sf: 0-0 GS: 0-1 Gd: 0-2 GF: 0-1 Fm: 0-0
Distance: 5f/6f: 0-2 7f-8f: 0-2 9f-13f: 0-0 14f+: 0-0
Track : LH: 0-0 RH: 0-1 Tight: 0-0 Gall: 0-0
Aids: Bl: 0-0 Vi: 0-0 Tstrap: 0-0
Best Rating: 62 5/01 Sals 6f gd-sft

Hidden Peace (USA)

84 **52**

3-y-o ch c Gilded Time (USA)-Sanctuary (Welsh Pageant)
Sir Michael Stoute Maktoum Al Maktoum

Placings:0 (0789)
2001: 6^{0}GS

	Starts	1st	2nd	3rd	Win & Pl
Career Total (Turf)	1	0	0	0	

Going (Turf): Sf: 0-0 GS: 0-1 Gd: 0-0 GF: 0-0 Fm: 0-0
Distance: 5f/6f: 0-1 7f-8f: 0-0 9f-13f: 0-0 14f+: 0-0
Track : LH: 0-0 RH: 0-0 Tight: 0-0 Gall: 0-0
Aids: Bl: 0-0 Vi: 0-0 Tstrap: 0-0
Best Rating: 52 4/01 NmkR 6f gd-sft

Hiddendale (IRE)

99 **88**

2-y-o br f Indian Ridge-That'Ll Be The Day (IRE) (Thatching)
B J Meehan Mrs Susan Roy

Placings:431 (5343)
2001: 6^{4}GF, 6^{3}G, 6^{1}GS

	Starts	1st	2nd	3rd	Win & Pl
Career Total (Turf)	3	1	0	1	32221
88 10/01 NmkR 6f	D			G-S	£5798

Total win prize-money £5798

Going (Turf): Sf: 0-0 **GS: 1-1** Gd: 0-1 GF: 0-1 Fm: 0-0
Distance: **5f/6f: 1-1** 7f-8f: 0-2 9f-13f: 0-0 14f+: 0-0
Track : LH: 0-0 RH: 0-0 Tight: 0-0 Gall: 0-0
Aids: Bl: 0-0 Vi: 0-0 Tstrap: 0-0
Best Rating: 88 10/01 NmkR 6f gd-sft

A half-sister to useful Italian two-year-old That's The Way and 12-14 furlong-winner Majestic Bay. Made a promising debut when fourth of 21 in a competitive Newbury maiden on good to firm over six furlongs, and went on to be third to Madame Boulangere in a valuable auction race at Ascot in September. Got off the mark in a Newmarket maiden. Suited by six furlongs, but likely to get further.

Hideaway Heroine (IRE)

95 **78**

2-y-o ch f Hernando (FR)-Dulcinea (Selkirk (USA))
J W Hills The Phantom Partnership

Placings:0333 (5459)
2001: 7^{0}GF, 7^{3}G, 7^{3}S, 8^{3}G

	Starts	1st	2nd	3rd	Win & Pl
Career Total (Turf)	4	0	0	3	2945

Going (Turf): Sf: 0-1 GS: 0-0 Gd: 0-2 GF: 0-1 Fm: 0-0
Distance: 5f/6f: 0-0 7f-8f: 0-3 9f-13f: 0-1 14f+: 0-0
Track : LH: 0-2 RH: 0-1 Tight: 0-1 Gall: 0-2
Aids: Bl: 0-0 Vi: 0-0 Tstrap: 0-1
Best Rating: 78 10/01 Bath 1m5y good

A 40,000gns yearling, she improved on an encouraging debut at Newmarket when beaten favourite in a Kempton conditions event. Finished in the placings twice when contesting maiden auction races. Has run in a tonge tie.

High And Mighty

99 **86**

6-y-o b g Shirley Heights-Air Distingue (USA) (Sir Ivor)
G Barnett J C Bradbury

Placings:00/012331/26411/00240 (2305)
2001: 12^{0}S, 16^{0}S, 18^{2}GF, 16^{4}GF, 20^{0}GF

	Starts	1st	2nd	3rd	Win & Pl
Career Total (Turf)	18	4	3	2	83818
96 7/99 Gdwd 2m4f	C(0-95)H			G-F	£14410
91 6/99 Asct 2m4f	C(0-95)H			G-F	£29700
76 8/98 Sand 1m6f	D(0-80)H			G-F	£3225
71 5/98 Ches 1m4f66y	C(0-95)H			GD	£8549

Total win prize-money £55884

Going (Turf): Sf: 0-3 GS: 0-2 Gd: 1-3 **GF: 3-10** Fm: 0-0
Distance: 5f/6f: 0-0 7f-8f: 0-2 9f-13f: 1-7 **14f+: 3-9**
Track : LH: 1-6 **RH: 3-10 Tight: 2-8** Gall: 1-6
Aids: Bl: 0-0 **Vi: 3-10** Tstrap: 0-0
Best Rating: 85 5/01 Kemp 2m gd-fm

He stays forever and put up improved performances when completing a big race double at Royal Ascot and Glorious Goodwood in the middle of 1999. Absent after, he reappeared in the spring of 2001 and ran second in the Chester Cup. Effective on a sound surface.

High Barn

86 **32**

4-y-o b f Shirley Heights-Mountain Lodge (Blakeney)
J R Fanshawe Lord Halifax

Placings:043-00 (5263)
2001: 14^{0}HY, 13^{0}GS

	Starts	1st	2nd	3rd	Win & Pl
Career Total (Turf)	5	0	0	1	942

Going (Turf): Sf: 0-3 GS: 0-2 Gd: 0-0 GF: 0-0 Fm: 0-0
Distance: 5f/6f: 0-0 7f-8f: 0-0 9f-13f: 0-3 14f+: 0-2
Track : LH: 0-3 RH: 0-2 Tight: 0-1 Gall: 0-1
Aids: Bl: 0-0 Vi: 0-0 Tstrap: 0-0
Best Rating: 32 10/01 York 1m5f194y gd-sft

Some ability in maidens and looks a stayer.

High Beauty

(74) **36**

4-y-o br f High Kicker (USA)-Tendresse (IRE) (Tender King)
M J Ryan M J Ryan

Placings:000/04040050000653-0 (0261)
2001: 16^{0}SD

	Starts	1st	2nd	3rd	Win & Pl
Career Total (Turf)	16	0	0	1	327
Career Total (AW)	2	0	0	0	

Going (Turf): Sf: 0-6 GS: 0-0 Gd: 0-5 GF: 0-5 Fm: 0-0
Distance: 5f/6f: 0-1 7f-8f: 0-1 9f-13f: 0-13 14f+: 0-3
Track : LH: 0-11 RH: 0-4 Tight: 0-7 Gall: 0-1
Aids: Bl: 0-1 Vi: 0-0 Tstrap: 0-0

High Blade

97 **77**

3-y-o b f Kris-High Atlas (Shirley Heights)
Michael Cunningham (B W Hills 10/7) Jet Syndicate

Placings:3300 (5305a)
2001: 10^{3}G, 10^{3}GF, 12^{0}GY, 9^{0}G

	Starts	1st	2nd	3rd	Win & Pl
Career Total (Turf)	4	0	0	2	1569

Going (Turf): Sf: 0-0 GS: 0-0 Gd: 0-2 GF: 0-1 Fm: 0-0
Distance: 5f/6f: 0-0 7f-8f: 0-0 9f-13f: 0-4 14f+: 0-0
Track : LH: 0-2 RH: 0-0 Tight: 0-0 Gall: 0-1
Aids: Bl: 0-1 Vi: 0-0 Tstrap: 0-0
Best Rating: 77 6/01 York 1m2f85y good

High Chaparral (IRE)

109 **117+**

2-y-o b c Sadler's Wells (USA)-Kasora (IRE) (Darshaan)
A P O'Brien Michael Tabor

Placings:211 (5500)
2001: 7^{2}G, 7^{1}S, 8^{1}HY

	Starts	1st	2nd	3rd	Win & Pl
Career Total (Turf)	3	2	1	0	125900
117 10/01 Donc 1m	A			HVY	£114000
86 10/01 Tipp 7f				SFT	£9660

Total win prize-money £123660

Going (Turf): Sf: 2-2 GS: 0-0 Gd: 0-1 GF: 0-0 Fm: 0-0
Distance: 5f/6f: 0-0 **7f-8f: 2-3** 9f-13f: 0-0 14f+: 0-0
Track : **LH: 1-1** RH: 0-0 Tight: 0-0 Gall: 0-0
Aids: Bl: 0-0 Vi: 0-0 Tstrap: 0-0
Best Rating: 117 10/01 Donc 1m heavy

A half-brother to Irish mile winner Oriental Ben. Finished runner-up on his debut at Punchestown when slowly away then went one better when winning a seven-furlong maiden at Tipperary in October. Ended the season with a game victory in the Racing Post Trophy and looks to have a bright future.

High Diva

(90) (63)**73**

2-y-o b f Piccolo-Gifted (Shareef Dancer (USA))
J W Hills J W Robb

Placings:332 **(5197)**
2001: 7^{3}GF, 7^{3}GF, 8^{2}SD

	Starts	1st	2nd	3rd	Win & Pl
Career Total (Turf)	2	0	0	2	921
Career Total (AW)	1	0	1	0	828

Going (Turf): Sf: 0-0 GS: 0-0 Gd: 0-0 GF: 0-2 Fm: 0-0
Distance: 5f/6f: 0-0 7f-8f: 0-2 9f-13f: 0-1 14f+: 0-0
Track : LH: 0-2 RH: 0-0 Tight: 0-2 Gall: 0-0
Aids: Bl: 0-0 Vi: 0-0 Tstrap: 0-0
Best Rating: 73 8/01 Folk 7f gd-fm

High Drama

101(59) **40**

4-y-o b/br g In The Wings-Maestrale (Top Ville)
W R Muir C L A Edginton

Placings:00000-0043663001100 **(5188)**
2001: 10^{0}GS, 12^{0}SD, 14^{4}GF, 16^{3}F, 18^{6}GF, 16^{6}GF, 14^{3}GF, 16^{0}GS, 16^{0}GF, 16^{1}GF, 15^{1}GF, 17^{0}G, 15^{0}GS

	Starts	1st	2nd	3rd	Win & Pl
Career Total (Turf)	17	2	0	2	5951
Career Total (AW)	1	0	0	0	

40 9/01 Catt 1m7f177yF(0-65)H G-F £2684
38 9/01 Wwck 2m39y F(0-70)H G-F £2506
Total win prize-money £5191

Going (Turf): Sf: 0-0 GS: 0-3 Gd: 0-4 **GF: 2-9** Fm: 0-1
Distance: 5f/6f: 0-0 7f-8f: 0-0 9f-13f: 0-7 **14f+: 2-11**
Track : **LH: 2-11** RH: 0-2 **Tight: 1-10** Gall: 0-1
Aids: Bl: 0-1 Vi: 0-0 Tstrap: 0-0
Best Rating: 40 9/01 Catt 1m7f177y gd-fm

High Esteem

104(104) (49)**53**

5-y-o b g Common Grounds-Whittle Woods Girl (Emarati (USA))
M A Buckley Mrs N W Buckley & Mr G N Buckley

Placings:060/6000440/100050630-60035010401 **(5639)**
2001: 6^{6}SW, 6^{0}SD, 8^{0}SW, 7^{3}SD, 7^{5}SD, 6^{0}G, 5^{1}G, 5^{0}S, 5^{4}G, 5^{0}HY, 5^{1}G

	Starts	1st	2nd	3rd	Win & Pl
Career Total (Turf)	21	2	0	0	5549
Career Total (AW)	9	1	0	2	2824

53 11/01 Catt 5f F GD £2327
49 8/01 Ripn 5f F(0-60)H GD £2779
58 5/00 Sthl 6f F(0-60)H STD £2261
Total win prize-money £7368

Going (Turf): Sf: 0-5 GS: 0-2 **Gd: 2-9** GF: 0-3 Fm: 0-2
Distance: **5f/6f: 3-24** 7f-8f: 0-6 9f-13f: 0-0 14f+: 0-0
Track : **LH: 1-10** RH: 0-0 Tight: 0-3 Gall: 0-0
Aids: Bl: 0-0 Vi: 0-0 Tstrap: 0-0
Best Rating: 53 11/01 Catt 5f good

A plating class sprint handicapper, he has plenty of early pace and appreciated the step back to the minimum trip when winning a seller at Ripon in August and a claimer at Catterick in November. Acts on good ground and Fibresand.

High Finale

100 **83**

2-y-o b f Sure Blade (USA)-High Velocity (Frimley Park)
K T Ivory K T Ivory

Placings:022215050 **(4479)**
2001: 5^{0}S, 5^{2}GS, 5^{2}GF, 5^{2}GF, 5^{1}GF, 5^{5}GF, 5^{0}GF, 5^{5}GF, 5^{0}F

	Starts	1st	2nd	3rd	Win & Pl
Career Total (Turf)	9	1	3	0	7921

83 7/01 Ches 5f16y D G-F £4114
Total win prize-money £4115

Going (Turf): Sf: 0-1 GS: 0-1 Gd: 0-0 **GF: 1-6** Fm: 0-1
Distance: **5f/6f: 1-9** 7f-8f: 0-0 9f-13f: 0-0 14f+: 0-0
Track : **LH: 1-1** RH: 0-0 **Tight: 1-1** Gall: 0-0
Aids: Bl: 0-0 Vi: 0-1 Tstrap: 0-0
Best Rating: 83 8/01 Gdwd 5f gd-fm

She made up for three consecutive second places when bounding away with a Chester maiden though the race took little winning. Outclassed in a Group Three event next time. Has won on good to firm.

High Hoyland

87 **33**

5-y-o b g High Estate-Waffling (Lomond (USA))
Jedd O'Keeffe (M D Hammond 20/2) Mrs L J Gennard

Placings:3330022245020/0 **(2872)**
2001: 8^{0}GF

	Starts	1st	2nd	3rd	Win & Pl
Career Total (Turf)	13	0	3	3	7024
Career Total (AW)	1	0	1	0	660

Going (Turf): Sf: 0-4 GS: 0-1 Gd: 0-2 GF: 0-5 Fm: 0-1
Distance: 5f/6f: 0-0 7f-8f: 0-9 9f-13f: 0-5 14f+: 0-0
Track : LH: 0-8 RH: 0-1 Tight: 0-5 Gall: 0-1
Aids: Bl: 0-1 Vi: 0-0 Tstrap: 0-0
Best Rating: 33 7/01 Ripn 1m gd-fm

High Paddy

60 **9**

2-y-o b g Master Willie-Ivy Edith (Blakeney)
R Ingram Glen Antill

Placings:0 **(4671)**
2001: 8^{0}G

	Starts	1st	2nd	3rd	Win & Pl
Career Total (Turf)	1	0	0	0	

Going (Turf): Sf: 0-0 GS: 0-0 Gd: 0-1 GF: 0-0 Fm: 0-0
Distance: 5f/6f: 0-0 7f-8f: 0-0 9f-13f: 0-1 14f+: 0-0
Track : LH: 0-0 RH: 0-0 Tight: 0-0 Gall: 0-0
Aids: Bl: 0-0 Vi: 0-0 Tstrap: 0-0
Best Rating: 9 9/01 Chep 1m14y good

High Pasture (USA)

99 **60**

3-y-o b/br f El Gran Senor (USA)-Summer Retreat (USA) (Gone West (USA))
R Charlton K Abdulla

Placings:60-050 **(3218)**
2001: 8^{0}GF, 8^{5}G, 10^{0}GF

	Starts	1st	2nd	3rd	Win & Pl
Career Total (Turf)	5	0	0	0	0

Going (Turf): Sf: 0-2 GS: 0-0 Gd: 0-1 GF: 0-2 Fm: 0-0
Distance: 5f/6f: 0-1 7f-8f: 0-2 9f-13f: 0-2 14f+: 0-0
Track : LH: 0-3 RH: 0-1 Tight: 0-1 Gall: 0-2
Aids: Bl: 0-0 Vi: 0-0 Tstrap: 0-0
Best Rating: 60 6/01 Bath 1m5y good

High Pitched

122 **115+**

3-y-o ch c Indian Ridge-Place De L'Opera (Sadler's Wells (USA))
H R A Cecil L Marinopoulos

Placings:231111 **(5595)**
2001: 12^{2}GF, 12^{3}GF, 11^{1}G, 12^{1}G, 12^{1}S, 12^{1}GS

	Starts	1st	2nd	3rd	Win & Pl
Career Total (Turf)	6	4	1	1	48696

115 11/01 NmkR 1m4f A G-S £13804
103 10/01 NmkR 1m4f B(0-100)H SFT £9483
93 9/01 Donc 1m4f B(0-105)H GD £19012
79 8/01 Hayd 1m3f200yD GD £4407
Total win prize-money £46707

Going (Turf): Sf: 1-1 GS: 1-1 **Gd: 2-2** GF: 0-2 Fm: 0-0
Distance: 5f/6f: 0-0 7f-8f: 0-0 **9f-13f: 4-6** 14f+: 0-0
Track : LH: 2-2 RH: 2-4 Tight: 0-0 **Gall: 3-4**
Aids: Bl: 0-0 Vi: 0-0 Tstrap: 0-0
Best Rating: 115 11/01 NmkR 1m4f gd-sft

Somewhat fortunate to keep the race after getting off the mark at Haydock on his third start, although he showed he is a horse of real potential when taking a very hot handicap at Doncaster. Followed up at Newmarket when still looking green and won a Listed event at the same strack. Talented, though the steering has looked decidedly dodgy. Suited by middle distances and acts on good ground.

High Policy (IRE)

105(103) (63)**51**

5-y-o ch g Machiavellian (USA)-Road To The Top (Shirley Heights)
R Hollinshead Mrs Suzy Haslehurst

Placings:0/63/1060230-45040061203 **(5640)**
2001: 16^{4}SW, 16^{5}HY, 14^{0}S, 14^{4}GF, 14^{0}G, 14^{0}GF, 16^{6}GF, 16^{1}G, 17^{2}GS, 17^{0}S, 13^{3}G, 16^{1}SD, 16^{1}SD

	Starts	1st	2nd	3rd	Win & Pl
Career Total (Turf)	15	1	1	2	5236
Career Total (AW)	6	1	1	1	3739

49 9/01 Nott 2m9y F(0-65)H GD £2849
52 2/00 Wolv 1m4f D STD £2613
Total win prize-money £5463

Going (Turf): Sf: 0-4 GS: 0-1 **Gd: 1-3** GF: 0-6 Fm: 0-1
Distance: 5f/6f: 0-0 7f-8f: 0-1 9f-13f: 1-6 14f+: 1-14
Track : **LH: 2-18** RH: 0-1 **Tight: 1-8** Gall: 0-1
Aids: Bl: 0-0 Vi: 0-1 Tstrap: 0-0
Best Rating: 59 1/01 Wolv 2m46y slow

He got off the mark on Fibresand at the start of 2000, but did not win again until a big drop in the handicap helped him score over two miles at Nottingham in September. Stays well and best on good ground or faster on turf. Returned to the sand an improved horse and twice annihilated the opposition at Southwell.

High Prospect (IRE)

93 **50**

3-y-o b g Lycius (USA)-Pay The Bank (High Top)
N A Graham Second Millennium Racing

Placings:0006005 **(5294)**
2001: 10^{0}GS, 10^{0}GS, 10^{0}GF, 9^{6}GS, 9^{0}G, 9^{0}GS, 11^{5}S

	Starts	1st	2nd	3rd	Win & Pl
Career Total (Turf)	7	0	0	0	0

Going (Turf): Sf: 0-1 GS: 0-4 Gd: 0-1 GF: 0-1 Fm: 0-0
Distance: 5f/6f: 0-0 7f-8f: 0-0 9f-13f: 0-7 14f+: 0-0
Track : LH: 0-1 RH: 0-4 Tight: 0-3 Gall: 0-0
Aids: Bl: 0-0 Vi: 0-0 Tstrap: 0-0
Best Rating: 52 4/01 NmkR 1m2f gd-sft

High Rock Henry (IRE)

94 **76**

2-y-o ch c Pennekamp (USA)-Belsay (Belmez (USA))
J Noseda Lucayan Stud

Placings:5040 **(4841)**
2001: 6^{5}GS, 6^{0}G, 5^{4}GF, 6^{0}G

	Starts	1st	2nd	3rd	Win & Pl
Career Total (Turf)	4	0	0	0	266

Going (Turf): Sf: 0-0 GS: 0-1 Gd: 0-2 GF: 0-1 Fm: 0-0
Distance: 5f/6f: 0-2 7f-8f: 0-2 9f-13f: 0-0 14f+: 0-0
Track : LH: 0-1 RH: 0-0 Tight: 0-0 Gall: 0-0
Aids: Bl: 0-0 Vi: 0-0 Tstrap: 0-0
Best Rating: 76 8/01 Brig 5f213y gd-fm

High Show

79 **33**

3-y-o ch g Superlative-Just Like You (Sandhurst Prince)
N M Babbage B Babbage

Placings:00 **(4613)**
2001: 8^{0}G, 11^{0}F

	Starts	1st	2nd	3rd	Win & Pl
Career Total (Turf)	2	0	0	0	

Going (Turf): Sf: 0-0 GS: 0-0 Gd: 0-1 GF: 0-0 Fm: 0-1
Distance: 5f/6f: 0-0 7f-8f: 0-0 9f-13f: 0-2 14f+: 0-0
Track : LH: 0-1 RH: 0-1 Tight: 0-2 Gall: 0-0
Aids: Bl: 0-0 Vi: 0-0 Tstrap: 0-0
Best Rating: 33 8/01 Wind 1m67y good

High Sierra (IRE)

106 **95**

2-y-o b c Danehill (USA)-Direct Lady (IRE) (Fool's Holme (USA))
A P O'Brien Mrs John Magnier & Mr M Tabor

Placings:15 **(5002)**
2001: 8^{1}GF, 8^{5}S

	Starts	1st	2nd	3rd	Win & Pl
Career Total (Turf)	2	1	0	0	8625
86 8/01 Tral 1m				G-F	£8625

Total win prize-money £8625

Going (Turf): Sf: 0-1 GS: 0-0 Gd: 0-0 **GF: 1-1** Fm: 0-0
Distance: 5f/6f: 0-0 **7f-8f: 1-2** 9f-13f: 0-0 14f+: 0-0
Track : LH: 0-0 RH: 0-1 Tight: 0-0 Gall: 0-1
Aids: Bl: 0-0 Vi: 0-0 Tstrap: 0-0
Best Rating: 95 9/01 Asct 1m soft

A son of Danehill, he made a winning debut over a mile at Tralee in August on good to firm. Failed to handle the soft ground behind stablemate Mutinyonthebounty in the Royal Lodge at Ascot.

High Society Lady (IRE)

83(76) (17)**30**

3-y-o ch f General Monash (USA)-Bardia (Jalmood (USA))
N Bycroft The Country Stayers

Placings:000000000-0000000 **(2267)**
2001: 8^{0}SD, 8^{0}SW, 11^{0}SD, 8^{0}S, 7^{0}F, 8^{0}GF, 6^{0}G

	Starts	1st	2nd	3rd	Win & Pl
Career Total (Turf)	12	0	0	0	
Career Total (AW)	5	0	0	0	

Going (Turf): Sf: 0-3 GS: 0-0 Gd: 0-2 GF: 0-6 Fm: 0-1
Distance: 5f/6f: 0-5 7f-8f: 0-9 9f-13f: 0-3 14f+: 0-0
Track : LH: 0-7 RH: 0-4 Tight: 0-2 Gall: 0-2
Aids: Bl: 0-4 Vi: 0-0 Tstrap: 0-0
Best Rating: 30 5/01 Ripn 1m gd-fm

High Spot

97 **69**

3-y-o b f Shirley Heights-Rash Gift (Cadeaux Genereux)
R Charlton The Queen

Placings:05-3040 **(4382)**
2001: 10^{3}GF, 12^{0}GF, 11^{4}GS, 12^{0}GF

	Starts	1st	2nd	3rd	Win & Pl
Career Total (Turf)	6	0	0	1	726

Going (Turf): Sf: 0-1 GS: 0-1 Gd: 0-1 GF: 0-3 Fm: 0-0
Distance: 5f/6f: 0-0 7f-8f: 0-2 9f-13f: 0-4 14f+: 0-0
Track : LH: 0 2 RH: 0-3 Tight: 0-1 Gall: 0-2
Aids: Bl: 0-1 Vi: 0-1 Tstrap: 0-0
Best Rating: 74 7/01 Chep 1m2f36y gd-fm

High Sun

105 **49**

5-y-o b g High Estate-Clyde Goddess (IRE) (Scottish Reel)
P Monteith Mrs V Nyberg

Placings:550/00001030411/400000500550-302125532244060 **(5659)**
2001: 8^{3}GS, 8^{0}GS, 8^{2}GS, 8^{1}GF, 8^{2}GF, 9^{5}G, 9^{5}GS, 8^{3}F, 9^{2}G, 7^{2}GF, 9^{4}G, 9^{4}G, 8^{0}F, 8^{6}GF, 8^{0}G

	Starts	1st	2nd	3rd	Win & Pl
Career Total (Turf)	42	4	4	3	19324
48 5/01 Haml 1m65y E(0-70)H				G-F	£3948
61 10/99 NmkJ 1m E(0-70)H				G-S	£3728
54 10/99 Donc 7f E(0-70)H				G-S	£3048
50 8/99 Leic 1m8y F				G-F	£2511

Total win prize-money £13237

Going (Turf): Sf: 0-6 **GS: 2-8** Gd: 0-12 **GF: 2-13** Fm: 0-3
Distance: 5f/6f: 0-0 7f-8f: 2-21 9f-13f: 2-21 14f+: 0-0
Track : LH: 0-8 **RH: 1-22 Tight: 1-15** Gall: 0-3
Aids: Bl: 0-3 Vi: 0-0 Tstrap: 0-0
Best Rating: 49 9/01 Haml 1m1f36y good

High Tempo

82 **5**

3-y-o b g Piccolo-Reem Fever (IRE) (Fairy King (USA))
K R Burke Haven Partnership

Placings:000-P0000 **(4422)**
2001: 8^{P}HY, 8^{0}F, 7^{0}F, 9^{0}F, 10^{0}GF

	Starts	1st	2nd	3rd	Win & Pl
Career Total (Turf)	8	0	0	0	

Going (Turf): Sf: 0-3 GS: 0-1 Gd: 0-0 GF: 0-1 Fm: 0-3
Distance: 5f/6f: 0-0 7f-8f: 0-4 9f-13f: 0-4 14f+: 0-0
Track : LH: 0-3 RH: 0-1 Tight: 0 1 Gall: 0-1
Aids: Bl: 0-1 Vi: 0-0 Tstrap: 0-6
Best Rating: 5 9/01 Ripn 1m2f gd-fm

High Tension (USA)

84 **71**

6-y-o b h Sadler's Wells (USA)-Very Confidential (USA) (Fappiano (USA))
Miss Z C Davison Feel The Tension

Placings:43/0210/50 **(5600)**
2001: 12^{5}GF, 16^{0}GS

	Starts	1st	2nd	3rd	Win & Pl
Career Total (Turf)	8	1	1	1	6171
71 5/98 Nott 1m6f15y D(0-80)H				FRM	£4012

Total win prize-money £4013

Going (Turf): Sf: 0-0 GS: 0-1 Gd: 0-2 GF: 0-4 **Fm: 1-1**
Distance: 5f/6f: 0-0 7f-8f: 0-3 9f-13f: 0-2 **14f+: 1-3**
Track : **LH: 1-3** RH: 0-4 Tight: 0-1 Gall: 0-3
Aids: Bl: 0-0 Vi: 0-0 Tstrap: 0-0
Best Rating: 37 9/01 Kemp 1m4f gd-fm

High Yielder (IRE)

77 **20**

3-y-o b/br g Namaqualand (USA)-Cadisa (Top Ville)
Pat Mitchell Mrs Catherine Reed

Placings:00000 **(5557)**
2001: 9^{0}GS, 10^{0}GF, 14^{0}F, 11^{0}GF, 14^{0}S

	Starts	1st	2nd	3rd	Win & Pl
Career Total (Turf)	5	0	0	0	

Going (Turf): Sf: 0-1 GS: 0-1 Gd: 0-0 GF: 0-2 Fm: 0-1
Distance: 5f/6f: 0-0 7f-8f: 0-0 9f-13f: 0-3 14f+: 0-2
Track : LH: 0-3 RH: 0-2 Tight: 0-3 Gall: 0-1
Aids: Bl: 0-0 Vi: 0-0 Tstrap: 0-0
Best Rating: 20 9/01 Ling 1m3f106y gd-fm

Highbury Legend

(76) (6)**49**

6-y-o ch g Mazilier (USA)-Jans Contessa (Rabdan)
G Brown T And J A Curry

Placings:0040500/322000200134/05 **(0104)**
2001: 8^{0}SD, 12^{5}SW

	Starts	1st	2nd	3rd	Win & Pl
Career Total (Turf)	9	1	1	1	3416
Career Total (AW)	12	0	2	1	1785
49 6/98 Pont 1m4f8y F(0-60)H				GD	£2595

Total win prize-money £2595

Going (Turf): Sf: 0-0 GS: 0-3 **Gd: 1-3** GF: 0-1 Fm: 0-2
Distance: 5f/6f: 0-3 7f-8f: 0-4 **9f-13f: 1-14** 14f+: 0-0
Track : **LH: 1-15** RH: 0-3 Tight: 0-10 Gall: 0-0
Aids: Bl: 0-0 Vi: 0-2 Tstrap: 0-0
Best Rating: 6 1/01 Wolv 1m4f slow

Highcal

92 **33**

4-y-o gr g King's Signet (USA)-Guarded Expression (Siberian Express (USA))
Ronald Thompson J Lomas

Placings:000/0000110-00000 **(4858)**
2001: 12^{0}GF, 11^{0}GF, 12^{0}GS, 12^{0}G, 15^{0}GF

	Starts	1st	2nd	3rd	Win & Pl
Career Total (Turf)	15	2	0	0	5241
49 8/00 Brig 1m1f209yF(0-65)H				FRM	£2436
42 7/00 Ripn 1m2f F(0-60)H				G-F	£2804

Total win prize-money £5241

Going (Turf): Sf: 0-1 GS: 0-2 Gd: 0-3 **GF: 1-8 Fm: 1-1**
Distance: 5f/6f: 0-0 7f-8f: 0-3 **9f-13f: 2-11** 14f+: 0-1
Track : LH: 1-4 RH: 1-8 **Tight: 1-6** Gall: 0-1
Aids: Bl. 0-1 Vi. 0-0 Tstrap: 0-0
Best Rating: 43 5/01 Muss 1m4f gd-fm

Highdown (IRE)

104 **99**

2-y-o b c Selkirk (USA)-Rispoto (Mtoto)
M R Channon Mrs W W Fleming

Placings:20146015 **(5571a)**
2001: 5^{2}GF, 6^{0}GF, 6^{1}GF, 7^{4}G, 7^{6}GF, 6^{0}Y, 6^{1}S, 6^{5}HY

	Starts	1st	2nd	3rd	Win & Pl
Career Total (Turf)	8	2	1	0	18601
99 10/01 York 6f214y B				SFT	£8149
86 7/01 Gdwd 6f D				G-F	£4251

Total win prize-money £12400

Going (Turf): **Sf: 1-2** GS: 0-0 Gd: 0-1 **GF: 1-4** Fm: 0-0
Distance: 5f/6f: 1-5 7f-8f: 1-3 9f-13f: 0-0 14f+: 0-0
Track : **LH: 1-1** RH: 0-1 Tight: 0-0 **Gall: 1-1**
Aids: Bl: 0-0 Vi: 0-0 Tstrap: 0-0
Best Rating: 99 10/01 York 6f214y soft

He struggled when tried in Pattern company and was dropped back in grade when winning well at York. Stays seven furlongs and acts on any ground. Sold for 100,000 gns in the autumn.

Higher Circle (USA)

93 **84**

2-y-o ch f Diesis-Captive Island (Northfields (USA))
J H M Gosden R E Sangster

Placings:552 **(5147)**
2001: 6^{5}GF, 7^{5}G, 7^{2}G

	Starts	1st	2nd	3rd	Win & Pl
Career Total (Turf)	3	0	1	0	1116

Going (Turf): Sf: 0-0 GS: 0-0 Gd: 0-2 GF: 0-1 Fm: 0-0
Distance: 5f/6f: 0-0 7f-8f: 0-3 9f-13f: 0-0 14f+: 0-0
Track : LH: 0-0 RH: 0-1 Tight: 0-0 Gall: 0-0
Aids: Bl: 0-0 Vi: 0-0 Tstrap: 0-0
Best Rating: 84 10/01 Rdcr 7f good

Good debut run behind a nice sort, Brown Eyes, but failed to progress on that when disappointing next time, although showed improvement when dropped down to seven furlongs at Redcar.

Highest (IRE)

102 **100+**

2-y-o b c Selkirk (USA)-Pearl Kite (USA) (Silver Hawk (USA))
Sir Michael Stoute Highclere Thoroughbred Racing Ltd

Placings:2 **(5361)**
2001: 8^{2}GS

	Starts	1st	2nd	3rd	Win & Pl
Career Total (Turf)	1	0	1	0	1744

Going (Turf): Sf: 0-0 GS: 0-1 Gd: 0-0 GF: 0-0 Fm: 0-0
Distance: 5f/6f: 0-0 7f-8f: 0-1 9f-13f: 0-0 14f+: 0-0
Track : LH: 0-0 RH: 0-0 Tight: 0-0 Gall: 0-0
Aids: Bl: 0-0 Vi: 0-0 Tstrap: 0-0
Best Rating: 100 10/01 NmkR 1m gd-sft

Has stamina and speed in his pedigree. He was flying at the finish and only just denied on his Newmarket debut over a mile.

Highfield Fizz

101 (22)**31**

9-y-o b m Efisio-Jendor (Condorcet (FR))
C W Fairhurst Mrs P J Taylor-Garthwaite

Placings:063034401260/00050601060/020342525352322/05100221360356/006315/00P0016063413000-0605501006000 **(5170)**
2001: 16^{0}S, 13^{6}GF, 16^{0}F, 14^{5}F, 17^{5}GF, 14^{0}GF, 16^{1}GF, 16^{0}GF, 16^{0}F, 15^{6}GS, 14^{0}GF, 17^{0}G, 17^{0}GS

	Starts	1st	2nd	3rd	Win & Pl
Career Total (Turf)	85	8	9	10	41760
Career Total (AW)	2	0	0	0	

38	6/01	Muss	2m	E(0-70)H	G-F	£4095
38	8/00	Ayr	1m7f	E(0-70)H	GD	£2762
44	5/00	Rdcr	1m6f19y	E(0-70)H	G-S	£3672
44	5/99	Muss	2m	F(0-60)H	FRM	£2879
53	6/98	Muss	2m	D(0-75)H	G-F	£3434
50	4/98	Pont	2m1f22y	D(0-80)H	G-S	£3492
44	10/96	Rdcr	1m6f19y	D(0-80)H	G-F	£3951
57	9/95	Rdcr	1m3f	G	GD	£2917

Total win prize-money £27206

Going (Turf): Sf: 0-10 GS: 2-17 Gd: 2-18 **GF: 3-28** Fm: 1-12
Distance: 5f/6f: 0-0 7f-8f: 0-2 9f-13f: 1-17 **14f+: 7-68**
Track : **LH: 5-64** RH: 3-23 **Tight: 6-54** Gall: 0-8
Aids: Bl: 0-0 Vi: 0-3 Tstrap: 0-0
Best Rating: 50 5/01 Newc 2m19y firm

Has notched up eight career wins to date. Stays two miles. Acts on fast ground. Has never won in a visor.

Highland Flight

90 **46**

3-y-o gr f Missed Flight-In The Highlands (Petong)
Bob Jones The Highland Partnership

Placings:0400-00 **(4601)**
2001: 5^{0}G, 5^{0}GF

	Starts	1st	2nd	3rd	Win & Pl
Career Total (Turf)	6	0	0	0	237

Going (Turf): Sf: 0-1 GS: 0-0 Gd: 0-3 GF: 0-2 Fm: 0-0
Distance: 5f/6f: 0-6 7f-8f: 0-0 9f-13f: 0-0 14f+: 0-0
Track : LH: 0-0 RH: 0-0 Tight: 0-0 Gall: 0-0
Aids: Bl: 0-0 Vi: 0-0 Tstrap: 0-0
Best Rating: 46 5/01 Yarm 5f43y good

Highland Gait

87 **69**

2-y-o ch f Most Welcome-Miller's Gait (Mill Reef (USA))
T D Easterby Mrs Ian Wills

Placings:005 **(3039)**
2001: 6^{0}GF, 6^{0}GF, 6^{5}GF

	Starts	1st	2nd	3rd	Win & Pl
Career Total (Turf)	3	0	0	0	0

Going (Turf): Sf: 0-0 GS: 0-0 Gd: 0-0 GF: 0-3 Fm: 0-0
Distance: 5f/6f: 0-2 7f-8f: 0-1 9f-13f: 0-0 14f+: 0-0
Track : LH: 0-1 RH: 0-0 Tight: 0-0 Gall: 0-0
Aids: Bl: 0-0 Vi: 0-0 Tstrap: 0-0
Best Rating: 69 7/01 Nott 6f15y gd-fm

Highland Gold (IRE)

104 **55**

4-y-o ch g Indian Ridge-Anjuli (Northfields (USA))
Miss L A Perratt Miss L A Perratt

Placings:65/35000402-061022022645656 **(4829)**
2001: 9^{0}S, 8^{6}GS, 11^{1}G, 8^{0}GF, 12^{2}G, 13^{2}GS, 12^{0}GF, 14^{2}F, 13^{2}S, 10^{6}S, 11^{4}GS, 11^{5}GS, 14^{6}GF, 12^{5}G, 17^{6}G

	Starts	1st	2nd	3rd	Win & Pl
Career Total (Turf)	25	1	5	1	13372

49	5/01	Haml	1m3f16y	D	GD	£3588

Total win prize-money £3588

Going (Turf): Sf: 0-9 GS: 0-5 **Gd: 1-5** GF: 0-5 Fm: 0-1
Distance: 5f/6f: 0-0 7f-8f: 0-5 **9f-13f: 1-15** 14f+: 0-5
Track : LH: 0-8 **RH: 1-13 Tight: 1-13** Gall: 0-2
Aids: Bl: 0-0 Vi: 0-0 Tstrap: 0-0
Best Rating: 58 7/01 Haml 1m3f16y gd-sft

A big horse, he scored his first success over 11 furlongs on good ground at Hamilton in May, but has shown signs of temperament. Stays a mile and a half.

Highland Reel

111 **98**

4-y-o ch c Selkirk (USA)-Taj Victory (Final Straw)
D R C Elsworth Sir Gordon Brunton

Placings:3033102-20003006 **(3823)**
2001: 8^{2}S, 10^{0}S, 8^{0}GS, 8^{0}GF, 8^{3}GF, 7^{0}G, 8^{0}G, 8^{6}G

	Starts	1st	2nd	3rd	Win & Pl
Career Total (Turf)	15	1	2	4	30438

73	7/00	Wind	1m67y	D	G-F	£4218

Total win prize-money £4219

Going (Turf): Sf: 0-5 GS: 0-2 Gd: 0-4 GF: 0-3 Fm: 0-0
Distance: 5f/6f: 0-0 7f-8f: 0-7 9f-13f: 0-7 14f+: 0-0
Track : LH: 0-3 RH: 0-8 Tight: 0-3 Gall: 0-3
Aids: Bl: 0-0 Vi: 0-0 Tstrap: 0-0
Best Rating: 98 6/01 Epsm 1m114y gd-fm

Winner of a Windsor maiden last season, he was second in the Lincoln on his reappearance, but has not really built on that including when appearing not to get ten furlongs at Kempton in April. Better effort when possibly an unlucky third in a decent handicap at Epsom on Oaks day.

Highland Shot

100 **55**

3-y-o b f Selkirk (USA)-Optaria (Song)
I A Balding J C Smith

Placings:64 **(4989)**
2001: 6^{6}GF, 8^{4}HY

	Starts	1st	2nd	3rd	Win & Pl
Career Total (Turf)	2	0	0	0	354

Going (Turf): Sf: 0-1 GS: 0-0 Gd: 0-0 GF: 0-1 Fm: 0-0
Distance: 5f/6f: 0-0 7f-8f: 0-1 9f-13f: 0-1 14f+: 0-0
Track : LH: 0-1 RH: 0-0 Tight: 0-0 Gall: 0-0
Aids: Bl: 0-0 Vi: 0-0 Tstrap: 0-0
Best Rating: 55 9/01 Hayd 1m30y heavy

Highland Warrior

98 **74**

2-y-o b c Makbul-Highland Rowena (Roybén)
J S Goldie Frank & Annette Brady

Placings:4000 **(4116)**
2001: 6^{4}GF, 5^{0}GF, 5^{0}GF, 6^{0}G

	Starts	1st	2nd	3rd	Win & Pl
Career Total (Turf)	4	0	0	0	0

Going (Turf): Sf: 0-0 GS: 0-0 Gd: 0-1 GF: 0-3 Fm: 0-0
Distance: 5f/6f: 0-4 7f-8f: 0-0 9f-13f: 0-0 14f+: 0-0
Track : LH: 0-0 RH: 0-0 Tight: 0-0 Gall: 0-0
Aids: Bl: 0-0 Vi: 0-0 Tstrap: 0-0
Best Rating: 85 6/01 Ayr 6f gd-fm

Highland Welcome

(96) (42)

5-y-o b g Most Welcome-Highland Hannah (IRE) (Persian Heights)
W Jarvis J M Ratcliffe

Placings:45 **(0053)**
2001: 11^{4}SD, 12^{5}SD

	Starts	1st	2nd	3rd	Win & Pl
Career Total (Turf)	0	0	0	0	
Career Total (AW)	2	0	0	0	0

Going (Turf): Sf: 0-0 GS: 0-0 Gd: 0-0 GF: 0-0 Fm: 0-0
Distance: 5f/6f: 0-0 7f-8f: 0-0 9f-13f: 0-2 14f+: 0-0
Track : LH: 0-2 RH: 0-0 Tight: 0-0 Gall: 0-0
Aids: Bl: 0-0 Vi: 0-0 Tstrap: 0-0
Best Rating: 42 1/01 Sthl 1m3f stand

Highly Fancied

80 **3**

5-y-o b m High Kicker (USA)-Angie's Darling (Milford)
A C Whillans Mrs L M Whillans

Placings:320262344/0006500/000-00 **(3570)**
2001: 7^{0}GS, 12^{0}G

	Starts	1st	2nd	3rd	Win & Pl
Career Total (Turf)	21	0	3	2	4416

Going (Turf): Sf: 0-4 GS: 0-3 Gd: 0-7 GF: 0-4 Fm: 0-3
Distance: 5f/6f: 0-10 7f-8f: 0-8 9f-13f: 0-3 14f+: 0-0
Track : LH: 0-6 RH: 0-5 Tight: 0-4 Gall: 0-4
Aids: Bl: 0-0 Vi: 0-0 Tstrap: 0-2
Best Rating: 3 7/01 Ayr 7f gd-sft

Highly Pleased (USA)

(85) (43)**49**

6-y-o b g Hansel (USA)-Bint Alfalla (USA) (Nureyev (USA))
P Burgoyne (J C Fox 13/8) Mrs C C Regaldo-Gonzalez

Placings:30/23/000006/000-02 **(5617)**
2001: 8^{0}G, 8^{2}SD

	Starts	1st	2nd	3rd	Win & Pl
Career Total (Turf)	13	0	1	2	1751

	Starts	1st	2nd	3rd	Win & Pl
Career Total (AW)	2	0	1	0	872

Going (Turf): Sf: 0-0 GS: 0-1 Gd: 0-6 GF: 0-5 Fm: 0-1
Distance: 5f/6f: 0-0 7f-8f: 0-10 9f-13f: 0-5 14f+: 0-0
Track : LH: 0-3 RH: 0-6 Tight: 0-4 Gall: 0-1
Aids: Bl: 0-0 Vi: 0-0 Tstrap: 0-0
Best Rating: 43 11/01 Wolv 1m100y stand

Lightly raced for a six-year-old, he had shown little to enthuse about until running second in a weak Wolverhampton maiden in November.

Highly Sociable

(76) **24**
4-y-o b f Puissance-Come To Tea (IRE) (Be My Guest (USA))
B A McMahon The Highly Sociable Syndicate

Placings:5300/00-06 **(3237)**
2001: 6^{0}GF, 6^{6}SD

	Starts	1st	2nd	3rd	Win & Pl
Career Total (Turf)	7	0	0	1	420
Career Total (AW)	1	0	0	0	0

Going (Turf): Sf: 0-2 GS: 0-1 Gd: 0-2 GF: 0-2 Fm: 0-0
Distance: 5f/6f: 0-3 7f-8f: 0-5 9f-13f: 0-0 14f+: 0-0
Track : LH: 0-4 RH: 0-0 Tight: 0-1 Gall: 0-0
Aids: Bl: 0-0 Vi: 0-0 Tstrap: 0-0
Best Rating: 24 6/01 Nott 6f15y gd-fm

Hightori (FR)

121 (119)**127**
4-y-o b c Vettori (IRE)-High Mecene (FR) (Highest Honor (FR))
P Demercastel Gary A Tanaka

Placings:31511/15-**13**23310 **(5247a)**
2001: 10^{1}FT, 10^{3}FT, 9^{2}G, 10^{3}GF, 12^{3}GF, 12^{1}G, 12^{0}HO

	Starts	1st	2nd	3rd	Win & Pl
Career Total (Turf)	12	5	1	3	262974
Career Total (AW)	2	1	0	1	438251

121	9/01	Lonc	1m4f		GD	£38797
114	3/01	Ndas	1m2f		FST	£38251
114	9/00	Lonc	1m2f		G-S	£21134
105	11/99	StCl	1m		HLD	£23681
	10/99	Lonc	1m1f		HVY	£9688
	8/99	Lonc	1m		GD	£8611

Total win prize-money £140162

Going (Turf): Sf: 0-1 **GS: 1-1 Gd: 1-3** GF: 0-2 Fm: 0-0
Distance: 5f/6f: 0-0 7f-8f: 1-1 **9f-13f: 3-10** 14f+: 0-0
Track : LH: 1-1 **RH: 2-7** Tight: 0-0 Gall: 0-2
Aids: **Bl: 1-2** Vi: 0-0 Tstrap: 0-0
Best Rating: 127 7/01 Asct 1m4f gd-fm

Top-class French colt. A Group Three winner at two and three, he finished a creditable fifth in the Arc in 2000 and ran up to that form when filling third place in the Dubai World Cup in March 2001. His strong, late challenge just failed to overhaul Observatory in the Prix d'Ispahan on his return to Europe, over what is probably an inadequate trip for him, and ran well at Royal Ascot and when third behind Galileo in the King George. A narrow winner of the Prix Foy, he failed to improve on his previous effort in the Arc on unsuitably heavy ground. He is effective at ten to 12 furlongs and handles all but extremes of ground.

Hill Country (IRE)

115 **112**
3-y-o b c Danehill (USA)-Rose Of Jericho (USA) (Alleged (USA))
J H M Gosden R E Sangster & Mrs J Magnier

Placings:0132-01062 **(4699)**
2001: 11^{0}GF, 12^{1}GS, 12^{0}GF, 11^{6}G, 12^{2}GS

	Starts	1st	2nd	3rd	Win & Pl
Career Total (Turf)	9	2	2	1	36149

107	7/01	NmkJ	1m4f	C	G-S	£6076
91	9/00	Kemp	1m	D	GD	£4348

Total win prize-money £10424

Going (Turf): Sf: 0-2 **GS: 1-2 Gd: 1-2** GF: 0-3 Fm: 0-0
Distance: 5f/6f: 0-0 7f-8f: 1-4 9f-13f: 1-5 14f+: 0-0
Track : LH: 0-2 **RH: 2-5** Tight: 0-1 **Gall: 2-6**
Aids: Bl: 0-0 Vi: 0-0 Tstrap: 0-0
Best Rating: 112 9/01 Donc 1m4f gd-sft

A half-brother to Dr Devious, he showed useful form at two but was well beaten behind Asian Heights in the Predominate Stakes at Goodwood on his reappearance. Landed a decent conditions event at Newmarket next time, but disappointed in both the Gordon Stakes and Great Voltigeur, before going down by a head to Ekraar in a Listed contest. Suited by some give, and 12 furlongs.

Hill Farm Dancer

(101) (36)**36**
10-y-o ch m Gunner B-Loadplan Lass (Nicholas Bill)
W M Brisbourne M E Hughes

Placings:450/031510/**0632**2144063**34**/**2011204335000 41125/134460335/25201204506000/400140324030U06 054L403/55231435114520**60-**145604** **(0538)**
2001: 12^{1}SD, 12^{4}SW, 12^{5}SD, 14^{6}SD, 12^{0}SD, 12^{4}SD

	Starts	1st	2nd	3rd	Win & Pl
Career Total (Turf)	46	4	5	5	21809
Career Total (AW)	61	10	6	9	30596

35	2/01	Wolv	1m4f	G(0-70)H	STD	£1372
35	5/00	Haml	1m4f17y	F(0-60)H	FRM	£2898
48	4/00	Wolv	1m4f	G	STD	£1809
32	2/00	Wolv	1m4f	F(0-60)H	STD	£1722
54	4/99	Sthl	1m4f	G	STD	£1787
49	7/98	Muss	1m4f	F(0-65)H	GD	£3652
76	1/97	Wolv	1m4f	D(0-80)H	STD	£3452
70	11/96	Wolv	1m4f	F(0-65)	STD	£2085
62	11/96	Wolv	1m4f	G(0-65)H	STD	£2243
57	3/96	Wolv	1m4f	F	STD	£2085
53	2/96	Wolv	1m4f	E(0-70)H	STD	£2913
	5/95	Bath	1m3f144y	D(0-75)H	G-F	£3696
44	6/94	Wolv	1m4f	E(0-70)H	STD	£2898
52	5/94	Carl	1m4f	F	FRM	£2540

Total win prize-money £35156

Going (Turf): Sf: 0-4 GS: 0-4 Gd: 1-14 GF: 1-15 **Fm: 2-8**
Distance: 5f/6f: 0-0 7f-8f: 0-3 **9f-13f: 14-85** 14f+: 0-18
Track : **LH: 11-85** RH: 3-21 **Tight: 12-76** Gall: 0-1
Aids: Bl: 0-0 Vi: 0-0 Tstrap: 0-0
Best Rating: 36 2/01 Wolv 1m4f slow

Quite useful over middle distances on Fibresand on her day, she is not as good as she once was, but can win the odd modest event on Fibresand.

Hill Magic

101 **79d**
6-y-o br g Magic Ring (IRE)-Stock Hill Lass (Air Trooper)
L G Cottrell E Gadsden

Placings:2150030/521U060/10005/0000020-003 **(3978)**
2001: 6^{0}S, 6^{0}GF, 6^{3}F

	Starts	1st	2nd	3rd	Win & Pl
Career Total (Turf)	29	3	3	2	58292

100	4/99	Kemp	6f	C	GD	£5670
94	5/98	Ling	6f	B(0-110)H	GD	£36475
77	7/97	Bath	5f161y	D	GD	£3517

Total win prize-money £45664

Going (Turf): Sf: 0-7 GS: 0-4 **Gd: 3-10** GF: 0-7 Fm: 0-1
Distance: **5f/6f: 3-21** 7f-8f: 0-8 9f-13f: 0-0 14f+: 0-0
Track : **LH: 1-2** RH: 0-2 Tight: 0-0 **Gall: 1-4**
Aids: Bl: 0-0 Vi: 0-0 Tstrap: 0-0
Best Rating: 71 8/01 Sals 6f firm

Hill Welcome

(85) (55)**59**
3-y-o ch f Most Welcome-Tarvie (Swing Easy (USA))
B W Hills P Fetherston-Godley

Placings:340-0500 **(0365)**
2001: 7^{0}SD, 7^{5}SW, 11^{0}SD, 10^{0}SW

	Starts	1st	2nd	3rd	Win & Pl
Career Total (Turf)	2	0	0	1	793
Career Total (AW)	5	0	0	0	0

Going (Turf): Sf: 0-0 GS: 0-1 Gd: 0-0 GF: 0-0 Fm: 0-1
Distance: 5f/6f: 0-3 7f-8f: 0-2 9f-13f: 0-2 14f+: 0-0
Track : LH: 0-7 RH: 0-0 Tight: 0-4 Gall: 0-1
Aids: Bl: 0-0 Vi: 0-0 Tstrap: 0-1
Best Rating: 55 1/01 Wolv 7f slow

Hillesley Henry

6-y-o gr g Zambrano-Diddy Girl (Comedy Star (USA))
Dr P Pritchard Three Of A Kind Racing

Placings:0 **(1843)**
2001: 8^{0}GF

	Starts	1st	2nd	3rd	Win & Pl
Career Total (Turf)	1	0	0	0	

Going (Turf): Sf: 0-0 GS: 0-0 Gd: 0-0 GF: 0-1 Fm: 0-0
Distance: 5f/6f: 0-0 7f-8f: 0-0 9f-13f: 0-1 14f+: 0-0
Track : LH: 0-0 RH: 0-0 Tight: 0-0 Gall: 0-0
Aids: Bl: 0-0 Vi: 0-0 Tstrap: 0-0

Hills Of Gold

99 **98+**
2-y-o b c Danehill (USA)-Valley Of Gold (FR) (Shirley Heights)
B W Hills Maktoum Al Maktoum

Placings:1 **(4656)**
2001: 7^{1}GF

	Starts	1st	2nd	3rd	Win & Pl
Career Total (Turf)	1	1	0	0	7345

98	9/01	Donc	7f	C	G-F	£7345

Total win prize-money £7345

Going (Turf): Sf: 0-0 GS: 0-0 Gd: 0-0 **GF: 1-1** Fm: 0-0
Distance: 5f/6f: 0-0 **7f-8f: 1-1** 9f-13f: 0-0 14f+: 0-0
Track : LH: 0-0 RH: 0-0 Tight: 0-0 Gall: 0-0
Aids: Bl: 0-0 Vi: 0-0 Tstrap: 0-0
Best Rating: 98 9/01 Donc 7f gd-fm

By Danehill and out of a smart racemare who won the Italian Oaks, he confirmed his pedigree with a win on his racecourse debut over seven furlongs at Doncaster.

Hilltop Warning

112(100) (67)**95**
4-y-o b g Reprimand-Just Irene (Sagaro)
S P C Woods G Noble

Placings:223/015403-**6115134** **(4782)**
2001: 6^{6}SD, 7^{1}GF, 7^{1}GF, 7^{5}GF, 7^{1}GF, 7^{3}GF, 7^{4}G

	Starts	1st	2nd	3rd	Win & Pl
Career Total (Turf)	15	4	2	3	37294
Career Total (AW)	1	0	0	0	0

94	8/01	Epsm	7f	C(0-90)H	G-F	£8853
86	6/01	Yarm	7f3y	D(0-85)H	G-F	£4537
83	5/01	Gdwd	7f	C(0-90)H	G-F	£12480
77	6/00	Newb	7f	D	G-F	£4342

Total win prize-money £30212

Going (Turf): Sf: 0-1 GS: 0-2 Gd: 0-3 **GF: 4-9** Fm: 0-0
Distance: 5f/6f: 0-4 **7f-8f: 4-11** 9f-13f: 0-1 14f+: 0-0
Track : LH: 1-2 RH: 1-5 **Tight: 1-2** Gall: 0-0
Aids: Bl: 0-1 Vi: 0-0 Tstrap: 0-0

Best Rating: 95 8/01 Gdwd 7f gd-fm

He has looked better than ever this year, landing back-to-back handicaps at Goodwood and Yarmouth, and did not enjoy the run of the race at Newmarket next time. Returned to winning form at Epsom in August and is well suited by seven furlongs and fast ground.

Hilton Head

104 **71**

3-y-o b f Primo Dominie-Low Hill (Rousillon (USA))

T D Easterby Mr & Mrs John Poynton

Placings:1-6004200 **(4588)**

2001: 8^{6}G, 6^{0}GF, 6^{0}G, 6^{4}GF, 6^{2}G, 5^{0}GF, 5^{0}HY

				Starts	1st	2nd	3rd	Win & Pl
Career Total (Turf)				8	1	1	0	4637
71	10/00	Catt	5f	D			SFT	£2730

Total win prize-money £2730

Going (Turf): Sf: 1-2 GS: 0-0 Gd: 0-3 GF: 0-3 Fm: 0-0
Distance: 5f/6f: 1-7 7f-8f: 0-1 9f-13f: 0-0 14f+: 0-0
Track: LH: 0-2 RH: 0-0 Tight: 0-0 Gall: 0-1
Aids: Bl: 0-0 Vi: 0-0 Tstrap: 0-0
Best Rating: 71 8/01 Pont 6f good

Scored on her one and only outing at two over the minimum trip. Has stepped up in trip at three and has yet to win again.

Hilton Park (IRE)

77(80) (36)**27**

2-y-o b f Dolphin Street (FR)-Test Case (Busted)

P D Evans J E Abbey

Placings:0560 **(2049)**

2001: 5^{0}SD, 5^{5}SD, 6^{6}SD, 7^{0}GF

	Starts	1st	2nd	3rd	Win & Pl
Career Total (Turf)	1	0	0	0	
Career Total (AW)	3	0	0	0	0

Going (Turf): Sf: 0-0 GS: 0-0 Gd: 0-0 GF: 0-1 Fm: 0-0
Distance: 5f/6f: 0-3 7f-8f: 0-1 9f-13f: 0-0 14f+: 0-0
Track: LH: 0-1 RH: 0-0 Tight: 0-0 Gall: 0-0
Aids: Bl: 0-0 Vi: 0-1 Tstrap: 0-0
Best Rating: 36 5/01 Sthl 5f stand

Him Of Distinction

97 **80**

2-y-o br c Rainbow Quest (USA)-Air Of Distinction (IRE) (Distinctly North (USA))

J L Dunlop Normandie Stud Ltd

Placings:51 **(5262)**

2001: 7^{5}G, 7^{1}GS

				Starts	1st	2nd	3rd	Win & Pl
Career Total (Turf)				2	1	0	0	7653
80	10/01	York	7f202y	D			G-S	£7377

Total win prize-money £7378

Going (Turf): Sf: 0-0 GS: 1-1 Gd: 0-1 GF: 0-0 Fm: 0-0
Distance: 5f/6f: 0-0 7f-8f: 1-2 9f-13f: 0-0 14f+: 0-0
Track: LH: 1-1 RH: 0-1 Tight: 0-0 Gall: 1-2
Aids: Bl: 0-0 Vi: 0-0 Tstrap: 0-0
Best Rating: 80 10/01 York 7f202y gd-sft

He improved on his racing debut with a win at York in a fairly ordiinary-looking maiden in October over a mile.

Hinchley Wood (IRE)

56 **4**

2-y-o b g Fayruz-Audriano (IRE) (Cyrano De Bergerac)

K McAuliffe Mrs Fitri Hay

Placings:00 **(5248)**

2001: 8^{0}SW, 7^{0}S

	Starts	1st	2nd	3rd	Win & Pl
Career Total (Turf)	1	0	0	0	
Career Total (AW)	1	0	0	0	

Going (Turf): Sf: 0-1 GS: 0-0 Gd: 0-0 GF: 0-0 Fm: 0-0
Distance: 5f/6f: 0-0 7f-8f: 0-1 9f-13f: 0-1 14f+: 0-0
Track: LH: 0-2 RH: 0-0 Tight: 0-1 Gall: 0-1
Aids: Bl: 0-0 Vi: 0-0 Tstrap: 0-0
Best Rating: 4 10/01 York 7f202y soft

Hindi

(81) (43)**66**

5-y-o b g Indian Ridge-Tootsiepop (USA) (Robellino (USA))

N A Graham Douglas Guyer, Norman Fish & Paul Jacobs

Placings:00456/0200-0 **(0080)**

2001: 11^{0}SD

	Starts	1st	2nd	3rd	Win & Pl
Career Total (Turf)	9	0	1	0	1256
Career Total (AW)	1	0	0	0	

Going (Turf): Sf: 0-1 GS: 0-6 Gd: 0-1 GF: 0-1 Fm: 0-0
Distance: 5f/6f: 0-0 7f-8f: 0-0 9f-13f: 0-10 14f+: 0-0
Track: LH: 0-6 RH: 0-3 Tight: 0-3 Gall: 0-2
Aids: Bl: 0-1 Vi: 0-0 Tstrap: 0-0
Best Rating: 43 1/01 Sthl 1m3f stand

Hint Of Magic

101(98) (65)**45**

4-y-o b g Magic Ring (IRE)-Thames Glow (Kalaglow)

J G Portman J G B Portman

Placings:52/440000-61300000 **(4899)**

2001: 10^{6}SD, 8^{1}SW, 7^{3}GS, 7^{0}G, 8^{0}G, 8^{0}GF, 8^{0}GF, 8^{0}GS

				Starts	1st	2nd	3rd	Win & Pl
Career Total (Turf)				14	0	1	1	2116
Career Total (AW)				2	1	0	0	1859
65	3/01	Ling	1m	F(0-60)H			SLW	£1858

Total win prize-money £1859

Going (Turf): Sf: 0-4 GS: 0-3 Gd: 0-4 GF: 0-3 Fm: 0-0
Distance: 5f/6f: 0-0 7f-8f: 1-7 9f-13f: 0-9 14f+: 0-0
Track: LH: 1-8 RH: 0-4 Tight: 1-3 Gall: 0-3
Aids: Bl: 0-1 Vi: 0-0 Tstrap: 0-2
Best Rating: 65 5/01 Brig 7f214y gd-sft

Hiraeth

98(74) (24)**75**

3-y-o b f Petong-Floppie (FR) (Law Society (USA))

B Palling Mr Derek D & Mrs Jean P Clee

Placings:323-0100 **(5671)**

2001: 7^{0}S, 5^{1}GF, 7^{0}SD, 6^{0}HY

				Starts	1st	2nd	3rd	Win & Pl
Career Total (Turf)				6	1	1	2	5380
Career Total (AW)				1	0	0	0	
59	8/01	Catt	5f212y	D			G-F	£3066

Total win prize-money £3066

Going (Turf): Sf: 0-3 GS: 0-1 Gd: 0-0 GF: 1-1 Fm: 0-1
Distance: 5f/6f: 1-3 7f-8f: 0-4 9f-13f: 0-0 14f+: 0-0
Track: LH: 1-3 RH: 0-0 Tight: 1-1 Gall: 0-1
Aids: Bl: 0-0 Vi: 0-0 Tstrap: 0-0
Best Rating: 59 8/01 Catt 5f212y gd-fm

Placed form in ordinary maidens before taking a Catterick maiden on good to firm ground.

Hirapour (IRE)

108 **99**

5-y-o b g Kahyasi-Himaya (IRE) (Mouktar)

Mrs A J Perrett Michael H Watt

Placings:21/0130000-10510 **(5387)**

2001: 12^{1}GF, 12^{0}G, 13^{5}G, 16^{1}GF, 18^{0}GS

					Starts	1st	2nd	3rd	Win & Pl
Career Total (Turf)					14	4	1	1	29459
99	9/01	Newb	2m	C(0-100)H				G-F	£7052
89	6/01	NmkR	1m4f	C(0-90)				G-F	£6743
93	4/00	List	1m4f					SFT	£8625
93	8/99	Fair	1m5f					GD	£3036

Total win prize-money £25458

Going (Turf): Sf: 1-2 GS: 0-1 Gd: 1-5 GF: 2-3 Fm: 0-0
Distance: 5f/6f: 0-0 7f-8f: 0-0 9f-13f: 3-8 14f+: 1-6
Track: LH: 2-7 RH: 2-7 Tight: 0-1 Gall: 1-4
Aids: Bl: 0-2 Vi: 0-0 Tstrap: 0-0
Best Rating: 99 9/01 Newb 2m gd-fm

Formerly a useful handicapper for Dermot Weld in Ireland, he made all to win on his debut for Amanda Perrett at Newmarket in June. Highly tried afterwards, but was successfully stepped up to two miles at Newbury in September.

Hirvine (FR)

34

3-y-o ch g Snurge-Guadanella (FR) (Guadanini (FR))

T P Tate T P Tate

Placings:6 **(0684)**

2001: 12^{6}S

	Starts	1st	2nd	3rd	Win & Pl
Career Total (Turf)	1	0	0	0	0

Going (Turf): Sf: 0-1 GS: 0-0 Gd: 0-0 GF: 0-0 Fm: 0-0
Distance: 5f/6f: 0-0 7f-8f: 0-0 9f-13f: 0-1 14f+: 0-0
Track: LH: 0-0 RH: 0-0 Tight: 0-0 Gall: 0-0
Aids: Bl: 0-0 Vi: 0-0 Tstrap: 0-0
Best Rating: 34 4/01 Muss 1m4f soft

Historic Treble

102 **83**

2-y-o b c Lycius (USA)-Alfaaselah (GER) (Dancing Brave (USA))

B Hanbury A Merza

Placings:4422102 **(5333)**

2001: 6^{4}GF, 6^{4}F, 6^{2}GS, 6^{2}GF, 5^{1}HY, 5^{0}GS, 6^{2}HY

				Starts	1st	2nd	3rd	Win & Pl
Career Total (Turf)				7	1	3	0	9418
80	9/01	Hayd	5f	D			HVY	£5005

Total win prize-money £5005

Going (Turf): Sf: 1-2 GS: 0-2 Gd: 0-0 GF: 0-2 Fm: 0-1
Distance: 5f/6f: 1-7 7f-8f: 0-0 9f-13f: 0-0 14f+: 0-0
Track: LH: 0-0 RH: 0-0 Tight: 0-0 Gall: 0-0
Aids: Bl: 0-0 Vi: 0-0 Tstrap: 0-0
Best Rating: 83 10/01 Ling 6f heavy

Got off the mark in heavy ground at Haydock in September over five furlongs and has continued to run well since. Acts well with cut in the ground, and is effective over five and six furlongs.

Hit The Trail (IRE)

59 **52**

3-y-o b f Treasure Kay-Shoot The Dealer (IRE) (Common Grounds)

J L Eyre P Birchenough

Placings:4-00 **(1065)**

2001: 5^{0}S, 6^{0}GS

	Starts	1st	2nd	3rd	Win & Pl
Career Total (Turf)	3	0	0	0	242

Going (Turf): Sf: 0-2 GS: 0-1 Gd: 0-0 GF: 0-0 Fm: 0-0
Distance: 5f/6f: 0-3 7f-8f: 0-0 9f-13f: 0-0 14f+: 0-0
Track: LH: 0-2 RH: 0-0 Tight: 0-0 Gall: 0-0

Aids: Bl: 0-0 Vi: 0-0 Tstrap: 0-0
Best Rating: 4 4/01 Nott 5f13y soft

Ho Choi

100 **94**
2-y-o b c Pivotal-Witch Of Fife (USA) (Lear Fan (USA))
Miss L A Perratt Alan Guthrie

Placings:124 **(4659)**
2001: 6[1]GF, 6[2]G, 6[4]GF

	Starts	1st	2nd	3rd	Win & Pl
Career Total (Turf)	3	1	1	0	45942
94 6/01 Ayr 6f	E			G-F	£3262

Total win prize-money £3262

Going (Turf): Sf: 0-0 GS: 0-0 Gd: 0-1 **GF: 1-2** Fm: 0-0
Distance: **5f/6f: 1-3** 7f-8f: 0-0 9f-13f: 0-0 14f+: 0-0
Track : LH: 0-0 RH: 0-0 Tight: 0-0 Gall: 0-0
Aids: Bl: 0-0 Vi: 0-0 Tstrap: 0-0
Best Rating: 94 8/01 York 6f good

An impressive winner on his debut over six furlongs at Ayr and ran a blinder to chase home Rock Of Gibraltar in the Gimcrack. Ran well to finish fourth in the St Leger Yearling Stakes at Doncaster, but was still green there and will be even better with more experience. Acts on fast ground and should win a decent race or two.

Ho Leng (IRE)

107 **92**
6-y-o ch g Statoblest-Indigo Blue (IRE) (Bluebird (USA))
Miss L A Perratt Alan Guthrie

Placings:125/101040/04020210053/3030233450-0000000400 **(4849)**
2001: 6[0]GF, 5[0]GF, 6[0]GF, 6[0]F, 7[0]GF, 6[0]G, 6[0]G, 6[0]G, 6[4]GF, 5[0]GF, 6[0]GF

	Starts	1st	2nd	3rd	Win & Pl
Career Total (Turf)	41	4	4	5	107465
103 9/99 York 6f	B(0-105)H			G-F	£16976
105 7/98 NmkJ 7f	B(0-105)H			FRM	£23850
100 5/98 York 6f214y	B(0-105)H			GD	£23750
88 8/97 Haml 6f5y	D			G-F	£3550

Total win prize-money £68126

Going (Turf): Sf: 0-3 GS: 0-3 Gd: 1-15 **GF: 2-17** Fm: 1-3
Distance: 5f/6f: 1-20 **7f-8f: 3-21** 9f-13f: 0-0 14f+: 0-0
Track : **LH: 1-6** RH: 0-0 Tight: 0-0 **Gall: 1-5**
Aids: Bl: 0-0 Vi: 0-0 Tstrap: 0-0
Best Rating: 92 9/01 York 6f gd-fm

Best over six and seven furlongs, but does stay a mile. This former front-runner now goes well when held up behind a fast pace, but struggled this term and needs more help from the Handicapper as well as a sound surface.

Ho Pang Yau

101 **53**
3-y-o b/br g Pivotal-La Cabrilla (Carwhite)
Miss L A Perratt Alan Guthrie

Placings:0526-560640653533600 **(5273)**
2001: 7[5]GS, 7[6]GF, 8[0]GF, 8[6]GF, 8[4]GS, 7[0]GF, 6[6]S, 6[5]GS, 6[3]F, 6[5]GS, 5[3]GF, 6[3]G, 5[6]GF, 5[0]G, 5[0]HY

	Starts	1st	2nd	3rd	Win & Pl
Career Total (Turf)	19	0	1	3	2597

Going (Turf): Sf: 0-3 GS: 0-4 Gd: 0-2 GF: 0-8 Fm: 0-2
Distance: 5f/6f: 0-7 7f-8f: 0-10 9f-13f: 0-2 14f+: 0-0
Track : LH: 0-6 RH: 0-3 Tight: 0-4 Gall: 0-1
Aids: Bl: 0-1 Vi: 0-0 Tstrap: 0-0
Best Rating: 61 5/01 Ayr 7f gd-fm

Has shown ability without winning in ordinary events up to a mile, mainly on the Scottish circuit.

Ho Sec (IRE)

(58)
3-y-o ch g Goldmark (USA)-Londubh (Tumble Wind (USA))
J M P Eustace Kai Tak Racing

Placings:0 **(0036)**
2001: 7[0]SD

	Starts	1st	2nd	3rd	Win & Pl
Career Total (Turf)	0	0	0	0	
Career Total (AW)	1	0	0	0	

Going (Turf): Sf: 0-0 GS: 0-0 Gd: 0-0 GF: 0-0 Fm: 0-0
Distance: 5f/6f: 0-0 7f-8f: 0-1 9f-13f: 0-0 14f+: 0-0
Track : LH: 0-1 RH: 0-0 Tight: 0-0 Gall: 0-0
Aids: Bl: 0-0 Vi: 0-0 Tstrap: 0-0

Hoax (IRE)

101 **91**
2-y-o b c Robellino (USA)-Hocus (High Top)
R F Johnson Houghton R F Johnson Houghton

Placings:4141440220 **(5021)**
2001: 5[4]G, 6[1]GF, 6[4]GF, 7[1]GF, 7[4]GF, 7[4]GF, 7[0]G, 8[2]G, 7[2]G, 7[0]HY

	Starts	1st	2nd	3rd	Win & Pl
Career Total (Turf)	10	2	2	0	18677
85 6/01 Wwck 7f26y	E			G-F	£2926
79 5/01 Sthl 6f	D			G-F	£3406

Total win prize-money £6332

Going (Turf): Sf: 0-1 GS: 0-0 Gd: 0-4 **GF: 2-5** Fm: 0-0
Distance: 5f/6f: 1-3 7f-8f: 1-7 9f-13f: 0-0 14f+: 0-0
Track : **LH: 2-5** RH: 0-1 Tight: 0-2 Gall: 0-1
Aids: Bl: 0-1 Vi: 0-0 Tstrap: 0-0
Best Rating: 91 9/01 Donc 1m good

His two wins in minor company sandwiched a good fourth in a Listed race on Derby Day, but he has struggled to get his head in front in better events since then. Stays a mile, acts on fast ground.

Hoh Express

93 **66**
9-y-o b g Waajib-Tissue Paper (Touch Paper)
P R Webber Mrs Joan L Egan

Placings:22/0120341303/00563020304/000130360620/46306/0 **(2305)**
2001: 20[0]GF

	Starts	1st	2nd	3rd	Win & Pl
Career Total (Turf)	41	3	5	8	67502
88 5/97 Gdwd 1m4f	C(0-100)H			GD	£7310
97 8/95 Badn 1m				GD	£16461
81 5/95 Newb 1m	D			GD	£4662

Total win prize-money £28434

Going (Turf): Sf: 0-6 GS: 0-5 **Gd: 3-16** GF: 0-14 Fm: 0-0
Distance: 5f/6f: 0-0 **7f-8f: 2-8** 9f-13f: 1-30 14f+: 0-3
Track : LH: 1-16 RH: 1-16 **Tight: 1-10** Gall: 0-16
Aids: Bl: 0-0 Vi: 0-0 Tstrap: 0-0
Best Rating: 66 6/01 Asct 2m4f gd-fm

Hoh Gem

(99) **47**
5-y-o b g Be My Chief (USA)-Jennies' Gem (Sayf El Arab (USA))
Don Enrico Incisa (N Tinkler 9/2) Don Enrico Incisa

Placings:0000/01410204600445-036P **(0445)**
2001: 8[0]SD, 9[3]SD, 8[6]SW, 8[P]SD

	Starts	1st	2nd	3rd	Win & Pl
Career Total (Turf)	12	1	0	0	2362
Career Total (AW)	10	1	1	1	2689
47 5/00 Wwck 7f164y	G(0-65)H			HVY	£2136
49 5/00 Sthl 1m	G(0-70)H			STD	£1939

Total win prize-money £4075

Going (Turf): Sf: 1-6 GS: 0-0 Gd: 0-3 GF: 0-3 Fm: 0-0
Distance: 5f/6f: 0-2 **7f-8f: 2-9** 9f-13f: 0-11 14f+: 0-0
Track : **LH: 2-15** RH: 0-2 Tight: 0-7 Gall: 0-0
Aids: Bl: 0-0 Vi: 0-0 Tstrap: 0-0
Best Rating: 43 1/01 Wolv 1m1f79y stand

Hoh Invader (IRE)

(89) (41)**74**
9-y-o b g Accordion-Newgate Fairy (Flair Path)
Mrs A Duffield Exors Late Neil Midgley & Stewart Pinner

Placings:432260 **(5044)**
2001: 10[4]S, 12[3]GF, 10[2]G, 16[2]GF, 16[6]F, 14[0]SD

	Starts	1st	2nd	3rd	Win & Pl
Career Total (Turf)	5	0	2	1	2762
Career Total (AW)	1	0	0	0	

Going (Turf): Sf: 0-1 GS: 0-0 Gd: 0-1 GF: 0-2 Fm: 0-1
Distance: 5f/6f: 0-0 7f-8f: 0-0 9f-13f: 0-3 14f+: 0-3
Track : LH: 0-4 RH: 0-2 Tight: 0-2 Gall: 0-3
Aids: Bl: 0-0 Vi: 0-0 Tstrap: 0-0
Best Rating: 74 8/01 Ripn 2m gd-fm

Hoh No

98 **52d**
5-y-o b g Efisio-Primetta (Precocious)
R M Stronge (M L W Bell 27/8) Berkshire Commercial Components Ltd

Placings:000313/21004000/00003300 **(5039)**
2001: 10[0]G, 10[0]GF, 10[0]GF, 10[0]GF, 10[3]G, 10[3]GF, 12[0]G, 17[0]G

	Starts	1st	2nd	3rd	Win & Pl
Career Total (Turf)	22	2	1	4	15097
84 5/99 Nott 1m1f213yD(0-80)				FRM	£4137
75 9/98 Gdwd 1m	D(0-85)H			G-F	£3215

Total win prize-money £7353

Going (Turf): Sf: 0-0 GS: 0-1 Gd: 0-9 **GF: 1-10 Fm: 1-2**
Distance: 5f/6f: 0-3 7f-8f: 1-3 9f-13f: 1-15 14f+: 0-1
Track : LH: 1-8 RH: 1-10 Tight: 0-7 Gall: 0-10
Aids: Bl: 0-0 Vi: 0-0 Tstrap: 0-0
Best Rating: 60 5/01 Kemp 1m2f gd-fm

Won at Goodwood at two, and gained a courageous victory at Nottingham in 1999. He ran a couple of good races in modest company in the summer of 2001. Seems best on fast ground.

Hoh's Back

(100) (80)**81**
2-y-o b c Royal Applause-Paris Joelle (IRE) (Fairy King (USA))
S Kirk Mr D Allport & Mr R B Michaelson

Placings:0021 **(5610)**
2001: 8[0]GF, 8[0]G, 6[2]S, 8[1]SD

	Starts	1st	2nd	3rd	Win & Pl
Career Total (Turf)	3	0	1	0	838
Career Total (AW)	1	1	0	0	2835
80 11/01 Wolv 1m100y	E			STD	£2835

Total win prize-money £2835

Going (Turf): Sf: 0-1 GS: 0-0 Gd: 0-1 GF: 0-1 Fm: 0-0
Distance: 5f/6f: 0-0 7f-8f: 0-1 **9f-13f: 1-3** 14f+: 0-0
Track : **LH: 1-4** RH: 0-0 **Tight: 1-1** Gall: 0-0
Aids: Bl: 0-0 Vi: 0-0 Tstrap: 0-0
Best Rating: 81 10/01 Brig 6f209y soft

Showed his best form when second in an Brighton auction maiden over seven furlongs on soft ground prior to scoring at Wolverhampton on his sand debut.

Holbeck (IRE)

84 7

3-y-o b f Efisio-Autumn Fall (USA) (Sanglamore (USA))
R Wilman (M Johnston 27/7) Mrs Joanna Hughes

Placings:655-000 (5296)
2001: 5^{0}GF, 8^{0}F, 8^{0}S

	Starts	1st	2nd	3rd	Win & Pl
Career Total (Turf)	6	0	0	0	0

Going (Turf): Sf: 0-2 GS: 0-0 Gd: 0-1 GF: 0-1 Fm: 0-2
Distance: 5f/6f: 0-4 7f-8f: 0-1 9f-13f: 0-1 14f+: 0-0
Track : LH: 0-2 RH: 0-0 Tight: 0-2 Gall: 0-0
Aids: Bl: 0-0 Vi: 0-0 Tstrap: 0-0
Best Rating: 7 7/01 Thsk 1m firm

Holding Court

116 120

4-y-o b c Hernando (FR)-Indian Love Song (Be My Guest (USA))
M A Jarvis J R Good

Placings:6210/111655-3310 (5247a)
2001: 12^{3}G, 12^{3}GS, 12^{1}GS, 12^{0}HO

	Starts	1st	2nd	3rd	Win & Pl
Career Total (Turf)	14	5	1	2	356135

119	8/01	Deau	1m4f110y	G-S	£48497
120	6/00	Chan	1m4f	VS	£240154
104	5/00	Lonc	1m4f	GD	£21134
104	4/00	Hayd	1m2f120yC(0-100)H	HVY	£6613
89	10/99	Hayd	1m30y C	HVY	£5587

Total win prize-money £321987

Going (Turf): Sf: 2-4 GS: 1-3 Gd: 1-2 GF: 0-1 Fm: 0-0
Distance: 5f/6f: 0-0 7f-8f: 0-3 **9f-13f: 5-11** 14f+: 0-0
Track : LH: 2-5 RH: 2-7 Tight: 0-0 Gall: 0-3
Aids: **Bl: 1-3** Vi: 0-0 Tstrap: 0-0
Best Rating: 120 7/01 NmkJ 1m4f gd-sft

A progressive sort in soft ground at three, he won a handicap at Haydock and a Group Three at Longchamp before running away with the French Derby, beating Lord Flasheart, another mudlark, by six lengths. However, that victory must have taken a lot out of him for he failed to win again until taking the Grand Prix de Deauville, although he has run with credit in some top-class middle-distance events. Has been sold to Sauda Arabia and renamed Wakaad.

Holly Games

77 33

2-y-o b f Mind Games-Young Holly (Risk Me (FR))
M R Bosley C R Marks (banbury)

Placings:500 (4211)
2001: 5^{5}GF, 5^{0}GF, 5^{0}GF

	Starts	1st	2nd	3rd	Win & Pl
Career Total (Turf)	3	0	0	0	0

Going (Turf): Sf: 0-0 GS: 0-0 Gd: 0-0 GF: 0-3 Fm: 0-0
Distance: 5f/6f: 0-3 7f-8f: 0-0 9f-13f: 0-0 14f+: 0-0
Track : LH: 0-1 RH: 0-1 Tight: 0-0 Gall: 0-2
Aids: Bl: 0-0 Vi: 0-0 Tstrap: 0-0
Best Rating: 33 7/01 Wind 5f10y gd-fm

Holly Rose

77 56

2-y-o b f Charnwood Forest (IRE)-Divina Luna (Dowsing (USA))
Pat Mitchell Mrs Catherine Reed

Placings:600 (4644)
2001: 6^{6}GF, 6^{0}GF, 6^{0}GF

	Starts	1st	2nd	3rd	Win & Pl
Career Total (Turf)	3	0	0	0	0

Going (Turf): Sf: 0-0 GS: 0-0 Gd: 0-0 GF: 0-3 Fm: 0-0
Distance: 5f/6f: 0-3 7f-8f: 0-0 9f-13f: 0-0 14f+: 0-0
Track : LH: 0-0 RH: 0-0 Tight: 0-0 Gall: 0-0
Aids: Bl: 0-0 Vi: 0-0 Tstrap: 0-0
Best Rating: 56 9/01 Ling 6f gd-fm

Hollybell

95 78

2-y-o b f Beveled (USA)-Fayre Holly (IRE) (Fayruz)
J Gallagher Mrs D Yeats Brown

Placings:503510 (4894)
2001: 5^{5}GS, 5^{0}F, 5^{3}GF, 6^{5}G, 5^{1}F, 5^{0}GS

	Starts	1st	2nd	3rd	Win & Pl
Career Total (Turf)	6	1	0	1	3370

78	9/01	Bath	5f11y	E	FRM £2947

Total win prize-money £2947

Going (Turf): Sf: 0-0 GS: 0-2 Gd: 0-1 GF: 0-1 **Fm: 1-2**
Distance: **5f/6f: 1-5** 7f-8f: 0-1 9f-13f: 0-0 14f+: 0-0
Track : **LH: 1-3** RH: 0-0 Tight: 0-0 **Gall: 1-3**
Aids: Bl: 0-0 Vi: 0-0 Tstrap: 0-0
Best Rating: 78 9/01 Bath 5f11y firm

A hard puller in the past, she was given her head when successful at Bath in September. She does not want further than five furlongs.

Hollybush (IRE)

93 59

2-y-o b f Ali-Royal (IRE)-Another Baileys (Deploy)
J S Goldie William Goldie

Placings:56504 (5283)
2001: 6^{5}GS, 7^{6}GS, 6^{5}GS, 8^{0}G, 8^{4}HY

	Starts	1st	2nd	3rd	Win & Pl
Career Total (Turf)	5	0	0	0	296

Going (Turf): Sf: 0-1 GS: 0-3 Gd: 0-1 GF: 0-0 Fm: 0-0
Distance: 5f/6f: 0-2 7f-8f: 0-3 9f-13f: 0-0 14f+: 0-0
Track : LH: 0-3 RH: 0-0 Tight: 0-0 Gall: 0-0
Aids: Bl: 0-0 Vi: 0-0 Tstrap: 0-0
Best Rating: 59 7/01 Ayr 6f gd-sft

An exclusive Ayr specialist, her best effort to date was a fourth in a nursery. She is bred to need middle-distances.

Holy Island

104 70

4-y-o b f Deploy-Bells (Sadler's Wells (USA))
L M Cumani G Shiel

Placings:30-00112340 (5599)
2001: 9^{0}S, 12^{0}GF, 9^{1}G, 10^{1}GF, 11^{2}G, 9^{3}GF, 10^{4}S, 12^{0}GS

	Starts	1st	2nd	3rd	Win & Pl
Career Total (Turf)	10	2	1	2	8651

70	7/01	Yarm	1m2f21y E(0-70)H	G-F	£3248
64	7/01	Brig	1m1f209yF(0-60)H	GD	£2870

Total win prize-money £6118

Going (Turf): Sf: 0-4 GS: 0-1 **Gd: 1-2 GF: 1-3** Fm: 0-0
Distance: 5f/6f: 0-0 7f-8f: 0-0 **9f-13f: 2-10** 14f+: 0-0
Track : **LH: 2-7** RH: 0-3 **Tight: 1-3** Gall: 0-3
Aids: Bl: 0-0 Vi: 0-0 Tstrap: 0-0
Best Rating: 70 8/01 Leic 1m3f183y good

A nervy filly who appreciated the drop in class and distance to win at Brighton on her handicap debut. Followed up at Yarmouth. Suited by ten furlongs and fast ground.

Holy Orders (IRE)

108 94

4-y-o b h Unblest-Shadowglow (Shaadi (USA))
W P Mullins A McLuckie

Placings:044132/10-100 (3787a)
2001: 12^{1}G, 12^{0}G, 12^{0}GY

	Starts	1st	2nd	3rd	Win & Pl
Career Total (Turf)	11	3	1	1	53046

80	5/01	Curr	1m4f	H	GD	£39000
81	6/00	Naas	1m2f	(0-90)H	YLD	£6900
73	10/99	Fair	7f	H	G-Y	£4830

Total win prize-money £50730

Going (Turf): Sf: 0-2 GS: 0-0 **Gd: 1-3** GF: 0-1 Fm: 0-0
Distance: 5f/6f: 0-1 7f-8f: 1-2 **9f-13f: 2-8** 14f+: 0-0
Track : LH: 1-3 RH: 1-5 Tight: 0-0 Gall: 0-1
Aids: Bl: 0-0 Vi: 0-0 Tstrap: 0-0
Best Rating: 94 6/01 Asct 1m4f good

A decent handicapper, found his form when stepped up in trip. Has been hurdling this spring to great effect, winning twice from four starts. Reverted back to level in May 2001 to win a Curragh handicap over a mile and a half. In flying form at present. Has never won on ground faster than good.

Home By Socks (IRE)

86(70) (25)61

2-y-o ch f Desert King (IRE)-Propitious (IRE) (Doyoun)
M C Chapman G C R Pryke

Placings:00004006006 (5280)
2001: 5^{0}S, 5^{0}G, 6^{0}SD, 6^{0}GF, 7^{0}GF, 7^{4}GS, 7^{0}GF, 8^{0}GF, 8^{6}S, 9^{0}HY, 10^{0}GS, 9^{6}S

	Starts	1st	2nd	3rd	Win & Pl
Career Total (Turf)	11	0	0	0	151
Career Total (AW)	1	0	0	0	

Going (Turf): Sf: 0-4 GS: 0-2 Gd: 0-1 GF: 0-4 Fm: 0-0
Distance: 5f/6f: 0-3 7f-8f: 0-4 9f-13f: 0-5 14f+: 0-0
Track : LH: 0-5 RH: 0-3 Tight: 0-0 Gall: 0-1
Aids: Bl: 0-0 Vi: 0-0 Tstrap: 0-0
Best Rating: 70 8/01 Bevl 7f100y gd-sft

Home Coming

89(83) (32)57

3-y-o br g Primo Dominie-Carolside (Music Maestro)
S P C Woods Arashan Ali

Placings:60000 (3617)
2001: 8^{6}SW, 8^{0}G, 8^{0}GF, 6^{0}GF, 6^{0}F

	Starts	1st	2nd	3rd	Win & Pl
Career Total (Turf)	4	0	0	0	
Career Total (AW)	1	0	0	0	0

Going (Turf): Sf: 0-0 GS: 0-0 Gd: 0-1 GF: 0-2 Fm: 0-1
Distance: 5f/6f: 0-1 7f-8f: 0-4 9f-13f: 0-0 14f+: 0-0
Track : LH: 0-1 RH: 0-1 Tight: 0-0 Gall: 0-0
Aids: Bl: 0-0 Vi: 0-0 Tstrap: 0-0
Best Rating: 57 5/01 NmkR 1m good

Homelife (IRE)

102(104) (82)80

3-y-o b g Persian Bold-Share The Vision (Vision (USA))
P W D'Arcy Mrs Jean Mitchell

Placings:64066204-10160521050 (5692)
2001: 12^{1}SD, 10^{0}GS, 12^{1}SD, 12^{6}GF, 12^{0}GF, 14^{5}G, 16^{2}GS, 16^{1}G, 16^{0}S, 16^{5}HY, 16^{0}S

	Starts	1st	2nd	3rd	Win & Pl
Career Total (Turf)	17	1	2	0	8879
Career Total (AW)	2	2	0	0	7543

80	8/01	NmkJ	2m24y	C(0-90)H	GD £6760
82	3/01	Sthl	1m4f	D(0-80)H	STD £3757
78	3/01	Wolv	1m4f	D(0-85)H	STD £3786

Total win prize-money £14303

Going (Turf): Sf: 0-7 GS: 0-3 **Gd: 1-4** GF: 0-3 Fm: 0-0

Distance: 5f/6f: 0-1 7f-8f: 0-5 **9f-13f: 2-7** 14f+: 1-6
Track : **LH: 2-10** RH: 1-3 Tight: 1-5 Gall: 1-5
Aids: Bl: 0-0 Vi: 0-0 Tstrap: 0-0
Best Rating: 82 3/01 Sthl 1m4f stand

He acts on turf and Fibresand and scored over two miles at Newmarket in August, but has struggled since. Stays well.

Homely Sort (IRE)

(67) (21)**40**
2-y-o b f Petardia-Safe Home (Home Guard (USA))
M J Polglase R D Letby

Placings:00000000 **(5594)**
2001: 5^{0}SD, 6^{0}F, 5^{0}F, 6^{0}GF, 5^{0}SD, 6^{0}SD, 5^{0}S, 6^{0}GS

	Starts	1st	2nd	3rd	Win & Pl
Career Total (Turf)	5	0	0	0	
Career Total (AW)	3	0	0	0	

Going (Turf): Sf: 0-1 GS: 0-1 Gd: 0-0 GF: 0-1 Fm: 0-2
Distance: 5f/6f: 0-8 7f-8f: 0-0 9f-13f: 0-0 14f+: 0-0
Track : LH: 0-4 RH: 0-0 Tight: 0-2 Gall: 0-0
Aids: Bl: 0-3 Vi: 0-0 Tstrap: 0-0
Best Rating: 40 11/01 NmkR 6f gd-sft

Homespun

92 **88**
2-y-o b f Reprimand-Home Truth (Known Fact (USA))
B W Hills D J Deer

Placings:320 **(4723)**
2001: 6^{3}GF, 6^{2}G, 7^{0}GF

	Starts	1st	2nd	3rd	Win & Pl
Career Total (Turf)	3	0	1	1	2218

Going (Turf): Sf: 0-0 GS: 0-0 Gd: 0-1 GF: 0-2 Fm: 0-0
Distance: 5f/6f: 0-1 7f-8f: 0-2 9f-13f: 0-0 14f+: 0-0
Track : LH: 0-1 RH: 0-0 Tight: 0-0 Gall: 0-0
Aids: Bl: 0-0 Vi: 0-0 Tstrap: 0-0
Best Rating: 88 8/01 Gdwd 6f good

A half-sister to Susu and Cadeaux Cher, missed the break on her debut in what looked a decent Newbury maiden, but finished well to be third. A beaten favourite on her next two runs, she does not appear to be progressing as expected.

Honest Borderer

109 **80**
6-y-o b g Selkirk (USA)-Tell No Lies (High Line)
J L Dunlop Mrs A Johnstone

Placings:54/230410/350036/614340-4300060 **(4891)**
2001: 7^{4}G, 8^{3}GF, 7^{0}F, 8^{0}GS, 8^{0}GF, 10^{6}GF, 8^{0}GF

	Starts	1st	2nd	3rd	Win & Pl
Career Total (Turf)	27	2	1	5	24218
84 6/00 Ling 7f140y C(0-90)H				G-F	£7572
81 8/98 Ripn 1m1f D(0-80)H				G-F	£6060
				Total win prize-money	£13633

Going (Turf): Sf: 0-3 GS: 0-4 Gd: 0-7 **GF: 2-12** Fm: 0-1
Distance: 5f/6f: 0-0 7f-8f: 1-17 9f-13f: 1-10 14f+: 0-0
Track : LH: 0-4 **RH: 1-10 Tight: 1-6** Gall: 0-2
Aids: Bl: 0-2 Vi: 0-0 Tstrap: 0-0
Best Rating: 82 5/01 Ling 7f good

Ran a fine race on reappearance when drawn poorly and racing on the unfavoured part of the track at Lingfield. Has failed to progress since and was reported to be suffering from a fibrillating heart when finishing last at Newmarket. Best on a sound surface. Stays a mile.

Honest Obsession (IRE)

87 **57**
3-y-o b c Sadler's Wells (USA)-Valley Of Gold (FR) (Shirley Heights)
B W Hills Maktoum Al Maktoum

Placings:0-00 **(1812)**
2001: 7^{0}S, 8^{0}GF

	Starts	1st	2nd	3rd	Win & Pl
Career Total (Turf)	3	0	0	0	

Going (Turf): Sf: 0-2 GS: 0-0 Gd: 0-0 GF: 0-1 Fm: 0-0
Distance: 5f/6f: 0-0 7f-8f: 0-3 9f-13f: 0-0 14f+: 0-0
Track : LH: 0-0 RH: 0-0 Tight: 0-0 Gall: 0-0
Aids: Bl: 0-0 Vi: 0-0 Tstrap: 0-0
Best Rating: 57 6/01 NmkR 1m gd-fm

Honest Villain (USA)

74 **37**
4-y-o b g St Jovite (USA)-Villandry (USA) (Lyphard's Wish (FR))
J G Given (I A Balding 27/7) Colin G R Booth

Placings:300/0-0 **(3426)**
2001: 14^{0}GF

	Starts	1st	2nd	3rd	Win & Pl
Career Total (Turf)	5	0	0	1	499

Going (Turf): Sf: 0-1 GS: 0-0 Gd: 0-1 GF: 0-2 Fm: 0-1
Distance: 5f/6f: 0-3 7f-8f: 0-0 9f-13f: 0-0 14f+: 0-2
Track : LH: 0-1 RH: 0-2 Tight: 0-2 Gall: 0-1
Aids: Bl: 0-0 Vi: 0-0 Tstrap: 0-0
Best Rating: 5 7/01 Sals 1m6f15y gd-fm

Honest Warning

106(99) (62)**70**
4-y-o b c Mtoto-Peryllys (Warning)
J R Best (B Smart 30/7) Lacey/buckham

Placings:42450-0100060 **(4640)**
2001: 6^{0}GF, 7^{1}GF, 6^{0}G, 7^{0}GF, 7^{0}GF, 7^{6}GF, 7^{0}GF

	Starts	1st	2nd	3rd	Win & Pl
Career Total (Turf)	12	1	1	0	5747
70 6/01 Bevl 7f100y E(0-75)H				G-F	£4023
				Total win prize-money	£4024

Going (Turf): Sf: 0-1 GS: 0-0 Gd: 0-1 **GF: 1-9** Fm: 0-1
Distance: 5f/6f: 0-2 **7f-8f: 1-10** 9f-13f: 0-0 14f+: 0-0
Track : LH: 0-2 **RH: 1-2** Tight: 0-2 Gall: 0-1
Aids: Bl: 0-0 Vi: 0-0 Tstrap: 0-0
Best Rating: 70 6/01 Bevl 7f100y gd-fm

He looked to be going the wrong way after showing early promise in maiden company, but got off the mark in a handicap at Beverley in June. Suited by seven furlongs and fast ground.

Honesty Fair

112 **101**
4-y-o b f Reprimand-Truthful Image (Reesh)
J A Glover P And S Partnership

Placings:3600/41100046611-0000153315010 **(5365)**
2001: 6^{0}GF, 5^{0}GF, 5^{0}GF, 6^{0}GF, 5^{1}GS, 6^{5}G, 6^{3}G, 6^{3}G, 6^{1}GF, 7^{5}G, 6^{0}GF, 6^{1}G, 6^{0}GS

	Starts	1st	2nd	3rd	Win & Pl
Career Total (Turf)	28	7	0	3	79569
101 10/01 NmkR 6f B(0-105)H				GD	£8984
101 9/01 York 6f B(0-105)H				G-F	£16022
96 7/01 NmkJ 5f C(0-100)H				G-S	£6857
97 9/00 NmkR 6f B(0-105)H				GD	£9767
86 8/00 York 5f C(0-100)H				GD	£15827
87 5/00 Thsk 5f C(0-100)H				GD	£7241
74 5/00 Bevl 5f D				G-F	£4189
				Total win prize-money	£68889

Going (Turf): Sf: 0-0 GS: 1-4 **Gd: 4-11** GF: 2-13 Fm: 0-0
Distance: **5f/6f: 7-27** 7f-8f: 0-1 9f-13f: 0-0 14f+: 0-0
Track : LH: 0-1 RH: 0-1 Tight: 0-0 Gall: 0-1
Aids: Bl: 0-0 Vi: 0-0 Tstrap: 0-0
Best Rating: 101 10/01 NmkR 6f good

In fine form at the end of 2000, she found her form once dropped a few pounds and faced with an easier surface at Newmarket in July 2001. Good efforts in the Stewards' Cup and in valuable handicaps at Ascot, York and Newmarket, winning at both the latter venues. Effective at both five and six furlongs, she is suited by being held up.

Honey For Money (IRE)

87 **69**
2-y-o b f Alzao (USA)-Classical Flair (USA) (Riverman (USA))
J R Fanshawe Oliver Murphy

Placings:366 **(5110)**
2001: 6^{3}GF, 7^{6}GF, 6^{6}HY

	Starts	1st	2nd	3rd	Win & Pl
Career Total (Turf)	3	0	0	1	641

Going (Turf): Sf: 0-1 GS: 0-0 Gd: 0-0 GF: 0-2 Fm: 0-0
Distance: 5f/6f: 0-1 7f-8f: 0-2 9f-13f: 0-0 14f+: 0-0
Track : LH: 0-0 RH: 0-0 Tight: 0-0 Gall: 0-0
Aids: Bl: 0-0 Vi: 0-0 Tstrap: 0-0
Best Rating: 69 8/01 Folk 7f gd-fm

Honey's Gift

92(80) (41)**55**
2-y-o b f Terimon-Honeycroft (Crofter (USA))
G G Margarson John M Richards

Placings:246540300 **(5589)**
2001: 5^{2}HY, 5^{4}HY, 6^{6}SD, 6^{5}GF, 7^{4}GS, 7^{0}SD, 7^{3}GS, 8^{0}S, 7^{0}GS

	Starts	1st	2nd	3rd	Win & Pl
Career Total (Turf)	7	0	1	1	1872
Career Total (AW)	2	0	0	0	0

Going (Turf): Sf: 0-3 GS: 0-3 Gd: 0-0 GF: 0-1 Fm: 0-0
Distance: 5f/6f: 0-3 7f-8f: 0-5 9f-13f: 0-1 14f+: 0-0
Track : LH: 0-7 RH: 0-0 Tight: 0-2 Gall: 0-1
Aids: Bl: 0-0 Vi: 0-0 Tstrap: 0-0
Best Rating: 55 11/01 Brig 7f214y gd-sft

Little sign of ability until a good third at Catterick in a nursery over seven furlongs.

Honeymooner (IRE)

81 **51**
2-y-o ch f Pursuit Of Love-Bathe In Light (USA) (Sunshine Forever (USA))
J G Portman P G Lowe

Placings:00505 **(3954)**
2001: 5^{0}G, 6^{0}GF, 7^{5}F, 7^{0}GF, 6^{5}GF

	Starts	1st	2nd	3rd	Win & Pl
Career Total (Turf)	5	0	0	0	0

Going (Turf): Sf: 0-0 GS: 0-0 Gd: 0-1 GF: 0-3 Fm: 0-1
Distance: 5f/6f: 0-2 7f-8f: 0-3 9f-13f: 0-0 14f+: 0-0
Track : LH: 0-0 RH: 0-1 Tight: 0-0 Gall: 0-1
Aids: Bl: 0-0 Vi: 0-0 Tstrap: 0-0
Best Rating: 51 6/01 Sals 6f gd-fm

Honeypoint

79 **67d**
2-y-o b f Robellino (USA)-Short And Sharp (Sharpen Up)
D Morris D Morris

Placings:100 **(3316)**
2001: 6^{1}G, 7^{0}G, 7^{0}G

	Starts	1st	2nd	3rd	Win & Pl

Career Total (Turf) 3 1 0 0 1897
67 7/01 Yarm 6f3y G GD £1897
Total win prize-money £1897

Going (Turf): Sf: 0-0 GS: 0-0 **Gd: 1-3** GF: 0-0 Fm: 0-0
Distance: 5f/6f: 0-0 **7f-8f: 1-3** 9f-13f: 0-0 14f+: 0-0
Track : LH: 0-0 RH: 0-0 Tight: 0-0 Gall: 0-0
Aids: Bl: 0-0 Vi: 0-0 Tstrap: 0-0
Best Rating: 67 7/01 Yarm 6f3y good

Won a poor Yarmouth seller on her debut in July over six furlongs. Acts on good ground.

Honor Rouge (IRE)

89 **73+**
2-y-o ch f Highest Honor (FR)-Ayers Rock (IRE) (In The Wings)
P W Harris Honors List

Placings:0310 **(5229)**
2001: 7^{0}GF, 7^{3}GS, 8^{1}F, 7^{0}S

	Starts	1st	2nd	3rd	Win & Pl
Career Total (Turf)	4	1	0	1	3109

73 9/01 Muss 1m F FRM £2576
Total win prize-money £2576

Going (Turf): Sf: 0-1 GS: 0-1 Gd: 0-0 GF: 0-1 **Fm: 1-1**
Distance: 5f/6f: 0-0 **7f-8f: 1-4** 9f-13f: 0-0 14f+: 0-0
Track : LH: 0-2 **RH: 1-1 Tight: 1-2** Gall: 0-1
Aids: Bl: 0-0 Vi: 0-0 Tstrap: 0-0
Best Rating: 73 9/01 Muss 1m firm

She improved in each of her first three starts and relished the step up to a mile to win a modest race at Musselburgh.

Honor's Lad

65 **8**
2-y-o ch c Sabrehill (USA)-Ackcontent (USA) (Key To Content (USA))
C N Kellett Sean A Taylor

Placings:0 **(3704)**
2001: 5^{0}G

	Starts	1st	2nd	3rd	Win & Pl
Career Total (Turf)	1	0	0	0	

Going (Turf): Sf: 0-0 GS: 0-0 Gd: 0-1 GF: 0-0 Fm: 0-0
Distance: 5f/6f: 0-1 7f-8f: 0-0 9f-13f: 0-0 14f+: 0-0
Track : LH: 0-0 RH: 0-0 Tight: 0-0 Gall: 0-0
Aids: Bl: 0-0 Vi: 0-0 Tstrap: 0-0
Best Rating: 8 8/01 Leic 5f218y good

Hope Jo'Anna (USA)

82 **30**
3-y-o ch f Chimes Band (USA)-Banker's Bundles (USA) (Majestic Light (USA))
N A Graham Fieldspring Racing

Placings:000 **(5631)**
2001: 8^{0}G, 8^{0}GS, 10^{0}G

	Starts	1st	2nd	3rd	Win & Pl
Career Total (Turf)	3	0	0	0	

Going (Turf): Sf: 0-0 GS: 0-1 Gd: 0-2 GF: 0-0 Fm: 0-0
Distance: 5f/6f: 0-0 7f-8f: 0-0 9f-13f: 0-3 14f+: 0-0
Track : LH: 0-3 RH: 0-0 Tight: 0-1 Gall: 0-0
Aids: Bl: 0-0 Vi: 0-0 Tstrap: 0-0
Best Rating: 30 9/01 Nott 1m54y good

Hopeful Henry

91 (101) (47)**44**
5-y-o ch g Cadeaux Genereux-Fernlea (USA) (Sir Ivor)
G L Moore Danny Bloor

Placings:0/600005-12505 **(4159)**
2001: 6^{1}SD, 6^{2}SD, 7^{5}SW, 6^{0}SD, 6^{5}GF

	Starts	1st	2nd	3rd	Win & Pl
Career Total (Turf)	5	0	0	0	0
Career Total (AW)	7	1	1	0	2703

47 1/01 Ling 6f G(0-65)H STD £1869
Total win prize-money £1869

Going (Turf): Sf: 0-0 GS: 0-1 Gd: 0-1 GF: 0-3 Fm: 0-0
Distance: **5f/6f: 1-10** 7f-8f: 0-2 9f-13f: 0-0 14f+: 0-0
Track : **LH: 1-7** RH: 0-1 **Tight: 1-7** Gall: 0-1
Aids: Bl: 0-0 Vi: 0-0 Tstrap: 0-0
Best Rating: 47 1/01 Ling 6f stand

Hormuz (IRE)

108 (84)**62**
5-y-o b g Hamas (IRE)-Balqis (USA) (Advocator)
D Nicholls (J M Bradley 20/6) The Knavesmire Alliance

Placings:5/12100121050/000000105526-052420341010 **(4800)**
2001: 8^{0}F, 9^{5}GF, 8^{2}G, 9^{4}GF, 7^{2}G, 10^{0}G, 8^{3}F, 8^{4}GF, 8^{1}GS, 8^{0}G, 9^{1}GF, 10^{0}F

	Starts	1st	2nd	3rd	Win & Pl
Career Total (Turf)	32	5	4	1	32127
Career Total (AW)	4	2	1	0	7900

62 9/01 Ripn 1m1f D(0-80)H G-F £7995
60 8/01 Bevl 1m100y E(0-75)H G-S £3535
61 7/00 Ripn 1m E G-F £2600
86 7/99 Bevl 1m100y D(0-85)H SFT £5930
79 6/99 Ripn 1m2f E(0-75) G-F £2570
84 3/99 Ling 1m2f D(0-85)H STD £3555
72 1/99 Ling 1m2f D STD £3623
Total win prize-money £29810

Going (Turf): Sf: 1-1 GS: 1-4 Gd: 0-8 **GF: 3-14** Fm: 0-5
Distance: 5f/6f: 0-0 7f-8f: 1-11 **9f-13f: 6-25** 14f+: 0-0
Track : LH: 2-18 **RH: 5-16 Tight: 5-20** Gall: 0-4
Aids: Bl: 0-0 Vi: 0-0 Tstrap: 0-0
Best Rating: 62 9/01 Ripn 1m1f gd-fm

A multiple winner for Mark Johnston in his younger days, the Milton Bradley magic only worked once for him since then and he is now with Dandy Nicholls. Ran well during the summer and won at Beverley and Ripon. He stays an easy ten furlongs but is better at a mile. Suited by fast ground.

Hornby Boy

88(78) (35)**28**
3-y-o b g Dolphin Street (FR)-Miss Walsh (Distant Relative)
J Hetherton Mrs C A Brown

Placings:00-050060000 **(4187)**
2001: 7^{0}SW, 7^{5}SD, 6^{0}SW, 6^{0}SD, 8^{6}F, 7^{0}GF, 11^{0}GF, 8^{0}GS, 9^{0}GF

	Starts	1st	2nd	3rd	Win & Pl
Career Total (Turf)	6	0	0	0	0
Career Total (AW)	5	0	0	0	0

Going (Turf): Sf: 0-1 GS: 0-1 Gd: 0-0 GF: 0-3 Fm: 0-1
Distance: 5f/6f: 0-3 7f-8f: 0-5 9f-13f: 0-3 14f+: 0-0
Track : LH: 0-7 RH: 0-2 Tight: 0-2 Gall: 0-1
Aids: Bl: 0-1 Vi: 0-0 Tstrap: 0-0
Best Rating: 35 1/01 Sthl 7f stand

Horoscope (IRE)

96 **86**
2-y-o b g Eagle Eyed (USA)-Council Rock (General Assembly (USA))
W J Haggas Horoscope Partnership

Placings:4122 **(3638)**
2001: 5^{4}F, 5^{1}F, 6^{2}GF, 6^{2}GS

	Starts	1st	2nd	3rd	Win & Pl
Career Total (Turf)	4	1	2	0	11001

79 6/01 Nott 5f13y D FRM £3692
Total win prize-money £3693

Going (Turf): Sf: 0-0 GS: 0-1 Gd: 0-0 GF: 0-1 **Fm: 1-2**
Distance: **5f/6f: 1-4** 7f-8f: 0-0 9f-13f: 0-0 14f+: 0-0
Track : LH: 0-0 RH: 0-0 Tight: 0-0 Gall: 0-0
Aids: Bl: 0-0 Vi: 0-0 Tstrap: 0-0
Best Rating: 86 8/01 NmkJ 6f gd-sft

A half-brother to Superstar Leo, he won a five furlong Nottingham maiden before just failing over six at Lingfield.

Horsecalledcharlie

80 **43**
3-y-o ch g Charmer-Ordima (Sylvan Express)
J Akehurst The Shoestring Partnership

Placings:000 **(2113)**
2001: 7^{0}GS, 7^{0}GF, 6^{0}F

	Starts	1st	2nd	3rd	Win & Pl
Career Total (Turf)	3	0	0	0	

Going (Turf): Sf: 0-0 GS: 0-1 Gd: 0-0 GF: 0-1 Fm: 0-1
Distance: 5f/6f: 0-1 7f-8f: 0-2 9f-13f: 0-0 14f+: 0-0
Track : LH: 0-0 RH: 0-1 Tight: 0-0 Gall: 0-0
Aids: Bl: 0-0 Vi: 0-0 Tstrap: 0-0
Best Rating: 43 5/01 Gdwd 7f gd-fm

Horton Dancer

101(98) (31)**36**
4-y-o b g Rambo Dancer (CAN)-Horton Lady (Midyan (USA))
D W Barker (J Parkes 19/2) Robert E Cook

Placings:4/**600**4003035**050-400**300106 **(4800)**
2001: 12^{4}SD, 12^{0}SD, 11^{0}SD, 12^{3}G, 11^{0}G, 16^{0}GS, 9^{1}GF, 8^{0}GF, 10^{6}F

	Starts	1st	2nd	3rd	Win & Pl
Career Total (Turf)	15	1	0	3	3752
Career Total (AW)	8	0	0	0	0

26 8/01 Bevl 1m1f207yF(0-60)H G-F £2411
Total win prize-money £2412

Going (Turf): Sf: 0-0 GS: 0-3 Gd: 0-2 **GF: 1-8** Fm: 0-2
Distance: 5f/6f: 0-0 7f-8f: 0-1 **9f-13f: 1-16** 14f+: 0-6
Track : LH: 0-15 **RH: 1-6** Tight: 0-10 Gall: 0-1
Aids: Bl: 0-0 Vi: 0-6 Tstrap: 0-1
Best Rating: 36 9/01 Pont 1m2f6y firm

Hossrum (IRE)

68
3-y-o br c Definite Article-Petite Maxine (Sharpo)
E A L Dunlop Ahmed Buhaleeba

Placings:603-0 **(1628)**
2001: 8^{0}F

	Starts	1st	2nd	3rd	Win & Pl
Career Total (Turf)	4	0	0	1	506

Going (Turf): Sf: 0-0 GS: 0-0 Gd: 0-2 GF: 0-1 Fm: 0-1
Distance: 5f/6f: 0-1 7f-8f: 0-2 9f-13f: 0-1 14f+: 0-0
Track : LH: 0-0 RH: 0-1 Tight: 0-0 Gall: 0-0
Aids: Bl: 0-0 Vi: 0-0 Tstrap: 0-1
Best Rating: 36 9/01 Pont 1m2f6y firm

Hot Java (USA)

68 **14**
2-y-o b f Twining (USA)-Coffee Ice (Primo Dominie)
T D Easterby Hassan Ahmadi And M S Anderson

Placings:00 **(1302)**
2001: 5^{0}HY, 5^{0}GF

	Starts	1st	2nd	3rd	Win & Pl
Career Total (Turf)	2	0	0	0	

Going (Turf): Sf: 0-1 GS: 0-0 Gd: 0-0 GF: 0-1 Fm: 0-0
Distance: 5f/6f: 0-2 7f-8f: 0-0 9f-13f: 0-0 14f+: 0-0
Track : LH: 0-1 RH: 0-0 Tight: 0-0 Gall: 0-1
Aids: Bl: 0-0 Vi: 0-0 Tstrap: 0-0
Best Rating: 14 5/01 Thsk 5f gd-fm

Hot Jazz

96 **74**

2-y-o ch f Midyan (USA)-Fascinating Rhythm (Slip Anchor)
J R Fanshawe Helena Springfield Ltd

Placings:54 (5658)
2001: 7^{5}GF, 7^{4}G

	Starts	1st	2nd	3rd	Win & Pl
Career Total (Turf)	2	0	0	0	0

Going (Turf): Sf: 0-0 GS: 0-0 Gd: 0-1 GF: 0-1 Fm: 0-0
Distance: 5f/6f: 0-0 7f-8f: 0-2 9f-13f: 0-0 14f+: 0-0
Track : LH: 0-0 RH: 0-1 Tight: 0-0 Gall: 0-1
Aids: Bl: 0-0 Vi: 0-0 Tstrap: 0-0
Best Rating: 74 9/01 Kemp 7f gd-fm

Hot Pants

97(97) (72)**53**

3-y-o ch f Rudimentary (USA)-True Precision (Presidium)
K T Ivory Mrs J A Pearson

Placings:053064-**1**004406025460 (4785)
2001: 5^{1}SD, 5^{0}SW, 5^{0}SW, 5^{4}G, 5^{4}F, 6^{0}GF, 6^{6}F, 5^{0}GF, 5^{2}G, 5^{5}G, 5^{4}G, 6^{6}GF, 5^{0}G

	Starts	1st	2nd	3rd	Win & Pl
Career Total (Turf)	16	0	1	1	2099
Career Total (AW)	3	1	0	0	2856

72 1/01 Ling 5f D STD £2856
Total win prize-money £2856

Going (Turf): Sf: 0-0 GS: 0-0 Gd: 0-8 GF: 0-5 Fm: 0-2
Distance: 5f/6f: 1-18 7f-8f: 0-0 9f-13f: 0-0 14f+: 0-0
Track : LH: 1-5 RH: 0-1 Tight: 1-2 Gall: 0-1
Aids: Bl: 0-1 Vi: 0-0 Tstrap: 0-0
Best Rating: 72 1/01 Ling 5f stand

A winner of just the one maiden on the sand, she is becoming expensive to follow.

Hot Potato

88(86) (13)**28**

5-y-o b h Roman Warrior-My Song Of Songs (Norwick (USA))
J S Wainwright Mrs S A Donald

Placings:500065/560005/04600502060500-000 (1134)
2001: 8^{0}SW, 12^{0}SD, 9^{0}GS

	Starts	1st	2nd	3rd	Win & Pl
Career Total (Turf)	16	0	1	0	1260
Career Total (AW)	13	0	0	0	0

Going (Turf): Sf: 0-9 GS: 0-3 Gd: 0-2 GF: 0-2 Fm: 0-0
Distance: 5f/6f: 0-8 7f-8f: 0-7 9f-13f: 0-14 14f+: 0-0
Track : LH: 0-14 RH: 0-7 Tight: 0-9 Gall: 0-1
Aids: Bl: 0-0 Vi: 0-4 Tstrap: 0-0
Best Rating: 13 5/01 Haml 1m1f36y gd-sft

Hot Produxion (USA)

98 **78**

2-y-o ch c Tabasco Cat (USA)-Princess Harriet (USA) (Mt. Livermore (USA))
Mrs A J Perrett Michael H Watt

Placings:0532 (5168)
2001: 7^{0}G, 7^{5}GF, 8^{3}G, 10^{2}GS

	Starts	1st	2nd	3rd	Win & Pl
Career Total (Turf)	4	0	1	1	1888

Going (Turf): Sf: 0-0 GS: 0-1 Gd: 0-2 GF: 0-1 Fm: 0-0
Distance: 5f/6f: 0-0 7f-8f: 0-3 9f-13f: 0-1 14f+: 0-0
Track : LH: 0-1 RH: 0-2 Tight: 0-0 Gall: 0-0
Aids: Bl: 0-0 Vi: 0-0 Tstrap: 0-0
Best Rating: 78 10/01 Pont 1m2f6y gd-sft

A $100,000 yearling, he ran well when stepped up to ten furlongs on his fourth start. Seems to handle any ground.

Hot Tin Roof (IRE)

112 **106**

5-y-o b m Thatching-No Reservations (IRE) (Commanche Run)
T D Easterby Giles W Pritchard-Gordon

Placings:31230/211226140-3032103005 (5694)
2001: 6^{3}HY, 6^{0}GF, 6^{3}GF, 6^{2}GF, 6^{1}GS, 6^{0}S, 6^{3}GS, 6^{0}S, 7^{0}GS, 6^{5}S

	Starts	1st	2nd	3rd	Win & Pl
Career Total (Turf)	24	5	5	5	94950

77 8/01 NmkJ 6f C G-S £6188
109 7/00 York 6f A GD £17468
105 5/00 Nott 6f15y A GD £13862
102 5/00 Ling 7f A G-S £13485
74 6/99 Newc 6f D GD £3631
Total win prize-money £54635

Going (Turf): Sf: 0-4 GS: 2-7 Gd: 3-6 GF: 0-7 Fm: 0-0
Distance: 5f/6f: 3-13 7f-8f: 2-11 9f-13f: 0-0 14f+: 0-0
Track : LH: 0-3 RH: 0-0 Tight: 0-0 Gall: 0-0
Aids: Bl: 0-0 Vi: 0-0 Tstrap: 0-0
Best Rating: 107 6/01 Hayd 6f gd-fm

After making the frame in Listed events at Windsor and Haydock, she scored in fine style at Newmarket in August, after apparently having problems with a foot. Hold since, including in a Group One. She does not look comfortable on fast ground and appears best suited by good or softer.

Hotcallie Legend

91 **65**

2-y-o b c Faustus (USA)-Alice Holt (Free State)
Mrs A J Perrett Fielden Racing

Placings:000 (4158)
2001: 6^{0}GF, 6^{0}GF, 7^{0}GF

	Starts	1st	2nd	3rd	Win & Pl
Career Total (Turf)	3	0	0	0	

Going (Turf): Sf: 0-0 GS: 0-0 Gd: 0-0 GF: 0-3 Fm: 0-0
Distance: 5f/6f: 0-0 7f-8f: 0-3 9f-13f: 0-0 14f+: 0-0
Track : LH: 0-0 RH: 0-2 Tight: 0-2 Gall: 0-0
Aids: Bl: 0-0 Vi: 0-0 Tstrap: 0-0
Best Rating: 65 8/01 Ling 7f140y gd-fm

Hotelgenie Dot Com

103 **79**

3-y-o gr f Selkirk (USA)-Birch Creek (Carwhite)
M R Channon Mr Derek D & Mrs Jean P Clee

Placings:1223-000 (4682)
2001: 9^{0}S, 8^{0}G, 7^{0}G

	Starts	1st	2nd	3rd	Win & Pl
Career Total (Turf)	7	1	2	1	66795

79 7/00 Sand 7f16y D GD £6955
Total win prize-money £6955

Going (Turf): Sf: 0-1 GS: 0-1 Gd: 1-3 GF: 0-2 Fm: 0-0
Distance: 5f/6f: 0-0 7f-8f: 1-5 9f-13f: 0-2 14f+: 0-0
Track : LH: 0-0 RH: 1-4 Tight: 0-0 Gall: 0-1
Aids: Bl: 0-0 Vi: 0-1 Tstrap: 0-0
Best Rating: 79 9/01 Donc 7f good

A useful juvenile, but has had problems and showed little this season. Acts on fast ground.

Hoteliers' Dream

83 **37**

3-y-o b f Reprimand-Pride Of Britain (CAN) (Linkage (USA))
W S Kittow Pride Of Britain Limited

Placings:6000 (5664)
2001: 8^{6}F, 10^{0}G, 8^{0}G, 8^{0}HY

	Starts	1st	2nd	3rd	Win & Pl
Career Total (Turf)	4	0	0	0	0

Going (Turf): Sf: 0-1 GS: 0-0 Gd: 0-2 GF: 0-0 Fm: 0-1
Distance: 5f/6f: 0-0 7f-8f: 0-0 9f-13f: 0-4 14f+: 0-0
Track : LH: 0-0 RH: 0-2 Tight: 0-2 Gall: 0-0
Aids: Bl: 0-0 Vi: 0-0 Tstrap: 0-0
Best Rating: 37 8/01 Wind 1m2f7y good

House Doctor

91 **52**

2-y-o ch c Rudimentary (USA)-Persian Air (Persian Bold)
K McAuliffe Highgrove Developments Limited

Placings:00 (2963)
2001: 6^{0}GF, 6^{0}GF

	Starts	1st	2nd	3rd	Win & Pl
Career Total (Turf)	2	0	0	0	

Going (Turf): Sf: 0-0 GS: 0-0 Gd: 0-0 GF: 0-2 Fm: 0-0
Distance: 5f/6f: 0-0 7f-8f: 0-2 9f-13f: 0-0 14f+: 0-0
Track : LH: 0-0 RH: 0-1 Tight: 0-1 Gall: 0-0
Aids: Bl: 0-0 Vi: 0-0 Tstrap: 0-0
Best Rating: 52 7/01 Folk 6f189y gd-fm

House Of Dreams

101(94) (32)**51**

9-y-o b g Darshaan-Helens Dreamgirl (Caerleon (USA))
Mrs M Reveley J & M Leisure / Unos Restaurant

Placings:0/6036/662/053/13146100/5006624/012366-0020 (4009)
2001: 14^{0}GF, 15^{0}GS, 13^{2}G, 11^{0}G

	Starts	1st	2nd	3rd	Win & Pl
Career Total (Turf)	34	4	4	4	23984
Career Total (AW)	2	0	0	0	0

42 8/00 Rdcr 1m6f19y F FRM £2278
65 9/98 Thsk 1m4f D(0-80)H GD £7795
63 7/98 Carl 1m6f32y E(0-70)H G-F £2983
56 6/98 Catt 1m3f214yE(0-70)H G-S £3077
Total win prize-money £16134

Going (Turf): Sf: 0-5 GS: 1-6 Gd: 1-10 GF: 1-9 Fm: 1-4
Distance: 5f/6f: 0-0 7f-8f: 0-1 9f-13f: 2-21 14f+: 2-14
Track : LH: 3-28 RH: 1-8 Tight: 3-23 Gall: 0-3
Aids: Bl: 0-0 Vi: 0-0 Tstrap: 0-0
Best Rating: 41 8/01 Catt 1m5f175y good

Houseparty (IRE)

104 **88**

3-y-o b/br c Grand Lodge (USA)-Special Display (Welsh Pageant)
Sir Michael Stoute Highclere Thoroughbred Racing Ltd

Placings:3-2210 (4170)
2001: 8^{2}GF, 8^{2}GF, 10^{1}GS, 10^{0}G

	Starts	1st	2nd	3rd	Win & Pl
Career Total (Turf)	5	1	2	1	7992

86 8/01 Hayd 1m2f120yD G-S £4407
Total win prize-money £4407

Going (Turf): Sf: 0-1 GS: 1-1 Gd: 0-1 GF: 0-2 Fm: 0-0
Distance: 5f/6f: 0-0 7f-8f: 0-2 9f-13f: 1-3 14f+: 0-0

Track : LH: 1-2 RH: 0-1 Tight: 0-0 Gall: 0-1
Aids: Bl: 0-0 Vi: 0-0 Tstrap: 0-0
Best Rating: 88 8/01 York 1m2f85y good

Showed plenty of ability in three outings before scoring on his fourth at Haydock over ten and a half furlongs. Has won on good to soft.

Houston Park (IRE)

90 **73**
2-y-o ch c Persian Bold-Harina (Pentotal)
L M Cumani Miss G Gatto Roissard

Placings:500011 **(5739a)**
2001: 7^{5}G, 7^{0}GF, 5^{0}GF, 6^{0}GF, 9^{1}S, 8^{1}HY

	Starts	1st	2nd	3rd	Win & Pl
Career Total (Turf)	6	2	0	0	16428

11/01	Siro	1m		HVY	£9857
10/01	Siro	1m1f		SFT	£6571

Total win prize-money £16428

Going (Turf): Sf: 2-2 GS: 0-0 Gd: 0-1 GF: 0-3 Fm: 0-0
Distance: 5f/6f: 0-2 7f-8f: 1-3 9f-13f: 1-1 14f+: 0-0
Track : LH: 0-1 **RH: 2-2** Tight: 0-0 Gall: 0-0
Aids: Bl: 0-0 Vi: 0-0 Tstrap: 0-0
Best Rating: 73 8/01 Newb 7f gd-fm

Hout Bay

103(105) (49)**64**
4-y-o ch g Komaite (USA)-Maiden Pool (Sharpen Up)
S E Kettlewell Hout's Partnership

Placings:6440/6453005400342-32362210060150 **(4876)**
2001: 5^{3}SD, 5^{2}SD, 7^{3}SW, 5^{6}SD, 5^{2}GF, 6^{2}GF, 5^{1}F, 6^{0}GF, 5^{0}G, 6^{6}F, 6^{0}G, 5^{1}GF, 5^{5}GF, 6^{0}SD

	Starts	1st	2nd	3rd	Win & Pl
Career Total (Turf)	20	2	2	1	8154
Career Total (AW)	11	0	2	3	2217

64	8/01	Catt	5f	F(0-60)H	G-F	£2527
60	7/01	Brig	5f59y	F(0-60)H	FRM	£2296

Total win prize-money £4823

Going (Turf): Sf: 0-1 GS: 0-3 Gd: 0-6 **GF: 1-8 Fm: 1-2**
Distance: 5f/6f: 2-28 7f-8f: 0-3 9f-13f: 0-0 14f+: 0-0
Track : LH: 1-14 RH: 0-2 Tight: 0-11 Gall: 0-1
Aids: Bl: 0-0 Vi: 0-0 Tstrap: 0-0
Best Rating: 64 8/01 Catt 5f gd-fm

He has been very consistent this season, though his victory in a Brighton handicap in July was his first in 24 attempts. He added another victory at Catterick in August.

How Do I Know

104 **89**
3-y-o gr f Petong-Glenfield Portion (Mummy's Pet)
G A Butler Manny Bernstein (racing) Ltd

Placings:0221-14030 **(5391)**
2001: 6^{1}S, 6^{4}GS, 6^{0}F, 6^{3}G, 7^{0}GS

	Starts	1st	2nd	3rd	Win & Pl
Career Total (Turf)	9	2	2	1	13956

89	4/01	NmkR	6f	C(0-95)H	SFT	£7592
82	10/00	Rdcr	5f	F	SFT	£2404

Total win prize-money £9997

Going (Turf): Sf: 2-2 GS: 0-3 Gd: 0-2 GF: 0-1 Fm: 0-1
Distance: 5f/6f: 2-7 7f-8f: 0-2 9f-13f: 0-0 14f+: 0-0
Track : LH: 0-1 RH: 0-1 Tight: 0-0 Gall: 0-2
Aids: Bl: 0-0 Vi: 0-0 Tstrap: 0-0
Best Rating: 89 4/01 NmkR 6f soft

Howard's Lad (IRE)

100(68) (10)**47**
4-y-o b g Reprimand-Port Isaac (USA) (Seattle Song (USA))
I Semple Gordon McDowall

Placings:013400/0000510200004 0-00264002050 **(5288)**
2001: 9^{0}S, 7^{0}GF, 7^{2}F, 8^{6}GF, 7^{4}G, 8^{0}GF, 9^{0}G, 8^{2}GF, 9^{0}G, 6^{5}F, 6^{0}HY

	Starts	1st	2nd	3rd	Win & Pl
Career Total (Turf)	30	2	3	1	9461
Career Total (AW)	1	0	0	0	

58	7/00	Haml	6f5y	F(0-60)	G-F	£2240
73	7/99	Ayr	6f	D	GD	£3610

Total win prize-money £5850

Going (Turf): Sf: 0-4 GS: 0-2 **Gd: 1-7 GF: 1-14** Fm: 0-3
Distance: 5f/6f: 1-10 7f-8f: 1-14 9f-13f: 0-7 14f+: 0-0
Track : LH: 0-2 RH: 0-9 Tight: 0-8 Gall: 0-2
Aids: Bl: 1-7 Vi: 0-12 Tstrap: 0-0
Best Rating: 47 7/01 Muss 1m gd-fm

Howards Dream (IRE)

90 **35**
3-y-o b g King's Theatre (IRE)-Keiko (Generous (IRE))
D A Nolan (I Semple 22/8) Mrs J McFadyen-Murray

Placings:6-5505050 **(4164)**
2001: 10^{5}GF, 12^{5}G, 14^{0}F, 13^{5}GF, 13^{0}S, 14^{5}GF, 16^{0}GF

	Starts	1st	2nd	3rd	Win & Pl
Career Total (Turf)	8	0	0	0	0

Going (Turf): Sf: 0-1 GS: 0-1 Gd: 0-1 GF: 0-4 Fm: 0-1
Distance: 5f/6f: 0-0 7f-8f: 0-1 9f-13f: 0-2 14f+: 0-5
Track : LH: 0-3 RH: 0-5 Tight: 0-6 Gall: 0-0
Aids: Bl: 0-0 Vi: 0-0 Tstrap: 0-1
Best Rating: 51 5/01 Ayr 1m2f192y gd-fm

Howards Hero (IRE)

85 **52**
2-y-o gr g Paris House-Gold Braisim (IRE) (Jareer (USA))
I Semple Gordon McDowall

Placings:46464 **(4437)**
2001: 5^{4}GF, 5^{6}GF, 5^{4}GF, 6^{6}G, 5^{4}G

	Starts	1st	2nd	3rd	Win & Pl
Career Total (Turf)	5	0	0	0	595

Going (Turf): Sf: 0-0 GS: 0-0 Gd: 0-2 GF: 0-3 Fm: 0-0
Distance: 5f/6f: 0-4 7f-8f: 0-1 9f-13f: 0-0 14f+: 0-0
Track : LH: 0-0 RH: 0-0 Tight: 0-0 Gall: 0-0
Aids: Bl: 0-0 Vi: 0-0 Tstrap: 0-0
Best Rating: 52 9/01 Haml 5f4y good

Howards Heroine (IRE)

93 **66**
2-y-o ch f Danehill Dancer (IRE)-Romangoddess (IRE) (Rhoman Rule (USA))
I Semple Gordon McDowall

Placings:053306365 **(5662)**
2001: 5^{0}S, 6^{5}GF, 7^{3}GF, 7^{3}G, 6^{0}G, 6^{6}F, 7^{3}G, 7^{6}GS, 8^{5}G

	Starts	1st	2nd	3rd	Win & Pl
Career Total (Turf)	9	0	0	3	1223

Going (Turf): Sf: 0-1 GS: 0-1 Gd: 0-4 GF: 0-2 Fm: 0-1
Distance: 5f/6f: 0-2 7f-8f: 0-7 9f-13f: 0-0 14f+: 0-0
Track : LH: 0-1 RH: 0-2 Tight: 0-1 Gall: 0-1
Aids: Bl: 0-0 Vi: 0-0 Tstrap: 0-0
Best Rating: 66 9/01 Bevl 7f100y good

Has shown ability in maidens and nurseries on good ground.

Howe Timely

63 **4**
4-y-o b g Timeless Times (USA)-Adder Howe (Amboise)
N Bycroft Mrs Susan Johnson

Placings:00000 **(4616)**
2001: 6^{0}GF, 5^{0}GF, 10^{0}S, 7^{0}F, 8^{0}F

	Starts	1st	2nd	3rd	Win & Pl
Career Total (Turf)	5	0	0	0	

Going (Turf): Sf: 0-1 GS: 0-0 Gd: 0-0 GF: 0-2 Fm: 0-2
Distance: 5f/6f: 0-2 7f-8f: 0-2 9f-13f: 0-1 14f+: 0-0
Track : LH: 0-3 RH: 0-0 Tight: 0-1 Gall: 0-1
Aids: Bl: 0-0 Vi: 0-0 Tstrap: 0-0
Best Rating: 4 7/01 Bevl 5f gd-fm

Hub Hub

100 **51**
3-y-o b c Polish Precedent (USA)-Ghassanah (Pas De Seul)
R Hannon Sheikh Amin Dahlawi

Placings:04030000 **(5626)**
2001: 8^{0}GS, 6^{4}GF, 8^{0}GF, 7^{3}S, 8^{0}HY, 8^{0}G, 8^{0}GS, 8^{0}GS

	Starts	1st	2nd	3rd	Win & Pl
Career Total (Turf)	8	0	0	1	403

Going (Turf): Sf: 0-2 GS: 0-3 Gd: 0-1 GF: 0-2 Fm: 0-0
Distance: 5f/6f: 0-0 7f-8f: 0-4 9f-13f: 0-4 14f+: 0-0
Track : LH: 0-2 RH: 0-3 Tight: 0-2 Gall: 0-0
Aids: Bl: 0-0 Vi: 0-2 Tstrap: 0-0
Best Rating: 66 7/01 Folk 6f189y gd-fm

Hudood (USA)

101 **94**
6-y-o ch g Gone West (USA)-Fife (IRE) (Lomond (USA))
C E Brittain Sheikh Rashid Bin Mohammed Al Maktoum

Placings:1144/1/1335000053-0530 **(2164)**
2001: 10^{0}S, 10^{5}G, 12^{3}GF, 10^{0}G

	Starts	1st	2nd	3rd	Win & Pl
Career Total (Turf)	15	2	0	2	22213
Career Total (AW)	4	2	0	2	15480

2/00	Jebl	1m1f165y	FST	£4576
1/99	Jebl	1m	FST	£3682
7/98	Claf	1m	SFT	£6061
4/98	Amie	1m55y	GD	£3535

Total win prize-money £17854

Going (Turf): Sf: 0-1 GS: 0-0 Gd: 0-4 GF: 0-6 Fm: 0-0
Distance: 5f/6f: 0-0 7f-8f: 0-0 9f-13f: 0-11 14f+: 0-0
Track : LH: 0-1 RH: 0-9 Tight: 0-2 Gall: 0-6
Aids: Bl: 0-0 Vi: 0-0 Tstrap: 0-0
Best Rating: 90 5/01 NmkR 1m2f good

A winner in France and Dubai, he is a decent handicapper who was disqualified after finishing first at Newmarket in July 2000. He was unable to gain compensation despite running well after. Stays ten furlongs. Acts on fast ground.

Hufflepuff (IRE)

96 **86**
2-y-o b f Desert King (IRE)-Circle Of Chalk (FR) (Kris)
J L Dunlop Mrs T Brudenell

Placings:2126 **(3395)**
2001: 6^{2}GF, 6^{1}GF, 6^{2}GS, 7^{6}GF

	Starts	1st	2nd	3rd	Win & Pl
Career Total (Turf)	4	1	2	0	7628

74	6/01	Pont	6f	D	G-F	£5323

Total win prize-money £5324

Going (Turf): Sf: 0-0 GS: 0-1 Gd: 0-0 **GF: 1-3** Fm: 0-0
Distance: 5f/6f: 1-3 7f-8f: 0-1 9f-13f: 0-0 14f+: 0-0
Track : LH: 1-1 RH: 0-1 Tight: 0-0 Gall: 0-0
Aids: Bl: 0-0 Vi: 0-0 Tstrap: 0-0
Best Rating: 86 7/01 Hayd 6f gd-sft

Showed ability on her debut before scoring on her second outing at Pontefract and was just touched off at Haydock next time. Probably went off too quick when last of six in a Sandown Listed event on her first try over seven furlongs.

Hugh The Man (IRE)

81 **60**

2-y-o b c Hamas (IRE)-Run To Jenny (Runnett)
N P Littmoden Silver Knight Exhibitions Ltd

Placings:00 **(5689)**
2001: 7^{0}HY, 6^{0}S

	Starts	1st	2nd	3rd	Win & Pl
Career Total (Turf)	2	0	0	0	

Going (Turf): **Sf: 0-2 GS: 0-0 Gd: 0-0 GF: 0-0 Fm: 0-0**
Distance: 5f/6f: 0-1 7f-8f: 0-1 9f-13f: 0-0 14f+: 0-0
Track : LH: 0-0 RH: 0-0 Tight: 0-0 Gall: 0-0
Aids: Bl: 0-0 Vi: 0-0 Tstrap: 0-0
Best Rating: 60 10/01 Donc 7f heavy

Hugs Dancer (FR)

108 **69**

4-y-o b g Cadeaux Genereux-Embracing (Reference Point)
J G Given J G White

Placings:3340300-04131321000 **(5387)**
2001: 8^{0}G, 8^{4}F, 12^{1}GF, 12^{3}GF, 14^{1}F, 15^{3}GF, 16^{2}F, 21^{1}GF, 13^{0}GF, 15^{0}S, 18^{0}GS

	Starts	1st	2nd	3rd	Win & Pl
Career Total (Turf)	18	3	1	5	40391

69	8/01	Gdwd	2m5f	C(0-95)H	G-F	£24960
64	7/01	Muss	1m6f	E(0-75)H	FRM	£4212
59	6/01	Newc	1m4f93y	F(0-60)	G-F	£2541

Total win prize-money £31713

Going (Turf): Sf: 0-3 GS: 0-3 Gd: 0-2 **GF: 2-7** Fm: 1-3
Distance: 5f/6f: 0-0 7f-8f: 0-2 9f-13f: 1-9 **14f+: 2-7**
Track : LH: 1-11 RH: 1-4 Tight: 1-5 Gall: 1-5
Aids: Bl: 0-1 **Vi: 2-9** Tstrap: 0-0
Best Rating: 69 8/01 Gdwd 2m5f gd-fm

He landed a Newcastle classified stakes in June 2001 despite carrying head high and ran a blinder to finish third in the Cumberland Plate at the same track. Gained compensation by winning a 14-furlong handicap at Musselburgh just four days later and found the step up to 21 furlongs ideal in the Goodwood Handicap. He acts on fast ground, but has to be brought late as he does nothing in front. Regularly visored.

Hugwity

106(111) (76)**60**

9-y-o ch g Cadeaux Genereux-Nuit D'Ete (USA) (Super Concorde (USA))
G C Bravery Sawyer, Webb, Whatley

Placings:040/41110/002410260200**0645411/22160/112 4430**0336214015366-**0023541116**003244250 **(4640)**
2001: **10**^{0}SW, **12**^{0}SW, **12**^{2}SD, **12**^{3}SD, **14**^{5}SD, **11**^{4}SD, **10**^{1}SD, **10**^{1}SD, **8**^{1}SD, **8**^{6}SD, 10^{0}GF, 9^{0}GF, 8^{3}GF, 7^{2}G, 8^{4}G, 8^{4}GF, 7^{2}GF, 8^{5}S, 7^{0}GF

	Starts	1st	2nd	3rd	Win & Pl
Career Total (Turf)	41	6	6	4	41792
Career Total (AW)	30	8	4	2	30103

73	4/01	Sthl	1m	E(0-75)H	STD	£3031
66	4/01	Ling	1m2f	E(0 75)H	STD	£2954
63	3/01	Ling	1m2f	F(0-65)H	STD	£2432
55	7/00	Yarm	1m3y	F	G-F	£2373
74	5/00	Nott	1m54y	E(0-70)	GD	£3038
64	1/00	Ling	1m2f	F	STD	£2170
63	1/00	Ling	1m2f	F	STD	£2289
83	1/99	Ling	7f	D(0-85)H	STD	£3572
74	12/98	Ling	1m	D(0-80)H	STD	£3533
66	12/98	Sthl	1m	F	STD	£1987
80	7/98	Yarm	1m3y	D(0-75)H	GD	£3850
83	5/96	Gdwd	1m	C(0-100)H	GD	£9006
80	5/96	Ches	1m2f75y	C(0-90)H	GD	£11022
73	4/96	Leic	1m1f218yD		GD	£3704

Total win prize-money £54963

Going (Turf): Sf: 0-2 GS: 0-2 **Gd: 5-20** GF: 1-16 Fm: 0-1
Distance: 5f/6f: 0-1 7f-8f: 5-25 **9f-13f: 9-44** 14f+: 0-1
Track : **LH: 10-47** RH: 2-9 **Tight: 7-34** Gall: 0-4
Aids: Bl: 0-0 Vi: 0-0 Tstrap: 0-0
Best Rating: 73 4/01 Sthl 1m stand

Prolific winner between seven and ten furlongs on turf and sand. Not as good as he was, but still capable of winning in the right grade. Reported to have broken a blood vessel after his run at Nottingham in June.

Hume's Law

94(76) (26)**42**

3-y-o b c Puissance-Will Be Bold (Bold Lad (IRE))
A Berry Alan Berry

Placings:04610000-**00**000000000**0**5060000040006000 **(5629)**
2001: **6**^{0}SD, **7**^{0}SW, 6^{0}GF, 5^{0}GF, 6^{0}GF, 7^{0}G, 5^{0}F, 5^{0}GF, 5^{0}F, 7^{0}SD, 7^{5}GS, 6^{0}G, 8^{6}GF, 7^{0}GF, 7^{0}G, 6^{0}HY, 5^{0}GF, 8^{0}F, 6^{4}GF, 5^{0}G, 7^{0}GS, 7^{0}G, 5^{6}GS, 6^{0}S, 8^{0}HY, 5^{0}G

	Starts	1st	2nd	3rd	Win & Pl
Career Total (Turf)	31	1	0	0	4055
Career Total (AW)	3	0	0	0	

68	7/00	Bevl	5f	E	G-F	£3107

Total win prize-money £3107

Going (Turf): Sf: 0-5 GS: 0-4 Gd: 0-8 **GF: 1-10** Fm: 0-4
Distance: **5f/6f: 1-22** 7f-8f: 0-10 9f-13f: 0-2 14f+: 0-0
Track : LH: 0-7 RH: 0-2 Tight: 0-3 Gall: 0-0
Aids: Bl: 0-3 Vi: 0-0 Tstrap: 0-15
Best Rating: 46 6/01 Bevl 5f gd-fm

Scored once as a juvenile, but has not been given much chance to add to that lately, running solely for appearance money.

Hunting Ground

13-y-o b g Dancing Brave (USA)-Ack's Secret (USA) (Ack Ack (USA))
M Mullineaux I S Ross

Placings:2/260**05/4242**046000511150011/00/**0**/**0**60/056 00/0305/0 **(1108)**
2001: 16^{0}GF

	Starts	1st	2nd	3rd	Win & Pl
Career Total (Turf)	33	5	2	1	17355
Career Total (AW)	8	0	2	0	1649

59	9/93	Ayr	2m1f105y	D(0-75)H	G-F	£4299
56	9/93	Folk	1m7f92y	E(0-70)H	GD	£3106
56	8/93	Nott	2m9y	E(0-70)H	GD	£2959
48	7/93	Muss	1m7f16y	E(0-70)H	G-F	£2284
46	7/93	Muss	1m7f16y	E(0-70)H	GD	£2832

Total win prize-money £15482

Going (Turf): Sf: 0-3 GS: 0-1 **Gd: 3-13** GF: 2-13 Fm: 0-3
Distance: 5f/6f: 0-0 7f-8f: 0-0 9f-13f: 0-6 **14f+: 5-35**
Track : LH: 2-29 **RH: 3-12 Tight: 3-28** Gall: 0-1
Aids: **Bl: 5-24** Vi: 0-0 Tstrap: 0-0

Hunting Lion (IRE)

111 **110**

4-y-o b h Piccolo-Jalopy (Jalmood (USA))
M R Channon Jaber Abdullah

Placings:4123/0013-02 **(1139)**
2001: 6^{0}GS, 6^{2}G

	Starts	1st	2nd	3rd	Win & Pl
Career Total (Turf)	10	2	2	2	57673

108	6/00	NmkR	6f	B(0-105)H	G-F	£26000
76	7/99	Bath	5f161y	D	G-F	£3533

Total win prize-money £29534

Going (Turf): Sf: 0-0 GS: 0-2 Gd: 0-2 **GF: 2-6** Fm: 0-0
Distance: **5f/6f: 2-7** 7f-8f: 0-3 9f-13f: 0-0 14f+: 0-0
Track : **LH: 1-1** RH: 1-4 RH: 0-0 Tight: 0-0 **Gall: 1-1**
Aids: Bl: 0-0 Vi: 0-0 Tstrap: 0-0
Best Rating: 110 5/01 NmkR 6f good

A fast-ground performer, he bounced back to his best at Newmarket on his second run back after a long lay-off.

Hureya (USA)

105 **80+**

3-y-o b f Woodman (USA)-Istiqlal (USA) (Diesis)
J L Dunlop Hamdan Al Maktoum

Placings:54-2136 **(2727)**
2001: 7^{2}G, 8^{1}GF, 7^{3}G, 8^{6}GF

	Starts	1st	2nd	3rd	Win & Pl
Career Total (Turf)	6	1	1	1	6140

80	5/01	Yarm	1m3y	E(0-75)H	G-F	£3388

Total win prize-money £3388

Going (Turf): Sf: 0-0 GS: 0-1 Gd: 0-2 **GF: 1-3** Fm: 0-0
Distance: 5f/6f: 0-0 7f-8f: 0-4 **9f-13f: 1-2** 14f+: 0-0
Track : LH: 0-0 RH: 0-2 Tight: 0-0 Gall: 0-2
Aids: Bl: 0-0 Vi: 0-0 Tstrap: 0-0
Best Rating: 80 5/01 Yarm 1m3y gd-fm

She improved to win over a mile at Yarmouth in the summer, but has not cut much ice in handicaps since then. She acts on a sound surface.

Hurlingham Star (IRE)

(91) (30)**11**

3-y-o b g Distinctly North (USA)-Charrua (Sharpo)
W M Brisbourne (P D Evans 31/3) W J Hamilton

Placings:006**6050**10-446056000 **(5503)**
2001: **5**^{4}SD, **5**^{4}SD, **6**^{6}SW, **6**^{0}SD, **6**^{5}SW, **8**^{6}SD, **7**^{0}SD, **7**^{0}SD, 7^{0}HY

	Starts	1st	2nd	3rd	Win & Pl
Career Total (Turf)	5	0	0	0	0
Career Total (AW)	13	1	0	0	2216

56	12/00	Ling	6f	F	STD	£2215

Total win prize-money £2216

Going (Turf): **Sf: 0-1 GS: 0-1 Gd: 0-1 GF: 0-0 Fm: 0-1**
Distance: **5f/6f: 1-9** 7f-8f: 0-6 9f-13f: 0-2 14f+: 0-0
Track : **LH: 1-15** RH: 0-0 **Tight: 1-14** Gall: 0-0
Aids: Bl: 0-0 **Vi: 1-0** Tstrap. 0-0
Best Rating: 53 1/01 Ling 5f stand

Hurricane Coast

97 **76**

2-y-o b g Hurricane Sky (AUS)-Tread Carefully (Sharpo)
T D Easterby Mrs Ian Wills

Placings:00330 **(5229)**
2001: 7^{0}GF, 7^{0}G, 6^{3}F, 7^{3}S, 7^{0}S

	Starts	1st	2nd	3rd	Win & Pl
Career Total (Turf)	5	0	0	2	1108

Going (Turf): **Sf: 0-2 GS: 0-0 Gd: 0-1 GF: 0-1 Fm: 0-1**
Distance: 5f/6f: 0-1 7f-8f: 0-4 9f-13f: 0-0 14f+: 0-0
Track : LH: 0-2 RH: 0-1 Tight: 0-1 Gall: 0-1
Aids: Bl: 0-0 Vi: 0-0 Tstrap: 0-0
Best Rating: 76 9/01 Ches 7f2y soft

Showed his first sign of form when third in an above-average Newcastle maiden in September, but did not look to handle the soft ground or Chester's tight track next time. Sure to stay further as a three-year-old.

Hurricane Dan

(90) (65)**65**
2-y-o b g Emarati (USA)-Bellateena (Nomination)
M W Easterby M P Burke

Placings:02504043034000 **(5393)**
2001: 5⁰GS, 5²SD, 5⁵SW, 6⁰GF, 5⁴G, 7⁰G, 6⁴GF, 5³G, 6⁰G, 5³GF, 5⁴F, 6⁰GF, 6⁰S, 6⁰SD

	Starts	1st	2nd	3rd	Win & Pl
Career Total (Turf)	11	0	0	2	2936
Career Total (AW)	3	0	1	0	798

Going (Turf): Sf: 0-1 GS: 0-1 Gd: 0-4 GF: 0-4 Fm: 0-1
Distance: 5f/6f: 0-12 7f-8f: 0-2 9f-13f: 0-0 14f+: 0-0
Track : LH: 0-3 RH: 0-0 Tight: 0-2 Gall: 0-0
Aids: Bl: 0-8 Vi: 0-0 Tstrap: 0-0
Best Rating: 65 9/01 Muss 5f firm

Has yet to win but has run some solid races in nurseries. Suited by fast ground.

Hurricane Floyd (IRE)

113 **106**
3-y-o ch c Pennekamp (USA)-Mood Swings (IRE) (Shirley Heights)
J Noseda Lucayan Stud

Placings:2140-26652 **(4284)**
2001: 7²GF, 7⁶GF, 7⁶GF, 6⁵G, 6²G

	Starts	1st	2nd	3rd	Win & Pl
Career Total (Turf)	9	1	3	0	27785

98 8/00 NmkJ 6f D GD £4426
Total win prize-money £4427

Going (Turf): Sf: 0-0 GS: 0-0 **Gd: 1-5** GF: 0-4 Fm: 0-0
Distance: **5f/6f: 1-3** 7f-8f: 0-6 9f-13f: 0-0 14f+: 0-0
Track : LH: 0-1 RH: 0-0 Tight: 0-0 Gall: 0-1
Aids: Bl: 0-0 Vi: 0-1 Tstrap: 0-0
Best Rating: 106 7/01 Asct 7f gd-fm

He has run some decent races this term at six and seven furlongs, but his come-from-behind style requires luck in running and he has not been getting that. Not easy to catch right.

Hutch

94 **55**
3-y-o b g Rock Hopper-Polly's Teahouse (Shack (USA))
J D Bethell Robert Gibbons

Placings:5550 **(5167)**
2001: 12⁵G, 8⁵F, 10⁵F, 12⁰GS

	Starts	1st	2nd	3rd	Win & Pl
Career Total (Turf)	4	0	0	0	0

Going (Turf): Sf: 0-0 GS: 0-1 Gd: 0-1 GF: 0-0 Fm: 0-2
Distance: 5f/6f: 0-0 7f-8f: 0-1 9f-13f: 0-3 14f+: 0-0
Track : LH: 0-3 RH: 0-1 Tight: 0-1 Gall: 0-1
Aids: Bl: 0-0 Vi: 0-0 Tstrap: 0-0
Best Rating: 55 9/01 Pont 1m2f6y firm

Hutchies Lady

99 (21)**25**
9-y-o b m Efisio-Keep Mum (Mummy's Pet)
J S Goldie J S Goldie

Placings:00005600/1442460040000/00426B50000/460500/25400/3100254-3046502140365020050050400 **(4881)**
2001: 9³S, 9⁰GS, 11⁴G, 8⁶GF, 11⁵GF, 10⁰G, 16²GF, 9¹GF, 13⁴GS, 10⁰GF, 13³G, 9⁶GF, 11⁵S, 9⁰GS, 10²GS, 7⁰GS, 12⁰G, 9⁵GS, 11⁰G, 8⁰GF, 8⁵S, 7⁰G, 11⁴G, 9⁰G, 6⁰GF

	Starts	1st	2nd	3rd	Win & Pl
Career Total (Turf)	73	3	6	3	16906
Career Total (AW)	2	0	0	0	

37 6/01 Haml 1m1f36y E(0-75)H G-F £3640
37 9/00 Haml 1m3f16y F(0-70)H SFT £2926
41 5/96 Haml 1m65y E(0-70)H HVY £3595

Total win prize-money £10161

Going (Turf): Sf: 2-18 GS: 0-17 Gd: 0-18 GF: 1-18 Fm: 0-2
Distance: 5f/6f: 0-0 7f-8f: 0-13 **9f-13f: 3-56** 14f+: 0-6
Track : LH: 0-22 **RH: 3-45 Tight: 3-48** Gall: 0-2
Aids: Bl: 0-5 Vi: 0-1 Tstrap: 0-0
Best Rating: 37 8/01 Rdcr 1m gd-fm

Hwisprian

101 **78**
3-y-o b f Definite Article-No Islands (Lomond (USA))
M Blanshard Acorns To Oaks Racing

Placings:00-520 **(2512)**
2001: 10⁵GF, 10²G, 9⁰GF

	Starts	1st	2nd	3rd	Win & Pl
Career Total (Turf)	5	0	1	0	1330

Going (Turf): Sf: 0-0 GS: 0-0 Gd: 0-1 GF: 0-4 Fm: 0-0
Distance: 5f/6f: 0-0 7f-8f: 0-1 9f-13f: 0-4 14f+: 0-0
Track : LH: 0-0 RH: 0-1 Tight: 0-3 Gall: 0-0
Aids: Bl: 0-0 Vi: 0-0 Tstrap: 0-0
Best Rating: 78 6/01 Wind 1m2f7y good

Hyde Hall

96 **83**
3-y-o b f Barathea (IRE)-Catawba (Mill Reef (USA))
H R A Cecil Plantation Stud

Placings:0-2140 **(4300)**
2001: 10²GF, 10¹GF, 10⁴GS, 10⁰G

	Starts	1st	2nd	3rd	Win & Pl
Career Total (Turf)	5	1	1	0	5615

83 7/01 Pont 1m2f6y D G-F £3477
Total win prize-money £3478

Going (Turf): Sf: 0-0 GS: 0-1 Gd: 0-2 **GF: 1-2** Fm: 0-0
Distance: 5f/6f: 0-0 7f-8f: 0-1 **9f-13f: 1-4** 14f+: 0-0
Track : **LH: 1-4** RH: 0-0 Tight: 0-1 Gall: 0-1
Aids: Bl: 0-0 Vi: 0-0 Tstrap: 0-0
Best Rating: 83 8/01 Hayd 1m2f120y gd-sft

A half-sister to Yorkshire Oaks winner Catchascatchcan. Won a Pontefract maiden in July 2001 over ten furlongs. Fourth in handicap company on next outing. Has won on fast ground. Acts on good to soft.

Hyde Park (IRE)

101(77) (65?)**53**
7-y-o b g Alzao (USA)-Park Elect (Ahonoora)
D Nicholls Dandy Nicholls Racing Club

Placings:521/000611201025/0250340033340/0000100-05350616 **(4238)**
2001: 8⁰SD, 8⁵GS, 7³GF, 7⁵GF, 8⁰F, 8⁶GS, 7¹G, 7⁶GF

	Starts	1st	2nd	3rd	Win & Pl
Career Total (Turf)	33	5	2	4	27842
Career Total (AW)	10	1	2	1	5236

53 8/01 Catt 7f E(0-70)H GD £4517
50 8/00 Carl 7f214y E(0-70)H FRM £2912
70 10/98 Brig 7f214y E(0-70)H GD £2577
62 8/98 Ches 7f122y D(0-85)H G-S £8988
59 7/98 Pont 1m4y E(0-70)H G-F £3392
71 11/96 Ling 5f D STD £3318
Total win prize-money £25706

Going (Turf): Sf: 0-6 GS: 1-5 **Gd: 2-9** GF: 1-8 Fm: 1-5
Distance: 5f/6f: 1-6 **7f-8f: 4-31** 9f-13f: 1-6 14f+: 0-0
Track : **LH: 5-25** RH: 1-4 **Tight: 3-20** Gall: 0-2
Aids: Bl: 0-1 Vi: 0-0 Tstrap: 0-1
Best Rating: 53 8/01 Catt 7f good

Now with Dandy Nicholls he has a moderate strike rate, but won at Catterick in August.

Hyderabad

104 **95**
3-y-o ch c Deploy-Ajuga (USA) (The Minstrel (CAN))
B W Hills K Abdulla

Placings:0-20302100 **(5143)**
2001: 12²GS, 12⁰GF, 12³GF, 12⁰GF, 10²GS, 11¹G, 14⁰G, 14⁰G

	Starts	1st	2nd	3rd	Win & Pl
Career Total (Turf)	9	1	2	1	7012

92 8/01 Bath 1m3f144yD GD £3474
Total win prize-money £3474

Going (Turf): Sf: 0-1 GS: 0-2 **Gd: 1-3** GF: 0-3 Fm: 0-0
Distance: 5f/6f: 0-0 7f-8f: 0-1 **9f-13f: 1-6** 14f+: 0-2
Track : **LH: 1-3** RH: 0-5 **Tight: 1-2** Gall: 0-5
Aids: Bl: 0-0 Vi: 0-0 Tstrap: 0-0
Best Rating: 95 6/01 NmkR 1m4f gd-fm

He was highly tried on occasions before breaking his duck at Bath in August. Stays a mile and a half, goes well on easy ground and suited by forcing tactics.

Hyperactive (IRE)

97(97) (61)**49**
5-y-o b g Perugino (USA)-Hyannis (FR) (Esprit Du Nord (USA))
B Ellison Hyperactive Partnership

Placings:420/1/02000040-000055060 **(5450)**
2001: 7⁰SD, 8⁰GF, 7⁰GF, 7⁰F, 8⁵GF, 8⁵GF, 8⁰F, 7⁶GS, 8⁰HY

	Starts	1st	2nd	3rd	Win & Pl
Career Total (Turf)	18	1	2	0	7286
Career Total (AW)	3	0	0	0	0

70 10/99 Yarm 7f3y D G-F £4306
Total win prize-money £4307

Going (Turf): Sf: 0-2 GS: 0-1 Gd: 0-4 **GF: 1-9** Fm: 0-2
Distance: 5f/6f: 0-6 **7f-8f: 1-15** 9f-13f: 0-0 14f+: 0-0
Track : LH: 0-5 RH: 0-4 Tight: 0-4 Gall: 0-3
Aids: Bl: 0-3 Vi: 0-0 Tstrap: 0-0
Best Rating: 52 6/01 Newc 1m gd-fm

Hypersonic

74 **3**
4-y-o b g Marju (IRE)-Hi-Li (High Top)
C L Popham H J W Davies

Placings:5423/000-00 **(5465)**
2001: 9⁰GF, 10⁰G

	Starts	1st	2nd	3rd	Win & Pl
Career Total (Turf)	9	0	1	1	2066

Going (Turf): Sf: 0-3 GS: 0-0 Gd: 0-3 GF: 0-3 Fm: 0-0
Distance: 5f/6f: 0-2 7f-8f: 0-5 9f-13f: 0-2 14f+: 0-0
Track : LH: 0-4 RH: 0-0 Tight: 0-2 Gall: 0-0
Aids: Bl: 0-0 Vi: 0-0 Tstrap: 0-0
Best Rating: 3 5/01 Brig 1m1f209y gd-fm

Hypothesis (IRE)

84 **46**
4-y-o b g Sadler's Wells (USA)-Surmise (USA) (Alleged (USA))
A Bailey Sandybrow Stables Ltd

Placings:0/000 **(4478)**
2001: 12⁰S, 12⁰GS, 16⁰F

	Starts	1st	2nd	3rd	Win & Pl
Career Total (Turf)	4	0	0	0	

Going (Turf): Sf: 0-2 GS: 0-1 Gd: 0-0 GF: 0-0 Fm: 0-1
Distance: 5f/6f: 0-0 7f-8f: 0-1 9f-13f: 0-2 14f+: 0-1
Track : LH: 0-1 RH: 0-1 Tight: 0-2 Gall: 0-0
Aids: Bl: 0-0 Vi: 0-0 Tstrap: 0-1
Best Rating: 46 5/01 Thsk 1m4f gd-sft

I Can't Remember

100(101) (39)**42**

7-y-o gr g Petong-Glenfield Portion (Mummy's Pet)

S R Bowring J Doxey

Placings:501224154510425014/06606400600/6400460 512053/1616651510**0**/**6624**540506034002**000**-350603 **(2188)**

2001: 10^{3}S, 8^{5}GS, 12^{0}F, 9^{6}F, 12^{0}GF, 14^{3}GF

	Starts	1st	2nd	3rd	Win & Pl
Career Total (Turf)	68	9	5	3	40335
Career Total (AW)	10	0	1	1	800

61	8/99	Nott	1m6f15y	F(0-65)H	GD	£3025
64	8/99	Ripn	1m4f60y	E(0-70)H	G-F	£2814
64	6/99	Pont	1m4y	E(0-75)H	SFT	£3915
53	5/99	Nott	1m1f213yG		FRM	£2372
59	6/98	Ches	1m2f75y	D	G-S	£3629
80	10/96	Donc	1m	D	GD	£4035
79	8/96	Ches	7f2y	C	G-S	£5475
67	8/96	Ches	6f18y	D H	G-F	£4279
46	7/96	Catt	5f	G	G-S	£2469

Total win prize-money £32017

Going (Turf): Sf: 1-11 **GS: 3-9** Gd: 2-13 GF: 2-28 Fm: 1-7

Distance: 5f/6f: 1-9 7f-8f: 3-23 **9f-13f: 4-37** 14f+: 1-9

Track : **LH: 7-50** RH: 1-15 **Tight: 4-30** Gall: 1-10

Aids: Bl: 0-2 Vi: 0-2 Tstrap: 0-3

Best Rating: 42 5/01 Leic 1m1f218y firm

I Cried For You (IRE)

110 (43)**99**

6-y-o b g Statoblest-Fall Of The Hammer (IRE) (Auction Ring (USA))

J G Given One Stop Partnership

Placings:00033/631300605000/**00**411200000/1321200 410-0465420215 **(5607)**

2001: 7^{0}S, 8^{4}GS, 7^{6}G, 7^{5}G, 8^{4}GF, 7^{2}G, 7^{0}HY, 7^{2}S, 9^{1}G, 8^{5}GS

	Starts	1st	2nd	3rd	Win & Pl
Career Total (Turf)	46	7	5	5	141556
Career Total (AW)	2	0	0	0	

99	10/01	NmkR	1m1f	B H	GD	£69600
87	10/00	York	6f214y	D(0-85)H	HVY	£10887
78	8/00	Donc	7f	D(0-80)H	G-F	£4719
74	4/00	Ling	7f	E(0-70)	G-S	£3022
71	6/99	Wind	6f	D(0-80)H	G-F	£7425
65	5/99	Nott	6f15y	E(0-65)	FRM	£3052
72	5/98	Brig	5f59y	E(0-70)H	FRM	£2749

Total win prize-money £101456

Going (Turf): Sf: 1-11 GS: 1-7 Gd: 1-16 **GF: 2-8 Fm: 2-4**

Distance: 5f/6f: 2-23 **7f-8f: 4-24** 9f-13f: 1-1 14f+: 0-0

Track : **LH: 2-13** RH: 1-6 Tight: 0-2 **Gall: 2-7**

Aids: Bl: 0-5 Vi: 0-1 Tstrap: 0-0

Best Rating: 99 10/01 NmkR 1m1f good

He is a versatile performer who goes on extremes of ground as he ably demonstrated in 2000 when winning at Lingfield, Doncaster and York. Considered a seven-furlong specialist, he has run with credit in 2001, notably when runner-up at Ascot in September, but he was a revelation when stepped up to nine furlongs in the Cambridgeshire, always travelling well and quickening impressively to seal matters. He now has new options open to him, perhaps over ten furlongs. Acts on most surfaces.

I Do

102 **81+**

2-y-o ch f Selkirk (USA)-Acquiesce (Generous (IRE))

Sir Mark Prescott Miss K Rausing

Placings:400115 **(4538)**

2001: 7^{4}GF, 7^{0}G, 7^{0}GF, 7^{1}G, 6^{1}G, 7^{5}GF

	Starts	1st	2nd	3rd	Win & Pl
Career Total (Turf)	6	2	0	0	8110

81	9/01	Folk	6f189y	D(0-85)	GD	£3874
77	9/01	Sand	7f16y	E(0-75)H	GD	£3900

Total win prize-money £7774

Going (Turf): Sf: 0-0 GS: 0-0 **Gd: 2-3** GF: 0-3 Fm: 0-0

Distance: 5f/6f: 0-0 **7f-8f: 2-6** 9f-13f: 0-0 14f+: 0-0

Track : LH: 0-0 **RH: 2-4 Tight: 1-1** Gall: 0-1

Aids: Bl: 0-0 Vi: 0-0 Tstrap: 0-0

Best Rating: 81 9/01 Folk 6f189y good

A well-bred filly, she ran three times in six days in September, winning a brace of nurseries. Suited by making the running.

I Got Rhythm

99(90) (44)**43**

3-y-o gr f Lycius (USA)-Eurythmic (Pharly (FR))

Mrs M Reveley G Thomson

Placings:0040053-333531244 **(5093)**

2001: 11^{3}SD, 9^{3}S, 9^{3}S, 12^{5}G, 11^{3}GF, 15^{1}G, 14^{2}GF, 13^{4}GF, 16^{4}GS

	Starts	1st	2nd	3rd	Win & Pl
Career Total (Turf)	13	1	1	3	4097
Career Total (AW)	3	0	0	2	563

33	8/01	Catt	1m7f177yG	GD	£1855

Total win prize-money £1855

Going (Turf): Sf: 0-2 GS: 0-1 **Gd: 1-3** GF: 0-6 Fm: 0-1

Distance: 5f/6f: 0-4 7f-8f: 0-1 9f-13f: 0-7 **14f+: 1-4**

Track : **LH: 1-10** RH: 0-2 **Tight: 1-6** Gall: 0-2

Aids: Bl: 0-0 Vi: 0-0 Tstrap: 0-0

Best Rating: 44 7/01 Newc 1m4f93y good

Plating-class stayer, suited by good ground or faster.

I Promise You

95(97) (58)**60**

4-y-o b g Shareef Dancer (USA)-Abuzz (Absalom)

C E Brittain Mrs C E Brittain

Placings:064035/100035-0000004005 **(5626)**

2001: 6^{0}SD, 8^{0}GS, 8^{0}GF, 7^{0}GF, 7^{0}GF, 7^{0}G, 7^{4}F, 10^{0}GF, 7^{0}GF, 8^{5}GS

	Starts	1st	2nd	3rd	Win & Pl
Career Total (Turf)	21	1	0	2	8679
Career Total (AW)	1	0	0	0	

75	3/00	Leic	7f9y	C(0-90)H	GD	£7124

Total win prize-money £7124

Going (Turf): Sf: 0-1 GS: 0-5 **Gd: 1-6** GF: 0-7 Fm: 0-2

Distance: 5f/6f: 0-2 **7f-8f: 1-14** 9f-13f: 0-6 14f+: 0-0

Track : LH: 0-8 RH: 0-3 Tight: 0-5 Gall: 0-0

Aids: Bl: 0-2 Vi: 0-0 Tstrap: 0-0

Best Rating: 60 8/01 Brig 7f214y firm

I Swear

94 **82+**

2-y-o b c Barathea (IRE)-Karlafsha (Top Ville)

J L Dunlop The Thoroughbred Corporation

Placings:4 **(3026)**

2001: 6^{4}G

	Starts	1st	2nd	3rd	Win & Pl
Career Total (Turf)	1	0	0	0	543

Going (Turf): Sf: 0-0 GS: 0-0 Gd: 0-1 GF: 0-0 Fm: 0-0

Distance: 5f/6f: 0-0 7f-8f: 0-1 9f-13f: 0-0 14f+: 0-0

Track : LH: 0-1 RH: 0-0 Tight: 0-0 Gall: 0-1

Aids: Bl: 0-0 Vi: 0-0 Tstrap: 0-0

Best Rating: 82 7/01 York 6f214y good

I T Consultant

91(100) (59)**65**

3-y-o b c Rock City-Game Germaine (Mummy's Game)

A G Newcombe Ronnie De Beau-Lox

Placings:01-6010500 **(5619)**

2001: 6^{6}SD, 6^{0}SD, 6^{1}G, 6^{0}GS, 6^{5}SD, 6^{0}SD, 6^{0}SD

	Starts	1st	2nd	3rd	Win & Pl
Career Total (Turf)	3	1	0	0	3754
Career Total (AW)	6	1	0	0	2226

65	6/01	Thsk	6f	E(0-70)H	GD	£3753
59	11/00	Sthl	5f	F	STD	£2226

Total win prize-money £5980

Going (Turf): Sf: 0-0 GS: 0-1 **Gd: 1-2** GF: 0-0 Fm: 0-0

Distance: **5f/6f: 2-9** 7f-8f: 0-0 9f-13f: 0-0 14f+: 0-0

Track : LH: 0-5 RH: 0-0 Tight: 0-3 Gall: 0-0

Aids: Bl: 0-0 Vi: 0-0 Tstrap: 0-0

Best Rating: 65 6/01 Thsk 6f good

I Tina

(104) (56)**56**

5-y-o b m Lycius (USA)-Tintomara (IRE) (Niniski (USA))

J G Portman (M P Tregoning 31/1) R Axford

Placings:2364/6040502-10205103 **(4735)**

2001: 10^{1}SD, 12^{0}SW, 10^{2}SW, 10^{0}G, 10^{5}GF, 10^{1}GF, 9^{0}GF, 10^{3}F

	Starts	1st	2nd	3rd	Win & Pl
Career Total (Turf)	15	1	1	2	6029
Career Total (AW)	4	1	2	0	4927

56	8/01	Chep	1m2f36y	E(0-70)H	G-F	£2856
55	1/01	Ling	1m2f	D	STD	£2905

Total win prize-money £5761

Going (Turf): Sf: 0-2 GS: 0-4 Gd: 0-3 **GF: 1-5** Fm: 0-1

Distance: 5f/6f: 0-0 7f-8f: 0-0 **9f-13f: 2-17** 14f+: 0-2

Track : **LH: 2-13** RH: 0-5 **Tight: 1-11** Gall: 0-2

Aids: Bl: 0-0 Vi: 0-1 Tstrap: 0-0

Best Rating: 56 8/01 Chep 1m2f36y gd-fm

I Walked By Night

82 **47**

2-y-o ch c Primo Dominie-Malwiya (USA) (Shahrastani (USA))

H R A Cecil Colin Davey

Placings:0 **(5604)**

2001: 7^{0}GS

	Starts	1st	2nd	3rd	Win & Pl
Career Total (Turf)	1	0	0	0	

Going (Turf): Sf: 0-0 GS: 0-1 Gd: 0-0 GF: 0-0 Fm: 0-0

Distance: 5f/6f: 0-0 7f-8f: 0-1 9f-13f: 0-0 14f+: 0-0

Track : LH: 0-0 RH: 0-0 Tight: 0-0 Gall: 0-0

Aids: Bl: 0-0 Vi: 0-0 Tstrap: 0-0

Best Rating: 47 11/01 NmkR 7f gd-sft

I Wish

91 **57?**

3-y-o ch f Beveled (USA)-Ballystate (Ballacashtal (CAN))

M Madgwick J M T Gaisford

Placings:60 **(1378)**

2001: 8^{6}GS, 9^{0}GS

	Starts	1st	2nd	3rd	Win & Pl
Career Total (Turf)	2	0	0	0	0

Going (Turf): Sf: 0-0 GS: 0-2 Gd: 0-0 GF: 0-0 Fm: 0-0

Distance: 5f/6f: 0-0 7f-8f: 0-0 9f-13f: 0-2 14f+: 0-0

Track : LH: 0-0 RH: 0-2 Tight: 0-2 Gall: 0-0

Aids: Bl: 0-0 Vi: 0-0 Tstrap: 0-0

Best Rating: 57 4/01 Wind 1m67y gd-sft

I'm A Bird (IRE)

87 **55**

2-y-o b f Prince Of Birds (USA)-E Sharp (USA) (Diesis)

G A Swinbank Alan Swinbank

Placings:50660 **(2750)**

2001: 6^{5}F, 6^{0}F, 7^{6}GF, 6^{6}GF, 6^{0}GF

Starts 1st 2nd 3rd Win & Pl

	Starts	1st	2nd	3rd	Win & Pl
Career Total (Turf)	5	0	0	0	0

Going (Turf): Sf: 0-0 GS: 0-0 Gd: 0-0 GF: 0-3 Fm: 0-2

Distance: 5f/6f: 0-4 7f-8f: 0-1 9f-13f: 0-0 14f+: 0-0

Track : LH: 0-0 RH: 0-0 Tight: 0-0 Gall: 0-0

Aids: Bl: 0-0 Vi: 0-1 Tstrap: 0-0

Best Rating: 55 5/01 Newc 6f firm

I'm Lulu

(88) (47)**57**

3-y-o b f Piccolo-Everdene (Bustino)

Mrs A J Perrett S P Tindall

Placings:06064-3 **(0222)**

2001: 7^{3}SD

	Starts	1st	2nd	3rd	Win & Pl
Career Total (Turf)	3	0	0	0	0
Career Total (AW)	3	0	0	1	295

Going (Turf): Sf: 0-1 GS: 0-1 Gd: 0-0 GF: 0-1 Fm: 0-0

Distance: 5f/6f: 0-2 7f-8f: 0-4 9f-13f: 0-0 14f+: 0-0

Track : LH: 0-3 RH: 0-2 Tight: 0-3 Gall: 0-2

Aids: Bl: 0-1 Vi: 0-0 Tstrap: 0-0

Best Rating: 38 2/01 Ling 7f stand

I'm Sophie (IRE)

104(94) (40)**54**

4-y-o ch f Shalford (IRE)-Caisson (Shaadi (USA))

D Burchell Three Acres Racing

Placings:2/450006-53050100 **(5111)**

2001: 6^{5}SD, 8^{3}SW, 5^{0}SD, 5^{5}HY, 5^{0}GS, 5^{1}GF, 5^{0}G, 6^{0}HY

	Starts	1st	2nd	3rd	Win & Pl
Career Total (Turf)	7	1	1	0	3760
Career Total (AW)	8	0	0	1	1363

54 5/01 Brig 5f213y E(0-70)H G-F £2912

Total win prize-money £2912

Going (Turf): Sf: 0-3 GS: 0-1 Gd: 0-2 **GF: 1-1** Fm: 0-0

Distance: **5f/6f: 1-11** 7f-8f: 0-3 9f-13f: 0-1 14f+: 0-0

Track : **LH: 1-9** RH: 0-0 Tight: 0-3 Gall: 0-1

Aids: Bl: 0-0 Vi: 0-0 Tstrap: 0-0

Best Rating: 54 5/01 Brig 5f213y gd-fm

I'm The Guv'Nor (IRE)

45

2-y-o b c College Chapel-Star Of Aran (Artaius (USA))

J Akehurst Transoceanic

Placings:0 **(5667)**

2001: 8^{0}HY

	Starts	1st	2nd	3rd	Win & Pl
Career Total (Turf)	1	0	0	0	

Going (Turf): Sf: 0-1 GS: 0-0 Gd: 0-0 GF: 0-0 Fm: 0-0

Distance: 5f/6f: 0-0 7f-8f: 0-0 9f-13f: 0-1 14f+: 0-0

Track : LH: 0-0 RH: 0-1 Tight: 0-1 Gall: 0-0

Aids: Bl: 0-0 Vi: 0-0 Tstrap: 0-0

Iamatmewhitzend

4-y-o ch f Whittingham (IRE)-The Fernhill Flyer (IRE) (Red Sunset)

A Berry B Batey

Placings:6-0 **(0370)**

2001: 8^{0}SW

	Starts	1st	2nd	3rd	Win & Pl
Career Total (Turf)	1	0	0	0	0
Career Total (AW)	1	0	0	0	

Going (Turf): Sf: 0-1 GS: 0-0 Gd: 0-0 GF: 0-0 Fm: 0-0

Distance: 5f/6f: 0-0 7f-8f: 0-2 9f-13f: 0-0 14f+: 0-0

Track : LH: 0-1 RH: 0-1 Tight: 0-1 Gall: 0-0

Aids: Bl: 0-0 Vi: 0-0 Tstrap: 0-0

Ibis Rouge (IRE)

73 **6**

2-y-o ch f Forzando-Aquiletta (Bairn (USA))

C B B Booth J A Porteous

Placings:00 **(5370)**

2001: 6^{0}F, 7^{0}G

	Starts	1st	2nd	3rd	Win & Pl
Career Total (Turf)	2	0	0	0	

Going (Turf): Sf: 0-0 GS: 0-0 Gd: 0-1 GF: 0-0 Fm: 0-1

Distance: 5f/6f: 0-1 7f-8f: 0-1 9f-13f: 0-0 14f+: 0-0

Track : LH: 0-0 RH: 0-0 Tight: 0-0 Gall: 0-0

Aids: Bl: 0-0 Vi: 0-0 Tstrap: 0-0

Best Rating: 6 9/01 Newc 6f firm

Icaressa

89 **60**

3-y-o b f Anabaa (USA)-Dance Quest (FR) (Green Dancer (USA))

H R A Cecil Plantation Stud

Placings:0 **(0810)**

2001: 7^{0}S

	Starts	1st	2nd	3rd	Win & Pl
Career Total (Turf)	1	0	0	0	

Going (Turf): Sf: 0-1 GS: 0-0 Gd: 0-0 GF: 0-0 Fm: 0-0

Distance: 5f/6f: 0-0 7f-8f: 0-1 9f-13f: 0-0 14f+: 0-0

Track : LH: 0-0 RH: 0-0 Tight: 0-0 Gall: 0-0

Aids: Bl: 0-0 Vi: 0-0 Tstrap: 0-0

Best Rating: 60 4/01 NmkR 7f soft

Ice

109 **76**

5-y-o b g Polar Falcon (USA)-Sarabah (IRE) (Ela-Mana-Mou)

S E Kettlewell (M Johnston 2/9) Uncle Jacks Pub

Placings:2431121/411000040/516144000-60140040 **(5251)**

2001: 8^{6}GF, 8^{0}G, 7^{1}G, 10^{4}GF, 8^{0}G, 7^{0}G, 8^{4}GF, 7^{0}S

	Starts	1st	2nd	3rd	Win & Pl
Career Total (Turf)	33	8	2	1	79788

92	7/01	York	7f202y	B(0-100)H	GD	£9456
95	6/00	York	1m205y	C(0-100)H	G-F	£16968
89	6/00	Ling	1m1f	C(0-90)H	GD	£7117
98	5/99	York	7f202y	C(0-95)H	SFT	£7895
95	4/99	Diel	1m		HVY	£6288
95	10/98	York	7f202y	C H	GD	£7694
80	9/98	York	7f202y	C H	GD	£8870
74	8/98	Muss	7f30y	D	GD	£3262

Total win prize-money £67552

Going (Turf): Sf: 2-5 GS: 0-4 **Gd: 5-17** GF: 1-7 Fm: 0-0

Distance: 5f/6f: 0-2 **7f-8f: 6-16** 9f-13f: 2-15 14f+: 0-0

Track : **LH: 7-21** RH: 1-8 Tight: 2-4 **Gall: 5-13**

Aids: Bl: 0-0 **Vi: 7-29** Tstrap: 0-0

Best Rating: 92 7/01 Asct 1m2f gd-fm

A York specialist, he had appeared to need soft ground earlier in his career, but seems equally effective on good to firm nowadays. Looked as good as ever when gaining his fifth success at York in July. Best at around a mile, but ten furlongs just stretches his stamina.

Ice And Fire

95 **67**

2-y-o b c Cadeaux Genereux-Tanz (IRE) (Sadler's Wells (USA))

D R Loder Abdullah Saeed Belhab

Placings:30 **(4698)**

2001: 7^{3}GF, 7^{0}GS

	Starts	1st	2nd	3rd	Win & Pl
Career Total (Turf)	2	0	0	1	758

Going (Turf): Sf: 0-0 GS: 0-1 Gd: 0-0 GF: 0-1 Fm: 0-0

Distance: 5f/6f: 0-0 7f-8f: 0-2 9f-13f: 0-0 14f+: 0-0

Track : LH: 0-0 RH: 0-0 Tight: 0-0 Gall: 0-0

Aids: Bl: 0-0 Vi: 0-0 Tstrap: 0-0

Best Rating: 67 7/01 NmkJ 7f gd-fm

He finished a well-beaten third at Newmarket on his debut and set the pace until weakening when facing a stiff task next time.

Ice Crystal

51 **56**

4-y-o b g Slip Anchor-Crystal Fountain (Great Nephew)

S Woodman Fortune Racing

Placings:00400600-0 **(5330)**

2001: 16^{0}HY

	Starts	1st	2nd	3rd	Win & Pl
Career Total (Turf)	9	0	0	0	274

Going (Turf): Sf: 0-3 GS: 0-2 Gd: 0-3 GF: 0-1 Fm: 0-0

Distance: 5f/6f: 0-0 7f-8f: 0-0 9f-13f: 0-7 14f+: 0-2

Track : LH: 0-3 RH: 0-6 Tight: 0-3 Gall: 0-2

Aids: Bl: 0-0 Vi: 0-0 Tstrap: 0-0

Ice Dancer (IRE)

100 **106**

3-y-o b c Sadler's Wells (USA)-Tappiano (USA) (Fappiano (USA))

A P O'Brien Michael Tabor

Placings:2120051 **(5647a)**

2001: 10^{2}HY, 12^{1}G, 11^{2}GY, 12^{0}Y, 12^{0}GF, 10^{5}G, 10^{1}Y

	Starts	1st	2nd	3rd	Win & Pl
Career Total (Turf)	7	2	2	0	56820

104	10/01	Leop	1m2f	YLD	£26000
90	5/01	Leop	1m4f	GD	£8625

Total win prize-money £34625

Going (Turf): Sf: 0-1 GS: 0-0 **Gd: 1-2** GF: 0-1 Fm: 0-0

Distance: 5f/6f: 0-0 7f-8f: 0-0 **9f-13f: 2-7** 14f+: 0-0

Track : **LH: 1-2** RH: 0-1 Tight: 0-0 Gall: 0-1

Aids: Bl: 0-0 Vi: 0-0 Tstrap: 0-0

Best Rating: 106 7/01 Curr 1m4f yield

Unraced at two, he won twice at Leopardstown this season, but looked out of his depth in the Irish Derby. Used as a pacemaker by Coolmore.

Ice Maiden

99 **57d**

3-y-o b f Polar Falcon (USA)-Affair Of State (IRE) (Tate Gallery (USA))

M R Channon Stephen Crown & Brook Land

Placings:1340-0205 **(3365)**

2001: 8^{0}GF, 8^{2}GF, 8^{0}GF, 7^{5}G

	Starts	1st	2nd	3rd	Win & Pl
Career Total (Turf)	8	1	1	1	7188

75 4/00 NmkR 5f D G-S £4810

Total win prize-money £4810

Going (Turf): Sf: 0-0 **GS: 1-1** Gd: 0-2 GF: 0-5 Fm: 0-0

Distance: **5f/6f: 1-2** 7f-8f: 0-6 9f-13f: 0-0 14f+: 0-0

Track : LH: 0-0 RH: 0-1 Tight: 0-0 Gall: 0-1

Aids: Bl: 0-0 Vi: 0-0 Tstrap: 0-0

Best Rating: 55 7/01 Leic 7f9y good

Ice Pack

98(85) (14)**26**

5-y-o gr m Mukaddamah (USA)-Mrs Gray (Red Sunset)
Don Enrico Incisa Don Enrico Incisa

Placings:00/**32060220**/**6000343600**-**05605400** **(4164)**
2001: 14^{0}F, 16^{5}GF, 11^{6}GF, 16^{0}GF, 12^{5}GF, 15^{4}G, 16^{0}GS, 16^{0}GF

	Starts	1st	2nd	3rd	Win & Pl
Career Total (Turf)	20	0	0	2	857
Career Total (AW)	8	0	3	1	1974

Going (Turf): Sf: 0-2 GS: 0-2 Gd: 0-3 GF: 0-10 Fm: 0-3
Distance: 5f/6f: 0-0 7f-8f: 0-2 9f-13f: 0-12 14f+: 0-14
Track : LH: 0-21 RH: 0-6 Tight: 0-15 Gall: 0-3
Aids: Bl: 0-0 Vi: 0-4 Tstrap: 0-0
Best Rating: 31 6/01 Rdcr 2m4y gd-fm

Ice Prince

(105) (75)**63**
3-y-o b c Polar Falcon (USA)-The Jotter (Night Shift (USA))
J A Osborne Martyn Booth

Placings:006-221 **(0434)**
2001: 8^{2}SD, 8^{2}SD, 8^{1}SD

	Starts	1st	2nd	3rd	Win & Pl
Career Total (Turf)	2	0	0	0	
Career Total (AW)	4	1	2	0	5122
71 3/01 Wolv 1m100y D				STD	£2791

Total win prize-money £2792

Going (Turf): Sf: 0-1 GS: 0-0 Gd: 0-0 GF: 0-1 Fm: 0-0
Distance: 5f/6f: 0-0 7f-8f: 0-1 **9f-13f: 1-5** 14f+: 0-0
Track : **LH: 1-6** RH: 0-0 **Tight: 1-4** Gall: 0-0
Aids: Bl: 0-0 Vi: 0-0 Tstrap: 0-0
Best Rating: 75 2/01 Wolv 1m100y stand

Iceni Queen

72 **18**
3-y-o b f Formidable (USA)-Queen Warrior (Daring March)
W McKeown N Hooson

Placings:56000 **(5269)**
2001: 0^{5}F, 10^{6}F, 7^{0}G, 8^{0}GS, 10^{0}HY

	Starts	1st	2nd	3rd	Win & Pl
Career Total (Turf)	5	0	0	0	0

Going (Turf): Sf: 0-1 GS: 0-1 Gd: 0-1 GF: 0-0 Fm: 0-2
Distance: 5f/6f: 0-0 7f-8f: 0-1 9f-13f: 0-4 14f+: 0-0
Track : LH: 0-3 RH: 0-1 Tight: 0-1 Gall: 0-1
Aids: Bl: 0-0 Vi: 0-0 Tstrap: 0-0
Best Rating: 18 5/01 Newc 1m2f32y firm

Ichiban

(58)
4-y-o gr g Kasakov-First Slice (Primo Dominie)
J J Bridger Speedforce Racing Limited

Placings:5 **(0339)**
2001: 7^{5}SW

	Starts	1st	2nd	3rd	Win & Pl
Career Total (Turf)	0	0	0	0	
Career Total (AW)	1	0	0	0	0

Going (Turf): Sf: 0-0 GS: 0-0 Gd: 0-0 GF: 0-0 Fm: 0-0
Distance: 5f/6f: 0-0 7f-8f: 0-1 9f-13f: 0-0 14f+: 0-0
Track : LH: 0-1 RH: 0-0 Tight: 0-1 Gall: 0-0
Aids: Bl: 0-0 Vi: 0-0 Tstrap: 0-0

Icy

86 **59**
2-y-o b f Mind Games-Snow Eagle (IRE) (Polar Falcon (USA))
M W Easterby Guy Reed

Placings:50000 **(4772)**
2001: 6^{5}F, 6^{0}G, 5^{0}GF, 5^{0}GF, 7^{0}G

	Starts	1st	2nd	3rd	Win & Pl
Career Total (Turf)	5	0	0	0	0

Going (Turf): Sf: 0-0 GS: 0-0 Gd: 0-2 GF: 0-2 Fm: 0-1
Distance: 5f/6f: 0-4 7f-8f: 0-1 9f-13f: 0-0 14f+: 0-0
Track : LH: 0-0 RH: 0-1 Tight: 0-0 Gall: 0-0
Aids: Bl: 0-0 Vi: 0-0 Tstrap: 0-0
Best Rating: 59 7/01 York 6f good

Idle Power (IRE)

108 **90**
3-y-o b g Common Grounds-Idle Fancy (Mujtahid (USA))
P W Harris The Dreamers

Placings:2516610-0515300 **(5266)**
2001: 6^{0}S, 6^{5}GS, 6^{1}G, 5^{5}GS, 6^{3}G, 6^{0}G, 6^{0}GS

	Starts	1st	2nd	3rd	Win & Pl
Career Total (Turf)	14	3	1	1	23725
88 7/01 Yarm 6f3y C(0-95)H				GD	£7345
89 10/00 NmkR 6f C(0-95)				SFT	£7358
78 6/00 Kemp 5f D				G-F	£3445

Total win prize-money £18148

Going (Turf): Sf: 1-4 GS: 0-4 **Gd: 1-3 GF: 1-3** Fm: 0-0
Distance: **5f/6f: 2-11** 7f-8f: 1-3 9f-13f: 0-0 14f+: 0-0
Track : LH: 0-1 RH: 0-0 Tight: 0-0 Gall: 0-0
Aids: Bl: 0-0 Vi: 0-0 Tstrap: 0-0
Best Rating: 90 8/01 Gdwd 6f good

Suited by fast ground but has also scored on in soft, he was twice a winner as a juvenile. Returned to form with a gutsy display at Yarmouth in July, and has run well in handicaps since.

If By Chance

(106) (70)**38**
3-y-o ch c Risk Me (FR)-Out Of Harmony (Song)
D W P Arbuthnot G S Thompson & P Banfield

Placings:042055-1433066230000 **(5108)**
2001: 6^{1}SD, 6^{4}SW, 6^{3}SW, 6^{3}SD, 5^{0}GS, 5^{6}G, 6^{6}GF, 5^{2}GF, 5^{3}GF, 5^{0}GF, 5^{0}GF, 5^{0}G, 5^{0}GS

	Starts	1st	2nd	3rd	Win & Pl
Career Total (Turf)	14	0	1	1	2197
Career Total (AW)	5	1	1	2	5037
59 1/01 Ling 6f D				STD	£2940

Total win prize-money £2940

Going (Turf): Sf: 0-2 GS: 0-2 Gd: 0-3 GF: 0-7 Fm: 0-0
Distance: **5f/6f: 1-18** 7f-8f: 0-1 9f-13f: 0-0 14f+: 0-0
Track : **LH: 1-6** RH: 0-2 **Tight: 1-5** Gall: 0-3
Aids: Bl: 0-0 Vi: 0-1 Tstrap: 0-0
Best Rating: 70 1/01 Ling 6f slow

Has shown ordinary form on both turf and sand, but his winning form is on the latter.

Iffah (IRE)

106 **82**
3-y-o ch f Halling (USA)-Taroob (IRE) (Roberto (USA))
J L Dunlop Hamdan Al Maktoum

Placings:62-214240 **(3833)**
2001: 10^{2}S, 11^{1}F, 12^{4}GF, 11^{2}GF, 14^{4}GF, 14^{0}G

	Starts	1st	2nd	3rd	Win & Pl
Career Total (Turf)	8	1	3	0	8268
75 5/01 Brig 1m3f196yD				FRM	£3874

Total win prize-money £3874

Going (Turf): Sf: 0-1 GS: 0-0 Gd: 0-2 GF: 0-4 **Fm: 1-1**
Distance: 5f/6f: 0-0 7f-8f: 0-2 **9f-13f: 1-4** 14f+: 0-2
Track : **LH: 1-4** RH: 0-4 Tight: 0-1 Gall: 0-1
Aids: Bl: 0-0 Vi: 0-0 Tstrap: 0-0
Best Rating: 82 7/01 Sand 1m6f gd-fm

Iftitah (USA)

96(35) (108)**91**
5-y-o ch h Gone West (USA)-Mur Taasha (USA) (Riverman (USA))
J H M Gosden Hamdan Al Maktoum

Placings:1/5/243-600 **(3029)**
2001: 6^{6}GF, 6^{0}GF, 5^{0}GF

	Starts	1st	2nd	3rd	Win & Pl
Career Total (Turf)	7	1	0	1	8927
Career Total (AW)	1	0	1	0	30488
91 10/98 NmkR 7f B				GD	£6326

Total win prize-money £6326

Going (Turf): Sf: 0-1 GS: 0-0 **Gd: 1-1** GF: 0-4 Fm: 0-1
Distance: 5f/6f: 0-3 **7f-8f: 1-4** 9f-13f: 0-1 14f+: 0-0
Track : LH: 0-1 RH: 0-1 Tight: 0-1 Gall: 0-0
Aids: Bl: 0-0 Vi: 0-1 Tstrap: 0-1
Best Rating: 87 5/01 Gdwd 6f gd-fm

He ran a good second in the Godolphin Mile at Nad Al Sheba last season but only ran twice in Britain. Dropped to six furlongs on his return this year, he has shaped as though further would suit him better. Acts on fast ground.

Ignite (IRE)

60 **60**
4-y-o b g Bluebird (USA)-Save Me The Waltz (King's Lake (USA))
R T Phillips Flying Tiger Partnership

Placings:6303304340/0600-0 **(5622)**
2001: 14^{0}GS

	Starts	1st	2nd	3rd	Win & Pl
Career Total (Turf)	15	0	0	4	2816

Going (Turf): Sf: 0-4 GS: 0-2 Gd: 0-2 GF: 0-7 Fm: 0-0
Distance: 5f/6f: 0-8 7f-8f: 0-2 9f-13f: 0-4 14f+: 0-1
Track : LH: 0-4 RH: 0-3 Tight: 0-2 Gall: 0-4
Aids: Bl: 0-2 Vi: 0-0 Tstrap: 0-0

Iguassu Falls

80 **17**
3-y-o b f Machiavellian (USA)-Ivrea (Sadler's Wells (USA))
J Parkes (H-A Pantall 20/5) Mrs Lynn Parkes

Placings:3400000 **(5447)**
2001: 11^{3}, 12^{4}, 12^{0}GS, 12^{0}HY, 10^{0}G, 14^{0}G, 10^{0}HY

	Starts	1st	2nd	3rd	Win & Pl
Career Total (Turf)	7	0	0	1	1386

Going (Turf): Sf: 0-2 GS: 0-1 Gd: 0-2 GF: 0-0 Fm: 0-0
Distance: 5f/6f: 0-0 7f-8f: 0-0 9f-13f: 0-6 14f+: 0-1
Track : LH: 0-3 RH: 0-0 Tight: 0-1 Gall: 0-1
Aids: Bl: 0-3 Vi: 0-0 Tstrap: 0-1
Best Rating: 17 10/01 Newc 1m2f32y heavy

Ihtimaam (FR)

(87) (17)**28**
9-y-o b g Polish Precedent (USA)-Haebeh (USA) (Alydar (USA))
H E Haynes Mrs H E Haynes

Placings:533000/00000**1003313**/06006/2500/0/00-0 **(0038)**
2001: 16^{0}SD

	Starts	1st	2nd	3rd	Win & Pl
Career Total (Turf)	18	0	1	2	1965
Career Total (AW)	13	2	0	3	4837
63 11/96 Sthl 1m3f G				STD	£2085
53 7/96 Sthl 1m3f F				STD	£2031

Total win prize-money £4116

Going (Turf): Sf: 0-0 GS: 0-1 Gd: 0-6 GF: 0-8 Fm: 0-3

Distance: 5f/6f: 0-0 7f-8f: 0-6 **9f-13f: 2-22** 14f+: 0-2
Track : **LH: 2-21** RH: 0-6 Tight: 0-14 Gall: 0-1
Aids: Bl: 0-2 Vi: 0-2 Tstrap: 0-0
Best Rating: 53 7/96 Sthl 1m3f SD

Ikbal

96 **75**

3-y-o ch c Indian Ridge-Amaniy (USA) (Dayjur (USA))
E J Alston (M P Tregoning 19/4) George Iv Racing

Placings:0-0240 **(4569)**
2001: 8^{0}S, 8^{2}G, 8^{4}GF, 7^{0}HY

	Starts	1st	2nd	3rd	Win & Pl
Career Total (Turf)	5	0	1	0	1406

Going (Turf): Sf: 0-3 GS: 0-0 Gd: 0-1 GF: 0-1 Fm: 0-0
Distance: 5f/6f: 0-0 7f-8f: 0-3 9f-13f: 0-2 14f+: 0-0
Track : LH: 0-2 RH: 0-1 Tight: 0-0 Gall: 0-0
Aids: Bl: 0-0 Vi: 0-0 Tstrap: 0-0
Best Rating: 75 8/01 Pont 1m4y good

Ikenga (IRE)

96 **80**

2-y-o ch f Spectrum (IRE)-Thistle Hill (IRE) (Danehill (USA))
M L W Bell Innlaw Racing

Placings:3110 **(5390)**
2001: 8^{3}GF, 7^{1}G, 7^{1}GS, 7^{0}GS

	Starts	1st	2nd	3rd	Win & Pl
Career Total (Turf)	4	2	0	1	9630

80 10/01 Catt 7f D(0-85) G-S £5928
68 9/01 Bevl 7f100y E GD £3237
Total win prize-money £9166

Going (Turf): Sf: 0-0 **GS: 1-2 Gd: 1-1** GF: 0-1 Fm: 0-0
Distance: 5f/6f: 0-0 **7f-8f: 2-3** 9f-13f: 0-1 14f+: 0-0
Track : LH: 1-2 RH: 1-1 **Tight: 1-1** Gall: 0-0
Aids: Bl: 0-0 Vi: 0-0 Tstrap: 0-0
Best Rating: 80 10/01 Catt 7f gd-sft

Got off the mark at the second time of asking, and then followed up well in a nursery. Suited by seven furlongs, and appreciates cut in the ground.

Ikis Zeb T Bob

67 **8**

4-y-o b g Rock Hopper-Ikis Girl (Silver Hawk (USA))
S Gollings Ian K I Stewart

Placings:00 **(4636)**
2001: 11^{0}G, 9^{0}GF

	Starts	1st	2nd	3rd	Win & Pl
Career Total (Turf)	2	0	0	0	

Going (Turf): Sf: 0-0 GS: 0-0 Gd: 0-1 GF: 0-1 Fm: 0-0
Distance: 5f/6f: 0-0 7f-8f: 0-0 9f-13f: 0-2 14f+: 0-0
Track : LH: 0-1 RH: 0-1 Tight: 0-1 Gall: 0-0
Aids: Bl: 0-0 Vi: 0-0 Tstrap: 0-0
Best Rating: 8 9/01 Leic 1m1f218y gd-fm

Iktinas

89 **80**

2-y-o b c Unfuwain (USA)-Midway Lady (USA) (Alleged (USA))
B Hanbury Hamdan Al Maktoum

Placings:34 **(4222)**
2001: 6^{3}GS, 7^{4}GF

	Starts	1st	2nd	3rd	Win & Pl
Career Total (Turf)	2	0	0	1	1003

Going (Turf): Sf: 0-0 GS: 0-1 Gd: 0-0 GF: 0-1 Fm: 0-0
Distance: 5f/6f: 0-1 7f-8f: 0-1 9f-13f: 0-0 14f+: 0-0

Track : LH: 0-0 RH: 0-0 Tight: 0-0 Gall: 0-0
Aids: Bl: 0-0 Vi: 0-0 Tstrap: 0-0
Best Rating: 80 8/01 NmkJ 7f gd-fm

Il Cavaliere

105 **71**

6-y-o b g Mtoto-Kalmia (Miller's Mate)
Mrs M Reveley The Thoughtful Partnership

Placings:30403-5004622S12 **(5661)**
2001: 14^{5}G, 16^{0}GF, 15^{0}GF, 16^{4}F, 14^{6}G, 14^{2}GF, 14^{2}GF, 16^{S}GF, 14^{1}G, 16^{2}G

	Starts	1st	2nd	3rd	Win & Pl
Career Total (Turf)	15	1	3	2	12973

67 10/01 Rdcr 1m6f19y E(0-70)H GD £3374
Total win prize-money £3374

Going (Turf): Sf: 0-0 GS: 0-1 **Gd: 1-6** GF: 0-6 Fm: 0-2
Distance: 5f/6f: 0-0 7f-8f: 0-2 9f-13f: 0-2 **14f+: 1-11**
Track : **LH: 1-9** RH: 0-4 **Tight: 1-7** Gall: 0-3
Aids: Bl: 0-0 Vi: 0-0 Tstrap: 0-0
Best Rating: 71 11/01 Muss 2m good

An unexposed, lightly-raced type, he was successful in two bumpers in 1999 before switching to the level. He has shown some ability including a win in a modest staying handicap. Acts on fast ground and should continue to give a good account.

Il Destino

94 (69)**57d**

6-y-o b g Casteddu-At First Sight (He Loves Me)
J G M O'Shea K W Bell

Placings:0P12/0066034/2031262/65003034-66000 **(2452)**
2001: 12^{6}SD, 8^{6}G, 8^{0}GF, 10^{0}GF, 10^{0}F

	Starts	1st	2nd	3rd	Win & Pl
Career Total (Turf)	24	1	2	3	10805
Career Total (AW)	7	1	2	1	4415

55 7/99 Bath 1m2f46y D(0-80)H G-F £7197
62 11/97 Ling 7f F STD £2294
Total win prize-money £9492

Going (Turf): Sf: 0-0 GS: 0-4 Gd: 0-6 **GF: 1-13** Fm: 0-1
Distance: 5f/6f: 0-1 7f-8f: 1-8 9f-13f: 1-22 14f+: 0-0
Track : **LH: 2-19** RH: 0-5 **Tight: 2-17** Gall: 0-0
Aids: Bl: 0-1 Vi: 0-1 Tstrap: 0-0
Best Rating: 49 5/01 Wwck 1m22y good

Il Falco (FR)

7-y-o ch g Polar Falcon (USA)-Scimitarlia (USA) (Diesis)
R Curtis Mrs R A Smith

Placings:60560/0 **(1934)**
2001: 16^{0}GF

	Starts	1st	2nd	3rd	Win & Pl
Career Total (Turf)	6	0	0	0	0

Going (Turf): Sf: 0-1 GS: 0-0 Gd: 0-3 GF: 0-2 Fm: 0-0
Distance: 5f/6f: 0-0 7f-8f: 0-3 9f-13f: 0-2 14f+: 0-1
Track : LH: 0-1 RH: 0-2 Tight: 0-2 Gall: 0-0
Aids: Bl: 0-0 Vi: 0-0 Tstrap: 0-0

Ile Michel

107 **83**

4-y-o b g Machiavellian (USA)-Circe's Isle (Be My Guest (USA))
Lady Herries Seymour Racing Partnership

Placings:215/0-051040300 **(5344)**
2001: 7^{0}GF, 7^{5}GF, 8^{1}GF, 6^{0}G, 7^{4}GF, 7^{0}G, 7^{3}G, 7^{0}S, 8^{0}GS

	Starts	1st	2nd	3rd	Win & Pl
Career Total (Turf)	13	2	1	1	10071

78 6/01 Ayr 1m D(0-80) G-F £4010
76 9/99 Catt 5f212y D G-F £3057
Total win prize-money £7069

Going (Turf): Sf: 0-2 GS: 0-1 Gd: 0-3 **GF: 2-7** Fm: 0-0
Distance: 5f/6f: 1-2 7f-8f: 1-11 9f-13f: 0-0 14f+: 0-0
Track : **LH: 2-3** RH: 0-3 **Tight: 1-1** Gall: 0-1
Aids: Bl: 0-0 Vi: 0-0 Tstrap: 0-0
Best Rating: 83 9/01 Sand 7f16y good

A strong-looking sort, he scored a gutsy win at Ayr in June over a mile. Acts on fast ground.

Illegal (IRE)

94 **78**

2-y-o b c Eagle Eyed (USA)-Lady Bodmin (IRE) (Law Society (USA))
N P Littmoden Paul J Dixon

Placings:031060 **(4348a)**
2001: 5^{0}G, 5^{3}F, 7^{1}GF, 7^{0}GF, 7^{6}GS, 6^{0}GY

	Starts	1st	2nd	3rd	Win & Pl
Career Total (Turf)	6	1	0	1	4510

78 7/01 Wwck 7f26y E G-F £4095
Total win prize-money £4095

Going (Turf): Sf: 0-0 GS: 0-1 Gd: 0-1 **GF: 1-2** Fm: 0-1
Distance: 5f/6f: 0-3 **7f-8f: 1-3** 9f-13f: 0-0 14f+: 0-0
Track : **LH: 1-2** RH: 0-1 Tight: 0-0 Gall: 0-0
Aids: Bl: 0-0 Vi: 0-0 Tstrap: 0-0
Best Rating: 78 7/01 Wwck 7f26y gd-fm

Ran green when scoring at Brighton on his third run, but was well held afterwards.

Illegal Immigrant (CZE)

2-y-o br g Thatching-Silindhra (GER) (Windwurf (GER))
Miss J F Craze D G Clayton

Placings:00 **(5530)**
2001: 8^{0}SD, 8^{0}HY

	Starts	1st	2nd	3rd	Win & Pl
Career Total (Turf)	1	0	0	0	
Career Total (AW)	1	0	0	0	

Going (Turf): Sf: 0-1 GS: 0-0 Gd: 0-0 GF: 0-0 Fm: 0-0
Distance: 5f/6f: 0-0 7f-8f: 0-1 9f-13f: 0-1 14f+: 0-0
Track : LH: 0-2 RH: 0-0 Tight: 0-0 Gall: 0-0
Aids: Bl: 0-0 Vi: 0-0 Tstrap: 0-0

Illuminate

(78) (16)

8-y-o b g Marju (IRE)-Light Bee (USA) (Majestic Light (USA))
D C O'Brien J F Jennings

Placings:4/35045/**1000**/0200/6P/0 **(0088)**
2001: 12^{0}SD

	Starts	1st	2nd	3rd	Win & Pl
Career Total (Turf)	12	0	1	1	2092
Career Total (AW)	5	1	0	0	3258

64 2/97 Ling 1m4f D STD £3257
Total win prize-money £3258

Going (Turf): Sf: 0-1 GS: 0-1 Gd: 0-3 GF: 0-5 Fm: 0-2
Distance: 5f/6f: 0-0 7f-8f: 0-1 **9f-13f: 1-10** 14f+: 0-6
Track : **LH: 1-8** RH: 0-8 **Tight: 1-12** Gall: 0-1
Aids: Bl: 0-1 Vi: 0-0 Tstrap: 0-0
Best Rating: 16 1/01 Ling 1m4f stand

Illumination

103 **95**

3-y-o b f Saddlers' Hall (IRE)-Warning Light (High Top)
J R Fanshawe Cheveley Park Stud

Placings:31660 **(5339)**

2001: 10^{3}S, 10^{1}G, 11^{6}G, 10^{6}HY, 10^{0}GS

	Starts	1st	2nd	3rd	Win & Pl
Career Total (Turf)	**5**	**1**	**0**	**1**	**5058**

93 8/01 Wind 1m2f7y D GD £4108

Total win prize-money £4108

Going (Turf): Sf: 0-2 GS: 0-1 **Gd: 1-2** GF: 0-0 Fm: 0-0
Distance: 5f/6f: 0-0 7f-8f: 0-0 **9f-13f: 1-5** 14f+: 0-0
Track : LH: 0-2 RH: 0-1 **Tight: 1-1** Gall: 0-1
Aids: Bl: 0-0 Vi: 0-1 Tstrap: 0-0
Best Rating: 95 8/01 York 1m3f195y good

A big, lightly-raced filly, ran away with a maiden on her second start but failed to progress since in much more competitive events including when a visor was applied. Suited by good ground, and has won over ten furlongs but should stay further.

Illusionist

100(98) (71)**54**

3-y-o b g Mujtahid (USA)-Merlin's Fancy (Caerleon (USA))
Mrs N Macauley (E A L Dunlop 4/7) Stephen Roots

Placings:400-**2140**002620000 **(5131)**
2001: 7^{2}SW, 7^{1}SW, 6^{4}SD, 7^{0}SD, 8^{0}GS, 7^{0}F, 5^{2}GF, 6^{6}F, 7^{2}G, 7^{0}GF, 7^{0}GF, 7^{0}G, 7^{0}HY

	Starts	1st	2nd	3rd	Win & Pl
Career Total (Turf)	**12**	**0**	**2**	**0**	**2543**
Career Total (AW)	**4**	**1**	**1**	**0**	**3695**

59 2/01 Ling 7f D SLW £2863

Total win prize-money £2863

Going (Turf): Sf: 0-3 GS: 0-2 Gd: 0-2 GF: 0-3 Fm: 0-2
Distance: 5f/6f: 0-4 **7f-8f: 1-12** 9f-13f: 0-0 14f+: 0-0
Track : **LH: 1-7** RH: 0-2 **Tight: 1-5** Gall: 0-1
Aids: Bl: 0-0 Vi: 0-7 Tstrap: 0-0
Best Rating: 71 2/01 Ling 7f slow

Winner of an All-Weather maiden in the spring, he has shown ability in handicaps on turf this summer since fitted with a visor. Suited by a sharp, undulating track and waiting tactics.

Illusive (IRE)

99(107) (85)**71**

4-y-o b g Night Shift (USA)-Mirage (Red Sunset)
M Wigham P G McCarthy

Placings:0005**1021**/**4112**0355332000-**0251223**0030 **(3851)**
2001: 5^{0}SD, 7^{2}SW, 6^{5}SD, 6^{1}SD, 5^{2}SD, 5^{2}SW, 6^{3}SD, 6^{0}GF, 5^{0}GF, 5^{3}GF, 5^{0}G

	Starts	1st	2nd	3rd	Win & Pl
Career Total (Turf)	**18**	**0**	**1**	**4**	**5010**
Career Total (AW)	**15**	**5**	**5**	**1**	**34766**

82 3/01 Wolv 6f B(0-105)H STD £13455
83 2/00 Ling 6f D(0-80)H STD £3750
78 2/00 Ling 6f D(0-85)H STD £3785
70 11/99 Sthl 5f E(0-75)H STD £2814
64 10/99 Ling 6f D(0-85)H STD £3882

Total win prize-money £27689

Going (Turf): Sf: 0-1 GS: 0-2 Gd: 0-6 GF: 0-8 Fm: 0-1
Distance: **5f/6f: 5-29** 7f-8f: 0-4 9f-13f: 0-0 14f+: 0-0
Track : **LH: 4-17** RH: 0-1 **Tight: 4-12** Gall: 0-3
Aids: **Bl: 5-29** Vi: 0-0 Tstrap: 0-0
Best Rating: 85 4/01 Sthl 6f stand

He is an effective sort in sprint company on sand and acts on both Equitrack and Fibresand. He has shown ability on turf, but has yet to win on it. Suited by five and six furlongs.

Illustrious Duke

93(101) (77d)**56**

3-y-o b c Dancing Spree (USA)-Killick (Slip Anchor)
M Mullineaux Esprit De Corps Racing

Placings:000**4426**-**1115**0000 **(5416)**
2001: 8^{1}SD, 8^{1}SD, 8^{1}SW, 8^{5}SD, 7^{0}GF, 8^{0}GF, 7^{0}G, 9^{0}3D

	Starts	1st	2nd	3rd	Win & Pl
Career Total (Turf)	**6**	**0**	**0**	**0**	
Career Total (AW)	**9**	**3**	**1**	**0**	**8284**

74 2/01 Sthl 1m F(0-65)H SLW £1785
77 2/01 Sthl 1m E(0-70)H STD £2961
56 1/01 Wolv 1m100y D STD £2912

Total win prize-money £7658

Going (Turf): Sf: 0-2 GS: 0-0 Gd: 0-1 GF: 0-3 Fm: 0-0
Distance: 5f/6f: 0-1 **7f-8f: 2-10** 9f-13f: 1-4 14f+: 0-0
Track : **LH: 3-13** RH: 0-0 **Tight: 1-8** Gall: 0-0
Aids: Bl: 0-0 Vi: 0-0 Tstrap: 0-0
Best Rating: 77 2/01 Sthl 1m stand

A late foal whose dam won up to middle distances, was switched successfully to the All-Weather surfaces after three outings on turf. Prefers Fibresand and races prominently.

Ilton

82 **54**

2-y-o ch c Dr Devious (IRE)-Madame Crecy (USA) (Al Nasr (FR))
J D Bethell Www.Clarendon Racing.Oc.Uk

Placings:00 **(4794)**
2001: 7^{0}G, 7^{0}G

	Starts	1st	2nd	3rd	Win & Pl
Career Total (Turf)	**2**	**0**	**0**	**0**	

Going (Turf): Sf: 0-0 GS: 0-0 Gd: 0-2 GF: 0-0 Fm: 0-0
Distance: 5f/6f: 0-0 7f-8f: 0-2 9f-13f: 0-0 14f+: 0-0
Track : LH: 0-0 RH: 0-0 Tight: 0-0 Gall: 0-0
Aids: Bl: 0-0 Vi: 0-0 Tstrap: 0-0
Best Rating: 54 9/01 Ayr 7f50y good

Imaginative

77 **25**

4-y-o b g Last Tycoon-Imaginary (IRE) (Dancing Brave (USA))
W Jenks The Glazeley Partnership

Placings:61/616-0 **(4420)**
2001: 15^{0}G

	Starts	1st	2nd	3rd	Win & Pl
Career Total (Turf)	**6**	**2**	**0**	**0**	**20636**

10/00 Lonc 1m3f H SFT £16330
12/99 Cros 1m1f SFT £4306

Total win prize-money £20636

Going (Turf): Sf: 0-1 GS: 0-0 Gd: 0-1 GF: 0-0 Fm: 0-0
Distance: 5f/6f: 0-0 7f-8f: 0-0 9f-13f: 0-1 14f+: 0-1
Track : LH: 0-2 RH: 0-0 Tight: 0-1 Gall: 0-0
Aids: Bl: 0-2 Vi: 0-0 Tstrap: 0-0
Best Rating: 25 9/01 Ches 1m7f195y good

Imagine (IRE)

110 **120+**

3-y-o b f Sadler's Wells (USA)-Doff The Derby (USA) (Master Derby (USA))
A P O'Brien Mrs David Nagle & Mrs John Magnier

Placings:361412-2311 **(1975)**
2001: 7^{2}S, 7^{3}G, 8^{1}G, 12^{1}GF

	Starts	1st	2nd	3rd	Win & Pl
Career Total (Turf)	**10**	**4**	**2**	**2**	**418250**

114 6/01 Epsm 1m4f10y A G-F £211700
120 5/01 Curr 1m GD £126675
100 9/00 Curr 7f Y-S £32500
87 9/00 Gowr 1m GD £10475

Total win prize-money £381350

Going (Turf): Sf: 0-1 GS: 0-2 **Gd: 2-4** GF: 1-2 Fm: 0-0
Distance: 5f/6f: 0-0 **7f-8f: 3-9** 9f-13f: 1-1 14f+: 0-0
Track : LH: 1-1 RH: 1-2 **Tight: 1-1** Gall: 0-1
Aids: Bl: 0-0 Vi: 0-0 Tstrap: 0-0
Best Rating: 120 5/01 Curr 1m good

A half-sister to Generous, she has improved considerably from two to three. Came good on her third outing this term when landing the Irish 1,000 Guineas from Crystal Music, where she relished the soft ground. She followed up by winning the Oaks at Epsom over an extra half-mile, despite looking ill at ease on the course, but was subsequently retired after a setback.

Imari

99(91) (43)**51**

4-y-o gr f Rock City-Misty Goddess (IRE) (Godswalk (USA))
R G Frost J F O'Donovan

Placings:444640/2501326310-4006030 **(4735)**
2001: 13^{4}G, 14^{0}GF, 10^{0}F, 8^{6}GF, 9^{0}GF, 8^{3}G, 10^{0}F

	Starts	1st	2nd	3rd	Win & Pl
Career Total (Turf)	**20**	**2**	**1**	**3**	**7405**
Career Total (AW)	**3**	**0**	**1**	**0**	**546**

60 8/00 Yarm 1m2f21y F G-F £2184
58 6/00 Yarm 1m3y G(0-60)H GD £2075

Total win prize-money £4260

Going (Turf): Sf: 0-3 GS: 0-1 **Gd: 1-5 GF: 1-8** Fm: 0-3
Distance: 5f/6f: 0-4 7f-8f: 0-4 **9f-13f: 2-13** 14f+: 0-2
Track : **LH: 1-14** RH: 0-4 **Tight: 1-12** Gall: 0-0
Aids: Bl: 0-0 Vi: 0-0 Tstrap: 0-0
Best Rating: 60 5/01 Bath 1m5f22y good

Imbackagain (IRE)

(97) (42)**48**

6-y-o b g Mujadil (USA)-Ballinclogher (IRE) (Creative Plan (USA))
N P Littmoden Turf 2000 Limited

Placings:000/**16**05**0604**20/**0032360000**/**63000**2021460-**003601000** **(0714)**
2001: 7^{0}SW, 7^{0}SD, 7^{3}SW, 7^{6}SD, 7^{0}SW, 6^{1}SD, 6^{0}SD, 6^{0}SD, 7^{0}SD

	Starts	1st	2nd	3rd	Win & Pl
Career Total (Turf)	**12**	**0**	**3**	**0**	**2571**
Career Total (AW)	**32**	**3**	**1**	**4**	**7625**

42 2/01 Sthl 6f G STD £1855
42 6/00 Sthl 7f G(0-60)H STD £1830
64 1/98 Sthl 6f F(0-60)H STD £2085

Total win prize-money £5771

Going (Turf): Sf: 0-2 GS: 0-1 Gd: 0-2 GF: 0-5 Fm: 0-2
Distance: **5f/6f: 2-6** 7f-8f: 1-29 9f-13f: 0-9 14f+: 0-0
Track : **LH: 3-37** RH: 0-3 Tight: 0-17 Gall: 0-0
Aids: Bl: 0-0 **Vi: 1-7** Tstrap: 0-2
Best Rating: 42 2/01 Sthl 6f stand

Imbibing (IRE)

95 **86**

2-y-o ch c Halling (USA)-Polar Fizz (Polar Falcon (USA))
R F Johnson Houghton Anthony Pye-Jeary And Michael Smith

Placings:00 **(5361)**
2001: 7^{0}GF, 8^{0}GS

	Starts	1st	2nd	3rd	Win & Pl
Career Total (Turf)	**2**	**0**	**0**	**0**	

Going (Turf): Sf: 0-0 GS: 0-1 Gd: 0-0 GF: 0-1 Fm: 0-0
Distance: 5f/6f: 0-0 7f-8f: 0-2 9f-13f: 0-0 14f+: 0-0
Track : LH: 0-0 RH: 0-0 Tight: 0-0 Gall: 0-0
Aids: Bl: 0-0 Vi: 0-0 Tstrap: 0-0
Best Rating: 86 10/01 NmkR 1m gd-sft

Immaculate Charlie (IRE)

61

3-y-o ch f Rich Charlie-Miner's Society (Miners Lamp)

L Lungo Mrs Ann Fortune

Placings:32040-00 (1766)
2001: 11^{0}G, 8^{0}GF

	Starts	1st	2nd	3rd	Win & Pl
Career Total (Turf)	7	0	1	1	1321

Going (Turf): Sf: 0-1 GS: 0-1 Gd: 0-2 GF: 0-3 Fm: 0-0
Distance: 5f/6f: 0-2 7f-8f: 0-2 9f-13f: 0-3 14f+: 0-0
Track : LH: 0-3 RH: 0-3 Tight: 0-2 Gall: 0-2
Aids: Bl: 0-0 Vi: 0-1 Tstrap: 0-0

Imoya (IRE)

99 **92**

2-y-o b f Desert King (IRE)-Urgent Liaison (IRE) (High Estate)
B J Meehan Fieldspring Racing

Placings:0442 (5484)
2001: 6^{0}GF, 6^{4}GF, 7^{4}GF, 8^{2}HY

	Starts	1st	2nd	3rd	Win & Pl
Career Total (Turf)	4	0	1	0	2230

Going (Turf): Sf: 0-1 GS: 0-0 Gd: 0-0 GF: 0-3 Fm: 0-0
Distance: 5f/6f: 0-0 7f-8f: 0-4 9f-13f: 0-0 14f+: 0-0
Track : LH: 0-1 RH: 0-1 Tight: 0-0 Gall: 0-2
Aids: Bl: 0-0 Vi: 0-0 Tstrap: 0-0
Best Rating: 92 10/01 Donc 1m heavy

Impaldi (IRE)

99(83) **41**

6-y-o b m Imp Society (USA)-Jaldi (IRE) (Nordico (USA))
B Ellison Mrs Susan J Ellison

Placings:400/056600/064040240050/00500023303-0403000 (3672)
2001: 6^{0}HY, 5^{4}F, 6^{0}F, 5^{3}GF, 7^{0}G, 6^{0}F, 5^{0}G

	Starts	1st	2nd	3rd	Win & Pl
Career Total (Turf)	38	0	2	4	3958
Career Total (AW)	1	0	0	0	

Going (Turf): Sf: 0-3 GS: 0-1 Gd: 0-7 GF: 0-13 Fm: 0-7
Distance: 5f/6f: 0-29 7f-8f: 0-9 9f-13f: 0-0 14f+: 0-0
Track : LH: 0-8 RH: 0-2 Tight: 0-2 Gall: 0-0
Aids: Bl: 0-1 Vi: 0-0 Tstrap: 0-0
Best Rating: 41 6/01 Newc 5f gd-fm

Impavido (IRE)

87 **64**

2-y-o b c Sadler's Wells (USA)-Tis Juliet (USA) (Alydar (USA))
M Johnston Alessandro Gaucci

Placings:05 (5089)
2001: 8^{0}GF, 8^{5}GS

	Starts	1st	2nd	3rd	Win & Pl
Career Total (Turf)	2	0	0	0	0

Going (Turf): Sf: 0-0 GS: 0-1 Gd: 0-0 GF: 0-1 Fm: 0-0
Distance: 5f/6f: 0-0 7f-8f: 0-2 9f-13f: 0-0 14f+: 0-0
Track : LH: 0-1 RH: 0-0 Tight: 0-0 Gall: 0-1
Aids: Bl: 0-0 Vi: 0-0 Tstrap: 0-0
Best Rating: 64 10/01 Newc 1m gd-sft

Impeller (IRE)

103 **90**

2-y-o ch c Polish Precedent (USA)-Almaaseh (IRE) (Dancing Brave (USA))
W R Muir D G Clarke

Placings:4130 (5368)
2001: 6^{4}GF, 6^{1}F, 8^{3}F, 8^{0}GS

	Starts	1st	2nd	3rd	Win & Pl
Career Total (Turf)	4	1	0	1	5095

90 8/01 Sals 6f212y E FRM £3721
Total win prize-money £3721

Going (Turf): Sf: 0-0 GS: 0-1 Gd: 0-0 GF: 0-1 **Fm: 1-2**
Distance: 5f/6f: 0-1 **7f-8f: 1-2** 9f-13f: 0-1 14f+: 0-0
Track : LH: 0-1 RH: 0-0 Tight: 0-1 Gall: 0-0
Aids: Bl: 0-0 Vi: 0-0 Tstrap: 0-0
Best Rating: 90 8/01 Sals 6f212y firm

Won at the second time of asking in an auction maiden event over seven furlongs at Salisbury and ran well in a much tougher contest next time. Suited by five to seven furlongs and a sound surface.

Imperial Beauty (USA)

107 **119**

5-y-o b m Imperial Ballet (IRE)-Multimara (USA) (Arctic Tern (USA))
J E Hammond Mrs John Magnier & Mr M Tabor

Placings:212/012012/44-44031 (5244a)
2001: 5^{4}G, 5^{4}G, 5^{0}G, 6^{3}VS, 5^{1}HO

	Starts	1st	2nd	3rd	Win & Pl
Career Total (Turf)	16	4	4	1	191432

119 10/01 Lonc 5f HLD £48497
104 9/99 Newb 5f34y A G-S £28750
104 7/99 York 6f A G-F £15140
90 9/98 Sals 6f B GD £6491
Total win prize-money £98878

Going (Turf): Sf: 0-2 **GS: 1-1 Gd: 1-5 GF: 1-6** Fm: 0-0
Distance: **5f/6f: 4-14** 7f-8f: 0-2 9f-13f: 0-0 14f+: 0-0
Track : LH: 0-0 RH: 0-0 Tight: 0-0 Gall: 0-0
Aids: Bl: 0-0 Vi: 0-0 Tstrap: 0-0
Best Rating: 119 10/01 Lonc 5f holding

She developed into a high-class sprinter on soft ground in 1999, but was restricted to two outings last season. Sold for 950,000gns, she finally gained a group One victory when taking the Prix de l'Abbaye in 2001. Acts on all types of ground but well suited by cut.

Imperial Dancer

105 **99**

3-y-o b c Primo Dominie-Gorgeous Dancer (IRE) (Nordico (USA))
M R Channon Imperial Racing

Placings:4213024513250-30004143 (5605)
2001: 7^{3}GS, 8^{0}G, 8^{0}G, 6^{0}G, 7^{4}G, 8^{1}HY, 7^{4}HY, 8^{3}GS, 8^{5}HY

	Starts	1st	2nd	3rd	Win & Pl
Career Total (Turf)	21	3	3	4	47390

88 10/01 Ayr 1m C HVY £5956
101 8/00 York 6f214y C GD £11609
80 4/00 Wwck 5f D HVY £3096
Total win prize-money £20663

Going (Turf): **Sf: 2-5** GS: 0-2 Gd: 1-9 GF: 0-4 Fm: 0-0
Distance: 5f/6f: 1-8 **7f-8f: 2-13** 9f-13f: 0-0 14f+: 0-0
Track : **LH: 3-4** RH: 0-2 Tight: 0-0 **Gall: 2-5**
Aids: Bl: 0-0 Vi: 0-0 Tstrap: 0-0
Best Rating: 107 4/01 Newb 7f gd-sft

Third in the Greenham on his reappearance, but has been generally disappointing since. Apparently does not let himself down on fast ground, and clearly appreciated the heavy surface when winning a conditions race at Ayr in October.

Imperial Jewel (FR)

101 **59**

3-y-o b f Deploy-Imperial Prospect (USA) (Imperial Falcon (CAN))
J J Sheehan Mrs Eileen Sheehan

Placings:05350000 (5275)
2001: 8^{0}GF, 8^{5}GF, 8^{3}G, 8^{5}G, 10^{0}G, 8^{0}GF, 8^{0}GF, 8^{0}GS

	Starts	1st	2nd	3rd	Win & Pl
Career Total (Turf)	8	0	0	1	650

Going (Turf): Sf: 0-0 GS: 0-1 Gd: 0-3 GF: 0-4 Fm: 0-0
Distance: 5f/6f: 0-0 7f-8f: 0-1 9f-13f: 0-7 14f+: 0-0
Track : LH: 0-0 RH: 0-6 Tight: 0-2 Gall: 0-1
Aids: Bl: 0-1 Vi: 0-0 Tstrap: 0-0
Best Rating: 69 8/01 Wind 1m67y good

Showed improvement when third in a Windsor maiden in August 2001 over a mile, but has not cut much ice in handicaps. Acts on good ground.

Imperial Racer (IRE)

(66) (13)**58**

2-y-o b g Blues Traveller (IRE)-Reasonably French (Reasonable (FR))
M R Channon Imperial Racing

Placings:0000 (5410)
2001: 7^{0}G, 8^{0}G, 8^{0}G, 7^{0}SD

	Starts	1st	2nd	3rd	Win & Pl
Career Total (Turf)	3	0	0	0	
Career Total (AW)	1	0	0	0	

Going (Turf): Sf: 0-0 GS: 0-0 Gd: 0-3 GF: 0-0 Fm: 0-0
Distance: 5f/6f: 0-0 7f-8f: 0-4 9f-13f: 0-0 14f+: 0-0
Track : LH: 0-2 RH: 0-1 Tight: 0-0 Gall: 0-0
Aids: Bl: 0-0 Vi: 0-0 Tstrap: 0-0
Best Rating: 58 9/01 Kemp 1m good

Imperial Theatre (IRE)

94 **85**

2-y-o b c Sadler's Wells (USA)-Aunt Pearl (USA) (Seattle Slew (USA))
J H M Gosden R E Sangster & A K Collins

Placings:3 (5485)
2001: 7^{3}HY

	Starts	1st	2nd	3rd	Win & Pl
Career Total (Turf)	1	0	0	1	669

Going (Turf): Sf: 0-1 GS: 0-0 Gd: 0-0 GF: 0-0 Fm: 0-0
Distance: 5f/6f: 0-0 7f-8f: 0-1 9f-13f: 0-0 14f+: 0-0
Track : LH: 0-0 RH: 0-0 Tight: 0-0 Gall: 0-0
Aids: Bl: 0-0 Vi: 0-0 Tstrap: 0-0
Best Rating: 85 10/01 Donc 7f heavy

Impero

91 **66**

3-y-o b g Emperor Jones (USA)-Fight Right (FR) (Crystal Glitters (USA))
R J Armson (Miss B Sanders 7/8) R J Armson

Placings:5000-006 (3688)
2001: 11^{0}GF, 9^{0}GF, 11^{6}GF

	Starts	1st	2nd	3rd	Win & Pl
Career Total (Turf)	7	0	0	0	0

Going (Turf): Sf: 0-0 GS: 0-1 Gd: 0-1 GF: 0-5 Fm: 0-0
Distance: 5f/6f: 0-0 7f-8f: 0-3 9f-13f: 0-4 14f+: 0-0
Track : LH: 0-5 RH: 0-0 Tight: 0-3 Gall: 0-0
Aids: Bl: 0-0 Vi: 0-0 Tstrap: 0-1
Best Rating: 43 7/01 Nott 1m1f213y gd-fm

Impish Jude

96 **53**

3-y-o b f Imp Society (USA)-Miss Nanna (Vayrann)
J Mackie P A Bartlett

Placings:046600 (4571)
2001: 8^{0}G, 7^{4}GF, 8^{6}F, 7^{6}G, 8^{0}GF, 8^{0}HY

	Starts	1st	2nd	3rd	Win & Pl

Career Total (Turf) 6 0 0 0 329

Going (Turf): Sf: 0-1 GS: 0-0 Gd: 0-2 GF: 0-2 Fm: 0-1
Distance: 5f/6f: 0-0 7f-8f: 0-2 9f-13f: 0-4 14f+: 0-0
Track : LH: 0-5 RH: 0-0 Tight: 0-0 Gall: 0-0
Aids: Bl: 0-0 Vi: 0-0 Tstrap: 0-0
Best Rating: 53 6/01 Leic 7f9y good

Impish Lad

85(94) (57)34
3-y-o b g Imp Society (USA)-Madonna Da Rossi (Mtoto)
M J Polglase (B S Rothwell 22/1) The Lovatt Partnership

Placings:0513632300-02106226355640006000000 (5294)
2001: 7^0SD, 8^2SD, 8^1SW, 8^0SD, 8^6SD, 7^2SD, 7^2SW, 7^6SD, 7^3SD, 7^5SD, 7^5SW, 8^6HY, 11^4SD, 8^0HY, 9^0G, 7^0GF, 8^6S, 7^0GS, 10^0GF, 10^0G, 9^0GS, 11^0S

	Starts	1st	2nd	3rd	Win & Pl
Career Total (Turf)	17	0	1	2	1183
Career Total (AW)	15	2	3	2	5635

63	1/01	Sthl	1m	F(0-65)	SLW	£2205
56	5/00	Sthl	6f	G	STD	£1834

Total win prize-money £4039

Going (Turf): Sf: 0-5 GS: 0-2 Gd: 0-5 GF: 0-4 Fm: 0-1
Distance: 5f/6f: 1-3 7f-8f: 1-20 9f-13f: 0-9 14f+: 0-0
Track : LH: 2-21 RH: 0-5 Tight: 0-3 Gall: 0-0
Aids: Bl: 1-19 Vi: 0-2 Tstrap: 0-0
Best Rating: 64 2/01 Sthl 7f stand

Imprevue (IRE)

94(105) (67)62d
7-y-o ch m Priolo (USA)-Las Bela (Welsh Pageant)
R J O'Sullivan (Andrew Reid 18/8) P W Saunders

Placings:040/3224631/300400/0025002113114/6310062-22125105S6 (5026)
2001: 12^2SW, 12^2SW, 12^1SD, 10^2SD, 12^5SW, 12^1SD, 10^0SD, 12^5G, 10^SF, 9^6S

	Starts	1st	2nd	3rd	Win & Pl
Career Total (Turf)	32	4	3	5	18836
Career Total (AW)	14	4	5	0	13324

66	4/01	Ling	1m4f	E(0-70)H	STD	£2899
61	3/01	Ling	1m4f	F	STD	£2128
62	8/00	Yarm	1m2f21y	F(0-60)	G-F	£2912
61	11/99	Ling	1m2f	F(0-60)	STD	£1798
62	10/99	Nott	1m1f213y	F(0-60)	FRM	£3036
55	9/99	Brig	1m1f209y	F(0-65)H	G-F	£3241
53	7/99	Ling	1m2f	F(0-65)H	STD	£2261
85	10/97	Curr	1m4f		Y-S	£2740

Total win prize-money £21015

Going (Turf): Sf: 0-4 GS: 0-1 Gd: 0-11 GF: 2-5 Fm: 1-5
Distance: 5f/6f: 0-0 7f-8f: 0-3 9f-13f: 8-38 14f+: 0-5
Track : LH: 7-29 RH: 1-16 Tight: 5-20 Gall: 0-2
Aids: Bl: 8-27 Vi: 0-0 Tstrap: 0-0
Best Rating: 67 2/01 Ling 1m4f slow

Equally effective on turf and sand and won twice on the Lingfield Equitrack this season. Suited by ten to 12 furlongs.

Impreza

74(72) (15)4
3-y-o b f Mistertopogigo (IRE)-Little Redwing (Be My Chief (USA))
Miss A Stokell Ms Caron Stokell

Placings:04000000-000 (3694)
2001: 12^0GF, 12^0SD, 11^0G

	Starts	1st	2nd	3rd	Win & Pl
Career Total (Turf)	7	0	0	0	223
Career Total (AW)	4	0	0	0	

Going (Turf): Sf: 0-4 GS: 0-0 Gd: 0-2 GF: 0-1 Fm: 0-0
Distance: 5f/6f: 0-3 7f-8f: 0-3 9f-13f: 0-5 14f+: 0-0
Track : LH: 0-7 RH: 0-0 Tight: 0-4 Gall: 0-0
Aids: Bl: 0 0 Vi: 0-7 Tstrap: 0-0

Impulsive Air (IRE)

104(91) (36)46
9-y-o b g Try My Best (USA)-Tracy's Sundown (Red Sunset)
J R Weymes Don Raper

Placings:21325/560000000/5015132040/20605040221 16040/211000350000/0001020340405/5002004300000-55604005106150000 (4908)
2001: 11^5SD, 8^5SD, 9^6S, 8^0F, 9^4F, 8^0GF, 9^0G, 10^5GF, 9^1GF, 9^0G, 10^0GS, 9^1GF, 11^5GF, 10^0GF, 10^0F, 10^0GF, 9^0G

	Starts	1st	2nd	3rd	Win & Pl
Career Total (Turf)	92	10	9	5	57339
Career Total (AW)	3	0	0	0	0

46	7/01	Bevl	1m1f207y	E(0-75)H	G-F	£3801
48	6/99	Haml	1m1f36y	E(0-75)H	GD	£3485
68	6/98	Carl	7f214y	D(0-80)H	G-S	£3582
65	5/98	Ripn	1m	D(0-85)H	GD	£4143
62	8/97	Muss	7f30y	F(0-60)	G-F	£2802
63	8/97	Rdcr	1m	F(0-60)	FRM	£2696
64	8/96	Newc	1m	D(0-85)H	FRM	£7197
57	6/96	Carl	6f206y	D(0-80)H	FRM	£3533
68	4/94	Hayd	5f	D	GD	£3532

Total win prize-money £34775

Going (Turf): Sf: 0-8 GS: 1-13 Gd: 3-31 GF: 3-29 Fm: 3-11
Distance: 5f/6f: 1-6 7f-8f: 6-41 9f-13f: 3-48 14f+: 0-0
Track : LH: 2-45 RH: 6-27 Tight: 3-28 Gall: 1-14
Aids: Bl: 0-0 Vi: 0-6 Tstrap: 0-0
Best Rating: 50 7/01 Nott 1m1f213y gd-fm

A fair sort in modest handicap company, he scored at Beverley and Nottingham this season. Suited by ten furlongs and fast ground.

Imtihan (IRE)

85 66
2-y-o ch c Unfuwain (USA)-Azyaa (Kris)
B W Hills Hamdan Al Maktoum

Placings:00 (5361)
2001: 8^0S, 8^0GS

	Starts	1st	2nd	3rd	Win & Pl
Career Total (Turf)	2	0	0	0	

Going (Turf): Sf: 0-1 GS: 0-1 Gd: 0-0 GF: 0-0 Fm: 0-0
Distance: 5f/6f: 0-0 7f-8f: 0-2 9f-13f: 0-0 14f+: 0-0
Track : LH: 0-0 RH: 0-0 Tight: 0-0 Gall: 0-0
Aids: Bl: 0-0 Vi: 0-0 Tstrap: 0-0
Best Rating: 66 10/01 NmkR 1m gd-sft

Imtiyaz (USA)

94 88
2-y-o ro c Woodman (USA)-Shadayid (USA) (Shadeed (USA))
D R Loder Hamdan Al Maktoum

Placings:135 (5246a)
2001: 7^1S, 7^3G, 7^5HO

	Starts	1st	2nd	3rd	Win & Pl
Career Total (Turf)	3	1	0	1	12697

88	6/01	Sand	7f16y	D	SFT	£4329

Total win prize-money £4329

Going (Turf): Sf: 1-1 GS: 0-0 Gd: 0-1 GF: 0-0 Fm: 0-0
Distance: 5f/6f: 0-0 7f-8f: 1-3 9f-13f: 0-0 14f+: 0-0
Track : LH: 0-0 RH: 1-2 Tight: 0-0 Gall: 0-0
Aids: Bl: 0-0 Vi: 0-1 Tstrap: 0-0
Best Rating: 88 6/01 Sand 7f16y soft

Bred to be special, being out of a 1000 Guineas winner. Ran on in very good style over seven furlongs to record an impressive success at Sandown on his debut, but disappointed in Listed company on his next run, and was visored when last in the Grand Criterium.

In 'N' Out

97 77d
2-y-o ch g Dancing Spree (USA)-Aquarula (Dominion)
P D Evans (D Nicholls 8/5) P D Evans

Placings:11000 (5660)
2001: 5^1S, 5^1S, 5^0S, 5^0GF, 5^0G

	Starts	1st	2nd	3rd	Win & Pl
Career Total (Turf)	5	2	0	0	6314

77	4/01	Muss	5f	D	SFT	£3332
63	3/01	Donc	5f	F	SFT	£2982

Total win prize-money £6314

Going (Turf): Sf: 2-3 GS: 0-0 Gd: 0-1 GF: 0-1 Fm: 0-0
Distance: 5f/6f: 2-5 7f-8f: 0-0 9f-13f: 0-0 14f+: 0-0
Track : LH: 0-1 RH: 0-0 Tight: 0-1 Gall: 0-0
Aids: Bl: 0-0 Vi: 0-1 Tstrap: 0-0
Best Rating: 77 4/01 Muss 5f soft

A late April foal who has already been gelded, showed his appreciation for the soft ground when winning a seller at Doncaster and stepped up in class to take a novice event next time. He played up badly in the stalls at Newmarket and that run can be ignored, but he did not show much in his other two starts.

In A Twinkling (IRE)

90 39
4-y-o b f Brief Truce (USA)-Glim (USA) (Damascus (USA))
M Blanshard The Star Racing Partnership

Placings:3644600/0060-000 (1843)
2001: 7^0G, 9^0F, 8^0GF

	Starts	1st	2nd	3rd	Win & Pl
Career Total (Turf)	14	0	0	1	2564

Going (Turf): Sf: 0-2 GS: 0-1 Gd: 0-7 GF: 0-3 Fm: 0-1
Distance: 5f/6f: 0-7 7f-8f: 0-2 9f-13f: 0-5 14f+: 0-0
Track : LH: 0-2 RH: 0-4 Tight: 0-2 Gall: 0-0
Aids: Bl: 0-0 Vi: 0-0 Tstrap: 0-0
Best Rating: 39 5/01 Leic 1m1f218y firm

In Disguise

96 85
2-y-o ch c Nashwan (USA)-Conspiracy (Rudimentary (USA))
J L Dunlop The Earl Cadogan

Placings:6200 (5368)
2001: 7^6GF, 7^2G, 8^0GF, 8^0GS

	Starts	1st	2nd	3rd	Win & Pl
Career Total (Turf)	4	0	1	0	1299

Going (Turf): Sf: 0-0 GS: 0-1 Gd: 0-1 GF: 0-2 Fm: 0-0
Distance: 5f/6f: 0-0 7f-8f: 0-4 9f-13f: 0-0 14f+: 0-0
Track : LH: 0-0 RH: 0-0 Tight: 0-0 Gall: 0-0
Aids: Bl: 0-0 Vi: 0-0 Tstrap: 0-0
Best Rating: 85 8/01 NmkJ 7f good

In For The Craic (IRE)

83 63
2-y-o b c Our Emblem (USA)-Lucky State (USA) (State Dinner (USA))
S Kirk The Quiet Men

Placings:0 (4625)
2001: 8^0GF

	Starts	1st	2nd	3rd	Win & Pl
Career Total (Turf)	1	0	0	0	

Going (Turf): Sf: 0-0 GS: 0-0 Gd: 0-0 GF: 0-1 Fm: 0-0
Distance: 5f/6f: 0-0 7f-8f: 0-0 9f-13f: 0-1 14f+: 0-0
Track : LH: 0-1 RH: 0-0 Tight: 0-0 Gall: 0-0
Aids: Bl: 0-0 Vi: 0-0 Tstrap: 0-0
Best Rating: 63 9/01 Nott 1m54y gd-fm

In Good Faith

67 (55)**52**
9-y-o b g Beveled (USA)-Dulcidene (Behistoun)
R E Barr P Cartmell

Placings:013030110/00000/0003/200600/0/56/0-0 **(1830)**
2001: 10^{0}F

	Starts	1st	2nd	3rd	Win & Pl
Career Total (Turf)	25	3	0	2	15515
Career Total (AW)	4	0	1	1	933

87 10/94 York 7f202y C G-S £6524
79 9/94 Ayr 1m C G-S £5061
63 6/94 Pont 5f F G-F £2641
Total win prize-money £14227

Going (Turf): Sf: 0-3 **GS: 2-5** Gd: 0-8 GF: 1-6 Fm: 0-3
Distance: 5f/6f: 1-5 **7f-8f: 2-10** 9f-13f: 0-14 14f+: 0-0
Track : **LH: 3-19** RH: 0-6 Tight: 0-6 **Gall: 1-2**
Aids: Bl: 0-0 Vi: 0-1 Tstrap: 0-0

In Good Time

78 **46**
2-y-o b g Classic Cliche (IRE)-Primum Tempus (Primo Dominie)
E J Alston Springs Equestrian Ltd

Placings:60 **(4939)**
2001: 8^{6}G, 7^{0}S

	Starts	1st	2nd	3rd	Win & Pl
Career Total (Turf)	2	0	0	0	0

Going (Turf): Sf: 0-1 GS: 0-0 Gd: 0-1 GF: 0-0 Fm: 0-0
Distance: 5f/6f: 0-0 7f-8f: 0-1 9f-13f: 0-1 14f+: 0-0
Track : LH: 0-1 RH: 0-1 Tight: 0-2 Gall: 0-0
Aids: Bl: 0-0 Vi: 0-0 Tstrap: 0-0
Best Rating: 46 9/01 Ches 7f2y soft

In Luck

96 **63**
3-y-o b f In The Wings-Lucca (Sure Blade (USA))
B Smart John W Ford

Placings:43 **(2367)**
2001: 9^{4}GF, 9^{3}GF

	Starts	1st	2nd	3rd	Win & Pl
Career Total (Turf)	2	0	0	1	651

Going (Turf): Sf: 0-0 GS: 0-0 Gd: 0-0 GF: 0-2 Fm: 0-0
Distance: 5f/6f: 0-0 7f-8f: 0-0 9f-13f: 0-2 14f+: 0-0
Track : LH: 0-0 RH: 0-2 Tight: 0-2 Gall: 0-0
Aids: Bl: 0-0 Vi: 0-0 Tstrap: 0-0
Best Rating: 63 6/01 Folk 1m1f149y gd-fm

In Space (USA)

101 **98?**
2-y-o ch c Sky Classic (CAN)-Thrilling Day (Groom Dancer (USA))
S P C Woods Lucayan Stud

Placings:5515235 **(4781)**
2001: 5^{5}S, 5^{5}GS, 6^{1}GF, 6^{5}G, 7^{2}F, 7^{3}GF, 8^{5}G

	Starts	1st	2nd	3rd	Win & Pl
Career Total (Turf)	7	1	1	1	8763

76 7/01 Yarm 6f3y D G-F £3477
Total win prize-money £3478

Going (Turf): Sf: 0-1 GS: 0-1 Gd: 0-2 **GF: 1-2** Fm: 0-1
Distance: 5f/6f: 0-3 **7f-8f: 1-4** 9f-13f: 0-0 14f+: 0-0
Track : LH: 0-2 RH: 0-1 Tight: 0-1 Gall: 0-0
Aids: Bl: 0-0 Vi: 0-0 Tstrap: 0-0
Best Rating: 98 8/01 Newb 7f gd-fm

An expensive yearling, ran with promise on easy ground in the spring, but looked better when winning at Yarmouth over six furlongs on fast ground after a break. Out of his depth in the July Stakes. Stays seven furlongs. Acts on fast ground.

In Spirit (IRE)

(97) (81)**70**
3-y-o b g Distinctly North (USA)-June Goddess (Junius (USA))
D J S Cosgrove Crown Pkg & Mailing Svs Ltd

Placings:0220-1042010006 **(5416)**
2001: 7^{1}SD, 8^{0}GS, 9^{4}GS, 10^{2}GF, 9^{0}GF, 8^{1}GF, 10^{0}GF, 8^{0}GF, 8^{0}G, 9^{6}SD

	Starts	1st	2nd	3rd	Win & Pl
Career Total (Turf)	9	1	1	0	6071
Career Total (AW)	5	1	2	0	3920

70 6/01 Wwck 1m22y D(0-80)H G-F £4127
65 1/01 Sthl 7f D STD £2408
Total win prize-money £6536

Going (Turf): Sf: 0-0 GS: 0-3 Gd: 0-1 **GF: 1-5** Fm: 0-0
Distance: 5f/6f: 0-1 7f-8f: 1-6 9f-13f: 1-7 14f+: 0-0
Track : **LH: 1-5** RH: 0-6 Tight: 0-5 Gall: 0-0
Aids: **Bl: 1-4** Vi: 0-0 Tstrap: 0-0
Best Rating: 70 7/01 Sand 1m2f7y gd-fm

In The Arena (USA)

95(70) (15)**47**
4-y-o ch g Cadeaux Genereux-Tajfah (USA) (Shadeed (USA))
D Shaw Lee Westwood

Placings:00/4340010-00000 **(4907)**
2001: 7^{0}GS, 6^{0}SD, 5^{0}G, 8^{0}GF, 7^{0}G

	Starts	1st	2nd	3rd	Win & Pl
Career Total (Turf)	12	1	0	1	4666
Career Total (AW)	2	0	0	0	0

79 10/00 Yarm 7f3y D SFT £3360
Total win prize-money £3361

Going (Turf): Sf: 1-2 GS: 0-2 Gd: 0-6 GF: 0-2 Fm: 0-0
Distance: 5f/6f: 0-4 **7f-8f: 1-9** 9f-13f: 0-1 14f+: 0-0
Track : LH: 0-5 RH: 0-3 Tight: 0-2 Gall: 0-1
Aids: Bl: 0-0 Vi: 0-0 Tstrap: 0-0
Best Rating: 47 5/01 Ripn 1m gd-fm

In The Frame (IRE)

96 **64**
2-y-o b c Definite Article-Victorian Flower (Tate Gallery (USA))
R Hannon Patrick Latham

Placings:0060 **(4714)**
2001: 6^{0}GF, 6^{0}GF, 7^{6}GF, 7^{0}G

	Starts	1st	2nd	3rd	Win & Pl
Career Total (Turf)	4	0	0	0	0

Going (Turf): Sf: 0-0 GS: 0-0 Gd: 0-1 GF: 0-3 Fm: 0-0
Distance: 5f/6f: 0-1 7f-8f: 0-3 9f-13f: 0-0 14f+: 0-0
Track : LH: 0-0 RH: 0-0 Tight: 0-0 Gall: 0-0
Aids: Bl: 0-0 Vi: 0-0 Tstrap: 0-0
Best Rating: 64 7/01 Newb 7f gd-fm

In The Green

99 **68**
2-y-o b g Greensmith-Carn Maire (Northern Prospect (USA))
R A Fahey Giles W Pritchard-Gordon

Placings:3330610 **(5102)**
2001: 5^{3}GF, 5^{3}GF, 5^{3}GF, 5^{0}G, 5^{6}G, 5^{1}F, 5^{0}GS

	Starts	1st	2nd	3rd	Win & Pl
Career Total (Turf)	7	1	0	3	8054

68 9/01 Muss 5f C H FRM £6610
Total win prize-money £6611

Going (Turf): Sf: 0-0 GS: 0-1 Gd: 0-2 GF: 0-3 **Fm: 1-1**
Distance: **5f/6f: 1-7** 7f-8f: 0-0 9f-13f: 0-0 14f+: 0-0
Track : LH: 0-2 RH: 0-0 Tight: 0-2 Gall: 0-0
Aids: Bl: 0-0 Vi: 0-0 Tstrap: 0-0
Best Rating: 68 9/01 Muss 5f firm

Showed ability early and finally got off the mark over the minimum trip in a decent nursery at Musselburgh in September. Acts on firm ground.

In The Stars (IRE)

95 **68**
3-y-o ch c Definite Article-Astronomer Lady (IRE) (Montekin)
Mrs A J Perrett The Fancy Colours Partnership

Placings:400 **(5464)**
2001: 9^{4}GS, 10^{0}G, 11^{0}G

	Starts	1st	2nd	3rd	Win & Pl
Career Total (Turf)	3	0	0	0	0

Going (Turf): Sf: 0-0 GS: 0-1 Gd: 0-2 GF: 0-0 Fm: 0-0
Distance: 5f/6f: 0-0 7f-8f: 0-0 9f-13f: 0-3 14f+: 0-0
Track : LH: 0-1 RH: 0-1 Tight: 0-2 Gall: 0-0
Aids: Bl: 0-0 Vi: 0-0 Tstrap: 0-0
Best Rating: 68 8/01 Wind 1m2f7y good

In The Stocks

99 **44**
7-y-o b m Reprimand-Stock Hill Lass (Air Trooper)
L G Cottrell E Gadsden

Placings:600000140/4460561/0062015-0050512 **(5294)**
2001: 9^{0}G, 11^{0}GF, 10^{5}GF, 11^{0}GF, 12^{5}GS, 10^{1}GF, 11^{2}S

	Starts	1st	2nd	3rd	Win & Pl
Career Total (Turf)	30	4	2	0	11807

31 8/01 Wwck 1m2f188yG G-F £2136
47 9/00 Wwck 1m2f188yF(0-60)H G-F £2604
49 10/99 Ling 1m3f106yF(0-60)H G-F £2770
52 9/98 Bath 1m5y F(0-60)H GD £2444
Total win prize-money £9955

Going (Turf): Sf: 0-3 GS: 0-3 Gd: 1-8 **GF: 3-13** Fm: 0-3
Distance: 5f/6f: 0-0 7f-8f: 0-3 **9f-13f: 4-27** 14f+: 0-0
Track : **LH: 4-16** RH: 0-6 **Tight: 2-18** Gall: 0-0
Aids: Bl: 0-0 Vi: 0-0 Tstrap: 0-0
Best Rating: 44 6/01 Wwck 1m2f188y gd-fm

Fair plater at around a mile and a half who has shown her best form on fast ground.

In Xanadu (IRE)

92 **69+**
2-y-o b c Persian Bold-Dromoland (Cadeaux Genereux)
J L Dunlop Ian Cameron

Placings:000 **(5604)**
2001: 6^{0}GF, 7^{0}S, 7^{0}GS

	Starts	1st	2nd	3rd	Win & Pl
Career Total (Turf)	3	0	0	0	

Going (Turf): Sf: 0-1 GS: 0-1 Gd: 0-0 GF: 0-1 Fm: 0-0
Distance: 5f/6f: 0-0 7f-8f: 0-3 9f-13f: 0-0 14f+: 0-0
Track : LH: 0-0 RH: 0-0 Tight: 0-0 Gall: 0-0
Aids: Bl: 0-0 Vi: 0-0 Tstrap: 0-0
Best Rating: 69 11/01 NmkR 7f gd-sft

Inca Warrior (USA)

98 **85**

3-y-o ch c Diesis-Urus (USA) (Kris S (USA))

J W Hills Blenstock,Boase,Kerr-Dineen & Villareal

Placings:3324 **(3408)**

2001: 8^{3}GF, 8^{3}GF, 10^{2}GF, 10^{4}GF

	Starts	1st	2nd	3rd	Win & Pl
Career Total (Turf)	4	0	1	2	4255

Going (Turf): Sf: 0-0 GS: 0-0 Gd: 0-0 GF: 0-4 Fm: 0-0
Distance: 5f/6f: 0-0 7f-8f: 0-2 9f-13f: 0-2 14f+: 0-0
Track : LH: 0-1 RH: 0-3 Tight: 0-0 Gall: 0-2
Aids: Bl: 0-0 Vi: 0-0 Tstrap: 0-0
Best Rating: 85 7/01 Newb 1m2f6y gd-fm

Incantation

74 **33**

2-y-o b f Magic Ring (IRE)-Songsheet (Dominion)

Dr J D Scargill J P T Partnership

Placings:000 **(5022)**

2001: 7^{0}GF, 6^{0}GF, 7^{0}S

	Starts	1st	2nd	3rd	Win & Pl
Career Total (Turf)	3	0	0	0	

Going (Turf): Sf: 0-1 GS: 0-0 Gd: 0-0 GF: 0-2 Fm: 0-0
Distance: 5f/6f: 0-1 7f-8f: 0-2 9f-13f: 0-0 14f+: 0-0
Track : LH: 0-1 RH: 0-0 Tight: 0-0 Gall: 0-0
Aids: Bl: 0-0 Vi: 0-0 Tstrap: 0-0
Best Rating: 33 8/01 Ling 6f gd-fm

Inch By Inch

84 **57**

2-y-o b f Inchinor-Maid Welcome (Mummy's Pet)

P J Makin Mrs Anna L Sanders

Placings:00 **(5603)**

2001: 7^{0}GF, 7^{0}GS

	Starts	1st	2nd	3rd	Win & Pl
Career Total (Turf)	2	0	0	0	

Going (Turf): Sf: 0-0 GS: 0-1 Gd: 0-0 GF: 0-1 Fm: 0-0
Distance: 5f/6f: 0-0 7f-8f: 0-2 9f-13f: 0-0 14f+: 0-0
Track : LH: 0-0 RH: 0-0 Tight: 0-0 Gall: 0-0
Aids: Bl: 0-0 Vi: 0-0 Tstrap: 0-0
Best Rating: 57 11/01 NmkR 7f gd-sft

Inch High

59 **2**

3-y-o ch g Inchinor-Harrken Heights (IRE) (Belmez (USA))

J S Goldie Frank Brady

Placings:00 **(3071)**

2001: 7^{0}GF, 10^{0}S

	Starts	1st	2nd	3rd	Win & Pl
Career Total (Turf)	2	0	0	0	

Going (Turf): Sf: 0-1 GS: 0-0 Gd: 0-0 GF: 0-1 Fm: 0-0
Distance: 5f/6f: 0-0 7f-8f: 0-1 9f-13f: 0-1 14f+: 0-0
Track : LH: 0-2 RH: 0-0 Tight: 0-0 Gall: 0-0
Aids: Bl: 0-0 Vi: 0-0 Tstrap: 0-0
Best Rating: 2 7/01 Hayd 7f30y gd-fm

Inch Perfect

108(96) (78)**86**

6-y-o b g Inchinor-Scarlet Veil (Tyrnavos)

R A Fahey Exors Of The Late T P Staunton

Placings:43/100433111131/131310003-20055006 **(5057)**

2001: 8^{2}G, 11^{0}GS, 8^{0}GF, 10^{5}GF, 11^{5}G, 13^{0}GF, 12^{0}G, 12^{6}S

	Starts	1st	2nd	3rd	Win & Pl
Career Total (Turf)	25	7	1	5	47346
Career Total (AW)	6	2	0	2	5189

89	6/00	York	1m5f194y	C(0-95)H	GD	£9396
79	5/00	York	1m3f195y	C(0-95)H	G-F	£11960
74	4/00	Thsk	1m	F(0-65)H	SFT	£3614
64	11/99	Wolv	1m4f	F(0-60)H	STD	£2379
61	10/99	Bath	1m2f46y	E(0-70)H	SFT	£3178
59	10/99	Newc	1m2f32y	F(0-60)H	G-S	£2400
52	10/99	Pont	1m2f6y	E(0-70)H	GD	£4305
43	9/99	Rdcr	1m2f	G(0-60)H	G-F	£2220
54	3/99	Sthl	1m	G	STD	£1973

Total win prize-money £41425

Going (Turf): Sf: 2-4 GS: 1-3 **Gd: 2-12 GF: 2-5** Fm: 0-1
Distance: 5f/6f: 0-0 7f-8f: 2-7 **9f-13f: 6-19** 14f+: 1-5
Track : **LH: 9-26** RH: 0-2 **Tight: 4-7** Gall: 3-12
Aids: Bl: 0-0 Vi: 0-0 Tstrap: 0-1
Best Rating: 89 6/01 York 1m205y good

He has looked too high in the weights this term. Suited by eight to 13 furlongs and all type of ground.

Inchalong

91(78) (36)**43**

6-y-o b m Inchinor-Reshift (Night Shift (USA))

M Brittain Northgate Lodge Partnerships

Placings:53532652125236143332332O/004344012501 0000/**0**0000000206102**06**/000**0**-000 **(1728)**

2001: 7^{0}GF, 6^{0}G, 7^{0}GF

	Starts	1st	2nd	3rd	Win & Pl
Career Total (Turf)	58	5	9	9	44941
Career Total (AW)	4	0	0	0	0

61	9/99	Pont	6f	D(0-85)H	G-F	£8220
75	8/98	Ripn	6f	D(0-80)H	G-F	£3793
72	7/98	Wind	6f	E(0-70)H	G-F	£3192
70	8/97	Muss	7f30y	E	GD	£2576
61	6/97	Newc	6f	E	GD	£7262

Total win prize-money £25046

Going (Turf): Sf: 0-7 GS: 0-3 Gd: 2-27 **GF: 3-20** Fm: 0-1
Distance: **5f/6f: 4-31** 7f-8f: 1-31 9f-13f: 0-0 14f+: 0-0
Track : LH: 1-20 **RH: 2-3** Tight: 1-11 Gall: 1-5
Aids: Bl: 0-0 **Vi: 3-30** Tstrap: 0-0
Best Rating: 34 5/01 Ripn 6f good

A tough and speedy sprint handicapper, he won twice last summer over six furlongs and after a long losing run got back to winning ways when landing a Pontefract sprint in September. Needs decent ground on turf.

Inchcape

103 **95**

3-y-o b c Indian Ridge-Inchmurrin (Lomond (USA))

R Charlton A E Oppenheimer

Placings:3-13 **(1143)**

2001: 6^{1}GS, 7^{3}G

	Starts	1st	2nd	3rd	Win & Pl
Career Total (Turf)	3	1	0	2	7074

87	4/01	NmkR	6f	D	G-S	£4992

Total win prize-money £4992

Going (Turf): Sf: 0-1 **GS: 1-1** Gd: 0-1 GF: 0-0 Fm: 0-0
Distance: **5f/6f: 1-2** 7f-8f: 0-1 9f-13f: 0-0 14f+: 0-0
Track : LH: 0-0 RH: 0-0 Tight: 0-0 Gall: 0-0
Aids: Bl: 0-0 Vi: 0-0 Tstrap: 0-0
Best Rating: 95 5/01 NmkR 7f good

Won impressively on reappearance at three over six furlongs on good to soft. Did not lot himself down on the ground at Newmarket next timet. Seems best at six furlongs at present, appreciates cut in the ground.

Inchcoonan

(93) (38)**48**

3-y-o b f Emperor Jones (USA)-Miss Ivory Coast (USA) (Sir Ivor)

K R Burke David McKenzie

Placings:000610 **(4799)**

2001: 7^{0}S, 6^{0}G, 7^{0}GF, 8^{6}GF, 8^{1}GF, 10^{0}G

	Starts	1st	2nd	3rd	Win & Pl
Career Total (Turf)	6	1	0	0	2786

48	8/01	Muss	1m	E(0-70)H	G-F	£2786

Total win prize-money £2786

Going (Turf): Sf: 0-1 GS: 0-0 Gd: 0-2 **GF: 1-3** Fm: 0-0
Distance: 5f/6f: 0-1 **7f-8f: 1-4** 9f-13f: 0-1 14f+: 0-0
Track : LH: 0-2 **RH: 1-2 Tight: 1-1** Gall: 0-1
Aids: Bl: 0-0 Vi: 0-0 Tstrap: 0-0
Best Rating: 48 8/01 Muss 1m gd-fm

Inchdura

110 **85**

3-y-o ch c Inchinor-Sunshine Coast (Posse (USA))

R Charlton S M De Zoete

Placings:0-002101210 **(5607)**

2001: 8^{0}G, 8^{0}S, 7^{2}GF, 6^{1}GF, 7^{0}GF, 7^{1}GF, 7^{2}GF, 8^{1}GF, 8^{0}GS

	Starts	1st	2nd	3rd	Win & Pl
Career Total (Turf)	10	3	2	0	17926

85	9/01	Newb	1m	C(0-100)H	G-F	£7553
79	8/01	Ling	7f140y	E(0-75)H	G-F	£3374
75	6/01	Sals	6f212y	F(0-65)H	G-F	£3444

Total win prize-money £14371

Going (Turf): Sf: 0-2 GS: 0-1 Gd: 0-1 **GF: 3-6** Fm: 0-0
Distance: 5f/6f: 0-0 **7f-8f: 3-10** 9f-13f: 0-0 14f+: 0-0
Track : LH: 0-0 RH: 0-1 Tight: 0-0 Gall: 0-0
Aids: Bl: 0-0 Vi: 0-0 **Tstrap: 1-3**
Best Rating: 85 9/01 Newb 1m gd-fm

A winner three times this season at Salisbury, Lingfield and Newbury, his trainer has attributed his improvement to the combination of a tongue tie, fast ground and growing up. A mile is probably his best trip.

Inching Closer

104 **86**

4-y-o b g Inchinor-Maiyaasah (Kris)

Fordy Murphy (N A Callaghan 30/6) Mrs N L Spence

Placings:524/0013333-0622010 **(2607)**

2001: 12^{0}S, 12^{6}S, 12^{2}G, 12^{2}S, 14^{0}GF, 13^{1}GF, 16^{0}F

	Starts	1st	2nd	3rd	Win & Pl
Career Total (Turf)	17	2	3	4	23030

86	6/01	Newb	1m5f61y	D(0-85)H	G-F	£5200
81	6/00	Ayr	1m2f	D	G-F	£3770

Total win prize-money £8970

Going (Turf): Sf: 0-3 GS: 0-0 Gd: 0-7 **GF: 2-6** Fm: 0-1
Distance: 5f/6f: 0-1 7f-8f: 0-2 9f-13f: 1-11 14f+: 1-3
Track : **LH: 2-5** RH: 0-7 Tight: 0-4 **Gall: 1-6**
Aids: Bl: 0-0 Vi: 0-0 Tstrap: 0-0
Best Rating: 86 6/01 Newb 1m5f61y gd-fm

A half-brother to three winners, he is a consistent performer at up to a mile and a half and battled on well to win at Newbury in June. Suited by fast ground.

Inchinnan

105 **72**

4-y-o b f Inchinor-Westering (Auction Ring (USA))

C Weedon Atlantic Foods Ltd

Placings:35522552/21326-065332010 **(4983)**

2001: 9^{0}HY, 8^{6}S, 10^{5}GF, 9^{3}GF, 9^{3}GF, 10^{2}G, 10^{0}G, 10^{1}HY, 12^{0}G

	Starts	1st	2nd	3rd	Win & Pl
Career Total (Turf)	22	2	6	4	16508

70	9/01	Hayd	1m2f120y	E(0-80)H	HVY	£3374
61	4/00	Epsm	1m114y	E(0-70)	HVY	£4309

Total win prize-money £7684

Going (Turf): Sf: 2-5 GS: 0-3 Gd: 0-6 GF: 0-8 Fm: 0-0

Distance: 5f/6f: 0-0 7f-8f: 0-8 **9f-13f: 2-14** 14f+: 0-0
Track : **LH: 2-10** RH: 0-4 **Tight: 1-5** Gall: 0-2
Aids: Bl: 0-0 Vi: 0-0 Tstrap: 0-0
Best Rating: 70 9/01 Hayd 1m2f120y heavy

Has only two wins to her name at Epsom and Haydock. Stays ten furlongs. Loves the mud but handles a faster surface as well.

Inchiri

103 **107**
3-y-o b f Sadler's Wells (USA)-Inchyre (Shirley Heights)
G A Butler Woodcote Stud Ltd

Placings:54-314631055 **(5672a)**
2001: 12^{3}S, 10^{1}S, 11^{4}GF, 10^{6}GF, 10^{3}GF, 11^{1}G, 12^{0}G, 12^{5}GS, 10^{5}HO

	Starts	1st	2nd	3rd	Win & Pl
Career Total (Turf)	11	2	0	2	44182

100	8/01	York	1m3f195yA		GD	£30485
79	4/01	Ripn	1m2f	D	SFT	£4143

Total win prize-money £34629

Going (Turf): Sf: 1-3 GS: 0-2 **Gd: 1-2** GF: 0-3 Fm: 0-0
Distance: 5f/6f: 0-0 7f-8f: 0-2 **9f-13f: 2-9** 14f+: 0-0
Track : LH: 1-5 RH: 1-3 Tight: 1-2 Gall: 1-3
Aids: Bl: 0-0 Vi: 0-0 Tstrap: 0-0
Best Rating: 107 9/01 Lonc 1m4f good

Got off the mark over ten furlongs on her second start at three, but was held in listed company until springing a surprise at York, although she has struggled since. Has a bit of a mind of her own. Stays twelve furlongs.

Incline (IRE)

69 **12**
2-y-o b c Danehill (USA)-Shalwar Kameez (IRE) (Sadler's Wells (USA))
T G Mills Mrs Pauline Merrick

Placings:0 **(1267)**
2001: 5^{0}GS

	Starts	1st	2nd	3rd	Win & Pl
Career Total (Turf)	1	0	0	0	

Going (Turf): Sf: 0-0 GS: 0-1 Gd: 0-0 GF: 0-0 Fm: 0-0
Distance: 5f/6f: 0-1 7f-8f: 0-0 9f-13f: 0-0 14f+: 0-0
Track : LH: 0-0 RH: 0-0 Tight: 0-0 Gall: 0-0
Aids: Bl: 0-0 Vi: 0-0 Tstrap: 0-0
Best Rating: 12 5/01 Ling 5f gd-sft

Indaba (IRE)

108 **95**
3-y-o ch f Indian Ridge-Sedulous (Tap On Wood)
J Noseda Mrs K Sellars

Placings:22211321 **(5499)**
2001: 6^{2}GS, 6^{2}G, 6^{2}GS, 6^{1}G, 7^{1}S, 6^{3}G, 7^{2}GS, 7^{1}HY, 6^{3}HY

	Starts	1st	2nd	3rd	Win & Pl
Career Total (Turf)	8	3	4	1	29714

95	10/01	Donc	7f	B	HVY	£11163
82	9/01	Yarm	7f3y	D(0-80)	SFT	£4959
80	8/01	NmkJ	6f	D	GD	£4153

Total win prize-money £20278

Going (Turf): Sf: 2-2 GS: 0-3 Gd: 1-3 GF: 0-0 Fm: 0-0
Distance: 5f/6f: 1-5 **7f-8f: 2-3** 9f-13f: 0-0 14f+: 0-0
Track : LH: 0-1 RH: 0-0 Tight: 0-0 Gall: 0-0
Aids: Bl: 0-0 Vi: 0-0 Tstrap: 0-0
Best Rating: 95 10/01 Donc 7f heavy

Out of an useful Irish mare, she is very progressive and won her third race of the campaign in the mud at Doncaster. Seems suited by cut in the ground, yet to race on fast. Looks equally effective over six and seven furlongs.

Indefinite Stay

(68) **(6)38**
3-y-o b g Beveled (USA)-Wassl's Sister (Troy)
W R Muir The Four Willies Partnership

Placings:00-0000 **(4557)**
2001: 8^{0}S, 9^{0}G, 9^{0}GS, 9^{0}SW

	Starts	1st	2nd	3rd	Win & Pl
Career Total (Turf)	5	0	0	0	
Career Total (AW)	1	0	0	0	

Going (Turf): Sf: 0-2 GS: 0-2 Gd: 0-1 GF: 0-0 Fm: 0-0
Distance: 5f/6f: 0-0 7f-8f: 0-2 9f-13f: 0-4 14f+: 0-0
Track : LH: 0-2 RH: 0-2 Tight: 0-3 Gall: 0-0
Aids: Bl: 0-0 Vi: 0-0 Tstrap: 0-0
Best Rating: 38 8/01 Leic 1m1f218y good

Indelible

91(87) **(60)68**
2-y-o br f Polar Falcon (USA)-Ink Pot (USA) (Green Dancer (USA))
W J Haggas Cheveley Park Stud

Placings:43302 **(5370)**
2001: 6^{4}GF, 6^{3}SD, 5^{3}GF, 7^{0}GS, 7^{2}G

	Starts	1st	2nd	3rd	Win & Pl
Career Total (Turf)	4	0	1	1	1568
Career Total (AW)	1	0	0	1	342

Going (Turf): Sf: 0-0 GS: 0-1 Gd: 0-1 GF: 0-2 Fm: 0-0
Distance: 5f/6f: 0-3 7f-8f: 0-2 9f-13f: 0-0 14f+: 0-0
Track : LH: 0-1 RH: 0-1 Tight: 0-0 Gall: 0-0
Aids: Bl: 0-0 Vi: 0-0 Tstrap: 0-0
Best Rating: 68 6/01 NmkJ 6f gd-fm

Still a maiden, but has run some fair races on a sound surface, at both six and seven furlongs.

Independence

111 **113**
3-y-o b f Selkirk (USA)-Yukon Hope (USA) (Forty Niner (USA))
E A L Dunlop Cliveden Stud

Placings:30-2411311 **(5141)**
2001: 7^{2}GS, 7^{4}G, 7^{1}G, 8^{1}GF, 7^{3}GF, 8^{1}GY, 8^{1}G

	Starts	1st	2nd	3rd	Win & Pl
Career Total (Turf)	9	4	1	2	102689

113	10/01	NmkR	1m	A	GD	£34800
105	9/01	Curr	1m		G-Y	£42250
94	6/01	Asct	1m	A(0-105)H	G-F	£15544
90	6/01	Sand	7f16y	D(0-80)	GD	£4290

Total win prize-money £96884

Going (Turf): Sf: 0-0 GS: 0-2 **Gd: 2-3** GF: 1-3 Fm: 0-0
Distance: 5f/6f: 0-0 **7f-8f: 4-9** 9f-13f: 0-0 14f+: 0-0
Track : LH: 0-0 **RH: 1-3** Tight: 0-0 Gall: 0-0
Aids: Bl: 0-0 Vi: 0-0 Tstrap: 0-0
Best Rating: 113 10/01 NmkR 1m good

She showed ability in her early starts and got off the mark in a Sandown classified stakes in June 2001. Followed up in an Ascot Listed handicap. She showed a good turn of foot there and, after being poorly drawn at Goodwood, bounced back with a win at the Curragh. Decisive winner of the Sun Chariot Stakes in October. Stays a mile. Has won on fast ground, but acts on good to soft. Progressive.

Indian Bazaar (IRE)

107 **61**
5-y-o ch g Indian Ridge-Bazaar Promise (Native Bazaar)
J M Bradley Leeway (wholesale) Meats Ltd

Placings:000/0230/03201005600-0114103403305140 **(5111)**
2001: 5^{0}G, 5^{1}GF, 5^{1}G, 5^{4}G, 5^{1}F, 5^{0}GF, 5^{3}GF, 5^{4}GF, 5^{0}G, 5^{3}G, 5^{3}GF, 5^{0}GF, 5^{5}F, 5^{1}G, 5^{4}G, 6^{0}HY

	Starts	1st	2nd	3rd	Win & Pl
Career Total (Turf)	33	5	2	5	21248
Career Total (AW)	1	0	0	0	

59	9/01	Chep	5f16y	E(0-70)H	GD	£2996
50	6/01	Ling	5f	E(0-70)H	FRM	£3835
45	5/01	Yarm	5f43y	F(0-60)H	GD	£2765
47	5/01	Gdwd	5f	E(0-70)H	G-F	£3818
42	6/00	Bevl	5f	F(0-70)H	G-F	£2194

Total win prize-money £15610

Going (Turf): Sf: 0-6 GS: 0-4 **Gd: 2-8 GF: 2-11** Fm: 1-4
Distance: **5f/6f: 5-28** 7f-8f: 0-3 9f-13f: 0-3 14f+: 0-0
Track : LH: 0-6 RH: 0-3 Tight: 0-1 Gall: 0-4
Aids: Bl: 0-0 Vi: 0-0 Tstrap: 0-0
Best Rating: 61 9/01 Gdwd 5f good

Is in good form this season with four wins to his name over five furlongs on fast ground.

Indian Beat

99 **71**
4-y-o ch g Indian Ridge-Rappa Tap Tap (FR) (Tap On Wood)
Mrs L Stubbs D R Richards

Placings:0424500 **(4256)**
2001: 8^{0}GF, 10^{4}F, 9^{2}GF, 10^{4}GF, 10^{5}GF, 9^{0}G, 8^{0}GF

	Starts	1st	2nd	3rd	Win & Pl
Career Total (Turf)	7	0	1	0	1626

Going (Turf): Sf: 0-0 GS: 0-0 Gd: 0-1 GF: 0-5 Fm: 0-1
Distance: 5f/6f: 0-0 7f-8f: 0-2 9f-13f: 0-5 14f+: 0-0
Track : LH: 0-5 RH: 0-1 Tight: 0-4 Gall: 0-2
Aids: Bl: 0-0 Vi: 0-2 Tstrap: 0-0
Best Rating: 71 6/01 Donc 1m2f60y gd-fm

Indian Blaze

105(78) **(70)69**
7-y-o ch g Indian Ridge-Odile (Green Dancer (USA))
D R C Elsworth The Braves

Placings:0245/000002/**26**P000410**341**/**000**1220321010 6401**034**/00000-00021030 **(5671)**
2001: 8^{0}G, 8^{0}GF, 7^{0}F, 6^{2}GF, 8^{1}GF, 8^{0}GF, 8^{3}GF, 6^{0}HY

	Starts	1st	2nd	3rd	Win & Pl
Career Total (Turf)	45	6	6	2	32008
Career Total (AW)	11	1	1	2	4457

66	8/01	Kemp	1m	E(0-75)H	G-F	£4699
84	10/99	NmkJ	1m	D(0-85)H	GD	£6482
76	8/99	Kemp	1m	E(0-75)H	G-F	£3728
71	7/99	Kemp	7f	E(0-70)H	G-F	£2983
64	3/99	Folk	7f	E(0-70)H	SFT	£3101
63	12/98	Wolv	7f	F(0-60)H	SLW	£1903
62	11/98	Brig	5f213y	F(0-65)H	SFT	£1955

Total win prize-money £24854

Going (Turf): Sf: 2-12 GS: 0-4 Gd: 1-11 **GF: 3-16** Fm: 0-2
Distance: 5f/6f: 1-16 **7f-8f: 6-35** 9f-13f: 0-5 14f+: 0-0
Track : LH: 2-21 **RH: 3-17** Tight: 1-11 **Gall: 2-10**
Aids: Bl: 0-1 Vi: 0-0 Tstrap: 0-0
Best Rating: 69 9/01 Kemp 1m gd-fm

A winner four times during a busy 1999, he is best over seven furlongs or a mile on a decent surface.

Indian Brave

91(92) **(48)48d**
7-y-o b g Indian Ridge-Supreme Kingdom (Take A Reef)
P Howling (Jamie Poulton 13/2) Bvi Partnership

Placings:23/04/250500523/6403356300/**5**-000630 **(2313)**
2001: 8^{0}SD, 9^{0}SD, 12^{0}SW, 7^{6}GF, 7^{3}F, 8^{0}G

	Starts	1st	2nd	3rd	Win & Pl
Career Total (Turf)	26	0	3	6	7511

	Starts	1st	2nd	3rd	Win & Pl
Career Total (AW)	4	0	0	0	0

Going (Turf): Sf: 0-4 GS: 0-6 Gd: 0-7 GF: 0-6 Fm: 0-3
Distance: 5f/6f: 0-15 7f-8f: 0-9 9f-13f: 0-6 14f+: 0-0
Track : LH: 0-8 RH: 0-3 Tight: 0-5 Gall: 0-1
Aids: Bl: 0-1 Vi: 0-0 Tstrap: 0-0
Best Rating: 48 1/01 Sthl 1m stand

A maiden, despite some solid form in handicaps.

Indian Creek

110 **115**
3-y-o br c Indian Ridge-Blue Water (USA) (Bering)
D R C Elsworth Seymour Cohn

Placings:41153134 **(5597)**
2001: 8^{4}GS, 8^{1}GF, 9^{1}GF, 10^{5}GS, 9^{3}G, 10^{1}G, 10^{3}GS, 10^{4}GS

	Starts	1st	2nd	3rd	Win & Pl
Career Total (Turf)	8	3	0	2	83659

101	9/01	Asct	1m2f	B(0-95)	GD	£13520
100	7/01	Gdwd	1m1f192y	C(0-95)H	G-F	£9347
83	6/01	Gdwd	1m	D	G-F	£4602

Total win prize-money £27469

Going (Turf): Sf: 0-0 GS: 0-4 Gd: 1-2 **GF: 2-2** Fm: 0-0
Distance: 5f/6f: 0-0 7f-8f: 1-1 **9f-13f: 2-7** 14f+: 0-0
Track : LH: 0-0 **RH: 3-6** Tight: 1-3 Gall: 1-2
Aids: Bl: 0-0 Vi: 0-0 Tstrap: 0-0
Best Rating: 115 10/01 NmkR 1m2f gd-sft

Unraced as a juvenile, he improved from his debut to win twice at Goodwood in the summer of 2001, but was a touch disappointing on easier ground at Newmarket. Put that right when winning over ten furlongs at Ascot and ran his best race yet when third in the Champion Stakes. Sometimes slowly away. Acts on fast ground.

Indian Dance

(106) (68d)**48**
5-y-o ch g Indian Ridge-Petronella (USA) (Nureyev (USA))
P D Evans R J Hayward

Placings:6560030/00000300**43511112-0650000 (1181)**
2001: 7^{0}SD, 7^{6}SD, 9^{5}SW, 8^{0}SW, 7^{0}SD, 8^{0}SD, 8^{0}G

	Starts	1st	2nd	3rd	Win & Pl
Career Total (Turf)	15	0	0	2	940
Career Total (AW)	15	4	1	1	9032

76	12/00	Wolv	7f	E(0-70)H	STD	£2982
62	12/00	Wolv	1m1f79y	F(0-65)H	STD	£1750
62	12/00	Sthl	6f	F(0-60)H	STD	£1890
53	11/00	Sthl	7f	G	STD	£1512

Total win prize-money £8134

Going (Turf): Sf: 0-2 GS: 0-0 Gd: 0-6 GF: 0-7 Fm: 0-0
Distance: 5f/6f: 1-8 **7f-8f: 2-17** 9f-13f: 1-5 14f+: 0-0
Track : **LH: 4-18** RH: 0-2 **Tight: 2-9** Gall: 0-1
Aids: Bl: 0-0 Vi: 0-0 Tstrap: 0-6
Best Rating: 61 4/01 Sthl 1m stand

Indian Dreamer (IRE)

92 **84+**
2-y-o b c Indian Ridge-Truly A Dream (IRE) (Darshaan)
D R Loder Sheikh Mohammed

Placings:10 **(5053)**
2001: 7^{1}GF, 7^{0}S

	Starts	1st	2nd	3rd	Win & Pl
Career Total (Turf)	2	1	0	0	4173

84	9/01	Leic	7f9y	D	G-F	£4173

Total win prize-money £4173

Going (Turf): Sf: 0-1 GS: 0-0 Gd: 0-0 **GF: 1-1** Fm: 0-0
Distance: 5f/6f: 0-0 **7f-8f: 1-2** 9f-13f: 0-0 14f+: 0-0
Track : LH: 0-0 RH: 0-0 Tight: 0-0 Gall: 0-0
Aids: Bl: 0-0 Vi: 0-0 Tstrap: 0-0
Best Rating: 84 9/01 Leic 7f9y gd-fm

A 400,000gns half-brother to mile juvenile winner Truly Yours, looked likely to improve for the outing when taking a Leicester maiden on his debut, but unable to handle the step up in class in a sales race at Newmarket.

Indian File

109 **93**
3-y-o ch c Indian Ridge-Shining Water (Kalaglow)
B W Hills K Abdulla

Placings:0-2102110 **(4225)**
2001: 7^{2}S, 10^{1}GF, 10^{0}GF, 10^{2}G, 11^{1}GS, 12^{1}G, 14^{0}GF

	Starts	1st	2nd	3rd	Win & Pl
Career Total (Turf)	8	3	2	0	19076

93	8/01	NmkJ	1m4f	C(0-90)H	GD	£6873
88	8/01	Hayd	1m3f200y	D(0-85)H	G-S	£4504
80	5/01	Bath	1m2f46y	D	G-F	£3513

Total win prize-money £14892

Going (Turf): Sf: 0-1 **GS: 1-1 Gd: 1-2 GF: 1-4** Fm: 0-0
Distance: 5f/6f: 0-0 7f-8f: 0-2 **9f-13f: 3-5** 14f+: 0-1
Track : **LH: 2-4** RH: 1-2 Tight: 1-3 Gall: 1-2
Aids: Bl: 0-0 Vi: 0-0 Tstrap: 0-0
Best Rating: 93 8/01 NmkJ 1m4f good

A half-brother to Tenby, he won his maiden at Bath when stepped up to ten furlongs and appreciated the step up to 12 furlongs when just getting up to win at Haydock in August. Looked progressive when following up at Newmarket, but ran inexpilcably poorly next time. Had to be put down after an accident at home in the autumn.

Indian Gift

91 **60**
2-y-o ch f Cadeaux Genereux-Vanishing Trick (USA) (Gone West (USA))
E A L Dunlop Cliveden Stud

Placings:000 **(5561)**
2001: 7^{0}GF, 8^{0}HY, 7^{0}S

	Starts	1st	2nd	3rd	Win & Pl
Career Total (Turf)	3	0	0	0	

Going (Turf): Sf: 0-2 GS: 0-0 Gd: 0-0 GF: 0-1 Fm: 0-0
Distance: 5f/6f: 0-0 7f-8f: 0-2 9f-13f: 0-1 14f+: 0-0
Track : LH: 0-1 RH: 0-0 Tight: 0-0 Gall: 0-0
Aids: Bl: 0-0 Vi: 0-0 Tstrap: 0-0
Best Rating: 60 10/01 Nott 1m54y heavy

Indian Giver

105 **78**
3-y-o ch f Cadeaux Genereux-About Face (Midyan (USA))
R Hannon Geoff Howard-Spink & Lindy Regis

Placings:00-210 **(5608)**
2001: 8^{2}GS, 6^{1}GF, 7^{0}GS

	Starts	1st	2nd	3rd	Win & Pl
Career Total (Turf)	5	1	1	0	5039

72	6/01	Sals	6f212y	D	G-F	£3835

Total win prize-money £3835

Going (Turf): Sf: 0-0 GS: 0-3 Gd: 0-0 **GF: 1-2** Fm: 0-0
Distance: 5f/6f: 0-2 **7f-8f: 1-3** 9f-13f: 0-0 14f+: 0-0
Track : LH: 0-0 RH: 0-1 Tight: 0-0 Gall: 0-1
Aids: Bl: 0-0 Vi: 0-0 Tstrap: 0-0
Best Rating: 78 6/01 Sals 1m gd-sft

Unplaced at two. Appreciated step up to a mile on her reappearance in 2001. Scored next time out on drop back to seven. Has won on firm ground, acts on good to soft.

Indian Justice

43

2-y-o b g Bijou D'Inde-Legal Sound (Legal Eagle)
R A Fahey Reg Richardson

Placings:4 **(4257)**
2001: 7^{4}GF

	Starts	1st	2nd	3rd	Win & Pl
Career Total (Turf)	1	0	0	0	275

Going (Turf): Sf: 0-0 GS: 0-0 Gd: 0-0 GF: 0-1 Fm: 0-0
Distance: 5f/6f: 0-0 7f-8f: 0-1 9f-13f: 0-0 14f+: 0-0
Track : LH: 0-0 RH: 0-0 Tight: 0-0 Gall: 0-0
Aids: Bl: 0-0 Vi: 0-0 Tstrap: 0-0

Indian Music

103(103) (71)**64d**
4-y-o b g Indian Ridge-Dagny Juel (USA) (Danzig (USA))
A Berry Robert Aird

Placings:004001/004555326040-**3215103560600000 (5111)**
2001: 5^{3}SW, 6^{2}SD, 6^{1}SD, 5^{5}S, 5^{1}GS, 6^{0}G, 6^{3}SD, 5^{5}GF, 5^{6}GF, 5^{0}G, 6^{6}GF, 5^{0}SD, 5^{0}GS, 5^{0}GF, 5^{0}G, 6^{0}HY

	Starts	1st	2nd	3rd	Win & Pl
Career Total (Turf)	29	2	1	1	9899
Career Total (AW)	5	1	1	2	4189

67	4/01	Muss	5f	D(0-85)H	G-S	£4348
70	3/01	Sthl	6f	E(0-75)H	STD	£2268
74	11/99	Donc	5f	D(0-85)H	SFT	£3468

Total win prize-money £10086

Going (Turf): Sf: 1-9 GS: 1-3 Gd: 0-7 GF: 0-9 Fm: 0-1
Distance: **5f/6f: 3-31** 7f-8f: 0-3 9f-13f: 0-0 14f+: 0-0
Track : **LH: 1-8** RH: 0-2 Tight: 0-4 Gall: 0-2
Aids: Bl: 0-7 Vi: 0-0 Tstrap: 0-0
Best Rating: 71 5/01 Sthl 6f stand

He is a fair sort in modest sprint handicap company on turf and Fibresand. Probably best over the minimum trip and needs cut in the ground on turf.

Indian Plume

109 **88**
5-y-o b g Efisio-Boo Hoo (Mummy's Pet)
T G Mills E & S Racing

Placings:514/3400/01001003520-00313220 **(5133)**
2001: 7^{0}GS, 7^{0}G, 7^{3}GF, 8^{1}GF, 8^{3}GS, 8^{2}G, 8^{2}HY, 7^{0}G

	Starts	1st	2nd	3rd	Win & Pl
Career Total (Turf)	26	4	3	4	28972

83	7/01	Yarm	1m3y	D(0-80)H	G-F	£5073
81	5/00	Ripn	1m	D(0-85)H	GD	£5401
82	4/00	Muss	7f30y	D(0-75)	G-S	£4075
77	8/98	Pont	6f	D	G-F	£3191

Total win prize-money £17742

Going (Turf): Sf: 0-3 GS: 1-6 Gd: 1-13 **GF: 2-4** Fm: 0-0
Distance: 5f/6f: 1-2 **7f-8f: 2-19** 9f-13f: 1-5 14f+: 0-0
Track : LH: 1-9 **RH: 2-9 Tight: 2-8** Gall: 0-1
Aids: Bl: 0-0 Vi: 0-0 Tstrap: 0-0
Best Rating: 88 9/01 Hayd 1m30y heavy

A decent performer for Chris Thornton, he returned to form for his new connections at Yarmouth in July, and has continued to run well in similar events. Seems to act on any ground, and is best making the running. Stays a mile.

Indian Prince (IRE)

113(104) (82)**109**
3-y-o ch g Indian Ridge-Lingering Melody (IRE) (Nordico (USA))
B J Meehan Matham Investments

Placings:22430213200510 **(5365)**
2001: 6^{2}SD, 6^{2}GS, 6^{4}HY, 5^{3}G, 5^{0}GF, 6^{2}GS, 5^{1}F, 5^{3}G, 5^{2}GF, 5^{0}G, 5^{0}GF, 6^{5}GF, 5^{1}GS, 6^{0}GS

Starts 1st 2nd 3rd Win & Pl
Career Total (Turf) 13 2 3 2 30733
Career Total (AW) 1 0 1 0 1080
109 10/01 NmkR 5f A G-S £15486
93 7/01 Bath 5f11y C(0-95)H FRM £6938
Total win prize-money £22425

Going (Turf): Sf: 0-1 **GS: 1-4** Gd: 0-3 GF: 0-4 **Fm: 1-1**
Distance: **5f/6f: 2-13** 7f-8f: 0-1 9f-13f: 0-0 14f+: 0-0
Track : **LH: 1-2** RH: 0-0 Tight: 0-1 **Gall: 1-1**
Aids: Bl: 0-0 Vi: 0-0 Tstrap: 0-0
Best Rating: 109 10/01 NmkR 5f gd-sft

Running well in sprint handicaps earlier this season including a victory at Bath in July, but surpassed anything he had achieved before when winning a Newmarket Listed event in October at odds of 33/1. Best over five furlongs and acts on any ground.

Indian Shores

87(77) (39)**69**
2-y-o b f Forzando-Cottonwood (Teenoso (USA))
E J Alston P Currey

Placings:0534500 **(5364)**
2001: 5^{0}GF, 5^{5}GF, 6^{3}G, 5^{4}GF, 5^{5}F, 5^{0}SD, 6^{0}GS
Starts 1st 2nd 3rd Win & Pl
Career Total (Turf) 6 0 0 1 638
Career Total (AW) 1 0 0 0

Going (Turf): Sf: 0-0 GS: 0-1 Gd: 0-1 GF: 0-3 Fm: 0-1
Distance: 5f/6f: 0-7 7f-8f: 0-0 9f-13f: 0-0 14f+: 0-0
Track : LH: 0-3 RH: 0-0 Tight: 0-2 Gall: 0-0
Aids: Bl: 0-0 Vi: 0-0 Tstrap: 0-0
Best Rating: 69 8/01 Catt 5f gd-fm

Indian Silk (IRE)

100(102) (69)**72**
3-y-o b f Dolphin Street (FR)-Scammony (IRE) (Persian Bold)
J A Osborne Paul J Dixon

Placings:1411043000 **(5601)**
2001: 7^{1}SD, 7^{4}SD, 6^{1}HY, 7^{1}S, 8^{0}G, 7^{4}SD, 8^{3}G, 10^{0}G, 8^{0}SD, 8^{0}GS
Starts 1st 2nd 3rd Win & Pl
Career Total (Turf) 6 2 0 1 8623
Career Total (AW) 4 1 0 0 2134
72 5/01 Newb 7f D(0-80)H SFT £4940
68 3/01 Nott 6f15y E(0-70)H HVY £3094
59 2/01 Sthl 7f G STD £1834
Total win prize-money £9868

Going (Turf): Sf: 2-2 GS: 0-1 Gd: 0-3 GF: 0-0 Fm: 0-0
Distance: 5f/6f: 0-0 **7f-8f: 3-7** 9f-13f: 0-3 14f+: 0-0
Track : **LH: 1-5** RH: 0-1 Tight: 0-0 Gall: 0-0
Aids: Bl: 0-0 Vi: 0-0 **Tstrap: 3-9**
Best Rating: 72 5/01 Newb 7f soft

Suited by easy ground, he won three times in the spring. Held since. Usually has tongue tied.

Indian Solitaire (IRE)

96 **89**
2-y-o b c Bigstone (IRE)-Terrama Sioux (Relkino)
Mrs A J Perrett Atlantic Foods Ltd

Placings:231 **(5459)**
2001: 7^{2}G, 7^{3}F, 8^{1}G
Starts 1st 2nd 3rd Win & Pl
Career Total (Turf) 3 1 1 1 4187
89 10/01 Bath 1m5y E GD £3003
Total win prize-money £3003

Going (Turf): Sf: 0-0 GS: 0-0 **Gd: 1-2** GF: 0-0 Fm: 0-1
Distance: 5f/6f: 0-0 7f-8f: 0-2 **9f-13f: 1-1** 14f+: 0-0
Track : **LH: 1-1** RH: 0-0 **Tight: 1-1** Gall: 0-0
Aids: Bl: 0-0 Vi: 0-0 Tstrap: 0-0
Best Rating: 89 10/01 Bath 1m5y good

A half-brother to five winners including 12-furlong three-year-old scorer Dakota Brave, made a highly satisfactory debut and got off the mark two outings later with a cosy success over a mile at Bath. Best on an easy surface.

Indian Spark

114 **114**
7-y-o ch g Indian Ridge-Annes Gift (Ballymoss)
J S Goldie Frank Brady

Placings:12/02106260500/0006025421640100010/005534105300000000/041501102010-0000041032000
(5494)
2001: 6^{0}S, 5^{0}GS, 6^{0}S, 6^{0}GF, 5^{0}GF, 6^{4}GF, 5^{1}GF, 7^{0}GF, 5^{3}G, 5^{2}G, 6^{0}GF, 5^{0}HO, 6^{0}HY
Starts 1st 2nd 3rd Win & Pl
Career Total (Turf) 75 11 7 3 143561
107 6/01 Newc 5f B(0-105)H G-F £19500
106 7/00 Ches 5f16y A G-S £20300
100 6/00 York 6f B(0-100)H GD £9622
93 5/00 Hayd 5f B(0-105)H SFT £11154
87 4/00 Newc 5f D(0-80)H SFT £4160
87 6/99 York 6f B(0-100)H G-S £9524
87 10/98 Donc 5f B(0-100)H HVY £9397
84 9/98 Donc 5f D(0-80)H GD £3840
82 7/98 Thsk 6f D(0-80)H FRM £4570
99 5/97 Sals 6f B(0-100) G-F £7409
85 3/96 Donc 5f C GD £4710
Total win prize-money £104187

Going (Turf): Sf: 3-14 GS: 2-12 **Gd: 3-21** GF: 2-22 Fm: 1-5
Distance: **5f/6f: 11-66** 7f-8f: 0-9 9f-13f: 0-0 14f+: 0-0
Track : **LH: 1-3** RH: 0-0 **Tight: 1-1** Gall: 0-0
Aids: Bl: 0-0 Vi: 0-0 Tstrap: 0-0
Best Rating: 114 9/01 Leop 5f good

Not particularly consistent, but wins his share of useful sprint handicaps and did just that with a fine win in the Gosforth Park Cup at Newcastle in June when just given a bit of a chance by the Handicapper. Runner-up in a Leopardstown Group Three in September. He has won on fast ground, but looks better suited by cut.

Indian Sun

98(101) (55d)**42**
4-y-o ch g Indian Ridge-Star Tulip (Night Shift (USA))
P D Evans (Mrs L C Jewell 26/2) Treble Chance Partnership

Placings:0610/460020-100660020146000550510004
(5615)
2001: 8^{1}SW, 8^{0}SD, 9^{0}SD, 8^{6}SD, 6^{6}GS, 8^{0}GF, 8^{0}SD, 10^{2}GF, 12^{0}GF, 11^{1}SD, 11^{4}SD, 11^{6}F, 10^{0}GF, 8^{0}SD, 11^{0}GF, 16^{5}GF, 12^{5}SD, 15^{0}S, 11^{5}SD, 11^{1}S, 14^{0}SD, 14^{0}S, 12^{4}SD
Starts 1st 2nd 3rd Win & Pl
Career Total (Turf) 21 2 2 0 9167
Career Total (AW) 12 2 0 0 4102
42 10/01 Leic 1m3f183yF SFT £2786
46 6/01 Sthl 1m3f G STD £1960
49 2/01 Sthl 1m F SLW £2142
73 10/99 Ling 6f D HVY £3492
Total win prize-money £10381

Going (Turf): Sf: 2-8 GS: 0-2 Gd: 0-3 GF: 0-7 Fm: 0-1
Distance: 5f/6f: 1-3 7f-8f: 1-12 **9f-13f: 2-14** 14f+: 0-4
Track : **LH: 2-22** RH: 1-4 Tight: 0-13 Gall: 0-2
Aids: Bl: 0-1 Vi: 0-1 **Tstrap: 3-22**
Best Rating: 63 3/01 Wolv 1m100y stand

An inconsistent sort, he goes well in testing ground but also handles a faster surface and is a winner on the Southwell Fibresand. Stays 12 furlongs, seems best held up.

Indian Sunset

96(97) (33)**25**
8-y-o ch g Indian Ridge-Alanood (Northfields (USA))
J A Osborne (Trainer Unknown 11/2) Tom Macfarlane

Placings:00/030/046055 **(3579)**
2001: 14^{0}SD, 14^{4}SD, 17^{6}GF, 12^{0}GF, 16^{5}GF, 14^{5}GF
Starts 1st 2nd 3rd Win & Pl
Career Total (Turf) 8 0 0 1 423
Career Total (AW) 3 0 0 0 0

Going (Turf): Sf: 0-0 GS: 0-1 Gd: 0-0 GF: 0-6 Fm: 0-1
Distance: 5f/6f: 0-0 7f-8f: 0-3 9f-13f: 0-3 14f+: 0-5
Track : LH: 0-7 RH: 0-1 Tight: 0-3 Gall: 0-0
Aids: Bl: 0-0 Vi: 0-0 Tstrap: 0-0
Best Rating: 33 5/01 Sthl 1m6f stand

Indian Swinger (IRE)

(97) (44)**22**
5-y-o ch h Up And At 'Em-Seanee Squaw (Indian Ridge)
P Howling Richard Berenson

Placings:40016/23305/005220033000300-24 **(0078)**
2001: 8^{2}SD, 8^{4}SW
Starts 1st 2nd 3rd Win & Pl
Career Total (Turf) 6 0 0 0 232
Career Total (AW) 21 1 4 5 7572
69 10/98 Sthl 6f E(0-85) STD £3099
Total win prize-money £3099

Going (Turf): Sf: 0-2 GS: 0-0 Gd: 0-2 GF: 0-2 Fm: 0-0
Distance: **5f/6f: 1-6** 7f-8f: 0-12 9f-13f: 0-9 14f+: 0-0
Track : **LH: 1-23** RH: 0-2 Tight: 0-14 Gall: 0-1
Aids: Bl: 0-0 Vi: 0-0 Tstrap: 0-0
Best Rating: 44 1/01 Sthl 1m stand

Indian Warrior

100(98) (54)**45**
5-y-o b g Be My Chief (USA)-Wanton (Kris)
W J Musson Broughton Thermal Insulation

Placings:22310/600010/06660000602006-400513
(4415)
2001: 6^{4}SD, 6^{0}SD, 6^{0}F, 6^{5}F, 6^{1}GF, 7^{3}S
Starts 1st 2nd 3rd Win & Pl
Career Total (Turf) 25 3 3 2 13195
Career Total (AW) 6 0 0 0 0
45 8/01 Ling 6f G(0-60)H G-F £2191
55 10/99 Ling 7f F G-F £2633
81 8/98 Wwck 7f E G-F £3444
Total win prize-money £8268

Going (Turf): Sf: 0-3 GS: 0-3 Gd: 0-4 **GF: 3-12** Fm: 0-2
Distance: 5f/6f: 1-9 **7f-8f: 2-18** 9f-13f: 0-3 14f+: 0-0
Track : **LH: 1-13** RH: 0-5 Tight: 0-7 Gall: 0-4
Aids: Bl: 0-1 Vi: 0-2 Tstrap: 0-0
Best Rating: 45 8/01 Ling 6f gd-fm

Goes well at Lingfield and won there for the second time when landing a selling handicap in August.

Indiana Jones (IRE)

(71) **49**
4-y-o b g Emperor Jones (USA)-Broadway Rosie (Absalom)
D W Chapman Michael Hill

Placings:0000-00 **(0714)**
2001: 9^{0}SD, 7^{0}SD
Starts 1st 2nd 3rd Win & Pl
Career Total (Turf) 3 0 0 0
Career Total (AW) 3 0 0 0

Going (Turf): Sf: 0-1 GS: 0-2 Gd: 0-0 GF: 0-0 Fm: 0-0
Distance: 5f/6f: 0-1 7f-8f: 0-4 9f-13f: 0-1 14f+: 0-0
Track : LH: 0-3 RH: 0-0 Tight: 0-1 Gall: 0-0
Aids: Bl: 0-0 Vi: 0-0 Tstrap: 0-0

Indiana Springs (IRE)

101(98) (40)**44**

4-y-o b g Foxhound (USA)-Moss Agate (Alias Smith (USA))

J G Given Plyvine, Guy, Howles & Slater

Placings:000/00540060353000-05410 **(0345)**

2001: 11^{0}SD, 12^{5}SD, 16^{4}SD, 16^{1}SD, 16^{0}SD

	Starts	1st	2nd	3rd	Win & Pl
Career Total (Turf)	12	0	0	2	563
Career Total (AW)	10	1	0	0	1372

40 2/01 Wolv 2m46y G(0-60)H STD £1372

Total win prize-money £1372

Going (Turf): Sf: 0-3 GS: 0-2 Gd: 0-3 GF: 0-3 Fm: 0-1
Distance: 5f/6f: 0-0 7f-8f: 0-5 9f-13f: 0-14 14f+: 1-3
Track: LH: 1-15 RH: 0-3 Tight: 1-12 Gall: 0-0
Aids: Bl: 1-4 Vi: 0-6 Tstrap: 0-0
Best Rating: 40 2/01 Wolv 2m46y stand

Indigo Bay (IRE)

(103) (23)**30**

5-y-o b g Royal Academy (USA)-Cape Heights (Shirley Heights)

R Bastiman Miss Fee Gibson

Placings:0000/3103212000200/45100000051030206-00600000446000200 **(5615)**

2001: 16^{0}SD, 11^{0}SD, 11^{6}SD, 10^{0}HY, 12^{0}S, 9^{0}G, 8^{0}GF, 16^{0}GF, 13^{4}GF, 11^{4}GF, 12^{6}F, 11^{0}G, 11^{0}GF, 11^{0}G, 11^{2}G, 11^{0}S, 12^{0}SD

	Starts	1st	2nd	3rd	Win & Pl
Career Total (Turf)	37	3	3	3	13439
Career Total (AW)	14	1	2	0	3104

41 8/00 Muss 1m4f E(0-75)H GD £3412
56 2/00 Ling 1m5f F STD £2052
72 7/99 Ling 1m3f106yE(0-70)H FRM £2887
59 5/99 Brig 1m3f196yG(0-60)H FRM £1945

Total win prize-money £10297

Going (Turf): Sf: 0-7 GS: 0-1 Gd: 1-9 GF: 0-15 Fm: 2-5
Distance: 5f/6f: 0-0 7f-8f: 0-2 9f-13f: 4-41 14f+: 0-8
Track: LH: 3-37 RH: 1-12 Tight: 3-34 Gall: 0-1
Aids: Bl: 2-26 Vi: 1-6 Tstrap: 1-7
Best Rating: 37 5/01 Hayd 1m30y gd-fm

Indium

102(92) (46)**78**

7-y-o b g Groom Dancer (USA)-Gold Bracelet (Golden Fleece (USA))

D E Cantillon Mrs Edward Cantillon

Placings:033/55/050302000041000/5024002604100/40 4010500000-41230 **(3967)**

2001: 7^{4}GF, 8^{1}GF, 8^{2}GF, 10^{3}GS, 8^{0}GS

	Starts	1st	2nd	3rd	Win & Pl
Career Total (Turf)	47	4	4	4	67440
Career Total (AW)	3	0	0	0	193

72 7/01 Yarm 1m3y F G-F £2495
78 5/00 Newb 1m2f6y D(0-80)H G-F £4615
78 9/99 Asct 1m B H HVY £32300
77 9/98 Newb 1m7y C(0-100)H GD £18075

Total win prize-money £57486

Going (Turf): Sf: 1-4 GS: 0-8 Gd: 1-15 GF: 2-19 Fm: 0-1
Distance: 5f/6f: 0-0 7f-8f: 1-28 9f-13f: 3-22 14f+: 0-0
Track: LH: 2-15 RH: 0-14 Tight: 0-7 Gall: 2-8
Aids: Bl: 0-0 Vi: 0-0 Tstrap: 0-0
Best Rating: 73 6/01 Wwck 7f26y gd-fm

A useful handicapper, he has been revived by a change of yard this season. Stays ten furlongs, but is more effective at a mile and acts on any ground. He is best coming late off a fast pace.

Inducement

93 **85**

5-y-o ch g Sabrehill (USA)-Verchinina (Star Appeal)

Mrs A J Perrett J B Dale

Placings:33146/5516400/4153-00 **(5065)**

2001: 12^{0}S, 10^{0}S

	Starts	1st	2nd	3rd	Win & Pl
Career Total (Turf)	18	3	0	3	20498

83 8/00 Leic 1m1f218yD(0-85)H G-F £4046
85 6/99 Sand 1m1f C(0-95)H GD £7295
81 8/98 Bevl 1m100y D G-F £3250

Total win prize-money £14592

Going (Turf): Sf: 0-3 GS: 0-2 Gd: 1-6 GF: 2-7 Fm: 0-0
Distance: 5f/6f: 0-1 7f-8f: 0-3 9f-13f: 3-14 14f+: 0-0
Track: LH: 0-6 RH: 3-9 Tight: 0-0 Gall: 0-7
Aids: Bl: 0-0 Vi: 0-0 Tstrap: 0-0
Best Rating: 81 10/01 NmkR 1m2f soft

Successful on the flat, he more often than not runs over hurdles now.

Indy Rose (USA)

99 **86**

2-y-o b f A.P. Indy (USA)-Chelsey Flower (USA) (His Majesty (USA))

D R Loder Sheikh Mohammed

Placings:15500 **(5390)**

2001: 7^{1}G, 7^{5}GF, 7^{5}G, 7^{0}GY, 7^{0}GS

	Starts	1st	2nd	3rd	Win & Pl
Career Total (Turf)	5	1	0	0	4640

82 7/01 Yarm 7f3y D GD £3770

Total win prize-money £3770

Going (Turf): Sf: 0-0 GS: 0-1 Gd: 1-2 GF: 0-1 Fm: 0-0
Distance: 5f/6f: 0-0 7f-8f: 1-5 9f-13f: 0-0 14f+: 0-0
Track: LH: 0-0 RH: 0-1 Tight: 0-0 Gall: 0-0
Aids: Bl: 0-0 Vi: 0-1 Tstrap: 0-0
Best Rating: 86 9/01 Curr 7f gd-yld

A good-looking filly who is bred to stay middle distances. Got off the mark at Yarmouth over seven furlongs on her debut. She disappointed when odds on for a Listed event next time. Connections suspected she may have picked up a bug that was affecting the yard. However, she has struggled in Pattern races since, and does not appear to be progressing.

Inexpensive

97(95) (44)**37**

5-y-o b m Puissance-Sojourn (Be My Guest (USA))

M Kettle Johnny Wise

Placings:5/1-00000000 **(2876)**

2001: 8^{0}SW, 8^{0}S, 7^{0}G, 7^{0}F, 9^{0}GF, 7^{0}GF, 8^{0}GF, 8^{0}GF

	Starts	1st	2nd	3rd	Win & Pl
Career Total (Turf)	7	0	0	0	
Career Total (AW)	3	1	0	0	2765

44 11/00 Wolv 1m100y D STD £2765

Total win prize-money £2765

Going (Turf): Sf: 0-1 GS: 0-0 Gd: 0-1 GF: 0-4 Fm: 0-1
Distance: 5f/6f: 0-0 7f-8f: 0-4 9f-13f: 1-6 14f+: 0-0
Track: LH: 1-7 RH: 0-3 Tight: 1-7 Gall: 0-0
Aids: Bl: 0-1 Vi: 0-0 Tstrap: 0-2
Best Rating: 51 5/01 Brig 7f214y firm

Infamous (USA)

92(62) **21**

8-y-o ch g Diesis-Name And Fame (USA) (Arts And Letters (USA))

B J Llewellyn B J Llewellyn

Placings:6/1200022003/36/62400/22253/00 **(1483)**

2001: 16^{0}SD, 17^{0}GF

	Starts	1st	2nd	3rd	Win & Pl
Career Total (Turf)	16	1	4	1	9590
Career Total (AW)	9	0	3	2	2519

79 3/96 Leic 1m3f183yD SFT £3595

Total win prize-money £3596

Going (Turf): Sf: 1-2 GS: 0-3 Gd. 0-3 GF: 0-7 Fm: 0-1
Distance: 5f/6f: 0-0 7f-8f: 0-2 9f-13f: 1-15 14f+: 0-8
Track: LH: 0-17 RH: 1-6 Tight: 0-15 Gall: 0-3
Aids: Bl: 0-3 Vi: 0-0 Tstrap: 0-6
Best Rating: 21 5/01 Bath 2m1f34y gd-fm

Infinite Risk

80 **57**

2-y-o gr c Vettori (IRE)-Dolly Bevan (Another Realm)

R Hannon Kenneth Kornfeld

Placings:005 **(4889)**

2001: 6^{0}GF, 6^{0}GF, 8^{5}GF

	Starts	1st	2nd	3rd	Win & Pl
Career Total (Turf)	3	0	0	0	0

Going (Turf): Sf: 0-0 GS: 0-0 Gd: 0-0 GF: 0-3 Fm: 0-0
Distance: 5f/6f: 0-1 7f-8f: 0-2 9f-13f: 0-0 14f+: 0-0
Track: LH: 0-0 RH: 0-1 Tight: 0-0 Gall: 0-0
Aids: Bl: 0-0 Vi: 0-0 Tstrap: 0-0
Best Rating: 57 9/01 Kemp 1m gd-fm

Infinite Spirit (USA)

105 **92**

2-y-o ch f Maria's Mon (USA)-Eternal Reve (USA) (Diesis)

D R Loder Sheikh Mohammed

Placings:142 **(5401)**

2001: 6^{1}F, 7^{4}G, 8^{2}S

	Starts	1st	2nd	3rd	Win & Pl
Career Total (Turf)	3	1	1	0	10648

78 5/01 Rdcr 6f E FRM £3388

Total win prize-money £3388

Going (Turf): Sf: 0-1 GS: 0-0 Gd: 0-1 GF: 0-0 Fm: 1-1
Distance: 5f/6f: 1-1 7f-8f: 0-1 9f-13f: 0-1 14f+: 0-0
Track: LH: 0-1 RH: 0-0 Tight: 0-0 Gall: 0-0
Aids: Bl: 0-0 Vi: 0-0 Tstrap: 0-0
Best Rating: 92 10/01 Pont 1m4y soft

Winner of a Redcar maiden on her debut, she ran a fair race after a four-month absence in a Newmarket Listed race in October. She then bettered this effort to be runner-up to Bandari in similar company over a mile at Pontefract. Suited to cut in the ground.

Infotec (IRE)

102(74) (25)**63**

4-y-o b/br g Shalford (IRE)-Tomona (Linacre)

H Akbary Michael C Whatley

Placings:022/01052000-00200000 **(5288)**

2001: 6^{0}SW, 6^{0}SD, 7^{2}HY, 7^{0}G, 8^{0}G, 8^{0}GF, 5^{0}GS, 6^{0}HY

	Starts	1st	2nd	3rd	Win & Pl
Career Total (Turf)	17	1	4	0	8446
Career Total (AW)	2	0	0	0	

80 5/00 Wwck 6f168y D(0-80)H SFT £4277

Total win prize-money £4277

Going (Turf): Sf: 1-9 GS: 0-3 Gd: 0-3 GF: 0-2 Fm: 0-0
Distance: 5f/6f: 0-6 7f-8f: 1-11 9f-13f: 0-2 14f+: 0-0
Track: LH: 1-6 RH: 0-2 Tight: 0-2 Gall: 0-0
Aids: Bl: 0-0 Vi: 0-0 Tstrap: 0-0
Best Rating: 63 4/01 Wwck 7f26y heavy

A mud lover, he rarely shows anything approaching his best form on anything but testing ground. He is fairly handicapped at present and should not be dismissed when conditions are in his favour. Best form at around seven furlongs.

Infra Red

2-y-o ch c Most Welcome-Flying Wind (Forzando)

C Grant Havelock Racing

Placings:0 **(2789)**
2001: 6^0GF

	Starts	1st	2nd	3rd	Win & Pl
Career Total (Turf)	1	0	0	0	

Going (Turf): Sf: 0-0 GS: 0-0 Gd: 0-0 GF: 0-1 Fm: 0-0
Distance: 5f/6f: 0-1 7f-8f: 0-0 9f-13f: 0-0 14f+: 0-0
Track : LH: 0-0 RH: 0-0 Tight: 0-0 Gall: 0-0
Aids: Bl: 0-0 Vi: 0-0 Tstrap: 0-0

Inglemotte Miss

53
3-y-o ch f Hatim (USA)-Phantom Singer (Relkino)
Miss J F Craze J Lynam

Placings:5-00 **(1721)**
2001: 6^0HY, 8^0GF

	Starts	1st	2nd	3rd	Win & Pl
Career Total (Turf)	3	0	0	0	0

Going (Turf): Sf: 0-2 GS: 0-0 Gd: 0-0 GF: 0-1 Fm: 0-0
Distance: 5f/6f: 0-0 7f-8f: 0-2 9f-13f: 0-1 14f+: 0-0
Track : LH: 0-0 RH: 0-2 Tight: 0-2 Gall: 0-0
Aids: Bl: 0-0 Vi: 0-0 Tstrap: 0-0

Inglenook (IRE)

109 **106**
4-y-o b h Cadeaux Genereux-Spring (Sadler's Wells (USA))
J L Dunlop Seymour Cohn

Placings:5110441-4463 **(4976a)**
2001: 8^4Y, 10^4G, 10^6GS, 9^3HY

	Starts	1st	2nd	3rd	Win & Pl
Career Total (Turf)	11	3	0	1	46725

116	10/00	StCl	1m2f		HVY	£13449
115	5/00	Kemp	1m	A	SFT	£14885
100	5/00	Kemp	1m	D	G-S	£4758

Total win prize-money £33092

Going (Turf): Sf: 2-4 GS: 1-3 Gd: 0-2 GF: 0-1 Fm: 0-0
Distance: 5f/6f: 0-0 **7f-8f: 2-5** 9f-13f: 1-6 14f+: 0-0
Track : LH: 1-4 **RH: 2-3** Tight: 0-0 **Gall: 2-4**
Aids: Bl: 0-0 Vi: 0-0 Tstrap: 0-0
Best Rating: 109 7/01 Curr 1m yield

A lightly-raced sort. Useful colt at up to ten furlongs. Has won three times, twice in Listed company at three, but was not at his best this season. Suited by give underfoot and a strong pace. Has a history of knee problems.

Ingletonian

69
12-y-o b g Doc Marten-Dreamy Desire (Palm Track)
B Mactaggart Mrs Hilary Mactaggart

Placings:0 **(1108)**
2001: 16^0GF

	Starts	1st	2nd	3rd	Win & Pl
Career Total (Turf)	1	0	0	0	

Going (Turf): Sf: 0-0 GS: 0-0 Gd: 0-0 GF: 0-1 Fm: 0-0
Distance: 5f/6f: 0-0 7f-8f: 0-0 9f-13f: 0-0 14f+: 0-1
Track : LH: 0-0 RH: 0-1 Tight: 0-1 Gall: 0-0
Aids: Bl: 0-0 Vi: 0-0 Tstrap: 0-0

Inglis Drever

84 **58+**
2-y-o b c In The Wings-Cormorant Creek (Gorytus (USA))
Sir Mark Prescott P J D Pottinger

Placings:460 **(5491)**
2001: 6^4S, 6^6HY, 6^0HY

	Starts	1st	2nd	3rd	Win & Pl
Career Total (Turf)	3	0	0	0	310

Going (Turf): Sf: 0-3 GS: 0-0 Gd: 0-0 GF: 0-0 Fm: 0-0
Distance: 5f/6f: 0-2 7f-8f: 0-1 9f-13f: 0-0 14f+: 0-0
Track : LH: 0-1 RH: 0-0 Tight: 0-0 Gall: 0-0
Aids: Bl: 0-0 Vi: 0-0 Tstrap: 0-0
Best Rating: 58 10/01 Ling 6f heavy

Inigo Jones (IRE)

106 **94**
5-y-o b g Alzao (USA)-Kindjal (Kris)
P W Harris Mrs P W Harris

Placings:2322133/14560-0400 **(5501)**
2001: 12^0S, 12^4G, 10^0GF, 12^0HY

	Starts	1st	2nd	3rd	Win & Pl
Career Total (Turf)	16	2	3	3	24635

100	4/00	Hayd	1m3f200y	C(0-90)H	GD	£6565
73	8/99	Nott	1m6f15y	D	G-F	£4163

Total win prize-money £10729

Going (Turf): Sf: 0-3 GS: 0-1 **Gd: 1-4 GF: 1-7** Fm: 0-1
Distance: 5f/6f: 0-0 7f-8f: 0-0 9f-13f: 1-11 14f+: 1-5
Track : **LH: 2-12** RH: 0-4 Tight: 0-3 Gall: 0-9
Aids: Bl: 0-0 Vi: 0-0 Tstrap: 0-0
Best Rating: 94 8/01 Asct 1m4f good

Quite a headstrong sort, he is probably best when making the running though he was held up when winning at Haydock last season. Lightly raced of late.

Inishowen (IRE)

94 **92**
2-y-o b c Alhaarth (IRE)-Naaman (IRE) (Marju (IRE))
B W Hills John C Grant

Placings:14 **(5017)**
2001: 6^1G, 7^4S

	Starts	1st	2nd	3rd	Win & Pl
Career Total (Turf)	2	1	0	0	9745

92	9/01	Donc	6f	C	GD	£8697

Total win prize-money £8697

Going (Turf): Sf: 0-1 GS: 0-0 **Gd: 1-1** GF: 0-0 Fm: 0-0
Distance: **5f/6f: 1-1** 7f-8f: 0-1 9f-13f: 0-0 14f+: 0-0
Track : LH: 0-0 RH: 0-0 Tight: 0-0 Gall: 0-0
Aids: Bl: 0-0 Vi: 0-0 Tstrap: 0-0
Best Rating: 92 9/01 Donc 6f good

Winner of a conditions event on his debut, pulled too hard on soft ground next time.

Initiative

92(90) (30)**25**
5-y-o ch g Arazi (USA)-Dance Quest (FR) (Green Dancer (USA))
J Hetherton (B W Murray 22/7) Frank Reay

Placings:3/15/000300-000000 **(5534)**
2001: 6^0SD, 7^0SD, 8^0GF, 8^0SD, 8^0F, 11^0S

	Starts	1st	2nd	3rd	Win & Pl
Career Total (Turf)	11	1	0	2	5838
Career Total (AW)	4	0	0	0	

73	5/99	Thsk	1m	D	G-F	£3873

Total win prize-money £3873

Going (Turf): Sf: 0-2 GS: 0-1 Gd: 0-1 **GF: 1-6** Fm: 0-1
Distance: 5f/6f: 0-2 **7f-8f: 1-8** 9f-13f: 0-5 14f+: 0-0
Track : **LH: 1-12** RH: 0-0 **Tight: 1-4** Gall: 0-3
Aids: Bl: 0-2 Vi: 0-0 Tstrap: 0-0
Best Rating: 30 1/01 Sthl 6f stand

Injaaz

103 **94**
3-y-o ch f Sheikh Albadou-Ferber's Follies (USA) (Saratoga Six (USA))
J L Dunlop Kuwait Racing Syndicate Ii

Placings:01200-104530 **(3580)**
2001: 7^1GS, 6^0F, 7^4GF, 8^5GF, 8^3GF, 7^0GF

	Starts	1st	2nd	3rd	Win & Pl
Career Total (Turf)	11	2	1	1	18955

91	4/01	NmkR	7f	C(0-95)H	G-S	£7514
71	8/00	Leic	5f218y	E	G-F	£2925

Total win prize-money £10439

Going (Turf): Sf: 0-0 **GS: 1-2** Gd: 0-3 **GF: 1-5** Fm: 0-1
Distance: 5f/6f: 1-2 7f-8f: 1-9 9f-13f: 0-0 14f+: 0-0
Track : LH: 0-2 RH: 0-2 Tight: 0-1 Gall: 0-2
Aids: Bl: 0-2 Vi: 0-0 Tstrap: 0-0
Best Rating: 94 6/01 Asct 1m gd-fm

She won a Leicester maiden last season and landed a decent Newmarket handicap on her reappearance. Held in better company since, she may be best with some cut in the ground.

Injun

78 **34**
2-y-o ch c Efisio-Lassoo (Caerleon (USA))
C W Thornton Guy Reed

Placings:0 **(5627)**
2001: 7^0G

	Starts	1st	2nd	3rd	Win & Pl
Career Total (Turf)	1	0	0	0	

Going (Turf): Sf: 0-0 GS: 0-0 Gd: 0-1 GF: 0-0 Fm: 0-0
Distance: 5f/6f: 0-0 7f-8f: 0-1 9f-13f: 0-0 14f+: 0-0
Track : LH: 0-0 RH: 0-0 Tight: 0-0 Gall: 0-0
Aids: Bl: 0-0 Vi: 0-0 Tstrap: 0-0
Best Rating: 34 11/01 Rdcr 7f good

Inkwell

84(95) (34)**27**
7-y-o b g Relief Pitcher-Fragrant Hackette (Simply Great (FR))
M R Ewer-Hoad Phil Collins

Placings:00/042630035**030**/010403310051/000002204/5250000-0000 **(2234)**
2001: 9^0GF, 11^0F, 11^0GF, 7^0GF

	Starts	1st	2nd	3rd	Win & Pl
Career Total (Turf)	37	3	3	4	15326
Career Total (AW)	9	0	1	1	730

57	11/98	Brig	6f209y	F	SFT	£2473
41	8/98	Bath	1m5y	D(0-75)H	GD	£7425
43	4/98	Brig	7f214y	E(0-70)H	GD	£1680

Total win prize-money £11579

Going (Turf): Sf: 1-8 GS: 0-8 **Gd: 2-5** GF: 0-12 Fm: 0-4
Distance: 5f/6f: 0-1 **7f-8f: 2-13** 9f-13f: 1-32 14f+: 0-0
Track : **LH: 3-31** RH: 0-8 **Tight: 1-20** Gall: 0-1
Aids: **Bl: 2-20** Vi: 0-1 Tstrap: 0-1
Best Rating: 27 6/01 Wind 1m3f135y gd-fm

Innes

(85) (39)**55**
5-y-o b m Inchinor-Trachelium (Formidable (USA))
Miss S E Hall C Platts

Placings:0/630/4-0 **(0191)**
2001: 16^0SD

	Starts	1st	2nd	3rd	Win & Pl
Career Total (Turf)	4	0	0	1	307
Career Total (AW)	2	0	0	0	218

Going (Turf): Sf: 0-0 GS: 0-1 Gd: 0-0 GF: 0-2 Fm: 0-1
Distance: 5f/6f: 0-0 7f-8f: 0-1 9f-13f: 0-4 14f+: 0-1
Track : LH: 0-5 RH: 0-1 Tight: 0-2 Gall: 0-1

Aids: Bl: 0-0 Vi: 0-0 Tstrap: 0-0

Innkeeper

(96) (52d)**68**

4-y-o b g Night Shift (USA)-Riyoom (USA) (Vaguely Noble)

G L Moore Chris Wilkinson

Placings:442400/5200664000-205630 **(0479)**

2001: 8^{2}SD, 8^{0}SD, 8^{5}SD, 10^{6}SD, 6^{3}SD, 7^{0}SD

	Starts	1st	2nd	3rd	Win & Pl
Career Total (Turf)	14	0	2	0	3699
Career Total (AW)	8	0	1	1	1090

Going (Turf): Sf: 0-2 GS: 0-1 Gd: 0-4 GF: 0-6 Fm: 0-1
Distance: 5f/6f: 0-6 7f-8f: 0-13 9f-13f: 0-3 14f+: 0-0
Track : LH: 0-10 RH: 0-2 Tight: 0-8 Gall: 0-1
Aids: Bl: 0-6 Vi: 0-0 Tstrap: 0-0
Best Rating: 52 1/01 Ling 1m stand

Innocent (IRE)

86 **50**

3-y-o b g Lure (USA)-Miss Declared (USA) (Alleged (USA))

J A Osborne P Byrne

Placings:000 **(5374)**

2001: 6^{0}GF, 5^{0}G, 6^{0}G

	Starts	1st	2nd	3rd	Win & Pl
Career Total (Turf)	3	0	0	0	

Going (Turf): Sf: 0-0 GS: 0-0 Gd: 0-2 GF: 0-1 Fm: 0-0
Distance: 5f/6f: 0-3 7f-8f: 0-0 9f-13f: 0-0 14f+: 0-0
Track : LH: 0-0 RH: 0-0 Tight: 0-0 Gall: 0-0
Aids: Bl: 0-0 Vi: 0-0 Tstrap: 0-0
Best Rating: 50 8/01 Ling 6f gd-fm

Innovator (IRE)

91 **71**

2-y-o b c Entrepreneur-Midnight Angel (Machiavellian (USA))

R Hannon Highclere Thoroughbred Racing Ltd

Placings:05000 **(5176)**

2001: 6^{0}F, 7^{5}GF, 6^{0}F, 7^{0}G, 8^{0}HY

	Starts	1st	2nd	3rd	Win & Pl
Career Total (Turf)	5	0	0	0	0

Going (Turf): Sf: 0-1 GS: 0-0 Gd: 0-1 GF: 0-1 Fm: 0-2
Distance: 5f/6f: 0-1 7f-8f: 0-3 9f-13f: 0-1 14f+: 0-0
Track : LH: 0-1 RH: 0-2 Tight: 0-2 Gall: 0-1
Aids: Bl: 0-0 Vi: 0-1 Tstrap: 0-0
Best Rating: 71 8/01 Sals 6f212y firm

Inquisitive

90 **80**

2-y-o b f Nashwan (USA)-Ingenuity (Clever Trick (USA))

R Hannon The Queen

Placings:3460 **(4985)**

2001: 6^{3}GF, 7^{4}GF, 5^{6}GF, 6^{0}G

	Starts	1st	2nd	3rd	Win & Pl
Career Total (Turf)	4	0	0	1	7318

Going (Turf): Sf: 0-0 GS: 0-0 Gd: 0-1 GF: 0-3 Fm: 0-0
Distance: 5f/6f: 0-2 7f-8f: 0-2 9f-13f: 0-0 14f+: 0-0
Track : LH: 0-1 RH: 0-0 Tight: 0-0 Gall: 0-1
Aids: Bl: 0-0 Vi: 0-0 Tstrap: 0-0
Best Rating: 80 7/01 Newb 7f gd-fm

Made a promising debut when third of 19 in a Salisbury maiden and again went close next time when fourth in a similar event, but dissappointed at her first attempt at five furlongs. Suited by good to firm, goes well over six furlongs.

Insenor (USA)

95 **71**

4-y-o ch f El Gran Senor (USA)-Informatrice (USA) (Trempolino (USA))

E J O'Neill Mrs Luciana Moretti

Placings:62/23125-000606 **(3942)**

2001: 10^{0}GF, 10^{0}F, 8^{0}GF, 11^{6}G, 8^{0}GF, 10^{6}GF

	Starts	1st	2nd	3rd	Win & Pl
Career Total (Turf)	13	1	3	1	7505

78 8/00 Rosc 1m2f FRM £3450
Total win prize-money £3450

Going (Turf): Sf: 0-1 GS: 0-0 Gd: 0-3 GF: 0-5 **Fm: 1-3**
Distance: 5f/6f: 0-1 7f-8f: 0-2 **9f-13f: 1-10** 14f+: 0-0
Track : LH: 0-6 **RH: 1-4** Tight: 0-3 Gall: 0-1
Aids: Bl: 0-1 Vi: 0-0 Tstrap: 0-0
Best Rating: 74 5/01 York 1m2f85y gd-fm

Formerly trained in Ireland, she only has a victory in a Roscommon maiden to her name so far.

Insheen (IRE)

(85) (44)**44**

3-y-o b g Inzar (USA)-Moonshine Lady (Ballad Rock)

J S Moore Alan J Speyer

Placings:050-664 **(0223)**

2001: 10^{6}SD, 8^{6}SD, 12^{4}SD

	Starts	1st	2nd	3rd	Win & Pl
Career Total (Turf)	3	0	0	0	0
Career Total (AW)	3	0	0	0	0

Going (Turf): Sf: 0-0 GS: 0-2 Gd: 0-0 GF: 0-1 Fm: 0-0
Distance: 5f/6f: 0-3 7f-8f: 0-1 9f-13f: 0-2 14f+: 0-0
Track : LH: 0-4 RH: 0-1 Tight: 0-3 Gall: 0-2
Aids: Bl: 0-0 Vi: 0-0 Tstrap: 0-0
Best Rating: 44 2/01 Ling 1m4f stand

Insignis (IRE)

81 **48**

2-y-o b f Inzar (USA)-Negria (IRE) (Al Hareb (USA))

Mrs P N Dutfield The Bright And Early Partnership

Placings:05560 **(5079)**

2001: 6^{0}GF, 7^{5}GF, 6^{5}GF, 7^{6}GF, 5^{0}S

	Starts	1st	2nd	3rd	Win & Pl
Career Total (Turf)	5	0	0	0	0

Going (Turf): Sf: 0-1 GS: 0-0 Gd: 0-0 GF: 0-4 Fm: 0-0
Distance: 5f/6f: 0-3 7f-8f: 0-2 9f-13f: 0-0 14f+: 0-0
Track : LH: 0-2 RH: 0-0 Tight: 0-0 Gall: 0-0
Aids: Bl: 0-0 Vi: 0-0 Tstrap: 0-0
Best Rating: 48 6/01 Wwck 7f26y gd-fm

Inspector Blue

92 **66**

3-y-o ch g Royal Academy (USA)-Blue Siren (Bluebird (USA))

D R C Elsworth J C Smith

Placings:0-00000 **(4951)**

2001: 8^{0}GF, 7^{0}GS, 8^{0}GF, 8^{0}F, 8^{0}G

	Starts	1st	2nd	3rd	Win & Pl
Career Total (Turf)	6	0	0	0	

Going (Turf): Sf: 0-1 GS: 0-1 Gd: 0-1 GF: 0-2 Fm: 0-1
Distance: 5f/6f: 0-0 7f-8f: 0-5 9f-13f: 0-1 14f+: 0-0
Track : LH: 0-0 RH: 0-1 Tight: 0-0 Gall: 0-0
Aids: Bl: 0-0 Vi: 0-0 Tstrap: 0-0
Best Rating: 66 6/01 NmkR 1m gd-fm

Inspector General (IRE)

109 **91**

3-y-o b g Dilum (USA)-New Generation (Young Generation)

P F I Cole The Blenheim Partnership

Placings:1110-0000015600 **(5391)**

2001: 8^{0}S, 5^{0}S, 6^{0}GS, 6^{0}F, 8^{0}GF, 7^{1}G, 7^{5}GF, 8^{6}GS, 7^{0}G, 7^{0}GS

	Starts	1st	2nd	3rd	Win & Pl
Career Total (Turf)	14	4	0	0	23357

66	6/01	Hayd	7f30y	C(0-90)	GD	£7058
94	9/00	Sals	6f	C	SFT	£6252
82	5/00	Thsk	5f	D	GD	£3591
86	4/00	Newb	5f34y	D	SFT	£5005

Total win prize-money £21907

Going (Turf): Sf: 2-5 GS: 0-3 **Gd: 2-3** GF: 0-2 Fm: 0-1
Distance: 5f/6f: 3-6 7f-8f: 1-7 9f-13f: 0-1 14f+: 0-0
Track : LH: 1-3 RH: 0-3 Tight: 0-0 Gall: 0-1
Aids: Bl: 0-0 Vi: 0-0 Tstrap: 0-0
Best Rating: 92 5/01 York 6f214y firm

Tried over various trips this term, he was the gutsy winner of a conditions event over seven furlongs at Haydock in June, but is struggling in handicaps. Does not want the ground too fast.

Intangible (USA)

97 **81**

2-y-o ch f Diesis-Flamboyance (USA) (Zilzal (USA))

H R A Cecil Dr Catherine Wills

Placings:01 **(5468)**

2001: 8^{0}GF, 7^{1}S

	Starts	1st	2nd	3rd	Win & Pl
Career Total (Turf)	2	1	0	0	3572

81 10/01 Brig 7f214y D SFT £3571
Total win prize-money £3572

Going (Turf): Sf: 1-1 GS: 0-0 Gd: 0-0 GF: 0-1 Fm: 0-0
Distance: 5f/6f: 0-0 **7f-8f: 1-1** 9f-13f: 0-1 14f+: 0-0
Track : LH: 1-1 RH: 0-0 Tight: 0-0 Gall: 0-0
Aids: Bl: 0-0 Vi: 0-0 Tstrap: 0-0
Best Rating: 81 10/01 Brig 7f214y soft

By Diesis, she benefited from a softer surface to win a Brighton maiden over a mile.

Integrate (USA)

94 **63**

3-y-o b/br g You And I (USA)-September Kaper (USA) (Peterhof (USA))

M H Tompkins Kenneth Macpherson

Placings:030450 **(4542)**

2001: 10^{0}GF, 8^{3}GF, 7^{0}GS, 8^{4}GS, 8^{5}GF, 10^{0}GF

	Starts	1st	2nd	3rd	Win & Pl
Career Total (Turf)	6	0	0	1	821

Going (Turf): Sf: 0-0 GS: 0-2 Gd: 0-0 GF: 0-4 Fm: 0-0
Distance: 5f/6f: 0-0 7f-8f: 0-3 9f-13f: 0-3 14f+: 0-0
Track : LH: 0-3 RH: 0-2 Tight: 0-3 Gall: 0-1
Aids: Bl: 0-0 Vi: 0-0 Tstrap: 0-0
Best Rating: 63 8/01 Epsm 1m114y gd-fm

Internal Affair (USA)

(107) (65)**54**

6-y-o b g Nicholas (USA)-Gdynia (USA) (Sir Ivor)

D L Williams Miss L Horner

Placings:0/0100005/20025000615462 0/10141351566-0 **(0574)**

2001: 12^{0}SW

	Starts	1st	2nd	3rd	Win & Pl
Career Total (Turf)	18	0	2	0	2220
Career Total (AW)	17	6	1	1	16080

65 3/00 Sthl 1m E(0-70)H STD £2522
65 2/00 Wolv 1m100y E(0-75)H STD £2639
62 1/00 Wolv 1m100y F STD £2177
61 1/00 Wolv 1m100y F STD £2268
63 10/99 Wolv 1m100y F(0-60)H STD £2514
62 6/98 Wolv 5f F STD £2406
Total win prize-money £14526

Going (Turf): Sf: 0-9 GS: 0-1 Gd: 0-4 GF: 0-4 Fm: 0-0
Distance: 5f/6f: 1-5 7f-8f: 1-14 **9f-13f: 4-16** 14f+: 0-0
Track : **LH: 6-20** RH: 0-5 **Tight: 5-17** Gall: 0-1
Aids: Bl: 0-0 Vi: 0-0 Tstrap: 0-0
Best Rating: 28 3/01 Ling 1m4f slow

Internationalguest (IRE)

99 **73**

2-y-o b c Petardia-Banco Solo (Distant Relative)
G G Margarson John Guest

Placings:0054263 **(5379)**
2001: 5^{0}GS, 6^{0}GF, 6^{5}GF, 7^{4}G, 6^{2}G, 8^{6}GS, 7^{3}S

	Starts	1st	2nd	3rd	Win & Pl
Career Total (Turf)	7	0	1	1	1857

Going (Turf): Sf: 0-1 GS: 0-2 Gd: 0-2 GF: 0-2 Fm: 0-0
Distance: 5f/6f: 0-2 7f-8f: 0-5 9f-13f: 0-0 14f+: 0-0
Track : LH: 0-1 RH: 0-4 Tight: 0-3 Gall: 0-1
Aids: Bl: 0-5 Vi: 0-0 Tstrap: 0-0
Best Rating: 73 10/01 Catt 7f soft

Out of a half-sister to My Branch, has shown progressive form in maidens and nurseries.

Intersky Champagne

96 **87d**

2-y-o b g Emperor Jones (USA)-Champagne Grandy (Vaigly Great)
A Berry Interskyracing.Com

Placings:61200 **(3571)**
2001: 5^{6}S, 5^{1}F, 5^{2}G, 5^{0}G, 5^{0}G

	Starts	1st	2nd	3rd	Win & Pl
Career Total (Turf)	5	1	1	0	3852

87 6/01 Newc 5f E FRM £2912
Total win prize-money £2912

Going (Turf): Sf: 0-1 GS: 0-0 Gd: 0-3 GF: 0-0 **Fm: 1-1**
Distance: **5f/6f: 1-5** 7f-8f: 0-0 9f-13f: 0-0 14f+: 0-0
Track : LH: 0-1 RH: 0-0 Tight: 0-1 Gall: 0-0
Aids: Bl: 0-0 Vi: 0-0 Tstrap: 0-0
Best Rating: 87 6/01 Newc 5f firm

Winner of a maiden auction in the summer, he has not progressed from that.

Inthaar

(102) (50)**28**

4-y-o b g Nashwan (USA)-Twafeaj (USA) (Topsider (USA))
R Brotherton (G M Moore 21/6) The Joiners Arms Racing Club Quarndon

Placings:204060230010 **(3433)**
2001: 9^{2}SD, 8^{0}SW, 9^{4}SD, 11^{0}SD, 8^{6}SD, 9^{0}G, 8^{2}SD, 7^{3}SD, 7^{0}SD, 8^{0}GF, 12^{1}SD, 16^{0}SD

	Starts	1st	2nd	3rd	Win & Pl
Career Total (Turf)	2	0	0	0	
Career Total (AW)	10	1	2	1	3645

50 7/01 Sthl 1m4f G STD £1925
Total win prize-money £1925

Going (Turf): Sf: 0-0 GS: 0-0 Gd: 0-1 GF: 0-1 Fm: 0-0
Distance: 5f/6f: 0-0 7f-8f: 0-5 **9f-13f: 1-6** 14f+: 0-1
Track : **LH: 1-11** RH: 0-0 Tight: 0-2 Gall: 0-0
Aids: Bl: 0-3 **Vi: 1-3** Tstrap: 0-0
Best Rating: 51 2/01 Wolv 1m1f79y stand

Intothedrink

(69) (13)**19**

3-y-o b f River Falls-Miss Alkie (Noalcoholic (FR))
J A Osborne The Woolfie And Tom Partnership

Placings:000 **(1088)**
2001: 9^{0}GS, 7^{0}SD, 9^{0}SD

	Starts	1st	2nd	3rd	Win & Pl
Career Total (Turf)	1	0	0	0	
Career Total (AW)	2	0	0	0	

Going (Turf): Sf: 0-0 GS: 0-1 Gd: 0-0 GF: 0-0 Fm: 0-0
Distance: 5f/6f: 0-0 7f-8f: 0-1 9f-13f: 0-2 14f+: 0-0
Track : LH: 0-3 RH: 0-0 Tight: 0-1 Gall: 0-0
Aids: Bl: 0-0 Vi: 0-0 Tstrap: 0-0
Best Rating: 19 4/01 Brig 1m1f209y gd-sft

Intrepidous

108 **102**

3-y-o b f Polar Falcon (USA)-Silver Braid (USA) (Miswaki (USA))
B J Meehan Wyck Hall Stud

Placings:521010 **(5141)**
2001: 7^{5}GF, 8^{2}G, 8^{1}GF, 10^{0}GF, 8^{1}G, 8^{0}G

	Starts	1st	2nd	3rd	Win & Pl
Career Total (Turf)	6	2	1	0	21055

102 9/01 Sand 1m14y A GD £15470
85 7/01 Wind 1m67y D G-F £4299
Total win prize-money £19770

Going (Turf): Sf: 0-0 GS: 0-0 **Gd: 1-3 GF: 1-3** Fm: 0-0
Distance: 5f/6f: 0-0 7f-8f: 0-3 **9f-13f: 2-3** 14f+: 0-0
Track : LH: 0-1 **RH: 2-4 Tight: 1-2** Gall: 0-1
Aids: Bl: 0-0 Vi: 0-0 Tstrap: 0-0
Best Rating: 102 9/01 Sand 1m14y good

Progressive filly, made all and won going away when beating Panna by five lengths in a mile maiden at Windsor in July, but slipped badly when behind that filly at Ascot. Came back to make all in a Sandown Listed event. Stays a mile. Acts on fast and good ground.

Intricate Web (IRE)

110(109) (91)**82**

5-y-o b g Warning-In Anticipation (IRE) (Sadler's Wells (USA))
E J Alston Morris, Oliver, Pierce

Placings:5056301/600613305300062-121112020601055 **(5608)**
2001: 7^{1}SW, 7^{2}SW, 7^{1}SD, 7^{1}SD, 7^{1}G, 7^{2}GF, 7^{0}GF, 7^{2}F, 7^{0}G, 8^{6}GF, 7^{0}G, 7^{1}G, 7^{0}S, 7^{5}GS, 7^{5}GS

	Starts	1st	2nd	3rd	Win & Pl
Career Total (Turf)	31	4	2	4	29957
Career Total (AW)	6	3	2	0	22183

70 8/01 Ayr 7f50y D(0-80) GD £4030
82 5/01 Thsk 7f C(0-90)H GD £7475
91 3/01 Sthl 7f C(0-95)H STD £10374
87 2/01 Sthl 7f C(0-100)H STD £6857
84 1/01 Wolv 7f E(0-75)H SLW £2975
72 6/00 Carl 6f206y D(0-80)H G-F £4231
68 10/99 Rdcr 7f E(0-70)H GD £4666
Total win prize-money £40610

Going (Turf): Sf: 0-8 GS: 0-3 **Gd: 3-7** GF: 1-9 Fm: 0-3
Distance: 5f/6f: 0-0 **7f-8f: 7-35** 9f-13f: 0-2 14f+: 0-0
Track : **LH: 4-19** RH: 1-2 **Tight: 2-9** Gall: 0-3
Aids: Bl: 0-2 Vi: 0-1 Tstrap: 0-0
Best Rating: 91 3/01 Sthl 7f stand

A useful seven-furlong handicapper on turf and sand, he was in great heart early in 2001, winning four times over seven furlongs, and came back to form at Ayr in August. Suited by a turning left-hand track and needs fast ground on turf.

Invader

108(110) (98)**84**

5-y-o b h Danehill (USA)-Donya (Mill Reef (USA))
C E Brittain R J Swinbourne

Placings:0044/45/55002105-00140030540 **(5344)**
2001: 6^{0}SW, 7^{0}SD, 8^{1}SD, 10^{4}SD, 8^{0}GS, 8^{0}F, 9^{3}F, 10^{0}GF, 10^{5}GF, 8^{4}GF, 8^{0}GS

	Starts	1st	2nd	3rd	Win & Pl
Career Total (Turf)	19	1	1	1	10279
Career Total (AW)	6	1	0	0	36625

93 3/01 Wolv 1m100y B(0-105)H STD £32500
80 7/00 Sand 1m14y D G-F £4231
Total win prize-money £36732

Going (Turf): Sf: 0-1 GS: 0-4 Gd: 0-4 **GF: 1-8** Fm: 0-2
Distance: 5f/6f: 0-1 7f-8f: 0-11 **9f-13f: 2-13** 14f+: 0-0
Track : LH: 1-9 RH: 1-7 **Tight: 1-7** Gall: 0-4
Aids: Bl: 1-8 Vi: 1-4 Tstrap: 0-0
Best Rating: 93 3/01 Wolv 1m100y stand

Returned to winning ways in Lincoln Trial at Wolverhampton in March, but held since returning to turf. Races prominently, stays a mile, acts on a sound surface on turf and on Fibresand.

Inver Gold

101(106) (73)**67**

4-y-o ch h Arazi (USA)-Mary Martin (Be My Guest (USA))
A G Newcombe M Patel

Placings:624/1300430100054-5040500125 **(5100)**
2001: 9^{5}SW, 12^{0}SD, 10^{4}G, 11^{0}GS, 10^{5}G, 12^{0}GF, 12^{0}GY, 9^{1}SD, 10^{2}GF, 9^{5}GS

	Starts	1st	2nd	3rd	Win & Pl
Career Total (Turf)	13	0	1	1	4284
Career Total (AW)	12	3	1	1	12630

69 8/01 Wolv 1m1f79y D(0-85)H STD £3835
76 8/00 Wolv 1m100y D(0-85)H STD £3789
69 1/00 Sthl 7f D STD £2847
Total win prize-money £10472

Going (Turf): Sf: 0-1 GS: 0-4 Gd: 0-6 GF: 0-2 Fm: 0-0
Distance: 5f/6f: 0-0 7f-8f: 1-6 **9f-13f: 2-19** 14f+: 0-0
Track : **LH: 3-15** RH: 0-6 **Tight: 2-13** Gall: 0-2
Aids: Bl: 0-0 Vi: 0-0 Tstrap: 0-0
Best Rating: 69 8/01 Wolv 1m1f79y stand

He has only ever won on Fibresand and has never won on turf, but has shown enough to suggest he can win a race on that surface. Best at around ten furlongs.

Invermark

109 **110**

7-y-o b g Machiavellian (USA)-Applecross (Glint Of Gold)
J R Fanshawe Lady Wills

Placings:053/01524/66211410/3224/12 **(5385)**
2001: 14^{1}HY, 16^{2}GS

	Starts	1st	2nd	3rd	Win & Pl
Career Total (Turf)	22	5	5	2	171785

97 9/01 Hayd 1m6f C HVY £6467
109 10/98 Lonc 2m4f SFT £50505
100 8/98 Ches 1m5f89y A(0-110)H G-S £18624
88 7/98 Hayd 1m6f D(0-85)H GD £3374
78 7/97 Yarm 1m3f101yD G-F £3677
Total win prize-money £82648

Going (Turf): Sf: 2-7 GS: 1-2 Gd: 1-6 GF: 1-5 Fm: 0-0
Distance: 5f/6f: 0-0 7f-8f: 0-2 9f-13f: 1-8 **14f+: 4-12**
Track : **LH: 4-9** RH: 1-10 **Tight: 2-4** Gall: 0-6
Aids: Bl: 0-0 Vi: 0-0 Tstrap: 0-0
Best Rating: 110 10/01 NmkR 2m gd-sft

A grand stayer with a bright turn of foot, runner-up in the '99 Ascot Gold Cup, he was having his first run for two years when winning at Haydock in October. Runner-up at Newmarket next time, he acts on most types of ground but is especially effective on soft.

Investment Force (IRE)

102(90) (45)**66**

3-y-o b g Imperial Frontier (USA)-Superb Investment (IRE) (Hatim (USA))

M Johnston Markus Graff

Placings:005200-40626342 **(3617)**

2001: 8^{4}SD, 7^{0}SD, 6^{6}GF, 6^{2}GF, 6^{6}GS, 6^{3}GF, 6^{4}GF, 6^{2}F

	Starts	1st	2nd	3rd	Win & Pl
Career Total (Turf)	11	0	3	1	4232
Career Total (AW)	3	0	0	0	0

Going (Turf): Sf: 0-0 GS: 0-3 Gd: 0-2 GF: 0-5 Fm: 0-1
Distance: 5f/6f: 0-7 7f-8f: 0-7 9f-13f: 0-0 14f+: 0-0
Track : LH: 0-6 RH: 0-2 Tight: 0-4 Gall: 0-0
Aids: Bl: 0-4 Vi: 0-2 Tstrap: 0-0
Best Rating: 66 8/01 Thsk 6f firm

Often placed in varied company, but has still to win and has not always looked too enthusiastic. His best trip is still something of a mystery.

Investor (IRE)

100 **72**

2-y-o b c Marju (IRE)-Shine On Me (Machiavellian (USA))

P F I Cole Highclere Thoroughbred Racing Ltd

Placings:0231500 **(5379)**

2001: 6^{0}S, 6^{2}GF, 7^{3}GS, 7^{1}G, 7^{5}GS, 7^{0}GF, 7^{0}S

	Starts	1st	2nd	3rd	Win & Pl
Career Total (Turf)	7	1	1	1	6199
72 8/01 Ches 7f2y D				GD	£4348

Total win prize-money £4349

Going (Turf): Sf: 0-2 GS: 0-2 **Gd: 1-1** GF: 0-2 Fm: 0-0
Distance: 5f/6f: 0-0 **7f-8f: 1-7** 9f-13f: 0-0 14f+: 0-0
Track : **LH: 1-4** RH: 0-1 **Tight: 1-2** Gall: 0-0
Aids: Bl: 0-0 Vi: 0-1 Tstrap: 0-0
Best Rating: 72 8/01 Ches 7f2y good

Well fancied in decent soft-ground maiden on debut but was very coltish in the paddock. Showed plenty of speed that day but was found to have swallowed his tongue. Fitted with different bit after that, he got off the mark at Chester on fourth outing. Stays seven furlongs. Acts on a sound surface.

Investor Relations (IRE)

90 **65d**

3-y-o b g Goldmark (USA)-Debach Delight (Great Nephew)

N J Hawke (B J Meehan 7/5) N J McMullan

Placings:600-500 **(1180)**

2001: 9^{5}GS, 10^{0}GS, 8^{0}G

	Starts	1st	2nd	3rd	Win & Pl
Career Total (Turf)	6	0	0	0	0

Going (Turf): Sf: 0-0 GS: 0-3 Gd: 0-2 GF: 0-1 Fm: 0-0
Distance: 5f/6f: 0-1 7f-8f: 0-2 9f-13f: 0-3 14f+: 0-0
Track : LH: 0-2 RH: 0-0 Tight: 0-1 Gall: 0-0
Aids: Bl: 0-1 Vi: 0-0 Tstrap: 0-0
Best Rating: 54 4/01 Brig 1m1f209y gd-sft

Invictress (DEN)

92 **48**

6-y-o b m Prince Mab (FR)-Joe's Lake (DEN) (King's Lake (USA))

P J Hobbs Alan Stevens & Denise Winton

Placings:1/11112/0 **(2386)**

2001: 16^{0}GF

	Starts	1st	2nd	3rd	Win & Pl
Career Total (Turf)	7	5	1	0	18463
10/98 Klam 1m4f				SFT	£2662
9/98 Klam 1m4f				HRD	£10648
8/98 Klam 1m3f110y				SFT	£1331
5/98 Klam 1m1f				FRM	£710
11/97 Aarh 7f				GD	£894

Total win prize-money £16245

Going (Turf): Sf: 0-0 GS: 0-0 Gd: 0-0 GF: 0-1 Fm: 0-0
Distance: 5f/6f: 0-0 7f-8f: 0-0 9f-13f: 0-0 14f+: 0-1
Track : LH: 0-0 RH: 0-1 Tight: 0-0 Gall: 0-1
Aids: Bl: 0-0 Vi: 0-0 Tstrap: 0-0
Best Rating: 48 6/01 Asct 2m45y gd-fm

Invincible

102 **79**

3-y-o b f Slip Anchor-Blessed Honour (Ahonoora)

J R Fanshawe Cheveley Park Stud

Placings:4-13 **(2182)**

2001: 11^{1}GF, 11^{3}G

	Starts	1st	2nd	3rd	Win & Pl
Career Total (Turf)	3	1	0	1	3697
76 5/01 Haml 1m3f16y E				G-F	£2940

Total win prize-money £2940

Going (Turf): Sf: 0-0 GS: 0-1 Gd: 0-1 **GF: 1-1** Fm: 0-0
Distance: 5f/6f: 0-0 7f-8f: 0-0 **9f-13f: 1-3** 14f+: 0-0
Track : LH: 0-2 **RH: 1-1 Tight: 1-3** Gall: 0-0
Aids: Bl: 0-0 Vi: 0-0 Tstrap: 0-0
Best Rating: 79 6/01 Bath 1m3f144y good

Invincible Spirit (IRE)

110 **114+**

4-y-o b h Green Desert (USA)-Rafha (Kris)

J L Dunlop Prince A A Faisal

Placings:3116/46-410121 **(4760a)**

2001: 7^{4}G, 6^{1}GF, 6^{0}GF, 6^{1}GF, 6^{2}GS, 6^{1}G

	Starts	1st	2nd	3rd	Win & Pl
Career Total (Turf)	12	5	1	1	97649
113 9/01 Curr 6f				GD	£39000
114 7/01 Newb 6f8y A				G-F	£14645
113 5/01 Gdwd 6f B				G-F	£9526
106 8/99 Ripn 6f A				G-F	£13016
85 7/99 Gdwd 6f D				G-F	£7360

Total win prize-money £83547

Going (Turf): Sf: 0-0 GS: 0-3 Gd: 1-2 **GF: 4-6** Fm: 0-1
Distance: **5f/6f: 4-8** 7f-8f: 1-4 9f-13f: 0-0 14f+: 0-0
Track : LH: 0-1 RH: 0-0 Tight: 0-0 Gall: 0-1
Aids: Bl: 0-0 Vi: 0-0 Tstrap: 0-0
Best Rating: 114 8/01 Deau 6f gd-sft

He has done well this season, winning at Goodwood, Newbury and a Group Three at the Curragh as well as finishing second in a Deauville Group Two. Six furlongs on fast ground suits.

Inviramental

(98) (40)**44**

5-y-o b g Pursuit Of Love-Corn Futures (Nomination)

Mrs L C Jewell The Likely Bunch

Placings:0504/250000-030 **(0634)**

2001: 10^{0}SD, 8^{3}SW, 8^{0}SD

	Starts	1st	2nd	3rd	Win & Pl
Career Total (Turf)	2	0	0	0	
Career Total (AW)	11	0	1	1	817

Going (Turf): Sf: 0-2 GS: 0-0 Gd: 0-0 GF: 0-0 Fm: 0-0
Distance: 5f/6f: 0-1 7f-8f: 0-7 9f-13f: 0-5 14f+: 0-0
Track : LH: 0-13 RH: 0-0 Tight: 0-12 Gall: 0-1
Aids: Bl: 0-6 Vi: 0-2 Tstrap: 0-0
Best Rating: 43 3/01 Ling 1m2f stand

Invisible Force (IRE)

91(80) (33)**48**

4-y-o b g Imperial Frontier (USA)-Virginia Cottage (Lomond (USA))

B S Rothwell Jim Browne

Placings:40/60466134443-00 **(1000)**

2001: 10^{0}HY, 10^{0}S

	Starts	1st	2nd	3rd	Win & Pl
Career Total (Turf)	12	1	0	2	5208
Career Total (AW)	3	0	0	0	220
50 7/00 Carl 1m1f61y E(0-70)H				FRM	£2977

Total win prize-money £2977

Going (Turf): Sf: 0-4 GS: 0-1 Gd: 0-2 GF: 0-3 **Fm: 1-2**
Distance: 5f/6f: 0-3 7f-8f: 0-3 **9f-13f: 1-9** 14f+: 0-0
Track : LH: 0-6 **RH: 1-6** Tight: 0-4 Gall: 0-1
Aids: **Bl: 1-4** Vi: 0-4 Tstrap: 0-0
Best Rating: 24 4/01 Pont 1m2f6y heavy

Invitado (IRE)

78 **38**

2-y-o ch g Be My Guest (USA)-Lady Dulcinea (ARG) (General (FR))

J G Fitzgerald A Huddlestone

Placings:0000 **(5628)**

2001: 7^{0}GF, 8^{0}GS, 8^{0}G, 8^{0}G

	Starts	1st	2nd	3rd	Win & Pl
Career Total (Turf)	4	0	0	0	

Going (Turf): Sf: 0-0 GS: 0-1 Gd: 0-2 GF: 0-1 Fm: 0-0
Distance: 5f/6f: 0-0 7f-8f: 0-4 9f-13f: 0-0 14f+: 0-0
Track : LH: 0-2 RH: 0-0 Tight: 0-0 Gall: 0-2
Aids: Bl: 0-0 Vi: 0-0 Tstrap: 0-0
Best Rating: 38 10/01 Rdcr 1m good

Invitation

101 **78**

3-y-o b g Bin Ajwaad (IRE)-On Request (IRE) (Be My Guest (USA))

K O Cunningham-Brown Woodhaven Racing Syndicate

Placings:0-105630 **(5591)**

2001: 10^{1}G, 10^{0}GF, 12^{5}GF, 11^{6}HY, 10^{3}G, 9^{0}GS

	Starts	1st	2nd	3rd	Win & Pl
Career Total (Turf)	7	1	0	1	4388
71 5/01 Wind 1m2f7y E				GD	£3290

Total win prize-money £3290

Going (Turf): Sf: 0-2 GS: 0-1 **Gd: 1-2** GF: 0-2 Fm: 0-0
Distance: 5f/6f: 0-0 7f-8f: 0-1 **9f-13f: 1-6** 14f+: 0-0
Track : LH: 0-2 RH: 0-1 **Tight: 1-3** Gall: 0-0
Aids: Bl: 0-0 Vi: 0-0 Tstrap: 0-0
Best Rating: 78 10/01 NmkR 1m2f good

Won his maiden on his seasonal reappearance at Windsor but has not run to his best on fast ground since. Better run at Newmarket in October. He is usually slow out of the stalls. Stays twelve furlongs.

Inzacure (IRE)

86(102) (81)**61**

3-y-o b g Inzar (USA)-Whittingham Girl (Primo Dominie)

R M Beckett The Inzacure Partnership

Placings:0051111-00000 **(2216)**

2001: 6^{0}S, 6^{0}G, 6^{0}S, 7^{0}GF, 7^{0}G

	Starts	1st	2nd	3rd	Win & Pl
Career Total (Turf)	8	1	0	0	3636
Career Total (AW)	4	3	0	0	7630
81 12/00 Sthl 5f E(0-85)				STD	£2660
74 12/00 Ling 6f E(0-75)				STD	£2268
76 12/00 Sthl 6f E(0-75)				STD	£2702
57 9/00 Brig 5f213y D(0-85)				SFT	£3636

Total win prize-money £11266

Going (Turf): Sf: 1-3 GS: 0-0 Gd: 0-3 GF: 0-1 Fm: 0-1
Distance: **5f/6f: 4-8** 7f-8f: 0-4 9f-13f: 0-0 14f+: 0-0
Track : **LH: 3-3** RH: 0-2 **Tight: 1-2** Gall: 0-1
Aids: Bl: 0-0 Vi: 0-0 Tstrap: 0-0
Best Rating: 53 4/01 NmkR 6f soft

Ended last season with a four-timer of which three were on sand, but was not in the same form this season.

Inzarmood (IRE)

87(88) (28)**23**

3-y-o b f Inzar (USA)-Pepilin (Coquelin (USA))
K R Burke Mrs Elaine M Burke

Placings:000-000200 **(5284)**
2001: 8^{0}GF, 6^{0}GF, 8^{0}F, 9^{2}SD, 9^{0}GF, 9^{0}HY

	Starts	1st	2nd	3rd	Win & Pl
Career Total (Turf)	7	0	0	0	
Career Total (AW)	2	0	1	0	552

Going (Turf): Sf: 0-3 GS: 0-0 Gd: 0-0 GF: 0-3 Fm: 0-1
Distance: 5f/6f: 0-1 7f-8f: 0-4 9f-13f: 0-4 14f+: 0-0
Track : LH: 0-3 RH: 0-1 Tight: 0-3 Gall: 0-0
Aids: Bl: 0-0 Vi: 0-5 Tstrap: 0-0
Best Rating: 28 8/01 Wolv 1m1f79y stand

Ionian Spring (IRE)

107(110) (84)**78**

6-y-o b g Ela-Mana-Mou-Well Head (IRE) (Sadler's Wells (USA))
C G Cox (C R Egerton 22/5) Elite Racing Club

Placings:3221/0002-04421500161 **(5249)**
2001: 7^{0}SW, 10^{4}SW, 10^{4}SW, 12^{2}SD, 12^{1}SD, 12^{5}SD, 10^{0}G, 17^{0}GF, 10^{1}GF, 10^{6}G, 10^{1}S

	Starts	1st	2nd	3rd	Win & Pl
Career Total (Turf)	11	2	2	1	13495
Career Total (AW)	8	2	2	0	11151
78 10/01 York	1m2f85y	C(0-90)H		SFT	£7917
73 8/01 Chep	1m2f36y	E(0-70)H		G-F	£2863
84 3/01 Sthl	1m4f	D(0-85)H		STD	£3766
83 8/98 Wolv	1m1f79y	E		STD	£2872

Total win prize-money £17420

Going (Turf): Sf: 1-1 GS: 0-0 Gd: 0-5 **GF: 1-5** Fm: 0-0
Distance: 5f/6f: 0-0 7f-8f: 0-5 **9f-13f: 4-13** 14f+: 0-1
Track : **LH: 4-14** RH: 0-2 Tight: 1-8 Gall: 1-3
Aids: Bl: 0-0 Vi: 0-0 Tstrap: 0-0
Best Rating: 84 3/01 Sthl 1m4f stand

Missed the whole of 1999 and has done most of his running since on sand including winning at Southwell in March. Scored in good style on turf at Chepstow in August and York in October off much lower marks. Just about stays 12 furlongs, but probably better over shorter.

Ipanema Beach

(97) (58)**62**

4-y-o ch f Lion Cavern (USA)-Girl From Ipanema (Salse (USA))
Andrew Reid A S Reid

Placings:6/03601-000 **(5048)**
2001: 8^{0}GF, 7^{0}GF, 7^{0}SD

	Starts	1st	2nd	3rd	Win & Pl
Career Total (Turf)	7	0	0	1	600
Career Total (AW)	2	1	0	0	2899
58 10/00 Wolv	1m100y	D		STD	£2899

Total win prize-money £2899

Going (Turf): Sf: 0-2 GS: 0-1 Gd: 0-2 GF: 0-2 Fm: 0-0
Distance: 5f/6f: 0-1 7f-8f: 0-4 **9f-13f: 1-4** 14f+: 0-0
Track : **LH: 1-3** RH: 0-4 **Tight: 1-3** Gall: 0-1
Aids: Bl: 0-0 Vi: 0-0 Tstrap: 0-0
Best Rating: 33 7/01 Wind 1m67y gd-fm

Ireland's Eye (IRE)

104 **35**

6-y-o b g Shareef Dancer (USA)-So Romantic (IRE) (Teenoso (USA))
J R Norton Ejam Connection

Placings:40002360/3320660360-460 **(2040)**
2001: 14^{4}HY, 16^{6}G, 17^{0}GF

	Starts	1st	2nd	3rd	Win & Pl
Career Total (Turf)	20	0	2	4	3485
Career Total (AW)	1	0	0	0	

Going (Turf): Sf: 0-8 GS: 0-2 Gd: 0-4 GF: 0-5 Fm: 0-1
Distance: 5f/6f: 0-0 7f-8f: 0-0 9f-13f: 0-2 14f+: 0-19
Track : LH: 0-16 RH: 0-5 Tight: 0-10 Gall: 0-1
Aids: Bl: 0-0 Vi: 0-2 Tstrap: 0-0
Best Rating: 41 5/01 Nott 1m6f15y heavy

Iridescent

69 **49**

3-y-o b f Spectrum (IRE)-Ingenuity (Clever Trick (USA))
W M Brisbourne J Sankey

Placings:4-00 **(1939)**
2001: 11^{0}GF, 7^{0}GF

	Starts	1st	2nd	3rd	Win & Pl
Career Total (Turf)	3	0	0	0	510

Going (Turf): Sf: 0-0 GS: 0-0 Gd: 0-1 GF: 0-2 Fm: 0-0
Distance: 5f/6f: 0-1 7f-8f: 0-1 9f-13f: 0-1 14f+: 0-0
Track : LH: 0-2 RH: 0-0 Tight: 0-1 Gall: 0-0
Aids: Bl: 0-0 Vi: 0-0 Tstrap: 0-0
Best Rating: 8 6/01 Hayd 7f30y gd-fm

Irie Rasta (IRE)

87 **60**

2-y-o ch c Desert King (IRE)-Seeds Of Doubt (IRE) (Night Shift (USA))
S Kirk I A N Wight

Placings:065 **(4087)**
2001: 7^{0}GF, 7^{6}GF, 8^{5}S

	Starts	1st	2nd	3rd	Win & Pl
Career Total (Turf)	3	0	0	0	0

Going (Turf): Sf: 0-1 GS: 0-0 Gd: 0-0 GF: 0-2 Fm: 0-0
Distance: 5f/6f: 0-0 7f-8f: 0-2 9f-13f: 0-1 14f+: 0-0
Track : LH: 0-0 RH: 0-2 Tight: 0-0 Gall: 0-1
Aids: Bl: 0-0 Vi: 0-0 Tstrap: 0-0
Best Rating: 60 8/01 Sand 1m14y soft

Irina (IRE)

88 **75d**

5-y-o b m Polar Falcon (USA)-Bird Of Love (Ela-Mana-Mou)
E J O'Neill T F Brennan

Placings:351/036331000-5000 **(1999)**
2001: 7^{5}S, 5^{0}G, 10^{0}G, 6^{0}F

	Starts	1st	2nd	3rd	Win & Pl
Career Total (Turf)	16	2	0	4	16260
70 6/00 Navn	1m75y	(0-90)H		YLD	£9750
72 11/99 Cork	7f			SFT	£3795

Total win prize-money £13545

Going (Turf): Sf: 1-4 GS: 0-0 Gd: 0-3 GF: 0-0 Fm: 0-1
Distance: 5f/6f: 0-3 **7f-8f: 1-9** 9f-13f: 1-2 14f+: 0-0
Track : LH: 1-3 RH: 1-7 Tight: 0-0 Gall: 0-1
Aids: Bl: 0-0 Vi: 0-0 Tstrap: 0-0
Best Rating: 53 5/01 Hayd 7f30y soft

An ex-Irish handicapper who has won at seven furlongs and a mile on easy ground. Has been tried at various trips since coming to Britain.

Iris' Tempest (USA)

76 **34**

2-y-o b f Trempolino (USA)-Ivory Dance (CAN) (Sir Ivor)
Sir Michael Stoute Newsells Park Stud Limited

Placings:0 **(4886)**
2001: 7^{0}GF

	Starts	1st	2nd	3rd	Win & Pl
Career Total (Turf)	1	0	0	0	

Going (Turf): Sf: 0-0 GS: 0-0 Gd: 0-0 GF: 0-1 Fm: 0-0
Distance: 5f/6f: 0-0 7f-8f: 0-1 9f-13f: 0-0 14f+: 0-0
Track : LH: 0-0 RH: 0-1 Tight: 0-0 Gall: 0-1
Aids: Bl: 0-0 Vi: 0-0 Tstrap: 0-0
Best Rating: 34 9/01 Kemp 7f gd-fm

Irish Blessing (USA)

62 **73**

4-y-o b g Ghazi (USA)-Win For Leah (USA) (His Majesty (USA))
F Jordan The Bhiss Partnership

Placings:050/053413-0 **(5010)**
2001: 14^{0}HY

	Starts	1st	2nd	3rd	Win & Pl
Career Total (Turf)	10	1	0	2	5158
61 8/00 Slig	1m6f			YLD	£3967

Total win prize-money £3968

Going (Turf): Sf: 0-3 GS: 0-0 Gd: 0-1 GF: 0-2 Fm: 0-0
Distance: 5f/6f: 0-0 7f-8f: 0-2 9f-13f: 0-6 **14f+: 1-2**
Track : LH: 0-6 **RH: 1-4** Tight: 0-0 Gall: 0-0
Aids: **Bl: 1-5** Vi: 0-0 Tstrap: 0-0
Best Rating: 61 8/00 Slig 1m6f Y

He is a winner on the Flat in Ireland.

Irish Cream (IRE)

84(105) (41)**44**

5-y-o b m Petong-Another Baileys (Deploy)
J L Spearing Masonaires

Placings:10533150046**0**/31116000050006000**3**/201062 6202-435410 **(0585)**
2001: 16^{4}SD, 12^{3}SW, 12^{5}SD, 12^{4}SD, 12^{1}SD, 14^{0}HY

	Starts	1st	2nd	3rd	Win & Pl
Career Total (Turf)	18	1	0	3	4540
Career Total (AW)	28	6	4	2	16083
41 3/01 Wolv	1m4f	F(0-65)H		STD	£2324
47 3/00 Sthl	1m6f	F(0-60)		STD	£2124
66 3/99 Sthl	1m	F(0-65)		STD	£2341
75 2/99 Sthl	7f	G		STD	£1906
64 2/99 Sthl	7f	G		STD	£1847
67 7/98 Sthl	6f	F		STD	£2304
55 3/98 Haml	5f4y	E		HVY	£2736

Total win prize-money £15583

Going (Turf): Sf: 1-4 GS: 0-6 Gd: 0-6 GF: 0-2 Fm: 0-0
Distance: 5f/6f: 2-13 **7f-8f: 3-13** 9f-13f: 1-13 14f+: 1-7
Track : **LH: 6-34** RH: 0-4 **Tight: 1-18** Gall: 0-2
Aids: Bl: 0-5 **Vi: 5-29** Tstrap: 0-0
Best Rating: 41 3/01 Wolv 1m4f stand

She pops up from time to time in modest events on Fibresand.

Irish Distinction (IRE)

(78) (27)**72**

3-y-o b g Distinctly North (USA)-Shane's Girl (IRE) (Marktingo)
Simon Earle (A P Jarvis 27/8) Ambrose Turnbull

Placings:5-002560000 **(5407)**

2001: 8^{0}GS, 6^{0}GS, 11^{2}GF, 11^{5}GF, 10^{6}GF, 9^{0}G, 11^{0}G, 10^{0}GF, 12^{0}SD

	Starts	1st	2nd	3rd	Win & Pl
Career Total (Turf)	9	0	1	0	1434
Career Total (AW)	1	0	0	0	

Going (Turf): Sf: 0-0 GS: 0-2 Gd: 0-2 GF: 0-5 Fm: 0-0
Distance: 5f/6f: 0-2 7f-8f: 0-1 9f-13f: 0-7 14f+: 0-0
Track : LH: 0-5 RH: 0-1 Tight: 0-2 Gall: 0-1
Aids: Bl: 0-0 Vi: 0-0 Tstrap: 0-0
Best Rating: 72 5/01 Gdwd 1m3f gd-fm

Irish Paddy (IRE)

63 **12**

2-y-o b g Idris (IRE)-Ceili Queen (IRE) (Shareef Dancer (USA))
K McAuliffe Michael H Keogh

Placings:00 **(4722)**
2001: 8^{0}S, 7^{0}GF

	Starts	1st	2nd	3rd	Win & Pl
Career Total (Turf)	2	0	0	0	

Going (Turf): Sf: 0-1 GS: 0-0 Gd: 0-0 GF: 0-1 Fm: 0-0
Distance: 5f/6f: 0-0 7f-8f: 0-1 9f-13f: 0-1 14f+: 0-0
Track : LH: 0-1 RH: 0-1 Tight: 0-0 Gall: 0-0
Aids: Bl: 0-2 Vi: 0-0 Tstrap: 0-0
Best Rating: 12 8/01 Sand 1m14y soft

Irish Sea (USA)

105 **43**

8-y-o b g Zilzal (USA)-Dunkellin (USA) (Irish River (FR))
B J Llewellyn J V Rawlings

Placings:2634505500/33/01000 **(3411)**
2001: 17^{0}HY, 15^{1}HY, 18^{0}GF, 17^{0}G, 16^{0}GF

	Starts	1st	2nd	3rd	Win & Pl
Career Total (Turf)	16	1	1	3	5660
Career Total (AW)	1	0	0	0	

43 4/01 Folk 1m7f92y E(0-70)H HVY £3150
Total win prize-money £3150

Going (Turf): Sf: 1-2 GS: 0-0 Gd: 0-5 GF: 0-7 Fm: 0-2
Distance: 5f/6f: 0-0 7f-8f: 0-1 9f-13f: 0-9 **14f+: 1-7**
Track : LH: 0-12 **RH: 1-5 Tight: 1-10** Gall: 0-0
Aids: Bl: 0-1 Vi: 0-0 Tstrap: 0-0
Best Rating: 43 4/01 Folk 1m7f92y heavy

Irish Stream (USA)

102 **76**

3-y-o ch c Irish River (FR)-Euphonic (USA) (The Minstrel (CAN))
R Charlton K Abdulla

Placings:326-0P42 **(2393)**
2001: 6^{0}S, 6^{P}F, 6^{4}GF, 6^{2}GF

	Starts	1st	2nd	3rd	Win & Pl
Career Total (Turf)	7	0	2	1	3321

Going (Turf): Sf: 0-2 GS: 0-0 Gd: 0-1 GF: 0-3 Fm: 0-1
Distance: 5f/6f: 0-3 7f-8f: 0-4 9f-13f: 0-0 14f+: 0-0
Track : LH: 0-2 RH: 0-0 Tight: 0-0 Gall: 0-1
Aids: Bl: 0-1 Vi: 0-0 Tstrap: 0-0
Best Rating: 76 6/01 Kemp 6f gd-fm

Irish Vale

102 **96**

2-y-o ch c Wolfhound (USA)-Valencia (Kenmare (FR))
M Meade (R Charlton 16/6) Ladyswood Stud

Placings:631020610 **(5493)**
2001: 5^{6}G, 5^{3}GF, 5^{1}G, 5^{0}GF, 6^{2}G, 6^{0}G, 5^{6}S, 5^{1}G, 7^{0}HY

	Starts	1st	2nd	3rd	Win & Pl
Career Total (Turf)	9	2	1	1	17538

96	9/01	Ayr	5f	A	GD	£11484
81	6/01	Bath	5f11y	D	GD	£3337

Total win prize-money £14822

Going (Turf): Sf: 0-2 GS: 0-0 **Gd: 2-5** GF: 0-2 Fm: 0-0
Distance: **5f/6f: 2-8** 7f-8f: 0-1 9f-13f: 0-0 14f+: 0-0
Track : **LH: 1-2** RH: 0-0 Tight: 0-0 **Gall: 1-2**
Aids: Bl: 0-0 Vi: 0-0 Tstrap: 0-0
Best Rating: 96 9/01 Ayr 5f good

He has been busy this season and got off the mark in a novice event at Bath on his third start. He managed to win a Listed event at Ayr in September, but it may have been a weak race of its type as he had previously been exposed in decent company in the meantime. Suited by good ground and the minimum trip.

Iron Dragon (IRE)

84 **67**

3-y-o b c Royal Academy (USA)-Kerry Project (IRE) (Project Manager)
J Noseda Lucayan Stud

Placings:646-00 **(3259)**
2001: 6^{0}HY, 6^{0}GF

	Starts	1st	2nd	3rd	Win & Pl
Career Total (Turf)	5	0	0	0	270

Going (Turf): Sf: 0-1 GS: 0-0 Gd: 0-1 GF: 0-3 Fm: 0-0
Distance: 5f/6f: 0-3 7f-8f: 0-2 9f-13f: 0-0 14f+: 0-0
Track : LH: 0-0 RH: 0-0 Tight: 0-0 Gall: 0-0
Aids: Bl: 0-0 Vi: 0-0 Tstrap: 0-5
Best Rating: 38 7/01 Ripn 6f gd-fm

Iron Mountain (IRE)

106 **79**

6-y-o b g Scenic-Merlannah (IRE) (Shy Groom (USA))
N A Callaghan Gallagher Equine Ltd

Placings:05430256/000521231512050016 0/554414226 0/3534014305301-02250005230 **(5055)**
2001: 7^{0}GS, 10^{2}G, 9^{2}G, 10^{5}G, 8^{0}GS, 8^{0}GF, 8^{0}GF, 8^{5}GS, 8^{2}GS, 10^{3}G, 10^{0}S

	Starts	1st	2nd	3rd	Win & Pl
Career Total (Turf)	61	7	9	7	61820

78	10/00	Yarm	1m2f21y	D(0-85)H	SFT	£8222
73	7/00	NmkJ	1m	D(0-80)H	G-S	£9776
74	6/99	Gdwd	1m1f	E(0-70)H	G-S	£3988
69	10/98	Leic	1m1f218y	D(0-75)H	SFT	£7587
64	7/98	Bevl	1m1f207y	E(0-75)H	G-F	£3185
67	7/98	Brig	1m1f209y	F(0-65)H	GD	£2634
61	6/98	Yarm	1m2f21y	D(0-75)H	GD	£3947

Total win prize-money £39345

Going (Turf): Sf: 2-11 GS: 2-11 Gd: 2-21 GF: 1-17 Fm: 0-1
Distance: 5f/6f: 0-3 7f-8f: 1-16 **9f-13f: 6-42** 14f+: 0-0
Track : LH: 3-27 RH: 3-12 **Tight: 3-17** Gall: 0-6
Aids: Bl: 0-1 Vi: 0-0 Tstrap: 0-0
Best Rating: 79 9/01 Donc 1m2f60y good

A decent handicapper, he is effective from a mile to ten furlongs, but must have some cut in the ground and a strong pace to be seen to best effect. Does not win as often as he should but always capable of running well in face of stiff tasks.

Irony (IRE)

104 **100**

2-y-o gr c Mujadil (USA)-Cidaris (IRE) (Persian Bold)
J A Osborne John Nicholls Ltd/mobley Homes

Placings:1126526 **(5256)**
2001: 5^{1}GF, 5^{1}GF, 5^{2}GF, 5^{6}G, 5^{5}G, 6^{2}GF, 5^{6}GS

	Starts	1st	2nd	3rd	Win & Pl
Career Total (Turf)	7	2	2	0	45010

100	6/01	Asct	5f	B	G-F	£20300
76	5/01	Hayd	5f	E	G-F	£3360

Total win prize-money £23660

Going (Turf): Sf: 0-0 GS: 0-1 Gd: 0-2 **GF: 2-4** Fm: 0-0
Distance: **5f/6f: 2-6** 7f-8f: 0-1 9f-13f: 0-0 14f+: 0-0
Track : LH: 0-0 RH: 0-0 Tight: 0-0 Gall: 0-0
Aids: Bl: 0-0 Vi: 0-0 Tstrap: 0-0
Best Rating: 100 6/01 Asct 5f gd-fm

He looked in need of the run when winning with a bit to spare at Haydock on his debut and earned his big pay-day by winning the Windsor Castle at Ascot on his second start. He ran a close second in the Molecomb, but disappointed twice before a much better run over six furlongs in the Mill Reef. He looks to need genuinely fast ground.

Iroquois Chief (USA)

85 **67+**

2-y-o b c Known Fact (USA)-Celtic Shade (Lomond (USA))
M L W Bell Mrs Maureen Buckley

Placings:604 **(4801)**
2001: 6^{6}G, 7^{0}S, 5^{4}F

	Starts	1st	2nd	3rd	Win & Pl
Career Total (Turf)	3	0	0	0	311

Going (Turf): Sf: 0-1 GS: 0-0 Gd: 0-1 GF: 0-0 Fm: 0-1
Distance: 5f/6f: 0-2 7f-8f: 0-1 9f-13f: 0-0 14f+: 0-0
Track : LH: 0-1 RH: 0-1 Tight: 0-0 Gall: 0-0
Aids: Bl: 0-0 Vi: 0-0 Tstrap: 0-0
Best Rating: 67 9/01 Pont 5f firm

Showed little on his first two runs, but ran an eyecatching race on his third start where he hung left-handed throughout.

Irrevocable (IRE)

74 **38**

2-y-o b f Revoque (IRE)-Nellie's Away (IRE) (Magical Strike (USA))
N A Graham Matthews Breeding And Racing

Placings:00 **(5520)**
2001: 7^{0}GS, 8^{0}HY

	Starts	1st	2nd	3rd	Win & Pl
Career Total (Turf)	2	0	0	0	

Going (Turf): Sf: 0-1 GS: 0-1 Gd: 0-0 GF: 0-0 Fm: 0-0
Distance: 5f/6f: 0-0 7f-8f: 0-1 9f-13f: 0-1 14f+: 0-0
Track : LH: 0-0 RH: 0-1 Tight: 0-1 Gall: 0-0
Aids: Bl: 0-0 Vi: 0-0 Tstrap: 0-0
Best Rating: 38 10/01 Wind 1m67y heavy

Irsal

(100) (9)**15**

7-y-o ch g Nashwan (USA)-Amwag (USA) (El Gran Senor (USA))
D W Chapman David W Chapman

Placings:5/63363146/205060050/302000000-0600 **(0496)**
2001: 12^{0}SD, 11^{6}SD, 11^{0}SD, 8^{0}SD

	Starts	1st	2nd	3rd	Win & Pl
Career Total (Turf)	17	1	1	3	8435
Career Total (AW)	14	0	1	1	784

73	7/97	Sals	1m4f	D(0-85)H	G-F	£3730

Total win prize-money £3730

Going (Turf): Sf: 0-2 GS: 0-2 Gd: 0-2 **GF: 1-9** Fm: 0-2
Distance: 5f/6f: 0-0 7f-8f: 0-2 **9f-13f: 1-25** 14f+: 0-4
Track : LH: 0-20 **RH: 1-10 Tight: 1-14** Gall: 0-0
Aids: Bl: 0-10 Vi: 0-0 Tstrap: 0-0
Best Rating: 9 2/01 Sthl 1m3f stand

Irvington (IRE)

96 **77**

3-y-o br c Lahib (USA)-Snoozy Time (Cavo Doro)
R Hannon J A Lazzari

Placings:040515050 **(5688)**
2001: 7^{0}GF, 8^{4}GF, 8^{0}GF, 7^{5}GF, 9^{1}GF, 10^{5}G, 8^{0}GF, 8^{5}G, 7^{0}S

	Starts	1st	2nd	3rd	Win & Pl
Career Total (Turf)	9	1	0	0	6045

77 8/01 Newb 1m1f D G-F £6045
Total win prize-money £6045

Going (Turf): Sf: 0-1 GS: 0-0 Gd: 0-2 **GF: 1-6** Fm: 0-0
Distance: 5f/6f: 0-0 7f-8f: 0-7 **9f-13f: 1-2** 14f+: 0-0
Track : **LH: 1-2** RH: 0-3 Tight: 0-0 **Gall: 1-1**
Aids: Bl: 0-0 Vi: 0-0 Tstrap: 0-0
Best Rating: 77 9/01 Asct 1m good

He had already been well beaten in a handicap before getting off the mark in a maiden at Newbury in August 2001, but it looked a very weak event for the track, and he has since been well beaten in handicaps. Suited by nine furlongs and acts on good to firm.

Is Wonderful (USA)

103 **83**

3-y-o ch c Diesis-Falling In Love (IRE) (Sadler's Wells (USA))
Mrs A J Perrett Seymour Cohn

Placings:0-20210503 **(5039)**
2001: 10^{2}GS, 10^{0}S, 11^{2}G, 14^{1}G, 14^{0}G, 13^{5}G, 14^{0}HY, 17^{3}G

	Starts	1st	2nd	3rd	Win & Pl
Career Total (Turf)	9	1	2	1	8122

81 6/01 Yarm 1m6f17y D GD £4030
Total win prize-money £4030

Going (Turf): Sf: 0-3 GS: 0-1 **Gd: 1-5** GF: 0-0 Fm: 0-0
Distance: 5f/6f: 0-0 7f-8f: 0-1 9f-13f: 0-3 **14f+: 1-5**
Track : **LH: 1-6** RH: 0-1 **Tight: 1-5** Gall: 0-2
Aids: Bl: 0-0 Vi: 0-0 **Tstrap: 1-6**
Best Rating: 83 6/01 Bath 1m3f144y good

Showed his appreciation for fast ground and a tongue tie when getting off the mark at Yarmouth over fourteen furlongs. Held since.

Isabella D'Este (IRE)

102 **69**

3-y-o ch f Irish River (FR)-Vienna Charm (IRE) (Sadler's Wells (USA))
P W Harris Mrs A M Palmer & Mrs P W Harris

Placings:66404 **(4477)**
2001: 8^{6}G, 10^{6}GF, 9^{4}GF, 10^{0}G, 12^{4}F

	Starts	1st	2nd	3rd	Win & Pl
Career Total (Turf)	5	0	0	0	342

Going (Turf): Sf: 0-0 GS: 0-0 Gd: 0-2 GF: 0-2 Fm: 0-1
Distance: 5f/6f: 0-0 7f-8f: 0-0 9f-13f: 0-5 14f+: 0-0
Track : LH: 0-2 RH: 0-1 Tight: 0-1 Gall: 0-1
Aids: Bl: 0-0 Vi: 0-0 Tstrap: 0-0
Best Rating: 69 7/01 Kemp 1m2f gd-fm

Isadora

112 **103**

4-y-o b f Sadler's Wells (USA)-Ahead (Shirley Heights)
L M Cumani Gerald W Leigh - Cancer Bacup

Placings:1-204242 **(5680a)**
2001: 11^{2}GF, 11^{0}G, 14^{4}GF, 12^{2}G, 12^{4}GS, 12^{2}S

	Starts	1st	2nd	3rd	Win & Pl
Career Total (Turf)	7	1	3	0	28919

85 9/00 Chep 1m4f23y D G-S £4182
Total win prize-money £4183

Going (Turf): Sf: 0-1 **GS: 1-2** Gd: 0-2 GF: 0-2 Fm: 0-0
Distance: 5f/6f: 0-0 7f-8f: 0-0 **9f-13f: 1-6** 14f+: 0-1
Track : **LH: 1-3** RH: 0-3 Tight: 0-1 Gall: 0-4
Aids: Bl: 0-0 Vi: 0-0 Tstrap: 0-0
Best Rating: 103 9/01 Asct 1m4f good

She came back from a ten-month layoff when beaten a head at Windsor in July. She was not beaten far when stepped up to an extended one mile six furlongs in September and ran a decent race at Ascot. Suited by 11 to 14 furlongs and handles any ground.

Ischia

97 **64**

2-y-o ch f Lion Cavern (USA)-Royal Passion (Ahonoora)
M Johnston J R Good

Placings:6340 **(4941)**
2001: 7^{6}G, 7^{3}GF, 7^{4}HY, 7^{0}S

	Starts	1st	2nd	3rd	Win & Pl
Career Total (Turf)	4	0	0	1	956

Going (Turf): Sf: 0-2 GS: 0-0 Gd: 0-1 GF: 0-1 Fm: 0-0
Distance: 5f/6f: 0-0 7f-8f: 0-4 9f-13f: 0-0 14f+: 0-0
Track : LH: 0-3 RH: 0-1 Tight: 0-2 Gall: 0-0
Aids: Bl: 0-0 Vi: 0-0 Tstrap: 0-0
Best Rating: 64 8/01 Bevl 7f100y gd-fm

Ishaam

96 **67**

3-y-o ch f Selkirk (USA)-Elaine's Honor (USA) (Chief's Crown (USA))
Sir Michael Stoute Hamdan Al Maktoum

Placings:0-4301 **(3576)**
2001: 8^{4}GF, 9^{3}GF, 10^{0}G, 8^{1}GF

	Starts	1st	2nd	3rd	Win & Pl
Career Total (Turf)	5	1	0	1	4765

52 8/01 Wwck 1m22y D(0-75) G-F £4004
Total win prize-money £4004

Going (Turf): Sf: 0-1 GS: 0-0 Gd: 0-1 **GF: 1-3** Fm: 0-0
Distance: 5f/6f: 0-0 7f-8f: 0-2 **9f-13f: 1-3** 14f+: 0-0
Track : LH: 0-1 RH: 0-1 Tight: 0-3 Gall: 0-0
Aids: Bl: 0-0 Vi: 0-0 Tstrap: 0-0
Best Rating: 67 6/01 Wind 1m2f7y good

Ishiguru (USA)

109 **115+**

3-y-o b c Danzig (USA)-Strategic Maneuver (USA) (Cryptoclearance (USA))
A P O'Brien Mrs John Magnier

Placings:21-2020110 **(5244a)**
2001: 5^{2}Y, 5^{0}G, 5^{2}Y, 6^{0}G, 6^{1}GY, 5^{1}G, 5^{0}HO

	Starts	1st	2nd	3rd	Win & Pl
Career Total (Turf)	9	3	3	0	100866

115 9/01 Leop 5f GD £45650
110 8/01 Curr 6f G-Y £26000
104 10/00 Naas 6f YLD £9660
Total win prize-money £81310

Going (Turf): Sf: 0-1 GS: 0-0 **Gd: 1-3** GF: 0-0 Fm: 0-0
Distance: **5f/6f: 3-9** 7f-8f: 0-0 9f-13f: 0-0 14f+: 0-0
Track : LH: 0-0 RH: 0-0 Tight: 0-0 Gall: 0-0
Aids: Bl: 0-0 Vi: 0-0 Tstrap: 0-0
Best Rating: 115 9/01 Leop 5f good

Cost over $1m as a yearling. Regarded a potential top sprinter, he did not look up to that level at Royal Ascot or Newmarket but did score at the Curragh in August and Leopardstown in September. Seems best suited by an easy surface.

Iskan (GER)

62

6-y-o b g Perceive Arrogance (USA)-Ifakara (GER) (Athenagoras (GER))
J J O'Neill H Henderson

Placings:0/0 **(1133)**
2001: 8^{0}GS

	Starts	1st	2nd	3rd	Win & Pl
Career Total (Turf)	2	0	0	0	

Going (Turf): Sf: 0-0 GS: 0-1 Gd: 0-0 GF: 0-0 Fm: 0-0
Distance: 5f/6f: 0-0 7f-8f: 0-0 9f-13f: 0-1 14f+: 0-0
Track : LH: 0-0 RH: 0-1 Tight: 0-1 Gall: 0-0
Aids: Bl: 0-0 Vi: 0-0 Tstrap: 0-0

Island Destiny

94 **88+**

2-y-o ch f Kris-Balnaha (Lomond (USA))
G Wragg The Eclipse Partnership - 2

Placings:30 **(5594)**
2001: 6^{3}G, 6^{0}GS

	Starts	1st	2nd	3rd	Win & Pl
Career Total (Turf)	2	0	0	1	708

Going (Turf): Sf: 0-0 GS: 0-1 Gd: 0-1 GF: 0-0 Fm: 0-0
Distance: 5f/6f: 0-2 7f-8f: 0-0 9f-13f: 0-0 14f+: 0-0
Track : LH: 0-0 RH: 0-0 Tight: 0-0 Gall: 0-0
Aids: Bl: 0-0 Vi: 0-0 Tstrap: 0-0
Best Rating: 88 9/01 Kemp 6f good

An extravagant-actioned sister to Coronation Stakes winner Balisada from the family of Inchinor, finished well after an interrupted run on her debut and will be suited by further.

Island Flight

(78) (30)

2-y-o b f Missed Flight-Island Mead (Pharly (FR))
C W Thornton The Challengers

Placings:000500 **(5396)**
2001: 5^{0}S, 6^{0}G, 7^{0}GF, 7^{5}G, 8^{0}S, 8^{0}SD, 8^{0}SD

	Starts	1st	2nd	3rd	Win & Pl
Career Total (Turf)	5	0	0	0	
Career Total (AW)	1	0	0	0	

Going (Turf): Sf: 0-2 GS: 0-0 Gd: 0-2 GF: 0-1 Fm: 0-0
Distance: 5f/6f: 0-2 7f-8f: 0-2 9f-13f: 0-2 14f+: 0-0
Track : LH: 0-3 RH: 0-0 Tight: 0-2 Gall: 0-0
Aids: Bl: 0-0 Vi: 0-0 Tstrap: 0-0
Best Rating: 60 8/01 Thsk 7f good

Island House (IRE)

113 **117**

5-y-o ch h Grand Lodge (USA)-Fortitude (IRE) (Last Tycoon)
G Wragg Mollers Racing

Placings:04/0424112/1115414-0123364 **(5132)**
2001: 12^{0}G, 10^{1}S, 10^{2}GF, 10^{3}G, 10^{3}GS, 10^{6}VS, 12^{4}G

	Starts	1st	2nd	3rd	Win & Pl
Career Total (Turf)	23	7	3	2	122486

117 4/01 Sand 1m2f7y A SFT £24000
117 9/00 Ayr 1m2f192yA SFT £13641
115 6/00 Kemp 1m2f A G-F £14235
114 5/00 Gdwd 1m1f192yA SFT £22750
117 5/00 NmkR 1m2f B GD £10150
93 10/99 Ayr 1m C SFT £5968
82 9/99 Pont 1m4y D(0-80) G-F £4279
Total win prize-money £95026

Going (Turf): Sf: 4-6 GS: 0-2 Gd: 1-8 GF: 2-5 Fm: 0-1
Distance: 5f/6f: 0-0 7f-8f: 1-7 **9f-13f: 6-16** 14f+: 0-0
Track : LH: 3-12 RH: 3-4 Tight: 1-3 Gall: 1-7
Aids: Bl: 0-0 Vi: 0-0 Tstrap: 0-0
Best Rating: 117 6/01 Lonc 1m2f good

A decent Listed race performer from a mile to ten furlongs. He has a good wins to runs record and should have won at Chester in May, but his rider dropped his hands. Has run well without out winning since. Suited by most types of ground.

Island Light

100 **76+**

3-y-o b g Inchinor-Miss Prism (Niniski (USA))
A C Stewart Gibson, Goddard, Hamer & Hawkes

Placings:021 **(5528)**
2001: 8^0GF, 8^2GS, 8^1HY

	Starts	1st	2nd	3rd	Win & Pl
Career Total (Turf)	3	1	1	0	5379

76 10/01 Nott 1m54y D HVY £4264
Total win prize-money £4264

Going (Turf): Sf: 1-1 GS: 0-1 Gd: 0-0 GF: 0-1 Fm: 0-0
Distance: 5f/6f: 0-0 7f-8f: 0-0 **9f-13f: 1-3** 14f+: 0-0
Track : **LH: 1-2** RH: 0-0 Tight: 0-0 Gall: 0-0
Aids: Bl: 0-0 Vi: 0-0 Tstrap: 0-0
Best Rating: 76 10/01 Nott 1m54y heavy

Enjoyed the testing conditions when getting off the mark at Nottingham on his third start.

Island Mint (USA)

99 **80**

2-y-o b f Hennessy (USA)-Mintecy (USA) (Key To The Mint (USA))
B J Meehan John C Roberts A O

Placings:0650 **(4716)**
2001: 6^0G, 6^6GF, 6^5GF, 7^0G

	Starts	1st	2nd	3rd	Win & Pl
Career Total (Turf)	4	0	0	0	292

Going (Turf): Sf: 0-0 GS: 0-0 Gd: 0-2 GF: 0-2 Fm: 0-0
Distance: 5f/6f: 0-2 7f-8f: 0-2 9f-13f: 0-0 14f+: 0-0
Track : LH: 0-1 RH: 0-0 Tight: 0-1 Gall: 0-0
Aids: Bl: 0-0 Vi: 0-0 Tstrap: 0-0
Best Rating: 80 8/01 Gdwd 6f gd-fm

She has shown ability in good company over six furlongs on fast ground. Will be interesting in handicaps.

Island Of Paradise

88 **61**

2-y-o b f Turtle Island (IRE)-Mighty Squaw (Indian Ridge)
B R Millman Mrs V A Tory

Placings:0550 **(4428)**
2001: 5^0F, 5^5GF, 6^5GF, 7^0G

	Starts	1st	2nd	3rd	Win & Pl
Career Total (Turf)	4	0	0	0	0

Going (Turf): Sf: 0-0 GS: 0-0 Gd: 0-1 GF: 0-2 Fm: 0-1
Distance: 5f/6f: 0-2 7f-8f: 0-2 9f-13f: 0-0 14f+: 0-0
Track : LH: 0-1 RH: 0-1 Tight: 0-0 Gall: 0-1
Aids: Bl: 0-0 Vi: 0-0 Tstrap: 0-0
Best Rating: 61 7/01 Sals 6f212y gd-fm

Island Princess (IRE)

(79) (7)**72**

4-y-o b f Turtle Island (IRE)-Classic Dilemma (Sandhurst Prince)
K O Cunningham-Brown (S C Williams 27/6) Philip J Costello & John F Costello

Placings:50020/5040000-000 **(4606)**
2001: 16^0SD, 9^0HY, 12^0SD

	Starts	1st	2nd	3rd	Win & Pl
Career Total (Turf)	11	0	1	0	1413
Career Total (AW)	4	0	0	0	

Going (Turf): Sf: 0-5 GS: 0-1 Gd: 0-2 GF: 0-3 Fm: 0-0
Distance: 5f/6f: 0-2 7f-8f: 0-3 9f-13f: 0-9 14f+: 0-1
Track : LH: 0-8 RH: 0-5 Tight: 0-2 Gall: 0-4
Aids: Bl: 0-1 Vi: 0-0 Tstrap: 0-0
Best Rating: 30 5/01 Nott 1m1f213y heavy

Island Queen (IRE)

105 **78**

3-y-o b f Turtle Island (IRE)-Holy Devotion (Commanche Run)
R Hannon R A Bernard

Placings:43256-33001 **(3474)**
2001: 8^3GS, 8^3G, 9^0GF, 9^0GF, 10^1GF

	Starts	1st	2nd	3rd	Win & Pl
Career Total (Turf)	10	1	1	3	9502

52 7/01 NmkJ 1m2f E G-F £6873
Total win prize-money £6874

Going (Turf): Sf: 0-2 GS: 0-3 Gd: 0-1 **GF: 1-4** Fm: 0-0
Distance: 5f/6f: 0-1 7f-8f: 0-3 **9f-13f: 1-6** 14f+: 0-0
Track : LH: 0-4 **RH: 1-5** Tight: 0-3 **Gall: 1-4**
Aids: Bl: 0-0 Vi: 0-0 Tstrap: 0-0
Best Rating: 78 5/01 Wind 1m67y gd-sft

Won a claimer at Newmarket in July, but is a quirky filly and not one to trust entirely.

Island Sands (IRE)

121 **116**

5-y-o b/br h Turtle Island (IRE)-Tiavanita (USA) (J O Tobin (USA))
D R Loder Maktoum Al Maktoum

Placings:11/15/2-2310 **(2258)**
2001: 8^2HY, 8^3S, 8^1GF, 8^0G

	Starts	1st	2nd	3rd	Win & Pl
Career Total (Turf)	9	4	2	1	214127

76	5/01	Hayd	1m30y	C	G-F	£6873
118	5/99	NmkJ	1m	A	G-F	£171800
102	9/98	Sals	6f	C	HVY	£4630
102	8/98	Sals	6f	E	G-F	£3779

Total win prize-money £187083

Going (Turf): Sf: 1-3 GS: 0-0 Gd: 0-2 **GF: 3-4** Fm: 0-0
Distance: **5f/6f: 2-2** 7f-8f: 1-5 9f-13f: 1-2 14f+: 0-0
Track : **LH: 1-1** RH: 0-2 Tight: 0-0 Gall: 0-1
Aids: Bl: 0-0 Vi: 0-1 Tstrap: 0-0
Best Rating: 116 4/01 Sand 1m14y soft

Unbeaten in two races at two for David Elsworth, he joined Godolphin afterwards and won the 2000 Guineas in '99. Lightly-raced subsequently, he has run well in Pattern company and gained his first win since the Guineas in a Haydock conditions event. Not as good as he was, he has gone to stud.

Island Sound

113 **101**

4-y-o b g Turtle Island (IRE)-Ballet (Sharrood (USA))
D R C Elsworth Mrs Michael Meredith

Placings:411/253441-443000 **(5132)**
2001: 10^4S, 10^4S, 12^3GS, 12^0VS, 10^0GS, 12^0G

	Starts	1st	2nd	3rd	Win & Pl
Career Total (Turf)	15	3	1	2	37076

114	10/00	NmkR	1m2f	A	SFT	£13224
95	10/99	Newb	1m	C	G-S	£6376
98	9/99	Sals	1m	D	HVY	£3194

Total win prize-money £22794

Going (Turf): Sf: 2-5 GS: 1-4 Gd: 0-3 GF: 0-1 Fm: 0-0
Distance: 5f/6f: 0-0 **7f-8f: 2-4** 9f-13f: 1-11 14f+: 0-0
Track : LH: 0-4 RH: 0-6 Tight: 0-1 Gall: 0-5
Aids: Bl: 0-0 Vi: 0-1 Tstrap: 0-0
Best Rating: 108 4/01 Sand 1m2f7y soft

A winner twice at two, he ran well in Listed company in 2000, and ended the campaign with an impressive victory at that level at Newmarket. Has failed to progress this season. Suited by soft ground.

Island Stream (IRE)

81 **61**

2-y-o b g Turtle Island (IRE)-Tilbrook (IRE) (Don't Forget Me)
J L Eyre The Island Stream Partnership

Placings:060 **(5088)**
2001: 7^0HY, 7^6G, 6^0GS

	Starts	1st	2nd	3rd	Win & Pl
Career Total (Turf)	3	0	0	0	0

Going (Turf): Sf: 0-1 GS: 0-1 Gd: 0-1 GF: 0-0 Fm: 0-0
Distance: 5f/6f: 0-1 7f-8f: 0-2 9f-13f: 0-0 14f+: 0-0
Track : LH: 0-1 RH: 0-1 Tight: 0-0 Gall: 0-0
Aids: Bl: 0-0 Vi: 0-0 Tstrap: 0-0
Best Rating: 61 9/01 Bevl 7f100y good

Island Warrior (IRE)

6-y-o b g Warcraft (USA)-Only Flower (Warpath)
B P J Baugh (George Stewart 10/2) M N Dennis

Placings:5 **(4045)**
2001: 11^5HY

	Starts	1st	2nd	3rd	Win & Pl
Career Total (Turf)	1	0	0	0	271

Going (Turf): Sf: 0-1 GS: 0-0 Gd: 0-0 GF: 0-0 Fm: 0-0
Distance: 5f/6f: 0-0 7f-8f: 0-0 9f-13f: 0-1 14f+: 0-0
Track : LH: 0-1 RH: 0-0 Tight: 0-0 Gall: 0-0
Aids: Bl: 0-0 Vi: 0-0 Tstrap: 0-1

Isle Of Cebu

3

3-y-o b f Aragon-Salala (Connaught)
Miss J A Camacho Mrs S Camacho

Placings:0O **(4553)**
2001: 10^0G, 14^OSW

	Starts	1st	2nd	3rd	Win & Pl
Career Total (Turf)	1	0	0	0	
Career Total (AW)	1	0	0	0	

Going (Turf): Sf: 0-0 GS: 0-0 Gd: 0-1 GF: 0-0 Fm: 0-0
Distance: 5f/6f: 0-0 7f-8f: 0-0 9f-13f: 0-1 14f+: 0-1
Track : LH: 0-2 RH: 0-0 Tight: 0-1 Gall: 0-1
Aids: Bl: 0-0 Vi: 0-0 Tstrap: 0-0
Best Rating: 3 8/01 Newc 1m2f32y good

Islington (IRE)

106 **94**

2-y-o b f Sadler's Wells (USA)-Hellenic (Darshaan)
Sir Michael Stoute Lord Weinstock

Placings:63 **(5144)**
2001: 7^6G, 7^3G

	Starts	1st	2nd	3rd	Win & Pl
Career Total (Turf)	2	0	0	1	2420

Going (Turf): Sf: 0-0 GS: 0-0 Gd: 0-2 GF: 0-0 Fm: 0-0
Distance: 5f/6f: 0-0 7f-8f: 0-2 9f-13f: 0-0 14f+: 0-0
Track : LH: 0-0 RH: 0-0 Tight: 0-0 Gall: 0-0
Aids: Bl: 0-0 Vi: 0-0 Tstrap: 0-0
Best Rating: 94 10/01 NmkR 7f good

A sister to Group One winner Greek Dance, ran a fair race on her debut and will do better when tackling further next year.

Isthereanygoodinu (IRE)

4-y-o ch f Forest Wind (USA)-Solar Flash (IRE) (Shy Groom (USA))
P Howling Paul Howling

Placings:0 **(0447)**
2001: 11^{0}SD

	Starts	1st	2nd	3rd	Win & Pl
Career Total (Turf)	0	0	0	0	
Career Total (AW)	1	0	0	0	

Going (Turf): Sf: 0-0 GS: 0-0 Gd: 0-0 GF: 0-0 Fm: 0-0
Distance: 5f/6f: 0-0 7f-8f: 0-0 9f-13f: 0-1 14f+: 0-0
Track : LH: 0-1 RH: 0-0 Tight: 0-0 Gall: 0-0
Aids: Bl: 0-0 Vi: 0-0 Tstrap: 0-0

Istihsaan (IRE)

106 **63**
3-y-o b g Barathea (IRE)-Ghazwat (USA) (Riverman (USA))
R A Fahey Mrs Janis Macpherson

Placings:56-5001050000 **(5375)**
2001: 8^{5}S, 8^{0}GF, 9^{0}GF, 7^{1}GS, 7^{0}GS, 8^{5}GS, 9^{0}G, 8^{0}HY, 8^{0}GS, 7^{0}G

	Starts	1st	2nd	3rd	Win & Pl
Career Total (Turf)	12	1	0	0	3588

66	7/01	Ayr	7f	E(0-70)H	G-S	£3587

Total win prize-money £3588

Going (Turf): Sf: 0-3 **GS: 1-5** Gd: 0-2 GF: 0-2 Fm: 0-0
Distance: 5f/6f: 0-0 **7f-8f: 1-8** 9f-13f: 0-4 14f+: 0-0
Track : **LH: 1-6** RH: 0-4 Tight: 0-3 Gall: 0-2
Aids: Bl: 0-0 **Vi: 1-6** Tstrap: 0-0
Best Rating: 66 7/01 Ayr 7f gd-sft

Won over seven furlongs at Ayr in July when fitted with a visor for the first time. Likes a strong gallop. He stays a mile, but is unsuited by fast ground.

It Is As It Is

74 **32**
2-y-o b g Aragon-Hatimena (Hatim (USA))
J S Wainwright A D Bottomley

Placings:00 **(5370)**
2001: 5^{0}G, 7^{0}G

	Starts	1st	2nd	3rd	Win & Pl
Career Total (Turf)	2	0	0	0	

Going (Turf): Sf: 0-0 GS: 0-0 Gd: 0-2 GF: 0-0 Fm: 0-0
Distance: 5f/6f: 0-1 7f-8f: 0-1 9f-13f: 0-0 14f+: 0-0
Track : LH: 0-0 RH: 0-0 Tight: 0-0 Gall: 0-0
Aids: Bl: 0-0 Vi: 0-0 Tstrap: 0-0
Best Rating: 32 10/01 Rdcr 7f good

It Was Meant To Be

97 **68**
2-y-o b f Distant Relative-Belle Vue (Petong)
P C Haslam (K T Ivory 3/8) S A B Dinsmore

Placings:021010220 **(5185)**
2001: 5^{0}G, 5^{2}F, 6^{1}GF, 6^{0}GF, 7^{1}F, 7^{0}GS, 8^{2}G, 8^{2}G, 7^{0}GS

	Starts	1st	2nd	3rd	Win & Pl
Career Total (Turf)	9	2	3	0	9240

76	8/01	Thsk	7f	E	FRM	£3737
73	7/01	Ling	6f	E	G-F	£2968

Total win prize-money £6706

Going (Turf): Sf: 0-0 GS: 0-2 Gd: 0-3 **GF: 1-2 Fm: 1-2**
Distance: 5f/6f: 1-3 7f-8f: 1-6 9f-13f: 0-0 14f+: 0-0
Track : **LH: 1-6** RH: 0-2 **Tight: 1-2** Gall: 0-2
Aids: Bl: 0-0 Vi: 0-0 Tstrap: 0-0
Best Rating: 76 8/01 Thsk 7f firm

She won twice on fast ground early in the season and has since showed good form on Fibresand during November. Suited by six or seven furlongs.

It's A Secret

110 **91**
3-y-o b f Polish Precedent (USA)-Secret Obsession (USA) (Secretariat (USA))
W J Haggas Cheveley Park Stud

Placings:510102230 **(5339)**
2001: 7^{5}G, 8^{1}GF, 8^{0}GF, 9^{1}GF, 9^{0}GF, 10^{2}GF, 10^{2}GF, 8^{3}G, 10^{0}GS

	Starts	1st	2nd	3rd	Win & Pl
Career Total (Turf)	9	2	2	1	21749

85	6/01	Newc	1m1f9y	D(0-80)H	G-F	£7020
76	6/01	NmkR	1m	D	G-F	£5005

Total win prize-money £12025

Going (Turf): Sf: 0-0 GS: 0-1 Gd: 0-2 **GF: 2-6** Fm: 0-0
Distance: 5f/6f: 0-0 7f-8f: 1-4 9f-13f: 1-5 14f+: 0-0
Track : **LH: 1-2** RH: 0-2 Tight: 0-0 **Gall: 1-3**
Aids: Bl: 0-0 Vi: 0-0 Tstrap: 0-0
Best Rating: 91 8/01 Newc 1m2f32y gd-fm

Well regarded filly. Scored at Newmarket and Newcastle in June, and subsequently placed in Listed company. Has won over nine furlongs but stays ten. Acts on fast ground.

It's Allowed

88 **40**
4-y-o b f Piccolo-Double Flutter (Beldale Flutter (USA))
T D Barron Ian Armitage

Placings:0543343113220102/0050000-000F **(4859)**
2001: 7^{0}GF, 7^{0}G, 7^{0}GF, 7^{F}GF

	Starts	1st	2nd	3rd	Win & Pl
Career Total (Turf)	27	3	3	4	22546

81	10/99	Catt	7f	D(0-85)H	GD	£4796
78	8/99	Ling	6f	G	GD	£2215
71	7/99	Thsk	7f	E	FRM	£2965

Total win prize-money £9976

Going (Turf): Sf: 0-2 GS: 0-2 **Gd: 2-11** GF: 0-10 Fm: 1-2
Distance: 5f/6f: 1-10 **7f-8f: 2-17** 9f-13f: 0-0 14f+: 0-0
Track : **LH: 2-11** RH: 0-3 **Tight: 2-5** Gall: 0-3
Aids: Bl: 0-0 Vi: 0-0 Tstrap: 0-0
Best Rating: 40 8/01 Catt 7f good

It's Magic

102(102) (59)**66**
5-y-o b g Magic Ring (IRE)-Ryewater Dream (Touching Wood (USA))
B Hanbury Mrs Hazel Barber

Placings:500/006150116/0620660043-344 **(1810)**
2001: 7^{3}G, 8^{4}G, 8^{4}GF

	Starts	1st	2nd	3rd	Win & Pl
Career Total (Turf)	23	3	1	1	13627
Career Total (AW)	2	0	0	1	1027

73	8/99	Leic	1m8y	E(0-70)H	GD	£3311
69	8/99	Leic	1m8y	E(0-70)H	GD	£4042
69	5/99	Newc	1m3y	E(0-70)H	G-F	£2906

Total win prize-money £10259

Going (Turf): Sf: 0-2 GS: 0-3 **Gd: 2-9** GF: 1-8 Fm: 0-1
Distance: 5f/6f: 0-0 7f-8f: 0-11 **9f-13f: 3-14** 14f+: 0-0
Track : LH: 0-11 RH: 0-0 Tight: 0-6 Gall: 0-1
Aids: **Bl: 3-18** Vi: 0-0 Tstrap: 0-0
Best Rating: 61 6/01 NmkR 1m gd-fm

It's Our Secret (IRE)

104(99) (64)**69**
5-y-o ch g Be My Guest (USA)-Lady Dulcinea (ARG) (General (FR))
M H Tompkins Mrs M Barwell

Placings:050/2051600000/240050043146-10120426002 **(5659)**
2001: 7^{1}GS, 7^{0}G, 8^{1}GF, 8^{2}G, 9^{0}GS, 8^{4}GS, 8^{2}GF, 8^{6}G, 8^{0}G, 8^{0}GF, 8^{2}G

	Starts	1st	2nd	3rd	Win & Pl
Career Total (Turf)	31	3	5	0	14459
Career Total (AW)	5	1	0	1	2473

67	6/01	Ayr	1m	F(0-65)H	G-F	£2453
60	5/01	Brig	7f214y	E(0-70)H	G-S	£2891
64	11/00	Ling	1m2f	F(0-60)H	STD	£1820
70	5/99	Nott	1m54y	E(0-70)	FRM	£2966

Total win prize-money £10131

Going (Turf): Sf: 0-1 **GS: 1-8** Gd: 0-7 **GF: 1-14 Fm: 1-1**
Distance: 5f/6f: 0-2 7f-8f: 2-17 9f-13f: 2-17 14f+: 0-0
Track : **LH: 4-17** RH: 0-6 **Tight: 1-10** Gall: 0-0
Aids: Bl: 0-0 Vi: 0-1 Tstrap: 0-0
Best Rating: 69 8/01 Rdcr 1m gd-fm

Winner at Brighton in May and Ayr in June, he is effective over a mile on fast ground. Suited by hold up tactics off a strong pace.

It's Smee Again

91(76) (32)**36**
3-y-o ch f Mizoram (USA)-Mountain Dew (Pharly (FR))
Ronald Thompson B Bruce

Placings:44461000-000000 **(3624)**
2001: 10^{0}SW, 6^{0}S, 6^{0}GF, 5^{0}GF, 6^{0}GF, 6^{0}GF

	Starts	1st	2nd	3rd	Win & Pl
Career Total (Turf)	11	1	0	0	2789
Career Total (AW)	3	0	0	0	

60	8/00	Ripn	6f	F	GD	£2282

Total win prize-money £2282

Going (Turf): Sf: 0-2 GS: 0-0 **Gd: 1-1** GF: 0-7 Fm: 0-1
Distance: **5f/6f: 1-9** 7f-8f: 0-4 9f-13f: 0-1 14f+: 0-0
Track : LH: 0-6 RH: 0-0 Tight: 0-2 Gall: 0-2
Aids: Bl: 0-0 Vi: 0-0 Tstrap: 0-0
Best Rating: 36 6/01 Bevl 5f gd-fm

It's The Limit (USA)

73 **47**
2-y-o b c Boundary (USA)-Beside (USA) (Sportin' Life (USA))
Mrs A J Perrett John E Bodie

Placings:0 **(5056)**
2001: 8^{0}S

	Starts	1st	2nd	3rd	Win & Pl
Career Total (Turf)	1	0	0	0	

Going (Turf): Sf: 0-1 GS: 0-0 Gd: 0-0 GF: 0-0 Fm: 0-0
Distance: 5f/6f: 0-0 7f-8f: 0-1 9f-13f: 0-0 14f+: 0-0
Track : LH: 0-0 RH: 0-0 Tight: 0-0 Gall: 0-0
Aids: Bl: 0-0 Vi: 0-0 Tstrap: 0-0
Best Rating: 47 10/01 NmkR 1m soft

It'safact

98(84) (41)**64**
2-y-o ch f So Factual (USA)-Axed Again (Then Again)
P D Evans J G White

Placings:51136 **(3601)**
2001: 5^{5}SD, 5^{1}GF, 6^{1}GS, 6^{3}GF, 6^{6}G

	Starts	1st	2nd	3rd	Win & Pl
Career Total (Turf)	4	2	0	1	6713
Career Total (AW)	1	0	0	0	0

64	7/01	Ayr	6f	D	G-S	£3822
45	7/01	Bath	5f11y	F	G-F	£2240

Total win prize-money £6062

Going (Turf): Sf: 0-0 **GS: 1-1** Gd: 0-1 **GF: 1-2** Fm: 0-0
Distance: **5f/6f: 2-5** 7f-8f: 0-0 9f-13f: 0-0 14f+: 0-0
Track : **LH: 1-1** RH: 0-0 Tight: 0 0 **Gall: 1-1**
Aids: Bl: 0-0 Vi: 0-0 Tstrap: 0-0
Best Rating: 64 7/01 Ayr 6f gd-sft

Started off in sellers, winning over the minimum trip at Bath, and added to that in an Ayr nursery over six. She did not do badly in similar races afterwards. Acts on any ground.

Italian Affair

98(90) (47)51

3-y-o ch f Fumo Di Londra (IRE)-Sergentti (IRE) (Common Grounds)
A Bailey John A Duffy

Placings:020210504600**064**-0**2**40400 **(3821)**
2001: 6^{0}SW, 6^{2}SW, 5^{4}GF, 5^{0}GF, 5^{4}G, 5^{0}F, 5^{0}SD

	Starts	1st	2nd	3rd	Win & Pl
Career Total (Turf)	16	1	2	0	3711
Career Total (AW)	6	0	1	0	522

53 7/00 Yarm 6f3y G FRM £1897
Total win prize-money £1897

Going (Turf): Sf: 0-1 GS: 0-0 Gd: 0-5 GF: 0-5 **Fm: 1-5**
Distance: 5f/6f: 0-18 **7f-8f: 1-4** 9f-13f: 0-0 14f+: 0-0
Track : LH: 0-10 RH: 0-0 Tight: 0-8 Gall: 0-0
Aids: Bl: 0-0 Vi: 0-0 Tstrap: 0-0
Best Rating: 47 2/01 Ling 6f slow

Italian Counsel (IRE)

(84) (25)35

4-y-o b g Leading Counsel (USA)-Mullaghroe (Tarboosh (USA))
A J Martin (R Hollinshead 27/3) Onurb Draw Syndicate

Placings:0000/000-50000 **(5651a)**
2001: 6^{5}SD, 11^{0}SD, 12^{0}SD, 7^{0}F, 9^{0}HY

	Starts	1st	2nd	3rd	Win & Pl
Career Total (Turf)	8	0	0	0	
Career Total (AW)	4	0	0	0	0

Going (Turf): Sf: 0-2 GS: 0-0 Gd: 0-1 GF: 0-0 Fm: 0-1
Distance: 5f/6f: 0-3 7f-8f: 0-2 9f-13f: 0-7 14f+: 0-0
Track : LH: 0-6 RH: 0-4 Tight: 0-3 Gall: 0-0
Aids: Bl: 0-0 Vi: 0-0 Tstrap: 0-0
Best Rating: 25 3/01 Wolv 1m4f stand

Italian Mist (FR)

92 68

2-y-o b g Forzando-Digamist Girl (IRE) (Digamist (USA))
B J Meehan Thurloe Coolinn

Placings:03 **(3654)**
2001: 5^{0}GF, 5^{3}GF

	Starts	1st	2nd	3rd	Win & Pl
Career Total (Turf)	2	0	0	1	663

Going (Turf): Sf: 0-0 GS: 0-0 Gd: 0-0 GF: 0-2 Fm: 0-0
Distance: 5f/6f: 0-2 7f-8f: 0-0 9f-13f: 0-0 14f+: 0-0
Track : LH: 0-0 RH: 0-1 Tight: 0-0 Gall: 0-1
Aids: Bl: 0-0 Vi: 0-0 Tstrap: 0-0
Best Rating: 68 8/01 Newb 5f34y gd-fm

Italian Symphony (IRE)

87(103) (90)58

7-y-o b g Royal Academy (USA)-Terracotta Hut (Habitat)
J J Quinn Ms Jane Wolff

Placings:545663/2664055206**140106**/**21131521**100343 1034**22112333**1023/**466121435**300244314541441405 52521**0054344150**/**50500**455056351650000**451**-0 **(2042)**
2001: 6^{0}GF

	Starts	1st	2nd	3rd	Win & Pl
Career Total (Turf)	59	5	4	5	24278
Career Total (AW)	59	15	8	9	65605
65 12/00 Sthl 1m	F			STD	£1757
55 8/00 Yarm 7f3y	D(0-80)H			GD	£4062
94 12/99 Sthl 7f	C(0-95)H			SLW	£7132
57 11/99 Muss 1m	E(0-70)H			GD	£2957
48 8/99 Catt 7f	F(0-60)H			FRM	£2717
45 7/99 Wwck 6f168y	F(0-70)H			G-F	£2188
41 6/99 NmkJ 7f	E(0-70)H			G-F	£3566
95 2/99 Wolv 7f	C(0-100)H			STD	£6970
96 2/99 Ling 1m	C			STD	£5497
84 11/98 Ling 7f	D(0-85)			STD	£3485
74 10/98 Wolv 7f	F			STD	£2700
74 9/98 Wolv 6f	E(0-70)H			STD	£3003
73 7/98 Sthl 7f	F			STD	£2056
73 5/98 Sthl 7f	F			STD	£2448
60 4/98 Wolv 6f	G			STD	£1375
67 2/98 Wolv 7f	F			STD	£2085
72 2/98 Ling 7f	F(0-70)H			SLW	£2263
61 2/98 Wolv 6f	F(0-65)			STD	£2316
63 12/97 Ling 7f	E(0-70)H			STD	£2518
60 11/97 Wolv 6f	F(0-60)H			STD	£1932

Total win prize-money £63030

Going (Turf): Sf: 0-6 GS: 0-5 **Gd: 2-14 GF: 2-26** Fm: 1-8
Distance: 5f/6f: 4-13 **7f-8f: 16-81** 9f-13f: 0-24 14f+: 0-0
Track : **LH: 17-83** RH: 1-16 **Tight: 13-66** Gall: 0-1
Aids: Bl: 0-4 **Vi: 20-99** Tstrap: 0-0
Best Rating: 27 6/01 Pont 6f gd-fm

Amazingly tough and genuine, he is no better than fair on the turf and capable of much better form on sand. He has won over a mile, but seven furlongs is by far his best trip.

Itcanbedone Again (IRE)

92 74?

2-y-o b c Sri Pekan (USA)-Maradata (IRE) (Shardari)
R Hollinshead Michael R Oliver

Placings:4335404 **(5115)**
2001: 6^{4}G, 7^{3}GF, 7^{3}G, 6^{5}GS, 7^{4}GS, 6^{0}GS, 9^{4}HY

	Starts	1st	2nd	3rd	Win & Pl
Career Total (Turf)	7	0	0	2	2549

Going (Turf): Sf: 0-1 GS: 0-3 Gd: 0-2 GF: 0-1 Fm: 0-0
Distance: 5f/6f: 0-3 7f-8f: 0-3 9f-13f: 0-1 14f+: 0-0
Track : LH: 0-3 RH: 0-0 Tight: 0-2 Gall: 0-0
Aids: Bl: 0-0 Vi: 0-0 Tstrap: 0-0
Best Rating: 74 7/01 Donc 7f gd-fm

Fair efforts in maiden and nursery company so far. Suited by seven furlongs.

Ithrair (IRE)

96 74

2-y-o ch c Machiavellian (USA)-Saleemah (USA) (Storm Bird (CAN))
J L Dunlop Hamdan Al Maktoum

Placings:3406 **(5340)**
2001: 7^{3}GF, 7^{4}F, 7^{0}GF, 6^{6}GS

	Starts	1st	2nd	3rd	Win & Pl
Career Total (Turf)	4	0	0	1	742

Going (Turf): Sf: 0-0 GS: 0-1 Gd: 0-0 GF: 0-2 Fm: 0-1
Distance: 5f/6f: 0-1 7f-8f: 0-3 9f-13f: 0-0 14f+: 0-0
Track : LH: 0-0 RH: 0-0 Tight: 0-0 Gall: 0-0
Aids: Bl: 0-0 Vi: 0-0 Tstrap: 0-0
Best Rating: 74 9/01 Leic 7f9y gd-fm

A brother to the mile winner Medraar. Has shown good speed over seven furlongs, but missed the break when dropped back in distance. Acts on a sound surface but also handles cut.

Its Ecco Boy

107 75

3-y-o ch g Clantime-Laena (Roman Warrior)
K R Burke Jonathan Cowan

Placings:044-40544300 **(5688)**
2001: 8^{4}GF, 7^{0}GF, 8^{5}F, 6^{4}GS, 7^{4}F, 7^{3}GF, 7^{0}GS, 7^{0}S

	Starts	1st	2nd	3rd	Win & Pl
Career Total (Turf)	11	0	0	1	2223

Going (Turf): Sf: 0-2 GS: 0-2 Gd: 0-1 GF: 0-4 Fm: 0-2
Distance: 5f/6f: 0-2 7f-8f: 0-9 9f-13f: 0-0 14f+: 0-0
Track : LH: 0-5 RH: 0-0 Tight: 0-3 Gall: 0-1
Aids: Bl: 0-0 Vi: 0-0 Tstrap: 0-0
Best Rating: 75 9/01 Ling 7f gd-fm

He is still a maiden, but has run well in maiden and handicap company. Stays a mile but might be better over shorter.

Its Your Bid

105 53

3-y-o b f Dilum (USA)-By Arrangement (IRE) (Bold Arrangement)
S Woodman John Nicholson Auctioneers

Placings:0-000415**4** **(4523)**
2001: 8^{0}GS, 9^{0}GS, 10^{0}GF, 11^{4}GF, 12^{1}GF, 16^{5}GF, 16^{4}GF

	Starts	1st	2nd	3rd	Win & Pl
Career Total (Turf)	8	1	0	0	5051

53 8/01 Epsm 1m4f10y E(0-75)H G-F £5050
Total win prize-money £5051

Going (Turf): Sf: 0-1 GS: 0-2 Gd: 0-0 **GF: 1-5** Fm: 0-0
Distance: 5f/6f: 0-0 7f-8f: 0-1 **9f-13f: 1-5** 14f+: 0-2
Track : **LH: 1-4** RH: 0-2 **Tight: 1-6** Gall: 0-0
Aids: Bl: 0-0 Vi: 0-0 Tstrap: 0-0
Best Rating: 53 8/01 Epsm 1m4f10y gd-fm

Is often slowly away, but she ran a little better when stepped up in trip at Lingfield and confirmed that with a last-gasp victory in a handicap at Epsom in August. The form may not amount to much.

Itsanothergirl

106(86) (27)67

5-y-o b m Reprimand-Tasmim (Be My Guest (USA))
M W Easterby Joanne Widdop And Partners

Placings:6354314/42035/001220-**000000001014** **(5400)**
2001: 8^{0}SW, 8^{0}SW, 8^{0}SD, 8^{0}HY, 12^{0}S, 8^{0}S, 8^{0}GS, 7^{0}GF, 10^{1}HY, 8^{0}G, 10^{1}HY, 10^{4}S

	Starts	1st	2nd	3rd	Win & Pl
Career Total (Turf)	26	4	3	3	20875
Career Total (AW)	4	0	0	0	
60 10/01 Ayr 1m2f	D(0-80)H			HVY	£4176
55 8/01 Hayd 1m2f120y	E(0-70)H			HVY	£3374
72 4/00 Thsk 1m	D(0-80)H			G-S	£4517
74 10/98 Catt 7f	E(0-85)H			SFT	£3233

Total win prize-money £15301

Going (Turf): **Sf: 3-13** GS: 1-3 Gd: 0-2 GF: 0-7 Fm: 0-1
Distance: 5f/6f: 0-3 7f-8f: 2-12 9f-13f: 2-15 14f+: 0-0
Track : **LH: 4-20** RH: 0-5 **Tight: 2-9** Gall: 0-4
Aids: **Bl: 2-4** Vi: 0-0 Tstrap: 0-0
Best Rating: 61 10/01 Pont 1m2f6y soft

An able sort at her best, she stays ten furlongs and likes to get her toe in. Scored at Haydock over ten furlongs in August after an absence of three months. Had similar conditions when successful at Ayr.

Itsfornowt (IRE)

86 52

2-y-o b f Royal Abjar (USA)-Ewar Snowflake (Snow Chief (USA))
D W Barker D W Barker

Placings:00566 **(4184)**
2001: 6^{0}G, 6^{0}GF, 5^{5}GF, 5^{6}G, 5^{6}GF

	Starts	1st	2nd	3rd	Win & Pl
Career Total (Turf)	5	0	0	0	0

Going (Turf): Sf: 0-0 GS: 0-0 Gd: 0-2 GF: 0-3 Fm: 0-0
Distance: 5f/6f: 0-5 7f-8f: 0-0 9f-13f: 0-0 14f+: 0-0
Track : LH: 0-0 RH: 0-0 Tight: 0-0 Gall: 0-0
Aids: Bl: 0-0 Vi: 0-0 Tstrap: 0-0
Best Rating: 52 8/01 Muss 5f good

Itsgottabdun (IRE)

(101) (52d)**58**
4-y-o b g Foxhound (USA)-Lady Ingrid (Taufan (USA))
Andrew Reid A S Reid

Placings:066550203/4406142366430020000-00 **(0070)**
2001: 6^{0}SD, 8^{0}SD

	Starts	1st	2nd	3rd	Win & Pl
Career Total (Turf)	13	0	1	0	545
Career Total (AW)	16	1	2	3	4872

58	2/00	Ling	6f	G	STD	£1867

Total win prize-money £1867

Going (Turf): Sf: 0-2 GS: 0-3 Gd: 0-5 GF: 0-3 Fm: 0-0
Distance: **5f/6f: 1-20** 7f-8f: 0-9 9f-13f: 0-0 14f+: 0-0
Track : **LH: 1-20** RH: 0-3 **Tight: 1-16** Gall: 0-4
Aids: **Bl: 1-13** Vi: 0-1 Tstrap: 0-0
Best Rating: 29 1/01 Ling 1m stand

Ivan's Baby (IRE)

87(84) (38)**57d**
2-y-o b/br f Distinctly North (USA)-Alexander Goddess (IRE) (Alzao (USA))
B A Pearce (R Hannon 31/5) Custom Racing

Placings:2054060 **(2646)**
2001: 5^{2}G, 5^{0}GF, 5^{5}F, 6^{4}GF, 7^{0}F, 5^{6}GF, 5^{0}SD

	Starts	1st	2nd	3rd	Win & Pl
Career Total (Turf)	6	0	1	0	1419
Career Total (AW)	1	0	0	0	

Going (Turf): Sf: 0-0 GS: 0-0 Gd: 0-1 GF: 0-3 Fm: 0-2
Distance: 5f/6f: 0-6 7f-8f: 0-1 9f-13f: 0-0 14f+: 0-0
Track : LH: 0-2 RH: 0-0 Tight: 0-0 Gall: 0-2
Aids: Bl: 0-2 Vi: 0-1 Tstrap: 0-0
Best Rating: 57 5/01 Wwck 5f good

Ivor's Flutter

96 **60**
12-y-o b g Beldale Flutter (USA)-Rich Line (High Line)
D R C Elsworth W I M Perry

Placings:0/641323412/5/014/00/6361340/00/1100000/400/0600 **(4953)**
2001: 16^{0}GF, 14^{6}G, 16^{0}G, 16^{0}GS

	Starts	1st	2nd	3rd	Win & Pl
Career Total (Turf)	39	6	2	4	40636

86	4/98	Sand	2m78y	D(0-85)H	SFT	£5015
84	4/98	Kemp	2m	C(0-100)H	HVY	£10991
84	8/96	Sand	1m6f	D(0-80)H	GD	£3870
79	9/94	Bath	2m1f34y	D(0-80)H	GD	£3712
78	10/92	Asct	1m4f	D H	G-S	£3720
73	6/92	Wind	1m3f135yF	(0-70)H	GD	£2616

Total win prize-money £29925

Going (Turf): Sf: 2-4 GS: 1-11 **Gd: 3-15** GF: 0-7 Fm: 0-2
Distance: 5f/6f: 0-0 7f-8f: 0-1 9f-13f: 2-7 **14f+: 4-31**
Track : LH: 1-11 **RH: 4-25 Tight: 2-11** Gall: 1-16
Aids: Bl: 0-0 Vi: 0-0 Tstrap: 0-0
Best Rating: 60 8/01 Sand 1m6f good

Ivorsagoodun

93 **63**
2-y-o b f Piccolo-Malibasta (Auction Ring (USA))
Mrs P N Dutfield W I M Perry

Placings:06600 **(4725)**
2001: 5^{0}GF, 6^{6}GF, 5^{6}HD, 7^{0}G, 7^{0}GF

	Starts	1st	2nd	3rd	Win & Pl
Career Total (Turf)	5	0	0	0	0

Going (Turf): Sf: 0-0 GS: 0-0 Gd: 0-1 GF: 0-3 Fm: 0-1
Distance: 5f/6f: 0-3 7f-8f: 0-2 9f-13f: 0-0 14f+: 0-0
Track : LH: 0-3 RH: 0-1 Tight: 0-0 Gall: 0-2
Aids: Bl: 0-1 Vi: 0-0 Tstrap: 0-0
Best Rating: 63 6/01 Kemp 6f gd-fm

Showed ability in maiden auction races, but did not get the run of the race when tried over seven on her handicap debut.

Ivory Bay

95 **59**
2-y-o b c Piccolo-Fantasy Racing (IRE) (Tirol)
J Hetherton (I A Balding 1/10) J Hetherton

Placings:20200000 **(5660)**
2001: 6^{2}GF, 6^{0}GF, 5^{2}F, 5^{0}G, 5^{0}F, 6^{0}G, 5^{0}G, 5^{0}G

	Starts	1st	2nd	3rd	Win & Pl
Career Total (Turf)	8	0	2	0	3333

Going (Turf): Sf: 0-0 GS: 0-0 Gd: 0-4 GF: 0-2 Fm: 0-2
Distance: 5f/6f: 0-8 7f-8f: 0-0 9f-13f: 0-0 14f+: 0-0
Track : LH: 0-1 RH: 0-0 Tight: 0-0 Gall: 0-1
Aids: Bl: 0-1 Vi: 0-0 Tstrap: 0-0
Best Rating: 77 6/01 Ling 5f firm

Ivory Dawn

103 **63**
7-y-o b m Batshoof-Cradle Of Love (USA) (Roberto (USA))
K T Ivory Dean Ivory

Placings:036/020050210233020000/505065113340254 0/0060450301133003000/0022403015003020000-000005 **(3011)**
2001: 5^{0}GS, 6^{0}GF, 7^{0}GF, 6^{0}G, 6^{0}GF, 6^{5}GF

	Starts	1st	2nd	3rd	Win & Pl
Career Total (Turf)	81	6	8	11	47528

78	7/00	Ling	6f	D(0-80)H	G-F	£3984
76	7/99	Ling	6f	E(0-70)H	G-F	£3139
67	6/99	Brig	5f213y	E(0-70)H	GD	£3113
72	7/98	Ling	6f	E(0-70)H	G-F	£3287
64	7/98	Brig	5f213y	E(0-70)H	GD	£3165
70	6/97	Gdwd	6f	D(0-75)H	GD	£3882

Total win prize-money £20572

Going (Turf): Sf: 0-13 GS: 0-6 **Gd: 3-27 GF: 3-28** Fm: 0-6
Distance: **5f/6f: 6-64** 7f-8f: 0-16 9f-13f: 0-0 14f+: 0-0
Track : **LH: 2-12** RH: 0-7 Tight: 0-1 Gall: 0-7
Aids: Bl: 0-0 Vi: 0-5 Tstrap: 0-0
Best Rating: 63 5/01 Gdwd 6f gd-fm

Not a great strike rate, but tends to find her best form in the summer and has dropped to a handy mark. Suited by six furlongs and fast ground.

Ivory's Joy

111(89) (85)**95**
6-y-o b m Tina's Pet-Jacqui Joy (Music Boy)
K T Ivory K T Ivory

Placings:0461212413650/0402303326000545/32016200503330120010/56031604501210-0200260060205050 **(5502)**

2001: 5^{0}GS, 5^{2}GS, 5^{0}G, 5^{0}GF, 5^{2}GF, 5^{6}Y, 5^{0}GF, 5^{0}GF, 5^{6}G, 5^{0}G, 5^{2}GF, 5^{0}GS, 5^{5}GF, 5^{0}HO, 5^{5}GS, 5^{0}HY

	Starts	1st	2nd	3rd	Win & Pl
Career Total (Turf)	76	8	11	9	133066
Career Total (AW)	3	1	0	0	7003

106	9/00	Newb	5f34y	A	G-F	£23200
92	8/00	Hayd	5f	C(0-100)H	GD	£14885
83	6/00	Brig	5f59y	D(0-80)H	G-F	£6818
85	11/99	Wolv	5f	C(0-95)H	STD	£7002
76	9/99	Hayd	5f	C(0-90)H	SFT	£11186
74	5/99	Thsk	5f	D(0-80)H	SFT	£4315
73	9/97	Newb	5f34y	C	G-S	£4900
73	6/97	Gdwd	6f	E	SFT	£5287
65	6/97	Gdwd	5f	E	GD	£3427

Total win prize-money £81024

Going (Turf): Sf: 3-11 GS: 1-12 Gd: 2-25 GF: 2-24 Fm: 0-2
Distance: **5f/6f: 9-78** 7f-8f: 0-1 9f-13f: 0-0 14f+: 0-0
Track : **LH: 2-10** RH: 0-6 **Tight: 1-3** Gall: 0-9
Aids: **Bl: 1-4** Vi: 0-0 Tstrap: 0-0
Best Rating: 103 6/01 Epsm 5f gd-fm

Much improved in 2000, gaining a surprise success in Listed company at Newbury. Confirmed promise of that run second time out in 2001, when a game runner-up in Listed fillies' stakes at Bath in May but held since. Handles soft but best form on faster. Usually needs a run or two to hit form.

Izmail (IRE)

98 **93**
2-y-o b c Bluebird (USA)-My-Lorraine (IRE) (Mac's Imp (USA))
E A L Dunlop Mohammed Ali

Placings:51044240 **(4795)**
2001: 5^{5}G, 5^{1}GF, 5^{0}GF, 6^{4}G, 5^{4}G, 5^{2}G, 6^{4}G, 5^{0}G

	Starts	1st	2nd	3rd	Win & Pl
Career Total (Turf)	8	1	1	0	10550

89	6/01	Newc	5f	D	G-F	£2905

Total win prize-money £2905

Going (Turf): Sf: 0-0 GS: 0-0 Gd: 0-6 **GF: 1-2** Fm: 0-0
Distance: **5f/6f: 1-8** 7f-8f: 0-0 9f-13f: 0-0 14f+: 0-0
Track : LH: 0-0 RH: 0-0 Tight: 0-0 Gall: 0-0
Aids: Bl: 0-0 Vi: 0-0 Tstrap: 0-0
Best Rating: 93 8/01 York 5f good

Bred for speed and a close relation to Group Three winning sprinter Catch The Blues, scored in very easy fashion on his second start at two.

Izwah (USA)

95 **89**
2-y-o b f Bahri (USA)-Firdous (Nashwan (USA))
D R Loder Hamdan Al Maktoum

Placings:13 **(2615)**
2001: 5^{1}GF, 6^{3}GF

	Starts	1st	2nd	3rd	Win & Pl
Career Total (Turf)	2	1	0	1	6511

80	5/01	Sand	5f6y	D	G-F	£4231

Total win prize-money £4232

Going (Turf): Sf: 0-0 GS: 0-0 Gd: 0-0 **GF: 1-2** Fm: 0-0
Distance: **5f/6f: 1-2** 7f-8f: 0-0 9f-13f: 0-0 14f+: 0-0
Track : LH: 0-0 RH: 0-0 Tight: 0-0 Gall: 0-0
Aids: Bl: 0-0 Vi: 0-0 Tstrap: 0-0
Best Rating: 89 6/01 NmkJ 6f gd-fm

A debut winner, she won the maiden which her stable won with the high-class two-year-old Blue Duster seven years ago. She is by the champion miler Bahri, out of a daughter of Salsabil. She stretched out well on the ground and, although she will clearly need further in time, this was a pleasing start to her career.

Izzet Muzzy (FR)

104(109) (83)63
3-y-o ch g Piccolo-Texanne (BEL) (Efisio)
R Wilman (C N Kellett 16/3) Century Racing

Placings:50554600050214-22020406140140 **(5671)**
2001: 6^{2}SD, 6^{2}SD, 6^{0}SD, 7^{2}SD, 6^{0}SD, 6^{4}SD, 8^{0}SD, 6^{6}SW, 6^{1}SD, 5^{4}HY, 6^{0}G, 6^{1}SD, 6^{4}SD, 6^{0}HY

	Starts	1st	2nd	3rd	Win & Pl
Career Total (Turf)	10	0	0	0	749
Career Total (AW)	18	3	4	0	11692

83 10/01 Sthl 6f E(0-75)H STD £3532
79 9/01 Wolv 6f E(0-70)H STD £2943
71 12/00 Sthl 6f G STD £1855
Total win prize-money £8332

Going (Turf): Sf: 0-2 GS: 0-3 Gd: 0-2 GF: 0-3 Fm: 0-0
Distance: **5f/6f: 3-19** 7f-8f: 0-7 9f-13f: 0-2 14f+: 0-0
Track : **LH: 3-21** RH: 0-0 **Tight: 1-12** Gall: 0-1
Aids: Bl: 0-0 **Vi: 1-12** Tstrap: 0-0
Best Rating: 83 10/01 Sthl 6f stand

He is a regular on Fibresand and, after changing stables and being gelded, exceeded his previous form when bolting up at Wolverhampton in September. Gained a similar type of victory at Southwell the following month and on both occasions drifted violently to the right in the home straight. Suited by six furlongs and Fibresand.

J M W Turner

100 **85**
2-y-o b c Forzando-Noor El Houdah (IRE) (Fayruz)
N P Littmoden Richard Green (fine Paintings)

Placings:6531004510 **(5140)**
2001: 5^{6}GF, 6^{5}G, 6^{3}GF, 6^{1}G, 6^{0}GF, 6^{0}G, 7^{4}G, 6^{5}G, 6^{1}GF, 6^{0}G

	Starts	1st	2nd	3rd	Win & Pl
Career Total (Turf)	10	2	0	1	18031

85 9/01 Haml 6f5y C G-F £13926
75 6/01 Haml 6f5y F GD £2996
Total win prize-money £16922

Going (Turf): Sf: 0-0 GS: 0-0 **Gd: 1-6 GF: 1-4** Fm: 0-0
Distance: 5f/6f: 0-6 **7f-8f: 2-4** 9f-13f: 0-0 14f+: 0-0
Track : LH: 0-1 RH: 0-0 Tight: 0-1 Gall: 0-0
Aids: **Bl: 1-3** Vi: 0-0 Tstrap: 0-0
Best Rating: 85 9/01 Haml 6f5y gd-fm

Improved with each run before getting off the mark in a novice event at Hamilton in June, and then won a valuable nursery at the same track in September in second-time blinkers, before disappointing in a similar event at Newmarket. Suited by six furlongs and good or fast ground, and is unlikely to get much further.

J R Stevenson (USA)

110 **94**
5-y-o ch g Lyphard (USA)-While It Lasts (USA) (Foolish Pleasure (USA))
P R Webber Claret & Blue Army

Placings:1/355150/0006500-15066000 **(4710)**
2001: 7^{1}GS, 7^{5}S, 8^{0}GS, 8^{6}GF, 8^{6}GF, 8^{0}G, 10^{0}G, 8^{0}G

	Starts	1st	2nd	3rd	Win & Pl
Career Total (Turf)	22	3	0	1	19022

96 4/01 Brig 7f214y C(0-95)H G-S £6955
97 6/99 Gdwd 1m1f192yD G-S £4035
87 9/98 Ches 7f2y D GD £3355
Total win prize-money £14346

Going (Turf): Sf: 0-1 **GS: 2-4** Gd: 1-9 GF: 0-7 Fm: 0-1
Distance: 5f/6f: 0-0 **7f-8f: 2-7** 9f-13f: 1-15 14f+: 0-0
Track : **LH: 2-10** RH: 1-8 **Tight: 2-7** Gall: 0-8
Aids: Bl: 0-0 **Vi: 1-5** Tstrap: 0-0
Best Rating: 97 6/01 Epsm 1m114y gd-fm

He kicked off this season with a fine win over an extended seven furlongs at Brighton and has run well in big handicaps since. Best over a mile, he acts on good and soft ground and is usually held up.

J'Ubio

73 **38**
2-y-o b f Bijou D'Inde-Eternal Triangle (USA) (Barachois (CAN))
B A Pearce Sheridan Racing

Placings:000 **(3867)**
2001: 7^{0}GF, 6^{0}GS, 7^{0}G

	Starts	1st	2nd	3rd	Win & Pl
Career Total (Turf)	3	0	0	0	

Going (Turf): Sf: 0-0 GS: 0-1 Gd: 0-1 GF: 0-1 Fm: 0-0
Distance: 5f/6f: 0-1 7f-8f: 0-2 9f-13f: 0-0 14f+: 0-0
Track : LH: 0-0 RH: 0-1 Tight: 0-0 Gall: 0-1
Aids: Bl: 0-0 Vi: 0-0 Tstrap: 0-0
Best Rating: 38 7/01 Kemp 7f gd-fm

Jabaar (USA)

103 **78**
3-y-o gr c Silver Hawk (USA)-Sierra Madre (FR) (Baillamont (USA))
E A L Dunlop Hamdan Al Maktoum

Placings:51 **(5173)**
2001: 10^{5}GF, 8^{1}GS

	Starts	1st	2nd	3rd	Win & Pl
Career Total (Turf)	2	1	0	0	3624

69 10/01 Pont 1m4y D G-S £3623
Total win prize-money £3624

Going (Turf): Sf: 0-0 **GS: 1-1** Gd: 0-0 GF: 0-1 Fm: 0-0
Distance: 5f/6f: 0-0 7f-8f: 0-0 **9f-13f: 1-2** 14f+: 0-0
Track : **LH: 1-1** RH: 0-1 Tight: 0-0 Gall: 0-1
Aids: Bl: 0-0 Vi: 0-0 Tstrap: 0-0
Best Rating: 78 7/01 Asct 1m2f gd-fm

Jabulani (IRE)

84 **77**
2-y-o b c Marju (IRE)-Houwara (IRE) (Darshaan)
W Jarvis The Jabulani Partnership

Placings:5 **(5107)**
2001: 7^{5}GS

	Starts	1st	2nd	3rd	Win & Pl
Career Total (Turf)	1	0	0	0	0

Going (Turf): Sf: 0-0 GS: 0-1 Gd: 0-0 GF: 0-0 Fm: 0-0
Distance: 5f/6f: 0-0 7f-8f: 0-1 9f-13f: 0-0 14f+: 0-0
Track : LH: 0-0 RH: 0-0 Tight: 0-0 Gall: 0-0
Aids: Bl: 0-0 Vi: 0-0 Tstrap: 0-0
Best Rating: 77 10/01 NmkR 7f gd-sft

Jacana (USA)

88 **77**
3-y-o ch f Woodman (USA)-Storm Teal (USA) (Storm Bird (CAN))
J H M Gosden R E Sangster & Mrs J Magnier

Placings:25-40 **(3421)**
2001: 6^{4}GF, 6^{0}GF

	Starts	1st	2nd	3rd	Win & Pl
Career Total (Turf)	4	0	1	0	1958

Going (Turf): Sf: 0-0 GS: 0-0 Gd: 0-1 GF: 0-3 Fm: 0-0
Distance: 5f/6f: 0-2 7f-8f: 0-2 9f-13f: 0-0 14f+: 0-0
Track : LH: 0-0 RH: 0-0 Tight: 0-0 Gall: 0-0
Aids: Bl: 0-0 Vi: 0-0 Tstrap: 0-2
Best Rating: 67 6/01 Newb 6f8y gd-fm

Jack Carter (IRE)

91 **74**
2-y-o ch c Desert King (IRE)-Miss Garuda (Persian Bold)
M L W Bell Wafic Said & R P B Michaelson

Placings:0 **(4066)**
2001: 7^{0}GF

	Starts	1st	2nd	3rd	Win & Pl
Career Total (Turf)	1	0	0	0	

Going (Turf): Sf: 0-0 GS: 0-0 Gd: 0-0 GF: 0-1 Fm: 0-0
Distance: 5f/6f: 0-0 7f-8f: 0-1 9f-13f: 0-0 14f+: 0-0
Track : LH: 0-0 RH: 0-0 Tight: 0-0 Gall: 0-0
Aids: Bl: 0-0 Vi: 0-0 Tstrap: 0-0
Best Rating: 74 8/01 Newb 7f gd-fm

Jack Dawson (IRE)

108 **71**
4-y-o b g Persian Bold-Dream Of Jenny (Caerleon (USA))
John Berry The Premier Cru

Placings:000/00025012231200-0401310061 **(5033)**
2001: 10^{0}G, 10^{4}GF, 12^{0}F, 15^{1}GF, 14^{3}F, 15^{1}GF, 21^{0}GF, 13^{0}GF, 13^{6}GF, 16^{1}GF

	Starts	1st	2nd	3rd	Win & Pl
Career Total (Turf)	27	5	4	2	43642

65 9/01 Muss 2m C(0-90)H G-F £10237
71 7/01 Ches 1m7f195yD(0-80)H G-F £14560
67 6/01 Ayr 1m7f C(0-90)H G-F £6890
70 8/00 Rdcr 1m6f19y E(0-70)H FRM £3591
66 7/00 Chep 2m49y E(0-75)H G-F £3425
Total win prize-money £38705

Going (Turf): Sf: 0-2 GS: 0-2 Gd: 0-5 **GF: 4-11** Fm: 1-7
Distance: 5f/6f: 0-1 7f-8f: 0-4 9f-13f: 0-7 **14f+: 5-15**
Track : **LH: 4-19** RH: 1-4 **Tight: 3-7** Gall: 0-6
Aids: Bl: 0-0 Vi: 0-0 Tstrap: 0-0
Best Rating: 71 7/01 Ches 1m7f195y gd-fm

A fair staying handicapper, he scored over 15 furlongs at Ayr in June and over a similar trip at Chester before landing a competitve event at Musselburgh.He has quite a useful turn of foot for a stayer and loves fast ground, though he looks best going left-handed.

Jack Flush (IRE)

81 **41?**
7-y-o b g Broken Hearted-Clubhouse Turn (IRE) (King Of Clubs)
M E Sowersby Derek A Smith

Placings:6432050/0063124000/0005000/0/0 **(0705)**
2001: 10^{0}HY

	Starts	1st	2nd	3rd	Win & Pl
Career Total (Turf)	24	1	2	2	10647
Career Total (AW)	2	0	0	0	

64 5/97 Thsk 1m D(0-80)H G-S £7512
Total win prize-money £7512

Going (Turf): Sf: 0-3 **GS: 1-2** Gd: 0-9 GF: 0-5 Fm: 0-4
Distance: 5f/6f: 0-3 **7f-8f: 1-15** 9f-13f: 0-8 14f+: 0-0
Track : **LH: 1-14** RH: 0-4 **Tight: 1-6** Gall: 0-4
Aids: Bl: 0-1 Vi: 0-2 Tstrap: 0-2
Best Rating: 41 4/01 Pont 1m2f6y heavy

Jack The Track (IRE)

98 **84**
2-y-o b g Barathea (IRE)-Babushka (IRE) (Dance Of Life (USA))
J Noseda C Fox

Placings:10 **(5401)**
2001: 8^{1}GF, 8^{0}S

	Starts	1st	2nd	3rd	Win & Pl
Career Total (Turf)	2	1	0	0	4446

80 9/01 Kemp 1m D G-F £4446
Total win prize-money £4446

Going (Turf): Sf: 0-1 GS: 0-0 Gd: 0-0 **GF: 1-1** Fm: 0-0

Distance: 5f/6f: 0-0 **7f-8f: 1-1** 9f-13f: 0-1 14f+: 0-0
Track : LH: 0-1 **RH: 1-1** Tight: 0-0 Gall: 0-0
Aids: Bl: 0-0 Vi: 0-0 Tstrap: 0-0
Best Rating: 84 10/01 Pont 1m4y soft

He made a winning debut in a Kempton maiden, but it did not look a strong heat.

Jack To A King

90(107) (50)**31**
6-y-o b g Nawwar-Rudda Flash (General David)
M J Polglase M J Polglase

Placings:600/00506/152021200000000-24250600660 **(4466)**
2001: 5^{2}SD, 5^{4}SD, 5^{2}SW, 7^{5}SD, 5^{0}SD, 5^{6}SD, 5^{0}SD, 5^{0}SD, 5^{6}GF, 5^{6}SD, 5^{0}G

	Starts	1st	2nd	3rd	Win & Pl		
Career Total (Turf)	11	0	0	0	0		
Career Total (AW)	23	2	5	0	7898		
54	2/00	Wolv	5f	E(0-70)H		STD	£2213
49	1/00	Wolv	5f	F(0-60)H		STD	£2173

Total win prize-money £4387

Going (Turf): Sf: 0-2 GS: 0-0 Gd: 0-3 GF: 0-5 Fm: 0-1
Distance: 5f/6f: 2-29 7f-8f: 0-4 9f-13f: 0-1 14f+: 0-0
Track : LH: 2-20 RH: 0-1 **Tight: 2-16** Gall: 0-1
Aids: Bl: 2-23 Vi: 0-1 Tstrap: 1-10
Best Rating: 55 2/01 Wolv 5f slow

Jackerin (IRE)

102(107) (61)**54**
6-y-o b g Don't Forget Me-Meanz Beanz (High Top)
Miss J F Craze Holgate Racing Club

Placings:1130020/0002204034254410/000050500/655 4406640002045632-051242416P **(1962)**
2001: 5^{0}SD, 5^{5}SD, 6^{1}SD, 6^{2}SD, 5^{4}SD, 5^{2}SD, 6^{4}G, 5^{1}GF, 5^{6}F, 5^{P}GF

	Starts	1st	2nd	3rd	Win & Pl		
Career Total (Turf)	50	4	5	2	20991		
Career Total (AW)	11	1	3	1	3908		
50	5/01	Haml	5f4y	F(0-60)H		G-F	£3402
50	3/01	Ling	6f	G		STD	£1848
66	10/98	Ayr	5f	E(0-70)H		G-S	£2999
79	5/97	Donc	5f	D		GD	£3318
63	3/97	Donc	5f	F		G-F	£2511

Total win prize-money £14079

Going (Turf): Sf: 0-8 GS: 1-6 Gd: 1-12 **GF: 2-21** Fm: 0-3
Distance: 5f/6f: 5-58 7f-8f: 0-3 9f-13f: 0-0 14f+: 0-0
Track : LH: 1-18 RH: 0-1 **Tight: 1-7** Gall: 0-2
Aids: Bl: 3-40 Vi: 0-8 Tstrap: 0-2
Best Rating: 61 3/01 Ling 6f stand

Jackie's Baby

91(103) (73d)**77d**
5-y-o b g Then Again-Guarded Expression (Siberian Express (USA))
W G M Turner D & J Racing

Placings:431315312/0020002310/**0400**045400400-00 **(1459)**
2001: 5^{0}GF, 5^{0}G

	Starts	1st	2nd	3rd	Win & Pl		
Career Total (Turf)	24	2	2	3	18793		
Career Total (AW)	10	2	1	1	13027		
84	7/99	Bath	5f11y	C(0-90)H		FRM	£6710
84	8/98	Folk	5f	D H		G-F	£3622
76	7/98	Sthl	5f	E H		STD	£2924
68	5/98	Sthl	5f	F		STD	£2427

Total win prize-money £15684

Going (Turf): Sf: 0-0 GS: 0-1 Gd: 0-9 **GF: 1-11 Fm: 1-3**
Distance: 5f/6f: 4-34 7f-8f: 0-0 9f-13f: 0-0 14f+: 0-0
Track : LH: 1-19 RH: 0-1 Tight: 0-12 **Gall: 1-7**
Aids: Bl: 0-0 Vi: 0-0 Tstrap: 0-0
Best Rating: 56 5/01 Bath 5f11y good

Jacks Birthday (IRE)

98(65) **61d**
3-y-o b g Mukaddamah (USA)-High Concept (IRE) (Thatching)
R J O'Sullivan Jack Joseph

Placings:0500-0050 **(3808)**
2001: 6^{0}SD, 8^{0}GF, 10^{5}GF, 11^{0}GF

	Starts	1st	2nd	3rd	Win & Pl
Career Total (Turf)	7	0	0	0	0
Career Total (AW)	1	0	0	0	

Going (Turf): Sf: 0-1 GS: 0-1 Gd: 0-1 GF: 0-4 Fm: 0-0
Distance: 5f/6f: 0-5 7f-8f: 0-0 9f-13f: 0-3 14f+: 0-0
Track : LH: 0-3 RH: 0-1 Tight: 0-2 Gall: 0-0
Aids: Bl: 0-2 Vi: 0-0 Tstrap: 0-0
Best Rating: 50 7/01 Wwck 1m2f188y gd-fm

Jacksmiles

76(65) (1)**34**
2-y-o b c Puissance-Cassiar (Connaught)
J J Bridger Jack Farley

Placings:0000P0 **(4524)**
2001: 5^{0}S, 6^{0}GF, 5^{0}SD, 7^{0}G, 7^{P}GF, 6^{0}GF

	Starts	1st	2nd	3rd	Win & Pl
Career Total (Turf)	5	0	0	0	
Career Total (AW)	1	0	0	0	

Going (Turf): Sf: 0-1 GS: 0-0 Gd: 0-1 GF: 0-3 Fm: 0-0
Distance: 5f/6f: 0-4 7f-8f: 0-2 9f-13f: 0-0 14f+: 0-0
Track : LH: 0-2 RH: 0-0 Tight: 0-2 Gall: 0-0
Aids: Bl: 0-1 Vi: 0-0 Tstrap: 0-0
Best Rating: 34 9/01 Ling 6f gd-fm

Jacmar (IRE)

98 **24**
6-y-o br g High Estate-Inseyab (Persian Bold)
Miss L A Perratt Sutherland-Hay

Placings:21221410/40030000200/00304143550060000 0000/2641052103000005-000000540660605 **(4466)**
2001: 5^{0}S, 7^{0}GF, 6^{0}GF, 5^{0}G, 5^{0}GF, 6^{0}GF, 6^{5}GS, 6^{4}G, 5^{0}GF, 6^{6}G, 7^{6}GF, 7^{0}GS, 6^{6}GS, 5^{0}S, 5^{5}G

	Starts	1st	2nd	3rd	Win & Pl		
Career Total (Turf)	71	6	6	4	43372		
48	6/00	Haml	6f5y	D(0-80)H		G-F	£4043
47	5/00	Haml	5f4y	F(0-65)H		G-F	£2565
60	6/99	Haml	5f4y	E(0-70)H		G-S	£2827
93	9/97	Haml	6f5y	C		GD	£8335
81	8/97	Haml	6f5y	E		GD	£3241
79	6/97	Haml	6f5y	F		G-F	£2528

Total win prize-money £23540

Going (Turf): Sf: 0-16 GS: 1-12 Gd: 2-15 **GF: 3-20** Fm: 0-6
Distance: 5f/6f: 2-28 **7f-8f: 4-38** 9f-13f: 0-4 14f+: 0-0
Track : LH: 0-5 RH: 0-11 Tight: 0-8 Gall: 0-3
Aids: Bl: 0-0 Vi: 0-0 Tstrap: 0-0
Best Rating: 30 6/01 Haml 6f5y gd-sft

A modest sprint handicapper who does not let the grass grow under his feet, all six of his wins to date have come at Hamilton, a course on which he does most of his running. On the decline.

Jade Tiger

97(93) (31)**43**
5-y-o ch g Lion Cavern (USA)-Precious Jade (Northfields (USA))
F Jordan Miss Laura Jordan

Placings:62630/003120320460/**0406**-**00**0040403 **(4672)**
2001: 12^{0}SD, 8^{0}SD, 8^{0}GS, 8^{0}GF, 8^{4}G, 11^{0}GF, 9^{4}SD, 10^{0}GF, 8^{3}G

	Starts	1st	2nd	3rd	Win & Pl		
Career Total (Turf)	23	1	3	4	7625		
Career Total (AW)	7	0	0	0	0		
58	6/99	Leic	1m8y	F		GD	£2574

Total win prize-money £2574

Going (Turf): Sf: 0-1 GS: 0-5 **Gd: 1-7** GF: 0-9 Fm: 0-1
Distance: 5f/6f: 0-2 7f-8f: 0-5 **9f-13f: 1-23** 14f+: 0-0
Track : LH: 0-13 RH: 0-3 Tight: 0-12 Gall: 0-0
Aids: Bl: 0-1 Vi: 0-0 Tstrap: 0-0
Best Rating: 45 7/01 Chep 1m14y good

Jade Warrior

91 **73**
2-y-o b c Sabrehill (USA)-Jade Pet (Petong)
P Howling J Hammond

Placings:606 **(5682)**
2001: 7^{6}S, 7^{0}GF, 7^{6}S

	Starts	1st	2nd	3rd	Win & Pl
Career Total (Turf)	3	0	0	0	166

Going (Turf): Sf: 0-2 GS: 0-0 Gd: 0-0 GF: 0-1 Fm: 0-0
Distance: 5f/6f: 0-0 7f-8f: 0-3 9f-13f: 0-0 14f+: 0-0
Track : LH: 0-1 RH: 0-1 Tight: 0-0 Gall: 0-1
Aids: Bl: 0-0 Vi: 0-0 Tstrap: 0-0
Best Rating: 73 11/01 Donc 7f soft

Jade's Promise

86 **61**
2-y-o b g Definite Article-Zacinta (USA) (Hawkster (USA))
J R Best Alan Turner

Placings:060 **(4443)**
2001: 7^{0}G, 6^{6}G, 7^{0}G

	Starts	1st	2nd	3rd	Win & Pl
Career Total (Turf)	3	0	0	0	0

Going (Turf): Sf: 0-0 GS: 0-0 Gd: 0-3 GF: 0-0 Fm: 0-0
Distance: 5f/6f: 0-0 7f-8f: 0-3 9f-13f: 0-0 14f+: 0-0
Track : LH: 0-0 RH: 0-1 Tight: 0-0 Gall: 0-0
Aids: Bl: 0-0 Vi: 0-0 Tstrap: 0-0
Best Rating: 61 9/01 Sand 7f16y good

Jadeeron

87 **65+**
2-y-o b c Green Desert (USA)-Rain And Shine (FR) (Rainbow Quest (USA))
B Hanbury A Merza

Placings:000 **(3960)**
2001: 6^{0}GF, 7^{0}GF, 6^{0}G

	Starts	1st	2nd	3rd	Win & Pl
Career Total (Turf)	3	0	0	0	

Going (Turf): Sf: 0-0 GS: 0-0 Gd: 0-1 GF: 0-2 Fm: 0-0
Distance: 5f/6f: 0-1 7f-8f: 0-2 9f-13f: 0-0 14f+: 0-0
Track : LH: 0-0 RH: 0-0 Tight: 0-0 Gall: 0-0
Aids: Bl: 0-1 Vi: 0-0 Tstrap: 0-1
Best Rating: 65 6/01 NmkJ 6f gd-fm

Jahangir

90 **66**
2-y-o b c Zamindar (USA)-Imperial Jade (Lochnager)
W R Muir Perspicacious Punters Racing Club

Placings:60 **(3242)**
2001: 5^{6}GF, 5^{0}GF

	Starts	1st	2nd	3rd	Win & Pl
Career Total (Turf)	2	0	0	0	0

Going (Turf): Sf: 0-0 GS: 0-0 Gd: 0-0 GF: 0-2 Fm: 0-0
Distance: 5f/6f: 0-2 7f-8f: 0-0 9f-13f: 0-0 14f+: 0-0
Track: LH: 0-0 RH: 0-0 Tight: 0-0 Gall: 0-0
Aids: Bl: 0-0 Vi: 0-0 Tstrap: 0-0
Best Rating: 66 7/01 Newb 5f34y gd-fm

Jahash

105(75) (41)**48**
3-y-o ch g Hernando (FR)-Jalsun (Jalmood (USA))
Sir Mark Prescott J Hawkins

Placings:000-030214 **(4858)**
2001: 12^0GF, 12^3GS, 14^0GF, 16^2GF, 16^1GF, 15^4GF

	Starts	1st	2nd	3rd	Win & Pl
Career Total (Turf)	6	1	1	1	3560
Career Total (AW)	3	0	0	0	

48 8/01 Chep 2m49y F(0-60)H G-F £2394
Total win prize-money £2394

Going (Turf): Sf: 0-0 GS: 0-1 Gd: 0-0 **GF: 1-5** Fm: 0-0
Distance: 5f/6f: 0-0 7f-8f: 0-2 9f-13f: 0-3 **14f+: 1-4**
Track: **LH: 1-5** RH: 0-3 Tight: 0-6 Gall: 0-0
Aids: **Bl: 1-3** Vi: 0-0 Tstrap: 0-0
Best Rating: 48 8/01 Chep 2m49y gd-fm

Jailhouse Rocket

101(87) (30)**42**
4-y-o gr g Petong-Selvi (Mummy's Pet)
Miss B Sanders (C A Dwyer 26/1) Mrs Monica Caine

Placings:0121033/0000000-**0**000000200 **(5469)**
2001: 6^0SD, 8^0SD, 5^0F, 5^0G, 9^0GF, 8^0GF, 9^0GF, 8^2S, 8^0G, 9^0S

	Starts	1st	2nd	3rd	Win & Pl
Career Total (Turf)	22	2	2	2	9917
Career Total (AW)	2	0	0	0	

100 9/99 Bevl 5f D SFT £3393
76 8/99 Carl 5f F G-F £2710
Total win prize-money £6104

Going (Turf): **Sf: 1-7** GS: 0-0 Gd: 0-7 **GF: 1-7** Fm: 0-1
Distance: **5f/6f: 2-17** 7f-8f: 0-1 9f-13f: 0-6 14f+: 0-0
Track: LH: 0-6 **RH: 1-5** Tight: 0-3 **Gall: 1-2**
Aids: Bl: 0-0 Vi: 0-0 Tstrap: 0-0
Best Rating: 42 8/01 Chep 1m14y soft

Jalindi (IRE)

107 **74**
4-y-o ch f Indian Ridge-Jaljuli (Jalmood (USA))
E J O'Neill Paolo Crespi

Placings:605/1230-00204405 **(3578)**
2001: 12^0S, 10^0G, 7^2G, 7^0GF, 7^4G, 7^4GF, 6^0G, 7^5GF

	Starts	1st	2nd	3rd	Win & Pl
Career Total (Turf)	15	1	2	1	9012

70 5/00 Dund 7f166y FRM £3450
Total win prize-money £3450

Going (Turf): Sf: 0-1 GS: 0-0 Gd: 0-6 GF: 0-4 **Fm: 1-1**
Distance: 5f/6f: 0-0 **7f-8f: 1-12** 9f-13f: 0-3 14f+: 0-0
Track: **LH: 1-6** RH: 0-6 Tight: 0-1 Gall: 0-3
Aids: Bl: 0-1 Vi: 0-5 **Tstrap: 1-12**
Best Rating: 74 7/01 Donc 7f gd-fm

Fairly useful performer for John Oxx in Ireland, but has looked a difficult ride this year. Stays a mile but best form over seven furlongs on a sound surface. Has worn blinkers and a tongue strap on his last few outings.

Jalons Star (IRE)

96(86) (41)**66**
3-y-o b g Eagle Eyed (USA)-Regina St Cyr (IRE) (Doulab (USA))
G M McCourt (M Quinn 3/8) Jalons Partnership 2

Placings:5066-**4**0651250 **(1326)**
2001: 10^4SW, 10^0SW, 12^6SD, 10^5GS, 9^1S, 11^2GS, 12^5GS, 11^0G

	Starts	1st	2nd	3rd	Win & Pl
Career Total (Turf)	9	1	1	0	3720
Career Total (AW)	3	0	0	0	0

66 4/01 Nott 1m1f213yF(0-65)H SFT £2639
Total win prize-money £2639

Going (Turf): **Sf: 1-3** GS: 0-3 Gd: 0-2 GF: 0-1 Fm: 0-0
Distance: 5f/6f: 0-1 7f-8f: 0-3 **9f-13f: 1-8** 14f+: 0-0
Track: **LH: 1-8** RH: 0-0 Tight: 0-5 Gall: 0-2
Aids: Bl: 0-0 Vi: 0-0 Tstrap: 0-0
Best Rating: 66 4/01 Wind 1m3f135y gd-sft

Jalousie (IRE)

111(107) (84+)**100**
3-y-o b f Barathea (IRE)-Duende (High Top)
S P C Woods Dennis Yardy

Placings:0-1410112336 **(5257)**
2001: 11^1SD, 11^4G, 12^1SD, 12^0GF, 11^1G, 12^1GS, 13^2G, 14^3GF, 12^3G, 12^6GS

	Starts	1st	2nd	3rd	Win & Pl
Career Total (Turf)	9	2	1	2	29159
Career Total (AW)	2	2	0	0	7517

96 8/01 NmkJ 1m4f C G-S £6646
94 7/01 Leic 1m3f183yC(0-95)H GD £7020
84 6/01 Sthl 1m4f D(0-80)H STD £4114
65 4/01 Sthl 1m3f D STD £3402
Total win prize-money £21183

Going (Turf): Sf: 0-0 **GS: 1-3 Gd: 1-4** GF: 0-2 Fm: 0-0
Distance: 5f/6f: 0-0 7f-8f: 0-1 **9f-13f: 4-8** 14f+: 0-2
Track: LH: 2-4 RH: 2-6 Tight: 0-1 **Gall: 1-5**
Aids: Bl: 0-0 Vi: 0-0 Tstrap: 0-0
Best Rating: 100 9/01 Ches 1m5f89y good

She looked very smart when winning twice on the Southwell Fibresand this year, and showed she could also do it on turf when winning twice in the summer. Good efforts in pattern company since. On the upgrade, she acts on good and easy ground on turf.

Jamaican Flight (USA)

104(103) (51)**56?**
8-y-o b h Sunshine Forever (USA)-Kalamona (USA) (Hawaii)
Mrs S Lamyman P Lamyman

Placings:20/405132/2552226/**3125**22033331000/**00**52 4140011256**505/3344**3204006554423-**4**4040050 **(5600)**
2001: 11^4SW, 16^4SD, 12^0SD, 18^4S, 17^0HY, 16^0G, 12^5GS, 16^0GS

	Starts	1st	2nd	3rd	Win & Pl
Career Total (Turf)	58	5	12	7	42609
Career Total (AW)	15	1	2	3	11574

76 7/99 Donc 2m110y F(0-80)H G-F £2295
71 7/99 Carl 1m6f32y E(0-70)H FRM £2822
72 5/99 Pont 2m1f216yC GD £6040
78 8/98 Pont 2m1f216yC G-F £5454
79 2/98 Wolv 1m4f C(0-100)H STD £8091
57 7/96 Bevl 2m35y F G-F £2532
Total win prize-money £27234

Going (Turf): Sf: 0-8 GS: 0-8 Gd: 1-21 **GF: 3-16** Fm: 1-5
Distance: 5f/6f: 0-0 7f-8f: 0-3 9f-13f: 1-16 **14f+: 5-54**
Track: **LH: 4-52** RH: 2-20 **Tight: 2-26** Gall: 1-17
Aids: Bl: 0-0 Vi: 0-1 Tstrap: 0-0
Best Rating: 56 11/01 NmkR 2m gd-sft

A thorough stayer, he gets two miles well and is suited by soft ground. On the downgrade in recent years, he last won a race in 1999. At his best when able to gain an uncontested early lead.

James Dee (IRE)

101(104) (80)**61**
5-y-o b g Shalford (IRE)-Glendale Joy (IRE) (Glenstal (USA))
A P Jarvis Mrs Ann Jarvis

Placings:025230/**2044**1403024401/**0222**6200460-2550 **(2746)**
2001: 7^2SD, 5^5GS, 6^5GF, 7^0GF

	Starts	1st	2nd	3rd	Win & Pl
Career Total (Turf)	23	1	5	2	7970
Career Total (AW)	12	1	4	0	8681

76 9/99 Wolv 7f D(0-85)H STD £4013
62 5/99 Brig 6f209y F FRM £2543
Total win prize-money £6557

Going (Turf): Sf: 0-1 GS: 0-4 Gd: 0-9 GF: 0-8 **Fm: 1-1**
Distance: 5f/6f: 0-18 **7f-8f: 2-17** 9f-13f: 0-0 14f+: 0-0
Track: **LH: 2-20** RH: 0-0 **Tight: 1-9** Gall: 0-0
Aids: Bl: 0-0 Vi: 0-0 Tstrap: 0-0
Best Rating: 61 6/01 Gdwd 6f gd-fm

James Stark (IRE)

(104) (83)**83**
4-y-o b g Up And At 'Em-June Maid (Junius (USA))
N P Littmoden Paul J Dixon

Placings:05**116**/000020342445615310-000043005260000010 **(5688)**
2001: 6^0GF, 6^0GF, 6^0GF, 5^0GS, 5^4GS, 6^3GF, 6^0G, 6^0G, 5^5G, 7^2G, 7^6GS, 6^0G, 6^0G, 6^0GS, 7^0GS, 5^0HY, 6^1SD, 7^0S

	Starts	1st	2nd	3rd	Win & Pl
Career Total (Turf)	36	2	3	3	23543
Career Total (AW)	5	3	0	0	8823

72 11/01 Wolv 6f D(0-75) STD £3835
84 10/00 Pont 5f D(0-85)H HVY £7605
76 9/00 Gdwd 5f E(0-75)H GD £4043
83 11/99 Ling 6f E(0-85)H STD £2703
80 11/99 Sthl 5f F STD £2284
Total win prize-money £20472

Going (Turf): **Sf: 1-6** GS: 0-8 **Gd: 1-12** GF: 0-9 Fm: 0-1
Distance: **5f/6f: 5-34** 7f-8f: 0-7 9f-13f: 0-0 14f+: 0-0
Track: **LH: 3-9** RH: 0-4 **Tight: 2-4** Gall: 0-7
Aids: **Bl: 5-17** Vi: 0-15 Tstrap: 0-0
Best Rating: 85 9/01 Ches 7f122y good

A winner at Goodwood and Pontefract in 2000, he has been held in warm sprint-handicap company on turf since, though not disgraced. Acts well on the All-Weather and bounced back to form with two wins at Wolverhampton in November. Seems to act on any going.

Jamestown

93(103) (75)**68**
4-y-o b g Merdon Melody-Thabeh (Shareef Dancer (USA))
C Smith A E Needham

Placings:0520516/046140**4**21-**4**030104004 **(5384)**
2001: 9^4SD, 8^0SD, 8^3SW, 7^0SD, 7^1GS, 7^0GF, 8^4GS, 7^0GF, 7^0G, 7^4S

	Starts	1st	2nd	3rd	Win & Pl
Career Total (Turf)	19	3	1	0	14151
Career Total (AW)	7	1	1	1	4777

67 4/01 Muss 7f30y D(0-75) G-S £4465
75 12/00 Wolv 7f E(0-70) STD £2751
61 8/00 Bevl 7f100y E G-F £2380
74 9/99 Wwck 6f168y E SFT £2839
Total win prize-money £12437

Going (Turf): **Sf: 1-5 GS: 1-2** Gd: 0-3 **GF: 1-7** Fm: 0-2
Distance: 5f/6f: 0-5 **7f-8f: 4-16** 9f-13f: 0-5 14f+: 0-0
Track: **LH: 2-14** RH: 1-3 **Tight: 1-5** Gall: 0-2
Aids: Bl: 0-0 Vi: 0-0 Tstrap: 0-0
Best Rating: 73 2/01 Sthl 1m slow

Jamie Ann

41
4-y-o b f Son Pardo-Taine Sands (Record Run)
Miss Sheena West Gerald West

Placings:00/0 (5664)
2001: 8^{0}HY

	Starts	1st	2nd	3rd	Win & Pl
Career Total (Turf)	3	0	0	0	

Going (Turf): Sf: 0-1 GS: 0-0 Gd: 0-1 GF: 0-1 Fm: 0-0
Distance: 5f/6f: 0-0 7f-8f: 0-2 9f-13f: 0-1 14f+: 0-0
Track : LH: 0-1 RH: 0-1 Tight: 0-2 Gall: 0-0
Aids: Bl: 0-0 Vi: 0-0 Tstrap: 0-0

Jamie My Boy (IRE)

(63) **63**
3-y-o b g Common Grounds-House Of Fame (USA) (Trempolino (USA))
T Keddy Mrs Julie Mitchell

Placings:400-0000 (3015)
2001: 7^{0}S, 8^{0}G, 11^{0}SD, 7^{0}SD

	Starts	1st	2nd	3rd	Win & Pl
Career Total (Turf)	5	0	0	0	327
Career Total (AW)	2	0	0	0	

Going (Turf): Sf: 0-3 GS: 0-0 Gd: 0-2 GF: 0-0 Fm: 0-0
Distance: 5f/6f: 0-0 7f-8f: 0-5 9f-13f: 0-2 14f+: 0-0
Track : LH: 0-2 RH: 0-1 Tight: 0-0 Gall: 0-0
Aids: Bl: 0-1 Vi: 0-0 Tstrap: 0-0
Best Rating: 43 5/01 Wwck 1m22y good

Jammie Dodger

(88) (27) **39**
5-y-o b g Ardkinglass-Ling Lane (Slip Anchor)
D Burchell Mrs Ruth Burchell

Placings:0460530/000201U06000-066000000000 (0754)
2001: 12^{0}SD, 8^{6}SW, 9^{6}SW, 8^{0}SD, 6^{0}SD, 10^{0}SW, 7^{0}SD, 9^{0}SD, 6^{0}SD, 12^{0}SW, 8^{0}SD, 12^{0}SW

	Starts	1st	2nd	3rd	Win & Pl
Career Total (Turf)	18	1	1	1	3852
Career Total (AW)	13	0	0	0	157

36 7/00 Muss 1m F(0-60)H G-S £2660
Total win prize-money £2660

Going (Turf): Sf: 0-3 GS: 1-2 Gd: 0-8 GF: 0-4 Fm: 0-1
Distance: 5f/6f: 0-2 7f-8f: 1-13 9f-13f: 0-16 14f+: 0-0
Track : LH: 0-20 RH: 1-11 Tight: 1-22 Gall: 0-1
Aids: Bl: 0-0 Vi: 0-0 Tstrap: 0-0
Best Rating: 48 2/01 Sthl 6f stand

Jan Brueghel (USA)

92 **80**
2-y-o ch c Phone Trick (USA)-Sunk (USA) (Polish Navy (USA))
P F I Cole Richard Green (fine Paintings)

Placings:65 (5343)
2001: 5^{6}G, 6^{5}GS

	Starts	1st	2nd	3rd	Win & Pl
Career Total (Turf)	2	0	0	0	0

Going (Turf): Sf: 0-0 GS: 0-1 Gd: 0-1 GF: 0-0 Fm: 0-0
Distance: 5f/6f: 0-2 7f-8f: 0-0 9f-13f: 0-0 14f+: 0-0
Track : LH: 0-0 RH: 0-0 Tight: 0-0 Gall: 0-0
Aids: Bl: 0-0 Vi: 0-0 Tstrap: 0-0
Best Rating: 80 10/01 NmkR 6f gd-sft

Janefer John (IRE)

90 **37**
4-y-o ch f Magical Wonder (USA)-John's Vision (IRE) (Vision (USA))
D J S Cosgrove T C Quinn

Placings:5400060/00620-000 (3097)
2001: 5^{0}F, 6^{0}GF, 6^{0}G

	Starts	1st	2nd	3rd	Win & Pl
Career Total (Turf)	15	0	1	0	1648

Going (Turf): Sf: 0-5 GS: 0-0 Gd: 0-3 GF: 0-2 Fm: 0-2
Distance: 5f/6f: 0-9 7f-8f: 0-5 9f-13f: 0-0 14f+: 0-0
Track : LH: 0-3 RH: 0-2 Tight: 0-0 Gall: 0-0
Aids: Bl: 0-0 Vi: 0-0 Tstrap: 0-0
Best Rating: 37 7/01 Wind 6f gd-fm

Janglynyve

96 (6) **34**
7-y-o ch m Sharpo-Wollow Maid (Wollow)
C A Dwyer (Ferdy Murphy 26/4) D Farrow

Placings:40430/501121/000/0005065 (4093)
2001: 8^{0}GF, 12^{0}GF, 6^{0}GF, 8^{5}GF, 7^{0}GF, 10^{6}GS, 9^{5}G

	Starts	1st	2nd	3rd	Win & Pl
Career Total (Turf)	19	3	1	1	11851
Career Total (AW)	2	0	0	0	0

61 6/97 NmkJ 1m2f D SFT £3492
60 5/97 Leic 1m8y F GD £2595
59 5/97 NmkR 1m D GD £3785
Total win prize-money £9873

Going (Turf): Sf: 1-2 GS: 0-2 Gd: 2-8 GF: 0-6 Fm: 0-1
Distance: 5f/6f: 0-3 7f-8f: 1-10 9f-13f: 2-8 14f+: 0-0
Track : LH: 0-5 RH: 1-5 Tight: 0-2 Gall: 1-2
Aids: Bl: 0-0 Vi: 0-0 Tstrap: 0-0
Best Rating: 59 6/01 NmkJ 6f gd-fm

Janiceland (IRE)

100(104) (68) **65**
4-y-o b f Foxhound (USA)-Rebecca's Girl (IRE) (Nashamaa)
S E Kettlewell (M Wigham 30/9) Cable Media Consultancy Ltd

Placings:52206035022541/10553341100-32P353661030000 (5616)
2001: 7^{3}SD, 7^{2}SD, 8^{P}SD, 7^{3}SW, 7^{5}SW, 8^{3}SW, 6^{6}GF, 7^{6}GF, 6^{1}G, 7^{0}GF, 7^{3}GF, 7^{0}G, 7^{0}GF, 7^{0}SD

	Starts	1st	2nd	3rd	Win & Pl
Career Total (Turf)	17	1	2	3	6335
Career Total (AW)	22	4	3	4	13815

65 7/01 Brig 6f209y F(0-60)H GD £2646
61 11/00 Ling 7f E(0-70)H STD £2951
57 11/00 Ling 7f E(0-75) STD £2405
52 2/00 Ling 6f G STD £1817
66 11/99 Wolv 5f G STD £1829
Total win prize-money £11649

Going (Turf): Sf: 0-0 GS: 0-1 Gd: 1-4 GF: 0-12 Fm: 0-0
Distance: 5f/6f: 2-21 7f-8f: 3-18 9f-13f: 0-0 14f+: 0-0
Track : LH: 5-26 RH: 0-0 Tight: 4-18 Gall: 0-0
Aids: Bl: 0-0 Vi: 0-1 Tstrap: 0-0
Best Rating: 69 1/01 Ling 7f stand

She is only plating class and has been successful on both Fibresand and Equitrack at that level. Recorded her first win on Turf in a moderate Brighton handicap in 2001 when positively ridden.

Janoueix (IRE)

75 **24**
2-y-o b c Desert King (IRE)-Miniver (IRE) (Mujtahid (USA))
G A Butler Andy J Smith, Nigel R Smith

Placings:00 (5665)
2001: 7^{0}G, 6^{0}HY

	Starts	1st	2nd	3rd	Win & Pl
Career Total (Turf)	2	0	0	0	

Going (Turf): Sf: 0-1 GS: 0-0 Gd: 0-1 GF: 0-0 Fm: 0-0
Distance: 5f/6f: 0-1 7f-8f: 0-1 9f-13f: 0-0 14f+: 0-0
Track : LH: 0-1 RH: 0-0 Tight: 0-1 Gall: 0-0
Aids: Bl: 0-0 Vi: 0-0 Tstrap: 0-0
Best Rating: 24 8/01 Ches 7f2y good

Japan (IRE)

101(100) (62) **50**
3-y-o ch f Caerleon (USA)-Culture Vulture (USA) (Timeless Moment (USA))
P F I Cole Newgate Stud

Placings:521600500 (4622)
2001: 6^{5}SD, 6^{2}SD, 7^{1}SD, 6^{6}GS, 7^{0}S, 7^{0}G, 6^{5}GF, 6^{0}GF, 6^{0}GF

	Starts	1st	2nd	3rd	Win & Pl
Career Total (Turf)	6	0	0	0	0
Career Total (AW)	3	1	1	0	3303

62 3/01 Sthl 7f D STD £2471
Total win prize-money £2471

Going (Turf): Sf: 0-1 GS: 0-1 Gd: 0-1 GF: 0-3 Fm: 0-0
Distance: 5f/6f: 0-4 7f-8f: 1-5 9f-13f: 0-0 14f+: 0-0
Track : LH: 1-4 RH: 0-1 Tight: 0-0 Gall: 0-0
Aids: Bl: 0-1 Vi: 0-0 Tstrap: 0-0
Best Rating: 65 5/01 Brig 6f209y gd-sft

Unraced as a juvenile, she won on her third start on the Southwell All-Weather in March 2001. She has raced exclusively on turf since, but has made little impression.

Jardines Lookout (IRE)

109 **116**
4-y-o b g Fourstars Allstar (USA)-Foolish Flight (IRE) (Fool's Holme (USA))
A P Jarvis Ambrose Turnbull

Placings:5362120151-503025 (4681)
2001: 13^{5}GF, 16^{0}G, 20^{3}GF, 16^{0}G, 15^{2}G, 18^{5}G

	Starts	1st	2nd	3rd	Win & Pl
Career Total (Turf)	16	3	3	2	87093

85 11/00 Donc 1m6f132yC HVY £6922
104 9/00 NmkR 1m6f B(0-100)H SFT £15381
90 7/00 Sals 1m6f15y D GD £3718
Total win prize-money £26023

Going (Turf): Sf: 2-2 GS: 0-3 Gd: 1-6 GF: 0-4 Fm: 0-1
Distance: 5f/6f: 0-0 7f-8f: 0-0 9f-13f: 0-1 14f+: 3-15
Track : LH: 1-8 RH: 2-8 Tight: 1-5 Gall: 2-8
Aids: Bl: 0-0 Vi: 0-0 Tstrap: 0-0
Best Rating: 116 8/01 York 1m7f195y good

Unraced at two, he won well at Salisbury in 2000 but was unfortunate to be thrown out after winning the Melrose at the York Ebor meeting. He gained compensation with victories at Newmarket and Doncaster, but had looked out of his depth in Pattern company until finishing a fine third in this season's Ascot Gold Cup. Has won on good but prefers soft ground.

Jarn

107 **106**
4-y-o b h Green Desert (USA)-Alkariyh (USA) (Alydar (USA))
B Hanbury Hamdan Al Maktoum

Placings:10/1026-00164450 (4531)
2001: 6^{0}G, 7^{0}GF, 6^{1}GF, 6^{6}F, 5^{4}GF, 6^{4}G, 6^{5}G, 6^{0}GF

	Starts	1st	2nd	3rd	Win & Pl
Career Total (Turf)	14	3	1	0	25737

103 6/01 Yarm 6f3y C G-F £6003
107 5/00 Newb 6f8y B G-F £9198
97 9/99 Newb 6f8y D G-F £4792
Total win prize-money £19995

Going (Turf): Sf: 0-1 GS: 0-0 Gd: 0-4 GF: 3-7 Fm: 0-2
Distance: 5f/6f: 0-6 7f-8f: 3-8 9f-13f: 0-0 14f+: 0-0
Track : LH: 0-2 RH: 0-0 Tight: 0-1 Gall: 0-1
Aids: Bl: 1-6 Vi: 0-0 Tstrap: 2-10
Best Rating: 106 8/01 Ripn 6f good

Sharpened up by blinkers and tongue-strap when beating Palanzo by a short head at Yarmouth in June. Fair efforts since, but is not going to be easy to place. Usually wears a tongue-tie these days, goes well fresh and is suited by a flat track and fast ground. Best over six furlongs.

Jarv (IRE)

103(82) (44)**55**
3-y-o b f Inzar (USA)-Conditional Sale (IRE) (Petorius)
J Akehurst C Jarvis

Placings:000240-0066013500 **(5626)**
2001: 8^0S, 8^0GF, 8^6GF, 8^6G, 6^0GF, 7^1GF, 8^3G, 7^5HY, 8^0G, 8^0GS

	Starts	1st	2nd	3rd	Win & Pl
Career Total (Turf)	15	1	1	1	4428
Career Total (AW)	1	0	0	0	
53 9/01 Brig	7f214y	F(0-60)H		G-F	£2429

Total win prize-money £2429

Going (Turf): Sf: 0-4 GS: 0-2 Gd: 0-3 **GF: 1-6** Fm: 0-0
Distance: 5f/6f: 0-3 **7f-8f: 1-6** 9f-13f: 0-7 14f+: 0-0
Track : **LH: 1-10** RH: 0-3 Tight: 0-5 Gall: 0-1
Aids: **Bl: 1-8** Vi: 0-0 Tstrap: 0-0
Best Rating: 55 9/01 Epsm 1m114y good

Won a weak mile handicap at Brighton in September. Suited by fast ground.

Jaskini

(78) (19)
5-y-o b g Lion Cavern (USA)-Sharka (Shareef Dancer (USA))
A G Juckes (W M Brisbourne 18/1) M Ephgrave

Placings:213/4/0-0 **(0117)**
2001: 9^0SW

	Starts	1st	2nd	3rd	Win & Pl
Career Total (Turf)	4	1	1	1	18946
Career Total (AW)	2	0	0	0	
9/98 StCl 1m				VS	£9091

Total win prize-money £9091

Going (Turf): Sf: 0-0 GS: 0-0 Gd: 0-0 GF: 0-0 Fm: 0-0
Distance: 5f/6f: 0-0 7f-8f: 0-2 9f-13f: 0-1 14f+: 0-0
Track : LH: 0-3 RH: 0-0 Tight: 0-2 Gall: 0-0
Aids: Bl: 0-0 Vi: 0-0 Tstrap: 0-0

Jasmick (IRE)

109 **81**
3-y-o ch f Definite Article-Glass Minnow (IRE) (Alzao (USA))
H Morrison Melksham Craic

Placings:0-3434012540 **(5599)**
2001: 8^3G, 8^4GF, 10^3G, 9^4GF, 10^0G, 12^1GF, 11^2GF, 13^5GF, 14^4G, 12^0GS

	Starts	1st	2nd	3rd	Win & Pl
Career Total (Turf)	11	1	1	2	10070
74 8/01 Sals	1m4f	D(0-80)H		G-F	£4290

Total win prize-money £4290

Going (Turf): Sf: 0-0 GS: 0-1 Gd: 0-4 **GF: 1-6** Fm: 0-0
Distance: 5f/6f: 0-1 7f-8f: 0-1 **9f-13f: 1-7** 14f+: 0-2
Track : LH: 0-4 **RH: 1-6 Tight: 1-5** Gall: 0-5
Aids: Bl: 0-0 Vi: 0-0 Tstrap: 0-0
Best Rating: 81 10/01 NmkR 1m6f good

Has speed on her dam's side but was well suited by a mile and a half when scoring at Salisbury in August and has gone close in similar events since. Stays 14 furlongs, acts on fast ground.

Jasmine Breeze

87 **75**
2-y-o b f Saddlers' Hall (IRE)-Regal Peace (Known Fact (USA))
W Jarvis The Tea Clippers

Placings:0 **(4873)**
2001: 7^0G

	Starts	1st	2nd	3rd	Win & Pl
Career Total (Turf)	1	0	0	0	

Going (Turf): Sf: 0-0 GS: 0-0 Gd: 0-1 GF: 0-0 Fm: 0-0
Distance: 5f/6f: 0-0 7f-8f: 0-1 9f-13f: 0-0 14f+: 0-0
Track : LH: 0-0 RH: 0-0 Tight: 0-0 Gall: 0-0
Aids: Bl: 0-0 Vi: 0-0 Tstrap: 0-0
Best Rating: 75 9/01 NmkR 7f good

Jato Dancer (IRE)

93(95) (28)**25**
6-y-o b m Mukaddamah (USA)-Que Tranquila (Dominion)
R Hollinshead Mrs Norman Hill

Placings:01000/**3000**10200**00**/0000**000**/**5000**0540600 6-**43005445005436000** **(4319)**
2001: 12^4SW, 12^3SD, 7^0SW, 11^0SD, 12^5SW, 12^4SD, 12^4SD, 11^5SD, 7^0SD, 11^0SD, 8^5SD, 11^4SD, 11^3SD, 11^6GF, 11^0GS, 11^0G, 10^0GF

	Starts	1st	2nd	3rd	Win & Pl
Career Total (Turf)	23	2	1	0	6029
Career Total (AW)	30	0	0	3	930
49 5/98 Wind	1m67y	F		G-F	£2766
49 7/97 Brig	6f209y	G		FRM	£1984

Total win prize-money £4751

Going (Turf): Sf: 0-0 GS: 0-3 Gd: 0-7 **GF: 1-10 Fm: 1-3**
Distance: 5f/6f: 0-0 7f-8f: 1-20 9f-13f: 1-33 14f+: 0-0
Track : LH: 1-44 RH: 1-5 **Tight: 1-25** Gall: 0-0
Aids: Bl: 0-6 Vi: 0-0 Tstrap: 0-0
Best Rating: 37 1/01 Wolv 1m4f slow

Javelin

(91) (52)**62?**
5-y-o ch g Generous (IRE)-Moss (Alzao (USA))
Ian Williams Cockbury Court Partnership

Placings:0/400/540600-0 **(0618)**
2001: 10^0SD

	Starts	1st	2nd	3rd	Win & Pl
Career Total (Turf)	7	0	0	0	1507
Career Total (AW)	4	0	0	0	0

Going (Turf): Sf: 0-1 GS: 0-1 Gd: 0-1 GF: 0-0 Fm: 0-0
Distance: 5f/6f: 0-0 7f-8f: 0-0 9f-13f: 0-7 14f+: 0-0
Track : LH: 0-5 RH: 0-2 Tight: 0-4 Gall: 0-0
Aids: Bl: 0-0 Vi: 0-0 Tstrap: 0-0
Best Rating: 29 3/01 Ling 1m2f stand

Jawah (IRE)

100 **49**
7-y-o br g In The Wings-Saving Mercy (Lord Gayle (USA))
J R Jenkins The East India Dock Partnership

Placings:000/01525114/0000450023/10010/0000-0500 **(3966)**
2001: 14^0G, 14^5F, 16^0GF, 16^0GS

	Starts	1st	2nd	3rd	Win & Pl
Career Total (Turf)	34	5	2	1	26616
79 10/99 Donc	1m6f132yD(0-85)H			G-S	£4338
74 9/99 Hayd	1m6f	D(0-85)H		SFT	£7457
81 10/97 Nott	1m6f15y	D(0-80)H		GD	£4175
75 10/97 Donc	1m6f132yD(0-85)H			GD	£4435
62 7/97 Bell	1m6f	(0-85)H		G-Y	£2740

Total win prize-money £23146

Going (Turf): Sf: 1-8 GS: 1-5 **Gd: 2-10** GF: 0-6 Fm: 0-1
Distance: 5f/6f: 0-0 7f-8f: 0-2 9f-13f: 0-6 **14f+: 5-26**
Track : **LH: 5-19** RH: 0-13 Tight: 0-7 **Gall: 2-12**
Aids: Bl: 0-2 Vi: 0-3 Tstrap: 0-0
Best Rating: 49 5/01 Yarm 1m6f17y good

Jawhari

106(103) (43)**62**
7-y-o b g Lahib (USA)-Lady Of The Land (Wollow)
T G Mills T G Mills

Placings:24/1050/00002600/10600/0100-135210 **(5027)**
2001: 5^1SD, 6^3SD, 5^5SD, 5^2GF, 5^1GF, 5^0S

	Starts	1st	2nd	3rd	Win & Pl
Career Total (Turf)	23	3	3	0	14150
Career Total (AW)	6	2	0	1	4916
59 9/01 Brig	5f59y	F(0-60)		G-F	£2303
50 2/01 Wolv	5f	G		STD	£1841
68 2/00 Wolv	5f	E(0-70)H		STD	£2808
63 7/99 Catt	5f	D(0-85)H		GD	£4922
80 7/97 Ling	7f140y	D		G-F	£4110

Total win prize-money £15985

Going (Turf): Sf: 0-3 GS: 0-4 Gd: 1-8 **GF: 2-8** Fm: 0-0
Distance: **5f/6f: 4-21** 7f-8f: 1-8 9f-13f: 0-0 14f+: 0-0
Track : **LH: 3-11** RH: 0-2 **Tight: 2-7** Gall: 0-1
Aids: Bl: 0-1 Vi: 0-0 Tstrap: 0-0
Best Rating: 62 8/01 Brig 5f59y gd-fm

Sprint handicapper, effective over five furlongs on fast ground.

Jawhirji

78 **32**
4-y-o b g Owington-Dream Baby (Master Willie)
Mrs Lydia Pearce (J Pearce 24/2) Jeff Pearce

Placings:00 **(3855)**
2001: 7^0GF, 7^0GS

	Starts	1st	2nd	3rd	Win & Pl
Career Total (Turf)	2	0	0	0	

Going (Turf): Sf: 0-0 GS: 0-1 Gd: 0-0 GF: 0-1 Fm: 0-0
Distance: 5f/6f: 0-0 7f-8f: 0-2 9f-13f: 0-0 14f+: 0-0
Track : LH: 0-0 RH: 0-0 Tight: 0-0 Gall: 0-0
Aids: Bl: 0-0 Vi: 0-0 Tstrap: 0-0
Best Rating: 32 5/01 Yarm 7f3y gd-fm

Jawrjik (IRE)

88 **39**
3-y-o b g Blues Traveller (IRE)-Eva Fay (IRE) (Fayruz)
B S Rothwell Richard Brown

Placings:00-6 **(3935)**
2001: 11^6G

	Starts	1st	2nd	3rd	Win & Pl
Career Total (Turf)	3	0	0	0	0

Going (Turf): Sf: 0-1 GS: 0-1 Gd: 0-1 GF: 0-0 Fm: 0-0
Distance: 5f/6f: 0-0 7f-8f: 0-1 9f-13f: 0-2 14f+: 0-0
Track : LH: 0-2 RH: 0-1 Tight: 0-1 Gall: 0-1
Aids: Bl: 0-0 Vi: 0-0 Tstrap: 0-0
Best Rating: 39 8/01 Bevl 1m3f216y good

Jawwala (USA)

96 **80+**
2-y-o b f Green Dancer (USA)-Fetch N Carry (USA) (Alleged (USA))
J W Payne C Cotran

Placings:1 **(5559)**
2001: 8^1S

	Starts	1st	2nd	3rd	Win & Pl
Career Total (Turf)	1	1	0	0	4524
80 10/01 Yarm	1m3y	D		SFT	£4524

Total win prize-money £4524

Going (Turf): Sf: 1-1 GS: 0-0 Gd: 0-0 GF: 0-0 Fm: 0-0
Distance: 5f/6f: 0-0 7f-8f: 0-0 **9f-13f: 1-1** 14f+: 0-0
Track : LH: 0-0 RH: 0-0 Tight: 0-0 Gall: 0-0

Aids: Bl: 0-0 Vi: 0-0 Tstrap: 0-0
Best Rating: 80 10/01 Yarm 1m3y soft

She made a winning debut over a mile at Yarmouth in October and should find further success at three.

Jayanjay

94 **83**
2-y-o b c Piccolo-Morica (Moorestyle)
B R Johnson Peter Crate

Placings:044126 **(4668)**
2001: 5^0GF, 5^4GF, 5^4GF, 5^1S, 5^2G, 6^6GF

	Starts	1st	2nd	3rd	Win & Pl
Career Total (Turf)	6	1	1	0	8038

76 8/01 Sand 5f6y D SFT £5824
Total win prize-money £5824

Going (Turf): Sf: 1-1 GS: 0-0 Gd: 0-1 GF: 0-4 Fm: 0-0
Distance: 5f/6f: 1-6 7f-8f: 0-0 9f-13f: 0-0 14f+: 0-0
Track : LH: 0-0 RH: 0-0 Tight: 0-0 Gall: 0-0
Aids: Bl: 0-0 Vi: 0-0 Tstrap: 0-0
Best Rating: 83 9/01 Sand 5f6y good

Showed ability in maidens before winning a sandown nursery on soft ground. Narrowly beaten at the same track next time, he did not seem to stay six on his final run.

Jayannpee

100 **40**
10-y-o ch g Doulab (USA)-Amina (Brigadier Gerard)
I A Balding I A Balding

Placings:3200/011062110160/32653364000/01100104 10/24040500/000031003500/0000/000000000 **(4950)**
2001: 5^0G, 6^0GF, 5^0GF, 5^0G, 5^0GF, 6^0F, 5^0G, 6^0GF, 5^0G

	Starts	1st	2nd	3rd	Win & Pl
Career Total (Turf)	70	10	4	6	166068

84	6/98	Bath	5f161y	D(0-85)H	G-S	£3501
95	9/96	Taby	6f		GD	£34985
107	7/96	Newb	6f8y	A	G-F	£12724
104	5/96	York	6f	B(0-105)H	G-F	£11274
95	5/96	NmkR	6f	C(0-95)H	G-F	£24855
90	8/94	Sand	5f6y	B(0-100)H	GD	£6900
83	7/94	Gdwd	5f	C(0-90)H	FRM	£7830
76	7/94	Bath	5f11y	C(0-90)H	FRM	£5247
78	5/94	Bath	5f11y	F(0-65)	GD	£2617
70	5/94	Bath	5f161y	E(0-70)H	G-F	£3120

Total win prize-money £113055

Going (Turf): Sf: 0-6 GS: 1-8 Gd: 3-23 **GF: 4-30** Fm: 2-3
Distance: 5f/6f: 9-62 7f-8f: 1-8 9f-13f: 0-0 14f+: 0-0
Track : LH: 5-14 RH: 0-1 Tight: 0-4 **Gall: 4-9**
Aids: Bl: 0-0 Vi: 0-0 Tstrap: 0-13
Best Rating: 53 8/01 Thsk 6f firm

Jaycat (IRE)

96(72) (10)**37**
3-y-o ch f Catrail (USA)-Improviste (CAN) (The Minstrel (CAN))
G A Butler Julian, Andrew, Chris And Terry

Placings:00-32050000 **(5187)**
2001: 6^3S, 8^2S, 8^0G, 7^5S, 9^0GF, 8^0SD, 9^0G, 5^0GS

	Starts	1st	2nd	3rd	Win & Pl
Career Total (Turf)	9	0	1	1	1241
Career Total (AW)	1	0	0	0	

Going (Turf): Sf: 0-5 GS: 0-1 Gd: 0-2 GF: 0-1 Fm: 0-0
Distance: 5f/6f: 0-3 7f-8f: 0-2 9f-13f: 0-5 14f+: 0-0
Track : LH: 0-3 RH: 0-2 Tight: 0-2 Gall: 0-0
Aids: Bl: 0-1 Vi: 0-0 Tstrap: 0-0
Best Rating: 54 5/01 Newb 7f soft

Jazan (IRE)

85 **78**
2-y-o b f Danehill (USA)-Babita (Habitat)
C E Brittain Saeed Manana

Placings:20 **(5147)**
2001: 8^2G, 7^0G

	Starts	1st	2nd	3rd	Win & Pl
Career Total (Turf)	2	0	1	0	2321

Going (Turf): Sf: 0-0 GS: 0-0 Gd: 0-2 GF: 0-0 Fm: 0-0
Distance: 5f/6f: 0-0 7f-8f: 0-1 9f-13f: 0-1 14f+: 0-0
Track : LH: 0-0 RH: 0-1 Tight: 0-0 Gall: 0-0
Aids: Bl: 0-0 Vi: 0-0 Tstrap: 0-0
Best Rating: 78 9/01 Sand 1m14y good

Jazmeer

97 **81**
2-y-o ch f Sabrehill (USA)-Saabga (USA) (Woodman (USA))
M P Tregoning Sheikh Ahmed Al Maktoum

Placings:61 **(2563)**
2001: 6^6GF, 7^1GF

	Starts	1st	2nd	3rd	Win & Pl
Career Total (Turf)	2	1	0	0	4173

81 6/01 Gdwd 7f D G-F £4173
Total win prize-money £4173

Going (Turf): Sf: 0-0 GS: 0-0 Gd: 0-0 **GF: 1-2** Fm: 0-0
Distance: 5f/6f: 0-1 **7f-8f: 1-1** 9f-13f: 0-0 14f+: 0-0
Track : LH: 0-0 **RH: 1-1** Tight: 0-0 Gall: 0-0
Aids: Bl: 0-0 Vi: 0-0 Tstrap: 0-0
Best Rating: 81 6/01 Gdwd 7f gd-fm

Showed the benefit of her first run when taking what looked like an ordinary maiden at Goodwood.

Jazzaam

49
2-y-o ch f Fraam-Aldwick Colonnade (Kind Of Hush)
M D I Usher Midweek Racing

Placings:0 **(5666)**
2001: 6^0HY

	Starts	1st	2nd	3rd	Win & Pl
Career Total (Turf)	1	0	0	0	

Going (Turf): Sf: 0-1 GS: 0-0 Gd: 0-0 GF: 0-0 Fm: 0-0
Distance: 5f/6f: 0-1 7f-8f: 0-0 9f-13f: 0-0 14f+: 0-0
Track : LH: 0-0 RH: 0-0 Tight: 0-0 Gall: 0-0
Aids: Bl: 0-0 Vi: 0-0 Tstrap: 0-0
Best Rating: 49 11/01 Wind 6f heavy

Jazzy Millennium

101 **55**
4-y-o ch g Lion Cavern (USA)-Woodcrest (Niniski (USA))
B R Millman Millennium Millionaires Partnership

Placings:4220/035000-0000012141 **(5027)**
2001: 7^0G, 5^0F, 6^0GF, 9^0GF, 6^0G, 6^1GF, 7^2GS, 6^1F, 7^4G, 5^1S

	Starts	1st	2nd	3rd	Win & Pl
Career Total (Turf)	20	3	3	1	12037

55	9/01	Brig	5f213y	E(0-75)H	SFT	£2996
47	8/01	Ling	6f	F(0-65)H	FRM	£3048
37	7/01	Brig	6f209y	G	G-F	£1967

Total win prize-money £8012

Going (Turf): Sf: 1-3 GS: 0-3 Gd: 0-5 **GF: 1-7 Fm: 1-2**
Distance: 5f/6f: 2-7 7f-8f: 1-11 9f-13f: 0-2 14f+: 0-0
Track : LH: 2-4 RH: 0-6 Tight: 0-0 Gall: 0-3
Aids: Bl: 3-6 Vi: 0-0 Tstrap: 0-0
Best Rating: 55 9/01 Brig 5f213y soft

Improved for the fitting of blinkers. Effective at six and seven furlongs. Acts on fast and soft ground.

Je'Thame (IRE)

92 **38**
3-y-o ch f Definite Article-Victorian Flower (Tate Gallery (USA))
P L Gilligan Thame Partnership

Placings:00353320-0000 **(2597)**
2001: 10^0G, 8^0GF, 8^0GS, 7^0GF

	Starts	1st	2nd	3rd	Win & Pl
Career Total (Turf)	12	0	1	3	3312

Going (Turf): Sf: 0-3 GS: 0-3 Gd: 0-2 GF: 0-3 Fm: 0-0
Distance: 5f/6f: 0-4 7f-8f: 0-5 9f-13f: 0-2 14f+: 0-0
Track : LH: 0-1 RH: 0-3 Tight: 0-1 Gall: 0-3
Aids: Bl: 0-4 Vi: 0-0 Tstrap: 0-0
Best Rating: 38 5/01 NmkR 1m2f good

Jeba To

49
2-y-o b f Petong-Sunley Stars (Sallust)
M W Easterby Brig Racing Club

Placings:0 **(1858)**
2001: 6^0F

	Starts	1st	2nd	3rd	Win & Pl
Career Total (Turf)	1	0	0	0	

Going (Turf): Sf: 0-0 GS: 0-0 Gd: 0-0 GF: 0-0 Fm: 0-1
Distance: 5f/6f: 0-1 7f-8f: 0-0 9f-13f: 0-0 14f+: 0-0
Track : LH: 0-0 RH: 0-0 Tight: 0-0 Gall: 0-0
Aids: Bl: 0-0 Vi: 0-0 Tstrap: 0-0

Jedeydd

109 **91d**
4-y-o b g Shareef Dancer (USA)-Bilad (USA) (Riverman (USA))
B Hanbury A Merza

Placings:0-216220000 **(5523)**
2001: 8^2GF, 7^1GF, 7^6GF, 7^2GF, 6^2GF, 7^0GF, 8^0G, 7^0GS, 5^0HY

	Starts	1st	2nd	3rd	Win & Pl
Career Total (Turf)	10	1	3	0	9819

88 5/01 Yarm 7f3y D G-F £3672
Total win prize-money £3673

Going (Turf): Sf: 0-2 GS: 0-1 Gd: 0-1 **GF: 1-6** Fm: 0-0
Distance: 5f/6f: 0-1 **7f-8f: 1-8** 9f-13f: 0-1 14f+: 0-0
Track : LH: 0-3 RH: 0-2 Tight: 0-2 Gall: 0-2
Aids: Bl: 0-0 Vi: 0-0 Tstrap: 0-0
Best Rating: 91 7/01 Newb 6f8y gd-fm

Progressive form in three maiden runs, stepped back in trip each start, culminating in comfortable maiden win at Yarmouth over seven furlongs in May. He has run well in some decent races since though his form tailed off towards the end of the season. Suited by fast ground.

Jedi Knight

108 **90**
7-y-o b g Emarati (USA)-Hannie Caulder (Workboy)
M W Easterby Mr K Hodgson & Mrs J Hodgson

Placings:434/005021124004110026421/0063042424056 /00152610140/020-026460 **(3056)**
2001: 10^0HY, 10^2GF, 8^6GF, 10^4GF, 8^6G, 10^0G

	Starts	1st	2nd	3rd	Win & Pl
Career Total (Turf)	56	7	9	2	67160

87	8/99	Haml	1m1f36y	C(0-90)H	G-F	£6289
84	7/99	York	7f202y	B(0-100)H	G-F	£10255
84	5/99	Bevl	1m100y	D(0-85)H	GD	£4458
74	11/97	Rdcr	1m2f	E(0-70)H	GD	£3249
70	8/97	Thsk	1m	D(0-80)H	G-F	£4272
62	6/97	Carl	7f214y	D(0-80)H	FRM	£3582
62	6/97	Donc	7f	D(0-75)H	GD	£4142

Total win prize-money £36250

Going (Turf): Sf: 0-5 GS: 0-6 **Gd: 3-20 GF: 3-22** Fm: 1-

3

Distance: 5f/6f: 0-6 **7f-8f: 4-24** 9f-13f: 3-26 14f+: 0-0
Track : LH: 3-31 RH: 3-13 **Tight: 3-16** Gall: 1-12
Aids: Bl: 0-1 Vi: 0-0 Tstrap: 0-0
Best Rating: 88 6/01 Epsm 1m2f18y gd-fm

A winner of three of his ten starts in 1999. he has not managed to score since though he has run well in some decent handicaps. Effective from a mile to ten furlongs and likes fast ground.

Jeffrey Anotherred

103 (68) (51)**56**
7-y-o b g Emarati (USA)-First Pleasure (Dominion)
M Dods N A Riddell

Placings:3131210/020060360056/00002351014260040 0/3500061514603/00060420446-32350000 **(5608)**
2001: 7^{3}HY, 7^{2}G, 7^{3}G, 7^{5}GF, 6^{0}G, 7^{0}GS, 7^{0}GF, 7^{0}GS

			Starts	1st	2nd	3rd		Win & Pl
Career Total (Turf)			67	7	6	8		56842
Career Total (AW)			2	0	0	0		
75	7/99	Ayr	7f	C(0-95)H			SFT	£6450
71	6/99	Ayr	7f	C(0-90)H			G-S	£6687
84	7/98	Ayr	6f	C(0-90)H			SFT	£7294
70	7/98	Carl	5f207y	F(0-65)			G-F	£2346
96	11/96	Donc	7f	D			SFT	£4066
74	9/96	Kemp	6f	D			GD	£3777
69	8/96	Haml	5f4y	F			G-F	£2619

Total win prize-money £33241

Going (Turf): Sf: 3-15 GS: 1-14 Gd: 1-22 GF: 2-14 Fm: 0-2
Distance: **5f/6f: 4-27** 7f-8f: 3-41 9f-13f: 0-1 14f+: 0-0
Track : **LH: 2-25** RH: 1-6 Tight: 0-13 **Gall: 1-7**
Aids: Bl: 0-0 Vi: 0-4 Tstrap: 0-0
Best Rating: 69 6/01 Kemp 7f gd-fm

A seven-furlong handicapper, he has not won since July 1999 though he has been placed on several occasions.

Jelani (IRE)

103 **97**
2-y-o b c Darshaan-No Rehearsal (FR) (Baillamont (USA))
Andrew Turnell Paradime Ltd

Placings:122 **(5227)**
2001: 7^{1}HY, 7^{2}G, 6^{2}S

			Starts	1st	2nd	3rd		Win & Pl
Career Total (Turf)			3	1	2	0		9557
87	9/01	Hayd	7f30y	D			HVY	£4023

Total win prize-money £4024

Going (Turf): Sf: 1-2 GS: 0-0 Gd: 0-1 GF: 0-0 Fm: 0-0
Distance: 5f/6f: 0-0 **7f-8f: 1-3** 9f-13f: 0-0 14f+: 0-0
Track : **LH: 1-2** RH: 0-0 Tight: 0-0 Gall: 0-1
Aids: Bl: 0-0 Vi: 0-0 Tstrap: 0-0
Best Rating: 97 10/01 York 6f214y soft

Won readily on his Haydock debut and ran well on both of his subsequent starts..

Jelba

103(103) (69)**73**
3-y-o b f Pursuit Of Love-Gold Bracelet (Golden Fleece (USA))
N P Littmoden The Jelba Partnership

Placings:535054-050602222144046 **(5598)**
2001: 7^{0}S, 7^{5}GF, 10^{0}G, 7^{6}GF, 7^{0}GF, 6^{2}G, 6^{2}GF, 6^{2}GF, 6^{2}SD, 6^{1}GS, 7^{4}S, 8^{4}G, 7^{0}G, 6^{4}SD, 6^{6}GS

			Starts	1st	2nd	3rd		Win & Pl
Career Total (Turf)			19	1	3	1		10742
Career Total (AW)			2	0	1	0		1114
73	7/01	NmkJ	6f	D			G-S	£4075

Total win prize-money £4076

Going (Turf): Sf: 0-3 **GS: 1-2** Gd: 0-5 GF: 0-9 Fm: 0-0
Distance: **5f/6f: 1-10** 7f-8f: 0-9 9f-13f: 0-2 14f+: 0-0
Track : LH: 0-6 RH: 0-1 Tight: 0-3 Gall: 0-2
Aids: Bl: 0-2 **Vi: 1-10** Tstrap: 0-0
Best Rating: 74 5/01 Ches 7f122y gd-fm

A fair sprinter, she had been runner-up four times in a row before given an inspired ride by Keiren Fallon to get off the mark at Newmarket in July, but has been held since then. Handles most surfaces, including the new Polytrack, but well suited by cut. Most effective at six and seven furlongs.

Jellybeen (IRE)

77(103) (32?)**50**
5-y-o ch m Petardia-Lux Aeterna (Sandhurst Prince)
Miss A Stokell Ms Caron Stokell

Placings:00010/0026350/0000-036000 **(3938)**
2001: 9^{0}SD, 12^{3}SD, 16^{6}SD, 12^{0}SW, 13^{0}G, 11^{0}G

			Starts	1st	2nd	3rd		Win & Pl
Career Total (Turf)			10	0	1	1		1162
Career Total (AW)			12	1	0	1		2671
65	11/98	Wolv	1m1f79y	F			STD	£2179

Total win prize-money £2180

Going (Turf): Sf: 0-0 GS: 0-1 Gd: 0-6 GF: 0-3 Fm: 0-0
Distance: 5f/6f: 0-0 7f-8f: 0-4 **9f-13f: 1-9** 14f+: 0-9
Track : **LH: 1-19** RH: 0-3 **Tight: 1-16** Gall: 0-1
Aids: Bl: 0-2 Vi: 0-1 Tstrap: 0-1
Best Rating: 32 3/01 Wolv 1m4f stand

Jenko (IRE)

(95) (26)**44**
4-y-o b g College Chapel-Flicker Of Hope (IRE) (Baillamont (USA))
Miss J Feilden J W Jenkins

Placings:0460/000-0060 **(0457)**
2001: 8^{0}SD, 7^{0}SW, 8^{6}SW, 8^{0}SD

	Starts	1st	2nd	3rd	Win & Pl
Career Total (Turf)	7	0	0	0	230
Career Total (AW)	4	0	0	0	0

Going (Turf): Sf: 0-1 GS: 0-0 Gd: 0-3 GF: 0-3 Fm: 0-0
Distance: 5f/6f: 0-2 7f-8f: 0-7 9f-13f: 0-2 14f+: 0-0
Track : LH: 0-5 RH: 0-1 Tight: 0-2 Gall: 0-1
Aids: Bl: 0-5 Vi: 0-0 Tstrap: 0-0
Best Rating: 26 1/01 Sthl 1m stand

Jennash

(69) **48**
3-y-o b f Sabrehill (USA)-Kayartis (Kaytu)
C A Dwyer Mrs J A Cornwell

Placings:00-00 **(0962)**
2001: 11^{0}SD, 8^{0}HY

	Starts	1st	2nd	3rd	Win & Pl
Career Total (Turf)	3	0	0	0	
Career Total (AW)	1	0	0	0	

Going (Turf): Sf: 0-2 GS: 0-0 Gd: 0-1 GF: 0-0 Fm: 0-0
Distance: 5f/6f: 0-0 7f-8f: 0-1 9f-13f: 0-3 14f+: 0-0
Track : LH: 0-1 RH: 0-0 Tight: 0-0 Gall: 0-0
Aids: Bl: 0-0 Vi: 0-0 Tstrap: 0-0

Jennifer Jenkins

77(82) (46)**18**
3-y-o b f Komaite (USA)-Joemlujen (Forzando)
P D Evans J Powell-Tuck

Placings:00-00 **(5081)**
2001: 5^{0}GF, 9^{0}S

	Starts	1st	2nd	3rd	Win & Pl
Career Total (Turf)	3	0	0	0	
Career Total (AW)	1	0	0	0	

Going (Turf): Sf: 0-1 GS: 0-1 Gd: 0-0 GF: 0-1 Fm: 0-0
Distance: 5f/6f: 0-1 7f-8f: 0-1 9f-13f: 0-2 14f+: 0-0
Track : LH: 0-4 RH: 0-0 Tight: 0-3 Gall: 0-0
Aids: Bl: 0-0 Vi: 0-0 Tstrap: 0-0
Best Rating: 18 8/01 Catt 5f212y gd-fm

Jentzen (USA)

109 **106**
3-y-o b c Miswaki (USA)-Bold Jessie (Never So Bold)
R Hannon Jeffen Racing

Placings:41-41310304 **(4412)**
2001: 7^{4}GS, 7^{1}G, 7^{3}G, 7^{1}GF, 7^{0}GF, 6^{3}G, 6^{0}GY, 7^{4}GS

			Starts	1st	2nd	3rd	Win & Pl
Career Total (Turf)			10	3	0	2	54561
102	6/01	Epsm	7f	A		G-F	£22750
100	5/01	NmkR	7f	B(0-95)		GD	£10166
82	8/00	Sals	6f	D		GD	£3601

Total win prize-money £36517

Going (Turf): Sf: 0-0 GS: 0-2 **Gd: 2-4** GF: 1-3 Fm: 0-0
Distance: 5f/6f: 1-4 **7f-8f: 2-6** 9f-13f: 0-0 14f+: 0-0
Track : **LH: 1-2** RH: 0-0 **Tight: 1-2** Gall: 0-0
Aids: Bl: 0-0 Vi: 0-0 Tstrap: 0-0
Best Rating: 106 8/01 Asct 6f good

An improving sort, he won well at Newmarket in May 2001 before stepping up on that form in the Prix du Palais-Royal. He held on well to claim a Listed event at Epsom on Oaks day, but dhas been a little in-and-out since. He gives the impression that a drop to six furlongs will not inconvenience him.

Jepaje

86(101) (41)**41**
4-y-o b g Rambo Dancer (CAN)-Hi-Hunsley (Swing Easy (USA))
A Bailey Mrs V Farrington

Placings:0042040/000644502550-3302100000 **(2863)**
2001: 7^{3}SD, 7^{3}SW, 6^{0}SW, 7^{2}SW, 7^{1}SD, 7^{0}SW, 7^{0}GF, 6^{0}G, 8^{0}GF, 8^{0}GF

			Starts	1st	2nd	3rd		Win & Pl
Career Total (Turf)			18	0	2	0		2216
Career Total (AW)			11	1	1	2		3253
41	3/01	Ling	7f	F(0-60)H			STD	£2296

Total win prize-money £2296

Going (Turf): Sf: 0-4 GS: 0-3 Gd: 0-3 GF: 0-7 Fm: 0-1
Distance: 5f/6f: 0-11 **7f-8f: 1-17** 9f-13f: 0-1 14f+: 0-0
Track : **LH: 1-19** RH: 0-4 **Tight: 1-12** Gall: 0-3
Aids: Bl: 0-8 Vi: 0-0 Tstrap: 0-0
Best Rating: 41 3/01 Ling 7f stand

Jerpahni

92 **60**
2-y-o b f Distant Relative-Oublier L'Ennui (FR) (Bellman (FR))
G Wragg Mrs Claude Lilley

Placings:4000 **(4638)**
2001: 5^{4}GS, 6^{0}G, 6^{0}G, 7^{0}GF

	Starts	1st	2nd	3rd	Win & Pl
Career Total (Turf)	4	0	0	0	309

Going (Turf): Sf: 0-0 GS: 0-1 Gd: 0-2 GF: 0-1 Fm: 0-0
Distance: 5f/6f: 0-2 7f-8f: 0-2 9f-13f: 0-0 14f+: 0-0
Track : LH: 0-1 RH: 0-0 Tight: 0-0 Gall: 0-0
Aids: Bl: 0-0 Vi: 0-0 Tstrap: 0-0
Best Rating: 60 8/01 Yarm 6f3y good

Jervaulx Flicka

75 **33**

2-y-o b f Magic Ring (IRE)-Tirolina (IRE) (Thatching)
C W Fairhurst B Odner

Placings:6 **(3438)**
2001: 6^{6}F

	Starts	1st	2nd	3rd	Win & Pl
Career Total (Turf)	1	0	0	0	0

Going (Turf): Sf: 0-0 GS: 0-0 Gd: 0-0 GF: 0-0 Fm: 0-1
Distance: 5f/6f: 0-1 7f-8f: 0-0 9f-13f: 0-0 14f+: 0-0
Track : LH: 0-0 RH: 0-0 Tight: 0-0 Gall: 0-0
Aids: Bl: 0-0 Vi: 0-0 Tstrap: 0-0
Best Rating: 33 7/01 Thsk 6f firm

Jess Rebec's Pet (IRE)

(83) (24)**39**

4-y-o b f Petorius-Jess Rebec (Kala Shikari)
P D Evans Byron J Stokes

Placings:0000/00-000 **(0338)**
2001: 9^{0}SW, 12^{0}SD, 9^{0}SD

	Starts	1st	2nd	3rd	Win & Pl
Career Total (Turf)	5	0	0	0	
Career Total (AW)	4	0	0	0	

Going (Turf): Sf: 0-2 GS: 0-1 Gd: 0-0 GF: 0-2 Fm: 0-0
Distance: 5f/6f: 0-2 7f-8f: 0-2 9f-13f: 0-5 14f+: 0-0
Track : LH: 0-4 RH: 0-3 Tight: 0-3 Gall: 0-2
Aids: Bl: 0-0 Vi: 0-1 Tstrap: 0-0
Best Rating: 9 1/01 Wolv 1m1f79y slow

Jessica's Dream (IRE)

111 **107**

3-y-o b f Desert Style (IRE)-Ziffany (Taufan (USA))
J G Given Derek Hilton

Placings:561123110011 **(5482a)**
2001: 6^{5}F, 7^{6}GF, 6^{1}GF, 6^{1}GF, 6^{2}GS, 6^{3}GF, 5^{1}G, 5^{1}G, 5^{0}GF, 6^{0}GF, 5^{1}S, 5^{1}HY

	Starts	1st	2nd	3rd	Win & Pl
Career Total (Turf)	12	6	1	1	94875

107	10/01	Siro	5f		HVY	£35748
104	9/01	Asct	5f	B(0-105)H	SFT	£15422
96	9/01	Sand	5f6y	B(0-100)H	GD	£8700
92	8/01	York	5f	C(0-100)H	GD	£19977
81	7/01	Ripn	6f	D(0-80)H	G-F	£7442
63	6/01	Newc	6f	D	G-F	£5109

Total win prize-money £92400

Going (Turf): Sf: 2-2 GS: 0-1 **Gd: 2-2 GF: 2-6** Fm: 0-1
Distance: 5f/6f: 6-11 7f-8f: 0-1 9f-13f: 0-0 14f+: 0-0
Track : LH: 0-2 **RH: 1-1** Tight: 0-0 Gall: 0-0
Aids: Bl: 0-0 Vi: 0-0 Tstrap: 0-0
Best Rating: 107 10/01 Siro 5f heavy

Progressive sprinter, unraced as a juvenile, she won her maiden at Newcastle at the third attempt and followed up in a Ripon handicap, both times on firm ground. She took a competitive handicap over the minimum trip at the York Ebor meeting and a rated handicap at Sandown, and showed that she could handle softer ground when winning a decent handicap at Ascot in September. Crowned her season by taking an Italian Group Three in the autumn. Stays six furlongs but possibly best at five, acts on any ground.

Jessie

87 **79**

2-y-o ch f Pivotal-Bold Gem (Never So Bold)
B J Meehan F C T Wilson

Placings:61400 **(4962)**
2001: 6^{6}F, 7^{1}GS, 7^{4}G, 7^{0}GF, 8^{0}S

	Starts	1st	2nd	3rd	Win & Pl
Career Total (Turf)	5	1	0	0	4728

75	8/01	Epsm	7f	D	G-S	£4173

Total win prize-money £4173

Going (Turf): Sf: 0-1 **GS: 1-1** Gd: 0-1 GF: 0-1 Fm: 0-1
Distance: 5f/6f: 0-1 **7f-8f: 1-3** 9f-13f: 0-1 14f+: 0-0
Track : **LH: 1-2** RH: 0-1 **Tight: 1-1** Gall: 0-1
Aids: Bl: 0-0 Vi: 0-0 Tstrap: 0-0
Best Rating: 79 9/01 Kemp 7f good

Finished last on her Lingfield debut, but went on to win an Epsom maiden on much softer ground. Looked to put up a better performance in a Kempton conditions event.

Jessinca

98(105) (49)**38**

5-y-o b m Minshaanshu Amad (USA)-Noble Soul (Sayf El Arab (USA))
A P Jones The Lambourn Racing Club

Placings:U0506400**640/40/315100**01422000-**2522235**05000**0** **(4557)**
2001: 9^{2}SW, 8^{5}SD, 8^{2}SW, 7^{2}SW, 8^{2}SD, 7^{3}SD, 8^{5}SD, 7^{0}GF, 7^{5}GF, 8^{0}GF, 8^{0}G, 6^{0}GF, 9^{0}SW

	Starts	1st	2nd	3rd	Win & Pl
Career Total (Turf)	22	1	2	0	5319
Career Total (AW)	18	2	4	2	8176

47	5/00	Brig	7f214y	E(0-70)H	SFT	£2886
52	3/00	Wolv	1m100y	G(0-60)H	STD	£1572
52	2/00	Sthl	1m	E(0-70)H	STD	£2756

Total win prize-money £7215

Going (Turf): Sf: 1-3 GS: 0-2 Gd: 0-5 GF: 0-9 Fm: 0-3
Distance: 5f/6f: 0-6 **7f-8f: 2-23** 9f-13f: 1-11 14f+: 0-0
Track : **LH: 3-28** RH: 0-1 **Tight: 1-11** Gall: 0-4
Aids: Bl: 0-0 Vi: 0-2 Tstrap: 0-0
Best Rating: 49 3/01 Sthl 7f stand

A winner on All-Weather and soft turf, she is best at a mile. On a long losing run, but has been six-times runner-up during that period, meaning she gets little mercy from the Handicapper.

Jetstream Flyer

99(71) (3)**30**

3-y-o b f Distant Relative-Persian Air (Persian Bold)
J M P Eustace Guy And James Carstairs

Placings:0-3006000 **(4471)**
2001: 6^{3}GS, 8^{0}SD, 6^{0}G, 10^{6}GF, 8^{0}GS, 7^{0}GF, 6^{0}GF

	Starts	1st	2nd	3rd	Win & Pl
Career Total (Turf)	7	0	0	1	273
Career Total (AW)	1	0	0	0	

Going (Turf): Sf: 0-1 GS: 0-2 Gd: 0-1 GF: 0-3 Fm: 0-0
Distance: 5f/6f: 0-1 7f-8f: 0-5 9f-13f: 0-2 14f+: 0-0
Track : LH: 0-5 RH: 0-0 Tight: 0-1 Gall: 0-0
Aids: Bl: 0-2 Vi: 0-0 Tstrap: 0-0
Best Rating: 40 4/01 Brig 6f209y gd-sft

Jetta (IRE)

76 **48**

2-y-o b g Tagula (IRE)-Freedom's Flame (IRE) (Caerleon (USA))
A Berry Mrs A E Robertson

Placings:406 **(5029)**
2001: 5^{4}F, 5^{0}GF, 5^{6}GF

	Starts	1st	2nd	3rd	Win & Pl
Career Total (Turf)	3	0	0	0	0

Going (Turf): Sf: 0-0 GS: 0-0 Gd: 0-0 GF: 0-2 Fm: 0-1
Distance: 5f/6f: 0-3 7f-8f: 0-0 9f-13f: 0-0 14f+: 0-0
Track : LH: 0-0 RH: 0-0 Tight: 0-0 Gall: 0-0
Aids: Bl: 0-0 Vi: 0-0 Tstrap: 0-0
Best Rating: 48 9/01 Muss 5f gd-fm

Jevington Grey

42

2-y-o gr c Bal Harbour-Bercheba (Bellypha)
R M Flower M Lickert

Placings:0 **(2401)**
2001: 7^{0}F

	Starts	1st	2nd	3rd	Win & Pl
Career Total (Turf)	1	0	0	0	

Going (Turf): Sf: 0-0 GS: 0-0 Gd: 0-0 GF: 0-0 Fm: 0-1
Distance: 5f/6f: 0-0 7f-8f: 0-1 9f-13f: 0-0 14f+: 0-0
Track : LH: 0-0 RH: 0-0 Tight: 0-0 Gall: 0-0
Aids: Bl: 0-0 Vi: 0-0 Tstrap: 0-0

Jewel Of India

91 **74**

2-y-o ch c Bijou D'Inde-Low Hill (Rousillon (USA))
Sir Mark Prescott G Moore - Osborne House

Placings:34 **(4029)**
2001: 5^{3}F, 7^{4}G

	Starts	1st	2nd	3rd	Win & Pl
Career Total (Turf)	2	0	0	1	405

Going (Turf): Sf: 0-0 GS: 0-0 Gd: 0-1 GF: 0-0 Fm: 0-1
Distance: 5f/6f: 0-1 7f-8f: 0-1 9f-13f: 0-0 14f+: 0-0
Track : LH: 0-1 RH: 0-0 Tight: 0-0 Gall: 0-1
Aids: Bl: 0-0 Vi: 0-0 Tstrap: 0-0
Best Rating: 74 8/01 Newc 7f good

Jezadil (IRE)

99(99) (50)**48**

3-y-o b f Mujadil (USA)-Tender Time (Tender King)
Mrs L Stubbs (P S McEntee 8/9) O J Williams

Placings:0644340**114-6530**4056124006**1**02**06** **(5419)**
2001: 9^{6}SD, 12^{5}SD, 9^{3}SD, 11^{0}SD, 10^{4}GS, 11^{0}GS, 16^{5}GF, 9^{6}F, 11^{1}F, 11^{2}F, 11^{4}F, 11^{0}GF, 11^{0}GF, 16^{6}GF, 12^{1}SD, 10^{0}F, 9^{2}S, 12^{0}SD, 12^{6}SD

	Starts	1st	2nd	3rd	Win & Pl
Career Total (Turf)	19	1	2	1	5665
Career Total (AW)	10	3	0	1	6322

50	9/01	Wolv	1m4f	G(0-60)H	STD	£2002
48	6/01	Brig	1m3f196y	E(0-70)H	FRM	£2835
63	10/00	Wolv	1m100y	G(0-65)	STD	£1848
63	10/00	Wolv	1m100y	G	STD	£1897

Total win prize-money £8582

Going (Turf): Sf: 0-4 GS: 0-3 Gd: 0-2 GF: 0-5 **Fm: 1-5**
Distance: 5f/6f: 0-2 7f-8f: 0-5 **9f-13f: 4-20** 14f+: 0-2
Track : **LH: 4-24** RH: 0-1 **Tight: 3-17** Gall: 0-1
Aids: Bl: 0-1 Vi: 0-0 Tstrap: 0-0
Best Rating: 61 3/01 Wolv 1m1f79y stand

She has gained the majority of her wins on Fibresand and goes particularly well at Wolverhampton, but can act on turf as well and is suited by undulating tracks and fast ground.

Jezebel

105 **107**

4-y-o b f Owington-Just Ice (Polar Falcon (USA))
C F Wall Ettore Landi

Placings:11/253223-003 **(3640)**
2001: 5^{0}G, 6^{0}GF, 6^{3}GS

	Starts	1st	2nd	3rd	Win & Pl
Career Total (Turf)	11	2	3	3	47758

	6/99	Siro	6f		FRM	£16493
	6/99	Siro	5f		GD	£12758

Total win prize-money £29251

Going (Turf): Sf: 0-0 GS: 0-2 **Gd: 1-6** GF: 0-2 **Fm: 1-1**
Distance: 5f/6f: 2-10 7f-8f: 0-1 9f-13f: 0-0 14f+: 0-0
Track : LH: 0-1 **RH: 2-2** Tight: 0-0 Gall: 0-0
Aids: Bl: 0-0 Vi: 0-0 Tstrap: 0-0

Best Rating: 91 5/01 NmkR 5f good

Useful sprinter, but is proving difficult to place and has not won since her two-year-old days.

Jibereen

(103) (49)**49**

9-y-o b g Lugana Beach-Fashion Lover (Shiny Tenth)
J Pearce The Fantasy Fellowship

Placings:61421/0000001/6014/1145210601010004401/366650004021/20435200/04204310004000-3 (0005)
2001: 8^{3}SD

	Starts	1st	2nd	3rd	Win & Pl
Career Total (Turf)	36	5	2	0	21174
Career Total (AW)	35	7	4	4	23758

52	4/00	Sthl	1m3f	F	STD	£2310
86	1/99	Sthl	1m	F	STD	£2224
78	1/98	Sthl	1m	F(0-75)H	STD	£2083
62	7/97	NmkJ	1m	D(0-80)H	GD	£4698
56	6/97	NmkJ	7f	E(0-70)H	SFT	£3517
75	4/97	Sthl	1m	E(0-70)H	STD	£3096
73	1/97	Wolv	7f	F	STD	£2580
73	1/97	Sthl	7f	F	STD	£2294
67	12/96	Sthl	6f	E(0-70)H	SLW	£2616
77	10/95	Chep	7f16y	G(0-70)H	G-S	£2468
85	9/94	Brig	5f213y	D	GD	£3686
75	8/94	Sals	6f	E	G-S	£2897

Total win prize-money £34472

Going (Turf): Sf: 1-3 **GS: 2-7 Gd: 2-12** GF: 0-12 Fm: 0-2
Distance: 5f/6f: 3-8 **7f-8f: 8-46** 9f-13f: 1-17 14f+: 0-0
Track : **LH: 8-39** RH: 0-9 **Tight: 1-9** Gall: 0-2
Aids: Bl: 0-1 Vi: 0-0 Tstrap: 0-0
Best Rating: 43 1/01 Sthl 1m stand

A fair handicapper on his day, his best recent form has been on Fibresand. A mile at Southwell looks to be his ideal conditions.

Jimgareen (IRE)

68 **14**

4-y-o b/br f Lahib (USA)-Sharp Circle (IRE) (Sure Blade (USA))
M Johnston Dr J Walker

Placings:20400/0645006-000 **(1041)**
2001: 10^{0}HY, 8^{0}GS, 14^{0}HY

	Starts	1st	2nd	3rd	Win & Pl
Career Total (Turf)	15	0	1	0	1363

Going (Turf): Sf: 0-2 GS: 0-3 Gd: 0-4 GF: 0-5 Fm: 0-1
Distance: 5f/6f: 0-2 7f-8f: 0-4 9f-13f: 0-8 14f+: 0-1
Track : LH: 0-6 RH: 0-6 Tight: 0-6 Gall: 0-1
Aids: Bl: 0-2 Vi: 0-0 Tstrap: 0-0

Jimmy Floyd (IRE)

80 **51**

2-y-o b g Dolphin Street (FR)-Queen Sigi (IRE) (Fairy King (USA))
I A Balding Stamford Bridge Partnership

Placings:00 **(4837)**
2001: 8^{0}G, 8^{0}G

	Starts	1st	2nd	3rd	Win & Pl
Career Total (Turf)	2	0	0	0	

Going (Turf): Sf: 0-0 GS: 0-0 Gd: 0-2 GF: 0-0 Fm: 0-0
Distance: 5f/6f: 0-0 7f-8f: 0-1 9f-13f: 0-1 14f+: 0-0
Track : LH: 0-1 RH: 0-1 Tight: 0-0 Gall: 0-0
Aids: Bl: 0-0 Vi: 0-0 Tstrap: 0-0
Best Rating: 51 9/01 Kemp 1m good

Jimmy Swift (IRE)

68 **38**

6-y-o b g Petardia-Grade A Star (IRE) (Alzao (USA))
P R Hedger P R Hedger

Placings:4/0553423410520/300/40-0 **(1529)**
2001: 11^{0}F

	Starts	1st	2nd	3rd	Win & Pl
Career Total (Turf)	20	1	2	3	5512

88	8/98	Rosc	1m2f		G-Y	£2234

Total win prize-money £2234

Going (Turf): Sf: 0-6 GS: 0-0 Gd: 0-2 GF: 0-2 Fm: 0-1
Distance: 5f/6f: 0-2 7f-8f: 0-3 **9f-13f: 1-15** 14f+: 0-0
Track : LH: 0-11 **RH: 1-5** Tight: 0-1 Gall: 0-1
Aids: Bl: 0-1 Vi: 0-0 Tstrap: 0-2
Best Rating: 88 8/98 Rosc 1m2f GY

Jimoranni

60 **8**

2-y-o b f Rock City-Cornflower Blue (Tyrnavos)
J R Norton J B Thomson

Placings:0 **(1656)**
2001: 6^{0}F

	Starts	1st	2nd	3rd	Win & Pl
Career Total (Turf)	1	0	0	0	

Going (Turf): Sf: 0-0 GS: 0-0 Gd: 0-0 GF: 0-0 Fm: 0-1
Distance: 5f/6f: 0-1 7f-8f: 0-0 9f-13f: 0-0 14f+: 0-0
Track : LH: 0-0 RH: 0-0 Tight: 0-0 Gall: 0-0
Aids: Bl: 0-0 Vi: 0-0 Tstrap: 0-0
Best Rating: 8 5/01 Rdcr 6f firm

Jingle Rose (FR)

83 **24**

4-y-o b g Missolonghi (USA)-Quelle Etoile V (FR) (Mitsoupam (FR))
Miss Venetia Williams (P J Hobbs 2/8) Mrs R J Skan

Placings:363513-4 **(3388)**
2001: 11^{4}F

	Starts	1st	2nd	3rd	Win & Pl
Career Total (Turf)	7	1	0	3	4909

6/00	Angl	1m2f		HRD	£1921

Total win prize-money £1921

Going (Turf): Sf: 0-2 GS: 0-0 Gd: 0-0 GF: 0-0 Fm: 0-1
Distance: 5f/6f: 0-0 7f-8f: 0-0 9f-13f: 0-5 14f+: 0-0
Track : LH: 0-1 RH: 0-0 Tight: 0-1 Gall: 0-0
Aids: Bl: 0-0 Vi: 0-0 Tstrap: 0-0
Best Rating: 24 7/01 Bath 1m3f144y firm

Jingling Georgie

(72) (29)**66**

2-y-o b f Ali-Royal (IRE)-Golden Daring (IRE) (Night Shift (USA))
B Palling Celtic Racing

Placings:00500 **(5618)**
2001: 5^{0}SD, 7^{0}SD, 7^{5}GS, 8^{0}G, 8^{0}SD

	Starts	1st	2nd	3rd	Win & Pl
Career Total (Turf)	2	0	0	0	0
Career Total (AW)	3	0	0	0	

Going (Turf): Sf: 0-0 GS: 0-1 Gd: 0-1 GF: 0-0 Fm: 0-0
Distance: 5f/6f: 0-1 7f-8f: 0-2 9f-13f: 0-2 14f+: 0-0
Track : LH: 0-3 RH: 0-0 Tight: 0-2 Gall: 0-0
Aids: Bl: 0-0 Vi: 0-0 Tstrap: 0-0
Best Rating: 66 7/01 Wwck 7f26y gd-sft

Jo Mell

109(89) (61)**92**

8-y-o b g Efisio-Militia Girl (Rarity)
T D Easterby C H Newton Jnr Ltd

Placings:4413/00024353243/00000111061 1/04023012/50000000150/0101200-060000 **(3054)**
2001: 7^{0}S, 8^{6}G, 7^{0}GF, 8^{0}GF, 8^{0}G, 6^{0}G

	Starts	1st	2nd	3rd	Win & Pl
Career Total (Turf)	58	10	5	5	232589
Career Total (AW)	1	0	0	0	

95	5/00	Bevl	1m100y	C(0-95)H	GD	£6014
91	4/00	Bevl	7f100y	C(0-90)	HVY	£6435
86	9/99	Newc	7f	C(0-90)	SFT	£7164
106	8/98	Asct	7f	B H	G-F	£86000
104	10/97	Donc	7f	B	GD	£7643
103	9/97	Asct	7f	B H	G-F	£50005
92	7/97	York	7f202y	C(0-90)H	GD	£8350
85	7/97	Hayd	7f30y	C(0-95)	GD	£8027
80	6/97	Newc	7f	C(0-100)H	HVY	£13030
85	9/95	Ayr	7f	D	GD	£4807

Total win prize-money £197477

Going (Turf): Sf: 3-9 GS: 0-9 **Gd: 5-22** GF: 2-14 Fm: 0-4
Distance: 5f/6f: 0-6 **7f-8f: 9-45** 9f-13f: 1-8 14f+: 0-0
Track : **LH: 3-31** RH: 2-5 Tight: 0-5 **Gall: 1-15**
Aids: Bl: 0-0 Vi: 0-0 Tstrap: 0-0
Best Rating: 87 5/01 Thsk 1m good

Very useful 7f/1m front-running handicapper in his prime, best with an easy lead. Not just as good as he was but still retains plenty of fire in his belly. Tough and genuine. Has acted on any going in the past but might not want it too firm these days.

Jocko Glasses

88 **83+**

4-y-o ch g Inchinor-Corinthia (USA) (Empery (USA))
N J Henderson David J Jackson

Placings:5/0511-0 **(1144)**
2001: 12^{0}G

	Starts	1st	2nd	3rd	Win & Pl
Career Total (Turf)	6	2	0	0	8447

83	7/00	Wwck	1m2f188y	D(0-80)H	G-F	£3883
76	6/00	Pont	1m2f6y	E(0-75)H	G-F	£4563

Total win prize-money £8447

Going (Turf): Sf: 0-0 GS: 0-0 Gd: 0-2 **GF: 2-4** Fm: 0-0
Distance: 5f/6f: 0-0 7f-8f: 0-2 **9f-13f: 2-4** 14f+: 0-0
Track : **LH: 2-2** RH: 0-1 Tight: 0-1 Gall: 0-1
Aids: Bl: 0-0 Vi: 0-0 Tstrap: 0-0
Best Rating: 68 5/01 NmkR 1m4f good

Jodeeka

110 **89**

4-y-o ch f Fraam-Gold And Blue (IRE) (Bluebird (USA))
J A Glover S J Beard

Placings:5150-010102200 **(4658)**
2001: 6^{0}G, 5^{1}GF, 6^{0}G, 5^{1}GF, 5^{0}GF, 5^{2}GS, 5^{2}G, 6^{0}G, 5^{0}GF

	Starts	1st	2nd	3rd	Win & Pl
Career Total (Turf)	13	3	2	0	24502

85	7/01	Haml	5f4y	D(0-80)H	G-F	£7052
79	6/01	Ripn	5f	C(0-90)H	G-F	£7150
76	5/00	Donc	5f	E	G-S	£2899

Total win prize-money £17102

Going (Turf): Sf: 0-0 GS: 1-3 Gd: 0-4 **GF: 2-6** Fm: 0-0
Distance: **5f/6f: 3-13** 7f-8f: 0-0 9f-13f: 0-0 14f+: 0-0
Track : LH: 0-1 RH: 0-1 Tight: 0-0 Gall: 0-1
Aids: Bl: 0-0 Vi: 0-0 Tstrap: 0-0
Best Rating: 89 8/01 Hayd 5f good

Lightly raced, she looked progressive when winning at Ripon in June, but failed to see out the sixth furlong at York. Returned to winning form back over the minimum trip in a valuable handicap at Hamilton and has continued to run well since. Suited by the minimum trip.

Joe Taylor (CAN)

91 **20**

3-y-o b c Known Fact (USA)-Shore Mist (USA) (Coastal (USA))
C N Kellett (D W P Arbuthnot 11/5) Sean A Taylor

Placings:0-040000000 **(4319)**
2001: 7^{0}GS, 7^{4}GF, 8^{0}G, 7^{0}G, 8^{0}GF, 8^{0}GF, 9^{0}GF, 9^{0}GF, 10^{0}GF

	Starts	1st	2nd	3rd	Win & Pl
Career Total (Turf)	10	0	0	0	330

Going (Turf): Sf: 0-0 GS: 0-1 Gd: 0-2 GF: 0-7 Fm: 0-0
Distance: 5f/6f: 0-1 7f-8f: 0-3 9f-13f: 0-6 14f+: 0-0
Track : LH: 0-3 RH: 0-3 Tight: 0-0 Gall: 0-0
Aids: Bl: 0-0 Vi: 0-0 Tstrap: 0-0
Best Rating: 63 5/01 Bevl 7f100y gd-fm

Joel Ash

(74) **23**
6-y-o b g Crofthall-Lady Carol (Lord Gayle (USA))
D Shaw Miss Julie Tomkins

Placings:00/000/00000 **(2322)**
2001: 6^{0}G, 6^{0}GF, 5^{0}F, 5^{0}G, 5^{0}SD

	Starts	1st	2nd	3rd	Win & Pl
Career Total (Turf)	8	0	0	0	
Career Total (AW)	2	0	0	0	

Going (Turf): Sf: 0-0 GS: 0-0 Gd: 0-3 GF: 0-4 Fm: 0-1
Distance: 5f/6f: 0-8 7f-8f: 0-0 9f-13f: 0-2 14f+: 0-0
Track : LH: 0-3 RH: 0-1 Tight: 0-1 Gall: 0-1
Aids: Bl: 0-0 Vi: 0-0 Tstrap: 0-2
Best Rating: 23 6/01 Donc 5f firm

Joely Green

105(103) (52)**55**
4-y-o b g Binary Star (USA)-Comedy Lady (Comedy Star (USA))
N P Littmoden Paul J Dixon

Placings:02630610/23450000160-50345346 **(2115)**
2001: 12^{5}SD, 11^{0}SW, 9^{3}SD, 11^{4}SD, 11^{5}GF, 11^{3}GF, 12^{4}GF, 11^{6}F

	Starts	1st	2nd	3rd	Win & Pl
Career Total (Turf)	10	1	0	1	3625
Career Total (AW)	17	1	2	3	6563

60	7/00	Ling	1m3f106yE(0-75)H		G-F	£2842
67	11/99	Wolv	7f	D	STD	£2749

Total win prize-money £5591

Going (Turf): Sf: 0-0 GS: 0-0 Gd: 0-1 **GF: 1-8** Fm: 0-1
Distance: 5f/6f: 0-6 7f-8f: 1-6 9f-13f: 1-14 14f+: 0-1
Track : **LH: 2-21** RH: 0-3 **Tight: 2-13** Gall: 0-1
Aids: **Bl: 1-2** Vi: 0-11 Tstrap: 0-0
Best Rating: 57 6/01 NmkR 1m4f gd-fm

Joey The Jolly

71 **10**
5-y-o b g Belfort (FR)-Divine Penny (Divine Gift)
John A Harris David Pettifor

Placings:0000/0 **(4902)**
2001: 5^{0}G

	Starts	1st	2nd	3rd	Win & Pl
Career Total (Turf)	5	0	0	0	

Going (Turf): Sf: 0-1 GS: 0-1 Gd: 0-1 GF: 0-1 Fm: 0-1
Distance: 5f/6f: 0-1 7f-8f: 0-3 9f-13f: 0-1 14f+: 0-0
Track : LH: 0-2 RH: 0-1 Tight: 0-2 Gall: 0-0
Aids: Bl: 0-1 Vi: 0-0 Tstrap: 0-0

Joey The Schnoze

50
3-y-o ch g Zilzal (USA)-Linda's Design (Persian Bold)
S Magnier Fergus Jones

Placings:00 **(4857)**
2001: 5^{0}GF, 7^{0}GF

	Starts	1st	2nd	3rd	Win & Pl
Career Total (Turf)	2	0	0	0	

Going (Turf): Sf: 0-0 GS: 0-0 Gd: 0-0 GF: 0-2 Fm: 0-0
Distance: 5f/6f: 0-1 7f-8f: 0-1 9f-13f: 0-0 14f+: 0-0
Track : LH: 0-1 RH: 0-0 Tight: 0-1 Gall: 0-0
Aids: Bl: 0-0 Vi: 0-0 Tstrap: 0-1

Joey Tribbiani (IRE)

(92) (40)**45**
4-y-o b g Foxhound (USA)-Mardi Gras Belle (USA) (Masked Dancer (USA))
C N Allen Newmarketconnections.Com

Placings:063064/000000-05 **(0109)**
2001: 8^{0}SD, 8^{5}SD

	Starts	1st	2nd	3rd	Win & Pl
Career Total (Turf)	9	0	0	1	658
Career Total (AW)	5	0	0	0	0

Going (Turf): Sf: 0-3 GS: 0-2 Gd: 0-1 GF: 0-3 Fm: 0-0
Distance: 5f/6f: 0-3 7f-8f: 0-8 9f-13f: 0-2 14f+: 0-1
Track : LH: 0-8 RH: 0-1 Tight: 0-3 Gall: 0-1
Aids: Bl: 0-0 Vi: 0-0 Tstrap: 0-1
Best Rating: 36 1/01 Sthl 1m stand

Joey-Ho

80(50)
4-y-o b g Kasakov-Little Wilma (Zalazl (USA))
J J Bridger Speedforce Racing Limited

Placings:0000 **(1459)**
2001: 8^{0}SW, 7^{0}SD, 6^{0}GS, 5^{0}G

	Starts	1st	2nd	3rd	Win & Pl
Career Total (Turf)	2	0	0	0	
Career Total (AW)	2	0	0	0	

Going (Turf): Sf: 0-0 GS: 0-1 Gd: 0-1 GF: 0-0 Fm: 0-0
Distance: 5f/6f: 0-2 7f-8f: 0-2 9f-13f: 0-0 14f+: 0-0
Track : LH: 0-3 RH: 0-0 Tight: 0-2 Gall: 0-1
Aids: Bl: 0-0 Vi: 0-0 Tstrap: 0-0
Best Rating: 34 5/01 Bath 5f11y good

Johannesburg (USA)

111 (111+)**118+**
2-y-o b c Hennessy (USA)-Myth (USA) (Ogygian (USA))
A P O'Brien M Tabor & Mrs John Magnier

Placings:1111111 **(5578a)**
2001: 6^{1}F, 5^{1}GF, 6^{1}GY, 6^{1}Y, 6^{1}GS, 6^{1}GS, 8^{1}FT

	Starts	1st	2nd	3rd	Win & Pl
Career Total (Turf)	6	6	0	0	372705
Career Total (AW)	1	1	0	0	346667

111	10/01	Belm	1m110y		FST	£346667
118	10/01	NmkR	6f	A	G-S	£87000
115	8/01	Deau	6f		G-S	£77595
106	8/01	Leop	6f		YLD	£126450
112	7/01	Curr	6f63y		G-Y	£39000
94	6/01	Asct	5f	A	G-F	£33000
93	5/01	Fair	6f		FRM	£9660

Total win prize-money £719372

Going (Turf): Sf: 0-0 **GS: 2-2** Gd: 0-0 GF: 1-1 Fm: 1-1
Distance: **5f/6f: 5-5** 7f-8f: 1-1 9f-13f: 1-1 14f+: 0-0
Track : **LH: 1-1** RH: 0-0 Tight: 0-0 Gall: 0-0
Aids: Bl: 0-0 Vi: 0-0 Tstrap: 0-0
Best Rating: 118 10/01 NmkR 6f gd-sft

Scored with plenty in hand in a Fairyhouse maiden in May and has gone from strength to strength since, winning the Norfolk Stakes and Anglesey Stakes, both Group Threes, and a string of Group Ones, the Heinz 57 Phoenix Stakes, the Prix Morny and the Middle Park. However, he managed to exceed even those exploits with a brilliant win in the Breeders' Cup Juvenile, his first start on dirt and his first try beyond six furlongs. He was installed as favourite for the Kentucky Derby after that, but he has a sprint pedigree and there must be some doubt over his stamina.

Johannian

106 **103**
3-y-o b c Hernando (FR)-Photo Call (Chief Singer)
M A Jarvis J R Good

Placings:31053550 **(5501)**
2001: 10^{3}GF, 10^{1}GF, 16^{0}GF, 12^{5}GS, 11^{3}HY, 12^{5}GS, 10^{5}GS, 12^{0}HY

	Starts	1st	2nd	3rd	Win & Pl
Career Total (Turf)	8	1	0	2	7045

72	5/01	Hayd	1m2f120yD	G-F	£4225

Total win prize-money £4225

Going (Turf): Sf: 0-2 GS: 0-3 Gd: 0-0 **GF: 1-3** Fm: 0-0
Distance: 5f/6f: 0-0 7f-8f: 0-0 **9f-13f: 1-7** 14f+: 0-1
Track : **LH: 1-5** RH: 0-3 Tight: 0-1 Gall: 0-5
Aids: Bl: 0-0 Vi: 0-0 Tstrap: 0-0
Best Rating: 103 8/01 Hayd 1m3f200y heavy

Unraced at two, he looked good when winning a ten-furlong Haydock maiden on his second start at three, but did not seem to stay when down the field in the Queen's Vase. He finished a close third behind Yavana's Pace in a Haydock conditions event in August and has been panned by the Handicapper for that.

Johayro

101 (62)**55**
8-y-o ch g Clantime-Arroganza (Crofthall)
J S Goldie Frank Brady

Placings:2220051/**40**0000520600/61114050462043250 10020/0035422144000400000/5061115452501644000/ 04050000024300012200-0006660001400300200 **(4796)**
2001: 5^{0}GS, 5^{0}GF, 6^{0}G, 5^{6}G, 7^{6}GF, 7^{6}GF, 5^{0}GF, 6^{0}GF, 5^{0}GF, 6^{1}GF, 5^{4}G, 6^{0}G, 6^{0}GF, 5^{3}GF, 5^{0}GS, 6^{0}G, 5^{2}GF, 6^{0}G, 5^{0}G

	Starts	1st	2nd	3rd	Win & Pl
Career Total (Turf)	116	12	14	4	66398
Career Total (AW)	2	0	0	0	243

52	6/01	Haml	6f5y	F(0-60)H	G-F	£3080
56	8/00	Rdcr	6f	F(0-60)H	FRM	£3250
72	7/99	Thsk	6f	D(0-80)H	FRM	£4388
62	5/99	Muss	5f	E(0-75)H	FRM	£4357
58	5/99	Ayr	5f	E(0-70)H	GD	£2777
56	5/99	Muss	7f30y	E(0-70)H	G-F	£2866
65	7/98	Ayr	5f	C(0-90)H	GD	£6940
63	9/97	Rdcr	6f	E(0-80)H	FRM	£3288
54	4/97	Catt	5f212y	G	GD	£2258
61	4/97	Ripn	5f	E(0-70)H	G-F	£2705
59	4/97	Muss	5f	F(0-65)	G-F	£2582
73	10/95	Catt	5f	D	G-F	£4012

Total win prize-money £42508

Going (Turf): Sf: 0-8 GS: 0-10 Gd: 3-40 **GF: 5-47** Fm: 4-11
Distance: **5f/6f: 10-99** 7f-8f: 2-19 9f-13f: 0-0 14f+: 0-0
Track : LH: 1-11 RH: 1-4 **Tight: 2-11** Gall: 0-3
Aids: **Bl: 1-11** Vi: 0-6 Tstrap: 0-0
Best Rating: 55 8/01 Muss 5f gd-fm

Won an amateurs' handicap at Hamilton in June. Held off higher marks since.

John Ferneley

99(108) (94)**105**
6-y-o b g Polar Falcon (USA)-I'Ll Try (Try My Best (USA))
Mrs J R Ramsden J D Martin

Placings:0/1116/44133/312443-00 **(2610)**
2001: 6^{0}S, 7^{0}F

	Starts	1st	2nd	3rd	Win & Pl
Career Total (Turf)	17	5	1	3	100740
Career Total (AW)	1	0	0	1	5000

98	3/00	Donc	1m	B H	GD	£43761
86	10/99	York	7f202y	B(0-100)H	G-S	£10951
81	7/98	Sand	7f16y	D(0-85)H	G-F	£4924
81	6/98	Thsk	7f	D	GD	£3730
75	4/98	Folk	7f	F	SFT	£1720

Total win prize-money £65087

Going (Turf): Sf: 1-5 GS: 1-2 **Gd: 2-6** GF: 1-3 Fm: 0-1
Distance: 5f/6f: 0-2 **7f-8f: 5-13** 9f-13f: 0-3 14f+: 0-0
Track : **LH: 2-5** RH: 1-3 Tight: 1-2 Gall: 1-3
Aids: **Bl: 2-5** Vi: 0-0 Tstrap: 0-0
Best Rating: 93 6/01 Newc 7f firm

Winner of the Lincoln in 2000, he was beaten a neck in the Hunt Cup and continued to run well in top handicaps. He has joined Lynda Ramsden, but did not show much in two starts this term.

John Foley (IRE)

(95) (40)**53**
3-y-o b g Petardia-Fast Bay (Bay Express)
J W Unett (W M Brisbourne 9/8) Foley Steelstock

Placings:00252422600-30050 **(5407)**
2001: 8^{3}G, 8^{0}GF, 7^{0}GS, 8^{5}SD, 12^{0}SD

	Starts	1st	2nd	3rd	Win & Pl
Career Total (Turf)	7	0	1	1	1184
Career Total (AW)	9	0	3	0	2022

Going (Turf): Sf: 0-1 GS: 0-3 Gd: 0-1 GF: 0-1 Fm: 0-1
Distance: 5f/6f: 0-9 7f-8f: 0-3 9f-13f: 0-4 14f+: 0-0
Track : LH: 0-11 RH: 0-1 Tight: 0-7 Gall: 0-2
Aids: Bl: 0-1 Vi: 0-2 Tstrap: 0-0
Best Rating: 53 7/01 Haml 1m65y good

John Hunter (IRE)

102 **85**
4-y-o b c Unfuwain (USA)-Aigue (High Top)
B W Hills W J Gredley

Placings:261000000 **(5249)**
2001: 7^{2}S, 10^{6}G, 10^{1}F, 8^{0}G, 11^{0}G, 12^{0}G, 10^{0}GF, 10^{0}S, 10^{0}S

	Starts	1st	2nd	3rd	Win & Pl
Career Total (Turf)	9	1	1	0	4462

37	5/01	Rdcr	1m2f	D	FRM	£3066

Total win prize-money £3066

Going (Turf): Sf: 0-3 GS: 0-0 Gd: 0-4 GF: 0-1 **Fm: 1-1**
Distance: 5f/6f: 0-0 7f-8f: 0-1 **9f-13f: 1-8** 14f+: 0-0
Track : **LH: 1-5** RH: 0-2 **Tight: 1-2** Gall: 0-5
Aids: Bl: 0-0 Vi: 0-0 Tstrap: 0-1
Best Rating: 90 5/01 NmkR 1m2f good

Unraced at two, he showed a deal of promise on his debut and faced a massive task in a Newmarket conditions event next time. Landed odds of 1/5 at Redcar on his third start in workmanlike style, but the Handicapper overreacted and he has had little chance in decent handicaps since.

John O'Groats (IRE)

105 **82**
3-y-o b g Distinctly North (USA)-Bannons Dream (IRE) (Thatching)
M Dods Bernard Hathaway

Placings:4-11200000 **(5403)**
2001: 5^{1}S, 6^{1}S, 6^{2}GF, 6^{0}GS, 5^{0}GF, 6^{0}GF, 5^{0}GS, 5^{0}S

	Starts	1st	2nd	3rd	Win & Pl
Career Total (Turf)	9	2	1	0	9572

81	5/01	Hayd	6f	D(0-85)H	SFT	£6175
76	4/01	Nott	5f13y	F	SFT	£1897

Total win prize-money £8072

Going (Turf): Sf: 2-3 GS: 0-2 Gd: 0-0 GF: 0-3 Fm: 0-1
Distance: 5f/6f: 2-8 7f-8f: 0-1 9f-13f: 0-0 14f+: 0-0
Track : LH: 0-1 RH: 0-0 Tight: 0-0 Gall: 0-0
Aids: Bl: 0-0 Vi: 0-0 Tstrap: 0-0
Best Rating: 82 6/01 Newc 6f gd-fm

Very green on his sole start at two where he finished lame. Made up for that when making a winning reappearance in 2001 at Nottingham, followed up with another success over six furlongs at Haydock, but his form tailed off after that.

John Steed (IRE)

89 **35**
4-y-o b g Thatching-Trinity Hall (Hallgate)
N A Dunger (C Weedon 24/8) N A Dunger

Placings:600/040006-40 **(4210)**
2001: 11^{4}G, 11^{0}GF

	Starts	1st	2nd	3rd	Win & Pl
Career Total (Turf)	11	0	0	0	222

Going (Turf): Sf: 0-4 GS: 0-1 Gd: 0-4 GF: 0-2 Fm: 0-0
Distance: 5f/6f: 0-1 7f-8f: 0-3 9f-13f: 0-7 14f+: 0-0
Track : LH: 0-5 RH: 0-1 Tight: 0-5 Gall: 0-0
Aids: Bl: 0-0 Vi: 0-0 Tstrap: 0-0
Best Rating: 20 8/01 Brig 1m3f196y good

Johnny No Name (IRE)

(81)
4-y-o b g Fairy King (USA)-Zariysha (IRE) (Darshaan)
K R Burke Mrs Elaine M Burke

Placings:00000 **(1319)**
2001: 9^{0}SD, 6^{0}SD, 6^{0}HY, 5^{0}SD, 7^{0}SD

	Starts	1st	2nd	3rd	Win & Pl
Career Total (Turf)	1	0	0	0	
Career Total (AW)	4	0	0	0	

Going (Turf): Sf: 0-1 GS: 0-0 Gd: 0-0 GF: 0-0 Fm: 0-0
Distance: 5f/6f: 0-3 7f-8f: 0-1 9f-13f: 0-1 14f+: 0-0
Track : LH: 0-4 RH: 0-0 Tight: 0-2 Gall: 0-0
Aids: Bl: 0-1 Vi: 0-1 Tstrap: 0-0

Johnny Oscar

110 **83+**
4-y-o b g Belmez (USA)-Short Rations (Lorenzaccio)
J R Fanshawe J M Greetham

Placings:4330-0256316 **(4225)**
2001: 12^{0}S, 14^{2}GF, 14^{5}S, 16^{6}GF, 16^{3}GF, 14^{1}GS, 14^{6}GF

	Starts	1st	2nd	3rd	Win & Pl
Career Total (Turf)	11	1	1	3	9986

83	7/01	NmkJ	1m6f175yD(0-85)H	G-S	£6711

Total win prize-money £6711

Going (Turf): Sf: 0-3 **GS: 1-1** Gd: 0-1 GF: 0-6 Fm: 0-0
Distance: 5f/6f: 0-0 7f-8f: 0-0 9f-13f: 0-4 **14f+: 1-7**
Track : LH: 0-3 RH: 0-7 Tight: 0-1 Gall: 0-4
Aids: Bl: 0-0 Vi: 0-0 Tstrap: 0-0
Best Rating: 83 8/01 NmkJ 1m6f175y gd-fm

A half-brother to Arctic Owl, he won at Newmarket in July. Stays fourteen furlongs. Has an awkward action, but seems to act on any ground.

Johnny Reb

102 **60**
3-y-o b c Danehill (USA)-Dixie Eyes Blazing (USA) (Gone West (USA))
R Hannon Lindy Regis & Geoff Howard-Spink

Placings:260500-06106300 **(4951)**
2001: 8^{0}GF, 7^{6}GF, 8^{1}GF, 8^{0}GF, 7^{6}G, 7^{3}F, 7^{0}GF, 8^{0}G

	Starts	1st	2nd	3rd	Win & Pl
Career Total (Turf)	14	1	1	1	6314

72	6/01	Sals	1m	F(0-70)H	G-F	£3146

Total win prize-money £3147

Going (Turf): Sf: 0-2 GS: 0-1 Gd: 0-3 **GF: 1-7** Fm: 0-1
Distance: 5f/6f: 0-5 **7f-8f: 1-9** 9f-13f: 0-0 14f+: 0-0
Track : LH: 0-3 RH: 0-3 Tight: 0-1 Gall: 0-1
Aids: Bl: 0-0 Vi: 0-0 Tstrap: 0-3
Best Rating: 72 6/01 Sals 1m gd-fm

Fair colt, was suited by the mile, fast ground and making the running when getting off the mark in a small apprentice event at Salisbury in June 2001.

Johnny Staccato

97(77) (31)**45**
7-y-o b g Statoblest-Frasquita (Song)
C Drew C Drew

Placings:1466/403100003**000**/02000500**500/00**40250 000030/000000-0450215400 **(4558)**
2001: 5^{0}GS, 11^{4}F, 14^{5}GF, 10^{0}G, 10^{2}GF, 8^{1}GS, 10^{5}GF, 8^{4}GS, 9^{0}GF, 9^{0}SW

	Starts	1st	2nd	3rd	Win & Pl
Career Total (Turf)	49	3	3	3	17517
Career Total (AW)	8	0	0	0	

42	7/01	NmkJ	1m	E(0-75)H	G-S	£3532
88	6/97	Sand	5f6y	C	G-F	£4477
89	8/96	Wind	5f217y	E	SFT	£3257

Total win prize-money £11268

Going (Turf): Sf: 1-7 GS: 1-12 Gd: 0-12 **GF: 1-15** Fm: 0-3
Distance: 5f/6f: 2-34 7f-8f: 1-16 9f-13f: 0-6 14f+: 0-1
Track : LH: 0-25 **RH: 1-4** Tight: 0-9 **Gall: 1-7**
Aids: Bl: 0-1 Vi: 0-2 Tstrap: 0-0
Best Rating: 45 8/01 NmkJ 1m gd-sft

Johnson's Point

99 **61**
3-y-o ch f Sabrehill (USA)-Watership (USA) (Foolish Pleasure (USA))
M W Easterby J W P Curtis

Placings:2104-00000061623240 **(5263)**
2001: 10^{0}GS, 9^{0}S, 8^{0}S, 10^{0}GS, 9^{0}GF, 11^{0}GF, 12^{6}GF, 9^{1}GF, 12^{6}GF, 10^{2}GF, 12^{3}F, 11^{2}G, 9^{4}GF, 13^{0}GS

	Starts	1st	2nd	3rd	Win & Pl
Career Total (Turf)	18	2	3	1	11895

51	7/01	Bevl	1m1f207yE(0-70)H		G-F	£3458
72	8/00	Epsm	7f	D	G-F	£4212

Total win prize-money £7670

Going (Turf): Sf: 0-2 GS: 0-3 Gd: 0-3 **GF: 2-9** Fm: 0-1
Distance: 5f/6f: 0-0 7f-8f: 1-5 9f-13f: 1-12 14f+: 0-1
Track : LH: 1-9 RH: 1-8 **Tight: 1-7** Gall: 0-5
Aids: Bl: 0-3 Vi: 0-0 Tstrap: 0-0
Best Rating: 61 8/01 Bevl 1m1f207y gd-fm

Scored once at two over seven furlongs. Took advantage of tumbling down the weights when scoring at Beverley in July 2001. Running well since without winning. Stays a mile and a half. Has won at up to ten furlongs on fast ground.

Johnston's Diamond (IRE)

96(84) (37)**56**
3-y-o b g Tagula (IRE)-Toshair Flyer (Ballad Rock)
E J Alston Frank McKevitt

Placings:406-502 **(2724)**
2001: 7^{5}SD, 5^{0}G, 6^{2}GF

	Starts	1st	2nd	3rd	Win & Pl
Career Total (Turf)	5	0	1	0	1131
Career Total (AW)	1	0	0	0	0

Going (Turf): Sf: 0-1 GS: 0-0 Gd: 0-2 GF: 0-2 Fm: 0-0
Distance: 5f/6f: 0-4 7f-8f: 0-2 9f-13f: 0-0 14f+: 0-0
Track : LH: 0-3 RH: 0-1 Tight: 0-1 Gall: 0-1
Aids: Bl: 0-0 Vi: 0-0 Tstrap: 0-0
Best Rating: 52 7/01 Sthl 6f gd-fm

Join The Parade

95(89) (28)**35**
5-y-o b m Elmaamul (USA)-Summer Pageant (Chief's Crown (USA))
P Howling Peter Curtis

Placings:055023100/030200000-000000 **(5106)**
2001: 11^{0}GF, 10^{0}G, 10^{0}G, 9^{0}GF, 14^{0}G, 12^{0}GS

	Starts	1st	2nd	3rd	Win & Pl
Career Total (Turf)	21	1	2	2	5945
Career Total (AW)	3	0	0	0	

58 9/99 Leic 1m1f218yE(0-75)H FRM £3243
Total win prize-money £3243

Going (Turf): Sf: 0-0 GS: 0-2 Gd: 0-5 GF: 0-8 **Fm: 1-5**
Distance: 5f/6f: 0-0 7f-8f: 0-1 **9f-13f: 1-17** 14f+: 0-5
Track : LH: 0-17 **RH: 1-5** Tight: 0-12 Gall: 0-2
Aids: Bl: 0-0 Vi: 0-0 Tstrap: 0-0
Best Rating: 40 6/01 Yarm 1m2f21y good

Joint Instruction (IRE)

(96) (32)**65**
3-y-o b g Forzando-Edge Of Darkness (Vaigly Great)
D Nicholls J P Honeyman

Placings:45215202011000-0332000000 **(5418)**
2001: 6^{0}SD, 6^{3}SD, 6^{3}SD, 7^{2}SD, 7^{0}S, 7^{0}SD, 5^{0}HY, 6^{0}HY, 5^{0}G, 7^{0}SD

	Starts	1st	2nd	3rd	Win & Pl
Career Total (Turf)	18	3	3	0	9842
Career Total (AW)	6	0	1	2	1369

75 8/00 Wwck 6f21y E GD £2821
75 5/00 Brig 5f213y E SFT £2717
Total win prize-money £5538

Going (Turf): Sf: 2-9 GS: 0-1 Gd: 1-5 GF: 0-1 Fm: 0-2
Distance: 5f/6f: 1-12 **7f-8f: 2-12** 9f-13f: 0-0 14f+: 0-0
Track : **LH: 2-11** RH: 0-1 Tight: 0-4 Gall: 0-3
Aids: Bl: 0-0 Vi: 0-3 Tstrap: 0-0
Best Rating: 71 2/01 Wolv 6f stand

Triple winner in a busy juvenile campaign. Has run to a similar level of form on the All-Weather in 2001.

Jokesmith (IRE)

107 **95**
3-y-o b g Mujadil (USA)-Grinning (IRE) (Bellypha)
B J Meehan Kennet Valley Thoroughbred Ii

Placings:124001 **(5135)**
2001: 8^{1}S, 9^{2}GF, 10^{4}GF, 10^{0}G, 10^{0}HY, 10^{1}G

	Starts	1st	2nd	3rd	Win & Pl
Career Total (Turf)	6	2	1	0	16526

95 10/01 NmkR 1m2f C(0-100)H GD £7133
91 5/01 Newb 1m D SFT £5850
Total win prize-money £12984

Going (Turf): Sf: 1-2 GS: 0-0 **Gd: 1-2** GF: 0-2 Fm: 0-0
Distance: 5f/6f: 0-0 7f-8f: 1-1 9f-13f: 1-5 14f+: 0-0
Track : LH: 0-2 RH: 0-2 Tight: 0-1 Gall: 0-2
Aids: Bl: 0-0 Vi: 0-0 Tstrap: 0-0
Best Rating: 95 10/01 NmkR 1m2f good

A half-brother to a winner over seven and eight furlongs, he scored on his debut at Newbury over a mile. Just beaten on his subsequent outing at Salisbury by the smart Foreign Affairs but was then disappointing until winning at Newmarket in October. Stays nine furlongs. Acts on good to firm but has won on soft.

Jollands

96(60) (12)**50**
3-y-o b c Ezzoud (IRE)-Rainbow Fleet (Nomination)
D Marks D Marks

Placings:0300-012000600 **(2512)**
2001: 6^{0}SD, 7^{1}GS, 9^{2}S, 10^{0}GS, 9^{0}G, 10^{0}G, 11^{6}GF, 8^{0}GF, 9^{0}GF

	Starts	1st	2nd	3rd	Win & Pl
Career Total (Turf)	11	1	1	1	4568
Career Total (AW)	2	0	0	0	

73 4/01 Brig 7f214y E(0-70) G-S £2975
Total win prize-money £2975

Going (Turf): Sf: 0-1 **GS: 1-2** Gd: 0-3 GF: 0-5 Fm: 0-0
Distance: 5f/6f: 0-2 **7f-8f: 1-4** 9f-13f: 0-7 14f+: 0-0
Track : **LH: 1-7** RH: 0-2 Tight: 0-5 Gall: 0-0
Aids: Bl: 0-0 Vi: 0-2 Tstrap: 0-0
Best Rating: 79 4/01 Nott 1m1f213y soft

Winner of a mile classified event in the spring of 2001, he stays ten furlongs and acts on easy ground.

Jolly Sharp (USA)

102 **90**
4-y-o ch c Diesis-Milly Ha Ha (Dancing Brave (USA))
H R A Cecil Cliveden Stud

Placings:4/166-000 **(2261)**
2001: 12^{0}G, 14^{0}GF, 12^{0}G

	Starts	1st	2nd	3rd	Win & Pl
Career Total (Turf)	7	1	0	0	4625

89 4/00 Kemp 1m3f30y D SFT £4387
Total win prize-money £4388

Going (Turf): Sf: 1-2 GS: 0-0 Gd: 0-4 GF: 0-1 Fm: 0-0
Distance: 5f/6f: 0-0 7f-8f: 0-0 **9f-13f: 1-5** 14f+: 0-2
Track : LH: 0-3 **RH: 1-4** Tight: 0-2 Gall: 0-3
Aids: Bl: 0-0 Vi: 0-0 Tstrap: 0-0
Best Rating: 88 5/01 Gdwd 1m6f gd-fm

Jona Holley

43 (44)**51**
8-y-o b g Sharpo-Spurned (USA) (Robellino (USA))
A Streeter Malt 'N' Hops

Placings:00/00050/0542212041/0226/540650614/06-0 **(5448)**
2001: 10^{0}HY

	Starts	1st	2nd	3rd	Win & Pl
Career Total (Turf)	30	2	4	0	10909
Career Total (AW)	3	1	1	0	2998

51 10/99 Ayr 1m1f20y F SFT £2582
52 10/97 Sthl 1m G(0-70)H STD £1984
50 7/97 Folk 1m1f149yF(0-60)H SFT £3201
Total win prize-money £7769

Going (Turf): Sf: 2-11 GS: 0-4 Gd: 0-8 GF: 0-6 Fm: 0-1
Distance: 5f/6f: 0-0 7f-8f: 1-10 **9f-13f: 2-23** 14f+: 0-0
Track : **LH: 2-13** RH: 1-16 **Tight: 1-15** Gall: 0-3
Aids: **Bl: 1-7** Vi: 0-2 Tstrap: 0-0

Jonalton (IRE)

83 **54**
2-y-o b c Perugino (USA)-Vago Pequeno (IRE) (Posen (USA))
Mrs P Sly T Crowson

Placings:0000 **(5168)**
2001: 6^{0}GF, 8^{0}GS, 8^{0}GF, 10^{0}GS

	Starts	1st	2nd	3rd	Win & Pl
Career Total (Turf)	4	0	0	0	

Going (Turf): Sf: 0-0 GS: 0-2 Gd: 0-0 GF: 0-2 Fm: 0-0
Distance: 5f/6f: 0-0 7f-8f: 0-2 9f-13f: 0-2 14f+: 0-0
Track : LH: 0-2 RH: 0-0 Tight: 0-0 Gall: 0-0

Aids: Bl: 0-0 Vi: 0-0 Tstrap: 0-0
Best Rating: 54 8/01 NmkJ 1m gd-sft

Jones'Folly (IRE)

87(74) (38)**62**
2-y-o b c Anita's Prince-Dame's Folly (IRE) (King's Lake (USA))
B Palling Dominic Fagan

Placings:6500 **(5458)**
2001: 7^{6}GS, 8^{5}GF, 7^{0}SD, 5^{0}G

	Starts	1st	2nd	3rd	Win & Pl
Career Total (Turf)	3	0	0	0	0
Career Total (AW)	1	0	0	0	

Going (Turf): Sf: 0-0 GS: 0-1 Gd: 0-1 GF: 0-1 Fm: 0-0
Distance: 5f/6f: 0-1 7f-8f: 0-2 9f-13f: 0-1 14f+: 0-0
Track : LH: 0-2 RH: 0-0 Tight: 0-0 Gall: 0-1
Aids: Bl: 0-0 Vi: 0-0 Tstrap: 0-0
Best Rating: 62 7/01 Wwck 7f26y gd-sft

Jonesy

3-y-o b g Emperor Jones (USA)-Don't Jump (IRE) (Entitled)
J Gallagher B P Jones

Placings:00 **(2433)**
2001: 8^{0}F, 8^{0}GF

	Starts	1st	2nd	3rd	Win & Pl
Career Total (Turf)	2	0	0	0	

Going (Turf): Sf: 0-0 GS: 0-0 Gd: 0-0 GF: 0-1 Fm: 0-1
Distance: 5f/6f: 0-0 7f-8f: 0-0 9f-13f: 0-2 14f+: 0-0
Track : LH: 0-0 RH: 0-1 Tight: 0-1 Gall: 0-0
Aids: Bl: 0-0 Vi: 0-0 Tstrap: 0-0

Joni Wikabe (IRE)

(69) (25)
2-y-o b g Nicolotte-Shoot To Kill (Posse (USA))
R M H Cowell Celtic Connections

Placings:000 **(4069)**
2001: 5^{0}SD, 5^{0}GF, 6^{0}SD

	Starts	1st	2nd	3rd	Win & Pl
Career Total (Turf)	1	0	0	0	
Career Total (AW)	2	0	0	0	

Going (Turf): Sf: 0-0 GS: 0-0 Gd: 0-0 GF: 0-1 Fm: 0-0
Distance: 5f/6f: 0-3 7f-8f: 0-0 9f-13f: 0-0 14f+: 0-0
Track : LH: 0-1 RH: 0-0 Tight: 0-1 Gall: 0-0
Aids: Bl: 0-0 Vi: 0-0 Tstrap: 0-0
Best Rating: 25 8/01 Wolv 6f stand

Jonjo

79 **43**
3-y-o b g Charnwood Forest (IRE)-Katy-Q (IRE) (Taufan (USA))
J G Given Mr & Mrs D J Smart

Placings:040 **(4319)**
2001: 8^{0}GF, 10^{4}GS, 10^{0}GF

	Starts	1st	2nd	3rd	Win & Pl
Career Total (Turf)	3	0	0	0	339

Going (Turf): Sf: 0-0 GS: 0-1 Gd: 0-0 GF: 0-2 Fm: 0-0
Distance: 5f/6f: 0-0 7f-8f: 0-0 9f-13f: 0-3 14f+: 0-0
Track : LH: 0-3 RH: 0-0 Tight: 0-0 Gall: 0-0
Aids: Bl: 0-0 Vi: 0-0 Tstrap: 0-0
Best Rating: 43 6/01 Hayd 1m30y gd-fm

Jonloz

104(77) (41)33

4-y-o ch g Presidium-Stratford Lady (Touching Wood (USA))

A B Mulholland P Appleyard

Placings:600040/545660120-000400060 **(5294)**

2001: 12^{0}GF, 11^{0}GF, 14^{0}GF, 9^{4}GF, 12^{0}GF, 11^{0}GF, 12^{0}G, 11^{6}GF, 11^{0}S

	Starts	1st	2nd	3rd	Win & Pl
Career Total (Turf)	20	1	1	0	3215
Career Total (AW)	4	0	0	0	0

47 8/00 Bevl 1m3f216yF(0-60)H GD £2310

Total win prize-money £2310

Going (Turf): Sf: 0-4 GS: 0-1 **Gd: 1-6** GF: 0-9 Fm: 0-0

Distance: 5f/6f: 0-2 7f-8f: 0-8 **9f-13f: 1-15** 14f+: 0-1

Track : LH: 0-11 **RH: 1-9 Tight: 1-7** Gall: 0-0

Aids: Bl: 0-0 Vi: 0-0 Tstrap: 0-0

Best Rating: 38 7/01 Bevl 1m1f207y gd-fm

Jonny Ebeneezer

93

2-y-o b g Hurricane Sky (AUS)-Leap Of Faith (IRE) (Northiam (USA))

I A Wood John Purcell

Placings:0301 **(5588)**

2001: 6^{0}GF, 7^{3}S, 7^{0}GS, 5^{1}GS

	Starts	1st	2nd	3rd	Win & Pl
Career Total (Turf)	4	1	0	1	5932

93 11/01 Brig 5f213y D G-S £3627

Total win prize-money £3627

Going (Turf): Sf: 0-1 **GS: 1-2** Gd: 0-0 GF: 0-1 Fm: 0-0

Distance: **5f/6f: 1-1** 7f-8f: 0-3 9f-13f: 0-0 14f+: 0-0

Track : **LH: 1-1** RH: 0-0 Tight: 0-0 Gall: 0-0

Aids: Bl: 0-0 Vi: 0-0 Tstrap: 0-0

Best Rating: 93 11/01 Brig 5f213y gd-sft

Finished third in a conditions event at Ascot in September, before being well beaten in a very similar event over course and distance. Came good in a Brighton maiden in November.

Jools

105(102) (72)65

3-y-o b c Cadeaux Genereux-Madame Crecy (USA) (Al Nasr (FR))

Mrs N Macauley (W J Haggas 22/6) Diamond Racing Ltd

Placings:41060114540 **(4988)**

2001: 7^{4}SD, 7^{1}SW, 8^{0}SD, 10^{6}SW, 7^{0}F, 8^{1}GF, 8^{1}GF, 8^{4}GF, 8^{5}G, 7^{4}GF, 8^{0}G

	Starts	1st	2nd	3rd	Win & Pl
Career Total (Turf)	7	2	0	0	8216
Career Total (AW)	4	1	0	0	2373

56 6/01 NmkJ 1m E G-F £3474

44 6/01 NmkJ 1m E G-F £3591

72 1/01 Wolv 7f D SLW £2373

Total win prize-money £9438

Going (Turf): Sf: 0-0 GS: 0-0 Gd: 0-2 **GF: 2-4** Fm: 0-1

Distance: 5f/6f: 0-0 **7f-8f: 3-8** 9f-13f: 0-3 14f+: 0-0

Track : **LH: 1-4** RH: 0-1 **Tight: 1-3** Gall: 0-0

Aids: Bl: 0-0 Vi: 0-1 Tstrap: 0-0

Best Rating: 72 1/01 Wolv 7f slow

Won on Fibresand at the start of the year and a couple of fast-ground claimers at Newmarket in June.

Jordan's Ridge (IRE)

102 58

5-y-o b/br g Indian Ridge-Sadie Jordan (USA) (Hail The Pirates (USA))

P Monteith Allan W Melville

Placings:00452650/002-320 **(1138)**

2001: 16^{3}S, 14^{2}GS, 13^{0}G

	Starts	1st	2nd	3rd	Win & Pl
Career Total (Turf)	14	0	3	1	3477

Going (Turf): Sf: 0-4 GS: 0-1 Gd: 0-4 GF: 0-1 Fm: 0-0

Distance: 5f/6f: 0-0 7f-8f: 0-3 9f-13f: 0-6 14f+: 0-5

Track : LH: 0-1 RH: 0-11 Tight: 0-3 Gall: 0-3

Aids: Bl: 0-1 Vi: 0-2 Tstrap: 0-0

Best Rating: 56 4/01 Muss 1m6f gd-sft

Jorrocks (USA)

(115) (102)72d

7-y-o b g Rubiano (USA)-Perla Fina (USA) (Gallant Man)

R Hess Jr (M W Easterby 1/2) Duggan, Equils & Mowbray

Placings:23211614/4306030003/00005010/26000121-12110

2001: 8^{1}SD, 9^{2}SW, 7^{1}SW, 8^{1}SD, 10^{0}FT

	Starts	1st	2nd	3rd	Win & Pl
Career Total (Turf)	32	4	3	4	43621
Career Total (AW)	8	5	2	0	31828

102 2/01 Wolv 1m100y C STD £6177

91 1/01 Sthl 7f C(0-100)H SLW £8190

88 1/01 Sthl 1m C(0-90)H STD £8190

82 12/00 Sthl 1m D(0-85)H STD £3789

68 11/00 Sthl 7f F(0-60)H STD £2016

59 9/99 Bevl 7f100y E(0-70)H SFT £3350

94 9/97 Newb 7f64y C(0-95)H SFT £6287

85 8/97 Gdwd 7f C(0-100)H G-F £20535

77 7/97 Sand 7f16y D(0-85)H G-F £4299

Total win prize-money £62835

Going (Turf): Sf: 2-8 GS: 0-3 Gd: 0-9 **GF: 2-11** Fm: 0-1

Distance: 5f/6f: 0-1 **7f-8f: 8-27** 9f-13f: 1-12 14f+: 0-0

Track : **LH: 6-21** RH: 3-9 Tight: 1-7 Gall: 1-4

Aids: Bl: 0-1 Vi: 0-0 Tstrap: 0-0

Best Rating: 102 2/01 Wolv 1m100y stand

He showed some very smart form on Fibresand during the winter of 2000/2001, winning five times and ending Hail The Chief's winning run at Wolverhampton. Continued his career in the US afterwards.

Joseph William (IRE)

85(59) (17)59

2-y-o b c College Chapel-Murroe Star (Glenstal (USA))

C N Kellett Sean A Taylor

Placings:0000 **(5536)**

2001: 7^{0}F, 7^{0}S, 6^{0}SD, 6^{0}S

	Starts	1st	2nd	3rd	Win & Pl
Career Total (Turf)	3	0	0	0	
Career Total (AW)	1	0	0	0	

Going (Turf): Sf: 0-2 GS: 0-0 Gd: 0-0 GF: 0-0 Fm: 0-1

Distance: 5f/6f: 0-2 7f-8f: 0-2 9f-13f: 0-0 14f+: 0-0

Track : LH: 0-2 RH: 0-0 Tight: 0-2 Gall: 0-0

Aids: Bl: 0-0 Vi: 0-0 Tstrap: 0-0

Best Rating: 59 9/01 Ches 7f2y soft

Joy Of Norway

62(102) (65)34

3-y-o b g Halling (USA)-Triple Joy (Most Welcome)

Sir Mark Prescott Hesmonds Stud

Placings:44200 **(5131)**

2001: 7^{4}SW, 7^{4}SD, 8^{2}SD, 8^{0}GF, 7^{0}HY

	Starts	1st	2nd	3rd	Win & Pl
Career Total (Turf)	2	0	0	0	
Career Total (AW)	3	0	1	0	859

Going (Turf): Sf: 0-1 GS: 0-0 Gd: 0-0 GF: 0-1 Fm: 0-0

Distance: 5f/6f: 0-0 7f-8f: 0-3 9f-13f: 0-2 14f+: 0-0

Track : LH: 0-3 RH: 0-0 Tight: 0-3 Gall: 0-0

Aids: Bl: 0-1 Vi: 0-0 Tstrap: 0-1

Best Rating: 65 3/01 Wolv 1m100y stand

Joyce's Choice

95 74

2-y-o b c Mind Games-Madrina (Waajib)

A Berry Billy Parker

Placings:513040 **(5636)**

2001: 5^{5}GF, 5^{1}GS, 6^{3}G, 6^{0}GS, 5^{4}S, 5^{0}G

	Starts	1st	2nd	3rd	Win & Pl
Career Total (Turf)	6	1	0	1	5046

76 8/01 Thsk 5f E G-S £3692

Total win prize-money £3693

Going (Turf): Sf: 0-1 **GS: 1-2** Gd: 0-2 GF: 0-1 Fm: 0-0

Distance: **5f/6f: 1-5** 7f-8f: 0-1 9f-13f: 0 0 14f+: 0-0

Track : LH: 0-2 RH: 0-0 Tight: 0-2 Gall: 0-0

Aids: Bl: 0-0 Vi: 0-0 Tstrap: 0-0

Best Rating: 76 8/01 Thsk 5f gd-sft

Landed a Thirsk maiden on his second start when there was some cut in the ground.

Joyful Illusion

30

2-y-o b/br f Robellino (USA)-Sharp Falcon (IRE) (Shaadi (USA))

M D I Usher P Sweeting & Mr And Mrs J Purvis

Placings:000 **(3215)**

2001: 6^{0}GF, 5^{0}G, 7^{0}GF

	Starts	1st	2nd	3rd	Win & Pl
Career Total (Turf)	3	0	0	0	

Going (Turf): Sf: 0-0 GS: 0-0 Gd: 0-1 GF: 0-2 Fm: 0-0

Distance: 5f/6f: 0-2 7f-8f: 0-1 9f-13f: 0-0 14f+: 0-0

Track : LH: 0-0 RH: 0-0 Tight: 0-0 Gall: 0-0

Aids: Bl: 0-0 Vi: 0-0 Tstrap: 0-0

Best Rating: 30 6/01 Gdwd 6f gd-fm

Joyfull Dream (FR)

(84) (12)9

3-y-o ch f Midyan (USA)-Villa Maria Pia (FR) (Alwasmi (USA))

Mrs N Macauley (A Spanu 17/1) Mrs N Macauley

Placings:016046360005-20000000 **(4898)**

2001: 5^{2}SD, 7^{0}SD, 5^{0}SD, 6^{0}HY, 5^{0}SD, 9^{0}SD, 6^{0}S, 5^{0}GS

	Starts	1st	2nd	3rd	Win & Pl
Career Total (Turf)	15	1	0	1	9126
Career Total (AW)	5	0	1	0	

5/00 Chan 5f SFT £5764

Total win prize-money £5764

Going (Turf): Sf: 0-3 GS: 0-1 Gd: 0-0 GF: 0-0 Fm: 0-0

Distance: 5f/6f: 0-5 7f-8f: 0-3 9f-13f: 0-1 14f+: 0-0

Track : LH: 0-3 RH: 0-0 Tight: 0-3 Gall: 0-0

Aids: Bl: 0-1 Vi: 0-6 Tstrap: 0-0

Best Rating: 50 1/01 Ling 5f stand

Judge Davidson

94 82+

2-y-o b c Royal Applause-Without Warning (IRE) (Warning)

J R Fanshawe M Fisch

Placings:321 **(5633)**

2001: 6^{3}GF, 6^{2}GF, 7^{1}G

	Starts	1st	2nd	3rd	Win & Pl
Career Total (Turf)	3	1	1	1	4278

82 11/01 Catt 7f E GD £2884

Total win prize-money £2884

Going (Turf): Sf: 0-0 GS: 0-0 **Gd: 1-1** GF: 0-2 Fm: 0-0

Distance: 5f/6f: 0-1 **7f-8f: 1-2** 9f-13f: 0-0 14f+: 0-0

Track : **LH: 1-1** RH: 0-0 **Tight: 1-1** Gall: 0-0

Aids: Bl: 0-0 Vi: 0-0 Tstrap: 0-0
Best Rating: 82 11/01 Catt 7f good

Came good at the third attempt in a moderate back-end maiden at Catterick. Stays seven furlongs.

Judiam

94(99) (63)63

4-y-o b f Primo Dominie-Hoist (IRE) (Bluebird (USA))
C A Dwyer R West

Placings:05303021/45000510000-40 (5685)
2001: 5^{4}HY, 5^{0}S

	Starts	1st	2nd	3rd	Win & Pl
Career Total (Turf)	20	2	1	2	9461
Career Total (AW)	1	0	0	0	312

63 7/00 Kemp 5f E(0-75)H G-S £4329
74 10/99 Yarm 5f43y E(0-85)H G-S £2906
Total win prize-money £7235

Going (Turf): Sf: 0-6 **GS: 2-4** Gd: 0-3 GF: 0-6 Fm: 0-1
Distance: **5f/6f: 2-20** 7f-8f: 0-1 9f-13f: 0-0 14f+: 0-0
Track : LH: 0-2 RH: 0-1 Tight: 0-2 Gall: 0-1
Aids: Bl: 0-0 Vi: 0-0 Tstrap: 0-0
Best Rating: 39 10/01 Newb 5f34y heavy

Judicious (IRE)

104 86

4-y-o b c Fairy King (USA)-Kama Tashoof (Mtoto)
G Wragg Mollers Racing

Placings:00/0301622-0130 (2972)
2001: 8^{0}S, 7^{1}F, 8^{3}GF, 7^{0}G

	Starts	1st	2nd	3rd	Win & Pl
Career Total (Turf)	13	2	2	2	15350

57 6/01 Thsk 7f D(0-80) FRM £4478
76 8/00 Leic 1m8y E(0-70)H G-F £3623
Total win prize-money £8103

Going (Turf): Sf: 0-5 GS: 0-1 Gd: 0-2 **GF: 1-4 Fm: 1-1**
Distance: 5f/6f: 0-0 7f-8f: 1-8 9f-13f: 1-5 14f+: 0-0
Track : **LH: 1-4** RH: 0-0 **Tight: 1-2** Gall: 0-1
Aids: Bl: 0-0 Vi: 0-0 Tstrap: 0-0
Best Rating: 80 6/01 Newb 1m gd-fm

Has had problems with the stalls in the past and is loaded late now. Ran as if needing the run on his turf reappearance but made no mistake in a weak Thirsk classified event next time. He did not get the run of the race in his next start at Newbury and does need things to go his way. Best at around a mile.

Jufiscea

91 71

2-y-o b g Efisio-Jucea (Bluebird (USA))
M R Channon G M Eales

Placings:200 (4663)
2001: 6^{2}F, 5^{0}GF, 6^{0}GF

	Starts	1st	2nd	3rd	Win & Pl
Career Total (Turf)	3	0	1	0	1148

Going (Turf): Sf: 0-0 GS: 0-0 Gd: 0-0 GF: 0-2 Fm: 0-1
Distance: 5f/6f: 0-3 7f-8f: 0-0 9f-13f: 0-0 14f+: 0-0
Track : LH: 0-1 RH: 0-0 Tight: 0-0 Gall: 0-0
Aids: Bl: 0-0 Vi: 0-0 Tstrap: 0-0
Best Rating: 71 8/01 Brig 5f213y gd-fm

Juliet Turner (IRE)

60(54) 5

2-y-o b f General Monash (USA)-Solway Lass (IRE) (Anita's Prince)
J S Moore J S Moore

Placings:00 (2436)
2001: 6^{0}SD, 5^{0}G

	Starts	1st	2nd	3rd	Win & Pl
Career Total (Turf)	1	0	0	0	
Career Total (AW)	1	0	0	0	

Going (Turf): Sf: 0-0 GS: 0-0 Gd: 0-1 GF: 0-0 Fm: 0-0
Distance: 5f/6f: 0-2 7f-8f: 0-0 9f-13f: 0-0 14f+: 0-0
Track : LH: 0-1 RH: 0-0 Tight: 0-0 Gall: 0-0
Aids: Bl: 0-0 Vi: 0-0 Tstrap: 0-0
Best Rating: 5 6/01 Yarm 5f43y good

Julius (IRE)

107 92

4-y-o b f Persian Bold-Babushka (IRE) (Dance Of Life (USA))
M Johnston Mrs K E Daley

Placings:0336/121111040510-250 (2383)
2001: 9^{2}GF, 12^{5}GF, 10^{0}GF

	Starts	1st	2nd	3rd	Win & Pl
Career Total (Turf)	19	6	2	2	34389

88 9/00 NmkR 1m2f E(0-85)H G-S £5086
79 6/00 Newc 1m2f32y D(0-75) FRM £5617
91 6/00 Ches 1m4f66y D(0-85)H G-F £3731
82 6/00 Ripn 1m2f E(0-70) G-F £2746
82 6/00 Muss 1m4f E(0-75)H FRM £8658
64 6/00 Nott 1m1f213yF(0-70) G-F £2278
Total win prize-money £28118

Going (Turf): Sf: 0-1 GS: 1-2 Gd: 0-6 **GF: 3-8** Fm: 2-2
Distance: 5f/6f: 0-0 7f-8f: 0-4 **9f-13f: 6-15** 14f+: 0-0
Track : **LH: 3-8** RH: 2-10 **Tight: 3-7** Gall: 1-6
Aids: Bl: 0-0 Vi: 0-0 Tstrap: 0-0
Best Rating: 92 6/01 Epsm 1m4f10y gd-fm

She had a blinding time in 2000, winning no fewer than six times over trips ranging from ten to 12 furlongs. Not surprisingly, she rose swiftly in the handicap, but she has been running well this season. She has won with cut, but looks especially suited by fast ground.

Jumaireyah

107 89

3-y-o b f Fairy King (USA)-Donya (Mill Reef (USA))
L M Cumani Sheikh Mohammed Obaid Al Maktoum

Placings:1-5202100 (5669)
2001: 8^{5}GF, 10^{2}S, 10^{0}GS, 10^{2}HY, 10^{1}G, 12^{0}HY, 10^{0}HY

	Starts	1st	2nd	3rd	Win & Pl
Career Total (Turf)	8	2	2	0	32472

89 9/01 Donc 1m2f60y C(0-95)H GD £19987
75 10/00 Wind 1m67y D HVY £4166
Total win prize-money £24155

Going (Turf): Sf: 1-5 GS: 0-1 **Gd: 1-1** GF: 0-1 Fm: 0-0
Distance: 5f/6f: 0-0 7f-8f: 0-1 **9f-13f: 2-7** 14f+: 0-0
Track : LH: 1-4 RH: 1-2 Tight: 1-2 Gall: 1-2
Aids: Bl: 0-0 Vi: 0-0 Tstrap: 0-0
Best Rating: 89 9/01 Donc 1m2f60y good

Won a heavy-ground maiden in October of 2000 and after a fair effort on faster ground on her reappearance, was unlucky to be touched off at Haydock next time. Ran another good race on the same tack in September, before scoring in a competitive event at Doncaster, although she proved disappointing after that at Ascot when maybe not staying the 12 furlong trip. Stays ten furlongs and likely to need cut in the ground.

Jumbo Jade

66 22

5-y-o ch m Jumbo Hirt (USA)-Miss Mac (Smackover)
E J Alston M D Townson

Placings:0000 (2040)
2001: 9^{0}GS, 10^{0}S, 9^{0}GF, 17^{0}GF

	Starts	1st	2nd	3rd	Win & Pl
Career Total (Turf)	4	0	0	0	

Going (Turf): Sf: 0-1 GS: 0-1 Gd: 0-0 GF: 0-2 Fm: 0-0
Distance: 5f/6f: 0-0 7f-8f: 0-0 9f-13f: 0-3 14f+: 0-1
Track : LH: 0-2 RH: 0-1 Tight: 0-0 Gall: 0-1
Aids: Bl: 0-0 Vi: 0-0 Tstrap: 0-0
Best Rating: 22 5/01 Bevl 1m1f207y gd-fm

Jumbo Jet

68 44

4-y-o b g Emarati (USA)-Mithi Al Gamar (USA) (Blushing Groom (FR))
B R Millman Mrs A K H Ooi

Placings:40550-00 (1476)
2001: 7^{0}G, 6^{0}G

	Starts	1st	2nd	3rd	Win & Pl
Career Total (Turf)	7	0	0	0	208

Going (Turf): Sf: 0-0 GS: 0-3 Gd: 0-2 GF: 0-2 Fm: 0-0
Distance: 5f/6f: 0-2 7f-8f: 0-3 9f-13f: 0-2 14f+: 0-0
Track : LH: 0-0 RH: 0-3 Tight: 0-2 Gall: 0-1
Aids: Bl: 0-0 Vi: 0-0 Tstrap: 0-3
Best Rating: 22 5/01 Leic 7f9y good

Jumbo's Flyer

(88) (43)56

4-y-o ch g Jumbo Hirt (USA)-Fragrant Princess (Germont)
F P Murtagh (J L Eyre 6/2) T H Littleton

Placings:500/0524620030000-0 (0053)
2001: 12^{0}SD

	Starts	1st	2nd	3rd	Win & Pl
Career Total (Turf)	12	0	2	1	2772
Career Total (AW)	5	0	0	0	

Going (Turf): Sf: 0-1 GS: 0-1 Gd: 0-3 GF: 0-4 Fm: 0-3
Distance: 5f/6f: 0-0 7f-8f: 0-10 9f-13f: 0-7 14f+: 0-0
Track : LH: 0-8 RH: 0-8 Tight: 0-8 Gall: 0-1
Aids: Bl: 0-0 Vi: 0-0 Tstrap: 0-0
Best Rating: 24 1/01 Sthl 1m4f stand

Jumeirah Dream (USA)

96 78

2-y-o ch c Diesis-Golden Vale (USA) (Slew O'Gold (USA))
E A L Dunlop Jumeirah Racing

Placings:020 (4585)
2001: 6^{0}GF, 7^{2}GF, 7^{0}HY

	Starts	1st	2nd	3rd	Win & Pl
Career Total (Turf)	3	0	1	0	1285

Going (Turf): Sf: 0-1 GS: 0-0 Gd: 0-0 GF: 0-2 Fm: 0-0
Distance: 5f/6f: 0-0 7f-8f: 0-3 9f-13f: 0-0 14f+: 0-0
Track : LH: 0-1 RH: 0-1 Tight: 0-0 Gall: 0-1
Aids: Bl: 0-0 Vi: 0-0 Tstrap: 0-0
Best Rating: 78 7/01 Kemp 7f gd-fm

Jumeirah Song (USA)

84 60

2-y-o b c Sultry Song (USA)-Sunnytime Lady (USA) (Majestic Light (USA))
M R Channon Jumeirah Racing

Placings:00 (5040)
2001: 8^{0}G, 10^{0}G

	Starts	1st	2nd	3rd	Win & Pl
Career Total (Turf)	2	0	0	0	

Going (Turf): Sf: 0-0 GS: 0-0 Gd: 0-2 GF: 0-0 Fm: 0-0
Distance: 5f/6f: 0-0 7f-8f: 0-0 9f-13f: 0-2 14f+: 0-0

Track : LH: 0-2 RH: 0-0 Tight: 0-1 Gall: 0-0
Aids: Bl: 0-0 Vi: 0-0 Tstrap: 0-0
Best Rating: 60 10/01 Bath 1m2f46y good

Jump (USA)

92(100) (42)**19**
4-y-o b g Trempolino (USA)-Professional Dance (USA) (Nijinsky (CAN))
A W Carroll Dennis Deacon

Placings:05/260040000-0000 **(3301)**
2001: 14^{0}SD, 8^{0}SD, 9^{0}G, 11^{0}GF

	Starts	1st	2nd	3rd	Win & Pl
Career Total (Turf)	9	0	0	0	0
Career Total (AW)	6	0	1	0	876

Going (Turf): Sf: 0-0 GS: 0-1 Gd: 0-2 GF: 0-3 Fm: 0-3
Distance: 5f/6f: 0-1 7f-8f: 0-5 9f-13f: 0-8 14f+: 0-1
Track : LH: 0-10 RH: 0-2 Tight: 0-5 Gall: 0-0
Aids: Bl: 0-1 Vi: 0-0 Tstrap: 0-0
Best Rating: 21 3/01 Sthl 1m6f stand

Jungle Lion

96 **95**
3-y-o ch c Lion Cavern (USA)-Star Ridge (USA) (Storm Bird (CAN))
H R A Cecil Buckram Oak Holdings

Placings:1-40 **(4074)**
2001: 10^{4}GF, 8^{0}G

	Starts	1st	2nd	3rd	Win & Pl
Career Total (Turf)	3	1	0	0	4141
95 11/00 Donc 7f	D			HVY	£3331

Total win prize-money £3331

Going (Turf): Sf: 1-1 GS: 0-0 Gd: 0-1 GF: 0-1 Fm: 0-0
Distance: 5f/6f: 0-0 **7f-8f: 1-1** 9f-13f: 0-2 14f+: 0-0
Track : LH: 0-2 RH: 0-0 Tight: 0-1 Gall: 0-1
Aids: Bl: 0-0 Vi: 0-0 **Tstrap: 1-1**
Best Rating: 84 5/01 Donc 1m2f60y gd-fm

Junikay (IRE)

108 (36)**77**
7-y-o b g Treasure Kay-Junijo (Junius (USA))
R Ingram Ellangowan Racing Partners

Placings:44201/50000003560/001000660656320/0510 02663255044/021132041430-04105635010006 **(5463)**
2001: 10^{0}GS, 10^{4}G, 10^{1}GF, 10^{0}GF, 9^{5}GF, 10^{6}G, 10^{3}G, 9^{5}G, 10^{0}GF, 10^{1}G, 10^{0}G, 10^{0}GF, 10^{0}S, 11^{6}G

	Starts	1st	2nd	3rd	Win & Pl
Career Total (Turf)	71	8	6	6	48573
Career Total (AW)	1	0	0	0	

75	9/01	Kemp	1m2f	D(0-85)H	GD	£7800
74	5/01	Sthl	1m2f	E(0-75)H	G-F	£3003
72	8/00	Gdwd	1m1f	D(0-80)H	GD	£9789
61	5/00	Ling	1m1f	F(0-60)H	G-S	£2772
56	5/00	Nott	1m1f213y	F(0-60)H	G-F	£2625
54	5/99	Nott	1m1f213y	F(0-60)H	FRM	£2868
58	5/98	Brig	6f209y	E(0-70)H	GD	£3022
73	7/96	Baln	6f		GD	£3082

Total win prize-money £34962

Going (Turf): Sf: 0-8 GS: 1-5 **Gd: 4-30** GF: 2-20 Fm: 1-3
Distance: 5f/6f: 1-6 7f-8f: 1-14 **9f-13f: 6-52** 14f+: 0-0
Track : **LH: 4-38** RH: 3-24 **Tight: 2-26** Gall: 1-8
Aids: Bl: 0-4 Vi: 0-0 Tstrap: 0-0
Best Rating: 75 9/01 Kemp 1m2f good

A decent handicapper, he comes into form in May and he did the same thing this season when winning on turf at Southwell. Added a victory at Kempton in September, before disappointing afterwards. Acts on fast ground and is best over ten furlongs.

Junior Brief (IRE)

82(78) (18)**35**
3-y-o b g Case Law-Sharpnkeen (Keen)
K McAuliffe Highgrove Developments Limited

Placings:00000000-5000000 **(3080)**
2001: 11^{5}SD, 8^{0}SD, 7^{0}SD, 5^{0}F, 9^{0}SD, 11^{0}GF, 11^{0}GF

	Starts	1st	2nd	3rd	Win & Pl
Career Total (Turf)	9	0	0	0	
Career Total (AW)	6	0	0	0	0

Going (Turf): Sf: 0-2 GS: 0-0 Gd: 0-2 GF: 0-3 Fm: 0-1
Distance: 5f/6f: 0-4 7f-8f: 0-6 9f-13f: 0-5 14f+: 0-0
Track : LH: 0-10 RH: 0-0 Tight: 0-4 Gall: 0-1
Aids: Bl: 0-2 Vi: 0-6 Tstrap: 0-0
Best Rating: 35 7/01 Wind 1m3f135y gd-fm

Juniper (USA)

107 **104**
3-y-o b c Danzig (USA)-Montage (USA) (Alydar (USA))
A P O'Brien M Tabor,Mrs Magnier,Sir Alex Ferguson

Placings:31-306 **(2839)**
2001: 6^{3}GY, 6^{0}GF, 5^{6}GF

	Starts	1st	2nd	3rd	Win & Pl
Career Total (Turf)	5	1	0	2	29175
94 9/00 Curr 6f				YLD	£9800

Total win prize-money £9800

Going (Turf): Sf: 0-0 GS: 0-0 Gd: 0-1 GF: 0-2 Fm: 0-0
Distance: **5f/6f: 1-5** 7f-8f: 0-0 9f-13f: 0-0 14f+: 0-0
Track : LH: 0-0 RH: 0-0 Tight: 0-0 Gall: 0-0
Aids: Bl: 0-0 Vi: 0-0 Tstrap: 0-0
Best Rating: 104 5/01 Curr 6f gd-yld

Made his juvenile debut in the Group Two Gimcrack Stakes and was beaten only half a length into third. Made no mistake next time and reappeared to run a good third to the in-form Final Exam in a Group Three sprint at the Curragh on his return. Well beaten in the Cork and Orrery and found Sandown's five furlongs too short next time. Best with ease in the ground.

Junkanoo

90 **54+**
5-y-o ch g Generous (IRE)-Lupescu (Dixieland Band (USA))
Mrs M Reveley Lucayan Stud

Placings:40001 **(5531)**
2001: 12^{4}S, 10^{0}F, 8^{0}HY, 14^{0}G, 16^{1}HY

	Starts	1st	2nd	3rd	Win & Pl
Career Total (Turf)	5	1	0	0	2611
54 10/01 Nott 2m9y F(0-60)H				HVY	£2611

Total win prize-money £2611

Going (Turf): Sf: 1-3 GS: 0-0 Gd: 0-1 GF: 0-0 Fm: 0-1
Distance: 5f/6f: 0-0 7f-8f: 0-0 9f-13f: 0-3 **14f+: 1-2**
Track : **LH: 1-4** RH: 0-0 Tight: 0-1 Gall: 0-0
Aids: Bl: 0-0 Vi: 0-0 Tstrap: 0-0
Best Rating: 54 10/01 Nott 2m9y heavy

Juno Beach

101(91) (38)**65**
5-y-o ch m Jupiter Island-Kovalevskia (Ardross)
D Morris Bloomsbury Stud

Placings:340-1005 **(3478)**
2001: 14^{1}G, 14^{0}GF, 16^{0}GF, 14^{5}GF

	Starts	1st	2nd	3rd	Win & Pl
Career Total (Turf)	6	1	0	1	3662
Career Total (AW)	1	0	0	0	
65 5/01 Yarm 1m6f17y F(0-65)H				GD	£2712

Total win prize-money £2713

Going (Turf): Sf: 0-0 GS: 0-0 **Gd: 1-3** GF: 0-3 Fm: 0-0
Distance: 5f/6f: 0-0 7f-8f: 0-0 9f-13f: 0-3 **14f+: 1-4**
Track : **LH: 1-4** RH: 0-3 **Tight: 1-4** Gall: 0-2
Aids: Bl: 0-0 Vi: 0-0 Tstrap: 0-0
Best Rating: 65 5/01 Yarm 1m6f17y good

Jupiters Princess

94 **51**
3-y-o b f Jupiter Island-Capricious Lass (Corvaro (USA))
C E Brittain D Newland

Placings:0060600 **(3299)**
2001: 7^{0}S, 5^{0}G, 7^{6}GF, 9^{0}F, 11^{6}F, 12^{0}GF, 9^{0}GF

	Starts	1st	2nd	3rd	Win & Pl
Career Total (Turf)	7	0	0	0	0

Going (Turf): Sf: 0-1 GS: 0-0 Gd: 0-1 GF: 0-3 Fm: 0-2
Distance: 5f/6f: 0-1 7f-8f: 0-2 9f-13f: 0-4 14f+: 0-0
Track : LH: 0-4 RH: 0-1 Tight: 0-3 Gall: 0-0
Aids: Bl: 0-0 Vi: 0-0 Tstrap: 0-0
Best Rating: 58 5/01 Yarm 7f3y gd-fm

Just A Carat (IRE)

95 **61**
2-y-o b f Distinctly North (USA)-Justice System (USA) (Criminal Type (USA))
R Hannon Mrs Anna Doyle

Placings:615000 **(5467)**
2001: 5^{6}F, 5^{1}GF, 6^{5}GF, 7^{0}G, 6^{0}GY, 6^{0}S

	Starts	1st	2nd	3rd	Win & Pl
Career Total (Turf)	6	1	0	0	2282
56 6/01 Brig 5f59y F				G-F	£2282

Total win prize-money £2282

Going (Turf): Sf: 0-1 GS: 0-0 Gd: 0-1 **GF: 1-2** Fm: 0-1
Distance: **5f/6f: 1-4** 7f-8f: 0-2 9f-13f: 0-0 14f+: 0-0
Track : **LH: 1-3** RH: 0-1 Tight: 0-0 Gall: 0-1
Aids: Bl: 0-0 Vi: 0-0 Tstrap: 0-2
Best Rating: 61 8/01 Curr 6f gd-yld

She got off the mark in a very modest event at Brighton on her second start and added a seller on the Lingfield Polytrack in November. Basically moderate.

Just Arthur

56
3-y-o b g Aragon-Spark Out (Sparkler)
B P J Baugh L R Perry

Placings:005 **(3829)**
2001: 7^{0}GF, 9^{0}GS, 11^{5}G

	Starts	1st	2nd	3rd	Win & Pl
Career Total (Turf)	3	0	0	0	0

Going (Turf): Sf: 0-0 GS: 0-1 Gd: 0-1 GF: 0-1 Fm: 0-0
Distance: 5f/6f: 0-0 7f-8f: 0-1 9f-13f: 0-2 14f+: 0-0
Track : LH: 0-2 RH: 0-1 Tight: 0-0 Gall: 0-0
Aids: Bl: 0-0 Vi: 0-0 Tstrap: 0-0

Just Emerald

99 **73**
2-y-o ch f Emarati (USA)-Bichette (Lidhame)
G L Moore Bryan Pennick

Placings:035 **(5666)**
2001: 7^{0}GS, 6^{3}S, 6^{5}HY

	Starts	1st	2nd	3rd	Win & Pl
Career Total (Turf)	3	0	0	1	419

Going (Turf): Sf: 0-2 GS: 0-1 Gd: 0-0 GF: 0-0 Fm: 0-0
Distance: 5f/6f: 0-1 7f-8f: 0-2 9f-13f: 0-0 14f+: 0-0
Track : LH: 0-1 RH: 0-0 Tight: 0-0 Gall: 0-0
Aids: Bl: 0-0 Vi: 0-0 Tstrap: 0-0
Best Rating: 73 10/01 Leic 7f9y gd-sft

Just Ern

95 **71**
2-y-o ch g Young Ern-Just Run (IRE) (Runnett)
P C Haslam Lawrence Watts & N P Green

Placings:63600 **(5031)**
2001: 5^{6}GF, 6^{3}G, 6^{6}GF, 8^{0}G, 8^{0}GF

	Starts	1st	2nd	3rd	Win & Pl
Career Total (Turf)	5	0	0	1	620

Going (Turf): Sf: 0-0 GS: 0-0 Gd: 0-2 GF: 0-3 Fm: 0-0
Distance: 5f/6f: 0-3 7f-8f: 0-2 9f-13f: 0-0 14f+: 0-0
Track : LH: 0-1 RH: 0-1 Tight: 0-1 Gall: 0-0
Aids: Bl: 0-0 Vi: 0-0 Tstrap: 0-0
Best Rating: 71 8/01 Ripn 6f good

Just For You Jane (IRE)

62(88) (53)**27**
5-y-o b m Petardia-Steffi (Precocious)
T J Naughton G Stupple

Placings:0354233000/3423/0004300-0 **(2553)**
2001: 6^{0}GF

	Starts	1st	2nd	3rd	Win & Pl
Career Total (Turf)	16	0	1	4	2578
Career Total (AW)	6	0	1	2	1063

Going (Turf): Sf: 0-2 GS: 0-2 Gd: 0-2 GF: 0-6 Fm: 0-4
Distance: 5f/6f: 0-12 7f-8f: 0-9 9f-13f: 0-1 14f+: 0-0
Track : LH: 0-14 RH: 0-1 Tight: 0-7 Gall: 0-0
Aids: Bl: 0-12 Vi: 0-0 Tstrap: 0-0
Best Rating: 71 8/01 Ripn 6f good

Just Good Friends (IRE)

81 **22**
4-y-o b g Shalford (IRE)-Sinfonietta (Foolish Pleasure (USA))
Denys Smith B Batey

Placings:006600-00 **(4105)**
2001: 13^{0}S, 12^{0}S

	Starts	1st	2nd	3rd	Win & Pl
Career Total (Turf)	8	0	0	0	0

Going (Turf): Sf: 0-2 GS: 0-2 Gd: 0-0 GF: 0-1 Fm: 0-3
Distance: 5f/6f: 0-0 7f-8f: 0-5 9f-13f: 0-3 14f+: 0-0
Track : LH: 0-2 RH: 0-4 Tight: 0-6 Gall: 0-0
Aids: Bl: 0-1 Vi: 0-0 Tstrap: 0-1
Best Rating: 22 4/01 Muss 1m5f soft

Just James

101 **81**
2-y-o b c Spectrum (IRE)-Fairy Flight (IRE) (Fairy King (USA))
J Noseda Lucayan Stud

Placings:61 **(5689)**
2001: 7^{6}HY, 6^{1}S

	Starts	1st	2nd	3rd	Win & Pl
Career Total (Turf)	2	1	0	0	4817

81 11/01 Donc 6f D SFT £4816
Total win prize-money £4817

Going (Turf): Sf: 1-2 GS: 0-0 Gd: 0-0 GF: 0-0 Fm: 0-0
Distance: 5f/6f: 1-1 7f-8f: 0-1 9f-13f: 0-0 14f+: 0-0
Track : LH: 0-0 RH: 0-0 Tight: 0-0 Gall: 0-0
Aids: Bl: 0-0 Vi: 0-0 Tstrap: 0-0
Best Rating: 81 11/01 Donc 6f soft

Got off the mark on only his second start in an ordinary maiden at Doncaster over six furlongs in soft ground.

Just Jazz

59 **15**
2-y-o b g Alhijaz-Jersey Belle (Distant Relative)
J Balding J M Lacey

Placings:00 **(4313)**
2001: 5^{0}GF, 6^{0}G

	Starts	1st	2nd	3rd	Win & Pl
Career Total (Turf)	2	0	0	0	

Going (Turf): Sf: 0-0 GS: 0-0 Gd: 0-1 GF: 0-1 Fm: 0-0
Distance: 5f/6f: 0-2 7f-8f: 0-0 9f-13f: 0-0 14f+: 0-0
Track : LH: 0-1 RH: 0-0 Tight: 0-0 Gall: 0-0
Aids: Bl: 0-0 Vi: 0-0 Tstrap: 0-0
Best Rating: 15 8/01 Pont 5f gd-fm

Just Michael

98 **70**
2-y-o b c Bluegrass Prince (IRE)-Plucky Pet (Petong)
A Berry Peter M Dodd

Placings:040550006 **(5635)**
2001: 5^{0}G, 6^{4}GF, 5^{0}GF, 5^{5}GS, 7^{5}GF, 7^{0}GS, 7^{0}GS, 6^{0}HY, 7^{6}G

	Starts	1st	2nd	3rd	Win & Pl
Career Total (Turf)	9	0	0	0	262

Going (Turf): Sf: 0-1 GS: 0-3 Gd: 0-2 GF: 0-3 Fm: 0-0
Distance: 5f/6f: 0-5 7f-8f: 0-4 9f-13f: 0-0 14f+: 0-0
Track : LH: 0-3 RH: 0-0 Tight: 0-1 Gall: 0-0
Aids: Bl: 0-2 Vi: 0-0 Tstrap: 0-0
Best Rating: 70 10/01 Donc 6f heavy

Just Midas

98(81) (27)**54**
3-y-o b g Merdon Melody-Thabeh (Shareef Dancer (USA))
K R Burke D G & D J Robinson

Placings:000-0050060 **(5269)**
2001: 8^{0}HY, 8^{0}F, 8^{5}G, 8^{0}F, 8^{0}GF, 8^{6}SD, 10^{0}HY

	Starts	1st	2nd	3rd	Win & Pl
Career Total (Turf)	8	0	0	0	0
Career Total (AW)	2	0	0	0	0

Going (Turf): Sf: 0-3 GS: 0-0 Gd: 0-1 GF: 0-2 Fm: 0-2
Distance: 5f/6f: 0-0 7f-8f: 0-4 9f-13f: 0-6 14f+: 0-0
Track : LH: 0-8 RH: 0-0 Tight: 0-2 Gall: 0-0
Aids: Bl: 0-0 Vi: 0-0 Tstrap: 0-0
Best Rating: 54 6/01 Hayd 1m30y good

Just Missed

95 **59d**
3-y-o b f Inchinor-Lucky Round (Auction Ring (USA))
M W Easterby Guy Reed

Placings:005053-00 **(4906)**
2001: 10^{0}G, 9^{0}G

	Starts	1st	2nd	3rd	Win & Pl
Career Total (Turf)	8	0	0	1	500

Going (Turf): Sf: 0-3 GS: 0-0 Gd: 0-4 GF: 0-1 Fm: 0-0
Distance: 5f/6f: 0-3 7f-8f: 0-3 9f-13f: 0-2 14f+: 0-0
Track : LH: 0-5 RH: 0-1 Tight: 0-2 Gall: 0-1
Aids: Bl: 0-0 Vi: 0-0 Tstrap: 0-0
Best Rating: 44 8/01 Rdcr 1m2f good

Just Mo (IRE)

68(67) (5)**28**
2-y-o ch f Common Grounds-Nomadic Dancer (IRE) (Nabeel Dancer (USA))
K R Burke Maurice Charge

Placings:000 **(5128)**
2001: 5^{0}SW, 5^{0}F, 6^{0}HY

	Starts	1st	2nd	3rd	Win & Pl
Career Total (Turf)	2	0	0	0	
Career Total (AW)	1	0	0	0	

Going (Turf): Sf: 0-1 GS: 0-0 Gd: 0-0 GF: 0-0 Fm: 0-1
Distance: 5f/6f: 0-3 7f-8f: 0-0 9f-13f: 0-0 14f+: 0-0
Track : LH: 0-0 RH: 0-0 Tight: 0-0 Gall: 0-0
Aids: Bl: 0-0 Vi: 0-0 Tstrap: 0-0
Best Rating: 28 6/01 Nott 5f13y firm

Just Murphy (IRE)

105 **81**
3-y-o b g Namaqualand (USA)-Bui-Doi (IRE) (Dance Of Life (USA))
G A Swinbank B Valentine

Placings:603-5131635134 **(4963)**
2001: 6^{5}G, 8^{1}GF, 8^{3}GF, 10^{1}GF, 10^{6}GF, 11^{3}F, 10^{5}GS, 9^{1}S, 10^{3}HY, 10^{4}S

	Starts	1st	2nd	3rd	Win & Pl
Career Total (Turf)	13	3	0	4	20710

80 8/01 Haml 1m1f36y C(0-90)H SFT £6327
80 6/01 Pont 1m2f6y E(0-75)H G-F £4563
70 5/01 Thsk 1m D(0-80)H G-F £4966
Total win prize-money £15857

Going (Turf): Sf: 1-3 GS: 0-1 Gd: 0-3 **GF: 2-4** Fm: 0-2
Distance: 5f/6f: 0-4 7f-8f: 1-2 **9f-13f: 2-7** 14f+: 0-0
Track : LH: 2-7 RH: 1-4 **Tight: 2-3** Gall: 0-3
Aids: Bl: 0-0 Vi: 0-0 Tstrap: 0-0
Best Rating: 81 9/01 Hayd 1m2f120y heavy

Fair handicapper at around a mile. He has won three times in 2001 from a mile to nine furlongs. Carries his head high but it is a trait he inherited from his dam, though he has looked a bit reluctant to exert himself at times. Has won on fast ground and soft.

Just Nick

106 **84**
7-y-o b g Nicholas (USA)-Just Never Know (USA) (Riverman (USA))
W R Muir D G Clarke

Placings:34321/232350420/0340000/36521100-012003061 **(5344)**
2001: 8^{0}GS, 8^{1}GF, 8^{2}GF, 8^{0}GF, 8^{0}S, 9^{3}G, 9^{0}GF, 8^{6}S, 8^{1}GS

	Starts	1st	2nd	3rd	Win & Pl
Career Total (Turf)	38	5	6	7	59695

84 10/01 NmkR 1m D(0-85)H G-S £5980
72 5/01 Sand 1m14y D(0-80)H G-F £4641
73 7/00 Newb 1m C(0-100)H G-F £6987
68 7/00 Gdwd 1m C(0-90)H GD £14495
74 11/96 Folk 6f E SFT £2799
Total win prize-money £34904

Going (Turf): Sf: 1-8 GS: 1-5 Gd: 1-11 **GF: 2-14** Fm: 0-0
Distance: 5f/6f: 1-4 **7f-8f: 3-28** 9f-13f: 1-6 14f+: 0-0
Track : LH: 0-6 **RH: 2-14** Tight: 0-2 Gall: 0-4
Aids: Bl: 0-0 Vi: 0-0 Tstrap: 0-0
Best Rating: 84 10/01 NmkR 1m gd-sft

A decent handicapper, is most effective over a mile, with waiting tactics employed. Acts on any ground.

Just Serenade

91 **69**
2-y-o ch f Factual (USA)-Thimbalina (Salmon Leap (USA))
M J Ryan W J Wyatt

Placings:5055306 **(5562)**
2001: 6^{5}G, 6^{0}G, 6^{5}G, 5^{5}G, 5^{3}GF, 5^{0}GS, 5^{6}S

	Starts	1st	2nd	3rd	Win & Pl
Career Total (Turf)	7	0	0	1	580

Going (Turf): Sf: 0-1 GS: 0-1 Gd: 0-4 GF: 0-1 Fm: 0-0
Distance: 5f/6f: 0-6 7f-8f: 0-1 9f-13f: 0-0 14f+: 0-0
Track : LH: 0-0 RH: 0-0 Tight: 0-0 Gall: 0-0
Aids: Bl: 0-0 Vi: 0-0 Tstrap: 0-0
Best Rating: 74 8/01 Yarm 6f3y good

Just The Job Too (IRE)

91(101) (52)**41**
4-y-o b/br g Prince Of Birds (USA)-Bold Encounter (IRE) (Persian Bold)
P C Haslam A Stancliffe & J Trevillion

Placings:00/6410600-03150000 **(4469)**
2001: 8^{0}SD, 8^{3}SW, 12^{1}SD, 12^{5}SW, 11^{0}SD, 11^{0}SD, 14^{0}SD, 12^{0}G

	Starts	1st	2nd	3rd	Win & Pl
Career Total (Turf)	3	0	0	0	0
Career Total (AW)	14	2	0	1	4064

50	1/01	Wolv	1m4f	G(0-60)H	STD	£1379
56	2/00	Sthl	1m	F(0-60)H	STD	£2362

Total win prize-money £3742

Going (Turf): Sf: 0-2 GS: 0-0 Gd: 0-1 GF: 0-0 Fm: 0-0
Distance: 5f/6f: 0-1 7f-8f: 1-8 9f-13f: 1-7 14f+: 0-1
Track : **LH: 2-13** RH: 0-3 **Tight: 1-6** Gall: 0-0
Aids: Bl: 0-0 Vi: 0-0 Tstrap: 0-0
Best Rating: 52 2/01 Wolv 1m4f slow

Just The Trick (USA)

77(80) (45)**47**

2-y-o b/br f Phone Trick (USA)-Tammi's Pal (USA) (Lear Fan (USA))
W R Muir C L A Edgington

Placings:656600 **(5345)**
2001: 5^{6}S, 5^{5}GF, 5^{6}G, 5^{6}GF, 5^{0}SD, 6^{0}SD, 5^{6}SD

	Starts	1st	2nd	3rd	Win & Pl
Career Total (Turf)	**4**	**0**	**0**	**0**	**0**
Career Total (AW)	**2**	**0**	**0**	**0**	

Going (Turf): Sf: 0-1 GS: 0-0 Gd: 0-1 GF: 0-2 Fm: 0-0
Distance: 5f/6f: 0-6 7f-8f: 0-0 9f-13f: 0-0 14f+: 0-0
Track : LH: 0-4 RH: 0-0 Tight: 0-2 Gall: 0-1
Aids: Bl: 0-0 Vi: 0-0 Tstrap: 0-0
Best Rating: 47 7/01 Ches 5f16y gd-fm

Just Wiz

(102) (77)**50**

5-y-o b g Efisio-Jade Pet (Petong)
N P Littmoden Turf 2000 Limited

Placings:500053451/5204200231310/553002221-001 **(5166)**
2001: 10^{0}GF, 10^{0}F, 9^{1}SD

	Starts	1st	2nd	3rd	Win & Pl
Career Total (Turf)	**21**	**0**	**6**	**1**	**6023**
Career Total (AW)	**13**	**5**	**0**	**3**	**14688**

77	10/01	Wolv	1m1f79y	E(0-70)H	STD	£3031
72	9/00	Wolv	1m1f79y	E(0-70)H	STD	£3094
83	12/99	Ling	1m2f	D(0-80)H	STD	£3401
77	11/99	Ling	1m2f	G(0-75)H	STD	£1542
72	1/99	Sthl	7f	F(0-65)H	STD	£2316

Total win prize-money £13385

Going (Turf): Sf: 0-3 GS: 0-3 Gd: 0-2 GF: 0-8 Fm: 0-5
Distance: 5f/6f: 0-7 7f-8f: 1-6 **9f-13f: 4-21** 14f+: 0-0
Track : **LH: 5-21** RH: 0-4 **Tight: 4-15** Gall: 0-0
Aids: **Bl: 2-9** Vi: 1-8 Tstrap: 0-0
Best Rating: 77 10/01 Wolv 1m1f79y stand

Has ability on turf, but looks better on sand. Probably best over ten furlongs.

Just Woody (IRE)

101 **58**

3-y-o br g Charnwood Forest (IRE)-Zalamera (Rambo Dancer (CAN))
A Berry E Nisbet

Placings:30-005010030000 **(5657)**
2001: 7^{0}GS, 7^{0}GF, 8^{5}GF, 7^{0}G, 8^{1}GS, 8^{0}GF, 9^{0}G, 9^{3}GF, 9^{0}G, 8^{0}GF, 8^{0}GS, 8^{0}G

	Starts	1st	2nd	3rd	Win & Pl
Career Total (Turf)	**14**	**1**	**0**	**2**	**4353**

63	6/01	Haml	1m65y	E(0-65)	G-S	£2870

Total win prize-money £2870

Going (Turf): Sf: 0-1 **GS: 1-3** Gd: 0-5 GF: 0-5 Fm: 0-0
Distance: 5f/6f: 0-1 7f-8f: 0-6 **9f-13f: 1-7** 14f+: 0-0
Track : LH: 0-2 **RH: 1-7 Tight: 1-8** Gall: 0-0
Aids: Bl: 0-0 Vi: 0-0 Tstrap: 0-0
Best Rating: 63 6/01 Haml 1m65y gd-sft

Justafancy

105(74) (13)**53**

3-y-o b c Green Desert (USA)-Justsayno (USA) (Dr Blum (USA))
E A L Dunlop Salem Suhail

Placings:046350 **(3264)**
2001: 7^{0}SD, 7^{4}S, 6^{6}GS, 6^{3}GF, 7^{5}GF, 10^{0}GS

	Starts	1st	2nd	3rd	Win & Pl
Career Total (Turf)	**5**	**0**	**0**	**1**	**889**
Career Total (AW)	**1**	**0**	**0**	**0**	

Going (Turf): Sf: 0-1 GS: 0-2 Gd: 0-0 GF: 0-2 Fm: 0-0
Distance: 5f/6f: 0-2 7f-8f: 0-3 9f-13f: 0-1 14f+: 0-0
Track : LH: 0-4 RH: 0-1 Tight: 0-1 Gall: 0-1
Aids: Bl: 0-1 Vi: 0-0 Tstrap: 0-0
Best Rating: 81 4/01 Kemp 7f soft

Justalord

100(96) (68)**40**

3-y-o b g King's Signet (USA)-Just Lady (Emarati (USA))
T Keddy Bob Williams

Placings:616152424-1026000000000 **(4898)**
2001: 5^{1}SD, 6^{0}SW, 5^{2}SW, 5^{6}SD, 5^{0}GS, 5^{0}G, 5^{0}GF, 5^{0}F, 5^{0}G, 5^{0}GF, 5^{0}G, 5^{0}GF, 5^{0}GS

	Starts	1st	2nd	3rd	Win & Pl
Career Total (Turf)	**15**	**1**	**1**	**0**	**3856**
Career Total (AW)	**7**	**2**	**2**	**0**	**7737**

68	1/01	Ling	5f	E(0-70)H	STD	£2877
62	5/00	Thsk	5f	E	GD	£3006
68	4/00	Ling	5f	D	STD	£3472

Total win prize-money £9356

Going (Turf): Sf: 0-1 GS: 0-2 **Gd: 1-6** GF: 0-4 Fm: 0-1
Distance: **5f/6f: 3-21** 7f-8f: 0-0 9f-13f: 0-0 14f+: 0-0
Track : **LH: 2-12** RH: 0-0 **Tight: 2-8** Gall: 0-2
Aids: Bl: 0-0 Vi: 0-0 Tstrap: 0-0
Best Rating: 69 2/01 Ling 5f slow

Justinia

84 **24**

3-y-o b f Inchinor-Just Julia (Natroun (FR))
Miss S E Hall (E J O'Neill 28/5) Mrs Rosemary Moszkowicz

Placings:03500-0500 **(5634)**
2001: 6^{0}G, 11^{5}F, 10^{0}HY, 11^{0}G

	Starts	1st	2nd	3rd	Win & Pl
Career Total (Turf)	**9**	**0**	**0**	**1**	**550**

Going (Turf): Sf: 0-1 GS: 0-1 Gd: 0-3 GF: 0-2 Fm: 0-2
Distance: 5f/6f: 0-1 7f-8f: 0-5 9f-13f: 0-3 14f+: 0-0
Track : LH: 0-5 RH: 0-1 Tight: 0-2 Gall: 0-0
Aids: Bl: 0-0 Vi: 0-2 Tstrap: 0-0
Best Rating: 24 11/01 Catt 1m3f214y good

Justsilv

(55)

2-y-o ch f Democratic (USA)-Smocking (Night Shift (USA))
Miss K M George Miss K George

Placings:00 **(2583)**
2001: 6^{0}SD, 7^{0}SD

	Starts	1st	2nd	3rd	Win & Pl
Career Total (Turf)	**0**	**0**	**0**	**0**	
Career Total (AW)	**2**	**0**	**0**	**0**	

Going (Turf): Sf: 0-0 GS: 0-0 Gd: 0-0 GF: 0-0 Fm: 0-0
Distance: 5f/6f: 0-1 7f-8f: 0-1 9f-13f: 0-0 14f+: 0-0
Track : LH: 0-2 RH: 0-0 Tight: 0-0 Gall: 0-0
Aids: Bl: 0-0 Vi: 0-0 Tstrap: 0-0

Juthjoor (IRE)

86 **9**

3-y-o b c Marju (IRE)-Deyaajeer (USA) (Dayjur (USA))
J O'Reilly Burntwood Sports Ltd

Placings:0 **(3694)**
2001: 11^{0}G

	Starts	1st	2nd	3rd	Win & Pl
Career Total (Turf)	**1**	**0**	**0**	**0**	

Going (Turf): Sf: 0-0 GS: 0-0 Gd: 0-1 GF: 0-0 Fm: 0-0
Distance: 5f/6f: 0-0 7f-8f: 0-0 9f-13f: 0-1 14f+: 0-0
Track : LH: 0-1 RH: 0-0 Tight: 0-1 Gall: 0-0
Aids: Bl: 0-0 Vi: 0-0 Tstrap: 0-0
Best Rating: 9 8/01 Catt 1m3f214y good

Juwwi

106(110) (89)**85**

7-y-o ch g Mujtahid (USA)-Nouvelle Star (AUS) (Luskin Star (AUS))
J M Bradley Triumph Racing International

Placings:212/04/1100000603530620246350/005041632606210200026215 5/33532206015144150500000000004005025 65-1060365061200400410000000006 00 **(5630)**
2001: 5^{1}SD, 6^{0}SW, 5^{6}SW, 6^{0}SD, 5^{3}SW, 6^{6}SD, 5^{5}SD, 5^{0}GS, 5^{6}GF, 6^{1}GF, 6^{2}GF, 6^{0}GF, 6^{0}GF, 6^{4}G, 6^{0}GF, 6^{0}GF, 6^{4}G, 6^{1}G, 6^{0}GF, 6^{0}G, 6^{0}G, 6^{0}G, 6^{0}G, 6^{0}G, 5^{0}G, 6^{0}G, 5^{0}HY, 6^{6}GS, 6^{0}GS, 6^{0}G

	Starts	1st	2nd	3rd	Win & Pl
Career Total (Turf)	**88**	**8**	**9**	**3**	**90395**
Career Total (AW)	**30**	**4**	**4**	**5**	**40732**

90	7/01	York	6f	C(0-90)H	GD	£11943
87	5/01	Thsk	6f	C(0-95)H	G-F	£7865
89	1/01	Sthl	5f	C(0-100)H	STD	£13617
94	5/00	York	6f	B(0-105)H	FRM	£17005
91	4/00	Thsk	5f	C(0-90)H	G-S	£8011
83	3/00	Wind	6f	D(0-80)H	G-F	£7280
83	11/99	Sthl	6f	C(0-90)H	STD	£7100
72	9/99	Chep	5f16y	E(0-70)H	GD	£2962
70	5/99	Carl	5f207y	E(0-70)H	FRM	£3269
80	4/98	Ling	5f	C(0-90)H	STD	£5410
64	3/98	Wolv	5f	G	STD	£1882
79	6/96	Newb	6f8y	D	G-F	£3850

Total win prize-money £90200

Going (Turf): Sf: 0-22 GS: 1-11 Gd: 2-29 **GF: 3-21** Fm: 2-5
Distance: **5f/6f: 11-101** 7f-8f: 1-17 9f-13f: 0-0 14f+: 0-0
Track : **LH: 3-38** RH: 2-5 Tight: 2-27 Gall: 2-6
Aids: Bl: 0-0 Vi: 0-0 Tstrap: 0-0
Best Rating: 90 7/01 York 6f good

A very talented if somewhat exasperating sprint handicapper, he is often slow to start and leaves his finishing effort until the last second. He seems to go really well for an apprentice these days and he is suited by big fields and a strong pace. When he runs twice in 24 hours, he often runs better on the second day than on the first. Prefers six furlongs on fast ground.

Juyush (USA)

105 **75d**

9-y-o b g Silver Hawk (USA)-Silken Doll (USA) (Chieftain Ii)
R M Stronge (P F Nicholls 29/3) Robert Stronge

Placings:62133/153120/1030/5/060122000 **(5387)**
2001: 16^{0}S, 16^{6}GF, 14^{0}G, 16^{1}GF, 16^{2}GF, 16^{2}GF, 16^{0}GF, 16^{0}S, 18^{0}GS

	Starts	1st	2nd	3rd	Win & Pl
Career Total (Turf)	**25**	**5**	**4**	**4**	**78545**

59	6/01	Nott	2m9y	F	G-F	£2485
113	3/96	Donc	1m4f	B	G-S	£7553
93	6/95	Asct	1m4f	B	FRM	£9783
92	3/95	Donc	1m	C	G-F	£6420
92	7/94	Asct	7f	D	G-F	£11062

Total win prize-money £37304

Going (Turf): Sf: 0-3 GS: 1-4 Gd: 0-6 **GF: 3-11** Fm: 1-1
Distance: 5f/6f: 0-0 7f-8f: 2-7 9f-13f: 2-6 14f+: 1-12
Track : **LH: 2-11** RH: 1-11 Tight: 0-4 **Gall: 2-13**
Aids: Bl: 0-0 Vi: 0-0 Tstrap: 0-0
Best Rating: 80 5/01 Kemp 2m gd-fm

Better known as a hurdler/chaser, he showed he can still win in modest company when landing a Nottingham claimer in June, before running well at Newbury and Ascot.

Kadiskar (IRE)

104 **78+**

3-y-o b c Ashkalani (IRE)-Kadissya (USA) (Blushing Groom (FR))
Sir Michael Stoute H H Aga Khan

Placings:54 **(5464)**
2001: 12^{5}GF, 11^{4}G

	Starts	1st	2nd	3rd	Win & Pl
Career Total (Turf)	2	0	0	0	0

Going (Turf): Sf: 0-0 GS: 0-0 Gd: 0-1 GF: 0-1 Fm: 0-0
Distance: 5f/6f: 0-0 7f-8f: 0-0 9f-13f: 0-2 14f+: 0-0
Track : LH: 0-1 RH: 0-1 Tight: 0-1 Gall: 0-0
Aids: Bl: 0-0 Vi: 0-0 Tstrap: 0-0
Best Rating: 78 10/01 Bath 1m3f144y good

A half-brother to Derby winner Kahyasi, ran green on his racecourse debut at Kempton in September 2001.

Kafezah (FR)

106 **91**

3-y-o br f Pennekamp (USA)-Yakin (USA) (Nureyev (USA))
B Hanbury Hamdan Al Maktoum

Placings:44-535141666 **(5137)**
2001: 7^{5}S, 7^{3}GF, 6^{5}G, 7^{1}F, 7^{4}GS, 9^{1}GF, 8^{6}G, 9^{6}GS, 8^{6}G

	Starts	1st	2nd	3rd	Win & Pl
Career Total (Turf)	11	2	0	1	16860

91 8/01 Gdwd 1m1f C(0-90)H G-F £10985
83 7/01 Brig 7f214y D FRM £2989
Total win prize-money £13974

Going (Turf): Sf: 0-1 GS: 0-2 Gd: 0-4 **GF: 1-3 Fm: 1-1**
Distance: 5f/6f: 0-1 7f-8f: 1-8 9f-13f: 1-2 14f+: 0-0
Track : LH: 1-2 RH: 1-4 **Tight: 1-3** Gall: 0-2
Aids: **Bl: 1-2** Vi: 0-0 Tstrap: 0-0
Best Rating: 91 8/01 Gdwd 1m1f gd-fm

She ran with cedit in some decent maidens, but came into her own when stepped up to a mile at Brighton though she had little to beat. Responded well to first-time blinkers to win a valuable fillies' handicap at Glorious Goodwood, but they failed to have the same effect the second time at Ascot. Acts on fast ground.

Kafil (USA)

45(98) (53)**49d**

7-y-o b/br g Housebuster (USA)-Alchaasibiyeh (USA) (Seattle Slew (USA))
J J Bridger J J Bridger

Placings:00/0430022126/55003206026000010000/6300 00240002253656O/260000306030600O446-0 **(4279)**
2001: 7^{0}GF

	Starts	1st	2nd	3rd	Win & Pl
Career Total (Turf)	27	0	1	2	2377
Career Total (AW)	43	2	8	4	12449

59 10/98 Ling 7f F(0-65) STD £2070
68 11/97 Ling 1m D STD £3338
Total win prize-money £5409

Going (Turf): Sf: 0-5 GS: 0-4 Gd: 0-5 GF: 0-10 Fm: 0-2
Distance: 5f/6f: 0-1 **7f-8f: 2-36** 9f-13f: 0-32 14f+: 0-0
Track : **LH: 2-49** RH: 0-14 **Tight: 2-51** Gall: 0-1
Aids: Bl: 0-9 Vi: 0-0 Tstrap: 0-0
Best Rating: 68 11/97 Ling 1m SD

Does not win very often these days. Best on Equitrack.

Kagoshima (IRE)

108 **66**

6-y-o b g Shirley Heights-Kashteh (IRE) (Green Desert (USA))
J R Norton Keep On Running

Placings:6/65/0231210-0410 **(2410)**
2001: 16^{0}G, 16^{4}F, 17^{1}F, 17^{0}GF

	Starts	1st	2nd	3rd	Win & Pl
Career Total (Turf)	14	3	2	1	15657

64 6/01 Pont 2m1f22y D(0-80)H FRM £4446
58 7/00 Bevl 2m35y E(0-70)H G-F £3523
48 6/00 Pont 2m1f22y E(0-70)H G-F £3575
Total win prize-money £11544

Going (Turf): Sf: 0-1 GS: 0-1 Gd: 0-3 **GF: 2-7** Fm: 1-2
Distance: 5f/6f: 0-0 7f-8f: 0-0 9f-13f: 0-3 **14f+: 3-11**
Track : **LH: 2-9** RH: 1-5 **Tight: 1-5** Gall: 0-4
Aids: Bl: 0-0 **Vi: 3-10** Tstrap: 0-0
Best Rating: 64 6/01 Pont 2m1f22y firm

Kahtan

105 **107d**

6-y-o b h Nashwan (USA)-Harmless Albatross (Pas De Seul)
N J Henderson Trevor Hemmings

Placings:41/23136/343101/4464-2 **(2355)**
2001: 22^{2}GF

	Starts	1st	2nd	3rd	Win & Pl
Career Total (Turf)	18	4	2	4	76939

107 10/99 NmkJ 1m4f A G-S £14358
104 7/99 Ches 2m2f147yB(0-105)H G-F £14998
103 7/98 NmkJ 1m6f175yA FRM £10754
80 10/97 Newc 1m3y D G-F £3452
Total win prize-money £43563

Going (Turf): Sf: 0-1 GS: 1-3 Gd: 0-5 **GF: 2-6** Fm: 1-3
Distance: 5f/6f: 0-0 7f-8f: 0-1 9f-13f: 2-6 14f+: 2-11
Track : LH: 1-5 **RH: 2-11** Tight: 1-2 **Gall: 2-10**
Aids: Bl: 0-0 Vi: 0-0 Tstrap: 0-0
Best Rating: 83 6/01 Asct 2m6f34y gd-fm

Restricted to one start on the Flat in 2001 when runner-up in the Queen Alexandra Stakes at Ascot. Suited by fast ground and stays well.

Kahzima (USA)

98 **71**

2-y-o b f Gulch (USA)-Gharayib (USA) (Nureyev (USA))
E A L Dunlop Hamdan Al Maktoum

Placings:5314 **(3058)**
2001: 5^{5}GF, 6^{3}GF, 5^{1}GF, 5^{4}G

	Starts	1st	2nd	3rd	Win & Pl
Career Total (Turf)	4	1	0	1	5057

68 7/01 Kemp 5f D G-F £3688
Total win prize-money £3689

Going (Turf): Sf: 0-0 GS: 0-0 Gd: 0-1 **GF: 1-3** Fm: 0-0
Distance: **5f/6f: 1-4** 7f-8f: 0-0 9f-13f: 0-0 14f+: 0-0
Track : LH: 0-0 RH: 0-0 Tight: 0-0 Gall: 0-0
Aids: Bl: 0-0 Vi: 0-0 Tstrap: 0-0
Best Rating: 71 7/01 York 5f good

Not always the easiest in the stalls, she consoled connections with a win at Kempton over the minimum trip over firm ground.

Kai One

106 **85**

3-y-o b c Puissance-Kind Of Shy (Kind Of Hush)
R Hannon The Cayman 'A' Team

Placings:32333-1000 **(4445)**
2001: 7^{1}GF, 8^{0}GF, 7^{0}G, 8^{0}G

	Starts	1st	2nd	3rd	Win & Pl
Career Total (Turf)	9	1	1	4	9212

85 6/01 Hayd 7f30y D G-F £4543
Total win prize-money £4544

Going (Turf): Sf: 0-1 GS: 0-0 Gd: 0-3 **GF: 1-5** Fm: 0-0
Distance: 5f/6f: 0-3 **7f-8f: 1-5** 9f-13f: 0-1 14f+: 0-0
Track : **LH: 1-2** RH: 0-2 Tight: 0-0 Gall: 0-0
Aids: Bl: 0-0 Vi: 0-0 Tstrap: 0-0
Best Rating: 85 6/01 Hayd 7f30y gd-fm

Placed in his first five starts before running out an easy winner of a Haydock maiden in June,but well beaten subsequently.

Kaiapoi

107 **82**

4-y-o ch c Elmaamul (USA)-Salanka (IRE) (Persian Heights)
R Hollinshead J D Graham

Placings:501000/11U3502060-01502300 **(4942)**
2001: 9^{0}HY, 12^{1}GF, 12^{5}F, 11^{0}GS, 12^{2}G, 11^{3}GF, 10^{0}G, 15^{0}S

	Starts	1st	2nd	3rd	Win & Pl
Career Total (Turf)	24	4	2	2	28822

79 5/01 Ches 1m4f66y D(0-80)H G-F £7377
81 5/00 Ches 1m4f66y C(0-95)H GD £8391
74 3/00 Donc 1m2f60y D(0-85)H G-F £4485
75 9/99 Ches 7f2y D SFT £3533
Total win prize-money £23789

Going (Turf): Sf: 1-6 GS: 0-4 Gd: 1-7 **GF: 2-6** Fm: 0-1
Distance: 5f/6f: 0-0 7f-8f: 1-5 **9f-13f: 3-15** 14f+: 0-4
Track : **LH: 4-21** RH: 0-2 **Tight: 3-8** Gall: 1-8
Aids: Bl: 0-0 Vi: 0-0 Tstrap: 0-0
Best Rating: 82 6/01 Donc 1m4f firm

A useful middle-distance handicapper, he was winning for the third time at the track when scoring at Chester in May and is obviously suited by a tight left-handed course. Acts on fast ground.

Kaieteur (USA)

107 **98**

2-y-o b c Marlin (USA)-Strong Embrace (USA) (Regal Embrace (CAN))
B J Meehan Mrs Susan McCarthy

Placings:21 **(5460)**
2001: 7^{2}GF, 8^{1}G

	Starts	1st	2nd	3rd	Win & Pl
Career Total (Turf)	2	1	1	0	4772

91 10/01 Bath 1m5y E GD £2996
Total win prize-money £2996

Going (Turf): Sf: 0-0 GS: 0-0 **Gd: 1-1** GF: 0-1 Fm: 0-0
Distance: 5f/6f: 0-0 7f-8f: 0-1 **9f-13f: 1-1** 14f+: 0-0
Track : **LH: 1-1** RH: 0-0 **Tight: 1-1** Gall: 0-0
Aids: Bl: 0-0 Vi: 0-0 Tstrap: 0-0
Best Rating: 98 9/01 Newb 7f gd-fm

Related to winners in the US, made a very encouraging debut at Newbury in September. Went one better at Bath in October over a mile. Well regarded by connections.

Kailan Scamp

90 **16**

8-y-o gr m Palm Track-Noble Scamp (Scallywag)
J Parkes Mrs G M Z Spink

Placings:050-05 **(4268)**
2001: 9^{0}F, 9^{5}GF

	Starts	1st	2nd	3rd	Win & Pl
Career Total (Turf)	5	0	0	0	0

Going (Turf): Sf: 0-2 GS: 0-0 Gd: 0-0 GF: 0-2 Fm: 0-1
Distance: 5f/6f: 0-0 7f-8f: 0-0 9f-13f: 0-5 14f+: 0-0
Track : LH: 0-2 RH: 0-3 Tight: 0-2 Gall: 0-1
Aids: Bl: 0-0 Vi: 0-0 Tstrap: 0-4
Best Rating: 13 8/01 Bevl 1m1f207y gd-fm

Kala Sunrise

70

8-y-o ch h Kalaglow-Belle Of The Dawn (Bellypha)
C Smith A E Needham

Placings:410004/64006006401/5032026053402/0650/0 100500064240/0033501-P **(5265)**
2001: 8^{P}GS

	Starts	1st	2nd	3rd	Win & Pl
Career Total (Turf)	55	4	4	4	37860

59 8/00 Carl 7f214y D(0-75) FRM £3957
83 4/99 Leic 7f9y D(0-85)H GD £4100
86 10/96 York 7f202y B(0-100)H GD £8531
77 4/95 Pont 5f E FRM £3269
Total win prize-money £19859

Going (Turf): Sf: 0-1 GS: 0-9 **Gd: 2-22** GF: 0-19 **Fm: 2-4**
Distance: 5f/6f: 1-4 **7f-8f: 3-31** 9f-13f: 0-20 14f+: 0-0
Track : **LH: 2-28** RH: 1-9 Tight: 0-2 **Gall: 1-15**
Aids: Bl: 0-0 Vi: 0-0 Tstrap: 0-0
Best Rating: 77 4/95 Pont 5f F

Likes to come from off a strong pace and had things go his way when scoring his fourth career win at Carlisle in August 2000. Pulled up lame on only start in 2001. Best at seven furlongs to a mile on a sound surface.

Kalabell Prince

88 **57**
2-y-o br c Bluegrass Prince (IRE)-Shikabell (Kala Shikari)
J C Fox Lord Mutton Racing Partnership

Placings:00666000 **(5458)**
2001: 5^{0}GF, 6^{0}GF, 6^{6}GF, 7^{6}G, 7^{6}G, 6^{0}GF, 8^{0}GF, 5^{0}G

	Starts	1st	2nd	3rd	Win & Pl
Career Total (Turf)	8	0	0	0	0

Going (Turf): Sf: 0-0 GS: 0-0 Gd: 0-3 GF: 0-5 Fm: 0-0
Distance: 5f/6f: 0-2 7f-8f: 0-5 9f-13f: 0-1 14f+: 0-0
Track : LH: 0-2 RH: 0-0 Tight: 0-0 Gall: 0-1
Aids: Bl: 0-1 Vi: 0-0 Tstrap: 0-0
Best Rating: 57 8/01 Brig 6f209y gd-fm

Kalahari Ferrari

74 (12)**12**
5-y-o ch g Clantime-Royal Agnes (Royal Palace)
A G Hobbs Furnish With Abbey

Placings:444006/53532235330/00-0 **(5101)**
2001: 9^{0}GS

	Starts	1st	2nd	3rd	Win & Pl
Career Total (Turf)	19	0	2	5	3744
Career Total (AW)	1	0	0	0	0

Going (Turf): Sf: 0-4 GS: 0-3 Gd: 0-5 GF: 0-4 Fm: 0-3
Distance: 5f/6f: 0-4 7f-8f: 0-9 9f-13f: 0-7 14f+: 0-0
Track : LH: 0-7 RH: 0-6 Tight: 0-5 Gall: 0-1
Aids: Bl: 0-0 Vi: 0-1 Tstrap: 0-0

Kalanisi (IRE)

122 **128**
5-y-o b h Doyoun-Kalamba (IRE) (Green Dancer (USA))
Sir Michael Stoute H H Aga Khan

Placings:111/212211-32 **(2303)**
2001: 10^{3}G, 10^{2}GF

	Starts	1st	2nd	3rd	Win & Pl
Career Total (Turf)	11	6	4	1	1373089

125	11/00	Chur	1m4f		FRM	£786341
128	10/00	NmkR	1m2f	A	G-S	£232000
123	6/00	Asct	1m	A	G-F	£72000
109	5/99	Kemp	1m	A	G-F	£14200
112	5/99	NmkJ	7f	C	G-F	£6057
87	4/99	Folk	7f	D	SFT	£3110

Total win prize-money £1113709

Going (Turf): Sf: 1-1 GS: 1-1 Gd: 0-3 **GF: 3-5** Fm: 1-1
Distance: 5f/6f: 0-0 **7f-8f: 4-4** 9f-13f: 2-7 14f+: 0-0
Track : LH: 1-2 RH: 1-4 Tight: 0-1 **Gall: 1-3**
Aids: Bl: 0-0 Vi: 0-0 Tstrap: 0-0
Best Rating: 127 6/01 Asct 1m2f gd-fm

He improved throughout 2000, winning the Queen Anne over a mile on his second start, before twice going down narrowly to the 'iron horse' Giant's Causeway in the Eclipse and Juddmonte International. He gained his first Group One success in the Champion Stakes, then stepped up to a mile and a half in the Breeders' Cup Turf, when he produced a terrific late challenge to give Europe its only winner at the meeting. He put up a pleasing display on his reappearance in Ireland behind fantastic Light, especially as he looked in real need of the outing, but sustained an injury when chasing home the same horse at Royal Ascot and had to be retired to stud in Ireland.

Kalarram

73
4-y-o ch f Muhtarram (USA)-Kalandariya (Kris)
C B B Booth C B B Booth

Placings:5/0 **(3489)**
2001: 5^{0}GF

	Starts	1st	2nd	3rd	Win & Pl
Career Total (Turf)	2	0	0	0	0

Going (Turf): Sf: 0-1 GS: 0-0 Gd: 0-0 GF: 0-1 Fm: 0-0
Distance: 5f/6f: 0-1 7f-8f: 0-1 9f-13f: 0-0 14f+: 0-0
Track : LH: 0-0 RH: 0-0 Tight: 0-0 Gall: 0-0
Aids: Bl: 0-0 Vi: 0-0 Tstrap: 0-0

Kalingalinga

92(88) (40)**54**
4-y-o b g Zafonic (USA)-Bell Toll (High Line)
B J Curley Mrs B J Curley

Placings:650001000 **(5626)**
2001: 6^{6}SD, 9^{5}SD, 11^{0}SD, 10^{0}GS, 5^{0}G, 8^{1}GY, 8^{0}G, 8^{0}GS, 8^{0}GS

	Starts	1st	2nd	3rd	Win & Pl
Career Total (Turf)	6	1	0	0	8280
Career Total (AW)	3	0	0	0	0

54	8/01	Gway	1m100y	(0-60)H	G-Y	£8280

Total win prize-money £8280

Going (Turf): Sf: 0-0 GS: 0-3 Gd: 0-2 GF: 0-0 Fm: 0-0
Distance: 5f/6f: 0-2 7f-8f: 0-0 **9f-13f: 1-7** 14f+: 0-0
Track : LH: 0-5 RH: 0-0 Tight: 0-3 Gall: 0-0
Aids: Bl: 0-1 Vi: 0-0 Tstrap: 0-0
Best Rating: 54 8/01 Gway 1m100y gd-yld

Landed a gamble at Galway in August.

Kaloushka (IRE)

(80) (29)
3-y-o b f Inzar (USA)-Petova (IRE) (Petorius)
R Brotherton K Thrussell

Placings:5506 **(0610)**
2001: 7^{5}SD, 6^{5}SD, 9^{0}SD, 11^{6}SD

	Starts	1st	2nd	3rd	Win & Pl
Career Total (Turf)	0	0	0	0	
Career Total (AW)	4	0	0	0	0

Going (Turf): Sf: 0-0 GS: 0-0 Gd: 0-0 GF: 0-0 Fm: 0-0
Distance: 5f/6f: 0-1 7f-8f: 0-1 9f-13f: 0-2 14f+: 0-0
Track : LH: 0-4 RH: 0-0 Tight: 0-3 Gall: 0-0
Aids: Bl: 0-0 Vi: 0-0 Tstrap: 0-0
Best Rating: 29 2/01 Wolv 1m1f79y stand

Kaluana Court

105 **57**
5-y-o b m Batshoof-Fairfields Cone (Celtic Cone)
R J Price Derek & Cheryl Holder

Placings:0/000/0-05211100 **(4953)**
2001: 12^{0}GF, 12^{5}GF, 14^{2}GF, 17^{1}G, 14^{1}GF, 17^{1}GF, 16^{0}G, 16^{0}GS

	Starts	1st	2nd	3rd	Win & Pl
Career Total (Turf)	13	3	1	0	10459

57	8/01	Pont	2m1f22y	F(0-65)H	G-F	£3900
50	8/01	Wwck	1m6f213y	F(0-60)H	G-F	£2665
47	7/01	Bath	2m1f34y	E(0-70)H	GD	£2933

Total win prize-money £9499

Going (Turf): Sf: 0-3 GS: 0-2 Gd: 1-3 **GF: 2-5** Fm: 0-0
Distance: 5f/6f: 0-1 7f-8f: 0-1 9f-13f: 0-5 **14f+: 3-6**
Track : **LH: 2-6** RH: 0-4 **Tight: 1-4** Gall: 0-0
Aids: Bl: 0-0 Vi: 0-0 Tstrap: 0-0
Best Rating: 57 8/01 Pont 2m1f22y gd-fm

Fair staying handicapper, best on fast ground.

Kaluga (IRE)

95(74) (24)**48**
3-y-o ch f Tagula (IRE)-Another Baileys (Deploy)
P R Rodford (I A Balding 11/5) Mrs Christine Priest

Placings:00-0100 **(1280)**
2001: 11^{0}SD, 12^{1}S, 12^{0}SD, 14^{0}G

	Starts	1st	2nd	3rd	Win & Pl
Career Total (Turf)	4	1	0	0	2629
Career Total (AW)	2	0	0	0	

48	4/01	Pont	1m4f8y	F	SFT	£2628

Total win prize-money £2629

Going (Turf): Sf: 1-1 GS: 0-1 Gd: 0-1 GF: 0-1 Fm: 0-0
Distance: 5f/6f: 0-2 7f-8f: 0-0 **9f-13f: 1-3** 14f+: 0-1
Track : **LH: 1-5** RH: 0-0 Tight: 0-1 Gall: 0-0
Aids: Bl: 0-0 Vi: 0-2 Tstrap: 0-0
Best Rating: 48 4/01 Pont 1m4f8y soft

She showed none of her sire, Tagula's liking of a sound surface when winning a mile and a half Pontefract seller on soft ground for Ian Balding in April.

Kama Sutra

(99) (53) **58**
3-y-o b c Pursuit Of Love-Note Book (Mummy's Pet)
W Jarvis W J Simms

Placings:4-02 **(5374)**
2001: 7^{0}G, 6^{2}G

	Starts	1st	2nd	3rd	Win & Pl
Career Total (Turf)	3	0	1	0	1673

Going (Turf): Sf: 0-1 GS: 0-0 Gd: 0-2 GF: 0-0 Fm: 0-0
Distance: 5f/6f: 0-2 7f-8f: 0-1 9f-13f: 0-0 14f+: 0-0
Track : LH: 0-0 RH: 0-0 Tight: 0-0 Gall: 0-0
Aids: Bl: 0-0 Vi: 0-0 Tstrap: 0-0
Best Rating: 58 10/01 Rdcr 6f good

Has run well in all starts in maidens, but was outclassed when put into a conditions event, although when she was second in a Redcar maiden, she was beaten by a horse rated only 47.

Kama's Wheel

(81) (50)**60**
2-y-o ch f Magic Ring (IRE)-Tea And Scandals (USA) (Key To The Kingdom (USA))
John A Harris (J L Harris 14/5) Paddy Barrett

Placings:0534344004 **(5193)**
2001: 5^{0}SD, 5^{5}SD, 6^{3}G, 5^{4}GS, 6^{3}GF, 7^{4}G, 5^{4}G, 6^{0}S, 6^{0}G, 6^{4}SD

	Starts	1st	2nd	3rd	Win & Pl
Career Total (Turf)	7	0	0	2	808
Career Total (AW)	3	0	0	0	0

Going (Turf): Sf: 0-1 GS: 0-1 Gd: 0-4 GF: 0-1 Fm: 0-0
Distance: 5f/6f: 0-5 7f-8f: 0-5 9f-13f: 0-0 14f+: 0-0
Track : LH: 0-3 RH: 0-0 Tight: 0-2 Gall: 0-0
Aids: Bl: 0-0 Vi: 0-0 Tstrap: 0-0
Best Rating: 60 7/01 Yarm 6f3y good

Signs of ability, although improvement needed if she is to win a race.

Kamakazi Knight (IRE)

66 **25**
2-y-o b c Night Shift (USA)-Kaskazi (Dancing Brave (USA))
R M Flower Richard J Gurr

Placings:000 **(4889)**
2001: 7^{0}GF, 6^{11}G, 8^{0}GF

	Starts	1st	2nd	3rd	Win & Pl
Career Total (Turf)	3	0	0	0	

Going (Turf): Sf: 0-0 GS: 0-0 Gd: 0-1 GF: 0-2 Fm: 0-0
Distance: 5f/6f: 0-1 7f-8f: 0-2 9f-13f: 0-0 14f+: 0-0

Track : LH: 0-0 RH: 0-1 Tight: 0-0 Gall: 0-0
Aids: Bl: 0-0 Vi: 0-0 Tstrap: 0-0
Best Rating: 25 9/01 Kemp 1m gd-fm

Kameynn (IRE)

104 **84**

3-y-o b c Green Desert (USA)-Continuous (IRE) (Darshaan)
M P Tregoning Sheikh Ahmed Al Maktoum

Placings:43342110 **(4445)**
2001: 7^{4}S, 7^{3}GF, 8^{3}GF, 7^{4}GF, 7^{2}GS, 7^{1}G, 8^{1}GF, 8^{0}G

	Starts	1st	2nd	3rd	Win & Pl
Career Total (Turf)	8	2	1	2	13021

84	8/01	Bevl	1m100y	D(0-80)	G-F	£4241
80	8/01	Asct	7f	D	GD	£5395

Total win prize-money £9636

Going (Turf): Sf: 0-1 GS: 0-1 **Gd: 1-2 GF: 1-4** Fm: 0-0
Distance: 5f/6f: 0-0 7f-8f: 1-5 9f-13f: 1-3 14f+: 0-0
Track : LH: 0-0 **RH: 1-3** Tight: 0-1 Gall: 0-0
Aids: Bl: 0-0 Vi: 0-0 Tstrap: 0-0
Best Rating: 84 8/01 Bevl 1m100y gd-fm

A half-brother to a seven-furlong winner in Hong Kong, he was often placed before getting off the mark in a poor maiden at Ascot in August. Followed up in a soft race at Beverley.

Kandymal (IRE)

100(83) (31)**45**

3-y-o ch f Prince Of Birds (USA)-Gentle Papoose (Commanche Run)
R A Fahey Mrs Andrea M Mallinson

Placings:06066000-0200333256 **(5284)**
2001: 8^{0}F, 7^{2}GF, 8^{0}GF, 8^{0}GF, 7^{3}GS, 8^{3}F, 8^{3}S, 10^{2}GF, 8^{5}F, 9^{6}HY

	Starts	1st	2nd	3rd	Win & Pl
Career Total (Turf)	16	0	2	3	2650
Career Total (AW)	2	0	0	0	

Going (Turf): Sf: 0-4 GS: 0-1 Gd: 0-3 GF: 0-5 Fm: 0-3
Distance: 5f/6f: 0-5 7f-8f: 0-8 9f-13f: 0-5 14f+: 0-0
Track : LH: 0-9 RH: 0-4 Tight: 0-6 Gall: 0-2
Aids: Bl: 0-0 Vi: 0-1 Tstrap: 0-0
Best Rating: 46 6/01 Bevl 7f100y gd-fm

Kangarilla Road

(79) (56)**50**

2-y-o b g Magic Ring (IRE)-Kangra Valley (Indian Ridge)
Mrs J R Ramsden Manor Farm Stud (rutland)

Placings:06 **(5689)**
2001: 5^{0}S, 6^{6}S

	Starts	1st	2nd	3rd	Win & Pl
Career Total (Turf)	2	0	0	0	0

Going (Turf): Sf: 0-2 GS: 0-0 Gd: 0-0 GF: 0-0 Fm: 0-0
Distance: 5f/6f: 0-2 7f-8f: 0-0 9f-13f: 0-0 14f+: 0-0
Track : LH: 0-0 RH: 0-0 Tight: 0-0 Gall: 0-0
Aids: Bl: 0-0 Vi: 0-0 Tstrap: 0-0
Best Rating: 50 11/01 Donc 6f soft

Well beaten on debut, he improved at Doncaster when sixth.

Kanz Wood (USA)

(104) (70)

5-y-o ch g Woodman (USA)-Kanz (USA) (The Minstrel (CAN))
A W Carroll (W R Muir 8/9) P J Wilmott

Placings:53000/050/1004100-0200052P26 **(5626)**
2001: 8^{0}SD, 6^{2}SD, 6^{0}GF, 7^{0}GF, 7^{0}G, 6^{5}G, 7^{2}SD, 8^{P}GS, 8^{2}G, 8^{6}GS, 6^{3}SD

	Starts	1st	2nd	3rd	Win & Pl
Career Total (Turf)	19	1	1	1	8699
Career Total (AW)	6	1	2	0	4879

70	11/00	Sthl	1m	D(0-85)H	STD	£3165
65	5/00	Gdwd	1m	D(0-80)H	SFT	£6012

Total win prize-money £9179

Going (Turf): Sf: 1-2 GS: 0-2 Gd: 0-7 GF: 0-8 Fm: 0-0
Distance: 5f/6f: 0-3 **7f-8f: 2-14** 9f-13f: 0-8 14f+: 0-0
Track : LH: 1-10 RH: 1-5 Tight: 0-6 Gall: 0-2
Aids: Bl: 0-0 Vi: 0-0 Tstrap: 0-0
Best Rating: 70 9/01 Wolv 7f stand

Has been tried over a number of different trips, showing his best form at a mile. He is suited by Fibresand and soft ground.

Kanzina

95 **78**

2-y-o b f Machiavellian (USA)-Kanz (USA) (The Minstrel (CAN))
R Hannon D J Deer

Placings:00 **(5603)**
2001: 7^{0}GS, 7^{0}GS

	Starts	1st	2nd	3rd	Win & Pl
Career Total (Turf)	2	0	0	0	

Going (Turf): Sf: 0-0 GS: 0-2 Gd: 0-0 GF: 0-0 Fm: 0-0
Distance: 5f/6f: 0-0 7f-8f: 0-2 9f-13f: 0-0 14f+: 0-0
Track : LH: 0-0 RH: 0-0 Tight: 0-0 Gall: 0-0
Aids: Bl: 0-0 Vi: 0-0 Tstrap: 0-0
Best Rating: 78 11/01 NmkR 7f gd-sft

Kaparolo (USA)

79

2-y-o ch c El Prado (IRE)-Parliament House (USA) (General Assembly (USA))
Mrs A J Perrett John Connolly

Placings:3 **(5295)**
2001: 8^{3}S

	Starts	1st	2nd	3rd	Win & Pl
Career Total (Turf)	1	0	0	1	650

Going (Turf): Sf: 0-1 GS: 0-0 Gd: 0-0 GF: 0-0 Fm: 0-0
Distance: 5f/6f: 0-0 7f-8f: 0-0 9f-13f: 0-1 14f+: 0-0
Track : LH: 0-0 RH: 0-0 Tight: 0-0 Gall: 0-0
Aids: Bl: 0-0 Vi: 0-0 Tstrap: 0-0
Best Rating: 79 10/01 Leic 1m9y soft

Showed promise to finish third on his Leicester debut and should be suited by middle distances at three.

Karakum

93 **68**

2-y-o b c Mtoto-Magongo (Be My Chief (USA))
M A Jarvis Sheikh Ahmed Al Maktoum

Placings:64 **(3368)**
2001: 7^{6}GF, 7^{4}GF

	Starts	1st	2nd	3rd	Win & Pl
Career Total (Turf)	2	0	0	0	0

Going (Turf): Sf: 0-0 GS: 0-0 Gd: 0-0 GF: 0-2 Fm: 0-0
Distance: 5f/6f: 0-0 7f-8f: 0-2 9f-13f: 0-0 14f+: 0-0
Track : LH: 0-0 RH: 0-0 Tight: 0-0 Gall: 0-0
Aids: Bl: 0-0 Vi: 0-0 Tstrap: 0-0
Best Rating: 68 7/01 Ling 7f gd-fm

Karamah

94 **92+**

2-y-o b f Unfuwain (USA)-Azdihaar (USA) (Mr Prospector (USA))
J L Dunlop Hamdan Al Maktoum

Placings:2 **(2974)**
2001: 6^{2}G

	Starts	1st	2nd	3rd	Win & Pl
Career Total (Turf)	1	0	1	0	1716

Going (Turf): Sf: 0-0 GS: 0-0 Gd: 0-1 GF: 0-0 Fm: 0-0
Distance: 5f/6f: 0-1 7f-8f: 0-0 9f-13f: 0-0 14f+: 0-0
Track : LH: 0-0 RH: 0-0 Tight: 0-0 Gall: 0-0
Aids: Bl: 0-0 Vi: 0-0 Tstrap: 0-0
Best Rating: 92 7/01 NmkJ 6f good

A fine second to Gossamer on her debut.

Karameg (IRE)

107 **81**

5-y-o b m Danehill (USA)-House Of Queens (IRE) (King Of Clubs)
P W Harris Graham & Lynn Knight

Placings:040/40013523515/04220500-026542 **(4283)**
2001: 7^{0}S, 7^{2}G, 6^{6}GF, 6^{5}GF, 7^{4}G, 7^{2}G

	Starts	1st	2nd	3rd	Win & Pl
Career Total (Turf)	28	2	5	2	25295

78	10/99	NmkJ	7f	C(0-90)H	SFT	£8448
72	6/99	Donc	7f	E(0-70)H	G-F	£3152

Total win prize-money £11600

Going (Turf): Sf: 1-7 GS: 0-1 Gd: 0-9 **GF: 1-11** Fm: 0-0
Distance: 5f/6f: 0-5 **7f-8f: 2-21** 9f-13f: 0-2 14f+: 0-0
Track : LH: 0-6 RH: 0-3 Tight: 0-1 Gall: 0-3
Aids: Bl: 0-0 Vi: 0-0 Tstrap: 0-0
Best Rating: 81 7/01 Yarm 7f3y good

She was beaten only narrowly in a couple of races last summer, but did not manage to win during the campaign. Suited by seven furlongs and fast ground. She ran well again in 2001 without winning.

Karasta (IRE)

96 **108**

3-y-o b f Lake Coniston (IRE)-Karliyka (IRE) (Last Tycoon)
Sir Michael Stoute H H Aga Khan

Placings:112-060 **(2301)**
2001: 8^{0}G, 8^{6}G, 7^{0}GF

	Starts	1st	2nd	3rd	Win & Pl
Career Total (Turf)	6	2	1	0	62540

106	9/00	Donc	1m	A	G-F	£24000
90	8/00	NmkJ	7f	D	G-F	£4875

Total win prize-money £28875

Going (Turf): Sf: 0-0 GS: 0-0 Gd: 0-3 **GF: 2-3** Fm: 0-0
Distance: 5f/6f: 0-0 **7f-8f: 2-6** 9f-13f: 0-0 14f+: 0-0
Track : **LH: 1-1** RH: 0-1 Tight: 0-0 **Gall: 1-1**
Aids: Bl: 0-0 Vi: 0-0 Tstrap: 0-0
Best Rating: 108 5/01 Curr 1m good

She looked very decent in her first two starts at two, winning a Newmarket maiden and the Group Three May Hill Stakes at Doncaster. She lost no caste in defeat when runner-up in the Prix Marcel Boussac on her final start, where she went down to Amonita's better turn of foot. She ran no sort of a race in the 1000 Guineas first time out, but shaped a bit better to be sixth in the Irish equivalent. Retired to stud.

Kareeb (FR)

111 **82**

4-y-o b g Green Desert (USA)-Braari (USA) (Gulch (USA))
W R Muir J Bernstein

Placings:22324/650034361030-0446054252 **(4834)**
2001: 7^{0}GF, 8^{4}GF, 8^{4}GF, 8^{6}GF, 8^{0}G, 8^{5}GF, 6^{4}GF, 7^{2}GF, 7^{5}GF, 7^{2}GF

	Starts	1st	2nd	3rd	Win & Pl
Career Total (Turf)	27	1	5	4	23835

79	9/00	Newb	1m7y	C(0-100)H	G-F	£9165

Total win prize-money £9165

Going (Turf): Sf: 0-4 GS: 0-0 Gd: 0-6 **GF: 1-15** Fm: 0-2
Distance: 5f/6f: 0-8 7f-8f: 0-14 **9f-13f: 1-5** 14f+: 0-0
Track : **LH: 1-7** RH: 0-5 Tight: 0-4 **Gall: 1-4**
Aids: Bl: 0-4 Vi: 0-0 Tstrap: 0-0
Best Rating: 85 6/01 Epsm 1m114y gd-fm

He has a poor strike rate, but has run well this term without scoring. He is a consistent sort who earns little respite from the Handicapper.

Karin's Lad (IRE)

(60) **3**

4-y-o b g Up And At 'Em-Sharp Goodbye (Sharpo)
G M Moore (R Hollinshead 1/1) Mrs S E Cooper

Placings:500-00 **(0708)**
2001: 11^{0}SD, 17^{0}HY

	Starts	1st	2nd	3rd	Win & Pl
Career Total (Turf)	3	0	0	0	0
Career Total (AW)	2	0	0	0	

Going (Turf): Sf: 0-1 GS: 0-0 Gd: 0-0 GF: 0-2 Fm: 0-0
Distance: 5f/6f: 0-0 7f-8f: 0-0 9f-13f: 0-4 14f+: 0-1
Track : LH: 0-4 RH: 0-1 Tight: 0-1 Gall: 0-1
Aids: Bl: 0-0 Vi: 0-0 Tstrap: 0-0

Karindee

66(71) (8)

3-y-o ch f Karinga Bay-Jaydeebee (Buckley)
M Madgwick J D Brownrigg

Placings:0-0000 **(4094)**
2001: 6^{0}SW, 8^{0}SW, 9^{0}G, 9^{0}G

	Starts	1st	2nd	3rd	Win & Pl
Career Total (Turf)	2	0	0	0	
Career Total (AW)	3	0	0	0	

Going (Turf): Sf: 0-0 GS: 0-0 Gd: 0-2 GF: 0-0 Fm: 0-0
Distance: 5f/6f: 0-1 7f-8f: 0-2 9f-13f: 0-2 14f+: 0-0
Track : LH: 0-5 RH: 0-0 Tight: 0-3 Gall: 0-0
Aids: Bl: 0-0 Vi: 0-0 Tstrap: 0-0
Best Rating: 8 2/01 Ling 1m slow

Karitsa

93(87) (31)**55**

3-y-o b f Rudimentary (USA)-Desert Ditty (Green Desert (USA))
M R Channon Colin Brown Racing Iii

Placings:2510345-000603500000 **(5497)**
2001: 5^{0}S, 6^{0}S, 5^{0}GS, 5^{6}G, 5^{0}F, 6^{3}F, 5^{5}GF, 6^{0}GF, 5^{0}G, 5^{0}GF, 5^{0}SD, 5^{0}HY

	Starts	1st	2nd	3rd	Win & Pl
Career Total (Turf)	18	1	1	2	6761
Career Total (AW)	1	0	0	0	
70 7/00 Ches 5f16y	D			G-S	£4212

Total win prize-money £4212

Going (Turf): Sf: 0-5 **GS: 1-4** Gd: 0-3 GF: 0-4 Fm: 0-2
Distance: **5f/6f: 1-18** 7f-8f: 0-1 9f-13f: 0-0 14f+: 0-0
Track : **LH: 1-3** RH: 0-1 **Tight: 1-1** Gall: 0-1
Aids: Bl: 0-0 Vi: 0-0 Tstrap: 0-0
Best Rating: 55 6/01 Ling 6f firm

Karmafair (IRE)

86 **29**

5-y-o b m Always Fair (USA)-Karmisymixa (FR) (Linamix (FR))
C B B Booth The Foston Partnership

Placings:006 **(1108)**
2001: 12^{0}S, 12^{0}S, 16^{6}GF

	Starts	1st	2nd	3rd	Win & Pl
Career Total (Turf)	3	0	0	0	0

Going (Turf): Sf: 0-2 GS: 0-0 Gd: 0-0 GF: 0-1 Fm: 0-0
Distance: 5f/6f: 0-0 7f-8f: 0-0 9f-13f: 0-2 14f+: 0-1
Track : LH: 0-0 RH: 0-2 Tight: 0-2 Gall: 0-0
Aids: Bl: 0-0 Vi: 0-0 Tstrap: 0-0
Best Rating: 29 4/01 Muss 1m4f soft

Karminskey Park

93 **68**

2-y-o b f Sabrehill (USA)-Housefull (Habitat)
T J Etherington Wold House Partnership

Placings:03 **(3877)**
2001: 5^{0}GF, 5^{3}GS

	Starts	1st	2nd	3rd	Win & Pl
Career Total (Turf)	2	0	0	1	528

Going (Turf): Sf: 0-0 GS: 0-1 Gd: 0-0 GF: 0-1 Fm: 0-0
Distance: 5f/6f: 0-2 7f-8f: 0-0 9f-13f: 0-0 14f+: 0-0
Track : LH: 0-0 RH: 0-0 Tight: 0-0 Gall: 0-0
Aids: Bl: 0-0 Vi: 0-0 Tstrap: 0-0
Best Rating: 68 8/01 Thsk 5f gd-sft

Karowna

102 (26)**58**

5-y-o ch m Karinga Bay-Misowni (Niniski (USA))
Ian Williams (S A Brookshaw 4/8) The M28 Partnership

Placings:500/3443450/400-000 **(5263)**
2001: 12^{0}GF, 15^{0}GF, 13^{0}GS

	Starts	1st	2nd	3rd	Win & Pl
Career Total (Turf)	15	0	0	2	2638
Career Total (AW)	1	0	0	0	

Going (Turf): Sf: 0-0 GS: 0-4 Gd: 0-1 GF: 0-6 Fm: 0-3
Distance: 5f/6f: 0-1 7f-8f: 0-8 9f-13f: 0-2 14f+: 0-4
Track : LH: 0-12 RH: 0-1 Tight: 0-7 Gall: 0-2
Aids: Bl: 0-0 Vi: 0-0 Tstrap: 0-0
Best Rating: 58 7/01 Ches 1m7f195y gd-fm

Still a maiden on the Flat but has shown rather more over hurdles, and that included a win in a maiden hurdle at Huntingdon in April.

Karpasiana (USA)

101(108) (68+)**77+**

3-y-o ch f Woodman (USA)-Redwood Falls (IRE) (Dancing Brave (USA))
M A Jarvis Tigerland Ltd

Placings:0-50114101 **(4272)**
2001: 8^{5}SD, 6^{0}HY, 10^{1}SD, 11^{1}SD, 10^{4}G, 12^{1}SD, 14^{0}G, 9^{1}GF

	Starts	1st	2nd	3rd	Win & Pl
Career Total (Turf)	5	1	0	0	5325
Career Total (AW)	4	3	0	0	7938
77 8/01 Bevl 1m1f207y	D(0-80)H			G-F	£4910
68 6/01 Wolv 1m4f	E(0-75)H			STD	£2765
63 5/01 Sthl 1m3f	F(0-65)H			STD	£2359
65 5/01 Ling 1m2f	E(0-70)H			STD	£2814

Total win prize-money £12849

Going (Turf): Sf: 0-2 GS: 0-0 Gd: 0-2 **GF: 1-1** Fm: 0-0
Distance: 5f/6f: 0-1 7f-8f: 0-1 **9f-13f: 4-6** 14f+: 0-1
Track : **LH: 3-5** RH: 1-2 **Tight: 2-4** Gall: 0-0
Aids: Bl: 0-0 Vi: 0-0 Tstrap: 0-0
Best Rating: 77 8/01 Bevl 1m1f207y gd-fm

Enjoyed a good season on the sand and has shown decent form on fast ground on turf.

Karsavina (IRE)

102 **113**

3-y-o b f Sadler's Wells (USA)-Dumfries Pleasure (USA) (Pleasant Colony (USA))
A P O'Brien Joseph Allen

Placings:23-214345 **(4821a)**
2001: 10^{2}SH, 11^{1}G, 10^{4}Y, 12^{3}G, 11^{4}G, 12^{5}G

	Starts	1st	2nd	3rd	Win & Pl
Career Total (Turf)	8	1	2	2	60365
91 6/01 Naas 1m3f				GD	£11700

Total win prize-money £11700

Going (Turf): Sf: 0-1 GS: 0-0 **Gd: 1-4** GF: 0-0 Fm: 0-0
Distance: 5f/6f: 0-0 7f-8f: 0-1 **9f-13f: 1-7** 14f+: 0-0
Track : LH: 0-3 RH: 0-1 Tight: 0-0 Gall: 0-1
Aids: Bl: 0-0 Vi: 0-0 Tstrap: 0-0
Best Rating: 113 9/01 Lonc 1m4f good

Runner-up to Robolline in a Navan maiden over a mile on her debut, she stepped up to Listed class on her only other outing as a juvenile, finishing third to Vinnie Roe. Was slightly disappointing on her reappearance at three when stepped up to ten furlongs, but scored next time out at Naas over eleven furlongs. Subsequently ran with credit in top company. Acts on soft, has won on good ground.

Kasamba

97 **85**

2-y-o b f Salse (USA)-Kabayil (Dancing Brave (USA))
C G Cox Elite Racing Club

Placings:65100 **(5401)**
2001: 6^{6}GS, 6^{5}GF, 7^{1}GS, 7^{0}S, 8^{0}S

	Starts	1st	2nd	3rd	Win & Pl
Career Total (Turf)	5	1	0	0	4076
85 7/01 NmkJ 7f	D			G-S	£4075

Total win prize-money £4076

Going (Turf): Sf: 0-2 **GS: 1-2** Gd: 0-0 GF: 0-1 Fm: 0-0
Distance: 5f/6f: 0-2 **7f-8f: 1-2** 9f-13f: 0-1 14f+: 0-0
Track : LH: 0-2 RH: 0-0 Tight: 0-0 Gall: 0-0
Aids: Bl: 0-0 Vi: 0-0 Tstrap: 0-0
Best Rating: 85 7/01 NmkJ 7f gd-sft

Improved for the step up to seven furlongs when winning a Newmarket maiden on easy ground on her third start. Bred to stay further.

Kashmor (USA)

94 **86+**

2-y-o b c Nashwan (USA)-Millstream (USA) (Dayjur (USA))
D R Loder Sheikh Ahmed Al Maktoum

Placings:1 **(4964)**
2001: 8^{1}S

	Starts	1st	2nd	3rd	Win & Pl
Career Total (Turf)	1	1	0	0	4095
86 9/01 Pont 1m4y	D			SFT	£4095

Total win prize-money £4095

Going (Turf): Sf: 1-1 GS: 0-0 Gd: 0-0 GF: 0-0 Fm: 0-0
Distance: 5f/6f: 0-0 7f-8f: 0-0 **9f-13f: 1-1** 14f+: 0-0
Track : **LH: 1-1** RH: 0-0 Tight: 0-0 Gall: 0-0
Aids: Bl: 0-0 Vi: 0-0 Tstrap: 0-0
Best Rating: 86 9/01 Pont 1m4y soft

From a very good family, he relished the mud on his racecourse debut to land a moderate maiden over a mile in September.

Kashra (IRE)

95 **89d**

4-y-o b f Dancing Dissident (USA)-Tudor Loom (Sallust)
M Johnston K Towey

Placings:266121146/40002066-0600 **(4117)**
2001: 6^{0}F, 6^{6}G, 6^{0}G, 6^{0}G

	Starts	1st	2nd	3rd	Win & Pl
Career Total (Turf)	21	3	3	0	36037
87 8/99 NmkJ 6f	B H			G-F	£15790
72 7/99 Gdwd 6f	C H			G-F	£7595
58 7/99 Pont 6f	D H			G-S	£3785

Total win prize-money £27170

Going (Turf): Sf: 0-1 GS: 1-5 Gd: 0-8 **GF: 2-6** Fm: 0-1
Distance: **5f/6f: 3-18** 7f-8f: 0-3 9f-13f: 0-0 14f+: 0-0
Track : **LH: 1-3** RH: 0-2 Tight: 0-0 Gall: 0-1
Aids: Bl: 0-0 Vi: 0-0 Tstrap: 0-1
Best Rating: 78 8/01 Ripn 6f good

A useful filly when things go her way. Scored three times over six furlongs as a juvenile, but failed to score in 2000 and has not shown a great deal this term. Likes to hear her feet rattle.

Kass Alhawa

105(98) (57)44

8-y-o b g Shirley Heights-Silver Braid (USA) (Miswaki (USA))

D W Chapman T S Redman

Placings:4/25**000**050/**00344**3102014024240/**1245**0401 2366010230**22/423022**5202001534000643**10/206**24054 244225040**1430**-000000430**5255** **(5450)**

2001: 7^{0}GF, 8^{0}GF, 7^{0}GF, 8^{0}GF, 8^{0}GF, 8^{0}F, 8^{4}GF, 7^{3}G, 7^{0}G, 7^{5}G, **11^{2}SD**, 11^{5}S, 8^{5}HY

	Starts	1st	2nd	3rd	Win & Pl
Career Total (Turf)	74	5	12	7	38470
Career Total (AW)	31	3	8	2	14021

55	11/00	Wolv	1m100y	F(0-65)H	STD	£2478
55	11/99	Wolv	1m100y	F(0-65)H	STD	£2347
71	7/99	Bevl	1m100y	D(0-80)H	G-F	£4432
66	8/98	Bevl	7f100y	E(0-70)H	G-F	£4640
68	6/98	Bevl	7f100y	E(0-70)H	G-S	£3458
38	2/98	Sthl	6f	E(0-70)H	STD	£2801
63	8/97	Catt	7f	F(0-60)H	G-F	£3120
58	6/97	Rdcr	1m	G(0-70)H	GD	£2216

Total win prize-money £25495

Going (Turf): Sf: 0-7 GS: 1-11 Gd: 1-26 **GF: 3-26** Fm: 0-4
Distance: 5f/6f: 1-3 **7f-8f: 4-67** 9f-13f: 3-35 14f+: 0-0
Track : **LH: 4-60** RH: 3-33 **Tight: 3-45** Gall: 0-6
Aids: Bl: 0-9 Vi: 0-0 Tstrap: 0-0
Best Rating: 54 6/01 Bevl 7f100y gd-fm

He is a regular in modest handicaps at around a mile on turf and sand, but has a very moderate strike rate in recent seasons.

Kastanea

81(80) (9)38

3-y-o ch f Tharqaam (IRE)-Adana (FR) (Green Dancer (USA))

Mrs N Macauley Mr & Mrs R Harris

Placings:0-0000000 **(5113)**

2001: 9^{0}SW, 8^{0}SD, 11^{0}SD, 11^{0}SD, 11^{0}GF, 9^{0}GF, 8^{0}HY

	Starts	1st	2nd	3rd	Win & Pl
Career Total (Turf)	3	0	0	0	
Career Total (AW)	5	0	0	0	

Going (Turf): Sf: 0-1 GS: 0-0 Gd: 0-0 GF: 0-2 Fm: 0-0
Distance: 5f/6f: 0-0 7f-8f: 0-2 9f-13f: 0-6 14f+: 0-0
Track : LH: 0-6 RH: 0-2 Tight: 0-1 Gall: 0-0
Aids: Bl: 0-0 Vi: 0-0 Tstrap: 0-0
Best Rating: 38 6/01 Leic 1m3f183y gd-fm

Kat Slater (IRE)

(55) 9

2-y-o b f Eagle Eyed (USA)-Taniokey (Grundy)

G A Swinbank S A B Dinsmore

Placings:000 **(3018)**

2001: 5^{0}GF, 7^{0}F, 6^{0}SD

	Starts	1st	2nd	3rd	Win & Pl
Career Total (Turf)	2	0	0	0	
Career Total (AW)	1	0	0	0	

Going (Turf): Sf: 0-0 GS: 0-0 Gd: 0-0 GF: 0-1 Fm: 0-1
Distance: 5f/6f: 0-2 7f-8f: 0-1 9f-13f: 0-0 14f+: 0-0
Track : LH: 0-1 RH: 0-0 Tight: 0-0 Gall: 0-0
Aids: Bl: 0-0 Vi: 0-0 Tstrap: 0-0
Best Rating: 9 7/01 Muss 7f30y firm

Katali

85 29

4-y-o ch f Clantime-Portvally (Import)

A Bailey John Edwards

Placings:600 **(5503)**

2001: 7^{6}GF, 5^{0}F, 7^{0}HY

	Starts	1st	2nd	3rd	Win & Pl
Career Total (Turf)	3	0	0	0	0

Going (Turf): Sf: 0-1 GS: 0-0 Gd: 0-0 GF: 0-1 Fm: 0-1
Distance: 5f/6f: 0-1 7f-8f: 0-2 9f-13f: 0-0 14f+: 0-0
Track : LH: 0-1 RH: 0-0 Tight: 0-0 Gall: 0-0
Aids: Bl: 0-0 Vi: 0-0 Tstrap: 0-0
Best Rating: 29 8/01 Wwck 7f26y gd-fm

Katatonic (IRE)

(71) (41)

8-y-o b g Waajib-Miss Kate (FR) (Nonoalco (USA))

A G Juckes A C W Price

Placings:53/3/4 **(0334)**

2001: 12^{4}SD

	Starts	1st	2nd	3rd	Win & Pl
Career Total (Turf)	0	0	0	0	
Career Total (AW)	4	0	0	2	908

Going (Turf): Sf: 0-0 GS: 0-0 Gd: 0-0 GF: 0-0 Fm: 0-0
Distance: 5f/6f: 0-0 7f-8f: 0-2 9f-13f: 0-2 14f+: 0-0
Track : LH: 0-4 RH: 0-0 Tight: 0-4 Gall: 0-0
Aids: Bl: 0-0 Vi: 0-0 Tstrap: 0-0
Best Rating: 19 2/01 Wolv 1m4f stand

Kates Son (IRE)

(94) (43)59

4-y-o ch g Fayruz-Kates Choice (IRE) (Taufan (USA))

Noel T Chance Fizzgigg Partnership

Placings:660/030043-0205 **(4071)**

2001: 7^{0}GF, 7^{2}G, 8^{0}GF, 8^{5}SD

	Starts	1st	2nd	3rd	Win & Pl
Career Total (Turf)	12	0	1	2	2900
Career Total (AW)	1	0	0	0	0

Going (Turf): Sf: 0-1 GS: 0-0 Gd: 0-7 GF: 0-3 Fm: 0-0
Distance: 5f/6f: 0-1 7f-8f: 0-8 9f-13f: 0-4 14f+: 0-0
Track : LH: 0-3 RH: 0-9 Tight: 0-1 Gall: 0-1
Aids: Bl: 0-0 Vi: 0-0 Tstrap: 0-0
Best Rating: 54 7/01 Kemp 7f good

Kathakali (IRE)

102(111) (86d)55

4-y-o b c Dancing Dissident (USA)-She's A Dancer (IRE) (Alzao (USA))

S Dow M B N Clements

Placings:0065400/**2111**000005000**220**-000200003**10** **(5469)**

2001: 9^{0}SW, 10^{0}SD, 9^{0}G, 10^{2}G, 10^{0}GF, 9^{0}GF, 9^{0}GS, 10^{0}GF, 8^{3}G, 7^{1}S, 9^{0}S

	Starts	1st	2nd	3rd	Win & Pl
Career Total (Turf)	24	1	1	1	4712
Career Total (AW)	10	3	3	0	15496

46	9/01	Brig	7f214y	G	SFT	£2044
75	4/00	Ling	1m2f	E(0-75)H	STD	£2730
75	1/00	Ling	1m2f	C	STD	£6217
64	1/00	Ling	1m	E	STD	£2743

Total win prize-money £13735

Going (Turf): Sf: 1-2 GS: 0-3 Gd: 0-5 GF: 0-14 Fm: 0-0
Distance: 5f/6f: 0-4 7f-8f: 2-6 9f-13f: 2-24 14f+: 0-0
Track : **LH: 4-19** RH: 0-6 **Tight: 3-16** Gall: 0-3
Aids: Bl: 0-0 Vi: 0-1 Tstrap: 0-0
Best Rating: 60 5/01 Sand 1m2f7y good

Notched up a hat-trick in 2000 on Lingfield's Equitrack, and landed a soft-ground Brighton seller in September, but was very disappointing in a similar event back there in October. Best at around a mile.

Kathann

52 47d

3-y-o ch f Presidium-Travel Mystery (Godswalk (USA))

J A Glover Kenneth Paul Beecroft

Placings:000-00 **(2188)**

2001: 14^{0}G, 14^{0}GF

	Starts	1st	2nd	3rd	Win & Pl
Career Total (Turf)	5	0	0	0	

Going (Turf): Sf: 0-0 GS: 0-0 Gd: 0-1 GF: 0-4 Fm: 0-0
Distance: 5f/6f: 0-1 7f-8f: 0-2 9f-13f: 0-0 14f+: 0-2
Track : LH: 0-3 RH: 0-1 Tight: 0-0 Gall: 0-0
Aids: Bl: 0-0 Vi: 0-0 Tstrap: 0-0

Kathies Pet

(91) (29)53

6-y-o b m Tina's Pet-Unveiled (Sayf El Arab (USA))

R J Hodges Mrs E A Tucker

Placings:020002/6031501000000/0100454500/**0040** **(0983)**

2001: 8^{0}SD, 8^{0}SW, 8^{4}SD, 7^{0}SD

	Starts	1st	2nd	3rd	Win & Pl
Career Total (Turf)	28	3	2	1	11102
Career Total (AW)	5	0	0	0	0

55	5/99	Bath	5f161y	E(0-70)H	GD	£2970
66	6/98	Wind	6f	E(0-70)H	GD	£3011
61	5/98	Brig	5f213y	E(0-70)H	GD	£2892

Total win prize-money £8873

Going (Turf): Sf: 0-4 GS: 0-3 **Gd: 3-9** GF: 0-10 Fm: 0-2
Distance: **5f/6f: 3-19** 7f-8f: 0-10 9f-13f: 0-4 14f+: 0-0
Track : **LH: 2-17** RH: 1-5 Tight: 0-6 **Gall: 2-8**
Aids: Bl: 0-0 Vi: 0-0 Tstrap: 0-0
Best Rating: 29 2/01 Wolv 1m100y stand

Kathinka

88 72

2-y-o b f Bin Ajwaad (IRE)-Promissory (Caerleon (USA))

C E Brittain B H Voak

Placings:060 **(5609)**

2001: 7^{0}GS, 8^{6}HY, 8^{0}GS

	Starts	1st	2nd	3rd	Win & Pl
Career Total (Turf)	3	0	0	0	0

Going (Turf): Sf: 0-1 GS: 0-2 Gd: 0-0 GF: 0-0 Fm: 0-0
Distance: 5f/6f: 0-0 7f-8f: 0-2 9f-13f: 0-1 14f+: 0-0
Track : LH: 0-0 RH: 0-1 Tight: 0-1 Gall: 0-0
Aids: Bl: 0-0 Vi: 0-0 Tstrap: 0-0
Best Rating: 72 11/01 NmkR 1m gd-sft

Showed promise on debut when ninth of 20 in a Leicester maiden, but missed the break when claimer-ridden next time. Outclassed in Listed event on final start.

Kathology (IRE)

107(94) (74)81

4-y-o b g College Chapel-Wicken Wonder (IRE) (Distant Relative)

M Johnston Mcdowell Racing

Placings:042223/2114002000-00300200000 **(5090)**

2001: 5^{0}SD, 5^{0}GS, 6^{3}G, 7^{0}G, 6^{0}GF, 7^{2}G, 6^{0}GF, 6^{0}G, 7^{0}G, 6^{0}G, 5^{0}GS

	Starts	1st	2nd	3rd	Win & Pl
Career Total (Turf)	24	2	5	1	36432
Career Total (AW)	3	0	1	1	1045

93	5/00	Ches	5f16y	C(0-100)H	GD	£8801
87	4/00	Sand	5f6y	B(0-100)H	SFT	£9335

Total win prize-money £18136

Going (Turf): Sf: 1-4 GS: 0-5 **Gd: 1-8** GF: 0-7 Fm: 0-0
Distance: **5f/6f: 2-22** 7f-8f: 0-5 9f-13f: 0-0 14f+: 0-0
Track : **LH: 1-7** RH: 0-1 **Tight: 1-4** Gall: 0-1
Aids: Bl: 0-0 Vi: 0-0 Tstrap: 0-0
Best Rating: 90 5/01 NmkR 6f good

Useful sprint handicapper in 2000 for David Elsworth when he showed his form on ground ranging from good to firm to soft. Showed his best form for his current handler when runner-up at Haydock in June 2001, but was unplaced in the Wokingham and Stewards' Cup after having made the running, and continued to look held by the Handicapper afterwards. Handles most ground types, but seems best with cut.

Kathys Jack

3-y-o b g Silca Blanka (IRE)-Kathy Fair (IRE) (Nicholas Bill)
A D Smith Miss K Smith

Placings:00 **(5519)**
2001: 8^{0}GF, 6^{0}HY

	Starts	1st	2nd	3rd	Win & Pl
Career Total (Turf)	2	0	0	0	

Going (Turf): Sf: 0-1 GS: 0-0 Gd: 0-0 GF: 0-1 Fm: 0-0
Distance: 5f/6f: 0-1 7f-8f: 0-0 9f-13f: 0-1 14f+: 0-0
Track : LH: 0-0 RH: 0-0 Tight: 0-0 Gall: 0-0
Aids: Bl: 0-0 Vi: 0-0 Tstrap: 0-0

Katie Komaite

103 (22?)**34**
8-y-o b m Komaite (USA)-City To City (Windjammer (USA))
Mrs G S Rees Red Rose Partnership

Placings:64**0**30063/**6**0004050300/**0**204254212064/000 1640236/4505000010/40002352200-5005410 **(5101)**
2001: 12^{5}S, 10^{0}F, 10^{0}GF, 10^{5}HY, 12^{4}S, 11^{1}G, 9^{0}GS

	Starts	1st	2nd	3rd	Win & Pl
Career Total (Turf)	67	4	8	5	20949
Career Total (AW)	3	0	0	0	0

34	9/01	Haml	1m3f16y	F(0-70)H	GD	£3024
36	10/99	Newc	1m2f32y	F(0-60)H	G-S	£2410
43	6/98	Pont	1m4y	E(0-70)H	SFT	£3262
45	10/97	Nott	1m54y	E(0-70)H	G-S	£3005

Total win prize-money £11702

Going (Turf): Sf: 1-22 **GS: 2-7** Gd: 1-12 GF: 0-20 Fm: 0-6
Distance: 5f/6f: 0-9 7f-8f: 0-11 **9f-13f: 4-50** 14f+: 0-0
Track : **LH: 3-29** RH: 1-31 Tight: 1-30 Gall: 1-5
Aids: Bl: 0-2 **Vi: 3-31** Tstrap: 0-0
Best Rating: 43 5/01 Newc 1m4f93y soft

Moderate middle-distance handicapper, handles any ground.

Katie's Valentine

90(78) (51)**15**
4-y-o b f Balnibarbi-Ring Side (IRE) (Alzao (USA))
T A K Cuthbert Stephen Lowthian

Placings:045/32000-0400000 **(4881)**
2001: 5^{0}G, 6^{4}S, 7^{0}G, 6^{0}GS, 7^{0}G, 9^{0}G, 6^{0}GF

	Starts	1st	2nd	3rd	Win & Pl
Career Total (Turf)	12	0	1	1	1416
Career Total (AW)	3	0	0	0	246

Going (Turf): Sf: 0-3 GS: 0-2 Gd: 0-6 GF: 0-1 Fm: 0-0
Distance: 5f/6f: 0-6 7f-8f: 0-7 9f-13f: 0-2 14f+: 0-0
Track : LH: 0-4 RH: 0-2 Tight: 0-4 Gall: 0-1
Aids: Bl: 0-0 Vi: 0-2 Tstrap: 0-2
Best Rating: 45 7/01 Haml 6f5y soft

Katies Chimes (IRE)

92 **46**
4-y-o b f African Chimes-The Monks Sister (IRE) (Tony Nobles (USA))
R Ingram D G Wheatley

Placings:0040 **(4378)**
2001: 6^{0}F, 8^{0}G, 10^{4}GF, 10^{0}GF

	Starts	1st	2nd	3rd	Win & Pl
Career Total (Turf)	4	0	0	0	326

Going (Turf): Sf: 0-0 GS: 0-0 Gd: 0-1 GF: 0-2 Fm: 0-1
Distance: 5f/6f: 0-1 7f-8f: 0-0 9f-13f: 0-3 14f+: 0-0
Track : LH: 0-2 RH: 0-1 Tight: 0-3 Gall: 0-0
Aids: Bl: 0-0 Vi: 0-0 Tstrap: 0-0
Best Rating: 46 8/01 Wind 1m67y good

Katies Dolphin (IRE)

99(75) (36)**43**
3-y-o ch f Dolphin Street (FR)-Kuwah (IRE) (Be My Guest (USA))
J L Eyre K G Williams

Placings:62305600-000 **(4480)**
2001: 8^{0}GS, 6^{0}F, 7^{0}F

	Starts	1st	2nd	3rd	Win & Pl
Career Total (Turf)	10	0	1	1	1543
Career Total (AW)	1	0	0	0	

Going (Turf): Sf: 0-1 GS: 0-3 Gd: 0-2 GF: 0-2 Fm: 0-2
Distance: 5f/6f: 0-6 7f-8f: 0-4 9f-13f: 0-1 14f+: 0-0
Track : LH: 0-4 RH: 0-1 Tight: 0-1 Gall: 0-1
Aids: Bl: 0-2 Vi: 0-2 Tstrap: 0-0
Best Rating: 43 7/01 Thsk 6f firm

Katies Genie

87 **46**
3-y-o b f Syrtos-Reine De La Chasse (FR) (Ti King (FR))
B N Doran D G & D J Robinson

Placings:00300 **(3085)**
2001: 7^{0}GF, 8^{0}G, 8^{3}F, 8^{0}GF, 8^{0}GF

	Starts	1st	2nd	3rd	Win & Pl
Career Total (Turf)	5	0	0	1	1058

Going (Turf): Sf: 0-0 GS: 0-0 Gd: 0-1 GF: 0-3 Fm: 0-1
Distance: 5f/6f: 0-0 7f-8f: 0-1 9f-13f: 0-4 14f+: 0-0
Track : LH: 0-3 RH: 0-2 Tight: 0-4 Gall: 0-0
Aids: Bl: 0-0 Vi: 0-0 Tstrap: 0-0
Best Rating: 46 6/01 Bath 1m5y firm

Katies Tight Jeans

85 **37**
7-y-o b m Green Adventure (USA)-Haraka Sasa (Town And Country)
R E Peacock M F Harris

Placings:0000 **(3061)**
2001: 7^{0}GF, 10^{0}G, 6^{0}F, 5^{0}G

	Starts	1st	2nd	3rd	Win & Pl
Career Total (Turf)	4	0	0	0	

Going (Turf): Sf: 0-0 GS: 0-0 Gd: 0-2 GF: 0-1 Fm: 0-1
Distance: 5f/6f: 0-2 7f-8f: 0-1 9f-13f: 0-1 14f+: 0-0
Track : LH: 0-2 RH: 0-0 Tight: 0-1 Gall: 0-1
Aids: Bl: 0-0 Vi: 0-0 Tstrap: 0-0
Best Rating: 37 6/01 Wind 1m2f7y good

Kattegat

102 **69**
5-y-o b g Slip Anchor-Kirkton (Kris)
J A B Old W E Sturt

Placings:01/231/30-006 **(3250)**
2001: 16^{0}GS, 13^{0}GF, 14^{6}GS

	Starts	1st	2nd	3rd	Win & Pl
Career Total (Turf)	10	2	1	2	14241

90	10/99	Ayr	1m5f13y	C(0-95)H	SFT	£6488
81	10/98	Nott	1m54y	D	SFT	£3752

Total win prize-money £10242

Going (Turf): Sf: 2-3 GS: 0-5 Gd: 0-1 GF: 0-1 Fm: 0-0
Distance: 5f/6f: 0-0 7f-8f: 0-1 9f-13f: 1-2 14f+: 1-7
Track : **LH: 2-6** RH: 0-2 Tight: 0-1 Gall: 0-3
Aids: Bl: 0-0 Vi: 0-0 Tstrap: 0-0
Best Rating: 69 4/01 Newb 2m gd-sft

A winner on the Flat at two and three, but has been very lightly raced on the level in the last couple of years and has been seen more over hurdles. Likes soft ground. Stays two miles.

Katy Nowaitee

109 **103**
5-y-o b m Komaite (USA)-Cold Blow (Posse (USA))
P W Harris The Stable Maites

Placings:1512/111-6220 **(5142)**
2001: 9^{6}S, 9^{2}G, 9^{2}GF, 9^{0}G

	Starts	1st	2nd	3rd	Win & Pl
Career Total (Turf)	11	5	3	0	123673

104	10/00	NmkR	1m2f	A	SFT	£14326
107	9/00	NmkR	1m1f	B H	GD	£69600
92	3/00	Donc	1m	B H	GD	£14560
82	10/99	Rdcr	1m	D(0-85)H	GD	£6710
75	8/99	NmkJ	1m	D	G-F	£4620

Total win prize-money £109816

Going (Turf): Sf: 1-2 GS: 0-0 **Gd: 3-6** GF: 1-3 Fm: 0-0
Distance: 5f/6f: 0-0 **7f-8f: 3-3** 9f-13f: 2-8 14f+: 0-0
Track : LH: 0-2 RH: 0-1 Tight: 0-1 Gall: 0-0
Aids: Bl: 0-0 Vi: 0-0 Tstrap: 0-0
Best Rating: 105 4/01 NmkR 1m1f soft

Lightly-raced, she landed the Spring Mile at Doncaster early in 2000, but was then sidelined for six months. Returned to land an ante-post gamble in the Cambridgeshire before earning black type by taking a Listed event back at Newmarket. Ran reasonably without winning in 2001.

Katy O'Hara

80 **49**
2-y-o b f Komaite (USA)-Amy Leigh (IRE) (Imperial Frontier (USA))
Miss S E Hall C Platts

Placings:0000 **(5487)**
2001: 6^{0}GF, 6^{0}G, 6^{0}S, 6^{0}HY

	Starts	1st	2nd	3rd	Win & Pl
Career Total (Turf)	4	0	0	0	

Going (Turf): Sf: 0-2 GS: 0-0 Gd: 0-1 GF: 0-1 Fm: 0-0
Distance: 5f/6f: 0-4 7f-8f: 0-0 9f-13f: 0-0 14f+: 0-0
Track : LH: 0-1 RH: 0-0 Tight: 0-0 Gall: 0-0
Aids: Bl: 0-0 Vi: 0-0 Tstrap: 0-0
Best Rating: 49 10/01 Pont 6f soft

Kauri (USA)

85(101) (58)**39**
3-y-o b f Woodman (USA)-No Ordinary Storm (USA) (Storm Bird (CAN))
M Johnston J David Abell

Placings:0340-2313000 **(2867)**
2001: 12^{2}SD, 11^{3}SD, 11^{1}SD, 12^{3}SD, 9^{0}GF, 10^{0}GF, 12^{0}GF

	Starts	1st	2nd	3rd	Win & Pl
Career Total (Turf)	4	0	0	0	
Career Total (AW)	7	1	1	3	4023

58	4/01	Sthl	1m3f	F(0-65)H	STD	£2289

Total win prize-money £2289

Going (Turf): Sf: 0-0 GS: 0-0 Gd: 0-1 GF: 0-3 Fm: 0-0
Distance: 5f/6f: 0-3 7f-8f: 0-1 **9f-13f: 1-7** 14f+: 0-0
Track : **LH: 1-8** RH: 0-1 Tight: 0-4 Gall: 0-1
Aids: Bl: 0-0 Vi: 0-0 Tstrap: 0-1
Best Rating: 58 5/01 Wolv 1m4f stand

Fair middle-distance handicapper on the All-Weather, has looked less effective on turf.

Kawanbaik

82 **58**
2-y-o ch f Inchinor-Sky Music (Absalom)
K McAuliffe Mrs Fitri Hay

Placings:550 **(5250)**
2001: 6^{5}GS, 6^{5}G, 6^{0}S

	Starts	1st	2nd	3rd	Win & Pl
Career Total (Turf)	3	0	0	0	0

Going (Turf): Sf: 0-1 GS: 0-1 Gd: 0-1 GF: 0-0 Fm: 0-0

Distance: 5f/6f: 0-3 7f-8f: 0-0 9f-13f: 0-0 14f+: 0-0
Track : LH: 0-0 RH: 0-0 Tight: 0-0 Gall: 0-0
Aids: Bl: 0-1 Vi: 0-0 Tstrap: 0-0
Best Rating: 58 8/01 Gdwd 6f gd-sft

Kayo

109(100) (70)**98**
6-y-o b g Superpower-Shiny Kay (Star Appeal)
M Johnston J David Abell

Placings:4041010/1120126005510/466030030511103 0/000231220350400030-1650121P **(5391)**
2001: 6^{1}GF, 8^{6}SD, 7^{5}G, 6^{0}G, 8^{1}GF, 7^{2}G, 6^{1}S, 7^{P}GS

	Starts	1st	2nd	3rd	Win & Pl
Career Total (Turf)	47	11	6	4	113170
Career Total (AW)	16	2	0	2	7343

97	10/01	York	6f214y	B(0-105)H	SFT	£10516
59	8/01	Ripn	1m	F	G-F	£2786
99	7/01	Newb	6f8y	B(0-105)H	G-F	£9387
102	7/00	Newc	7f	C(0-100)H	FRM	£14170
93	10/99	Newc	6f	C(0-90)H	G-S	£7425
92	10/99	NmkJ	7f	C(0-100)H	GD	£8292
83	10/99	Rdcr	7f	D(0-85)H	GD	£6157
92	10/98	Wwck	1m	C(0-95)H	GD	£12254
86	6/98	Newb	7f	B(0-100)H	HVY	£7886
78	5/98	Sthl	7f	E(0-70)H	STD	£3106
72	4/98	Sthl	6f	E(0-70)H	STD	£3106
71	10/97	Ayr	1m	E(0-85)	SFT	£3073
66	9/97	Muss	1m	F	G-F	£2682

Total win prize-money £90844

Going (Turf): Sf: 3-12 GS: 1-6 **Gd: 3-17 GF: 3-11** Fm: 1-1
Distance: 5f/6f: 2-15 **7f-8f: 11-46** 9f-13f: 0-2 14f+: 0-0
Track : **LH: 5-30** RH: 2-4 **Tight: 2-10** Gall: 1-4
Aids: Bl: 0-1 Vi: 0-0 Tstrap: 0-0
Best Rating: 99 7/01 Newb 6f8y gd-fm

A useful six and seven-furlong handicapper, he showed himself as good as ever when winning on his belated Newbury reappearance and went on to win a weak contest at Ripon and a decent York handicap. Pulled up at Newmarket in October.

Kayseri (IRE)

100 **82**
2-y-o b c Alzao (USA)-Ms Calera (USA) (Diesis)
M A Jarvis Sheikh Ahmed Al Maktoum

Placings:021 **(5168)**
2001: 7^{0}GF, 8^{2}G, 10^{1}GS

	Starts	1st	2nd	3rd	Win & Pl
Career Total (Turf)	3	1	1	0	5323

82	10/01	Pont	1m2f6y	D	G-S	£3984

Total win prize-money £3985

Going (Turf): Sf: 0-0 **GS: 1-1** Gd: 0-1 GF: 0-1 Fm: 0-0
Distance: 5f/6f: 0-0 7f-8f: 0-1 **9f-13f: 1-2** 14f+: 0-0
Track : **LH: 1-2** RH: 0-0 Tight: 0-1 Gall: 0-0
Aids: Bl: 0-0 Vi: 0-0 Tstrap: 0-0
Best Rating: 82 10/01 Pont 1m2f6y gd-sft

A IR105,000gns son of a half-sister to an Irish St Leger winner, showed his appreciation of a distance of ground when winning a ten-furlong Pontefract maiden as a juvenile.

Kazana

94(97) (70)**63d**
3-y-o b f Salse (USA)-Sea Ballad (USA) (Bering)
G L Moore (S P C Woods 7/7) Leydens Farm Stud

Placings:42-100406 **(5082)**
2001: 8^{1}SD, 9^{0}GS, 9^{0}GF, 11^{4}GF, 7^{0}G, 7^{6}S

	Starts	1st	2nd	3rd	Win & Pl
Career Total (Turf)	7	0	1	0	2178
Career Total (AW)	1	1	0	0	2828

70	3/01	Ling	1m	D	STD	£2828

Total win prize-money £2828

Going (Turf): Sf: 0-1 GS: 0-1 Gd: 0-2 GF: 0-3 Fm: 0-0
Distance: 5f/6f: 0-0 **7f-8f: 1-4** 9f-13f: 0-4 14f+: 0-0
Track : **LH: 1-5** RH: 0-2 **Tight: 1-3** Gall: 0-1
Aids: Bl: 0-0 Vi: 0-0 Tstrap: 0-0
Best Rating: 70 3/01 Ling 1m stand

Fulfilled some of the promise of her juvenile career when scoring on the Lingfield Equitrack first time up this season, but has not done so well back on turf.

Kazeem

80 **76**
3-y-o b f Darshaan-Kanz (USA) (The Minstrel (CAN))
B W Hills D J Deer

Placings:66-0 **(0840)**
2001: 10^{0}GS

	Starts	1st	2nd	3rd	Win & Pl
Career Total (Turf)	3	0	0	0	0

Going (Turf): Sf: 0-0 GS: 0-1 Gd: 0-1 GF: 0-1 Fm: 0-0
Distance: 5f/6f: 0-0 7f-8f: 0-2 9f-13f: 0-1 14f+: 0-0
Track : LH: 0-2 RH: 0-0 Tight: 0-0 Gall: 0-2
Aids: Bl: 0-0 Vi: 0-0 Tstrap: 0-0
Best Rating: 49 4/01 Newb 1m2f6y gd-sft

Kebreya (USA)

85 **68**
2-y-o ch c Affirmed (USA)-Minifah (USA) (Nureyev (USA))
J L Dunlop Hamdan Al Maktoum

Placings:65 **(5623)**
2001: 8^{6}S, 8^{5}GS

	Starts	1st	2nd	3rd	Win & Pl
Career Total (Turf)	2	0	0	0	0

Going (Turf): Sf: 0-1 GS: 0-1 Gd: 0-0 GF: 0-0 Fm: 0-0
Distance: 5f/6f: 0-0 7f-8f: 0-0 9f-13f: 0-2 14f+: 0-0
Track : LH: 0-1 RH: 0-1 Tight: 0-0 Gall: 0-0
Aids: Bl: 0-0 Vi: 0-0 Tstrap: 0-0
Best Rating: 68 11/01 Nott 1m54y gd-sft

Kee Ring

98(96) (37)**49**
5-y-o ch g Keen-Rose And The Ring (Welsh Pageant)
P R Chamings Mrs J E L Wright

Placings:20/6005035/6060600-05025440 **(2966)**
2001: 6^{0}SD, 6^{5}SD, 5^{0}SD, 6^{2}SD, 5^{5}F, 6^{4}F, 5^{4}F, 5^{0}GF

	Starts	1st	2nd	3rd	Win & Pl
Career Total (Turf)	20	0	1	1	1377
Career Total (AW)	4	0	1	0	492

Going (Turf): Sf: 0-0 GS: 0-5 Gd: 0-1 GF: 0-9 Fm: 0-5
Distance: 5f/6f: 0-16 7f-8f: 0-8 9f-13f: 0-0 14f+: 0-0
Track : LH: 0-13 RH: 0-2 Tight: 0-4 Gall: 0-2
Aids: Bl: 0-13 Vi: 0-0 Tstrap: 0-0
Best Rating: 49 6/01 Ling 6f firm

Keen Hands

(108) (71)**38**
5-y-o ch g Keen-Broken Vow (IRE) (Local Suitor (USA))
Mrs N Macauley Andy Peake

Placings:00602/21502111060036 4024/1041050551040 060000000-50106403220000000 **(5612)**
2001: 6^{5}SD, 7^{0}SD, 7^{1}SW, 6^{0}SD, 8^{6}SW, 8^{4}SW, 8^{0}SD, 7^{3}SD, 6^{2}SD, 7^{2}SD, 6^{0}SD, 6^{0}G, 6^{0}SD, 8^{0}G, 8^{0}SD, 6^{0}SD, 6^{0}SD

	Starts	1st	2nd	3rd	Win & Pl
Career Total (Turf)	9	0	0	0	258
Career Total (AW)	53	8	6	2	35210

76	1/01	Wolv	7f	D(0-80)H	SLW	£3835
78	5/00	Sthl	6f	D(0-85)H	STD	£3835
78	2/00	Sthl	6f	D(0-80)H	STD	£4270
71	1/00	Sthl	6f	E(0-70)H	STD	£3835
72	4/99	Sthl	6f	E(0-70)H	STD	£7298
71	3/99	Sthl	5f	G	STD	£1838
61	3/99	Sthl	7f	G	STD	£1813
55	1/99	Wolv	5f	G	STD	£1861

Total win prize-money £28588

Going (Turf): Sf: 0-0 GS: 0-2 Gd: 0-2 GF: 0-3 Fm: 0-2
Distance: **5f/6f: 6-40** 7f-8f: 2-19 9f-13f: 0-3 14f+: 0-0
Track : **LH: 7-51** RH: 0-2 **Tight: 2-22** Gall: 0-2
Aids: Bl: 0-0 **Vi: 8-58** Tstrap: 0-0
Best Rating: 76 1/01 Wolv 7f slow

Apparently resents being hit with the whip, but has been successful on Fibresand in the past couple of years. Six furlongs at Southwell seem to be his ideal conditions.

Keep Dreaming

(85) (24)**18**
3-y-o b f Mistertopogigo (IRE)-Ominous (Dominion)
M Johnston S Harris

Placings:0006-050 **(0325)**
2001: 7^{0}SD, 11^{5}SD, 8^{0}SD

	Starts	1st	2nd	3rd	Win & Pl
Career Total (Turf)	3	0	0	0	0
Career Total (AW)	4	0	0	0	0

Going (Turf): Sf: 0-0 GS: 0-0 Gd: 0-2 GF: 0-1 Fm: 0-0
Distance: 5f/6f: 0-3 7f-8f: 0-3 9f-13f: 0-1 14f+: 0-0
Track : LH: 0-3 RH: 0-1 Tight: 0-1 Gall: 0-0
Aids: Bl: 0-0 Vi: 0-0 Tstrap: 0-0
Best Rating: 23 2/01 Sthl 1m3f stand

Keep Ikis

104 **63**
7-y-o ch m Anshan-Santee Sioux (Dancing Brave (USA))
Mrs M Reveley T McGoran

Placings:66000023/143151-034630 **(3549)**
2001: 16^{0}GF, 16^{3}F, 17^{4}F, 17^{6}GF, 16^{3}GF, 21^{0}GF

	Starts	1st	2nd	3rd	Win & Pl
Career Total (Turf)	20	3	1	4	15218

63	8/00	Pont	2m1f22y	F(0-65)H	G-F	£3802
51	7/00	Catt	1m7f177y	E(0-75)H	G-F	£3493
45	5/00	Ripn	2m	E(0-75)H	GD	£3549

Total win prize-money £10846

Going (Turf): Sf: 0-3 GS: 0-0 Gd: 1-2 **GF: 2-12** Fm: 0-3
Distance: 5f/6f: 0-0 7f-8f: 0-0 9f-13f: 0-2 **14f+: 3-18**
Track : **LH: 2-14** RH: 1-5 **Tight: 2-8** Gall: 0-1
Aids: Bl: 0-0 Vi: 0-0 Tstrap: 0-0
Best Rating: 65 5/01 Newc 2m19y firm

A staying handicapper, successful three times in 2000, she is rather short of gears.

Keep Tapping (IRE)

98(100) (59)**57**
4-y-o b g Mac's Imp (USA)-Mystery Bid (Auction Ring (USA))
N P Littmoden The Wayfarers

Placings:54201030000/30004-350000005 **(2556)**
2001: 6^{3}SW, 6^{5}SD, 7^{0}SD, 5^{0}SD, 6^{0}G, 5^{0}GF, 5^{0}GF, 5^{0}F, 6^{5}GF

	Starts	1st	2nd	3rd	Win & Pl
Career Total (Turf)	17	1	1	2	7154
Career Total (AW)	8	0	0	1	247

80	6/99	Sand	5f6y	D	GD	£3403

Total win prize-money £3404

Going (Turf): Sf: 0-1 GS: 0-1 **Gd: 1-5** GF: 0-9 Fm: 0-1
Distance: **5f/6f: 1-21** 7f-8f: 0-4 9f-13f: 0-0 14f+: 0-0
Track : LH: 0-11 RH: 0-0 Tight: 0-7 Gall: 0-1
Aids: Bl: 0-3 Vi: 0-8 Tstrap: 0-0
Best Rating: 59 1/01 Wolv 6f slow

He won an ordinary maiden at Sandown in June, but has had his limitations exposed in useful company.

Keep The Peace (IRE)

95 **66**
3-y-o br g Petardia-Eiras Mood (Jalmood (USA))
I A Balding Miss A V Hill

Placings:00-5020 **(2843)**
2001: 6^{5}G, 8^{0}GF, 8^{2}GS, 10^{0}GF

	Starts	1st	2nd	3rd	Win & Pl
Career Total (Turf)	6	0	1	0	862

Going (Turf): Sf: 0-0 GS: 0-1 Gd: 0-1 GF: 0-4 Fm: 0-0
Distance: 5f/6f: 0-1 7f-8f: 0-3 9f-13f: 0-2 14f+: 0-0
Track : LH: 0-0 RH: 0-2 Tight: 0-1 Gall: 0-0
Aids: Bl: 0-0 Vi: 0-2 Tstrap: 0-0
Best Rating: 64 6/01 Sals 1m gd-sft

Keep The Silver

(96) (82)**79**
2-y-o gr c Petong-Marjorie's Memory (IRE) (Fairy King (USA))
A P Jarvis Christopher Shankland

Placings:00021352 **(5408)**
2001: 5^{0}GS, 5^{0}GF, 5^{0}S, 6^{2}GF, 5^{1}G, 5^{3}G, 6^{5}GF, 6^{2}SD

	Starts	1st	2nd	3rd	Win & Pl
Career Total (Turf)	7	1	1	1	10902
Career Total (AW)	1	0	1	0	1128
73 7/01 York 5f	C			GD	£8944

Total win prize-money £8944

Going (Turf): Sf: 0-1 GS: 0-1 **Gd: 1-2** GF: 0-3 Fm: 0-0
Distance: **5f/6f: 1-7** 7f-8f: 0-1 9f-13f: 0-0 14f+: 0-0
Track : LH: 0-2 RH: 0-0 Tight: 0-1 Gall: 0-0
Aids: Bl: 0-0 Vi: 0-0 Tstrap: 0-0
Best Rating: 82 10/01 Sthl 6f stand

Winner of a nursery at York in July, he has run with credit since. A stiff five furlongs would probably suit him best at present. Acts on a sound surface.

Keepers Hill (IRE)

88 **97**
2-y-o b f Danehill (USA)-Asnieres (USA) (Spend A Buck (USA))
M Halford Kilboy Estate

Placings:2202 **(3350a)**
2001: 5^{2}G, 5^{2}GY, 5^{0}GF, 5^{2}G

	Starts	1st	2nd	3rd	Win & Pl
Career Total (Turf)	4	0	3	0	12790

Going (Turf): Sf: 0-0 GS: 0-0 Gd: 0-2 GF: 0-1 Fm: 0-0
Distance: 5f/6f: 0-4 7f-8f: 0-0 9f-13f: 0-0 14f+: 0-0
Track : LH: 0-0 RH: 0-0 Tight: 0-0 Gall: 0-0
Aids: Bl: 0-0 Vi: 0-0 Tstrap: 0-0
Best Rating: 97 5/01 Curr 5f gd-yld

Her dam is a half-sister to the Breeders' Cup Classic winner Arcangues and Agathe (dam of Prix de Diane winner Aquarreliste) and to the dam of 1000 Guineas winner Cape Verdi. She has yet to win a race but has shown plenty of speed in decent company and should find a race. Acts on a sound surface.

Keetchy (IRE)

95 **77**
2-y-o b c Darshaan-Ezana (Ela-Mana-Mou)
J L Dunlop Michael H Watt

Placings:603 **(5040)**
2001: 8^{6}G, 8^{0}GF, 10^{3}G

	Starts	1st	2nd	3rd	Win & Pl
Career Total (Turf)	3	0	0	1	541

Going (Turf): Sf: 0-0 GS: 0-0 Gd: 0-2 GF: 0-1 Fm: 0-0
Distance: 5f/6f: 0-0 7f-8f: 0-2 9f-13f: 0-1 14f+: 0-0
Track : LH: 0-1 RH: 0-0 Tight: 0-1 Gall: 0-0
Aids: Bl: 0-0 Vi: 0-0 Tstrap: 0-0
Best Rating: 77 10/01 Bath 1m2f46y good

Kelburne (USA)

107 **84**
4-y-o b g Red Ransom (USA)-Golden Klair (Damister (USA))
I Semple Kelburne Construction Ltd

Placings:5440000-0116101102050 **(5366)**
2001: 8^{0}G, 8^{1}GF, 8^{1}GF, 9^{6}GF, 9^{1}GF, 10^{0}S, 8^{1}GF, 8^{1}GF, 7^{0}G, 9^{2}G, 8^{0}GF, 8^{5}G, 8^{0}GS

	Starts	1st	2nd	3rd	Win & Pl
Career Total (Turf)	21	5	1	0	32592
84 7/01 Gdwd 1m	D(0-85)H			G-F	£11960
84 7/01 Asct 1m	C(0-90)H			G-F	£6873
72 7/01 Haml 1m1f36y	E(0-75)H			G-F	£3688
58 6/01 Haml 1m65y	F(0-60)			G-F	£2842
52 6/01 Newc 1m	F(0-60)H			G-F	£3010

Total win prize-money £28375

Going (Turf): Sf: 0-3 GS: 0-1 Gd: 0-5 **GF: 5-9** Fm: 0-3
Distance: 5f/6f: 0-0 **7f-8f: 3-7** 9f-13f: 2-14 14f+: 0-0
Track : LH: 1-8 **RH: 3-9 Tight: 2-5** Gall: 1-3
Aids: Bl: 0-0 Vi: 0-0 Tstrap: 0-0
Best Rating: 86 9/01 Haml 1m1f36y good

A big, long-striding horse, he has won five times this season at Newcastle, Ascot, Goodwood and Hamilton twice, rising dramatically in the handicap as a result. He has had excuses for his defeats and is best on fast ground.

Kelsey Rose

102(92) (70+)**94**
2-y-o b f Most Welcome-Duxyana (IRE) (Cyrano De Bergerac)
P D Evans Swift Racing

Placings:2251155402613356 **(5021)**
2001: 5^{2}SD, 5^{2}GS, 5^{5}S, 5^{1}SD, 5^{1}GS, 5^{5}GF, 5^{5}GF, 5^{4}GF, 5^{0}GF, 5^{2}G, 5^{6}GF, 5^{1}GF, 6^{3}G, 6^{3}GS, 6^{5}GF, 7^{6}HY

	Starts	1st	2nd	3rd	Win & Pl
Career Total (Turf)	14	2	2	2	19271
Career Total (AW)	2	1	1	0	3616
85 7/01 Yarm 5f43y	C			G-F	£5481
68 5/01 Thsk 5f	D			G-S	£3679
70 4/01 Sthl 5f	E			STD	£2957

Total win prize-money £12118

Going (Turf): Sf: 0-2 **GS: 1-3** Gd: 0-2 **GF: 1-7** Fm: 0-0
Distance: **5f/6f: 3-14** 7f-8f: 0-2 9f-13f: 0-0 14f+: 0-0
Track : LH: 0-4 RH: 0-0 Tight: 0-3 Gall: 0-0
Aids: Bl: 0-0 Vi: 0-0 Tstrap: 0-0
Best Rating: 94 9/01 Ayr 6f gd-fm

Consistent early-season juvenile over five furlongs, showing form on good to soft/Fibresand. A pacy sort, she has retained her form well, and scored again in a Yarmouth conditions event in July. Suited by any going and five to six furlongs.

Keltech Gold (IRE)

97 **58**
4-y-o b g Petorius-Creggan Vale Lass (Simply Great (FR))
B Palling D Brennan

Placings:50/021510-000003 **(5626)**
2001: 8^{0}F, 8^{0}GF, 8^{0}G, 7^{0}GS, 7^{0}S, 8^{3}GS

	Starts	1st	2nd	3rd	Win & Pl
Career Total (Turf)	14	2	1	1	11148
74 8/00 Chep 1m14y	C(0-90)H			G-F	£6483
74 6/00 Bath 1m5y	E(0-70)H			G-S	£2849

Total win prize-money £9333

Going (Turf): Sf: 0-4 **GS: 1-4** Gd: 0-2 **GF: 1-3** Fm: 0-1
Distance: 5f/6f: 0-0 7f-8f: 0-7 **9f-13f: 2-7** 14f+: 0-0
Track : **LH: 1-7** RH: 0-2 **Tight: 1-4** Gall: 0-2
Aids: Bl: 0-1 Vi: 0-0 Tstrap: 0-0
Best Rating: 58 11/01 Nott 1m54y gd-sft

Twice a winner over a mile last term, he showed nothing this season until dropped in the weights in the autumn. Stays a mile, likes to front-run and acts on fast and easy ground.

Keltic Flute

2-y-o b g Piccolo-Nanny Doon (Dominion)
D Morris T Mohan

Placings:06 **(4947)**
2001: 8^{0}G, 8^{6}G

	Starts	1st	2nd	3rd	Win & Pl
Career Total (Turf)	2	0	0	0	0

Going (Turf): Sf: 0-0 GS: 0-0 Gd: 0-2 GF: 0-0 Fm: 0-0
Distance: 5f/6f: 0-0 7f-8f: 0-1 9f-13f: 0-1 14f+: 0-0
Track : LH: 0-0 RH: 0-1 Tight: 0-0 Gall: 0-0
Aids: Bl: 0-0 Vi: 0-0 Tstrap: 0-0
Best Rating: 49 9/01 Gdwd 1m good

Keltos (FR)

107 **115+**
3-y-o gr c Kendor (FR)-Loxandra (Last Tycoon)
C Laffon-Parias Gary A Tanaka

Placings:2-115161 **(5678a)**
2001: 8^{1}HY, 8^{1}HY, 8^{5}G, 8^{1}G, 8^{6}G, 8^{1}HO

	Starts	1st	2nd	3rd	Win & Pl
Career Total (Turf)	7	4	1	0	63768
105 11/01 StCl 1m				HLD	£21339
106 5/01 Chan 1m				GD	£13579
4/01 Lonc 1m				HVY	£8923
3/01 StCl 1m				HVY	£7953

Total win prize-money £51794

Going (Turf): **Sf: 2-2** GS: 0-0 Gd: 1-3 GF: 0-0 Fm: 0-0
Distance: 5f/6f: 0-0 **7f-8f: 4-6** 9f-13f: 0-0 14f+: 0-0
Track : **LH: 1-1** RH: 0-1 Tight: 0-0 Gall: 0-1
Aids: Bl: 0-0 Vi: 0-0 Tstrap: 0-0
Best Rating: 115 6/01 Asct 1m good

French miler and half-brother to miler Iridanos, a dual Listed winner who was placed in Group Two over a mile. Clearly a smart colt, as he showed when beaten only three length into sixth behind Noverre in the Poule d'Essai des Poulains. Followed up at odds-on in Listed event at Chantilly, beating Spanish Don by 3/4 length and won a Group Three at Saint Cloud in November. Suited by cut.

Ken's Dream

88 **70**
2-y-o b c Bin Ajwaad (IRE)-Shoag (USA) (Affirmed (USA))
Ms A E Embiricos Michael Underwood

Placings:50 **(5684)**
2001: 8^{5}S, 8^{0}S

	Starts	1st	2nd	3rd	Win & Pl
Career Total (Turf)	2	0	0	0	0

Going (Turf): Sf: 0-2 GS: 0-0 Gd: 0-0 GF: 0-0 Fm: 0-0
Distance: 5f/6f: 0-0 7f-8f: 0-1 9f-13f: 0-1 14f+: 0-0
Track : LH: 0-0 RH: 0-0 Tight: 0-0 Gall: 0-0
Aids: Bl: 0-0 Vi: 0-0 Tstrap: 0-0
Best Rating: 70 10/01 Yarm 1m3y soft

Kennet

103(110) (57)**67**
6-y-o b g Kylian (USA)-Marwell Mitzi (Interrex (CAN))
P D Cundell Miss M C Fraser

Placings:26U02402605/26322200/1030013346310/5600002022311365000-355000430 **(2756)**
2001: 12^{3}SD, 16^{5}SW, 14^{5}SW, 11^{0}SD, 10^{0}G, 11^{0}F, 13^{4}GF, 13^{3}GF, 13^{0}GF

	Starts	1st	2nd	3rd	Win & Pl
Career Total (Turf)	45	4	8	8	28295
Career Total (AW)	15	1	2	1	6605
71 8/00 Bath 1m5f22y	E(0-75)H			GD	£3493
70 8/00 Wind 1m3f135y	E(0-70)H			GD	£2996
71 10/99 Brig 1m3f196y	E(0-70)			G-S	£2688
72 5/99 Wind 1m2f7y	D(0-75)			GD	£3655
73 2/99 Ling 1m2f	D			STD	£3623

Total win prize-money £16458

Going (Turf): Sf: 0-3 GS: 1-7 **Gd: 3-16** GF: 0-17 Fm: 0-1
Distance: 5f/6f: 0-9 7f-8f: 0-11 **9f-13f: 4-30** 14f+: 1-9
Track : **LH: 3-32** RH: 0-7 **Tight: 4-15** Gall: 0-10
Aids: Bl: 0-1 Vi: 0-2 Tstrap: 0-0
Best Rating: 67 6/01 Newb 1m5f61y gd-fm

He has run some fair races in his time on turf and sand, but last five wins have been on turf. Handles most surfaces and a turning track.

Kennythorpe Boppy (IRE)

95 **52**
3-y-o ch g Aragon-Spark (IRE) (Flash Of Steel)
J S Wainwright R C Bond

Placings:5050-003000 **(5226)**
2001: 8^{0}GF, 11^{0}GF, 11^{3}GF, 12^{0}GF, 11^{0}G, 11^{0}S

	Starts	1st	2nd	3rd	Win & Pl
Career Total (Turf)	10	0	0	1	528

Going (Turf): Sf: 0-1 GS: 0-1 Gd: 0-2 GF: 0-6 Fm: 0-0
Distance: 5f/6f: 0-0 7f-8f: 0-4 9f-13f: 0-6 14f+: 0-0
Track : LH: 0-3 RH: 0-6 Tight: 0-4 Gall: 0-2
Aids: Bl: 0-0 Vi: 0-1 Tstrap: 0-0
Best Rating: 56 6/01 Bevl 1m3f216y gd-fm

Kent

(103) (65)**46**
6-y-o b g Kylian (USA)-Precious Caroline (IRE) (The Noble Player (USA))
P D Cundell Miss M C Fraser

Placings:03000005/12164004-12112360 **(1719)**
2001: 16^{1}SD, 16^{2}SW, 16^{1}SD, 16^{1}SD, 16^{2}SD, 16^{3}SD, 17^{6}GF, 13^{0}GF

	Starts	1st	2nd	3rd	Win & Pl
Career Total (Turf)	8	0	0	1	481
Career Total (AW)	16	5	3	1	14295

60	2/01	Sthl	2m	F(0-80)H	STD	£2212
60	1/01	Sthl	2m	E(0-70)H	STD	£2429
47	1/01	Sthl	2m	F(0-60)H	STD	£1750
53	2/00	Sthl	2m	E(0-70)H	STD	£2821
44	1/00	Sthl	2m	F(0-60)H	STD	£2373

Total win prize-money £11585

Going (Turf): Sf: 0-1 GS: 0-2 Gd: 0-2 GF: 0-3 Fm: 0-0
Distance: 5f/6f: 0-0 7f-8f: 0-2 9f-13f: 0-6 **14f+: 5-16**
Track : **LH: 5-19** RH: 0-3 Tight: 0-4 Gall: 0-2
Aids: **Bl: 2-4** Vi: 0-3 Tstrap: 0-0
Best Rating: 65 3/01 Sthl 2m stand

Kentucky Bound (IRE)

94 **21**
3-y-o b g Charnwood Forest (IRE)-Blown-Over (Ron's Victory (USA))
J W Payne C Cotran

Placings:000-00000 **(4601)**
2001: 6^{0}GF, 6^{0}F, 7^{0}GF, 6^{0}GF, 5^{0}GF

	Starts	1st	2nd	3rd	Win & Pl
Career Total (Turf)	8	0	0	0	

Going (Turf): Sf: 0-2 GS: 0-0 Gd: 0-0 GF: 0-5 Fm: 0-1
Distance: 5f/6f: 0-6 7f-8f: 0-2 9f-13f: 0-0 14f+: 0-0
Track : LH: 0-0 RH: 0-0 Tight: 0-0 Gall: 0-0
Aids: Bl: 0-2 Vi: 0-0 Tstrap: 0-0
Best Rating: 50 8/01 NmkJ 7f gd-fm

Kentucky Bullet (USA)

(108) (54)**40**
5-y-o b g Housebuster (USA)-Exactly So (Caro)
A G Newcombe Mrs B J Sherwin

Placings:65151060000660000/03-2260526506 **(4606)**
2001: 9^{2}SW, 11^{2}SW, 12^{6}SD, 11^{0}GS, 9^{5}F, 12^{2}GF, 9^{6}G, 9^{5}SD, 11^{0}GF, 12^{6}SD

	Starts	1st	2nd	3rd	Win & Pl
Career Total (Turf)	16	1	1	0	5297
Career Total (AW)	13	1	2	1	4122

71	3/99	Donc	7f	D(0-85)H	G-S	£4494
69	2/99	Sthl	7f	D	STD	£2853

Total win prize-money £7347

Going (Turf): Sf: 0-0 **GS: 1-3** Gd: 0-4 GF: 0-8 Fm: 0-1
Distance: 5f/6f: 0-3 **7f-8f: 2-11** 9f-13f: 0-15 14f+: 0-0
Track : **LH: 1-18** RH: 0-6 Tight: 0-14 Gall: 0-1
Aids: Bl: 0-7 Vi: 0-0 **Tstrap: 1-10**
Best Rating: 63 1/01 Sthl 1m3f slow

Kepler (USA)

102+
2-y-o ch c Spinning World (USA)-Perfect Arc (USA) (Brown Arc (USA))
P F I Cole Frank Stella

Placings:1 **(5666)**
2001: 6^{1}HY

	Starts	1st	2nd	3rd	Win & Pl
Career Total (Turf)	1	1	0	0	3754

102	11/01	Wind	6f	D	HVY	£3753

Total win prize-money £3754

Going (Turf): Sf: 1-1 GS: 0-0 Gd: 0-0 GF: 0-0 Fm: 0-0
Distance: **5f/6f: 1-1** 7f-8f: 0-0 9f-13f: 0-0 14f+: 0-0
Track : LH: 0-0 RH: 0-0 Tight: 0-0 Gall: 0-0
Aids: Bl: 0-0 Vi: 0-0 Tstrap: 0-0
Best Rating: 102 11/01 Wind 6f heavy

Got off the mark in good style at Windsor in November 2001, and acts in heavy ground.

Kerala (IRE)

64 **20**
2-y-o b f Mujadil (USA)-Kalisz (IRE) (Polish Precedent (USA))
Don Enrico Incisa Don Enrico Incisa

Placings:0 **(5372)**
2001: 6^{0}G

	Starts	1st	2nd	3rd	Win & Pl
Career Total (Turf)	1	0	0	0	

Going (Turf): Sf: 0-0 GS: 0-0 Gd: 0-1 GF: 0-0 Fm: 0-0
Distance: 5f/6f: 0-1 7f-8f: 0-0 9f-13f: 0-0 14f+: 0-0
Track : LH: 0-0 RH: 0-0 Tight: 0-0 Gall: 0-0
Aids: Bl: 0-0 Vi: 0-0 Tstrap: 0-0
Best Rating: 20 10/01 Rdcr 6f good

Kerouni (IRE)

20
3-y-o ch c Rainbow Quest (USA)-Kerita (Formidable (USA))
Sir Michael Stoute H H Aga Khan

Placings:0 **(1669)**
2001: 10^{0}GF

	Starts	1st	2nd	3rd	Win & Pl
Career Total (Turf)	1	0	0	0	

Going (Turf): Sf: 0-0 GS: 0-0 Gd: 0-0 GF: 0-1 Fm: 0-0
Distance: 5f/6f: 0-0 7f-8f: 0-0 9f-13f: 0-1 14f+: 0-0
Track : LH: 0-0 RH: 0-1 Tight: 0-0 Gall: 0-0
Aids: Bl: 0-0 Vi: 0-0 Tstrap: 0-0

Kestle Imp (IRE)

(92) (41)
3-y-o b f Imp Society (USA)-Dark Truffle (Deploy)
R M H Cowell Mr & Mrs D A Gamble

Placings:200-05 **(0140)**
2001: 10^{0}SD, 9^{5}SW

	Starts	1st	2nd	3rd	Win & Pl
Career Total (Turf)	0	0	0	0	
Career Total (AW)	5	0	1	0	782

Going (Turf): Sf: 0-0 GS: 0-0 Gd: 0-0 GF: 0-0 Fm: 0-0
Distance: 5f/6f: 0-0 7f-8f: 0-1 9f-13f: 0-4 14f+: 0-0
Track : LH: 0-5 RH: 0-0 Tight: 0-4 Gall: 0-0
Aids: Bl: 0-0 Vi: 0-2 Tstrap: 0-0
Best Rating: 22 1/01 Wolv 1m1f79y slow

Kestle Sky (IRE)

(59) **12**
2-y-o b f Woodborough (USA)-Dark Truffle (Deploy)
M R Ewer-Hoad Mr & Mrs D A Gamble

Placings:0000 **(5410)**
2001: 6^{0}GF, 7^{0}GF, 5^{0}S, 7^{0}SD

	Starts	1st	2nd	3rd	Win & Pl
Career Total (Turf)	3	0	0	0	
Career Total (AW)	1	0	0	0	

Going (Turf): Sf: 0-1 GS: 0-0 Gd: 0-0 GF: 0-2 Fm: 0-0
Distance: 5f/6f: 0-2 7f-8f: 0-2 9f-13f: 0-0 14f+: 0-0
Track : LH: 0-2 RH: 0-0 Tight: 0-0 Gall: 0-0
Aids: Bl: 0-0 Vi: 0-0 Tstrap: 0-0
Best Rating: 12 9/01 Ling 7f gd-fm

Kestral

107(101) (48)**68**
5-y-o ch g Ardkinglass-Shiny Kay (Star Appeal)
T J Etherington The R And R Partnership

Placings:0000/04500440000/50606232123003-1450121410030 **(4848)**
2001: 8^{1}SD, 8^{4}SD, 8^{5}SD, 8^{0}SW, 9^{1}F, 8^{2}GF, 8^{1}F, 8^{4}GF, 8^{1}G, 7^{0}GF, 8^{0}G, 9^{3}GF, 8^{0}GF

	Starts	1st	2nd	3rd	Win & Pl
Career Total (Turf)	33	4	4	3	26446
Career Total (AW)	9	1	0	1	2056

68	7/01	Donc	1m	D(0-85)H	GD	£4348
66	6/01	Thsk	1m	D(0-80)H	FRM	£7572
59	5/01	Rdcr	1m1f	E(0-70)H	FRM	£3192
48	1/01	Sthl	1m	F(0-60)H	STD	£1778
54	8/00	Newc	1m1f9y	E(0-70)H	FRM	£2989

Total win prize-money £19881

Going (Turf): Sf: 0-1 GS: 0-3 Gd: 1-10 GF: 0-12 **Fm: 3-7**
Distance: 5f/6f: 0-5 **7f-8f: 3-23** 9f-13f: 2-14 14f+: 0-0
Track : **LH: 5-22** RH: 0-15 Tight: 2-13 Gall: 2-7
Aids: Bl: 0-0 Vi: 0-0 Tstrap: 0-2
Best Rating: 68 7/01 Donc 1m good

A half-brother to Kayo, he is a fair handicapper over eight and nine furlongs. Acts on fast ground and has looked an improved performer this year, scoring four times including once on Fibresand. Enjoys a fast-run race.

Kew

92 **60**
2-y-o b c Royal Applause-Cutleaf (Kris)
J J Bridger (Sir Mark Prescott 17/8) Connaught Racing

Placings:05300 **(4954)**
2001: 6^{0}GF, 6^{5}GF, 7^{3}G, 7^{0}GF, 8^{0}GS

	Starts	1st	2nd	3rd	Win & Pl
Career Total (Turf)	5	0	0	1	282

Going (Turf): Sf: 0-0 GS: 0-1 Gd: 0-1 GF: 0-3 Fm: 0-0
Distance: 5f/6f: 0-1 7f-8f: 0-4 9f-13f: 0-0 14f+: 0-0
Track : LH: 0-2 RH: 0-1 Tight: 0-1 Gall: 0-0
Aids: Bl: 0-0 Vi: 0-2 Tstrap: 0-0
Best Rating: 60 8/01 Catt 7f good

Kew Green (USA)

102 **72**
3-y-o b/br c Brocco (USA)-Jump With Joy (USA) (Linkage (USA))
W J Haggas Peter S Jensen

Placings:021 **(3185)**
2001: 7^{0}GS, 7^{2}GF, 9^{1}GS

	Starts	1st	2nd	3rd	Win & Pl
Career Total (Turf)	3	1	1	0	3922

68 7/01 Leic 1m1f218yF G-S £2523
Total win prize-money £2524

Going (Turf): Sf: 0-0 **GS: 1-2** Gd: 0-0 GF: 0-1 Fm: 0-0
Distance: 5f/6f: 0-0 7f-8f: 0-2 **9f-13f: 1-1** 14f+: 0-0
Track : LH: 0-1 **RH: 1-1** Tight: 0-0 Gall: 0-0
Aids: Bl: 0-0 Vi: 0-0 Tstrap: 0-0
Best Rating: 72 6/01 Hayd 7f30y gd-fm

Kewarra

(86) (45)**59d**
7-y-o b g Distant Relative-Shalati (FR) (High Line)
A Streeter Dr C V Macphail

Placings:0544/0023533101100/100203300/30050/003-000 **(4727)**
2001: 12^0SD, 14^0GF, 10^0GF

	Starts	1st	2nd	3rd	Win & Pl
Career Total (Turf)	36	4	2	7	35850
Career Total (AW)	1	0	0	0	

90 4/98 Epsm 1m2f18y B(0-105)H SFT £10698
84 10/97 NmkR 1m2f C(0-100)H G-F £6160
78 9/97 Chep 1m2f36y D(0-80)H GD £3946
75 8/97 Chep 1m2f36y D(0-85)H GD £5381
Total win prize-money £26186

Going (Turf): Sf: 1-4 GS: 0-1 **Gd: 2-15** GF: 1-16 Fm: 0-0
Distance: 5f/6f: 0-3 7f-8f: 0-4 **9f-13f: 4-29** 14f+: 0-1
Track : **LH: 3-20** RH: 0-7 **Tight: 1-14** Gall: 0-6
Aids: Bl: 0-1 Vi: 0-1 Tstrap: 0-0
Best Rating: 45 2/01 Wolv 1m4f stand

Key To The City (IRE)

(79) (18)
7-y-o b g Shalford (IRE)-Green Wings (General Assembly (USA))
C P Morlock (D G Bridgwater 29/7) West Lancs Antiques Export Racing

Placings:050021002/23040040/**2042102/00** **(2172)**
2001: 7^0SD, 11^0SD

	Starts	1st	2nd	3rd	Win & Pl
Career Total (Turf)	19	2	3	1	8471
Career Total (AW)	7	0	3	0	1879

50 3/99 Haml 1m1f36y F(0-65) HVY £2192
76 9/97 Dund 1m1f (0-75)H Y-S £2226
Total win prize-money £4418

Going (Turf): **Sf: 1-2** GS: 0-0 Gd: 0-4 GF: 0-1 Fm: 0-0
Distance: 5f/6f: 0-5 7f-8f: 0-10 **9f-13f: 2-11** 14f+: 0-0
Track : LH: 1-14 RH: 1-8 **Tight: 1-7** Gall: 0-0
Aids: Bl: 0-5 Vi: 0-0 Tstrap: 0-0
Best Rating: 18 4/01 Sthl 7f stand

He has shown ability on Equitrack, but is prone to breaking blood vessels.

Key Virtue (USA)

94 **84**
2-y-o ch f Atticus (USA)-Questionablevirtue (USA) (Key To The Mint (USA))
Mrs A J Perrett P Garvey

Placings:30 **(5277)**
2001: 7^3GF, 7^0GS

	Starts	1st	2nd	3rd	Win & Pl
Career Total (Turf)	2	0	0	1	693

Going (Turf): Sf: 0-0 GS: 0-1 Gd: 0-0 GF: 0-1 Fm: 0-0
Distance: 5f/6f: 0-0 7f-8f: 0-2 9f-13f: 0-0 14f+: 0-0
Track : LH: 0-0 RH: 0-1 Tight: 0-0 Gall: 0-1
Aids: Bl: 0-0 Vi: 0-0 Tstrap: 0-0
Best Rating: 84 9/01 Kemp 7f gd-fm

A half-sister to top-class miler Among Men. Showed promise on her debut at Kempton over seven furlongs but soon beaten and eased on next start on an easier surface.

Kez

105(78) (37)**74**
5-y-o b g Polar Falcon (USA)-Briggsmaid (Elegant Air)
P R Webber Dennis Yardy

Placings:033321000/00204-311410150306 **(5465)**
2001: 11^3GF, 9^1F, 11^1F, 10^4GF, 10^1G, 10^0GF, 10^1GF, 12^5GF, 9^0GS, 10^3GF, 9^0GF, 10^6G

	Starts	1st	2nd	3rd	Win & Pl
Career Total (Turf)	25	5	2	5	20032
Career Total (AW)	1	0	0	0	

74 7/01 Epsm 1m2f18y D(0-80)H G-F £4212
70 7/01 Yarm 1m2f21y F(0-75)H GD £2660
62 6/01 Ling 1m3f106yE(0-75)H FRM £2899
57 5/01 Brig 1m1f209yF(0-65)H FRM £2639
63 8/99 Brig 1m3f196yE FRM £2684
Total win prize-money £15094

Going (Turf): Sf: 0-0 GS: 0-5 Gd: 1-5 GF: 1-8 **Fm: 3-7**
Distance: 5f/6f: 0-0 7f-8f: 0-1 **9f-13f: 5-25** 14f+: 0-0
Track : **LH: 5-19** RH: 0-4 **Tight: 3-11** Gall: 0-3
Aids: Bl: 0-0 Vi: 0-1 Tstrap: 0-0
Best Rating: 74 7/01 Epsm 1m2f18y gd-fm

Useful handicapper. His four wins this season have been at up to eleven furlongs on firm and good ground. Goes well at Brighton and Epsom. Does not want to be in front too soon.

Khaled (IRE)

96(73) (41)**41**
6-y-o b g Petorius-Felin Special (Lyphard's Special (USA))
T Keddy P Harper

Placings:031/50/03000-00060 **(4802)**
2001: 8^0GS, 6^0G, 6^0GF, 9^6GS, 8^0F

	Starts	1st	2nd	3rd	Win & Pl
Career Total (Turf)	12	1	0	2	5555
Career Total (AW)	3	0	0	0	0

75 8/98 Wwck 1m D G-F £3980
Total win prize-money £3980

Going (Turf): Sf: 0-0 GS: 0-4 Gd: 0-4 **GF: 1-3** Fm: 0-1
Distance: 5f/6f: 0-2 **7f-8f: 1-8** 9f-13f: 0-5 14f+: 0-0
Track : **LH: 1-5** RH: 0-2 Tight: 0-5 Gall: 0-0
Aids: Bl: 0-0 Vi: 0-0 Tstrap: 0-0
Best Rating: 41 8/01 NmkJ 6f good

Fair two-year-old, but on the downgrade since. Little to enthuse about this season.

Khalik (IRE)

100(78) (25)**66**
7-y-o b g Lear Fan (USA)-Silver Dollar (Shirley Heights)
Miss Gay Kelleway A P Griffin

Placings:042/03430000/1100200/31400363-5000 **(5671)**
2001: 5^5G, 5^0SD, 5^0G, 6^0HY

	Starts	1st	2nd	3rd	Win & Pl
Career Total (Turf)	28	3	2	5	14169
Career Total (AW)	2	0	0	0	

67 5/00 Bath 5f11y E(0-70)H G-S £2758
63 8/99 Ling 6f F(0-65)H GD £2763
58 8/99 Sals 6f E(0-80)H G-S £2778
Total win prize-money £8300

Going (Turf): Sf: 0-4 **GS: 2-9** Gd: 1-11 GF: 0-4 Fm: 0-0
Distance: **5f/6f: 3-23** 7f-8f: 0-6 9f-13f: 0-1 14f+: 0-0
Track : **LH: 1-5** RH: 0-6 Tight: 0-1 **Gall: 1-7**
Aids: Bl: 0-6 Vi: 0-0 **Tstrap: 3-18**
Best Rating: 66 8/01 Wind 5f10y good

He has won over five furlongs but looks better over six on ground no faster than good. Goes well fresh.

Khaysar (IRE)

81 **68**
3-y-o br c Pennekamp (USA)-Khaytada (IRE) (Doyoun)
R Curtis (John M Oxx 27/5) Katie Curtis & Exors Of Late David Auer

Placings:306-6006 **(5622)**
2001: 8^6GF, 8^0G, 9^0HY, 14^6GS

	Starts	1st	2nd	3rd	Win & Pl
Career Total (Turf)	7	0	0	1	700

Going (Turf): Sf: 0-1 GS: 0-1 Gd: 0-2 GF: 0-1 Fm: 0-0
Distance: 5f/6f: 0-1 7f-8f: 0-3 9f-13f: 0-1 14f+: 0-1
Track : LH: 0-2 RH: 0-0 Tight: 0-0 Gall: 0-0
Aids: Bl: 0-0 Vi: 0-0 Tstrap: 0-0
Best Rating: 68 5/01 Navn 1m gd-fm

Khayyam (USA)

77
3-y-o b c Affirmed (USA)-True Celebrity (USA) (Lyphard (USA))
P F I Cole Newgate Stud

Placings:04-02613540 **(5171)**
2001: 6^0GF, 8^2GF, 9^6G, 8^1GF, 8^3G, 8^5G, 7^4G, 8^0GS

	Starts	1st	2nd	3rd	Win & Pl
Career Total (Turf)	10	1	1	1	12371

74 8/01 Newb 1m D G-F £9009
Total win prize-money £9009

Going (Turf): Sf: 0-1 GS: 0-1 Gd: 0-4 **GF: 1-3** Fm: 0-1
Distance: 5f/6f: 0-1 **7f-8f: 1-5** 9f-13f: 0-4 14f+: 0-0
Track : LH: 0-2 RH: 0-3 Tight: 0-0 Gall: 0-0
Aids: Bl: 0-0 Vi: 0-0 Tstrap: 0-0
Best Rating: 77 9/01 Kemp 1m good

Got off the mark in a valuable Newbury claimer, having been dropped back to a mile, but has been well held since in handicaps, and another try in a claimer. Suited by a sound surface.

Khazayin (USA)

105 **76**
3-y-o b f Bahri (USA)-Thawakib (IRE) (Sadler's Wells (USA))
J L Dunlop Hamdan Al Maktoum

Placings:022 **(4636)**
2001: 8^0GS, 10^2GF, 9^2GF

	Starts	1st	2nd	3rd	Win & Pl
Career Total (Turf)	3	0	2	0	2590

Going (Turf): Sf: 0-0 GS: 0-1 Gd: 0-0 GF: 0-2 Fm: 0-0
Distance: 5f/6f: 0-0 7f-8f: 0-1 9f-13f: 0-2 14f+: 0-0
Track : LH: 0-0 RH: 0-2 Tight: 0-0 Gall: 0-1
Aids: Bl: 0-0 Vi: 0-0 Tstrap: 0-0
Best Rating: 76 7/01 Kemp 1m2f gd-fm

A sister to Sakhee, she has shown ability in maiden company.

Khitaam (IRE)

102 **86**
3-y-o b c Charnwood Forest (IRE)-Queen's Ransom (IRE) (Last Tycoon)
B Hanbury Hamdan Al Maktoum

Placings:24-40210 **(3472)**
2001: 7^4S, 7^0G, 7^2GF, 8^1GF, 8^0GF

	Starts	1st	2nd	3rd	Win & Pl
Career Total (Turf)	7	1	2	0	8100

86 7/01 Wwck 1m22y D G-F £3883
Total win prize-money £3884

Going (Turf): Sf: 0-1 GS: 0-0 Gd: 0-2 **GF: 1-4** Fm: 0-0
Distance: 5f/6f: 0-0 7f-8f: 0-6 **9f-13f: 1-1** 14f+: 0-0
Track : LH: 0-2 RH: 0-2 Tight: 0-0 Gall: 0-3
Aids: Bl: 0-0 Vi: 0-0 Tstrap: 0-0
Best Rating: 86 7/01 Wwck 1m22y gd-fm

A big, strong colt, shaped well on both his outings at two. Had grown into an attractive colt at three but was a bit too keen when second at Haydock in May. Scored at Warwick over a mile in July as a result of settling better. Needs a strong pace and fast ground.

Khuchn (IRE)

89(94) (38)**34**
5-y-o b h Unfuwain (USA)-Stay Sharpe (USA) (Sharpen

Up)
M Brittain Mel Brittain

Placings:50010/00505265422P-60600 **(3293)**
2001: 11^{6}SD, 10^{0}HY, 11^{6}GF, 9^{0}GF, 9^{0}GF

	Starts	1st	2nd	3rd	Win & Pl
Career Total (Turf)	21	1	3	0	6685
Career Total (AW)	1	0	0	0	0

63 7/99 Nott 1m1f213yF(0-60) G-F £2652
Total win prize-money £2653

Going (Turf): Sf: 0-3 GS: 0-5 Gd: 0-5 **GF: 1-7** Fm: 0-1
Distance: 5f/6f: 0-0 7f-8f: 0-1 **9f-13f: 1-21** 14f+: 0-0
Track : **LH: 1-7** RH: 0-15 Tight: 0-3 Gall: 0-1
Aids: Bl: 0-0 Vi: 0-0 Tstrap: 0-1
Best Rating: 38 2/01 Sthl 1m3f stand

Khulan (USA)

104 **103d**
3-y-o b f Bahri (USA)-Jawlaat (USA) (Dayjur (USA))
J L Dunlop Hamdan Al Maktoum

Placings:120-403 **(2576)**
2001: 7^{4}GS, 6^{0}GF, 6^{3}GF

	Starts	1st	2nd	3rd	Win & Pl
Career Total (Turf)	6	1	1	1	26276

95 7/00 NmkJ 6f D G-S £5785
Total win prize-money £5785

Going (Turf): Sf: 0-0 **GS: 1-3** Gd: 0-1 GF: 0-2 Fm: 0-0
Distance: **5f/6f: 1-5** 7f-8f: 0-1 9f-13f: 0-0 14f+: 0-0
Track : LH: 0-0 RH: 0-0 Tight: 0-0 Gall: 0-0
Aids: Bl: 0-0 Vi: 0-0 Tstrap: 0-0
Best Rating: 95 4/01 NmkR 7f gd-sft

Highly impressive in a Newmarket maiden at two, she still looked green when beaten by Enthused in the Lowther and disappointed when finishing last in the Cheveley Park. She does not stay seven furlongs and has been disappointing this year in decent sprint company.

Ki Chi Saga (USA)

71 (99) (18) **9**
9-y-o ch g Miswaki (USA)-Cedilla (USA) (Caro)
Jean-Rene Auvray Lambourn Racing Limited

Placings:110/06660000/0201420600000000/513440110 42300243/5236336503000100044020/60044006030-00 **(1076)**
2001: 10^{0}SD, 11^{0}GS

	Starts	1st	2nd	3rd	Win & Pl
Career Total (Turf)	26	2	0	1	4059
Career Total (AW)	52	5	6	7	15752

54 8/99 Ling 1m4f G STD £1987
64 4/98 Ling 1m2f G STD £1725
57 3/98 Ling 1m F(0-60)H STD £1892
51 2/98 Ling 1m G SLW £1472
61 3/97 Ling 1m F STD £2473
5/95 Jage 6f GD £2332
4/95 Klam 7f SFT £1047
Total win prize-money £12930

Going (Turf): Sf: 0-5 GS: 0-3 Gd: 0-6 GF: 0-8 Fm: 0-1
Distance: 5f/6f: 0-0 **7f-8f: 3-24** 9f-13f: 2-49 14f+: 0-2
Track : **LH: 5-62** RH: 0-7 **Tight: 5-56** Gall: 0-2
Aids: **Bl: 2-37** Vi: 0-4 Tstrap: 0-6
Best Rating: 5 4/01 Ling 1m2f stand

He shows his best form on Equitrack, but is basically a plater these days. He looks to need a mile and a half now.

Kid'Z'Play (IRE)

101 **79**
5-y-o b g Rudimentary (USA)-Saka Saka (Camden Town)
J S Goldie Liam McGuigan

Placings:00/4001024/014040014P320-110100003000 **(4109)**
2001: 10^{1}S, 9^{1}S, 10^{0}S, 12^{1}GS, 12^{0}GF, 11^{0}F, 16^{0}GF, 12^{0}GF, 9^{3}GS, 12^{0}GF, 13^{0}S, 9^{0}S

	Starts	1st	2nd	3rd	Win & Pl
Career Total (Turf)	34	6	2	2	21421

79 4/01 Muss 1m4f D(0-85)H G-S £4153
76 4/01 Muss 1m1f E(0-75)H SFT £2922
62 3/01 Donc 1m2f60y E(0-75)H SFT £3262
57 9/00 Ayr 1m2f192yE(0-70)H SFT £2600
57 6/00 Muss 1m1f F(0-60)H FRM £2618
50 8/99 Haml 1m65y F(0-65)H G-F £2892
Total win prize-money £18449

Going (Turf): Sf: 3-11 GS: 1-4 Gd: 0-5 GF: 1-11 Fm: 1-3
Distance: 5f/6f: 0-3 7f-8f: 0-5 **9f-13f: 6-23** 14f+: 0-3
Track : LH: 2-11 RH: 2-17 **Tight: 2-14** Gall: 1-6
Aids: Bl: 0-0 Vi: 0-0 Tstrap: 0-0
Best Rating: 79 4/01 Muss 1m4f gd-sft

He is suited by forcing the pace and used those tactics to good effect when winning at Doncaster at the start of the 2001 season, then scored twice at Musselburgh in April. Best at around ten furlongs, he has won on fast ground but likes to get his toe in.

Kidology (IRE)

74
5-y-o b g Petardia-Loveville (USA) (Assert)
R Johnson (W Storey 29/5) Foster Watson

Placings:000/0-0 **(1657)**
2001: 9^{0}F

	Starts	1st	2nd	3rd	Win & Pl
Career Total (Turf)	5	0	0	0	

Going (Turf): Sf: 0-3 GS: 0-0 Gd: 0-0 GF: 0-1 Fm: 0-1
Distance: 5f/6f: 0-0 7f-8f: 0-0 9f-13f: 0-5 14f+: 0-0
Track : LH: 0-4 RH: 0-0 Tight: 0-2 Gall: 0-1
Aids: Bl: 0-0 Vi: 0-0 Tstrap: 0-4

Kier Park (IRE)

110 **111**
4-y-o b c Foxhound (USA)-Merlannah (IRE) (Shy Groom (USA))
M A Jarvis H R H Sultan Ahmad Shah

Placings:4211/2-00203560 **(5244a)**
2001: 5^{0}S, 5^{0}G, 6^{2}GF, 5^{0}G, 6^{3}S, 5^{5}G, 6^{6}HY, 5^{0}HO

	Starts	1st	2nd	3rd	Win & Pl
Career Total (Turf)	13	2	3	1	59963

101 10/99 Asct 5f A G-S £23825
86 10/99 Ling 5f D HVY £4110
Total win prize-money £27935

Going (Turf): Sf: 1-4 GS: 1-1 Gd: 0-5 GF: 0-2 Fm: 0-0
Distance: **5f/6f: 2-12** 7f-8f: 0-1 9f-13f: 0-0 14f+: 0-0
Track : LH: 0-0 RH: 0-0 Tight: 0-0 Gall: 0-0
Aids: Bl: 0-0 Vi: 0-0 Tstrap: 0-0
Best Rating: 111 8/01 Deau 6f110y soft

Put up a smart performance when going down by a neck to Pipalong (who was favoured by the weights) in the Palace House Stakes of 2000. Injured shortly afterwards, he remains a sprinter of potential and put in a career best effort when third in a Group One at Deauville. Beaten at a similar level since, both his wins came with give in the ground, but he has run well on a quicker surface.

Kierchem (IRE)

100 (57?) **36**
10-y-o b g Mazaad-Smashing Gale (Lord Gayle (USA))
C Grant Mrs M Hunter

Placings:120/0000/40/030/26014600430360-04420 **(3282)**
2001: 8^{0}F, 10^{4}F, 10^{4}GF, 10^{2}F, 8^{0}F

	Starts	1st	2nd	3rd	Win & Pl
Career Total (Turf)	29	2	3	3	9889
Career Total (AW)	2	0	0	0	218

35 6/00 Ripn 1m F(0-60)H G-F £2352
72 4/93 Ripn 5f D GD £3172
Total win prize-money £5525

Going (Turf): Sf: 0-8 GS: 0-2 **Gd: 1-7 GF: 1-8** Fm: 0-4
Distance: 5f/6f: 1-3 7f-8f: 1-9 9f-13f: 0-17 14f+: 0-2
Track : LH: 0-15 **RH: 1-8 Tight: 1-11** Gall: 0-2
Aids: Bl: 0-1 Vi: 0-0 Tstrap: 0-0
Best Rating: 36 7/01 Newc 1m2f32y firm

Kigema (IRE)

(92) (10)
4-y-o ch f Case Law-Grace De Bois (Tap On Wood)
C N Allen Green Square Racing

Placings:5044155061/46226-000 **(0280)**
2001: 7^{0}SD, 8^{0}SD, 8^{0}SW

	Starts	1st	2nd	3rd	Win & Pl
Career Total (Turf)	5	1	0	0	2400
Career Total (AW)	13	1	2	0	3639

56 1/00 Ling 1m F STD £2194
58 6/99 Brig 5f213y G G-F £1882
Total win prize-money £4077

Going (Turf): Sf: 0-0 GS: 0-1 Gd: 0-2 **GF: 1-1** Fm: 0-1
Distance: 5f/6f: 1-6 7f-8f: 1-10 9f-13f: 0-2 14f+: 0-0
Track : **LH: 2-16** RH: 0-0 **Tight: 1-11** Gall: 0-0
Aids: Bl: 0-0 Vi: 0-0 Tstrap: 0-0
Best Rating: 1 1/01 Ling 7f stand

Kilbarchan

100 **38**
3-y-o ch f Selkirk (USA)-Haitienne (FR) (Green Dancer (USA))
Miss L A Perratt Dr J Walker

Placings:355-500060600 **(4266)**
2001: 8^{5}S, 5^{0}GS, 8^{0}F, 8^{0}F, 9^{6}GF, 7^{0}GS, 6^{6}F, 6^{0}GS, 7^{0}GF

	Starts	1st	2nd	3rd	Win & Pl
Career Total (Turf)	12	0	0	1	583

Going (Turf): Sf: 0-1 GS: 0-4 Gd: 0-0 GF: 0-4 Fm: 0-3
Distance: 5f/6f: 0-3 7f-8f: 0-7 9f-13f: 0-2 14f+: 0-0
Track : LH: 0-2 RH: 0-5 Tight: 0-3 Gall: 0-1
Aids: Bl: 0-0 Vi: 0-0 Tstrap: 0-0
Best Rating: 38 8/01 Thsk 6f firm

Kilcreggan

101 (98) (47) **51**
7-y-o b g Landyap (USA)-Lehmans Lot (Oats)
Mrs M Reveley C Anderson

Placings:65405364610/03360640-40 **(3866)**
2001: 16^{4}F, 16^{0}GF

	Starts	1st	2nd	3rd	Win & Pl
Career Total (Turf)	18	1	0	3	5626
Career Total (AW)	3	0	0	0	0

60 10/99 Rdcr 1m6f19y E(0-70)H GD £3315
Total win prize-money £3316

Going (Turf): Sf: 0-0 GS: 0-1 **Gd: 1-5** GF: 0-6 Fm: 0-6
Distance: 5f/6f: 0-0 7f-8f: 0-1 9f-13f: 0-9 **14f+: 1-11**
Track : **LH: 1-17** RH: 0-3 **Tight: 1-12** Gall: 0-1
Aids: Bl: 0-0 Vi: 0-0 Tstrap: 0-0
Best Rating: 48 7/01 Rdcr 2m4y firm

Has won just once, back in 1999, at Redcar. He is a tricky ride who has to be held up and produced late. Stays two miles. Acts on fast ground.

Kilcullen Lad (IRE)

(104) (61) **71**
7-y-o b g Fayruz-Royal Home (Royal Palace)
P M Mooney Ms Ann Cully

Placings:0102102**2115**/2140002040/0100020450**454**/0 0601052006 0/052300603505001-4304000500060 **(5642a)**
2001: 5^{4}Y, 5^{3}GF, 5^{0}G, 5^{4}GF, 6^{0}GY, 6^{0}S, 5^{0}GF, 5^{5}GY, 5^{0}G, 5^{0}F, 5^{0}S, 5^{6}S, 6^{0}Y

	Starts	1st	2nd	3rd	Win & Pl
Career Total (Turf)	67	5	7	3	44222
Career Total (AW)	7	3	1	0	8065

61 11/00 Ling 5f F(0-60)H STD £1767
74 8/99 Brig 5f59y D(0-80)H SFT £11759
81 5/98 Rdcr 5f C(0-90)H G-F £7100
74 5/97 Ling 6f D(0-85)H G-F £5952
75 12/96 Ling 6f E(0-75) STD £2995
77 11/96 Ling 5f E STD £2232
53 9/96 Rdcr 5f E(0-75) FRM £3172
48 6/96 Ling 6f F FRM £2571
Total win prize-money £37551

Going (Turf): Sf: 1-10 GS: 0-4 Gd: 0-17 **GF: 2-28 Fm: 2-4**
Distance: **5f/6f: 8-71** 7f-8f: 0-3 9f-13f: 0-0 14f+: 0-0
Track : **LH: 4-16** RH: 0-4 **Tight: 3-8** Gall: 0-9
Aids: Bl: 0-13 **Vi: 5-43** Tstrap: 0-0
Best Rating: 71 7/01 Curr 5f good

Suited by a sharp five furlongs, he likes decent ground but can go on soft. Now trained in Ireland.

Kildare Chiller (IRE)

88(100) (54)**54**
7-y-o ch g Shahrastani (USA)-Ballycuirke (Taufan (USA))
P R Hedger P R Hedger

Placings:0000/051601/052050001/0-46 **(1074)**
2001: 11^{4}SD, 11^{6}GS

	Starts	1st	2nd	3rd	Win & Pl
Career Total (Turf)	21	3	1	0	11285
Career Total (AW)	1	0	0	0	0

54	10/99	Curr	1m1f	(0-80)H	Y-S	£3622
54	11/98	Curr	1m1f	(0-80)H	HVY	£3437
65	7/98	Klny	1m3f	(0-65)H	G-Y	£3437

Total win prize-money £10499

Going (Turf): Sf: 1-3 GS: 0-1 Gd: 0-5 GF: 0-1 Fm: 0-0
Distance: 5f/6f: 0-0 7f-8f: 0-2 **9f-13f: 3-20** 14f+: 0-0
Track : LH: 1-8 **RH: 2-14** Tight: 0-0 Gall: 0-0
Aids: Bl: 0-0 Vi: 0-0 Tstrap: 0-0
Best Rating: 54 2/01 Sthl 1m3f stand

Formerly a winner on the Flat and over hurdles in Ireland, he seems to handle anything between good to soft and good to firm going.

Kildrummy

101 **63?**
3-y-o br g Timeless Times (USA)-Rynavey (Rousillon (USA))
Denys Smith Evelyn Duchess Of Sutherland

Placings:63432230645 **(4885)**
2001: 9^{6}GS, 8^{3}S, 7^{4}G, 7^{3}GF, 10^{2}F, 9^{2}GF, 8^{3}GF, 9^{0}G, 8^{6}GS, 7^{4}F, 9^{5}GF

	Starts	1st	2nd	3rd	Win & Pl
Career Total (Turf)	11	0	2	3	2918

Going (Turf): Sf: 0-1 GS: 0-2 Gd: 0-2 GF: 0-4 Fm: 0-2
Distance: 5f/6f: 0-0 7f-8f: 0-3 9f-13f: 0-8 14f+: 0-0
Track : LH: 0-4 RH: 0-3 Tight: 0-4 Gall: 0-1
Aids: Bl: 0-1 Vi: 0-1 Tstrap: 0-0
Best Rating: 68 5/01 Thsk 7f good

Exposed maiden. Stays ten furlongs. Acts on fast ground.

Kilkenny Castle (IRE)

105 **80**
5-y-o b g Grand Lodge (USA)-Shahaamh (IRE) (Reference Point)
S Dow T G Parker

Placings:22421/000300 **(5607)**
2001: 8^{0}GF, 8^{0}GF, 9^{0}G, 7^{3}G, 8^{0}GS, 8^{0}GS

	Starts	1st	2nd	3rd	Win & Pl
Career Total (Turf)	13	1	3	1	7521

85	10/99	Punc	7f110y	G-Y	£3450

Total win prize-money £3450

Going (Turf): Sf: 0-0 GS: 0-2 Gd: 0-3 GF: 0-3 Fm: 0-0
Distance: 5f/6f: 0-0 **7f-8f: 1-10** 9f-13f: 0-3 14f+: 0-0
Track : LH: 0-4 **RH: 1-4** Tight: 0-0 Gall: 0-1
Aids: **Bl: 1-1** Vi: 0-0 Tstrap: 0-0
Best Rating: 80 10/01 NmkR 7f good

Useful juvenile in Ireland when he showed his best form around a mile on an easy surface and won a seven-furlong maiden at Punchestown back in 1999. Now with Simon Dow, he did not really fire until racing on a rain-softened surface at Newmarket in October.

Killarney

102 **62**
3-y-o gr f Pursuit Of Love-Laune (AUS) (Kenmare (FR))
R Hannon Plantation Stud

Placings:0-05003040 **(4707)**
2001: 7^{0}GF, 8^{5}F, 8^{0}GF, 9^{0}GF, 10^{3}GF, 9^{0}G, 10^{4}G, 10^{0}G

	Starts	1st	2nd	3rd	Win & Pl
Career Total (Turf)	9	0	0	1	1004

Going (Turf): Sf: 0-1 GS: 0-0 Gd: 0-3 GF: 0-4 Fm: 0-1
Distance: 5f/6f: 0-1 7f-8f: 0-2 9f-13f: 0-6 14f+: 0-0
Track : LH: 0-4 RH: 0-3 Tight: 0-4 Gall: 0-0
Aids: Bl: 0-1 Vi: 0-0 Tstrap: 0-0
Best Rating: 68 5/01 Gdwd 7f gd-fm

Has shown ability in maidens and handicaps at around ten furlongs. Has looked short of pace and may be best ridden positively.

Killarney Jazz

(107) (47)
6-y-o b g Alhijaz-Killarney Belle (USA) (Irish Castle (USA))
G C H Chung G C H Chung

Placings:240/46111045/4343442044/0030150250-52642344440 **(3428)**
2001: 6^{5}SD, 7^{2}SD, 7^{6}SW, 6^{4}SD, 7^{2}SD, 6^{3}SD, 7^{4}SD, 6^{4}SD, 7^{4}SD, 7^{4}SD, 8^{0}SD

	Starts	1st	2nd	3rd	Win & Pl
Career Total (Turf)	4	0	0	0	246
Career Total (AW)	38	4	5	4	13108

54	4/00	Sthl	1m	G	STD	£1925
71	5/98	Sthl	1m	F	STD	£2343
69	3/98	Sthl	1m	F(0-65)	STD	£2200
62	2/98	Sthl	1m	F(0-60)H	STD	£1735

Total win prize-money £8204

Going (Turf): Sf: 0-2 GS: 0-0 Gd: 0-1 GF: 0-0 Fm: 0-1
Distance: 5f/6f: 0-9 **7f-8f: 4-27** 9f-13f: 0-6 14f+: 0-0
Track : **LH: 4-40** RH: 0-0 Tight: 0-13 Gall: 0-0
Aids: **Bl: 2-16** Vi: 1-8 Tstrap: 0-6
Best Rating: 50 4/01 Sthl 7f stand

Kilmeena Lad

104(104) (77)**75**
5-y-o b g Minshaanshu Amad (USA)-Kilmeena Glen (Beveled (USA))
J C Fox (E A Wheeler 14/2) Mrs J A Cleary

Placings:0010/003000101004/410005000020453 5-06611 **(3147)**
2001: 6^{0}SD, 7^{6}SW, 6^{6}GF, 6^{1}GF, 7^{1}G

	Starts	1st	2nd	3rd	Win & Pl
Career Total (Turf)	26	4	1	1	20274
Career Total (AW)	11	2	0	1	11494

65	7/01	Kemp	7f	E(0-70)H	GD	£4875
62	7/01	Kemp	6f	D(0-80)H	G-F	£5876
80	2/00	Ling	7f	C(0-90)H	STD	£6630
75	10/99	Ling	6f	E(0-75)H	STD	£2988
70	8/99	NmkJ	6f	F(0-80)H	GD	£3696
80	10/98	Newb	6f8y	D	HVY	£4276

Total win prize-money £28341

Going (Turf): Sf: 1-6 GS: 0-5 **Gd: 2-11** GF: 1-4 Fm: 0-0
Distance: 5f/6f: 3-20 7f-8f: 3-17 9f-13f: 0-0 14f+: 0-0
Track : **LH: 2-13** RH: 1-4 **Tight: 2-10** Gall: 1-6
Aids: Bl: 0-3 Vi: 0-0 Tstrap: 0-0
Best Rating: 66 2/01 Ling 7f slow

A fair handicapper for Eric Wheeler, his new yard got a tune out of him almost straight away with an easy win at Kempton in July and he followed up in similar style at the same venue a fortnight later.

Kilmeena Star

93 **48**
3-y-o b c So Factual (USA)-Kilmeena Glen (Beveled (USA))
J C Fox (E A Wheeler 16/7) Mrs J A Cleary

Placings:05-0605040 **(5593)**
2001: 6^{0}GS, 6^{6}F, 5^{0}GF, 6^{5}GF, 5^{0}GF, 5^{4}GF, 5^{0}GS

	Starts	1st	2nd	3rd	Win & Pl
Career Total (Turf)	9	0	0	0	0

Going (Turf): Sf: 0-2 GS: 0-2 Gd: 0-0 GF: 0-4 Fm: 0-1
Distance: 5f/6f: 0-8 7f-8f: 0-1 9f-10f: 0-0 14f+: 0-0
Track : LH: 0-3 RH: 0-1 Tight: 0-0 Gall: 0-1
Aids: Bl: 0-0 Vi: 0-0 Tstrap: 0-0
Best Rating: 48 6/01 Nott 6f15y gd-fm

Kilmeny (IRE)

103(102) (81+)**71+**
3-y-o b f Royal Abjar (USA)-Mouchez Le Nez (IRE) (Cyrano De Bergerac)
H Morrison The Hon Miss Katie Trenchard

Placings:4121005010 **(5608)**
2001: 8^{4}SD, 8^{1}SD, 8^{2}F, 8^{1}G, 9^{0}S, 7^{0}GF, 7^{5}F, 8^{0}G, 8^{1}SD, 7^{0}GS

	Starts	1st	2nd	3rd	Win & Pl
Career Total (Turf)	7	1	1	0	4524
Career Total (AW)	3	2	0	0	5430

81	10/01	Sthl	1m	G(0-75)H	STD	£2268
71	8/01	Hayd	1m30y	E(0-70)H	GD	£3654
66	3/01	Sthl	1m	D	STD	£2947

Total win prize-money £8869

Going (Turf): Sf: 0-1 GS: 0-1 **Gd: 1-2** GF: 0-1 Fm: 0-2
Distance: 5f/6f: 0-0 **7f-8f: 2-7** 9f-13f: 1-3 14f+: 0-0
Track : **LH: 3-6** RH: 0-1 Tight: 0-2 Gall: 0-2
Aids: Bl: 0-0 Vi: 0-0 Tstrap: 0-0
Best Rating: 81 10/01 Sthl 1m stand

A winner on the Southwell Fibresand in the spring, she took a Haydock handicap on only her second run on turf and added another victory back at Southwell in October. Likes to race prominently and is still open to improvement.

Kilmory

54 **4**
2-y-o b f Puissance-Lizzy Cantle (Homing)
G G Margarson The Symphony Partnership

Placings:00 **(2664)**
2001: 5^{0}G, 6^{0}G

	Starts	1st	2nd	3rd	Win & Pl
Career Total (Turf)	2	0	0	0	

Going (Turf): Sf: 0-0 GS: 0-0 Gd: 0-2 GF: 0-0 Fm: 0-0
Distance: 5f/6f: 0-1 7f-8f: 0-1 9f-13f: 0-0 14f+: 0-0
Track : LH: 0-0 RH: 0-0 Tight: 0-0 Gall: 0-0
Aids: Bl: 0-0 Vi: 0-0 Tstrap: 0-0
Best Rating: 4 7/01 Yarm 6f3y good

Kimoe Warrior

87(90) (35)**47**
3-y-o ch g Royal Abjar (USA)-Thewaari (USA) (Eskimo (USA))
M Mullineaux Michael Mullineaux

Placings:50050-3000605 **(4993)**
2001: 8^{3}HY, 11^{0}G, 10^{0}GF, 8^{0}SD, 6^{6}SD, 7^{0}GF, 7^{5}HY

	Starts	1st	2nd	3rd	Win & Pl
Career Total (Turf)	10	0	0	1	436
Career Total (AW)	2	0	0	0	0

Going (Turf): Sf: 0-4 GS: 0-2 Gd: 0-2 GF: 0-2 Fm: 0-0
Distance: 5f/6f: 0-4 7f-8f: 0-5 9f-13f: 0-3 14f+: 0-0
Track : LH: 0-7 RH: 0-1 Tight: 0-5 Gall: 0-1
Aids: Bl: 0-0 Vi: 0-0 Tstrap: 0-0
Best Rating: 47 9/01 Hayd 7f30y heavy

Kinan (USA)

103 **63**
5-y-o b g Dixieland Band (USA)-Alsharta (USA) (Mr Prospector (USA))
T D Barron North Yorkshire Cycling Club

Placings:6261/0050/010036060-0000053 **(4907)**
2001: 7^{0}S, 8^{0}G, 8^{0}GS, 8^{0}GF, 8^{0}GF, 8^{5}GS, 7^{3}G

	Starts	1st	2nd	3rd	Win & Pl
Career Total (Turf)	24	2	1	2	13217

85	7/00	Epsm	7f	D(0-85)H	G-S	£7247
85	9/98	Nott	6f15y	D	GD	£3336

Total win prize-money £10585

Going (Turf): Sf: 0-5 **GS: 1-5 Gd: 1-7** GF: 0-7 Fm: 0-0
Distance: 5f/6f: 0-7 **7f-8f: 2-15** 9f-13f: 0-2 14f+: 0-0
Track : **LH: 1-10** RH: 0-3 **Tight: 1-3** Gall: 0-2
Aids: Bl: 0-0 Vi: 0-0 Tstrap: 0-0
Best Rating: 63 7/01 Ayr 1m gd-sft

Out of form for the most part of this season though he was running better in the autumn. Goes well with cut in the ground.

Kind Emperor

103(97) (68d)**55**

4-y-o br g Emperor Jones (USA)-Kind Lady (Kind Of Hush)
P L Gilligan John Peters

Placings:3222504200020**3**/**44**2530004L0200-01002 **(3317)**
2001: 6^{0}HY, 8^{1}G, 8^{0}GF, 8^{0}GF, 7^{2}G

	Starts	1st	2nd	3rd	Win & Pl
Career Total (Turf)	28	1	8	2	15432
Career Total (AW)	5	0	0	1	724
55 5/01 Yarm 1m3y E(0-70)H				GD	£3416

Total win prize-money £3416

Going (Turf): Sf: 0-4 GS: 0-6 **Gd: 1-8** GF: 0-8 Fm: 0-1
Distance: 5f/6f: 0-25 7f-8f: 0-4 **9f-13f: 1-3** 14f+: 0-0
Track : LH: 0-5 RH: 0-2 Tight: 0-3 Gall: 0-2
Aids: Bl: 0-0 Vi: 0-1 Tstrap: 0-0
Best Rating: 55 7/01 Yarm 7f3y good

Kept on making the frame and was the proverbial bridesmaid until getting off the mark at thirteenth attempt at Yarmouth in May 2001. Has plenty of early dash. Stays a mile. Acts on a sound surface. Best when racing up with the pace.

Kind Of Loving

90 **70**

2-y-o ch f Diesis-Gentilesse (Generous (IRE))
J L Dunlop Michael L Page

Placings:0 **(5603)**
2001: 7^{0}GS

	Starts	1st	2nd	3rd	Win & Pl
Career Total (Turf)	1	0	0	0	

Going (Turf): Sf: 0-0 GS: 0-1 Gd: 0-0 GF: 0-0 Fm: 0-0
Distance: 5f/6f: 0-0 7f-8f: 0-1 9f-13f: 0-0 14f+: 0-0
Track : LH: 0-0 RH: 0-0 Tight: 0-0 Gall: 0-0
Aids: Bl: 0-0 Vi: 0-0 Tstrap: 0-0
Best Rating: 70 11/01 NmkR 7f gd-sft

Kindred Falls

69

4-y-o b f Bin Ajwaad (IRE)-Rising River (Warning)
P R Hedger Mrs Gina Webster

Placings:000 **(5664)**
2001: 12^{0}GS, 11^{0}S, 8^{0}HY

	Starts	1st	2nd	3rd	Win & Pl
Career Total (Turf)	3	0	0	0	

Going (Turf): Sf: 0-2 GS: 0-1 Gd: 0-0 GF: 0-0 Fm: 0-0
Distance: 5f/6f: 0-0 7f-8f: 0-0 9f-13f: 0-3 14f+: 0-0
Track : LH: 0-0 RH: 0-3 Tight: 0-1 Gall: 0-1
Aids: Bl: 0-0 Vi: 0-0 Tstrap: 0-0

King Carew (IRE)

105 **83**

3-y-o b c Fairy King (USA)-Kareena (Riverman (USA))
M R Channon John Carey

Placings:25-001504000 **(5607)**
2001: 12^{0}GF, 12^{0}GF, 8^{1}F, 10^{5}GF, 9^{0}G, 10^{4}GF, 8^{0}GF, 8^{0}GS, 8^{0}GS

	Starts	1st	2nd	3rd	Win & Pl
Career Total (Turf)	11	1	1	0	12180
78 6/01 Newc 1m D				FRM	£6776

Total win prize-money £6776

Going (Turf): Sf: 0-2 GS: 0-2 Gd: 0-1 GF: 0-5 **Fm: 1-1**
Distance: 5f/6f: 0-0 **7f-8f: 1-6** 9f-13f: 0-5 14f+: 0-0
Track : **LH: 1-4** RH: 0-3 Tight: 0-3 **Gall: 1-4**
Aids: Bl: 0-0 Vi: 0-1 Tstrap: 0-0
Best Rating: 101 6/01 Epsm 1m4f10y gd-fm

Showed promise on his debut in soft ground at Ascot as a juvenile, but was well beaten behind Nayef on even softer ground at the same track next time. He was very highly tried in his early starts this season, including in the Derby, but managed to get off the mark in a Newcastle maiden in June, though the form amounts to little, and he has since struggled in handicap company. Suited by a mile and acts well on firm ground.

King Creole

89 **74+**

2-y-o b c Slip Anchor-Myrrh (Salse (USA))
J Noseda B E Nielsen

Placings:00 **(5361)**
2001: 8^{0}G, 8^{0}GS

	Starts	1st	2nd	3rd	Win & Pl
Career Total (Turf)	2	0	0	0	

Going (Turf): Sf: 0-0 GS: 0-1 Gd: 0-1 GF: 0-0 Fm: 0-0
Distance: 5f/6f: 0-0 7f-8f: 0-1 9f-13f: 0-1 14f+: 0-0
Track : LH: 0-1 RH: 0-0 Tight: 0-0 Gall: 0-0
Aids: Bl: 0-0 Vi: 0-0 Tstrap: 0-0
Best Rating: 74 10/01 NmkR 1m gd-sft

A half-brother to an Italian seven-furlong winner, is out of a lightly-raced half-sister to the stayers Celeric and Sesame. Made a promisng debut at Nottingham in September. Was apparently unsuited by the softer surface and undulating course at Newmarket on his second start.

King Eider

85 **70**

2-y-o b/br g Mtoto-Hen Harrier (Polar Falcon (USA))
J L Dunlop Sir Thomas Pilkington

Placings:005 **(5684)**
2001: 7^{0}GS, 8^{0}S, 8^{5}S

	Starts	1st	2nd	3rd	Win & Pl
Career Total (Turf)	3	0	0	0	0

Going (Turf): Sf: 0-2 GS: 0-1 Gd: 0-0 GF: 0-0 Fm: 0-0
Distance: 5f/6f: 0-0 7f-8f: 0-2 9f-13f: 0-1 14f+: 0-0
Track : LH: 0-0 RH: 0-0 Tight: 0-0 Gall: 0-0
Aids: Bl: 0-0 Vi: 0-0 Tstrap: 0-0
Best Rating: 70 10/01 Leic 1m9y soft

King Flyer (IRE)

110(98) (62)**80**

5-y-o b g Ezzoud (IRE)-Al Guswa (Shernazar)
Miss J Feilden In The Know (2)

Placings:54003/**236**12320/**6**05211221-03302222104 **(4803)**
2001: 12^{0}G, 14^{3}GF, 14^{3}GF, 20^{0}GF, 16^{2}GF, 14^{2}GF, 16^{2}G, 14^{2}GF, 13^{1}GF, 14^{0}GS, 17^{4}F

	Starts	1st	2nd	3rd	Win & Pl
Career Total (Turf)	27	5	9	3	64175
Career Total (AW)	6	0	1	2	1367
80 9/01 York 1m5f194yC(0-95)H				G-F	£18931
73 9/00 Yarm 2m2f51y C(0-95)H				GF	£6890
67 8/00 Sand 1m6f C(0-90)H				GD	£6955
65 7/00 NmkJ 1m6f175yD(0-85)H				GD	£7020
56 6/99 NmkJ 1m2f E				G-F	£3200

Total win prize-money £42996

Going (Turf): Sf: 0-1 GS: 0-1 Gd: 2-8 **GF: 3-15** Fm: 0-2
Distance: 5f/6f: 0-1 7f-8f: 0-3 9f-13f: 1-11 **14f+: 4-18**
Track : LH: 2-14 **RH: 3-18** Tight: 1-8 **Gall: 3-12**
Aids: Bl: 0-1 Vi: 0-0 **Tstrap: 4-22**
Best Rating: 80 9/01 York 1m5f194y gd-fm

A fair All-Weather performer, he is just as effective on turf and ended a frustrating run of four consecutive second placings with a narrow victory over 14 furlongs at York in September 2000. After four consecutive second placings, he went one better at York in September 2001. Stays two and a quarter miles and acts on a sound surface.

King For A Day

100 **34**

5-y-o b g Machiavellian (USA)-Dizzy Heights (USA) (Danzig (USA))
Bob Jones Mrs Joan Marioni

Placings:063/600000/0041440-0050 **(4181)**
2001: 14^{0}G, 14^{0}GF, 16^{5}GF, 12^{0}GF

	Starts	1st	2nd	3rd	Win & Pl
Career Total (Turf)	20	1	0	1	3776
41 7/00 Yarm 1m6f17y E(0-70)H				G-F	£2873

Total win prize-money £2873

Going (Turf): Sf: 0-3 GS: 0-0 Gd: 0-10 **GF: 1-6** Fm: 0-1
Distance: 5f/6f: 0-0 7f-8f: 0-4 9f-13f: 0-6 **14f+: 1-10**
Track : **LH: 1-10** RH: 0-5 **Tight: 1-11** Gall: 0-0
Aids: Bl: 0-2 **Vi: 1-9** Tstrap: 0-0
Best Rating: 34 5/01 Yarm 1m6f17y good

King Harson

101 **93**

2-y-o b c Greensmith-Safari Park (Absalom)
J D Bethell C J Burley

Placings:13306001 **(5487)**
2001: 5^{1}F, 5^{3}G, 5^{3}GF, 5^{0}GF, 5^{6}GF, 6^{0}G, 5^{0}GS, 6^{1}HY

	Starts	1st	2nd	3rd	Win & Pl
Career Total (Turf)	8	2	0	2	24984
93 10/01 Donc 6f B				HVY	£19655
64 6/01 Pont 5f F				FRM	£3558

Total win prize-money £23214

Going (Turf): Sf: 1-1 GS: 0-1 Gd: 0-2 GF: 0-3 **Fm: 1-1**
Distance: **5f/6f: 2-8** 7f-8f: 0-0 9f-13f: 0-0 14f+: 0-0
Track : **LH: 1-1** RH: 0-1 Tight: 0-0 Gall: 0-1
Aids: **Bl: 1-1** Vi: 0-2 Tstrap: 0-0
Best Rating: 93 10/01 Donc 6f heavy

Won his debut on firm ground and capped the season with success in a valuable sales race at Doncaster on heavy ground. Acts well on extremes of going.

King Nicholas (USA)

83 **55**

2-y-o b c Nicholas (USA)-Lifetime Honour (USA) (Kingmambo (USA))
M A Jarvis F H Lee

Placings:00 **(5689)**
2001: 6^{0}GS, 6^{0}S

	Starts	1st	2nd	3rd	Win & Pl
Career Total (Turf)	2	0	0	0	

Going (Turf): Sf: 0-1 GS: 0-1 Gd: 0-0 GF: 0-0 Fm: 0-0
Distance: 5f/6f: 0-2 7f-8f: 0-0 9f-13f: 0-0 14f+: 0-0
Track : LH: 0-0 RH: 0-0 Tight: 0-0 Gall: 0-0
Aids: Bl: 0-0 Vi: 0-0 Tstrap: 0-0
Best Rating: 55 11/01 NmkR 6f gd-sft

King O' The Mana (IRE)

99 **110**

4-y-o b h Turtle Island (IRE)-Olivia Jane (IRE) (Ela-Mana-Mou)
R Hannon D Boocock

Placings:61216/04132340-54 **(4591)**
2001: 10^{5}GF, 12^{4}G

	Starts	1st	2nd	3rd	Win & Pl
Career Total (Turf)	15	3	2	2	68376
102 5/00 Bath 1m2f46y B(0-95)				G-S	£10166
100 8/99 Newc 1m3y B H				GD	£28270
84 7/99 Wwck 6f168y E				G-F	£4712

Total win prize-money £43148

Going (Turf): Sf: 0-2 **GS: 1-5 Gd: 1-5 GF: 1-3** Fm: 0-0
Distance: 5f/6f: 0-0 7f-8f: 1-6 **9f-13f: 2-8** 14f+: 0-1
Track : **LH: 2-7** RH: 0-4 **Tight: 1-4** Gall: 0-5
Aids: Bl: 0-0 Vi: 0-0 Tstrap: 0-0
Best Rating: 93 8/01 Wind 1m2f7y gd-fm

He has developed into a decent middle-distance performer if just short of Pattern class, performing well behind Mutamam in last season's Cumberland Lodge and over 15 furlongs in France. Lightly raced this season. Acts on most ground, although does not want it heavy.

King Of Adoc

59 **16**

2-y-o ch c Dr Devious (IRE)-Urchin (IRE) (Fairy King (USA))

S Kirk J J Whelan

Placings:00 **(5459)**

2001: 6^{0}HY, 8^{0}G

	Starts	1st	2nd	3rd	Win & Pl
Career Total (Turf)	2	0	0	0	

Going (Turf): Sf: 0-1 GS: 0-0 Gd: 0-1 GF: 0-0 Fm: 0-0
Distance: 5f/6f: 0-1 7f-8f: 0-0 9f-13f: 0-1 14f+: 0-0
Track : LH: 0-1 RH: 0-0 Tight: 0-1 Gall: 0-0
Aids: Bl: 0-0 Vi: 0-0 Tstrap: 0-0
Best Rating: 16 10/01 Bath 1m5y good

King Of Happiness (USA)

109 **89+**

2-y-o ch c Spinning World (USA)-Mystery Rays (USA) (Nijinsky (CAN))

Sir Michael Stoute Saeed Suhail

Placings:1 **(3622)**

2001: 7^{1}GF

	Starts	1st	2nd	3rd	Win & Pl
Career Total (Turf)	1	1	0	0	4583

89	8/01	Donc	7f	D	G-F	£4582

Total win prize-money £4583

Going (Turf): Sf: 0-0 GS: 0-0 Gd: 0-0 **GF: 1-1** Fm: 0-0
Distance: 5f/6f: 0-0 **7f-8f: 1-1** 9f-13f: 0-0 14f+: 0-0
Track : LH: 0-0 RH: 0-0 Tight: 0-0 Gall: 0-0
Aids: Bl: 0-0 Vi: 0-0 Tstrap: 0-0
Best Rating: 89 8/01 Donc 7f gd-fm

A half-brother to four winners, he made a winning debut in what looked a hot maiden at Doncaster in August and can go on to much better things.

King Of Mommur (IRE)

95 **42**

6-y-o b g Fairy King (USA)-Monoglow (Kalaglow)

B G Powell The Three Bears Racing

Placings:003630/003500060/34-34 **(4614)**

2001: 11^{3}F, 13^{4}F

	Starts	1st	2nd	3rd	Win & Pl
Career Total (Turf)	19	0	0	5	3108

Going (Turf): Sf: 0-2 GS: 0-1 Gd: 0-4 GF: 0-8 Fm: 0-4
Distance: 5f/6f: 0-0 7f-8f: 0-1 9f-13f: 0-10 14f+: 0-8
Track : LH: 0-9 RH: 0-8 Tight: 0-2 Gall: 0-6
Aids: Bl: 0-5 Vi: 0-0 Tstrap: 0-2
Best Rating: 42 9/01 Bath 1m5f22y firm

King Of Peru

105(108) (72)**63**

8-y-o b g Inca Chief (USA)-Julie's Star (IRE) (Thatching)

D Nicholls The Gardening Partnership

Placings:2140110/6301000525/33040046600/0203045 00/0000002130536033200022/5564422011424-0160000003220303 **(3379)**

2001: 5^{0}SD, 5^{1}SD, 6^{6}SD, 5^{0}SD, 5^{0}S, 6^{0}HY, 5^{0}S, 5^{0}GF, 5^{3}GF, 5^{2}GF, 5^{2}G, 5^{0}F, 5^{3}SD, 6^{0}SD, 5^{3}GF

	Starts	1st	2nd	3rd	Win & Pl
Career Total (Turf)	75	7	11	9	61990
Career Total (AW)	12	1	1	2	6164

67	1/01	Sthl	5f	F	STD	£2184
63	8/00	Kemp	5f	E	G-F	£2795
61	7/00	Catt	5f	F	G-F	£2236
61	5/99	Brig	5f213y	E(0-70)H	FRM	£4221
97	5/96	Gdwd	7f	C(0-100)H	GD	£10867

93	9/95	NmkR	6f	C	G-F	£8350
86	9/95	Ayr	6f	D	GD	£5010
75	7/95	Hayd	6f	D	G-F	£3746

Total win prize-money £39412

Going (Turf): Sf: 0-10 GS: 0-8 Gd: 2-24 **GF: 4-28** Fm: 1-5
Distance: **5f/6f: 7-72** 7f-8f: 1-14 9f-13f: 0-1 14f+: 0-0
Track : LH: 1-23 RH: 1-6 Tight: 0-12 Gall: 0-9
Aids: Bl: 0-5 Vi: 0-15 Tstrap: 0-0
Best Rating: 67 1/01 Sthl 5f stand

Suited by the minimum trip on both turf and Fibresand, he won at Southwell in January. Has made the frame several times afterwards without winning. A bit of a character.

King Of The Tweed (IRE)

85 **77**

2-y-o b g Robellino (USA)-River Tweed (Selkirk (USA))

J J Sheehan Mrs Eileen Sheehan

Placings:060 **(4830)**

2001: 5^{0}GF, 5^{6}G, 6^{0}GF

	Starts	1st	2nd	3rd	Win & Pl
Career Total (Turf)	3	0	0	0	0

Going (Turf): Sf: 0-0 GS: 0-0 Gd: 0-1 GF: 0-2 Fm: 0-0
Distance: 5f/6f: 0-2 7f-8f: 0-1 9f-13f: 0-0 14f+: 0-0
Track : LH: 0-0 RH: 0-1 Tight: 0-0 Gall: 0-1
Aids: Bl: 0-0 Vi: 0-0 Tstrap: 0-0
Best Rating: 77 9/01 Folk 5f good

King Of Trumps

93 **67**

2-y-o ch c First Trump-Sea Of Stone (USA) (Sanglamore (USA))

T G Mills Mrs A K Petersen

Placings:0660 **(5467)**

2001: 7^{0}F, 7^{6}GF, 7^{6}G, 6^{0}S

	Starts	1st	2nd	3rd	Win & Pl
Career Total (Turf)	4	0	0	0	0

Going (Turf): Sf: 0-1 GS: 0-0 Gd: 0-1 GF: 0-1 Fm: 0-1
Distance: 5f/6f: 0-0 7f-8f: 0-4 9f-13f: 0-0 14f+: 0-0
Track : LH: 0-3 RH: 0-0 Tight: 0-2 Gall: 0-0
Aids: Bl: 0-0 Vi: 0-0 Tstrap: 0-0
Best Rating: 67 7/01 Epsm 7f gd-fm

King Priam (IRE)

(109) (87)**71**

6-y-o b g Priolo (USA)-Barinia (Corvaro (USA))

M J Polglase Mark Lewis

Placings:0/455230312650/2324635123400000205400011135011152/31362000500-0330050010300002010022 **(5632)**

2001: 8^{0}SD, 8^{3}S, 10^{3}HY, 10^{0}G, 7^{0}GF, 8^{5}F, 8^{0}GF, 10^{0}G, 12^{1}SD, 8^{0}GF, 8^{3}GF, 9^{0}G, 10^{0}GF, 8^{0}G, 10^{0}G, 9^{2}G, 10^{0}S, 10^{1}G, 8^{0}GS, 8^{0}GS, 10^{2}G, 10^{2}G

	Starts	1st	2nd	3rd	Win & Pl
Career Total (Turf)	58	5	8	6	59233
Career Total (AW)	22	6	3	5	44960

67	10/01	Rdcr	1m2f	D(0-80)H	GD	£5346
66	6/01	Sthl	1m4f	F	STD	£2303
97	2/00	Wolv	1m100y	C	STD	£5887
91	12/99	Wolv	1m1f79y	C(0-95)H	STD	£6320
89	12/99	Wolv	1m100y	C(0-100)H	STD	£7035
79	11/99	Sthl	1m	C(0-95)H	STD	£7165
75	10/99	York	1m2f85y	D(0-85)H	G-S	£7798
69	9/99	Hayd	1m30y	D(0-85)H	SFT	£4481
66	9/99	Leic	1m8y	F(0-60)	GD	£3078
72	3/99	Sthl	1m	D(0-80)H	STD	£3158
66	10/98	NmkR	1m4f	E	GD	£4110

Total win prize-money £56682

Going (Turf): Sf: 1-14 GS: 1-8 **Gd: 3-22** GF: 0-14 Fm: 0-1
Distance: 5f/6f: 0-0 7f-8f: 2-15 **9f-13f: 9-65** 14f+: 0-0
Track : **LH: 9-55** RH: 1-16 **Tight: 4-29** Gall: 2-17
Aids: **Bl: 11-72** Vi: 0-0 Tstrap: 0-1
Best Rating: 88 3/01 Donc 1m soft

Kept very busy, he ran third in the 2001 Lincoln and won at Southwell on the Fibresand in June. Had rather lost his form since until a good second at Nottingham in September. Won a Redcar handicap in October. Stays a mile, acts on an easy surface, and is usually held up.

King Solomon (FR)

98 **88**

2-y-o gr c Simon Du Desert (FR)-All Square (FR) (Holst (USA))

P F I Cole The Blenheim Partnership

Placings:321 **(5674a)**

2001: 6^{3}GS, 7^{2}S, 8^{1}HO

	Starts	1st	2nd	3rd	Win & Pl
Career Total (Turf)	3	1	1	1	12200

88	11/01	MsnL	1m		HLD	£8923

Total win prize-money £8923

Going (Turf): Sf: 0-1 GS: 0-1 Gd: 0-0 GF: 0-0 Fm: 0-0
Distance: 5f/6f: 0-0 **7f-8f: 1-3** 9f-13f: 0-0 14f+: 0-0
Track : LH: 0-1 RH: 0-0 Tight: 0-0 Gall: 0-1
Aids: Bl: 0-0 Vi: 0-0 Tstrap: 0-0
Best Rating: 88 11/01 MsnL 1m holding

King Spinner (IRE)

(103) (68)**68**

4-y-o b g Mujadil (USA)-Money Spinner (USA) (Teenoso (USA))

A P Jarvis Grant & Bowman Limited

Placings:3451/003-00003001 **(5411)**

2001: 10^{0}GS, 10^{0}G, 9^{0}GF, 10^{0}GS, 12^{3}G, 11^{0}G, 12^{0}GS, 14^{1}SD

	Starts	1st	2nd	3rd	Win & Pl
Career Total (Turf)	14	1	0	3	6088
Career Total (AW)	1	1	0	0	3024

68	10/01	Sthl	1m6f	E(0-70)H	STD	£3024
72	10/99	Yarm	1m3y	D	G-S	£3297

Total win prize-money £6322

Going (Turf): Sf: 0-0 **GS: 1-6** Gd: 0-7 GF: 0-1 Fm: 0-0
Distance: 5f/6f: 0-0 7f-8f: 0-3 9f-13f: 1-11 14f+: 1-1
Track : **LH: 1-6** RH: 0-4 Tight: 0-1 Gall: 0-6
Aids: Bl: 0-0 **Vi: 1-1** Tstrap: 0-0
Best Rating: 68 10/01 Sthl 1m6f stand

Lightly raced, he won once at two when making all, but had shown little since until stepped up to 14 furlongs on the Southwell Fibresand in October.

King Tut

83(91) (37)**48**

5-y-o ch g Anshan-Fahrenheit (Mount Hagen (FR))

J G Given A Clarke

Placings:6000/220400200-00 **(1064)**

2001: 8^{0}HY, 8^{0}GS

	Starts	1st	2nd	3rd	Win & Pl
Career Total (Turf)	12	0	3	0	2563
Career Total (AW)	3	0	0	0	

Going (Turf): Sf: 0-3 GS: 0-1 Gd: 0-3 GF: 0-4 Fm: 0-1
Distance: 5f/6f: 0-0 7f-8f: 0-8 9f-13f: 0-7 14f+: 0-0
Track : LH: 0-10 RH: 0-1 Tight: 0-2 Gall: 0-2
Aids: Bl: 0-0 Vi: 0-0 Tstrap: 0-0
Best Rating: 9 4/01 Nott 1m54y heavy

King's Ballet (USA)

98 **92**

3-y-o b c Imperial Ballet (IRE)-Multimara (USA) (Arctic Tern (USA))

P J Makin Admin Of The Late C Stelling

Placings:010-00010 **(5258)**

2001: 5^{0}GF, 6^{0}GS, 5^{0}G, 5^{1}S, 5^{0}GS

	Starts	1st	2nd	3rd	Win & Pl
Career Total (Turf)	8	2	0	0	8821

92	9/01	Ches	5f16y	D(0-85)H	SFT	£4186
88	9/00	Hayd	5f	D	SFT	£4634

Total win prize-money £8821

Going (Turf): **Sf: 2-3** GS: 0-2 Gd: 0-1 GF: 0-2 Fm: 0-0

Distance: **5f/6f: 2-8** 7f-8f: 0-0 9f-13f: 0-0 14f+: 0-0
Track : **LH: 1-1** RH: 0-0 **Tight: 1-1** Gall: 0-0
Aids: Bl: 0-0 Vi: 0-0 Tstrap: 0-0
Best Rating: 92 9/01 Ches 5f16y soft

A full-brother to Imperial Beauty, he won a soft ground maiden as a juvenile, but had shown nothing in handicaps this season until faced with soft ground at Chester in September. A soft-ground five furlongs are his ideal conditions.

King's Chambers

94(66) **30**

5-y-o ch g Sabrehill (USA)-Flower Girl (Pharly (FR))
J Parkes P J Cronin

Placings:0/00/000552-04020 **(4855)**
2001: 10^{0}S, 12^{4}GF, 16^{0}F, 16^{2}GS, 11^{0}GF

	Starts	1st	2nd	3rd	Win & Pl
Career Total (Turf)	10	0	2	0	1323
Career Total (AW)	4	0	0	0	

Going (Turf): Sf: 0-2 GS: 0-2 Gd: 0-1 GF: 0-3 Fm: 0-2
Distance: 5f/6f: 0-2 7f-8f: 0-3 9f-13f: 0-6 14f+: 0-3
Track : LH: 0-7 RH: 0-5 Tight: 0-9 Gall: 0-0
Aids: Bl: 0-6 Vi: 0-0 Tstrap: 0-7
Best Rating: 30 8/01 Bevl 2m35y gd-sft

King's Crest

103(81) (50)**73**

3-y-o b g Deploy-Classic Beauty (IRE) (Fairy King (USA))
S C Williams Mrs M Craggs & Mrs H Ashworth

Placings:066414520-5303112100 **(5152)**
2001: 9^{5}HY, 12^{3}GS, 13^{0}GF, 10^{3}G, 9^{1}G, 12^{1}GF, 12^{2}G, 11^{1}GF, 12^{0}G, 14^{0}G

	Starts	1st	2nd	3rd	Win & Pl
Career Total (Turf)	17	4	2	2	20904
Career Total (AW)	2	0	0	0	0

73	8/01	Catt	1m3f214y	F(0-65)H	G-F	£2464
69	8/01	Folk	1m4f	E(0-70)H	G-F	£3220
64	8/01	Brig	1m1f209y	F(0-65)H	GD	£2380
65	9/00	Muss	1m	D(0-80)	G-S	£5232

Total win prize-money £13297

Going (Turf): Sf: 0-3 GS: 1-4 Gd: 1-6 **GF: 2-4** Fm: 0-0
Distance: 5f/6f: 0-3 7f-8f: 1-4 **9f-13f: 3-10** 14f+: 0-2
Track : LH: 2-11 RH: 2-5 **Tight: 3-8** Gall: 0-4
Aids: Bl: 0-0 Vi: 0-0 Tstrap: 0-0
Best Rating: 73 8/01 Catt 1m3f214y gd-fm

He won over a mile as a two-year-old, suggesting he would get further this term. He duly came good over ten furlongs at Brighton in August, followed up over two furlongs further at Folkestone and scored again at Catterick. Needs to come late in a strongly-run race.

King's Envoy (USA)

91 **68**

2-y-o b c Royal Academy (USA)-Island Of Silver (USA) (Forty Niner (USA))
E A L Dunlop Maktoum Al Maktoum

Placings:506 **(4443)**
2001: 7^{5}GF, 7^{0}G, 7^{6}G

	Starts	1st	2nd	3rd	Win & Pl
Career Total (Turf)	3	0	0	0	0

Going (Turf): Sf: 0-0 GS: 0-0 Gd: 0-2 GF: 0-1 Fm: 0-0
Distance: 5f/6f: 0-0 7f-8f: 0-3 9f-13f: 0-0 14f+: 0-0
Track : LH: 0-0 RH: 0-1 Tight: 0-0 Gall: 0-0
Aids: Bl: 0-0 Vi: 0-0 Tstrap: 0-0
Best Rating: 68 9/01 Sand 7f16y good

King's Ironbridge (IRE)

106 **117**

3-y-o b c King's Theatre (IRE)-Dream Chaser (Record Token)
B J Meehan (R Hannon 5/5) Johnsey Estates (1990) Ltd

Placings:21510-1064 **(3981)**
2001: 8^{1}S, 8^{0}G, 7^{6}G, 8^{4}F

	Starts	1st	2nd	3rd	Win & Pl
Career Total (Turf)	9	3	1	0	49488

117	4/01	NmkR	1m	A	SFT	£23200
106	8/00	Sand	7f16y	A	GD	£18000
87	7/00	NmkJ	7f	D	G-F	£5148

Total win prize-money £46348

Going (Turf): Sf: 1-1 GS: 0-2 **Gd: 1-3 GF: 1-2** Fm: 0-1
Distance: 5f/6f: 0-0 **7f-8f: 3-9** 9f-13f: 0-0 14f+: 0-0
Track : LH: 0-0 **RH: 1-2** Tight: 0-0 Gall: 0-0
Aids: Bl: 0-0 Vi: 0-0 Tstrap: 0-0
Best Rating: 117 4/01 NmkR 1m soft

He won the Solario Stakes at Sandown as a juvenile, beating Storming Home, but looked outclassed in the Dewhurst. Usually races prominently, but was held up when making a winning reappearance in the Craven on soft ground. He ran well below that form in the 2000 Guineas and left Richard Hannon after the race. Disappointed subsequently.

King's Mill (IRE)

103 **104**

4-y-o b c Doyoun-Adarika (King's Lake (USA))
N A Graham First Millennium Racing

Placings:0223/111055-05060 **(4172)**
2001: 10^{0}S, 10^{5}G, 12^{0}GF, 12^{6}GF, 13^{0}G

	Starts	1st	2nd	3rd	Win & Pl
Career Total (Turf)	15	3	2	1	33865

99	5/00	York	1m2f85y	B(0-100)H	G-F	£16504
94	4/00	NmkR	1m2f	C(0-95)H	G-S	£7631
93	4/00	Sthl	1m2f	F	G-S	£2404

Total win prize-money £26540

Going (Turf): Sf: 0-2 **GS: 2-2** Gd: 0-6 GF: 1-5 Fm: 0-0
Distance: 5f/6f: 0-0 7f-8f: 0-4 **9f-13f: 3-10** 14f+: 0-1
Track : **LH: 1-4** RH: 0-6 Tight: 0-1 **Gall: 1-6**
Aids: Bl: 0-0 Vi: 0-0 Tstrap: 0-0
Best Rating: 100 5/01 NmkR 1m2f good

He completed a hat-trick in his first three starts of last season, winning over ten furlongs at Southwell, Newmarket and York. He rose in the handicap as a result, but was far from disgraced in a couple of very valuable handicaps and a Haydock Group Three.

King's Regards (IRE)

102 **80**

3-y-o b c Machiavellian (USA)-Hagwah (USA) (Dancing Brave (USA))
Sir Michael Stoute Abdulla Buhaleeba

Placings:052444 **(4180)**
2001: 8^{0}S, 10^{5}GF, 10^{2}GF, 11^{4}GF, 9^{4}GF, 9^{4}GF

	Starts	1st	2nd	3rd	Win & Pl
Career Total (Turf)	6	0	1	0	2236

Going (Turf): Sf: 0-1 GS: 0-0 Gd: 0-0 GF: 0-5 Fm: 0-0
Distance: 5f/6f: 0-0 7f-8f: 0-1 9f-13f: 0-5 14f+: 0-0
Track : LH: 0-1 RH: 0-3 Tight: 0-3 Gall: 0-1
Aids: Bl: 0-0 Vi: 0-2 Tstrap: 0-1
Best Rating: 80 7/01 Wind 1m3f135y gd-fm

He has a little bit of ability, but is still a maiden and looks one-paced.

King's Secret (USA)

102 **76**

3-y-o ch c Kingmambo (USA)-Mystery Rays (USA) (Nijinsky (CAN))
Sir Michael Stoute Saeed Suhail

Placings:32-34 **(4447)**
2001: 10^{3}G, 9^{4}G

	Starts	1st	2nd	3rd	Win & Pl
Career Total (Turf)	4	0	1	2	2640

Going (Turf): Sf: 0-1 GS: 0-0 Gd: 0-2 GF: 0-1 Fm: 0-0
Distance: 5f/6f: 0-0 7f-8f: 0-2 9f-13f: 0-2 14f+: 0-0
Track : LH: 0-1 RH: 0-2 Tight: 0-1 Gall: 0-1
Aids: Bl: 0-0 Vi: 0-0 Tstrap: 0-1
Best Rating: 76 9/01 Sand 1m1f good

King's Thought

93 **74**

2-y-o b c King's Theatre (IRE)-Lora's Guest (Be My Guest (USA))
E A L Dunlop Abdulla Buhaleeba

Placings:4 **(5290)**
2001: 7^{4}S

	Starts	1st	2nd	3rd	Win & Pl
Career Total (Turf)	1	0	0	0	315

Going (Turf): Sf: 0-1 GS: 0-0 Gd: 0-0 GF: 0-0 Fm: 0-0
Distance: 5f/6f: 0-0 7f-8f: 0-1 9f-13f: 0-0 14f+: 0-0
Track : LH: 0-0 RH: 0-0 Tight: 0-0 Gall: 0-0
Aids: Bl: 0-0 Vi: 0-0 Tstrap: 0-0
Best Rating: 74 10/01 Leic 7f9y soft

King's Travel (FR)

98 **94?**

5-y-o gr g Balleroy (USA)-Travel Free (Be My Guest (USA))
G M McCourt P Ince

Placings:122266/4 **(1233)**
2001: 10^{4}GF

	Starts	1st	2nd	3rd	Win & Pl
Career Total (Turf)	7	1	3	0	25908

3/99	StCl	1m		HLD	£9688

Total win prize-money £9688

Going (Turf): Sf: 0-1 GS: 0-0 Gd: 0-0 GF: 0-1 Fm: 0-0
Distance: 5f/6f: 0-0 7f-8f: 0-2 9f-13f: 0-2 14f+: 0-0
Track : LH: 0-1 RH: 0-0 Tight: 0-1 Gall: 0-0
Aids: Bl: 0-0 Vi: 0-0 Tstrap: 0-0
Best Rating: 94 5/01 Ches 1m2f75y gd-fm

King's Welcome

105 **95**

3-y-o b c Most Welcome-Reine De Thebes (FR) (Darshaan)
C W Fairhurst G H & S Leggott

Placings:313-2622 **(2012)**
2001: 10^{2}HY, 10^{6}S, 10^{2}F, 11^{2}GF

	Starts	1st	2nd	3rd	Win & Pl
Career Total (Turf)	7	1	3	2	16587

73	8/00	Thsk	7f	E	GD	£3103

Total win prize-money £3104

Going (Turf): Sf: 0-3 GS: 0-0 **Gd: 1-1** GF: 0-2 Fm: 0-1
Distance: 5f/6f: 0-0 **7f-8f: 1-2** 9f-13f: 0-5 14f+: 0-0
Track : **LH: 1-5** RH: 0-0 **Tight: 1-1** Gall: 0-1
Aids: Bl: 0-0 Vi: 0-0 Tstrap: 0-0
Best Rating: 95 6/01 Hayd 1m3f200y gd-fm

Useful at two, he has developed into a decent middle-distance performer. Goes well in testing conditions .

Kingchip Boy

85(96) (34)**16**

12-y-o b g Petong-Silk St James (Pas De Seul)
M J Ryan M J Ryan

Placings:000001/6064112100423/0100022351641/523223500521441006/000106460063000020/0111222221603050352 02/011104504050000000/011014634004040000 0500055/010145115041000 0/30005600504-645000000 **(1564)**
2001: 8^{6}SD, 8^{4}SD, 8^{5}SD, 8^{0}SD, 8^{0}SW, 7^{0}SD, 6^{0}GS, 9^{0}G, 5^{0}F

	Starts	1st	2nd	3rd	Win & Pl
Career Total (Turf)	88	8	10	6	48042
Career Total (AW)	79	17	6	3	48605

59	5/99	Wolv	1m1f79y	F	STD	£1717
64	3/99	Sthl	1m	F(0-65)	STD	£2193
67	2/99	Wolv	1m100y	G	STD	£1897
63	2/99	Sthl	7f	F(0-60)H	STD	£1945
57	1/99	Sthl	1m	F(0-65)H	STD	£2008
68	2/98	Sthl	7f	F	STD	£2085
71	2/98	Sthl	7f	F(0-60)H	STD	£1735
61	1/98	Sthl	1m	F(0-65)H	STD	£1735

79	2/97	Sthl	1m	D(0-85)H	STD	£4143
75	2/97	Sthl	1m	D(0-80)H	STD	£3517
68	1/97	Sthl	7f	E(0-70)H	STD	£3231
69	4/96	Sthl	1m	G(0-70)H	STD	£2070
66	1/96	Sthl	1m	F(0-65)H	STD	£2471
67	1/96	Sthl	1m	E(0-70)H	STD	£3189
57	1/96	Sthl	1m	F(0-65)H	STD	£2222
74	5/95	Gdwd	1m	D(0-80)H	G-F	£4342
74	9/94	Brig	7f214y	D(0-80)H	GD	£4109
65	8/94	Epsm	7f	E(0-70)H	G-F	£4207
57	11/93	Ling	1m	D(0-75)H	STD	£3611
57	9/93	Brig	7f214y	D(0-80)H	G-F	£4079
53	5/93	Gdwd	1m	D(0-80)H	G-F	£3882
65	8/92	Brig	7f214y	F(0-70)H	FRM	£2758
57	7/92	Sand	1m14y	E(0-70)H	GD	£3197
53	7/92	Yarm	1m3y	F(0-60)H	FRM	£2448
60	11/91	Ling	1m	F	STD	£2186

Total win prizo money £70986

Going (Turf): Sf: 0-9 GS: 0-14 Gd: 2-21 **GF: 4-31** Fm: 2-13
Distance: 5f/6f: 0-5 **7f-8f: 21-124** 9f-13f: 4-38 14f+: 0-0
Track : LH: 21-119 RH: 3-30 **Tight: 5-38** Gall: 0-5
Aids: Bl: 0-13 **Vi: 11-84** Tstrap: 0-0
Best Rating: 34 1/01 Sthl 1m stand

Kingfisher Eve (IRE)

81 **12**

3-y-o b f Hamas (IRE)-Houwara (IRE) (Darshaan)
C Grant Henry Bell

Placings:0-0 **(4084)**
2001: 8^{0}GF

	Starts	1st	2nd	3rd	Win & Pl
Career Total (Turf)	2	0	0	0	

Going (Turf): Sf: 0-0 GS: 0-0 Gd: 0-0 GF: 0-2 Fm: 0-0
Distance: 5f/6f: 0-0 7f-8f: 0-0 9f-13f: 0-2 14f+: 0-0
Track : LH: 0-1 RH: 0-1 Tight: 0-0 Gall: 0-0
Aids: Bl: 0-0 Vi: 0-0 Tstrap: 0-0
Best Rating: 12 8/01 Pont 1m4y gd-fm

Kingfishers Bonnet

94(76) (24)**31**

5-y-o b m Hamas (IRE)-Mainmast (Bustino)
J M Bradley (S G Knight 23/1) E R Griffiths

Placings:3300400/050662002624/013540300-500000 **(5026)**
2001: 9^{5}HY, 11^{0}GS, 11^{0}GS, 11^{0}G, 9^{0}F, 9^{0}S

	Starts	1st	2nd	3rd	Win & Pl
Career Total (Turf)	32	1	3	4	7160
Career Total (AW)	2	0	0	0	

55 4/00 Wwck 1m2f110yF(0-60)H HVY £2478
Total win prize-money £2478

Going (Turf): Sf: 1-10 GS: 0-4 Gd: 0-12 GF: 0-5 Fm: 0-1
Distance: 5f/6f: 0-5 7f-8f: 0-3 **9f-13f: 1-26** 14f+: 0-0
Track : LH: 1-17 RH: 0-11 Tight: 0-12 Gall: 0-1
Aids: Bl: 0-0 Vi: 0-0 Tstrap: 0-0
Best Rating: 40 5/01 Bath 1m3f144y gd-sft

Kings Of Europe (USA)

105 **68**

3-y-o b g Rainbow Quest (USA)-Bemissed (USA) (Nijinsky (CAN))
B W Hills Manchester United Racing Club

Placings:420-33414530 **(5114)**
2001: 11^{3}F, 14^{3}G, 14^{4}GF, 12^{1}GF, 14^{4}G, 14^{5}G, 16^{3}GF, 16^{0}HY

	Starts	1st	2nd	3rd	Win & Pl
Career Total (Turf)	11	1	1	3	6599

51 7/01 Newc 1m4f93y D G-F £2954
Total win prize-money £2954

Going (Turf): Sf: 0-2 GS: 0-0 Gd: 0-3 **GF: 1-5** Fm: 0-1
Distance: 5f/6f: 0-0 7f-8f: 0-1 **9f-13f: 1-4** 14f+: 0-6
Track : LH: 1-8 RH: 0-0 Tight: 0-1 **Gall: 1-1**
Aids: Bl: 1-2 Vi: 0-2 Tstrap: 0-0
Best Rating: 80 6/01 Hayd 1m6f good

Has not gone on from promising juvenile form but managed to break his duck in a poor maiden at Newcastle in first-time blinkers.

Kings Signal (USA)

101 **72**

3-y-o b c Red Ransom (USA)-Star Of Albion (Ajdal (USA))
M R Channon P J Sheehan

Placings:0-0043226416000 **(4734)**
2001: 8^{0}G, 10^{0}S, 7^{4}GF, 7^{3}F, 6^{2}GF, 7^{2}G, 8^{6}GF, 7^{4}GF, 8^{1}GF, 9^{6}F, 8^{0}GF, 8^{0}GF, 8^{0}F

	Starts	1st	2nd	3rd	Win & Pl
Career Total (Turf)	14	1	2	1	7592

72 7/01 Nott 1m54y E(0-70) G-F £3206
Total win prize-money £3206

Going (Turf): Sf: 0-2 GS: 0-0 Gd: 0-2 **GF: 1-7** Fm: 0-3
Distance: 5f/6f: 0-0 7f-8f: 0-9 **9f-13f: 1-5** 14f+: 0-0
Track : LH: 1-5 RH: 0-0 Tight: 0-1 Gall: 0-1
Aids: Bl: 0-0 Vi: 0-0 Tstrap: 0-0
Best Rating: 72 7/01 Nott 1m54y gd-fm

Ran once at two. Best over seven furlongs and fast ground this term. Proved more suited to hold-up tactics when scoring at Nottingham in July. Should stay further. Acts on fast ground.

Kings To Open

89(99) (43)**37**

4-y-o b g First Trump-Shadiyama (Nishapour (FR))
P W Hiatt P Burton

Placings:0/06000620-0650 **(5042)**
2001: 12^{0}SD, 9^{6}SD, 12^{5}SD, 8^{0}G

	Starts	1st	2nd	3rd	Win & Pl
Career Total (Turf)	6	0	0	0	0
Career Total (AW)	7	0	1	0	776

Going (Turf): Sf: 0-2 GS: 0-0 Gd: 0-2 GF: 0-1 Fm: 0-1
Distance: 5f/6f: 0-0 7f-8f: 0-3 9f-13f: 0-10 14f+: 0-0
Track : LH: 0-13 RH: 0-0 Tight: 0-9 Gall: 0-0
Aids: Bl: 0-1 Vi: 0-0 Tstrap: 0-1
Best Rating: 43 2/01 Wolv 1m1f79y stand

Kingsade (IRE)

103 **64**

3-y-o b f King's Theatre (IRE)-Haiti Mill (Free State)
B Smart Adrienne And Michael Barnett

Placings:30520 **(4105)**
2001: 8^{3}GS, 10^{0}G, 11^{5}HD, 11^{2}GF, 12^{0}S

	Starts	1st	2nd	3rd	Win & Pl
Career Total (Turf)	5	0	1	1	1388

Going (Turf): Sf: 0-1 GS: 0-1 Gd: 0-1 GF: 0-1 Fm: 0-1
Distance: 5f/6f: 0-0 7f-8f: 0-0 9f-13f: 0-5 14f+: 0-0
Track : LH: 0-2 RH: 0-2 Tight: 0-5 Gall: 0-0
Aids: Bl: 0-0 Vi: 0-0 Tstrap: 0-0
Best Rating: 64 8/01 Bath 1m3f144y gd-fm

Kingsclere

105 **43**

4-y-o b g Fairy King (USA)-Spurned (USA) (Robellino (USA))
I A Balding Mike Charlton And Rodger Sargent

Placings:114323/15050-0000650 **(4805)**
2001: 8^{0}GS, 10^{0}G, 8^{0}G, 10^{0}GF, 8^{6}GF, 7^{5}G, 8^{0}F

	Starts	1st	2nd	3rd	Win & Pl
Career Total (Turf)	18	3	1	2	56530

110 4/00 Kemp 1m A SFT £15145
93 7/99 York 6f214y B G-F £8091
85 6/99 Newb 6f8y C GD £6192
Total win prize-money £29428

Going (Turf): Sf: 1-2 GS: 0-1 **Gd: 1-8 GF: 1-6** Fm: 0-1
Distance: 5f/6f: 0-0 **7f-8f: 3-10** 9f-13f: 0-8 14f+: 0-0
Track : LH: 1-5 RH: 1-9 Tight: 0-4 **Gall: 2-6**
Aids: Bl: 0-2 Vi: 0-0 Tstrap: 0-3
Best Rating: 79 7/01 Gdwd 1m gd-fm

Was a useful three-year-old and was unlucky not to win the Chester Vase but has gone the wrong way since a wayward effort in the 2000 Derby. Stays 12 furlongs, possibly better suited by shorter, acts on any ground. Has shown the odd sign of form and has been tried in blinkers.

Kingscross

104 **73**

3-y-o ch g King's Signet (USA)-Calamanco (Clantime)
M Blanshard Mrs D Ellis

Placings:00-00010 **(5252)**
2001: 6^{0}G, 5^{0}G, 5^{0}GS, 5^{1}GS, 5^{0}S

	Starts	1st	2nd	3rd	Win & Pl
Career Total (Turf)	7	1	0	0	4992

70 10/01 NmkR 5f D(0-85)H G-S £4992
Total win prize-money £4992

Going (Turf): Sf: 0-2 **GS: 1-2** Gd: 0-3 GF: 0-0 Fm: 0-0
Distance: 5f/6f: 1-6 7f-8f: 0-1 9f-13f: 0-0 14f+: 0-0
Track : LH: 0-0 RH: 0-0 Tight: 0-0 Gall: 0-0
Aids: Bl: 0-0 Vi: 0-0 Tstrap: 0-0
Best Rating: 70 10/01 NmkR 5f gd-sft

Lightly-raced sprinter, unlucky in running twice before getting off the mark in a Newmarket handicap. Suited by five furlongs and cut in the ground.

Kingsdon (IRE)

98 **71d**

4-y-o b g Brief Truce (USA)-Richly Deserved (IRE) (King's Lake (USA))
D Nicholls Mike Browne

Placings:21231/6300654405-0000620306 **(5384)**
2001: 8^{0}S, 10^{0}S, 10^{0}GF, 10^{0}G, 7^{6}F, 10^{2}GF, 8^{0}GF, 8^{3}GS, 8^{0}GS, 7^{6}S

	Starts	1st	2nd	3rd	Win & Pl
Career Total (Turf)	25	2	3	3	15888

93 9/99 Sals 6f212y D HVY £3980
81 8/99 Kemp 6f E G-S £3956
Total win prize-money £7937

Going (Turf): Sf: 1-8 GS: 1-5 Gd: 0-5 GF: 0-6 Fm: 0-1
Distance: 5f/6f: 1-2 7f-8f: 1-13 9f-13f: 0-10 14f+: 0-0
Track : LH: 0-11 RH: 0-4 Tight: 0-7 Gall: 0-3
Aids: Bl: 0-0 Vi: 0-3 Tstrap: 0-7
Best Rating: 73 5/01 Ches 1m2f75y gd-fm

He gradually dropped in the weights and finished second over ten furlongs at Newcastle in June 2001. That was on fast ground, but he does like to get his toe in.

Kingsdown Trix (IRE)

98(86) (22)**40**

7-y-o b g Contract Law (USA)-Three Of Trumps (Tyrnavos)
R J Smith The Kingsdowners

Placings:060054/61416150004/0000 **(2743)**
2001: 12^{0}SW, 16^{0}SD, 16^{0}SD, 18^{0}GF

	Starts	1st	2nd	3rd	Win & Pl
Career Total (Turf)	9	0	0	0	0
Career Total (AW)	12	3	0	0	6548

57 5/97 Wolv 1m4f G STD £1984
57 3/97 Ling 1m4f G(0-60)H STD £1984
55 2/97 Ling 1m2f F(0-65)H STD £2383
Total win prize-money £6354

Going (Turf): Sf: 0-0 GS: 0-0 Gd: 0-2 GF: 0-5 Fm: 0-2
Distance: 5f/6f: 0-2 7f-8f: 0-5 **9f-13f: 3-11** 14f+: 0-3
Track : LH: 3-18 RH: 0-1 **Tight: 3-12** Gall: 0-0
Aids: Bl: 0-0 Vi: 0-0 Tstrap: 0-0
Best Rating: 40 7/01 Chep 2m2f gd-fm

Kingston Bill

93(84) (31)**60**

4-y-o b g Then Again-Tricata (Electric)
W G M Turner Miss Corinne J Overton

Placings:1360/0063 **(2047)**
2001: 11^{0}SD, 6^{0}GF, 8^{6}F, 11^{3}GF

	Starts	1st	2nd	3rd	Win & Pl
Career Total (Turf)	7	1	0	2	3507
Career Total (AW)	1	0	0	0	

72 3/99 Newc 5f D G-S £3009

Total win prize-money £3009

Going (Turf): Sf: 0-2 **GS: 1-1** Gd: 0-1 GF: 0-2 Fm: 0-1
Distance: **5f/6f: 1-2** 7f-8f: 0-3 9f-13f: 0-3 14f+: 0-0
Track : LH: 0-4 RH: 0-1 Tight: 0-2 Gall: 0-0
Aids: Bl: 0-0 Vi: 0-0 Tstrap: 0-0
Best Rating: 47 5/01 Brig 6f209y gd-fm

Kingston Blue

89 **59**
2-y-o b c Bluegrass Prince (IRE)-Miss Pokey (Uncle Pokey)
W G M Turner Miss Corinne J Overton

Placings:0000 **(5530)**
2001: 6^{0}GF, 8^{0}G, 10^{0}G, 8^{0}HY

	Starts	1st	2nd	3rd	Win & Pl
Career Total (Turf)	4	0	0	0	

Going (Turf): Sf: 0-1 GS: 0-0 Gd: 0-2 GF: 0-1 Fm: 0-0
Distance: 5f/6f: 0-0 7f-8f: 0-2 9f-13f: 0-2 14f+: 0-0
Track : LH: 0-3 RH: 0-0 Tight: 0-1 Gall: 0-1
Aids: Bl: 0-0 Vi: 0-0 Tstrap: 0-0
Best Rating: 59 10/01 Bath 1m2f46y good

Kingston Game

77(82) (47)**51**
2-y-o b c Mind Games-Valmaranda (USA) (Sir Ivor)
A Berry Kingston Bloodstock Ltd

Placings:00060 **(5530)**
2001: 5^{0}GF, 5^{0}GF, 6^{0}F, 6^{6}SD, 8^{0}HY

	Starts	1st	2nd	3rd	Win & Pl
Career Total (Turf)	4	0	0	0	
Career Total (AW)	1	0	0	0	0

Going (Turf): Sf: 0-1 GS: 0-0 Gd: 0-0 GF: 0-2 Fm: 0-1
Distance: 5f/6f: 0-4 7f-8f: 0-0 9f-13f: 0-1 14f+: 0-0
Track : LH: 0-3 RH: 0-0 Tight: 0-1 Gall: 0-0
Aids: Bl: 0-2 Vi: 0-0 Tstrap: 0-0
Best Rating: 51 8/01 Pont 5f gd-fm

Kingston Wish (IRE)

94 **55**
2-y-o b c Mujadil (USA)-Well Wisher (USA) (Sanglamore (USA))
A Berry Kingston Bloodstock Ltd

Placings:300 **(2307)**
2001: 5^{3}S, 5^{0}GF, 6^{0}GS

	Starts	1st	2nd	3rd	Win & Pl
Career Total (Turf)	3	0	0	1	373

Going (Turf): Sf: 0-1 GS: 0-1 Gd: 0-0 GF: 0-1 Fm: 0-0
Distance: 5f/6f: 0-2 7f-8f: 0-1 9f-13f: 0-0 14f+: 0-0
Track : LH: 0-0 RH: 0-0 Tight: 0-0 Gall: 0-0
Aids: Bl: 0-0 Vi: 0-0 Tstrap: 0-0
Best Rating: 55 5/01 Ripn 5f gd-fm

Kinnino

100(97) (43)**47**
7-y-o b g Polish Precedent (USA)-On Tiptoes (Shareef Dancer (USA))
G L Moore Exors Of The Late Mr A Moore

Placings:06000560/530000505020/134032144660-531314 **(3610)**
2001: 8^{5}SD, 10^{3}SD, 10^{1}SW, 10^{3}SD, 10^{1}GF, 9^{4}G

	Starts	1st	2nd	3rd	Win & Pl
Career Total (Turf)	21	2	1	0	6219
Career Total (AW)	17	2	1	5	5743

47	6/01	Wwck	1m2f188y	G(0-60)H	G-F	£2212
43	3/01	Ling	1m2f	G	SLW	£1949
45	8/00	Nott	1m1f213y	E(0-75)H	G-F	£2938
41	1/00	Wolv	1m100y	F(0-75)H	STD	£1949

Total win prize-money £9050

Going (Turf): Sf: 0-3 GS: 0-1 Gd: 0-5 **GF: 2-8** Fm: 0-4
Distance: 5f/6f: 0-0 7f-8f: 0-15 **9f-13f: 4-23** 14f+: 0-0
Track : **LH: 4-30** RH: 0-6 **Tight: 2-21** Gall: 0-1
Aids: **Bl: 1-9** Vi: 0-0 Tstrap: 0-0
Best Rating: 47 8/01 Nott 1m1f213y good

Kinsman (IRE)

(109) (87)**76**
4-y-o b g Distant Relative-Besito (Wassl)
Andrew Reid R Marshall,S Ironside,R Gurney,A Reid

Placings:00006215/300623160100511341-4510P06000 **(2961)**
2001: 7^{4}SD, 7^{5}SD, 8^{1}SW, 10^{0}SW, 8^{P}SD, 7^{0}GF, 6^{6}F, 8^{0}GF, 8^{0}GF, 6^{0}GF

	Starts	1st	2nd	3rd	Win & Pl
Career Total (Turf)	22	3	2	0	12372
Career Total (AW)	14	4	0	3	20449

87	2/01	Ling	1m	C(0-95)H	SLW	£6695
82	12/00	Ling	7f	D(0-80)H	STD	£3851
78	12/00	Ling	7f	D(0-80)H	STD	£3201
73	11/00	Ling	7f	D(0-80)H	STD	£4078
69	8/00	Epsm	6f	E(0-70)H	GD	£4270
69	6/00	Brig	5f213y	E(0-75)H	FRM	£2899
69	9/99	Brig	5f213y	D(0-85)H	SFT	£3403

Total win prize-money £28400

Going (Turf): **Sf: 1-5** GS: 0-1 **Gd: 1-6** GF: 0-8 **Fm: 1-2**
Distance: 5f/6f: 3-12 **7f-8f: 4-21** 9f-13f: 0-3 14f+: 0-0
Track : **LH: 7-26** RH: 0-2 **Tight: 5-20** Gall: 0-2
Aids: Bl: 0-4 **Vi: 3-12** Tstrap: 0-0
Best Rating: 87 2/01 Ling 1m slow

Ran well on the All-Weather during the spring of 2001. Best over seven furlongs and a mile. Needs to come late off a fast pace. Best on a sound surface.

Kippax Blues (IRE)

72 **16**
3-y-o b c Grand Lodge (USA)-Bird In Blue (IRE) (Bluebird (USA))
J L Eyre S Pinner

Placings:000 **(2271)**
2001: 9^{0}GS, 10^{0}GF, 7^{0}G

	Starts	1st	2nd	3rd	Win & Pl
Career Total (Turf)	3	0	0	0	

Going (Turf): Sf: 0-0 GS: 0-1 Gd: 0-1 GF: 0-1 Fm: 0-0
Distance: 5f/6f: 0-0 7f-8f: 0-1 9f-13f: 0-2 14f+: 0-0
Track : LH: 0-2 RH: 0-0 Tight: 0-1 Gall: 0-0
Aids: Bl: 0-0 Vi: 0-0 Tstrap: 0-3
Best Rating: 16 6/01 Thsk 7f good

Kirat

89 **47**
3-y-o b c Darshaan-Kafsa (IRE) (Vayrann)
R Charlton Simon Keswick

Placings:0 **(1669)**
2001: 10^{0}GF

	Starts	1st	2nd	3rd	Win & Pl
Career Total (Turf)	1	0	0	0	

Going (Turf): Sf: 0-0 GS: 0-0 Gd: 0-0 GF: 0-1 Fm: 0-0
Distance: 5f/6f: 0-0 7f-8f: 0-0 9f-13f: 0-1 14f+: 0-0
Track : LH: 0-0 RH: 0-1 Tight: 0-0 Gall: 0-0
Aids: Bl: 0-0 Vi: 0-0 Tstrap: 0-0
Best Rating: 47 5/01 Sand 1m2f7y gd-fm

Kirikou

96 **60d**
3-y-o b g Mtoto-Nevis (Connaught)
D J Wintle (R F Johnson Houghton 27/6) R K Davies Engineering Ltd

Placings:6051000 **(5190)**
2001: 10^{6}GF, 10^{0}GF, 10^{5}G, 10^{1}GF, 9^{0}G, 10^{0}S, 11^{0}GS

	Starts	1st	2nd	3rd	Win & Pl
Career Total (Turf)	7	1	0	0	1859

44	6/01	Wwck	1m2f188yG		G-F	£1859

Total win prize-money £1859

Going (Turf): Sf: 0-1 GS: 0-1 Gd: 0-2 **GF: 1-3** Fm: 0-0
Distance: 5f/6f: 0-0 7f-8f: 0-0 **9f-13f: 1-7** 14f+: 0-0
Track : **LH: 1-4** RH: 0-1 Tight: 0-5 Gall: 0-0
Aids: Bl: 0-0 Vi: 0-0 Tstrap: 0-0
Best Rating: 65 5/01 Bath 1m2f46y gd-fm

A poor performer whose best effort to date was winning a Warwick seller over a mile on fast ground in the summer of 2001. He has run dismally since then.

Kirisnippa

(108) (61)**47**
6-y-o b g Beveled (USA)-Kiri Te (Liboi (USA))
R Curtis (Derrick Morris 25/1) D A Drake

Placings:04P3U060/5131605320403504201-010400 **(2544)**
2001: 11^{0}SD, 12^{1}SD, 12^{0}SW, 12^{4}SD, 14^{0}SD, 14^{0}GF

	Starts	1st	2nd	3rd	Win & Pl
Career Total (Turf)	18	0	2	3	4649
Career Total (AW)	15	4	0	1	15880

61	1/01	Wolv	1m4f	D(0-80)H	STD	£5460
53	11/00	Wolv	1m4f	D(0-80)H	STD	£3711
53	2/00	Sthl	1m3f	E(0-70)H	STD	£2782
46	1/00	Sthl	1m3f	E(0-70)H	STD	£2977

Total win prize-money £14931

Going (Turf): **Sf: 0-1 GS: 0-2 Gd: 0-6 GF: 0-6 Fm: 0-2**
Distance: 5f/6f: 0-0 7f-8f: 0-3 **9f-13f: 4-24** 14f+: 0-5
Track : **LH: 4-23** RH: 0-5 **Tight: 2-10** Gall: 0-2
Aids: Bl: 0-1 Vi: 0-1 Tstrap: 0-0
Best Rating: 61 1/01 Wolv 1m4f stand

Kirkby's Treasure

(96) (64)**69**
3-y-o ro g Mind Games-Gem Of Gold (Jellaby)
A Berry Kirkby Lonsdale Racing

Placings:036650-40404462400222210 **(5612)**
2001: 5^{4}GS, 6^{0}G, 6^{4}S, 6^{0}GF, 6^{4}GF, 7^{4}GF, 7^{6}GF, 6^{2}S, 5^{4}GF, 6^{0}F, 5^{0}G, 5^{2}GF, 5^{2}GF, 6^{2}GF, 5^{2}G, 7^{2}GF, 5^{1}GS, 6^{0}SD

	Starts	1st	2nd	3rd	Win & Pl
Career Total (Turf)	23	1	6	1	10935
Career Total (AW)	1	0	0	0	

50	10/01	Catt	5f212y	F	G-S	£2306

Total win prize-money £2307

Going (Turf): Sf: 0-3 **GS: 1-3** Gd: 0-5 GF: 0-11 Fm: 0-1
Distance: **5f/6f: 1-20** 7f-8f: 0-4 9f-13f: 0-0 14f+: 0-0
Track : **LH: 1-7** RH: 0-1 **Tight: 1-4** Gall: 0-1
Aids: Bl: 0-0 Vi: 0-0 Tstrap: 0-0
Best Rating: 69 9/01 Catt 7f gd-fm

Was second five times in a row before finally getting off the mark at Catterick in October over six furlongs.

Kirov

84 **78**
2-y-o b f Darshaan-Dance To The Top (Sadler's Wells (USA))
Sir Michael Stoute Cheveley Park Stud

Placings:0 **(4871)**
2001: 8^{0}G

	Starts	1st	2nd	3rd	Win & Pl
Career Total (Turf)	1	0	0	0	

Going (Turf): Sf: 0-0 GS: 0-0 Gd: 0-1 GF: 0-0 Fm: 0-0
Distance: 5f/6f: 0-0 7f-8f: 0-1 9f-13f: 0-0 14f+: 0-0
Track : LH: 0-0 RH: 0-0 Tight: 0-0 Gall: 0-0
Aids: Bl: 0-0 Vi: 0-0 Tstrap: 0-0
Best Rating: 78 9/01 NmkR 1m good

Kirovski (IRE)

107 **89**
4-y-o b g Common Grounds-Nordic Doll (IRE) (Royal Academy (USA))
P W Harris Batten, Bowstead, Gregory & Manning

Placings:060/21113-00000206 **(5607)**
2001: 8^{0}S, 8^{0}GF, 8^{0}GF, 8^{0}GF, 9^{0}G, 10^{2}GF, 9^{0}G, 8^{6}GS

	Starts	1st	2nd	3rd	Win & Pl
Career Total (Turf)	16	3	2	1	59405

90	8/00	Asct	1m	C(0-100)H	G-F	£8404
82	7/00	NmkJ	1m	C(0-90)H	GD	£11310
78	6/00	Carl	7f214y	D(0-80)H	G-F	£14950

Total win prize-money £34665

Going (Turf): Sf: 0-2 GS: 0-2 Gd: 1-4 **GF: 2-8** Fm: 0-0
Distance: 5f/6f: 0-0 **7f-8f: 3-10** 9f-13f: 0-6 14f+: 0-0
Track : LH: 0-3 **RH: 1-5** Tight: 0-0 Gall: 0-1
Aids: Bl: 0-0 Vi: 0-0 Tstrap: 0-0
Best Rating: 89 9/01 Newb 1m2f6y gd-fm

Progressive, he completed a hat-trick in 2000 before a fine effort in a hot handicap on his last run of the season. Took his time to come to hand this term but ran well at Newbury in September, before disappointing at Newmarket in October. Stays a mile. Acts on fast ground.

Kirtle

93 **89**
2-y-o b f Hector Protector (USA)-Kyle Rhea (In The Wings)
J R Fanshawe Lady Wills

Placings:63 **(5147)**
2001: 6^{6}GF, 7^{3}G

	Starts	1st	2nd	3rd	Win & Pl
Career Total (Turf)	2	0	0	1	558

Going (Turf): Sf: 0-0 GS: 0-0 Gd: 0-1 GF: 0-1 Fm: 0-0
Distance: 5f/6f: 0-0 7f-8f: 0-2 9f-13f: 0-0 14f+: 0-0
Track : LH: 0-0 RH: 0-0 Tight: 0-0 Gall: 0-0
Aids: Bl: 0-0 Vi: 0-0 Tstrap: 0-0
Best Rating: 89 9/01 Sals 6f212y gd-fm

Was not beaten far on her debut running, and again went close behind a progressive sort at Redcar.

Kismet

87 **35**
3-y-o b f Tirol-Belamcanda (Belmez (USA))
Don Enrico Incisa Don Enrico Incisa

Placings:660 **(5174)**
2001: 7^{6}G, 8^{6}F, 8^{0}GS

	Starts	1st	2nd	3rd	Win & Pl
Career Total (Turf)	3	0	0	0	0

Going (Turf): Sf: 0-0 GS: 0-1 Gd: 0-1 GF: 0-0 Fm: 0-1
Distance: 5f/6f: 0-0 7f-8f: 0-2 9f-13f: 0-1 14f+: 0-0
Track : LH: 0-2 RH: 0-0 Tight: 0-0 Gall: 0-1
Aids: Bl: 0-0 Vi: 0-0 Tstrap: 0-0
Best Rating: 35 10/01 Pont 1m4y gd-sft

Kiss Curl

75 **10**
3-y-o ch f Beveled (USA)-Laquette (Bairn (USA))
M Madgwick Miss E M L Coller

Placings:00-0000 **(4361)**
2001: 8^{0}GS, 6^{0}GF, 9^{0}G, 11^{0}GF

	Starts	1st	2nd	3rd	Win & Pl
Career Total (Turf)	6	0	0	0	

Going (Turf): Sf: 0-1 GS: 0-2 Gd: 0-1 GF: 0-2 Fm: 0-0
Distance: 5f/6f: 0-1 7f-8f: 0-3 9f-13f: 0-2 14f+: 0-0
Track : LH: 0-3 RH: 0-2 Tight: 0-0 Gall: 0-2
Aids: Bl: 0-0 Vi: 0-0 Tstrap: 0-0
Best Rating: 10 8/01 Brig 1m1f209y good

Kissed By Moonlite

75(85) (16)
5-y-o gr m Petong-Rose Bouquet (General Assembly (USA))
R Hollinshead A Fairfield

Placings:000/0660200/060-000 **(2188)**
2001: 6^{0}SD, 7^{0}SD, 14^{0}GF

	Starts	1st	2nd	3rd	Win & Pl
Career Total (Turf)	13	0	1	0	1216
Career Total (AW)	3	0	0	0	

Going (Turf): Sf: 0-1 GS: 0-1 Gd: 0-4 GF: 0-7 Fm: 0-0
Distance: 5f/6f: 0-2 7f-8f: 0-7 9f-13f: 0-5 14f+: 0-2
Track : LH: 0-7 RH: 0-3 Tight: 0-3 Gall: 0-1
Aids: Bl: 0-0 Vi: 0-0 Tstrap: 0-0
Best Rating: 16 5/01 Sthl 7f stand

Kissing Time

(85) (32)**54**
4-y-o b f Lugana Beach-Princess Athena (Ahonoora)
P F I Cole W H Ponsonby

Placings:01506/05000-55005032060 **(5350)**
2001: 5^{5}GF, 5^{5}GF, 5^{0}GF, 8^{0}GF, 8^{5}GF, 8^{0}S, 5^{3}GF, 5^{2}GF, 5^{0}G, 5^{6}G, 5^{0}SD

	Starts	1st	2nd	3rd	Win & Pl
Career Total (Turf)	20	1	1	1	5380
Career Total (AW)	1	0	0	0	

80 8/99 Bath 5f11y D GD £4318
Total win prize-money £4319

Going (Turf): Sf: 0-3 GS: 0-2 **Gd: 1-4** GF: 0-11 Fm: 0-0
Distance: **5f/6f: 1-17** 7f-8f: 0-1 9f-13f: 0-3 14f+: 0-0
Track : **LH: 1-6** RH: 0-4 Tight: 0-2 **Gall: 1-5**
Aids: Bl: 0-1 Vi: 0-1 Tstrap: 0-0
Best Rating: 62 5/01 Ling 5f gd-fm

A fair juvenile in 1999, she has struggled since but has dropped down the weights as a result. Stays a mile but probably best at sprint distances. Unsuited by soft ground.

Kitchener (USA)

(94) (53)**71**
3-y-o br g Lord At War (ARG)-Visiting Bee (USA) (Drone (USA))
P W Harris R J Spencer & Mrs P W Harris

Placings:3000 **(5330)**
2001: 11^{3}G, 11^{0}GF, 12^{0}GF, 16^{0}HY

	Starts	1st	2nd	3rd	Win & Pl
Career Total (Turf)	4	0	0	1	678

Going (Turf): Sf: 0-1 GS: 0-0 Gd: 0-1 GF: 0-2 Fm: 0-0
Distance: 5f/6f: 0-0 7f-8f: 0-0 9f-13f: 0-3 14f+: 0-1
Track : LH: 0-3 RH: 0-1 Tight: 0-2 Gall: 0-0
Aids: Bl: 0-0 Vi: 0-0 Tstrap: 0-0
Best Rating: 71 9/01 Kemp 1m4f gd-fm

Kite Mark

80 **56**
3-y-o ch f Mark Of Esteem (IRE)-Shadywood (Habitat)
H R A Cecil Cliveden Stud

Placings:6 **(1385)**
2001: 9^{6}S

	Starts	1st	2nd	3rd	Win & Pl
Career Total (Turf)	1	0	0	0	0

Going (Turf): Sf: 0-1 GS: 0-0 Gd: 0-0 GF: 0-0 Fm: 0-0
Distance: 5f/6f: 0-0 7f-8f: 0-0 9f-13f: 0-1 14f+: 0-0
Track : LH: 0-0 RH: 0-1 Tight: 0-1 Gall: 0-0
Aids: Bl: 0-0 Vi: 0-0 Tstrap: 0-0
Best Rating: 56 5/01 Sals 1m1f198y soft

Kitty Bankes

(72) **29**
3-y-o b f Forzando-St Kitts (Tragic Role (USA))
W G M Turner Mrs J Lightbowne

Placings:0-00 **(4070)**
2001: 11^{0}F, 9^{0}SD

	Starts	1st	2nd	3rd	Win & Pl
Career Total (Turf)	2	0	0	0	
Career Total (AW)	1	0	0	0	

Going (Turf): Sf: 0-0 GS: 0-1 Gd: 0-0 GF: 0-0 Fm: 0-1
Distance: 5f/6f: 0-0 7f-8f: 0-0 9f-13f: 0-3 14f+: 0-0
Track : LH: 0-3 RH: 0-0 Tight: 0-3 Gall: 0-0
Aids: Bl: 0-0 Vi: 0-0 Tstrap: 0-0

Kittylee

64 **15**
2-y-o b f Bal Harbour-Courtesy Call (Northfields (USA))
R M Whitaker The High Hopers

Placings:0 **(5526)**
2001: 5^{0}S

	Starts	1st	2nd	3rd	Win & Pl
Career Total (Turf)	1	0	0	0	

Going (Turf): Sf: 0-1 GS: 0-0 Gd: 0-0 GF: 0-0 Fm: 0-0
Distance: 5f/6f: 0-1 7f-8f: 0-0 9f-13f: 0-0 14f+: 0-0
Track : LH: 0-0 RH: 0-0 Tight: 0-0 Gall: 0-0
Aids: Bl: 0-0 Vi: 0-0 Tstrap: 0-0
Best Rating: 15 10/01 Nott 5f13y soft

Kivotos (USA)

93 **61**
3-y-o gr g Trempolino (USA)-Authorized Staff (USA) (Relaunch (USA))
Mrs J R Ramsden Mrs J R Ramsden

Placings:64-600 **(1446)**
2001: 8^{6}HY, 10^{0}GS, 8^{0}GF

	Starts	1st	2nd	3rd	Win & Pl
Career Total (Turf)	5	0	0	0	0

Going (Turf): Sf: 0-1 GS: 0-2 Gd: 0-1 GF: 0-1 Fm: 0-0
Distance: 5f/6f: 0-0 7f-8f: 0-3 9f-13f: 0-2 14f+: 0-0
Track : LH: 0-4 RH: 0-1 Tight: 0-1 Gall: 0-0
Aids: Bl: 0-0 Vi: 0-0 Tstrap: 0-0
Best Rating: 48 5/01 Pont 1m2f6y gd-sft

Knave's Ash (USA)

82 **30**
10-y-o ch g Miswaki (USA)-Quiet Rendezvous (USA) (Nureyev (USA))
M Todhunter P G Airey

Placings:641/1300/040013441/0650060/000261000230160/000003213023/00003600606-0 **(2125)**
2001: 8^{0}GF

	Starts	1st	2nd	3rd	Win & Pl
Career Total (Turf)	62	7	4	7	70565

53	7/99	Rdcr	1m	G(0-60)H	FRM	£2500
68	9/98	Newc	1m	E(0-70)H	GD	£3235
61	7/98	Thsk	1m	E(0-70)H	FRM	£2809
98	9/95	Pont	1m2f6y	B(0-95)H	GD	£9400
93	7/95	Donc	1m2f60y	B(0-105)H	G-F	£10656
82	5/94	York	6f214y	B(0-105)H	FRM	£19087
78	8/93	Haml	6f5y	D	GD	£4163

Total win prize-money £51854

Going (Turf): Sf: 0-3 GS: 0-9 **Gd: 3-14** GF: 1-30 **Fm: 3-6**
Distance: 5f/6f: 0-5 **7f-8f: 5-33** 9f-13f: 2-24 14f+: 0-0
Track : **LH: 5-30** RH: 0-15 Tight: 1-18 **Gall: 3-10**
Aids: Bl: 0-0 Vi: 0-0 Tstrap: 0-0
Best Rating: 12 6/01 Haml 1m65y gd-fm

Knavesmire Dream

(80) (41)
2-y-o b c Mujadil (USA)-Dreams Are Free (IRE) (Caerleon (USA))
M Johnston The Knavesmire Partnership

Placings:06400600 **(5618)**
2001: 5^{0}GF, 7^{6}F, 7^{4}G, 7^{0}G, 7^{0}G, 8^{6}GF, 7^{0}G, 8^{0}SD

	Starts	1st	2nd	3rd	Win & Pl
Career Total (Turf)	7	0	0	0	321
Career Total (AW)	1	0	0	0	

Going (Turf): Sf: 0-0 GS: 0-0 Gd: 0-4 GF: 0-2 Fm: 0-1
Distance: 5f/6f: 0-1 7f-8f: 0-5 9f-13f: 0-2 14f+: 0-0
Track : LH: 0-3 RH: 0-0 Tight: 0-3 Gall: 0-0
Aids: Bl: 0-3 Vi: 0-0 Tstrap: 0-0
Best Rating: 66 7/01 Epsm 7f good

Knavesmire Omen

(90) (67)**74**
2-y-o b c Robellino (USA)-Signs (Risk Me (FR))

M Johnston The Knavesmire Partnership

Placings:65233003 **(5342)**
2001: 6^{6}GF, 7^{5}GF, 7^{2}G, 7^{3}GF, 7^{3}G, 7^{0}G, 6^{0}S, 7^{3}GS

	Starts	1st	2nd	3rd	Win & Pl
Career Total (Turf)	8	0	1	3	2376

Going (Turf): Sf: 0-1 GS: 0-1 Gd: 0-3 GF: 0-3 Fm: 0-0
Distance: 5f/6f: 0-2 7f-8f: 0-6 9f-13f: 0-0 14f+: 0-0
Track : LH: 0-2 RH: 0-0 Tight: 0-2 Gall: 0-0
Aids: Bl: 0-1 Vi: 0-0 Tstrap: 0-0
Best Rating: 74 8/01 Ayr 7f50y good

Has shown ability in ordinary events up to seven furlongs. Acts on any ground.

Knight Crossing (IRE)

101(77) (21)**50**
3-y-o b g Doyoun-Princess Sarara (USA) (Trempolino (USA))
Mrs A Duffield Miss Betty Duxbury

Placings:50-00030 **(4857)**
2001: 7^{0}SD, 9^{0}GF, 10^{0}F, 8^{3}GF, 7^{0}GF

	Starts	1st	2nd	3rd	Win & Pl
Career Total (Turf)	6	0	0	1	786
Career Total (AW)	1	0	0	0	0

Going (Turf): Sf: 0-2 GS: 0-0 Gd: 0-0 GF: 0-3 Fm: 0-1
Distance: 5f/6f: 0-2 7f-8f: 0-3 9f-13f: 0-2 14f+: 0-0
Track : LH: 0-5 RH: 0-0 Tight: 0-2 Gall: 0-2
Aids: Bl: 0-0 Vi: 0-0 Tstrap: 0-0
Best Rating: 50 8/01 Newc 1m gd-fm

Knight Of Silver

(85) (24)
4-y-o gr g Presidium-Misty Rocket (Roan Rocket)
S Mellor The Knight Of Silver Partnership

Placings:0053000/0 **(0618)**
2001: 10^{0}SD

	Starts	1st	2nd	3rd	Win & Pl
Career Total (Turf)	7	0	0	1	510
Career Total (AW)	1	0	0	0	0

Going (Turf): Sf: 0-1 GS: 0-1 Gd: 0-2 GF: 0-3 Fm: 0-0
Distance: 5f/6f: 0-3 7f-8f: 0-3 9f-13f: 0-2 14f+: 0-0
Track : LH: 0-2 RH: 0-1 Tight: 0-2 Gall: 0-1
Aids: Bl: 0-0 Vi: 0-0 Tstrap: 0-0
Best Rating: 24 3/01 Ling 1m2f stand

Knight's Emperor (IRE)

105 **56**
4-y-o b g Grand Lodge (USA)-So Kind (Kind Of Hush)
J L Spearing M Olden

Placings:0/40060-0226000 **(3957)**
2001: 7^{0}GF, 8^{2}G, 8^{2}GF, 7^{6}GF, 8^{0}GF, 8^{0}G, 9^{0}GF

	Starts	1st	2nd	3rd	Win & Pl
Career Total (Turf)	13	0	2	0	2647

Going (Turf): Sf: 0-0 GS: 0-1 Gd: 0-4 GF: 0-7 Fm: 0-1
Distance: 5f/6f: 0-1 7f-8f: 0-5 9f-13f: 0-7 14f+: 0-0
Track : LH: 0-3 RH: 0-4 Tight: 0-2 Gall: 0-1
Aids: Bl: 0-1 Vi: 0-0 Tstrap: 0-0
Best Rating: 56 6/01 Bevl 7f100y gd-fm

Knighted

104 **69**
5-y-o b g Bigstone (IRE)-Missed Again (High Top)
T D Easterby Elite Racing Club

Placings:363/00/10500 **(5692)**
2001: 18^{1}S, 16^{0}HY, 16^{5}S, 16^{0}GF, 16^{0}S

	Starts	1st	2nd	3rd	Win & Pl		
Career Total (Turf)	10	1	0	2	8241		
68	3/01	Donc	2m2f	C(0-90)H		SFT	£7312

Total win prize-money £7313

Going (Turf): Sf: 1-4 GS: 0-0 Gd: 0-3 GF: 0-3 Fm: 0-0					

Going (Turf): Sf: 1-4 GS: 0-0 Gd: 0-3 GF: 0-3 Fm: 0-0
Distance: 5f/6f: 0-0 7f-8f: 0-3 9f-13f: 0-2 **14f+: 1-5**
Track : **LH: 1-5** RH: 0-4 Tight: 0-3 **Gall: 1-3**
Aids: Bl: 0-0 Vi: 0-0 Tstrap: 0-0
Best Rating: 69 4/01 Ripn 2m soft

Lightly raced, he was fit from a hurdling campaign when scoring on his seasonal bow in 2001 over two miles two. He relishes a test of stamina. Best with give.

Knock (IRE)

103(100) (75)**76**
3-y-o b c Mujadil (USA)-Beechwood (USA) (Blushing Groom (FR))
R Hannon Mrs Suzanne Costello-Haloute

Placings:41524304**31**-**5**30010460 **(4279)**
2001: 6^{5}SW, 6^{3}GS, 6^{0}GF, 6^{0}G, 7^{1}GF, 7^{0}GS, 7^{4}GF, 8^{6}GF, 7^{0}GF

	Starts	1st	2nd	3rd	Win & Pl		
Career Total (Turf)	16	2	1	2	13069		
Career Total (AW)	3	1	0	1	3802		
68	6/01	Gdwd	7f	D(0-75)		G-F	£4631
75	12/00	Ling	7f	D		STD	£3406
74	6/00	Brig	5f213y	E		G-F	£2886

Total win prize-money £10923

Going (Turf): Sf: 0-2 GS: 0-2 Gd: 0-4 **GF: 2-8** Fm: 0-0
Distance: 5f/6f: 1-8 **7f-8f: 2-10** 9f-13f: 0-1 14f+: 0-0
Track : **LH: 2-9** RH: 1-4 **Tight: 1-5** Gall: 0-1
Aids: Bl: 0-0 Vi: 0-0 Tstrap: 0-0
Best Rating: 77 5/01 Brig 6f209y gd-sft

Knockdoo (IRE)

102 **45**
8-y-o ch g Be My Native (USA)-Ashken (Artaius (USA))
J J O'Neill Strathayr Publishing Ltd

Placings:000/113065/000/0403-22 **(0879)**
2001: 17^{2}HY, 21^{2}S

	Starts	1st	2nd	3rd	Win & Pl		
Career Total (Turf)	18	2	2	2	10179		
60	4/98	Cork	1m4f	(0-90)H		SH	£4795
66	4/98	Naas	1m3f	(0-70)H		SH	£2740

Total win prize-money £7535

Going (Turf): Sf: 0-3 GS: 0-0 Gd: 0-2 GF: 0-0 Fm: 0-1
Distance: 5f/6f: 0-0 7f-8f: 0-1 **9f-13f: 2-11** 14f+: 0-5
Track : LH: 1-8 RH: 1-9 Tight: 0-0 Gall: 0-0
Aids: Bl: 0-0 Vi: 0-1 Tstrap: 0-0
Best Rating: 45 4/01 Pont 2m5f122y soft

Knockemback Nellie

104(96) (51)**61**
5-y-o b m Forzando-Sea Clover (IRE) (Ela-Mana-Mou)
P W Harris Resplendent Racing Limited

Placings:060002024/55005/000121005005002**00**-05310205250 **(4950)**
2001: 5^{0}HY, 5^{5}GF, 5^{3}G, 5^{1}F, 5^{0}GF, 5^{2}GF, 5^{0}GF, 5^{5}F, 5^{2}G, 5^{5}G, 5^{0}G

	Starts	1st	2nd	3rd	Win & Pl		
Career Total (Turf)	39	3	5	1	13542		
Career Total (AW)	3	0	1	0	505		
61	6/01	Brig	5f59y	F(0-65)H		FRM	£2254
66	6/00	Sand	5f6y	E		G-F	£3493
65	5/00	Ling	5f	E(0-70)H		HVY	£2912

Total win prize-money £8660

Going (Turf): Sf: 1-4 GS: 0-5 Gd: 0-10 **GF: 1-14 Fm: 1-6**
Distance: **5f/6f: 3-39** 7f-8f: 0-3 9f-13f: 0-0 14f+: 0-0
Track : **LH: 1-13** RH: 0-6 Tight: 0-4 Gall: 0-10
Aids: **Bl: 3-26** Vi: 0-0 Tstrap: 0-3
Best Rating: 61 8/01 Leic 5f2y good

Knockholt

106 **91**
5-y-o b g Be My Chief (USA)-Saffron Crocus (Shareef Dancer (USA))
S P C Woods S P C Woods

Placings:61623101/000100-00420 **(3246)**
2001: 16^{0}G, 14^{0}GF, 16^{4}G, 14^{2}GF, 13^{0}GF

	Starts	1st	2nd	3rd	Win & Pl		
Career Total (Turf)	19	4	2	1	53767		
95	7/00	Newb	2m	B(0-105)H		G-F	£10156
97	9/99	Donc	1m6f132y	B(0-105)H		G-F	£20812
91	7/99	Gdwd	1m6f	C(0-95)H		FRM	£9750
83	5/99	Sals	1m4f	D		G-F	£3647

Total win prize-money £44368

Going (Turf): Sf: 0-1 GS: 0-1 Gd: 0-7 **GF: 3-9** Fm: 1-1
Distance: 5f/6f: 0-0 7f-8f: 0-0 9f-13f: 1-3 **14f+: 3-16**
Track : LH: 2-7 RH: 2-11 **Tight: 2-5** Gall: 1-10
Aids: Bl: 0-0 Vi: 0-3 Tstrap: 0-0
Best Rating: 93 5/01 Gdwd 1m6f gd-fm

A tough stayer who is best when allowed to dominate in small fields. Prefers fast ground and is on a winning mark. Has won over two miles.

Knocktopher Abbey

105 **76**
4-y-o ch g Pursuit Of Love-Kukri (Kris)
B R Millman Seasons Holidays

Placings:420331600/50536500-023602660 **(5019)**
2001: 8^{0}GF, 7^{2}F, 7^{3}F, 8^{6}GF, 8^{0}GF, 8^{2}GF, 8^{6}G, 7^{6}GF, 8^{0}S

	Starts	1st	2nd	3rd	Win & Pl		
Career Total (Turf)	26	1	3	4	10836		
70	7/99	Chep	6f16y	E		G-F	£2794

Total win prize-money £2794

Going (Turf): Sf: 0-4 GS: 0-3 Gd: 0-5 **GF: 1-11** Fm: 0-3
Distance: 5f/6f: 0-5 **7f-8f: 1-16** 9f-13f: 0-5 14f+: 0-0
Track : LH: 0-6 RH: 0-5 Tight: 0-3 Gall: 0-4
Aids: Bl: 0-0 Vi: 0-0 Tstrap: 0-0
Best Rating: 76 7/01 Asct 1m gd-fm

A useful performer, but he has not won since his two-year-old days. Stays a mile and acts on an easy surface, but probably better on faster ground.

Knotty Ash Girl (IRE)

92 **72**
2-y-o ch f Ashkalani (IRE)-Camisha (IRE) (Shernazar)
B A McMahon W D McClennon

Placings:4332 **(5115)**
2001: 6^{4}GS, 6^{3}G, 7^{3}HY, 9^{2}HY

	Starts	1st	2nd	3rd	Win & Pl
Career Total (Turf)	4	0	1	2	2123

Going (Turf): Sf: 0-2 GS: 0-1 Gd: 0-1 GF: 0-0 Fm: 0-0
Distance: 5f/6f: 0-1 7f-8f: 0-2 9f-13f: 0-1 14f+: 0-0
Track : LH: 0-2 RH: 0-0 Tight: 0-0 Gall: 0-0
Aids: Bl: 0-0 Vi: 0-0 Tstrap: 0-0
Best Rating: 72 10/01 Nott 1m1f213y heavy

In the frame in maidens, and in a nursery when stepped up to ten furlongs.

Knotty Hill

96(90) (24)**23**
9-y-o b g Green Ruby (USA)-Esilam (Frimley Park)
R Craggs Ray Craggs

Placings:5263003B/**1020**2030000/**54020120000**/0/0-000006 **(4255)**
2001: 8^{0}SD, 7^{0}SW, 6^{0}SD, 6^{0}G, 8^{0}S, 6^{6}GF

	Starts	1st	2nd	3rd	Win & Pl		
Career Total (Turf)	28	1	4	3	8762		
Career Total (AW)	10	1	1	0	5903		
59	5/98	Haml	6f5y	F(0-60)		SFT	£2696
79	2/97	Sthl	7f	D		STD	£3969

Total win prize-money £6665

Going (Turf): Sf: 1-6 GS: 0-4 Gd: 0-7 GF: 0-9 Fm: 0-2
Distance: 5f/6f: 0-14 **7f-8f: 2-23** 9f-13f: 0-1 14f+: 0-0
Track : **LH: 1-18** RH: 0-2 Tight: 0-6 Gall: 0-2
Aids: Bl: 0-0 Vi: 0-0 Tstrap: 0-0
Best Rating: 32 8/01 Rdcr 6f gd-fm

On the downgrade since last winning a race in May 1998.

Known Maneuver (USA)

98(98) (78+)68

3-y-o b c Known Fact (USA)-Northernmaneuver (USA) (Al Nasr (FR))

P F I Cole The Blandford Partnership

Placings:10503 (4952)

2001: 6^{1}SD, 6^{0}GF, 12^{5}GF, 8^{0}GF, 11^{3}G

	Starts	1st	2nd	3rd	Win & Pl
Career Total (Turf)	4	0	0	1	794
Career Total (AW)	1	1	0	0	2786

78 6/01 Sthl 6f D STD £2786

Total win prize-money £2786

Going (Turf): Sf: 0-0 GS: 0-0 Gd: 0-1 GF: 0-3 Fm: 0-0
Distance: 5f/6f: 1-2 7f-8f: 0-0 9f-13f: 0-3 14f+: 0-0
Track : LH: 1-2 RH: 0-1 Tight: 0-1 Gall: 0-1
Aids: Bl: 0-0 Vi: 0-0 Tstrap: 0-0
Best Rating: 78 6/01 Sthl 6f stand

Made a winning debut on the Southwell Fibresand, but has shown little since being stepped up in trip. Suited by six furlongs plus.

Koincidental (IRE)

63 49d

4-y-o b f Mtoto-Floris (Master Willie)

C Grant W Raw

Placings:6000550-0 (0741)

2001: 14^{0}GS

	Starts	1st	2nd	3rd	Win & Pl
Career Total (Turf)	8	0	0	0	0

Going (Turf): Sf: 0-1 GS: 0-1 Gd: 0-3 GF: 0-3 Fm: 0-0
Distance: 5f/6f: 0-0 7f-8f: 0-2 9f-13f: 0-5 14f+: 0-1
Track : LH: 0-3 RH: 0-3 Tight: 0-3 Gall: 0-0
Aids: Bl: 0-0 Vi: 0-0 Tstrap: 0-0

Kokopelli Star

69 43

2-y-o b f Hernando (FR)-Celebrity (Troy)

B Smart J A Griffin

Placings:0 (5460)

2001: 8^{0}G

	Starts	1st	2nd	3rd	Win & Pl
Career Total (Turf)	1	0	0	0	

Going (Turf): Sf: 0-0 GS: 0-0 Gd: 0-1 GF: 0-0 Fm: 0-0
Distance: 5f/6f: 0-0 7f-8f: 0-0 9f-13f: 0-1 14f+: 0-0
Track : LH: 0-1 RH: 0-0 Tight: 0-1 Gall: 0-0
Aids: Bl: 0-0 Vi: 0-0 Tstrap: 0-0
Best Rating: 43 10/01 Bath 1m5y good

Kollegio (IRE)

83 50

2-y-o b c College Chapel-Steal 'Em (Efisio)

P W Harris Bain, Edrich, Gregory & Hassett

Placings:0000 (5127)

2001: 6^{0}G, 5^{0}GF, 5^{0}GF, 7^{0}HY

	Starts	1st	2nd	3rd	Win & Pl
Career Total (Turf)	4	0	0	0	

Going (Turf): Sf: 0-1 GS: 0-0 Gd: 0-1 GF: 0-2 Fm: 0-0
Distance: 5f/6f: 0-3 7f-8f: 0-1 9f-13f: 0-0 14f+: 0-0
Track : LH: 0-0 RH: 0-0 Tight: 0-0 Gall: 0-0
Aids: Bl: 0-0 Vi: 0-0 Tstrap: 0-0
Best Rating: 50 8/01 Folk 6f good

Komaluna

90(100) (38)43d

3-y-o ch g Komaite (USA)-Sugar Token (Record Token)

D Shaw Mrs P A Barratt

Placings:00000-4603 (2236)

2001: 5^{4}SD, 6^{6}SD, 7^{0}G, 5^{3}GF

	Starts	1st	2nd	3rd	Win & Pl
Career Total (Turf)	7	0	0	1	326
Career Total (AW)	2	0	0	0	0

Going (Turf): Sf: 0-1 GS: 0-0 Gd: 0-4 GF: 0-2 Fm: 0-0
Distance: 5f/6f: 0-8 7f-8f: 0-1 9f-13f: 0-0 14f+: 0-0
Track : LH: 0-3 RH: 0-0 Tight: 0-0 Gall: 0-0
Aids: Bl: 0-0 Vi: 0-0 Tstrap: 0-1
Best Rating: 40 6/01 Brig 5f213y gd-fm

Komaseph

(99) (27)

9-y-o b g Komaite (USA)-Starkist (So Blessed)

R F Marvin Mrs M A Marvin

Placings:026000/1620100000/000050/3606400000000 2-040600 (0490)

2001: 8^{0}SD, 6^{4}SW, 6^{0}SW, 6^{6}SD, 7^{0}SW, 6^{0}SD

	Starts	1st	2nd	3rd	Win & Pl
Career Total (Turf)	7	0	0	0	0
Career Total (AW)	35	2	3	1	6952

58 8/98 Sthl 6f F(0-65)H STD £2721
51 1/98 Sthl 6f F(0-55) STD £2085

Total win prize-money £4806

Going (Turf): Sf: 0-1 GS: 0-0 Gd: 0-2 GF: 0-4 Fm: 0-0
Distance: 5f/6f: 2-30 7f-8f: 0-11 9f-13f: 0-1 14f+: 0-0
Track : LH: 2-33 RH: 0-0 Tight: 0-4 Gall: 0-0
Aids: Bl: 0-7 Vi: 0-2 Tstrap: 0-12
Best Rating: 27 2/01 Sthl 6f slow

Komedera

88 63

2-y-o b g Danzig Connection (USA)-Musica (Primo Dominie)

A Berry J M Ranson

Placings:2660 (4801)

2001: 6^{2}GF, 5^{6}GS, 5^{6}GF, 5^{0}F

	Starts	1st	2nd	3rd	Win & Pl
Career Total (Turf)	4	0	1	0	872

Going (Turf): Sf: 0-0 GS: 0-1 Gd: 0-0 GF: 0-2 Fm: 0-1
Distance: 5f/6f: 0-4 7f-8f: 0-0 9f-13f: 0-0 14f+: 0-0
Track : LH: 0-1 RH: 0-0 Tight: 0-0 Gall: 0-0
Aids: Bl: 0-0 Vi: 0-0 Tstrap: 0-0
Best Rating: 63 7/01 Newc 6f gd-fm

A half-brother to five-furlong winner Coco de Mer. He ran with credit on his debut at Newcastle, but has been disappointing since. Stays six furlongs. Acts on fast ground.

Komena

84 45

3-y-o b f Komaite (USA)-Mena (Blakeney)

J W Payne The Frankland Lodgers

Placings:42140-000 (5608)

2001: 7^{0}GF, 7^{0}GS, 7^{0}GS

	Starts	1st	2nd	3rd	Win & Pl
Career Total (Turf)	8	1	1	0	5209

82 8/00 Brig 5f213y F FRM £2341

Total win prize-money £2342

Going (Turf): Sf: 0-0 GS: 0-3 Gd: 0-2 GF: 0-2 **Fm: 1-1**
Distance: **5f/6f: 1-3** 7f-8f: 0-5 9f-13f: 0-0 14f+: 0-0
Track : **LH: 1-2** RH: 0-1 Tight: 1-1 Gall: 0-1
Aids: Bl: 0-0 Vi: 0-0 Tstrap: 0-0
Best Rating: 45 6/01 Epsm 7f gd-fm

Kompliment

92 78

3-y-o ch g Komaite (USA)-Eladale (IRE) (Ela-Mana-Mou)

Mrs H Dalton Ray Bailey

Placings:5130-000 (2742)

2001: 5^{0}F, 6^{0}GF, 5^{0}GF

	Starts	1st	2nd	3rd	Win & Pl
Career Total (Turf)	7	1	0	1	8711

82 5/00 Ches 5f16y D GD £7085

Total win prize-money £7085

Going (Turf): Sf: 0-1 GS: 0-1 **Gd: 1-1** GF: 0-3 Fm: 0-1
Distance: **5f/6f: 1-7** 7f-8f: 0-0 9f-13f: 0-0 14f+: 0-0
Track : **LH: 1-1** RH: 0-1 **Tight: 1-1** Gall: 0-1
Aids: Bl: 0-0 Vi: 0-0 Tstrap: 0-0
Best Rating: 74 6/01 Kemp 6f gd-fm

Konica

87 69

2-y-o b f Desert King (IRE)-Haboobti (Habitat)

P S Felgate S J Booth

Placings:606 (5109)

2001: 6^{0}GF, 5^{0}HY, 6^{0}HY

	Starts	1st	2nd	3rd	Win & Pl
Career Total (Turf)	3	0	0	0	0

Going (Turf): Sf: 0-2 GS: 0-0 Gd: 0-0 GF: 0-1 Fm: 0-0
Distance: 5f/6f: 0-1 7f-8f: 0-2 9f-13f: 0-0 14f+: 0-0
Track : LH: 0-0 RH: 0-0 Tight: 0-0 Gall: 0-0
Aids: Bl: 0-0 Vi: 0-0 Tstrap: 0-0
Best Rating: 69 10/01 Nott 6f15y heavy

Konker

100 70

6-y-o ch g Selkirk (USA)-Helens Dreamgirl (Caerleon (USA))

Mrs M Reveley J & M Leisure / Unos Restaurant

Placings:605/3351500/06/0031-3114 (5538)

2001: 9^{3}HY, 12^{1}GS, 10^{1}HY, 10^{4}S

	Starts	1st	2nd	3rd	Win & Pl
Career Total (Turf)	20	4	0	4	14795

70 10/01 Newc 1m2f32y F(0-60)H HVY £2751
58 10/01 Pont 1m4f8y F(0-60)H G-S £3143
56 10/00 Newc 1m2f32y F(0-60)H HVY £3090
69 5/98 Newb 1m2f6y E GD £3168

Total win prize-money £12153

Going (Turf): Sf: 2-7 GS: 1-3 Gd: 1-3 GF: 0-6 Fm: 0-1
Distance: 5f/6f: 0-1 7f-8f: 0-1 **9f-13f: 4-18** 14f+: 0-0
Track : **LH: 4-14** RH: 0-5 Tight: 0-6 **Gall: 3-5**
Aids: Bl: 0-0 Vi: 0-0 Tstrap: 0-0
Best Rating: 70 10/01 Newc 1m2f32y heavy

Kool (IRE)

100 94

2-y-o b c Danehill Dancer (IRE)-New Rochelle (IRE) (Lafontaine (USA))

P F I Cole Andy J Smith

Placings:6222120 (5140)

2001: 5^{6}GS, 5^{2}GF, 5^{2}GF, 5^{2}GF, 5^{1}GF, 6^{2}GS, 6^{0}G

	Starts	1st	2nd	3rd	Win & Pl
Career Total (Turf)	7	1	4	0	19801

79 8/01 Pont 5f D G-F £5902

Total win prize-money £5902

Going (Turf): Sf: 0-0 GS: 0-2 Gd: 0-1 **GF: 1-4** Fm: 0-0
Distance: **5f/6f: 1-7** 7f-8f: 0-0 9f-13f: 0-0 14f+: 0-0
Track : **LH: 1-2** RH: 0-1 Tight: 0-0 Gall: 0-2
Aids: Bl: 0-0 Vi: 0-0 Tstrap: 0-0
Best Rating: 94 9/01 Donc 6f gd-sft

A 72,000gns half-brother to mile juvenile winner Tower Of Song, he has shown plenty of promise although he hung right and threw away the advantage on his fourth run. Finally got off the mark at Pontefract in August, before finishing second in a Doncaster Sales race, in which he had won the race on his side, but he was disappointing after that in a Newmarket nursery. A free-running sort, he has proved most effective at five and six furlongs on most ground.

Koori

(70) (14)

3-y-o b f Komaite (USA)-Unadorned (Never So Bold)

B A Pearce Richard J Gray

Placings:0-0 (0090)

2001: 6^{0}SD

	Starts	1st	2nd	3rd	Win & Pl
Career Total (Turf)	1	0	0	0	

Career Total (AW) 1 0 0 0

Going (Turf): Sf: 0-0 GS: 0-0 Gd: 0-1 GF: 0-0 Fm: 0-0
Distance: 5f/6f: 0-2 7f-8f: 0-0 9f-13f: 0-0 14f+: 0-0
Track : LH: 0-1 RH: 0-0 Tight: 0-1 Gall: 0-0
Aids: Bl: 0-0 Vi: 0-0 Tstrap: 0-0
Best Rating: 14 1/01 Ling 6f stand

Kootenay (IRE)

96 **98**
2-y-o ch f Selkirk (USA)-Llia (Shirley Heights)
J L Dunlop Capt J Macdonald-Buchanan

Placings:41312 (5356a)
2001: 7^{4}GF, 7^{1}G, 7^{3}GS, 7^{1}HY, 8^{2}GS

	Starts	1st	2nd	3rd	Win & Pl
Career Total (Turf)	5	2	1	1	81766

98 9/01 Siro 7f110y HVY £41071
86 8/01 Gdwd 7f D GD £10676
Total win prize-money £51747

Going (Turf): Sf: 1-1 GS: 0-2 Gd: 1-1 GF: 0-1 Fm: 0-0
Distance: 5f/6f: 0-0 7f-8f: 2-5 9f-13f: 0-0 14f+: 0-0
Track : LH: 0-0 RH: 2-5 Tight: 0-0 Gall: 0-1
Aids: Bl: 0-0 Vi: 0-0 Tstrap: 0-0
Best Rating: 98 9/01 Siro 7f110y heavy

Improved from her debut to win over seven furlongs at Goodwood next time. Scored in Listed company at Sandown, and is suited by soft ground. Should get further than a mile at three.

Kosevo (IRE)

85(99) (27)**40**
7-y-o b g Shareef Dancer (USA)-Kallista (Zeddaan)
J Balding (D Shaw 14/6) K Nicholls

Placings:5/005455/0420211050205005226 0/32055030 20452563551026000/000005200000003000610466200-0200000600000 (4255)
2001: 6^{0}SD, 6^{2}SD, 5^{0}SD, 6^{0}SW, 5^{0}SD, 6^{0}SD, 5^{0}SW, 5^{6}SD, 5^{0}SD, 7^{0}F, 5^{0}GF, 6^{0}GF, 5^{0}S, 6^{0}GF

	Starts	1st	2nd	3rd	Win & Pl
Career Total (Turf)	43	2	1	2	12130
Career Total (AW)	50	2	11	2	13890

40 9/00 Yarm 6f3y F(0-60)H G-F £2135
58 7/99 Hayd 5f D(0-80)H FRM £7555
54 7/98 Sthl 7f D(0-80)H STD £3590
58 7/98 Sthl 7f G STD £1987
Total win prize-money £15268

Going (Turf): Sf: 0-4 GS: 0-1 Gd: 0-9 GF: 1-24 Fm: 1-5
Distance: 5f/6f: 1-60 7f-8f: 3-30 9f-13f: 0-3 14f+: 0-0
Track : LH: 2-53 RH: 0-3 Tight: 0-21 Gall: 0-1
Aids: Bl: 3-34 Vi: 1-51 Tstrap: 0-0
Best Rating: 46 1/01 Ling 6f stand

A moderate sprinter with a low strike rate. He runs regularly on the All-Weather, but his last two wins have been on fast ground on turf.

Kosmic Lady

(95) (47)**52**
4-y-o b f Cosmonaut-Ktolo (Tolomeo)
P W Hiatt P J Morgan

Placings:00003054-01200200 (5592)
2001: 8^{0}SD, 6^{1}GS, 8^{2}G, 10^{0}GS, 10^{0}S, 8^{2}GF, 7^{0}S, 6^{0}GS

	Starts	1st	2nd	3rd	Win & Pl
Career Total (Turf)	12	1	2	1	3424
Career Total (AW)	4	0	0	0	0

44 4/01 Brig 6f209y G G-S £1911
Total win prize-money £1911

Going (Turf): Sf: 0-5 GS: 1-4 Gd: 0-1 GF: 0-2 Fm: 0-0
Distance: 5f/6f: 0-0 7f-8f: 1-7 9f-13f: 0-9 14f+: 0-0
Track : LH: 1-10 RH: 0-1 Tight: 0-4 Gall: 0-1
Aids: Bl: 0-1 Vi: 0-0 Tstrap: 0-2
Best Rating: 52 5/01 Wwck 1m22y gd-fm

Kotori (IRE)

82 **57**
2-y-o gr g Charnwood Forest (IRE)-La Kermesse (USA) (Storm Bird (CAN))
M S Saunders D Naylor

Placings:000 (5037)
2001: 5^{0}GS, 5^{0}S, 5^{0}G

	Starts	1st	2nd	3rd	Win & Pl
Career Total (Turf)	3	0	0	0	

Going (Turf): Sf: 0-1 GS: 0-1 Gd: 0-1 GF: 0-0 Fm: 0-0
Distance: 5f/6f: 0-3 7f-8f: 0-0 9f-13f: 0-0 14f+: 0-0
Track : LH: 0-1 RH: 0-1 Tight: 0-0 Gall: 0-2
Aids: Bl: 0-0 Vi: 0-0 Tstrap: 0-0
Best Rating: 57 8/01 Chep 5f16y soft

Krato (USA)

103 **84d**
5-y-o b h Theatrical-Claxton's Slew (USA) (Seattle Slew (USA))
T D Easterby M P Burke

Placings:51P0/312361-00006600 (4315)
2001: 6^{0}S, 5^{0}G, 5^{0}GF, 8^{0}GF, 8^{6}GF, 7^{6}G, 9^{0}GS, 8^{0}G

	Starts	1st	2nd	3rd	Win & Pl
Career Total (Turf)	18	3	1	2	49060

9/00 Belm 1m FRM £16829
3/00 Gulf 1m110y FRM £13537
10/99 Belm 1m110y SFT £15181
Total win prize-money £45547

Going (Turf): Sf: 1-2 GS: 0-1 Gd: 0-3 GF: 0-3 Fm: 2-8
Distance: 5f/6f: 0-3 7f-8f: 1-8 9f-13f: 2-6 14f+: 0-0
Track : LH: 0-2 RH: 0-2 Tight: 0-1 Gall: 0-2
Aids: Bl: 2-4 Vi: 0-0 Tstrap: 0-0
Best Rating: 84 6/01 Newc 1m gd-fm

A five-length winner of an allowance race over a mile on turf at Belmont Park last term, he had earlier been third, half a length behind Barrister, in the same grade at Saratoga. Has cut little ice in Britain so far.

Kriskova (USA)

105 **97**
2-y-o br c Kris S (USA)-Tereshkova (USA) (Mr Prospector (USA))
D R Loder Maktoum Al Maktoum

Placings:13 (4781)
2001: 7^{1}GF, 8^{3}G

	Starts	1st	2nd	3rd	Win & Pl
Career Total (Turf)	2	1	0	1	8905

87 7/01 Sand 7f16y D G-F £6825
Total win prize-money £6825

Going (Turf): Sf: 0-0 GS: 0-0 Gd: 0-1 GF: 1-1 Fm: 0-0
Distance: 5f/6f: 0-0 7f-8f: 1-2 9f-13f: 0-0 14f+: 0-0
Track : LH: 0-0 RH: 1-2 Tight: 0-0 Gall: 0-0
Aids: Bl: 0-0 Vi: 0-0 Tstrap: 0-0
Best Rating: 97 9/01 Gdwd 1m good

A game winner over seven furlongs at Sandown first time out. Dam won the Prix Cabourg and ran second in Group One at two, and is a sister to the Middle Park winner Lycius and half-sister to high-class US turf performer Akabir. Third to Henri Labasque in a Listed event over a mile at Goodwood.

Kristensen

93 **69**
2-y-o ch g Kris S (USA)-Papaha (FR) (Green Desert (USA))
Mrs J R Ramsden Mrs J R Ramsden

Placings:330305 (4856)
2001: 6^{3}GF, 5^{3}F, 5^{0}GF, 6^{3}GF, 7^{0}G, 7^{5}GF

	Starts	1st	2nd	3rd	Win & Pl
Career Total (Turf)	6	0	0	3	2327

Going (Turf): Sf: 0-0 GS: 0-0 Gd: 0-1 GF: 0-4 Fm: 0-1
Distance: 5f/6f: 0-4 7f-8f: 0-2 9f-13f: 0-0 14f+: 0-0
Track : LH: 0-2 RH: 0-0 Tight: 0-1 Gall: 0-0
Aids: Bl: 0-0 Vi: 0-0 Tstrap: 0-0
Best Rating: 69 9/01 York 6f gd-fm

Kristineau

88 **62d**
3-y-o ch f Cadeaux Genereux-Kantikoy (Alzao (USA))
C F Wall Kieran D Scott

Placings:00-520000 (4908)
2001: 7^{5}S, 8^{2}S, 8^{0}HY, 8^{0}G, 9^{0}GF, 9^{0}G

	Starts	1st	2nd	3rd	Win & Pl
Career Total (Turf)	8	0	1	0	584

Going (Turf): Sf: 0-5 GS: 0-0 Gd: 0-2 GF: 0-1 Fm: 0-0
Distance: 5f/6f: 0-0 7f-8f: 0-3 9f-13f: 0-5 14f+: 0-0
Track : LH: 0-3 RH: 0-1 Tight: 0-0 Gall: 0-0
Aids: Bl: 0-0 Vi: 0-0 Tstrap: 0-0
Best Rating: 62 4/01 Nott 1m54y soft

Kroisos (IRE)

86(100) (43)**44**
3-y-o b g Kris-Lydia Maria (Dancing Brave (USA))
P W Harris Kris Connections

Placings:005020 (4483)
2001: 11^{0}GF, 12^{0}GF, 12^{5}GF, 16^{0}GF, 12^{2}SD, 14^{0}S

	Starts	1st	2nd	3rd	Win & Pl
Career Total (Turf)	5	0	0	0	0
Career Total (AW)	1	0	1	0	520

Going (Turf): Sf: 0-1 GS: 0-0 Gd: 0-0 GF: 0-4 Fm: 0-0
Distance: 5f/6f: 0-0 7f-8f: 0-0 9f-13f: 0-4 14f+: 0-2
Track : LH: 0-2 RH: 0-4 Tight: 0-3 Gall: 0-0
Aids: Bl: 0-0 Vi: 0-0 Tstrap: 0-0
Best Rating: 52 6/01 Leic 1m3f183y gd-fm

Krugerrand (USA)

104 **77**
2-y-o ch c Gulch (USA)-Nasers Pride (USA) (Al Nasr (FR))
M L W Bell Highclere Thoroughbred Racing Ltd

Placings:321 (4722)
2001: 6^{3}GF, 6^{2}GS, 7^{1}GF

	Starts	1st	2nd	3rd	Win & Pl
Career Total (Turf)	3	1	1	1	5560

77 9/01 Wwck 7f26y D G-F £3932
Total win prize-money £3933

Going (Turf): Sf: 0-0 GS: 0-1 Gd: 0-0 GF: 1-2 Fm: 0-0
Distance: 5f/6f: 0-1 7f-8f: 1-2 9f-13f: 0-0 14f+: 0-0
Track : LH: 1-1 RH: 0-0 Tight: 0-0 Gall: 0-0
Aids: Bl: 0-0 Vi: 0-0 Tstrap: 1-1
Best Rating: 77 9/01 Wwck 7f26y gd-fm

Showed ability on his debut and was just touched off at odds-on at Lingfield next time. Got off the mark at odds of 1/4 at Warwick next time but made very hard work of it.

Krystal Max (IRE)

102(106) (75)**62**
8-y-o b g Classic Music (USA)-Lake Isle (IRE) (Caerleon (USA))
P S McEntee M A Shipman

Placings:14346611/11605000/231500000/2111036/111 13222420/2511126-623043160060 0236000 (4075)
2001: 6^{6}SD, 5^{2}SD, 6^{3}SD, 5^{0}SW, 5^{4}SW, 7^{3}SW, 6^{1}SW, 5^{6}SW, 6^{0}SD, 6^{0}SD, 5^{6}F, 6^{0}GF, 6^{0}GF, 5^{2}GF, 5^{3}G, 6^{6}G, 5^{0}G, 5^{0}G, 5^{0}G

	Starts	1st	2nd	3rd	Win & Pl
Career Total (Turf)	21	1	1	2	6497
Career Total (AW)	48	16	9	5	58336

75 2/01 Ling 6f D(0-80)H SLW £3727
74 7/00 Ling 7f F STD £2299
59 7/00 Ling 5f F STD £2236
67 1/00 Ling 6f F STD £2009
78 2/99 Wolv 6f F STD £2067
70 1/99 Ling 5f E STD £2545
70 1/99 Ling 5f E STD £2583
66 1/99 Ling 6f E STD £2608
79 3/98 Ling 5f D(0-85)H STD £3355

75	3/98	Sthl	5f	D(0-85)H	STD	£3517
65	2/98	Ling	6f	C(0-90)H	SLW	£5353
67	1/97	Ling	5f	E	STD	£2726
82	2/96	Ling	7f	F	STD	£2517
82	1/96	Ling	5f	D(0-80)H	STD	£3655
84	12/95	Ling	6f	D	STD	£3420
84	12/95	Sthl	5f	E(0-75)	STD	£3038
78	6/95	Rdcr	5f	D	FRM	£3598

Total win prize-money £51260

Going (Turf): Sf: 0-0 GS: 0-2 Gd: 0-9 GF: 0-7 **Fm: 1-3**
Distance: **5f/6f: 15-60** 7f-8f: 2-9 9f-13f: 0-0 14f+: 0-0
Track : **LH: 14-54** RH: 0-1 **Tight: 14-43** Gall: 0-4
Aids: Bl: 0-1 Vi: 0-0 Tstrap: 0-0
Best Rating: 75 2/01 Ling 6f slow

Kulachi (IRE)

103 **94**
2-y-o b c Royal Applause-Silly View (IRE) (Scenic)
M R Channon Sheikh Ahmed Al Maktoum

Placings:14100 **(4833)**
2001: 6^{1}GF, 5^{4}GF, 6^{1}GF, 6^{0}G, 6^{0}GF

	Starts	1st	2nd	3rd	Win & Pl
Career Total (Turf)	5	2	0	0	18590

94	7/01	Newb	6f8y	A	G-F	£11275
84	6/01	Gdwd	6f	D	G-F	£4290

Total win prize-money £15565

Going (Turf): Sf: 0-0 GS: 0-0 Gd: 0-1 **GF: 2-4** Fm: 0-0
Distance: 5f/6f: 1-3 7f-8f: 1-2 9f-13f: 0-0 14f+: 0-0
Track : LH: 0-0 RH: 0-0 Tight: 0-0 Gall: 0-0
Aids: Bl: 0-0 Vi: 0-0 Tstrap: 0-0
Best Rating: 94 7/01 Newb 6f8y gd-fm

A half-brother to a winner in Sweden, he was impressive when winning over six furlongs on his Goodwood debut and confirmed that promise when running well in the Norfolk Stakes over five furlongs at Royal Ascot. He won a Listed race when stepped back up to 6f, but disappointed when stepped up to Group Two company in his next two starts.

Kumakawa

(106) (70)**60**
3-y-o ch g Dancing Spree (USA)-Maria Cappuccini (Siberian Express (USA))
M J Polglase Nilesh Unadkat

Placings:00001312i-324000002005000 **(5413)**
2001: 8^{3}SD, 7^{2}SD, 9^{4}SD, 10^{0}GS, 10^{0}S, 8^{0}GF, 7^{0}G, 8^{0}F, 7^{2}SD, 8^{0}SD, 8^{0}SD, 8^{5}SD, 7^{0}SD, 8^{0}SD, 8^{0}SD

	Starts	1st	2nd	3rd	Win & Pl
Career Total (Turf)	10	1	0	0	1939
Career Total (AW)	14	2	3	2	9218

78	12/00	Sthl	7f	E(0-75)	STD	£2205
71	11/00	Sthl	1m	F	STD	£2303
52	9/00	Leic	1m8y	G(0-65)	G-F	£1939

Total win prize-money £6447

Going (Turf): Sf: 0-1 GS: 0-1 Gd: 0-2 **GF: 1-4** Fm: 0-2
Distance: 5f/6f: 0-3 **7f-8f: 2-14** 9f-13f: 1-7 14f+: 0-0
Track : **LH: 2-16** RH: 0-2 Tight: 0-6 Gall: 0-2
Aids: Bl: 0-1 Vi: 0-1 Tstrap: 0-0
Best Rating: 85 6/01 Sthl 7f stand

Kumon Eileen

(85) (14)**46**
5-y-o ch m Anshan-Katie Eileen (USA) (Bering)
J R Jenkins The Royston Raiders

Placings:00/00-0 **(0249)**
2001: 13^{0}SW

	Starts	1st	2nd	3rd	Win & Pl
Career Total (Turf)	2	0	0	0	
Career Total (AW)	3	0	0	0	

Going (Turf): Sf: 0-0 GS: 0-0 Gd: 0-0 GF: 0-2 Fm: 0-0
Distance: 5f/6f: 0-0 7f-8f: 0-0 9f-13f: 0-5 14f+: 0-0
Track : LH: 0-3 RH: 0-2 Tight: 0-3 Gall: 0-1
Aids: Bl: 0-0 Vi: 0-1 Tstrap: 0-0

Kundalila

89 **29**
3-y-o b f River Falls-Kalou (K-Battery)
A C Whillans Miss E Johnston

Placings:0400-0P050 **(3308)**
2001: 8^{0}GF, 8^{P}GF, 8^{0}GF, 8^{5}GS, 7^{0}GS

	Starts	1st	2nd	3rd	Win & Pl
Career Total (Turf)	9	0	0	0	288

Going (Turf): Sf: 0-1 GS: 0-2 Gd: 0-1 GF: 0-5 Fm: 0-0
Distance: 5f/6f: 0-1 7f-8f: 0-5 9f-13f: 0-3 14f+: 0-0
Track : LH: 0-3 RH: 0-5 Tight: 0-4 Gall: 0-0
Aids: Bl: 0-0 Vi: 0-0 Tstrap: 0-0
Best Rating: 40 5/01 Ayr 1m gd-fm

Kundooz

96 **96**
2-y-o b c Sabrehill (USA)-Reem Albaraari (Sadler's Wells (USA))
M A Jarvis Sheikh Ahmed Al Maktoum

Placings:142 **(4943)**
2001: 7^{1}GF, 7^{4}GS, 7^{2}S

	Starts	1st	2nd	3rd	Win & Pl
Career Total (Turf)	3	1	1	0	9450

87	7/01	Donc	7f	C	G-F	£6825

Total win prize-money £6825

Going (Turf): Sf: 0-1 GS: 0-1 Gd: 0-0 **GF: 1-1** Fm: 0-0
Distance: 5f/6f: 0-0 **7f-8f: 1-3** 9f-13f: 0-0 14f+: 0-0
Track : LH: 0-1 RH: 0-0 Tight: 0-1 Gall: 0-0
Aids: Bl: 0-0 Vi: 0-0 Tstrap: 0-0
Best Rating: 96 8/01 NmkJ 7f gd-sft

A half-brother to Morshdi, he scored over seven furlongs at Doncaster in July, producing useful turn of foot. Good efforts since and will stay middle distances in time.

Kuster

108 **91**
5-y-o b h Indian Ridge-Ustka (Lomond (USA))
L M Cumani Lord Vestey

Placings:0/120/42405-56064100 **(5142)**
2001: 10^{5}FT, 12^{6}FT, 8^{0}GF, 10^{6}GF, 12^{4}GF, 9^{1}GF, 13^{0}G, 9^{0}G

	Starts	1st	2nd	3rd	Win & Pl
Career Total (Turf)	15	2	2	0	42266
Career Total (AW)	2	0	0	0	437

87	7/01	Gdwd	1m1f192yB	H	G-F	£32500
86	4/99	Epsm	1m114y	D	SFT	£4279

Total win prize-money £36780

Going (Turf): Sf: 1-6 GS: 0-1 Gd: 0-4 **GF: 1-4** Fm: 0-0
Distance: 5f/6f: 0-0 7f-8f: 0-1 **9f-13f: 2-15** 14f+: 0-1
Track : LH: 1-6 RH: 1-6 **Tight: 2-5** Gall: 0-6
Aids: **Bl: 1-3** Vi: 0-0 Tstrap: 0-0
Best Rating: 87 7/01 Gdwd 1m1f192y gd-fm

Appreciated the step up to middle distances last season and ran well without winning. Had two runs at Nad Al Sheba this spring, and had been running reasonably until scoring in first-time blinkers at Glorious Goodwood. Acts on fast, but best with cut.

Kustom Kit Kevin

91(95) (61)**20**
5-y-o b g Local Suitor (USA)-Sweet Revival (Claude Monet (USA))
S R Bowring Charterhouse Holdings Plc

Placings:60/322010000300000-00 **(3282)**
2001: 7^{0}GF, 8^{0}F

	Starts	1st	2nd	3rd	Win & Pl
Career Total (Turf)	13	0	0	1	357
Career Total (AW)	6	1	2	1	3781

59	2/00	Sthl	1m	F(0-60)H	STD	£1806

Total win prize-money £1806

Going (Turf): Sf: 0-1 GS: 0-2 Gd: 0-2 GF: 0-6 Fm: 0-2
Distance: 5f/6f: 0-0 **7f-8f: 1-12** 9f-13f: 0-7 14f+: 0-0
Track : **LH: 1-12** RH: 0-0 Tight: 0-2 Gall: 0-1
Aids: Bl: 0-1 Vi: 0-0 Tstrap: 0-5
Best Rating: 13 5/01 Thsk 7f gd-fm

Kut O Island (USA)

(90) (50)**61**
3-y-o br g Woodman (USA)-Cherry Jubilee (USA) (Coastal (USA))
G A Butler Mrs A K H Ooi

Placings:00-5 **(0487)**
2001: 8^{5}SD

	Starts	1st	2nd	3rd	Win & Pl
Career Total (Turf)	2	0	0	0	
Career Total (AW)	1	0	0	0	0

Going (Turf): Sf: 0-0 GS: 0-1 Gd: 0-1 GF: 0-0 Fm: 0-0
Distance: 5f/6f: 0-0 7f-8f: 0-3 9f-13f: 0-0 14f+: 0-0
Track : LH: 0-1 RH: 0-1 Tight: 0-0 Gall: 0-1
Aids: Bl: 0-0 Vi: 0-0 Tstrap: 0-2
Best Rating: 50 3/01 Sthl 1m stand

Kuuipo

104(92) (29)**42**
4-y-o b f Puissance-Yankee Special (Bold Lad (IRE))
B S Rothwell S P Hudson

Placings:46630600/0006026504-0400522000 **(2379)**
2001: 11^{0}SD, 9^{4}SW, 8^{0}SD, 9^{0}SD, 10^{5}HY, 8^{2}S, 9^{2}S, 10^{0}F, 8^{0}F, 8^{0}GF

	Starts	1st	2nd	3rd	Win & Pl
Career Total (Turf)	23	0	3	1	3724
Career Total (AW)	5	0	0	0	0

Going (Turf): Sf: 0-5 GS: 0-5 Gd: 0-3 GF: 0-7 Fm: 0-3
Distance: 5f/6f: 0-8 7f-8f: 0-6 9f-13f: 0-14 14f+: 0-0
Track : LH: 0-17 RH: 0-2 Tight: 0-5 Gall: 0-1
Aids: Bl: 0-0 Vi: 0-1 Tstrap: 0-20
Best Rating: 45 4/01 Ripn 1m soft

Kuwait Dawn (IRE)

89(95) (60)**48**
5-y-o b m Pips Pride-Red Note (Rusticaro (FR))
D Nicholls John E Lund

Placings:24000/100406000000/00060000-640000 **(2269)**
2001: 7^{6}SD, 7^{4}SD, 8^{0}SD, 9^{0}HY, 8^{0}F, 8^{0}G

	Starts	1st	2nd	3rd	Win & Pl
Career Total (Turf)	28	1	1	0	20377
Career Total (AW)	3	0	0	0	0

99	3/99	Donc	1m	C	G-S	£6775

Total win prize-money £6775

Going (Turf): Sf: 0-4 **GS: 1-5** Gd: 0-10 GF: 0-7 Fm: 0-2
Distance: 5f/6f: 0-2 **7f-8f: 1-21** 9f-13f: 0-8 14f+: 0-0
Track : LH: 0-10 RH: 0-7 Tight: 0-4 Gall: 0-3
Aids: Bl: 0-0 Vi: 0-2 Tstrap: 0-0
Best Rating: 60 4/01 Sthl 7f stand

Little to write home about this season.

Kuwait Flavour (IRE)

92(82) (21)**46**
5-y-o b g Bluebird (USA)-Plume Magique (Kenmare (FR))
G Prodromou George Prodromou

Placings:4/3/60450-000 **(4632)**
2001: 9^{0}SD, 10^{0}GF, 7^{0}GF

	Starts	1st	2nd	3rd	Win & Pl
Career Total (Turf)	8	0	0	1	1181
Career Total (AW)	2	0	0	0	0

Going (Turf): Sf: 0-1 GS: 0-1 Gd: 0-2 GF: 0-4 Fm: 0-0
Distance: 5f/6f: 0-2 7f-8f: 0-4 9f-13f: 0-4 14f+: 0-0
Track : LH: 0-5 RH: 0-2 Tight: 0-3 Gall: 0-0
Aids: Bl: 0-0 Vi: 0-0 Tstrap: 0-0

Best Rating: 46 9/01 Leic 7f9y gd-fm

Kuwait Millennium

87 **69**

4-y-o b g Salse (USA)-Lyphartissima (FR) (Lightning (FR))

M C Pipe Greenfield Stud

Placings:545-0 **(2305)**

2001: 20^{0}GF

	Starts	1st	2nd	3rd	Win & Pl
Career Total (Turf)	4	0	0	0	294

Going (Turf): Sf: 0-1 GS: 0-0 Gd: 0-1 GF: 0-2 Fm: 0-0
Distance: 5f/6f: 0-0 7f-8f: 0-0 9f-13f: 0-3 14f+: 0-1
Track : LH: 0-2 RH: 0-2 Tight: 0-1 Gall: 0-1
Aids: Bl: 0-0 Vi: 0-1 Tstrap: 0-0
Best Rating: 51 6/01 Asct 2m4f gd-fm

Kuwait Rose

107(66) (57)**68**

5-y-o b g Inchinor-Black Ivor (USA) (Sir Ivor)

Ferdy Murphy (K A Ryan 21/9) Mrs N L Spence

Placings:03626/4540250100-032051 **(4436)**

2001: 7^{0}GF, 9^{3}F, 8^{2}GF, 8^{0}GF, 7^{5}GF, 9^{1}G

	Starts	1st	2nd	3rd	Win & Pl
Career Total (Turf)	18	2	2	2	10353
Career Total (AW)	3	0	1	0	864

56 9/01 Haml 1m1f36y E GD £3206
70 8/00 Wwck 7f26y D GD £4225
Total win prize-money £7431

Going (Turf): Sf: 0-4 GS: 0-1 **Gd: 2-4** GF: 0-7 Fm: 0-2
Distance: 5f/6f: 0-6 7f-8f: 1-13 9f-13f: 1-2 14f+: 0-0
Track : LH: 1-10 RH: 1-3 **Tight: 1-4** Gall: 0-1
Aids: Bl: 0-1 Vi: 0-0 Tstrap: 0-0
Best Rating: 68 7/01 Ripn 1m gd-fm

Kuwait Thunder (IRE)

102(102) (39)**41**

5-y-o ch g Mac's Imp (USA)-Romangoddess (IRE) (Rhoman Rule (USA))

J L Eyre The Flowerpot Men

Placings:3543/3004050000/**0044**0600505026**00**-**0**35**2**5**0**313 **(4482)**

2001: 11^{0}SD, 11^{3}SD, 9^{5}F, 8^{2}GF, 8^{5}SD, 10^{0}GF, 8^{3}F, 7^{1}F, 8^{3}F

	Starts	1st	2nd	3rd	Win & Pl
Career Total (Turf)	30	1	2	5	8004
Career Total (AW)	9	0	0	1	337

37 8/01 Thsk 7f E(0-70)H FRM £3552
Total win prize-money £3552

Going (Turf): Sf: 0-6 GS: 0-4 Gd: 0-5 GF: 0-8 **Fm: 1-7**
Distance: 5f/6f: 0-8 **7f-8f: 1-19** 9f-13f: 0-12 14f+: 0-0
Track : **LH: 1-18** RH: 0-7 **Tight: 1-13** Gall: 0-3
Aids: Bl: 0-0 Vi: 0-13 Tstrap: 0-0
Best Rating: 41 9/01 Muss 1m firm

He had become a very frustrating sort, but finally got off the mark at the 38th attempt in an apprentice maiden handicap at Thirsk in August.

Kuwait Trooper (USA)

109(94) (51)**110**

4-y-o b h Cozzene (USA)-Super Fan (USA) (Lear Fan (USA))

G A Butler Sheikh Khaled Duaij Al Sabah

Placings:604/103105220-3003 **(4055)**

2001: 11^{3}G, 20^{0}GF, 14^{0}HO, 13^{3}GF

	Starts	1st	2nd	3rd	Win & Pl
Career Total (Turf)	13	2	2	3	37353
Career Total (AW)	3	0	0	0	216

96 5/00 York 1m5f194yB G-F £9222
65 3/00 Muss 1m4f F(0-60) GD £2576
Total win prize-money £11798

Going (Turf): Sf: 0-1 GS: 0-0 **Gd: 1-5 GF: 1-6** Fm: 0-0
Distance: 5f/6f: 0-0 7f-8f: 0-1 9f-13f: 1-8 14f+: 1-7
Track : LH: 1-6 RH: 1-6 Tight: 1-9 Gall: 1-5
Aids: Bl: 0-3 Vi: 0-0 Tstrap: 0-1
Best Rating: 110 8/01 Newb 1m5f61y gd-fm

He got off the mark in a Musselburgh classified event early on last season and added a York conditions event when stepped up to 14 furlongs. He was far from disgraced, though comfortably beaten, when runner-up in a Goodwood Listed event and a Kempton Group Three later in the campaign. Ran over an inadequate trip on his reappearance, but the Ascot Gold Cup trip looked too far. Tailed off in France before a better effort in the Geoffrey Freer. Best suited by good or faster, but lacks a change of gear.

Kuzi

68 **27**

2-y-o br f Bin Ajwaad (IRE)-Petonellajill (Petong)

M Mullineaux I S Ross

Placings:000 **(1656)**

2001: 5^{0}S, 5^{0}GF, 6^{0}F

	Starts	1st	2nd	3rd	Win & Pl
Career Total (Turf)	3	0	0	0	

Going (Turf): Sf: 0-1 GS: 0-0 Gd: 0-0 GF: 0-1 Fm: 0-1
Distance: 5f/6f: 0-3 7f-8f: 0-0 9f-13f: 0-0 14f+: 0-0
Track : LH: 0-1 RH: 0-0 Tight: 0-1 Gall: 0-0
Aids: Bl: 0-0 Vi: 0-0 Tstrap: 0-0
Best Rating: 27 4/01 Nott 5f13y soft

Kwaheri

95 **54d**

3-y-o b f Efisio-Fleeting Affair (Hotfoot)

Mrs P N Dutfield Simon Dutfield

Placings:040-0500 **(3874)**

2001: 11^{0}G, 14^{5}GS, 11^{0}GF, 12^{0}G

	Starts	1st	2nd	3rd	Win & Pl
Career Total (Turf)	7	0	0	0	342

Going (Turf): Sf: 0-0 GS: 0-1 Gd: 0-2 GF: 0-4 Fm: 0-0
Distance: 5f/6f: 0-1 7f-8f: 0-2 9f-13f: 0-3 14f+: 0-1
Track : LH: 0-0 RH: 0-2 Tight: 0-4 Gall: 0-0
Aids: Bl: 0-0 Vi: 0-0 Tstrap: 0-0
Best Rating: 54 5/01 Wind 1m3f135y good

Kwikpoint

76 **34**

7-y-o ch g Never So Bold-Try The Duchess (Try My Best (USA))

R F Fisher Great Head House Estates Limited

Placings:455/00400/006/00 **(4167)**

2001: 8^{0}GF, 7^{0}GF

	Starts	1st	2nd	3rd	Win & Pl
Career Total (Turf)	13	0	0	0	252

Going (Turf): Sf: 0-0 GS: 0-2 Gd: 0-2 GF: 0-8 Fm: 0-1
Distance: 5f/6f: 0-5 7f-8f: 0-7 9f-13f: 0-1 14f+: 0-0
Track : LH: 0-3 RH: 0-6 Tight: 0-2 Gall: 0-3
Aids: Bl: 0-1 Vi: 0-0 Tstrap: 0-0
Best Rating: 21 8/01 Muss 7f30y gd-fm

Kyda (USA)

105 **72**

3-y-o b f Gulch (USA)-Trampoli (USA) (Trempolino (USA))

H R A Cecil Newgate Stud

Placings:243232 **(5670)**

2001: 10^{2}GF, 10^{4}GF, 10^{3}S, 8^{2}GF, 7^{3}S, 8^{2}HY

	Starts	1st	2nd	3rd	Win & Pl
Career Total (Turf)	6	0	3	2	4597

Going (Turf): Sf: 0-3 GS: 0-0 Gd: 0-0 GF: 0-3 Fm: 0-0
Distance: 5f/6f: 0-0 7f-8f: 0-1 9f-13f: 0-5 14f+: 0-0
Track : LH: 0-4 RH: 0-2 Tight: 0-2 Gall: 0-1
Aids: Bl: 0-0 Vi: 0-0 Tstrap: 0-0
Best Rating: 76 5/01 Ling 1m2f gd-fm

She has made the frame in maidens, but has looked one-paced and irresolute on occasions.

Kylkenny

107(111) (61)**59**

6-y-o b g Kylian (USA)-Fashion Flow (Balidar)

H Morrison H Morrison

Placings:055/00-**110302**002110 **(5249)**

2001: 12^{1}SD, 12^{1}SD, 12^{0}SW, 11^{3}SW, 10^{0}S, 11^{2}SD, 11^{0}GF, 12^{0}GF, 9^{2}GF, 10^{1}F, 10^{1}S, 10^{0}S

	Starts	1st	2nd	3rd	Win & Pl
Career Total (Turf)	12	2	1	0	9410
Career Total (AW)	5	2	1	1	11186

59 10/01 NmkR 1m2f E(0-85)H SFT £5297
52 9/01 Pont 1m2f6y E(0-70)H FRM £3178
61 2/01 Sthl 1m4f D(0-85)H STD £8287
59 1/01 Sthl 1m4f G(0-60)H STD £1463
Total win prize-money £18227

Going (Turf): Sf: 1-6 GS: 0-2 Gd: 0-0 GF: 0-3 **Fm: 1-1**
Distance: 5f/6f: 0-0 7f-8f: 0-0 **9f-13f: 4-17** 14f+: 0-0
Track : **LH: 3-11** RH: 0-3 Tight: 0-6 Gall: 0-2
Aids: Bl: 0-0 Vi: 0-0 Tstrap: 0-0
Best Rating: 61 2/01 Sthl 1m4f stand

He won twice over 12 furlongs on Fibresand earlier in the year and hit form on turf in the autumn including wins at Pontefract and Newmarket over ten furlongs.

Kyllachy

113 **104**

3-y-o b c Pivotal-Pretty Poppy (Song)

H Candy Thurloe Thoroughbreds V

Placings:122-1244 **(5018)**

2001: 5^{1}S, 5^{2}GS, 5^{4}G, 5^{4}S

	Starts	1st	2nd	3rd	Win & Pl
Career Total (Turf)	7	2	3	0	21409

102 4/01 Sand 5f6y B(0-100)H SFT £9500
82 8/00 Chep 5f16y E G-F £2800
Total win prize-money £12300

Going (Turf): Sf: 1-4 GS: 0-1 Gd: 0-1 **GF: 1-1** Fm: 0-0
Distance: **5f/6f: 2-7** 7f-8f: 0-0 9f-13f: 0-0 14f+: 0-0
Track : LH: 0-0 RH: 0-0 Tight: 0-0 Gall: 0-0
Aids: Bl: 0-0 Vi: 0-0 Tstrap: 0-0
Best Rating: 104 8/01 Deau 5f gd-sft

Got off the mark at the first time of asking as a two year old, and followed that succes up with a win in a competitive handicap as a three-year-old. He has gone close since and looks a consistent sort who is suited by good to firm, and soft. Only ever tried at five furlongs.

Kylmax

71 **29**

2-y-o b g Classic Cliche (IRE)-Dame Lorraine (Damister (USA))

H A McWilliams J J Wright

Placings:00 **(5371)**

2001: 7^{0}G, 8^{0}G

	Starts	1st	2nd	3rd	Win & Pl
Career Total (Turf)	2	0	0	0	

Going (Turf): Sf: 0-0 GS: 0-0 Gd: 0-2 GF: 0-0 Fm: 0-0
Distance: 5f/6f: 0-0 7f-8f: 0-2 9f-13f: 0-0 14f+: 0-0
Track : LH: 0-0 RH: 0-0 Tight: 0-0 Gall: 0-0
Aids: Bl: 0-0 Vi: 0-0 Tstrap: 0-0
Best Rating: 29 10/01 Rdcr 1m good

L For Leisure

71 **36**

2-y-o ch g Cosmonaut-York Street (USA) (Diamond Shoal)

W G M Turner Tony Taylor

Placings:000 **(5459)**

2001: 8^{0}GF, 10^{0}G, 8^{0}G

	Starts	1st	2nd	3rd	Win & Pl
Career Total (Turf)	3	0	0	0	

Going (Turf): Sf: 0-0 GS: 0-0 Gd: 0-2 GF: 0-1 Fm: 0-0
Distance: 5f/6f: 0-0 7f-8f: 0-0 9f-13f: 0-3 14f+: 0-0
Track : LH: 0-2 RH: 0-1 Tight: 0-2 Gall: 0-0
Aids: Bl: 0-0 Vi: 0-0 Tstrap: 0-0
Best Rating: 36 10/01 Bath 1m2f46y good

L'Affaire Monique

84 **71+**

2-y-o b f Machiavellian (USA)-Much Too Risky (Bustino)

Sir Michael Stoute J M Greetham

Placings:0 **(5107)**

2001: 7^{0}GS

	Starts	1st	2nd	3rd	Win & Pl
Career Total (Turf)	1	0	0	0	

Going (Turf): Sf: 0-0 GS: 0-1 Gd: 0-0 GF: 0-0 Fm: 0-0
Distance: 5f/6f: 0-0 7f-8f: 0-1 9f-13f: 0-0 14f+: 0-0
Track : LH: 0-0 RH: 0-0 Tight: 0-0 Gall: 0-0
Aids: Bl: 0-0 Vi: 0-0 Tstrap: 0-0
Best Rating: 71 10/01 NmkR 7f gd-sft

L'Amour (USA)

95 **87**

3-y-o ch f Gone West (USA)-Midnight Air (USA) (Green Dancer (USA))

H R A Cecil H R H Prince Fahd Salman

Placings:010 **(1532)**

2001: 8^{0}S, 8^{1}G, 9^{0}GF

	Starts	1st	2nd	3rd	Win & Pl
Career Total (Turf)	3	1	0	0	3060

79 5/01 Wwck 1m22y D GD £3060
Total win prize-money £3060

Going (Turf): Sf: 0-1 GS: 0-0 **Gd: 1-1** GF: 0-1 Fm: 0-0
Distance: 5f/6f: 0-0 7f-8f: 0-1 **9f-13f: 1-2** 14f+: 0-0
Track : LH: 0-0 RH: 0-1 Tight: 0-1 Gall: 0-0
Aids: Bl: 0-0 Vi: 0-0 Tstrap: 0-0
Best Rating: 87 5/01 Gdwd 1m1f192y gd-fm

Took a fair fillies' maiden on her second outing, but was out of her depth in Listed company next time.

L'Ancress Princess

4-y-o b f Rock City-Premier Princess (Hard Fought)

Mrs A M Naughton D M Drury

Placings:0/5-6 **(2926)**

2001: 12^{6}GF

	Starts	1st	2nd	3rd	Win & Pl
Career Total (Turf)	1	0	0	0	0
Career Total (AW)	2	0	0	0	0

Going (Turf): Sf: 0-0 GS: 0-0 Gd: 0-0 GF: 0-1 Fm: 0-0
Distance: 5f/6f: 0-0 7f-8f: 0-1 9f-13f: 0-2 14f+: 0-0
Track : LH: 0-3 RH: 0-0 Tight: 0-2 Gall: 0-1
Aids: Bl: 0-0 Vi: 0-0 Tstrap: 0-0

L'Evangile

108 **96**

3-y-o b f Danehill (USA)-Dubai Lady (Kris)

J W Hills Wood Hall Stud Limited

Placings:032422 **(5600)**

2001: 7^{0}G, 10^{3}GF, 12^{2}G, 12^{4}G, 11^{2}G, 16^{2}GS

	Starts	1st	2nd	3rd	Win & Pl
Career Total (Turf)	6	0	3	1	9400

Going (Turf): Sf: 0-0 GS: 0-1 Gd: 0-4 GF: 0-1 Fm: 0-0
Distance: 5f/6f: 0-0 7f-8f: 0-1 9f-13f: 0-4 14f+: 0-1
Track : LH: 0-2 RH: 0-2 Tight: 0-1 Gall: 0-2
Aids: Bl: 0-0 Vi: 0-0 Tstrap: 0-0
Best Rating: 96 11/01 NmkR 2m gd-sft

A full-sister to the very useful ten-furlong winner Ela-Aristokrati, she improved considerably for her debut over seven furlongs, when third to Playtime in a good maiden at Newmarket in June, and went close again when second in a maiden at Chepstow. Ran well at Ascot, but was well beaten back in maiden company at Bath. Suited by middle distances on good to firm and good ground.

L'Ouest (USA)

89 **63**

4-y-o br c Gone West (USA)-La Carene (FR) (Kenmare (FR))

G Wragg Baron G Von Ullmann

Placings:03-60 **(3679)**

2001: 7^{6}S, 8^{0}G

	Starts	1st	2nd	3rd	Win & Pl
Career Total (Turf)	4	0	0	1	710

Going (Turf): Sf: 0-3 GS: 0-0 Gd: 0-1 GF: 0-0 Fm: 0-0
Distance: 5f/6f: 0-0 7f-8f: 0-2 9f-13f: 0-2 14f+: 0-0
Track : LH: 0-1 RH: 0-2 Tight: 0-1 Gall: 0-1
Aids: Bl: 0-0 Vi: 0-0 Tstrap: 0-0
Best Rating: 63 4/01 Kemp 7f soft

La Birba (IRE)

78(92) (28)**9**

4-y-o b f Prince Of Birds (USA)-Ariadne (Bustino)

D Morris I W Harfitt & Partners

Placings:0004/00-0000 **(1670)**

2001: 9^{0}SW, 11^{0}SW, 11^{0}GS, 14^{0}G

	Starts	1st	2nd	3rd	Win & Pl
Career Total (Turf)	7	0	0	0	
Career Total (AW)	3	0	0	0	0

Going (Turf): Sf: 0-1 GS: 0-3 Gd: 0-2 GF: 0-1 Fm: 0-0
Distance: 5f/6f: 0-4 7f-8f: 0-2 9f-13f: 0-3 14f+: 0-1
Track : LH: 0-7 RH: 0-0 Tight: 0-3 Gall: 0-1
Aids: Bl: 0-2 Vi: 0-0 Tstrap: 0-0
Best Rating: 24 1/01 Wolv 1m1f79y slow

La Koca (FR)

83 **44**

3-y-o b f Thatching-Green Maid (USA) (Green Dancer (USA))

H J Collingridge The Headquarters Partnership Vi

Placings:0060 **(3961)**

2001: 8^{0}G, 8^{0}G, 7^{6}GS, 6^{0}G

	Starts	1st	2nd	3rd	Win & Pl
Career Total (Turf)	4	0	0	0	0

Going (Turf): Sf: 0-0 GS: 0-1 Gd: 0-3 GF: 0-0 Fm: 0-0
Distance: 5f/6f: 0-0 7f-8f: 0-2 9f-13f: 0-2 14f+: 0-0
Track : LH: 0-1 RH: 0-0 Tight: 0-0 Gall: 0-1
Aids: Bl: 0-0 Vi: 0-0 Tstrap: 0-0
Best Rating: 44 7/01 NmkJ 7f gd-sft

La Martina

102 **83**

2-y-o b f Atraf-Dance Steppe (Rambo Dancer (CAN))

M G Quinlan Mario Lanfranchi

Placings:13 **(3395)**

2001: 7^{1}G, 7^{3}GF

	Starts	1st	2nd	3rd	Win & Pl
Career Total (Turf)	2	1	0	1	8721

6/01 Siro 7f GD £6571
Total win prize-money £6571

Going (Turf): Sf: 0-0 GS: 0-0 **Gd: 1-1** GF: 0-1 Fm: 0-0
Distance: 5f/6f: 0-0 **7f-8f: 1-2** 9f-13f: 0-0 14f+: 0-0
Track : LH: 0-0 RH: 0-1 Tight: 0-0 Gall: 0-0
Aids: Bl: 0-0 Vi: 0-0 Tstrap: 0-0
Best Rating: 83 7/01 Sand 7f16y gd-fm

La Mondotte (IRE)

(99) (59)**54**

3-y-o b f Alzao (USA)-Saucy Maid (IRE) (Sure Blade (USA))

J A Osborne Wood Hall Stud Limited

Placings:5-34040052 **(5407)**

2001: 11^{3}SD, 11^{4}SD, 14^{0}G, 11^{4}GF, 10^{0}G, 12^{0}GS, 12^{5}SD, 12^{2}SD

	Starts	1st	2nd	3rd	Win & Pl
Career Total (Turf)	5	0	0	0	0
Career Total (AW)	4	0	1	1	690

Going (Turf): Sf: 0-1 GS: 0-1 Gd: 0-2 GF: 0-1 Fm: 0-0
Distance: 5f/6f: 0-0 7f-8f: 0-0 9f-13f: 0-8 14f+: 0-1
Track : LH: 0-9 RH: 0-0 Tight: 0-3 Gall: 0-0
Aids: Bl: 0-0 Vi: 0-0 Tstrap: 0-0
Best Rating: 59 10/01 Sthl 1m4f stand

Still a maiden, but despite showing enough ability to suggest he can win a race, also looks a very difficult ride.

La Notte

106 **83**

3-y-o b f Factual (USA)-Miss Mirror (Magic Mirror)

W Jarvis A L Harrison

Placings:3133-050 **(4872)**

2001: 7^{0}G, 8^{5}GF, 7^{0}G

	Starts	1st	2nd	3rd	Win & Pl
Career Total (Turf)	7	1	0	3	5209

70 9/00 Ling 6f F G-F £2593
Total win prize-money £2594

Going (Turf): Sf: 0-2 GS: 0-0 Gd: 0-2 **GF: 1-3** Fm: 0-0
Distance: **5f/6f: 1-1** 7f-8f: 0-5 9f-13f: 0-1 14f+: 0-0
Track : LH: 0-2 RH: 0-0 Tight: 0-1 Gall: 0-0
Aids: Bl: 0-0 Vi: 0-0 Tstrap: 0-0
Best Rating: 84 5/01 NmkR 7f good

La Paola (IRE)

95(80) (35)**36**

5-y-o ch m Common Grounds-Lotte Lenta (Gorytus (USA))

P Howling (Jamie Poulton 13/2) Bvi Partnership

Placings:00120/00004100/0006000 **(3840)**

2001: 6^{0}SD, 8^{0}SW, 7^{0}GF, 6^{6}F, 5^{0}G, 6^{0}GF, 7^{0}G

	Starts	1st	2nd	3rd	Win & Pl
Career Total (Turf)	17	2	1	0	7630
Career Total (AW)	3		0	0	0

57 8/99 Folk 6f F(0-60) G-S £2972
72 9/98 Sand 5f6y E G-S £3680
Total win prize-money £6652

Going (Turf): Sf: 0-2 **GS: 2-2** Gd: 0-7 GF: 0-5 Fm: 0-1

Distance: 5f/6f: **2-16** 7f-8f: 0-3 9f-13f: 0-1 14f+: 0-0
Track : LH: 0-7 RH: 0-3 Tight: 0-2 Gall: 0-3
Aids: Bl: 0-1 Vi: 0-0 Tstrap: 0-0
Best Rating: 36 6/01 Sand 5f6y good

La Passione (USA)

104 **84**

3-y-o ch f Gulch (USA)-Larking (USA) (Green Forest (USA))
H R A Cecil M Tabor & Mrs John Magnier

Placings:2-02015 (5470)
2001: 8⁰GS, 9²GF, 8⁰GF, 8¹HY, 7⁵S

	Starts	1st	2nd	3rd	Win & Pl
Career Total (Turf)	6	1	2	0	7297

62 9/01 Hayd 1m30y D HVY £4602
Total win prize-money £4602

Going (Turf): Sf: 1-3 GS: 0-1 Gd: 0-0 GF: 0-2 Fm: 0-0
Distance: 5f/6f: 0-1 7f-8f: 0-3 **9f-13f: 1-2** 14f+: 0-0
Track : **LH: 1-2** RH: 0-2 Tight: 0-1 Gall: 0-0
Aids: Bl: 0-0 Vi: 0-0 Tstrap: 0-0
Best Rating: 84 5/01 Gdwd 1m1f gd-fm

Got off the mark at the fifth attempt in a Haydock maiden, but was hampered on her attempt to follow up at Brighton a month later.

La Paz

92 **77**

2-y-o b f Nashwan (USA)-Las Flores (IRE) (Sadler's Wells (USA))
J H M Gosden George Strawbridge

Placings:5 (5484)
2001: 8⁵HY

	Starts	1st	2nd	3rd	Win & Pl
Career Total (Turf)	1	0	0	0	0

Going (Turf): Sf: 0-1 GS: 0-0 Gd: 0-0 GF: 0-0 Fm: 0-0
Distance: 5f/6f: 0-0 7f-8f: 0-1 9f-13f: 0-0 14f+: 0-0
Track : LH: 0-1 RH: 0-0 Tight: 0-0 Gall: 0-1
Aids: Bl: 0-0 Vi: 0-0 Tstrap: 0-0
Best Rating: 77 10/01 Donc 1m heavy

La Perla

(93) (67)**66**

2-y-o gr f Royal Applause-Lammastide (Martinmas)
M C Chapman (W J Haggas 10/8) W P Gaff

Placings:423254200603 (5635)
2001: 5⁴G, 5²F, 6³SD, 7²SD, 7⁵GS, 6⁴GF, 7²G, 6⁰G, 8⁰GF, 8⁶HY, 7⁰S, 7³G,

	Starts	1st	2nd	3rd	Win & Pl
Career Total (Turf)	10	0	2	1	2589
Career Total (AW)	2	0	1	1	1300

Going (Turf): Sf: 0-2 GS: 0-1 Gd: 0-4 GF: 0-2 Fm: 0-1
Distance: 5f/6f: 0-4 7f-8f: 0-6 9f-13f: 0-2 14f+: 0-0
Track : LH: 0-9 RH: 0-0 Tight: 0-1 Gall: 0-3
Aids: Bl: 0-1 Vi: 0-0 Tstrap: 0-0
Best Rating: 67 7/01 Sthl 7f stand

Exposed maiden. Best trip probably seven furlongs.

La Reine Roxanne

87 **53**

2-y-o b f Cyrano De Bergerac-Sylvandra (Mazilier (USA))
L R James C Raine

Placings:5000 (5399)
2001: 5⁵GF, 6⁰G, 5⁰GS, 6⁰S

	Starts	1st	2nd	3rd	Win & Pl
Career Total (Turf)	4	0	0	0	0

Going (Turf): Sf: 0-1 GS: 0-1 Gd: 0-1 GF: 0-1 Fm: 0-0
Distance: 5f/6f: 0-4 7f-8f: 0-0 9f-13f: 0-0 14f+: 0-0
Track : LH: 0-1 RH: 0-0 Tight: 0-0 Gall: 0-0
Aids: Bl: 0-0 Vi: 0-0 Tstrap: 0-0
Best Rating: 53 7/01 Bevl 5f gd-fm

La Speziana (IRE)

104 **81**

4-y-o b f Perugino (USA)-Election Special (Chief Singer)
D R C Elsworth Pampas Partnership

Placings:466/113-206000 (5391)
2001: 8²S, 8⁰GS, 7⁶G, 8⁰GF, 8⁰S, 7⁰GS

	Starts	1st	2nd	3rd	Win & Pl
Career Total (Turf)	12	2	1	1	17117

91 5/00 Sand 7f16y C(0-95)H HVY £7020
69 5/00 Newb 7f D(0-80)H G-F £4693
Total win prize-money £11713

Going (Turf): Sf: 1-4 GS: 0-3 Gd: 0-2 **GF: 1-3** Fm: 0-0
Distance: 5f/6f: 0-1 **7f-8f: 2-8** 9f-13f: 0-3 14f+: 0-0
Track : LH: 0-2 **RH: 1-5** Tight: 0-1 Gall: 0-1
Aids: Bl: 0-0 Vi: 0-0 Tstrap: 0-0
Best Rating: 81 4/01 Sand 1m14y soft

Very useful handicapper. Won twice in nine days in May 2000 before a shoulder injury curtailed her season. She confirmed that she retained her ability with fine second at Sandown in April, but has not really gone on from there.

La Sylphide

(103) (63)**49**

4-y-o ch f Rudimentary (USA)-Primitive Gift (Primitive Rising (USA))
Mrs A Duffield Mrs S E Turnbull

Placings:360-11100 (5616)
2001: 7¹SD, 8¹SD, 7¹SD, 6⁰G, 7⁰SD

	Starts	1st	2nd	3rd	Win & Pl
Career Total (Turf)	4	0	0	1	798
Career Total (AW)	4	3	0	0	7112

63 6/01 Sthl 7f F(0-65)H STD £2366
59 5/01 Sthl 1m E(0-70)H STD £2905
52 4/01 Sthl 7f F(0-60)H STD £1841
Total win prize-money £7112

Going (Turf): Sf: 0-0 GS: 0-0 Gd: 0-1 GF: 0-3 Fm: 0-0
Distance: 5f/6f: 0-0 **7f-8f: 3-5** 9f-13f: 0-3 14f+: 0-0
Track : **LH: 3-5** RH: 0-1 Tight: 0-2 Gall: 0-0
Aids: Bl: 0-0 Vi: 0-0 Tstrap: 0-0
Best Rating: 63 6/01 Sthl 7f stand

All of her wins to date have come on the Southwell Fibresand.

La Tania

84 **65**

2-y-o b f Polish Precedent (USA)-Highsplasher (USA) (Bucksplasher (USA))
C F Wall S Fustok

Placings:05 (4485)
2001: 7⁰GF, 8⁵S

	Starts	1st	2nd	3rd	Win & Pl
Career Total (Turf)	2	0	0	0	0

Going (Turf): Sf: 0-1 GS: 0-0 Gd: 0-0 GF: 0-1 Fm: 0-0
Distance: 5f/6f: 0-0 7f-8f: 0-1 9f-13f: 0-1 14f+: 0-0
Track : LH: 0-0 RH: 0-1 Tight: 0-0 Gall: 0-1
Aids: Bl: 0-0 Vi: 0-0 Tstrap: 0-0
Best Rating: 65 9/01 Yarm 1m3y soft

La Traviata

98 **47**

3-y-o b f Spectrum (IRE)-Opera Lover (IRE) (Sadler's Wells (USA))
Sir Mark Prescott Cheveley Park Stud

Placings:000-10 (5532)
2001: 9¹S, 9⁰HY

	Starts	1st	2nd	3rd	Win & Pl
Career Total (Turf)	5	1	0	0	2373

47 10/01 Brig 1m1f209yF(0-60)H SFT £2373
Total win prize-money £2373

Going (Turf): Sf: 1-5 GS: 0-0 Gd: 0-0 GF: 0-0 Fm: 0-0
Distance: 5f/6f: 0-0 7f-8f: 0-3 **9f-13f: 1-2** 14f+: 0-0
Track : **LH: 1-3** RH: 0-1 Tight: 0-0 Gall: 0-1
Aids: Bl: 0-0 Vi: 0-0 Tstrap: 0-0
Best Rating: 47 10/01 Brig 1m1f209y soft

She showed nothing in three starts at two, but was always going to appreciate middle distances and came back from a break of a year to just win a ten-furlong handicap at Brighton in October.

La Yolam

107 **80+**

3-y-o ch f Unfuwain (USA)-Massorah (FR) (Habitat)
B Hanbury Ahmed Buhaleeba

Placings:63155 (4828)
2001: 7⁶GF, 8³G, 10¹G, 10⁵GF, 10⁵G

	Starts	1st	2nd	3rd	Win & Pl
Career Total (Turf)	5	1	0	1	4981

67 8/01 Yarm 1m2f21y D GD £3688
Total win prize-money £3689

Going (Turf): Sf: 0-0 GS: 0-0 **Gd: 1-3** GF: 0-2 Fm: 0-0
Distance: 5f/6f: 0-0 7f-8f: 0-1 **9f-13f: 1-4** 14f+: 0-0
Track : **LH: 1-3** RH: 0-0 **Tight: 1-1** Gall: 0-1
Aids: Bl: 0-0 Vi: 0-0 Tstrap: 0-0
Best Rating: 80 8/01 Newc 1m2f32y gd-fm

Got off the mark at the third attempt when running away with a Yarmouth maiden in August, but has found life tough in handicap company since.

Labasheeda (IRE)

(70) (5)**75**

3-y-o ch f Lahib (USA)-Hebat (Kris)
J Cullinan John Geraghty

Placings:2400 (5416)
2001: 10²GF, 11⁴G, 9⁰GF, 9⁰SD

	Starts	1st	2nd	3rd	Win & Pl
Career Total (Turf)	3	0	1	0	2038
Career Total (AW)	1	0	0	0	

Going (Turf): Sf: 0-0 GS: 0-0 Gd: 0-1 GF: 0-2 Fm: 0-0
Distance: 5f/6f: 0-0 7f-8f: 0-0 9f-13f: 0-4 14f+: 0-0
Track : LH: 0-2 RH: 0-2 Tight: 0-1 Gall: 0-2
Aids: Bl: 0-0 Vi: 0-0 Tstrap: 0-0
Best Rating: 75 6/01 Kemp 1m2f gd-fm

Labrett

110(108) (79+)**84**

4-y-o b g Tragic Role (USA)-Play The Game (Mummy's Game)
B J Meehan Mrs E A Lerpiniere

Placings:54143145000/00004401140000-121353050000000 (5391)
2001: 6¹SD, 5²GS, 7¹G, 7³GF, 6⁵GF, 6³G, 7⁰G, 6⁵GF, 7⁰GF, 6⁰G, 6⁰G, 7⁰GF, 6⁰G, 6⁰GS, 7⁰GS

	Starts	1st	2nd	3rd	Win & Pl
Career Total (Turf)	39	5	1	3	22864

Career Total (AW)	1	1	0	0		3900
84	5/01	Ling	7f	F(0-75)H	GD	£2772
79	4/01	Ling	6f	D(0-80)H	STD	£3900
60	8/00	Bath	5f161y	E	G-F	£2736
75	7/00	Kemp	6f	E	G-F	£2795
82	6/99	Ches	5f16y	D	G-F	£3415
72	5/99	Rdcr	5f	F	SFT	£2407

Total win prize-money £18027

Going (Turf): Sf: 1-7 GS: 0-5 Gd: 1-10 **GF: 3-17** Fm: 0-0
Distance: **5f/6f: 5-31** 7f-8f: 1-9 9f-13f: 0-0 14f+: 0-0
Track : **LH: 3-7** RH: 0-3 **Tight: 2-3** Gall: 1-2
Aids: **Bl: 3-20** Vi: 0-0 Tstrap: 0-0
Best Rating: 88 6/01 Wind 6f gd-fm

A decent fast-finishing handicapper who was in great heart in the first half of this term, winning at Lingfield on both the turf and All-weather and running some fine races in defeat. Best at six furlongs but stays seven. Acts on a sound surface and can come from behind with a late rattle.

Lady Abai

38

4-y-o b f Bin Ajwaad (IRE)-Charmed I'm Sure (Nicholas Bill)
J Cullinan Young Roman Racing Club

Placings:000-0 **(1076)**
2001: 11⁰GS

	Starts	1st	2nd	3rd	Win & Pl
Career Total (Turf)	4	0	0	0	

Going (Turf): Sf: 0-0 GS: 0-1 Gd: 0-2 GF: 0-1 Fm: 0-0
Distance: 5f/6f: 0-0 7f-8f: 0-0 9f-13f: 0-4 14f+: 0-0
Track : LH: 0-3 RH: 0-1 Tight: 0-1 Gall: 0-0
Aids: Bl: 0-0 Vi: 0-0 Tstrap: 0-0

Lady Alruna (IRE)

96 89

2-y-o ch f Alhaarth (IRE)-In Tranquility (IRE) (Shalford (IRE))
P J Makin John Gale & George Darling

Placings:533 **(5038)**
2001: 6⁵F, 5³F, 5³G

	Starts	1st	2nd	3rd	Win & Pl
Career Total (Turf)	3	0	0	2	971

Going (Turf): Sf: 0-0 GS: 0-0 Gd: 0-1 GF: 0-0 Fm: 0-2
Distance: 5f/6f: 0-3 7f-8f: 0-0 9f-13f: 0-0 14f+: 0-0
Track : LH: 0-2 RH: 0-0 Tight: 0-0 Gall: 0-2
Aids: Bl: 0-0 Vi: 0-0 Tstrap: 0-0
Best Rating: 89 10/01 Bath 5f161y good

Lady Anastasia (IRE)

95 41

4-y-o b f Unblest-Cry In The Dark (Godswalk (USA))
P L Gilligan Mrs Anastasia Keane

Placings:0-6000 **(5469)**
2001: 9⁶G, 7⁰G, 10⁰HY, 9⁰S

	Starts	1st	2nd	3rd	Win & Pl
Career Total (Turf)	5	0	0	0	0

Going (Turf): Sf: 0-2 GS: 0-0 Gd: 0-2 GF: 0-0 Fm: 0-0
Distance: 5f/6f: 0-0 7f-8f: 0-1 9f-13f: 0-3 14f+: 0-0
Track : LH: 0-1 RH: 0-1 Tight: 0-2 Gall: 0-0
Aids: Bl: 0-0 Vi: 0-0 Tstrap: 0-0
Best Rating: 41 10/01 Wind 1m2f7y heavy

Lady Angola (USA)

(99) (79) 76

3-y-o ch f Lord At War (ARG)-Benguela (USA) (Little Current (USA))
J L Dunlop T Ricketts (susan Abbott Racing)

Placings:400-0201 **(5394)**
2001: 10⁰GS, 10²GF, 9⁰GF, 12¹SD

	Starts	1st	2nd	3rd	Win & Pl		
Career Total (Turf)	6	0	1	0	2645		
Career Total (AW)	1	1	0	0	3474		
79	10/01	Wolv	1m4f	E(0-75)H	STD	£3474	

Total win prize-money £3474

Going (Turf): Sf: 0-2 GS: 0-1 Gd: 0-0 GF: 0-3 Fm: 0-0
Distance: 5f/6f: 0-0 7f-8f: 0-2 **9f-13f: 1-5** 14f+: 0-0
Track : **LH: 1-3** RH: 0-3 **Tight: 1-4** Gall: 0-2
Aids: Bl: 0-0 Vi: 0-0 Tstrap: 0-0
Best Rating: 79 10/01 Wolv 1m4f stand

Lightly-raced but with fair form on turf, she got off the mark when stepped up to 12 furlongs on her Fibresand debut.

Lady Ansell

92(95) (62+)75

2-y-o b f Puissance-Rare Indigo (Timeless Times (USA))
A Berry Ansells Of Watford

Placings:102 **(1785)**
2001: 5¹SD, 5⁰GF, 5²F

	Starts	1st	2nd	3rd	Win & Pl		
Career Total (Turf)	2	0	1	0	671		
Career Total (AW)	1	1	0	0	2317		
62	4/01	Sthl	5f	F	STD	£2317	

Total win prize-money £2317

Going (Turf): Sf: 0-0 GS: 0-0 Gd: 0-0 GF: 0-1 Fm: 0-1
Distance: **5f/6f: 1-3** 7f-8f: 0-0 9f-13f: 0-0 14f+: 0-0
Track : LH: 0-1 RH: 0-0 Tight: 0-1 Gall: 0-0
Aids: Bl: 0-0 Vi: 0-0 Tstrap: 0-0
Best Rating: 75 6/01 Nott 5f13y firm

Lady Arnica

73 41

2-y-o b f Ezzoud (IRE)-Brand (Shareef Dancer (USA))
I A Balding Queen Elizabeth

Placings:0 **(5602)**
2001: 7⁰GS

	Starts	1st	2nd	3rd	Win & Pl
Career Total (Turf)	1	0	0	0	

Going (Turf): Sf: 0-0 GS: 0-1 Gd: 0-0 GF: 0-0 Fm: 0-0
Distance: 5f/6f: 0-0 7f-8f: 0-1 9f-13f: 0-0 14f+: 0-0
Track : LH: 0-0 RH: 0-0 Tight: 0-0 Gall: 0-0
Aids: Bl: 0-0 Vi: 0-0 Tstrap: 0-0
Best Rating: 41 11/01 NmkR 7f gd-sft

Lady Base

82 39

3-y-o b f Blushing Flame (USA)-Lady Marguerrite (Blakeney)
W S Kittow Midd Shire Racing

Placings:0 **(2251)**
2001: 12⁰GF

	Starts	1st	2nd	3rd	Win & Pl
Career Total (Turf)	1	0	0	0	

Going (Turf): Sf: 0-0 GS: 0-0 Gd: 0-0 GF: 0-1 Fm: 0-0
Distance: 5f/6f: 0-0 7f-8f: 0-0 9f-13f: 0-1 14f+: 0-0
Track : LH: 0-1 RH: 0-0 Tight: 0-0 Gall: 0-0
Aids: Bl: 0-0 Vi: 0-0 Tstrap: 0-0
Best Rating: 39 6/01 Wwck 1m4f134y gd-fm

Lady Bathwick (IRE)

(73) (30)63

2-y-o ch f General Monash (USA)-Forget Paris (IRE) (Broken Hearted)
B R Millman Mrs S Clifford

Placings:22000 **(4878)**
2001: 5²GS, 6²GF, 7⁰GF, 8⁰GF, 7⁰SD

	Starts	1st	2nd	3rd	Win & Pl
Career Total (Turf)	4	0	2	0	1123
Career Total (AW)	1	0	0	0	

Going (Turf): Sf: 0-0 GS: 0-1 Gd: 0-0 GF: 0-3 Fm: 0-0
Distance: 5f/6f: 0-2 7f-8f: 0-2 9f-13f: 0-1 14f+: 0-0
Track : LH: 0-2 RH: 0-0 Tight: 0-1 Gall: 0-0
Aids: Bl: 0-0 Vi: 0-0 Tstrap: 0-0
Best Rating: 63 8/01 Ling 6f gd-fm

Lady Bear (IRE)

(101) (72)78

3-y-o b f Grand Lodge (USA)-Boristova (IRE) (Royal Academy (USA))
R A Fahey A & K Lingerie

Placings:633441021-1400400500364 **(5681)**
2001: 8¹S, 10⁴GS, 10⁰F, 10⁰GF, 7⁴GF, 6⁰G, 8⁰GF, 9⁵S, 8⁰G, 8⁰GF, 8³S, 8⁶GS, 8⁴S

	Starts	1st	2nd	3rd	Win & Pl		
Career Total (Turf)	21	3	1	2	28274		
Career Total (AW)	1	0	0	1	427		
84	4/01	Ripn	1m	C(0-90)H	SFT	£7124	
78	10/00	York	7f202y	C H	SFT	£7020	
69	8/00	Muss	7f30y	D	G-F	£4127	

Total win prize-money £18272

Going (Turf): **Sf: 2-5** GS: 0-3 Gd: 0-2 GF: 1-10 Fm: 0-1
Distance: 5f/6f: 0-2 **7f-8f: 3-14** 9f-13f: 0-6 14f+: 0-0
Track : LH: 1-11 **RH: 2-5 Tight: 2-6** Gall: 1-4
Aids: Bl: 0-0 **Vi: 1-4** Tstrap: 0-0
Best Rating: 85 5/01 Pont 1m2f6y gd-sft

She made a winning reappearance in April over a mile at Ripon, but went up in the handicap and was held over a variety of trips after. Has won on fast ground, but looks much better suited by soft.

Lady Blue

82 10

5-y-o b m Puissance-Blueit (FR) (Bold Lad (IRE))
P T Dalton Mrs Christina M Griffin

Placings:0 **(4778)**
2001: 5⁰G

	Starts	1st	2nd	3rd	Win & Pl
Career Total (Turf)	1	0	0	0	

Going (Turf): Sf: 0-0 GS: 0-0 Gd: 0-1 GF: 0-0 Fm: 0-0
Distance: 5f/6f: 0-1 7f-8f: 0-0 9f-13f: 0-0 14f+: 0-0
Track : LH: 0-0 RH: 0-0 Tight: 0-0 Gall: 0-0
Aids: Bl: 0-0 Vi: 0-0 Tstrap: 0-0
Best Rating: 10 9/01 Bevl 5f good

Lady Boxer

(112) 90

5-y-o b m Komaite (USA)-Lady Broker (Petorius)
M Mullineaux Esprit De Corps Racing

Placings:13560/04100/00P001011000-300050003300 **(5694)**
2001: 6³S, 7⁰GF, 6⁰GF, 7⁰G, 6⁵HY, 6⁰G, 6⁰S, 6⁰G, 5³GS, 6³HY, 7⁰S, 6⁰S

	Starts	1st	2nd	3rd	Win & Pl		
Career Total (Turf)	34	6	0	4	43536		
86	9/00	Ches	6f18y	D(0-80)	SFT	£4465	
81	9/00	Ayr	6f	B H	SFT	£11635	
75	8/00	Ches	7f122y	C(0-100)H	GD	£14820	
75	9/99	Ches	6f18y	D(0-80)	SFT	£3896	

.74	6/98	Leic	5f218y	E	SFT	£3470

Total win prize-money £38287

Going (Turf): Sf: 4-16 GS: 0-4 Gd: 1-9 GF: 0-5 Fm: 0-0
Distance: 5f/6f: 2-18 **7f-8f: 3-16** 9f-13f: 0-0 14f+: 0-0
Track : **LH: 3-10** RH: 0-0 **Tight: 3-9** Gall: 0-0
Aids: Bl: 0-0 Vi: 0-0 Tstrap: 0-0
Best Rating: 90 5/01 Hayd 6f soft

A decent handicapper, she landed the Ayr Silver Cup in 2000. Ran well first time out this season but was held after. Six furlongs and soft conditions bring out the best in her.

Lady Breanne (IRE)

100(104) (50)**48**

5-y-o b m Woods Of Windsor (USA)-Tootsie Roll (Comedy Star (USA))
G L Moore Brighton Racing Club

Placings:030/4602**636**/000**5-231324**103006 **(4162)**
2001: 8^{2}SD, **9^{3}SW, 7^{1}SW, 8^{3}SD, 8^{2}SD, 8^{4}SW, 8^{1}SD**, 7^{0}GF, 9^{3}GF, 9^{0}GF, 8^{0}GF, 10^{6}GF

	Starts	1st	2nd	3rd	Win & Pl
Career Total (Turf)	**15**	**0**	**1**	**2**	**2498**
Career Total (AW)	**11**	**2**	**2**	**3**	**6097**

50	4/01	Ling	1m	F(0-65)H	STD	£2422
47	1/01	Ling	7f	F(0-60)H	SLW	£1701

Total win prize-money £4123

Going (Turf): Sf: 0-0 GS: 0-0 Gd: 0-2 GF: 0-9 Fm: 0-1
Distance: 5f/6f: 0-3 **7f-8f: 2-17** 9f-13f: 0-6 14f+: 0-0
Track : **LH: 2-14** RH: 0-5 **Tight: 2-13** Gall: 0-0
Aids: **Bl: 2-13** Vi: 0-0 Tstrap: 0-0
Best Rating: 50 4/01 Ling 1m stand

Lady Coldunell

102(107) (64)**66d**

5-y-o b m Deploy-Beau's Delight (USA) (Lypheor)
H J Collingridge D T Thom

Placings:00/**00**2224314015250**5**/032**3-5221**2060056 **(3404)**
2001: **14^{5}SD, 16^{2}SW, 16^{2}SW, 13^{1}SD**, 16^{2}F, 14^{0}G, 14^{6}S, 16^{0}G, 16^{0}GF, 16^{5}GF, 16^{6}GF

	Starts	1st	2nd	3rd	Win & Pl
Career Total (Turf)	**24**	**1**	**6**	**2**	**11766**
Career Total (AW)	**9**	**2**	**2**	**1**	**9069**

64	4/01	Ling	1m5f	E(0-75)H	STD	£2817
55	8/99	Epsm	1m4f10y	D(0-80)H	GD	£4065
62	7/99	Ling	1m4f	E(0-70)H	STD	£3492

Total win prize-money £10376

Going (Turf): Sf: 0-4 GS: 0-2 **Gd: 1-9** GF: 0-4 Fm: 0-5
Distance: 5f/6f: 0-0 7f-8f: 0-3 **9f-13f: 3-12** 14f+: 0-18
Track : **LH: 3-20** RH: 0-11 **Tight: 3-14** Gall: 0-6
Aids: Bl: 0-2 Vi: 0-3 Tstrap: 0-0
Best Rating: 66 5/01 Newc 2m19y firm

A fair staying handicapper, her successes on turf have come over a mile and a half, but has won over a bit further on sand and has performed creditably at up to two miles. Best suited by a decent pace.

Lady Cyrano

(87) (24)**49**

4-y-o b f Cyrano De Bergerac-Hazy Kay (IRE) (Treasure Kay)
Mrs N Macauley Exors Of The Late J Teasdale

Placings:0033643000/362060200000-0 **(0307)**
2001: 6^{0}SD

	Starts	1st	2nd	3rd	Win & Pl
Career Total (Turf)	**10**	**0**	**1**	**1**	**970**
Career Total (AW)	**13**	**0**	**1**	**3**	**1359**

Going (Turf): Sf: 0-0 GS: 0-2 Gd: 0-2 GF: 0-5 Fm: 0-1
Distance: 5f/6f: 0-11 7f-8f: 0-9 9f-13f: 0-3 14f+: 0-0
Track : LH: 0-11 RH: 0-0 Tight: 0-1 Gall: 0-0
Aids: Bl: 0-1 Vi: 0-5 Tstrap: 0-0

Lady Dancer

50

3-y-o b f Aragon-Hi-Hunsley (Swing Easy (USA))
A Smith Rosswood Racing

Placings:00 **(1582)**
2001: 6^{0}GS, 6^{0}F

	Starts	1st	2nd	3rd	Win & Pl
Career Total (Turf)	**2**	**0**	**0**	**0**	

Going (Turf): Sf: 0-0 GS: 0-1 Gd: 0-0 GF: 0-0 Fm: 0-1
Distance: 5f/6f: 0-2 7f-8f: 0-0 9f-13f: 0-0 14f+: 0-0
Track : LH: 0-2 RH: 0-0 Tight: 0-0 Gall: 0-0
Aids: Bl: 0-0 Vi: 0-0 Tstrap: 0-0

Lady De Bathe

84 **71**

2-y-o b f Robellino (USA)-Langtry Lady (Pas De Seul)
I A Balding Mrs G M Tregaskes

Placings:50 **(4771)**
2001: 7^{5}GS, 7^{0}G

	Starts	1st	2nd	3rd	Win & Pl
Career Total (Turf)	**2**	**0**	**0**	**0**	**0**

Going (Turf): Sf: 0-0 GS: 0-1 Gd: 0-1 GF: 0-0 Fm: 0-0
Distance: 5f/6f: 0-0 7f-8f: 0-2 9f-13f: 0-0 14f+: 0-0
Track : LH: 0-1 RH: 0-1 Tight: 0-1 Gall: 0-0
Aids: Bl: 0-0 Vi: 0-0 Tstrap: 0-0
Best Rating: 71 8/01 Epsm 7f gd-sft

Lady Devika

92 **63**

2-y-o b f Sri Pekan (USA)-The Frog Lady (IRE) (Al Hareb (USA))
R Hannon The Waney Racing Group Inc

Placings:0 **(4864)**
2001: 7^{0}GF

	Starts	1st	2nd	3rd	Win & Pl
Career Total (Turf)	**1**	**0**	**0**	**0**	

Going (Turf): Sf: 0-0 GS: 0-0 Gd: 0-0 GF: 0-1 Fm: 0-0
Distance: 5f/6f: 0-0 7f-8f: 0-1 9f-13f: 0-0 14f+: 0-0
Track : LH: 0-0 RH: 0-0 Tight: 0-0 Gall: 0-0
Aids: Bl: 0-0 Vi: 0-0 Tstrap: 0-0
Best Rating: 63 9/01 Newb 7f gd-fm

Lady Dominatrix (IRE)

103 **86**

2-y-o b f Danehill Dancer (IRE)-Spout House (IRE) (Flash Of Steel)
Mrs P N Dutfield J Dutfield

Placings:1200020 **(4680)**
2001: 5^{1}G, 5^{2}S, 5^{0}GF, 6^{0}GF, 5^{0}GF, 7^{2}G, 8^{0}G

	Starts	1st	2nd	3rd	Win & Pl
Career Total (Turf)	**7**	**1**	**2**	**0**	**10581**

73	5/01	Donc	5f	E	GD	£3640

Total win prize-money £3640

Going (Turf): Sf: 0-1 GS: 0-0 **Gd: 1-3** GF: 0-3 Fm: 0-0
Distance: **5f/6f: 1-5** 7f-8f: 0-2 9f-13f: 0-0 14f+: 0-0
Track : LH: 0-1 RH: 0-0 Tight: 0-0 Gall: 0-1
Aids: Bl: 0-0 Vi: 0-0 Tstrap: 0-0
Best Rating: 86 8/01 NmkJ 7f good

A February foal who got off the mark at Doncaster on her debut. Showed good early speed on her next start when runner-up at Newbury. Was out of her depth in good class contests later. Acts on good and soft ground.

Lady Eberspacher (IRE)

82 **31**

3-y-o b f Royal Abjar (USA)-Samriah (IRE) (Wassl)
Mrs P N Dutfield The Hot Air Partnership

Placings:042440-00000 **(5273)**
2001: 8^{0}GS, 6^{0}GF, 6^{0}F, 6^{0}GF, 5^{0}HY

	Starts	1st	2nd	3rd	Win & Pl
Career Total (Turf)	**11**	**0**	**1**	**0**	**1867**

Going (Turf): Sf: 0-2 GS: 0-2 Gd: 0-2 GF: 0-4 Fm: 0-1
Distance: 5f/6f: 0-10 7f-8f: 0-0 9f-13f: 0-1 14f+: 0-0
Track : LH: 0-1 RH: 0-2 Tight: 0-1 Gall: 0-2
Aids: Bl: 0-0 Vi: 0-0 Tstrap: 0-2
Best Rating: 31 6/01 Ling 6f firm

Lady El Ee

88 **60**

2-y-o b f Komaite (USA)-Mountain Harvest (FR) (Shirley Heights)
Miss L A Perratt David R Sutherland

Placings:000 **(5268)**
2001: 6^{0}G, 5^{0}GF, 7^{0}HY

	Starts	1st	2nd	3rd	Win & Pl
Career Total (Turf)	**3**	**0**	**0**	**0**	

Going (Turf): Sf: 0-1 GS: 0-0 Gd: 0-1 GF: 0-1 Fm: 0-0
Distance: 5f/6f: 0-2 7f-8f: 0-1 9f-13f: 0-0 14f+: 0-0
Track : LH: 0-0 RH: 0-0 Tight: 0-0 Gall: 0-0
Aids: Bl: 0-0 Vi: 0-0 Tstrap: 0-0
Best Rating: 60 9/01 Ayr 6f good

Lady Fearless

87(77) (22)**42?**

4-y-o b f Cosmonaut-Lady Broker (Petorius)
M Mullineaux Esprit De Corps Racing

Placings:06/0060-00 **(1068)**
2001: 7^{0}SD, 6^{0}GS

	Starts	1st	2nd	3rd	Win & Pl
Career Total (Turf)	**6**	**0**	**0**	**0**	**0**
Career Total (AW)	**2**	**0**	**0**	**0**	

Going (Turf): Sf: 0-3 GS: 0-3 Gd: 0-0 GF: 0-0 Fm: 0-0
Distance: 5f/6f: 0-3 7f-8f: 0-3 9f-13f: 0-1 14f+: 0-1
Track : LH: 0-6 RH: 0-0 Tight: 0-1 Gall: 0-0
Aids: Bl: 0-0 Vi: 0-0 Tstrap: 0-0
Best Rating: 42 5/01 Pont 6f gd-sft

Lady High Havens (IRE)

98 **94**

2-y-o b f Bluebird (USA)-Blanche Dubois (Nashwan (USA))
P W D'Arcy Mrs A Lovat

Placings:4212120 **(4680)**
2001: 6^{4}GS, 6^{2}GF, 6^{1}GF, 6^{2}GS, 7^{1}GF, 7^{2}GS, 8^{0}G

	Starts	1st	2nd	3rd	Win & Pl
Career Total (Turf)	**7**	**2**	**3**	**0**	**40299**

90	7/01	Asct	7f	B	G-F	£14202
84	6/01	Asct	6f	D	G-F	£5434

Total win prize-money £19637

Going (Turf): Sf: 0-0 GS: 0-3 Gd: 0-1 **GF: 2-3** Fm: 0-0
Distance: 5f/6f: 1-4 7f-8f: 1-3 9f-13f: 0-0 14f+: 0-0
Track : LH: 0-1 RH: 0-0 Tight: 0-0 Gall: 0-1
Aids: Bl: 0-0 Vi: 0-0 Tstrap: 0-0
Best Rating: 94 8/01 Deau 7f gd-sft

She came up against some decent sorts on her first two starts, but made no mistake when winning an Ascot novice event on her third outing. Battled on well when only narrowly denied in the Cherry Hinton, and justified favouritism next time when stepped up to seven furlongs. Acts on good to soft but best on good to firm.

Lady Hopper

38

2-y-o ch f Muhtarram (USA)-Lady Sheriff (Taufan (USA))
M W Easterby E J Mangan

Placings:0 (1858)
2001: 6^{0}F

	Starts	1st	2nd	3rd	Win & Pl
Career Total (Turf)	1	0	0	0	

Going (Turf): Sf: 0-0 GS: 0-0 Gd: 0-0 GF: 0-0 Fm: 0-1
Distance: 5f/6f: 0-1 7f-8f: 0-0 9f-13f: 0-0 14f+: 0-0
Track : LH: 0-0 RH: 0-0 Tight: 0-0 Gall: 0-0
Aids: Bl: 0-0 Vi: 0-0 Tstrap: 0-0

Lady In The Night (IRE)

97 46

3-y-o ch f Royal Academy (USA)-Pig Tail (Habitat)
J A R Toller M E Wates

Placings:400-030 (5129)
2001: 6^{0}GF, 7^{3}F, 7^{0}HY

	Starts	1st	2nd	3rd	Win & Pl
Career Total (Turf)	6	0	0	1	911

Going (Turf): Sf: 0-1 GS: 0-0 Gd: 0-1 GF: 0-3 Fm: 0-1
Distance: 5f/6f: 0-3 7f-8f: 0-3 9f-13f: 0-0 14f+: 0-0
Track : LH: 0-2 RH: 0-1 Tight: 0-1 Gall: 0-1
Aids: Bl: 0-0 Vi: 0-0 Tstrap: 0-0
Best Rating: 46 8/01 Thsk 7f firm

Lady Inch

(80) (30)

3-y-o b f Inchinor-Head Turner (My Dad Tom (USA))
Mrs L Wadham (B Smart 30/3) The Dyball Partnership

Placings:00-000 (0611)
2001: 8^{0}SD, 9^{0}SD, 11^{0}SD

	Starts	1st	2nd	3rd	Win & Pl
Career Total (Turf)	1	0	0	0	
Career Total (AW)	4	0	0	0	

Going (Turf): Sf: 0-1 GS: 0-0 Gd: 0-0 GF: 0-0 Fm: 0-0
Distance: 5f/6f: 0-0 7f-8f: 0-1 9f-13f: 0 4 14f+: 0-0
Track : LH: 0-4 RH: 0-0 Tight: 0-2 Gall: 0-0
Aids: Bl: 0-0 Vi: 0-0 Tstrap: 0-0
Best Rating: 30 2/01 Wolv 1m1f79y stand

Lady Ingabelle (IRE)

89(68) 69

3-y-o b f Catrail (USA)-Lady Anna Livia (Ahonoora)
T G Mills Kentavr (uk) Ltd

Placings:054000 (2876)
2001: 9^{0}SW, 10^{5}S, 9^{4}S, 9^{0}GF, 11^{0}GF, 8^{0}GF

	Starts	1st	2nd	3rd	Win & Pl
Career Total (Turf)	5	0	0	0	235
Career Total (AW)	1	0	0	0	

Going (Turf): Sf: 0-2 GS: 0-0 Gd: 0-0 GF: 0-3 Fm: 0-0
Distance: 5f/6f: 0-0 7f-8f: 0-0 9f-13f: 0-6 14f+: 0-0
Track : LH: 0-1 RH: 0-4 Tight: 0-5 Gall: 0-0
Aids: Bl: 0-0 Vi: 0-1 Tstrap: 0-0
Best Rating: 69 5/01 Sals 1m1f198y soft

Lady Irene (IRE)

84(65) (25)23

5-y-o br m Tirol-Felsen (IRE) (Ballad Rock)
T J Naughton Mrs L Archer

Placings:62560040420/00-0 (1529)
2001: 11^{0}F

	Starts	1st	2nd	3rd	Win & Pl
Career Total (Turf)	8	0	1	0	750
Career Total (AW)	6	0	1	0	943

Going (Turf): Sf: 0-3 GS: 0-1 Gd: 0-2 GF: 0-1 Fm: 0-1
Distance: 5f/6f: 0-0 7f-8f: 0-3 9f-13f: 0-10 14f+: 0-1
Track : LH: 0-10 RH: 0-2 Tight: 0-10 Gall: 0-0
Aids: Bl: 0-1 Vi: 0-0 Tstrap: 0-0
Best Rating: 16 5/01 Brig 1m3f196y firm

Lady Jeannie

(96) (52)58

4-y-o b f Emarati (USA)-Cottonwood (Teenoso (USA))
M J Haynes G R Sanford & Partners

Placings:06000020-060461020 (4891)
2001: 7^{0}SD, 8^{6}S, 7^{0}GS, 6^{4}GF, 6^{6}F, 8^{1}GF, 8^{0}G, 7^{2}GF, 8^{0}GF

	Starts	1st	2nd	3rd	Win & Pl
Career Total (Turf)	13	1	1	0	4946
Career Total (AW)	4	0	1	0	660

58	7/01	Wind	1m67y	D(0-80)H	G-F	£4030

Total win prize-money £4030

Going (Turf): Sf: 0-2 GS: 0-3 Gd: 0-2 **GF: 1-5** Fm: 0-1
Distance: 5f/6f: 0-5 7f-8f: 0-8 **9f-13f: 1-4** 14f+: 0-0
Track : LH: 0-5 **RH: 1-6 Tight: 1-7** Gall: 0-2
Aids: Bl: 0-0 Vi: 0-0 Tstrap: 0-0
Best Rating: 58 7/01 Wind 1m67y gd-fm

Lady Jones

105 58

4-y-o b/br f Emperor Jones (USA)-So Beguiling (USA) (Woodman (USA))
P L Gilligan Mrs Jean Routledge

Placings:500100/013005601-005100 (5599)
2001: 10^{0}GF, 10^{0}G, 9^{5}G, 14^{1}GS, 10^{0}HY, 12^{0}GS

	Starts	1st	2nd	3rd	Win & Pl
Career Total (Turf)	21	4	0	1	12344

58	10/01	Sals	1m6f15y	E(0-70)H	G-S	£3626
58	10/00	Nott	1m1f213y	F(0-65)H	SFT	£2991
59	6/00	Hayd	1m30y	E(0-70)H	G-S	£2996
57	9/99	Brig	6f209y	F	G-F	£2304

Total win prize-money £11918

Going (Turf): Sf: 1-4 **GS: 2-5** Gd: 0-4 GF: 1-6 Fm: 0-1
Distance: 5f/6f: 0-1 7f-8f: 1-5 **9f-13f: 2-13** 14f+: 1-1
Track : **LH: 3-12** RH: 1-5 **Tight: 1-3** Gall: 0-4
Aids: Bl: 0-0 Vi: 0-0 Tstrap: 0-0
Best Rating: 58 10/01 Sals 1m6f15y gd-sft

Lightly raced, she has gained stamina with age, and won over 14 furlongs at Salisbury in October. She is very effective with cut in the ground.

Lady Kinvarrah (IRE)

105 73

3-y-o b f Brief Truce (USA)-Al Corniche (IRE) (Bluebird (USA))
P J Makin John Gale & George Darling

Placings:060310-0163400 (5486)
2001: 8^{0}G, 9^{1}GF, 10^{6}GF, 9^{3}GS, 10^{4}G, 11^{0}G, 10^{0}HY

	Starts	1st	2nd	3rd	Win & Pl
Career Total (Turf)	13	2	0	2	10224

73	7/01	Kemp	1m1f	D(0-80)H	G-F	£4426
71	9/00	Leic	5f218y	E(0-75)	G-S	£2990

Total win prize-money £7417

Going (Turf): Sf: 0-2 **GS: 1-4** Gd: 0-5 **GF: 1-2** Fm: 0-0
Distance: 5f/6f: 1-4 7f-8f: 0-2 9f-13f: 1-7 14f+: 0-0
Track : LH: 0-4 **RH: 1-5** Tight: 0-1 Gall: 0-4
Aids: Bl: 0-0 Vi: 0-0 Tstrap: 0-0
Best Rating: 73 7/01 Kemp 1m1f gd-fm

From the family of Irish 1000 Guineas winner Nicer, she is a half-sister to a mile and a quarter winner. Relished the step up in trip when winning a nine-furlong handicap at Kempton in July.

Lady Lahar

107 (73)108

3-y-o b f Fraam-Brigadiers Bird (IRE) (Mujadil (USA))
M R Channon Barry Walters Catering

Placings:134104-4134250 (5339)
2001: 8^{4}FT, 8^{1}G, 8^{3}G, 8^{4}G, 10^{2}GS, 8^{5}GF, 10^{0}GS

	Starts	1st	2nd	3rd	Win & Pl
Career Total (Turf)	12	3	1	2	67969
Career Total (AW)	1	0	0	0	6666

74	6/01	Haml	1m65y	C	GD	£7377
108	8/00	Curr	7f		GD	£32500
79	6/00	Chep	6f16y	D	G-F	£3419

Total win prize-money £43297

Going (Turf): Sf: 0-1 GS: 0-4 **Gd: 2-4** GF: 1-3 Fm: 0-0
Distance: 5f/6f: 0-2 **7f-8f: 2-7** 9f-13f: 1-4 14f+: 0-0
Track : LH: 0-1 **RH: 1-3 Tight: 1-1** Gall: 0-1
Aids: Bl: 0-0 Vi: 0-0 Tstrap: 0-0
Best Rating: 108 8/01 Deau 1m2f gd-sft

Performed with credit in Group company in 2000 and scored on her second start at three, but was far from impressive. Fine efforts since in pattern company. Stays ten furlongs and handles any ground.

Lady Lap Dancer

98 40

3-y-o b f Shareef Dancer (USA)-Jelabna (Jalmood (USA))
Mrs M Reveley Mrs C Strang Steel

Placings:352 (3461)
2001: 8^{3}F, 9^{5}GF, 11^{2}F

	Starts	1st	2nd	3rd	Win & Pl
Career Total (Turf)	3	0	1	1	1199

Going (Turf): Sf: 0-0 GS: 0-0 Gd: 0-0 GF: 0-1 Fm: 0-2
Distance: 5f/6f: 0-0 7f-8f: 0-1 9f-13f: 0-2 14f+: 0-0
Track : LH: 0-2 RH: 0-0 Tight: 0-1 Gall: 0-1
Aids: Bl: 0-0 Vi: 0-0 Tstrap: 0-0
Best Rating: 40 7/01 Newc 1m firm

Lady Laureate

104(72) (23)73

3-y-o b f Sir Harry Lewis (USA)-Cyrillic (Rock City)
G C Bravery Blackfoot Bloodstock

Placings:0560-005221130210100 (5661)
2001: 11^{0}SD, 10^{0}GS, 11^{5}G, 14^{2}F, 11^{2}F, 11^{1}F, 11^{1}GF, 11^{3}G, 12^{0}F, 12^{2}GF, 11^{1}GF, 12^{0}G, 17^{1}G, 14^{0}G, 16^{0}G

	Starts	1st	2nd	3rd	Win & Pl
Career Total (Turf)	17	4	3	1	16708
Career Total (AW)	2	0	0	0	0

73	10/01	Bath	2m1f34y	D(0-80)H	GD	£3883
70	9/01	Brig	1m3f196y	E(0-70)H	G-F	£2786
66	7/01	Ling	1m3f106y	E(0-70)H	G-F	£3688
59	6/01	Ling	1m3f106y	E(0-70)H	FRM	£3614

Total win prize-money £13973

Going (Turf): Sf: 0-1 GS: 0-2 Gd: 1-6 **GF: 2-4** Fm: 1-4
Distance: 5f/6f: 0-1 7f-8f: 0-2 **9f-13f: 3-12** 14f+: 1-4
Track : **LH: 4-15** RH: 0-2 **Tight: 3-13** Gall: 0-0

Aids: Bl: 0-0 Vi: 0-0 Tstrap: 0-0
Best Rating: 73 10/01 Bath 2m1f34y good

A likeable filly, she has progressed well in 2001, winning three middle-distance handicaps and one over 17 furlongs, although she looks high enough in the handicap now.

Lady Lauren

85 **26**

5-y-o b m Cyrano De Bergerac-Wandering Stranger (Petong)

J O'Reilly Burntwood Sports Ltd

Placings:333540/0000000/00 (1921)

2001: 7^0S, 5^0GF

	Starts	1st	2nd	3rd	Win & Pl
Career Total (Turf)	14	0	0	3	1295
Career Total (AW)	1	0	0	0	

Going (Turf): Sf: 0-2 GS: 0-0 Gd: 0-3 GF: 0-8 Fm: 0-1
Distance: 5f/6f: 0-11 7f-8f: 0-3 9f-13f: 0-1 14f+: 0-0
Track: LH: 0-2 RH: 0-0 Tight: 0-1 Gall: 0-0
Aids: Bl: 0-2 Vi: 0-0 Tstrap: 0-0
Best Rating: 26 6/01 Newc 5f gd-fm

Lady Lenor

100(94) (72)**51**

3-y-o b f Presidium-Sparkling Roberta (Kind Of Hush)

Mrs G S Rees Longlands Racing

Placings:023-0050005 (5273)

2001: 6^0S, 6^0GF, 5^5G, 6^0F, 5^0GF, 5^0GS, 5^5HY

	Starts	1st	2nd	3rd	Win & Pl
Career Total (Turf)	9	0	1	0	840
Career Total (AW)	1	0	0	1	323

Going (Turf): Sf: 0-3 GS: 0-1 Gd: 0-2 GF: 0-2 Fm: 0-1
Distance: 5f/6f: 0-10 7f-8f: 0-0 9f-13f: 0-0 14f+: 0-0
Track: LH: 0-1 RH: 0-1 Tight: 0-1 Gall: 0-1
Aids: Bl: 0-0 Vi: 0-0 Tstrap: 0-0
Best Rating: 51 10/01 Newc 5f gd-sft

Lady Lindsay (IRE)

88 **85**

2-y-o ch f Danehill Dancer (IRE)-Jungle Jezebel (Thatching)

R Guest Graham Robinson

Placings:11 (4209)

2001: 6^1GF, 5^1GF

	Starts	1st	2nd	3rd	Win & Pl
Career Total (Turf)	2	2	0	0	6671

85	8/01	Bath	5f161y	E	G-F	£2982
85	7/01	Wind	6f	D	G-F	£3688

Total win prize-money £6671

Going (Turf): Sf: 0-0 GS: 0-0 Gd: 0-0 **GF: 2-2** Fm: 0-0
Distance: 5f/6f: 2-2 7f-8f: 0-0 9f-13f: 0-0 14f+: 0-0
Track: LH: 1-1 RH: 0-0 Tight: 0-0 **Gall: 1-1**
Aids: Bl: 0-0 Vi: 0-0 Tstrap: 0-0
Best Rating: 85 8/01 Bath 5f161y gd-fm

Winner of her two starts on firm ground.

Lady Links

106 **88**

2-y-o b f Bahamian Bounty-Sparky's Song (Electric)

R Hannon Coriolan Partnership Ii

Placings:2346411 (5736a)

2001: 5^2GF, 5^3GF, 6^4G, 6^6G, 6^4G, 6^1HY, 6^1HY

	Starts	1st	2nd	3rd	Win & Pl
Career Total (Turf)	7	2	1	1	49908

87	11/01	StCl	6f		HVY	£13579
72	10/01	Ling	6f	D	HVY	£4147

Total win prize-money £17726

Going (Turf): Sf: 2-2 GS: 0-0 Gd: 0-3 GF: 0-2 Fm: 0-0
Distance: 5f/6f: 2-6 7f-8f: 0-1 9f-13f: 0-0 14f+: 0-0
Track: LH: 0-0 RH: 0-0 Tight: 0-0 Gall: 0-0
Aids: Bl: 0-0 Vi: 0-0 Tstrap: 0-0
Best Rating: 88 10/01 Rdcr 6f good

She finally got off the mark in a heavy-ground conditions event at Lingfield in October, and followed up in a French Listed race. She had earlier run fine races in the Weatherbys Super Sprint, Watership Down Stud Sales Stakes and Betabet Two-Year-Old Trophy.

Lady Miletrian (IRE)

108 **109**

3-y-o b f Barathea (IRE)-Local Custom (IRE) (Be My Native (USA))

M R Channon Miletrian Plc

Placings:520-144352000 (3580)

2001: 8^1S, 8^4S, 7^4GS, 7^3G, 9^5G, 8^2GF, 8^0GF, 8^0G, 7^0GF

	Starts	1st	2nd	3rd	Win & Pl
Career Total (Turf)	12	1	2	1	17131

79	4/01	Muss	1m	D	SFT	£2828

Total win prize-money £2828

Going (Turf): Sf: 1-2 GS: 0-2 Gd: 0-3 GF: 0-5 Fm: 0-0
Distance: 5f/6f: 0-3 **7f-8f: 1-7** 9f-13f: 0-2 14f+: 0-0
Track: LH: 0-1 **RH: 1-5 Tight: 1-2** Gall: 0-2
Aids: Bl: 0-0 Vi: 0-0 Tstrap: 0-0
Best Rating: 109 6/01 Asct 1m gd-fm

She hinted at ability at two and had little difficulty in getting off the mark in a modest Musselburgh maiden on her reappearance before running well in Guineas trials at Kempton and Newbury. Subsequently ran with credit in a Listed events at Baden-Baden and Epsom, but still looks short of Group company. Has won on soft ground and acts on good to firm.

Lady Netbetsports (IRE)

101 **78**

2-y-o b f In The Wings-Auntie Maureen (IRE) (Roi Danzig (USA))

B S Rothwell Full Time Whistle Limited

Placings:20243 (5282)

2001: 6^2GF, 7^0GF, 8^2GF, 8^4HY, 8^3HY

	Starts	1st	2nd	3rd	Win & Pl
Career Total (Turf)	5	0	2	1	3202

Going (Turf): Sf: 0-2 GS: 0-0 Gd: 0-0 GF: 0-3 Fm: 0-0
Distance: 5f/6f: 0-1 7f-8f: 0-2 9f-13f: 0-2 14f+: 0-0
Track: LH: 0-3 RH: 0-0 Tight: 0-0 Gall: 0-0
Aids: Bl: 0-0 Vi: 0-0 Tstrap: 0-0
Best Rating: 78 10/01 Ayr 1m heavy

Has shown ability in maidens on varying ground.

Lady Of Gdansk (IRE)

74 **24**

2-y-o ch f Danehill Dancer (IRE)-Rebecca's Girl (IRE) (Nashamaa)

H J Collingridge The Headquarters Partnership Vii

Placings:0 (5689)

2001: 6^0S

	Starts	1st	2nd	3rd	Win & Pl
Career Total (Turf)	1	0	0	0	

Going (Turf): Sf: 0-1 GS: 0-0 Gd: 0-0 GF: 0-0 Fm: 0-0
Distance: 5f/6f: 0-1 7f-8f: 0-0 9f-13f: 0-0 14f+: 0-0
Track: LH: 0-0 RH: 0-0 Tight: 0-0 Gall: 0-0
Aids: Bl: 0-0 Vi: 0-0 Tstrap: 0-0
Best Rating: 24 11/01 Donc 6f soft

Lady Of Kildare (IRE)

105 **96**

3-y-o b f Mujadil (USA)-Dancing Sunset (IRE) (Red Sunset)

T J Taaffe Gerard P Callanan

Placings:0220110-55650 (4349a)

2001: 7^5G, 6^5GY, 6^6GS, 7^5GF, 6^0GY

	Starts	1st	2nd	3rd	Win & Pl
Career Total (Turf)	12	2	2	0	27713

94	9/00	Curr	6f	GD	£19500
82	8/00	Tipp	7f	GD	£5865

Total win prize-money £25365

Going (Turf): Sf: 0-0 GS: 0-1 **Gd: 2-3** GF: 0-3 Fm: 0-0
Distance: 5f/6f: 1-6 7f-8f: 1-6 9f-13f: 0-0 14f+: 0-0
Track: LH: 1-2 RH: 0-3 Tight: 0-0 Gall: 0-0
Aids: Bl: 0-1 Vi: 0-0 Tstrap: 0-0
Best Rating: 96 5/01 Curr 7f good

Scored twice as a juvenile over six and seven furlongs on good ground, including a Listed event. Stepped up to Group class this term without success.

Lady Of Ta'Pinu

(60) (14)

2-y-o ch f Greensmith-Pitcairn Princess (Capricorn Line)

C N Kellett Willwewontwe Club

Placings:500 (5163)

2001: 5^5G, 6^0G, 6^0SD

	Starts	1st	2nd	3rd	Win & Pl
Career Total (Turf)	2	0	0	0	0
Career Total (AW)	1	0	0	0	

Going (Turf): Sf: 0-0 GS: 0-0 Gd: 0-2 GF: 0-0 Fm: 0-0
Distance: 5f/6f: 0-2 7f-8f: 0-1 9f-13f: 0-0 14f+: 0-0
Track: LH: 0-2 RH: 0-0 Tight: 0-1 Gall: 0-1
Aids: Bl: 0-0 Vi: 0-0 Tstrap: 0-0
Best Rating: 14 10/01 Wolv 6f stand

Lady Of The Braes

54 **14**

2-y-o b f Mind Games-Mary From Dunlow (Nicholas Bill)

H A McWilliams G P Bernacchi

Placings:06000 (4435)

2001: 5^0S, 5^6G, 5^0GF, 5^0GF, 5^0G

	Starts	1st	2nd	3rd	Win & Pl
Career Total (Turf)	5	0	0	0	0

Going (Turf): Sf: 0-1 GS: 0-0 Gd: 0-2 GF: 0-2 Fm: 0-0
Distance: 5f/6f: 0-5 7f-8f: 0-0 9f-13f: 0-0 14f+: 0-0
Track: LH: 0-1 RH: 0-0 Tight: 0-0 Gall: 0-0
Aids: Bl: 0-0 Vi: 0-0 Tstrap: 0-0

No signs of ability to date.

Lady Of Windsor (IRE)

97(95) (58)**39**

4-y-o ch f Woods Of Windsor (USA)-North Lady (Northfields (USA))

I Semple Raeburn Brick Limited

Placings:44432240404/510230060404l-0000400 (5659)

2001: 7^0SW, 7^0GS, 8^0GF, 7^0GF, 8^4GF, 7^0GF, 8^0G

	Starts	1st	2nd	3rd	Win & Pl
Career Total (Turf)	29	2	3	2	11482
Career Total (AW)	2	0	0	0	0

64 10/00 Muss 7f30y E(0-70)H SFT £2268
73 5/00 Muss 1m E(0-70) FRM £3081
Total win prize money £5349

Going (Turf): Sf: 1-4 GS: 0-5 Gd: 0-8 GF: 0-8 **Fm: 1-3**
Distance: 5f/6f: 0-4 **7f-8f: 2-24** 9f-13f: 0-3 14f+: 0-0
Track : LH: 0-10 **RH: 2-14 Tight: 2-14** Gall: 0-0
Aids: Bl: 1-6 Vi: 1-22 Tstrap: 0-0
Best Rating: 47 4/01 Muss 7f30y gd-sft

Below par this year, she is best when able to dominate.

Lady Pahia (IRE)

106 **78**

3-y-o ch f Pivotal-Appledorn (Doulab (USA))
A P Jarvis Ambrose Turnbull

Placings:4-0301125000 **(5267)**
2001: 7⁰S, 7³GF, 7⁰G, 7¹GF, 7¹GF, 8²GS, 7⁵GF, 7⁰GS, 8⁰G, 6⁰GS

	Starts	1st	2nd	3rd	Win & Pl
Career Total (Turf)	11	2	1	1	10475

78 6/01 Gdwd 7f D(0-85)H G-F £4936
73 6/01 Kemp 7f E(0-75)H G-F £3786
Total win prize-money £8723

Going (Turf): Sf: 0-1 GS: 0-3 Gd: 0-2 **GF: 2-5** Fm: 0-0
Distance: 5f/6f: 0-0 **7f-8f: 2-10** 9f-13f: 0-1 14f+: 0-0
Track : LH: 0-3 **RH: 2-5** Tight: 0-0 **Gall: 1-4**
Aids: Bl: 0-0 Vi: 0-0 Tstrap: 0-0
Best Rating: 78 6/01 Gdwd 7f gd-fm

Decent handicapper, she won at Kempton and Goodwood in June, both victories coming on fast ground over seven furlongs, although she has looked held by the Handicapper since.

Lady Pekan

100(79) (45)**84**

2-y-o b f Sri Pekan (USA)-Cloudberry (Night Shift (USA))
J Balding (P S McEntee 15/5) P S J Croft

Placings:042623412100 **(4659)**
2001: 5⁰S, 5⁴SD, 5²GF, 6⁶F, 5²GF, 5³GF, 5⁴GF, 5¹GF, 5²G, 5¹GS, 5⁰GF, 6⁰GF

	Starts	1st	2nd	3rd	Win & Pl
Career Total (Turf)	11	2	3	1	20537
Career Total (AW)	1	0	0	0	0

84 8/01 Sand 5f6y D G-S £4095
77 7/01 Kemp 5f D G-F £5590
Total win prize-money £9685

Going (Turf): Sf: 0-1 **GS: 1-1** Gd: 0-1 **GF: 1-7** Fm: 0-1
Distance: **5f/6f: 2-12** 7f-8f: 0-9 9f-13f: 0-0 14f+: 0-0
Track : LH: 0-0 RH: 0-0 Tight: 0-0 Gall: 0-0
Aids: Bl: 0-0 Vi: 0-0 Tstrap: 0-0
Best Rating: 84 8/01 Sand 5f6y gd-sft

Had a busy time as a juvenile winning twice at the minimum trip on varying ground.

Lady Rath (IRE)

59(35)

3-y-o b f Standiford (USA)-Jalopy (Jalmood (USA))
L A Dace Noel Monaghan

Placings:0000 **(1484)**
2001: 6⁰SD, 7⁰S, 6⁰GF, 5⁰GF

	Starts	1st	2nd	3rd	Win & Pl
Career Total (Turf)	3	0	0	0	
Career Total (AW)	1	0	0	0	

Going (Turf): Sf: 0-1 GS: 0-0 Gd: 0-0 GF: 0-2 Fm: 0-0
Distance: 5f/6f: 0-2 7f-8f: 0-2 9f-13f: 0-0 14f+: 0-0
Track : LH: 0-3 RH: 0-1 Tight: 0-1 Gall: 0-2
Aids: Bl: 0-0 Vi: 0-0 Tstrap: 0-0

Lady Rock

(97) (55)**56**

3-y-o b f Mistertopogigo (IRE)-Bollin Victoria (Jalmood (USA))
R Bastiman New Kids On The Block Limited

Placings:0046366-0001600434 **(5619)**
2001: 5⁰G, 6⁰GF, 5⁰GF, 6¹GF, 6⁶S, 6⁰GF, 6⁰F, 7⁴GF, 6³SD, 6⁴SD

	Starts	1st	2nd	3rd	Win & Pl
Career Total (Turf)	15	1	0	1	4729
Career Total (AW)	2	0	0	1	352

56 7/01 Sthl 6f E(0-70)H G-F £3542
Total win prize-money £3542

Going (Turf): Sf: 0-2 GS: 0-1 Gd: 0-4 **GF: 1-7** Fm: 0-1
Distance: **5f/6f: 1-15** 7f-8f: 0-2 9f-13f: 0-0 14f+: 0-0
Track : **LH: 1-6** RH: 0-0 Tight: 0-2 Gall: 0-0
Aids: Bl: 0-0 Vi: 0-0 Tstrap: 0-0
Best Rating: 56 9/01 Catt 7f gd-fm

Front running handicapper, suited by fast ground on turf but acts on Fibresand.

Lady Sandrovitch (IRE)

(91) (36)**28**

4-y-o b f Desert Style (IRE)-Mauras Pride (IRE) (Cadeaux Genereux)
R A Fahey J M Flynn

Placings:5443/0600-40 **(0199)**
2001: 7⁴SW, 6⁰SD

	Starts	1st	2nd	3rd	Win & Pl
Career Total (Turf)	3	0	0	0	0
Career Total (AW)	7	0	0	1	250

Going (Turf): Sf: 0-1 GS: 0-0 Gd: 0-0 GF: 0-1 Fm: 0-1
Distance: 5f/6f: 0-8 7f-8f: 0-2 9f-13f: 0-0 14f+: 0-0
Track : LH: 0-6 RH: 0-0 Tight: 0-4 Gall: 0-0
Aids: Bl: 0-1 Vi: 0-0 Tstrap: 0-0
Best Rating: 25 1/01 Wolv 7f slow

Lady Santana (IRE)

(80) (15)**66**

4-y-o b f Doyoun-Santana Lady (IRE) (Blakeney)
Mrs Merrita Jones Exors Of The Late F J Sainsbury

Placings:000/50-0 **(0347)**
2001: 9⁰SD

	Starts	1st	2nd	3rd	Win & Pl
Career Total (Turf)	4	0	0	0	
Career Total (AW)	2	0	0	0	

Going (Turf): Sf: 0-1 GS: 0-0 Gd: 0-0 GF: 0-3 Fm: 0-0
Distance: 5f/6f: 0-3 7f-8f: 0-0 9f-13f: 0-3 14f+: 0-0
Track : LH: 0-2 RH: 0-2 Tight: 0-3 Gall: 0-2
Aids: Bl: 0-0 Vi: 0-0 Tstrap: 0-0
Best Rating: 15 2/01 Wolv 1m1f79y stand

Lady Sapphire

79(69) (21)**33**

2-y-o b f Dancing Spree (USA)-Lady Broker (Petorius)
M Mullineaux Esprit De Corps Racing

Placings:0000000 **(5689)**
2001: 5⁰GF, 5⁰GF, 5⁰GF, 7⁰HY, 6⁰G, 6⁰SD, 6⁰S

	Starts	1st	2nd	3rd	Win & Pl
Career Total (Turf)	6	0	0	0	
Career Total (AW)	1	0	0	0	

Going (Turf): Sf: 0-2 GS: 0-0 Gd: 0-1 GF: 0-3 Fm: 0-0
Distance: 5f/6f: 0-6 7f-8f: 0-1 9f-13f: 0-0 14f+: 0-0

Track : LH: 0-4 RH: 0-0 Tight: 0-3 Gall: 0-0
Aids: Bl: 0-0 Vi: 0-0 Tstrap: 0-0
Best Rating: 33 5/01 Hayd 5f gd-fm

Lady Sharp Shot (IRE)

76(87) (34)**28**

3-y-o b f Son Of Sharp Shot (IRE)-Ski For Gold (Shirley Heights)
J L Dunlop Windflower Overseas Holdings Inc

Placings:50-40 **(4614)**
2001: 11⁴SD, 13⁰F

	Starts	1st	2nd	3rd	Win & Pl
Career Total (Turf)	3	0	0	0	0
Career Total (AW)	1	0	0	0	0

Going (Turf): Sf: 0-1 GS: 0-1 Gd: 0-0 GF: 0-0 Fm: 0-1
Distance: 5f/6f: 0-0 7f-8f: 0-0 9f-13f: 0-3 14f+: 0-1
Track : LH: 0-4 RH: 0-0 Tight: 0-2 Gall: 0-0
Aids: Bl: 0-0 Vi: 0-0 Tstrap: 0-0
Best Rating: 34 4/01 Sthl 1m3f stand

Lady Sophia

86(68) (23)**49**

2-y-o ch f Atraf-Miss Lear (Lear Fan (USA))
Andrew Reid (W G M Turner 4/6) A S Reid

Placings:05630000 **(4630)**
2001: 5⁰G, 5⁵GF, 6⁶F, 7³GF, 7⁰SD, 6⁰GF, 6⁰GF, 8⁰GF

	Starts	1st	2nd	3rd	Win & Pl
Career Total (Turf)	7	0	0	1	265
Career Total (AW)	1	0	0	0	

Going (Turf): Sf: 0-0 GS: 0-0 Gd: 0-1 GF: 0-5 Fm: 0-1
Distance: 5f/6f: 0-5 7f-8f: 0-2 9f-13f: 0-1 14f+: 0-0
Track : LH: 0-2 RH: 0-0 Tight: 0-0 Gall: 0-1
Aids: Bl: 0-0 Vi: 0-2 Tstrap: 0-0
Best Rating: 49 9/01 Ling 6f gd-fm

Lady Stratagem

89 **72**

2-y-o gr f Mark Of Esteem (IRE)-Grey Angel (Kenmare (FR))
R Hannon R V Lewis

Placings:0600 **(5602)**
2001: 7⁰GF, 6⁶GS, 6⁰GF, 7⁰GS

	Starts	1st	2nd	3rd	Win & Pl
Career Total (Turf)	4	0	0	0	0

Going (Turf): Sf: 0-0 GS: 0-2 Gd: 0-0 GF: 0-2 Fm: 0-0
Distance: 5f/6f: 0-1 7f-8f: 0-3 9f-13f: 0-0 14f+: 0-0
Track : LH: 0-0 RH: 0-0 Tight: 0-0 Gall: 0-0
Aids: Bl: 0-0 Vi: 0-0 Tstrap: 0-0
Best Rating: 72 11/01 NmkR 7f gd-sft

Lady Tilly

79(71) **6**

4-y-o b f Puissance-Lady Of Itatiba (BEL) (King Of Macedon)
A C Whillans Miss E Johnston

Placings:60030560/0544000-500 **(3310)**
2001: 8⁵G, 9⁰GS, 7⁰GS

	Starts	1st	2nd	3rd	Win & Pl
Career Total (Turf)	17	0	0	1	868
Career Total (AW)	1	0	0	0	

Going (Turf): Sf: 0-3 GS: 0-4 Gd: 0-3 GF: 0-6 Fm: 0-1
Distance: 5f/6f: 0-4 7f-8f: 0-12 9f-13f: 0-2 14f+: 0-0
Track : LH: 0-7 RH: 0-4 Tight: 0-8 Gall: 0-0
Aids: Bl: 0-1 Vi: 0-0 Tstrap: 0-0

Best Rating: 6 6/01 Haml 1m65y good

Lady Two K (IRE)

102 **81**

4-y-o b f Grand Lodge (USA)-Princess Pavlova (IRE) (Sadler's Wells (USA))

J Mackie Gwen K Dot.Com

Placings:04601-22000 **(5501)**

2001: 11^{2}GS, 12^{0}G, 10^{0}HY, 11^{0}S, 12^{0}HY

	Starts	1st	2nd	3rd	Win & Pl
Career Total (Turf)	10	1	2	0	7386

74 10/00 Bath 1m3f144yE(0-70)H G-S £3669

Total win prize-money £3669

Going (Turf): Sf: 0-5 **GS: 1-2** Gd: 0-2 GF: 0-1 Fm: 0-0
Distance: 5f/6f: 0-0 7f-8f: 0-1 **9f-13f: 1-9** 14f+: 0-0
Track : **LH: 1-8** RH: 0-1 **Tight: 1-3** Gall: 0-2
Aids: Bl: 0-0 Vi: 0-0 Tstrap: 0-0
Best Rating: 81 5/01 Bath 1m3f144y gd-sft

Got off the mark in a competitive handicap at Bath on her final run of 2000 and was twice denied by narrow margins in the spring, the first of them due to jockey error. Suited by good and good to soft and middle distances.

Lady Ward (IRE)

99(76) (33)**59**

3-y-o b f Mujadil (USA)-Sans Ceriph (IRE) (Thatching)

M H Tompkins Lillypop Racing Club

Placings:036500-4011300 **(4872)**

2001: 8^{4}GF, 7^{0}GF, 8^{1}GF, 8^{1}S, 10^{3}G, 8^{0}HY, 7^{0}G

	Starts	1st	2nd	3rd	Win & Pl
Career Total (Turf)	12	2	0	2	5929
Career Total (AW)	1	0	0	0	

59 8/01 Nott 1m54y F SFT £2486
50 8/01 Leic 1m9y F G-F £2513

Total win prize-money £4999

Going (Turf): **Sf: 1-2** GS: 0-0 Gd: 0-4 **GF: 1-6** Fm: 0-0
Distance: 5f/6f: 0-3 7f-8f: 0-6 **9f-13f: 2-4** 14f+: 0-0
Track : **LH: 1-5** RH: 0-2 Tight: 0-2 Gall: 0-1
Aids: Bl: 0-0 Vi: 0-0 Tstrap: 0-0
Best Rating: 59 8/01 Nott 1m54y soft

Moderate miler, winner of two claimers within a week in August. Seems to handle any ground.

Lady's Secret (IRE)

96 **77+**

2-y-o b f Alzao (USA)-Kaaba (Darshaan)

B W Hills Mrs E Roberts

Placings:40 **(5144)**

2001: 7^{4}GF, 7^{0}G

	Starts	1st	2nd	3rd	Win & Pl
Career Total (Turf)	2	0	0	0	834

Going (Turf): **Sf: 0-0 GS: 0-0 Gd: 0-1 GF: 0-1 Fm: 0-0**
Distance: 5f/6f: 0-0 7f-8f: 0-2 9f-13f: 0-0 14f+: 0-0
Track : LH: 0-0 RH: 0-0 Tight: 0-0 Gall: 0-0
Aids: Bl: 0-0 Vi: 0-0 Tstrap: 0-0
Best Rating: 77 9/01 Newb 7f gd-fm

Lady-Love

89(63) (11)**31**

4-y-o b f Pursuit Of Love-Lady Day (FR) (Lightning (FR))

Denys Smith D Morland

Placings:1060/5020020-000000000U0 **(4481)**

2001: 7^{0}GF, 8^{0}F, 6^{0}GF, 8^{0}GF, 8^{0}GF, 5^{0}GF, 6^{0}G, 6^{0}F, 5^{0}S, 5^{U}GF, 8^{0}F

	Starts	1st	2nd	3rd	Win & Pl
Career Total (Turf)	21	1	2	0	4421
Career Total (AW)	1	0	0	0	

74 6/99 Muss 5f E GD £2801

Total win prize-money £2801

Going (Turf): Sf: 0-2 GS: 0-2 **Gd: 1-3** GF: 0-7 Fm: 0-6
Distance: **5f/6f: 1-10** 7f-8f: 0-10 9f-13f: 0-1 14f+: 0-0
Track : LH: 0-3 RH: 0-4 Tight: 0-5 Gall: 0-1
Aids: Bl: 0-3 Vi: 0-1 Tstrap: 0-0
Best Rating: 58 5/01 Muss 7f30y gd-fm

Ladychatterly

(97) (72)**72**

2-y-o ch f Botanic (USA)-Gay Sarah (Last Fandango)

J W Hills J W Hills

Placings:321 **(5163)**

2001: 5^{3}G, 6^{2}G, 6^{1}SD

	Starts	1st	2nd	3rd	Win & Pl
Career Total (Turf)	2	0	1	1	10377
Career Total (AW)	1	1	0	0	3059

72 10/01 Wolv 6f F STD £3059

Total win prize-money £3059

Going (Turf): **Sf: 0-0 GS: 0-0 Gd: 0-2 GF: 0-0 Fm: 0-0**
Distance: **5f/6f: 1-3** 7f-8f: 0-0 9f-13f: 0-0 14f+: 0-0
Track : **LH: 1-1** RH: 0-0 **Tight: 1-1** Gall: 0-0
Aids: Bl: 0-0 Vi: 0-0 Tstrap: 0-0
Best Rating: 72 10/01 Wolv 6f stand

Improved on her debut with a good second in a valuable sales event at Kempton, before getting off the mark on the sand at Wolverhampton over six furlongs.

Ladycromby (IRE)

(83) (16)

3-y-o ch f Lycius (USA)-Havinia (Habitat)

E J O'Neill Mrs Patrick O'Neill

Placings:0000 **(4066)**

2001: 8^{0}S, 10^{0}G, 7^{0}GF, 12^{0}SD

	Starts	1st	2nd	3rd	Win & Pl
Career Total (Turf)	3	0	0	0	
Career Total (AW)	1	0	0	0	

Going (Turf): **Sf: 0-1 GS: 0-0 Gd: 0-1 GF: 0-1 Fm: 0-0**
Distance: 5f/6f: 0-0 7f-8f: 0-2 9f-13f: 0-2 14f+: 0-0
Track : LH: 0-1 RH: 0-0 Tight: 0-2 Gall: 0-0
Aids: Bl: 0-0 Vi: 0-0 Tstrap: 0-0
Best Rating: 47 4/01 NmkR 1m soft

Ladywell Blaise (IRE)

104(93) (36)**33**

4-y-o b f Turtle Island (IRE)-Duly Elected (Persian Bold)

J J Bridger W Wood

Placings:5/314640601200000000-0000600040243500300000 **(4715)**

2001: 7^{0}SW, 6^{0}SD, 7^{0}SW, 8^{0}SD, 8^{6}S, 6^{0}HY, 8^{0}GS, 7^{0}GS, 6^{4}G, 5^{0}GF, 7^{2}F, 6^{4}GF, 7^{3}GF, 7^{5}GF, 8^{0}GF, 7^{0}GS, 9^{3}GF, 7^{0}G, 7^{0}GF, 7^{0}GF, 7^{0}GF, 6^{0}G

	Starts	1st	2nd	3rd	Win & Pl
Career Total (Turf)	32	1	2	2	4307
Career Total (AW)	10	1	0	1	3220

61 1/00 Ling 6f D STD £2782

Total win prize-money £2782

Going (Turf): Sf: 0-5 GS: 0-3 Gd: 0-6 **GF: 1-16** Fm: 0-2
Distance: 5f/6f: 1-11 7f-8f: 1-26 9f-13f: 0-5 14f+: 0-0
Track : **LH: 1-14** RH: 0-12 **Tight: 1-14** Gall: 0-3
Aids: Bl: 0-1 Vi: 0-0 Tstrap: 0-0
Best Rating: 63 4/01 Kemp 1m soft

Claiming-class filly. Best over seven on fast ground, she races prominently.

Lafayette (IRE)

104 **85**

3-y-o b c General Monash (USA)-Bezee (Belmez (USA))

A C Stewart Racing For Gold

Placings:00-01241010 **(5135)**

2001: 7^{0}G, 10^{1}GF, 11^{2}G, 12^{4}GF, 9^{1}G, 10^{0}G, 10^{1}S, 10^{0}G

	Starts	1st	2nd	3rd	Win & Pl
Career Total (Turf)	10	3	1	0	17616

85 9/01 Pont 1m2f6y C(0-95)H SFT £6351
76 8/01 Bevl 1m1f207yE(0-70)H GD £5070
64 5/01 Sand 1m2f7y D(0-80)H G-F £4446

Total win prize-money £15867

Going (Turf): **Sf: 1-2** GS: 0-0 **Gd: 1-6 GF: 1-2** Fm: 0-0
Distance: 5f/6f: 0-0 7f-8f: 0-3 **9f-13f: 3-7** 14f+: 0-0
Track : LH: 1-1 **RH: 2-5** Tight: 0-1 Gall: 0-1
Aids: Bl: 0-0 Vi: 0-0 Tstrap: 0-0
Best Rating: 85 9/01 Pont 1m2f6y soft

He has won over ten furlongs at Sandown, Beverley and Pontefract this season and ran well when tried over further. Handles any ground.

Laffah (USA)

103 **63**

6-y-o b g Silver Hawk (USA)-Sakiyah (USA) (Secretariat (USA))

G L Moore Richard Green (fine Paintings)

Placings:00/006440/13411010-000400 **(3549)**

2001: 16^{0}S, 14^{0}GF, 20^{0}GF, 16^{4}GF, 18^{0}GF, 21^{0}GF

	Starts	1st	2nd	3rd	Win & Pl
Career Total (Turf)	22	4	0	1	31521

69 9/00 Gdwd 2m D(0-85)H GD £7328
68 8/00 Gdwd 2m4f C(0-95)H G-F £17225
64 7/00 Bath 2m1f34y E(0-70)H FRM £2749
52 7/00 Chep 2m2f E(0-70)H G-F £2749

Total win prize-money £30054

Going (Turf): Sf: 0-4 GS: 0-1 Gd: 1-4 **GF: 2-12** Fm: 1-1
Distance: 5f/6f: 0-0 7f-8f: 0-2 9f-13f: 0-6 **14f+: 4-14**
Track : LH: 2-6 RH: 2-12 **Tight: 3-7** Gall: 0-4
Aids: Bl: 0-1 Vi: 0-1 **Tstrap: 4-14**
Best Rating: 63 6/01 Asct 2m45y gd-fm

He is an out-and-out stayer and enjoyed a good 2000, winning four times at Chepstow, Bath and Goodwood twice. Acts well on fast ground, but has yet to hit form this season.

Laggan Minstrel (IRE)

105(99) (73)**77**

3-y-o b c Mark Of Esteem (IRE)-Next Episode (USA) (Nijinsky (CAN))

R Hannon Stonethorn Stud Farms Limited

Placings:00233-3152210 **(3636)**

2001: 7^{3}SW, 8^{1}GS, 8^{5}G, 8^{2}GF, 8^{2}GF, 7^{1}GF, 7^{0}GS

	Starts	1st	2nd	3rd	Win & Pl
Career Total (Turf)	8	2	2	0	8724
Career Total (AW)	4	0	1	3	1849

77 7/01 Ling 7f140y E(0-75)H G-F £3416
73 5/01 Sals 1m E(0-70)H G-S £3402

Total win prize-money £6818

Going (Turf): Sf: 0-1 **GS: 1-2** Gd: 0-2 **GF: 1-3** Fm: 0-0
Distance: 5f/6f: 0-0 **7f-8f: 2-9** 9f-13f: 0-3 14f+: 0-0
Track : LH: 0-6 RH: 0-2 Tight: 0-6 Gall: 0-0
Aids: Bl: 0-0 Vi: 0-0 Tstrap: 0-0
Best Rating: 77 7/01 Ling 7f140y gd-fm

Fair mile handicapper, acts on fast and easy ground, usually held up. In good form at present. Has won twice so far this season, once on All-Weather.

Lago

99(60) **51**

3-y-o b g Maelstrom Lake-Jugendliebe (IRE) (Persian Bold)

M W Easterby B Bargh T Swain J Walsh & P Bown

Placings:0-0042045 **(4259)**

2001: 8^{0}SW, 5^{0}S, 10^{4}GF, 12^{2}GF, 10^{0}GF, 14^{5}S, 14^{5}GF

	Starts	1st	2nd	3rd	Win & Pl
Career Total (Turf)	7	0	1	0	1461
Career Total (AW)	1	0	0	0	

Going (Turf): **Sf:** 0-2 **GS:** 0-0 **Gd:** 0-0 **GF:** 0-5 **Fm:** 0-0
Distance: 5f/6f: 0-1 7f-8f: 0-1 9f-13f: 0-4 14f+: 0-2
Track : LH: 0-5 RH: 0-1 Tight: 0-2 Gall: 0-0
Aids: Bl: 0-0 Vi: 0-0 Tstrap: 0-0
Best Rating: 51 7/01 Haml 1m4f17y gd-fm

His best effort so far came when runner-up in a modest handicap over 12 furlongs at Hamilton in July.

Lago Di Como

99(102) (57)**52?**

4-y-o b c Piccolo-Farmer's Pet (Sharrood (USA))

T J Naughton Miss R A Moody

Placings:00003/041000-00051120 **(4704)**

2001: 8^{0}S, 11^{0}GS, 11^{0}F, 11^{5}G, 10^{1}F, 9^{1}GF, 9^{2}SW, 8^{0}G

	Starts	1st	2nd	3rd	Win & Pl
Career Total (Turf)	15	3	0	0	6846
Career Total (AW)	4	0	1	1	1100

52	8/01	Brig	1m1f209yF(0-65)H		G-F	£2436
39	8/01	Ling	1m2f	G	FRM	£2086
60	7/00	Ling	1m1f	F	G-F	£2324

Total win prize-money £6846

Going (Turf): Sf: 0-3 GS: 0-2 Gd: 0-4 **GF: 2-3** Fm: 1-3
Distance: 5f/6f: 0-0 7f-8f: 0-4 **9f-13f: 3-15** 14f+: 0-0
Track : **LH: 3-16** RH: 0-1 **Tight: 2-14** Gall: 0-0
Aids: Bl: 0-1 Vi: 0-1 Tstrap: 0-0
Best Rating: 55 9/01 Wolv 1m1f79y slow

Appreciated the drop back to ten furlongs to win a Lingfield seller and followed up with a runaway win in an amateurs' event at Brighton. Goes on fast ground and likes to make the running.

Lago Di Levico

89(95) (38)**26**

4-y-o ch g Pelder (IRE)-Langton Herring (Nearly A Hand)

H S Howe M R Lavis

Placings:0/1546000-435000 **(4291)**

2001: 6^{4}SW, 7^{3}SW, 8^{5}SD, 10^{0}SW, 9^{0}GF, 7^{0}GF

	Starts	1st	2nd	3rd	Win & Pl
Career Total (Turf)	10	1	0	0	1939
Career Total (AW)	5	0	0	1	412

66	3/00	Nott	1m54y	G	GD	£1939

Total win prize-money £1939

Going (Turf): Sf: 0-0 GS: 0-3 **Gd: 1-2** GF: 0-2 Fm: 0-2
Distance: 5f/6f: 0-2 7f-8f: 0-6 **9f-13f: 1-6** 14f+: 0-0
Track : **LH: 1-10** RH: 0-0 Tight: 0-4 Gall: 0-0
Aids: Bl: 0-0 Vi: 0-1 Tstrap: 0-2
Best Rating: 38 2/01 Ling 6f slow

Lago Di Varano

106 **82**

9-y-o b g Clantime-On The Record (Record Token)

R M Whitaker The Pbt Group

Placings:1225551140/23500404/012004152054443002
3/052000001005000/36042104622020030 06/00003100
53601000064/066035315053001200 2650-
100006002400 **(5630)**

2001: 6^{1}GS, 6^{0}G, 6^{0}G, 6^{0}GF, 6^{0}GF, 6^{6}G, 5^{0}G, 6^{0}S, 5^{2}GS, 6^{4}GS, 5^{0}S, 6^{0}G

	Starts	1st	2nd	3rd	Win & Pl
Career Total (Turf)	124	12	14	10	148343

80	4/01	Wind	6f	C(0-90)	G-S	£6776
84	8/00	Ripn	6f	C(0-95)H	GD	£6370
79	6/00	Hayd	5f	D(0-80)H	G-S	£4043
86	8/99	Sand	5f6y	B(0-100)H	GD	£8625
80	6/99	York	5f	C(0-100)H	G-S	£7310
84	6/98	Ripn	5f	D(0-80)H	SFT	£3501
80	7/97	Newc	5f	C(0-95)H	GD	£5147
84	6/96	Donc	5f	C(0-90)H	G-F	£5343
73	4/96	Ripn	5f	F	G-F	£2599
98	9/94	Ayr	5f	A	G-S	£7556
93	9/94	Chep	5f16y	C	G-S	£4714
71	4/94	Newc	5f	E	GD	£2762

Total win prize-money £64749

Going (Turf): Sf: 1-14 **GS: 5-18** Gd: 4-57 GF: 2-31 Fm: 0-4
Distance: **5f/6f: 12-117** 7f-8f: 0-7 9f-13f: 0-0 14f+: 0-0
Track : LH: 0-11 RH: 0-0 Tight: 0-7 Gall: 0-0
Aids: **Bl: 8-53** Vi: 3-57 Tstrap: 0-0
Best Rating: 83 6/01 York 6f good

A veteran sprint handicapper, he wins his share every year and is effective at five furlongs or six. Has won on a fast surface, but best on easier ground.

Lagudin (IRE)

112 **109**

3-y-o b c Eagle Eyed (USA)-Liaison (USA) (Blushing Groom (FR))

L M Cumani Miss G Gatto Roissard

Placings:121-3432131 **(5597)**

2001: 8^{3}G, 8^{4}G, 7^{3}G, 10^{2}G, 10^{1}GS, 9^{3}GS, 10^{1}GS

	Starts	1st	2nd	3rd	Win & Pl
Career Total (Turf)	10	4	2	3	65071

107	11/01	NmkR	1m2f	A	G-S	£14161
109	9/01	Donc	1m2f60y	B	G-S	£13000
94	10/00	Yarm	7f3y	D	SFT	£3786
88	9/00	NmkR	7f	D	SFT	£5590

Total win prize-money £36537

Going (Turf): **Sf: 2-3 GS: 2-3** Gd: 0-4 GF: 0-0 Fm: 0-0
Distance: 5f/6f: 0-0 7f-8f: 2-6 9f-13f: 2-4 14f+: 0-0
Track : **LH: 1-2** RH: 0-2 Tight: 0-0 **Gall: 1-2**
Aids: Bl: 0-0 Vi: 0-0 Tstrap: 0-0
Best Rating: 109 9/01 Donc 1m2f60y gd-sft

A winner on soft ground at Newmarket and Yarmouth at two, he got off the mark at Doncaster's St Leger meeting and improved to win a Newmarket Listed event. Relishes cut in the ground and stays ten furlongs.

Laguna Bay (IRE)

(86) (11)**40d**

7-y-o b m Arcane (USA)-Meg Daughter (IRE) (Doulab (USA))

G M McCourt Christopher Shankland

Placings:040/6204514250/000/02515540/00-0 **(0311)**

2001: 16^{0}SD

	Starts	1st	2nd	3rd	Win & Pl
Career Total (Turf)	24	2	3	0	8267
Career Total (AW)	3	0	0	0	

46	6/99	Bath	2m1f34y	F(0-60)H	FRM	£2346
54	8/97	Yarm	1m2f21y	F	G-F	£2623

Total win prize-money £4970

Going (Turf): Sf: 0-1 GS: 0-2 Gd: 0-5 **GF: 1-13 Fm: 1-3**
Distance: 5f/6f: 0-0 7f-8f: 0-3 9f-13f: 1-12 14f+: 1-12
Track : **LH: 2-16** RH: 0-10 **Tight: 2-15** Gall: 0-2
Aids: Bl: 0-0 Vi: 0-0 Tstrap: 0-0
Best Rating: 5 2/01 Sthl 2m stand

Laguna Seca

82 **56**

2-y-o b f General Monash (USA)-Cavatina (Chief Singer)

R Guest Rae Guest Racing Partnership Ii

Placings:3 **(5533)**

2001: 5^{3}S

	Starts	1st	2nd	3rd	Win & Pl
Career Total (Turf)	1	0	0	1	406

Going (Turf): **Sf: 0-1 GS: 0-0 Gd: 0-0 GF: 0-0 Fm: 0-0**
Distance: 5f/6f: 0-1 7f-8f: 0-0 9f-13f: 0-0 14f+: 0-0
Track : LH: 0-0 RH: 0-0 Tight: 0-0 Gall: 0-0
Aids: Bl: 0-0 Vi: 0-0 Tstrap: 0-0
Best Rating: 56 10/01 Rdcr 5f soft

Lahaay

99(98) (59)**68**

4-y-o ch g Lahib (USA)-Jasarah (IRE) (Green Desert (USA))

J Akehurst Epsom Downs Racing Club

Placings:05/00453601-0406510 **(5465)**

2001: 10^{0}SD, 10^{4}SD, 10^{0}F, 10^{6}GF, 8^{5}GF, 9^{1}G, 10^{0}G

	Starts	1st	2nd	3rd	Win & Pl
Career Total (Turf)	14	1	0	1	3682
Career Total (AW)	3	1	0	0	2834

66	8/01	Folk	1m1f149yF(0-65)H		GD	£2590
56	12/00	Ling	1m2f	D	STD	£2834

Total win prize-money £5424

Going (Turf): Sf: 0-4 GS: 0-0 **Gd: 1-3** GF: 0-5 Fm: 0-2
Distance: 5f/6f: 0-0 7f-8f: 0-7 **9f-13f: 2-10** 14f+: 0-0
Track : LH: 1-10 RH: 1-4 **Tight: 2-8** Gall: 0-0
Aids: Bl: 0-0 Vi: 0-0 Tstrap: 0-0
Best Rating: 66 8/01 Folk 1m1f149y good

Lahberhorn (USA)

92 **76**

2-y-o ch c Affirmed (USA)-Skiable (IRE) (Niniski (USA))

B W Hills K Abdulla

Placings:0 **(4056)**

2001: 7^{0}GF

	Starts	1st	2nd	3rd	Win & Pl
Career Total (Turf)	1	0	0	0	

Going (Turf): **Sf: 0-0 GS: 0-0 Gd: 0-0 GF: 0-1 Fm: 0-0**
Distance: 5f/6f: 0-0 7f-8f: 0-1 9f-13f: 0-0 14f+: 0-0
Track : LH: 0-0 RH: 0-0 Tight: 0-0 Gall: 0-0
Aids: Bl: 0-0 Vi: 0-0 Tstrap: 0-0
Best Rating: 76 8/01 Newb 7f gd-fm

Lahinch (IRE)

109 **100**

2-y-o b f Danehill Dancer (IRE)-Dublah (USA) (Private Account (USA))

A P O'Brien Mrs E M Stockwell

Placings:041412 **(5390)**

2001: 7^{0}S, 6^{4}GY, 5^{1}G, 6^{4}S, 5^{1}S, 7^{2}GS

	Starts	1st	2nd	3rd	Win & Pl
Career Total (Turf)	6	2	1	0	60475

94	10/01	Tipp	5f		SFT	£29250
91	9/01	Curr	5f		GD	£11375

Total win prize-money £40625

Going (Turf): **Sf: 1-3** GS: 0-1 **Gd: 1-1** GF: 0-0 Fm: 0-0
Distance: **5f/6f: 2-4** 7f-8f: 0-2 9f-13f: 0-0 14f+: 0-0
Track : LH: 0-0 RH: 0-0 Tight: 0-0 Gall: 0-0
Aids: Bl: 0-0 Vi: 0-0 Tstrap: 0-0
Best Rating: 100 10/01 NmkR 7f gd-sft

A half-sister to several winning juveniles including the useful Perugino Bay, she was beaten in Pattern company on her first two starts before dropping back to five furlongs to take a Curragh maiden. Ran a good race to be fourth in the Cheveley Park and has since scored in listed company at Tipperary. A narrow second in the Group Two Rockfel Stakes at Newmarket, she handles good and easy ground, yet to encounter fast.

Lahooq

98 **80+**

2-y-o b c Indian Ridge-Woodsia (Woodman (USA))
D R Loder Sheikh Mohammed

Placings:10 **(5002)**
2001: 8^{1}G, 8^{0}S

	Starts	1st	2nd	3rd	Win & Pl
Career Total (Turf)	2	1	0	0	4329

80 9/01 Kemp 1m D GD £4329
Total win prize-money £4329

Going (Turf): Sf: 0-1 GS: 0-0 **Gd: 1-1** GF: 0-0 Fm: 0-0
Distance: 5f/6f: 0-0 **7f-8f: 1-2** 9f-13f: 0-0 14f+: 0-0
Track : LH: 0-0 **RH: 1-2** Tight: 0-0 Gall: 0-1
Aids: Bl: 0-0 Vi: 0-0 Tstrap: 0-0
Best Rating: 80 9/01 Kemp 1m good

Well regarded, he made a comfortable winning debut at Kempton in September on fast ground but failed to handle soft in the Royal Lodge.

Lai See (IRE)

85(85) (47)**61**

3-y-o b g Tagula (IRE)-Sevens Are Wild (Petorius)
A P Jarvis St Davids Racing Syndicate 2

Placings:0002225550-000000 **(5461)**
2001: 6^{0}SW, 5^{0}SW, 8^{0}GS, 5^{0}SD, 6^{0}GF, 8^{0}G

	Starts	1st	2nd	3rd	Win & Pl
Career Total (Turf)	12	0	3	0	3716
Career Total (AW)	4	0	0	0	0

Going (Turf): Sf: 0-1 GS: 0-1 Gd: 0-5 GF: 0-5 Fm: 0-0
Distance: 5f/6f: 0-13 7f-8f: 0-2 9f-13f: 0-1 14f+: 0-0
Track : LH: 0-6 RH: 0-0 Tight: 0-3 Gall: 0-1
Aids: Bl: 0-0 Vi: 0-1 Tstrap: 0-0
Best Rating: 40 2/01 Ling 5f slow

Lailani

116 **117**

3-y-o b f Unfuwain (USA)-Lailati (USA) (Mr Prospector (USA))
E A L Dunlop Maktoum Al Maktoum

Placings:00-11111110 **(5577a)**
2001: 8^{1}GS, 10^{1}G, 10^{1}GF, 10^{1}GF, 12^{1}G, 9^{1}G, 10^{1}G, 10^{0}F

	Starts	1st	2nd	3rd	Win & Pl
Career Total (Turf)	10	7	0	0	539499

117 9/01 Belm 1m2f GD £300000
114 8/01 Gdwd 1m1f192yA GD £78300
113 7/01 Curr 1m4f GD £126675
107 6/01 Epsm 1m2f18y C(0-100)H G-F £19500
94 5/01 Hayd 1m2f120yC(0-95)H G-F £6196
89 5/01 NmkR 1m2f D(0-85)H GD £5382
86 4/01 Wind 1m67y D G-S £3445
Total win prize-money £539499

Going (Turf): Sf: 0-1 GS: 1-1 **Gd: 4-5** GF: 2-2 Fm: 0-1
Distance: 5f/6f: 0-0 7f-8f: 0-2 **9f-13f: 7-8** 14f+: 0-0
Track : **LH: 3-5** RH: 2-2 **Tight: 3-3** Gall: 0-1
Aids: Bl: 0-0 Vi: 0-0 Tstrap: 0-0
Best Rating: 117 9/01 Belm 1m2f good

Showed little in two outings at two, but has been a revelation this season winning seven times. She started out winning a Windsor maiden before adding a Newmarket handicap and a Haydock rated stakes. She then won a very hot handicap at Epsom on Oaks day and managed to bridge the class gap with a clear-cut victory in the Irish Oaks and a game victory in the Nassau Stakes. Notched up her seventh consecutive win with an impressive performance at Belmont Park, but was well below par in the Breeders' Cup Filly and Mare Turf. Stayed 12 furlongs and proven on all ground. Retired.

Laissezaller (USA)

104 **91**

2-y-o gr/ro c End Sweep (USA)-Laissez Faire (USA) (Talinum (USA))
Mrs A J Perrett Seymour Cohn

Placings:123 **(5596)**
2001: 7^{1}GF, 7^{2}GF, 8^{3}GS

	Starts	1st	2nd	3rd	Win & Pl
Career Total (Turf)	3	1	1	1	9738

78 7/01 Newb 7f D G-F £4472
Total win prize-money £4472

Going (Turf): Sf: 0-0 GS: 0-1 Gd: 0-0 **GF: 1-2** Fm: 0-0
Distance: 5f/6f: 0-0 **7f-8f: 1-3** 9f-13f: 0-0 14f+: 0-0
Track : LH: 0-0 RH: 0-0 Tight: 0-0 Gall: 0-0
Aids: Bl: 0-0 Vi: 0-0 Tstrap: 0-0
Best Rating: 91 11/01 NmkR 1m gd-sft

Out of a mare from the family of Dahlia, he was an impressive maiden winner first time out at Newbury in July, before being beaten in better class on the same track. He had an excuse there as he had got loose beforer the start. Ran to a similar level on soft on his final run.

Lajadhal (FR)

(3)

12-y-o gr g Bellypha-Rose D'Amour (USA) (Lines Of Power (USA))
P D Purdy P D Purdy

Placings:050/0000/000006400000/0005005/000/00/00-0P **(2821)**
2001: 14^{0}GF, 18^{P}GF

	Starts	1st	2nd	3rd	Win & Pl
Career Total (Turf)	25	0	0	0	
Career Total (AW)	11	0	0	0	174

Going (Turf): Sf: 0-2 GS: 0-3 Gd: 0-5 GF: 0-11 Fm: 0-4
Distance: 5f/6f: 0-0 7f-8f: 0-0 9f-13f: 0-17 14f+: 0-19
Track : LH: 0-28 RH: 0-7 Tight: 0-23 Gall: 0-0
Aids: Bl: 0-5 Vi: 0-8 Tstrap: 0-0

Lakatoi

85 **63**

2-y-o b f Saddlers' Hall (IRE)-Bireme (Grundy)
B W Hills M H Dixon

Placings:00 **(5602)**
2001: 7^{0}GS, 7^{0}GS

	Starts	1st	2nd	3rd	Win & Pl
Career Total (Turf)	2	0	0	0	

Going (Turf): Sf: 0-0 GS: 0-2 Gd: 0-0 GF: 0-0 Fm: 0-0
Distance: 5f/6f: 0-0 7f-8f: 0-2 9f-13f: 0-0 14f+: 0-0
Track : LH: 0-0 RH: 0-0 Tight: 0-0 Gall: 0-0
Aids: Bl: 0-0 Vi: 0-0 Tstrap: 0-0
Best Rating: 63 11/01 NmkR 7f gd-sft

Lake Dorset (IRE)

95 **60+**

3-y-o b c Night Shift (USA)-Lara's Dream (Dominion)
L M Cumani Allevamento Gialloblu

Placings:200040 **(4472)**
2001: 9^{2}GF, 8^{0}GS, 7^{0}GS, 7^{0}GS, 9^{4}G, 9^{0}GF

	Starts	1st	2nd	3rd	Win & Pl
Career Total (Turf)	6	0	1	0	2891

Going (Turf): Sf: 0-0 GS: 0-3 Gd: 0-1 GF: 0-2 Fm: 0-0
Distance: 5f/6f: 0-0 7f-8f: 0-3 9f-13f: 0-3 14f+: 0-0
Track : LH: 0-1 RH: 0-2 Tight: 0-0 Gall: 0-0
Aids: Bl: 0-0 Vi: 0-0 Tstrap: 0-0
Best Rating: 60 8/01 Leic 1m1f218y good

Lake Eyre (IRE)

88 **61**

2-y-o b f Bluebird (USA)-Pooh Wee (Music Boy)
D Shaw J C Fretwell

Placings:005 **(4939)**
2001: 6^{0}G, 6^{0}G, 7^{5}S

	Starts	1st	2nd	3rd	Win & Pl
Career Total (Turf)	3	0	0	0	0

Going (Turf): Sf: 0-1 GS: 0-0 Gd: 0-2 GF: 0-0 Fm: 0-0
Distance: 5f/6f: 0-1 7f-8f: 0-2 9f-13f: 0-0 14f+: 0-0
Track : LH: 0-1 RH: 0-0 Tight: 0-1 Gall: 0-0
Aids: Bl: 0-0 Vi: 0-0 Tstrap: 0-0
Best Rating: 61 9/01 Ches 7f2y soft

A half-sister to useful juvenile sprinter Pacifica. Ran her best race in three attempts on soft ground at Chester in September. Now qualifies for handicaps.

Lake Kinneret (IRE)

102 **70**

3-y-o b f Danehill (USA)-Dancing Shadow (Dancer's Image (USA))
Sir Michael Stoute Lord Weinstock

Placings:0-02150 **(4445)**
2001: 10^{0}G, 8^{2}GF, 8^{1}G, 8^{5}GF, 8^{0}G

	Starts	1st	2nd	3rd	Win & Pl
Career Total (Turf)	6	1	1	0	4840

70 8/01 Pont 1m4y D GD £3510
Total win prize-money £3510

Going (Turf): Sf: 0-1 GS: 0-0 **Gd: 1-3** GF: 0-2 Fm: 0-0
Distance: 5f/6f: 0-0 7f-8f: 0-1 **9f-13f: 1-5** 14f+: 0-0
Track : **LH: 1-2** RH: 0-2 Tight: 0-1 Gall: 0-0
Aids: Bl: 0-0 Vi: 0-0 Tstrap: 0-0
Best Rating: 70 8/01 Pont 1m4y good

Lake Sunbeam

96(91) (71)**59d**

5-y-o b g Nashwan (USA)-Moon Drop (Dominion)
W R Muir Perspicacious Punters Racing Club

Placings:3/610536045/56113200-3202 **(5023)**
2001: 8^{3}GF, 7^{2}GF, 8^{0}GF, 7^{2}S

	Starts	1st	2nd	3rd	Win & Pl
Career Total (Turf)	19	3	3	4	18484
Career Total (AW)	3	0	0	0	0

71 7/00 Sand 1m14y E G-F £2795
43 7/00 Epsm 1m114y E G-S £2782
86 6/99 Sals 6f212y C G-F £5809
Total win prize-money £11386

Going (Turf): Sf: 0-2 GS: 1-1 Gd: 0-6 **GF: 2-9** Fm: 0-1
Distance: 5f/6f: 0-0 7f-8f: 1-11 **9f-13f: 2-11** 14f+: 0-0
Track : LH: 1-12 RH: 1-5 **Tight: 1-8** Gall: 0-4
Aids: Bl: 0-0 Vi: 0-0 Tstrap: 0-0
Best Rating: 59 8/01 Epsm 1m114y gd-fm

He has gone the wrong way and was beaten in a seller in September.

Lake Verdi (IRE)

99 **87**

2-y-o ch c Lake Coniston (IRE)-Shore Lark (USA) (Storm Bird (CAN))
B Hanbury P Wilden

Placings:141044000 **(5364)**
2001: 5^{1}G, 5^{4}G, 6^{1}GF, 6^{0}GF, 6^{4}GF, 7^{4}GF, 6^{0}GF, 7^{0}G, 6^{0}GS

	Starts	1st	2nd	3rd	Win & Pl
Career Total (Turf)	9	2	0	0	14801

84 6/01 Newb 6f8y C G-F £5672
70 5/01 NmkR 5f D GD £6841
Total win prize-money £12513

Going (Turf): Sf: 0-0 GS: 0-1 **Gd: 1-3 GF: 1-5** Fm: 0-0
Distance: 5f/6f: 1-6 7f-8f: 1-3 9f-13f: 0-0 14f+: 0-0
Track : LH: 0-1 RH: 0-1 Tight: 0-1 Gall: 0-1
Aids: Bl: 0-0 Vi: 0-0 **Tstrap: 2-4**
Best Rating: 87 9/01 Epsm 7f good

Won well on his debut and scored in better company at Newbury. Ran disappointingly at Royal Ascot but has since acquitted himself well. He has yet to convince over seven furlongs. The tongue strap he wore in his early races has been dispensed with.

Lakeland Paddy (IRE)

(92) (41)**58**
4-y-o b g Lake Coniston (IRE)-Inshad (Indian King (USA))
M Blanshard Mrs R G Wellman

Placings:0544256/336410000-000 **(3188)**
2001: 6^{0}GF, 8^{0}G, 5^{0}GS

	Starts	1st	2nd	3rd	Win & Pl
Career Total (Turf)	19	1	1	2	9080

74 6/00 Newb 6f8y D G-F £4498
Total win prize-money £4498

Going (Turf): Sf: 0-6 GS: 0-1 Gd: 0-6 **GF: 1-6** Fm: 0-0
Distance: 5f/6f: 0-12 **7f-8f: 1-6** 9f-13f: 0-1 14f+: 0-0
Track : LH: 0-2 RH: 0-4 Tight: 0-2 Gall: 0-3
Aids: Bl: 0-0 Vi: 0-0 Tstrap: 0-0
Best Rating: 58 7/01 Leic 5f218y gd-sft

Lakota Brave

101(103) (67)**57**
7-y-o ch g Anshan-Pushkinia (FR) (Pharly (FR))
C N Allen Newmarketconnections.Com

Placings:0/6416-050 **(1538)**
2001: 7^{0}SD, 8^{5}SD, 7^{0}GF

	Starts	1st	2nd	3rd	Win & Pl
Career Total (Turf)	5	0	0	0	274
Career Total (AW)	3	1	0	0	2786

60 8/00 Ling 1m E(0-65) STD £2786
Total win prize-money £2786

Going (Turf): Sf: 0-0 GS: 0-0 Gd: 0-2 GF: 0-3 Fm: 0-0
Distance: 5f/6f: 0-0 **7f-8f: 1-6** 9f-13f: 0-2 14f+: 0-0
Track : **LH: 1-3** RH: 0-3 **Tight: 1-3** Gall: 0-0
Aids: Bl: 0-0 Vi: 0-0 **Tstrap: 1-6**
Best Rating: 67 5/01 Ling 1m stand

Lambadora

99(69) (19)**47**
3-y-o ch f Suave Dancer (USA)-Lust (Pursuit Of Love)
Miss J A Camacho Miss J A Camacho

Placings:06-0352600 **(4164)**
2001: 8^{0}GF, 14^{3}F, 14^{5}GF, 16^{2}F, 16^{0}GF, 14^{0}S, 16^{0}GF

	Starts	1st	2nd	3rd	Win & Pl
Career Total (Turf)	7	0	1	1	1112
Career Total (AW)	2	0	0	0	0

Going (Turf): Sf: 0-1 GS: 0-0 Gd: 0-0 GF: 0-4 Fm: 0-2
Distance: 5f/6f: 0-1 7f-8f: 0-2 9f-13f: 0-0 14f+: 0-6
Track : LH: 0-7 RH: 0-2 Tight: 0-7 Gall: 0-0
Aids: Bl: 0-0 Vi: 0-0 Tstrap: 0-0
Best Rating: 47 6/01 Thsk 2m firm

Lambay Island (IRE)

(58) **72**
3-y-o b g Turtle Island (IRE)-Ullapool (Dominion)
Sean Gannon (Noel T Chance 5/1) Sean Gannon

Placings:000-00040 **(5543a)**
2001: 7^{0}SD, 10^{0}SH, 14^{0}G, 12^{4}G, 13^{0}Y

	Starts	1st	2nd	3rd	Win & Pl
Career Total (Turf)	7	0	0	0	320
Career Total (AW)	1	0	0	0	

Going (Turf): Sf: 0-2 GS: 0-0 Gd: 0-2 GF: 0-0 Fm: 0-0
Distance: 5f/6f: 0-0 7f-8f: 0-3 9f-13f: 0-3 14f+: 0-1
Track : LH: 0-1 RH: 0-1 Tight: 0-0 Gall: 0-0
Aids: Bl: 0-0 Vi: 0-0 Tstrap: 0-0
Best Rating: 72 4/01 Navn 1m2f sft-hvy

Lambrook

(78) (42)**60**
2-y-o b g Emarati (USA)-Shalverton (IRE) (Shalford (IRE))
W R Muir Dulverton Equine

Placings:60200 **(3480)**
2001: 5^{6}SD, 5^{0}SW, 5^{2}G, 5^{0}HD, 5^{0}GF

	Starts	1st	2nd	3rd	Win & Pl
Career Total (Turf)	3	0	1	0	798
Career Total (AW)	2	0	0	0	0

Going (Turf): Sf: 0-0 GS: 0-0 Gd: 0-1 GF: 0-1 Fm: 0-1
Distance: 5f/6f: 0-5 7f-8f: 0-0 9f-13f: 0-0 14f+: 0-0
Track : LH: 0-2 RH: 0-0 Tight: 0-0 Gall: 0-2
Aids: Bl: 0-0 Vi: 0-0 Tstrap: 0-0
Best Rating: 60 6/01 Bath 5f11y good

Lammoski (IRE)

90(88) (26)**26**
4-y-o ch g Hamas (IRE)-Penny In My Shoe (USA) (Sir Ivor)
M C Chapman G C R Pryke

Placings:0000050000000005/0005005000403 0-000005000 **(4450)**
2001: 6^{0}SD, 5^{0}SD, 6^{0}G, 5^{0}G, 5^{0}GF, 11^{5}GF, 11^{0}GF, 8^{0}GS, 8^{0}GF

	Starts	1st	2nd	3rd	Win & Pl
Career Total (Turf)	26	0	0	1	263
Career Total (AW)	11	0	0	0	0

Going (Turf): Sf: 0-2 GS: 0-1 Gd: 0-10 GF: 0-12 Fm: 0-1
Distance: 5f/6f: 0-25 7f-8f: 0-3 9f-13f: 0-6 14f+: 0-3
Track : LH: 0-11 RH: 0-5 Tight: 0-5 Gall: 0-1
Aids: Bl: 0-6 Vi: 0-2 Tstrap: 0-2
Best Rating: 26 8/01 Bevl 1m100y gd-sft

Lamzig

71 **48**
2-y-o b c Danzig Connection (USA)-Lamsonetti (Never So Bold)
Mrs Lydia Pearce Ian Hall

Placings:0 **(5367)**
2001: 8^{0}GS

	Starts	1st	2nd	3rd	Win & Pl
Career Total (Turf)	1	0	0	0	

Going (Turf): Sf: 0-0 GS: 0-1 Gd: 0-0 GF: 0-0 Fm: 0-0
Distance: 5f/6f: 0-0 7f-8f: 0-1 9f-13f: 0-0 14f+: 0-0
Track : LH: 0-0 RH: 0-0 Tight: 0-0 Gall: 0-0
Aids: Bl: 0-0 Vi: 0-0 Tstrap: 0-0
Best Rating: 48 10/01 NmkR 1m gd-sft

Behind from halfway on his Newmarket debut over a mile in October.

Lance Feather (IRE)

81 **53**
3-y-o b c Petardia-Fantasticus (IRE) (Lycius (USA))
J L Eyre Tony Fawcett

Placings:600-00 **(3594)**
2001: 10^{0}GF, 10^{0}GS

	Starts	1st	2nd	3rd	Win & Pl
Career Total (Turf)	5	0	0	0	0

Going (Turf): Sf: 0-0 GS: 0-2 Gd: 0-1 GF: 0-2 Fm: 0-0
Distance: 5f/6f: 0-0 7f-8f: 0-2 9f-13f: 0-3 14f+: 0-0
Track : LH: 0-5 RH: 0-0 Tight: 0-3 Gall: 0-0
Aids: Bl: 0-0 Vi: 0-0 Tstrap: 0-0
Best Rating: 16 6/01 Rdcr 1m2f gd-fm

Lancer (USA)

107(37) (34)**45**
9-y-o ch g Diesis-Last Bird (USA) (Sea-Bird Ii)
Mrs Lydia Pearce Chris Marsh

Placings:13/566040/**240**0225136125640221/05531206 5420**0420**/616606503261534-345264016101 **(5471)**
2001: 12^{3}GS, 11^{4}GS, 11^{5}GS, 14^{2}G, 12^{6}GF, 14^{4}GF, 14^{0}GF, 12^{1}G, 11^{6}GF, 11^{1}G, 11^{0}S, 11^{1}S

	Starts	1st	2nd	3rd	Win & Pl
Career Total (Turf)	64	10	10	6	91817
Career Total (AW)	6	0	1	0	488

45 10/01 Brig 1m3f196yE(0-70)H SFT £3069
34 9/01 Bevl 1m3f216yG GD £2415
44 8/01 Folk 1m4f G GD £1918
56 10/00 Pont 1m4f8y F(0-60)H HVY £2278
65 4/00 Wwck 1m4f56y D(0-80)H SFT £7117
70 5/99 Folk 1m4f E(0-80) G-F £2684
71 10/98 York 1m3f195yE(0-70)H GD £7132
63 6/98 Folk 1m4f F(0-65)H G-F £2784
60 5/98 Leic 1m3f183yF(0-65)H GD £2410
64 7/94 Bevl 7f100y D G-F £3529
Total win prize-money £35343

Going (Turf): Sf: 3-10 GS: 0-8 **Gd: 4-20** GF: 3-22 Fm: 0-4
Distance: 5f/6f: 0-0 7f-8f: 1-3 **9f-13f: 9-54** 14f+: 0-13
Track : LH: 4-38 **RH: 6-28 Tight: 4-24** Gall: 1-21
Aids: Bl: 0-2 **Vi: 8-48** Tstrap: 0-0
Best Rating: 56 5/01 Yarm 1m6f17y good

An able performer at around a mile and a half, he is best held up for a late run, and was running well in the second half of the season.

Land Girl

66
3-y-o b f General Monash (USA)-Charming Madam (General Holme (USA))
Miss S E Hall C Platts

Placings:0-0 **(4436)**
2001: 9^{0}G

	Starts	1st	2nd	3rd	Win & Pl
Career Total (Turf)	2	0	0	0	

Going (Turf): Sf: 0-0 GS: 0-0 Gd: 0-1 GF: 0-1 Fm: 0-0
Distance: 5f/6f: 0-1 7f-8f: 0-0 9f-13f: 0-1 14f+: 0-0
Track : LH: 0-0 RH: 0-1 Tight: 0-1 Gall: 0-0
Aids: Bl: 0-0 Vi: 0-0 Tstrap: 0-0

Land Of Fantasy

79 **63**

2-y-o ch c Hernando (FR)-Height Of Folly (Shirley Heights)
S Dow G Steinberg

Placings:0 **(4575)**
2001: 8^{0}G

	Starts	1st	2nd	3rd	Win & Pl
Career Total (Turf)	1	0	0	0	

Going (Turf): Sf: 0-0 GS: 0-0 Gd: 0-1 GF: 0-0 Fm: 0-0
Distance: 5f/6f: 0-0 7f-8f: 0-1 9f-13f: 0-0 14f+: 0-0
Track : LH: 0-0 RH: 0-1 Tight: 0-0 Gall: 0-0
Aids: Bl: 0-0 Vi: 0-0 Tstrap: 0-0
Best Rating: 63 9/01 Kemp 1m good

Landican Lad

(77) (15)

4-y-o b g Petong-Dancing Daughter (Dance In Time (CAN))
Miss C J E Caroe (A C Whillans 30/1) Miss C J E Caroe

Placings:0050000-0 **(0199)**
2001: 6^{0}SD

	Starts	1st	2nd	3rd	Win & Pl
Career Total (Turf)	7	0	0	0	0
Career Total (AW)	1	0	0	0	

Going (Turf): Sf: 0-3 GS: 0-0 Gd: 0-1 GF: 0-3 Fm: 0-0
Distance: 5f/6f: 0-5 7f-8f: 0-1 9f-13f: 0-2 14f+: 0-0
Track : LH: 0-4 RH: 0-2 Tight: 0-3 Gall: 0-2
Aids: Bl: 0-0 Vi: 0-0 Tstrap: 0-0
Best Rating: 15 1/01 Wolv 6f stand

Landing Slot (USA)

(93) (38)**96**

6-y-o b g Personal Hope (USA)-Durability (USA) (Affirmed (USA))
E W Tuer E Tuer

Placings:2333/1200010/0 **(0054)**
2001: 11^{0}SD

	Starts	1st	2nd	3rd	Win & Pl
Career Total (Turf)	11	2	2	3	13930
Career Total (AW)	1	0	0	0	

96 8/99 Leop 1m1f (0-100)H GD £6900
95 5/99 Fair 1m1f GD £3300
Total win prize-money £10200

Going (Turf): Sf: 0-2 GS: 0-0 **Gd: 2-5** GF: 0-3 Fm: 0-0
Distance: 5f/6f: 0-0 7f-8f: 0-2 **9f-13f: 2-10** 14f+: 0-0
Track : LH: 1-4 RH: 1-7 Tight: 0-0 Gall: 0-1
Aids: **Bl: 1-3** Vi: 0-0 Tstrap: 0-0
Best Rating: 38 1/01 Sthl 1m3f stand

He does not appear to stay beyond a mile and a quarter and has run his best races when ridden forcefully.

Landings

98 **57**

2-y-o ch f Deploy-Sandblaster (Most Welcome)
Miss L A Perratt (W G M Turner 25/7) R N Racing Services

Placings:0100 **(5031)**
2001: 6^{0}GF, 7^{1}GF, 8^{0}G, 8^{0}GF

	Starts	1st	2nd	3rd	Win & Pl
Career Total (Turf)	4	1	0	0	1841

55 7/01 Muss 7f30y G G-F £1841
Total win prize-money £1841

Going (Turf): Sf: 0-0 GS: 0-0 Gd: 0-1 **GF: 1-3** Fm: 0-0
Distance: 5f/6f: 0-0 **7f-8f: 1-4** 9f-13f: 0-0 14f+: 0-0
Track : LH: 0-1 RH: 0-2 Tight: 0-2 Gall: 0-0
Aids: Bl: 0-0 Vi: 0-0 Tstrap: 0-0
Best Rating: 57 9/01 Muss 1m gd-fm

She surprised everybody with a 50/1 win in a Musselburgh seller in the summer of 2001, but has since failed to build on that form. He stays seven furlongs on firm ground, but should get further as a three-year-old.

Landseer

108 **109**

2-y-o b c Danehill (USA)-Sabria (USA) (Miswaki (USA))
A P O'Brien M Tabor & Mrs John Magnier

Placings:411222 **(5677a)**
2001: 5^{4}S, 7^{1}G, 6^{1}GF, 7^{2}S, 7^{2}GS, 8^{2}HO

	Starts	1st	2nd	3rd	Win & Pl
Career Total (Turf)	6	2	3	0	221198

104 6/01 Asct 6f A G-F £36000
88 5/01 Gowr 7f GD £9660
Total win prize-money £45660

Going (Turf): Sf: 0-2 GS: 0-1 **Gd: 1-1 GF: 1-1** Fm: 0-0
Distance: 5f/6f: 1-2 7f-8f: 1-4 9f-13f: 0-0 14f+: 0-0
Track : LH: 0-1 RH: 0-0 Tight: 0-0 Gall: 0-0
Aids: Bl: 0-0 Vi: 0-0 Tstrap: 0-0
Best Rating: 109 11/01 StCl 1m holding

A 260,000gns half-brother to two winners, he got off the mark on his second start in a Gowran Park maiden over seven furlongs and was successfully dropped back to six in the Coventry Stakes at Royal Ascot. Came back from a break to be touched off in a valuable sales event when he did not get the run of the race, lost out by a short head to stablemate Rock Of Gibraltar in the Dewhurst and was narrowly beaten in the Criterium International. Acts on a sound surface but also handles cut and will stay further in time.

Lane Cove (IRE)

85 **58**

2-y-o b f Turtle Island (IRE)-Shining Creek (CAN) (Bering)
P J Makin Martin Wesson Partners Ii

Placings:00 **(5588)**
2001: 5^{0}G, 5^{0}GS

	Starts	1st	2nd	3rd	Win & Pl
Career Total (Turf)	2	0	0	0	

Going (Turf): Sf: 0-0 GS: 0-1 Gd: 0-1 GF: 0-0 Fm: 0-0
Distance: 5f/6f: 0-2 7f-8f: 0-0 9f-13f: 0-0 14f+: 0-0
Track : LH: 0-2 RH: 0-0 Tight: 0-0 Gall: 0-1
Aids: Bl: 0-0 Vi: 0-0 Tstrap: 0-0
Best Rating: 58 11/01 Brig 5f213y gd-sft

Lanesborough (USA)

96 **82**

3-y-o ch c Irish River (FR)-Hot Option (USA) (Explodent (USA))
G A Butler Mr & Mrs J Amerman

Placings:51-000 **(4109)**
2001: 7^{0}GF, 8^{0}G, 9^{0}S

	Starts	1st	2nd	3rd	Win & Pl
Career Total (Turf)	5	1	0	0	4029

82 10/00 Rdcr 7f D SFT £3510
Total win prize-money £3510

Going (Turf): **Sf: 1-3** GS: 0-0 Gd: 0-1 GF: 0-1 Fm: 0-0
Distance: 5f/6f: 0-0 **7f-8f: 1-4** 9f-13f: 0-1 14f+: 0-0
Track : LH: 0-0 RH: 0-1 Tight: 0-1 Gall: 0-0
Aids: Bl: 0-1 Vi: 0-0 Tstrap: 0-0
Best Rating: 70 8/01 Haml 1m1f36y soft

Only small, he got off the mark on second start as a juvenile over seven furlongs on soft ground. Well beaten this season.

Lanoso (IRE)

91(73) (41)**52**

3-y-o b g Charnwood Forest (IRE)-Silver Spark (USA) (Silver Hawk (USA))
C R Egerton Ian S P Hogg

Placings:00-000 **(2519)**
2001: 8^{0}GF, 8^{0}GF, 12^{0}GF

	Starts	1st	2nd	3rd	Win & Pl
Career Total (Turf)	4	0	0	0	
Career Total (AW)	1	0	0	0	

Going (Turf): Sf: 0-1 GS: 0-0 Gd: 0-0 GF: 0-3 Fm: 0-0
Distance: 5f/6f: 0-1 7f-8f: 0-2 9f-13f: 0-2 14f+: 0-0
Track : LH: 0-2 RH: 0-2 Tight: 0-1 Gall: 0-0
Aids: Bl: 0-0 Vi: 0-0 Tstrap: 0-0
Best Rating: 52 5/01 Kemp 1m gd-fm

Lantic Bay

80 **30**

4-y-o b f Afzal-Silent Dancer (Quiet Fling (USA))
J C Tuck J C Tuck

Placings:040-60 **(3741)**
2001: 11^{6}F, 10^{0}S

	Starts	1st	2nd	3rd	Win & Pl
Career Total (Turf)	5	0	0	0	0

Going (Turf): Sf: 0-1 GS: 0-1 Gd: 0-1 GF: 0-0 Fm: 0-2
Distance: 5f/6f: 0-0 7f-8f: 0-0 9f-13f: 0-5 14f+: 0-0
Track : LH: 0-3 RH: 0-1 Tight: 0-3 Gall: 0-0
Aids: Bl: 0-0 Vi: 0-0 Tstrap: 0-0
Best Rating: 14 7/01 Bath 1m3f144y firm

Lanzerac

97 **74**

4-y-o b g Lycius (USA)-Watership (USA) (Foolish Pleasure (USA))
John A Harris (J L Harris 28/5) Cleartherm Ltd

Placings:555 **(5637)**
2001: 12^{5}GF, 12^{5}G, 11^{5}G

	Starts	1st	2nd	3rd	Win & Pl
Career Total (Turf)	3	0	0	0	0

Going (Turf): Sf: 0-0 GS: 0-0 Gd: 0-2 GF: 0-1 Fm: 0-0
Distance: 5f/6f: 0-0 7f-8f: 0-0 9f-13f: 0-3 14f+: 0-0
Track : LH: 0-2 RH: 0-1 Tight: 0-1 Gall: 0-2
Aids: Bl: 0-0 Vi: 0-0 Tstrap: 0-0
Best Rating: 74 8/01 NmkJ 1m4f good

Lanzlo (FR)

81 **63**

4-y-o b/br g Le Balafre (FR)-L'Eternite (FR) (Cariellor (FR))
P J Hobbs Winton Bloodstock Ltd

Placings:00500/25-0 **(4296)**
2001: 12^{0}G

	Starts	1st	2nd	3rd	Win & Pl
Career Total (Turf)	8	0	1	0	888

Going (Turf): Sf: 0-2 GS: 0-2 Gd: 0-2 GF: 0-2 Fm: 0-0
Distance: 5f/6f: 0-0 7f-8f: 0-4 9f-13f: 0-4 14f+: 0-0
Track : LH: 0-3 RH: 0-1 Tight: 0-3 Gall: 0-0
Aids: Bl: 0-0 Vi: 0-0 Tstrap: 0-0
Best Rating: 50 8/01 Epsm 1m4f10y good

Lapadar (IRE)

(93) (70)**65**

2-y-o b/br f Woodborough (USA)-Indescent Blue (Bluebird (USA))

J R Weymes P W Lonsdale

Placings:0340203 **(5610)**

2001: 7^{0}G, 7^{3}SD, 7^{4}GS, 7^{0}SD, 8^{2}SD, 8^{0}S, 8^{3}SD

	Starts	1st	2nd	3rd	Win & Pl
Career Total (Turf)	3	0	0	0	0
Career Total (AW)	4	0	1	2	1900

Going (Turf): **Sf: 0-1 GS: 0-1 Gd: 0-1 GF: 0-0 Fm: 0-0**
Distance: 5f/6f: 0-0 7f-8f: 0-5 9f-13f: 0-2 14f+: 0-0
Track : LH: 0-6 RH: 0-0 Tight: 0-3 Gall: 0-0
Aids: Bl: 0-0 Vi: 0-0 Tstrap: 0-0
Best Rating: 66 11/01 Wolv 1m100y stand

She has shown her best form to date on Fibresand.

Lapwing (IRE)

110 **93**

3-y-o b c Tagula (IRE)-Wasaif (IRE) (Lomond (USA))

B W Hills The Hon Mrs J M Corbett & Mr C Wright

Placings:4116-42100423230 **(5391)**

2001: 7^{4}G, 6^{2}F, 8^{1}GF, 8^{0}GF, 7^{0}GF, 7^{4}G, 8^{2}GF, 8^{3}G, 7^{2}G, 6^{3}S, 7^{0}GS

	Starts	1st	2nd	3rd	Win & Pl
Career Total (Turf)	15	3	3	2	37438

90	6/01	NmkR	1m	C(0-95)H	G-F	£6938
75	9/00	Wwck	7f26y	C(0-95)	G-F	£7247
70	8/00	Ayr	6f	D	G-F	£3464

Total win prize-money £17652

Going (Turf): Sf: 0-2 GS: 0-1 Gd: 0-4 **GF: 3-7** Fm: 0-1
Distance: 5f/6f: 1-2 **7f-8f: 2-13** 9f-13f: 0-0 14f+: 0-0
Track : **LH: 1-6** RH: 0-3 Tight: 0-3 Gall: 0-2
Aids: Bl: 0-0 Vi: 0-0 Tstrap: 0-0
Best Rating: 93 10/01 York 6f214y soft

Winner of an Ayr maiden and Warwick nursery last season, he has been running in some very competitive three-year-old handicaps this season and won in good style at Newmarket in July, but has since found a rise in the weights difficult to overcome. Needs fast ground and stays a mile.

Lara Falana

103 **54**

3-y-o b f Tagula (IRE)-Victoria Mill (Free State)

J A Osborne Mrs C A Waters

Placings:0-0021142 **(4734)**

2001: 7^{0}GF, 6^{0}GF, 8^{2}G, 7^{1}F, 10^{1}G, 9^{4}GS, 8^{2}F

	Starts	1st	2nd	3rd	Win & Pl
Career Total (Turf)	8	2	2	0	8823

51	8/01	Ripn	1m2f	E(0-70)H	GD	£3766
51	8/01	Brig	7f214y	E(0-70)H	FRM	£2968

Total win prize-money £6734

Going (Turf): Sf: 0-1 GS: 0-1 **Gd: 1-2** GF: 0-2 **Fm: 1-2**
Distance: 5f/6f: 0-0 7f-8f: 1-4 9f-13f: 1-4 14f+: 0-0
Track : LH: 1-3 RH: 1-2 **Tight: 1-2** Gall: 0-0
Aids: Bl: 0-0 Vi: 0-0 Tstrap: 0-1
Best Rating: 54 9/01 Chep 1m14y firm

Capable handicapper on good/fast ground. Does not appear to handle soft. Stays ten furlongs.

Lara Ruby (IRE)

87 **42**

2-y-o b f Sri Pekan (USA)-Atisayin (USA) (Al Nasr (FR))

P L Gilligan Russ Dalton

Placings:00000 **(4215)**

2001: 5^{0}G, 5^{0}GF, 7^{0}G, 6^{0}GF, 8^{0}G

	Starts	1st	2nd	3rd	Win & Pl
Career Total (Turf)	5	0	0	0	

Going (Turf): **Sf: 0-0 GS: 0-0 Gd: 0-3 GF: 0-2 Fm: 0-0**
Distance: 5f/6f: 0-3 7f-8f: 0-2 9f-13f: 0-0 14f+: 0-0
Track : LH: 0-2 RH: 0-1 Tight: 0-0 Gall: 0-3
Aids: Bl: 0-1 Vi: 0-0 Tstrap: 0-0
Best Rating: 42 7/01 Yarm 7f3y good

Lara's Delight

83 **10**

6-y-o b m Then Again-Sarah Dream (IRE) (Strong Gale)

M J Weeden Mrs S Frost

Placings:006-0000 **(4048)**

2001: 6^{0}GF, 9^{0}GF, 10^{0}S, 10^{0}F

	Starts	1st	2nd	3rd	Win & Pl
Career Total (Turf)	7	0	0	0	0

Going (Turf): **Sf: 0-2 GS: 0-0 Gd: 0-0 GF: 0-2 Fm: 0-3**
Distance: 5f/6f: 0-0 7f-8f: 0-1 9f-13f: 0-6 14f+: 0-0
Track : LH: 0-5 RH: 0-1 Tight: 0-4 Gall: 0-0
Aids: Bl: 0-0 Vi: 0-0 Tstrap: 0-0
Best Rating: 10 8/01 Chep 1m2f36y soft

Larkwood Sienna (IRE)

62 **11**

2-y-o ch f Woodborough (USA)-Luisa Di Camerata (IRE) (Marju (IRE))

C A Dwyer Larkwood Stud

Placings:60 **(2664)**

2001: 5^{6}G, 6^{0}G

	Starts	1st	2nd	3rd	Win & Pl
Career Total (Turf)	2	0	0	0	0

Going (Turf): **Sf: 0-0 GS: 0-0 Gd: 0-2 GF: 0-0 Fm: 0-0**
Distance: 5f/6f: 0-1 7f-8f: 0-1 9f-13f: 0-0 14f+: 0-0
Track : LH: 0-0 RH: 0-0 Tight: 0-0 Gall: 0-0
Aids: Bl: 0-0 Vi: 0-1 Tstrap: 0-0
Best Rating: 11 7/01 Yarm 6f3y good

Larousse

101 **63**

3-y-o ch f Unfuwain (USA)-Allespagne (USA) (Trempolino (USA))

S C Williams Alasdair Simpson

Placings:60-051313 **(4483)**

2001: 6^{0}GS, 10^{5}G, 11^{1}GF, 12^{3}GF, 12^{1}GS, 14^{3}S

	Starts	1st	2nd	3rd	Win & Pl
Career Total (Turf)	8	2	0	2	11166

59	8/01	NmkJ	1m4f	E(0-70)H	G-S	£5018
54	6/01	Bevl	1m3f216yF(0-60)H		G-F	£4673

Total win prize-money £9692

Going (Turf): Sf: 0-3 **GS: 1-2** Gd: 0-1 **GF: 1-2** Fm: 0-0
Distance: 5f/6f: 0-1 7f-8f: 0-1 **9f-13f: 2-5** 14f+: 0-1
Track : LH: 0-1 **RH: 2-3** Tight: 1-3 Gall: 1-1
Aids: Bl: 0-0 Vi: 0-0 Tstrap: 0-0
Best Rating: 63 9/01 Yarm 1m6f17y soft

She has improved for the step up in trip this season. Well suited by waiting tactics and handles any ground.

Las Ramblas (IRE)

96(104) (66)**70**

4-y-o b g Thatching-Raise A Warning (Warning)

Andrew Reid A S Reid

Placings:3203100/000042305000-204020 **(1608)**

2001: 6^{2}SD, 5^{0}SW, 6^{4}SD, 7^{0}HY, 6^{2}G, 6^{0}GF

	Starts	1st	2nd	3rd	Win & Pl
Career Total (Turf)	22	1	3	3	10872
Career Total (AW)	3	0	1	0	996

92	8/99	NmkJ	6f	D	G-F	£4581

Total win prize-money £4581

Going (Turf): Sf: 0-3 GS: 0-4 Gd: 0-5 **GF: 1-10** Fm: 0-0
Distance: **5f/6f: 1-21** 7f-8f: 0-4 9f-13f: 0-0 14f+: 0-0
Track : LH: 0-4 RH: 0-0 Tight: 0-2 Gall: 0-0
Aids: Bl: 0-1 Vi: 0-9 Tstrap: 0-0
Best Rating: 68 5/01 Nott 6f15y good

Lascombes

99 **92**

2-y-o b c Bluebird (USA)-Arinaga (Warning)

J Noseda Kilboy Estate

Placings:40104150 **(5493)**

2001: 6^{4}GF, 6^{0}GF, 7^{1}G, 6^{0}G, 7^{4}HY, 7^{1}S, 8^{5}GS, 7^{0}HY

	Starts	1st	2nd	3rd	Win & Pl
Career Total (Turf)	8	2	0	0	10783

92	9/01	Ches	7f122y	C	SFT	£5676
76	8/01	Hayd	7f30y	D	GD	£4355

Total win prize-money £10031

Going (Turf): **Sf: 1-3** GS: 0-1 **Gd: 1-2** GF: 0-2 Fm: 0-0
Distance: 5f/6f: 0-1 **7f-8f: 2-7** 9f-13f: 0-0 14f+: 0-0
Track : **LH: 2-4** RH: 0-1 **Tight: 1-1** Gall: 0-2
Aids: Bl: 0-0 Vi: 0-1 Tstrap: 0-0
Best Rating: 92 9/01 Ches 7f122y soft

Bred for speed, he was given a fine ride when scoring over seven furlongs at Haydock in August and was ridden the same way when winning at Chester the following month. Not quite up to Listed class, carries his head rather high and could be a bit of a thinker, but goes well for Darryll Holland. Acts on good and soft ground.

Laser Crystal (IRE)

84 **55**

2-y-o b f King's Theatre (IRE)-Solar Crystal (IRE) (Alzao (USA))

D R C Elsworth Michael Poland

Placings:6 **(3635)**

2001: 7^{6}GS

	Starts	1st	2nd	3rd	Win & Pl
Career Total (Turf)	1	0	0	0	0

Going (Turf): **Sf: 0-0 GS: 0-1 Gd: 0-0 GF: 0-0 Fm: 0-0**
Distance: 5f/6f: 0-0 7f-8f: 0-1 9f-13f: 0-0 14f+: 0-0
Track : LH: 0-0 RH: 0-0 Tight: 0-0 Gall: 0-0
Aids: Bl: 0-0 Vi: 0-0 Tstrap: 0-0
Best Rating: 55 8/01 NmkJ 7f gd-sft

Last Exhibit

15

3-y-o b f Royal Academy (USA)-Noirmant (Dominion)

R Guest Rae Guest

Placings:6 **(5519)**

2001: 6^{6}HY

	Starts	1st	2nd	3rd	Win & Pl
Career Total (Turf)	1	0	0	0	0

Going (Turf): **Sf: 0-1 GS: 0-0 Gd: 0-0 GF: 0-0 Fm: 0-0**
Distance: 5f/6f: 0-1 7f-8f: 0-0 9f-13f: 0-0 14f+: 0-0
Track : LH: 0-0 RH: 0-0 Tight: 0-0 Gall: 0-0
Aids: Bl: 0-0 Vi: 0-0 Tstrap: 0-0
Best Rating: 15 10/01 Wind 6f heavy

Last Gesture

90 **64**

2-y-o b c Jester-Suile Mor (Satin Wood)

B R Millman Mrs R T H Heeley

Placings:01200 (4638)
2001: 6^{0}GF, 6^{1}GF, 7^{2}GF, 7^{0}G, 7^{0}GF

	Starts	1st	2nd	3rd	Win & Pl
Career Total (Turf)	5	1	1	0	2574

64 8/01 Brig 6f209y G G-F £1897
Total win prize-money £1897

Going (Turf): Sf: 0-0 GS: 0-0 Gd: 0-1 **GF: 1-4** Fm: 0-0
Distance: 5f/6f: 0-0 **7f-8f: 1-5** 9f-13f: 0-0 14f+: 0-0
Track : **LH: 1-2** RH: 0-0 Tight: 0-1 Gall: 0-0
Aids: Bl: 0-0 Vi: 0-0 Tstrap: 0-0
Best Rating: 64 8/01 Folk 7f gd-fm

A plating-class winner, he went the wrong way following his Brighton victory over seven furlongs in August.

Last Impression

79 **69**
3-y-o b f Imp Society (USA)-Figment (Posse (USA))
J S Goldie W M Johnstone

Placings:142-000 (1291)
2001: 5^{0}GS, 6^{0}G, 6^{0}F

	Starts	1st	2nd	3rd	Win & Pl
Career Total (Turf)	6	1	1	0	3582

53 6/00 Haml 5f4y E GD £2730
Total win prize-money £2730

Going (Turf): Sf: 0-0 GS: 0-1 **Gd: 1-3** GF: 0-1 Fm: 0-1
Distance: **5f/6f: 1-3** 7f-8f: 0-3 9f-13f: 0-0 14f+: 0-0
Track : LH: 0-0 RH: 0-0 Tight: 0-0 Gall: 0-0
Aids: Bl: 0-0 Vi: 0-0 Tstrap: 0-0
Best Rating: 33 4/01 Muss 5f gd-sft

Last Master

73 **51**
2-y-o b c Master Willie-Oatfield (Great Nephew)
H Candy R Barnett

Placings:0 (5095)
2001: 8^{0}GS

	Starts	1st	2nd	3rd	Win & Pl
Career Total (Turf)	1	0	0	0	

Going (Turf): Sf: 0-0 GS: 0-1 Gd: 0-0 GF: 0-0 Fm: 0-0
Distance: 5f/6f: 0-0 7f-8f: 0-1 9f-13f: 0-0 14f+: 0-0
Track : LH: 0-0 RH: 0-0 Tight: 0-0 Gall: 0-0
Aids: Bl: 0-0 Vi: 0-0 Tstrap: 0-0
Best Rating: 51 10/01 Sals 1m gd-sft

Last Of The Mice

101(92) (57)**64**
3-y-o b g Deploy-Top Mouse (High Top)
J A Osborne Lady Vestey

Placings:6-055010 (2967)
2001: 8^{0}GS, 9^{5}SD, 10^{5}GF, 11^{0}G, 11^{1}GF, 12^{0}GF

	Starts	1st	2nd	3rd	Win & Pl
Career Total (Turf)	6	1	0	0	3220
Career Total (AW)	1	0	0	0	0

64 6/01 Wind 1m3f135yE(0-75)H G-F £3220
Total win prize-money £3220

Going (Turf): Sf: 0-0 GS: 0-1 Gd: 0-1 **GF: 1-4** Fm: 0-0
Distance: 5f/6f: 0-0 7f-8f: 0-0 **9f-13f: 1-7** 14f+: 0-0
Track : LH: 0-1 RH: 0-5 **Tight: 1-4** Gall: 0-0
Aids: **Bl: 1-2** Vi: 0-0 Tstrap: 0-0
Best Rating: 64 6/01 Wind 1m3f135y gd-fm

Last Symphony

98(82) (27)**61**
4-y-o b g Last Tycoon-Dancing Heights (IRE) (High Estate)
P Mitchell Mrs P Mitchell Mrs S Sheldon Mrs L Kidby

Placings:061-06000000 (4303)
2001: 8^{0}SW, 7^{6}GF, 8^{0}GF, 9^{0}G, 10^{0}GS, 8^{0}G, 8^{0}GF, 7^{0}GF

	Starts	1st	2nd	3rd	Win & Pl
Career Total (Turf)	10	1	0	0	4004
Career Total (AW)	1	0	0	0	

77 5/00 Hayd 7f30y D SFT £4004
Total win prize-money £4004

Going (Turf): Sf: 1-1 GS: 0-2 Gd: 0-3 GF: 0-4 Fm: 0-0
Distance: 5f/6f: 0-0 **7f-8f: 1-6** 9f-13f: 0-5 14f+: 0-0
Track : **LH: 1-5** RH: 0-4 Tight: 0-5 Gall: 0-1
Aids: Bl: 0-0 Vi: 0-2 Tstrap: 0-0
Best Rating: 61 7/01 Kemp 1m1f good

Won Kempton maiden over seven furlongs in 2000 but found life tougher in handicap company. Has not looked an easy ride in the past. Won on soft ground.

Lastman (USA)

89 **35**
6-y-o b/br g Fabulous Dancer (USA)-Rivala (USA) (Riverman (USA))
J J O'Neill Darren C Mercer

Placings:234/5/52202-0 (2811)
2001: 12^{0}GF

	Starts	1st	2nd	3rd	Win & Pl
Career Total (Turf)	10	0	4	1	13124

Going (Turf): Sf: 0-3 GS: 0-0 Gd: 0-3 GF: 0-2 Fm: 0-0
Distance: 5f/6f: 0-0 7f-8f: 0-0 9f-13f: 0-5 14f+: 0-3
Track : LH: 0-4 RH: 0-4 Tight: 0-4 Gall: 0-2
Aids: Bl: 0-0 Vi: 0-0 Tstrap: 0-0
Best Rating: 35 7/01 Wwck 1m4f134y gd-fm

Lastofthecash

75(74) (19)**21**
5-y-o b g Ballacashtal (CAN)-Blue Empress (Blue Cashmere)
Dr P Pritchard Three Of A Kind Racing

Placings:06-06 (4214)
2001: 7^{0}S, 5^{6}GF

	Starts	1st	2nd	3rd	Win & Pl
Career Total (Turf)	2	0	0	0	
Career Total (AW)	2	0	0	0	

Going (Turf): Sf: 0-1 GS: 0-0 Gd: 0-0 GF: 0-1 Fm: 0-0
Distance: 5f/6f: 0-1 7f-8f: 0-3 9f-13f: 0-0 14f+: 0-0
Track : LH: 0-3 RH: 0-0 Tight: 0-2 Gall: 0-1
Aids: Bl: 0-0 Vi: 0-0 Tstrap: 0-0
Best Rating: 21 8/01 Bath 5f11y gd-fm

Late Arrival

95 **49**
4-y-o b g Emperor Jones (USA)-Try Vickers (USA) (Fuzzbuster (USA))
A Crook (D Morris 25/5) The Adbrokes Partnership

Placings:040/4200023-000526 (4240)
2001: 8^{0}GS, 8^{0}F, 9^{0}GF, 12^{5}GS, 9^{2}G, 9^{6}GF

	Starts	1st	2nd	3rd	Win & Pl
Career Total (Turf)	16	0	3	1	3275

Going (Turf): Sf: 0-2 GS: 0-4 Gd: 0-2 GF: 0-7 Fm: 0-1
Distance: 5f/6f: 0-1 7f-8f: 0-4 9f-13f: 0-11 14f+: 0-0
Track : LH: 0-8 RH: 0-3 Tight: 0-4 Gall: 0-0
Aids: Bl: 0-3 Vi: 0-1 Tstrap: 0-0
Best Rating: 49 8/01 Muss 1m1f good

Late Night Out

114(34) (88)**117**
6-y-o b g Lahib (USA)-Chain Dance (Shareef Dancer (USA))
W Jarvis J M Greetham

Placings:315/3616/3144004524/012100-123123314 (5386)
2001: 7^{1}S, 8^{2}G, 7^{3}GF, 8^{1}GF, 8^{2}GF, 8^{3}GF, 8^{3}G, 7^{1}GS, 7^{4}GS

	Starts	1st	2nd	3rd	Win & Pl
Career Total (Turf)	31	8	4	6	176085
Career Total (AW)	1	0	0	0	

105 9/01 Gdwd 7f A G-S £22200
108 7/01 Gdwd 1m A G-F £19623
110 5/01 Hayd 7f30y A SFT £17615
109 8/00 York 6f214y A GD £22717
97 7/00 Ches 7f2y B G-S £9570
99 5/99 Hayd 7f30y A(0-110)H GD £12149
94 10/98 Rdcr 7f C G-S £4996
88 10/97 Nott 6f15y D GD £3785
Total win prize-money £112657

Going (Turf): Sf: 1-6 **GS: 3-7 Gd: 3-9** GF: 1-7 Fm: 0-0
Distance: 5f/6f: 0-4 **7f-8f: 8-28** 9f-13f: 0-0 14f+: 0-0
Track : **LH: 4-13** RH: 2-6 Tight: 1-1 Gall: 1-5
Aids: Bl: 0-0 Vi: 0-0 Tstrap: 0-0
Best Rating: 117 8/01 Gdwd 1m gd-fm

Generally suited by hold-up tactics, he goes particularly well at Haydock. He has a fine record in Listed company and finally bridged the gap to Group Three class after several fine efforts at Goodwood in September. Best over seven furlongs although he stays a mile.

Late Summer (USA)

98 **68**
3-y-o b f Gone West (USA)-Sun And Shade (Ajdal (USA))
H R A Cecil Cliveden Stud

Placings:6-446040 (5141)
2001: 10^{4}GF, 10^{4}GF, 8^{6}GF, 10^{0}GF, 8^{4}GF, 8^{0}G

	Starts	1st	2nd	3rd	Win & Pl
Career Total (Turf)	7	0	0	0	1035

Going (Turf): Sf: 0-1 GS: 0-0 Gd: 0-1 GF: 0-5 Fm: 0-0
Distance: 5f/6f: 0-0 7f-8f: 0-2 9f-13f: 0-5 14f+: 0-0
Track : LH: 0-1 RH: 0-2 Tight: 0-1 Gall: 0-2
Aids: Bl: 0-0 Vi: 0-0 Tstrap: 0-0
Best Rating: 79 6/01 NmkR 1m2f gd-fm

A disappointing filly, she has ability but has not lived up to expectations.

Latensaani

96(63) (21)**42**
3-y-o b g Shaamit (IRE)-Intoxication (Great Nephew)
W J Haggas & Mrs Peter Lumley

Placings:00-04303 (4473)
2001: 6^{0}HY, 12^{4}GF, 16^{3}GF, 15^{0}G, 11^{3}GF

	Starts	1st	2nd	3rd	Win & Pl
Career Total (Turf)	6	0	0	2	798
Career Total (AW)	1	0	0	0	

Going (Turf): Sf: 0-2 GS: 0-0 Gd: 0-1 GF: 0-3 Fm: 0-0
Distance: 5f/6f: 0-1 7f-8f: 0-2 9f-13f: 0-2 14f+: 0-2
Track : LH: 0-3 RH: 0-3 Tight: 0-4 Gall: 0-0
Aids: Bl: 0-0 Vi: 0-0 Tstrap: 0-0
Best Rating: 42 9/01 Brig 1m3f196y gd-fm

Latin Bay

83(96) (42)**33**
6-y-o b g Superlative-Hugging (Beveled (USA))
A E Jones Mrs Susan Pullin

Placings:000500/5300014006/11000300/002-600

(4280)
2001: 13^{6}GF, 13^{0}G, 9^{0}GS

	Starts	1st	2nd	3rd	Win & Pl
Career Total (Turf)	24	1	0	2	3698
Career Total (AW)	6	2	1	0	4413

54 1/99 Ling 1m4f G(0-60)H STD £1946
56 1/99 Ling 1m5f G(0-60)H STD £1900
45 8/98 Kemp 1m1f E(0-70)H G-F £2733
Total win prize-money £6580

Going (Turf): Sf: 0-1 GS: 0-6 Gd: 0-6 **GF: 1-10** Fm: 0-1
Distance: 5f/6f: 0-2 7f-8f: 0-9 **9f-13f: 3-15** 14f+: 0-4
Track : **LH: 2-17** RH: 1-8 **Tight: 2-14** Gall: 0-1
Aids: Bl: 0-0 Vi: 0-0 Tstrap: 0-2
Best Rating: 33 7/01 Newb 1m5f61y gd-fm

Latin Lynx (USA)

94 **93**
2-y-o br f Forest Wildcat (USA)-Senita Lane (CAN) (Ascot Knight (CAN))
D R Loder Sheikh Mohammed

Placings:144 **(4387a)**
2001: 5^{1}GF, 5^{4}GF, 5^{4}GS

	Starts	1st	2nd	3rd	Win & Pl
Career Total (Turf)	3	1	0	0	8837

82 6/01 Leic 5f2y D G-F £3484
Total win prize-money £3484

Going (Turf): Sf: 0-0 GS: 0-1 Gd: 0-0 **GF: 1-2** Fm: 0-0
Distance: **5f/6f: 1-3** 7f-8f: 0-0 9f-13f: 0-0 14f+: 0-0
Track : LH: 0-0 RH: 0-0 Tight: 0-0 Gall: 0-0
Aids: Bl: 0-0 Vi: 0-0 Tstrap: 0-0
Best Rating: 93 6/01 Asct 5f gd-fm

Her dam was a stakes winner over six furlongs in the USA, and she was a most impressive four length winner at Leicester on her debut, before a fine effort in the Queen Mary. Returning after two months off she was beaten on easy ground at Deauville.

Latino Bay (IRE)

(94) (33)**51**
4-y-o ch g Perugino (USA)-Slightly Latin (Ahonoora)
Cathal McCarthy (N P Littmoden 23/1) Cathal McCarthy

Placings:000/06000126200-050040 **(4128a)**
2001: 7^{0}SW, 7^{5}SW, 7^{0}SD, 13^{0}F, 12^{4}F, 16^{0}G

	Starts	1st	2nd	3rd	Win & Pl
Career Total (Turf)	9	0	0	0	280
Career Total (AW)	11	1	2	0	3040

48 10/00 Wolv 7f F STD £2233
Total win prize-money £2233

Going (Turf): **Sf: 0-0 GS: 0-0 Gd: 0-4 GF: 0-3 Fm: 0-2**
Distance: 5f/6f: 0-0 **7f-8f: 1-15** 9f-13f: 0-4 14f+: 0-1
Track : **LH: 1-10** RH: 0-0 **Tight: 1-9** Gall: 0-0
Aids: Bl: 0-1 Vi: 0-0 Tstrap: 0-0
Best Rating: 32 7/01 DRoy 1m4f68y firm

Latterly (USA)

(93)
6-y-o b g Cryptoclearance (USA)-Latest Scandal (USA) (Two Davids (USA))
F Jordan F Jordan

Placings:6/56000/003050050/060 **(0346)**
2001: 14^{0}SD, 12^{6}SW, 16^{0}SD

	Starts	1st	2nd	3rd	Win & Pl
Career Total (Turf)	15	0	0	1	287
Career Total (AW)	3	0	0	0	0

Going (Turf): **Sf: 0-2 GS: 0-0 Gd: 0-5 GF: 0-1 Fm: 0-1**
Distance: 5f/6f: 0-0 7f-8f: 0-2 9f-13f: 0-11 14f+: 0-5
Track : LH: 0-10 RH: 0-7 Tight: 0-3 Gall: 0-0
Aids: Bl: 0-4 Vi: 0-0 Tstrap: 0-0
Best Rating: 14 2/01 Wolv 1m4f slow

Laughing Girl (USA)

102 **85**
3-y-o ch f Woodman (USA)-Milly Ha Ha (Dancing Brave (USA))
H R A Cecil Cliveden Stud

Placings:3314 **(5226)**
2001: 10^{3}G, 12^{3}GF, 9^{1}GF, 11^{4}S

	Starts	1st	2nd	3rd	Win & Pl
Career Total (Turf)	4	1	0	2	6100

69 9/01 Leic 1m1f218yD G-F £3991
Total win prize-money £3991

Going (Turf): Sf: 0-1 GS: 0-0 Gd: 0-1 **GF: 1-2** Fm: 0-0
Distance: 5f/6f: 0-0 7f-8f: 0-0 **9f-13f: 1-4** 14f+: 0-0
Track : LH: 0-2 **RH: 1-2** Tight: 0-0 Gall: 0-3
Aids: Bl: 0-0 Vi: 0-0 Tstrap: 0-0
Best Rating: 85 7/01 NmkJ 1m2f good

Laund View Leona

83(83) (35)**8**
3-y-o ch f Piccolo-Punta Leona (IRE) (Shernazar)
R Bastiman Laund View Racing

Placings:000-5606000000U000000 **(5625)**
2001: 7^{5}SD, 7^{6}SD, 8^{0}SD, 7^{6}SD, 8^{0}HY, 8^{0}G, 7^{0}G, 8^{0}GF, 8^{0}GF, 7^{0}GF, 6^{U}F, 7^{0}GF, 5^{0}GS, 6^{0}S, 7^{0}GS, 7^{0}HY, 8^{0}GS

	Starts	1st	2nd	3rd	Win & Pl
Career Total (Turf)	14	0	0	0	
Career Total (AW)	6	0	0	0	0

Going (Turf): **Sf: 0-4 GS: 0-3 Gd: 0-2 GF: 0-4 Fm: 0-1**
Distance: 5f/6f: 0-4 7f-8f: 0-13 9f-13f: 0-3 14f+: 0-0
Track : LH: 0-10 RH: 0-2 Tight: 0-2 Gall: 0-0
Aids: Bl: 0-0 Vi: 0-0 Tstrap: 0-0
Best Rating: 35 1/01 Sthl 7f stand

A poor performer who is a regular in 'appearance money' events.

Laura Beth

95 **67**
2-y-o b f Danehill Dancer (IRE)-Cantata (IRE) (Saddlers' Hall (IRE))
A Dickman Mike Smallman

Placings:4450 **(3585)**
2001: 6^{4}GF, 6^{4}F, 6^{5}GF, 5^{0}G

	Starts	1st	2nd	3rd	Win & Pl
Career Total (Turf)	4	0	0	0	300

Going (Turf): **Sf: 0-0 GS: 0-0 Gd: 0-1 GF: 0-2 Fm: 0-1**
Distance: 5f/6f: 0-4 7f-8f: 0-0 9f-13f: 0-0 14f+: 0-0
Track : LH: 0-1 RH: 0-0 Tight: 0-1 Gall: 0-0
Aids: Bl: 0-0 Vi: 0-0 Tstrap: 0-0
Best Rating: 67 6/01 Thsk 6f firm

Laurel Dawn

104(108) (85)**59**
3-y-o gr c Paris House-Madrina (Waajib)
A Berry Laurel (leisure) Limited

Placings:4012134533-1040040000060 **(5381)**
2001: 5^{1}SD, 5^{0}GF, 5^{4}F, 5^{0}GF, 5^{0}GF, 5^{4}GF, 5^{0}G, 5^{0}F, 6^{0}G, 5^{0}GF, 5^{0}GS, 5^{6}G, 5^{0}S

	Starts	1st	2nd	3rd	Win & Pl
Career Total (Turf)	19	1	1	1	13995
Career Total (AW)	4	2	0	2	6864

85 4/01 Ling 5f D(0-80)H STD £3874
80 7/00 York 5f C GD £8827
69 6/00 Ling 5f F STD £2215
Total win prize-money £14917

Going (Turf): Sf: 0-1 GS: 0-2 **Gd: 1-6** GF: 0-7 Fm: 0-3
Distance: **5f/6f: 3-23** 7f-8f: 0-0 9f-13f: 0-0 14f+: 0-0
Track : **LH: 2-6** RH: 0-0 **Tight: 2-5** Gall: 0-1
Aids: Bl: 0-0 Vi: 0-0 Tstrap: 0-0
Best Rating: 85 4/01 Ling 5f stand

A speedy, fair sprinter, he is a winner on Equitrack and turf. Usually races prominently and acts best on fast ground.

Laurie Shearer

(26)
5-y-o b/br m Show-A-Leg-Grand Teton (Bustino)
R C Spicer Mrs A J Chinn

Placings:0-0 **(0053)**
2001: 12^{0}SD

	Starts	1st	2nd	3rd	Win & Pl
Career Total (Turf)	0	0	0	0	
Career Total (AW)	2	0	0	0	

Going (Turf): **Sf: 0-0 GS: 0-0 Gd: 0-0 GF: 0-0 Fm: 0-0**
Distance: 5f/6f: 0-0 7f-8f: 0-0 9f-13f: 0-2 14f+: 0-0
Track : LH: 0-2 RH: 0-0 Tight: 0-1 Gall: 0-0
Aids: Bl: 0-0 Vi: 0-0 Tstrap: 0-0

Laurieston Flo (IRE)

(88) (46)**46**
3-y-o b f Nicolotte-Brown Foam (Horage)
J W Mullins (B J Meehan 3/5) Mrs Caroline Taylor

Placings:0-3043 **(1088)**
2001: 8^{3}SD, 9^{0}GS, 12^{4}S, 9^{3}SD

	Starts	1st	2nd	3rd	Win & Pl
Career Total (Turf)	3	0	0	0	0
Career Total (AW)	2	0	0	2	674

Going (Turf): **Sf: 0-2 GS: 0-1 Gd: 0-0 GF: 0-0 Fm: 0-0**
Distance: 5f/6f: 0-0 7f-8f: 0-1 9f-13f: 0-4 14f+: 0-0
Track : LH: 0-4 RH: 0-1 Tight: 0-3 Gall: 0-0
Aids: Bl: 0-2 Vi: 0-0 Tstrap: 0-0
Best Rating: 46 3/01 Ling 1m stand

Lautrec

(81) (9)**54**
5-y-o b g Shareef Dancer (USA)-Pride Of Paris (Troy)
R M Stronge Robert Stronge

Placings:603/43360/50-060 **(0511)**
2001: 11^{0}SD, 12^{6}SW, 12^{0}SD

	Starts	1st	2nd	3rd	Win & Pl
Career Total (Turf)	7	0	0	3	1705
Career Total (AW)	6	0	0	0	0

Going (Turf): **Sf: 0-0 GS: 0-0 Gd: 0-3 GF: 0-3 Fm: 0-1**
Distance: 5f/6f: 0-0 7f-8f: 0-4 9f-13f: 0-9 14f+: 0-0
Track : LH: 0-8 RH: 0-3 Tight: 0-6 Gall: 0-0
Aids: Bl: 0-1 Vi: 0-1 Tstrap: 0-0
Best Rating: 9 2/01 Wolv 1m4f slow

Lavys Dream

(96) (57+)**38**
2-y-o b f Lugana Beach-Gaelic Air (Ballad Rock)
M J Polglase Mark Lewis

Placings:20000 **(5195)**
2001: 5^{2}SD, 5^{0}G, 5^{0}GF, 6^{0}SW, 6^{0}SD

	Starts	1st	2nd	3rd	Win & Pl
Career Total (Turf)	2	0	0	0	
Career Total (AW)	3	0	1	0	534

Going (Turf): Sf: 0-0 GS: 0-0 Gd: 0-1 GF: 0-1 Fm: 0-0
Distance: 5f/6f: 0-5 7f-8f: 0-0 9f-13f: 0-0 14f+: 0-0
Track : LH: 0-4 RH: 0-0 Tight: 0-3 Gall: 0-1
Aids: Bl: 0-0 Vi: 0-0 Tstrap: 0-0
Best Rating: 57 7/01 Wolv 5f stand

Law Breaker (IRE)

105(104) (73)**72**

3-y-o ch g Case Law-Revelette (Runnett)
J Cullinan Alan Spargo Ltd Toolmakers

Placings:04053032-32321303000 **(4527)**
2001: 6^{3}SD, 5^{2}SW, 6^{3}SD, 5^{2}SW, 5^{1}SD, 5^{3}SD, 5^{0}GS, 5^{3}G, 5^{0}G, 6^{0}GF, 6^{0}GF

	Starts	1st	2nd	3rd	Win & Pl
Career Total (Turf)	11	0	0	3	2286
Career Total (AW)	8	1	3	3	8040

73	3/01	Sthl	5f	E(0-70)H	STD	£2450

Total win prize-money £2450

Going (Turf): Sf: 0-2 GS: 0-1 Gd: 0-3 GF: 0-5 Fm: 0-0
Distance: 5f/6f: 1-17 7f-8f: 0-2 9f-13f: 0-0 14f+: 0-0
Track : LH: 0-6 RH: 0-4 Tight: 0-4 Gall: 0-4
Aids: Bl: 0-0 Vi: 0-1 Tstrap: 0-0
Best Rating: 73 4/01 Ling 5f stand

Fair sprint handicapper, effective on soft ground and Fibresand.

Law Commission

(95) (58)**59**

11-y-o ch g Ela-Mana-Mou-Adjala (Northfields (USA))
S Kirk Raymond Tooth

Placings:503214/566000/000200/0003610/0410141250/6000066221005/0500050/0150006000/6014200-00440006105 **(5406)**
2001: 5^{0}G, 6^{0}GF, 7^{4}G, 7^{4}GF, 8^{0}GF, 6^{0}GF, 8^{0}GF, 7^{6}GF, 7^{1}G, 6^{0}S, 8^{5}SD

	Starts	1st	2nd	3rd	Win & Pl
Career Total (Turf)	83	9	6	2	102521
Career Total (AW)	1	0	0	0	0

59	9/01	Chep	7f16y	F(0-65)H	GD	£2499
61	7/00	Bath	5f161y	E(0-70)	FRM	£3347
85	5/99	Newb	7f	D(0-85)H	G-F	£5637
93	9/97	Gdwd	7f	B(0-105)H	GD	£9529
91	8/96	Asct	7f	C(0-95)H	G-F	£6318
81	7/96	Kemp	6f	E	G-F	£3046
81	6/96	Folk	6f	D(0-85)H	G-F	£3590
79	8/95	Sals	6f	D(0-80)H	FRM	£3944
87	10/92	NmkR	7f	C	G-F	£8675

Total win prize-money £46589

Going (Turf): Sf: 0-9 GS: 0-8 Gd: 2-23 GF: 5-38 Fm: 2-5
Distance: 5f/6f: 4-19 7f-8f: 5-62 9f-13f: 0-3 14f+: 0-0
Track : LH: 1-12 RH: 1-14 Tight: 0-3 Gall: 1-12
Aids: Bl: 0-0 Vi: 0-0 Tstrap: 0-0
Best Rating: 62 7/01 Kemp 7f good

Not as good as he was, despite winning at Newbury on his second start of the season. Best suited by fast ground, but needs everything to go his way.

Lawful Contract (IRE)

62

6-y-o br g Contract Law (USA)-Lucciola (FR) (Auction Ring (USA))
Graeme Roe G B Perry & Roe Racing

Placings:0000/0500/0 **(4319)**
2001: 10^{0}GF

	Starts	1st	2nd	3rd	Win & Pl
Career Total (Turf)	5	0	0	0	
Career Total (AW)	4	0	0	0	0

Going (Turf): Sf: 0-0 GS: 0-0 Gd: 0-4 GF: 0-1 Fm: 0-0
Distance: 5f/6f: 0-5 7f-8f: 0-1 9f-13f: 0-3 14f+: 0-0
Track : LH: 0-5 RH: 0-0 Tight: 0-1 Gall: 0-0
Aids: Bl: 0-0 Vi: 0-0 Tstrap: 0-0

Lay Down Sally (IRE)

95(88) (44)**55**

3-y-o ch f General Monash (USA)-Sally Fay (IRE) (Fayruz)
J White Nick Quesnel

Placings:00040-0043060 **(5412)**
2001: 6^{0}G, 5^{0}GF, 6^{4}GF, 5^{3}GF, 5^{0}GS, 5^{6}F, 6^{0}SD

	Starts	1st	2nd	3rd	Win & Pl
Career Total (Turf)	9	0	0	1	712
Career Total (AW)	3	0	0	0	219

Going (Turf): Sf: 0-2 GS: 0-1 Gd: 0-2 GF: 0-3 Fm: 0-1
Distance: 5f/6f: 0-11 7f-8f: 0-1 9f-13f: 0-0 14f+: 0-0
Track : LH: 0-4 RH: 0-2 Tight: 0-0 Gall: 0-3
Aids: Bl: 0-2 Vi: 0-0 Tstrap: 0-0
Best Rating: 55 7/01 Sals 6f gd-fm

Layan

101(98) (35)**55**

4-y-o b f Puissance-Most Uppitty (Absalom)
J Balding Rowley Racing

Placings:624006/5660342030343030-602240364 **(3259)**
2001: 6^{6}SD, 6^{0}SD, 5^{2}SD, 6^{2}G, 5^{4}GF, 6^{0}F, 5^{3}G, 5^{6}SD, 6^{4}GF

	Starts	1st	2nd	3rd	Win & Pl
Career Total (Turf)	21	0	2	4	4452
Career Total (AW)	11	0	2	2	1662

Going (Turf): Sf: 0-3 GS: 0-2 Gd: 0-6 GF: 0-7 Fm: 0-3
Distance: 5f/6f: 0-31 7f-8f: 0-1 9f-13f: 0-0 14f+: 0-0
Track : LH: 0-10 RH: 0-0 Tight: 0-3 Gall: 0-1
Aids: Bl: 0-0 Vi: 0-0 Tstrap: 0-0
Best Rating: 45 7/01 Ripn 6f gd-fm

Lazzaz

97(89) (55)**50**

3-y-o b g Muhtarram (USA)-Astern (USA) (Polish Navy (USA))
P W Hiatt (Miss H M Irving 22/6) Phil Kelly

Placings:044-0005302 **(5278)**
2001: 9^{0}S, 9^{0}GS, 11^{0}GF, 11^{5}GF, 10^{3}GF, 9^{0}G, 9^{2}GS

	Starts	1st	2nd	3rd	Win & Pl
Career Total (Turf)	9	0	1	1	1132
Career Total (AW)	1	0	0	0	179

Going (Turf): Sf: 0-1 GS: 0-2 Gd: 0-2 GF: 0-4 Fm: 0-0
Distance: 5f/6f: 0-0 7f-8f: 0-2 9f-13f: 0-8 14f+: 0-0
Track : LH: 0-5 RH: 0-2 Tight: 0-4 Gall: 0-0
Aids: Bl: 0-0 Vi: 0-0 Tstrap: 0-0
Best Rating: 59 4/01 Nott 1m1f213y soft

His best race was when he came second in a seller at Leicester in October.

Le Cavalier (USA)

97(101) (34)**21**

4-y-o b g Mister Baileys-Secret Deed (USA) (Shadeed (USA))
A Bailey (C N Allen 19/3) Ms Jayne Morton

Placings:50300400/02222265000040-006433335050003002 **(4606)**
2001: 11^{0}SD, 12^{0}SD, 12^{6}SW, 13^{4}SD, 13^{3}SW, 12^{3}SW, 16^{3}SW, 16^{3}SD, 12^{5}SD, 14^{0}SD, 13^{5}SD, 9^{0}S, 11^{0}G, 10^{0}GF, 9^{3}SD, 10^{0}G, 14^{0}SW, 12^{2}SD

	Starts	1st	2nd	3rd	Win & Pl
Career Total (Turf)	11	0	0	1	702
Career Total (AW)	29	0	6	5	7149

Going (Turf): Sf: 0-2 GS: 0-1 Gd: 0-4 GF: 0-4 Fm: 0-0
Distance: 5f/6f: 0-0 7f-8f: 0-4 9f-13f: 0-31 14f+: 0-5
Track : LH: 0-33 RH: 0-5 Tight: 0-28 Gall: 0-1
Aids: Bl: 0-5 Vi: 0-3 Tstrap: 0-1
Best Rating: 47 2/01 Ling 2m slow

Le Fantasme

105 **65**

3-y-o b c Fairy King (USA)-La Splendide (FR) (Slip Anchor)
S Dow D G Churston

Placings:0-004064415 **(5591)**
2001: 8^{0}GS, 8^{0}GS, 7^{4}G, 9^{0}G, 7^{6}G, 8^{4}G, 7^{4}S, 8^{1}G, 9^{5}GS

	Starts	1st	2nd	3rd	Win & Pl
Career Total (Turf)	10	1	0	0	3319

63	10/01	Bath	1m5y	F(0-60)H	GD	£2429

Total win prize-money £2429

Going (Turf): Sf: 0-2 GS: 0-3 Gd: 1-5 GF: 0-0 Fm: 0-0
Distance: 5f/6f: 0-0 7f-8f: 0-7 9f-13f: 1-3 14f+: 0-0
Track : LH: 1-4 RH: 0-5 Tight: 1-2 Gall: 0-1
Aids: Bl: 0-0 Vi: 0-0 Tstrap: 0-0
Best Rating: 65 11/01 Brig 1m1f209y gd-sft

A fair handicapper with one win to his name over a mile at Bath. Has not always looked a straightforward ride. Acts on good and good to soft.

Le Follie (CHI)

89 **45**

4-y-o ch f Hussonet (USA)-Whisper Loud (CHI) (Worldwatch (USA))
B W Hills Wafic Said

Placings:06-0 **(3882)**
2001: 8^{0}G

	Starts	1st	2nd	3rd	Win & Pl
Career Total (Turf)	3	0	0	0	0

Going (Turf): Sf: 0-0 GS: 0-0 Gd: 0-2 GF: 0-1 Fm: 0-0
Distance: 5f/6f: 0-1 7f-8f: 0-0 9f-13f: 0-2 14f+: 0-0
Track : LH: 0-0 RH: 0-2 Tight: 0-2 Gall: 0-0
Aids: Bl: 0-0 Vi: 0-0 Tstrap: 0-0
Best Rating: 45 8/01 Wind 1m67y good

Le Meridien (IRE)

103 **57**

3-y-o ch f Magical Wonder (USA)-Dutch Queen (Ahonoora)
J S Wainwright J S Wainwright

Placings:044040-043046601 **(4236)**
2001: 5^{0}S, 6^{4}G, 6^{3}GF, 6^{0}F, 5^{4}F, 6^{6}GF, 5^{6}G, 6^{0}F, 5^{1}GF

	Starts	1st	2nd	3rd	Win & Pl
Career Total (Turf)	15	1	0	1	5988

57	8/01	Bevl	5f	D	G-F	£4400

Total win prize-money £4401

Going (Turf): Sf: 0-2 GS: 0-1 Gd: 0-3 GF: 1-5 Fm: 0-4
Distance: 5f/6f: 1-14 7f-8f: 0-1 9f-13f: 0-1 14f+: 0-0
Track : LH: 0-1 RH: 0-0 Tight: 0-0 Gall: 0-0
Aids: Bl: 0-0 Vi: 0-2 Tstrap: 1-1
Best Rating: 58 5/01 Hayd 6f gd-fm

Modest maiden. Seems to handle firm and soft alike.

Le Ruban Bleu (IRE)

72 **34**

2-y-o ch c Bluebird (USA)-Minervitta (Warrshan (USA))
H J Collingridge The Headquarters Partnership Viii

Placings:00 (5527)
2001: 7^{0}GF, 8^{0}HY

	Starts	1st	2nd	3rd	Win & Pl
Career Total (Turf)	2	0	0	0	

Going (Turf): Sf: 0-1 GS: 0-0 Gd: 0-0 GF: 0-1 Fm: 0-0
Distance: 5f/6f: 0-0 7f-8f: 0-1 9f-13f: 0-1 14f+: 0-0
Track: LH: 0-1 RH: 0-1 Tight: 0-0 Gall: 0-1
Aids: Bl: 0-0 Vi: 0-0 Tstrap: 0-0
Best Rating: 34 10/01 Nott 1m54y heavy

Le Sauvage (IRE)

(85) (37)
6-y-o b g Tirol-Cistus (Sun Prince)
D W Barker The Ebor Partnership

Placings:0063/205000560/0-0 (0037)
2001: 16^{0}SD

	Starts	1st	2nd	3rd	Win & Pl
Career Total (Turf)	9	0	0	0	0
Career Total (AW)	6	0	1	1	861

Going (Turf): Sf: 0-2 GS: 0-0 Gd: 0-4 GF: 0-3 Fm: 0-0
Distance: 5f/6f: 0-0 7f-8f: 0-0 9f-13f: 0-6 14f+: 0-9
Track: LH: 0-9 RH: 0-6 Tight: 0-5 Gall: 0-1
Aids: Bl: 0-0 Vi: 0-0 Tstrap: 0-0
Best Rating: 9 1/01 Sthl 2m stand

Leadership

97 82
2-y-o b c Selkirk (USA)-Louella (USA) (El Gran Senor (USA))
Sir Michael Stoute K Abdulla

Placings:210 (5229)
2001: 6^{2}GF, 7^{1}G, 7^{0}S

	Starts	1st	2nd	3rd	Win & Pl
Career Total (Turf)	3	1	1	0	5591

82 9/01 Sand 7f16y D GD £4270
Total win prize-money £4271

Going (Turf): Sf: 0-1 GS: 0-0 **Gd: 1-1** GF: 0-1 Fm: 0-0
Distance: 5f/6f: 0-0 **7f-8f: 1-3** 9f-13f: 0-0 14f+: 0-0
Track: LH: 0-1 **RH: 1-1** Tight: 0-0 Gall: 0-1
Aids: Bl: 0-0 Vi: 0-0 Tstrap: 0-0
Best Rating: 82 9/01 Sand 7f16y good

By Selkirk, his dam is a daughter of a winner in the US and a half-sister to useful winners Himself and Don Bosio, he made a pleasing debut and then won a maiden at Sandown next time. He looked unhappy on soft in October. He has been effective over seven furlongs and is suited to a firm surface. He should stay a mile as a three-year-old.

Leanadis Rose

29
3-y-o b f Namaqualand (USA)-Fiorini (Formidable (USA))
M F Barraclough (J M Jefferson 3/8) M F Barraclough

Placings:560-0 (3001)
2001: 11^{0}S

	Starts	1st	2nd	3rd	Win & Pl
Career Total (Turf)	4	0	0	0	0

Going (Turf): Sf: 0-2 GS: 0-0 Gd: 0-0 GF: 0-2 Fm: 0-0
Distance: 5f/6f: 0-1 7f-8f: 0-1 9f-13f: 0-2 14f+: 0-0
Track: LH: 0-0 RH: 0-2 Tight: 0-1 Gall: 0-0
Aids: Bl: 0-0 Vi: 0-0 Tstrap: 0-0

Leaping Charlie

98(89) (51)59
5-y-o b g Puissance-Impala Lass (Kampala)
Mrs A Duffield Starnotes Racing

Placings:0030/00001605020/0500-005140010000 (5639)
2001: 5^{0}SD, 6^{0}SD, 5^{5}S, 5^{1}GF, 5^{4}GF, 5^{0}GF, 5^{0}F, 5^{1}GF, 5^{0}G, 5^{0}GF, 6^{0}F, 5^{0}G

	Starts	1st	2nd	3rd	Win & Pl
Career Total (Turf)	27	3	1	1	11203
Career Total (AW)	4	0	0	0	0

59 7/01 Bevl 5f F(0-60)H G-F £4200
55 5/01 Ayr 5f E(0-70)H G-F £3136
58 6/99 Haml 5f4y F(0-65)H GD £2388
Total win prize-money £9724

Going (Turf): Sf: 0-9 GS: 0-1 Gd: 1-6 **GF: 2-8** Fm: 0-3
Distance: 5f/6f: 3-30 7f-8f: 0-1 9f-13f: 0-0 14f+: 0-0
Track: LH: 0-9 RH: 0-0 Tight: 0-0 Gall: 0-0
Aids: Bl: 0-1 Vi: 0-0 Tstrap: 0-0
Best Rating: 59 7/01 Bevl 5f gd-fm

Fair sprinter, best at the minimum trip on fast ground and had conditions in his favour when winning at Ayr and Beverley this season. Seems best delivered late.

Lear Spear (USA)

110(33) (118)118
6-y-o b h Lear Fan (USA)-Golden Gorse (USA) (His Majesty (USA))
H R A Cecil Raymond Tooth

Placings:633/0200313314/546110103/2031-3 (2613)
2001: 12^{3}GF

	Starts	1st	2nd	3rd	Win & Pl
Career Total (Turf)	25	6	1	8	362077
Career Total (AW)	2	0	1	0	11647

108 9/00 Donc 1m4f A G-F £14579
118 9/99 Gdwd 1m1f192yA G-F £22500
120 6/99 Asct 1m2f A G-F £88945
110 6/99 Epsm 1m114y A GD £31100
96 10/98 NmkR 1m1f B H GD £51700
75 8/98 Sand 1m14y D GD £4221
Total win prize-money £213046

Going (Turf): Sf: 0-1 GS: 0-2 **Gd: 3-12 GF: 3-10** Fm: 0-0
Distance: 5f/6f: 0-0 7f-8f: 0-6 **9f-13f: 6-21** 14f+: 0-0
Track: LH: 2-7 **RH: 3-14** Tight: 2-4 Gall: 2-7
Aids: Bl: 0-0 Vi: 0-0 Tstrap: 0-0
Best Rating: 112 6/01 NmkJ 1m4f gd-fm

Tough and genuine, he is a high-class performer at around ten furlongs but has just been found wanting at the top level. Lightly-raced in recent seasons, he has reportedly returned. Acts on fast ground.

Learned Lad (FR)

97 73
3-y-o ch c Royal Academy (USA)-Blushing Storm (USA) (Blushing Groom (FR))
D R C Elsworth J C Smith

Placings:05-565500 (5083)
2001: 12^{5}GF, 11^{6}HD, 11^{5}GF, 11^{5}F, 12^{0}GF, 7^{0}S

	Starts	1st	2nd	3rd	Win & Pl
Career Total (Turf)	8	0	0	0	285

Going (Turf): Sf: 0-2 GS: 0-0 Gd: 0-0 GF: 0-4 Fm: 0-2
Distance: 5f/6f: 0-0 7f-8f: 0-3 9f-13f: 0-5 14f+: 0-0
Track: LH: 0-4 RH: 0-2 Tight: 0-2 Gall: 0-0
Aids: Bl: 0-0 Vi: 0-0 Tstrap: 0-0
Best Rating: 73 9/01 Kemp 1m4f gd-fm

Lease

101 88
3-y-o ch g Lycius (USA)-Risanda (Kris)
Mrs A J Perrett K Abdulla

Placings:156 (4706)
2001: 10^{1}F, 12^{5}GF, 10^{6}G

	Starts	1st	2nd	3rd	Win & Pl
Career Total (Turf)	3	1	0	0	3500

88 6/01 Ling 1m2f D FRM £3122
Total win prize-money £3122

Going (Turf): Sf: 0-0 GS: 0-0 Gd: 0-1 GF: 0-1 **Fm: 1-1**
Distance: 5f/6f: 0-0 7f-8f: 0-0 **9f-13f: 1-3** 14f+: 0-0
Track: LH: 1-3 RH: 0-0 **Tight: 1-2** Gall: 0-1
Aids: Bl: 0-0 Vi: 0-0 Tstrap: 0-0
Best Rating: 88 6/01 Ling 1m2f firm

Leatherback (IRE)

104 75
3-y-o b g Turtle Island (IRE)-Phyllode (Pharly (FR))
N A Callaghan M Tabor

Placings:0000111-0050513 (5525)
2001: 10^{0}S, 10^{0}G, 12^{5}G, 12^{0}G, 10^{5}S, 10^{1}HY, 11^{3}HY

	Starts	1st	2nd	3rd	Win & Pl
Career Total (Turf)	14	4	0	1	17507

75 10/01 Donc 1m2f60y D(0-85)H HVY £5369
75 11/00 Donc 7f D(0-85) HVY £4777
67 10/00 Brig 7f214y D(0-85) SFT £3536
58 10/00 Pont 1m4y E(0-75) HVY £3198
Total win prize-money £16881

Going (Turf): Sf: 4-7 GS: 0-1 Gd: 0-4 GF: 0-2 Fm: 0-0
Distance: 5f/6f: 0-3 7f-8f: 2-3 9f-13f: 2-8 14f+: 0-0
Track: LH: 3-5 RH: 0-2 Tight: 0-2 **Gall: 1-4**
Aids: Bl: 0-0 Vi: 0-0 Tstrap: 0-0
Best Rating: 75 10/01 Donc 1m2f60y heavy

A tough individual, he notched up a hat-trick of wins at the back-end of the 2000 season on testing ground, but has found life harder over middle distances this term and was banned under the non-tiers' rule after his effort at Windsor in June. Suited by cut in the ground and bounced back to form on heavy ground in October.

Ledgendry Line

94 51
8-y-o b g Mtoto-Eider (Niniski (USA))
Mrs M Reveley The Home & Away Partnership

Placings:304440/320140643/2/503532240/5641500-04 (5402)
2001: 14^{0}G, 17^{4}S

	Starts	1st	2nd	3rd	Win & Pl
Career Total (Turf)	34	2	4	5	14401

77 6/97 Ayr 1m5f13y E(0-70)H GD £2956
Total win prize-money £2957

Going (Turf): Sf: 1-9 GS: 0-4 **Gd: 1-17** GF: 0-3 Fm: 0-1
Distance: 5f/6f: 0-0 7f-8f: 0-0 9f-13f: 0-11 **14f+: 2-23**
Track: LH: 2-32 RH: 0-2 Tight: 0-4 Gall: 0-10
Aids: Bl: 0-0 Vi: 0-0 Tstrap: 0-0
Best Rating: 41 10/01 Pont 2m1f216y soft

Can win races on the Flat but tends to use it as a pipe opener for a jumps campaign.

Leen

98(92) (23)39
4-y-o b f Distant Relative-St James's Antigua (IRE) (Law Society (USA))
M J Polglase R D Lotby

Placings:62140/0000060204000-01660500 (2955)
2001: 5^{0}S, 7^{1}S, 9^{6}GF, 9^{6}SD, 7^{0}GF, 7^{6}G, 6^{0}GF, 7^{0}GF

	Starts	1st	2nd	3rd	Win & Pl
Career Total (Turf)	20	2	2	0	7655
Career Total (AW)	6	0	0	0	0

48 5/01 Newc 7f F SFT £2079

73	9/99	Bath	5f11y	E	G-F	£3571

Total win prize-money £5650

Going (Turf): **Sf: 1-4** GS: 0-1 Gd: 0-2 **GF: 1-12** Fm: 0-1
Distance: 5f/6f: 1-7 7f-8f: 1-13 9f-13f: 0-5 14f+: 0-1
Track : **LH: 1-9** RH: 0-2 Tight: 0-3 **Gall: 1-3**
Aids: Bl: 0-0 Vi: 0-1 Tstrap: 0-0
Best Rating: 52 4/01 Nott 5f13y soft

Plating-class performer with a low strike rate.

Leeside (IRE)

(90) (70)**69**
3-y-o ch g Brief Truce (USA)-Pennine Music (IRE) (Pennine Walk)
D G McArdle Channonrock Racing Syndicate

Placings:5512-0556562006 **(4746a)**
2001: 7^{0}S, 8^{5}SH, 8^{5}G, 8^{6}G, 9^{5}G, 8^{6}GF, 9^{2}F, 8^{0}S, 8^{0}G, 8^{6}G

	Starts	1st	2nd	3rd	Win & Pl
Career Total (Turf)	13	1	1	0	4905
Career Total (AW)	1	0	1	0	542
79 9/00 Dund 7f166y				G-F	£3450

Total win prize-money £3450

Going (Turf): Sf: 0-2 GS: 0-0 Gd: 0-6 **GF: 1-2** Fm: 0-2
Distance: 5f/6f: 0-0 **7f-8f: 1-7** 9f-13f: 0-7 14f+: 0-0
Track : **LH: 1-3** RH: 0-1 Tight: 0-1 Gall: 0-0
Aids: Bl: 0-3 Vi: 0-0 Tstrap: 0-9
Best Rating: 69 6/01 Baln 1m1f good

Legal Approach

98 **93**
2-y-o b c Zafonic (USA)-Legaya (Shirley Heights)
M Johnston Maktoum Al Maktoum

Placings:11 **(5017)**
2001: 7^{1}G, 7^{1}S

	Starts	1st	2nd	3rd	Win & Pl
Career Total (Turf)	2	2	0	0	17009
93 9/01 Asct 7f B				SFT	£12465
81 9/01 Ayr 7f50y D				GD	£4543

Total win prize-money £17009

Going (Turf): **Sf: 1-1** GS: 0-0 **Gd: 1-1** GF: 0-0 Fm: 0-0
Distance: 5f/6f: 0-0 **7f-8f: 2-2** 9f-13f: 0-0 14f+: 0-0
Track : LH: 0-0 RH: 0-0 Tight: 0-0 Gall: 0-0
Aids: Bl: 0-0 Vi: 0-0 Tstrap: 0-0
Best Rating: 93 9/01 Asct 7f soft

He made a winning debut at Ayr despite being weak in the market and followed up with a brave victory in soft ground at Ascot. Still has plenty of scope.

Legal Coup

72 **26**
3-y-o gr f Contract Law (USA)-What A Coup (Malicious)
B A Pearce The Lawbreakers

Placings:000 **(5024)**
2001: 9^{0}G, 11^{0}GF, 11^{0}S

	Starts	1st	2nd	3rd	Win & Pl
Career Total (Turf)	3	0	0	0	

Going (Turf): Sf: 0-1 GS: 0-0 Gd: 0-1 GF: 0-1 Fm: 0-0
Distance: 5f/6f: 0-0 7f-8f: 0-0 9f-13f: 0-3 14f+: 0-0
Track : LH: 0-2 RH: 0-1 Tight: 0-2 Gall: 0-0
Aids: Bl: 0-0 Vi: 0-0 Tstrap: 0-0
Best Rating: 26 9/01 Ling 1m3f106y gd-fm

Legal Lunch (USA)

99(82) (62)**69**
6-y-o b g Alleged (USA)-Dinner Surprise (USA) (Lyphard (USA))
R M Stronge Berkshire Commercial Components Ltd

Placings:2/41050530/0020526350055233/4205313561 50-20036 **(5039)**
2001: 18^{2}S, 13^{0}GF, 16^{0}GF, 16^{3}G, 17^{6}G

	Starts	1st	2nd	3rd	Win & Pl
Career Total (Turf)	40	3	6	5	30401
Career Total (AW)	2	0	0	2	760
70 7/00 Epsm 1m4f10y E(0-70)H				G-F	£5232
69 5/00 Donc 1m4f D(0-85)H				G-S	£4231
90 5/98 Hayd 1m2f120yD				G-F	£3680

Total win prize-money £13145

Going (Turf): Sf: 0-6 GS: 1-7 Gd: 0-12 **GF: 2-13** Fm: 0-2
Distance: 5f/6f: 0-0 7f-8f: 0-1 **9f-13f: 3-23** 14f+: 0-18
Track : **LH: 3-29** RH: 0-12 Tight: 1-11 Gall: 1-18
Aids: **Bl: 2-5** Vi: 0-14 Tstrap: 0-0
Best Rating: 69 9/01 Nott 2m9y good

A winner of a couple of mile and a half handicaps last season, he has shown form over further this term. Does not really relish a battle.

Legal Native (IRE)

84 **6**
5-y-o br m Be My Native (USA)-Tullahought (Jaazeiro (USA))
R J Price E G Bevan

Placings:0 **(5041)**
2001: 10^{0}G

	Starts	1st	2nd	3rd	Win & Pl
Career Total (Turf)	1	0	0	0	

Going (Turf): Sf: 0-0 GS: 0-0 Gd: 0-1 GF: 0-0 Fm: 0-0
Distance: 5f/6f: 0-0 7f-8f: 0-0 9f-13f: 0-1 14f+: 0-0
Track : LH: 0-1 RH: 0-0 Tight: 0-1 Gall: 0-0
Aids: Bl: 0-0 Vi: 0-0 Tstrap: 0-0

Legal Set (IRE)

103(102) (72)**74**
5-y-o gr g Second Set (IRE)-Tiffany's Case (IRE) (Thatching)
K R Burke Platinum Racing Club Limited

Placings:00/0300/2003360230**0**-0514221033 **(5503)**
2001: 9^{0}GF, 7^{5}GF, 7^{1}GS, 8^{4}GF, 7^{2}G, 6^{2}F, 6^{1}G, 6^{0}SD, 6^{3}S, 7^{3}HY

	Starts	1st	2nd	3rd	Win & Pl
Career Total (Turf)	25	2	4	6	16601
Career Total (AW)	2	0	0	0	
72 8/01 Ayr 6f E(0-70)H				GD	£3290
61 7/01 Ling 7f F				G-S	£2453

Total win prize-money £5744

Going (Turf): Sf: 0-2 **GS: 1-4 Gd: 1-7** GF: 0-10 Fm: 0-2
Distance: 5f/6f: 1-4 7f-8f: 1-13 9f-13f: 0-10 14f+: 0-0
Track : LH: 0-5 RH: 0-10 Tight: 0-9 Gall: 0-2
Aids: Bl: 0-0 Vi: 0-2 Tstrap: 0-1
Best Rating: 74 8/01 NmkJ 7f good

A fair handicapper over a mile who does not find much off the bridle, he got off the mark at the 20th attempt with an easy win in a Lingfield claimer. Dropped to six furlongs to win an Ayr handicap. Suited by some cut and racing prominently.

Legal Venture (IRE)

84(99) (44d)**31**
5-y-o ch g Case Law-We Two (Glenstal (USA))
Julian Poulton Russell Reed

Placings:0004133245202605/0432340010602000U/003 40204600-0 **(4322)**
2001: 5^{0}GF

	Starts	1st	2nd	3rd	Win & Pl
Career Total (Turf)	19	1	1	2	4388
Career Total (AW)	26	1	5	3	5346
60 5/99 Wolv 5f G				STD	£1840
64 7/98 Ling 5f G				G-F	£1725

Total win prize-money £3565

Going (Turf): Sf: 0-2 GS: 0-1 Gd: 0-6 **GF: 1-8** Fm: 0-2
Distance: **5f/6f: 2-45** 7f-8f: 0-0 9f-13f: 0-0 14f+: 0-0
Track : **LH: 1-28** RH: 0-0 **Tight: 1-23** Gall: 0-2
Aids: **Bl: 1-21** Vi: 0-5 Tstrap: 0-0
Best Rating: 14 8/01 Wwck 5f gd-fm

He has been successful in selling company on sand, but is very moderate.

Legendary Lover (IRE)

103 (38)**58**
7-y-o b g Fairy King (USA)-Broken Romance (IRE) (Ela-Mana-Mou)
J R Jenkins S C Finance Limited

Placings:03640/026066/530-160 **(4580)**
2001: 11^{1}GS, 11^{6}G, 16^{0}G

	Starts	1st	2nd	3rd	Win & Pl
Career Total (Turf)	16	1	1	2	4978
Career Total (AW)	1	0	0	0	0
58 5/01 Wind 1m3f135yF(0-60)				G-S	£2516

Total win prize-money £2517

Going (Turf): Sf: 0-2 **GS: 1-4** Gd: 0-6 GF: 0-4 Fm: 0-0
Distance: 5f/6f: 0-0 7f-8f: 0-1 **9f-13f: 1-12** 14f+: 0-4
Track : LH: 0-5 RH: 0-9 **Tight: 1-6** Gall: 0-2
Aids: Bl: 0-0 Vi: 0-1 Tstrap: 0-0
Best Rating: 58 5/01 Wind 1m3f135y gd-sft

Ran well to finish runner-up at Sandown in July, but has not shown that sort of form otherwise. Surprise winner of a modest event at Windsor, he acts on any ground and looks inconsistent.

Leggit (IRE)

103(94) (59d)**56d**
3-y-o b f Night Shift (USA)-Scales Of Justice (Final Straw)
Andrew Reid L R Gotch

Placings:00052**503**-**000**00430045232500 **(5026)**
2001: 8^{0}SW, 7^{0}SD, 8^{0}SD, 7^{0}GS, 8^{0}HY, 8^{0}G, 5^{4}F, 11^{3}GF, 6^{0}GF, 10^{0}GF, 8^{4}GF, 9^{5}GF, 9^{2}G, 9^{3}GF, 9^{2}G, 10^{5}G, 9^{0}G, 9^{0}S

	Starts	1st	2nd	3rd	Win & Pl
Career Total (Turf)	20	0	3	2	3697
Career Total (AW)	6	0	0	1	388

Going (Turf): Sf: 0-2 GS: 0-1 Gd: 0-6 GF: 0-9 Fm: 0-1
Distance: 5f/6f: 0-5 7f-8f: 0-7 9f-13f: 0-13 14f+: 0-0
Track : LH: 0-16 RH: 0-4 Tight: 0-8 Gall: 0-3
Aids: Bl: 0-0 Vi: 0-1 Tstrap: 0-3
Best Rating: 57 4/01 Brig 7f214y gd-sft

Leggy Lady

86(102) (40)**50d**
5-y-o b m Sir Harry Lewis (USA)-Lady Minstrel (Tudor Music)
B J Llewellyn Thomas Leonard

Placings:0604/05304-02146 **(0893)**
2001: 16^{0}SD, 16^{2}SD, 16^{1}SD, 16^{4}SD, 15^{6}HY

	Starts	1st	2nd	3rd	Win & Pl
Career Total (Turf)	7	0	0	1	436
Career Total (AW)	7	1	1	0	2093
40 2/01 Wolv 2m46y F(0-60)H				STD	£1701

Total win prize-money £1701

Going (Turf): Sf: 0-1 GS: 0-0 Gd: 0-1 GF: 0-4 Fm: 0-1
Distance: 5f/6f: 0-0 7f-8f: 0-0 9f-13f: 0-3 **14f+: 1-11**
Track : **LH: 1-11** RH: 0-3 **Tight: 1-9** Gall: 0-0
Aids: Bl: 0-0 Vi: 0-0 Tstrap: 0-0

Best Rating: 40 2/01 Wolv 2m46y stand

Leggy Lou (IRE)

111 **99**

2-y-o b f Mujadil (USA)-Alzeam (IRE) (Alzao (USA))
J Noseda Lucayan Stud

Placings:53110 **(4191)**
2001: 5^{5}F, 5^{3}GF, 5^{1}GF, 6^{1}GF, 6^{0}G

	Starts	1st	2nd	3rd	Win & Pl
Career Total (Turf)	5	2	0	1	31028

99 7/01 Asct 6f A G-F £24000
75 7/01 Wind 5f10y E G-F £3178
Total win prize-money £27178

Going (Turf): Sf: 0-0 GS: 0-0 Gd: 0-1 **GF: 2-3** Fm: 0-1
Distance: **5f/6f: 2-5** 7f-8f: 0-0 9f-13f: 0-0 14f+: 0-0
Track : LH: 0-0 **RH: 1-1** Tight: 0-0 **Gall: 1-1**
Aids: Bl: 0-0 Vi: 0-0 Tstrap: 0-0
Best Rating: 99 7/01 Asct 6f gd-fm

She comes from the family of Salsabil and Marju and followed up her promising debut fifth with a much improved performance at Ascot in the Windsor Castle Stakes, winning her race on the stands' side. Had to fight hard to win her maiden at Windsor in July, but was most impressive when upped to six furlongs in the Princess Margaret at Ascot. Finished lame when last in the Lowther, she is suited by five or six furlongs on fast ground. Wears a Monty Roberts blanket for stalls entry.

Legs Be Frendly (IRE)

(93) (13)**66**

6-y-o b g Fayruz-Thalssa (Rusticaro (FR))
D Nicholls V Greaves

Placings:2322242201/0000/020000/35004-000 **(0143)**
2001: 6^{0}SD, 7^{0}SD, 6^{0}SW

	Starts	1st	2nd	3rd	Win & Pl
Career Total (Turf)	22	1	6	2	15599
Career Total (AW)	6	0	1	0	627

64 10/97 Ling 5f C GD £4653
Total win prize-money £4653

Going (Turf): Sf: 0-5 GS: 0-3 **Gd: 1-9** GF: 0-4 Fm: 0-1
Distance: **5f/6f: 1-23** 7f-8f: 0-5 9f-13f: 0-0 14f+: 0-0
Track : LH: 0-6 RH: 0-1 Tight: 0-1 Gall: 0-1
Aids: **Bl: 1-13** Vi: 0-1 Tstrap: 0-0
Best Rating: 48 1/01 Sthl 6f stand

Leila

91 **26**

6-y-o b m Aragon-Carpe Diem (Good Times (ITY))
Miss E C Lavelle D F Jordan

Placings:040-00 **(1483)**
2001: 11^{0}GS, 17^{0}GF

	Starts	1st	2nd	3rd	Win & Pl
Career Total (Turf)	5	0	0	0	218

Going (Turf): Sf: 0-0 GS: 0-1 Gd: 0-1 GF: 0-3 Fm: 0-0
Distance: 5f/6f: 0-0 7f-8f: 0-0 9f-13f: 0-3 14f+: 0-2
Track : LH: 0-4 RH: 0-0 Tight: 0-4 Gall: 0-0
Aids: Bl: 0-0 Vi: 0-0 Tstrap: 0-0
Best Rating: 20 5/01 Bath 2m1f34y gd-fm

Lemarate (USA)

94(82) (27)**59d**

4-y-o b c Gulch (USA)-Sayyedati (Shadeed (USA))
D W Chapman (C E Brittain 13/8) Michael Hill

Placings:00-606000000 **(5448)**
2001: 7^{0}S, 8^{0}GF, 8^{6}GF, 10^{0}F, 10^{0}GF, 9^{0}G, 9^{0}G, 8^{0}SD, 10^{0}HY

	Starts	1st	2nd	3rd	Win & Pl
Career Total (Turf)	10	0	0	0	0
Career Total (AW)	1	0	0	0	

Going (Turf): Sf: 0-3 GS: 0-0 Gd: 0-2 GF: 0-4 Fm: 0-1
Distance: 5f/6f: 0-0 7f-8f: 0-3 9f-13f: 0-8 14f+: 0-0
Track : LH: 0-5 RH: 0-5 Tight: 0-3 Gall: 0-2
Aids: Bl: 0-2 Vi: 0-0 Tstrap: 0-0
Best Rating: 64 4/01 Kemp 7f soft

Lemon Bridge (IRE)

101 **75**

6-y-o b g Shalford (IRE)-Sharply (Sharpman)
C N Allen Lemon Connections

Placings:0/323135460/220/55-001600104 **(3609)**
2001: 12^{0}S, 12^{0}G, 13^{1}GF, 14^{6}GF, 14^{0}GF, 16^{0}GF, 14^{1}GF, 15^{0}GF, 12^{4}GS

	Starts	1st	2nd	3rd	Win & Pl
Career Total (Turf)	24	3	3	3	21767

70 6/01 Donc 1m6f132yD(0-80)H G-F £4914
70 5/01 York 1m5f194yC(0-90)H G-F £7442
79 6/98 Gdwd 1m1f192yE G-F £3850
Total win prize-money £16207

Going (Turf): Sf: 0-7 GS: 0-2 Gd: 0-5 **GF: 3-10** Fm: 0-0
Distance: 5f/6f: 0-0 7f-8f: 0-2 9f-13f: 1-16 **14f+: 2-6**
Track : **LH: 2-8** RH: 1-14 Tight: 1-6 **Gall: 2-12**
Aids: Bl: 0-0 Vi: 0-0 Tstrap: 0-0
Best Rating: 70 6/01 Donc 1m6f132y gd-fm

Scored for the first time in three years at York in May 2001 over fourteen furlongs, and at Doncaster the following month. Not the most consistent, he likes fast ground and has plenty of ability.

Lemuria (IRE)

(63) (10)

2-y-o b f Idris (IRE)-Tiempo (King Of Spain)
Miss J F Craze (M H Tompkins 13/6) Holgate Racing Club

Placings:04400 **(5165)**
2001: 5^{0}GS, 5^{4}GF, 5^{4}F, 5^{0}GF, 5^{0}SD

	Starts	1st	2nd	3rd	Win & Pl
Career Total (Turf)	4	0	0	0	0
Career Total (AW)	1	0	0	0	

Going (Turf): Sf: 0-0 GS: 0-1 Gd: 0-0 GF: 0-2 Fm: 0-1
Distance: 5f/6f: 0-5 7f-8f: 0-0 9f-13f: 0-0 14f+: 0-0
Track : LH: 0-2 RH: 0-0 Tight: 0-1 Gall: 0-0
Aids: Bl: 0-0 Vi: 0-0 Tstrap: 0-0
Best Rating: 38 6/01 Ling 5f firm

Lenango (GER)

(54)

8-y-o b g Acatenango (GER)-Lekana (GER) (Ile De Bourbon (USA))
R G Frost Terry Sanders

Placings:11/0 **(0266)**
2001: 12^{0}SW

	Starts	1st	2nd	3rd	Win & Pl
Career Total (Turf)	2	2	0	0	2727
Career Total (AW)	1	0	0	0	

7/97 Aabe 1m2f110y SFT £1591
6/97 Aikn 1m1f110y GD £1136
Total win prize-money £2727

Going (Turf): Sf: 0-0 GS: 0-0 Gd: 0-0 GF: 0-0 Fm: 0-0
Distance: 5f/6f: 0-0 7f-8f: 0-0 9f-13f: 0-1 14f+: 0-0
Track : LH: 0-1 RH: 0-0 Tight: 0-0 Gall: 0-0
Aids: Bl: 0-0 Vi: 0-0 Tstrap: 0-0

Lengai (USA)

97 **79**

2-y-o b c Dixieland Band (USA)-La Pepite (USA) (Mr Prospector (USA))
E A L Dunlop Khalid Ali

Placings:425 **(4794)**
2001: 6^{4}GF, 6^{2}GF, 7^{5}G

	Starts	1st	2nd	3rd	Win & Pl
Career Total (Turf)	3	0	1	0	1601

Going (Turf): Sf: 0-0 GS: 0-0 Gd: 0-1 GF: 0-2 Fm: 0-0
Distance: 5f/6f: 0-0 7f-8f: 0-3 9f-13f: 0-0 14f+: 0-0
Track : LH: 0-0 RH: 0-0 Tight: 0-0 Gall: 0-0
Aids: Bl: 0-0 Vi: 0-0 Tstrap: 0-0
Best Rating: 79 7/01 Sals 6f212y gd-fm

Has shown ability in maidens.

Lennel

108 **74**

3-y-o b g Presidium-Ladykirk (Slip Anchor)
Denys Smith Evelyn Duchess Of Sutherland

Placings:63555-21414000 **(5146)**
2001: 8^{2}S, 8^{1}S, 9^{4}S, 8^{1}GF, 10^{4}GF, 8^{0}GF, 8^{0}G, 8^{0}G

	Starts	1st	2nd	3rd	Win & Pl
Career Total (Turf)	13	2	1	1	8119

74 5/01 Muss 1m E(0-70) G-F £3220
70 4/01 Muss 1m D SFT £2828
Total win prize-money £6048

Going (Turf): Sf: 1-5 GS: 0-0 Gd: 0-3 **GF: 1-5** Fm: 0-0
Distance: 5f/6f: 0-4 **7f-8f: 2-7** 9f-13f: 0-2 14f+: 0-0
Track : LH: 0-4 **RH: 2-5 Tight: 2-4** Gall: 0-1
Aids: Bl: 0-0 Vi: 0-0 Tstrap: 0-0
Best Rating: 74 5/01 Muss 1m gd-fm

He was twice successful over a mile at Musselburgh in the spring and seems equally effective on fast ground and soft. May be a shade high in the handicap at present.

Lenny The Lion

89 **40**

4-y-o b g Bin Ajwaad (IRE)-Patriotic (Hotfoot)
Mrs M Reveley A D Simmons

Placings:0065/05530000-0 **(1408)**
2001: 11^{0}G

	Starts	1st	2nd	3rd	Win & Pl
Career Total (Turf)	13	0	0	1	348

Going (Turf): Sf: 0-3 GS: 0-3 Gd: 0-1 GF: 0-5 Fm: 0-1
Distance: 5f/6f: 0-0 7f-8f: 0-4 9f-13f: 0-9 14f+: 0-0
Track : LH: 0-6 RH: 0-4 Tight: 0-6 Gall: 0-0
Aids: Bl: 0-2 Vi: 0-0 Tstrap: 0-0
Best Rating: 29 5/01 Haml 1m3f16y good

Leo's Luckyman (USA)

102 **102**

2-y-o b c Woodman (USA)-Leo's Lucky Lady (USA) (Seattle Slew (USA))
M Johnston Mrs S J Brookhouse

Placings:1363 **(4698)**
2001: 7^{1}GF, 7^{3}GF, 7^{6}G, 7^{3}GS

	Starts	1st	2nd	3rd	Win & Pl
Career Total (Turf)	4	1	0	2	20910

96 6/01 Ayr 7f D G-F £3659
Total win prize-money £3660

Going (Turf): Sf: 0-0 GS: 0-1 Gd: 0-1 **GF: 1-2** Fm: 0-0
Distance: 5f/6f: 0-0 **7f-8f: 1-4** 9f-13f: 0-0 14f+: 0-0
Track : **LH: 1-1** RH: 0-1 Tight: 0-0 Gall: 0-0
Aids: Bl: 0-0 Vi: 0-0 Tstrap: 0-0
Best Rating: 102 8/01 Gdwd 7f gd-fm

Bred along similar lines to top-class pair Bosra Sham and Hector Protector, he made $50,000 at the sales. Well regarded, he bolted up in a modest maiden at Ayr on his debut, but was found out in Group company subsequently.

Leonica

96 **81**

2-y-o b f Lion Cavern (USA)-South Shore (Caerleon (USA))
M L W Bell B H Farr

Placings:322 **(3852)**
2001: 6^{3}GF, 6^{2}GF, 6^{2}G

	Starts	1st	2nd	3rd	Win & Pl
Career Total (Turf)	3	0	2	1	5150

Going (Turf): Sf: 0-0 GS: 0-0 Gd: 0-1 GF: 0-2 Fm: 0-0
Distance: 5f/6f: 0-3 7f-8f: 0-0 9f-13f: 0-0 14f+: 0-0
Track : LH: 0-0 RH: 0-0 Tight: 0-0 Gall: 0-0
Aids: Bl: 0-0 Vi: 0-0 Tstrap: 0-0
Best Rating: 81 8/01 Asct 6f good

Apparently well regarded, has faced stiff tasks. Sure to improve.

Leonora Truce (IRE)

89(86) (56)**56**

2-y-o b f Brief Truce (USA)-Eleonora D'Arborea (Prince Sabo)
K McAuliffe Mrs S D Fidler

Placings:4303600 **(5487)**
2001: 5^{4}SD, 5^{3}SD, 5^{0}F, 6^{3}GF, 6^{6}SD, 6^{0}HY, 6^{0}HY

	Starts	1st	2nd	3rd	Win & Pl
Career Total (Turf)	4	0	0	1	326
Career Total (AW)	3	0	0	1	341

Going (Turf): Sf: 0-2 GS: 0-0 Gd: 0-0 GF: 0-1 Fm: 0-1
Distance: 5f/6f: 0-6 7f-8f: 0-1 9f-13f: 0-0 14f+: 0-0
Track : LH: 0-1 RH: 0-0 Tight: 0-0 Gall: 0-0
Aids: Bl: 0-0 Vi: 0-3 Tstrap: 0-0
Best Rating: 56 7/01 Chep 6f16y gd-fm

Leophin Dancer (USA)

98 (63) (4)**65**

3-y-o b g Green Dancer (USA)-Happy Gal (FR) (Habitat)
M Johnston F Gillespie

Placings:42260 **(5348)**
2001: 8^{4}GF, 9^{2}GF, 10^{2}F, 11^{6}GS, 12^{0}SD

	Starts	1st	2nd	3rd	Win & Pl
Career Total (Turf)	4	0	2	0	2825
Career Total (AW)	1	0	0	0	

Going (Turf): Sf: 0-0 GS: 0-1 Gd: 0-0 GF: 0-2 Fm: 0-1
Distance: 5f/6f: 0-0 7f-8f: 0-0 9f-13f: 0-5 14f+: 0-0
Track : LH: 0-5 RH: 0-0 Tight: 0-2 Gall: 0-0
Aids: Bl: 0-0 Vi: 0-0 Tstrap: 0-0
Best Rating: 65 10/01 Catt 1m3f214y gd-sft

Still a maiden and looked well held on handicap debut, so a drop in the handicap and a bit of improvement are both needed.

Leopold

78 **41**

2-y-o b c Lion Cavern (USA)-Warning Star (Warning)
M L W Bell Cheveley Park Stud

Placings:000 **(5128)**
2001: 6^{0}GF, 7^{0}S, 6^{0}HY

	Starts	1st	2nd	3rd	Win & Pl
Career Total (Turf)	3	0	0	0	

Going (Turf): Sf: 0-2 GS: 0-0 Gd: 0-0 GF: 0-1 Fm: 0-0
Distance: 5f/6f: 0-2 7f-8f: 0-1 9f-13f: 0-0 14f+: 0-0
Track : LH: 0-1 RH: 0-0 Tight: 0-1 Gall: 0-0
Aids: Bl: 0-0 Vi: 0-0 Tstrap: 0-0
Best Rating: 41 10/01 Ling 6f heavy

Leozian

104(90) (78)**86**

3-y-o b g Lion Cavern (USA)-Alzianah (Alzao (USA))
E A L Dunlop Littleton Manor Racing

Placings:20410-0041401000000 **(5108)**
2001: 6^{0}S, 6^{0}G, 5^{4}G, 5^{1}F, 5^{4}GF, 5^{0}GF, 5^{1}GF, 5^{0}GF, 6^{0}G, 5^{0}G, 5^{0}G, 5^{0}G, 5^{0}GS

	Starts	1st	2nd	3rd	Win & Pl
Career Total (Turf)	17	3	1	0	19265
Career Total (AW)	1	0	0	0	

86	7/01	Chep	5f16y	C(0-100)H	G-F	£6516
83	6/01	Brig	5f59y	D(0-80)H	FRM	£6792
74	9/00	Ling	5f	D	SFT	£3909

Total win prize-money £17219

Going (Turf): Sf: 1-2 GS: 0-1 Gd: 0-7 GF: 1-6 Fm: 1-1
Distance: 5f/6f: 3-17 7f-8f: 0-1 9f-13f: 0-0 14f+: 0-0
Track : LH: 1-2 RH: 0-1 Tight: 0-1 Gall: 0-1
Aids: Bl: 0-0 Vi: 0-0 Tstrap: 0-0
Best Rating: 86 8/01 York 5f good

Looked a decent sprint handicapper when scoring at Brighton in June and, despite disappointing on his next two starts, ran well to beat some seasoned handicappers at Chepstow in July. Seems to like fast ground.

Lermontov (USA)

106 **85**

4-y-o b/br g Alleged (USA)-Prospect Dalia (USA) (Mr Prospector (USA))
W R Muir (D Nicholls 31/7) Fayzad Thoroughbred Limited

Placings:112/4000-000002255460 **(5693)**
2001: 8^{0}GF, 12^{0}G, 10^{0}GF, 10^{0}G, 8^{0}G, 14^{0}GF, 8^{2}GF, 9^{2}G, 10^{5}G, 8^{5}G, 10^{4}GS, 10^{6}S, 12^{0}S

	Starts	1st	2nd	3rd	Win & Pl
Career Total (Turf)	20	2	3	0	80415

100	10/99	Curr	1m	Y-S	£27950
80	6/99	Gowr	7f	GD	£4125

Total win prize-money £32075

Going (Turf): Sf: 0-3 GS: 0-3 Gd: 1-9 GF: 0-4 Fm: 0-0
Distance: 5f/6f: 0-0 7f-8f: 2-5 9f-13f: 0-13 14f+: 0-2
Track : LH: 0-9 RH: 2-9 Tight: 0-6 Gall: 1-8
Aids: Bl: 0-0 Vi: 0-0 Tstrap: 0-0
Best Rating: 91 6/01 Epsm 1m114y gd-fm

Won the Beresford Stakes at the Curragh in '99 before chasing home Aristotle in the Racing Post Trophy when with Aidan O'Brien. Has run one or two good races since joining William Muir, finishing runner-up in handicaps at Windsor and Sandown. Not the most straightforward of rides.

Lesmacadam (IRE)

82(80) (6)**7**

10-y-o b m Digamist (USA)-Fiodoir (Weavers Hall)
D A Nolan (P J Lally 22/2) Mrs J McFadyen-Murray

Placings:0000/0006350000/000000/00000000-0000006000 **(3281)**
2001: 6^{0}SD, 7^{0}SD, 9^{0}SD, 11^{0}G, 8^{0}GF, 14^{0}G, 8^{6}G, 12^{0}GF, 12^{0}GF, 16^{0}F

	Starts	1st	2nd	3rd	Win & Pl
Career Total (Turf)	35	0	0	1	461
Career Total (AW)	4	0	0	0	

Going (Turf): Sf: 0-2 GS: 0-0 Gd: 0-11 GF: 0-10 Fm: 0-2
Distance: 5f/6f: 0-3 7f-8f: 0-16 9f-13f: 0-12 14f+: 0-4
Track : LH: 0-14 RH: 0-20 Tight: 0-9 Gall: 0-0
Aids: Bl: 0-2 Vi: 0-0 Tstrap: 0-2
Best Rating: 7 7/01 Haml 1m4f17y gd-fm

Let Me Go (GER)

87(78) (8)**54**

3-y-o ch g Java Gold (USA)-Leventina (GER) (Kris)
S P C Woods G V Wright

Placings:005000 **(3019)**
2001: 11^{0}S, 11^{0}SD, 11^{5}GF, 14^{0}GF, 12^{0}GF, 12^{0}SD

	Starts	1st	2nd	3rd	Win & Pl
Career Total (Turf)	4	0	0	0	0
Career Total (AW)	2	0	0	0	

Going (Turf): Sf: 0-1 GS: 0-0 Gd: 0-0 GF: 0-3 Fm: 0-0
Distance: 5f/6f: 0-0 7f-8f: 0-0 9f-13f: 0-5 14f+: 0-1
Track : LH: 0-5 RH: 0-1 Tight: 0-2 Gall: 0-0
Aids: Bl: 0-3 Vi: 0-0 Tstrap: 0-0
Best Rating: 54 4/01 Kemp 1m3f30y soft

Let Rip

7-y-o b g Nalchik (USA)-Delbounty (Bounteous)
Mrs A Price (W M Brisbourne 18/1) Mrs B Brown

Placings:0 **(0120)**
2001: 14^{0}SW

	Starts	1st	2nd	3rd	Win & Pl
Career Total (Turf)	0	0	0	0	
Career Total (AW)	1	0	0	0	

Going (Turf): Sf: 0-0 GS: 0-0 Gd: 0-0 GF: 0-0 Fm: 0-0
Distance: 5f/6f: 0-0 7f-8f: 0-0 9f-13f: 0-0 14f+: 0-1
Track : LH: 0-1 RH: 0-0 Tight: 0-1 Gall: 0-0
Aids: Bl: 0-0 Vi: 0-0 Tstrap: 0-0

Lethals Lady

110 **114**

3-y-o b f Rudimentary (USA)-Madiyla (Darshaan)
Robert Collet Ecurie Vallin

Placings:004424132-3613244000 **(5353a)**
2001: 8^{3}HY, 9^{6}HY, 8^{1}S, 8^{3}G, 8^{2}G, 8^{4}GF, 8^{4}S, 8^{0}GS, 8^{0}GS, 7^{0}VS

	Starts	1st	2nd	3rd	Win & Pl
Career Total (Turf)	19	2	3	3	83989

5/01	Toul	1m	SFT	£12609
11/00	Toul	1m	G-S	£6724

Total win prize-money £19333

Going (Turf): Sf: 1-5 GS: 1-3 Gd: 0-2 GF: 0-1 Fm: 0-0
Distance: 5f/6f: 0-0 7f-8f: 2-13 9f-13f: 0-1 14f+: 0-0
Track : LH: 0-0 RH: 0-3 Tight: 0-0 Gall: 0-1
Aids: Bl: 0-0 Vi: 0-0 Tstrap: 0-0
Best Rating: 116 5/01 Lonc 1m good

Useful filly, a close third in the French 1000 Guineas and runner-up to Banks Hill in a Group Two. Finished fourth in the Coronation Stakes at Royal Ascot and has faced some stiff tasks since.

Lets Reflect

89 **35**

4-y-o b f Mtoto-Lets Fall In Love (USA) (Northern Baby (CAN))
L R James D Hilton Cox

Placings:54050-60 **(1637)**

2001: 10^{6}G, 7^{0}F

	Starts	1st	2nd	3rd	Win & Pl
Career Total (Turf)	7	0	0	0	275

Going (Turf): Sf: 0-2 GS: 0-0 Gd: 0-1 GF: 0-3 Fm: 0-1
Distance: 5f/6f: 0-0 7f-8f: 0-2 9f-13f: 0-5 14f+: 0-0
Track : LH: 0-3 RH: 0-3 Tight: 0-3 Gall: 0-0
Aids: Bl: 0-0 Vi: 0-0 Tstrap: 0-0
Best Rating: 35 5/01 Ripn 1m2f good

Level Headed

100(103) (51)**62**

6-y-o b m Beveled (USA)-Snowline (Bay Express)
P W Hiatt Anthony Harrison

Placings:0064/0000**50**/035044134101100320-1530330051035 **(3013)**
2001: 9^{1}SW, 11^{5}SW, 9^{3}SD, 10^{0}SD, 9^{3}SD, 10^{3}SW, 8^{0}F, 9^{0}F, 9^{5}GF, 9^{1}GF, 8^{0}GF, 9^{3}GF, 10^{5}GF

	Starts	1st	2nd	3rd	Win & Pl		
Career Total (Turf)	28	5	0	3	17086		
Career Total (AW)	13	1	1	4	3818		
62	6/01	Folk	1m1f149yE(0-70)H			G-F	£3542
49	1/01	Wolv	1m1f79y F(0-65)H			SLW	£1715
57	9/00	Brig	1m1f209yE(0-75)H			G-S	£3822
60	9/00	Bevl	1m1f207yF(0-60)H			HVY	£2184
43	8/00	Ling	1m2f F(0-65)H			G-F	£2604
38	7/00	Bath	1m2f46y E(0-70)H			FRM	£3620

Total win prize-money £17488

Going (Turf): Sf: 1-4 GS: 1-6 Gd: 0-4 **GF: 2-9** Fm: 1-4
Distance: 5f/6f: 0-3 7f-8f: 0-5 **9f-13f: 6-32** 14f+: 0-0
Track : **LH: 4-30** RH: 2-6 **Tight: 4-22** Gall: 0-0
Aids: Bl: 0-2 Vi: 0-0 Tstrap: 0-0
Best Rating: 62 6/01 Folk 1m1f149y gd-fm

Levendi (IRE)

82 **20**

4-y-o b g Mukaddamah (USA)-Christle Mill (Pas De Seul)
J S Wainwright Wishingwell Group

Placings:000-000 **(1790)**
2001: 8^{0}S, 5^{0}G, 8^{0}F

	Starts	1st	2nd	3rd	Win & Pl
Career Total (Turf)	6	0	0	0	

Going (Turf): Sf: 0-4 GS: 0-0 Gd: 0-1 GF: 0-0 Fm: 0-1
Distance: 5f/6f: 0-2 7f-8f: 0-2 9f-13f: 0-2 14f+: 0-0
Track : LH: 0-3 RH: 0-0 Tight: 0-0 Gall: 0-0
Aids: Bl: 0-0 Vi: 0-0 Tstrap: 0-0
Best Rating: 20 5/01 Bevl 5f good

Lewis Island (IRE)

90 **77**

2-y-o b c Turtle Island (IRE)-Phyllode (Pharly (FR))
T G Mills J J Devaney

Placings:322 **(4889)**
2001: 7^{3}S, 8^{2}HY, 8^{2}GF

	Starts	1st	2nd	3rd	Win & Pl
Career Total (Turf)	3	0	2	1	3564

Going (Turf): Sf: 0-2 GS: 0-0 Gd: 0-0 GF: 0-1 Fm: 0-0
Distance: 5f/6f: 0-0 7f-8f: 0-2 9f-13f: 0-1 14f+: 0-0
Track : LH: 0-1 RH: 0-2 Tight: 0-0 Gall: 0-0
Aids: Dl: 0-0 Vi: 0-0 Tstrap: 0-0
Best Rating: 77 9/01 Kemp 1m gd-fm

Liberty Bound

101(102) (64)**60**

3-y-o b f Primo Dominie-Tshusick (Dancing Brave (USA))
D Shaw J C Fretwell

Placings:400-234025651 **(5349)**
2001: 6^{2}SW, 5^{3}S, 6^{4}SW, 6^{0}SD, 6^{2}F, 5^{5}GF, 5^{6}GS, 5^{5}GS, 5^{1}SD

	Starts	1st	2nd	3rd	Win & Pl		
Career Total (Turf)	8	0	1	1	1372		
Career Total (AW)	4	1	1	0	3276		
64	10/01	Sthl	5f	F(0-60)H		STD	£2338

Total win prize-money £2338

Going (Turf): Sf: 0-2 GS: 0-4 Gd: 0-0 GF: 0-1 Fm: 0-1
Distance: **5f/6f: 1-11** 7f-8f: 0-1 9f-13f: 0-0 14f+: 0-0
Track : LH: 0-3 RH: 0-0 Tight: 0-1 Gall: 0-0
Aids: Bl: 0-0 Vi: 0-1 Tstrap: 0-0
Best Rating: 64 10/01 Sthl 5f stand

Bits and pieces of form on sand on turf before getting off the mark over the minimum trip on the Southwell Fibresand in October.

Licence To Thrill

96(108) (76)**62**

4-y-o ch f Wolfhound (USA)-Crime Of Passion (Dragonara Palace (USA))
D W P Arbuthnot Christopher Wright

Placings:025/110200-00335 **(3689)**
2001: 5^{0}GS, 5^{0}GF, 5^{3}HD, 5^{3}GF, 5^{5}GF

	Starts	1st	2nd	3rd	Win & Pl		
Career Total (Turf)	10	0	1	2	6258		
Career Total (AW)	4	2	1	0	7820		
76	3/00	Ling	5f	D(0-85)H		STD	£4056
69	2/00	Ling	5f	D		STD	£2704

Total win prize-money £6760

Going (Turf): Sf: 0-0 GS: 0-3 Gd: 0-1 GF: 0-5 Fm: 0-1
Distance: **5f/6f: 2-14** 7f-8f: 0-0 9f-13f: 0-0 14f+: 0-0
Track : **LH: 2-7** RH: 0-3 **Tight: 2-5** Gall: 0-5
Aids: Bl: 0-0 Vi: 0-0 Tstrap: 0-0
Best Rating: 62 7/01 Wind 5f10y gd-fm

Fair sprint handicapper whose wins have been on Equitrack.

Lieuday

90 **77**

2-y-o b g Atraf-Figment (Posse (USA))
J L Eyre Billy Parker

Placings:24 **(5405)**
2001: 6^{2}G, 6^{4}S

	Starts	1st	2nd	3rd	Win & Pl
Career Total (Turf)	2	0	1	0	1515

Going (Turf): Sf: 0-1 GS: 0-0 Gd: 0-1 GF: 0-0 Fm: 0-0
Distance: 5f/6f: 0-2 7f-8f: 0-0 9f-13f: 0-0 14f+: 0-0
Track : LH. 0-1 RH. 0-0 Tight. 0-0 Gall. 0-0
Aids: Bl: 0-0 Vi: 0-0 Tstrap: 0-0
Best Rating: 77 10/01 Pont 6f soft

He showed ability to finish runner-up on his Ripon debut and ran well when fourth at Pontefract.

Life Is Beautiful (IRE)

94 **69**

2-y-o b f Septieme Ciel (USA)-Palombella (FR) (Groom Dancer (USA))
M L W Bell Christopher Wright

Placings:646004 **(5342)**
2001: 5^{6}G, 5^{4}GF, 6^{6}GF, 6^{0}GF, 8^{0}S, 7^{4}GS

	Starts	1st	2nd	3rd	Win & Pl
Career Total (Turf)	6	0	0	0	718

Going (Turf): Sf: 0-1 GS: 0-1 Gd: 0-1 GF: 0-3 Fm: 0-0
Distance: 5f/6f: 0-3 7f-8f: 0-2 9f-13f: 0-1 14f+: 0-0
Track : LH: 0-1 RH: 0-1 Tight: 0-0 Gall: 0-1
Aids: Bl: 0-0 Vi: 0-0 Tstrap: 0-0
Best Rating: 69 7/01 Nott 6f15y gd-fm

She has shown a little ability in maidens and nurseries.

Life Is Life (FR)

110 **113**

5-y-o b m Mansonnien (FR)-La Vie Immobile (USA) (Alleged (USA))
M A Jarvis Mr & Mrs Raymond Anderson Green

Placings:43102/3250-4104 **(4681)**
2001: 16^{4}G, 22^{1}GF, 16^{0}G, 18^{4}G

	Starts	1st	2nd	3rd	Win & Pl		
Career Total (Turf)	13	2	2	2	58553		
81	6/01	Asct	2m6f34y	B		G-F	£20300
84	9/99	Kemp	1m4f	D		HVY	£4070

Total win prize-money £24370

Going (Turf): Sf: 1-3 GS: 0-1 Gd: 0-5 **GF: 1-3** Fm: 0-0
Distance: 5f/6f: 0-0 7f-8f: 0-0 9f-13f: 1-5 14f+: 1-7
Track : LH: 0-4 **RH: 2-8** Tight: 0-2 **Gall: 1-6**
Aids: Bl: 0-0 Vi: 0-0 Tstrap: 0-0
Best Rating: 110 5/01 Sand 2m78y good

An ex-French mare, she has run well in Pattern company in recent seasons but seemed to find the marathon trip ideal when easily winning the Queen Alexandra at Royal Ascot.

Life Match (FR)

83

3-y-o b c Polish Precedent (USA)-Life Watch (USA) (Highland Park (USA))
A P O'Brien Mrs John Magnier

Placings:4001 **(5433a)**
2001: 11^{4}GY, 14^{0}G, 10^{0}GF, 13^{1}S

	Starts	1st	2nd	3rd	Win & Pl		
Career Total (Turf)	4	1	0	0	6530		
83	10/01	Navn	1m5f			SFT	£6210

Total win prize-money £6210

Going (Turf): Sf: 1-1 GS: 0-0 Gd: 0-1 GF: 0-1 Fm: 0-0
Distance: 5f/6f: 0-0 7f-8f: 0-0 **9f-13f: 1-3** 14f+: 0-1
Track : LH: 0-1 RH: 0-0 Tight: 0-0 Gall: 0-1
Aids: Bl: 0-0 Vi: 0-0 Tstrap: 0-0
Best Rating: 83 10/01 Navn 1m5f soft

Lifford Lady

96(80) (44)**42**

3-y-o b f Syrtos-Sally Maxwell (Roscoe Blake)
B N Doran The Lifford Lady Partnership

Placings:000600-1665005000 **(5524)**
2001: 8^{1}S, 8^{6}HY, 7^{6}GF, 9^{5}G, 10^{0}GF, 10^{0}GF, 8^{5}GF, 10^{0}GF, 7^{0}GF, 10^{0}HY

	Starts	1st	2nd	3rd	Win & Pl		
Career Total (Turf)	14	1	0	0	2044		
Career Total (AW)	2	0	0	0			
56	4/01	Nott	1m54y	F(0-60)H		SFT	£2044

Total win prize-money £2044

Going (Turf): Sf: 1-3 GS: 0-1 Gd: 0-1 GF: 0-9 Fm: 0-0
Distance: 5f/6f: 0-2 7f-8f: 0-6 **9f-13f: 1-8** 14f+: 0-0
Track : **LH: 1-10** RH: 0-0 Tight: 0-4 Gall: 0-0
Aids: Bl: 0-0 Vi: 0-0 Tstrap: 0-0
Best Rating: 56 4/01 Nott 1m54y soft

Light Brigade

85 **66**

2-y-o b g Kris-Mafatin (IRE) (Sadler's Wells (USA))
J M P Eustace Charles Curtis

Placings:005 (4099)
2001: 7^{0}GF, 7^{0}GF, 6^{5}G

	Starts	1st	2nd	3rd	Win & Pl
Career Total (Turf)	3	0	0	0	0

Going (Turf): Sf: 0-0 GS: 0-0 Gd: 0-1 GF: 0-2 Fm: 0-0
Distance: 5f/6f: 0-0 7f-8f: 0-3 9f-13f: 0-0 14f+: 0-0
Track : LH: 0-1 RH: 0-0 Tight: 0-0 Gall: 0-0
Aids: Bl: 0-0 Vi: 0-0 Tstrap: 0-0
Best Rating: 66 8/01 Nott 6f15y good

Light Duties

73

3-y-o gr c Dancing Spree (USA)-Goody Four Shoes (Blazing Saddles (AUS))
A G Newcombe K Atcherley

Placings:0 (4362)
2001: 7^{0}GF

	Starts	1st	2nd	3rd	Win & Pl
Career Total (Turf)	1	0	0	0	

Going (Turf): Sf: 0-0 GS: 0-0 Gd: 0-0 GF: 0-1 Fm: 0-0
Distance: 5f/6f: 0-0 7f-8f: 0-1 9f-13f: 0-0 14f+: 0-0
Track : LH: 0-1 RH: 0-0 Tight: 0-0 Gall: 0-0
Aids: Bl: 0-0 Vi: 0-0 Tstrap: 0-0

Light Evidence

(101) (62)

3-y-o ch f Factual (USA)-Blazing Sunset (Blazing Saddles (AUS))
R Hollinshead G J Sargent

Placings:050614332-4600 (0327)
2001: 6^{4}SW, 7^{6}SD, 9^{0}SD, 6^{0}SD

	Starts	1st	2nd	3rd	Win & Pl
Career Total (Turf)	3	0	0	0	0
Career Total (AW)	10	1	1	2	3032

58	11/00	Wolv	5f	G	STD	£1869

Total win prize-money £1869

Going (Turf): Sf: 0-1 GS: 0-0 Gd: 0-2 GF: 0-0 Fm: 0-0
Distance: 5f/6f: 1-10 7f-8f: 0-2 9f-13f: 0-1 14f+: 0-0
Track : LH: 1-10 RH: 0-1 Tight: 1-8 Gall: 0-1
Aids: Bl: 0-0 Vi: 0-0 Tstrap: 0-0
Best Rating: 55 1/01 Wolv 6f slow

Light Of Dawn (USA)

84 57

3-y-o b/br f Dynaformer (USA)-Dixie Morn (USA) (Dixieland Band (USA))
P W Harris The Early Risers

Placings:0 (1167)
2001: 8^{0}GS

	Starts	1st	2nd	3rd	Win & Pl
Career Total (Turf)	1	0	0	0	

Going (Turf): Sf: 0-0 GS: 0-1 Gd: 0-0 GF: 0-0 Fm: 0-0
Distance: 5f/6f: 0-0 7f-8f: 0-1 9f-13f: 0-0 14f+: 0-0
Track : LH: 0-0 RH: 0-1 Tight: 0-0 Gall: 0-0
Aids: Bl: 0-0 Vi: 0-0 Tstrap: 0-0
Best Rating: 57 5/01 Kemp 1m gd-sft

Light Of Fashion

3-y-o b f Common Grounds-May Light (Midyan (USA))
B Smart Dr J A E Hobby

Placings:005-0P (1015)
2001: 8^{0}S, 7^{P}SD

	Starts	1st	2nd	3rd	Win & Pl
Career Total (Turf)	4	0	0	0	0
Career Total (AW)	1	0	0	0	

Going (Turf): Sf: 0-2 GS: 0-0 Gd: 0-0 GF: 0-1 Fm: 0-1
Distance: 5f/6f: 0-1 7f-8f: 0-3 9f-13f: 0-1 14f+: 0-0
Track : LH: 0-4 RH: 0-0 Tight: 0-0 Gall: 0-1
Aids: Bl: 0-0 Vi: 0-0 Tstrap: 0-0

Light Programme

101(95) (15)50

7-y-o b g El Gran Senor (USA)-Nashmeel (USA) (Blushing Groom (FR))
A L Forbes Tony Forbes

Placings:21/00/00-0625340 (5044)
2001: 11^{0}SD, 10^{6}GF, 12^{2}GS, 9^{5}GF, 11^{3}G, 16^{4}GF, 14^{0}SD

	Starts	1st	2nd	3rd	Win & Pl
Career Total (Turf)	10	1	2	1	8033
Career Total (AW)	3	0	0	0	

87	7/97	NmkJ	1m2f	D	G-F	£5481

Total win prize-money £5481

Going (Turf): Sf: 0-1 GS: 0-4 Gd: 0-1 GF: 1-4 Fm: 0-0
Distance: 5f/6f: 0-0 7f-8f: 0-0 9f-13f: 1-11 14f+: 0-2
Track : LH: 0-8 RH: 1-4 Tight: 0-3 Gall: 1-5
Aids: Bl: 0-0 Vi: 0-0 Tstrap: 0-1
Best Rating: 50 7/01 Bevl 1m1f207y gd-fm

Fair staying handicapper. Lightly raced for his years. Acts best with ease in the ground.

Light Scent (USA)

100 85

2-y-o ch c Silver Hawk (USA)-Music Lane (USA) (Miswaki (USA))
Sir Michael Stoute Saeed Suhail

Placings:52 (4087)
2001: 7^{5}GF, 8^{2}S

	Starts	1st	2nd	3rd	Win & Pl
Career Total (Turf)	2	0	1	0	1338

Going (Turf): Sf: 0-1 GS: 0-0 Gd: 0-0 GF: 0-1 Fm: 0-0
Distance: 5f/6f: 0-0 7f-8f: 0-1 9f-13f: 0-1 14f+: 0-0
Track : LH: 0-0 RH: 0-1 Tight: 0-0 Gall: 0-0
Aids: Bl: 0-0 Vi: 0-0 Tstrap: 0-0
Best Rating: 85 8/01 Sand 1m14y soft

Light The Rocket (IRE)

99 54

5-y-o ch g Pips Pride-Coolrain Lady (IRE) (Common Grounds)
W J Musson Tprc Limited

Placings:0201140/2260002002/5000-00000000 (5181)
2001: 6^{0}GS, 6^{0}G, 6^{0}GF, 5^{0}GS, 6^{0}GF, 6^{0}G, 6^{0}G, 6^{0}HY

	Starts	1st	2nd	3rd	Win & Pl
Career Total (Turf)	27	2	5	0	25566
Career Total (AW)	2	0	0	0	

90	8/98	Asct	5f	B	G-F	£6197
83	8/98	Sand	5f6y	D	GD	£4260

Total win prize-money £10458

Going (Turf): Sf: 0-3 GS: 0-4 Gd: 1-9 GF: 1-9 Fm: 0-1
Distance: 5f/6f: 2-25 7f-8f: 0-1 9f-13f: 0-0 14f+: 0-0
Track : LH: 0-0 RH: 0-0 Tight: 0-0 Gall: 0-0
Aids: Bl: 0-1 Vi: 0-0 Tstrap: 0-0
Best Rating: 55 5/01 NmkR 6f good

Very useful sprint handicapper in his prime but has not looked the same horse since returning from foreign shores and is falling down the handicap. Best at five furlongs, he seems to act on any ground.

Lightning Blaze

95(56) 40

5-y-o ch m Cosmonaut-Royal Deed (USA) (Shadeed (USA))
P S McEntee Racing Thoroughbreds Plc

Placings:03101211300/50642500/0005-004004000 (4284)
2001: 6^{0}GF, 5^{0}F, 5^{4}GF, 6^{0}SD, 5^{0}GF, 6^{4}GS, 5^{0}G, 5^{0}G, 6^{0}G

	Starts	1st	2nd	3rd	Win & Pl
Career Total (Turf)	31	3	2	2	9638
Career Total (AW)	2	1	0	0	1725

64	7/98	Folk	5f	F	G-F	£2322
64	7/98	Bevl	5f	F	G-F	£2407
74	6/98	Folk	5f	F	G-F	£2070
62	6/98	Wolv	5f	G	STD	£1725

Total win prize-money £8525

Going (Turf): Sf: 0-0 GS: 0-2 Gd: 0-8 GF: 3-18 Fm: 0-3
Distance: 5f/6f: 4-32 7f-8f: 0-1 9f-13f: 0-0 14f+: 0-0
Track : LH: 1-8 RH: 0-0 Tight: 1-1 Gall: 0-2
Aids: Bl: 0-0 Vi: 0-0 Tstrap: 0-0
Best Rating: 40 8/01 Nott 5f13y good

Lightning Ridge

83 10

3-y-o b f Lightning Dealer-Amazing News (Mazilier (USA))
D R C Elsworth Quakers Yard Racing Club

Placings:0000 (5524)
2001: 10^{0}GF, 11^{0}GF, 8^{0}GF, 10^{0}HY

	Starts	1st	2nd	3rd	Win & Pl
Career Total (Turf)	4	0	0	0	

Going (Turf): Sf: 0-1 GS: 0-0 Gd: 0-0 GF: 0-3 Fm: 0-0
Distance: 5f/6f: 0-0 7f-8f: 0-0 9f-13f: 0-4 14f+: 0-0
Track : LH: 0-1 RH: 0-1 Tight: 0-2 Gall: 0-1
Aids: Bl: 0-0 Vi: 0-0 Tstrap: 0-0
Best Rating: 10 7/01 Sand 1m14y gd-fm

Lightning Star (USA)

83 35

6-y-o b g El Gran Senor (USA)-Cuz's Star (USA) (Galaxy Libra)
T P McGovern Ashley Carr Racing (5)

Placings:510/036/40-060 (3678)
2001: 20^{0}GF, 12^{6}GF, 11^{0}G

	Starts	1st	2nd	3rd	Win & Pl
Career Total (Turf)	11	1	0	1	6731

81	8/97	Gway	1m100y		G-Y	£5480

Total win prize-money £5480

Going (Turf): Sf: 0-3 GS: 0-0 Gd: 0-2 GF: 0-3 Fm: 0-0
Distance: 5f/6f: 0-0 7f-8f: 0-2 9f-13f: 1-7 14f+: 0-2
Track : LH: 0-4 RH: 1-4 Tight: 0-3 Gall: 0-1
Aids: Bl: 0-5 Vi: 0-0 Tstrap: 0-0
Best Rating: 54 7/01 Epsm 1m4f10y gd-fm

Ligne Gagnante (IRE)

101 96

5-y-o b g Turtle Island (IRE)-Lightino (Bustino)
M Johnston The Winning Line

Placings:0640/1113532/602230-0 (4115)
2001: 11^{0}G

	Starts	1st	2nd	3rd	Win & Pl
Career Total (Turf)	18	3	3	3	59155

83	6/99	Newc	1m4f93y	B(0-105)H	GD	£8938
85	6/99	Gdwd	1m4f	C(0-95)H	G-S	£8412
72	5/99	Ayr	1m1f20y	E(0-75)	GD	£2588

Total win prize-money £19938

Going (Turf): Sf: 0-3 GS: 1-1 Gd: 2-8 GF: 0-4 Fm: 0-2
Distance: 5f/6f: 0-2 7f-8f: 0-2 9f-13f: 3-11 14f+: 0-3
Track : LH: 2-12 RH: 1-4 Tight: 1-5 Gall: 1-8

Aids: Bl: 0-0 Vi: 0-0 Tstrap: 0-0
Best Rating: 88 8/01 York 1m3f195y good

Decent middle-distance stayer, he has paid the penalty for a hat-trick in 1999.

Lihou Island

98 **89**

2-y-o b f Beveled (USA)-Foreign Mistress (Darshaan)
N P Littmoden Trojan Racing

Placings:353140052 **(5496)**
2001: 5^3GF, 5^5GF, 5^3G, 6^1GS, 6^4G, 6^0GF, 6^0GS, 7^5S, 7^2HY

	Starts	1st	2nd	3rd	Win & Pl
Career Total (Turf)	9	1	1	2	24701
80 8/01 NmkJ 6f	B			G-S	£19500

Total win prize-money £19500

Going (Turf): Sf: 0-2 **GS: 1-2** Gd: 0-3 GF: 0-2 Fm: 0-0
Distance: **5f/6f: 1-7** 7f-8f: 0-2 9f-13f: 0-0 14f+: 0-0
Track : LH: 0-1 RH: 0-1 Tight: 0-0 Gall: 0-2
Aids: Bl: 0-0 Vi: 0-0 Tstrap: 0-0
Best Rating: 89 10/01 Newb 7f heavy

A half-sister to mile-winner Pink Ticket, she got off the mark on her fourth start at Newmarket in August. Ran well afterwards in nurseries. Stays seven furlongs and appreciates cut in the ground.

Likely Lady (IRE)

64

2-y-o b f Revoque (IRE)-Harmer (IRE) (Alzao (USA))
N P Littmoden Miss Vanessa Church

Placings:0640 **(5628)**
2001: 6^0GF, 5^6G, 5^4GF, 8^0G

	Starts	1st	2nd	3rd	Win & Pl
Career Total (Turf)	4	0	0	0	473

Going (Turf): Sf: 0-0 GS: 0-0 Gd: 0-2 GF: 0-2 Fm: 0-0
Distance: 5f/6f: 0-3 7f-8f: 0-1 9f-13f: 0-0 14f+: 0-0
Track : LH: 0-0 RH: 0-0 Tight: 0-0 Gall: 0-0
Aids: Bl: 0-0 Vi: 0-0 Tstrap: 0-0
Best Rating: 64 7/01 Chep 5f16y good

A half-sister to National Stakes Winner Amaretto Bay and a mile winner in Germany, she has shown little to date.

Lil's Jessy (IRE)

107 **105**

3-y-o b f Kris-Lobmille (Mill Reef (USA))
J Noseda Razza Pallorsi

Placings:5101130-10000 **(4682)**
2001: 7^1GS, 8^0G, 8^0GF, 8^0G, 7^0G

	Starts	1st	2nd	3rd	Win & Pl
Career Total (Turf)	12	4	0	1	40631
100 4/01 NmkR 7f	A			G-S	£20300
89 9/00 Donc 7f	D(0-85)			G-F	£7995
86 8/00 Ches 7f2y	C			GD	£6240
75 7/00 Yarm 7f3y	D			FRM	£3750

Total win prize-money £38286

Going (Turf): Sf: 0-0 **GS: 1-2 Gd: 1-5 GF: 1-4 Fm: 1-1**
Distance: 5f/6f: 0-1 **7f-8f: 4-11** 9f-13f: 0-0 14f+: 0-0
Track : **LH: 1-1** RH: 0-2 **Tight: 1-1** Gall: 0-1
Aids: Bl: 0-0 Vi: 0-0 Tstrap: 0-0
Best Rating: 105 6/01 Asct 1m gd-fm

Tries hard and developed into a useful juvenile. Showed a good turn of foot to take the Nell Gwyn on her reappearance, but the form of that race has not worked out at all and she has been well held in Group company this term. Has yet to prove she stays a mile.

Lilium

116 **110**

3-y-o b f Nashwan (USA)-Satin Flower (USA) (Shadeed (USA))
Sir Michael Stoute Sheikh Mohammed

Placings:110-6413 **(5257)**
2001: 9^6GF, 10^4F, 12^1G, 12^3GS

	Starts	1st	2nd	3rd	Win & Pl
Career Total (Turf)	7	3	0	1	46133
110 9/01 Asct 1m4f	A			GD	£22750
100 9/00 NmkR 7f	A			GD	£12365
82 9/00 Wwck 7f26y	D			G-F	£3965

Total win prize-money £39081

Going (Turf): Sf: 0-0 GS: 0-2 **Gd: 2-2** GF: 1-2 Fm: 0-1
Distance: 5f/6f: 0-0 **7f-8f: 2-3** 9f-13f: 1-4 14f+: 0-0
Track : LH: 1-2 RH: 1-3 Tight: 0-1 **Gall: 1-3**
Aids: Bl: 0-0 Vi: 0-0 Tstrap: 0-0
Best Rating: 110 9/01 Asct 1m4f good

Useful at two, she disappointed in her first two runs in 2001 but came back from a break to score on her first try over 12 furlongs. Acts on good and good to firm. Should continue to improve now that she has found her trip.

Lilleman

98(98) (80)**72**

3-y-o b g Distant Relative-Lillemor (Connaught)
G A Butler M Berger

Placings:502230-100000 **(4588)**
2001: 5^1SD, 5^0S, 5^0GF, 5^0GF, 5^0S, 5^0HY

	Starts	1st	2nd	3rd	Win & Pl
Career Total (Turf)	9	0	1	0	1035
Career Total (AW)	3	1	1	1	4093
59 3/01 Ling 5f	D			STD	£2828

Total win prize-money £2828

Going (Turf): Sf: 0-4 GS: 0-1 Gd: 0-1 GF: 0-3 Fm: 0-0
Distance: **5f/6f: 1-11** 7f-8f: 0-1 9f-13f: 0-0 14f+: 0-0
Track : **LH: 1-4** RH: 0-0 **Tight: 1-3** Gall: 0-0
Aids: Bl: 0-1 Vi: 0-0 Tstrap: 0-1
Best Rating: 69 4/01 Sand 5f6y soft

Showed ability in a very warm maiden at the York Ebor meeting in 2000, but has spurned some good opportunities afterwards. Got off the mark on the All-Weather, but has struggled in handicaps since.

Lilli's Lad

70 **18**

3-y-o ch g Selkirk (USA)-Langtry Lady (Pas De Seul)
P W Harris C Brosnan, T Mansfield & Mrs P W Harris

Placings:00 **(3149)**
2001: 9^0GF, 12^0G

	Starts	1st	2nd	3rd	Win & Pl
Career Total (Turf)	2	0	0	0	

Going (Turf): Sf: 0-0 GS: 0-0 Gd: 0-1 GF: 0-1 Fm: 0-0
Distance: 5f/6f: 0-0 7f-8f: 0-0 9f-13f: 0-2 14f+: 0-0
Track : LH: 0-0 RH: 0-2 Tight: 0-1 Gall: 0-0
Aids: Bl: 0-0 Vi: 0-0 Tstrap: 0-0
Best Rating: 18 6/01 Sals 1m1f198y gd-fm

Lillian Violet

78(58) (3)**44**

2-y-o b f Beveled (USA)-Grey Twig (Godswalk (USA))
J S Moore W J Wyatt

Placings:000 **(2056)**
2001: 5^0G, 6^0SD, 6^0GF

	Starts	1st	2nd	3rd	Win & Pl
Career Total (Turf)	2	0	0	0	
Career Total (AW)	1	0	0	0	

Going (Turf): Sf: 0-0 GS: 0-0 Gd: 0-1 GF: 0-1 Fm: 0-0
Distance: 5f/6f: 0-3 7f-8f: 0-0 9f-13f: 0-0 14f+: 0-0
Track : LH: 0-1 RH: 0-1 Tight: 0-0 Gall: 0-1
Aids: Bl: 0-0 Vi: 0-0 Tstrap: 0-0
Best Rating: 44 6/01 Sals 6f gd-fm

Lillies Bordello (IRE)

104 **82**

2-y-o b f Danehill Dancer (IRE)-Lunulae (Tumble Wind (USA))
K A Ryan Mrs Gillian Quinn

Placings:32201305 **(4795)**
2001: 5^3GF, 5^2GF, 6^2GF, 5^0GF, 5^1G, 6^3G, 5^0GF, 5^5G

	Starts	1st	2nd	3rd	Win & Pl
Career Total (Turf)	8	1	2	2	7696
81 8/01 Muss 5f	E			GD	£3276

Total win prize-money £3276

Going (Turf): Sf: 0-0 GS: 0-0 **Gd: 1-3** GF: 0-5 Fm: 0-0
Distance: **5f/6f: 1-8** 7f-8f: 0-0 9f-13f: 0-0 14f+: 0-0
Track : LH: 0-1 RH: 0-0 Tight: 0-0 Gall: 0-0
Aids: Bl: 0-0 Vi: 0-0 Tstrap: 0-0
Best Rating: 82 9/01 Ayr 5f good

She has faced some very stiff tasks this season and only has a victory in a Musselburgh maiden to her name.

Lily Of The Guild (IRE)

82 **59**

2-y-o ch f Lycius (USA)-Secreto Bold (Never So Bold)
W S Kittow Racing Guild 2000

Placings:0000 **(4894)**
2001: 5^0F, 6^0GF, 5^0F, 5^0GS

	Starts	1st	2nd	3rd	Win & Pl
Career Total (Turf)	4	0	0	0	

Going (Turf): Sf: 0-0 GS: 0-1 Gd: 0-0 GF: 0-1 Fm: 0-2
Distance: 5f/6f: 0-3 7f-8f: 0-1 9f-13f: 0-0 14f+: 0-0
Track : LH: 0-1 RH: 0-0 Tight: 0-0 Gall: 0-1
Aids: Bl: 0-0 Vi: 0-0 Tstrap: 0-0
Best Rating: 59 9/01 Bath 5f11y firm

Limbo Lad

83 **55**

2-y-o b g Millkom-Bumble Boogie (IRE) (Bluebird (USA))
P C Haslam Mrs B Hawkins

Placings:060 **(4595)**
2001: 6^0GF, 8^6G, 7^0GF

	Starts	1st	2nd	3rd	Win & Pl
Career Total (Turf)	3	0	0	0	0

Going (Turf): Sf: 0-0 GS: 0-0 Gd: 0-1 GF: 0-2 Fm: 0-0
Distance: 5f/6f: 0-1 7f-8f: 0-2 9f-13f: 0-0 14f+: 0-0
Track : LH: 0-2 RH: 0-0 Tight: 0-1 Gall: 0-1
Aids: Bl: 0-0 Vi: 0-0 Tstrap: 0-0
Best Rating: 55 8/01 Newc 1m good

Limburg (IRE)

77(84) (33)**45**

3-y-o b/br g Hamas (IRE)-Tambora (Darshaan)
W R Muir Dulverton Equine

Placings:000-5000 **(2991)**
2001: 8^5SD, 7^0GF, 8^0SD, 8^0G

	Starts	1st	2nd	3rd	Win & Pl
Career Total (Turf)	5	0	0	0	
Career Total (AW)	2	0	0	0	0

Going (Turf): Sf: 0-0 GS: 0-1 Gd: 0-1 GF: 0-3 Fm: 0-0

Distance: 5f/6f: 0-1 7f-8f: 0-5 9f-13f: 0-1 14f+: 0-0
Track : LH: 0-3 RH: 0-0 Tight: 0-0 Gall: 0-0
Aids: Bl: 0-0 Vi: 0-0 Tstrap: 0-0
Best Rating: 33 4/01 Sthl 1m stand

Lime Gardens

108 **110**

3-y-o b f Sadler's Wells (USA)-Hatton Gardens (Auction Ring (USA))
M J Grassick J Higgins

Placings:10-20510 **(4821a)**
2001: 10^{2}GF, 12^{0}GF, 12^{5}G, 12^{1}G, 12^{0}G

	Starts	1st	2nd	3rd	Win & Pl
Career Total (Turf)	7	2	1	0	36264

108 8/01 Deau 1m4f110y GD £21339
95 10/00 Leop 7f HVY £9750
Total win prize-money £31089

Going (Turf): Sf: 0-1 GS: 0-0 **Gd: 1-3** GF: 0-2 Fm: 0-0
Distance: 5f/6f: 0-0 7f-8f: 0-0 **9f-13f: 1-6** 14f+: 0-0
Track : LH: 0-1 RH: 0-2 Tight: 0-0 Gall: 0-1
Aids: Bl: 0-0 Vi: 0-0 Tstrap: 0-0
Best Rating: 110 7/01 Curr 1m4f good

Impressive maiden winner as a juvenile and has run to similar level in two Listed runs since. Looked in need of further when just failing over ten furlongs on seasonal bow and improve when stepped up in trip, putting up creditable efforts in the Ribblesdale and Irish Oaks. Won a Group Three at Deauville in August and looks to be improving.

Lincoln Dancer (IRE)

104 **87**

4-y-o b h Turtle Island (IRE)-Double Grange (IRE) (Double Schwartz)
M A Jarvis Michael Baker

Placings:1310/4012002-4020030 **(5694)**
2001: 7^{4}GF, 6^{0}G, 6^{2}GS, 6^{0}HY, 8^{0}GS, 7^{3}HY, 6^{0}S

	Starts	1st	2nd	3rd	Win & Pl
Career Total (Turf)	18	3	3	2	76789

115 5/00 Hayd 6f A(0-110)H SFT £13885
100 5/99 York 6f B SFT £9035
82 4/99 Wwck 5f D GD £2762
Total win prize-money £25683

Going (Turf): Sf: 2-9 GS: 0-4 Gd: 1-3 GF: 0-2 Fm: 0-0
Distance: 5f/6f: 3-12 7f-8f: 0-6 9f-13f: 0-0 14f+: 0-0
Track : LH: 1-3 RH: 0-1 Tight: 0-0 **Gall: 1-2**
Aids: Bl: 0-0 Vi: 0-0 Tstrap: 0-0
Best Rating: 102 6/01 Hayd 7f30y gd-fm

He had operations for a chipped fetlock and colic over the winter but ran a fair race at Haydock on his reappearance in 2001, given that the ground was on the fast side and the distance further than he would have liked. Made no show in the July Cup, in which he had finished second in 2000, but ran better at Yarmouth. Down the field in the Haydock Sprint Cup and in lesser contests since, he is suited by soft ground and a flat track and has yet to win beyond six furlongs.

Lincoln Dean

100 (72)**36**

5-y-o b g Mtoto-Play With Me (IRE) (Alzao (USA))
J S Goldie Clayton Bigley Partnership Ltd

Placings:005/**1**02**0**5040/0003204-501002000304000**0** **(5284)**
2001: 8^{5}GS, 8^{0}GS, 8^{1}GS, 8^{0}GF, 8^{0}G, 8^{2}GF, 9^{0}G, 9^{0}GF, 10^{0}F, 11^{3}GS, 10^{0}G, 10^{4}G, 9^{0}G, 10^{0}F, 8^{0}GF, 9^{0}HY

	Starts	1st	2nd	3rd	Win & Pl
Career Total (Turf)	30	1	2	2	9487
Career Total (AW)	4	1	1	0	4625

45 5/01 Haml 1m65y E(0-70)H G-S £3867
70 1/99 Ling 1m D(0-80)H STD £3543
Total win prize-money £7411

Going (Turf): Sf: 0-4 **GS: 1-4** Gd: 0-6 GF: 0-10 Fm: 0-6
Distance: 5f/6f: 0-1 7f-8f: 1-9 9f-13f: 1-24 14f+: 0-0
Track : LH: 1-15 RH: 1-14 **Tight: 2-19** Gall: 0-5
Aids: Bl: 0-0 Vi: 0-0 Tstrap: 0-0
Best Rating: 46 6/01 Newc 1m gd-fm

Moderate handicapper, suited by a mile and cut in the ground. Likes to make the running.

Lindinis (USA)

94 **49**

3-y-o b c Distant View (USA)-Annual Dance (USA) (Nostalgia (USA))
S Kirk Jeffen Racing

Placings:050 **(5631)**
2001: 8^{0}HY, 8^{5}HY, 10^{0}G

	Starts	1st	2nd	3rd	Win & Pl
Career Total (Turf)	3	0	0	0	0

Going (Turf): Sf: 0-2 GS: 0-0 Gd: 0-1 GF: 0-0 Fm: 0-0
Distance: 5f/6f: 0-0 7f-8f: 0-0 9f-13f: 0-3 14f+: 0-0
Track : LH: 0-3 RH: 0-0 Tight: 0-1 Gall: 0-0
Aids: Bl: 0-0 Vi: 0-0 Tstrap: 0-0
Best Rating: 49 11/01 Rdcr 1m2f good

Line Rider (USA)

94 **87**

2-y-o b c Danzig (USA)-Freewheel (USA) (Arctic Tern (USA))
A P O'Brien M Tabor & Mrs John Magnier

Placings:42103006 **(5104)**
2001: 5^{4}GF, 5^{2}Y, 6^{1}GF, 6^{0}GY, 7^{3}GF, 6^{0}Y, 6^{0}GS, 6^{6}GS

	Starts	1st	2nd	3rd	Win & Pl
Career Total (Turf)	8	1	1	1	22460

87 7/01 Leop 6f G-F £10400
Total win prize-money £10400

Going (Turf): Sf: 0-0 GS: 0-2 Gd: 0-0 **GF: 1-3** Fm: 0-0
Distance: 5f/6f: 1-6 7f-8f: 0-2 9f-13f: 0-0 14f+: 0-0
Track : LH: 0-0 RH: 0-0 Tight: 0-0 Gall: 0-0
Aids: Bl: 0-0 Vi: 0-0 Tstrap: 0-0
Best Rating: 87 7/01 Curr 7f gd-fm

Impressive winner of a Leopardstown maiden in July over six furlongs, he has yet to prove he stays seven. Has acted as a pacemaker on a number of occasions since.

Linea-G

104(100) (66)**59**

7-y-o ch m Keen-Horton Line (High Line)
Mrs M Reveley W Ginzel

Placings:550/4000/**1**23**1**25**1**20/605631-323411134**0**0 **(3712)**
2001: 16^{3}SW, 12^{2}SW, 16^{3}SD, 13^{4}S, 13^{1}GF, 14^{1}GF, 13^{1}GF, 14^{3}F, 12^{4}GF, 12^{0}GF, 14^{0}G

	Starts	1st	2nd	3rd	Win & Pl
Career Total (Turf)	23	5	2	2	17139
Career Total (AW)	10	2	2	3	6258

50 6/01 Ayr 1m5f13y F(0-60) G-F £2369
56 5/01 Muss 1m6f F(0-60) G-F £3430
60 5/01 Ayr 1m5f13y E(0-70)H G-F £3528
63 12/00 Sthl 1m6f F(0-65)H STD £1799
66 8/99 Bevl 1m3f216yF(0-60) GD £2267
54 5/99 Newc 1m4f93y E(0-70)H G-F £2794
57 3/99 Sthl 1m4f F STD £2034
Total win prize-money £18223

Going (Turf): Sf: 0-1 GS: 0-1 Gd: 1-7 **GF: 4-13** Fm: 0-1
Distance: 5f/6f: 0-0 7f-8f: 0-1 9f-13f: 3-19 **14f+: 4-13**
Track : LH: 5-25 RH: 2-7 **Tight: 2-12** Gall: 1-3
Aids: Bl: 0-0 Vi: 0-0 Tstrap: 0-0
Best Rating: 66 1/01 Wolv 2m46y slow

A half-sister to Angus-G, she is most consistent and has won three fairly modest events this season. She does not have much in the way of a turn of foot, but tries hard and is suited by a test of stamina.

Linens Girl

77(71) (6)**22**

5-y-o br m Thowra (FR)-Stocktina (Tina's Pet)
B G Powell D & J Newell

Placings:P540/00 **(1525)**
2001: 8^{0}SW, 7^{0}F

	Starts	1st	2nd	3rd	Win & Pl
Career Total (Turf)	5	0	0	0	264
Career Total (AW)	1	0	0	0	

Going (Turf): Sf: 0-0 GS: 0-0 Gd: 0-2 GF: 0-1 Fm: 0-2
Distance: 5f/6f: 0-1 7f-8f: 0-5 9f-13f: 0-0 14f+: 0-0
Track : LH: 0-5 RH: 0-0 Tight: 0-2 Gall: 0-0
Aids: Bl: 0-0 Vi: 0-0 Tstrap: 0-0
Best Rating: 22 5/01 Brig 7f214y firm

Lingo (IRE)

82 **75**

2-y-o b c Poliglote-Sea Ring (FR) (Bering)
Mrs J R Ramsden Swisspartners

Placings:300 **(4536)**
2001: 6^{3}G, 6^{0}G, 6^{0}GF

	Starts	1st	2nd	3rd	Win & Pl
Career Total (Turf)	3	0	0	1	384

Going (Turf): Sf: 0-0 GS: 0-0 Gd: 0-2 GF: 0-1 Fm: 0-0
Distance: 5f/6f: 0-3 7f-8f: 0-0 9f-13f: 0-0 14f+: 0-0
Track : LH: 0-0 RH: 0-0 Tight: 0-0 Gall: 0-0
Aids: Bl: 0-0 Vi: 0-0 Tstrap: 0-0
Best Rating: 75 8/01 Newc 6f good

Linus

99 **66**

3-y-o b g Bin Ajwaad (IRE)-Land Line (High Line)
S Kirk Raymond Tooth

Placings:06035 **(3669)**
2001: 10^{0}G, 11^{6}GF, 12^{0}GF, 12^{3}G, 14^{5}S

	Starts	1st	2nd	3rd	Win & Pl
Career Total (Turf)	5	0	0	1	426

Going (Turf): Sf: 0-1 GS: 0-0 Gd: 0-2 GF: 0-2 Fm: 0-0
Distance: 5f/6f: 0-0 7f-8f: 0-0 9f-13f: 0-4 14f+: 0-1
Track : LH: 0-3 RH: 0-1 Tight: 0-1 Gall: 0-0
Aids: Bl: 0-0 Vi: 0-0 Tstrap: 0-0
Best Rating: 66 6/01 Wwck 1m4f134y gd-fm

Lion Of Judah

88 **38**

4-y-o b c Caerleon (USA)-Lyndonville (IRE) (Top Ville)
R Brotherton R D Evans

Placings:5-000060 **(1938)**
2001: 12^{0}S, 8^{0}S, 7^{0}G, 9^{0}G, 8^{6}GF, 11^{0}GF

	Starts	1st	2nd	3rd	Win & Pl
Career Total (Turf)	7	0	0	0	178

Going (Turf): Sf: 0-3 GS: 0-0 Gd: 0-2 GF: 0-2 Fm: 0-0
Distance: 5f/6f: 0-0 7f-8f: 0-1 9f-13f: 0-6 14f+: 0-0
Track : LH: 0-6 RH: 0-0 Tight: 0-1 Gall: 0-1
Aids: Bl: 0-0 Vi: 0-0 Tstrap: 0-0
Best Rating: 38 5/01 Hayd 1m30y gd-fm

Lion Song

48(72) (27)26

3-y-o b g Savahra Sound-Lucky Candy (Lucky Wednesday)

M J Polglase (N P Littmoden 6/1) Paul J Dixon

Placings:00-06 **(0581)**

2001: 5^{0}SD, 8^{6}HY

	Starts	1st	2nd	3rd	Win & Pl
Career Total (Turf)	3	0	0	0	0
Career Total (AW)	1	0	0	0	

Going (Turf): Sf: 0-2 GS: 0-0 Gd: 0-1 GF: 0-0 Fm: 0-0
Distance: 5f/6f: 0-3 7f-8f: 0-0 9f-13f: 0-1 14f+: 0-0
Track : LH: 0-3 RH: 0-0 Tight: 0-1 Gall: 0-1
Aids: Bl: 0-1 Vi: 0-0 Tstrap: 0-0
Best Rating: 27 1/01 Ling 5f stand

Lion's Domane

106(93) (48)66

4-y-o b g Lion Cavern (USA)-Vilany (Never So Bold)

I Semple (P C Haslam 26/1) Belstane Racing Partnership (two)

Placings:000/260610-0001643611404100 **(5659)**

2001: 8^{0}SD, 8^{0}SD, 8^{0}GS, 7^{1}GF, 8^{6}GF, 8^{4}F, 7^{3}G, 6^{6}G, 7^{1}GF, 7^{1}GF, 7^{4}GF, 7^{0}G, 7^{4}G, 7^{1}GF, 6^{0}GF, 8^{0}G

	Starts	1st	2nd	3rd	Win & Pl
Career Total (Turf)	20	5	0	1	16429
Career Total (AW)	5	0	1	0	657

66	8/01	Muss	7f30y	E(0-65)	G-F	£2835
57	7/01	Muss	7f30y	F(0-65)H	G-F	£2366
54	7/01	Ches	7f122y	E(0-70)H	G-F	£3374
42	5/01	Thsk	7f	G	G-F	£3185
47	8/00	Thsk	7f	E(0-70)H	GD	£2814

Total win prize-money £14575

Going (Turf): Sf: 0-1 GS: 0-2 Gd: 1-7 **GF: 4-9** Fm: 0-1
Distance: 5f/6f: 0-3 **7f-8f: 5-20** 9f-13f: 0-2 14f+: 0-0
Track : **LH: 3-11** RH: 0-3 **Tight: 3-10** Gall: 0-1
Aids: Bl: 0-0 Vi: 0-0 Tstrap: 0-0
Best Rating: 66 8/01 Muss 7f30y gd-fm

Fair seven-furlong handicapper on fast ground. Suited by sharp tracks. In good form in 2001.

Lionardo

96 59

5-y-o b h Lion Cavern (USA)-Pravolo (Fool's Holme (USA))

Paul Smith R Vanslembrouck

Placings:50/0211501/0011011-1604010

2001: 8^{1}GS, 7^{6}G, 8^{0}G, 8^{4}GS, 8^{0}S, 8^{1}G, 10^{0}S

	Starts	1st	2nd	3rd	Win & Pl
Career Total (Turf)	22	8	1	0	20683
Career Total (AW)	1	1	0	0	1562

8/01	Deau	1m	H	GD	£7759
5/01	Comp	1m		G-S	£2522
8/00	Oste	1m2f		SFT	£1171
8/00	Oste	1m		SFT	£1562
6/00	Oste	1m		G-S	£1562
5/00	Ster	1m110y	H	SFT	£1562
10/99	Oste	1m		SFT	£1050
8/99	Oste	1m1f	H	GD	£1749
7/99	Oste	1m	H	FRM	£1749

Total win prize-money £20686

Going (Turf): Sf: 2-5 GS: 1-2 Gd: 1-3 GF: 0-3 Fm: 0-0
Distance: 5f/6f: 0-1 **7f-8f: 3-8** 9f-13f: 1-4 14f+: 0-0
Track : LH: 0-0 RH: 0-3 Tight: 0-1 Gall: 0-0
Aids: Bl: 0-0 Vi: 0-0 Tstrap: 0-0
Best Rating: 59 6/01 Wind 1m67y good

Lionel Andros

102 46

3-y-o b g Lion Cavern (USA)-Guyum (Rousillon (USA))

R J Hodges Miss R Dobson

Placings:05-06200040 **(4052)**

2001: 6^{0}GS, 5^{6}HY, 5^{2}F, 5^{0}G, 5^{0}GF, 5^{0}GF, 5^{4}F, 6^{0}F

	Starts	1st	2nd	3rd	Win & Pl
Career Total (Turf)	10	0	1	0	656

Going (Turf): Sf: 0-1 GS: 0-1 Gd: 0-2 GF: 0-2 Fm: 0-4
Distance: 5f/6f: 0-8 7f-8f: 0-2 9f-13f: 0-0 14f+: 0-0
Track : LH: 0-7 RH: 0-0 Tight: 0-0 Gall: 0-5
Aids: Bl: 0-1 Vi: 0-0 Tstrap: 0-0
Best Rating: 46 6/01 Bath 5f11y firm

Lipica (IRE)

88 98

3-y-o b f Night Shift (USA)-Top Knot (High Top)

K R Burke Paul & Jenny Green

Placings:313-00 **(3413)**

2001: 8^{0}S, 10^{0}GF

	Starts	1st	2nd	3rd	Win & Pl
Career Total (Turf)	5	1	0	2	6118

78	9/00	Kemp	7f	D	SFT	£3038

Total win prize-money £3039

Going (Turf): Sf: 1-3 GS: 0-0 Gd: 0-1 GF: 0-1 Fm: 0-0
Distance: 5f/6f: 0-0 **7f-8f: 1-4** 9f-13f: 0-1 14f+: 0-0
Track : LH: 0-2 **RH: 1-2** Tight: 0-0 **Gall: 1-2**
Aids: Bl: 0-0 Vi: 0-0 Tstrap: 0-1
Best Rating: 64 7/01 Chep 1m2f36y gd-fm

A robust sort, she finished third to Tobougg in 2000. She scored nicely on her second run at Kempton and ran well to finish third in a Newbury Listed event on her final start. She appreciates getting her toe in. Swallowed her tongue on her return to action and only seen once more.

Lipstick

103 97+

2-y-o b f Zamindar (USA)-Final Shot (Dalsaan)

M R Channon John Breslin

Placings:5112 **(4985)**

2001: 5^{5}GF, 5^{1}GF, 6^{1}G, 6^{2}G

	Starts	1st	2nd	3rd	Win & Pl
Career Total (Turf)	4	2	1	0	69843

89	9/01	Kemp	6f	A	GD	£13910
90	8/01	Bath	5f11y	D	G-F	£3464

Total win prize-money £17375

Going (Turf): Sf: 0-0 GS: 0-0 **Gd: 1-2 GF: 1-2** Fm: 0-0
Distance: **5f/6f: 2-3** 7f-8f: 0-1 9f-13f: 0-0 14f+: 0-0
Track : **LH: 1-1** RH: 0-0 Tight: 0-0 **Gall: 1-1**
Aids: Bl: 0-0 Vi: 0-0 Tstrap: 0-0
Best Rating: 97 9/01 Asct 6f110y good

A half-sister to six winners, the majority of whom won as juveniles, she showed inexperience on her debut. Dropped in class next time, she won in taking style before showing gameness when winning a Listed event at Kempton over six furlongs and running well in a valuable sales race. Suited by a good/fast surface.

Liquidambar

81 56

2-y-o ch f Atraf-Precious Ballerina (Ballacashtal (CAN))

J R Norton J Wightman

Placings:040 **(5635)**

2001: 7^{0}G, 7^{4}S, 7^{0}G

	Starts	1st	2nd	3rd	Win & Pl
Career Total (Turf)	3	0	0	0	0

Going (Turf): Sf: 0-1 GS: 0-0 Gd: 0-2 GF: 0-0 Fm: 0-0
Distance: 5f/6f: 0-0 7f-8f: 0-3 9f-13f: 0-0 14f+: 0-0
Track : LH: 0-2 RH: 0-0 Tight: 0-2 Gall: 0-0
Aids: Bl: 0-0 Vi: 0-0 Tstrap: 0-0
Best Rating: 56 10/01 Rdcr 7f good

Liquorice

90 48

3-y-o b f Robellino (USA)-Missed Blessing (So Blessed)

W J Haggas W J Haggas

Placings:5 **(3853)**

2001: 7^{5}G

	Starts	1st	2nd	3rd	Win & Pl
Career Total (Turf)	1	0	0	0	0

Going (Turf): Sf: 0-0 GS: 0-0 Gd: 0-1 GF: 0-0 Fm: 0-0
Distance: 5f/6f: 0-0 7f-8f: 0-1 9f-13f: 0-0 14f+: 0-0
Track : LH: 0-0 RH: 0-0 Tight: 0-0 Gall: 0-0
Aids: Bl: 0-0 Vi: 0-0 Tstrap: 0-1
Best Rating: 48 8/01 Asct 7f good

Lisa's Looney

85(73) (16)51

2-y-o b f Bahamian Bounty-Starfida (Soviet Star (USA))

Mrs C A Dunnett Mrs Christine Dunnett

Placings:000000 **(5410)**

2001: 5^{0}G, 5^{0}GS, 6^{0}GF, 6^{0}GF, 7^{0}GS, 7^{0}SD

	Starts	1st	2nd	3rd	Win & Pl
Career Total (Turf)	5	0	0	0	
Career Total (AW)	1	0	0	0	

Going (Turf): Sf: 0-0 GS: 0-2 Gd: 0-1 GF: 0-2 Fm: 0-0
Distance: 5f/6f: 0-3 7f-8f: 0-3 9f-13f: 0-0 14f+: 0-0
Track : LH: 0-1 RH: 0-0 Tight: 0-0 Gall: 0-0
Aids: Bl: 0-0 Vi: 0-0 Tstrap: 0-0
Best Rating: 51 9/01 Wwck 6f21y gd-fm

Moderate form to date but has been slowly away on most of her starts.

Lishtar (IRE)

90 78

2-y-o b c Mtoto-Lilissa (IRE) (Doyoun)

Sir Michael Stoute H H Aga Khan

Placings:3 **(5684)**

2001: 8^{3}S

	Starts	1st	2nd	3rd	Win & Pl
Career Total (Turf)	1	0	0	1	720

Going (Turf): Sf: 0-1 GS: 0-0 Gd: 0-0 GF: 0-0 Fm: 0-0
Distance: 5f/6f: 0-0 7f-8f: 0-1 9f-13f: 0-0 14f+: 0-0
Track : LH: 0-0 RH: 0-0 Tight: 0-0 Gall: 0-0
Aids: Bl: 0-0 Vi: 0-0 Tstrap: 0-0
Best Rating: 78 11/01 Donc 1m soft

He is closely related to Irish nine-furlong Listed winner Livadiya and is a half-brother to decent middle-distance winner Lidakiya. Despite being very green going to post for his debut, he showed promise in the race itself.

Lisianski (IRE)

103 75

3-y-o b g Fairy King (USA)-Tough Lady (Bay Express)

I A Balding Exors Of The Late Robert Hitchins

Placings:0000311100 **(4986)**

2001: 8^{0}GS, 8^{0}GF, 7^{0}GF, 6^{0}GF, 5^{3}GF, 5^{1}G, 5^{1}G, 5^{1}GF, 5^{0}GS, 6^{0}G

	Starts	1st	2nd	3rd	Win & Pl
Career Total (Turf)	10	3	0	1	11039

75	9/01	Sals	5f	E(0-80)H	G-F	£3031
71	8/01	Gdwd	5f	D(0-80)H	GD	£4543
64	8/01	Folk	5f	E(0-70)H	GD	£3010

Total win prize-money £10585

Going (Turf): Sf: 0-0 GS: 0-2 **Gd: 2-3** GF: 1-5 Fm: 0-0
Distance: **5f/6f: 3-7** 7f-8f: 0-2 9f-13f: 0-1 14f+: 0-0
Track : LH: 0-1 RH: 0-2 Tight: 0-1 Gall: 0-0
Aids: Bl: 0-0 **Vi: 3-5** Tstrap: 0-0
Best Rating: 75 9/01 Sals 5f gd-fm

Improved for application of a visor and notched up a hat-trick over the minimum trip between August and September 2001. Equally at home racing in front or held up. Acts on fast ground.

Lissome (USA)

40

2-y-o b f Lear Fan (USA)-Miss Otis (USA) (One For All (USA))
I A Balding Blue Ridge Stables

Placings:0 **(3680)**
2001: 6^{0}G

	Starts	1st	2nd	3rd	Win & Pl
Career Total (Turf)	1	0	0	0	

Going (Turf): Sf: 0-0 GS: 0-0 Gd: 0-1 GF: 0-0 Fm: 0-0
Distance: 5f/6f: 0-1 7f-8f: 0-0 9f-13f: 0-0 14f+: 0-0
Track : LH: 0-0 RH: 0-0 Tight: 0-0 Gall: 0-0
Aids: Bl: 0-0 Vi: 0-0 Tstrap: 0-0
Best Rating: 40 8/01 Wind 6f good

Litany

76 **38**

2-y-o b f Colonel Collins (USA)-Hymn Book (IRE) (Darshaan)
J G Smyth-Osbourne J H Henderson

Placings:0000 **(3804)**
2001: 6^{0}GF, 7^{0}GF, 7^{0}G, 6^{0}GF

	Starts	1st	2nd	3rd	Win & Pl
Career Total (Turf)	4	0	0	0	

Going (Turf): Sf: 0-0 GS: 0-0 Gd: 0-1 GF: 0-3 Fm: 0-0
Distance: 5f/6f: 0-1 7f-8f: 0-3 9f-13f: 0-0 14f+: 0-0
Track : LH: 0-1 RH: 0-1 Tight: 0-1 Gall: 0-0
Aids: Bl: 0-0 Vi: 0-1 Tstrap: 0-0
Best Rating: 38 6/01 Folk 6f189y gd-fm

Literary Society (USA)

99 **85d**

8-y-o ch h Runaway Groom (CAN)-Dancing Gull (USA) (Northern Dancer)
J A R Toller Lady Celina Carter

Placings:63/0031210024/25103102/115010/003U3300/0004-50000 **(5138)**
2001: 6^{5}G, 6^{0}GF, 5^{0}GF, 6^{0}GF, 6^{0}G

	Starts	1st	2nd	3rd	Win & Pl
Career Total (Turf)	43	7	4	6	69274

94	8/98	York	6f	C(0-100)H	G-F	£17090
91	6/98	Yarm	6f3y	C(0-90)	GD	£7513
86	5/98	NmkR	5f	C(0-100)H	G-F	£5796
77	7/97	Newb	6f8y	C(0-90)H	G-F	£5735
74	5/97	NmkR	5f	C(0-100)H	G-F	£5628
67	8/96	Thsk	5f	D(0-80)H	GD	£4027
61	7/96	Brig	5f59y	F	FRM	£2381

Total win prize-money £48172

Going (Turf): Sf: 0-1 GS: 0-1 Gd: 2-17 **GF: 4-21** Fm: 1-3
Distance: **5f/6f: 5-41** 7f-8f: 2-2 9f-13f: 0-0 14f+: 0-0
Track : **LH: 1-3** RH: 0-2 Tight: 0-1 Gall: 0-3
Aids: Bl: 0-0 Vi: 0-0 Tstrap: 0-0
Best Rating: 85 5/01 NmkR 6f good

Formerly a useful sprint-handicapper, but despite some fair efforts as he drops down the handicap he has not won since 1998 and is not quite the horse he was. Suited by six furlongs and fast ground.

Lithgow Flash (IRE)

104(96) (75)**78**

3-y-o b f Mark Of Esteem (IRE)-Innocence (Unfuwain (USA))
J H M Gosden P G & J M Maher

Placings:663523 **(5394)**
2001: 10^{6}GF, 10^{6}GF, 11^{3}G, 11^{5}GF, 11^{2}F, 12^{3}SD

	Starts	1st	2nd	3rd	Win & Pl
Career Total (Turf)	5	0	1	1	2411
Career Total (AW)	1	0	0	1	535

Going (Turf): Sf: 0-0 GS: 0-0 Gd: 0-1 GF: 0-3 Fm: 0-1
Distance: 5f/6f: 0-0 7f-8f: 0-0 9f-13f: 0-6 14f+: 0-0
Track : LH: 0-4 RH: 0-1 Tight: 0-3 Gall: 0-2
Aids: Bl: 0-0 Vi: 0-0 Tstrap: 0-0
Best Rating: 78 8/01 Bath 1m3f144y gd-fm

Lightly-raced maiden, stays 12 furlongs, progressing with racing.

Little Acorn

62(96) (65)

7-y-o b g Unfuwain (USA)-Plaything (High Top)
D Moffatt John C Naylor

Placings:05/2112322O/300000102/6-0 **(5010)**
2001: 14^{0}HY

	Starts	1st	2nd	3rd	Win & Pl
Career Total (Turf)	18	3	4	2	21673
Career Total (AW)	3	0	1	0	1030

82	9/98	Gdwd	2m	C(0-90)H	G-S	£7448
76	4/97	Carl	1m4f	D(0-75)H	GD	£3566
66	3/97	Catt	1m3f214y	D(0-75)H	GD	£3457

Total win prize-money £14473

Going (Turf): Sf: 0-5 GS: 1-3 **Gd: 2-7** GF: 0-3 Fm: 0-0
Distance: 5f/6f: 0-0 7f-8f: 0-1 **9f-13f: 2-7** 14f+: 1-13
Track : LH: 1-13 **RH: 2-8 Tight: 2-7** Gall: 0-6
Aids: Bl: 0-1 Vi: 0-0 Tstrap: 0-0

A fair stayer a couple of season ago, but has been lightly raced of late and has obviously had problems.

Little Amin

112 **87**

5-y-o b g Unfuwain (USA)-Ghassanah (Pas De Seul)
K R Burke Asterlane Ltd

Placings:30/120344160/00016326650-0112530 **(4192)**
2001: 7^{0}G, 8^{1}GF, 8^{1}GF, 9^{2}GF, 10^{5}GF, 8^{3}G, 7^{0}G

	Starts	1st	2nd	3rd	Win & Pl
Career Total (Turf)	29	5	3	4	67254

86	6/01	Epsm	1m114y	B(0-105)H	G-F	£29000
80	5/01	Gdwd	1m	D(0-80)H	G-F	£6467
75	6/00	Bevl	1m100y	D(0-80)H	G-S	£4576
78	8/99	Hayd	1m3f200y	D(0-85)H	G-S	£3954
73	3/99	Newc	7f	D	G-S	£3615

Total win prize-money £47614

Going (Turf): Sf: 0-4 **GS: 3-4** Gd: 0-11 GF: 2-10 Fm: 0-0
Distance: 5f/6f: 0-2 7f-8f: 2-8 **9f-13f: 3-19** 14f+: 0-0
Track : LH: 2-13 RH: 2-11 **Tight: 1-10** Gall: 0-5
Aids: Bl: 0-0 Vi: 0-0 Tstrap: 0-0
Best Rating: 87 8/01 Gdwd 1m good

A decent handicapper, best at around a mile but stays 12 furlongs. He has shown with victories at Goodwood and Epsom in 2001 that he acts on a fast surface. Held off higher marks.

Little Bluebell

48

2-y-o ch f Greensmith-Bluebell Copse (Formidable (USA))
W G M Turner Major R P Thorman

Placings:000 **(5458)**
2001: 5^{0}S, 5^{0}HY, 5^{0}G

	Starts	1st	2nd	3rd	Win & Pl
Career Total (Turf)	3	0	0	0	

Going (Turf): Sf: 0-2 GS: 0-0 Gd: 0-1 GF: 0-0 Fm: 0-0
Distance: 5f/6f: 0-3 7f-8f: 0-0 9f-13f: 0-0 14f+: 0-0
Track : LH: 0-2 RH: 0-0 Tight: 0-0 Gall: 0-1
Aids: Bl: 0-0 Vi: 0-0 Tstrap: 0-0

Little Brave

(100) (79)**64**

6-y-o b g Kahyasi-Littlemisstrouble (USA) (My Gallant (USA))
J M P Eustace Guy And James Carstairs

Placings:50/10066322 4/06016110024/4605143336-52 **(0321)**
2001: 16^{5}SW, 16^{2}SD

	Starts	1st	2nd	3rd	Win & Pl
Career Total (Turf)	28	3	2	4	20764
Career Total (AW)	6	2	2	0	8383

67	7/00	Ling	2m	E(0-70)H	G-F	£2922
60	9/99	Yarm	2m2f51y	C(0-95)H	SFT	£6897
57	8/99	Wwck	1m7f181y	D(0-80)H	GD	£4199
78	7/99	Ling	2m	E(0-70)	STD	£3172
68	3/98	Sthl	1m	D	STD	£3436

Total win prize-money £20629

Going (Turf): Sf: 1-4 GS: 0-4 **Gd: 1-6 GF: 1-12** Fm: 0-2
Distance: 5f/6f: 0-0 7f-8f: 1-3 9f-13f: 0-4 **14f+: 4-27**
Track : **LH: 5-22** RH: 0-9 **Tight: 3-13** Gall: 0-5
Aids: Bl: 0-0 Vi: 0-0 Tstrap: 0-0
Best Rating: 72 2/01 Wolv 2m46y stand

Little Callian

88(95) (48)**35**

3-y-o ch f Charmer-Eucharis (Tickled Pink)
T M Jones Richard L Page

Placings:60436250-252300000 **(4950)**
2001: 5^{2}SW, 5^{5}SW, 5^{2}SD, 5^{3}S, 5^{0}GS, 5^{0}GS, 5^{0}GF, 5^{0}GF, 5^{0}G

	Starts	1st	2nd	3rd	Win & Pl
Career Total (Turf)	14	0	1	2	2115
Career Total (AW)	3	0	2	0	1632

Going (Turf): Sf: 0-1 GS: 0-2 Gd: 0-5 GF: 0-6 Fm: 0-0
Distance: 5f/6f: 0-16 7f-8f: 0-1 9f-13f: 0-0 14f+: 0-0
Track : LH: 0-6 RH: 0-3 Tight: 0-4 Gall: 0-4
Aids: Bl: 0-0 Vi: 0-1 Tstrap: 0-0
Best Rating: 60 4/01 Nott 5f13y soft

Little Chapel (IRE)

78 **13**

5-y-o b m College Chapel-Istaraka (IRE) (Darshaan)
G H Yardley Philip Jones

Placings:023000/40050/40000-00 **(4046)**
2001: 12^{0}G, 10^{0}HY

	Starts	1st	2nd	3rd	Win & Pl
Career Total (Turf)	18	0	1	1	9146

Going (Turf): Sf: 0-4 GS: 0-2 Gd: 0-6 GF: 0-5 Fm: 0-1
Distance: 5f/6f: 0-7 7f-8f: 0-7 9f-13f: 0-4 14f+: 0-0

Track : LH: 0-6 RH: 0-1 Tight: 0-2 Gall: 0-1
Aids: Bl: 0-0 Vi: 0-0 Tstrap: 0-0
Best Rating: 60 4/01 Nott 5f13y soft

Little Cinnamon

79 **19**

5-y-o ch h Timeless Times (USA)-Belltina (Belfort (FR))
J Balding Ms Kim Jansen

Placings:50640/00006/000 **(4619)**
2001: 5^{0}GF, 5^{0}G, 5^{0}F

	Starts	1st	2nd	3rd	Win & Pl
Career Total (Turf)	13	0	0	0	255

Going (Turf): Sf: 0-1 GS: 0-1 Gd: 0-3 GF: 0-5 Fm: 0-3
Distance: 5f/6f: 0-11 7f-8f: 0-2 9f-13f: 0-0 14f+: 0-0
Track : LH: 0-2 RH: 0-3 Tight: 0-1 Gall: 0-3
Aids: Bl: 0-1 Vi: 0-0 Tstrap: 0-0
Best Rating: 19 8/01 Ripn 5f good

Little Daisy

43

3-y-o ch f Factual (USA)-Twice In Bundoran (IRE) (Bold Arrangement)
A B Mulholland Ms Kim Jansen

Placings:0 **(5281)**
2001: 7^{0}S

	Starts	1st	2nd	3rd	Win & Pl
Career Total (Turf)	1	0	0	0	

Going (Turf): Sf: 0-1 GS: 0-0 Gd: 0-0 GF: 0-0 Fm: 0-0
Distance: 5f/6f: 0-0 7f-8f: 0-1 9f-13f: 0-0 14f+: 0-0
Track : LH: 0-0 RH: 0-0 Tight: 0-0 Gall: 0-0
Aids: Bl: 0-0 Vi: 0-0 Tstrap: 0-0

Little Docker (IRE)

95 **41**

4-y-o b g Vettori (IRE)-Fair Maid Of Kent (USA) (Diesis)
T D Easterby C H Stevens

Placings:4/3542-00 **(5151)**
2001: 15^{0}S, 10^{0}G

	Starts	1st	2nd	3rd	Win & Pl
Career Total (Turf)	7	0	1	1	2119

Going (Turf): Sf: 0-1 GS: 0-1 Gd: 0-2 GF: 0-2 Fm: 0-1
Distance: 5f/6f: 0-0 7f-8f: 0-1 9f-13f: 0-4 14f+: 0-2
Track : LH: 0-6 RH: 0-1 Tight: 0-4 Gall: 0-2
Aids: Bl: 0-0 Vi: 0-0 Tstrap: 0-0
Best Rating: 41 10/01 Rdcr 1m2f good

Little Edward

108 **77+**

3-y-o gr g King's Signet (USA)-Cedar Lady (Telsmoss)
B G Powell J W Mursell

Placings:21 **(3723)**
2001: 6^{2}GF, 5^{1}GS

	Starts	1st	2nd	3rd	Win & Pl
Career Total (Turf)	2	1	1	0	5485

77 8/01 Sand 5f6y D G-S £4329
Total win prize-money £4329

Going (Turf): Sf: 0-0 **GS: 1-1** Gd: 0-0 GF: 0-1 Fm: 0-0
Distance: 5f/6f: 1-2 7f-8f: 0-0 9f-13f: 0-0 14f+: 0-0
Track : LH: 0-0 RH: 0-0 Tight: 0-0 Gall: 0-0
Aids: Bl: 0-0 Vi: 0-0 Tstrap: 0-0
Best Rating: 77 8/01 Sand 5f6y gd-sft

A Sandown maiden winner over five furlongs, he has plenty of speed but should stay further in time.

Little Emma

81 **22**

3-y-o b f Safawan-Little Vixen (Aragon)
C W Fairhurst Twinacre Nurseries Ltd

Placings:0000 **(3255)**
2001: 6^{0}F, 6^{0}GF, 8^{0}F, 8^{0}GF

	Starts	1st	2nd	3rd	Win & Pl
Career Total (Turf)	4	0	0	0	

Going (Turf): Sf: 0-0 GS: 0-0 Gd: 0-0 GF: 0-2 Fm: 0-2
Distance: 5f/6f: 0-2 7f-8f: 0-2 9f-13f: 0-0 14f+: 0-0
Track : LH: 0-2 RH: 0-0 Tight: 0-0 Gall: 0-1
Aids: Bl: 0-0 Vi: 0-0 Tstrap: 0-0
Best Rating: 22 5/01 Pont 6f firm

Little Fox (IRE)

101 (57)**48**

6-y-o br m Persian Bold-Dance Land (IRE) (Nordance (USA))
J J Bridger C Mussell

Placings:40240/063264220 **(5471)**
2001: 11^{0}GS, 7^{6}F, 9^{3}F, 10^{2}F, 14^{6}GF, 9^{4}GF, 10^{2}GF, 8^{2}G, 11^{0}S

	Starts	1st	2nd	3rd	Win & Pl
Career Total (Turf)	11	0	3	1	3721
Career Total (AW)	3	0	1	0	772

Going (Turf): Sf: 0-1 GS: 0-1 Gd: 0-1 GF: 0-4 Fm: 0-4
Distance: 5f/6f: 0-0 7f-8f: 0-1 9f-13f: 0-11 14f+: 0-2
Track : LH: 0-12 RH: 0-1 Tight: 0-9 Gall: 0-0
Aids: Bl: 0-0 Vi: 0-0 Tstrap: 0-0
Best Rating: 48 10/01 Bath 1m5y good

Little John

104 **55**

5-y-o b g Warrshan (USA)-Silver Venture (USA) (Silver Hawk (USA))
Miss L A Perratt T P Finch

Placings:444/425503446/3432524235-00665052324422223332223 **(4164)**
2001: 12^{0}GS, 9^{0}S, 13^{6}S, 12^{6}GS, 9^{5}GS, 8^{0}GF, 12^{5}F, 11^{2}G, 13^{3}GF, 12^{2}GF, 12^{4}GF, 14^{4}G, 14^{2}G, 13^{2}G, 16^{2}F, 11^{2}GF, 12^{3}G, 13^{3}G, 14^{3}GF, 16^{2}F, 12^{2}F, 14^{2}G, 16^{3}GF

	Starts	1st	2nd	3rd	Win & Pl
Career Total (Turf)	45	0	13	9	20902

Going (Turf): Sf: 0-6 GS: 0-8 Gd: 0-8 GF: 0-18 Fm: 0-5
Distance: 5f/6f: 0-0 7f-8f: 0-5 9f-13f: 0-30 14f+: 0-10
Track : LH: 0-16 RH: 0-27 Tight: 0-31 Gall: 0-4
Aids: Bl: 0-2 Vi: 0-4 Tstrap: 0-0
Best Rating: 55 8/01 Muss 2m gd-fm

Seems destined to be the bridesmaid and is not one to trust. Stays two miles and acts on fast ground.

Little Kenny

8-y-o b m Warning-Tarvie (Swing Easy (USA))
R J Price Vizard Racing

Placings:60050/03544363/0 **(0247)**
2001: 16^{0}SD

	Starts	1st	2nd	3rd	Win & Pl
Career Total (Turf)	12	0	0	3	1324
Career Total (AW)	2	0	0	0	0

Going (Turf): Sf: 0-0 GS: 0-1 Gd: 0-3 GF: 0-7 Fm: 0-1
Distance: 5f/6f: 0-2 7f-8f: 0-5 9f-13f: 0-6 14f+: 0-1
Track : LH: 0-6 RH: 0-4 Tight: 0-5 Gall: 0-1
Aids: Bl: 0-1 Vi: 0-6 Tstrap: 0-0

Little Les

85 **34**

5-y-o b g Jumbo Hirt (USA)-Hand On Heart (IRE) (Taufan (USA))
F P Murtagh (J L Eyre 1/8) L Irving

Placings:606406-005 **(3568)**
2001: 7^{0}G, 6^{0}GF, 9^{5}G

	Starts	1st	2nd	3rd	Win & Pl
Career Total (Turf)	9	0	0	0	263

Going (Turf): Sf: 0-1 GS: 0-0 Gd: 0-3 GF: 0-4 Fm: 0-1
Distance: 5f/6f: 0-1 7f-8f: 0-5 9f-13f: 0-3 14f+: 0-0
Track : LH: 0-3 RH: 0-2 Tight: 0-2 Gall: 0-0
Aids: Bl: 0-0 Vi: 0-0 Tstrap: 0-0
Best Rating: 34 7/01 Haml 6f5y gd-fm

Little Nobby

81(85) (54)**59**

2-y-o b g Makbul-Simply Style (Bairn (USA))
R Hollinshead Miss B Connop

Placings:500036 **(5614)**
2001: 6^{5}F, 5^{0}G, 6^{0}GS, 6^{0}SD, 7^{3}HY, 6^{6}SD

	Starts	1st	2nd	3rd	Win & Pl
Career Total (Turf)	4	0	0	1	382
Career Total (AW)	2	0	0	0	0

Going (Turf): Sf: 0-1 GS: 0-1 Gd: 0-1 GF: 0-0 Fm: 0-1
Distance: 5f/6f: 0-5 7f-8f: 0-1 9f-13f: 0-0 14f+: 0-0
Track : LH: 0-3 RH: 0-0 Tight: 0-2 Gall: 0-0
Aids: Bl: 0-0 Vi: 0-0 Tstrap: 0-0
Best Rating: 59 6/01 Donc 6f firm

Little Oak (IRE)

85 **36**

3-y-o b f Tagula (IRE)-Blue Goose (Belmez (USA))
G A Swinbank J A Kavanagh

Placings:500 **(4368)**
2001: 8^{5}GS, 7^{0}G, 5^{0}GF

	Starts	1st	2nd	3rd	Win & Pl
Career Total (Turf)	3	0	0	0	0

Going (Turf): Sf: 0-0 GS: 0-1 Gd: 0-1 GF: 0-1 Fm: 0-0
Distance: 5f/6f: 0-1 7f-8f: 0-2 9f-13f: 0-0 14f+: 0-0
Track : LH: 0-2 RH: 0-0 Tight: 0-1 Gall: 0-0
Aids: Bl: 0-0 Vi: 0-0 Tstrap: 0-0
Best Rating: 36 8/01 Catt 5f212y gd-fm

Little Pearl (IRE)

99(92) (34)**52**

3-y-o b f Bigstone (IRE)-Congress Lady (General Assembly (USA))
T D Easterby T H Bennett

Placings:5500440110 **(3637)**
2001: 7^{5}SD, 8^{5}SD, 8^{0}SD, 8^{0}SD, 10^{4}S, 12^{4}SD, 16^{0}F, 12^{1}GF, 12^{1}GF, 12^{0}GS

	Starts	1st	2nd	3rd	Win & Pl
Career Total (Turf)	5	2	0	0	5520
Career Total (AW)	5	0	0	0	0

52 7/01 Muss 1m4f F(0-65)H G-F £2786
43 7/01 Pont 1m4f8y F(0-60)H G-F £2733
Total win prize-money £5520

Going (Turf): Sf: 0-1 GS: 0-1 Gd: 0-0 **GF: 2-2** Fm: 0-1
Distance: 5f/6f: 0-0 7f-8f: 0-4 **9f-13f: 2-5** 14f+: 0-1
Track : LH: 1-7 RH: 0-2 Tight: 0-2 Gall: 0-1
Aids: Bl: 0-0 Vi: 0-0 Tstrap: 0-0
Best Rating: 52 7/01 Muss 1m4f gd-fm

Landed a weak seller at Pontefract in July, and followed up in a Musselburgh handicap. Well handicapped, and on the upgrade.

Little Pippin

101 **79**

5-y-o ch m Rudimentary (USA)-Accuracy (Gunner B)
G B Balding Miss B Swire

Placings:0603/30431140/40-44300 **(5010)**
2001: 12^{4}S, 14^{4}GS, 12^{3}GF, 12^{0}G, 14^{0}HY

	Starts	1st	2nd	3rd	Win & Pl
Career Total (Turf)	19	2	0	4	13533

80 8/99 Kemp 1m4f D(0-85)H SFT £5129
75 8/99 Sals 1m4f E(0-75)H G-S £2883
Total win prize-money £8013

Going (Turf): Sf: 1-7 GS: 1-6 Gd: 0-3 GF: 0-3 Fm: 0-0
Distance: 5f/6f: 0-1 7f-8f: 0-3 **9f-13f: 2-11** 14f+: 0-4
Track : LH: 0-7 **RH: 2-8 Tight: 1-4** Gall: 0-3
Aids: Bl: 0-0 Vi: 0-0 Tstrap: 0-1
Best Rating: 79 5/01 Sals 1m6f15y gd-sft

Took time in getting off the mark, but won two handicaps over a mile and a half in August 1999. Has not won since, but has run well and is very effective on soft ground.

Little Pixie (USA)

92 **44**

3-y-o ch f Woodman (USA)-Tryarra (IRE) (Persian Heights)
N Tinkler Mr James Marshall & Mrs Susan Marshall

Placings:0-6000100050 **(4734)**
2001: 10^{6}S, 10^{0}S, 8^{0}F, 8^{0}GF, 7^{1}G, 7^{0}GF, 7^{0}GS, 7^{0}GS, 7^{5}GF, 8^{0}F

	Starts	1st	2nd	3rd	Win & Pl
Career Total (Turf)	11	1	0	0	3290

44 6/01 Hayd 7f30y E(0-70)H GD £3290
Total win prize-money £3290

Going (Turf): Sf: 0-3 GS: 0-2 **Gd: 1-1** GF: 0-3 Fm: 0-2
Distance: 5f/6f: 0-0 **7f-8f: 1-8** 9f-13f: 0-3 14f+: 0-0
Track : **LH: 1-6** RH: 0-2 Tight: 0-2 Gall: 0-3
Aids: Bl: 0-0 Vi: 0-0 Tstrap: 0-0
Best Rating: 44 8/01 Muss 7f30y gd-fm

Little Robs' Girl

91 **55**

2-y-o ch f Cosmonaut-David James' Girl (Faustus (USA))
A Bailey One In Ten Racing Club

Placings:60 **(5029)**
2001: 5^{6}HY, 5^{0}GF

	Starts	1st	2nd	3rd	Win & Pl
Career Total (Turf)	2	0	0	0	0

Going (Turf): Sf: 0-1 GS: 0-0 Gd: 0-0 GF: 0-1 Fm: 0-0
Distance: 5f/6f: 0-2 7f-8f: 0-0 9f-13f: 0-0 14f+: 0-0
Track : LH: 0-0 RH: 0-0 Tight: 0-0 Gall: 0-0
Aids: Bl: 0-0 Vi: 0-0 Tstrap: 0-0
Best Rating: 55 9/01 Hayd 5f heavy

Little Rock

117 **119**

5-y-o b h Warning-Much Too Risky (Bustino)
Sir Michael Stoute J M Greetham

Placings:1/12401/161345-42046 **(5247a)**
2001: 10^{4}HO, 12^{2}GS, 12^{0}S, 12^{4}G, 12^{6}HO, 10^{3}HY

	Starts	1st	2nd	3rd	Win & Pl
Career Total (Turf)	17	5	2	1	131513

117 7/00 NmkJ 1m4f A G-S £34800
112 4/00 Sand 1m2f7y A HVY £24000
112 10/99 NmkJ 1m2f A G-S £13894
91 4/99 Sand 1m14y C G-S £5409
86 10/98 Leic 7f9y D SFT £3301
Total win prize-money £81405

Going (Turf): Sf: 2-3 **GS: 3-7** Gd: 0-3 GF: 0-2 Fm: 0-0
Distance: 5f/6f: 0-0 7f-8f: 1-2 **9f-13f: 4-14** 14f+: 0-1
Track : LH: 0-1 **RH: 4-12** Tight: 0-1 **Gall: 2-5**
Aids: Bl: 0-0 Vi: 0-0 Tstrap: 0-0
Best Rating: 119 10/01 Lonc 1m4f holding

A very smart colt, he reached new heights in the first half of last season with victories in the Group Three Gordon Richards Stakes at Sandown and Group Two Princess Of Wales' Stakes at Newmarket. Ran well again in the Princess of Wales' Stakes this season when runner-up in a stronger renewal. Genuine efforts in the Prix Foy and Arc in the autumn. Just below the very best middle-distance performers, his victories have come with cut in the ground.

Little Task

90(90) (62)**28**

3-y-o b g Environment Friend-Lucky Thing (Green Desert (USA))
J S Wainwright (H A McWilliams 27/7) Keith Jackson

Placings:302426060155-0060000 **(4450)**
2001: 10^{0}GF, 10^{0}GF, 12^{6}F, 12^{0}G, 8^{0}F, 7^{0}GF, 8^{0}GF

	Starts	1st	2nd	3rd	Win & Pl
Career Total (Turf)	16	0	2	1	3091
Career Total (AW)	3	1	0	0	1967

62 10/00 Sthl 7f G STD £1967
Total win prize-money £1967

Going (Turf): Sf: 0-2 GS: 0-0 Gd: 0-3 GF: 0-8 Fm: 0-3
Distance: 5f/6f: 0-3 **7f-8f: 1-10** 9f-13f: 0-6 14f+: 0-0
Track : **LH: 1-14** RH: 0-2 Tight: 0-4 Gall: 0-6
Aids: **Bl: 1-6** Vi: 0-0 Tstrap: 0-0
Best Rating: 28 6/01 Pont 1m2f6y gd-fm

Little Tobias (IRE)

96 **57**

2-y-o ch g Millkom-Barbara Frietchie (IRE) (Try My Best (USA))
Andrew Turnell Mrs Claire Hollowood

Placings:0550 **(5169)**
2001: 5^{0}GF, 6^{5}GF, 6^{5}F, 6^{0}GS

	Starts	1st	2nd	3rd	Win & Pl
Career Total (Turf)	4	0	0	0	0

Going (Turf): Sf: 0-0 GS: 0-1 Gd: 0-0 GF: 0-2 Fm: 0-1
Distance: 5f/6f: 0-3 7f-8f: 0-1 9f-13f: 0-0 14f+: 0-0
Track : LH: 0-1 RH: 0-0 Tight: 0-0 Gall: 0-0
Aids: Bl: 0-0 Vi: 0-0 Tstrap: 0-0
Best Rating: 57 9/01 Newc 6f firm

Little Tumbler (IRE)

102 **53**

6-y-o b m Cyrano De Bergerac-Glass Minnow (IRE) (Alzao (USA))
S Woodman Mrs W Edgar

Placings:224500/1440000/4051000/565022-00224015 **(4704)**
2001: 9^{0}F, 9^{0}GF, 10^{2}F, 9^{2}GF, 7^{4}G, 9^{0}GF, 9^{1}GF, 8^{5}G

	Starts	1st	2nd	3rd	Win & Pl
Career Total (Turf)	33	3	6	0	13694
Career Total (AW)	1	0	0	0	

53 9/01 Brig 1m1f209yE(0-70)H G-F £2947
49 8/99 Brig 1m1f209yF(0-60)H FRM £3256
61 5/98 Ling 6f F(0-65)H G-F £2070
Total win prize-money £8273

Going (Turf): Sf: 0-1 GS: 0-0 Gd: 0-8 **GF: 2-18** Fm: 1-6
Distance: 5f/6f: 1-7 7f-8f: 0-9 **9f-13f: 2-18** 14f+: 0-0
Track : **LH: 2-15** RH: 0-10 Tight: 0-8 Gall: 0-1
Aids: Bl: 0-0 Vi: 0-0 Tstrap: 0-0
Best Rating: 53 9/01 Brig 1m1f209y gd-fm

Deserved her win at Brighton in September, having run a string of good races. Suited by ten furlongs and fast ground.

Little Woodstock (IRE)

(89) (68)**56**

2-y-o ch g Woodborough (USA)-Penultimate Cress (IRE) (My Generation)
D J S Cosgrove The Cosgrove Group

Placings:034203 **(4878)**
2001: 5^{0}GS, 5^{3}GF, 5^{4}GF, 5^{2}GF, 5^{0}F, 7^{3}SD

	Starts	1st	2nd	3rd	Win & Pl
Career Total (Turf)	5	0	1	1	1391
Career Total (AW)	1	0	0	1	285

Going (Turf): Sf: 0-0 GS: 0-1 Gd: 0-0 GF: 0-3 Fm: 0-1
Distance: 5f/6f: 0-5 7f-8f: 0-1 9f-13f: 0-0 14f+: 0-0
Track : LH: 0-6 RH: 0-0 Tight: 0-1 Gall: 0-0
Aids: Bl: 0-3 Vi: 0-0 Tstrap: 0-0
Best Rating: 68 9/01 Wolv 7f stand

Littleton Boreas (USA)

76 **53**

2-y-o b/br c Foxhound (USA)-Susita Song (USA) (Seattle Song (USA))
R J White Littleton Manor Racing

Placings:00 **(4158)**
2001: 6^{0}GS, 7^{0}GF

	Starts	1st	2nd	3rd	Win & Pl
Career Total (Turf)	2	0	0	0	

Going (Turf): Sf: 0-0 GS: 0-1 Gd: 0-0 GF: 0-1 Fm: 0-0
Distance: 5f/6f: 0-1 7f-8f: 0-1 9f-13f: 0-0 14f+: 0-0
Track : LH: 0-0 RH: 0-0 Tight: 0-0 Gall: 0-0
Aids: Bl: 0-0 Vi: 0-0 Tstrap: 0-0
Best Rating: 53 8/01 Hayd 6f gd-sft

Littleton Tzar (IRE)

96(95) (73)**73**

2-y-o b c Inzar (USA)-Solo Symphony (IRE) (Fayruz)
R J White Littleton Manor Racing

Placings:0405345 **(5588)**
2001: 6^{0}GF, 6^{4}G, 6^{0}G, 5^{5}F, 5^{3}S, 6^{4}SD, 5^{5}GS

	Starts	1st	2nd	3rd	Win & Pl
Career Total (Turf)	6	0	0	1	558
Career Total (AW)	1	0	0	0	282

Going (Turf): Sf: 0-1 GS: 0-1 Gd: 0-2 GF: 0-1 Fm: 0-1
Distance: 5f/6f: 0-7 7f-8f: 0-0 9f-13f: 0-0 14f+: 0-0
Track : LH: 0-3 RH: 0-0 Tight: 0-0 Gall: 0-0
Aids: Bl: 0-0 Vi: 0-0 Tstrap: 0-0
Best Rating: 73 11/01 Brig 5f213y gd-sft

Some ability in maiden and nursery company, but looks one-paced.

Littleton Zeus (IRE)

86 **55**

2-y-o ch g Woodborough (USA)-La Fandango (IRE) (Taufan (USA))
R J White Littleton Manor Racing

Placings:000 **(5080)**
2001: 6^{0}GF, 6^{0}GF, 6^{0}S

	Starts	1st	2nd	3rd	Win & Pl
Career Total (Turf)	3	0	0	0	

Going (Turf): Sf: 0-1 GS: 0-0 Gd: 0-0 GF: 0-2 Fm: 0-0
Distance: 5f/6f: 0-1 7f-8f: 0-2 9f-13f: 0-0 14f+: 0-0
Track : LH: 0-1 RH: 0-0 Tight: 0-0 Gall: 0-0
Aids: Bl: 0-0 Vi: 0-0 Tstrap: 0-0
Best Rating: 55 10/01 Brig 6f209y soft

Lituus (USA)

65
8-y-o gr g El Gran Senor (USA)-Liturgism (USA) (Native Charger)
Miss Gay Kelleway (S Seemar 8/3) E Oertel

Placings:0/500544/**P5**0000 **(4305)**
2001: 10^{P}FT, 10^{5}FT, 8^{0}F, 7^{0}FT, 8^{0}GS, 12^{0}GF

	Starts	1st	2nd	3rd	Win & Pl
Career Total (Turf)	10	0	0	0	556
Career Total (AW)	3	0	0	0	175

Going (Turf): Sf: 0-0 GS: 0-1 Gd: 0-1 GF: 0-6 Fm: 0-2
Distance: 5f/6f: 0-0 7f-8f: 0-6 9f-13f: 0-7 14f+: 0-0
Track : LH: 0-1 RH: 0-4 Tight: 0-3 Gall: 0-1
Aids: Bl: 0-1 Vi: 0-1 Tstrap: 0-1

Largely disappointing maiden.

Litzinsky

105 **73**
3-y-o b g Muhtarram (USA)-Boulevard Girl (Nicholas Bill)
C B B Booth Mrs A M Lyons

Placings:0-24505414003 **(5692)**
2001: 10^{2}HY, 11^{4}GS, 13^{5}F, 14^{0}GF, 11^{5}S, 13^{4}GS, 16^{1}HY, 15^{4}G, 14^{0}HY, 18^{0}GS, 16^{3}S

	Starts	1st	2nd	3rd	Win & Pl
Career Total (Turf)	12	1	1	1	7051
73 8/01 Hayd 2m45y	E(0-75)H			HVY	£3122

Total win prize-money £3122

Going (Turf): Sf: 1-6 GS: 0-3 Gd: 0-1 GF: 0-1 Fm: 0-1
Distance: 5f/6f: 0-0 7f-8f: 0-1 9f-13f: 0-3 **14f+: 1-8**
Track : **LH: 1-10** RH: 0-1 Tight: 0-1 Gall: 0-4
Aids: Bl: 0-0 Vi: 0-0 Tstrap: 0-0
Best Rating: 75 5/01 York 1m5f194y firm

A fair staying handicapper. Appreciated the step up to two miles and heavy ground when getting off the mark at Haydock in August, he had looked held after that until a good third on the last day of the season in a competitive Doncaster handicap. Goes well in very soft ground.

Live Danger (USA)

79 **52**
2-y-o b c Affirmed (USA)-Personal Colors (USA) (Danzig (USA))
M R Channon Jaber Abdullah

Placings:6 **(4442)**
2001: 7^{6}G

	Starts	1st	2nd	3rd	Win & Pl
Career Total (Turf)	1	0	0	0	0

Going (Turf): Sf: 0-0 GS: 0-0 Gd: 0-1 GF: 0-0 Fm: 0-0
Distance: 5f/6f: 0-0 7f-8f: 0-1 9f-13f: 0-0 14f+: 0-0
Track : LH: 0-0 RH: 0-1 Tight: 0-0 Gall: 0-0
Aids: Bl: 0-0 Vi: 0-0 Tstrap: 0-0
Best Rating: 52 9/01 Sand 7f16y good

Live In Lover (IRE)

56(78) (39)**9**
3-y-o b g Up And At 'Em-Inesse (Simply Great (FR))
P C Haslam Mrs B Hawkins

Placings:000-000 **(4422)**
2001: 7^{0}GD, 7^{0}GD, 10^{0}GF

	Starts	1st	2nd	3rd	Win & Pl
Career Total (Turf)	4	0	0	0	
Career Total (AW)	2	0	0	0	

Going (Turf): Sf: 0-1 GS: 0-0 Gd: 0-1 GF: 0-2 Fm: 0-0
Distance: 5f/6f: 0-2 7f-8f: 0-3 9f-13f: 0-1 14f+: 0-0
Track : LH: 0-4 RH: 0-1 Tight: 0-1 Gall: 0-1
Aids: Bl: 0-0 Vi: 0-0 Tstrap: 0-0
Best Rating: 39 1/01 Sthl 7f stand

Live The Dream

94(86) (36)**50**
3-y-o b f Exit To Nowhere (USA)-Inveraven (Alias Smith (USA))
M C Pipe (J Hetherton 22/9) The Reims Partnership

Placings:004-0500041 **(4854)**
2001: 8^{0}SD, 8^{5}SD, 11^{0}SD, 10^{0}G, 9^{0}GF, 16^{4}F, 13^{1}GF

	Starts	1st	2nd	3rd	Win & Pl
Career Total (Turf)	7	1	0	0	1876
Career Total (AW)	3	0	0	0	0
36 9/01 Catt 1m5f175yG				G-F	£1876

Total win prize-money £1876

Going (Turf): Sf: 0-0 GS: 0-0 Gd: 0-2 **GF: 1-4** Fm: 0-1
Distance: 5f/6f: 0-1 7f-8f: 0-4 9f-13f: 0-3 **14f+: 1-2**
Track : **LH: 1-6** RH: 0-3 **Tight: 1-5** Gall: 0-0
Aids: Bl: 0-0 Vi: 0-0 Tstrap: 0-0
Best Rating: 48 9/01 Muss 2m firm

She took some time to come into form but she was bought by Martin Pipe after winning a seller.

Live To Tell

88 **42**
5-y-o ch m Primo Dominie-Dreams Are Free (IRE) (Caerleon (USA))
W G M Turner Paul Thorman

Placings:416001622100/6000 **(5462)**
2001: 5^{6}GF, 5^{0}G, 6^{0}HY, 5^{0}G

	Starts	1st	2nd	3rd	Win & Pl
Career Total (Turf)	12	2	2	0	8205
Career Total (AW)	4	1	0	0	2926
60 10/99 Ayr 5f	E(0-70)H			SFT	£2921
49 8/99 Wwck 5f	F(0-60)H			GD	£2594
49 2/99 Wolv 6f	D			STD	£2723

Total win prize-money £8238

Going (Turf): Sf: 1-4 GS: 0-1 **Gd: 1-4** GF: 0-3 Fm: 0-0
Distance: **5f/6f: 3-16** 7f-8f: 0-0 9f-13f: 0-0 14f+: 0-0
Track : **LH: 2-7** RH: 0-0 Tight: 1-4 Gall: 1-3
Aids: Bl: 0-0 Vi: 0-0 Tstrap: 0-0
Best Rating: 42 7/01 Chep 5f16y gd-fm

Lively Felix

(90) (25)
4-y-o b g Presidium-Full Of Life (Wolverlife)
W Clay (S Mellor 17/3) W Clay

Placings:004056-0 **(0271)**
2001: 7^{0}SW

	Starts	1st	2nd	3rd	Win & Pl
Career Total (Turf)	6	0	0	0	325
Career Total (AW)	1	0	0	0	

Going (Turf): Sf: 0-1 GS: 0-1 Gd: 0-2 GF: 0-1 Fm: 0-0
Distance: 5f/6f: 0-0 7f-8f: 0-2 9f-13f: 0-4 14f+: 0-0
Track : LH: 0-4 RH: 0-1 Tight: 0-4 Gall: 0-0
Aids: Bl: 0-0 Vi: 0-0 Tstrap: 0-0
Best Rating: 25 2/01 Ling 7f slow

Lively Lady

98(68) (59)**77**
5-y-o b m Beveled (USA)-In The Papers (Aragon)
J R Jenkins Mrs Jean Powell

Placings:142036024/1002102501/4103300003-60006000 **(5523)**
2001: 6^{6}GS, 5^{0}GS, 5^{0}SD, 6^{0}G, 5^{6}G, 5^{0}HY, 5^{0}S, 5^{0}HY

	Starts	1st	2nd	3rd	Win & Pl
Career Total (Turf)	33	5	4	3	31890
Career Total (AW)	4	0	0	1	416
89 4/00 Kemp 5f	C(0-95)H			SFT	£7377
78 11/99 Donc 5f	D(0-80)H			SFT	£7295
75 6/99 Kemp 6f	D(0-85)H			GD	£3875
71 3/99 Nott 6f15y	E(0-70)H			G-S	£3297
67 4/98 Folk 5f	G			SFT	£1725

Total win prize-money £23570

Going (Turf): Sf: 3-15 GS: 1-6 Gd: 1-11 GF: 0-1 Fm: 0-0
Distance: **5f/6f: 4-34** 7f-8f: 1-3 9f-13f: 0-0 14f+: 0-0
Track : LH: 0-5 RH: 0-4 Tight: 0-1 Gall: 0-5
Aids: Bl: 0-3 **Vi: 4-24** Tstrap: 0-0
Best Rating: 77 8/01 Yarm 5f43y good

Useful sprint handicapper. She is at her best in soft ground but rather needs things her own way. Has run well in a visor and probably best over five furlongs.

Livius (IRE)

110 **78**
7-y-o b g Alzao (USA)-Marie De Beaujeu (FR) (Kenmare (FR))
C A Dwyer George Taiano And Partners

Placings:2/3442020/021/34160-0406446000 **(5106)**
2001: 12^{0}S, 12^{4}G, 12^{0}GF, 12^{6}GF, 11^{4}GS, 12^{4}G, 12^{6}G, 14^{0}GS, 12^{0}GF, 12^{0}GS

	Starts	1st	2nd	3rd	Win & Pl
Career Total (Turf)	26	2	4	2	33061
89 8/00 Gdwd 1m4f	D(0-85)H			GD	£15275
82 8/99 Asct 1m4f	D(0-85)H			GD	£5602

Total win prize-money £20877

Going (Turf): Sf: 0-4 GS: 0-5 **Gd: 2-12** GF: 0-5 Fm: 0-0
Distance: 5f/6f: 0-0 7f-8f: 0-0 **9f-13f: 2-22** 14f+: 0-4
Track : LH: 0-8 **RH: 2-17** Tight: 1-9 Gall: 1-15
Aids: Bl: 0-1 Vi: 0-0 Tstrap: 0-0
Best Rating: 87 6/01 Epsm 1m4f10y gd-fm

He has been difficult to train but took a valuable handicap at Goodwood in 2000. Short of a turn of foot, he likes to come late off a strong pace and a fast-run mile and a half on good ground seems to suit him best.

Lizzey Letti

98(93) (62)**91**
3-y-o ch f Grand Lodge (USA)-Crystal Ring (IRE) (Kris)
G Wragg Gestut Schlenderhan

Placings:01-3051 **(5476a)**
2001: 10^{3}GF, 10^{0}G, 10^{5}GF, 10^{1}S

	Starts	1st	2nd	3rd	Win & Pl
Career Total (Turf)	5	1	0	1	7650
Career Total (AW)	1	1	0	0	2327
91 10/01 Gels 1m2f				SFT	£6515
62 11/00 Ling 1m	D			STD	£2327

Total win prize-money £8842

Going (Turf): Sf: 1-1 GS: 0-0 Gd: 0-1 GF: 0-2 Fm: 0-1
Distance: 5f/6f: 0-0 7f-8f: 1-2 9f-13f: 1-4 14f+: 0-0
Track : **LH: 1-3** RH: 0-1 **Tight: 1-2** Gall: 0-2
Aids: Bl: 0-0 Vi: 0-0 Tstrap: 0-0
Best Rating: 91 10/01 Gels 1m2f soft

Lightly-raced, she did not look up to Pattern Class until winning a German Listed event.

Lloyd

90(88) (76)**56**

2-y-o b g Glory Of Dancer-Broughtons Bird (IRE) (Exhibitioner)

J O'Reilly J Saul

Placings:0060**6**204 **(5415)**

2001: 5^{0}GS, 6^{0}GF, 7^{6}G, 8^{0}G, 7^{6}SD, 6^{2}SD, 6^{0}SD, 6^{4}SD

	Starts	1st	2nd	3rd	Win & Pl
Career Total (Turf)	4	0	0	0	0
Career Total (AW)	4	0	1	0	874

Going (Turf): Sf: 0-0 GS: 0-1 Gd: 0-2 GF: 0-1 Fm: 0-0
Distance: 5f/6f: 0-5 7f-8f: 0-3 9f-13f: 0-0 14f+: 0-0
Track : LH: 0-6 RH: 0-0 Tight: 0-3 Gall: 0-1
Aids: Bl: 0-0 Vi: 0-0 Tstrap: 0-4
Best Rating: 76 10/01 Wolv 6f stand

Signs of ability and looks best at Wolverhampton, but has no scope.

Loblite Leader (IRE)

101(54) **44**

4-y-o b g Tirol-Cyrano Beauty (IRE) (Cyrano De Bergerac)

G A Swinbank (D Eddy 18/5) Montagu Bloodstock Ltd

Placings:0640450/00040-01043110 **(5010)**

2001: 9^{0}GS, 11^{1}G, 10^{0}GF, 9^{4}GF, 11^{3}S, 14^{1}G, 14^{0}HY

	Starts	1st	2nd	3rd	Win & Pl
Career Total (Turf)	19	3	0	1	9846
Career Total (AW)	1	0	0	0	

44	8/01	Muss	1m6f	E(0-70)H	G-F	£2758
44	8/01	Newc	1m6f97y	F(0-65)H	GD	£3038
36	5/01	Haml	1m3f16y	F(0-60)H	GD	£2912

Total win prize-money £8708

Going (Turf): Sf: 0-6 GS: 0-3 **Gd: 2-4** GF: 1-6 Fm: 0-0
Distance: 5f/6f: 0-0 7f-8f: 0-7 9f-13f: 1-9 **14f+: 2-4**
Track : LH: 1-7 **RH: 2-6 Tight: 2-8** Gall: 1-2
Aids: Bl: 0-0 Vi: 0-0 Tstrap: 0-0
Best Rating: 44 8/01 Muss 1m6f gd-fm

He is only modest, but was well placed to win three weak events this season at Hamilton, Newcastle and Musselburgh. Stays 14 furlongs.

Lobuche (IRE)

(75) (32)**26**

6-y-o b g Petardia-Lhotse (IRE) (Shernazar)

M C Chapman K D Blanch

Placings:04200666/**5202513**04000000/00**6**00000/0-0 **(0443)**

2001: 7^{0}SD

	Starts	1st	2nd	3rd	Win & Pl
Career Total (Turf)	21	1	1	0	3991
Career Total (AW)	12	0	2	1	1395

67	6/98	Yarm	6f3y	E(0-70)H	SFT	£3054

Total win prize-money £3054

Going (Turf): Sf: 1-2 GS: 0-4 Gd: 0-5 GF: 0-6 Fm: 0-4
Distance: 5f/6f: 0-7 **7f-8f: 1-15** 9f-13f: 0-9 14f+: 0-2
Track : LH: 0-22 RH: 0-2 Tight: 0-9 Gall: 0-1
Aids: Bl: 0-2 Vi: 0-0 Tstrap: 0-7

Loch Ailort

(100) (38)

5-y-o b m Be My Chief (USA)-Lochbelle (Robellino (USA))

Miss V Haigh Tune Pack Produce Ltd

Placings:0622-3550250 **(0471)**

2001: 11^{3}SD, 8^{5}SD, 9^{5}SW, 9^{0}SD, 8^{2}SW, 11^{5}SD, 8^{0}SD

	Starts	1st	2nd	3rd	Win & Pl
Career Total (Turf)	1	0	0	0	
Career Total (AW)	10	0	3	1	1805

Going (Turf): Sf: 0-1 GS: 0-0 Gd: 0-0 GF: 0-0 Fm: 0-0
Distance: 5f/6f: 0-1 7f-8f: 0-6 9f-13f: 0-4 14f+: 0-0
Track : LH: 0-10 RH: 0-0 Tight: 0-2 Gall: 0-0
Aids: Bl: 0-0 Vi: 0-11 Tstrap: 0-0
Best Rating: 38 2/01 Sthl 1m slow

Loch Inch

99(95) (55)**56**

4-y-o ch g Inchinor-Carrie Kool (Prince Sabo)

K McAuliffe Folly Road Racing Partners (1996)

Placings:3510460010/000-0006000 **(5497)**

2001: 6^{0}GF, 6^{0}GF, 6^{0}GF, 6^{6}SD, 6^{0}HY, 5^{0}S, 5^{0}HY

	Starts	1st	2nd	3rd	Win & Pl
Career Total (Turf)	18	2	0	1	13955
Career Total (AW)	2	0	0	0	0

87	10/99	Wind	6f	D(0-85)H	SFT	£3663
78	8/99	Nott	6f15y	E	G-F	£3590

Total win prize-money £7254

Going (Turf): Sf: 1-9 GS: 0-0 Gd: 0-2 **GF: 1-7** Fm: 0-0
Distance: 5f/6f: 1-12 7f-8f: 1-8 9f-13f: 0-0 14f+: 0-0
Track : LH: 0-4 **RH: 1-1** Tight: 0-2 **Gall: 1-2**
Aids: **Bl: 1-8** Vi: 0-1 Tstrap: 0-0
Best Rating: 56 7/01 Wind 6f gd-fm

Loch Laird

103 **65**

6-y-o b g Beveled (USA)-Daisy Loch (Lochnager)

M Madgwick Miss E M L Coller

Placings:223/3220/10106000/5000006-535000050 **(4950)**

2001: 7^{5}G, 6^{3}S, 6^{5}GF, 6^{0}GF, 6^{0}GF, 7^{0}GF, 6^{0}G, 7^{5}GF, 5^{0}G

	Starts	1st	2nd	3rd	Win & Pl
Career Total (Turf)	31	2	4	3	12955

79	6/99	Gdwd	6f	D(0-80)H	SFT	£4235
81	5/99	Sals	6f	D	G-F	£3208

Total win prize-money £7444

Going (Turf): Sf: 1-4 GS: 0-1 Gd: 0-9 **GF: 1-16** Fm: 0-1
Distance: **5f/6f: 2-24** 7f-8f: 0-7 9f-13f: 0-0 14f+: 0-0
Track : LH: 0-2 RH: 0-4 Tight: 0-0 Gall: 0-4
Aids: Bl: 0-2 Vi: 0-1 Tstrap: 0-0
Best Rating: 67 5/01 Sals 6f212y soft

A fair sprinter, he showed good form early in his career, but is without a win since June 1999 despite tumbling in the handicap.

Loch Maree

91 **61**

2-y-o b f Primo Dominie-Aurora Bay (IRE) (Night Shift (USA))

M W Easterby Mrs E Rhind

Placings:63000 **(5536)**

2001: 5^{6}GS, 6^{3}G, 6^{0}GF, 6^{0}GS, 6^{0}S

	Starts	1st	2nd	3rd	Win & Pl
Career Total (Turf)	5	0	0	1	694

Going (Turf): Sf: 0-1 GS: 0-2 Gd: 0-1 GF: 0-1 Fm: 0-0
Distance: 5f/6f: 0-5 7f-8f: 0-0 9f-13f: 0-0 14f+: 0-0
Track : LH: 0-1 RH: 0-0 Tight: 0-0 Gall: 0-0
Aids: Bl: 0-0 Vi: 0-0 Tstrap: 0-0
Best Rating: 61 8/01 Thsk 6f good

Locharia

101 **83+**

2-y-o b f Wolfhound (USA)-Lochbelle (Robellino (USA))

Mrs L Stubbs M S & C S Griffiths

Placings:3014 **(5256)**

2001: 5^{3}GF, 5^{0}G, 5^{1}GF, 5^{4}GS

	Starts	1st	2nd	3rd	Win & Pl
Career Total (Turf)	4	1	0	1	7045

83	9/01	Muss	5f	D	G-F	£4192

Total win prize-money £4193

Going (Turf): Sf: 0-0 GS: 0-1 Gd: 0-1 **GF: 1-2** Fm: 0-0
Distance: **5f/6f: 1-4** 7f-8f: 0-0 9f-13f: 0-0 14f+: 0-0
Track : LH: 0-0 RH: 0-0 Tight: 0-0 Gall: 0-0
Aids: Bl: 0-0 Vi: 0-0 Tstrap: 0-0
Best Rating: 83 9/01 Muss 5f gd-fm

Out of a half-sister to Lochsong and Lochangel, she made an encouraging debut over five furlongs at Lingfield, but was outclassed next time at Doncaster in a Group Three before running out a convincing winner of a Musselburgh maiden. Suited by the minimum trip and decent ground.

Lochridge

100 **82**

2-y-o ch f Indian Ridge-Lochsong (Song)

I A Balding J C Smith

Placings:32 **(4886)**

2001: 6^{3}GF, 7^{2}GF

	Starts	1st	2nd	3rd	Win & Pl
Career Total (Turf)	2	0	1	1	2264

Going (Turf): Sf: 0-0 GS: 0-0 Gd: 0-0 GF: 0-2 Fm: 0-0
Distance: 5f/6f: 0-0 7f-8f: 0-2 9f-13f: 0-0 14f+: 0-0
Track : LH: 0-0 RH: 0-1 Tight: 0-0 Gall: 0-1
Aids: Bl: 0-0 Vi: 0-0 Tstrap: 0-0
Best Rating: 82 9/01 Kemp 7f gd-fm

Bred to be fast, she has shown ability in races beyond sprint trips.

Lochsprite

(71) (17)

3-y-o ch f So Factual (USA)-Lochspring (IRE) (Precocious)

I A Balding J C Smith

Placings:023-6230 **(5048)**

2001: 6^{6}GS, 5^{2}GF, 5^{3}GF, 7^{0}SD

	Starts	1st	2nd	3rd	Win & Pl
Career Total (Turf)	6	0	2	2	2802
Career Total (AW)	1	0	0	0	

Going (Turf): Sf: 0-2 GS: 0-1 Gd: 0-0 GF: 0-3 Fm: 0-0
Distance: 5f/6f: 0-6 7f-8f: 0-1 9f-13f: 0-0 14f+: 0-0
Track : LH: 0-3 RH: 0-0 Tight: 0-0 Gall: 0-2
Aids: Bl: 0-0 Vi: 0-0 Tstrap: 0-0
Best Rating: 64 5/01 Bath 5f11y gd-fm

Lock Inn

39

2-y-o b g Dolphin Street (FR)-Highest Bid (FR) (Highest Honor (FR))

Miss D A McHale The Lion Partners

Placings:0 **(5361)**

2001: 8^{0}GS

	Starts	1st	2nd	3rd	Win & Pl
Career Total (Turf)	1	0	0	0	

Going (Turf): Sf: 0-0 GS: 0-1 Gd: 0-0 GF: 0-0 Fm: 0-0
Distance: 5f/6f: 0-0 7f-8f: 0-1 9f-13f: 0-0 14f+: 0-0
Track : LH: 0-0 RH: 0-0 Tight: 0-0 Gall: 0-0
Aids: Bl: 0-0 Vi: 0-0 Tstrap: 0-0

Lockstock (IRE)

(97) (64)**64**

3-y-o b g Inchinor-Hisalah (Marju (IRE))

M S Saunders Chris Scott

Placings:04003002 **(3817)**

2001: 7^{0}SD, 8^{4}GS, 10^{0}GS, 7^{0}GF, 8^{3}GS, 8^{0}GF, 8^{0}G, 9^{2}SD

	Starts	1st	2nd	3rd	Win & Pl
Career Total (Turf)	6	0	0	1	786
Career Total (AW)	2	0	1	0	874

Going (Turf): Sf: 0-0 GS: 0-3 Gd: 0-1 GF: 0-2 Fm: 0-0
Distance: 5f/6f: 0-0 7f-8f: 0-5 9f-13f: 0-3 14f+: 0-0
Track : LH: 0-5 RH: 0-0 Tight: 0-4 Gall: 0-0
Aids: Bl: 0-0 Vi: 0-0 Tstrap: 0-0
Best Rating: 64 8/01 Wolv 1m1f79y stand

Locombe Hill (IRE)

106 **55**

5 y o b g Barathea (IRE)-Roberts Pride (Roberto (USA))

M Blanshard Stanley Hinton

Placings:11626/400310/3030040-0065600 **(5101)**

2001: 8^{0}GS, 7^{0}G, 10^{6}G, 8^{5}G, 8^{6}G, 10^{0}G, 9^{0}GS

	Starts	1st	2nd	3rd	Win & Pl
Career Total (Turf)	25	3	1	3	22102

95 9/99 Kemp 1m4f C(0-95) HVY £7002
95 7/98 Newb 6f8y D G-F £3571
85 6/98 Newb 6f8y D SFT £3785
Total win prize-money £14359

Going (Turf): Sf: 2-7 GS: 0-3 Gd: 0-11 GF: 1-4 Fm: 0-0
Distance: 5f/6f: 0-1 **7f-8f: 2-10** 9f-13f: 1-13 14f+: 0-1
Track : LH: 0-4 **RH: 1-14** Tight: 0-7 Gall: 0-8
Aids: Bl: 0-0 Vi: 0-0 Tstrap: 0-0
Best Rating: 65 4/01 Newb 1m gd-sft

A very useful sort at two, he has not really lived up to that early promise. Gained two of his three victories in the mud.

Locomotive

81 **68**

2-y-o b g Bin Ajwaad (IRE)-Saluti Tutti (Trojan Fen)

C F Wall S Fustok

Placings:04 **(5095)**

2001: 7^{0}S, 8^{4}GS

	Starts	1st	2nd	3rd	Win & Pl
Career Total (Turf)	2	0	0	0	348

Going (Turf): Sf: 0-1 GS: 0-1 Gd: 0-0 GF: 0-0 Fm: 0-0
Distance: 5f/6f: 0-0 7f-8f: 0-2 9f-13f: 0-0 14f+: 0-0
Track : LH: 0-0 RH: 0-0 Tight: 0-0 Gall: 0-0
Aids: Bl: 0-0 Vi: 0-0 Tstrap: 0-0
Best Rating: 68 10/01 Sals 1m gd-sft

Lodestone (IRE)

70

3-y-o b c Distant Relative-Magnetic Point (USA) (Bering)

J M Bradley Mrs H Raw

Placings:006 **(2555)**

2001: 8^{0}S, 6^{0}GF, 6^{6}GF

	Starts	1st	2nd	3rd	Win & Pl
Career Total (Turf)	3	0	0	0	0

Going (Turf): Sf: 0-1 GS: 0-0 Gd: 0-0 GF: 0-2 Fm: 0-0
Distance: 5f/6f: 0-0 7f-8f: 0-3 9f-13f: 0-0 14f+: 0-0
Track : LH: 0-1 RH: 0-2 Tight: 0-2 Gall: 0-0
Aids: Bl: 0-0 Vi: 0-0 Tstrap: 0-0

Logo's Dream

86(70) (31)**50**

2-y-o b c Mind Games-Yukosan (Absalom)

B A McMahon Mrs B B Whitehorn

Placings:300 **(3018)**

2001: 5^{3}HY, 5^{0}GF, 6^{0}SD

	Starts	1st	2nd	3rd	Win & Pl
Career Total (Turf)	2	0	0	1	333
Career Total (AW)	1	0	0	0	

Going (Turf): Sf: 0-1 GS: 0-0 Gd: 0-0 GF: 0-1 Fm: 0-0
Distance: 5f/6f: 0-3 7f-8f: 0-0 9f-13f: 0-0 14f+: 0-0
Track : LH: 0-1 RH: 0-0 Tight: 0-0 Gall: 0-0
Aids: Bl: 0-0 Vi: 0-0 Tstrap: 0-0
Best Rating: 50 5/01 Hayd 5f gd-fm

Lokomotiv

93(88) (27)**12**

5-y-o b g Salse (USA)-Rainbow's End (My Swallow)

M Madgwick (J M Bradley 24/8) M Madgwick

Placings:061/0005425300/60001052610-000000 **(3734)**

2001: 11^{0}GF, 9^{0}GF, 12^{0}GF, 11^{0}GF, 12^{0}GS, 11^{0}G

	Starts	1st	2nd	3rd	Win & Pl
Career Total (Turf)	28	3	2	1	8312
Career Total (AW)	2	0	0	0	0

45 9/00 Yarm 1m2f21y G G-F £2065
39 7/00 Ayr 1m2f192yF FRM £2282
67 7/98 Yarm 7f3y G G-F £1987
Total win prize-money £6335

Going (Turf): Sf: 0-2 GS: 0-3 Gd: 0-4 **GF: 2-13** Fm: 1-6
Distance: 5f/6f: 0-1 7f-8f: 1-8 **9f-13f: 2-21** 14f+: 0-0
Track : **LH: 2-16** RH: 0-7 **Tight: 1-10** Gall: 0-0
Aids: **Bl: 2-15** Vi: 0-2 Tstrap: 0-0
Best Rating: 43 6/01 Bevl 1m1f207y gd-fm

Londolozi Lad (IRE)

(78) (47)

2-y-o b g Ali-Royal (IRE)-Ashdown (Pharly (FR))

P C Haslam David H Morgan

Placings:000 **(4551)**

2001: 6^{0}GF, 6^{0}G, 8^{0}SW

	Starts	1st	2nd	3rd	Win & Pl
Career Total (Turf)	2	0	0	0	
Career Total (AW)	1	0	0	0	

Going (Turf): Sf: 0-0 GS: 0-0 Gd: 0-1 GF: 0-1 Fm: 0-0
Distance: 5f/6f: 0-2 7f-8f: 0-0 9f-13f: 0-1 14f+: 0-0
Track : LH: 0-1 RH: 0-0 Tight: 0-1 Gall: 0-0
Aids: Bl: 0-0 Vi: 0-0 Tstrap: 0-0
Best Rating: 47 9/01 Wolv 1m100y slow

London Eye

93(96) (55)**46**

3-y-o b f Distinctly North (USA)-Clonavon Girl (IRE) (Be My Guest (USA))

K T Ivory J B Waterfall

Placings:0603320016440560-3202000000 **(4715)**

2001: 7^{3}SD, 8^{2}SD, 8^{0}SD, 7^{2}SD, 8^{0}SW, 6^{0}F, 5^{0}GF, 7^{0}GF, 6^{0}GF, 6^{0}G

	Starts	1st	2nd	3rd	Win & Pl
Career Total (Turf)	17	1	1	2	4080
Career Total (AW)	9	0	2	1	1641

57 7/00 Brig 5f59y F FRM £2236
Total win prize-money £2237

Going (Turf): Sf: 0-2 GS: 0-1 Gd: 0-3 GF: 0-8 **Fm: 1-3**
Distance: **5f/6f: 1-19** 7f-8f: 0-7 9f-13f: 0-0 14f+: 0-0
Track : **LH: 1-15** RH: 0-1 Tight: 0-9 Gall: 0-1
Aids: **Bl: 1-22** Vi: 0-0 Tstrap: 0-0
Best Rating: 55 2/01 Ling 7f stand

London Follies (IRE)

98 **71**

2-y-o b g Danehill Dancer (IRE)-Savona (IRE) (Cyrano De Bergerac)

N A Callaghan M Tabor

Placings:04110046 **(5467)**

2001: 7^{0}GF, 6^{4}GF, 5^{1}F, 6^{1}S, 6^{0}G, 6^{0}G, 6^{4}GS, 6^{6}S

	Starts	1st	2nd	3rd	Win & Pl
Career Total (Turf)	8	2	0	0	5880

71 8/01 Chep 6f16y D SFT £3510
72 7/01 Brig 5f213y G FRM £1820
Total win prize-money £5330

Going (Turf): Sf: 1-2 GS: 0-1 Gd: 0-2 GF: 0-2 **Fm: 1-1**
Distance: 5f/6f: 1-5 7f-8f: 1-3 9f-13f: 0-0 14f+: 0-0
Track : **LH: 1-2** RH: 0-0 Tight: 0-0 Gall: 0-0
Aids: Bl: 0-0 Vi: 0-0 Tstrap: 0-0
Best Rating: 76 7/01 Ling 6f gd-fm

Dropped in class to win a Brighton seller on very fast ground on his third start and conditions could not have been more different when he followed up in a Chepstow nursery. Well beatensubsequently. Six furlongs is his trip at present.

London Lights

(90) (29)

7-y-o b g Slip Anchor-Pageantry (Welsh Pageant)

Lady Connell (D J Wintle 16/4) Lady Connell

Placings:35/050/000 **(0120)**

2001: 12^{0}SD, 12^{0}SD, 14^{0}SW

	Starts	1st	2nd	3rd	Win & Pl
Career Total (Turf)	5	0	0	1	493
Career Total (AW)	3	0	0	0	

Going (Turf): Sf: 0-1 GS: 0-0 Gd: 0-0 GF: 0-3 Fm: 0-0
Distance: 5f/6f: 0-0 7f-8f: 0-0 9f-13f: 0-6 14f+: 0-2
Track : LH: 0-3 RH: 0-5 Tight: 0-1 Gall: 0-0
Aids: Bl: 0-0 Vi: 0-0 Tstrap: 0-0
Best Rating: 29 1/01 Sthl 1m4f stand

Londoner (USA)

104 **106**

3-y-o ch c Sky Classic (CAN)-Love And Affection (USA) (Exclusive Era (USA))

H R A Cecil H R H Prince Fahd Salman

Placings:114-303 **(2959)**

2001: 10^{3}GF, 12^{0}GF, 10^{3}GF

	Starts	1st	2nd	3rd	Win & Pl
Career Total (Turf)	6	2	0	2	16020

92 8/00 Yarm 7f3y D GD £4134
92 7/00 NmkJ 7f D G-S £6207
Total win prize-money £10342

Going (Turf): Sf: 0-0 **GS: 1-1 Gd: 1-2** GF: 0-3 Fm: 0-0
Distance: 5f/6f: 0-0 **7f-8f: 2-3** 9f-13f: 0-3 14f+: 0-0
Track : LH: 0-2 RH: 0-2 Tight: 0-1 Gall: 0-2
Aids: Bl: 0-0 Vi: 0-0 Tstrap: 0-0
Best Rating: 106 6/01 Asct 1m4f gd-fm

A rangy colt, won two from his three starts at two over seven furlongs. Effective on good and good to soft, he has yet to encounter extremes of going. Good third in the Glasgow Stakes at York, where he was beaten by Musha Merr and the subsequent Listed winner Potemkin, but he has since been disappointing. Sold to Martin Pipe in the autumn.

Lone Chief (USA)

96 **84**

2-y-o b c Cozzene (USA)-Alcando (Alzao (USA))
T D Barron T D Barron

Placings:1230 **(4309)**
2001: 6^{1}GF, 5^{2}GF, 7^{3}F, 8^{0}GF

	Starts	1st	2nd	3rd	Win & Pl
Career Total (Turf)	4	1	1	1	6704

77	6/01	Ripn	6f	D	G-F	£4420

Total win prize-money £4420

Going (Turf): Sf: 0-0 GS: 0-0 Gd: 0-0 **GF: 1-3** Fm: 0-1
Distance: **5f/6f: 1-2** 7f-8f: 0-1 9f-13f: 0-1 14f+: 0-0
Track : LH: 0-1 RH: 0-0 Tight: 0-1 Gall: 0-0
Aids: Bl: 0-0 Vi: 0-0 Tstrap: 0-0
Best Rating: 84 7/01 Thsk 7f firm

A winner over six furlongs on his debut, he has performed well over five and seven furlongs since. Acts on fast ground. Has made the running.

Lone Piper

105(109) (46)**66**
6-y-o b g Warning-Shamisen (Diesis)
Jedd O'Keeffe P Smith

Placings:360/5100010/020/40000000300-000000022150035020100 **(5685)**
2001: 6^{0}S, 7^{0}GS, 8^{0}S, 5^{0}GS, 5^{0}G, 5^{0}GF, 6^{0}G, 5^{2}F, 5^{2}F, 5^{1}G, 5^{3}GF, 6^{0}F, 6^{0}G, 5^{3}GF, 5^{3}GF, 6^{0}SW, 5^{2}G, 5^{0}G, 5^{1}G, 5^{0}S, 5^{0}S, 5^{0}S

	Starts	1st	2nd	3rd	Win & Pl
Career Total (Turf)	44	4	4	3	44385
Career Total (AW)	2	0	0	0	864

66	9/01	Gdwd	5f	E(0-70)H	GD	£4364
51	7/01	Donc	5f	F(0-65)H	GD	£3981
101	9/98	York	6f	B(0-105)H	GD	£19151
99	5/98	NmkR	7f	C	GD	£5133

Total win prize-money £32631

Going (Turf): Sf: 0-8 GS: 0-6 **Gd: 4-16** GF: 0-11 Fm: 0-3
Distance: **5f/6f: 3-33** 7f-8f: 1-13 9f-13f: 0-0 14f+: 0-0
Track : LH: 0-4 RH: 0-3 Tight: 0-3 Gall: 0-1
Aids: Bl: 0-0 Vi: 0-4 Tstrap: 0-4
Best Rating: 66 9/01 Gdwd 5f good

He was a decent sprint handicapper a few years ago, but lost the plot and changed stables. A dramatic drop in the handicap finally helped him rediscover a bit of form and he ended a losing run of almost three years at Doncaster in July 2001, and added to that off a higher mark at Goodwood in July. Acts on a sound surface.

Loner

93 **61d**
3-y-o b g Magic Ring (IRE)-Jolis Absent (Primo Dominie)
M Wigham Miss Arabella Smallman

Placings:0462150400-0000 **(4721)**
2001: 7^{0}GF, 9^{0}GF, 10^{0}GF, 12^{0}G

	Starts	1st	2nd	3rd	Win & Pl
Career Total (Turf)	14	1	1	0	9781

77	8/00	Gdwd	7f	C	GD	£7020

Total win prize-money £7020

Going (Turf): Sf: 0-2 GS: 0-0 **Gd: 1-6** GF: 0-5 Fm: 0-0
Distance: 5f/6f: 0-5 **7f-8f: 1-5** 9f-13f: 0-3 14f+: 0-0
Track : LH: 0-5 **RH: 1-2** Tight: 0-4 Gall: 0-2
Aids: Bl: 0-0 Vi: 0-0 Tstrap: 0-0
Best Rating: 52 5/01 York 7f202y gd-fm

Long Tall Sally (IRE)

95 **69**
2-y-o b f Danehill Dancer (IRE)-Miss Galwegian (Sandford Lad)
D W P Arbuthnot Noel Cronin

Placings:64340 **(4894)**
2001: 5^{6}G, 5^{4}GF, 5^{3}GF, 6^{4}G, 5^{0}GS

	Starts	1st	2nd	3rd	Win & Pl
Career Total (Turf)	5	0	0	1	3033

Going (Turf): Sf: 0-0 GS: 0-1 Gd: 0-2 GF: 0-2 Fm: 0-0
Distance: 5f/6f: 0-5 7f-8f: 0-0 9f-13f: 0-0 14f+: 0-0
Track : LH: 0-3 RH: 0-0 Tight: 0-0 Gall: 0-3
Aids: Bl: 0-0 Vi: 0-0 Tstrap: 0-0
Best Rating: 69 8/01 Bath 5f11y gd-fm

Speedy filly, ran several good races against decent opposition in the late summer. Capable of winning an ordinary event over sprint distances.

Long Weekend (IRE)

81(76) (36)**65**
3-y-o b c Flying Spur (AUS)-Friday Night (USA) (Trempolino (USA))
D Shaw The Denton Partnership

Placings:0540-600 **(1177)**
2001: 7^{6}SD, 9^{0}SW, 7^{0}G

	Starts	1st	2nd	3rd	Win & Pl
Career Total (Turf)	5	0	0	0	296
Career Total (AW)	2	0	0	0	0

Going (Turf): Sf: 0-1 GS: 0-0 Gd: 0-1 GF: 0-3 Fm: 0-0
Distance: 5f/6f: 0-2 7f-8f: 0-4 9f-13f: 0-1 14f+: 0-0
Track : LH: 0-4 RH: 0-0 Tight: 0-2 Gall: 0-0
Aids: Bl: 0-1 Vi: 0-0 Tstrap: 0-0
Best Rating: 36 1/01 Sthl 7f stand

Longchamp Du Lac

87 **36**
3-y-o b g Lake Coniston (IRE)-Kaprisky (IRE) (Red Sunset)
A Berry The Property Racing Partnership

Placings:00-0000 **(2499)**
2001: 6^{0}HY, 6^{0}F, 7^{0}G, 9^{0}G

	Starts	1st	2nd	3rd	Win & Pl
Career Total (Turf)	6	0	0	0	

Going (Turf): Sf: 0-1 GS: 0-1 Gd: 0-2 GF: 0-1 Fm: 0-1
Distance: 5f/6f: 0-3 7f-8f: 0-2 9f-13f: 0-1 14f+: 0-0
Track : LH: 0-1 RH: 0-1 Tight: 0-1 Gall: 0-0
Aids: Bl: 0-1 Vi: 0-0 Tstrap: 0-0
Best Rating: 36 4/01 Wwck 6f21y heavy

Look And Learn (FR)

(84) (40)
6-y-o ch g Rock Hopper-Lailati (USA) (Mr Prospector (USA))
R F Marvin R A B Saville

Placings:1012/00 **(0438)**
2001: 6^{0}SD, 9^{0}SD

	Starts	1st	2nd	3rd	Win & Pl
Career Total (Turf)	4	2	1	0	10403
Career Total (AW)	2	0	0	0	

8/98	Deau	1m4f	G-S	£5555
5/98	Lisi	1m1f110y	GD	£2020

Total win prize-money £7575

Going (Turf): Sf: 0-0 GS: 0-0 **Gd: 1-1** GF: 0-0 Fm: 0-0
Distance: 5f/6f: 0-1 7f-8f: 0-0 **9f-13f: 1-2** 14f+: 0-0
Track : LH: 0-2 RH: 0-0 Tight: 0-1 Gall: 0-0
Aids: Bl: 0-0 Vi: 0-0 Tstrap: 0-2
Best Rating: 40 2/01 Sthl 6f stand

Look Away Now

94(87) (52)**75**
2-y-o ch c Timeless Times (USA)-Petite Elite (Anfield)
W A O'Gorman Peter Bonner

Placings:520 **(2428)**
2001: 5^{5}SD, 6^{2}GF, 6^{0}GF

	Starts	1st	2nd	3rd	Win & Pl
Career Total (Turf)	2	0	1	0	990
Career Total (AW)	1	0	0	0	0

Going (Turf): Sf: 0-0 GS: 0-0 Gd: 0-0 GF: 0-2 Fm: 0-0
Distance: 5f/6f: 0-2 7f-8f: 0-1 9f-13f: 0-0 14f+: 0-0
Track : LH: 0-0 RH: 0-0 Tight: 0-0 Gall: 0-0
Aids: Bl: 0-0 Vi: 0-0 Tstrap: 0-0
Best Rating: 75 6/01 Yarm 6f3y gd-fm

Look First (IRE)

104(99) (76)**68**
3-y-o b c Namaqualand (USA)-Be Prepared (IRE) (Be My Guest (USA))
A P Jarvis Christopher Shankland

Placings:231026-511006012 **(2488)**
2001: 10^{5}SD, 8^{1}SD, 8^{1}SD, 12^{0}SD, 10^{0}GS, 12^{6}SD, 8^{0}F, 8^{1}F, 10^{2}HD

	Starts	1st	2nd	3rd	Win & Pl
Career Total (Turf)	9	2	3	1	7452
Career Total (AW)	6	2	0	0	4865

49	5/01	Leic	1m9y	F	FRM	£2492
76	2/01	Sthl	1m	E(0-70)H	STD	£2975
64	1/01	Sthl	1m	G(0-60)H	STD	£1890
63	8/00	Brig	6f209y	F	GD	£2194

Total win prize-money £9552

Going (Turf): Sf: 0-1 GS: 0-3 **Gd: 1-1** GF: 0-0 **Fm: 1-4**
Distance: 5f/6f: 0-0 **7f-8f: 3-7** 9f-13f: 1-8 14f+: 0-0
Track : **LH: 3-11** RH: 0-1 Tight: 0-6 Gall: 0-1
Aids: Bl: 0-0 **Vi: 1-2** Tstrap: 0-0
Best Rating: 76 2/01 Sthl 1m stand

Claiming-class miler, effective on fast ground and Fibresand.

Look Here Now

98 **72d**
4-y-o gr g Ardkinglass-Where's Carol (Anfield)
B A McMahon S L Edwards

Placings:150000160-000000 **(3445)**
2001: 6^{0}S, 6^{0}G, 6^{0}G, 6^{0}GF, 7^{0}GS, 7^{0}GF

	Starts	1st	2nd	3rd	Win & Pl
Career Total (Turf)	15	2	0	0	12656

75	10/00	York	6f	D(0-75)	SFT	£8092
77	3/00	Donc	6f	D	GD	£4309

Total win prize-money £12403

Going (Turf): Sf: 1-5 GS: 0-1 **Gd: 1-6** GF: 0-3 Fm: 0-0
Distance: **5f/6f: 2-9** 7f-8f: 0-6 9f-13f: 0-0 14f+: 0-0
Track : LH: 0-3 RH: 0-0 Tight: 0-2 Gall: 0-1
Aids: Bl: 0-0 Vi: 0-0 Tstrap: 0-0
Best Rating: 63 6/01 Wind 6f good

Fair sprinter.

Looking For Love (IRE)

105 **76**
3-y-o b f Tagula (IRE)-Mousseux (IRE) (Jareer (USA))
J G Portman Out To Grass Partnership

Placings:03332321-443403601060 **(5145)**
2001: 9^{4}S, 9^{4}GS, 10^{3}G, 9^{4}GF, 8^{0}GF, 8^{3}GF, 8^{6}GF, 8^{0}G, 7^{1}GF, 7^{0}G, 7^{6}GS, 7^{0}G

	Starts	1st	2nd	3rd	Win & Pl
Career Total (Turf)	20	2	2	6	15083

62	8/01	Gdwd	7f	D(0-75)	G-F	£4173
80	10/00	Newb	7f	D(0-85)	SFT	£4602

Total win prize-money £8775

Going (Turf): **Sf: 1-3** GS: 0-3 Gd: 0-8 **GF: 1-6** Fm: 0-0
Distance: 5f/6f: 0-3 **7f-8f: 2-10** 9f-13f: 0-7 14f+: 0-0
Track : LH. 0-3 **RH: 1-10** Tight: 0-4 Gall: 0-2
Aids: Bl: 0-0 Vi: 0-0 Tstrap: 0-0
Best Rating: 82 5/01 NmkR 1m2f good

Consistent and genuine, she won over seven furlongs at Goodwood in August but stays further.

Loop The Loup

105 **80**

5-y-o b g Petit Loup (USA)-Mithi Al Gamar (USA) (Blushing Groom (FR))
Mrs M Reveley And Mrs J D Cotton

Placings:03/50112122/500001-60060 **(5263)**
2001: 13^{6}GF, 16^{0}F, 13^{0}G, 14^{6}GS, 13^{0}GS

	Starts	1st	2nd	3rd	Win & Pl
Career Total (Turf)	21	4	3	1	39517

88	10/00	Donc	1m6f132yD(0-85)H		GD	£4660
95	8/99	York	1m5f194yB(0-100)H		GD	£20266
84	7/99	Sals	1m4f	D(0-85)H	G-S	£3857
84	6/99	Ling	1m3f106yF		G-S	£2219

Total win prize-money £31004

Going (Turf): Sf: 0-3 **GS: 2-6 Gd: 2-7** GF: 0-3 Fm: 0-2
Distance: 5f/6f: 0-0 7f-8f: 0-1 9f-13f: 2-8 14f+: 2-12
Track : **LH: 3-13** RH: 1-5 Tight: 2-4 Gall: 2-11
Aids: Bl: 0-2 Vi: 0-0 Tstrap: 0-0
Best Rating: 87 5/01 York 1m5f194y gd-fm

He has been around a few yards in his life and was a progressive stayer in 1999, but lost his way until a drop in the handicap enabled him to win at Doncaster at the end of 2000. No form this season.

Loose Chippins (IRE)

59(75) (4)**82**

3-y-o b f Bigstone (IRE)-Fortune Teller (Troy)
G L Moore G G N Productions Limited

Placings:00-000 **(1317)**
2001: 5^{0}SD, 8^{0}G, 8^{0}SD

	Starts	1st	2nd	3rd	Win & Pl
Career Total (Turf)	3	0	0	0	
Career Total (AW)	2	0	0	0	

Going (Turf): **Sf: 0-1 GS: 0-0 Gd: 0-2 GF: 0-0 Fm: 0-0**
Distance: 5f/6f: 0-1 7f-8f: 0-3 9f-13f: 0-1 14f+: 0-0
Track : LH: 0-2 RH: 0-0 Tight: 0-1 Gall: 0-0
Aids: Bl: 0-0 Vi: 0-0 Tstrap: 0-0
Best Rating: 41 5/01 Wwck 1m22y good

Lord Advocate

96 (26)**23**

13-y-o br g Law Society (USA)-Kereolle (Riverman (USA))
D A Nolan Mrs J McFadyen-Murray

Placings:0000/5300301/0612020000020225403024 0/2565001631000 0/350000/3121026365434310 0/065163112535423362000505/42065201150502500020 0/0666614442050/04555053642506 0/0006066056-005400500056 **(5033)**
2001: 13^{0}G, 12^{0}GF, 13^{5}GS, 13^{4}G, 12^{0}GF, 13^{0}G, 10^{5}GS, 13^{0}GS, 7^{0}G, 11^{0}G, 10^{5}GF, 16^{6}GF

	Starts	1st	2nd	3rd	Win & Pl
Career Total (Turf)	145	11	14	13	57263
Career Total (AW)	21	2	4	1	7541

44	6/98	Haml	1m5f9y	F(0-60)H	GD	£2346
57	6/97	Haml	1m5f9y	D(0-80)H	GD	£4123
43	6/97	Haml	1m5f9y	E(0-70)H	G-F	£3051
53	6/96	Haml	1m5f9y	D(0-80)H	GD	£4513
47	5/96	Muss	1m3f32y	F(0-65)H	GD	£2707
43	5/96	Haml	1m5f9y	D(0-75)H	SFT	£3811
35	8/95	Muss	1m4f31y	E(0-70)H	G-F	£3139
37	6/95	Haml	1m5f9y	E(0-70)H	FRM	£3741
36	5/95	Haml	1m3f16y	G(0-60)H	G-F	£2731
41	7/93	Muss	1m7f16y	F	G-F	£2353
26	6/93	Muss	1m7f16y	F	GD	£2377
45	1/92	Sthl	1m4f	F(0-70)H	STD	£2382
59	12/91	Ling	1m2f	F	STD	£2324

Total win prize-money £39602

Going (Turf): Sf: 1-22 GS: 0-20 **Gd: 5-38** GF: 4-47 Fm: 1-18
Distance: 5f/6f: 0-3 7f-8f: 0-2 9f-13f: 5-85 **14f+: 8-76**
Track : LH: 2-41 **RH: 11-123 Tight: 12-124** Gall: 0-6
Aids: **Bl: 8-72** Vi: 5-82 Tstrap: 0-0
Best Rating: 46 9/01 Muss 2m gd-fm

Veteran stayer, all of his wins since '92 have been in Scotland, and he hardly ever runs south of the border. Has not won since 1998 and is an exceedingly limited performer these days.

Lord Alaska (IRE)

110 **88+**

4-y-o b g Sir Harry Lewis (USA)-Anchorage (IRE) (Slip Anchor)
J A R Toller Mrs Claire Smith

Placings:00501112-1 **(1305)**
2001: 16^{1}GF

	Starts	1st	2nd	3rd	Win & Pl
Career Total (Turf)	9	4	1	0	19172

88	5/01	Thsk	2m	C(0-90)H	G-F	£7241
74	9/00	Wwck	2m39y	F(0-70)H	G-F	£2467
69	8/00	Muss	2m	F(0-65)H	G-F	£2873
59	8/00	Folk	2m93y	F(0-70)H	G-F	£2268

Total win prize-money £14850

Going (Turf): Sf: 0-0 GS: 0-2 Gd: 0-2 **GF: 4-5** Fm: 0-0
Distance: 5f/6f: 0-0 7f-8f: 0-0 9f-13f: 0-4 **14f+: 4-5**
Track : LH: 2-4 RH: 2-3 **Tight: 3-7** Gall: 0-1
Aids: Bl: 0-0 Vi: 0-0 Tstrap: 0-0
Best Rating: 88 5/01 Thsk 2m gd-fm

Lord Ashmore

97 **55**

2-y-o gr g Greensmith-Flair Lady (Chilibang)
W G M Turner Mrs M S Teversham

Placings:032602000 **(5458)**
2001: 5^{0}HD, 5^{3}GF, 5^{2}GF, 5^{6}F, 5^{0}GF, 5^{2}GF, 5^{0}F, 5^{0}HY, 5^{0}G

	Starts	1st	2nd	3rd	Win & Pl
Career Total (Turf)	9	0	2	1	1722

Going (Turf): **Sf: 0-1 GS: 0-0 Gd: 0-1 GF: 0-4 Fm: 0-3**
Distance: 5f/6f: 0-9 7f-8f: 0-0 9f-13f: 0-0 14f+: 0-0
Track : LH: 0-5 RH: 0-0 Tight: 0-0 Gall: 0-4
Aids: Bl: 0-0 Vi: 0-1 Tstrap: 0-0
Best Rating: 55 10/01 Ling 5f heavy

Lord Bankes

(71) (1)

4-y-o b g Presidium-Marfen (Lochnager)
W G M Turner T Lightbowne

Placings:225004060/0 **(5350)**
2001: 5^{0}SD

	Starts	1st	2nd	3rd	Win & Pl
Career Total (Turf)	8	0	2	0	2651
Career Total (AW)	2	0	0	0	

Going (Turf): **Sf: 0-2 GS: 0-2 Gd: 0-3 GF: 0-1 Fm: 0-0**
Distance: 5f/6f: 0-9 7f-8f: 0-1 9f-13f: 0-0 14f+: 0-0
Track : LH: 0-4 RH: 0-0 Tight: 0-1 Gall: 0-2
Aids: Bl: 0-1 Vi: 0-0 Tstrap: 0-0
Best Rating: 1 10/01 Sthl 5f stand

Lord Chamberlain

96 **52**

8-y-o b g Be My Chief (USA)-Metaphysique (FR) (Law Society (USA))
J M Bradley W C Harries

Placings:056 **(5670)**
2001: 11^{0}S, 11^{5}G, 8^{6}HY

	Starts	1st	2nd	3rd	Win & Pl
Career Total (Turf)	3	0	0	0	0

Going (Turf): **Sf: 0-2 GS: 0-0 Gd: 0-1 GF: 0-0 Fm: 0-0**
Distance: 5f/6f: 0-0 7f-8f: 0-0 9f-13f: 0-3 14f+: 0-0
Track : LH: 0-1 RH: 0-2 Tight: 0-2 Gall: 0-0
Aids: Bl: 0-0 Vi: 0-0 Tstrap: 0-0
Best Rating: 52 11/01 Catt 1m3f214y good

Lord Conyers (IRE)

83 **58**

2-y-o b f Inzar (USA)-Primelta (Primo Dominie)
Miss V Haigh The Lord Conyers Racing Partnership

Placings:004 **(4774)**
2001: 6^{0}GF, 8^{0}GF, 7^{4}G

	Starts	1st	2nd	3rd	Win & Pl
Career Total (Turf)	3	0	0	0	0

Going (Turf): **Sf: 0-0 GS: 0-0 Gd: 0-1 GF: 0-2 Fm: 0-0**
Distance: 5f/6f: 0-1 7f-8f: 0-1 9f-13f: 0-1 14f+: 0-0
Track : LH: 0-1 RH: 0-1 Tight: 0-0 Gall: 0-0
Aids: Bl: 0-0 Vi: 0-0 Tstrap: 0-0
Best Rating: 58 9/01 Bevl 7f100y good

Lord Dundee (IRE)

96 **71**

3-y-o ch c Polish Precedent (USA)-Easy To Copy (USA) (Affirmed (USA))
H R A Cecil Angus Dundee Plc

Placings:3 **(1847)**
2001: 11^{3}GF

	Starts	1st	2nd	3rd	Win & Pl
Career Total (Turf)	1	0	0	1	658

Going (Turf): **Sf: 0-0 GS: 0-0 Gd: 0-0 GF: 0-1 Fm: 0-0**
Distance: 5f/6f: 0-0 7f-8f: 0-0 9f-13f: 0-1 14f+: 0-0
Track : LH: 0-0 RH: 0-1 Tight: 0-0 Gall: 0-0
Aids: Bl: 0-0 Vi: 0-1 Tstrap: 0-0
Best Rating: 71 6/01 Leic 1m3f183y gd-fm

Lord Eurolink (IRE)

112(105) (67)**80**

7-y-o b g Danehill (USA)-Lady Eurolink (Kala Shikari)
M H Tompkins Icon-Ctt

Placings:31030/3/60450/30531110446450 1236-6010310503 **(5249)**
2001: 7^{6}GF, 8^{0}GF, 10^{1}GF, 10^{0}GF, 10^{3}G, 9^{1}GS, 10^{0}HY, 12^{5}GF, 12^{0}G, 10^{3}S

	Starts	1st	2nd	3rd	Win & Pl
Career Total (Turf)	28	4	1	6	28538
Career Total (AW)	11	3	0	2	7545

77	8/01	Bevl	1m1f207yC(0-90)H		G-S	£7150
70	6/01	Newb	1m2f6y	E(0-75)H	G-F	£3472
61	9/00	York	1m205y	E	GD	£6214
67	3/00	Wolv	1m100y	E(0-75)H	STD	£2786
65	3/00	Sthl	1m	F(0-60)	STD	£1722
48	2/00	Wolv	1m100y	G	STD	£1922
83	5/97	Donc	1m	D	GD	£4435

Total win prize-money £27702

Going (Turf): Sf: 0-7 GS: 1-5 **Gd: 2-7** GF: 1-9 Fm: 0-0

Distance: 5f/6f: 0-0 7f-8f: 2-8 **9f-13f: 5-31** 14f+: 0-0
Track : **LH: 5-28** RH: 1-7 Tight: 2-15 Gall: 2-11
Aids: Bl: 0-0 **Vi: 4-15** Tstrap: 3-8
Best Rating: 80 10/01 York 1m2f85y soft

He is equally effective on turf and sand and has scored at Newbury and Beverley so far this season. Ten furlongs is his best trip and he goes well for an inexperienced rider.

Lord Fernando

93 **65**

2-y-o ch g Forzando-Lady Lacey (Kampala)
G B Balding The Pj Partnership

Placings:000300200 **(5589)**
2001: 5[0]G, 5[0]S, 5[0]GF, 7[3]GS, 7[0]GF, 7[0]G, 7[2]HY, 6[0]GS, 7[0]GS

	Starts	1st	2nd	3rd	Win & Pl
Career Total (Turf)	9	0	1	1	1353

Going (Turf): Sf: 0-2 GS: 0-3 Gd: 0-2 GF: 0-2 Fm: 0-0
Distance: 5f/6f: 0-4 7f-8f: 0-5 9f-13f: 0-0 14f+: 0-0
Track : LH: 0-2 RH: 0-0 Tight: 0-0 Gall: 0-1
Aids: Bl: 0-0 Vi: 0-0 Tstrap: 0-0
Best Rating: 76 7/01 Wwck 7f26y gd-sft

Still a maiden, but has shown enough to suggest he can win a race before long.

Lord Gg (IRE)

88(81) (50)**61**

2-y-o b g Fayruz-Cnoc Ban (IRE) (On Your Mark)
J S Moore Wilwyn Racing (wwwwilwyncom)

Placings:000000 **(5038)**
2001: 6[0]GF, 6[0]GF, 6[0]GF, 6[0]SD, 8[0]SW, 5[0]G

	Starts	1st	2nd	3rd	Win & Pl
Career Total (Turf)	4	0	0	0	
Career Total (AW)	2	0	0	0	

Going (Turf): Sf: 0-0 GS: 0-0 Gd: 0-1 GF: 0-3 Fm: 0-0
Distance: 5f/6f: 0-4 7f-8f: 0-1 9f-13f: 0-1 14f+: 0-0
Track : LH: 0-3 RH: 0-0 Tight: 0-2 Gall: 0-1
Aids: Bl: 0-0 Vi: 0-3 Tstrap: 0-0
Best Rating: 61 7/01 Ling 6f gd-fm

Lord Gizzmo

(102) (45)**33**

4-y-o ch g Democratic (USA)-Figrant (USA) (L'Emigrant (USA))
R M Beckett The Paddy Pipers

Placings:060062-421406 **(0636)**
2001: 9[4]SW, 11[2]SD, 12[1]SD, 12[4]SD, 11[0]SD, 13[6]SD

	Starts	1st	2nd	3rd	Win & Pl
Career Total (Turf)	4	0	0	0	0
Career Total (AW)	8	1	2	0	3836

52	2/01	Wolv	1m4f	F(0-65)H	STD	£2296

Total win prize-money £2296

Going (Turf): Sf: 0-1 GS: 0-0 Gd: 0-1 GF: 0-2 Fm: 0-0
Distance: 5f/6f: 0-0 7f-8f: 0-2 **9f-13f: 1-10** 14f+: 0-0
Track : **LH: 1-10** RH: 0-1 **Tight: 1-7** Gall: 0-1
Aids: Bl: 0-0 Vi: 0-0 Tstrap: 0-0
Best Rating: 54 2/01 Sthl 1m3f stand

Lord Invincible

85(78) (38)**47**

3-y-o b c Dancing Spree (USA)-Lady Broker (Petorius)
M Mullineaux Esprit De Corps Racing

Placings:5600 **(4185)**
2001: 6[5]SD, 5[6]G, 8[0]G, 7[0]GF

	Starts	1st	2nd	3rd	Win & Pl
Career Total (Turf)	3	0	0	0	0
Career Total (AW)	1	0	0	0	0

Going (Turf): Sf: 0-0 GS: 0-0 Gd: 0-2 GF: 0-1 Fm: 0-0
Distance: 5f/6f: 0-2 7f-8f: 0-1 9f-13f: 0-1 14f+: 0-0
Track : LH: 0-2 RH: 0-0 Tight: 0-1 Gall: 0-0
Aids: Bl: 0-0 Vi: 0-0 Tstrap: 0-0
Best Rating: 47 8/01 Nott 1m54y good

Lord Jim (IRE)

105 (83)**93**

9-y-o b g Kahyasi-Sarah Georgina (Persian Bold)
G A Butler Mrs S Y Thomas

Placings:0540/144302604/511223/05300/034/5-10 **(2305)**
2001: 12[1]GF, 20[0]GF

	Starts	1st	2nd	3rd	Win & Pl
Career Total (Turf)	29	4	3	4	77853
Career Total (AW)	1	0	0	0	728

93	6/01	Epsm	1m4f10y	B(0-105)H	G-F	£29000
97	8/96	Leop	1m6f		GD	£9675
90	6/96	Sals	1m6f	C	G-F	£4799
72	3/95	Leic	1m3f183yD		SFT	£3698

Total win prize-money £47173

Going (Turf): Sf: 1-4 GS: 0-5 Gd: 1-10 **GF: 2-9** Fm: 0-1
Distance: 5f/6f: 0-0 7f-8f: 0-1 9f-13f: 2-10 14f+: 2-19
Track : LH: 2-14 RH: 2-13 **Tight: 2-6** Gall: 0-12
Aids: Bl: 1-5 Vi: 1-6 Tstrap: 0-0
Best Rating: 93 6/01 Epsm 1m4f10y gd-fm

He only ran once last season, but bounced right back to form when coming from an unpromising position to gain a slightly fortunate win at Epsom over a mile and a half on Derby Day. Ideally needs further and is best on a sound surface.

Lord Joshua (IRE)

106 **83+**

3-y-o b c King's Theatre (IRE)-Lady Joshua (IRE) (Royal Academy (USA))
G A Butler Mrs A E Butler

Placings:3-05421020001 **(5463)**
2001: 8[0]S, 7[5]S, 9[4]G, 11[2]G, 14[1]GF, 12[0]GF, 13[2]GF, 13[0]GF, 14[0]HY, 16[0]S, 11[1]G

	Starts	1st	2nd	3rd	Win & Pl
Career Total (Turf)	12	2	2	1	12846

83	10/01	Bath	1m3f144yD(0-80)H		GD	£4004
79	6/01	Kemp	1m6f92y	D(0-75)	G-F	£4114

Total win prize-money £8119

Going (Turf): Sf: 0-5 GS: 0-0 **Gd: 1-3 GF: 1-4** Fm: 0-0
Distance: 5f/6f: 0-0 7f-8f: 0-3 9f-13f: 1-4 14f+: 1-5
Track : LH: 1-4 RH: 1-5 **Tight: 1-3** Gall: 0-4
Aids: Bl: 0-0 Vi: 0-0 Tstrap: 0-0
Best Rating: 83 10/01 Bath 1m3f144y good

A backward sort last term, he gradually improved as he was stepped up in trip and got off the mark in a 14-furlong classified stakes at Kempton in June. Struggled off higher marks until given a chance by the Handicapper at Bath in October. Acts on good or fast ground, does not seem to handle soft. Has joined Nicky Henderson.

Lord Kintyre

111 **95**

6-y-o b g Makbul-Highland Rowena (Royben)
B R Millman M Calvert

Placings:4141242/2523030/50/244021115-00043006003 **(5502)**
2001: 5[0]GS, 5[0]G, 5[0]GF, 5[4]GF, 5[3]GF, 5[0]G, 5[0]GS, 5[6]G, 5[0]S, 5[0]GS, 5[3]HY

	Starts	1st	2nd	3rd	Win & Pl
Career Total (Turf)	36	5	6	4	176263

105	9/00	Donc	5f	A	G-F	£14508
105	8/00	Nott	5f13y	C	GD	£6351
103	7/00	NmkJ	5f	C	GD	£6426
98	7/97	Newb	5f34y	B	G-F	£74671
80	6/97	Wind	5f217y	E	G-F	£3257

Total win prize-money £105215

Going (Turf): Sf: 0-6 GS: 0-4 Gd: 2-14 **GF: 3-11** Fm: 0-1
Distance: **5f/6f: 5-36** 7f-8f: 0-0 9f-13f: 0-0 14f+: 0-0
Track : LH: 0-1 **RH: 1-1** Tight: 0-0 **Gall: 1-2**
Aids: Bl: 0-0 Vi: 0-0 Tstrap: 0-0
Best Rating: 105 7/01 Asct 5f gd-fm

Useful sprinter who falls just short at Group level. Best on a sound surface at up to six furlongs but does handle slower. One or two promising runs in 2001, but generally below his best.

Lord Lamb

102 **89**

9-y-o gr g Dunbeath (USA)-Caroline Lamb (Hotfoot)
Mrs M Reveley A Sharratt & J Renton

Placings:054310/323/2-5 **(1941)**
2001: 16[5]G

	Starts	1st	2nd	3rd	Win & Pl
Career Total (Turf)	11	1	2	3	18087

69	9/98	Hayd	1m6f	D(0-85)H	G-F	£7262

Total win prize-money £7263

Going (Turf): Sf: 0-2 GS: 0-2 Gd: 0-4 **GF: 1-2** Fm: 0-1
Distance: 5f/6f: 0-0 7f-8f: 0-1 9f-13f: 0-5 **14f+: 1-5**
Track : **LH: 1-7** RH: 0-3 Tight: 0-1 Gall: 0-5
Aids: Bl: 0-0 Vi: 0-0 Tstrap: 0-0
Best Rating: 82 6/01 Hayd 2m45y good

Useful stayer. Lightly-raced on the Flat in recent seasons.

Lord Liam (USA)

91(86) (55)**56**

3-y-o b g Foxhound (USA)-Crackling Sike (Salse (USA))
T Keddy Mrs Hayley Keddy

Placings:534560-00400000 **(4366)**
2001: 6[0]GS, 6[0]GS, 8[4]F, 8[0]GF, 7[0]G, 5[0]GS, 7[0]GF, 9[0]GF

	Starts	1st	2nd	3rd	Win & Pl
Career Total (Turf)	12	0	0	1	819
Career Total (AW)	2	0	0	0	0

Going (Turf): Sf: 0-0 GS: 0-3 Gd: 0-3 GF: 0-5 Fm: 0-1
Distance: 5f/6f: 0-6 7f-8f: 0-5 9f-13f: 0-3 14f+: 0-0
Track : LH: 0-6 RH: 0-1 Tight: 0-4 Gall: 0-0
Aids: Bl: 0-0 Vi: 0-0 Tstrap: 0-8
Best Rating: 66 4/01 NmkR 6f gd-sft

Lord Melbourne (IRE)

73 **43**

2-y-o b f Lycius (USA)-Adana (IRE) (Classic Music (USA))
J A Osborne The Memory Lane Partnership

Placings:0 **(4639)**
2001: 6[0]GF

	Starts	1st	2nd	3rd	Win & Pl
Career Total (Turf)	1	0	0	0	

Going (Turf): Sf: 0-0 GS: 0-0 Gd: 0-0 GF: 0-1 Fm: 0-0
Distance: 5f/6f: 0-1 7f-8f: 0-0 9f-13f: 0-0 14f+: 0-0
Track : LH: 0-0 RH: 0-0 Tight: 0-0 Gall: 0-0
Aids: Bl: 0-0 Vi: 0-0 Tstrap: 0-0
Best Rating: 43 9/01 Ling 6f gd-fm

Lord Merlin (IRE)

98 **92**

2-y-o b c Turtle Island (IRE)-My-O-My (IRE) (Waajib)
D Nicholls Neil Smith

Placings:1330 **(5256)**
2001: 5^{1}GS, 5^{3}GF, 6^{3}GY, 5^{0}GS

	Starts	1st	2nd	3rd	Win & Pl
Career Total (Turf)	4	1	0	2	33339

72 5/01 Pont 5f D G-S £4013
Total win prize-money £4014

Going (Turf): Sf: 0-0 **GS: 1-2** Gd: 0-0 GF: 0-1 Fm: 0-0
Distance: **5f/6f: 1-4** 7f-8f: 0-0 9f-13f: 0-0 14f+: 0-0
Track : **LH: 1-1** RH: 0-0 Tight: 0-0 Gall: 0-0
Aids: Bl: 0-0 Vi: 0-0 Tstrap: 0-0
Best Rating: 92 8/01 Curr 6f gd-yld

Whose dam was a listed winner over five furlongs, is the first debutant juvenile scorer David Nicholls has sent out. Handles soft ground well, as do most of the progeny of Turtle Island, but coped with faster ground at Ascot. Ran a good race when tried at six in the Curragh. However, he has three times had to be withdrawn after becoming upset in the stalls.

Lord Of Love

65 **46**

6-y-o b g Noble Patriarch-Gymcrak Lovebird (Taufan (USA))
D Burchell (D L Williams 16/4) Mouse Racing

Placings:0054303604/0644456/0 **(5170)**
2001: 17^{0}GS

	Starts	1st	2nd	3rd	Win & Pl
Career Total (Turf)	18	0	0	2	1892

Going (Turf): Sf: 0-1 GS: 0-7 Gd: 0-4 GF: 0-5 Fm: 0-1
Distance: 5f/6f: 0-3 7f-8f: 0-9 9f-13f: 0-5 14f+: 0-1
Track : LH: 0-6 RH: 0-10 Tight: 0-4 Gall: 0-4
Aids: Bl: 0-0 Vi: 0-0 Tstrap: 0-0

Lord Of Methley

96 **73**

2-y-o gr c Zilzal (USA)-Paradise Waters (Celestial Storm (USA))
R M Whitaker D Samuel

Placings:05450 **(5690)**
2001: 6^{0}G, 7^{5}G, 7^{4}G, 7^{5}HY, 7^{0}S

	Starts	1st	2nd	3rd	Win & Pl
Career Total (Turf)	5	0	0	0	291

Going (Turf): Sf: 0-2 GS: 0-0 Gd: 0-3 GF: 0-0 Fm: 0-0
Distance: 5f/6f: 0-1 7f-8f: 0-4 9f-13f: 0-0 14f+: 0-0
Track : LH: 0-3 RH: 0-0 Tight: 0-1 Gall: 0-0
Aids: Bl: 0-0 Vi: 0-0 Tstrap: 0-0
Best Rating: 73 8/01 Thsk 7f good

Has shown promise on all starts so far, although he needs to improve if he is going to win a race.

Lord Of The East

94 **73**

2-y-o b g Emarati (USA)-Fairy Free (Rousillon (USA))
B R Millman Mrs G Austen Smith/c Lewis/m Calvert

Placings:6002552 **(4623)**
2001: 5^{6}F, 6^{0}GF, 5^{0}GF, 5^{2}GF, 5^{5}S, 6^{5}GF, 5^{2}GF

	Starts	1st	2nd	3rd	Win & Pl
Career Total (Turf)	7	0	2	0	1882

Going (Turf): Sf: 0-1 GS: 0-0 Gd: 0-0 GF: 0-5 Fm: 0-1
Distance: 5f/6f: 0-6 7f-8f: 0-1 9f-13f: 0-0 14f+: 0-0
Track : LH: 0-0 RH: 0-1 Tight: 0-0 Gall: 0-1
Aids: Bl: 0-0 Vi: 0-0 Tstrap: 0-4
Best Rating: 73 7/01 Folk 5f gd fm

Lord Omni (USA)

92(105) (72)**72**

4-y-o ch g El Prado (IRE)-Muskoka Ice (USA) (It's Freezing (USA))
R H Buckler (T D Barron 28/7) Mrs Liz Jones

Placings:604/615-**0310**000 **(3445)**
2001: 7^{0}SW, 6^{3}SW, 6^{1}SD, 7^{0}SD, 6^{0}G, 6^{0}F, 7^{0}GF

	Starts	1st	2nd	3rd	Win & Pl
Career Total (Turf)	9	1	0	0	3074
Career Total (AW)	4	1	0	1	4392

72 2/01 Sthl 6f D(0-80)H STD £3796
72 6/00 Thsk 6f E(0-70)H FRM £2827
Total win prize-money £6624

Going (Turf): Sf: 0-2 GS: 0-0 Gd: 0-3 GF: 0-2 **Fm: 1-2**
Distance: **5f/6f: 2-7** 7f-8f: 0-6 9f-13f: 0-0 14f+: 0-0
Track : **LH: 1-4** RH: 0-1 Tight: 0-1 Gall: 0-0
Aids: Bl: 0-0 Vi: 0-0 Tstrap: 0-1
Best Rating: 72 2/01 Sthl 6f stand

Really came to himself last season. Suited by six and seven furlongs. Acts on firm and Fibresand.

Lord Pacal (IRE)

109 **85**

4-y-o b g Indian Ridge-Please Believe Me (Try My Best (USA))
N A Callaghan Paul & Jenny Green

Placings:14542034/00002214102-0004402500 **(5133)**
2001: 7^{0}S, 6^{0}G, 6^{0}GF, 7^{4}GF, 7^{4}F, 6^{0}G, 6^{2}GS, 6^{5}G, 7^{0}GS, 7^{0}G

	Starts	1st	2nd	3rd	Win & Pl
Career Total (Turf)	29	3	5	1	40423

86 8/00 NmkJ 7f C(0-90)H G-F £7221
81 7/00 Yarm 6f3y C(0-95)H G-F £6955
95 5/99 Newb 5f34y D G-F £4224
Total win prize-money £18401

Going (Turf): Sf: 0-4 GS: 0-5 Gd: 0-11 **GF: 3-8** Fm: 0-1
Distance: 5f/6f: 1-16 **7f-8f: 2-13** 9f-13f: 0-0 14f+: 0-0
Track : LH: 0-3 RH: 0-0 Tight: 0-3 Gall: 0-0
Aids: Bl: 0-1 Vi: 0-0 Tstrap: 0-0
Best Rating: 87 6/01 Newc 7f firm

He is a fairly useful handicapper who stays up to seven furlongs. He took time to return to his best this season but put in a couple of much better efforts during midsummer as the Handicapper relented. He has run well with cut in the ground, but his wins have been on a fast surface.

Lord Pierce

101(102) (88+)**87**

3-y-o b g Tragic Role (USA)-Mirkan Honey (Ballymore)
M Johnston Hertford Offset Limited

Placings:51 **(5286)**
2001: 11^{5}S, 10^{1}HY

	Starts	1st	2nd	3rd	Win & Pl
Career Total (Turf)	2	1	0	0	4079

87 10/01 Ayr 1m2f D HVY £4078
Total win prize-money £4079

Going (Turf): Sf: 1-2 GS: 0-0 Gd: 0-0 GF: 0-0 Fm: 0-0
Distance: 5f/6f: 0-0 7f-8f: 0-0 **9f-13f: 1-2** 14f+: 0-0
Track : **LH: 1-1** RH: 0-1 Tight: 0-0 Gall: 0-0
Aids: Bl: 0-0 Vi: 0-0 Tstrap: 0-0
Best Rating: 87 10/01 Ayr 1m2f heavy

A powerful galloper with a markedly round action, he relished the conditions at Ayr over ten furlongs to land a fair maiden. Looks a very useful stayer in the making.

Lord Protector (IRE)

109(99) (78+)**93**

3-y-o b c Nicolotte-Scared (Royal Academy (USA))
D W P Arbuthnot Derrick C Broomfield

Placings:425-132620 **(4053)**
2001: 7^{1}SD, 6^{3}F, 8^{2}GF, 8^{6}GF, 8^{2}GS, 7^{0}GF

	Starts	1st	2nd	3rd	Win & Pl
Career Total (Turf)	8	0	3	1	26114
Career Total (AW)	1	1	0	0	1799

78 4/01 Sthl 7f F STD £1799
Total win prize-money £1799

Going (Turf): Sf: 0-1 GS: 0-1 Gd: 0-1 GF: 0-4 Fm: 0-1
Distance: 5f/6f: 0-0 **7f-8f: 1-8** 9f-13f: 0-1 14f+: 0-0
Track : **LH: 1-4** RH: 0-0 Tight: 0-0 Gall: 0-2
Aids: Bl: 0-0 Vi: 0-0 Tstrap: 0-0
Best Rating: 93 7/01 NmkJ 1m gd-sft

He landed a Fibresand maiden on his reappearance and has run well in some very warm handicaps since. Effective on fast ground, but handles good to soft. Stays a mile.

Lord Stradbroke (USA)

83 **56**

2-y-o b c Lear Fan (USA)-Encorenous (USA) (Diesis)
M A Jarvis Tigerland Ltd

Placings:05 **(5527)**
2001: 8^{0}GS, 8^{5}HY

	Starts	1st	2nd	3rd	Win & Pl
Career Total (Turf)	2	0	0	0	0

Going (Turf): Sf: 0-1 GS: 0-1 Gd: 0-0 GF: 0-0 Fm: 0-0
Distance: 5f/6f: 0-0 7f-8f: 0-1 9f-13f: 0-1 14f+: 0-0
Track : LH: 0-1 RH: 0-0 Tight: 0-0 Gall: 0-0
Aids: Bl: 0-0 Vi: 0-0 Tstrap: 0-0
Best Rating: 56 10/01 Nott 1m54y heavy

Lordofenchantment (IRE)

105(78) (42)**56**

4-y-o ch g Soviet Lad (USA)-Sauvignon (IRE) (Alzao (USA))
Don Enrico Incisa Mrs Christine Cawley

Placings:06501566/0522055240-0020216501 **(4907)**
2001: 6^{0}SD, 6^{0}G, 7^{2}GF, 6^{0}GF, 7^{2}GF, 7^{1}GF, 7^{6}GF, 7^{5}G, 7^{0}GF, 7^{1}G

	Starts	1st	2nd	3rd	Win & Pl
Career Total (Turf)	26	3	5	0	14959
Career Total (AW)	2	0	0	0	0

56 9/01 Bevl 7f100y E(0-70)H GD £3535
55 7/01 Sthl 7f D(0-80)H G-F £4329
67 8/99 Ripn 6f F G-F £2253
Total win prize-money £10117

Going (Turf): Sf: 0-3 GS: 0-5 Gd: 1-10 **GF: 2-8** Fm: 0-0
Distance: 5f/6f: 1-16 **7f-8f: 2-12** 9f-13f: 0-0 14f+: 0-0
Track : LH: 1-8 RH: 1-6 Tight: 0-1 Gall: 0-1
Aids: Bl: 0-0 **Vi: 1-6** Tstrap: 0-0
Best Rating: 56 9/01 Bevl 7f100y good

Improving gelding, he won his first handicap on turf at Southwell in July and scored again at Beverley in September. Suited by seven furlongs, but should stay a mile.

Lorenzino (IRE)

82 **43**

4-y-o ch g Thunder Gulch (USA)-Russian Ballet (USA) (Nijinsky (CAN))
J J O'Neill P Piller

Placings:5/04663-00 (4572)

2001: 10^{0}S, 10^{0}HY

	Starts	1st	2nd	3rd	Win & Pl
Career Total (Turf)	8	0	0	1	1200

Going (Turf): Sf: 0-4 GS: 0-0 Gd: 0-0 GF: 0-1 Fm: 0-0
Distance: 5f/6f: 0-0 7f-8f: 0-4 9f-13f: 0-3 14f+: 0-0
Track : LH: 0-5 RH: 0-1 Tight: 0-0 Gall: 0-1
Aids: Bl: 0-0 Vi: 0-0 Tstrap: 0-0
Best Rating: 43 9/01 Hayd 1m2f120y heavy

Lori's Dancer

85(59) (7)**69**

2-y-o ch f Zilzal (USA)-Brush Away (Ahonoora)
W Jarvis Stephen Purner

Placings:06 (5417)

2001: 7^{0}GF, 7^{6}SD

	Starts	1st	2nd	3rd	Win & Pl
Career Total (Turf)	1	0	0	0	
Career Total (AW)	1	0	0	0	0

Going (Turf): Sf: 0-0 GS: 0-0 Gd: 0-0 GF: 0-1 Fm: 0-0
Distance: 5f/6f: 0-0 7f-8f: 0-2 9f-13f: 0-0 14f+: 0-0
Track : LH: 0-1 RH: 0-0 Tight: 0-1 Gall: 0-0
Aids: Bl: 0-0 Vi: 0-0 Tstrap: 0-0
Best Rating: 69 8/01 NmkJ 7f gd-fm

Lost At Sea (IRE)

103 **84**

3-y-o b c Exit To Nowhere (USA)-Night At Sea (Night Shift (USA))
K R Burke David H Morgan

Placings:020165-060050 (4315)

2001: 7^{0}G, 7^{6}GF, 8^{0}GF, 6^{0}GF, 7^{5}GF, 8^{0}G

	Starts	1st	2nd	3rd	Win & Pl
Career Total (Turf)	12	1	1	0	6408

78	7/00	Yarm	7f3y	E	GD	£2821

Total win prize-money £2821

Going (Turf): Sf: 0-0 GS: 0-0 Gd: 0-4 GF: 0-7 Fm: 0-0
Distance: 5f/6f: 0-5 7f-8f: 0-6 9f-13f: 0-0 14f+: 0-0
Track : LH: 0-1 RH: 0-3 Tight: 0-1 Gall: 0-0
Aids: Bl: 0-0 Vi: 0-0 Tstrap: 0-8
Best Rating: 84 5/01 Gdwd 7f gd-fm

Scored once as a juvenile over seven furlongs on good ground. Has tended to race keenly but showed signs of improvement when dropped out the back.

Lost In Hook (IRE)

86(103) **24**

4-y-o b f Dancing Dissident (USA)-Rathbawn Realm (Doulab (USA))
P S McEntee (A P Jarvis 5/5) Travel Spot Ltd

Placings:16452/300000-1600000000 (5397)

2001: 6^{1}FT, 6^{6}FT, 8^{0}FT, 7^{0}GF, 5^{0}GF, 6^{0}G, 8^{0}GS, 7^{0}G, 7^{0}G, 8^{0}SD

	Starts	1st	2nd	3rd	Win & Pl
Career Total (Turf)	16	1	1	0	4642
Career Total (AW)	5	1	0	1	2153

	2/01	Mija	6f		FST	£1529
94	7/99	Ripn	5f	F	GD	£2762

Total win prize-money £4291

Going (Turf): Sf: 0-2 GS: 0-2 **Gd: 1-9** GF: 0-3 Fm: 0-0
Distance: **5f/6f: 2-14** 7f-8f: 0-6 9f-13f: 0-1 14f+: 0-0
Track : LH: 0-4 RH: 0-0 Tight: 0-3 Gall: 0-0
Aids: Bl: 0-1 Vi: 0-1 Tstrap: 0-2
Best Rating: 25 6/01 NmkJ 7f gd-fm

Lost Spirit

98(109) (47)**49**

5-y-o b g Strolling Along (USA)-Shoag (USA) (Affirmed (USA))
P W Hiatt P W Hiatt

Placings:0260/5631153000660/1202506003506401135210064-01241011100002060600 (5407)

2001: 10^{0}SD, 13^{1}SD, 12^{2}SD, 12^{4}SW, 12^{1}SD, 12^{0}SW, 12^{1}SW, 12^{1}SW, 12^{1}SW, 12^{0}SD, 12^{0}SD, 12^{0}SD, 12^{0}SD, 12^{2}GF, 12^{0}GF, 11^{6}G, 12^{0}GF, 12^{6}GF, 12^{0}SD, 12^{0}SD

	Starts	1st	2nd	3rd	Win & Pl
Career Total (Turf)	23	3	3	3	13072
Career Total (AW)	40	8	3	1	37802

68	2/01	Ling	1m4f	C(0-95)H	SLW	£6678
60	2/01	Ling	1m4f	C(0-100)H	SLW	£10634
60	2/01	Ling	1m4f	D(0-80)H	SLW	£3737
50	1/01	Sthl	1m4f	G(0-60)H	STD	£1456
50	1/01	Ling	1m5f	E(0-70)H	STD	£2905
41	8/00	Folk	1m4f	E(0-70)H	G-F	£3108
37	8/00	Bevl	1m3f216y	E(0-70)H	GD	£4121
31	7/00	Wwck	1m4f134y	G(0-60)H	G-F	£2027
47	1/00	Ling	1m4f	E(0-70)H	STD	£3607
63	3/99	Wolv	1m4f	D(0-85)H	SLW	£3517
73	2/99	Sthl	1m4f	F	STD	£2028

Total win prize-money £43823

Going (Turf): Sf: 0-4 GS: 0-2 Gd: 1-5 **GF: 2-10** Fm: 0-2
Distance: 5f/6f: 0-1 7f-8f: 0-4 **9f-13f: 11-57** 14f+: 0-1
Track : **LH: 9-51** RH: 2-8 **Tight: 8-40** Gall: 0-0
Aids: Bl: 0-2 Vi: 0-0 Tstrap: 0-0
Best Rating: 68 2/01 Ling 1m4f slow

Best when able to dominate, he improved out of all recognition to win five times in the space of six weeks on the sand earlier in the year. Adopted front-running tactics on his return to the turf when second at Southwell.

Lots Of Love (USA)

104 **96**

3-y-o b g Woodman (USA)-Accountable Lady (USA) (The Minstrel (CAN))
M Johnston M Doyle

Placings:14-16011200 (5607)

2001: 7^{1}GS, 10^{6}GS, 7^{0}G, 7^{1}HY, 7^{1}HY, 7^{2}S, 8^{0}GS, 8^{0}GS

	Starts	1st	2nd	3rd	Win & Pl
Career Total (Turf)	10	4	1	0	32485

96	9/01	Hayd	7f30y	C(0-95)H	HVY	£14397
93	9/01	Hayd	7f30y	C(0-90)H	HVY	£7897
84	7/01	Ling	7f140y	C(0-90)	G-S	£7052
90	8/00	Newc	7f	D	G-S	£2814

Total win prize-money £32163

Going (Turf): Sf: 2-3 GS: 2-6 Gd: 0-1 GF: 0-0 Fm: 0-0
Distance: 5f/6f: 0-0 **7f-8f: 4-9** 9f-13f: 0-1 14f+: 0-0
Track : **LH: 2-5** RH: 0-0 Tight: 0-0 Gall: 0-2
Aids: Bl: 0-0 Vi: 0-0 Tstrap: 0-0
Best Rating: 96 10/01 York 7f202y soft

A winner on his Newcastle debut at two, he was beaten at long odds-on at Leicester next time and was off the track for ten months before winning a valuable Lingfield classified event on his return in July. Appeared not to stay longer distances afterwards, but scored at Haydock when dropped back in trip and followed up over the same course and distance. He is suited by seven furlongs and soft ground.

Lots Of Magic

104 **79d**

5-y-o b h Magic Ring (IRE)-Pounelta (Tachypous)
R Hannon Peter Valentine

Placings:22414/14140/6000-003005050 (4872)

2001: 7^{0}G, 7^{0}G, 7^{3}F, 7^{0}GF, 6^{0}GF, 7^{5}G, 7^{0}GF, 6^{5}G, 7^{0}G

	Starts	1st	2nd	3rd	Win & Pl
Career Total (Turf)	23	3	2	1	57832

115	6/99	Asct	7f	A	G-F	£41700
97	5/99	Ling	7f	D	G-F	£3968
85	9/98	Epsm	7f	E	GD	£3452

Total win prize-money £49122

Going (Turf): Sf: 0-0 GS: 0-0 Gd: 1-13 **GF: 2-9** Fm: 0-1
Distance: 5f/6f: 0-4 **7f-8f: 3-18** 9f-13f: 0-1 14f+: 0-0
Track : **LH: 1-5** RH: 0-6 **Tight: 1-3** Gall: 0-1
Aids: Bl: 0-0 Vi: 0-0 Tstrap: 0-5
Best Rating: 95 5/01 NmkR 7f good

A seven furlong specialist, he made all for a shock victory in the Jersey Stakes at Royal Ascot in 1999, but was off the track for three months afterwards due to a lung infection. Largely out of form since, he has worn a tongue tie in recent races. Suited by fast ground.

Lotus Eater

65 **14**

2-y-o gr f Linamix (FR)-La Adrada (Arazi (USA))
S C Williams D A Shekells

Placings:0 (5594)

2001: 6^{0}GS

	Starts	1st	2nd	3rd	Win & Pl
Career Total (Turf)	1	0	0	0	

Going (Turf): Sf: 0-0 GS: 0-1 Gd: 0-0 GF: 0-0 Fm: 0-0
Distance: 5f/6f: 0-1 7f-8f: 0-0 9f-13f: 0-0 14f+: 0-0
Track : LH: 0-0 RH: 0-0 Tight: 0-0 Gall: 0-0
Aids: Bl: 0-0 Vi: 0-0 Tstrap: 0-0
Best Rating: 14 11/01 NmkR 6f gd-sft

Lou's Wish

92(105) (29)**32**

4-y-o b g Thatching-Shamaka (Kris)
M J Polglase Brian Androlia

Placings:00500600/31263600000002-063005050000 (5225)

2001: 16^{0}SD, 11^{6}SD, 11^{3}SD, 9^{0}SD, 8^{0}SD, 12^{5}SD, 11^{0}SD, 11^{5}SD, 12^{0}SD, 8^{0}SD, 8^{0}G, 10^{0}S

	Starts	1st	2nd	3rd	Win & Pl
Career Total (Turf)	12	0	0	0	0
Career Total (AW)	23	1	2	3	5190

65	1/00	Wolv	7f	G(0-60)H	STD	£1904

Total win prize-money £1905

Going (Turf): Sf: 0-2 GS: 0-2 Gd: 0-3 GF: 0-4 Fm: 0-1
Distance: 5f/6f: 0-4 **7f-8f: 1-17** 9f-13f: 0-13 14f+: 0-1
Track : **LH: 1-28** RH: 0-0 **Tight: 1-6** Gall: 0-3
Aids: **Bl: 1-22** Vi: 0-0 Tstrap: 0-0
Best Rating: 42 2/01 Sthl 1m3f stand

Loud And Proud

87 **49**

2-y-o b g Polish Precedent (USA)-Echo Cove (Slip Anchor)
R A Fahey Jim Blair

Placings:000 (5527)

2001: 7^{0}GF, 8^{0}GS, 8^{0}HY

	Starts	1st	2nd	3rd	Win & Pl
Career Total (Turf)	3	0	0	0	

Going (Turf): Sf: 0-1 GS: 0-1 Gd: 0-0 GF: 0-1 Fm: 0-0
Distance: 5f/6f: 0-0 7f-8f: 0-2 9f-13f: 0-1 14f+: 0-0
Track : LH: 0-3 RH: 0-0 Tight: 0-0 Gall: 0-2
Aids: Bl: 0-0 Vi: 0-0 Tstrap: 0-0
Best Rating: 49 9/01 York 7f202y gd-fm

Lough Bow (IRE)

92 **49**

3-y-o b g Nicolotte-Gale Force Seven (Strong Gale)
M W Easterby Mrs Anne Jarvis

Placings:00-000 **(4542)**
2001: 8^{0}GF, 10^{0}G, 10^{0}GF

	Starts	1st	2nd	3rd	Win & Pl
Career Total (Turf)	5	0	0	0	

Going (Turf): Sf: 0-0 GS: 0-0 Gd: 0-1 GF: 0-4 Fm: 0-0
Distance: 5f/6f: 0-0 7f-8f: 0-1 9f-13f: 0-4 14f+: 0-0
Track : LH: 0-1 RH: 0-4 Tight: 0-2 Gall: 0-0
Aids: Bl: 0-0 Vi: 0-0 Tstrap: 0-0
Best Rating: 41 8/01 Ripn 1m2f good

Loughlorien (IRE)

95(67) (18)**61d**
2-y-o b g Lake Coniston (IRE)-Fey Lady (IRE) (Fairy King (USA))
K A Ryan Pendle Inn Too Partnership

Placings:004256000 **(4990)**
2001: 5^{0}SW, 5^{0}GF, 5^{4}GF, 5^{2}GF, 5^{5}G, 6^{6}GS, 5^{0}F, 5^{0}G, 6^{0}HY

	Starts	1st	2nd	3rd	Win & Pl
Career Total (Turf)	8	0	1	0	1008
Career Total (AW)	1	0	0	0	

Going (Turf): Sf: 0-1 GS: 0-1 Gd: 0-2 GF: 0-3 Fm: 0-1
Distance: 5f/6f: 0-9 7f-8f: 0-0 9f-13f: 0-0 14f+: 0-0
Track : LH: 0-2 RH: 0-0 Tight: 0-2 Gall: 0-0
Aids: Bl: 0-4 Vi: 0-1 Tstrap: 0-0
Best Rating: 69 6/01 Rdcr 5f gd-fm

Louis Georgio

83 **62+**
2-y-o b c Royal Applause-Swellegant (Midyan (USA))
J Noseda L P Calvente

Placings:60 **(5125)**
2001: 5^{6}F, 5^{0}HY

	Starts	1st	2nd	3rd	Win & Pl
Career Total (Turf)	2	0	0	0	0

Going (Turf): Sf: 0-1 GS: 0-0 Gd: 0-0 GF: 0-0 Fm: 0-1
Distance: 5f/6f: 0-2 7f-8f: 0-0 9f-13f: 0-0 14f+: 0-0
Track : LH: 0-1 RH: 0-0 Tight: 0-0 Gall: 0-0
Aids: Bl: 0-0 Vi: 0-0 Tstrap: 0-0
Best Rating: 62 9/01 Pont 5f firm

Loup Cervier (IRE)

92(90) (27)**22**
4-y-o b g Wolfhound (USA)-Luth D'Or (FR) (Noir Et Or)
S Dow S Dow

Placings:00000034400000-00000000 **(4020)**
2001: 8^{0}SD, 7^{0}SW, 9^{0}F, 8^{0}GF, 9^{0}F, 6^{0}GF, 11^{0}G, 16^{0}G

	Starts	1st	2nd	3rd	Win & Pl
Career Total (Turf)	17	0	0	1	488
Career Total (AW)	5	0	0	0	

Going (Turf): Sf: 0-0 GS: 0-1 Gd: 0-5 GF: 0-7 Fm: 0-4
Distance: 5f/6f: 0-3 7f-8f: 0-6 9f-13f: 0-11 14f+: 0-2
Track : LH: 0-13 RH: 0-3 Tight: 0-8 Gall: 0-0
Aids: Bl: 0-0 Vi: 0-1 Tstrap: 0-1
Best Rating: 27 1/01 Ling 1m stand

Louvolite (IRE)

98 **74**
2-y-o b f Fayruz-Non Dimenticar Me (IRE) (Don't Forget Me)
J A Glover Sports Mania

Placings:0315 **(1903)**
2001: 5^{0}G, 5^{3}GF, 5^{1}F, 5^{5}GF

	Starts	1st	2nd	3rd	Win & Pl
Career Total (Turf)	4	1	0	1	4078
74 5/01 Rdcr 5f		E		FRM	£2954

Total win prize-money £2954

Going (Turf): Sf: 0-0 GS: 0-0 Gd: 0-1 GF: 0-2 Fm: 1-1
Distance: 5f/6f: 1-4 7f-8f: 0-0 9f-13f: 0-0 14f+: 0-0
Track : LH: 0-0 RH: 0-0 Tight: 0-0 Gall: 0-0
Aids: Bl: 0-0 Vi: 0-0 Tstrap: 0-0
Best Rating: 74 6/01 Bevl 5f gd-fm

A keen sort with bags of toe, she got off the mark at the third attempt in an auction event at Redcar in May.

Love (IRE)

94(65) (1)**31**
3-y-o b g Royal Academy (USA)-Kentmere (FR) (Galetto (FR))
M Johnston M Doyle

Placings:505-03000000 **(5273)**
2001: 9^{0}GF, 9^{3}GF, 8^{0}G, 8^{0}GF, 7^{0}G, 8^{0}SD, 8^{0}F, 5^{0}HY

	Starts	1st	2nd	3rd	Win & Pl
Career Total (Turf)	10	0	0	1	675
Career Total (AW)	1	0	0	0	

Going (Turf): Sf: 0-1 GS: 0-1 Gd: 0-2 GF: 0-5 Fm: 0-1
Distance: 5f/6f: 0-4 7f-8f: 0-2 9f-13f: 0-5 14f+: 0-0
Track : LH: 0-4 RH: 0-2 Tight: 0-3 Gall: 0-1
Aids: Bl: 0-4 Vi: 0-0 Tstrap: 0-5
Best Rating: 68 7/01 Muss 1m1f gd-fm

Love Diamonds (IRE)

91(98) (61)**41**
5-y-o b g Royal Academy (USA)-Baby Diamonds (Habitat)
Miss C Dyson (R Dickin 17/7) Miss C Dyson

Placings:50502213/21245000025300**0/206**000**326014**
-44300 **(3096)**
2001: 8^{4}SD, 9^{4}SW, 9^{3}SD, 8^{0}SD, 9^{0}G

	Starts	1st	2nd	3rd	Win & Pl
Career Total (Turf)	18	0	1	2	1570
Career Total (AW)	23	3	6	3	15070
61 12/00 Wolv 1m1f79y		F(0-65)H		STD	£1757
76 1/99 Ling 1m		E(0-75)H		STD	£2710
58 12/98 Ling 1m		E H		STD	£2925

Total win prize-money £7392

Going (Turf): Sf: 0-4 GS: 0-2 Gd: 0-6 GF: 0-5 Fm: 0-1
Distance: 5f/6f: 0-1 **7f-8f: 2-19** 9f-13f: 1-21 14f+: 0-0
Track : LH: 3-28 RH: 0-11 **Tight: 3-19** Gall: 0-1
Aids: Bl: 0-1 Vi: 0-1 Tstrap: 0-0
Best Rating: 59 1/01 Sthl 1m stand

Love Everlasting

115 **107**
3-y-o b f Pursuit Of Love-In Perpetuity (Great Nephew)
M Johnston Mr & Mrs G Middlebrook

Placings:342125-60351213425 **(5595)**
2001: 10^{6}G, 8^{0}GF, 8^{3}GF, 10^{5}F, 11^{1}G, 12^{2}GS, 12^{1}GF, 11^{3}G, 12^{4}S, 12^{2}GS, 12^{5}GS

	Starts	1st	2nd	3rd	Win & Pl
Career Total (Turf)	17	3	4	3	69079
106 8/01 Newb 1m4f5y		A		G-F	£15660
101 7/01 York 1m3f195yB(0-100)H				GD	£11126
70 9/00 Bevl 7f100y		D		G-F	£3705

Total win prize-money £30491

Going (Turf): Sf: 0-2 GS: 0-4 Gd: 1-5 **GF: 2-5** Fm: 0-1
Distance: 5f/6f: 0-2 7f-8f: 1-5 **9f-13f: 2-10** 14f+: 0-0
Track : LH: 2-6 RH: 1-4 Tight: 0-0 **Gall: 2-8**
Aids: Bl: 0-0 Vi: 0-0 Tstrap: 0-0
Best Rating: 107 10/01 Asct 1m4f gd-sft

She bolted up in a York rated stakes on her first try over 12 furlongs at York in July and ran well in a Newmarket Listed event when possibly a little unlucky. Made no mistake in a similar event at Newbury and has since run well in Pattern races. Acts on any ground, though her trainer believes she is suited by cut.

Love In The Mist

86(92) (68)**69**
2-y-o gr f Pursuit Of Love-Misty Goddess (IRE) (Godswalk (USA))
N P Littmoden J R Good

Placings:60663 **(5618)**
2001: 5^{6}S, 8^{0}SD, 7^{6}G, 8^{6}G, 8^{3}SD

	Starts	1st	2nd	3rd	Win & Pl
Career Total (Turf)	3	0	0	0	0
Career Total (AW)	2	0	0	1	276

Going (Turf): Sf: 0-1 GS: 0-0 Gd: 0-2 GF: 0-0 Fm: 0-0
Distance: 5f/6f: 0-1 7f-8f: 0-2 9f-13f: 0-2 14f+: 0-0
Track : LH: 0-2 RH: 0-0 Tight: 0-2 Gall: 0-0
Aids: Bl: 0-0 Vi: 0-0 Tstrap: 0-0
Best Rating: 69 10/01 Rdcr 7f good

Love Kiss (IRE)

95 **39**
6-y-o b g Brief Truce (USA)-Pendulina (Prince Tenderfoot (USA))
W Storey K Knox

Placings:043/0/600/0020064146-0000000 **(4617)**
2001: 7^{0}GF, 8^{0}F, 10^{0}F, 10^{0}GF, 9^{0}GF, 8^{0}F, 10^{0}F

	Starts	1st	2nd	3rd	Win & Pl
Career Total (Turf)	24	1	1	1	6189
60 10/00 Ayr 1m2f		D(0-80)H		HVY	£4013

Total win prize-money £4014

Going (Turf): Sf: 1-6 GS: 0-2 Gd: 0-4 GF: 0-5 Fm: 0-7
Distance: 5f/6f: 0-1 7f-8f: 0-10 **9f-13f: 1-12** 14f+: 0-1
Track : LH: 1-14 RH: 0-5 Tight: 0-10 Gall: 0-5
Aids: Bl: 0-0 Vi: 0-0 Tstrap: 0-1
Best Rating: 39 9/01 Ripn 1m1f gd-fm

Love Regardless (USA)

111 **86+**
2-y-o b/br c Storm Bird (CAN)-Circus Toons (USA) (Wild Again (USA))
M Johnston M Doyle

Placings:1 **(4615)**
2001: 6^{1}F

	Starts	1st	2nd	3rd	Win & Pl
Career Total (Turf)	1	1	0	0	2863
86 9/01 Newc 6f		D		FRM	£2863

Total win prize-money £2863

Going (Turf): Sf: 0-0 GS: 0-0 Gd: 0-0 GF: 0-0 **Fm: 1-1**
Distance: 5f/6f: 1-1 7f-8f: 0-0 9f-13f: 0-0 14f+: 0-0
Track : LH: 0-0 RH: 0-0 Tight: 0-0 Gall: 0-0
Aids: Bl: 0-0 Vi: 0-0 Tstrap: 0-0
Best Rating: 86 9/01 Newc 6f firm

A son of a Stakes winner in America, made an impressive debut at Newcastle in September, and looks sure to go on to better things.

Love Song

104 **75**
3-y-o b f Kris-Heart's Harmony (Blushing Groom (FR))
Sir Michael Stoute Mrs Denis Haynes

Placings:00436510 **(5179)**
2001: 7^{0}S, 7^{0}G, 10^{4}GF, 10^{3}GF, 9^{6}GF, 9^{5}GF, 10^{1}S, 10^{0}HY

	Starts	1st	2nd	3rd	Win & Pl
Career Total (Turf)	8	1	0	1	4856

47 9/01 Pont 1m2f6y E(0-70) SFT £3721
Total win prize-money £3721

Going (Turf): Sf: 1-3 GS: 0-0 Gd: 0-1 GF: 0-4 Fm: 0-0
Distance: 5f/6f: 0-0 7f-8f: 0-2 **9f-13f: 1-6** 14f+: 0-0
Track : **LH: 1-3** RH: 0-2 Tight: 0-2 Gall: 0-0
Aids: Bl: 0-0 Vi: 0-0 Tstrap: 0-0
Best Rating: 75 6/01 Pont 1m2f6y gd-fm

Love Thee Forever

84 **41**
2-y-o ch f Millkom-Exceptional Beauty (Sallust)
N P Littmoden Mrs Gillian Curley

Placings:0 (3704)
2001: 5⁰G

	Starts	1st	2nd	3rd	Win & Pl
Career Total (Turf)	1	0	0	0	

Going (Turf): Sf: 0-0 GS: 0-0 Gd: 0-1 GF: 0-0 Fm: 0-0
Distance: 5f/6f: 0-1 7f-8f: 0-0 9f-13f: 0-0 14f+: 0-0
Track : LH: 0-0 RH: 0-0 Tight: 0-0 Gall: 0-0
Aids: Bl: 0-0 Vi: 0-0 Tstrap: 0-0
Best Rating: 41 8/01 Leic 5f218y good

Love Thing

100 **65**
3-y-o b f Phountzi (USA)-Devils Dirge (Song)
R A Fahey Giles W Pritchard-Gordon

Placings:60100-206642250 (5449)
2001: 6²G, 7⁰GF, 5⁶GF, 6⁶F, 6⁴G, 6²G, 6²G, 6⁵F, 6⁰HY

	Starts	1st	2nd	3rd	Win & Pl
Career Total (Turf)	14	1	3	0	11765

65 8/00 Ripn 6f E G-F £4371
Total win prize-money £4371

Going (Turf): Sf: 0-2 GS: 0-1 Gd: 0-5 **GF: 1-4** Fm: 0-2
Distance: **5f/6f: 1-11** 7f-8f: 0-3 9f-13f: 0-0 14f+: 0-0
Track : LH: 0-1 RH: 0-1 Tight: 0-0 Gall: 0-1
Aids: Bl: 0-2 **Vi: 1-9** Tstrap: 0-0
Best Rating: 65 9/01 Pont 6f firm

Fair 6f performer, effective on any going.

Love Tune

91(92) (54)**49**
3-y-o b f Alhijaz-Heights Of Love (Persian Heights)
K R Burke Haven Partnership

Placings:53622200-6450000 (4233)
2001: 5⁶S, 5⁴GS, 5⁵HY, 5⁰GF, 5⁰F, 5⁰G, 5⁰G

	Starts	1st	2nd	3rd	Win & Pl
Career Total (Turf)	14	0	3	0	3727
Career Total (AW)	1	0	0	1	319

Going (Turf): Sf: 0-4 GS: 0-3 Gd: 0-5 GF: 0-1 Fm: 0-1
Distance: 5f/6f: 0-13 7f-8f: 0-2 9f-13f: 0-0 14f+: 0-0
Track : LH: 0-2 RH: 0-1 Tight: 0-2 Gall: 0-1
Aids: Bl: 0-0 Vi: 0-1 Tstrap: 0-0
Best Rating: 55 4/01 Muss 5f gd-sft

Love You Too

108 **74**
4-y-o ch f Be My Chief (USA)-Nagida (Skyliner)
K T Ivory Mike Perkins

Placings:10064540/040500-00341203100 (4283)
2001: 6⁰G, 5⁰F, 6³GF, 6⁴GF, 6¹GF, 6²GF, 6⁰GF, 6³GS, 6¹GF, 7⁰GF, 7⁰G

	Starts	1st	2nd	3rd	Win & Pl
Career Total (Turf)	25	3	1	2	20917

74 7/01 Sals 6f212y D(0-80)H G-F £5466
69 6/01 Sals 6f E(0-70)H G-F £3750
64 6/99 Donc 6f E GD £3777
Total win prize-money £12996

Going (Turf): Sf: 0-0 GS: 0-4 Gd: 1-9 **GF: 2-10** Fm: 0-2
Distance: **5f/6f: 2-15** 7f-8f: 1-8 9f-13f: 0-2 14f+: 0-0
Track : LH: 0-2 RH: 0-1 Tight: 0-3 Gall: 0-0
Aids: Bl: 0-0 **Vi: 2-9** Tstrap: 0-0
Best Rating: 74 7/01 Sals 6f212y gd-fm

She is suited by fast ground and and is effective at six or seven furlongs.

Love's Design (IRE)

104(109) (86+)**76**
4-y-o b/br g Pursuit Of Love-Cephista (Shirley Heights)
Miss J Feilden In The Know (3)

Placings:0631/30000-**460131110404010000** (4452)
2001: 7⁴SD, 9⁶SW, 8⁰SD, 8¹SW, 7³SD, 8¹SW, 8¹SD, 7¹SD, 8⁰GS, 6⁴F, 9⁰GF, 8⁴HD, 8⁰GF, 7¹G, 7⁰GF, 7⁰G, 7⁰GF, 7⁰GF

	Starts	1st	2nd	3rd	Win & Pl
Career Total (Turf)	19	2	0	2	9044
Career Total (AW)	8	4	0	1	9434

76 7/01 Brig 7f214y D(0-80)H GD £4046
86 4/01 Ling 7f E(0-75)H STD £3052
71 4/01 Ling 1m F(0-60)H STD £2324
72 3/01 Ling 1m F(0-60)H SLW £1858
45 2/01 Ling 1m G SLW £1883
67 11/99 Muss 7f30y E GD £3225
Total win prize-money £16389

Going (Turf): Sf: 0-2 GS: 0-2 **Gd: 2-6** GF: 0-7 Fm: 0-2
Distance: 5f/6f: 0-5 **7f-8f: 6-18** 9f-13f: 0-4 14f+: 0-0
Track : **LH: 5-15** RH: 1-3 **Tight: 5-9** Gall: 0-2
Aids: Bl: 0-0 **Vi: 6-20** Tstrap: 0-0
Best Rating: 86 4/01 Ling 7f stand

Best known as an Equitrack specialist, he has also won on turf. Stays a mile and best suited by hold-up tactics.

Loveleaves

95 **90**
2-y-o b f Polar Falcon (USA)-Rash (Pursuit Of Love)
M A Jarvis Mrs Mary Taylor

Placings:2 (5491)
2001: 6²HY

	Starts	1st	2nd	3rd	Win & Pl
Career Total (Turf)	1	0	1	0	1688

Going (Turf): Sf: 0-1 GS: 0-0 Gd: 0-0 GF: 0-0 Fm: 0-0
Distance: 5f/6f: 0-0 7f-8f: 0-1 9f-13f: 0-0 14f+: 0-0
Track : LH: 0-0 RH: 0-0 Tight: 0-0 Gall: 0-0
Aids: Bl: 0-0 Vi: 0-0 Tstrap: 0-0
Best Rating: 90 10/01 Newb 6f8y heavy

Finished runner-up in a bog on her Newbury debut and should come into her own at three.

Loves To Dare (IRE)

(59) **37**
2-y-o b f Desert King (IRE)-Loves To Dance (FR) (Sadler's Wells (USA))
B J Meehan (Robert Collet 30/4) E H Jones (paints) Ltd

Placings:0000 (5410)
2001: 5⁰HY, 7⁰GF, 7⁰GS, 7⁰SD

	Starts	1st	2nd	3rd	Win & Pl
Career Total (Turf)	3	0	0	0	0
Career Total (AW)	1	0	0	0	

Going (Turf): Sf: 0-1 GS: 0-1 Gd: 0-0 GF: 0-1 Fm: 0-0
Distance: 5f/6f: 0-1 7f-8f: 0-3 9f-13f: 0-0 14f+: 0-0
Track : LH: 0-1 RH: 0-0 Tight: 0-0 Gall: 0-0
Aids: Bl: 0-1 Vi: 0-0 Tstrap: 0-0
Best Rating: 37 9/01 Newb 7f gd-fm

Low On Funds (USA)

93(87) (22)**32**
4-y-o b g Eagle Eyed (USA)-Miss Sanmar (USA) (Recitation (USA))
I A Wood (T G Mills 17/1) Mrs Michelle Potter

Placings:606/00-000064054 (4093)
2001: 8⁰SD, 8⁰GF, 6⁰GF, 7⁰GS, 8⁶SD, 9⁴GF, 10⁰GS, 10⁵F, 9⁴G

	Starts	1st	2nd	3rd	Win & Pl
Career Total (Turf)	10	0	0	0	0
Career Total (AW)	4	0	0	0	0

Going (Turf): Sf: 0-0 GS: 0-2 Gd: 0-3 GF: 0-4 Fm: 0-1
Distance: 5f/6f: 0-2 7f-8f: 0-5 9f-13f: 0-6 14f+: 0-1
Track : LH: 0-7 RH: 0-2 Tight: 0-5 Gall: 0-1
Aids: Bl: 0-2 Vi: 0-1 Tstrap: 0-2
Best Rating: 32 7/01 Sals 1m1f198y gd-fm

Loweswater (USA)

101 **101**
2-y-o b c Nureyev (USA)-River Empress (USA) (Riverman (USA))
J H M Gosden Manton Racing Partnership

Placings:215 (3550)
2001: 6²GF, 6¹GF, 7⁵GF

	Starts	1st	2nd	3rd	Win & Pl
Career Total (Turf)	3	1	1	0	5974

84 7/01 Donc 6f D G-F £4465
Total win prize-money £4466

Going (Turf): Sf: 0-0 GS: 0-0 Gd: 0-0 **GF: 1-3** Fm: 0-0
Distance: **5f/6f: 1-2** 7f-8f: 0-1 9f-13f: 0-0 14f+: 0-0
Track : LH: 0-0 RH: 0-1 Tight: 0-0 Gall: 0-0
Aids: Bl: 0-0 Vi: 0-0 Tstrap: 0-0
Best Rating: 101 8/01 Gdwd 7f gd-fm

A 330,000gns fourth foal from a decent American family, he finished best of all when runner-up on his Newmarket debut and had to work hard to get the better of a potentially useful sort at Doncaster next time. Never got into the race when held up in a Group Three over seven furlongs at Goodwood, and may be better ridden closer to the pace.

Lowry (USA)

76 **43**
3-y-o b/br g Gulch (USA)-Aviara (USA) (Cox's Ridge (USA))
J S King D Goodenough Removals & Transport

Placings:006 (2545)
2001: 10⁰GS, 10⁰GF, 9⁶GF

	Starts	1st	2nd	3rd	Win & Pl
Career Total (Turf)	3	0	0	0	0

Going (Turf): Sf: 0-0 GS: 0-1 Gd: 0-0 GF: 0-2 Fm: 0-0
Distance: 5f/6f: 0-0 7f-8f: 0-0 9f-13f: 0-3 14f+: 0-0
Track : LH: 0-2 RH: 0-1 Tight: 0-3 Gall: 0-0
Aids: Bl: 0-0 Vi: 0-0 Tstrap: 0-0
Best Rating: 43 5/01 Bath 1m2f46y gd-fm

Loxley

85 **47**
2-y-o b g Ezzoud (IRE)-Shewillifshewants (IRE) (Alzao (USA))
M A Buckley Mrs D J Buckley

Placings:500 (4398)
2001: 7⁵GF, 7⁰G, 7⁰G

	Starts	1st	2nd	3rd	Win & Pl
Career Total (Turf)	3	0	0	0	0

Going (Turf): Sf: 0-0 GS: 0-0 Gd: 0-2 GF: 0-1 Fm: 0-0
Distance: 5f/6f: 0-0 7f-8f: 0-3 9f-13f: 0-0 14f+: 0-0
Track : LH: 0-1 RH: 0-0 Tight: 0-1 Gall: 0-0
Aids: Bl: 0-0 Vi: 0-0 Tstrap: 0-0
Best Rating: 47 8/01 Ayr 7f50y good

Loyal Tycoon (IRE)

104 **78**

3-y-o br c Royal Abjar (USA)-Rosy Lydgate (Last Tycoon)
S Dow Michael A J Hall & Miss M Shields

Placings:31620-00053100000 **(5138)**
2001: 7^{0}GS, 7^{0}G, 7^{0}GF, 6^{5}GF, 7^{3}G, 6^{1}F, 6^{0}GS, 5^{0}G, 7^{0}GF, 6^{0}G, 6^{0}G

	Starts	1st	2nd	3rd	Win & Pl
Career Total (Turf)	16	2	1	2	10996

84 6/01 Ling 6f D(0-85)H FRM £3991
78 7/00 Leic 7f9y E G-F £3055
Total win prize-money £7046

Going (Turf): Sf: 0-2 GS: 0-2 Gd: 0-7 **GF: 1-4 Fm: 1-1**
Distance: 5f/6f: 1-7 7f-8f: 1-9 9f-13f: 0-0 14f+: 0-0
Track : LH: 0-3 RH: 0-3 Tight: 0-0 Gall: 0-3
Aids: Bl: 0-0 Vi: 0-0 Tstrap: 0-0
Best Rating: 84 6/01 Ling 6f firm

Appreciated the step up to seven furlongs when bolting up in a Leicester maiden auction event on his second start at two, but was found out when tried in Pattern company. Returned to form when dropped to six furlongs off a reasonable mark at Lingfield in July. Suited by fast ground.

Lubohenrik (IRE)

87 **4**

4-y-o b f Perugino (USA)-Febian John (FR) (Shafaraz (FR))
P Monteith The Friar Tuck Racing Club

Placings:0000/005-0000 **(2865)**
2001: 5^{0}GS, 5^{0}G, 6^{0}GF, 5^{0}GF

	Starts	1st	2nd	3rd	Win & Pl
Career Total (Turf)	11	0	0	0	0

Going (Turf): Sf: 0-1 GS: 0-2 Gd: 0-5 GF: 0-3 Fm: 0-0
Distance: 5f/6f: 0-7 7f-8f: 0-3 9f-13f: 0-1 14f+: 0-0
Track : LH: 0-0 RH: 0-3 Tight: 0-3 Gall: 0-0
Aids: Bl: 0-0 Vi: 0-1 Tstrap: 0-0
Best Rating: 4 7/01 Haml 6f5y gd-fm

Lucayan Chief (IRE)

109 **102**

3-y-o b c With Approval (CAN)-Littleladyleah (USA) (Shareef Dancer (USA))
S P C Woods Lucayan Stud

Placings:51323-4660606 **(4869)**
2001: 9^{4}S, 10^{6}G, 10^{6}GF, 12^{0}GF, 14^{6}G, 14^{0}GF, 14^{6}G

	Starts	1st	2nd	3rd	Win & Pl
Career Total (Turf)	12	1	1	2	14247

83 8/00 Bevl 7f100y D GD £3285
Total win prize-money £3285

Going (Turf): Sf: 0-3 GS: 0-0 **Gd: 1-4** GF: 0-5 Fm: 0-0
Distance: 5f/6f: 0-0 **7f-8f: 1-4** 9f-13f: 0-5 14f+: 0-3
Track : LH: 0-1 **RH: 1-7** Tight: 0-1 Gall: 0-4
Aids: Bl: 0-0 Vi: 0-1 Tstrap: 0-0
Best Rating: 102 6/01 Asct 1m4f gd-fm

Won a Beverley maiden at two and posted some creditable efforts in Pattern company, but does not look up to that level and his high handicap mark will not help his chances in that sphere either. Acts on an easy surface, but has tried various trips this season without success.

Lucayan Legacy (IRE)

93 **76**

2-y-o b c Persian Bold-Catherinofaragon (USA) (Chief's Crown (USA))
S P C Woods Lucayan Stud

Placings:21100 **(5280)**
2001: 7^{2}GF, 7^{1}G, 7^{1}GS, 8^{0}GF, 9^{0}S

	Starts	1st	2nd	3rd	Win & Pl
Career Total (Turf)	5	2	1	0	7791

76 8/01 Yarm 7f3y D G-S £4452
76 7/01 Newc 7f F GD £2359
Total win prize-money £6811

Going (Turf): Sf: 0-1 **GS: 1-1 Gd: 1-1** GF: 0-2 Fm: 0-0
Distance: 5f/6f: 0-0 **7f-8f: 2-3** 9f-13f: 0-2 14f+: 0-0
Track : LH: 0-1 RH: 0-1 Tight: 0-0 Gall: 0-0
Aids: Bl: 0-0 Vi: 0-0 Tstrap: 0-0
Best Rating: 76 8/01 Yarm 7f3y gd-sft

Came off second-best to a Loder juvenile on his Southwell debut but duly won his maiden at Newcastle in July. Followed up at Yarmouth but well beaten subsequently. He is bred to stay further and a step up to a mile should prove beneficial. Has won on good and easy ground.

Lucayan Monarch

79(93) (66)**64**

3-y-o ch c Cadeaux Genereux-Flight Soundly (IRE) (Caerleon (USA))
D Nicholls (J Noseda 25/5) Lucayan Stud

Placings:41500 **(4896)**
2001: 8^{4}SW, 9^{1}SD, 9^{5}S, 8^{0}F, 9^{0}GS

	Starts	1st	2nd	3rd	Win & Pl
Career Total (Turf)	3	0	0	0	0
Career Total (AW)	2	1	0	0	2891

66 3/01 Wolv 1m1f79y D STD £2891
Total win prize-money £2891

Going (Turf): Sf: 0-1 GS: 0-1 Gd: 0-0 GF: 0-0 Fm: 0-1
Distance: 5f/6f: 0-0 7f-8f: 0-1 **9f-13f: 1-4** 14f+: 0-0
Track : **LH: 1-4** RH: 0-1 **Tight: 1-2** Gall: 0-0
Aids: Bl: 0-0 Vi: 0-0 Tstrap: 0-0
Best Rating: 66 3/01 Wolv 1m1f79y stand

Lucefer (IRE)

95(87) (45)**69**

3-y-o b g Lycius (USA)-Maharani (USA) (Red Ransom (USA))
G C H Chung Gigginstown House

Placings:02022-10000 **(5616)**
2001: 7^{1}F, 7^{0}GF, 7^{0}HY, 9^{0}S, 7^{0}SD

	Starts	1st	2nd	3rd	Win & Pl
Career Total (Turf)	9	1	3	0	5527
Career Total (AW)	1	0	0	0	

51 9/01 Muss 7f30y F FRM £2649
Total win prize-money £2650

Going (Turf): Sf: 0-4 GS: 0-2 Gd: 0-0 GF: 0-2 **Fm: 1-1**
Distance: 5f/6f: 0-0 **7f-8f: 1-9** 9f-13f: 0-1 14f+: 0-0
Track : LH: 0-5 RH: 0-1 Tight: 0-2 Gall: 0-0
Aids: Bl: 0-1 Vi: 0-0 Tstrap: 0-1
Best Rating: 69 9/01 Ayr 7f50y gd-fm

Faced some stiff tasks at two, but showed the benefit of a long break when returning to win a maiden at Musselburgh in September. Despite his win coming on fast ground, he may be best with some cut.

Lucid Dreams (IRE)

80 **41**

2-y-o b g Sri Pekan (USA)-Scenaria (IRE) (Scenic)
M L W Bell Cable Media Consultancy Ltd

Placings:00 **(5684)**
2001: 7^{0}S, 8^{0}S

	Starts	1st	2nd	3rd	Win & Pl
Career Total (Turf)	2	0	0	0	

Going (Turf): Sf: 0-2 GS: 0-0 Gd: 0-0 GF: 0-0 Fm: 0-0
Distance: 5f/6f: 0-0 7f-8f: 0-2 9f-13f: 0-0 14f+: 0-0
Track : LH: 0-1 RH: 0-0 Tight: 0-0 Gall: 0-0
Aids: Bl: 0-0 Vi: 0-0 Tstrap: 0-0
Best Rating: 41 10/01 Leic 7f9y soft

Lucido (IRE)

113 **112**

5-y-o b h Royal Academy (USA)-Lady Ambassador (General Assembly (USA))
J L Dunlop Mrs H Focke

Placings:413/11003/546-1166 **(2883)**
2001: 12^{1}S, 12^{1}GS, 12^{6}GF, 12^{6}GS

	Starts	1st	2nd	3rd	Win & Pl
Career Total (Turf)	15	5	0	2	102803

112 4/01 Newb 1m4f5y A G-S £20300
90 3/01 Donc 1m4f B SFT £11017
120 5/99 Ling 1m3f106yA G-F £32127
105 4/99 Newb 1m2f6y B G-F £9180
82 9/98 Sals 1m D HVY £3239
Total win prize-money £75866

Going (Turf): Sf: 2-4 GS: 1-5 Gd: 0-3 **GF: 2-3** Fm: 0-0
Distance: 5f/6f: 0-0 7f-8f: 1-3 **9f-13f: 4-12** 14f+: 0-0
Track : **LH: 4-5** RH: 0-8 Tight: 1-2 **Gall: 3-8**
Aids: Bl: 0-0 Vi: 0-0 Tstrap: 0-0
Best Rating: 112 4/01 Newb 1m4f5y gd-sft

He took the scalp of Daliapour in the Lingfield Derby Trial as a three-year-old but beat just one home in the Derby itself. Lightly raced since, he has had his problems, but returned in great heart, following up his Doncaster reappearance win with a smooth success in the Group 3 John Porter at Newbury. Probably found the the ground too fast when well beaten in the Hardwicke at Royal Ascot.

Lucille (IRE)

101 **65**

3-y-o b f Sadler's Wells (USA)-Lady Ambassador (General Assembly (USA))
J L Dunlop Mrs H Focke

Placings:0-0355 **(5010)**
2001: 10^{0}GF, 12^{3}G, 12^{5}G, 14^{5}HY

	Starts	1st	2nd	3rd	Win & Pl
Career Total (Turf)	5	0	0	1	645

Going (Turf): Sf: 0-1 GS: 0-0 Gd: 0-3 GF: 0-1 Fm: 0-0
Distance: 5f/6f: 0-0 7f-8f: 0-1 9f-13f: 0-3 14f+: 0-1
Track : LH: 0-3 RH: 0-2 Tight: 0-0 Gall: 0-3
Aids: Bl: 0-0 Vi: 0-0 Tstrap: 0-1
Best Rating: 65 9/01 Hayd 1m6f heavy

Better than she has shown, has a high knee action and may be better on an easy surface.

Luck And Dough

72 **16**

2-y-o b g Forzando-Lucky Song (Lucky Wednesday)
M W Easterby T R Deston

Placings:000 **(3375)**
2001: 7^{0}G, 6^{0}G, 7^{0}GF

	Starts	1st	2nd	3rd	Win & Pl
Career Total (Turf)	3	0	0	0	

Going (Turf): Sf: 0-0 GS: 0-0 Gd: 0-2 GF: 0-1 Fm: 0-0
Distance: 5f/6f: 0-1 7f-8f: 0-2 9f-13f: 0-0 14f+: 0-0
Track : LH: 0-1 RH: 0-0 Tight: 0-1 Gall: 0-0
Aids: Bl: 0-0 Vi: 0-0 Tstrap: 0-0
Best Rating: 16 6/01 Thsk 7f good

Lucky Archer

103(88) (50)**60**
8-y-o b g North Briton-Preobrajenska (Double Form)
Ian Williams James Burley, Andrew Wyer, Philippa Wyer

Placings:65356003523002/050/111250025/061005155 0/00-401001050 **(4550)**
2001: 8^{4}SD, 8^{0}GF, 8^{1}GF, 8^{0}G, 9^{0}GF, 8^{1}GF, 8^{0}GF, 8^{5}GF, 8^{0}GF

	Starts	1st	2nd	3rd	Win & Pl
Career Total (Turf)	46	7	4	3	39235
Career Total (AW)	1	0	0	0	0

53	7/01	Sand	1m14y	E	G-F	£3883
49	6/01	Leic	1m9y	F	G-F	£2618
73	8/99	Bath	1m5y	D(0-80)H	HRD	£7100
71	6/99	Yarm	1m3y	D(0-80)H	GD	£5390
71	6/98	Carl	7f214y	D(0-80)H	G-S	£7620
67	5/98	Yarm	7f3y	E(0-70)H	FRM	£3442
59	5/98	Nott	1m54y	G(0-70)H	FRM	£1899

Total win prize-money £31954

Going (Turf): Sf: 0-1 GS: 1-4 Gd: 1-11 GF: 2-26 **Fm: 3-4**
Distance: 5f/6f: 0-2 7f-8f: 2-27 **9f-13f: 5-18** 14f+: 0-0
Track : LH: 2-14 RH: 2-10 **Tight: 1-9** Gall: 0-3
Aids: Bl: 0-1 Vi: 0-0 Tstrap: 0-0
Best Rating: 60 8/01 Bath 1m5y gd-fm

He won his first three starts last season, including the Carlisle Bell, before the Handicapper grabbed him. Returned to winning form at Yarmouth in June and also won at Bath in August. He always runs a game race, attacking from the front.

Lucky Bea

(87) (26)
8-y-o b g Lochnager-Knocksharry (Palm Track)
K A Ryan Steve Ryan

Placings:002320005050/335150230300000/5/00/0040-0 **(0002)**
2001: 8^{0}SD

	Starts	1st	2nd	3rd	Win & Pl
Career Total (Turf)	29	1	3	5	8298
Career Total (AW)	6	0	0	0	0

56 5/96 Newc 1m D(0-80)H GD £3631
Total win prize-money £3631

Going (Turf): Sf: 0-0 GS: 0-5 **Gd: 1-7** GF: 0-10 Fm: 0-7
Distance: 5f/6f: 0-9 **7f-8f: 1-16** 9f-13f: 0-10 14f+: 0-0
Track : **LH: 1-17** RH: 0-7 Tight: 0-9 **Gall: 1-2**
Aids: Bl: 0-5 Vi: 0-0 Tstrap: 0-0
Best Rating: 23 1/01 Sthl 1m stand

Lucky Boy

41
3-y-o b g Magic Ring (IRE)-Etourdie (USA) (Arctic Tern (USA))
W G M Turner Mrs Tracy Turner

Placings:0 **(2941)**
2001: 10^{0}GF

	Starts	1st	2nd	3rd	Win & Pl
Career Total (Turf)	1	0	0	0	

Going (Turf): Sf: 0-0 GS: 0-0 Gd: 0-0 GF: 0-1 Fm: 0-0
Distance: 5f/6f: 0-0 7f-8f: 0-0 9f-13f: 0-1 14f+: 0-0
Track : LH: 0-1 RH: 0-0 Tight: 0-1 Gall: 0-0
Aids: Bl: 0-0 Vi: 0-0 Tstrap: 0-0

Lucky Break (IRE)

102 **71**
3-y-o ch c Brief Truce (USA)-Paradise Forum (Prince Sabo)
C A Horgan Mrs B Sumner

Placings:000-63056 **(3957)**
2001: 7^{6}G, 8^{3}G, 10^{0}GF, 7^{5}GF, 9^{6}GF

	Starts	1st	2nd	3rd	Win & Pl
Career Total (Turf)	8	0	0	1	1215

Going (Turf): Sf: 0-0 GS: 0-0 Gd: 0-3 GF: 0-4 Fm: 0-0
Distance: 5f/6f: 0-1 7f-8f: 0-3 9f-13f: 0-3 14f+: 0-0
Track : LH: 0-0 RH: 0-4 Tight: 0-1 Gall: 0-0
Aids: Bl: 0-0 Vi: 0-0 Tstrap: 0-0
Best Rating: 71 6/01 Sand 1m14y good

Lucky Chrystal (IRE)

103(87) (42)**63**
3-y-o b g Lucky Guest-Chrysilia (USA) (Tilt Up (USA))
E A L Dunlop Anamoine Ltd

Placings:5-5503310 **(3941)**
2001: 7^{5}SD, 5^{5}S, 6^{0}GF, 6^{3}GF, 7^{3}GF, 8^{1}G, 8^{0}GF

	Starts	1st	2nd	3rd	Win & Pl
Career Total (Turf)	7	1	0	2	4823
Career Total (AW)	1	0	0	0	0

59 7/01 Epsm 1m114y E(0-70)H GD £3867
Total win prize-money £3868

Going (Turf): Sf: 0-1 GS: 0-0 **Gd: 1-1** GF: 0-4 Fm: 0-0
Distance: 5f/6f: 0-1 7f-8f: 0-4 **9f-13f: 1-2** 14f+: 0-0
Track : **LH: 1-5** RH: 0-0 **Tight: 1-2** Gall: 0-0
Aids: Bl: 0-0 Vi: 0-0 Tstrap: 0-0
Best Rating: 59 7/01 Epsm 1m114y good

Handles fast ground, but won a maiden handicap at Epsom on rain-softened ground when stepped up to an extended mile.

Lucky Cove

87(90) (48)**24**
5-y-o gr g Lugana Beach-Port Na Blath (On Your Mark)
N Tinkler Mrs Christine Cawley

Placings:33024/003003/000000040-0006000 **(5629)**
2001: 5^{0}S, 5^{0}SD, 5^{0}GF, 5^{6}SD, 5^{0}GF, 6^{0}G, 5^{0}G

	Starts	1st	2nd	3rd	Win & Pl
Career Total (Turf)	21	0	1	1	1869
Career Total (AW)	7	0	0	3	920

Going (Turf): Sf: 0-5 GS: 0-2 Gd: 0-5 GF: 0-9 Fm: 0-0
Distance: 5f/6f: 0-28 7f-8f: 0-0 9f-13f: 0-0 14f+: 0-0
Track : LH: 0-4 RH: 0-1 Tight: 0-1 Gall: 0-1
Aids: Bl: 0-6 Vi: 0-0 Tstrap: 0-0
Best Rating: 25 7/01 Sthl 5f stand

Lucky For George

70
3-y-o b c Theatrical Charmer-Jeed Amaya (Taufan (USA))
Ms A E Embiricos Mrs Jacquie Mikhailides

Placings:0F5-00 **(5294)**
2001: 12^{0}GS, 11^{0}S

	Starts	1st	2nd	3rd	Win & Pl
Career Total (Turf)	5	0	0	0	865

Going (Turf): Sf: 0-2 GS: 0-1 Gd: 0-1 GF: 0-0 Fm: 0-0
Distance: 5f/6f: 0-0 7f-8f: 0-1 9f-13f: 0-3 14f+: 0-0
Track : LH: 0-0 RH: 0-2 Tight: 0-0 Gall: 0-1
Aids: Bl: 0-0 Vi: 0-0 Tstrap: 0-0

Lucky Gitano (IRE)

98 **87**
5-y-o b/br g Lucky Guest-April Wind (Windjammer (USA))
J L Dunlop Anamoine Ltd

Placings:325/32/00246411-006 **(1418)**
2001: 8^{0}S, 8^{0}S, 8^{6}GS

	Starts	1st	2nd	3rd	Win & Pl
Career Total (Turf)	16	2	3	2	12419

87	11/00	Donc	7f	E(0-90)H	HVY	£3916
75	10/00	Rdcr	1m	E(0-75)H	SFT	£4030

Total win prize-money £7946

Going (Turf): **Sf: 2-7** GS: 0-2 Gd: 0-4 GF: 0-2 Fm: 0-1
Distance: 5f/6f: 0-0 **7f-8f: 2-6** 9f-13f: 0-10 14f+: 0-0
Track : LH: 0-6 RH: 0-3 Tight: 0-3 Gall: 0-2
Aids: Bl: 0-0 Vi: 0-0 Tstrap: 0-0
Best Rating: 73 5/01 NmkR 1m gd-sft

Useful handicapper on his day. Out of form in 2001.

Lucky Heather (IRE)

92 **41**
4-y-o b f Soviet Lad (USA)-Idrak (Young Generation)
R J Baker Graham Brown

Placings:0600/010 **(4210)**
2001: 11^{0}GF, 10^{1}S, 11^{0}GF

	Starts	1st	2nd	3rd	Win & Pl
Career Total (Turf)	7	1	0	0	2394

41 8/01 Chep 1m2f36y F SFT £2394
Total win prize-money £2394

Going (Turf): **Sf: 1-2** GS: 0-0 Gd: 0-1 GF: 0-3 Fm: 0-1
Distance: 5f/6f: 0-4 7f-8f: 0-0 **9f-13f: 1-3** 14f+: 0-0
Track : **LH: 1-4** RH: 0-1 Tight: 0-2 Gall: 0-3
Aids: Bl: 0-0 Vi: 0-0 Tstrap: 0-0
Best Rating: 41 8/01 Chep 1m2f36y soft

Lucky Hettie

95(94) (48)**51**
3-y-o b f Alzao (USA)-Halo's Charm (USA) (Halo (USA))
C R Egerton Alan Stubbs

Placings:05-045250 **(3805)**
2001: 6^{0}HY, 8^{4}GF, 9^{5}GF, 8^{2}SD, 6^{5}GF, 7^{0}GF

	Starts	1st	2nd	3rd	Win & Pl
Career Total (Turf)	6	0	0	0	318
Career Total (AW)	2	0	1	0	656

Going (Turf): Sf: 0-2 GS: 0-0 Gd: 0-0 GF: 0-4 Fm: 0-0
Distance: 5f/6f: 0-1 7f-8f: 0-4 9f-13f: 0-3 14f+: 0-0
Track : LH: 0-3 RH: 0-2 Tight: 0-2 Gall: 0-0
Aids: Bl: 0-1 Vi: 0-0 Tstrap: 0-0
Best Rating: 51 6/01 Haml 1m65y gd-fm

Lucky Jacasa

86 **60**
2-y-o b f Whittingham (IRE)-Lucky Dip (Tirol)
Mrs P N Dutfield Mrs Jasmine B Chesters

Placings:4 **(1380)**
2001: 5^{4}S

	Starts	1st	2nd	3rd	Win & Pl
Career Total (Turf)	1	0	0	0	290

Going (Turf): Sf: 0-1 GS: 0-0 Gd: 0-0 GF: 0-0 Fm: 0-0
Distance: 5f/6f: 0-1 7f-8f: 0-0 9f-13f: 0-0 14f+: 0-0
Track : LH: 0-0 RH: 0-0 Tight: 0-0 Gall: 0-0
Aids: Bl: 0-0 Vi: 0-0 Tstrap: 0-0
Best Rating: 59 5/01 Sals 5f soft

Lucky Judge

107(68) **69**
4-y-o b g Saddlers' Hall (IRE)-Lady Lydia (Ela-Mana-Mou)
G A Swinbank Mrs I Gibson

Placings:0/504642330-15325535 **(5033)**
2001: 13^{1}G, 16^{5}F, 14^{3}G, 16^{2}GF, 16^{5}F, 13^{5}GS, 16^{3}G, 16^{5}GF

Starts 1st 2nd 3rd Win & Pl
Career Total (Turf) 17 1 2 4 8024
Career Total (AW) 1 0 0 0
67 5/01 Haml 1m5f9y E(0-70)H GD £3010
Total win prize-money £3819

Going (Turf): Sf: 0-1 GS: 0-3 **Gd: 1-5** GF: 0-6 Fm: 0-2
Distance: 5f/6f: 0-0 7f-8f: 0-1 9f-13f: 0-4 **14f+: 1-13**
Track : LH: 0-9 **RH: 1-9 Tight: 1-13** Gall: 0-3
Aids: Bl: 0-0 Vi: 0-1 Tstrap: 0-0
Best Rating: 69 8/01 Thsk 2m good

Fair stayer, he has only won once, but has run some decent races since scoring in the spring.

Lucky Lilly (IRE)

3-y-o b f Definite Article-Nordic Doll (IRE) (Royal Academy (USA))
P J Hobbs Ms C Hehir

Placings:00 **(5464)**
2001: 7^{0}S, 11^{0}G
Starts 1st 2nd 3rd Win & Pl
Career Total (Turf) 2 0 0 0

Going (Turf): Sf: 0-1 GS: 0-0 Gd: 0-1 GF: 0-0 Fm: 0-0
Distance: 5f/6f: 0-0 7f-8f: 0-1 9f-13f: 0-1 14f+: 0-0
Track : LH: 0-1 RH: 0-0 Tight: 0-1 Gall: 0-0
Aids: Bl: 0-0 Vi: 0-0 Tstrap: 0-0
Best Rating: 7 10/01 Bath 1m3f144y good

Lucky Man

93 **80**
2-y-o b c Robellino (USA)-Vannozza (Kris)
G C Bravery Sawyer, Webb, Whatley

Placings:3600 **(4695)**
2001: 6^{3}GF, 6^{6}G, 7^{0}GF, 6^{0}GS
Starts 1st 2nd 3rd Win & Pl
Career Total (Turf) 4 0 0 1 1776

Going (Turf): Sf: 0-0 GS: 0-1 Gd: 0-1 GF: 0-2 Fm: 0-0
Distance: 5f/6f: 0-2 7f-8f: 0-2 9f-13f: 0-0 14f+: 0-0
Track : LH: 0-0 RH: 0-0 Tight: 0-0 Gall: 0-0
Aids: Bl: 0-0 Vi: 0-0 Tstrap: 0-0
Best Rating: 80 9/01 Donc 6f gd-sft

Showed some ability in maidens.

Lucky Princess

65 **12**
2-y-o b f Bijou D'Inde-Thinkluckybelucky (Maystreak)
J D Czerpak K C Payne

Placings:0400 **(5110)**
2001: 5^{0}G, 6^{4}G, 6^{0}G, 6^{0}HY
Starts 1st 2nd 3rd Win & Pl
Career Total (Turf) 4 0 0 0 313

Going (Turf): Sf: 0-1 GS: 0-0 Gd: 0-3 GF: 0-0 Fm: 0-0
Distance: 5f/6f: 0-3 7f-8f: 0-1 9f-13f: 0-0 14f+: 0-0
Track : LH: 0-1 RH: 0-0 Tight: 0-0 Gall: 0-1
Aids: Bl: 0-0 Vi: 0-1 Tstrap: 0-0
Best Rating: 12 8/01 Hayd 6f good

A half-sister to smart six to eight furlong performer Hornbeam. Has not shown much on turf this season.

Lucky Rainbow (USA)

105 **77**
3-y-o b f Rainbow Quest (USA)-Tinaca (USA) (Manila (USA))
J L Dunlop Wafic Said

Placings:241 **(5182)**

2001: 10^{2}S, 11^{4}GF, 10^{1}HY
Starts 1st 2nd 3rd Win & Pl
Career Total (Turf) 3 1 1 0 4641
51 10/01 Wind 1m2f7y D HVY £3024
Total win prize-money £3024

Going (Turf): Sf: 1-2 GS: 0-0 Gd: 0-0 GF: 0-1 Fm: 0-0
Distance: 5f/6f: 0-0 7f-8f: 0-0 **9f-13f: 1-3** 14f+: 0-0
Track : LH: 0-1 RH: 0-1 **Tight: 1-1** Gall: 0-0
Aids: Bl: 0-0 Vi: 0-0 Tstrap: 0-0
Best Rating: 77 5/01 Hayd 1m3f200y gd-fm

Lightly-raced, had shown ability on soft ground before overcoming an absence to score on heavy at Windsor in October.

Lucky Star

96(99) (61)**41**
4-y-o b f Emarati (USA)-Child Star (FR) (Bellypha)
Mrs Merrita Jones (D Marks 27/6) D Marks

Placings:0666/131400-004500U **(3409)**
2001: 7^{0}SD, 7^{0}G, 5^{4}F, 7^{5}GF, 6^{0}F, 6^{0}GF, 12^{U}GF
Starts 1st 2nd 3rd Win & Pl
Career Total (Turf) 11 0 0 0 0
Career Total (AW) 6 2 0 1 5366
58 3/00 Wolv 1m100y F(0-60) STD £2236
61 1/00 Ling 7f F(0-65)H STD £2756
Total win prize-money £4993

Going (Turf): Sf: 0-0 GS: 0-0 Gd: 0-1 GF: 0-8 Fm: 0-2
Distance: 5f/6f: 0-3 7f-8f: 1-10 9f-13f: 1-4 14f+: 0-0
Track : LH: 2-13 RH: 0-0 **Tight: 2-6** Gall: 0-0
Aids: Bl: 0-0 Vi: 0-1 Tstrap: 0-0
Best Rating: 41 5/01 Sthl 7f gd-fm

Lucky's Son (IRE)

96(82) (15)**44**
4-y-o gr g Lucky Guest-April Wind (Windjammer (USA))
P Howling Arkland International (uk) Ltd

Placings:0000216000-0060 **(2421)**
2001: 7^{0}SD, 5^{0}G, 5^{6}G, 6^{0}GF
Starts 1st 2nd 3rd Win & Pl
Career Total (Turf) 11 1 1 0 4818
Career Total (AW) 3 0 0 0
43 8/00 Thsk 6f E(0-70)H GD £4137
Total win prize-money £4137

Going (Turf): Sf: 0-0 GS: 0-1 **Gd: 1-5** GF: 0-4 Fm: 0-1
Distance: 5f/6f: 1-7 7f-8f: 0-4 9f-13f: 0-3 14f+: 0-0
Track : LH: 0-5 RH: 0-1 Tight: 0-3 Gall: 0-0
Aids: Bl: 0-0 Vi: 0-0 Tstrap: 0-2
Best Rating: 44 6/01 Sand 5f6y good

Lucy Tufty

(50)
10-y-o b m Vin St Benet-Manor Farm Toots (Royalty)
G Prodromou George Prodromou

Placings:0545/40410/00346/1600/0-0 **(0171)**
2001: 12^{0}SD
Starts 1st 2nd 3rd Win & Pl
Career Total (Turf) 15 2 0 0 5189
Career Total (AW) 5 0 0 1 260
44 4/98 Ripn 1m4f60y F(0-60)H SFT £2358
44 11/96 Folk 1m4f G(0-60)H SFT £2616
Total win prize-money £4974

Going (Turf): Sf: 2-4 GS: 0-0 Gd: 0-6 GF: 0-2 Fm: 0-3
Distance: 5f/6f: 0-0 7f-8f: 0-0 **9f-13f: 2-15** 14f+: 0-5
Track : LH: 0-14 **RH: 2-6 Tight: 2-11** Gall: 0-1
Aids: Bl: 0-0 Vi: 0-0 Tstrap: 0-0
Best Rating: 44 11/96 Folk 1m4f S

Ludere (IRE)

(86) (38)**40**
6-y-o ch g Desse Zenny (USA)-White Jasmin (Jalmood (USA))
B J Llewellyn The Trade Import Agency Ltd

Placings:00500/534061254355/022400/41-0 **(0258)**
2001: 16^{0}SD
Starts 1st 2nd 3rd Win & Pl
Career Total (Turf) 20 2 3 1 9711
Career Total (AW) 6 0 0 1 235
40 8/00 Catt 1m7f177yG G-F £1806
40 5/98 Muss 1m4f F GD £2372
Total win prize-money £4179

Going (Turf): Sf: 0-3 GS: 0-0 **Gd: 1-6 GF: 1-6** Fm: 0-5
Distance: 5f/6f: 0-1 7f-8f: 0-5 9f-13f: 1-12 14f+: 1-8
Track : LH: 1-10 RH: 1-15 **Tight: 2-19** Gall: 0-0
Aids: Bl: 0-1 Vi: 0-0 Tstrap: 0-0
Best Rating: 18 2/01 Wolv 2m46y stand

Ludynosa (USA)

95 **84**
2-y-o b f Cadeaux Genereux-Boubskaia (Niniski (USA))
L M Cumani Equibreed Srl

Placings:4 **(5602)**
2001: 7^{4}GS
Starts 1st 2nd 3rd Win & Pl
Career Total (Turf) 1 0 0 0 325

Going (Turf): Sf: 0-0 GS: 0-1 Gd: 0-0 GF: 0-0 Fm: 0-0
Distance: 5f/6f: 0-0 7f-8f: 0-1 9f-13f: 0-0 14f+: 0-0
Track : LH: 0-0 RH: 0-0 Tight: 0-0 Gall: 0-0
Aids: Bl: 0-0 Vi: 0-0 Tstrap: 0-0
Best Rating: 84 11/01 NmkR 7f gd-sft

Lugana Mist

72 **36**
2-y-o gr f Lugana Beach-Swallow Bay (Penmarric (USA))
J C Fox Lord Mutton Racing Partnership

Placings:0000 **(5331)**
2001: 6^{0}GF, 6^{0}GS, 6^{0}GF, 5^{0}HY
Starts 1st 2nd 3rd Win & Pl
Career Total (Turf) 4 0 0 0

Going (Turf): Sf: 0-1 GS: 0-1 Gd: 0-0 GF: 0-2 Fm: 0-0
Distance: 5f/6f: 0-3 7f-8f: 0-1 9f-13f: 0-0 14f+: 0-0
Track : LH: 0-0 RH: 0-0 Tight: 0-0 Gall: 0-0
Aids: Bl: 0-0 Vi: 0-0 Tstrap: 0-0
Best Rating: 36 9/01 Sals 6f212y gd-fm

Luluwa (IRE)

90 **81**
2-y-o b/br f Zafonic (USA)-Affection Affirmed (USA) (Affirmed (USA))
H R A Cecil Newgate Stud

Placings:5 **(5367)**
2001: 8^{5}GS
Starts 1st 2nd 3rd Win & Pl
Career Total (Turf) 1 0 0 0 0

Going (Turf): Sf: 0-0 GS: 0-1 Gd: 0-0 GF: 0-0 Fm: 0-0
Distance: 5f/6f: 0-0 7f-8f: 0-1 9f-13f: 0-0 14f+: 0-0
Track : LH: 0-0 RH: 0-0 Tight: 0-0 Gall: 0-0
Aids: Bl: 0-0 Vi: 0-0 Tstrap: 0-0
Best Rating: 81 10/01 NmkR 1m gd-sft

Was not knocked about on her Newmarket debut over a mile but showed ability.

Lumiere D'Espoir (FR)

101 **82**
3-y-o br f Saumarez-Light Of Hope (USA) (Lyphard (USA))
S Dow Byerley Bloodstock

Placings:04-6110 **(2325)**

2001: 10^6GS, 10^1GS, 14^1G, 12^0GF

	Starts	1st	2nd	3rd	Win & Pl
Career Total (Turf)	6	2	0	0	7353

78 5/01 Donc 1m6f132yD(0-80)H GD £4114
73 5/01 Bath 1m2f46y E(0-75)H G-S £3017
Total win prize-money £7132

Going (Turf): Sf: 0-1 **GS: 1-3 Gd: 1-1** GF: 0-1 Fm: 0-0
Distance: 5f/6f: 0-0 7f-8f: 0-1 9f-13f: 1-4 14f+: 1-1
Track : **LH: 2-4** RH: 0-1 Tight: 1-1 Gall: 1-3
Aids: Bl: 0-0 Vi: 0-0 Tstrap: 0-0
Best Rating: 82 6/01 Asct 1m4f gd-fm

An improving filly, won consecutive handicaps within a week in early May, over ten furlongs at Bath and 14 furlongs at Doncaster.

Lumiere Du Soleil

99(85) (29)**51**
3-y-o b f Tragic Role (USA)-Pounelta (Tachypous)
K A Ryan Tony Fawcett

Placings:506-0600503 **(3749)**
2001: 6^0G, 8^6F, 8^0GF, 14^0F, 8^5SD, 8^0GF, 8^3GS

	Starts	1st	2nd	3rd	Win & Pl
Career Total (Turf)	9	0	0	1	376
Career Total (AW)	1	0	0	0	0

Going (Turf): Sf: 0-1 GS: 0-2 Gd: 0-1 GF: 0-3 Fm: 0-2
Distance: 5f/6f: 0-2 7f-8f: 0-4 9f-13f: 0-3 14f+: 0-1
Track : LH: 0-4 RH: 0-3 Tight: 0-3 Gall: 0-0
Aids: Bl: 0-1 Vi: 0-1 Tstrap: 0-1
Best Rating: 51 5/01 Haml 1m65y firm

Luming (USA)

96 **60**
3-y-o b f Miesque's Son (USA)-Lucky State (USA) (State Dinner (USA))
R Guest The Escapologists

Placings:524 **(4306)**
2001: 8^5G, 9^2GF, 9^4GF

	Starts	1st	2nd	3rd	Win & Pl
Career Total (Turf)	3	0	1	0	876

Going (Turf): Sf: 0-0 GS: 0-0 Gd: 0-1 GF: 0-2 Fm: 0-0
Distance: 5f/6f: 0-0 7f-8f: 0-0 9f-13f: 0-3 14f+: 0-0
Track : LH: 0-2 RH: 0-1 Tight: 0-2 Gall: 0-0
Aids: Bl: 0-0 Vi: 0-0 Tstrap: 0-0
Best Rating: 60 8/01 Folk 1m1f149y gd-fm

Luna Moth (USA)

96 **74**
2-y-o b f Silver Hawk (USA)-Night And Dreams (USA) (Fappiano (USA))
E A L Dunlop Maktoum Al Maktoum

Placings:063 **(5623)**
2001: 7^0GF, 7^6GF, 8^3GS

	Starts	1st	2nd	3rd	Win & Pl
Career Total (Turf)	3	0	0	1	570

Going (Turf): Sf: 0-0 GS: 0-1 Gd: 0-0 GF: 0-2 Fm: 0-0
Distance: 5f/6f: 0-0 7f-8f: 0-2 9f-13f: 0-1 14f+: 0-0
Track : LH: 0-1 RH: 0-1 Tight: 0-0 Gall: 0-1
Aids: Bl: 0-0 Vi: 0-0 Tstrap: 0-0
Best Rating: 74 11/01 Nott 1m54y gd-sft

Luna Nova

91 **39**
3-y-o b g Aragon-Lucidity (Vision (USA))
C W Thornton Guy Reed

Placings:000000 **(3949)**
2001: 7^0S, 6^0G, 7^0GF, 9^0GF, 11^0GF, 8^0GS

	Starts	1st	2nd	3rd	Win & Pl
Career Total (Turf)	6	0	0	0	

Going (Turf): Sf: 0-1 GS: 0-1 Gd: 0-1 GF: 0-3 Fm: 0-0
Distance: 5f/6f: 0-0 7f-8f: 0-2 9f-13f: 0-3 14f+: 0-0
Track : LH: 0-2 RH: 0-2 Tight: 0-2 Gall: 0-0
Aids: Bl: 0-1 Vi: 0-0 Tstrap: 0-0
Best Rating: 42 5/01 Rdcr 7f soft

Luna Wain

87 **40**
4-y-o b g Unfuwain (USA)-Lunafairy (FR) (Always Fair (USA))
G L Moore Phil Collins

Placings:000 **(2545)**
2001: 6^0HY, 10^0G, 9^0GF

	Starts	1st	2nd	3rd	Win & Pl
Career Total (Turf)	3	0	0	0	

Going (Turf): Sf: 0-1 GS: 0-0 Gd: 0-1 GF: 0-1 Fm: 0-0
Distance: 5f/6f: 0-0 7f-8f: 0-1 9f-13f: 0-2 14f+: 0-0
Track : LH: 0-1 RH: 0-2 Tight: 0-3 Gall: 0-0
Aids: Bl: 0-0 Vi: 0-0 Tstrap: 0-0
Best Rating: 40 5/01 Ling 1m2f good

Lunacy (IRE)

91 **77**
2-y-o b f Alzao (USA)-Lunar Ridge (Indian Ridge)
G C Bravery The Tt Partnership

Placings:2 **(4723)**
2001: 7^2GF

	Starts	1st	2nd	3rd	Win & Pl
Career Total (Turf)	1	0	1	0	1215

Going (Turf): Sf: 0-0 GS: 0-0 Gd: 0-0 GF: 0-1 Fm: 0-0
Distance: 5f/6f: 0-0 7f-8f: 0-1 9f-13f: 0-0 14f+: 0-0
Track : LH: 0-1 RH: 0-0 Tight: 0-0 Gall: 0-0
Aids: Bl: 0-0 Vi: 0-0 Tstrap: 0-0
Best Rating: 77 9/01 Wwck 7f26y gd-fm

Lunajaz

84(83) (44)**29**
4-y-o ch g Alhijaz-Lunagraphe (USA) (Time For A Change (USA))
T M Jones Robert Le Blanc

Placings:0005/0000-000 **(2602)**
2001: 7^0F, 7^0GF, 11^0F

	Starts	1st	2nd	3rd	Win & Pl
Career Total (Turf)	8	0	0	0	
Career Total (AW)	3	0	0	0	0

Going (Turf): Sf: 0-0 GS: 0-1 Gd: 0-1 GF: 0-2 Fm: 0-4
Distance: 5f/6f: 0-1 7f-8f: 0-8 9f-13f: 0-2 14f+: 0-0
Track : LH: 0-7 RH: 0-0 Tight: 0-4 Gall: 0-0
Aids: Bl: 0-0 Vi: 0-1 Tstrap: 0-0
Best Rating: 29 6/01 Ling 7f firm

Lunalux

96(88) (44)**21**
4-y-o b f Emarati (USA)-Ragged Moon (Raga Navarro (ITY))
C Smith C Smith

Placings:0605634550/0240052600-00000450000 **(5149)**
2001: 5^0GS, 5^0HY, 5^0G, 5^0G, 5^0G, 6^4F, 6^5GF, 5^0GF, 5^0GF, 5^0G, 7^0G

	Starts	1st	2nd	3rd	Win & Pl
Career Total (Turf)	28	0	2	1	2192
Career Total (AW)	3	0	0	0	0

Going (Turf): Sf: 0-3 GS: 0-3 Gd: 0-9 GF: 0-11 Fm: 0-2
Distance: 5f/6f: 0-28 7f-8f: 0-3 9f-13f: 0-0 14f+: 0-0
Track : LH: 0-4 RH: 0-1 Tight: 0-0 Gall: 0-2
Aids: Bl: 0-5 Vi: 0-6 Tstrap: 0-0
Best Rating: 44 6/01 Ling 6f firm

Lunar Crystal (IRE)

102 **93**
3-y-o b c Shirley Heights-Solar Crystal (IRE) (Alzao (USA))
D R C Elsworth Michael Poland

Placings:140-56405 **(3467)**
2001: 8^5S, 10^6GF, 8^4GF, 8^0GF, 10^5GF

	Starts	1st	2nd	3rd	Win & Pl
Career Total (Turf)	8	1	0	0	14416

87 9/00 Asct 7f B SFT £12035
Total win prize-money £12035

Going (Turf): Sf: 1-4 GS: 0-0 Gd: 0-0 GF: 0-4 Fm: 0-0
Distance: 5f/6f: 0-0 **7f-8f: 1-5** 9f-13f: 0-3 14f+: 0-0
Track : LH: 0-1 RH: 0-4 Tight: 0-1 Gall: 0-2
Aids: Bl: 0-0 Vi: 0-0 Tstrap: 0-0
Best Rating: 93 5/01 Ches 1m2f75y gd-fm

He made a winning debut in soft ground at Ascot as a juvenile and has run respectably in decent company since, but it is proving difficult identifying his best trip. Looks harshly handicapped at present.

Lunar Leo

113 **89**
3-y-o b g Muhtarram (USA)-Moon Mistress (Storm Cat (USA))
S C Williams Bruce W Wyatt

Placings:413635-01304 **(4231)**
2001: 6^0GF, 7^1GF, 7^3G, 7^0G, 8^4G

	Starts	1st	2nd	3rd	Win & Pl
Career Total (Turf)	11	2	0	3	37680

88 7/01 Sand 7f16y C(0-100)H G-F £23200
81 7/00 Wwck 6f168y E G-F £3568
Total win prize-money £26769

Going (Turf): Sf: 0-1 GS: 0-0 Gd: 0-6 **GF: 2-4** Fm: 0-0
Distance: 5f/6f: 0-4 **7f-8f: 2-7** 9f-13f: 0-0 14f+: 0-0
Track : LH: 1-4 RH: 1-2 Tight: 0-1 Gall: 0-2
Aids: Bl: 0-0 Vi: 0-0 **Tstrap: 1-5**
Best Rating: 89 8/01 Gdwd 7f good

A game and consistent performer, he responded well to pressure and got up in the final stride when winning a very valuable seven-furlong handicap at Sandown in July. He showed that it was no fluke with another solid effort at Goodwood next time.

Lunar Lord

108(69) (6)**51**
5-y-o b g Elmaamul (USA)-Cache (Bustino)
D Burchell Brian Williams

Placings:000/0050/0042022440330-31330 **(5170)**
2001: 14^3HY, 14^1S, 14^3GF, 12^3GF, 17^0GS

	Starts	1st	2nd	3rd	Win & Pl
Career Total (Turf)	23	1	3	5	8640
Career Total (AW)	2	0	0	0	

51 4/01 Nott 1m6f15y F(0-60)H SFT £2649
Total win prize-money £2650

Going (Turf): Sf: 1-11 GS: 0-2 Gd: 0-1 GF: 0-7 Fm: 0-2
Distance: 5f/6f: 0-1 7f-8f: 0-2 9f-13f: 0-17 **14f+: 1-5**
Track : **LH: 1-19** RH: 0-3 Tight: 0-5 Gall: 0-0
Aids: Bl: 0-0 Vi: 0-0 Tstrap: 0-0
Best Rating: 87 4/01 Nott 1m6f15y heavy

Lunar Sovereign (USA)

100 **95**
2-y-o br c Cobra King (USA)-January Moon (USA) (Apalachee (USA))
D R Loder Sheikh Mohammed

Placings:12 (5363)
2001: 7^{1}GG, 7^{2}GS

	Starts	1st	2nd	3rd	Win & Pl
Career Total (Turf)	**2**	**1**	**1**	**0**	**7728**

78 9/01 Leic 7f9y D G-S £4647
Total win prize-money £4648

Going (Turf): Sf: 0-0 **GS: 1-2** Gd: 0-0 GF: 0-0 Fm: 0-0
Distance: 5f/6f: 0-0 **7f-8f: 1-2** 9f-13f: 0-0 14f+: 0-0
Track : LH: 0-0 RH: 0-0 Tight: 0-0 Gall: 0-0
Aids: Bl: 0-0 Vi: 0-0 Tstrap: 0-0
Best Rating: 95 10/01 NmkR 7f gd-sft

An American bred $140,000 yearling whose dam was a sprint winner, only had to be pushed out by Dettori to win on his debut at Leicester in September. Improved on that when runner-up in decent event at Newmarket on second start and will even better suited by a sounder surface. Should stay a mile.

Lunch Date

(68) (23)
2-y-o b f Robellino (USA)-Darkness At Noon (USA) (Night Shift (USA))
K McAuliffe Miss J Hall

Placings:405 (1474)
2001: 5^{4}SD, 5^{0}SD, 6^{5}SD

	Starts	1st	2nd	3rd	Win & Pl
Career Total (Turf)	**0**	**0**	**0**	**0**	
Career Total (AW)	**3**	**0**	**0**	**0**	**0**

Going (Turf): Sf: 0-0 GS: 0-0 Gd: 0-0 GF: 0-0 Fm: 0-0
Distance: 5f/6f: 0-3 7f-8f: 0-0 9f-13f: 0-0 14f+: 0-0
Track : LH: 0-2 RH: 0-0 Tight: 0-1 Gall: 0-0
Aids: Bl: 0-0 Vi: 0-3 Tstrap: 0-0
Best Rating: 23 5/01 Sthl 6f stand

Lunch Party

98(99) (55)**50**
9-y-o b g Beveled (USA)-Crystal Sprite (Crystal Glitters (USA))
R A Fahey Stephen Laidlaw

Placings:12000/00001041/3112614050/4511020060/4061050-05000024 (4904)
2001: 6^{0}GF, 7^{5}GF, 6^{0}GF, 7^{0}G, 8^{0}GS, 7^{0}G, 8^{2}F, 7^{4}G

	Starts	1st	2nd	3rd	Win & Pl
Career Total (Turf)	**46**	**9**	**4**	**1**	**32557**
Career Total (AW)	**2**	**0**	**0**	**0**	**0**

58	8/00	Catt	7f	F(0-60)H	G-F	£2677
64	6/99	Thsk	7f	F(0-70)H	G-F	£3481
62	5/99	Catt	7f	F(0-60)	FRM	£2556
63	8/98	Catt	7f	E(0-70)H	G-F	£3194
57	5/98	Catt	7f	D(0-85)H	G-S	£4370
49	5/98	Muss	7f30y	E(0-70)H	G-F	£3057
49	11/97	Muss	1m	E(0-70)H	G-S	£3116
42	9/97	Yarm	7f3y	E(0-70)H	G-F	£3191
57	5/96	Thsk	7f	G	G-F	£1970

Total win prize-money £27615

Going (Turf): Sf: 0-2 GS: 2-11 Gd: 0-15 **GF: 6-13** Fm: 1-5
Distance: 5f/6f: 0-5 **7f-8f: 9-42** 9f-13f: 0-1 14f+: 0-0
Track : **LH: 6-26** RH: 2-13 **Tight: 8-34** Gall: 0-1
Aids: Bl: 0-0 Vi: 0-0 Tstrap: 0-2
Best Rating: 50 9/01 Muss 1m firm

Modest handicapper. Acts on any ground.

Lunevision (FR)

89 **56**
3-y-o b f Solid Illusion (USA)-Lumiere Celeste (FR) (Always Fair (USA))
H J Collingridge The Headquarters Partnership Iv

Placings:3230-06600 (3300)
2001: 7^{0}GS, 6^{6}G, 6^{6}GF, 8^{0}GF, 5^{0}GF

	Starts	1st	2nd	3rd	Win & Pl
Career Total (Turf)	**9**	**0**	**1**	**2**	**2446**

Going (Turf): Sf: 0-1 GS: 0-1 Gd: 0-2 GF: 0-5 Fm: 0-0
Distance: 5f/6f: 0-4 7f-8f: 0-4 9f-13f: 0-1 14f+: 0-0
Track : LH: 0-1 RH: 0-1 Tight: 0-0 Gall: 0-0
Aids: Bl: 0-0 Vi: 0-0 Tstrap: 0-1
Best Rating: 56 4/01 NmkR 7f gd-sft

Lupine (IRE)

105 **82**
2-y-o b/br f Lake Coniston (IRE)-Prosaic Star (IRE) (Common Grounds)
M R Channon G W Robinson

Placings:414 (2615)
2001: 5^{4}G, 5^{1}GF, 6^{4}GF

	Starts	1st	2nd	3rd	Win & Pl
Career Total (Turf)	**3**	**1**	**0**	**0**	**5017**

82 6/01 Hayd 5f D G-F £3640
Total win prize-money £3640

Going (Turf): Sf: 0-0 GS: 0-0 Gd: 0-1 **GF: 1-2** Fm: 0-0
Distance: **5f/6f: 1-3** 7f-8f: 0-0 9f-13f: 0-0 14f+: 0-0
Track : LH: 0-0 RH: 0-1 Tight: 0-0 Gall: 0-1
Aids: Bl: 0-0 Vi: 0-0 Tstrap: 0-0
Best Rating: 82 6/01 NmkJ 6f gd-fm

She learned a good deal from her debut and showed a useful turn of foot to take a Haydock maiden on her next start. Did not disgrace herself in Listed company on final start.

Lurdi (IRE)

103 **77**
3-y-o b c Lure (USA)-Headrest (Habitat)
J R Fanshawe Abdulla Al Khalifa

Placings:3004103 (4570)
2001: 7^{3}G, 7^{0}GS, 8^{0}GF, 8^{4}GF, 9^{1}GF, 11^{0}GF, 11^{3}HY

	Starts	1st	2nd	3rd	Win & Pl
Career Total (Turf)	**7**	**1**	**0**	**2**	**1862**

Going (Turf): Sf: 0-1 GS: 0-1 Gd: 0-1 **GF: 1-4** Fm: 0-0
Distance: 5f/6f: 0-0 7f-8f: 0-2 **9f-13f: 1-5** 14f+: 0-0
Track : **LH: 1-4** RH: 0-1 Tight: 0-2 Gall: 0-0
Aids: Bl: 0-0 Vi: 0-1 Tstrap: 0-0
Best Rating: 77 5/01 Thsk 7f good

Half-brother to a mile and a quarter Group Two winner, he dead-heated for first place on his first attempt at ten furlongs, giving weight and a beating to older rivals. He has improvement in him. Acts on fast ground.

Lurina (IRE)

105 **114**
3-y-o b f Lure (USA)-Alligatrix (USA) (Alleged (USA))
J H M Gosden Mrs Shirley H Taylor

Placings:2-130 (2352)
2001: 7^{1}G, 8^{3}G, 8^{0}GF

	Starts	1st	2nd	3rd	Win & Pl
Career Total (Turf)	**4**	**1**	**1**	**1**	**13963**

87 5/01 NmkR 7f D GD £7117
Total win prize-money £7118

Going (Turf): Sf: 0-1 GS: 0-0 **Gd: 1-2** GF: 0-1 Fm: 0-0
Distance: 5f/6f: 0-0 **7f-8f: 1-4** 9f-13f: 0-0 14f+: 0-0
Track : LH: 0-0 RH: 0-1 Tight: 0-0 Gall: 0-1
Aids: Bl: 0-0 Vi: 0-0 Tstrap: 0-0
Best Rating: 114 6/01 Chan 1m good

A half-sister to Alidiva, ran a good third to Banks Hill in the Prix Sandringham over a mile at Chantilly in June after winning a maiden at the Guineas meeting. Not seen after running unplaced in the Coronation Stakes.

Lushs Lad

94(91) (52)**54**
3-y-o b c Wolfhound (USA)-Helsinki (Machiavellian (USA))
G L Moore Chris Wilkinson

Placings:0-635105000 (2876)
2001: 5^{6}SW, 7^{3}SW, 7^{5}SD, 7^{1}SD, 7^{0}G, 8^{5}GS, 6^{0}GF, 8^{0}GF, 8^{0}GF

	Starts	1st	2nd	3rd	Win & Pl
Career Total (Turf)	**6**	**0**	**0**	**0**	**0**
Career Total (AW)	**4**	**1**	**0**	**1**	**3104**

40 3/01 Ling 7f E STD £2695
Total win prize-money £2695

Going (Turf): Sf: 0-0 GS: 0-1 Gd: 0-1 GF: 0-3 Fm: 0-0
Distance: 5f/6f: 0-1 **7f-8f: 1-8** 9f-13f: 0-1 14f+: 0-0
Track : **LH: 1-6** RH: 0-1 **Tight: 1-5** Gall: 0-0
Aids: Bl: 0-0 Vi: 0-0 Tstrap: 0-1
Best Rating: 54 5/01 Sals 1m gd-sft

Lusong (IRE)

88(99) (51)**52**
4-y-o ch c Fayruz-Mildred Anne (IRE) (Thatching)
R Hannon Taylor Homer Racing

Placings:22634055006-640 (2057)
2001: 8^{6}SD, 7^{4}SW, 6^{0}GF

	Starts	1st	2nd	3rd	Win & Pl
Career Total (Turf)	**7**	**0**	**0**	**1**	**1008**
Career Total (AW)	**7**	**0**	**2**	**0**	**1684**

Going (Turf): Sf: 0-0 GS: 0-0 Gd: 0-2 GF: 0-3 Fm: 0-2
Distance: 5f/6f: 0-7 7f-8f: 0-7 9f-13f: 0-0 14f+: 0-0
Track : LH: 0-8 RH: 0-1 Tight: 0-7 Gall: 0-1
Aids: Bl: 0-1 Vi: 0-0 Tstrap: 0-0
Best Rating: 51 1/01 Ling 7f slow

Lutine Bell

86(85) (5)**13**
6-y-o b g Fairy King (USA)-Bell Toll (High Line)
H J Collingridge D T Thom

Placings:0/00/0005-00 (1577)
2001: 7^{0}GF, 8^{0}F

	Starts	1st	2nd	3rd	Win & Pl
Career Total (Turf)	**5**	**0**	**0**	**0**	
Career Total (AW)	**4**	**0**	**0**	**0**	**0**

Going (Turf): Sf: 0-1 GS: 0-0 Gd: 0-1 GF: 0-2 Fm: 0-1
Distance: 5f/6f: 0-0 7f-8f: 0-3 9f-13f: 0-4 14f+: 0-2
Track : LH: 0-7 RH: 0-0 Tight: 0-5 Gall: 0-0
Aids: Bl: 0-0 Vi: 0-0 Tstrap: 0-1
Best Rating: 13 5/01 Pont 1m4y firm

Luxor

93(77) (34)**50**
4-y-o ch g Grand Lodge (USA)-Escrime (USA) (Sharpen Up)
P Mitchell Gordon Li

Placings:421000-000400000 (4667)
2001: 12^{0}SD, 10^{0}S, 10^{0}G, 7^{4}F, 10^{0}GS, 8^{0}GS, 7^{0}G, 9^{0}GS, 8^{0}GF

	Starts	1st	2nd	3rd	Win & Pl
Career Total (Turf)	**14**	**1**	**1**	**0**	**6263**
Career Total (AW)	**1**	**0**	**0**	**0**	

89 6/00 NmkJ 1m2f D G-F £5050
Total win prize-money £5051

Going (Turf): Sf: 0-2 GS: 0-4 Gd: 0-2 **GF: 1-5** Fm: 0-1
Distance: 5f/6f: 0-0 7f-8f: 0-4 **9f-13f: 1-11** 14f+: 0-0
Track : LH: 0-8 **RH: 1-4** Tight: 0-6 **Gall: 1-5**
Aids: Bl: 0-0 Vi: 0-4 Tstrap: 0-5
Best Rating: 50 8/01 NmkJ 1m gd-sft

Lycheel

92(93) A(48)**43**
3-y-o ch g Lycius (USA)-Talon D'Aiguille (USA) (Big Spruce (USA))
W R Muir Mrs E Clowes And Mrs D Edginton

Placings:0-04500000 **(4802)**
2001: 8^{0}SD, 8^{4}SW, 8^{5}GF, 8^{0}S, 10^{0}GF, 9^{0}GS, 8^{0}F, 8^{0}F

	Starts	1st	2nd	3rd	Win & Pl
Career Total (Turf)	7	0	0	0	0
Career Total (AW)	2	0	0	0	0

Going (Turf): Sf: 0-1 GS: 0-2 Gd: 0-0 GF: 0-2 Fm: 0-2
Distance: 5f/6f: 0-0 7f-8f: 0-2 9f-13f: 0-7 14f+: 0-0
Track : LH: 0-7 RH: 0-1 Tight: 0-3 Gall: 0-0
Aids: Bl: 0-1 Vi: 0-0 Tstrap: 0-0
Best Rating: 53 8/01 Leic 1m9y gd-fm

Lycian (IRE)

106(93) (66)**66**
6-y-o b g Lycius (USA)-Perfect Time (IRE) (Dance Of Life (USA))
J A R Toller A Ilsley

Placings:0004/12153215/153062l200/60340114-0603 **(4635)**
2001: 10^{0}G, 10^{6}GF, 9^{0}GF, 9^{3}GF

	Starts	1st	2nd	3rd	Win & Pl
Career Total (Turf)	27	5	2	3	27721
Career Total (AW)	7	2	2	1	7811

66	9/00	Yarm	1m2f21y	C(0-90)H	G-F	£7702
66	9/00	Leic	1m1f218y	E(0-75)H	G-F	£2977
60	6/99	Gdwd	1m1f	D(0-80)H	G-F	£5215
70	1/99	Ling	1m	E(0-70)H	STD	£2646
63	12/98	Ling	1m	D(0-85)H	STD	£3030
57	7/98	Brig	7f214y	D(0-80)H	G-F	£3533
48	5/98	Bath	1m5y	E(0-70)H	G-F	£3039

Total win prize-money £28144

Going (Turf): Sf: 0-0 GS: 0-1 Gd: 0-7 **GF: 5-16** Fm: 0-3
Distance: 5f/6f: 0-0 7f-8f: 3-16 **9f-13f: 4-18** 14f+: 0-0
Track : **LH: 5-20** RH: 2-5 **Tight: 5-15** Gall: 0-2
Aids: Bl: 0-0 Vi: 0-0 Tstrap: 0-0
Best Rating: 61 9/01 Leic 1m1f218y gd-fm

A useful handicapper at around ten furlongs. Acts on fast ground.

Lyciat Sparkle (IRE)

95(69) (24)**28**
3-y-o b g Lycius (USA)-Benguiat (FR) (Exceller (USA))
Mrs G S Rees The Most Wanted Partnership

Placings:0000-500460 **(5269)**
2001: 8^{5}GF, 11^{0}GF, 8^{0}GS, 10^{4}GF, 13^{6}GF, 10^{0}HY

	Starts	1st	2nd	3rd	Win & Pl
Career Total (Turf)	7	0	0	0	0
Career Total (AW)	3	0	0	0	

Going (Turf): Sf: 0-2 GS: 0-1 Gd: 0-0 GF: 0-4 Fm: 0-0
Distance: 5f/6f: 0-3 7f-8f: 0-2 9f-13f: 0-4 14f+: 0-1
Track : LH: 0-7 RH: 0-2 Tight: 0-4 Gall: 0-0
Aids: Bl: 0-0 Vi: 0-0 Tstrap: 0-0
Best Rating: 29 6/01 Muss 1m gd-fm

Lydia's Look (IRE)

107(96) (42)**57**
4-y-o b f Distant View (USA)-Mrs Croesus (USA) (Key To The Mint (USA))
T J Etherington Callers And Clerks

Placings:54100000-404141020 **(4804)**
2001: 5^{4}GF, 5^{0}GF, 5^{4}SD, 5^{1}G, 5^{4}GF, 6^{1}F, 6^{0}F, 5^{2}G, 6^{0}F

	Starts	1st	2nd	3rd	Win & Pl
Career Total (Turf)	10	2	1	0	10806
Career Total (AW)	7	1	0	0	2958

57	7/01	Thsk	6f	D(0-80)H	FRM	£4394
46	6/01	Haml	5f4y	E(0-75)H	GD	£4875
54	3/00	Sthl	5f	D	STD	£2743

Total win prize-money £12012

Going (Turf): Sf: 0-0 GS: 0-1 **Gd: 1-3** GF: 0-3 **Fm: 1-3**
Distance: **5f/6f: 3-15** 7f-8f: 0-2 9f-13f: 0-0 14f+: 0-0
Track : LH: 0-5 RH: 0-0 Tight: 0-0 Gall: 0-0
Aids: Bl: 0-0 Vi: 0-0 Tstrap: 0-0
Best Rating: 57 7/01 Thsk 6f firm

Lygeton Lad

85(91) (47)**42**
3-y-o b g Shaamit (IRE)-Smartie Lee (Dominion)
Miss Gay Kelleway J McGonagle & B J McGonagle

Placings:6040 **(4872)**
2001: 9^{6}SD, 8^{0}GF, 9^{4}SD, 7^{0}G

	Starts	1st	2nd	3rd	Win & Pl
Career Total (Turf)	2	0	0	0	
Career Total (AW)	2	0	0	0	0

Going (Turf): Sf: 0-0 GS: 0-0 Gd: 0-1 GF: 0-1 Fm: 0-0
Distance: 5f/6f: 0-0 7f-8f: 0-1 9f-13f: 0-3 14f+: 0-0
Track : LH: 0-3 RH: 0-0 Tight: 0-2 Gall: 0-0
Aids: Bl: 0-0 Vi: 0-0 Tstrap: 0-2
Best Rating: 42 7/01 Nott 1m54y gd-fm

Lynton Lad

(99) (47d)
9-y-o b g Superpower-House Maid (Habitat)
M J Gingell (P S McEntee 5/2) Gentlemen Don't Work On Mondays

Placings:21361/50000025/2000/440240/030125/66001 005004006-24500 **(0285)**
2001: 9^{2}SD, 8^{4}SW, 9^{5}SW, 6^{0}SD, 9^{0}SW

	Starts	1st	2nd	3rd	Win & Pl
Career Total (Turf)	37	4	5	2	26368
Career Total (AW)	11	0	1	0	1128

56	7/00	Pont	1m4y	E(0-70)H	G-F	£3341
56	5/99	Ayr	1m	F(0-65)H	GD	£2500
85	10/94	Yarm	6f3y	C	GD	£4831
74	9/94	Hayd	5f	D	GD	£3662

Total win prize-money £14336

Going (Turf): Sf: 0-9 GS: 0-4 **Gd: 3-12** GF: 1-11 Fm: 0-1
Distance: 5f/6f: 1-10 **7f-8f: 2-25** 9f-13f: 1-13 14f+: 0-0
Track : **LH: 2-24** RH: 0-5 Tight: 0-11 Gall: 0-2
Aids: Bl: 0-8 Vi: 0-4 Tstrap: 0-0
Best Rating: 47 1/01 Wolv 1m1f79y stand

Lyric Maestro

92 **76**
2-y-o b c Merdon Melody-Dubitable (Formidable (USA))
S Dow T G Parker

Placings:003 **(4574)**
2001: 6^{0}GS, 7^{0}G, 8^{3}G

	Starts	1st	2nd	3rd	Win & Pl
Career Total (Turf)	3	0	0	1	666

Going (Turf): Sf: 0-0 GS: 0-1 Gd: 0-2 GF: 0-0 Fm: 0-0
Distance: 5f/6f: 0-1 7f-8f: 0-2 9f-13f: 0-0 14f+: 0-0
Track : LH: 0-0 RH: 0-1 Tight: 0-0 Gall: 0-0
Aids: Bl: 0-0 Vi: 0-0 Tstrap: 0-0
Best Rating: 76 9/01 Kemp 1m good

Improved on previous efforts when third at Kempton in September.

Lyrical

103 **76**
3-y-o b f Shirley Heights-La Sky (IRE) (Law Society (USA))
H R A Cecil Lordship Stud

Placings:U424 **(4673)**
2001: 10^{U}S, 10^{4}G, 12^{2}GS, 12^{4}G

	Starts	1st	2nd	3rd	Win & Pl
Career Total (Turf)	4	0	1	0	1636

Going (Turf): Sf: 0-1 GS: 0-1 Gd: 0-2 GF: 0-0 Fm: 0-0
Distance: 5f/6f: 0-0 7f-8f: 0-0 9f-13f: 0-4 14f+: 0-0
Track : LH: 0-3 RH: 0-1 Tight: 0-2 Gall: 0-0
Aids: Bl: 0-0 Vi: 0-0 Tstrap: 0-0
Best Rating: 76 8/01 Ches 1m4f66y gd-sft

Lyrical Lad

84 **59**
2-y-o b g Primo Dominie-Lyrical Bid (USA) (Lyphard (USA))
P W Harris Partners In Prime

Placings:040 **(5295)**
2001: 6^{0}GF, 8^{4}GF, 8^{0}S

	Starts	1st	2nd	3rd	Win & Pl
Career Total (Turf)	3	0	0	0	342

Going (Turf): Sf: 0-1 GS: 0-0 Gd: 0-0 GF: 0-2 Fm: 0-0
Distance: 5f/6f: 0-0 7f-8f: 0-2 9f-13f: 0-1 14f+: 0-0
Track : LH: 0-0 RH: 0-1 Tight: 0-0 Gall: 0-0
Aids: Bl: 0-0 Vi: 0-0 Tstrap: 0-0
Best Rating: 59 9/01 Kemp 1m gd-fm

Lyrical Way

80 **65**
2-y-o b c Vettori (IRE)-Fortunate (Reference Point)
P R Chamings Mrs Alexandra J Chandris

Placings:060 **(5094)**
2001: 7^{0}GF, 7^{6}F, 8^{0}GS

	Starts	1st	2nd	3rd	Win & Pl
Career Total (Turf)	3	0	0	0	0

Going (Turf): Sf: 0-0 GS: 0-1 Gd: 0-0 GF: 0-1 Fm: 0-1
Distance: 5f/6f: 0-0 7f-8f: 0-3 9f-13f: 0-0 14f+: 0-0
Track : LH: 0-1 RH: 0-0 Tight: 0-0 Gall: 0-0
Aids: Bl: 0-0 Vi: 0-0 Tstrap: 0-0
Best Rating: 65 9/01 Chep 7f16y firm

Lyringo

(65)
7-y-o b m Rustingo-Lyricist (Averof)
P D Evans S R Brown

Placings:0 **(1997)**
2001: 14^{0}SD

	Starts	1st	2nd	3rd	Win & Pl
Career Total (Turf)	0	0	0	0	
Career Total (AW)	1	0	0	0	

Going (Turf): Sf: 0-0 GS: 0-0 Gd: 0-0 GF: 0-0 Fm: 0-0
Distance: 5f/6f: 0-0 7f-8f: 0-0 9f-13f: 0-0 14f+: 0-1
Track : LH: 0-1 RH: 0-0 Tight: 0-0 Gall: 0-0
Aids: Bl: 0-0 Vi: 0-0 Tstrap: 0-0

Lysander's Quest (IRE)

86 **62**
3-y-o br c King's Theatre (IRE)-Haramayda (FR) (Doyoun)
L Montague Hall Mrs E N Nield

Placings:456-0000 **(4952)**
2001: 10^{0}S, 9^{0}GF, 12^{0}GF, 11^{0}G

	Starts	1st	2nd	3rd	Win & Pl
Career Total (Turf)	7	0	0	0	506

Going (Turf): Sf: 0-2 GS: 0-0 Gd: 0-1 GF: 0-4 Fm: 0-0
Distance: 5f/6f: 0-0 7f-8f: 0-2 9f-13f: 0-5 14f+: 0-0
Track : LH: 0-0 RH: 0-4 Tight: 0-1 Gall: 0-0
Aids: Bl: 0-0 Vi: 0-0 Tstrap: 0-0
Best Rating: 62 4/01 NmkR 1m2f soft

M For Magic

84 **70**

2-y-o ch g First Trump-Celestine (Skyliner)
J L Spearing M Olden

Placings:655530 **(5689)**
2001: 5^{6}F, 6^{5}GF, 6^{5}G, 6^{5}GF, 6^{3}HY, 6^{0}S

	Starts	1st	2nd	3rd	Win & Pl
Career Total (Turf)	6	0	0	1	628

Going (Turf): Sf: 0-2 GS: 0-0 Gd: 0-1 GF: 0-2 Fm: 0-1
Distance: 5f/6f: 0-5 7f-8f: 0-1 9f-13f: 0-0 14f+: 0-0
Track : LH: 0-0 RH: 0-0 Tight: 0-0 Gall: 0-0
Aids: Bl: 0-2 Vi: 0-0 Tstrap: 0-0
Best Rating: 76 8/01 Sals 6f gd-fm

A half-brother to five-furlong juvenile winners Prix Star and Ringside Jack, has shown moderate form in maidens. Best on a sound surface.

M'Auld Segoisha (IRE)

101(87) (55)**60**

3-y-o ro f Dolphin Street (FR)-September Tide (IRE) (Thatching)
J G Fitzgerald Tim Kilroe

Placings:0022-242000 **(5375)**
2001: 7^{2}GF, 8^{4}SD, 7^{2}S, 7^{0}GS, 7^{0}G, 7^{0}G

	Starts	1st	2nd	3rd	Win & Pl
Career Total (Turf)	9	0	4	0	10892
Career Total (AW)	1	0	0	0	0

Going (Turf): Sf: 0-1 GS: 0-3 Gd: 0-4 GF: 0-1 Fm: 0-0
Distance: 5f/6f: 0-3 7f-8f: 0-7 9f-13f: 0-1 14f+: 0-0
Track : LH: 0-2 RH: 0-2 Tight: 0-0 Gall: 0-0
Aids: Bl: 0-0 Vi: 0-0 Tstrap: 0-1
Best Rating: 60 10/01 Rdcr 7f good

She has finished runner-up in varied company, but is still a maiden and does not look progressive.

Ma Belle Bleue

100 **62**

2-y-o b f Bluegrass Prince (IRE)-My Bonus (Cyrano De Bergerac)
Miss A Stokell (T D Easterby 22/9) T J Ford

Placings:5040006000 **(5633)**
2001: 5^{5}GF, 5^{0}GF, 5^{4}GF, 7^{0}F, 6^{0}G, 7^{0}G, 6^{6}G, 5^{0}GF, 6^{0}HY, 7^{0}G

	Starts	1st	2nd	3rd	Win & Pl
Career Total (Turf)	10	0	0	0	0

Going (Turf): Sf: 0-1 GS: 0-0 Gd: 0-4 GF: 0-4 Fm: 0-1
Distance: 5f/6f: 0-6 7f-8f: 0-4 9f-13f: 0-0 14f+: 0-0
Track : LH: 0-4 RH: 0-0 Tight: 0-4 Gall: 0-0
Aids: Bl: 0-1 Vi: 0-0 Tstrap: 0-0
Best Rating: 73 6/01 Hayd 5f gd-fm

Ma Jolie

98 **77**

3-y-o ch f Shalford (IRE)-Scalford Brook (Handsome Sailor)
H Akbary Charles Alan McKechnie

Placings:0344-04401000 **(5254)**
2001: 7^{0}S, 7^{4}S, 7^{4}F, 7^{0}GS, 8^{1}GF, 7^{0}GF, 7^{0}HY, 6^{0}S

	Starts	1st	2nd	3rd	Win & Pl
Career Total (Turf)	12	1	0	1	9169
77 8/01 Donc 1m	D(0-85)H			G-F	£4270

Total win prize-money £4271

Going (Turf): Sf: 0-6 GS: 0-2 Gd: 0-1 **GF: 1-2** Fm: 0-1
Distance: 5f/6f: 0-2 **7f-8f: 1-9** 9f-13f: 0-1 14f+: 0-0
Track : **LH: 1-5** RH: 0-0 Tight: 0-1 **Gall: 1-2**
Aids: Bl: 0-0 Vi: 0-0 Tstrap: 0-0
Best Rating: 77 8/01 Donc 1m gd-fm

She got off the mark at the ninth attempt when winning a slowly-run fillies' handicap at Doncaster in August.

Ma Vie

99 **62**

4-y-o b f Salse (USA)-One Life (USA) (L'Emigrant (USA))
J R Fanshawe The Earl Of Lonsdale

Placings:600/020225-1 **(3965)**
2001: 10^{1}G

	Starts	1st	2nd	3rd	Win & Pl
Career Total (Turf)	10	1	3	0	6526
50 8/01 Yarm 1m2f21y F(0-60)				GD	£3220

Total win prize-money £3220

Going (Turf): Sf: 0-2 GS: 0-2 **Gd: 1-3** GF: 0-1 Fm: 0-1
Distance: 5f/6f: 0-1 7f-8f: 0-3 **9f-13f: 1-5** 14f+: 0-0
Track : **LH: 1-3** RH: 0-3 **Tight: 1-2** Gall: 0-2
Aids: Bl: 0-0 Vi: 0-3 Tstrap: 0-0
Best Rating: 50 8/01 Yarm 1m2f21y good

Mabrum (IRE)

78 **49**

2-y-o b c Alhaarth (IRE)-Absaar (USA) (Alleged (USA))
J L Dunlop Hamdan Al Maktoum

Placings:6 **(3854)**
2001: 7^{6}GS

	Starts	1st	2nd	3rd	Win & Pl
Career Total (Turf)	1	0	0	0	0

Going (Turf): Sf: 0-0 GS: 0-1 Gd: 0-0 GF: 0-0 Fm: 0-0
Distance: 5f/6f: 0-0 7f-8f: 0-1 9f-13f: 0-0 14f+: 0-0
Track : LH: 0-0 RH: 0-0 Tight: 0-0 Gall: 0-0
Aids: Bl: 0-0 Vi: 0-0 Tstrap: 0-0
Best Rating: 49 8/01 Leic 7f9y gd-sft

Mac Be Lucky

104 **59**

4-y-o b g Magic Ring (IRE)-Take Heart (Electric)
T D Barron Alex Gorrie Combi (uk)

Placings:320/002023-000000 **(5092)**
2001: 7^{0}G, 8^{0}GF, 7^{0}G, 7^{0}GS, 7^{0}G, 8^{0}GS

	Starts	1st	2nd	3rd	Win & Pl
Career Total (Turf)	15	0	3	2	4156

Going (Turf): Sf: 0-6 GS: 0-3 Gd: 0-5 GF: 0-1 Fm: 0-0
Distance: 5f/6f: 0-1 7f-8f: 0-9 9f-13f: 0-5 14f+: 0-0
Track : LH: 0-8 RH: 0-3 Tight: 0-2 Gall: 0-2
Aids: Bl: 0-0 Vi: 0-0 Tstrap: 0-0
Best Rating: 61 5/01 Ripn 1m gd-fm

He has some ability in varied company in his career but remains a maiden.

Mac's Dream (USA)

97(85) (33)**39**

6-y-o b g Mister Frisky (USA)-Annie's Dream (USA) (Droll Role (USA))
A W Carroll J R Barr

Placings:0400**060**/000030205/000505**000**-003000000 **(4872)**
2001: 6^{0}GS, 6^{0}S, 8^{3}GF, 8^{0}GF, 9^{0}G, 8^{0}G, 10^{0}S, 7^{0}GF, 7^{0}G

	Starts	1st	2nd	3rd	Win & Pl
Career Total (Turf)	29	0	1	2	2553
Career Total (AW)	6	0	0	0	0

Going (Turf): Sf: 0-4 GS: 0-1 Gd: 0-12 GF: 0-9 Fm: 0-3
Distance: 5f/6f: 0-4 7f-8f: 0-17 9f-13f: 0-14 14f+: 0-0
Track : LH: 0-17 RH: 0-2 Tight: 0-9 Gall: 0-2
Aids: Bl: 0-0 Vi: 0-0 Tstrap: 0-27
Best Rating: 56 5/01 Hayd 6f soft

Poor plater who has shown little worthwhile form this season.

Macadamia (IRE)

99 **79+**

2-y-o b f Classic Cliche (IRE)-Cashew (Sharrood (USA))
J R Fanshawe Lord Vestey

Placings:41 **(5371)**
2001: 7^{4}F, 8^{1}G

	Starts	1st	2nd	3rd	Win & Pl
Career Total (Turf)	2	1	0	0	3850
79 10/01 Rdcr 1m E				GD	£3850

Total win prize-money £3850

Going (Turf): Sf: 0-0 GS: 0-0 **Gd: 1-1** GF: 0-0 Fm: 0-1
Distance: 5f/6f: 0-0 **7f-8f: 1-2** 9f-13f: 0-0 14f+: 0-0
Track : LH: 0-0 RH: 0-0 Tight: 0-0 Gall: 0-0
Aids: Bl: 0-0 Vi: 0-0 Tstrap: 0-0
Best Rating: 79 10/01 Rdcr 1m good

Got off the mark on only her second attempt. Acts on good ground, and is suited by a mile.

Macaroon (IRE)

111(94) (52)**97**

3-y-o ch f Tagula (IRE)-Almond Flower (IRE) (Alzao (USA))
M L W Bell The Fitzrovians

Placings:312331304101 **(5473a)**
2001: 6^{3}HY, 7^{1}SD, 8^{2}G, 7^{3}G, 7^{3}GF, 7^{1}GF, 6^{3}GS, 7^{0}G, 7^{4}GF, 6^{1}GF, 6^{0}G, 7^{1}VS

	Starts	1st	2nd	3rd	Win & Pl
Career Total (Turf)	11	3	1	4	39667
Career Total (AW)	1	1	0	0	1806
97 10/01 MsnL 7f				VS	£13579
90 9/01 Sals 6f212y	C(0-95)H			G-F	£12447
81 6/01 Ling 7f	C(0-95)H			G-F	£7150
52 4/01 Sthl 7f	F			STD	£1806

Total win prize-money £34983

Going (Turf): Sf: 0-1 GS: 0-1 Gd: 0-4 **GF: 2-4** Fm: 0-0
Distance: 5f/6f: 0-3 **7f-8f: 4-9** 9f-13f: 0-0 14f+: 0-0
Track : **LH: 1-2** RH: 0-3 Tight: 0-1 Gall: 0-0
Aids: Bl: 0-0 Vi: 0-0 Tstrap: 0-0
Best Rating: 97 10/01 MsnL 7f v soft

Unraced at two, she is very consistent and got off the mark on her only start so far on Fibresand at Southwell in April. She has run well in much better races on turf since then, including a victory in a decent little handicap at Lingfield in June, and when making all to win another decent handicap at Salisbury in September. Gained black type when leading throughout to win a Listed race in France in October. Suited by seven furlongs, any ground and forcing tactics.

Macaw (IRE)

97 **86**

2-y-o b c Bluebird (USA)-No Quest (IRE) (Rainbow Quest (USA))
J H M Gosden Anthony Speelman

Placings:422 **(5268)**
2001: 6^{4}GF, 6^{2}GS, 7^{2}HY

	Starts	1st	2nd	3rd	Win & Pl
Career Total (Turf)	3	0	2	0	2544

Going (Turf): Sf: 0-1 GS: 0-1 Gd: 0-0 GF: 0-1 Fm: 0-0
Distance: 5f/6f: 0-1 7f-8f: 0-2 9f-13f: 0-0 14f+: 0-0
Track : LH: 0-0 RH: 0-0 Tight: 0-0 Gall: 0-0
Aids: Bl: 0-0 Vi: 0-0 Tstrap: 0-0
Best Rating: 86 10/01 Ayr 7f50y heavy

A good-bodied colt, is out of a half-sister to Poule d'Essai des Poulains winner No Pass No Sale. Soundly beaten on his first start. Improved for that to finish runner-up at Salisbury after a ten-week break. Again finished second at Ayr in the mud just over a week later over seven furlongs.

Macdune (FR)

93 **60**

3-y-o b c Machiavellian (USA)-Sandhill (IRE) (Danehill (USA))
E A L Dunlop Patrick Milmo

Placings:00-0004 (5593)
2001: 8^0S, 7^0G, 7^0HY, 5^4GS

	Starts	1st	2nd	3rd	Win & Pl
Career Total (Turf)	6	0	0	0	0

Going (Turf): Sf: 0-2 GS: 0-1 Gd: 0-3 GF: 0-0 Fm: 0-0
Distance: 5f/6f: 0-1 7f-8f: 0-5 9f-13f: 0-0 14f+: 0-0
Track : LH: 0-1 RH: 0-1 Tight: 0-0 Gall: 0-0
Aids: Bl: 0-0 Vi: 0-0 Tstrap: 0-0
Best Rating: 60 11/01 Brig 5f213y gd-sft

Showed speed on his debut at two. Made little impact this season but appreciated the drop back to six on his final start.

Maceo (GER)

102 **72**

7-y-o ch g Acatenango (GER)-Metropolitan Star (USA) (Lyphard (USA))
Mrs M Reveley Les De La Haye

Placings:416/31111213/530205/04114555/0311445 (5640)
2001: 10^0G, 10^3GF, 13^1GS, 13^1G, 12^4G, 13^4HY, 13^5G

	Starts	1st	2nd	3rd	Win & Pl
Career Total (Turf)	32	10	2	4	87006

72	8/01	Catt	1m5f175y	E(0-70)H	GD	£4143
69	7/01	Ayr	1m5f13y	E(0-70)	G-S	£3045
	6/99	Vien	1m2f			£4000
	5/99	Muni	1m2f			£4223
	9/97	Hopp	1m6f			£11811
	8/97	Hopp	1m4f	H	GD	£7874

Total win prize-money £59190

Going (Turf): Sf: 1-7 GS: 1-1 **Gd: 4-9** GF: 0-1 Fm: 0-0
Distance: 5f/6f: 0-0 7f-8f: 1-4 **9f-13f: 6-18** 14f+: 3-7
Track : **LH: 2-7** RH: 1-2 **Tight: 1-2** Gall: 0-2
Aids: Bl: 0-0 Vi: 0-0 Tstrap: 0-0
Best Rating: 72 8/01 Catt 1m5f175y good

High class performer in his native Germany. Now with Mary Reveley, he notched up back-to-back victories at Ayr and Catterick over 13 furlongs during the summer. Has won on good and good to soft ground.

Maconachie

91 **73**

2-y-o b g Bahamian Bounty-Madurai (Chilibang)
J L Dunlop Mrs Simon Boscawen

Placings:043 (5526)
2001: 6^0S, 6^4HY, 5^3S

	Starts	1st	2nd	3rd	Win & Pl
Career Total (Turf)	3	0	0	1	889

Going (Turf): Sf: 0-3 GS: 0-0 Gd: 0-0 GF: 0-0 Fm: 0-0
Distance: 5f/6f: 0-2 7f-8f: 0-1 9f-13f: 0-0 14f+: 0-0
Track : LH: 0-0 RH: 0-0 Tight: 0-0 Gall: 0-0
Aids: Bl: 0-0 Vi: 0-0 Tstrap: 0-0
Best Rating: 73 10/01 Nott 5f13y soft

Macs Miesque (USA)

87 **64**

3-y-o b c Miesque's Son (USA)-Santella (USA) (Coastal (USA))
W A O'Gorman Michael McDonnell

Placings:00 (1146)
2001: 7^0S, 8^0G

	Starts	1st	2nd	3rd	Win & Pl
Career Total (Turf)	2	0	0	0	

Going (Turf): Sf: 0-1 GS: 0-0 Gd: 0-1 GF: 0-0 Fm: 0-0
Distance: 5f/6f: 0-0 7f-8f: 0-2 9f-13f: 0-0 14f+: 0-0
Track : LH: 0-0 RH: 0-0 Tight: 0-0 Gall: 0-0
Aids: Bl: 0-0 Vi: 0-0 Tstrap: 0-0
Best Rating: 64 5/01 NmkR 1m good

Mactire

89 **60**

2-y-o b c Celtic Swing-High Desire (IRE) (High Estate)
J C Fox Miss Lorna Goddard

Placings:0000300 (5130)
2001: 6^0S, 6^0GF, 6^0GF, 6^0GF, 7^3GF, 6^0GS, 7^0HY

	Starts	1st	2nd	3rd	Win & Pl
Career Total (Turf)	7	0	0	1	654

Going (Turf): Sf: 0-2 GS: 0-1 Gd: 0-0 GF: 0-4 Fm: 0-0
Distance: 5f/6f: 0-0 7f-8f: 0-7 9f-13f: 0-0 14f+: 0-0
Track : LH: 0-0 RH: 0-1 Tight: 0-0 Gall: 0-0
Aids: Bl: 0-0 Vi: 0-0 Tstrap: 0-0
Best Rating: 60 5/01 Newb 6f8y soft

Mad Carew (USA)

92 **72**

2-y-o ch c Rahy (USA)-Poppy Carew (IRE) (Danehill (USA))
P W Harris Mrs P W Harris

Placings:0450 (5176)
2001: 7^0GF, 8^4G, 8^5GF, 8^0HY

	Starts	1st	2nd	3rd	Win & Pl
Career Total (Turf)	4	0	0	0	333

Going (Turf): Sf: 0-1 GS: 0-0 Gd: 0-1 GF: 0-2 Fm: 0-0
Distance: 5f/6f: 0-0 7f-8f: 0-3 9f-13f: 0-1 14f+: 0-0
Track : LH: 0-0 RH: 0-3 Tight: 0-1 Gall: 0-0
Aids: Bl: 0-0 Vi: 0-0 Tstrap: 0-0
Best Rating: 72 9/01 Kemp 1m gd-fm

Mad Genius

2-y-o b g Makbul-Rinca (Unfuwain (USA))
T H Caldwell J S Camilleri

Placings:0 (5415)
2001: 6^0SD

	Starts	1st	2nd	3rd	Win & Pl
Career Total (Turf)	0	0	0	0	
Career Total (AW)	1	0	0	0	

Going (Turf): Sf: 0-0 GS: 0-0 Gd: 0-0 GF: 0-0 Fm: 0-0
Distance: 5f/6f: 0-1 7f-8f: 0-0 9f-13f: 0-0 14f+: 0-0
Track : LH: 0-1 RH: 0-0 Tight: 0-1 Gall: 0-0
Aids: Bl: 0-0 Vi: 0-0 Tstrap: 0-0

Mad Habit

89 **35**

3-y-o b g Minshaanshu Amad (USA)-Shady Habitat (Sharpo)
W R Muir F Hope

Placings:000-0 (3080)
2001: 11^0GF

	Starts	1st	2nd	3rd	Win & Pl
Career Total (Turf)	4	0	0	0	

Going (Turf): Sf: 0-1 GS: 0-0 Gd: 0-1 GF: 0-2 Fm: 0-0
Distance: 5f/6f: 0-0 7f-8f: 0-2 9f-13f: 0-2 14f+: 0-0
Track : LH: 0-1 RH: 0-2 Tight: 0-2 Gall: 0-2
Aids: Bl: 0-1 Vi: 0-0 Tstrap: 0-0
Best Rating: 23 7/01 Wind 1m3f135y gd-fm

Mad Mick (IRE)

6-y-o b g Homo Sapien-Yougotit (Orange Reef)
K McAuliffe K W J McAuliffe

Placings:00 (2172)
2001: 11^0F, 11^0SD

	Starts	1st	2nd	3rd	Win & Pl
Career Total (Turf)	1	0	0	0	
Career Total (AW)	1	0	0	0	

Going (Turf): Sf: 0-0 GS: 0-0 Gd: 0-0 GF: 0-0 Fm: 0-1
Distance: 5f/6f: 0-0 7f-8f: 0-0 9f-13f: 0-2 14f+: 0-0
Track : LH: 0-2 RH: 0-0 Tight: 0-0 Gall: 0-0
Aids: Bl: 0-1 Vi: 0-0 Tstrap: 0-0

Madam Elsa (IRE)

(97) (58)**60**

3-y-o b f Lycius (USA)-Extra Time (Shadeed (USA))
R M Beckett The Elsa Partners

Placings:006400301 (5348)
2001: 7^0SD, 7^0S, 7^6G, 8^4GF, 10^0G, 9^0GF, 10^3GS, 9^0G, 12^1SD

	Starts	1st	2nd	3rd	Win & Pl
Career Total (Turf)	7	0	0	1	628
Career Total (AW)	2	1	0	0	3552

58	10/01	Sthl	1m4f	E(0-75)H	STD	£3552

Total win prize-money £3552

Going (Turf): Sf: 0-1 GS: 0-1 Gd: 0-3 GF: 0-2 Fm: 0-0
Distance: 5f/6f: 0-0 7f-8f: 0-3 **9f-13f: 1-6** 14f+: 0-0
Track : **LH: 1-4** RH: 0-2 Tight: 0-2 Gall: 0-1
Aids: Bl: 0-0 Vi: 0-1 Tstrap: 0-0
Best Rating: 60 5/01 Yarm 1m3y gd-fm

Had not shown much ability until winning at 33-1 at Southwell over 12 furlongs in October.

Madam Jenkov

(69) (24)**57**

2-y-o ch f Baryshnikov (AUS)-Joemlujen (Forzando)
P D Evans J Powell-Tuck

Placings:0000 (5351)
2001: 7^0GF, 6^0GF, 7^0SD, 8^0SD

	Starts	1st	2nd	3rd	Win & Pl
Career Total (Turf)	2	0	0	0	
Career Total (AW)	2	0	0	0	

Going (Turf): Sf: 0-0 GS: 0-0 Gd: 0-0 GF: 0-2 Fm: 0-0
Distance: 5f/6f: 0-1 7f-8f: 0-3 9f-13f: 0-0 14f+: 0-0
Track : LH: 0-2 RH: 0-0 Tight: 0-1 Gall: 0-0
Aids: Bl: 0-0 Vi: 0-0 Tstrap: 0-0
Best Rating: 57 8/01 Folk 7f gd-fm

Madam Shoolay

66 **14**

7-y-o b m Tragic Role (USA)-Lady Alone (Mr Fluorocarbon)
D Mullarkey Dune Racing

Placings:0 (2576)
2001: 6^0GF

	Starts	1st	2nd	3rd	Win & Pl
Career Total (Turf)	1	0	0	0	

Going (Turf): Sf: 0-0 GS: 0-0 Gd: 0-0 GF: 0-1 Fm: 0-0

Distance: 5f/6f: 0-1 7f-8f: 0-0 9f-13f: 0-0 14f+: 0-0
Track : LH: 0-0 RH: 0-0 Tight: 0-0 Gall: 0-0
Aids: Bl: 0-0 Vi: 0-0 Tstrap: 0-0

Madame Boulangere

97 **89**

2-y-o b f Royal Applause-Jazz (Sharrood (USA))
R Hannon The Mystery Partnership

Placings:213531 **(4985)**
2001: 5^{2}GS, 6^{1}F, 6^{3}GF, 7^{5}GS, 6^{3}GS, 6^{1}G

	Starts	1st	2nd	3rd	Win & Pl
Career Total (Turf)	**6**	**2**	**1**	**2**	**145666**

89	9/01	Asct	6f110y	B	GD	£129950
69	5/01	York	6f	D	FRM	£6922

Total win prize-money £136873

Going (Turf): Sf: 0-0 GS: 0-3 **Gd: 1-1** GF: 0-1 **Fm: 1-1**
Distance: 5f/6f: 1-4 7f-8f: 1-2 9f-13f: 0-0 14f+: 0-0
Track : LH: 0-0 RH: 0-1 Tight: 0-0 Gall: 0-0
Aids: Bl: 0-0 Vi: 0-0 Tstrap: 0-0
Best Rating: 89 9/01 Asct 6f110y good

Showed promse on her debut and battled on well to win over six furlongs at York, but was not herself when a well-beaten third of four at Windsor on her next start. Out of her depth in a Group Three at Goodwood, but bounced back to form with a good third in a competitive sales race at Doncaster next time. Suited by six furlongs, she had her biggest pay-day when winning a valuable sales race at Ascot in September. Handles most ground.

Madame Butterfly

72(89) (55)**36**

3-y-o b f Reprimand-Mill D'Art (Artaius (USA))
D J S Cosgrove Eridge Lodge Racing

Placings:005-600 **(2041)**
2001: 7^{6}SD, 10^{0}SW, 8^{0}GF

	Starts	1st	2nd	3rd	Win & Pl
Career Total (Turf)	**2**	**0**	**0**	**0**	
Career Total (AW)	**4**	**0**	**0**	**0**	**0**

Going (Turf): Sf: 0-0 GS: 0-0 Gd: 0-0 GF: 0-1 Fm: 0-0
Distance: 5f/6f: 0-0 7f-8f: 0-2 9f-13f: 0-3 14f+: 0-0
Track : LH: 0-5 RH: 0-0 Tight: 0-4 Gall: 0-0
Aids: Bl: 0-4 Vi: 0-0 Tstrap: 0-0
Best Rating: 40 1/01 Ling 7f stand

Madame Jones (IRE)

(105) (73) **66**

6-y-o ch m Lycius (USA)-Gold Braisim (IRE) (Jareer (USA))
P D Evans (A T Murphy 6/1) J E Abbey

Placings:0330/21130005456100/**000**/0050000**0033-4461113132510460001**2345**00**6450**2**2134**1**10241364**22**
5053 **(5657)**
2001: **12**^{4}SD, **9**^{4}SW, **9**^{6}SD, **8**^{1}SW, **9**^{1}SD, **9**^{1}SD, **7**^{3}SD, **7**^{1}SW, **8**^{3}SD, **8**^{2}SD, **8**^{5}SD, **8**^{1}SD, **8**^{0}SD, **9**^{4}SD, **8**^{6}SD, **8**^{0}SD, **8**^{0}SD, **8**^{0}SD, **8**^{1}SD, 7^{2}F, 8^{3}GF, 8^{4}GF, 8^{5}GF, **8**^{0}SD, 8^{0}GF, 8^{6}HD, 7^{4}GF, 7^{5}GF, 8^{4}G, **8**^{0}SD, 8^{2}GF, 8^{1}G, 8^{3}G, 7^{4}G, **8**^{1}SD, 7^{1}G, 8^{0}G, 8^{2}SF, 8^{4}GF, 8^{1}GF, 7^{3}GF, 10^{6}SF, 8^{4}HY, **7**^{2}SD, **8**^{2}SD, **8**^{5}SD, 8^{0}SF, **8**^{5}SD, 8^{3}G

	Starts	1st	2nd	3rd	Win & Pl
Career Total (Turf)	**47**	**6**	**4**	**7**	**34754**
Career Total (AW)	**34**	**7**	**4**	**4**	**23944**

66	9/01	Nott	1m54y	E(0-75)H	G-F	£3395
58	8/01	Yarm	7f3y	D(0-80)H	GD	£4283
60	8/01	Wolv	1m100y	E(0-70)H	STD	£2835
52	8/01	Nott	1m54y	D(0-80)H	GD	£4712
50	5/01	Sthl	1m	D(0-80)H	STD	£4026
50	3/01	Sthl	1m	F(0-60)H	STD	£1827
42	2/01	Sthl	7f	E(0-70)H	SLW	£2980
47	2/01	Wolv	1m1f79y	F(0-60)H	STD	£1757
43	2/01	Wolv	1m1f79y	E(0-70)H	STD	£2975
37	2/01	Sthl	1m	E(0-70)H	SLW	£2940
68	9/98	Ches	6f18y	D(0-80)	GD	£3837
68	6/98	Gdwd	6f	D(0-80)H	GD	£5580
64	5/98	Nott	6f15y	F(0-65)	FRM	£2616

Total win prize-money £43777

Going (Turf): Sf: 0-8 GS: 0-4 **Gd: 4-13** GF: 1-18 Fm: 1-4
Distance: 5f/6f: 1-15 **7f-8f: 7-36** 9f-13f: 5-30 14f+: 0-0
Track : **LH: 10-54** RH: 0-8 **Tight: 4-37** Gall: 0-2
Aids: Bl: 0-2 **Vi: 10-49** Tstrap: 0-0
Best Rating: 73 10/01 Wolv 1m100y stand

Ultra-tough and genuine mare, who thrives on her racing and is effective on turf and Fibresand. Her ten handicap wins in 2001 stands as a modern-day record. Best at around a mile. Acts on a sound surface. Has only just failed to add to her tally this term and does not look to have finished just yet.

Madame Maxi

103 **58**

7-y-o ch m Ron's Victory (USA)-New Pastures (Formidable (USA))
H S Howe George Searle

Placings:600/2100**0**/**56**300/2561000 **(5608)**
2001: 8^{2}GF, 8^{5}G, 8^{6}GF, 7^{1}G, 7^{0}GF, 8^{0}GS, 7^{0}GS

	Starts	1st	2nd	3rd	Win & Pl
Career Total (Turf)	**17**	**2**	**2**	**1**	**11599**
Career Total (AW)	**3**	**0**	**0**	**0**	**0**

58	9/01	Sand	7f16y	D(0-80)H	GD	£5200
54	9/98	Bath	1m5y	F(0-60)H	G-S	£2706

Total win prize-money £7906

Going (Turf): Sf: 0-2 **GS: 1-4 Gd: 1-6** GF: 0-5 Fm: 0-0
Distance: 5f/6f: 0-0 7f-8f: 1-8 9f-13f: 1-12 14f+: 0-0
Track : LH: 1-9 RH: 1-6 **Tight: 1-8** Gall: 0-1
Aids: Bl: 0-2 Vi: 0-0 Tstrap: 0-0
Best Rating: 58 9/01 Sand 7f16y good

A Bath specialist, she returned from almost two years off in August and made all to win at Sandown in September. Suited by a mile and acts on easy and fast ground.

Madame Maxine (USA)

8

2-y-o b/br f Dayjur (USA)-Political Parody (USA) (Doonesbury (USA))
B J Meehan Mrs Susan Roy

Placings:0 **(5491)**
2001: 6^{0}HY

	Starts	1st	2nd	3rd	Win & Pl
Career Total (Turf)	**1**	**0**	**0**	**0**	

Going (Turf): Sf: 0-1 GS: 0-0 Gd: 0-0 GF: 0-0 Fm: 0-0
Distance: 5f/6f: 0-0 7f-8f: 0-1 9f-13f: 0-0 14f+: 0-0
Track : LH: 0-0 RH: 0-0 Tight: 0-0 Gall: 0-0
Aids: Bl: 0-0 Vi: 0-0 Tstrap: 0-0
Best Rating: 8 10/01 Newb 6f8y heavy

A half-sister to the mile and nine furlong Group Three winner Panis, she needed every yard of the six-furlong trip when scoring on her sand debut at Southwell in November.

Madame Roux

99 **56**

3-y-o b f Rudimentary (USA)-Foreign Mistress (Darshaan)
G Wragg Ashley Carr Racing (6)

Placings:400-53 **(4840)**
2001: 7^{5}GF, 6^{3}G

	Starts	1st	2nd	3rd	Win & Pl
Career Total (Turf)	**5**	**0**	**0**	**1**	**477**

Going (Turf): Sf: 0-0 GS: 0-0 Gd: 0-2 GF: 0-3 Fm: 0-0
Distance: 5f/6f: 0-3 7f-8f: 0-2 9f-13f: 0-0 14f+: 0-0
Track : LH: 0-1 RH: 0-0 Tight: 0-0 Gall: 0-0
Aids: Bl: 0-0 Vi: 0-0 Tstrap: 0-0
Best Rating: 55 9/01 Nott 6f15y good

Maddora (IRE)

97 **64**

2-y-o b f Mark Of Esteem (IRE)-Almuhtarama (IRE) (Rainbow Quest (USA))
M P Tregoning Sheikh Ahmed Al Maktoum

Placings:46 **(5095)**
2001: 7^{4}GF, 8^{6}GS

	Starts	1st	2nd	3rd	Win & Pl
Career Total (Turf)	**2**	**0**	**0**	**0**	**323**

Going (Turf): Sf: 0-0 GS: 0-1 Gd: 0-0 GF: 0-1 Fm: 0-0
Distance: 5f/6f: 0-0 7f-8f: 0-2 9f-13f: 0-0 14f+: 0-0
Track : LH: 0-0 RH: 0-1 Tight: 0-0 Gall: 0-0
Aids: Bl: 0-0 Vi: 0-0 Tstrap: 0-0
Best Rating: 64 8/01 Bevl 7f100y gd-fm

Failed to improve on her debut when beaten at Salisbury on soft ground. Bred to stay middle distances.

Madeline Bassett (IRE)

102 **77**

3-y-o b f Kahyasi-Impressive Lady (Mr Fluorocarbon)
G A Butler The Blewbury Hill Partnership

Placings:0-06401220 **(5599)**
2001: 8^{0}G, 7^{6}GF, 10^{4}GF, 10^{0}G, 12^{1}GS, 12^{2}G, 11^{2}S, 12^{0}GS

	Starts	1st	2nd	3rd	Win & Pl
Career Total (Turf)	**9**	**1**	**2**	**0**	**6499**

72	9/01	Folk	1m4f	E(0-70)	G-S	£2835

Total win prize-money £2835

Going (Turf): Sf: 0-1 **GS: 1-2** Gd: 0-4 GF: 0-2 Fm: 0-0
Distance: 5f/6f: 0-0 7f-8f: 0-2 **9f-13f: 1-7** 14f+: 0-0
Track : LH: 0-1 **RH: 1-6 Tight: 1-5** Gall: 0-2
Aids: Bl: 0-0 Vi: 0-0 Tstrap: 0-0
Best Rating: 77 10/01 Leic 1m3f183y soft

A half-sister to Compton Arrow, she appreciated the step up to 12 furlongs when winning at Folkestone in September.

Madiba

80 **74**

2-y-o b c Emperor Jones (USA)-Priluki (Lycius (USA))
R Guest Rae Guest

Placings:4 **(5561)**
2001: 7^{4}S

	Starts	1st	2nd	3rd	Win & Pl
Career Total (Turf)	**1**	**0**	**0**	**0**	**350**

Going (Turf): Sf: 0-1 GS: 0-0 Gd: 0-0 GF: 0-0 Fm: 0-0
Distance: 5f/6f: 0-0 7f-8f: 0-1 9f-13f: 0-0 14f+: 0-0
Track : LH: 0-0 RH: 0-0 Tight: 0-0 Gall: 0-0
Aids: Bl: 0-0 Vi: 0-0 Tstrap: 0-0
Best Rating: 74 10/01 Yarm 7f3y soft

Madies Pride (IRE)

95(64) **53**

3-y-o b f Fayruz-June Lady (Junius (USA))
J J Quinn Pride Of Yorkshire Racing Club

Placings:400-001000 **(4965)**
2001: 5^{0}S, 6^{0}S, 5^{1}GF, 5^{0}G, 5^{0}SW, 5^{0}S

	Starts	1st	2nd	3rd	Win & Pl
Career Total (Turf)	**8**	**1**	**0**	**0**	**3024**
Career Total (AW)	**1**	**0**	**0**	**0**	

53	6/01	Bevl	5f	F(0-65)H	G-F	£2807

Total win prize-money £2807

Going (Turf): Sf: 0-3 GS: 0-1 Gd: 0-2 **GF: 1-1** Fm: 0-1
Distance: **5f/6f: 1-9** 7f-8f: 0-0 9f-13f: 0-0 14f+: 0-0

Track : LH: 0-2 RH: 0-1 Tight: 0-1 Gall: 0-1
Aids: Bl: 0-0 Vi: 0-0 Tstrap: 0-0
Best Rating: 53 6/01 Bevl 5f gd-fm

Bar a surprising win when claiming 5lb from a plum draw at Beverley in June, she could not have run any worse.

Madonna Fan (IRE)

93 **72**
3-y-o b g Lear Fan (USA)-Madonna Sprite (Saint Cyrien (FR))
L M Cumani Robert H Smith

Placings:00550 **(4776)**
2001: 8^0GF, 7^0GS, 10^5G, 10^5GF, 11^0G

	Starts	1st	2nd	3rd	Win & Pl
Career Total (Turf)	5	0	0	0	0

Going (Turf): Sf: 0-0 GS: 0-1 Gd: 0-2 GF: 0-2 Fm: 0-0
Distance: 5f/6f: 0-0 7f-8f: 0-2 9f-13f: 0-3 14f+: 0-0
Track : LH: 0-1 RH: 0-1 Tight: 0-2 Gall: 0-0
Aids: Bl: 0-0 Vi: 0-0 Tstrap: 0-0
Best Rating: 72 8/01 Wind 1m2f7y good

Madrasee

97(93) (70)**60**
3-y-o b f Beveled (USA)-Pendona (Blue Cashmere)
L Montague Hall (M Blanshard 13/8) J Daniels

Placings:263032045-034305040041 **(5593)**
2001: 6^0SW, 7^3SW, 6^4SW, 7^3SD, 5^0GS, 5^5G, 5^0F, 6^4G, 5^0F, 6^0G, 5^4S, 5^1GS

	Starts	1st	2nd	3rd	Win & Pl
Career Total (Turf)	17	1	2	2	6019
Career Total (AW)	4	0	0	2	1246

60 11/01 Brig 5f213y F(0-65)H G-S £2359
Total win prize-money £2359

Going (Turf): Sf: 0-3 **GS: 1-2** Gd: 0-6 GF: 0-3 Fm: 0-2
Distance: **5f/6f: 1-16** 7f-8f: 0-4 9f-13f: 0-0 14f+: 0-0
Track : **LH: 1-9** RH: 0-2 Tight: 0-4 Gall: 0-3
Aids: Bl: 0-0 Vi: 0-0 Tstrap: 0-0
Best Rating: 70 2/01 Ling 7f slow

Finally got off the mark at the 21st attempt in a handicap at Brighton. Has plenty of speed and has performed with some credit on the Equitrack surface.

Magdaleon

96 **48**
3-y-o b f Lion Cavern (USA)-Magdala (IRE) (Sadler's Wells (USA))
R Charlton Golden Arrow S.A & Geoff Howard-Spink

Placings:0-05600 **(4736)**
2001: 7^0GS, 6^5GF, 7^6GF, 6^0GF, 6^0F

	Starts	1st	2nd	3rd	Win & Pl
Career Total (Turf)	6	0	0	0	0

Going (Turf): Sf: 0-1 GS: 0-1 Gd: 0-0 GF: 0-3 Fm: 0-1
Distance: 5f/6f: 0-2 7f-8f: 0-4 9f-13f: 0-0 14f+: 0-0
Track : LH: 0-0 RH: 0-0 Tight: 0-0 Gall: 0-0
Aids: Bl: 0-0 Vi: 0-0 Tstrap: 0-0
Best Rating: 48 8/01 Sals 6f gd-fm

Magelta

103(105) (69+)**52**
4-y-o b c Magic Ring (IRE)-Pounelta (Tachypous)
R Hannon Peter Valentine

Placings:043/00200011-06500303 **(4471)**
2001: 7^0GF, 6^0GF, 8^5GF, 9^0GF, 7^0GS, 6^3F, 6^0G, 6^3GF

	Starts	1st	2nd	3rd	Win & Pl
Career Total (Turf)	17	0	1	3	2927
Career Total (AW)	2	2	0	0	5043

69 12/00 Ling 1m E(0-75)H STD £2327
58 12/00 Wolv 7f D STD £2716
Total win prize-money £5043

Going (Turf): Sf: 0-1 GS: 0-3 Gd: 0-2 GF: 0-10 Fm: 0-1
Distance: 5f/6f: 0-6 **7f-8f: 2-12** 9f-13f: 0-1 14f+: 0-0
Track : **LH: 2-7** RH: 0-6 **Tight: 2-5** Gall: 0-2
Aids: Bl: 0-0 Vi: 0-0 Tstrap: 0-3
Best Rating: 65 6/01 Folk 6f189y gd-fm

Magenta (IRE)

75 **36**
2-y-o b/br f Spectrum (IRE)-Bird In My Hand (IRE) (Bluebird (USA))
M L W Bell Highclere Thoroughbred Racing Ltd

Placings:5 **(2665)**
2001: 7^5G

	Starts	1st	2nd	3rd	Win & Pl
Career Total (Turf)	1	0	0	0	0

Going (Turf): Sf: 0-0 GS: 0-0 Gd: 0-1 GF: 0-0 Fm: 0-0
Distance: 5f/6f: 0-0 7f-8f: 0-1 9f-13f: 0-0 14f+: 0-0
Track : LH: 0-0 RH: 0-0 Tight: 0-0 Gall: 0-0
Aids: Bl: 0-0 Vi: 0-0 Tstrap: 0-0
Best Rating: 36 7/01 Yarm 7f3y good

Maggie Flynn

(83) (38)
3-y-o b f Imp Society (USA)-Lonely Street (Frimley Park)
A P Jarvis Terence P Lyons Ii

Placings:00-6 **(0453)**
2001: 7^6SD

	Starts	1st	2nd	3rd	Win & Pl
Career Total (Turf)	0	0	0	0	
Career Total (AW)	3	0	0	0	0

Going (Turf): Sf: 0-0 GS: 0-0 Gd: 0-0 GF: 0-0 Fm: 0-0
Distance: 5f/6f: 0-1 7f-8f: 0-2 9f-13f: 0-0 14f+: 0-0
Track : LH: 0-3 RH: 0-0 Tight: 0-3 Gall: 0-0
Aids: Bl: 0-0 Vi: 0-0 Tstrap: 0-0
Best Rating: 38 3/01 Wolv 7f stand

Magic Air

99(87) (27)**35**
3-y-o b f Magic Ring (IRE)-Exhibit Air (IRE) (Exhibitioner)
J S Moore Derek E Theobald

Placings:0-0504030060 **(3701)**
2001: 8^0SW, 10^5SW, 8^0S, 6^4GF, 6^0S, 7^3GF, 8^0GF, 7^0GS, 6^6GF, 6^0GF

	Starts	1st	2nd	3rd	Win & Pl
Career Total (Turf)	9	0	0	1	354
Career Total (AW)	2	0	0	0	0

Going (Turf): Sf: 0-2 GS: 0-1 Gd: 0-0 GF: 0-6 Fm: 0-0
Distance: 5f/6f: 0-1 7f-8f: 0-8 9f-13f: 0-2 14f+: 0-0
Track : LH: 0-5 RH: 0-1 Tight: 0-2 Gall: 0-0
Aids: Bl: 0-2 Vi: 0-0 Tstrap: 0-0
Best Rating: 38 6/01 Bevl 7f100y gd-fm

Magic Arrow (USA)

87(86) (29)**28**
5-y-o b g Defensive Play (USA)-Magic Blue (USA) (Cure The Blues (USA))
I Emmerson Ian Emmerson

Placings:0/16150/4600 **(2815)**
2001: 14^4SD, 14^6G, 17^0GF, 16^0GF

	Starts	1st	2nd	3rd	Win & Pl
Career Total (Turf)	6	0	0	0	0
Career Total (AW)	4	2	0	0	7305

72 5/99 Wolv 1m6f166yD(0-85)H STD £3597
69 2/99 Ling 1m4f D STD £3707
Total win prize-money £7305

Going (Turf): Sf: 0-1 GS: 0-1 Gd: 0-1 GF: 0-2 Fm: 0-1
Distance: 5f/6f: 0-0 7f-8f: 0-0 9f-13f: 1-2 14f+: 1-8
Track : **LH: 2-7** RH: 0-3 **Tight: 2-6** Gall: 0-0
Aids: Bl: 0-0 Vi: 0-0 Tstrap: 0-0
Best Rating: 29 6/01 Sthl 1m6f stand

Winner of 12 and 14-furlong events on the All-Weather in 1999, he has disappointed on turf and looks moderate at best.

Magic Babe

83(95) (47d)**19**
4-y-o b f Magic Ring (IRE)-Head Turner (My Dad Tom (USA))
Jamie Poulton Mrs J Wotherspoon

Placings:00040000/02412450000-5000060 **(5026)**
2001: 7^5SD, 8^0SW, 7^0GF, 6^0GF, 6^0F, 9^6GF, 9^0S

	Starts	1st	2nd	3rd	Win & Pl
Career Total (Turf)	22	1	2	0	5883
Career Total (AW)	4	0	0	0	0

59 6/00 Newb 7f E(0-75)H G-F £3302
Total win prize-money £3302

Going (Turf): Sf: 0-3 GS: 0-1 Gd: 0-4 **GF: 1-11** Fm: 0-3
Distance: 5f/6f: 0-8 **7f-8f: 1-16** 9f-13f: 0-2 14f+: 0-0
Track : LH: 0-10 RH: 0-7 Tight: 0-8 Gall: 0-2
Aids: Bl: 0-1 Vi: 0-0 Tstrap: 0-0
Best Rating: 22 1/01 Ling 7f stand

Magic Bengie

85 **54**
2-y-o b g Magic Ring (IRE)-Zinzi (Song)
Mrs L Stubbs Maurice Parker

Placings:000 **(5594)**
2001: 7^0GF, 6^0HY, 6^0GS

	Starts	1st	2nd	3rd	Win & Pl
Career Total (Turf)	3	0	0	0	

Going (Turf): Sf: 0-1 GS: 0-1 Gd: 0-0 GF: 0-1 Fm: 0-0
Distance: 5f/6f: 0-2 7f-8f: 0-1 9f-13f: 0-0 14f+: 0-0
Track : LH: 0-0 RH: 0-0 Tight: 0-0 Gall: 0-0
Aids: Bl: 0-0 Vi: 0-0 Tstrap: 0-0
Best Rating: 54 9/01 Newb 7f gd-fm

Magic Box

99 **66**
3-y-o b g Magic Ring (IRE)-Princess Poquito (Hard Fought)
Miss Kate Milligan (A P Jarvis 2/9) R A W Racing

Placings:644341-60000030 **(4450)**
2001: 9^6GS, 10^0F, 8^0GF, 8^0GF, 7^0G, 8^0GF, 8^3S, 8^0GF

	Starts	1st	2nd	3rd	Win & Pl
Career Total (Turf)	14	1	0	2	5417

68 8/00 Yarm 1m3y E G-F £3510
Total win prize-money £3510

Going (Turf): Sf: 0-2 GS: 0-1 Gd: 0-1 **GF: 1-8** Fm: 0-2
Distance: 5f/6f: 0-4 7f-8f: 0-4 **9f-13f: 1-6** 14f+: 0-0
Track : LH: 0-3 RH: 0-2 Tight: 0-1 Gall: 0-2
Aids: Bl: 0-0 Vi: 0-1 Tstrap: 0-0
Best Rating: 74 6/01 Kemp 1m gd-fm

Gained his only success last summer over a mile on fast ground as a juvenile. Has stepped up in trip this term to little effect.

Magic Charm

95(86) (46)**38**
3-y-o b f Magic Ring (IRE)-Loch Clair (IRE) (Lomond (USA))
N P Littmoden Wetherby Racing Bureau 46

Placings:006-02300060 **(5081)**

2001: 7^{0}SD, 7^{2}SW, 8^{3}GF, 8^{0}GF, 9^{0}G, 9^{0}GF, 10^{6}G, 9^{0}S

	Starts	1st	2nd	3rd	Win & Pl
Career Total (Turf)	6	0	0	1	372
Career Total (AW)	5	0	1	0	532

Going (Turf): Sf: 0-1 GS: 0-0 Gd: 0-2 GF: 0-3 Fm: 0-0
Distance: 5f/6f: 0-1 7f-8f: 0-4 9f-13f: 0-6 14f+: 0-0
Track : LH: 0-9 RH: 0-1 Tight: 0-3 Gall: 0-0
Aids: Bl: 0-0 Vi: 0-0 Tstrap: 0-0
Best Rating: 44 1/01 Wolv 7f slow

Magic Eagle

(107) (65) **57**

4-y-o b g Magic Ring (IRE)-Shadow Bird (Martinmas)
G L Moore The Straight Forward Partnership Ii

Placings:6000000165-1040024 **(5592)**
2001: 7^{1}SD, 7^{0}SW, 6^{4}GF, 5^{0}G, 7^{0}SD, 6^{2}SD, 6^{4}GS

	Starts	1st	2nd	3rd	Win & Pl
Career Total (Turf)	9	0	0	0	0
Career Total (AW)	8	2	1	0	4694

65	1/01	Sthl	7f	E(0-70)H	STD	£2478
55	11/00	Sthl	1m	G(0-60)H	STD	£1512

Total win prize-money £3990

Going (Turf): Sf: 0-0 GS: 0-5 Gd: 0-1 GF: 0-3 Fm: 0-0
Distance: 5f/6f: 0-4 7f-8f: 2-12 9f-13f: 0-1 14f+: 0-0
Track : LH: 2-11 RH: 0-2 Tight: 0-3 Gall: 0-3
Aids: Bl: 0-0 Vi: 0-0 Tstrap: 0-0
Best Rating: 65 1/01 Sthl 7f stand

Fibresand handicapper, stays a mile, likes it at Southwell and goes well fresh.

Magic Feathers

93(82) (46) **40**

3-y-o b g Anabaa (USA)-Plume Magique (Kenmare (FR))
M E Sowersby (E A L Dunlop 31/3) A Milner

Placings:0003 **(4854)**
2001: 8^{0}SD, 9^{0}GF, 10^{0}GF, 13^{3}GF

	Starts	1st	2nd	3rd	Win & Pl
Career Total (Turf)	3	0	0	1	268
Career Total (AW)	1	0	0	0	

Going (Turf): Sf: 0-0 GS: 0-0 Gd: 0-0 GF: 0-3 Fm: 0-0
Distance: 5f/6f: 0-0 7f-8f: 0-1 9f-13f: 0-2 14f+: 0-1
Track : LH: 0-3 RH: 0-1 Tight: 0-2 Gall: 0-1
Aids: Bl: 0-0 Vi: 0-0 Tstrap: 0-0
Best Rating: 46 3/01 Ling 1m stand

Magic Flute

107 **66**

5-y-o ch m Magic Ring (IRE)-Megan's Flight (Welsh Pageant)
R J Baker Mrs Jayne Thompson

Placings:055P20/206000-3410 **(4667)**
2001: 8^{3}G, 8^{4}HD, 8^{1}G, 8^{0}GF

	Starts	1st	2nd	3rd	Win & Pl
Career Total (Turf)	16	1	2	1	9862

66	7/01	Bath	1m5y	D(0-80)H	GD	£7068

Total win prize-money £7069

Going (Turf): Sf: 0-0 GS: 0-2 Gd: 1-5 GF: 0-7 Fm: 0-2
Distance: 5f/6f: 0-0 7f-8f: 0-10 9f-13f: 1-6 14f+: 0-0
Track : LH: 1-5 RH: 0-7 Tight: 1-3 Gall: 0-2
Aids: Bl: 0-0 Vi: 0-0 Tstrap: 0-1
Best Rating: 66 7/01 Bath 1m5y good

Magic Gem (IRE)

86(91) (49) **47**

3-y-o gr g Petong-Fairy Magic (IRE) (Fairy King (USA))
J A Osborne A Edward

Placings:05504060-2040600 **(4675)**

2001: 5^{2}SD, 6^{0}SW, 5^{4}SW, 5^{0}SW, 5^{6}G, 6^{0}F, 7^{0}G

	Starts	1st	2nd	3rd	Win & Pl
Career Total (Turf)	7	0	0	0	0
Career Total (AW)	9	0	1	0	209

Going (Turf): Sf: 0-0 GS: 0-0 Gd: 0-4 GF: 0-2 Fm: 0-1
Distance: 5f/6f: 0-15 7f-8f: 0-1 9f-13f: 0-0 14f+: 0-0
Track : LH: 0-10 RH: 0-1 Tight: 0-9 Gall: 0-1
Aids: Bl: 0-1 Vi: 0-0 Tstrap: 0-1
Best Rating: 49 1/01 Ling 5f stand

Magic Hanne

56 **20**

2-y-o ch f Magic Ring (IRE)-Sunfleet (Red Sunset)
S E Kettlewell Middleham Park Racing Vi

Placings:4 **(5446)**
2001: 7^{4}HY

	Starts	1st	2nd	3rd	Win & Pl
Career Total (Turf)	1	0	0	0	0

Going (Turf): Sf: 0-1 GS: 0-0 Gd: 0-0 GF: 0-0 Fm: 0-0
Distance: 5f/6f: 0-0 7f-8f: 0-1 9f-13f: 0-0 14f+: 0-0
Track : LH: 0-0 RH: 0-0 Tight: 0-0 Gall: 0-0
Aids: Bl: 0-0 Vi: 0-0 Tstrap: 0-0
Best Rating: 20 10/01 Newc 7f heavy

Magic Harp (IRE)

82 **49**

3-y-o b f Common Grounds-Princess Of Zurich (IRE) (Law Society (USA))
M A Jarvis Gary Seidler & Andy J Smith

Placings:0-0 **(1268)**
2001: 7^{0}GS

	Starts	1st	2nd	3rd	Win & Pl
Career Total (Turf)	2	0	0	0	

Going (Turf): Sf: 0-0 GS: 0-2 Gd: 0-0 GF: 0-0 Fm: 0-0
Distance: 5f/6f: 0-1 7f-8f: 0-1 9f-13f: 0-0 14f+: 0-0
Track : LH: 0-0 RH: 0-1 Tight: 0-0 Gall: 0-1
Aids: Bl: 0-0 Vi: 0-0 Tstrap: 0-0
Best Rating: 24 5/01 Ling 7f gd-sft

Magic Lodge

86 **72**

2-y-o b c Grand Lodge (USA)-Samsung Spirit (Statoblest)
M R Channon T S M Cunningham

Placings:6060 **(4460)**
2001: 6^{6}GF, 7^{0}G, 6^{6}GF, 6^{0}G

	Starts	1st	2nd	3rd	Win & Pl
Career Total (Turf)	4	0	0	0	0

Going (Turf): Sf: 0-0 GS: 0-0 Gd: 0-2 GF: 0-2 Fm: 0-0
Distance: 5f/6f: 0-1 7f-8f: 0-3 9f-13f: 0-0 14f+: 0-0
Track : LH: 0-0 RH: 0-2 Tight: 0-1 Gall: 0-0
Aids: Bl: 0-0 Vi: 0-0 Tstrap: 0-0
Best Rating: 72 8/01 Sals 6f gd-fm

Magic Maid

76 **46**

2-y-o b f Presidium-Mrs Magic (Magic Mirror)
H S Howe R J Parish

Placings:000 **(4608)**
2001: 5^{0}GF, 6^{0}F, 5^{0}F

	Starts	1st	2nd	3rd	Win & Pl
Career Total (Turf)	3	0	0	0	

Going (Turf): Sf: 0-0 GS: 0-0 Gd: 0-0 GF: 0-1 Fm: 0-2
Distance: 5f/6f: 0-2 7f-8f: 0-1 9f-13f: 0-0 14f+: 0-0

Track : LH: 0-2 RH: 0-0 Tight: 0-0 Gall: 0-2
Aids: Bl: 0-0 Vi: 0-0 Tstrap: 0-0
Best Rating: 46 9/01 Bath 5f11y firm

Magic Mill (IRE)

102 (75) **47**

8-y-o b g Simply Great (FR)-Rosy O'Leary (Majetta)
J S Goldie A S Scott

Placings:31/063055620/14450502/040/400005-33355220005 **(5284)**
2001: 7^{3}S, 7^{3}S, 7^{3}GF, 8^{5}GF, 6^{5}G, 8^{2}GS, 7^{2}GS, 6^{0}GS, 9^{0}G, 9^{0}G, 9^{5}HY

	Starts	1st	2nd	3rd	Win & Pl
Career Total (Turf)	37	2	3	5	16493
Career Total (AW)	2	0	1	0	759

87	4/98	Newc	7f	D(0-85)H	SFT	£3501
82	10/95	Rdcr	7f	D	FRM	£4042

Total win prize-money £7543

Going (Turf): Sf: 1-10 GS: 0-5 Gd: 0-12 GF: 0-9 Fm: 1-1
Distance: 5f/6f: 0-2 7f-8f: 2-29 9f-13f: 0-8 14f+: 0-0
Track : LH: 0-18 RH: 0-2 Tight: 0-6 Gall: 0-1
Aids: Bl: 0-0 Vi: 0-2 Tstrap: 0-0
Best Rating: 54 7/01 Ayr 1m gd-sft

Runs plenty of decent races but is hard to win with. Suited by seven furlongs. Acts on any ground. Has not won for over three years

Magic Music (IRE)

96 **66**

2-y-o b f Magic Ring (IRE)-Chiming Melody (Cure The Blues (USA))
A Bailey Ray Bailey

Placings:60303 **(5446)**
2001: 6^{6}G, 7^{0}GF, 6^{3}G, 6^{0}GF, 7^{3}HY

	Starts	1st	2nd	3rd	Win & Pl
Career Total (Turf)	5	0	0	2	5434

Going (Turf): Sf: 0-1 GS: 0-0 Gd: 0-2 GF: 0-2 Fm: 0-0
Distance: 5f/6f: 0-3 7f-8f: 0-2 9f-13f: 0-0 14f+: 0-0
Track : LH: 0-0 RH: 0-0 Tight: 0-0 Gall: 0-0
Aids: Bl: 0-0 Vi: 0-0 Tstrap: 0-0
Best Rating: 66 10/01 Newc 7f heavy

Ran her best race when third in a Kempton sales race.

Magic Of Love

109 **94**

4-y-o b f Magic Ring (IRE)-Mistitled (USA) (Miswaki (USA))
M L W Bell Mrs Maureen Buckley

Placings:1131/3304600-5062345066 **(5136)**
2001: 6^{5}G, 6^{0}GF, 5^{6}GF, 6^{2}GF, 5^{3}G, 6^{4}G, 6^{5}GF, 5^{0}GF, 7^{6}G, 6^{6}G

	Starts	1st	2nd	3rd	Win & Pl
Career Total (Turf)	21	3	1	4	78361

82	10/99	NmkJ	6f	B	GD	£49000
86	8/99	Ling	6f	F	GD	£2532
86	7/99	Bevl	5f	F	G-F	£2495

Total win prize-money £54027

Going (Turf): Sf: 0-0 GS: 0-1 Gd: 2-10 GF: 1-10 Fm: 0-0
Distance: 5f/6f: 3-18 7f-8f: 0-3 9f-13f: 0-0 14f+: 0-0
Track : LH: 0-3 RH: 0-0 Tight: 0-1 Gall: 0-1
Aids: Bl: 0-0 Vi: 0-0 Tstrap: 0-0
Best Rating: 97 8/01 Asct 6f good

Useful sprinter who avoids soft ground. Usually held up, and probably better suited by six furlongs than five. Ran with credit without winning this term.

Magic Rainbow

104(104) (91) **83**

6-y-o b g Magic Ring (IRE)-Blues Indigo (Music Boy)
M L W Bell P T Fenwick

Placings:415/1041040060/1456142030/1060065150-050010 (4868)
2001: 6⁰G, 6⁵GF, 5⁰GF, 5⁰GF, 5¹GF, 5⁰G

	Starts	1st	2nd	3rd	Win & Pl
Career Total (Turf)	34	5	1	1	93452
Career Total (AW)	5	3	0	0	17700

78	8/01	Bath	5f11y	D(0-80)	G-F	£3997
85	7/00	Asct	5f	B H	G-F	£46400
82	3/00	Ling	7f	C	STD	£6061
85	5/99	Kemp	6f	C(0-95)H	G-F	£6970
94	3/99	Ling	6f	C(0-95)H	STD	£6126
84	5/98	NmkR	6f	B(0-105)H	G-F	£22450
80	3/98	Sthl	6f	D(0-85)H	STD	£4924
76	6/97	Leic	5f2y	F	GD	£2532

Total win prize-money £99463

Going (Turf): Sf: 0-2 GS: 0-1 Gd: 1-12 **GF: 4-19** Fm: 0-0
Distance: **5f/6f: 7-35** 7f-8f: 1-4 9f-13f: 0-0 14f+: 0-0
Track : **LH: 4-9** RH: 0-0 **Tight: 2-6** Gall: 1-2
Aids: Bl: 0-0 Vi: 0-0 Tstrap: 0-0
Best Rating: 83 5/01 Kemp 6f gd-fm

An effective if not altogether consistent sprinter, he is struggling in handicaps but managed to win a classified event at Bath in August. Suited by fast ground and five or six furlongs on turf, but has won over seven furlongs on sand.

Magic Songbird

91 **60**

2-y-o b f Magic Ring (IRE)-Winsong Melody (Music Maestro)
C A Dwyer The Fairy Story Partnership

Placings:000 (4524)
2001: 6⁰G, 5⁰GF, 6⁰GF

	Starts	1st	2nd	3rd	Win & Pl
Career Total (Turf)	3	0	0	0	

Going (Turf): Sf: 0-0 GS: 0-0 Gd: 0-1 GF: 0-2 Fm: 0-0
Distance: 5f/6f: 0-3 7f-8f: 0-0 9f-13f: 0-0 14f+: 0-0
Track : LH: 0-0 RH: 0-1 Tight: 0-0 Gall: 0-1
Aids: Bl: 0-0 Vi: 0-0 Tstrap: 0-0
Best Rating: 60 9/01 Ling 6f gd-fm

Magic Sound

(83) (16)**40**

3-y-o ch g Savahra Sound-Ace Girl (Stanford)
Mrs A Duffield Paul J Dixon

Placings:06030 (5374)
2001: 7⁰SD, 5⁶GF, 5⁰G, 5³F, 6⁰G

	Starts	1st	2nd	3rd	Win & Pl
Career Total (Turf)	4	0	0	1	408
Career Total (AW)	1	0	0	0	

Going (Turf): Sf: 0-0 GS: 0-0 Gd: 0-2 GF: 0-1 Fm: 0-1
Distance: 5f/6f: 0-4 7f-8f: 0-1 9f-13f: 0-0 14f+: 0-0
Track : LH: 0-1 RH: 0-0 Tight: 0-0 Gall: 0-0
Aids: Bl: 0-0 Vi: 0-0 Tstrap: 0-0
Best Rating: 40 10/01 Rdcr 6f good

Lightly-raced sprinter, suited by five-furlongs and fast ground.

Magic To Do (IRE)

79 **25**

3-y-o b c Spectrum (IRE)-Smouldering (IRE) (Caerleon (USA))
R F Johnson Houghton Anthony Pye-Jeary

Placings:0-0 (5464)
2001: 11⁰G

	Starts	1st	2nd	3rd	Win & Pl
Career Total (Turf)	2	0	0	0	

Going (Turf): Sf: 0-0 GS: 0-0 Gd: 0-2 GF: 0-0 Fm: 0-0
Distance: 5f/6f: 0-0 7f-8f: 0-1 9f-13f: 0-1 14f+: 0-0
Track : LH: 0-1 RH: 0-0 Tight: 0-1 Gall: 0-0
Aids: Bl: 0-0 Vi: 0-0 Tstrap: 0-0
Best Rating: 25 10/01 Bath 1m3f144y good

Magic Trick

87

2-y-o b c Magic Ring (IRE)-Les Amis (Alzao (USA))
B W Hills Lee Jackson

Placings:313430060 (5140)
2001: 5³GS, 5¹S, 5³GF, 6⁴F, 6³G, 7⁰G, 6⁰GF, 6⁶GF, 6⁰G

	Starts	1st	2nd	3rd	Win & Pl
Career Total (Turf)	9	1	0	3	17321

69	4/01	NmkR	5f	D	SFT	£4784

Total win prize-money £4784

Going (Turf): Sf: 1-1 GS: 0-1 Gd: 0-3 GF: 0-3 Fm: 0-1
Distance: **5f/6f: 1-8** 7f-8f: 0-1 9f-13f: 0-0 14f+: 0-0
Track : LH: 0-2 RH: 0-0 Tight: 0-1 Gall: 0-0
Aids: Bl: 0-0 Vi: 0-0 Tstrap: 0-0
Best Rating: 87 9/01 Donc 6f gd-fm

A sharp sort on breeding who ran well to finish third in the Brocklesby, he duly followed up when dominating the field in a Newmarket maiden at the Craven Meeting. Fair efforts since but looks exposed. Only win came on soft ground.

Magic Waters

99 **69**

3-y-o b g Ezzoud (IRE)-Paradise Waters (Celestial Storm (USA))
T D Easterby D F Sills

Placings:0-423060344 (4542)
2001: 8⁴S, 10²GS, 11³GF, 10⁰GF, 12⁶GF, 16⁰GF, 10³F, 14⁴GF, 10⁴GF

	Starts	1st	2nd	3rd	Win & Pl
Career Total (Turf)	10	0	1	2	3232

Going (Turf): Sf: 0-1 GS: 0-1 Gd: 0-0 GF: 0-6 Fm: 0-2
Distance: 5f/6f: 0-1 7f-8f: 0-1 9f-13f: 0-6 14f+: 0-2
Track : LH: 0-5 RH: 0-4 Tight: 0-7 Gall: 0-0
Aids: Bl: 0-1 Vi: 0-0 Tstrap: 0-0
Best Rating: 69 5/01 Haml 1m3f16y gd-fm

Bred to stay middle distances. Improved for step up to ten furlongs at three. Probably best suited by give underfoot.

Magic's Beauty

84 **67d**

2-y-o b f Magic Ring (IRE)-Tocco Jewel (Reesh)
M J Ryan M Byron

Placings:0050 (5078)
2001: 6⁰G, 6⁰GF, 5⁵GF, 5⁰S

	Starts	1st	2nd	3rd	Win & Pl
Career Total (Turf)	4	0	0	0	0

Going (Turf): Sf: 0-1 GS: 0-0 Gd: 0-1 GF: 0-2 Fm: 0-0
Distance: 5f/6f: 0-3 7f-8f: 0-1 9f-13f: 0-0 14f+: 0-0
Track : LH: 0-1 RH: 0-0 Tight: 0-0 Gall: 0-0
Aids: Bl: 0-0 Vi: 0-0 Tstrap: 0-0
Best Rating: 67 8/01 Yarm 6f3y good

Magical Bailiwick (IRE)

89 **51**

5-y-o ch g Magical Wonder (USA)-Alpine Dance (USA) (Apalachee (USA))
R J Baker Islands Racing Connection

Placings:4530/000000216-0 (5626)
2001: 8⁰GS

	Starts	1st	2nd	3rd	Win & Pl
Career Total (Turf)	14	1	1	1	4690

51	9/00	Bath	1m5y	F(0-60)H	SFT	£2695

Total win prize-money £2695

Going (Turf): Sf: 1-2 GS: 0-3 Gd: 0-4 GF: 0-4 Fm: 0-1
Distance: 5f/6f: 0-0 7f-8f: 0-4 **9f-13f: 1-10** 14f+: 0-0
Track : **LH: 1-3** RH: 0-8 **Tight: 1-7** Gall: 0-0
Aids: **Bl: 1-6** Vi: 0-0 Tstrap: 0-0
Best Rating: 38 11/01 Nott 1m54y gd-sft

Magical Day

88 **56**

2-y-o ch f Halling (USA)-Ahla (Unfuwain (USA))
Mrs J R Ramsden L C And A E Sigsworth

Placings:050 (4774)
2001: 6⁰G, 7⁵GF, 7⁰G

	Starts	1st	2nd	3rd	Win & Pl
Career Total (Turf)	3	0	0	0	0

Going (Turf): Sf: 0-0 GS: 0-0 Gd: 0-2 GF: 0-1 Fm: 0-0
Distance: 5f/6f: 0-1 7f-8f: 0-2 9f-13f: 0-0 14f+: 0-0
Track : LH: 0-1 RH: 0-1 Tight: 0-1 Gall: 0-0
Aids: Bl: 0-0 Vi: 0-0 Tstrap: 0-0
Best Rating: 56 9/01 Bevl 7f100y good

Magical Flute

62(96) (79)**76**

3-y-o ch f Piccolo-Stride Home (Absalom)
M R Channon Peter Taplin

Placings:031320-0 (0526)
2001: 7⁰S

	Starts	1st	2nd	3rd	Win & Pl
Career Total (Turf)	6	1	0	2	4230
Career Total (AW)	1	0	1	0	1156

67	7/00	Bath	5f161y	F	FRM	£2464

Total win prize-money £2464

Going (Turf): Sf: 0-2 GS: 0-0 Gd: 0-1 GF: 0-1 **Fm: 1-2**
Distance: **5f/6f: 1-4** 7f-8f: 0-3 9f-13f: 0-0 14f+: 0-0
Track : **LH: 1-3** RH: 0-0 Tight: 0-2 **Gall: 1-1**
Aids: Bl: 0-0 Vi: 0-0 Tstrap: 0-0
Best Rating: 67 7/00 Bath 5f161y F

Fair form on fast ground in the summer of 2000. Yet to prove as effective on an easier surface since.

Magical Fool

79 **45**

2-y-o b g Magic Ring (IRE)-Vera's First (IRE) (Exodal (USA))
N Wilson Steven Downes

Placings:000 (4774)
2001: 6⁰G, 5⁰GF, 7⁰G

	Starts	1st	2nd	3rd	Win & Pl
Career Total (Turf)	3	0	0	0	

Going (Turf): Sf: 0-0 GS: 0-0 Gd: 0-2 GF: 0-1 Fm: 0-0
Distance: 5f/6f: 0-2 7f-8f: 0-1 9f-13f: 0-0 14f+: 0-0
Track : LH: 0-0 RH: 0-1 Tight: 0-0 Gall: 0-0
Aids: Bl: 0-0 Vi: 0-0 Tstrap: 0-0
Best Rating: 45 7/01 York 6f good

Magical Knight

93 **67**

3-y-o b g Sir Harry Lewis (USA)-Formal Affair (Rousillon (USA))
R T Phillips The Old Foresters Partnership

Placings:064 (4636)

2001: 8^{0}GF, 8^{6}GF, 9^{4}GF

	Starts	1st	2nd	3rd	Win & Pl
Career Total (Turf)	3	0	0	0	307

Going (Turf): Sf: 0-0 GS: 0-0 Gd: 0-0 GF: 0-3 Fm: 0-0
Distance: 5f/6f: 0-0 7f-8f: 0-1 9f-13f: 0-2 14f+: 0-0
Track : LH: 0-0 RH: 0-2 Tight: 0-0 Gall: 0-0
Aids: Bl: 0-0 Vi: 0-0 Tstrap: 0-0
Best Rating: 67 5/01 Kemp 1m gd-fm

Magical Myth

82 **48**
2-y-o b f Robellino (USA)-Sinking (Midyan (USA))
D Nicholls Neil Smith

Placings:0 **(3089)**
2001: 5^{0}GF

	Starts	1st	2nd	3rd	Win & Pl
Career Total (Turf)	1	0	0	0	

Going (Turf): Sf: 0-0 GS: 0-0 Gd: 0-0 GF: 0-1 Fm: 0-0
Distance: 5f/6f: 0-1 7f-8f: 0-0 9f-13f: 0-0 14f+: 0-0
Track : LH: 0-0 RH: 0-0 Tight: 0-0 Gall: 0-0
Aids: Bl: 0-0 Vi: 0-0 Tstrap: 0-0
Best Rating: 48 7/01 Bevl 5f gd-fm

Magical Nature (IRE)

82 **56**
2-y-o ch f Petardia-Sweet Nature (IRE) (Classic Secret (USA))
N P Littmoden Nick Littmoden

Placings:05 **(4639)**
2001: 5^{0}G, 6^{5}GF

	Starts	1st	2nd	3rd	Win & Pl
Career Total (Turf)	2	0	0	0	0

Going (Turf): Sf: 0-0 GS: 0-0 Gd: 0-1 GF: 0-1 Fm: 0-0
Distance: 5f/6f: 0-2 7f-8f: 0-0 9f-13f: 0-0 14f+: 0-0
Track : LH: 0-0 RH: 0-0 Tight: 0-0 Gall: 0-0
Aids: Bl: 0-0 Vi: 0-0 Tstrap: 0-0
Best Rating: 56 9/01 Ling 6f gd-fm

Magical Power (IRE)

(91) (74)
2-y-o ch c Magic Ring (IRE)-Try Vickers (USA) (Fuzzbuster (USA))
W R Muir T W Langley

Placings:0025 **(5610)**
2001: 6^{0}G, 7^{0}S, 7^{2}SD

	Starts	1st	2nd	3rd	Win & Pl
Career Total (Turf)	2	0	0	0	
Career Total (AW)	2	0	1	0	830

Going (Turf): Sf: 0-1 GS: 0-0 Gd: 0-1 GF: 0-0 Fm: 0-0
Distance: 5f/6f: 0-0 7f-8f: 0-3 9f-13f: 0-1 14f+: 0-0
Track : LH: 0-3 RH: 0-0 Tight: 0-2 Gall: 0-1
Aids: Bl: 0-0 Vi: 0-0 Tstrap: 0-0
Best Rating: 74 10/01 Wolv 7f stand

Improved no end when switched to sand, finishing runner-up in a maiden on the Wolverhampton Fibresand in October.

Magical River

96(85) (32)**40**
4-y-o ch f Lahib (USA)-Awtaar (USA) (Lyphard (USA))
J M Bradley Mrs A M Johnson

Placings:030600/000-0010600 **(4283)**
2001: 8^{0}SW, 7^{0}GS, 5^{1}GF, 6^{0}GF, 7^{6}GF, 6^{0}G, 7^{0}G

	Starts	1st	2nd	3rd	Win & Pl
Career Total (Turf)	14	1	0	1	3191
Career Total (AW)	2		0	0	0

40 7/01 Brig 5f213y F(0-60)H G-F £2681
Total win prize-money £2681

Going (Turf): Sf: 0-0 GS: 0-2 Gd: 0-6 GF: 1-4 Fm: 0-2
Distance: **5f/6f: 1-6** 7f-8f: 0-10 9f-13f: 0-0 14f+: 0-0
Track : **LH: 1-7** RH: 0-1 Tight: 0-1 Gall: 0-1
Aids: Bl: 0-0 Vi: 0-0 Tstrap: 0-0
Best Rating: 40 7/01 Brig 5f213y gd-fm

Magical Shadows

80(76) (37)**33**
2-y-o b g Whittingham (IRE)-She Knew The Rules (IRE) (Jamesmead)
D Burchell Philip Kirby

Placings:65500 **(2215)**
2001: 5^{6}SD, 5^{5}SD, 5^{5}G, 5^{0}GF, 5^{0}G

	Starts	1st	2nd	3rd	Win & Pl
Career Total (Turf)	3	0	0	0	0
Career Total (AW)	2	0	0	0	0

Going (Turf): Sf: 0-0 GS: 0-0 Gd: 0-2 GF: 0-1 Fm: 0-0
Distance: 5f/6f: 0-5 7f-8f: 0-0 9f-13f: 0-0 14f+: 0-0
Track : LH: 0-3 RH: 0-0 Tight: 0-2 Gall: 0-1
Aids: Bl: 0-0 Vi: 0-0 Tstrap: 0-0
Best Rating: 37 4/01 Sthl 5f stand

Magique Etoile (IRE)

86(92) (50)**20**
5-y-o b m Magical Wonder (USA)-She's A Dancer (IRE) (Alzao (USA))
Dr J R J Naylor Gallery Racing

Placings:00060406**6333**/0552503**32**/0062**26604-0000** **(4642)**
2001: 6^{0}GF, 6^{0}G, 10^{0}GF, 10^{0}GF

	Starts	1st	2nd	3rd	Win & Pl
Career Total (Turf)	24	0	2	1	2578
Career Total (AW)	10	0	2	4	2850

Going (Turf): Sf: 0-1 GS: 0-5 Gd: 0-5 GF: 0-10 Fm: 0-3
Distance: 5f/6f: 0-16 7f-8f: 0-14 9f-13f: 0-4 14f+: 0-0
Track : LH: 0-18 RH: 0-3 Tight: 0-13 Gall: 0-1
Aids: Bl: 0-1 Vi: 0-9 Tstrap: 0-0
Best Rating: 19 9/01 Ling 1m2f gd-fm

Magnanimous

81(62) (2)**52d**
3-y-o ch g Presidium-Mayor (Laxton)
N Tinkler The Penniless Partnership

Placings:000030-0000 **(2050)**
2001: 5^{0}S, 5^{0}G, 6^{0}GF, 6^{0}GF

	Starts	1st	2nd	3rd	Win & Pl
Career Total (Turf)	10	0	0	1	393
Career Total (AW)	1	0	0	0	

Going (Turf): Sf: 0-2 GS: 0-1 Gd: 0-4 GF: 0-3 Fm: 0-0
Distance: 5f/6f: 0-11 7f-8f: 0-0 9f-13f: 0-0 14f+: 0-0
Track : LH: 0-1 RH: 0-0 Tight: 0-0 Gall: 0-0
Aids: Bl: 0-0 Vi: 0-5 Tstrap: 0-0
Best Rating: 29 5/01 Bevl 5f good

Magnusson

103 **78**
3-y-o b c Primo Dominie-Nunsharpa (Sharpo)
J H M Gosden P D Savill

Placings:32-321 **(4842)**
2001: 6^{3}GF, 8^{2}G, 8^{1}G

	Starts	1st	2nd	3rd	Win & Pl
Career Total (Turf)	5	1	2	2	7917

76 9/01 Nott 1m54y D GD £4176
Total win prize-money £4176

Going (Turf): Sf: 0-0 GS: 0-0 **Gd: 1-3** GF: 0-2 Fm: 0-0
Distance: 5f/6f: 0-1 7f-8f: 0-2 **9f-13f: 1-2** 14f+: 0-0
Track : **LH: 1-2** RH: 0-2 Tight: 0-2 Gall: 0-0
Aids: Bl: 0-0 Vi: 0-0 Tstrap. 0-0
Best Rating: 76 9/01 Nott 1m54y good

Mags Crystal Dream

47
4-y-o b g Holly Buoy-Keep Mum (Mummy's Pet)
J S Goldie Magteam

Placings:04 **(3078)**
2001: 16^{0}GF, 10^{4}GS

	Starts	1st	2nd	3rd	Win & Pl
Career Total (Turf)	2	0	0	0	309

Going (Turf): Sf: 0-0 GS: 0-1 Gd: 0-0 GF: 0-1 Fm: 0-0
Distance: 5f/6f: 0-0 7f-8f: 0-0 9f-13f: 0-1 14f+: 0-1
Track : LH: 0-1 RH: 0-1 Tight: 0-1 Gall: 0-0
Aids: Bl: 0-0 Vi: 0-0 Tstrap: 0-0

Magzaa (IRE)

98 **82**
3-y-o gr c Marju (IRE)-Labibeh (USA) (Lyphard (USA))
Luke Comer (J L Dunlop 6/7) Luke Comer

Placings:003-22200006 **(3918a)**
2001: 9^{2}G, 9^{2}GF, 12^{2}GF, 12^{0}Y, 12^{0}GY, 12^{0}GY, 7^{0}GY, 13^{6}GY

	Starts	1st	2nd	3rd	Win & Pl
Career Total (Turf)	11	0	3	1	4730

Going (Turf): Sf: 0-2 GS: 0-0 Gd: 0-1 GF: 0-3 Fm: 0-0
Distance: 5f/6f: 0-0 7f-8f: 0-3 9f-13f: 0-8 14f+: 0-0
Track : LH: 0-1 RH: 0-3 Tight: 0-1 Gall: 0-0
Aids: Bl: 0-2 Vi: 0-0 Tstrap: 0-0
Best Rating: 82 7/01 Sals 1m4f gd-fm

Mahala

(84) (26)
4-y-o b f Lugana Beach-Little Nutmeg (Gabitat)
J Balding Ms Kim Jansen

Placings:060-0 **(0026)**
2001: 6^{0}SD

	Starts	1st	2nd	3rd	Win & Pl
Career Total (Turf)	0	0	0	0	
Career Total (AW)	4	0	0	0	0

Going (Turf): Sf: 0-0 GS: 0-0 Gd: 0-0 GF: 0-0 Fm: 0-0
Distance: 5f/6f: 0-2 7f-8f: 0-2 9f-13f: 0-0 14f+: 0-0
Track : LH: 0-4 RH: 0-0 Tight: 0-2 Gall: 0-0
Aids: Bl: 0-0 Vi: 0-0 Tstrap: 0-0
Best Rating: 17 1/01 Sthl 6f stand

Mahfooth (USA)

108(30) (108)**111**
4-y-o ch h Diesis-I Certainly Am (USA) (Affirmed (USA))
Saeed Bin Suroor Godolphin

Placings:3/0212-210610 **(2987a)**
2001: 8^{2}G, 8^{1}G, 8^{0}G, 7^{6}G, 8^{1}G, 8^{0}G

	Starts	1st	2nd	3rd	Win & Pl
Career Total (Turf)	10	3	3	1	67015
Career Total (AW)	1	0	0	0	

111 6/01 Chan 1m GD £21339
109 3/01 Ndas 1m195y GD £21858
104 7/00 Hayd 7f30y D G-F £4101
Total win prize-money £47299

Going (Turf): Sf: 0-1 GS: 0-1 **Gd: 2-7** GF: 1-1 Fm: 0-0
Distance: 5f/6f: 0-0 **7f-8f: 2-8** 9f-13f: 1-3 14f+: 0-0
Track : **LH: 1-3** RH: 0-1 Tight: 0-0 Gall: 0-2
Aids: Bl: 0-0 Vi: 0-0 Tstrap: 0-0
Best Rating: 111 6/01 Chan 1m good

Winner of a Haydock maiden last year, he won at Nad al Sheba in March, but was held in his next two starts before bouncing back with a narrow victory in a Chantilly Group Three in June. Suited by a mile.

Mahlstick (IRE)

95(77) (16)41

3-y-o b g Tagula (IRE)-Guv's Joy (IRE) (Thatching)

D W P Arbuthnot The Chelsea Arts Racing Club

Placings:000-05000 **(5503)**

2001: 8^{0}SD, 6^{5}GF, 6^{0}F, 9^{0}GF, 7^{0}HY

	Starts	1st	2nd	3rd	Win & Pl
Career Total (Turf)	7	0	0	0	0
Career Total (AW)	1	0	0	0	

Going (Turf): Sf: 0-4 GS: 0-0 Gd: 0-0 GF: 0-2 Fm: 0-1
Distance: 5f/6f: 0-4 7f-8f: 0-3 9f-13f: 0-1 14f+: 0-0
Track : LH: 0-2 RH: 0-1 Tight: 0-1 Gall: 0-1
Aids: Bl: 0-0 Vi: 0-2 Tstrap: 0-0
Best Rating: 41 7/01 Kemp 1m1f gd-fm

Mahsusie (IRE)

102 90

2-y-o gr f Mukaddamah (USA)-La Susiane (Persepolis (FR))

Francis Ennis Mrs Norah Kennedy

Placings:3115500 **(4659)**

2001: 5^{3}S, 6^{1}G, 5^{1}GY, 6^{5}GF, 7^{5}S, 7^{0}GY, 6^{0}GF

	Starts	1st	2nd	3rd	Win & Pl
Career Total (Turf)	7	2	0	1	39665
99 5/01 Curr 5f				G-Y	£29250
85 5/01 Leop 6f				GD	£8625

Total win prize-money £37875

Going (Turf): Sf: 0-2 GS: 0-0 **Gd: 1-1** GF: 0-2 Fm: 0-0
Distance: 5f/6f: 2-5 7f-8f: 0-2 9f-13f: 0-0 14f+: 0-0
Track : LH: 0-0 RH: 0-0 Tight: 0-0 Gall: 0-0
Aids: Bl: 0-0 Vi: 0-0 Tstrap: 0-0
Best Rating: 99 5/01 Curr 5f gd-yld

She won at Leopardstown and the Curragh this season and subsequently ran quite well in Group company.

Mai Tai (IRE)

94(103) (54)40

6-y-o b m Scenic-Oystons Propweekly (Swing Easy (USA))

D W Barker Keith Nicholson

Placings:35/6034403600000/2013031600000304314/ 2540102566625000-000026201130 **(2414)**

2001: 7^{0}SD, 8^{0}SD, 11^{0}SW, 8^{0}SW, 9^{0}S, 8^{2}SD, 8^{6}SW, 7^{2}S, 7^{0}S, 8^{1}SD, 7^{1}SD, 7^{3}SD, 8^{0}GF

	Starts	1st	2nd	3rd	Win & Pl
Career Total (Turf)	33	1	2	4	11350
Career Total (AW)	31	5	4	4	15785
54 6/01 Sthl 7f	F(0-65)H			STD	£2359
39 5/01 Sthl 1m	G			STD	£1925
54 4/00 Sthl 7f	F(0-60)H			STD	£2425
52 12/99 Ling 1m	E(0-70)H			STD	£2303
54 5/99 Rdcr 7f	D(0-80)H			SFT	£7610
56 2/99 Sthl 7f	F			STD	£1850

Total win prize-money £18474

Going (Turf): Sf: 1-9 GS: 0-3 Gd: 0-7 GF: 0-13 Fm: 0-1
Distance: 5f/6f: 0-5 **7f-8f: 6-55** 9f-13f: 0-4 14f+: 0-0
Track : LH: 5-39 RH: 0-10 **Tight: 1-10** Gall: 0-5
Aids: Bl: 0-1 **Vi: 4-26** Tstrap: 0-0
Best Rating: 54 6/01 Sthl 7f stand

Maid For Freedom (USA)

95 68

3-y-o gr f Trempolino (USA)-Spectacular Native (USA) (Spectacular Bid (USA))

G A Butler Chris Brasher

Placings:6-05 **(1228)**

2001: 7^{0}S, 7^{5}GF

	Starts	1st	2nd	3rd	Win & Pl
Career Total (Turf)	3	0	0	0	0

Going (Turf): Sf: 0-2 GS: 0-0 Gd: 0-0 GF: 0-1 Fm: 0-0
Distance: 5f/6f: 0-0 7f-8f: 0-3 9f-13f: 0-0 14f+: 0-0
Track : LH: 0-1 RH: 0-0 Tight: 0-1 Gall: 0-0
Aids: Bl: 0-0 Vi: 0-0 Tstrap: 0-0
Best Rating: 68 4/01 NmkR 7f soft

Maid For Romance

104 76

3-y-o ch f Pursuit Of Love-High Savannah (Rousillon (USA))

D R C Elsworth Normandie Stud Ltd

Placings:3 **(3385)**

2001: 10^{3}GF

	Starts	1st	2nd	3rd	Win & Pl
Career Total (Turf)	1	0	0	1	666

Going (Turf): Sf: 0-0 GS: 0-0 Gd: 0-0 GF: 0-1 Fm: 0-0
Distance: 5f/6f: 0-0 7f-8f: 0-0 9f-13f: 0-1 14f+: 0-0
Track : LH: 0-0 RH: 0-1 Tight: 0-0 Gall: 0-0
Aids: Bl: 0-0 Vi: 0-0 Tstrap: 0-0
Best Rating: 76 7/01 Sand 1m2f7y gd-fm

Maid For Running

94 78

2-y-o b f Namaqualand (USA)-Scarlet Lake (Reprimand)

G A Butler Chris Brasher

Placings:21050 **(5150)**

2001: 5^{2}G, 5^{1}GS, 7^{0}G, 6^{5}G, 6^{0}G

	Starts	1st	2nd	3rd	Win & Pl
Career Total (Turf)	5	1	1	0	10911
74 8/01 Haml 5f4y	E			G-S	£3477

Total win prize-money £3478

Going (Turf): Sf: 0-0 **GS: 1-1** Gd: 0-4 GF: 0-0 Fm: 0-0
Distance: 5f/6f: 1-3 7f-8f: 0-2 9f-13f: 0-0 14f+: 0-0
Track : LH: 0-0 RH: 0-0 Tight: 0-0 Gall: 0-0
Aids: Bl: 0-0 Vi: 0-0 Tstrap: 0-0
Best Rating: 78 9/01 Asct 6f110y good

Came on from her debut to win a maiden auction event at Hamilton on her second start and appeared to appreciate the easier ground, although disappointed next time time when finding little luck in running. Effective at five furlongs on good to soft, but seems to stay seven.

Maid Of Arc (USA)

89(81) (43)44

3-y-o b f Patton (USA)-Holy Speed (CAN) (Afleet (CAN))

Lady Herries Chris Hardy

Placings:022446315-00000 **(4302)**

2001: 6^{0}G, 5^{0}F, 7^{0}GF, 7^{0}G, 6^{0}GF

	Starts	1st	2nd	3rd	Win & Pl
Career Total (Turf)	13	1	2	1	4118
Career Total (AW)	1	0	0	0	0
59 8/00 Ling 6f	G			G-F	£1960

Total win prize-money £1960

Going (Turf): Sf: 0-1 GS: 0-1 Gd: 0-2 **GF: 1-6** Fm: 0-3
Distance: 5f/6f: 1-6 7f-8f: 0-8 9f-13f: 0-0 14f+: 0-0
Track : LH: 0-9 RH: 0-1 Tight: 0-3 Gall: 0-2
Aids: Bl: 0-0 Vi: 0-0 Tstrap: 0-8
Best Rating: 38 8/01 Brig 7f214y good

Maid To Love (IRE)

(98) (38)

4-y-o ch f Petardia-Lomond Heights (IRE) (Lomond (USA))

M C Pipe (I A Wood 19/5) Sandicroft Stud Syndicate

Placings:3300223/4225000-60004002343 **(1451)**

2001: 8^{6}SW, 8^{0}SD, 8^{0}SW, 7^{0}SD, 8^{4}SD, 11^{0}SD, 8^{0}SD, 10^{2}SD, 12^{3}SD, 10^{4}SD, 12^{3}SD

	Starts	1st	2nd	3rd	Win & Pl
Career Total (Turf)	5	0	0	2	843
Career Total (AW)	20	0	5	3	4284

Going (Turf): Sf: 0-1 GS: 0-0 Gd: 0-1 GF: 0-3 Fm: 0-0
Distance: 5f/6f: 0-2 7f-8f: 0-15 9f-13f: 0-8 14f+: 0-0
Track : LH: 0-21 RH: 0-0 Tight: 0-12 Gall: 0-0
Aids: Bl: 0-8 Vi: 0-2 Tstrap: 0-1
Best Rating: 46 1/01 Sthl 1m slow

Poor maiden.

Maid To Perfection

101 90

2-y-o b f Sadler's Wells (USA)-Maid For The Hills (Indian Ridge)

J L Dunlop Normandie Stud Ltd

Placings:51 **(5603)**

2001: 7^{5}G, 7^{1}GS

	Starts	1st	2nd	3rd	Win & Pl
Career Total (Turf)	2	1	0	0	4490
90 11/01 NmkR 7f	D			G-S	£4212

Total win prize-money £4212

Going (Turf): Sf: 0-0 **GS: 1-1** Gd: 0-1 GF: 0-0 Fm: 0-0
Distance: 5f/6f: 0-0 **7f-8f: 1-2** 9f-13f: 0-0 14f+: 0-0
Track : LH: 0-0 RH: 0-1 Tight: 0-0 Gall: 0-1
Aids: Bl: 0-0 Vi: 0-0 Tstrap: 0-0
Best Rating: 90 11/01 NmkR 7f gd-sft

A daughter of Sadler's Wells out of a Listed juvenile winner, benefited from her debut when taking a back-end Newmarket maiden. Likely to go on from that.

Maiden Voyage

88 43

3-y-o b f Slip Anchor-Elaine Tully (IRE) (Persian Bold)

Mrs J R Ramsden R J McAlpine

Placings:560 **(4989)**

2001: 10^{5}GF, 9^{6}GF, 8^{0}HY

	Starts	1st	2nd	3rd	Win & Pl
Career Total (Turf)	3	0	0	0	0

Going (Turf): Sf: 0-1 GS: 0-0 Gd: 0-0 GF: 0-2 Fm: 0-0
Distance: 5f/6f: 0-0 7f-8f: 0-0 9f-13f: 0-3 14f+: 0-0
Track : LH: 0-2 RH: 0-1 Tight: 0-0 Gall: 0-1
Aids: Bl: 0-0 Vi: 0-0 Tstrap: 0-0
Best Rating: 43 9/01 Leic 1m1f218y gd-fm

Maimana (IRE)

102 81

2-y-o b/br f Desert King (IRE)-Staff Approved (Teenoso (USA))

M A Jarvis Sheikh Ahmed Al Maktoum

Placings:032 **(5112)**

2001: 7^{0}GS, 8^{3}S, 8^{2}HY

	Starts	1st	2nd	3rd	Win & Pl
Career Total (Turf)	3	0	1	1	1940

Going (Turf): Sf: 0-2 GS: 0-1 Gd: 0-0 GF: 0-0 Fm: 0-0
Distance: 5f/6f: 0-0 7f-8f: 0-1 9f-13f: 0-2 14f+: 0-0
Track : LH: 0-1 RH: 0-0 Tight: 0-0 Gall: 0-0
Aids: Bl: 0-0 Vi: 0-0 Tstrap: 0-0
Best Rating: 81 10/01 Nott 1m54y heavy

Touched off in a Nottingham maiden on her third run.

Maine Lobster (USA)

101 **71**

3-y-o ch f Woodman (USA)-Capades (USA) (Overskate (CAN))

J L Dunlop Robin F Scully

Placings:03250-555 **(1777)**

2001: 8^{5}GS, 9^{5}G, 9^{5}F

	Starts	1st	2nd	3rd	Win & Pl
Career Total (Turf)	8	0	1	1	1891

Going (Turf): Sf: 0-1 GS: 0-1 Gd: 0-1 GF: 0-4 Fm: 0-1
Distance: 5f/6f: 0-2 7f-8f: 0-3 9f-13f: 0-3 14f+: 0-0
Track : LH: 0-1 RH: 0-3 Tight: 0-1 Gall: 0-1
Aids: Bl: 0-0 Vi: 0-0 Tstrap: 0-0
Best Rating: 71 4/01 Wind 1m67y gd-sft

Mairi's Wedding

91 **62**

2-y-o b f Atraf-Crofters Ceilidh (Scottish Reel)

J S Goldie Paul Murphy

Placings:66450606 **(5185)**

2001: 5^{6}GF, 5^{6}GF, 5^{4}GF, 5^{5}G, 6^{0}G, 5^{6}F, 6^{0}G, 7^{6}GS

	Starts	1st	2nd	3rd	Win & Pl
Career Total (Turf)	8	0	0	0	0

Going (Turf): Sf: 0-0 GS: 0-1 Gd: 0-3 GF: 0-3 Fm: 0-1
Distance: 5f/6f: 0-6 7f-8f: 0-2 9f-13f: 0-0 14f+: 0-0
Track : LH: 0-1 RH: 0-0 Tight: 0-1 Gall: 0-0
Aids: Bl: 0-0 Vi: 0-0 Tstrap: 0-0
Best Rating: 62 7/01 Muss 5f gd-fm

Signs of ability in all starts to date, but improvement needed to win a race.

Majestic Bay (IRE)

104 **86**

5-y-o b g Unfuwain (USA)-That'Ll Be The Day (IRE) (Thatching)

P W Harris The Quiet Ones

Placings:52423/301314100-601630 **(5010)**

2001: 12^{6}GS, 13^{0}G, 13^{1}GF, 13^{6}GF, 14^{3}HY, 14^{0}HY

	Starts	1st	2nd	3rd	Win & Pl
Career Total (Turf)	20	4	2	4	44506

84	7/01	Newb	1m5f61y	C(0-90)H	G-F	£7247
85	9/00	Hayd	1m6f	D(0-85)H	HVY	£21108
79	7/00	Rdcr	2m4y	D(0-85)H	G-F	£4823
74	6/00	Yarm	1m6f17y	D	FRM	£3068

Total win prize-money £36248

Going (Turf): Sf: 1-6 GS: 0-2 Gd: 0-4 GF: 2-7 Fm: 1-1
Distance: 5f/6f: 0-0 7f-8f: 0-0 9f-13f: 0-7 14f+: 4-13
Track : LH: 3-13 RH: 0-6 Tight: 2-3 Gall: 0-7
Aids: Bl: 0-1 Vi: 0-0 Tstrap: 0-0
Best Rating: 86 9/01 Hayd 1m6f heavy

Won three times in the summer of 2000 at up to two miles, and returned to form when storming home over 13 furlongs at Newbury in July. Has won on fast ground and heavy.

Majestic Quest (IRE)

104(64) **52d**

3-y-o b g Piccolo-Teanarco (IRE) (Kafu)

J Neville Brian K Symonds

Placings:421000-00003000 **(4527)**

2001: 6^{0}F, 6^{0}GF, 6^{0}GF, 6^{0}SD, 7^{3}G, 7^{0}GF, 6^{0}F, 6^{0}GF

	Starts	1st	2nd	3rd	Win & Pl
Career Total (Turf)	13	1	1	1	5158
Career Total (AW)	1	0	0	0	

69	7/00	Ripn	5f	D	G-F	£3367

Total win prize-money £3367

Going (Turf): Sf: 0-1 GS: 0-1 Gd: 0-3 GF: 1-6 Fm: 0-2
Distance: 5f/6f: 1-10 7f-8f: 0-4 9f-13f: 0-0 14f+: 0-0
Track : LH: 0-2 RH: 0-0 Tight: 0-0 Gall: 0-0
Aids: Bl: 0-0 Vi: 0-0 Tstrap: 0-0
Best Rating: 52 7/01 Chep 7f16y good

Majestic Wind (IRE)

(89) (49)

4-y-o ch g College Chapel-Columbian Sand (IRE) (Salmon Leap (USA))

M G Quinlan Mrs C M Bathe

Placings:0/600004-36000 **(0375)**

2001: 6^{3}SD, 7^{6}SD, 9^{0}SW, 6^{0}SD, 12^{0}SD

	Starts	1st	2nd	3rd	Win & Pl
Career Total (Turf)	7	0	0	0	240
Career Total (AW)	5	0	0	1	418

Going (Turf): Sf: 0-1 GS: 0-0 Gd: 0-2 GF: 0-1 Fm: 0-0
Distance: 5f/6f: 0-3 7f-8f: 0-6 9f-13f: 0-3 14f+: 0-0
Track : LH: 0-6 RH: 0-4 Tight: 0-4 Gall: 0-0
Aids: Bl: 0-2 Vi: 0-0 Tstrap: 0-4
Best Rating: 49 1/01 Sthl 6f stand

Majhool

86 **78d**

2-y-o b c Mark Of Esteem (IRE)-Be Peace (USA) (Septieme Ciel (USA))

G L Moore Lancing Racing Syndicate

Placings:2000 **(5127)**

2001: 6^{2}GF, 6^{0}G, 6^{0}GF, 7^{0}HY

	Starts	1st	2nd	3rd	Win & Pl
Career Total (Turf)	4	0	1	0	1508

Going (Turf): Sf: 0-1 GS: 0-0 Gd: 0-1 GF: 0-2 Fm: 0-0
Distance: 5f/6f: 0-2 7f-8f: 0-2 9f-13f: 0-0 14f+: 0-0
Track : LH: 0-0 RH: 0-0 Tight: 0-0 Gall: 0-0
Aids: Bl: 0-0 Vi: 0-0 Tstrap: 0-0
Best Rating: 78 8/01 NmkJ 6f gd-fm

Major Attraction

105(91) (26)**51d**

6-y-o gr g Major Jacko-My Friend Melody (Sizzling Melody)

W M Brisbourne Mrs A E Burrows

Placings:00/64340/00060001001-05200122304560 **(4469)**

2001: 12^{0}GS, 13^{5}GF, 12^{2}F, 10^{0}G, 12^{0}GF, 10^{1}GF, 12^{2}GF, 12^{2}GF, 12^{3}G, 12^{0}G, 12^{4}G, 11^{5}G, 12^{6}GS, 12^{0}G

	Starts	1st	2nd	3rd	Win & Pl
Career Total (Turf)	23	3	3	1	14721
Career Total (AW)	10	0	0	1	276

52	6/01	Ayr	1m2f192y	F(0-60)H	G-F	£4176
46	7/00	Hayd	1m3f200y	E(0-70)	G-F	£2856
35	5/00	Haml	1m3f16y	F(0-60)H	G-F	£2926

Total win prize-money £9958

Going (Turf): Sf: 0-2 GS: 0-2 Gd: 0-9 GF: 3-9 Fm: 0-1
Distance: 5f/6f: 0-0 7f-8f: 0-3 9f-13f: 3-27 14f+: 0-3
Track : LH: 2-25 RH: 1-8 Tight: 1-21 Gall: 0-2
Aids: Bl: 0-2 Vi: 0-1 Tstrap: 0-0
Best Rating: 56 7/01 Ches 1m4f66y good

Major Drive (IRE)

100 **82**

3-y-o b c Sadler's Wells (USA)-Puck's Castle (Shirley Heights)

J H M Gosden R E Sangster And C Brook Johnson

Placings:00620 **(4958)**

2001: 8^{0}S, 10^{0}GS, 10^{6}GF, 9^{2}GF, 9^{0}GS

	Starts	1st	2nd	3rd	Win & Pl
Career Total (Turf)	5	0	1	0	3260

Going (Turf): Sf: 0-1 GS: 0-2 Gd: 0-0 GF: 0-2 Fm: 0-0
Distance: 5f/6f: 0-0 7f-8f: 0-1 9f-13f: 0-4 14f+: 0-0
Track : LH: 0-2 RH: 0-2 Tight: 0-3 Gall: 0-0
Aids: Bl: 0-0 Vi: 0-0 Tstrap: 0-0
Best Rating: 82 6/01 Gdwd 1m1f192y gd-fm

Major Laugh

(100) (84)**83**

2-y-o ch c Colonel Collins (USA)-Joytime (John De Coombe)

B W Hills R Wainwright

Placings:34021315501 **(5364)**

2001: 5^{3}GS, 5^{4}GF, 6^{0}G, 6^{2}GF, 7^{1}SD, 7^{3}GS, 7^{1}G, 6^{5}G, 6^{5}GF, 6^{0}G, 6^{1}GS

	Starts	1st	2nd	3rd	Win & Pl
Career Total (Turf)	10	2	1	2	63666
Career Total (AW)	1	1	0	0	3073

83	10/01	NmkR	6f	B	G-S	£57875
82	8/01	NmkJ	7f	D	GD	£4065
73	7/01	Sthl	7f	D	STD	£3073

Total win prize-money £65014

Going (Turf): Sf: 0-0 GS: 1-3 Gd: 1-4 GF: 0-3 Fm: 0-0
Distance: 5f/6f: 1-6 7f-8f: 2-5 9f-13f: 0-0 14f+: 0-0
Track : LH: 1-5 RH: 0-0 Tight: 0-0 Gall: 0-3
Aids: Bl: 0-0 Vi: 0-0 Tstrap: 0-0
Best Rating: 83 10/01 NmkR 6f gd-sft

Had run well in maidens before getting off the mark when stepped up in trip and tried on the All-Weather. Scored on Turf two outings later over a stiff seven at Newmarket, and took a sales event at the same track in October back at six. Will get further than seven in time.

Major Review (IRE)

99 **49d**

3-y-o b f Definite Article-Fresh Look (IRE) (Alzao (USA))

M L W Bell W H Ponsonby

Placings:0-0405000 **(5278)**

2001: 10^{0}GF, 8^{4}GF, 9^{0}GF, 10^{5}GF, 11^{0}G, 16^{0}GF, 9^{0}GS

	Starts	1st	2nd	3rd	Win & Pl
Career Total (Turf)	8	0	0	0	267

Going (Turf): Sf: 0-0 GS: 0-1 Gd: 0-2 GF: 0-5 Fm: 0-0
Distance: 5f/6f: 0-0 7f-8f: 0-2 9f-13f: 0-5 14f+: 0-1
Track : LH: 0-2 RH: 0-3 Tight: 0-3 Gall: 0-0
Aids: Bl: 0-1 Vi: 0-0 Tstrap: 0-0
Best Rating: 49 8/01 Wind 1m3f135y good

Makarim (IRE)

(109) (86)**79**

5-y-o ch g Generous (IRE)-Emmaline (USA) (Affirmed (USA))

M R Bosley Mrs Jean M O'Connor

Placings:46100650/5042111-1332022144233 **(5164)**

2001: 16^{1}SD, 16^{3}SW, 16^{3}SD, 12^{2}SD, 11^{0}GS, 14^{2}GF, 14^{2}GF, 12^{1}GF, 12^{4}G, 12^{4}GF, 14^{2}G, 13^{3}GF, 12^{3}SD

	Starts	1st	2nd	3rd	Win & Pl
Career Total (Turf)	14	2	3	1	21920
Career Total (AW)	14	4	2	3	15553

79	7/01	Kemp	1m4f	D(0-80)H	G-F	£7159
80	1/01	Sthl	2m	E(0-75)H	STD	£2926
80	12/00	Sthl	1m6f	E(0-75)H	STD	£2737
75	12/00	Wolv	1m6f166y	D(0-80)H	STD	£3672
62	11/00	Sthl	1m6f	G(0-65)	STD	£1939
79	8/99	Bath	1m3f144y	D	GD	£5836

Total win prize-money £24271

Going (Turf): Sf: 0-0 GS: 0-1 Gd: 1-6 GF: 1-6 Fm: 0-1
Distance: 5f/6f: 0-0 7f-8f: 0-0 9f-13f: 2-14 14f+: 4-14
Track : LH: 5-21 RH: 1-7 Tight: 2-11 Gall: 0-4
Aids: Bl: 0-1 Vi: 0-0 Tstrap: 0-0
Best Rating: 86 3/01 Wolv 2m46y stand

He has had a few trainers in his time, but enjoyed a purple patch on Fibresand in the winter of 2000 with four victories from between 14 furlongs and two miles. He is not just a stayer and ran very well when dropped to 12 furlongs afterwards and won over that trip on turf at Kempton in July and has since gone well in some decent handicaps. Not an easy ride, but George Baker gets on very well with him.

Makasseb

(103) (73) **80**

4-y-o ch g Kris-Shefoog (Kefaah (USA))

M R Channon Ahmed Al Shafar

Placings:632215/00604401003**334-41** **(0038)**

2001: 16^{4}SD, 16^{1}SD

	Starts	1st	2nd	3rd	Win & Pl
Career Total (Turf)	16	2	2	1	18794
Career Total (AW)	6	1	0	3	3667

71	1/01	Ling	2m	F(0-70)H	STD	£2275
75	8/00	Ripn	2m	E(0-75)H	GD	£3458
83	11/99	MsnL	1m1f		HVY	£9688

Total win prize-money £15421

Going (Turf): Sf: 1-6 GS: 0-2 **Gd: 1-5** GF: 0-3 Fm: 0-0
Distance: 5f/6f: 0-0 7f-8f: 0-5 9f-13f: 1-9 **14f+: 2-8**
Track : LH: 1-16 **RH: 2-6 Tight: 2-7** Gall: 0-4
Aids: Bl: 0-0 Vi: 0-0 Tstrap: 0-0
Best Rating: 71 1/01 Ling 2m stand

Makboola (IRE)

102 **82**

3-y-o b f Mujtahid (USA)-Haddeyah (USA) (Dayjur (USA))

J L Dunlop Khalil Alsayegh

Placings:312-60030 **(2758)**

2001: 8^{6}GS, 9^{0}GS, 9^{0}GF, 8^{3}G, 8^{0}GF

	Starts	1st	2nd	3rd	Win & Pl
Career Total (Turf)	8	1	1	2	6829

64	6/00	Rdcr	6f	E	GD	£2887

Total win prize-money £2888

Going (Turf): Sf: 0-1 GS: 0-2 **Gd: 1-3** GF: 0-2 Fm: 0-0
Distance: **5f/6f: 1-3** 7f-8f: 0-2 9f-13f: 0-3 14f+: 0-0
Track : LH: 0-1 RH: 0-3 Tight: 0-2 Gall: 0-1
Aids: Bl: 0-0 Vi: 0-0 Tstrap: 0-0
Best Rating: 82 6/01 Bath 1m5y good

Shaped well at two, winning a Redcar maiden over six furlongs. She looks the type who will come into her own at three. Her win came on a sound surface.

Make My Hay

81 **50**

2-y-o b g Bluegrass Prince (IRE)-Shashi (IRE) (Shaadi (USA))

M Kettle Mrs Irene Clifford

Placings:0 **(5290)**

2001: 7^{0}S

	Starts	1st	2nd	3rd	Win & Pl
Career Total (Turf)	1	0	0	0	

Going (Turf): Sf: 0-1 GS: 0-0 Gd: 0-0 GF: 0-0 Fm: 0-0
Distance: 5f/6f: 0-0 7f-8f: 0-1 9f-13f: 0-0 14f+: 0-0
Track : LH: 0-0 RH: 0-0 Tight: 0-0 Gall: 0-0
Aids: Bl: 0-0 Vi: 0-0 Tstrap: 0-0
Best Rating: 50 10/01 Leic 7f9y soft

Make The Call

64

4-y-o b f Syrtos-Dawn Call (Rymer)

B N Doran T D Galer

Placings:0 **(2251)**

2001: 12^{0}GF

	Starts	1st	2nd	3rd	Win & Pl
Career Total (Turf)	1	0	0	0	

Going (Turf): Sf: 0-0 GS: 0-0 Gd: 0-0 GF: 0-1 Fm: 0-0
Distance: 5f/6f: 0-0 7f-8f: 0-0 9f-13f: 0-1 14f+: 0-0
Track : LH: 0-1 RH: 0-0 Tight: 0-0 Gall: 0-0
Aids: Bl: 0-0 Vi: 0-0 Tstrap: 0-0

Makelovelast (IRE)

100 **75**

3-y-o b f Darshaan-Touch And Love (IRE) (Green Desert (USA))

B W Hills Maktoum Al Maktoum

Placings:00344 **(2926)**

2001: 8^{0}S, 10^{0}GF, 12^{3}GF, 10^{4}GF, 12^{4}GF

	Starts	1st	2nd	3rd	Win & Pl
Career Total (Turf)	5	0	0	1	844

Going (Turf): Sf: 0-1 GS: 0-0 Gd: 0-0 GF: 0-4 Fm: 0-0
Distance: 5f/6f: 0-0 7f-8f: 0-1 9f-13f: 0-4 14f+: 0-0
Track : LH: 0-3 RH: 0-0 Tight: 0-0 Gall: 0-1
Aids: Bl: 0-0 Vi: 0-0 Tstrap: 0-0
Best Rating: 75 6/01 Wwck 1m4f134y gd-fm

Making Waves (IRE)

78 **53**

2-y-o b f Danehill (USA)-Wavey (Kris)

J H M Gosden George Strawbridge

Placings:0 **(5147)**

2001: 7^{0}G

	Starts	1st	2nd	3rd	Win & Pl
Career Total (Turf)	1	0	0	0	

Going (Turf): Sf: 0-0 GS: 0-0 Gd: 0-1 GF: 0-0 Fm: 0-0
Distance: 5f/6f: 0-0 7f-8f: 0-1 9f-13f: 0-0 14f+: 0-0
Track : LH: 0-0 RH: 0-0 Tight: 0-0 Gall: 0-0
Aids: Bl: 0-0 Vi: 0-0 Tstrap: 0-0
Best Rating: 53 10/01 Rdcr 7f good

Maknaas

105(108) (77) **49**

5-y-o ch h Wolfhound (USA)-White-Wash (Final Straw)

P S McEntee Travel Spot Ltd

Placings:00/00034531/415111100-023030 **(4728)**

2001: 16^{0}GF, 16^{2}GF, 16^{3}G, 16^{0}G, 14^{3}SW, 16^{0}GF

	Starts	1st	2nd	3rd	Win & Pl
Career Total (Turf)	13	0	1	2	1183
Career Total (AW)	12	6	0	2	17158

77	3/00	Wolv	2m46y	D(0-85)H	STD	£3828
75	3/00	Ling	2m	F(0-70)H	STD	£2173
65	3/00	Wolv	2m46y	D(0-80)H	STD	£3750
61	2/00	Wolv	2m46y	F(0-65)H	STD	£2352
53	1/00	Ling	2m	F(0-70)H	STD	£2278
49	12/99	Wolv	2m46y	F(0-65)H	STD	£1913

Total win prize-money £16299

Going (Turf): Sf: 0-2 GS: 0-3 Gd: 0-4 GF: 0-4 Fm: 0-0
Distance: 5f/6f: 0-1 7f-8f: 0-4 9f-13f: 0-4 **14f+: 6-16**
Track : **LH: 6-18** RH: 0-2 **Tight: 6-14** Gall: 0-0
Aids: Bl: 0-4 Vi: 0-0 Tstrap: 0-0
Best Rating: 49 8/01 Bevl 2m35y good

In brilliant form on sand in the winter of 1999/2000, winning six times over two miles. He returned from over a year off in July 2001, and ran well at Yarmouth on his second outing. Stays two miles well.

Maktavish

100 **92**

2-y-o b c Makbul-La Belle Vie (Indian King (USA))

B R Millman Robin Lawson

Placings:122010 **(5150)**

2001: 5^{1}S, 5^{2}G, 5^{2}GF, 5^{0}GF, 5^{1}G, 6^{0}G

	Starts	1st	2nd	3rd	Win & Pl
Career Total (Turf)	6	2	2	0	13395

92	9/01	Bevl	5f	D	GD	£3776
85	4/01	Nott	5f13y	D	SFT	£2926

Total win prize-money £6703

Going (Turf): Sf: 1-1 GS: 0-0 **Gd: 1-3** GF: 0-2 Fm: 0-0
Distance: **5f/6f: 2-6** 7f-8f: 0-0 9f-13f: 0-0 14f+: 0-0
Track : LH: 0-0 RH: 0-1 Tight: 0-0 Gall: 0-1
Aids: Bl: 0-0 Vi: 0-0 Tstrap: 0-0
Best Rating: 92 9/01 Bevl 5f good

Twice successful over five furlongs, needs cut in the ground to perform at his best. He looks Listed class at least.

Malaah (IRE)

103(107) (65) **49**

5-y-o gr g Pips Pride-Lingdale Lass (Petong)

Julian Poulton Mrs Elizabeth Reed

Placings:0/00066/0005005600**0340-1225250040060** **(4525)**

2001: 8^{1}SD, 8^{2}SD, 7^{2}SD, 8^{5}SD, 7^{2}SW, 7^{5}SD, 6^{0}HY, 8^{0}SD, 7^{4}GF, 8^{0}GF, 7^{0}G, 6^{6}F, 7^{0}GF

	Starts	1st	2nd	3rd	Win & Pl
Career Total (Turf)	22	0	0	0	330
Career Total (AW)	11	1	3	1	5575

56	1/01	Ling	1m	D	STD	£2877

Total win prize-money £2877

Going (Turf): Sf: 0-2 GS: 0-1 Gd: 0-5 GF: 0-11 Fm: 0-3
Distance: 5f/6f: 0-11 **7f-8f: 1-19** 9f-13f: 0-3 14f+: 0-0
Track : **LH: 1-16** RH: 0-2 **Tight: 1-12** Gall: 0-3
Aids: Bl: 0-16 Vi: 0-0 Tstrap: 0-0
Best Rating: 67 1/01 Ling 7f stand

Maladerie (IRE)

97(56) (44) **39**

7-y-o b g Thatching-Native Melody (Tudor Music)

M Dods B Woollett

Placings:421344/000000206320250/543022622036126 5140150/00606613002330505000000/0002000000400 -06054420063 **(5027)**

2001: 7^{0}GF, 6^{6}G, 5^{0}F, 5^{5}GS, 6^{4}F, 6^{4}GF, 6^{2}F, 5^{0}G, 6^{0}G, 6^{6}F, 5^{3}S

	Starts	1st	2nd	3rd	Win & Pl
Career Total (Turf)	90	5	12	8	45973
Career Total (AW)	1	0	0	0	

69	6/99	Bath	5f161y	D(0-85)H	GD	£3850
70	10/98	York	5f	D(0-80)H	GD	£7434
68	9/98	Hayd	5f	C(0-95)H	GD	£5767
60	8/98	Wind	5f10y	E(0-70)H	G-F	£2932
76	6/96	Wind	5f217y	D	G-F	£3403

Total win prize-money £23390

Going (Turf): Sf: 0-7 GS: 0-9 **Gd: 3-32** GF: 2-27 Fm: 0-14
Distance: **5f/6f: 5-65** 7f-8f: 0-23 9f-13f: 0-2 14f+: 0-0
Track : LH: 1-19 **RH: 2-11** Tight: 0-3 **Gall: 3-10**
Aids: Bl: 0-1 **Vi: 4-55** Tstrap: 0-0
Best Rating: 45 7/01 Ling 6f firm

Decent handicapper in his prime but on the downgrade and has endured a hectic schedule over the last few years. Wins are infrequent these days. Effective from five furlongs to a mile

Malarkey

104(100) (64) **67**

4-y-o b g Mukaddamah (USA)-Malwiya (USA) (Shahrastani (USA))

J A Osborne John Livock

Placings:05545325-**130**46520340640 **(5387)**

2001: 9^{1}SD, 10^{3}SD, 8^{0}SW, 9^{4}G, 11^{6}F, 14^{5}GF, 17^{2}G, 16^{0}GF, 17^{3}G, 14^{4}GF, 14^{0}F, 16^{6}GF, 17^{4}G, 18^{0}GS

	Starts	1st	2nd	3rd	Win & Pl
Career Total (Turf)	19	0	2	2	3428
Career Total (AW)	3	1	0	1	3319

64 2/01 Wolv 1m1f79y D STD £2926

Total win prize-money £2926

Going (Turf): Sf: 0-0 GS: 0-2 Gd: 0-6 GF: 0-8 Fm: 0-2
Distance: 5f/6f: 0-2 7f-8f: 0-3 **9f-13f: 1-7** 14f+: 0-9
Track : **LH: 1-8** RH: 0-9 **Tight: 1-10** Gall: 0-2
Aids: Bl: 0-1 Vi: 0-0 Tstrap: 0-0
Best Rating: 72 7/01 Bath 2m1f34y good

Got off the mark on his All-Weather debut at Wolverhampton in the spring and has continued to run well in modest handicap company since without scoring. Stays two miles and acts on a sound surface.

Malchik

(101) (55)**33**

5-y-o ch g Absalom-Very Good (Noalto)
P Howling I G Mirzoian

Placings:000000301000063/3243365000026530000505/5560020033312026000000-20311000000066 **(4558)**
2001: 8^{2}SW, 9^{0}SD, 8^{3}SD, 9^{1}SD, 8^{1}SD, 9^{0}SD, 12^{0}SD, 11^{0}GF, 8^{0}GS, 11^{0}GF, 9^{6}SD, 9^{6}SW

	Starts	1st	2nd	3rd	Win & Pl
Career Total (Turf)	23	1	0	1	2610
Career Total (AW)	47	3	6	9	12718

55 2/01 Wolv 1m100y G STD £1820
43 2/01 Wolv 1m1f79y G STD £1848
55 4/00 Wolv 1m1f79y G STD £1913
59 9/98 Leic 1m8y G(0-65)H G-S £2080

Total win prize-money £7662

Going (Turf): Sf: 0-2 **GS: 1-5** Gd: 0-6 GF: 0-9 Fm: 0-1
Distance: 5f/6f: 0-5 7f-8f: 0-22 **9f-13f: 4-41** 14f+: 0-2
Track : **LH: 3-51** RH: 0-4 **Tight: 3-51** Gall: 0-3
Aids: Bl: 0-1 Vi: 0-0 Tstrap: 0-0
Best Rating: 55 2/01 Wolv 1m100y stand

Malhub (USA)

112 **112**

3-y-o b c Kingmambo (USA)-Arjuzah (IRE) (Ahonoora)
J H M Gosden Hamdan Al Maktoum

Placings:1-1050 **(5386)**
2001: 7^{1}GF, 8^{0}G, 8^{5}GS, 7^{0}GS

	Starts	1st	2nd	3rd	Win & Pl
Career Total (Turf)	5	2	0	0	19817

112 6/01 NmkR 7f A G-F £14036
91 9/00 NmkR 7f D GD £5086

Total win prize-money £19122

Going (Turf): Sf: 0-0 GS: 0-2 **Gd: 1-2 GF: 1-1** Fm: 0-0
Distance: 5f/6f: 0-0 **7f-8f: 2-5** 9f-13f: 0-0 14f+: 0-0
Track : LH: 0-0 RH: 0-1 Tight: 0-0 Gall: 0-1
Aids: Bl: 0-0 Vi: 0-0 **Tstrap: 1-4**
Best Rating: 112 6/01 NmkR 7f gd-fm

Won his two-year-old debut at Newmarket over seven furlongs, and made a successful reappearance in a Listed event over the same course and distance in June. Well beaten in the St James's Palace Stakes at Royal Ascot, and might have found the yielding ground against him on his next two starts in October. Regularly tongue tied.

Mallard (IRE)

91 **53**

3-y-o b g Tagula (IRE)-Frill (Henbit (USA))
N A Graham Audrey Scotney,Malcolm Joyce,Paul Jacobs

Placings:060 **(5174)**
2001: 10^{0}GS, 8^{6}G, 8^{0}GS

	Starts	1st	2nd	3rd	Win & Pl
Career Total (Turf)	3	0	0	0	0

Going (Turf): Sf: 0-0 GS: 0-2 Gd: 0-1 GF: 0-0 Fm: 0-0
Distance: 5f/6f: 0-0 7f-8f: 0-0 9f-13f: 0-3 14f+: 0-0
Track : LH: 0-2 RH: 0-1 Tight: 0-0 Gall: 0-0
Aids: Bl: 0-0 Vi: 0-0 Tstrap: 0-0
Best Rating: 53 9/01 Nott 1m54y good

Mallia

(104) (59)**50**

8-y-o b g Statoblest-Pronetta (USA) (Mr Prospector (USA))
T D Barron H T Duddin

Placings:421/5210/0000000020020110/01030000515/23020513201301464002000046 0/4055164140444400006-0315332150000200044601 **(5619)**
2001: 6^{0}SD, 6^{3}SD, 6^{1}SD, 6^{5}SD, 6^{3}SD, 6^{3}SD, 6^{2}SD, 6^{1}SD, 6^{5}HY, 6^{0}SD, 6^{0}G, 6^{0}GS, 6^{0}GF, 6^{2}F, 6^{0}GF, 6^{0}G, 6^{0}G, 6^{4}G, 6^{4}SW, 6^{6}SD, 6^{0}SD, 6^{1}SD

	Starts	1st	2nd	3rd	Win & Pl
Career Total (Turf)	60	4	7	2	69524
Career Total (AW)	40	10	3	5	30351

59 11/01 Wolv 6f F(0-60)H STD £2380
58 3/01 Wolv 6f D(0-80)H STD £3181
59 1/01 Wolv 6f G STD £1904
68 3/00 Wolv 6f F STD £2236
62 2/00 Wolv 6f F STD £2135
74 7/99 Hayd 6f D(0-80)H G-S £7587
74 5/99 Wolv 6f D(0-85)H STD £3616
69 3/99 Wolv 6f F STD £2284
63 12/98 Wolv 6f F STD £1934
70 4/98 Ripn 6f C(0-95)H SFT £5836
77 12/97 Wolv 6f D(0-75)H STD £2473
70 11/97 Sthl 6f E(0-70)H STD £2531
84 6/96 York 6f B(0-105)H GD £34238
78 5/95 Haml 5f4y F GD £2759

Total win prize-money £75100

Going (Turf): Sf: 1-12 GS: 1-11 **Gd: 2-20** GF: 0-12 Fm: 0-5
Distance: **5f/6f: 14-90** 7f-8f: 0-10 9f-13f: 0-0 14f+: 0-0
Track : **LH: 10-43** RH: 0-0 **Tight: 9-21** Gall: 0-0
Aids: **Bl: 10-72** Vi: 0-3 Tstrap: 0-0
Best Rating: 59 11/01 Wolv 6f stand

A Wolverhampton specialist, he has won nine times over six furlongs at Dunstall Park. Not as good as he was, he still has the ability to win claimers and minor handicaps on the sand. Usually held up for a late run.

Malmand (USA)

85 **62**

2-y-o ch c Distant View (USA)-Bidski (USA) (Explosive Bid (USA))
M A Jarvis Sheikh Ahmed Al Maktoum

Placings:40 **(5468)**
2001: 6^{4}G, 7^{0}S

	Starts	1st	2nd	3rd	Win & Pl
Career Total (Turf)	2	0	0	0	288

Going (Turf): Sf: 0-1 GS: 0-0 Gd: 0-1 GF: 0-0 Fm: 0-0
Distance: 5f/6f: 0-0 7f-8f: 0-2 9f-13f: 0-0 14f+: 0-0
Track : LH: 0-1 RH: 0-0 Tight: 0-0 Gall: 0-0
Aids: Bl: 0-0 Vi: 0-0 Tstrap: 0-0
Best Rating: 62 10/01 Brig 7f214y soft

Malumla (IRE)

70 **33**

2-y-o b f Marju (IRE)-Pearl Shell (USA) (Bering)
J Nicol J P Hill

Placings:0 **(5684)**
2001: 8^{0}S

	Starts	1st	2nd	3rd	Win & Pl
Career Total (Turf)	1	0	0	0	

Going (Turf): Sf: 0-1 GS: 0-0 Gd: 0-0 GF: 0-0 Fm: 0-0
Distance: 5f/6f: 0-0 7f-8f: 0-1 9f-13f: 0-0 14f+: 0-0
Track : LH: 0-0 RH: 0-0 Tight: 0-0 Gall: 0-0
Aids: Bl: 0-0 Vi. 0-0 Tstrap: 0-0
Best Rating: 33 11/01 Donc 1m soft

Mamboesque (USA)

100(83) (22)**47**

3-y-o b g Miesque's Son (USA)-Brawl (USA) (Fit To Fight (USA))
T D Barron Nigel Shields

Placings:00000501 **(5278)**
2001: 7^{0}SD, 8^{0}S, 7^{0}S, 8^{0}GF, 12^{0}SD, 8^{5}GS, 9^{0}GF, 9^{1}GS

	Starts	1st	2nd	3rd	Win & Pl
Career Total (Turf)	6	1	0	0	1974
Career Total (AW)	2	0	0	0	

47 10/01 Leic 1m1f218yG G-S £1974

Total win prize-money £1974

Going (Turf): Sf: 0-2 **GS: 1-2** Gd: 0-0 GF: 0-2 Fm: 0-0
Distance: 5f/6f: 0-0 7f-8f: 0-4 **9f-13f: 1-4** 14f+: 0-0
Track : LH. 0-3 **RH: 1-4** Tight: 0-2 Gall: 0-1
Aids: **Bl: 1-3** Vi: 0-0 Tstrap: 0-0
Best Rating: 47 10/01 Leic 1m1f218y gd-sft

Had to be dropped into poor company in order to notch up a win in an unimpressive seller in October. Has worn blinkers.

Mamcazma

99(102) (71)**66**

3-y-o b/br c Terimon-Merryhill Maid (IRE) (M Double M (USA))
D Morris (A Smith 27/7) H A Cushing

Placings:060410-05222 **(4483)**
2001: 8^{0}G, 12^{5}SD, 11^{2}SD, 12^{2}G, 14^{2}S

	Starts	1st	2nd	3rd	Win & Pl
Career Total (Turf)	6	0	2	0	2388
Career Total (AW)	5	1	1	0	3362

66 11/00 Sthl 1m F STD £2261

Total win prize-money £2261

Going (Turf): Sf: 0-2 GS: 0-1 Gd: 0-3 GF: 0-0 Fm: 0-0
Distance: 5f/6f: 0-2 **7f-8f: 1-4** 9f-13f: 0-4 14f+: 0-1
Track : **LH: 1-8** RH: 0-1 Tight: 0-3 Gall: 0-1
Aids: Bl: 0-0 Vi: 0-0 Tstrap: 0-0
Best Rating: 71 7/01 Sthl 1m3f stand

His form on sand has been better than on turf so far and he broke his maiden over a mile at Southwell towards the end of 2000.

Mameha

100 **100**

3-y-o b f Rainbow Quest (USA)-Musetta (IRE) (Cadeaux Genereux)
C E Brittain B H Voak

Placings:035-0503 **(2450)**
2001: 8^{0}G, 9^{5}GF, 12^{0}GF, 10^{3}F

	Starts	1st	2nd	3rd	Win & Pl
Career Total (Turf)	7	0	0	2	6056

Going (Turf): Sf: 0-0 GS: 0-1 Gd: 0-1 GF: 0-4 Fm: 0-1
Distance: 5f/6f: 0-1 7f-8f: 0-3 9f-13f: 0-3 14f+: 0-0
Track : LH: 0-3 RH: 0-2 Tight: 0-3 Gall: 0-1
Aids: Bl: 0-0 Vi: 0-0 Tstrap: 0-0
Best Rating: 98 5/01 Gdwd 1m1f192y gd-fm

A keen sort, her best run was when she was beaten three lengths into fifth behind Foodbroker Fancy in the Lupe Stakes at Goodwood in May. At 100-1, she was out of her depth in the Oaks at Epsom next time. Probably best suited by a sound surface.

Mameyuki

84 **70+**

2-y-o ch f Zafonic (USA)-Musetta (IRE) (Cadeaux Genereux)
C E Brittain B H Voak

Placings:01 **(3082)**
2001: 6^{0}GF, 6^{1}GF

	Starts	1st	2nd	3rd	Win & Pl
Career Total (Turf)	2	1	0	0	5519

70	7/01	Wind	6f	C	G-F	£5518

Total win prize-money £5519

Going (Turf): Sf: 0-0 GS: 0-0 Gd: 0-0 **GF: 1-2** Fm: 0-0
Distance: **5f/6f: 1-2** 7f-8f: 0-0 9f-13f: 0-0 14f+: 0-0
Track : LH: 0-0 RH: 0-0 Tight: 0-0 Gall: 0-0
Aids: Bl: 0-0 Vi: 0-0 Tstrap: 0-0
Best Rating: 70 7/01 Wind 6f gd-fm

Improved from her debut to win a Windsor conditions event on her second start and should have no problem getting seven furlongs.

Mamma's Boy

99 (50)**44**

6-y-o b g Rock City-Henpot (IRE) (Alzao (USA))
A Berry Mrs J M Berry

Placings:23343503/3042315026140/000110350634066 400/004111004601600-0411360003000 **(4482)**
2001: 8^{0}GS, 8^{4}GS, 7^{1}GF, 7^{1}GF, 7^{3}F, 9^{6}G, 7^{0}F, 8^{0}F, 8^{0}GF, 7^{3}GF, 7^{0}G, 8^{0}GF, 8^{0}F

	Starts	1st	2nd	3rd	Win & Pl
Career Total (Turf)	66	10	3	10	35576
Career Total (AW)	1	0	0	0	0

54	5/01	Muss	7f30y	E(0-70)H	G-F	£3122
52	5/01	Muss	7f30y	F(0-65)H	G-F	£2324
52	8/00	Muss	1m	F(0-60)H	G-F	£2002
54	6/00	Muss	7f30y	F	FRM	£2394
52	6/00	Muss	7f30y	F	FRM	£2380
54	5/00	Rdcr	7f	F	G-S	£2499
61	5/99	Muss	7f30y	F	FRM	£2332
55	5/99	Thsk	7f	E	G-S	£2932
63	9/98	Sand	5f6y	E	G-S	£3035
72	6/98	Donc	6f	E(0-70)H	GD	£4305

Total win prize-money £27326

Going (Turf): Sf: 0-8 **GS: 3-17** Gd: 1-15 **GF: 3-15 Fm: 3-11**
Distance: 5f/6f: 2-27 **7f-8f: 8-38** 9f-13f: 0-2 14f+: 0-0
Track : LH: 1-16 **RH: 4-17 Tight: 5-23** Gall: 0-0
Aids: Bl: 0-1 Vi: 0-0 Tstrap: 0-0
Best Rating: 57 6/01 Donc 7f firm

Mammas F-C (IRE)

103(92) (34)**67**

5-y-o ch m Case Law-Wasaif (IRE) (Lomond (USA))
J M Bradley J M Kearney

Placings:2202611620100/4445242411314020/0055F-00010531314145660 **(4804)**
2001: 6^{0}SD, 6^{0}HY, 5^{0}G, 5^{1}GF, 5^{0}F, 5^{5}GF, 5^{3}GF, 6^{1}GF, 6^{3}GF, 5^{1}F, 6^{4}GF, 5^{1}GF, 5^{4}GF, 6^{5}GF, 5^{6}F, 5^{6}G, 6^{0}F

	Starts	1st	2nd	3rd	Win & Pl
Career Total (Turf)	37	9	5	3	39058
Career Total (AW)	14	1	2	0	3567

67	8/01	Bath	5f11y	D(0-85)H	G-F	£3727
64	7/01	Ling	5f	E(0-65)H	FRM	£3220
59	7/01	Pont	6f	D(0-85)H	G-F	£7085
53	5/01	Ling	5f	E(0-70)H	G-F	£3010
58	8/99	Ripn	6f	D(0-80)H	G-F	£5265
49	8/99	Bath	5f161y	E	HRD	£2892
46	7/99	Folk	7f	F(0-55)	G-F	£2067
65	9/98	Hayd	6f	F	GD	£2556
60	6/98	Muss	5f	E	G-F	£2688
66	6/98	Sthl	5f	F	STD	£2343

Total win prize-money £34857

Going (Turf): Sf: 0-3 GS: 0-2 Gd: 1-8 **GF: 6-19** Fm: 2-5
Distance: **5f/6f: 9-46** 7f-8f: 1-5 9f-13f: 0-0 14f+: 0-0
Track : **LH: 3-22** RH: 0-2 Tight: 0-8 **Gall: 2-10**
Aids: Bl: 0-0 Vi: 0-0 Tstrap: 0-0
Best Rating: 67 8/01 Bath 5f11y gd-fm

Fair sprinter, effective at up to seven furlongs, but better over shorter. Suited by fast ground and hold-up tactics.

Mamool (IRE)

101 **101**

2-y-o b c In The Wings-Genovefa (USA) (Woodman (USA))
D R Loder Sheikh Mohammed

Placings:2214 **(5480a)**
2001: 7^{2}GS, 7^{2}GF, 8^{1}G, 8^{4}HY

	Starts	1st	2nd	3rd	Win & Pl
Career Total (Turf)	4	1	2	0	26278

84	9/01	Gdwd	1m	D	GD	£4303

Total win prize-money £4303

Going (Turf): Sf: 0-1 GS: 0-1 **Gd: 1-1** GF: 0-1 Fm: 0-0
Distance: 5f/6f: 0-0 **7f-8f: 1-4** 9f-13f: 0-0 14f+: 0-0
Track : LH: 0-0 **RH: 1-2** Tight: 0-0 Gall: 0-0
Aids: Bl: 0-0 Vi: 0-0 Tstrap: 0-0
Best Rating: 101 8/01 Newb 7f gd-fm

A half-brother to Ejlaal who was a winner over a mile as a juvenile. He showed ability on his debut at Newmarket over seven furlongs, then gave Funfair Wane a good race in a Listed event at Newbury. Ran away with a Goodwood maiden before a reasonable effort in an Italian Group One. Handles fast and easy ground, and open to improvement.

Mamore Gap (IRE)

103(94) (67)**83**

3-y-o b c General Monash (USA)-Ravensdale Rose (IRE) (Henbit (USA))
R Hannon The South-Western Partnership Ii

Placings:22311-00314260 **(5344)**
2001: 7^{0}GS, 8^{0}G, 8^{3}GF, 8^{1}GS, 8^{4}G, 9^{2}GS, 8^{6}G, 8^{0}GS

	Starts	1st	2nd	3rd	Win & Pl
Career Total (Turf)	12	3	2	2	21474
Career Total (AW)	1	0	1	0	985

68	7/01	Wwck	1m22y	C(0-85)	G-S	£7052
82	8/00	Newb	7f	D	G-F	£4368
77	7/00	Brig	6f209y	E	FRM	£2703

Total win prize-money £14124

Going (Turf): Sf: 0-0 **GS: 1-5** Gd: 0-3 **GF: 1-3 Fm: 1-1**
Distance: 5f/6f: 0-3 **7f-8f: 2-8** 9f-13f: 1-2 14f+: 0-0
Track : **LH: 1-3** RH: 0-3 Tight: 0-3 Gall: 0-1
Aids: Bl: 0-0 Vi: 0-0 Tstrap: 0-0
Best Rating: 83 8/01 Gdwd 1m1f gd-sft

Scored twice as a juvenile in the summer of 2000 over seven furlongs on fast ground and proved he stays a mile when winning at Warwick in July 2001 on an easier surface, but has been well held since. Gives the impression that he should stay further.

Mamounia (IRE)

99 **89**

2-y-o b f Green Desert (USA)-Maroussie (FR) (Saumarez)
B W Hills Burton Agnes Bloodstock

Placings:322 **(5588)**
2001: 6^{3}S, 6^{2}S, 5^{2}GS

	Starts	1st	2nd	3rd	Win & Pl
Career Total (Turf)	3	0	2	1	4116

Going (Turf): **Sf: 0-2 GS: 0-1 Gd: 0-0 GF: 0-0 Fm: 0-0**
Distance: 5f/6f: 0-3 7f-8f: 0-0 9f-13f: 0-0 14f+: 0-0
Track : LH: 0-2 RH: 0-0 Tight: 0-0 Gall: 0-0
Aids: Bl: 0-0 Vi: 0-0 Tstrap: 0-0
Best Rating: 89 10/01 York 6f soft

Mamzug (IRE)

(87) (41)**66**

4-y-o b g Hamas (IRE)-Bellissi (IRE) (Bluebird (USA))
B Hanbury Christopher Cooke

Placings:0/414235-052000000 **(4876)**
2001: 8^{0}HY, 10^{5}GF, 8^{2}GF, 8^{0}G, 9^{0}GF, 10^{0}GF, 7^{0}G, 7^{0}G, 6^{0}SD

	Starts	1st	2nd	3rd	Win & Pl
Career Total (Turf)	15	1	2	1	7833
Career Total (AW)	1	0	0	0	

77	5/00	Bath	1m5y	F	G-F	£1876

Total win prize-money £1876

Going (Turf): Sf: 0-1 GS: 0-1 Gd: 0-5 **GF: 1-8** Fm: 0-0
Distance: 5f/6f: 0-1 7f-8f: 0-6 **9f-13f: 1-9** 14f+: 0-0
Track : **LH: 1-6** RH: 0-3 **Tight: 1-6** Gall: 0-0
Aids: Bl: 0-2 Vi: 0-0 Tstrap: 0-5
Best Rating: 82 5/01 Bevl 1m100y gd-fm

Consistent performer around a mile in decent handicap company last season. Disappointing for most of this term. Best on a sound surface.

Man From Havana (USA)

98 **77**

2-y-o b g Green Dancer (USA)-Charmie Carmie (USA) (Lyphard (USA))
P F I Cole Christopher Wright

Placings:4340 **(4584)**
2001: 7^{4}S, 7^{3}GF, 7^{4}GF, 8^{0}HY

	Starts	1st	2nd	3rd	Win & Pl
Career Total (Turf)	4	0	0	1	1382

Going (Turf): **Sf: 0-2 GS: 0-0 Gd: 0-0 GF: 0-2 Fm: 0-0**
Distance: 5f/6f: 0-0 7f-8f: 0-3 9f-13f: 0-1 14f+: 0-0
Track : LH: 0-2 RH: 0-2 Tight: 0-1 Gall: 0-0
Aids: Bl: 0-0 Vi: 0-0 Tstrap: 0-0
Best Rating: 77 7/01 Epsm 7f gd-fm

Man O'Mystery (USA)

108 **108**

4-y-o b h Diesis-Eurostorm (USA) (Storm Bird (CAN))
J Noseda Ecurie Pharos

Placings:0/1242642-04223 **(3815)**
2001: 10^{0}S, 10^{4}G, 10^{2}GF, 10^{2}G, 10^{3}G

	Starts	1st	2nd	3rd	Win & Pl
Career Total (Turf)	13	1	5	1	78477

86	3/00	Leic	1m8y	D	GD	£4004

Total win prize-money £4004

Going (Turf): Sf: 0-3 GS: 0-1 **Gd: 1-7** GF: 0-2 Fm: 0-0
Distance: 5f/6f: 0-0 7f-8f: 0-2 **9f-13f: 1-11** 14f+: 0-0
Track : LH: 0-3 RH: 0-4 Tight: 0-0 Gall: 0-5
Aids: Bl: 0-0 Vi: 0-0 Tstrap: 0-0
Best Rating: 108 7/01 York 1m2f85y good

He ran some fine races without much in the way of luck last season, including being beaten just a head in the John Smith's Cup and finishing fourth in the Cambridgeshire. He has plenty of ability, but his career record reads just one victory in a Leicester maiden. Acts on a sound surface and stays ten furlongs.

Man Of Distinction

45 **84**

3-y-o b c Spectrum (IRE)-Air Of Distinction (IRE) (Distinctly North (USA))
D R C Elsworth Nicholas Cooper

Placings:512-30 **(1163)**
2001: 6^{3}GS, 9^{0}GS

	Starts	1st	2nd	3rd	Win & Pl
Career Total (Turf)	5	1	1	1	6462

80	6/00	Kemp	6f	E	G-F	£3883

Total win prize-money £3884

Going (Turf): Sf: 0-0 GS: 0-3 Gd: 0-0 **GF: 1-2** Fm: 0-0
Distance: **5f/6f: 1-3** 7f-8f: 0-1 9f-13f: 0-1 14f+: 0-0
Track : LH: 0-0 RH: 0-1 Tight: 0-0 Gall: 0-0
Aids: Bl: 0-0 Vi: 0-0 Tstrap: 0-0
Best Rating: 68 4/01 Wind 6f gd-sft

Man The Gate

95(89) (63)**66**
2-y-o b c Elmaamul (USA)-Girl At The Gate (Formidable (USA))
P W Harris John G Morley

Placings:460 **(5466)**
2001: 7^{4}SD, 8^{6}SD, 6^{0}S

	Starts	1st	2nd	3rd	Win & Pl
Career Total (Turf)	1	0	0	0	
Career Total (AW)	2	0	0	0	269

Going (Turf): Sf: 0-1 GS: 0-0 Gd: 0-0 GF: 0-0 Fm: 0-0
Distance: 5f/6f: 0-0 7f-8f: 0-3 9f-13f: 0-0 14f+: 0-0
Track : LH: 0-3 RH: 0-0 Tight: 0-1 Gall: 0-0
Aids: Bl: 0-0 Vi: 0-0 Tstrap: 0-0
Best Rating: 66 10/01 Brig 6f209y soft

Mana D'Argent (IRE)

106(106) (83)**84**
4-y-o b g Ela-Mana-Mou-Petite-D-Argent (Noalto)
M Johnston Daniel A Couper

Placings:633/20456303132346-35004022520046520 **(5693)**
2001: 14^{3}SD, 18^{5}GF, 13^{0}GF, 12^{0}GF, 20^{4}GF, 16^{0}F, 11^{2}G, 12^{2}GF, 14^{5}GF, 12^{2}G, 13^{0}G, 12^{0}G, 13^{4}GF, 12^{6}HY, 13^{5}HY, 12^{4}HY, 12^{0}S

	Starts	1st	2nd	3rd	Win & Pl
Career Total (Turf)	33	1	6	6	42889
Career Total (AW)	1	0	0	1	598

80 7/00 Asct 1m4f D(0-85)H G-F £6890
Total win prize-money £6890

Going (Turf): Sf: 0-8 GS: 0-2 Gd: 0-11 **GF: 1-10** Fm: 0-2
Distance: 5f/6f: 0-2 7f-8f: 0-9 **9f-13f: 1-12** 14f+: 0-11
Track : LH: 0-21 **RH: 1-7** Tight: 0-6 **Gall: 1-15**
Aids: Bl: 0-4 Vi: 0-6 Tstrap: 0-0
Best Rating: 89 8/01 Asct 1m4f good

Consistent on good to fast ground, he has run a number of good races this term but has become hard to win with. Effective between a mile and a half and two and a half miles, he has been tried in headgear this term.

Mana Pools (IRE)

56
2-y-o b f Brief Truce (USA)-Pipers Pool (IRE) (Mtoto)
J A Glover H J P Farr

Placings:0000044 **(5628)**
2001: 5^{0}F, 6^{0}GF, 5^{0}GF, 7^{0}GS, 5^{0}GS, 8^{4}HY, 8^{4}G

	Starts	1st	2nd	3rd	Win & Pl
Career Total (Turf)	7	0	0	0	0

Going (Turf): Sf: 0-1 GS: 0-2 Gd: 0-1 GF: 0-2 Fm: 0-1
Distance: 5f/6f: 0-4 7f-8f: 0-2 9f-13f: 0-1 14f+: 0-0
Track : LH: 0-2 RH: 0-0 Tight: 0-0 Gall: 0-0
Aids: Bl: 0-2 Vi: 0-1 Tstrap: 0-0
Best Rating: 56 7/01 Wwck 7f26y gd-sft

Moderate maiden, who has been unsuccessfully dropped down to selling company.

Mana-Mou Bay (IRE)

107 **93**
4-y-o b g Ela-Mana-Mou-Summerhill (Habitat)
R Hannon N A Woodcock

Placings:21/024500-4504013 **(5042)**
2001: 8^{4}GS, 8^{5}G, 8^{0}GF, 9^{4}GF, 8^{0}GF, 8^{1}GF, 8^{3}G

	Starts	1st	2nd	3rd	Win & Pl
Career Total (Turf)	15	2	2	1	25984

92 8/01 Wind 1m67y C(0-95)H G-F £6264
93 8/99 Newb 7f A GD £11795
Total win prize-money £18059

Going (Turf): Sf: 0-1 GS: 0-1 **Gd: 1-7 GF: 1-6** Fm: 0-0
Distance: 5f/6f: 0-1 7f-8f: 1-9 9f-13f: 1-5 14f+: 0-0
Track : LH: 0-2 **RH: 1-7 Tight: 1-5** Gall: 0-1
Aids: Bl: 0-0 **Vi: 1-2** Tstrap: 0-0
Best Rating: 93 5/01 Wind 1m67y good

He was starting to become disappointing, but a drop in the handicap and a first-time visor saw him score over a mile at Windsor in August.

Mananan McLir (USA)

101 **87**
2-y-o b c Royal Academy (USA)-St Lucinda (CAN) (St Jovite (USA))
J H M Gosden Action Bloodstock

Placings:0224010 **(5260)**
2001: 6^{0}GF, 6^{2}G, 6^{2}GF, 7^{4}GF, 7^{0}G, 8^{1}GF, 7^{0}GS

	Starts	1st	2nd	3rd	Win & Pl
Career Total (Turf)	7	1	2	0	7536

87 9/01 Kemp 1m D G-F £4465
Total win prize-money £4466

Going (Turf): Sf: 0-0 GS: 0-1 Gd: 0-2 **GF: 1-4** Fm: 0-0
Distance: 5f/6f: 0-3 **7f-8f: 1-4** 9f-13f: 0-0 14f+: 0-0
Track : LH: 0-0 **RH: 1-2** Tight: 0-0 Gall: 0-0
Aids: Bl: 0-0 **Vi: 1-2** Tstrap: 0-0
Best Rating: 87 9/01 Kemp 1m gd-fm

He showed some ability in maiden company in his early starts, but had the help of a first-time visor when making all to win at Kempton in September. Has been sold to race in the USA.

Mandelson (USA)

91(83) (40)**57**
2-y-o ch c Spinning World (USA)-Draconienne (USA) (Trempolino (USA))
Sir Mark Prescott Neil Greig - Osborne House Ii

Placings:060004 **(5130)**
2001: 7^{0}GS, 6^{6}HY, 6^{0}GF, 6^{0}SW, 7^{0}GF, 7^{4}HY

	Starts	1st	2nd	3rd	Win & Pl
Career Total (Turf)	5	0	0	0	0
Career Total (AW)	1	0	0	0	

Going (Turf): Sf: 0-2 GS: 0-1 Gd: 0-0 GF: 0-2 Fm: 0-0
Distance: 5f/6f: 0-3 7f-8f: 0-3 9f-13f: 0-0 14f+: 0-0
Track : LH: 0-1 RH: 0-0 Tight: 0-1 Gall: 0-0
Aids: Bl: 0-1 Vi: 0-0 Tstrap: 0-0
Best Rating: 64 8/01 NmkJ 6f gd-fm

A half-brother to a two-year-old winner in America. Not very big but well put together.

Manderina

58 **8**
2-y-o b f Mind Games-Millaine (Formidable (USA))
A Berry T G Holdcroft

Placings:500 **(4801)**
2001: 6^{5}G, 6^{0}GF, 5^{0}F

	Starts	1st	2nd	3rd	Win & Pl
Career Total (Turf)	3	0	0	0	0

Going (Turf): Sf: 0-0 GS: 0-0 Gd: 0-1 GF: 0-1 Fm: 0-1
Distance: 5f/6f: 0-3 7f-8f: 0-0 9f-13f: 0-0 14f+: 0-0
Track : LH: 0-1 RH: 0-1 Tight: 0-0 Gall: 0-0
Aids: Bl: 0-0 Vi: 0-0 Tstrap: 0-0
Best Rating: 8 9/01 Pont 5f firm

Mandoob

104 **64**
4-y-o b g Zafonic (USA)-Thaidah (CAN) (Vice Regent (CAN))
B R Johnson Kevin Nolan

Placings:5/0456-0001015 **(5465)**
2001: 12^{0}GF, 9^{0}GF, 9^{0}G, 6^{1}GF, 8^{0}G, 9^{1}HY, 10^{5}G

	Starts	1st	2nd	3rd	Win & Pl
Career Total (Turf)	12	2	0	0	6331

64 10/01 Nott 1m1f213yE(0-70)H HVY £3710
58 9/01 Brig 6f209y F G-F £2352
Total win prize-money £6062

Going (Turf): Sf: 1-1 GS: 0-0 Gd: 0-7 **GF: 1-4** Fm: 0-0
Distance: 5f/6f: 0-0 7f-8f: 1-4 9f-13f: 1-8 14f+: 0-0
Track : **LH: 2-4** RH: 0-6 Tight: 0-2 Gall: 0-0
Aids: Bl: 0-0 Vi: 0-0 Tstrap: 0-0
Best Rating: 64 10/01 Nott 1m1f213y heavy

He has changed stables this term, and landed a minor gamble in a seller at Brighton in September. Added a handicap in testing ground at Nottingham in October. Effective seven to ten furlongs.

Mandown

89 **66**
2-y-o b c Danehill Dancer (IRE)-Golden Decoy (Decoy Boy)
K McAuliffe E P Jameson

Placings:000 **(5487)**
2001: 5^{0}S, 7^{0}GS, 6^{0}HY

	Starts	1st	2nd	3rd	Win & Pl
Career Total (Turf)	3	0	0	0	

Going (Turf): Sf: 0-2 GS: 0-1 Gd: 0-0 GF: 0-0 Fm: 0-0
Distance: 5f/6f: 0-2 7f-8f: 0-1 9f-13f: 0-0 14f+: 0-0
Track : LH: 0-1 RH: 0-0 Tight: 0-0 Gall: 0-1
Aids: Bl: 0-0 Vi: 0-0 Tstrap: 0-0
Best Rating: 66 10/01 Donc 6f heavy

Quite a cheaply-bought late foal, has speed in his pedigree. Yet to race on ground better than good to soft.

Mandy's Collection

(87) (49)**65**
2-y-o ch f Forzando-Instinction (Never So Bold)
A G Newcombe Mrs Mandy McRoberts

Placings:00 **(5415)**
2001: 6^{0}G, 6^{0}SD

	Starts	1st	2nd	3rd	Win & Pl
Career Total (Turf)	1	0	0	0	
Career Total (AW)	1	0	0	0	

Going (Turf): Sf: 0-0 GS: 0-0 Gd: 0-1 GF: 0-0 Fm: 0-0
Distance: 5f/6f: 0-2 7f-8f: 0-0 9f-13f: 0-0 14f+: 0-0
Track : LH: 0-1 RH: 0-0 Tight: 0-1 Gall: 0-0
Aids: Bl: 0-0 Vi: 0-0 Tstrap: 0-0
Best Rating: 65 7/01 Kemp 6f good

Mangus (IRE)

(109) (58)**42**
7-y-o b g Mac's Imp (USA)-Holly Bird (Runnett)
K O Cunningham-Brown Danebury Racing Stables Limited

Placings:55443/22120506/0500101006044/420034033 0202014/650005000005-033240560403 **(5349)**
2001: 5^{0}SW, 5^{3}SW, 5^{3}SD, 5^{2}SD, 5^{4}GS, 5^{0}GF, 5^{5}SD, 5^{6}GF, 5^{0}SD, 5^{4}SW, 5^{0}G, 5^{3}SD

	Starts	1st	2nd	3rd	Win & Pl
Career Total (Turf)	42	2	3	4	11889
Career Total (AW)	24	2	4	3	13878

77	12/99	Wolv	5f	D(0-85)H	STD	£3740
74	6/98	Wolv	5f	D(0-80)H	STD	£3492
72	5/98	Ling	5f	E(0-70)H	G-F	£3002
72	4/97	Wwck	5f	E(0-70)H	G-F	£2940

Total win prize-money £13175

Going (Turf): Sf: 0-6 GS: 0-6 Gd: 0-10 **GF: 2-18** Fm: 0-2
Distance: **5f/6f: 4-66** 7f-8f: 0-0 9f-13f: 0-0 14f+: 0-0
Track : **LH: 3-36** RH: 0-4 **Tight: 2-23** Gall: 1-12
Aids: Bl: 0-0 Vi: 0-0 Tstrap: 0-0
Best Rating: 58 4/01 Ling 5f stand

A fair sort in modest company over the minimum trip, he is suited by fast ground on turf and can go on Fibresand too.

Maniatis

112 **99**
4-y-o b c Slip Anchor-Tamassos (Dance In Time (CAN))
P F I Cole Athos Christodoulou

Placings:0321-020220 **(4172)**
2001: 12^{0}S, 11^{2}F, 12^{0}G, 13^{2}G, 12^{2}G, 13^{0}G

	Starts	1st	2nd	3rd	Win & Pl
Career Total (Turf)	10	1	4	1	27340

92	10/00	Bath	1m3f144yD	G-S	£4033

Total win prize-money £4033

Going (Turf): Sf: 0-4 **GS: 1-1** Gd: 0-4 GF: 0-0 Fm: 0-1
Distance: 5f/6f: 0-0 7f-8f: 0-0 **9f-13f: 1-8** 14f+: 0-2
Track : **LH: 1-5** RH: 0-5 **Tight: 1-2** Gall: 0-5
Aids: Bl: 0-0 Vi: 0-0 Tstrap: 0-0
Best Rating: 99 8/01 Gdwd 1m4f good

Winner of a Bath maiden last season, he has run some fine races without winning this term, including when making nearly all the running at Glorious Goodwood. Suited by 12 furlongs and fast ground.

Manicani (IRE)

96 **78+**
3-y-o ch c Tagula (IRE)-Pluvia (USA) (Raise A Native)
I A Balding Robert Hitchins

Placings:0-52 **(0758)**
2001: 8^{5}HY, 7^{2}S

	Starts	1st	2nd	3rd	Win & Pl
Career Total (Turf)	3	0	1	0	1170

Going (Turf): Sf: 0-2 GS: 0-0 Gd: 0-1 GF: 0-0 Fm: 0-0
Distance: 5f/6f: 0-1 7f-8f: 0-1 9f-13f: 0-1 14f+: 0-0
Track : LH: 0-1 RH: 0-1 Tight: 0-0 Gall: 0-1
Aids: Bl: 0-0 Vi: 0-0 Tstrap: 0-0
Best Rating: 78 4/01 Kemp 7f soft

Manikato (USA)

96(98) (39)**38**
7-y-o b g Clever Trick (USA)-Pasampsi (USA) (Crow (FR))
R Curtis Mrs K M Curtis

Placings:404424020/0244065042**4/33444000/50**600/46 1530-44 **(2669)**
2001: 9^{4}F, 10^{4}G

	Starts	1st	2nd	3rd	Win & Pl
Career Total (Turf)	26	1	3	0	8377
Career Total (AW)	15	0	1	3	3471

37	8/00	Chep	1m14y	E(0-70)H	G-F	£2814

Total win prize-money £2814

Going (Turf): Sf: 0-1 GS: 0-3 Gd: 0-8 **GF: 1-9** Fm: 0-5
Distance: 5f/6f: 0-6 7f-8f: 0-15 **9f-13f: 1-20** 14f+: 0-0
Track : LH: 0-27 RH: 0-6 Tight: 0-23 Gall: 0-0
Aids: Bl: 0-0 Vi: 0-7 Tstrap: 0-0
Best Rating: 36 5/01 Leic 1m1f218y firm

Manileno

(86) (23)
7-y-o ch g K-Battery-Andalucia (Rheingold)
Miss S J Wilton John Pointon And Sons

Placings:45/0331113/**11/511640/00605** **(1997)**
2001: 14^{0}SD, 12^{0}SD, 12^{6}SD, 14^{0}SD, 14^{5}SD

	Starts	1st	2nd	3rd	Win & Pl
Career Total (Turf)	10	3	0	3	8783
Career Total (AW)	12	4	0	0	8848

62	2/99	Wolv	1m6f166yF	STD	£2067
55	2/99	Wolv	2m46y G	STD	£1446
73	6/98	Sthl	1m6f F	STD	£2532
74	6/98	Sthl	2m F	STD	£2553
65	7/97	Wwck	1m6f194yE(0-70)H	SFT	£3174
55	6/97	Ling	1m3f106yF(0-70)H	GD	£2277
48	5/97	Brig	1m3f196yG(0-60)H	FRM	£1984

Total win prize-money £16035

Going (Turf): Sf: 1-2 GS: 0-1 **Gd: 1-2** GF: 0-3 **Fm: 1-2**
Distance: 5f/6f: 0-0 7f-8f: 0-1 9f-13f: 2-8 **14f+: 5-13**
Track : **LH: 7-19** RH: 0-3 **Tight: 3-10** Gall: 0-1
Aids: Bl: 0-3 Vi: 0-0 Tstrap: 0-0
Best Rating: 23 5/01 Sthl 1m6f stand

Nowhere near as good as he was. Best form on Fibresand at around two miles.

Manon Lyn

89 **33**
3-y-o b f Awesome-Sea Challenger (Seaepic (USA))
D Burchell Lyn Phillips

Placings:00000 **(4734)**
2001: 8^{0}GF, 5^{0}G, 7^{0}G, 7^{0}GF, 8^{0}F

	Starts	1st	2nd	3rd	Win & Pl
Career Total (Turf)	5	0	0	0	

Going (Turf): Sf: 0-0 GS: 0-0 Gd: 0-2 GF: 0-2 Fm: 0-1
Distance: 5f/6f: 0-1 7f-8f: 0-2 9f-13f: 0-2 14f+: 0-0
Track : LH: 0-1 RH: 0-0 Tight: 0-0 Gall: 0-1
Aids: Bl: 0-0 Vi: 0-0 Tstrap: 0-0
Best Rating: 33 7/01 Chep 7f16y good

Manor From Heaven

76 **36**
3-y-o ch f Most Welcome-Manor Adventure (Smackover)
R Hannon Mrs Julie Martin

Placings:006 **(5522)**
2001: 8^{0}G, 8^{0}GF, 6^{6}HY

	Starts	1st	2nd	3rd	Win & Pl
Career Total (Turf)	3	0	0	0	0

Going (Turf): Sf: 0-1 GS: 0-0 Gd: 0-1 GF: 0-1 Fm: 0-0
Distance: 5f/6f: 0-1 7f-8f: 0-0 9f-13f: 0-2 14f+: 0-0
Track : LH: 0-0 RH: 0-1 Tight: 0-0 Gall: 0-0
Aids: Bl: 0-0 Vi: 0-0 Tstrap: 0-0
Best Rating: 36 9/01 Sand 1m14y good

Manor Lake

98 **60**
3-y-o b f Puissance-Harifa (Local Suitor (USA))
R F Johnson Houghton R F Johnson Houghton

Placings:5-00350660 **(3372)**
2001: 5^{0}S, 6^{0}HY, 5^{3}GF, 5^{5}GF, 7^{0}F, 6^{6}GF, 5^{6}GS, 5^{0}F

	Starts	1st	2nd	3rd	Win & Pl
Career Total (Turf)	9	0	0	1	416

Going (Turf): Sf: 0-3 GS: 0-1 Gd: 0-0 GF: 0-3 Fm: 0-2
Distance: 5f/6f: 0-6 7f-8f: 0-3 9f-13f: 0-0 14f+: 0-0
Track : LH: 0-3 RH: 0-0 Tight: 0-0 Gall: 0-2
Aids: Bl: 0-1 Vi: 0-0 Tstrap: 0-0
Best Rating: 60 5/01 Bath 5f11y gd-fm

Manorbier

103(107) (86)**98d**
5-y-o ch g Shalford (IRE)-La Pirouette (USA) (Kennedy Road (CAN))
K A Ryan Uncle Jacks Pub

Placings:61250/**0141**120414050-0550005 **(1827)**
2001: 5^{0}SD, 6^{5}SD, 6^{5}S, 6^{0}GS, 6^{0}S, 6^{0}GF, 6^{5}F

	Starts	1st	2nd	3rd	Win & Pl
Career Total (Turf)	19	3	2	0	26184
Career Total (AW)	6	2	0	0	3828

86	5/00	Thsk	6f	C(0-95)H	GD	£8216
75	3/00	Donc	6f	C(0-90)H	GD	£7735
61	3/00	Wolv	6f	G	STD	£1913
51	2/00	Wolv	5f	G	STD	£1913
79	8/98	Chep	5f16y	E	G-F	£3290

Total win prize-money £23069

Going (Turf): Sf: 0-3 GS: 0-3 **Gd: 2-8** GF: 1-3 Fm: 0-1
Distance: **5f/6f: 5-22** 7f-8f: 0-3 9f-13f: 0-0 14f+: 0-0
Track : **LH: 2-10** RH: 0-0 **Tight: 2-6** Gall: 0-1
Aids: Bl: 0-0 Vi: 0-0 Tstrap: 0-0
Best Rating: 96 4/01 NmkR 6f gd-sft

Useful sprinter, improved from winning sellers on Fibresand to running well in Pattern class in 2000. High in the weights as a result. Generally comes from off the pace.

Mantilla

101(99) (27d)**37**
4-y-o b f Son Pardo-Well Tried (IRE) (Thatching)
R Hollinshead Mrs A D Williams

Placings:534/023-555530000 **(4800)**
2001: 8^{5}SW, 9^{5}SW, 9^{5}SD, 7^{5}F, 7^{3}GF, 8^{0}G, 10^{0}G, 9^{0}GF, 10^{0}F

	Starts	1st	2nd	3rd	Win & Pl
Career Total (Turf)	8	0	0	2	829
Career Total (AW)	7	0	1	1	1433

Going (Turf): Sf: 0-2 GS: 0-0 Gd: 0-2 GF: 0-2 Fm: 0-2
Distance: 5f/6f: 0-3 7f-8f: 0-4 9f-13f: 0-8 14f+: 0-0
Track : LH: 0-9 RH: 0-3 Tight: 0-7 Gall: 0-0
Aids: Bl: 0-0 Vi: 0-0 Tstrap: 0-0
Best Rating: 37 6/01 Bevl 7f100y gd-fm

Mantles Pride

103(88) (75)**72**
6-y-o br g Petong-State Romance (Free State)
M Dods (J A Glover 30/10) Mrs C E Dods

Placings:520155/33000000320/35306101130/0041060 0500022010-40031042301100 **(5681)**
2001: 7^{4}GS, 7^{0}HY, 7^{0}GF, 8^{3}F, 7^{1}GF, 7^{0}GF, 7^{4}GF, 7^{2}GS, 8^{3}F, 7^{0}GF, 7^{1}GF, 7^{1}G, 7^{0}S, 8^{0}S

	Starts	1st	2nd	3rd	Win & Pl
Career Total (Turf)	58	9	5	8	57856
Career Total (AW)	1	0	0	0	

65	9/01	NmkR	7f	E	GD	£5330
69	9/01	Rdcr	7f	E(0-70)	G-F	£2996
70	6/01	Bev	7f100y	E(0-70)	G-F	£2637
74	10/00	Donc	7f	E	SFT	£3786
84	5/00	Donc	7f	C(0-100)H	G-S	£7475
79	9/99	Hayd	7f30y	C(0-90)H	G-F	£6970
76	8/99	Rdcr	7f	D(0-80)H	GD	£5238
69	7/99	Carl	6f206y	E(0-70)H	FRM	£2944
83	9/97	Folk	5f	D(0-85)	FRM	£3322

Total win prize-money £38061

Going (Turf): Sf: 1-13 GS: 1-7 Gd: 2-19 **GF: 3-13** Fm: 2-6
Distance: 5f/6f: 1-14 **7f-8f: 8-45** 9f-13f: 0-0 14f+: 0-0
Track : LH: 1-18 **RH: 2-6** Tight: 0-11 Gall: 0-2
Aids: **Bl: 8-36** Vi: 0-9 Tstrap: 0-0
Best Rating: 72 8/01 Thsk 1m firm

A decent handicapper and a true seven-furlong specialist, he wins in his turn. He is a shade quirky. Has a good season in 2001 winning three times.

Manuka Too (IRE)

101 **63**

3-y-o ch f First Trump-Kukri (Kris)

C F Wall The Lively Partners

Placings:0500-0323312 **(4183)**

2001: 7^{0}F, 9^{3}GF, 9^{2}G, 10^{3}GF, 11^{3}F, 14^{1}GS, 16^{2}GF

	Starts	1st	2nd	3rd	Win & Pl
Career Total (Turf)	11	1	2	3	5167

61 8/01 Yarm 1m6f17y F(0-75)H G-S £2422

Total win prize-money £2422

Going (Turf): Sf: 0-1 **GS: 1-1** Gd: 0-1 GF: 0-6 Fm: 0-2
Distance: 5f/6f: 0-1 7f-8f: 0-4 9f-13f: 0-4 **14f+: 1-2**
Track : **LH: 1-5** RH: 0-3 **Tight: 1-3** Gall: 0-1
Aids: Bl: 0-0 Vi: 0-0 Tstrap: 0-0
Best Rating: 63 8/01 Folk 2m93y gd-fm

Has been running well since faced with middle distances this season. Does not have a great deal in the way of acceleration.

Manzoni

106 (50)**67**

5-y-o b g Warrshan (USA)-Arc Empress Jane (IRE) (Rainbow Quest (USA))

M W Easterby Bodfari Stud Ltd

Placings:0500/0043122/0060010-211411060 **(5170)**

2001: 10^{2}F, 14^{1}G, 14^{1}GF, 11^{4}GF, 14^{1}GF, 15^{1}G, 14^{0}GF, 15^{6}S, 17^{0}GS

	Starts	1st	2nd	3rd	Win & Pl
Career Total (Turf)	25	5	3	0	20604
Career Total (AW)	2	1	0	1	2574

67 9/01 Ches 1m7f195yD(0-85)H GD £4407
53 8/01 Muss 1m6f E(0-75)H G-F £3080
49 6/01 Rdcr 1m6f19y F(0-60)H G-F £3528
52 6/01 Muss 1m6f F(0-60)H GD £2485
46 8/00 Muss 1m6f E(0-75)H G-F £3445
50 7/99 Sthl 1m4f F(0-60)H STD £2263

Total win prize-money £19209

Going (Turf): Sf: 0-4 GS: 0-4 Gd: 2-7 **GF: 3-8** Fm: 0-2
Distance: 5f/6f: 0-4 7f-8f: 0-1 9f-13f: 1-13 **14f+: 5-9**
Track : LH: 3-15 RH: 3-9 **Tight: 5-13** Gall: 0-2
Aids: **Bl: 1-2** Vi: 0-1 Tstrap: 0-0
Best Rating: 67 9/01 Ches 1m7f195y good

Improved stayer in 2001, winning four times on fast ground in the summer. Raised 15lb as a result, he is suited by forcing tactics.

Map Boy

61 **1**

3-y-o b g Chaddleworth (IRE)-Chaconia Girl (Bay Express)

Jamie Poulton (B R Johnson 24/6) M C Trevena

Placings:0-0 **(4446)**

2001: 9^{0}G

	Starts	1st	2nd	3rd	Win & Pl
Career Total (Turf)	2	0	0	0	

Going (Turf): Sf: 0-1 GS: 0-0 Gd: 0-1 GF: 0-0 Fm: 0-0
Distance: 5f/6f: 0-1 7f-8f: 0-0 9f-13f: 0-1 14f+: 0-0
Track : LH: 0-0 RH: 0-1 Tight: 0-0 Gall: 0-0
Aids: Bl: 0-0 Vi: 0-0 Tstrap: 0-0
Best Rating: 1 9/01 Sand 1m1f good

Maple House

91(84) (42)**55**

2-y-o ch f Emperor Fountain-Strathrusdale (Blazing Saddles (AUS))

M W Easterby Steve Hull

Placings:0024650 **(5253)**

2001: 5^{0}GF, 6^{0}F, 6^{2}F, **6**^{4}SD, 7^{6}G, 7^{5}GF, 6^{0}S

	Starts	1st	2nd	3rd	Win & Pl
Career Total (Turf)	6	0	1	0	915
Career Total (AW)	1	0	0	0	0

Going (Turf): Sf: 0-1 GS: 0-0 Gd: 0-1 GF: 0-2 Fm: 0-2
Distance: 5f/6f: 0-5 7f-8f: 0-2 9f-13f: 0-0 14f+: 0-0
Track : LH: 0-1 RH: 0-0 Tight: 0-0 Gall: 0-0
Aids: Bl: 0-0 Vi: 0-0 Tstrap: 0-0
Best Rating: 55 8/01 Muss 7f30y gd-fm

Maraami

91 **85**

2-y-o b f Selkirk (USA)-Tansy (Shareef Dancer (USA))

D R Loder Sheikh Mohammed

Placings:36 **(5372)**

2001: 6^{3}G, 6^{6}G

	Starts	1st	2nd	3rd	Win & Pl
Career Total (Turf)	2	0	0	1	864

Going (Turf): Sf: 0-0 GS: 0-0 Gd: 0-2 GF: 0-0 Fm: 0-0
Distance: 5f/6f: 0-2 7f-8f: 0-0 9f-13f: 0-0 14f+: 0-0
Track : LH: 0-0 RH: 0-0 Tight: 0-0 Gall: 0-0
Aids: Bl: 0-0 Vi: 0-0 Tstrap: 0-0
Best Rating: 85 10/01 NmkR 6f good

Ran well on her debut , but did not progress from there next time at Redcar on ground that was too soft.

Marabar

102 **80**

3-y-o b f Sri Pekan (USA)-Erbaya (IRE) (El Gran Senor (USA))

P J Makin Prof C D Green

Placings:63-13 **(4622)**

2001: 6^{1}GF, 6^{3}GF

	Starts	1st	2nd	3rd	Win & Pl
Career Total (Turf)	4	1	0	2	4761

77 8/01 Ling 6f D G-F £3598

Total win prize-money £3598

Going (Turf): Sf: 0-1 GS: 0-0 Gd: 0-0 **GF: 1-3** Fm: 0-0
Distance: **5f/6f: 1-2** 7f-8f: 0-2 9f-13f: 0-0 14f+: 0-0
Track : LH: 0-1 RH: 0-0 Tight: 0-0 Gall: 0-1
Aids: Bl: 0-0 Vi: 0-0 Tstrap: 0-0
Best Rating: 80 9/01 Nott 6f15y gd-fm

Showed ability at two and was off the track for 11 months before easily winning a Lingfield maiden in August.

Maragun (GER)

91 **52**

5-y-o b g General Assembly (USA)-Marcelia (GER) (Priamos (GER))

M C Pipe Stuart Mercer & Emlyn Hughes

Placings:4031411/00332106-0 **(1384)**

2001: 12^{0}S

	Starts	1st	2nd	3rd	Win & Pl
Career Total (Turf)	16	4	1	3	14794

8/00 Mulh 1m3f H £3774
11/99 Colo 1m1f55y H SFT £2888
10/99 Gels 1m1f H SFT £1985

Total win prize-money £10632

Going (Turf): Sf: 2-5 GS: 0-0 Gd: 1-5 GF: 0-0 Fm: 0-0
Distance: 5f/6f: 0-0 7f-8f: 0-4 **9f-13f: 4-12** 14f+: 0-0
Track : LH: 0-0 RH: 0-1 Tight: 0-1 Gall: 0-0
Aids: Bl: 0-0 Vi: 0-0 Tstrap: 0-0
Best Rating: 52 5/01 Sals 1m4f soft

Marakabei

93 **55**

3-y-o ch f Hernando (FR)-Kirsten (Kris)

R Guest Mrs Jane Poulter

Placings:8050 **(5448)**

2001: 10^{6}S, 8^{0}G, 12^{5}GF, 10^{0}HY

	Starts	1st	2nd	3rd	Win & Pl
Career Total (Turf)	4	0	0	0	0

Going (Turf): Sf: 0-2 GS: 0-0 Gd: 0-1 GF: 0-1 Fm: 0-0
Distance: 5f/6f: 0-0 7f-8f: 0-0 9f-13f: 0-4 14f+: 0-0
Track : LH: 0-2 RH: 0-1 Tight: 0-1 Gall: 0-1
Aids: Bl: 0-0 Vi: 0-0 Tstrap: 0-0
Best Rating: 55 8/01 Wind 1m67y good

Still a maiden and seems to be of moderate ability.

Marakash (IRE)

90 **72+**

2-y-o b c Ashkalani (IRE)-Marilaya (IRE) (Shernazar)

Sir Michael Stoute H H Aga Khan

Placings:4 **(5620)**

2001: 8^{4}GS

	Starts	1st	2nd	3rd	Win & Pl
Career Total (Turf)	1	0	0	0	286

Going (Turf): Sf: 0-0 GS: 0-1 Gd: 0-0 GF: 0-0 Fm: 0-0
Distance: 5f/6f: 0-0 7f-8f: 0-0 9f-13f: 0-1 14f+: 0-0
Track : LH: 0-1 RH: 0-0 Tight: 0-0 Gall: 0-0
Aids: Bl: 0-0 Vi: 0-0 Tstrap: 0-0
Best Rating: 72 11/01 Nott 1m54y gd-sft

Marani

110 **101**

3-y-o ch f Ashkalani (IRE)-Aquamarine (Shardari)

J H M Gosden K Abdulla

Placings:5-130 **(2827)**

2001: 9^{1}GF, 12^{3}GF, 11^{0}GS

	Starts	1st	2nd	3rd	Win & Pl
Career Total (Turf)	4	1	0	1	20920

85 5/01 Gdwd 1m1f D G-F £5395

Total win prize-money £5395

Going (Turf): Sf: 0-0 GS: 0-1 Gd: 0-1 **GF: 1-2** Fm: 0-0
Distance: 5f/6f: 0-0 7f-8f: 0-1 **9f-13f: 1-3** 14f+: 0-0
Track : LH: 0-2 **RH: 1-2 Tight: 1-1** Gall: 0-2
Aids: Bl: 0-0 Vi: 0-0 Tstrap: 0-0
Best Rating: 101 6/01 Asct 1m4f gd-fm

She looks potential Group class and is bred to be so, her dam being closely related to the St. Leger winner Toulon. Impressive when winning at Goodwood in May, she finished a fine third in the Ribblesdale next time on her first attempt over 12 furlongs and may well have been in season when disappointing in the Lancashire Oaks.

Maranilla (IRE)

96 **84**

2-y-o b c Desert King (IRE)-Queen Moranbon (USA) (Bering)

E J O'Neill Dr Karen Sanderson

Placings:562 **(5682)**

2001: 7^{5}GF, 7^{6}GF, 7^{2}S

	Starts	1st	2nd	3rd	Win & Pl
Career Total (Turf)	3	0	1	0	1458

Going (Turf): Sf: 0-1 GS: 0-0 Gd: 0-0 GF: 0-2 Fm: 0-0
Distance: 5f/6f: 0-0 7f-8f: 0-3 9f-13f: 0-0 14f+: 0-0
Track : LH: 0-1 RH: 0-0 Tight: 0-0 Gall: 0-0
Aids: Bl: 0-0 Vi: 0-0 Tstrap: 0-0
Best Rating: 84 11/01 Donc 7f soft

He has shown ability in three outings in maiden company and had no problem with the soft ground on his final start at Doncaster.

Marcassin

(61)
7-y-o b g Unfuwain (USA)-Coir 'A' Ghaill (Jalmood (USA))
Bob Jones Miss J M Rutherford

Placings:0 **(0053)**
2001: 12[0]SD

	Starts	1st	2nd	3rd	Win & Pl
Career Total (Turf)	0	0	0	0	
Career Total (AW)	1	0	0	0	

Going (Turf): Sf: 0-0 GS: 0-0 Gd: 0-0 GF: 0-0 Fm: 0-0
Distance: 5f/6f: 0-0 7f-8f: 0-0 9f-13f: 0-1 14f+: 0-0
Track : LH: 0-1 RH: 0-0 Tight: 0-0 Gall: 0-0
Aids: Bl: 0-0 Vi: 0-0 Tstrap: 0-0

Marching Orders (IRE)

82 **52**
5-y-o b g Nashwan (USA)-Minstrels Folly (USA) (The Minstrel (CAN))
R Ford Richard Ford

Placings:35214010/000600-0 **(4572)**
2001: 10[0]HY

	Starts	1st	2nd	3rd	Win & Pl
Career Total (Turf)	15	2	1	1	10436

86 10/99 Cork 1m (60-90)H Y-S £5865
86 8/99 Fair 1m1f GD £3036
Total win prize-money £8901

Going (Turf): Sf: 0-4 GS: 0-2 **Gd: 1-3** GF: 0-2 Fm: 0-0
Distance: 5f/6f: 0-0 7f-8f: 1-3 9f-13f: 1-12 14f+: 0-0
Track : LH: 0-5 **RH: 2-8** Tight: 0-2 Gall: 0-1
Aids: **Bl: 1-5** Vi: 0-1 Tstrap: 0-0
Best Rating: 35 9/01 Hayd 1m2f120y heavy

Marcosa

(84) (56)**36**
2-y-o b f Cosmonaut-Maria Cappuccini (Siberian Express (USA))
J G Given D Bass

Placings:604 **(3574)**
2001: 6[6]SD, 6[0]SD, 6[4]GF

	Starts	1st	2nd	3rd	Win & Pl
Career Total (Turf)	1	0	0	0	0
Career Total (AW)	2	0	0	0	0

Going (Turf): Sf: 0-0 GS: 0-0 Gd: 0-0 GF: 0-1 Fm: 0-0
Distance: 5f/6f: 0-2 7f-8f: 0-1 9f-13f: 0-0 14f+: 0-0
Track : LH: 0-2 RH: 0-0 Tight: 0-1 Gall: 0-0
Aids: Bl: 0-0 Vi: 0-0 Tstrap: 0-0
Best Rating: 56 6/01 Wolv 6f stand

Marcovina (IRE)

87 **44**
3-y-o ch g Erin's Isle-Irish Call (USA) (Irish River (FR))
M Todhunter (J S Bolger 19/5) Ugm Racing Club

Placings:000-500 **(3693)**
2001: 12[5]HY, 12[0]G, 13[0]G

	Starts	1st	2nd	3rd	Win & Pl
Career Total (Turf)	6	0	0	0	

Going (Turf): Sf: 0-3 GS: 0-0 Gd: 0-2 GF: 0-0 Fm: 0-0
Distance: 5f/6f: 0-3 7f-8f: 0-0 9f-13f: 0-2 14f+: 0-1
Track : LH: 0-1 RH: 0-0 Tight: 0-1 Gall: 0-0
Aids: Bl: 0-1 Vi: 0-0 Tstrap: 0-0
Best Rating: 44 5/01 Clon 1m4f good

Marcus Aurelius (IRE)

100 **87**
2-y-o b c Alzao (USA)-Kaguyahime (Distant Relative)
T D Barron C A Washbourn

Placings:212 **(5378)**
2001: 5[2]GF, 5[1]G, 5[2]S

	Starts	1st	2nd	3rd	Win & Pl
Career Total (Turf)	3	1	2	0	7216

82 9/01 Bevl 5f D GD £4225
Total win prize-money £4225

Going (Turf): Sf: 0-1 GS: 0-0 **Gd: 1-1** GF: 0-1 Fm: 0-0
Distance: **5f/6f: 1-3** 7f-8f: 0-0 9f-13f: 0-0 14f+: 0-0
Track : LH: 0-1 RH: 0-0 Tight: 0-0 Gall: 0-0
Aids: Bl: 0-0 Vi: 0-0 Tstrap: 0-0
Best Rating: 87 10/01 Catt 5f soft

His dam is a half-sister to St James's Palace Stakes winner Bijou d'Inde. He got off the mark when taking advantage of a good draw at Beverley, and will stay further.

Marcus Maximus (USA)

94(95) (75)**85**
6-y-o ch g Woodman (USA)-Star Pastures (Northfields (USA))
N A Callaghan N A Callaghan

Placings:114/01/63-000650 **(2133)**
2001: 12[0]S, 10[0]G, 13[0]GF, 10[6]GF, 12[5]GF, 10[0]GF

	Starts	1st	2nd	3rd	Win & Pl
Career Total (Turf)	12	3	0	0	19507
Career Total (AW)	1	0	0	1	564

119 5/99 Newc 1m4f93y C FRM £5658
105 9/98 Donc 1m2f60y B GD £9600
77 7/98 Yarm 1m3f101yD G-F £3557
Total win prize-money £18816

Going (Turf): Sf: 0-2 GS: 0-0 **Gd: 1-4 GF: 1-5 Fm: 1-1**
Distance: 5f/6f: 0-0 7f-8f: 0-0 **9f-13f: 3-12** 14f+: 0-1
Track : **LH: 3-8** RH: 0-3 Tight: 1-3 **Gall: 2-8**
Aids: Bl: 0-0 Vi: 0-0 Tstrap: 0-0
Best Rating: 85 5/01 Newb 1m2f6y gd-fm

Mare Of Wetwang

97(91) (33)**45**
3-y-o ch f River Falls-Kudos Blue (Elmaamul (USA))
J D Bethell Richard Whiteley

Placings:60000025-40425051 **(4422)**
2001: 8[4]SD, 8[0]SD, 11[4]SD, 12[2]S, 9[5]G, 14[0]F, 11[5]GF, 10[1]GF

	Starts	1st	2nd	3rd	Win & Pl
Career Total (Turf)	11	1	1	0	3506
Career Total (AW)	5	0	1	0	658

38 9/01 Ripn 1m2f F(0-60)H G-F £2754
Total win prize-money £2755

Going (Turf): Sf: 0-1 GS: 0-1 Gd: 0-5 **GF: 1-3** Fm: 0-1
Distance: 5f/6f: 0-4 7f-8f: 0-6 **9f-13f: 1-5** 14f+: 0-1
Track : LH: 0-8 **RH: 1-4 Tight: 1-4** Gall: 0-1
Aids: Bl: 0-0 Vi: 0-0 Tstrap: 0-0
Best Rating: 40 5/01 Bevl 1m1f207y good

Plating class. Only win came in an apprentice seller at Ripon at the back-end of 2001 season. Stays a mile and a half. Acts on a sound surface. Handles soft.

Marechal George

94 **78**
2-y-o b/br c Deerhound (USA)-Lady Of Limerick (IRE) (Thatching)
A Berry Chris & Antonia Deuters

Placings:6053150340 **(5102)**
2001: 6[6]GF, 6[0]GS, 5[5]F, 5[3]GF, 5[1]GF, 5[5]F, 5[0]GF, 5[3]F, 6[4]GF, 5[0]GS

	Starts	1st	2nd	3rd	Win & Pl
Career Total (Turf)	10	1	0	2	4209

78 8/01 Catt 5f F G-F £2359
Total win prize-money £2359

Going (Turf): Sf: 0-0 GS: 0-2 Gd: 0-0 **GF: 1-5** Fm: 0-3
Distance: **5f/6f: 1-8** 7f-8f: 0-2 9f-13f: 0-0 14f+: 0-0
Track : LH: 0-0 RH: 0-0 Tight: 0-0 Gall: 0-0
Aids: Bl: 0-0 Vi: 0-0 Tstrap: 0-0
Best Rating: 78 9/01 Chep 5f16y firm

Winner of a Catterick maiden at the minimum trip on fast ground, he has struggled in nurseries since. Acts over five furlongs.

Marengo

(101) (52)**48**
7-y-o b g Never So Bold-Born To Dance (Dancing Brave (USA))
M J Polglase Mr Androlia,Mrs Reeve,Dr Cody,Mr Young

Placings:300/20326050000/11143500/0200000650340 530103/003062232150402400006365000105043-3200312540565505002016004320 **(5630)**
2001: 6[3]SD, 7[2]SD, 6[0]SD, 6[0]SW, 6[3]SD, 6[1]SD, 7[2]SW, 6[5]SD, 5[4]SD, 6[0]SD, 6[5]HY, 6[6]SD, 7[5]GF, 6[5]GF, 6[0]SD, 6[5]SD, 5[0]GF, 5[0]GS, 7[2]SD, 6[0]SD, 5[1]GF, 5[6]G, 6[0]SD, 6[0]GS, 6[4]G, 7[3]G, 5[2]SD, 6[0]G

	Starts	1st	2nd	3rd	Win & Pl
Career Total (Turf)	56	3	5	7	21802
Career Total (AW)	46	5	6	6	21120

42 8/01 Wwck 5f110y F G-F £2430
58 2/01 Sthl 6f G STD £1890
56 9/00 Sthl 6f F(0-60)H STD £2016
63 5/00 Donc 6f E G-S £2522
56 12/99 Sthl 6f D(0-85)H STD £5017
65 4/98 Epsm 6f C(0-95)H SFT £6937
66 4/98 Wolv 6f E(0-70)H STD £2709
53 3/98 Sthl 6f D(0-75)H STD £3387
Total win prize-money £26910

Going (Turf): Sf: 1-7 GS: 1-14 Gd: 0-14 **GF: 1-15** Fm: 0-5
Distance: **5f/6f: 8-87** 7f-8f: 0-14 9f-13f: 0-0 14f+: 0-0
Track : **LH: 6-64** RH: 0-5 **Tight: 2-23** Gall: 0-6
Aids: Bl: 0-0 Vi: 0-4 Tstrap: 0-0
Best Rating: 59 1/01 Sthl 6f stand

A regular on the Fibresand, he wins in his turn and also managed to win an apprentice claimer on turf at Warwick during the summer. Best at six furlongs.

Margaret's Dancer

85(52) (35)**21**
6-y-o b g Rambo Dancer (CAN)-Cateryne (Ballymoss)
J L Eyre J Bladen

Placings:00400000/00313011020/04020006550/00610 30-00000 **(3276)**
2001: 8[0]GS, 7[0]GF, 8[0]GF, 8[0]GF, 8[0]F

	Starts	1st	2nd	3rd	Win & Pl
Career Total (Turf)	36	4	2	3	15171
Career Total (AW)	6	0	0	0	

46 8/00 Thsk 1m F(0-60)H GD £3027
62 9/98 Bevl 1m100y D(0-75)H G-F £3824
57 9/98 Thsk 1m F GD £2705
49 6/98 Pont 1m4y F SFT £2469
Total win prize-money £12027

Going (Turf): Sf: 1-10 GS: 0-5 **Gd: 2-6** GF: 1-14 Fm: 0-1
Distance: 5f/6f: 0-6 7f-8f: 2-17 9f-13f: 2-19 14f+: 0-0
Track : **LH: 3-21** RH: 1-10 **Tight: 2-12** Gall: 0-3
Aids: Bl: 0-5 Vi: 0-0 **Tstrap: 1-22**
Best Rating: 21 6/01 Newc 1m gd-fm

Margot

87 **36**
3-y-o b f Sadler's Wells (USA)-Glatisant (Rainbow Quest (USA))
J H M Gosden Ms Emily Oppenheimer

Placings:00 (5464)
2001: 10^{0}G, 11^{0}G

	Starts	1st	2nd	3rd	Win & Pl
Career Total (Turf)	2	0	0	0	

Going (Turf): Sf: 0-0 GS: 0-0 Gd: 0-2 GF: 0-0 Fm: 0-0
Distance: 5f/6f: 0-0 7f-8f: 0-0 9f-13f: 0-2 14f+: 0-0
Track : LH: 0-2 RH: 0-0 Tight: 0-2 Gall: 0-0
Aids: Bl: 0-1 Vi: 0-0 Tstrap: 0-0
Best Rating: 36 10/01 Bath 1m3f144y good

Marhoob (USA)

111 (77)**114**
3-y-o b c Mr Prospector (USA)-Flagbird (USA) (Nureyev (USA))
Saeed Bin Suroor Godolphin

Placings:10126 (5362)
2001: 8^{1}FT, 9^{0}FT, 10^{1}G, 9^{2}G, 9^{6}GS

	Starts	1st	2nd	3rd	Win & Pl
Career Total (Turf)	3	1	1	0	12459
Career Total (AW)	2	1	0	0	4554

114	8/01	Epsm	1m2f18y	C	GD	£6634
	2/01	Ndas	1m		FST	£4554

Total win prize-money £11188

Going (Turf): Sf: 0-0 GS: 0-1 **Gd: 1-2** GF: 0-0 Fm: 0-0
Distance: 5f/6f: 0-0 7f-8f: 1-1 9f-13f: 1-4 14f+: 0-0
Track : **LH: 1-1** RH: 0-1 **Tight: 1-2** Gall: 0-0
Aids: Bl: 0-0 Vi: 0-0 **Tstrap: 1-3**
Best Rating: 114 8/01 Epsm 1m2f18y good

He won a mile maiden at Nad Al Sheba, finished well beaten behind Express Tour in the strongly contested UAE Derby. Having his first run since when impressing in a conditions race at Epsom. Disappointed at Newmarket in Listed company two runs later but could have found the ground a bit on the easy side for him. Suited by ten furlongs and a sound surface.

Mariana

(93) (20)**29**
6-y-o ch m Anshan-Maria Cappuccini (Siberian Express (USA))
T T Clement C Holcroft

Placings:305000/**4240**040002**000**/**33**4040000/**5040**003 030000-00 (0099)
2001: 11^{0}SD, 12^{0}SD

	Starts	1st	2nd	3rd	Win & Pl
Career Total (Turf)	21	0	1	2	1148
Career Total (AW)	22	0	1	3	2199

Going (Turf): Sf: 0-2 GS: 0-7 Gd: 0-7 GF: 0-3 Fm: 0-2
Distance: 5f/6f: 0-8 7f-8f: 0-22 9f-13f: 0-11 14f+: 0-2
Track : LH: 0-32 RH: 0-1 Tight: 0-15 Gall: 0-4
Aids: Bl: 0-3 Vi: 0-12 Tstrap: 0-0
Best Rating: 20 1/01 Sthl 1m3f stand

Marie De Court

78 **37**
2-y-o b f Muhtarram (USA)-Marie De Sologne (Lashkari)
M G Quinlan Mrs C A Dyke

Placings:000 (5128)
2001: 7^{0}GF, 7^{0}F, 6^{0}HY

	Starts	1st	2nd	3rd	Win & Pl
Career Total (Turf)	3	0	0	0	

Going (Turf): Sf: 0-1 GS: 0-0 Gd: 0-0 GF: 0-1 Fm: 0-1
Distance: 5f/6f: 0-1 7f-8f: 0-2 9f-13f: 0-0 14f+: 0-0
Track : LH: 0-1 RH: 0-0 Tight: 0-0 Gall: 0-0
Aids: Bl: 0-0 Vi: 0-0 Tstrap: 0-0
Best Rating: 37 8/01 Wwck 7f26y gd-fm

A half-sister to useful french filly Minervitta who won over ten furlongs. Unplaced so far in three starts.

Marienbard (IRE)

112 **119**
4-y-o b h Caerleon (USA)-Marienbad (FR) (Darshaan)
Saeed Bin Suroor Godolphin

Placings:111262-15230 (5735a)
2001: 13^{1}GF, 20^{5}GF, 12^{2}GS, 14^{3}GF, 16^{0}GS

	Starts	1st	2nd	3rd	Win & Pl
Career Total (Turf)	11	4	3	1	191265

110	5/01	York	1m5f194yA	G-F	£78300
109	7/00	Hayd	1m3f200yA	G-F	£15015
93	6/00	Wind	1m3f135yC	G-F	£7566
70	6/00	Leic	1m3f183yD	G-S	£3984

Total win prize-money £104866

Going (Turf): Sf: 0-1 GS: 1-3 Gd: 0-1 **GF: 3-6** Fm: 0-0
Distance: 5f/6f: 0-0 7f-8f: 0-0 **9f-13f: 3-6** 14f+: 1-5
Track : **LH: 2-6** RH: 1-3 Tight: 1-1 Gall: 1-5
Aids: Bl: 0-2 **Vi: 1-3** Tstrap: 0-0
Best Rating: 119 8/01 Deau 1m4f110y gd-sft

Unraced at two, he won his first three starts last season in progressively better company and was not disgraced when in the frame in both the Great Voltigeur and Perpetual Stakes. He took the Yorkshire Cup first time this season, but ran like a non-stayer in the Ascot Gold Cup. Best with give in the ground.

Marigliano (USA)

89 (69)**57**
8-y-o b g Riverman (USA)-Mount Holyoke (Golden Fleece (USA))
K A Morgan T R Pryke,B Jones,M Scaife,S Alcock

Placings:3/313/0/4131**0**300240/06/0-0 (1279)
2001: 9^{0}G

	Starts	1st	2nd	3rd	Win & Pl
Career Total (Turf)	18	2	1	5	10022
Career Total (AW)	2	1	0	0	2077

69	7/98	Sthl	7f	F	STD	£2077
73	6/98	Muss	7f30y	F	SFT	£2302
69	5/96	Bevl	7f100y	D	G-F	£3561

Total win prize-money £7941

Going (Turf): Sf: 1-4 GS: 0-2 Gd: 0-4 **GF: 1-7** Fm: 0-1
Distance: 5f/6f: 0-1 **7f-8f: 3-14** 9f-13f: 0-5 14f+: 0-0
Track : LH: 1-6 **RH: 2-3 Tight: 1-1** Gall: 0-2
Aids: Bl: 0-0 Vi: 0-0 Tstrap: 0-0
Best Rating: 39 5/01 Nott 1m1f213y good

Mariinsky

105 **90**
2-y-o b c Royal Applause-Mainly Dry (The Brianstan)
B J Meehan Mr & Mrs David Brown

Placings:414 (4713)
2001: 5^{4}S, 5^{1}GF, 5^{4}G

	Starts	1st	2nd	3rd	Win & Pl
Career Total (Turf)	3	1	0	0	6991

90	8/01	Ling	5f	D	G-F	£4241

Total win prize-money £4241

Going (Turf): Sf: 0-1 GS: 0-0 Gd: 0-1 **GF: 1-1** Fm: 0-0
Distance: **5f/6f: 1-3** 7f-8f: 0-0 9f-13f: 0-0 14f+: 0-0
Track : LH: 0-0 RH: 0-0 Tight: 0-0 Gall: 0-0
Aids: Bl: 0-0 Vi: 0-0 Tstrap: 0-0
Best Rating: 90 9/01 Donc 5f good

A half-brother to several good sprinters including Bolshoi, he showed ability in soft ground on his debut, but looked much more effective on faster ground when winning at Lingfield next time and ran a cracker in the Flying Childers.

Marika

110 **94**
3-y-o b f Marju (IRE)-Nordica (Northfields (USA))
B W Hills O F Waller

Placings:5-513 (2970)
2001: 11^{5}GF, 8^{1}GF, 8^{3}G

	Starts	1st	2nd	3rd	Win & Pl
Career Total (Turf)	4	1	0	1	5738

85	6/01	Hayd	1m30y	D	G-F	£4433

Total win prize-money £4433

Going (Turf): Sf: 0-0 GS: 0-0 Gd: 0-1 **GF: 1-3** Fm: 0-0
Distance: 5f/6f: 0-1 7f-8f: 0-1 **9f-13f: 1-2** 14f+: 0-1
Track : **LH: 1-2** RH: 0-1 Tight: 0-1 Gall: 0-1
Aids: Bl: 0-0 Vi: 0-0 Tstrap: 0-0
Best Rating: 94 7/01 NmkJ 1m good

She showed ability in her only start at two, but faced a stiff task in the Cheshire Oaks on her reappearance. She made no mistake in a Haydock maiden next time and looks progressive. Stays a mile. Acts on fast ground.

Marino Street

96(97) (42)**59**
8-y-o b m Totem (USA)-Demerger (Dominion)
B A McMahon Roy Penton

Placings:543**5252**/**3252253503**531654050**600**/0320**604** 000/**4033053**343020040/65112560/211566201-**6**5006 (2521)
2001: 5^{6}SD, 6^{5}SD, 6^{0}F, 5^{0}G, 5^{6}GF

	Starts	1st	2nd	3rd	Win & Pl
Career Total (Turf)	48	5	5	5	20523
Career Total (AW)	29	1	5	6	8333

42	11/00	Sthl	5f	E(0-70)H	STD	£2226
54	6/00	Wwck	5f	E(0-70)H	G-F	£2980
51	6/00	Nott	6f15y	F(0-60)H	G-F	£2593
43	7/99	Hayd	5f	E(0-70)H	G-S	£2766
37	6/99	Wwck	5f	E(0-70)H	G-F	£3052
48	7/96	Leic	5f2y	F	GD	£2571

Total win prize-money £16190

Going (Turf): Sf: 0-2 GS: 1-4 Gd: 1-10 **GF: 3-18** Fm: 0-11
Distance: **5f/6f: 5-58** 7f-8f: 1-15 9f-13f: 0-1 14f+: 0-0
Track : **LH: 2-40** RH: 0-4 Tight: 0-27 **Gall: 2-11**
Aids: Bl: 0-5 **Vi: 1-32** Tstrap: 0-0
Best Rating: 49 6/01 Leic 5f218y good

She shows only modest form on turf and sand these days.

Marino Tino (IRE)

42
2-y-o ch f Fayruz-Zestino (Shack (USA))
C Weedon Colin Weedon

Placings:0 (2937)
2001: 6^{0}GF

	Starts	1st	2nd	3rd	Win & Pl
Career Total (Turf)	1	0	0	0	

Going (Turf): Sf: 0-0 GS: 0-0 Gd: 0-0 GF: 0-1 Fm: 0-0
Distance: 5f/6f: 0-1 7f-8f: 0-0 9f-13f: 0-0 14f+: 0-0
Track : LH: 0-0 RH: 0-0 Tight: 0-0 Gall: 0-0
Aids: Bl: 0-0 Vi: 0-0 Tstrap: 0-0
Best Rating: 42 7/01 Ling 6f gd-fm

Marino Wood (IRE)

91 **55**
2-y-o ch f Woodpas (USA)-Forgren (IRE) (Thatching)
J S Moore Ernest H Moore

Placings:34300530 (4184)
2001: 5^{3}F, 5^{4}GF, 5^{3}F, 6^{0}G, 5^{0}GS, 5^{5}GF, 5^{3}GF, 5^{0}GF

	Starts	1st	2nd	3rd	Win & Pl
Career Total (Turf)	8	0	0	3	963

Going (Turf): Sf: 0-0 GS: 0-1 Gd: 0-1 GF: 0-4 Fm: 0-2
Distance: 5f/6f: 0-8 7f-8f: 0-0 9f-13f: 0-0 14f+: 0-0
Track : LH: 0-1 RH: 0-0 Tight: 0-0 Gall: 0-1
Aids: Bl: 0-0 Vi: 0-0 Tstrap: 0-0
Best Rating: 55 8/01 Bath 5f11y gd-fm

Marion Haste (IRE)

91 **60**

2-y-o ch f Ali-Royal (IRE)-Coryana (Sassafras (FR))
A Berry Mrs Julie Mitchell

Placings:13650P00 **(5270)**
2001: 5^{1}HY, 5^{3}F, 5^{6}G, 5^{5}G, 6^{0}GS, 6^{P}HY, 5^{0}GS, 6^{0}HY

	Starts	1st	2nd	3rd	Win & Pl
Career Total (Turf)	8	1	0	1	2740

58 5/01 Nott 5f13y F HVY £2327
Total win prize-money £2328

Going (Turf): Sf: 1-3 GS: 0-2 Gd: 0-2 GF: 0-0 Fm: 0-1
Distance: **5f/6f: 1-8** 7f-8f: 0-0 9f-13f: 0-0 14f+: 0-0
Track : LH: 0-1 RH: 0-0 Tight: 0-0 Gall: 0-0
Aids: Bl: 0-0 Vi: 0-0 Tstrap: 0-0
Best Rating: 60 10/01 NmkR 5f gd-sft

Got off the mark at the first time of asking, but has since been well held. Acts over five furlongs and is suited by heavy ground.

Mariska

90 **72**

2-y-o b f Magic Ring (IRE)-Prima Silk (Primo Dominie)
N A Callaghan Norcroft Park Stud

Placings:54066 **(5331)**
2001: 6^{5}GS, 6^{4}F, 6^{0}G, 5^{6}GS, 5^{6}HY

	Starts	1st	2nd	3rd	Win & Pl
Career Total (Turf)	5	0	0	0	0

Going (Turf): Sf: 0-1 GS: 0-2 Gd: 0-1 GF: 0-0 Fm: 0-1
Distance: 5f/6f: 0-4 7f-8f: 0-1 9f-13f: 0-0 14f+: 0-0
Track : LH: 0-1 RH: 0-0 Tight: 0-0 Gall: 0-0
Aids: Bl: 0-0 Vi: 0-0 Tstrap: 0-0
Best Rating: 72 9/01 Donc 6f good

Maritsa (IRE)

94 **53**

3-y-o b f Danehill (USA)-Marwell (Habitat)
Sir Mark Prescott Sir Edmund Loder

Placings:3 **(2569)**
2001: 6^{3}GF

	Starts	1st	2nd	3rd	Win & Pl
Career Total (Turf)	1	0	0	1	786

Going (Turf): Sf: 0-0 GS: 0-0 Gd: 0-0 GF: 0-1 Fm: 0-0
Distance: 5f/6f: 0-1 7f-8f: 0-0 9f-13f: 0-0 14f+: 0-0
Track : LH: 0-0 RH: 0-0 Tight: 0-0 Gall: 0-0
Aids: Bl: 0-1 Vi: 0-0 Tstrap: 0-0
Best Rating: 53 6/01 Newc 6f gd-fm

Maritun Lad

(108) (59)**54d**

4-y-o b g Presidium-Girl Next Door (Local Suitor (USA))
D Shaw M G Vines

Placings:0654/3164006234-0000 **(2170)**
2001: 5^{0}SD, 5^{0}SD, 5^{0}G, 5^{0}SD

	Starts	1st	2nd	3rd	Win & Pl
Career Total (Turf)	5	0	0	0	0
Career Total (AW)	13	1	1	2	4618

60 3/00 Wolv 5f D STD £2704
Total win prize-money £2704

Going (Turf): Sf: 0-1 GS: 0-0 Gd: 0-4 GF: 0-0 Fm: 0-0
Distance: **5f/6f: 1-17** 7f-8f: 0-1 9f-13f: 0-0 14f+: 0-0
Track : **LH: 1-10** RH: 0-1 **Tight: 1-10** Gall: 0-1
Aids: **Bl: 1-12** Vi: 0-2 Tstrap: 0-0
Best Rating: 38 1/01 Wolv 5f stand

Marjeune

(98) (62d)**53**

4-y-o b f Marju (IRE)-Ann Veronica (IRE) (Sadler's Wells (USA))
J G Portman (J G Smyth-Osbourne 1/10) The Breakaways

Placings:50041/02330-20046006 **(5044)**
2001: 16^{2}SD, 12^{0}S, 14^{0}HY, 16^{4}SD, 16^{6}GF, 16^{0}GF, 12^{0}S, 14^{6}SD

	Starts	1st	2nd	3rd	Win & Pl
Career Total (Turf)	15	1	1	2	5963
Career Total (AW)	3	0	1	0	666

65 10/99 Nott 1m1f213yE(0-75)H SFT £3139
Total win prize-money £3139

Going (Turf): Sf: 1-7 GS: 0-0 Gd: 0-2 GF: 0-6 Fm: 0-0
Distance: 5f/6f: 0-0 7f-8f: 0-3 **9f-13f: 1-7** 14f+: 0-8
Track : **LH: 1-11** RH: 0-4 Tight: 0-3 Gall: 0-1
Aids: Bl: 0-1 Vi: 0-0 Tstrap: 0-0
Best Rating: 63 4/01 Sthl 2m stand

Marjurita (IRE)

98 **66**

2-y-o b f Marju (IRE)-Unfuwaanah (Unfuwain (USA))
N P Littmoden Paul J Dixon

Placings:63005310 **(5487)**
2001: 6^{6}GF, 6^{3}GF, 5^{0}GF, 5^{0}GF, 5^{5}G, 5^{3}GF, 6^{1}G, 6^{0}HY

	Starts	1st	2nd	3rd	Win & Pl
Career Total (Turf)	8	1	0	2	5384

66 9/01 Haml 6f5y D(0-85) GD £4290
Total win prize-money £4290

Going (Turf): Sf: 0-1 GS: 0-0 **Gd: 1-2** GF: 0-5 Fm: 0-0
Distance: 5f/6f: 0-7 **7f-8f: 1-1** 9f-13f: 0-0 14f+: 0-0
Track : LH: 0-3 RH: 0-0 Tight: 0-1 Gall: 0-0
Aids: Bl: 0-0 Vi: 0-0 Tstrap: 0-0
Best Rating: 76 6/01 Pont 6f gd-fm

She did not seem to stay six furlongs early in her career, but got stronger with time and stayed every yard of the trip to win a Hamilton nursery in September.

Mark It

79 **55**

2-y-o b g Botanic (USA)-Everdene (Bustino)
Mrs A J Perrett S P Tindall

Placings:5 **(5459)**
2001: 8^{5}G

	Starts	1st	2nd	3rd	Win & Pl
Career Total (Turf)	1	0	0	0	0

Going (Turf): Sf: 0-0 GS: 0-0 Gd: 0-1 GF: 0-0 Fm: 0-0
Distance: 5f/6f: 0-0 7f-8f: 0-0 9f-13f: 0-1 14f+: 0-0
Track : LH: 0-1 RH: 0-0 Tight: 0-1 Gall: 0-0
Aids: Bl: 0-0 Vi: 0-0 Tstrap: 0-0
Best Rating: 55 10/01 Bath 1m5y good

Mark Of Prophet (IRE)

96 **59**

6-y-o b g Scenic-Sure Flyer (IRE) (Sure Blade (USA))
E Stanners P Cunningham

Placings:050/0021021/4-5 **(2268)**
2001: 12^{5}G

	Starts	1st	2nd	3rd	Win & Pl
Career Total (Turf)	12	2	2	0	13698

75 10/98 NmkR 1m6f C(0-95)H GD £7700
72 8/98 Leic 1m3f183yE(0-70) G-F £2805
Total win prize-money £10505

Going (Turf): Sf: 0-2 GS: 0-0 **Gd: 1-6 GF: 1-4** Fm: 0-0
Distance: 5f/6f: 0-0 7f-8f: 0-4 9f-13f: 1-6 14f+: 1-2
Track : LH: 0-2 **RH: 2-7** Tight: 0-2 **Gall: 1-4**
Aids: Bl: 0-0 Vi: 0-0 Tstrap: 0-0
Best Rating: 59 6/01 Thsk 1m4f good

Mark Of Respect

77 **52**

2-y-o b f Mark Of Esteem (IRE)-Bassmaat (USA) (Cadeaux Genereux)
B J Meehan Total (bloodstock) Ltd

Placings:000 **(3955)**
2001: 7^{0}GF, 7^{0}G, 6^{0}GF

	Starts	1st	2nd	3rd	Win & Pl
Career Total (Turf)	3	0	0	0	

Going (Turf): Sf: 0-0 GS: 0-0 Gd: 0-1 GF: 0-2 Fm: 0-0
Distance: 5f/6f: 0-0 7f-8f: 0-3 9f-13f: 0-0 14f+: 0-0
Track : LH: 0-0 RH: 0-1 Tight: 0-0 Gall: 0-1
Aids: Bl: 0-0 Vi: 0-0 Tstrap: 0-0
Best Rating: 52 7/01 Kemp 7f gd-fm

Mark One

103(86) (29)**79**

3-y-o b f Mark Of Esteem (IRE)-One Wild Oat (Shareef Dancer (USA))
J G Burns (B W Hills 9/7) Anthony F O'Callaghan

Placings:325-4431041603 **(5556a)**
2001: 12^{4}SD, 9^{4}GF, 11^{3}HD, 10^{1}GF, 10^{0}GF, 9^{4}G, 12^{1}GY, 12^{6}GF, 14^{0}S, 12^{3}SH, 12^{0}S

	Starts	1st	2nd	3rd	Win & Pl
Career Total (Turf)	12	2	1	3	16489
Career Total (AW)	1	0	0	0	0

79 8/01 Tram 1m4f (0-80)H G-Y £9750
76 7/01 Bath 1m2f46y D G-F £2926
Total win prize-money £12676

Going (Turf): Sf: 0-1 GS: 0-0 Gd: 0-1 **GF: 1-7** Fm: 0-1
Distance: 5f/6f: 0-0 7f-8f: 0-2 **9f-13f: 2-10** 14f+: 0-1
Track : **LH: 1-4** RH: 0-5 **Tight: 1-5** Gall: 0-0
Aids: Bl: 0-0 Vi: 0-0 Tstrap: 0-0
Best Rating: 79 8/01 Tram 1m4f gd-yld

Won a Bath maiden for Barry Hills before moving to Ireland. Stays 12 furlongs, acts on any ground.

Market Avenue

97 **61**

2-y-o b f Factual (USA)-The Lady Vanishes (Robin Des Pins (USA))
R A Fahey Market Avenue Racing Club

Placings:0432000 **(5487)**
2001: 5^{0}GF, 6^{4}GF, 5^{3}GF, 7^{2}GS, 7^{0}G, 6^{0}GS, 6^{0}HY

	Starts	1st	2nd	3rd	Win & Pl
Career Total (Turf)	7	0	1	1	2707

Going (Turf): Sf: 0-1 GS: 0-2 Gd: 0-1 GF: 0-3 Fm: 0-0
Distance: 5f/6f: 0-5 7f-8f: 0-2 9f-13f: 0-0 14f+: 0-0
Track : LH: 0-3 RH: 0-0 Tight: 0-1 Gall: 0-0
Aids: Bl: 0-0 Vi: 0-0 Tstrap: 0-0
Best Rating: 61 9/01 Donc 7f good

Marking Time (IRE)

96(59) (8)**46**

3-y-o b g Goldmark (USA)-Tamarsiya (USA) (Shahrastani (USA))
K R Burke Mrs Elaine M Burke

Placings:0-043102 **(4854)**
2001: 10^{0}SD, 9^{4}F, 11^{3}GF, 14^{1}GF, 16^{0}F, 13^{2}GF

	Starts	1st	2nd	3rd	Win & Pl
Career Total (Turf)	5	1	1	1	3226
Career Total (AW)	2	0	0	0	

44 6/01 Nott 1m6f15y G(0-60)H G-F £2144
Total win prize-money £2145

Going (Turf): Sf: 0-0 GS: 0-0 Gd: 0-0 **GF: 1-3** Fm: 0-2
Distance: 5f/6f: 0-1 7f-8f: 0-0 9f-13f: 0-3 **14f+: 1-3**
Track : **LH: 1-4** RH: 0-2 Tight: 0-5 Gall: 0-0
Aids: Bl: 0-0 Vi: 0-0 Tstrap: 0-0
Best Rating: 46 9/01 Catt 1m5f175y gd-fm

A half-brother to a juvenile winner in Italy. Only win to date came in a Nottingham selling handicap. Stays a mile and six furlongs. Acts on a sound surface.

Markova's Dance

87 **63**
2-y-o ch f Mark Of Esteem (IRE)-Tanouma (USA) (Miswaki (USA))
J G Smyth-Osbourne Howard Barton Stud

Placings:350 **(5053)**
2001: 6^{3}GF, 7^{5}HY, 7^{0}S

	Starts	1st	2nd	3rd	Win & Pl
Career Total (Turf)	3	0	0	1	625

Going (Turf): Sf: 0-2 GS: 0-0 Gd: 0-0 GF: 0-1 Fm: 0-0
Distance: 5f/6f: 0-0 7f-8f: 0-3 9f-13f: 0-0 14f+: 0-0
Track : LH: 0-1 RH: 0-0 Tight: 0-0 Gall: 0-0
Aids: Bl: 0-0 Vi: 0-0 Tstrap: 0-0
Best Rating: 63 10/01 NmkR 7f soft

125,000gns half-sister to high-class juvenile Tamnia and Group-winning middle-distance horses Azzilfi and Khamaseen, she needed the run on her debut and pulled too hard on heavy ground next time. Likely to do better in due course.

Markusha

102(95) (63)**63**
3-y-o b g Alhijaz-Shafir (IRE) (Shaadi (USA))
Mrs J R Ramsden Nigel Munton

Placings:4303-02003350023 **(5490)**
2001: 6^{0}GF, 7^{2}F, 8^{0}GF, 8^{0}G, 8^{3}GF, 10^{3}G, 10^{5}G, 10^{0}G, 8^{0}GS, 8^{2}SD, 7^{3}HY

	Starts	1st	2nd	3rd	Win & Pl
Career Total (Turf)	13	0	1	4	5501
Career Total (AW)	2	0	1	1	1087

Going (Turf): Sf: 0-3 GS: 0-1 Gd: 0-4 GF: 0-4 Fm: 0-1
Distance: 5f/6f: 0-5 7f-8f: 0-5 9f-13f: 0-5 14f+: 0-0
Track : LH: 0-7 RH: 0-1 Tight: 0-2 Gall: 0-2
Aids: Bl: 0-0 Vi: 0-0 Tstrap: 0-0
Best Rating: 72 6/01 Donc 7f firm

Lightly raced, he is still a maiden but has shown a bit of promise in handicap company. Has shown form between seven and ten furlongs, but gives the impression that he needs to be stepped up still further in trip. Handles any ground, including Fibresand.

Marlo

94(84) (79)**100**
2-y-o b c Hector Protector (USA)-Tender Moment (IRE) (Caerleon (USA))
B W Hills Ray Richards

Placings:3113 **(5636)**
2001: 6^{3}HY, 6^{1}SD, 6^{1}HY, 5^{3}G

	Starts	1st	2nd	3rd	Win & Pl
Career Total (Turf)	3	1	0	2	5018
Career Total (AW)	1	1	0	0	2975

100	10/01	Wind	6f	D(0-85)	HVY	£3835
79	10/01	Sthl	6f	E	STD	£2975

Total win prize-money £6810

Going (Turf): Sf: 1-2 GS: 0-0 Gd: 0-1 GF: 0-0 Fm: 0-0
Distance: 5f/6f: 2-4 7f-8f: 0-0 9f-13f: 0-0 14f+: 0-0
Track : LH: 1-2 RH: 0-0 Tight: 0-1 Gall: 0-0
Aids: Bl: 0-0 Vi: 0-0 Tstrap: 0-0

Best Rating: 100 10/01 Wind 6f heavy

A half-brother to winning miler Spring Fever, he made an encouraging debut when third in a six-furlong heavy-ground maiden at Windsor, and followed up with a win on the sand at Southwell. Bred to get a mile, he spread-eagled his field in a nursery back at the Berkshire course and is clearly well suited by soft ground. Conditions were against him when subsequently beaten at Catterick.

Marmaduke (IRE)

98(103) (54)**56**
5-y-o ch g Perugino (USA)-Sympathy (Precocious)
M Pitman Martin Butler

Placings:10/55534000/03660340-15515 **(4983)**
2001: 11^{1}SD, 11^{5}SW, 12^{5}SD, 11^{1}G, 12^{5}G

	Starts	1st	2nd	3rd	Win & Pl
Career Total (Turf)	16	2	0	3	14477
Career Total (AW)	7	1	0	0	1764

56	8/01	Wind	1m3f135y	E(0-75)H	GD	£2898
52	2/01	Sthl	1m3f	F(0-65)H	STD	£1764
	10/98	Siro	7f110y		SFT	£8596

Total win prize-money £13258

Going (Turf): Sf: 1-3 GS: 0-2 **Gd: 1-6** GF: 0-4 Fm: 0-1
Distance: 5f/6f: 0-1 7f-8f: 1-8 **9f-13f: 2-12** 14f+: 0-2
Track : LH: 1-14 RH: 1-5 **Tight: 1-13** Gall: 0-2
Aids: Bl: 0-0 Vi: 0-4 Tstrap: 0-0
Best Rating: 56 8/01 Wind 1m3f135y good

Marnie

103(108) (70)**60**
4-y-o ch f First Trump-Miss Aboyne (Lochnager)
J Akehurst The Grass Is Greener Partnership

Placings:3050/006022100051-2321300 **(5608)**
2001: 7^{2}SD, 7^{3}SD, 7^{2}SW, 8^{1}SW, 7^{3}G, 6^{0}GF, 7^{0}GS

	Starts	1st	2nd	3rd	Win & Pl
Career Total (Turf)	15	1	2	2	6060
Career Total (AW)	8	2	2	1	10813

70	2/01	Ling	1m	E(0-75)H	SLW	£2933
60	12/00	Ling	7f	E(0-70)H	STD	£2353
57	7/00	Brig	5f213y	F(0-60)H	FRM	£2383

Total win prize-money £7670

Going (Turf): Sf: 0-3 GS: 0-2 Gd: 0-4 GF: 0-5 **Fm: 1-1**
Distance: 5f/6f: 1-5 **7f-8f: 2-17** 9f-13f: 0-1 14f+: 0-0
Track : LH: 3-13 RH: 0-1 **Tight: 2-8** Gall: 0-1
Aids: Bl: 0-0 Vi: 0-0 Tstrap: 0-0
Best Rating: 70 2/01 Ling 1m slow

Marnor (USA)

104 **69**
5-y-o ch h Diesis-Love's Reward (Nonoalco (USA))
M W Easterby M P Burke

Placings:213/0000002060 **(5344)**
2001: 6^{0}HY, 6^{0}G, 5^{0}G, 5^{0}G, 5^{0}GS, 10^{0}G, 8^{2}GF, 8^{0}HY, 10^{6}G, 8^{0}GS

	Starts	1st	2nd	3rd	Win & Pl
Career Total (Turf)	13	1	2	1	13325

84	6/99	NmkJ	1m2f	D	G-F	£4737

Total win prize-money £4737

Going (Turf): Sf: 0-2 GS: 0-2 Gd: 0-6 **GF: 1-3** Fm: 0-0
Distance: 5f/6f: 0-4 7f-8f: 0-3 **9f-13f: 1-6** 14f+: 0-0
Track : LH: 0-5 **RH: 1-2** Tight: 0-1 **Gall: 1-3**
Aids: Bl: 0-1 Vi: 0-0 Tstrap: 0-0
Best Rating: 76 9/01 Ayr 1m gd-fm

A full-brother to high-class sprinter Keen Hunter, he ran three times for Henry Cecil in 1999, winning a Newmarket maiden, but was then off the track for nearly two years and had shown little for Mick Easterby prior to finishing runner-up at Ayr in September. He is now down to a realistic mark.

Maromito (IRE)

105(105) (59)**73**
4-y-o b g Up And At 'Em-Amtico (Bairn (USA))
R Bastiman Peter Beaton-Brown

Placings:10/00000200-021245244 **(4718)**
2001: 6^{0}SD, 5^{2}SD, 5^{1}GF, 5^{2}GF, 5^{4}SD, 5^{5}GF, 5^{2}GF, 5^{4}G, 5^{4}G

	Starts	1st	2nd	3rd	Win & Pl
Career Total (Turf)	16	2	3	0	14143
Career Total (AW)	3	0	1	0	674

70	5/01	Muss	5f	F(0-65)H	G-F	£3220
80	6/99	Ling	5f	E	G-F	£3817

Total win prize-money £7038

Going (Turf): Sf: 0-2 GS: 0-1 Gd: 0-5 **GF: 2-7** Fm: 0-1
Distance: 5f/6f: 2-19 7f-8f: 0-0 9f-13f: 0-0 14f+: 0-0
Track : LH: 0-3 RH: 0-0 Tight: 0-1 Gall: 0-0
Aids: Bl: 0-0 Vi: 0-0 Tstrap: 0-0
Best Rating: 73 9/01 Epsm 5f good

He won his first race since he was a two-year-old at Musselburgh in May 2001 and has run well off a higher mark since. Suited by fast ground, an easy track and the minimum trip.

Maron

(104) (49)**46**
4-y-o b g Puissance-Will Be Bold (Bold Lad (IRE))
A Berry J Laughton

Placings:032301443000/0032100005000-042601216520000500 **(4556)**
2001: 6^{0}SD, 6^{4}SD, 5^{2}SD, 6^{6}SD, 5^{0}SD, 5^{1}SD, 5^{2}SD, 6^{1}SD, 5^{6}SD, 5^{5}SD, 6^{2}SD, 6^{0}G, 5^{0}G, 5^{0}GF, 6^{0}SD, 6^{5}SD, 5^{0}GF, 5^{0}SW

	Starts	1st	2nd	3rd	Win & Pl
Career Total (Turf)	24	2	2	4	10215
Career Total (AW)	19	2	3	0	5166

60	3/01	Ling	6f	F(0-65)H	STD	£1722
54	2/01	Wolv	5f	F(0-60)H	STD	£1701
58	7/00	Catt	5f212y	E(0-70)H	G-F	£3347
71	7/99	Haml	5f4y	E	G-F	£2626

Total win prize-money £9397

Going (Turf): Sf: 0-2 GS: 0-5 Gd: 0-7 **GF: 2-9** Fm: 0-1
Distance: 5f/6f: 4-38 7f-8f: 0-5 9f-13f: 0-0 14f+: 0-0
Track : LH: 3-22 RH: 0-1 **Tight: 3-14** Gall: 0-2
Aids: Bl: 0-0 Vi: 0-0 Tstrap: 0-0
Best Rating: 65 2/01 Sthl 6f stand

Twice a winner on the sand earlier in the year, he could not reproduce that level of form on turf.

Marquise

79 **59**
2-y-o gr f Petong-Jewel (IRE) (Cyrano De Bergerac)
R Hannon Lady Tennant

Placings:000 **(4724)**
2001: 6^{0}GF, 5^{0}F, 6^{0}GF

	Starts	1st	2nd	3rd	Win & Pl
Career Total (Turf)	3	0	0	0	

Going (Turf): Sf: 0-0 GS: 0-0 Gd: 0-0 GF: 0-2 Fm: 0-1
Distance: 5f/6f: 0-1 7f-8f: 0-2 9f-13f: 0-0 14f+: 0-0
Track : LH: 0-1 RH: 0-0 Tight: 0-0 Gall: 0-1
Aids: Bl: 0-0 Vi: 0-0 Tstrap: 0-0
Best Rating: 59 8/01 Newb 6f8y gd-fm

Marrakech (IRE)

107 **96**
4-y-o ch f Barathea (IRE)-Nashkara (Shirley Heights)
P W Harris Millennium Crossing

Placings:410-4150 **(5693)**
2001: 10^{4}S, 12^{1}GF, 11^{5}G, 12^{0}S

	Starts	1st	2nd	3rd	Win & Pl
Career Total (Turf)	7	2	0	0	14357

95	7/01	Asct	1m4f	C(0-95)H	G-F	£8927
84	8/00	Sand	1m14y	D	GD	£3900

Total win prize-money £12828

Going (Turf): Sf: 0-2 GS: 0-0 **Gd: 1-2 GF: 1-3** Fm: 0-0
Distance: 5f/6f: 0-0 7f-8f: 0-0 **9f-13f: 2-7** 14f+: 0-0
Track : LH: 0-5 **RH: 2-2** Tight: 0-1 **Gall: 1-4**
Aids: Bl: 0-0 Vi: 0-0 Tstrap: 0-0
Best Rating: 96 8/01 York 1m3f195y good

Lightly raced, she won an Ascot handicap in July and did not run badly in a Listed race at York. Might stay further than 12 furlongs.

Marrel

104(105) (53)**53**
3-y-o b g Shareef Dancer (USA)-Upper Caen (High Top)
B Hanbury H B E Van Cutsem

Placings:003-040331404 **(4371)**
2001: 11^{0}GS, 11^{4}F, 14^{0}G, 12^{3}SD, 12^{3}SD, 16^{1}GF, 16^{4}GF, 16^{0}G, 11^{4}GF

	Starts	1st	2nd	3rd	Win & Pl
Career Total (Turf)	9	1	0	0	3071
Career Total (AW)	3	0	0	3	1177

53 7/01 Bevl 2m35y F(0-65)H G-F £2800
Total win prize-money £2800

Going (Turf): Sf: 0-1 GS: 0-1 Gd: 0-2 **GF: 1-4** Fm: 0-1
Distance: 5f/6f: 0-0 7f-8f: 0-1 9f-13f: 0-7 **14f+: 1-4**
Track : LH: 0-9 **RH: 1-2 Tight: 1-8** Gall: 0-0
Aids: Bl: 0-2 Vi: 0-0 Tstrap: 0-0
Best Rating: 53 7/01 Bevl 2m35y gd-fm

Marriforth

86 **51**
2-y-o ch f Wolfhound (USA)-Ghassanah (Pas De Seul)
J D Bethell Www.Clarendon Racing.Oc.Uk

Placings:660060 **(4985)**
2001: 5^{6}S, 6^{6}F, 6^{0}GF, 6^{0}G, 7^{6}G, 6^{0}G

	Starts	1st	2nd	3rd	Win & Pl
Career Total (Turf)	6	0	0	0	0

Going (Turf): Sf: 0-1 GS: 0-0 Gd: 0-3 GF: 0-1 Fm: 0-1
Distance: 5f/6f: 0-3 7f-8f: 0-3 9f-13f: 0-0 14f+: 0-0
Track : LH: 0-1 RH: 0-1 Tight: 0-0 Gall: 0-0
Aids: Bl: 0-2 Vi: 0-0 Tstrap: 0-0
Best Rating: 60 5/01 Rdcr 6f firm

Has shown little ability in all starts to date including a seller. Has been tried in blinkers.

Marsad (IRE)

110 **95**
7-y-o ch g Fayruz-Broad Haven (IRE) (Be My Guest (USA))
J Akehurst Canisbay Bloodstock Ltd

Placings:6332402/060/133/10564330/50002000-02120205655 **(5494)**
2001: 6^{0}S, 7^{2}S, 6^{1}G, 6^{2}GF, 6^{0}GF, 6^{2}GF, 6^{0}G, 6^{5}G, 6^{6}GF, 6^{5}GS, 6^{5}HY, 6^{6}HY

	Starts	1st	2nd	3rd	Win & Pl
Career Total (Turf)	40	3	6	6	69910

90 5/01 NmkR 6f C(0-95)H GD £26000
91 3/99 Donc 6f C(0-90)H G-S £6828
79 4/98 Kemp 6f D(0-85)H SFT £3842
Total win prize-money £36672

Going (Turf): Sf: 1-10 GS: 1-6 Gd: 1-12 GF: 0-12 Fm: 0-0
Distance: **5f/6f: 3-34** 7f-8f: 0-6 9f-13f: 0-0 14f+: 0-0
Track : LH: 0-1 RH: 0-4 Tight: 0-1 Gall: 0-4
Aids: Bl: 0-0 Vi: 0-0 Tstrap: 0-0
Best Rating: 95 10/01 Sals 6f gd-sft

He is a useful handicapper when on song as he showed at Newmarket in May and has run well in some competitive sprint handicaps since. Best at around six furlongs with cut in the ground, although he handles faster going, but has a poor strike rate.

Marshal Bond

(95) (53)**70**
3-y-o b g Celtic Swing-Arminda (Blakeney)
B Smart R C Bond

Placings:6200-**4**11**4**050504303 **(5538)**
2001: 8^{4}SD, 8^{1}S, 9^{1}GS, 10^{4}S, 10^{0}GS, 10^{5}GF, 11^{0}G, 10^{5}HD, 9^{0}GF, 10^{4}G, 9^{3}GF, 12^{0}GS, 10^{3}S

	Starts	1st	2nd	3rd	Win & Pl
Career Total (Turf)	16	2	1	2	8632
Career Total (AW)	1	0	0	0	0

74 4/01 Brig 1m1f209yE(0-70)H G-S £2996
67 3/01 Muss 1m E(0-70)H SFT £3108
Total win prize-money £6104

Going (Turf): Sf: 1-4 GS: 1-4 Gd: 0-3 GF: 0-4 Fm: 0-1
Distance: 5f/6f: 0-0 7f-8f: 1-6 9f-13f: 1-11 14f+: 0-0
Track : LH: 1-10 RH: 1-5 **Tight: 1-4** Gall: 0-1
Aids: Bl: 0-0 Vi: 0-0 Tstrap: 0-0
Best Rating: 76 4/01 NmkR 1m2f soft

A half-brother to Carburton, appreciated the step up to a mile when scoring twice at the beginning of his three-year-old campaign on soft ground. He has struggled this season on faster surfaces, but has dropped in the weights as a result.

Marshall Neigh (USA)

(74) (39)
2-y-o ch c French Deputy (USA)-Jamie De Vil (USA) (Digression (USA))
P F I Cole The Presidential Partnership

Placings:00 **(5351)**
2001: 7^{0}SD, 8^{0}SD

	Starts	1st	2nd	3rd	Win & Pl
Career Total (Turf)	0	0	0	0	
Career Total (AW)	2	0	0	0	

Going (Turf): Sf: 0-0 GS: 0-0 Gd: 0-0 GF: 0-0 Fm: 0-0
Distance: 5f/6f: 0-0 7f-8f: 0-2 9f-13f: 0-0 14f+: 0-0
Track : LH: 0-2 RH: 0-0 Tight: 0-0 Gall: 0-0
Aids: Bl: 0-0 Vi: 0-0 Tstrap: 0-1
Best Rating: 39 10/01 Sthl 7f stand

Marshall Rooster

85 **66**
2-y-o gr g Greensmith-Petinata (Petong)
T D Barron Tim D Barron

Placings:2 **(5533)**
2001: 5^{2}S

	Starts	1st	2nd	3rd	Win & Pl
Career Total (Turf)	1	0	1	0	811

Going (Turf): Sf: 0-1 GS: 0-0 Gd: 0-0 GF: 0-0 Fm: 0-0
Distance: 5f/6f: 0-1 7f-8f: 0-0 9f-13f: 0-0 14f+: 0-0
Track : LH: 0-0 RH: 0-0 Tight: 0-0 Gall: 0-0
Aids: Bl: 0-0 Vi: 0-0 Tstrap: 0-0
Best Rating: 66 10/01 Rdcr 5f soft

Marshallspark (IRE)

(83) (57)**85**
2-y-o b g Fayruz-Lindas Delight (Batshoof)
R A Fahey Exors Of The Late T P Staunton

Placings:024 **(5345)**
2001: 6^{0}G, 6^{2}GS, 6^{4}SD

	Starts	1st	2nd	3rd	Win & Pl
Career Total (Turf)	2	0	1	0	866
Career Total (AW)	1	0	0	0	0

Going (Turf): Sf: 0-0 GS: 0-1 Gd: 0-1 GF: 0-0 Fm: 0-0
Distance: 5f/6f: 0-3 7f-8f: 0-0 9f-13f: 0-0 14f+: 0-0
Track : LH: 0-1 RH: 0-0 Tight: 0-0 Gall: 0-0
Aids: Bl: 0-0 Vi: 0-0 Tstrap: 0-0
Best Rating: 85 10/01 Newc 6f gd-sft

A half-brother to useful sprinter Fromsong, he improved on his debut run to finish second in a Newcastle maiden, but was a shade disappointing next time on the Southwell Fibresand when fourth.

Marshman (IRE)

100 **78**
2-y-o ch c College Chapel-Gold Fly (IRE) (Be My Guest (USA))
M H Tompkins J H Ellis

Placings:3123360615 **(5636)**
2001: 5^{3}GS, 5^{1}GF, 5^{2}GF, 6^{3}GF, 5^{3}G, 6^{6}G, 6^{0}GF, 6^{6}G, 6^{1}S, 5^{5}G

	Starts	1st	2nd	3rd	Win & Pl
Career Total (Turf)	10	2	1	3	13475

78 10/01 York 6f C SFT £7137
74 5/01 Haml 5f4y E G-F £2996
Total win prize-money £10133

Going (Turf): Sf: 1-1 GS: 0-1 Gd: 0-4 **GF: 1-4** Fm: 0-0
Distance: **5f/6f: 2-9** 7f-8f: 0-1 9f-13f: 0-0 14f+: 0-0
Track : LH: 0-3 RH: 0-0 Tight: 0-1 Gall: 0-0
Aids: Bl: 0-0 Vi: 0-0 Tstrap: 0-0
Best Rating: 78 10/01 York 6f soft

Got off the mark at Hamilton over the minimum trip, he then put in some fair efforts after that over five and six furlongs before winning a competitive nursery at York. A consistent sort, he acts on fast ground and stays six furlongs.

Martello

(96) (59)**65**
5-y-o b g Polish Precedent (USA)-Round Tower (High Top)
R Charlton Beckhampton Stables Ltd

Placings:4006005/4202-2356 **(0508)**
2001: 8^{2}SD, 8^{3}SD, 8^{5}SW, 8^{6}SD

	Starts	1st	2nd	3rd	Win & Pl
Career Total (Turf)	10	0	1	0	1241
Career Total (AW)	5	0	2	1	1471

Going (Turf): Sf: 0-4 GS: 0-1 Gd: 0-1 GF: 0-4 Fm: 0-0
Distance: 5f/6f: 0-0 7f-8f: 0-5 9f-13f: 0-10 14f+: 0-0
Track : LH: 0-10 RH: 0-3 Tight: 0-5 Gall: 0-0
Aids: Bl: 0-2 Vi: 0-1 Tstrap: 0-0
Best Rating: 65 1/01 Sthl 1m stand

Martha Daly

(74) (38)**64**
2-y-o b f Royal Applause-Primulette (Mummy's Pet)
R M Whitaker (M R Channon 22/5) Paul & Justine Rhodes

Placings:461150006 **(5193)**
2001: 5^{4}S, 5^{6}GS, 5^{1}GF, 5^{1}GF, 5^{5}G, 5^{0}GF, 6^{0}GF, 6^{0}G, 6^{6}SD

	Starts	1st	2nd	3rd	Win & Pl
Career Total (Turf)	8	2	0	0	8414
Career Total (AW)	1	0	0	0	0

68 6/01 Muss 5f E G-F £5382
48 5/01 Bevl 5f F G-F £2667
Total win prize-money £8049

Going (Turf): Sf: 0-1 GS: 0-1 Gd: 0-2 **GF: 2-4** Fm: 0-0
Distance: **5f/6f: 2-8** 7f-8f: 0-1 9f-13f: 0-0 14f+: 0-0
Track : LH: 0-2 RH: 0-0 Tight: 0-1 Gall: 0-1
Aids: Bl: 0-0 Vi: 0-0 Tstrap: 0-0
Best Rating: 68 6/01 Muss 5f gd-fm

A half-sister to six juvenile winners. She is only small but scored back-to back wins over five furlongs in selling company in May and June 2001. Acts on a sound surface.

Martha P Perkins (IRE)

(61) (2)**27**

3-y-o b f Fayruz-Cake Contract (IRE) (Contract Law (USA))

T J Naughton (J A Osborne 29/8) Mrs Byron Paterson

Placings:050-000 **(5409)**

2001: 7^{0}G, 7^{0}GF, 6^{0}SD

	Starts	1st	2nd	3rd	Win & Pl
Career Total (Turf)	5	0	0	0	0
Career Total (AW)	1	0	0	0	

Going (Turf): Sf: 0-0 GS: 0-0 Gd: 0-4 GF: 0-1 Fm: 0-0
Distance: 5f/6f: 0-4 7f-8f: 0-2 9f-13f: 0-0 14f+: 0-0
Track : LH: 0-4 RH: 0-0 Tight: 0-0 Gall: 0-1
Aids: Bl: 0-0 Vi: 0-0 Tstrap: 0-0
Best Rating: 2 10/01 Sthl 6f stand

Martha Reilly (IRE)

93(53) (44)**41d**

5-y-o ch m Rainbows For Life (CAN)-Debach Delight (Great Nephew)

Mrs Barbara Waring
Charlsworth,Shapter,Haggerty,Mcdonnell

Placings:000000055/613000400346/2003155-005 **(0879)**

2001: 16^{0}HY, 17^{0}HY, 21^{5}S

	Starts	1st	2nd	3rd	Win & Pl
Career Total (Turf)	19	1	1	1	5163
Career Total (AW)	12	1	0	2	2384

48	10/00	Pont	2m1f22y	E(0-70)H	HVY	£3737
59	2/99	Sthl	1m	G	STD	£1830

Total win prize-money £5568

Going (Turf): Sf: 1-8 GS: 0-3 Gd: 0-1 GF: 0-7 Fm: 0-0
Distance: 5f/6f: 0-1 7f-8f: 1-10 9f-13f: 0-9 14f+: 1-11
Track : LH: 2-22 RH: 0-2 Tight: 0-11 Gall: 0-0
Aids: Bl: 0-4 Vi: 0-0 Tstrap: 0-0
Best Rating: 19 4/01 Pont 2m5f122y soft

Martial Eagle (IRE)

(88) (31)**12**

5-y-o b g Sadler's Wells (USA)-Twine (Thatching)

N Tinkler The Izz That Right Partnership

Placings:0/1/006-0000 **(0345)**

2001: 12^{0}SW, 16^{0}SD, 16^{0}SW, 16^{0}SD

	Starts	1st	2nd	3rd	Win & Pl
Career Total (Turf)	4	1	0	0	3438
Career Total (AW)	5	0	0	0	0

70	6/99	Cork	1m6f	G-F	£3437

Total win prize-money £3438

Going (Turf): Sf: 0-2 GS: 0-0 Gd: 0-0 GF: 1-1 Fm: 0-0
Distance: 5f/6f: 0-0 7f-8f: 0-1 9f-13f: 0-3 14f+: 1-5
Track : LH: 0-8 RH: 1-1 Tight: 0-2 Gall: 0-2
Aids: Bl: 0-2 Vi: 0-0 Tstrap: 0-3
Best Rating: 31 2/01 Sthl 2m slow

Martin House (IRE)

96 **87**

2-y-o b c Mujadil (USA)-Dolcezza (FR) (Lichine (USA))

J D Bethell M J Dawson

Placings:144 **(5227)**

2001: 6^{1}G, 7^{4}G, 6^{4}S

	Starts	1st	2nd	3rd	Win & Pl
Career Total (Turf)	3	1	0	0	10759

85	7/01	York	6f214y	D	GD	£7052

Total win prize-money £7053

Going (Turf): Sf: 0-1 GS: 0-0 Gd: 1-2 GF: 0-0 Fm: 0-0
Distance: 5f/6f: 0-0 7f-8f: 1-3 9f-13f: 0-0 14f+: 0-0
Track : LH: 1-2 RH: 0-0 Tight: 0-0 Gall: 1-2
Aids: Bl: 0-0 Vi: 0-0 Tstrap: 0-0
Best Rating: 87 8/01 Asct 7f good

A half-brother to three winners abroad, he made the perfect start when winning over seven furlongs at York (good) in July and will be even better over further.

Martin's Pearl (IRE)

102 **50**

4-y-o gr g Petong-Mainly Dry (The Brianstan)

W R Muir Mrs Barbara Jean Martin

Placings:00-06000 **(3730)**

2001: 7^{0}GS, 7^{6}GF, 8^{0}G, 6^{0}GF, 8^{0}GS

	Starts	1st	2nd	3rd	Win & Pl
Career Total (Turf)	7	0	0	0	0

Going (Turf): Sf: 0-1 GS: 0-2 Gd: 0-1 GF: 0-3 Fm: 0-0
Distance: 5f/6f: 0-1 7f-8f: 0-4 9f-13f: 0-2 14f+: 0-0
Track : LH: 0-1 RH: 0-1 Tight: 0-0 Gall: 0-0
Aids: Bl: 0-1 Vi: 0-0 Tstrap: 0-0
Best Rating: 50 6/01 Bevl 7f100y gd-fm

Martin's Sunset

107 **74**

3-y-o ch c Royal Academy (USA)-Mainly Sunset (Red Sunset)

W R Muir Mrs Barbara Jean Martin

Placings:003-0002004060 **(5669)**

2001: 9^{0}GF, 8^{0}GF, 8^{0}G, 8^{2}G, 8^{0}S, 10^{0}G, 8^{4}GF, 8^{0}S, 9^{6}GS, 10^{0}HY

	Starts	1st	2nd	3rd	Win & Pl
Career Total (Turf)	13	0	1	1	3637

Going (Turf): Sf: 0-4 GS: 0-1 Gd: 0-3 GF: 0-5 Fm: 0-0
Distance: 5f/6f: 0-0 7f-8f: 0-7 9f-13f: 0-6 14f+: 0-0
Track : LH: 0-2 RH: 0-4 Tight: 0-2 Gall: 0-0
Aids: Bl: 0-2 Vi: 0-4 Tstrap: 0-0
Best Rating: 76 6/01 Newb 1m gd-fm

Still a maiden, has gone close on occasions. Suited by all goings. Has been tried at a variety of trips and a mile seems to suit well.

Martinez (IRE)

(81) (24)

5-y-o b g Tirol-Elka (USA) (Val De L'Orne (FR))

C W Thornton Guy Reed

Placings:0/060-0 **(1470)**

2001: 16^{0}SD

	Starts	1st	2nd	3rd	Win & Pl
Career Total (Turf)	1	0	0	0	
Career Total (AW)	4	0	0	0	0

Going (Turf): Sf: 0-0 GS: 0-0 Gd: 0-1 GF: 0-0 Fm: 0-0
Distance: 5f/6f: 0-1 7f-8f: 0-0 9f-13f: 0-3 14f+: 0-1
Track : LH: 0-4 RH: 0-0 Tight: 0-3 Gall: 0-0
Aids: Bl: 0-0 Vi: 0-0 Tstrap: 0-0

Marton Mere

100(80) (8)**46**

5-y-o ch g Cadeaux Genereux-Hyatti (Habitat)

A J Lockwood A J Lockwood

Placings:0002056/001005100-0000626 **(2887)**

2001: 9^{0}G, 8^{0}F, 7^{0}GF, 7^{0}GF, 8^{6}G, 7^{2}GF, 10^{6}GF

	Starts	1st	2nd	3rd	Win & Pl
Career Total (Turf)	19	2	2	0	7770
Career Total (AW)	5	0	0	0	

59	8/00	Bevl	1m100y	E	G-F	£3062
50	7/00	Bevl	7f100y	F(0-60)H	GD	£2576

Total win prize-money £5639

Going (Turf): Sf: 0-1 GS: 0-0 Gd: 1-6 GF: 1-9 Fm: 0-3
Distance: 5f/6f: 0-1 7f-8f: 1-15 9f-13f: 1-8 14f+: 0-0
Track : LH: 0-9 RH: 2-11 Tight: 0-3 Gall: 0-1
Aids: Bl: 0-0 Vi: 0-0 Tstrap: 0-0
Best Rating: 46 7/01 Bevl 7f100y gd-fm

Marvel

84(63) **36**

4-y-o b f Rudimentary (USA)-Maravilla (Mandrake Major)

N Tinkler (Don Enrico Incisa 23/4) Don Enrico Incisa

Placings:610/000203606-006 **(1168)**

2001: 8^{0}SW, 8^{0}S, 7^{6}S

	Starts	1st	2nd	3rd	Win & Pl
Career Total (Turf)	14	1	1	1	5400
Career Total (AW)	1	0	0	0	

63	10/99	Ayr	7f	D	SFT	£3652

Total win prize-money £3652

Going (Turf): Sf: 1-7 GS: 0-3 Gd: 0-2 GF: 0-2 Fm: 0-0
Distance: 5f/6f: 0-1 7f-8f: 1-6 9f-13f: 0-8 14f+: 0-0
Track : LH: 1-8 RH: 0-3 Tight: 0-2 Gall: 0-1
Aids: Bl: 0-0 Vi: 0-0 Tstrap: 0-0
Best Rating: 16 4/01 Nott 1m54y soft

Marweh

101 **95**

6-y-o b g Prince Sabo-Born To Dance (Dancing Brave (USA))

Mrs J R Ramsden B Lynam

Placings:25/32344011/30111-4000 **(5266)**

2001: 6^{4}GF, 5^{0}GF, 7^{0}G, 6^{0}GS

	Starts	1st	2nd	3rd	Win & Pl
Career Total (Turf)	19	5	2	3	80510

95	11/00	MsnL	6f		HVY	£13449
80	10/00	MsnL	6f110y		SFT	£7685
	8/00	Deau	6f	H	GD	£16330
	11/99	MsnL	6f	H	HVY	£18299
	10/99	Deau	6f	H	GD	£8611

Total win prize-money £64374

Going (Turf): Sf: 2-3 GS: 0-3 Gd: 0-3 GF: 0-2 Fm: 0-0
Distance: 5f/6f: 1-7 7f-8f: 1-4 9f-13f: 0-0 14f+: 0-0
Track : LH: 0-0 RH: 0-0 Tight: 0-0 Gall: 0-0
Aids: Bl: 0-0 Vi: 0-0 Tstrap: 0-0
Best Rating: 83 10/01 NmkR 7f good

Unraced at two, he ran a blinder in a Newmarket maiden on his debut and then raced in France for John Hammond where he won five races including a Listed event at Maisons-Laffitte. Caught the wrath of the Stewards under the non-triers' rule on his first start for Lynda Ramsden when fourth at Doncaster in August, but has failed to figure since. Best on soft ground.

Mary Doll (IRE)

90(80) (42)**55**

2-y-o b f Distinctly North (USA)-Robin Red Breast (Red Alert)

D W Chapman (P C Haslam 1/8) Roland M Wheatley

Placings:62445660 **(5621)**

2001: 5^{6}SD, 5^{2}GF, 5^{4}GF, 5^{4}GF, 5^{5}GS, 5^{6}G, 5^{6}SD, 5^{0}GS

	Starts	1st	2nd	3rd	Win & Pl
Career Total (Turf)	6	0	1	0	1554
Career Total (AW)	2	0	0	0	0

Going (Turf): Sf: 0-0 GS: 0-2 Gd: 0-1 GF: 0-3 Fm: 0-0
Distance: 5f/6f: 0-8 7f-8f: 0-0 9f-13f: 0-0 14f+: 0-0
Track : LH: 0-1 RH: 0-0 Tight: 0-1 Gall: 0-0
Aids: Bl: 0-0 Vi: 0-0 Tstrap: 0-0
Best Rating: 57 5/01 Hayd 5f gd-fm

Mary Hannah

77 **14**

8-y-o b m Lugana Beach-Bloomsbury Girl (Weepers

Boy)
J Balding Miss Greta Naden

Placings:00042/1000/0 **(5148)**
2001: 5^{0}G

	Starts	1st	2nd	3rd	Win & Pl		
Career Total (Turf)	2	0	0	0			
Career Total (AW)	8	1	1	0	2999		

47	1/99	Wolv	5f	F(0-60)H	STD	£2284

Total win prize-money £2285

Going (Turf): Sf: 0-0 GS: 0-1 Gd: 0-1 GF: 0-0 Fm: 0-0
Distance: **5f/6f: 1-9** 7f-8f: 0-0 9f-13f: 0-1 14f+: 0-0
Track : **LH: 1-7** RH: 0-0 **Tight: 1-6** Gall: 0-0
Aids: Bl: 0-0 Vi: 0-0 Tstrap: 0-0
Best Rating: 13 10/01 Rdcr 5f good

Mary Jane

107(96) (60)**60**

6-y-o br m Tina's Pet-Fair Attempt (IRE) (Try My Best (USA))
N Tinkler Executive Network (pertemps Group)

Placings:0316/041430006050144I/513034211025215 /00000065-0326242001230434O5 **(5451)**
2001: 5^{0}S, 5^{3}F, 5^{2}GF, 5^{6}GF, 5^{2}G, 5^{4}GF, 5^{2}GF, 5^{0}SD, 5^{0}SD, 5^{1}G, 5^{2}GF, 5^{3}GF, 5^{0}SW, 5^{4}G, 5^{3}S, 5^{4}GS, 5^{0}S, 5^{5}HY

	Starts	1st	2nd	3rd	Win & Pl
Career Total (Turf)	41	4	7	4	25971
Career Total (AW)	21	5	0	3	12060

60	8/01	Thsk	5f	E(0-70)H	GD	£3835
59	9/99	Leic	5f2y	D(0-80)H	GD	£5020
54	7/99	Chep	5f16y	E(0-70)H	G-F	£2836
66	7/99	Wolv	5f	F(0-65)H	STD	£2626
62	1/99	Wolv	5f	F(0-65)H	STD	£2233
57	12/98	Sthl	5f	F	STD	£1850
57	11/98	Sthl	6f	F	STD	£1945
54	2/98	Wolv	5f	F	STD	£2085
68	10/97	Rdcr	5f	F	G-F	£2598

Total win prize-money £25029

Going (Turf): Sf: 0-8 GS: 0-3 **Gd: 2-9 GF: 2-19** Fm: 0-2
Distance: **5f/6f: 9-60** 7f-8f: 0-2 9f-13f: 0-0 14f+: 0-0
Track : **LH: 4-23** RH: 0-0 **Tight: 3-18** Gall: 0-2
Aids: Bl: 0-1 Vi: 0-0 Tstrap: 0-0
Best Rating: 60 10/01 Newc 5f gd-sft

She is a speedy front-runner who has a good record over sprint trips on Fibresand, but she can go on turf too as she showed when winning at Thirsk in August.

Maryinsky (IRE)

106 **103**

2-y-o b f Sadler's Wells (USA)-Blush With Pride (USA) (Blushing Groom (FR))
A P O'Brien Michael Tabor

Placings:221 **(5306a)**
2001: 7^{2}GF, 8^{2}S, 7^{1}YS

	Starts	1st	2nd	3rd	Win & Pl
Career Total (Turf)	3	1	2	0	58410

102	10/01	Gowr	7f	Y-S	£9660

Total win prize-money £9660

Going (Turf): Sf: 0-1 GS: 0-0 Gd: 0-0 GF: 0-1 Fm: 0-0
Distance: 5f/6f: 0-0 **7f-8f: 1-3** 9f-13f: 0-0 14f+: 0-0
Track : LH: 0-0 RH: 0-1 Tight: 0-0 Gall: 0-1
Aids: Bl: 0-0 Vi: 0-0 Tstrap: 0-0
Best Rating: 103 9/01 Asct 1m soft

A Sadler's Wells half-sister to Turnberry Isle out of a Kentucky Oaks winner, she was narrowly beaten on her Curragh debut when relatively unfancied, but improved considerably on that when encountering soft ground in the Fillies' Mile. She will come into her own over further next year and should be able to win her share of races.

Marzelle (FR)

105 **69**

3-y-o b f Sillery (USA)-Marzipan (IRE) (Green Desert (USA))
S Dow J & S Kelly

Placings:425552620 **(5026)**
2001: 10^{4}S, 9^{2}F, 10^{5}GF, 11^{5}GF, 10^{5}GF, 10^{2}G, 11^{6}GF, 10^{2}G, 9^{0}S

	Starts	1st	2nd	3rd	Win & Pl
Career Total (Turf)	9	0	3	0	3702

Going (Turf): Sf: 0-2 GS: 0-0 Gd: 0-2 GF: 0-4 Fm: 0-1
Distance: 5f/6f: 0-0 7f-8f: 0-0 9f-13f: 0-9 14f+: 0-0
Track : LH: 0-5 RH: 0-3 Tight: 0-2 Gall: 0-3
Aids: Bl: 0-0 Vi: 0-0 Tstrap: 0-0
Best Rating: 74 5/01 Brig 1m1f209y firm

Still a maiden but has run some good races in both handicaps and maidens and it will not be long before he gets off the mark. Suited by most types of ground and ten to 11 furlongs.

Mashhoor (USA)

93 **69**

3-y-o b c Thunder Gulch (USA)-Memorive (USA) (Riverman (USA))
C E Brittain Saeed Manana

Placings:040 **(4673)**
2001: 10^{0}S, 11^{4}G, 12^{0}G

	Starts	1st	2nd	3rd	Win & Pl
Career Total (Turf)	3	0	0	0	282

Going (Turf): Sf: 0-1 GS: 0-0 Gd: 0-2 GF: 0-0 Fm: 0-0
Distance: 5f/6f: 0-0 7f-8f: 0-0 9f-13f: 0-3 14f+: 0-0
Track : LH: 0-2 RH: 0-1 Tight: 0-1 Gall: 0-0
Aids: Bl: 0-0 Vi: 0-0 Tstrap: 0-0
Best Rating: 69 7/01 Yarm 1m3f101y good

Masilia (IRE)

111 **102**

4-y-o b f Kahyasi-Masmouda (Dalsaan)
John M Oxx H H Aga Khan

Placings:4/111222 **(5322a)**
2001: 16^{1}GF, 12^{1}F, 12^{1}GY, 12^{2}YS, 14^{2}GF, 12^{2}Y, 12^{6}HY

	Starts	1st	2nd	3rd	Win & Pl
Career Total (Turf)	7	3	3	0	61955

93	7/01	Curr	1m4f	H	G-Y	£32500
89	6/01	Downr	1m4f68y		FRM	£19750
60	5/01	Clon	2m		G-F	£4830

Total win prize-money £37330

Going (Turf): Sf: 0-1 GS: 0-0 Gd: 0-0 **GF: 1-2 Fm: 1-1**
Distance: 5f/6f: 0-0 7f-8f: 0-1 **9f-13f: 2-4** 14f+: 1-2
Track : LH: 0-1 RH: 0-1 Tight: 0-0 Gall: 0-1
Aids: Bl: 0-0 Vi: 0-0 Tstrap: 0-0
Best Rating: 102 10/01 Curr 1m4f yield

Ran once at two, did not run at three but switched to race in Ireland and has won three times in 2001. Has won over a mile and a half to two miles and seems to handle any ground

Masque Tonnerre (USA)

95(96) (52)**58**

3-y-o b c Thunder Gulch (USA)-Veiled Lady (USA) (Professor Blue (USA))
M A Jarvis R Meredith

Placings:00-0400 **(2809)**
2001: 11^{0}SD, 11^{4}GF, 11^{0}GF, 10^{0}GF

	Starts	1st	2nd	3rd	Win & Pl
Career Total (Turf)	5	0	0	0	294
Career Total (AW)	1	0	0	0	

Going (Turf): Sf: 0-1 GS: 0-0 Gd: 0-0 GF: 0-4 Fm: 0-0
Distance: 5f/6f: 0-0 7f-8f: 0-1 9f-13f: 0-5 14f+: 0-0
Track : LH: 0-2 RH: 0-2 Tight: 0-2 Gall: 0-0
Aids: Bl: 0-0 Vi: 0-0 Tstrap: 0-1
Best Rating: 58 5/01 Bevl 1m3f216y gd-fm

Massarra

100 **96**

2-y-o b f Danehill (USA)-Rafha (Kris)
J L Dunlop Prince A A Faisal

Placings:211206 **(5054)**
2001: 6^{2}GF, 6^{1}GF, 6^{1}GF, 5^{2}GS, 6^{0}G, 6^{6}S

	Starts	1st	2nd	3rd	Win & Pl
Career Total (Turf)	6	2	2	0	33944

90	6/01	NmkJ	6f	A	G-F	£12328
78	6/01	Gdwd	6f	D	G-F	£4397

Total win prize-money £16725

Going (Turf): Sf: 0-1 GS: 0-1 Gd: 0-1 **GF: 2-3** Fm: 0-0
Distance: **5f/6f: 2-6** 7f-8f: 0-0 9f-13f: 0-0 14f+: 0-0
Track : LH: 0-0 RH: 0-0 Tight: 0-0 Gall: 0-0
Aids: Bl: 0-0 Vi: 0-0 Tstrap: 0-0
Best Rating: 96 7/01 MsnL 5f110y gd-sft

She is a half-sister to smart middle distance performers Al Widyan and Sadian, and to the sprinter Invincible Spirit. Their dam Rafha acted on a sound surface, but it was soft when she won the Prix de Diane at Chantilly. Showed the benefit of her Goodwood debut when running away with a similar event over the same course and distance next time and was given a fine tactical ride to follow up in a Newmarket Listed event. Narrowly beaten in the Prix Robert Papin in July, she failed to settle when well beaten in the Lowther and Cheveley Park. Suited by front-running tactics and fast ground.

Massenet (IRE)

78 **27**

6-y-o b g Caerleon (USA)-Massawippi (Be My Native (USA))
D J Wintle Hugh M Duffy

Placings:033/0 **(0643)**
2001: 9^{0}HY

	Starts	1st	2nd	3rd	Win & Pl
Career Total (Turf)	4	0	0	2	1049

Going (Turf): Sf: 0-1 GS: 0-0 Gd: 0-1 GF: 0-2 Fm: 0-0
Distance: 5f/6f: 0-0 7f-8f: 0-0 9f-13f: 0-4 14f+: 0-0
Track : LH: 0-2 RH: 0-1 Tight: 0-2 Gall: 0-0
Aids: Bl: 0-0 Vi: 0-0 Tstrap: 0-0
Best Rating: 27 4/01 Nott 1m1f213y heavy

Massey

(103) (71)**37**

5-y-o br g Machiavellian (USA)-Massaraat (USA) (Nureyev (USA))
T D Barron J Edward Boynton

Placings:1600000000000011-140042 **(5347)**
2001: 9^{1}SW, 11^{4}SD, 11^{0}S, 9^{0}F, 8^{4}SD, 8^{2}SD

	Starts	1st	2nd	3rd	Win & Pl
Career Total (Turf)	12	0	0	0	0
Career Total (AW)	10	4	1	0	8711

71	1/01	Wolv	1m1f79y	G(0-60)H	SLW	£1337
58	12/00	Sthl	1m3f	G(0-70)H	STD	£1400
49	11/00	Sthl	1m3f	G	STD	£1967
66	3/00	Wolv	1m4f	D	STD	£2730

Total win prize-money £7434

Going (Turf): Sf: 0-2 GS: 0-1 Gd: 0-1 GF: 0-6 Fm: 0-2
Distance: 5f/6f: 0-0 7f-8f: 0-6 **9f-13f: 4-16** 14f+: 0-0
Track : **LH: 4-16** RH: 0-3 **Tight: 2-11** Gall: 0-1
Aids: Bl: 0-0 **Vi: 1-6** Tstrap: 0-0
Best Rating: 71 1/01 Wolv 1m1f79y slow

Notched up a hat-trick of wins at the end of 2000, beginning of 2001, but looked well held since then until finishing a good second to an unexposed sort at Southwell in October.

Master Beveled

95 (63)**56**

11-y-o b g Beveled (USA)-Miss Anniversary (Tachypous)

P D Evans Mrs E J Williams

Placings:000504040313114332401132U0000132121/0000000000556600/26450600011005/3442505002555346/040603201006/0/30340-050 **(3678)**

2001: 15^{0}GF, 9^{5}G, 11^{0}G

	Starts	1st	2nd	3rd	Win & Pl
Career Total (Turf)	82	9	6	7	77114
Career Total (AW)	20	2	2	4	10270

72	9/98	Ayr	1m2f192y	E(0-70)H	G-S	£2570
67	10/96	Wwck	1m	E(0-70)	FRM	£3807
74	10/96	Hayd	1m2f120y	E(0-70)	SFT	£3139
85	10/94	NmkR	1m	C(0-100)H	SFT	£23880
71	10/94	York	1m205y	D(0-80)H	G-S	£10722
64	9/94	Hayd	1m30y	F(0-65)	GD	£3785
58	5/94	Donc	7f	E(0-70)H	G-F	£2615
63	5/94	Kemp	1m	E(0-75)H	HVY	£3366
55	12/93	Ling	1m	E(0-70)H	STD	£3002
51	12/93	Ling	7f	E(0-70)H	STD	£3210
50	10/93	NmkR	1m1f	E(0-70)H	GD	£4500

Total win prize-money £64598

Going (Turf): Sf: 3-11 GS: 2-9 Gd: 2-31 GF: 1-26 Fm: 1-5

Distance: 5f/6f: 0-3 **7f-8f: 6-34** 9f-13f: 5-64 14f+: 0-1

Track : **LH: 7-72** RH: 1-9 Tight: 2-31 Gall: 2-23

Aids: Bl: 0-6 Vi: 0-14 Tstrap: 0-0

Best Rating: 51 8/01 Nott 1m1f213y good

A multiple winner over on the Flat and over hurdles. He was retired in November 2001.

Master Blue

91 **41**

3-y-o b g Mind Games-Sandicroft Jewel (Grey Desire)

J R Norton The Blueblood Partnership

Placings:60500 **(4618)**

2001: 7^{6}G, 6^{0}F, 6^{5}GF, 6^{0}S, 6^{0}F

	Starts	1st	2nd	3rd	Win & Pl
Career Total (Turf)	5	0	0	0	0

Going (Turf): Sf: 0-1 GS: 0-0 Gd: 0-1 GF: 0-1 Fm: 0-2

Distance: 5f/6f: 0-3 7f-8f: 0-2 9f-13f: 0-0 14f+: 0-0

Track : LH: 0-1 RH: 0-0 Tight: 0-1 Gall: 0-0

Aids: Bl: 0-0 Vi: 0-0 Tstrap: 0-0

Best Rating: 41 5/01 Thsk 7f good

Master Cooper (IRE)

107 **78**

7-y-o b g Kahyasi-Arabian Princess (Taufan (USA))

D R C Elsworth D S Dunne

Placings:5233062/011010543/3/00402022250-100 **(1428)**

2001: 10^{1}G, 11^{0}F, 12^{0}S

	Starts	1st	2nd	3rd	Win & Pl
Career Total (Turf)	31	4	6	4	31346

75	5/01	NmkR	1m2f	D(0-85)H	GD	£7328
86	7/98	Leop	1m2f	(0-80)H	G-F	£5843
78	5/98	Rosc	1m4f	(0-75)	GD	£3253
78	5/98	Clon	1m2f	(0-65)	GD	£2740

Total win prize-money £19167

Going (Turf): Sf: 0-3 GS: 0-1 **Gd: 3-10** GF: 1-6 Fm: 0-1

Distance: 5f/6f: 0-0 7f-8f: 0-2 **9f-13f: 4-28** 14f+: 0-0

Track : LH: 1-11 **RH: 2-17** Tight: 0-1 Gall: 0-3

Aids: Bl: 0-7 Vi: 0-0 Tstrap: 0-0

Best Rating: 78 5/01 York 1m3f195y firm

Ex-Irish handicapper, he won well at Newmarket in May Suited by ten furlongs.

Master Ellis (IRE)

78 **45**

2-y-o b g Turtle Island (IRE)-Take No Chances (IRE) (Thatching)

P D Evans Mrs M Gittins

Placings:005 **(4464)**

2001: 7^{0}G, 8^{0}S, 8^{5}G

	Starts	1st	2nd	3rd	Win & Pl
Career Total (Turf)	3	0	0	0	0

Going (Turf): Sf: 0-1 GS: 0-0 Gd: 0-2 GF: 0-0 Fm: 0-0

Distance: 5f/6f: 0-0 7f-8f: 0-1 9f-13f: 0-2 14f+: 0-0

Track : LH: 0-1 RH: 0-2 Tight: 0-2 Gall: 0-0

Aids: Bl: 0-0 Vi: 0-0 Tstrap: 0-0

Best Rating: 45 9/01 Haml 1m65y good

Master Fellow

88 **39**

3-y-o ch g First Trump-Take Charge (Last Tycoon)

J G Given R H Jennings

Placings:640-00000 **(5188)**

2001: 8^{0}GF, 9^{0}G, 8^{0}GF, 10^{0}GF, 15^{0}GS

	Starts	1st	2nd	3rd	Win & Pl
Career Total (Turf)	8	0	0	0	257

Going (Turf): Sf: 0-2 GS: 0-2 Gd: 0-1 GF: 0-3 Fm: 0-0

Distance: 5f/6f: 0-2 7f-8f: 0-3 9f-13f: 0-2 14f+: 0-1

Track : LH: 0-6 RH: 0-0 Tight: 0-2 Gall: 0-1

Aids: Bl: 0-0 Vi: 0-0 Tstrap: 0-0

Best Rating: 44 5/01 Thsk 1m gd-fm

Master Gatemaker

(91) (57)**50**

3-y-o b g Tragic Role (USA)-Girl At The Gate (Formidable (USA))

P W Harris John G Morley

Placings:03-00000 **(2650)**

2001: 8^{0}HY, 9^{0}G, 10^{0}GF, 9^{0}GF, 8^{0}SD

	Starts	1st	2nd	3rd	Win & Pl
Career Total (Turf)	5	0	0	0	
Career Total (AW)	2	0	0	1	444

Going (Turf): Sf: 0-1 GS: 0-0 Gd: 0-1 GF: 0-3 Fm: 0-0

Distance: 5f/6f: 0-0 7f-8f: 0-2 9f-13f: 0-5 14f+: 0-0

Track : LH: 0-4 RH: 0-2 Tight: 0-1 Gall: 0-0

Aids: Bl: 0-0 Vi: 0-1 Tstrap: 0-0

Best Rating: 47 5/01 Leic 1m1f218y good

Master George

99 **72**

4-y-o b g Mtoto-Topwinder (USA) (Topsider (USA))

I A Balding David R Watson & Duncan Lofts

Placings:2/1625043-0000 **(4027)**

2001: 16^{0}GF, 13^{0}GF, 14^{0}GF, 13^{0}GF

	Starts	1st	2nd	3rd	Win & Pl
Career Total (Turf)	12	1	2	1	12441

72	4/00	Wind	1m2f7y	D	HVY	£4043

Total win prize-money £4043

Going (Turf): Sf: 1-2 GS: 0-1 Gd: 0-2 GF: 0-7 Fm: 0-0

Distance: 5f/6f: 0-0 7f-8f: 0-1 **9f-13f: 1-5** 14f+: 0-6

Track : LH: 0-4 RH: 0-4 **Tight: 1-3** Gall: 0-5

Aids: Bl: 0-0 Vi: 0-1 Tstrap: 0-0

Best Rating: 72 7/01 Sand 2m78y gd-fm

Master Henry (GER)

(83)

7-y-o b g Mille Balles (FR)-Maribelle (GER) (Windwurf (GER))

Ian Williams Thurlestone Hotel Racing Club

Placings:024/6660165-0 **(0620)**

2001: 8^{0}SD

	Starts	1st	2nd	3rd	Win & Pl
Career Total (Turf)	10	1	1	0	6912
Career Total (AW)	1		0	0	0

63	7/00	Muss	1m1f	E(0-65)	FRM	£3094

Total win prize-money £3094

Going (Turf): Sf: 0-0 GS: 0-3 Gd: 0-1 GF: 0-2 **Fm: 1-1**

Distance: 5f/6f: 0-2 7f-8f: 0-4 **9f-13f: 1-2** 14f+: 0-0

Track : LH: 0-3 **RH: 1-3 Tight: 1-4** Gall: 0-1

Aids: Bl: 0-0 Vi: 0-0 Tstrap: 0-0

Best Rating: 41 4/01 Ling 1m stand

Master In Law (IRE)

95 **89**

2-y-o ch c Polish Precedent (USA)-Clara Bow (USA) (Coastal (USA))

G C Bravery M I L Racing

Placings:21 **(5295)**

2001: 7^{2}GF, 8^{1}S, 10^{0}HY

	Starts	1st	2nd	3rd	Win & Pl
Career Total (Turf)	2	1	1	0	5435

89	10/01	Leic	1m9y	D	SFT	£4225

Total win prize-money £4225

Going (Turf): Sf: 1-1 GS: 0-0 Gd: 0-0 GF: 0-1 Fm: 0-0

Distance: 5f/6f: 0-0 7f-8f: 0-1 **9f-13f: 1-1** 14f+: 0-0

Track : LH: 0-1 RH: 0-0 Tight: 0-0 Gall: 0-0

Aids: Bl: 0-0 Vi: 0-0 Tstrap: 0-0

Best Rating: 89 10/01 Leic 1m9y soft

He showed promise to finish runner-up on his Warwick debut and went one better on much softer ground over an extra furlong at Leicester. Should win more races.

Master Luke

104(104) (63)**51**

4-y-o b g Contract Law (USA)-Flying Wind (Forzando)

G L Moore Bryan Pennick

Placings:00020231303-50004300 **(5292)**

2001: 6^{5}HY, 5^{0}GS, 7^{0}G, 7^{0}SD, 6^{4}GF, 5^{3}G, 5^{0}S, 7^{0}S

	Starts	1st	2nd	3rd	Win & Pl
Career Total (Turf)	13	0	2	2	2755
Career Total (AW)	6	1	0	2	3850

51	11/00	Ling	6f	D	STD	£2860

Total win prize-money £2860

Going (Turf): Sf: 0-4 GS: 0-2 Gd: 0-4 GF: 0-2 Fm: 0-1

Distance: **5f/6f: 1-11** 7f-8f: 0-7 9f-13f: 0-1 14f+: 0-0

Track : **LH: 1-10** RH: 0-2 **Tight: 1-6** Gall: 0-2

Aids: **Bl: 1-16** Vi: 0-0 Tstrap: 0-0

Best Rating: 51 6/01 Sthl 7f stand

Master McGrath (IRE)

101 **67**

3-y-o b c Common Grounds-Darabaka (IRE) (Doyoun)

J Noseda Mrs Nicky Chambers

Placings:4401 **(4483)**

2001: 10^{4}GS, 10^{4}S, 11^{0}G, 14^{1}S

	Starts	1st	2nd	3rd	Win & Pl
Career Total (Turf)	4	1	0	0	5200

67	9/01	Yarm	1m6f17y	E(0-70)H	SFT	£4543

Total win prize-money £4544

Going (Turf): Sf: 1-2 GS: 0-1 Gd: 0-1 GF: 0-0 Fm: 0-0

Distance: 5f/6f: 0-0 7f-8f: 0-0 9f-13f: 0-3 **14f+: 1-1**

Track : **LH: 1-3** RH: 0-0 **Tight: 1-3** Gall: 0-0

Aids: Bl: 0-0 **Vi: 1-1** Tstrap: 0-0

Best Rating: 67 9/01 Yarm 1m6f17y soft

He had the assistance of Kieren Fallon and a first-time visor when stepping up successfully in distance at Yarmouth. A half-brother to Far Cry, he has taken time to mature, but will surely make his mark in staying events.

Master Robbie

97 96

2-y-o b c Piccolo-Victoria's Secret (IRE) (Law Society (USA))

M R Channon Alec Tuckerman

Placings:321520 (5256)

2001: 5^{3}GF, 6^{2}GF, 6^{1}G, 6^{5}G, 5^{2}G, 5^{0}GS

	Starts	1st	2nd	3rd	Win & Pl
Career Total (Turf)	6	1	2	1	10974

96 8/01 Gdwd 6f E GD £4397

Total win prize-money £4397

Going (Turf): Sf: 0-0 GS: 0-1 **Gd: 1-3** GF: 0-2 Fm: 0-0
Distance: **5f/6f: 1-5** 7f-8f: 0-1 9f-13f: 0-0 14f+: 0-0
Track : LH: 0-1 RH: 0-0 Tight: 0-0 Gall: 0-0
Aids: Bl: 0-0 Vi: 0-0 Tstrap: 0-0
Best Rating: 96 9/01 Ayr 5f good

A useful sprint juvenile, he scored at Goodwood on his third start and ran his best race when runner-up in a Listed event at Ayr.

Master Soden (USA)

108(101) (63)75

4-y-o b g Pembroke (USA)-Lady Member (FR) (Saint Estephe (FR))

T G Mills Albert Soden Ltd

Placings:0001/5-410011021043 (4872)

2001: 11^{4}SD, 8^{1}SW, 8^{0}SD, 6^{0}S, 7^{1}F, 6^{1}GF, 6^{0}G, 8^{2}GF, 7^{1}G, 7^{0}GS, 6^{4}GF, 7^{3}G

	Starts	1st	2nd	3rd	Win & Pl
Career Total (Turf)	14	4	1	1	14840
Career Total (AW)	3	1	0	0	2968

75 7/01 Yarm 7f3y E(0-75)H GD £3444
68 6/01 Sals 6f212y F G-F £3332
53 5/01 Rdcr 7f F FRM £2891
63 2/01 Wolv 1m100y E(0-75)H SLW £2968
59 11/99 Rdcr 1m E(0-75)H G-S £3640

Total win prize-money £16275

Going (Turf): Sf: 0-1 **GS: 1-3 Gd: 1-3 GF: 1-6 Fm: 1-1**
Distance: 5f/6f: 0-3 **7f-8f: 4-10** 9f-13f: 1-4 14f+: 0-0
Track : **LH: 1-4** RH: 0-1 **Tight: 1-2** Gall: 0-1
Aids: Bl: 0-0 Vi: 0-0 Tstrap: 0-0
Best Rating: 75 7/01 Yarm 7f3y good

Seems to act on any ground but very effective on fast ground in 2001. Best suited by making the running.

Master Sun (IRE)

86 57

2-y-o b c Grand Lodge (USA)-Mersada (IRE) (Heraldiste (USA))

R Charlton Michael Pescod

Placings:00 (5682)

2001: 7^{0}GS, 7^{0}S

	Starts	1st	2nd	3rd	Win & Pl
Career Total (Turf)	2	0	0	0	

Going (Turf): Sf: 0-1 GS: 0-1 Gd: 0-0 GF: 0-0 Fm: 0-0
Distance: 5f/6f: 0-0 7f-8f: 0-2 9f-13f: 0-0 14f+: 0-0
Track : LH: 0-0 RH: 0-0 Tight: 0-0 Gall: 0-0
Aids: Bl: 0-0 Vi: 0-0 Tstrap: 0-0
Best Rating: 57 11/01 NmkR 7f gd-sft

Master T (USA)

94 74

2-y-o b c Trempolino (USA)-Our Little C (USA) (Marquetry (USA))

G L Moore Lancing Racing Syndicate

Placings:6450 (5022)

2001: 7^{6}G, 7^{4}GF, 7^{5}GF, 7^{0}S

	Starts	1st	2nd	3rd	Win & Pl
Career Total (Turf)	4	0	0	0	0

Going (Turf): Sf: 0-1 GS: 0-0 Gd: 0-1 GF: 0-2 Fm: 0-0
Distance: 5f/6f: 0-0 7f-8f: 0-4 9f-13f: 0-0 14f+: 0-0
Track : LH: 0-2 RH: 0-0 Tight: 0-0 Gall: 0-1
Aids: Bl: 0-0 Vi: 0-0 Tstrap: 0-0
Best Rating: 74 8/01 Ling 7f140y gd-fm

Master Trump

(52) 43

3-y-o b g First Trump-Anhaar (Ela-Mana-Mou)

J J O'Neill Mrs Jonjo O'Neill

Placings:600 (3817)

2001: 10^{6}GF, 14^{0}G, 9^{0}SD

	Starts	1st	2nd	3rd	Win & Pl
Career Total (Turf)	2	0	0	0	0
Career Total (AW)	1	0	0	0	

Going (Turf): Sf: 0-0 GS: 0-0 Gd: 0-1 GF: 0-1 Fm: 0-0
Distance: 5f/6f: 0-0 7f-8f: 0-0 9f-13f: 0-2 14f+: 0-1
Track : LH: 0-3 RH: 0-0 Tight: 0-1 Gall: 0-0
Aids: Bl: 0-0 Vi: 0-0 Tstrap: 0-0
Best Rating: 43 6/01 Hayd 1m6f good

Masterful (USA)

107 116+

3-y-o b c Danzig (USA)-Moonlight Serenade (FR) (Dictus (FR))

J H M Gosden Sheikh Mohammed

Placings:4-2221121 (4197a)

2001: 6^{2}GF, 7^{2}GF, 7^{2}GF, 8^{1}GF, 10^{1}GF, 9^{2}G, 10^{1}S

	Starts	1st	2nd	3rd	Win & Pl
Career Total (Turf)	8	3	4	0	59201

116 8/01 Deau 1m2f SFT £29098
102 7/01 Asct 1m2f B(0-95) G-F £10010
90 7/01 Asct 1m D G-F £5486

Total win prize-money £44594

Going (Turf): Sf: 1-1 GS: 0-0 Gd: 0-2 **GF: 2-5** Fm: 0-0
Distance: 5f/6f: 0-1 7f-8f: 1-4 **9f-13f: 2-3** 14f+: 0-0
Track : LH: 0-1 **RH: 1-2** Tight: 0-1 **Gall: 1-1**
Aids: Bl: 0-0 Vi: 0-0 Tstrap: 0-0
Best Rating: 116 8/01 Deau 1m2f soft

He finished runner-up in three consecutive maidens before easily winning a similar event at Ascot in July, then followed up in a handicap on the same track. He has improved given a longer trip and with forcing tactics employed.

Mastermind (IRE)

115 108

4-y-o ch g Dolphin Street (FR)-Glenarff (USA) (Irish River (FR))

Mrs J R Ramsden J D Martin

Placings:21/04023-41003 (2700a)

2001: 8^{4}S, 8^{1}GS, 7^{0}GF, 8^{0}GF, 8^{3}Y

	Starts	1st	2nd	3rd	Win & Pl
Career Total (Turf)	12	2	2	2	40063

108 4/01 Newb 1m B(0-105)H G-S £16796
86 7/99 NmkJ 6f D G-F £4386

Total win prize-money £21183

Going (Turf): Sf: 0-1 **GS: 1-1** Gd: 0-3 **GF: 1-4** Fm: 0-1
Distance: 5f/6f: 1-2 7f-8f: 1-6 9f-13f: 0-4 14f+: 0-0
Track : LH: 0-3 RH: 0-2 Tight: 0-0 Gall: 0-4
Aids: Bl: 0-0 Vi: 0-0 Tstrap: 0-0
Best Rating: 108 4/01 Newb 1m gd-sft

He contested the 2000 Guineas and the French Derby for Paul Cole last season before showing useful form in handicaps. Relatively unexposed, he made his debut for the Ramsdens in the Lincoln where he finished a good fourth, before winning the Spring Cup at Newbury. Best effort since to finish third in a Curragh Listed event in July. Sold for 380,000 gns to the Middle East.

Masterpiece (USA)

87(85) (47)66d

4-y-o b/br g Nureyev (USA)-Lovely Gemstone (USA) (Alydar (USA))

K R Burke Lifestyle Bloodstock (uk) Ltd

Placings:01/0444-0000000 (1466)

2001: 8^{0}SW, 8^{0}SD, 8^{0}S, 9^{0}S, 8^{0}S, 11^{0}S, 7^{0}GF

	Starts	1st	2nd	3rd	Win & Pl
Career Total (Turf)	11	1	0	0	6340
Career Total (AW)	2	0	0	0	

78 10/99 Ling 7f D HVY £4760

Total win prize-money £4760

Going (Turf): Sf: 1-5 GS: 0-2 Gd: 0-1 GF: 0-3 Fm: 0-0
Distance: 5f/6f: 0-0 **7f-8f: 1-9** 9f-13f: 0-4 14f+: 0-0
Track : LH: 0-5 RH: 0-3 Tight: 0-4 Gall: 0-0
Aids: Bl: 0-1 Vi: 0-1 Tstrap: 0-2
Best Rating: 56 5/01 Muss 7f30y gd-fm

Material Witness (IRE)

78

4-y-o b g Barathea (IRE)-Dial Dream (Gay Mecene (USA))

W R Muir M J Caddy

Placings:32/223021-00532000 (5265)

2001: 8^{0}GS, 8^{0}GS, 8^{5}G, 7^{3}G, 8^{2}G, 10^{0}G, 8^{0}HY, 8^{0}GS

	Starts	1st	2nd	3rd	Win & Pl
Career Total (Turf)	16	1	5	3	20074

77 9/00 Catt 7f D SFT £2860

Total win prize-money £2860

Going (Turf): Sf: 1-3 GS: 0-6 Gd: 0-5 GF: 0-1 Fm: 0-0
Distance: 5f/6f: 0-1 **7f-8f: 1-8** 9f-13f: 0-6 14f+: 0-0
Track : **LH: 1-6** RH: 0-3 **Tight: 1-2** Gall: 0-3
Aids: Bl: 0-1 Vi: 0-0 Tstrap: 0-0
Best Rating: 79 9/01 Haml 1m65y good

Took a long time to get off the mark and finally scored at the back end of 2000 over seven furlongs at Catterick. Running well in the summer, he carries his head high but seems honest enough. Stays a mile and is best on an easy surface.

Mathmagician

(80) (53)13

2-y-o ch c Hector Protector (USA)-Inherent Magic (IRE) (Magical Wonder (USA))

W R Muir J Bernstein

Placings:0046000 (5410)

2001: 5^{0}G, 5^{0}SD, 6^{4}SD, 7^{6}SD, 7^{0}G, 7^{0}HY, 7^{0}SD

	Starts	1st	2nd	3rd	Win & Pl
Career Total (Turf)	3	0	0	0	
Career Total (AW)	4	0	0	0	

Going (Turf): Sf: 0-1 GS: 0-0 Gd: 0-2 GF: 0-0 Fm: 0-0
Distance: 5f/6f: 0-3 7f-8f: 0-4 9f-13f: 0-3 14f+: 0-0
Track : LH: 0-5 RH: 0-0 Tight: 0-0 Gall: 0-1
Aids: Bl: 0-0 Vi: 0-0 Tstrap: 0-0
Best Rating: 53 5/01 Sthl 6f stand

Matins (IRE)

80(75) (35)30

2-y-o ch f College Chapel-Krayyalei (IRE) (Krayyan)

W J Haggas Anglia Bloodstock 2000

Placings:60 (5466)

2001: 6^{6}SD, 6^{0}S

	Starts	1st	2nd	3rd	Win & Pl
Career Total (Turf)	1	0	0	0	

	Starts	1st	2nd	3rd	Win & Pl
Career Total (AW)	1	0	0	0	0

Going (Turf): Sf: 0-1 GS: 0-0 Gd: 0-0 GF: 0-0 Fm: 0-0
Distance: 5f/6f: 0-1 7f-8f: 0-1 9f-13f: 0-0 14f+: 0-0
Track : LH: 0-2 RH: 0-0 Tight: 0-0 Gall: 0-0
Aids: Bl: 0-0 Vi: 0-0 Tstrap: 0-0
Best Rating: 35 10/01 Sthl 6f stand

Shown little worthwhile form to date.

Matlock (IRE)

102(95) (85)**83**

3-y-o b c Barathea (IRE)-Palio Flyer (Slip Anchor)
P F I Cole W J Smith And M D Dudley

Placings:14343-3000 **(1949)**
2001: 8^{3}S, 7^{0}GF, 10^{0}GF, 8^{0}GF

	Starts	1st	2nd	3rd	Win & Pl
Career Total (Turf)	8	1	0	2	7248
Career Total (AW)	1	0	0	1	536

85 7/00 Sand 7f16y D G-F £4309
Total win prize-money £4310

Going (Turf): Sf: 0-4 GS: 0-0 Gd: 0-0 **GF: 1-4** Fm: 0-0
Distance: 5f/6f: 0-0 **7f-8f: 1-7** 9f-13f: 0-2 14f+: 0-0
Track : LH: 0-3 **RH: 1-3** Tight: 0-1 Gall: 0-0
Aids: Bl: 0-0 Vi: 0-0 Tstrap: 0-0
Best Rating: 83 4/01 Kemp 1m soft

Matoaka (USA)

109 **92**

3-y-o b f A.P. Indy (USA)-Appointed One (USA) (Danzig (USA))
Sir Michael Stoute Cheveley Park Stud

Placings:24-20130 **(3597)**
2001: 9^{2}GS, 8^{0}GF, 6^{1}GF, 7^{3}GS, 7^{0}G

	Starts	1st	2nd	3rd	Win & Pl
Career Total (Turf)	7	1	2	1	9219

67 6/01 Folk 6f189y D G-F £3122
Total win prize-money £3122

Going (Turf): Sf: 0-0 GS: 0-3 Gd: 0-2 **GF: 1-2** Fm: 0-0
Distance: 5f/6f: 0-0 **7f-8f: 1-5** 9f-13f: 0-2 14f+: 0-0
Track : LH: 0-1 **RH: 1-4 Tight: 1-3** Gall: 0-1
Aids: Bl: 0-0 Vi: 0-0 Tstrap: 0-0
Best Rating: 92 7/01 NmkJ 7f gd-sft

A good-looking, scopey filly, she showed ability in her early starts but did not get off the mark until finding a non-event at Folkestone. She looked in need of a mile at least when third in a Newmarket handicap next time.

Matron (IRE)

89 **88d**

3-y-o b f Dr Devious (IRE)-Matrona (USA) (Woodman (USA))
L M Cumani Fittocks Stud

Placings:22-6 **(5281)**
2001: 7^{6}S

	Starts	1st	2nd	3rd	Win & Pl
Career Total (Turf)	3	0	2	0	2330

Going (Turf): Sf: 0-3 GS: 0-0 Gd: 0-0 GF: 0-0 Fm: 0-0
Distance: 5f/6f: 0-1 7f-8f: 0-2 9f-13f: 0-0 14f+: 0-0
Track : LH: 0-0 RH: 0-0 Tight: 0-0 Gall: 0-0
Aids: Bl: 0-0 Vi: 0-0 Tstrap: 0-0
Best Rating: 54 10/01 Leic 7f9y soft

Mattan

88 **49**

5-y-o b g Chaddleworth (IRE)-Gilded Omen (Faustus (USA))
P F Nicholls (B J Llewellyn 10/5) Mel Fordham

Placings:33/00 **(0879)**
2001: 14^{0}HY, 21^{0}S

	Starts	1st	2nd	3rd	Win & Pl
Career Total (Turf)	4	0	0	2	1060

Going (Turf): Sf: 0-2 GS: 0-0 Gd: 0-1 GF: 0-1 Fm: 0-0
Distance: 5f/6f: 0-0 7f-8f: 0-0 9f-13f: 0-1 14f+: 0-3
Track : LH: 0-4 RH: 0-0 Tight: 0-1 Gall: 0-0
Aids: Bl: 0-0 Vi: 0-0 Tstrap: 0-0
Best Rating: 32 4/01 Nott 1m6f15y heavy

Matty Tun

71(88) (55)**34**

2-y-o b g Lugana Beach-B Grade (Lucky Wednesday)
Miss J F Craze Mrs O Tunstall

Placings:460 **(4064)**
2001: 5^{4}SD, 5^{6}SD, 6^{0}G

	Starts	1st	2nd	3rd	Win & Pl
Career Total (Turf)	1	0	0	0	
Career Total (AW)	2	0	0	0	0

Going (Turf): Sf: 0-0 GS: 0-0 Gd: 0-1 GF: 0-0 Fm: 0-0
Distance: 5f/6f: 0-3 7f-8f: 0-0 9f-13f: 0-0 14f+: 0-0
Track : LH: 0-0 RH: 0-0 Tight: 0-0 Gall: 0-0
Aids: Bl: 0-0 Vi: 0-0 Tstrap: 0-0
Best Rating: 55 5/01 Sthl 5f stand

Maunby Roller (IRE)

65

2-y-o b g Flying Spur (AUS)-Brown Foam (Horage)
P C Haslam Maunby Investment Management

Placings:66 **(5533)**
2001: 6^{6}S, 5^{6}S

	Starts	1st	2nd	3rd	Win & Pl
Career Total (Turf)	2	0	0	0	0

Going (Turf): Sf: 0-2 GS: 0-0 Gd: 0-0 GF: 0-0 Fm: 0-0
Distance: 5f/6f: 0-2 7f-8f: 0-0 9f-13f: 0-0 14f+: 0-0
Track : LH: 0-1 RH: 0-0 Tight: 0-0 Gall: 0-0
Aids: Bl: 0-0 Vi: 0-0 Tstrap: 0-0
Best Rating: 65 10/01 Pont 6f soft

Maunsell's Road (IRE)

92 **77**

2-y-o b c Desert Style (IRE)-Zara's Birthday (IRE) (Waajib)
S Kirk The South Western Partnership Iii

Placings:02200 **(5496)**
2001: 7^{0}GS, 8^{2}GF, 7^{2}F, 7^{0}S, 7^{0}HY

	Starts	1st	2nd	3rd	Win & Pl
Career Total (Turf)	5	0	2	0	1742

Going (Turf): Sf: 0-2 GS: 0-1 Gd: 0-0 GF: 0-1 Fm: 0-1
Distance: 5f/6f: 0-0 7f-8f: 0-4 9f-13f: 0-1 14f+: 0-0
Track : LH: 0-1 RH: 0-0 Tight: 0-0 Gall: 0-1
Aids: Bl: 0-0 Vi: 0-0 Tstrap: 0-0
Best Rating: 77 9/01 Chep 7f16y firm

Maurangi

70

10-y-o b g Warning-Spin Dry (High Top)
B W Murray M E Foxton

Placings:320/0013100/0056404/006000/5004450000/4 3/0 **(1000)**
2001: 10^{0}S

	Starts	1st	2nd	3rd	Win & Pl
Career Total (Turf)	34	2	1	3	9727
Career Total (AW)	2	0	0	0	

59 7/94 Bevl 1m100y F(0-65)H G-F £3413
53 6/94 Ayr 1m F(0-70)H G-S £2582
Total win prize-money £5995

Going (Turf): Sf: 0-3 **GS: 1-4** Gd: 0-10 **GF: 1-13** Fm: 0-4
Distance: 5f/6f: 0-0 7f-8f: 1-14 9f-13f: 1-20 14f+: 0-2
Track : LH: 1-26 RH: 1-7 Tight: 0-7 Gall: 0-7
Aids: **Bl: 1-9** Vi: 0-0 Tstrap: 0-0
Best Rating: 53 6/94 Ayr 1m GS

Mauri Moon

110 **102**

3-y-o b f Green Desert (USA)-Dazzling Heights (Shirley Heights)
G Wragg Peter R Pritchard

Placings:511-204100 **(5141)**
2001: 8^{2}S, 7^{0}G, 10^{4}GF, 7^{1}GF, 7^{0}G, 8^{0}G

	Starts	1st	2nd	3rd	Win & Pl
Career Total (Turf)	9	3	1	0	41717

102 8/01 Gdwd 7f A G-F £22750
93 8/00 Ches 6f18y B GD £9371
80 7/00 Nott 6f15y D G-F £3623
Total win prize-money £35745

Going (Turf): Sf: 0-1 GS: 0-0 Gd: 1-4 **GF: 2-4** Fm: 0-0
Distance: 5f/6f: 0-1 **7f-8f: 3-7** 9f-13f: 0-1 14f+: 0-0
Track : LH: 1-2 RH: 1-2 **Tight: 1-1** Gall: 0-1
Aids: Bl: 0-0 Vi: 0-0 Tstrap: 0-0
Best Rating: 102 8/01 Gdwd 7f gd-fm

Twice a winner at two, she has ability, but also showed a lot of temperament and that has to be a worry. Battled on well when making all over seven in Listed company at Goodwood, but does not look an easy ride. A mile looks her limit.

Mawdsley

92(72) (9)**27**

4-y-o b f Piccolo-Legendary Dancer (Shareef Dancer (USA))
A B Mulholland Andrew Lloyd

Placings:0/060-00000000 **(4599)**
2001: 8^{0}GF, 7^{0}GF, 10^{0}F, 8^{0}GF, 12^{0}G, 10^{0}G, 9^{0}GF, 8^{0}GF

	Starts	1st	2nd	3rd	Win & Pl
Career Total (Turf)	11	0	0	0	0
Career Total (AW)	1	0	0	0	

Going (Turf): Sf: 0-0 GS: 0-0 Gd: 0-3 GF: 0-7 Fm: 0-1
Distance: 5f/6f: 0-2 7f-8f: 0-6 9f-13f: 0-4 14f+: 0-0
Track : LH: 0-5 RH: 0-3 Tight: 0-4 Gall: 0-2
Aids: Bl: 0-0 Vi: 0-3 Tstrap: 0-0
Best Rating: 27 8/01 Bevl 1m1f207y gd-fm

Mawhoob (USA)

99 **80**

3-y-o gr c Dayjur (USA)-Asl (USA) (Caro)
Mrs N Macauley (J L Dunlop 1/6) West Indies Capital Company Limited

Placings:643-25 **(4239)**
2001: 8^{2}F, 8^{5}GF

	Starts	1st	2nd	3rd	Win & Pl
Career Total (Turf)	5	0	1	1	2209

Going (Turf): Sf: 0-0 GS: 0-1 Gd: 0-0 GF: 0-3 Fm: 0-1
Distance: 5f/6f: 0-1 7f-8f: 0-2 9f-13f: 0-2 14f+: 0-0
Track : LH: 0-1 RH: 0-1 Tight: 0-0 Gall: 0-0
Aids: Bl: 0-0 Vi: 0-0 Tstrap: 0-0
Best Rating: 80 6/01 Nott 1m54y firm

Mawingo (IRE)

90(101) (62)**65**

8-y-o b g Taufan (USA)-Tappen Zee (Sandhurst Prince)
G Wragg Mrs Claude Lilley

Placings:65/6151156/302032/5000/0300354/00205-230

(3965)

2001: 10^{2}SD, 11^{3}SD, 10^{0}G

	Starts	1st	2nd	3rd	Win & Pl
Career Total (Turf)	29	3	3	4	27836
Career Total (AW)	5	0	1	1	1218

80	6/96	NmkJ	1m	C(0-90)H	GD	£5900
74	6/96	NmkJ	1m	C(0-90)H	GD	£8155
65	5/96	Wwck	7f	D(0-80)H	FRM	£4357

Total win prize-money £18413

Going (Turf): Sf: 0-3 GS: 0-3 **Gd: 2-7** GF: 0-15 Fm: 1-1
Distance: 5f/6f: 0-0 **7f-8f: 3-20** 9f-13f: 0-14 14f+: 0-0
Track : **LH: 1-16** RH: 0-5 Tight: 0-12 Gall: 0-3
Aids: Bl: 0-2 Vi: 0-0 Tstrap: 0-0
Best Rating: 62 2/01 Sthl 1m3f stand

Nowhere near as good as he was, has been lightly raced over the past two seasons. Stays ten furlongs. Best on fast ground.

Mawjud

(69) **34**

8-y-o b h Mujtahid (USA)-Elfaslah (IRE) (Green Desert (USA))
A W Carroll Michael Gates

Placings:1/30/000 (5419)
2001: 7^{0}GF, 5^{0}S, 12^{0}SD

	Starts	1st	2nd	3rd	Win & Pl
Career Total (Turf)	5	1	0	1	5835
Career Total (AW)	1	0	0	0	

88	10/95	Yarm	7f3y	D	FRM	£4932

Total win prize-money £4932

Going (Turf): Sf: 0-1 GS: 0-1 Gd: 0-1 GF: 0-1 **Fm: 1-1**
Distance: 5f/6f: 0-1 **7f-8f: 1-3** 9f-13f: 0-2 14f+: 0-0
Track : LH: 0-4 RH: 0-1 Tight: 0-1 Gall: 0-2
Aids: Bl: 0-0 Vi: 0-0 Tstrap: 0-0
Best Rating: 34 9/01 York 7f202y gd-fm

Max (FR)

85(94) (21)**35**

6-y-o gr g L'Emigrant (USA)-Miss Mendez (FR) (Bellypha)
J J Bridger J J Bridger

Placings:12110/600003000000540-05600000 **(2748)**
2001: 10^{0}SD, 12^{5}SW, 12^{6}SD, 12^{0}SW, 6^{0}GS, 7^{0}GS, 11^{0}GF, 8^{0}GF

	Starts	1st	2nd	3rd	Win & Pl
Career Total (Turf)	20	3	1	1	3096
Career Total (AW)	9	0	0	0	289

	11/99	Oste	1m110y	H	YLD	£1050
	11/99	Oste	1m		GD	£787
	9/99	Oste	1m	H	FRM	£700

Total win prize-money £2537

Going (Turf): Sf: 0-3 GS: 0-4 Gd: 0-4 GF: 0-3 Fm: 0-2
Distance: 5f/6f: 0-0 7f-8f: 0-5 9f-13f: 0-20 14f+: 0-0
Track : LH: 0-19 RH: 0-4 Tight: 0-18 Gall: 0-0
Aids: Bl: 0-3 Vi: 0-0 Tstrap: 0-3
Best Rating: 50 5/01 Ling 7f140y gd-sft

Max Bee Jay

79(67) (7)**20**

3-y-o b g Imp Society (USA)-Dulzura (Daring March)
A P Jarvis Mrs D B Brazier

Placings:0-0000 (3706)
2001: 7^{0}SD, 5^{0}G, 6^{0}GF, 7^{0}G

	Starts	1st	2nd	3rd	Win & Pl
Career Total (Turf)	3	0	0	0	
Career Total (AW)	2	0	0	0	

Going (Turf): Sf: 0-0 GS: 0-0 Gd: 0-2 GF: 0-1 Fm: 0-0
Distance: 5f/6f: 0-2 7f-8f: 0-3 9f-13f: 0-0 14f+: 0-0
Track : LH: 0-3 RH: 0-0 Tight: 0-1 Gall: 0-0
Aids: Bl: 0-0 Vi: 0-0 Tstrap: 0-0
Best Rating: 20 8/01 Leic 7f9y good

May Ball

106 **100**

4-y-o b f Cadeaux Genereux-Minute Waltz (Sadler's Wells (USA))
J H M Gosden Lord Hartington

Placings:1241136-30153 (5678a)
2001: 7^{3}S, 7^{0}G, 7^{1}G, 7^{5}GS, 8^{3}HO

	Starts	1st	2nd	3rd	Win & Pl
Career Total (Turf)	12	4	1	3	42850

65	10/01	Rdcr	7f	C	GD	£6815
102	8/00	Deau	1m		G-S	£13449
78	7/00	Asct	1m	D	GD	£5382
24	5/00	NmkR	1m	G	GD	£0

Total win prize-money £25646

Going (Turf): Sf: 0-3 GS: 1-2 **Gd: 3-6** GF: 0-0 Fm: 0-0
Distance: 5f/6f: 0-0 **7f-8f: 4-10** 9f-13f: 0-2 14f+: 0-0
Track : LH: 0-3 **RH: 1-2** Tight: 0-1 Gall: 0-1
Aids: Bl: 0-0 Vi: 0-0 Tstrap: 0-0
Best Rating: 99 11/01 StCl 1m holding

Won at the first time of asking in the two runner Challenge Whip at Newmarket, she still qualified for maidens and was a well beaten second in one after that, before scoring in July, she then followed up in Deauville. She began the 2001 season in May looking well held, but came back looking as good as ever in October winning a conditions event.

May I Say (IRE)

(81) (15)**20**

5-y-o b m Night Shift (USA)-Monoglow (Kalaglow)
R Brotherton (Mrs A Duffield 28/4) Ms Gerardine P O'Reilly

Placings:03025/0050200/1105-0000 (5469)
2001: 9^{0}SD, 9^{0}S, 10^{0}S, 9^{0}S

	Starts	1st	2nd	3rd	Win & Pl
Career Total (Turf)	18	2	2	1	5342
Career Total (AW)	2	0	0	0	

	7/00	Colo	1m	H	SFT	£1935
	4/00	Brem	1m		SFT	£1129

Total win prize-money £3064

Going (Turf): Sf: 2-8 GS: 0-2 Gd: 0-1 GF: 0-6 Fm: 0-1
Distance: 5f/6f: 0-0 **7f-8f: 2-5** 9f-13f: 0-15 14f+: 0-0
Track : LH: 0-8 RH: 0-5 Tight: 0-5 Gall: 0-0
Aids: Bl: 0-1 Vi: 0-1 Tstrap: 0-3
Best Rating: 20 10/01 Brig 1m1f209y soft

May King Mayhem

102 (35)**55**

8-y-o ch g Great Commotion (USA)-Queen Ranavalona (Sure Blade (USA))
Mrs A L M King S J Harrison

Placings:50/040060/05006030251365/630F653063410 031/56600116/65111120-032 (1876)
2001: 9^{0}G, 12^{3}F, 11^{2}F

	Starts	1st	2nd	3rd	Win & Pl
Career Total (Turf)	52	9	3	6	36452
Career Total (AW)	5	0	0	1	338

48	6/00	NmkJ	1m4f	D(0-80)H	G-F	£4862
55	6/00	Kemp	1m4f	E(0-75)H	G-F	£3334
50	6/00	NmkR	1m4f	F(0-60)H	G-F	£5128
47	6/00	Ling	1m3f106y	E(0-75)H	GD	£2842
40	6/99	NmkJ	1m4f	F(0-60)H	GD	£4727
39	5/99	Leic	1m3f183y	F(0-65)H	GD	£2368
42	10/98	Pont	1m4f8y	F(0-60)H	GD	£2242
34	8/98	Hayd	1m3f200y	F(0-60)H	GD	£2906
47	7/97	Carl	1m4f	E(0-70)H	GD	£2931

Total win prize-money £31344

Going (Turf): Sf: 0-6 GS: 0-4 **Gd: 6-22** GF: 3-14 Fm: 0-6
Distance: 5f/6f: 0-0 7f-8f: 0-3 **9f-13f: 9-42** 14f+: 0-12
Track : LH: 3-32 **RH: 6-23** Tight: 1-14 **Gall: 3-7**
Aids: **Bl: 8-27** Vi: 0-1 Tstrap: 0-0
Best Rating: 49 6/01 Ling 1m3f106y firm

May Princess

93 **58**

3-y-o ch f Prince Sabo-Mim (Midyan (USA))
D Morris P J Turner

Placings:0005-503000 (4459)
2001: 6^{5}GF, 8^{0}GF, 7^{3}GF, 8^{0}GF, 7^{0}GF, 7^{0}G

	Starts	1st	2nd	3rd	Win & Pl
Career Total (Turf)	10	0	0	1	488

Going (Turf): Sf: 0-1 GS: 0-0 Gd: 0-3 GF: 0-6 Fm: 0-0
Distance: 5f/6f: 0-2 7f-8f: 0-6 9f-13f: 0-2 14f+: 0-0
Track : LH: 0-2 RH: 0-0 Tight: 0-0 Gall: 0-0
Aids: Bl: 0-0 Vi: 0-0 Tstrap: 0-0
Best Rating: 58 7/01 Ling 7f140y gd-fm

May Queen Megan

102(96) (40)**46**

8-y-o gr m Petorius-Siva (FR) (Bellypha)
Mrs A L M King All The Kings Horses

Placings:363/6046062104/000064426320/0F15010030 50/50042032605504/465-**01501**501000 (4366)
2001: 8^{0}SD, 9^{1}SD, 9^{5}SD, 9^{0}SD, 8^{1}F, 9^{5}F, 9^{0}GF, 8^{1}GF, 8^{0}GF, 8^{0}GS, 9^{0}GF

	Starts	1st	2nd	3rd	Win & Pl
Career Total (Turf)	60	5	5	5	23312
Career Total (AW)	5	1	0	0	1414

46	7/01	Pont	1m4y	E(0-70)H	G-F	£3672
39	6/01	Nott	1m54y	G(0-70)H	FRM	£2144
40	1/01	Wolv	1m1f79y	G(0-65)H	STD	£1414
52	7/98	Ling	1m1f	E(0-70)H	G-F	£3028
48	6/98	Nott	1m54y	E(0-70)H	GD	£3652
52	7/96	Ling	6f	E(0-70)H	G-F	£3343

Total win prize-money £17255

Going (Turf): Sf: 0-1 GS: 0-5 Gd: 1-12 **GF: 3-28** Fm: 1-14
Distance: 5f/6f: 1-13 7f-8f: 0-17 **9f-13f: 5-35** 14f+: 0-0
Track : **LH: 5-37** RH: 0-10 **Tight: 2-15** Gall: 0-3
Aids: Bl: 0-1 Vi: 0-0 Tstrap: 0-0
Best Rating: 46 7/01 Pont 1m4y gd-fm

Maybe Baby (IRE)

86 **51**

2-y-o b g Lake Coniston (IRE)-Nadedge (IRE) (Petorius)
J L Eyre John Roberts (wakefield)

Placings:000 (4801)
2001: 6^{0}G, 6^{0}G, 5^{0}F

	Starts	1st	2nd	3rd	Win & Pl
Career Total (Turf)	3	0	0	0	

Going (Turf): Sf: 0-0 GS: 0-0 Gd: 0-2 GF: 0-0 Fm: 0-1
Distance: 5f/6f: 0-3 7f-8f: 0-0 9f-13f: 0-0 14f+: 0-0
Track : LH: 0-1 RH: 0-0 Tight: 0-0 Gall: 0-0
Aids: Bl: 0-0 Vi: 0-0 Tstrap: 0-0
Best Rating: 51 9/01 Kemp 6f good

Maybe Shades

47 **18**

2-y-o b f Thornberry (USA)-My Moody Girl (IRE) (Alzao (USA))
G F H Charles-Jones The Maybe Syndicate

Placings:00 (5175)
2001: 6^{0}GF, 6^{0}HY

	Starts	1st	2nd	3rd	Win & Pl
Career Total (Turf)	2	0	0	0	

Going (Turf): Sf: 0-1 GS: 0-0 Gd: 0-0 GF: 0-1 Fm: 0-0

Distance: 5f/6f: 0-2 7f-8f: 0-0 9f-13f: 0-0 14f+: 0-0
Track : LH: 0-0 RH: 0-0 Tight: 0-0 Gall: 0-0
Aids: Bl: 0-0 Vi: 0-0 Tstrap: 0-0
Best Rating: 18 10/01 Wind 6f heavy

Maycocks Bay

108(87) (49)**70**

3-y-o b f Muhtarram (USA)-Beacon (High Top)
J A Glover Lady Bamford

Placings:0-3532335402 **(5624)**
2001: 7[3]G, 7[5]GF, 8[3]GF, 10[2]G, 9[3]GF, 10[3]GF, 9[5]GF, 11[4]GS, 12[0]SD, 9[2]GS

	Starts	1st	2nd	3rd	Win & Pl
Career Total (Turf)	10	0	2	4	5782
Career Total (AW)	1	0	0	0	

Going (Turf): Sf: 0-1 GS: 0-2 Gd: 0-2 GF: 0-5 Fm: 0-0
Distance: 5f/6f: 0-1 7f-8f: 0-3 9f-13f: 0-7 14f+: 0-0
Track : LH: 0-8 RH: 0-2 Tight: 0-4 Gall: 0-1
Aids: Bl: 0-0 Vi: 0-0 Tstrap: 0-0
Best Rating: 70 11/01 Nott 1m1f213y gd-sft

Lightly-raced filly, has shown ability in ordinary events. Stays a ten furlongs, but has tended to pull and needs to learn to settle. Seemed to appreciate being allowed to bowl along when touched off at Nottingham in November.

Maylane

99 **111**

7-y-o b g Mtoto-Possessive Dancer (Shareef Dancer (USA))
A C Stewart Sheikh Ahmed Al Maktoum

Placings:521/U5I211U/00/03511/046335-00 **(2613)**
2001: 11[0]G, 12[0]GF

	Starts	1st	2nd	3rd	Win & Pl
Career Total (Turf)	25	6	2	3	101254

107	11/99	Donc	1m4f	A	SFT	£14330
102	10/99	Hayd	1m3f200y	C	HVY	£5808
112	9/97	Epsm	1m4f10y	A	GD	£18840
102	7/97	Gdwd	1m4f	B(0-105)H	G-F	£36100
93	6/97	Gdwd	1m1f	C	GD	£5336
83	10/96	Ling	7f	D	G-S	£4079

Total win prize-money £84493

Going (Turf): Sf: 2-3 GS: 1-3 **Gd: 2-8** GF: 1-10 Fm: 0-1
Distance: 5f/6f: 0-0 7f-8f: 1-5 **9f-13f: 5-18** 14f+: 0-2
Track : **LH: 3-11** RH: 2-10 **Tight: 3-5** Gall: 1-9
Aids: Bl: 0-2 Vi: 0-0 Tstrap: 0-0
Best Rating: 86 6/01 NmkJ 1m4f gd-fm

He is a very talented individual, but is a monkey. He is habitually slow out of the gates and reluctant to race, but when he is persuaded to take part, he has the ability to compete at Listed class.

Mayreau Legend (IRE)

92 **59**

2-y-o b c Distinctly North (USA)-Crystal River (Jester)
M H Tompkins The Three Carats

Placings:5400002 **(5536)**
2001: 6[5]GF, 6[4]G, 6[0]G, 7[0]G, 8[0]G, 7[0]GS, 6[2]S

	Starts	1st	2nd	3rd	Win & Pl
Career Total (Turf)	7	0	1	0	1243

Going (Turf): Sf: 0-1 GS: 0-1 Gd: 0-4 GF: 0-1 Fm: 0-0
Distance: 5f/6f: 0-4 7f-8f: 0-3 9f-13f: 0-0 14f+: 0-0
Track : LH: 0-2 RH: 0-1 Tight: 0-0 Gall: 0-0
Aids: Bl: 0-0 Vi: 0-0 Tstrap: 0-0
Best Rating: 72 8/01 Pont 6f good

Maysboyo

64(72) (15)**13**

3-y-o b g Makbul-Maysimp (IRE) (Mac's Imp (USA))
B P J Baugh Mrs Joan M Chrimes

Placings:30000-0000000 **(3749)**
2001: 8[0]SD, 8[0]F, 8[0]G, 10[0]GF, 7[0]GF, 9[0]SD, 8[0]CS

	Starts	1st	2nd	3rd	Win & Pl
Career Total (Turf)	9	0	0	1	406
Career Total (AW)	3	0	0	0	

Going (Turf): Sf: 0-1 GS: 0-2 Gd: 0-2 GF: 0-3 Fm: 0-1
Distance: 5f/6f: 0-4 7f-8f: 0-3 9f-13f: 0-5 14f+: 0-0
Track : LH: 0-7 RH: 0-1 Tight: 0-5 Gall: 0-0
Aids: Bl: 0-0 Vi: 0-2 Tstrap: 0-0
Best Rating: 13 6/01 Ches 7f122y gd-fm

Maytime

98 **47**

3-y-o ch f Pivotal-May Hinton (Main Reef)
H Morrison Ian Cameron

Placings:00500-00020505 **(5129)**
2001: 5[0]GF, 5[0]GF, 6[0]GF, 8[2]GF, 7[0]GS, 8[5]GS, 8[0]G, 7[5]HY

	Starts	1st	2nd	3rd	Win & Pl
Career Total (Turf)	13	0	1	0	1008

Going (Turf): Sf: 0-1 GS: 0-3 Gd: 0-1 GF: 0-8 Fm: 0-0
Distance: 5f/6f: 0-6 7f-8f: 0-5 9f-13f: 0-2 14f+: 0-0
Track : LH: 0-3 RH: 0-0 Tight: 0-1 Gall: 0-0
Aids: Bl: 0-1 Vi: 0-0 Tstrap: 0-0
Best Rating: 47 7/01 Sals 1m gd-fm

Mayville Thunder

107(106) (95+)**111**

3-y-o ch c Zilzal (USA)-Mountain Lodge (Blakeney)
G A Butler Mayville Farms Ltd

Placings:31-10 **(1119)**
2001: 10[1]SD, 8[0]G

	Starts	1st	2nd	3rd	Win & Pl
Career Total (Turf)	3	1	0	1	3141
Career Total (AW)	1	1	0	0	3731

95	3/01	Ling	1m2f	D(0-85)H	STD	£3731
76	11/00	Muss	7f30y	E	G-S	£2307

Total win prize-money £6039

Going (Turf): Sf: 0-0 **GS: 1-1** Gd: 0-1 GF: 0-1 Fm: 0-0
Distance: 5f/6f: 0-0 7f-8f: 1-3 9f-13f: 1-1 14f+: 0-0
Track : LH: 1-1 RH: 1-1 **Tight: 2-2** Gall: 0-0
Aids: Bl: 0-0 Vi: 0-0 Tstrap: 0-0
Best Rating: 111 5/01 NmkR 1m good

Promising colt, made his debut behind West Order and Halawan in above average maiden at Newbury, followed up with hard fought win in maiden at Musselburgh, and reappeared for smooth win in AW handicap at Lingfield, beating Buddeliea by 3/4 length (pair nine lengths clear). Ran a blinder in the Guineas to finish seventh and, as a half-brother to Gordon Stakes winner Compton Ace, should come into his own over middle distances.

Mazury (USA)

91 **69**

2-y-o b c Langfuhr (CAN)-Assurgent (USA) (Damascus (USA))
M Johnston Abdullah Saeed Belhab

Placings:03 **(5537)**
2001: 6[0]GS, 7[3]S

	Starts	1st	2nd	3rd	Win & Pl
Career Total (Turf)	2	0	0	1	484

Going (Turf): Sf: 0-1 GS: 0-1 Gd: 0-0 GF: 0-0 Fm: 0-0
Distance: 5f/6f: 0-1 7f-8f: 0-1 9f-13f: 0-0 14f+: 0-0
Track : LH: 0-0 RH: 0-0 Tight: 0-0 Gall: 0-0
Aids: Bl: 0-0 Vi: 0-0 Tstrap: 0-0
Best Rating: 69 10/01 Rdcr 7f soft

Mbele

107 **111**

4-y-o b c Mtoto-Majestic Image (Niniski (USA))
W R Muir Mr And Mrs John Wilson

Placings:2/321612-5660 **(3582)**
2001: 16[5]G, 20[6]GF, 14[6]HO, 16[0]G

	Starts	1st	2nd	3rd	Win & Pl
Career Total (Turf)	11	2	3	1	28071

96	9/00	Asct	2m45y	C(0-95)H	G-S	£14137
75	5/00	Nott	1m6f15y	D	G-S	£3289

Total win prize-money £17427

Going (Turf): Sf: 0-3 **GS: 2-2** Gd: 0-2 GF: 0-3 Fm: 0-0
Distance: 5f/6f: 0-0 7f-8f: 0-0 9f-13f: 0-3 **14f+: 2-8**
Track : LH: 1-2 RH: 1-8 Tight: 0-3 **Gall: 1-4**
Aids: Bl: 0-1 Vi: 0-0 Tstrap: 0-0
Best Rating: 111 5/01 Sand 2m78y good

Progressed into a decent stayer in the autumn of 2000, and made a promising reappearance at Sandown having suffered a minor stress fracture in the interim. Did not seem to stay in the Ascot Gold Cup and was then a little disappointing in France. Stays two miles and is best with cut in the ground.

Mcbain (USA)

103 **74**

2-y-o br c Lear Fan (USA)-River City Moon (USA) (Riverman (USA))
R F Johnson Houghton C W Sumner

Placings:04260211 **(5668)**
2001: 5[0]GS, 6[4]GF, 6[2]GF, 6[6]GF, 7[0]GF, 8[2]GS, 8[1]G, 8[1]HY

	Starts	1st	2nd	3rd	Win & Pl
Career Total (Turf)	8	2	2	0	12875

74	11/01	Wind	1m67y	C(0-95)	HVY	£6522
74	11/01	Rdcr	1m	E(0-75)	GD	£3122

Total win prize-money £9645

Going (Turf): Sf: 1-1 GS: 0-2 **Gd: 1-1** GF: 0-4 Fm: 0-0
Distance: 5f/6f: 0-3 7f-8f: 1-4 9f-13f: 1-1 14f+: 0-0
Track : LH: 0-2 **RH: 1-1 Tight: 1-2** Gall: 0-0
Aids: Bl: 0-0 Vi: 0-0 Tstrap: 0-0
Best Rating: 74 11/01 Wind 1m67y heavy

Has performed with credit in decent company. Was a fair second in a Newmarket nursery over a mile, doing all his best work late on, he then went one better next time at Redcar in November. Followed up Windsor and obviously likes to get his toe in. He should stay middle distances next season.

Mcgillycuddy Reeks (IRE)

108 (31)**75**

10-y-o b m Kefaah (USA)-Kilvarnet (Furry Glen)
Don Enrico Incisa Don Enrico Incisa

Placings:343/4602550313/0606463334/645623011112 2001064/05106404106606063/03050142140300600/32 52310564550-64541225005242 **(5686)**
2001: 11[6]S, 11[4]F, 10[5]F, 10[4]GF, 12[1]G, 10[2]GF, 12[2]GF, 10[5]GF, 11[0]G, 11[0]GF, 10[5]S, 10[2]S, 12[4]HY, 10[2]S

	Starts	1st	2nd	3rd	Win & Pl
Career Total (Turf)	101	12	11	13	87840
Career Total (AW)	2	0	0	0	0

67	6/01	Thsk	1m4f	D(0-80)H	GD	£4322
77	7/00	Donc	1m2f60y	B(0-105)H	GD	£10481
73	7/99	Donc	1m2f60y	D(0-85)H	G-F	£4013
70	6/99	Bevl	1m1f207y	D(0-80)H	G-F	£3673
77	8/98	Thsk	1m4f	D(0-80)H	GD	£4890
73	6/98	Newc	1m2f32y	D(0-85)H	SFT	£3615
71	10/97	York	1m2f85y	D(0-85)H	GD	£6680
65	8/97	Nott	1m1f213y	E(0-70)H	G-F	£3434
59	7/97	Bevl	1m1f207y	E(0-75)H	GD	£3185
51	7/97	Bevl	1m1f207y	D(0-80)H	G-F	£4235
45	7/97	Pont	1m4y	E(0-70)H	GD	£3353
48	8/94	Wind	1m2f7y	G	G-F	£2782

Total win prize-money £54666

Going (Turf): Sf: 1-18 GS: 0-12 **Gd: 6-25** GF: 5-37 Fm: 0-9
Distance: 5f/6f: 0-1 7f-8f: 0-9 **9f-13f: 12-93** 14f+: 0-0
Track : **LH: 8-72** RH: 3-28 Tight: 3-27 **Gall: 4-40**
Aids: Bl: 0-0 Vi: 0-0 Tstrap: 0-5
Best Rating: 75 8/01 Donc 1m2f60y gd-fm

A fairly useful veteran middle-distance handicapper who is best coming off a strong pace on fast ground. A winner at Thirsk in June, she seems as good as ever and is capable of winning more races when things fall into place for her. Best on flat tracks, a mile and a half is her maximum trip.

Mcquillan

(90) (36)
4-y-o b g Maledetto (IRE)-Macs Maharanee (Indian King (USA))
P S Felgate P S Felgate

Placings:00/0000-6030 **(1996)**
2001: 6^{6}SD, 7^{0}SD, 6^{3}SD, 7^{0}SD

	Starts	1st	2nd	3rd	Win & Pl
Career Total (Turf)	4	0	0	0	
Career Total (AW)	6	0	0	1	196

Going (Turf): Sf: 0-1 GS: 0-0 Gd: 0-2 GF: 0-1 Fm: 0-0
Distance: 5f/6f: 0-5 7f-8f: 0-4 9f-13f: 0-1 14f+: 0-0
Track : LH: 0-8 RH: 0-0 Tight: 0-5 Gall: 0-0
Aids: Bl: 0-0 Vi: 0-0 Tstrap: 0-0
Best Rating: 36 5/01 Wolv 6f stand

Mea Culpa (IRE)

46 **52**
3-y-o b f Blues Traveller (IRE)-Tolomena (Tolomeo)
T D Easterby Mrs Sue Tindall

Placings:500-0 **(1081)**
2001: 7^{0}S

	Starts	1st	2nd	3rd	Win & Pl
Career Total (Turf)	4	0	0	0	0

Going (Turf): Sf: 0-1 GS: 0-0 Gd: 0-1 GF: 0-2 Fm: 0-0
Distance: 5f/6f: 0-3 7f-8f: 0-1 9f-13f: 0-0 14f+: 0-0
Track : LH: 0-0 RH: 0-0 Tight: 0-0 Gall: 0-0
Aids: Bl: 0-0 Vi: 0-0 Tstrap: 0-0

Measure Up

95 **80**
2-y-o ch c Inchinor-Victoria Blue (Old Vic)
R Hannon Raymond Tooth

Placings:045 **(4534)**
2001: 6^{0}GF, 6^{4}GF, 6^{5}GF

	Starts	1st	2nd	3rd	Win & Pl
Career Total (Turf)	3	0	0	0	279

Going (Turf): Sf: 0-0 GS: 0-0 Gd: 0-0 GF: 0-3 Fm: 0-0
Distance: 5f/6f: 0-1 7f-8f: 0-2 9f-13f: 0-0 14f+: 0-0
Track : LH: 0-2 RH: 0-0 Tight: 0-1 Gall: 0-1
Aids: Bl: 0-0 Vi: 0-0 Tstrap: 0-0
Best Rating: 80 8/01 Epsm 6f gd-fm

Medelai

88(102) (32)**28**
5-y-o b m Marju (IRE)-No Islands (Lomond (USA))
Ms A E Embiricos The New Twelve

Placings:06340210/00500502/010400-000060 (3966)
2001: 16^{0}SD, 16^{0}SD, 16^{0}SD, 16^{0}GF, 16^{6}GF, 16^{0}GS

	Starts	1st	2nd	3rd	Win & Pl
Career Total (Turf)	19	1	1	1	3653
Career Total (AW)	9	1	1	0	2857

42	1/00	Wolv	2m46y	F(0-65)H	STD	£2320
56	10/98	Nott	1m54y	G	SFT	£2197

Total win prize-money £4519

Going (Turf): Sf: 1-3 GS: 0-2 Gd: 0-5 GF: 0-7 Fm: 0-2
Distance: 5f/6f: 0-1 7f-8f: 0-5 9f-13f: 1-6 14f+: 1-16
Track : **LH: 2-16** RH: 0-10 **Tight: 1-15** Gall: 0-0
Aids: Bl: 0-0 Vi: 0-0 Tstrap: 0-0
Best Rating: 32 2/01 Wolv 2m46y stand

Media Buyer (USA)

(98) (60)
3-y-o b g Green Dancer (USA)-California Rush (USA) (Forty Niner (USA))
R J Price E G Bevan

Placings:000320030-3450 **(0440)**
2001: 7^{3}SD, 6^{4}SD, 8^{5}SD, 8^{0}SD

	Starts	1st	2nd	3rd	Win & Pl
Career Total (Turf)	8	0	1	2	2216
Career Total (AW)	5	0	0	1	414

Going (Turf): Sf: 0-2 GS: 0-1 Gd: 0-3 GF: 0-2 Fm: 0-0
Distance: 5f/6f: 0-2 7f-8f: 0-8 9f-13f: 0-3 14f+: 0-0
Track : LH: 0-9 RH: 0-1 Tight: 0-7 Gall: 0-0
Aids: Bl: 0-5 Vi: 0-0 Tstrap: 0-0
Best Rating: 60 2/01 Wolv 7f stand

Medicean

115 **126**
4-y-o ch h Machiavellian (USA)-Mystic Goddess (USA) (Storm Bird (CAN))
Sir Michael Stoute Cheveley Park Stud

Placings:31130314-1113 **(4113)**
2001: 8^{1}S, 8^{1}G, 10^{1}GF, 10^{3}G

	Starts	1st	2nd	3rd	Win & Pl
Career Total (Turf)	12	6	0	4	547055

120	7/01	Sand	1m2f7y	A	G-F	£200100
126	6/01	Asct	1m	A	GD	£72000
119	5/01	Newb	1m	A	SFT	£87000
123	8/00	Gdwd	1m	A	GD	£46400
105	6/00	Ayr	1m	C(0-90)	G-F	£7598
91	4/00	Sand	1m14y	C	SFT	£6307

Total win prize-money £419405

Going (Turf): Sf: 2-2 GS: 0-2 **Gd: 2-4 GF: 2-4** Fm: 0-0
Distance: 5f/6f: 0-0 **7f-8f: 4-8** 9f-13f: 2-4 14f+: 0-0
Track : LH: 1-3 **RH: 3-6** Tight: 0-0 Gall: 0-4
Aids: Bl: 0-0 Vi: 0-0 Tstrap: 0-0
Best Rating: 126 6/01 Asct 1m good

A high-class miler, he won the Celebration Mile at three and was in the frame in a trio of Group Ones in 2000. Got a win in the top grade under his belt when successful in the Lockinge on his return, and defied a Group One penalty when winning the Queen Anne. Followed up with a gutsy win in the Eclipse Stakes at Sandown on his first attempt at ten furlongs, he seemed to run flat when third to Sakhee in the Juddmonte International. Best on top of the ground, but effective on an easy surface, he retires to the Cheveley Park Stud as a consistent top-class performer.

Mediterranean

109 **108**
3-y-o b c Sadler's Wells (USA)-Pato (High Top)
A P O'Brien Mrs John Magnier & Mr M Tabor

Placings:1-0261P **(4711)**
2001: 16^{0}GF, 14^{2}Y, 14^{6}G, 13^{1}G, 14^{P}G

	Starts	1st	2nd	3rd	Win & Pl
Career Total (Turf)	6	2	1	0	141400

108	8/01	York	1m5f194y	B H	GD	£120250
87	10/00	Leop	1m		HVY	£9750

Total win prize-money £130000

Going (Turf): Sf: 0-0 GS: 0-0 **Gd: 1-3** GF: 0-1 Fm: 0-0
Distance: 5f/6f: 0-0 7f-8f: 0-0 9f-13f: 0-0 **14f+: 1-5**
Track : **LH: 1-2** RH: 0-1 Tight: 0-0 **Gall: 1-3**
Aids: Bl: 0-0 Vi: 0-0 Tstrap: 0-0
Best Rating: 108 8/01 York 1m5f194y good

A half-brother to Classic Cliche and My Emma. Won a mile maiden at Leopardstown last October, scoring easily by four lengths from Delude. Well beaten in the Queen's Vase at Ascot. Not suited by slow pace in Curragh Cup at end of June, but appreciated the good gallop when winning the Ebor at York. He was retired having broken down in the St Leger.

Medkhan (IRE)

93 **38**
4-y-o ch g Lahib (USA)-Safayn (USA) (Lyphard (USA))
F Jordan Miss L M Rochford

Placings:62404-65000 **(5043)**
2001: 12^{6}GF, 10^{5}GF, 10^{0}GF, 12^{0}GS, 8^{0}G

	Starts	1st	2nd	3rd	Win & Pl
Career Total (Turf)	10	0	1	0	1280

Going (Turf): Sf: 0-1 GS: 0-1 Gd: 0-2 GF: 0-3 Fm: 0-2
Distance: 5f/6f: 0-0 7f-8f: 0-1 9f-13f: 0-9 14f+: 0-0
Track : LH: 0-6 RH: 0-2 Tight: 0-3 Gall: 0-1
Aids: Bl: 0-2 Vi: 0-0 Tstrap: 0-0
Best Rating: 66 6/01 Wwck 1m4f134y gd-fm

Medraar

103 **83+**
3-y-o b c Machiavellian (USA)-Saleemah (USA) (Storm Bird (CAN))
J L Dunlop Hamdan Al Maktoum

Placings:0-12424 **(2994)**
2001: 8^{1}S, 8^{2}S, 8^{4}G, 8^{2}F, 8^{4}G

	Starts	1st	2nd	3rd	Win & Pl
Career Total (Turf)	6	1	2	0	8014

69	4/01	Ripn	1m	D	SFT	£3575

Total win prize-money £3575

Going (Turf): Sf: 1-3 GS: 0-0 Gd: 0-2 GF: 0-0 Fm: 0-1
Distance: 5f/6f: 0-0 **7f-8f: 1-4** 9f-13f: 0-2 14f+: 0-0
Track : LH: 0-2 **RH: 1-2 Tight: 1-2** Gall: 0-1
Aids: Bl: 0-0 Vi: 0-0 Tstrap: 0-0
Best Rating: 83 5/01 Newc 1m soft

Mega (IRE)

85(84) (31)**45**
5-y-o b m Petardia-Gobolino (Don)
M H Tompkins Mystic Meg Limited

Placings:0/00000/540-000 **(3707)**
2001: 10^{0}GF, 14^{0}G, 11^{0}G

	Starts	1st	2nd	3rd	Win & Pl
Career Total (Turf)	9	0	0	0	
Career Total (AW)	3	0	0	0	0

Going (Turf): Sf: 0-1 GS: 0-1 Gd: 0-4 GF: 0-2 Fm: 0-1
Distance: 5f/6f: 0-1 7f-8f: 0-3 9f-13f: 0-7 14f+: 0-1
Track : LH: 0-6 RH: 0-2 Tight: 0-3 Gall: 0-2
Aids: Bl: 0-1 Vi: 0-1 Tstrap: 0-0
Best Rating: 45 6/01 Donc 1m2f60y gd-fm

Mehmaas

(79) (65?)**65**
5-y-o b g Distant Relative-Guest List (Be My Guest (USA))
R E Barr Middleham Park Racing Xxiv

Placings:05022/051504/033100000530406-004330241 03303320066 **(5659)**
2001: 8^{0}GS, 7^{0}F, 8^{4}GF, 8^{3}F, 7^{3}GF, 7^{0}GF, 8^{2}F, 7^{4}GF, 7^{1}F, 7^{0}GF, 7^{3}GF, 8^{3}GF, 6^{0}GF, 7^{3}GF, 8^{3}G, 7^{2}G, 8^{0}G, 7^{0}S, 7^{6}S, 8^{6}G

	Starts	1st	2nd	3rd	Win & Pl

	Starts	1st	2nd	3rd	Win & Pl
Career Total (Turf)	45	3	3	9	19746
Career Total (AW)	1	0	1	0	657

62	7/01	Rdcr	7f	G(0-70)	FRM	£1876
02	0/00	Bevl	7f100y	E(0-70)H	G-F	£4576
75	8/99	Brig	6f209y	F	G-F	£2550

Total win prize-money £9003

Going (Turf): Sf: 0-7 GS: 0-5 Gd: 0-6 **GF: 2-18** Fm: 1-9
Distance: 5f/6f: 0-1 **7f-8f: 3-35** 9f-13f: 0-10 14f+: 0-0
Track : LH: 1-14 RH: 1-12 Tight: 0-11 Gall: 0-3
Aids: Bl: 0-3 **Vi: 2-33** Tstrap: 0-0
Best Rating: 65 9/01 Bevl 7f100y good

Fair handicapper who pays his way. Stays a mile, but better over shorter. Acts on fast ground.

Meiying

86 **34**
3-y-o br f Cyrano De Bergerac-Hong Kong Girl (Petong)
M Kettle J D Eggleton

Placings:60000 **(4733)**
2001: 6⁰GF, 5⁰GF, 6⁰GF, 5⁰F, 7⁰F

	Starts	1st	2nd	3rd	Win & Pl
Career Total (Turf)	5	0	0	0	0

Going (Turf): Sf: 0-0 GS: 0-0 Gd: 0-0 GF: 0-3 Fm: 0-2
Distance: 5f/6f: 0-4 7f-8f: 0-1 9f-13f: 0-0 14f+: 0-0
Track : LH: 0-1 RH: 0-0 Tight: 0-0 Gall: 0-1
Aids: Bl: 0-0 Vi: 0-0 Tstrap: 0-0
Best Rating: 34 9/01 Bath 5f161y firm

Melanzana

106(74) (21)**83**
4-y-o b f Alzao (USA)-Melody Park (Music Boy)
E A L Dunlop The Serendipity Partnership

Placings:31/4256000-0100405230 **(4590)**
2001: 7⁰SD, 5¹G, 6⁰F, 6⁰G, 6⁴GF, 6⁰GF, 6⁵GS, 6²G, 6³G, 6⁰G

	Starts	1st	2nd	3rd	Win & Pl
Career Total (Turf)	18	2	2	2	13657
Career Total (AW)	1	0	0	0	

81	5/01	Leic	5f218y	D(0-80)H	GD	£3874
85	9/99	Rdcr	6f	D	G-F	£3270

Total win prize-money £7144

Going (Turf): Sf: 0-1 GS: 0-2 **Gd: 1-9 GF: 1-5** Fm: 0-1
Distance: **5f/6f: 2-16** 7f-8f: 0-3 9f-13f: 0-0 14f+: 0-0
Track : LH: 0-1 RH: 0-0 Tight: 0-0 Gall: 0-0
Aids: Bl: 0-0 Vi: 0-0 Tstrap: 0-0
Best Rating: 83 8/01 NmkJ 6f good

Decent sprinter, suited by six furlongs and scored over that trip at Leicester in May. Acts on any ground. Usually held up.

Melledgan (IRE)

(95) (41)**46**
4-y-o b f Catrail (USA)-Dark Hyacinth (IRE) (Darshaan)
Miss S J Wilton (R Guest 17/9) John Pointon And Sons

Placings:6400-003010003100 **(5407)**
2001: 6⁰HY, 5⁰GF, 7³SD, 8⁰GF, 7¹G, 7⁰GF, 8⁰GS, 7⁰G, 8³F, 10¹GF, 10⁰S, 12⁰SD

	Starts	1st	2nd	3rd	Win & Pl
Career Total (Turf)	14	2	0	1	6063
Career Total (AW)	2	0	0	1	336

46	9/01	Wwck	1m2f188y	F(0-60)H	G-F	£2915
43	6/01	Muss	7f30y	F	GD	£2453

Total win prize-money £5370

Going (Turf): Sf: 0-3 GS: 0-1 **Gd: 1-3 GF: 1-6** Fm: 0-1
Distance: 5f/6f: 0-5 7f-8f: 1-7 9f-13f: 1-4 14f+: 0-0
Track : **LH: 1-7** RH: 0-0 Tight: 0-1 Gall: 0-2
Aids: Bl: 0-0 Vi: 0-0 Tstrap: 0-0
Best Rating: 46 9/01 Wwck 1m2f188y gd-fm

Mellow Park (IRE)

95 **80**
2-y-o b f In The Wings-Park Special (Relkino)
J Noseda Mrs Seamus Burns

Placings:5 **(5603)**
2001: 7⁵GS

	Starts	1st	2nd	3rd	Win & Pl
Career Total (Turf)	1	0	0	0	0

Going (Turf): Sf: 0-0 GS: 0-1 Gd: 0-0 GF: 0-0 Fm: 0-0
Distance: 5f/6f: 0-0 7f-8f: 0-1 9f-13f: 0-0 14f+: 0-0
Track : LH: 0-0 RH: 0-0 Tight: 0-0 Gall: 0-0
Aids: Bl: 0-0 Vi: 0-0 Tstrap: 0-0
Best Rating: 80 11/01 NmkR 7f gd-sft

Melodian

109(46) **65**
6-y-o b h Grey Desire-Mere Melody (Dunphy)
M Brittain Mel Brittain

Placings:0/0001300/40213110350/0231041000013220 0-100500000 **(5624)**
2001: 8¹S, 8⁰GS, 8⁰G, 8⁵G, 8⁰G, 8⁰S, 8⁰S, 6⁰GS, 9⁰GS

	Starts	1st	2nd	3rd	Win & Pl
Career Total (Turf)	46	8	4	5	51638
Career Total (AW)	1	0	0	0	

85	3/01	Donc	1m	B H	SFT	£14560
69	9/00	Bevl	7f100y	E(0-70)H	HVY	£2769
69	6/00	Bevl	7f100y	E(0-70)H	G-S	£5018
65	4/00	Newc	7f	D(0-85)H	SFT	£4078
53	8/99	Catt	7f	E(0-70)H	G-F	£4588
52	7/99	Donc	7f	E(0-70)H	G-F	£3126
48	7/99	Bevl	7f100y	E(0-70)H	G-F	£4177
41	7/98	Newc	7f	F(0-65)H	GD	£2431

Total win prize-money £40749

Going (Turf): Sf: 3-12 GS: 1-9 Gd: 1-11 **GF: 3-13** Fm: 0-1
Distance: 5f/6f: 0-4 **7f-8f: 8-36** 9f-13f: 0-7 14f+: 0-0
Track : LH: 1-16 **RH: 3-13 Tight: 1-7** Gall: 0-5
Aids: **Bl: 8-42** Vi: 0-0 Tstrap: 0-0
Best Rating: 85 3/01 Donc 1m soft

Fairly useful handicapper at up to a mile and best when the mud is flying. He revelled in the mud when winning the Spring Mile at Doncaster on his reappearance, but was clobbered by the Handicapper and has struggled since.

Melody Lady

90(84) (21)**49**
5-y-o ch m Dilum (USA)-Ansellady (Absalom)
K A Ryan R Sunter

Placings:005300/00202/00220350-00 **(2632)**
2001: 12⁰GF, 16⁰F

	Starts	1st	2nd	3rd	Win & Pl
Career Total (Turf)	19	0	4	2	4435
Career Total (AW)	2	0	0	0	

Going (Turf): Sf: 0-1 GS: 0-2 Gd: 0-7 GF: 0-4 Fm: 0-4
Distance: 5f/6f: 0-5 7f-8f: 0-2 9f-13f: 0-12 14f+: 0-1
Track : LH: 0-12 RH: 0-4 Tight: 0-7 Gall: 0-2
Aids: Bl: 0-3 Vi: 0-0 Tstrap: 0-1
Best Rating: 26 7/01 Muss 2m firm

Melomania (USA)

67(84) (34)
9-y-o b g Shadeed (USA)-Medley Of Song (USA) (Secretariat (USA))
T T Clement Mrs P Haddow

Placings:40000/0/100306000006/00-0000 **(1810)**
2001: 8⁰SW, 12⁰SD, 10⁰SW, 8⁰GF

	Starts	1st	2nd	3rd	Win & Pl
Career Total (Turf)	10	0	0	0	253
Career Total (AW)	14	1	0	1	2453

43	2/99	Ling	1m	E(0-75)H	STD	£2220

Total win prize-money £2221

Going (Turf): Sf: 0-0 GS: 0-1 Gd: 0-5 GF: 0-3 Fm: 0-1
Distance: 5f/6f: 0-1 **7f-8f: 1-9** 9f-13f: 0-13 14f+: 0-1
Track : **LH: 1-16** RH: 0-4 **Tight: 1-13** Gall: 0-1
Aids: Bl: 0-3 Vi: 0-1 Tstrap: 0-3
Best Rating: 34 2/01 Ling 1m slow

Mels Baby (IRE)

96 **34**
8-y-o br g Contract Law (USA)-Launch The Raft (Home Guard (USA))
J L Eyre Ms Melanie Jayne Eyre

Placings:004650006/2640226222351116/4231500/400 00P/00-060000 **(4399)**
2001: 10⁰HY, 12⁶GF, 9⁰G, 10⁰GF, 10⁰G, 10⁰G

	Starts	1st	2nd	3rd	Win & Pl
Career Total (Turf)	40	4	6	2	25242
Career Total (AW)	6	0	1	0	656

76	5/97	Bevl	1m1f207y	D(0-80)H	SFT	£7035
68	11/96	Donc	1m	E(0-80)H	SFT	£4175
62	10/96	Pont	1m4y	D(0-80)H	GD	£5526
63	9/96	Rdcr	1m	E(0-70)H	FRM	£3787

Total win prize-money £20524

Going (Turf): Sf: 2-7 GS: 0-4 **Gd: 1-13** GF: 0-8 **Fm: 1-8**
Distance: 5f/6f: 0-6 7f-8f: 2-14 9f-13f: 2-26 14f+: 0-0
Track : **LH: 1-24 RH: 1-10** Tight: 0-13 Gall: 0-5
Aids: Bl: 0-3 Vi: 0-2 Tstrap: 0-0
Best Rating: 34 8/01 Newc 1m2f32y good

Melstair

6-y-o b g Terimon-Kevins Lady (Alzao (USA))
A R Dicken Gravy Boys Racing

Placings:0 **(0684)**
2001: 12⁰S

	Starts	1st	2nd	3rd	Win & Pl
Career Total (Turf)	1	0	0	0	

Going (Turf): Sf: 0-1 GS: 0-0 Gd: 0-0 GF: 0-0 Fm: 0-0
Distance: 5f/6f: 0-0 7f-8f: 0-0 9f-13f: 0-1 14f+: 0-0
Track : LH: 0-0 RH: 0-0 Tight: 0-0 Gall: 0-0
Aids: Bl: 0-0 Vi: 0-0 Tstrap: 0-0

Memameda

92(80) (27)**25**
5-y-o b m Cigar-Mamzooj (IRE) (Shareef Dancer (USA))
K A Ryan The One And Only Racing

Placings:60-U000500 **(3949)**
2001: 12ᵁSD, 12⁰SW, 7⁰F, 8⁰GF, 8⁵F, 14⁰GF, 8⁰GS

	Starts	1st	2nd	3rd	Win & Pl
Career Total (Turf)	5	0	0	0	0
Career Total (AW)	4	0	0	0	0

Going (Turf): Sf: 0-0 GS: 0-1 Gd: 0-0 GF: 0-2 Fm: 0-2
Distance: 5f/6f: 0-0 7f-8f: 0-3 9f-13f: 0-5 14f+: 0-1
Track : LH: 0-5 RH: 0-1 Tight: 0-2 Gall: 0-0
Aids: Bl: 0-0 Vi: 0-0 Tstrap: 0-0
Best Rating: 25 7/01 Rdcr 1m firm

Memphis Dancer

6-y-o b m Shareef Dancer (USA)-Wollow Maid (Wollow)
M W Easterby Peter Armitage

Placings:00/206002/6/0 **(0879)**
2001: 21⁰S

	Starts	1st	2nd	3rd	Win & Pl
Career Total (Turf)	10	0	2	0	1750

Going (Turf): Sf: 0-1 GS: 0-3 Gd: 0-3 GF: 0-3 Fm: 0-0

Distance: 5f/6f: 0-0 7f-8f: 0-3 9f-13f: 0-6 14f+: 0-1
Track : LH: 0-4 RH: 0-3 Tight: 0-2 Gall: 0-2
Aids: Bl: 0-0 Vi: 0-0 Tstrap: 0-0

Memsahib

81 **37**

3-y-o b f Alzao (USA)-Indian Queen (Electric)
D R C Elsworth Sir Gordon Brunton

Placings:0-00 **(4893)**
2001: 12^{0}G, 12^{0}GF

	Starts	1st	2nd	3rd	Win & Pl
Career Total (Turf)	3	0	0	0	

Going (Turf): Sf: 0-1 GS: 0-0 Gd: 0-1 GF: 0-1 Fm: 0-0
Distance: 5f/6f: 0-0 7f-8f: 0-0 9f-13f: 0-3 14f+: 0-0
Track : LH: 0-1 RH: 0-2 Tight: 0-1 Gall: 0-0
Aids: Bl: 0-0 Vi: 0-0 Tstrap: 0-0
Best Rating: 37 9/01 Kemp 1m4f gd-fm

Men Of Wickenby

(58)

7-y-o b g Shirley Heights-Radiant Bride (USA) (Blushing Groom (FR))
G A Swinbank J P Slattery

Placings:0650/0401500050/0-0 **(2172)**
2001: 11^{0}SD

	Starts	1st	2nd	3rd	Win & Pl
Career Total (Turf)	14	1	0	0	2853
Career Total (AW)	2	0	0	0	0

39 6/99 Haml 1m1f36y E G-S £2853
Total win prize-money £2853

Going (Turf): Sf: 0-2 **GS: 1-2** Gd: 0-4 GF: 0-5 Fm: 0-1
Distance: 5f/6f: 0-0 7f-8f: 0-0 **9f-13f: 1-16** 14f+: 0-0
Track : LH: 0-5 **RH: 1-11 Tight: 1-11** Gall: 0-0
Aids: Bl: 0-0 Vi: 0-0 Tstrap: 0-0

Menaggio (USA)

106 **85**

3-y-o b c Danehill (USA)-Mayenne (USA) (Nureyev (USA))
P W Harris Mrs P W Harris

Placings:160 **(5344)**
2001: 8^{1}GF, 8^{6}GS, 8^{0}GS

	Starts	1st	2nd	3rd	Win & Pl
Career Total (Turf)	3	1	0	0	4823

85 8/01 NmkJ 1m D G-F £4823
Total win prize-money £4823

Going (Turf): Sf: 0-0 GS: 0-2 Gd: 0-0 **GF: 1-1** Fm: 0-0
Distance: 5f/6f: 0-0 **7f-8f: 1-3** 9f-13f: 0-0 14f+: 0-0
Track : LH: 0-1 RH: 0-0 Tight: 0-0 Gall: 0-1
Aids: Bl: 0-0 Vi: 0-0 Tstrap: 0-0
Best Rating: 85 8/01 NmkJ 1m gd-fm

Got off the mark on his first attempt at Newmarket, but has been disappointing since. Acts well on good to firm, and is suited by a mile.

Mental Pressure

109 **68**

8-y-o ch g Polar Falcon (USA)-Hysterical (High Top)
Mrs M Reveley The Mary Reveley Racing Club

Placings:03/6232223/0000/32521343-215135205 **(5661)**
2001: 16^{2}GF, 14^{1}F, 16^{5}GF, 16^{1}F, 16^{3}GF, 13^{5}GF, 16^{2}GF, 14^{0}G, 16^{5}G

	Starts	1st	2nd	3rd	Win & Pl
Career Total (Turf)	30	3	8	7	30906

68 7/01 Rdcr 2m4y E(0-75)H FRM £4829
64 5/01 Rdcr 1m6f19y E(0-70)H FRM £3607
62 8/00 Rdcr 2m4y E(0-75)H FRM £2886
Total win prize-money £11324

Going (Turf): Sf: 0-1 GS: 0-2 Gd: 0-12 GF: 0-10 **Fm: 3-5**
Distance: 5f/6f: 0-0 7f-8f: 0-2 9f-13f: 0-5 **14f+: 3-23**
Track : **LH: 3-20** RH: 0-9 **Tight: 3-19** Gall: 0-4
Aids: Bl: 0-0 Vi: 0-0 Tstrap: 0-0
Best Rating: 70 5/01 Thsk 2m gd-fm

Has won twice this year, and has also had some good placed efforts. Goes well on a fast surface, and is a good stayer.

Mer Lock

65 **14**

3-y-o b f Piccolo-Sojourn (Be My Guest (USA))
T J Naughton Bonus Partnership

Placings:0-0 **(4160)**
2001: 6^{0}GF

	Starts	1st	2nd	3rd	Win & Pl
Career Total (Turf)	2	0	0	0	

Going (Turf): Sf: 0-0 GS: 0-0 Gd: 0-0 GF: 0-2 Fm: 0-0
Distance: 5f/6f: 0-2 7f-8f: 0-0 9f-13f: 0-0 14f+: 0-0
Track : LH: 0-0 RH: 0-0 Tight: 0-0 Gall: 0-0
Aids: Bl: 0-0 Vi: 0-0 Tstrap: 0-0
Best Rating: 3 8/01 Ling 6f gd-fm

Mer Made

93(78) (28)**30**

3-y-o b f Prince Sabo-Blue Zulu (IRE) (Don't Forget Me)
T J Naughton Mr & Mrs D J Flahive

Placings:500-0006 **(4365)**
2001: 6^{0}GF, 5^{0}F, 6^{0}GF, 7^{6}GF

	Starts	1st	2nd	3rd	Win & Pl
Career Total (Turf)	6	0	0	0	0
Career Total (AW)	1	0	0	0	

Going (Turf): Sf: 0-0 GS: 0-1 Gd: 0-0 GF: 0-4 Fm: 0-1
Distance: 5f/6f: 0-4 7f-8f: 0-3 9f-13f: 0-0 14f+: 0-0
Track : LH: 0-3 RH: 0-1 Tight: 0-1 Gall: 0-1
Aids: Bl: 0-1 Vi: 0-0 Tstrap: 0-0
Best Rating: 30 8/01 Brig 7f214y gd-fm

Meranti

96 (16)**38**

8-y-o b g Puissance-Sorrowful (Moorestyle)
J M Bradley J M Bradley

Placings:06404450/52404000/01410602100000/00300 161550000/0040000/000-06003650 **(3672)**
2001: 6^{0}GF, 6^{6}GF, 6^{0}GF, 5^{0}G, 7^{3}GS, 7^{6}GS, 6^{5}F, 5^{0}G

	Starts	1st	2nd	3rd	Win & Pl
Career Total (Turf)	61	5	2	2	21811
Career Total (AW)	1	0	0	0	

66 7/98 Thsk 6f D(0-80)H GD £4118
54 7/98 Sals 6f E(0-70)H G-F £3176
60 7/97 Sals 6f E(0-70)H G-F £3210
55 4/97 Thsk 7f E(0-70)H G-F £3471
57 4/97 Nott 6f15y E(0-70)H G-F £3382
Total win prize-money £17359

Going (Turf): Sf: 0-3 GS: 0-3 Gd: 1-21 **GF: 4-26** Fm: 0-8
Distance: **5f/6f: 3-41** 7f-8f: 2-21 9f-13f: 0-0 14f+: 0-0
Track : **LH: 1-12** RH: 0-6 **Tight: 1-4** Gall: 0-9
Aids: Bl: 0-1 Vi: 0-0 Tstrap: 0-0
Best Rating: 38 7/01 Ling 7f gd-sft

Mercede (IRE)

(18)**29**

4-y-o b f Perugino (USA)-Miss Busybody (IRE) (Phardante (FR))
J Balding (N P Littmoden 19/8) Josef Fusenich

Placings:000/000506-0024001600 **(5538)**
2001: 10^{0}, 8^{0}, 8^{2}, 8^{4}, 10^{0}, 8^{0}, 8^{1}G, 8^{6}G, 8^{0}S, 10^{0}S

	Starts	1st	2nd	3rd	Win & Pl
Career Total (Turf)	17	1	1	0	2019
Career Total (AW)	2	0	0	0	

7/01 Mulh 1m H GD £1368
Total win prize-money £1368

Going (Turf): Sf: 0-6 GS: 0-0 **Gd: 1-2** GF: 0-1 Fm: 0-0
Distance: 5f/6f: 0-1 **7f-8f: 1-6** 9f-13f: 0-12 14f+: 0-0
Track : LH: 0-3 RH: 0-1 Tight: 0-2 Gall: 0-0
Aids: Bl: 0-0 Vi: 0-0 Tstrap: 0-0
Best Rating: 29 10/01 Rdcr 1m2f soft

Mercernary (IRE)

64(67) (19)**19**

2-y-o b g General Monash (USA)-Battle Rage (IRE) (Shernazar)
A Berry Paul J Dixon

Placings:000 **(2664)**
2001: 5^{0}S, 5^{0}SD, 6^{0}G

	Starts	1st	2nd	3rd	Win & Pl
Career Total (Turf)	2	0	0	0	
Career Total (AW)	1	0	0	0	

Going (Turf): Sf: 0-1 GS: 0-0 Gd: 0-1 GF: 0-0 Fm: 0-0
Distance: 5f/6f: 0-2 7f-8f: 0-1 9f-13f: 0-0 14f+: 0-0
Track : LH: 0-0 RH: 0-0 Tight: 0-0 Gall: 0-0
Aids: Bl: 0-0 Vi: 0-0 Tstrap: 0-0
Best Rating: 19 7/01 Yarm 6f3y good

There is stamina on the dam's side and he has been well and truly outpaced so far.

Merchant Prince

95(88) (35)**33**

5-y-o b g Flying Tyke-Bellinote (FR) (Noir Et Or)
A Smith Alfred Smith

Placings:0/00000/50000050-0050 **(4778)**
2001: 7^{0}F, 8^{0}GF, 10^{5}G, 5^{0}G

	Starts	1st	2nd	3rd	Win & Pl
Career Total (Turf)	12	0	0	0	0
Career Total (AW)	6	0	0	0	0

Going (Turf): Sf: 0-3 GS: 0-0 Gd: 0-5 GF: 0-1 Fm: 0-3
Distance: 5f/6f: 0-9 7f-8f: 0-4 9f-13f: 0-5 14f+: 0-0
Track : LH: 0-9 RH: 0-1 Tight: 0-4 Gall: 0-1
Aids: Bl: 0-1 Vi: 0-1 Tstrap: 0-0
Best Rating: 33 8/01 Newc 1m2f32y good

Merchant Princess

69 **17**

2-y-o ch f Dashing Blade-Running Tycoon (IRE) (Last Tycoon)
I A Balding J C Smith

Placings:5 **(5096)**
2001: 6^{5}GS

	Starts	1st	2nd	3rd	Win & Pl
Career Total (Turf)	1	0	0	0	272

Going (Turf): Sf: 0-0 GS: 0-1 Gd: 0-0 GF: 0-0 Fm: 0-0
Distance: 5f/6f: 0-1 7f-8f: 0-0 9f-13f: 0-0 14f+: 0-0
Track : LH: 0-0 RH: 0-0 Tight: 0-0 Gall: 0-0
Aids: Bl: 0-0 Vi: 0-0 Tstrap: 0-0
Best Rating: 17 10/01 Sals 6f gd-sft

Mercury Rising (IRE)

80

3-y-o b c Sadler's Wells (USA)-Silwana (FR) (Nashwan (USA))
J W Hills The Jampot Partnership

Placings:4302 **(5525)**
2001: 8^{4}S, 10^{3}S, 12^{0}GF, 11^{2}HY

	Starts	1st	2nd	3rd	Win & Pl

	Starts	1st	2nd	3rd	Win & Pl
Career Total (Turf)	4	0	1	1	2245

Going (Turf): Sf: 0-3 GS: 0-0 Gd: 0-0 GF: 0-1 Fm: 0-0
Distance: 5f/6f: 0-0 7f-8f: 0-1 9f-13f: 0-3 14f+: 0-0
Track : LH: 0-1 RH: 0-1 Tight: 0-1 Gall: 0-1
Aids: Bl: 0-0 Vi: 0-0 Tstrap: 0-0
Best Rating: 80 10/01 Wind 1m3f135y heavy

Ran with great promise on his first three starts, and confirmed that with a good second on his handicap debut at Windsor. There are races to be won with him.

Merdiff

47
2-y-o b c Machiavellian (USA)-Balwa (USA) (Danzig (USA))
M A Jarvis Sheikh Ahmed Al Maktoum

Placings:0 (5559)
2001: 8^{0}S

	Starts	1st	2nd	3rd	Win & Pl
Career Total (Turf)	1	0	0	0	

Going (Turf): Sf: 0-1 GS: 0-0 Gd: 0-0 GF: 0-0 Fm: 0-0
Distance: 5f/6f: 0-0 7f-8f: 0-0 9f-13f: 0-1 14f+: 0-0
Track : LH: 0-0 RH: 0-0 Tight: 0-0 Gall: 0-0
Aids: Bl: 0-0 Vi: 0-0 Tstrap: 0-0

Merely A Monarch

(97) (68) **72**
2-y-o b g Reprimand-Ruby Princess (IRE) (Mac's Imp (USA))
I A Wood Miss Jacqueline Goodearl

Placings:0101 (5408)
2001: 6^{0}GF, 6^{1}GF, 6^{0}G, 6^{1}SD

	Starts	1st	2nd	3rd	Win & Pl
Career Total (Turf)	3	1	0	0	2061
Career Total (AW)	1	1	0	0	3666

68 10/01 Sthl 6f D(0-85) STD £3666
72 9/01 Ling 6f G G-F £2060
Total win prize-money £5727

Going (Turf): Sf: 0-0 GS: 0-0 Gd: 0-1 **GF: 1-2** Fm: 0-0
Distance: 5f/6f: 2-3 7f-8f: 0-1 9f-13f: 0-0 14f+: 0-0
Track : LH: 1-1 RH: 0-0 Tight: 0-0 Gall: 0-0
Aids: Bl: 0-0 Vi: 0-0 Tstrap: 0-0
Best Rating: 72 9/01 Ling 6f gd-fm

He tended to hang in his early starts, but has plenty of ability and has landed a Lingfield maiden on turf and a nursery on the Southwell Fibresand so far. Stays six furlongs. Acts on good to firm and Southwell's Fibresand.

Meriden Mist

98(93) (60) **72**
3-y-o b f Distinctly North (USA)-Bring On The Choir (Chief Singer)
P W Harris Mr G E Williams & Mr B Lawrence

Placings:52441405426-66253000 (5465)
2001: 7^{6}GS, 8^{6}G, 8^{2}GF, 7^{5}G, 8^{3}G, 8^{0}G, 10^{0}HY, 10^{0}G

	Starts	1st	2nd	3rd	Win & Pl
Career Total (Turf)	18	1	3	1	9941
Career Total (AW)	1	0	0	0	0

68 7/00 Brig 6f209y D FRM £3523
Total win prize-money £3523

Going (Turf): Sf: 0 2 GS: 0-1 Gd: 0-9 GF: 0-5 **Fm: 1-1**
Distance: 5f/6f: 0-3 **7f-8f: 1-13** 9f-13f: 0-3 14f+: 0-0
Track : LH: 1-8 RH: 0-2 Tight: 0-4 Gall: 0-2
Aids: Bl: 0 0 Vi: 0-0 Tstrap: 0-0
Best Rating: 73 7/01 Donc 1m gd-fm

Won a maiden on fast ground at Brighton as a two-year-old and goes well there, but has been held in handicap company since.

Merlin's Mistress

79
3-y-o b f Magic Ring (IRE)-Jubilata (USA) (The Minstrel (CAN))
W G M Turner I W T Loftus

Placings:00 (3691)
2001: 11^{0}F, 15^{0}G

	Starts	1st	2nd	3rd	Win & Pl
Career Total (Turf)	2	0	0	0	

Going (Turf): Sf: 0-0 GS: 0-0 Gd: 0-1 GF: 0-0 Fm: 0-1
Distance: 5f/6f: 0-0 7f-8f: 0-0 9f-13f: 0-1 14f+: 0-1
Track : LH: 0-2 RH: 0-0 Tight: 0-2 Gall: 0-0
Aids: Bl: 0-0 Vi: 0-0 Tstrap: 0-0

Merly Notty

92(72) **23**
5-y-o ch m Inchinor-Rambadale (Vaigly Great)
W Storey Tony Stafford

Placings:000/0005/246-000000 (4478)
2001: 12^{0}SD, 12^{0}GF, 10^{0}GF, 12^{0}GF, 12^{0}G, 16^{0}F

	Starts	1st	2nd	3rd	Win & Pl
Career Total (Turf)	15	0	1	0	752
Career Total (AW)	1	0	0	0	

Going (Turf): Sf: 0-2 GS: 0-1 Gd: 0-3 GF: 0-6 Fm: 0-3
Distance: 5f/6f: 0-2 7f-8f: 0-3 9f-13f: 0-9 14f+: 0-2
Track : LH: 0-6 RH: 0-6 Tight: 0-7 Gall: 0-4
Aids: Bl: 0-0 Vi: 0-0 Tstrap: 0-0
Best Rating: 23 7/01 Newc 1m4f93y good

Merryvale Man

106(99) (47) **59**
4-y-o b g Rudimentary (USA)-Salu (Ardross)
J M Jefferson Arthur Symons Key

Placings:0003500**2**/**05312**1020505**300**-00610530414 (5640)
2001: 13^{0}GF, 12^{0}SD, 13^{6}GS, 11^{1}S, 11^{0}G, 12^{5}S, 10^{3}HY, 10^{0}G, 14^{4}SD, 10^{1}HY, 13^{4}G

	Starts	1st	2nd	3rd	Win & Pl
Career Total (Turf)	23	3	1	2	10832
Career Total (AW)	11	1	2	2	4753

55 10/01 Newc 1m2f32y F(0-60)H HVY £2758
52 7/01 Haml 1m3f16y F(0-70)H SFT £2842
72 3/00 Catt 1m3f214yE(0-75)H GD £2814
60 2/00 Sthl 1m3f E STD £2613
Total win prize-money £11028

Going (Turf): Sf: 2-8 GS: 0-3 Gd: 1-8 GF: 0-3 Fm: 0-0
Distance: 5f/6f: 0-2 7f-8f: 0-7 **9f-13f: 4-16** 14f+: 0-8
Track : LH: 3-24 RH: 1-4 **Tight: 2-11** Gall: 1-4
Aids: Bl: 0-1 Vi: 0-0 Tstrap: 0-0
Best Rating: 59 11/01 Catt 1m5f175y good

Mersey Mirage

100(86) (49) **71**
4-y-o b c King's Signet (USA)-Kirriemuir (Lochnager)
R Hannon Speedlith Group

Placings:4401302/014300-00000425550 (5181)
2001: 7^{0}S, 6^{0}G, 6^{0}GF, 7^{0}GF, 6^{0}GF, 6^{0}G, 6^{4}GF, 5^{2}GF, 6^{5}G, 6^{5}F, 7^{5}GF, 6^{0}HY

	Starts	1st	2nd	3rd	Win & Pl
Career Total (Turf)	24	2	2	2	19731
Career Total (AW)	1	0	0	0	

86 8/00 Leic 5f218y B(0-105)H G-F £9639
74 7/99 Brig 5f213y D FRM £3777
Total win prize-money £13418

Going (Turf): Sf: 0-5 GS: 0-2 Gd: 0-6 **GF: 1-9 Fm: 1-2**
Distance: 5f/6f: 2-17 7f-8f: 0-8 9f-13f: 0-0 14f+: 0-0
Track : LH: 1-5 RH: 0-1 Tight: 0-2 Gall: 0-0
Aids: Bl: 0-0 Vi: 0-2 Tstrap: 0-0
Best Rating: 71 7/01 Wind 6f gd-fm

He has not found his form in 2001 but has come down the weights as a consequence. Best at five and six furlongs and an easy seven on fast ground.

Mersey Sound (IRE)

109 **94**
3-y-o b c Ela-Mana-Mou-Coral Sound (IRE) (Glow (USA))
D R C Elsworth Terry Neill

Placings:3-440 (2329)
2001: 10^{4}GF, 10^{4}GF, 12^{0}GF

	Starts	1st	2nd	3rd	Win & Pl
Career Total (Turf)	4	0	0	1	3737

Going (Turf): Sf: 0-0 GS: 0-0 Gd: 0-0 GF: 0-4 Fm: 0-0
Distance: 5f/6f: 0-0 7f-8f: 0-1 9f-13f: 0-3 14f+: 0-0
Track : LH: 0-1 RH: 0-2 Tight: 0-0 Gall: 0-2
Aids: Bl: 0-0 Vi: 0-0 Tstrap: 0-0
Best Rating: 94 6/01 Asct 1m4f gd-fm

He showed plenty of promise when third behind Nayef at Newbury in his only start at two but has failed to improve on that effort this term, finishing fourth in the Glasgow Stakes at York before flopping in a decent maiden last time. Should have no trouble winning races but may need his sights lowered to do so.

Meshaheer (USA)

106 **107+**
2-y-o b c Nureyev (USA)-Race The Wild Wind (USA) (Sunny's Halo (CAN))
D R Loder Hamdan Al Maktoum

Placings:1313 (4394a)
2001: 6^{1}GF, 6^{3}GF, 6^{1}G, 6^{3}GS

	Starts	1st	2nd	3rd	Win & Pl
Career Total (Turf)	4	2	0	2	50724

101 7/01 NmkJ 6f A GD £23800
93 5/01 Donc 6f D G-F £4504
Total win prize-money £28305

Going (Turf): Sf: 0-0 GS: 0-1 **Gd: 1-1 GF: 1-2** Fm: 0-0
Distance: 5f/6f: 2-4 7f-8f: 0-0 9f-13f: 0-0 14f+: 0-0
Track : LH: 0-0 RH: 0-0 Tight: 0-0 Gall: 0-0
Aids: Bl: 0-0 Vi: 0-0 Tstrap: 0-0
Best Rating: 107 8/01 Deau 6f gd-sft

An imposing£500,000 yearling, brother to King Charlemagne. Hacked up over six furlongs on his debut at Doncaster. Endured a nightmare passage when an unlucky loser in the Coventry Stakes at Royal Ascot, and made amends with a smooth win in the July Stakes at Newmarket. He found Johannesburg too good for him in France.

Mesmeric (IRE)

109 **104**
3-y-o b c Sadler's Wells (USA)-Mesmerize (Mill Reef (USA))
E A L Dunlop Maktoum Al Maktoum

Placings:24643211012 (5693)
2001: 8^{2}G, 10^{4}G, 10^{6}GF, 12^{4}GF, 10^{3}GS, 12^{2}G, 12^{1}G, 13^{1}GF, 12^{0}S, 12^{1}GS, 12^{2}S

	Starts	1st	2nd	3rd	Win & Pl
Career Total (Turf)	11	3	3	1	37705

100 10/01 NmkR 1m4f B(0-100)H G-S £9245
90 9/01 Newb 1m5f61y C(0-100)H G-F £14625
91 9/01 Chep 1m4f23y D GD £2926
Total win prize-money £26796

Going (Turf): Sf: 0-2 **GS: 1-2 Gd: 1-4 GF: 1-3** Fm: 0-0
Distance: 5f/6f: 0-0 7f-8f: 0-1 **9f-13f: 2-9** 14f+: 1-1
Track : LH: 2-5 RH: 1-4 Tight: 0-2 **Gall: 2-6**

Aids: Bl: 0-0 **Vi: 2-5** Tstrap: 0-0
Best Rating: 104 11/01 Donc 1m4f soft

After narrowly missing the target on a number of occasions, he finally came good in a Chepstow maiden in September 2001 and followed up in a slowly-run Newbury Autumn Cup, but was well beaten next time at Newmarket on soft ground. Usually wears a visor, but it was dispensed with when taking a handicap at the Cesarewitch meeting. Just beaten into second in the November Handicap. 12 furlongs is probably his best trip, and he is suited by good and good to firm ground. Has been quirky in the past, but seemed a reformed character in the latter stages of 2001 season.

Mesmeric Lady

(67) (22)**60**
2-y-o ch f Zilzal (USA)-Blue Brocade (Reform)
R Hannon Deauville Daze Partnership

Placings:600000 **(5410)**
2001: 5^{6}GF, 5^{0}G, 5^{0}GF, 7^{0}G, 6^{0}SD, 7^{0}SD

	Starts	1st	2nd	3rd	Win & Pl
Career Total (Turf)	4	0	0	0	0
Career Total (AW)	2	0	0	0	

Going (Turf): Sf: 0-0 GS: 0-0 Gd: 0-2 GF: 0-2 Fm: 0-0
Distance: 5f/6f: 0-4 7f-8f: 0-2 9f-13f: 0-0 14f+: 0-0
Track : LH: 0-2 RH: 0-1 Tight: 0-1 Gall: 0-0
Aids: Bl: 0-0 Vi: 0-0 Tstrap: 0-0
Best Rating: 60 8/01 Leic 5f218y gd-fm

Metalico

(89) (61)
2-y-o b f Piccolo-Pewter Lass (Dowsing (USA))
M Blanshard Mrs Elaine Wood

Placings:056 **(5420)**
2001: 6^{0}GF, 8^{5}SD, 7^{6}SD

	Starts	1st	2nd	3rd	Win & Pl
Career Total (Turf)	1	0	0	0	
Career Total (AW)	2	0	0	0	0

Going (Turf): Sf: 0-0 GS: 0-0 Gd: 0-0 GF: 0-1 Fm: 0-0
Distance: 5f/6f: 0-0 7f-8f: 0-2 9f-13f: 0-1 14f+: 0-0
Track : LH: 0-2 RH: 0-0 Tight: 0-2 Gall: 0-0
Aids: Bl: 0-0 Vi: 0-0 Tstrap: 0-0
Best Rating: 61 10/01 Wolv 1m100y stand

Meteor Strike (USA)

76(96) (55)
7-y-o ch g Lomond (USA)-Meteoric (High Line)
D Burchell (G M McCourt 9/8) Raglan Racing Club

Placings:1200/051/2640300/**6216**0354U0-000 **(4901)**
2001: 10^{0}GF, 11^{0}G, 11^{0}G

	Starts	1st	2nd	3rd	Win & Pl
Career Total (Turf)	20	1	2	2	6242
Career Total (AW)	7	2	1	0	9325

33	1/00	Sthl	1m3f	G	STD	£1909
82	12/98	Ling	1m4f	C(0-100)H	STD	£6872
75	7/97	Bath	1m2f46y	D	GD	£3101

Total win prize-money £11884

Going (Turf): Sf: 0-0 GS: 0-1 **Gd: 1-7** GF: 0-8 Fm: 0-4
Distance: 5f/6f: 0-0 7f-8f: 0-0 **9f-13f: 3-26** 14f+: 0-1
Track : **LH: 3-22** RH: 0-4 **Tight: 2-13** Gall: 0-5
Aids: Bl: 0-2 Vi: 0-0 **Tstrap: 1-10**
Best Rating: 75 7/97 Bath 1m2f46y G

Meteorite (IRE)

102 **59**
5-y-o b g Bigstone (IRE)-Winning Appeal (FR) (Law Society (USA))
J M P Eustace Mrs T S Matthews

Placings:0/55404256040/40 **(3318)**
2001: 14^{4}GF, 14^{0}G

	Starts	1st	2nd	3rd	Win & Pl
Career Total (Turf)	14	0	1	0	2325

Going (Turf): Sf: 0-0 GS: 0-4 Gd: 0-4 GF: 0-6 Fm: 0-0
Distance: 5f/6f: 0-0 7f-8f: 0-0 9f-13f: 0-5 14f+: 0-9
Track : LH: 0-7 RH: 0-5 Tight: 0-6 Gall: 0-1
Aids: Bl: 0-0 Vi: 0-0 Tstrap: 0-0
Best Rating: 59 7/01 Yarm 1m6f17y gd-fm

He has put up one or two fair efforts in modest staying events, but remains a maiden.

Meticulous

74 **34**
3-y-o gr g Eagle Eyed (USA)-Careful (IRE) (Distinctly North (USA))
R F Johnson Houghton Woodway Racing

Placings:00 **(2433)**
2001: 8^{0}F, 8^{0}GF

	Starts	1st	2nd	3rd	Win & Pl
Career Total (Turf)	2	0	0	0	

Going (Turf): Sf: 0-0 GS: 0-0 Gd: 0-0 GF: 0-1 Fm: 0-1
Distance: 5f/6f: 0-0 7f-8f: 0-0 9f-13f: 0-2 14f+: 0-0
Track : LH: 0-1 RH: 0-1 Tight: 0-1 Gall: 0-0
Aids: Bl: 0-0 Vi: 0-0 Tstrap: 0-0
Best Rating: 34 6/01 Nott 1m54y firm

Mexican (USA)

97 **82**
2-y-o b c Pine Bluff (USA)-Cuando Quiere (USA) (Affirmed (USA))
C E Brittain Saeed Manana

Placings:430 **(4873)**
2001: 7^{4}GF, 7^{3}S, 7^{0}G

	Starts	1st	2nd	3rd	Win & Pl
Career Total (Turf)	3	0	0	1	1189

Going (Turf): Sf: 0-1 GS: 0-0 Gd: 0-1 GF: 0-1 Fm: 0-0
Distance: 5f/6f: 0-0 7f-8f: 0-3 9f-13f: 0-0 14f+: 0-0
Track : LH: 0-0 RH: 0-0 Tight: 0-0 Gall: 0-0
Aids: Bl: 0-0 Vi: 0-0 Tstrap: 0-0
Best Rating: 82 9/01 Yarm 7f3y soft

An expensive yearling, he looked likely to come on for his Ascot debut when he was not far behind the subsequent Acomb winner Comfy, but did not look to cope with the soft ground next time, and failed to sparkle at Newmarket.

Mi Castano (IRE)

(73) (36)**66**
2-y-o ch c Fayruz-Tadasna (IRE) (Thatching)
N P Littmoden W R Hornby

Placings:04000 **(5192)**
2001: 6^{0}GS, 5^{4}G, 6^{0}GF, 6^{0}G, 8^{0}SD

	Starts	1st	2nd	3rd	Win & Pl
Career Total (Turf)	4	0	0	0	0
Career Total (AW)	1	0	0	0	0

Going (Turf): Sf: 0-0 GS: 0-1 Gd: 0-2 GF: 0-1 Fm: 0-0
Distance: 5f/6f: 0-3 7f-8f: 0-1 9f-13f: 0-1 14f+: 0-0
Track : LH: 0-2 RH: 0-0 Tight: 0-1 Gall: 0-1
Aids: Bl: 0-0 Vi: 0-0 Tstrap: 0-0
Best Rating: 66 8/01 Bath 5f11y good

Mi Favorita

(91) (37)**41**
3-y-o b f Piccolo-Mistook (USA) (Phone Trick (USA))
Don Enrico Incisa (B J Meehan 2/7) Don Enrico Incisa

Placings:0-000**2**000**6**04**2 (5412)**
2001: 7^{0}S, 6^{0}GS, 5^{0}F, 7^{0}G, 6^{2}SD, 6^{0}SD, 6^{0}GF, 5^{0}G, 5^{6}GF, 6^{0}GF, 5^{4}GS, 6^{2}SD

	Starts	1st	2nd	3rd	Win & Pl
Career Total (Turf)	10	0	0	0	0
Career Total (AW)	3	0	2	0	1294

Going (Turf): Sf: 0-1 GS: 0-2 Gd: 0-2 GF: 0-4 Fm: 0-1
Distance: 5f/6f: 0-11 7f-8f: 0-2 9f-13f: 0-0 14f+: 0-0
Track : LH: 0-8 RH: 0-0 Tight: 0-2 Gall: 0-0
Aids: Bl: 0-2 Vi: 0-3 Tstrap: 0-0
Best Rating: 44 5/01 Pont 6f gd-sft

Mi Odds

97(114) (82)**58**
5-y-o b g Sure Blade (USA)-Vado Via (Ardross)
Mrs N Macauley G Wiltshire

Placings:30506002211-3124130245400 **(2834)**
2001: 11^{3}SD, 11^{1}SD, 12^{2}SD, 12^{4}SD, 11^{1}SW, 10^{3}SW, 10^{0}SW, 9^{2}SD, 12^{4}SD, 12^{5}GF, 9^{4}F, 10^{0}G, 7^{0}GF

	Starts	1st	2nd	3rd	Win & Pl
Career Total (Turf)	7	0	0	0	0
Career Total (AW)	17	4	4	3	21493

79	2/01	Sthl	1m3f	D(0-85)H	SLW	£3737
74	1/01	Sthl	1m3f	D(0-80)H	STD	£3766
66	12/00	Wolv	1m4f	F(0-60)H	STD	£1764
48	12/00	Sthl	1m3f	F	STD	£2247

Total win prize-money £11516

Going (Turf): Sf: 0-1 GS: 0-0 Gd: 0-2 GF: 0-3 Fm: 0-1
Distance: 5f/6f: 0-0 7f-8f: 0-1 **9f-13f: 4-21** 14f+: 0-2
Track : **LH: 4-23** RH: 0-0 **Tight: 1-10** Gall: 0-0
Aids: Bl: 0-0 Vi: 0-0 Tstrap: 0-0
Best Rating: 82 3/01 Wolv 1m1f79y stand

Mia

(80) (21)
4-y-o b f Contract Law (USA)-Sianiski (Niniski (USA))
T D Barron Nigel Shields

Placings:060 **(0185)**
2001: 8^{0}SW, 7^{6}SW, 7^{0}SD

	Starts	1st	2nd	3rd	Win & Pl
Career Total (Turf)	0	0	0	0	
Career Total (AW)	3	0	0	0	0

Going (Turf): Sf: 0-0 GS: 0-0 Gd: 0-0 GF: 0-0 Fm: 0-0
Distance: 5f/6f: 0-0 7f-8f: 0-2 9f-13f: 0-1 14f+: 0-0
Track : LH: 0-3 RH: 0-0 Tight: 0-2 Gall: 0-0
Aids: Bl: 0-0 Vi: 0-0 Tstrap: 0-0
Best Rating: 21 1/01 Sthl 7f slow

Mia's Reform

85(89) (56)**47**
2-y-o b c Lugana Beach-Lady Caroline Lamb (IRE) (Contract Law (USA))
H A McWilliams Reform Health Studio Blackpool

Placings:600052650 **(4437)**
2001: 5^{6}GS, 5^{0}G, 5^{0}GF, 5^{0}GF, 5^{5}GF, 5^{2}SD, 5^{6}SD, 5^{5}GF, 5^{0}G

	Starts	1st	2nd	3rd	Win & Pl
Career Total (Turf)	7	0	0	0	
Career Total (AW)	2	0	1	0	546

Going (Turf): Sf: 0-0 GS: 0-1 Gd: 0-2 GF: 0-4 Fm: 0-0
Distance: 5f/6f: 0-9 7f-8f: 0-0 9f-13f: 0-0 14f+: 0-0
Track : LH: 0-1 RH: 0-0 Tight: 0-1 Gall: 0-0
Aids: Bl: 0-1 Vi: 0-0 Tstrap: 0-0
Best Rating: 56 7/01 Sthl 5f stand

Mice Design (IRE)

(100) (48d)**46**

4-y-o b g Presidium-Diplomatist (Dominion)
N P Littmoden Mice Group Plc

Placings:0543003-16005 **(4553)**
2001: 16^{1}SD, 16^{6}SD, 16^{0}SW, 11^{0}G, 14^{5}SW

	Starts	1st	2nd	3rd	Win & Pl
Career Total (Turf)	5	0	0	1	418
Career Total (AW)	7	1	0	1	2007

48 1/01 Sthl 2m F(0-60)H STD £1750
Total win prize-money £1750

Going (Turf): Sf: 0-0 GS: 0-0 Gd: 0-3 GF: 0-1 Fm: 0-1
Distance: 5f/6f: 0-0 7f-8f: 0-0 9f-13f: 0-6 **14f+: 1-6**
Track : **LH: 1-10** RH: 0-1 Tight: 0-5 Gall: 0-0
Aids: Bl: 0-0 Vi: 0-0 Tstrap: 0-0
Best Rating: 48 1/01 Sthl 2m stand

A modest stayer on Fibresand. Won over two miles in January 2001.

Mice Ideas (IRE)

(109) (37)**31**
5-y-o ch g Fayruz-Tender Encounter (Prince Tenderfoot (USA))
N P Littmoden Mice Group Plc

Placings:040425/054054/1605123616 0015-10356000636 **(5050)**
2001: 11^{1}SW, 12^{0}SD, 11^{3}SD, 11^{5}SD, 11^{6}SD, 11^{0}F, 11^{0}SD, 9^{0}GF, 10^{6}F, 12^{3}SD, 11^{6}SD

	Starts	1st	2nd	3rd	Win & Pl
Career Total (Turf)	18	1	1	1	6095
Career Total (AW)	19	4	1	2	9239

59 1/01 Sthl 1m3f E(0-70)H SLW £2184
44 12/00 Sthl 1m3f G(0-60) STD £1939
45 6/00 Bevl 1m1f207yE(0-70)H G-F £4628
45 3/00 Sthl 1m3f G STD £1509
49 1/00 Sthl 1m3f F STD £2159
Total win prize-money £12420

Going (Turf): Sf: 0-1 GS: 0-3 Gd: 0-7 **GF: 1-5** Fm: 0-2
Distance: 5f/6f: 0-1 7f-8f: 0-4 **9f-13f: 5-29** 14f+: 0-3
Track : **LH: 4-31** RH: 1-4 Tight: 0-8 Gall: 0-0
Aids: Bl: 0-0 Vi: 0-0 Tstrap: 0-0
Best Rating: 59 1/01 Sthl 1m3f slow

Mice World (IRE)

(89) (34)
4-y-o b g River Falls-Naglaa (USA) (State Dinner (USA))
N P Littmoden Mice Group Plc

Placings:000/050 **(0304)**
2001: 16^{0}SD, 13^{5}SW, 16^{0}SD

	Starts	1st	2nd	3rd	Win & Pl
Career Total (Turf)	3	0	0	0	
Career Total (AW)	3	0	0	0	0

Going (Turf): Sf: 0-1 GS: 0-1 Gd: 0-1 GF: 0-0 Fm: 0-0
Distance: 5f/6f: 0-0 7f-8f: 0-1 9f-13f: 0-3 14f+: 0-2
Track : LH: 0-3 RH: 0-0 Tight: 0-1 Gall: 0-0
Aids: Bl: 0-0 Vi: 0-0 Tstrap: 0-0
Best Rating: 34 2/01 Ling 1m5f slow

Michael Maher

85 **55**
2-y-o b c Indian Ridge-Well Proud (IRE) (Sadler's Wells (USA))
M A Jarvis W J Gredley

Placings:0 **(5604)**
2001: 7^{0}GS

	Starts	1st	2nd	3rd	Win & Pl
Career Total (Turf)	1	0	0	0	

Going (Turf): Sf: 0-0 GS: 0-1 Gd: 0-0 GF: 0-0 Fm: 0-0
Distance: 5f/6f: 0-0 7f-8f: 0-1 9f-13f: 0-0 14f+: 0-0
Track : LH: 0-0 RH: 0-0 Tight: 0-0 Gall: 0-0
Aids: Bl: 0-0 Vi: 0-0 Tstrap: 0-0
Best Rating: 55 11/01 NmkR 7f gd-sft

Michaels Dream (IRE)

99(81) (50)**56**
2-y-o b g Spectrum (IRE)-Stormswept (USA) (Storm Bird (CAN))
R A Fahey Exors Of The Late M J Paver

Placings:055300500 **(5404)**
2001: 6^{0}GF, 6^{5}GF, 6^{5}SD, 7^{3}F, 7^{0}G, 6^{0}G, 8^{5}GF, 9^{0}HY, 8^{0}S

	Starts	1st	2nd	3rd	Win & Pl
Career Total (Turf)	8	0	0	1	540
Career Total (AW)	1	0	0	0	0

Going (Turf): Sf: 0-2 GS: 0-0 Gd: 0-2 GF: 0-3 Fm: 0-1
Distance: 5f/6f: 0-3 7f-8f: 0-4 9f-13f: 0-2 14f+: 0-0
Track : LH: 0-4 RH: 0-1 Tight: 0-1 Gall: 0-1
Aids: Bl: 0-1 Vi: 0-3 Tstrap: 0-0
Best Rating: 69 7/01 Rdcr 7f firm

Michaels Girl

90(96) (63)**66**
2-y-o ch f Bluebird (USA)-Bonnie Lassie (Efisio)
M C Chapman W P Gaff

Placings:02145000 **(5636)**
2001: 5^{0}GS, 5^{2}SW, 5^{1}SD, 6^{4}F, 5^{5}F, 5^{0}GF, 5^{0}GF, 5^{0}G

	Starts	1st	2nd	3rd	Win & Pl
Career Total (Turf)	6	0	0	0	533
Career Total (AW)	2	1	1	0	3265

69 5/01 Wolv 5f F STD £2331
Total win prize-money £2331

Going (Turf): Sf: 0-0 GS: 0-1 Gd: 0-1 GF: 0-2 Fm: 0-2
Distance: **5f/6f: 1-8** 7f-8f: 0-0 9f-13f: 0-0 14f+: 0-0
Track : **LH: 1-2** RH: 0-1 **Tight: 1-2** Gall: 0-1
Aids: Bl: 0-0 Vi: 0-0 Tstrap: 0-0
Best Rating: 69 5/01 Wolv 5f stand

A late foal, showed plenty of dash in the Brocklesby and ran out a 1 1/4 lengths winner from Galaxy Jewel in a five furlong maiden at Wolverhampton in May. She is bred to get further.

Mickley (IRE)

(100) (61)**62**
4-y-o b g Ezzoud (IRE)-Dawsha (IRE) (Slip Anchor)
P R Hedger (M D Hammond 10/3) Jay Dee Bloodstock Limited

Placings:05115400/25453631100-**05000000 3033** **(5419)**
2001: 10^{0}SW, 16^{5}SD, 14^{0}GF, 14^{0}S, 9^{0}GF, 11^{0}G, 11^{0}GF, 12^{0}GF, 12^{3}SD, 12^{0}SD, 14^{3}SD, 12^{3}SD

	Starts	1st	2nd	3rd	Win & Pl
Career Total (Turf)	25	4	1	2	24538
Career Total (AW)	6	0	0	3	1132

82 8/00 Ripn 1m4f60y C(0-90)H G-F £7020
77 7/00 Thsk 1m4f D(0-80)H FRM £3893
82 7/99 Ches 7f2y D H G-F £3972
76 6/99 Muss 7f30y F SFT £2584
Total win prize-money £17470

Going (Turf): Sf: 1-4 GS: 0-5 Gd: 0-5 **GF: 2-8** Fm: 1-3
Distance: 5f/6f: 0-2 7f-8f: 2-5 9f-13f: 2-19 14f+: 0-5
Track : LH: 2-15 RH: 2-10 **Tight: 4-17** Gall: 0-2
Aids: Bl: 0-5 **Vi: 2-9** Tstrap: 0-0
Best Rating: 76 3/01 Wolv 2m46y stand

A decent handicapper in 2000, he is a modest performer in staying events on Fibresand these days.

Micklow Magic

104 **73d**
3-y-o b f Farfelu-Scotto's Regret (Celtic Cone)
C Grant Exors Of The Late F Taylor

Placings:225-1304030 **(4804)**
2001: 8^{1}GF, 8^{3}F, 10^{0}GF, 8^{4}G, 8^{0}GS, 7^{3}GF, 6^{0}F

	Starts	1st	2nd	3rd	Win & Pl
Career Total (Turf)	10	1	2	2	8242

59 5/01 Thsk 1m D G-F £4582
Total win prize-money £4583

Going (Turf): Sf: 0-1 GS: 0-2 Gd: 0-1 **GF: 1-4** Fm: 0-2
Distance: 5f/6f: 0-3 **7f-8f: 1-5** 9f-13f: 0-2 14f+: 0-0
Track : **LH: 1-7** RH: 0-0 **Tight: 1-3** Gall: 0-1
Aids: Bl: 0-0 Vi: 0-0 Tstrap: 0-0
Best Rating: 73 7/01 Donc 1m good

Placed twice from three starts at two. Made a winning reappearance at three when stepped up to a mile at Thirsk. Has struggled in handicap company since. Acts on fast ground.

Middlethorpe

97(79) (32)**66**
4-y-o b g Noble Patriarch-Prime Property (IRE) (Tirol)
M W Easterby J H Quickfall & A G Black

Placings:64053300/05103013136-0010560 **(5293)**
2001: 12^{0}S, 11^{0}F, 12^{1}G, 14^{0}HY, 10^{5}S, 11^{6}S, 9^{0}S

	Starts	1st	2nd	3rd	Win & Pl
Career Total (Turf)	25	4	0	5	25557
Career Total (AW)	1	0	0	0	

68 8/01 Pont 1m4f8y C(0-90)H GD £7052
61 9/00 Chep 1m2f36y D(0-80)H G-S £4329
66 8/00 York 1m2f85y E(0-70)H GD £6344
56 6/00 Bevl 1m3f216yF(0-60)H G-S £3835
Total win prize-money £21561

Going (Turf): Sf: 0-7 **GS: 2-6 Gd: 2-7** GF: 0-4 Fm: 0-1
Distance: 5f/6f: 0-2 7f-8f: 0-7 **9f-13f: 4-16** 14f+: 0-1
Track : **LH: 3-17** RH: 1-7 Tight: 1-8 Gall: 1-7
Aids: **Bl: 3-11** Vi: 0-0 Tstrap: 0-0
Best Rating: 68 8/01 Pont 1m4f8y good

A winner three times last season, returned from a three-month break to score at Pontefract in August 2001. Effective from ten to 12 furlongs and does not want the ground too fast.

Middleton Grey

(107) (80)**69**
3-y-o gr g Ashkalani (IRE)-Petula (Petong)
D W P Arbuthnot Derrick C Broomfield

Placings:506401 **(5347)**
2001: 6^{5}GF, 6^{0}G, 6^{6}GF, 6^{4}GF, 7^{0}GF, 8^{1}SD

	Starts	1st	2nd	3rd	Win & Pl
Career Total (Turf)	5	0	0	0	358
Career Total (AW)	1	1	0	0	3455

73 10/01 Sthl 1m E(0-70) STD £3454
Total win prize-money £3455

Going (Turf): Sf: 0-0 GS: 0-0 Gd: 0-1 GF: 0-4 Fm: 0-0
Distance: 5f/6f: 0-3 **7f-8f: 1-3** 9f-13f: 0-0 14f+: 0-0
Track : **LH: 1-2** RH: 0-0 Tight: 0-1 Gall: 0-0
Aids: Bl: 0-0 Vi: 0-0 Tstrap: 0-0
Best Rating: 73 10/01 Sthl 1m stand

Had shown signs of ability on turf, and improved for his first try on Fibresand to win a classified event over a mile. Followed up in a handicap over the same course and distance and is clearly going the right way.

Midhish Two (IRE)

76(90) (40)**28**
5-y-o b g Midhish-Tudor Loom (Sallust)
P Mitchell (B Ellison 21/6) Philip Mitchell

Placings:4140/65310606/0000000060**6-005000** **(5694)**
2001: 5^{0}SD, 5^{0}GF, 6^{5}GF, 5^{0}GF, 7^{0}SD, 6^{0}S

	Starts	1st	2nd	3rd	Win & Pl
Career Total (Turf)	25	2	0	1	41829

Career Total (AW)	4	0	0	0	0

84 5/99 Ling 6f B(0-105)H G-F £36312
71 6/98 Newc 6f D SFT £3517
Total win prize-money £39831

Going (Turf): Sf: 1-4 GS: 0-4 Gd: 0-5 **GF: 1-11** Fm: 0-1
Distance: **5f/6f: 2-18** 7f-8f: 0-10 9f-13f: 0-1 14f+: 0-0
Track : LH: 0-6 RH: 0-5 Tight: 0-4 Gall: 0-5
Aids: Bl: 0-2 Vi: 0-1 Tstrap: 0-1
Best Rating: 28 5/01 Haml 6f5y gd-fm

Sprint handicapper whose handicap mark has been in freefall since the start of 2000. Effective between five and seven furlong, handles good to firm/soft.

Midnight Arrow

88 **79d**

3-y-o b f Robellino (USA)-Princess Oberon (IRE) (Fairy King (USA))
I A Balding R P B Michaelson & Wafic Said

Placings:1500400-00 **(1433)**
2001: 8^{0}GS, 7^{0}S

	Starts	1st	2nd	3rd	Win & Pl
Career Total (Turf)	9	1	0	0	6011

79 5/00 NmkR 5f D GD £5525
Total win prize-money £5525

Going (Turf): Sf: 0-2 GS: 0-2 **Gd: 1-1** GF: 0-4 Fm: 0-0
Distance: **5f/6f: 1-6** 7f-8f: 0-2 9f-13f: 0-1 14f+: 0-0
Track : LH: 0-0 RH: 0-1 Tight: 0-1 Gall: 0-0
Aids: Bl: 0-1 Vi: 0-0 Tstrap: 0-0
Best Rating: 48 4/01 Wind 1m67y gd-sft

Midnight Cafe (IRE)

92 **60**

2-y-o b f Sri Pekan (USA)-Midnight Heights (Persian Heights)
J L Dunlop J Higgins

Placings:000 **(3368)**
2001: 6^{0}GF, 6^{0}GF, 7^{0}GF

	Starts	1st	2nd	3rd	Win & Pl
Career Total (Turf)	3	0	0	0	

Going (Turf): Sf: 0-0 GS: 0-0 Gd: 0-0 GF: 0-3 Fm: 0-0
Distance: 5f/6f: 0-1 7f-8f: 0-2 9f-13f: 0-0 14f+: 0-0
Track : LH: 0-0 RH: 0-1 Tight: 0-1 Gall: 0-0
Aids: Bl: 0-0 Vi: 0-0 Tstrap: 0-0
Best Rating: 60 6/01 Wind 6f gd-fm

Midnight Coup

90 **51**

5-y-o br g First Trump-Anhaar (Ela-Mana-Mou)
B G Powell (G T Hourigan 8/6) Mark Barrett Racing

Placings:00/0031135/00 **(4953)**
2001: 16^{0}GF, 16^{0}GS

	Starts	1st	2nd	3rd	Win & Pl
Career Total (Turf)	11	2	0	2	7961

71 6/99 Slig 2m (0-70)H YLD £3437
71 5/99 Gowr 1m6f (0-75)H GD £3781
Total win prize-money £7219

Going (Turf): Sf: 0-3 GS: 0-1 **Gd: 1-2** GF: 0-3 Fm: 0-0
Distance: 5f/6f: 0-0 7f-8f: 0-3 9f-13f: 0-3 **14f+: 2-5**
Track : LH: 0-3 **RH: 2-6** Tight: 0-1 Gall: 0-1
Aids: Bl: 0-0 Vi: 0-0 Tstrap: 0-0
Best Rating: 51 9/01 Wwck 2m39y gd-fm

Midnight Creek

103 **72**

3-y-o br g Tragic Role (USA)-Greek Night Out (IRE) (Ela-Mana-Mou)
Mrs A J Perrett Fred And Sacha Cotton

Placings:523-0441304 **(5471)**
2001: 11^{0}G, 14^{4}GF, 16^{4}G, 12^{1}GF, 12^{3}GS, 11^{0}G, 11^{4}S

	Starts	1st	2nd	3rd	Win & Pl
Career Total (Turf)	10	1	1	2	6148

70 8/01 Gdwd 1m4f E(0-70)H G-F £4426
Total win prize-money £4427

Going (Turf): Sf: 0-2 GS: 0-2 Gd: 0-4 **GF: 1-2** Fm: 0-0
Distance: 5f/6f: 0-0 7f-8f: 0-3 **9f-13f: 1-5** 14f+: 0-2
Track : LH: 0-4 **RH: 1-4 Tight: 1-4** Gall: 0-0
Aids: Bl: 0-0 Vi: 0-0 Tstrap: 0-0
Best Rating: 72 9/01 Folk 1m4f gd-sft

Moderate handicapper who has won once this season. Suited by 12 furlongs and good to firm ground.

Midnight Escape

81 **82**

8-y-o b g Aragon-Executive Lady (Night Shift (USA))
C F Wall Mervyn Ayers

Placings:4143/110001/0052103/610500/003000040/00 4561000-0 **(1594)**
2001: 6^{0}GF

	Starts	1st	2nd	3rd	Win & Pl
Career Total (Turf)	42	7	1	3	82417

82 7/00 Kemp 6f D(0-80) G-F £6909
110 5/98 Kemp 5f A GD £10371
99 9/97 Leop 5f GD £19500
89 10/96 NmkR 5f B(0-100)H GD £8966
91 6/96 Asct 5f B(0-105)H G-F £14265
87 5/96 Wind 5f10y C(0-95)H GD £5270
0 6/95 Ling 5f E G-F £3473
Total win prize-money £68759

Going (Turf): Sf: 0-4 GS: 0-3 **Gd: 4-19** GF: 3-15 Fm: 0-1
Distance: **5f/6f: 7-41** 7f-8f: 0-1 9f-13f: 0-0 14f+: 0-0
Track : LH: 0-1 **RH: 1-2** Tight: 0-1 **Gall: 1-2**
Aids: Bl: 0-0 Vi: 0-0 Tstrap: 0-0
Best Rating: 38 5/01 Donc 6f gd-fm

Midnight Parkes

81 **44**

2-y-o br c Polar Falcon (USA)-Summerhill Spruce (Windjammer (USA))
M A Jarvis Joseph Heler

Placings:50 **(5343)**
2001: 6^{5}S, 6^{0}GS

	Starts	1st	2nd	3rd	Win & Pl
Career Total (Turf)	2	0	0	0	0

Going (Turf): Sf: 0-1 GS: 0-1 Gd: 0-0 GF: 0-0 Fm: 0-0
Distance: 5f/6f: 0-2 7f-8f: 0-0 9f-13f: 0-0 14f+: 0-0
Track : LH: 0-1 RH: 0-0 Tight: 0-0 Gall: 0-0
Aids: Bl: 0-0 Vi: 0-0 Tstrap: 0-0
Best Rating: 44 9/01 Pont 6f soft

Midnight Venture

110 **71**

3-y-o b g Night Shift (USA)-Front Line Romance (Caerleon (USA))
Mrs L Stubbs The Midnight Venture Partnership

Placings:0302210-000401 **(4959)**
2001: 6^{0}GS, 6^{0}G, 6^{0}GF, 6^{4}GF, 6^{0}GF, 7^{1}GS

	Starts	1st	2nd	3rd	Win & Pl
Career Total (Turf)	13	2	2	1	12102

71 9/01 Gdwd 7f D(0-85)H G-S £5216
74 8/00 Gdwd 6f E GD £4290
Total win prize-money £9506

Going (Turf): Sf: 0-1 **GS: 1-3 Gd: 1-4** GF: 0-4 Fm: 0-1
Distance: 5f/6f: 1-12 7f-8f: 1-1 9f-13f: 0-0 14f+: 0-0
Track : LH: 0-1 **RH: 1-2** Tight: 0-0 Gall: 0-2
Aids: Bl: 0-0 Vi: 0-0 Tstrap: 0-0
Best Rating: 71 9/01 Gdwd 7f gd-sft

He got off the mark as a juvenile at Goodwood and returned to winning ways at the same track in September on his first attempt at seven furlongs.

Midnight Watch (USA)

(102) (16)**30**

7-y-o b g Capote (USA)-Midnight Air (USA) (Green Dancer (USA))
I A Wood Mrs Joyce Wood

Placings:2/6463/0/00/**0001322022500-000** **(3238)**
2001: 9^{0}SW, 8^{0}SD, 8^{0}SD

	Starts	1st	2nd	3rd	Win & Pl
Career Total (Turf)	9	0	1	1	2520
Career Total (AW)	15	1	4	1	4101

36 2/00 Wolv 1m100y G(0-70)H STD £1551
Total win prize-money £1551

Going (Turf): Sf: 0-2 GS: 0-0 Gd: 0-5 GF: 0-2 Fm: 0-0
Distance: 5f/6f: 0-0 7f-8f: 0-6 **9f-13f: 1-15** 14f+: 0-3
Track : **LH: 1-20** RH: 0-3 **Tight: 1-10** Gall: 0-1
Aids: Bl: 0-1 Vi: 0-0 Tstrap: 0-5
Best Rating: 16 7/01 Sthl 1m stand

Midshipman

(104) (73)**77d**

3-y-o b c Executive Man-Midler (Comedy Star (USA))
P W D'Arcy (Mrs D Haine 25/5) Hethersett Racing

Placings:051-000062 **(5560)**
2001: 6^{0}S, 7^{0}G, 8^{0}F, 6^{0}G, 6^{6}SD, 7^{2}S

	Starts	1st	2nd	3rd	Win & Pl
Career Total (Turf)	8	1	1	0	5082
Career Total (AW)	1	0	0	0	0

77 9/00 Nott 6f15y D G-S £3217
Total win prize-money £3218

Going (Turf): Sf: 0-2 **GS: 1-1** Gd: 0-2 GF: 0-2 Fm: 0-1
Distance: 5f/6f: 0-5 **7f-8f: 1-3** 9f-13f: 0-1 14f+: 0-0
Track : LH: 0-2 RH: 0-0 Tight: 0-0 Gall: 0-0
Aids: Bl: 0-0 Vi: 0-0 Tstrap: 0-0
Best Rating: 82 5/01 NmkR 7f good

He only had the three outings at two, winning the last of them when appreciating the softer surface over six furlongs at Nottingham. Ran his best race of this season at Yarmouth in October and looks likely to have a good winter on the sand judged on his second at Southwell in November.

Midy's Risk (FR)

102(91) (53)**72**

4-y-o gr g Take Risks (FR)-Martine Midy (FR) (Lashkari)
Mrs N Smith Tony Hayward And Barry Fulton

Placings:02-2230 **(3027)**
2001: 10^{2}SD, 10^{2}G, 10^{3}G, 12^{0}GF

	Starts	1st	2nd	3rd	Win & Pl
Career Total (Turf)	5	0	2	1	4784
Career Total (AW)	1	0	1	0	784

Going (Turf): Sf: 0-0 GS: 0-0 Gd: 0-2 GF: 0-1 Fm: 0-0
Distance: 5f/6f: 0-0 7f-8f: 0-0 9f-13f: 0-4 14f+: 0-0
Track : LH: 0-2 RH: 0-1 Tight: 0-3 Gall: 0-1
Aids: Bl: 0-0 Vi: 0-0 Tstrap: 0-0
Best Rating: 72 6/01 Wind 1m2f7y good

Started his career in France, where he ran twice on the level and once over hurdles. Runner-up on his British debut on the All-Weather behind a useful sort, he ran well to finish third at Windsor on his third run for a mark. Has shown a tendency to edge left under pressure. Should be suited by a mile and a half.

Mighty Magic

(88) (28)**45**

6-y-o b m Magic Ring (IRE)-Mighty Flash (Rolfe (USA))
N R Mitchell (Mrs P N Dutfield 13/1) Mrs V A Tory

Placings:345000/00002424305/6522300/00-0 **(0088)**
2001: 12^{0}SD

	Starts	1st	2nd	3rd	Win & Pl
Career Total (Turf)	25	0	4	3	5899
Career Total (AW)	2	0	0	0	

Going (Turf): Sf: 0-4 GS: 0-2 Gd: 0-7 GF: 0-9 Fm: 0-3
Distance: 5f/6f: 0-8 7f-8f: 0-7 9f-13f: 0-9 14f+: 0-3
Track : LH: 0-9 RH: 0-9 Tight: 0-9 Gall: 0-5
Aids: Bl: 0-1 Vi: 0-1 Tstrap: 0-0
Best Rating: 23 1/01 Ling 1m4f stand

Mighty Max

3-y-o b g Well Beloved-Jokers High (USA) (Vaguely Noble)
G A Ham Max Pro Bets

Placings:0 **(4076)**
2001: 11^{0}G

	Starts	1st	2nd	3rd	Win & Pl
Career Total (Turf)	1	0	0	0	

Going (Turf): Sf: 0-0 GS: 0-0 Gd: 0-1 GF: 0-0 Fm: 0-0
Distance: 5f/6f: 0-0 7f-8f: 0-0 9f-13f: 0-1 14f+: 0-0
Track : LH: 0-1 RH: 0-0 Tight: 0-1 Gall: 0-0
Aids: Bl: 0-0 Vi: 0-0 Tstrap: 0-0

Migwar

(100) (20)**20**
8-y-o b g Unfuwain (USA)-Pick Of The Pops (High Top)
R Craggs Ray Craggs

Placings:05/22110/0/6000**1**/164000000**0401**/0603**0000-0** **(1585)**
2001: 14^{0}SD

	Starts	1st	2nd	3rd	Win & Pl
Career Total (Turf)	14	2	2	0	22712
Career Total (AW)	20	3	0	1	6665

55	12/99	Ling	1m2f	E(0-70)H	STD	£2391
64	1/99	Sthl	1m4f	G	STD	£1838
65	1/99	Sthl	1m3f	G	STD	£1903
95	5/96	Rdcr	1m2f	B(0-105)H	G-F	£14655
85	5/96	Donc	1m2f60y	C(0-90)H	G-F	£5952

Total win prize-money £26740

Going (Turf): Sf: 0-3 GS: 0-3 Gd: 0-2 **GF: 2-6** Fm: 0-0
Distance: 5f/6f: 0-0 7f-8f: 0-4 **9f-13f: 5-29** 14f+: 0-1
Track : **LH: 5-27** RH: 0-4 **Tight: 2-14** Gall: 1-5
Aids: Bl: 0-2 **Vi: 1-5** Tstrap: 0-1

Mike's Double (IRE)

(95) (32d)**25**
7-y-o br g Cyrano De Bergerac-Glass Minnow (IRE) (Alzao (USA))
Mrs N Macauley D S Allan

Placings:640032/35320145243043/24663531201040060000040406441/30205330600000050605U60/523050000000336-6050 **(0285)**
2001: 7^{6}SD, 7^{0}SD, 7^{5}SW, 9^{0}SW

	Starts	1st	2nd	3rd	Win & Pl
Career Total (Turf)	38	1	2	6	12741
Career Total (AW)	53	3	5	7	11158

60	12/98	Wolv	6f	F(0-65)H	STD	£1882
61	5/98	Thsk	6f	D(0-75)H	GD	£7961
62	4/98	Wolv	7f	F(0-60)H	STD	£2427
62	7/97	Wolv	6f	F	STD	£2277

Total win prize-money £14547

Going (Turf): Sf: 0-10 GS: 0-8 **Gd: 1-9** GF: 0-9 Fm: 0-2
Distance: **5f/6f: 3-37** 7f-8f: 1-45 9f-13f: 0-9 14f+: 0-0
Track : **LH: 3-62** RH: 0-2 **Tight: 3-43** Gall: 0-1
Aids: Bl: 0-12 **Vi: 2-62** Tstrap: 0-0
Best Rating: 25 1/01 Wolv 7f slow

He runs a lot, but his recent strike-rate hardly sets the pulse racing. Effective on soft ground and on Fibresand.

Milady Lillie (IRE)

(103) (48)**53**
5-y-o b m Distinctly North (USA)-Millingdale Lillie (Tumble Wind (USA))
K T Ivory K T Ivory

Placings:006/44510463603/600020406600**60535-40** **(0092)**
2001: 7^{4}SD, 8^{0}SD

	Starts	1st	2nd	3rd	Win & Pl
Career Total (Turf)	26	1	1	2	5832
Career Total (AW)	7	0	0	1	524

59	5/99	Brig	6f209y	E(0-65)	FRM	£2859

Total win prize-money £2860

Going (Turf): Sf: 0-2 GS: 0-0 Gd: 0-8 GF: 0-12 **Fm: 1-4**
Distance: 5f/6f: 0-11 **7f-8f: 1-21** 9f-13f: 0-1 14f+: 0-0
Track : **LH: 1-18** RH: 0-5 Tight: 0-7 Gall: 0-5
Aids: Bl: 0-1 Vi: 0-0 **Tstrap: 1-4**
Best Rating: 43 1/01 Sthl 7f stand

Milan

115 **128+**
3-y-o b c Sadler's Wells (USA)-Kithanga (IRE) (Darshaan)
A P O'Brien M Tabor & Mrs John Magnier

Placings:1-23541152 **(5579a)**
2001: 10^{2}S, 10^{3}G, 12^{5}G, 12^{4}GF, 11^{1}G, 14^{1}G, 12^{5}HO, 12^{2}F

	Starts	1st	2nd	3rd	Win & Pl
Career Total (Turf)	9	3	2	1	677304

124	9/01	Donc	1m6f132yA		GD	£222000
118	8/01	York	1m3f195yA		GD	£87000
105	10/00	Curr	7f		Y-S	£9750

Total win prize-money £318750

Going (Turf): Sf: 0-1 GS: 0-0 **Gd: 2-4** GF: 0-1 Fm: 0-1
Distance: 5f/6f: 0-0 7f-8f: 1-1 9f-13f: 1-7 14f+: 1-1
Track : **LH: 2-3** RH: 0-2 Tight: 0-0 **Gall: 2-3**
Aids: Bl: 0-0 Vi: 0-0 Tstrap: 0-0
Best Rating: 128 10/01 Belm 1m4f firm

Winner of his only start at two, he made a promising return to action behind stablemate Galileo and was beaten less than half a length when a fast-finishing third in the Prix Lupin. Came from well off the pace to finish fifth to Anabaa Blue in Prix du Jockey Club at Chantilly, but may have been feeling the ground when disappointing at Royal Ascot. Came back an improved colt after a two-month break to win the Great Voltigeur before running out an impressive winner of the St Leger. Unable to pose a threat when fifth in the Arc, but was possibly an unlucky loser when a fast-finishing runner-up in the Breeders' Cup Turf. Suited by good ground or easier, he is likely to be a major contender for the top middle-distance races in 2002.

Miles

82 **48**
3-y-o ch f Selkirk (USA)-Tricorne (Green Desert (USA))
M A Jarvis N R A Springer

Placings:00 **(4842)**
2001: 8^{0}GF, 8^{0}G

	Starts	1st	2nd	3rd	Win & Pl
Career Total (Turf)	2	0	0	0	

Going (Turf): Sf: 0-0 GS: 0-0 Gd: 0-1 GF: 0-1 Fm: 0-0
Distance: 5f/6f: 0-0 7f-8f: 0-0 9f-13f: 0-2 14f+: 0-0
Track : LH: 0-2 RH: 0-0 Tight: 0-0 Gall: 0-0
Aids: Bl: 0-0 Vi: 0-0 Tstrap: 0-0
Best Rating: 48 6/01 Hayd 1m30y gd-fm

Miletrian (IRE)

113 **102**
4-y-o b f Marju (IRE)-Warg (Dancing Brave (USA))
M R Channon Miletrian Plc

Placings:02514/04016441-20000640 **(4984)**
2001: 12^{2}G, 12^{0}G, 13^{0}GF, 16^{0}G, 16^{0}G, 14^{6}GF, 11^{4}GF, 12^{0}G

	Starts	1st	2nd	3rd	Win & Pl
Career Total (Turf)	21	3	2	0	152977

113	9/00	Donc	1m6f132yA		G-F	£24000
111	6/00	Asct	1m4f	A	G-F	£81000
78	9/99	Rdcr	1m1f	D	G-F	£3111

Total win prize-money £108111

Going (Turf): Sf: 0-1 GS: 0-2 Gd: 0-9 **GF: 3-9** Fm: 0-0
Distance: 5f/6f: 0-0 7f-8f: 0-3 **9f-13f: 2-13** 14f+: 1-5
Track : **LH: 2-8** RH: 1-8 Tight: 1-3 **Gall: 2-9**
Aids: Bl: 0-0 Vi: 0-0 Tstrap: 0-0
Best Rating: 114 2/01 Ndas 1m4f good

Showed her best side by winning both the Ribblesdale and Park Hill last season, but was just found out when taking on the very best and looked moody on one occasion. Held in decent races this season, including a couple of outings at Nad Al Sheba. Suited by 12 to 14 furlongs on good to firm ground.

Miliana (IRE)

103 **104**
4-y-o b f Polar Falcon (USA)-Mirana (IRE) (Ela-Mana-Mou)
A De Royer Dupre H H Aga Khan

Placings:15-1431 **(5672a)**
2001: 10^{1}G, 8^{4}GF, 10^{3}GF, 10^{1}HO

	Starts	1st	2nd	3rd	Win & Pl
Career Total (Turf)	6	3	0	1	42217

104	10/01	StCl	1m2f110y	HLD	£21339
	5/01	Lonc	1m2f	GD	£7759
	11/00	Toul	1m2f110y	G-S	£6724

Total win prize-money £35822

Going (Turf): Sf: 0-1 **GS: 1-1 Gd: 1-1** GF: 0-2 Fm: 0-0
Distance: 5f/6f: 0-0 7f-8f: 0-0 **9f-13f: 3-6** 14f+: 0-0
Track : **LH: 1-3** RH: 0-0 Tight: 0-1 Gall: 0-0
Aids: Bl: 0-0 Vi: 0-0 Tstrap: 0-0
Best Rating: 104 10/01 StCl 1m2f110y holding

A French-trained filly, she won her first start in May of this year over ten furlongs at Longchamp on good ground. Won a Group Three in October and is clearly suited by give.

Mill Afrique

97 **33**
5-y-o b m Mtoto-Milinetta (Milford)
Mrs M Reveley R Meredith

Placings:005/00244000/000-20 **(3966)**
2001: 14^{2}GF, 16^{0}GS

	Starts	1st	2nd	3rd	Win & Pl
Career Total (Turf)	16	0	2	0	1633

Going (Turf): Sf: 0-3 GS: 0-2 Gd: 0-3 GF: 0-7 Fm: 0-1
Distance: 5f/6f: 0-1 7f-8f: 0-0 9f-13f: 0-13 14f+: 0-2
Track : LH: 0-9 RH: 0-4 Tight: 0-6 Gall: 0-1
Aids: Bl: 0-1 Vi: 0-0 Tstrap: 0-0
Best Rating: 32 7/01 Nott 1m6f15y gd-fm

Mill Dot Kom

81(84) (53)**43**
2-y-o ch c Millkom-Bear To Dance (Rambo Dancer (CAN))
W G M Turner T Lightbowne

Placings:303555 **(2436)**
2001: 5^{3}SD, 5^{0}SD, 6^{3}SD, 6^{5}SD, 7^{5}GF, 5^{5}G

	Starts	1st	2nd	3rd	Win & Pl
Career Total (Turf)	2	0	0	0	0

	Starts	1st	2nd	3rd	Win & Pl
Career Total (AW)	4	0	0	2	520

Going (Turf): Sf: 0-0 GS: 0-0 Gd: 0-1 GF: 0-1 Fm: 0-0
Distance: 5f/6f: 0-5 7f-8f: 0-1 9f-13f: 0-0 14f+: 0-0
Track : LH: 0-2 RH: 0-0 Tight: 0-0 Gall: 0-0
Aids: Bl: 0-0 Vi: 0-1 Tstrap: 0-0
Best Rating: 53 5/01 Sthl 6f stand

Mill Lord (IRE)

71

8-y-o b g Aristocracy-Millflower (Millfontaine)
C J Drewe W P Long

Placings:0 **(2047)**
2001: 11^{0}GF

	Starts	1st	2nd	3rd	Win & Pl
Career Total (Turf)	1	0	0	0	

Going (Turf): Sf: 0-0 GS: 0-0 Gd: 0-0 GF: 0-1 Fm: 0-0
Distance: 5f/6f: 0-0 7f-8f: 0-0 9f-13f: 0-1 14f+: 0-0
Track : LH: 0-0 RH: 0-0 Tight: 0-1 Gall: 0-0
Aids: Bl: 0-0 Vi: 0-1 Tstrap: 0-0
Best Rating: 16 6/01 Wind 1m3f135y gd-fm

Millenary

116 **122**

4-y-o b h Rainbow Quest (USA)-Ballerina (IRE) (Dancing Brave (USA))
J L Dunlop L Neil Jones

Placings:35/11011-13522 **(4758a)**
2001: 12^{1}G, 12^{3}GF, 12^{5}GF, 13^{2}GF, 14^{2}GF

	Starts	1st	2nd	3rd	Win & Pl
Career Total (Turf)	12	5	2	2	432953

122	5/01	NmkR	1m4f	A	GD	£34800
120	9/00	Donc	1m6f132yA		G-F	£222000
116	8/00	Gdwd	1m4f	A	G-F	£29000
105	5/00	Ches	1m4f66y	A	GD	£36000
83	4/00	Newb	1m3f5y	D	SFT	£5200

Total win prize-money £327000

Going (Turf): Sf: 1-1 GS: 0-0 **Gd: 2-4 GF: 2-6** Fm: 0-0
Distance: 5f/6f: 0-0 7f-8f: 0-2 **9f-13f: 4-7** 14f+: 1-3
Track : **LH: 3-5** RH: 2-5 Tight: 2-3 **Gall: 3-5**
Aids: Bl: 0-0 Vi: 0-0 Tstrap: 0-0
Best Rating: 122 7/01 Asct 1m4f gd-fm

Won last year's St Leger when staying on strongly to beat Air Marshall. He had earlier landed two Group Three races, at Chester in May and at Goodwood in August, but was below form on testing ground in the French Derby. Very impressive when winning the Jockey Club Stakes on his return, he found the moderate pace of the Coronation Cup against him and was far from disgraced in the King George VI and Queen Elizabeth Diamond Stakes. Was beaten by St Leger hopeful Mr Combustible at Newbury, and does not look up to winning another Group One.

Millenium Moonbeam (USA)

102 **78**

4-y-o ch c Phone Trick (USA)-Shywing (USA) (Wing Out (USA))
G G Margarson (M Pitman 10/8) & Mrs John Harris

Placings:614/060-050500500 **(5344)**
2001: 7^{0}G, 7^{5}F, 6^{0}GF, 6^{5}G, 6^{0}GF, 6^{0}G, 7^{5}GS, 7^{0}S, 8^{0}GS

	Starts	1st	2nd	3rd	Win & Pl
Career Total (Turf)	15	1	0	0	12241

86	8/99	Sals	6f	D	G-S	£3844

Total win prize-money £3844

Going (Turf): Sf: 0-1 **GS: 1-3** Gd: 0-6 GF: 0-4 Fm: 0-1
Distance: **5f/6f: 1-6** 7f-8f: 0-8 9f-13f: 0-1 14f+: 0-0
Track : LH: 0-0 RH: 0-1 Tight: 0-1 Gall: 0-0
Aids: Bl: 0-0 Vi: 0-0 Tstrap: 0-1

Best Rating: 86 5/01 NmkR 7f good

He showed decent form as a juvenile, but has been out of his depth in the main since and still remains too high in the handicap. Had his first run for his new stable at Doncaster in September.

Millennia Star (USA)

(84) (37)

3-y-o b f Hennessy (USA)-Woodyoubelieveit (USA) (Woodman (USA))
J H M Gosden Gary Seidler & Andy J Smith

Placings:3 **(5617)**
2001: 8^{3}SD

	Starts	1st	2nd	3rd	Win & Pl
Career Total (Turf)	0	0	0	0	
Career Total (AW)	1	0	0	1	436

Going (Turf): Sf: 0-0 GS: 0-0 Gd: 0-0 GF: 0-0 Fm: 0-0
Distance: 5f/6f: 0-0 7f-8f: 0-0 9f-13f: 0-1 14f+: 0-0
Track : LH: 0-1 RH: 0-0 Tight: 0-1 Gall: 0-0
Aids: Bl: 0-0 Vi: 0-0 Tstrap: 0-0
Best Rating: 37 11/01 Wolv 1m100y stand

She is related to a US Grade Three winner and was hardly thrown in at the deep end on her debut. However, she was weak in the market and proved most disappointing in the race itself.

Millennium Bug

100(67) **45**

5-y-o b m Rock Hopper-So Precise (FR) (Balidar)
M Madgwick Carrington Network Services Ltd

Placings:066/0-0333250 **(3298)**
2001: 11^{0}GS, 11^{3}GS, 11^{3}GS, 11^{3}F, 12^{2}GS, 11^{5}GF, 11^{0}GF

	Starts	1st	2nd	3rd	Win & Pl
Career Total (Turf)	10	0	1	3	3088
Career Total (AW)	1	0	0	0	

Going (Turf): Sf: 0-0 GS: 0-4 Gd: 0-1 GF: 0-4 Fm: 0-1
Distance: 5f/6f: 0-0 7f-8f: 0-0 9f-13f: 0-11 14f+: 0-0
Track : LH: 0-6 RH: 0-3 Tight: 0-6 Gall: 0-0
Aids: Bl: 0-0 Vi: 0-0 Tstrap: 0-0
Best Rating: 48 5/01 Bath 1m3f144y gd-sft

Millennium Cadeaux (IRE)

104 **74**

3-y-o ch g Cadeaux Genereux-Quest Of Fire (FR) (Rainbow Quest (USA))
E A L Dunlop Khalifa Sultan

Placings:5-063260 **(5114)**
2001: 10^{0}GF, 9^{6}GF, 11^{3}G, 12^{2}GF, 14^{6}G, 16^{0}HY

	Starts	1st	2nd	3rd	Win & Pl
Career Total (Turf)	7	0	1	1	1407

Going (Turf): Sf: 0-1 GS: 0-1 Gd: 0-2 GF: 0-3 Fm: 0-0
Distance: 5f/6f: 0-0 7f-8f: 0-1 9f-13f: 0-4 14f+: 0-2
Track : LH: 0-4 RH: 0-2 Tight: 0-2 Gall: 0-1
Aids: Bl: 0-0 Vi: 0-0 Tstrap: 0-0
Best Rating: 74 7/01 Yarm 1m3f101y good

Millennium Dawn (IRE)

91 **50**

3-y-o b/br f Cadeaux Genereux-Rasaael (Warning)
B Hanbury A Merza

Placings:0 **(4248)**
2001: 8^{0}GF

	Starts	1st	2nd	3rd	Win & Pl
Career Total (Turf)	1	0	0	0	

Going (Turf): Sf: 0-0 GS: 0-0 Gd: 0-0 GF: 0-1 Fm: 0-0
Distance: 5f/6f: 0-0 7f-8f: 0-1 9f-13f: 0-0 14f+: 0-0
Track : LH: 0-0 RH: 0-0 Tight: 0-0 Gall: 0-0
Aids: Bl: 0-0 Vi: 0-0 Tstrap: 0-0
Best Rating: 50 8/01 NmkJ 1m gd-fm

Millennium Dragon

92 **91+**

2-y-o b c Mark Of Esteem (IRE)-Feather Bride (IRE) (Groom Dancer (USA))
M A Jarvis Sheikh Hamdan Bin Mohammed Al Maktoum

Placings:215 **(5493)**
2001: 7^{2}S, 7^{1}GS, 7^{5}HY

	Starts	1st	2nd	3rd	Win & Pl
Career Total (Turf)	3	1	1	0	8053

91	10/01	NmkR	7f	D	G-S	£5850

Total win prize-money £5850

Going (Turf): Sf: 0-2 **GS: 1-1** Gd: 0-0 GF: 0-0 Fm: 0-0
Distance: 5f/6f: 0-0 **7f-8f: 1-3** 9f-13f: 0-0 14f+: 0-0
Track : LH: 0-0 RH: 0-0 Tight: 0-0 Gall: 0-0
Aids: Bl: 0-0 Vi: 0-0 Tstrap: 0-0
Best Rating: 91 10/01 NmkR 7f gd-sft

He made a promising debut at Yarmouth in September and then got off the mark in a decent Newmarket maiden a month later. Handles soft ground well and should stay a mile.

Millennium Force

104 **81**

3-y-o b c Bin Ajwaad (IRE)-Jumairah Sun (IRE) (Scenic)
M R Channon A Merza

Placings:6604424331203 **(5529)**
2001: 8^{0}GS, 8^{6}GF, 10^{0}GF, 10^{4}S, 9^{4}GF, 8^{2}GF, 8^{4}GF, 8^{3}GF, 9^{3}G, 7^{1}GF, 7^{2}HY, 7^{0}GS, 8^{3}HY

	Starts	1st	2nd	3rd	Win & Pl
Career Total (Turf)	13	1	2	3	13579

76	9/01	Catt	7f	D	G-F	£3654

Total win prize-money £3654

Going (Turf): Sf: 0-3 GS: 0-2 Gd: 0-1 **GF: 1-7** Fm: 0-0
Distance: 5f/6f: 0-0 **7f-8f: 1-6** 9f-13f: 0-7 14f+: 0-0
Track : **LH: 1-5** RH: 0-5 **Tight: 1-3** Gall: 0-0
Aids: Bl: 0-0 Vi: 0-1 Tstrap: 0-0
Best Rating: 81 10/01 Nott 1m54y heavy

He showed ability in his early starts, but did not get off the mark until landing a seven-furlong maiden at Catterick in September.

Millennium Hall

91 **76**

2-y-o b c Saddlers' Hall (IRE)-Millazure (USA) (Dayjur (USA))
L M Cumani Mrs Luca Cumani/Iancen Farm Partnership

Placings:003 **(5559)**
2001: 8^{0}G, 7^{0}GF, 8^{3}S

	Starts	1st	2nd	3rd	Win & Pl
Career Total (Turf)	3	0	0	1	696

Going (Turf): Sf: 0-1 GS: 0-0 Gd: 0-1 GF: 0-1 Fm: 0-0
Distance: 5f/6f: 0-0 7f-8f: 0-2 9f-13f: 0-1 14f+: 0-0
Track : LH: 0-1 RH: 0-1 Tight: 0-0 Gall: 0-0
Aids: Bl: 0-0 Vi: 0-0 Tstrap: 0-0
Best Rating: 76 10/01 Yarm 1m3y soft

He ran his best race to date on his third start and would be interesting in handicap company.

Millennium King

81 77

2-y-o b c Piccolo-Zabelina (USA) (Diesis)

W Jarvis N S Yong

Placings:150 (4449)

2001: 6^{1}GS, 6^{5}G, 6^{0}GF

	Starts	1st	2nd	3rd	Win & Pl
Career Total (Turf)	3	1	0	0	4272

77 7/01 NmkJ 6f D G-S £4026

Total win prize-money £4027

Going (Turf): Sf: 0-0 **GS: 1-1** Gd: 0-1 GF: 0-1 Fm: 0-0
Distance: **5f/6f: 1-3** 7f-8f: 0-0 9f-13f: 0-0 14f+: 0-0
Track : LH: 0-0 RH: 0-0 Tight: 0-0 Gall: 0-0
Aids: Bl: 0-0 Vi: 0-0 Tstrap: 0-0
Best Rating: 77 7/01 NmkJ 6f gd-sft

A half-brother to middle-distance winner Zorba and a winner in France. Made a winning debut over six furlongs at Newmarket despite the trip possibly being on the short side. Sure to improve. Stays six furlongs. Acts on good to soft ground.

Millennium Knight

103(79) (40)71d

3-y-o ch g Kris-High Stepping (IRE) (Taufan (USA))

B Hanbury B Hanbury

Placings:35000 (5330)

2001: 14^{3}GF, 14^{5}G, 11^{0}G, 14^{0}SD, 16^{0}HY

	Starts	1st	2nd	3rd	Win & Pl
Career Total (Turf)	4	0	0	1	490
Career Total (AW)	1	0	0	0	

Going (Turf): Sf: 0-1 GS: 0-0 Gd: 0-2 GF: 0-1 Fm: 0-0
Distance: 5f/6f: 0-0 7f-8f: 0-0 9f-13f: 0-1 14f+: 0-4
Track : LH: 0-5 RH: 0-0 Tight: 0-4 Gall: 0-0
Aids: Bl: 0-0 Vi: 0-0 Tstrap: 0-0
Best Rating: 72 6/01 Rdcr 1m6f19y gd-fm

Millennium Lady (USA)

(87) (45)73

3-y-o ch f Woodman (USA)-Salina Cookie (USA) (Seattle Dancer (USA))

B W Hills C Wright & The Hon Mrs J M Corbett

Placings:053-4000 (4879)

2001: 12^{4}GF, 8^{0}SD, 8^{0}SD, 12^{0}SD

	Starts	1st	2nd	3rd	Win & Pl
Career Total (Turf)	4	0	0	1	891
Career Total (AW)	3	0	0	0	

Going (Turf): Sf: 0-1 GS: 0-0 Gd: 0-0 GF: 0-3 Fm: 0-0
Distance: 5f/6f: 0-1 7f-8f: 0-2 9f-13f: 0-4 14f+: 0-0
Track : LH: 0-4 RH: 0-2 Tight: 0-4 Gall: 0-1
Aids: Bl: 0-0 Vi: 0-0 Tstrap: 0-0
Best Rating: 45 9/01 Wolv 1m100y stand

Millennium Magic

(103) (64)77

3-y-o b f Magic Ring (IRE)-Country Spirit (Sayf El Arab (USA))

J G Portman The Goose Partnership

Placings:1342000004-501 (0366)

2001: 8^{5}SW, 10^{0}SW, 8^{1}SW

	Starts	1st	2nd	3rd	Win & Pl
Career Total (Turf)	9	1	1	1	5450
Career Total (AW)	4	1	0	0	2898

64 2/01 Ling 1m E SLW £2898
77 3/00 Sand 5f6y D G-F £3428

Total win prize-money £6327

Going (Turf): Sf: 0-2 GS: 0-0 Gd: 0-3 **GF: 1-4** Fm: 0-0
Distance: 5f/6f: 1-9 7f-8f: 1-2 9f-13f: 0-2 14f+: 0-0
Track : **LH: 1-4** RH: 0-1 **Tight: 1-4** Gall: 0-1
Aids: Bl: 0-0 Vi: 0-0 Tstrap: 0-0
Best Rating: 64 2/01 Ling 1m slow

Made a winning debut at two. Switched to the All-Weather over the winter of 2000, winning a claimer over a mile in February 2001. Acts on fast ground.

Millfields Dreams

34

2-y-o b c Dreams End-Millfields Lady (Sayf El Arab (USA))

R Brotherton R D Evans

Placings:0 (2128)

2001: 6^{0}GF

	Starts	1st	2nd	3rd	Win & Pl
Career Total (Turf)	1	0	0	0	

Going (Turf): Sf: 0-0 GS: 0-0 Gd: 0-0 GF: 0-1 Fm: 0-0
Distance: 5f/6f: 0-0 7f-8f: 0-1 9f-13f: 0-0 14f+: 0-0
Track : LH: 0-0 RH: 0-0 Tight: 0-0 Gall: 0-0
Aids: Bl: 0-0 Vi: 0-0 Tstrap: 0-0

Milliken Park (IRE)

100 56

3-y-o ch f Fumo Di Londra (IRE)-Miss Ironwood (Junius (USA))

Miss L A Perratt Dr J Walker

Placings:6123000-54000 (4439)

2001: 5^{5}GF, 5^{4}F, 6^{0}GF, 6^{0}GF, 6^{0}G

	Starts	1st	2nd	3rd	Win & Pl
Career Total (Turf)	12	1	1	1	5705

69 7/00 Haml 6f5y E G-F £2808

Total win prize-money £2808

Going (Turf): Sf: 0-3 GS: 0-0 Gd: 0-1 **GF: 1-6** Fm: 0-2
Distance: 5f/6f: 0-9 **7f-8f: 1-3** 9f-13f: 0-0 14f+: 0-0
Track : LH: 0-0 RH: 0-0 Tight: 0-0 Gall: 0-0
Aids: Bl: 0-0 Vi: 0-0 Tstrap: 0-0
Best Rating: 56 5/01 Ayr 5f gd-fm

Million Percent

100 90

2-y-o b c Ashkalani (IRE)-Royal Jade (Last Tycoon)

K R Burke Platinum Racing Club Limited

Placings:31041260 (5150)

2001: 5^{3}S, 6^{1}GF, 6^{0}GF, 6^{4}GY, 6^{1}G, 6^{2}G, 6^{6}G, 6^{0}G

	Starts	1st	2nd	3rd	Win & Pl
Career Total (Turf)	8	2	1	1	14984

86 8/01 Ripn 6f D GD £4143
80 5/01 Yarm 6f3y D G-F £3570

Total win prize-money £7714

Going (Turf): Sf: 0-1 GS: 0-0 **Gd: 1-4 GF: 1-2** Fm: 0-0
Distance: 5f/6f: 1-6 7f-8f: 1-2 9f-13f: 0-0 14f+: 0-0
Track : LH: 0-0 RH: 0-0 Tight: 0-0 Gall: 0-0
Aids: Bl: 0-0 Vi: 0-0 Tstrap: 0-0
Best Rating: 90 8/01 Ripn 6f good

His dam won over seven furlongs and he himself is a winner over six furlongs at Yarmouth and Ripon this season. He faced some impossible tasks in between but should win more races if not too highly tried. Has won on good and good to firm ground.

Millions

101(82) (23)46

4-y-o b g Bering-Miznah (IRE) (Sadler's Wells (USA))

Ferdy Murphy (K A Ryan 21/5) Platinum Racing Club Limited

Placings:000/5200-**000**003000 (1465)

2001: 8^{0}SD, 8^{0}SW, 12^{0}SD, 7^{0}SW, 10^{0}S, 8^{3}S, 8^{0}GS, 11^{0}G, 12^{0}GF

	Starts	1st	2nd	3rd	Win & Pl
Career Total (Turf)	12	0	1	1	1444
Career Total (AW)	4	0	0	0	

Going (Turf): Sf: 0-4 GS: 0-2 Gd: 0-4 GF: 0-2 Fm: 0-0
Distance: 5f/6f: 0-0 7f-8f: 0-4 9f-13f: 0-12 14f+: 0-0
Track : LH: 0-9 RH: 0-3 Tight: 0-7 Gall: 0-1
Aids: Bl: 0-3 Vi: 0-0 Tstrap: 0-0
Best Rating: 46 4/01 Ripn 1m soft

Has not shown a lot since leaving Michael Stoute's yard, but did well to finish seventh after a slow start at Doncaster on his reappearance on turf. Appears to be suited by soft ground.

Millkom Elegance

92 62

2-y-o b f Millkom-Premier Princess (Hard Fought)

K A Ryan Yorkshire Racing Club lv

Placings:500 (3843)

2001: 7^{5}GF, 7^{0}GF, 7^{0}G

	Starts	1st	2nd	3rd	Win & Pl
Career Total (Turf)	3	0	0	0	0

Going (Turf): Sf: 0-0 GS: 0-0 Gd: 0-1 GF: 0-2 Fm: 0-0
Distance: 5f/6f: 0-0 7f-8f: 0-3 9f-13f: 0-0 14f+: 0-0
Track : LH: 0-0 RH: 0-1 Tight: 0-0 Gall: 0-0
Aids: Bl: 0-0 Vi: 0-0 Tstrap: 0-0
Best Rating: 62 6/01 Bevl 7f100y gd-fm

Millsec

94(83) (21)11

4-y-o b f Petong-Harmony Park (Music Boy)

R Bastiman Chris Mills

Placings:0062/0000-000000000 (5686)

2001: 6^{0}HY, 6^{0}S, 5^{0}G, 8^{0}GS, 5^{0}G, 7^{0}GS, 6^{0}G, 7^{0}HY, 10^{0}S

	Starts	1st	2nd	3rd	Win & Pl
Career Total (Turf)	16	0	1	0	768
Career Total (AW)	1	0	0	0	

Going (Turf): Sf: 0-8 GS: 0-2 Gd: 0-5 GF: 0-1 Fm: 0-0
Distance: 5f/6f: 0-10 7f-8f: 0-6 9f-13f: 0-1 14f+: 0-0
Track : LH: 0-5 RH: 0-0 Tight: 0-2 Gall: 0-1
Aids: Bl: 0-1 Vi: 0-0 Tstrap: 0-0
Best Rating: 46 5/01 Hayd 6f soft

Poor performer who has run most of his recent races in 'appearance money' contests.

Milly's Lass

82 31

3-y-o b f Mind Games-Millie's Lady (IRE) (Common Grounds)

M R Channon Ken Lock Racing Ltd

Placings:3121320302502-00 (5685)

2001: 5^{0}HY, 5^{0}S

	Starts	1st	2nd	3rd	Win & Pl
Career Total (Turf)	15	2	4	3	13053

72 5/00 Nott 5f13y F G-S £2331
69 4/00 Leic 5f2y F G-S £2464

Total win prize-money £4795

Going (Turf): Sf: 0-4 **GS: 2-2** Gd: 0-2 GF: 0-7 Fm: 0-0
Distance: **5f/6f: 2-15** 7f-8f: 0-0 9f-13f: 0-0 14f+: 0-0
Track : LH: 0-0 RH: 0-2 Tight: 0-0 Gall: 0-2
Aids: Bl: 0-0 Vi: 0-0 Tstrap: 0-0
Best Rating: 31 10/01 Wind 5f10y heavy

Millys Filly

94 44

3-y-o b f Polish Precedent (USA)-Lemon's Mill (USA) (Roberto (USA))

R Charlton R Waters

Placings:U6 (5634)
2001: 12^{U}GF, 11^{6}G

	Starts	1st	2nd	3rd	Win & Pl
Career Total (Turf)	2	0	0	0	0

Going (Turf): Sf: 0-0 GS: 0-0 Gd: 0-1 GF: 0-1 Fm: 0-0
Distance: 5f/6f: 0-0 7f-8f: 0-0 9f-13f: 0-2 14f+: 0-0
Track : LH: 0-1 RH: 0-1 Tight: 0-1 Gall: 0-0
Aids: Bl: 0-0 Vi: 0-0 Tstrap: 0-0
Best Rating: 44 11/01 Catt 1m3f214y good

Min Mirri

105 **74**

3-y-o b f Selkirk (USA)-Sulitelma (USA) (The Minstrel (CAN))
M R Channon Dominion Partners

Placings:45310-5542003046 (4486)
2001: 10^{5}GF, 7^{5}GF, 7^{4}GF, 7^{2}GF, 7^{0}GS, 7^{0}GF, 8^{3}GF, 7^{0}GF, 7^{4}G, 7^{6}S

	Starts	1st	2nd	3rd	Win & Pl
Career Total (Turf)	15	1	1	2	9140

79	9/00	Thsk	1m	D	GD	£3939

Total win prize-money £3939

Going (Turf): Sf: 0-2 GS: 0-1 **Gd: 1-2** GF: 0-10 Fm: 0-0
Distance: 5f/6f: 0-2 **7f-8f: 1-12** 9f-13f: 0-1 14f+: 0-0
Track : **LH: 1-4** RH: 0-2 **Tight: 1-3** Gall: 0-1
Aids: Bl: 0-0 Vi: 0-0 Tstrap: 0-0
Best Rating: 83 6/01 Ling 7f gd-fm

Won a Thirsk maiden at two over a mile. Has run some game races in defeat this season. Her only win has come on good ground.

Minardi (USA)

108 **116**

3-y-o br c Boundary (USA)-Yarn (USA) (Mr Prospector (USA))
A P O'Brien M Tabor & Mrs John Magnier

Placings:211-43060 (4583)
2001: 8^{4}G, 8^{3}GY, 8^{0}G, 6^{6}S, 6^{0}HY

	Starts	1st	2nd	3rd	Win & Pl
Career Total (Turf)	8	2	1	1	225660

121	9/00	NmkR	6f	A	GD	£89320
119	8/00	Leop	6f		GD	£98350

Total win prize-money £187670

Going (Turf): Sf: 0-2 GS: 0-0 **Gd: 2-4** GF: 0-1 Fm: 0-0
Distance: **5f/6f: 2-4** 7f-8f: 0-4 9f-13f: 0-0 14f+: 0-0
Track : LH: 0-0 RH: 0-1 Tight: 0-0 Gall: 0-1
Aids: Bl: 0-0 Vi: 0-0 Tstrap: 0-0
Best Rating: 116 5/01 Curr 1m gd-yld

Officially the top-rated juvenile of 2000 after winning two Group Ones, the Heinz 57 at Leopardstown and the Middle Park. Finished fourth on his seasonal debut in the 2000 Guineas and has since looked a non-stayer in both the Irish version and the St James's Palace. Did not improve for the drop back to shorter on his subsequent starts, although the ground was against him on both occasions. Retired to stud.

Minashki (IRE)

93 **100**

2-y-o b c Ashkalani (IRE)-Blushing Minstrel (IRE) (Nicholas (USA))
H Rogers Mrs Christine Kiernan

Placings:4120120 (4713)
2001: 5^{4}G, 5^{1}GF, 6^{2}Y, 6^{0}Y, 5^{1}YS, 6^{2}GY, 5^{0}G

	Starts	1st	2nd	3rd	Win & Pl
Career Total (Turf)	7	2	2	0	51160

100	8/01	Tipp	5f	Y-S	£13000
98	5/01	Tipp	5f	G-F	£9660

Total win prize-money £22660

Going (Turf): Sf: 0-0 GS: 0-0 Gd: 0-2 **GF: 1-1** Fm: 0-0
Distance: **5f/6f: 2-6** 7f-8f: 0-1 9f-13f: 0-0 14f+: 0-0
Track : LH: 0-0 RH: 0-0 Tight: 0-0 Gall: 0-0
Aids: Bl: 0-0 Vi: 0-0 Tstrap: 0-0
Best Rating: 100 9/01 Curr 6f gd-yld

Twice a winner over five furlongs at Tipperary, and ran two good races in defeat at the Curragh. Acts on fast and easy ground, and stays six furlongs.

Mind Over Matter

81(66) (22)**48**

3-y-o b g Muhtarram (USA)-Veuve (Tirol)
Patrick J Flynn (C A Cyzer 29/6) Ms Geraldine M Reilly

Placings:00-600003 (4129a)
2001: 9^{6}GS, 11^{0}SD, 14^{0}G, 11^{0}GF, 10^{0}GF, 12^{3}GY

	Starts	1st	2nd	3rd	Win & Pl
Career Total (Turf)	6	0	0	1	560
Career Total (AW)	2	0	0	0	

Going (Turf): Sf: 0-0 GS: 0-1 Gd: 0-2 GF: 0-2 Fm: 0-0
Distance: 5f/6f: 0-0 7f-8f: 0-2 9f-13f: 0-5 14f+: 0-1
Track : LH: 0-5 RH: 0-1 Tight: 0-1 Gall: 0-1
Aids: Bl: 0-0 Vi: 0-0 Tstrap: 0-0
Best Rating: 48 4/01 Brig 1m1f209y gd-sft

Mind Song

101 **49**

3-y-o b f Barathea (IRE)-Discomatic (USA) (Roberto (USA))
H R A Cecil K Abdulla

Placings:30 (5464)
2001: 10^{3}G, 11^{0}G

	Starts	1st	2nd	3rd	Win & Pl
Career Total (Turf)	2	0	0	1	432

Going (Turf): Sf: 0-0 GS: 0-0 Gd: 0-2 GF: 0-0 Fm: 0-0
Distance: 5f/6f: 0-0 7f-8f: 0-0 9f-13f: 0-2 14f+: 0-0
Track : LH: 0-2 RH: 0-0 Tight: 0-2 Gall: 0-0
Aids: Bl: 0-0 Vi: 0-0 Tstrap: 0-0
Best Rating: 49 10/01 Bath 1m3f144y good

Mind The Silver

97(95) (38)**40**

4-y-o gr g Petong-Marjorie's Memory (IRE) (Fairy King (USA))
J M Bradley The Soane Rangers

Placings:656/00600400100-0000000000060 (4386)
2001: 8^{0}SD, 8^{0}SD, 8^{0}SW, 6^{0}GF, 8^{0}G, 8^{0}GF, 8^{0}G, 8^{0}G, 7^{0}G, 8^{0}S, 8^{0}G, 6^{6}GF, 6^{0}GF

	Starts	1st	2nd	3rd	Win & Pl
Career Total (Turf)	22	1	0	0	2477
Career Total (AW)	5	0	0	0	

55	9/00	Yarm	1m3y	F(0-60)H	G-F	£2198

Total win prize-money £2198

Going (Turf): Sf: 0-1 GS: 0-2 Gd: 0-5 **GF: 1-14** Fm: 0-0
Distance: 5f/6f: 0-3 7f-8f: 0-15 **9f-13f: 1-9** 14f+: 0-0
Track : LH: 0-9 RH: 0-1 Tight: 0-5 Gall: 0-1
Aids: Bl: 0-4 Vi: 0-1 Tstrap: 0-0
Best Rating: 46 6/01 Newc 1m gd-fm

Mindahra

(64) (7)

3-y-o b f Mind Games-Indiahra (Indian Ridge)
M Mullineaux P J Lawton

Placings:0-0000 (5409)
2001: 7^{0}GF, 5^{0}GF, 5^{0}G, 6^{0}SD

	Starts	1st	2nd	3rd	Win & Pl
Career Total (Turf)	4	0	0	0	
Career Total (AW)	1	0	0	0	

Going (Turf): Sf: 0-1 GS: 0-0 Gd: 0-1 GF: 0-2 Fm: 0-0
Distance: 5f/6f: 0-4 7f-8f: 0-1 9f-13f: 0-0 14f+: 0-0
Track : LH: 0-2 RH: 0-0 Tight: 0-1 Gall: 0-0
Aids: Bl: 0-0 Vi: 0-1 Tstrap: 0-0
Best Rating: 7 10/01 Sthl 6f stand

Mindanao

102 **74**

5-y-o b m Most Welcome-Salala (Connaught)
Miss J A Camacho Mrs S Camacho

Placings:00/0122121/42-60010113 (5373)
2001: 12^{6}S, 10^{0}GF, 11^{0}GS, 11^{1}GF, 10^{0}S, 11^{1}G, 11^{1}S, 14^{3}G

	Starts	1st	2nd	3rd	Win & Pl
Career Total (Turf)	19	6	4	1	39553

74	10/01	York	1m3f195y	E(0-75)H	SFT	£7605
37	8/01	Catt	1m3f214y	F	GD	£2422
55	6/01	Bevl	1m3f216y	F	G-F	£2352
90	10/99	Ayr	1m2f	D(0-80)H	SFT	£4081
69	8/99	Ripn	1m2f	D(0-80)H	GD	£7392
58	6/99	Newc	1m1f9y	E(0-75)H	GD	£7490

Total win prize-money £31343

Going (Turf): Sf: 2-5 GS: 0-5 **Gd: 3-5** GF: 1-3 Fm: 0-1
Distance: 5f/6f: 0-2 7f-8f: 0-1 **9f-13f: 6-15** 14f+: 0-1
Track : **LH: 4-13** RH: 2-5 **Tight: 3-8** Gall: 2-4
Aids: Bl: 0-0 Vi: 0-0 Tstrap: 0-0
Best Rating: 77 6/01 Ayr 1m2f gd-fm

A winner three times in 1999 between nine and ten furlongs, she only ran twice in 2000, where she was not far away on each occasion. She returned from nearly a year off in April of 2001, and has since won a further three times, two of which were claimers, and is well handicapped on her best form. She acts on most ground.

Minderoo

98(85) (45)**56**

3-y-o b c Efisio-Mindomica (Dominion)
B W Hills Guy Reed And Mrs Ailsa Daniels

Placings:0004050 (5281)
2001: 6^{0}GS, 6^{0}GS, 5^{0}GF, 5^{4}GS, 7^{0}GF, 8^{5}SD, 7^{0}S

	Starts	1st	2nd	3rd	Win & Pl
Career Total (Turf)	6	0	0	0	333
Career Total (AW)	1	0	0	0	0

Going (Turf): Sf: 0-1 GS: 0-3 Gd: 0-0 GF: 0-2 Fm: 0-0
Distance: 5f/6f: 0-4 7f-8f: 0-2 9f-13f: 0-1 14f+: 0-0
Track : LH: 0-2 RH: 0-0 Tight: 0-1 Gall: 0-1
Aids: Bl: 0-0 Vi: 0-0 Tstrap: 0-0
Best Rating: 65 5/01 Sals 6f gd-sft

Mine (IRE)

100 **77**

3-y-o b c Primo Dominie-Ellebanna (Tina's Pet)
J D Bethell M J Dawson

Placings:30-34121 (3876)
2001: 7^{3}GF, 6^{4}GF, 8^{1}GF, 8^{2}GF, 8^{1}GS

	Starts	1st	2nd	3rd	Win & Pl
Career Total (Turf)	7	2	1	2	13497

77	8/01	Thsk	1m	D(0-80)H	G-S	£4706
71	7/01	Donc	1m	D(0-80)H	G-F	£5141

Total win prize-money £9848

Going (Turf): Sf: 0-0 **GS: 1-1** Gd: 0-0 **GF: 1-6** Fm: 0-0
Distance: 5f/6f: 0-2 **7f-8f: 2-4** 9f-13f: 0-1 14f+: 0-0
Track : **LH: 1-3** RH: 0-0 **Tight: 1-1** Gall: 0-0
Aids: Bl: 0-0 Vi: 0-0 Tstrap: 0-0
Best Rating: 77 8/01 Thsk 1m gd-sft

Mine Forever

86 **57**

2-y-o br g Royal Academy (USA)-Overseas Romance (USA) (Assert)
A Berry Clayton Bigley Partnership Ltd

Placings:064400500 (5370)

2001: 5^{0}GF, 5^{6}GF, 7^{4}GF, 7^{4}GF, 7^{0}F, 7^{0}G, 8^{5}G, 6^{0}G, 7^{0}G

	Starts	1st	2nd	3rd	Win & Pl
Career Total (Turf)	9	0	0	0	0

Going (Turf): Sf: 0-0 GS: 0-0 Gd: 0-4 GF: 0-4 Fm: 0-1

Distance: 5f/6f: 0-3 7f-8f: 0-6 9f-13f: 0-0 14f+: 0-0

Track : LH: 0-3 RH: 0-1 Tight: 0-2 Gall: 0-1

Aids: Bl: 0-0 Vi: 0-0 Tstrap: 0-0

Best Rating: 57 8/01 Newc 1m good

Mine Host

97 **93**

2-y-o b c Elmaamul (USA)-Divina Mia (Dowsing (USA))

M L W Bell Nicholas R Hodges

Placings:140 (4348a)

2001: 6^{1}G, 7^{4}GF, 6^{0}GY

	Starts	1st	2nd	3rd	Win & Pl
Career Total (Turf)	3	1	0	0	5403
83 5/01 Yarm 6f3y E				GD	£3528

Total win prize-money £3528

Going (Turf): Sf: 0-0 GS: 0-0 **Gd: 1-1** GF: 0-1 Fm: 0-0

Distance: 5f/6f: 0-1 **7f-8f: 1-2** 9f-13f: 0-0 14f+: 0-0

Track : LH: 0-0 RH: 0-0 Tight: 0-0 Gall: 0-0

Aids: Bl: 0-0 Vi: 0-0 Tstrap: 0-0

Best Rating: 93 6/01 Asct 7f gd-fm

A half-brother to five-furlong two-year-old winner So Divine, won well on his debut despite showing signs of greenness. He ran with credit when stepped up in trip and class at Ascot.

Mingling

104 **78**

4-y-o b g Wolfhound (USA)-On The Tide (Slip Anchor)

M H Tompkins Mrs Beryl Lockey

Placings:450/352365-26541102330 (4855)

2001: 12^{2}GF, 12^{6}GF, 9^{5}F, 10^{4}G, 10^{1}GF, 10^{1}G, 10^{0}GF, 11^{2}GS, 12^{3}GF, 10^{3}F, 11^{0}GF

	Starts	1st	2nd	3rd	Win & Pl
Career Total (Turf)	20	2	3	4	18133
78 7/01 Sand 1m2f7y D(0-85)H				GD	£5746
56 6/01 Newc 1m2f32y D(0-75)				G-F	£5109

Total win prize-money £10855

Going (Turf): Sf: 0-0 GS: 0-3 **Gd: 1-5 GF: 1-9** Fm: 0-3

Distance: 5f/6f: 0-0 7f-8f: 0-3 **9f-13f: 2-17** 14f+: 0-0

Track : LH: 1-11 RH: 1-5 Tight: 0-7 **Gall: 1-4**

Aids: Bl: 0-0 Vi: 0-1 Tstrap: 0-0

Best Rating: 80 5/01 Muss 1m4f gd-fm

A consistent sort, he had a good chance at the weights when finally getting off the mark under a well-judged ride at Newcastle, and followed up in determined fashion at Sandown. Has yet to win beyond ten furlongs but stays 12. At his best on good ground or faster.

Mingora (USA)

90 **83**

2-y-o b f Mtoto-Silk Braid (USA) (Danzig (USA))

D R Loder Sheikh Ahmed Al Maktoum

Placings:2 (5107)

2001: 7^{2}GS

	Starts	1st	2nd	3rd	Win & Pl
Career Total (Turf)	1	0	1	0	1800

Going (Turf): Sf: 0-0 GS: 0-1 Gd: 0-0 GF: 0-0 Fm: 0-0

Distance: 5f/6f: 0-0 7f-8f: 0-1 9f-13f: 0-0 14f+: 0 0

Track : LH: 0-0 RH: 0-0 Tight: 0-0 Gall: 0-0

Aids: Bl: 0-0 Vi: 0-0 Tstrap: 0-0

Best Rating: 83 10/01 NmkR 7f gd-sft

Mini Lodge (IRE)

87 **76**

5-y-o ch g Grand Lodge (USA)-Mirea (USA) (The Minstrel (CAN))

J G Fitzgerald Marquesa De Moratalla

Placings:1022/60600/012232-000 (5693)

2001: 10^{0}S, 10^{0}S, 12^{0}S

	Starts	1st	2nd	3rd	Win & Pl
Career Total (Turf)	18	2	5	1	21239
64 7/00 Ripn 1m2f D(0-80)H				G-F	£4875
78 7/98 Newc 7f D				GD	£3208

Total win prize-money £8084

Going (Turf): Sf: 0-4 GS: 0-3 **Gd: 1-6 GF: 1-5** Fm: 0-0

Distance: 5f/6f: 0-0 7f-8f: 1-5 9f-13f: 1-13 14f+: 0-0

Track : LH: 0-10 **RH: 1-5 Tight: 1-3** Gall: 0-6

Aids: Bl: 0-0 Vi: 0-3 Tstrap: 0-0

Best Rating: 45 10/01 NmkR 1m2f soft

Lightly raced this season, she has shown nothing to suggest that she is as good as she was, although she is better on fast ground.

Minihaha

100 **67**

3-y-o ch f First Trump-Indian Lament (Indian Ridge)

Mrs A J Perrett J H Richmond-Watson

Placings:0-2531004 (5465)

2001: 6^{2}GF, 8^{5}GF, 8^{3}G, 9^{1}G, 9^{0}GF, 10^{0}S, 10^{4}G

	Starts	1st	2nd	3rd	Win & Pl
Career Total (Turf)	8	1	1	1	4541
64 8/01 Folk 1m1f149yE				GD	£2947

Total win prize-money £2947

Going (Turf): Sf: 0-2 GS: 0-0 **Gd: 1-3** GF: 0-3 Fm: 0-0

Distance: 5f/6f: 0-0 7f-8f: 0-3 **9f-13f: 1-5** 14f+: 0-0

Track : LH: 0-3 **RH: 1-3 Tight: 1-2** Gall: 0-0

Aids: Bl: 0-0 Vi: 0-0 Tstrap: 0-0

Best Rating: 67 7/01 Kemp 1m gd-fm

Fair front-running handicapper, winner of a ten-furlong maiden at Folkestone in August 2001. Needs good ground or faster.

Ministry Of Magic (USA)

63

3-y-o ch f Pine Bluff (USA)-Record Setter (USA) (Damascus (USA))

B J Meehan Mrs Susan Roy

Placings:002 (5522)

2001: 10^{0}GS, 8^{0}S, 6^{2}HY

	Starts	1st	2nd	3rd	Win & Pl
Career Total (Turf)	3	0	1	0	868

Going (Turf): Sf: 0-2 GS: 0-1 Gd: 0-0 GF: 0-0 Fm: 0-0

Distance: 5f/6f: 0-1 7f-8f: 0-1 9f-13f: 0-1 14f+: 0-0

Track : LH: 0-1 RH: 0-0 Tight: 0-0 Gall: 0-1

Aids: Bl: 0-0 Vi: 0-0 Tstrap: 0-0

Best Rating: 63 5/01 Newb 1m soft

Minivet

105 **76**

6-y-o b g Midyan (USA)-Bronzewing (Beldale Flutter (USA))

T D Easterby The Pertemps Professionals

Placings:3/0232133622/13030642125/000550 (3609)

2001: 11^{0}F, 12^{0}GF, 11^{0}GS, 10^{5}GF, 10^{5}S, 12^{0}GS

	Starts	1st	2nd	3rd	Win & Pl
Career Total (Turf)	28	3	6	6	33723
83 9/99 Hayd 1m3f200yC(0-90)H				SFT	£7490
79 4/99 NmkJ 1m4f C(0-95)H				GD	£6492
44 8/98 Rdcr 1m1f E				FRM	£3650

Total win prize-money £17632

Going (Turf): Sf: 1-5 GS: 0-5 **Gd: 1-10** GF: 0-6 **Fm: 1-2**

Distance: 5f/6f: 0-0 7f-8f: 0-3 **9f-13f: 3-22** 14f+: 0-3

Track : **LH: 2-19** RH: 1-8 Tight: 1-8 Gall: 1-12

Aids: Bl: 0-1 Vi: 0-0 Tstrap: 0-0

Best Rating: 77 5/01 York 1m3f195y firm

A decent middle-distance handicapper a couple of seasons ago, he has enjoyed more success over hurdles of late. Runs his best races on good or easier ground. Stays a mile and a half.

Minnie Bloo Min (IRE)

95(92) (52)**49**

2-y-o b f Blues Traveller (IRE)-White Jasmin (Jalmood (USA))

Miss V Haigh A Zacharia

Placings:2221300460 (5331)

2001: 5^{2}GF, 6^{2}G, 5^{2}G, 5^{1}SD, 6^{3}SD, 7^{0}GF, 5^{0}G, 6^{4}SW, 7^{6}HY, 5^{0}HY

	Starts	1st	2nd	3rd	Win & Pl
Career Total (Turf)	7	0	3	0	2081
Career Total (AW)	3	1	0	1	2307
52 7/01 Sthl 5f G				STD	£1911

Total win prize-money £1911

Going (Turf): Sf: 0-2 GS: 0-0 Gd: 0-3 GF: 0-2 Fm: 0-0

Distance: **5f/6f: 1-8** 7f-8f: 0-2 9f-13f: 0-0 14f+: 0-0

Track : LH: 0-3 RH: 0-0 Tight: 0-2 Gall: 0-0

Aids: Bl: 0-0 Vi: 0-0 Tstrap: 0-0

Best Rating: 52 7/01 Sthl 5f stand

Plating-class juvenile. Had done little wrong despite being three-times runner-up before getting off the mark at Southwell, on her first try on the All-Weather. Bred to get further in time.

Minskip Merlin

92 **72**

2-y-o b c Sea Raven (IRE)-Minskip Miss (Lucky Wednesday)

T D Barron Minskip Merlin Partnership

Placings:6622 (4852)

2001: 6^{6}F, 5^{6}GS, 6^{2}G, 5^{2}GF

	Starts	1st	2nd	3rd	Win & Pl
Career Total (Turf)	4	0	2	0	2423

Going (Turf): Sf: 0-0 GS: 0-1 Gd: 0-1 GF: 0-1 Fm: 0-1

Distance: 5f/6f: 0-4 7f-8f: 0-0 9f-13f: 0-0 14f+: 0-0

Track : LH: 0 1 RH: 0-0 Tight: 0-1 Gall: 0-0

Aids: Bl: 0-0 Vi: 0-0 Tstrap: 0-0

Best Rating: 72 9/01 Catt 5f212y gd-fm

Mint Approval (USA)

73 **37**

2-y-o gr/ro g With Approval (CAN)-Mint Bell (USA) (Key To The Mint (USA))

B J Meehan Matham Investments

Placings:000 (2715)

2001: 5^{0}GS, 5^{0}S, 5^{0}GF

	Starts	1st	2nd	3rd	Win & Pl
Career Total (Turf)	3	0	0	0	

Going (Turf): Sf: 0-1 GS: 0-1 Gd: 0-0 GF: 0-1 Fm: 0-0

Distance: 5f/6f: 0-3 7f-8f: 0-0 9f-13f: 0-0 14f+: 0-0

Track : LH: 0-0 RH: 0-1 Tight: 0-0 Gall: 0-1

Aids: Bl: 0-0 Vi: 0-0 Tstrap: 0-0

Best Rating: 37 5/01 Sals 5f soft

Mint Cake

91 **54d**

2-y-o b f Namaqualand (USA)-Caroline Connors (Fairy King (USA))

N Tinkler Merewood Racing

Placings:040000 **(4793)**
2001: 6^{0}GF, 6^{4}GF, 6^{0}GF, 5^{0}G, 8^{0}G, 8^{0}G

	Starts	1st	2nd	3rd	Win & Pl
Career Total (Turf)	6	0	0	0	396

Going (Turf): **Sf: 0-0 GS: 0-0 Gd: 0-3 GF: 0-3 Fm: 0-0**
Distance: 5f/6f: 0-4 7f-8f: 0-2 9f-13f: 0-0 14f+: 0-0
Track : LH: 0-2 RH: 0-0 Tight: 0-0 Gall: 0-1
Aids: Bl: 0-0 Vi: 0-0 Tstrap: 0-0
Best Rating: 54 6/01 Newc 6f gd-fm

Mint Julep (IRE)

(62) (9)**58**
3-y-o br g Piccolo-Kingdom Princess (Forzando)
K R Burke Michael S Wilson

Placings:0600000 **(5198)**
2001: 8^{0}S, 8^{6}GF, 8^{0}GF, 7^{0}F, 7^{0}G, 8^{0}F, 9^{0}SD

	Starts	1st	2nd	3rd	Win & Pl
Career Total (Turf)	6	0	0	0	0
Career Total (AW)	1	0	0	0	

Going (Turf): **Sf: 0-1 GS: 0-0 Gd: 0-1 GF: 0-2 Fm: 0-2**
Distance: 5f/6f: 0-0 7f-8f: 0-5 9f-13f: 0-2 14f+: 0-0
Track : LH: 0-2 RH: 0-3 Tight: 0-4 Gall: 0-0
Aids: Bl: 0-0 Vi: 0-0 Tstrap: 0-0
Best Rating: 58 7/01 Kemp 1m gd-fm

Mint Leaf (IRE)

74(87) **16**
4-y-o b f Sri Pekan (USA)-Suaad (IRE) (Fool's Holme (USA))
Julian Poulton (Jamie Poulton 25/1) Mrs H Shaw

Placings:5446220/00000000**0**-00 **(1767)**
2001: 9^{0}GF, 10^{0}F

	Starts	1st	2nd	3rd	Win & Pl
Career Total (Turf)	16	0	2	0	2640
Career Total (AW)	2	0	0	0	

Going (Turf): **Sf: 0-2 GS: 0-2 Gd: 0-3 GF: 0-6 Fm: 0-1**
Distance: 5f/6f: 0-10 7f-8f: 0-4 9f-13f: 0-4 14f+: 0-0
Track : LH: 0-9 RH: 0-2 Tight: 0-6 Gall: 0-2
Aids: Bl: 0-2 Vi: 0-0 Tstrap: 0-8

Mint Royale (IRE)

86 **56d**
3-y-o ch f Cadeaux Genereux-Clarentia (Ballad Rock)
T D Easterby R J Cornelius

Placings:0-50000 **(3259)**
2001: 6^{5}S, 6^{0}HY, 6^{0}S, 5^{0}GF, 6^{0}GF

	Starts	1st	2nd	3rd	Win & Pl
Career Total (Turf)	6	0	0	0	0

Going (Turf): **Sf: 0-3 GS: 0-0 Gd: 0-1 GF: 0-2 Fm: 0-0**
Distance: 5f/6f: 0-6 7f-8f: 0-0 9f-13f: 0-0 14f+: 0-0
Track : LH: 0-1 RH: 0-0 Tight: 0-0 Gall: 0-0
Aids: Bl: 0-0 Vi: 0-0 Tstrap: 0-0
Best Rating: 44 6/01 Bevl 5f gd-fm

Minus Four (IRE)

(91) (31)**39**
3-y-o b c Standiford (USA)-Minibar (Dominion)
L A Dace Noel Monaghan

Placings:000-50 **(5050)**
2001: 9^{5}GS, 11^{0}SD

	Starts	1st	2nd	3rd	Win & Pl
Career Total (Turf)	3	0	0	0	0
Career Total (AW)	2	0	0	0	

Going (Turf): **Sf: 0-1 GS: 0-2 Gd: 0-0 GF: 0-0 Fm: 0-0**
Distance: 5f/6f: 0-1 7f-8f: 0-2 9f-13f: 0-2 14f+: 0-0
Track : LH: 0-2 RH: 0-1 Tight: 0-0 Gall: 0-0
Aids: Bl: 0-0 Vi: 0-0 Tstrap: 0-0
Best Rating: 39 9/01 Leic 1m1f218y gd-sft

Minuscolo

92 **40**
3-y-o b f Piccolo-Wrangbrook (Shirley Heights)
J A Osborne Harry Sibley

Placings:00635-0000 **(4899)**
2001: 5^{0}G, 6^{0}GF, 7^{0}GF, 8^{0}GS

	Starts	1st	2nd	3rd	Win & Pl
Career Total (Turf)	9	0	0	1	568

Going (Turf): **Sf: 0-0 GS: 0-2 Gd: 0-2 GF: 0-5 Fm: 0-0**
Distance: 5f/6f: 0-6 7f-8f: 0-2 9f-13f: 0-1 14f+: 0-0
Track : LH: 0-0 RH: 0-2 Tight: 0-0 Gall: 0-2
Aids: Bl: 0-0 Vi: 0-0 Tstrap: 0-0
Best Rating: 40 5/01 Wind 5f10y good

Miracle Island

99(97) (73d)**62**
6-y-o b g Jupiter Island-Running Game (Run The Gantlet (USA))
K R Burke Champagne Racing

Placings:22144/00/0-60002660 **(4296)**
2001: 8^{6}SD, 9^{0}SW, 16^{0}GF, 10^{0}GF, 11^{2}G, 10^{6}G, 11^{6}G, 12^{0}G

	Starts	1st	2nd	3rd	Win & Pl
Career Total (Turf)	9	0	1	0	1002
Career Total (AW)	7	1	2	0	5130

73 2/98 Wolv 1m1f79y D STD £3468
Total win prize-money £3469

Going (Turf): **Sf: 0-0 GS: 0-1 Gd: 0-5 GF: 0-3 Fm: 0-0**
Distance: 5f/6f: 0-0 7f-8f: 0-1 **9f-13f: 1-14** 14f+: 0-1
Track : **LH: 1-11** RH: 0-4 **Tight: 1-7** Gall: 0-3
Aids: Bl: 0-0 Vi: 0-1 Tstrap: 0-5
Best Rating: 64 2/01 Sthl 1m stand

Suited by an easy track, it is a long time since he scored on the Flat. Handles Fibresand and likes some give on turf.

Mirafiori (IRE)

(80) (37)**55**
2-y-o br f Inzar (USA)-Monaco Lady (Manado)
G C H Chung G C H Chung

Placings:001000 **(5618)**
2001: 5^{0}SD, 6^{0}F, 7^{1}GF, 8^{0}GF, 8^{0}G, 8^{0}SD

	Starts	1st	2nd	3rd	Win & Pl
Career Total (Turf)	4	1	0	0	2370
Career Total (AW)	2	0	0	0	

55 8/01 Folk 7f F G-F £2369
Total win prize-money £2370

Going (Turf): Sf: 0-0 GS: 0-0 Gd: 0-1 **GF: 1-2** Fm: 0-1
Distance: 5f/6f: 0-1 **7f-8f: 1-3** 9f-13f: 0-2 14f+: 0-0
Track : LH: 0-3 RH: 0-0 Tight: 0-1 Gall: 0-0
Aids: Bl: 0-0 Vi: 0-0 Tstrap: 0-0
Best Rating: 55 8/01 Folk 7f gd-fm

Well beaten in maiden company previously, he appreciated the drop in class and step up in trip when wearing down Last Gesture in the closing stages at Folkestone in August 2001. Needs to be covered up.

Misalliance

47(94) (35)**35**
6-y-o ch m Elmaamul (USA)-Cabaret Artiste (Shareef Dancer (USA))
M E Sowersby T J Stubbins

Placings:0410/00560350/0400/00330-00 **(0708)**
2001: 12^{0}SD, 17^{0}HY

	Starts	1st	2nd	3rd	Win & Pl
Career Total (Turf)	18	1	0	1	3002
Career Total (AW)	5	0	0	2	625

71 10/97 Newc 7f F G-F £2239
Total win prize-money £2239

Going (Turf): Sf: 0-3 GS: 0-4 Gd: 0-1 **GF: 1-10** Fm: 0-0
Distance: 5f/6f: 0-0 **7f-8f: 1-8** 9f-13f: 0-12 14f+: 0-3
Track : LH: 0-13 RH: 0-7 Tight: 0-4 Gall: 0-2
Aids: Bl: 0-1 Vi: 0-0 Tstrap: 0-2
Best Rating: 71 10/97 Newc 7f GF

Misbehaviour

90 **69**
2-y-o b g Tragic Role (USA)-Exotic Forest (Dominion)
J G Portman The Naughty Boys

Placings:03300 **(5364)**
2001: 5^{0}G, 6^{3}G, 6^{3}GF, 5^{0}GF, 6^{0}GS

	Starts	1st	2nd	3rd	Win & Pl
Career Total (Turf)	5	0	0	2	904

Going (Turf): **Sf: 0-0 GS: 0-1 Gd: 0-2 GF: 0-2 Fm: 0-0**
Distance: 5f/6f: 0-5 7f-8f: 0-0 9f-13f: 0-0 14f+: 0-0
Track : LH: 0-0 RH: 0-0 Tight: 0-0 Gall: 0-0
Aids: Bl: 0-0 Vi: 0-0 Tstrap: 0-0
Best Rating: 69 8/01 Ling 6f gd-fm

A speedy sort. Placed twice over six furlongs on a sound surface.

Mischief

(102) (30)**36**
5-y-o ch g Generous (IRE)-Knight's Baroness (Rainbow Quest (USA))
K Bell (M Quinn 27/1) Mrs Angela Ellis

Placings:5303/0556203000506165000435**2**-**00636**2020 **(5622)**
2001: 16^{0}SD, 13^{0}SD, 14^{6}SW, 16^{3}SD, 16^{6}SD, 15^{2}GF, 14^{0}GS, 9^{2}GF, 14^{0}GS

	Starts	1st	2nd	3rd	Win & Pl
Career Total (Turf)	18	1	2	2	6411
Career Total (AW)	18	0	2	3	2376

33 7/00 Carl 1m6f32y E(0-70)H FRM £2758
Total win prize-money £2758

Going (Turf): Sf: 0-7 GS: 0-2 Gd: 0-3 GF: 0-4 **Fm: 1-2**
Distance: 5f/6f: 0-0 7f-8f: 0-0 9f-13f: 0-16 **14f+: 1-20**
Track : LH: 0-28 **RH: 1-8** Tight: 0-23 Gall: 0-1
Aids: Bl: 0-3 **Vi: 1-21** Tstrap: 0-0
Best Rating: 36 7/01 Folk 1m7f92y gd-fm

Mischievious (IRE)

58 **29**
2-y-o ch f Dr Devious (IRE)-Last Affaire (IRE) (Roi Danzig (USA))
H J Collingridge G B Amy

Placings:000 **(3811)**
2001: 6^{0}GF, 7^{0}GF, 7^{0}G

	Starts	1st	2nd	3rd	Win & Pl
Career Total (Turf)	3	0	0	0	

Going (Turf): **Sf: 0-0 GS: 0-0 Gd: 0-1 GF: 0-2 Fm: 0-0**
Distance: 5f/6f: 0-1 7f-8f: 0-2 9f-13f: 0-0 14f+: 0-0
Track : LH: 0-0 RH: 0-0 Tight: 0-0 Gall: 0-0
Aids: Bl: 0-0 Vi: 0-0 Tstrap: 0-0
Best Rating: 29 6/01 Wind 6f gd-fm

Misck (IRE)

87 **68**
2-y-o ch f Desert King (IRE)-Sedra (Nebbiolo)
J L Dunlop M Alqatami & K M Al-Mudhaf

Placings:00 (5602)
2001: 7^{0}GS, 7^{0}GS

	Starts	1st	2nd	3rd	Win & Pl
Career Total (Turf)	2	0	0	0	

Going (Turf): Sf: 0-0 GS: 0-2 Gd: 0-0 GF: 0-0 Fm: 0-0
Distance: 5f/6f: 0-0 7f-8f: 0-2 9f-13f: 0-0 14f+: 0-0
Track : LH: 0-0 RH: 0-0 Tight: 0-0 Gall: 0-0
Aids: Bl: 0-0 Vi: 0-0 Tstrap: 0-0
Best Rating: 68 11/01 NmkR 7f gd-sft

Misconduct

97 (48)**56**
7-y-o gr m Risk Me (FR)-Grey Cree (Creetown)
J G Portman The Playmates

Placings:0000323/5002151104/20/23240-50 (3984)
2001: 11^{5}GS, 14^{0}F

	Starts	1st	2nd	3rd	Win & Pl
Career Total (Turf)	16	2	3	1	10160
Career Total (AW)	10	1	2	2	4550

48	8/98	Ling	1m2f	F(0-65)H	STD	£2070
47	7/98	Bath	1m2f46y	E(0-70)H	GD	£2944
42	6/98	Sals	1m1f198y	F(0-65)H	G-F	£2626

Total win prize-money £7640

Going (Turf): Sf: 0-4 GS: 0-1 **Gd: 1-8 GF: 1-2** Fm: 0-1
Distance: 5f/6f: 0-2 7f-8f: 0-9 **9f-13f: 3-11** 14f+: 0-4
Track : **LH: 2-16** RH: 1-8 **Tight: 3-18** Gall: 0-0
Aids: Bl: 0-0 Vi: 0-0 Tstrap: 0-0
Best Rating: 49 5/01 Bath 1m3f144y gd-sft

Lightly raced on the Flat in recent years. Best form around 12 to 14 furlongs. Handles give.

Misdemeanor

57(75) (31)**55**
3-y-o b f Presidium-Fair Madame (Monseigneur (USA))
J S Wainwright J S Wainwright

Placings:05600-0 (0875)
2001: 9^{0}S

	Starts	1st	2nd	3rd	Win & Pl
Career Total (Turf)	4	0	0	0	149
Career Total (AW)	2	0	0	0	0

Going (Turf): Sf: 0-2 GS: 0-0 Gd: 0-1 GF: 0-1 Fm: 0-0
Distance: 5f/6f: 0-2 7f-8f: 0-2 9f-13f: 0-2 14f+: 0-0
Track : LH: 0-3 RH: 0-0 Tight: 0-1 Gall: 0-0
Aids: Bl: 0-0 Vi: 0-0 Tstrap: 0-0
Best Rating: 16 4/01 Nott 1m1f213y soft

Mishead

20
3-y-o ch c Unfuwain (USA)-Green Jannat (USA) (Alydar (USA))
M C Chapman (Sir Michael Stoute 17/4) N Malbon

Placings:00000 (5634)
2001: 10^{0}GS, 10^{0}G, 5^{0}G, 7^{0}GF, 11^{0}G

	Starts	1st	2nd	3rd	Win & Pl
Career Total (Turf)	5	0	0	0	0

Going (Turf): Sf: 0-0 GS: 0-1 Gd: 0-3 GF: 0-1 Fm: 0-0
Distance: 5f/6f: 0-1 7f-8f: 0-1 9f-13f: 0-3 14f+: 0-0
Track : LH: 0-2 RH: 0-1 Tight: 0-2 Gall: 0-1
Aids: Bl: 0-0 Vi: 0-0 Tstrap: 0-0
Best Rating: 46 4/01 NmkR 1m2f gd-sft

Mishka

(102) (67)**73**
3-y-o b g Mistertopogigo (IRE)-Walsham Witch (Music Maestro)
Julian Poulton The Sutton Family

Placings:0035-230304524350030 (5523)
2001: 6^{2}SD, 5^{3}S, 6^{0}GS, 5^{3}F, 5^{0}GF, 5^{4}GF, 6^{5}GF, 5^{2}GS, 5^{4}S, 5^{3}G, 5^{5}F, 5^{0}G, 5^{0}GS, 5^{3}S, 5^{0}HY

	Starts	1st	2nd	3rd	Win & Pl
Career Total (Turf)	18	0	1	5	6502
Career Total (AW)	1	0	1	0	1200

Going (Turf): Sf: 0-4 GS: 0-3 Gd: 0-4 GF: 0-5 Fm: 0-2
Distance: 5f/6f: 0-19 7f-8f: 0-0 9f-13f: 0-0 14f+: 0-0
Track : LH: 0-2 RH: 0-2 Tight: 0-1 Gall: 0-3
Aids: Bl: 0-2 Vi: 0-3 Tstrap: 0-0
Best Rating: 73 10/01 York 5f soft

Still a maiden, but has run with some credit in 2001. Seems to act on most surfaces but is proving difficult to win with.

Misraah (IRE)

115 **115**
4-y-o ch g Lure (USA)-Dwell (USA) (Habitat)
Sir Michael Stoute Hamdan Al Maktoum

Placings:41/1044-50251345 (4054)
2001: 6^{5}GS, 6^{0}GF, 5^{2}GF, 6^{5}GF, 5^{1}GF, 6^{3}G, 7^{4}GF, 7^{5}GF

	Starts	1st	2nd	3rd	Win & Pl
Career Total (Turf)	14	3	1	1	76619

106	7/01	Sand	5f6y	A	G-F	£19500
104	4/00	NmkR	7f	C	G-S	£6948
92	10/99	Leic	7f9y	D	GD	£3687

Total win prize-money £30136

Going (Turf): Sf: 0-0 **GS: 1-4 Gd: 1-3 GF: 1-7** Fm: 0-0
Distance: **5f/6f: 1-6 7f-8f: 2-8** 9f-13f: 0-0 14f+: 0-0
Track : LH: 0-1 RH: 0-0 Tight: 0-0 Gall: 0-1
Aids: Bl: 0-0 Vi: 0-0 Tstrap: 0-0
Best Rating: 115 7/01 NmkJ 6f good

Made a winning reappearance in 2000 but ran poorly in the Guineas. Has since been dropped back to sprint distances. Came from last to first to win Listed event over five furlongs at Sandown in July and finished a fine third behind Mozart in the July Cup. Came home first of the far side group in the Tote International Handicap at Ascot. Six furlongs looks his best trip.

Miss All Alone

62(78) (35)**35**
6-y-o ch m Crofthall-Uninvited (Be My Guest (USA))
J A Glover Countrywide Classics Limited

Placings:0/6325223202/33205400/00-0 (1041)
2001: 14^{0}HY

	Starts	1st	2nd	3rd	Win & Pl
Career Total (Turf)	12	0	1	2	2257
Career Total (AW)	10	0	5	2	3558

Going (Turf): Sf: 0-4 GS: 0-2 Gd: 0-2 GF: 0-2 Fm: 0-2
Distance: 5f/6f: 0-1 7f-8f: 0-11 9f-13f: 0-8 14f+: 0-1
Track : LH: 0-15 RH: 0-3 Tight: 0-2 Gall: 0-1
Aids: Bl: 0-7 Vi: 0-3 Tstrap: 0-0

Miss Amazer

95(77) (28)**62**
2-y-o b f Shaamit (IRE)-Kiss On Time (Lead On Time (USA))
J M Bradley Mrs A M Johnson

Placings:006300560 (4384)
2001: 5^{0}SD, 5^{0}SD, 5^{6}HY, 5^{3}F, 5^{0}HD, 5^{0}GS, 6^{5}S, 6^{6}GF, 6^{0}GF

	Starts	1st	2nd	3rd	Win & Pl
Career Total (Turf)	7	0	0	1	533
Career Total (AW)	2	0	0	0	0

Going (Turf): Sf: 0-2 GS: 0-1 Gd: 0-0 GF: 0-2 Fm: 0-2
Distance: 5f/6f: 0-6 7f-8f: 0-3 9f-13f: 0-0 14f+: 0-0
Track : LH: 0-3 RH: 0-0 Tight: 0-0 Gall: 0-3
Aids: Bl: 0-0 Vi: 0-0 Tstrap: 0-0
Best Rating: 62 8/01 Sals 6f212y gd-fm

Miss Amber Nectar

(80) (8)**44**
4-y-o b f Theatrical Charmer-Avenmore Star (Comedy Star (USA))
E A Wheeler M V Kirby

Placings:0000-0 (0020)
2001: 12^{0}SD

	Starts	1st	2nd	3rd	Win & Pl
Career Total (Turf)	4	0	0	0	
Career Total (AW)	1	0	0	0	

Going (Turf): Sf: 0-0 GS: 0-1 Gd: 0-3 GF: 0-0 Fm: 0-0
Distance: 5f/6f: 0-0 7f-8f: 0-0 9f-13f: 0-5 14f+: 0-0
Track : LH: 0-2 RH: 0-2 Tight: 0-4 Gall: 0-0
Aids: Bl: 0-0 Vi: 0-0 Tstrap: 0-0
Best Rating: 8 1/01 Ling 1m4f stand

Miss Bananas

(102) (41)**39**
6-y-o b m Risk Me (FR)-Astrid Gilberto (Runnett)
C N Kellett W Meah

Placings:500243/2410000003030/0054200002050010000/6001500400000100005-014660 (0499)
2001: 6^{0}SD, 5^{1}SD, 6^{4}SW, 5^{6}SW, 5^{6}SD, 5^{0}SD

	Starts	1st	2nd	3rd	Win & Pl
Career Total (Turf)	25	3	0	0	8416
Career Total (AW)	38	2	4	3	9936

43	1/01	Sthl	5f	E(0-70)H	STD	£2457
39	8/00	Leic	5f2y	E(0-70)H	G-F	£2808
55	4/00	Pont	6f	F	G-S	£2394
40	8/99	Leic	5f2y	E(0-70)H	GD	£3213
63	2/98	Ling	5f	D(0-85)H	SLW	£3355

Total win prize-money £14228

Going (Turf): Sf: 0-5 **GS: 1-3 Gd: 1-5 GF: 1-11** Fm: 0-1
Distance: **5f/6f: 5-58** 7f-8f: 0-5 9f-13f: 0-0 14f+: 0-0
Track : **LH: 2-39** RH: 0-0 **Tight: 1-28** Gall: 0-1
Aids: Bl: 0-0 Vi: 0-0 **Tstrap: 1-7**
Best Rating: 43 1/01 Sthl 5f stand

Miss Beady (IRE)

92 **53**
3-y-o b f Eagle Eyed (USA)-Regal Fanfare (IRE) (Taufan (USA))
Don Enrico Incisa Don Enrico Incisa

Placings:0055004-0605460 (4400)
2001: 7^{0}S, 6^{6}G, 6^{0}F, 6^{5}GF, 7^{4}G, 8^{6}GF, 6^{0}G

	Starts	1st	2nd	3rd	Win & Pl
Career Total (Turf)	14	0	0	0	225

Going (Turf): Sf: 0-4 GS: 0-0 Gd: 0-3 GF: 0-5 Fm: 0-2
Distance: 5f/6f: 0-11 7f-8f: 0-3 9f-13f: 0-0 14f+: 0-0
Track : LH: 0-3 RH: 0-0 Tight: 0-1 Gall: 0-1
Aids: Bl: 0-1 Vi: 0-0 Tstrap: 0-0
Best Rating: 53 7/01 Newc 7f good

Miss Beetee (IRE)

97(88) (25)**47**
3-y-o b f Brief Truce (USA)-Majestic Amber (USA) (Majestic Light (USA))
J J Bridger The Hop-Pickers Partnership

Placings:4440-0000000 (3176)
2001: 6^{0}GS, 5^{0}G, 6^{0}F, 6^{0}GF, 6^{0}SD, 8^{0}SD, 8^{0}G

	Starts	1st	2nd	3rd	Win & Pl
Career Total (Turf)	9	0	0	0	869
Career Total (AW)	2	0	0	0	

Going (Turf): Sf: 0-2 GS: 0-2 Gd: 0-3 GF: 0-1 Fm: 0-1

Distance: 5f/6f: 0-7 7f-8f: 0-2 9f-13f: 0-2 14f+: 0-0
Track : LH: 0-3 RH: 0-2 Tight: 0-2 Gall: 0-2
Aids: Bl: 0-0 Vi: 0-0 Tstrap: 0-0
Best Rating: 47 5/01 Wind 5f10y good

Miss Brief (IRE)

91(90) (46)**34**
3-y-o b f Brief Truce (USA)-Preponderance (IRE) (Cyrano De Bergerac)
P D Evans Crewe And Nantwich Racing Club

Placings:02442000-**65**00500 **(3706)**
2001: 5^{6}SD, 5^{5}SW, 5^{0}SD, 5^{0}GF, 8^{5}GF, 6^{0}GF, 7^{0}G

	Starts	1st	2nd	3rd	Win & Pl
Career Total (Turf)	12	0	2	0	4614
Career Total (AW)	3	0	0	0	0

Going (Turf): Sf: 0-1 GS: 0-1 Gd: 0-3 GF: 0-6 Fm: 0-1
Distance: 5f/6f: 0-12 7f-8f: 0-2 9f-13f: 0-1 14f+: 0-0
Track : LH: 0-8 RH: 0-0 Tight: 0-6 Gall: 0-1
Aids: Bl: 0-0 Vi: 0-2 Tstrap: 0-4
Best Rating: 46 1/01 Ling 5f stand

Miss C

(91) (69)**69**
2-y-o b f Tachyon Park-Fallal (IRE) (Fayruz)
R Hollinshead D Coppenhall

Placings:31403 **(5194)**
2001: 5^{3}GF, 5^{1}GF, 5^{4}GF, 5^{0}GF, 5^{3}SD

	Starts	1st	2nd	3rd	Win & Pl
Career Total (Turf)	4	1	0	1	3208
Career Total (AW)	1	0	0	1	542

69 6/01 Bevl 5f F G-F £2408
Total win prize-money £2408

Going (Turf): Sf: 0-0 GS: 0-0 Gd: 0-0 **GF: 1-4** Fm: 0-0
Distance: 5f/6f: 1-5 7f-8f: 0-0 9f-13f: 0-0 14f+: 0-0
Track : LH: 0-2 RH: 0-0 Tight: 0-2 Gall: 0-0
Aids: Bl: 0-0 Vi: 0-0 Tstrap: 0-0
Best Rating: 69 10/01 Wolv 5f stand

A tall, speedily-bred filly, showed promise on her debut and went on to win a Beverley claimer next time. Lightly raced in the 2001 season, and was placed on the All-Weather in October. Has only run over five furlongs. Acts on fast ground.

Miss Cash

89 **32**
4-y-o b f Rock Hopper-Miss Cashtal (IRE) (Ballacashtal (CAN))
M E Sowersby R D Seldon

Placings:424-30 **(4537)**
2001: 9^{3}GF, 9^{0}GF

	Starts	1st	2nd	3rd	Win & Pl
Career Total (Turf)	5	0	1	1	1809

Going (Turf): Sf: 0-1 GS: 0-0 Gd: 0-0 GF: 0-4 Fm: 0-0
Distance: 5f/6f: 0-0 7f-8f: 0-0 9f-13f: 0-5 14f+: 0-0
Track : LH: 0-3 RH: 0-2 Tight: 0-2 Gall: 0-0
Aids: Bl: 0-0 Vi: 0-0 Tstrap: 0-0
Best Rating: 25 9/01 Rdcr 1m1f gd-fm

Miss Concept (IRE)

2-y-o b f Frimaire-Hard Sweet (Hard Fought)
F Jordan Tony Cocum

Placings:0 **(4670)**
2001: 7^{0}G

	Starts	1st	2nd	3rd	Win & Pl
Career Total (Turf)	1	0	0	0	

Going (Turf): Sf: 0-0 GS: 0-0 Gd: 0-1 GF: 0-0 Fm: 0-0
Distance: 5f/6f: 0-0 7f-8f: 0-1 9f-13f: 0-0 14f+: 0-0
Track : LH: 0-0 RH: 0-0 Tight: 0-0 Gall: 0-0
Aids: Bl: 0-0 Vi: 0-0 Tstrap: 0-0

Miss Corniche

96 **88**
2-y-o b f Hernando (FR)-Miss Beaulieu (Northfields (USA))
G Wragg J L C Pearce

Placings:21 **(5561)**
2001: 7^{2}GF, 7^{1}S

	Starts	1st	2nd	3rd	Win & Pl
Career Total (Turf)	2	1	1	0	5930

88 10/01 Yarm 7f3y D SFT £4543
Total win prize-money £4544

Going (Turf): Sf: 1-1 GS: 0-0 Gd: 0-0 GF: 0-1 Fm: 0-0
Distance: 5f/6f: 0-0 **7f-8f: 1-2** 9f-13f: 0-0 14f+: 0-0
Track : LH: 0-0 RH: 0-1 Tight: 0-0 Gall: 0-1
Aids: Bl: 0-0 Vi: 0-0 Tstrap: 0-0
Best Rating: 88 10/01 Yarm 7f3y soft

Second of 12 on debut in a Kempton maiden behind the Pattern-class Red Rioja, she made no mistake in a soft-ground maiden at Yarmouth next time. She should make her mark in decent company at three.

Miss Croisette

92 **68**
2-y-o ch f Hernando (FR)-Miss Riviera (Kris)
G Wragg J L C Pearce

Placings:00 **(5594)**
2001: 6^{0}GF, 6^{0}GS

	Starts	1st	2nd	3rd	Win & Pl
Career Total (Turf)	2	0	0	0	

Going (Turf): Sf: 0-0 GS: 0-1 Gd: 0-0 GF: 0-1 Fm: 0-0
Distance: 5f/6f: 0-2 7f-8f: 0-0 9f-13f: 0-0 14f+: 0-0
Track : LH: 0-0 RH: 0-0 Tight: 0-0 Gall: 0-0
Aids: Bl: 0-0 Vi: 0-0 Tstrap: 0-0
Best Rating: 68 8/01 Gdwd 6f gd-fm

Miss Damask

(101) (66)**57**
3-y-o b f Barathea (IRE)-Startino (Bustino)
J A Osborne Hertford Offset Limited

Placings:2052 **(5611)**
2001: 8^{2}SW, 8^{0}GF, 7^{5}S, 8^{2}SD

	Starts	1st	2nd	3rd	Win & Pl
Career Total (Turf)	2	0	0	0	0
Career Total (AW)	2	0	2	0	1622

Going (Turf): Sf: 0-1 GS: 0-0 Gd: 0-0 GF: 0-1 Fm: 0-0
Distance: 5f/6f: 0-0 7f-8f: 0-2 9f-13f: 0-2 14f+: 0-0
Track : LH: 0-2 RH: 0-1 Tight: 0-2 Gall: 0-0
Aids: Bl: 0-0 Vi: 0-0 Tstrap: 0-0
Best Rating: 66 11/01 Wolv 1m100y stand

She has shown her best form on Fibresand. Stays a mile.

Miss Damina

(80) (28)**31**
3-y-o b f Primo Dominie-So Beguiling (USA) (Woodman (USA))
J D Czerpak (P L Gilligan 22/9) Z Kulaib

Placings:00040400-6600030006 **(5617)**
2001: 8^{6}GF, 8^{6}G, 7^{0}GF, 8^{0}F, 7^{0}GF, 9^{3}G, 10^{0}GF, 13^{0}GF, 12^{0}SD, 8^{6}SD

	Starts	1st	2nd	3rd	Win & Pl
Career Total (Turf)	15	0	0	1	604
Career Total (AW)	3	0	0	0	0

Going (Turf): Sf: 0-1 GS: 0-1 Gd: 0-3 GF: 0-7 Fm: 0-2
Distance: 5f/6f: 0-4 7f-8f: 0-4 9f-13f: 0-8 14f+: 0-1
Track : LH: 0-8 RH: 0-2 Tight: 0-4 Gall: 0-2
Aids: Bl: 0-1 Vi: 0-1 Tstrap: 0-0
Best Rating: 47 5/01 Yarm 1m3y gd-fm

Miss Devious (IRE)

98(90) (37)**39**
3-y-o ch f Dr Devious (IRE)-Lothlorien (USA) (Woodman (USA))
Miss J Feilden (R Guest 13/6) Ms Anne Dawson

Placings:000-**0424**3030240**33** **(5085)**
2001: 8^{0}SD, 11^{4}SD, 12^{2}SD, 12^{4}SD, 12^{3}SD, 14^{0}G, 16^{3}GF, 11^{0}GF, 16^{2}G, 15^{4}G, 16^{0}GF, 13^{3}F, 11^{3}S

	Starts	1st	2nd	3rd	Win & Pl
Career Total (Turf)	11	0	1	3	1907
Career Total (AW)	5	0	1	1	1163

Going (Turf): Sf: 0-2 GS: 0-0 Gd: 0-5 GF: 0-3 Fm: 0-1
Distance: 5f/6f: 0-1 7f-8f: 0-3 9f-13f: 0-6 14f+: 0-6
Track : LH: 0-12 RH: 0-1 Tight: 0-7 Gall: 0-0
Aids: Bl: 0-0 Vi: 0-0 Tstrap: 0-0
Best Rating: 39 10/01 Brig 1m3f196y soft

Often in the frame, but looks short of pace and ideally needs two miles.

Miss Dordogne

101 **90**
4-y-o b/br f Brief Truce (USA)-Miss Bergerac (Bold Lad (IRE))
G Wragg J L C Pearce

Placings:25210-46 **(0975)**
2001: 8^{4}S, 8^{6}S

	Starts	1st	2nd	3rd	Win & Pl
Career Total (Turf)	7	1	2	0	8229

53 7/00 Ches 7f122y D SFT £4396
Total win prize-money £4396

Going (Turf): Sf: 1-3 GS: 0-2 Gd: 0-1 GF: 0-1 Fm: 0-0
Distance: 5f/6f: 0-0 **7f-8f: 1-5** 9f-13f: 0-2 14f+: 0-0
Track : LH: 1-2 RH: 0-4 **Tight: 1-1** Gall: 0-0
Aids: Bl: 0-0 Vi: 0-0 Tstrap: 0-0
Best Rating: 75 4/01 Kemp 1m soft

She had little difficutly landing odds of 1/7 in a four-runner soft-ground Chester maiden in 2001, but was well beaten in a Deauville Listed event on her only subsequent start. Disappointing in two starts this year. Best with give.

Miss Equinox

96 **34**
3-y-o b f Presidium-Miss Nelski (Most Secret)
N Tinkler Contract Natural Gas Ltd

Placings:50223132050-006130360000 **(5172)**
2001: 6^{0}GF, 7^{0}GF, 7^{6}G, 5^{1}F, 5^{3}F, 5^{0}GF, 6^{3}S, 5^{6}G, 6^{0}GF, 6^{0}F, 5^{0}GS, 6^{0}GS

	Starts	1st	2nd	3rd	Win & Pl
Career Total (Turf)	23	2	3	4	5201

42 7/01 Muss 5f G FRM £1724
56 7/00 Newc 6f G G-F £1869
Total win prize-money £1869

Going (Turf): Sf: 0-3 GS: 0-2 Gd: 0-5 **GF: 1-9 Fm: 1-4**
Distance: 5f/6f: 2-17 7f-8f: 0-6 9f-13f: 0-0 14f+: 0-0
Track : LH: 0-3 RH: 0-1 Tight: 0-1 Gall: 0-0
Aids: Bl: 0-0 Vi: 0-0 Tstrap: 0-0
Best Rating: 43 7/01 Rdcr 5f firm

A winner of a six-furlong seller at two, she dead-heated with Sean's Honor in a selling handicap over five furlongs at Musselburgh in July.

Miss Fara (FR)

105 **81**

6-y-o ch m Galetto (FR)-Faracha (FR) (Kenmare (FR))
M C Pipe Mrs Christine Painting

Placings:66032023/20/0-222114 **(4860)**
2001: 11^{2}GS, 13^{2}GF, 12^{2}GF, 13^{1}GF, 14^{1}G, 13^{4}GF

				Starts	1st	2nd	3rd	Win & Pl
Career Total (Turf)				17	2	6	2	22790
80	9/01	Kemp	1m6f92y	D(0-80)H			GD	£6214
77	8/01	Bath	1m5f22y	D(0-80)H			G-F	£4095

Total win prize-money £10309

Going (Turf): Sf: 0-0 GS: 0-2 **Gd: 1-1 GF: 1-10** Fm: 0-0
Distance: 5f/6f: 0-0 7f-8f: 0-1 9f-13f: 0-8 **14f+: 2-4**
Track : LH: 1-5 RH: 1-5 **Tight: 1-6** Gall: 0-3
Aids: Bl: 0-0 Vi: 0-0 Tstrap: 0-0
Best Rating: 81 9/01 Newb 1m5f61y gd-fm

She is quite a decent hurdler and has been running with credit on the Flat too. Not winning out of turn when scoring at Bath in August over a mile and five furlongs before following that victory up with a win at Kempton. She was then fourth at Newbury on the Flat before making a succesful return to hurdling. Stays well.

Miss Fit (IRE)

(90) (59) **59**

5-y-o b m Hamas (IRE)-Soucaro (Rusticaro (FR))
Mrs G S Rees Mrs G S Rees

Placings:11120/564035510205003/0500005500-52003600205 **(5350)**
2001: 5^{5}G, 5^{2}F, 5^{0}F, 6^{0}F, 5^{3}GF, 5^{6}GS, 5^{0}G, 6^{0}F, 5^{2}G, 6^{0}F, 5^{5}SD

				Starts	1st	2nd	3rd	Win & Pl
Career Total (Turf)				39	3	4	3	20084
Career Total (AW)				2	1	0	0	2318
82	7/99	Ches	5f16y	C(0-95)H			G-F	£8325
76	8/98	Rdcr	5f	E			G-F	£2931
77	7/98	Carl	5f207y	F			G-F	£2360
70	6/98	Sthl	5f	F			STD	£2318

Total win prize-money £15934

Going (Turf): Sf: 0-3 GS: 0-5 Gd: 0-10 **GF: 3-15** Fm: 0-6
Distance: **5f/6f: 4-40** 7f-8f: 0-1 9f-13f: 0-0 14f+: 0-0
Track : LH: 1-5 RH: 1-2 Tight: 1-3 Gall: 1-3
Aids: Bl: 0-0 Vi: 0-1 Tstrap: 0-9
Best Rating: 59 8/01 Catt 5f good

Rattled up a hat-trick in her first three starts at two, but has not won since scoring at Chester in July 1999. She has run some creditable races this season and still has the ability to win. Suited by fast ground and the minimum trip.

Miss Flirtatious

(103) (75) **68**

4-y-o b f Piccolo-By Candlelight (IRE) (Roi Danzig (USA))
D Haydn Jones Jack Brown (bookmaker) Ltd

Placings:06654002/000030056-400111211110 **(3494)**
2001: 7^{4}SD, 6^{0}SW, 7^{0}SD, 6^{1}SD, 6^{1}SD, 5^{1}G, 6^{2}GF, 6^{1}SD, 5^{1}SD, 6^{1}SD, 5^{1}GF, 6^{0}GF

				Starts	1st	2nd	3rd	Win & Pl
Career Total (Turf)				17	2	2	0	8689
Career Total (AW)				12	5	0	1	12780
68	7/01	Chep	5f16y	E(0-70)H			G-F	£2870
75	7/01	Sthl	6f	E(0-70)H			STD	£2878
66	7/01	Sthl	5f	F(0-65)H			STD	£2373
56	7/01	Sthl	6f	F(0-60)H			STD	£2352
46	6/01	Leic	5f218y	E(0-75)H			GD	£3770
49	5/01	Wolv	6f	E(0-70)H			STD	£3010
44	4/01	Sthl	6f	G			STD	£1925

Total win prize-money £19178

Going (Turf): Sf: 0-0 GS: 0-3 **Gd: 1-3 GF: 1-11** Fm: 0-0
Distance: **5f/6f: 7-20** 7f-8f: 0-8 9f-13f: 0-1 14f+: 0-0
Track : **LH: 4-14** RH: 0-4 **Tight: 1-7** Gall: 0-6
Aids: **Bl: 7-18** Vi: 0-1 Tstrap: 0-0
Best Rating: 75 7/01 Sthl 6f stand

Improving sprinter, suited by Fibresand but acts on turf. Speedy, and best when making the running.

Miss George

107 **85**

3-y-o b f Pivotal-Brightside (IRE) (Last Tycoon)
K T Ivory Mrs A Shone

Placings:0442410 **(3633)**
2001: 7^{0}S, 7^{4}G, 7^{4}GF, 6^{2}GF, 5^{4}GF, 5^{1}GF, 5^{0}G

				Starts	1st	2nd	3rd	Win & Pl
Career Total (Turf)				7	1	1	0	7498
85	7/01	Bevl	5f	D			G-F	£4134

Total win prize-money £4134

Going (Turf): Sf: 0-1 GS: 0-0 Gd: 0-2 **GF: 1-4** Fm: 0-0
Distance: **5f/6f: 1-4** 7f-8f: 0-3 9f-13f: 0-0 14f+: 0-0
Track : LH: 0-0 RH: 0-0 Tight: 0-0 Gall: 0-0
Aids: Bl: 0-0 Vi: 0-0 Tstrap: 0-0
Best Rating: 85 7/01 Bevl 5f gd-fm

Miss Gigi

97 **78**

2-y-o br f Deploy-Sunley Sinner (Try My Best (USA))
M R Channon John B Sunley

Placings:32340 **(5248)**
2001: 7^{3}G, 7^{2}GF, 8^{3}G, 8^{4}S, 7^{0}S

	Starts	1st	2nd	3rd	Win & Pl
Career Total (Turf)	5	0	1	2	1874

Going (Turf): Sf: 0-2 GS: 0-0 Gd: 0-2 GF: 0-1 Fm: 0-0
Distance: 5f/6f: 0-0 7f-8f: 0-3 9f-13f: 0-2 14f+: 0-0
Track : LH: 0-2 RH: 0-0 Tight: 0-0 Gall: 0-1
Aids: Bl: 0-0 Vi: 0-0 Tstrap: 0-0
Best Rating: 78 9/01 Pont 1m4y soft

Miss Glory Be

86(92) (43) **39**

3-y-o b f Glory Of Dancer-Miss Blondie (USA) (Stop The Music (USA))
Miss Gay Kelleway Khalid Abdullah Al Ghurair

Placings:000300 **(4302)**
2001: 5^{0}G, 5^{0}GF, 5^{0}F, 8^{3}SD, 6^{0}GF, 6^{0}GF

	Starts	1st	2nd	3rd	Win & Pl
Career Total (Turf)	5	0	0	0	
Career Total (AW)	1	0	0	1	328

Going (Turf): Sf: 0-0 GS: 0-0 Gd: 0-1 GF: 0-3 Fm: 0-1
Distance: 5f/6f: 0-4 7f-8f: 0-1 9f-13f: 0-1 14f+: 0-0
Track : LH: 0-3 RH: 0-0 Tight: 0-1 Gall: 0-0
Aids: Bl: 0-0 Vi: 0-0 Tstrap: 0-0
Best Rating: 43 7/01 Wolv 1m100y stand

Miss Hit

89(105) (74) **67**

6-y-o b m Efisio-Jennies' Gem (Sayf El Arab (USA))
G A Butler D R Windebank

Placings:0/452301001/1004544221400/102050360-000 **(2510)**
2001: 6^{0}SD, 6^{0}GF, 6^{0}GF

				Starts	1st	2nd	3rd	Win & Pl
Career Total (Turf)				27	3	4	1	16896
Career Total (AW)				9	2	0	1	7525
69	4/00	Brig	5f59y	E(0-75)H			G-S	£2702
68	8/99	Sals	6f	E(0-70)H			GD	£3095
71	1/99	Ling	5f	D(0-80)H			STD	£3606
71	12/98	Wolv	5f	E(0-70)H			STD	£2871
63	10/98	NmkR	5f	D(0-80)H			GD	£5088

Total win prize-money £17362

Going (Turf): Sf: 0-3 GS: 1-3 **Gd: 2-9** GF: 0-11 Fm: 0-1
Distance: **5f/6f: 5-34** 7f-8f: 0-2 9f-13f: 0-0 14f+: 0-0
Track : **LH: 3-15** RH: 0-4 **Tight: 2-8** Gall: 0-7
Aids: Bl: 0-0 Vi: 0-0 Tstrap: 0-1
Best Rating: 55 4/01 Sthl 6f stand

Miss Indigo

101 **65**

3-y-o b f Indian Ridge-Monaiya (Shareef Dancer (USA))
J H M Gosden Lady Bamford

Placings:4640 **(5461)**
2001: 8^{4}GF, 8^{6}GF, 10^{4}G, 8^{0}G

	Starts	1st	2nd	3rd	Win & Pl
Career Total (Turf)	4	0	0	0	422

Going (Turf): Sf: 0-0 GS: 0-0 Gd: 0-2 GF: 0-2 Fm: 0-0
Distance: 5f/6f: 0-0 7f-8f: 0-2 9f-13f: 0-2 14f+: 0-0
Track : LH: 0-2 RH: 0-1 Tight: 0-2 Gall: 0-1
Aids: Bl: 0-0 Vi: 0-0 Tstrap: 0-0
Best Rating: 65 7/01 Asct 1m gd-fm

Miss Inform

100(99) (48) **46**

3-y-o b f So Factual (USA)-As Sharp As (Handsome Sailor)
K O Cunningham-Brown Woodhaven Racing Syndicate

Placings:3500002-20640405 **(5522)**
2001: 5^{2}HY, 5^{0}GS, 5^{6}GF, 5^{4}SD, 5^{0}G, 6^{4}F, 5^{0}G, 6^{5}HY

	Starts	1st	2nd	3rd	Win & Pl
Career Total (Turf)	14	0	2	1	1812
Career Total (AW)	1	0	0	0	0

Going (Turf): Sf: 0-2 GS: 0-4 Gd: 0-4 GF: 0-3 Fm: 0-1
Distance: 5f/6f: 0-14 7f-8f: 0-1 9f-13f: 0-0 14f+: 0-0
Track : LH: 0-2 RH: 0-2 Tight: 0-1 Gall: 0-3
Aids: Bl: 0-0 Vi: 0-0 Tstrap: 0-0
Best Rating: 48 8/01 Wolv 5f stand

Miss Jingles

95 **66**

2-y-o b f Muhtarram (USA)-Flamingo Times (Good Times (ITY))
J A Gilbert (S C Williams 24/7) Terry Connors

Placings:04001060 **(5368)**
2001: 7^{0}G, 7^{4}G, 7^{0}G, 7^{0}G, 7^{1}GF, 7^{0}G, 7^{6}S, 8^{0}GS

				Starts	1st	2nd	3rd	Win & Pl
Career Total (Turf)				8	1	0	0	4427
58	8/01	Muss	7f30y	D			G-F	£4426

Total win prize-money £4427

Going (Turf): Sf: 0-1 GS: 0-1 Gd: 0-5 **GF: 1-1** Fm: 0-0
Distance: 5f/6f: 0-0 **7f-8f: 1-8** 9f-13f: 0-0 14f+: 0-0
Track : LH: 0-1 RH: 0-1 Tight: 0-1 Gall: 0-0
Aids: Bl: 0-0 Vi: 0-0 Tstrap: 0-0
Best Rating: 66 8/01 NmkJ 7f good

Won an ordinary nursery at Musselburgh over seven furlongs. Acts on fast ground.

Miss Lippy

80 **12**

4-y-o b f Emperor Jones (USA)-Anatroccolo (Ile De Bourbon (USA))
P J Hobbs Colin Brown Racing Ii

Placings:0 **(2402)**
2001: 6^{0}F

	Starts	1st	2nd	3rd	Win & Pl
Career Total (Turf)	1	0	0	0	

Going (Turf): Sf: 0-0 GS: 0-0 Gd: 0-0 GF: 0-0 Fm: 0-1
Distance: 5f/6f: 0-1 7f-8f: 0-0 9f-13f: 0-0 14f+: 0-0
Track : LH: 0-0 RH: 0-0 Tight: 0-0 Gall: 0-0
Aids: Bl: 0-0 Vi: 0-0 Tstrap: 0-0
Best Rating: 12 6/01 Ling 6f firm

Miss Lorilaw (FR)

107 **95**

4-y-o b f Homme De Loi (IRE)-Miss Lorika (FR) (Bikala)
J W Hills David A Caruth

Placings:1/3360100-5540035 **(4987)**
2001: 12^{5}GF, 11^{5}G, 11^{4}GS, 13^{0}S, 15^{0}G, 10^{3}GF, 10^{5}G

		Starts	1st	2nd	3rd	Win & Pl
Career Total (Turf)		15	2	0	3	28328
103 8/00 Newb 1m4f5y	A				G-F	£13166
75 10/99 York 7f202y	E				G-S	£8162

Total win prize-money £21328

Going (Turf): Sf: 0-3 **GS: 1-2** Gd: 0-5 **GF: 1-5** Fm: 0-0
Distance: 5f/6f: 0-0 7f-8f: 1-1 9f-13f: 1-11 14f+: 0-3
Track : **LH: 2-6** RH: 0-7 Tight: 0-1 **Gall: 2-10**
Aids: Bl: 0-0 Vi: 0-0 Tstrap: 0-0
Best Rating: 100 6/01 Hamb 1m3f good

She won a Newbury Listed event in 2000, but it was a very weak race of its type and she has struggled in Pattern company otherwise. She has tried picking up more black type on the continent, but has been well held there too. Stays a mile and a half. Acts on fast ground.

Miss Manette

90 **29**

4-y-o br f Dilum (USA)-Lucy Manette (Final Straw)
P Monteith (R Curtis 29/6) Mrs E McLoughlin

Placings:6000-000 **(4481)**
2001: 6^{0}GF, 9^{0}GF, 8^{0}F

	Starts	1st	2nd	3rd	Win & Pl
Career Total (Turf)	7	0	0	0	0

Going (Turf): Sf: 0-2 GS: 0-0 Gd: 0-1 GF: 0-2 Fm: 0-2
Distance: 5f/6f: 0-0 7f-8f: 0-2 9f-13f: 0-5 14f+: 0-0
Track : LH: 0-2 RH: 0-5 Tight: 0-7 Gall: 0-0
Aids: Bl: 0-0 Vi: 0-0 Tstrap: 0-0
Best Rating: 29 6/01 Folk 6f189y gd-fm

Miss Marple

99(69) (7)**56d**

4-y-o b f Puissance-Juliet Bravo (Glow (USA))
J M Bradley Mrs Marion C Morgan

Placings:030-000300 **(2510)**
2001: 6^{0}SD, 5^{0}GF, 5^{0}GF, 5^{3}GF, 5^{0}G, 6^{0}GF

	Starts	1st	2nd	3rd	Win & Pl
Career Total (Turf)	7	0	0	2	1055
Career Total (AW)	2	0	0	0	

Going (Turf): Sf: 0-0 GS: 0-0 Gd: 0-2 GF: 0-5 Fm: 0-0
Distance: 5f/6f: 0-8 7f-8f: 0-1 9f-13f: 0-0 14f+: 0-0
Track : LH: 0-6 RH: 0-0 Tight: 0-0 Gall: 0-2
Aids: Bl: 0-0 Vi: 0-0 Tstrap: 0-0
Best Rating: 49 6/01 Bevl 5f gd-fm

Miss Moore (IRE)

77 **44**

2-y-o b f Tagula (IRE)-Thatcherite (Final Straw)
I A Balding Much Moore Partnership

Placings:0000 **(5342)**
2001: 5^{0}G, 6^{0}G, 6^{0}HY, 7^{0}GS

	Starts	1st	2nd	3rd	Win & Pl
Career Total (Turf)	4	0	0	0	

Going (Turf): Sf: 0-1 GS: 0-1 Gd: 0-2 GF: 0-0 Fm: 0-0
Distance: 5f/6f: 0-2 7f-8f: 0-2 9f-13f: 0-0 14f+: 0-0
Track : LH: 0-0 RH: 0-0 Tight: 0-0 Gall: 0-0
Aids: Bl: 0-0 Vi: 0-1 Tstrap: 0-0
Best Rating: 44 7/01 Sand 5f6y good

Miss Moselle (IRE)

104 **71**

3-y-o b f Zieten (USA)-Topseys Tipple (IRE) (Hatim (USA))
P W Harris Mrs G A Godfrey

Placings:300-5066212020 **(5400)**
2001: 9^{5}GF, 10^{0}GF, 11^{6}GF, 10^{6}GF, 9^{2}GF, 10^{1}GF, 10^{2}S, 10^{0}G, 10^{2}S, 10^{0}S

		Starts	1st	2nd	3rd	Win & Pl
Career Total (Turf)		13	1	3	1	11141
67 8/01 Epsm 1m2f18y	D(0-80)H				G-F	£5850

Total win prize-money £5850

Going (Turf): Sf: 0-5 GS: 0-0 Gd: 0-1 **GF: 1-7** Fm: 0-0
Distance: 5f/6f: 0-0 7f-8f: 0-3 **9f-13f: 1-10** 14f+: 0-0
Track : **LH: 1-8** RH: 0-2 **Tight: 1-4** Gall: 0-2
Aids: Bl: 0-0 **Vi: 1-7** Tstrap: 0-0
Best Rating: 78 5/01 Gdwd 1m1f gd-fm

Did not look the most genuine of horses, but was resolute enough when getting off the mark in a four-runner handicap at Epsom in August.

Miss Mougins

95 **67+**

3-y-o b/br f Polar Falcon (USA)-Miss Bergerac (Bold Lad (IRE))
G Wragg J L C Pearce

Placings:00 **(1533)**
2001: 7^{0}G, 7^{0}GF

	Starts	1st	2nd	3rd	Win & Pl
Career Total (Turf)	2	0	0	0	

Going (Turf): Sf: 0-0 GS: 0-0 Gd: 0-1 GF: 0-1 Fm: 0-0
Distance: 5f/6f: 0-0 7f-8f: 0-2 9f-13f: 0-0 14f+: 0-0
Track : LH: 0-0 RH: 0-1 Tight: 0-0 Gall: 0-0
Aids: Bl: 0-0 Vi: 0-0 Tstrap: 0-0
Best Rating: 67 5/01 NmkR 7f good

Miss Ninotchka (IRE)

84(47) **25**

4-y-o b f Petardia-Sin Sceal Eile (IRE) (Pitskelly)
N Wilson J B Slatcher

Placings:00-060 **(2038)**
2001: 9^{0}GF, 5^{6}GF, 5^{0}GF

	Starts	1st	2nd	3rd	Win & Pl
Career Total (Turf)	3	0	0	0	0
Career Total (AW)	2	0	0	0	

Going (Turf): Sf: 0-0 GS: 0-0 Gd: 0-0 GF: 0-3 Fm: 0-0
Distance: 5f/6f: 0-2 7f-8f: 0-2 9f-13f: 0-1 14f+: 0-0
Track : LH: 0-3 RH: 0-1 Tight: 0-0 Gall: 0-0
Aids: Bl: 0-0 Vi: 0-0 Tstrap: 0-0
Best Rating: 25 6/01 Pont 5f gd-fm

Miss Opulence (IRE)

98 **75**

2-y-o b f Kylian (USA)-Oriental Splendour (Runnett)
Miss V Haigh Miss V Haigh

Placings:0120F0 **(5052)**
2001: 7^{0}GF, 7^{1}G, 7^{2}G, 8^{0}G, 7^{F}G, 7^{0}S

		Starts	1st	2nd	3rd	Win & Pl
Career Total (Turf)		6	1	1	0	4266
75 8/01 Newc 7f	E				GD	£3066

Total win prize-money £3066

Going (Turf): Sf: 0-1 GS: 0-0 **Gd: 1-4** GF: 0-1 Fm: 0-0
Distance: 5f/6f: 0-0 **7f-8f: 1-6** 9f-13f: 0-0 14f+: 0-0
Track : LH: 0-1 RH: 0-1 Tight: 0-1 Gall: 0-0
Aids: Bl: 0-0 Vi: 0-0 Tstrap: 0-0
Best Rating: 75 9/01 Sand 7f16y good

Winner of a median auction event at Newcastle on her second start, she has not performed badly in nursery company since and was in the process of running a big race when falling at Doncaster in September.

Miss Peaches

87 **64**

3-y-o b f Emperor Jones (USA)-Dear Person (Rainbow Quest (USA))
G G Margarson P E Axon & E M Thornton

Placings:064 **(5519)**
2001: 7^{0}S, 8^{6}G, 6^{4}HY

	Starts	1st	2nd	3rd	Win & Pl
Career Total (Turf)	3	0	0	0	0

Going (Turf): Sf: 0-2 GS: 0-0 Gd: 0-1 GF: 0-0 Fm: 0-0
Distance: 5f/6f: 0-1 7f-8f: 0-2 9f-13f: 0-0 14f+: 0-0
Track : LH: 0-0 RH: 0-0 Tight: 0-0 Gall: 0-0
Aids: Bl: 0-0 Vi: 0-0 Tstrap: 0-0
Best Rating: 64 5/01 NmkR 1m good

Miss Phantine (IRE)

82 **38**

3-y-o ch f Be My Guest (USA)-Rosananti (Blushing Groom (FR))
R Hollinshead Geoff Lloyd

Placings:00-000 **(4893)**
2001: 10^{0}G, 9^{0}GF, 12^{0}GF

	Starts	1st	2nd	3rd	Win & Pl
Career Total (Turf)	5	0	0	0	

Going (Turf): Sf: 0-1 GS: 0-0 Gd: 0-1 GF: 0-3 Fm: 0-0
Distance: 5f/6f: 0-0 7f-8f: 0-2 9f-13f: 0-3 14f+: 0-0
Track : LH: 0-0 RH: 0-3 Tight: 0-1 Gall: 0-1
Aids: Bl: 0-0 Vi: 0-0 Tstrap: 0-0
Best Rating: 38 8/01 Wind 1m2f7y good

Miss Pinkerton

94 **76**

2-y-o b f Danehill (USA)-Rebecca Sharp (Machiavellian (USA))
G Wragg A E Oppenheimer

Placings:01 **(4839)**
2001: 5^{0}GF, 6^{1}G

		Starts	1st	2nd	3rd	Win & Pl
Career Total (Turf)		2	1	0	0	3738
76 9/01 Nott 6f15y	D				GD	£3737

Total win prize-money £3738

Going (Turf): Sf: 0-0 GS: 0-0 **Gd: 1-1** GF: 0-1 Fm: 0-0
Distance: 5f/6f: 0-1 **7f-8f: 1-1** 9f-13f: 0-0 14f+: 0-0
Track : LH: 0-0 RH: 0-0 Tight: 0-0 Gall: 0-0
Aids: Bl: 0-0 Vi: 0-0 Tstrap: 0-0
Best Rating: 76 9/01 Nott 6f15y good

First foal of Coronation Stakes winner Rebecca Sharp. She showed the benefit of the experience gained at Lingfield on her debut to score at Nottingham over six furlongs on her only other outing. Acts on a sound surface. Should stay further.

Miss Pitz

100 **75**

3-y-o b f Cadeaux Genereux-Catch The Sun (Kalaglow)
E A L Dunlop John D Pitt

Placings:660-0135345 **(5272)**
2001: 9^{0}GF, 10^{1}GF, 10^{3}GF, 11^{5}HY, 10^{3}G, 10^{4}S, 10^{5}HY

Starts	1st	2nd	3rd	Win & Pl

	Starts	1st	2nd	3rd	Win & Pl
Career Total (Turf)	10	1	0	2	5101

69 7/01 Newc 1m2f32y E(0-70)H G-F £3024
Total win prize-money £3024

Going (Turf): Sf: 0-3 GS: 0-1 Gd: 0-1 GF: **1-5** Fm: 0-0
Distance: 5f/6f: 0-0 7f-8f: 0-3 **9f-13f: 1-7** 14f+: 0-0
Track : **LH: 1-6** RH: 0-2 Tight: 0-1 **Gall: 1-2**
Aids: Bl: 0-0 Vi: 0-0 Tstrap: 0-0
Best Rating: 75 9/01 Ayr 1m2f good

A scopey sort, she tended to race too keenly on her juvenile starts. Badly hampered on three-year-old debut over nine furlongs, she made up for that in a small Newcastle handicap next time. Suited by a sound surface, but has not looked a straightforward ride.

Miss Polly

94 **25**

3-y-o b f Democratic (USA)-My Pretty Niece (Great Nephew)
J R Best Edward Charles Brooke

Placings:000-00000 **(4707)**
2001: 11^{0}G, 11^{0}F, 8^{0}G, 9^{0}GF, 10^{0}G

	Starts	1st	2nd	3rd	Win & Pl
Career Total (Turf)	8	0	0	0	

Going (Turf): Sf: 0-3 GS: 0-0 Gd: 0-3 GF: 0-1 Fm: 0-1
Distance: 5f/6f: 0-1 7f-8f: 0-2 9f-13f: 0-5 14f+: 0-0
Track : LH: 0-4 RH: 0-2 Tight: 0-5 Gall: 0-1
Aids: Bl: 0-0 Vi: 0-0 Tstrap: 0-0
Best Rating: 25 7/01 Folk 1m1f149y gd-fm

Miss Progressive (IRE)

94(79) (47)**42**

3-y-o b f Common Grounds-Kaweah Maid (General Assembly (USA))
N Tinkler J P Hardiman

Placings:6000025130-0002000 **(2225)**
2001: 8^{0}SD, 8^{0}SD, 8^{0}S, 6^{2}HY, 6^{0}S, 6^{0}GF, 7^{0}G

	Starts	1st	2nd	3rd	Win & Pl
Career Total (Turf)	13	1	1	1	4259
Career Total (AW)	4	0	1	0	532

40 8/00 Sand 7f16y E GD £3250
Total win prize-money £3250

Going (Turf): Sf: 0-5 GS: 0-1 **Gd: 1-5** GF: 0-1 Fm: 0-1
Distance: 5f/6f: 0-6 **7f-8f: 1-10** 9f-13f: 0-1 14f+: 0-0
Track : LH: 0-7 **RH: 1-1** Tight: 0-3 Gall: 0-0
Aids: Bl: 0-0 Vi: 0-0 Tstrap: 0-0
Best Rating: 42 5/01 Nott 6f15y heavy

Miss Sadie (IRE)

(72) (16)**48**

2-y-o b f Distinctly North (USA)-Raggy (Smoggy)
J J Quinn The Westwood Partnership

Placings:0440 **(2646)**
2001: 5^{0}S, 5^{4}F, 5^{4}GF, 5^{0}SD

	Starts	1st	2nd	3rd	Win & Pl
Career Total (Turf)	3	0	0	0	274
Career Total (AW)	1	0	0	0	

Going (Turf): Sf: 0-1 GS: 0-0 Gd: 0-0 GF: 0-1 Fm: 0-1
Distance: 5f/6f: 0-4 7f-8f: 0-0 9f-13f: 0-0 14f+: 0-0
Track : LH: 0-1 RH: 0-0 Tight: 0-0 Gall: 0-0
Aids: Bl: 0-0 Vi: 0-0 Tstrap: 0-0
Best Rating: 48 6/01 Pont 5f firm

Miss Samantha

74(69) (12)**21**

3-y-o b f Emarati (USA)-Puella Bona (Handsome Sailor)
M D I Usher Mrs J Black

Placings:000 **(4446)**

2001: 7^{0}GS, 6^{0}SD, 9^{0}G

	Starts	1st	2nd	3rd	Win & Pl
Career Total (Turf)	2	0	0	0	
Career Total (AW)	1	0	0	0	

Going (Turf): Sf: 0-0 GS: 0-1 Gd: 0-1 GF: 0-0 Fm: 0-0
Distance: 5f/6f: 0-1 7f-8f: 0-1 9f-13f: 0-1 14f+: 0-0
Track : LH: 0-1 RH: 0-1 Tight: 0-0 Gall: 0-0
Aids: Bl: 0-0 Vi: 0-0 Tstrap: 0-0
Best Rating: 21 9/01 Sand 1m1f good

Miss Skicap

90(89) (35)**43**

4-y-o b f Welsh Captain-Miss Nelski (Most Secret)
W Clay (Miss S J Wilton 10/4) Lee Heath

Placings:421/400-0000000 **(1985)**
2001: 7^{0}SW, 9^{0}SD, 7^{0}SD, 7^{0}G, 7^{0}F, 10^{0}F, 10^{0}G

	Starts	1st	2nd	3rd	Win & Pl
Career Total (Turf)	5	0	0	0	
Career Total (AW)	8	1	1	0	3176

74 12/99 Wolv 6f F STD £2284
Total win prize-money £2285

Going (Turf): Sf: 0-0 GS: 0-1 Gd: 0-2 GF: 0-0 Fm: 0-2
Distance: **5f/6f: 1-5** 7f-8f: 0-4 9f-13f: 0-4 14f+: 0-0
Track : **LH: 1-10** RH: 0-0 **Tight: 1-5** Gall: 0-0
Aids: Bl: 0-4 Vi: 0-0 Tstrap: 0-0
Best Rating: 43 6/01 Hayd 1m2f120y good

Miss Sutton

81(95) (50)**41**

3-y-o b f Formidable (USA)-Saysana (Sayf El Arab (USA))
T G Mills M J Joyce

Placings:544-523140030 **(3434)**
2001: 8^{5}SW, 8^{2}SD, 8^{3}SD, 7^{1}SW, 7^{4}SD, 7^{0}SD, 8^{0}GS, 7^{3}SD, 8^{0}F

	Starts	1st	2nd	3rd	Win & Pl
Career Total (Turf)	4	0	0	0	0
Career Total (AW)	8	1	1	2	3071

50 2/01 Sthl 7f G SLW £1883
Total win prize-money £1883

Going (Turf): Sf: 0-0 GS: 0-1 Gd: 0-1 GF: 0-1 Fm: 0-1
Distance: 5f/6f: 0-2 **7f-8f: 1-10** 9f-13f: 0-0 14f+: 0-0
Track : **LH: 1-9** RH: 0-1 Tight: 0-2 Gall: 0-1
Aids: Bl: 0-0 **Vi: 1-6** Tstrap: 0-0
Best Rating: 50 2/01 Sthl 7f slow

Miss T

76 **44**

2-y-o b f Sabrehill (USA)-Pourville (USA) (Manila (USA))
J R Fanshawe Andrew & Julia Turner

Placings:0 **(5684)**
2001: 8^{0}S

	Starts	1st	2nd	3rd	Win & Pl
Career Total (Turf)	1	0	0	0	

Going (Turf): Sf: 0-1 GS: 0-0 Gd: 0-0 GF: 0-0 Fm: 0-0
Distance: 5f/6f: 0-0 7f-8f: 0-1 9f-13f: 0-0 14f+: 0-0
Track : LH: 0-0 RH: 0-0 Tight: 0-0 Gall: 0-0
Aids: Bl: 0-0 Vi: 0-0 Tstrap: 0-0
Best Rating: 44 11/01 Donc 1m soft

Miss Tango

94 **56**

4-y-o b f Batshoof-Spring Flyer (IRE) (Waajib)
M C Pipe Codan Trust Company Limited

Placings:533335/0204 **(2704)**
2001: 12^{0}GF, 11^{2}F, 12^{0}GF, 11^{4}F

	Starts	1st	2nd	3rd	Win & Pl
Career Total (Turf)	9	0	1	4	2898
Career Total (AW)	1	0	0	0	0

Going (Turf): Sf: 0-0 GS: 0-0 Gd: 0-1 GF: 0-4 Fm: 0-4
Distance: 5f/6f: 0-5 7f-8f: 0-1 9f-13f: 0-4 14f+: 0-0
Track : LH: 0-6 RH: 0-2 Tight: 0-4 Gall: 0-0
Aids: Bl: 0-0 Vi: 0-1 Tstrap: 0-0
Best Rating: 56 5/01 Leic 1m3f183y firm

Miss Teak (USA)

104 **64**

3-y-o b f Woodman (USA)-Miss Profile (IRE) (Sadler's Wells (USA))
G A Butler Beetle N Wedge Partnership

Placings:4-24052650 **(5254)**
2001: 8^{2}S, 9^{4}GF, 10^{0}GF, 10^{5}GF, 8^{2}S, 8^{6}G, 6^{5}S, 6^{0}S

	Starts	1st	2nd	3rd	Win & Pl
Career Total (Turf)	9	0	2	0	4480

Going (Turf): Sf: 0-4 GS: 0-0 Gd: 0-1 GF: 0-4 Fm: 0-0
Distance: 5f/6f: 0-1 7f-8f: 0-3 9f-13f: 0-5 14f+: 0-0
Track : LH: 0-1 RH: 0-5 Tight: 0-3 Gall: 0-1
Aids: Bl: 0-1 Vi: 0-0 Tstrap: 0-1
Best Rating: 99 5/01 Gdwd 1m1f192y gd-fm

She has run some game races in defeat including when fourth in the Lupe, but is still to win and has become disappointing. Has a tendency to race keenly.

Miss Texas

64 **21**

2-y-o ch f Master Willie-Houston (GER) (Surumu (GER))
D Morris Bloomsbury Stud

Placings:0 **(5484)**
2001: 8^{0}HY

	Starts	1st	2nd	3rd	Win & Pl
Career Total (Turf)	1	0	0	0	

Going (Turf): Sf: 0-1 GS: 0-0 Gd: 0-0 GF: 0-0 Fm: 0-0
Distance: 5f/6f: 0-0 7f-8f: 0-1 9f-13f: 0-0 14f+: 0-0
Track : LH: 0-1 RH: 0-0 Tight: 0-0 Gall: 0-1
Aids: Bl: 0-0 Vi: 0-0 Tstrap: 0-0
Best Rating: 21 10/01 Donc 1m heavy

Miss Topogino

85(78) (34)**18**

3-y-o b f Mistertopogigo (IRE)-Bitch (Risk Me (FR))
J Parkes R Naylor

Placings:0560-060 **(5374)**
2001: 9^{0}GF, 5^{6}GS, 6^{0}G

	Starts	1st	2nd	3rd	Win & Pl
Career Total (Turf)	5	0	0	0	0
Career Total (AW)	2	0	0	0	0

Going (Turf): Sf: 0-1 GS: 0-1 Gd: 0-1 GF: 0-2 Fm: 0-0
Distance: 5f/6f: 0-6 7f-8f: 0-0 9f-13f: 0-1 14f+: 0-0
Track : LH: 0-2 RH: 0-1 Tight: 0-2 Gall: 0-0
Aids: Bl: 0-0 Vi: 0-0 Tstrap: 0-0
Best Rating: 18 10/01 Catt 5f212y gd-sft

Miss Tress (IRE)

85 **59**

3-y-o b f Salse (USA)-Circulate (High Top)
P W Harris Michael Smith & Chris Murphy

Placings:46400-00 **(3424)**
2001: 8^{0}G, 8^{0}GF

	Starts	1st	2nd	3rd	Win & Pl
Career Total (Turf)	7	0	0	0	654

Going (Turf): Sf: 0-3 GS: 0-0 Gd: 0-1 GF: 0-3 Fm: 0-0
Distance: 5f/6f: 0-0 7f-8f: 0-5 9f-13f: 0-2 14f+: 0-0

Track : LH: 0-2 RH: 0-2 Tight: 0-0 Gall: 0-1
Aids: Bl: 0-0 Vi: 0-0 Tstrap: 0-0
Best Rating: 38 7/01 Chep 1m14y good

Miss Uluwatu (IRE)

96 **66**

2-y-o b f Night Shift (USA)-Miss Kinabalu (Shirley Heights)
E J O'Neill Mrs Julie Mitchell

Placings:06250 **(5052)**
2001: 6⁰GF, 7⁶GF, 7²GF, 7⁵G, 7⁰S

	Starts	1st	2nd	3rd	Win & Pl
Career Total (Turf)	5	0	1	0	2480

Going (Turf): Sf: 0-1 GS: 0-0 Gd: 0-1 GF: 0-3 Fm: 0-0
Distance: 5f/6f: 0-1 7f-8f: 0-4 9f-13f: 0-0 14f+: 0-0
Track : LH: 0-4 RH: 0-0 Tight: 0-2 Gall: 0-1
Aids: Bl: 0-0 Vi: 0-0 Tstrap: 0-0
Best Rating: 66 9/01 Epsm 7f good

Improved for the step up to a mile at York on her third start and ran very well on her nursery debut at Epsom.

Miss Valentine

42

2-y-o b f Cosmonaut-Miss Mariner (Rock Hopper)
J F Coupland J F Coupland

Placings:0 **(3854)**
2001: 7⁰GS

	Starts	1st	2nd	3rd	Win & Pl
Career Total (Turf)	1	0	0	0	

Going (Turf): Sf: 0-0 GS: 0-1 Gd: 0-0 GF: 0-0 Fm: 0-0
Distance: 5f/6f: 0-0 7f-8f: 0-1 9f-13f: 0-0 14f+: 0-0
Track : LH: 0-0 RH: 0-0 Tight: 0-0 Gall: 0-0
Aids: Bl: 0-0 Vi: 0-0 Tstrap: 0-0

Miss World (IRE)

90(95) (23)**11**

4-y-o b f Mujadil (USA)-Great Land (USA) (Friend's Choice (USA))
P S McEntee Mrs B A McEntee

Placings:0460404144623215/40500000000-3400520000050650 **(4284)**
2001: 12⁰SD, 12⁴SD, 16⁰SD, 9⁰SW, 9⁵SD, 12²SD, 11⁰SD, 12⁰SD, 10⁰G, 9⁰F, 11⁰F, 12⁰SD, 9⁵GF, 12⁰GS, 10⁶G, 9⁵SD, 6⁰G

	Starts	1st	2nd	3rd	Win & Pl
Career Total (Turf)	17	0	0	0	703
Career Total (AW)	27	2	3	2	8189

77 12/99 Sthl 1m E(0-85)H SLW £2668
69 9/99 Wolv 7f G STD £2066
Total win prize-money £4734

Going (Turf): Sf: 0-1 GS: 0-2 Gd: 0-6 GF: 0-6 Fm: 0-2
Distance: 5f/6f: 0-3 **7f-8f: 2-15** 9f-13f: 0-25 14f+: 0-1
Track : **LH: 2-34** RH: 0-5 **Tight: 1-24** Gall: 0-2
Aids: Bl: 0-6 Vi: 0-1 **Tstrap: 2-32**
Best Rating: 31 8/01 Yarm 6f3y good

Showed little ability on turf and is at her best on sand, though she is totally exposed.

Missed The Boat (IRE)

(67)

11-y-o b g Cyrano De Bergerac-Lady Portobello (Porto Bello)
G A Ham Ms J C Hutley

Placings:04520603/356233306440/030/0100/0064/0/0-00 **(2323)**
2001: 12⁰SD, 16⁰SD

	Starts	1st	2nd	3rd	Win & Pl
Career Total (Turf)	22	1	2	3	6094
Career Total (AW)	13	0	0	3	893

44 9/95 Bath 1m5f22y E(0-70)H HRD £3181
Total win prize-money £3181

Going (Turf): Sf: 0-2 GS: 0-2 Gd: 0-9 GF: 0-3 **Fm: 1-6**
Distance: 5f/6f: 0-9 7f-8f: 0-10 9f-13f: 0-12 **14f+: 1-4**
Track : **LH: 1-25** RH: 0-4 **Tight: 1-22** Gall: 0-1
Aids: Bl: 0-5 Vi: 0-2 Tstrap: 0-0

Missile Toe (IRE)

101 (23)**59**

8-y-o b g Exactly Sharp (USA)-Debach Dust (Indian King (USA))
D Morris Stag And Huntsman

Placings:225615553/006500542203/062000/0555300/6542010000/554116530-10300326 **(4535)**
2001: 10¹GS, 8⁰GF, 10³GF, 10⁰GF, 10⁰GF, 9³GF, 10²GF, 10⁶GF

	Starts	1st	2nd	3rd	Win & Pl
Career Total (Turf)	57	5	6	6	28212
Career Total (AW)	4	0	1	0	694

55 5/01 Wind 1m2f7y F(0-60)H G-S £2674
54 6/00 Newc 1m2f32y E(0-75)H FRM £3640
49 6/00 NmkJ 1m E(0-70)H G-F £4030
46 7/99 NmkJ 1m2f E(0-70)H G-F £4207
65 7/95 Newc 6f E G-F £3166
Total win prize-money £17719

Going (Turf): Sf: 0-3 GS: 1-4 Gd: 0-15 **GF: 3-29** Fm: 1-6
Distance: 5f/6f: 1-12 7f-8f: 1-13 **9f-13f: 3-36** 14f+: 0-0
Track : LH: 1-25 RH: 1-5 Tight: 1-14 **Gall: 2-8**
Aids: Bl: 0-2 Vi: 0-1 Tstrap: 0-0
Best Rating: 56 9/01 York 1m2f85y gd-fm

A fair handicapper. Wins have come from eight to ten furlongs. Probably best suited by a sound surface.

Missing

87 **56**

2-y-o b f Singspiel (IRE)-Misbelief (Shirley Heights)
T D Easterby And Mrs J D Cotton

Placings:56 **(4307)**
2001: 7⁵G, 7⁶GF

	Starts	1st	2nd	3rd	Win & Pl
Career Total (Turf)	2	0	0	0	0

Going (Turf): Sf: 0-0 GS: 0-0 Gd: 0-1 GF: 0-1 Fm: 0-0
Distance: 5f/6f: 0-0 7f-8f: 0-2 9f-13f: 0-0 14f+: 0-0
Track : LH: 0-0 RH: 0-1 Tight: 0-0 Gall: 0-0
Aids: Bl: 0-0 Vi: 0-0 Tstrap: 0-0
Best Rating: 56 8/01 Newc 7f gd-fm

Missing Drink (IRE)

(76) (27)**59**

3-y-o ch g Idris (IRE)-Miss Tuko (Good Times (ITY))
P D Evans R J Hayward

Placings:05050000-0 **(2488)**
2001: 10⁰HD

	Starts	1st	2nd	3rd	Win & Pl
Career Total (Turf)	7	0	0	0	221
Career Total (AW)	2	0	0	0	

Going (Turf): Sf: 0-0 GS: 0-0 Gd: 0-1 GF: 0-3 Fm: 0-2
Distance: 5f/6f: 0-4 7f-8f: 0-3 9f-13f: 0-1 14f+: 0-0
Track : LH: 0-4 RH: 0-2 Tight: 0-2 Gall: 0-2
Aids: Bl: 0-0 Vi: 0-0 Tstrap: 0-1

Mission Hills

98(99) (36)**53**

6-y-o b m Faustus (USA)-Hot Case (Upper Case (USA))
B G Powell P M T Partnership

Placings:000/02010/020600/04404-00360 **(3734)**
2001: 12⁰SW, 10⁰SD, 10³SD, 9⁶F, 11⁰G

	Starts	1st	2nd	3rd	Win & Pl
Career Total (Turf)	21	1	2	0	6031
Career Total (AW)	3	0	0	1	402

75 7/98 Klny 1m100y (0-75)H GD £3437
Total win prize-money £3438

Going (Turf): Sf: 0-1 GS: 0-0 **Gd: 1-5** GF: 0-4 Fm: 0-1
Distance: 5f/6f: 0-0 7f-8f: 0-8 **9f-13f: 1-16** 14f+: 0-0
Track : **LH: 1-13** RH: 0-11 Tight: 0-3 Gall: 0-0
Aids: Bl: 0-0 Vi: 0-0 Tstrap: 0-0
Best Rating: 41 5/01 Brig 1m1f209y firm

Mission To Mars

54

2-y-o b c Muhtarram (USA)-Ideal Candidate (Celestial Storm (USA))
C A Cyzer Mrs E A Cyzer

Placings:00 **(5623)**
2001: 6⁰S, 8⁰GS

	Starts	1st	2nd	3rd	Win & Pl
Career Total (Turf)	2	0	0	0	

Going (Turf): Sf: 0-1 GS: 0-1 Gd: 0-0 GF: 0-0 Fm: 0-0
Distance: 5f/6f: 0-0 7f-8f: 0-1 9f-13f: 0-1 14f+: 0-0
Track : LH: 0-2 RH: 0-0 Tight: 0-0 Gall: 0-0
Aids: Bl: 0-0 Vi: 0-0 Tstrap: 0-0
Best Rating: 54 11/01 Nott 1m54y gd-sft

Missouri

105 **76**

3-y-o b f Charnwood Forest (IRE)-Medway (IRE) (Shernazar)
M H Tompkins Pollards Stables

Placings:6-24023210 **(5661)**
2001: 10²GF, 12⁴GF, 10⁰G, 11²G, 10³GF, 11²GF, 15¹G, 16⁰G

	Starts	1st	2nd	3rd	Win & Pl
Career Total (Turf)	9	1	3	1	10780

76 9/01 Ayr 1m7f C(0-95)H GD £7117
Total win prize-money £7118

Going (Turf): Sf: 0-0 GS: 0-0 **Gd: 1-4** GF: 0-5 Fm: 0-0
Distance: 5f/6f: 0-0 7f-8f: 0-1 9f-13f: 0-6 **14f+: 1-2**
Track : **LH: 1-4** RH: 0-4 Tight: 0-4 Gall: 0-1
Aids: Bl: 0-0 Vi: 0-0 Tstrap: 0-0
Best Rating: 76 9/01 Ayr 1m7f good

She ran well in maidens, but found one or two too good, and was successfully switched to handicap company and a longer trip with an easy win at Ayr in September.

Mist 'n Rain

84 **72**

2-y-o b f Ezzoud (IRE)-Uncharted Waters (Celestial Storm (USA))
C A Cyzer Mrs E A Cyzer

Placings:6 **(4593)**
2001: 7⁶G

	Starts	1st	2nd	3rd	Win & Pl
Career Total (Turf)	1	0	0	0	167

Going (Turf): Sf: 0-0 GS: 0-0 Gd: 0-1 GF: 0-0 Fm: 0-0
Distance: 5f/6f: 0-0 7f-8f: 0-1 9f-13f: 0-0 14f+: 0-0
Track : LH: 0-0 RH: 0-1 Tight: 0-0 Gall: 0-1
Aids: Bl: 0-0 Vi: 0-0 Tstrap: 0-0
Best Rating: 72 9/01 Kemp 7f good

Mist Of Time (IRE)

99 **74**

2-y-o b f Danehill (USA)-Lothlorien (USA) (Woodman (USA))
J H M Gosden R E Sangster & Mrs J Magnier

Placings:4 (4038)
2001: 7^{4}G

	Starts	1st	2nd	3rd	Win & Pl
Career Total (Turf)	1	0	0	0	320

Going (Turf): Sf: 0-0 GS: 0-0 Gd: 0-1 GF: 0-0 Fm: 0-0
Distance: 5f/6f: 0-0 7f-8f: 0-1 9f-13f: 0-0 14f+: 0-0
Track : LH: 0-0 RH: 0-0 Tight: 0-0 Gall: 0-0
Aids: Bl: 0-0 Vi: 0-0 Tstrap: 0-0
Best Rating: 74 8/01 NmkJ 7f good

Mistanoora

89 **71?**
2-y-o b c Topanoora-Mistinguett (IRE) (Doyoun)
M R Channon A M J Duggan

Placings:400 (5095)
2001: 8^{4}GF, 7^{0}F, 8^{0}GS

	Starts	1st	2nd	3rd	Win & Pl
Career Total (Turf)	3	0	0	0	267

Going (Turf): Sf: 0-0 GS: 0-1 Gd: 0-0 GF: 0-1 Fm: 0-1
Distance: 5f/6f: 0-0 7f-8f: 0-2 9f-13f: 0-1 14f+: 0-0
Track : LH: 0-0 RH: 0-0 Tight: 0-0 Gall: 0-0
Aids: Bl: 0-0 Vi: 0-0 Tstrap: 0-0
Best Rating: 71 8/01 Chep 1m14y gd-fm

Mister Benji

99 **96**
2-y-o b c Catrail (USA)-Katy-Q (IRE) (Taufan (USA))
J G Given Mr & Mrs D J Smart

Placings:110050 (5150)
2001: 5^{1}GS, 6^{1}F, 6^{0}GF, 6^{0}GF, 6^{5}G, 6^{0}G

	Starts	1st	2nd	3rd	Win & Pl			
Career Total (Turf)	6	2	0	0	9045			
90	5/01	Pont	6f	C			FRM	£6119
76	4/01	Muss	5f	E			G-S	£2926

Total win prize-money £9045

Going (Turf): Sf: 0-0 **GS: 1-1** Gd: 0-2 GF: 0-2 **Fm: 1-1**
Distance: **5f/6f: 2-5** 7f-8f: 0-1 9f-13f: 0-0 14f+: 0-0
Track : **LH: 1-1** RH: 0-0 Tight: 0-0 Gall: 0-0
Aids: Bl: 0-0 Vi: 0-0 Tstrap: 0-0
Best Rating: 96 9/01 Donc 6f good

He won his first two starts on contrasting ground, but he has found life tougher up in class. Six furlongs suits him well.

Mister Bucket (IRE)

(81) (7)**61**
3-y-o ch g Superlative-Rose Bouquet (General Assembly (USA))
P W Harris R Dagg, S Williams & Mrs P W Harris

Placings:4-03000 (4553)
2001: 9^{0}GS, 10^{3}GF, 9^{0}GF, 12^{0}GF, 14^{0}SW

	Starts	1st	2nd	3rd	Win & Pl
Career Total (Turf)	5	0	0	1	418
Career Total (AW)	1	0	0	0	

Going (Turf): Sf: 0-0 GS: 0-1 Gd: 0-1 GF: 0-3 Fm: 0-0
Distance: 5f/6f: 0-0 7f-8f: 0-1 9f-13f: 0-4 14f+: 0-1
Track : LH: 0-4 RH: 0-1 Tight: 0-4 Gall: 0-0
Aids: Bl: 0-0 Vi: 0-0 Tstrap: 0-0
Best Rating: 61 7/01 Bath 1m2f46y gd-fm

Mister Clinton (IRE)

105 **64**
4-y-o ch g Lion Cavern (USA)-Thewaari (USA) (Eskimo (USA))
K T Ivory J B Waterfall

Placings:000/41031604-06541500022105 (5025)
2001: 7^{0}GS, 6^{6}F, 7^{5}GF, 7^{4}GF, 6^{1}GF, 6^{5}GF, 6^{0}GF, 7^{0}G, 6^{0}GS, 5^{2}G, 6^{2}GF, 7^{1}GF, 7^{0}GF, 6^{5}S

	Starts	1st	2nd	3rd	Win & Pl	
Career Total (Turf)	25	4	2	1	16172	
56	9/01	Ling	7f140y	E(0-65)	G-F	£3206
59	6/01	Nott	6f15y	F(0-60)H	G-F	£2600
67	6/00	Sals	6f212y	F(0-65)H	G-F	£2786
67	5/00	Brig	6f209y	D	FRM	£3818

Total win prize-money £12412

Going (Turf): Sf: 0-3 GS: 0-3 Gd: 0-4 **GF: 3-13** Fm: 1-2
Distance: 5f/6f: 0-7 **7f-8f: 4-17** 9f-13f: 0-1 14f+: 0-0
Track : **LH: 1-7** RH: 0-5 Tight: 0-1 Gall: 0-2
Aids: Bl: 0-0 Vi: 0-0 Tstrap: 0-0
Best Rating: 64 8/01 Folk 6f gd-fm

Needs a strongly-run race to be seen to best effect.

Mister Cosmi

103 **98**
2-y-o b c Royal Applause-Degree (Warning)
M Johnston Miss Elisabetta Tulliani

Placings:1241053 (5480a)
2001: 5^{1}GF, 6^{2}GF, 6^{4}GF, 6^{1}GF, 6^{0}G, 6^{5}GF, 8^{3}HY

	Starts	1st	2nd	3rd	Win & Pl	
Career Total (Turf)	7	2	1	1	82259	
97	7/01	Gdwd	6f	A	G-F	£43500
82	6/01	Haml	5f4y	E	G-F	£3542

Total win prize-money £47043

Going (Turf): Sf: 0-1 GS: 0-0 Gd: 0-1 **GF: 2-5** Fm: 0-0
Distance: **5f/6f: 2-4** 7f-8f: 0-3 9f-13f: 0-0 14f+: 0-0
Track : LH: 0-0 RH: 0-1 Tight: 0-0 Gall: 0-0
Aids: Bl: 0-0 Vi: 0-0 Tstrap: 0-0
Best Rating: 98 10/01 Siro 1m heavy

He won going away at Hamilton over five furlongs on his debut, but then caught a tartar over an extra furlong at Goodwood. Not beaten far though only fourth of seven in a Newbury Listed event next time, he returned to form under a positive ride to win the Richmond Stakes at Goodwood. Beaten at a similar level afterwards, he stayed a mile on heavy ground when third in a Group One in Italy in the autumn. His wins have been on fast ground using forcing tactics.

Mister Doc

88 **55d**
3-y-o ch g Most Welcome-Red Poppy (IRE) (Coquelin (USA))
D W Barker L H Gilmurray & T J Docherty

Placings:0-530000 (2360)
2001: 11^{5}G, 10^{3}GF, 11^{0}GF, 14^{0}F, 10^{0}GF, 10^{0}GF

	Starts	1st	2nd	3rd	Win & Pl
Career Total (Turf)	7	0	0	1	582

Going (Turf): Sf: 0-0 GS: 0-0 Gd: 0-2 GF: 0-4 Fm: 0-1
Distance: 5f/6f: 0-0 7f-8f: 0-1 9f-13f: 0-5 14f+: 0-1
Track : LH: 0-5 RH: 0-2 Tight: 0-4 Gall: 0-0
Aids: Bl: 0-0 Vi: 0-0 Tstrap: 0-0
Best Rating: 55 5/01 Ayr 1m2f192y gd-fm

Mister Falcon (FR)

89 **46**
4-y-o b g Passing Sale (FR)-Falcon Crest (FR) (Cadoudal (FR))
M C Pipe Telefocus Limited

Placings:0/4000433541-0 (0585)
2001: 14^{0}HY

	Starts	1st	2nd	3rd	Win & Pl	
Career Total (Turf)	12	1	0	2	12683	
	10/00	MsnL	1m5f		HVY	£5764

Total win prize-money £5764

Going (Turf): Sf: 0-2 GS: 0-0 Gd: 0-0 GF: 0-0 Fm: 0-0
Distance: 5f/6f: 0-0 7f-8f: 0-0 9f-13f: 0-4 14f+: 0-1
Track : LH: 0-1 RH: 0-0 Tight: 0-0 Gall: 0-0
Aids: Bl: 0-0 Vi: 0-1 Tstrap: 0-0
Best Rating: 46 3/01 Nott 1m6f15y heavy

Mister Havana

92(89) (39)**32**
4-y-o br g Pelder (IRE)-Cee Beat (Bairn (USA))
E A Wheeler E A Wheeler

Placings:00-00000 (5330)
2001: 11^{0}SD, 11^{0}GS, 8^{0}GF, 11^{0}GF, 16^{0}HY

	Starts	1st	2nd	3rd	Win & Pl
Career Total (Turf)	5	0	0	0	
Career Total (AW)	2	0	0	0	

Going (Turf): Sf: 0-1 GS: 0-1 Gd: 0-0 GF: 0-2 Fm: 0-1
Distance: 5f/6f: 0-0 7f-8f: 0-2 9f-13f: 0-4 14f+: 0-1
Track : LH: 0-4 RH: 0-0 Tight: 0-5 Gall: 0-0
Aids: Bl: 0-0 Vi: 0-0 Tstrap: 0-0
Best Rating: 39 4/01 Sthl 1m3f stand

Mister John

52
2-y-o b c Unfuwain (USA)-Natural Key (Safawan)
M Wigham John Smallman

Placings:0 (3473)
2001: 7^{0}GF

	Starts	1st	2nd	3rd	Win & Pl
Career Total (Turf)	1	0	0	0	

Going (Turf): Sf: 0-0 GS: 0-0 Gd: 0-0 GF: 0-1 Fm: 0-0
Distance: 5f/6f: 0-0 7f-8f: 0-1 9f-13f: 0-0 14f+: 0-0
Track : LH: 0-0 RH: 0-0 Tight: 0-0 Gall: 0-0
Aids: Bl: 0-0 Vi: 0-0 Tstrap: 0-0

Mister Mal (IRE)

109(98) (70)**87**
5-y-o b g Scenic-Fashion Parade (Mount Hagen (FR))
D Nicholls Mrs Andrea M Mallinson

Placings:0/33211200313/05001020650030-40120020 (2396)
2001: 6^{4}S, 7^{0}SD, 5^{1}GS, 6^{2}G, 6^{0}GF, 6^{0}F, 6^{2}G, 6^{0}GF

	Starts	1st	2nd	3rd	Win & Pl	
Career Total (Turf)	32	5	4	4	29432	
Career Total (AW)	4	0	1	1	1651	
79	5/01	Brig	5f213y	D(0-80)H	G-S	£4163
76	8/00	Newc	7f	D(0-85)H	GD	£3835
72	10/99	Rdcr	7f	D(0-85)H	SFT	£4640
70	6/99	Leic	7f9y	E(0-75)H	G-S	£3730
61	6/99	Catt	7f	G(0-60)	GD	£1825

Total win prize-money £18194

Going (Turf): Sf: 1-11 **GS: 2-4 Gd: 2-9** GF: 0-6 Fm: 0-2
Distance: 5f/6f: 1-13 **7f-8f: 4-21** 9f-13f: 0-2 14f+: 0-0
Track : **LH: 2-17** RH: 0-1 **Tight: 1-7** Gall: 0-1
Aids: Bl: 0-1 Vi: 0-1 Tstrap: 0-0
Best Rating: 87 6/01 York 6f good

He is a capable handicapper on his day and is equally effective over six or seven furlongs. Best when able to dominate and prefers the ground good or softer.

Mister McGoldrick

95(88) (39)**70d**
4-y-o b g Sabrehill (USA)-Anchor Inn (Be My Guest (USA))
J G Given Richard Longley

Placings:010-60 (5624)
2001: 12^{6}SD, 9^{0}GS

	Starts	1st	2nd	3rd	Win & Pl
Career Total (Turf)	4	1	0	0	4375
Career Total (AW)	1	0	0	0	0

70 9/00 Hayd 1m2f120yD HVY £4374
Total win prize-money £4375

Going (Turf): Sf: 1-2 GS: 0-1 Gd: 0-0 GF: 0-1 Fm: 0-0
Distance: 5f/6f: 0-0 7f-8f: 0-0 **9f-13f: 1-5** 14f+: 0-0
Track : **LH: 1-5** RH: 0-0 Tight: 0-1 Gall: 0-1
Aids: Bl: 0-0 Vi: 0-0 Tstrap: 0-0
Best Rating: 40 11/01 Nott 1m1f213y gd-sft

Mister Moussac

77 **56**
2-y-o b g Kasakov-Salu (Ardross)
J M Jefferson Arthur Symons Key

Placings:04 **(5445)**
2001: 7^{0}G, 6^{4}HY

	Starts	1st	2nd	3rd	Win & Pl
Career Total (Turf)	2	0	0	0	0

Going (Turf): Sf: 0-1 GS: 0-0 Gd: 0-1 GF: 0-0 Fm: 0-0
Distance: 5f/6f: 0-1 7f-8f: 0-1 9f-13f: 0-0 14f+: 0-0
Track : LH: 0-0 RH: 0-0 Tight: 0-0 Gall: 0-0
Aids: Bl: 0-0 Vi: 0-0 Tstrap: 0-0
Best Rating: 56 9/01 Ayr 7f50y good

Mister Pq

98(80) **34**
5-y-o ch g Ardkinglass-Well Off (Welsh Pageant)
J G Smyth-Osbourne Pq International/euromedia

Placings:0500/00010540/6000-000 **(3579)**
2001: 18^{0}GF, 16^{0}GF, 14^{0}GF

	Starts	1st	2nd	3rd	Win & Pl
Career Total (Turf)	17	1	0	0	4900
Career Total (AW)	2	0	0	0	

51 8/99 Brig 1m3f196yE(0-70)H G-S £4900
Total win prize-money £4900

Going (Turf): Sf: 0-2 **GS: 1-2** Gd: 0-2 GF: 0-10 Fm: 0-1
Distance: 5f/6f: 0-1 7f-8f: 0-3 **9f-13f: 1-9** 14f+: 0-6
Track : **LH: 1-9** RH: 0-5 Tight: 0-5 Gall: 0-1
Aids: Bl: 0-1 Vi: 0-0 Tstrap: 0-0
Best Rating: 34 7/01 Chep 2m2f gd-fm

Mister Putt (USA)

98(92) (44)**65**
3-y-o b/br g Mister Baileys-Theresita (GER) (Surumu (GER))
Mrs N Smith (J A Osborne 7/7) Tony Hayward

Placings:66003300 **(2821)**
2001: 8^{6}SW, 8^{6}GS, 11^{0}SD, 11^{0}G, 11^{3}F, 14^{3}GF, 14^{0}G, 18^{0}GF

	Starts	1st	2nd	3rd	Win & Pl
Career Total (Turf)	6	0	0	2	1188
Career Total (AW)	2	0	0	0	0

Going (Turf): Sf: 0-0 GS: 0-1 Gd: 0-2 GF: 0-2 Fm: 0-1
Distance: 5f/6f: 0-0 7f-8f: 0-2 9f-13f: 0-3 14f+: 0-3
Track : LH: 0-4 RH: 0-2 Tight: 0-3 Gall: 0-0
Aids: Bl: 0-0 Vi: 0-0 Tstrap: 0-0
Best Rating: 65 6/01 Gdwd 1m6f gd-fm

Staying maiden, has shown ability at various trips without winning. Handles fast ground.

Mister Rambo

107 **63**
6-y-o b g Rambo Dancer (CAN)-Ozra (Red Alert)
D Nicholls Middleham Park Racing Xxv

Placings:1/2550144505/203004010540/010520605506 0-054104062000305 **(5384)**
2001: 8^{0}S, 8^{5}HY, 7^{4}G, 7^{1}GF, 8^{0}GF, 7^{4}GF, 7^{0}GF, 7^{6}GS, 7^{2}F, 8^{0}GF, 7^{0}GF, 6^{0}GF, 7^{3}GF, 7^{0}G, 7^{5}S

	Starts	1st	2nd	3rd	Win & Pl
Career Total (Turf)	51	5	4	2	46368

73 5/01 Ches 7f122y C(0-90)H G-F £9282
81 4/00 Wwck 7f164y D(0-80)H SFT £4303
84 7/99 Asct 7f C(0-95)H G-F £7360
91 6/98 Fmk 7f165y GD £6757
87 10/97 Newb 6f8y D GD £4276
Total win prize-money £31978

Going (Turf): Sf: 1-10 GS: 0-7 **Gd: 2-16 GF: 2-17** Fm: 0-1
Distance: 5f/6f: 0-4 **7f-8f: 5-45** 9f-13f: 0-2 14f+: 0-0
Track : **LH: 3-17** RH: 0-13 **Tight: 1-9** Gall: 0-6
Aids: Bl: 0-4 Vi: 0-0 Tstrap: 0-0
Best Rating: 73 5/01 Ches 7f122y gd-fm

Formerly a useful seven-furlong performer for Brian Meehan. Has shaped well for David Nicholls and won well at Chester in May. Suited by fast ground.

Mister Sanders

96 **45**
3-y-o ch g Cosmonaut-Arroganza (Crofthall)
R M Whitaker Paul & Justine Rhodes

Placings:06000-0000003034006 **(5593)**
2001: 8^{0}G, 6^{0}GF, 6^{0}F, 7^{0}GF, 7^{0}GF, 8^{0}GF, 11^{3}F, 9^{0}GF, 6^{3}GF, 8^{4}F, 7^{0}G, 6^{0}S, 5^{6}GS

	Starts	1st	2nd	3rd	Win & Pl
Career Total (Turf)	18	0	0	2	605

Going (Turf): Sf: 0-2 GS: 0-1 Gd: 0-4 GF: 0-8 Fm: 0-3
Distance: 5f/6f: 0-7 7f-8f: 0-8 9f-13f: 0-3 14f+: 0-0
Track : LH: 0-5 RH: 0-4 Tight: 0-4 Gall: 0-0
Aids: Bl: 0-0 Vi: 0-6 Tstrap: 0-0
Best Rating: 53 5/01 Ripn 6f gd-fm

Mister Waterline (IRE)

88(100) (68)**68**
2-y-o b c Mujadil (USA)-Cree's Figurine (Creetown)
P D Evans M W Lawrence

Placings:0234004 **(3033)**
2001: 5^{0}GS, 5^{2}SD, 5^{3}SW, 5^{4}GF, 5^{0}G, 6^{0}GF, 5^{4}GF

	Starts	1st	2nd	3rd	Win & Pl
Career Total (Turf)	5	0	0	0	874
Career Total (AW)	2	0	1	1	1307

Going (Turf): Sf: 0-0 GS: 0-1 Gd: 0-1 GF: 0-3 Fm: 0-0
Distance: 5f/6f: 0-7 7f-8f: 0-0 9f-13f: 0-0 14f+: 0-0
Track : LH: 0-4 RH: 0-0 Tight: 0-3 Gall: 0-1
Aids: Bl: 0-0 Vi: 0-0 Tstrap: 0-2
Best Rating: 68 6/01 Asct 6f gd-fm

Mister Webb

100(93) (32)**36**
4-y-o b g Whittingham (IRE)-Ruda (FR) (Free Round (USA))
Dr J R J Naylor (B Smart 10/4) Norman E Webb

Placings:64/500400-0000 **(5098)**
2001: 14^{0}SD, 13^{0}F, 16^{0}G, 14^{0}GS

	Starts	1st	2nd	3rd	Win & Pl
Career Total (Turf)	10	0	0	0	451
Career Total (AW)	2	0	0	0	

Going (Turf): Sf: 0-2 GS: 0-2 Gd: 0-2 GF: 0-3 Fm: 0-1
Distance: 5f/6f: 0-0 7f-8f: 0-1 9f-13f: 0-4 14f+: 0-7
Track : LH: 0-7 RH: 0-3 Tight: 0-6 Gall: 0-0
Aids: Bl: 0-0 Vi: 0-0 Tstrap: 0-0
Best Rating: 36 10/01 Sals 1m6f15y gd-sft

Mister Westsound

91 (41)**23**
9-y-o b g Cyrano De Bergerac-Captivate (Mansingh (USA))
Miss L A Perratt David Sutherland-Ian Hay

Placings:61300/40052223301126042260/23534356056 0U0040/0000041120030/00352620500541536/03100/40 0000000633-000060 **(3161)**
2001: 7^{0}GF, 7^{0}S, 6^{0}GF, 7^{0}G, 5^{6}GS, 6^{0}G

	Starts	1st	2nd	3rd	Win & Pl
Career Total (Turf)	93	7	10	12	43741
Career Total (AW)	2	0	0	0	0

57 5/99 Ayr 6f D(0-85)H GD £3736
50 10/98 Ayr 6f E(0-70)H HVY £3408
49 6/97 Ayr 7f E(0-70)H GD £3093
49 6/97 Haml 6f5y D(0-80)H G-S £3533
56 8/95 Haml 6f5y E(0-70)H FRM £3758
51 8/95 Ayr 6f D(0-75)H G-F £3809
73 7/94 Muss 5f F G-F £2563
Total win prize-money £23906

Going (Turf): Sf: 1-15 GS: 1-8 **Gd: 2-24 GF: 2-34** Fm: 1-12
Distance: **5f/6f: 4-46** 7f-8f: 3-46 9f-13f: 0-3 14f+: 0-0
Track : **LH: 1-14** RH: 0-11 Tight: 0-5 Gall: 0-7
Aids: **Bl: 6-82** Vi: 0-2 Tstrap: 0-0
Best Rating: 23 6/01 Haml 5f4y gd-sft

Misterah

108 **98+**
2-y-o b f Alhaarth (IRE)-Jasarah (IRE) (Green Desert (USA))
M P Tregoning Hamdan Al Maktoum

Placings:1213 **(5390)**
2001: 6^{1}GF, 6^{2}GF, 6^{1}GF, 7^{3}GS

	Starts	1st	2nd	3rd	Win & Pl
Career Total (Turf)	4	2	1	1	27290

98 9/01 Ayr 6f A G-F £12713
92 8/01 Newb 6f8y D G-F £5622
Total win prize-money £18337

Going (Turf): Sf: 0-0 GS: 0-1 Gd: 0-0 **GF: 2-3** Fm: 0-0
Distance: 5f/6f: 1-2 7f-8f: 1-2 9f-13f: 0-0 14f+: 0-0
Track : LH: 0-0 RH: 0-0 Tight: 0-0 Gall: 0-0
Aids: Bl: 0-0 Vi: 0-0 Tstrap: 0-0
Best Rating: 98 10/01 NmkR 7f gd-sft

A half-sister to the useful juvenile Muqtarb, she won like a decent filly on her debut. Only beaten a neck next time at Salisbury, she raced closer to the pace when taking a Listed event at Ayr. Lost little in defeat when third at Newmarket. Progressive, she will stay a mile and looks sure to win more races.

Mistral Sky

70 **46**
2-y-o b c Hurricane Sky (AUS)-Dusk In Daytona (Beveled (USA))
R Hannon A Ezen

Placings:00 **(5491)**
2001: 6^{0}GF, 6^{0}HY

	Starts	1st	2nd	3rd	Win & Pl
Career Total (Turf)	2	0	0	0	

Going (Turf): Sf: 0-1 GS: 0-0 Gd: 0-0 GF: 0-1 Fm: 0-0
Distance: 5f/6f: 0-1 7f-8f: 0-1 9f-13f: 0-0 14f+: 0-0
Track : LH: 0-0 RH: 0-0 Tight: 0-0 Gall: 0-0
Aids: Bl: 0-0 Vi: 0-0 Tstrap: 0-0
Best Rating: 46 10/01 Newb 6f8y heavy

Mistress Mouse

76(61) (13)**33**
2-y-o br f Mistertopogigo (IRE)-Perfidy (FR) (Persian Bold)
T M Jones Mrs R A Jennings

Placings:65600 **(5487)**
2001: 5^{6}SD, 5^{5}SD, 6^{6}GF, 6^{0}G, 6^{0}HY

	Starts	1st	2nd	3rd	Win & Pl
Career Total (Turf)	3	0	0	0	0

Career Total (AW) 2 0 0 0 0

Going (Turf): Sf: 0-1 GS: 0-0 Gd: 0-1 GF: 0-1 Fm: 0-0
Distance: 5f/6f: 0-5 7f-8f: 0-0 9f-13f: 0-0 14f+: 0-0
Track : LH: 0-2 RH: 0-0 Tight: 0-2 Gall: 0-0
Aids: Bl: 0-0 Vi: 0-0 Tstrap: 0-0
Best Rating: 33 5/01 Gdwd 6f gd-fm

Mistress Ofthehall

65 **7**
3-y-o b f Son Pardo-Covent Garden Girl (Sizzling Melody)
P D Evans J R B Williams

Placings:000 **(1073)**
2001: 8^{0}S, 8^{0}GS, 9^{0}GS

	Starts	1st	2nd	3rd	Win & Pl
Career Total (Turf)	3	0	0	0	

Going (Turf): Sf: 0-1 GS: 0-2 Gd: 0-0 GF: 0-0 Fm: 0-0
Distance: 5f/6f: 0-0 7f-8f: 0-1 9f-13f: 0-2 14f+: 0-0
Track : LH: 0-1 RH: 0-2 Tight: 0-2 Gall: 0-0
Aids: Bl: 0-0 Vi: 0-0 Tstrap: 0-0
Best Rating: 7 4/01 Ripn 1m soft

Misty Boy

105(93) (45)**48**
4-y-o br g Polar Falcon (USA)-Misty Silks (Scottish Reel)
M J Ryan M J Baxter

Placings:060/0005-0050144F **(3188)**
2001: 7^{0}SD, 5^{0}GF, 5^{5}G, 7^{0}SD, 6^{1}GF, 6^{4}GF, 6^{4}GF, 5^{F}GS

	Starts	1st	2nd	3rd	Win & Pl
Career Total (Turf)	13	1	0	0	3542
Career Total (AW)	2	0	0	0	
48 6/01 Yarm 6f3y		E(0-70)H		G-F	£3248

Total win prize-money £3248

Going (Turf): Sf: 0-3 GS: 0-2 Gd: 0-3 **GF: 1-5** Fm: 0-0
Distance: 5f/6f: 0-6 **7f-8f: 1-9** 9f-13f: 0-0 14f+: 0-0
Track : LH: 0-3 RH: 0-2 Tight: 0-0 Gall: 0-1
Aids: **Bl: 1-8** Vi: 0-0 Tstrap: 0-0
Best Rating: 48 7/01 Yarm 6f3y gd-fm

Misty Dancer

95 **76**
2-y-o gr c Vettori (IRE)-Light Fantastic (Deploy)
G L Moore Pinks Gym & Leisure Wear Ltd

Placings:32 **(4783)**
2001: 7^{3}G, 8^{2}G

	Starts	1st	2nd	3rd	Win & Pl
Career Total (Turf)	2	0	1	1	2028

Going (Turf): Sf: 0-0 GS: 0-0 Gd: 0-2 GF: 0-0 Fm: 0-0
Distance: 5f/6f: 0-0 7f-8f: 0-2 9f-13f: 0-0 14f+: 0-0
Track : LH: 0-0 RH: 0-2 Tight: 0-0 Gall: 0-0
Aids: Bl: 0-0 Vi: 0-0 Tstrap: 0-0
Best Rating: 76 9/01 Gdwd 1m good

Misty Eyed (IRE)

115 **111**
3-y-o gr f Paris House-Bold As Love (Lomond (USA))
Mrs P N Dutfield Mrs Jan Fuller

Placings:51011125-023633 **(4861)**
2001: 5^{0}GF, 5^{2}G, 6^{8}GS, 5^{6}G, 5^{3}GS, 5^{3}GF

	Starts	1st	2nd	3rd	Win & Pl
Career Total (Turf)	14	4	2	3	103509
106 8/00 Gdwd 5f		A		GD	£24000
96 7/00 Sand 5f6y		A		GD	£13910
87 7/00 Wind 5f10y		E		GD	£3474
78 6/00 Wind 5f10y		D		GD	£5005

Total win prize-money £46389

Going (Turf): Sf: 0-0 GS: 0-3 **Gd: 4-6** GF: 0-5 Fm: 0-0
Distance: **5f/6f: 4-13** 7f-8f: 0-1 9f-13f: 0-0 14f+: 0-0
Track : LH: 0-0 **RH: 2-3** Tight: 0-0 **Gall: 2-3**
Aids: Bl: 0-0 Vi: 0-0 Tstrap: 0-0
Best Rating: 111 6/01 Asct 5f good

A speedy filly, she improved for her seasonal debut when runner-up in the King's Stand, and did not get the best of runs in France next time. A never-dangerous sixth in the Nunthorpe at York, before going close in Listed event when coming with a late surge, she has a decent sprint in her.

Misty Magic

95(89) (35)**31**
4-y-o b f Distinctly North (USA)-Meadmore Magic (Mansingh (USA))
K T Ivory R D Hartshorn

Placings:030/004326300**6000**-00060006 **(4299)**
2001: 7^{0}GF, 6^{0}F, 6^{0}GF, 6^{6}G, 5^{0}GF, 6^{0}F, 7^{0}GF, 6^{6}G

	Starts	1st	2nd	3rd	Win & Pl
Career Total (Turf)	20	0	1	3	2475
Career Total (AW)	4	0	0	0	0

Going (Turf): Sf: 0-1 GS: 0-2 Gd: 0-4 GF: 0-10 Fm: 0-3
Distance: 5f/6f: 0-7 7f-8f: 0-10 9f-13f: 0-7 14f+: 0-0
Track : LH: 0-14 RH: 0-0 Tight: 0-5 Gall: 0-0
Aids: Bl: 0-7 Vi: 0-0 Tstrap: 0-0
Best Rating: 31 8/01 Epsm 6f good

Misty Man (USA)

98 **49**
3-y-o ch g El Gran Senor (USA)-Miasma (USA) (Lear Fan (USA))
Miss J Feilden R J Creese

Placings:2 **(5664)**
2001: 8^{2}HY

	Starts	1st	2nd	3rd	Win & Pl
Career Total (Turf)	1	0	1	0	896

Going (Turf): Sf: 0-1 GS: 0-0 Gd: 0-0 GF: 0-0 Fm: 0-0
Distance: 5f/6f: 0-0 7f-8f: 0-0 9f-13f: 0-1 14f+: 0-0
Track : LH: 0-0 RH: 0-1 Tight: 0-1 Gall: 0-0
Aids: Bl: 0-0 Vi: 0-0 Tstrap: 0-1
Best Rating: 49 11/01 Wind 1m67y heavy

Good run on debut at Windsor in November when a never-nearer second.

Mitawa (IRE)

97 **72**
2-y-o b f Alhaarth (IRE)-Susquehanna Days (USA) (Chief's Crown (USA))
B W Hills Mrs C F Van Straubenzee

Placings:6100 **(5052)**
2001: 5^{6}G, 7^{1}GS, 7^{0}G, 7^{0}S

	Starts	1st	2nd	3rd	Win & Pl
Career Total (Turf)	4	1	0	0	3523
72 7/01 Ayr 7f		D		G-S	£3523

Total win prize-money £3523

Going (Turf): Sf: 0-1 **GS: 1-1** Gd: 0-2 GF: 0-0 Fm: 0-0
Distance: 5f/6f: 0-1 **7f-8f: 1-3** 9f-13f: 0-0 14f+: 0-0
Track : **LH: 1-1** RH: 0-0 Tight: 0-0 Gall: 0-0
Aids: Bl: 0-0 Vi: 0-0 Tstrap: 0-0
Best Rating: 72 7/01 Ayr 7f gd-sft

She showed promise on her debut and got off the mark over seven furlongs at Ayr on her second start. Disappointing on her nursery debut at Doncaster next time, but is better than that.

Mitcham (IRE)

112 **95**
5-y-o br g Hamas (IRE)-Arab Scimetar (IRE) (Sure Blade (USA))
T G Mills T G Mills

Placings:412/23151040/040000-002000006003 **(4780)**
2001: 5^{0}GS, 5^{0}GF, 5^{2}GF, 5^{0}GF, 6^{0}GF, 5^{0}GF, 5^{0}GF, 5^{0}GF, 6^{6}G, 6^{0}G, 6^{0}G, 6^{3}G

	Starts	1st	2nd	3rd	Win & Pl
Career Total (Turf)	29	3	3	2	121391
118 6/99 Asct 5f		A		G-F	£80050
106 5/99 NmkJ 6f		B(0-105)H		GD	£22450
81 9/98 Wwck 6f		E		G-F	£2859

Total win prize-money £105359

Going (Turf): Sf: 0-2 GS: 0-2 Gd: 1-11 **GF: 2-14** Fm: 0-0
Distance: **5f/6f: 3-26** 7f-8f: 0-3 9f-13f: 0-0 14f+: 0-0
Track : **LH: 1-2** RH: 0-2 Tight: 0-0 Gall: 0-1
Aids: Bl: 0-1 Vi: 0-0 Tstrap: 0-0
Best Rating: 95 8/01 Gdwd 6f good

Winner of the King's Stand Stakes in 1999, he has not reached those heights since but has been running creditably in handicap company this season. He is probably best suited by a fast-run five furlongs on good to firm ground.

Mitchells Mayhem

(72)
4-y-o b f Mistertopogigo (IRE)-Mayday Kitty (Interrex (CAN))
Mrs N Macauley Mrs N Macauley

Placings:6/500-0 **(0427)**
2001: 5^{0}SD

	Starts	1st	2nd	3rd	Win & Pl
Career Total (Turf)	2	0	0	0	0
Career Total (AW)	3	0	0	0	0

Going (Turf): Sf: 0-0 GS: 0-0 Gd: 0-0 GF: 0-1 Fm: 0-1
Distance: 5f/6f: 0-5 7f-8f: 0-0 9f-13f: 0-0 14f+: 0-0
Track : LH: 0-3 RH: 0-0 Tight: 0-3 Gall: 0-0
Aids: Bl: 0-0 Vi: 0-0 Tstrap: 0-0

Mithraic (IRE)

93 **35**
9-y-o b g Kefaah (USA)-Persian's Glory (Prince Tenderfoot (USA))
W S Cunningham Mrs Vicky Cunningham

Placings:20603/52221105/3313/5610-30 **(4031)**
2001: 12^{3}G, 10^{0}G

	Starts	1st	2nd	3rd	Win & Pl
Career Total (Turf)	23	4	4	5	13889
35 8/00 Newc 1m4f93y		G		GD	£1890
46 8/99 Newc 1m4f93y		G		FRM	£1871
59 7/96 Muss 1m3f32y		F(0-55)		G-F	£2619
59 7/96 Haml 1m3f16y		F		G-F	£2535

Total win prize-money £8916

Going (Turf): Sf: 0-1 GS: 0-1 Gd: 1-8 **GF: 2-9** Fm: 1-4
Distance: 5f/6f: 0-0 7f-8f: 0-2 **9f-13f: 4-20** 14f+: 0-1
Track : LH: 2-18 RH: 2-5 Tight: 2-14 Gall: 2-5
Aids: Bl: 0-3 Vi: 0-0 Tstrap: 0-0
Best Rating: 28 8/01 Newc 1m2f32y good

Mitrebeenjane

62 **27**
2-y-o b f Beveled (USA)-Jane Herring (Nishapour (FR))
D J S Ffrench Davis Mrs Patrick McCarthy

Placings:00 **(5491)**
2001: 6^{0}GF, 6^{0}HY

	Starts	1st	2nd	3rd	Win & Pl
Career Total (Turf)	2	0	0	0	

Going (Turf): Sf: 0-1 GS: 0-0 Gd: 0-0 GF: 0-1 Fm: 0-0

Distance: 5f/6f: 0-0 7f-8f: 0-2 9f-13f: 0-0 14f+: 0-0
Track : LH: 0-0 RH: 0-0 Tight: 0-0 Gall: 0-0
Aids: Bl: 0-0 Vi: 0-0 Tstrap: 0-0
Best Rating: 27 8/01 Sals 6f212y gd-fm

Mitsuki

100 **87?**

2-y-o b f Puissance-Surrealist (ITY) (Night Shift (USA))
J D Bethell (A Berry 15/6) John E Lund

Placings:0012401034 **(4795)**
2001: 5^{0}GF, 5^{0}GF, 6^{1}F, 6^{2}G, 6^{4}G, 5^{0}G, 5^{1}F, 6^{0}G, 5^{3}F, 5^{4}G

	Starts	1st	2nd	3rd	Win & Pl
Career Total (Turf)	10	2	1	1	14530

68 8/01 Thsk 5f C FRM £7020
59 6/01 Thsk 6f E FRM £3202
Total win prize-money £10223

Going (Turf): Sf: 0-0 GS: 0-0 Gd: 0-5 GF: 0-2 **Fm: 2-3**
Distance: **5f/6f: 2-9** 7f-8f: 0-1 9f-13f: 0-0 14f+: 0-0
Track : LH: 0-1 RH: 0-0 Tight: 0-1 Gall: 0-0
Aids: Bl: 0-0 Vi: 0-0 Tstrap: 0-0
Best Rating: 87 9/01 Ayr 5f good

Won a six-furlong seller at Thirsk on her third start and a five-furlong nursery at the same course during the summer of 2001. Fourth in a Listed race at the back-end of the 2001 season, beaten just a length. Acts on fast ground.

Mixed Marriage (IRE)

96 **65d**

3-y-o ch c Indian Ridge-Marie De Flandre (FR) (Crystal Palace (FR))
J W Hills Mountgrange Stud

Placings:006000 **(4614)**
2001: 8^{0}S, 8^{0}GS, 10^{6}G, 12^{0}GS, 16^{0}HY, 13^{0}F

	Starts	1st	2nd	3rd	Win & Pl
Career Total (Turf)	6	0	0	0	0

Going (Turf): Sf: 0-2 GS: 0-2 Gd: 0-1 GF: 0-0 Fm: 0-1
Distance: 5f/6f: 0-0 7f-8f: 0-1 9f-13f: 0-3 14f+: 0-2
Track : LH: 0-2 RH: 0-3 Tight: 0-2 Gall: 0-1
Aids: Bl: 0-0 Vi: 0-0 Tstrap: 0-0
Best Rating: 69 5/01 Wind 1m67y gd-sft

Lightly-raced over a mile and ten furlongs, his best effort was on easy ground.

Mizhar (USA)

(115) (81)**78**

5-y-o b/br g Dayjur (USA)-Futuh (USA) (Diesis)
D Shaw (D Nicholls 19/1) J H Knight

Placings:0411/006/00000224-**4000145**006461300 **(5685)**
2001: 5^{4}SD, 6^{0}SW, 6^{0}SD, 7^{0}SW, 5^{1}SD, 6^{4}SD, 5^{5}SD, 5^{0}GS, 5^{0}GS, 6^{6}GF, 6^{4}GF, 6^{6}F, 5^{1}SD, 6^{3}F, 6^{0}G, 5^{0}S

	Starts	1st	2nd	3rd	Win & Pl
Career Total (Turf)	24	2	2	1	18318
Career Total (AW)	8	2	0	0	13942

81 6/01 Wolv 5f D(0-80)H STD £3727
78 2/01 Wolv 5f C(0-100)H STD £8131
94 10/98 NmkR 6f C H GD £6004
82 9/98 Nott 6f15y D GD £3306
Total win prize-money £21171

Going (Turf): Sf: 0-1 GS: 0-2 **Gd: 2-11** GF: 0-6 Fm: 0-4
Distance: **5f/6f: 3-28** 7f-8f: 1-4 9f-13f: 0-0 14f+: 0-0
Track : **LH: 2-8** RH: 0-0 **Tight: 2-5** Gall: 0-0
Aids: Bl: 1-10 Vi: 1-7 Tstrap: 0-0
Best Rating: 81 6/01 Wolv 5f stand

Fairly useful sprinter on his day, but does not win as often as he should. Now with Derek Shaw, he ran well on turf and especially on Fibresand this year and seems to go well for a girl, especially Dawn Watson.

Mizillablack (IRE)

103 **86**

2-y-o b f Eagle Eyed (USA)-Sketch Pad (Warning)
Mrs P N Dutfield Mrs S Thornton

Placings:314045033 **(5150)**
2001: 5^{3}GS, 5^{1}GS, 5^{4}GF, 5^{0}GF, 5^{4}G, 5^{5}GF, 5^{0}GF, 5^{3}GF, 6^{3}G

	Starts	1st	2nd	3rd	Win & Pl
Career Total (Turf)	9	1	0	3	34345

78 5/01 Sals 5f C G-S £6264
Total win prize-money £6264

Going (Turf): Sf: 0-0 **GS: 1-2** Gd: 0-2 GF: 0-5 Fm: 0-0
Distance: **5f/6f: 1-9** 7f-8f: 0-0 9f-13f: 0-0 14f+: 0-0
Track : LH: 0-0 RH: 0-1 Tight: 0-0 Gall: 0-1
Aids: Bl: 0-0 Vi: 0-0 Tstrap: 0-0
Best Rating: 86 10/01 Rdcr 6f good

She has been running with credit in some of the top two-year-old races since winning a conditions event at Salisbury on her second start. Has won on good to soft but has performed to a consistent level on faster.

Mobaader (USA)

101 **76+**

3-y-o b c Danzig (USA)-Retrospective (USA) (Easy Goer (USA))
Saeed Bin Suroor Godolphin

Placings:12 **(5091)**
2001: 8^{1}GF, 7^{2}GS

	Starts	1st	2nd	3rd	Win & Pl
Career Total (Turf)	2	1	1	0	6714

76 6/01 Nott 1m54y D G-F £3902
Total win prize-money £3903

Going (Turf): Sf: 0-0 GS: 0-1 Gd: 0-0 **GF: 1-1** Fm: 0-0
Distance: 5f/6f: 0-0 7f-8f: 0-1 **9f-13f: 1-1** 14f+: 0-0
Track : **LH: 1-1** RH: 0-0 Tight: 0-0 Gall: 0-0
Aids: Bl: 0-0 Vi: 0-0 Tstrap: 0-0
Best Rating: 76 6/01 Nott 1m54y gd-fm

Made a winning debut at Nottingham in June, but was beaten at odds-on in softer groundin October.

Mobil-One Dot Com

86 **44**

3-y-o b g Magic Ring (IRE)-Not So Generous (IRE) (Fayruz)
J S Goldie W M Johnstone

Placings:033 **(1551)**
2001: 9^{0}GS, 9^{3}F, 10^{3}F

	Starts	1st	2nd	3rd	Win & Pl
Career Total (Turf)	3	0	0	2	943

Going (Turf): Sf: 0-0 GS: 0-1 Gd: 0-0 GF: 0-0 Fm: 0-2
Distance: 5f/6f: 0-0 7f-8f: 0-0 9f-13f: 0-3 14f+: 0-0
Track : LH: 0-1 RH: 0-2 Tight: 0-2 Gall: 0-1
Aids: Bl: 0-0 Vi: 0-0 Tstrap: 0-0
Best Rating: 44 5/01 Newc 1m2f32y firm

Mobo-Baco

(95) (50?)**50**

4-y-o ch g Bandmaster (USA)-Darakah (Doulab (USA))
R J Hodges Frome Racing

Placings:040600005-5040014 **(4735)**
2001: 7^{5}SD, 6^{0}GF, 5^{4}HD, 6^{0}GF, 6^{0}GF, 8^{1}F, 10^{4}F

	Starts	1st	2nd	3rd	Win & Pl
Career Total (Turf)	15	1	0	0	2492
Career Total (AW)	1	0	0	0	0

48 9/01 Bath 1m5y F(0-60)H FRM £2492
Total win prize-money £2492

Going (Turf): Sf: 0-2 GS: 0-4 Gd: 0-1 GF: 0-4 **Fm: 1-4**

Distance: 5f/6f: 0-6 7f-8f: 0-6 **9f-13f: 1-4** 14f+: 0-0
Track : **LH: 1-6** RH: 0-1 **Tight: 1-3** Gall: 0-1
Aids: Bl: 0-0 Vi: 0-0 Tstrap: 0-0
Best Rating: 50 6/01 Bath 5f161y hard

Got off the mark when stepped back up to a mile for the first time this season. Appreciated forcing tactics on that occasion.

Mobtaker (IRE)

104 **71**

3-y-o b c Marju (IRE)-Absaar (USA) (Alleged (USA))
B W Hills Hamdan Al Maktoum

Placings:0-2100 **(5171)**
2001: 8^{2}GS, 8^{1}GF, 8^{0}GF, 8^{0}GS

	Starts	1st	2nd	3rd	Win & Pl
Career Total (Turf)	5	1	1	0	5395

62 8/01 Pont 1m4y D G-F £4309
Total win prize-money £4310

Going (Turf): Sf: 0-0 GS: 0-2 Gd: 0-1 **GF: 1-2** Fm: 0-0
Distance: 5f/6f: 0-0 7f-8f: 0-3 **9f-13f: 1-2** 14f+: 0-0
Track : **LH: 1-3** RH: 0-1 Tight: 0-0 Gall: 0-0
Aids: Bl: 0-0 Vi: 0-0 Tstrap: 0-0
Best Rating: 71 8/01 Ayr 1m gd-sft

Got off the mark on his third attempt after a promising run in his previous maiden, although he failed to progress after that. Suited by a mile and is effective on good to firm ground.

Model Queen (USA)

104 **80**

3-y-o ch f Kingmambo (USA)-Model Bride (USA) (Blushing Groom (FR))
B W Hills K Abdulla

Placings:3-01344 **(3982)**
2001: 7^{0}GS, 7^{1}GF, 10^{3}GF, 10^{4}GS, 8^{4}F

	Starts	1st	2nd	3rd	Win & Pl
Career Total (Turf)	6	1	0	2	6219

70 6/01 Bevl 7f100y D G-F £4026
Total win prize-money £4027

Going (Turf): Sf: 0-1 GS: 0-2 Gd: 0-0 **GF: 1-2** Fm: 0-1
Distance: 5f/6f: 0-0 **7f-8f: 1-4** 9f-13f: 0-2 14f+: 0-0
Track : LH: 0-3 **RH: 1-1** Tight: 0-0 Gall: 0-1
Aids: Bl: 0-0 Vi: 0-0 Tstrap: 0-0
Best Rating: 80 7/01 Donc 1m2f60y gd-fm

She got off the mark in a Beverley maiden in June and has run pretty well in handicaps since, though she has looked one-paced. Best on fast ground.

Modem (IRE)

101(96) (51d)**46**

4-y-o b g Midhish-Holy Water (Monseigneur (USA))
D Shaw Dr J Charlesworth

Placings:000/**1364000064**-0040016 **(5292)**
2001: 6^{0}SD, 7^{0}GF, 7^{4}GS, 7^{0}G, 8^{0}GS, 8^{1}GS, 7^{6}S

	Starts	1st	2nd	3rd	Win & Pl
Career Total (Turf)	11	1	0	0	3308
Career Total (AW)	9	1	0	1	2250

46 8/01 Thsk 1m F(0-60)H G-S £3307
64 1/00 Sthl 7f G STD £1500
Total win prize-money £4809

Going (Turf): Sf: 0-2 **GS: 1-5** Gd: 0-3 GF: 0-1 Fm: 0-0
Distance: 5f/6f: 0-3 **7f-8f: 2-15** 9f-13f: 0-2 14f+: 0-0
Track : **LH: 2-12** RH: 0-0 **Tight: 1-4** Gall: 0-1
Aids: Bl: 0-1 **Vi: 1-7** Tstrap: 0-0
Best Rating: 46 8/01 Thsk 1m gd-sft

Modesty

86 **47**

3-y-o b f Bin Ajwaad (IRE)-Penny Dip (Cadeaux

Genereux)
B N Doran R P & M Berrow

Placings:000-400 (5462)
2001: 6^{4}G, 5^{0}GF, 5^{0}G

	Starts	1st	2nd	3rd	Win & Pl
Career Total (Turf)	6	0	0	0	0

Going (Turf): Sf: 0-1 GS: 0-0 Gd: 0-3 GF: 0-1 Fm: 0-1
Distance: 5f/6f: 0-5 7f-8f: 0-1 9f-13f: 0-0 14f+: 0-0
Track : LH: 0-3 RH: 0-0 Tight: 0-0 Gall: 0-3
Aids: Bl: 0-0 Vi: 0-0 Tstrap: 0-0
Best Rating: 47 5/01 Nott 6f15y good

Modigliani (USA)

107 **108**

3-y-o b c Danzig (USA)-Hot Princess (Hot Spark)
A P O'Brien Mrs John Magnier

Placings:134255-100 (2328)
2001: 7^{1}G, 8^{0}G, 6^{0}GF

	Starts	1st	2nd	3rd	Win & Pl
Career Total (Turf)	9	2	1	1	65750

108 5/01 Curr 7f GD £45500
82 3/00 Curr 5f SFT £6900
Total win prize-money £52400

Going (Turf): Sf: 1-1 GS: 0-0 **Gd: 1-3** GF: 0-2 Fm: 0-0
Distance: 5f/6f: 1-6 7f-8f: 1-2 9f-13f: 0-0 14f+: 0-0
Track : LH: 0-0 RH: 0-0 Tight: 0-0 Gall: 0-0
Aids: Bl: 0-2 Vi: 0-0 Tstrap: 0-0
Best Rating: 108 5/01 Lonc 1m good

Third in the Coventry as a juvenile, he was unable to build on that promise in the second half of the season, but he came back to his best on his reappearance, winning a Group Three over seven furlongs at the Curragh, where he got an uncontested lead. He tried the same tactics in the French Guineas but did not see out the trip. Dropped back to six in the Cork and Orrery where he showed tremendous speed early on but could only manage seventh place. Has the speed for five furlongs.

Modrik (USA)

111 **95**

3-y-o ch c Dixieland Band (USA)-Seattle Summer (USA) (Seattle Slew (USA))
N A Graham Hamdan Al Maktoum

Placings:03421-34253 (3750)
2001: 8^{3}GS, 8^{4}G, 10^{2}F, 10^{5}G, 10^{3}GS

	Starts	1st	2nd	3rd	Win & Pl
Career Total (Turf)	10	1	2	3	15038

90 10/00 Donc 7f C(0-95) SFT £6844
Total win prize-money £6845

Going (Turf): Sf: 1-2 GS: 0-2 Gd: 0-4 GF: 0-1 Fm: 0-1
Distance: 5f/6f: 0-1 **7f-8f: 1-6** 9f-13f: 0-3 14f+: 0-0
Track : LH: 0-2 RH: 0-2 Tight: 0-0 Gall: 0-2
Aids: Bl: 0-1 Vi: 0-0 Tstrap: 0-0
Best Rating: 95 7/01 NmkJ 1m2f good

Fairly useful handicapper. Game winner of Doncaster nursery over seven furlongs as a juvenile. Ran well in face of stiff task on reappearance and has performed to a consistent level all season. Seems best suited by cut in the ground. Stays a mile and a quarter.

Modus Operandi (USA)

106(103) (62)**54**

5-y-o b g Known Fact (USA)-Proud Lou (USA) (Proud Clarion)
T Keddy Mrs Julie Mitchell

Placings:0415/64000004-515305 (4270)
2001: 12^{5}SD, 12^{1}SW, 11^{5}SD, 12^{3}SW, 11^{0}G, 11^{5}GF

	Starts	1st	2nd	3rd	Win & Pl
Career Total (Turf)	10	1	0	0	3293
Career Total (AW)	8	1	0	1	4444

59 1/01 Sthl 1m4f E(0-70)H SLW £2996
79 6/99 Rdcr 1m2f D FRM £2960
Total win prizo money £5956

Going (Turf): Sf: 0-1 GS: 0-0 Gd: 0-2 GF: 0-6 Fm: 1-1
Distance: 5f/6f: 0-0 7f-8f: 0-2 **9f-13f: 2-16** 14f+: 0-0
Track : **LH: 2-10** RH: 0-6 **Tight: 1-9** Gall: 0-3
Aids: Bl: 0-0 Vi: 0-0 Tstrap: 0-0
Best Rating: 59 1/01 Sthl 1m4f slow

Scored once at three then given a chance by the Handicapper when scoring on All-Weather at Southwell in January 2001. Stays a mile and a half. Acts on fast ground.

Mojave Flower (IRE)

92(39) **58**

2-y-o b f Desert Style (IRE)-Torrmana (IRE) (Ela-Mana-Mou)
M J Haynes Sfb Racing

Placings:0400005 (5667)
2001: 5^{0}SD, 6^{4}GF, 6^{0}GF, 6^{0}GF, 6^{0}GF, 6^{0}GF, 8^{5}HY

	Starts	1st	2nd	3rd	Win & Pl
Career Total (Turf)	6	0	0	0	0
Career Total (AW)	1	0	0	0	

Going (Turf): Sf: 0-1 GS: 0-0 Gd: 0-0 GF: 0-5 Fm: 0-0
Distance: 5f/6f: 0-6 7f-8f: 0-0 9f-13f: 0-1 14f+: 0-0
Track : LH: 0-1 RH: 0-1 Tight: 0-2 Gall: 0-0
Aids: Bl: 0-2 Vi: 0-0 Tstrap: 0-0
Best Rating: 58 9/01 Ling 6f gd-fm

Moderate maiden.

Mojo

72(29)

5-y-o gr g Mtoto-Pepper Star (IRE) (Salt Dome (USA))
G M Moore (Miss L C Siddall 10/8) Mrs S E Cooper

Placings:0000 (3801)
2001: 10^{0}GF, 6^{0}SD, 10^{0}S, 6^{0}G

	Starts	1st	2nd	3rd	Win & Pl
Career Total (Turf)	3	0	0	0	
Career Total (AW)	1	0	0	0	

Going (Turf): Sf: 0-1 GS: 0-0 Gd: 0-1 GF: 0-1 Fm: 0-0
Distance: 5f/6f: 0-2 7f-8f: 0-0 9f-13f: 0-2 14f+: 0-0
Track : LH: 0-3 RH: 0-0 Tight: 0-1 Gall: 0-0
Aids: Bl: 0-0 Vi: 0-0 Tstrap: 0-0

Mojo Man

88 **76**

2-y-o b c Millkom-Prima Sinfonia (Fairy King (USA))
R Hannon Speedlith Group

Placings:5405 (5295)
2001: 7^{5}G, 8^{4}HY, 7^{0}HY, 8^{5}S

	Starts	1st	2nd	3rd	Win & Pl
Career Total (Turf)	4	0	0	0	0

Going (Turf): Sf: 0-3 GS: 0-0 Gd: 0-1 GF: 0-0 Fm: 0-0
Distance: 5f/6f: 0-0 7f-8f: 0-2 9f-13f: 0-2 14f+: 0-0
Track : LH: 0-2 RH: 0-1 Tight: 0-0 Gall: 0-0
Aids: Bl: 0-0 Vi: 0-0 Tstrap: 0-0
Best Rating: 76 10/01 Leic 1m9y soft

Showed a hint of ability on his Sandown debut and may not have been suited by the mud subsequently.

Molaaf

97 **70**

2-y-o b f Shareef Dancer (USA)-Amber Fizz (USA) (Effervescing (USA))
C E Brittain Saeed Manana

Placings:56300 (4327)
2001: 6^{5}GS, 5^{6}GF, 7^{3}GF, 6^{0}GF, 6^{0}GF

	Starts	1st	2nd	3rd	Win & Pl
Career Total (Turf)	5	0	0	1	775

Going (Turf): Sf: 0-0 GS: 0-1 Gd: 0-0 GF: 0-4 Fm: 0-0
Distance: 5f/6f: 0-4 7f-8f: 0-1 9f-13f: 0-0 14f+: 0-0
Track : LH: 0-1 RH: 0-0 Tight: 0-0 Gall: 0-0
Aids: Bl: 0-0 Vi: 0-0 Tstrap: 0-0
Best Rating: 70 7/01 Sthl 7f gd-fm

Fair efforts in varied company so far, though nothing to get too excited about.

Molakem

93 **58**

3-y-o b c Darshaan-Calpella (Ajdal (USA))
C E Brittain Saeed Manana

Placings:0400 (5279)
2001: 10^{0}GF, 12^{4}GF, 9^{0}GS, 11^{0}S

	Starts	1st	2nd	3rd	Win & Pl
Career Total (Turf)	4	0	0	0	279

Going (Turf): Sf: 0-1 GS: 0-1 Gd: 0-0 GF: 0-2 Fm: 0-0
Distance: 5f/6f: 0-0 7f-8f: 0-0 9f-13f: 0-4 14f+: 0-0
Track : LH: 0-2 RH: 0-2 Tight: 0-2 Gall: 0-0
Aids: Bl: 0-0 Vi: 0-0 Tstrap: 0-0
Best Rating: 58 9/01 Gdwd 1m1f192y gd-sft

Molly Malone

101 **56**

4-y-o gr f Formidable (USA)-Pharland (FR) (Bellypha)
J C Tuck G S Tuck

Placings:6000-5304505 (3809)
2001: 5^{5}G, 6^{3}F, 5^{0}G, 6^{4}GF, 8^{5}GF, 8^{0}G, 7^{5}GF

	Starts	1st	2nd	3rd	Win & Pl
Career Total (Turf)	11	0	0	1	982

Going (Turf): Sf: 0-2 GS: 0-0 Gd: 0-4 GF: 0-4 Fm: 0-1
Distance: 5f/6f: 0-5 7f-8f: 0-4 9f-13f: 0-2 14f+: 0-0
Track : LH: 0-2 RH: 0-2 Tight: 0-1 Gall: 0-1
Aids: Bl: 0-1 Vi: 0-0 Tstrap: 0-0
Best Rating: 56 7/01 Sals 1m gd-fm

Molly's Secret

(100) (49)**55**

3-y-o b f Minshaanshu Amad (USA)-Secret Miss (Beveled (USA))
C G Cox The Two M's Partnership

Placings:6550100 (4734)
2001: 7^{6}SD, 8^{5}G, 6^{5}GF, 8^{0}GF, 8^{1}GF, 10^{0}S, 8^{0}F

	Starts	1st	2nd	3rd	Win & Pl
Career Total (Turf)	6	1	0	0	4505
Career Total (AW)	1	0	0	0	0

54 8/01 Epsm 1m114y E(0-75)H G-F £4504
Total win prize-money £4505

Going (Turf): Sf: 0-1 GS: 0-0 Gd: 0-1 **GF: 1-3** Fm: 0-1
Distance: 5f/6f: 0-0 7f-8f: 0-2 **9f-13f: 1-5** 14f+: 0-0
Track : **LH: 1-4** RH: 0-0 **Tight: 1-3** Gall: 0-0
Aids: Bl: 0-0 Vi: 0-0 Tstrap: 0-0
Best Rating: 55 6/01 Sals 6f212y gd-fm

Improved on previous efforts to land a small Epsom handicap in August. Suited by a mile and fast ground.

Moloko (USA)

92 **62**

2-y-o b/br f Boundary (USA)-Future Starlet (USA) (Theatrical)

J W Hills Christopher Wright

Placings:000 (5666)
2001: 7^{0}GF, 6^{0}HY, 6^{0}HY

	Starts	1st	2nd	3rd	Win & Pl
Career Total (Turf)	3	0	0	0	

Going (Turf): Sf: 0-2 GS: 0-0 Gd: 0-0 GF: 0-1 Fm: 0-0
Distance: 5f/6f: 0-2 7f-8f: 0-1 9f-13f: 0-0 14f+: 0-0
Track : LH: 0-0 RH: 0-0 Tight: 0-0 Gall: 0-0
Aids: Bl: 0-0 Vi: 0-0 Tstrap: 0-2
Best Rating: 62 9/01 Newb 7f gd-fm

Molomo

102 **103**
4-y-o b f Barathea (IRE)-Nishan (Nashwan (USA))
Noel Meade Barouche Stud Ltd

Placings:3220-315250425 (5339)
2001: 10^{3}G, 12^{1}GF, 10^{5}GF, 10^{2}Y, 10^{5}GF, 12^{0}YS, 10^{4}GF, 9^{2}G, 10^{5}GS

	Starts	1st	2nd	3rd	Win & Pl
Career Total (Turf)	13	1	4	2	51070

81 5/01 Rosc 1m4f G-F £6900
Total win prize-money £6900

Going (Turf): Sf: 0-0 GS: 0-1 Gd: 0-3 **GF: 1-5** Fm: 0-0
Distance: 5f/6f: 0-0 7f-8f: 0-1 **9f-13f: 1-12** 14f+: 0-0
Track : LH: 0-0 RH: 0-4 Tight: 0-0 Gall: 0-1
Aids: Bl: 0-0 Vi: 0-0 Tstrap: 0-0
Best Rating: 104 6/01 Curr 1m2f yield

She has managed to make the frame in Group company in Ireland, the best of which was her second place in the Group Two Pretty Polly Stakes at The Curragh, but her only victory so far came in an ordinary event at Roscommon. Best over ten to 12 furlongs, seems to handle any ground.

Moment

87 **71**
2-y-o ch f Nashwan (USA)-Well Away (IRE) (Sadler's Wells (USA))
J H M Gosden K Abdulla

Placings:0 (5274)
2001: 7^{0}GS

	Starts	1st	2nd	3rd	Win & Pl
Career Total (Turf)	1	0	0	0	

Going (Turf): Sf: 0-0 GS: 0-1 Gd: 0-0 GF: 0-0 Fm: 0-0
Distance: 5f/6f: 0-0 7f-8f: 0-1 9f-13f: 0-0 14f+: 0-0
Track : LH: 0-0 RH: 0-0 Tight: 0-0 Gall: 0-0
Aids: Bl: 0-0 Vi: 0-0 Tstrap: 0-0
Best Rating: 71 10/01 Leic 7f9y gd-sft

Momentous Jones

99 (48)**44**
4-y-o b g Emperor Jones (USA)-Ivory Moment (USA) (Sir Ivor)
M Madgwick Peter Taplin

Placings:0552/00-004 (5330)
2001: 10^{0}F, 14^{0}GS, 16^{4}HY

	Starts	1st	2nd	3rd	Win & Pl
Career Total (Turf)	8	0	1	0	654
Career Total (AW)	1	0	0	0	0

Going (Turf): Sf: 0-1 GS: 0-2 Gd: 0-3 GF: 0-1 Fm: 0-1
Distance: 5f/6f: 0-0 7f-8f: 0-2 9f-13f: 0-5 14f+: 0-2
Track : LH: 0-5 RH: 0-4 Tight: 0-6 Gall: 0-0
Aids: Bl: 0-0 Vi: 0-0 Tstrap: 0-0
Best Rating: 44 10/01 Sals 1m6f15y gd-sft

Moments In Time

86(83) (15)**22**
3-y-o b f Emperor Jones (USA)-Dame Helene (USA) (Sir Ivor)
M J Ryan Four Jays Racing Partnership

Placings:646500-00060 (5534)
2001: 9^{0}GS, 11^{0}GS, 11^{0}F, 12^{6}SD, 11^{0}S

	Starts	1st	2nd	3rd	Win & Pl
Career Total (Turf)	10	0	0	0	324
Career Total (AW)	1	0	0	0	0

Going (Turf): Sf: 0-1 GS: 0-3 Gd: 0-2 GF: 0-3 Fm: 0-1
Distance: 5f/6f: 0-1 7f-8f: 0-4 9f-13f: 0-6 14f+: 0-0
Track : LH: 0-5 RH: 0-1 Tight: 0-4 Gall: 0-0
Aids: Bl: 0-2 Vi: 0-0 Tstrap: 0-0
Best Rating: 22 4/01 Brig 1m1f209y gd-sft

Momentum (USA)

110 **112**
3-y-o b c Nureyev (USA)-Imprudent Love (USA) (Foolish Pleasure (USA))
J W Hills Letsgogolfin Syndicate

Placings:3210121 (4530)
2001: 8^{3}GF, 8^{2}F, 9^{1}GF, 10^{0}G, 8^{1}GF, 8^{2}F, 8^{1}GF

	Starts	1st	2nd	3rd	Win & Pl
Career Total (Turf)	7	3	2	1	44006

112 9/01 York 1m205y A G-F £21742
93 7/01 NmkJ 1m C(0-90)H G-F £10634
74 6/01 Gdwd 1m1f D G-F £4231
Total win prize-money £36609

Going (Turf): Sf: 0-0 GS: 0-0 Gd: 0-1 **GF: 3-4** Fm: 0-2
Distance: 5f/6f: 0-0 7f-8f: 1-4 **9f-13f: 2-3** 14f+: 0-0
Track : LH: 1-2 RH: 1-3 Tight: 1-2 Gall: 1-2
Aids: Bl: 0-0 Vi: 0-0 **Tstrap: 3-7**
Best Rating: 112 9/01 York 1m205y gd-fm

He ran well over a mile before a step up to nine furlongs brought about success. Scored again at Newmarket a month later in a Class C handicap, before running well in a Listed event at Salisbury and winning at York. Has gone to race in the USA. .

Mon Petite (IRE)

97(72) (30)**58**
2-y-o ch f General Monash (USA)-Wide Outside (IRE) (Don't Forget Me)
J A Glover Mrs R Morley

Placings:000101350 (3968)
2001: 5^{0}S, 5^{0}SD, 5^{0}GF, 6^{1}G, 6^{0}GF, 7^{1}G, 7^{3}F, 7^{5}G, 7^{0}GS

	Starts	1st	2nd	3rd	Win & Pl
Career Total (Turf)	8	2	0	1	5466
Career Total (AW)	1	0	0	0	

58 7/01 Yarm 7f3y G GD £2002
50 6/01 Thsk 6f G GD £2730
Total win prize-money £4732

Going (Turf): Sf: 0-1 GS: 0-1 **Gd: 2-3** GF: 0-2 Fm: 0-1
Distance: 5f/6f: 1-5 7f-8f: 1-4 9f-13f: 0-0 14f+: 0-0
Track : LH: 0-1 RH: 0-1 Tight: 0-0 Gall: 0-0
Aids: Bl: 0-0 **Vi: 2-6** Tstrap: 0-0
Best Rating: 58 7/01 Rdcr 7f firm

Only small, she took sellers at Thirsk and Yarmouth. Runs in a visor, suited by good ground and being held up.

Mon Prefere (FR)

(102) (66)**32**
6-y-o ch g Pistolet Bleu (IRE)-Salve (Sallust)
R Brotherton (I A Wood 13/2) J Laughton

Placings:15/052/003-51213600 (5166)
2001: 10^{5}SD, 9^{1}SW, 12^{2}SD, 10^{1}SD, 12^{3}SW, 10^{6}SD, 10^{0}S, 9^{0}SD

	Starts	1st	2nd	3rd	Win & Pl
Career Total (Turf)	7	1	1	0	11984
Career Total (AW)	9	2	1	2	5889

66 3/01 Ling 1m2f E STD £2751
57 2/01 Wolv 1m1f79y F SLW £2128
3/98 MsnL 1m2f110y HLD £8081
Total win prize-money £12960

Going (Turf): Sf: 0-2 GS: 0-0 Gd: 0-0 GF: 0-0 Fm: 0-0
Distance: 5f/6f: 0-0 7f-8f: 0-2 **9f-13f: 2-9** 14f+: 0-0
Track : **LH: 2-10** RH: 0-0 **Tight: 2-7** Gall: 0-0
Aids: Bl: 0-0 Vi: 0-0 Tstrap: 0-0
Best Rating: 66 3/01 Ling 1m2f stand

Mon Secret (IRE)

100(78) (47)**63d**
3-y-o b c General Monash (USA)-Ron's Secret (Efisio)
J L Eyre Pinnacle Monash Partnership

Placings:03241400000-6040400 (5172)
2001: 6^{6}G, 6^{0}GF, 7^{4}GF, 7^{0}G, 7^{4}GF, 7^{0}G, 6^{0}GS

	Starts	1st	2nd	3rd	Win & Pl
Career Total (Turf)	16	1	1	1	6283
Career Total (AW)	2	0	0	0	

71 6/00 Carl 5f207y D G-F £4030
Total win prize-money £4030

Going (Turf): Sf: 0-2 GS: 0-2 Gd: 0-8 **GF: 1-4** Fm: 0-0
Distance: **5f/6f: 1-12** 7f-8f: 0-6 9f-13f: 0-0 14f+: 0-0
Track : LH: 0-5 **RH: 1-1** Tight: 0-3 **Gall: 1-1**
Aids: Bl: 0-0 Vi: 0-0 Tstrap: 0-0
Best Rating: 63 7/01 Newc 7f gd-fm

Fairly useful juvenile sprinter, he has found life tougher this year and a drop into claiming company on his final start failed to bring about any improvement. Best on fast ground.

Monacle

80(98) (44)**43**
7-y-o b g Saddlers' Hall (IRE)-Endless Joy (Law Society (USA))
John Berry Chris Benest

Placings:0650005/**0361054003F**/3412542-5540 (0585)
2001: 16^{5}SD, 16^{5}SD, 13^{4}SD, 14^{0}HY

	Starts	1st	2nd	3rd	Win & Pl
Career Total (Turf)	21	2	1	1	6913
Career Total (AW)	8	0	1	2	1214

41 7/00 Yarm 2m E(0-70)H GD £3493
39 5/99 Yarm 1m3f101yF(0-70)H FRM £2070
Total win prize-money £5564

Going (Turf): Sf: 0-3 GS: 0-0 Gd: 0-7 GF: 0-7 **Fm: 1-3**
Distance: 5f/6f: 0-0 7f-8f: 0-1 **9f-13f: 1-13** 14f+: 0-14
Track : **LH: 1-25** RH: 0-2 **Tight: 1-14** Gall: 0-1
Aids: Bl: 0-2 Vi: 0-0 Tstrap: 0-0
Best Rating: 30 3/01 Ling 1m5f stand

Monalinga (IRE)

88(79) (19)**45**
3-y-o ch g General Monash (USA)-Malinga (USA) (Alwasmi (USA))
M Brittain Northgate Millennium

Placings:00000 (1850)
2001: 7^{0}S, 8^{0}SW, 8^{0}GS, 6^{0}S, 6^{0}F

	Starts	1st	2nd	3rd	Win & Pl
Career Total (Turf)	4	0	0	0	
Career Total (AW)	1	0	0	0	

Going (Turf): Sf: 0-2 GS: 0-1 Gd: 0-0 GF: 0-0 Fm: 0-1
Distance: 5f/6f: 0-2 7f-8f: 0-3 9f-13f: 0-0 14f+: 0-0
Track : LH: 0-1 RH: 0-0 Tight: 0-0 Gall: 0-0
Aids: Bl: 0-1 Vi: 0-0 Tstrap: 0-0
Best Rating: 45 3/01 Donc 7f soft

Monarchoftheglen (USA)

98 **99**

2-y-o b c A.P. Indy (USA)-Milliardaire (USA) (Alydar (USA))
A P O'Brien Mrs John Magnier

Placings:1344 **(4912a)**
2001: 6^{1}Y, 7^{3}GF, 7^{4}G, 7^{4}GF

	Starts	1st	2nd	3rd	Win & Pl
Career Total (Turf)	**4**	**1**	**0**	**1**	**25150**

93	5/01	Curr	6f		YLD	£10400

Total win prize-money £10400

Going (Turf): Sf: 0-0 GS: 0-0 Gd: 0-1 GF: 0-2 Fm: 0-0
Distance: **5f/6f: 1-1** 7f-8f: 0-3 9f-13f: 0-0 14f+: 0-0
Track : LH: 0-0 RH: 0-0 Tight: 0-0 Gall: 0-0
Aids: Bl: 0-1 Vi: 0-0 Tstrap: 0-0
Best Rating: 99 6/01 Asct 7f gd-fm

Succesful on his debut, he found life more difficult when stepped up to Pattern company on his next starts.

Monash Freeway (IRE)

96 **39**

3-y-o ch c General Monash (USA)-Pennine Pearl (IRE) (Pennine Walk)
Miss Jacqueline S Doyle A W Regan

Placings:000-000040 **(4290)**
2001: 11^{0}GS, 12^{0}GS, 8^{0}GF, 11^{0}F, 9^{4}G, 16^{0}GF

	Starts	1st	2nd	3rd	Win & Pl
Career Total (Turf)	**9**	**0**	**0**	**0**	**0**

Going (Turf): Sf: 0-0 GS: 0-3 Gd: 0-1 GF: 0-4 Fm: 0-1
Distance: 5f/6f: 0-1 7f-8f: 0-2 9f-13f: 0-5 14f+: 0-1
Track : LH: 0-3 RH: 0-1 Tight: 0-3 Gall: 0-0
Aids: Bl: 0-3 Vi: 0-0 Tstrap: 0-0
Best Rating: 39 6/01 Leic 1m9y gd-fm

Monash Lady (IRE)

96(103) (73)**41**

3-y-o ch f General Monash (USA)-Don't Be That Way (IRE) (Dance Of Life (USA))
J S Moore G Patterson

Placings:466**202**-**1116**0604**6**0360 **(4900)**
2001: 10^{1}SD, 10^{1}SD, 10^{1}SD, 10^{6}SW, 12^{0}SD, 9^{6}S, 10^{0}GS, 11^{4}G, 11^{6}G, 10^{0}GF, 10^{3}G, 12^{6}GF, 8^{0}GS

	Starts	1st	2nd	3rd	Win & Pl
Career Total (Turf)	**11**	**0**	**0**	**1**	**530**
Career Total (AW)	**8**	**3**	**2**	**0**	**11757**

73	1/01	Ling	1m2f	C	STD	£5988
57	1/01	Ling	1m2f	F(0-65)H	STD	£2205
55	1/01	Ling	1m2f	F	STD	£2177

Total win prize-money £10370

Going (Turf): Sf: 0-2 GS: 0-2 Gd: 0-4 GF: 0-3 Fm: 0-0
Distance: 5f/6f: 0-2 7f-8f: 0-3 **9f-13f: 3-14** 14f+: 0-0
Track : **LH: 3-11** RH: 0-2 **Tight: 3-11** Gall: 0-2
Aids: Bl: 0-0 Vi: 0-0 Tstrap: 0-0
Best Rating: 73 1/01 Ling 1m2f stand

Monash Prince (IRE)

95 **88**

2-y-o b c General Monash (USA)-Elinor Dashwood (IRE) (Fool's Holme (USA))
C Collins Confusion Syndicate

Placings:0063 **(5588)**
2001: 6^{0}S, 6^{0}S, 6^{6}S, 5^{3}GS

	Starts	1st	2nd	3rd	Win & Pl
Career Total (Turf)	**4**	**0**	**0**	**1**	**558**

Going (Turf): Sf: 0-3 GS: 0-1 Gd: 0-0 GF: 0-0 Fm: 0-0
Distance: 5f/6f: 0-4 7f-8f: 0-0 9f-13f: 0-0 14f+: 0-0
Track : LH: 0-1 RH: 0-0 Tight: 0-0 Gall: 0-0
Aids: Bl: 0-0 Vi: 0-0 Tstrap: 0-0
Best Rating: 88 10/01 Curr 6f soft

Monduru

98(93) (36)**49**

4-y-o b g Lion Cavern (USA)-Bint Albadou (IRE) (Green Desert (USA))
W R Muir J Haim

Placings:0/035000**0**-000204653 **(5469)**
2001: 8^{0}GF, 10^{0}GF, 8^{0}GS, 10^{2}G, 10^{0}HY, 10^{4}GF, 9^{6}G, 11^{5}SD, 9^{3}S

	Starts	1st	2nd	3rd	Win & Pl
Career Total (Turf)	**15**	**0**	**1**	**2**	**1894**
Career Total (AW)	**2**	**0**	**0**	**0**	**0**

Going (Turf): Sf: 0-6 GS: 0-2 Gd: 0-4 GF: 0-3 Fm: 0-0
Distance: 5f/6f: 0-1 7f-8f: 0-3 9f-13f: 0-13 14f+: 0-0
Track : LH: 0-6 RH: 0-5 Tight: 0-6 Gall: 0-1
Aids: Bl: 0-0 Vi: 0-0 Tstrap: 0-0
Best Rating: 52 8/01 Yarm 1m2f21y good

Still a maiden, but has gone close once or twice. Seems best on a sound surface.

Monica Geller

107(93) (56)**72**

3-y-o b f Komaite (USA)-Rion River (IRE) (Taufan (USA))
C N Allen Newmarketconnections.Com

Placings:0630362166-**0200**3100000 **(5669)**
2001: **8**^{0}SW, **8**^{2}SD, **8**^{0}SD, **10**^{0}SW, 9^{3}S, 9^{1}GS, 9^{0}GF, 8^{0}S, 8^{0}GS, 7^{0}S, 10^{0}HY

	Starts	1st	2nd	3rd	Win & Pl
Career Total (Turf)	**13**	**2**	**1**	**2**	**14602**
Career Total (AW)	**8**	**0**	**1**	**1**	**842**

77	5/01	Kemp	1m1f	C(0-90)H	G-S	£7475
61	9/00	Gdwd	1m	D(0-85)	SFT	£4416

Total win prize-money £11892

Going (Turf): Sf: 1-6 GS: 1-3 Gd: 0-0 GF: 0-4 Fm: 0-0
Distance: 5f/6f: 0-3 7f-8f: 1-11 9f-13f: 1-7 14f+: 0-0
Track : LH: 0-10 **RH: 2-4** Tight: 0-5 Gall: 0-2
Aids: Bl: 0-0 Vi: 0-0 Tstrap: 0-0
Best Rating: 77 5/01 Kemp 1m1f gd-sft

A modest handicapper, she is usually kept busy and landed a Kempton handicap in May 2001. Suited by cut in the ground and is effective over nine furlongs. Often slowly away.

Monksford

96 **79d**

2-y-o b g Minster Son-Mortify (Prince Sabo)
Denys Smith Evelyn Duchess Of Sutherland

Placings:223400 **(4882)**
2001: 5^{2}GF, 6^{2}GS, 6^{3}GS, 5^{4}GF, 6^{0}F, 6^{0}GF

	Starts	1st	2nd	3rd	Win & Pl
Career Total (Turf)	**6**	**0**	**2**	**1**	**2877**

Going (Turf): Sf: 0-0 GS: 0-2 Gd: 0-0 GF: 0-3 Fm: 0-1
Distance: 5f/6f: 0-4 7f-8f: 0-2 9f-13f: 0-0 14f+: 0-0
Track : LH: 0-0 RH: 0-0 Tight: 0-0 Gall: 0-0
Aids: Bl: 0-0 Vi: 0-0 Tstrap: 0-0
Best Rating: 79 7/01 Ayr 6f gd-sft

Monkston Point (IRE)

117 **111**

5-y-o b g Fayruz-Doon Belle (Ardoon)
D W P Arbuthnot Derrick C Broomfield

Placings:13133413/560000200/11013000000-011430634 **(5694)**
2001: 5^{0}GS, 5^{1}GS, 6^{1}S, 6^{4}GF, 6^{3}HY, 6^{0}S, 6^{6}GS, 5^{3}HY, 6^{4}S

	Starts	1st	2nd	3rd	Win & Pl
Career Total (Turf)	**37**	**8**	**1**	**7**	**139102**

108	5/01	Hayd	6f	C	SFT	£6496
106	4/01	Newb	5f34y	B(0-110)H	G-S	£9609
106	5/00	Kemp	5f	A	SFT	£14755
106	4/00	Kemp	6f	C	SFT	£6235
99	4/00	Newb	5f34y	B(0-110)H	SFT	£9108
99	9/90	Ayr	5f	A	G S	£9702
93	6/98	Bath	5f11y	D	G-S	£3436
88	4/98	Bath	5f11y	E	SFT	£3355

Total win prize-money £62696

Going (Turf): Sf: 5-17 GS: 3-8 Gd: 0-4 GF: 0-6 Fm: 0-0
Distance: **5f/6f: 8-35** 7f-8f: 0-2 9f-13f: 0-0 14f+: 0-0
Track : **LH: 2-2** RH: 0-0 Tight: 0-0 **Gall: 2-2**
Aids: Bl: 0-1 **Vi: 5-19** Tstrap: 0-0
Best Rating: 111 9/01 Hayd 6f heavy

Pattern-class sprinter who thrives on an easy surface. He was back to form at Newbury in April, landing the same race for second year in a row and running on resolutely to win going away and followed up with the minimum of fuss at Haydock. Ran arguably his best race when a staying-on third in the Group One Sprint Cup at Haydock.

Monnavanna (IRE)

111 **112**

3-y-o ch f Machiavellian (USA)-Mezzogiorno (Unfuwain (USA))
G Wragg Mrs R Philipps

Placings:312010120 **(5105)**
2001: 7^{3}GS, 7^{1}GF, 8^{2}GF, 8^{0}GF, 7^{1}GS, 8^{0}S, 6^{1}GF, 6^{2}VS, 5^{0}GS

	Starts	1st	2nd	3rd	Win & Pl
Career Total (Turf)	**9**	**3**	**2**	**1**	**56633**

97	8/01	Pont	6f	A	G-F	£21937
112	7/01	Deau	7f		G-S	£13579
92	5/01	Ches	7f2y	D	G-F	£7182

Total win prize-money £42700

Going (Turf): Sf: 0-1 GS: 1-3 Gd: 0-0 **GF: 2-4** Fm: 0-0
Distance: 5f/6f: 1-3 **7f-8f: 2-6** 9f-13f: 0-0 14f+: 0-0
Track : **LH: 2-2** RH: 0-2 **Tight: 1-1** Gall: 0-1
Aids: Bl: 0-0 Vi: 0-0 Tstrap: 0-0
Best Rating: 112 7/01 Deau 7f gd-sft

Out of an Oaks-placed mare, she did not race at two. Ran with promise on her debut and followed up by running away with a maiden at Chester. Blossomed further in the second half of the season with victories in Listed events at Deauville and Pontefract. A progressive filly, she can go on to better things.

Mono Lady (IRE)

96(107) (69)**75**

8-y-o b m Polish Patriot (USA)-Phylella (Persian Bold)
D Haydn Jones Monolithic Refractories Ltd

Placings:04640/040616**46**/**1132**035**1**32021/026201500 0/**30**215420/**0204514**43**5**-**30**1005 **(3141)**
2001: **12**^{3}SD, **12**^{0}SW, 11^{1}GF, 12^{0}F, 12^{0}GS, 12^{5}G

	Starts	1st	2nd	3rd	Win & Pl
Career Total (Turf)	**42**	**5**	**6**	**3**	**34736**
Career Total (AW)	**18**	**4**	**2**	**3**	**14457**

75	5/01	Brig	1m3f196y	E(0-70)H	G-F	£2849
69	6/00	Wolv	1m4f	E(0-75)H	STD	£2684
68	5/99	Ches	1m4f66y	D(0-80)H	G-F	£7340
74	8/98	Leic	1m3f183y	D(0-85)H	GD	£7002
68	9/97	Brig	1m3f196y	E(0-70)H	G-F	£3174
71	5/97	Ling	1m2f	E(0-70)H	STD	£3018
58	1/97	Sthl	1m	E(0-70)H	STD	£2817
52	1/97	Wolv	1m1f79y	E(0-70)H	SLW	£2453
57	10/96	Folk	1m1f149y	F(0-60)H	G-S	£3343

Total win prize-money £34682

Going (Turf): Sf: 0-6 GS: 1-4 Gd: 1-15 **GF: 3-16** Fm: 0-1
Distance: 5f/6f: 0-4 7f-8f: 1-5 **9f-13f: 8-51** 14f+: 0-0
Track : **LH: 7-42** RH: 2-11 **Tight: 5-30** Gall: 0-8
Aids: **Bl: 7-30** Vi: 0-6 Tstrap: 0-0
Best Rating: 75 5/01 Brig 1m3f196y gd-fm

Fair handicapper at a mile and a half on a fast surface. Effective on the All-Weather, she has won at all three venues in her time. She has paid her way over the years. Was reluctant to race on her last two starts of 2001 season.

Monolith

104 **81**

3-y-o b c Bigstone (IRE)-Ancara (Dancing Brave (USA))

Mrs A J Perrett K Abdulla

Placings:4361 **(5180)**

2001: 9^{4}GF, 10^{3}G, 11^{6}G, 10^{1}HY

	Starts	1st	2nd	3rd	Win & Pl
Career Total (Turf)	4	1	0	1	3966

68 10/01 Wind 1m2f7y D HVY £3038

Total win prize-money £3038

Going (Turf): Sf: 1-1 GS: 0-0 Gd: 0-2 GF: 0-1 Fm: 0-0
Distance: 5f/6f: 0-0 7f-8f: 0-0 **9f-13f: 1-4** 14f+: 0-0
Track : LH: 0-1 RH: 0-2 **Tight: 1-3** Gall: 0-0
Aids: Bl: 0-0 Vi: 0-0 Tstrap: 0-0
Best Rating: 81 7/01 Sand 1m2f7y good

Lightly-raced, had shown ability in maidens before winning over ten furlongs on heavy ground at Windsor.

Monsal Dale (IRE)

85 **60**

2-y-o ch c Desert King (IRE)-Zanella (IRE) (Nordico (USA))

J A R Toller Duke Of Devonshire

Placings:60 **(2370)**

2001: 6^{6}GF, 6^{0}GF

	Starts	1st	2nd	3rd	Win & Pl
Career Total (Turf)	2	0	0	0	0

Going (Turf): Sf: 0-0 GS: 0-0 Gd: 0-0 GF: 0-2 Fm: 0-0
Distance: 5f/6f: 0-2 7f-8f: 0-0 9f-13f: 0-0 14f+: 0-0
Track : LH: 0-0 RH: 0-0 Tight: 0-0 Gall: 0-0
Aids: Bl: 0-0 Vi: 0-0 Tstrap: 0-0
Best Rating: 60 6/01 NmkJ 6f gd-fm

Monsieur Le Blanc (IRE)

103 **79**

3-y-o b g Alzao (USA)-Dedara (Head For Heights)

I A Balding Kennet Valley Thoroughbreds Iv

Placings:63560-0204565 **(3858)**

2001: 10^{0}S, 11^{2}G, 11^{0}GF, 13^{4}GF, 14^{5}GF, 12^{6}S, 11^{5}GS

	Starts	1st	2nd	3rd	Win & Pl
Career Total (Turf)	12	0	1	1	2684

Going (Turf): Sf: 0-2 GS: 0-1 Gd: 0-3 GF: 0-6 Fm: 0-0
Distance: 5f/6f: 0-0 7f-8f: 0-4 9f-13f: 0-6 14f+: 0-2
Track : LH: 0-1 RH: 0-4 Tight: 0-1 Gall: 0-1
Aids: Bl: 0-1 Vi: 0-5 Tstrap: 0-0
Best Rating: 79 6/01 Newb 1m5f61y gd-fm

Showed some good form without winning as a juvenile, but struggled in 2001, running his best race when fourth over 13 furlongs at Newbury. Suited by fast ground.

Mont Rocher (FR)

107 **115**

6-y-o gr g Caerleon (USA)-Cuixmala (FR) (Highest Honor (FR))

J E Hammond Tsega Ltd

Placings:4/062011111/123200-261310 **(5477a)**

2001: 8^{2}HY, 10^{6}GS, 12^{1}GS, 12^{3}G, 9^{1}G, 12^{0}HY

	Starts	1st	2nd	3rd	Win & Pl
Career Total (Turf)	22	8	4	2	139168

109 9/01 Gdwd 1m1f192yA GD £17615
5/01 Bord 1m4f G-S £5335
7/00 Bord 1m4f G-S £7685
12/99 Toul 1m4f VS £21529
9/99 Toul 1m4f G-S £19376
7/99 MsnL 1m7f110y H GD £15070
6/99 Lonc 1m7f110y H GD £15070
6/99 Comp 1m6f G-S £4844

Total win prize-money £106524

Going (Turf): Sf: 0-2 **GS: 3-5** Gd: 1-5 GF: 0-0 Fm: 0-0
Distance: 5f/6f: 0-0 7f-8f: 0-1 **9f-13f: 3-11** 14f+: 1-1
Track : LH: 0-1 **RH: 1-5 Tight: 1-1** Gall: 0-0
Aids: Bl: 0-1 Vi: 0-0 **Tstrap: 1-1**
Best Rating: 115 6/01 Chan 1m4f good

Placed in Group company in France earlier in the year, he appreciated the rain-softened ground when successful in a Listed race at Goodwood in September. Stays 12 furlongs. Needs a right-handed track.

Montagu Breezer (IRE)

78 **24**

3-y-o b g Paris House-Forever 'N' Ever (Jasmine Star)

Jamie Poulton Mrs M Liston

Placings:000 **(2557)**

2001: 6^{0}GS, 6^{0}F, 5^{0}GF

	Starts	1st	2nd	3rd	Win & Pl
Career Total (Turf)	3	0	0	0	

Going (Turf): Sf: 0-0 GS: 0-1 Gd: 0-0 GF: 0-1 Fm: 0-1
Distance: 5f/6f: 0-3 7f-8f: 0-0 9f-13f: 0-0 14f+: 0-0
Track : LH: 0-0 RH: 0-0 Tight: 0-0 Gall: 0-0
Aids: Bl: 0-0 Vi: 0-0 Tstrap: 0-0
Best Rating: 24 6/01 Folk 5f gd-fm

Montana Lady (IRE)

96 **76**

4-y-o ch f Be My Guest (USA)-Invisible Halo (USA) (Halo (USA))

E J O'Neill T F Brennan

Placings:600/10224004-000 **(2389)**

2001: 6^{0}S, 7^{0}F, 7^{0}GF

	Starts	1st	2nd	3rd	Win & Pl
Career Total (Turf)	14	1	2	0	10440

65 6/00 Cork 7f (0-85)H GD £6900

Total win prize-money £6900

Going (Turf): Sf: 0-3 GS: 0-0 **Gd: 1-4** GF: 0-1 Fm: 0-1
Distance: 5f/6f: 0-0 **7f-8f: 1-10** 9f-13f: 0-2 14f+: 0-0
Track : LH: 0-3 **RH: 1-6** Tight: 0-0 Gall: 0-0
Aids: Bl: 0-2 Vi: 0-0 **Tstrap: 1-5**
Best Rating: 59 5/01 Sals 6f212y soft

An able seven-furlong handicapper in Ireland, has only the one success to his name. Now trained in this country. Best suited to a sound surface.

Montana Miss (IRE)

99(102) (77)**76**

3-y-o b f Earl Of Barking (IRE)-Cupid Miss (Anita's Prince)

B Palling Mrs A L Stacey

Placings:411630-0220030000 **(4898)**

2001: 8^{0}GS, 8^{2}SD, 7^{2}GF, 8^{0}F, 8^{0}GF, 7^{3}GF, 8^{0}S, 7^{0}GF, 7^{0}SD, 5^{0}GS

	Starts	1st	2nd	3rd	Win & Pl
Career Total (Turf)	14	2	1	2	7838
Career Total (AW)	2	0	1	0	1239

78 7/00 Catt 7f F G-F £2289
58 6/00 Bevl 7f100y E G-F £2835

Total win prize-money £5124

Going (Turf): Sf: 0-3 GS: 0-2 Gd: 0-1 **GF: 2-7** Fm: 0-1
Distance: 5f/6f: 0-1 **7f-8f: 2-11** 9f-13f: 0-4 14f+: 0-0
Track : LH: 1-6 RH: 1-4 **Tight: 1-5** Gall: 0-1
Aids: Bl: 0-1 Vi: 0-0 Tstrap: 0-0
Best Rating: 77 5/01 Sthl 1m stand

A winner at Beverley and Catterick on her second and third starts at two, she has been mainly held in handicap company since then. Suited by fast ground.

Montana Moon (IRE)

(79) (40)**72**

2-y-o b g Ajraas (USA)-Batilde (IRE) (Victory Piper (USA))

R A Fahey Mrs Una Towell

Placings:0260 **(5342)**

2001: 5^{0}GF, 6^{2}G, 7^{6}GS, 7^{0}GS

	Starts	1st	2nd	3rd	Win & Pl
Career Total (Turf)	4	0	1	0	1228

Going (Turf): Sf: 0-0 GS: 0-2 Gd: 0-1 GF: 0-1 Fm: 0-0
Distance: 5f/6f: 0-2 7f-8f: 0-2 9f-13f: 0-0 14f+: 0-0
Track : LH: 0-0 RH: 0-0 Tight: 0-0 Gall: 0-0
Aids: Bl: 0-0 Vi: 0-0 Tstrap: 0-0
Best Rating: 72 9/01 Ayr 6f good

Montauroux (IRE)

39

2-y-o b g Eagle Eyed (USA)-Lyrical Vision (IRE) (Vision (USA))

T M Jones Richard L Page

Placings:0 **(5343)**

2001: 6^{0}GS

	Starts	1st	2nd	3rd	Win & Pl
Career Total (Turf)	1	0	0	0	

Going (Turf): Sf: 0-0 GS: 0-1 Gd: 0-0 GF: 0-0 Fm: 0-0
Distance: 5f/6f: 0-1 7f-8f: 0-0 9f-13f: 0-0 14f+: 0-0
Track : LH: 0-0 RH: 0-0 Tight: 0-0 Gall: 0-0
Aids: Bl: 0-0 Vi: 0-0 Tstrap: 0-0

Monte Carlo (IRE)

96 **79**

4-y-o b g Rainbows For Life (CAN)-Roberts Pride (Roberto (USA))

L Montague Hall J Daniels

Placings:43311/06-06500 **(5008)**

2001: 12^{0}G, 10^{6}G, 13^{5}GF, 21^{0}GF, 16^{0}S

	Starts	1st	2nd	3rd	Win & Pl
Career Total (Turf)	12	2	0	2	16057

104 10/99 NmkJ 1m2f A SFT £11189
77 9/99 Epsm 1m114y D G-F £3485

Total win prize-money £14674

Going (Turf): Sf: 1-3 GS: 0-1 Gd: 0-2 **GF: 1-4** Fm: 0-1
Distance: 5f/6f: 0-0 7f-8f: 0-2 **9f-13f: 2-7** 14f+: 0-3
Track : LH: 1-1 RH: 1-6 Tight: 1-2 Gall: 1-3
Aids: Bl: 0-0 Vi: 0-0 Tstrap: 0-0
Best Rating: 79 7/01 Newb 1m5f61y gd-fm

Highly tried in two runs in April 2000, he missed the rest of the campaign and has shown little this term. Won over a mile and ten furlongs as a juvenile.

Monte Mayor Golf (IRE)

(103) (84)**56**

3-y-o b f Case Law-Nishiki (USA) (Brogan (USA))

D Haydn Jones Mrs E M Haydn Jones

Placings:05060012222-32 **(0262)**

2001: 8^{3}SD, 8^{2}SD

	Starts	1st	2nd	3rd	Win & Pl
Career Total (Turf)	5	0	0	0	0
Career Total (AW)	8	1	5	1	7642

69 10/00 Wolv 7f E STD £2219

Total win prize-money £2219

Going (Turf): Sf: 0-0 GS: 0-1 Gd: 0-2 GF: 0-1 Fm: 0-1
Distance: 5f/6f: 0-3 **7f-8f: 1-6** 9f-13f: 0-4 14f+: 0-0
Track : LH: 1-11 RH: 0-0 **Tight: 1-7** Gall: 0-2

Aids: Bl: 0-0 Vi: 0-0 Tstrap: 0-0
Best Rating: 80 2/01 Wolv 1m100y stand

Monte Mayor Lady (IRE)

(53) (3)**19**
2-y-o b f Brief Truce (USA)-Busker (Bustino)
D Haydn Jones Mrs E M Haydn Jones

Placings:000 **(5396)**
2001: 6^{0}G, 6^{0}GF, 8^{0}SD

	Starts	1st	2nd	3rd	Win & Pl
Career Total (Turf)	2	0	0	0	
Career Total (AW)	1	0	0	0	

Going (Turf): Sf: 0-0 GS: 0-0 Gd: 0-1 GF: 0-1 Fm: 0-0
Distance: 5f/6f: 0-1 7f-8f: 0-1 9f-13f: 0-1 14f+: 0-0
Track : LH: 0-1 RH: 0-0 Tight: 0-1 Gall: 0-0
Aids: Bl: 0-1 Vi: 0-0 Tstrap: 0-0
Best Rating: 19 9/01 Folk 6f good

Montecassino Abbey (IRE)

99 **79**
2-y-o b c Danehill (USA)-Battle Mountain (IRE) (Dancing Brave (USA))
P W Harris Mrs P W Harris

Placings:423 **(4838)**
2001: 5^{4}GF, 6^{2}G, 6^{3}G

	Starts	1st	2nd	3rd	Win & Pl
Career Total (Turf)	3	0	1	1	1705

Going (Turf): Sf: 0-0 GS: 0-0 Gd: 0-2 GF: 0-1 Fm: 0-0
Distance: 5f/6f: 0-2 7f-8f: 0-1 9f-13f: 0-0 14f+: 0-0
Track : LH: 0-0 RH: 0-0 Tight: 0-0 Gall: 0-0
Aids: Bl: 0-0 Vi: 0-0 Tstrap: 0-0
Best Rating: 79 9/01 Nott 6f15y good

His dam is a half-sister to Big Stone. He showed ability in maiden races and should make his mark at three.

Montecastillo (IRE)

100 **105**
4-y-o b g Fairy King (USA)-Arcade (Rousillon (USA))
Charles O'Brien Painestown Syndicate

Placings:6/2105-523200363141 **(5218a)**
2001: 7^{5}S, 8^{2}S, 8^{3}G, 8^{2}GY, 8^{0}GY, 8^{0}GF, 8^{3}Y, 9^{6}G, 8^{3}GF, 7^{1}S, 7^{4}G, 7^{1}S

	Starts	1st	2nd	3rd	Win & Pl
Career Total (Turf)	17	3	3	3	94940
105 10/01 Tipp 7f				SFT	£42250
93 8/01 Tipp 7f				SFT	£9670
84 5/00 Leop 1m				GD	£5520

Total win prize-money £57440

Going (Turf): Sf: 2-4 GS: 0-0 Gd: 1-5 GF: 0-2 Fm: 0-1
Distance: 5f/6f: 0-0 **7f-8f: 3-15** 9f-13f: 0-2 14f+: 0-0
Track : **LH: 2-5** RH: 0-2 Tight: 0-0 Gall: 0-1
Aids: Bl: 0-3 Vi: 0-1 **Tstrap: 1-4**
Best Rating: 105 10/01 Tipp 7f soft

Stays a mile well, but his recent wins have been over seven. He scored a surprise victory in a Group Three on his final start of the season. Seems to act on any ground, but prefers give. Sold to the USA.

Montecristo

104 (80)**84**
8-y-o br g Warning-Sutosky (Great Nephew)
R Guest Rae Guest

Placings:5000/**41216**33106/**4056**504**111113**/**13**134413 13/20001100/35545304-51532436 **(5661)**
2001: 16^{5}S, 12^{1}GF, 11^{5}GS, 16^{3}GF, 16^{2}SD, 16^{4}GF, 13^{3}HY, 16^{6}G

	Starts	1st	2nd	3rd	Win & Pl
Career Total (Turf)	46	10	1	9	69858
Career Total (AW)	15	5	2	2	22401
83 5/01 Sthl 1m4f D(0-80)				G-F	£2526
90 9/99 Haml 1m5f9y C(0-100)H				SFT	£14200
90 8/99 Newb 1m4f5y C(0-90)				GD	£7002
86 9/98 Epsm 1m4f10y C(0-90)H				SFT	£5602
82 7/98 Brig 1m3f196yD(0-80)H				GD	£7035
77 3/98 Wwck 1m4f115yD(0-85)H				G-S	£3532
71 2/98 Wolv 1m4f D(0-80)H				STD	£3387
73 11/97 Wolv 1m4f F(0-60)				STD	£1946
74 11/97 Nott 1m6f15y G(0-70)				GD	£1984
51 10/97 Sthl 1m4f F(0-60)				STD	£2277
70 9/97 Newb 1m4f5y E(0-70)H				SFT	£4708
65 8/97 Haml 1m3f16y F(0-70)H				G-F	£2556
65 4/96 Bevl 1m1f207yF				G-F	£2721
54 2/96 Ling 1m4f E				STD	£2763
70 2/96 Ling 1m2f F(0-65)H				STD	£2612

Total win prize-money £62329

Going (Turf): Sf: 3-13 GS: 1-7 **Gd: 3-11 GF: 3-13** Fm: 0-2
Distance: 5f/6f: 0-0 7f-8f: 0-3 **9f-13f: 13-45** 14f+: 2-13
Track : **LH: 12-42** RH: 3-16 **Tight: 7-29** Gall: 2-14
Aids: Bl: 0-0 Vi: 0-0 Tstrap: 0-0
Best Rating: 84 11/01 Muss 2m good

An able handicapper with a multitude of wins to his name, though his win at Southwell in May 2001 was his first since September 1999. Likes to come off a strong pace and stays two miles, but better over shorter.

Montessori Mio (FR)

63
2-y-o b c Robellino (USA)-Child's Play (USA) (Sharpen Up)
M Johnston P D Savill

Placings:54 **(5662)**
2001: 7^{5}S, 8^{4}G

	Starts	1st	2nd	3rd	Win & Pl
Career Total (Turf)	2	0	0	0	335

Going (Turf): Sf: 0-1 GS: 0-0 Gd: 0-1 GF: 0-0 Fm: 0-0
Distance: 5f/6f: 0-0 7f-8f: 0-2 9f-13f: 0-0 14f+: 0-0
Track : LH: 0-1 RH: 0-1 Tight: 0-2 Gall: 0-0
Aids: Bl: 0-0 Vi: 0-0 Tstrap: 0-0
Best Rating: 63 11/01 Muss 1m good

A brother to the useful seven furlong to a mile and a quarter winner Sharp Play, he has shaped as if requiring a greater test of stamina than he has been offered to date.

Montev Lady

102(86) (30)**49**
3-y-o gr f Greensmith-Flair Lady (Chilibang)
W G M Turner Mrs M S Teversham

Placings:01400-03006060050 **(5592)**
2001: 5^{0}HD, 5^{3}GF, 5^{0}F, 5^{0}F, 5^{6}GF, 5^{0}G, 5^{6}GF, 6^{0}F, 5^{0}GS, 7^{5}SD, 6^{0}GS

	Starts	1st	2nd	3rd	Win & Pl
Career Total (Turf)	14	1	0	1	2852
Career Total (AW)	2	0	0	0	0
60 8/00 Bath 5f11y F				G-F	£2247

Total win prize-money £2247

Going (Turf): Sf: 0-1 GS: 0-3 Gd: 0-1 **GF: 1-5** Fm: 0-4
Distance: **5f/6f: 1-12** 7f-8f: 0-4 9f-13f: 0-0 14f+: 0-0
Track : **LH: 1-9** RH: 0-0 Tight: 0-3 **Gall: 1-4**
Aids: Bl: 0-0 Vi: 0-1 Tstrap: 0-0
Best Rating: 50 7/01 Ling 5f gd-fm

Montoya (IRE)

(84) (54)**79**
2-y-o b c Kylian (USA)-Saborinie (Prince Sabo)
P D Cundell Peter Dimmock

Placings:5504 **(5047)**
2001: 6^{5}GF, 7^{5}GF, 6^{0}G, 8^{4}SD

	Starts	1st	2nd	3rd	Win & Pl
Career Total (Turf)	3	0	0	0	0
Career Total (AW)	1	0	0	0	264

Going (Turf): Sf: 0-0 GS: 0-0 Gd: 0-1 GF: 0-2 Fm: 0-0
Distance: 5f/6f: 0-1 7f-8f: 0-3 9f-13f: 0-0 14f+: 0-0
Track : LH: 0-1 RH: 0-0 Tight: 0-0 Gall: 0-0
Aids: Bl: 0-0 Vi: 0-0 Tstrap: 0-0
Best Rating: 79 8/01 Newb 7f gd-fm

Yet to win a race and has shown little in terms of ability.

Montrave

82 **9**
12-y-o ch g Netherkelly-Streakella (Firestreak)
Miss Lucinda V Russell D St Clair

Placings:0/6024/6 **(5285)**
2001: 13^{6}HY

	Starts	1st	2nd	3rd	Win & Pl
Career Total (Turf)	6	0	1	0	624

Going (Turf): Sf: 0-1 GS: 0-1 Gd: 0-3 GF: 0-0 Fm: 0-1
Distance: 5f/6f: 0-0 7f-8f: 0-0 9f-13f: 0-3 14f+: 0-3
Track : LH: 0-4 RH: 0-2 Tight: 0-2 Gall: 0-0
Aids: Bl: 0-0 Vi: 0-0 Tstrap: 0-0
Best Rating: 9 10/01 Ayr 1m5f13y heavy

Monts Memory

(89) (58)**59**
2-y-o ch g Fraam-Miss Derby (USA) (Master Derby (USA))
K A Ryan The Three Bills

Placings:523404002 **(5410)**
2001: 6^{5}GF, 6^{2}SD, 7^{3}GF, 6^{4}G, 7^{0}GS, 7^{4}HY, 8^{0}G, 7^{0}G, 7^{2}SD

	Starts	1st	2nd	3rd	Win & Pl
Career Total (Turf)	7	0	0	1	838
Career Total (AW)	2	0	2	0	1116

Going (Turf): Sf: 0-1 GS: 0-1 Gd: 0-3 GF: 0-2 Fm: 0-0
Distance: 5f/6f: 0-3 7f-8f: 0-6 9f-13f: 0-0 14f+: 0-0
Track : LH: 0-5 RH: 0-1 Tight: 0-0 Gall: 0-0
Aids: Bl: 0-2 Vi: 0-0 Tstrap: 0-0
Best Rating: 59 9/01 Hayd 7f30y heavy

He has managed to finish runner-up in a couple of Fibresand sellers.

Monturani (IRE)

97 **83+**
2-y-o b f Indian Ridge-Mezzogiorno (Unfuwain (USA))
G Wragg Mrs R Philipps

Placings:3 **(5603)**
2001: 7^{3}GS

	Starts	1st	2nd	3rd	Win & Pl
Career Total (Turf)	1	0	0	1	648

Going (Turf): Sf: 0-0 GS: 0-1 Gd: 0-0 GF: 0-0 Fm: 0-0
Distance: 5f/6f: 0-0 7f-8f: 0-1 9f-13f: 0-0 14f+: 0-0
Track : LH: 0-0 RH: 0-0 Tight: 0-0 Gall: 0-0
Aids: Bl: 0-0 Vi: 0-0 Tstrap: 0-0
Best Rating: 83 11/01 NmkR 7f gd-sft

Moo-Az (USA)

19
4-y-o b g Red Ransom (USA)-Fappies Cosy Miss (USA) (Fappiano (USA))
C A Dwyer David L Bowkett

Placings:1-00 (5560)
2001: 10^{0}S, 7^{0}S

	Starts	1st	2nd	3rd	Win & Pl
Career Total (Turf)	3	1	0	0	4319

85	8/00	Thsk	1m	D		GD	£4319

Total win prize-money £4319

Going (Turf): Sf: 0-2 GS: 0-0 **Gd: 1-1** GF: 0-0 Fm: 0-0
Distance: 5f/6f: 0-0 **7f-8f: 1-2** 9f-13f: 0-1 14f+: 0-0
Track : **LH: 1-2** RH: 0-0 **Tight: 1-1** Gall: 0-1
Aids: Bl: 0-0 Vi: 0-0 Tstrap: 0-0
Best Rating: 19 10/01 York 1m2f85y soft

Moocha Cha Man

(102) (49d)
5-y-o b g Sizzling Melody-Nilu (IRE) (Ballad Rock)
B A McMahon Mrs J McMahon

Placings:351060/205003061240/005000516155-50564 (0462)
2001: 7^{5}SD, 6^{0}SW, 6^{5}SD, 6^{6}SD, 6^{4}SD

	Starts	1st	2nd	3rd	Win & Pl
Career Total (Turf)	17	1	2	2	5301
Career Total (AW)	18	3	0	0	7124

47	11/00	Sthl	6f	F		STD	£1757
62	9/00	Wolv	6f	E(0-70)H		STD	£3132
65	8/99	Pont	5f	F		G-F	£2238
65	7/98	Wolv	5f	F		STD	£2234

Total win prize-money £9362

Going (Turf): Sf: 0-4 GS: 0-3 Gd: 0-3 **GF: 1-7** Fm: 0-0
Distance: **5f/6f: 4-29** 7f-8f: 0-6 9f-13f: 0-0 14f+: 0-0
Track : **LH: 4-22** RH: 0-0 **Tight: 2-13** Gall: 0-1
Aids: **Bl: 3-18** Vi: 0-1 Tstrap: 0-0
Best Rating: 49 1/01 Sthl 7f stand

Moojaz

105 **75**
3-y-o b f Lahib (USA)-Numuthej (USA) (Nureyev (USA))
A C Stewart Hamdan Al Maktoum

Placings:3100 (5171)
2001: 8^{3}GF, 8^{1}G, 7^{0}GF, 8^{0}GS

	Starts	1st	2nd	3rd	Win & Pl
Career Total (Turf)	4	1	0	1	3773

75	8/01	Wind	1m67y	D		GD	£3108

Total win prize-money £3108

Going (Turf): Sf: 0-0 GS: 0-1 **Gd: 1-1** GF: 0-2 Fm: 0-0
Distance: 5f/6f: 0-0 7f-8f: 0-1 **9f-13f: 1-3** 14f+: 0-0
Track : LH: 0-1 **RH: 1-2 Tight: 1-2** Gall: 0-0
Aids: Bl: 0-0 Vi: 0-0 Tstrap: 0-0
Best Rating: 75 8/01 Wind 1m67y good

Just got home on her second run in a Windsor maiden on good ground, but was very disappointing on her handicap debut. Acts well over a mile.

Moon At Night

106(58) **43**
6-y-o gr g Pursuit Of Love-La Nureyeva (USA) (Nureyev (USA))
W S Kittow H C Seymour

Placings:000001/3600110/1030000-063000 (4951)
2001: 7^{0}G, 7^{6}G, 8^{3}G, 8^{0}GF, 7^{0}G, 8^{0}G

	Starts	1st	2nd	3rd	Win & Pl
Career Total (Turf)	25	4	0	3	14466
Career Total (AW)	1	0	0	0	0

69	5/00	Brig	7f214y	E(0-70)H		G-F	£2947
60	8/99	Brig	7f214y	E(0-70)H		G-S	£3256
60	7/99	Chep	7f16y	E(0-70)H		G-F	£2962
55	9/98	Gdwd	1m	E(0-60)H		G-F	£4011

Total win prize-money £13176

Going (Turf): Sf: 0-2 GS: 1-1 Gd: 0-10 **GF: 3-12** Fm: 0-0
Distance: 5f/6f: 0-2 **7f-8f: 4-19** 9f-13f: 0-5 14f+: 0-0
Track : **LH: 2-11** RH: 1-8 Tight: 0-6 Gall: 0-3
Aids: Bl: 0-0 Vi: 0-1 Tstrap: 0-0
Best Rating: 54 8/01 Wind 1m67y good

Moon Ballad (IRE)

97 **101**
2-y-o ch c Singspiel (IRE)-Velvet Moon (IRE) (Shaadi (USA))
D R Loder Sheikh Mohammed

Placings:2 (4873)
2001: 7^{2}G

	Starts	1st	2nd	3rd	Win & Pl
Career Total (Turf)	1	0	1	0	1792

Going (Turf): Sf: 0-0 GS: 0-0 Gd: 0-1 GF: 0-0 Fm: 0-0
Distance: 5f/6f: 0-0 7f-8f: 0-1 9f-13f: 0-0 14f+: 0-0
Track : LH: 0-0 RH: 0-0 Tight: 0-0 Gall: 0-0
Aids: Bl: 0-0 Vi: 0-0 Tstrap: 0-0
Best Rating: 101 9/01 NmkR 7f good

Disqualified from first on his debut at Newmarket, he is well bred out of a Lowther Stakes winner.

Moon Colony

97 **49**
8-y-o b g Top Ville-Honeymooning (USA) (Blushing Groom (FR))
A L Forbes Tony Forbes

Placings:060222163/2300116040/0030650/06-03206 (3693)
2001: 16^{0}GF, 14^{3}GF, 14^{2}GF, 11^{0}GF, 13^{6}G

	Starts	1st	2nd	3rd	Win & Pl
Career Total (Turf)	32	3	5	4	23105
Career Total (AW)	1	0	0	0	

79	7/98	NmkJ	1m4f	D(0-80)H		GD	£4854
74	7/98	Donc	1m4f	D(0-80)H		G-F	£4776
81	10/97	Nott	1m6f15y	D		SFT	£4207

Total win prize-money £13838

Going (Turf): Sf: 1-5 GS: 0-3 **Gd: 1-11 GF: 1-13** Fm: 0-0
Distance: 5f/6f: 0-0 7f-8f: 0-0 **9f-13f: 2-14** 14f+: 1-19
Track : **LH: 2-19** RH: 1-13 Tight: 0-12 **Gall: 2-9**
Aids: Bl: 0-1 Vi: 0-0 Tstrap: 0-6
Best Rating: 49 7/01 Nott 1m6f15y gd-fm

Moon Emperor

110(106) (96)**103**
4-y-o b g Emperor Jones (USA)-Sir Hollow (USA) (Sir Ivor)
J R Jenkins Christopher Shankland & Robert Ellis

Placings:3545/1050-106556241646 (5385)
2001: 12^{1}SD, 12^{0}SD, 10^{6}SD, 10^{5}S, 12^{5}G, 12^{6}GF, 13^{2}G, 16^{4}G, 16^{1}G, 13^{6}G, 14^{4}GS, 16^{6}GS

	Starts	1st	2nd	3rd	Win & Pl
Career Total (Turf)	17	2	1	1	36980
Career Total (AW)	3	1	0	0	8801

97	8/01	Asct	2m45y	B(0-100)H		GD	£25000
96	1/01	Ling	1m4f	C(0-100)H		STD	£7975
84	4/00	Ripn	1m	D		SFT	£3588

Total win prize-money £36564

Going (Turf): Sf: 1-3 GS: 0-4 **Gd: 1-5** GF: 0-5 Fm: 0-0
Distance: 5f/6f: 0-0 7f-8f: 1-7 9f-13f: 1-7 14f+: 1-6
Track : LH: 1-7 **RH: 2-10 Tight: 2-5** Gall: 1-9
Aids: Bl: 0-0 Vi: 0-0 Tstrap: 0-0
Best Rating: 103 9/01 Donc 1m6f132y gd-sft

A winner over hurdles and on the All-Weather, he stays well and returned to winning form over two miles at Ascot in August 2001. Held off higher marks since. He does not want the ground any faster than good.

Moon Goddess

111 **90+**
3-y-o ch f Rainbow Quest (USA)-Mystic Goddess (USA) (Storm Bird (CAN))
Sir Michael Stoute Cheveley Park Stud

Placings:21350 (5339)
2001: 8^{2}GF, 8^{1}G, 9^{3}GF, 10^{5}G, 10^{0}GS

	Starts	1st	2nd	3rd	Win & Pl
Career Total (Turf)	5	1	1	1	7325

82	6/01	Yarm	1m3y	D		GD	£4095

Total win prize-money £4095

Going (Turf): Sf: 0-0 GS: 0-1 **Gd: 1-2** GF: 0-2 Fm: 0-0
Distance: 5f/6f: 0-0 7f-8f: 0-1 **9f-13f: 1-4** 14f+: 0-0
Track : LH: 0-1 RH: 0-1 Tight: 0-1 Gall: 0-1
Aids: Bl: 0-0 Vi: 0-0 Tstrap: 0-0
Best Rating: 90 10/01 NmkR 1m2f gd-sft

A progressive filly, she got off the mark by the minimum margin at Yarmouth in June 2001 on her second start and did not get the run of the race when third in a decent handicap at Glorious Goodwood. Had a poor draw when beaten at Doncaster and did not run badly in Listed company at Newmarket in October. Has won over mile but should get ten furlongs. Acts on a sound surface.

Moon Master

96(88) (34)**34**
3-y-o b c Primo Dominie-Sickle Moon (Shirley Heights)
J A Osborne Thehasbeenscom

Placings:40-604 (4360)
2001: 6^{6}SD, 7^{0}SD, 9^{4}GF

	Starts	1st	2nd	3rd	Win & Pl
Career Total (Turf)	3	0	0	0	284
Career Total (AW)	2	0	0	0	0

Going (Turf): Sf: 0-1 GS: 0-1 Gd: 0-0 GF: 0-1 Fm: 0-0
Distance: 5f/6f: 0-2 7f-8f: 0-2 9f-13f: 0-1 14f+: 0-0
Track : LH: 0-3 RH: 0-0 Tight: 0-0 Gall: 0-0
Aids: Bl: 0-0 Vi: 0-0 Tstrap: 0-1
Best Rating: 36 3/01 Sthl 6f stand

Moon Parade (ARG)

108 **82**
5-y-o b h Parade Marshal (USA)-Moon Fitz (ARG) (Fitzcarraldo (ARG))
Diego Lowther Moon Parade Hb

Placings:1/41400143/200-03660220 (3443)
2001: 8^{0}HY, 6^{3}SD, 8^{6}FT, 10^{6}G, 9^{0}G, 8^{2}G, 8^{2}G, 7^{0}GF

	Starts	1st	2nd	3rd	Win & Pl
Career Total (Turf)	4	0	1	0	1788
Career Total (AW)	16	3	2	2	38245

10/99	Plat	1m2f	FST	£12099
3/99	Plat	6f	SLP	£7562
11/98	Plmo	4f	FST	£6051

Total win prize-money £25712

Going (Turf): Sf: 0-1 GS: 0-0 Gd: 0-4 GF: 0-1 Fm: 0-0
Distance: 5f/6f: 1-3 7f-8f: 0-7 9f-13f: 1-9 14f+: 0-0
Track : LH: 0-0 RH: 0-0 Tight: 0-0 Gall: 0-0
Aids: Bl: 0-1 Vi: 0-0 Tstrap: 0-0
Best Rating: 82 7/01 Asct 7f gd-fm

Trained in Sweden and difficult to evaluate.

Moon Royale

98 **48**
3-y-o ch f Royal Abjar (USA)-Ragged Moon (Raga Navarro (ITY))
Denys Smith B Batey

Placings:50-0010001300 (5657)
2001: 10^{0}HY, 8^{0}GF, 8^{1}GF, 8^{0}GF, 8^{0}GF, 9^{0}GF, 8^{1}F, 7^{3}GF, 8^{0}GF, 8^{0}G

	Starts	1st	2nd	3rd	Win & Pl
Career Total (Turf)	12	2	0	1	6378

48	7/01	Thsk	1m	F(0-60)H		FRM	£3080
48	6/01	Pont	1m4y	F		G-F	£2828

Total win prize-money £5908

Going (Turf): Sf: 0-2 GS: 0-0 Gd: 0-2 **GF: 1-7 Fm: 1-1**
Distance: 5f/6f: 0-1 7f-8f: 1-8 9f-13f: 1-3 14f+: 0-0
Track : **LH: 2-7** RH: 0-3 **Tight: 1-7** Gall: 0-1
Aids: Bl: 0-0 Vi: 0-0 Tstrap: 0-0
Best Rating: 48 7/01 Thsk 1m firm

A winner of fast-ground sellers at Pontefract and Thirsk in 2001.

Moon Safari (USA)

103 **97?**

2-y-o b f Mr Prospector (USA)-Video (USA) (Nijinsky (CAN))
A P O'Brien M Tabor & Mrs John Magnier

Placings:53106 **(5003)**
2001: 6^5G, 8^3YS, 7^1S, 7^0GY, 8^6S

	Starts	1st	2nd	3rd	Win & Pl
Career Total (Turf)	5	1	0	1	14190
85 8/01 Tipp 7f				SFT	£9660

Total win prize-money £9660

Going (Turf): Sf: 1-2 GS: 0-0 Gd: 0-1 GF: 0-0 Fm: 0-0
Distance: 5f/6f: 0-1 **7f-8f: 1-3** 9f-13f: 0-1 14f+: 0-0
Track : LH: 0-0 RH: 0-1 Tight: 0-0 Gall: 0-1
Aids: Bl: 0-0 Vi: 0-0 Tstrap: 0-0
Best Rating: 97 9/01 Asct 1m soft

Winner of a Tipperary maiden but out of her depth in the Moyglare Stud Stakes, and the Fillies' Mile at Ascot.

Moon Solitaire (IRE)

108 **106**

4-y-o b c Night Shift (USA)-Gay Fantastic (Ela-Mana-Mou)
E A L Dunlop Maktoum Al Maktoum

Placings:6/4131301330-3133040 **(4170)**
2001: 10^3S, 10^1G, 12^3GF, 12^3GF, 12^0G, 12^4G, 10^0G

	Starts	1st	2nd	3rd	Win & Pl
Career Total (Turf)	18	4	0	7	101124
104 5/01 NmkR 1m2f	B(0-100)H			GD	£9471
100 7/00 NmkJ 1m2f	B(0-105)H			GD	£26000
94 5/00 Gdwd 1m1f	B(0-105)H			GD	£32500
76 4/00 Folk 7f	D			SFT	£2632

Total win prize-money £70603

Going (Turf): Sf: 1-3 GS: 0-2 **Gd: 3-9** GF: 0-4 Fm: 0-0
Distance: 5f/6f: 0-0 7f-8f: 1-5 **9f-13f: 3-13** 14f+: 0-0
Track : LH: 0-5 **RH: 2-6** Tight: 1-5 Gall: 1-5
Aids: Bl: 0-0 Vi: 0-3 Tstrap: 0-3
Best Rating: 106 6/01 Epsm 1m4f10y gd-fm

Made every yard and kept on very gamely to land a handicap at Newmarket in May. Held since in some very competitive events over a mile and a half, he is best at ten furlongs, acts on any ground and races prominently.

Moona's Magic (IRE)

92 **66**

2-y-o b f Inzar (USA)-Moona (USA) (Lear Fan (USA))
R Hannon Jubert Family

Placings:0600 **(4841)**
2001: 6^0GF, 6^6G, 6^0GF, 6^0G

	Starts	1st	2nd	3rd	Win & Pl
Career Total (Turf)	4	0	0	0	0

Going (Turf): Sf: 0-0 GS: 0-0 Gd: 0-2 GF: 0-2 Fm: 0-0
Distance: 5f/6f: 0-2 7f-8f: 0-2 9f-13f: 0-0 14f+: 0-0
Track : LH: 0-0 RH: 0-0 Tight: 0-0 Gall: 0-0
Aids: Bl: 0-0 Vi: 0-0 Tstrap: 0-0
Best Rating: 66 8/01 Sals 6f212y gd-fm

Mooncell

78(66) (25)**42**

2-y-o b g Exit To Nowhere (USA)-Lady Liska (USA) (Diesis)
M W Easterby David & Steven Dudley

Placings:000 **(5371)**
2001: 7^0GF, 8^0SD, 8^0G

	Starts	1st	2nd	3rd	Win & Pl
Career Total (Turf)	2	0	0	0	
Career Total (AW)	1	0	0	0	

Going (Turf): Sf: 0-0 GS: 0-0 Gd: 0-1 GF: 0-1 Fm: 0-0
Distance: 5f/6f: 0-0 7f-8f: 0-3 9f-13f: 0-0 14f+: 0-0
Track : LH: 0-2 RH: 0-0 Tight: 0-1 Gall: 0-0
Aids: Bl: 0-0 Vi: 0-0 Tstrap: 0-0
Best Rating: 42 10/01 Rdcr 1m good

Moonjaz

111 **96**

4-y-o ch c Nashwan (USA)-Harayir (USA) (Gulch (USA))
M P Tregoning Hamdan Al Maktoum

Placings:3-312 **(3513)**
2001: 10^3GF, 12^1GF, 14^2GF

	Starts	1st	2nd	3rd	Win & Pl
Career Total (Turf)	4	1	1	2	14981
78 7/01 Pont 1m4f8y D				G-F	£3623

Total win prize-money £3624

Going (Turf): Sf: 0-1 GS: 0-0 Gd: 0-0 **GF: 1-3** Fm: 0-0
Distance: 5f/6f: 0-0 7f-8f: 0-0 **9f-13f: 1-3** 14f+: 0-1
Track : **LH: 1-1** RH: 0-3 Tight: 0-1 Gall: 0-0
Aids: Bl: 0-0 Vi: 0-0 Tstrap: 0-0
Best Rating: 96 7/01 Gdwd 1m6f gd-fm

Bred in the purple, he was a comfortable winner of a Pontefract maiden on his third career start and ran a cracker when stepped up to 14 furlongs at Goodwood on his handicap bow. He should win a nice prize over that sort of trip.

Moonlight Dancer

109(92) (65)**75**

3-y-o b g Polar Falcon (USA)-Guanhumara (Caerleon (USA))
K R Burke The Jonah'S

Placings:4220250506-005601121 **(3280)**
2001: 7^0SD, 7^0SW, 8^5SW, 7^6SD, 8^0GF, 8^1GF, 8^1GF, 9^2GF, 9^1F

	Starts	1st	2nd	3rd	Win & Pl
Career Total (Turf)	14	3	4	0	15022
Career Total (AW)	5	0	0	0	0
47 7/01 Rdcr 1m1f	E(0-70)			FRM	£4111
69 6/01 Muss 1m	F(0-65)H			G-F	£2474
68 6/01 Wind 1m67y	E(0-70)H			G-F	£3482

Total win prize-money £10069

Going (Turf): Sf: 0-1 GS: 0-1 Gd: 0-2 **GF: 2-8** Fm: 1-2
Distance: 5f/6f: 0-8 7f-8f: 1-8 **9f-13f: 2-3** 14f+: 0-0
Track : LH: 1-10 **RH: 2-3 Tight: 3-9** Gall: 0-1
Aids: Bl: 0-0 Vi: 0-0 Tstrap: 0-0
Best Rating: 74 7/01 Muss 1m1f gd-fm

Successful three times at araound a mile on fast ground in 2001. He is genuine and consistent.

Moonlight Invader (IRE)

70

7-y-o br g Darshaan-Mashmoon (USA) (Habitat)
J G Portman A S B Portman

Placings:60/004/00/0 **(0879)**
2001: 21^0S

	Starts	1st	2nd	3rd	Win & Pl
Career Total (Turf)	8	0	0	0	0

Going (Turf): Sf: 0-3 GS: 0-2 Gd: 0-1 GF: 0-2 Fm: 0-0
Distance: 5f/6f: 0-0 7f-8f: 0-1 9f-13f: 0-3 14f+: 0-4
Track : LH: 0-5 RH: 0-3 Tight: 0-3 Gall: 0-1
Aids: Bl: 0-0 Vi: 0-0 Tstrap: 0-0

Moonlight Monty

73(77) (8)**50d**

5-y-o ch g Elmaamul (USA)-Lovers Light (Grundy)
Rodger Sweeney (B Ellison 22/6) Mrs J B Sweeney

Placings:0300/50/300-0 **(0500)**
2001: 12^0GS

	Starts	1st	2nd	3rd	Win & Pl
Career Total (Turf)	9	0	0	2	1159
Career Total (AW)	1	0	0	0	

Going (Turf): Sf: 0-2 GS: 0-1 Gd: 0-4 GF: 0-1 Fm: 0-1
Distance: 5f/6f: 0-0 7f-8f: 0-2 9f-13f: 0-5 14f+: 0-3
Track : LH: 0-10 RH: 0-0 Tight: 0-4 Gall: 0-2
Aids: Bl: 0-0 Vi: 0-0 Tstrap: 0-0

Moonlight Song (IRE)

(106) (63)**50**

4-y-o b f Mujadil (USA)-Model Show (IRE) (Dominion)
John A Harris (J L Harris 26/3) Paddy Barrett

Placings:140/000122201**433-124000200**0545034 **(5659)**
2001: 7^1SD, 8^2SD, 7^4SD, 7^0SD, 7^0SD, 7^2SD, 7^0SD, 6^0G, 7^0G, 7^5G, 8^4S, 8^5GF, 7^0GF, 7^3S, 8^4G

	Starts	1st	2nd	3rd	Win & Pl
Career Total (Turf)	18	1	3	1	8411
Career Total (AW)	13	3	2	2	10517
58 1/01 Sthl 7f	F			STD	£2261
68 9/00 Sthl 7f	E(0-70)H			STD	£2954
61 7/00 Sthl 7f	F			STD	£2247
10/99 Hopp 7f				GD	£2527

Total win prize-money £9989

Going (Turf): Sf: 0-3 GS: 0-2 Gd: 0-5 GF: 0-6 Fm: 0-0
Distance: 5f/6f: 0-5 **7f-8f: 3-23** 9f-13f: 0-1 14f+: 0-0
Track : **LH: 3-16** RH: 0-2 Tight: 0-6 Gall: 0-0
Aids: Bl: 0-0 Vi: 0-0 Tstrap: 0-0
Best Rating: 68 1/01 Sthl 1m stand

Her wins at home have come at Southwell on the Fibresand.

Moonlighting

75

4-y-o b f Lugana Beach-White Flash (Sure Blade (USA))
D R C Elsworth Del & Jake Partnership

Placings:0 **(3425)**
2001: 9^0GF

	Starts	1st	2nd	3rd	Win & Pl
Career Total (Turf)	1	0	0	0	

Going (Turf): Sf: 0-0 GS: 0-0 Gd: 0-0 GF: 0-1 Fm: 0-0
Distance: 5f/6f: 0-0 7f-8f: 0-0 9f-13f: 0-1 14f+: 0-0
Track : LH: 0-0 RH: 0-1 Tight: 0-1 Gall: 0-0
Aids: Bl: 0-0 Vi: 0-0 Tstrap: 0-0

Moonraking

(91) (27)**20**

8-y-o gr g Rusticaro (FR)-Lunaire (Try My Best (USA))
W Clay (Miss S J Wilton 19/1) J R Greenleaf

Placings:02026/31353060312/22211500/011253005 0/355-63000 **(5050)**
2001: 12^6SW, 11^3SW, 10^0GF, 10^0GF, 11^0SD

	Starts	1st	2nd	3rd	Win & Pl
Career Total (Turf)	15	0	0	3	1824
Career Total (AW)	27	6	7	4	20372
68 2/99 Sthl 1m4f	F			STD	£2263
57 2/99 Sthl 1m	F			STD	£1619
68 3/98 Sthl 1m	D(0-85)H			STD	£3452

60	2/98	Sthl	1m3f	F(0-65)H	STD	£1735
54	12/97	Sthl	1m3f	F(0-65)H	STD	£1944
56	3/97	Sthl	1m4f	F(0-70)H	STD	£2671

Total win prize-money £13686

Going (Turf): Sf: 0-5 GS: 0-3 Gd: 0-3 GF: 0-4 Fm: 0-0
Distance: 5f/6f: 0-0 7f-8f: 2-6 **9f-13f: 4-30** 14f+: 0-6
Track : **LH: 6-37** RH: 0-5 Tight: 0-13 Gall: 0-2
Aids: **Bl: 4-21** Vi: 0-2 Tstrap: 0-0
Best Rating: 27 1/01 Sthl 1m3f slow

Moorlands Again

96 **50**

6-y-o b g Then Again-Sandford Springs (USA) (Robellino (USA))
J M Bradley Mrs Lynda M Williams

Placings:6504543-00460005 **(5400)**
2001: 8^0G, 9^0GS, 9^4GF, 10^6GF, 9^0G, 8^0G, 11^0S, 10^5S

	Starts	1st	2nd	3rd	Win & Pl
Career Total (Turf)	15	0	0	1	1665

Going (Turf): Sf: 0-3 GS: 0-3 Gd: 0-4 GF: 0-5 Fm: 0-0
Distance: 5f/6f: 0-0 7f-8f: 0-2 9f-13f: 0-13 14f+: 0-0
Track : LH: 0-10 RH: 0-3 Tight: 0-5 Gall: 0-2
Aids: Bl: 0-1 Vi: 0-0 Tstrap: 0-0
Best Rating: 52 8/01 Bevl 1m1f207y gd-fm

Moortop Lady

78(65) (13)**34**

2-y-o b f Mtoto-Octavia Girl (Octavo (USA))
J L Eyre Sunpak Potatoes

Placings:0000 **(5168)**
2001: 5^0SD, 5^0S, 5^0SD, 10^0GS

	Starts	1st	2nd	3rd	Win & Pl
Career Total (Turf)	2	0	0	0	
Career Total (AW)	2	0	0	0	

Going (Turf): Sf: 0-1 GS: 0-1 Gd: 0-0 GF: 0-0 Fm: 0-0
Distance: 5f/6f: 0-3 7f-8f: 0-0 9f-13f: 0-1 14f+: 0-0
Track : LH: 0-2 RH: 0-0 Tight: 0-0 Gall: 0-0
Aids: Bl: 0-0 Vi: 0-0 Tstrap: 0-0
Best Rating: 34 10/01 Pont 1m2f6y gd-sft

Moose Malloy

98 **33**

4-y-o ch g Formidable (USA)-Jolimo (Fortissimo)
M J Ryan Extraman Ltd

Placings:600/00000-6 **(3497)**
2001: 16^6GF

	Starts	1st	2nd	3rd	Win & Pl
Career Total (Turf)	9	0	0	0	100

Going (Turf): Sf: 0-2 GS: 0-2 Gd: 0-1 GF: 0-4 Fm: 0-0
Distance: 5f/6f: 0-0 7f-8f: 0-4 9f-13f: 0-4 14f+: 0-1
Track : LH: 0-4 RH: 0-2 Tight: 0-3 Gall: 0-2
Aids: Bl: 0-0 Vi: 0-0 Tstrap: 0-0
Best Rating: 29 7/01 Yarm 2m gd-fm

Mootafayill (USA)

104 **96**

3-y-o b c Danzig (USA)-Ruznama (USA) (Forty Niner (USA))
B W Hills Hamdan Al Maktoum

Placings:222-23 **(2954)**
2001: 7^2GF, 8^3GF

	Starts	1st	2nd	3rd	Win & Pl
Career Total (Turf)	5	0	4	1	6604

Going (Turf): Sf: 0-1 GS: 0-0 Gd: 0-0 GF: 0-4 Fm: 0-0
Distance: 5f/6f: 0-2 7f-8f: 0-3 9f-13f: 0-0 14f+: 0-0

Track : LH: 0-1 RH: 0-0 Tight: 0-0 Gall: 0-1
Aids: Bl: 0-0 Vi: 0-0 Tstrap: 0-0
Best Rating: 82 5/01 Yarm 7f3y gd-fm

Moppy May (IRE)

81 **64**

2-y-o b f Alhaarth (IRE)-Lacinia (Groom Dancer (USA))
T G Mills J E Harley

Placings:05 **(4703)**
2001: 6^0GF, 7^5G

	Starts	1st	2nd	3rd	Win & Pl
Career Total (Turf)	2	0	0	0	0

Going (Turf): Sf: 0-0 GS: 0-0 Gd: 0-1 GF: 0-1 Fm: 0-0
Distance: 5f/6f: 0-0 7f-8f: 0-2 9f-13f: 0-0 14f+: 0-0
Track : LH: 0-1 RH: 0-0 Tight: 0-1 Gall: 0-0
Aids: Bl: 0-0 Vi: 0-0 Tstrap: 0-0
Best Rating: 64 8/01 Sals 6f212y gd-fm

Moqui Marble (GER)

94 **59?**

5-y-o b g Petit Loup (USA)-Margo's New Hope (USA) (Cannonade (USA))
John Berry (Ronald O'Leary 14/5) P M Harley

Placings:00 **(3944)**
2001: 6^0GS, 8^0GF

	Starts	1st	2nd	3rd	Win & Pl
Career Total (Turf)	2	0	0	0	

Going (Turf): Sf: 0-0 GS: 0-1 Gd: 0-0 GF: 0-1 Fm: 0-0
Distance: 5f/6f: 0-0 7f-8f: 0-1 9f-13f: 0-1 14f+: 0-0
Track : LH: 0-1 RH: 0-0 Tight: 0-1 Gall: 0-0
Aids: Bl: 0-0 Vi: 0-0 Tstrap: 0-0
Best Rating: 59 8/01 Yarm 6f3y gd-sft

Morahib

86 **48+**

3-y-o ch c Nashwan (USA)-Irish Valley (USA) (Irish River (FR))
Saeed Bin Suroor Godolphin

Placings:5 **(4414)**
2001: 10^5S

	Starts	1st	2nd	3rd	Win & Pl
Career Total (Turf)	1	0	0	0	0

Going (Turf): Sf: 0-1 GS: 0-0 Gd: 0-0 GF: 0-0 Fm: 0-0
Distance: 5f/6f: 0-0 7f-8f: 0-0 9f-13f: 0-1 14f+: 0-0
Track : LH: 0-1 RH: 0-0 Tight: 0-1 Gall: 0-0
Aids: Bl: 0-0 Vi: 0-0 Tstrap: 0-0
Best Rating: 48 8/01 Epsm 1m2f18y soft

More Modern (USA)

104 **91**

3-y-o ch c Mt. Livermore (USA)-A La Mode (USA) (Known Fact (USA))
R Charlton K Abdulla

Placings:4-31021106 **(4782)**
2001: 7^3S, 7^1GS, 8^0GF, 7^2GF, 7^1F, 7^1GF, 7^0GS, 7^6G

	Starts	1st	2nd	3rd	Win & Pl
Career Total (Turf)	9	3	1	1	17979

91	8/01	Kemp	7f	D(0-85)H	G-F	£7312
89	7/01	Ling	7f	D(0-80)	FRM	£4127
69	5/01	Ling	7f	D	G-S	£4147

Total win prize-money £15588

Going (Turf): Sf: 0-2 **GS: 1-2** Gd: 0-1 **GF: 1-3 Fm: 1-1**
Distance: 5f/6f: 0-1 **7f-8f: 3-7** 9f-13f: 0-1 14f+: 0-0
Track : LH: 0-3 **RH: 1-3** Tight: 0-1 **Gall: 1-2**
Aids: **Bl: 2-4** Vi: 0-0 Tstrap: 0-0
Best Rating: 91 8/01 Kemp 7f gd-fm

More Sirens (IRE)

104 **76**

3-y-o ch f Night Shift (USA)-Lower The Tone (IRE) (Phone Trick (USA))
Mrs J R Ramsden Mrs J R Ramsden

Placings:03-034120 **(2621)**
2001: 8^0GF, 7^3GF, 10^4GF, 8^1F, 8^2GF, 8^0GF

	Starts	1st	2nd	3rd	Win & Pl
Career Total (Turf)	8	1	1	2	8534

70	6/01	Nott	1m54y	D(0-80)H	FRM	£4283

Total win prize-money £4284

Going (Turf): Sf: 0-0 GS: 0-0 Gd: 0-0 GF: 0-5 **Fm: 1-1**
Distance: 5f/6f: 0-0 7f-8f: 0-3 **9f-13f: 1-3** 14f+: 0-0
Track : **LH: 1-4** RH: 0-2 Tight: 0-2 Gall: 0-1
Aids: Bl: 0-0 Vi: 0-0 Tstrap: 0-0
Best Rating: 76 6/01 Pont 1m4y gd-fm

Lightly raced. Placed third in France as a juvenile. Scored over a mile at Nottingham. Acts on fast ground.

More Specific

95 **63**

2-y-o ch c Definite Article-Blue Lamp (USA) (Shadeed (USA))
A P Jarvis The Aston Partnership

Placings:326440 **(5690)**
2001: 7^3F, 7^2GS, 6^6GF, 8^4G, 7^4S, 7^0S

	Starts	1st	2nd	3rd	Win & Pl
Career Total (Turf)	6	0	1	1	2605

Going (Turf): Sf: 0-2 GS: 0-1 Gd: 0-1 GF: 0-1 Fm: 0-1
Distance: 5f/6f: 0-1 7f-8f: 0-5 9f-13f: 0-0 14f+: 0-0
Track : LH: 0-2 RH: 0-0 Tight: 0-0 Gall: 0-1
Aids: Bl: 0-0 Vi: 0-0 Tstrap: 0-0
Best Rating: 83 7/01 Wwck 7f26y gd-sft

20,000gns first foal, dam placed over ten furlongs. Promise shown on all but one of his starts so far, although he was a little disappointing at Doncaster in November.

Moreover (IRE)

99(93) (53)**66**

3-y-o b f Caerleon (USA)-Overcall (Bustino)
Sir Mark Prescott Sir Edmund Loder

Placings:406-235322 **(5383)**
2001: 12^2F, 11^3G, **12^5SD**, 12^3F, **14^2SD**, 13^2S

	Starts	1st	2nd	3rd	Win & Pl
Career Total (Turf)	6	0	2	2	2863
Career Total (AW)	3	0	1	0	662

Going (Turf): Sf: 0-3 GS: 0-0 Gd: 0-1 GF: 0-0 Fm: 0-2
Distance: 5f/6f: 0-0 7f-8f: 0-3 9f-13f: 0-4 14f+: 0-2
Track : LH: 0-5 RH: 0-1 Tight: 0-5 Gall: 0-0
Aids: Bl: 0-1 Vi: 0-0 Tstrap: 0-0
Best Rating: 66 8/01 Leic 1m3f183y good

Morgan Le Fay

(99) (48)**52**

6-y-o b m Magic Ring (IRE)-Melody Park (Music Boy)
Don Enrico Incisa Don Enrico Incisa

Placings:00302202030/5230/10054405-236530000 **(4621)**
2001: 6^2SD, 6^3SD, 6^6SD, 8^5SW, 6^3SW, 7^0SD, 6^0G, 6^0G, 6^0F

	Starts	1st	2nd	3rd	Win & Pl
Career Total (Turf)	22	1	4	3	9446
Career Total (AW)	10	0	1	2	1714

60	5/00	Thsk	6f	D	GD	£3737

Total win prize-money £3738

Going (Turf): Sf: 0-2 GS: 0-3 **Gd: 1-12** GF: 0-3 Fm: 0-2

Distance: **5f/6f: 1-16** 7f-8f: 0-15 9f-13f: 0-1 14f+: 0-0
Track : LH: 0-15 RH: 0-2 Tight: 0-1 Gall: 0-1
Aids: Bl: 0-0 Vi: 0-0 Tstrap: 0-0
Best Rating: 56 1/01 Sthl 6f stand

Morgans Orchard (IRE)

(109) (69)**60**
5-y-o ch g Forest Wind (USA)-Regina St Cyr (IRE) (Doulab (USA))
A G Newcombe After Hours Partnership

Placings:053/**15215**52023260000-**32**6546100 **(5411)**
2001: 12^{3}SD, 14^{2}SD, 13^{6}GF, 12^{5}GF, 12^{4}GF, 15^{6}GF, 12^{1}GF, 12^{0}G, 14^{0}SD

				Starts	1st	2nd	3rd	Win & Pl
Career Total (Turf)				18	1	3	1	16439
Career Total (AW)				9	2	2	2	6546
56 8/01	Kemp	1m4f	E(0-75)H				G-F	£3523
65 2/00	Wolv	1m4f	G(0-60)H				STD	£1456
61 1/00	Sthl	1m4f	F(0-60)H				STD	£1806

Total win prize-money £6785

Going (Turf): Sf: 0-3 GS: 0-1 Gd: 0-5 **GF: 1-9** Fm: 0-0
Distance: 5f/6f: 0-0 7f-8f: 0-0 **9f-13f: 3-19** 14f+: 0-8
Track : **LH: 2-22** RH: 1-4 **Tight: 1-9** Gall: 0-9
Aids: Bl: 0-0 Vi: 0-0 Tstrap: 0-0
Best Rating: 69 4/01 Sthl 1m6f stand

Better on the All-Weather than on turf, he scored twice on the sand last season. He stays a mile and a half well but lacks a turn of foot. The switch to front-running tactics worked admirably at Kempton in early August. Acts on fast ground.

Mornin Reserves

90 **63**
2-y-o b c Atraf-Pusey Street Girl (Gildoran)
M R Channon A Ball & W Harrison-Allan

Placings:30 **(2936)**
2001: 5^{3}G, 6^{0}GF

	Starts	1st	2nd	3rd	Win & Pl
Career Total (Turf)	2	0	0	1	399

Going (Turf): Sf: 0-0 GS: 0-0 Gd: 0-1 GF: 0-1 Fm: 0-0
Distance: 5f/6f: 0-2 7f-8f: 0-0 9f-13f: 0-0 14f+: 0-0
Track : LH: 0-1 RH: 0-0 Tight: 0-0 Gall: 0-1
Aids: Bl: 0-0 Vi: 0-0 Tstrap: 0-0
Best Rating: 63 7/01 Ling 6f gd-fm

Morning Sky (IRE)

96 **85**
2-y-o b f Machiavellian (USA)-Dizzy Heights (USA) (Danzig (USA))
E A L Dunlop Maktoum Al Maktoum

Placings:001 **(4278)**
2001: 6^{0}GF, 7^{0}GS, 6^{1}GS

				Starts	1st	2nd	3rd	Win & Pl
Career Total (Turf)				3	1	0	0	4329
85 8/01	Gdwd	6f	D				G-S	£4329

Total win prize-money £4329

Going (Turf): Sf: 0-0 **GS: 1-2** Gd: 0-0 GF: 0-1 Fm: 0-0
Distance: **5f/6f: 1-2** 7f-8f: 0-1 9f-13f: 0-0 14f+: 0-0
Track : LH: 0-0 RH: 0-0 Tight: 0-0 Gall: 0-0
Aids: Bl: 0-0 Vi: 0-0 Tstrap: 0-0
Best Rating: 85 8/01 Gdwd 6f gd-sft

Stepped up on her initial runs when taking a Goodwood maiden. Looks to need seven furlongs plus.

Morning Sunset

93 **58**
2-y-o b f Zafonic (USA)-Eclipsing (IRE) (Baillamont (USA))
P W Harris B Lawrence

Placings:0 **(3410)**
2001: 6^{0}GF

	Starts	1st	2nd	3rd	Win & Pl
Career Total (Turf)	1	0	0	0	

Going (Turf): Sf: 0-0 GS: 0-0 Gd: 0-0 GF: 0-1 Fm: 0-0
Distance: 5f/6f: 0-0 7f-8f: 0-1 9f-13f: 0-0 14f+: 0-0
Track : LH: 0-0 RH: 0-0 Tight: 0-0 Gall: 0-0
Aids: Bl: 0-0 Vi: 0-0 Tstrap: 0-0
Best Rating: 58 7/01 Chep 6f16y gd-fm

Mornings Minion

110 **86**
4-y-o b g Polar Falcon (USA)-Fair Dominion (Dominion)
R Charlton Exors Of The Late D A Shirley

Placings:441530-6000211505 **(5251)**
2001: 8^{6}GS, 10^{0}G, 10^{0}S, 8^{0}GF, 8^{2}GF, 8^{1}GS, 8^{1}GS, 8^{5}G, 8^{0}S, 7^{5}S

				Starts	1st	2nd	3rd	Win & Pl
Career Total (Turf)				16	3	1	1	22724
86 8/01	Leic	1m9y	D(0-85)H				G-S	£7202
81 8/01	NmkJ	1m	D(0-80)H				G-S	£4202
86 7/00	Wwck	7f164y	D				GD	£3006

Total win prize-money £14410

Going (Turf): Sf: 0-5 **GS: 2-4** Gd: 1-3 GF: 0-4 Fm: 0-0
Distance: 5f/6f: 0-0 **7f-8f: 2-12** 9f-13f: 1-4 14f+: 0-0
Track : **LH: 1-5** RH: 0-2 Tight: 0-1 Gall: 0-2
Aids: Bl: 0-0 Vi: 0-1 Tstrap: 0-0
Best Rating: 86 8/01 Leic 1m9y gd-sft

Unraced at two, he got off the mark in a Warwick maiden on his third start last season and has run in some decent handicaps since. He dropped a few pounds in the handicap and found his form in August with wins at Newmarket and Leicester. A mile looks as far as he wants.

Morocco (IRE)

90 **35**
12-y-o b g Cyrano De Bergerac-Lightning Laser (Monseigneur (USA))
J A Osborne Martin Myers

Placings:05100/0603124220/100/006300066103300/000150302140302055/01500555013430/4362006/010440030/0006/030-000 **(3666)**
2001: 7^{0}GF, 8^{0}F, 8^{0}S

				Starts	1st	2nd	3rd	Win & Pl
Career Total (Turf)				91	9	6	11	44132
58 7/98	Leic	7f9y	D(0-80)H				GD	£4012
56 9/96	Ling	7f	E(0-70)H				FRM	£3889
52 5/96	Sals	6f212y	D(0-80)H				G-F	£4337
65 8/95	Carl	6f206y	F(0-60)				HRD	£2773
57 6/95	Muss	1m16y	F(0-60)H				G-F	£2970
53 8/94	Bath	1m5y	G				G-F	£2423
71 5/93	Newb	7f64y	C(0-90)H				G-S	£6056
72 6/92	Wwck	7f	F(0-80)H				FRM	£2363
72 7/91	Bath	5f161y	F				G-F	£2924

Total win prize-money £31750

Going (Turf): Sf: 0-9 GS: 1-12 Gd: 1-24 **GF: 4-28** Fm: 3-18
Distance: 5f/6f: 1-9 **7f-8f: 6-67** 9f-13f: 2-15 14f+: 0-0
Track : **LH: 4-28** RH: 2-20 Tight: 2-17 Gall: 2-6
Aids: Bl: 0-1 Vi: 0-3 Tstrap: 0-0
Best Rating: 35 7/01 Rdcr 1m firm

Morouj (USA)

104 **84**
2-y-o b f Gone West (USA)-Chicarica (USA) (The Minstrel (CAN))
D R Loder Sheikh Mohammed

Placings:4251 **(5183)**
2001: 6^{4}G, 5^{2}GF, 6^{5}GF, 5^{1}GS

				Starts	1st	2nd	3rd	Win & Pl
Career Total (Turf)				4	1	1	0	5571
83 10/01	Catt	5f	D				G-S	£3444

Total win prize-money £3444

Going (Turf): Sf: 0-0 **GS: 1-1** Gd: 0-1 GF: 0-2 Fm: 0-0
Distance: **5f/6f: 1-4** 7f-8f: 0-0 9f-13f: 0-0 14f+: 0-0
Track : LH: 0-0 RH: 0-0 Tight: 0-0 Gall: 0-0
Aids: Bl: 0-0 **Vi: 1-1** Tstrap: 0-0
Best Rating: 84 9/01 Sals 6f gd-fm

A daughter of a Cherry Hinton winner, she ran into Pattern-class performers on all three runs, before getting off the mark in the soft at Catterick over five furlongs. Races keenly and seems to struggle to get six furlongs.

Morris Dancing (USA)

93 **72+**
2-y-o b c Rahy (USA)-Summer Dance (Sadler's Wells (USA))
Sir Michael Stoute Cheveley Park Stud

Placings:54 **(5559)**
2001: 7^{5}S, 8^{4}S

	Starts	1st	2nd	3rd	Win & Pl
Career Total (Turf)	2	0	0	0	348

Going (Turf): Sf: 0-2 GS: 0-0 Gd: 0-0 GF: 0-0 Fm: 0-0
Distance: 5f/6f: 0-0 7f-8f: 0-1 9f-13f: 0-1 14f+: 0-0
Track : LH: 0-0 RH: 0-0 Tight: 0-0 Gall: 0-0
Aids: Bl: 0-0 Vi: 0-0 Tstrap: 0-0
Best Rating: 72 10/01 Yarm 1m3y soft

From the family of Opera House and Kayf Tara, hinted at ability at two but will not come into his own until tackling longer distances later on.

Morro Castle (USA)

104 **85**
3-y-o b/br c Kris S (USA)-Fuerza (USA) (Distinctive Pro (USA))
C E Brittain Saeed Manana

Placings:43010 **(4863)**
2001: 10^{4}G, 11^{3}G, 12^{0}G, 9^{1}G, 10^{0}GF

				Starts	1st	2nd	3rd	Win & Pl
Career Total (Turf)				5	1	0	1	5254
85 9/01	Sand	1m1f	D				GD	£4192

Total win prize-money £4193

Going (Turf): Sf: 0-0 GS: 0-0 **Gd: 1-4** GF: 0-1 Fm: 0-0
Distance: 5f/6f: 0-0 7f-8f: 0-0 **9f-13f: 1-5** 14f+: 0-0
Track : LH: 0-2 **RH: 1-3** Tight: 0-1 Gall: 0-3
Aids: Bl: 0-0 Vi: 0-0 Tstrap: 0-0
Best Rating: 85 9/01 Sand 1m1f good

He showed promise before scoring in a Sandown maiden over nine furlongs. Races prominently. Has not stayed a mile and a half in the past but should do so in time. Has won on good ground.

Morshdi

109 **122**
3-y-o b c Slip Anchor-Reem Albaraari (Sadler's Wells (USA))
M A Jarvis Darley Stud Management Snc

Placings:510-31201 **(4563a)**
2001: 10^{3}G, 12^{1}GF, 12^{2}Y, 12^{0}GF, 12^{1}GS

				Starts	1st	2nd	3rd	Win & Pl
Career Total (Turf)				8	3	1	1	918214
121 9/01	Badn	1m4f					G-S	£325733
116 5/01	Capa	1m4f					G-F	£412102
92 9/00	Hayd	1m30y	E				SFT	£3066

Total win prize-money £740901

Going (Turf): Sf: 1-2 GS: 1-1 Gd: 0-1 **GF: 1-3** Fm: 0-0
Distance: 5f/6f: 0-0 7f-8f: 0-1 **9f-13f: 3-7** 14f+: 0-0
Track : **LH: 1-1** RH: 0-1 Tight: 0-0 Gall: 0-1
Aids: Bl: 0-0 Vi: 0-0 Tstrap: 0-0

Best Rating: 122 7/01 Curr 1m4f yield

Smart and progressive middle-distance performer, out of a half-sister to champion sprinter Habibti. Was quite impressive winning the Derby Italiano in May when he came with a strong run to beat Falbrav. Improved on that performance when chasing home Galileo in the Irish Derby, and gained another Group One when taking the Grosser Preis von Baden. Stays a mile and a half well and may get further. Won on soft at two but looks better on top of the ground.

Morshid (USA)

106 **77**

3-y-o b g Gulch (USA)-Possessive Dancer (Shareef Dancer (USA))

M R Channon Sheikh Ahmed Al Maktoum

Placings:033-024640 **(2336)**

2001: 10[0]GS, 12[2]S, 14[4]G, 10[6]GF, 10[4]GF, 12[0]GF

	Starts	1st	2nd	3rd	Win & Pl
Career Total (Turf)	9	0	1	2	3486

Going (Turf): Sf: 0-2 GS: 0-1 Gd: 0-2 GF: 0-4 Fm: 0-0
Distance: 5f/6f: 0-0 7f-8f: 0-2 9f-13f: 0-6 14f+: 0-1
Track : LH: 0-5 RH: 0-3 Tight: 0-3 Gall: 0-3
Aids: Bl: 0-0 Vi: 0-2 Tstrap: 0-0
Best Rating: 77 4/01 Ripn 1m4f60y soft

Morton (IRE)

57

2-y-o b g Lake Coniston (IRE)-Tannerrun (IRE) (Runnett)

R F Marvin Miss Janine L Mann

Placings:0 **(2619)**

2001: 5[0]GF

	Starts	1st	2nd	3rd	Win & Pl
Career Total (Turf)	1	0	0	0	

Going (Turf): Sf: 0-0 GS: 0-0 Gd: 0-0 GF: 0-1 Fm: 0-0
Distance: 5f/6f: 0-1 7f-8f: 0-0 9f-13f: 0-0 14f+: 0-0
Track : LH: 0-0 RH: 0-0 Tight: 0-0 Gall: 0-0
Aids: Bl: 0-0 Vi: 0-0 Tstrap: 0-0

Mosaahim (IRE)

86 **77**

3-y-o b c Nashwan (USA)-Azdihaar (USA) (Mr Prospector (USA))

J L Dunlop Hamdan Al Maktoum

Placings:25-0 **(0855)**

2001: 8[0]GS

	Starts	1st	2nd	3rd	Win & Pl
Career Total (Turf)	3	0	1	0	1368

Going (Turf): Sf: 0-0 GS: 0-1 Gd: 0-1 GF: 0-1 Fm: 0-0
Distance: 5f/6f: 0-0 7f-8f: 0-3 9f-13f: 0-0 14f+: 0-0
Track : LH: 0-0 RH: 0-0 Tight: 0-0 Gall: 0-0
Aids: Bl: 0-0 Vi: 0-0 Tstrap: 0-0
Best Rating: 54 4/01 Newb 1m gd-sft

Mosayter (USA)

107 **92**

3-y-o b c Storm Cat (USA)-Bashayer (USA) (Mr Prospector (USA))

M P Tregoning Hamdan Al Maktoum

Placings:4-63110 **(4664)**

2001: 10[6]GF, 8[3]F, 8[1]F, 8[1]G, 9[0]GF

				Starts	1st	2nd	3rd	Win & Pl
Career Total (Turf)				6	2	0	1	13193
92	8/01	Thsk	1m	C(0-90)			GD	£7203
86	8/01	Thsk	1m	D			FRM	£4462

Total win prize-money £11667

Going (Turf): Sf: 0-0 GS: 0-0 **Gd: 1-2** GF: 0-2 **Fm: 1-2**
Distance: 5f/6f: 0-0 **7f-8f: 2-4** 9f-13f: 0-2 14f+: 0-0
Track : **LH: 2-4** RH: 0-1 **Tight: 2-4** Gall: 0-1
Aids: Bl: 0-0 Vi: 0-0 Tstrap: 0-0
Best Rating: 92 8/01 Thsk 1m good

He showed plenty of ability when fourth of 17 in a maiden at Newmarket on his only outing at two, but did not look fully fit when last in the Glasgow Stakes on his seasonal reappearance. Won a three-runner affair at Thirsk with ease, the time of which was decent and returned there three weeks later to take a classified event. Suited by fast ground.

Mosca

104 **73**

3-y-o ch f Most Welcome-Moidart (Electric)

J R Fanshawe Dr Catherine Wills

Placings:0-641 **(3426)**

2001: 10[6]GF, 14[4]GF, 14[1]GF

				Starts	1st	2nd	3rd	Win & Pl
Career Total (Turf)				4	1	0	0	4235
73	7/01	Sals	1m6f15y	E(0-70)H			G-F	£3955

Total win prize-money £3955

Going (Turf): Sf: 0-0 GS: 0-1 Gd: 0-0 **GF: 1-3** Fm: 0-0
Distance: 5f/6f: 0-0 7f-8f: 0-0 9f-13f: 0-2 **14f+: 1-2**
Track : LH: 0-1 **RH: 1-3 Tight: 1-4** Gall: 0-0
Aids: Bl: 0-0 Vi: 0-0 Tstrap: 0-0
Best Rating: 73 7/01 Sals 1m6f15y gd-fm

Bred to stay well, she scored at Salisbury on her handicap debut.

Moselle

111 **103**

4-y-o b f Mtoto-Miquette (FR) (Fabulous Dancer (USA))

W J Haggas Mr & Mrs G Middlebrook/mr & Mrs P Brain

Placings:3/201362530-41005010 **(4910a)**

2001: 9[4]G, 10[1]GF, 10[0]G, 12[0]G, 11[5]GS, 12[0]G, 10[1]GF, 10[0]GF

				Starts	1st	2nd	3rd	Win & Pl
Career Total (Turf)				18	3	2	3	51491
103	8/01	Newc	1m2f32y	A(0-105)H			G-F	£15352
101	5/01	York	1m2f85y	A			G-F	£18270
88	6/00	Yarm	1m3y	D			FRM	£3558

Total win prize-money £37182

Going (Turf): Sf: 0-1 GS: 0-2 Gd: 0-9 **GF: 2-4** Fm: 1-2
Distance: 5f/6f: 0-0 7f-8f: 0-4 **9f-13f: 3-14** 14f+: 0-0
Track : **LH: 2-6** RH: 0-5 Tight: 0-2 **Gall: 2-5**
Aids: Bl: 0-0 Vi: 0-0 Tstrap: 0-0
Best Rating: 103 8/01 Newc 1m2f32y gd-fm

Won a Yarmouth maiden in June 2000, but did not score again until nearly a year later in a Listed event at York. She ideally needs ten furlongs and fast ground and had conditions in her favour when winning a Listed handicap at Newcastle in August.

Mosspat

84 **43**

2-y-o b g Reprimand-Queen And Country (Town And Country)

W G M Turner Mossie O'Connell

Placings:30550 **(2397)**

2001: 5[3]GS, 5[0]S, 5[5]F, 7[5]GF, 7[0]GF

	Starts	1st	2nd	3rd	Win & Pl
Career Total (Turf)	5	0	0	1	651

Going (Turf): Sf: 0-1 GS: 0-1 Gd: 0-0 GF: 0-2 Fm: 0-1
Distance: 5f/6f: 0-3 7f-8f: 0-2 9f-13f: 0-0 14f+: 0-0
Track : LH: 0-1 RH: 0-0 Tight: 0-0 Gall: 0-0
Aids: Bl: 0-0 Vi: 0-1 Tstrap: 0-0
Best Rating: 43 5/01 Haml 5f4y gd-sft

Most Stylish

101(106) (60)**50**

4-y-o ch f Most Welcome-Corman-Style (Ahonoora)

L Lungo Elite Racing Club

Placings:52344640-150 **(5152)**

2001: 12[1]G, 11[5]G, 14[0]G

				Starts	1st	2nd	3rd	Win & Pl
Career Total (Turf)				9	1	0	1	2636
Career Total (AW)				2	0	1	0	634
38	8/01	Newc	1m4f93y G				GD	£1841

Total win prize-money £1841

Going (Turf): Sf: 0-4 GS: 0-0 **Gd: 1-4** GF: 0-1 Fm: 0-0
Distance: 5f/6f: 0-0 7f-8f: 0-2 **9f-13f: 1-8** 14f+: 0-1
Track : **LH: 1-7** RH: 0-4 Tight: 0-5 **Gall: 1-1**
Aids: Bl: 0-0 Vi: 0-0 Tstrap: 0-0
Best Rating: 50 10/01 Rdcr 1m6f19y good

A winning hurdler, got off the mark in a 12-furlong seller at Newcastle. Seems to handle any ground.

Most-Saucy

(108) (80)**61**

5-y-o br m Most Welcome-So Saucy (Teenoso (USA))

I A Wood Nigel Shields

Placings:034021014/3005**2054-1242000420040062**1560 **(5681)**

2001: 8[1]SD, 8[2]SW, 8[4]SD, 8[2]SW, 8[0]SD, 8[0]SD, 8[0]G, 7[4]GF, 8[2]GF, 10[0]S, 8[0]SD, 8[4]SD, 7[0]G, 7[0]GF, 6[6]F, 8[2]GS, 7[1]SD, 8[5]GS, 7[6]S, 8[0]S

				Starts	1st	2nd	3rd	Win & Pl
Career Total (Turf)				23	2	3	2	13899
Career Total (AW)				14	2	3	0	15949
72	10/01	Sthl	7f	E(0-70)H			STD	£3640
78	1/01	Ling	1m	D(0-80)H			STD	£5447
76	8/99	Ling	7f140y	E(0-75)H			G-F	£3517
72	7/99	Leic	7f9y	D(0-80)H			G-F	£4597

Total win prize-money £17202

Going (Turf): Sf: 0-6 GS: 0-3 Gd: 0-5 **GF: 2-8** Fm: 0-1
Distance: 5f/6f: 0-1 **7f-8f: 4-22** 9f-13f: 0-14 14f+: 0-0
Track : **LH: 2-22** RH: 0-7 **Tight: 1-14** Gall: 0-3
Aids: Bl: 0-0 Vi: 0-0 Tstrap: 0-0
Best Rating: 84 1/01 Wolv 1m100y slow

Has won four times at seven furlongs to a mile.Showed little on turf until finishing a good second at Leicester, and got her head in front off a decent mark at Southwell. Suited by most going, and handles the All-Weather.

Mostabshir (IRE)

103 **84**

3-y-o b c Unfuwain (USA)-Istibshar (USA) (Mr Prospector (USA))

J H M Gosden Hamdan Al Maktoum

Placings:0-3334410 **(5143)**

2001: 10[3]GF, 11[3]GF, 11[3]GF, 12[4]GF, 12[4]G, 12[1]GF, 14[0]G

				Starts	1st	2nd	3rd	Win & Pl
Career Total (Turf)				8	1	0	3	7021
84	9/01	Kemp	1m4f	D			G-F	£4257

Total win prize-money £4258

Going (Turf): Sf: 0-1 GS: 0-0 Gd: 0-2 **GF: 1-5** Fm: 0-0
Distance: 5f/6f: 0-0 7f-8f: 0-1 **9f-13f: 1-6** 14f+: 0-1
Track : LH: 0-1 **RH: 1-4** Tight: 0-2 Gall: 0-2
Aids: Bl: 0-0 Vi: 0-0 **Tstrap: 1-5**
Best Rating: 86 7/01 Wind 1m3f135y gd-fm

He is not blessed with much in the way of a turn of foot but, allowed an uncontested lead, got off the mark in a 12-furlong maiden at Kempton. Suited by fast ground and front-running tactics.

Mostarsil (USA)

106 **80**

3-y-o ch c Kingmambo (USA)-Naazeq (Nashwan (USA))
A C Stewart Hamdan Al Maktoum

Placings:61625 **(4066)**
2001: 10^{6}GF, 12^{1}GF, 10^{6}G, 10^{2}GS, 12^{5}G

	Starts	1st	2nd	3rd		Win & Pl
Career Total (Turf)	5	1	1	0		6257
80 6/01 Pont 1m4f8y	D				G-F	£3688

Total win prize-money £3689

Going (Turf): Sf: 0-0 GS: 0-1 Gd: 0-2 **GF: 1-2** Fm: 0-0
Distance: 5f/6f: 0-0 7f-8f: 0-0 **9f-13f: 1-5** 14f+: 0-0
Track : **LH: 1-2** RH: 0-3 Tight: 0-2 Gall: 0-1
Aids: Bl: 0-0 Vi: 0-0 Tstrap: 0-0
Best Rating: 80 8/01 NmkJ 1m2f gd-sft

Scrambled home in a maiden but did not look at ease dropped in trip at Chester. Ran far too free at Ripon in August. Stays a mile and a half. Acts on good to firm.

Mot Juste

107 **114**

3-y-o b f Mtoto-Bunting (Shaadi (USA))
E A L Dunlop Sheikh Mohammed

Placings:1-1420420 **(5577a)**
2001: 10^{1}G, 12^{4}GF, 12^{2}G, 11^{0}G, 12^{4}G, 10^{2}HO, 10^{0}F

	Starts	1st	2nd	3rd		Win & Pl
Career Total (Turf)	8	2	2	0		115467
100 5/01 NmkR 1m2f	A				GD	£15254
76 9/00 Yarm 1m3y	D				G-F	£3620

Total win prize-money £18875

Going (Turf): Sf: 0-0 GS: 0-0 **Gd: 1-4 GF: 1-2** Fm: 0-1
Distance: 5f/6f: 0-0 7f-8f: 0-0 **9f-13f: 2-8** 14f+: 0-0
Track : LH: 0-3 RH: 0-2 Tight: 0-1 Gall: 0-1
Aids: Bl: 0-0 Vi: 0-0 Tstrap: 0-0
Best Rating: 114 10/01 Lonc 1m2f holding

A very lean-looking, leggy filly who is bred to stay, knew what was required and landed the spoils comfortably on her one and only outing at two in an above-average maiden. Made all to win on her reappearance at three when stepped up to ten furlongs in the Pretty Polly Stakes, and improved again when stepped up to a mile and a half in the Oaks. Again raced prominently when just beaten in the Irish version, and ran further good races when in the frame in the Vermeille and Prix de l'Opera, but finished last in the Breeders' Cup Filly and Mare Turf.

Moten Swing

94 **77**

2-y-o b c Kris-Lady Bankes (IRE) (Alzao (USA))
R Hannon Bob Lalemant

Placings:4014 **(4428)**
2001: 5^{4}F, 6^{0}GF, 6^{1}GF, 7^{4}G

	Starts	1st	2nd	3rd		Win & Pl
Career Total (Turf)	4	1	0	0		4116
77 7/01 Sals 6f	D				G-F	£3815

Total win prize-money £3816

Going (Turf): Sf: 0-0 GS: 0-0 Gd: 0-1 **GF: 1-2** Fm: 0-1
Distance: **5f/6f: 1-2** 7f-8f: 0-2 9f-13f: 0-0 14f+: 0-0
Track : LH: 0-0 RH: 0-1 Tight: 0-0 Gall: 0-0
Aids: Bl: 0-0 Vi: 0-0 Tstrap: 0-0
Best Rating: 77 7/01 Sals 6f gd-fm

Battled back well to win at Salisbury on his third run before a good effort in a Sandown nursery when stepped up to seven furlongs.

Moth Hil (USA)

40

2-y-o b c Danzig (USA)-Siyadah (USA) (Mr Prospector (USA))
J L Dunlop Hamdan Al Maktoum

Placings:0 **(5527)**
2001: 8^{0}HY

	Starts	1st	2nd	3rd	Win & Pl
Career Total (Turf)	1	0	0	0	

Going (Turf): Sf: 0-1 GS: 0-0 Gd: 0-0 GF: 0-0 Fm: 0-0
Distance: 5f/6f: 0-0 7f-8f: 0-0 9f-13f: 0-1 14f+: 0-0
Track : LH: 0-1 RH: 0-0 Tight: 0-0 Gall: 0-0
Aids: Bl: 0-0 Vi: 0-0 Tstrap: 0-0

Mother Corrigan (IRE)

92(82) (12)**32**

5-y-o gr m Paris House-Missed Opportunity (IRE) (Exhibitioner)
M Brittain Mel Brittain

Placings:0/0046/01000000000-0000 **(3847)**
2001: 8^{0}SD, 6^{0}F, 5^{0}GF, 6^{0}G

	Starts	1st	2nd	3rd		Win & Pl
Career Total (Turf)	18	1	0	0		8000
Career Total (AW)	2	0	0	0		
58 5/00 Rdcr 7f	D(0-80)H				G F	£7702

Total win prize-money £7703

Going (Turf): Sf: 0-1 GS: 0-2 Gd: 0-3 **GF: 1-7** Fm: 0-4
Distance: 5f/6f: 0-8 **7f-8f: 1-8** 9f-13f: 0-3 14f+: 0-0
Track : LH: 0-6 RH: 0-4 Tight: 0-2 Gall: 0-2
Aids: Bl: 0-1 **Vi: 1-12** Tstrap: 0-0
Best Rating: 32 8/01 Rdcr 6f good

Mother Molly (USA)

89(68) **35**

4-y-o b/br f Irish River (FR)-Charming Molly (USA) (Diesis)
P S McEntee Eclipse-Rogers Partnership

Placings:2/300-000 **(3836)**
2001: 8^{0}GF, 7^{0}GF, 10^{0}G

	Starts	1st	2nd	3rd	Win & Pl
Career Total (Turf)	5	0	1	1	1720
Career Total (AW)	2	0	0	0	

Going (Turf): Sf: 0-1 GS: 0-0 Gd: 0-1 GF: 0-3 Fm: 0-0
Distance: 5f/6f: 0-1 7f-8f: 0-3 9f-13f: 0-3 14f+: 0-0
Track : LH: 0-3 RH: 0-2 Tight: 0-4 Gall: 0-1
Aids: Bl: 0-0 Vi: 0-0 Tstrap: 0-0
Best Rating: 35 7/01 Wind 1m67y gd-fm

Lightly-raced maiden, moderate recent form.

Motto (FR)

109 **89**

3-y-o b f Mtoto-Coigach (Niniski (USA))
H R A Cecil Dr Catherine Wills

Placings:6-4210004 **(5686)**
2001: 10^{4}GF, 9^{2}GF, 11^{1}GF, 14^{0}GF, 12^{0}G, 12^{0}GS, 10^{4}S

	Starts	1st	2nd	3rd		Win & Pl
Career Total (Turf)	8	1	1	0		5963
83 8/01 Brig 1m3f196yD					G-F	£3711

Total win prize-money £3712

Going (Turf): Sf: 0-2 GS: 0-1 Gd: 0-1 **GF: 1-4** Fm: 0-0
Distance: 5f/6f: 0-1 7f-8f: 0-0 **9f-13f: 1-6** 14f+: 0-1
Track : **LH: 1-4** RH: 0-3 Tight: 0-0 Gall: 0-5
Aids: Bl: 0-0 Vi: 0-0 Tstrap: 0-0
Best Rating: 89 9/01 Donc 1m6f132y gd-fm

Dam won the Park Hill Stakes. Had one run at two, and made a belated return at three, but proved well suited by step up to a mile and a half when scoring at Brighton in August, but has struggled in better company since. Acts on fast ground, and stays 12 furlongs, may eventually get further.

Mount Abu (IRE)

112 **123**

4-y-o b h Foxhound (USA)-Twany Angel (Double Form)
J H M Gosden Gary Seidler & Andy J Smith

Placings:41526/4116310-3164261 **(5353a)**
2001: 7^{3}G, 7^{1}GF, 6^{6}G, 6^{4}S, 6^{2}HY, 6^{6}S, 7^{1}VS

	Starts	1st	2nd	3rd		Win & Pl
Career Total (Turf)	19	6	2	2		182102
123 10/01 Lonc 7f					VS	£48497
114 6/01 Hayd 7f30y	A				G-F	£16770
113 9/00 Gdwd 7f	A				SFT	£22800
112 6/00 Ling 6f	A				G-S	£15718
113 5/00 Asct 6f	A				G-S	£15470
70 5/99 Newb 6f8y	D				SFT	£4965

Total win prize-money £124220

Going (Turf): **Sf: 2-5 GS: 2-5** Gd: 0-5 GF: 1-2 Fm: 0-0
Distance: 5f/6f: 2-10 **7f-8f: 4-9** 9f-13f: 0-0 14f+: 0-0
Track : LH: 1-1 **RH: 2-3** Tight: 0-0 Gall: 0-0
Aids: Bl: 0-0 Vi: 0-0 Tstrap: 0-0
Best Rating: 123 10/01 Lonc 7f v soft

A pottery mover, he is suited by easy ground. Only just managed to stay Goodwood's easy seven furlongs when taking a Group Three in the autumn of 2000, but appears to be acquiring extra stamina with age judging by his performances this term. He took a Listed race at Haydock on ground that may not have suited, but ran his best races in the autumn, when a good second in the Group One Stanley Leisure Sprint Cup in September back at six furlongs, and when winning the Prix de la Foret the following month.

Mount Elbrus

102 **68+**

3-y-o b f Barathea (IRE)-El Jazirah (Kris)
J H M Gosden Sheikh Mohammed

Placings:31 **(4631)**
2001: 8^{3}GS, 9^{1}GF

	Starts	1st	2nd	3rd		Win & Pl
Career Total (Turf)	2	1	0	1		4606
60 9/01 Leic 1m1f218yD					G-F	£4004

Total win prize-money £4004

Going (Turf): Sf: 0-0 GS: 0-1 Gd: 0-0 **GF: 1-1** Fm: 0-0
Distance: 5f/6f: 0-0 7f-8f: 0-1 **9f-13f: 1-1** 14f+: 0-0
Track : LH: 0-0 **RH: 1-1** Tight: 0-0 Gall: 0-0
Aids: Bl: 0-0 Vi: 0-0 Tstrap: 0-0
Best Rating: 68 6/01 Sals 1m gd-sft

She got off the mark on her second start on turf at Leicester.

Mount Joy

107 **100**

2-y-o br c Mtoto-Nightitude (Night Shift (USA))
Saeed Bin Suroor (B W Hills 4/8) Godolphin

Placings:24 **(5500)**
2001: 7^{2}GF, 8^{4}HY

	Starts	1st	2nd	3rd	Win & Pl
Career Total (Turf)	2	0	1	0	11860

Going (Turf): Sf: 0-1 GS: 0-0 Gd: 0-0 GF: 0-1 Fm: 0-0
Distance: 5f/6f: 0-0 7f-8f: 0-2 9f-13f: 0-0 14f+: 0-0
Track : LH: 0-0 RH: 0-0 Tight: 0-0 Gall: 0-0
Aids: Bl: 0-0 Vi: 0-0 Tstrap: 0-0
Best Rating: 100 10/01 Donc 1m heavy

A half-brother to a Listed winner in Italy, he pulled hard when runner-up on his debut at Doncaster, but showed plenty of ability and was snapped up by Godolphin. Far from disgraced in the Racing Post Trophy on his only other start.

Mount Park (IRE)

100(97) (36)**37**

4-y-o b f Colonel Collins (USA)-Make Hay (Nomination)
D W Chapman David W Chapman

Placings:00253/**000006**000000105000-**0**4006**0**000 **(3695)**
2001: **6**^{0}SD, 5^{4}S, 5^{0}GF, 5^{0}GF, 5^{6}G, 6^{0}GF, **5**^{0}SD, 5^{0}GF, 5^{0}G

	Starts	1st	2nd	3rd	Win & Pl
Career Total (Turf)	**24**	**1**	**1**	**1**	**4481**
Career Total (AW)	**8**	**0**	**0**	**0**	**0**

49	7/00	Rdcr	5f	F(0-60)H	G-F	£2404

Total win prize-money £2405

Going (Turf): Sf: 0-5 GS: 0-2 Gd: 0-5 **GF: 1-9** Fm: 0-3
Distance: **5f/6f: 1-22** 7f-8f: 0-10 9f-13f: 0-0 14f+: 0-0
Track : LH: 0-11 RH: 0-3 Tight: 0-3 Gall: 0-3
Aids: **Bl: 1-20** Vi: 0-0 Tstrap: 0-0
Best Rating: 41 5/01 Rdcr 5f soft

Mount Royale (IRE)

99(93) (45)**55**

3-y-o ch g Wolfhound (USA)-Mahabba (USA) (Elocutionist (USA))
N Tinkler Langton Partnership

Placings:0000-606**3**03**1**20220 **(4736)**
2001: 8^{6}S, 8^{0}GF, 7^{6}G, **6**^{3}SD, 6^{0}F, 6^{3}GF, **7**^{1}SD, 7^{2}GS, 6^{0}S, 7^{2}GF, 7^{2}G, 6^{0}F

	Starts	1st	2nd	3rd	Win & Pl
Career Total (Turf)	**14**	**0**	**3**	**1**	**2990**
Career Total (AW)	**2**	**1**	**0**	**1**	**2600**

43	7/01	Sthl	7f	F	STD	£2275

Total win prize-money £2275

Going (Turf): Sf: 0-5 GS: 0-1 Gd: 0-2 GF: 0-4 Fm: 0-2
Distance: 5f/6f: 0-4 **7f-8f: 1-11** 9f-13f: 0-1 14f+: 0-0
Track : **LH: 1-8** RH: 0-1 Tight: 0-1 Gall: 0-1
Aids: Bl: 0-0 Vi: 0-0 **Tstrap: 1-5**
Best Rating: 55 9/01 Folk 7f good

A half-brother to nine winners. Got off the mark when dropping to claiming company on the All-Weather in July 2001. Stays seven furlongs. Acts on a sound surface.

Mount Street (IRE)

96 **95+**

2-y-o b f Pennekamp (USA)-Highland Gift (IRE) (Generous (IRE))
Sir Michael Stoute Lord Weinstock

Placings:2 **(4384)**
2001: 6^{2}GF

	Starts	1st	2nd	3rd	Win & Pl
Career Total (Turf)	**1**	**0**	**1**	**0**	**1440**

Going (Turf): Sf: 0-0 GS: 0-0 Gd: 0-0 GF: 0-1 Fm: 0-0
Distance: 5f/6f: 0-0 7f-8f: 0-1 9f-13f: 0-0 14f+: 0-0
Track : LH: 0-0 RH: 0-0 Tight: 0-0 Gall: 0-0
Aids: Bl: 0-0 Vi: 0-0 Tstrap: 0-0
Best Rating: 95 8/01 Sals 6f212y gd-fm

Mountrath Rock

91 **30**

4-y-o b f Rock Hopper-Point Of Law (Law Society (USA))
Miss B Sanders Racingclubcouk

Placings:0220/00044015665-60 **(5023)**
2001: 7^{6}GF, 7^{0}S

	Starts	1st	2nd	3rd	Win & Pl
Career Total (Turf)	**17**	**1**	**2**	**0**	**3245**

49	6/00	Nott	1m54y	G(0-60)H	G-F	£2094

Total win prize-money £2094

Going (Turf): Sf: 0-3 GS: 0-1 Gd: 0-4 **GF: 1-8** Fm: 0-1
Distance: 5f/6f: 0-2 7f-8f: 0-5 **9f-13f: 1-10** 14f+: 0-0
Track : **LH: 1-8** RH: 0-5 Tight: 0-5 Gall: 0-0
Aids: Bl: 0-3 **Vi: 1-6** Tstrap: 0-2
Best Rating: 26 8/01 Brig 7f214y gd-fm

Mousehole

106 **67**

9-y-o b g Statoblest-Alo Ez (Alzao (USA))
R Guest Mrs Janet Linskey

Placings:0/003212400/00521236052/00420212310/000 6332120105000/001042311123606/0000020210000-00301240204000 **(5462)**
2001: 5^{0}HY, 5^{0}GS, 5^{3}GF, 5^{0}GF, 5^{1}F, 5^{2}F, 5^{4}GF, 5^{0}GF, 5^{2}GF, 5^{0}G, 5^{4}GF, 5^{0}G, 5^{0}G, 5^{0}G

	Starts	1st	2nd	3rd	Win & Pl
Career Total (Turf)	**92**	**12**	**16**	**8**	**62084**

66	6/01	Nott	5f13y	D(0-85)H	FRM	£4088
71	7/00	Sand	5f6y	D(0-80)H	G-F	£4348
71	8/99	Wind	5f10y	E(0-70)H	G-F	£2766
66	7/99	Nott	5f13y	E(0-65)	G-F	£3021
65	7/99	Wind	5f10y	E(0-70)H	G-F	£2710
61	5/99	Nott	5f13y	E(0-70)H	FRM	£3431
77	8/98	Bath	5f11y	E(0-70)	FRM	£2775
70	7/98	Carl	5f	F(0-65)	G-F	£2542
72	8/97	Bath	5f11y	E(0-70)	GD	£2820
63	7/97	Wwck	5f	E(0-70)	G-F	£3018
63	6/96	Wind	5f10y	F(0-60)	G-F	£2717
65	6/95	Thsk	6f	E(0-70)H	G-F	£3634

Total win prize-money £37872

Going (Turf): Sf: 0-8 GS: 0-6 Gd: 1-32 **GF: 8-40** Fm: 3-6
Distance: **5f/6f: 12-88** 7f-8f: 0-4 9f-13f: 0-0 14f+: 0-0
Track : LH: 3-11 **RH: 4-10** Tight: 0-1 **Gall: 7-18**
Aids: **Bl: 1-7** Vi: 0-0 Tstrap: 0-0
Best Rating: 74 7/01 Sand 5f6y gd-fm

Fair sprint handicapper who needs everything to fall his way to score. Best when able to come from behind over five furlongs on fast ground.

Mouton (IRE)

(97) (36?)**29**

5-y-o b m Dolphin Street (FR)-The Queen Of Soul (Chief Singer)
J J Bridger W Wood

Placings:02/5322/**505**00006000**0035-00560** **(0421)**
2001: **6**^{0}SD, **7**^{0}SD, **6**^{5}SD, **7**^{6}SW, **6**^{0}SD

	Starts	1st	2nd	3rd	Win & Pl
Career Total (Turf)	**13**	**0**	**3**	**1**	**3131**
Career Total (AW)	**13**	**0**	**0**	**1**	**390**

Going (Turf): Sf: 0-1 GS: 0-2 Gd: 0-4 GF: 0-5 Fm: 0-1
Distance: 5f/6f: 0-9 7f-8f: 0-11 9f-13f: 0-6 14f+: 0-0
Track : LH: 0-16 RH: 0-7 Tight: 0-18 Gall: 0-2
Aids: Bl: 0-0 Vi: 0-0 Tstrap: 0-0
Best Rating: 36 1/01 Ling 6f stand

Mouwadh (USA)

100 **68**

3-y-o b/br f Nureyev (USA)-Min Alhawa (USA) (Riverman (USA))
M P Tregoning Hamdan Al Maktoum

Placings:40 **(4842)**
2001: 8^{4}G, 8^{0}G

	Starts	1st	2nd	3rd	Win & Pl
Career Total (Turf)	**2**	**0**	**0**	**0**	**325**

Going (Turf): Sf: 0-0 GS: 0-0 Gd: 0-2 GF: 0-0 Fm: 0-0
Distance: 5f/6f: 0-0 7f-8f: 0-0 9f-13f: 0-2 14f+: 0-0
Track : LH: 0-1 RH: 0-1 Tight: 0-1 Gall: 0-0
Aids: Bl: 0-0 Vi: 0-0 Tstrap: 0-0
Best Rating: 68 8/01 Wind 1m67y good

Movie King (IRE)

92 **67**

2-y-o ch c Catrail (USA)-Marilyn (IRE) (King's Lake (USA))
A P Jarvis Jarvis Associates

Placings:300 **(2745)**
2001: 5^{3}GF, 6^{0}G, 7^{0}GF

	Starts	1st	2nd	3rd	Win & Pl
Career Total (Turf)	**3**	**0**	**0**	**1**	**428**

Going (Turf): Sf: 0-0 GS: 0-0 Gd: 0-1 GF: 0-2 Fm: 0-0
Distance: 5f/6f: 0-1 7f-8f: 0-2 9f-13f: 0-0 14f+: 0-0
Track : LH: 0-1 RH: 0-0 Tight: 0-1 Gall: 0-0
Aids: Bl: 0-0 Vi: 0-0 Tstrap: 0-0
Best Rating: 67 5/01 Haml 5f4y gd-fm

Moving Experience (IRE)

103 **64**

4-y-o b f Nicolotte-Sound Performance (IRE) (Ahonoora)
D W P Arbuthnot The Moving Partnership

Placings:04/04060-123510 **(5275)**
2001: 7^{1}GF, 9^{2}GF, 9^{3}GF, 8^{5}GF, 8^{1}G, 8^{0}GS

	Starts	1st	2nd	3rd	Win & Pl
Career Total (Turf)	**13**	**2**	**1**	**1**	**10435**

64	9/01	Gdwd	1m	E(0-65)H	GD	£4819
57	6/01	Brig	7f214y	E(0-70)H	G-F	£2856

Total win prize-money £7676

Going (Turf): Sf: 0-3 GS: 0-4 **Gd: 1-2 GF: 1-4** Fm: 0-0
Distance: 5f/6f: 0-1 **7f-8f: 2-3** 9f-13f: 0-9 14f+: 0-0
Track : LH: 1-3 RH: 1-7 Tight: 0-6 Gall: 0-1
Aids: Bl: 0-0 Vi: 0-0 Tstrap: 0-0
Best Rating: 64 9/01 Gdwd 1m good

Moderate handicapper who is best suited by hold-up tactics and seven to nine furlongs. She acts well on a sound surface.

Mowaadah (IRE)

108 **89**

3-y-o b f Alzao (USA)-Mahrah (USA) (Vaguely Noble)
A C Stewart Hamdan Al Maktoum

Placings:221110 **(5607)**
2001: 8^{2}GF, 8^{2}GF, 8^{1}GF, 8^{1}G, 8^{1}S, 8^{0}GS

	Starts	1st	2nd	3rd	Win & Pl
Career Total (Turf)	**6**	**3**	**2**	**0**	**32138**

89	9/01	Asct	1m	A(0-105)H	SFT	£18560
84	9/01	Kemp	1m	D(0-85)H	GD	£6266
80	8/01	Pont	1m4y	D	G-F	£4290

Total win prize-money £29116

Going (Turf): Sf: 1-1 GS: 0-1 **Gd: 1-1 GF: 1-3** Fm: 0-0
Distance: 5f/6f: 0-0 **7f-8f: 2-5** 9f-13f: 1-1 14f+: 0-0
Track : LH: 1-1 RH: 1-2 Tight: 0-0 Gall: 0-1
Aids: Bl: 0-0 Vi: 0-0 Tstrap: 0-0
Best Rating: 89 9/01 Asct 1m soft

Unraced at two, she finished runner-up in her first two starts, but made no mistake at Pontefract in August before taking a Kempton handicap the following month. Given a fine ride when just holding on in Listed event at Ascot, she is suited by a mile and, although effective on soft ground, appears best on fast.

Mowbray (USA)

103 **93**

6-y-o b/br g Opening Verse (USA)-Peppy Raja (USA) (Raja Baba (USA))
G L Moore Graham Parker

Placings:21142/442614/400201305/5604403050-60 **(1541)**
2001: 16^{6}GS, 14^{0}GF

	Starts	1st	2nd	3rd	Win & Pl
Career Total (Turf)	**32**	**4**	**4**	**2**	**140949**

94	7/99	Gdwd	1m6f	B(0-105)H	G-F	£32250
100	10/98	Leic	1m3f183yC		HVY	£5591
97	8/97	Kemp	7f	C	GD	£4393
77	8/97	Catt	7f	D	G-F	£3411

Total win prize-money £45647

Going (Turf):	Sf: 1-6 GS: 0-2 Gd: 1-11 **GF: 2-11** Fm: 0-1
Distance:	5f/6f: 0-0 **7f-8f: 2-5** 9f-13f: 1-12 14f+: 1-15
Track :	LH: 1-14 **RH: 3-18 Tight: 2-10** Gall: 1-16
Aids:	Bl: 0-3 Vi: 0-1 Tstrap: 0-0
Best Rating: 87	5/01 Gdwd 1m6f gd-fm

He carries his head high and is a tricky customer. Best around a mile and three-quarters, he is not one to rely on.

Mowelga

80 **104**

7-y-o ch g Most Welcome-Galactic Miss (Damister (USA))

Lady Herries L G Lazarus

Placings:031/123110/1020-0 **(5132)**

2001: 12^{0}G

	Starts	1st	2nd	3rd	Win & Pl
Career Total (Turf)	**14**	**5**	**2**	**2**	**47526**

98	4/00	NmkR	1m4f	C(0-95)H	G-S	£7553
92	8/98	Newb	1m4f5y	C(0-90)	GD	£7889
92	8/98	Pont	1m4f8y	C(0-90)H	G-F	£7440
81	5/98	Donc	1m2f60y	C(0-90)H	G-F	£8025
61	10/97	Newb	1m2f6y	D	GD	£3938

Total win prize-money £34846

Going (Turf):	Sf: 0-2 GS: 1-1 **Gd: 2-5 GF: 2-6** Fm: 0-0
Distance:	5f/6f: 0-0 7f-8f: 0-1 **9f-13f: 5-12** 14f+: 0-1
Track :	**LH: 4-8** RH: 1-5 Tight: 0-1 **Gall: 4-10**
Aids:	Bl: 0-0 Vi: 0-0 Tstrap: 0-0
Best Rating: 40	10/01 NmkR 1m4f good

A very useful middle-distance handicapper at his best, he was in fine form in 1998 and successfully returned from missing a season to win at Newmarket at the start of the 2000 season. Off the track after September of that year for another year, he returned in a Listed race, but was well held. Best held up off a fast pace. A mile and a half is his trip. Has won on fast and good ground.

Moyne Pleasure (IRE)

97 (107) (88) **78d**

3-y-o b c Exit To Nowhere (USA)-Ilanga (IRE) (Common Grounds)

J A Osborne Berkeley Land Limited

Placings:0511063-35110000030600 **(3679)**

2001: 7^{3}SD, 7^{5}SD, 8^{1}SD, 9^{1}SD, 10^{0}SD, 8^{0}GS, 9^{0}GS, 8^{0}GF, 10^{3}GF, 8^{0}GF, 8^{6}G, 9^{0}GF, 8^{0}G

	Starts	1st	2nd	3rd	Win & Pl
Career Total (Turf)	**9**	**0**	**0**	**1**	**986**
Career Total (AW)	**11**	**4**	**0**	**2**	**15459**

83	3/01	Wolv	1m1f79y	C	STD	£6090
88	2/01	Wolv	1m100y	D(0-80)H	STD	£3805
82	11/00	Sthl	7f	E(0-75)	STD	£2884
69	10/00	Wolv	6f	F	STD	£1757

Total win prize-money £14537

Going (Turf):	**Sf: 0-0 GS: 0-3 Gd: 0-2 GF: 0-4 Fm: 0-0**
Distance:	5f/6f: 1-2 7f-8f: 1-10 **9f-13f: 2-8** 14f+: 0-0
Track :	**LH: 4-14** RH: 0-3 **Tight: 3-13** Gall: 0-0
Aids:	Bl: 0-0 Vi: 0-0 Tstrap: 0-0
Best Rating: 88	2/01 Wolv 1m100y stand

Only had the one outing on turf before switching to the artificial surfaces. Prefers Wolverhampton over eight and nine furlongs. Not so good on turf this season.

Moynoe Princess (IRE)

(88) (11) **36**

7-y-o b m Distinctly North (USA)-First String (FR) (What A Guest)

P D Evans P D Evans

Placings:05565/6064/0/0000/360-000 **(0161)**

2001: 14^{0}SD, 11^{0}SD, 16^{0}SD

	Starts	1st	2nd	3rd	Win & Pl
Career Total (Turf)	**17**	**0**	**0**	**1**	**560**
Career Total (AW)	**3**	**0**	**0**	**0**	

Going (Turf):	**Sf: 0-1 GS: 0-0 Gd: 0-3 GF: 0-6 Fm: 0-0**
Distance:	5f/6f: 0-1 7f-8f: 0-4 9f-13f: 0-13 14f+: 0-2
Track :	LH: 0-5 RH: 0-15 Tight: 0-1 Gall: 0-0
Aids:	Bl: 0-0 Vi: 0-1 Tstrap: 0-0
Best Rating: 11	1/01 Sthl 1m6f stand

Mozart (IRE)

(99) **127**

3-y-o b c Danehill (USA)-Victoria Cross (USA) (Spectacular Bid (USA))

A P O'Brien Mrs John Magnier & Mr M Tabor

Placings:114-3321110 **(5576a)**

2001: 8^{3}S, 7^{3}G, 8^{2}GY, 7^{1}GF, 6^{1}G, 5^{1}G, 6^{0}FT

	Starts	1st	2nd	3rd	Win & Pl
Career Total (Turf)	**9**	**5**	**1**	**2**	**582875**
Career Total (AW)	**1**	**0**	**0**	**0**	

123	8/01	York	5f	A	GD	£107300
127	7/01	NmkJ	6f	A	GD	£133400
109	6/01	Asct	7f	A	G-F	£42000
109	9/00	NmkR	7f	B	G-S	£229200
80	7/00	Curr	7f		GD	£6900

Total win prize-money £518800

Going (Turf):	Sf: 0-1 GS: 1-2 **Gd: 3-4** GF: 1-1 Fm: 0-0
Distance:	5f/6f: 2-3 **7f-8f: 3-7** 9f-13f: 0-0 14f+: 0-0
Track :	LH: 0-1 RH: 0-0 Tight: 0-0 Gall: 0-0
Aids:	Bl: 0-0 Vi: 0-0 Tstrap: 0-1
Best Rating: 127	7/01 NmkJ 6f good

Winner of two of his three races and fourth in the Dewhurst as a juvenile, he was below par earlier this season but ran a cracker in the Irish Guineas, only swallowed up inside the last by stablemate Black Minnaloushe. He landed a massive gamble in the Jersey Stakes, before being dropped in trip and stamping himself an outstanding sprinter by making all in the July Cup and then taking the Nunthorpe. He failed to act on the dirt when well beaten in the Breeders' Cup Sprint, but was still the champion European sprinter. He has retired to Coolmore Stud in Ireland.

Mr Blue Sky (IRE)

(93) (76) **76**

2-y-o b c Blues Traveller (IRE)-Faypool (IRE) (Fayruz)

G C H Chung Wilwyn Racing (wwwwilwyncom)

Placings:63551 **(5417)**

2001: 5^{6}G, 6^{3}G, 5^{5}G, 6^{5}HY, 7^{1}SD

	Starts	1st	2nd	3rd	Win & Pl
Career Total (Turf)	**4**	**0**	**0**	**1**	**614**
Career Total (AW)	**1**	**1**	**0**	**0**	**2905**

76	10/01	Wolv	7f	E	STD	£2905

Total win prize-money £2905

Going (Turf):	**Sf: 0-1 GS: 0-0 Gd: 0-3 GF: 0-0 Fm: 0-0**
Distance:	5f/6f: 0-4 **7f-8f: 1-1** 9f-13f: 0-0 14f+: 0-0
Track :	**LH: 1-2** RH: 0-0 **Tight: 1-1** Gall: 0-1
Aids:	Bl: 0-0 Vi: 0-0 Tstrap: 0-0
Best Rating: 76	10/01 Wolv 7f stand

Got off the mark when stepped up to seven furlongs on the Wolverhampton Fibresand in October.

Mr Bountiful (IRE)

(88) (37) **51**

3-y-o b g Mukaddamah (USA)-Nawadder (Kris)

Mrs J R Ramsden Mrs Claire Hollowood

Placings:0000-0020000260 **(5350)**

2001: 6^{0}HY, 5^{0}GF, 5^{7}GF, 6^{0}GF, 7^{0}GF, 6^{0}F, 5^{0}GF, 5^{7}GF, 5^{6}S, 5^{0}SD

	Starts	1st	2nd	3rd	Win & Pl
Career Total (Turf)	**12**	**0**	**2**	**0**	**1953**
Career Total (AW)	**2**	**0**	**0**	**0**	

Going (Turf):	**Sf: 0-2 GS: 0-0 Gd: 0-2 GF: 0-7 Fm: 0-1**
Distance:	5f/6f: 0-12 7f-8f: 0-2 9f-13f: 0-0 14f+: 0-0
Track :	LH: 0-2 RH: 0-1 Tight: 0-1 Gall: 0-1
Aids:	Bl: 0-0 Vi: 0-0 Tstrap: 0-0
Best Rating: 55	6/01 Newc 5f gd-fm

He ran a fine race to finish runner-up at Newcastle in June, and again at Thirsk in September, but does not look the easiest of rides. He is at his best over five furlongs.

Mr Busby

(89) (25)

8-y-o b g La Grange Music-Top-Anna (IRE) (Ela-Mana-Mou)

John A Harris (J L Harris 16/4) D Wilcox & Mrs A Sedgwick

Placings:5 **(0287)**

2001: 12^{5}SW

	Starts	1st	2nd	3rd	Win & Pl
Career Total (Turf)	**0**	**0**	**0**	**0**	
Career Total (AW)	**1**	**0**	**0**	**0**	**0**

Going (Turf):	**Sf: 0-0 GS: 0-0 Gd: 0-0 GF: 0-0 Fm: 0-0**
Distance:	5f/6f: 0-0 7f-8f: 0-0 9f-13f: 0-1 14f+: 0-0
Track :	LH: 0-1 RH: 0-0 Tight: 0-1 Gall: 0-0
Aids:	Bl: 0-0 Vi: 0-0 Tstrap: 0-0
Best Rating: 25	2/01 Wolv 1m4f slow

Mr Carrigann (IRE)

91 **29**

8-y-o b g Commanche Run-Madam's Well (Pitpan)

M Tate P J Kennedy

Placings:00 **(2624)**

2001: 7^{0}GF, 12^{0}GF

	Starts	1st	2nd	3rd	Win & Pl
Career Total (Turf)	**2**	**0**	**0**	**0**	

Going (Turf):	**Sf: 0-0 GS: 0-0 Gd: 0-0 GF: 0-2 Fm: 0-0**
Distance:	5f/6f: 0-0 7f-8f: 0-1 9f-13f: 0-1 14f+: 0-0
Track :	LH: 0-2 RH: 0-0 Tight: 0-0 Gall: 0-1
Aids:	Bl: 0-0 Vi: 0-0 Tstrap: 0-0
Best Rating: 29	5/01 Wwck 7f26y gd-fm

Lightly raced. Stays two and a half miles over hurldes. Acts on a sound surface.

Mr Chestnut Tree

(75) (31) **61**

2-y-o b g Forzando-Sure Flyer (IRE) (Sure Blade (USA))

M R Channon Noel Wabe

Placings:003603200 **(5410)**

2001: 5^{0}GS, 5^{0}GF, 6^{3}GF, 6^{6}GF, 6^{0}GF, 7^{3}GF, 8^{2}GF, 7^{0}G, 7^{0}SD

	Starts	1st	2nd	3rd	Win & Pl
Career Total (Turf)	**8**	**0**	**1**	**2**	**1556**
Career Total (AW)	**1**	**0**	**0**	**0**	

Going (Turf):	**Sf: 0-0 GS: 0-1 Gd: 0-1 GF: 0-6 Fm: 0-0**
Distance:	5f/6f: 0-3 7f-8f: 0-5 9f-13f: 0-1 14f+: 0-0
Track :	LH: 0-4 RH: 0-1 Tight: 0-0 Gall: 0-2
Aids:	Bl: 0-0 Vi: 0-1 Tstrap: 0-0
Best Rating: 61	9/01 Leic 1m9y gd-fm

Beaten in sellers before a good run in a nursery. Just touched off in a selling nursery at Leicester and should be capable of winning in that grade. Stays a mile and acts on fast ground.

Mr Combustible (IRE)

110 **117**

3-y-o b c Hernando (FR)-Warg (Dancing Brave (USA))

B W Hills R A N Bonnycastle

Placings:02-214613 **(4711)**
2001: 10^{2}S, 12^{1}GF, 12^{4}GF, 12^{0}Y, 13^{1}GF, 14^{3}G

	Starts	1st	2nd	3rd	Win & Pl
Career Total (Turf)	8	2	2	1	179137

117 8/01 Newb 1m5f61y A G-F £35700
108 5/01 Ches 1m4f66y A G-F £36000
Total win prize-money £71700

Going (Turf): Sf: 0-1 GS: 0-2 Gd: 0-1 **GF: 2-3** Fm: 0-0
Distance: 5f/6f: 0-0 7f-8f: 0-1 9f-13f: 1-5 14f+: 1-2
Track : **LH: 2-6** RH: 0-0 Tight: 1-2 Gall: 1-3
Aids: Bl: 0-0 Vi: 0-0 Tstrap: 0-0
Best Rating: 117 8/01 Newb 1m5f61y gd-fm

Smart middle-distance performer, half-brother to Ribblesdale winner Miletrian. Ran out a very game winner of the Chester Vase in May, making all and holding off a strong challenge from Snowstorm. Stepped up on that effort with a fine fourth in the Derby, beaten five lengths behind Galileo, but could not improve on that in the Irish version. Beat Millenary fair and square at Newbury when stepped up in trip and finished third to Milan in the St Leger.

Mr Cospector

96 **62**

4-y-o b g Cosmonaut-L'Ancressaan (Dalsaan)
T H Caldwell R Cabrera-Vargas

Placings:5400/100400-2006 **(2790)**
2001: 9^{2}HY, 8^{0}S, 10^{0}G, 14^{6}GF

	Starts	1st	2nd	3rd	Win & Pl
Career Total (Turf)	14	1	1	0	5136

80 4/00 Hayd 7f30y D HVY £4043
Total win prize-money £4043

Going (Turf): **Sf: 1-5** GS: 0-2 Gd: 0-3 GF: 0-4 Fm: 0-0
Distance: 5f/6f: 0-3 **7f-8f: 1-4** 9f-13f: 0-6 14f+: 0-1
Track : **LH: 1-10** RH: 0-2 Tight: 0-1 Gall: 0-1
Aids: Bl: 0-0 Vi: 0-0 Tstrap: 0-0
Best Rating: 62 4/01 Nott 1m1f213y heavy

Mr Dinos (IRE)

102 **93**

2-y-o b c Desert King (IRE)-Spear Dance (Gay Fandango (USA))
P F I Cole C Shiacolas

Placings:2 **(3407)**
2001: 7^{2}GF

	Starts	1st	2nd	3rd	Win & Pl
Career Total (Turf)	1	0	1	0	2100

Going (Turf): Sf: 0-0 GS: 0-0 Gd: 0-0 GF: 0-1 Fm: 0-0
Distance: 5f/6f: 0-0 7f-8f: 0-1 9f-13f: 0-0 14f+: 0-0
Track : LH: 0-0 RH: 0-0 Tight: 0-0 Gall: 0-0
Aids: Bl: 0-0 Vi: 0-0 Tstrap: 0-0
Best Rating: 93 7/01 Asct 7f gd-fm

Mr Ed (IRE)

104 **70**

3-y-o ch g In The Wings-Center Moriches (IRE) (Magical Wonder (USA))
D R C Elsworth Del & Jake Partnership

Placings:0-652010 **(4952)**
2001: 9^{6}F, 9^{5}GF, 11^{2}GF, 14^{0}GF, 9^{1}GF, 11^{0}G

	Starts	1st	2nd	3rd	Win & Pl
Career Total (Turf)	7	1	1	0	4700

67 8/01 Sals 1m1f198yE(0-70)H G-F £3430
Total win prize-money £3430

Going (Turf): Sf: 0-0 GS: 0-0 Gd: 0-1 **GF: 1-5** Fm: 0-1
Distance: 5f/6f: 0-1 7f-8f: 0-0 **9f-13f: 1-5** 14f+: 0-1
Track : LH: 0-1 **RH: 1-4 Tight: 1-4** Gall: 0-1
Aids: Bl: 0-0 Vi: 0-0 Tstrap: 0-0
Best Rating: 70 7/01 Wind 1m3f135y gd-fm

A fair handicapper with just one success to his name over ten furlongs at Salisbury in the summer of 2001. Acts on a sound surface. Failed to stay a mile and six but should stay a mile and a half.

Mr Fitzer

37

2-y-o b g Robellino (USA)-Tiszta Sharok (Song)
M C Chapman Leo Fitzpatrick

Placings:0000 **(4325)**
2001: 5^{0}HD, 5^{0}GF, 7^{0}G, 5^{0}GF

	Starts	1st	2nd	3rd	Win & Pl
Career Total (Turf)	4	0	0	0	

Going (Turf): Sf: 0-0 GS: 0-0 Gd: 0-1 GF: 0-2 Fm: 0-1
Distance: 5f/6f: 0-3 7f-8f: 0-1 9f-13f: 0-0 14f+: 0-0
Track : LH: 0-1 RH: 0-0 Tight: 0-0 Gall: 0-1
Aids: Bl: 0-0 Vi: 0-0 Tstrap: 0-0
Best Rating: 37 7/01 Bevl 5f gd-fm

Mr Fortywinks (IRE)

106(97) (70)**62**

7-y-o ch g Fool's Holme (USA)-Dream On (Absalom)
J L Eyre Miss Nuala Cassidy

Placings:5030/061222413/213212000400/2252101143 0300/20413414025-1305200040 **(5661)**
2001: 16^{1}S, 16^{3}GF, 16^{0}GF, 15^{5}GF, 13^{2}G, 16^{0}GS, 15^{0}S, 14^{0}G, 13^{4}GS, 16^{0}G

	Starts	1st	2nd	3rd	Win & Pl
Career Total (Turf)	52	8	10	5	48631
Career Total (AW)	8	2	2	2	7077

65 4/01 Ripn 2m C(0-90)H SFT £7150
63 9/00 Rdcr 1m6f19y E(0-70)H SFT £3133
61 6/00 Newc 1m4f93y F(0-60) SFT £2649
62 7/99 Carl 1m4f E(0-70)H GD £2840
61 6/99 Ripn 1m4f60y E(0-70)H G-F £2814
57 5/99 Haml 1m5f9y E(0-70)H SFT £2801
58 4/98 Nott 1m1f213yF(0-75)H SFT £2616
61 1/98 Sthl 1m3f G(0-65)H STD £1735
63 11/97 Wolv 1m4f F(0-60)H STD £2294
44 8/97 Haml 1m1f36y F GD £2514
Total win prize-money £30547

Going (Turf): Sf: 5-12 GS: 0-6 Gd: 2-16 GF: 1-16 Fm: 0-2
Distance: 5f/6f: 0-6 7f-8f: 0-0 **9f-13f: 7-26** 14f+: 3-28
Track : LH: 5-32 RH: 5-24 **Tight: 6-35** Gall: 1-9
Aids: Bl: 0-0 Vi: 0-0 Tstrap: 0-1
Best Rating: 68 5/01 Thsk 2m gd-fm

An able if modest middle-distance performer. Notched up ten career wins at Ripon in April 2001 at up to two miles. Looked held by the Handicapper during the summer but has slipped back to a winning mark now. Suited by soft ground.

Mr George Smith

(94) (31)**31**

4-y-o b g Prince Sabo-Nellie's Gamble (Mummy's Game)
G L Moore George Smith Ltd

Placings:0000313/0-0060 **(0479)**
2001: 7^{0}SD, 8^{0}SW, 7^{6}SW, 7^{0}SD

	Starts	1st	2nd	3rd	Win & Pl
Career Total (Turf)	5	0	0	0	
Career Total (AW)	7	1	0	2	3583

56 12/99 Ling 7f E(0-75)H STD £2791
Total win prize-money £2792

Going (Turf): Sf: 0-1 GS: 0-0 Gd: 0-1 GF: 0-3 Fm: 0-0
Distance: 5f/6f: 0-3 **7f-8f: 1-8** 9f-13f: 0-1 14f+: 0-0
Track : **LH: 1-9** RH: 0-2 **Tight: 1-8** Gall: 0-1
Aids: Bl: 0-1 Vi: 0-0 Tstrap: 0-0
Best Rating: 31 1/01 Ling 7f stand

Mr Gisby (USA)

92 **72**

3-y-o b g Chief's Crown (USA)-Double Lock (Home Guard (USA))
D R C Elsworth Nightmare Partnership

Placings:4550 **(5106)**
2001: 10^{4}GF, 9^{5}GF, 9^{5}G, 12^{0}GS

	Starts	1st	2nd	3rd	Win & Pl
Career Total (Turf)	4	0	0	0	306

Going (Turf): Sf: 0-0 GS: 0-1 Gd: 0-1 GF: 0-2 Fm: 0-0
Distance: 5f/6f: 0-0 7f-8f: 0-0 9f-13f: 0-4 14f+: 0-0
Track : LH: 0-1 RH: 0-2 Tight: 0-2 Gall: 0-2
Aids: Bl: 0-0 Vi: 0-0 Tstrap: 0-0
Best Rating: 72 7/01 Wind 1m2f7y gd-fm

Mr Lear (USA)

77 **53**

2-y-o b c Lear Fan (USA)-Majestic Mae (USA) (Crow (FR))
T D Barron Christine Townley & Ms Laura Townley

Placings:600 **(3491)**
2001: 5^{6}GF, 5^{0}GF, 5^{0}GF

	Starts	1st	2nd	3rd	Win & Pl
Career Total (Turf)	3	0	0	0	0

Going (Turf): Sf: 0-0 GS: 0-0 Gd: 0-0 GF: 0-3 Fm: 0-0
Distance: 5f/6f: 0-3 7f-8f: 0-0 9f-13f: 0-0 14f+: 0-0
Track : LH: 0-0 RH: 0-1 Tight: 0-0 Gall: 0-1
Aids: Bl: 0-0 Vi: 0-0 Tstrap: 0-0
Best Rating: 53 6/01 Newc 5f gd-fm

Mr Mahoose (USA)

105(84) (55)**96+**

3-y-o b g Rakeen (USA)-Golden Hen (USA) (Native Prospector (USA))
W J Haggas Wentworth Racing (pty) Ltd

Placings:3-511216 **(5005)**
2001: 8^{5}SD, 6^{1}GF, 7^{1}S, 7^{2}GF, 7^{1}GF, 7^{6}S

	Starts	1st	2nd	3rd	Win & Pl
Career Total (Turf)	6	3	1	1	18793
Career Total (AW)	1	0	0	0	0

96 8/01 NmkJ 7f C(0-90)H G-F £7036
64 7/01 Hayd 7f30y D(0-75) SFT £4446
65 6/01 Newc 6f E G-F £3234
Total win prize-money £14716

Going (Turf): Sf: 1-2 GS: 0-1 Gd: 0-0 **GF: 2-3** Fm: 0-0
Distance: 5f/6f: 1-2 **7f-8f: 2-5** 9f-13f: 0-0 14f+: 0-0
Track : **LH: 1-2** RH: 0-1 Tight: 0-0 Gall: 0-1
Aids: Bl: 0-0 Vi: 0-0 Tstrap: 0-0
Best Rating: 96 8/01 NmkJ 7f gd-fm

Got off the mark over six furlongs at Newcastle on his second start at three and followed up in good style over an extra furlong at Haydock on very different ground. Consistent sort who took a competitive handicap at Newmarket in August. Suited by six to seven furlongs on soft or good to firm. Looks progressive.

Mr Micky (IRE)

84 **45**

3-y-o b g Rudimentary (USA)-Top Berry (High Top)
T D Easterby David & Steven Dudley

Placings:0600 **(5190)**
2001: 10^{0}GS, 12^{6}GF, 10^{0}GF, 11^{0}GS

	Starts	1st	2nd	3rd	Win & Pl
Career Total (Turf)	4	0	0	0	0

Going (Turf): Sf: 0-0 GS: 0-2 Gd: 0-0 GF: 0-2 Fm: 0-0
Distance: 5f/6f: 0-0 7f-8f: 0-0 9f-13f: 0-4 14f+: 0-0
Track : LH: 0-4 RH: 0-0 Tight: 0-2 Gall: 0-0
Aids: Bl: 0-0 Vi: 0-0 Tstrap: 0-0
Best Rating: 45 5/01 Thsk 1m4f gd-fm

Mr Midaz

93 **67**

2-y-o ch c Danzig Connection (USA)-Marmy (Midyan (USA))
Jedd O'Keeffe Peter Charter

Placings:430020 **(5340)**
2001: 5^{4}GF, 5^{3}G, 7^{0}GS, 6^{0}GF, 7^{2}GF, 6^{0}GS

	Starts	1st	2nd	3rd	Win & Pl
Career Total (Turf)	6	0	1	1	1830

Going (Turf): Sf: 0-0 GS: 0-2 Gd: 0-1 GF: 0-3 Fm: 0-0
Distance: 5f/6f: 0-4 7f-8f: 0-2 9f-13f: 0-0 14f+: 0-0
Track : LH: 0-1 RH: 0-0 Tight: 0-1 Gall: 0-0
Aids: Bl: 0-0 Vi: 0-0 Tstrap: 0-0
Best Rating: 67 9/01 Rdcr 7f gd-fm

A February foal who was cheaply bought. Ran his best race when returned to seven furlongs in September on a sound surface.

Mr Monroe

44

2-y-o b c Mistertopogigo (IRE)-Highland Heights (IRE) (Lomond (USA))
C Smith C Smith

Placings:5 **(5596)**
2001: 8^{5}GS

	Starts	1st	2nd	3rd	Win & Pl
Career Total (Turf)	1	0	0	0	234

Going (Turf): Sf: 0-0 GS: 0-1 Gd: 0-0 GF: 0-0 Fm: 0-0
Distance: 5f/6f: 0-0 7f-8f: 0-1 9f-13f: 0-0 14f+: 0-0
Track : LH: 0-0 RH: 0-0 Tight: 0-0 Gall: 0-0
Aids: Bl: 0-0 Vi: 0-0 Tstrap: 0-0
Best Rating: 44 11/01 NmkR 1m gd-sft

Mr Oboe

95 **44**

3-y-o b g Charnwood Forest (IRE)-Miss Clarinet (Pharly (FR))
Andrew Turnell Dr John Hollowood

Placings:660 **(5286)**
2001: 11^{6}G, 8^{6}HY, 10^{0}HY

	Starts	1st	2nd	3rd	Win & Pl
Career Total (Turf)	3	0	0	0	0

Going (Turf): Sf: 0-2 GS: 0-0 Gd: 0-1 GF: 0-0 Fm: 0-0
Distance: 5f/6f: 0-0 7f-8f: 0-0 9f-13f: 0-3 14f+: 0-0
Track : LH: 0-2 RH: 0-1 Tight: 0-1 Gall: 0-0
Aids: Bl: 0-0 Vi: 0-0 Tstrap: 0-0
Best Rating: 44 9/01 Hayd 1m30y heavy

Mr Perry (IRE)

(90) (33)**42**

5-y-o br g Perugino (USA)-Elegant Tune (USA) (Alysheba (USA))
R M Stronge (A Crook 16/5) Peter J Douglas Engineering

Placings:20602041500/002300600000**6**56-00 **(0796)**
2001: 8^{0}SW, 6^{0}SD

	Starts	1st	2nd	3rd	Win & Pl
Career Total (Turf)	21	0	2	1	2415
Career Total (AW)	7	1	1	0	3744

66 9/99 Wolv 1m100y E(0-70)H STD £2967
Total win prize-money £2967

Going (Turf): Sf: 0-6 GS: 0-4 Gd: 0-3 GF: 0-4 Fm: 0-4
Distance: 5f/6f: 0-1 7f-8f: 0-15 **9f-13f: 1-12** 14f+: 0-0
Track : **LH: 1-16** RH: 0-0 **Tight: 1-16** Gall. 0-2
Aids: Bl: 0-5 Vi: 0-3 Tstrap: 0-0
Best Rating: 15 4/01 Sthl 6f stand

Mr Pertemps

103(81) (48)**49**

3-y-o b g Primo Dominie-Amber Mill (Doulab (USA))
S C Williams Pertemps Flexipeople Owners Syndicate

Placings:0602-02 **(5129)**
2001: 5^{0}G, 7^{2}HY

	Starts	1st	2nd	3rd	Win & Pl
Career Total (Turf)	5	0	2	0	2321
Career Total (AW)	1	0	0	0	0

Going (Turf): Sf: 0-3 GS: 0-0 Gd: 0-1 GF: 0-1 Fm: 0-0
Distance: 5f/6f: 0-4 7f-8f: 0-2 9f-13f: 0-0 14f+: 0-0
Track : LH: 0-1 RH: 0-0 Tight: 0-0 Gall: 0-0
Aids: Bl: 0-0 Vi: 0-0 Tstrap: 0-0
Best Rating: 49 10/01 Ling 7f heavy

Mr Piano Man (IRE)

88 **66d**

3-y-o gr g Paris House-Winter March (Ballad Rock)
J L Eyre Mrs S J Yates

Placings:3050-00 **(1593)**
2001: 6^{0}GF, 5^{0}GF

	Starts	1st	2nd	3rd	Win & Pl
Career Total (Turf)	6	0	0	1	450

Going (Turf): Sf: 0-0 GS: 0-0 Gd: 0-2 GF: 0-4 Fm: 0-0
Distance: 5f/6f: 0-6 7f-8f: 0-0 9f-13f: 0-0 14f+: 0-0
Track : LH: 0-3 RH: 0-0 Tight: 0-1 Gall: 0-0
Aids: Bl: 0-0 Vi: 0-0 Tstrap: 0-0
Best Rating: 49 5/01 Thsk 6f gd-fm

Mr Pitz

98 **80+**

2-y-o ch c Hector Protector (USA)-Moogie (Young Generation)
E A L Dunlop John D Pitt

Placings:4221 **(4294)**
2001: 7^{4}GF, 7^{2}GS, 7^{2}GF, 7^{1}G

	Starts	1st	2nd	3rd	Win & Pl
Career Total (Turf)	4	1	2	0	7210

80 8/01 Epsm 7f E GD £4494
Total win prize-money £4494

Going (Turf): Sf: 0-0 GS: 0-1 **Gd: 1-1** GF: 0-2 Fm: 0-0
Distance: 5f/6f: 0-0 **7f-8f: 1-4** 9f-13f: 0-0 14f+: 0-0
Track : **LH: 1-4** RH: 0-0 **Tight: 1-2** Gall: 0-0
Aids: Bl: 0-0 Vi: 0-0 Tstrap: 0-0
Best Rating: 80 8/01 Epsm 7f good

30,000gns half-sister to very smart juvenile Catwalk and other winning sprinters. Deservedly got off the mark in a three-runner maiden at Epsom.

Mr Ricciolo (IRE)

2-y-o b g Highest Honor (FR)-Just Rainbow (FR) (Rainbow Quest (USA))
B J Curley Mrs B J Curley

Placings:0 **(4888)**
2001: 8^{0}GF

	Starts	1st	2nd	3rd	Win & Pl
Career Total (Turf)	1	0	0	0	

Going (Turf): Sf: 0-0 GS: 0-0 Gd: 0-0 GF: 0-1 Fm: 0-0
Distance: 5f/6f: 0-0 7f-8f: 0-1 9f-13f: 0-0 14f+: 0-0
Track : LH: 0-0 RH: 0-1 Tight: 0-0 Gall: 0-0
Aids: Bl: 0-0 Vi: 0-0 Tstrap: 0-0

Mr Sandancer

102 **101d**

2-y-o b c Zafonic (USA)-Um Lardaff (Mill Reef (USA))
J G Given A Mordain

Placings:140266 **(5500)**
2001: 6^{1}F, 7^{4}GF, 7^{0}G, 7^{2}GF, 8^{6}GS, 8^{6}HY

	Starts	1st	2nd	3rd	Win & Pl
Career Total (Turf)	6	1	1	0	11835

86 6/01 Newc 6f D FRM £6825
Total win prize-money £6825

Going (Turf): Sf: 0-1 GS: 0-1 Gd: 0-1 GF: 0-2 **Fm: 1-1**
Distance: **5f/6f: 1-1** 7f-8f: 0-5 9f-13f: 0-0 14f+: 0-0
Track : LH: 0-0 RH: 0-3 Tight: 0-0 Gall: 0-1
Aids: Bl: 0-0 Vi: 0-0 Tstrap: 0-0
Best Rating: 101 9/01 Donc 7f gd-fm

A February foal, he has already changed hands three times. Given a tough introduction, he knew his job and never flinched under pressure. Ran well in a Group Three at Goodwood but hung left in a similar race at Sandown. Better effort when dropped in grade at Sandown, but was comfortably held in a Listed event at Ascot. Best on fast ground.

Mr Speaker (IRE)

97(88) (28)**51**

8-y-o ch g Statoblest-Casting Vote (USA) (Monteverdi)
C F Wall Hintlesham Thoroughbreds

Placings:0**0**036/0001040/200020006/**0**610**3**/00130/**500**
000-00631 **(4489)**
2001: 10^{0}GS, 7^{0}GF, 8^{6}S, 7^{3}G, 8^{1}S

	Starts	1st	2nd	3rd	Win & Pl
Career Total (Turf)	36	4	2	3	15308
Career Total (AW)	6	0	0	1	364

51	9/01	Yarm	1m3y	F(0-80)H	SFT	£2282
56	10/99	Brig	7f214y	E(0-70)H	G-S	£2840
60	9/98	Bevl	7f100y	E(0-70)H	G-F	£3393
60	7/96	Chep	6f16y	F(0-65)H	G-F	£2845

Total win prize-money £11360

Going (Turf): Sf: 1-9 GS: 1-6 Gd: 0-8 **GF: 2-11** Fm: 0-2
Distance: 5f/6f: 0-9 **7f-8f: 3-21** 9f-13f: 1-12 14f+: 0-0
Track : LH: 1-13 RH: 1-7 Tight: 0-10 Gall: 0-2
Aids: Bl: 0-0 Vi: 0-0 Tstrap: 0-0
Best Rating: 51 9/01 Yarm 1m3y soft

Mr Spliffy (IRE)

56

2-y-o b g Fayruz-Johns Conquerer (IRE) (Conquering Hero (USA))
M C Chapman Miss C T Hickford

Placings:000000 **(5183)**
2001: 5^{0}GS, 6^{0}G, 5^{0}GF, 7^{0}G, 5^{0}G, 5^{0}GS

	Starts	1st	2nd	3rd	Win & Pl
Career Total (Turf)	6	0	0	0	

Going (Turf): Sf: 0-0 GS: 0-2 Gd: 0-3 GF: 0-1 Fm: 0-0
Distance: 5f/6f: 0-5 7f-8f: 0-1 9f-13f: 0-0 14f+: 0-0
Track : LH: 0-0 RH: 0-1 Tight: 0-0 Gall: 0-1
Aids: Bl: 0-0 Vi: 0-0 Tstrap: 0-0
Best Rating: 56 10/01 Catt 5f gd-sft

Mr Squiggle (IRE)

100(74) (33)**45**

3-y-o b g Persian Bold-Soul Fire (IRE) (Exactly Sharp (USA))
A Dickman Mike Smallman

Placings:066-000100 **(4422)**

2001: 7^{0}GF, 8^{0}GF, 8^{0}GF, 11^{1}F, 11^{0}G, 10^{0}GF

	Starts	1st	2nd	3rd	Win & Pl
Career Total (Turf)	8	1	0	0	1960
Career Total (AW)	1	0	0	0	0

45	7/01	Rdcr	1m3f	G	FRM	£1960

Total win prize-money £1960

Going (Turf): Sf: 0-0 GS: 0-0 Gd: 0-2 GF: 0-5 **Fm: 1-1**
Distance: 5f/6f: 0-2 7f-8f: 0-3 **9f-13f: 1-4** 14f+: 0-0
Track : **LH: 1-4** RH: 0-3 **Tight: 1-4** Gall: 0-0
Aids: Bl: 0-0 Vi: 0-0 Tstrap: 0-0
Best Rating: 45 7/01 Rdcr 1m3f firm

Plating class. Won at Redcar in summer of 2001. Stays a mile. Acts on fast ground.

Mr Stylish

(102) (81) **67**

5-y-o b g Mazilier (USA)-Moore Stylish (Moorestyle)
J S Moore Alan J Speyer

Placings:05032223404/023305053301011**240**-060602 0604040003310 **(5612)**
2001: 5^{0}SD, 6^{6}G, 5^{0}G, 6^{6}GF, 5^{0}GF, 6^{2}GF, 6^{0}GF, 6^{6}S, 7^{0}GF, 6^{4}F, 5^{0}G, 5^{4}F, 5^{0}G, 5^{0}G, 6^{0}G, 6^{3}HY, 5^{3}S, 6^{1}SD, 6^{0}SD

	Starts	1st	2nd	3rd	Win & Pl
Career Total (Turf)	40	2	5	8	19387
Career Total (AW)	8	2	1	0	8905

76	10/01	Wolv	6f	E(0-75)H	STD	£3475
76	11/00	Wolv	6f	E(0-75)H	STD	£2982
76	10/00	Bath	5f11y	E(0-75)H	G-S	£3630
65	9/00	Bevl	5f	D	G-F	£4212

Total win prize-money £14300

Going (Turf): Sf: 0-7 **GS: 1-3** Gd: 0-11 **GF: 1-14** Fm: 0-5
Distance: **5f/6f: 4-38** 7f-8f: 0-10 9f-13f: 0-0 14f+: 0-0
Track : **LH: 3-16** RH: 0-3 **Tight: 2-6** Gall: 1-10
Aids: Bl: 0-1 Vi: 4-29 Tstrap: 4-30
Best Rating: 76 10/01 Wolv 6f stand

Quirky sprinter, fairly useful handicapper on his day, but has a poor wins-to-runs ratio. Best over six furlongs on good to soft or faster on turf and seems well suited by Fibresand.

Mr Toad (IRE)

105 **89**

2-y-o b c Marju (IRE)-Zany (Junius (USA))
J A Osborne Michael Buckley

Placings:03102513635 **(5104)**
2001: 5^{0}F, 6^{3}GF, 6^{1}GF, 6^{0}GF, 5^{2}G, 6^{5}GF, 6^{1}GS, 6^{3}G, 6^{6}G, 7^{3}G, 6^{5}GS

	Starts	1st	2nd	3rd	Win & Pl
Career Total (Turf)	11	2	1	3	17560

89	8/01	Epsm	6f	D	G-S	£4868
83	6/01	Kemp	6f	E	G-F	£3786

Total win prize-money £8655

Going (Turf): Sf: 0-0 **GS: 1-2** Gd: 0-4 **GF: 1-4** Fm: 0-1
Distance: **5f/6f: 2-10** 7f-8f: 0-1 9f-13f: 0-0 14f+: 0-0
Track : **LH: 1-1** RH: 0-1 **Tight: 1-1** Gall: 0-0
Aids: Bl: 0-0 Vi: 0-0 **Tstrap: 1-7**
Best Rating: 89 9/01 Donc 6f good

A half-brother to the speedy juvenile Zany Zanna, he won a Kempton maiden in June before facing some stiff tasks, but showed he could handle soft ground when winning an Epsom nursery under top weight in August. Very tough.

Mr Top Flight (IRE)

49

2-y-o b g Night Shift (USA)-Native Rhythm (IRE) (Lycius (USA))
Mrs G S Rees P Bamford

Placings:00 **(5689)**
2001: 7^{0}G, 6^{0}S

	Starts	1st	2nd	3rd	Win & Pl
Career Total (Turf)	2	0	0	0	

Going (Turf): Sf: 0-1 GS: 0-0 Gd: 0-1 GF: 0-0 Fm: 0-0
Distance: 5f/6f: 0-1 7f-8f: 0-1 9f-13f: 0-0 14f+: 0-0
Track : LH: 0-1 RH: 0-0 Tight: 0-1 Gall: 0-0
Aids: Bl: 0-0 Vi: 0-0 Tstrap: 0-0
Best Rating: 49 11/01 Donc 6f soft

Moderate form in maidens.

Mr Wensleydale

91 **63**

2-y-o b c Alzao (USA)-Third Watch (Slip Anchor)
G L Moore Rodger Sargent

Placings:00506 **(5589)**
2001: 7^{0}G, 7^{0}G, 8^{5}G, 8^{0}HY, 7^{6}GS

	Starts	1st	2nd	3rd	Win & Pl
Career Total (Turf)	5	0	0	0	0

Going (Turf): Sf: 0-1 GS: 0-1 Gd: 0-3 GF: 0-0 Fm: 0-0
Distance: 5f/6f: 0-0 7f-8f: 0-3 9f-13f: 0-2 14f+: 0-0
Track : LH: 0-2 RH: 0-2 Tight: 0-2 Gall: 0-0
Aids: Bl: 0-0 Vi: 0-0 Tstrap: 0-0
Best Rating: 68 8/01 NmkJ 7f good

Mr Whizz

53

4-y-o ch g Manhal-Panienka (POL) (Dom Racine (FR))
M R Bosley The Milk Sheiks

Placings:1 **(5519)**
2001: 6^{1}HY

	Starts	1st	2nd	3rd	Win & Pl
Career Total (Turf)	1	1	0	0	3052

53	10/01	Wind	6f	D	HVY	£3052

Total win prize-money £3052

Going (Turf): Sf: 1-1 GS: 0-0 Gd: 0-0 GF: 0-0 Fm: 0-0
Distance: **5f/6f: 1-1** 7f-8f: 0-0 9f-13f: 0-0 14f+: 0-0
Track : LH: 0-0 RH: 0-0 Tight: 0-0 Gall: 0-0
Aids: Bl: 0-0 Vi: 0-0 Tstrap: 0-0
Best Rating: 53 10/01 Wind 6f heavy

He was making a belated racecourse debut when successful in a poor heavy-ground end-of-season maiden at Windsor in October. He is a half-brother to the sprinter Whizz Kid, who is similarly at home in the mud.

Mrs Anna

95 **70**

2-y-o b f Charnwood Forest (IRE)-Jezyah (USA) (Chief's Crown (USA))
T D Easterby Mrs Jean P Connew

Placings:43530 **(4454)**
2001: 5^{4}S, 6^{3}F, 6^{5}GF, 7^{3}GF, 6^{0}GF

	Starts	1st	2nd	3rd	Win & Pl
Career Total (Turf)	5	0	0	2	1205

Going (Turf): Sf: 0-1 GS: 0-0 Gd: 0-0 GF: 0-3 Fm: 0-1
Distance: 5f/6f: 0-4 7f-8f: 0-1 9f-13f: 0-0 14f+: 0-0
Track : LH: 0-1 RH: 0-1 Tight: 0-0 Gall: 0-0
Aids: Bl: 0-0 Vi: 0-0 Tstrap: 0-0
Best Rating: 70 6/01 Bevl 7f100y gd-fm

Mrs Cube

79 **50**

2-y-o ch f Missed Flight-Norska (Northfields (USA))
J M Bradley R Miles

Placings:0000 **(3680)**
2001: 5^{0}F, 5^{0}GF, 6^{0}GF, 6^{0}G

	Starts	1st	2nd	3rd	Win & Pl
Career Total (Turf)	4	0	0	0	

Going (Turf): Sf: 0-0 GS: 0-0 Gd: 0-1 GF: 0-2 Fm: 0-1
Distance: 5f/6f: 0-3 7f-8f: 0-1 9f-13f: 0-0 14f+: 0-0
Track : LH: 0-2 RH: 0-0 Tight: 0-0 Gall: 0-2
Aids: Bl: 0-0 Vi: 0-0 Tstrap: 0-0
Best Rating: 50 8/01 Wind 6f good

Mrs Johnson (IRE)

42

3-y-o b f Brief Truce (USA)-Zara Whetei (IRE) (Lomond (USA))
J A Osborne The Woolfie And Tom Partnership

Placings:00 **(4896)**
2001: 8^{0}GF, 9^{0}GS

	Starts	1st	2nd	3rd	Win & Pl
Career Total (Turf)	2	0	0	0	

Going (Turf): Sf: 0-0 GS: 0-1 Gd: 0-0 GF: 0-1 Fm: 0-0
Distance: 5f/6f: 0-0 7f-8f: 0-1 9f-13f: 0-1 14f+: 0-0
Track : LH: 0-0 RH: 0-1 Tight: 0-0 Gall: 0-0
Aids: Bl: 0-0 Vi: 0-0 Tstrap: 0-0
Best Rating: 42 8/01 Sals 1m gd-fm

Mrs Kanning

82 **65**

2-y-o ch f Distant View (USA)-Red Hot Dancer (USA) (Seattle Dancer (USA))
M H Tompkins G J Burke

Placings:000 **(5484)**
2001: 5^{0}GF, 8^{0}GS, 8^{0}HY

	Starts	1st	2nd	3rd	Win & Pl
Career Total (Turf)	3	0	0	0	

Going (Turf): Sf: 0-1 GS: 0-1 Gd: 0-0 GF: 0-1 Fm: 0-0
Distance: 5f/6f: 0-1 7f-8f: 0-2 9f-13f: 0-0 14f+: 0-0
Track : LH: 0-1 RH: 0-0 Tight: 0-0 Gall: 0-1
Aids: Bl: 0-0 Vi: 0-0 Tstrap: 0-0
Best Rating: 65 10/01 NmkR 1m gd-sft

Mrs Nash

93 **70**

3-y-o b f Night Shift (USA)-Nashkara (Shirley Heights)
R Charlton Mountgrange Stud

Placings:020 **(5180)**
2001: 8^{0}GF, 9^{2}GF, 10^{0}HY

	Starts	1st	2nd	3rd	Win & Pl
Career Total (Turf)	3	0	1	0	1860

Going (Turf): Sf: 0-1 GS: 0-0 Gd: 0-0 GF: 0-2 Fm: 0-0
Distance: 5f/6f: 0-0 7f-8f: 0-1 9f-13f: 0-2 14f+: 0-0
Track : LH: 0-1 RH: 0-1 Tight: 0-1 Gall: 0-1
Aids: Bl: 0-0 Vi: 0-0 Tstrap: 0-0
Best Rating: 70 8/01 Newb 1m1f gd-fm

Mrs Plum

(83) (72) **46**

2-y-o b f Emarati (USA)-Aubade (Henbit (USA))
D Morris The Brookfield Stud & Partners

Placings:36 **(5627)**
2001: 6^{3}SD, 7^{6}G, 6^{4}SD

	Starts	1st	2nd	3rd	Win & Pl
Career Total (Turf)	1	0	0	0	0
Career Total (AW)	1	0	0	1	425

Going (Turf): Sf: 0-0 GS: 0-0 Gd: 0-1 GF: 0-0 Fm: 0-0
Distance: 5f/6f: 0-1 7f-8f: 0-1 9f-13f: 0-0 14f+: 0-0
Track : LH: 0-1 RH: 0-0 Tight: 0-0 Gall: 0-0
Aids: Bl: 0-0 Vi: 0-0 Tstrap: 0-0

Best Rating: 72 10/01 Sthl 6f stand

Made a very encouraging debut at Southwell over six furlongs when finishing a close third, but was disappointing next time at Hedcar.

Mrs Pooters (IRE)

76

2-y-o b f Petardia-Mrs Hooters (Glint Of Gold)
D W P Arbuthnot K A Alexander

Placings:03 (5666)
2001: 7^{0}GF, 6^{3}HY

	Starts	1st	2nd	3rd	Win & Pl
Career Total (Turf)	2	0	0	1	578

Going (Turf): Sf: 0-1 GS: 0-0 Gd: 0-0 GF: 0-1 Fm: 0-0
Distance: 5f/6f: 0-1 7f-8f: 0-1 9f-13f: 0-0 14f+: 0-0
Track : LH: 0-0 RH: 0-0 Tight: 0-0 Gall: 0-0
Aids: Bl: 0-0 Vi: 0-0 Tstrap: 0-0
Best Rating: 76 11/01 Wind 6f heavy

Mrs Tiggywinkle

93(93) (56)**35**

3-y-o b f Magic Ring (IRE)-Upper Sister (Upper Case (USA))
Miss L A Perratt (J M Bradley 19/2) T P Finch

Placings:6400060263624-3000300520 (5273)
2001: 6^{3}SD, 6^{0}SD, 6^{0}SW, 8^{0}SD, 5^{3}GF, 6^{0}GF, 6^{0}G, 5^{5}F, 5^{2}GS, 5^{0}HY

	Starts	1st	2nd	3rd	Win & Pl
Career Total (Turf)	10	0	1	1	1087
Career Total (AW)	13	0	2	2	1872

Going (Turf): Sf: 0-2 GS: 0-1 Gd: 0-3 GF: 0-3 Fm: 0-1
Distance: 5f/6f: 0-18 7f-8f: 0-4 9f-13f: 0-1 14f+: 0-0
Track : LH: 0-14 RH: 0-0 Tight: 0-6 Gall: 0-1
Aids: Bl: 0-3 Vi: 0-0 Tstrap: 0-0
Best Rating: 56 1/01 Sthl 6f stand

Moderate maiden, has done most of her racing on Fibresand. Appears to stay seven furlongs.

Mshinda

(79) (11)**53**

3-y-o b f Mtoto-Nibabu (FR) (Nishapour (FR))
P J Makin Lady Davis

Placings:425 (5412)
2001: 6^{4}GF, 5^{2}F, 6^{5}SD

	Starts	1st	2nd	3rd	Win & Pl
Career Total (Turf)	2	0	1	0	1386
Career Total (AW)	1	0	0	0	0

Going (Turf): Sf: 0-0 GS: 0-0 Gd: 0-0 GF: 0-1 Fm: 0-1
Distance: 5f/6f: 0-2 7f-8f: 0-1 9f-13f: 0-0 14f+: 0-0
Track : LH: 0-2 RH: 0-0 Tight: 0-0 Gall: 0-1
Aids: Bl: 0-0 Vi: 0-0 Tstrap: 0-0
Best Rating: 53 6/01 Sals 6f212y gd-fm

Mu-Tadil

(98) (22)**16**

9-y-o gr g Be My Chief (USA)-Inveraven (Alias Smith (USA))
J Gallagher Mrs V W Jones

Placings:50/50/0/6S32630/045340200/00006040000-5400000044P (4552)
2001: 16^{5}SD, 16^{4}SD, 21^{0}S, 17^{0}GF, 17^{0}G, 16^{0}GF, 14^{0}GF, 16^{0}GF, 14^{4}GF, 16^{4}GS, 14^{P}SW

	Starts	1st	2nd	3rd	Win & Pl
Career Total (Turf)	36	0	2	3	3591
Career Total (AW)	7	0	0	0	0

Going (Turf): Sf: 0-3 GS: 0-7 Gd: 0-9 GF: 0-13 Fm: 0-4
Distance: 5f/6f: 0-0 7f-8f: 0-0 9f-13f: 0-2 14f+: 0-41
Track : LH: 0-34 RH: 0-7 Tight: 0-27 Gall: 0-0
Aids: Bl: 0-2 Vi: 0-0 Tstrap: 0-0
Best Rating: 22 2/01 Wolv 2m46y stand

Mubaah

90 **75**

2-y-o ch c Cadeaux Genereux-Numuthej (USA) (Nureyev (USA))
A C Stewart Hamdan Al Maktoum

Placings:54 (5588)
2001: 6^{5}HY, 5^{4}GS

	Starts	1st	2nd	3rd	Win & Pl
Career Total (Turf)	2	0	0	0	279

Going (Turf): Sf: 0-1 GS: 0-1 Gd: 0-0 GF: 0-0 Fm: 0-0
Distance: 5f/6f: 0-2 7f-8f: 0-0 9f-13f: 0-0 14f+: 0-0
Track : LH: 0-1 RH: 0-0 Tight: 0-0 Gall: 0-0
Aids: Bl: 0-0 Vi: 0-0 Tstrap: 0-0
Best Rating: 75 11/01 Brig 5f213y gd-sft

Mubkera (IRE)

106 **75**

2-y-o ch f Nashwan (USA)-Na-Ayim (IRE) (Shirley Heights)
E A L Dunlop Hamdan Al Maktoum

Placings:1 (4287)
2001: 8^{1}GF

	Starts	1st	2nd	3rd	Win & Pl			
Career Total (Turf)	1	1	0	0	3465			
75	8/01	Chep	1m14y	D		G-F	£3464	

Total win prize-money £3465

Going (Turf): Sf: 0-0 GS: 0-0 Gd: 0-0 **GF: 1-1** Fm: 0-0
Distance: 5f/6f: 0-0 7f-8f: 0-0 **9f-13f: 1-1** 14f+: 0-0
Track : LH: 0-0 RH: 0-0 Tight: 0-0 Gall: 0-0
Aids: Bl: 0-0 Vi: 0-0 Tstrap: 0-0
Best Rating: 75 8/01 Chep 1m14y gd-fm

A late foal who is a full-sister to the useful Hishma, made an impressive winning debut at Chepstow in August 2001. Acts on fast ground. Stays a mile.

Mubtaker (USA)

118 **119+**

4-y-o ch c Silver Hawk (USA)-Gazayil (USA) (Irish River (FR))
M P Tregoning Hamdan Al Maktoum

Placings:2/13-32121213 (5595)
2001: 10^{3}S, 10^{2}G, 9^{1}GF, 11^{2}G, 12^{1}GF, 11^{2}GF, 12^{1}G, 12^{3}GS

	Starts	1st	2nd	3rd	Win & Pl		
Career Total (Turf)	11	4	4	3	87807		
119	10/01	NmkR	1m4f	A		GD	£15834
116	6/01	NmkJ	1m4f	A		G-F	£13572
110	5/01	Gdwd	1m1f192y	A		G-F	£22750
102	10/00	Newb	1m2f6y	D		HVY	£5174

Total win prize-money £57330

Going (Turf): Sf: 1-3 GS: 0-1 Gd: 1-3 **GF: 2-3** Fm: 0-0
Distance: 5f/6f: 0-0 7f-8f: 0-0 **9f-13f: 4-10** 14f+: 0-0
Track : LH: 1-3 **RH: 3-6** Tight: 1-1 **Gall: 3-7**
Aids: Bl: 0-0 Vi: 0-0 Tstrap: 0-0
Best Rating: 119 10/01 NmkR 1m4f good

A progressive sort, he put up an eyecatching performance when just pipped by Zindabad in a conditions stakes over ten furlongs at Newmarket in May. Duly landed a conditions race at Goodwood and was a touch unlucky when narrowly beaten again by Zindabad at Leicester. He put up a taking display to land a Newmarket Listed race in June and was then second to Grandera at Newbury before bolting up at Newmarket. Seems most effective on fast ground.

Much Too Much (IRE)

(84) (46)**53**

3-y-o b f Mujadil (USA)-Spoilt Again (Mummy's Pet)
K McAuliffe Mrs H Raw

Placings:00300 (4874)
2001: 6^{0}G, 6^{0}F, 6^{3}SD, 6^{0}SD, 8^{0}SD

	Starts	1st	2nd	3rd	Win & Pl
Career Total (Turf)	2	0	0	0	
Career Total (AW)	3	0	0	1	421

Going (Turf): Sf: 0-0 GS: 0-0 Gd: 0-1 GF: 0-0 Fm: 0-1
Distance: 5f/6f: 0-4 7f-8f: 0-0 9f-13f: 0-1 14f+: 0-0
Track : LH: 0-3 RH: 0-0 Tight: 0-2 Gall: 0-0
Aids: Bl: 0-0 Vi: 0-0 Tstrap: 0-0
Best Rating: 53 6/01 Wind 6f good

Muchana Yetu

88 **46**

4-y-o b f Mtoto-Bobbie Dee (Blakeney)
Mrs P N Dutfield Mrs Nerys Dutfield

Placings:3054/06065056-40 (2991)
2001: 6^{4}GF, 8^{0}G

	Starts	1st	2nd	3rd	Win & Pl
Career Total (Turf)	14	0	0	1	1123

Going (Turf): Sf: 0-2 GS: 0-3 Gd: 0-2 GF: 0-6 Fm: 0-1
Distance: 5f/6f: 0-3 7f-8f: 0-2 9f-13f: 0-8 14f+: 0-1
Track : LH: 0-3 RH: 0-5 Tight: 0-7 Gall: 0-0
Aids: Bl: 0-1 Vi: 0-0 Tstrap: 0-2
Best Rating: 21 7/01 Chep 1m14y good

Muchea

115 **96**

7-y-o ch h Shalford (IRE)-Bargouzine (Hotfoot)
M R Channon Andy J Smith

Placings:3113212/306063/15201503646/000/02205300 4125050-0335305040062 (5625)
2001: 8^{0}GS, 8^{3}GS, 7^{3}GF, 8^{5}G, 8^{3}GF, 7^{0}GF, 8^{5}G, 7^{0}G, 8^{4}G, 7^{0}S, 6^{0}S, 6^{6}HY, 8^{2}GS

	Starts	1st	2nd	3rd	Win & Pl		
Career Total (Turf)	55	6	7	9	267990		
99	8/00	Gdwd	7f	B(0-105)H		GD	£9616
115	6/98	NmkJ	7f	A		GD	£20000
111	4/98	Curr	7f			HVY	£19500
104	8/96	Badn	6f			GD	£45045
84	4/96	NmkR	5f	C		G-F	£5524
93	3/96	Catt	5f	D		G-S	£3125

Total win prize-money £102812

Going (Turf): Sf: 1-7 GS: 1-12 **Gd: 3-19** GF: 1-12 Fm: 0-1
Distance: 5f/6f: 3-9 7f-8f: 3-40 9f-13f: 0-3 14f+: 0-0
Track : LH: 0-8 **RH: 1-13** Tight: 0-0 Gall: 0-4
Aids: Bl: 0-0 Vi: 0-5 Tstrap: 0-0
Best Rating: 105 6/01 Asct 1m gd-fm

A winner twice at Group Three level in 1998, he won a good handicap at Goodwood in 2000, but he has been running well in good handicaps this season without quite being able to win. Suited by seven furlongs or a mile and he does seem to enjoy the hustle and bustle of big-field handicaps.

Mucho Gusto

91(73) (26)**39**

3-y-o b g Casteddu-Heather Honey (Insan (USA))
R F Marvin Joe Singh

Placings:05-00004 (4631)
2001: 6^{0}SD, 7^{0}GS, 8^{0}GF, 7^{0}GF, 9^{4}GF

	Starts	1st	2nd	3rd	Win & Pl
Career Total (Turf)	6	0	0	0	308

Career Total (AW) 1 0 0 0

Going (Turf): Sf: 0-0 GS: 0-1 Gd: 0-0 GF: 0-5 Fm: 0-0
Distance: 5f/6f: 0-1 7f-8f: 0-4 9f-13f: 0-2 14f+: 0-0
Track : LH: 0-2 RH: 0-2 Tight: 0-0 Gall: 0-0
Aids: Bl: 0-0 Vi: 0-0 Tstrap: 0-1
Best Rating: 39 9/01 Leic 1m1f218y gd-fm

Muddy Water

(103) (48)**43**
5-y-o b m Salse (USA)-Rainbow Fleet (Nomination)
I A Wood (D Marks 27/2) Neardown Stables

Placings:06/23606462/010032500000-25345136036 (5397)
2001: 8²SW, 8⁵SD, 7³GF, 8⁴GF, 8⁵G, 8¹SD, 7³GF, 7⁶G, 8⁰F, 7³S, 8⁶SD

	Starts	1st	2nd	3rd	Win & Pl
Career Total (Turf)	15	1	1	3	3818
Career Total (AW)	18	1	3	2	5539

48 7/01 Sthl 1m F(0-65) STD £2303
61 4/00 Folk 6f G(0-60)H SFT £1879
Total win prize-money £4183

Going (Turf): Sf: 1-4 GS: 0-1 Gd: 0-2 GF: 0-6 Fm: 0-2
Distance: 5f/6f: 1-9 7f-8f: 1-17 9f-13f: 0-7 14f+: 0-0
Track : LH: 1-23 RH: 0-1 Tight: 0-9 Gall: 0-0
Aids: Bl: 0-0 Vi: 0-0 Tstrap: 0-2
Best Rating: 48 7/01 Sthl 1m stand

Moderate plater, best at a mile, acts on any going and surface. Caused a surprise when taking a Fibresand claimer when her stable was at the top of its form.

Mudlark

(84)
9-y-o b g Salse (USA)-Mortal Sin (USA) (Green Forest (USA))
J R Norton (J Norton 12/1) J Norton

Placings:050/335/055/0/325324005/0 (0083)
2001: 16⁰SD

	Starts	1st	2nd	3rd	Win & Pl
Career Total (Turf)	9	0	0	2	1039
Career Total (AW)	11	0	2	2	2059

Going (Turf): Sf: 0-2 GS: 0-3 Gd: 0-1 GF: 0-3 Fm: 0-0
Distance: 5f/6f: 0-1 7f-8f: 0-3 9f-13f: 0-3 14f+: 0-13
Track : LH: 0-15 RH: 0-3 Tight: 0-2 Gall: 0-1
Aids: Bl: 0-4 Vi: 0-12 Tstrap: 0-0
Best Rating: 13 1/01 Sthl 2m stand

Muffin Man

101 **44**
4-y-o b c Timeless Times (USA)-Allesca (Alleging (USA))
M D I Usher Miss D G Kerr

Placings:0544045524000/00046040-0006305000 (3610)
2001: 7⁰G, 5⁰F, 7⁰GF, 8⁶GF, 8³HD, 9⁰GF, 10⁵GF, 8⁰G, 9⁰GF, 9⁰G

	Starts	1st	2nd	3rd	Win & Pl
Career Total (Turf)	31	0	1	1	3522

Going (Turf): Sf: 0-2 GS: 0-0 Gd: 0-11 GF: 0-15 Fm: 0-3
Distance: 5f/6f: 0-10 7f-8f: 0-14 9f-13f: 0-7 14f+: 0-0
Track : LH: 0-11 RH: 0-3 Tight: 0-5 Gall: 0-4
Aids: Bl: 0-0 Vi: 0-0 Tstrap: 0-0
Best Rating: 44 7/01 Bath 1m2f46y gd-fm

Muffit (IRE)

(81) (60)**60**
2-y-o b f Alhaarth (IRE)-Calash (Indian King (USA))
M R Channon Tim Corby

Placings:000126403520203 (5396)
2001: 6⁰GF, 6⁰GF, 7⁰GF, 6¹GF, 7²GF, 7⁶GF, 6⁴G, 7⁰GF, 7³GF, 7⁵HY, 6²GS, 7⁰GS, 8²HY, 7⁰GS, 8³SD

	Starts	1st	2nd	3rd	Win & Pl
Career Total (Turf)	14	1	3	1	6618
Career Total (AW)	1	0	0	1	279

63 8/01 Ling 6f G G-F £2033
Total win prize-money £2034

Going (Turf): Sf: 0-2 GS: 0-3 Gd: 0-1 GF: 1-8 Fm: 0-0
Distance: 5f/6f: 1-3 7f-8f: 0-11 9f-13f: 0-1 14f+: 0-0
Track : LH: 0-5 RH: 0-1 Tight: 0-4 Gall: 0-0
Aids: Bl: 0-0 Vi: 0-0 Tstrap: 0-0
Best Rating: 63 9/01 Folk 6f189y good

Kept busy, she won at Lingfield in August. Appreciated the step up in trip in a nursery at Ayr, and ran up to her best in the testing ground. Acts on any ground, stays a mile.

Mufreh (USA)

(84) (41)**28**
3-y-o br c Dayjur (USA)-Mathkurh (USA) (Riverman (USA))
A G Newcombe (N A Graham 6/7) Advanced Marketing Services Ltd

Placings:354 (5617)
2001: 6³GF, 7⁵HY, 8⁴SD

	Starts	1st	2nd	3rd	Win & Pl
Career Total (Turf)	2	0	0	1	548
Career Total (AW)	1	0	0	0	0

Going (Turf): Sf: 0-1 GS: 0-0 Gd: 0-0 GF: 0-1 Fm: 0-0
Distance: 5f/6f: 0-0 7f-8f: 0-2 9f-13f: 0-1 14f+: 0-0
Track : LH: 0-1 RH: 0-0 Tight: 0-1 Gall: 0-0
Aids: Bl: 0-0 Vi: 0-0 Tstrap: 0-0
Best Rating: 41 11/01 Wolv 1m100y stand

Mugharreb (USA)

106 **113**
3-y-o b c Gone West (USA)-Marling (IRE) (Lomond (USA))
B Hanbury Hamdan Al Maktoum

Placings:3-1632010 (5365)
2001: 8¹G, 8⁶GY, 8³GF, 6²GF, 6⁰G, 6¹GF, 6⁰GS

	Starts	1st	2nd	3rd	Win & Pl
Career Total (Turf)	8	2	1	2	32268

113 8/01 NmkJ 6f A G-F £14815
101 5/01 NmkR 1m D GD £6402
Total win prize-money £21219

Going (Turf): Sf: 0-1 GS: 0-1 Gd: 1-2 GF: 1-3 Fm: 0-0
Distance: 5f/6f: 1-4 7f-8f: 1-3 9f-13f: 0-1 14f+: 0-0
Track : LH: 0-0 RH: 0-1 Tight: 0-0 Gall: 0-0
Aids: Bl: 0-0 Vi: 0-0 Tstrap: 0-0
Best Rating: 113 8/01 NmkJ 6f gd-fm

An impeccably bred colt, he impressed when beating Askham by five lengths in a good time at Newmarket in May, but had to settle for sixth behind Black Minnaloushe in the Irish 2000 Guineas. Ran a bit flat when third to Vicious Knight in a conditions race at Sandown in July and was then dropped back to six furlongs. Ran well at Newbury before a good winner of a Listed contest at Newmarket in August. Acts on soft ground, but suited by faster.

Muhareb (USA)

90 **78**
2-y-o ch c Thunder Gulch (USA)-Queen Of Spirit (USA) (Deputy Minister (CAN))
C E Brittain Saeed Manana

Placings:04 (5623)
2001: 7⁰GS, 8⁴GS

	Starts	1st	2nd	3rd	Win & Pl
Career Total (Turf)	2	0	0	0	285

Going (Turf): Sf: 0-0 GS: 0-2 Gd: 0-0 GF: 0-0 Fm: 0-0
Distance: 5f/6f: 0-0 7f-8f: 0-1 9f-13f: 0-1 14f+: 0-0
Track : LH: 0-1 RH: 0-0 Tight: 0-0 Gall: 0-0
Aids: Bl: 0-0 Vi: 0-0 Tstrap: 0-0
Best Rating: 78 11/01 Nott 1m54y gd-sft

Muhtafel

90 **65**
7-y-o b g Nashwan (USA)-The Perfect Life (IRE) (Try My Best (USA))
J R Jenkins R M Ellis

Placings:2125/60000053212130/62/00 (2877)
2001: 9⁰GF, 11⁰GF

	Starts	1st	2nd	3rd	Win & Pl
Career Total (Turf)	21	3	5	2	25023
Career Total (AW)	1	0	0	0	0

86 8/98 Chep 1m2f36y C(0-95)H G-F £5283
77 7/98 NmkJ 1m2f E(0-75)H G-F £4077
81 6/97 Rdcr 1m D GD £3691
Total win prize-money £13053

Going (Turf): Sf: 0-1 GS: 0-1 Gd: 1-7 GF: 2-11 Fm: 0-1
Distance: 5f/6f: 0-0 7f-8f: 1-5 9f-13f: 2-17 14f+: 0-0
Track : LH: 1-8 RH: 1-9 Tight: 0-4 Gall: 1-9
Aids: Bl: 0-0 Vi: 1-4 Tstrap: 0-3
Best Rating: 65 6/01 Gdwd 1m1f gd-fm

Has had plenty of trainers. A decent handicapper in 1998 over ten furlongs on fast ground. He was absent from the track for over two years before reappearing in June 2001

Muja Farewell

105 **92**
3-y-o ch f Mujtahid (USA)-Highland Rhapsody (IRE) (Kris)
T D Barron T Hollins P Huntbach D Rutter W Carson

Placings:122101-5100 (4176)
2001: 6⁵GS, 5¹GF, 5⁰GF, 5⁰G

	Starts	1st	2nd	3rd	Win & Pl
Career Total (Turf)	10	4	2	0	35267

92 6/01 Asct 5f B(0-105)H G-F £18070
84 9/00 NmkR 5f C(0-95) GD £7254
74 6/00 Wind 5f10y C G-F £5253
65 5/00 Rdcr 5f E G-S £2535
Total win prize-money £33113

Going (Turf): Sf: 0-0 GS: 1-4 Gd: 1-3 GF: 2-3 Fm: 0-0
Distance: 5f/6f: 4-10 7f-8f: 0-0 9f-13f: 0-0 14f+: 0-0
Track : LH: 0-0 RH: 1-1 Tight: 0-0 Gall: 1-1
Aids: Bl: 0-0 Vi: 0-0 Tstrap: 0-0
Best Rating: 92 6/01 Asct 5f gd-fm

Won on her debut at two. Only out of the frame once in six outings as a juvenile. A tough filly who is blessed with tremendous speed, she is at her best over five furlongs. Has won on good to firm and good to soft over the minimum trip.

Muja's Magic (IRE)

(103) (54d)**49**
6-y-o b m Mujadil (USA)-Grave Error (Northern Treat (USA))
Mrs N Macauley Mrs N Macauley

Placings:04050630000233102/350651460205300/0000562250501653401/2440205005010020000-0304406050 (0694)
2001: 6⁰SD, 7³SW, 7⁰SD, 8⁴SW, 8⁴SD, 7⁰SD, 7⁶SD, 7⁰SD, 7⁵SD, 8⁰SD

	Starts	1st	2nd	3rd	Win & Pl
Career Total (Turf)	48	3	4	3	19573
Career Total (AW)	32	2	4	4	9936

52 7/00 Yarm 6f3y E(0-70)H G-F £3526
64 12/99 Wolv 7f F(0-60)H STD £1934
45 8/99 Bevl 5f E(0-75)H GD £4614
59 6/98 Brig 5f213y D(0-80)H GD £6970
58 12/97 Ling 6f E STD £2700
Total win prize-money £19745

Going (Turf): Sf: 0-3 GS: 0-3 **Gd: 2-11** GF: 1-24 Fm: 0-7
Distance: **5f/6f: 3-47** 7f-8f: 2-30 9f-13f: 0-3 14f+: 0-0
Track : **LH: 3-48** RH: 0-2 **Tight: 2-18** Gall: 0-6
Aids: Bl: 0-5 **Vi: 4-59** Tstrap: 0-0
Best Rating: 57 1/01 Sthl 1m slow

Mujaaled (IRE)

79(64)
4-y-o b g Elmaamul (USA)-Balaabol (USA) (Sadler's Wells (USA))
D W Chapman Michael Hill

Placings:00-000 **(1637)**
2001: 8^{0}SD, 7^{0}GF, 7^{0}F

	Starts	1st	2nd	3rd	Win & Pl
Career Total (Turf)	4	0	0	0	
Career Total (AW)	1	0	0	0	

Going (Turf): Sf: 0-0 GS: 0-0 Gd: 0-0 GF: 0-3 Fm: 0-1
Distance: 5f/6f: 0-0 7f-8f: 0-4 9f-13f: 0-1 14f+: 0-0
Track : LH: 0-3 RH: 0-1 Tight: 0-2 Gall: 0-0
Aids: Bl: 0-0 Vi: 0-0 Tstrap: 0-0

Mujadilly

91 **52**
3-y-o b f Mujadil (USA)-Casbah Girl (Native Bazaar)
W M Brisbourne H B Hughes

Placings:6660 **(5593)**
2001: 6^{6}S, 7^{6}GF, 8^{6}S, 5^{0}GS

	Starts	1st	2nd	3rd	Win & Pl
Career Total (Turf)	4	0	0	0	158

Going (Turf): Sf: 0-2 GS: 0-1 Gd: 0-0 GF: 0-1 Fm: 0-0
Distance: 5f/6f: 0-2 7f-8f: 0-1 9f-13f: 0-1 14f+: 0-0
Track : LH: 0-2 RH: 0-0 Tight: 0-1 Gall: 0-0
Aids: Bl: 0-0 Vi: 0-0 Tstrap: 0-0
Best Rating: 52 5/01 Ches 7f2y gd-fm

Mujado (IRE)

105 **94**
3-y-o b f Mujadil (USA)-Unaria (Prince Tenderfoot (USA))
W J Haggas Lael Stable

Placings:2210-00150 **(3825)**
2001: 6^{0}GF, 5^{0}GF, 6^{1}G, 6^{5}G, 6^{0}G

	Starts	1st	2nd	3rd	Win & Pl
Career Total (Turf)	9	2	2	0	17103

94 6/01 Yarm 6f3y B(0-95) GD £8972
84 8/00 Wind 6f D G-F £3854
Total win prize-money £12828

Going (Turf): Sf: 0-0 GS: 0-1 **Gd: 1-4 GF: 1-4** Fm: 0-0
Distance: 5f/6f: 1-8 7f-8f: 1-1 9f-13f: 0-0 14f+: 0-0
Track : LH: 0-0 **RH: 1-1** Tight: 0-0 **Gall: 1-1**
Aids: Bl: 0-0 Vi: 0-0 **Tstrap: 1-4**
Best Rating: 94 7/01 York 6f good

A speedy filly, she disappointed when well backed at Haydock on her return and did not get much luck in running next time, but she landed a minor event at Yarmouth in June. Has gone to the USA.

Mujagem (IRE)

95(105) (46)**36**
5-y-o br m Mujadil (USA)-Lili Bengam (Welsh Saint)
M W Easterby C F Spence

Placings:5460000/0146020035-6P0 **(5287)**
2001: 5^{6}G, 5^{P}SW, 6^{0}HY

	Starts	1st	2nd	3rd	Win & Pl
Caroor Total (Turf)	14	0	0	1	679
Career Total (AW)	6	1	1	0	3619

46 5/00 Sthl 1m E(0-70)H STD £2756
Total win prize-money £2756

Going (Turf): Sf: 0-6 GS: 0-2 Gd: 0-4 GF: 0-1 Fm: 0-1
Distance: 5f/6f: 0-12 **7f-8f: 1-7** 9f-13f: 0-1 14f+: 0-0
Track : **LH: 1-7** RH: 0-0 Tight: 0-1 Gall: 0-0
Aids: Bl: 0-6 Vi: 0-0 Tstrap: 0-0
Best Rating: 26 8/01 Thsk 5f good

Mujalia (IRE)

82(99) (60)
3-y-o b g Mujtahid (USA)-Danalia (IRE) (Danehill (USA))
Jamie Poulton (S Dow 8/5) Ormonde Racing

Placings:00000-251300R0 **(5524)**
2001: 10^{2}SD, 9^{5}SW, 10^{1}SW, 10^{3}SW, 9^{0}GS, 6^{0}GF, 9^{R}GS, 10^{0}HY

	Starts	1st	2nd	3rd	Win & Pl
Career Total (Turf)	9	0	0	0	
Career Total (AW)	4	1	1	1	3623

53 2/01 Ling 1m2f E SLW £2576
Total win prize-money £2576

Going (Turf): Sf: 0-3 GS: 0-3 Gd: 0-1 GF: 0-2 Fm: 0-0
Distance: 5f/6f: 0-2 7f-8f: 0-4 **9f-13f: 1-7** 14f+: 0-0
Track : **LH: 1-6** RH: 0-4 **Tight: 1-5** Gall: 0-1
Aids: Bl: 0-0 Vi: 0-0 Tstrap: 0-0
Best Rating: 60 2/01 Ling 1m2f slow

Won a claimer over ten furlongs in spring of 2001 on the All-Weather. Has refused to race.

Mujasina (IRE)

92 **70**
2-y-o b c Mujadil (USA)-Camassina (IRE) (Taufan (USA))
J L Eyre A S Scott

Placings:4144000 **(5283)**
2001: 5^{4}GF, 5^{1}GF, 5^{4}GF, 6^{4}GF, 7^{0}GS, 7^{0}GF, 8^{0}HY

	Starts	1st	2nd	3rd	Win & Pl
Career Total (Turf)	7	1	0	0	3207

56 5/01 Muss 5f F G-F £2674
Total win prize-money £2674

Going (Turf): Sf: 0-1 GS: 0-1 Gd: 0-0 **GF: 1-5** Fm: 0-0
Distance: **5f/6f: 1-4** 7f-8f: 0-3 9f-13f: 0-0 14f+: 0-0
Track : LH: 0-4 RH: 0-0 Tight: 0-0 Gall: 0-0
Aids: Bl: 0-0 Vi: 0-0 Tstrap: 0-5
Best Rating: 70 9/01 Wwck 7f26y gd-fm

A March foal. Won a maiden auction race over five furlongs on his second start at Musselburgh but well beaten in nurseries after that. Acts on a sound surface.

Mujkari (IRE)

102(101) (47)**40**
5-y-o ch g Mujtahid (USA)-Hot Curry (USA) (Sharpen Up)
J M Bradley Robert Bailey

Placings:006000/060052160/0000040023000034-0102335046502 **(4293)**
2001: 9^{0}SW, 10^{1}SD, 12^{0}SW, 13^{2}SW, 11^{3}F, 12^{3}GF, 11^{5}GF, 10^{0}F, 12^{4}GF, 11^{6}GF, 12^{5}G, 13^{0}G, 10^{2}GF

	Starts	1st	2nd	3rd	Win & Pl
Career Total (Turf)	32	1	3	3	6855
Career Total (AW)	12	1	1	1	4926

47 1/01 Ling 1m2f D(0-80)H STD £3757
41 8/99 Brig 6f209y F(0-60)H FRM £3273
Total win prize-money £7031

Going (Turf): Sf: 0-4 GS: 0-2 Gd: 0-8 GF: 0-12 **Fm: 1-6**
Distance: 5f/6f: 0-2 7f-8f: 1-22 9f-13f: 1-19 14f+: 0-1
Track : **LH: 2-27** RH: 0-6 **Tight: 1-20** Gall: 0-0
Aids: Bl: 0-3 **Vi: 2-31** Tstrap: 0-0
Best Rating: 47 1/01 Ling 1m2f stand

Muklah (IRE)

103 **97+**
2-y-o b f Singspiel (IRE)-Maraatib (IRE) (Green Desert (USA))
B W Hills Hamdan Al Maktoum

Placings:211 **(3838)**
2001: 7^{2}GF, 7^{1}GF, 7^{1}G

	Starts	1st	2nd	3rd	Win & Pl
Career Total (Turf)	3	2	1	0	17671

97 8/01 NmkJ 7f A GD £12064
76 7/01 Kemp 7f D G-F £4329
Total win prize-money £16393

Going (Turf): Sf: 0-0 GS: 0-0 **Gd: 1-1 GF: 1-2** Fm: 0-0
Distance: 5f/6f: 0-0 **7f-8f: 2-3** 9f-13f: 0-0 14f+: 0-0
Track : LH: 0-0 **RH: 1-1** Tight: 0-0 **Gall: 1-1**
Aids: Bl: 0-0 Vi: 0-0 Tstrap: 0-0
Best Rating: 97 8/01 NmkJ 7f good

Just came off second-best to a David Loder hotpot on her Doncaster debut. Made amends with a pillar-to-post victory at Kempton next time, and took the Sweet Solera Stakes back at Newmarket. Acts over seven furlongs on fast ground and should stay further.

Mulabee (USA)

97 **88**
2-y-o br c Gulch (USA)-Shir Dar (FR) (Lead On Time (USA))
E A L Dunlop Mohammed Jaber

Placings:6241 **(4374)**
2001: 6^{6}GF, 7^{2}GF, 7^{4}G, 7^{1}GF

	Starts	1st	2nd	3rd	Win & Pl
Career Total (Turf)	4	1	1	0	4835

88 8/01 Ling 7f E G-F £3192
Total win prize-money £3192

Going (Turf): Sf: 0-0 GS: 0-0 Gd: 0-1 **GF: 1-3** Fm: 0-0
Distance: 5f/6f: 0-0 **7f-8f: 1-4** 9f-13f: 0-0 14f+: 0-0
Track : LH: 0-0 RH: 0-2 Tight: 0-0 Gall: 0-1
Aids: Bl: 0-0 Vi: 0-0 Tstrap: 0-0
Best Rating: 88 8/01 Ling 7f gd-fm

He showed ability in maiden company before making a successful if narrow winning nursery debut at Lingfield in August. Suited by seven furlongs.

Muldoon (IRE)

87(86) (46)**67**
2-y-o b c Fumo Di Londra (IRE)-Caroline's Mark (On Your Mark)
B Palling Mrs M M Palling

Placings:404360006 **(5458)**
2001: 5^{4}GS, 5^{0}G, 5^{4}SD, 5^{3}SD, 5^{6}S, 6^{0}SW, 5^{0}S, 5^{0}HY, 5^{6}G

	Starts	1st	2nd	3rd	Win & Pl
Career Total (Turf)	6	0	0	0	0
Career Total (AW)	3	0	0	1	324

Going (Turf): Sf: 0-3 GS: 0-1 Gd: 0-2 GF: 0-0 Fm: 0-0
Distance: 5f/6f: 0-9 7f-8f: 0-0 9f-13f: 0-0 14f+: 0-0
Track : LH: 0-5 RH: 0-1 Tight: 0-2 Gall: 0-3
Aids: Bl: 0-0 Vi: 0-0 Tstrap: 0-0
Best Rating: 67 8/01 Chep 5f16y soft

Mull Of Kintyre (USA)

107 **110**
4-y-o b h Danzig (USA)-Retrospective (USA) (Easy Goer (USA))

A P O'Brien Mrs John Magnier

Placings:1214/62346 **(5353a)**
2001: 8^{6}G, 7^{2}G, 7^{3}G, 6^{4}HY, 7^{6}VS

	Starts	1st	2nd	3rd	Win & Pl
Career Total (Turf)	8	2	2	1	109061
Career Total (AW)	1	0	0	0	33263

106 8/99 York 6f A GD £71565
91 6/99 Leop 6f GD £5156
Total win prize-money £76721

Going (Turf): Sf: 0-1 GS: 0-0 **Gd: 2-6** GF: 0-0 Fm: 0-0
Distance: **5f/6f: 2-4** 7f-8f: 0-4 9f-13f: 0-1 14f+: 0-0
Track : LH: 0-1 RH: 0-2 Tight: 0-0 Gall: 0-0
Aids: Bl: 0-0 Vi: 0-0 Tstrap: 0-0
Best Rating: 110 9/01 Hayd 6f heavy

He was a leading two-year-old in 1999, winning the Gimcrack at York. Fourth at the Breeders' Cup on his final start, he was not seen for 18 months after injuring a pedal bone. Promising return at Royal Ascot and just beaten in a Curragh Group Three, but a little disappointing at Goodwood. Ran quite well when dropped back to six in Haydock's Sprint Cup. Retired to stud.

Mullaghmore (IRE)

101(104) (67)51
5-y-o b g Petardia-Comfrey Glen (Glenstal (USA))
M Kettle Greenacres

Placings:00/030653604/151550005130-0543500 **(5098)**
2001: 10^{0}SD, 9^{5}F, 11^{4}GF, 9^{3}GF, 8^{5}GF, 9^{0}G, 14^{0}GS

	Starts	1st	2nd	3rd	Win & Pl
Career Total (Turf)	25	1	0	4	4898
Career Total (AW)	5	2	0	0	4800

49 8/00 Bath 1m5y F(0-65)H FRM £2977
67 3/00 Ling 1m2f F(0-65)H STD £1991
61 1/00 Ling 1m D STD £2808
Total win prize-money £7777

Going (Turf): Sf: 0-2 GS: 0-2 Gd: 0-10 GF: 0-8 **Fm: 1-3**
Distance: 5f/6f: 0-0 7f-8f: 1-9 **9f-13f: 2-20** 14f+: 0-1
Track : **LH: 3-15** RH: 0-9 **Tight: 3-15** Gall: 0-2
Aids: **Bl: 2-12** Vi: 0-1 Tstrap: 0-4
Best Rating: 51 7/01 Wind 1m67y gd-fm

Found his form when tried on Equitrack last season, winning twice on it. Stays ten furlongs. Often slow to start.

Mulling It Over (IRE)

82 45
3-y-o b f Blues Traveller (IRE)-Wonderment (Mummy's Pet)
T D Easterby Anglia Bloodstock Syndicate 1999

Placings:30003-6 **(1640)**
2001: 6^{6}F

	Starts	1st	2nd	3rd	Win & Pl
Career Total (Turf)	6	0	0	2	1147

Going (Turf): Sf: 0-1 GS: 0-1 Gd: 0-0 GF: 0-3 Fm: 0-1
Distance: 5f/6f: 0-4 7f-8f: 0-2 9f-13f: 0-0 14f+: 0-0
Track : LH: 0-1 RH: 0-0 Tight: 0-1 Gall: 0-0
Aids: Bl: 0-0 Vi: 0-0 Tstrap: 0-0
Best Rating: 45 5/01 Rdcr 6f firm

Mulsanne

69
3-y-o b c Clantime-Prim Lass (Reprimand)
P A Pritchard P A Pritchard

Placings:00000-000 **(3204)**
2001: 7^{0}GF, 6^{0}GF, 7^{0}G

	Starts	1st	2nd	3rd	Win & Pl
Career Total (Turf)	8	0	0	0	

Going (Turf): Sf: 0-1 GS: 0-0 Gd: 0-3 GF: 0-4 Fm: 0-0
Distance: 5f/6f: 0-2 7f-8f: 0-6 9f-13f: 0-0 14f+: 0-0
Track : LH: 0-2 RH: 0-1 Tight: 0-0 Gall: 0-2
Aids: Bl: 0-0 Vi: 0-0 Tstrap: 0-0
Best Rating: 3 6/01 Wwck 7f26y gd-fm

Multiploy

83 54
2-y-o b f Deploy-Multi-Sofft (Northern State (USA))
I A Wood M I Forbes

Placings:06000 **(4158)**
2001: 5^{0}F, 6^{6}GF, 6^{0}GF, 7^{0}GF, 7^{0}GF

	Starts	1st	2nd	3rd	Win & Pl
Career Total (Turf)	5	0	0	0	0

Going (Turf): Sf: 0-0 GS: 0-0 Gd: 0-0 GF: 0-4 Fm: 0-1
Distance: 5f/6f: 0-3 7f-8f: 0-2 9f-13f: 0-0 14f+: 0-0
Track : LH: 0-1 RH: 0-0 Tight: 0-0 Gall: 0-1
Aids: Bl: 0-0 Vi: 0-0 Tstrap: 0-0
Best Rating: 54 6/01 Gdwd 6f gd-fm

A half-sister to a couple of juvenile winners. Unplaced so far at up to seven furlongs but should do better over further in time.

Mumbling (IRE)

107 84
3-y-o ch g Dr Devious (IRE)-Valley Lights (IRE) (Dance Of Life (USA))
M H Tompkins Mrs Beryl Lockey

Placings:00-0111304350 **(5486)**
2001: 10^{0}GS, 10^{1}GS, 12^{1}F, 10^{1}GF, 14^{3}GS, 12^{0}GF, 11^{4}GF, 13^{3}GF, 11^{5}S, 10^{0}HY

	Starts	1st	2nd	3rd	Win & Pl
Career Total (Turf)	12	3	0	2	18105

81 5/01 Ayr 1m2f192yD(0-80)H G-F £3887
76 5/01 Haml 1m4f17y E(0-75)H FRM £3248
72 5/01 Pont 1m2f6y D(0-85)H G-S £7247
Total win prize-money £14383

Going (Turf): Sf: 0-3 **GS: 1-3** Gd: 0-1 **GF: 1-4 Fm: 1-1**
Distance: 5f/6f: 0-0 7f-8f: 0-2 **9f-13f: 3-8** 14f+: 0-2
Track : **LH: 2-6** RH: 1-3 **Tight: 1-2** Gall: 0-4
Aids: Bl: 0-1 Vi: 0-0 Tstrap: 0-0
Best Rating: 84 6/01 Sals 1m6f15y gd-sft

Progressed well in May, winning three times at middle-distances, but never figured in the King George V Handicap at Royal Ascot. Did not appear to stay 14 furlongs when upped in trip. Has won on fast ground and soft.

Munadil

101 85
3-y-o ch c Nashwan (USA)-Bintalshaati (Kris)
M P Tregoning Hamdan Al Maktoum

Placings:63-52160 **(5344)**
2001: 11^{5}GF, 10^{2}GF, 10^{1}GF, 10^{6}S, 8^{0}GS

	Starts	1st	2nd	3rd	Win & Pl
Career Total (Turf)	7	1	1	1	7671

85 8/01 Epsm 1m2f18y D G-F £4231
Total win prize-money £4232

Going (Turf): Sf: 0-2 GS: 0-2 Gd: 0-0 **GF: 1-3** Fm: 0-0
Distance: 5f/6f: 0-0 7f-8f: 0-3 **9f-13f: 1-4** 14f+: 0-0
Track : **LH: 1-2** RH: 0-1 **Tight: 1-1** Gall: 0-1
Aids: Bl: 0-0 Vi: 0-0 **Tstrap: 1-2**
Best Rating: 85 8/01 Epsm 1m2f18y gd-fm

Only raced on soft ground as a juvenile, but he has been running on much faster ground this term, eventually getting off the mark in a four-runner maiden at Epsom in August.

Munchie

81 38
2-y-o ch f Bluegrass Prince (IRE)-Hoyland Common (IRE) (Common Grounds)
N Tinkler Bezwell Fixings Limited

Placings:0000 **(3842)**
2001: 7^{0}G, 5^{0}GF, 5^{0}GF, 6^{0}G

	Starts	1st	2nd	3rd	Win & Pl
Career Total (Turf)	4	0	0	0	

Going (Turf): Sf: 0-0 GS: 0-0 Gd: 0-2 GF: 0-2 Fm: 0-0
Distance: 5f/6f: 0-3 7f-8f: 0-1 9f-13f: 0-0 14f+: 0-0
Track : LH: 0-0 RH: 0-0 Tight: 0-0 Gall: 0-0
Aids: Bl: 0-0 Vi: 0-0 Tstrap: 0-0
Best Rating: 38 7/01 Bevl 5f gd-fm

Mundo Raro

93(89) (53)49
6-y-o b g Zafonic (USA)-Star Spectacle (Spectacular Bid (USA))
J G Fitzgerald Marquesa De Moratalla

Placings:231020/620000/0000500 **(5450)**
2001: 10^{0}S, 8^{0}SD, 8^{0}SD, 7^{0}GF, 8^{5}G, 9^{0}G, 8^{0}HY

	Starts	1st	2nd	3rd	Win & Pl
Career Total (Turf)	17	1	3	1	11826
Career Total (AW)	2	0	0	0	

87 8/98 Pont 1m4y D G-F £3566
Total win prize-money £3566

Going (Turf): Sf: 0-3 GS: 0-3 Gd: 0-7 **GF: 1-4** Fm: 0-0
Distance: 5f/6f: 0-0 7f-8f: 0-11 **9f-13f: 1-8** 14f+: 0-0
Track : **LH: 1-11** RH: 0-5 Tight: 0-2 Gall: 0-4
Aids: Bl: 0-0 Vi: 0-0 Tstrap: 0-0
Best Rating: 53 6/01 Sthl 1m stand

Mungo Park

106 78
7-y-o b g Selkirk (USA)-River Dove (USA) (Riverman (USA))
M Dods Mrs R Olivier

Placings:0040/000013300013/241201510051440563/0
41046020654245200/20202222510000-
53432250062000 **(5630)**
2001: 5^{5}S, 5^{3}G, 5^{4}GF, 5^{3}G, 5^{2}GS, 5^{2}GF, 5^{5}GF, 6^{0}S, 5^{0}GF, 5^{6}G, 5^{2}G, 5^{0}GS, 5^{0}S, 6^{0}G

	Starts	1st	2nd	3rd	Win & Pl
Career Total (Turf)	80	8	14	6	70028

83 8/00 Bevl 5f D(0-80)H G-F £7904
82 4/99 Thsk 5f D(0-80) GD £3795
80 7/98 Newc 5f C(0-95)H GD £5361
76 6/98 Nott 5f13y D(0-85)H GD £4240
75 5/98 Bevl 5f D(0-80)H GD £4458
70 4/98 Newc 5f D(0-80)H SFT £3420
60 10/97 Newc 5f E(0-70)H G-F £2986
51 5/97 Carl 5f F FRM £2710
Total win prize-money £34875

Going (Turf): Sf: 1-13 GS: 0-9 **Gd: 4-34** GF: 2-21 Fm: 1-3
Distance: **5f/6f: 8-73** 7f-8f: 0-4 9f-13f: 0-3 14f+: 0-0
Track : LH: 0-14 **RH: 1-5** Tight: 0-0 **Gall: 1-8**
Aids: Bl: 0-8 Vi: 0-1 Tstrap: 0-0
Best Rating: 81 6/01 Sals 5f gd-fm

He has been a useful come-from-behind sprinter in his time, but wins very rarely these days and more often than not throws away races he ought to have won. Not one to trust.

Munir

116 116
3-y-o ch c Indian Ridge-Al Bahathri (USA) (Blushing Groom (FR))
B W Hills Hamdan Al Maktoum

Placings:31-1602441 **(5386)**

2001: 7^{1}GS, 8^{6}G, 7^{0}GF, 7^{2}G, 8^{4}GF, 7^{4}GS, 7^{1}GS

	Starts	1st	2nd	3rd	Win & Pl
Career Total (Turf)	9	3	1	1	108787

116	10/01	NmkR	7f	A	G-S	£58000
114	4/01	Newb	7f	A	G-S	£23200
90	10/00	Newb	6f8y	D	HVY	£5102

Total win prize-money £86303

Going (Turf): Sf: 1-2 **GS: 2-3** Gd: 0-2 GF: 0-2 Fm: 0-0
Distance: 5f/6f: 0-1 **7f-8f: 3-8** 9f-13f: 0-0 14f+: 0-0
Track : LH: 0-1 RH: 0-3 Tight: 0-0 Gall: 0-1
Aids: Bl: 0-1 Vi: 0-0 Tstrap: 0-0
Best Rating: 116 10/01 NmkR 7f gd-sft

A scopey son of top-class miler Al Bahathri, he won the the Greenham decisively on his reappearance. He failed to see the mile out when sixth in the 2000 Guineas, but did not shape badly back over seven in the Jersey Stakes, and confirmed that that is his trip at Goodwood. Ran below-par in first-time blinkers at the end of September before springing a surprise in the Group Two Challenge Stakes at Newmarket. Goes well on soft and has looked unsuited by fast ground. Usually held up.

Munjiz (IRE)

112(30) (65)**110**

5-y-o b h Marju (IRE)-Absaar (USA) (Alleged (USA))
B W Hills Hamdan Al Maktoum

Placings:4213/1626262/300-3416013405 **(5365)**
2001: 6^{3}S, 5^{4}GS, 6^{1}G, 6^{6}GF, 6^{0}GF, 5^{1}G, 6^{3}Y, 6^{4}GF, 6^{0}S, 6^{5}GS

	Starts	1st	2nd	3rd	Win & Pl
Career Total (Turf)	22	4	4	3	75019
Career Total (AW)	2	0	0	1	1631

90	7/01	Bath	5f161y	C	GD	£6075
108	5/01	NmkR	6f	B(0-110)H	GD	£9309
94	4/99	NmkJ	6f	C(0-95)H	GD	£7772
88	9/98	Gdwd	6f	D	G-S	£4825

Total win prize-money £27981

Going (Turf): Sf: 0-3 GS: 1-5 **Gd: 3-8** GF: 0-4 Fm: 0-1
Distance: **5f/6f: 4-21** 7f-8f: 0-2 9f-13f: 0-0 14f+: 0-0
Track : **LH: 1-4** RH: 0-0 Tight: 0-1 **Gall: 1-2**
Aids: Bl: 0-0 Vi: 0-0 Tstrap: 0-0
Best Rating: 110 10/01 NmkR 6f gd-sft

Pattern-class sprinter, best at six furlongs with cut in the ground. Tends to race prominently, but came from just off the pace when landing the odds at Bath in July. Good efforts in Pattern races since, but will probably need to find a weak one to score. Sold to the USA.

Munqith (USA)

100 **83**

2-y-o b c Bahri (USA)-Indihash (USA) (Gulch (USA))
E A L Dunlop Hamdan Al Maktoum

Placings:4 **(5604)**
2001: 7^{4}GS

	Starts	1st	2nd	3rd	Win & Pl
Career Total (Turf)	1	0	0	0	337

Going (Turf): Sf: 0-0 GS: 0-1 Gd: 0-0 GF: 0-0 Fm: 0-0
Distance: 5f/6f: 0-0 7f-8f: 0-1 9f-13f: 0-0 14f+: 0-0
Track : LH: 0-0 RH: 0-0 Tight: 0-0 Gall: 0-0
Aids: Bl: 0-0 Vi: 0-0 Tstrap: 0-0
Best Rating: 83 11/01 NmkR 7f gd-sft

Muqtarb (IRE)

90 **50**

5-y-o ch g Cadeaux Genereux-Jasarah (IRE) (Green Desert (USA))
W J Musson Cogtree Partnership

Placings:15/40/00-000000 **(5450)**
2001: 6^{0}G, 6^{0}GF, 6^{0}G, 6^{0}F, 5^{0}G, 8^{0}HY

	Starts	1st	2nd	3rd	Win & Pl
Career Total (Turf)	12	1	0	0	7796

89	7/98	Asct	6f	D	G-F	£6775

Total win prize-money £6775

Going (Turf): Sf: 0-1 GS: 0-1 Gd: 0-5 **GF: 1-4** Fm: 0-1
Distance: **5f/6f: 1-8** 7f-8f: 0-4 9f-13f: 0-0 14f+: 0-0
Track : LH: 0-2 RH: 0-1 Tight: 0-0 Gall: 0-3
Aids: Bl: 0-0 Vi: 0-0 Tstrap: 0-5
Best Rating: 53 5/01 Donc 6f good

A useful juvenile sprinter, but has shown nothing in the last three seasons.

Murdinga

19

2-y-o br g Emperor Jones (USA)-Tintinara (Selkirk (USA))
Lady Herries D K R & Mrs J B C Oliver

Placings:0 **(5290)**
2001: 7^{0}S

	Starts	1st	2nd	3rd	Win & Pl
Career Total (Turf)	1	0	0	0	

Going (Turf): Sf: 0-1 GS: 0-0 Gd: 0-0 GF: 0-0 Fm: 0-0
Distance: 5f/6f: 0-0 7f-8f: 0-1 9f-13f: 0-0 14f+: 0-0
Track : LH: 0-0 RH: 0-0 Tight: 0-0 Gall: 0-0
Aids: Bl: 0-0 Vi: 0-0 Tstrap: 0-0
Best Rating: 19 10/01 Leic 7f9y soft

Improved on his debut run to finish second at Lingfield in November.

Murghem (IRE)

108(99) (102)**111**

6-y-o b h Common Grounds-Fabulous Pet (Somethingfabulous (USA))
M Johnston A Al-Rostamani

Placings:2502132223/40641320320/2242111121466-05025 **(5322a)**
2001: 12^{0}G, 12^{5}GS, 16^{0}G, 14^{2}HY, 12^{5}Y

	Starts	1st	2nd	3rd	Win & Pl
Career Total (Turf)	38	7	11	4	218232
Career Total (AW)	1	0	1	0	1990

117	8/00	Newb	1m5f61y	A	G-F	£36000
112	8/00	Gdwd	1m4f	A(0-110)H	GD	£29000
113	7/00	NmkJ	1m4f	A	G-F	£13764
111	6/00	Leic	1m3f183y	A	G-F	£12945
107	6/00	Epsm	1m4f10y	B(0-105)H	GD	£29000
93	8/99	Sand	1m6f	C(0-90)H	G-S	£6464
80	7/98	Kemp	1m4f	D	G-F	£3566

Total win prize-money £130741

Going (Turf): Sf: 0-7 GS: 1-3 Gd: 2-16 **GF: 4-10** Fm: 0-1
Distance: 5f/6f: 0-0 7f-8f: 0-1 **9f-13f: 5-26** 14f+: 2-12
Track : LH: 2-20 **RH: 5-18** Tight: 2-6 Gall: 2-16
Aids: Bl: 0-1 Vi: 0-0 Tstrap: 0-0
Best Rating: 105 4/01 Newb 1m4f5y gd-sft

He ran his best race in 2000 when beating Savoire Vivre by 1 1/4 lengths in a 13-furlong Group Two at Newbury. Went globe-trotting after that, was highly tried, but ran below form. Ran poorly at Nad Al Sheba in March and well beaten in first two starts back home before running well at Haydock in September, and was not beaten far in Listed event at The Curragh. He is suited by a mile and a half plus, prefers a sound surface and has done best from the front in small fields.

Murjana (IRE)

105 **80**

3-y-o b f Pleasant Colony (USA)-Golden Reef (USA) (Mr Prospector (USA))
B W Hills Hamdan Al Maktoum

Placings:02223210 **(4855)**
2001: 8^{0}G, 8^{2}F, 10^{2}GF, 10^{2}G, 10^{3}GF, 8^{2}GF, 10^{1}GF, 11^{0}GF

	Starts	1st	2nd	3rd	Win & Pl
Career Total (Turf)	8	1	4	1	9030

75	9/01	Ripn	1m2f	D	G-F	£3484

Total win prize-money £3484

Going (Turf): Sf: 0-0 GS: 0-0 Gd: 0-2 **GF: 1-5** Fm: 0-1
Distance: 5f/6f: 0-0 7f-8f: 0-0 **9f-13f: 1-8** 14f+: 0-0
Track : LH: 0-5 **RH: 1-3 Tight: 1-3** Gall: 0-1
Aids: Bl: 0-0 Vi: 0-0 Tstrap: 0-0
Best Rating: 80 7/01 Pont 1m2f6y gd-fm

Murrendi (IRE)

103 **65**

3-y-o b g Ashkalani (IRE)-Formaestre (IRE) (Formidable (USA))
M R Channon The Dapper Boys

Placings:505423-066025641000 **(5269)**
2001: 9^{0}S, 10^{6}G, 9^{6}GF, 9^{0}S, 9^{2}GF, 10^{5}G, 10^{6}GF, 11^{4}GF, 10^{1}G, 9^{0}GF, 10^{0}GF, 10^{0}HY

	Starts	1st	2nd	3rd	Win & Pl
Career Total (Turf)	18	1	2	1	6276

65	8/01	Yarm	1m2f21y	F	GD	£2359

Total win prize-money £2359

Going (Turf): Sf: 0-3 GS: 0-1 **Gd: 1-6** GF: 0-8 Fm: 0-0
Distance: 5f/6f: 0-0 7f-8f: 0-4 **9f-13f: 1-14** 14f+: 0-0
Track : **LH: 1-9** RH: 0-7 **Tight: 1-7** Gall: 0-1
Aids: Bl: 0-0 Vi: 0-0 Tstrap: 0-0
Best Rating: 74 6/01 Gdwd 1m1f192y gd-fm

Ran well at two without winning. Has looked moderate this season at three. Tends to race keenly. Ran his better races on good ground.

Murron Wallace

(90) (27)

7-y-o gr m Reprimand-Fair Eleanor (Saritamer (USA))
D Haydn Jones Barry Adams

Placings:6555/55532110/0000064-0 **(0060)**
2001: 12^{0}SW

	Starts	1st	2nd	3rd	Win & Pl
Career Total (Turf)	14	2	1	1	6179
Career Total (AW)	6	0	0	0	0

50	9/97	Bath	1m5y	G(0-60)H	GD	£2556
44	8/97	Haml	1m65y	F(0-65)H	GD	£2528

Total win prize-money £5084

Going (Turf): Sf: 0-1 GS: 0-2 **Gd: 2-7** GF: 0-4 Fm: 0-0
Distance: 5f/6f: 0-2 7f-8f: 0-6 **9f-13f: 2-12** 14f+: 0-0
Track : LH: 1-10 RH: 1-5 **Tight: 2-10** Gall: 0-0
Aids: Bl: 0-2 Vi: 0-0 Tstrap: 0-0
Best Rating: 44 8/97 Haml 1m65y G

Murzim

85 **62**

2-y-o b c Salse (USA)-Guilty Secret (IRE) (Kris)
G A Butler Abdulla Al Khalifa

Placings:000 **(5459)**
2001: 10^{0}G, 7^{0}S, 8^{0}G

	Starts	1st	2nd	3rd	Win & Pl
Career Total (Turf)	3	0	0	0	

Going (Turf): Sf: 0-1 GS: 0-0 Gd: 0-2 GF: 0-0 Fm: 0-0
Distance: 5f/6f: 0-0 7f-8f: 0-1 9f-13f: 0-2 14f+: 0-0
Track : LH: 0-3 RH: 0-0 Tight: 0-2 Gall: 0-1
Aids: Bl: 0-0 Vi: 0-0 Tstrap: 0-0
Best Rating: 62 10/01 Bath 1m2f46y good

Mush (IRE)

(99) (42)**72**

4-y-o b c Thatching-Petite Jameel (IRE) (Ahonoora)
N P Littmoden Turf 2000 Limited

Placings:03/210-05233500 **(5406)**

2001: 8^{0}G, 9^{5}GF, 8^{2}G, 8^{3}F, 8^{3}GF, 8^{5}G, 7^{0}GF, 8^{0}SD

	Starts	1st	2nd	3rd	Win & Pl
Career Total (Turf)	12	1	2	3	7651
Career Total (AW)	1	0	0	0	

76 9/00 Wwck 1m22y F G-F £2488

Total win prize-money £2489

Going (Turf): Sf: 0-1 GS: 0-0 Gd: 0-5 **GF: 1-5** Fm: 0-1
Distance: 5f/6f: 0-1 7f-8f: 0-6 **9f-13f: 1-6** 14f+: 0-0
Track : **LH: 1-6** RH: 0-3 Tight: 0-5 Gall: 0-0
Aids: Bl: 0-0 Vi: 0-0 Tstrap: 0-0
Best Rating: 72 6/01 Kemp 1m1f gd-fm

Fair performer around a mile on fast ground.

Musha Merr (IRE)

106 **112**

3-y-o b c Sadler's Wells (USA)-Valdara (Darshaan)
Saeed Bin Suroor Godolphin

Placings:2-106 **(2350)**
2001: 10^{1}GF, 12^{0}G, 12^{6}GF

	Starts	1st	2nd	3rd	Win & Pl
Career Total (Turf)	4	1	1	0	21902

107 5/01 York 1m2f85y A G-F £18444

Total win prize-money £18444

Going (Turf): Sf: 0-0 GS: 0-0 Gd: 0-1 **GF: 1-2** Fm: 0-0
Distance: 5f/6f: 0-0 7f-8f: 0-0 **9f-13f: 1-3** 14f+: 0-0
Track : **LH: 1-1** RH: 0-1 Tight: 0-0 **Gall: 1-2**
Aids: Bl: 0-0 Vi: 0-1 Tstrap: 0-0
Best Rating: 110 6/01 Asct 1m4f gd-fm

Pattern-class colt, who finished runner-up behind the useful Equerry at Deauville in his only start at two, when trained in France by David Loder. Beaten a short head by Wareed in strongly-run private trial at Nad Al Sheba early this year, and beat Potemkin in the Glasgow Stakes at York in May. Raced in a visor and disappointed when unplaced in Prix du Jockey Club at Chantilly the following month, and found the ground too fast when sixth in the King Edward VII Stakes.

Music Club (USA)

103 **95+**

2-y-o b f Dixieland Band (USA)-Long View (USA) (Damascus (USA))
J H M Gosden W S Farish Iii

Placings:1 **(5361)**
2001: 8^{1}GS

	Starts	1st	2nd	3rd	Win & Pl
Career Total (Turf)	1	1	0	0	5668

95 10/01 NmkR 1m D G-S £5668

Total win prize-money £5668

Going (Turf): Sf: 0-0 **GS: 1-1** Gd: 0-0 GF: 0-0 Fm: 0-0
Distance: 5f/6f: 0-0 **7f-8f: 1-1** 9f-13f: 0-0 14f+: 0-0
Track : LH: 0-0 RH: 0-0 Tight: 0-0 Gall: 0-0
Aids: Bl: 0-0 Vi: 0-0 Tstrap: 0-0
Best Rating: 95 10/01 NmkR 1m gd-sft

A half-sister to winners in America, she is bred to stay and scored a smooth victory in a Newmarket maiden over a mile on good to soft ground.

Music Maid (IRE)

100 **68**

3-y-o b f Inzar (USA)-Richardstown Lass (IRE) (Muscatite)
H S Howe R J Parish

Placings:61300100-05663500 **(4988)**
2001: 7^{0}GF, 7^{5}GF, 7^{6}GF, 8^{6}GF, 8^{3}F, 7^{5}GF, 6^{0}GF, 8^{0}G

	Starts	1st	2nd	3rd	Win & Pl
Career Total (Turf)	16	2	0	2	10350

78 8/00 Epsm 7f D GD £4800
76 6/00 Ling 7f E G-F £3136

Total win prize-money £7936

Going (Turf): Sf: 0-2 GS: 0-0 **Gd: 1-3 GF: 1-10** Fm: 0-1
Distance: 5f/6f: 0-3 **7f-8f: 2-13** 9f-13f: 0-0 14f+: 0-0
Track : **LH: 1-4** RH: 0-3 **Tight: 1-3** Gall: 0-1
Aids: Bl: 0-0 Vi: 0-0 Tstrap: 0-0
Best Rating: 68 8/01 Sals 1m firm

She is not very consistent, but managed to win over seven furlongs at Lingfield and Epsom last season and obviously handles a sharp downhill track. She was tried in Listed company, but is nowhere near that class and has only shown glimpses of form back in less exalted company since.

Musical Flute

90 **62d**

2-y-o b f Piccolo-Stride Home (Absalom)
M R Channon Peter Taplin

Placings:445550 **(4488)**
2001: 5^{4}F, 5^{4}G, 6^{5}GF, 6^{5}GF, 7^{5}GF, 6^{0}S

	Starts	1st	2nd	3rd	Win & Pl
Career Total (Turf)	6	0	0	0	523

Going (Turf): Sf: 0-1 GS: 0-0 Gd: 0-1 GF: 0-3 Fm: 0-1
Distance: 5f/6f: 0-2 7f-8f: 0-4 9f-13f: 0-0 14f+: 0-0
Track : LH: 0-2 RH: 0-1 Tight: 0-1 Gall: 0-2
Aids: Bl: 0-0 Vi: 0-0 Tstrap: 0-0
Best Rating: 63 6/01 Bath 5f11y good

Musical Heath (IRE)

104 **79**

4-y-o b g Common Grounds-Song Of The Glens (Horage)
P W Harris The Highlanders

Placings:42210-001300 **(5344)**
2001: 8^{0}GS, 8^{0}GF, 8^{1}GF, 7^{3}GF, 8^{0}GF, 8^{0}GS

	Starts	1st	2nd	3rd	Win & Pl
Career Total (Turf)	11	2	2	1	13513

76 7/01 Epsm 1m114y D(0-85)H G-F £5564
78 9/00 Epsm 1m114y D GD £4192

Total win prize-money £9757

Going (Turf): Sf: 0-1 GS: 0-2 **Gd: 1-1 GF: 1-7** Fm: 0-0
Distance: 5f/6f: 0-0 7f-8f: 0-7 **9f-13f: 2-4** 14f+: 0-0
Track : **LH: 2-5** RH: 0-3 **Tight: 2-3** Gall: 0-1
Aids: Bl: 0-0 Vi: 0-0 **Tstrap: 1-5**
Best Rating: 79 9/01 Ling 7f140y gd-fm

Winner of an Epsom maiden over a mile and half a furlong in autumn of 2000. Scored in handicap over course and distance in July 2001. Acts on a sound surface.

Musical Mayhem (IRE)

89 **35**

8-y-o b g Shernazar-Minstrels Folly (USA) (The Minstrel (CAN))
D J Wintle A A Wintle

Placings:111/2154/100/0 **(3187)**
2001: 11^{0}GS

	Starts	1st	2nd	3rd	Win & Pl
Career Total (Turf)	11	5	1	0	22410

4/99 Leop 1m6f GD £0
92 7/98 Gway 2m (0-80)H YLD £5500
78 8/97 Tral 1m4f G-Y £6850
78 8/97 Slig 1m4f Y-S £2940
46 7/97 Gway 1m4f YLD £4795

Total win prize-money £20085

Going (Turf): Sf: 0-1 GS: 0-1 Gd: 0-1 GF: 0-2 Fm: 0-0
Distance: 5f/6f: 0-0 7f-8f: 0-0 **9f-13f: 3-4** 14f+: 1-6
Track : LH: 1-2 **RH: 3-8** Tight: 0-0 Gall: 0-1
Aids: Bl: 0-1 Vi: 0-0 Tstrap: 0-0
Best Rating: 35 7/01 Leic 1m3f183y gd-sft

Must Be Magic

107(101) (62)**60**

4-y-o b g Magic Ring (IRE)-Sequin Lady (Star Appeal)
H J Collingridge The Headquarters Partnership Iii

Placings:04300/063431006200-4200015202 **(4900)**
2001: 12^{4}SW, 10^{2}SD, 8^{0}S, 9^{0}G, 9^{0}F, 9^{1}GF, 10^{5}G, 8^{2}GF, 10^{0}G, 8^{2}GS

	Starts	1st	2nd	3rd	Win & Pl
Career Total (Turf)	20	2	2	3	15961
Career Total (AW)	7	0	2	0	1358

60 6/01 Kemp 1m1f D(0-80)H G-F £7865
64 7/00 Epsm 1m114y E(0-70)H G-F £3656

Total win prize-money £11521

Going (Turf): Sf: 0-5 GS: 0-2 Gd: 0-7 **GF: 2-5** Fm: 0-1
Distance: 5f/6f: 0-0 7f-8f: 0-7 **9f-13f: 2-20** 14f+: 0-0
Track : LH: 1-19 RH: 1-4 **Tight: 1-13** Gall: 0-0
Aids: Bl: 0-0 **Vi: 1-10** Tstrap: 0-0
Best Rating: 60 6/01 Kemp 1m1f gd-fm

A useful handicapper at around a mile. Acts on fast ground. Usually comes good at around June/July time.

Mustang

(96) (30)**40**

8-y-o ch g Thatching-Lassoo (Caerleon (USA))
J Pearce Chris Marsh

Placings:04/06/5444001642642l0/22220242660046/40 4454/300250306105450000-600 **(0164)**
2001: 8^{6}SD, 8^{0}SW, 9^{0}SD

	Starts	1st	2nd	3rd	Win & Pl
Career Total (Turf)	19	1	1	1	3506
Career Total (AW)	40	2	8	1	11687

40 6/00 Brig 7f214y G FRM £1943
45 11/97 Ling 7f E(0-70)H STD £2466
32 3/97 Wolv 7f F(0-65)H STD £2433

Total win prize-money £6842

Going (Turf): Sf: 0-1 GS: 0-3 Gd: 0-7 GF: 0-5 **Fm: 1-3**
Distance: 5f/6f: 0-5 **7f-8f: 3-35** 9f-13f: 0-19 14f+: 0-0
Track : **LH: 3-48** RH: 0-5 **Tight: 2-28** Gall: 0-2
Aids: **Bl: 3-26** Vi: 0-15 Tstrap: 0-0
Best Rating: 30 1/01 Sthl 1m stand

He has done most of his racing on sand in recent seasons, and is a winner on both Fibresand and Equitrack.

Mutabari (USA)

(100) (51)**38**

7-y-o ch g Seeking The Gold (USA)-Cagey Exuberance (USA) (Exuberant (USA))
R Hollinshead G J Sargent

Placings:530/30040540/66000502/10511025064440550 5600/342530400406500601-60 **(0565)**
2001: 7^{6}SD, 7^{0}SD

	Starts	1st	2nd	3rd	Win & Pl
Career Total (Turf)	33	0	0	2	2577
Career Total (AW)	27	4	3	2	11865

51 12/00 Wolv 7f F(0-60)H STD £1757
61 3/99 Wolv 7f F(0-60)H STD £1698
55 2/99 Ling 7f E(0-70)H STD £2946
54 1/99 Sthl 7f E(0-70)H STD £2463

Total win prize-money £8864

Going (Turf): Sf: 0-7 GS: 0-9 Gd: 0-7 GF: 0-6 Fm: 0-4
Distance: 5f/6f: 0-7 **7f-8f: 4-35** 9f-13f: 0-17 14f+: 0-1
Track : **LH: 4-38** RH: 0-9 **Tight: 3-20** Gall: 0-1
Aids: Bl: 0-0 **Vi: 2-19** Tstrap: 0-0
Best Rating: 45 3/01 Wolv 7f stand

Mutabassir (IRE)

104(92) (62)62

7-y-o ch g Soviet Star (USA)-Anghaam (USA) (Diesis)

G L Moore George Smith Ltd

Placings:5/204053511112112/2124430/65430251500-00114400 **(4640)**

2001: 8^{0}GF, 6^{0}F, 7^{1}GF, 6^{1}F, 7^{4}G, 7^{4}GF, 7^{0}GF, 7^{0}GF

	Starts	1st	2nd	3rd	Win & Pl
Career Total (Turf)	33	7	3	3	27359
Career Total (AW)	8	2	3	0	7666

7/01 Brig 6f209y E(0-70)H FRM £2793
45 6/01 Brig 7f214y G G-F £1974
62 8/00 Brig 7f214y E(0-70)H FRM £3094
73 4/99 Brig 7f214y E(0-70)H G-F £2866
53 11/98 Sthl 7f F(0-60)H STD £2008
53 11/98 Ling 7f E(0-75)H STD £2502
57 9/98 Folk 7f E(0-70)H G-F £3675
52 9/98 Epsm 7f E(0-70)H GD £2944
50 8/98 Brig 6f209y F(0-60)H FRM £2729
Total win prize-money £24586

Going (Turf): Sf: 0-3 GS: 0-2 Gd: 1-11 **GF: 3-10 Fm: 3-7**
Distance: 5f/6f: 0-1 **7f-8f: 9-34** 9f-13f: 0-6 14f+: 0-0
Track : **LH: 8-28** RH: 0-6 **Tight: 2-11** Gall: 0-1
Aids: Bl: 0-0 Vi: 0-0 Tstrap: 0-0
Best Rating: 62 7/01 Folk 7f gd-fm

A fair handicapper in modest company, he reserves his best form for Brighton these days and has an admirable record there.

Mutadarra (IRE)

99(92) (31)51

8-y-o ch g Mujtahid (USA)-Silver Echo (Caerleon (USA))

G M McCourt Mccourt Fine Meats Ltd

Placings:2/23100/0050214000/050220/0210460000/400002510200-300 **(3496)**

2001: 9^{3}GF, 9^{0}GF, 11^{0}GF

	Starts	1st	2nd	3rd	Win & Pl
Career Total (Turf)	42	4	8	2	32412
Career Total (AW)	5	0	0	0	0

60 7/00 Wind 1m2f7y E(0-70)H SFT £3570
66 6/99 Sand 1m2f7y C(0-100)H GD £7100
69 7/97 NmkJ 1m2f D(0-75)H GD £4932
80 5/96 Pont 6f D GD £3728
Total win prize-money £19331

Going (Turf): Sf: 1-3 GS: 0-5 **Gd: 3-14** GF: 0-18 Fm: 0-2
Distance: 5f/6f: 1-2 7f-8f: 0-5 **9f-13f: 3-39** 14f+: 0-1
Track : LH: 1-15 **RH: 2-22** Tight: 1-17 Gall: 1-10
Aids: Bl: 0-1 Vi: 0-0 Tstrap: 0-0
Best Rating: 51 6/01 Gdwd 1m1f gd-fm

Lightly raced this season, he looks best on good ground at around ten furlongs.

Mutafaweq (USA)

113 118

5-y-o b h Silver Hawk (USA)-The Caretaker (Caerleon (USA))

Saeed Bin Suroor Godolphin

Placings:21/11541/301031-013006 **(5120a)**

2001: 12^{0}G, 12^{1}GF, 12^{3}GF, 12^{0}GS, 11^{0}F, 12^{6}G

	Starts	1st	2nd	3rd	Win & Pl
Career Total (Turf)	19	7	1	3	978447

124 6/01 Epsm 1m4f10y A G-F £150000
125 10/00 Wood 1m4f FRM £379747
113 7/00 Duss 1m4f GD £64516
126 9/99 Donc 1m6f132yA G-F £218500
112 6/99 Asct 1m4f A G-F £77160
104 5/99 Donc 1m2f60y B G-F £8593
87 10/98 NmkR 1m D GD £7632
Total win prize-money £906148

Going (Turf): Sf: 0-0 GS: 0-2 Gd: 2-7 **GF: 4-6** Fm: 1-2
Distance: 5f/6f: 0-0 7f-8f: 1-1 **9f-13f: 5-16** 14f+: 1-2
Track : **LH: 4-8** RH: 2-6 Tight: 1-1 **Gall: 3-6**
Aids: Bl: 0-0 Vi: 0-0 Tstrap: 0-0
Best Rating: 124 6/01 Epsm 1m4f10y gd-fm

He proved that stamina was his forte when outbattling the triple Oaks-winner Ramruma in the 1999 St Leger. He has since been globetrotting for Godolphin and picked up Group Ones at Dusseldorf and Woodbine last season. Very game winner of the Coronation Cup this term, but did not show the same level of form in the Hardwicke and did not have things go his way in Germany and America subsequently. Suited by at least 12 furlongs and fast ground.

Mutahadeth

93(99) (32)33

7-y-o ch g Rudimentary (USA)-Music In My Life (IRE) (Law Society (USA))

D Shaw K G Radford

Placings:0056/51252003530300 4/102036002050 03/03641120040403/256034446044001-000000500 **(3967)**

2001: 8^{0}SD, 8^{0}SD, 9^{0}SD, 9^{0}SD, 11^{0}SD, 7^{0}S, 8^{5}GS, 8^{0}F, 8^{0}GS

	Starts	1st	2nd	3rd	Win & Pl
Career Total (Turf)	21	0	1	2	2302
Career Total (AW)	50	5	5	6	16206

46 12/00 Wolv 1m100y F(0-60)H STD £1830
60 3/99 Sthl 1m E(0-70)H STD £2346
60 2/99 Wolv 1m100y F(0-55) STD £2165
68 1/98 Sthl 7f F(0-65) STD £1735
60 2/97 Sthl 1m F(0-65)H STD £2294
Total win prize-money £10373

Going (Turf): Sf: 0-2 GS: 0-3 Gd: 0-5 GF: 0-9 Fm: 0-2
Distance: 5f/6f: 0-3 **7f-8f: 3-48** 9f-13f: 2-20 14f+: 0-0
Track : **LH: 5-59** RH: 0-6 **Tight: 2-22** Gall: 0-1
Aids: **Bl: 4-49** Vi: 0-1 Tstrap: 0-0
Best Rating: 33 7/01 Hayd 7f30y soft

His best form has been in modest company at around a mile on Fibresand.

Mutakarrim

109 104

4-y-o ch c Mujtahid (USA)-Alyakkh (IRE) (Sadler's Wells (USA))

D K Weld Hamdan Al Maktoum

Placings:521111-253201 **(4748a)**

2001: 10^{2}S, 12^{5}G, 12^{3}Y, 12^{2}GY, 13^{0}G, 12^{1}GF

	Starts	1st	2nd	3rd	Win & Pl
Career Total (Turf)	12	5	3	1	65447

104 9/01 Gway 1m4f G-F £29250
89 9/00 List 1m4f SH £8280
89 9/00 Fair 1m4f (0-90)H G-F £4485
80 8/00 Dpat 1m3f208y G-F £2932
78 8/00 Tram 1m4f G-F £4140
Total win prize-money £49087

Going (Turf): Sf: 0-1 GS: 0-0 Gd: 0-2 **GF: 4-4** Fm: 0-1
Distance: 5f/6f: 0-0 7f-8f: 0-0 **9f-13f: 5-10** 14f+: 0-1
Track : LH: 1-2 **RH: 4-6** Tight: 0-0 Gall: 0-2
Aids: **Bl: 5-10** Vi: 0-0 Tstrap: 0-0
Best Rating: 104 9/01 Gway 1m4f gd-fm

Unraced at two, he scored four times on the bounce over a mile and a half in Ireland in 2000 and ran right up to his best on his seasonal bow. Has won on fast ground and soft. Took a Listed event at Galway on his final start of the season. Sold to go hurdling.

Mutamam

118 124

6-y-o b h Darshaan-Petal Girl (Caerleon (USA))

A C Stewart Hamdan Al Maktoum

Placings:113/201114/0/214114-10110 **(5579a)**

2001: 12^{1}GS, 12^{0}GF, 12^{1}G, 12^{1}G, 12^{0}F

	Starts	1st	2nd	3rd	Win & Pl
Career Total (Turf)	21	11	2	1	712189

120 9/01 Wood 1m4f GD £400000
117 9/01 Kemp 1m4f A GD £21000
118 7/01 NmkJ 1m4f A G-S £34800
120 9/00 Asct 1m4f A G-S £32400
124 9/00 Kemp 1m4f A GD £21000
106 5/00 Gdwd 1m4f B SFT £10753
118 9/98 Gdwd 1m1f192yA G-S £22450
113 8/98 Hayd 1m2f120yA GD £19600
116 7/98 Sand 1m2f7y C GD £5180
102 9/97 Ches 7f122y C GD £5120
86 8/97 Ling 7f140y D G-S £3143
Total win prize-money £575446

Going (Turf): Sf: 1-1 GS: 4-4 **Gd: 6-10** GF: 0-4 Fm: 0-2
Distance: 5f/6f: 0-0 7f-8f: 2-3 **9f-13f: 9-18** 14f+: 0-0
Track : LH: 3-8 **RH: 7-10 Tight: 3-5** Gall: 2-5
Aids: Bl: 0-0 Vi: 0-0 Tstrap: 0-0
Best Rating: 120 9/01 Wood 1m4f good

He came back this season as good as ever with a fine victory in the Princess Of Wales Stakes at the Newmarket July meeting, but may not have got over that when well behind Galileo in the King George. Repeated his September Stakes victory next time and beat the 2000 Derby runner-up Daliapour in the Canadian International. He may still have been feeling the effects of that when well beaten in the Breeders' Cup Turf. He is suited by 12 furlongs, forcing tactics and easy ground. Retired to the National Stud.

Mutamarkiz (IRE)

102 88

4-y-o b c Rainbow Quest (USA)-Pharaoh's Delight (Fairy King (USA))

M P Tregoning Hamdan Al Maktoum

Placings:150 **(1605)**

2001: 7^{1}S, 8^{5}GS, 10^{0}GF

	Starts	1st	2nd	3rd	Win & Pl
Career Total (Turf)	3	1	0	0	4024

88 4/01 Kemp 7f D SFT £3763
Total win prize-money £3764

Going (Turf): Sf: 1-1 GS: 0-1 Gd: 0-0 GF: 0-1 Fm: 0-0
Distance: 5f/6f: 0-0 **7f-8f: 1-2** 9f-13f: 0-1 14f+: 0-0
Track : LH: 0-0 **RH: 1-3** Tight: 0-0 **Gall: 1-2**
Aids: Bl: 0-0 Vi: 0-0 Tstrap: 0-0
Best Rating: 88 4/01 Kemp 7f soft

Mutarafaa (USA)

100 79

2-y-o b c Red Ransom (USA)-Mashaarif (USA) (Mr Prospector (USA))

J H M Gosden Hamdan Al Maktoum

Placings:20560 **(5368)**

2001: 6^{2}GF, 6^{0}GF, 7^{5}G, 7^{6}G, 8^{0}GS

	Starts	1st	2nd	3rd	Win & Pl
Career Total (Turf)	5	0	1	0	1320

Going (Turf): Sf: 0-0 GS: 0-1 Gd: 0-2 GF: 0-2 Fm: 0-0
Distance: 5f/6f: 0-2 7f-8f: 0-3 9f-13f: 0-0 14f+: 0-0
Track : LH: 0-2 RH: 0-0 Tight: 0-2 Gall: 0-0
Aids: Bl: 0-0 Vi: 0-0 Tstrap: 0-0
Best Rating: 79 6/01 Gdwd 6f gd-fm

Has not progressed from a good effort on his

Goodwood debut and was disappointing in handicaps.

Mutarased (USA)

103 **87**

3-y-o b c Storm Cat (USA)-Sajjaya (USA) (Blushing Groom (FR))

R J White (J L Dunlop 30/6) Littleton Manor Racing

Placings:012-040 **(3848)**

2001: 7^0GF, 7^4GF, 8^0G

	Starts	1st	2nd	3rd	Win & Pl
Career Total (Turf)	6	1	1	0	5438

79	9/00	Brig	6f209y	D	SFT	£3807

Total win prize-money £3808

Going (Turf): Sf: 1-2 GS: 0-0 Gd: 0-1 GF: 0-3 Fm: 0-0
Distance: 5f/6f: 0-0 **7f-8f: 1-6** 9f-13f: 0-0 14f+: 0-0
Track : **LH: 1-1** RH: 0-1 Tight: 0-0 Gall: 0-0
Aids: Bl: 0-0 Vi: 0-0 Tstrap: 0-0
Best Rating: 87 6/01 Ling 7f gd-fm

A winner in soft ground as a juvenile, he has been held on a fast surface in 2001.

Mutared (IRE)

95 **60**

3-y-o b c Marju (IRE)-Shahaada (USA) (Private Account (USA))

M Wigham (J E Hammond 17/1) The Rob'Em Blind Partnership

Placings:0-00602 **(5681)**

2001: 7^0VS, 7^0G, 6^6G, 11^0G, 8^2S

	Starts	1st	2nd	3rd	Win & Pl
Career Total (Turf)	6	0	1	0	1446

Going (Turf): Sf: 0-2 GS: 0-0 Gd: 0-3 GF: 0-0 Fm: 0-0
Distance: 5f/6f: 0-1 7f-8f: 0-4 9f-13f: 0-1 14f+: 0-0
Track : LH: 0-1 RH: 0-0 Tight: 0-1 Gall: 0-0
Aids: Bl: 0-0 Vi: 0-0 Tstrap: 0-0
Best Rating: 60 11/01 Donc 1m soft

Signs of ability in maiden company, and put up an improved display on first start in handicap company when runner-up at Doncaster. Acts on soft.

Mutasawwar

107(110) (66)**61**

7-y-o ch g Clantime-Keen Melody (USA) (Sharpen Up)

J M Bradley Clifton Hunt

Placings:00/42400**625**/**14266**00064100**002**/**403500**/500 0400**222**000**316263-506**032222401036360 **(4253)**

2001: 5^5SD, 6^0SD, 5^6SD, 5^0GS, 5^3S, 5^2GF, 5^2G, 5^2GF, 5^2F, 5^4F, 5^0GF, 5^1GF, 5^0S, 5^3GF, 5^6GF, 5^3G, 5^6G, 5^0GF

	Starts	1st	2nd	3rd	Win & Pl
Career Total (Turf)	45	2	7	3	21914
Career Total (AW)	25	2	5	3	9182

57	7/01	Bevl	5f	D(0-80)H	G-F	£7787
67	11/00	Wolv	5f	F(0-60)H	STD	£2320
55	9/98	Chep	5f16y	E(0-70)H	G-S	£3109
61	1/98	Ling	6f	F(0-80)H	STD	£2377

Total win prize-money £15594

Going (Turf): Sf: 0-9 **GS: 1-7** Gd: 0-8 **GF: 1-17** Fm: 0-4
Distance: **5f/6f: 4-63** 7f-8f: 0-7 9f-13f: 0-0 14f+: 0-0
Track : **LH: 2-36** RH: 0-3 **Tight: 2-23** Gall: 0-10
Aids: **Bl: 1-7** Vi: 0-0 Tstrap: 0-0
Best Rating: 61 8/01 Wind 5f10y good

Has a poor wins-to-runs ratio, but runs consistently well. Scored in July 2001 at Beverley. Fast-ground and five furlongs suit him well.

Mutawaqed (IRE)

73 **40**

3-y-o ch g Zafonic (USA)-Waqood (USA) (Riverman (USA))

M P Tregoning Hamdan Al Maktoum

Placings:0-00 **(1167)**

2001: 6^0HY, 8^0GS

	Starts	1st	2nd	3rd	Win & Pl
Career Total (Turf)	3	0	0	0	

Going (Turf): Sf: 0-1 GS: 0-1 Gd: 0-1 GF: 0-0 Fm: 0-0
Distance: 5f/6f: 0-0 7f-8f: 0-3 9f-13f: 0-0 14f+: 0-0
Track : LH: 0-0 RH: 0-2 Tight: 0-1 Gall: 0-0
Aids: Bl: 0-0 Vi: 0-0 Tstrap: 0-0
Best Rating: 40 5/01 Kemp 1m gd-sft

Muted Gift

86 **22**

3-y-o ch f King's Signet (USA)-Ballet On Ice (FR) (Fijar Tango (FR))

W G M Turner Darren Coombes

Placings:0-40506 **(1564)**

2001: 5^4HY, 6^0HY, 6^5GF, 6^0S, 5^6F

	Starts	1st	2nd	3rd	Win & Pl
Career Total (Turf)	6	0	0	0	0

Going (Turf): Sf: 0-3 GS: 0-0 Gd: 0-0 GF: 0-2 Fm: 0-1
Distance: 5f/6f: 0-3 7f-8f: 0-3 9f-13f: 0-0 14f+: 0-0
Track : LH: 0-2 RH: 0-0 Tight: 0-0 Gall: 0-0
Aids: Bl: 0-0 Vi: 0-0 Tstrap: 0-0
Best Rating: 22 5/01 Brig 5f213y firm

Muthaaber

106 **96**

3-y-o br c Machiavellian (USA)-Raheefa (USA) (Riverman (USA))

J H M Gosden Hamdan Al Maktoum

Placings:52-103452 **(4059)**

2001: 7^1GF, 7^0G, 8^3GF, 8^4GF, 9^5G, 10^2GF

	Starts	1st	2nd	3rd	Win & Pl
Career Total (Turf)	8	1	2	1	15218

82	5/01	Hayd	7f30y	D	G-F	£4277

Total win prize-money £4277

Going (Turf): Sf: 0-1 GS: 0-0 Gd: 0-2 **GF: 1-5** Fm: 0-0
Distance: 5f/6f: 0-0 **7f-8f: 1-6** 9f-13f: 0-2 14f+: 0-0
Track : **LH: 1-3** RH: 0-1 Tight: 0-1 Gall: 0-1
Aids: Bl: 0-0 Vi: 0-0 Tstrap: 0-0
Best Rating: 96 8/01 Newb 1m2f6y gd-fm

Showed ability at two and scored on his reappearance over seven furlongs at Haydock. Ran very well to finish a fine third in the Britannia and fourth in a valuable Newbury handicap since. Stays a mile, has won on good to firm, but is suited by an easy surface as well.

Mutiny

87 **54**

3-y-o ch c Selkirk (USA)-Indian Love Song (Be My Guest (USA))

M Johnston J R Good

Placings:000 **(2376)**

2001: 10^0GF, 11^0GF, 14^0GF

	Starts	1st	2nd	3rd	Win & Pl
Career Total (Turf)	3	0	0	0	

Going (Turf): Sf: 0-0 GS: 0-0 Gd: 0-0 GF: 0-3 Fm: 0-0
Distance: 5f/6f: 0-0 7f-8f: 0-0 9f-13f: 0-2 14f+: 0-1
Track : LH: 0-2 RH: 0-1 Tight: 0-1 Gall: 0-0
Aids: Bl: 0-0 Vi: 0-0 Tstrap: 0-0
Best Rating: 54 6/01 Leic 1m3f183y gd-fm

Mutinyonthebounty

112 **106**

2-y-o b c Sadler's Wells (USA)-Threatening (Warning)

A P O'Brien M Tabor & Mrs John Magnier

Placings:3114 **(5677a)**

2001: 7^3GF, 8^1G, 8^1S, 8^4HO

	Starts	1st	2nd	3rd	Win & Pl
Career Total (Turf)	4	2	0	1	90224

106	9/01	Asct	1m	A	SFT	£72000
78	8/01	Gowr	1m		GD	£9660

Total win prize-money £81660

Going (Turf): Sf: 1-1 GS: 0-0 **Gd: 1-1** GF: 0-1 Fm: 0-0
Distance: 5f/6f: 0-0 **7f-8f: 2-4** 9f-13f: 0-0 14f+: 0-0
Track : LH: 0-1 **RH: 1-1** Tight: 0-0 **Gall: 1-1**
Aids: Bl: 0-0 Vi: 0-0 Tstrap: 0-0
Best Rating: 106 9/01 Asct 1m soft

Comfortable winner at Gowran on his second start, he improved dramatically to win the Royal Lodge on his next start. The soft ground was clearly in his favour that day and placed the emphasis on stamina. His dam is a half-sister to Classic Cliche and My Emma. Far from disgraced when fourth in the Criterium at Saint Cloud on his final start.

Muwakleh

110 (113+)**119**

3-y-o b f Machiavellian (USA)-Elfaslah (IRE) (Green Desert (USA))

Saeed Bin Suroor Godolphin

Placings:112 **(1142)**

2001: 8^1FT, 8^1FT, 8^2G

	Starts	1st	2nd	3rd	Win & Pl
Career Total (Turf)	1	0	1	0	66000
Career Total (AW)	2	2	0	0	180000

113	3/01	Ndas	1m	FST £100000
105	2/01	Ndas	1m	FST £80000

Total win prize-money £180000

Going (Turf): Sf: 0-0 GS: 0-0 Gd: 0-1 GF: 0-0 Fm: 0-0
Distance: 5f/6f: 0-0 **7f-8f: 2-3** 9f-13f: 0-0 14f+: 0-0
Track : LH: 0-0 RH: 0-0 Tight: 0-0 Gall: 0-0
Aids: Bl: 0-0 Vi: 0-0 Tstrap: 0-0
Best Rating: 119 5/01 NmkR 1m good

High class filly, ran a cracking race to be second to Ameerat in 1000 Guineas, where she failed by only a neck in her attempt to make all. Sustained an injury in that event and had to be retired. She had won on her two previous races, both at Nad Al Sheba, where she was an impressive winner of the UAE 1000 Guineas. She would probably have stayed a mile and a quarter, being a sister to the Dubai World Cup winner Almutawakel.

Muyassir (IRE)

(91) (70)**83**

6-y-o b h Brief Truce (USA)-Twine (Thatching)

P J Makin William Otley

Placings:0040/2030**0014**/362140/011355-01600 **(5344)**

2001: 8^0GF, 8^1GF, 8^6GF, 9^0G, 8^0GS

	Starts	1st	2nd	3rd	Win & Pl
Career Total (Turf)	26	4	2	3	39775
Career Total (AW)	2	1	0	0	3158

83	7/01	Kemp	1m	C(0-95)H	G-F	£9590
83	6/00	Gdwd	1m1f	C(0-90)H	G-F	£8463
79	6/00	Kemp	1m	D(0-80)H	G-F	£7507

72 7/99 NmkJ 1m D(0-80)H GD £8350
69 10/98 Ling 1m2f E(0-70)H STD £3157
Total win prize-money £37070

Going (Turf): Sf: 0-0 GS: 0-4 Gd: 1-6 **GF: 3-14** Fm: 0-2
Distance: 5f/6f: 0-2 **7f-8f: 3-12** 9f-13f: 2-14 14f+: 0-0
Track : LH: 1-7 **RH: 3-10 Tight: 2-10** Gall: 0-2
Aids: Bl: 0-0 Vi: 0-0 Tstrap: 0-0
Best Rating: 83 7/01 Kemp 1m gd-fm

Useful mile handicapper when on song, best on a sound surface. Winner at Kempton in July. Has been ridden by Seb Sanders on all five of his wins. Usually held up. Capable of going well fresh.

My American Beauty

107 **87**
3-y-o ch f Wolfhound (USA)-Hooray Lady (Ahonoora)
T D Easterby Peter G Gorvin

Placings:603100-001141130 **(4826)**
2001: 6^{0}G, 5^{0}F, 5^{1}GF, 5^{1}GF, 6^{4}GF, 5^{1}GF, 5^{1}G, 5^{3}G, 6^{0}G

	Starts	1st	2nd	3rd	Win & Pl
Career Total (Turf)	15	5	0	2	37622

80 8/01 Bevl 5f D(0-80)H GD £9399
71 7/01 Nott 5f13y D(0-85)H G-F £5489
66 6/01 Ayr 5f D(0-85)H G-F £7410
63 6/01 Pont 5f E(0-65) G-F £3108
69 9/00 York 6f C GD £8079
Total win prize-money £33486

Going (Turf): Sf: 0-1 GS: 0-0 Gd: 2-7 **GF: 3-5** Fm: 0-2
Distance: **5f/6f: 5-15** 7f-8f: 0-0 9f-13f: 0-0 14f+: 0-0
Track : **LH: 1-2** RH: 0-0 Tight: 0-0 Gall: 0-0
Aids: Bl: 0-0 Vi: 0-0 Tstrap: 0-0
Best Rating: 87 8/01 York 5f good

Winner at six furlongs as a juvenile, she has been in fine form this season with four victories over the minimum trip. Gradually climbing the handicap, she is suited by fast ground.

My Bayard

(82) (49)
2-y-o ch c Efisio-Bay Bay (Bay Express)
P F I Cole Penelope, Viscountess Portman

Placings:05 **(4875)**
2001: 6^{0}GF, 8^{5}SD

	Starts	1st	2nd	3rd	Win & Pl
Career Total (Turf)	1	0	0	0	
Career Total (AW)	1	0	0	0	0

Going (Turf): Sf: 0-0 GS: 0-0 Gd: 0-0 GF: 0-1 Fm: 0-0
Distance: 5f/6f: 0-1 7f-8f: 0-0 9f-13f: 0-1 14f+: 0-0
Track : LH: 0-1 RH: 0-0 Tight: 0-1 Gall: 0-0
Aids: Bl: 0-0 Vi: 0-0 Tstrap: 0-0
Best Rating: 49 9/01 Wolv 1m100y stand

My Bold Boyo

95(102) (48)**41**
6-y-o b g Never So Bold-My Rosie (Forzando)
K Bishop E T Roberts

Placings:43431500/6650000/4405000-045 **(4293)**
2001: 12^{0}GF, 8^{4}S, 10^{5}GF

	Starts	1st	2nd	3rd	Win & Pl
Career Total (Turf)	21	1	0	2	3425
Career Total (AW)	4	0	0	0	290

76 8/98 Ling 7f140y F GD £2070
Total win prize-money £2070

Going (Turf): Sf: 0-7 GS: 0-1 **Gd: 1-6** GF: 0-5 Fm: 0-2
Distance: 5f/6f: 0-1 **7f-8f: 1-12** 9f-13f: 0-12 14f+: 0-0
Track : LH: 0-10 RH: 0-4 Tight: 0-10 Gall: 0-1
Aids: Bl: 0-6 Vi: 0-0 Tstrap: 0-0
Best Rating: 33 8/01 Chep 1m2f36y gd-fm

My Brother

104 (14)**52**
7-y-o b g Lugana Beach-Lucky Love (Mummy's Pet)
Dr J R J Naylor Robert & Cora Till

Placings:0/00/5P000/15-256600 **(4950)**
2001: 6^{2}GF, 6^{5}GF, 7^{6}GF, 5^{6}G, 6^{0}F, 5^{0}G

	Starts	1st	2nd	3rd	Win & Pl
Career Total (Turf)	15	1	1	0	4660
Career Total (AW)	1	0	0	0	

39 6/00 Gdwd 6f E(0-70)H GD £3250
Total win prize-money £3250

Going (Turf): Sf: 0-0 GS: 0-0 **Gd: 1-5** GF: 0-9 Fm: 0-1
Distance: **5f/6f: 1-6** 7f-8f: 0-9 9f-13f: 0-1 14f+: 0-0
Track : LH: 0-3 RH: 0-3 Tight: 0-1 Gall: 0-3
Aids: Bl: 0-0 Vi: 0-1 Tstrap: 0-0
Best Rating: 52 7/01 Wind 6f gd-fm

My Dancer (IRE)

97 **80**
2-y-o b f Alhaarth (IRE)-Dance Land (IRE) (Nordance (USA))
R Hannon Jubert Family

Placings:200130 **(3601)**
2001: 5^{2}GF, 5^{0}GF, 5^{0}GF, 5^{1}GF, 5^{3}GF, 6^{0}G

	Starts	1st	2nd	3rd	Win & Pl
Career Total (Turf)	6	1	1	1	6496

80 7/01 Bath 5f11y D G-F £3415
Total win prize-money £3416

Going (Turf): Sf: 0-0 GS: 0-0 Gd: 0-1 **GF: 1-5** Fm: 0-0
Distance: **5f/6f: 1-6** 7f-8f: 0-0 9f-13f: 0-0 14f+: 0-0
Track : **LH: 1-2** RH: 0-0 Tight: 0-1 **Gall: 1-1**
Aids: Bl: 0-0 Vi: 0-0 Tstrap: 0-0
Best Rating: 80 7/01 Bath 5f11y gd-fm

A half-sister to a mile and a half winner. She showed plenty of speed to win over the minimum trip at Bath in the summer of 2001. Acts on a sound surface. Should stay further.

My Dilemma

79(62)
5-y-o b m Pursuit Of Love-Butosky (Busted)
J A Gilbert C L Jennison, M D Bromley, N S A Dragone

Placings:403/000060/0-0 **(3707)**
2001: 11^{0}G

	Starts	1st	2nd	3rd	Win & Pl
Career Total (Turf)	7	0	0	1	596
Career Total (AW)	4	0	0	0	238

Going (Turf): Sf: 0-0 GS: 0-2 Gd: 0-3 GF: 0-1 Fm: 0-1
Distance: 5f/6f: 0-0 7f-8f: 0-6 9f-13f: 0-5 14f+: 0-0
Track : LH: 0-8 RH: 0-1 Tight: 0-3 Gall: 0-0
Aids: Bl: 0-1 Vi: 0-0 Tstrap: 0-0
Best Rating: 24 8/01 Leic 1m3f183y good

My Ding A Ling

(67) (5)
2-y-o b f Librate-Dawn Bell (Belfort (FR))
J M Bradley J M Bradley

Placings:50 **(1019)**
2001: 5^{5}HY, 5^{0}SD

	Starts	1st	2nd	3rd	Win & Pl
Career Total (Turf)	1	0	0	0	0
Career Total (AW)	1	0	0	0	

Going (Turf): Sf: 0-1 GS: 0-0 Gd: 0-0 GF: 0-0 Fm: 0-0
Distance: 5f/0f. 0-2 7f-8f. 0-0 9f-13f: 0-0 14f+: 0-0
Track : LH: 0-1 RH: 0-0 Tight: 0-0 Gall: 0-1
Aids: Bl: 0-0 Vi: 0-0 Tstrap: 0-0
Best Rating: 5 4/01 Sthl 5f stand

My Friend Jack

96(88) (57)**38**
3-y-o b g Petong-Spring Collection (Tina's Pet)
J Akehurst The Grass Is Greener Partnership Ii

Placings:5060303-434000 **(4363)**
2001: 6^{4}SD, 6^{3}SW, 6^{4}SW, 5^{0}GF, 5^{0}G, 6^{0}GF

	Starts	1st	2nd	3rd	Win & Pl
Career Total (Turf)	7	0	0	0	0
Career Total (AW)	6	0	0	3	846

Going (Turf): Sf: 0-1 GS: 0-1 Gd: 0-2 GF: 0-3 Fm: 0-0
Distance: 5f/6f: 0 13 7f-8f: 0-0 9f-13f: 0-0 14f+: 0-0
Track : LH: 0-10 RH: 0-0 Tight: 0-6 Gall: 0-2
Aids: Bl: 0-0 Vi: 0-0 Tstrap: 0-0
Best Rating: 40 1/01 Ling 6f stand

My Lady

74 **26**
4-y-o b f Derrylin-Brianstan Rose (The Brianstan)
B P J Baugh E Dytcher-Boon

Placings:0/50 **(4084)**
2001: 10^{5}GS, 8^{0}GF

	Starts	1st	2nd	3rd	Win & Pl
Career Total (Turf)	3	0	0	0	0

Going (Turf): Sf: 0-0 GS: 0-1 Gd: 0-1 GF: 0-1 Fm: 0-0
Distance: 5f/6f: 0-0 7f-8f: 0-1 9f-13f: 0-2 14f+: 0-0
Track : LH: 0-3 RH: 0-0 Tight: 0-0 Gall: 0-0
Aids: Bl: 0-0 Vi: 0-0 Tstrap: 0-0
Best Rating: 26 8/01 Hayd 1m2f120y gd-sft

My Last Bean (IRE)

(101) (63)**71d**
4-y-o gr g Soviet Lad (USA)-Meanz Beanz (High Top)
B Smart B Smart

Placings:54-30303 **(2584)**
2001: 12^{3}SD, 12^{0}SW, 11^{3}SD, 14^{0}GS, 12^{3}SD

	Starts	1st	2nd	3rd	Win & Pl
Career Total (Turf)	3	0	0	0	310
Career Total (AW)	4	0	0	3	1245

Going (Turf): Sf: 0-0 GS: 0-3 Gd: 0-0 GF: 0-0 Fm: 0-0
Distance: 5f/6f: 0-0 7f-8f: 0-0 9f-13f: 0-6 14f+: 0-1
Track : LH: 0-6 RH: 0-1 Tight: 0-4 Gall: 0-0
Aids: Bl: 0-0 Vi: 0-0 Tstrap: 0-0
Best Rating: 63 3/01 Wolv 1m4f stand

He has showed a bit of form on sand, but looks moderate.

My Legal Eagle (IRE)

106(101) (41)**48**
7-y-o b g Law Society (USA)-Majestic Nurse (On Your Mark)
R J Price E G Bevan

Placings:6500/4/030041304/0653330425002130405320 4/0322222136060040640O-62422205 **(5531)**
2001: 12^{6}SD, 14^{2}HY, 17^{4}GF, 16^{2}GF, 15^{2}S, 17^{2}G, 17^{0}GS, 16^{5}HY

	Starts	1st	2nd	3rd	Win & Pl
Career Total (Turf)	47	3	8	6	23059
Career Total (AW)	18	0	4	3	3807

59 4/00 Nott 1m6f15y E(0-70)H SFT £3157
49 9/99 Sals 1m1f198yF(0-70)H HVY £2708
47 7/98 Thsk 7f F(0-70)H GD £2550
Total win prize-money £8416

Going (Turf): Sf: 2-18 GS: 0-6 Gd: 1-14 GF: 0-6 Fm: 0-2
Distance: 5f/6f: 0-1 7f-8f: 1-7 9f-13f: 1-30 14f+: 1-27
Track : **LH: 2-57** RH: 1-6 **Tight: 2-29** Gall: 0-2
Aids: Bl: 0-11 Vi: 0-0 Tstrap: 0-0
Best Rating: 48 9/01 Ches 1m7f195y soft

One-paced stayer. Moderate strike rate but consistent enough. Suited by plenty of cut in the ground.

My Line

99 **47+**
4-y-o b g Perpendicular-My Desire (Grey Desire)
Mrs M Reveley J And A Spensley

Placings:0000-261 **(5188)**
2001: 15²G, 16⁶G, 15¹GS

	Starts	1st	2nd	3rd	Win & Pl
Career Total (Turf)	7	1	1	0	3730

47 10/01 Catt 1m7f177yF(0-60)H G-S £2786
Total win prize-money £2786

Going (Turf): Sf: 0-1 **GS: 1-1** Gd: 0-2 GF: 0-2 Fm: 0-1
Distance: 5f/6f: 0-0 7f-8f: 0-0 9f-13f: 0-4 **14f+: 1-3**
Track : **LH: 1-6** RH: 0-1 **Tight: 1-5** Gall: 0-0
Aids: Bl: 0-0 Vi: 0-0 Tstrap: 0-0
Best Rating: 47 10/01 Catt 1m7f177y gd-sft

Got off the mark at the seventh attempt, and looks to be well handicapped. Acts well with cut in the ground, and looks like an out an out stayer.

My Lucy Locket (IRE)

105 **87**
3-y-o b f Mujadil (USA)-First Nadia (Auction Ring (USA))
R Hannon Mrs H F Prendergast

Placings:33210502-541210400 **(5607)**
2001: 7⁵G, 7⁴GF, 8¹GF, 7²F, 8¹F, 8⁰GF, 8⁴S, 7⁰GS, 8⁰GS

	Starts	1st	2nd	3rd	Win & Pl
Career Total (Turf)	17	3	3	2	21490

86 8/01 Sals 1m D(0-85)H FRM £4322
82 7/01 Wind 1m67y D(0-85)H G-F £3861
79 7/00 Ches 5f16y D SFT £5586
Total win prize-money £13771

Going (Turf): Sf: 1-4 GS: 0-2 Gd: 0-4 **GF: 1-5 Fm: 1-2**
Distance: 5f/6f: 1-7 7f-8f: 1-9 9f-13f: 1-1 14f+: 0-0
Track : LH: 1-3 RH: 1-4 **Tight: 2-2** Gall: 0-4
Aids: Bl: 0-0 Vi: 0-0 Tstrap: 0-0
Best Rating: 87 9/01 Asct 1m soft

She won on soft ground over the minimum trip at Chester at two, but stayed the mile well on faster ground when winning at Windsor in July. Added another victory at Salisbury in August, but she has been well held since on ground that has been too soft. She looks ideally suited by a mile and fast ground. All three of her wins have been gained when carrying top weight.

My Man Friday

98(102) (36)**40**
5-y-o b g Lugana Beach-My Ruby Ring (Blushing Scribe (USA))
Dr J R J Naylor Mrs Marion Wickham

Placings:005/00053400/00605-0520005 **(5519)**
2001: 8⁰SW, 10⁵SD, 7²SW, 8⁰SW, 5⁰G, 5⁵S, 6⁵HY

	Starts	1st	2nd	3rd	Win & Pl
Career Total (Turf)	16	0	0	1	890
Career Total (AW)	7	0	1	0	636

Going (Turf): Sf: 0-2 GS: 0-1 Gd: 0-8 GF: 0-4 Fm: 0-1
Distance: 5f/6f: 0-8 7f-8f: 0-10 9f-13f: 0-5 14f+: 0-0
Track : LH: 0-11 RH: 0-3 Tight: 0-10 Gall: 0-2
Aids: Bl: 0-0 Vi: 0-0 Tstrap: 0-0
Best Rating: 36 10/01 Wind 6f heavy

My Mate Henry

49
2-y-o ch g Pursuit Of Love-Gopi (Marju (IRE))
M Madgwick Thoroughbred Racing Gb

Placings:0 **(3393)**
2001: 5⁰GF

	Starts	1st	2nd	3rd	Win & Pl
Career Total (Turf)	1	0	0	0	

Going (Turf): Sf: 0-0 GS: 0-0 Gd: 0-0 GF: 0-1 Fm: 0-0
Distance: 5f/6f: 0-1 7f-8f: 0-0 9f-13f: 0-0 14f+: 0-0
Track : LH: 0-0 RH: 0-0 Tight: 0-0 Gall: 0-0
Aids: Bl: 0-0 Vi: 0-0 Tstrap: 0-0

My Only Sunshine

96 **77**
2-y-o b g First Trump-Fiveofive (IRE) (Fairy King (USA))
G G Margarson Mrs T A Foreman

Placings:46210 **(5364)**
2001: 5⁴G, 5⁶GF, 7²GF, 7¹GF, 6⁰GS

	Starts	1st	2nd	3rd	Win & Pl
Career Total (Turf)	5	1	1	0	6166

77 8/01 Folk 7f E G-F £2947
Total win prize-money £2947

Going (Turf): Sf: 0-0 GS: 0-1 Gd: 0-1 **GF: 1-3** Fm: 0-0
Distance: 5f/6f: 0-3 **7f-8f: 1-2** 9f-13f: 0-0 14f+: 0-0
Track : LH: 0-0 RH: 0-1 Tight: 0-0 Gall: 0-1
Aids: Bl: 0-0 Vi: 0-0 Tstrap: 0-0
Best Rating: 77 8/01 Folk 7f gd-fm

Improved on his third start when stepped up to seven furlongs, and confirmed that when winning a Folkestone maiden. Progressive.

My Petal

87 **33**
5-y-o gr m Petong-Najariya (Northfields (USA))
J M Bradley Jubert Family

Placings:2110/0000/00-00 **(4897)**
2001: 5⁰F, 5⁰GS

	Starts	1st	2nd	3rd	Win & Pl
Career Total (Turf)	12	2	1	0	19099

85 7/98 Gdwd 6f C H G-F £7546
67 7/98 Newb 5f34y D G-F £3493
Total win prize-money £11039

Going (Turf): Sf: 0-0 GS: 0-3 Gd: 0-2 **GF: 2-5** Fm: 0-2
Distance: **5f/6f: 2-9** 7f-8f: 0-3 9f-13f: 0-0 14f+: 0-0
Track : LH: 0-4 RH: 0-1 Tight: 0-1 Gall: 0-3
Aids: Bl: 0-1 Vi: 0-0 Tstrap: 0-0
Best Rating: 33 9/01 Bath 5f161y firm

My Place

(93) (64d)**72**
3-y-o b f Environment Friend-Verchinina (Star Appeal)
B W Hills W J Gredley

Placings:30462-40 **(0084)**
2001: 8⁴SD, 8⁰SD

	Starts	1st	2nd	3rd	Win & Pl
Career Total (Turf)	4	0	0	1	1244
Career Total (AW)	3	0	1	0	868

Going (Turf): Sf: 0-1 GS: 0-1 Gd: 0-1 GF: 0-0 Fm: 0-0
Distance: 5f/6f: 0-0 7f-8f: 0-5 9f-13f: 0-1 14f+: 0-0
Track : LH: 0-6 RH: 0-0 Tight: 0-3 Gall: 0-1
Aids: Bl: 0-0 Vi: 0-0 Tstrap: 0-0
Best Rating: 20 1/01 Ling 1m stand

My Pledge (IRE)

102 **61**
6-y-o b g Waajib-Pollys Glow (IRE) (Glow (USA))
C A Horgan Mrs B Sumner

Placings:0/40106/00450/2103440-20 **(3808)**
2001: 11²GF, 11⁰GF

	Starts	1st	2nd	3rd	Win & Pl
Career Total (Turf)	20	2	2	1	11175

59 6/00 Kemp 1m4f D(0-85)H G-F £4153
71 6/98 Wind 1m2f7y D(0-80)H SFT £3668
Total win prize-money £7823

Going (Turf): Sf: 1-1 GS: 0-2 Gd: 0-6 **GF: 1-10** Fm: 0-0
Distance: 5f/6f: 0-0 7f-8f: 0-3 **9f-13f: 2-13** 14f+: 0-3
Track : LH: 0-3 **RH: 1-12 Tight: 1-6** Gall: 0-4
Aids: Bl: 0-0 Vi: 0-0 Tstrap: 0-2
Best Rating: 60 7/01 Wind 1m3f135y gd-fm

My Poppet

69(71)
6-y-o b m Midyan (USA)-Pretty Poppy (Song)
N J Hawke (S G Knight 19/5) Gordon C Fox

Placings:0/00/000 **(2553)**
2001: 6⁰GS, 5⁰SD, 6⁰GF

	Starts	1st	2nd	3rd	Win & Pl
Career Total (Turf)	5	0	0	0	
Career Total (AW)	1	0	0	0	

Going (Turf): Sf: 0-0 GS: 0-1 Gd: 0-0 GF: 0-3 Fm: 0-1
Distance: 5f/6f: 0-4 7f-8f: 0-0 9f-13f: 0-2 14f+: 0-0
Track : LH: 0-1 RH: 0-2 Tight: 0-3 Gall: 0-0
Aids: Bl: 0-0 Vi: 0-0 Tstrap: 0-0

My Raggedy Man

95 **76**
2-y-o b c Forzando-Ragged Moon (Raga Navarro (ITY))
R Hannon The Waney Racing Group Inc

Placings:45012 **(5404)**
2001: 5⁴F, 7⁵G, 7⁰G, 7¹HY, 8²S

	Starts	1st	2nd	3rd	Win & Pl
Career Total (Turf)	5	1	1	0	4548

74 10/01 Ling 7f E(0-75) HVY £3272
Total win prize-money £3273

Going (Turf): Sf: 1-2 GS: 0-0 Gd: 0-2 GF: 0-0 Fm: 0-1
Distance: 5f/6f: 0-1 **7f-8f: 1-3** 9f-13f: 0-1 14f+: 0-0
Track : LH: 0-3 RH: 0-0 Tight: 0-1 Gall: 0-1
Aids: Bl: 0-0 Vi: 0-0 Tstrap: 0-0
Best Rating: 76 10/01 Pont 1m4y soft

Came good on his debut in handicap company over seven furlongs in heavy ground, and followed up with second in a similar event at Pontefract. He should stay further in time.

My Retreat (USA)

73(107) (82)**76d**
4-y-o b c Hermitage (USA)-My Jessica Ann (USA) (Native Rythm)

B W Hills Ms A Soltesova

Placings:52/100505211-0040 **(5503)**
2001: 8^0SD, 8^0GS, 7^4SD, 7^0HY

	Starts	1st	2nd	3rd	Win & Pl
Career Total (Turf)	12	2	2	0	8815
Career Total (AW)	3	1	0	0	3712

82	11/00	Wolv	1m1f79y	D(0-85)H	STD	£3711
76	11/00	Muss	1m	E(0-70)H	G-S	£3052
80	4/00	Wwck	7f164y	D	HVY	£3948

Total win prize-money £10713

Going (Turf): Sf: 1-3 **GS: 1-3** Gd: 0-0 GF: 0-4 Fm: 0-2
Distance: 5f/6f: 0-1 **7f-8f: 2-8** 9f-13f: 1-6 14f+: 0-0
Track : **LH: 2-10** RH: 1-2 **Tight: 2-4** Gall: 0-1
Aids: Bl: 0-1 Vi: 0-0 Tstrap: 0-0
Best Rating: 74 10/01 Wolv 7f stand

He likes to be up with the pace and goes well in testing consitions. Handles the Fibresand at Wolverhampton.

My Sharp Grey

82 **53**

2-y-o gr f Tragic Role (USA)-Sharp Anne (Belfort (FR))
K O Cunningham-Brown Barry M Fletcher

Placings:3606 **(3883)**
2001: 6^3GF, 6^6GF, 5^0G, 6^6G

	Starts	1st	2nd	3rd	Win & Pl
Career Total (Turf)	4	0	0	1	1163

Going (Turf): Sf: 0-0 GS: 0-0 Gd: 0-2 GF: 0-2 Fm: 0-0
Distance: 5f/6f: 0-4 7f-8f: 0-0 9f-13f: 0-0 14f+: 0-0
Track : LH: 0-1 RH: 0-0 Tight: 0-0 Gall: 0-1
Aids: Bl: 0-0 Vi: 0-0 Tstrap: 0-0
Best Rating: 53 6/01 Sals 6f gd-fm

Signs of ability in ordinary maidens and a nursery.

My Tess

(109) (82)**64**

5-y-o br m Lugana Beach-Barachois Princess (USA) (Barachois (CAN))
B A McMahon J D Graham

Placings:635/630100530614/452213242501235-40300003 **(5688)**
2001: 7^4SW, 6^0SD, 7^3SD, 7^0SD, 8^0HY, 8^0G, 7^0HY, 7^3S

	Starts	1st	2nd	3rd	Win & Pl
Career Total (Turf)	21	1	2	3	8183
Career Total (AW)	17	3	3	4	22763

77	11/00	Sthl	7f	D(0-85)H	STD	£3705
77	2/00	Sthl	7f	E(0-70)H	STD	£3558
66	11/99	Wolv	1m100y	D(0-85)H	STD	£8286
77	4/99	Nott	1m54y	D	HVY	£4356

Total win prize-money £19907

Going (Turf): Sf: 1-11 GS: 0-3 Gd: 0-3 GF: 0-4 Fm: 0-0
Distance: 5f/6f: 0-1 7f-8f: 2-21 9f-13f: 2-16 14f+: 0-0
Track : **LH: 4-29** RH: 0-0 **Tight: 1-12** Gall: 0-3
Aids: Bl: 0-0 Vi: 0-0 Tstrap: 0-0
Best Rating: 79 2/01 Sthl 7f stand

Decent handicapper on Fibresand, and is also effective on turf, as she showed on the last day of the 2001 season when third at Doncaster.

My Trivet (IRE)

90 **29**

10-y-o b g Thatching-Blue Scholar (Blue Cashmere)
M H Tompkins Mrs Jane Bailey

Placings:005/534230000/6200002/650012054/00320355210/32023000003460/00206050106/00040050300-00 **(2165)**
2001: 5^0G, 5^0G

	Starts	1st	2nd	3rd	Win & Pl
Career Total (Turf)	77	3	9	8	19131

65	8/99	Tral	5f	(0-78)H	YLD	£4002
65	10/97	Curr	5f	(0-90)H	Y-S	£2740
56	5/96	Layt	6f	(0-70)H	STD	£1712

Total win prize-money £8455

Going (Turf): Sf: 0-10 GS: 0-0 Gd: 0-10 GF: 0-5 Fm: 0-1
Distance: **5f/6f: 3-53** 7f-8f: 0-3 9f-13f: 0-0 14f+: 0-0
Track : **LH: 2-18** RH: 0-6 Tight: 0-0 Gall: 0-0
Aids: Bl: 1-11 Vi: 0-0 Tstrap: 1-11
Best Rating: 29 6/01 Sand 5f6y good

My Very Own (IRE)

104(101) (69)**72**

3-y-o ch g Persian Bold-Cossack Princess (IRE) (Lomond (USA))
N P Littmoden Mrs Gillian Curley

Placings:06220321-0420000 **(5624)**
2001: 9^0SW, 10^4G, 12^2GS, 11^0G, 11^0GF, 14^0G, 9^0GS

	Starts	1st	2nd	3rd	Win & Pl
Career Total (Turf)	9	0	2	0	3969
Career Total (AW)	6	1	2	1	3966

69	12/00	Sthl	1m	D	STD	£2184

Total win prize-money £2184

Going (Turf): Sf: 0-1 GS: 0-2 Gd: 0-4 GF: 0-2 Fm: 0-0
Distance: 5f/6f: 0-1 **7f-8f: 1-4** 9f-13f: 0-9 14f+: 0-1
Track : **LH: 1-11** RH: 0-2 Tight: 0-6 Gall: 0-5
Aids: Bl: 0-0 Vi: 0-0 Tstrap: 0-0
Best Rating: 75 8/01 NmkJ 1m4f gd-sft

He won his maiden over a mile on the sand at the end of last year, but showed improvement when stepped up to middle distances and ran his best race so far when narrowly beaten over 12 furlongs at Newmarket in August. Handles some cut in the ground.

Mybotye

102(84) (11)**54**

8-y-o br g Rambo Dancer (CAN)-Sigh (Highland Melody)
A B Mulholland J F Wright

Placings:011/330516000/000002316354/4505634/00000/4101000-404600 **(4904)**
2001: 7^4GF, 7^0SD, 7^4GF, 7^6GF, 7^0GF, 7^0G

	Starts	1st	2nd	3rd	Win & Pl
Career Total (Turf)	46	6	1	5	25995
Career Total (AW)	4	0	0	0	0

54	6/00	Catt	7f	F(0-60)	SFT	£2352
54	5/00	Rdcr	7f	F	G-S	£2520
64	9/97	Chep	7f16y	F(0-60)H	GD	£3037
77	6/96	Rdcr	7f	D(0-80)H	FRM	£3736
65	8/95	Rdcr	6f	C	G-F	£6450
61	6/95	Pont	5f	F	GD	£2717

Total win prize-money £20814

Going (Turf): Sf: 1-9 GS: 1-4 **Gd: 2-12** GF: 1-18 Fm: 1-3
Distance: 5f/6f: 2-4 **7f-8f: 4-42** 9f-13f: 0-4 14f+: 0-0
Track : **LH: 2-19** RH: 0-10 **Tight: 1-11** Gall: 0-3
Aids: Bl: 0-2 Vi: 0-0 **Tstrap: 2-18**
Best Rating: 54 7/01 Donc 7f gd-fm

Myhat

91 **46**

3-y-o ch f Factual (USA)-Rose Elegance (Bairn (USA))
K T Ivory Dean Ivory

Placings:213265000-000000 **(3668)**
2001: 8^0GS, 7^0F, 6^0GF, 7^0GF, 6^0GF, 6^0S

	Starts	1st	2nd	3rd	Win & Pl
Career Total (Turf)	15	1	2	1	8194

78	6/00	Wind	6f	E	GD	£3802

Total win prize-money £3803

Going (Turf): Sf: 0-2 GS: 0-3 **Gd: 1-4** GF: 0-5 Fm: 0-1
Distance: **5f/6f: 1-8** 7f 8f: 0 7 9f-13f: 0-0 14f+: 0-0
Track : LH: 0-1 **RH: 1-4** Tight: 0-0 **Gall: 1-4**
Aids: Bl: 0-1 Vi: 0-0 Tstrap: 0-0
Best Rating: 46 7/01 Ling 7f gd-fm

Mysteri Dancer

102(92) (74)**78**

3-y-o b g Rudimentary (USA)-Mystery Ship (Decoy Boy)
R J O'Sullivan Jack Joseph

Placings:0223-0006333146 **(5470)**
2001: 8^0GS, 6^0S, 6^0GF, 6^6GF, 6^3GF, 7^3G, 7^3GF, 7^1GF, 7^4GF, 7^6S

	Starts	1st	2nd	3rd	Win & Pl
Career Total (Turf)	13	1	2	3	8422
Career Total (AW)	1	0	0	1	250

78	8/01	Ling	7f140y	D(0-80)H	G-F	£4322

Total win prize-money £4323

Going (Turf): Sf: 0-3 GS: 0-1 Gd: 0-2 **GF: 1-7** Fm: 0-0
Distance: 5f/6f: 0-6 **7f-8f: 1-8** 9f-13f: 0-0 14f+: 0-0
Track : LH: 0-3 RH: 0-3 Tight: 0-2 Gall: 0-2
Aids: Bl: 0-0 Vi: 0-0 Tstrap: 0-0
Best Rating: 78 8/01 Ling 7f140y gd-fm

Running well before getting off the mark in a handicap at Lingfield in August, although not up to his best after that. Suited by seven furlongs and fast ground.

Mysterious Force

95 **67**

2-y-o b f Forzando-Mystique (Mystiko (USA))
D W Barker (J L Dunlop 29/6) Keith Nicholson

Placings:03300 **(4538)**
2001: 6^0GF, 6^3GF, 7^3GF, 7^0GF, 7^0GF

	Starts	1st	2nd	3rd	Win & Pl
Career Total (Turf)	5	0	0	2	809

Going (Turf): Sf: 0-0 GS: 0-0 Gd: 0-0 GF: 0-5 Fm: 0-0
Distance: 5f/6f: 0-1 7f-8f: 0-4 9f-13f: 0-0 14f+: 0-0
Track : LH: 0-1 RH: 0-1 Tight: 0-2 Gall: 0-0
Aids: Bl: 0-0 Vi: 0-0 Tstrap: 0-0
Best Rating: 67 6/01 Folk 6f189y gd-fm

Mysterium

(104) (62)**57**

7-y-o gr g Mystiko (USA)-Way To Go (Troy)
N P Littmoden Alcester Associates

Placings:06/1500230/40/563435403315041240/212400025110003 11-005 **(5419)**
2001: 9^0SW, 12^0SD, 12^5SD

	Starts	1st	2nd	3rd	Win & Pl
Career Total (Turf)	16	3	1	2	12570
Career Total (AW)	33	5	4	4	16028

62	11/00	Wolv	1m4f	F(0-60)H	STD	£2562
57	10/00	Wolv	1m4f	F(0-60)H	STD	£2530
57	8/00	NmkJ	1m2f	F(0-65)H	G-F	£4862
51	7/00	Wind	1m3f135y	E(0-70)H	G-F	£3192
50	1/00	Wolv	1m1f79y	E(0-70)H	STD	£2619
49	11/99	Wolv	1m1f79y	F(0-65)H	STD	£1945
43	7/99	Yarm	1m3f101y	E(0-70)H	G-F	£3045
59	2/97	Wolv	7f	E	STD	£2804

Total win prize-money £23560

Going (Turf): Sf: 0-0 GS: 0-0 Gd: 0-6 **GF: 2-6** Fm: 0-3
Distance: 5f/6f: 0-1 7f-8f: 1-3 **9f-13f: 6-44** 14f+: 0-0
Track : **LH: 6-46** RH: 1-1 **Tight: 6-35** Gall: 1-2
Aids: Bl: 0-0 Vi: 0-1 Tstrap: 0-0
Best Rating: 46 10/01 Wolv 1m4f stand

Mystic Forest

99 **73**

2-y-o b c Charnwood Forest (IRE)-Mystic Beauty (IRE) (Alzao (USA))

B J Meehan Walter Mariti

Placings:0563610 **(5368)**

2001: 6^0GF, 6^5GF, 6^6GF, 7^3G, 7^6GF, 8^1GS, 8^0GS

	Starts	1st	2nd	3rd	Win & Pl
Career Total (Turf)	7	1	0	1	5131

72 9/01 Gdwd 1m D(0-85)H G-S £4530

Total win prize-money £4531

Going (Turf): Sf: 0-0 **GS: 1-2** Gd: 0-1 GF: 0-4 Fm: 0-0
Distance: 5f/6f: 0-3 **7f-8f: 1-4** 9f-13f: 0-0 14f+: 0-0
Track : LH: 0-0 **RH: 1-2** Tight: 0-0 Gall: 0-0
Aids: Bl: 0-0 Vi: 0-0 Tstrap: 0-0
Best Rating: 73 9/01 Sand 7f16y good

A January foal from the family of Bluebird, he showed promise in six-furlong maidens before running well in a nursery when stepped up to seven, and showed his appreciation for a mile and soft ground when winning at Goodwood in September.

Mystic Man (FR)

101 **75**

3-y-o b c Cadeaux Genereux-Shawanni (Shareef Dancer (USA))

E A L Dunlop Maktoum Al Maktoum

Placings:0355401 **(5083)**

2001: 8^0GF, 7^3GS, 8^5GF, 8^5G, 8^4G, 7^0GF, 7^1S

	Starts	1st	2nd	3rd	Win & Pl
Career Total (Turf)	7	1	0	1	4132

73 10/01 Brig 7f214y D SFT £3052

Total win prize-money £3052

Going (Turf): Sf: 1-1 GS: 0-1 Gd: 0-2 GF: 0-3 Fm: 0-0
Distance: 5f/6f: 0-0 **7f-8f: 1-4** 9f-13f: 0-3 14f+: 0-0
Track : LH: 1-2 RH: 0-3 Tight: 0-3 Gall: 0-1
Aids: Bl: 0-0 Vi: 0-0 **Tstrap: 1-1**
Best Rating: 75 6/01 Wind 1m67y gd-fm

He has shown ability in maiden company over seven furlongs to a mile and got off the mark at Brighton in October. Suited by cut in the ground.

Mystic Venture (IRE)

90 **64**

2-y-o b g Woodborough (USA)-Paganina (FR) (Galetto (FR))

K A Ryan T Fawcett And Mrs C Reilly

Placings:53212054 **(5370)**

2001: 5^5GF, 5^3S, 6^2G, 5^1GF, 6^2G, 6^0G, 7^5G, 7^4G

	Starts	1st	2nd	3rd	Win & Pl
Career Total (Turf)	8	1	2	1	4735

57 8/01 Muss 5f F G-F £2674

Total win prize-money £2674

Going (Turf): Sf: 0-1 GS: 0-0 Gd: 0-5 **GF: 1-2** Fm: 0-0
Distance: 5f/6f: 1-6 7f-8f: 0-2 9f-13f: 0-0 14f+: 0-0
Track : LH: 0-1 RH: 0-1 Tight: 0-0 Gall: 0-0
Aids: Bl: 0-0 Vi: 0-0 Tstrap: 0-0
Best Rating: 64 10/01 Rdcr 7f good

Got off the mark in August of 2001 in a Musselburgh seller, although he has been held since in both sellers and claimers. Acts on a sound surface.

Mystic Witch

89 **56**

2-y-o b f Mistertopogigo (IRE)-Walsham Witch (Music Maestro)

E J Alston J Yates

Placings:05600 **(5487)**

2001: 5^0GS, 5^5GF, 6^6GF, 6^0S, 6^0HY

	Starts	1st	2nd	3rd	Win & Pl
Career Total (Turf)	5	0	0	0	0

Going (Turf): Sf: 0-2 GS: 0-1 Gd: 0-0 GF: 0-2 Fm: 0-0
Distance: 5f/6f: 0-4 7f-8f: 0-1 9f-13f: 0-0 14f+: 0-0
Track : LH: 0-1 RH: 0-0 Tight: 0-0 Gall: 0-0
Aids: Bl: 0-0 Vi: 0-0 Tstrap: 0-0
Best Rating: 56 9/01 Wwck 6f21y gd-fm

Mythic

93 **80**

2-y-o ch f Zafonic (USA)-Fetlar (Pharly (FR))

J R Fanshawe Dr Catherine Wills

Placings:6 **(5602)**

2001: 7^6GS

	Starts	1st	2nd	3rd	Win & Pl
Career Total (Turf)	1	0	0	0	0

Going (Turf): Sf: 0-0 GS: 0-1 Gd: 0-0 GF: 0-0 Fm: 0-0
Distance: 5f/6f: 0-0 7f-8f: 0-1 9f-13f: 0-0 14f+: 0-0
Track : LH: 0-0 RH: 0-0 Tight: 0-0 Gall: 0-0
Aids: Bl: 0-0 Vi: 0-0 Tstrap: 0-0
Best Rating: 80 11/01 NmkR 7f gd-sft

Mythical King (IRE)

107(74) (29)**72**

4-y-o b c Fairy King (USA)-Whatcombe (USA) (Alleged (USA))

B Palling Glyn And Albert Yemm

Placings:350/33142000-0516352300020 **(5293)**

2001: 10^0G, 10^5GF, 10^1GF, 9^6GF, 9^3GF, 10^5GF, 11^2G, 12^5G, 12^0G, 10^0F, 8^0GF, 10^2G, 9^0S

	Starts	1st	2nd	3rd	Win & Pl
Career Total (Turf)	23	2	3	5	19941
Career Total (AW)	1	0	0	0	

82 6/01 Ches 1m2f75y D(0-80)H G-F £4426
83 6/00 Gdwd 1m1f192yD(0-80)H GD £4387

Total win prize-money £8815

Going (Turf): Sf: 0-2 GS: 0-1 **Gd: 1-8 GF: 1-11** Fm: 0-1
Distance: 5f/6f: 0-0 7f-8f: 0-4 **9f-13f: 2-20** 14f+: 0-0
Track : LH: 1-10 RH: 1-12 **Tight: 2-9** Gall: 0-5
Aids: Bl: 0-0 Vi: 0-0 Tstrap: 0-0
Best Rating: 82 7/01 Leic 1m3f183y good

He likes to dominate, but needs a sharp track to show his best and had conditions to suit when winning at Chester in June, but he looked held by the Handicapper afterwards. Now back to a realistic mark. Suited by ten furlongs and fast ground.

Mytton's Again

(105) (68)**66d**

4-y-o b g Rambo Dancer (CAN)-Sigh (Highland Melody)

A Bailey Gordon Mytton

Placings:52050501004260/40026650063116400006502-12244100013054330236004000006 **(5688)**

2001: 8^1SD, 8^2SD, 8^2SW, 8^4SW, 8^4SD, 8^1SD, 8^0GS, 8^0GF, 7^0G, 7^1GF, 8^3GF, 8^0GF, 8^5G, 8^4GF, 8^3GF, 7^3GF, 8^0G, 6^2G, 7^3F, 7^6G, 7^0SD, 6^0GF, 8^4GF, 7^0G, 7^0S, 7^0S, 8^0G, 7^6S

	Starts	1st	2nd	3rd	Win & Pl
Career Total (Turf)	49	4	4	5	26794
Career Total (AW)	16	2	3	0	6598

66 5/01 Ayr 7f D(0-80)H G-F £4485
68 3/01 Ling 1m E(0-70)H STD £2772
61 1/01 Sthl 1m F(0-65)H STD £1820
64 8/00 Muss 7f30y E(0-70)H G-F £3094
48 8/00 Ayr 7f F GD £2282
72 9/99 Ches 7f2y C(0-95)H HVY £6320

Total win prize-money £20773

Going (Turf): Sf: 1-9 GS: 0-9 Gd: 1-15 **GF: 2-14** Fm: 0-2
Distance: 5f/6f: 0-7 **7f-8f: 6-47** 9f-13f: 0-11 14f+: 0-0
Track : LH: 5-40 RH: 1-8 **Tight: 3-30** Gall: 0-2
Aids: Bl: 4-36 Vi: 0-0 Tstrap: 0-0
Best Rating: 69 7/01 Gdwd 1m gd-fm

A fair handicapper over a mile, he scored twice on sand in the spring and added a win on turf at a Ayr in May, and he has continued to run well since then without winning. Acts on fast ground and likes to come from off the pace.

Mytton's Moment (IRE)

(99) (44)**44**

5-y-o b g Waajib-Late Swallow (My Swallow)

A Bailey Gordon Mytton

Placings:0044040/00001054633/44550-0 **(0776)**

2001: 14^0S

	Starts	1st	2nd	3rd	Win & Pl
Career Total (Turf)	19	1	0	1	5415
Career Total (AW)	5	0	0	1	218

69 6/99 NmkJ 1m E GD £3622

Total win prize-money £3623

Going (Turf): Sf: 0-4 GS: 0-4 **Gd: 1-8** GF: 0-3 Fm: 0-0
Distance: 5f/6f: 0-2 **7f-8f: 1-9** 9f-13f: 0-11 14f+: 0-2
Track : LH: 0-18 RH: 0-4 Tight: 0-10 Gall: 0-2
Aids: Bl: 1-15 Vi: 0-0 Tstrap: 0-0
Best Rating: 69 6/99 NmkJ 1m G

Myttons Mistake

103(89) (40)**56**

8-y-o b g Rambo Dancer (CAN)-Hi-Hunsley (Swing Easy (USA))

R J Baker P Slade

Placings:1140003/33233200543000000303/62243004144421001001650/0300220631310000/003404056001500 0/022421366660-1500 **(4213)**

2001: 7^1GF, 6^5G, 8^0S, 8^0GF

	Starts	1st	2nd	3rd	Win & Pl
Career Total (Turf)	78	11	7	7	55804
Career Total (AW)	18	0	3	7	5834

56 7/01 Kemp 7f E(0-75)H G-F £3591
60 6/00 Wwck 7f164y D(0-80)H G-F £3948
44 8/99 Brig 5f213y F G-S £2305
70 8/98 Kemp 7f E(0-70)H G-F £3022
67 7/98 Bath 5f161y D(0-80)H GD £3631
78 10/97 Leic 1m8y G(0-70)H GD £2207
64 9/97 Sand 7f16y D(0-80)H G-F £3810
60 8/97 Bevl 7f100y E(0-70)H GD £4890
58 7/97 Ches 7f122y F(0-70)H G-F £2848
85 7/95 Bevl 5f C G-F £4412
74 6/95 Ayr 7f D FRM £4162

Total win prize-money £38830

Going (Turf): Sf: 0-6 GS: 1-11 Gd: 3-20 **GF: 6-32** Fm: 1-9
Distance: 5f/6f: 3-33 **7f-8f: 7-54** 9f-13f: 1-9 14f+: 0-0
Track : LH: 5-57 RH: 4-12 Tight: 1-31 **Gall: 3-10**
Aids: Bl: 0-3 Vi: 0-0 Tstrap: 0-0
Best Rating: 56 7/01 Kemp 7f gd-fm

Probably best on a sound surface. Goes well round Kempton and scored in a girl apprentices' handicap at the Sunbury track in July.

Nacho Venture (FR)

102(96) (70)81

2-y-o b f Rainbow Quest (USA)-Pearl Venture (Salse (USA))

S P C Woods Seiichi Wada

Placings:02334 **(5606)**

2001: 7^{0}GF, 8^{2}S, 8^{3}SD, 8^{3}HY, 10^{4}GS

	Starts	1st	2nd	3rd	Win & Pl
Career Total (Turf)	4	0	1	1	2927
Career Total (AW)	1	0	0	1	568

Going (Turf): Sf: 0-2 GS: 0-1 Gd: 0-0 GF: 0-1 Fm: 0-0
Distance: 5f/6f: 0-0 7f-8f: 0-1 9f-13f: 0-4 14f+: 0-0
Track : LH: 0-2 RH: 0-0 Tight: 0-1 Gall: 0-0
Aids: Bl: 0-0 Vi: 0-0 Tstrap: 0-0
Best Rating: 81 11/01 NmkR 1m2f gd-sft

Out of a staying mare, he has shown ability in maidens and will come into his own when faced with a distance of ground as a three-year-old.

Nadour Al Bahr (IRE)

107(106) (95)96

6-y-o b g Be My Guest (USA)-Nona (GER) (Cortez (GER))

T G Mills T G Mills

Placings:11/12235/6556-06042135502 **(5261)**

2001: 12^{0}GS, 10^{6}S, 10^{0}G, 10^{4}G, 10^{2}GF, 10^{1}GF, 12^{3}G, 10^{5}GF, 10^{5}GF, 9^{0}G, 10^{2}GS

	Starts	1st	2nd	3rd	Win & Pl
Career Total (Turf)	20	4	4	2	195949
Career Total (AW)	2	0	0	0	750

96	7/01	Asct	1m2f	B(0-105)H	G-F	£15082
96	4/98	Frnk	1m2f		GD	£15202
	9/97	Colo	1m1f110y		GD	£9091
	7/97	Kref	7f		GD	£2273

Total win prize-money £41649

Going (Turf): Sf: 0-4 GS: 0-4 **Gd: 1-6 GF: 1-4** Fm: 0-0
Distance: 5f/6f: 0-0 7f-8f: 0-0 **9f-13f: 2-20** 14f+: 0-0
Track : LH: 1-8 RH: 1-9 Tight: 0-4 **Gall: 1-9**
Aids: Bl: 0-1 Vi: 0-0 Tstrap: 0-0
Best Rating: 96 10/01 Asct 1m2f gd-sft

Showed high-class form in '98 when German-trained and was off the course for two years before making his British debut at Ascot in September 2000. Given a chance by the Handicapper, he won well at Ascot in July and has run very well since. Effective from ten to 12 furlongs and acts on any ground.

Nafisah (IRE)

114 107

3-y-o ch f Lahib (USA)-Alyakkh (IRE) (Sadler's Wells (USA))

B Hanbury Hamdan Al Maktoum

Placings:22125-1212265 **(4984)**

2001: 8^{1}GS, 10^{2}S, 10^{1}GF, 12^{2}GF, 12^{2}GF, 11^{6}G, 12^{5}G

	Starts	1st	2nd	3rd	Win & Pl
Career Total (Turf)	12	3	6	0	78960

102	6/01	Newb	1m2f6y	A	G-F	£13595
108	4/01	Newb	1m	B(0-100)H	G-S	£9438
83	9/00	Kemp	7f	D	SFT	£3038

Total win prize-money £26073

Going (Turf): Sf: 1-3 GS: 1-1 Gd: 0-3 **GF: 1-5** Fm: 0-0
Distance: 5f/6f: 0-0 **7f-8f: 2-6** 9f-13f: 1-6 14f+: 0-0
Track : LH: 1-4 RH: 1-3 Tight: 0-0 **Gall: 2-7**
Aids: Bl: 0-0 Vi: 0-0 Tstrap: 0-0
Best Rating: 108 4/01 Newb 1m gd-sft

Very useful filly. Showed good juvenile form and won a decent handicap at Newbury on seasonal reappearance. Took another step in the right direction with a fine second in Listed event over ten furlongs at Newbury in May, and made all to win a similar event at the same course. Improved on that when just beaten in the Ribblesdale. Her limitations were exposed afterwards. Seems to stay 12 furlongs, handles any ground and is suited by making the running.

Nafith

95(105) (6)26

5-y-o ch g Elmaamul (USA)-Wanisa (USA) (Topsider (USA))

L R James (E L James 9/1) L R Lloyd-James

Placings:66/65000/**32130600-00**100 **(4169)**

2001: 9^{0}SW, 11^{0}SD, 16^{1}GF, 16^{0}GF, 14^{0}GF

	Starts	1st	2nd	3rd	Win & Pl
Career Total (Turf)	13	1	0	0	3038
Career Total (AW)	7	1	1	2	4291

26	5/01	Muss	2m	F	G-F	£3038
51	2/00	Wolv	1m1f79y	D	STD	£2730

Total win prize-money £5768

Going (Turf): Sf: 0-2 GS: 0-3 Gd: 0-4 **GF: 1-4** Fm: 0-0
Distance: 5f/6f: 0-0 7f-8f: 0-4 9f-13f: 1-13 14f+: 1-3
Track : LH: 1-12 RH: 1-4 **Tight: 2-13** Gall: 0-1
Aids: Bl: 0-1 Vi: 0-0 Tstrap: 0-1
Best Rating: 26 5/01 Muss 2m gd-fm

Naheef (IRE)

105 107+

2-y-o b c Marju (IRE)-Golden Digger (USA) (Mr Prospector (USA))

D R Loder Maktoum Al Maktoum

Placings:112 **(4912a)**

2001: 7^{1}G, 7^{1}GF, 7^{2}GF

	Starts	1st	2nd	3rd	Win & Pl
Career Total (Turf)	3	2	1	0	82173

107	8/01	Gdwd	7f	A	G-F	£30000
84	7/01	Epsm	7f	E	GD	£4173

Total win prize-money £34173

Going (Turf): Sf: 0-0 GS: 0-0 **Gd: 1-1 GF: 1-2** Fm: 0-0
Distance: 5f/6f: 0-0 **7f-8f: 2-3** 9f-13f: 0-0 14f+: 0-0
Track : LH: 1-1 RH: 1-1 **Tight: 1-1** Gall: 0-0
Aids: Bl: 0-0 Vi: 0-0 Tstrap: 0-0
Best Rating: 107 9/01 Curr 7f gd-fm

Out of a half-sister to Always Fair and Faithful Son, won easily on his Epsom debut and was very impressive when following up in the Group Three Vintage Stakes at Goodwood. He should improve further and will stay a mile. No match for Hawk Wing in the National Stakes at the Curragh.

Naj-De

104 70

3-y-o ch g Zafonic (USA)-River Jig (USA) (Irish River (FR))

P F I Cole Newgate Stud

Placings:5-0200500 **(5179)**

2001: 7^{0}S, 7^{2}GF, 7^{0}GF, 7^{0}GS, 8^{5}G, 8^{0}GF, 10^{0}HY

	Starts	1st	2nd	3rd	Win & Pl
Career Total (Turf)	8	0	1	0	1235

Going (Turf): Sf: 0-2 GS: 0-1 Gd: 0-2 GF: 0-3 Fm: 0-0
Distance: 5f/6f: 0-1 7f-8f: 0-5 9f-13f: 0-2 14f+: 0-0
Track : LH: 0-2 RH: 0-3 Tight: 0-3 Gall: 0-1
Aids: Bl: 0-1 Vi: 0-0 Tstrap: 0-0
Best Rating: 70 8/01 Wind 1m67y good

Has shown ability in maiden company, but has played up in the stalls on more than one occasion. Acts on fast ground.

Najah (IRE)

113 105

3-y-o b f Nashwan (USA)-Mehthaaf (USA) (Nureyev (USA))

Saeed Bin Suroor Godolphin

Placings:20011 **(5582a)**

2001: 8^{2}G, 12^{0}GF, 12^{0}GF, 10^{1}G, 10^{1}G

	Starts	1st	2nd	3rd	Win & Pl
Career Total (Turf)	5	2	1	0	56675

103	10/01	Capa	1m2f		GD	£44151
68	10/01	Bath	1m2f46y	D	GD	£3024

Total win prize-money £47175

Going (Turf): Sf: 0-0 GS: 0-0 **Gd: 2-3** GF: 0-2 Fm: 0-0
Distance: 5f/6f: 0-0 7f-8f: 0-1 **9f-13f: 2-4** 14f+: 0-0
Track : LH: 1-2 RH: 1-2 **Tight: 1-2** Gall: 0-1
Aids: Bl: 0-0 Vi: 0-0 Tstrap: 0-0
Best Rating: 105 5/01 Leop 1m good

Second in the Godolphin Fillies' Trial in Dubai in April before finishing runner-up in the 1,000 Guineas Trial at Leopardstown. Well beaten in the Oaks and the Ribblesdale, she was dropped in class to get off the mark at Bath. Suited by ten furlongs on good ground and was a clear winner of an Italian Group Two in the autumn.

Najda (IRE)

88 60

3-y-o b f Halling (USA)-Danishkada (Thatch (USA))

H R A Cecil Newgate Stud

Placings:00 **(4306)**

2001: 10^{0}G, 9^{0}GF

	Starts	1st	2nd	3rd	Win & Pl
Career Total (Turf)	2	0	0	0	

Going (Turf): Sf: 0-0 GS: 0-0 Gd: 0-1 GF: 0-1 Fm: 0-0
Distance: 5f/6f: 0-0 7f-8f: 0-0 9f-13f: 0-2 14f+: 0-0
Track : LH: 0-0 RH: 0-1 Tight: 0-2 Gall: 0-0
Aids: Bl: 0-0 Vi: 0-0 Tstrap: 0-0
Best Rating: 60 8/01 Wind 1m2f7y good

Naked Oat

99(109) (73)48

6-y-o b g Imp Society (USA)-Bajina (Dancing Brave (USA))

B Smart The Dyball Partnership

Placings:6506050**354/32430232/410**5610600/**0000000** 16000666-**1300103**1063300405 **(5191)**

2001: 9^{1}SW, 9^{3}SW, 9^{0}SD, 9^{0}SD, 9^{1}SD, 9^{0}SD, 11^{3}SD, 11^{1}SD, 10^{0}GS, 11^{6}GF, 10^{3}GF, 12^{3}GF, 9^{0}GF, 9^{0}GF, 9^{4}G, 9^{0}GS, 12^{5}SD, 13^{6}SD

	Starts	1st	2nd	3rd	Win & Pl
Career Total (Turf)	32	2	0	2	4689
Career Total (AW)	28	4	3	6	14429

73	4/01	Sthl	1m3f	E(0-70)H	STD	£2989
63	3/01	Wolv	1m1f79y	F	STD	£2296
49	1/01	Wolv	1m1f79y	G(0-60)H	SLW	£1337
40	6/00	Brig	1m1f209y	G	FRM	£1943
56	5/99	Wwck	1m	G(0-70)H	GD	£1934
69	2/99	Wolv	1m1f79y	D	STD	£2721

Total win prize-money £13221

Going (Turf): Sf: 0-6 GS: 0-6 **Gd: 1-8** GF: 0-10 **Fm: 1-2**
Distance: 5f/6f: 0-1 7f-8f: 1-15 **9f-13f: 5-44** 14f+: 0-0
Track : **LH: 6-48** RH: 0-8 **Tight: 3-31** Gall: 0-0
Aids: Bl: 0-1 Vi: 0-0 Tstrap: 0-0
Best Rating: 73 4/01 Sthl 1m3f stand

Nakwa (IRE)

104(84) (47)71d

3-y-o b g Namaqualand (USA)-Cajo (IRE) (Tirol)

E J Alston Alan Dick

Placings:00-50130600 **(5538)**

2001: 8^{5}S, 8^{0}SD, 8^{1}S, 8^{3}F, 10^{0}GF, 8^{6}G, 8^{0}GS, 10^{0}S

	Starts	1st	2nd	3rd	Win & Pl
Career Total (Turf)	9	1	0	1	4358
Career Total (AW)	1	0	0	0	

71	5/01	Newc	1m	D(0-80)H	SFT	£3922

Total win prize-money £3923

Going (Turf): Sf: 1-4 GS: 0-1 Gd: 0-2 GF: 0-1 Fm: 0-1
Distance: 5f/6f: 0-1 **7f-8f: 1-6** 9f-13f: 0-3 14f+: 0-0
Track : **LH: 1-8** RH: 0-0 Tight: 0-2 **Gall: 1-2**
Aids: Bl: 0-0 Vi: 0-0 Tstrap: 0-0
Best Rating: 71 5/01 Newc 1m firm

A half-brother to useful juvenile Fairy Gem. Won a handicap at Newcastle over a mile. Acts on soft ground. Handles fast.

Namllams

94 **54**

3-y-o b c Magic Ring (IRE)-White Flash (Sure Blade (USA))
A Dickman Mike Smallman

Placings:005-000004000 **(4542)**
2001: 5^{0}GF, 6^{0}G, 6^{0}F, 8^{0}F, 10^{4}F, 12^{0}G, 10^{0}G, 10^{0}GF

	Starts	1st	2nd	3rd	Win & Pl
Career Total (Turf)	12	0	0	0	404

Going (Turf): Sf: 0-0 GS: 0-0 Gd: 0-4 GF: 0-4 Fm: 0-4
Distance: 5f/6f: 0-6 7f-8f: 0-2 9f-13f: 0-4 14f+: 0-0
Track : LH: 0-4 RH: 0-1 Tight: 0-3 Gall: 0-2
Aids: Bl: 0-0 Vi: 0-2 Tstrap: 0-0
Best Rating: 56 6/01 Thsk 6f good

Modest form in varied company so far.

Nancy's Boy

82 **71?**

3-y-o b g Perpendicular-Derry's Delight (Mufrij)
J Hetherton R G Fell

Placings:004-00 **(3087)**
2001: 10^{0}GF, 7^{0}GF

	Starts	1st	2nd	3rd	Win & Pl
Career Total (Turf)	5	0	0	0	179

Going (Turf): Sf: 0-2 GS: 0-1 Gd: 0-0 GF: 0-2 Fm: 0-0
Distance: 5f/6f: 0-1 7f-8f: 0-3 9f-13f: 0-1 14f+: 0-0
Track : LH: 0-1 RH: 0-3 Tight: 0-2 Gall: 0-0
Aids: Bl: 0-0 Vi: 0-0 Tstrap: 0-0
Best Rating: 27 7/01 Bevl 7f100y gd-fm

Nandoo

98 **74**

2-y-o b f Forzando-Ascend (IRE) (Glint Of Gold)
P W Harris Board, Keats, Stanford & Wooder

Placings:0565 **(4428)**
2001: 6^{0}GF, 7^{5}GF, 6^{6}F, 7^{5}G

	Starts	1st	2nd	3rd	Win & Pl
Career Total (Turf)	4	0	0	0	0

Going (Turf): Sf: 0-0 GS: 0-0 Gd: 0-1 GF: 0-2 Fm: 0-1
Distance: 5f/6f: 0-1 7f-8f: 0-3 9f-13f: 0-0 14f+: 0-0
Track : LH: 0-0 RH: 0-1 Tight: 0-0 Gall: 0-0
Aids: Bl: 0-0 Vi: 0-0 Tstrap: 0-0
Best Rating: 74 8/01 Sals 6f212y firm

Nanette

97 **65**

3-y-o b f Hernando (FR)-No Restraint (Habitat)
S C Williams Tyrnest Ltd

Placings:330 **(4958)**
2001: 7^{3}S, 9^{3}GF, 9^{0}GS

	Starts	1st	2nd	3rd	Win & Pl
Career Total (Turf)	3	0	0	2	865

Going (Turf): Sf: 0-1 GS: 0-1 Gd: 0-0 GF: 0-1 Fm: 0-0
Distance: 5f/6f: 0-0 7f-8f: 0-1 9f-13f: 0-2 14f+: 0-0

Track : LH: 0-0 RH: 0-2 Tight: 0-2 Gall: 0-0
Aids: Bl: 0-0 Vi: 0-0 Tstrap: 0-0
Best Rating: 65 8/01 Chep 7f16y soft

Napa Valley

75(67) (14)**29**

2-y-o ch f Most Welcome-Eccolina (Formidable (USA))
M Blanshard Lady Page

Placings:000 **(4067)**
2001: 7^{0}GF, 7^{0}GF, 7^{0}SD

	Starts	1st	2nd	3rd	Win & Pl
Career Total (Turf)	2	0	0	0	
Career Total (AW)	1	0	0	0	

Going (Turf): Sf: 0-0 GS: 0-0 Gd: 0-0 GF: 0-2 Fm: 0-0
Distance: 5f/6f: 0-0 7f-8f: 0-3 9f-13f: 0-0 14f+: 0-0
Track : LH: 0-1 RH: 0-1 Tight: 0-1 Gall: 0-1
Aids: Bl: 0-0 Vi: 0-0 Tstrap: 0-0
Best Rating: 29 7/01 Kemp 7f gd-fm

Napier Star

71(98) (40)**33**

8-y-o b m Inca Chief (USA)-America Star (Norwick (USA))
A B Mulholland P M Heaton

Placings:050/045001536015224204431320/230021633 0260003606300/0/00/260400-0000 **(1079)**
2001: 7^{0}SD, 6^{0}HY, 7^{0}SD, 7^{0}S

	Starts	1st	2nd	3rd	Win & Pl
Career Total (Turf)	11	0	0	0	
Career Total (AW)	51	4	8	8	18591

63	5/97	Wolv	5f	F(0-65)H	STD	£2277
61	11/96	Wolv	5f	F(0-60)H	STD	£2085
51	7/96	Wolv	5f	F(0-60)H	STD	£2519
57	4/96	Sthl	6f	F	STD	£2381

Total win prize-money £9262

Going (Turf): Sf: 0-2 GS: 0-1 Gd: 0-3 GF: 0-5 Fm: 0-0
Distance: **5f/6f: 4-48** 7f-8f: 0-14 9f-13f: 0-0 14f+: 0-0
Track : **LH: 4-47** RH: 0-1 **Tight: 3-31** Gall: 0-1
Aids: Bl: 0-1 **Vi: 2-35** Tstrap: 0-12
Best Rating: 24 4/01 Sthl 7f stand

Naseem Reef (IRE)

63 **18**

2-y-o b c College Chapel-Bay Supreme (Martinmas)
A Berry Jaber Abdullah

Placings:0 **(4853)**
2001: 5^{0}GF

	Starts	1st	2nd	3rd	Win & Pl
Career Total (Turf)	1	0	0	0	

Going (Turf): Sf: 0-0 GS: 0-0 Gd: 0-0 GF: 0-1 Fm: 0-0
Distance: 5f/6f: 0-1 7f-8f: 0-0 9f-13f: 0-0 14f+: 0-0
Track : LH: 0-1 RH: 0-0 Tight: 0-1 Gall: 0-0
Aids: Bl: 0-0 Vi: 0-0 Tstrap: 0-0
Best Rating: 18 9/01 Catt 5f212y gd-fm

Nash Me (IRE)

100 **72+**

3-y-o b c Nashwan (USA)-Queen's View (FR) (Lomond (USA))
D R Loder Sheikh Mohammed

Placings:10 **(4699)**
2001: 10^{1}GF, 12^{0}GS

	Starts	1st	2nd	3rd	Win & Pl
Career Total (Turf)	2	1	0	0	6640

72	9/01	York	1m2f85y	D	G-F	£6639

Total win prize-money £6640

Going (Turf): Sf: 0-0 GS: 0-1 Gd: 0-0 **GF: 1-1** Fm: 0-0
Distance: 5f/6f: 0-0 7f-8f: 0-0 **9f-13f: 1-2** 14f+: 0-0

Track : **LH: 1-2** RH: 0-0 Tight: 0-0 **Gall: 1-2**
Aids: Bl: 0-0 Vi: 0-0 Tstrap: 0-0
Best Rating: 72 9/01 York 1m2f85y gd-fm

A half-brother to Dubai Two Thousand, he did not race at two, but made a winning debut when easily landing a very modest York maiden over ten furlongs in September 2001 but was well beaten in a Doncaster Listed race. He is likely to need further.

Nashaab (USA)

110(105) (81+)**87**

4-y-o b g Zafonic (USA)-Tajannub (USA) (Dixieland Band (USA))
P D Evans M W Lawrence

Placings:553431-106051053D0010200 **(5251)**
2001: 8^{1}SD, 6^{0}S, 8^{6}HY, 10^{0}S, 8^{5}GF, 8^{1}F, 9^{0}F, 8^{5}GF, 8^{3}G, 8^{1}GF, 8^{0}G, 8^{0}GF, 7^{1}G, 8^{0}S, 7^{2}GS, 8^{0}S, 7^{0}S

	Starts	1st	2nd	3rd	Win & Pl
Career Total (Turf)	19	3	1	2	31690
Career Total (AW)	4	2	0	1	6999

84	8/01	Ches	7f122y	C(0-90)H	GD	£9204
77	7/01	Donc	1m	D(0-80)H	G-F	£7962
72	5/01	Leic	1m9y	D(0-85)H	FRM	£7488
81	1/01	Sthl	1m	D(0-80)H	STD	£3874
70	12/00	Wolv	1m100y	D	STD	£2736

Total win prize-money £31266

Going (Turf): Sf: 0-6 GS: 0-1 **Gd: 1-3 GF: 1-6 Fm: 1-2**
Distance: 5f/6f: 0-1 **7f-8f: 3-9** 9f-13f: 2-12 14f+: 0-0
Track : **LH: 4-13** RH: 0-4 **Tight: 2-6** Gall: 1-4
Aids: Bl: 0-0 Vi: 0-1 Tstrap: 0-0
Best Rating: 87 9/01 Donc 7f gd-sft

Fairly useful mile handicapper, effective on Fibresand and a sound surface. Finished first four times and was unfortunate to be demoted after passing the post first at Doncaster in July, but he was reinstated on appeal. Likes to come fast and late off a decent pace. Fitted with a 'pricker' to prevent him from hanging when scoring at Chester in July. Best on fast ground.

Nashira

86 **76d**

3-y-o ch f Prince Sabo-Aldevonie (Green Desert (USA))
C R Egerton Mrs R F Lowe

Placings:310-00 **(4988)**
2001: 8^{0}G, 8^{0}G

	Starts	1st	2nd	3rd	Win & Pl
Career Total (Turf)	5	1	0	1	3376

76	6/00	Bath	5f11y	E	G-F	£2828

Total win prize-money £2828

Going (Turf): Sf: 0-1 GS: 0-1 Gd: 0-2 **GF: 1-1** Fm: 0-0
Distance: **5f/6f: 1-3** 7f-8f: 0-1 9f-13f: 0-1 14f+: 0-0
Track : **LH: 1-3** RH: 0-0 Tight: 0-1 **Gall: 1-2**
Aids: Bl: 0-0 Vi: 0-0 Tstrap: 0-0
Best Rating: 57 9/01 Epsm 1m114y good

She won a Bath maiden on her second start at two in 2000, but was well beaten in the Redcar Two-Year-Old Trophy and was off the track for a year afterwards. No form since.

Nasmatt

109 **85**

3-y-o b f Danehill (USA)-Society Lady (USA) (Mr Prospector (USA))
M R Channon Sheikh Ahmed Al Maktoum

Placings:33142-40525 **(3640)**
2001: 6^{4}GF, 6^{0}GS, 6^{5}G, 5^{2}G, 6^{5}GS

	Starts	1st	2nd	3rd	Win & Pl
Career Total (Turf)	10	1	2	2	18032

88	9/00	Yarm	6f3y	D	G-F	£3558

Total win prize-money £3559

Going (Turf): Sf: 0-1 GS: 0-2 Gd: 0-4 **GF: 1-3** Fm: 0-0
Distance: 5f/6f: 0-7 **7f-8f: 1-3** 9f-13f: 0-0 14f+: 0-0
Track : LH: 0-1 RH: 0-0 Tight: 0-0 Gall: 0-1
Aids: Bl: 0-0 Vi: 0-0 Tstrap: 0-0
Best Rating: 95 6/01 NmkR 6f gd-fm

A half-sister to Bint Allayl, won once as a juvenile and was placed at Listed level. Failed to reproduce that form in 2001. Handles any ground.

Nassau Night

86 **60**

2-y-o b g Bahamian Bounty-Leave At Dawn (Slip Anchor)
R M H Cowell Mrs J M Penney

Placings:0 (3696)
2001: 6^{0}GF

	Starts	1st	2nd	3rd	Win & Pl
Career Total (Turf)	1	0	0	0	

Going (Turf): Sf: 0-0 GS: 0-0 Gd: 0-0 GF: 0-1 Fm: 0-0
Distance: 5f/6f: 0-0 7f-8f: 0-1 9f-13f: 0-0 14f+: 0-0
Track : LH: 0-1 RH: 0-0 Tight: 0-0 Gall: 0-0
Aids: Bl: 0-0 Vi: 0-0 Tstrap: 0-0
Best Rating: 60 8/01 Brig 6f209y gd-fm

Nasty Nick

2-y-o gr g Petong-Silver Spell (Aragon)
M Wigham Wilwyn Executive Racing Wwwwilwyncom

Placings:0 (3476)
2001: 6^{0}GF

	Starts	1st	2nd	3rd	Win & Pl
Career Total (Turf)	1	0	0	0	

Going (Turf): Sf: 0-0 GS: 0-0 Gd: 0-0 GF: 0-1 Fm: 0-0
Distance: 5f/6f: 0-1 7f-8f: 0-0 9f-13f: 0-0 14f+: 0-0
Track : LH: 0-0 RH: 0-0 Tight: 0-0 Gall: 0-0
Aids: Bl: 0-0 Vi: 0-0 Tstrap: 0-0

Natalie Jay

104(90) (67)**71**

5-y-o b m Ballacashtal (CAN)-Falls Of Lora (Scottish Rifle)
M R Channon M Channon

Placings:3633/060201500525/30430106331316-050055100 (4547)
2001: 10^{0}GF, 8^{5}GF, 9^{0}GF, 9^{0}GF, 8^{5}G, 8^{5}F, 6^{1}GF, 7^{0}GF, 6^{0}GF

	Starts	1st	2nd	3rd	Win & Pl
Career Total (Turf)	37	5	1	8	23925
Career Total (AW)	2	0	1	0	583

74	8/01	Sals	6f212y	E(0-75)H	G-F	£3094
80	11/00	Donc	1m	E(0-80)H	HVY	£4680
66	8/00	Sals	1m	D(0-85)H	G-F	£3783
67	8/99	Sals	1m	D(0-85)H	G-S	£5589

Total win prize-money £17146

Going (Turf): Sf: 2-8 GS: 1-6 Gd: 0-9 **GF: 2-12** Fm: 0-2
Distance: 5f/6f: 0-0 **7f-8f: 4-20** 9f-13f: 1-19 14f+: 0-0
Track : LH: 0-12 RH: 0-11 Tight: 0-10 Gall: 0-4
Aids: Bl: 0-0 Vi: 0-0 Tstrap: 0-0
Best Rating: 74 8/01 Sals 6f212y gd-fm

Fair mile handicapper, handles fast but goes very well on really soft ground.

Nathan's Boy

103(97) (52)**58**

5-y-o gr g Tragic Role (USA)-Gold Belt (IRE) (Bellypha)
A Streeter (R Hollinshead 26/6) Mrs J Hughes

Placings:00303622/4100223400/**50**-65530435060 (4404)
2001: 12^{6}SW, 11^{5}SD, 10^{5}S, 8^{3}G, 10^{0}G, 10^{4}GF, 9^{3}GF, 9^{5}GF, 11^{0}GF, 10^{6}HY, 12^{0}GS

	Starts	1st	2nd	3rd	Win & Pl
Career Total (Turf)	26	1	4	5	14259
Career Total (AW)	5	0	0	0	0

78	4/99	Bevl	1m1f207yD(0-85)H		GD	£4048

Total win prize-money £4049

Going (Turf): Sf: 0-4 GS: 0-1 **Gd: 1-12** GF: 0-8 Fm: 0-1
Distance: 5f/6f: 0-3 7f-8f: 0-5 **9f-13f: 1-23** 14f+: 0-0
Track : LH: 0-17 **RH: 1-10** Tight: 0-8 Gall: 0-4
Aids: Bl: 0-0 Vi: 0-1 Tstrap: 0-0
Best Rating: 62 6/01 Bevl 1m1f207y gd-fm

Natiain

66 **30**

2-y-o ch g Danzig Connection (USA)-Fen Princess (IRE) (Trojan Fen)
P C Haslam Wilson Imports

Placings:00 (5623)
2001: 6^{0}S, 8^{0}GS

	Starts	1st	2nd	3rd	Win & Pl
Career Total (Turf)	2	0	0	0	

Going (Turf): Sf: 0-1 GS: 0-1 Gd: 0-0 GF: 0-0 Fm: 0-0
Distance: 5f/6f: 0-1 7f-8f: 0-0 9f-13f: 0-1 14f+: 0-0
Track : LH: 0-2 RH: 0-0 Tight: 0-0 Gall: 0-0
Aids: Bl: 0-0 Vi: 0-0 Tstrap: 0-0
Best Rating: 30 11/01 Nott 1m54y gd-sft

Nation (USA)

105 **86+**

3-y-o b c Miesque's Son (USA)-Erica's Fault (USA) (Muttering (USA))
Sir Michael Stoute Highclere Thoroughbred Racing Ltd

Placings:23-402136 (5226)
2001: 10^{4}GF, 12^{0}GF, 9^{2}GF, 10^{1}S, 10^{3}HY, 11^{6}S

	Starts	1st	2nd	3rd	Win & Pl
Career Total (Turf)	8	1	2	2	8841

85	8/01	Epsm	1m2f18y	D	SFT	£4192

Total win prize-money £4193

Going (Turf): Sf: 1-3 GS: 0-0 Gd: 0-0 GF: 0-5 Fm: 0-0
Distance: 5f/6f: 0-0 7f-8f: 0-2 **9f-13f: 1-6** 14f+: 0-0
Track : **LH: 1-6** RH: 0-1 **Tight: 1-3** Gall: 0-1
Aids: Bl: 0-0 Vi: 0-0 Tstrap: 0-0
Best Rating: 86 9/01 Hayd 1m2f120y heavy

In the frame in maidens and beaten in a handicap before winning a soft-ground Epsom maiden in September when forcing tactics seemed to bring about improvement. Stays ten furlongs. Handles any ground.

National Dance

103(101) (70)**66**

4-y-o b g Deploy-Fairy Flax (IRE) (Dancing Brave (USA))
Mrs J R Ramsden Michael Payton

Placings:45/**142**05402014-0060600 (4469)
2001: 9^{0}HY, 12^{0}GF, 12^{6}F, 10^{0}GF, 9^{6}GS, 11^{0}GF, 12^{0}G

	Starts	1st	2nd	3rd	Win & Pl
Career Total (Turf)	17	1	1	0	19467
Career Total (AW)	3	1	1	0	4630

	9/00	Chan	1m2f	H	GD	£9606
60	1/00	Sthl	1m	D	STD	£2847

Total win prize-money £12453

Going (Turf): Sf: 0-1 GS: 0-1 Gd: 0-1 GF: 0-3 Fm: 0-1
Distance: 5f/6f: 0-0 **7f-8f: 1-2** 9f-13f: 0-10 14f+: 0-0
Track : **LH: 1-8** RH: 0-2 Tight: 0-4 Gall: 0-2
Aids: Bl: 0-0 Vi: 0-0 Tstrap: 0-0
Best Rating: 66 5/01 Donc 1m4f gd-fm

National Park

109 **91+**

2-y-o gr g Common Grounds-Success Story (Sharrood (USA))
R Hannon The Queen

Placings:201214 (5260)
2001: 5^{2}G, 6^{0}S, 6^{1}F, 6^{2}GS, 7^{1}S, 7^{4}GS

	Starts	1st	2nd	3rd	Win & Pl
Career Total (Turf)	6	2	2	0	13979

91	9/01	Ches	7f2y	C(0-95)	SFT	£6815
67	8/01	Ling	6f	D	FRM	£3731

Total win prize-money £10546

Going (Turf): Sf: 1-2 GS: 0-2 Gd: 0-1 GF: 0-0 **Fm: 1-1**
Distance: 5f/6f: 1-3 7f-8f: 1-3 9f-13f: 0-0 14f+: 0-0
Track : **LH: 1-3** RH: 0-0 **Tight: 1-2** Gall: 0-1
Aids: Bl: 0-0 Vi: 0-0 Tstrap: 0-0
Best Rating: 91 9/01 Ches 7f2y soft

Winner of a fast-ground Lingfield maiden in August, he showed he could handle soft ground when runner-up at Epsom, and confirmed that by making all in a Chester nursery. Well suited by a sharp track and forcing tactics.

Native Force (IRE)

102 **75**

3-y-o b f Indian Ridge-La Pellegrina (IRE) (Be My Guest (USA))
J H M Gosden R E Sangster

Placings:0-51 (4090)
2001: 8^{5}GF, 8^{1}S

	Starts	1st	2nd	3rd	Win & Pl
Career Total (Turf)	3	1	0	0	4349

75	8/01	Sand	1m14y	D	SFT	£4348

Total win prize-money £4349

Going (Turf): Sf: 1-1 GS: 0-0 Gd: 0-1 GF: 0-1 Fm: 0-0
Distance: 5f/6f: 0-0 7f-8f: 0-2 **9f-13f: 1-1** 14f+: 0-0
Track : LH: 0-1 **RH: 1-2** Tight: 0-0 Gall: 0-1
Aids: Bl: 0-0 Vi: 0-0 Tstrap: 0-0
Best Rating: 75 8/01 Sand 1m14y soft

Got off the mark in a soft-ground maiden at Sandown in August.

Native Title

102 **79**

3-y-o b c Pivotal-Bermuda Lily (Dunbeath (USA))
M Blanshard C McKenna

Placings:54-222160000 (5560)
2001: 8^{2}GS, 8^{2}GS, 7^{2}GS, 7^{1}GF, 6^{6}GS, 6^{0}GF, 7^{0}G, 6^{0}GS, 7^{0}S

	Starts	1st	2nd	3rd	Win & Pl
Career Total (Turf)	11	1	3	0	9599

84	6/01	Newb	7f	D	G-F	£4654

Total win prize-money £4654

Going (Turf): Sf: 0-1 GS: 0-5 Gd: 0-3 **GF: 1-2** Fm: 0-0
Distance: 5f/6f: 0-1 **7f-8f: 1-10** 9f-13f: 0-0 14f+: 0-0
Track : LH: 0-1 RH: 0-1 Tight: 0-0 Gall: 0-1
Aids: Bl: 0-0 Vi: 0-0 Tstrap: 0-0
Best Rating: 84 6/01 Newb 7f gd-fm

He finished runner-up in his first three starts of this season on easy ground and deservedly got off the mark over seven furlongs at Newbury in June on fast going. He has failed to build on that since in handicap company having been dropped in trip.

Natmsky (IRE)

84(83) (72)**60**

2-y-o b g Shadeed (USA)-Cockney Lass (Camden Town)
K A Ryan Steer Arms Belton Racing Club

Placings:00000 (5610)
2001: 6^{0}GF, 8^{0}GF, 7^{0}GF, 8^{0}S, 8^{0}SD, 6^{3}SD

	Starts	1st	2nd	3rd	Win & Pl
Career Total (Turf)	4	0	0	0	
Career Total (AW)	1	0	0	0	

Going (Turf): Sf: 0-1 GS: 0-0 Gd: 0-0 GF: 0-3 Fm: 0-0
Distance: 5f/6f: 0-1 7f-8f: 0-1 9f-13f: 0-3 14f+: 0-0
Track : LH: 0-4 RH: 0-1 Tight: 0-2 Gall: 0-0
Aids: Bl: 0-0 Vi: 0-0 Tstrap: 0-0
Best Rating: 60 8/01 Bevl 1m100y gd-fm

Natsmagirl (IRE)

103(92) (41)**38**
4-y-o b f Blues Traveller (IRE)-Top The Rest (Top Ville)
R E Barr M O'Hair

Placings:65310524426300050/5056246-030000660 **(4617)**
2001: 5^{0}S, 9^{3}F, 8^{0}GF, 8^{0}GF, 10^{0}GF, 12^{0}G, 9^{6}GS, 9^{6}GF, 10^{0}F

	Starts	1st	2nd	3rd	Win & Pl
Career Total (Turf)	30	1	3	3	7741
Career Total (AW)	3	0	0	0	0

63 6/99 Thsk 6f E G-F £2722
Total win prize-money £2723

Going (Turf): Sf: 0-1 GS: 0-1 Gd: 0-7 **GF: 1-14** Fm: 0-6
Distance: **5f/6f: 1-16** 7f-8f: 0-9 9f-13f: 0-7 14f+: 0-0
Track : LH: 0-12 RH: 0-5 Tight: 0-8 Gall: 0-4
Aids: Bl: 0-0 Vi: 0-2 Tstrap: 0-0
Best Rating: 40 5/01 Rdcr 1m1f firm

Natural (IRE)

102 **64d**
4-y-o b g Bigstone (IRE)-You Make Me Real (USA) (Give Me Strength (USA))
John Berry Late Mrs Dinham, Mrs A Veale, C Berry

Placings:0/0620-0031000 **(5382)**
2001: 7^{0}G, 10^{0}GF, 9^{3}GF, 11^{1}GS, 11^{0}G, 14^{0}GS, 11^{0}S

	Starts	1st	2nd	3rd	Win & Pl
Career Total (Turf)	12	1	1	1	5141

64 7/01 Haml 1m3f16y E(0-70)H G-S £3601
Total win prize-money £3601

Going (Turf): Sf: 0-2 **GS: 1-3** Gd: 0-2 GF: 0-5 Fm: 0-0
Distance: 5f/6f: 0-1 7f-8f: 0-3 **9f-13f: 1-7** 14f+: 0-1
Track : LH: 0-5 **RH: 1-4 Tight: 1-4** Gall: 0-1
Aids: Bl: 0-0 Vi: 0-1 Tstrap: 0-0
Best Rating: 64 7/01 Haml 1m3f16y gd-sft

Natural Dancer

83 **57**
2-y-o b f Shareef Dancer (USA)-Naturally Fresh (Thatching)
C N Allen G S Shropshire

Placings:0 **(5361)**
2001: 8^{0}GS

	Starts	1st	2nd	3rd	Win & Pl
Career Total (Turf)	1	0	0	0	

Going (Turf): Sf: 0-0 GS: 0-1 Gd: 0-0 GF: 0-0 Fm: 0-0
Distance: 5f/6f: 0-0 7f-8f: 0-1 9f-13f: 0-0 14f+: 0-0
Track : LH: 0-0 RH: 0-0 Tight: 0-0 Gall: 0-0
Aids: Bl: 0-0 Vi: 0-0 Tstrap: 0-0
Best Rating: 57 10/01 NmkR 1m gd-sft

Nature (IRE)

82(87) (50)**40**
2-y-o b f Bluebird (USA)-Nawaji (USA) (Trempolino (USA))
R Hannon The Royal Ascot Racing Club

Placings:05606 **(5195)**
2001: 5^{0}GF, 6^{5}GF, 7^{6}GF, 6^{0}G, 6^{6}SD

	Starts	1st	2nd	3rd	Win & Pl
Career Total (Turf)	4	0	0	0	0
Career Total (AW)	1	0	0	0	0

Going (Turf): Sf: 0-0 GS: 0-0 Gd: 0-1 GF: 0-3 Fm: 0-0
Distance: 5f/6f: 0-3 7f-8f: 0-2 9f-13f: 0-0 14f+: 0-0
Track : LH: 0-1 RH: 0-2 Tight: 0-2 Gall: 0-1
Aids: Bl: 0-0 Vi: 0-0 Tstrap: 0-0
Best Rating: 50 10/01 Wolv 6f stand

Naughty Knight

107(96) (56)**45**
3-y-o ch g King's Signet (USA)-Maid Of Mischief (Be My Chief (USA))
P W D'Arcy (A Berry 12/2) Walt Sylvester

Placings:05011350000466-1233566306 **(5418)**
2001: 7^{1}SD, 7^{2}SD, 8^{3}SW, 7^{3}SD, 6^{5}SW, 8^{6}GF, 8^{6}GS, 7^{3}GF, 8^{0}GF, 7^{6}SD, 8^{0}SD

	Starts	1st	2nd	3rd	Win & Pl
Career Total (Turf)	13	2	0	2	5561
Career Total (AW)	11	1	1	2	3076

53 1/01 Sthl 7f G STD £1939
51 5/00 Leic 5f2y F SFT £2257
51 5/00 Bevl 5f F GD £2296
Total win prize-money £6493

Going (Turf): **Sf: 1-4** GS: 0-1 **Gd: 1-4** GF: 0-4 Fm: 0-0
Distance: **5f/6f: 2-14** 7f-8f: 1-8 9f-13f: 0-2 14f+: 0-0
Track : **LH: 1-14** RH: 0-2 Tight: 0-6 Gall: 0-1
Aids: **Bl: 1-8** Vi: 0-4 Tstrap: 0-0
Best Rating: 64 1/01 Sthl 7f stand

Plating class. Normally runs blinkered or visored. Appreciates easy ground. Seven furlongs is probably his limit.

Naughty Nell

92 **66**
2-y-o b f Danehill Dancer (IRE)-Hana Marie (Formidable (USA))
J Noseda Mrs K J Crangle

Placings:0 **(4886)**
2001: 7^{0}GF

	Starts	1st	2nd	3rd	Win & Pl
Career Total (Turf)	1	0	0	0	

Going (Turf): Sf: 0-0 GS: 0-0 Gd: 0-0 GF: 0-1 Fm: 0-0
Distance: 5f/6f: 0-0 7f-8f: 0-1 9f-13f: 0-0 14f+: 0-0
Track : LH: 0-0 RH: 0-1 Tight: 0-0 Gall: 0-1
Aids: Bl: 0-0 Vi: 0-0 Tstrap: 0-0
Best Rating: 66 9/01 Kemp 7f gd-fm

Nautical Light

98(76) (14)**40**
4-y-o b f Slip Anchor-Lighted Glitter (FR) (Crystal Glitters (USA))
D W P Arbuthnot Alan A Wright

Placings:0-0P0000000 **(5469)**
2001: 8^{0}G, 9^{0}GF, 9^{0}GF, 8^{0}SD, 8^{0}G, 10^{0}GF, 10^{0}GF, 11^{0}S, 9^{0}S

	Starts	1st	2nd	3rd	Win & Pl
Career Total (Turf)	9	0	0	0	
Career Total (AW)	1	0	0	0	

Going (Turf): Sf: 0-2 GS: 0-0 Gd: 0-3 GF: 0-4 Fm: 0-0
Distance: 5f/6f: 0-0 7f-8f: 0-0 9f-13f: 0-10 14f+: 0-0
Track : LH: 0-5 RH: 0-4 Tight: 0-7 Gall: 0-0
Aids: Bl: 0-0 Vi: 0-0 Tstrap: 0-0
Best Rating: 56 5/01 Wind 1m67y good

Nautical Star

95(89) (24)**57d**
6-y-o b g Slip Anchor-Comic Talent (Pharly (FR))
A C Whillans (J W Hills 6/9) Mrs Helen Greggan

Placings:510/140331/052201/000000-0045034 **(4552)**
2001: 12^{0}GS, 14^{0}GF, 16^{4}GF, 12^{5}G, 12^{0}GF, 12^{3}G, 14^{4}SW

	Starts	1st	2nd	3rd	Win & Pl
Career Total (Turf)	27	4	2	3	44106
Career Total (AW)	1	0	0	0	0

94 6/99 Gdwd 1m4f C(0-95) G-F £8742
94 8/98 Epsm 1m4f10y C(0-90)H G-F £10357
91 4/98 NmkR 1m2f C(0-95)H SFT £6212
80 8/97 Ayr 7f D G-F £3688
Total win prize-money £29000

Going (Turf): Sf: 1-3 GS: 0-4 Gd: 0-10 **GF: 3-10** Fm: 0-0
Distance: 5f/6f: 0-0 7f-8f: 1-3 **9f-13f: 3-22** 14f+: 0-3
Track : **LH: 2-11** RH: 1-15 **Tight: 2-10** Gall: 0-9
Aids: Bl: 0-0 Vi: 0-2 Tstrap: 0-0
Best Rating: 57 7/01 Chep 1m4f23y good

Usually allowed to race up with the pace, he enjoys turning tracks and does particularly well at Epsom. 12 furlongs is his limit, and he acts on any ground. Appears to be on the downgrade.

Nautical Warning

98(107) (75)**49**
6-y-o b/br g Warning-Night At Sea (Night Shift (USA))
Jamie Poulton (B R Johnson 13/6) M C Trevena

Placings:6000/150400/01351201412/14000006-066000 **(4448)**
2001: 7^{0}SD, 8^{6}SD, 8^{6}SD, 7^{0}F, 5^{0}GF, 5^{0}G, 7^{5}SD

	Starts	1st	2nd	3rd	Win & Pl
Career Total (Turf)	16	1	0	0	4595
Career Total (AW)	19	5	2	1	24465

80 1/00 Ling 7f B H STD £10725
75 11/99 Ling 1m E(0-75)H STD £2437
53 7/99 Ling 7f140y D(0-80)H FRM £3984
71 6/99 Ling 1m E(0-65) STD £2782
71 2/99 Ling 1m E(0-70)H STD £2684
63 1/98 Ling 7f F(0-60)H STD £2274
Total win prize-money £24888

Going (Turf): Sf: 0-1 GS: 0-4 Gd: 0-5 GF: 0-4 **Fm: 1-2**
Distance: 5f/6f: 0-5 **7f-8f: 6-27** 9f-13f: 0-3 14f+: 0-0
Track : **LH: 5-22** RH: 0-2 **Tight: 5-17** Gall: 0-1
Aids: Bl: 0-0 Vi: 0-2 **Tstrap: 4-24**
Best Rating: 65 1/01 Ling 7f stand

Moderate handicapper. He became the first winner trained by Jeremy Noseda when winning a modest apprentice handicap on the Lingfield Equitrack in January '98, and his best form since has been on that surface, including victory in the Ladbroke All-Weather Trophy Final.

Navarre Samson (FR)

106 **59**
6-y-o b/br g Ganges (USA)-L'Eternite (FR) (Cariellor (FR))
P J Hobbs Winton Bloodstock Ltd

Placings:023002/04-10 **(4020)**
2001: 16^{1}GF, 16^{0}G

	Starts	1st	2nd	3rd	Win & Pl
Career Total (Turf)	10	1	2	1	7136

45 7/01 Chep 2m49y F G-F £2394
Total win prize-money £2394

Going (Turf): Sf: 0-0 GS: 0-0 Gd: 0-2 **GF: 1-2** Fm: 0-0
Distance: 5f/6f: 0-0 7f-8f: 0-0 9f-13f: 0-1 **14f+: 1-3**
Track : **LH: 1-3** RH: 0-1 Tight: 0-2 Gall: 0-0
Aids: Bl: 0-0 Vi: 0-0 **Tstrap: 1-3**
Best Rating: 45 7/01 Chep 2m49y gd-fm

Naviasky (IRE)

104 **76**
6-y-o b/br g Scenic-Black Molly (IRE) (High Top)
Miss Venetia Williams (D Nicholls 18/10) Oakview Racing

Placings:66160050/00441332050/3311016/00040466340-00060002001203000 **(5344)**
2001: 6^{0}GF, 8^{0}G, 7^{0}F, 8^{6}F, 7^{0}GF, 8^{0}GF, 9^{0}G, 8^{2}G, 7^{0}G, 9^{0}G, 7^{1}GF, 7^{2}GF, 7^{0}GF, 8^{3}GF, 8^{0}S, 6^{0}GS, 8^{0}GS

	Starts	1st	2nd	3rd	Win & Pl		
Career Total (Turf)	55	6	3	6	62507		

65	8/01	Brig	7f214y	E	G-F	£2765
81	8/99	Leic	1m8y	C(0-95)H	G-F	£9378
73	7/99	Gdwd	1m	D(0-85)H	G-F	£11535
69	6/99	Gdwd	1m	C(0-90)H	G-F	£14330
66	6/98	Carl	7f214y	E(0-70)H	G-S	£2970
79	8/97	Thsk	5f	E	G-F	£3382

Total win prize-money £44361

Going (Turf): Sf: 0-5 GS: 1-8 Gd: 0-16 **GF: 5-23** Fm: 0-3
Distance: 5f/6f: 1-4 **7f-8f: 4-37** 9f-13f: 1-14 14f+: 0-0
Track : LH: 1-18 **RH: 3-19** Tight: 0-13 Gall: 0-5
Aids: Bl: 0-0 Vi: 0-0 Tstrap: 0-0
Best Rating: 76 9/01 Gdwd 1m gd-fm

Formerly a useful handicapper, he became quirky but easily landed a Brighton claimer in August 2001. Has gone well in handicaps since and is suited by undulating tracks and fast ground.

Nawader (USA)

91(73) (8)**40**
5-y-o b/br h Silver Hawk (USA)-Music Lane (USA) (Miswaki (USA))
M C Chapman G C R Pryke

Placings:40005600 **(5044)**
2001: 6^4GF, 6^0GS, 5^0GF, 7^0G, 10^5G, 8^6S, 9^0G, 14^0SD

	Starts	1st	2nd	3rd	Win & Pl
Career Total (Turf)	7	0	0	0	0
Career Total (AW)	1	0	0	0	

Going (Turf): Sf: 0-1 GS: 0-1 Gd: 0-3 GF: 0-2 Fm: 0-0
Distance: 5f/6f: 0-3 7f-8f: 0-1 9f-13f: 0-3 14f+: 0-1
Track : LH: 0-3 RH: 0-2 Tight: 0-1 Gall: 0-1
Aids: Bl: 0-0 Vi: 0-0 Tstrap: 0-0
Best Rating: 40 9/01 Yarm 1m3y soft

Nayef (USA)

114 **123**
3-y-o b c Gulch (USA)-Height Of Fashion (FR) (Bustino)
M P Tregoning Hamdan Al Maktoum

Placings:11-3031111 **(5389)**
2001: 8^3S, 8^0G, 12^3GF, 10^1G, 9^1GF, 12^1S, 10^1GS

	Starts	1st	2nd	3rd	Win & Pl
Career Total (Turf)	9	6	0	2	375067

123	10/01	NmkR	1m2f	A	G-S	£259840
121	9/01	Asct	1m4f	A	SFT	£32400
121	9/01	Gdwd	1m1f192y	A	G-F	£26200
116	8/01	Hayd	1m2f120y	A	GD	£23800
119	10/00	Asct	1m	A	HVY	£13487
98	9/00	Newb	1m	B	G-F	£9439

Total win prize-money £365167

Going (Turf): Sf: 2-3 GS: 1-1 Gd: 1-2 **GF: 2-3** Fm: 0-0
Distance: 5f/6f: 0-0 7f-8f: 2-4 **9f-13f: 4-5** 14f+: 0-0
Track : LH: 1-1 **RH: 3-4** Tight: 1-2 **Gall: 2-2**
Aids: Bl: 0-0 Vi: 0-0 Tstrap: 0-0
Best Rating: 123 10/01 NmkR 1m2f gd-sft

A half-brother to Nashwan, he was winter favourite for the Classics after being unbeaten in two races at two, but looked short of pace in the Craven and was only eighth in the Guineas. Returned from an absence to run a decent race in the Gordon Stakes on his first attempt at 12 furlongs and went on to gain easy wins in Group Threes at Haydock and Goodwood. Completed the hat trick in the Cumberland Lodge at Ascot and proved himself a Group One performer in the Dubai Champion Stakes. Ten furlongs is probably his best trip and he looks more the finished article now. He is to stay in training with the Dubai World Cup as the first target.

Nayyel

103 **88+**
2-y-o br c Zafonic (USA)-The Perfect Life (IRE) (Try My Best (USA))
J L Dunlop Hamdan Al Maktoum

Placings:21 **(3382)**
2001: 7^2GF, 7^1GF

	Starts	1st	2nd	3rd	Win & Pl
Career Total (Turf)	2	1	1	0	5627

88	7/01	Sand	7f16y	D	G-F	£4251

Total win prize-money £4251

Going (Turf): Sf: 0-0 GS: 0-0 Gd: 0-0 **GF: 1-2** Fm: 0-0
Distance: 5f/6f: 0-0 **7f-8f: 1-2** 9f-13f: 0-0 14f+: 0-0
Track : LH: 0-0 **RH: 1-1** Tight: 0-0 Gall: 0-0
Aids: Bl: 0-0 Vi: 0-0 Tstrap: 0-0
Best Rating: 88 7/01 Sand 7f16y gd-fm

Out of a sister to the champion sprinter/miler Last Tycoon who has also produced the Gordon Stakes winner Rabah, he was an eyecatching runner-up to Laissezaller in maiden at Newbury on his debut, and got off the mark in a small Sandown maiden.

Nazareth (IRE)

96 **79**
2-y-o b c Woodborough (USA)-Tinos Island (IRE) (Alzao (USA))
R Guest Rae Guest Racing Partnership

Placings:36232 **(4725)**
2001: 7^3GF, 7^6G, 7^2G, 7^3GF, 7^2GF

	Starts	1st	2nd	3rd	Win & Pl
Career Total (Turf)	5	0	2	2	4069

Going (Turf): Sf: 0-0 GS: 0-0 Gd: 0-2 GF: 0-3 Fm: 0-0
Distance: 5f/6f: 0-0 7f-8f: 0-5 9f-13f: 0-0 14f+: 0-0
Track : LH: 0-3 RH: 0-0 Tight: 0-0 Gall: 0-0
Aids: Bl: 0-0 Vi: 0-0 Tstrap: 0-0
Best Rating: 79 9/01 Wwck 7f26y gd-fm

Good place efforts so far. Suited by good and good to firm, he has only been tried at seven furlongs.

Ndola

67 **22**
2-y-o b g Emperor Jones (USA)-Lykoa (Shirley Heights)
B J Curley Mrs B J Curley

Placings:000 **(5527)**
2001: 8^0G, 8^0GS, 8^0HY

	Starts	1st	2nd	3rd	Win & Pl
Career Total (Turf)	3	0	0	0	

Going (Turf): Sf: 0-1 GS: 0-1 Gd: 0-1 GF: 0-0 Fm: 0-0
Distance: 5f/6f: 0-0 7f-8f: 0-1 9f-13f: 0-2 14f+: 0-0
Track : LH: 0-3 RH: 0-0 Tight: 0-0 Gall: 0-1
Aids: Bl: 0-0 Vi: 0-0 Tstrap: 0-0
Best Rating: 22 9/01 Nott 1m54y good

Near Miss (USA)

92 **62**
3-y-o b f Capote (USA)-Devon Diva (USA) (The Minstrel (CAN))
H R A Cecil K Abdulla

Placings:5 **(2668)**
2001: 11^5G

	Starts	1st	2nd	3rd	Win & Pl
Career Total (Turf)	1	0	0	0	0

Going (Turf): Sf: 0-0 GS: 0-0 Gd: 0-1 GF: 0-0 Fm: 0-0
Distance: 5f/6f: 0-0 7f-8f: 0-0 9f-13f: 0-1 14f+: 0-0
Track : LH: 0-1 RH: 0-0 Tight: 0-1 Gall: 0-0
Aids: Bl: 0-0 Vi: 0-0 Tstrap: 0-0
Best Rating: 62 7/01 Yarm 1m3f101y good

Nearly A Fool

100 **83**
3-y-o b g Komaite (USA)-Greenway Lady (Prince Daniel (USA))
B A McMahon Nearly A Fool Partnership

Placings:14331333302-040000060 **(3633)**
2001: 6^0GS, 5^4GF, 6^0GF, 6^0GS, 5^0GF, 5^0GF, 5^0G, 5^6F, 5^0G

	Starts	1st	2nd	3rd	Win & Pl
Career Total (Turf)	20	2	1	6	23024

83	6/00	Bath	5f11y	D	G-F	£3376
81	3/00	Donc	5f	D	G-F	£5694

Total win prize-money £9071

Going (Turf): Sf: 0-2 GS: 0-2 Gd: 0-7 **GF: 2-8** Fm: 0-1
Distance: 5f/6f: 2-20 7f-8f: 0-0 9f-13f: 0-0 14f+: 0-0
Track : LH: 1-5 RH: 0-1 Tight: 0-3 **Gall: 1-3**
Aids: Bl: 0-0 Vi: 0-0 Tstrap: 0-0
Best Rating: 93 5/01 Ches 5f16y gd-fm

Landed the 2000 Brocklesby in style on his debut and has run some good races afterwards in decent company afterwards. Has shown little in 2001.

Needwood Blade

114(71) (1)**103**
3-y-o ch c Pivotal-Finlaggan (Be My Chief (USA))
B A McMahon R L Bedding

Placings:00-01121045U3052 **(5228)**
2001: 6^0SD, 6^1S, 6^1S, 6^2GF, 6^1F, 8^0GF, 7^4G, 7^5GF, 6^UG, 6^3G, 6^0GF, 7^5S, 6^2S

	Starts	1st	2nd	3rd	Win & Pl
Career Total (Turf)	14	3	2	1	50691
Career Total (AW)	1	0	0	0	

100	5/01	York	6f214y	B(0-105)H	FRM	£22750
92	4/01	Ripn	6f	D(0-80)H	SFT	£4566
72	3/01	Donc	6f	D	SFT	£4270

Total win prize-money £31587

Going (Turf): Sf: 2-5 GS: 0-1 Gd: 0-3 GF: 0-4 Fm: 1-1
Distance: 5f/6f: 2-6 7f-8f: 1-9 9f-13f: 0-0 14f+: 0-0
Track : LH: 1-5 RH: 0-0 Tight: 0-1 **Gall: 1-3**
Aids: Bl: 0-0 Vi: 0-0 Tstrap: 0-0
Best Rating: 103 8/01 York 6f214y good

Having failed to take to the sand on his seasonal reappearance, he caused something of an upset on his next run when turning over an odds-on shot rated 38lb his superior at Doncaster, but showed that win was no fluke with a ten-length victory at Ripon and when landing a valuable handicap at York. Some good efforts in defeat since. Effective at up to seven furlongs, but did not seem to stay a mile when tried over it.

Needwood Brave

94 **52**
3-y-o b g Lion Cavern (USA)-Woodcrest (Niniski (USA))
J G Fitzgerald Tim Kilroe

Placings:000-00000 **(4270)**
2001: 9^0GF, 10^0GF, 10^0GF, 8^0G, 11^0GF

	Starts	1st	2nd	3rd	Win & Pl
Career Total (Turf)	8	0	0	0	

Going (Turf): Sf: 0-1 GS: 0-1 Gd: 0-1 GF: 0-5 Fm: 0-0
Distance: 5f/6f: 0-0 7f-8f: 0-2 9f-13f: 0-6 14f+: 0-0
Track : LH: 0-5 RH: 0-2 Tight: 0-1 Gall: 0-1
Aids: Bl: 0-2 Vi: 0-0 Tstrap: 0-0
Best Rating: 52 6/01 Newc 1m2f32y gd-fm

Needwood Maestro

93(64) (8)**31**
5-y-o b g Sizzling Melody-Needwood Poppy (Rolfe (USA))
J Mackie Trying To Buy Fun Partnership

Placings:3340000040/50031-00 **(5106)**
2001: 11^0G, 12^0GS

	Starts	1st	2nd	3rd	Win & Pl
Career Total (Turf)	15	1	0	3	3716
Career Total (AW)	2	0	0	0	

37 9/00 Haml 1m4f17y E SFT £2834
Total win prize-money £2834

Going (Turf): **Sf: 1-5** GS: 0-5 Gd: 0-3 GF: 0-1 Fm: 0-1
Distance: 5f/6f: 0-0 7f-8f: 0-0 **9f-13f: 1-15** 14f+: 0-2
Track: LH: 0-10 **RH: 1-7 Tight: 1-7** Gall: 0-1
Aids: Bl: 0-0 **Vi: 1-5** Tstrap: 0-1
Best Rating: 31 8/01 Hayd 1m3f200y good

Needwood Missile

73 **7**
5-y-o b g Sizzling Melody-Sea Dart (Air Trooper)
J L Spearing Bryan Mathieson

Placings:0 **(1409)**
2001: 12^{0}G

	Starts	1st	2nd	3rd	Win & Pl
Career Total (Turf)	1	0	0	0	

Going (Turf): Sf: 0-0 GS: 0-0 Gd: 0-1 GF: 0-0 Fm: 0-0
Distance: 5f/6f: 0-0 7f-8f: 0-0 9f-13f: 0-1 14f+: 0-0
Track: LH: 0-0 RH: 0-1 Tight: 0-1 Gall: 0-0
Aids: Bl: 0-0 Vi: 0-0 Tstrap: 0-0
Best Rating: 7 5/01 Haml 1m4f17y good

Needwood Mystic

104 (9)**60**
6-y-o b m Rolfe (USA)-Enchanting Kate (Enchantment)
Mrs A J Perrett Dene Jesmond Enterprises

Placings:504000/06000133215000/4001050-121010 **(5026)**
2001: 11^{1}GS, 11^{2}GS, 11^{1}G, 12^{0}GF, 11^{1}GF, 9^{0}S

	Starts	1st	2nd	3rd	Win & Pl
Career Total (Turf)	32	6	2	2	18962
Career Total (AW)	1	0	0	0	

60 8/01 Brig 1m3f196yE(0-70)H G-F £2807
55 5/01 Brig 1m3f196yE(0-70)H GD £2884
53 4/01 Brig 1m3f196yF(0-65)H G-S £2394
53 7/00 Catt 1m3f214yE(0-75)H G-F £3185
48 8/99 Wwck 1m4f56y F(0-60)H GD £2809
40 6/99 Wwck 1m4f56y F(0-60)H G-F £2408
Total win prize-money £16488

Going (Turf): Sf: 0-5 GS: 1-8 Gd: 2-4 **GF: 3-14** Fm: 0-1
Distance: 5f/6f: 0-0 7f-8f: 0-1 **9f-13f: 6-30** 14f+: 0-2
Track: **LH: 6-22** RH: 0-11 **Tight: 1-7** Gall: 0-4
Aids: Bl: 0-0 Vi: 0-0 Tstrap: 0-0
Best Rating: 60 8/01 Brig 1m3f196y gd-fm

A game front-running mare, she has developed a love affair with Brighton and won three times over 12 furlongs there this season. Very much suited by fast ground and dictating the pace.

Needwood Spirit

104(77) (17)**52**
6-y-o b g Rolfe (USA)-Needwood Nymph (Bold Owl)
Mrs A M Naughton (H Alexander 16/5) Famous Five Racing

Placings:54/4400365441/4415200345/02000-06330032 **(5402)**
2001: 16^{0}SD, 13^{6}G, 16^{3}GS, 17^{3}GF, 16^{0}GF, 17^{0}G, 17^{3}GS, 17^{2}S

	Starts	1st	2nd	3rd	Win & Pl
Career Total (Turf)	33	2	3	5	17012
Career Total (AW)	2	0	0	0	0

66 4/99 Folk 1m7f92y E(0-70)H SFT £2905
61 10/98 Catt 1m5f175yF(0-60) SFT £2845
Total win prize-money £5750

Going (Turf): **Sf: 2-15** GS: 0-8 Gd: 0-6 GF: 0-3 Fm: 0-1
Distance: 5f/6f: 0-0 7f-8f: 0-1 9f-13f: 0-9 **14f+: 2-25**
Track: LH: 1-24 RH: 1-10 **Tight: 2-16** Gall: 0-4
Aids: Bl: 0-0 Vi: 0-1 Tstrap: 0-0

Best Rating: 52 8/01 Pont 2m1f22y gd-fm

A modest staying handicapper who goes well in soft ground.

Needwood Trickster (IRE)

86(103) (49)**48**
4-y-o gr g Fayruz-Istaraka (IRE) (Darshaan)
R Brotherton Mrs S Arcourt-Rippingale

Placings:0336000621050-04403420500 **(4733)**
2001: 5^{0}SD, 6^{4}SW, 5^{4}SW, 5^{0}SW, 6^{3}SD, 7^{4}SD, 6^{2}SD, 5^{0}SD, 6^{5}SD, 5^{0}F, 7^{0}F

	Starts	1st	2nd	3rd	Win & Pl
Career Total (Turf)	10	0	0	2	780
Career Total (AW)	14	1	2	1	4585

57 11/00 Wolv 6f D STD £2697
Total win prize-money £2698

Going (Turf): Sf: 0-1 GS: 0-1 Gd: 0-1 GF: 0-5 Fm: 0-2
Distance: **5f/6f: 1-20** 7f-8f: 0-4 9f-13f: 0-0 14f+: 0-0
Track: **LH: 1-15** RH: 0-0 **Tight: 1-11** Gall: 0-0
Aids: Bl: 0-0 Vi: 0-0 Tstrap: 0-2
Best Rating: 49 3/01 Sthl 6f stand

Needwood Trident

(91) (32)**42**
4-y-o b f Minshaanshu Amad (USA)-Needwood Nymph (Bold Owl)
J Pearce Miss Sarah Diane Warren

Placings:00/050042040-500 **(0346)**
2001: 14^{5}SD, 16^{0}SD, 16^{0}SD

	Starts	1st	2nd	3rd	Win & Pl
Career Total (Turf)	10	0	1	0	845
Career Total (AW)	4	0	0	0	0

Going (Turf): Sf: 0-3 GS: 0-1 Gd: 0-3 GF: 0-3 Fm: 0-0
Distance: 5f/6f: 0-1 7f-8f: 0-2 9f-13f: 0-3 14f+: 0-8
Track: LH: 0-8 RH: 0-3 Tight: 0-5 Gall: 0-3
Aids: Bl: 0-0 Vi: 0-0 Tstrap: 0-0
Best Rating: 19 2/01 Wolv 2m46y stand

Needwood Trooper

95(80) (10)**40**
4-y-o br g Puissance-Blueit (FR) (Bold Lad (IRE))
J Balding (R Brotherton 24/1) Mrs David Hodgkinson

Placings:0/443-0000000 **(4601)**
2001: 6^{0}SD, 5^{0}F, 5^{0}F, 5^{0}SD, 5^{0}GS, 5^{0}S, 5^{0}GF

	Starts	1st	2nd	3rd	Win & Pl
Career Total (Turf)	9	0	0	1	1290
Career Total (AW)	2	0	0	0	

Going (Turf): Sf: 0-1 GS: 0-1 Gd: 0-2 GF: 0-3 Fm: 0-2
Distance: 5f/6f: 0-11 7f-8f: 0-0 9f-13f: 0-0 14f+: 0-0
Track: LH: 0-1 RH: 0-0 Tight: 0-1 Gall: 0-0
Aids: Bl: 0-1 Vi: 0-0 Tstrap: 0-0
Best Rating: 43 6/01 Thsk 5f firm

Needwood Truffle (IRE)

(76) (29)
4-y-o ch f Brief Truce (USA)-Green Wings (General Assembly (USA))
J Hetherton J G Johnson

Placings:6353100/0000-00 **(0115)**
2001: 6^{0}SD, 9^{0}SW

	Starts	1st	2nd	3rd	Win & Pl
Career Total (Turf)	10	1	0	2	8338
Career Total (AW)	3	0	0	0	

76 7/99 Gdwd 5f C H G-F £7107
Total win prize-money £7108

Going (Turf): Sf: 0-1 GS: 0-1 Gd: 0-5 **GF: 1-2** Fm: 0-1
Distance: **5f/6f: 1-9** 7f-8f: 0-3 9f-13f: 0-1 14f+: 0-0
Track: LH: 0-4 RH: 0-1 Tight: 0-2 Gall: 0-1
Aids: Bl: 0-0 Vi: 0-0 Tstrap: 0-0
Best Rating: 16 1/01 Wolv 1m1f79y slow

Negligee

99 **89+**
2-y-o gr f Night Shift (USA)-Vax Star (Petong)
B W Hills The Hon Mrs J M Corbett & Mr C Wright

Placings:61100 **(5264)**
2001: 6^{6}GF, 6^{1}GF, 6^{1}GS, 6^{0}GF, 6^{0}GS

	Starts	1st	2nd	3rd	Win & Pl
Career Total (Turf)	5	2	0	0	13784

89 8/01 Ches 6f18y B G-S £9526
85 8/01 Sals 6f D G-F £4257
Total win prize-money £13784

Going (Turf): Sf: 0-0 **GS: 1-2** Gd: 0-0 **GF: 1-3** Fm: 0-0
Distance: 5f/6f: 1-4 7f-8f: 1-1 9f-13f: 0-0 14f+: 0-0
Track: **LH: 1-1** RH: 0-0 **Tight: 1-1** Gall: 0-0
Aids: Bl: 0-0 Vi: 0-0 Tstrap: 0-0
Best Rating: 89 8/01 Ches 6f18y gd-sft

Out of a decent sprinter, she improved from her debut to take a maiden at Salisbury. Followed up by beating four previous winners at Chester, but her limitations were exposed in Listed company subsequently.

Nellie Melba

92(95) (63)**76**
2-y-o b f Hurricane Sky (AUS)-Persuasion (Batshoof)
D J Coakley Countess Of Lonsdale

Placings:445 **(5277)**
2001: 6^{4}GF, 7^{4}GF, 7^{5}GS

	Starts	1st	2nd	3rd	Win & Pl
Career Total (Turf)	3	0	0	0	579

Going (Turf): Sf: 0-0 GS: 0-1 Gd: 0-0 GF: 0-2 Fm: 0-0
Distance: 5f/6f: 0-1 7f-8f: 0-2 9f-13f: 0-0 14f+: 0-0
Track: LH: 0-1 RH: 0-0 Tight: 0-0 Gall: 0-0
Aids: Bl: 0-0 Vi: 0-0 Tstrap: 0-0
Best Rating: 76 10/01 Leic 7f9y gd-sft

Nelsons Flagship

84 **51**
3-y-o b g Petong-Marie's Crusader (IRE) (Last Tycoon)
J Akehurst Fraser Miller

Placings:000-00 **(1612)**
2001: 9^{0}GS, 10^{0}GF

	Starts	1st	2nd	3rd	Win & Pl
Career Total (Turf)	5	0	0	0	

Going (Turf): Sf: 0-0 GS: 0-1 Gd: 0-0 GF: 0-4 Fm: 0-0
Distance: 5f/6f: 0-2 7f-8f: 0-1 9f-13f: 0-2 14f+: 0-0
Track: LH: 0-2 RH: 0-1 Tight: 0-1 Gall: 0-1
Aids: Bl: 0-0 Vi: 0-0 Tstrap: 0-0
Best Rating: 34 5/01 Ling 1m2f gd-fm

Nemo Fugat (IRE)

95 **79**
2-y-o b c Danehill Dancer (IRE)-Do The Right Thing (Busted)
R Hannon Dr A Haloute

Placings:2413 **(5096)**
2001: 6^{2}GF, 6^{4}G, 6^{1}GF, 6^{3}GS

	Starts	1st	2nd	3rd	Win & Pl
Career Total (Turf)	4	1	1	1	7838

76 9/01 Ling 6f F G-F £3206
Total win prize-money £3206

Going (Turf): Sf: 0-0 GS: 0-1 Gd: 0-1 **GF: 1-2** Fm: 0-0
Distance: **5f/6f: 1-4** 7f-8f: 0-0 9f-13f: 0-0 14f+: 0-0
Track: LH: 0-0 RH: 0-0 Tight: 0-0 Gall: 0-0

Aids: Bl: 0-0 Vi: 0-0 Tstrap: 0-0
Best Rating: 79 8/01 York 6f good

Showed ability in decent maiden company before easily winning a Lingfield maiden on his third start, but was beaten on easy ground next time. Suited by fast ground.

Neptune

99(98) (34)**34d**
5-y-o b g Dolphin Street (FR)-Seal Indigo (IRE) (Glenstal (USA))
J C Fox S J V Construction

Placings:00060**540**/332-040 (3318)
2001: 12^{0}GF, 12^{4}GF, 14^{0}G

	Starts	1st	2nd	3rd	Win & Pl
Career Total (Turf)	9	0	0	0	0
Career Total (AW)	5	0	1	2	899

Going (Turf): **Sf: 0-1 GS: 0-2 Gd: 0-2 GF: 0-4 Fm: 0-0**
Distance: 5f/6f: 0-0 7f-8f: 0-3 9f-13f: 0-9 14f+: 0-2
Track : LH: 0-11 RH: 0-2 Tight: 0-4 Gall: 0-2
Aids: Bl: 0-0 Vi: 0-0 Tstrap: 0-0
Best Rating: 31 6/01 Wwck 1m4f134y gd-fm

Neptune's Gift

91(94) (62)**62**
2-y-o b f Lugana Beach-Not So Generous (IRE) (Fayruz)
A Berry William Burns

Placings:250360003 (5660)
2001: 5^{2}GF, 5^{5}G, 5^{0}GF, 5^{3}G, 5^{6}G, 5^{0}G, 5^{0}GS, 6^{0}HY, 5^{3}G, 5^{1}SD, 5^{3}SD

	Starts	1st	2nd	3rd	Win & Pl
Career Total (Turf)	9	0	1	2	1232

Going (Turf): **Sf: 0-1 GS: 0-1 Gd: 0-5 GF: 0-2 Fm: 0-0**
Distance: 5f/6f: 0-9 7f-8f: 0-0 9f-13f: 0-0 14f+: 0-0
Track : LH: 0-0 RH: 0-0 Tight: 0-0 Gall: 0-0
Aids: Bl: 0-0 Vi: 0-0 Tstrap: 0-0
Best Rating: 68 8/01 Muss 5f good

Modest form as a juvenile over sprint trips. Seems best on fast ground.

Neronian (IRE)

89(92) (41)**28**
7-y-o ch g Mujtahid (USA)-Nimieza (USA) (Nijinsky (CAN))
J A Gilbert (Miss D A McHale 23/1) Terry Connors

Placings:604213/0240045**06056**/**4305**001030050-050000000 (2018)
2001: 9^{0}SD, 8^{5}SW, 12^{0}SW, 6^{0}GS, 7^{0}GS, 6^{0}G, 10^{0}G, 8^{0}GF, 12^{0}GF

	Starts	1st	2nd	3rd	Win & Pl
Career Total (Turf)	27	2	2	2	9065
Career Total (AW)	13	0	0	1	225

33 6/00 Brig 6f209y E(0-75)H FRM £2877
71 6/97 Bevl 1m100y E G-F £2812
Total win prize-money £5689

Going (Turf): Sf: 0-2 GS: 0-2 Gd: 0-6 **GF: 1-12 Fm: 1-5**
Distance: 5f/6f: 0-1 7f-8f: 1-16 9f-13f: 1-23 14f+: 0-0
Track : LH: 1-28 RH: 1-7 Tight: 0-16 Gall: 0-3
Aids: Bl: 0-3 Vi: 0-2 Tstrap: 0-0
Best Rating: 46 5/01 Ling 7f140y gd-sft

Netherhall

(94) (39)**40**
5-y-o ch g Rudimentary (USA)-Legal Precedent (Star Appeal)
R D Wylie M R Johnson

Placings:00000/432211056/0-460 (0304)
2001: 16^{4}SW, 16^{6}SW, 16^{0}SD

	Starts	1st	2nd	3rd	Win & Pl
Career Total (Turf)	5	0	0	0	
Career Total (AW)	13	2	2	1	6147

49 6/99 Sthl 1m4f F(0-65)H STD £2263
44 6/99 Wolv 1m6f166yF(0-60)H STD £2276
Total win prize-money £4540

Going (Turf): **Sf: 0-0 GS: 0-2 Gd: 0-1 GF: 0-2 Fm: 0-0**
Distance: 5f/6f: 0-3 7f-8f: 0-2 9f-13f: 1-6 14f+: 1-7
Track : **LH: 2-13** RH: 0-2 **Tight: 1-5** Gall: 0-0
Aids: Bl: 0-0 Vi: 0-0 Tstrap: 0-0
Best Rating: 39 1/01 Wolv 2m46y slow

Nettles

(66) (19)**62**
3-y-o br g Cyrano De Bergerac-Sylvandra (Mazilier (USA))
R Williams (Denys Smith 26/1) R Williams

Placings:0000620**00**-0 (0176)
2001: 7^{0}SD

	Starts	1st	2nd	3rd	Win & Pl
Career Total (Turf)	8	0	1	0	548
Career Total (AW)	2	0	0	0	

Going (Turf): **Sf: 0-1 GS: 0-4 Gd: 0-0 GF: 0-2 Fm: 0-1**
Distance: 5f/6f: 0-6 7f-8f: 0-4 9f-13f: 0-0 14f+: 0-0
Track : LH: 0-4 RH: 0-1 Tight: 0-2 Gall: 0-1
Aids: Bl: 0-3 Vi: 0-0 Tstrap: 0-0
Best Rating: 39 1/01 Wolv 2m46y slow

Nettleton Knight

81 **35**
3-y-o b g Beveled (USA)-Mybella Ann (Anfield)
J M Bradley Paul De Weck

Placings:0000 (3701)
2001: 9^{0}GF, 8^{0}GF, 8^{0}GF, 6^{0}GF

	Starts	1st	2nd	3rd	Win & Pl
Career Total (Turf)	4	0	0	0	

Going (Turf): **Sf: 0-0 GS: 0-0 Gd: 0-0 GF: 0-4 Fm: 0-0**
Distance: 5f/6f: 0-0 7f-8f: 0-1 9f-13f: 0-3 14f+: 0-0
Track : LH: 0-2 RH: 0-1 Tight: 0-1 Gall: 0-0
Aids: Bl: 0-0 Vi: 0-0 Tstrap: 0-0
Best Rating: 35 6/01 Nott 1m54y gd-fm

Never Can Tell

(65) (30)**39**
5-y-o ch g Emarati (USA)-Farmer's Pet (Sharrood (USA))
M Mullineaux (B P J Baugh 15/3) Mrs Renee Farrington-Kirkham

Placings:00420/500000/0 (0457)
2001: 8^{0}SD

	Starts	1st	2nd	3rd	Win & Pl
Career Total (Turf)	9	0	1	0	1897
Career Total (AW)	3	0	0	0	

Going (Turf): **Sf: 0-1 GS: 0-1 Gd: 0-3 GF: 0-4 Fm: 0-0**
Distance: 5f/6f: 0-3 7f-8f: 0-5 9f-13f: 0-3 14f+: 0-4
Track : LH: 0-4 RH: 0-0 Tight: 0-3 Gall: 0-0
Aids: Bl: 0-0 Vi: 0-1 Tstrap: 0-0
Best Rating: 35 6/01 Nott 1m54y gd-fm

Never Diss Miss

101 **70**
4-y-o b f Owington-Pennine Pink (IRE) (Pennine Walk)
N A Graham Tim Fenner

Placings:0140300/5132503-00340 (2851)
2001: 12^{0}GS, 12^{0}S, 10^{3}GF, 10^{4}G, 10^{0}G

	Starts	1st	2nd	3rd	Win & Pl
Career Total (Turf)	19	2	1	4	13529

77 5/00 Bevl 1m1f207yD(0-80)H GD £4303
79 4/99 Sand 5f6y E G-S £3566
Total win prize-money £7869

Going (Turf): Sf: 0-4 **GS: 1-4 Gd: 1-7** GF: 0-4 Fm: 0-0
Distance: 5f/6f: 1-6 7f-8f: 0-2 9f-13f: 1-11 14f+: 0-0
Track : LH: 0-2 **RH: 1-8** Tight: 0-5 Gall: 0-2
Aids: Bl: 0-0 Vi: 0-0 Tstrap: 0-0
Best Rating: 70 6/01 Wind 1m2f7y gd-fm

Never End

93 **80**
3-y-o b f Alzao (USA)-Eternal (Kris)
B W Hills K Abdulla

Placings:1-00 (2741)
2001: 8^{0}S, 10^{0}GF

	Starts	1st	2nd	3rd	Win & Pl
Career Total (Turf)	3	1	0	0	3510

80 10/00 Ling 7f D HVY £3510
Total win prize-money £3510

Going (Turf): **Sf: 1-2** GS: 0-0 Gd: 0-0 GF: 0-1 Fm: 0-0
Distance: 5f/6f: 0-0 **7f-8f: 1-2** 9f-13f: 0-1 14f+: 0-0
Track : LH: 0-1 RH: 0-1 Tight: 0-0 Gall: 0-0
Aids: Bl: 0-0 Vi: 0-0 Tstrap: 0-0
Best Rating: 61 7/01 Chep 1m2f36y gd-fm

Never Ending Story

87 **48**
3-y-o b f Deploy-Bold Gem (Never So Bold)
E J Alston Mrs Carol P McPhail

Placings:000000 (4404)
2001: 7^{0}GF, 7^{0}GF, 8^{0}GF, 12^{0}G, 16^{0}HY, 12^{0}GS

	Starts	1st	2nd	3rd	Win & Pl
Career Total (Turf)	6	0	0	0	

Going (Turf): **Sf: 0-1 GS: 0-1 Gd: 0-1 GF: 0-3 Fm: 0-0**
Distance: 5f/6f: 0-0 7f-8f: 0-2 9f-13f: 0-3 14f+: 0-1
Track : LH: 0-6 RH: 0-0 Tight: 0-3 Gall: 0-0
Aids: Bl: 0-0 Vi: 0-0 Tstrap: 0-0
Best Rating: 48 8/01 Ches 1m4f66y good

Never Fear

(79)
3-y-o b f Mistertopogigo (IRE)-Never Say So (Prince Sabo)
Mrs S Lamyman P Lamyman

Placings:000-00000 (0878)
2001: 6^{0}SD, 6^{0}SW, 5^{0}SW, 5^{0}SD, 12^{0}S

	Starts	1st	2nd	3rd	Win & Pl
Career Total (Turf)	3	0	0	0	
Career Total (AW)	5	0	0	0	

Going (Turf): **Sf: 0-1 GS: 0-0 Gd: 0-1 GF: 0-1 Fm: 0-0**
Distance: 5f/6f: 0-7 7f-8f: 0-0 9f-13f: 0-1 14f+: 0-0
Track : LH: 0-4 RH: 0-0 Tight: 0-1 Gall: 0-0
Aids: Bl: 0-0 Vi: 0-2 Tstrap: 0-0

Never Promise (FR)

102(82) (35)**63**
3-y-o b f Cadeaux Genereux-Yazeanhaa (USA) (Zilzal (USA))
B W Hills Maktoum Al Maktoum

Placings:00-54031250 (4707)
2001: 9^{5}SD, 10^{4}F, 8^{0}GF, 10^{3}HD, 10^{1}G, 9^{2}GF, 9^{5}G, 10^{0}G

	Starts	1st	2nd	3rd	Win & Pl
Career Total (Turf)	9	1	1	1	4810
Career Total (AW)	1	0	0	0	0

63 7/01 Chep 1m2f36y E(0-70)H GD £3234
Total win prize-money £3234

Going (Turf): Sf: 0-1 GS: 0-0 **Gd: 1-3** GF: 0-3 Fm: 0-2

Distance: 5f/6f: 0-0 7f-8f: 0-3 **9f-13f: 1-7** 14f+: 0-0
Track : **LH: 1-7** RH: 0-1 Tight: 0-4 Gall: 0-1
Aids: **Bl: 1-7** Vi: 0-1 Tstrap: 0-0
Best Rating: 63 7/01 Folk 1m1f149y gd-fm

Got off the mark in a handicap at Chepstow in July. Suited by ten furlongs and good/fast ground.

New Caladonia (USA)

95 **61**
2-y-o ch c Trempolino (USA)-Tea Cozzy (USA) (Irish River (FR))
I A Balding Exors Of The Late Robert Hitchins

Placings:066 **(3368)**
2001: 6^{0}GF, 6^{6}GF, 7^{6}GF

	Starts	1st	2nd	3rd	Win & Pl
Career Total (Turf)	3	0	0	0	0

Going (Turf): Sf: 0-0 GS: 0-0 Gd: 0-0 GF: 0-3 Fm: 0-0
Distance: 5f/6f: 0-0 7f-8f: 0-3 9f-13f: 0-0 14f+: 0-0
Track : LH: 0-0 RH: 0-1 Tight: 0-1 Gall: 0-0
Aids: Bl: 0-0 Vi: 0-0 Tstrap: 0-0
Best Rating: 61 7/01 Folk 6f189y gd-fm

New Development

47
5-y-o b g Sizzling Melody-Silver's Girl (Sweet Monday)
N B Mason (T Wall 26/7) N B Mason

Placings:0 **(3388)**
2001: 11^{0}F

	Starts	1st	2nd	3rd	Win & Pl
Career Total (Turf)	1	0	0	0	

Going (Turf): Sf: 0-0 GS: 0-0 Gd: 0-0 GF: 0-0 Fm: 0-1
Distance: 5f/6f: 0-0 7f-8f: 0-0 9f-13f: 0-1 14f+: 0-0
Track : LH: 0-1 RH: 0-0 Tight: 0-1 Gall: 0-0
Aids: Bl: 0-0 Vi: 0-0 Tstrap: 0-0

New Horizon (IRE)

94(88) (44)**47**
3-y-o b g General Monash (USA)-Gulf Craft (IRE) (Petorius)
D Brace (J A Osborne 12/8) David Brace

Placings:530020 **(3855)**
2001: 7^{5}SD, 8^{3}SW, 8^{0}GS, 6^{0}F, 7^{2}G, 7^{0}GS

	Starts	1st	2nd	3rd	Win & Pl
Career Total (Turf)	4	0	1	0	724
Career Total (AW)	2	0	0	1	397

Going (Turf): Sf: 0-0 GS: 0-2 Gd: 0-1 GF: 0-0 Fm: 0-1
Distance: 5f/6f: 0-1 7f-8f: 0-5 9f-13f: 0-0 14f+: 0-0
Track : LH: 0-2 RH: 0-0 Tight: 0-1 Gall: 0-0
Aids: Bl: 0-3 Vi: 0-0 Tstrap: 0-0
Best Rating: 47 8/01 Leic 7f9y good

New Options

97 (94)**98**
4-y-o b g Formidable (USA)-No Comebacks (Last Tycoon)
Rune Haugen

Placings:1003/05001**1111111**-42605430 **(4693a)**
2001: 6^{4}SD, 4^{2}S, 5^{6}G, 6^{0}G, 5^{5}GF, 6^{4}SD, 5^{3}G, 5^{0}S

	Starts	1st	2nd	3rd	Win & Pl
Career Total (Turf)	14	2	1	1	5718
Career Total (AW)	10	7	0	1	20207

12/00	Taby	6f	H	GD	£3655
11/00	Taby	6f	H	GD	£3655
10/00	Jage	6f	H	SLW	£3655
10/00	Jage	6f	H	GD	£1754
9/00	Jage	6f	H	GD	£1754
9/00	Ovrl	5f110y	H	SLP	£1157
9/00	Jage	6f	H	SLW	£1754
8/00	Fyns	5f110y	H	GD	£1692
8/99	Ovrl	4f110y		GD	£1972

Total win prize-money £21048

Going (Turf): Sf: 0-2 GS: 0-0 **Gd: 6-10** GF: 0-1 Fm: 0-0
Distance: **5f/6f: 8-19** 7f-8f: 0-3 9f-13f: 0-0 14f+: 0-0
Track : LH: 0-3 RH: 0-0 Tight: 0-1 Gall: 0-0
Aids: **Bl: 8-14** Vi: 0-1 Tstrap: 0-0
Best Rating: 98 7/01 Ches 5f16y gd-fm

Useful Norwegian sprinter. Ran with credit when sent over to Chester in July. Often wears blinkers.

New Prospective

7
3-y-o b c Cadeaux Genereux-Amazing Bay (Mazilier (USA))
D Nicholls N J Jones

Placings:5 **(2222)**
2001: 9^{5}G

	Starts	1st	2nd	3rd	Win & Pl
Career Total (Turf)	1	0	0	0	0

Going (Turf): Sf: 0-0 GS: 0-0 Gd: 0-1 GF: 0-0 Fm: 0-0
Distance: 5f/6f: 0-0 7f-8f: 0-0 9f-13f: 0-1 14f+: 0-0
Track : LH: 0-0 RH: 0-0 Tight: 0-0 Gall: 0-0
Aids: Bl: 0-0 Vi: 0-0 Tstrap: 0-1
Best Rating: 7 6/01 Muss 1m1f good

New Wonder

(90) (50)**54**
3-y-o b f Presidium-Miss Tri Colour (Shavian)
J G Given Nigel Hardy

Placings:304203-06 **(0253)**
2001: 6^{0}SW, 5^{6}SW

	Starts	1st	2nd	3rd	Win & Pl
Career Total (Turf)	5	0	1	1	1199
Career Total (AW)	3	0	0	1	319

Going (Turf): Sf: 0-0 GS: 0-2 Gd: 0-1 GF: 0-1 Fm: 0-1
Distance: 5f/6f: 0-8 7f-8f: 0-0 9f-13f: 0-0 14f+: 0-0
Track : LH: 0-3 RH: 0-0 Tight: 0-3 Gall: 0-0
Aids: Bl: 0-0 Vi: 0-0 Tstrap: 0-0
Best Rating: 25 2/01 Ling 5f slow

Newpark Lady (IRE)

100 **98**
4-y-o b f Foxhound (USA)-Toledana (IRE) (Sure Blade (USA))
K F O'Brien Sax Syndicate

Placings:421540/4443064-46200116600 **(5214a)**
2001: 5^{4}S, 6^{6}G, 5^{2}GF, 6^{0}F, 6^{0}Y, 5^{1}G, 6^{1}G, 6^{6}GF, 5^{6}G, 5^{0}G, 5^{0}S

	Starts	1st	2nd	3rd	Win & Pl
Career Total (Turf)	24	3	2	1	67011

98	7/01	Leop	6f		GD	£12025
98	7/01	Curr	5f	H	GD	£39000
70	6/99	Bell	5f		G-F	£3437

Total win prize-money £54463

Going (Turf): Sf: 0-2 GS: 0-0 **Gd: 2-11** GF: 1-3 Fm: 0-2
Distance: **5f/6f: 3-20** 7f-8f: 0-4 9f-13f: 0-0 14f+: 0-0
Track : LH: 0-4 RH: 0-1 Tight: 0-0 Gall: 0-0
Aids: Bl: 0-1 Vi: 0-0 Tstrap: 0-0
Best Rating: 98 7/01 Leop 6f good

Newryman

87 **19**
6-y-o ch g Statoblest-With Love (Be My Guest (USA))
G P Kelly (M E Sowersby 27/2) A M McArdle

Placings:000-000005005040000000000000000 **(5226)**
2001: 6^{0}S, 8^{0}GF, 10^{0}GF, 7^{0}F, 8^{0}GF, 9^{5}G, 10^{0}GF, 7^{0}GF, 10^{5}GF, 10^{0}GF, 10^{4}GF, 6^{0}GF, 12^{0}F, 6^{0}GF, 10^{0}S, 8^{0}G, 6^{0}GF, 8^{0}GF, 8^{0}GF, 9^{0}GF, 8^{0}GF, 6^{0}HY, 10^{0}GF, 8^{0}F, 6^{0}GF, 14^{0}HY, 11^{0}S

	Starts	1st	2nd	3rd	Win & Pl
Career Total (Turf)	29	0	0	0	545
Career Total (AW)	1	0	0	0	

Going (Turf): Sf: 0-5 GS: 0-0 Gd: 0-3 GF: 0-18 Fm: 0-3
Distance: 5f/6f: 0-6 7f-8f: 0-7 9f-13f: 0-16 14f+: 0-1
Track : LH: 0-15 RH: 0-4 Tight: 0-3 Gall: 0-6
Aids: Bl: 0-0 Vi: 0-0 Tstrap: 0-0
Best Rating: 25 7/01 Donc 6f gd-fm

Very moderate, regular in appearance-money contests in 2001.

Newscaster

(100) (56d)
5-y-o b g Bluebird (USA)-Sharp Girl (FR) (Sharpman)
T E Powell Vogue Development Company (kent) Ltd

Placings:65421/50-0 **(0089)**
2001: 10^{0}SD

	Starts	1st	2nd	3rd	Win & Pl
Career Total (Turf)	4	1	0	0	3087
Career Total (AW)	4	0	1	0	808

65	8/99	Sand	1m1f	E	GD	£2801

Total win prize-money £2801

Going (Turf): Sf: 0-1 GS: 0-0 **Gd: 1-1** GF: 0-2 Fm: 0-0
Distance: 5f/6f: 0-1 7f-8f: 0-2 **9f-13f: 1-5** 14f+: 0-0
Track : LH: 0-4 **RH: 1-2** Tight: 0-5 Gall: 0-0
Aids: Bl: 0-0 Vi: 0-0 Tstrap: 0-0
Best Rating: 65 8/99 Sand 1m1f G

Newsimplejoy

92 **58**
3-y-o b f Marju (IRE)-Hesperia (Slip Anchor)
M L W Bell Wattlefield Hall Stud Ltd

Placings:000 **(2438)**
2001: 7^{0}GF, 7^{0}GF, 8^{0}G

	Starts	1st	2nd	3rd	Win & Pl
Career Total (Turf)	3	0	0	0	

Going (Turf): Sf: 0-0 GS: 0-0 Gd: 0-1 GF: 0-2 Fm: 0-0
Distance: 5f/6f: 0-0 7f-8f: 0-2 9f-13f: 0-1 14f+: 0-0
Track : LH: 0-0 RH: 0-0 Tight: 0-0 Gall: 0-0
Aids: Bl: 0-0 Vi: 0-0 Tstrap: 0-0
Best Rating: 58 6/01 Yarm 7f3y gd-fm

Next Chapter (IRE)

100(85) (36)**46**
3-y-o b/br f Cois Na Tine (IRE)-Book Choice (North Summit)
A P Jarvis Mrs Ann Jarvis

Placings:0-0053130 **(4290)**
2001: 8^{0}SW, 9^{0}SD, 12^{5}F, 11^{3}G, 16^{1}GF, 14^{3}GF, 16^{0}GF

	Starts	1st	2nd	3rd	Win & Pl
Career Total (Turf)	6	1	0	2	3202
Career Total (AW)	2	0	0	0	

38	5/01	Yarm	2m	F	G-F	£2327

Total win prize-money £2328

Going (Turf): Sf: 0-0 GS: 0-0 Gd: 0-1 **GF: 1-4** Fm: 0-1
Distance: 5f/6f: 0-0 7f-8f: 0-2 9f-13f: 0-3 **14f+: 1-3**
Track : **LH: 1-6** RH: 0-2 **Tight: 1-4** Gall: 0-1
Aids: Bl: 0-0 Vi: 0-0 Tstrap: 0-0
Best Rating: 46 6/01 Yarm 1m6f17y gd-fm

Next Flight (IRE)

96 **79**
2-y-o b c Woodborough (USA)-Sans Ceriph (IRE) (Thatching)
A P Jarvis A L R Morton

Placings:536 **(4282)**

2001: 7^{5}G, 8^{3}G, 8^{6}G

	Starts	1st	2nd	3rd	Win & Pl
Career Total (Turf)	3	0	0	1	632

Going (Turf): Sf: 0-0 GS: 0-0 Gd: 0-3 GF: 0-0 Fm: 0-0
Distance: 5f/6f: 0-0 7f-8f: 0-2 9f-13f: 0-1 14f+: 0-0
Track : LH: 0-0 RH: 0-1 Tight: 0-0 Gall: 0-0
Aids: Bl: 0-0 Vi: 0-0 Tstrap: 0-0
Best Rating: 79 8/01 NmkJ 1m good

Niagara (IRE)

109 **74**

4-y-o b g Rainbows For Life (CAN)-Highbrook (USA) (Alphabatim (USA))
M H Tompkins Pollards Stables

Placings:421460/00360-0211443104 **(5293)**
2001: 7^{0}GF, 9^{2}GS, 9^{1}GF, 10^{1}GF, 10^{4}GF, 11^{4}G, 11^{3}GF, 9^{1}G, 9^{0}GF, 9^{4}S

	Starts	1st	2nd	3rd	Win & Pl
Career Total (Turf)	21	4	2	2	25243

74	9/01	Haml	1m1f36y	B H	GD	£10627
70	7/01	Wind	1m2f7y	E(0-65)	G-F	£3094
66	6/01	Ayr	1m1f20y	D(0-85)H	G-F	£4049
84	5/99	Ayr	6f	E	GD	£2940

Total win prize-money £20713

Going (Turf): Sf: 0-1 GS: 0-2 **Gd: 2-10 GF: 2-6** Fm: 0-2
Distance: 5f/6f: 1-4 7f-8f: 0-4 **9f-13f: 3-13** 14f+: 0-0
Track : LH: 0-7 **RH: 1-6 Tight: 2-8** Gall: 0-3
Aids: Bl: 0-0 Vi: 0-0 Tstrap: 0-0
Best Rating: 74 9/01 Haml 1m1f36y good

Niamh (IRE)

32(27)

2-y-o br f Atraf-Island Girl (IRE) (Elbio)
D Shaw Moneyleague Ltd

Placings:000 **(3432)**
2001: 5^{0}S, 7^{0}G, 7^{0}SD

	Starts	1st	2nd	3rd	Win & Pl
Career Total (Turf)	2	0	0	0	
Career Total (AW)	1	0	0	0	

Going (Turf): Sf: 0-1 GS: 0-0 Gd: 0-1 GF: 0-0 Fm: 0-0
Distance: 5f/6f: 0-1 7f-8f: 0-2 9f-13f: 0-0 14f+: 0-0
Track : LH: 0-1 RH: 0-0 Tight: 0-0 Gall: 0-0
Aids: Bl: 0-0 Vi: 0-0 Tstrap: 0-0
Best Rating: 74 9/01 Haml 1m1f36y good

Nicander (USA)

97 **58**

3-y-o b c Rahy (USA)-Night Secret (Nijinsky (CAN))
M P Tregoning Sheikh Mohammed

Placings:0-000630 **(3156)**
2001: 11^{0}S, 10^{0}GS, 11^{0}G, 9^{6}GF, 12^{3}GF, 16^{0}GS

	Starts	1st	2nd	3rd	Win & Pl
Career Total (Turf)	7	0	0	1	690

Going (Turf): Sf: 0-2 GS: 0-2 Gd: 0-1 GF: 0-2 Fm: 0-0
Distance: 5f/6f: 0-0 7f-8f: 0-1 9f-13f: 0-5 14f+: 0-1
Track : LH: 0-2 RH: 0-2 Tight: 0-4 Gall: 0-0
Aids: Bl: 0-3 Vi: 0-0 Tstrap: 0-0
Best Rating: 58 7/01 Epsm 1m4f10y gd-fm

Nice Balance (USA)

71(106) (27)**10**

6-y-o b g Shadeed (USA)-Fellwaati (USA) (Alydar (USA))
M C Chapman Rasen Goes Racing

Placings:06005050/614315653000000**0-0055004006** **(3430)**
2001: 8^{0}SD, 11^{0}SD, 9^{5}SD, 8^{5}SD, 8^{0}SW, 8^{0}SD, 8^{4}SD, 8^{0}SD, 8^{0}GS, 8^{6}SD, 8^{0}SD

	Starts	1st	2nd	3rd	Win & Pl
Career Total (Turf)	9	0	0	0	0
Career Total (AW)	25	2	0	2	5002

43	1/00	Sthl	1m	F(0-65)H	STD	£2520
30	1/00	Sthl	1m	F(0-60)H	STD	£1638

Total win prize-money £4158

Going (Turf): Sf: 0-0 GS: 0-1 Gd: 0-3 GF: 0-4 Fm: 0-1
Distance: 5f/6f: 0-1 **7f-8f: 2-23** 9f-13f: 0-10 14f+: 0-0
Track : **LH: 2-28** RH: 0-2 Tight: 0-5 Gall: 0-1
Aids: Bl: 0-2 Vi: 0-0 Tstrap: 0-1
Best Rating: 30 3/01 Sthl 1m stand

Nice One Clare (IRE)

116 **113**

5-y-o b m Mukaddamah (USA)-Sarah-Clare (Reach)
J W Payne Oremsa Partnership

Placings:13211/53202-31424115 **(5386)**
2001: 6^{3}G, 6^{1}GF, 7^{4}GF, 7^{2}GF, 6^{4}GF, 7^{1}G, 6^{1}S, 7^{5}GS

	Starts	1st	2nd	3rd	Win & Pl
Career Total (Turf)	18	6	4	3	219367

113	9/01	Asct	6f	A	SFT	£60000
97	9/01	Donc	7f	A	GD	£18362
108	6/01	Asct	6f	B(0-110)H	G-F	£58000
87	8/99	NmkJ	7f	C(0-90)H	G-F	£7928
86	8/99	Kemp	7f	C(0-90)H	G-F	£7035
78	5/99	Folk	7f	F	G-F	£2370

Total win prize-money £153697

Going (Turf): Sf: 1-1 GS: 0-3 Gd: 1-2 **GF: 4-12** Fm: 0-0
Distance: 5f/6f: 2-5 **7f-8f: 4-13** 9f-13f: 0-0 14f+: 0-0
Track : LH: 0-2 **RH: 1-1** Tight: 0-0 **Gall: 1-1**
Aids: Bl: 0-0 Vi: 0-0 Tstrap: 0-0
Best Rating: 113 10/01 NmkR 7f gd-sft

High-class mare, suited by six to seven furlongs, she acts on fast ground but handles an easy surface. Won the 2001 Wokingham with the benefit of a prep race at Newmarket, and ran well when a close second in the Tote International Handicap on the same track. Stepped up in class, she scored in Listed company at Doncaster, and enjoyed her finest hour when returning to Ascot to take the Group Two Diadem Stakes.

Nichol Fifty

101(98) (55)**45**

7-y-o b g Old Vic-Jawaher (IRE) (Dancing Brave (USA))
D Nicholls (M H Tompkins 12/6) A A Bloodstock Ltd

Placings:0/005215413/0/1061022500/403-56304004200 **(5402)**
2001: 16^{5}SW, 12^{6}SW, 12^{3}F, 14^{0}G, 16^{4}GF, 11^{0}G, 12^{0}S, 10^{4}G, 15^{2}GF, 12^{0}GS, 17^{0}S

	Starts	1st	2nd	3rd	Win & Pl
Career Total (Turf)	32	4	4	2	25478
Career Total (AW)	3	0	0	1	577

77	6/99	Kemp	1m6f92y	D(0-75)	GD	£3582
75	4/99	Nott	1m6f15y	D(0-80)H	SFT	£8391
73	10/97	Leic	1m3f183y	E(0-70)	GD	£2833
67	7/97	Ches	1m4f66y	E(0-70)	G-F	£3767

Total win prize-money £18575

Going (Turf): Sf: 1-5 GS: 0-8 **Gd: 2-14** GF: 1-4 Fm: 0-1
Distance: 5f/6f: 0-0 7f-8f: 0-2 9f-13f: 2-14 14f+: 2-19
Track : LH: 2-23 RH: 2-11 **Tight: 1-12** Gall: 0-5
Aids: Bl: 0-2 Vi: 0-0 Tstrap: 0-0
Best Rating: 51 5/01 Yarm 1m6f17y good

Niciara (IRE)

(98) (52?)

4-y-o b g Soviet Lad (USA)-Verusa (IRE) (Petorius)
M C Chapman W P Gaff

Placings:000033P0/053246050040332**3224000-0** **(0149)**
2001: 11^{0}SW

	Starts	1st	2nd	3rd	Win & Pl
Career Total (Turf)	15	0	2	2	1989
Career Total (AW)	16	0	2	4	3280

Going (Turf): Sf: 0-2 GS: 0-2 Gd: 0-5 GF: 0-5 Fm: 0-0
Distance: 5f/6f: 0-2 7f-8f: 0-11 9f-13f: 0-9 14f+: 0-8
Track : LH: 0-24 RH: 0-2 Tight: 0-3 Gall: 0-2
Aids: Bl: 0-10 Vi: 0-1 Tstrap: 0-0
Best Rating: 27 1/01 Sthl 1m3f slow

Nickles

(93) (35)**52**

6-y-o b g Lugana Beach-Instinction (Never So Bold)
S R Bowring Roland M Wheatley

Placings:330/40300130000/06401000-**0040** **(0442)**
2001: 5^{0}SD, 5^{0}SD, 5^{4}SD, 6^{0}SD

	Starts	1st	2nd	3rd	Win & Pl
Career Total (Turf)	22	2	0	4	7544
Career Total (AW)	4	0	0	0	0

51	8/00	Wwck	5f	F	GD	£2446
57	8/99	Ling	5f	E	GD	£2988

Total win prize-money £5435

Going (Turf): Sf: 0-4 GS: 0-8 **Gd: 2-4** GF: 0-4 Fm: 0-2
Distance: **5f/6f: 2-26** 7f-8f: 0-0 9f-13f: 0-0 14f+: 0-0
Track : **LH: 1-11** RH: 0-0 Tight: 0-3 **Gall: 1-6**
Aids: Bl: 0-0 Vi: 0-0 Tstrap: 0-0
Best Rating: 35 2/01 Wolv 5f stand

Nicklette

68 **37**

2-y-o b f Nicolotte-Cayla (Tumble Wind (USA))
C N Allen Mrs A M Upsdell

Placings:0 **(5367)**
2001: 8^{0}GS

	Starts	1st	2nd	3rd	Win & Pl
Career Total (Turf)	1	0	0	0	

Going (Turf): Sf: 0-0 GS: 0-1 Gd: 0-0 GF: 0-0 Fm: 0-0
Distance: 5f/6f: 0-0 7f-8f: 0-1 9f-13f: 0-0 14f+: 0-0
Track : LH: 0-0 RH: 0-0 Tight: 0-0 Gall: 0-0
Aids: Bl: 0-0 Vi: 0-0 Tstrap: 0-0
Best Rating: 37 10/01 NmkR 1m gd-sft

Nicobar

123 **118**

4-y-o b h Indian Ridge-Duchess Of Alba (Belmez (USA))
I A Balding Exors Of The Late Robert Hitchins

Placings:31525/316105010-311664 **(5353a)**
2001: 8^{3}GS, 8^{1}S, 8^{1}G, 8^{6}GF, 8^{6}GF, 7^{4}VS

	Starts	1st	2nd	3rd	Win & Pl
Career Total (Turf)	20	6	1	3	159971

118	5/01	Siro	1m		GD	£46427
118	4/01	Sand	1m14y	A	SFT	£36000
110	9/00	Epsm	7f	A	GD	£15340
115	6/00	Epsm	7f	A	G-S	£22750
105	5/00	Ches	7f122y	C(0-100)H	GD	£18785
94	8/99	Hayd	7f30y	D	G-S	£4045

Total win prize-money £143348

Going (Turf): Sf: 1-1 GS: 2-5 **Gd: 3-7** GF: 0-6 Fm: 0-0
Distance: 5f/6f: 0-0 **7f-8f: 5-17** 9f-13f: 1-3 14f+: 0-0
Track : **LH: 4-8** RH: 1-6 **Tight: 3-5** Gall: 0-4
Aids: Bl: 0-0 Vi: 0-0 Tstrap: 0-1
Best Rating: 118 5/01 Siro 1m good

A keen individual, he has given trouble at the start. He improved considerably this season, winning the Group Two Masai Mile at Sandown and a similar event at San Siro. All of his wins have come on good or softer and he has never shown his best on fast ground.

Nicol (IRE)

(63)

3-y-o b f Nicolotte-Frensham Manor (Le Johnstan)

K McAuliffe Mrs J A Hall

Placings:0-0 **(0357)**
2001: 11^{0}SW

	Starts	1st	2nd	3rd	Win & Pl
Career Total (Turf)	0	0	0	0	
Career Total (AW)	2	0	0	0	

Going (Turf): Sf: 0-0 GS: 0-0 Gd: 0-0 GF: 0-0 Fm: 0-0
Distance: 5f/6f: 0-1 7f-8f: 0-0 9f-13f: 0-1 14f+: 0-0
Track : LH: 0-2 RH: 0-0 Tight: 0-1 Gall: 0-0
Aids: Bl: 0-0 Vi: 0-0 Tstrap: 0-0

Nicolai

99(90) (38)**55**
4-y-o b g Piccolo-Fair Eleanor (Saritamer (USA))
M L W Bell Mrs Anne Yearley

Placings:0000410-01400 **(3293)**
2001: 10^{0}SD, 10^{1}GF, 9^{4}GF, 10^{0}GF, 9^{0}GF

	Starts	1st	2nd	3rd	Win & Pl
Career Total (Turf)	11	2	0	0	5006
Career Total (AW)	1	0	0	0	0

55	5/01	Yarm	1m2f21y	F(0-60)H	G-F	£2254
52	8/00	Bevl	1m1f207y	F(0-60)H	FRM	£2236

Total win prize-money £4491

Going (Turf): Sf: 0-3 GS: 0-0 Gd: 0-1 **GF: 1-6 Fm: 1-1**
Distance: 5f/6f: 0-3 7f-8f: 0-0 **9f-13f: 2-9** 14f+: 0-0
Track : LH: 1-3 RH: 1-5 **Tight: 1-3** Gall: 0-0
Aids: Bl: 0-0 Vi: 0-0 Tstrap: 0-0
Best Rating: 55 5/01 Yarm 1m2f21y gd-fm

Nicole's Dancer

(84) (14)
4-y-o b f Rambo Dancer (CAN)-Emma Woodford (Master Willie)
N Hamilton John Hopkins (t/a South Hatch Racing)

Placings:000-0 **(0096)**
2001: 7^{0}SD

	Starts	1st	2nd	3rd	Win & Pl
Career Total (Turf)	0	0	0	0	
Career Total (AW)	4	0	0	0	

Going (Turf): Sf: 0-0 GS: 0-0 Gd: 0-0 GF: 0-0 Fm: 0-0
Distance: 5f/6f: 0-1 7f-8f: 0-3 9f-13f: 0-0 14f+: 0-0
Track : LH: 0-4 RH: 0-0 Tight: 0-3 Gall: 0-0
Aids: Bl: 0-0 Vi: 0-0 Tstrap: 0-0
Best Rating: 55 5/01 Yarm 1m2f21y gd-fm

Nieve Lady

95 **74**
2-y-o b f Komaite (USA)-Nikoola Eve (Roscoe Blake)
D Shaw Cooper & Holgate

Placings:0502040 **(5253)**
2001: 6^{0}S, 5^{5}G, 6^{0}G, 5^{2}GS, 5^{0}G, 5^{4}GS, 6^{0}S

	Starts	1st	2nd	3rd	Win & Pl
Career Total (Turf)	7	0	1	0	1606

Going (Turf): Sf: 0-2 GS: 0-2 Gd: 0-3 GF: 0-0 Fm: 0-0
Distance: 5f/6f: 0-7 7f-8f: 0-0 9f-13f: 0-0 14f+: 0-0
Track : LH: 0-0 RH: 0-0 Tight: 0-0 Gall: 0-0
Aids: Bl: 0-0 Vi: 0-0 Tstrap: 0-0
Best Rating: 74 10/01 NmkR 5f gd-sft

Has shown ability in maidens and nurseries.

Nifty Alice

95 **43**
3-y-o ch f First Trump-Nifty Fifty (IRE) (Runnett)
E J Alston (A Berry 13/8) Mrs Norma Peebles

Placings:1244100103-00600000 **(5630)**
2001: 5^{0}S, 5^{0}GF, 5^{6}GF, 5^{0}GF, 5^{0}GS, 5^{0}G, 5^{0}HY, 6^{0}G

	Starts	1st	2nd	3rd	Win & Pl
Career Total (Turf)	18	3	1	1	17254

82	8/00	Muss	5f	C	G-F	£6288
72	6/00	Ayr	5f	E	GD	£2828
64	3/00	Muss	5f	F	GD	£2646

Total win prize-money £11763

Going (Turf): Sf: 0-3 GS: 0-2 **Gd: 2-8** GF: 1-5 Fm: 0-0
Distance: **5f/6f: 3-18** 7f-8f: 0-0 9f-13f: 0-0 14f+: 0-0
Track : LH: 0-1 RH: 0-0 Tight: 0-1 Gall: 0-0
Aids: Bl: 0-0 Vi: 0-0 Tstrap: 0-0
Best Rating: 68 5/01 Ayr 5f gd-fm

Won a Musselburgh maiden on her debut in 2000, scored twice more at the minimum trip. Has hung in the past and shown signs of temperament. Best on a sound surface, she has shown little in 2001.

Nifty Dan

82 **49**
2-y-o b g Suave Dancer (USA)-Nifty Fifty (IRE) (Runnett)
A Berry Roy Peebles

Placings:060 **(3073)**
2001: 5^{0}GS, 6^{6}F, 6^{0}GS

	Starts	1st	2nd	3rd	Win & Pl
Career Total (Turf)	3	0	0	0	0

Going (Turf): Sf: 0-0 GS: 0-2 Gd: 0-0 GF: 0-0 Fm: 0-1
Distance: 5f/6f: 0-3 7f-8f: 0-0 9f-13f: 0-0 14f+: 0-0
Track : LH: 0-0 RH: 0-0 Tight: 0-0 Gall: 0-0
Aids: Bl: 0-0 Vi: 0-0 Tstrap: 0-0
Best Rating: 49 6/01 Donc 6f firm

Nifty Major

102 **42**
4-y-o b g Be My Chief (USA)-Nifty Fifty (IRE) (Runnett)
A Berry Roy Peebles

Placings:612545150/02000005R300-6304000000R5000 **(5451)**
2001: 5^{6}GS, 5^{3}GS, 5^{0}GF, 5^{4}F, 6^{0}G, 5^{0}F, 5^{0}GF, 5^{0}GS, 5^{0}G, 5^{0}G, 5^{R}GF, 5^{5}G, 5^{0}GS, 6^{0}HY, 5^{0}HY

	Starts	1st	2nd	3rd	Win & Pl
Career Total (Turf)	36	2	2	2	10943

84	8/99	Muss	5f	E H	G-S	£3127
71	4/99	Muss	5f	F	G-F	£2682

Total win prize-money £5810

Going (Turf): Sf: 0-8 **GS: 1-9** Gd: 0-10 **GF: 1-6** Fm: 0-3
Distance: **5f/6f: 2-36** 7f-8f: 0-0 9f-13f: 0-0 14f+: 0-0
Track : LH: 0-4 RH: 0-0 Tight: 0-3 Gall: 0-0
Aids: Bl: 0-0 Vi: 0-1 Tstrap: 0-0
Best Rating: 66 5/01 Thsk 5f gd-sft

Frustrating sprint handicapper who has refused to race on occasions. On the downgrade.

Nifty Norman

89(110) (31)**31**
7-y-o b g Rock City-Nifty Fifty (IRE) (Runnett)
D Nicholls D Nicholls

Placings:02203/101060/200000000/05015221305334126040040665/1323634630613153004-6400000 **(5349)**
2001: 6^{6}, 6^{4}, 6^{0}HY, 5^{0}S, 6^{0}G, 6^{0}G, 5^{0}SD

	Starts	1st	2nd	3rd	Win & Pl
Career Total (Turf)	46	4	4	4	22570
Career Total (AW)	26	4	3	6	14078

66	7/00	Folk	5f	E(0-70)H	GD	£2791
65	6/00	Sthl	6f	F(0-65)H	STD	£2296
59	1/00	Wolv	5f	F	STD	£2310
67	6/99	Ches	5f16y	D(0-85)H	SFT	£4279
69	3/99	Sthl	5f	E(0-75)H	STD	£2684
58	2/99	Sthl	6f	E(0-75)H	STD	£2450
73	6/97	Ayr	5f	C(0-90)H	GD	£5312
82	5/97	Bevl	5f	D	HVY	£3631

Total win prize-money £25756

Going (Turf): Sf: 2-13 GS: 0-9 **Gd: 2-13** GF: 0-10 Fm: 0-1
Distance: **5f/6f: 8-69** 7f-8f: 0-3 9f-13f: 0-0 14f+: 0-0
Track : **LH: 4-25** RH: 0-1 **Tight: 2-13** Gall: 0-2
Aids: **Bl: 1-9** Vi: 0-0 Tstrap: 0-0
Best Rating: 28 5/01 Wind 6f good

He is pretty inconsistent these days, but capable of winning modest events on turf or sand as long as he hits the traps running, something he does not always do.

Nigel's Lad (IRE)

105 **74**
9-y-o b g Dominion Royale-Back To Earth (FR) (Vayrann)
P C Haslam N C Dunnington & Mark Watson

Placings:0253/31214021316100542621/0005660320000/041110560/1100/0501530/6420 **(1826)**
2001: 16^{6}S, 16^{4}GF, 16^{2}GF, 17^{0}F

	Starts	1st	2nd	3rd	Win & Pl
Career Total (Turf)	49	10	6	3	56673
Career Total (AW)	12	2	1	2	10004

81	6/99	Pont	2m1f22y	D(0-80)H	GD	£4347
84	6/98	Haml	1m5f9y	D(0-80)H	SFT	£5040
76	5/98	Ripn	2m	D(0-75)H	GD	£3517
77	6/97	Pont	2m1f22y	D(0-80)H	G-F	£4560
79	5/97	Catt	1m7f177y	E(0-70)H	G-F	£2820
85	5/97	Ripn	2m	D(0-75)H	G-F	£3452
87	9/95	NmkR	1m2f	C(0-100)H	GD	£8285
87	5/95	Newc	1m	D(0-85)H	GD	£3656
75	5/95	Haml	1m1f36y	E(0-70)H	G-F	£3209
72	4/95	Nott	1m1f213y	E	GD	£3302
75	1/95	Ling	1m2f	(0-70)H	STD	£3268
60	1/95	Ling	1m2f	(0-75)H	STD	£3881

Total win prize-money £49342

Going (Turf): Sf: 1-6 GS: 0-7 **Gd: 5-12** GF: 4-21 Fm: 0-3
Distance: 5f/6f: 0-1 7f-8f: 1-6 9f-13f: 5-34 **14f+: 6-20**
Track : **LH: 7-35** RH: 4-20 **Tight: 7-30** Gall: 1-11
Aids: Bl: 0-0 Vi: 0-1 Tstrap: 0-0
Best Rating: 74 5/01 Thsk 2m gd-fm

Night Aurora

96 **89**
2-y-o ch c Pennekamp (USA)-India Atlanta (Ahonoora)
E A L Dunlop Saeed Suhail

Placings:5214 **(4824)**
2001: 7^{5}S, 6^{2}G, 7^{1}GS, 7^{4}G

	Starts	1st	2nd	3rd	Win & Pl
Career Total (Turf)	4	1	1	0	7015

84	8/01	Leic	7f9y	D	G-S	£4290

Total win prize-money £4290

Going (Turf): Sf: 0-1 **GS: 1-1** Gd: 0-2 GF: 0-0 Fm: 0-0
Distance: 5f/6f: 0-0 **7f-8f: 1-4** 9f-13f: 0-0 14f+: 0-0
Track : LH: 0-1 RH: 0-1 Tight: 0-0 Gall: 0-1
Aids: Bl: 0-0 Vi: 0-0 Tstrap: 0-0
Best Rating: 89 9/01 Ayr 7f50y good

A half-brother to smart juvenile and top class miler Ventiquattrofogli. Got off the mark on his third outing, with the minimum of fuss.

Night Cap (IRE)

74(73) (37)**41**
2-y-o ch c Night Shift (USA)-Classic Design (Busted)
Sir Mark Prescott W E Sturt-Osborne House V

Placings:000 **(5526)**
2001: 6^{0}HY, 6^{0}SD, 5^{0}S

	Starts	1st	2nd	3rd	Win & Pl
Career Total (Turf)	2	0	0	0	
Career Total (AW)	1	0	0	0	

Going (Turf): Sf: 0-2 GS: 0-0 Gd: 0-0 GF: 0-0 Fm: 0-0
Distance: 5f/6f: 0-3 7f-8f: 0-0 9f-13f: 0-0 14f+: 0-0
Track : LH: 0-1 RH: 0-0 Tight: 0-0 Gall: 0-0
Aids: Bl: 0-0 Vi: 0-0 Tstrap: 0-0
Best Rating: 41 10/01 Wind 6f heavy

Has been well beaten on all starts to date, will be better over further than the six furlongs it has been running over this season.

Night City

87(107) (40)**57**

10-y-o b g Kris-Night Secret (Nijinsky (CAN))
A G Juckes (K R Burke 21/5) A C W Price

Placings:2/15/40002201/10404/04040020101/3313136 100122111001101235/325022140015110326/52260214 0644152252-00501605200 **(5046)**
2001: 9^{0}SW, 12^{0}SW, 8^{5}SW, 12^{0}SD, 10^{1}SD, 10^{6}SW, 10^{0}S, 16^{5}GF, 11^{2}SD, 11^{0}F, 11^{0}SD

	Starts	1st	2nd	3rd	Win & Pl
Career Total (Turf)	58	14	11	0	84000
Career Total (AW)	41	8	7	7	31534

40	3/01	Ling	1m2f	G	STD	£1855
51	6/00	Catt	1m5f175y	F	G-S	£2341
59	3/00	Ling	1m4f	F	STD	£2101
70	11/99	Ling	1m	F	STD	£1787
74	10/99	Brig	1m1f209y	C(0-90)H	G-S	£6612
69	10/99	York	1m2f85y	D	G-S	£7018
67	6/99	Haml	1m3f16y	E(0-70)	GD	£3550
84	12/98	Ling	1m4f	D(0-85)H	STD	£7002
77	10/98	York	1m2f85y	D	GD	£7174
75	10/98	Brig	1m3f196y	F	GD	£2295
77	8/98	Ling	1m3f106y	D(0-80)H	FRM	£7375
66	8/98	Catt	1m3f214y	F	GD	£2318
55	7/98	Haml	1m4f17y	E(0-70)	FRM	£3387
71	5/98	Thsk	1m4f	F	GD	£2582
75	3/98	Haml	1m3f16y	D(0-75)H	HVY	£7392
75	2/98	Ling	1m4f	F	SLW	£2232
83	1/98	Ling	1m4f	E	STD	£2712
73	12/97	Ling	1m5f	G(0-75)H	STD	£1998
68	11/97	Ling	1m4f	F	STD	£2646
102	5/96	Newb	1m1f	B(0-105)H	SFT	£9529
84	10/95	Chep	1m14y	C	SFT	£4904
	4/94	Curr	1m		HVY	£3450

Total win prize-money £92270

Going (Turf): Sf: 3-13 GS: 3-8 **Gd: 5-13** GF: 0-17 Fm: 2-4
Distance: 5f/6f: 0-0 7f-8f: 1-6 **9f-13f: 19-86** 14f+: 1-4
Track : **LH: 17-76** RH: 3-10 **Tight: 15-61** Gall: 3-11
Aids: Bl: 0-1 Vi: 0-1 Tstrap: 0-0
Best Rating: 40 5/01 Sthl 1m3f stand

He has been a real money-spinner for connections in recent seasons in middle-distance events on both turf and sand. Now plating class, he remains a difficult horse to pass if allowed an uncontested early lead.

Night Driver (IRE)

89 **68**

2-y-o b g Night Shift (USA)-Highshaan (Pistolet Bleu (IRE))
B W Hills S W Transport (swindon) Ltd

Placings:0520 **(5379)**
2001: 7^{0}S, 7^{5}GF, 6^{2}GF, 7^{0}S

	Starts	1st	2nd	3rd	Win & Pl
Career Total (Turf)	4	0	1	0	1763

Going (Turf): Sf: 0-2 GS: 0-0 Gd: 0-0 GF: 0-2 Fm: 0-0
Distance: 5f/6f: 0-1 7f-8f: 0-3 9f-13f: 0-0 14f+: 0-0
Track : LH: 0-1 RH: 0-1 Tight: 0-1 Gall: 0-0
Aids: Bl: 0-0 Vi: 0-0 Tstrap: 0-0
Best Rating: 68 7/01 NmkJ 6f gd-fm

Night Fall (IRE)

98(91) (54)**57**

3-y-o ch f Night Shift (USA)-Tumble (Mtoto)
M Blanshard Vino Veritas

Placings:56140603-042365060 **(4473)**
2001: 7^{0}G, 9^{4}F, 11^{2}F, 11^{3}F, 12^{6}GF, 11^{5}GF, 14^{0}F, 11^{6}GF, 11^{0}GF

	Starts	1st	2nd	3rd	Win & Pl
Career Total (Turf)	15	1	1	1	6219
Career Total (AW)	2	0	0	1	318

70	6/00	Gdwd	7f	D	G-F	£4056

Total win prize-money £4056

Going (Turf): Sf: 0-0 GS: 0-0 Gd: 0-4 **GF: 1-7** Fm: 0-4
Distance: 5f/6f: 0-2 **7f-8f: 1-7** 9f-13f: 0-7 14f+: 0-1
Track : LH: 0-10 **RH: 1-5** Tight: 0-5 Gall: 0-1
Aids: Bl: 0-0 Vi: 0-0 Tstrap: 0-3
Best Rating: 66 6/01 Brig 1m3f196y firm

Night Flight

106(99) (80)**87**

7-y-o gr g Night Shift (USA)-Ancestry (Persepolis (FR))
R A Fahey C H Stevens

Placings:23520/100330000/425160350030/320011341 000006/00200600012030-0000045046652000 **(4826)**
2001: 6^{0}SD, 5^{0}GS, 5^{0}S, 6^{0}G, 5^{0}GF, 5^{4}GF, 6^{5}G, 5^{0}GF, 5^{4}G, 5^{6}GF, 5^{6}G, 6^{5}G, 6^{2}G, 6^{0}GF, 5^{0}GF, 6^{0}G

	Starts	1st	2nd	3rd	Win & Pl
Career Total (Turf)	68	6	7	7	125984
Career Total (AW)	3	0	0	1	1236

90	8/00	York	6f	C(0-100)H	GD	£17290
100	7/99	Asct	5f	B(0-105)H	G-F	£29050
91	5/99	Hayd	5f	B(0-105)H	GD	£10076
85	5/99	York	5f	B(0-105)H	G-S	£18925
80	6/98	Newc	6f	D(0-75)H	GD	£4357
82	4/97	Pont	6f	D(0-80)H	GD	£5481

Total win prize-money £85181

Going (Turf): Sf: 0-12 GS: 1-7 **Gd: 4-27** GF: 1-17 Fm: 0-5
Distance: **5f/6f: 6-67** 7f-8f: 0-4 9f-13f: 0-0 14f+: 0-0
Track : **LH: 1-7** RH: 0-0 Tight: 0-4 Gall: 0-1
Aids: Bl: 0-0 Vi: 0-0 Tstrap: 0-0
Best Rating: 87 8/01 York 6f good

He scored three times in 1999, but has only managed one win since. Probably best over six furlongs these days and needs a strongly-run race. Acts on a sound surface but at his best with some give.

Night Haven

110 **97**

3-y-o gr f Night Shift (USA)-Noble Haven (Indian King (USA))
M L W Bell B H Farr

Placings:22145-1103200 **(3857)**
2001: 6^{1}GS, 5^{1}F, 6^{0}GF, 6^{3}G, 6^{2}G, 7^{0}GF, 5^{0}GS

	Starts	1st	2nd	3rd	Win & Pl
Career Total (Turf)	12	3	3	1	29616

90	5/01	Leic	5f218y	C(0-90)	FRM	£6942
88	5/01	Sals	6f	B(0-100)H	G-S	£9204
75	8/00	Newc	5f	D	G-F	£3386

Total win prize-money £19534

Going (Turf): Sf: 0-1 **GS: 1-2** Gd: 0-3 **GF: 1-4 Fm: 1-2**
Distance: **5f/6f: 3-9** 7f-8f: 0-3 9f-13f: 0-0 14f+: 0-0
Track : LH: 0-0 RH: 0-1 Tight: 0-0 Gall: 0-0
Aids: Bl: 0-0 Vi: 0-0 Tstrap: 0-0
Best Rating: 97 7/01 York 6f good

A winner once at two, she won her first two races at three at Salisbury and Leicester and has put in some decent efforts since, especially when runner-up in a York Listed event in July. Suited by six furlongs and being held up for a late run.

Night Market

97 **67**

3-y-o ch c Inchinor-Night Transaction (Tina's Pet)
B Smart The Quartet

Placings:2206 **(4468)**
2001: 8^{2}GF, 9^{2}GF, 8^{0}G, 9^{6}G

	Starts	1st	2nd	3rd	Win & Pl
Career Total (Turf)	4	0	2	0	2134

Going (Turf): Sf: 0-0 GS: 0-0 Gd: 0-2 GF: 0-2 Fm: 0-0
Distance: 5f/6f: 0-0 7f-8f: 0-0 9f-13f: 0-4 14f+: 0-0
Track : LH: 0-1 RH: 0-2 Tight: 0-1 Gall: 0-0
Aids: Bl: 0-0 Vi: 0-0 Tstrap: 0-0
Best Rating: 67 6/01 Bevl 1m100y gd-fm

Night Of Glass

81 **33**

8-y-o b g Mazilier (USA)-Donna Elvira (Chief Singer)
Miss J F Craze K Silvester And Mr B Silvester

Placings:000/005023100/360253023100/11111320330 00031500/3503153050354/040-0000 **(5376)**
2001: 8^{0}G, 7^{0}GS, 7^{0}G, 9^{0}G

	Starts	1st	2nd	3rd	Win & Pl
Career Total (Turf)	62	9	4	12	74056
Career Total (AW)	1	0	0	0	

92	5/99	Bevl	1m100y	C(0-95)H	GD	£5512
88	9/98	Muss	7f30y	D(0-85)H	GD	£5966
87	5/98	Bevl	1m100y	D(0-85)H	GD	£4536
85	5/98	Thsk	7f	C(0-90)H	GD	£5995
79	4/98	Carl	7f214y	D(0-85)H	G-S	£3566
74	4/98	Thsk	7f	E(0-70)H	G-S	£3358
68	4/98	Catt	7f	D(0-80)H	GD	£3808
65	10/97	Catt	7f	E(0-70)H	SFT	£3772
58	9/96	Yarm	1m3y	F(0-60)H	G-F	£3548

Total win prize-money £40061

Going (Turf): Sf: 1-7 GS: 2-8 **Gd: 5-30** GF: 1-15 Fm: 0-2
Distance: 5f/6f: 0-2 **7f-8f: 6-42** 9f-13f: 3-19 14f+: 0-0
Track : LH: 4-29 RH: 4-14 **Tight: 5-13** Gall: 0-10
Aids: **Bl: 7-24** Vi: 2-23 Tstrap: 0-1
Best Rating: 33 9/01 Donc 7f gd-sft

Night Of Nights

98(64) (12)**46**

3-y-o b/br f Never So Bold-Shamasiya (FR) (Vayrann)
M Dods D B Stanley

Placings:00-020005 **(4480)**
2001: 7^{0}GS, 6^{2}F, 6^{0}G, 5^{0}GF, 7^{0}G, 7^{5}F

	Starts	1st	2nd	3rd	Win & Pl
Career Total (Turf)	7	0	1	0	708
Career Total (AW)	1	0	0	0	

Going (Turf): Sf: 0-0 GS: 0-2 Gd: 0-2 GF: 0-1 Fm: 0-2
Distance: 5f/6f: 0-5 7f-8f: 0-3 9f-13f: 0-0 14f+: 0-0
Track : LH: 0-1 RH: 0-0 Tight: 0-1 Gall: 0-0
Aids: Bl: 0-0 Vi: 0-0 Tstrap: 0-0
Best Rating: 46 6/01 Newc 6f firm

Night Omen (IRE)

92(65) **33**

4-y-o ch g Night Shift (USA)-Propitious (IRE) (Doyoun)
S C Williams C J M Remmerswaal

Placings:05/0-000022000 **(4621)**
2001: 8^{0}S, 7^{0}GF, 5^{0}SD, 8^{0}GF, 6^{2}GF, 7^{2}F, 7^{0}G, 7^{0}GF, 6^{0}F

	Starts	1st	2nd	3rd	Win & Pl
Career Total (Turf)	11	0	2	0	1770
Career Total (AW)	1	0	0	0	

Going (Turf): Sf: 0-1 GS: 0-1 Gd: 0-2 GF: 0-5 Fm: 0-2
Distance: 5f/6f: 0-5 7f-8f: 0-5 9f-13f: 0-2 14f+: 0-0
Track : LH: 0-4 RH: 0-1 Tight: 0-1 Gall: 0-0
Aids: Bl: 0-0 Vi: 0-0 Tstrap: 0-3
Best Rating: 35 8/01 Thsk 7f firm

Night On The Town

100(97) (63)**65**

3-y-o b g Dancing Spree (USA)-Ling Lane (Slip Anchor)
B Smart Anglia Bloodstock Syndicate 1999

Placings:002-1L602 (2432)
2001: 8^{1}SD, 9^{L}S, 10^{6}GS, 9^{0}GF, 11^{2}GF

	Starts	1st	2nd	3rd	Win & Pl
Career Total (Turf)	6	0	1	0	920
Career Total (AW)	2	1	1	0	3670

63 1/01 Sthl 1m D STD £3024
Total win prize-money £3024

Going (Turf): Sf: 0-1 GS: 0-2 Gd: 0-0 GF: 0-3 Fm: 0-0
Distance: 5f/6f: 0-0 **7f-8f: 1-3** 9f-13f: 0-5 14f+: 0-0
Track : **LH: 1-4** RH: 0-3 Tight: 0-3 Gall: 0-0
Aids: Bl: 0-0 Vi: 0-0 Tstrap: 0-0
Best Rating: 65 5/01 Bath 1m2f46y gd-sft

Night Passion

94 **86**

2-y-o b c Night Shift (USA)-Nedaarah (Reference Point)
K R Burke Mrs Elaine M Burke

Placings:421 (5268)
2001: 8^{4}G, 7^{2}G, 7^{1}HY

	Starts	1st	2nd	3rd	Win & Pl
Career Total (Turf)	3	1	1	0	5473

86 10/01 Ayr 7f50y D HVY £3802
Total win prize-money £3803

Going (Turf): Sf: 1-1 GS: 0-0 Gd: 0-2 GF: 0-0 Fm: 0-0
Distance: 5f/6f: 0-0 **7f-8f: 1-2** 9f-13f: 0-1 14f+: 0-0
Track : LH: 0-0 RH: 0-0 Tight: 0-0 Gall: 0-0
Aids: Bl: 0-0 Vi: 0-0 Tstrap: 0-0
Best Rating: 86 10/01 Ayr 7f50y heavy

Out of a winner on the All-Weather, showed distinct promise on his Yarmouth debut. Had a habit of hanging left on his first two starts but put that behind him when scoring over seven furlongs on heavy ground at Ayr in October. Sold to the USA in the autumn.

Night Rhapsody (IRE)

99 **76**

4-y-o ch f Mujtahid (USA)-Double On (IRE) (Doubletour (USA))
K R Burke M J Halligan

Placings:0660166-3000 (3839)
2001: 10^{3}G, 8^{0}GF, 8^{0}G, 8^{0}G

	Starts	1st	2nd	3rd	Win & Pl
Career Total (Turf)	11	1	0	1	5466

66 8/00 Tral 1m (0-75)H Y-S £4830
Total win prize-money £4830

Going (Turf): Sf: 0-1 GS: 0-0 Gd: 0-6 GF: 0-1 Fm: 0-0
Distance: 5f/6f: 0-1 **7f-8f: 1-7** 9f-13f: 0-3 14f+: 0-0
Track : **LH: 1-5** RH: 0-4 Tight: 0-2 Gall: 0-0
Aids: **Bl: 1-4** Vi: 0-1 Tstrap: 0-0
Best Rating: 76 5/01 Ripn 1m2f good

Night Runner

93 **59**

2-y-o b c Polar Falcon (USA)-Christmas Kiss (Taufan (USA))
T D Easterby C H Stevens

Placings:5504000 (4823)
2001: 5^{5}S, 5^{5}F, 6^{0}GF, 7^{4}GF, 8^{0}GF, 7^{0}HY, 6^{0}G

	Starts	1st	2nd	3rd	Win & Pl
Career Total (Turf)	7	0	0	0	380

Going (Turf): Sf: 0-2 GS: 0-0 Gd: 0-1 GF: 0-3 Fm: 0-1
Distance: 5f/6f: 0-4 7f-8f: 0-2 9f-13f: 0-1 14f+: 0-0
Track : LH: 0-1 RH: 0-0 Tight: 0-0 Gall: 0-0
Aids: Bl: 0-1 Vi: 0-0 Tstrap: 0-0
Best Rating: 75 7/01 Newc 7f gd-fm

Has shown ability in maidens. Has a pronounced knee action which suggests some give in the ground may suit.

Night Shift Blue's (IRE)

97 **70**

2-y-o b c Night Shift (USA)-Tommelise (USA) (Dayjur (USA))
M Johnston S Kimberley

Placings:32025 (5536)
2001: 5^{3}GF, 5^{2}G, 5^{0}G, 6^{2}HY, 6^{5}S

	Starts	1st	2nd	3rd	Win & Pl
Career Total (Turf)	5	0	2	1	2531

Going (Turf): Sf: 0-2 GS: 0-0 Gd: 0-2 GF: 0-1 Fm: 0-0
Distance: 5f/6f: 0-5 7f-8f: 0-0 9f-13f: 0-0 14f+: 0-0
Track : LH: 0-0 RH: 0-0 Tight: 0-0 Gall: 0-0
Aids: Bl: 0-0 Vi: 0-0 Tstrap: 0-0
Best Rating: 70 10/01 Ayr 6f heavy

Placed form at sprint distances. Acts on any ground.

Night Shifter (IRE)

15 **51d**

4-y-o b f Night Shift (USA)-Atsuko (IRE) (Mtoto)
Jamie Poulton Glendale Partnership Ltd

Placings:04001263/0000000-0 (1036)
2001: 6^{0}HY

	Starts	1st	2nd	3rd	Win & Pl
Career Total (Turf)	16	1	1	1	5344

69 8/99 Ling 5f EH GD £2912
Total win prize-money £2912

Going (Turf): Sf: 0-2 GS: 0-1 **Gd: 1-7** GF: 0-5 Fm: 0-1
Distance: **5f/6f: 1-10** 7f-8f: 0-4 9f-13f: 0-2 14f+: 0-0
Track : LH: 0-2 RH: 0-6 Tight: 0-4 Gall: 0-4
Aids: Bl: 0-0 Vi: 0-0 Tstrap: 0-0
Best Rating: 69 8/99 Ling 5f G

Night Sight (USA)

100(111) (87)**60d**

4-y-o b g Eagle Eyed (USA)-El Hamo (USA) (Search For Gold (USA))
M C Chapman David Fravigar-Alan Mann

Placings:00223221-0503411500600030000 (5376)
2001: 8^{0}SD, 6^{5}SD, 7^{0}SW, 11^{3}SW, 12^{4}SD, 11^{1}SW, 12^{1}SD, 12^{5}S, 10^{0}S, 10^{0}G, 12^{6}GF, 8^{0}GS, 14^{0}GF, 11^{0}G, 10^{3}GF, 11^{0}GF, 9^{0}HY, 10^{0}S, 9^{0}G, 8^{0}SD, 7^{6}SD, 8^{0}SD

	Starts	1st	2nd	3rd	Win & Pl
Career Total (Turf)	19	0	4	2	7433
Career Total (AW)	8	3	0	1	13879

87 3/01 Sthl 1m4f C(0-100)H STD £6776
79 2/01 Sthl 1m3f D(0-85)H SLW £3776
55 12/00 Sthl 7f D STD £2751
Total win prize-money £13304

Going (Turf): Sf: 0-4 GS: 0-3 Gd: 0-5 GF: 0-5 Fm: 0-2
Distance: 5f/6f: 0-1 7f-8f: 1-10 **9f-13f: 2-15** 14f+: 0-1
Track : **LH: 3-18** RH: 0-6 Tight: 0-8 Gall: 0-6
Aids: Bl: 0-1 Vi: 0-0 Tstrap: 0-0
Best Rating: 87 3/01 Sthl 1m4f stand

A maiden on turf, he took to Fibresand during the winter of 2000-01, winning three times. Has done little of note on turf since. Stays a mile and a half on sand.

Nightwatchman (IRE)

84 **52**

2-y-o b c Hector Protector (USA)-Nightlark (IRE) (Night Shift (USA))
W R Muir Trouble Free Partnership

Placings:000 (5604)
2001: 7^{0}G, 8^{0}GS, 7^{0}GS

	Starts	1st	2nd	3rd	Win & Pl
Career Total (Turf)	3	0	0	0	

Going (Turf): Sf: 0-0 GS: 0-2 Gd: 0-1 GF: 0-0 Fm: 0-0
Distance: 5f/6f: 0-0 7f-8f: 0-3 9f-13f: 0-0 14f+: 0-0
Track : LH: 0-0 RH: 0-1 Tight: 0-0 Gall: 0-0
Aids: Bl: 0-0 Vi: 0-0 Tstrap: 0-0
Best Rating: 52 11/01 NmkR 7f gd-sft

Nigrasine

107(86) (88)**84**

7-y-o b/br h Mon Tresor-Early Gales (Precocious)
J L Eyre Sunpak Potatoes

Placings:115242/05010003/5301404520203/00101242430400/03045104000-000620105001050 (5267)
2001: 5^{0}S, 6^{0}G, 7^{0}GF, 7^{6}GF, 8^{2}GF, 8^{0}GF, 6^{1}GF, 6^{0}G, 7^{5}G, 6^{0}G, 6^{0}GF, 8^{1}F, 8^{0}S, 8^{5}G, 6^{0}GS, 8^{0}SD

	Starts	1st	2nd	3rd	Win & Pl
Career Total (Turf)	66	9	7	5	126827
Career Total (AW)	1	0	0	0	

59	9/01	Pont	1m4y	D(0-80)	FRM	£4719
84	7/01	Pont	6f	D(0-80)H	G-F	£7442
101	6/00	Yarm	6f3y	C	G-F	£6090
114	6/99	Yarm	6f3y	C	GD	£5756
113	4/99	Thsk	6f	C	GD	£6276
107	6/98	Hayd	7f30y	A	GD	£12640
103	7/97	Hayd	6f	C(0-100)H	GD	£5322
101	7/96	Pont	6f	C	G-F	£4660
73	6/96	Rdcr	6f	D	G-F	£3491

Total win prize-money £56399

Going (Turf): Sf: 0-7 GS: 0-9 **Gd: 4-29 GF: 4-18** Fm: 1-2
Distance: **5f/6f: 5-34** 7f-8f: 3-31 9f-13f: 1-2 14f+: 0-0
Track : **LH: 4-16** RH: 0-1 Tight: 0-5 Gall: 0-6
Aids: **Bl: 4-29** Vi: 1-13 Tstrap: 0-0
Best Rating: 84 7/01 Pont 6f gd-fm

He is the veteran of many tough battles, but retains his enthusiasm and a steady drop in the handicap, together with a drop back to six furlongs, enabled him to return to winning form at Pontefract in July and scored again at that track in September. Acts on most types of ground. Effective at six to eight furlongs.

Nikita's Star (IRE)

86(97) (39)**20**

8-y-o ch g Soviet Lad (USA)-Sally Chase (Sallust)
M Brittain Northgate Lodge Racing Club

Placings:04050300/12100011525401/542206006052/54346303435641/44611202003263/00-65203002050 (3879)
2001: 16^{6}SD, 16^{5}SD, 16^{2}SD, 12^{0}S, 14^{3}SD, 16^{0}SD, 14^{0}SD, 16^{2}SD, 16^{0}GF, 16^{5}SD, 16^{0}GS

	Starts	1st	2nd	3rd	Win & Pl
Career Total (Turf)	29	1	2	1	5769
Career Total (AW)	46	7	8	7	28145

68	2/99	Sthl	1m4f	F(0-60)	STD	£2018
58	2/99	Wolv	1m4f	F(0-60)H	STD	£1945
57	12/98	Sthl	1m4f	F(0-60)H	STD	£1861
75	11/96	Wolv	1m4f	D(0-85)H	STD	£3074
64	7/96	Folk	1m4f	E(0-70)H	G-F	£2961
64	7/96	Sthl	1m3f	F	STD	£2381
69	3/96	Wolv	1m4f	D(0-80)H	STD	£3436
55	2/96	Wolv	1m1f79y	D	STD	£3452

Total win prize-money £21131

Going (Turf): Sf: 0-2 GS: 0-6 Gd: 0-7 **GF: 1-10** Fm: 0-4
Distance: 5f/6f: 0-2 7f-8f: 0-6 **9f-13f: 8-34** 14f+: 0-33
Track : **LH: 7-57** RH: 1-13 **Tight: 5-39** Gall: 0-5
Aids: Bl: 0-6 Vi: 0-5 Tstrap: 0-0
Best Rating: 39 7/01 Wolv 2m46y stand

Nikitin

94 **74d**

2-y-o b g Emarati (USA)-Choral Sundown (Night Shift (USA))

R M Beckett Pedro Rosas

Placings:54000 **(5589)**

2001: 6^{5}G, 6^{4}G, 6^{0}GF, 8^{0}GS, 7^{0}GS

	Starts	1st	2nd	3rd	Win & Pl
Career Total (Turf)	5	0	0	0	0

Going (Turf): Sf: 0-0 GS: 0-2 Gd: 0-2 GF: 0-1 Fm: 0-0
Distance: 5f/6f: 0-3 7f-8f: 0-2 9f-13f: 0-0 14f+: 0-0
Track : LH: 0-1 RH: 0-0 Tight: 0-0 Gall: 0-0
Aids: Bl: 0-0 Vi: 0-1 Tstrap: 0-0
Best Rating: 74 9/01 Folk 6f good

Nimble Traveller (IRE)

76 **44**

2-y-o b f Blues Traveller (IRE)-Be Nimble (Wattlefield)

K R Burke B Batey

Placings:000 **(5378)**

2001: 6^{0}GF, 5^{0}GS, 5^{0}S

	Starts	1st	2nd	3rd	Win & Pl
Career Total (Turf)	3	0	0	0	

Going (Turf): Sf: 0-1 GS: 0-1 Gd: 0-0 GF: 0-1 Fm: 0-0
Distance: 5f/6f: 0-3 7f-8f: 0-0 9f-13f: 0-0 14f+: 0-0
Track : LH: 0-0 RH: 0-0 Tight: 0-0 Gall: 0-0
Aids: Bl: 0-0 Vi: 0-0 Tstrap: 0-0
Best Rating: 44 10/01 Catt 5f gd-sft

Nimello (USA)

113(113) (96+)**105d**

5-y-o b g Kingmambo (USA)-Zakota (IRE) (Polish Precedent (USA))

P F I Cole C Shiacolas

Placings:1/520/0100043-111003 **(5625)**

2001: 8^{1}SD, 8^{1}S, 8^{1}GS, 7^{0}GF, 7^{0}G, 8^{3}GS

	Starts	1st	2nd	3rd	Win & Pl
Career Total (Turf)	16	4	1	2	94648
Career Total (AW)	1	1	0	0	13423

105	5/01	Kemp	1m	B(0-110)H	G-S	£29000
101	3/01	Donc	1m	B H	SFT	£41957
96	3/01	Wolv	1m100y	B H	STD	£13422
89	4/00	Sand	1m14y	C(0-95)H	SFT	£9883
87	7/98	NmkJ	7f	D	G-F	£5299

Total win prize-money £99563

Going (Turf): Sf: 2-5 GS: 1-2 Gd: 0-3 GF: 1-5 Fm: 0-1
Distance: 5f/6f: 0-0 **7f-8f: 3-11** 9f-13f: 2-6 14f+: 0-0
Track : LH: 1-7 **RH: 2-3 Tight: 1-1** Gall: 0-3
Aids: Bl: 0-3 Vi: 0-0 Tstrap: 0-0
Best Rating: 105 5/01 Kemp 1m gd-sft

He showed useful form in handicaps in 2000, but looked even better (after being gelded) on his seasonal bow when bolting up at Wolverhampton before taking the Lincoln in similar style. Coming back after a break, he landed a good handicap at Kempton. Does not want the ground too fast.

Nineacres

106(109) (88)**80**

10-y-o b g Sayf El Arab (USA)-Mayor (Laxton)

J M Bradley J M Bradley

Placings:245040213200052221 0/631505003 60/006023/340306/00004102/32261440130522101103041302210101000-00000603026560050065 **(5381)**

2001: 5^{0}SD, 5^{0}S, 5^{0}GF, 5^{0}GF, 5^{0}GF, 5^{6}GF, 5^{0}GF, 5^{3}GS, 5^{0}GF, 5^{2}GF, 5^{6}S, 5^{5}GF, 6^{6}G, 5^{0}G, 5^{0}G, 6^{5}GF, 6^{0}G, 6^{0}G, 5^{6}S, 5^{5}S

	Starts	1st	2nd	3rd	Win & Pl
Career Total (Turf)	70	8	8	8	62051
Career Total (AW)	35	5	7	3	22177

88	11/00	Wolv	5f	C(0-95)H	STD	£6808
92	10/00	Wind	5f10y	C(0-90)H	HVY	£7247
85	10/00	York	5f	D(0-80)H	SFT	£7195
73	8/00	Chep	6f16y	E(0-75)H	G-F	£2814
65	6/00	Wind	6f	D(0-80)H	G F	£7707
65	6/00	Bath	5f161y	D(0-85)H	G-F	£3838
59	5/00	Bath	5f161y	E(0-70)H	G-F	£2847
53	3/00	Sthl	6f	F(0-65)H	GD	£2436
56	2/00	Wolv	5f	F(0-60)H	STD	£1855
50	12/99	Wolv	6f	F	STD	£1798
56	1/95	Ling	5f	F(0-70)H	STD	£2663
56	12/94	Ling	5f	F(0-60)H	STD	£2564
44	6/94	Muss	5f	E(0-70)H	FRM	£2762

Total win prize-money £52599

Going (Turf): Sf: 2-16 GS: 0-7 Gd: 1-14 **GF: 4-27** Fm: 1-6
Distance: **5f/6f: 12-92** 7f-8f: 1-13 9f-13f: 0-0 14f+: 0 0
Track : **LH: 8-44** RH: 2-6 **Tight: 5-28** Gall: 4-10
Aids: **Bl: 12-70** Vi: 0-14 Tstrap: 0-0
Best Rating: 83 8/01 Ripn 6f good

Victorious a record-equalling nine times in handicap company in 2000, he failed to win this term but remains a useful sort in modest sprint handicaps. Suited by fast ground, he seems equally effective on turf and sand these days.

Nineteenninetynine

(82) (25)**58**

4-y-o b g Warning-Flower Girl (Pharly (FR))

Mrs N Macauley Shirebrook Park Management Ltd

Placings:506/0050-0 **(0053)**

2001: 12^{0}SD

	Starts	1st	2nd	3rd	Win & Pl
Career Total (Turf)	5	0	0	0	80
Career Total (AW)	3	0	0	0	

Going (Turf): Sf: 0-0 GS: 0-3 Gd: 0-0 GF: 0-2 Fm: 0-0
Distance: 5f/6f: 0-0 7f-8f: 0-5 9f-13f: 0-3 14f+: 0-0
Track : LH: 0-3 RH: 0-0 Tight: 0-0 Gall: 0-0
Aids: Bl: 0-0 Vi: 0-3 Tstrap: 0-0
Best Rating: 12 1/01 Sthl 1m4f stand

Ninnolo (IRE)

99(71) (17)**71**

4-y-o b g Perugino (USA)-Primo Stampari (Primo Dominie)

C N Allen Newmarketconnections.Com

Placings:5300523-6 **(1664)**

2001: 8^{6}GF

	Starts	1st	2nd	3rd	Win & Pl
Career Total (Turf)	7	0	1	2	2749
Career Total (AW)	1	0	0	0	

Going (Turf): Sf: 0-0 GS: 0-0 Gd: 0-4 GF: 0-3 Fm: 0-0
Distance: 5f/6f: 0-0 7f-8f: 0-0 9f-13f: 0-7 14f+: 0-1
Track : LH: 0-4 RH: 0-3 Tight: 0-5 Gall: 0-1
Aids: Bl: 0-0 Vi: 0-0 Tstrap: 0-4
Best Rating: 60 5/01 Sand 1m14y gd-fm

Nirvana

97 **76**

2-y-o b f Marju (IRE)-Charming Life (NZ) (Sir Tristram)

J L Dunlop Plantation Stud

Placings:62 **(5371)**

2001: 7^{6}GF, 8^{2}G

	Starts	1st	2nd	3rd	Win & Pl
Career Total (Turf)	2	0	1	0	1350

Going (Turf): Sf: 0-0 GS: 0-0 Gd: 0-1 GF: 0-1 Fm: 0-0
Distance: 5f/6f: 0-0 7f-8f: 0-2 9f-13f: 0-0 14f+: 0-0
Track : LH: 0-0 RH: 0-0 Tight: 0-0 Gall: 0-0
Aids: Bl: 0-0 Vi: 0-0 Tstrap: 0-0
Best Rating: 76 10/01 Rdcr 1m good

Finished behind the Rockfel winner Distant Valley on her debut, and was then second to another nice sort at Redacr in October.

Nisa Time

61

3-y-o ch f Timeless Times (USA)-Stork Hill (Crofthall)

N Tinkler Ian Blakey

Placings:000 **(1281)**

2001: 5^{0}S, 6^{0}HY, 9^{0}G

	Starts	1st	2nd	3rd	Win & Pl
Career Total (Turf)	3	0	0	0	

Going (Turf): Sf: 0-2 GS: 0-0 Gd: 0-1 GF: 0-0 Fm: 0-0
Distance: 5f/6f: 0-1 7f-8f: 0-1 9f-13f: 0-1 14f+: 0-0
Track : LH: 0-0 RH: 0-1 Tight: 0-0 Gall: 0-0
Aids: Bl: 0-0 Vi: 0-0 Tstrap: 0-0

Nisr

107 **80**

4-y-o b g Grand Lodge (USA)-Tharwa (IRE) (Last Tycoon)

J W Payne C Cotran

Placings:002/6010-3156 **(5391)**

2001: 7^{3}GF, 7^{1}GF, 7^{5}GF, 7^{6}GS

	Starts	1st	2nd	3rd	Win & Pl
Career Total (Turf)	11	2	1	1	14588

80	7/01	Folk	7f	D(0-80)H	G-F	£6864
78	6/00	Pont	6f	D(0-80)	G-F	£5772

Total win prize-money £12636

Going (Turf): Sf: 0-1 GS: 0-3 Gd: 0-2 **GF: 2-5** Fm: 0-0
Distance: 5f/6f: 1-6 7f-8f: 1-5 9f-13f: 0-0 14f+: 0-0
Track : **LH: 1-2** RH: 0-1 Tight: 0-1 Gall: 0-1
Aids: Bl: 0-0 Vi: 0-0 Tstrap: 0-0
Best Rating: 80 10/01 NmkR 7f gd-sft

Took a seven-furlong handicap at Folkestone and was not disgraced in a better race back at Newbury. Suited by fast ground.

Nite Owl Lady (IRE)

81(62) (8)**48**

2-y-o b f Elbio-Persian Royale (Persian Bold)

J O'Reilly Burntwood Sports Ltd

Placings:60600 **(5393)**

2001: 5^{6}GF, 7^{0}GF, 6^{6}G, 5^{0}GF, 6^{0}SD

	Starts	1st	2nd	3rd	Win & Pl
Career Total (Turf)	4	0	0	0	0
Career Total (AW)	1	0	0	0	

Going (Turf): Sf: 0-0 GS: 0-0 Gd: 0-1 GF: 0-3 Fm: 0-0
Distance: 5f/6f: 0-4 7f-8f: 0-1 9f-13f: 0-0 14f+: 0-0
Track : LH: 0-1 RH: 0-1 Tight: 0-1 Gall: 0-0
Aids: Bl: 0-0 Vi: 0-0 Tstrap: 0-0
Best Rating: 48 8/01 Rdcr 6f good

Nite-Owl Fizz

92 **28**

3-y-o b g Efisio-Nite-Owl Dancer (Robellino (USA))

J O'Reilly J Saul

Placings:00 **(4266)**

2001: 8^{0}S, 7^{0}GF

	Starts	1st	2nd	3rd	Win & Pl
Career Total (Turf)	2	0	0	0	

Going (Turf): Sf: 0-1 GS: 0-0 Gd: 0-0 GF: 0-1 Fm: 0-0
Distance: 5f/6f: 0-0 7f-8f: 0-1 9f-13f: 0-1 14f+: 0-0

Track : LH: 0-1 RH: 0-1 Tight: 0-0 Gall: 0-0
Aids: Bl: 0-0 Vi: 0-0 Tstrap: 0-0
Best Rating: 28 8/01 Bevl 7f100y gd-fm

Nite-Owl Mate

(106) (71)**33**
4-y-o b g Komaite (USA)-Nite-Owl Dancer (Robellino (USA))
J O'Reilly J Saul

Placings:33000100000-0 **(0473)**
2001: 7^{0}SD

	Starts	1st	2nd	3rd	Win & Pl
Career Total (Turf)	5	0	0	0	
Career Total (AW)	7	1	0	2	3647
71 7/00 Wolv 6f	E(0-70)H			STD	£2785

Total win prize-money £2785

Going (Turf): Sf: 0-0 GS: 0-0 Gd: 0-3 GF: 0-1 Fm: 0-1
Distance: **5f/6f: 1-9** 7f-8f: 0-3 9f-13f: 0-0 14f+: 0-0
Track : **LH: 1-8** RH: 0-0 **Tight: 1-4** Gall: 0-0
Aids: Bl: 0-1 Vi: 0-0 **Tstrap: 1-6**
Best Rating: 71 7/00 Wolv 6f SD

Nivernais

100 **79**
2-y-o b g Forzando-Funny Wave (Lugana Beach)
H Candy M J M Tricks

Placings:612 **(4730)**
2001: 5^{6}GF, 5^{1}G, 5^{2}F

	Starts	1st	2nd	3rd	Win & Pl
Career Total (Turf)	3	1	1	0	3469
76 8/01 Folk 5f	F			GD	£2639

Total win prize-money £2639

Going (Turf): Sf: 0-0 GS: 0-0 **Gd: 1-1** GF: 0-1 Fm: 0-1
Distance: **5f/6f: 1-3** 7f-8f: 0-0 9f-13f: 0-0 14f+: 0-0
Track : LH: 0-0 RH: 0-1 Tight: 0-0 Gall: 0-1
Aids: Bl: 0-0 Vi: 0-0 Tstrap: 0-0
Best Rating: 79 9/01 Chep 5f16y firm

Only cost 2,000 guineas as a foal and has already been gelded. He has shown plenty of ability at an ordinary level on decent ground. Described as a laid-back individual.

Niyabah (IRE)

107 **75**
3-y-o ch f Nashwan (USA)-Gharam (USA) (Green Dancer (USA))
A C Stewart Hamdan Al Maktoum

Placings:6-21 **(5631)**
2001: 8^{2}GS, 10^{1}G

	Starts	1st	2nd	3rd	Win & Pl
Career Total (Turf)	3	1	1	0	4638
69 11/01 Rdcr 1m2f	D			GD	£3528

Total win prize-money £3528

Going (Turf): Sf: 0-1 GS: 0-1 **Gd: 1-1** GF: 0-0 Fm: 0-0
Distance: 5f/6f: 0-0 7f-8f: 0-1 **9f-13f: 1-2** 14f+: 0-0
Track : **LH: 1-2** RH: 0-0 **Tight: 1-1** Gall: 0-0
Aids: Bl: 0-0 Vi: 0-0 Tstrap: 0-0
Best Rating: 75 10/01 Pont 1m4y gd-sft

Quite a well bred filly, but lightly-raced, she was second on her reappearance this year, and went one better next time at Redcar.

No Argument

94 **59**
2-y-o b c Young Ern-As Sharp As (Handsome Sailor)
N A Callaghan N A Callaghan

Placings:064324 **(4321)**
2001: 6^{0}GF, 6^{6}GS, 6^{4}GS, 7^{3}G, 7^{2}G, 6^{4}GF

	Starts	1st	2nd	3rd	Win & Pl
Career Total (Turf)	6	0	1	1	1863

Going (Turf): Sf: 0-0 GS: 0-2 Gd: 0-2 GF: 0-2 Fm: 0-0
Distance: 5f/6f: 0-2 7f-8f: 0-4 9f-13f: 0-0 14f+: 0-0
Track : LH: 0-0 RH: 0-0 Tight: 0-0 Gall: 0-0
Aids: Bl: 0-0 Vi: 0-0 Tstrap: 0-0
Best Rating: 59 8/01 Folk 7f good

Likes to race prominently, and has progressed with racing to run well in ordinary nurseries. Suited by seven furlongs and good ground.

No Diss Grace

52(71) (36)**37**
3-y-o b g Cigar-Llanelly (FR) (Kenmare (FR))
P C Haslam Kary-On Racing Partnership

Placings:500-00 **(1721)**
2001: 7^{0}SD, 8^{0}GF

	Starts	1st	2nd	3rd	Win & Pl
Career Total (Turf)	2	0	0	0	0
Career Total (AW)	3	0	0	0	

Going (Turf): Sf: 0-0 GS: 0-0 Gd: 0-1 GF: 0-1 Fm: 0-0
Distance: 5f/6f: 0-2 7f-8f: 0-3 9f-13f: 0-0 14f+: 0-0
Track : LH: 0-2 RH: 0-1 Tight: 0-1 Gall: 0-0
Aids: Bl: 0-0 Vi: 0-0 Tstrap: 0-0
Best Rating: 10 1/01 Sthl 7f stand

No Excuse Needed

113 **121**
3-y-o ch c Machiavellian (USA)-Nawaiet (USA) (Zilzal (USA))
Sir Michael Stoute Maktoum Al Maktoum

Placings:115-5210 **(5389)**
2001: 8^{5}G, 8^{2}GF, 8^{1}GF, 10^{0}GS

	Starts	1st	2nd	3rd	Win & Pl
Career Total (Turf)	7	3	1	0	150930
121 8/01 Gdwd 1m	A			G-F	£46400
113 8/00 Gdwd 7f	A			G-F	£30000
80 7/00 Sand 7f16y	D			GD	£7280

Total win prize-money £83680

Going (Turf): Sf: 0-1 GS: 0-1 **Gd: 1-2 GF: 2-3** Fm: 0-0
Distance: 5f/6f: 0-0 **7f-8f: 3-6** 9f-13f: 0-1 14f+: 0-0
Track : LH: 0-0 **RH: 3-6** Tight: 0-0 Gall: 0-2
Aids: Bl: 0-0 Vi: 0-0 Tstrap: 0-0
Best Rating: 121 8/01 Gdwd 1m gd-fm

Won his first two races as a juvenile in 2000, included the Vintage Stakes at Glorious Goodwood, but floundered in the soft ground on his final start. Incurred an injury in Dubai in March, but ran a fine race on his return at Royal Ascot after meeting trouble in running. Showed what he is capable of when second in the Sussex Stakes and got his reward in the Celebration Mile over the same course and distance. Ran no race in the Champion Stakes, confirming his dislike of soft ground. Suited by a mile, fast ground and hold-up tactics.

No Illusions

91 **63**
2-y-o b c Bluegrass Prince (IRE)-Dancing Years (USA) (Fred Astaire (USA))
R Ingram Burton & Smith Moving

Placings:0600600 **(4178)**
2001: 5^{0}GS, 6^{6}GF, 6^{0}G, 7^{0}GF, 7^{6}GF, 6^{0}GF, 7^{0}GF

	Starts	1st	2nd	3rd	Win & Pl
Career Total (Turf)	7	0	0	0	0

Going (Turf): Sf: 0-0 GS: 0-1 Gd: 0-1 GF: 0-5 Fm: 0-0
Distance: 5f/6f: 0-4 7f-8f: 0-3 9f-13f: 0-0 14f+: 0-0
Track : LH: 0-3 RH: 0-0 Tight: 0-2 Gall: 0-0
Aids: Bl: 0-0 Vi: 0-3 Tstrap: 0-0
Best Rating: 63 8/01 Epsm 6f gd-fm

No Joke

94 **51**
3-y-o b/br f Bin Ajwaad (IRE)-Round Midnight (Star Appeal)
C F Wall S Fustok

Placings:000600 **(5450)**
2001: 6^{0}GS, 8^{0}G, 7^{0}GF, 9^{6}GF, 10^{0}G, 8^{0}HY

	Starts	1st	2nd	3rd	Win & Pl
Career Total (Turf)	6	0	0	0	0

Going (Turf): Sf: 0-1 GS: 0-1 Gd: 0-2 GF: 0-2 Fm: 0-0
Distance: 5f/6f: 0-1 7f-8f: 0-2 9f-13f: 0-3 14f+: 0-0
Track : LH: 0-3 RH: 0-2 Tight: 0-2 Gall: 0-1
Aids: Bl: 0-0 Vi: 0-0 Tstrap: 0-0
Best Rating: 57 5/01 Wind 1m67y good

No Language Please (IRE)

95(81) (18)**47**
7-y-o ch g Arapahos (FR)-Strong Language (Formidable (USA))
R Curtis Mrs G Fletcher

Placings:130-063036 **(3727)**
2001: 10^{0}S, 11^{6}GS, 11^{3}F, 12^{0}GF, 16^{3}GF, 14^{6}GS

	Starts	1st	2nd	3rd	Win & Pl
Career Total (Turf)	8	1	0	3	3400
Career Total (AW)	1	0	0	0	
42 6/00 Brig 1m3f196yF				G-F	£2289

Total win prize-money £2289

Going (Turf): Sf: 0-1 GS: 0-2 Gd: 0-0 **GF: 1-3** Fm: 0-2
Distance: 5f/6f: 0-0 7f-8f: 0-0 **9f-13f: 1-7** 14f+: 0-2
Track : **LH: 1-7** RH: 0-2 Tight: 0-3 Gall: 0-2
Aids: Bl: 0-0 Vi: 0-0 Tstrap: 0-0
Best Rating: 47 6/01 Brig 1m3f196y firm

No Mercy

103(102) (54)**48**
5-y-o ch g Faustus (USA)-Nashville Blues (IRE) (Try My Best (USA))
B A Pearce Richard J Gray

Placings:044/143334/502050-0000243000 (4463)
2001: 7^{0}GS, 10^{0}G, 13^{0}GF, 9^{0}GF, 8^{2}SD, 10^{4}GF, 10^{3}GF, 11^{0}F, 9^{0}GS, 9^{0}GS

	Starts	1st	2nd	3rd	Win & Pl
Career Total (Turf)	23	0	1	4	5251
Career Total (AW)	2	1	1	0	3230
73 4/99 Ling 1m2f	E			STD	£2558

Total win prize-money £2558

Going (Turf): Sf: 0-1 GS: 0-4 Gd: 0-8 GF: 0-8 Fm: 0-2
Distance: 5f/6f: 0-0 7f-8f: 0-5 **9f-13f: 1-19** 14f+: 0-1
Track : **LH: 1-13** RH: 0-9 **Tight: 1-15** Gall: 0-3
Aids: Bl: 0-1 Vi: 0-1 Tstrap: 0-3
Best Rating: 54 7/01 Sthl 1m stand

No Name City (IRE)

84(100) (60)**54d**
3-y-o ch c Royal Abjar (USA)-Broadway Gal (USA) (Foolish Pleasure (USA))
J W Hills The Wandering Stars

Placings:0030-5306 **(5461)**
2001: 8^{5}SD, 8^{3}SW, 8^{0}GS, 8^{6}G

	Starts	1st	2nd	3rd	Win & Pl
Career Total (Turf)	4	0	0	0	0
Career Total (AW)	4	0	0	2	556

Going (Turf): Sf: 0-0 GS: 0-1 Gd: 0-2 GF: 0-1 Fm: 0-0
Distance: 5f/6f: 0-0 7f-8f: 0-3 9f-13f: 0-5 14f+: 0-0
Track : LH: 0-5 RH: 0-0 Tight: 0-5 Gall: 0-0
Aids: Bl: 0-0 Vi: 0-0 Tstrap: 0-0

Best Rating: 60 2/01 Wolv 1m100y stand

No Nellie No

65

7-y-o ch m Formidable (USA)-Now In Session (USA) (Diesis)
M A Allen J Bigg

Placings:0/000 **(2941)**
2001: 11^{0}GF, 11^{0}SD, 10^{0}GF

	Starts	1st	2nd	3rd	Win & Pl
Career Total (Turf)	3	0	0	0	
Career Total (AW)	1	0	0	0	

Going (Turf): Sf: 0-0 GS: 0-1 Gd: 0-0 GF: 0-2 Fm: 0-0
Distance: 5f/6f: 0-0 7f-8f: 0-0 9f-13f: 0-4 14f+: 0-0
Track : LH: 0-3 RH: 0-0 Tight: 0-3 Gall: 0-0
Aids: Bl: 0-0 Vi: 0-0 Tstrap: 0-3

No Question

97(97) (74)77

2-y-o b f Salse (USA)-Opalette (Sharrood (USA))
B W Hills Enton Thoroughbred Racing

Placings:5422 **(5610)**
2001: 7^{5}GF, 8^{4}GF, 8^{2}SD, 8^{2}SD

	Starts	1st	2nd	3rd	Win & Pl
Career Total (Turf)	2	0	0	0	344
Career Total (AW)	2	0	2	0	1640

Going (Turf): Sf: 0-0 GS: 0-0 Gd: 0-0 GF: 0-2 Fm: 0-0
Distance: 5f/6f: 0-0 7f-8f: 0-2 9f-13f: 0-2 14f+: 0-0
Track : LH: 0-2 RH: 0-1 Tight: 0-2 Gall: 0-0
Aids: Bl: 0-0 Vi: 0-0 Tstrap: 0-0
Best Rating: 77 9/01 Kemp 1m gd-fm

She has shown ability in maidens, twice finishing runner-up over the extended mile at Wolverhampton.

No Sam No

95(79) (23)43

3-y-o b f Reprimand-Samjamalifran (Blakeney)
Mrs K Walton (J A Osborne 1/9) Mrs K Walton

Placings:0-60042600 **(4422)**
2001: 7^{6}SD, 6^{0}G, 8^{0}SD, 8^{4}GF, 8^{2}GS, 10^{6}G, 9^{0}G, 10^{0}GF

	Starts	1st	2nd	3rd	Win & Pl
Career Total (Turf)	7	0	1	0	617
Career Total (AW)	2	0	0	0	0

Going (Turf): Sf: 0-0 GS: 0-2 Gd: 0-3 GF: 0-2 Fm: 0-0
Distance: 5f/6f: 0-1 7f-8f: 0-2 9f-13f: 0-6 14f+: 0-0
Track : LH: 0-6 RH: 0-1 Tight: 0-3 Gall: 0-0
Aids: Bl: 0-0 Vi: 0-0 Tstrap: 0-0
Best Rating: 43 8/01 Yarm 1m3y gd-sft

No Surrender

88(85) (12)20

3-y-o ch f Brief Truce (USA)-Furry Dance (USA) (Nureyev (USA))
D W Chapman David W Chapman

Placings:60000435-5005000000 **(3279)**
2001: 7^{5}SD, 7^{0}SW, 6^{0}SW, 6^{5}SD, 5^{0}SD, 5^{0}GF, 5^{0}G, 6^{0}GF, 5^{0}SD, 5^{0}F

	Starts	1st	2nd	3rd	Win & Pl
Career Total (Turf)	6	0	0	0	0
Career Total (AW)	12	0	0	1	265

Going (Turf): Sf: 0-1 GS: 0-0 Gd: 0-1 GF: 0-2 Fm: 0-2
Distance: 5f/6f: 0-11 7f-8f: 0-5 9f-13f: 0-2 14f+: 0-0
Track : LH: 0-13 RH: 0-0 Tight: 0-8 Gall: 0-0
Aids: Bl: 0-11 Vi: 0-0 Tstrap: 0-0
Best Rating: 33 1/01 Wolv 7f slow

Nobelist

109 93

6-y-o b g Bering-Noble Peregrine (Lomond (USA))
C E Brittain Sheikh Rashid Bin Mohammed Al Maktoum

Placings:1/234/61000060-0616 **(3477)**
2001: 7^{0}GF, 10^{6}F, 11^{1}F, 10^{6}GF

	Starts	1st	2nd	3rd	Win & Pl
Career Total (Turf)	16	3	1	1	32194

34 6/01 Ling 1m3f106yG FRM £1960
102 5/00 Rdcr 1m2f B(0-105)H G-S £11066
10/97 MsnL 7f110y GD £7856
Total win prize-money £20882

Going (Turf): Sf: 0-2 **GS: 1-1** Gd: 0-5 GF: 0-4 **Fm: 1-2**
Distance: 5f/6f: 0-0 7f-8f: 0-2 **9f-13f: 2-12** 14f+: 0-0
Track : **LH: 2-8** RH: 0-6 **Tight: 2-5** Gall: 0-7
Aids: Bl: 0-0 **Vi: 1-7** Tstrap: 0-0
Best Rating: 93 5/01 Rdcr 1m2f firm

Nobilissime

90 80

2-y-o b f Halling (USA)-Keswa (King's Lake (USA))
W Jarvis Bassam Freiha

Placings:10 **(4985)**
2001: 6^{1}GF, 6^{0}G

	Starts	1st	2nd	3rd	Win & Pl
Career Total (Turf)	2	1	0	0	11399

80 8/01 NmkJ 6f D G-F £4901
Total win prize-money £4901

Going (Turf): Sf: 0-0 GS: 0-0 Gd: 0-1 **GF: 1-1** Fm: 0-0
Distance: **5f/6f: 1-1** 7f-8f: 0-1 9f-13f: 0-0 14f+: 0-0
Track : LH: 0-0 RH: 0-0 Tight: 0-0 Gall: 0-0
Aids: Bl: 0-0 Vi: 0-0 Tstrap: 0-0
Best Rating: 80 8/01 NmkJ 6f gd-fm

Won at the first time of asking over six furlongs at Newmarket on good to firm, and did not run too badly in an Ascot Sales race.

Noble Academy (USA)

97 78

2-y-o b/br c Royal Academy (USA)-Aristocratique (Cadeaux Genereux)
R Hannon Mrs Toni S Tipper

Placings:02600 **(5689)**
2001: 6^{0}G, 7^{2}G, 7^{6}GF, 6^{0}G, 6^{0}S

	Starts	1st	2nd	3rd	Win & Pl
Career Total (Turf)	5	0	1	0	1096

Going (Turf): Sf: 0-1 GS: 0-0 Gd: 0-3 GF: 0-1 Fm: 0-0
Distance: 5f/6f: 0-2 7f-8f: 0-3 9f-13f: 0-0 14f+: 0-0
Track : LH: 0-0 RH: 0-0 Tight: 0-0 Gall: 0-0
Aids: Bl: 0-0 Vi: 0-0 Tstrap: 0-0
Best Rating: 78 9/01 Newb 7f gd-fm

He has shown plenty of ability in maiden company, but probably needs to find a modest event of that type to get off the mark.

Noble Arc

42(67)

3-y-o b c Noble Patriarch-Time For Joy (Good Times (ITY))
B S Rothwell Peter Bailey

Placings:0-0 **(0328)**
2001: 6^{0}SD

	Starts	1st	2nd	3rd	Win & Pl
Career Total (Turf)	1	0	0	0	
Career Total (AW)	1	0	0	0	

Going (Turf): Sf: 0-1 GS: 0-0 Gd: 0-0 GF: 0-0 Fm: 0-0
Distance: 5f/6f: 0-1 7f-8f: 0-1 9f-13f: 0-0 14f+: 0-0
Track : LH: 0-1 RH: 0-0 Tight: 0-0 Gall: 0-0
Aids: Bl: 0-0 Vi: 0-0 Tstrap: 0-0
Best Rating: 78 9/01 Newb 7f gd-fm

Noble Calling (FR)

100(103) (67)58

4-y-o b c Caller I.D. (USA)-Specificity (USA) (Alleged (USA))
R J Hodges R J Hodges

Placings:0600/3020623224-606104445 **(4550)**
2001: 8^{6}G, 10^{0}GF, 9^{6}GF, 9^{1}GF, 9^{0}G, 10^{4}GF, 11^{4}G, 8^{4}G, 8^{5}GF

	Starts	1st	2nd	3rd	Win & Pl
Career Total (Turf)	20	1	2	2	9163
Career Total (AW)	3	0	2	0	3351

58 7/01 Gdwd 1m1f F(0-65)H G-F £5427
Total win prize-money £5428

Going (Turf): Sf: 0-1 GS: 0-1 Gd: 0-10 **GF: 1-7** Fm: 0-1
Distance: 5f/6f: 0-0 7f-8f: 0-3 **9f-13f: 1-19** 14f+: 0-1
Track : LH: 0-11 **RH: 1-4 Tight: 1-13** Gall: 0-0
Aids: Bl: 0-4 **Vi: 1-11** Tstrap: 0-0
Best Rating: 58 7/01 Wind 1m2f7y gd-fm

Noble Cyrano

100(112) (37)47

6-y-o ch g Generous (IRE)-Miss Bergerac (Bold Lad (IRE))
Jedd O'Keeffe Wetherby Racing Bureau 38

Placings:30/501002/10004000-50001620000 **(5411)**
2001: 9^{5}S, 8^{0}GS, 9^{0}GF, 11^{0}F, 12^{1}GF, 12^{6}G, 14^{2}G, 14^{0}GF, 14^{0}GF, 16^{0}G, 14^{0}SD

	Starts	1st	2nd	3rd	Win & Pl
Career Total (Turf)	21	2	1	1	7132
Career Total (AW)	6	1	1	0	7642

48 6/01 Newc 1m4f93y F G-F £2436
68 1/00 Sthl 1m C(0-90)H STD £7117
58 8/99 Hayd 1m30y E(0-70)H G-S £3018
Total win prize-money £12572

Going (Turf): Sf: 0-3 **GS: 1-3** Gd: 0-6 **GF: 1-8** Fm: 0-1
Distance: 5f/6f: 0-0 7f-8f: 1-8 **9f-13f: 2-14** 14f+: 0-5
Track : **LH: 3-16** RH: 0-8 Tight: 0-7 **Gall: 1-3**
Aids: Bl: 0-0 Vi: 0-0 Tstrap: 0-0
Best Rating: 48 6/01 Newc 1m4f93y gd-fm

Modest handicapper, stays 12 furlongs acts on any ground on turf and has also won on the All-Weather.

Noble Investment

(92) (25)24

7-y-o b g Shirley Heights-Noble Destiny (Dancing Brave (USA))
B J Llewellyn The Ffrancasal Partnership

Placings:0450/0540/3016F0000-0 **(0319)**
2001: 8^{0}SD

	Starts	1st	2nd	3rd	Win & Pl
Career Total (Turf)	9	0	0	0	250
Career Total (AW)	9	1	0	1	2530

44 2/00 Sthl 1m F STD £2002
Total win prize-money £2002

Going (Turf): Sf: 0-2 GS: 0-1 Gd: 0-3 GF: 0-3 Fm: 0-0
Distance: 5f/6f: 0-1 **7f-8f: 1-9** 9f-13f: 0-8 14f+: 0-0
Track : **LH: 1-12** RH: 0-1 Tight: 0-8 Gall: 0-0
Aids: Bl: 0-2 Vi: 0-0 Tstrap: 0-0
Best Rating: 44 2/00 Sthl 1m SD

Noble Locks (IRE)

94(92) (52)30

3-y-o ch g Night Shift (USA)-Imperial Graf (USA) (Blushing John (USA))
K A Ryan Paul J Dixon

Placings:2-250530000000 **(5539)**
2001: 7^{2}SD, 6^{5}SD, 6^{0}SD, 7^{5}S, 6^{3}G, 7^{0}G, 7^{0}G, 7^{0}GF, 7^{0}GF, 6^{0}SD, 7^{0}G, 8^{0}S

	Starts	1st	2nd	3rd	Win & Pl
Career Total (Turf)	8	0	0	1	593
Career Total (AW)	5	0	2	0	1232

Going (Turf): Sf: 0-2 GS: 0-0 Gd: 0-4 GF: 0-2 Fm: 0-0
Distance: 5f/6f: 0-4 7f-8f: 0-9 9f-13f: 0-0 14f+: 0-0
Track : LH: 0-6 RH: 0-0 Tight: 0-1 Gall: 0-0
Aids: Bl: 0-1 Vi: 0-0 Tstrap: 0-1
Best Rating: 64 1/01 Sthl 7f stand

Noble Nick

97(95) (76)**76**
2-y-o b/br c Primo Dominie-Pericardia (Petong)
S P C Woods (M R Channon 2/8) Lucayan Stud

Placings:434202330 **(5340)**
2001: 5^{4}GF, 5^{3}GF, 6^{4}GF, 6^{2}GF, 5^{0}G, 6^{2}GF, 6^{3}SW, 6^{3}G, 6^{0}GS

	Starts	1st	2nd	3rd	Win & Pl
Career Total (Turf)	8	0	2	2	4564
Career Total (AW)	1	0	0	1	402

Going (Turf): Sf: 0-0 GS: 0-1 Gd: 0-2 GF: 0-5 Fm: 0-0
Distance: 5f/6f: 0-8 7f-8f: 0-1 9f-13f: 0-0 14f+: 0-0
Track : LH: 0-1 RH: 0-0 Tight: 0-1 Gall: 0-0
Aids: Bl: 0-0 Vi: 0-0 Tstrap: 0-0
Best Rating: 76 10/01 NmkR 6f good

Probably best at six furlongs, he has made the frame a number of times on turf and on Fibresand. Suited by a sound surface.

Noble Pasao (IRE)

103(95) (75d)**73**
4-y-o b g Alzao (USA)-Belle Passe (Be My Guest (USA))
Andrew Turnell Mrs Claire Hollowood

Placings:000010/**260**03055313300-03612500 **(5230)**
2001: 8^{0}F, 9^{3}GF, 10^{6}F, 8^{1}F, 10^{2}GF, 11^{5}GF, 13^{0}GF, 11^{0}S

	Starts	1st	2nd	3rd	Win & Pl
Career Total (Turf)	25	3	1	5	14775
Career Total (AW)	3	0	1	0	1202

69	7/01	Thsk	1m	E(0-70)H	FRM	£3542
67	7/00	Thsk	1m	E(0-70)H	FRM	£2801
71	9/99	Muss	1m	E(0-75)H	GD	£4396

Total win prize-money £10742

Going (Turf): Sf: 0-1 GS: 0-5 Gd: 1-5 GF: 0-8 **Fm: 2-6**
Distance: 5f/6f: 0-4 **7f-8f: 3-13** 9f-13f: 0-10 14f+: 0-1
Track : **LH: 2-18** RH: 1-5 **Tight: 3-11** Gall: 0-4
Aids: Bl: 0-1 Vi: 0-0 Tstrap: 0-0
Best Rating: 73 9/01 York 1m3f195y gd-fm

A useful handicapper at between a mile and twelve furlongs, he finds his form in the summer. Acts on fast ground and is usually held up these days.

Noble Pursuit

107 **83**
4-y-o b g Pursuit Of Love-Noble Peregrine (Lomond (USA))
T G Mills Mrs Stephanie Merrydew

Placings:412/4041030-0000015543000 **(5608)**
2001: 8^{0}S, 8^{0}S, 7^{0}G, 8^{0}GF, 8^{0}GF, 7^{1}F, 8^{5}GF, 8^{5}GF, 7^{4}GF, 7^{3}GS, 8^{0}S, 8^{0}GS, 7^{0}GS

	Starts	1st	2nd	3rd	Win & Pl
Career Total (Turf)	23	3	1	2	24176

80	6/01	Ling	7f140y	C(0-90)H	FRM	£7637
85	6/00	Ripn	1m	C(0-90)H	G-F	£6987
76	8/99	Sals	6f212y	E	G-S	£3350

Total win prize-money £17976

Going (Turf): Sf: 0-4 **GS: 1-4** Gd: 0-6 **GF: 1-8 Fm: 1-1**
Distance: 5f/6f: 0-0 **7f-8f: 3-18** 9f-13f: 0-5 14f+: 0-0
Track : LH: 0-3 **RH: 1-10 Tight: 1-5** Gall: 0-0
Aids: Bl: 0-0 Vi: 0-0 Tstrap: 0-0
Best Rating: 83 7/01 Gdwd 1m gd-fm

He seemed to lose his way after winning at Ripon last season, but a steady drop in the weights and a return to a more positive ride saw him return to winning form at Lingfield in June, but struggled afterwards. Suited by most types of ground and stays a mile.

Noble View (USA)

86 **72**
2-y-o ch f Distant View (USA)-Proud Lou (USA) (Proud Clarion)
B W Hills K Abdulla

Placings:44 **(3307)**
2001: 5^{4}GF, 6^{4}GS

	Starts	1st	2nd	3rd	Win & Pl
Career Total (Turf)	2	0	0	0	327

Going (Turf): Sf: 0-0 GS: 0-1 Gd: 0-0 GF: 0-1 Fm: 0-0
Distance: 5f/6f: 0-2 7f-8f: 0-0 9f-13f: 0-0 14f+: 0-0
Track : LH: 0-0 RH: 0-0 Tight: 0-0 Gall: 0-0
Aids: Bl: 0-0 Vi: 0-0 Tstrap: 0-0
Best Rating: 72 7/01 Ayr 6f gd-sft

Nod's Nephew

(100) (51)
4-y-o b g Efisio-Nordan Raider (Domynsky)
Miss J A Camacho Brian Nordan

Placings:00/41**040**0100-0500023040 **(5449)**
2001: 7^{0}SD, 7^{5}GF, 7^{0}GF, 7^{0}GF, 6^{0}G, 6^{2}G, 7^{3}G, 7^{0}GF, 7^{4}G, 6^{0}HY, 7^{4}SD

	Starts	1st	2nd	3rd	Win & Pl
Career Total (Turf)	17	2	1	1	7091
Career Total (AW)	4	0	0	0	213

64	8/00	Bevl	7f100y	E	G-F	£2394
63	4/00	Bevl	7f100y	E(0-75)H	HVY	£3224

Total win prize-money £5618

Going (Turf): Sf: 1-3 GS: 0-1 Gd: 0-8 **GF: 1-5** Fm: 0-0
Distance: 5f/6f: 0-5 **7f-8f: 2-15** 9f-13f: 0-1 14f+: 0-0
Track : LH: 0-7 **RH: 2-8** Tight: 0-4 Gall: 0-1
Aids: Bl: 0-0 Vi: 0-0 Tstrap: 0-0
Best Rating: 53 8/01 Catt 7f good

Front runner. Twice a winner over seven and a half furlongs at Beverley in 2000, he made all the running on both occasions. Has won on good to firm and heavy.

Noels Ganador (USA)

(95) (79)
2-y-o b c Our Emblem (USA)-Carolita (USA) (Caro)
Eddie Creighton Noel Cronin

Placings:533 **(4069)**
2001: 5^{5}SD, 6^{3}GF, 6^{3}SD

	Starts	1st	2nd	3rd	Win & Pl
Career Total (Turf)	1	0	0	1	433
Career Total (AW)	2	0	0	1	3630

Going (Turf): Sf: 0-0 GS: 0-0 Gd: 0-0 GF: 0-1 Fm: 0-0
Distance: 5f/6f: 0-2 7f-8f: 0-1 9f-13f: 0-0 14f+: 0-0
Track : LH: 0-2 RH: 0-0 Tight: 0-1 Gall: 0-0
Aids: Bl: 0-0 Vi: 0-0 Tstrap: 0-0
Best Rating: 79 8/01 Wolv 6f stand

Noirie

84(96) (24)**23**
7-y-o br g Warning-Callipoli (USA) (Green Dancer (USA))
M Brittain Miss Debi J Woods

Placings:64/40000050/014060/004000300/230200000-000 **(1174)**
2001: 12^{0}SW, 11^{0}SD, 12^{0}S

	Starts	1st	2nd	3rd	Win & Pl
Career Total (Turf)	33	1	2	2	6473
Career Total (AW)	4	0	0	0	

40	6/98	Pont	1m2f6y	F(0-70)H	HVY	£2237

Total win prize-money £2237

Going (Turf): Sf: 1-10 GS: 0-2 Gd: 0-14 GF: 0-7 Fm: 0-0
Distance: 5f/6f: 0-1 7f-8f: 0-8 **9f-13f: 1-24** 14f+: 0-4
Track : **LH: 1-21** RH: 0-12 Tight: 0-6 Gall: 0-7
Aids: Bl: 0-1 Vi: 0-2 Tstrap: 0-0
Best Rating: 11 1/01 Sthl 1m4f slow

Nominator Lad

(101) (70)**76**
7-y-o b g Nomination-Ankara's Princess (USA) (Ankara (USA))
B A McMahon (R N Bevis 14/3) J D Graham

Placings:02030/45150010/061044521006/001020000/0 0044160600-00P **(3563)**
2001: 8^{0}SD, 8^{0}SD, 9^{P}GF

	Starts	1st	2nd	3rd	Win & Pl
Career Total (Turf)	39	5	3	1	45336
Career Total (AW)	9	1	0	0	4198

76	8/00	Hayd	1m2f120y	E(0-75)H	GD	£3250
82	4/99	Pont	1m4y	D(0-85)H	SFT	£7360
79	9/98	Ayr	1m	C(0-100)H	G-S	£20080
70	6/98	Wolv	1m100y	D(0-85)H	STD	£3460
71	9/97	Hayd	7f30y	D(0-80)H	GD	£3858
72	7/97	Nott	1m54y	E	G-F	£3070

Total win prize-money £41079

Going (Turf): Sf: 1-8 GS: 1-9 **Gd: 2-12** GF: 1-10 Fm: 0-0
Distance: 5f/6f: 0-1 7f-8f: 2-25 **9f-13f: 4-22** 14f+: 0-0
Track : **LH: 6-35** RH: 0-5 **Tight: 1-10** Gall: 0-8
Aids: **Bl: 1-5** Vi: 0-0 Tstrap: 0-0
Best Rating: 55 6/01 Sthl 1m stand

Useful handicapper, effective at eight to ten furlongs. Handles any ground.

Nomore Mr Niceguy

105(98) (79)**63**
7-y-o b h Rambo Dancer (CAN)-Lariston Gale (Pas De Seul)
E J Alston Mrs Carol P McPhail

Placings:024140605**331**/**432**3125326400040/**2**0654031 2400300040**311**/**53**4002401326065200/**0**000020400664 603500**00**-034455624640**0** **(5414)**
2001: 7^{0}GF, 7^{3}GF, 7^{4}GF, 8^{4}GF, 8^{5}F, 8^{5}GS, 7^{6}G, 7^{2}GF, 7^{4}G, 8^{6}S, 6^{4}GF, 7^{0}G, 6^{0}SD

	Starts	1st	2nd	3rd	Win & Pl
Career Total (Turf)	85	3	9	8	79542
Career Total (AW)	16	4	2	4	35379

86	6/99	Ches	6f18y	B(0-100)H	G-F	£9272
94	12/98	Ling	1m	D	STD	£3517
94	11/98	Wolv	7f	C(0-100)H	STD	£8458
90	6/98	Ches	7f2y	C(0-95)H	G-S	£10548
88	3/97	Wolv	7f	C(0-100)H	STD	£5352
84	12/96	Wolv	7f	D(0-85)	STD	£3598
67	7/96	Haml	5f4y		GD	£3225

Total win prize-money £43974

Going (Turf): Sf: 0-10 **GS: 1-15 Gd: 1-31 GF: 1-26** Fm: 0-2
Distance: 5f/6f: 1-19 **7f-8f: 6-75** 9f-13f: 0-7 14f+: 0-0
Track : **LH: 6-61** RH: 0-6 **Tight: 6-43** Gall: 0-7
Aids: Bl: 0-1 Vi: 0-0 Tstrap: 0-0
Best Rating: 70 7/01 Bevl 7f100y gd-fm

Tough and genuine, he has been on a long losing run since winning in June 1999. Effective from six furlongs to a mile, he is ideally suited by a sharp left-handed track. He takes plenty of stoking.

Non Vintage (IRE)

76(39) **23**

10-y-o ch g Shy Groom (USA)-Great Alexandra (Runnett)

M C Chapman Rasen Goes Racing

Placings:02336315/65306034214004/530540200324/00020000/40/06/0/00-0 **(2188)**

2001: 14^{0}GF

	Starts	1st	2nd	3rd	Win & Pl
Career Total (Turf)	44	2	5	6	27382
Career Total (AW)	6	0	0	1	522

69	8/94	Pont	2m1f216y	C	G-F	£4777
80	10/93	Donc	1m	D	GD	£4435

Total win prize-money £9213

Going (Turf): Sf: 0-2 GS: 0-7 **Gd: 1-12 GF: 1-20** Fm: 0-3
Distance: 5f/6f: 0-2 7f-8f: 1-11 9f-13f: 0-20 14f+: 1-17
Track : **LH: 2-37** RH: 0-10 Tight: 0-11 **Gall: 1-16**
Aids: **Bl: 1-12** Vi: 0-0 Tstrap: 0-0
Best Rating: 80 10/93 Donc 1m G

Noon Gun

110(103) (70)**100+**

3-y-o ch c Ashkalani (IRE)-Lady Kris (IRE) (Kris)

W R Muir J Bernstein

Placings:44-10011 **(4383)**

2001: 7^{1}SD, 7^{0}GS, 8^{0}GF, 8^{1}GF, 8^{1}GF

	Starts	1st	2nd	3rd	Win & Pl
Career Total (Turf)	5	2	0	0	14069
Career Total (AW)	2	1	0	0	2464

100	8/01	Sals	1m	C(0-90)	G-F	£7812
88	7/01	Sals	1m	D(0-85)H	G-F	£6032
70	3/01	Sthl	7f	D	STD	£2464

Total win prize-money £16308

Going (Turf): Sf: 0-1 GS: 0-1 Gd: 0-0 **GF: 2-3** Fm: 0-0
Distance: 5f/6f: 0-1 **7f-8f: 3-6** 9f-13f: 0-0 14f+: 0-0
Track : **LH: 1-3** RH: 0-0 Tight: 0-1 Gall: 0-1
Aids: Bl: 0-0 Vi: 0-0 Tstrap: 0-0
Best Rating: 100 8/01 Sals 1m gd-fm

He won a small race on the All-Weather on his return to action this season. Well beaten in hot handicaps in his next two starts, he appreciated the drop in grade to win twice over a mile at Salisbury. Acts on fast ground.

Nooshman (USA)

114 (102)**109**

4-y-o ch g Woodman (USA)-Knoosh (USA) (Storm Bird (CAN))

Saeed Bin Suroor Godolphin

Placings:252/15013202-352223 **(4696)**

2001: 9^{3}FT, 10^{5}FT, 9^{2}GF, 10^{2}GF, 12^{2}GS, 10^{3}GS

	Starts	1st	2nd	3rd	Win & Pl
Career Total (Turf)	15	2	7	2	81028
Career Total (AW)	2	0	0	1	26388

97	7/00	Gdwd	1m1f192y	C(0-95)H	GD	£9262
84	5/00	Thsk	7f	C(0-90)H	GD	£7247

Total win prize-money £16511

Going (Turf): Sf: 0-2 GS: 0-3 **Gd: 2-6** GF: 0-4 Fm: 0-0
Distance: 5f/6f: 0-0 7f-8f: 1-5 9f-13f: 1-12 14f+: 0-0
Track : LH: 1-8 RH: 1-4 **Tight: 2-3** Gall: 0-6
Aids: Bl: 0-0 Vi: 0-0 Tstrap: 0-0
Best Rating: 109 5/01 Gdwd 1m1f192y gd-fm

Runner-up in the Cambridgeshire in 2000 when he also won handicaps over seven furlongs at Thirsk and over ten furlongs at Goodwood. He has just kept missing out in Listed and conditions events since, but is totally genuine. Best on fast ground.

Norcroft Lady

92 **61**

3-y-o ch f Mujtahid (USA)-Polytess (IRE) (Polish Patriot (USA))

N A Callaghan Norcroft Park Stud

Placings:141006-00006 **(4303)**

2001: 8^{0}G, 9^{0}GF, 7^{0}GS, 7^{0}GS, 7^{6}GF

	Starts	1st	2nd	3rd	Win & Pl
Career Total (Turf)	11	2	0	0	7815

84	7/00	Ling	6f	D	GD	£3679
70	6/00	Yarm	6f3y	D	GD	£3493

Total win prize-money £7173

Going (Turf): Sf: 0-0 GS: 0-2 **Gd: 2-4** GF: 0-5 Fm: 0-0
Distance: 5f/6f: 1-2 7f-8f: 1-8 9f-13f: 0-1 14f+: 0-0
Track : LH: 0-1 RH: 0-1 Tight: 0-1 Gall: 0-0
Aids: Bl: 0-0 Vi: 0-0 Tstrap: 0-0
Best Rating: 61 7/01 NmkJ 7f gd-sft

Twice a winner over six furlongs as a juvenile in 2000, she was tried at longer trips this season but does not appear to have trained on.

Nordic Hero (IRE)

(72)

8-y-o b g Nordico (USA)-Postscript (Final Straw)

J Balding Miss Alison J Newby & David V Norman

Placings:364005/000 **(1451)**

2001: 12^{0}SD, 11^{0}SD, 12^{0}SD

	Starts	1st	2nd	3rd	Win & Pl
Career Total (Turf)	1	0	0	0	0
Career Total (AW)	8	0	0	1	357

Going (Turf): Sf: 0-0 GS: 0-1 Gd: 0-0 GF: 0-0 Fm: 0-0
Distance: 5f/6f: 0-0 7f-8f: 0-0 9f-13f: 0-9 14f+: 0-0
Track : LH: 0-8 RH: 0-1 Tight: 0-4 Gall: 0-0
Aids: Bl: 0-0 Vi: 0-0 Tstrap: 0-0

Nordic Sabre

89 **46**

3-y-o b f Sabrehill (USA)-Nordico Princess (Nordico (USA))

Mrs L Stubbs K F F Potatoes Ltd

Placings:614-00000 **(3961)**

2001: 5^{0}GF, 6^{0}GF, 5^{0}GF, 5^{0}GF, 6^{0}G

	Starts	1st	2nd	3rd	Win & Pl
Career Total (Turf)	8	1	0	0	3056

74	8/00	Muss	5f	E	GD	£2795

Total win prize-money £2795

Going (Turf): Sf: 0-0 GS: 0-0 **Gd: 1-3** GF: 0-5 Fm: 0-0
Distance: **5f/6f: 1-7** 7f-8f: 0-1 9f-13f: 0-0 14f+: 0-0
Track : LH: 0-1 RH: 0-0 Tight: 0-1 Gall: 0-0
Aids: Bl: 0-1 Vi: 0-0 Tstrap: 0-0
Best Rating: 59 5/01 Ches 5f16y gd-fm

Norfolk Reed (IRE)

107 **85**

4-y-o b g Thatching-Sawaki (Song)

R Hannon The South-Western Partnership

Placings:1020/45000031000-61514440020 **(5366)**

2001: 7^{6}GS, 7^{1}G, 7^{5}GF, 8^{1}G, 8^{4}GF, 8^{4}GF, 8^{4}GF, 8^{0}GF, 8^{0}GF, 8^{2}S, 8^{0}GS

	Starts	1st	2nd	3rd	Win & Pl
Career Total (Turf)	26	4	2	1	39470

86	6/01	Wind	1m67y	C(0-90)H	GD	£7299
53	5/01	Wwck	7f26y	D(0-80)	GD	£4331
84	9/00	Donc	7f	C(0-90)H	G-F	£7605
69	5/99	Ling	5f	D	G-F	£3114

Total win prize-money £22351

Going (Turf): Sf: 0-2 GS: 0-5 **Gd: 2-5 GF: 2-14** Fm: 0-0
Distance: 5f/6f: 1-6 **7f-8f: 2-18** 9f-13f: 1-2 14f+: 0-0
Track : LH: 1-4 RH: 1-6 **Tight: 1-3** Gall: 0-0
Aids: Bl: 0-1 **Vi: 1-5** Tstrap: 0-0
Best Rating: 86 6/01 Wind 1m67y good

Useful seven furlong/mile handicapper who usually pays his way. In great heart earlier this term, winning at Warwick and Windsor, best on a sound surface.

Norman Conquest (USA)

65

7-y-o ch g Miswaki (USA)-Grand Luxe (CAN) (Sir Ivor)

A Crook B & K Associates

Placings:504/560660/0/00 **(4478)**

2001: 12^{0}S, 16^{0}F

	Starts	1st	2nd	3rd	Win & Pl
Career Total (Turf)	12	0	0	0	219

Going (Turf): Sf: 0-1 GS: 0-2 Gd: 0-5 GF: 0-2 Fm: 0-2
Distance: 5f/6f: 0-0 7f-8f: 0-4 9f-13f: 0-6 14f+: 0-2
Track : LH: 0-3 RH: 0-6 Tight: 0-5 Gall: 0-2
Aids: Bl: 0-0 Vi: 0-1 Tstrap: 0-0

North (IRE)

92(72) (7)**65**

3-y-o br g Mukaddamah (USA)-Flamenco (USA) (Dance Spell (USA))

Miss J A Camacho Fourgreys Partnership

Placings:05 **(0825)**

2001: 11^{0}SD, 8^{5}S

	Starts	1st	2nd	3rd	Win & Pl
Career Total (Turf)	1	0	0	0	0
Career Total (AW)	1	0	0	0	

Going (Turf): Sf: 0-1 GS: 0-0 Gd: 0-0 GF: 0-0 Fm: 0-0
Distance: 5f/6f: 0-0 7f-8f: 0-1 9f-13f: 0-1 14f+: 0-0
Track : LH: 0-1 RH: 0-1 Tight: 0-1 Gall: 0-0
Aids: Bl: 0-0 Vi: 0-0 Tstrap: 0-0
Best Rating: 65 4/01 Ripn 1m soft

North Ardar

(95) (10)**43**

11-y-o b g Ardar-Langwaite (Seaepic (USA))

R Brotherton Roy Brotherton

Placings:5464/312305133142200/55650022315526053/05521122040/11112136144006 60/6065/514166/0055633123000 0246/500003350-460 **(0346)**

2001: 12^{4}SW, 11^{6}SD, 16^{0}SD

	Starts	1st	2nd	3rd	Win & Pl
Career Total (Turf)	55	10	10	9	43016
Career Total (AW)	47	5	2	3	13891

50	6/99	Sthl	1m3f	G(0-112)	STD	£2008
46	2/98	Ling	1m4f	E(0-70)H	STD	£2805
41	1/98	Ling	1m2f	F(0-60)H	STD	£2316
57	9/96	Sthl	1m	G(0-70)H	STD	£2070
60	8/96	Haml	1m65y	G	G-F	£2402
57	7/96	Ripn	1m2f	F	GD	£2706
60	6/96	Rdcr	1m2f	F	FRM	£2826
53	6/96	Pont	1m2f6y	G	G-F	£2469
60	5/96	Catt	1m2f39y	G	GD	£2406
58	7/95	Muss	1m3f32y	D(0-80)H	G-F	£3517
54	6/95	Thsk	1m4f	D(0-80)H	G-F	£4051
60	6/94	Pont	1m2f6y	G	G-F	£2553
62	7/93	Catt	7f	E(0-70)H	G-F	£2950
57	7/93	Catt	7f	D(0-80)H	G-F	£3406
61	4/93	Sthl	7f	E	STD	£2743

Total win prize-money £41232

Going (Turf): Sf: 0-5 GS: 0-5 Gd: 2-13 **GF: 7-26** Fm: 1-6
Distance: 5f/6f: 0-2 7f-8f: 4-33 **9f-13f: 11-66** 14f+: 0-1
Track : **LH: 12-76** RH: 3-17 **Tight: 10-49** Gall: 0-3
Aids: Bl: 0-0 Vi: 0-1 Tstrap: 0-0
Best Rating: 10 1/01 Wolv 1m4f slow

He runs almost exclusively on sand these days, and is only able to make an impact at the very lowest level over middle distances.

	Starts	1st	2nd	3rd	Win & Pl
Career Total (Turf)	22	2	2	1	14569

69 7/99 Sals 1m6f15y E(0-70)H FRM £3306
72 8/96 Bevl 2m35y D GD £3847
Total win prize-money £7153

Going (Turf): Sf: 0-0 GS: 0-1 **Gd: 1-6** GF: 0-12 **Fm: 1-3**
Distance: 5f/6f: 0-0 7f-8f: 0-1 9f-13f: 0-5 **14f+: 2-16**
Track : LH: 0-0 **RH: 2-19 Tight: 2-10** Gall: 0-6
Aids: Bl: 0-1 Vi: 0-0 Tstrap: 0-0
Best Rating: 58 6/01 Asct 2m4f gd-fm

E J Alston The Burlington Partnership

Placings:0 **(0709)**
2001: 5^{0}SD

	Starts	1st	2nd	3rd	Win & Pl
Career Total (Turf)	0	0	0	0	
Career Total (AW)	1	0	0	0	

Going (Turf): Sf: 0-0 GS: 0-0 Gd: 0-0 GF: 0-0 Fm: 0-0
Distance: 5f/6f: 0-1 7f-8f: 0-0 9f-13f: 0-0 14f+: 0-0
Track : LH: 0-0 RH: 0-0 Tight: 0-0 Gall: 0-0
Aids: Bl: 0-0 Vi: 0-0 Tstrap: 0-0
Best Rating: 5 4/01 Sthl 5f stand

North By North (IRE)

97(92) (48)**57**
3-y-o b g Distinctly North (USA)-Winscarlet North (Garland Knight)
M H Tompkins Flint Fairyhouse Partnership

Placings:00-04526045 **(4459)**
2001: 6^{0}GS, 8^{4}F, 8^{5}GF, 7^{2}SD, 7^{6}GS, 7^{0}GS, 7^{4}GF, 7^{5}G

	Starts	1st	2nd	3rd	Win & Pl
Career Total (Turf)	9	0	0	0	279
Career Total (AW)	1	0	1	0	650

Going (Turf): Sf: 0-1 GS: 0-3 Gd: 0-1 GF: 0-3 Fm: 0-1
Distance: 5f/6f: 0-2 7f-8f: 0-6 9f-13f: 0-2 14f+: 0-0
Track : LH: 0-2 RH: 0-1 Tight: 0-0 Gall: 0-0
Aids: Bl: 0-0 Vi: 0-0 Tstrap: 0-0
Best Rating: 57 5/01 Haml 1m65y firm

North Cider Rose (IRE)

76 **35**
2-y-o ch f Goldmark (USA)-Scotia Rose (Tap On Wood)
G M McCourt (M Quinn 20/7) Mrs S G Davies

Placings:0000 **(5530)**
2001: 5^{0}GF, 7^{0}GF, 7^{0}GF, 8^{0}HY

	Starts	1st	2nd	3rd	Win & Pl
Career Total (Turf)	4	0	0	0	

Going (Turf): Sf: 0-1 GS: 0-0 Gd: 0-0 GF: 0-3 Fm: 0-0
Distance: 5f/6f: 0-1 7f-8f: 0-2 9f-13f: 0-1 14f+: 0-0
Track : LH: 0-3 RH: 0-0 Tight: 0-0 Gall: 0-1
Aids: Bl: 0-0 Vi: 0-0 Tstrap: 0-0
Best Rating: 35 7/01 Wwck 7f26y gd-fm

North Of Kala (IRE)

97 (33)**46**
8-y-o b g Distinctly North (USA)-Hi Kala (Kampala)
G L Moore B Lennard

Placings:0/00006/**0500**/13300-130 **(3556)**
2001: 12^{1}GF, 13^{3}GF, 12^{0}GF

	Starts	1st	2nd	3rd	Win & Pl
Career Total (Turf)	15	2	0	3	4423
Career Total (AW)	3	0	0	0	0

42 6/00 Sals 1m4f E(0-70)H G-F £2989
Total win prize-money £2989

Going (Turf): Sf: 0-3 GS: 0-0 Gd: 0-1 **GF: 2-6** Fm: 0-3
Distance: 5f/6f: 0-0 7f-8f: 0-0 **9f-13f: 2-12** 14f+: 0-6
Track : LH: 0-5 **RH: 2-13 Tight: 2-7** Gall: 0-1
Aids: Bl: 0-1 Vi: 0-0 Tstrap: 0-0
Best Rating: 46 7/01 Newb 1m5f61y gd-fm

North Point (IRE)

101(90) (49)**75**
3-y-o b c Definite Article-Friendly Song (Song)
A P Jarvis Ambrose Turnbull

Placings:005-4210 **(2157)**
2001: 8^{4}SD, 9^{2}F, 9^{1}GF, 9^{0}GF

	Starts	1st	2nd	3rd	Win & Pl
Career Total (Turf)	6	1	1	0	5380
Career Total (AW)	1	0	0	0	0

75 6/01 Leic 1m1f218yD(0-80)H G-F £4290
Total win prize-money £4290

Going (Turf): Sf: 0-1 GS: 0-0 Gd: 0-2 **GF: 1-2** Fm: 0-1
Distance: 5f/6f: 0-0 7f-8f: 0-4 **9f-13f: 1-3** 14f+: 0-0
Track : LH: 0-1 **RH: 1-3** Tight: 0-2 Gall: 0-0
Aids: Bl: 0-0 Vi: 0-0 Tstrap: 0-0
Best Rating: 75 6/01 Leic 1m1f218y gd-fm

Northern Danzig

(65) (5)
2-y-o b f Danzig Connection (USA)-Kristiana (Kris)

Northern Desert (IRE)

89 **71+**
2-y-o b c Desert Style (IRE)-Rosie's Guest (IRE) (Be My Guest (USA))
G Wragg Mollers Racing

Placings:22 **(5126)**
2001: 6^{2}GF, 6^{2}HY

	Starts	1st	2nd	3rd	Win & Pl
Career Total (Turf)	2	0	2	0	2441

Going (Turf): Sf: 0-1 GS: 0-0 Gd: 0-0 GF: 0-1 Fm: 0-0
Distance: 5f/6f: 0-2 7f-8f: 0-0 9f-13f: 0-0 14f+: 0-0
Track : LH: 0-0 RH: 0-0 Tight: 0-0 Gall: 0-0
Aids: Bl: 0-0 Vi: 0-0 Tstrap: 0-0
Best Rating: 71 9/01 Ling 6f gd-fm

Northern Echo

94(84) (36)**48**
4-y-o b g Pursuit Of Love-Stop Press (USA) (Sharpen Up)
M Dods The Northern Echo Partnership

Placings:0/00053200620**0**-04030 **(2809)**
2001: 12^{0}S, 14^{4}GF, 17^{0}GF, 13^{3}GF, 10^{0}GF

	Starts	1st	2nd	3rd	Win & Pl
Career Total (Turf)	17	0	2	2	2489
Career Total (AW)	1	0	0	0	

Going (Turf): Sf: 0-4 GS: 0-1 Gd: 0-3 GF: 0-7 Fm: 0-2
Distance: 5f/6f: 0-4 7f-8f: 0-4 9f-13f: 0-7 14f+: 0-3
Track : LH: 0-10 RH: 0-6 Tight: 0-4 Gall: 0-5
Aids: Bl: 0-5 Vi: 0-1 Tstrap: 0-0
Best Rating: 48 5/01 Muss 1m6f gd-fm

Northern Exposure

71 **31**
2-y-o ch f Polar Falcon (USA)-Lucky Round (Auction Ring (USA))
John Berry Dr St John Collier & Mrs Sherry Collier

Placings:0 **(4839)**
2001: 6^{0}G

	Starts	1st	2nd	3rd	Win & Pl
Career Total (Turf)	1	0	0	0	

Going (Turf): Sf: 0-0 GS: 0-0 Gd: 0-1 GF: 0-0 Fm: 0-0
Distance: 5f/6f: 0-0 7f-8f: 0-1 9f-13f: 0-0 14f+: 0-0
Track : LH: 0-0 RH: 0-0 Tight: 0-0 Gall: 0-0
Aids: Bl: 0-0 Vi: 0-0 Tstrap: 0-0
Best Rating: 31 9/01 Nott 6f15y good

Northern Fleet

97
8-y-o b g Slip Anchor-Kamkova (USA) (Northern Dancer)
Mark Campion Mrs J Howell

Placings:4/234125/4000/5100/4500-050 **(2305)**
2001: 11^{0}F, 11^{5}GF, 20^{0}GF

Starts 1st 2nd 3rd Win & Pl

Northern Games

92 **70**
2-y-o b c Mind Games-Northern Sal (Aragon)
A Berry R E Robinson

Placings:0566 **(4731)**
2001: 6^{0}S, 6^{5}G, 7^{6}G, 7^{6}F

	Starts	1st	2nd	3rd	Win & Pl
Career Total (Turf)	4	0	0	0	0

Going (Turf): Sf: 0-1 GS: 0-0 Gd: 0-2 GF: 0-0 Fm: 0-1
Distance: 5f/6f: 0-2 7f-8f: 0-2 9f-13f: 0-0 14f+: 0-0
Track : LH: 0-1 RH: 0-0 Tight: 0-1 Gall: 0-0
Aids: Bl: 0-0 Vi: 0-0 Tstrap: 0-0
Best Rating: 70 9/01 Chep 7f16y firm

Northern Gold

(93) (42+)
3-y-o b g Goldmark (USA)-Scottish Royal (IRE) (Night Shift (USA))
J G Given The Klondike Club

Placings:1 **(1088)**
2001: 9^{1}SD

	Starts	1st	2nd	3rd	Win & Pl
Career Total (Turf)	0	0	0	0	
Career Total (AW)	1	1	0	0	1876

42 5/01 Wolv 1m1f79y G STD £1876
Total win prize-money £1876

Going (Turf): Sf: 0-0 GS: 0-0 Gd: 0-0 GF: 0-0 Fm: 0-0
Distance: 5f/6f: 0-0 7f-8f: 0-0 **9f-13f: 1-1** 14f+: 0-0
Track : **LH: 1-1** RH: 0-0 **Tight: 1-1** Gall: 0-0
Aids: Bl: 0-0 Vi: 0-0 Tstrap: 0-0
Best Rating: 42 5/01 Wolv 1m1f79y stand

First foal of an unraced mare. Won on his only start in a seller on the All-Weather at Wolverhampton. Stays nine furlongs, should get further.

Northern Motto

92(90) (47)**43**
8-y-o b g Mtoto-Soulful (FR) (Zino)
J S Goldie Alf Chadwick

Placings:000/04000420014/10044310600/3001351410 200/405311042440/50003334436002**0**6-0 **(4858)**
2001: 15^{0}GF

	Starts	1st	2nd	3rd	Win & Pl
Career Total (Turf)	60	7	4	7	53471
Career Total (AW)	7	1	0	1	3442

54 7/99 Ches 1m7f195yD(0-80)H G-F £14850
53 6/99 Muss 2m E(0-75)H GD £3420
60 7/98 Ches 1m7f195yD(0-80)H G-F £7025
58 5/98 Muss 2m F(0-60)H G-S £2900
59 4/98 Muss 2m D(0-75)H G-S £3652
55 6/97 Donc 1m4f D(0-80)H GD £6004
57 2/97 Wolv 1m4f E(0-70)H STD £2814
54 11/96 Muss 1m7f16y E(0-70)H G-S £3598
Total win prize-money £44264

Going (Turf): Sf: 0-4 **GS: 3-14** Gd: 2-16 GF: 2-20 Fm: 0-6
Distance: 5f/6f: 0-0 7f-8f: 0-3 9f-13f: 2-15 **14f+: 6-49**
Track : LH: 4-34 RH: 4-32 **Tight: 7-42** Gall: 1-8
Aids: Bl: 0-1 Vi: 0-2 Tstrap: 0-0
Best Rating: 24 9/01 Catt 1m7f177y gd-fm

Northern Nymph

90 **67**

2-y-o b g Makbul-Needwood Sprite (Joshua)
R Hollinshead Tim Leadbeater

Placings:60 **(4416)**
2001: 6^{6}G, 7^{0}G

	Starts	1st	2nd	3rd	Win & Pl
Career Total (Turf)	2	0	0	0	0

Going (Turf): Sf: 0-0 GS: 0-0 Gd: 0-2 GF: 0-0 Fm: 0-0
Distance: 5f/6f: 0-1 7f-8f: 0-1 9f-13f: 0-0 14f+: 0-0
Track : LH: 0-1 RH: 0-0 Tight: 0-1 Gall: 0-0
Aids: Bl: 0-0 Vi: 0-0 Tstrap: 0-0
Best Rating: 67 9/01 Ches 7f2y good

Northern Raider (IRE)

91 **28**

3-y-o b g College Chapel-Pepper And Salt (IRE) (Double Schwartz)
Andrew Turnell Dr John Hollowood

Placings:32000 **(4896)**
2001: 11^{3}G, 10^{2}GS, 11^{0}G, 16^{0}GF, 9^{0}GS

	Starts	1st	2nd	3rd	Win & Pl
Career Total (Turf)	5	0	1	1	1786

Going (Turf): Sf: 0-0 GS: 0-2 Gd: 0-2 GF: 0-1 Fm: 0-0
Distance: 5f/6f: 0-0 7f-8f: 0-0 9f-13f: 0-4 14f+: 0-1
Track : LH: 0-2 RH: 0-3 Tight: 0-2 Gall: 0-0
Aids: Bl: 0-2 Vi: 0-0 Tstrap: 0-0
Best Rating: 28 9/01 Wwck 2m39y gd-fm

Northern Svengali (IRE)

102(98) (56)**64d**

5-y-o b g Distinctly North (USA)-Trilby's Dream (IRE) (Mansooj)
T D Barron Timothy Cox

Placings:020222201015353/0444/304000600405030 2150-600001031500000004000336 **(5639)**
2001: 5^{6}S, 5^{0}GS, 5^{0}GS, 6^{0}GF, 5^{0}GF, 5^{1}F, 5^{0}GF, 5^{3}F, 5^{1}GF, 5^{5}F, 5^{0}GF, 5^{0}F, 5^{0}G, 5^{0}GF, 5^{0}GF, 5^{4}G, 5^{0}G, 5^{0}GS, 5^{0}SD, 6^{3}SD, 6^{3}SD, 5^{6}G, 6^{3}SD

	Starts	1st	2nd	3rd	Win & Pl
Career Total (Turf)	56	5	7	2	29891
Career Total (AW)	8	0	0	5	2070

62	6/01	Haml	5f4y	F(0-60)H	G-F	£3965
59	6/01	Newc	5f	E(0-70)H	FRM	£3332
66	8/00	Thsk	5f	E(0-70)H	G-F	£3685
82	10/98	Catt	5f	E(0-85)H	G-S	£3174
80	9/98	Catt	5f212y	D	G-F	£3704

Total win prize-money £17862

Going (Turf): Sf: 0-4 GS: 1-8 Gd: 0-16 **GF: 3-21** Fm: 1-7
Distance: 5f/6f: 5-58 7f-8f: 0-6 9f-13f: 0-0 14f+: 0-0
Track : LH: 1-15 RH: 0-1 **Tight: 1-9** Gall: 0-1
Aids: Bl: 0-2 Vi: 0-0 Tstrap: 0-0
Best Rating: 64 6/01 Newc 5f firm

A fair sprint handicapper, he scored twice this term over five furlongs on fast ground, but looked held by the Handicapper subsequently. Acts on Fibresand.

Northern Tara (IRE)

101 **83**

2-y-o b f Fayruz-Mitsubishi Style (Try My Best (USA))
J J Quinn Tara Leisure

Placings:230126300 **(5378)**
2001: 5^{2}S, 5^{3}GF, 5^{0}GF, 5^{1}GF, 5^{2}G, 6^{6}G, 5^{3}GF, 5^{0}G, 5^{0}S

	Starts	1st	2nd	3rd	Win & Pl
Career Total (Turf)	9	1	2	2	9710

83	7/01	Ripn	5f	D	G-F	£4225

Total win prize-money £4225

Going (Turf): Sf: 0-2 GS: 0-0 Gd: 0-3 **GF: 1-4** Fm: 0-0
Distance: 5f/6f: 1-9 7f-8f: 0-0 9f-13f: 0-0 14f+: 0-0
Track : LH: 0-2 RH: 0-0 Tight: 0-1 Gall: 0-0
Aids: Bl: 0-0 Vi: 0-0 Tstrap: 0-0
Best Rating: 83 8/01 Ripn 5f gd-fm

She ran with credit in some very hot races in her early starts, but had to fight hard to break her maiden at Ripon in July. Held since.

Northern Times (USA)

95(96) (41)**54**

4-y-o ch g Cahill Road (USA)-Northern Nation (USA) (Northrop (USA))
R Brotherton Ms Gerardine P O'Reilly

Placings:0/510100000006-63432100 **(5046)**
2001: 8^{6}SW, 14^{3}SW, 14^{4}SD, 12^{3}SD, 11^{2}SD, 10^{1}SD, 8^{0}SD, 11^{0}SD

	Starts	1st	2nd	3rd	Win & Pl
Career Total (Turf)	6	1	0	0	1926
Career Total (AW)	15	2	1	2	4919

33	4/01	Ling	1m2f	G	STD	£1960
64	4/00	Ling	7f	G(0-60)H	G-S	£1926
54	2/00	Sthl	7f	G	STD	£1842

Total win prize-money £5728

Going (Turf): Sf: 0-1 **GS: 1-4** Gd: 0-0 GF: 0-1 Fm: 0-0
Distance: 5f/6f: 0-2 **7f-8f: 2-6** 9f-13f: 1-11 14f+: 0-2
Track : LH: 2-16 RH: 0-1 **Tight: 1-8** Gall: 0-0
Aids: Bl: 1-6 Vi: 0-3 Tstrap: 0-0
Best Rating: 45 2/01 Sthl 1m4f stand

Northern Union (CAN)

90 (90)**82**

10-y-o b g Alwasmi (USA)-Loving Cup (USA) (Big Spruce (USA))
A Parker Mr & Mrs Raymond Anderson Green

Placings:00/11/01B/12/0 **(2355)**
2001: 22^{0}GF

	Starts	1st	2nd	3rd	Win & Pl
Career Total (Turf)	8	3	0	0	12030
Career Total (AW)	2	1	1	0	6921

83	2/96	Wolv	1m4f	C(0-90)H	STD	£5329
82	6/95	Wind	1m2f7y	D(0-80)H	GD	£4500
82	4/94	Wind	1m3f135y	D(0-80)H	GD	£3655
79	4/94	Leic	1m8y	D	HVY	£3874

Total win prize-money £17360

Going (Turf): Sf: 1-3 GS: 0-0 **Gd: 2-2** GF: 0-3 Fm: 0-0
Distance: 5f/6f: 0-0 7f-8f: 0-2 **9f-13f: 4-7** 14f+: 0-1
Track : LH: 1-3 RH: 0-4 **Tight: 3-5** Gall: 0-3
Aids: Bl: 0-0 Vi: 0-0 Tstrap: 0-0
Best Rating: 54 6/01 Asct 2m6f34y gd-fm

Northfields Dancer (IRE)

95 **87**

3-y-o ch c Dr Devious (IRE)-Heartland (Northfields (USA))
K F O'Brien (R Hannon 21/6) John Michael

Placings:022022125-0500021000 **(5431a)**
2001: 8^{0}S, 10^{5}S, 7^{0}GS, 8^{0}GF, 8^{0}GF, 8^{2}G, 8^{1}G, 7^{0}G, 8^{0}Y, 10^{0}S

	Starts	1st	2nd	3rd	Win & Pl
Career Total (Turf)	19	2	6	0	26830

87	8/01	Tral	1m	(0-85)H	GD	£6210
76	9/00	Gdwd	1m	D	HVY	£3250

Total win prize-money £9460

Going (Turf): Sf: 1-6 GS: 0-1 **Gd: 1-4** GF: 0-7 Fm: 0-0
Distance: 5f/6f: 0-0 **7f-8f: 2-16** 9f-13f: 0-3 14f+: 0-0
Track : LH: 0-4 **RH: 1-5** Tight: 0-1 Gall: 0-3
Aids: Bl: 1-5 Vi: 0-0 Tstrap: 0-0
Best Rating: 87 8/01 Tral 1m good

Useful handicapper. Now racing in Ireland.

Northgate (IRE)

107(92) (27)**46**

5-y-o b g Thatching-Tender Time (Tender King)
M Brittain Mel Brittain

Placings:0600/044045200/05421420060-50300303500 **(4884)**
2001: 8^{5}GF, 8^{0}F, 7^{3}GF, 7^{0}GF, 7^{0}F, 8^{3}GF, 7^{0}GF, 7^{3}G, 7^{5}GF, 8^{0}GF, 8^{0}GF

	Starts	1st	2nd	3rd	Win & Pl
Career Total (Turf)	35	1	3	3	9560
Career Total (AW)	1	0	0	0	

48	6/00	Bevl	7f100y	E(0-75)H	G-F	£3818

Total win prize-money £3819

Going (Turf): Sf: 0-2 GS: 0-3 Gd: 0-9 **GF: 1-16** Fm: 0-5
Distance: 5f/6f: 0-2 **7f-8f: 1-27** 9f-13f: 0-7 14f+: 0-0
Track : LH: 0-8 **RH: 1-13** Tight: 0-11 Gall: 0-2
Aids: Bl: 1-28 Vi: 0-0 Tstrap: 0-0
Best Rating: 48 7/01 Ripn 1m gd-fm

Northside Lodge (IRE)

104 **57**

3-y-o b g Grand Lodge (USA)-Alongside (Slip Anchor)
P W Harris The Grandees

Placings:06600100 **(5632)**
2001: 9^{0}GS, 10^{6}S, 10^{6}GF, 12^{0}GF, 12^{0}GF, 10^{1}GF, 10^{0}G, 10^{0}G

	Starts	1st	2nd	3rd	Win & Pl
Career Total (Turf)	8	1	0	0	4030

57	9/01	Rdcr	1m2f	E(0-70)H	G-F	£4030

Total win prize-money £4030

Going (Turf): Sf: 0-1 GS: 0-1 Gd: 0-2 **GF: 1-4** Fm: 0-0
Distance: 5f/6f: 0-0 7f-8f: 0-0 **9f-13f: 1-8** 14f+: 0-0
Track : LH: 1-5 RH: 0-3 **Tight: 1-5** Gall: 0-1
Aids: Bl: 1-3 Vi: 0-0 Tstrap: 0-0
Best Rating: 62 6/01 Sand 1m2f7y soft

Left his previous form behind when landing a Redcar handicap.

Norton (IRE)

109 **88**

4-y-o ch c Barathea (IRE)-Primrose Valley (Mill Reef (USA))
T G Mills T G Mills

Placings:501/030-006154460 **(5607)**
2001: 10^{0}GF, 10^{0}S, 8^{6}GF, 8^{1}G, 7^{5}HY, 7^{4}GF, 7^{4}S, 8^{6}GS, 8^{0}GS

	Starts	1st	2nd	3rd	Win & Pl
Career Total (Turf)	15	2	0	1	16865

87	8/01	Hayd	1m30y	C(0-90)H	GD	£6699
84	11/99	Rdcr	7f	D	G-S	£3452

Total win prize-money £10152

Going (Turf): Sf: 0-3 **GS: 1-6 Gd: 1-2** GF: 0-4 Fm: 0-0
Distance: 5f/6f: 0-0 7f-8f: 1-9 9f-13f: 1-6 14f+: 0-0
Track : LH: 1-4 RH: 0-4 Tight: 0-1 Gall: 0-3
Aids: Bl: 0-0 Vi: 0-0 Tstrap: 0-0
Best Rating: 88 9/01 Asct 7f soft

A half-brother to Turtle Valley, he has not lived up to initial expectations, but returned to winning ways in a Haydock handicap in August, and ran some good races afterwards without winning. Suited by a mile and some cut in the ground.

Norway (USA)

97 **82**

3-y-o ch c Storm Cat (USA)-Weekend Surprise (USA) (Secretariat (USA))
A P O'Brien Michael Tabor

Placings:3-62500 **(2689a)**
2001: 7^{6}S, 8^{2}GF, 8^{5}G, 12^{0}GF, 10^{0}Y

	Starts	1st	2nd	3rd	Win & Pl
Career Total (Turf)	6	0	1	1	2475

Going (Turf): Sf: 0-1 GS: 0-0 Gd: 0-1 GF: 0-2 Fm: 0-0
Distance: 5f/6f: 0-0 7f-8f: 0-3 9f-13f: 0-2 14f+: 0-0
Track : LH: 0-0 RH: 0-1 Tight: 0-0 Gall: 0-1
Aids: Bl: 0-0 Vi: 0-0 Tstrap: 0-0
Best Rating: 82 5/01 Curr 1m good

Norwood Origo

92 75
2-y-o ch c Elmaamul (USA)-Miller's Creek (USA) (Star De Naskra (USA))
M L W Bell Norwood Partition Systems Ltd

Placings:02 (2554)
2001: 6^{0}GF, 6^{2}GF

	Starts	1st	2nd	3rd	Win & Pl
Career Total (Turf)	2	0	1	0	713

Going (Turf): Sf: 0-0 GS: 0-0 Gd: 0-0 GF: 0-2 Fm: 0-0
Distance: 5f/6f: 0-1 7f-8f: 0-1 9f-13f: 0-0 14f+: 0-0
Track : LH: 0-0 RH: 0-1 Tight: 0-1 Gall: 0-0
Aids: Bl: 0-0 Vi: 0-0 Tstrap: 0-0
Best Rating: 75 6/01 Folk 6f189y gd-fm

Nose The Trade

111(109) (90+)92
3-y-o b g Cyrano De Bergerac-Iolite (Forzando)
J A Osborne Martyn Booth

Placings:514-4111550010 (5607)
2001: 7^{4}SD, 8^{1}SD, 8^{1}SD, 8^{1}SD, 10^{5}SD, 9^{5}GF, 8^{0}GF, 7^{0}GF, 7^{1}GS, 8^{0}GS

	Starts	1st	2nd	3rd	Win & Pl
Career Total (Turf)	8	2	0	0	13920
Career Total (AW)	5	3	0	0	18897

92 10/01 NmkR 7f C(0-100)H G-S £7296
90 2/01 Wolv 1m100y C(0-100)H STD £8053
81 2/01 Wolv 1m100y D(0-85)H STD £3766
78 1/01 Wolv 1m100y D(0-85)H STD £5434
76 10/00 NmkR 7f E SFT £6097
Total win prize-money £30648

Going (Turf): Sf: 1-3 GS: 1-2 Gd: 0-0 GF: 0-3 Fm: 0-0
Distance: 5f/6f: 0-1 7f-8f: 2-7 9f-13f: 3-5 14f+: 0-0
Track : LH: 3-5 RH: 0-2 Tight: 3-6 Gall: 0-0
Aids: Bl: 0-1 Vi: 0-0 Tstrap: 0-0
Best Rating: 92 10/01 NmkR 7f gd-sft

He was switched to the All-Weather this year and notched up a hat-trick when stepped up to a mile at Wolverhampton. Rather lost his way on turf but returned from a break to win in good style at Newmarket. Best when held up for a late run. Showed temperament at Sandown when blinkered for the first time.

Nosey Native

101(86) (36)43
8-y-o b g Cyrano De Bergerac-Native Flair (Be My Native (USA))
Mrs Lydia Pearce (J Pearce 5/2) Jeff Pearce

Placings:5231/50506306624F105/0003010004640366/456360051521565/53000/0032262411-00000046 (4281)
2001: 12^{0}SD, 16^{0}SD, 14^{0}HY, 10^{0}F, 12^{0}GF, 13^{0}GF, 14^{4}GS, 14^{6}G

	Starts	1st	2nd	3rd	Win & Pl
Career Total (Turf)	56	7	6	4	28104
Career Total (AW)	17	0	0	3	1050

47 8/00 Catt 1m3f214yF(0-75)H G-S £2268
47 8/00 Yarm 1m6f17y F(0-75)H GD £2236
46 8/98 Catt 1m3f214yF(0-80)H G-F £2242
41 6/98 Ripn 1m4f60y E(0-70)H SFT £2814
58 6/97 Ripn 1m4f60y E(0-70)H GD £2908
71 10/96 Hayd 1m2f120yD(0-80)H SFT £4212
82 10/95 Yarm 1m3y D(0-85) G-F £4110
Total win prize-money £20793

Going (Turf): Sf: 2-8 GS: 1-6 Gd: 2-13 GF: 2-26 Fm: 0-3
Distance: 5f/6f: 0-0 7f-8f: 0-3 9f-13f: 6-48 14f+: 1-22
Track : LH: 4-54 RH: 2-16 Tight: 5-29 Gall: 0-13
Aids: Bl: 0-0 Vi: 0-5 Tstrap: 0-0
Best Rating: 43 8/01 Yarm 1m6f17y good

Nosy Be

97(94) (68)68
3-y-o b g Cyrano De Bergerac-Blossomville (Petong)
P J Makin Ten Of Hearts

Placings:5323-400 (4016)
2001: 6^{4}SD, 7^{0}GF, 7^{0}G

	Starts	1st	2nd	3rd	Win & Pl
Career Total (Turf)	5	0	1	1	1118
Career Total (AW)	2	0	0	1	251

Going (Turf): Sf: 0-0 GS: 0-0 Gd: 0-3 GF: 0-1 Fm: 0-0
Distance: 5f/6f: 0-4 7f-8f: 0-2 9f-13f: 0-0 14f+: 0-0
Track : LH: 0-2 RH: 0-1 Tight: 0-2 Gall: 0-1
Aids: Bl: 0-0 Vi: 0-0 Tstrap: 0-0
Best Rating: 67 8/01 Kemp 7f gd-fm

Has shown ability in maidens on turf and sand.

Not Fade Away

86 23
3-y-o b g Ezzoud (IRE)-Green Flower (USA) (Fappiano (USA))
R M Beckett The Hon W E Beckett

Placings:0-00 (5294)
2001: 10^{0}HY, 11^{0}S

	Starts	1st	2nd	3rd	Win & Pl
Career Total (Turf)	3	0	0	0	

Going (Turf): Sf: 0-3 GS: 0-0 Gd: 0-0 GF: 0-0 Fm: 0-0
Distance: 5f/6f: 0-0 7f-8f: 0-0 9f-13f: 0-3 14f+: 0-0
Track : LH: 0-1 RH: 0-1 Tight: 0-1 Gall: 0-0
Aids: Bl: 0-0 Vi: 0-0 Tstrap: 0-0
Best Rating: 23 10/01 Leic 1m3f183y soft

Not Just A Dream

94 51
3-y-o b f Mujadil (USA)-Red Cloud (IRE) (Taufan (USA))
A Berry Norman Jackson

Placings:430460-460000 (4159)
2001: 6^{4}G, 7^{6}GF, 7^{0}GF, 6^{0}GF, 6^{0}G, 6^{0}GF

	Starts	1st	2nd	3rd	Win & Pl
Career Total (Turf)	12	0	0	1	830

Going (Turf): Sf: 0-2 GS: 0-0 Gd: 0-2 GF: 0-7 Fm: 0-1
Distance: 5f/6f: 0-7 7f-8f: 0-5 9f-13f: 0-0 14f+: 0-0
Track : LH: 0-3 RH: 0-2 Tight: 0-2 Gall: 0-0
Aids: Bl: 0-0 Vi: 0-0 Tstrap: 0-0
Best Rating: 55 5/01 Ripn 6f good

Not Proven

85 60
2-y-o br c Mark Of Esteem (IRE)-Free City (USA) (Danzig (USA))
J G Fitzgerald Marquesa De Moratalla

Placings:004 (5527)
2001: 7^{0}G, 8^{0}GS, 8^{4}HY

	Starts	1st	2nd	3rd	Win & Pl
Career Total (Turf)	3	0	0	0	305

Going (Turf): Sf: 0-1 GS: 0-1 Gd: 0-1 GF: 0-0 Fm: 0-0
Distance: 5f/6f: 0-0 7f-8f: 0-2 9f-13f: 0-1 14f+: 0-0
Track : LH: 0-2 RH: 0-1 Tight: 0-0 Gall: 0-1
Aids: Bl: 0-0 Vi: 0-0 Tstrap: 0-0
Best Rating: 60 10/01 Nott 1m54y heavy

Notation (IRE)

94(100) (30?)17
7-y-o b g Arazi (USA)-Grace Note (FR) (Top Ville)
D W Chapman J M Chapman

Placings:0000000101/44322000463000/00040000/00040000400501140003006-000605062400000050 (4105)
2001: 14^{0}SD, 16^{0}SD, 12^{0}SD, 16^{6}SD, 16^{0}SD, 8^{5}SD, 11^{0}SD, 12^{6}SD, 16^{2}GF, 11^{4}SD, 11^{0}G, 11^{0}F, 12^{0}GF, 13^{0}GF, 16^{0}GF, 12^{0}GS, 16^{5}GS, 12^{0}S

	Starts	1st	2nd	3rd	Win & Pl
Career Total (Turf)	32	2	1	1	7968
Career Total (AW)	43	2	2	2	6390

28 8/00 Bevl 1m3f216yE(0-75)H G-F £3835
32 8/00 Haml 1m4f17y F(0-60)H SFT £2408
51 12/97 Sthl 1m6f F(0-65)H STD £2294
43 11/97 Sthl 1m6f F(0-60)H STD £1944
Total win prize-money £10481

Going (Turf): Sf: 1-5 GS: 0-7 Gd: 0-3 GF: 1-12 Fm: 0-3
Distance: 5f/6f: 0-0 7f-8f: 0-2 9f-13f: 2-22 14f+: 2-49
Track : LH: 2-48 RH: 2-23 Tight: 2-35 Gall: 0-0
Aids: Bl: 0-24 Vi: 0-0 Tstrap: 0-0
Best Rating: 30 5/01 Sthl 1m3f stand

Notecard

105 80+
3-y-o b c Zafonic (USA)-Lead Note (USA) (Nijinsky (CAN))
B W Hills K Abdulla

Placings:160 (4662)
2001: 8^{1}GF, 8^{6}G, 10^{0}GF

	Starts	1st	2nd	3rd	Win & Pl
Career Total (Turf)	3	1	0	0	4613

80 7/01 Donc 1m D G-F £4426
Total win prize-money £4427

Going (Turf): Sf: 0-0 GS: 0-0 Gd: 0-1 GF: 1-2 Fm: 0-0
Distance: 5f/6f: 0-0 7f-8f: 1-1 9f-13f: 0-2 14f+: 0-0
Track : LH: 0-2 RH: 0-0 Tight: 0-1 Gall: 0-1
Aids: Bl: 0-0 Vi: 0-0 Tstrap: 0-0
Best Rating: 80 7/01 Donc 1m gd-fm

Unraced at two, her dam is a winning half-sister to Rainbow Quest and she made a winning debut at Doncaster in July, but failed to shine in better company afterwards. Sure to improve.

Nothing Daunted

105 93
4-y-o ch c Selkirk (USA)-Khubza (Green Desert (USA))
E A L Dunlop Ahmed Buhaleeba

Placings:62132/30-20000 (5391)
2001: 7^{2}S, 7^{0}G, 8^{0}GF, 7^{0}G, 7^{0}GS

	Starts	1st	2nd	3rd	Win & Pl
Career Total (Turf)	12	1	3	2	14828

85 8/99 Gdwd 7f D GD £4440
Total win prize-money £4440

Going (Turf): Sf: 0-3 GS: 0-3 Gd: 1-4 GF: 0-2 Fm: 0-0
Distance: 5f/6f: 0-3 7f-8f: 1-9 9f-13f: 0-0 14f+: 0-0
Track : LH: 0-1 RH: 1-3 Tight: 0-0 Gall: 0-0
Aids: Bl: 0-0 Vi: 0-1 Tstrap: 0-0
Best Rating: 99 4/01 NmkR 7f soft

Decent handicapper on his day who lost his way in 2001. Effective at six to eight furlongs. Appreciates cut.

Notional (IRE)

6
5-y-o b m Lucky Guest-Sportin' Notion (USA) (Sportin' Life (USA))
J L Spearing (A Sadik 15/9) A Sadik

Placings:5/4624233000/00 (5463)
2001: 8^{0}GS, 11^{0}G

	Starts	1st	2nd	3rd	Win & Pl
Career Total (Turf)	11	0	2	2	3052
Career Total (AW)	2	0	0	0	

Going (Turf): Sf: 0-0 GS: 0-1 Gd: 0-3 GF: 0-6 Fm: 0-0
Distance: 5f/6f: 0-0 7f-8f: 0-2 9f-13f: 0-11 14f+: 0-0
Track : LH: 0-6 RH: 0-6 Tight: 0-3 Gall: 0-0
Aids: Bl: 0-1 Vi: 0-0 Tstrap: 0-2
Best Rating: 6 10/01 Leic 1m9y gd-sft

Nouf

106(80) (40)**74**

5-y-o b m Efisio-Miss Witch (High Line)
K A Ryan Mrs N L Spence

Placings:104/00206600512050-0015130 (4828)
2001: 8^{0}G, 7^{0}F, 8^{1}GF, 8^{5}G, 8^{1}GF, 9^{3}G, 10^{0}G

	Starts	1st	2nd	3rd	Win & Pl
Career Total (Turf)	23	4	2	1	27093
Career Total (AW)	1	0	0	0	

74 8/01 Rdcr 1m D(0-85)H G-F £5625
72 6/01 Hayd 1m30y C(0-95)H G-F £7312
76 9/00 Hayd 1m30y D(0-85)H HVY £5031
93 3/99 Donc 7f D G-S £4396
Total win prize-money £22367

Going (Turf): Sf: 1-4 GS: 1-3 Gd: 0-11 **GF: 2-4** Fm: 0-1
Distance: 5f/6f: 0-0 7f-8f: 2-10 9f-13f: 2-14 14f+: 0-0
Track : **LH: 2-9** RH: 0-3 Tight: 0-5 Gall: 0-3
Aids: Bl: 0-0 Vi: 0-0 Tstrap: 0-0
Best Rating: 74 9/01 Haml 1m1f36y good

She is a fair handicapper over a mile. Likes Haydock. Acts on fast ground and stays ten furlongs.

Noukari (IRE)

106(105) (60)**64**

8-y-o b g Darshaan-Noufiyla (Top Ville)
P D Evans J E Abbey

Placings:65/202**213061**5/**1225534433**5243522301042 2
163114501**311142/0544532**140102005-**40400**35035 (1764)
2001: 12^{4}SD, 12^{0}SD, 13^{4}SD, 12^{0}SW, 11^{0}SD, 16^{3}GF, 12^{5}GF, 13^{0}GF, 12^{3}GF, 13^{5}GF

	Starts	1st	2nd	3rd	Win & Pl
Career Total (Turf)	41	6	8	6	40067
Career Total (AW)	38	7	5	6	23851

78 5/00 Ches 1m2f75y C(0-95)H GD £12246
75 3/00 Catt 1m5f175yD(0-80)H GD £4309
79 12/99 Ling 1m4f D(0-85)H STD £3837
76 11/99 Ling 1m4f G(0-70)H STD £1982
72 11/99 Ling 1m4f G(0-80)H STD £1873
69 10/99 Ling 1m4f G(0-65) STD £2075
69 8/99 Pont 1m4f8y F(0-65) GD £2154
68 8/99 Catt 1m3f214yF(0-75)H G-F £2269
63 7/99 NmkJ 1m2f E(0-75)H G-F £4045
45 6/99 Ches 1m2f75y E G-F £3551
66 1/99 Ling 1m5f F(0-65)H STD £2107
63 12/98 Ling 1m5f G(0-80)H STD £1737
61 11/98 Sthl 1m4f G(0-65)H STD £1563
Total win prize-money £43755

Going (Turf): Sf: 0-3 GS: 0-4 **Gd: 3-9 GF: 3-20** Fm: 0-2
Distance: 5f/6f: 0-0 7f-8f: 0-1 **9f-13f: 12-67** 14f+: 1-11
Track : **LH: 12-69** RH: 1-9 **Tight: 10-49** Gall: 1-7
Aids: Bl: 0-0 Vi: 0-4 Tstrap: 0-0
Best Rating: 64 5/01 Donc 1m4f gd-fm

Multiple winner, most effective over a mile and a half on Equitrack. Likes a sharp track on turf.

Nova Zembla

(55)

2-y-o b f Young Ern-Candarela (Damister (USA))
W G M Turner Ian Murray Tough

Placings:0 (0604)
2001: 5^{0}SD

	Starts	1st	2nd	3rd	Win & Pl
Career Total (Turf)	0	0	0	0	
Career Total (AW)	1	0	0	0	

Going (Turf): Sf: 0-0 GS: 0-0 Gd: 0-0 GF: 0-0 Fm: 0-0
Distance: 5f/6f: 0-1 7f-8f: 0-0 9f-13f: 0-0 14f+: 0-0
Track : LH: 0-0 RH: 0-0 Tight: 0-0 Gall: 0-0
Aids: Bl: 0-0 Vi: 0-0 Tstrap: 0-0

Novak

77 **58**

2-y-o b c Revoque (IRE)-Most Uppitty (Absalom)
B J Meehan T G Holdcroft

Placings:000 (5343)
2001: 8^{0}GF, 7^{0}GS, 6^{0}GS

	Starts	1st	2nd	3rd	Win & Pl
Career Total (Turf)	3	0	0	0	

Going (Turf): Sf: 0-0 GS: 0-2 Gd: 0-0 GF: 0-1 Fm: 0-0
Distance: 5f/6f: 0-1 7f-8f: 0-2 9f-13f: 0-0 14f+: 0-0
Track : LH: 0-0 RH: 0-1 Tight: 0-0 Gall: 0-0
Aids: Bl: 0-0 Vi: 0-0 Tstrap: 0-0
Best Rating: 58 10/01 NmkR 7f gd-sft

Noverre (USA)

117(34) (115)**125**

3-y-o b c Rahy (USA)-Danseur Fabuleux (USA) (Northern Dancer)
Saeed Bin Suroor Godolphin

Placings:1113120-2021320 (5575a)
2001: 8^{2}FT, 8^{0}G, 8^{2}G, 8^{1}GF, 8^{3}GS, 8^{2}S, 8^{0}F

	Starts	1st	2nd	3rd	Win & Pl
Career Total (Turf)	12	5	3	2	484563
Career Total (AW)	2	0	1	0	33333

125 8/01 Gdwd 1m A G-F £159500
113 9/00 Donc 7f A G-F £60000
108 7/00 NmkJ 6f A GD £20300
6/00 MsnL 5f110y GD £13449
5/00 Chan 5f SFT £8646
Total win prize-money £261895

Going (Turf): Sf: 0-1 GS: 0-3 Gd: 1-3 **GF: 2-2** Fm: 0-1
Distance: 5f/6f: 1-2 **7f-8f: 2-9** 9f-13f: 0-1 14f+: 0-0
Track : LH: 0-2 **RH: 1-3** Tight: 0-0 Gall: 0-2
Aids: Bl: 0-0 Vi: 0-0 **Tstrap: 1-3**
Best Rating: 125 8/01 Gdwd 1m gd-fm

Closely related to Arazi, he was a precocious juvenile, winner of the July Stakes and the Champagne Stakes. Runner-up in the UAE 2000 Guineas at Nad Al Sheba on his reappearance, he put up a gutsy performance to beat Vahorimix by a head in the Poule d'Essai des Poulains at Longchamp in May, but was later disqualified after testing positive to a banned substance. Did nothing wrong when second in the St James's Palace Stakes and ran out a most decisive winner of the Sussex Stakes at Goodwood. Beaten by a slow pace in France next time, he had a pacemaker in the Queen Elizabeth II Stakes but gave him too much of a head-start on the soft ground. He may have had excuses for a below-par effort in the Breeders' Cup Mile on very fast ground. He is a very tough individual who is suited by good/fast ground and a strong pace. He reportedly stays in training in 2002.

Now Is The Hour

(100) (41)**34**

5-y-o ch g Timeless Times (USA)-Macs Maharanee (Indian King (USA))
P S Felgate John S Martin

Placings:004060/4000060/**662003**6560615-50000 (2644)
2001: 8^{5}SD, 7^{0}SD, 7^{0}SD, 7^{0}SD, 6^{0}SD

	Starts	1st	2nd	3rd	Win & Pl
Career Total (Turf)	15	0	0	1	546
Career Total (AW)	16	1	1	0	2617

40 12/00 Wolv 6f G STD £1841
Total win prize-money £1841

Going (Turf): Sf: 0-1 GS: 0-0 Gd: 0-5 GF: 0-7 Fm: 0-2
Distance: **5f/6f: 1-23** 7f-8f: 0-7 9f-13f: 0-1 14f+: 0-0
Track : **LH: 1-18** RH: 0-0 **Tight: 1-11** Gall: 0-0
Aids: Bl: 0-1 Vi: 0-0 Tstrap: 0-0
Best Rating: 41 3/01 Wolv 6f stand

Now Look Here

112 **106**

5-y-o b g Reprimand-Where's Carol (Anfield)
B A McMahon S L Edwards

Placings:634/1043003033/23334402005024-10300002 (5494)
2001: 6^{1}S, 6^{0}GS, 5^{3}G, 6^{0}GF, 7^{0}GF, 6^{0}G, 7^{0}GS, 6^{2}HY

	Starts	1st	2nd	3rd	Win & Pl
Career Total (Turf)	35	2	4	9	62100

105 3/01 Donc 6f A SFT £15873
83 4/99 Hayd 7f30y D SFT £3598
Total win prize-money £19472

Going (Turf): Sf: 2-10 GS: 0-7 Gd: 0-7 GF: 0-10 Fm: 0-1
Distance: 5f/6f: 1-24 7f-8f: 1-11 9f-13f: 0-0 14f+: 0-0
Track : **LH: 1-5** RH: 0-0 Tight: 0-0 Gall: 0-2
Aids: Bl: 0-1 Vi: 0-0 Tstrap: 0-0
Best Rating: 106 5/01 York 6f gd-fm

A Pattern-class gelding, he is effective at distances between five and seven furlongs. Seems suited by a flat track, appreciates soft ground and goes particularly well fresh having gained his two wins, on his seasonal reappearance.

Nowell House

107(85) (20)**87**

5-y-o ch g Polar Falcon (USA)-Langtry Lady (Pas De Seul)
M W Easterby Bernard Bargh & John Walsh

Placings:0330000/04031211/000001104-0215006330 (5693)
2001: 11^{0}SD, 13^{2}S, 12^{1}S, 12^{5}S, 11^{0}F, 13^{0}G, 14^{6}HY, 12^{3}GS, 12^{3}HY, 12^{0}S

	Starts	1st	2nd	3rd	Win & Pl
Career Total (Turf)	33	6	2	5	37321
Career Total (AW)	1	0	0	0	

88 4/01 NmkR 1m4f C(0-95)H SFT £7618
77 9/00 Rdcr 1m2f D(0-80)H SFT £5573
71 9/00 Catt 1m3f214yD(0-80)H SFT £4621
63 10/99 Rdcr 1m2f E(0-70)H GD £4583
64 10/99 Pont 1m4f8y F(0-60)H SFT £2249
55 9/99 Bevl 1m3f216yE(0-70)H GD £3174
Total win prize-money £27821

Going (Turf): Sf: 4-15 GS: 0-4 Gd: 2-9 GF: 0-3 Fm: 0-2
Distance: 5f/6f: 0-7 7f-8f: 0-3 **9f-13f: 6-21** 14f+: 0-3
Track : **LH: 4-19** RH: 2-8 **Tight: 4-8** Gall: 1-11
Aids: Bl: 0-0 Vi: 0-1 Tstrap: 0-0
Best Rating: 88 4/01 NmkR 1m4f soft

Effective between ten and 12 furlongs, although yet to conclusively prove he gets further, he usually runs his best races in the autumn and relishes testing conditions.

Nowt But Trouble (IRE)

85(77) (25)**60d**

3-y-o ch g Midhish-Shinadeosee (IRE) (Adonijah)
D Nicholls Stableinsidercom

Placings:63500-00000 (2635)

2001: 6^{0}SD, 6^{0}SD, 6^{0}GF, 6^{0}F, 5^{0}F

	Starts	1st	2nd	3rd	Win & Pl
Career Total (Turf)	8	0	0	1	404
Career Total (AW)	2	0	0	0	

Going (Turf): Sf: 0-0 GS: 0-1 Gd: 0-0 GF: 0-2 Fm: 0-5
Distance: 5f/6f: 0-8 7f-8f: 0-2 9f-13f: 0-0 14f+: 0-0
Track : LH: 0-3 RH: 0-0 Tight: 0-1 Gall: 0-0
Aids: Bl: 0-1 Vi: 0-0 Tstrap: 0-0
Best Rating: 32 6/01 Ches 6f18y gd-fm

Nowt Flash (IRE)

90(96) (35)**32**

4-y-o ch g Petardia-Mantlepiece (IRE) (Common Grounds)

B S Rothwell Brian Rothwell

Placings:600602/010061052250040400000-000000 **(3855)**

2001: 8^{0}SD, 8^{0}GF, 6^{0}G, 8^{0}F, 7^{0}GS, 7^{0}GS

	Starts	1st	2nd	3rd	Win & Pl
Career Total (Turf)	18	0	2	0	2653
Career Total (AW)	14	2	1	0	4455

66 2/00 Sthl 7f G STD £1825
68 1/00 Sthl 6f F(0-60) STD £2111
Total win prize-money £3937

Going (Turf): Sf: 0-3 GS: 0-3 Gd: 0-4 GF: 0-6 Fm: 0-1
Distance: 5f/6f: 1-12 7f-8f: 1-15 9f-13f: 0-4 14f+: 0-0
Track : LH: 2-21 RH: 0-1 Tight: 0-6 Gall: 0-2
Aids: Bl: 0-1 Vi: 0-1 Tstrap: 0-0
Best Rating: 32 7/01 Rdcr 1m firm

Nu To Me

83 **60d**

2-y-o b f So Factual (USA)-Mubadara (IRE) (Lahib (USA))

J R Weymes John Weymes Racing

Placings:640000 **(4615)**

2001: 6^{6}GF, 7^{4}GF, 6^{0}GF, 7^{0}G, 7^{0}GF, 6^{0}F

	Starts	1st	2nd	3rd	Win & Pl
Career Total (Turf)	6	0	0	0	0

Going (Turf): Sf: 0-0 GS: 0-0 Gd: 0-1 GF: 0-4 Fm: 0-1
Distance: 5f/6f: 0-3 7f-8f: 0-3 9f-13f: 0-0 14f+: 0-0
Track : LH: 0-2 RH: 0-0 Tight: 0-0 Gall: 0-0
Aids: Bl: 0-0 Vi: 0-0 Tstrap: 0-0
Best Rating: 60 6/01 Muss 7f30y gd-fm

Nuclear Debate (USA)

118 (123)**121**

6-y-o b g Geiger Counter (USA)-I'm An Issue (USA) (Cox's Ridge (USA))

J E Hammond J R Chester

Placings:622305/321510024/2014133120/61110-2430210 **(5244a)**

2001: 6^{2}FT, 6^{4}FT, 5^{3}GF, 5^{0}G, 5^{2}G, 6^{1}HY, 5^{0}HO

	Starts	1st	2nd	3rd	Win & Pl
Career Total (Turf)	35	9	7	5	447372
Career Total (AW)	2	0	1	0	73953

121 9/01 Hayd 6f A HVY £87000
121 8/00 York 5f A GD £101500
118 6/00 Asct 5f A G-F £81000
110 6/00 Chan 5f G-S £28818
96 8/99 Deau 5f VS £15070
6/99 MsnL 5f GD £15070
97 6/98 Newc 5f B(0-105)H GD £17775
88 5/98 Thsk 6f D GD £3210
Total win prize-money £349443

Going (Turf): Sf: 1-4 GS: 2-5 Gd: 3-12 GF: 1-9 Fm: 0-0
Distance: 5f/6f: 8-35 7f-8f: 0-0 9f-13f: 0-0 14f+: 0-0
Track : LH: 0-1 RH: 1-2 Tight: 0-0 Gall: 0-1
Aids: Bl: 0-0 Vi: 0-0 Tstrap: 0-0
Best Rating: 123 3/01 Ndas 6f fast

A useful sprint handicapper when trained by Lynda Ramsden, he showed his wellbeing with a game victory in a Group Two at Chantilly in June 2000 before beating Agnes World in the King's Stand at Ascot. Particularly impressive when winning the Nunthorpe to complete the hat-trick, he looked the best sprinter around last summer. He finished second to Mozart in the Nunthorpe this season before producing a devastating turn of foot to win the Stanley Leisure Sprint Cup on soft ground. Suited by a stiff five furlongs, his style of racing means he does not always get the best of runs. Sold for 180,000 gns to join Darrell Vienna in USA.

Nucleon Count (IRE)

92(58) **55**

5-y-o b g Nucleon (USA)-Clare's Hope (IRE) (Erin's Hope)

J G Given (M D Hammond 20/1) The G-Guck Group

Placings:06000 **(2890)**

2001: 11^{0}SD, 8^{6}GF, 7^{0}GF, 9^{0}G, 6^{0}GF

	Starts	1st	2nd	3rd	Win & Pl
Career Total (Turf)	4	0	0	0	0
Career Total (AW)	1	0	0	0	

Going (Turf): Sf: 0-0 GS: 0-0 Gd: 0-1 GF: 0-3 Fm: 0-0
Distance: 5f/6f: 0-1 7f-8f: 0-2 9f-13f: 0-2 14f+: 0-0
Track : LH: 0-5 RH: 0-0 Tight: 0-1 Gall: 0-0
Aids: Bl: 0-0 Vi: 0-0 Tstrap: 0-0
Best Rating: 55 5/01 Thsk 1m gd-fm

Nugget (IRE)

83(87) (68)**52**

3-y-o b g Goldmark (USA)-Folly Vision (IRE) (Vision (USA))

P Mitchell C F Ransom

Placings:05-00006 **(2648)**

2001: 8^{0}SD, 8^{0}G, 10^{0}GF, 8^{0}GF, 12^{6}SD

	Starts	1st	2nd	3rd	Win & Pl
Career Total (Turf)	4	0	0	0	
Career Total (AW)	3	0	0	0	0

Going (Turf): Sf: 0-0 GS: 0-1 Gd: 0-1 GF: 0-2 Fm: 0-0
Distance: 5f/6f: 0-0 7f-8f: 0-3 9f-13f: 0-4 14f+: 0-0
Track : LH: 0-3 RH: 0-2 Tight: 0-3 Gall: 0-0
Aids: Bl: 0-0 Vi: 0-0 Tstrap: 0-0
Best Rating: 54 3/01 Ling 1m stand

Numerate

93(99) (52)**69**

3-y-o b f Bishop Of Cashel-Half A Dozen (USA) (Saratoga Six (USA))

M Wigham (M L W Bell 3/7) Cable Media Consultancy Ltd

Placings:3100-406335 **(5613)**

2001: 7^{4}GS, 7^{0}SD, 8^{6}GF, 9^{3}GS, 10^{3}HY, 9^{5}SD, 8^{6}SD

	Starts	1st	2nd	3rd	Win & Pl
Career Total (Turf)	8	1	0	3	4520
Career Total (AW)	2	0	0	0	0

65 5/00 Rdcr 6f E G-S £2990
Total win prize-money £2990

Going (Turf): Sf: 0-3 GS: 1-3 Gd: 0-1 GF: 0-1 Fm: 0-0
Distance: 5f/6f: 1-1 7f-8f: 0-5 9f-13f: 0-4 14f+: 0-0
Track : LH: 0-2 RH: 0-2 Tight: 0-3 Gall: 0-0
Aids: Bl: 0-0 Vi: 0-0 Tstrap: 0-0
Best Rating: 69 4/01 NmkR 7f gd-sft

Made all to win on easy ground in the spring of 2000, but was absent for four months and ran badly on her return on softer ground, and she has since been dropped down to sellers without success.

Nutmeg (IRE)

100(89) (30)**41**

4-y-o ch f Lake Coniston (IRE)-Overdue Reaction (Be My Guest (USA))

M H Tompkins Mystic Meg Limited

Placings:000045/40066000-064400 **(4621)**

2001: 8^{0}SD, 7^{6}GF, 7^{4}GF, 6^{4}G, 6^{0}G, 6^{0}F

	Starts	1st	2nd	3rd	Win & Pl
Career Total (Turf)	17	0	0	0	233
Career Total (AW)	3	0	0	0	

Going (Turf): Sf: 0-2 GS: 0-3 Gd: 0-5 GF: 0-5 Fm: 0-2
Distance: 5f/6f: 0-6 7f-8f: 0-11 9f-13f: 0-3 14f+: 0-0
Track : LH: 0-6 RH: 0-4 Tight: 0-3 Gall: 0-1
Aids: Bl: 0-1 Vi: 0-0 Tstrap: 0-0
Best Rating: 41 8/01 Folk 6f good

Nutwood

95 **63**

3-y-o br c Charnwood Forest (IRE)-Ma Pavlova (USA) (Irish River (FR))

R Charlton D J Deer

Placings:400 **(4958)**

2001: 8^{4}GF, 11^{0}GF, 9^{0}GS

	Starts	1st	2nd	3rd	Win & Pl
Career Total (Turf)	3	0	0	0	282

Going (Turf): Sf: 0-0 GS: 0-1 Gd: 0-0 GF: 0-2 Fm: 0-0
Distance: 5f/6f: 0-0 7f-8f: 0-1 9f-13f: 0-2 14f+: 0-0
Track : LH: 0-1 RH: 0-1 Tight: 0-2 Gall: 0-0
Aids: Bl: 0-0 Vi: 0-0 Tstrap: 0-0
Best Rating: 63 8/01 Sals 1m gd-fm

Nysaean (IRE)

100 **84**

2-y-o b c Sadler's Wells (USA)-Irish Arms (FR) (Irish River (FR))

R Hannon Jeffen Racing

Placings:3 **(5604)**

2001: 7^{3}GS

	Starts	1st	2nd	3rd	Win & Pl
Career Total (Turf)	1	0	0	1	674

Going (Turf): Sf: 0-0 GS: 0-1 Gd: 0-0 GF: 0-0 Fm: 0-0
Distance: 5f/6f: 0-0 7f-8f: 0-1 9f-13f: 0-0 14f+: 0-0
Track : LH: 0-0 RH: 0-0 Tight: 0-0 Gall: 0-0
Aids: Bl: 0-0 Vi: 0-0 Tstrap: 0-0
Best Rating: 84 11/01 NmkR 7f gd-sft

A FF6m yearling, made a promising debut and will appreciate middle distances in 2001.

Nzame (IRE)

104 **71**

3-y-o b c Darshaan-Dawnsio (IRE) (Tate Gallery (USA))

J L Dunlop Lady Clague

Placings:50-201443334 **(5525)**

2001: 8^{2}HY, 9^{0}GF, 11^{1}G, 14^{4}GF, 12^{4}GF, 10^{3}GF, 12^{3}GF, 11^{3}S, 11^{4}HY

	Starts	1st	2nd	3rd	Win & Pl
Career Total (Turf)	11	1	1	3	9623

76 6/01 Sand 1m3f91y E(0-75)H GD £4582
Total win prize-money £4583

Going (Turf): Sf: 0-3 GS: 0-0 Gd: 1-3 GF: 0-5 Fm: 0-0
Distance: 5f/6f: 0-0 7f-8f: 0-2 9f-13f: 1-8 14f+: 0-1
Track : LH: 0-3 RH: 1-6 Tight: 0-5 Gall: 0-2
Aids: Bl: 0-0 Vi: 0-4 Tstrap: 0-0
Best Rating: 76 6/01 Sand 1m3f91y good

Appreciated the step up to eleven furlongs when scoring in handicap company in June, although she has been well held since. Seems best on a sound surface, and is effective over middle distances.

O B Comfort

101(89) (40)**68d**
3-y-o b g College Chapel-Crystal Magic (Mazilier (USA))
Mrs J R Ramsden Mrs J R Ramsden

Placings:60014000000 **(5392)**
2001: 5^{6}S, 7^{0}G, 6^{0}GF, 6^{1}F, 6^{4}GF, 6^{0}GF, 6^{0}GF, 7^{0}G, 6^{0}G, 6^{0}G, 6^{0}SD

	Starts	1st	2nd	3rd	Win & Pl
Career Total (Turf)	10	1	0	0	2805
Career Total (AW)	1	0	0	0	

63 6/01 Newc 6f F(0-60) FRM £2464
Total win prize-money £2464

Going (Turf): Sf: 0-1 GS: 0-0 Gd: 0-4 GF: 0-4 **Fm: 1-1**
Distance: **5f/6f: 1-9** 7f-8f: 0-2 9f-13f: 0-0 14f+: 0-0
Track : LH: 0-3 RH: 0-0 Tight: 0-2 Gall: 0-0
Aids: Bl: 0-0 Vi: 0-0 Tstrap: 0-0
Best Rating: 68 6/01 Donc 6f gd-fm

Unraced as a juvenile, won a weak maiden at the fourth attempt, and has performed with credit in all-aged handicaps since. Suited by six furlongs and fast ground on turf.

O I Bandi

70 **46**
2-y-o ch c Spectrum (IRE)-Nottash (IRE) (Royal Academy (USA))
J R Fanshawe Lord Vestey

Placings:00 **(3960)**
2001: 6^{0}GF, 6^{0}G

	Starts	1st	2nd	3rd	Win & Pl
Career Total (Turf)	2	0	0	0	

Going (Turf): Sf: 0-0 GS: 0-0 Gd: 0-1 GF: 0-1 Fm: 0-0
Distance: 5f/6f: 0-0 7f-8f: 0-2 9f-13f: 0-0 14f+: 0-0
Track : LH: 0-0 RH: 0-0 Tight: 0-0 Gall: 0-0
Aids: Bl: 0-0 Vi: 0-0 Tstrap: 0-0
Best Rating: 46 8/01 Yarm 6f3y good

Oakley Joy

(82) (43)
3-y-o ch f Beveled (USA)-Lillicara (FR) (Caracolero (USA))
R Hannon Brian C Oakley

Placings:00-0 **(0185)**
2001: 7^{0}SD

	Starts	1st	2nd	3rd	Win & Pl
Career Total (Turf)	0	0	0	0	
Career Total (AW)	3	0	0	0	

Going (Turf): Sf: 0-0 GS: 0-0 Gd: 0-0 GF: 0-0 Fm: 0-0
Distance: 5f/6f: 0-1 7f-8f: 0-2 9f-13f: 0-0 14f+: 0-0
Track : LH: 0-3 RH: 0-0 Tight: 0-3 Gall: 0-0
Aids: Bl: 0-0 Vi: 0-0 Tstrap: 0-0

Oakley Rambo

94 **80**
2-y-o br c Muhtarram (USA)-Westminster Waltz (Dance In Time (CAN))
R Hannon Brian C Oakley

Placings:62210 **(5099)**
2001: 6^{6}GF, 6^{2}GF, 7^{2}HY, 7^{1}F, 6^{0}GS

	Starts	1st	2nd	3rd	Win & Pl
Career Total (Turf)	5	1	2	0	4814

80 9/01 Chep 7f16y F FRM £2366
Total win prize-money £2366

Going (Turf): Sf: 0-1 GS: 0-1 Gd: 0-0 GF: 0-2 **Fm: 1-1**
Distance: 5f/6f: 0-1 **7f-8f: 1-4** 9f-13f: 0-0 14f+: 0-0
Track : LH: 0-1 RH: 0-0 Tight: 0-0 Gall: 0-0
Aids: Bl: 0-0 Vi: 0-0 Tstrap: 0-0
Best Rating: 80 9/01 Chep 7f16y firm

A half-brother to several winners at eight to ten furlongs. Got off the mark on fast ground at Chepstow in a maiden auction event in September over seven furlongs.

Oakwell Ace

102(89) (26)**50**
5-y-o b m Clantime-Fardella (ITY) (Molvedo)
J Balding J A Bower

Placings:0100000030/500525045-**0**60124505240 **(4618)**
2001: 7^{0}SD, 7^{6}SD, 7^{0}SD, 6^{1}G, 6^{2}F, 5^{4}G, 6^{5}GF, 5^{0}G, 6^{5}F, 6^{2}GS, 5^{4}GF, 6^{0}F

	Starts	1st	2nd	3rd	Win & Pl
Career Total (Turf)	27	2	3	1	9953
Career Total (AW)	4	0	0	0	0

46 5/01 Donc 6f E GD £2973
59 6/99 Wwck 6f168y F HVY £2521
Total win prize-money £5496

Going (Turf): Sf: 1-6 GS: 0-3 **Gd: 1-10** GF: 0-5 Fm: 0-3
Distance: 5f/6f: 1-10 7f-8f: 1-14 9f-13f: 0-7 14f+: 0-0
Track : **LH: 1-13** RH: 0-4 Tight: 0-3 Gall: 0-0
Aids: Bl: 0-0 Vi: 0-2 Tstrap: 0-0
Best Rating: 50 8/01 Catt 5f212y gd-fm

Oare Kite

103(105) (39)**51**
6-y-o b m Batshoof-Portvasco (Sharpo)
P S Felgate P S Felgate

Placings:663/000050320210/060502641400366/35424 6320100005-**0362004340004**20361 **(4897)**
2001: 8^{0}SW, 6^{3}SD, 6^{6}SD, 6^{2}SD, 7^{0}SD, 6^{0}SD, 5^{4}G, 6^{3}SD, 7^{4}GF, 5^{0}G, 6^{0}GF, 6^{0}SD, 6^{4}GF, 5^{2}F, 5^{0}G, 6^{3}GF, 7^{6}G, 5^{1}GS

	Starts	1st	2nd	3rd	Win & Pl
Career Total (Turf)	44	4	4	4	17474
Career Total (AW)	19	0	3	4	4094

51 9/01 Leic 5f2y D(0-80)H G-S £4745
48 6/00 Leic 5f218y E(0-75)H G-F £3068
48 8/99 Leic 7f9y F G-F £2452
62 10/98 Leic 7f9y F G-S £2400
Total win prize-money £12666

Going (Turf): Sf: 0-5 **GS: 2-7** Gd: 0-8 **GF: 2-20** Fm: 0-3
Distance: 5f/6f: 2-23 7f-8f: 2-35 9f-13f: 0-4 14f+: 0-0
Track : LH: 0-30 RH: 0-2 Tight: 0-10 Gall: 0-2
Aids: Bl: 2-32 Vi: 2-18 Tstrap: 0-0
Best Rating: 51 9/01 Leic 5f2y gd-sft

Oare Pintail

91(84) (3)**59**
4-y-o b f Distant Relative-Oare Sparrow (Night Shift (USA))
R M Beckett Hard Times Club

Placings:6060/0040-00 **(3010)**
2001: 5^{0}SD, 5^{0}GF

	Starts	1st	2nd	3rd	Win & Pl
Career Total (Turf)	9	0	0	0	218
Career Total (AW)	1	0	0	0	

Going (Turf): Sf: 0-2 GS: 0-0 Gd: 0-4 GF: 0-3 Fm: 0-0
Distance: 5f/6f: 0-5 7f-8f: 0-5 9f-13f: 0-0 14f+: 0-0
Track : LH: 0-3 RH: 0-0 Tight: 0-1 Gall: 0-1
Aids: Bl: 0-0 Vi: 0-0 Tstrap: 0-1
Best Rating: 26 7/01 Ling 5f gd-fm

Oases

97 **99+**
2-y-o ch g Zilzal (USA)-Markievicz (IRE) (Doyoun)
B J Meehan Gallagher Equine Ltd

Placings:1 **(5491)**
2001: 6^{1}HY

	Starts	1st	2nd	3rd	Win & Pl
Career Total (Turf)	1	1	0	0	5486

99 10/01 Newb 6f8y D HVY £5486
Total win prize-money £5486

Going (Turf): Sf: 1-1 GS: 0-0 Gd: 0-0 GF: 0-0 Fm: 0-0
Distance: 5f/6f: 0-0 **7f-8f: 1-1** 9f-13f: 0-0 14f+: 0-0
Track : LH: 0-0 RH: 0-0 Tight: 0-0 Gall: 0-0
Aids: Bl: 0-0 Vi: 0-0 Tstrap: 0-0
Best Rating: 99 10/01 Newb 6f8y heavy

Made a winning debut in awful ground at Newbury in October.

Obee Good

83 **17**
3-y-o b g Zambrano-Tout De Val (Tout Ensemble)
W G M Turner Mrs Carolyn Price

Placings:0000 **(4009)**
2001: 10^{0}GF, 10^{0}GF, 11^{0}GF, 11^{0}G

	Starts	1st	2nd	3rd	Win & Pl
Career Total (Turf)	4	0	0	0	

Going (Turf): Sf: 0-0 GS: 0-0 Gd: 0-1 GF: 0-3 Fm: 0-0
Distance: 5f/6f: 0-0 7f-8f: 0-0 9f-13f: 0-4 14f+: 0-0
Track : LH: 0-3 RH: 0-0 Tight: 0-3 Gall: 0-0
Aids: Bl: 0-0 Vi: 0-0 Tstrap: 0-0
Best Rating: 17 6/01 Wwck 1m2f188y gd-fm

Observatory (USA)

120 **128**
4-y-o ch h Distant View (USA)-Stellaria (USA) (Roberto (USA))
J H M Gosden K Abdulla

Placings:141/21121-14 **(2303)**
2001: 9^{1}G, 10^{4}GF

	Starts	1st	2nd	3rd	Win & Pl
Career Total (Turf)	10	6	2	0	369145

123 5/01 Lonc 1m1f55y GD £48497
128 9/00 Asct 1m A G-S £200100
119 8/00 Gdwd 7f A GD £30000
115 6/00 Asct 7f A G-F £42000
91 10/99 Yarm 6f3y C G-F £5933
82 6/99 Yarm 6f3y D GD £4386
Total win prize-money £330916

Going (Turf): Sf: 0-0 GS: 1-1 **Gd: 3-4** GF: 2-5 Fm: 0-0
Distance: 5f/6f: 0-0 **7f-8f: 5-8** 9f-13f: 1-2 14f+: 0-0
Track : LH: 0-0 **RH: 2-4** Tight: 0-0 **Gall: 1-2**
Aids: Bl: 0-0 Vi: 0-0 Tstrap: 0-0
Best Rating: 124 6/01 Asct 1m2f gd-fm

High class miler, beat Giant's Causeway in the Queen Elizabeth II Stakes at Ascot in 2000. Had earlier landed Jersey Stakes and run second to Medicean in Celebration Mile. Best on fast ground, he made a winning reappearance in the Prix d'Ispahan at Longchamp, but injured his pelvis at Royal Ascot next time and had to be retired.

Occam (IRE)

101(89) (30)**38**
7-y-o ch g Sharp Victor (USA)-Monterana (Sallust)
A Bailey Sandybrow Stables Ltd

Placings:4/0440/050/0040100 **(5448)**
2001: 6^{0}G, 8^{0}S, 10^{4}G, 9^{0}G, 11^{1}S, 15^{0}GS, 10^{0}HY, 14^{4}SD

	Starts	1st	2nd	3rd	Win & Pl
Career Total (Turf)	14	1	0	0	2651
Career Total (AW)	1	0	0	0	

38 10/01 Brig 1m3f196yF(0-70)H SFT £2373
Total win prize-money £2373

Going (Turf): Sf: 1-4 GS: 0-2 Gd: 0-5 GF: 0-3 Fm: 0-0
Distance: 5f/6f: 0-1 7f-8f: 0-1 **9f-13f: 1-12** 14f+: 0-1

Track : LH: 1-10 RH: 0-1 Tight: 0-3 Gall: 0-1
Aids: Bl: 0-0 Vi: 0-0 Tstrap: 0-0
Best Rating: 38 10/01 Brig 1m3f196y soft

Only modest, but received a good ride when winning a 12-furlong amateur riders' maiden handicap on easy ground at Brighton in October 2001.

Ocean Avenue (IRE)

83 **58**

2-y-o b c Dolphin Street (FR)-Trinity Hall (Hallgate)
C A Horgan A Kinghorn

Placings:60 **(5468)**
2001: 8^{6}G, 7^{0}S

	Starts	1st	2nd	3rd	Win & Pl
Career Total (Turf)	2	0	0	0	0

Going (Turf): Sf: 0-1 GS: 0-0 Gd: 0-1 GF: 0-0 Fm: 0-0
Distance: 5f/6f: 0-0 7f-8f: 0-2 9f-13f: 0-0 14f+: 0-0
Track : LH: 0-1 RH: 0-1 Tight: 0-0 Gall: 0-0
Aids: Bl: 0-0 Vi: 0-0 Tstrap: 0-0
Best Rating: 58 10/01 Brig 7f214y soft

Ocean Drive (IRE)

98 **44**

5-y-o b/br g Dolphin Street (FR)-Blonde Goddess (IRE) (Godswalk (USA))
Miss L A Perratt Sutherland-Hay

Placings:364/0605034145460030/05654342245424005 2-0404 **(1405)**
2001: 10^{0}S, 8^{4}GS, 9^{0}GF, 13^{4}G

	Starts	1st	2nd	3rd	Win & Pl
Career Total (Turf)	41	1	4	4	10059

59	6/99	Haml	1m4f17y	E(0-70)		GD	£2621

Total win prize-money £2621

Going (Turf): Sf: 0-7 GS: 0-7 **Gd: 1-12** GF: 0-9 Fm: 0-6
Distance: 5f/6f: 0-0 7f-8f: 0-4 **9f-13f: 1-30** 14f+: 0-7
Track : LH: 0-17 **RH: 1-22 Tight: 1-23** Gall: 0-3
Aids: Bl: 0-0 Vi: 0-0 Tstrap: 0-0
Best Rating: 42 5/01 Haml 1m65y gd-sft

Ocean Estates

(84) (36)

3-y-o ch f Inchinor-Colleen Liath (Another Realm)
K T Ivory Ocean Estates Marbella

Placings:0-00 **(0614)**
2001: 9^{0}SD, 8^{0}SD

	Starts	1st	2nd	3rd	Win & Pl
Career Total (Turf)	0	0	0	0	
Career Total (AW)	3	0	0	0	

Going (Turf): Sf: 0-0 GS: 0-0 Gd: 0-0 GF: 0-0 Fm: 0-0
Distance: 5f/6f: 0-0 7f-8f: 0-2 9f-13f: 0-1 14f+: 0-0
Track : LH: 0-3 RH: 0-0 Tight: 0-2 Gall: 0-0
Aids: Bl: 0-0 Vi: 0-0 Tstrap: 0-0
Best Rating: 36 2/01 Wolv 1m1f79y stand

Ocean Line (IRE)

(103) (38)**47**

6-y-o b g Kefaah (USA)-Tropic Sea (IRE) (Sure Blade (USA))
J J O'Neill The Cartmel Syndicate

Placings:0003/**0**00450/000**4**52514130/**23220**4001203-0 **(0461)**
2001: 12^{0}SD

	Starts	1st	2nd	3rd	Win & Pl
Career Total (Turf)	26	2	2	3	7507
Career Total (AW)	9	1	3	1	4580

38	7/00	Ling	1m2f	G		STD	£1928
50	8/99	Brig	1m1f209yF			G-F	£2274
39	7/99	Wind	1m3f135yF(0-60)H			G-F	£2507

Total win prize-money £6710

Going (Turf): Sf: 0-2 GS: 0-1 Gd: 0-4 **GF: 2-16** Fm: 0-3
Distance: 5f/6f: 0-0 7f-8f: 0-6 **9f-13f: 3-27** 14f+: 0-2
Track : **LH: 2-27** RH: 0-4 **Tight: 2-16** Gall: 0-1
Aids: Bl: 0-0 Vi: 0-0 Tstrap: 0-0
Best Rating: 39 7/99 Wind 1m3f135y GF

Ocean Love (IRE)

94 **44**

3-y-o b f Dolphin Street (FR)-Scuba Diver (King's Lake (USA))
M L W Bell J M Ratcliffe

Placings:523-00030 **(3949)**
2001: 11^{0}GS, 9^{0}G, 11^{0}GF, 8^{3}G, 8^{0}GS

	Starts	1st	2nd	3rd	Win & Pl
Career Total (Turf)	8	0	1	2	1564

Going (Turf): Sf: 0-0 GS: 0-2 Gd: 0-3 GF: 0-3 Fm: 0-0
Distance: 5f/6f: 0-0 7f-8f: 0-2 9f-13f: 0-6 14f+: 0-0
Track : LH: 0-1 RH: 0-4 Tight: 0-4 Gall: 0-0
Aids: Bl: 0-1 Vi: 0-0 Tstrap: 0-0
Best Rating: 44 7/01 Leic 1m9y good

Ocean Rain (IRE)

99 **54**

4-y-o ch g Lake Coniston (IRE)-Alicedale (USA) (Trempolino (USA))
C G Cox Stephen W Barrow

Placings:02105/0500403460-00060605 **(4609)**
2001: 8^{0}GS, 8^{0}G, 8^{0}F, 7^{6}GF, 9^{0}G, 10^{6}G, 9^{0}G, 8^{5}F

	Starts	1st	2nd	3rd	Win & Pl
Career Total (Turf)	23	1	1	1	5645

76	8/99	Hayd	6f	E		G-S	£3060

Total win prize-money £3060

Going (Turf): Sf: 0-1 **GS: 1-4** Gd: 0-10 GF: 0-5 Fm: 0-3
Distance: **5f/6f: 1-4** 7f-8f: 0-11 9f-13f: 0-8 14f+: 0-0
Track : LH: 0-12 RH: 0-0 Tight: 0-5 Gall: 0-2
Aids: Bl: 0-1 Vi: 0-9 Tstrap: 0-0
Best Rating: 57 7/01 Hayd 7f30y gd-fm

Ocean Road

95 **64**

3-y-o ch g Inchinor-Executive Lady (Night Shift (USA))
Mrs A J Perrett Bernard Keay

Placings:060-00 **(2254)**
2001: 7^{0}G, 10^{0}G

	Starts	1st	2nd	3rd	Win & Pl
Career Total (Turf)	5	0	0	0	0

Going (Turf): Sf: 0-0 GS: 0-0 Gd: 0-4 GF: 0-1 Fm: 0-0
Distance: 5f/6f: 0-0 7f-8f: 0-4 9f-13f: 0-1 14f+: 0-0
Track : LH: 0-2 RH: 0-1 Tight: 0-1 Gall: 0-1
Aids: Bl: 0-0 Vi: 0-0 Tstrap: 0-0
Best Rating: 58 6/01 Wind 1m2f7y good

Ocean Song

91(99) (32)**25**

4-y-o b f Savahra Sound-Marina Plata (Julio Mariner)
S R Bowring Simon Mapletoft

Placings:2460030030-04000000 **(5394)**
2001: 8^{0}SW, 11^{4}SD, 11^{0}S, 10^{0}F, 12^{0}GF, 8^{0}GF, 11^{0}SD, 12^{0}SD, 16^{5}SD

	Starts	1st	2nd	3rd	Win & Pl
Career Total (Turf)	11	0	0	1	470
Career Total (AW)	7	0	1	1	1372

Going (Turf): Sf: 0-1 GS: 0-1 Gd: 0-3 GF: 0-5 Fm: 0-1
Distance: 5f/6f: 0-0 7f-8f: 0-7 9f-13f: 0-10 14f+: 0-1
Track : LH: 0-13 RH: 0-1 Tight: 0-4 Gall: 0-1
Aids: Bl: 0-5 Vi: 0-0 Tstrap: 0-0
Best Rating: 46 2/01 Sthl 1m3f stand

Ocean Sound (IRE)

102 **91**

2-y-o b c Mujadil (USA)-Ossana (USA) (Tejano (USA))
B W Hills Mrs Belinda Harvey

Placings:03120304 **(4943)**
2001: 5^{0}G, 6^{3}GF, 6^{1}GF, 6^{2}G, 6^{0}GF, 7^{3}G, 6^{0}GY, 7^{4}S

	Starts	1st	2nd	3rd	Win & Pl
Career Total (Turf)	8	1	1	2	11926

85	5/01	Ayr	6f	D		G-F	£3958

Total win prize-money £3959

Going (Turf): Sf: 0-1 GS: 0-0 Gd: 0-3 **GF: 1-3** Fm: 0-0
Distance: **5f/6f: 1-6** 7f-8f: 0-2 9f-13f: 0-0 14f+: 0-0
Track : LH: 0-1 RH: 0-0 Tight: 0-1 Gall: 0-0
Aids: Bl: 0-1 Vi: 0-0 Tstrap: 0-0
Best Rating: 91 8/01 Asct 7f good

Showed a decent level of form in 2001 but his limitations were exposed in high-class events. Sold to USA.

Ocean Tide

105 **74**

4-y-o b g Deploy-Dancing Tide (Pharly (FR))
J G Given J E Titley

Placings:400-031114056 **(4115)**
2001: 7^{0}GF, 12^{3}GF, 13^{1}GF, 13^{1}GS, 12^{1}GF, 14^{4}GF, 14^{0}GF, 16^{5}GF, 11^{6}G

	Starts	1st	2nd	3rd	Win & Pl
Career Total (Turf)	12	3	0	1	14573

69	6/01	NmkJ	1m4f	D(0-80)H		G-F	£6906
74	6/01	Haml	1m5f9y	F(0-65)H		G-S	£2730
74	6/01	Haml	1m5f9y	F(0-60)H		G-F	£3318

Total win prize-money £12954

Going (Turf): Sf: 0-3 GS: 1-1 Gd: 0-1 **GF: 2-7** Fm: 0-0
Distance: 5f/6f: 0-0 7f-8f: 0-1 9f-13f: 1-6 **14f+: 2-5**
Track : LH: 0-6 **RH: 3-6 Tight: 2-3** Gall: 1-4
Aids: Bl: 0-0 **Vi: 3-7** Tstrap: 0-0
Best Rating: 74 6/01 Haml 1m5f9y gd-sft

He was a revelation in a first-time visor and won easily at Hamilton. He completed a hat-trick at Newmarket, and a mile and a half on fast ground is ideal for him. The Handicapper looks to have his measure now.

Octane (USA)

100 **72**

5-y-o b g Cryptoclearance (USA)-Something True (USA) (Sir Ivor)
W M Brisbourne Christopher Chell

Placings:60500/003132021145-003 **(2787)**
2001: 12^{0}G, 12^{0}GF, 10^{3}GF

	Starts	1st	2nd	3rd	Win & Pl
Career Total (Turf)	20	3	2	3	24223

71	7/00	Sand	1m2f7y	D(0-80)H		GD	£7085
57	7/00	Hayd	1m2f120yE(0-75)H			G-F	£3136
47	5/00	Muss	1m4f	F(0-65)H		FRM	£5300

Total win prize-money £15522

Going (Turf): Sf: 0-1 GS: 0-0 **Gd: 1-7 GF: 1-7 Fm: 1-5**
Distance: 5f/6f: 0-0 7f-8f: 0-2 **9f-13f: 3-17** 14f+: 0-1
Track : LH: 1-4 **RH: 2-11 Tight: 1-8** Gall: 0-4
Aids: Bl: 0-2 Vi: 0-0 Tstrap: 0-1
Best Rating: 70 7/01 Hayd 1m2f120y gd-fm

A winner three times at distances between ten and 12 furlongs in 2000, he shot up the handicap while in blistering form last July. Lightly raced in 2001. Acts on fast ground.

Octavius Caesar (USA)

103 **91**

4-y-o ch c Affirmed (USA)-Secret Imperatrice (USA) (Secretariat (USA))
P F I Cole Sir George Meyrick

Placings:20/3126-201000 **(5338)**
2001: 12^{2}GF, 12^{0}GF, 12^{1}G, 11^{0}G, 12^{0}G, 12^{0}GS

	Starts	1st	2nd	3rd	Win & Pl
Career Total (Turf)	12	2	3	1	17137

91	8/01	Ches	1m4f66y	C(0-90)H	GD	£7247
80	8/00	Bath	1m3f144yD		GD	£5499

Total win prize-money £12747

Going (Turf): Sf: 0-0 GS: 0-1 **Gd: 2-6** GF: 0-4 Fm: 0-1
Distance: 5f/6f: 0-0 7f-8f: 0-0 **9f-13f: 2-11** 14f+: 0-1
Track : **LH: 2-7** RH: 0-5 **Tight: 2-4** Gall: 0-5
Aids: Bl: 0-0 Vi: 0-0 **Tstrap: 1-3**
Best Rating: 91 8/01 Ches 1m4f66y good

An impressive winner at Bath last season, he returned to winning form at Chester in August 2001 when fitted with a tongue-strap for the first time, but he has since looked well held. He is suited by forcing tactics and middle distances. He acts on good ground, and may be most effective on a sharp track.

Octennial

78 **62**
2-y-o gr c Octagonal (NZ)-Laune (AUS) (Kenmare (FR))
R Hannon I A N Wight

Placings:00 **(5665)**
2001: 6^{0}HY, 6^{0}HY

	Starts	1st	2nd	3rd	Win & Pl
Career Total (Turf)	2	0	0	0	

Going (Turf): Sf: 0-2 GS: 0-0 Gd: 0-0 GF: 0-0 Fm: 0-0
Distance: 5f/6f: 0-1 7f-8f: 0-1 9f-13f: 0-0 14f+: 0-0
Track : LH: 0-0 RH: 0-0 Tight: 0-0 Gall: 0-0
Aids: Bl: 0-0 Vi: 0-0 Tstrap: 0-0
Best Rating: 62 10/01 Newb 6f8y heavy

Oddsanends

41(100) (60)**40**
5-y-o b g Alhijaz-Jans Contessa (Rabdan)
B R Johnson Peter Crate

Placings:54413/46022/05100050-0 **(0890)**
2001: 6^{0}HY

	Starts	1st	2nd	3rd	Win & Pl
Career Total (Turf)	8	1	0	0	5550
Career Total (AW)	11	1	2	1	7187

56	3/00	Sthl	7f	F(0-60)	STD	£2278
73	8/98	Asct	7f	C	G-F	£5550

Total win prize-money £7829

Going (Turf): Sf: 0-2 GS: 0-2 Gd: 0-3 **GF: 1-1** Fm: 0-0
Distance: 5f/6f: 0-4 **7f-8f: 2-15** 9f-13f: 0-0 14f+: 0-0
Track : **LH: 1-14** RH: 0-0 Tight: 0-6 Gall: 0-0
Aids: Bl: 0-1 Vi: 0-0 Tstrap: 0-0
Best Rating: 73 8/98 Asct 7f GF

Odyn Dancer

(99) (34)**22**
4-y-o b f Minshaanshu Amad (USA)-Themeda (Sure Blade (USA))
M D I Usher M D I Usher

Placings:0025400036/6620604003104220-3065 **(0261)**
2001: 16^{3}SD, 11^{0}SD, 12^{6}SD, 16^{5}SD

	Starts	1st	2nd	3rd	Win & Pl
Career Total (Turf)	5	0	0	0	
Career Total (AW)	25	1	4	3	5176

39	9/00	Wolv	1m4f	G(0-60)H	STD	£1897

Total win prize-money £1897

Going (Turf): Sf: 0-1 GS: 0-0 Gd: 0-2 GF: 0-2 Fm: 0-0
Distance: 5f/6f: 0-1 7f-8f: 0-7 **9f-13f: 1-15** 14f+: 0-7
Track : **LH: 1-28** RH: 0-1 **Tight: 1-17** Gall: 0-0
Aids: Bl: 0-0 Vi: 0-1 Tstrap: 0-0
Best Rating: 34 1/01 Sthl 2m stand

Off Hire

102(106) (62)**60**
5-y-o b g Clantime-Lady Pennington (Blue Cashmere)
C Smith John Martin-Hoyes

Placings:0001433/420060003/1421060441560044-55115322350403 **(4080)**
2001: 5^{5}SD, 5^{5}SW, 5^{1}SD, 5^{1}SD, 5^{5}SD, 5^{3}SD, 5^{2}S, 5^{2}S, 5^{3}GS, 5^{5}G, 5^{0}GF, 5^{4}SD, 5^{0}GF, 5^{3}GF

	Starts	1st	2nd	3rd	Win & Pl
Career Total (Turf)	22	2	3	2	9726
Career Total (AW)	24	4	1	4	10894

61	2/01	Wolv	5f	E(0-70)H	STD	£2940
56	2/01	Wolv	5f	F(0-60)H	STD	£1701
51	7/00	Bevl	5f	F(0-60)H	G-F	£3302
58	2/00	Wolv	5f	E(0-70)H	STD	£2213
50	1/00	Wolv	5f	F	STD	£2103
48	11/98	Muss	5f	F(0-65)H	SFT	£2745

Total win prize-money £15006

Going (Turf): Sf: 1-7 GS: 0-5 Gd: 0-2 **GF: 1-7** Fm: 0-1
Distance: **5f/6f: 6-44** 7f-8f: 0-1 9f-13f: 0-1 14f+: 0-0
Track : **LH: 4-20** RH: 0-0 **Tight: 4-11** Gall: 0-2
Aids: Bl: 0-0 **Vi: 5-32** Tstrap: 0-0
Best Rating: 62 3/01 Sthl 5f stand

Offa's Dyke (IRE)

95(102) (81)**80**
2-y-o b c Emperor Jones (USA)-Fakhira (IRE) (Jareer (USA))
S P C Woods G A Roberts

Placings:40416152 **(5504)**
2001: 7^{4}G, 7^{0}GF, 7^{4}G, 7^{1}SD, 8^{6}G, 8^{1}SD, 7^{5}GF, 7^{2}HY

	Starts	1st	2nd	3rd	Win & Pl
Career Total (Turf)	6	0	1	0	2025
Career Total (AW)	2	2	0	0	5639

81	9/01	Wolv	1m100y	E	STD	£2817
81	8/01	Wolv	7f	E	STD	£2821

Total win prize-money £5639

Going (Turf): Sf: 0-1 GS: 0-0 Gd: 0-3 GF: 0-2 Fm: 0-0
Distance: 5f/6f: 0-0 7f-8f: 1-6 9f-13f: 1-2 14f+: 0-0
Track : **LH: 2-5** RH: 0-0 **Tight: 2-4** Gall: 0-0
Aids: Bl: 0-0 Vi: 0-0 Tstrap: 0-0
Best Rating: 81 9/01 Wolv 1m100y stand

Hinted at ability in three runs in turf maidens before winning twice on the Wolverhampton Fibresand.

Official Flame (USA)

96 **86**
2-y-o ch c Deputy Minister (CAN)-Fire The Groom (USA) (Blushing Groom (FR))
D R Loder Sheikh Mohammed

Placings:100 **(5104)**
2001: 6^{1}G, 6^{0}GF, 6^{0}GS

	Starts	1st	2nd	3rd	Win & Pl
Career Total (Turf)	3	1	0	0	17813

86	8/01	York	6f	D	GD	£17813

Total win prize-money £17813

Going (Turf): Sf: 0-0 GS: 0-1 **Gd: 1-1** GF: 0-1 Fm: 0-0
Distance: **5f/6f: 1-2** 7f-8f: 0-1 9f-13f: 0-0 14f+: 0-0
Track : LH: 0-0 RH: 0-0 Tight: 0-0 Gall: 0-0
Aids: Bl: 0-0 Vi: 0-1 Tstrap: 0-0
Best Rating: 86 8/01 York 6f good

A half-brother to top-class sprinter Stravinsky, he made a successful debut at the York Ebor meeting, a race whose form was repeatedly boosted afterwards, but was out of his depth in Group races subsequently.

Oh Jamila

91 **30**
3-y-o b f Ezzoud (IRE)-True Bird (IRE) (In The Wings)
W R Muir Wooburn Racing

Placings:0-0600 **(3734)**
2001: 11^{0}GF, 10^{6}GF, 11^{0}GF, 11^{0}G

	Starts	1st	2nd	3rd	Win & Pl
Career Total (Turf)	5	0	0	0	0

Going (Turf): Sf: 0-0 GS: 0-1 Gd: 0-1 GF: 0-3 Fm: 0-0
Distance: 5f/6f: 0-0 7f-8f: 0-0 9f-13f: 0-5 14f+: 0-0
Track : LH: 0-4 RH: 0-0 Tight: 0-3 Gall: 0-0
Aids: Bl: 0-2 Vi: 0-0 Tstrap: 0-0
Best Rating: 30 6/01 Wwck 1m2f188y gd-fm

Oh No Not Him

104 **43**
5-y-o b g Reprimand-Lucky Mill (Midyan (USA))
W M Brisbourne Mugs Inc

Placings:005/000/0-6000L100300U **(4884)**
2001: 7^{6}F, 8^{0}GF, 8^{0}GF, 10^{0}GF, 8^{L}GF, 8^{1}GF, 8^{0}F, 12^{0}G, 8^{3}G, 10^{0}GF, 10^{0}GF, 8^{U}GF

	Starts	1st	2nd	3rd	Win & Pl
Career Total (Turf)	17	1	0	1	3248
Career Total (AW)	2	0	0	0	

43	7/01	Ripn	1m	E	G-F	£2800

Total win prize-money £2800

Going (Turf): Sf: 0-3 GS: 0-2 Gd: 0-2 **GF: 1-8** Fm: 0-2
Distance: 5f/6f: 0-0 **7f-8f: 1-8** 9f-13f: 0-11 14f+: 0-0
Track : LH: 0-9 RH: 0-3 Tight: 0-7 Gall: 0-0
Aids: Bl: 0-4 Vi: 0-0 Tstrap: 0-0
Best Rating: 43 7/01 Ripn 1m gd-fm

Oh So Dusty

83(95) (68)**61**
3-y-o b f Piccolo-Dark Eyed Lady (IRE) (Exhibitioner)
J Hetherton K C West

Placings:6104446-045000 **(5413)**
2001: 6^{0}SD, 5^{4}SD, 6^{5}SD, 5^{0}GS, 6^{0}SD, 8^{0}SD

	Starts	1st	2nd	3rd	Win & Pl
Career Total (Turf)	8	1	0	0	5064
Career Total (AW)	5	0	0	0	288

79	6/00	Newb	5f34y	D	G-F	£3776

Total win prize-money £3777

Going (Turf): Sf: 0-1 GS: 0-1 Gd: 0-1 **GF: 1-4** Fm: 0-0
Distance: **5f/6f: 1-11** 7f-8f: 0-1 9f-13f: 0-0 14f+: 0-0
Track : LH: 0-7 RH: 0-1 Tight: 0-2 Gall: 0-2
Aids: Bl: 0-1 Vi: 0-0 Tstrap: 0-0
Best Rating: 68 3/01 Ling 5f stand

Ok Twiggy

88 **24**
4-y-o b f Kylian (USA)-B B Glen (Hadeer)
J Akehurst Ok Partnership

Placings:60-0 **(5180)**
2001: 10^{0}HY

	Starts	1st	2nd	3rd	Win & Pl
Career Total (Turf)	3	0	0	0	0

Going (Turf): Sf: 0-3 GS: 0-0 Gd: 0-0 GF: 0-0 Fm: 0-0
Distance: 5f/6f: 0-0 7f-8f: 0-0 9f-13f: 0-3 14f+: 0-0
Track : LH: 0-0 RH: 0-1 Tight: 0-2 Gall: 0-0
Aids: Bl: 0-0 Vi: 0-0 Tstrap: 0-0
Best Rating: 24 10/01 Wind 1m2f7y heavy

Old Blue Eyes

100 **93**
2-y-o b c Whittingham (IRE)-Special One (Aragon)
P W Harris The Special Ones

Placings:412122 (5150)
2001: 5^{4}GF, 5^{1}GF, 5^{2}GF, 5^{1}G, 6^{2}GF, 6^{2}G

	Starts	1st	2nd	3rd	Win & Pl
Career Total (Turf)	6	2	3	0	108933

82 8/01 Newc 5f D GD £2912
75 7/01 Sand 5f6y E G-F £3802
Total win prize-money £6715

Going (Turf): Sf: 0-0 GS: 0-0 **Gd: 1-2 GF: 1-4** Fm: 0-0
Distance: **5f/6f: 2-6** 7f-8f: 0-0 9f-13f: 0-0 14f+: 0-0
Track : LH: 0-0 RH: 0-1 Tight: 0-0 Gall: 0-1
Aids: Bl: 0-0 Vi: 0-0 Tstrap: 0-0
Best Rating: 93 10/01 Rdcr 6f good

A genuine juvenile in 2001, winning twice at the minimum trip and finishing runner-up in two valuable sales races. Suited by good/fast ground and front-running tactics.

Old California (IRE)

98 **92**
2-y-o b c Sadler's Wells (USA)-Turban (Glint Of Gold)
J L Dunlop L Neil Jones

Placings:003 (5361)
2001: 7^{0}GF, 8^{0}GS, 8^{3}GS

	Starts	1st	2nd	3rd	Win & Pl
Career Total (Turf)	3	0	0	1	872

Going (Turf): Sf: 0-0 GS: 0-2 Gd: 0-0 GF: 0-1 Fm: 0-0
Distance: 5f/6f: 0-0 7f-8f: 0-3 9f-13f: 0-0 14f+: 0-0
Track : LH: 0-0 RH: 0-0 Tight: 0-0 Gall: 0-0
Aids: Bl: 0-0 Vi: 0-0 Tstrap: 0-0
Best Rating: 92 10/01 NmkR 1m gd-sft

Showed ability as a juvenile and will appreciate middle-distances in time.

Old Feathers (IRE)

91(100) (58)**59**
4-y-o b g Hernando (FR)-Undiscovered (Tap On Wood)
J G Fitzgerald Marquesa De Moratalla

Placings:666/0060013-1400 (1283)
2001: 16^{1}SD, 16^{4}SD, 21^{0}S, 16^{0}G

	Starts	1st	2nd	3rd	Win & Pl
Career Total (Turf)	12	1	0	1	3326
Career Total (AW)	2	1	0	0	1820

58 3/01 Sthl 2m F(0-60)H STD £1820
55 8/00 Catt 1m7f177yE(0-70)H G-S £2884
Total win prize-money £4704

Going (Turf): Sf: 0-2 **GS: 1-1** Gd: 0-3 GF: 0-6 Fm: 0-0
Distance: 5f/6f: 0-1 7f-8f: 0-1 9f-13f: 0-5 **14f+: 2-7**
Track : **LH: 2-7** RH: 0-7 **Tight: 1-6** Gall: 0-0
Aids: Bl: 0-0 Vi: 0-1 Tstrap: 0-0
Best Rating: 58 3/01 Sthl 2m stand

Old Hush Wing (IRE)

88(85) (38)**40**
8-y-o b g Tirol-Saneena (Kris)
S E Kettlewell Mrs B Ramsden

Placings:0030**630**/**602614**/**0525**/**32110**/**56000000-00** (1138)
2001: 16^{0}SD, 13^{0}G

	Starts	1st	2nd	3rd	Win & Pl
Career Total (Turf)	19	3	1	1	9799
Career Total (AW)	13	0	2	2	1984

53 4/99 Pont 2m1f22y E(0-75)H SFT £3366
49 3/99 Newc 2m19y E(0-70)H G-S £2571
44 7/97 Haml 1m5f9y F(0-60)H G-F £2780
Total win prize-money £8718

Going (Turf): Sf: 1-5 GS: 1-3 Gd: 0-5 **GF: 1-6** Fm: 0-0
Distance: 5f/6f: 0-2 7f-8f: 0-1 9f-13f: 0-6 **14f+: 3-23**
Track : **LH: 2-22** RH: 1-8 Tight: 1-14 Gall: 1-4
Aids: Bl: 0-1 Vi: 0-1 Tstrap: 0-0
Best Rating: 9 1/01 Sthl 2m stand

Old Opium

100(85) (63+)**74**
2-y-o b f Dilum (USA)-Ancient Secret (Warrshan (USA))
P S McEntee (S Kirk 20/10) N C Brown & Miss S Walcott

Placings:441632 (5690)
2001: 6^{4}HY, 6^{4}SD, 8^{1}SD, 8^{6}G, 8^{3}HY, 7^{2}S

	Starts	1st	2nd	3rd	Win & Pl
Career Total (Turf)	4	0	1	1	2708
Career Total (AW)	2	1	0	0	1953

63 10/01 Wolv 1m100y G STD £1953
Total win prize-money £1953

Going (Turf): Sf: 0-3 GS: 0-0 Gd: 0-1 GF: 0-0 Fm: 0-0
Distance: 5f/6f: 0-1 7f-8f: 0-3 **9f-13f: 1-2** 14f+: 0-0
Track : **LH: 1-2** RH: 0-1 **Tight: 1-2** Gall: 0-0
Aids: Bl: 0-0 Vi: 0-0 Tstrap: 0-0
Best Rating: 74 11/01 Donc 7f soft

Had shown promise on her first two runs before getting off the mark in a Wolverhampton seller over a mile in October, and she has improved for new stable, running well in nurseries.

Old Red (IRE)

93 (62?)**38**
11-y-o ch g Ela-Mana-Mou-Sea Port (Averof)
Mrs M Reveley A Flannigan

Placings:03000/125246212303/410/00/00532151/26/06 5 (4829)
2001: 14^{0}G, 14^{6}GF, 17^{5}G

	Starts	1st	2nd	3rd	Win & Pl
Career Total (Turf)	34	4	6	4	65659
Career Total (AW)	1	1	0	0	3202

48 9/98 Nott 2m9y F(0-65)H GD £3057
42 8/98 Nott 2m9y F(0-65)H G-F £2679
74 10/95 NmkR 2m2f B H G-F £46170
71 8/94 Rdcr 1m6f19y E(0-70)H G-F £3626
62 3/94 Sthl 1m3f D STD £3201
Total win prize-money £58734

Going (Turf): Sf: 0-6 GS: 0-1 Gd: 1-15 **GF: 3-10** Fm: 0-2
Distance: 5f/6f: 0-0 7f-8f: 0-0 9f-13f: 1-7 **14f+: 4-28**
Track : **LH: 4-27** RH: 1-8 Tight: 1-12 Gall: 1-12
Aids: Bl: 0-0 Vi: 0-0 Tstrap: 0-0
Best Rating: 38 9/01 Ayr 2m1f105y good

Old Rouvel (USA)

100 **60**
10-y-o b g Riverman (USA)-Marie De Russy (FR) (Sassafras (FR))
A King Mrs R D Cowell

Placings:6/1242553413/25436555/2520150/05/0 (0856)
2001: 16^{0}GS

	Starts	1st	2nd	3rd	Win & Pl
Career Total (Turf)	28	2	5	3	55006
Career Total (AW)	1	1	0	0	3589

60 9/97 Pont 2m1f216yC G-S £4612
76 10/95 Donc 2m110y C G-F £5601
61 2/95 Ling 1m4f D STD £3589
Total win prize-money £13804

Going (Turf): Sf: 0-4 **GS: 1-3** Gd: 0-8 **GF: 1-12** Fm: 0-0
Distance: 5f/6f: 0-0 7f-8f: 0-0 9f-13f: 1-1 **14f+: 2-27**
Track : **LH: 3-16** RH: 0-12 Tight: 1-3 Gall: 1-17
Aids: Bl: 0-0 Vi: 0-1 Tstrap: 0-0
Best Rating: 60 4/01 Newb 2m gd-sft

Olde Oak

86(6) **26**
7-y-o ch g Precocious-Quisissanno (Be My Guest (USA))
B Ellison (J S Wainwright 22/7) Mrs Jean Stapleton

Placings:000000000 (3932)
2001: 8^{0}SW, 7^{0}GF, 10^{0}GF, 9^{0}F, 10^{0}GF, 7^{0}GF, 10^{0}S, 8^{0}F, 8^{0}G

	Starts	1st	2nd	3rd	Win & Pl
Career Total (Turf)	8	0	0	0	
Career Total (AW)	1	0	0	0	

Going (Turf): Sf: 0-1 GS: 0-0 Gd: 0-1 GF: 0-4 Fm: 0-2
Distance: 5f/6f: 0-0 7f-8f: 0-3 9f-13f: 0-6 14f+: 0-0
Track : LH: 0-5 RH: 0-2 Tight: 0-3 Gall: 0-1
Aids: Bl: 0-0 Vi: 0-0 Tstrap: 0-1
Best Rating: 37 6/01 Nott 1m1f213y firm

Olden Times

109 **119**
3-y-o b c Darshaan-Garah (Ajdal (USA))
J L Dunlop Prince A A Faisal

Placings:4-151344 (4688a)
2001: 9^{1}S, 10^{5}GF, 9^{1}G, 8^{3}G, 8^{4}GF, 8^{4}GS

	Starts	1st	2nd	3rd	Win & Pl
Career Total (Turf)	7	2	0	1	116062

115 6/01 Chan 1m1f GD £48497
105 4/01 NmkR 1m1f A SFT £13398
Total win prize-money £61895

Going (Turf): Sf: 1-1 GS: 0-1 **Gd: 1-3** GF: 0-2 Fm: 0-0
Distance: 5f/6f: 0-0 7f-8f: 0-4 **9f-13f: 2-3** 14f+: 0-0
Track : LH: 0-2 RH: 0-3 Tight: 0-0 Gall: 0-3
Aids: Bl: 0-0 Vi: 0-0 Tstrap: 0-0
Best Rating: 119 6/01 Asct 1m good

High-class at around a mile. Recorded a game performance to win the Prix Jean Prat at Chantilly in June. He landed a Listed event at Newmarket first time out, and ran a cracker when a close third in the St James's Palace Stakes and performed well without matching that effort in the Sussex Stakes and Prix du Moulin. Seems to need to get his toe in, but is probably just below the very top class.

Oldenway

91 **66**
2-y-o b c Most Welcome-Sickle Moon (Shirley Heights)
R A Fahey Exors Of The Late T P Staunton

Placings:03505 (5283)
2001: 6^{0}G, 5^{3}GF, 6^{5}GF, 6^{0}G, 8^{5}HY

	Starts	1st	2nd	3rd	Win & Pl
Career Total (Turf)	5	0	0	1	492

Going (Turf): Sf: 0-1 GS: 0-0 Gd: 0-2 GF: 0-2 Fm: 0-0
Distance: 5f/6f: 0-4 7f-8f: 0-1 9f-13f: 0-0 14f+: 0-0
Track : LH: 0-1 RH: 0-0 Tight: 0-0 Gall: 0-0
Aids: Bl: 0-0 Vi: 0-0 Tstrap: 0-0
Best Rating: 66 9/01 York 6f gd-fm

Ran his best race to date in a maiden auction over five furlongs on a sound surface.

Olenka

82(95) **23**
3-y-o gr f Grand Lodge (USA)-Sarouel (IRE) (Kendor (FR))
Mrs J R Ramsden Nigel Munton

Placings:1-00 (5400)
2001: 6^{0}S, 10^{0}S, 6^{0}SD

	Starts	1st	2nd	3rd	Win & Pl
Career Total (Turf)	3	1	0	0	2782

74 7/00 Catt 5f212y D G-F £2782
Total win prize-money £2782

Going (Turf): Sf: 0-2 GS: 0-0 Gd: 0-0 **GF: 1-1** Fm: 0-0
Distance: **5f/6f: 1-2** 7f-8f: 0-0 9f-13f: 0-1 14f+: 0-0
Track : **LH: 1-2** RH: 0-0 **Tight: 1-1** Gall: 0-0
Aids: Bl: 0-0 Vi: 0-0 Tstrap: 0-0

Best Rating: 23 10/01 York 6f soft

Olimolimoo (IRE)

95 **79**

2-y-o gr g Ali-Royal (IRE)-Classy (Kalaglow)
M J Haynes Mrs Sally Pettis

Placings:420 **(5260)**
2001: 6^{4}GF, 7^{2}G, 7^{0}GS

	Starts	1st	2nd	3rd	Win & Pl
Career Total (Turf)	3	0	1	0	1314

Going (Turf): Sf: 0-0 GS: 0-1 Gd: 0-1 GF: 0-1 Fm: 0-0
Distance: 5f/6f: 0-1 7f-8f: 0-2 9f-13f: 0-0 14f+: 0-0
Track : LH: 0-0 RH: 0-1 Tight: 0-0 Gall: 0-0
Aids: Bl: 0-0 Vi: 0-0 Tstrap: 0-0
Best Rating: 79 9/01 Sand 7f16y good

Oliranar

77(88) (30)

5-y-o gr g Gran Alba (USA)-April Rain (Lepanto (GER))
J R Best R Blake, N Webberley, A Paine, R Sackett

Placings:300-00 **(3840)**
2001: 8^{0}SD, 7^{0}G

	Starts	1st	2nd	3rd	Win & Pl
Career Total (Turf)	1	0	0	0	
Career Total (AW)	4	0	0	1	191

Going (Turf): Sf: 0-0 GS: 0-0 Gd: 0-1 GF: 0-0 Fm: 0-0
Distance: 5f/6f: 0-0 7f-8f: 0-5 9f-13f: 0-0 14f+: 0-0
Track : LH: 0-4 RH: 0-0 Tight: 0-4 Gall: 0-0
Aids: Bl: 0-0 Vi: 0-0 Tstrap: 0-0
Best Rating: 18 8/01 NmkJ 7f good

Olivers Trail

93 **41**

3-y-o ch c Catrail (USA)-Carmenoura (IRE) (Carmelite House (USA))
A Smith Alfred Smith

Placings:0-00 **(4031)**
2001: 7^{0}GS, 10^{0}G

	Starts	1st	2nd	3rd	Win & Pl
Career Total (Turf)	3	0	0	0	

Going (Turf): Sf: 0-1 GS: 0-1 Gd: 0-1 GF: 0-0 Fm: 0-0
Distance: 5f/6f: 0-0 7f-8f: 0-2 9f-13f: 0-1 14f+: 0-0
Track : LH: 0-1 RH: 0-0 Tight: 0-0 Gall: 0-1
Aids: Bl: 0-0 Vi: 0-0 Tstrap: 0-0
Best Rating: 28 8/01 Newc 1m2f32y good

Olivia Grace

108(100) (53+)**81**

3-y-o ch f Pivotal-Sheila's Secret (IRE) (Bluebird (USA))
T G Mills Sherwoods Transport Ltd

Placings:161 **(5462)**
2001: 5^{1}SD, 6^{6}GF, 5^{1}G

	Starts	1st	2nd	3rd	Win & Pl
Career Total (Turf)	2	1	0	0	3045
Career Total (AW)	1	1	0	0	2968

81 10/01 Bath 5f11y E(0-75)H GD £3045
53 4/01 Ling 5f D STD £2968
Total win prize-money £6013

Going (Turf): Sf: 0-0 GS: 0-0 **Gd: 1-1** GF: 0-1 Fm: 0-0
Distance: 5f/6f: 2-3 7f-8f: 0-0 9f-13f: 0-0 14f+: 0-0
Track : LH: 2-2 RH: 0-0 Tight: 1-1 Gall: 1-1
Aids: Bl: 0-0 Vi: 0-0 Tstrap: 0-0
Best Rating: 81 10/01 Bath 5f11y good

She is bred for speed and duly got off the mark at the first time of asking in a sand maiden. She did not get home over six furlongs at Kempton, but made all to win a handicap back over five at Bath. Looks capable of making up into a decent handicapper.

Olivia Rose (IRE)

99(90) (58)**78**

2-y-o b f Mujadil (USA)-Santana Lady (IRE) (Blakeney)
M Johnston C G Maybury

Placings:0422 **(5635)**
2001: 7^{0}GS, 6^{4}S, 6^{2}HY, 7^{2}G

	Starts	1st	2nd	3rd	Win & Pl
Career Total (Turf)	4	0	2	0	2267

Going (Turf): Sf: 0-2 GS: 0-1 Gd: 0-1 GF: 0-0 Fm: 0-0
Distance: 5f/6f: 0-2 7f-8f: 0-2 9f-13f: 0-0 14f+: 0-0
Track : LH: 0-1 RH: 0-0 Tight: 0-1 Gall: 0-0
Aids: Bl: 0-0 Vi: 0-0 Tstrap: 0-0
Best Rating: 78 10/01 Newc 6f heavy

A half-sister to decent handicapper Port Moresby, she looks to have a race in her based on her performances in maiden company.

Olivo (IRE)

107 **37**

7-y-o ch g Priolo (USA)-Honourable Sheba (USA) (Roberto (USA))
C A Horgan J L Harrison

Placings:336/03012000/441620400/2006/0004463 **(3481)**
2001: 11^{0}GF, 13^{0}GF, 12^{0}GF, 18^{4}GF, 16^{4}GF, 17^{6}G, 15^{3}GF

	Starts	1st	2nd	3rd	Win & Pl
Career Total (Turf)	31	2	3	4	15593

67 7/98 Sals 1m6f15y G(0-65) G-F £2290
69 7/97 Brig 7f214y D(0-80)H FRM £3518
Total win prize-money £5808

Going (Turf): Sf: 0-0 GS: 0-2 Gd: 0-6 **GF: 1-21 Fm: 1-2**
Distance: 5f/6f: 0-1 7f-8f: 1-7 9f-13f: 0-8 14f+: 1-15
Track : LH: 1-12 RH: 1-15 **Tight: 1-10** Gall: 0-7
Aids: Bl: 0-0 Vi: 0-0 Tstrap: 0-0
Best Rating: 39 5/01 Brig 1m3f196y gd-fm

Oloroso

92(95) (33)**29**

4-y-o b g Piccolo-Saunders Lass (Hillandale)
J Neville Charles Saunders Ltd

Placings:00-300503 **(2649)**
2001: 8^{3}SW, 9^{0}SD, 11^{0}GS, 8^{5}F, 6^{0}GF, 11^{3}SD

	Starts	1st	2nd	3rd	Win & Pl
Career Total (Turf)	5	0	0	0	0
Career Total (AW)	3	0	0	2	420

Going (Turf): Sf: 0-1 GS: 0-2 Gd: 0-0 GF: 0-1 Fm: 0-1
Distance: 5f/6f: 0-0 7f-8f: 0-1 9f-13f: 0-7 14f+: 0-0
Track : LH: 0-7 RH: 0-0 Tight: 0-3 Gall: 0-0
Aids: Bl: 0-0 Vi: 0-0 Tstrap: 0-0
Best Rating: 33 7/01 Sthl 1m3f stand

Oly's Gill (IRE)

88(91) (10)**10**

3-y-o b f Eagle Eyed (USA)-Jealous One (USA) (Raise A Native)
A Berry Alan Berry

Placings:40000005056-524006000050005000 (1986)
2001: 5^{5}SD, 6^{2}SW, 7^{4}SD, 7^{0}SD, 5^{0}SD, 6^{6}SD, 6^{0}SD, 5^{0}S, 5^{0}GS, 5^{0}S, 6^{5}HY, 6^{0}S, 7^{0}G, 5^{0}G, 5^{5}F, 7^{0}F, 8^{0}GF, 7^{0}GF, 7^{0}G

	Starts	1st	2nd	3rd	Win & Pl
Career Total (Turf)	16	0	0	0	543
Career Total (AW)	14	0	1	0	528

Going (Turf): Sf: 0-6 GS: 0-2 Gd: 0-3 GF: 0-3 Fm: 0-2
Distance: 5f/6f: 0-20 7f-8f: 0-10 9f-13f: 0-0 14f+: 0-0
Track : LH: 0-16 RH: 0-2 Tight: 0-12 Gall: 0-0
Aids: Bl: 0-0 Vi: 0-0 Tstrap: 0-0
Best Rating: 55 3/01 Wolv 7f stand

Oly's Whit

93 **51**

3-y-o ch g Whittingham (IRE)-Nellie O'Dowd (USA) (Diesis)
J J O'Neill A & G Oliver

Placings:46-53 **(1292)**
2001: 10^{5}HY, 12^{3}F

	Starts	1st	2nd	3rd	Win & Pl
Career Total (Turf)	4	0	0	1	682

Going (Turf): Sf: 0-2 GS: 0-0 Gd: 0-0 GF: 0-0 Fm: 0-2
Distance: 5f/6f: 0-2 7f-8f: 0-0 9f-13f: 0-2 14f+: 0-0
Track : LH: 0-1 RH: 0-3 Tight: 0-1 Gall: 0-2
Aids: Bl: 0-0 Vi: 0-1 Tstrap: 0-0
Best Rating: 51 5/01 Haml 1m4f17y firm

Olympic Pride (IRE)

(67)

3-y-o b f Up And At 'Em-So Far Away (Robellino (USA))
C N Allen Robert McLachlan

Placings:00-0 **(0978)**
2001: 7^{0}SD

	Starts	1st	2nd	3rd	Win & Pl
Career Total (Turf)	2	0	0	0	
Career Total (AW)	1	0	0	0	

Going (Turf): Sf: 0-1 GS: 0-0 Gd: 0-0 GF: 0-1 Fm: 0-0
Distance: 5f/6f: 0-0 7f-8f: 0-2 9f-13f: 0-1 14f+: 0-0
Track : LH: 0-1 RH: 0-0 Tight: 0-0 Gall: 0-0
Aids: Bl: 0-0 Vi: 0-0 Tstrap: 0-0

Omey Strand (IRE)

101(87) (67)**89**

2-y-o b g Desert Style (IRE)-Ex-Imager (Exhibitioner)
B J Meehan The Second Tumbleweed Partnership

Placings:40402 **(5045)**
2001: 6^{4}GF, 6^{0}GS, 6^{4}F, 8^{0}F, 8^{2}SD

	Starts	1st	2nd	3rd	Win & Pl
Career Total (Turf)	4	0	0	0	586
Career Total (AW)	1	0	1	0	1060

Going (Turf): Sf: 0-0 GS: 0-1 Gd: 0-0 GF: 0-1 Fm: 0-2
Distance: 5f/6f: 0-2 7f-8f: 0-2 9f-13f: 0-1 14f+: 0-0
Track : LH: 0-2 RH: 0-0 Tight: 0-1 Gall: 0-0
Aids: Bl: 0-1 Vi: 0-0 Tstrap: 0-0
Best Rating: 89 8/01 Sals 6f212y firm

Has shown promise on turf and Fibresand and looks capable of winning a small race.

Omni Cosmo Touch (USA)

5-y-o b g Trempolino (USA)-Wooden Pudden (USA) (Top Ville)
O Sherwood It Wasn't Us

Placings:14/063-R **(5463)**
2001: 11^{R}G

	Starts	1st	2nd	3rd	Win & Pl
Career Total (Turf)	6	1	0	1	5409

80 7/99 Gway 1m100y G-F £4468
Total win prize-money £4469

Going (Turf): Sf: 0-0 GS: 0-0 Gd: 0-3 **GF: 1-1** Fm: 0-0
Distance: 5f/6f: 0-0 7f-8f: 0-1 **9f-13f: 1-4** 14f+: 0-1
Track : LH: 0-1 **RH: 1-3** Tight: 0-1 Gall: 0-1

Aids: Bl: 0-0 Vi: 0-0 Tstrap: 0-0

Omniheat

106(93) (62)**74**

4-y-o b f Ezzoud (IRE)-Lady Bequick (Sharpen Up)
M J Ryan Mrs E Delaney

Placings:5540461/3231654000504360-006056422202200311 **(5632)**
2001: 8^{0}GS, 8^{0}GS, 7^{6}G, 7^{0}F, 8^{5}G, 7^{6}GF, 9^{4}GF, 9^{2}GF, 9^{2}G, 9^{2}GF, 9^{0}GF, 9^{2}GF, 9^{2}GF, 9^{0}GF, 10^{0}HY, 8^{3}GS, 10^{1}S, 10^{1}G

	Starts	1st	2nd	3rd	Win & Pl
Career Total (Turf)	39	4	6	4	29620
Career Total (AW)	2	0	0	0	0

74 11/01 Rdcr 1m2f E(0-75)H GD £3290
69 10/01 Rdcr 1m2f E(0-65) SFT £3304
74 6/00 Brig 1m1f209yE(0-75)H G-F £2808
67 11/99 Donc 7f D(0-85)H SFT £4611
Total win prize-money £14013

Going (Turf): **Sf: 2-7** GS: 0-4 Gd: 1-7 GF: 1-18 Fm: 0-3
Distance: 5f/6f: 0-1 7f-8f: 1-20 **9f-13f: 3-20** 14f+: 0-0
Track : **LH: 3-18** RH: 0-11 **Tight: 2-9** Gall: 0-1
Aids: **Bl: 1-9** Vi: 0-1 Tstrap: 0-0
Best Rating: 74 11/01 Rdcr 1m2f good

Had finished runner-up on numerous occasions, until winning two on the trot, including at Redcar in November when eased right down. Suited by nine to ten furlongs, acts on any ground.

Omniscient (IRE)

99 **77?**

2-y-o br f Distinctly North (USA)-Mystic Shadow (IRE) (Mtoto)
Mrs P N Dutfield The Carpetbaggers

Placings:0300015 **(5496)**
2001: 5^{0}GF, 5^{3}F, 6^{0}GF, 6^{0}G, 9^{0}HY, 7^{1}G, 7^{5}HY

	Starts	1st	2nd	3rd	Win & Pl
Career Total (Turf)	7	1	0	1	3010

77 10/01 Rdcr 7f F GD £2674
Total win prize-money £2674

Going (Turf): Sf: 0-2 GS: 0-0 **Gd: 1-2** GF: 0-2 Fm: 0-1
Distance: 5f/6f: 0-3 **7f-8f: 1-3** 9f-13f: 0-1 14f+: 0-0
Track : LH: 0-2 RH: 0-0 Tight: 0-0 Gall: 0-1
Aids: Bl: 0-0 Vi: 0-0 Tstrap: 0-0
Best Rating: 77 10/01 Rdcr 7f good

Had not shown a great deal of ability until dropping down to a claimer at Redcar in October. Acts on good ground, and is suited by seven furlongs.

On Coo Lay (IRE)

97(78) (39)**52**

2-y-o b f Definite Article-Glass Minnow (IRE) (Alzao (USA))
P D Evans Mrs S G Allan

Placings:405443600603 **(5667)**
2001: 6^{4}G, 7^{0}SD, 6^{5}GF, 7^{4}GF, 6^{4}G, 8^{3}G, 8^{6}SD, 8^{0}SD, 8^{0}SD, 8^{6}HY, 8^{0}G, 8^{3}HY

	Starts	1st	2nd	3rd	Win & Pl
Career Total (Turf)	8	0	0	2	846
Career Total (AW)	4	0	0	0	0

Going (Turf): Sf: 0-2 GS: 0-0 Gd: 0-4 GF: 0-2 Fm: 0-0
Distance: 5f/6f: 0-2 7f-8f: 0-6 9f-13f: 0-4 14f+: 0-0
Track : LH: 0-6 RH: 0-1 Tight: 0-3 Gall: 0-0
Aids: Bl: 0-0 Vi: 0-3 Tstrap: 0-0
Best Rating: 52 11/01 Wind 1m67y heavy

Moderate form on turf and All-Weather.

On Guard

94(102) (64)**67d**

3-y-o b g Sabrehill (USA)-With Care (Warning)
Mrs N Macauley (W Jarvis 4/5) West Indies Capital Company Limited

Placings:621-0000240 **(5413)**
2001: 7^{0}GS, 8^{0}GF, 7^{0}SD, 6^{0}SD, 9^{2}SD, 9^{4}SD, 8^{0}SD

	Starts	1st	2nd	3rd	Win & Pl
Career Total (Turf)	3	0	0	0	0
Career Total (AW)	7	1	2	0	4225

72 12/00 Sthl 7f D STD £2709
Total win prize-money £2709

Going (Turf): Sf: 0-1 GS: 0-1 Gd: 0-0 GF: 0-1 Fm: 0-0
Distance: 5f/6f: 0-3 **7f-8f: 1-5** 9f-13f: 0-2 14f+: 0-0
Track : **LH: 1-7** RH: 0-1 Tight: 0-5 Gall: 0-0
Aids: Bl: 0-0 Vi: 0-2 Tstrap: 0-0
Best Rating: 67 4/01 NmkR 7f gd-sft

Appeared not to handle soft ground on his debut in 2000, but took to Fibresand and scored late in the year over seven furlongs. Showed little on turf or All-Weather this season until stepped up in trip in the autumn.

On My Honour

89 **35**

3-y-o b f Pyramus (USA)-Princess Matilda (Habitat)
J C Fox The Slaney Partnership

Placings:00-000000050 **(4610)**
2001: 8^{0}GS, 6^{0}GS, 6^{0}F, 6^{0}GF, 6^{0}GF, 7^{0}GS, 8^{0}S, 6^{5}F, 5^{0}F

	Starts	1st	2nd	3rd	Win & Pl
Career Total (Turf)	11	0	0	0	0

Going (Turf): Sf: 0-3 GS: 0-3 Gd: 0-0 GF: 0-2 Fm: 0-3
Distance: 5f/6f: 0-5 7f-8f: 0-5 9f-13f: 0-1 14f+: 0-0
Track : LH: 0-1 RH: 0-1 Tight: 0-0 Gall: 0-2
Aids: Bl: 0-2 Vi: 0-0 Tstrap: 0-0
Best Rating: 35 8/01 Sals 6f212y firm

On Porpoise

81(75) **41**

5-y-o b g Dolphin Street (FR)-Floppie (FR) (Law Society (USA))
P W D'Arcy Mrs Sue D'Arcy

Placings:000/000010-00 **(3415)**
2001: 8^{0}GS, 10^{0}GF

	Starts	1st	2nd	3rd	Win & Pl
Career Total (Turf)	10	1	0	0	2044
Career Total (AW)	1	0	0	0	

41 8/00 Yarm 1m3y G(0-60)H GD £2044
Total win prize-money £2044

Going (Turf): Sf: 0-3 GS: 0-3 **Gd: 1-1** GF: 0-2 Fm: 0-1
Distance: 5f/6f: 0-0 7f-8f: 0-3 **9f-13f: 1-8** 14f+: 0-0
Track : LH: 0-5 RH: 0-2 Tight: 0-2 Gall: 0-1
Aids: Bl: 0-0 Vi: 0-0 Tstrap: 0-0
Best Rating: 16 7/01 NmkJ 1m gd-sft

On Shade

85 **11**

4-y-o ch f Polar Falcon (USA)-Vagrant Maid (USA) (Honest Pleasure (USA))
N Tinkler Philip J Grundy

Placings:60/006-000 **(2379)**
2001: 11^{0}S, 10^{0}F, 8^{0}GF

	Starts	1st	2nd	3rd	Win & Pl
Career Total (Turf)	8	0	0	0	0

Going (Turf): Sf: 0-2 GS: 0-3 Gd: 0-1 GF: 0-1 Fm: 0-1
Distance: 5f/6f: 0-0 7f-8f: 0-3 9f-13f: 0-5 14f+: 0-0
Track : LH: 0-5 RH: 0-0 Tight: 0-1 Gall: 0-1
Aids: Bl: 0-0 Vi: 0-0 Tstrap: 0-0
Best Rating: 11 6/01 Rdcr 1m gd-fm

On The Fairway (IRE)

91 **43**

2-y-o b f Danehill Dancer (IRE)-Asta Madera (IRE) (Toca Madera)
T D Easterby Ruth Baldwin And Jill Kershaw

Placings:400 **(4615)**
2001: 7^{4}GF, 6^{0}GF, 6^{0}F

	Starts	1st	2nd	3rd	Win & Pl
Career Total (Turf)	3	0	0	0	0

Going (Turf): Sf: 0-0 GS: 0-0 Gd: 0-0 GF: 0-2 Fm: 0-1
Distance: 5f/6f: 0-2 7f-8f: 0-1 9f-13f: 0-0 14f+: 0-0
Track : LH: 0-1 RH: 0-0 Tight: 0-0 Gall: 0-0
Aids: Bl: 0-0 Vi: 0-0 Tstrap: 0-0
Best Rating: 43 9/01 Newc 6f firm

On The Line

(73) (33)

3-y-o ch f Alhijaz-Join The Clan (Clantime)
Mrs N Macauley J Redden

Placings:00-0 **(0174)**
2001: 8^{0}SD

	Starts	1st	2nd	3rd	Win & Pl
Career Total (Turf)	0	0	0	0	
Career Total (AW)	3	0	0	0	

Going (Turf): Sf: 0-0 GS: 0-0 Gd: 0-0 GF: 0-0 Fm: 0-0
Distance: 5f/6f: 0-2 7f-8f: 0-1 9f-13f: 0-0 14f+: 0-0
Track : LH: 0-2 RH: 0-0 Tight: 0-0 Gall: 0-0
Aids: Bl: 0-0 Vi: 0-1 Tstrap: 0-0

On The Take (IRE)

4-y-o b g Kahyasi-Malmada (USA) (Fappiano (USA))
B J Curley Mrs B J Curley

Placings:000 **(0423)**
2001: 9^{0}SD, 12^{0}SW, 12^{0}SD

	Starts	1st	2nd	3rd	Win & Pl
Career Total (Turf)	0	0	0	0	
Career Total (AW)	3	0	0	0	

Going (Turf): Sf: 0-0 GS: 0-0 Gd: 0-0 GF: 0-0 Fm: 0-0
Distance: 5f/6f: 0-0 7f-8f: 0-0 9f-13f: 0-3 14f+: 0-0
Track : LH: 0-3 RH: 0-0 Tight: 0-2 Gall: 0-0
Aids: Bl: 0-1 Vi: 0-0 Tstrap: 0-0

On The Trail

98(108) (58)**53**

4-y-o ch g Catrail (USA)-From The Rooftops (IRE) (Thatching)
T D Barron (S Dow 23/1) Nigel Shields

Placings:06/000000-11200000060 **(5349)**
2001: 7^{1}SW, 7^{1}SW, 7^{2}SD, 5^{0}F, 5^{0}F, 6^{0}GF, 6^{0}SD, 6^{0}F, 5^{0}GF, 5^{6}SW, 5^{0}SD

	Starts	1st	2nd	3rd	Win & Pl
Career Total (Turf)	11	0	0	0	0
Career Total (AW)	8	2	1	0	5810

54 1/01 Wolv 7f G SLW £1365
49 1/01 Wolv 7f G SLW £1925
Total win prize-money £3290

Going (Turf): Sf: 0-1 GS: 0-2 Gd: 0-2 GF: 0-3 Fm: 0-3
Distance: 5f/6f: 0-14 **7f-8f: 2-4** 9f-13f: 0-1 14f+: 0-0
Track : **LH: 2-8** RH: 0-2 **Tight: 2-6** Gall: 0-2
Aids: Bl: 0-0 Vi: 0-0 **Tstrap: 2-5**
Best Rating: 58 2/01 Ling 7f stand

He won a couple of sellers over seven furlongs on the Wolverhampton Fibresand at the start of 2001 and ran very well in a much better race on Equitrack next time, but has shown precious little since. Best when able to dominate.

Once More For Luck (IRE)

99 (62)**45**

10-y-o b g Petorius-Mrs Lucky (Royal Match)

Mrs M Reveley The Mary Reveley Racing Club

Placings:01530015/52033600/42044222230310/34621/1014/02114314/3304/06031252300-6351223430305 **(5534)**

2001: 12^{6}GF, 11^{3}GF, 10^{5}GF, 11^{1}GF, 11^{2}GF, 12^{2}GS, 11^{3}GF, 11^{4}G, 14^{3}G, 12^{0}GF, 11^{3}G, 11^{0}S, 11^{5}S

	Starts	1st	2nd	3rd	Win & Pl
Career Total (Turf)	73	10	12	15	68285
Career Total (AW)	2	1	0	0	2294

47	6/01	Bevl	1m3f216y	F	G-F	£2352
63	6/00	Haml	1m5f9y	F(0-65)H	G-F	£2632
78	10/98	Catt	1m3f214y	F	SFT	£2337
67	9/98	Muss	1m4f	E(0-70)H	G-S	£7532
67	9/98	York	1m2f85y	E(0-70)H	GD	£5182
53	10/97	Ayr	1m5f13y	F	SFT	£2637
62	2/97	Sthl	1m4f	F	STD	£2294
67	10/96	Rdcr	1m3f	F	G-F	£2047
61	10/95	Catt	1m3f214y	F	G-F	£3083
74	10/93	NmkR	1m	E	GD	£3548
70	7/93	Haml	5f4y	F	G-S	£1970

Total win prize-money £36416

Going (Turf): Sf: 2-11 GS: 2-13 Gd: 2-19 **GF: 4-27** Fm: 0-3
Distance: 5f/6f: 1-5 7f-8f: 1-10 **9f-13f: 7-49** 14f+: 2-11
Track : **LH: 6-46** RH: 3-17 **Tight: 6-29** Gall: 1-15
Aids: Bl: 0-0 Vi: 0-0 Tstrap: 0-0
Best Rating: 51 7/01 Haml 1m4f17y gd-sft

Plating-class middle-distance stayer. Best on fast ground.

Once Removed

(89) (32)

3-y-o b f Distant Relative-Hakone (IRE) (Alzao (USA))

C N Allen Mrs A M Upsdell

Placings:0440234050-**00433050** **(0493)**

2001: 6^{0}SD, 7^{0}SD, 7^{4}SD, 5^{3}SW, 6^{3}SW, 5^{0}SD, 6^{5}SD, 6^{0}SD

	Starts	1st	2nd	3rd	Win & Pl
Career Total (Turf)	10	0	1	1	1772
Career Total (AW)	8	0	0	2	524

Going (Turf): **Sf: 0-0 GS: 0-3 Gd: 0-4 GF: 0-2 Fm: 0-1**
Distance: 5f/6f: 0-15 7f-8f: 0-3 9f-13f: 0-0 14f+: 0-0
Track : LH: 0-11 RH: 0-3 Tight: 0-8 Gall: 0-4
Aids: Bl: 0-1 Vi: 0-0 Tstrap: 0-0
Best Rating: 43 2/01 Ling 5f slow

One Beloved

82(77) (1)**60d**

3-y-o b f Piccolo-Eternal Flame (Primo Dominie)

A G Juckes A C W Price

Placings:003245-00 **(1845)**

2001: 5^{0}SD, 5^{0}GF

	Starts	1st	2nd	3rd	Win & Pl
Career Total (Turf)	7	0	1	1	1036
Career Total (AW)	1	0	0	0	

Going (Turf): **Sf: 0-1 GS: 0-1 Gd: 0-1 GF: 0-2 Fm: 0-2**
Distance: 5f/6f: 0-7 7f-8f: 0-1 9f-13f: 0-0 14f+: 0-0
Track : LH: 0-4 RH: 0-1 Tight: 0-1 Gall: 0-3
Aids: Bl: 0-0 Vi: 0-0 Tstrap: 0-0
Best Rating: 7 6/01 Leic 5f218y gd-fm

One Dinar (FR)

106(116) (79)**67**

6-y-o b h Generous (IRE)-Lypharitissima (FR) (Lightning (FR))

D Nicholls Mrs T L Lund

Placings:00/0055004/23554024610/**212**0503603200-451200 **(5539)**

2001: 9^{4}S, 8^{5}S, 8^{1}S, 9^{2}GF, 8^{0}G, 8^{0}S, 8^{0}SD, 8^{0}SD

	Starts	1st	2nd	3rd	Win & Pl
Career Total (Turf)	32	2	4	2	13680
Career Total (AW)	7	1	2	1	9295

67	4/01	Ripn	1m	E(0-70)H	SFT	£3633
75	2/00	Wolv	1m100y	C(0-100)H	STD	£6695
72	9/99	Ling	7f	D	G-F	£3744

Total win prize-money £14072

Going (Turf): **Sf: 1-7** GS: 0-3 Gd: 0-12 **GF: 1-9** Fm: 0-1
Distance: 5f/6f: 0-0 **7f-8f: 2-22** 9f-13f: 1-17 14f+: 0-0
Track : LH: 1-13 RH: 1-14 **Tight: 2-10** Gall: 0-1
Aids: Bl: 0-0 Vi: 0-1 Tstrap: 0-0
Best Rating: 67 4/01 Ripn 1m soft

Fair handicapper at around a mile. Handles any ground on turf and Fibresand.

One For Me

92 **44**

3-y-o br f Tragic Role (USA)-Chantallee's Pride (Mansooj)

Jean-Rene Auvray M J Lewin

Placings:0000 **(5601)**

2001: 7^{0}GF, 9^{0}G, 10^{0}HY, 8^{0}GS

	Starts	1st	2nd	3rd	Win & Pl
Career Total (Turf)	4	0	0	0	

Going (Turf): **Sf: 0-1 GS: 0-1 Gd: 0-1 GF: 0-1 Fm: 0-0**
Distance: 5f/6f: 0-0 7f-8f: 0-2 9f-13f: 0-2 14f+: 0-0
Track : LH: 0-0 RH: 0-1 Tight: 0-2 Gall: 0-0
Aids: Bl: 0-0 Vi: 0-0 Tstrap: 0-0
Best Rating: 44 9/01 Gdwd 1m1f192y good

One For Us

83 **75**

2-y-o ch c Superlative-One For Jeannie (Clantime)

Bruce Hellier Doncaster Racing Club

Placings:623106 **(5487)**

2001: 5^{6}, 5^{2}, 5^{3}S, 5^{1}G, 6^{0}G, 6^{6}HY

	Starts	1st	2nd	3rd	Win & Pl
Career Total (Turf)	6	1	1	1	7952

7/01	Hopp	5f	GD	£1954

Total win prize-money £1954

Going (Turf): Sf: 0-2 GS: 0-0 **Gd: 1-2** GF: 0-0 Fm: 0-0
Distance: **5f/6f: 1-6** 7f-8f: 0-0 9f-13f: 0-0 14f+: 0-0
Track : LH: 0-1 RH: 0-0 Tight: 0-0 Gall: 0-0
Aids: Bl: 0-0 Vi: 0-0 Tstrap: 0-0
Best Rating: 75 10/01 Donc 6f heavy

One Life To Live (IRE)

(89) (27)

8-y-o gr g Classic Music (USA)-Fine Flame (Le Prince)

J S Wainwright (D W Barker 9/2) Philip E Clark

Placings:50000/460/42500/40/056-0 **(0266)**

2001: 12^{0}SW

	Starts	1st	2nd	3rd	Win & Pl
Career Total (Turf)	13	0	1	0	1759
Career Total (AW)	6	0	0	0	0

Going (Turf): **Sf: 0-3 GS: 0-4 Gd: 0-3 GF: 0-3 Fm: 0-0**
Distance: 5f/6f: 0-2 7f-8f: 0-4 9f-13f: 0-10 14f+: 0-3
Track : LH: 0-12 RH: 0-6 Tight: 0-8 Gall: 0-2
Aids: Bl: 0-1 Vi: 0-3 Tstrap: 0-0

One Mind

92 **46**

3-y-o b c Mind Games-Cafe Solo (Nomination)

R Hannon Mrs D M Wight

Placings:0-0500 **(5131)**

2001: 6^{0}GF, 7^{5}S, 6^{0}GF, 7^{0}HY

	Starts	1st	2nd	3rd	Win & Pl
Career Total (Turf)	5	0	0	0	0

Going (Turf): **Sf: 0-3 GS: 0-0 Gd: 0-0 GF: 0-2 Fm: 0-0**
Distance: 5f/6f: 0-3 7f-8f: 0-2 9f-13f: 0-0 14f+: 0-0
Track : LH: 0-0 RH: 0-0 Tight: 0-0 Gall: 0-0
Aids: Bl: 0-0 Vi: 0-0 Tstrap: 0-0
Best Rating: 46 7/01 Sals 6f gd-fm

One Quick Lion

(94) (35)

5-y-o b g Lion Cavern (USA)-One Quick Bid (USA) (Commemorate (USA))

J Pearce Jeff Pearce

Placings:065/**0400-6030** **(0272)**

2001: 8^{6}SW, 12^{0}SW, 7^{3}SW, 8^{0}SW

	Starts	1st	2nd	3rd	Win & Pl
Career Total (Turf)	3	0	0	0	0
Career Total (AW)	8	0	0	1	411

Going (Turf): **Sf: 0-0 GS: 0-2 Gd: 0-0 GF: 0-1 Fm: 0-0**
Distance: 5f/6f: 0-0 7f-8f: 0-6 9f-13f: 0-5 14f+: 0-0
Track : LH: 0-8 RH: 0-2 Tight: 0-8 Gall: 0-0
Aids: Bl: 0-0 Vi: 0-0 Tstrap: 0-0
Best Rating: 35 1/01 Wolv 7f slow

One To Go (IRE)

(84) (30)

6-y-o b g Petorius-Caroline's Mark (On Your Mark)

Mrs A J Bowlby Hillview Racing

Placings:060042/40402232**00002100/6000/00** **(0352)**

2001: 8^{0}SD, 7^{0}SD

	Starts	1st	2nd	3rd	Win & Pl
Career Total (Turf)	21	1	4	1	5850
Career Total (AW)	7	0	1	0	642

51	10/98	Catt	5f212y	F	GD	£2304

Total win prize-money £2304

Going (Turf): Sf: 0-4 GS: 0-6 **Gd: 1-3** GF: 0-8 Fm: 0-0
Distance: **5f/6f: 1-12** 7f-8f: 0-12 9f-13f: 0-3 14f+: 0-0
Track : **LH: 1-12** RH: 0-5 **Tight: 1-11** Gall: 0-0
Aids: Bl: 0-1 Vi: 0-0 Tstrap: 0-0
Best Rating: 21 1/01 Sthl 1m stand

Ones Enough

86 **21**

5-y-o b g Reprimand-Sea Fairy (Wollow)

T P McGovern Heart Of The South Racing

Placings:3636511/05000000/000100400-00 **(3153)**

2001: 6^{0}GF, 7^{0}GS

	Starts	1st	2nd	3rd	Win & Pl
Career Total (Turf)	26	3	0	2	9856

46	6/00	Bath	5f161y	F(0-60)H	G-F	£2310
88	10/98	Ling	5f	D	HVY	£3272
70	9/98	Folk	5f	F	G-F	£2831

Total win prize-money £8414

Going (Turf): Sf: 1-5 GS: 0-4 Gd: 0-6 **GF: 2-8** Fm: 0-3
Distance: **5f/6f: 3-17** 7f-8f: 0-9 9f-13f: 0-0 14f+: 0-0
Track : **LH: 1-8** RH: 0-2 Tight: 0-2 **Gall: 1-4**
Aids: Bl: 0-2 Vi: 0-0 **Tstrap: 1-6**
Best Rating: 21 7/01 Ling 7f gd-sft

Online Investor

108 **89**

2-y-o b c Puissance-Anytime Baby (Bairn (USA))

C G Cox S P Lansdown Racing

Placings:4102 **(3242)**

2001: 5^{4}GS, 5^{1}GF, 5^{0}GF, 5^{2}GF

	Starts	1st	2nd	3rd	Win & Pl
Career Total (Turf)	4	1	1	0	33165

70 5/01 Bath 5f161y E G-F £3465
Total win prize-money £3465

Going (Turf): Sf: 0-0 GS: 0-1 Gd: 0-0 **GF: 1-3** Fm: 0-0
Distance: **5f/6f: 1-4** 7f-8f: 0-0 9f-13f: 0-0 14f+: 0-0
Track : **LH: 1-2** RH: 0-0 Tight: 0-0 **Gall: 1-2**
Aids: Bl: 0-0 Vi: 0-0 Tstrap: 0-0
Best Rating: 89 7/01 Newb 5f34y gd-fm

Useful sort, dam from same family as Petong. Looked the type to appreciate six furlongs when winning a maiden at Bath in May. Bolted before the start when tenth at Ascot next time, but came back to finish runner-up in the Weatherbys Super Sprint. Suited by fast ground.

Only For Gold

107(101) (54)**82**
6-y-o b g Presidium-Calvanne Miss (Martinmas)
A Berry Mr John Milner & Mr Stephen Milner

Placings:114/0000604000/250660000220233**6**/662302 00561**406-215**1021213562300 **(5535)**
2001: 7^{2}SW, 7^{1}SD, 7^{5}SD, 7^{1}HY, 8^{0}GF, 7^{2}G, 7^{1}GF, 7^{2}GF, 7^{1}GS, 7^{3}G, 8^{5}S, 7^{6}G, 7^{2}HY, 6^{3}G, 6^{0}GS, 7^{0}S

	Starts	1st	2nd	3rd	Win & Pl
Career Total (Turf)	52	6	9	5	52771
Career Total (AW)	7	1	1	0	4070

79 7/01 Ayr 7f C(0-95)H G-S £7182
57 7/01 Sthl 7f E(0-65) G-F £3094
59 4/01 Wwck 7f26y D(0-80)H HVY £4127
54 2/01 Wolv 7f F(0-60)H STD £1757
56 10/00 Newc 7f F(0-60)H HVY £1834
84 6/97 Bevl 5f B G-F £8729
84 5/97 Ches 5f16y D SFT £6930
Total win prize-money £33657

Going (Turf): Sf: 3-13 GS: 1-9 Gd: 0-12 GF: 2-15 Fm: 0-3
Distance: 5f/6f: 2-14 **7f-8f: 5-42** 9f-13f: 0-3 14f+: 0-0
Track : **LH: 5-34** RH: 0-5 **Tight: 2-22** Gall: 0-3
Aids: Bl: 0-0 Vi: 0-1 Tstrap: 0-0
Best Rating: 82 9/01 Ayr 6f good

He has rediscovered the art of winning in the last couple of seasons and has won four times so far this year on all sorts of ground as well as Fibresand. He has risen almost two stone in the ratings as a result. All his wins in 2001 have been on sharpish left-handed tracks. A true seven-furlong specialist.

Only For Sue

87 **59**
2-y-o ch g Pivotal-Barbary Court (Grundy)
W S Kittow Ms Susan Arnesen

Placings:5 **(4895)**
2001: 7^{5}GS

	Starts	1st	2nd	3rd	Win & Pl
Career Total (Turf)	1	0	0	0	0

Going (Turf): Sf: 0-0 GS: 0-1 Gd: 0-0 GF: 0-0 Fm: 0-0
Distance: 5f/6f: 0-0 7f-8f: 0-1 9f-13f: 0-0 14f+: 0-0
Track : LH: 0-0 RH: 0-0 Tight: 0-0 Gall: 0-0
Aids: Bl: 0-0 Vi: 0-0 Tstrap: 0-0
Best Rating: 59 9/01 Leic 7f9y gd-sft

Only One Legend (IRE)

102 **73d**
3-y-o b g Eagle Eyed (USA)-Afifah (Nashwan (USA))
T D Easterby The Four Ball Partnership

Placings:0331052-5003020006000 **(5535)**
2001: 6^{5}S, 7^{0}G, 6^{0}GF, 6^{3}GF, 5^{0}G, 6^{2}GF, 5^{0}G, 6^{0}G, 5^{0}G, 6^{6}GF, 5^{0}HY, 6^{0}GS, 7^{0}S

	Starts	1st	2nd	3rd	Win & Pl
Career Total (Turf)	20	1	2	3	8423

76 7/00 Donc 5f D GD £3510
Total win prize-money £3510

Going (Turf): Sf: 0-5 GS: 0-1 **Gd: 1-8** GF: 0-4 Fm: 0-2
Distance: **5f/6f: 1-17** 7f-8f: 0-3 9f-13f: 0-0 14f+: 0-0
Track : LH: 0-3 RH: 0-1 Tight: 0-1 Gall: 0-1
Aids: Bl: 0-0 Vi: 0-0 Tstrap: 0-0
Best Rating: 78 7/01 Newc 6f gd-fm

He has run a couple of decent races over five and six furlongs but has only flattered to deceive.

Only Penang (IRE)

98 **74**
2-y-o b f Perugino (USA)-Unalaska (IRE) (High Estate)
B R Millman Mrs A K H Ooi

Placings:01502 **(4954)**
2001: 6^{0}GF, 7^{1}GF, 8^{5}GF, 8^{0}G, 8^{2}GS

	Starts	1st	2nd	3rd	Win & Pl
Career Total (Turf)	5	1	1	0	5892

86 7/01 Newb 7f E G-F £4498
Total win prize-money £4498

Going (Turf): Sf: 0-0 GS: 0-1 Gd: 0-1 **GF: 1-3** Fm: 0-0
Distance: 5f/6f: 0-1 **7f-8f: 1-4** 9f-13f: 0-0 14f+: 0-0
Track : LH: 0-0 RH: 0-1 Tight: 0-0 Gall: 0-0
Aids: Bl: 0-0 Vi: 0-0 Tstrap: 0-0
Best Rating: 86 7/01 Newb 7f gd-fm

Fair juvenile in 2001. Stays a mile and acts on any ground.

Only When Provoked (IRE)

81(75) (6)**23**
3-y-o b g General Monash (USA)-Lyzia (IRE) (Lycius (USA))
A Streeter The Saturday Lunchtime Syndicate

Placings:00000-000 **(2188)**
2001: 12^{0}SD, 12^{0}SD, 14^{0}GF

	Starts	1st	2nd	3rd	Win & Pl
Career Total (Turf)	5	0	0	0	
Career Total (AW)	3	0	0	0	

Going (Turf): Sf: 0-1 GS: 0-0 Gd: 0-1 GF: 0-3 Fm: 0-0
Distance: 5f/6f: 0-1 7f-8f: 0-3 9f-13f: 0-3 14f+: 0-1
Track : LH: 0-6 RH: 0-1 Tight: 0-1 Gall: 0-1
Aids: Bl: 0-0 Vi: 0-2 Tstrap: 0-0
Best Rating: 10 6/01 Nott 1m6f15y gd-fm

Only Words (USA)

96(90) (21)**42**
4-y-o ch g Shuailaan (USA)-Conversation Piece (USA) (Seeking The Gold (USA))
A J Lockwood Mrs Lynne Lumley

Placings:6006-00000000240046 **(5637)**
2001: 9^{0}S, 9^{0}G, 12^{0}F, 7^{0}SD, 7^{0}GF, 10^{0}GF, 8^{0}F, 8^{0}GF, 9^{2}GF, 9^{4}GF, 9^{0}GF, 10^{0}S, 13^{4}S, 11^{6}G

	Starts	1st	2nd	3rd	Win & Pl
Career Total (Turf)	17	0	1	0	1024
Career Total (AW)	1	0	0	0	

Going (Turf): Sf: 0-4 GS: 0-0 Gd: 0-3 GF: 0-8 Fm: 0-2
Distance: 5f/6f: 0-0 7f-8f: 0-5 9f-13f: 0-12 14f+: 0-1
Track : LH: 0-8 RH: 0-6 Tight: 0-6 Gall: 0-1
Aids: Bl: 0-0 Vi: 0-0 Tstrap: 0-2
Best Rating: 42 10/01 Catt 1m5f175y soft

Onlytime Will Tell

104(93) (63)**80**
3-y-o ch g Efisio-Prejudice (Young Generation)
D Nicholls (C A Dwyer 17/5) J Hair & D Faulkner

Placings:0634-34110260131 **(5490)**
2001: 7^{3}GS, 8^{4}HY, 6^{1}GF, 6^{1}S, 8^{0}GF, 7^{2}GF, 8^{6}GS, 9^{0}G, 6^{1}GS, 6^{3}SD, 7^{1}HY

	Starts	1st	2nd	3rd	Win & Pl
Career Total (Turf)	12	4	1	1	13264
Career Total (AW)	3	0	0	2	873

79 10/01 Donc 7f E(0-80)H HVY £3276
70 10/01 Pont 6f E G-S £3416
80 5/01 Sals 6f212y F SFT £3290
70 5/01 Brig 6f209y F G-F £1799
Total win prize-money £11781

Going (Turf): Sf: 2-5 GS: 1-3 Gd: 0-1 GF: 1-3 Fm: 0-0
Distance: 5f/6f: 1-2 **7f-8f: 3-11** 9f-13f: 0-2 14f+: 0-0
Track : **LH: 2-8** RH: 0-2 Tight: 0-2 Gall: 0-0
Aids: Bl: 0-0 Vi: 0-0 Tstrap: 0-0
Best Rating: 80 5/01 Sals 6f212y soft

He was successful in three claimers and an apprentice handicap. Suited by a stiff six or seven furlongs, he handles any ground.

Oomph

104(98) (59)**77**
3-y-o b f Shareef Dancer (USA)-Seductress (Known Fact (USA))
W Jarvis J M Greetham

Placings:4366-30130 **(4988)**
2001: 7^{3}GF, 7^{0}GF, 7^{1}G, 7^{3}S, 8^{0}G

	Starts	1st	2nd	3rd	Win & Pl
Career Total (Turf)	9	1	0	3	6925

62 7/01 Newc 7f F GD £2285
Total win prize-money £2286

Going (Turf): Sf: 0-3 GS: 0-0 **Gd: 1-3** GF: 0-3 Fm: 0-0
Distance: 5f/6f: 0-2 **7f-8f: 1-7** 9f-13f: 0-0 14f+: 0-0
Track : LH: 0-1 RH: 0-0 Tight: 0-0 Gall: 0-0
Aids: Bl: 0-0 Vi: 0-0 Tstrap: 0-0
Best Rating: 77 9/01 Yarm 7f3y soft

Ran in decent company at two, but did not win until landing a median auction maiden at Newcastle in July 2001 and made hard work of that.

Opal's Helmsman (USA)

75 **49**
2-y-o b c Helmsman (USA)-Opal's Notebook (USA) (Notebook (USA))
R M Beckett A D Simmons

Placings:000 **(5175)**
2001: 5^{0}G, 6^{0}GF, 6^{0}HY

	Starts	1st	2nd	3rd	Win & Pl
Career Total (Turf)	3	0	0	0	

Going (Turf): Sf: 0-1 GS: 0-0 Gd: 0-1 GF: 0-1 Fm: 0-0
Distance: 5f/6f: 0-3 7f-8f: 0-0 9f-13f: 0-0 14f+: 0-0
Track : LH: 0-1 RH: 0-0 Tight: 0-0 Gall: 0-1
Aids: Bl: 0-0 Vi: 0-0 Tstrap: 0-0
Best Rating: 49 8/01 Bath 5f11y good

Open Arms

97 **48**
5-y-o ch g Most Welcome-Amber Fizz (USA) (Effervescing (USA))
Mrs A L M King Aiden Murphy

Placings:544203/3/0001300-00000 **(4906)**
2001: 8^{0}G, 9^{0}GF, 9^{0}G, 10^{0}GF, 9^{0}G

	Starts	1st	2nd	3rd	Win & Pl
Career Total (Turf)	19	1	1	3	5475

65 8/00 Bevl 1m100y E(0-75)H G-F £2873
Total win prize-money £2873

Going (Turf): Sf: 0-2 GS: 0-5 Gd: 0-5 **GF: 1-6** Fm: 0-1
Distance: 5f/6f: 0-0 7f-8f: 0-4 **9f-13f: 1-15** 14f+: 0-0
Track : LH: 0-9 **RH: 1-5** Tight: 0-3 Gall: 0-2

Aids: Bl: 0-1 Vi: 0-0 Tstrap: 0-0
Best Rating: 58 8/01 Nott 1m1f213y good

Open Ground (IRE)

80(101) (51)**44**
4-y-o ch g Common Grounds-Poplina (USA) (Roberto (USA))
Ian Williams The Net Partnership

Placings:00630/016104-100 **(5531)**
2001: 13^{1}SD, 14^{0}G, 16^{0}HY

	Starts	1st	2nd	3rd	Win & Pl
Career Total (Turf)	9	2	0	0	4670
Career Total (AW)	5	1	0	1	2744

51 3/01 Ling 1m5f F(0-60)H STD £2324
46 5/00 Yarm 2m F GD £2205
58 4/00 Pont 1m4f8y F HVY £2247
Total win prize-money £6776

Going (Turf): **Sf: 1-3** GS: 0-2 **Gd: 1-3** GF: 0-1 Fm: 0-0
Distance: 5f/6f: 0-0 7f-8f: 0-3 **9f-13f: 2-5** 14f+: 1-6
Track : **LH: 3-12** RH: 0-0 **Tight: 2-6** Gall: 0-1
Aids: Bl: 0-0 Vi: 0-0 Tstrap: 0-0
Best Rating: 51 3/01 Ling 1m5f stand

Open Warfare (IRE)

103 **54**
3-y-o b/br f General Monash (USA)-Pipe Opener (Prince Sabo)
G A Swinbank (D Eddy 9/4) Mrs Michele Rutter

Placings:3341353335003010-R203000 **(4965)**
2001: 7^{R}SD, 6^{2}G, 5^{0}G, 6^{3}G, 5^{0}GF, 5^{0}GF, 5^{0}S

	Starts	1st	2nd	3rd	Win & Pl
Career Total (Turf)	22	2	1	8	12497
Career Total (AW)	1	0	0	0	

64 10/00 Nott 6f15y F SFT £2878
63 5/00 Hayd 5f D GD £3867
Total win prize-money £6746

Going (Turf): **Sf: 1-6** GS: 0-2 **Gd: 1-8** GF: 0-5 Fm: 0-0
Distance: 5f/6f: 1-19 7f-8f: 1-4 9f-13f: 0-0 14f+: 0-0
Track : LH: 0-7 RH: 0-1 Tight: 0-1 Gall: 0-3
Aids: Bl: 0-0 Vi: 0-0 Tstrap: 0-0
Best Rating: 56 8/01 Catt 5f good

Opening Ceremony (USA)

100 **96**
2-y-o br f Quest For Fame-Gleam Of Light (IRE) (Danehill (USA))
Mrs A J Perrett K Abdulla

Placings:1 **(5274)**
2001: 7^{1}GS

	Starts	1st	2nd	3rd	Win & Pl
Career Total (Turf)	1	1	0	0	4069

96 10/01 Leic 7f9y D G-S £4069
Total win prize-money £4069

Going (Turf): Sf: 0-0 **GS: 1-1** Gd: 0-0 GF: 0-0 Fm: 0-0
Distance: 5f/6f: 0-0 **7f-8f: 1-1** 9f-13f: 0-0 14f+: 0-0
Track : LH: 0-0 RH: 0-0 Tight: 0-0 Gall: 0-0
Aids: Bl: 0-0 Vi: 0-0 Tstrap: 0-0
Best Rating: 96 10/01 Leic 7f9y gd-sft

Half-sister to the useful two-year-old seven-furlong winner, Gleaming Blade, showed the right attitude to win on her debut on yielding ground.

Operation Envy

(81) (44)**62**
3-y-o b g Makbul-Safe Bid (Sure Blade (USA))
R M Flower M Lickert

Placings:4604000000-0 **(0069)**
2001: 10^{0}SD

	Starts	1st	2nd	3rd	Win & Pl
Career Total (Turf)	7	0	0	0	211
Career Total (AW)	4	0	0	0	0

Going (Turf): **Sf: 0-0 GS: 0-2 Gd: 0-1 GF: 0-1 Fm: 0-2**
Distance: 5f/6f: 0-5 7f-8f: 0-4 9f-13f: 0-1 14f+: 0-0
Track : LH: 0-7 RH: 0-0 Tight: 0-4 Gall: 0-0
Aids: Bl: 0-0 Vi: 0-0 Tstrap: 0-0
Best Rating: 10 1/01 Ling 1m2f stand

Opium

68 **31**
2-y-o b f Polish Precedent (USA)-Brecon Beacons (IRE) (Shirley Heights)
R Hannon Lindy Regis & Geoff Howard-Spink

Placings:0 **(5277)**
2001: 7^{0}GS

	Starts	1st	2nd	3rd	Win & Pl
Career Total (Turf)	1	0	0	0	

Going (Turf): **Sf: 0-0 GS: 0-1 Gd: 0-0 GF: 0-0 Fm: 0-0**
Distance: 5f/6f: 0-0 7f-8f: 0-1 9f-13f: 0-0 14f+: 0-0
Track : LH: 0-0 RH: 0-0 Tight: 0-0 Gall: 0-0
Aids: Bl: 0-0 Vi: 0-0 Tstrap: 0-0
Best Rating: 31 10/01 Leic 7f9y gd-sft

Opportune (GER)

102 **58**
6-y-o br g Shirley Heights-On The Tiles (Thatch (USA))
W M Brisbourne The Ox Hill Flyers

Placings:0000500/00314/50-311313231304 **(5167)**
2001: 13^{3}GS, 12^{1}GF, 14^{1}GF, 14^{3}GF, 13^{1}G, 14^{3}GF, 13^{2}G, 13^{3}GF, 16^{1}GF, 16^{3}GF, 16^{0}S, 12^{4}GS

	Starts	1st	2nd	3rd	Win & Pl
Career Total (Turf)	25	5	1	6	22686
Career Total (AW)	1	0	0	0	0

58 8/01 Wwck 2m39y D(0-80)H G-F £4160
49 7/01 Haml 1m5f9y E(0-70)H GD £5398
35 7/01 Wwck 1m6f213yE(0-70)H G-F £3360
43 7/01 Haml 1m4f17y F(0-70)H G-F £2744
49 5/98 Bevl 1m1f207yF GD £2425
Total win prize-money £18087

Going (Turf): Sf: 0-2 GS: 0-4 Gd: 2-8 **GF: 3-11** Fm: 0-0
Distance: 5f/6f: 0-0 7f-8f: 0-4 9f-13f: 2-11 **14f+: 3-11**
Track : LH: 1-10 **RH: 3-11 Tight: 2-7** Gall: 0-2
Aids: Bl: 0-0 Vi: 0-0 Tstrap: 0-0
Best Rating: 58 8/01 Wwck 2m39y gd-fm

He returned from a long layoff in August 2000 and was in great form during July 2001, winning three times in modest handicap company before taking a Warwick handicap the following month on his first attempt at two miles. Effective on fast ground between 12 and 16 furlongs.

Optimaite

108 **87**
4-y-o b g Komaite (USA)-Leprechaun Lady (Royal Blend)
B R Millman Always Hopeful Partnership

Placings:11002040/310505006-0162040420 **(5142)**
2001: 12^{0}S, 9^{1}GF, 10^{6}GF, 10^{2}GF, 12^{0}G, 12^{4}GF, 12^{0}G, 10^{4}G, 12^{2}GF, 9^{0}G

	Starts	1st	2nd	3rd	Win & Pl
Career Total (Turf)	27	4	3	1	36626

91 6/01 Folk 1m1f149yC G-F £6500
103 5/00 Sals 1m4f B(0-95) GD £8681
94 4/99 Asct 5f B GD £7282
81 4/99 Wind 5f10y E G-F £2704
Total win prize-money £25257

Going (Turf): Sf: 0-3 GS: 0-3 **Gd: 2-6 GF: 2-14** Fm: 0-1
Distance: 5f/6f: 2-6 7f-8f: 0-2 9f-13f: 2-17 14f+: 0-2
Track : LH: 0-11 **RH: 3-10 Tight: 2-7** Gall: 1-10
Aids: Bl: 0-0 Vi: 0-1 **Tstrap: 1-9**
Best Rating: 91 7/01 Sand 1m2f7y gd-fm

Decent handicapper, stays a mile and a half, goes on decent ground. Best form in the spring.

Optimax

73(66) (3)**22**
4-y-o ch g Rudimentary (USA)-Zipperti Do (Precocious)
P D Evans (M G Quinlan 27/7) Ms K Sadler

Placings:0000 **(5083)**
2001: 7^{0}GS, 7^{0}F, 8^{0}SD, 7^{0}S

	Starts	1st	2nd	3rd	Win & Pl
Career Total (Turf)	3	0	0	0	
Career Total (AW)	1	0	0	0	

Going (Turf): **Sf: 0-1 GS: 0-1 Gd: 0-0 GF: 0-0 Fm: 0-1**
Distance: 5f/6f: 0-0 7f-8f: 0-4 9f-13f: 0-0 14f+: 0-0
Track : LH: 0-2 RH: 0-0 Tight: 0-0 Gall: 0-0
Aids: Bl: 0-0 Vi: 0-0 Tstrap: 0-1
Best Rating: 22 6/01 Ling 7f firm

Or Royal (FR)

105(102) (52)**49**
10-y-o gr g Kendor (FR)-Pomme Royale (FR) (Shergar)
R Lee Mrs C Lee

Placings:231/530000001402 **(5411)**
2001: 12^{5}SW, 14^{3}S, 18^{0}GF, 16^{0}SD, 16^{0}GF, 12^{0}GF, 18^{0}GF, 11^{0}G, 14^{1}SW, 14^{4}SD, 15^{0}GS, 14^{2}SD

	Starts	1st	2nd	3rd	Win & Pl
Career Total (Turf)	10	1	1	2	18895
Career Total (AW)	5	1	1	0	3146

52 9/01 Wolv 1m6f166yF SLW £2282
6/94 Evry 1m4f GD £9153
Total win prize-money £11435

Going (Turf): Sf: 0-1 GS: 0-1 **Gd: 1-3** GF: 0-5 Fm: 0-0
Distance: 5f/6f: 0-0 7f-8f: 0-0 9f-13f: 1-6 14f+: 1-9
Track : **LH: 1-11** RH: 0-1 **Tight: 1-4** Gall: 0-1
Aids: Bl: 0-5 Vi: 0-2 Tstrap: 0-0
Best Rating: 71 5/01 Ches 2m2f147y gd-fm

Better known as a jumper, this quirky individual has enjoyed a renaissance in modest staying events on Fibresand of late.

Orake Prince

89 **62**
2-y-o b c Bluegrass Prince (IRE)-Kiri Te (Liboi (USA))
J G Portman Madhatter Racing

Placings:00 **(5460)**
2001: 6^{0}S, 8^{0}G

	Starts	1st	2nd	3rd	Win & Pl
Career Total (Turf)	2	0	0	0	

Going (Turf): **Sf: 0-1 GS: 0-0 Gd: 0-1 GF: 0-0 Fm: 0-0**
Distance: 5f/6f: 0-0 7f-8f: 0-1 9f-13f: 0-1 14f+: 0-0
Track : LH: 0-2 RH: 0-0 Tight: 0-1 Gall: 0-0
Aids: Bl: 0-0 Vi: 0-0 Tstrap: 0-0
Best Rating: 62 10/01 Brig 6f209y soft

Orange Place (IRE)

82
10-y-o ch g Nordance (USA)-Little Red Hut (Habitat)
B J Llewellyn Lodge Cross Partnership

Placings:011240/1601400/600/643653100/0320020300 44/5000005660/0 **(0500)**
2001: 12^{0}GS

	Starts	1st	2nd	3rd	Win & Pl
Career Total (Turf)	39	5	3	4	41221
Career Total (AW)	9	0	0	0	0

74 5/96 Gdwd 7f C(0-90)H SFT £8850

89	6/94	Epsm	7f	C(0-90)H	GD	£11210
85	4/94	Kemp	7f	B(0-100)H	SFT	£6196
79	7/93	Ling	7f	D	GD	£3201
66	6/93	Wwck	7f	F	G-S	£2070

Total win prize-money £31528

Going (Turf): Sf: 2-5 GS: 1-12 **Gd: 2-11** GF: 0-8 Fm: 0-3
Distance: 5f/6f: 0-2 **7f-8f: 5-38** 9f-13f: 0-8 14f+: 0-0
Track : LH: 2-24 RH: 2-9 Tight: 1-14 Gall: 1-3
Aids: Bl: 0-4 Vi: 0-1 Tstrap: 0-0

Orange Tree Lad

94(95) (64)**64**
3-y-o b g Tragic Role (USA)-Adorable Cherub (USA) (Halo (USA))
M L W Bell Jay Dee Bloodstock Limited

Placings:0232000-042 **(2768)**
2001: 6^{0}GF, 5^{4}GF, 6^{2}GF

	Starts	1st	2nd	3rd	Win & Pl
Career Total (Turf)	9	0	2	1	2668
Career Total (AW)	1	0	1	0	626

Going (Turf): Sf: 0-1 GS: 0-1 Gd: 0-2 GF: 0-5 Fm: 0-0
Distance: 5f/6f: 0-8 7f-8f: 0-2 9f-13f: 0-0 14f+: 0-0
Track : LH: 0-2 RH: 0-0 Tight: 0-0 Gall: 0-0
Aids: Bl: 0-0 Vi: 0-0 Tstrap: 0-0
Best Rating: 57 7/01 Sthl 6f gd-fm

Orangerie (IRE)

104(76) (43)**82**
3-y-o b g Darshaan-Fleur D'Oranger (Northfields (USA))
Sir Mark Prescott W E Sturt - Osborne House

Placings:050-3123253 **(5114)**
2001: 14^{3}G, 16^{1}G, 14^{2}S, 13^{3}GS, 16^{2}GF, 15^{5}G, 16^{3}HY

	Starts	1st	2nd	3rd	Win & Pl
Career Total (Turf)	9	1	2	3	7335
Career Total (AW)	1	0	0	0	

67	8/01	Nott	2m9y	F(0-65)H	GD	£2802

Total win prize-money £2803

Going (Turf): Sf: 0-2 GS: 0-1 **Gd: 1-4** GF: 0-2 Fm: 0-0
Distance: 5f/6f: 0-2 7f-8f: 0-1 9f-13f: 0-0 **14f+: 1-7**
Track : **LH: 1-6** RH: 0-2 Tight: 0-3 Gall: 0-0
Aids: Bl: 0-0 Vi: 0-0 Tstrap: 0-0
Best Rating: 82 9/01 Gdwd 2m gd-fm

Decent if one-paced staying handicapper.

Orangetree County (IRE)

89 **35**
3-y-o b/br f Dolphin Street (FR)-Empress Kim (Formidable (USA))
C A Dwyer D Farrow

Placings:6-5000400 **(5601)**
2001: 7^{5}G, 5^{0}GF, 7^{0}GF, 10^{0}GF, 5^{4}G, 5^{0}G, 8^{0}GS

	Starts	1st	2nd	3rd	Win & Pl
Career Total (Turf)	8	0	0	0	275

Going (Turf): Sf: 0-1 GS: 0-1 Gd: 0-3 GF: 0-3 Fm: 0-0
Distance: 5f/6f: 0-4 7f-8f: 0-3 9f-13f: 0-1 14f+: 0-0
Track : LH: 0-0 RH: 0-1 Tight: 0-0 Gall: 0-1
Aids: Bl: 0-0 Vi: 0-0 Tstrap: 0-0
Best Rating: 35 8/01 Leic 5f2y good

Orangino

94 **44**
3-y-o b c Primo Dominie-Sweet Jaffa (Never So Bold)
C W Thornton Guy Reed

Placings:00-000300 **(3178)**
2001: 6^{0}GS, 6^{0}GF, 7^{0}G, 5^{3}GF, 6^{0}GF, 6^{0}GS

	Starts	1st	2nd	3rd	Win & Pl
Career Total (Turf)	8	0	0	1	474

Going (Turf): Sf: 0-1 GS: 0-3 Gd: 0-1 GF: 0-3 Fm: 0-0
Distance: 5f/6f: 0-6 7f-8f: 0-2 9f-13f: 0-0 14f+: 0-0
Track : LH: 0-3 RH: 0-0 Tight: 0-0 Gall: 0-0
Aids: Bl: 0-3 Vi: 0-0 Tstrap: 0-0
Best Rating: 44 5/01 Hayd 6f gd-fm

Orchestra Stall

116d
9-y-o b g Old Vic-Blue Brocade (Reform)
J L Dunlop The Hon Sir David Sieff

Placings:0/3/2141012/310121/6110-0 **(1122)**
2001: 16^{0}G

	Starts	1st	2nd	3rd	Win & Pl
Career Total (Turf)	20	8	3	2	162103

112	9/00	Lonc	1m7f110y		G-S	£21134
114	5/00	Asct	2m45y	A	G-S	£25200
116	9/97	Lonc	1m7f110y		GD	£24691
107	6/97	Curr	1m6f		YLD	£18000
111	4/97	Asct	2m45y	A	G-F	£25240
96	11/96	NmkR	2m	A(0-105)H	GD	£10912
87	8/96	Newc	2m19y	C(0-100)H	GD	£10503
82	4/96	Ripn	2m	C(0-90)H	GD	£6937

Total win prize-money £142620

Going (Turf): Sf: 0-7 GS: 2-2 **Gd: 4-8** GF: 1-2 Fm: 0-0
Distance: 5f/6f: 0-0 7f-8f: 0-1 9f-13f: 0-3 **14f+: 8-16**
Track : LH: 1-5 **RH: 7-14** Tight: 1-1 **Gall: 4-7**
Aids: Bl: 0-0 Vi: 0-0 Tstrap: 0-0
Best Rating: 82 4/96 Ripn 2m G

Returned from two years off to run away with Ascot's Sagaro Stakes in 2000, and later added the Prix Gladiateur. Well beaten on his return , he had further problems and did not reappear.

Order

106 **88**
5-y-o b g Deploy-Gong (Bustino)
R M Beckett A D G Oldrey

Placings:2110 **(2949)**
2001: 12^{2}GS, 12^{1}G, 14^{1}G, 16^{0}G

	Starts	1st	2nd	3rd	Win & Pl
Career Total (Turf)	4	2	1	0	8954

88	6/01	Hayd	1m6f	D(0-85)H	GD	£4140
55	5/01	Haml	1m4f17y	E	GD	£3395

Total win prize-money £7536

Going (Turf): Sf: 0-0 GS: 0-1 **Gd: 2-3** GF: 0-0 Fm: 0-0
Distance: 5f/6f: 0-0 7f-8f: 0-0 9f-13f: 1-2 14f+: 1-2
Track : LH: 1-2 RH: 1-2 **Tight: 1-2** Gall: 0-1
Aids: Bl: 0-0 Vi: 0-0 Tstrap: 0-0
Best Rating: 88 6/01 Hayd 1m6f good

Ran well on flat debut and subsequently won twice over twelve and fourteen furlongs. Best on good ground.

Oreana (FR)

97 **79**
3-y-o b f Anabaa (USA)-Lavinia Fontana (IRE) (Sharpo)
J L Dunlop Cyril Humphris

Placings:051-000 **(4568)**
2001: 5^{0}S, 6^{0}G, 6^{0}HY

	Starts	1st	2nd	3rd	Win & Pl
Career Total (Turf)	6	1	0	0	3348

95	11/00	Donc	6f	D	HVY	£3347

Total win prize-money £3348

Going (Turf): Sf: 1-3 GS: 0-1 Gd: 0-1 GF: 0-1 Fm: 0-0
Distance: **5f/6f: 1-4** 7f-8f: 0-2 9f-13f: 0-0 14f+: 0-0
Track : LH: 0-0 RH: 0-1 Tight: 0-0 Gall: 0-1
Aids: Bl: 0-0 Vi: 0-0 Tstrap: 0-0
Best Rating: 79 4/01 Sand 5f6y soft

Won on heavy ground last term but cut no ice this season.

Oriental Empress

76(64) (19)**34**
2-y-o b f Emperor Fountain-Beijing (USA) (Northjet)
C W Thornton Mrs C Wilson

Placings:00 **(5371)**
2001: 7^{0}GS, 8^{0}G

	Starts	1st	2nd	3rd	Win & Pl
Career Total (Turf)	2	0	0	0	

Going (Turf): Sf: 0-0 GS: 0-1 Gd: 0-1 GF: 0-0 Fm: 0-0
Distance: 5f/6f: 0-0 7f-8f: 0-2 9f-13f: 0-0 14f+: 0-0
Track : LH: 0-0 RH: 0-0 Tight: 0-0 Gall: 0-0
Aids: Bl: 0-0 Vi: 0-0 Tstrap: 0-0
Best Rating: 34 10/01 Rdcr 1m good

Oriental Mist (IRE)

99 **59**
3-y-o gr g Balla Cove-Donna Katrina (King's Lake (USA))
Miss L A Perratt Oriental Mist Partnership

Placings:54330446010-000343004 **(5269)**
2001: 8^{0}S, 8^{0}F, 7^{0}GF, 8^{3}G, 8^{4}HY, 15^{3}G, 10^{0}HY, 11^{0}GS, 10^{4}HY

	Starts	1st	2nd	3rd	Win & Pl
Career Total (Turf)	20	1	0	4	7190

66	10/00	Ayr	1m	D(0-85)	HVY	£3672

Total win prize-money £3673

Going (Turf): Sf: 1-7 GS: 0-2 Gd: 0-6 GF: 0-3 Fm: 0-2
Distance: 5f/6f: 0-5 **7f-8f: 1-8** 9f-13f: 0-6 14f+: 0-1
Track : **LH: 1-9** RH: 0-4 Tight: 0-5 Gall: 0-1
Aids: Bl: 0-0 Vi: 0-0 Tstrap: 0-0
Best Rating: 68 8/01 Ayr 1m good

Oriental Moon (IRE)

92(70) (28)**72**
2-y-o ch f Spectrum (IRE)-La Grande Cascade (USA) (Beaudelaire (USA))
G C H Chung Greg Chung Racing Club

Placings:0050200 **(5283)**
2001: 6^{0}GF, 7^{0}SD, 7^{5}GS, 7^{0}GF, 7^{2}G, 7^{0}S, 8^{0}HY

	Starts	1st	2nd	3rd	Win & Pl
Career Total (Turf)	6	0	1	0	2480
Career Total (AW)	1	0	0	0	

Going (Turf): Sf: 0-2 GS: 0-1 Gd: 0-1 GF: 0-2 Fm: 0-0
Distance: 5f/6f: 0-0 7f-8f: 0-7 9f-13f: 0-0 14f+: 0-0
Track : LH: 0-2 RH: 0-1 Tight: 0-0 Gall: 0-0
Aids: Bl: 0-0 Vi: 0-0 Tstrap: 0-0
Best Rating: 72 9/01 Donc 7f good

She had shown little ability in maiden company, prior to finishing runner-up in a decent Doncaster nursery in September 2001.

Orientor

5 **117**
3-y-o b c Inchinor-Orient (Bay Express)
J S Goldie S Bruce

Placings:3203-21433100155223 **(5694)**
2001: 6^{2}S, 7^{1}S, 6^{4}F, 6^{3}GF, 6^{3}GF, 6^{1}GS, 6^{0}GF, 7^{0}GF, 6^{1}G, 6^{5}G, 6^{5}HY, 6^{2}S, 6^{2}GS, 6^{3}S

	Starts	1st	2nd	3rd	Win & Pl
Career Total (Turf)	18	3	4	5	147210

117	8/01	Asct	6f	B	GD	£50000
108	6/01	York	6f	B(0-105)H	G-S	£44460
82	5/01	Rdcr	7f	E	SFT	£3388

Total win prize-money £97848

Going (Turf): Sf: 1-9 GS: 1-2 Gd: 1-2 GF: 0-4 Fm: 0-1

Distance: 5f/6f: 2-14 7f-8f: 1-4 9f-13f: 0-0 14f+: 0-0
Track : LH: 0-2 RH: 0-0 Tight: 0-0 Gall: 0-2
Aids: Bl: 0-0 Vi: 0-0 Tstrap: 0-0
Best Rating: 117 8/01 Asct 6f good

High-class sprinter, he has run well in competitive handicaps, gaining a much-deserved success when winning a valuable handicap at York in June and putting up his best performance with a runaway success in a valuable event on Shergar Cup day at Ascot. Ran well in Group and Listed races afterwards. Suited by an easy surface and likes to come late off a strong pace.

Orinoco's Flight (IRE)

94 **48**
3-y-o ch g Spectrum (IRE)-Silk Route (USA) (Shahrastani (USA))
J G Given C D Carr

Placings:40 **(5631)**
2001: 8^{4}HY, 10^{0}G

	Starts	1st	2nd	3rd	Win & Pl
Career Total (Turf)	2	0	0	0	328

Going (Turf): Sf: 0-1 GS: 0-0 Gd: 0-1 GF: 0-0 Fm: 0-0
Distance: 5f/6f: 0-0 7f-8f: 0-0 9f-13f: 0-2 14f+: 0-0
Track : LH: 0-2 RH: 0-0 Tight: 0-1 Gall: 0-0
Aids: Bl: 0-0 Vi: 0-0 Tstrap: 0-0
Best Rating: 48 11/01 Rdcr 1m2f good

Orinocovsky (IRE)

87 **71**
2-y-o ch c Grand Lodge (USA)-Brillantina (FR) (Crystal Glitters (USA))
P F I Cole Andy J Smith

Placings:3 **(4889)**
2001: 8^{3}GF

	Starts	1st	2nd	3rd	Win & Pl
Career Total (Turf)	1	0	0	1	684

Going (Turf): Sf: 0-0 GS: 0-0 Gd: 0-0 GF: 0-1 Fm: 0-0
Distance: 5f/6f: 0-0 7f-8f: 0-1 9f-13f: 0-0 14f+: 0-0
Track : LH: 0-0 RH: 0-1 Tight: 0-0 Gall: 0-0
Aids: Bl: 0-0 Vi: 0-0 Tstrap: 0-0
Best Rating: 71 9/01 Kemp 1m gd-fm

Oriole

102(59) (42)**42**
8-y-o b g Mazilier (USA)-Odilese (Mummy's Pet)
Don Enrico Incisa Don Enrico Incisa

Placings:00624020146000/000034160000/000100231 3030/05002100001450/004250500045/0000040010-00000600 **(5535)**
2001: 8^{0}F, 7^{0}GF, 7^{0}GF, 8^{0}GS, 7^{0}F, 8^{6}GF, 8^{0}G, 7^{0}S

	Starts	1st	2nd	3rd	Win & Pl
Career Total (Turf)	81	7	5	4	31683
Career Total (AW)	4	0	0	0	0

46	10/00	Newc	7f	F(0-60)H	HVY	£1834
49	8/98	Rdcr	7f	D(0-75)H	FRM	£3728
50	6/98	Carl	6f206y	D(0-80)H	G-S	£3647
52	8/97	Rdcr	7f	D(0-75)H	FRM	£3663
39	5/97	Rdcr	1m	E(0-70)H	GD	£3054
49	7/96	Ayr	7f	E(0-70)H	G-S	£2957
62	7/95	Thsk	6f	D	G-F	£3850

Total win prize-money £22736

Going (Turf): Sf: 1-12 **GS: 2-6** Gd: 1-23 GF: 1-30 **Fm: 2-10**
Distance: 5f/6f: 1-13 **7f-8f: 6-68** 9f-13f: 0-4 14f+: 0-0
Track : LH: 1-18 RH: 1-8 Tight: 0-4 Gall: 0-6
Aids: Bl: 0-2 **Vi: 3-12** Tstrap: 0-0
Best Rating: 44 7/01 Donc 7f gd-fm

Moderate seven-furlong handicapper. Acts on any ground.

Orlando Sunrise (IRE)

99 **48**
4-y-o ch f Dolphin Street (FR)-Miss Belgravia (USA) (Smarten (USA))
Ian Williams Charles Eden

Placings:05045-000540 **(4635)**
2001: 9^{0}F, 11^{0}GF, 12^{0}GF, 10^{5}F, 10^{4}GF, 9^{0}GF

	Starts	1st	2nd	3rd	Win & Pl
Career Total (Turf)	11	0	0	0	0

Going (Turf): Sf: 0-1 GS: 0-0 Gd: 0-1 GF: 0-7 Fm: 0-2
Distance: 5f/6f: 0-0 7f-8f: 0-3 9f-13f: 0-8 14f+: 0-0
Track : LH: 0-4 RH: 0-4 Tight: 0-2 Gall: 0-0
Aids: Bl: 0-1 Vi: 0-0 Tstrap: 0-0
Best Rating: 55 5/01 Leic 1m1f218y firm

Orlass (IRE)

98(92) (57)**80**
2-y-o br f Hamas (IRE)-Rockbourne (Midyan (USA))
M G Quinlan P J McBride

Placings:22161023 **(5736a)**
2001: 5^{2}SD, 5^{2}SD, 6^{1}GF, 6^{6}GF, 6^{1}HY, 5^{0}GS, 6^{2}GS, 6^{3}HY

	Starts	1st	2nd	3rd	Win & Pl
Career Total (Turf)	6	2	1	1	12744
Career Total (AW)	2	0	2	0	1350

71	9/01	Hayd	6f	D(0-85)	HVY	£4420
57	7/01	Hayd	6f	F	G-F	£2632

Total win prize-money £7052

Going (Turf): Sf: 1-2 GS: 0-2 Gd: 0-0 **GF: 1-2** Fm: 0-0
Distance: **5f/6f: 2-8** 7f-8f: 0-0 9f-13f: 0-0 14f+: 0-0
Track : LH: 0-0 RH: 0-0 Tight: 0-0 Gall: 0-0
Aids: Bl: 0-0 Vi: 0-0 Tstrap: 0-0
Best Rating: 80 11/01 StCl 6f heavy

She got off the mark in a maiden claimer at Haydock and followed up with success in a nursery at that same course before a two narrow defeats in similar races at Newmarket. Handles most types of ground but suited by cut and best at six furlongs.

Orleans (IRE)

(69) **43**
6-y-o b g Scenic-Guest House (What A Guest)
G A Ham G A Ham

Placings:000/00305/00 **(0642)**
2001: 12^{0}SD, 16^{0}HY

	Starts	1st	2nd	3rd	Win & Pl
Career Total (Turf)	9	0	0	1	405
Career Total (AW)	1	0	0	0	

Going (Turf): Sf: 0-2 GS: 0-4 Gd: 0-3 GF: 0-0 Fm: 0-0
Distance: 5f/6f: 0-0 7f-8f: 0-3 9f-13f: 0-6 14f+: 0-1
Track : LH: 0-4 RH: 0-5 Tight: 0-2 Gall: 0-0
Aids: Bl: 0-0 Vi: 0-0 Tstrap: 0-0

Ormelie (IRE)

76 **96**
6-y-o gr g Jade Hunter (USA)-Trolley Song (USA) (Caro)
C A Dwyer M M Foulger

Placings:5133150/6551/053302-0 **(0807)**
2001: 12^{0}S

	Starts	1st	2nd	3rd	Win & Pl
Career Total (Turf)	18	3	1	4	53803

93	7/99	Gdwd	1m1f192yB H		G-F	£35500
88	8/98	Newb	1m5f61y	C(0-90)H	G-F	£5413
74	5/98	Ayr	1m2f	D	GD	£3444

Total win prize-money £44358

Going (Turf): Sf: 0-5 GS: 0-1 Gd: 1-1 **GF: 2-11** Fm: 0-0
Distance: 5f/6f: 0-0 7f-8f: 0-2 **9f-13f: 2-12** 14f+: 1-4

Track : **LH: 2-7** RH: 1-9 Tight: 1-3 Gall: 1-10
Aids: Bl: 0-1 Vi: 0-0 Tstrap: 0-0
Best Rating: 41 4/01 NmkR 1m4f soft

A lazy individual, he looked sharper when blinkered at Newmarket in September 2000. Sold to Chris Dwyer for 12,000 gns, he ran just once this season.

Orthodox

91 **74**
2-y-o gr c Baryshnikov (AUS)-Sancta (So Blessed)
G L Moore R Kiernan

Placings:04 **(5040)**
2001: 7^{0}G, 10^{4}G

	Starts	1st	2nd	3rd	Win & Pl
Career Total (Turf)	2	0	0	0	270

Going (Turf): Sf: 0-0 GS: 0-0 Gd: 0-2 GF: 0-0 Fm: 0-0
Distance: 5f/6f: 0-0 7f-8f: 0-1 9f-13f: 0-1 14f+: 0-0
Track : LH: 0-1 RH: 0-1 Tight: 0-1 Gall: 0-0
Aids: Bl: 0-0 Vi: 0-0 Tstrap: 0-0
Best Rating: 74 10/01 Bath 1m2f46y good

Oscar Pepper (USA)

106(108) (95)**66**
4-y-o b g Brunswick (USA)-Princess Baja (USA) (Conquistador Cielo (USA))
T D Barron Ian Armitage

Placings:05000/1122030362612-54120230000 **(4451)**
2001: 7^{5}SW, 6^{4}SD, 7^{1}SD, 7^{2}SD, 7^{0}GF, 7^{2}GF, 7^{3}GF, 7^{0}GF, 7^{0}GF, 6^{0}G, 6^{0}GF

	Starts	1st	2nd	3rd	Win & Pl
Career Total (Turf)	18	0	1	3	3435
Career Total (AW)	11	4	5	0	24226

79	3/01	Wolv	7f	C	STD	£6075
83	11/00	Sthl	6f	D(0-80)H	STD	£3250
67	1/00	Sthl	6f	E(0-70)H	STD	£2782
66	1/00	Sthl	6f	F(0-65)H	STD	£2331

Total win prize-money £14438

Going (Turf): Sf: 0-1 GS: 0-0 Gd: 0-3 GF: 0-13 Fm: 0-0
Distance: **5f/6f: 3-10** 7f-8f: 1-17 9f-13f: 0-1 14f+: 0-0
Track : **LH: 4-21** RH: 0-2 **Tight: 1-7** Gall: 0-3
Aids: Bl: 0-0 Vi: 0-0 Tstrap: 0-0
Best Rating: 95 3/01 Sthl 7f stand

He is useful on sand over six and seven furlongs, but is not quite as effective on turf.

Oscietra

96 **33**
5-y-o b m Robellino (USA)-Top Treat (USA) (Topsider (USA))
W M Brisbourne (G B Balding 5/1) Mark Brisbourne

Placings:05651406 0/0555600306-000032 **(5534)**
2001: 10^{0}F, 12^{0}GF, 9^{0}GF, 10^{0}HY, 9^{3}HY, 11^{2}S

	Starts	1st	2nd	3rd	Win & Pl
Career Total (Turf)	25	1	1	2	4738

67	8/99	Kemp	1m1f	E(0-70)H	G-S	£2739

Total win prize-money £2740

Going (Turf): Sf: 0-7 **GS: 1-7** Gd: 0-3 GF: 0-5 Fm: 0-3
Distance: 5f/6f: 0-0 7f-8f: 0-5 **9f-13f: 1-20** 14f+: 0-0
Track : LH: 0-8 **RH: 1-11** Tight: 0-6 Gall: 0-4
Aids: Bl: 0-0 Vi: 0-4 Tstrap: 0-0
Best Rating: 33 7/01 Kemp 1m1f gd-fm

Very moderate handicapper. Has only one win to her name . Likes to get her toe in.

Oshiponga

101(86) (35)**70**
3-y-o ch f Barathea (IRE)-Ingozi (Warning)
R Charlton A E Oppenheimer

Placings:000130 (3658)
2001: 7^{0}SD, 7^{0}S, 7^{0}G, 9^{1}GF, 9^{3}GF, 10^{0}GF

	Starts	1st	2nd	3rd	Win & Pl
Career Total (Turf)	5	1	0	1	4330
Career Total (AW)	1	0	0	0	

70 6/01 Rdcr 1m1f E(0-75)H G-F £3836
Total win prize-money £3836

Going (Turf): Sf: 0-1 GS: 0-1 Gd: 0-1 **GF: 1-3** Fm: 0-0
Distance: 5f/6f: 0-0 7f-8f: 0-3 **9f-13f: 1-3** 14f+: 0-0
Track : **LH: 1-3** RH: 0-1 **Tight: 1-1** Gall: 0-1
Aids: Bl: 0-1 Vi: 0-0 Tstrap: 0-0
Best Rating: 70 6/01 Rdcr 1m1f gd-fm

Ostara (IRE)

101(65) (1)53
4-y-o b g Petorius-Onde De Choc (USA) (L'Enjoleur (CAN))
R C Spicer (K A Ryan 28/8) Sean Michael Toynton

Placings:000240/030051100-000003045 (4675)
2001: 8^{0}SD, 8^{0}S, 8^{0}F, 7^{0}G, 10^{0}GF, 8^{3}GF, 8^{0}G, 8^{4}GF, 7^{5}G

	Starts	1st	2nd	3rd	Win & Pl
Career Total (Turf)	23	2	1	2	8404
Career Total (AW)	1	0	0	0	

64 8/00 Thsk 1m D(0-80)H GD £4121
55 8/00 Hayd 1m30y F G-S £2492
Total win prize-money £6613

Going (Turf): Sf: 0-4 **GS: 1-5 Gd: 1-4** GF: 0-7 Fm: 0-3
Distance: 5f/6f: 0-5 7f-8f: 1-14 9f-13f: 1-5 14f+: 0-0
Track : **LH: 2-13** RH: 0-3 **Tight: 1-9** Gall: 0-1
Aids: Bl: 0-1 Vi: 0-0 Tstrap: 0-0
Best Rating: 58 4/01 Ripn 1m soft

A fair handicapper. Best at around a mile on a sound surface.

Other Club

(102) (54)54
7-y-o ch g Kris-Tura (Northfields (USA))
J G Portman The Other Clubbers

Placings:66/32/10100/13 (1014)
2001: 11^{1}SD, 11^{3}SD

	Starts	1st	2nd	3rd	Win & Pl
Career Total (Turf)	3	0	0	0	62
Career Total (AW)	8	3	1	2	10144

49 3/01 Sthl 1m3f E(0-70)H STD £2310
61 6/98 Wolv 1m100y F STD £2511
61 1/98 Wolv 1m100y D STD £3403
Total win prize-money £8225

Going (Turf): Sf: 0-1 GS: 0-1 Gd: 0-1 GF: 0-0 Fm: 0-0
Distance: 5f/6f: 0-0 7f-8f: 0-4 **9f-13f: 3-7** 14f+: 0-0
Track : **LH: 3-9** RH: 0-0 **Tight: 2-5** Gall: 0-0
Aids: Bl: 0-0 Vi: 0-0 Tstrap: 0-0
Best Rating: 49 3/01 Sthl 1m3f stand

Other Routes

84 43
2-y-o ch c Efisio-Rainbow Fleet (Nomination)
G L Moore Brighthelm Racing

Placings:000 (5466)
2001: 6^{0}GF, 6^{0}HY, 6^{0}S

	Starts	1st	2nd	3rd	Win & Pl
Career Total (Turf)	3	0	0	0	

Going (Turf): Sf: 0-2 GS: 0-0 Gd: 0-0 GF: 0-1 Fm: 0-0
Distance: 5f/6f: 0-2 7f-8f: 0-1 9f-13f: 0-0 14f+: 0-0
Track : LH: 0-1 RH: 0-0 Tight: 0-0 Gall: 0-0
Aids: Bl: 0-0 Vi: 0-0 Tstrap: 0-0
Best Rating: 43 10/01 Brig 6f209y soft

Otime (IRE)

88(103) (56)45
4-y-o b g Mujadil (USA)-Kick The Habit (Habitat)
Andrew Reid A S Reid

Placings:01400513014/60206625000102-04506500 (3730)
2001: 8^{0}SD, 6^{4}SD, 6^{5}SD, 7^{0}SD, 8^{6}SW, 7^{5}F, 6^{0}GF, 8^{0}GS

	Starts	1st	2nd	3rd	Win & Pl
Career Total (Turf)	14	1	1	0	3321
Career Total (AW)	19	3	2	1	8662

41 11/00 Ling 1m F STD £1820
76 12/99 Ling 6f E(0-75)H STD £2615
66 11/99 Ling 6f F STD £2137
66 8/99 Bath 5f11y F HRD £2276
Total win prize-money £8849

Going (Turf): Sf: 0-2 GS: 0-2 Gd: 0-3 GF: 0-5 **Fm: 1-2**
Distance: **5f/6f: 3-15** 7f-8f: 1-17 9f-13f: 0-1 14f+: 0-0
Track : **LH: 4-22** RH: 0-0 **Tight: 3-17** Gall: 1-2
Aids: Bl: 0-5 Vi: 1-11 Tstrap: 1-10
Best Rating: 56 1/01 Ling 6f stand

Ouest Banque (USA)

100 81
2-y-o b f Red Ransom (USA)-Mrs West (USA) (Gone West (USA))
J L Dunlop S Khaled

Placings:23233 (4427)
2001: 6^{2}GS, 6^{3}GF, 7^{2}GF, 7^{3}G, 8^{3}GF

	Starts	1st	2nd	3rd	Win & Pl
Career Total (Turf)	5	0	2	3	4871

Going (Turf): Sf: 0-0 GS: 0-1 Gd: 0-1 GF: 0-3 Fm: 0-0
Distance: 5f/6f: 0-2 7f-8f: 0-3 9f-13f: 0-0 14f+: 0-0
Track : LH: 0-0 RH: 0-1 Tight: 0-1 Gall: 0-0
Aids: Bl: 0-0 Vi: 0-0 Tstrap: 0-0
Best Rating: 81 9/01 Ripn 1m gd-fm

Oulton Broad

75 (54)38
5-y-o b g Midyan (USA)-Lady Quachita (USA) (Sovereign Dancer (USA))
M R Ewer-Hoad J A Ewer,G Brice,R Barnett,A Pullinger

Placings:000/3025005/0 (2962)
2001: 16^{0}GF

	Starts	1st	2nd	3rd	Win & Pl
Career Total (Turf)	8	0	1	0	585
Career Total (AW)	3	0	0	1	379

Going (Turf): Sf: 0-2 GS: 0-1 Gd: 0-2 GF: 0-1 Fm: 0-2
Distance: 5f/6f: 0-0 7f-8f: 0-4 9f-13f: 0-6 14f+: 0-1
Track : LH: 0-6 RH: 0-2 Tight: 0-2 Gall: 0-0
Aids: Bl: 0-0 Vi: 0-1 Tstrap: 0-0
Best Rating: 22 7/01 Folk 2m93y gd-fm

Oundle Scoundrel (FR)

85 62
2-y-o b c Spinning World (USA)-Tidal Treasure (USA) (Crafty Prospector (USA))
M Johnston M P Burke

Placings:00 (5604)
2001: 7^{0}HY, 7^{0}GS

	Starts	1st	2nd	3rd	Win & Pl
Career Total (Turf)	2	0	0	0	

Going (Turf): Sf: 0-1 GS: 0-1 Gd: 0-0 GF: 0-0 Fm: 0-0
Distance: 5f/6f: 0-0 7f-8f: 0-2 9f-13f: 0-0 14f+: 0-0
Track : LH: 0-0 RH: 0-0 Tight: 0-0 Gall: 0-0
Aids: Bl: 0-0 Vi: 0-0 Tstrap: 0-0
Best Rating: 62 10/01 Donc 7f heavy

Our Albert (IRE)

86 17
8-y-o b g Durgam (USA)-Power Girl (Tyrant (USA))
J Balding Mrs J A Beighton

Placings:050/000/00/00 (4778)
2001: 5^{0}F, 5^{0}G

	Starts	1st	2nd	3rd	Win & Pl
Career Total (Turf)	10	0	0	0	

Going (Turf): Sf: 0-0 GS: 0-0 Gd: 0-5 GF: 0-4 Fm: 0-1
Distance: 5f/6f: 0-5 7f-8f: 0-4 9f-13f: 0-1 14f+: 0-0
Track : LH: 0-2 RH: 0-1 Tight: 0-1 Gall: 0-0
Aids: Bl: 0-0 Vi: 0-1 Tstrap: 0-0
Best Rating: 17 9/01 Bevl 5f good

Our Chelsea Blue (USA)

103 73
3-y-o ch f Distant View (USA)-Eastern Connection (USA) (Danzig Connection (USA))
T G Mills M J Legg

Placings:043022 (4060)
2001: 6^{0}GS, 5^{4}F, 5^{3}GF, 5^{0}GF, 5^{2}G, 5^{2}G

	Starts	1st	2nd	3rd	Win & Pl
Career Total (Turf)	6	0	2	1	4208

Going (Turf): Sf: 0-0 GS: 0-1 Gd: 0-2 GF: 0-2 Fm: 0-1
Distance: 5f/6f: 0-6 7f-8f: 0-0 9f-13f: 0-0 14f+: 0-0
Track : LH: 0-0 RH: 0-0 Tight: 0-0 Gall: 0-0
Aids: Bl: 0-0 Vi: 0-0 Tstrap: 0-3
Best Rating: 73 8/01 Gdwd 5f good

She has shown ability in maiden races but will have to learn to settle if she is to fulfil her potential.

Our Colonel

95(96) (59)67
3-y-o b c Darshaan-Dance By Night (Northfields (USA))
G A Butler Des Swan

Placings:63630 (2158)
2001: 10^{6}S, 11^{3}SD, 11^{6}SD, 14^{3}G, 14^{0}GF

	Starts	1st	2nd	3rd	Win & Pl
Career Total (Turf)	3	0	0	1	426
Career Total (AW)	2	0	0	1	0

Going (Turf): Sf: 0-1 GS: 0-0 Gd: 0-1 GF: 0-1 Fm: 0-0
Distance: 5f/6f: 0-0 7f-8f: 0-0 9f-13f: 0-3 14f+: 0-2
Track : LH: 0-4 RH: 0-1 Tight: 0-1 Gall: 0-1
Aids: Bl: 0-0 Vi: 0-0 Tstrap: 0-0
Best Rating: 67 5/01 Nott 1m6f15y good

Our Destiny

101(85) (53)56
3-y-o b g Mujadil (USA)-Superspring (Superlative)
M A Buckley Drew Kerr

Placings:0136300-0004550050300304 (5375)
2001: 7^{0}SD, 6^{0}SD, 8^{0}GF, 6^{4}GF, 6^{5}GF, 7^{5}G, 6^{0}F, 7^{0}GF, 5^{5}GF, 5^{0}GF, 6^{3}GF, 6^{0}G, 6^{0}F, 5^{3}GS, 7^{0}S, 7^{4}G

	Starts	1st	2nd	3rd	Win & Pl
Career Total (Turf)	21	1	0	4	5097
Career Total (AW)	2	0	0	0	

75 7/00 Hayd 6f E G-F £3038
Total win prize-money £3038

Going (Turf): Sf: 0-2 GS: 0-1 Gd: 0-5 **GF: 1-11** Fm: 0-2
Distance: **5f/6f: 1-15** 7f-8f: 0-8 9f-13f: 0-0 14f+: 0-0
Track : LH: 0-4 RH: 0-0 Tight: 0-1 Gall: 0-0
Aids: Bl: 0-0 Vi: 0-5 Tstrap: 0-0
Best Rating: 64 5/01 Ripn 6f gd-fm

Despite a couple of fair efforts in big-field handicaps, has not shown a great deal this season. Suited by six furlongs and fast ground

Our Emily (IRE)

82 **15**

3-y-o b f Charnwood Forest (IRE)-Lacinia (Groom Dancer (USA))

T Keddy Mrs Julie Mitchell

Placings:00-000 **(4854)**

2001: 11^{0}G, 14^{0}S, 13^{0}GF

	Starts	1st	2nd	3rd	Win & Pl
Career Total (Turf)	5	0	0	0	

Going (Turf): Sf: 0-3 GS: 0-0 Gd: 0-1 GF: 0-1 Fm: 0-0
Distance: 5f/6f: 0-0 7f-8f: 0-1 9f-13f: 0-2 14f+: 0-2
Track : LH: 0-4 RH: 0-0 Tight: 0-2 Gall: 0-0
Aids: Bl: 0-1 Vi: 0-0 Tstrap: 0-0
Best Rating: 49 7/01 Yarm 1m3f101y good

Our First Lady

(97) (61)

4-y-o b f Alzao (USA)-Eclipsing (IRE) (Baillamont (USA))

D W P Arbuthnot Derrick C Broomfield

Placings:0/0220-020 **(4891)**

2001: 7^{0}GF, 7^{2}GF, 8^{0}GF, 7^{0}SD

	Starts	1st	2nd	3rd	Win & Pl
Career Total (Turf)	7	0	3	0	3349
Career Total (AW)	1	0	0	0	

Going (Turf): Sf: 0-1 GS: 0-1 Gd: 0-2 GF: 0-3 Fm: 0-0
Distance: 5f/6f: 0-1 7f-8f: 0-7 9f-13f: 0-0 14f+: 0-0
Track : LH: 0-2 RH: 0-2 Tight: 0-1 Gall: 0-2
Aids: Bl: 0-0 Vi: 0-0 Tstrap: 0-1
Best Rating: 69 9/01 Leic 7f9y gd-fm

Our Fred

106(109) (82)**75**

4-y-o ch g Prince Sabo-Sheila's Secret (IRE) (Bluebird (USA))

T G Mills Sherwoods Transport Ltd

Placings:3433/440211200**0-23**00042203003 **(4944)**

2001: 5^{2}SW, 5^{3}SD, 5^{0}GS, 5^{0}GF, 5^{0}F, 5^{4}GF, 5^{2}GF, 5^{2}GS, 5^{0}GF, 5^{3}GF, 5^{0}GF, 5^{0}G, 5^{3}S

	Starts	1st	2nd	3rd	Win & Pl
Career Total (Turf)	23	2	4	5	18050
Career Total (AW)	4	0	1	1	3049

80	8/00	Thsk	5f	D(0-80)H	GD	£4303
70	7/00	Leic	5f2y	F	G-F	£2366

Total win prize-money £6669

Going (Turf): Sf: 0-2 GS: 0-4 **Gd: 1-7 GF: 1-9** Fm: 0-1
Distance: **5f/6f: 2-27** 7f-8f: 0-0 9f-13f: 0-0 14f+: 0-0
Track : LH: 0-8 RH: 0-1 Tight: 0-4 Gall: 0-3
Aids: **Bl: 2-17** Vi: 0-0 Tstrap: 0-0
Best Rating: 82 1/01 Wolv 5f slow

Blinkers brought about improvement in 2000 season and he scored over the minimum trip on fast ground. Took time to come back to form in 2001 but ran well in summer of 2001 in sprint handicaps. Plenty of early pace, likes to make all. Acts on fast ground, but also handles cut.

Our Glenard

97 **74+**

2-y-o b c Royal Applause-Loucoum (FR) (Iron Duke (FR))

B W Hills John C Grant

Placings:5500 **(5340)**

2001: 5^{5}G, 5^{5}GF, 5^{0}G, 6^{0}GS

	Starts	1st	2nd	3rd	Win & Pl
Career Total (Turf)	4	0	0	0	0

Going (Turf): Sf: 0-0 GS: 0-1 Gd: 0-2 GF: 0-1 Fm: 0-0

Distance: 5f/6f: 0-4 7f-8f: 0-0 9f-13f: 0-0 14f+: 0-0
Track : LH: 0-1 RH: 0-0 Tight: 0-0 Gall: 0-1
Aids: Bl: 0-0 Vi: 0-0 Tstrap: 0-0
Best Rating: 74 9/01 Folk 5f good

A half-brother to seven winners, he has shown a tendency to start slowly.

Our Indulgence (IRE)

94(59) **35**

3-y-o ch g Prince Of Birds (USA)-Megan's Dream (IRE) (Fayruz)

T D Easterby Mrs Barabara Woodworth

Placings:000-04**0**06506 **(4031)**

2001: 8^{0}HY, 6^{4}F, 6^{U}GF, **6**^{U}SD, 6^{6}GF, 8^{5}F, 8^{0}GS, 10^{6}G

	Starts	1st	2nd	3rd	Win & Pl
Career Total (Turf)	10	0	0	0	0
Career Total (AW)	1	0	0	0	

Going (Turf): Sf: 0-1 GS: 0-1 Gd: 0-2 GF: 0-4 Fm: 0-2
Distance: 5f/6f: 0-6 7f-8f: 0-2 9f-13f: 0-3 14f+: 0-0
Track : LH: 0-6 RH: 0-1 Tight: 0-1 Gall: 0-1
Aids: Bl: 0-0 Vi: 0-0 Tstrap: 0-0
Best Rating: 53 6/01 Newc 6f firm

Our Krissie

99 **67**

3-y-o b f Kris-Shehana (USA) (The Minstrel (CAN))

M Johnston J Henderson (co Durham)

Placings:6634000 **(5013)**

2001: 10^{6}GF, 12^{6}GF, 11^{3}G, 12^{4}GF, 10^{0}GF, 11^{0}GF, 10^{0}HY

	Starts	1st	2nd	3rd	Win & Pl
Career Total (Turf)	7	0	0	1	717

Going (Turf): Sf: 0-1 GS: 0-0 Gd: 0-1 GF: 0-5 Fm: 0-0
Distance: 5f/6f: 0-0 7f-8f: 0-0 9f-13f: 0-7 14f+: 0-0
Track : LH: 0-5 RH: 0-1 Tight: 0-4 Gall: 0-2
Aids: Bl: 0-2 Vi: 0-0 Tstrap: 0-0
Best Rating: 67 8/01 Newc 1m4f93y gd-fm

Lightly raced maiden. Stays a mile and a half.

Our Lad

73 **11**

3-y-o ch c Phountzi (USA)-Lady Kalliste (Another Realm)

S Dow Ken Butler

Placings:000 **(3153)**

2001: 10^{0}GF, 10^{0}G, 7^{0}GS

	Starts	1st	2nd	3rd	Win & Pl
Career Total (Turf)	3	0	0	0	

Going (Turf): Sf: 0-0 GS: 0-1 Gd: 0-1 GF: 0-1 Fm: 0-0
Distance: 5f/6f: 0-0 7f-8f: 0-1 9f-13f: 0-2 14f+: 0-0
Track : LH: 0-0 RH: 0-1 Tight: 0-1 Gall: 0-0
Aids: Bl: 0-0 Vi: 0-0 Tstrap: 0-0
Best Rating: 11 6/01 Wind 1m2f7y good

Our Monogram

99 **54**

5-y-o b g Deploy-Darling Splodge (Elegant Air)

A C Stewart The Foxons Fillies Partnership

Placings:00540/00031150-031 **(4330)**

2001: 17^{0}GF, 14^{3}F, 16^{1}GF

	Starts	1st	2nd	3rd	Win & Pl
Career Total (Turf)	16	3	0	2	11455

53	8/01	Ripn	2m	E(0-75)H	G-F	£3542
53	8/00	Bath	2m1f34y	E(0-75)H	FRM	£3088
48	8/00	Sand	2m78y	E(0-70)H	G-F	£3623

Total win prize-money £10255

Going (Turf): Sf: 0-4 GS: 0-0 Gd: 0-2 **GF: 2-8** Fm: 1-2

Distance: 5f/6f: 0-0 7f-8f: 0-0 9f-13f: 0-3 **14f+: 3-13**
Track : **LH: 1-10 RH: 2-6 Tight: 2-6** Gall: 0-3
Aids: Bl: 0-0 Vi: 0-0 Tstrap: 0-0
Best Rating: 53 8/01 Ripn 2m gd-fm

Our Rosy

92 **52**

3-y-o ch f First Trump-Cadeau Elegant (Cadeaux Genereux)

G G Margarson Mrs T A Foreman

Placings:60 **(3841)**

2001: 6^{6}GF, 6^{0}G

	Starts	1st	2nd	3rd	Win & Pl
Career Total (Turf)	2	0	0	0	0

Going (Turf): Sf: 0-0 GS: 0-0 Gd: 0-1 GF: 0-1 Fm: 0-0
Distance: 5f/6f: 0-2 7f-8f: 0-0 9f-13f: 0-0 14f+: 0-0
Track : LH: 0-0 RH: 0-0 Tight: 0-0 Gall: 0-0
Aids: Bl: 0-0 Vi: 0-0 Tstrap: 0-0
Best Rating: 52 7/01 Sals 6f gd-fm

Our Shellby (IRE)

88(81) (15)**29**

3-y-o b/br f Petardia-Davenport Goddess (IRE) (Classic Secret (USA))

J L Eyre Billy Parker

Placings:000-6600 **(2639)**

2001: 11^{6}SD, 14^{6}G, 14^{0}G, 12^{0}GF

	Starts	1st	2nd	3rd	Win & Pl
Career Total (Turf)	5	0	0	0	0
Career Total (AW)	2	0	0	0	0

Going (Turf): Sf: 0-1 GS: 0-0 Gd: 0-2 GF: 0-2 Fm: 0-0
Distance: 5f/6f: 0-0 7f-8f: 0-2 9f-13f: 0-3 14f+: 0-2
Track : LH: 0-5 RH: 0-2 Tight: 0-1 Gall: 0-0
Aids: Bl: 0-0 Vi: 0-0 Tstrap: 0-0
Best Rating: 29 5/01 Nott 1m6f15y good

Our Weddingpresent (USA)

83 **60**

2-y-o ch c Known Fact (USA)-All A Lark (General Assembly (USA))

M C Pipe Lord Donoughmore & Countess Donoughmore

Placings:000 **(5588)**

2001: 6^{0}HY, 7^{0}GS, 5^{0}GS

	Starts	1st	2nd	3rd	Win & Pl
Career Total (Turf)	3	0	0	0	

Going (Turf): Sf: 0-1 GS: 0-2 Gd: 0-0 GF: 0-0 Fm: 0-0
Distance: 5f/6f: 0-2 7f-8f: 0-1 9f-13f: 0-0 14f+: 0-0
Track : LH: 0-2 RH: 0-0 Tight: 0-0 Gall: 0-1
Aids: Bl: 0-0 Vi: 0-0 Tstrap: 0-0
Best Rating: 60 11/01 Brig 5f213y gd-sft

Out For A Stroll

86 **60**

2-y-o b g Zamindar (USA)-The Jotter (Night Shift (USA))

S C Williams The Suffolk Ramblers Racing Club

Placings:0050 **(4730)**

2001: 5^{0}GS, 5^{0}GF, 5^{5}GF, 5^{0}F

	Starts	1st	2nd	3rd	Win & Pl
Career Total (Turf)	4	0	0	0	0

Going (Turf): Sf: 0-0 GS: 0-1 Gd: 0-0 GF: 0-2 Fm: 0-1
Distance: 5f/6f: 0-4 7f-8f: 0-0 9f-13f: 0-0 14f+: 0-0
Track : LH: 0-1 RH: 0-0 Tight: 0-0 Gall: 0-0
Aids: Bl: 0-0 Vi: 0-0 Tstrap: 0-0
Best Rating: 60 7/01 Ripn 5f gd-fm

Has shown enough in maidens to suggest he will be interesting in handicaps. Has been withdrawn on several occasions with vets certificates.

Out Of Danger (IRE)

77 **38**

2-y-o b f Darnay-Achtung Lady (IRE) (Warning)
A Berry Gordon B Cunningham

Placings:4660 **(4215)**
2001: 5^{4}GF, 5^{6}GF, 7^{6}GF, 8^{0}G

	Starts	1st	2nd	3rd	Win & Pl
Career Total (Turf)	4	0	0	0	0

Going (Turf): Sf: 0-0 GS: 0-0 Gd: 0-1 GF: 0-3 Fm: 0-0
Distance: 5f/6f: 0-2 7f-8f: 0-2 9f-13f: 0-0 14f+: 0-0
Track : LH: 0-1 RH: 0-0 Tight: 0-0 Gall: 0-1
Aids: Bl: 0-0 Vi: 0-0 Tstrap: 0-0
Best Rating: 38 6/01 Muss 5f gd-fm

Out Of Retirement

80 **41**

3-y-o b g Beveled (USA)-Incatinka (Inca Chief (USA))
G C H Chung V E Murphy & K M Farr

Placings:00 **(5670)**
2001: 7^{0}GF, 8^{0}HY

	Starts	1st	2nd	3rd	Win & Pl
Career Total (Turf)	2	0	0	0	

Going (Turf): Sf: 0-1 GS: 0-0 Gd: 0-0 GF: 0-1 Fm: 0-0
Distance: 5f/6f: 0-0 7f-8f: 0-1 9f-13f: 0-1 14f+: 0-0
Track : LH: 0-0 RH: 0-1 Tight: 0-1 Gall: 0-0
Aids: Bl: 0-0 Vi: 0-0 Tstrap: 0-0
Best Rating: 41 6/01 Newb 7f gd-fm

Out Of Season (IRE)

93 **63**

2-y-o ch f Brief Truce (USA)-Red Partridge (Solinus)
W G M Turner Vale Racing

Placings:042 **(4524)**
2001: 5^{0}G, 5^{4}GF, 6^{2}GF

	Starts	1st	2nd	3rd	Win & Pl
Career Total (Turf)	3	0	1	0	855

Going (Turf): Sf: 0-0 GS: 0-0 Gd: 0-1 GF: 0-2 Fm: 0-0
Distance: 5f/6f: 0-3 7f-8f: 0-0 9f-13f: 0-0 14f+: 0-0
Track : LH: 0-2 RH: 0-0 Tight: 0-0 Gall: 0-2
Aids: Bl: 0-0 Vi: 0-0 Tstrap: 0-0
Best Rating: 63 9/01 Ling 6f gd-fm

Out Of Sight (IRE)

94(110)

7-y-o ch g Salse (USA)-Starr Danias (USA) (Sensitive Prince (USA))
B A McMahon D J Allen

Placings:555600/0414/460/4650001/**2103**000143400-00000U **(4557)**
2001: 8^{0}SW, 7^{0}SD, 10^{0}G, 10^{0}G, 10^{0}HY, 9^{0}SW

	Starts	1st	2nd	3rd	Win & Pl
Career Total (Turf)	32	2	0	1	16116
Career Total (AW)	8	2	1	1	11069

51 7/00 Nott 1m54y E(0-70) G-F £2879
74 2/00 Sthl 7f C(0-100)H STD £6532
67 11/99 Sthl 7f F(0-60)H STD £2008
79 5/97 York 7f202y C(0-95)H GD £8285
Total win prize-money £19706

Going (Turf): Sf: 0-9 GS: 0-3 **Gd: 1-10 GF: 1-10** Fm: 0-0
Distance: 5f/6f: 0-4 **7f-8f: 3-19** 9f-13f: 1-17 14f+: 0-0
Track : **LH: 4-23** RH: 0-6 Tight: 0-5 **Gall: 1-6**
Aids: Bl: 0-0 Vi: 0-0 Tstrap: 0-0
Best Rating: 53 2/01 Sthl 1m slow

Average handicapper. Best suited by a sound surface. (DEAD)

Outlaw

85 **56**

2-y-o b c Danehill (USA)-Sabaah Elfull (Kris)
Sir Michael Stoute Mohammed Al Nabouda

Placings:00 **(4416)**
2001: 7^{0}GS, 7^{0}G

	Starts	1st	2nd	3rd	Win & Pl
Career Total (Turf)	2	0	0	0	

Going (Turf): Sf: 0-0 GS: 0-1 Gd: 0-1 GF: 0-0 Fm: 0-0
Distance: 5f/6f: 0-0 7f-8f: 0-2 9f-13f: 0-0 14f+: 0-0
Track : LH: 0-1 RH: 0-0 Tight: 0-1 Gall: 0-0
Aids: Bl: 0-0 Vi: 0-0 Tstrap: 0-0
Best Rating: 56 9/01 Ches 7f2y good

Outrageouse

85(65) **42**

3-y-o b g Be My Chief (USA)-Pink Brief (IRE) (Ela-Mana-Mou)
Andrew Reid A S Reid

Placings:04-0000000 **(5114)**
2001: 8^{0}SD, 10^{0}GF, 7^{0}F, 6^{0}GF, 10^{0}GF, 13^{0}F, 16^{0}HY

	Starts	1st	2nd	3rd	Win & Pl
Career Total (Turf)	8	0	0	0	270
Career Total (AW)	1	0	0	0	

Going (Turf): Sf: 0-1 GS: 0-0 Gd: 0-1 GF: 0-4 Fm: 0-2
Distance: 5f/6f: 0-0 7f-8f: 0-4 9f-13f: 0-3 14f+: 0-2
Track : LH: 0-7 RH: 0-0 Tight: 0-2 Gall: 0-1
Aids: Bl: 0-0 Vi: 0-0 Tstrap: 0-0
Best Rating: 42 9/01 York 1m2f85y gd-fm

Outstanding Talent

96(101) (30)**40**

4-y-o gr f Environment Friend-Chaleureuse (Final Straw)
A W Carroll Group 1 Racing (1994) Ltd

Placings:04300/6002400-**4542010064465** **(4606)**
2001: 9^{4}SD, 7^{5}SD, 9^{4}SD, 9^{2}SD, 8^{0}SD, 9^{1}SD, 8^{0}SD, 8^{0}SD, 11^{6}GF, 12^{4}SD, 12^{4}G, 10^{6}F, 12^{5}SD

	Starts	1st	2nd	3rd	Win & Pl
Career Total (Turf)	15	0	1	1	1259
Career Total (AW)	10	1	1	0	3477

49 3/01 Wolv 1m1f79y E(0-70)H STD £2975
Total win prize-money £2975

Going (Turf): Sf: 0-2 GS: 0-2 Gd: 0-5 GF: 0-5 Fm: 0-1
Distance: 5f/6f: 0-5 7f-8f: 0-8 **9f-13f: 1-12** 14f+: 0-0
Track : **LH: 1-14** RH: 0-3 **Tight: 1-11** Gall: 0-2
Aids: Bl: 0-0 Vi: 0-0 Tstrap: 0-0
Best Rating: 49 3/01 Wolv 1m1f79y stand

Ovambo (IRE)

105 **101**

3-y-o b g Namaqualand (USA)-Razana (IRE) (Kahyasi)
P J Makin R A Henley

Placings:33-01112 **(4194)**
2001: 10^{0}GS, 10^{1}G, 12^{1}GF, 12^{1}GF, 13^{2}G

	Starts	1st	2nd	3rd	Win & Pl
Career Total (Turf)	7	3	1	2	64309

97 8/01 Gdwd 1m4f C(0-100)H G-F £45500
90 7/01 Sals 1m4f D(0-85)H G-F £4407
80 6/01 Wind 1m2f7y D(0-80)H GD £4322
Total win prize-money £54230

Going (Turf): Sf: 0-1 GS: 0-2 Gd: 1-2 **GF: 2-2** Fm: 0-0
Distance: 5f/6f: 0-0 7f-8f: 0-1 **9f-13f: 3-5** 14f+: 0-1
Track : LH: 0-2 **RH: 2-2 Tight: 3-5** Gall: 0-1
Aids: Bl: 0-0 Vi: 0-0 Tstrap: 0-0
Best Rating: 101 8/01 York 1m5f194y good

A most progressive gelding, he won handicaps at Windsor and Salisbury in the summer of 2001 and competed the hat-trick in fine style in the Tote Gold Trophy at Glorious Goodwood. Ran his best race when touched off in the Melrose at York. He stays 14 furlongs and appreciates a decent surface.

Overload (USA)

99 **88**

2-y-o b f Forest Wildcat (USA)-Magical Avie (USA) (Lord Avie (USA))
C R Egerton T M Bennett

Placings:310 **(5569a)**
2001: 7^{3}GF, 6^{1}HY, 8^{0}HO

	Starts	1st	2nd	3rd	Win & Pl
Career Total (Turf)	3	1	0	1	4772

88 10/01 Wind 6f D HVY £4078
Total win prize-money £4079

Going (Turf): Sf: 1-1 GS: 0-0 Gd: 0-0 GF: 0-1 Fm: 0-0
Distance: **5f/6f: 1-1** 7f-8f: 0-2 9f-13f: 0-0 14f+: 0-0
Track : LH: 0-0 RH: 0-2 Tight: 0-0 Gall: 0-1
Aids: Bl: 0-0 Vi: 0-0 Tstrap: 0-0
Best Rating: 88 10/01 Wind 6f heavy

Out of a multiple winner in America, showed ability on her debut run at Kempton over seven before dropping back to six to take a heavy-ground Windsor maiden.

Oversman

48(80)

8-y-o b g Keen-Jamaican Punch (IRE) (Shareef Dancer (USA))
B J Llewellyn Mackworth Snooker Club Pt

Placings:03000/213/302330/20-60 **(3064)**
2001: 12^{6}SD, 17^{0}G

	Starts	1st	2nd	3rd	Win & Pl
Career Total (Turf)	10	0	2	3	3357
Career Total (AW)	8	1	1	2	4391

46 2/96 Sthl 1m4f E STD £2900
Total win prize-money £2900

Going (Turf): Sf: 0-0 GS: 0-1 Gd: 0-5 GF: 0-2 Fm: 0-2
Distance: 5f/6f: 0-1 7f-8f: 0-4 **9f-13f: 1-10** 14f+: 0-3
Track : **LH: 1-15** RH: 0-1 Tight: 0-8 Gall: 0-1
Aids: Bl: 0-7 Vi: 0-0 Tstrap: 0-7

Overspect

100 **89**

3-y-o b c Spectrum (IRE)-Portelet (Night Shift (USA))
P F I Cole Alessandro Gaucci

Placings:1316-440 **(4709)**
2001: 8^{4}G, 10^{4}G, 12^{0}G

	Starts	1st	2nd	3rd	Win & Pl
Career Total (Turf)	7	2	0	1	14550

105 9/00 Donc 7f C GD £7020
5/00 Siro 6f GD £5693
Total win prize-money £12713

Going (Turf): Sf: 0-1 GS: 0-0 **Gd: 2-6** GF: 0-0 Fm: 0-0
Distance: 5f/6f: 1-1 7f-8f: 1-3 9f-13f: 0-3 14f+: 0-0
Track : LH: 0-4 **RH: 1-1** Tight: 0-3 Gall: 0-1
Aids: Bl: 0-0 Vi: 0-0 Tstrap: 0-0
Best Rating: 89 8/01 Epsm 1m2f18y good

Showed little sparkle at various trips in 2001.

Ozawa (IRE)

85(93) (29)**20**

4-y-o gr g Brief Truce (USA)-Classy (Kalaglow)
M E Sowersby (J W Payne 2/7) Racing Ladies

Placings:0/0000-06500000 (4805)
2001: 8^{0}SW, 8^{6}SD, 9^{5}S, 11^{0}SD, 10^{0}GF, 8^{0}SD, 9^{0}GF, 8^{0}F

	Starts	1st	2nd	3rd	Win & Pl
Career Total (Turf)	9	0	0	0	0
Career Total (AW)	4	0	0	0	0

Going (Turf): Sf: 0-2 GS: 0-0 Gd: 0-3 GF: 0-3 Fm: 0-1
Distance: 5f/6f: 0-3 7f-8f: 0-3 9f-13f: 0-7 14f+: 0-0
Track : LH: 0-7 RH: 0-2 Tight: 0-4 Gall: 0-1
Aids: Bl: 0-0 Vi: 0-0 Tstrap: 0-1
Best Rating: 29 6/01 Sthl 1m3f stand

Paarl Rock

78(100) (51)58
6-y-o ch h Common Grounds-Markievicz (IRE) (Doyoun)
G Barnett J C Bradbury

Placings:000/00003000/0003214416051-1450 (1004)
2001: 16^{1}SW, 16^{4}SD, 16^{5}SD, 12^{0}S

	Starts	1st	2nd	3rd	Win & Pl
Career Total (Turf)	21	2	1	2	10221
Career Total (AW)	7	2	0	0	4652

51	1/01	Wolv	2m46y	E(0-75)H	SLW	£2863
47	12/00	Wolv	2m46y	F(0-60)H	STD	£1788
58	8/00	Nott	1m1f213y	E(0-75)H	GD	£3107
54	8/00	Leic	1m1f218y	D(0-80)H	G-F	£3906

Total win prize-money £11666

Going (Turf): Sf: 0-3 GS: 0-3 Gd: 1-7 GF: 1-8 Fm: 0-0
Distance: 5f/6f: 0-2 7f-8f: 0-6 9f-13f: 2-16 14f+: 2-4
Track : LH: 3-20 RH: 1-5 Tight: 2-10 Gall: 0-0
Aids: Bl: 0-4 Vi: 4-14 Tstrap: 0-0
Best Rating: 51 1/01 Wolv 2m46y slow

Pachara

99 86
2-y-o b c Mind Games-Miss Mercy (IRE) (Law Society (USA))
M L W Bell Billy Maguire

Placings:321330234 (5498)
2001: 5^{3}S, 5^{2}GF, 5^{1}GF, 6^{3}G, 6^{3}GF, 6^{0}GF, 6^{2}GS, 5^{3}GS, 6^{4}HY

	Starts	1st	2nd	3rd	Win & Pl
Career Total (Turf)	9	1	2	4	24181

74	5/01	Wwck	5f	E	G-F	£2979

Total win prize-money £2979

Going (Turf): Sf: 0-2 GS: 0-2 Gd: 0-1 GF: 1-4 Fm: 0-0
Distance: 5f/6f: 1-9 7f-8f: 0-0 9f-13f: 0-0 14f+: 0-0
Track : LH: 1-2 RH: 0-0 Tight: 0-1 Gall: 1-1
Aids: Bl: 0-0 Vi: 0-0 Tstrap: 0-0
Best Rating: 86 10/01 Asct 5f gd-sft

Sprint bred, he was a staying-on third at Newmarket on his debut and ran well from a bad draw at Chester. Still showed signs of greenness when winning at Warwick and has run well in competitive events since. Effective at five and six furlongs and handles any ground.

Pachinco

3-y-o ch c Bluebird (USA)-Lady Philippa (IRE) (Taufan (USA))
P Mitchell Gordon Li

Placings:0-P (5024)
2001: 11^{P}S

	Starts	1st	2nd	3rd	Win & Pl
Career Total (Turf)	2	0	0	0	

Going (Turf): Sf: 0-2 GS: 0-0 Gd: 0-0 GF: 0-0 Fm: 0-0
Distance: 5f/6f: 0-0 7f-8f: 0-0 9f-13f: 0-2 14f+: 0-0
Track : LH: 0-1 RH: 0-0 Tight: 0-0 Gall: 0-0
Aids: Bl: 0-0 Vi: 0-0 Tstrap: 0-1

Pacific Alliance (IRE)

96(99) (65)48
5-y-o b g Fayruz-La Gravotte (FR) (Habitat)
J G Given Mrs D E Armitage

Placings:50/4130014/344003111 00-000006000050 (5230)
2001: 8^{0}S, 8^{0}SD, 8^{0}GF, 7^{0}G, 8^{0}G, 8^{6}G, 7^{0}G, 8^{0}GF, 8^{0}GF, 9^{0}G, 12^{5}GS, 11^{0}S

	Starts	1st	2nd	3rd	Win & Pl
Career Total (Turf)	25	4	0	1	24458
Career Total (AW)	7	1	0	2	3428

80	9/00	Muss	1m	D(0-75)	G-S	£4446
74	9/00	York	7f202y	D(0-80)H	GD	£12577
69	8/00	Muss	1m	F(0-60)H	G-F	£1988
63	6/99	Sand	1m14y	D(0-80)H	GD	£4416
68	2/99	Ling	1m	F	STD	£2058

Total win prize-money £25486

Going (Turf): Sf: 0-4 GS: 1-3 Gd: 2-8 GF: 1-9 Fm: 0-1
Distance: 5f/6f: 0-2 7f-8f: 4-17 9f-13f: 1-13 14f+: 0-0
Track : LH: 2-19 RH: 3-7 Tight: 3-11 Gall: 1-3
Aids: Bl: 2-10 Vi: 0-0 Tstrap: 0-0
Best Rating: 58 8/01 Hayd 1m30y good

He bounced right back to his very best when completing a hat-trick in the summer of 2000, but on a long losing run since. Suited by a mile.

Pacific Place (IRE)

98 38
4-y-o gr g College Chapel-Kaitlin (IRE) (Salmon Leap (USA))
J S Goldie John Breslin

Placings:00/024232200000-00006506U5060500 (5287)
2001: 5^{0}GF, 5^{0}GF, 6^{0}F, 6^{0}G, 5^{6}F, 5^{5}F, 6^{0}GF, 5^{6}G, 6^{U}G, 5^{5}S, 5^{0}GF, 5^{6}G, 6^{0}F, 6^{5}GF, 7^{0}GS, 6^{0}HY

	Starts	1st	2nd	3rd	Win & Pl
Career Total (Turf)	30	0	4	1	4691

Going (Turf): Sf: 0-5 GS: 0-2 Gd: 0-6 GF: 0-11 Fm: 0-6
Distance: 5f/6f: 0-24 7f-8f: 0-6 9f-13f: 0-0 14f+: 0-0
Track : LH: 0-3 RH: 0-2 Tight: 0-0 Gall: 0-2
Aids: Bl: 0-0 Vi: 0-1 Tstrap: 0-0
Best Rating: 44 7/01 Newc 5f firm

Pacific Shore (USA)

100 75
3-y-o b f Gone West (USA)-Youm Jadeed (IRE) (Sadler's Wells (USA))
Sir Michael Stoute Maktoum Al Maktoum

Placings:4346 (4885)
2001: 8^{4}F, 8^{3}F, 10^{4}GF, 9^{6}GF

	Starts	1st	2nd	3rd	Win & Pl
Career Total (Turf)	4	0	0	1	1639

Going (Turf): Sf: 0-0 GS: 0-0 Gd: 0-0 GF: 0-2 Fm: 0-2
Distance: 5f/6f: 0-0 7f-8f: 0-2 9f-13f: 0-2 14f+: 0-0
Track : LH: 0-2 RH: 0-2 Tight: 0-3 Gall: 0-1
Aids: Bl: 0-0 Vi: 0-0 Tstrap: 0-0
Best Rating: 75 6/01 Thsk 1m firm

Pacifyc (IRE)

95(77) (3)28
6-y-o b g Brief Truce (USA)-Ocean Blue (IRE) (Bluebird (USA))
John A Harris (Exors Of The Late J L Harris 2/7)
Exors Of The Late J L Harris

Placings:03000000/0000 (4079)
2001: 11^{0}SD, 11^{0}GS, 14^{0}GF, 17^{0}GF

	Starts	1st	2nd	3rd	Win & Pl
Career Total (Turf)	11	0	0	1	448
Career Total (AW)	1	0	0	0	

Going (Turf): Sf: 0-1 GS: 0-1 Gd: 0-4 GF: 0-5 Fm: 0-0
Distance: 5f/6f: 0-0 7f-0f: 0-2 9f-13f: 0-0 14f+: 0-4
Track : LH: 0-5 RH: 0-5 Tight: 0-3 Gall: 0-3
Aids: Bl: 0-0 Vi: 0-1 Tstrap: 0-1
Best Rating: 28 7/01 Nott 1m6f15y gd-fm

Paddy McGoon (USA)

(68) 53
6-y-o ch g Irish River (FR)-Flame McGoon (USA) (Staff Writer (USA))
S E H Sherwood Mrs Richard Pilkington

Placings:00/5535/00/6040-0 (0099)
2001: 12^{0}SD

	Starts	1st	2nd	3rd	Win & Pl
Career Total (Turf)	11	0	0	1	840
Career Total (AW)	2	0	0	0	

Going (Turf): Sf: 0-3 GS: 0-2 Gd: 0-3 GF: 0-1 Fm: 0-2
Distance: 5f/6f: 0-1 7f-8f: 0-1 9f-13f: 0-11 14f+: 0-0
Track : LH: 0-5 RH: 0-4 Tight: 0-6 Gall: 0-0
Aids: Bl: 0-1 Vi: 0-0 Tstrap: 0-0
Best Rating: 28 7/01 Nott 1m6f15y gd-fm

Paddy Mul

96 33
4-y-o ch c Democratic (USA)-My Pretty Niece (Great Nephew)
W Storey Gremlin Racing

Placings:0000/003040-30 (4800)
2001: 10^{3}GF, 10^{0}F

	Starts	1st	2nd	3rd	Win & Pl
Career Total (Turf)	12	0	0	2	887

Going (Turf): Sf: 0-5 GS: 0-0 Gd: 0-1 GF: 0-4 Fm: 0-2
Distance: 5f/6f: 0-1 7f-8f: 0-4 9f-13f: 0-6 14f+: 0-1
Track : LH: 0-7 RH: 0-2 Tight: 0-5 Gall: 0-2
Aids: Bl: 0-0 Vi: 0-1 Tstrap: 0-11
Best Rating: 29 6/01 Rdcr 1m2f gd-fm

Paddy's Rice

63 17
10-y-o ch g Hadeer-Requiem (Song)
A P Jones Mrs Hazel Skuse

Placings:40/600165000/3015230260/100534200/00100 4/00100500/0060-00 (1810)
2001: 7^{0}GF, 8^{0}GF

	Starts	1st	2nd	3rd	Win & Pl
Career Total (Turf)	50	5	3	3	20826

54	6/98	Bath	1m5y	E(0-70)H	G-S	£3053
52	5/97	Brig	7f214y	F(0-60)H	FRM	£3108
60	6/96	Wwck	7f	F(0-60)	FRM	£3190
49	5/95	Ling	6f	D(0-80)H	FRM	£4378
43	7/94	Wind	5f217y	G(0-60)H	G-F	£2673

Total win prize-money £16403

Going (Turf): Sf: 0-2 GS: 1-3 Gd: 0-11 GF: 1-18 Fm: 3-14
Distance: 5f/6f: 2-15 7f-8f: 2-24 9f-13f: 1-9 14f+: 0-0
Track : LH: 3-19 RH: 1-8 Tight: 1-9 Gall: 1-5
Aids: Bl: 0-2 Vi: 0-0 Tstrap: 0-1
Best Rating: 43 7/94 Wind 5f217y GF

Paddywack (IRE)

(109) (63)56
4-y-o b g Bigstone (IRE)-Millie's Return (IRE) (Ballad Rock)
D W Chapman David W Chapman

Placings:00063001060/0524112220020U005013-036 (0221)
2001: 6^{0}SW, 6^{3}SD, 6^{6}SD

	Starts	1st	2nd	3rd	Win & Pl

Career Total (Turf) 11 1 1 1 4523
Career Total (AW) 23 3 4 2 11841
61 11/00 Wolv 6f F(0-65)H STD £1778
54 3/00 Ling 7f F(0-60)H STD £2808
48 3/00 Wolv 6f E(0-70)H STD £2717
57 10/99 Rdcr 6f E(0-75)H SFT £3330
Total win prize-money £10634

Going (Turf): Sf: 1-2 GS: 0-0 Gd: 0-4 GF: 0-5 Fm: 0-0
Distance: **5f/6f: 3-27** 7f-8f: 1-7 9f-13f: 0-0 14f+: 0-0
Track : **LH: 3-22** RH: 0-2 **Tight: 3-15** Gall: 0-2
Aids: **Bl: 4-28** Vi: 0-0 Tstrap: 0-0
Best Rating: 63 1/01 Wolv 6f stand

Pagan Prince

107 **64**
4-y-o br c Primo Dominie-Mory Kante (USA) (Icecapade (USA))
J A R Toller The Gap Partnership

Placings:056-405453164 **(5376)**
2001: 7^{4}GS, 8^{0}G, 8^{5}G, 10^{4}GF, 10^{5}GF, 9^{3}G, 8^{1}G, 8^{6}GF, 9^{4}G
Starts 1st 2nd 3rd Win & Pl
Career Total (Turf) 12 1 0 1 4978
62 8/01 Sand 1m14y E(0-80)H GD £3445
Total win prize-money £3445

Going (Turf): Sf: 0-0 GS: 0-1 **Gd: 1-5** GF: 0-6 Fm: 0-0
Distance: 5f/6f: 0-0 7f-8f: 0-4 **9f-13f: 1-8** 14f+: 0-0
Track : LH: 0-3 **RH: 1-4** Tight: 0-6 Gall: 0-0
Aids: Bl: 0-0 Vi: 0-0 Tstrap: 0-0
Best Rating: 64 7/01 Wind 1m2f7y gd-fm

Finally got off the mark at Sandown over a mile in summer of 2001, following a string of consistent efforts in handicap company, and he has continued to run well since.

Pagan Princess

98 **58**
3-y-o b f Mujtahid (USA)-Dalu (IRE) (Dancing Brave (USA))
J A R Toller The Gap Partnership

Placings:00046 **(4899)**
2001: 10^{0}GF, 10^{0}GF, 7^{0}GF, 8^{4}S, 8^{6}GS
Starts 1st 2nd 3rd Win & Pl
Career Total (Turf) 5 0 0 0 0

Going (Turf): Sf: 0-1 GS: 0-1 Gd: 0-0 GF: 0-3 Fm: 0-0
Distance: 5f/6f: 0-0 7f-8f: 0-1 9f-13f: 0-4 14f+: 0-0
Track : LH: 0-2 RH: 0-1 Tight: 0-0 Gall: 0-1
Aids: Bl: 0-0 Vi: 0-0 Tstrap: 0-0
Best Rating: 65 6/01 NmkR 1m2f gd-fm

Page Nouvelle (FR)

99 **88**
3-y-o b f Spectrum (IRE)-Page Bleue (IRE) (Sadler's Wells (USA))
B W Hills E D Kessly

Placings:310-450 **(4660)**
2001: 12^{4}GF, 9^{5}GF, 14^{0}GF
Starts 1st 2nd 3rd Win & Pl
Career Total (Turf) 6 1 0 1 6336
75 8/00 Bevl 7f100y D G-F £4121
Total win prize-money £4121

Going (Turf): Sf: 0-0 GS: 0-1 Gd: 0-1 **GF: 1-4** Fm: 0-0
Distance: 5f/6f: 0-0 **7f-8f: 1-3** 9f-13f: 0-2 14f+: 0-1
Track : LH: 0-2 **RH: 1-4** Tight: 0-1 Gall: 0-2
Aids: Bl: 0-0 Vi: 0-0 Tstrap: 0-0
Best Rating: 88 5/01 Wwck 1m4f134y gd-fm

A close-coupled half-sister to a German Group Three winner. Did just enough to win her maiden at Beverley on her second start at two. Stepped up in trip this term, but looks short of toe.

Pageant

101(104) (37)**45**
4-y-o br f Inchinor-Positive Attitude (Red Sunset)
J M Bradley (Mrs Lydia Pearce 20/7) Saracen Racing

Placings:443/512625550**2562-20030500**0**02266**025240 **(5592)**
2001: 8^{2}SD, 8^{0}SW, 8^{0}SD, 8^{3}SW, 9^{0}SD, 8^{5}SD, 8^{0}S, 10^{0}SD, 7^{0}SD, 7^{0}GF, 8^{2}GF, 7^{2}GF, 8^{6}GF, 8^{6}SD, 7^{0}G, 8^{2}F, 7^{5}G, 8^{2}F, 7^{4}S, 6^{0}GS
Starts 1st 2nd 3rd Win & Pl
Career Total (Turf) 22 1 6 1 9620
Career Total (AW) 14 0 3 1 2167
75 6/00 Yarm 6f3y D GD £3802
Total win prize-money £3803

Going (Turf): Sf: 0-5 GS: 0-1 **Gd: 1-4** GF: 0-10 Fm: 0-2
Distance: 5f/6f: 0-1 **7f-8f: 1-27** 9f-13f: 0-8 14f+: 0-0
Track : LH: 0-21 RH: 0-5 Tight: 0-10 Gall: 0-1
Aids: Bl: 0-0 Vi: 0-0 Tstrap: 0-0
Best Rating: 55 1/01 Sthl 1m stand

Pageboy

90(97) (39)**38**
12-y-o b g Tina's Pet-Edwins' Princess (Owen Dudley)
P C Haslam Mrs A Haslam

Placings:00210240/0523023430/0000251000040/**230 21110002000/125060000**34340004/**126550**012401206/ **1600000001/505000000/05422005**0066/4453-0 **(0023)**
2001: 7^{0}SD
Starts 1st 2nd 3rd Win & Pl
Career Total (Turf) 76 6 8 6 37548
Career Total (AW) 38 5 6 1 21930
75 1/98 Ling 6f E(0-70)H STD £2845
75 1/97 Ling 6f D(0-80)H STD £3306
65 9/96 Wolv 6f E(0-70)H STD £3003
66 8/96 Haml 6f5y E(0-70)H G-F £3631
63 1/96 Ling 6f E(0-70)H STD £3103
63 1/95 Ling 6f E(0-70)H STD £3009
73 5/94 Haml 6f5y F(0-60)H FRM £3850
64 5/94 Haml 6f5y E(0-70)H FRM £3687
57 5/94 Thsk 6f D(0-75)H FRM £4207
57 7/93 Haml 5f4y G(0-70)H G-F £1970
67 8/91 Pont 6f E G-F £3054
Total win prize-money £35668

Going (Turf): Sf: 0-3 GS: 0-4 Gd: 0-30 **GF: 3-29 Fm: 3-10**
Distance: **5f/6f: 8-87** 7f-8f: 3-26 9f-13f: 0-1 14f+: 0-0
Track : **LH: 6-53** RH: 0-2 **Tight: 5-38** Gall: 0-3
Aids: **Bl: 2-24** Vi: 0-7 Tstrap: 0-0
Best Rating: 28 1/01 Sthl 7f stand

Paid Up

101 **45**
3-y-o b g Mind Games-Indian Summer (Young Generation)
M W Easterby The Shooting Syndicate

Placings:460-0002600004 **(5273)**
2001: 7^{0}S, 8^{0}GS, 8^{0}S, 5^{2}GF, 5^{6}G, 5^{0}GF, 5^{0}GF, 6^{0}G, 5^{0}GF, 5^{4}HY
Starts 1st 2nd 3rd Win & Pl
Career Total (Turf) 13 0 1 0 1027

Going (Turf): Sf: 0-3 GS: 0-1 Gd: 0-4 GF: 0-5 Fm: 0-0
Distance: 5f/6f: 0-10 7f-8f: 0-2 9f-13f: 0-1 14f+: 0-0
Track : LH: 0-2 RH: 0-1 Tight: 0-1 Gall: 0-0
Aids: Bl: 0-1 Vi: 0-0 Tstrap: 0-0
Best Rating: 53 6/01 Bevl 5f gd-fm

Painted Room (USA)

99 **98d**
3-y-o ch c Woodman (USA)-All At Sea (USA) (Riverman (USA))
H R A Cecil K Abdulla

Placings:22-534 **(1602)**
2001: 8^{5}S, 8^{3}G, 10^{4}GF
Starts 1st 2nd 3rd Win & Pl
Career Total (Turf) 5 0 2 1 6466

Going (Turf): Sf: 0-2 GS: 0-1 Gd: 0-1 GF: 0-1 Fm: 0-0
Distance: 5f/6f: 0-0 7f-8f: 0-4 9f-13f: 0-1 14f+: 0-0
Track : LH: 0-1 RH: 0-0 Tight: 0-0 Gall: 0-0
Aids: Bl: 0-0 Vi: 0-0 Tstrap: 0-0
Best Rating: 98 4/01 NmkR 1m soft

Pairing (IRE)

92 **85**
3-y-o ch g Rudimentary (USA)-Splicing (Sharpo)
H Morrison The Beach Club

Placings:4100-0 **(5598)**
2001: 6^{0}GS
Starts 1st 2nd 3rd Win & Pl
Career Total (Turf) 5 1 0 0 3448
85 7/00 Ling 6f E GD £3185
Total win prize-money £3185

Going (Turf): Sf: 0-1 GS: 0-1 **Gd: 1-1** GF: 0-2 Fm: 0-0
Distance: **5f/6f: 1-3** 7f-8f: 0-2 9f-13f: 0-0 14f+: 0-0
Track : LH: 0-0 RH: 0-0 Tight: 0-0 Gall: 0-0
Aids: Bl: 0-0 Vi: 0-0 Tstrap: 0-0
Best Rating: 61 11/01 NmkR 6f gd-sft

Pairumani Star (IRE)

106 **105**
6-y-o ch h Caerleon (USA)-Dawn Star (High Line)
J L Dunlop Windflower Overseas Holdings Inc

Placings:066/221316123/46111200/012140-2420 **(3582)**
2001: 13^{2}GF, 14^{4}GF, 15^{2}S, 16^{0}G
Starts 1st 2nd 3rd Win & Pl
Career Total (Turf) 30 8 7 2 125379
103 7/00 Leop 1m6f GD £16250
103 5/00 Gdwd 1m6f B(0-100)H SFT £9785
90 7/99 Newb 2m B(0-105)H G-F £10211
92 6/99 Sals 1m6f15y C FRM £6248
90 6/99 York 1m5f194yB(0-100)H G-S £10006
87 8/98 Gdwd 1m4f D(0-85)H G-F £7448
86 7/98 Sals 1m4f D(0-85)H GD £3610
80 6/98 Hayd 1m6f D(0-80)H GD £3550
Total win prize-money £67111

Going (Turf): Sf: 1-3 GS: 1-5 **Gd: 3-11** GF: 2-8 Fm: 1-2
Distance: 5f/6f: 0-0 7f-8f: 0-1 9f-13f: 2-6 **14f+: 6-22**
Track : LH: 4-11 RH: 4-15 **Tight: 4-12** Gall: 1-8
Aids: **Bl: 1-2** Vi: 0-0 Tstrap: 0-0
Best Rating: 102 6/01 Chan 1m7f soft

A smart stayer, he has graduated from successful handicapper to Pattern performer.

Paiyda

95 **82**
3-y-o b f Danehill (USA)-Meadow Pipit (CAN) (Meadowlake (USA))
E A L Dunlop Mohammed Ali

Placings:1-60 **(4987)**
2001: 7^{6}GF, 10^{0}G
Starts 1st 2nd 3rd Win & Pl
Career Total (Turf) 3 1 0 0 3751
82 10/00 Ling 7f D SFT £3542
Total win prize-money £3543

Going (Turf): Sf: 1-1 GS: 0-0 Gd: 0-1 GF: 0-1 Fm: 0-0
Distance: 5f/6f: 0-0 **7f-8f: 1-2** 9f-13f: 0-1 14f+: 0-0
Track : LH: 0-0 RH: 0-1 Tight: 0-0 Gall: 0-1
Aids: Bl: 0-0 Vi: 0-0 Tstrap: 0-0
Best Rating: 55 9/01 Asct 1m2f good

Comfortable winner of a soft ground Lingfield maiden on her only run as a juvenile in 2000. Made a belated reappearance giving little appearance.

Palace Affair

110 **109**

3-y-o ch f Pursuit Of Love-Palace Street (USA) (Secreto (USA))
G B Balding Miss B Swire

Placings:510-2150100 **(4081)**
2001: 7^{2}S, 7^{1}G, 7^{5}GF, 7^{0}GF, 6^{1}G, 7^{0}GF, 6^{0}GF

	Starts	1st	2nd	3rd	Win & Pl
Career Total (Turf)	10	3	1	0	43574

108	7/01	York	6f	A	GD	£17468
102	5/01	Ling	7f	A	GD	£14674
95	9/00	Kemp	6f	D	GD	£4602

Total win prize-money £36745

Going (Turf): Sf: 0-2 GS: 0-0 **Gd: 3-4** GF: 0-4 Fm: 0-0
Distance: **5f/6f: 2-5** 7f-8f: 1-5 9f-13f: 0-0 14f+: 0-0
Track : LH: 0-1 RH: 0-3 Tight: 0-0 Gall: 0-1
Aids: **Bl: 1-3** Vi: 0-0 Tstrap: 0-0
Best Rating: 109 5/01 Gdwd 7f gd-fm

A winner once at two, she finished runner-up in the Free Handicap on her seasonal reappearance in 2001 and showed plenty of guts to get up in a Listed event at Lingfield subsequently. Found the ground too lively in her next two starts, but dropped back to six furlongs successfully in another Listed event at York in July. She needs the ground good or softer.

Palace Lake

85(93) (48)**33**

2-y-o b f Whittingham (IRE)-Oh Whataknight (Primo Dominie)
N P Littmoden Barry Minty

Placings:0445 **(1183)**
2001: 5^{0}S, 5^{4}SD, 5^{4}SD, 5^{5}GF

	Starts	1st	2nd	3rd	Win & Pl
Career Total (Turf)	2	0	0	0	0
Career Total (AW)	2	0	0	0	0

Going (Turf): Sf: 0-1 GS: 0-0 Gd: 0-0 GF: 0-1 Fm: 0-0
Distance: 5f/6f: 0-4 7f-8f: 0-0 9f-13f: 0-0 14f+: 0-0
Track : LH: 0-1 RH: 0-0 Tight: 0-0 Gall: 0-0
Aids: Bl: 0-0 Vi: 0-0 Tstrap: 0-0
Best Rating: 48 4/01 Sthl 5f stand

Palacegate Touch

98(106) (51)**50**

11-y-o gr g Petong-Dancing Chimes (London Bells (CAN))
A Berry A B Parr

Placings:01110/65010221110006/105300000402/150024055040/0125430411312310610/036101351023160005212/3014235061554411103 00/41331502500300233356006325/342050130030336500400003 4134-24225121415322000 4050 **(5639)**
2001: 6^{2}SW, 7^{4}SD, 6^{2}SD, 6^{2}SD, 6^{5}SD, 7^{1}SD, 6^{2}SD, 6^{1}SD, 5^{4}SD, 7^{1}SD, 6^{5}SD, 6^{3}GF, 7^{2}SD, 7^{2}GF, 6^{0}GF, 7^{0}SD, 6^{0}F, 7^{4}SD, 6^{0}G, 7^{5}SD, 5^{0}G

	Starts	1st	2nd	3rd	Win & Pl
Career Total (Turf)	127	22	7	16	104848
Career Total (AW)	52	10	13	9	33636

61	4/01	Sthl	7f	G	STD	£1939
55	3/01	Wolv	6f	F	STD	£2268
49	2/01	Wolv	7f	G	STD	£1855
59	10/00	Wolv	6f	F(0-60)H	STD	£2590
57	5/00	Wolv	6f	G	STD	£1512
67	3/99	Ling	6f	F	STD	£2107
63	1/99	Ling	6f	F	STD	£2107
58	7/98	Catt	5f212y	F	GD	£2332
55	7/98	Catt	5f212y	G	FRM	£1968
60	7/98	Haml	6f5y	E	FRM	£2818
64	6/98	Wwck	6f	F	GD	£2056
72	1/98	Ling	6f	F	STD	£2158
76	11/97	Ling	7f	G(0-75)H	STD	£1648
72	8/97	Hayd	6f	F	G-F	£2640
78	7/97	Haml	6f5y	D(0-85)H	G-S	£5831
64	5/97	Catt	5f	F	G-F	£2530
75	5/97	Donc	5f	E	GD	£2966
78	10/96	Catt	5f	D(0-85)H	GD	£4110
75	9/96	Sand	5f6y	E	G-F	£3111
65	8/96	Catt	5f	F	G-F	£2721
72	7/96	Wwck	5f	E(0-70)	FRM	£2988
66	7/96	Ling	5f	F	STD	£2381
65	4/96	Carl	6f206y	F	G-S	£2283
90	4/95	Ripn	6f	C(0-90)H	G-S	£5888
84	4/94	Ripn	6f	C(0-90)H	G-S	£5796
86	8/93	Ches	7f2y	B(0-95)H	G-S	£6434
73	8/93	Haml	6f5y	F	GD	£2579
74	8/93	Hayd	6f	F	SFT	£2465
73	6/93	Ripn	6f	F	GD	£2684
74	10/92	NmkR	6f	D	G-S	£6368
73	9/92	Hayd	6f	D	G-S	£4050
51	9/92	Yarm	6f3y	F	GD	£2973

Total win prize-money £98161

Going (Turf): Sf: 1-19 GS: 6-17 **Gd: 8-39** GF: 4-41 Fm: 3-11
Distance: 5f/6f: 23-134 7f-8f: 9-45 9f-13f: 0-0 14f+: 0-0
Track : LH: 15-80 RH: 1-9 **Tight: 12-60** Gall: 1-8
Aids: Bl: 20-117 Vi: 3-18 Tstrap: 0-0
Best Rating: 61 5/01 Sthl 7f stand

Veteran sprinter, he can still win in claiming company, either on turf or sand.

Palais (IRE)

(92) (8)**28**

6-y-o b g Darshaan-Dance Festival (Nureyev (USA))
J L Harris J South

Placings:456643/12505405000/00000-0000 **(0546)**
2001: 11^{0}SD, 16^{0}SD, 11^{0}SD, 11^{0}SD

	Starts	1st	2nd	3rd	Win & Pl
Career Total (Turf)	13	0	0	0	683
Career Total (AW)	13	1	1	1	4982

65	1/99	Sthl	1m3f	D	STD	£2892

Total win prize-money £2892

Going (Turf): Sf: 0-0 GS: 0-4 Gd: 0-2 GF: 0-7 Fm: 0-0
Distance: 5f/6f: 0-0 7f-8f: 0-2 **9f-13f: 1-17** 14f+: 0-7
Track : **LH: 1-22** RH: 0-4 Tight: 0-2 Gall: 0-1
Aids: Bl: 0-0 Vi: 0-4 Tstrap: 0-0
Best Rating: 7 3/01 Sthl 1m3f stand

Palamedes

84 **75+**

2-y-o b c Sadler's Wells (USA)-Kristal Bridge (Kris)
P W Harris Mrs P W Harris

Placings:0 **(5107)**
2001: 7^{0}GS

	Starts	1st	2nd	3rd	Win & Pl
Career Total (Turf)	1	0	0	0	

Going (Turf): Sf: 0-0 GS: 0-1 Gd: 0-0 GF: 0-0 Fm: 0-0
Distance: 5f/6f: 0-0 7f-8f: 0-1 9f-13f: 0-0 14f+: 0-0
Track : LH: 0-0 RH: 0-0 Tight: 0-0 Gall: 0-0
Aids: Bl: 0-0 Vi: 0-0 Tstrap: 0-0
Best Rating: 75 10/01 NmkR 7f gd-sft

Palanzo (IRE)

109 **105**

3-y-o b g Green Desert (USA)-Karpacka (IRE) (Rousillon (USA))
P W Harris Mrs P W Harris

Placings:210-5521220464 **(5494)**
2001: 7^{5}S, 8^{5}G, 6^{2}GF, 6^{1}GF, 6^{2}GF, 6^{2}GF, 6^{0}G, 6^{4}G, 6^{6}G, 6^{4}HY

	Starts	1st	2nd	3rd	Win & Pl
Career Total (Turf)	13	2	4	0	58029

107	6/01	NmkR	6f	B(0-105)H	G-F	£32500
96	9/00	Newb	6f8y	D	G-F	£5486

Total win prize-money £37986

Going (Turf): Sf: 0-2 GS: 0-0 Gd: 0-5 **GF: 2-6** Fm: 0-0
Distance: 5f/6f: 1-6 7f-8f: 1-7 9f-13f: 0-0 14f+: 0-0
Track : LH: 0-1 RH: 0-0 Tight: 0-0 Gall: 0-1
Aids: Bl: 0-1 Vi: 0-0 Tstrap: 0-0
Best Rating: 107 6/01 Yarm 6f3y gd-fm

Lightly-raced as a juvenile, he won a valuable handicap over six furlongs at Newmarket in May 2001. That win resulted in a very high handicap mark which has forced him to run in conditions events, but he has continued to perform with credit.

Palatial

105 **95**

3-y-o b f Green Desert (USA)-White Palace (Shirley Heights)
J R Fanshawe Cheveley Park Stud

Placings:222111-0205160 **(5365)**
2001: 7^{0}GS, 8^{2}GF, 8^{0}GF, 8^{5}G, 7^{1}G, 8^{6}GS, 6^{0}GS

	Starts	1st	2nd	3rd	Win & Pl
Career Total (Turf)	13	4	4	0	50280

84	9/01	NmkR	7f	B(0-95)	GD	£8798
93	9/00	NmkR	7f	B	G-S	£20800
85	9/00	Newb	7f		G-F	£9674
84	8/00	NmkJ	7f	D	G-F	£4143

Total win prize-money £43417

Going (Turf): Sf: 0-0 GS: 1-4 Gd: 1-3 **GF: 2-6** Fm: 0-0
Distance: 5f/6f: 0-1 **7f-8f: 4-12** 9f-13f: 0-0 14f+: 0-0
Track : LH: 0-1 RH: 0-1 Tight: 0-1 Gall: 0-1
Aids: Bl: 0-0 Vi: 0-0 Tstrap: 0-0
Best Rating: 95 10/01 NmkR 1m gd-sft

Concluded her two-year-old season by running up a hat-trick of victories over seven furlongs, and consequently proved hard to place earlier this year, before running out a cosy winner of a classified stakes over seven at Newmarket in September. Suited by a straight seven and acts on any ground.

Palatial Poise

81 **32**

3-y-o b f Rock Hopper-Kamaress (Kampala)
N Bycroft N Bycroft

Placings:06600 **(4422)**
2001: 10^{0}S, 9^{6}GF, 8^{6}GF, 9^{0}GF, 10^{0}GF

	Starts	1st	2nd	3rd	Win & Pl
Career Total (Turf)	5	0	0	0	0

Going (Turf): Sf: 0-1 GS: 0-0 Gd: 0-0 GF: 0-4 Fm: 0-0
Distance: 5f/6f: 0-0 7f-8f: 0-0 9f-13f: 0-5 14f+: 0-0
Track : LH: 0-3 RH: 0-2 Tight: 0-2 Gall: 0-0
Aids: Bl: 0-3 Vi: 0-0 Tstrap: 0-0
Best Rating: 32 8/01 Pont 1m4y gd-fm

Palawan

101(97) (78)**73**

5-y-o br g Polar Falcon (USA)-Krameria (Kris)
I A Balding Exors Of The Late Robert Hitchins

Placings:00/25220/211203010625305-000545304 **(3386)**
2001: 6^{0}SD, 5^{0}SD, 5^{0}GS, 5^{5}GF, 5^{4}GF, 5^{5}G, 6^{3}GF, 5^{0}GF, 5^{4}GF

	Starts	1st	2nd	3rd	Win & Pl
Career Total (Turf)	26	1	5	3	13823
Career Total (AW)	5	2	1	0	4970

69	6/00	Wind	5f10y	D(0-75)	G-F	£3802
78	2/00	Sthl	7f	G(0-75)H	STD	£1526
55	2/00	Wolv	7f	D	STD	£2704

Total win prize-money £8033

Going (Turf): Sf: 0-4 GS: 0-3 Gd: 0-7 **GF: 1-11** Fm: 0-1
Distance: 5f/6f: 1-23 **7f-8f: 2-8** 9f-13f: 0-0 14f+: 0-0
Track : **LH: 2-8** RH: 1-5 Tight: 1-3 Gall: 1-6
Aids: Bl: 0-0 Vi: 0-1 Tstrap: 0-0
Best Rating: 73 6/01 Wind 6f gd-fm

Fair handicapper, but with a low strike rate.

Palisandra (USA)

81(72) (7)**54+**
3-y-o b f Chief's Crown (USA)-Placer Queen (Habitat)
P W Harris Mrs P W Harris

Placings:0000 **(3233)**
2001: 7^{0}GS, 7^{0}G, 8^{0}GF, 12^{0}SD

	Starts	1st	2nd	3rd	Win & Pl
Career Total (Turf)	3	0	0	0	
Career Total (AW)	1	0	0	0	

Going (Turf): Sf: 0-0 GS: 0-1 Gd: 0-1 GF: 0-1 Fm: 0-0
Distance: 5f/6f: 0-0 7f-8f: 0-2 9f-13f: 0-2 14f+: 0-0
Track : LH: 0-1 RH: 0-1 Tight: 0-1 Gall: 0-0
Aids: Bl: 0-0 Vi: 0-0 Tstrap: 0-0
Best Rating: 54 4/01 Newb 7f gd-sft

Pallium (IRE)

85 (45)**5**
13-y-o b g Try My Best (USA)-Jungle Gardenia (Nonoalco (USA))
D A Nolan Mrs J McFadyen-Murray

Placings:50226/03331320100/3040505041300/000460201000055**240/55035**0406353522324000/050210016450/050040320000/43606221400025056/000520340604006/000500000500/0000000-00006000 **(4881)**
2001: 5^{0}GS, 5^{0}GF, 6^{0}G, 7^{0}GS, 5^{6}GF, 7^{0}GF, 7^{0}G, 6^{0}GF

	Starts	1st	2nd	3rd	Win & Pl
Career Total (Turf)	146	7	13	12	44556
Career Total (AW)	8	0	1	1	1922

47	7/97	Haml	5f4y	F(0-65)H	G-F	£2640
56	7/95	Ripn	5f	F(0-60)H	G-F	£2944
53	7/95	Muss	5f	F(0-60)H	G-F	£2815
64	8/93	Carl	5f	D(0-80)H	G-F	£4175
69	9/92	Bevl	5f	D(0-95)H	G-F	£3561
73	8/91	Hayd	5f	F	FRM	£2898
69	5/91	Wolv	5f	F(0-70)H	GD	£2822

Total win prize-money £21855

Going (Turf): Sf: 0-13 GS: 0-19 Gd: 1-39 **GF: 5-58** Fm: 1-17
Distance: **5f/6f: 7-140** 7f-8f: 0-14 9f-13f: 0-0 14f+: 0-0
Track : LH: 1-9 RH: 1-11 Tight: 0-4 **Gall: 1-10**
Aids: **Bl: 1-51** Vi: 0-14 Tstrap: 0-27
Best Rating: 11 7/01 Muss 5f gd-fm

Palua

111 **81**
4-y-o b g Sri Pekan (USA)-Reticent Bride (IRE) (Shy Groom (USA))
I A Balding Exors Of The Late Robert Hitchins

Placings:0030/34320332432-30062 **(5387)**
2001: 16^{3}GS, 14^{0}HY, 12^{0}G, 16^{6}S, 18^{2}GS

	Starts	1st	2nd	3rd	Win & Pl
Career Total (Turf)	20	0	4	7	33753

Going (Turf): Sf: 0-3 GS: 0-5 Gd: 0-4 GF: 0-8 Fm: 0-0
Distance: 5f/6f: 0-1 7f-8f: 0-3 9f-13f: 0-8 14f+: 0-8
Track : LH: 0-10 RH: 0-6 Tight: 0-6 Gall: 0-5
Aids: Bl: 0-6 Vi: 0-0 Tstrap: 0-0
Best Rating: 81 10/01 NmkR 2m2f gd-sft

He is a good mover who has been consistently placed but does not look too keen to get his head in front. Touched off by a stablemate in the Cesarewitch. Has raced on all bar extremes of going. Stays two miles plus.

Palvic Lady

90(97) (28)**29**
5-y-o b m Cotation-Palvic Grey (Kampala)
L R James (C Smith 13/3) R Arbon

Placings:000/0636005310/00**0000206-620000**000000 **(3509)**
2001: 5^{6}SD, 6^{2}SW, 5^{0}SD, 6^{0}SD, 6^{0}SD, 5^{0}SD, 5^{0}G, 5^{0}GF, 6^{0}SD, 5^{0}F, 7^{0}GF, 5^{0}SD, 5^{0}GF

	Starts	1st	2nd	3rd	Win & Pl
Career Total (Turf)	20	1	0	2	5070
Career Total (AW)	15	0	2	0	1018

61	9/99	Bevl	5f	D	GD	£3923

Total win prize-money £3924

Going (Turf): Sf: 0-0 GS: 0-3 **Gd: 1-7** GF: 0-8 Fm: 0-2
Distance: **5f/6f: 1-28** 7f-8f: 0-6 9f-13f: 0-1 14f+: 0-0
Track : LH: 0-10 RH: 0-0 Tight: 0-1 Gall: 0-0
Aids: Bl: 0-11 Vi: 0-2 Tstrap: 0-0
Best Rating: 41 1/01 Sthl 5f stand

Pamela Anshan

(68)
4-y-o b f Anshan-Have Form (Haveroid)
P R Rodford (J Cullinan 14/3) Mrs Christine Priest

Placings:000/0000600-00 **(0450)**
2001: 7^{0}SW, 9^{0}SD

	Starts	1st	2nd	3rd	Win & Pl
Career Total (Turf)	10	0	0	0	0
Career Total (AW)	2	0	0	0	

Going (Turf): Sf: 0-3 GS: 0-3 Gd: 0-0 GF: 0-4 Fm: 0-0
Distance: 5f/6f: 0-3 7f-8f: 0-6 9f-13f: 0-3 14f+: 0-0
Track : LH: 0-5 RH: 0-1 Tight: 0-2 Gall: 0-1
Aids: Bl: 0-0 Vi: 0-4 Tstrap: 0-0

Pan Jammer

110 **113**
3-y-o b c Piccolo-Ingerence (FR) (Akarad (FR))
M R Channon Ms Lynn Bell

Placings:41231406-04035352 **(3828)**
2001: 7^{0}S, 6^{4}G, 6^{0}GF, 7^{3}GF, 7^{5}GF, 6^{3}F, 6^{5}GF, 6^{2}G

	Starts	1st	2nd	3rd	Win & Pl
Career Total (Turf)	16	2	2	3	72192

104	7/00	Curr	6f63y		GD	£27300
71	5/00	Sals	5f	D	GD	£3542

Total win prize-money £30843

Going (Turf): Sf: 0-1 GS: 0-0 **Gd: 2-7** GF: 0-6 Fm: 0-1
Distance: 5f/6f: 1-10 7f-8f: 1-6 9f-13f: 0-0 14f+: 0-0
Track : LH: 0-1 RH: 0-0 Tight: 0-1 Gall: 0-0
Aids: Bl: 0-0 Vi: 0-0 Tstrap: 0-0
Best Rating: 113 6/01 Newc 6f firm

Showed plenty of ability in the first half of 2000, including winning a Group Three at the Curragh. He has been struggling to regain that kind of form as a three-year-old, but shaped well when third in a Listed event at Epsom on Oaks day and in a Group Three at Newcastle. Best on fast ground.

Panamint (USA)

98 **59**
3-y-o br f Silver Hawk (USA)-Kamsi (USA) (Afleet (CAN))
J R Fanshawe Philip Newton

Placings:000 **(3305)**
2001: 10^{0}GF, 10^{0}GF, 10^{0}GF

	Starts	1st	2nd	3rd	Win & Pl
Career Total (Turf)	3	0	0	0	

Going (Turf): Sf: 0-0 GS: 0-0 Gd: 0-0 GF: 0-3 Fm: 0-0
Distance: 5f/6f: 0-0 7f-8f: 0-0 9f-13f: 0-3 14f+: 0-0
Track : LH: 0-0 RH: 0-2 Tight: 0-1 Gall: 0-2
Aids: Bl: 0-0 Vi: 0-0 Tstrap: 0-0
Best Rating: 59 7/01 Kemp 1m2f gd-fm

Pancakehill

88 **71**
2-y-o ch f Sabrehill (USA)-Sawlah (Known Fact (USA))
G A Butler Nicholas Jones

Placings:066 **(4939)**
2001: 6^{0}GF, 7^{6}GF, 7^{6}S

	Starts	1st	2nd	3rd	Win & Pl
Career Total (Turf)	3	0	0	0	0

Going (Turf): Sf: 0-1 GS: 0-0 Gd: 0-0 GF: 0-2 Fm: 0-0
Distance: 5f/6f: 0-1 7f-8f: 0-2 9f-13f: 0-0 14f+: 0-0
Track : LH: 0-2 RH: 0-0 Tight: 0-1 Gall: 0-0
Aids: Bl: 0-0 Vi: 0-0 Tstrap: 0-0
Best Rating: 71 9/01 Wwck 7f26y gd-fm

Pandjojoe (IRE)

109(100) (54)**65**
5-y-o b g Archway (IRE)-Vital Princess (Prince Sabo)
R A Fahey Northumbria Leisure Ltd

Placings:05605/1114500000/0556060030**240-00**150000 **(5288)**
2001: 7^{0}SD, 6^{0}SD, 6^{1}S, 7^{5}GS, 7^{0}G, 6^{0}G, 6^{0}G, 6^{0}HY

	Starts	1st	2nd	3rd	Win & Pl
Career Total (Turf)	31	4	0	1	30158
Career Total (AW)	5	0	1	0	508

65	7/01	Haml	6f5y	C(0-100)H	SFT	£19175
73	5/99	Hayd	6f	E(0-70)H	GD	£3088
74	5/99	Wind	6f	D(0-80)H	GD	£4201
64	5/99	Newc	6f	E(0-70)H	G-F	£2906

Total win prize-money £29371

Going (Turf): Sf: 1-8 GS: 0-3 **Gd: 2-10** GF: 1-8 Fm: 0-2
Distance: **5f/6f: 3-30** 7f-8f: 1-6 9f-13f: 0-0 14f+: 0-0
Track : LH: 0-7 **RH: 1-3** Tight: 0-3 **Gall: 1-3**
Aids: Bl: 0-1 Vi: 0-0 Tstrap: 0-0
Best Rating: 65 7/01 Haml 6f5y soft

He notched up a hat-trick as a three-year-old, but went up in the ratings and did not win again until landing a valuable handicap on soft ground at Hamilton in July 2001 when backed at long odds. Best over six furlongs.

Pango

93 **69**
2-y-o ch c Bluegrass Prince (IRE)-Riverine (Risk Me (FR))
H Morrison Pangfield Partners

Placings:630 **(5290)**
2001: 6^{6}GF, 7^{3}GF, 7^{0}S

	Starts	1st	2nd	3rd	Win & Pl
Career Total (Turf)	3	0	0	1	446

Going (Turf): Sf: 0-1 GS: 0-0 Gd: 0-0 GF: 0-2 Fm: 0-0
Distance: 5f/6f: 0-1 7f-8f: 0-2 9f-13f: 0-0 14f+: 0-0
Track : LH: 0-0 RH: 0-0 Tight: 0-0 Gall: 0-0
Aids: Bl: 0-0 Vi: 0-0 Tstrap: 0-0
Best Rating: 69 7/01 Ling 7f gd-fm

Panjandrum

94(103) (62)**60**
3-y-o b g Polar Falcon (USA)-Rengaine (FR) (Music Boy)
P D Evans (P F I Cole 19/5) Mrs S G Allan

Placings:00101620046 **(3239)**
2001: 5^{0}SD, 5^{0}SD, 5^{1}SD, 5^{0}GS, 5^{1}SD, 6^{6}GF, 6^{2}GF, 5^{0}GF, 5^{0}GF, 6^{4}SD, 6^{6}SD

	Starts	1st	2nd	3rd	Win & Pl
Career Total (Turf)	5	0	1	0	1110
Career Total (AW)	6	2	0	0	3668

62	5/01	Wolv	5f	G	STD	£1876
47	4/01	Sthl	5f	F	STD	£1792

Total win prize-money £3668

Going (Turf): Sf: 0-0 GS: 0-1 Gd: 0-0 GF: 0-4 Fm: 0-0
Distance: 5f/6f: 2-10 7f-8f: 0-1 9f-13f: 0-0 14f+: 0-0
Track : LH: 1-6 RH: 0-1 Tight: 1-4 Gall: 0-2
Aids: Bl: 0-0 Vi: 0-1 Tstrap: 0-0
Best Rating: 62 5/01 Wolv 5f stand

A half-brother to three winners. Has won a claimer and a seller on the All-Weather over five furlongs. Best effort on turf at Chester in a six-furlong claimer on fast ground.

Panna

102 **100**

3-y-o b f Polish Precedent (USA)-Gull Nook (Mill Reef (USA))
G Wragg Lord Halifax

Placings:4-0212 **(4190)**
2001: 8^{0}G, 8^{2}GF, 10^{1}GF, 11^{2}G

	Starts	1st	2nd	3rd	Win & Pl
Career Total (Turf)	5	1	2	0	19404

89	7/01	Asct	1m2f	C(0-90)H	G-F	£8326

Total win prize-money £8327

Going (Turf): Sf: 0-1 GS: 0-0 Gd: 0-2 **GF: 1-2** Fm: 0-0
Distance: 5f/6f: 0-0 7f-8f: 0-1 **9f-13f: 1-4** 14f+: 0-0
Track : LH: 0-1 **RH: 1-2** Tight: 0-1 **Gall: 1-2**
Aids: Bl: 0-0 Vi: 0-0 Tstrap: 0-0
Best Rating: 100 8/01 York 1m3f195y good

A lightly-raced half-sister to Pentire, she won her handicap in runaway fashion, and was touched off in a Listed race at York.

Panooras Lord (IRE)

90 (15)**38**

7-y-o b g Topanoora-Ladyship (Windjammer (USA))
J S Wainwright J S Wainwright

Placings:00/00/0-50000002000 **(5226)**
2001: 10^{5}HY, 12^{0}S, 10^{0}F, 9^{0}F, 10^{0}GF, 16^{0}F, 8^{0}GF, 9^{2}GF, 9^{0}G, 12^{0}GF, 11^{0}S

	Starts	1st	2nd	3rd	Win & Pl
Career Total (Turf)	14	0	1	0	1347
Career Total (AW)	2	0	0	0	

Going (Turf): Sf: 0-3 GS: 0-0 Gd: 0-1 GF: 0-7 Fm: 0-3
Distance: 5f/6f: 0-0 7f-8f: 0-3 9f-13f: 0-11 14f+: 0-2
Track : LH: 0-7 RH: 0-6 Tight: 0-7 Gall: 0-1
Aids: Bl: 0-0 Vi: 0-0 Tstrap: 0-0
Best Rating: 55 4/01 Pont 1m2f6y heavy

Pantar (IRE)

111(105) (86)**98**

6-y-o b g Shirley Heights-Spring Daffodil (Pharly (FR))
I A Balding Exors Of The Late Robert Hitchins

Placings:00/0342130503/5450560330/0321436300236 10-0030321406036 **(5142)**
2001: 8^{0}SD, 8^{0}S, 8^{3}S, 8^{0}GS, 8^{3}GF, 10^{2}F, 10^{1}G, 10^{4}GF, 10^{0}G, 9^{6}GF, 7^{0}G, 9^{3}GF, 9^{6}G

	Starts	1st	2nd	3rd	Win & Pl
Career Total (Turf)	44	3	3	11	102508
Career Total (AW)	6	1	1	1	8240

100	6/01	Sand	1m2f7y	C(0-100)H	GD	£10676
96	9/00	Gdwd	1m1f	C(0-100)H	GD	£12285
86	3/00	Wolv	1m1f79y	C	STD	£6061
96	6/98	Gdwd	1m	C(0-90)H	GD	£14980

Total win prize-money £44002

Going (Turf): Sf: 0-7 GS: 0-5 **Gd: 3-16** GF: 0-16 Fm: 0-1
Distance: 5f/6f: 0-0 7f-8f: 1-24 **9f-13f: 3-26** 14f+: 0-0
Track : LH: 1-13 **RH: 3-18 Tight: 2-12** Gall: 0-8
Aids: **Bl: 1-10** Vi: 0-0 Tstrap: 0-0
Best Rating: 100 6/01 Sand 1m2f7y good

Often runs well in big handicaps and got some reward with a win at Sandown in June. Unlucky in running when third at Goodwood in September. Best over nine/ten furlongs on a sound surface.

Pants

93 **76**

2-y-o b f Pivotal-Queenbird (Warning)
Andrew Reid A S Reid

Placings:4334006 **(5022)**
2001: 6^{4}GF, 6^{3}G, 6^{3}G, 6^{4}GS, 6^{0}GF, 6^{0}G, 7^{6}S

	Starts	1st	2nd	3rd	Win & Pl
Career Total (Turf)	7	0	0	2	2486

Going (Turf): Sf: 0-1 GS: 0-1 Gd: 0-3 GF: 0-2 Fm: 0-0
Distance: 5f/6f: 0-4 7f-8f: 0-3 9f-13f: 0-0 14f+: 0-0
Track : LH: 0-2 RH: 0-0 Tight: 0-1 Gall: 0-0
Aids: Bl: 0-0 Vi: 0-0 Tstrap: 0-0
Best Rating: 76 8/01 Ches 6f18y gd-sft

Fair maiden. Does not appear to handle fast ground.

Papa Mio

84(87) (45)**54**

2-y-o br f Ventiquattrofogli (IRE)-Judys Girl (IRE) (Simply Great (FR))
M W Easterby Harold Winton

Placings:063300 **(4630)**
2001: 5^{0}S, 5^{6}GS, 5^{3}SD, 6^{3}G, 7^{0}G, 8^{0}GF

	Starts	1st	2nd	3rd	Win & Pl
Career Total (Turf)	5	0	0	1	345
Career Total (AW)	1	0	0	1	261

Going (Turf): Sf: 0-1 GS: 0-1 Gd: 0-2 GF: 0-1 Fm: 0-0
Distance: 5f/6f: 0-4 7f-8f: 0-1 9f-13f: 0-1 14f+: 0-0
Track : LH: 0-1 RH: 0-0 Tight: 0-1 Gall: 0-0
Aids: Bl: 0-0 Vi: 0-0 Tstrap: 0-0
Best Rating: 54 8/01 Rdcr 6f good

Papagena (USA)

(92) (43)

4-y-o b/br f Robellino (USA)-Morning Crown (USA) (Chief's Crown (USA))
C W Thornton Simon Brown

Placings:0062030564/62430000-006 **(0215)**
2001: 12^{0}SD, 12^{0}SD, 11^{6}SD

	Starts	1st	2nd	3rd	Win & Pl
Career Total (Turf)	9	0	1	1	2643
Career Total (AW)	12	0	1	1	1196

Going (Turf): Sf: 0-3 GS: 0-2 Gd: 0-1 GF: 0-2 Fm: 0-1
Distance: 5f/6f: 0-8 7f-8f: 0-4 9f-13f: 0-9 14f+: 0-0
Track : LH: 0-13 RH: 0-1 Tight: 0-5 Gall: 0-0
Aids: Bl: 0-11 Vi: 0-0 Tstrap: 0-0
Best Rating: 29 2/01 Sthl 1m3f stand

Paper Chase (FR)

96 **85**

2-y-o ch f Machiavellian (USA)-Papering (IRE) (Shaadi (USA))
D R Loder Sheikh Mohammed

Placings:20 **(3584)**
2001: 7^{2}GS, 7^{0}G

	Starts	1st	2nd	3rd	Win & Pl
Career Total (Turf)	2	0	1	0	1254

Going (Turf): Sf: 0-0 GS: 0-1 Gd: 0-1 GF: 0-0 Fm: 0-0
Distance: 5f/6f: 0-0 7f-8f: 0-2 9f-13f: 0-0 14f+: 0-0
Track : LH: 0-0 RH: 0-1 Tight: 0-0 Gall: 0-0
Aids: Bl: 0-0 Vi: 0-0 Tstrap: 0-0
Best Rating: 85 7/01 NmkJ 7f gd-sft

Paperweight

84(105) (68)**56**

5-y-o b m In The Wings-Crystal Reay (Sovereign Dancer (USA))
Miss K M George Stableline

Placings:25230/42303440024611-264420002 **(1993)**
2001: 10^{2}SD, 9^{6}SW, 9^{4}SW, 9^{4}SD, 9^{2}SD, 11^{0}SD, 9^{0}HY, 11^{0}GS, 12^{2}SD

	Starts	1st	2nd	3rd	Win & Pl
Career Total (Turf)	10	0	2	1	3460
Career Total (AW)	18	2	5	2	10860

68	12/00	Wolv	1m1f79y	E(0-70)H	STD	£2212
44	12/00	Wolv	1m1f79y	D	STD	£2716

Total win prize-money £4928

Going (Turf): Sf: 0-3 GS: 0-3 Gd: 0-1 GF: 0-3 Fm: 0-0
Distance: 5f/6f: 0-0 7f-8f: 0-0 **9f-13f: 2-28** 14f+: 0-0
Track : **LH: 2-23** RH: 0-2 **Tight: 2-21** Gall: 0-2
Aids: Bl: 0-1 Vi: 0-1 Tstrap: 0-0
Best Rating: 67 2/01 Wolv 1m1f79y stand

Papi Special (IRE)

100 **51**

4-y-o b g Tragic Role (USA)-Practical (Ballymore)
I Semple Mrs E Chung

Placings:0422/00240102000-2603536600 **(2866)**
2001: 16^{2}S, 14^{6}GS, 13^{0}G, 13^{3}GF, 13^{5}G, 14^{3}GF, 16^{6}GF, 14^{6}G, 17^{0}GF, 16^{0}GF

	Starts	1st	2nd	3rd	Win & Pl
Career Total (Turf)	25	1	5	2	9852

56	7/00	Haml	1m5f9y	E(0-75)H	G-F	£3087

Total win prize-money £3088

Going (Turf): Sf: 0-7 GS: 0-1 Gd: 0-6 **GF: 1-11** Fm: 0-0
Distance: 5f/6f: 0-0 7f-8f: 0-2 9f-13f: 0-8 **14f+: 1-15**
Track : LH: 0-7 **RH: 1-18 Tight: 1-18** Gall: 0-2
Aids: Bl: 0-2 Vi: 0-17 Tstrap: 0-0
Best Rating: 51 6/01 Muss 2m gd-fm

Papingo

75 **21**

3-y-o b f Charnwood Forest (IRE)-Maracuja (USA) (Riverman (USA))
K R Burke David McKenzie

Placings:0 **(2873)**
2001: 8^{0}GF

	Starts	1st	2nd	3rd	Win & Pl
Career Total (Turf)	1	0	0	0	

Going (Turf): Sf: 0-0 GS: 0-0 Gd: 0-0 GF: 0-1 Fm: 0-0
Distance: 5f/6f: 0-0 7f-8f: 0-1 9f-13f: 0-0 14f+: 0-0
Track : LH: 0-0 RH: 0-1 Tight: 0-1 Gall: 0-0
Aids: Bl: 0-0 Vi: 0-0 Tstrap: 0-0
Best Rating: 21 7/01 Ripn 1m gd-fm

Para Glider (FR)

107(102) (75)**85**

3-y-o b c Jeune Homme (USA)-Idee Folle (FR) (Crystal Palace (FR))
G C Bravery Khalifa Dasmal

Placings:50-32314024 **(5486)**
2001: 9^{3}SD, 8^{2}SW, 8^{3}GS, 8^{1}SD, 8^{4}G, 8^{0}GF, 10^{2}HY, 10^{4}HY

	Starts	1st	2nd	3rd	Win & Pl
Career Total (Turf)	7	0	1	1	3366
Career Total (AW)	3	1	1	1	4245

75	4/01	Sthl	1m	E(0-75)H	STD	£2999

Total win prize-money £3000

Going (Turf): Sf: 0-4 GS: 0-1 Gd: 0-1 GF: 0-1 Fm: 0-0
Distance: 5f/6f: 0-1 **7f-8f: 1-4** 9f-13f: 0-5 14f+: 0-0
Track : **LH: 1-4** RH: 0-2 Tight: 0-4 Gall: 0-1
Aids: Bl: 0-0 Vi: 0-0 Tstrap: 0-0
Best Rating: 82 10/01 Wind 1m2f7y heavy

Got off the mark in a Southwell handicap, but has found a few too good since back on turf. Suited by a mile on Fibresand. Best at around ten furlongs on soft ground.

Parachute

91 **65**

2-y-o ch c Hector Protector (USA)-Shortfall (Last Tycoon)
Sir Mark Prescott W E Sturt - Osborne House Ii

Placings:0600 (5536)
2001: 7^{0}S, 6^{6}S, 6^{0}HY, 6^{0}S

	Starts	1st	2nd	3rd	Win & Pl
Career Total (Turf)	4	0	0	0	0

Going (Turf): Sf: 0-4 GS: 0-0 Gd: 0-0 GF: 0-0 Fm: 0-0
Distance: 5f/6f: 0-2 7f-8f: 0-2 9f-13f: 0-0 14f+: 0-0
Track : LH: 0-2 RH: 0-0 Tight: 0-1 Gall: 0-0
Aids: Bl: 0-0 Vi: 0-0 Tstrap: 0-0
Best Rating: 65 10/01 Brig 6f209y soft

A 100,000gns yearling from a good middle-distance family, is the type to improve significantly when allowed a stiffer test in due course. Yet to race on ground better than soft.

Parade (IRE)

(101) (65)

3-y-o ch g Lycius (USA)-Cheviot Amble (IRE) (Pennine Walk)
W J Haggas Highclere Thoroughbred Racing Ltd

Placings:23 (0299)
2001: 7^{2}SW, 7^{3}SD

	Starts	1st	2nd	3rd	Win & Pl
Career Total (Turf)	0	0	0	0	
Career Total (AW)	2	0	1	1	1088

Going (Turf): Sf: 0-0 GS: 0-0 Gd: 0-0 GF: 0-0 Fm: 0-0
Distance: 5f/6f: 0-0 7f-8f: 0-2 9f-13f: 0-0 14f+: 0-0
Track : LH: 0-2 RH: 0-0 Tight: 0-2 Gall: 0-0
Aids: Bl: 0-0 Vi: 0-0 Tstrap: 0-0
Best Rating: 65 2/01 Wolv 7f stand

Paradise Blue (IRE)

95 **57**

3-y-o gr f Bluebird (USA)-Safka (USA) (Irish River (FR))
R Hannon J G Davis

Placings:045000 (4840)
2001: 7^{0}GS, 6^{4}GS, 6^{5}GS, 7^{0}GF, 7^{0}G, 6^{0}G

	Starts	1st	2nd	3rd	Win & Pl
Career Total (Turf)	6	0	0	0	238

Going (Turf): Sf: 0-0 GS: 0-3 Gd: 0-2 GF: 0-1 Fm: 0-0
Distance: 5f/6f: 0-2 7f-8f: 0-4 9f-13f: 0-0 14f+: 0-0
Track : LH: 0-0 RH: 0-0 Tight: 0-0 Gall: 0-0
Aids: Bl: 0-0 Vi: 0-0 Tstrap: 0-0
Best Rating: 57 8/01 Ling 7f gd-fm

Paradise Garden (USA)

99(30) (63)**31**

4-y-o b g Septieme Ciel (USA)-Water Course (USA) (Irish River (FR))
P L Clinton (Denys Smith 7/9) P L Clinton

Placings:31224/0304000-001000 (5622)
2001: 12^{0}GS, 11^{0}G, 10^{1}GS, 9^{0}G, 16^{0}HY, 14^{0}GS

	Starts	1st	2nd	3rd	Win & Pl
Career Total (Turf)	17	2	2	2	16329
Career Total (AW)	1	0	0	0	

35 7/01 Ayr 1m2f192yF G-S £2464
68 8/99 Newc 1m3y F GD £2253
Total win prize-money £4717

Going (Turf): Sf: 0-3 GS: 1-4 Gd: 1-9 GF: 0-1 Fm: 0-0
Distance: 5f/6f: 0-0 7f-8f: 0-5 **9f-13f: 2-11** 14f+: 0-2
Track : **LH: 1-12** RH: 0-3 Tight: 0-4 Gall: 0-4
Aids: Bl: 0-0 Vi: 0-0 Tstrap: 0-0
Best Rating: 49 4/01 Muss 1m4f gd-sft

Paradiso Paradis (IRE)

83 **34**

3-y-o b f Tagula (IRE)-Shanamara (IRE) (Shernazar)
J A Osborne Mrs E Roberts

Placings:06 (4096)
2001: 8^{0}G, 6^{6}G

	Starts	1st	2nd	3rd	Win & Pl
Career Total (Turf)	2	0	0	0	0

Going (Turf): Sf: 0-0 GS: 0-0 Gd: 0-2 GF: 0-0 Fm: 0-0
Distance: 5f/6f: 0-0 7f-8f: 0-1 9f-13f: 0-1 14f+: 0-0
Track : LH: 0-1 RH: 0-1 Tight: 0-1 Gall: 0-0
Aids: Bl: 0-0 Vi: 0-0 Tstrap: 0-0
Best Rating: 34 8/01 Wind 1m67y good

Paragon Of Virtue

81 **45**

4-y-o ch g Cadeaux Genereux-Madame Dubois (Legend Of France (USA))
P Mitchell J Morton

Placings:0233-0 (5607)
2001: 8^{0}GS

	Starts	1st	2nd	3rd	Win & Pl
Career Total (Turf)	5	0	1	2	3089

Going (Turf): Sf: 0-0 GS: 0-3 Gd: 0-2 GF: 0-0 Fm: 0-0
Distance: 5f/6f: 0-0 7f-8f: 0-3 9f-13f: 0-2 14f+: 0-0
Track : LH: 0-3 RH: 0-0 Tight: 0-1 Gall: 0-1
Aids: Bl: 0-0 Vi: 0-0 Tstrap: 0-0
Best Rating: 45 11/01 NmkR 1m gd-sft

Parasol (IRE)

109 **102**

2-y-o br c Halling (USA)-Bunting (Shaadi (USA))
M R Channon Mohammed Al Nabouda

Placings:12436 (5388)
2001: 6^{1}G, 7^{2}GF, 8^{4}GS, 8^{3}S, 7^{6}GS

	Starts	1st	2nd	3rd	Win & Pl
Career Total (Turf)	5	1	1	1	36525

80 6/01 Hayd 6f D GD £4465
Total win prize-money £4466

Going (Turf): Sf: 0-1 GS: 0-2 **Gd: 1-1** GF: 0-1 Fm: 0-0
Distance: **5f/6f: 1-1** 7f-8f: 0-4 9f-13f: 0-0 14f+: 0-0
Track : LH: 0-0 RH: 0-1 Tight: 0-0 Gall: 0-1
Aids: Bl: 0-0 Vi: 0-0 Tstrap: 0-0
Best Rating: 102 10/01 NmkR 7f gd-sft

He made all to win at Haydock on his debut and was only just caught in the Chesham next time. He was first past the post in a Listed event at Deauville in August, but was demoted for causing interference. Ran good races in top juvenile company in the autumn on easy ground.

Pardishar (IRE)

110 **99**

3-y-o b c Kahyasi-Parapa (IRE) (Akarad (FR))
Sir Michael Stoute H H Aga Khan

Placings:134 (4045)
2001: 10^{1}G, 9^{3}G, 11^{4}HY

	Starts	1st	2nd	3rd	Win & Pl
Career Total (Turf)	3	1	0	1	5983

89 7/01 Sand 1m2f7y D GD £4241
Total win prize-money £4241

Going (Turf): Sf: 0-1 GS: 0-0 **Gd: 1-2** GF: 0-0 Fm: 0-0
Distance: 5f/6f: 0-0 7f-8f: 0-0 **9f-13f: 1-3** 14f+: 0-0
Track : LH: 0-1 **RH: 1-2** Tight: 0-0 Gall: 0-0
Aids: Bl: 0-0 Vi: 0-0 Tstrap: 0-0
Best Rating: 99 8/01 Sand 1m1f good

Won at the first time of asking, but found his subsequent races a little bit too competitive.

Paris Flash (IRE)

83 **50**

2-y-o gr f Paris House-Flash Donna (USA) (Well Decorated (USA))
A B Mulholland Miss K Watson

Placings:00 (5370)
2001: 7^{0}HY, 7^{0}G

	Starts	1st	2nd	3rd	Win & Pl
Career Total (Turf)	2	0	0	0	

Going (Turf): Sf: 0-1 GS: 0-0 Gd: 0-1 GF: 0-0 Fm: 0-0
Distance: 5f/6f: 0-0 7f-8f: 0-2 9f-13f: 0-0 14f+: 0-0
Track : LH: 0-1 RH: 0-0 Tight: 0-0 Gall: 0-0
Aids: Bl: 0-0 Vi: 0-0 Tstrap: 0-0
Best Rating: 50 10/01 Rdcr 7f good

Paris Knight (IRE)

93(78) (35)**20**

3-y-o b g Paris House-Bykova (Petoski)
B J Llewellyn (A Berry 2/9) B J Llewellyn

Placings:50600000 (5524)
2001: 6^{5}SD, 6^{0}GF, 6^{6}SD, 7^{0}GS, 6^{0}F, 7^{0}GS, 7^{0}GF, 10^{0}HY

	Starts	1st	2nd	3rd	Win & Pl
Career Total (Turf)	6	0	0	0	
Career Total (AW)	2	0	0	0	0

Going (Turf): Sf: 0-1 GS: 0-2 Gd: 0-0 GF: 0-2 Fm: 0-1
Distance: 5f/6f: 0-4 7f-8f: 0-3 9f-13f: 0-1 14f+: 0-0
Track : LH: 0-3 RH: 0-1 Tight: 0-2 Gall: 0-0
Aids: Bl: 0-0 Vi: 0-0 Tstrap: 0-0
Best Rating: 35 6/01 Sthl 6f stand

Parisian Eire (IRE)

83 **53**

2-y-o gr c Paris House-La Fille De Feu (Never So Bold)
M R Channon Brian Chandler

Placings:00 (4379)
2001: 5^{0}GF, 6^{0}GF

	Starts	1st	2nd	3rd	Win & Pl
Career Total (Turf)	2	0	0	0	

Going (Turf): Sf: 0-0 GS: 0-0 Gd: 0-0 GF: 0-2 Fm: 0-0
Distance: 5f/6f: 0-2 7f-8f: 0-0 9f-13f: 0-0 14f+: 0-0
Track : LH: 0-0 RH: 0-0 Tight: 0-0 Gall: 0-0
Aids: Bl: 0-0 Vi: 0-0 Tstrap: 0-0
Best Rating: 53 8/01 Ling 6f gd-fm

Parisian Elegance

102(94) (67+)**90**

2-y-o b f Zilzal (USA)-Tshusick (Dancing Brave (USA))
R M H Cowell Mike Charlton And Rodger Sargent

Placings:411033600 (4833)
2001: 5^{4}GS, 5^{1}SW, 5^{1}GF, 5^{0}GF, 6^{3}GF, 6^{3}GF, 6^{6}G, 5^{0}S, 6^{0}GF

	Starts	1st	2nd	3rd	Win & Pl
Career Total (Turf)	8	1	0	2	11752
Career Total (AW)	1	1	0	0	3269

87 5/01 Thsk 5f D G-F £4218
67 4/01 Sthl 5f D GLW £3269
Total win prize-money £7488

Going (Turf): Sf: 0-1 GS: 0-1 Gd: 0-1 **GF: 1-5** Fm: 0-0
Distance: **5f/6f: 2-7** 7f-8f: 0-2 9f-13f: 0-0 14f+: 0-0
Track : LH: 0-0 RH: 0-0 Tight: 0-0 Gall: 0-0
Aids: Bl: 0-0 Vi: 0-0 Tstrap: 0-0
Best Rating: 90 9/01 Chan 5f110y soft

Useful sprinting juvenile in 2001, who ran well in Pattern company after two victories in the spring.

Parisian Lady (IRE)

91 (99) (50) **41**
6-y-o b m Paris House-Mia Gigi (Hard Fought)
A G Newcombe Advanced Marketing Services Ltd

Placings:11420/43004000/0000**400106/634**4202U40-0400 **(3096)**
2001: 11^{0}F, 12^{4}GF, 12^{0}G, 9^{0}G

	Starts	1st	2nd	3rd	Win & Pl
Career Total (Turf)	28	2	3	1	17603
Career Total (AW)	9	1	0	1	2983

55 12/99 Ling 1m E(0-70)H STD £2303
93 7/97 Sals 6f F G-F £2847
80 6/97 Sals 6f F G-F £2602
Total win prize-money £7752

Going (Turf): Sf: 0-2 GS: 0-2 Gd: 0-7 **GF: 2-14** Fm: 0-3
Distance: **5f/6f: 2-8** 7f-8f: 1-14 9f-13f: 0-15 14f+: 0-0
Track : **LH: 1-21** RH: 0-2 **Tight: 1-11** Gall: 0-2
Aids: Bl: 0-3 Vi: 0-0 Tstrap: 0-0
Best Rating: 41 7/01 Epsm 1m4f10y gd-fm

Parisien Star (IRE)

109 **90**
5-y-o ch g Paris House-Auction Maid (IRE) (Auction Ring (USA))
N Hamilton John Hopkins (t/a South Hatch Racing)

Placings:00031124/5402026000/40451240-05200204450 **(5669)**
2001: 7^{0}S, 8^{5}GF, 10^{2}GF, 8^{0}GF, 10^{0}G, 9^{2}GF, 8^{0}G, 8^{4}S, 10^{4}G, 9^{5}GF, 10^{0}HY

	Starts	1st	2nd	3rd	Win & Pl
Career Total (Turf)	37	3	6	1	75299

84 8/00 Gdwd 1m D(0-85)H G-F £11700
82 9/98 Newb 7f64y C H GD £5702
76 9/98 Epsm 6f D H GD £3452
Total win prize-money £20856

Going (Turf): Sf: 0-6 GS: 0-5 **Gd: 2-12** GF: 1-13 Fm: 0-1
Distance: 5f/6f: 1-5 **7f-8f: 2-20** 9f-13f: 0-12 14f+: 0-0
Track : **LH: 2-11** RH: 1-16 Tight: 1-12 Gall: 1-5
Aids: Bl: 0-0 Vi: 0-0 Tstrap: 0-0
Best Rating: 90 7/01 Gdwd 1m1f192y gd-fm

Ended a long losing run when winning at Goodwood in August 2000. He failed by a whisker to follow-up over course and distance two days later and paid the price with a hike in the ratings. Has won at up to a mile on a sound surface and looks suited by a switchback track.

Parisienne Hill

91 (4) **17**
5-y-o b m Lapierre-Snarry Hill (Vitiges (FR))
B W Murray B Murray

Placings:000/000660**0**000/0000000-000000300000600 **(5149)**
2001: 12^{0}S, 14^{0}HY, 10^{0}HY, 8^{0}GF, 10^{0}GF, 8^{0}GF, 10^{3}GF, 12^{0}F, 10^{0}S, 9^{0}F, 8^{0}GF, 8^{0}GF, 9^{6}GF, 8^{0}GF, 8^{0}F, 7^{0}G

	Starts	1st	2nd	3rd	Win & Pl
Career Total (Turf)	35	0	0	1	1090
Career Total (AW)	1	0	0	0	

Going (Turf): Sf: 0-6 GS: 0-1 Gd: 0-7 GF: 0-16 Fm: 0-5
Distance: 5f/6f: 0-1 7f-8f: 0-6 9f-13f: 0-25 14f+: 0-4
Track : LH: 0-19 RH: 0-13 Tight: 0-9 Gall: 0-6
Aids: Bl: 0-0 Vi: 0-0 Tstrap: 0-0
Best Rating: 24 7/01 Donc 1m2f60y gd-fm

Poor individual. Stays a mile and a half but is pretty paceless. Best on a sound surface.

Park City

70 **24**
2-y-o b c Slip Anchor-Cryptal (Persian Bold)
P Howling Mrs A K Petersen

Placings:0 **(4534)**
2001: 6^{0}GF

	Starts	1st	2nd	3rd	Win & Pl
Career Total (Turf)	1	0	0	0	

Going (Turf): Sf: 0-0 GS: 0-0 Gd: 0-0 GF: 0-1 Fm: 0-0
Distance: 5f/6f: 0-0 7f-8f: 0-1 9f-13f: 0-0 14f+: 0-0
Track : LH: 0-1 RH: 0-0 Tight: 0-0 Gall: 0-1
Aids: Bl: 0-0 Vi: 0-0 Tstrap: 0-0
Best Rating: 24 9/01 York 6f214y gd-fm

Parker

112 (105) (72) **81**
4-y-o b g Magic Ring (IRE)-Miss Loving (Northfields (USA))
B Palling Lamb Brook Associates

Placings:304/2463532-**15352**012000 **(4640)**
2001: 8^{1}SD, 7^{5}SW, 8^{3}SD, 7^{5}SD, 8^{2}SD, 8^{0}GF, 7^{1}GF, 7^{2}GF, 7^{0}F, 7^{0}G, 7^{0}GF

	Starts	1st	2nd	3rd	Win & Pl
Career Total (Turf)	16	1	3	3	15843
Career Total (AW)	5	1	1	1	4957

81 6/01 Ches 7f2y C(0-95)H G-F £11115
68 1/01 Ling 1m D STD £2891
Total win prize-money £14006

Going (Turf): Sf: 0-1 GS: 0-1 Gd: 0-2 **GF: 1-11** Fm: 0-1
Distance: 5f/6f: 0-1 **7f-8f: 2-18** 9f-13f: 0-2 14f+: 0-0
Track : **LH: 2-8** RH: 0-3 **Tight: 2-5** Gall: 0-0
Aids: Bl: 0-0 Vi: 0-0 Tstrap: 0-0
Best Rating: 81 6/01 Ches 7f2y gd-fm

A winner over a mile on the sand at Lingfield, he scored his second ever success at Chester over seven furlongs in the summer of 2001, beating Brevity. A game individual. Acts on fast ground. Likes a sharp, left-handed track.

Parkside (IRE)

102 **71d**
5-y-o b g Common Grounds-Warg (Dancing Brave (USA))
W R Muir The Parkside Partnership

Placings:56130/05030000-0 **(1096)**
2001: 10^{0}G

	Starts	1st	2nd	3rd	Win & Pl
Career Total (Turf)	14	1	0	2	7633

85 8/99 Wwck 7f164y D GD £4334
Total win prize-money £4334

Going (Turf): Sf: 0-3 GS: 0-2 **Gd: 1-7** GF: 0-2 Fm: 0-0
Distance: 5f/6f: 0-0 **7f-8f: 1-8** 9f-13f: 0-6 14f+: 0-0
Track : **LH: 1-3** RH: 0-3 Tight: 0-0 Gall: 0-1
Aids: Bl: 0-0 Vi: 0-0 Tstrap: 0-0
Best Rating: 58 5/01 NmkR 1m2f good

Parkside Prophecy

94 (88) (56) **49d**
3-y-o ch g Aragon-Fairgroundprincess (Kalaglow)
M R Channon Mrs Jean Keegan

Placings:603-0060 **(3255)**
2001: 8^{0}SD, 8^{0}GF, 7^{6}GF, 8^{0}GF

	Starts	1st	2nd	3rd	Win & Pl
Career Total (Turf)	4	0	0	0	0
Career Total (AW)	3	0	0	1	268

Going (Turf): Sf: 0-0 GS: 0-1 Gd: 0-0 GF: 0-3 Fm: 0-0
Distance: 5f/6f: 0-1 7f-8f: 0-5 9f-13f: 0-1 14f+: 0-1
Track : LH: 0-5 RH: 0-0 Tight: 0-1 Gall: 0-1
Aids: Bl: 0-0 Vi: 0-0 Tstrap: 0-0
Best Rating: 44 6/01 Nott 1m54y gd-fm

Parkside Prospect

79 (95) (28) **50**
4-y-o b f Piccolo-Banner (USA) (Known Fact (USA))
E A Wheeler Graham Racing

Placings:033341000502**1231/45000000-050** **(0250)**
2001: 6^{0}SD, 7^{5}SD, 6^{0}SW

	Starts	1st	2nd	3rd	Win & Pl
Career Total (Turf)	14	2	0	3	9516
Career Total (AW)	13	1	2	1	4157

59 12/99 Ling 6f F STD £2085
50 11/99 Muss 5f F(0-65)H GD £2738
60 6/99 Newc 6f E GD £5204
Total win prize-money £10027

Going (Turf): Sf: 0-4 GS: 0-0 **Gd: 2-6** GF: 0-1 Fm: 0-3
Distance: **5f/6f: 3-20** 7f-8f: 0-7 9f-13f: 0-0 14f+: 0-0
Track : **LH: 1-12** RH: 0-3 **Tight: 1-11** Gall: 0-1
Aids: Bl: 0-4 Vi: 0-0 Tstrap: 0-0
Best Rating: 28 1/01 Ling 7f stand

Parkside Pursuit

101 (90) (47) **864**
3-y-o b g Pursuit Of Love-Ivory Bride (Domynsky)
J M Bradley (M R Channon 26/7) Ye Olde Monken Holt

Placings:001-00113301050**0** **(5352)**
2001: 7^{0}S, 6^{0}GF, 5^{1}G, 5^{1}HD, 6^{3}GS, 5^{3}GF, 6^{0}GS, 5^{1}F, 5^{0}GF, 5^{5}GF, 5^{0}GS, 5^{0}S, 6^{0}SD

	Starts	1st	2nd	3rd	Win & Pl
Career Total (Turf)	15	4	0	2	12124
Career Total (AW)	1	0	0	0	

62 7/01 Bath 5f11y F FRM £2366
62 6/01 Bath 5f161y E(0-70) HRD £2758
50 6/01 Bath 5f161y F GD £2310
68 6/00 Rdcr 5f D FRM £2860
Total win prize-money £10294

Going (Turf): Sf: 0-2 GS: 0-3 Gd: 1-1 GF: 0-6 **Fm: 3-3**
Distance: **5f/6f: 4-13** 7f-8f: 0-3 9f-13f: 0-0 14f+: 0-0
Track : **LH: 3-5** RH: 0-0 Tight: 0-0 **Gall: 3-3**
Aids: Bl: 0-0 Vi: 0-0 Tstrap: 0-0
Best Rating: 70 7/01 Hayd 6f gd-sft

Fair sprinter.

Parndon Belle

70 **14**
2-y-o ch f Clan Of Roses-Joara (FR) (Radetzky)
J S Wainwright Lawn, Thomas

Placings:00 **(4229)**
2001: 5^{0}GF, 7^{0}G

	Starts	1st	2nd	3rd	Win & Pl
Career Total (Turf)	2	0	0	0	

Going (Turf): Sf: 0-0 GS: 0-0 Gd: 0-1 GF: 0-1 Fm: 0-0
Distance: 5f/6f: 0-1 7f-8f: 0-1 9f-13f: 0-0 14f+: 0-0
Track : LH: 0-1 RH: 0-0 Tight: 0-1 Gall: 0-0
Aids: Bl: 0-0 Vi: 0-0 Tstrap: 0-0
Best Rating: 14 8/01 Thsk 7f good

Parsifal

96 **88**
2-y-o b c Sadler's Wells (USA)-Moss (USA) (Woodman (USA))

L M Cumani G Howard-Spink,Raimon B/stock,D Simpson

Placings:00 **(5559)**
2001: 8^{0}GS, 8^{0}S

	Starts	1st	2nd	3rd	Win & Pl
Career Total (Turf)	2	0	0	0	

Going (Turf): Sf: 0-1 GS: 0-1 Gd: 0-0 GF: 0-0 Fm: 0-0
Distance: 5f/6f: 0-0 7f-8f: 0-1 9f-13f: 0-1 14f+: 0-0
Track : LH: 0-0 RH: 0-0 Tight: 0-0 Gall: 0-0
Aids: Bl: 0-0 Vi: 0-0 Tstrap: 0-0
Best Rating: 88 10/01 NmkR 1m gd-sft

Bred to stay, he was staying on seventh on his Newmarket debut and should do better as a three-year-old.

Parting Shot

103 **65**

3-y-o b g Young Ern-Tribal Lady (Absalom)
T D Easterby C H Stevens

Placings:0-20142064200 **(5146)**
2001: 8^{2}S, 7^{0}G, 7^{1}GF, 8^{4}GF, 7^{2}GF, 6^{0}GF, 7^{6}GF, 7^{4}GF, 7^{2}GF, 7^{0}GF, 8^{0}G

	Starts	1st	2nd	3rd	Win & Pl
Career Total (Turf)	12	1	3	0	8582

70 5/01 Bevl 7f100y D G-F £4290
Total win prize-money £4290

Going (Turf): Sf: 0-1 GS: 0-0 Gd: 0-2 **GF: 1-8** Fm: 0-1
Distance: 5f/6f: 0-2 **7f-8f: 1-10** 9f-13f: 0-0 14f+: 0-0
Track : LH: 0-3 **RH: 1-2** Tight: 0-3 Gall: 0-1
Aids: Bl: 0-0 Vi: 0-0 Tstrap: 0-0
Best Rating: 74 6/01 Newc 1m gd-fm

A maiden winner over the extended seven furlongs at Beverley in May 2001, he has found life tougher in handicap company since.

Partner (IRE)

81(81) (28)**38**

3-y-o b g Turtle Island (IRE)-Sorara (Aragon)
C E Brittain R N Khan

Placings:0000 **(5524)**
2001: 8^{0}GF, 8^{0}HY, 7^{0}SD, 10^{0}HY

	Starts	1st	2nd	3rd	Win & Pl
Career Total (Turf)	3	0	0	0	
Career Total (AW)	1	0	0	0	

Going (Turf): Sf: 0-2 GS: 0-0 Gd: 0-0 GF: 0-1 Fm: 0-0
Distance: 5f/6f: 0-0 7f-8f: 0-1 9f-13f: 0-3 14f+: 0-0
Track : LH: 0-2 RH: 0-0 Tight: 0-2 Gall: 0-0
Aids: Bl: 0-0 Vi: 0-0 Tstrap: 0-0
Best Rating: 38 10/01 Nott 1m54y heavy

Party Charmer

95 **62**

3-y-o b f Charmer-Party Game (Red Alert)
C E Brittain Michael Clarke

Placings:140650-000P **(5688)**
2001: 6^{0}G, 8^{0}G, 5^{0}GS, 7^{P}S

	Starts	1st	2nd	3rd	Win & Pl
Career Total (Turf)	10	1	0	0	6350

76 5/00 Wwck 5f D SFT £3556
Total win prize-money £3557

Going (Turf): Sf: 1-3 GS: 0-1 Gd: 0-4 GF: 0-2 Fm: 0-0
Distance: **5f/6f: 1-7** 7f-8f: 0-3 9f-13f: 0-0 14f+: 0-0
Track : **LH: 1-1** RH: 0-1 Tight: 0-0 **Gall: 1-2**
Aids: Bl: 0-0 Vi: 0-0 Tstrap: 0-0
Best Rating: 62 9/01 Asct 6f good

Got off the mark at her first attempt as a two-year-old on soft ground over five furlongs, but has since struggled in better company. Well beaten in 2001.

Party Ploy

103(96) (62)**73**

3-y-o b g Deploy-Party Treat (IRE) (Millfontaine)
K R Burke Clive Batt

Placings:000-01345P323 **(5622)**
2001: 8^{0}GS, 11^{1}G, 11^{3}G, 12^{4}GF, 12^{5}GF, 12^{P}GS, 11^{3}GS, 12^{2}SD, 14^{3}GS

	Starts	1st	2nd	3rd	Win & Pl
Career Total (Turf)	10	1	0	3	5161
Career Total (AW)	2	0	1	0	1093

65 5/01 Wind 1m3f135yE(0-70)H GD £3272
Total win prize-money £3273

Going (Turf): Sf: 0-0 GS: 0-4 **Gd: 1-2** GF: 0-3 Fm: 0-0
Distance: 5f/6f: 0-0 7f-8f: 0-1 **9f-13f: 1-9** 14f+: 0-1
Track : LH: 0-4 RH: 0-4 **Tight: 1-7** Gall: 0-1
Aids: Bl: 0-0 Vi: 0-0 Tstrap: 0-0
Best Rating: 73 5/01 Wind 1m3f135y good

Winner of a Windsor handicap in the spring, he has been beaten off a higher mark since. Needs a good gallop.

Partytime (IRE)

101 **87**

2-y-o ch f Tagula (IRE)-Camarat (Ahonoora)
R Hannon Lady Davis

Placings:23110020 **(5256)**
2001: 5^{2}G, 5^{3}S, 5^{1}F, 5^{1}GS, 5^{0}GF, 5^{0}GF, 6^{2}GY, 5^{0}GS

	Starts	1st	2nd	3rd	Win & Pl
Career Total (Turf)	8	2	2	1	47076

55 6/01 Sals 5f D G-S £4368
76 5/01 Leic 5f2y F FRM £2586
Total win prize-money £6955

Going (Turf): Sf: 0-1 **GS: 1-2** Gd: 0-1 GF: 0-2 **Fm: 1-1**
Distance: **5f/6f: 2-8** 7f-8f: 0-0 9f-13f: 0-0 14f+: 0-0
Track : LH: 0-0 RH: 0-0 Tight: 0-0 Gall: 0-0
Aids: Bl: 0-0 Vi: 0-0 Tstrap: 0-0
Best Rating: 87 8/01 Curr 6f gd-yld

A useful juvenile, she ran out a two-length winner at Leicester in May and won a non-event at Salisbury next time. Down the field in both the Queen Mary and Weatherbys Super Sprint, but ran better to finish runner-up in a valuable sales race at the Curragh despite suffering a gashed off-hind hoof. Acts on any ground.

Parvenue (FR)

80

3-y-o b f Ezzoud (IRE)-Patria (USA) (Mr Prospector (USA))
E A L Dunlop Hesmonds Stud

Placings:124-5 **(0963)**
2001: 8^{5}HY

	Starts	1st	2nd	3rd	Win & Pl
Career Total (Turf)	4	1	1	0	3845

65 5/00 Nott 6f15y E GD £2646
Total win prize-money £2646

Going (Turf): Sf: 0-1 GS: 0-0 **Gd: 1-2** GF: 0-1 Fm: 0-0
Distance: 5f/6f: 0-0 **7f-8f: 1-3** 9f-13f: 0-1 14f+: 0-0
Track : LH: 0-1 RH: 0-0 Tight: 0-1 Gall: 0-0
Aids: Bl: 0-0 Vi: 0-0 Tstrap: 0-0
Best Rating: 61 4/01 Wwck 1m22y heavy

Pas De Probleme (IRE)

102(80) (19)**61**

5-y-o ch g Ela-Mana-Mou-Torriglia (USA) (Nijinsky (CAN))
J G Portman Captain Francis Burne

Placings:2650/66050/0153146000-6043600 **(5534)**
2001: 10^{6}S, 10^{0}G, 9^{4}G, 10^{3}G, 9^{6}GS, 11^{0}SD, 11^{0}S

	Starts	1st	2nd	3rd	Win & Pl
Career Total (Turf)	25	2	1	2	13022
Career Total (AW)	1	0	0	0	

68 5/00 Sand 1m2f7y D(0-80)H HVY £5369
64 4/00 Wwck 1m2f110yD(0-80)H HVY £4066
Total win prize-money £9435

Going (Turf): Sf: 2-10 GS: 0-1 Gd: 0-8 GF: 0-6 Fm: 0-0
Distance: 5f/6f: 0-3 7f-8f: 0-1 **9f-13f: 2-21** 14f+: 0-1
Track : LH: 1-13 RH: 1-8 Tight: 0-4 Gall: 0-3
Aids: Bl: 0-0 Vi: 0-0 Tstrap: 0-0
Best Rating: 61 5/01 Sand 1m2f7y good

A fair handicapper, in winning form in 2000 over ten furlongs on heavy ground. Has slipped down the weights in 2001 but that failed to spark a revival. His wins have been on heavy ground.

Pas De Surprise

103(91) (55)**70d**

3-y-o b g Dancing Spree (USA)-Supreme Rose (Frimley Park)
J G Portman Captain Francis Burne

Placings:0-505060006 **(5046)**
2001: 10^{5}GS, 10^{0}G, 8^{5}GF, 8^{0}G, 8^{6}GF, 8^{0}G, 8^{0}GF, 7^{0}GF, 11^{6}SD

	Starts	1st	2nd	3rd	Win & Pl
Career Total (Turf)	9	0	0	0	0
Career Total (AW)	1	0	0	0	0

Going (Turf): Sf: 0-1 GS: 0-1 Gd: 0-3 GF: 0-4 Fm: 0-0
Distance: 5f/6f: 0-0 7f-8f: 0-4 9f-13f: 0-6 14f+: 0-0
Track : LH: 0-4 RH: 0-2 Tight: 0-4 Gall: 0-0
Aids: Bl: 0-1 Vi: 0-0 Tstrap: 0-0
Best Rating: 70 6/01 Sand 1m14y good

Pasada Llamada

81 **47**

2-y-o b g College Chapel-First Play (Primo Dominie)
S E Kettlewell Middleham Park Racing Xii

Placings:300 **(5030)**
2001: 5^{3}G, 6^{0}GF, 5^{0}GF

	Starts	1st	2nd	3rd	Win & Pl
Career Total (Turf)	3	0	0	1	416

Going (Turf): Sf: 0-0 GS: 0-0 Gd: 0-1 GF: 0-2 Fm: 0-0
Distance: 5f/6f: 0-3 7f-8f: 0-0 9f-13f: 0-0 14f+: 0-0
Track : LH: 0-0 RH: 0-0 Tight: 0-0 Gall: 0-0
Aids: Bl: 0-0 Vi: 0-0 Tstrap: 0-0
Best Rating: 47 8/01 Newc 5f good

Pasithea (IRE)

109 **84**

3-y-o b f Celtic Swing-Midnight's Reward (Night Shift (USA))
T D Easterby Lady Legard

Placings:453310222-403344210400 **(5691)**
2001: 8^{4}S, 8^{0}S, 7^{3}S, 8^{3}GF, 8^{4}G, 8^{4}GS, 9^{2}GS, 11^{1}HY, 12^{0}G, 10^{4}HY, 11^{0}S, 12^{0}S

	Starts	1st	2nd	3rd	Win & Pl
Career Total (Turf)	21	2	4	4	23296

83 9/01 Hayd 1m3f200yD(0-80)H HVY £5850
74 8/00 Bevl 7f100y D G-F £3818
Total win prize-money £9669

Going (Turf): Sf: 1-10 GS: 0-2 Gd: 0-6 **GF: 1-3** Fm: 0-0
Distance: 5f/6f: 0-4 7f-8f: 1-11 9f-13f: 1-6 14f+: 0-0
Track : LH: 1-9 RH: 1-4 Tight: 0-4 Gall: 0-4
Aids: Bl: 0-0 Vi: 0-0 Tstrap: 0-0
Best Rating: 84 9/01 Hayd 1m2f120y heavy

Scored once as a juvenile over seven furlongs and ran consistently well the remainder of the season. Bred to stay, she ran well this term and scored at Haydock in September on her first attempt over 12 furlongs, although she was well beaten in better races afterwards. Best with ease in the ground and a consistent sort.

Paso Doble

102 **75**

3-y-o b g Dancing Spree (USA)-Delta Tempo (IRE) (Bluebird (USA))
B R Millman J A Pickford

Placings:034222-0033 **(2525)**
2001: 9^{0}GS, 7^{0}G, 6^{3}F, 8^{3}GF

	Starts	1st	2nd	3rd	Win & Pl
Career Total (Turf)	10	0	3	3	4907

Going (Turf): Sf: 0-0 GS: 0-2 Gd: 0-1 GF: 0-6 Fm: 0-1
Distance: 5f/6f: 0-2 7f-8f: 0-6 9f-13f: 0-2 14f+: 0-0
Track : LH: 0-2 RH: 0-3 Tight: 0-0 Gall: 0-1
Aids: Bl: 0-0 Vi: 0-0 Tstrap: 0-0
Best Rating: 74 6/01 Wwck 1m22y gd-fm

Passerine

95(77) (29)**28**

3-y-o b f Distant Relative-Oare Sparrow (Night Shift (USA))
J R Weymes White Rose Poultry Ltd

Placings:63406000 **(5409)**
2001: 5^{6}S, 6^{3}G, 6^{4}F, 5^{0}GF, 5^{6}GF, 6^{0}SD, 5^{0}GS, 6^{0}SD, 7^{0}SD

	Starts	1st	2nd	3rd	Win & Pl
Career Total (Turf)	6	0	0	1	540
Career Total (AW)	2	0	0	0	

Going (Turf): Sf: 0-1 GS: 0-1 Gd: 0-1 GF: 0-2 Fm: 0-1
Distance: 5f/6f: 0-8 7f-8f: 0-0 9f-13f: 0-0 14f+: 0-0
Track : LH: 0-3 RH: 0-0 Tight: 0-1 Gall: 0-0
Aids: Bl: 0-1 Vi: 0-0 Tstrap: 0-0
Best Rating: 58 5/01 Ripn 6f good

Passing Glance

104 **87**

2-y-o b c Polar Falcon (USA)-Spurned (USA) (Robellino (USA))
I A Balding Kingsclere Stud And M E Wates

Placings:513 **(3243)**
2001: 6^{5}GF, 6^{1}GF, 7^{3}GF

	Starts	1st	2nd	3rd	Win & Pl
Career Total (Turf)	3	1	0	1	5921

87	6/01	Sals	6f212y	D	G-F	£3802

Total win prize-money £3803

Going (Turf): Sf: 0-0 GS: 0-0 Gd: 0-0 **GF: 1-3** Fm: 0-0
Distance: 5f/6f: 0-1 **7f-8f: 1-2** 9f-13f: 0-0 14f+: 0-0
Track : LH: 0-0 RH: 0-0 Tight: 0-0 Gall: 0-0
Aids: Bl: 0-0 Vi: 0-0 Tstrap: 0-0
Best Rating: 87 7/01 Newb 7f gd-fm

A half-brother to the useful Overbrook, Hidden Meadow and Kingsclere, improved for the step up in trip to get off the mark at Salisbury. Pulled that day but relaxed once in front. Disappointed next time and not seen again.

Passion For Life

105 **84**

8-y-o br g Charmer-Party Game (Red Alert)
J Akehurst Canisbay Bloodstock Ltd

Placings:31124/31161602/60000405/0060/130002061/100000-000301060 **(5560)**
2001: 6^{0}GF, 6^{0}GF, 6^{0}GF, 5^{0}GF, 6^{3}G, 6^{0}G, 6^{1}GS, 6^{0}HY, 6^{0}S, 7^{0}S

	Starts	1st	2nd	3rd	Win & Pl
Career Total (Turf)	50	9	3	4	107021

84	10/01	Sals	6f	C(0-95)H	G-S	£9952
89	3/00	Kemp	6f	C(0-100)H	GD	£10822
82	9/99	Sals	6f	C(0-95)H	HVY	£10112
85	4/99	Kemp	6f	D(0-85)H	GD	£4572
112	6/96	Badn	6f		GD	£33784
115	4/96	NmkR	6f	A	G-F	£11662
103	4/96	Kemp	6f	C(0-90)H	GD	£5426
74	4/95	Wwck	5f	D	G-F	£4023
86	4/95	Hayd	5f	E	GD	£3338

Total win prize-money £93696

Going (Turf): Sf: 1-10 GS: 1-4 **Gd: 5-20** GF: 2-15 Fm: 0-1
Distance: **5f/6f: 9-48** 7f-8f: 0-2 9f-13f: 0-0 14f+: 0-0
Track : **LH: 1-1** RH: 0-3 Tight: 0-0 **Gall: 1-2**
Aids: Bl: 0-2 Vi: 0-0 Tstrap: 0-0
Best Rating: 84 10/01 Sals 6f gd-sft

Front-running sprint handicapper. He needs to dominate and runs nowhere near his best if taken on. Has winning form on fast ground but prefers an easier surface these days. Needs a rail on his right-hand side. Best at six furlongs and goes well at Kempton and Salisbury.

Pastel

104 **86**

2-y-o ch f Lion Cavern (USA)-Dancing Spirit (IRE) (Ahonoora)
B J Meehan Wyck Hall Stud

Placings:221622250 **(4985)**
2001: 5^{2}GS, 5^{2}G, 5^{1}GF, 5^{6}GF, 6^{2}GF, 6^{2}GF, 5^{2}GF, 6^{5}G, 6^{0}G

	Starts	1st	2nd	3rd	Win & Pl
Career Total (Turf)	9	1	5	0	31382

73	5/01	Gdwd	5f	E	G-F	£3802

Total win prize-money £3803

Going (Turf): Sf: 0-0 GS: 0-1 Gd: 0-3 **GF: 1-5** Fm: 0-0
Distance: **5f/6f: 1-8** 7f-8f: 0-1 9f-13f: 0-0 14f+: 0-0
Track : LH: 0-0 RH: 0-2 Tight: 0-0 Gall: 0-2
Aids: **Bl: 1-1** Vi: 0-0 Tstrap: 0-0
Best Rating: 86 8/01 Newb 5f34y gd-fm

A half-sister to three winners from six to eight furlongs, she raced in blinkers for the only time when upsetting High Finale by a short-head in a five-furlong maiden at Goodwood in May. She continued to run well in Pattern events afterwards, possibly her best effort being when second to Leggy Lou in the Princess Margaret. Effective at five and six furlongs, she has won on good to firm but acts on good to soft.

Pastiche

81 **7**

7-y-o b m Kylian (USA)-Titian Beauty (Auction Ring (USA))
Mrs L C Jewell Mrs Val Morgan

Placings:4/14500/000 **(4472)**
2001: 15^{0}GF, 11^{0}GF, 9^{0}GF

	Starts	1st	2nd	3rd	Win & Pl
Career Total (Turf)	6	0	0	0	0
Career Total (AW)	3	1	0	0	3648

53	1/97	Ling	1m	D	STD	£3290

Total win prize-money £3290

Going (Turf): Sf: 0-0 GS: 0-1 Gd: 0-1 GF: 0-3 Fm: 0-1
Distance: 5f/6f: 0-0 **7f-8f: 1-4** 9f-13f: 0-4 14f+: 0-1
Track : **LH: 1-6** RH: 0-2 **Tight: 1-6** Gall: 0-0
Aids: Bl: 0-0 Vi: 0-0 Tstrap: 0-0
Best Rating: 7 8/01 Ling 1m3f106y gd-fm

Pastichio Medley

80 **51**

2-y-o b c Celtic Swing-Blue Nile (IRE) (Bluebird (USA))
T D Easterby Ron George

Placings:050 **(3878)**
2001: 6^{0}GF, 7^{5}GF, 7^{0}GS

	Starts	1st	2nd	3rd	Win & Pl
Career Total (Turf)	3	0	0	0	0

Going (Turf): Sf: 0-0 GS: 0-1 Gd: 0-0 GF: 0-2 Fm: 0-0
Distance: 5f/6f: 0-1 7f-8f: 0-2 9f-13f: 0-0 14f+: 0-0
Track : LH: 0-1 RH: 0-1 Tight: 0-1 Gall: 0-0
Aids: Bl: 0-1 Vi: 0-0 Tstrap: 0-0
Best Rating: 51 7/01 Bevl 7f100y gd-fm

Pat The Builder (IRE)

78(92) (49)**57**

3-y-o b g Common Grounds-Demoiselle (Midyan (USA))
K R Burke James Ryan

Placings:5404610**340-104600** **(2635)**
2001: 5^{1}SD, 5^{0}SW, 5^{4}SW, 5^{6}SD, 7^{0}SD, 5^{0}F

	Starts	1st	2nd	3rd	Win & Pl
Career Total (Turf)	7	0	0	0	0
Career Total (AW)	9	2	0	1	3928

59	1/01	Ling	5f	G	STD	£1806
63	10/00	Ling	5f	G	STD	£1855

Total win prize-money £3661

Going (Turf): Sf: 0-1 GS: 0-0 Gd: 0-1 GF: 0-2 Fm: 0-2
Distance: **5f/6f: 2-14** 7f-8f: 0-1 9f-13f: 0-0 14f+: 0-0
Track : **LH: 2-11** RH: 0-0 **Tight: 2-8** Gall: 0-1
Aids: Bl: 0-0 Vi: 0-1 Tstrap: 0-0
Best Rating: 59 1/01 Ling 5f stand

Moderate All-Weather sprinter. Likes to dominate.

Patavellian (IRE)

96 **71**

3-y-o b g Machiavellian (USA)-Alessia (Caerleon (USA))
W R Muir D J Deer

Placings:032000 **(5608)**
2001: 10^{0}GF, 10^{3}S, 9^{2}G, 8^{0}G, 8^{0}G, 7^{0}GS

	Starts	1st	2nd	3rd	Win & Pl
Career Total (Turf)	6	0	1	1	1923

Going (Turf): Sf: 0-1 GS: 0-1 Gd: 0-3 GF: 0-1 Fm: 0-0
Distance: 5f/6f: 0-0 7f-8f: 0-3 9f-13f: 0-3 14f+: 0-0
Track : LH: 0-1 RH: 0-2 Tight: 0-1 Gall: 0-0
Aids: Bl: 0-0 Vi: 0-0 Tstrap: 0-0
Best Rating: 71 8/01 Sand 1m1f good

Fair performer. Looks best suited by a soft surface.

Path Of Honour (IRE)

(55) **50**

2-y-o b f Marju (IRE)-Zorilla (Belmez (USA))
M Johnston J W Robb

Placings:000 **(5345)**
2001: 8^{0}HY, 7^{0}G, 6^{0}SD

	Starts	1st	2nd	3rd	Win & Pl
Career Total (Turf)	2	0	0	0	
Career Total (AW)	1	0	0	0	

Going (Turf): Sf: 0-1 GS: 0-0 Gd: 0-1 GF: 0-0 Fm: 0-0
Distance: 5f/6f: 0-1 7f-8f: 0-1 9f-13f: 0-1 14f+: 0-0
Track : LH: 0-2 RH: 0-0 Tight: 0-0 Gall: 0-0
Aids: Bl: 0-0 Vi: 0-0 Tstrap: 0-0
Best Rating: 50 10/01 Rdcr 7f good

Well beaten in all starts so far.

Patientes Virtis

73 **26**

2-y-o ch f Lion Cavern (USA)-Alzianah (Alzao (USA))
Miss Gay Kelleway A P Griffin

Placings:0 **(5125)**
2001: 5^{0}HY

	Starts	1st	2nd	3rd	Win & Pl
Career Total (Turf)	1	0	0	0	

Going (Turf): Sf: 0-1 GS: 0-0 Gd: 0-0 GF: 0-0 Fm: 0-0
Distance: 5f/6f: 0-1 7f-8f: 0-0 9f-13f: 0-0 14f+: 0-0
Track: LH: 0-0 RH: 0-0 Tight: 0-0 Gall: 0-0
Aids: Bl: 0-0 Vi: 0-0 Tstrap: 0-0
Best Rating: 26 10/01 Ling 5f heavy

Patricia Philomena (IRE)

97 **62**

3-y-o br f Prince Of Birds (USA)-Jeewan (Touching Wood (USA))
T D Barron Miss Pauline Laycock

Placings:33250 **(4267)**
2001: 7^{3}GF, 7^{3}G, 7^{2}G, 7^{5}F, 7^{0}GF

	Starts	1st	2nd	3rd	Win & Pl
Career Total (Turf)	5	0	1	2	1886

Going (Turf): Sf: 0-0 GS: 0-0 Gd: 0-2 GF: 0-2 Fm: 0-1
Distance: 5f/6f: 0-0 7f-8f: 0-5 9f-13f: 0-0 14f+: 0-0
Track: LH: 0-2 RH: 0-2 Tight: 0-2 Gall: 0-0
Aids: Bl: 0-0 Vi: 0-0 Tstrap: 0-0
Best Rating: 62 7/01 Newc 7f good

Patrician Fox (IRE)

103(86) (51)**46**

3-y-o b f Nicolotte-Peace Mission (Dunbeath (USA))
J J Quinn C R Galloway & R W North

Placings:00343260200-104015000000 **(4840)**
2001: 5^{1}S, 5^{0}SD, 6^{4}S, 6^{0}S, 5^{1}GF, 5^{5}G, 5^{0}GF, 6^{0}GS, 5^{0}GF, 5^{0}G, 5^{0}HY, 6^{0}G

	Starts	1st	2nd	3rd	Win & Pl
Career Total (Turf)	20	2	2	1	8789
Career Total (AW)	3	0	0	1	323

66 6/01 Bevl 5f E(0-70)H G-F £3430
63 4/01 Nott 5f13y E(0-75)H SFT £2940
Total win prize-money £6370

Going (Turf): Sf: 1-6 GS: 0-3 Gd: 0-7 GF: 1-4 Fm: 0-0
Distance: 5f/6f: 2-19 7f-8f: 0-4 9f-13f: 0-0 14f+: 0-0
Track: LH: 0-2 RH: 0-0 Tight: 0-0 Gall: 0-0
Aids: Bl: 0-0 Vi: 0-1 Tstrap: 0-0
Best Rating: 66 6/01 Bevl 5f gd-fm

Modest sprinter, had seemed best suited by soft ground until winning on fast ground at Beverley in June 2000 where the high draw would have helped.

Patrington Boy

71 **8**

8-y-o b g Sayf El Arab (USA)-Gunnard (Gunner B)
G T Gaines Largesse Racing

Placings:6/0 **(4324)**
2001: 7^{0}GF

	Starts	1st	2nd	3rd	Win & Pl
Career Total (Turf)	2	0	0	0	

Going (Turf): Sf: 0-0 GS: 0-0 Gd: 0-0 GF: 0-2 Fm: 0-0
Distance: 5f/6f: 0-1 7f-8f: 0-1 9f-13f: 0-0 14f+: 0-0
Track: LH: 0-1 RH: 0-0 Tight: 0-0 Gall: 0-0
Aids: Bl: 0-0 Vi: 0-0 Tstrap: 0-0
Best Rating: 8 8/01 Wwck 7f26y gd-fm

Patrita Park

89 (38)**40**

7-y-o br m Flying Tyke-Bellinote (FR) (Noir Et Or)
A Smith Park Racing Partnership

Placings:00505/00000/36506051/32223240/06-0 **(2887)**
2001: 10^{0}GF

	Starts	1st	2nd	3rd	Win & Pl
Career Total (Turf)	27	1	4	3	7437
Career Total (AW)	2	0	0	0	0

33 9/98 Brig 1m1f209yF(0-65)H G-F £2473

Total win prize-money £2474

Going (Turf): Sf: 0-3 GS: 0-3 Gd: 0-4 **GF: 1-14** Fm: 0-3
Distance: 5f/6f: 0-3 7f-8f: 0-7 **9f-13f: 1-17** 14f+: 0-2
Track: **LH: 1-12** RH: 0-9 Tight: 0-8 Gall: 0-2
Aids: Bl: 0-0 Vi: 0-0 Tstrap: 0-0
Best Rating: 37 7/01 Pont 1m2f6y gd-fm

Patrivalor (USA)

90 **52**

3-y-o b c Diesis-False Image (USA) (Danzig (USA))
L M Cumani M J Dawson

Placings:00030 **(4908)**
2001: 7^{0}S, 8^{0}G, 8^{0}G, 8^{3}F, 9^{0}G

	Starts	1st	2nd	3rd	Win & Pl
Career Total (Turf)	5	0	0	1	365

Going (Turf): Sf: 0-1 GS: 0-0 Gd: 0-3 GF: 0-0 Fm: 0-1
Distance: 5f/6f: 0-0 7f-8f: 0-3 9f-13f: 0-2 14f+: 0-0
Track: LH: 0-0 RH: 0-3 Tight: 0-2 Gall: 0-0
Aids: Bl: 0-0 Vi: 0-0 Tstrap: 0-0
Best Rating: 52 5/01 NmkR 1m good

Has shown little in terms of ability and improvement is needed to win a race.

Patsy Culsyth

102(86) (26)**47**

6-y-o b m Tragic Role (USA)-Regal Salute (Dara Monarch)
Don Enrico Incisa Don Enrico Incisa

Placings:665225241302/0064010/2000000/100360300-064320313250 **(5288)**
2001: 6^{0}SD, 7^{6}SD, 6^{4}HY, 5^{3}S, 7^{2}GF, 6^{0}F, 7^{3}GF, 6^{1}G, 7^{3}GS, 8^{2}GF, 6^{5}F, 6^{0}HY

	Starts	1st	2nd	3rd	Win & Pl
Career Total (Turf)	43	4	7	6	17943
Career Total (AW)	4	0	0	0	0

38 7/01 Newc 6f G GD £1939
50 3/00 Newc 6f G GD £1862
50 8/98 Ayr 7f G(0-60)H G-S £2038
62 8/97 Bevl 5f E GD £2925
Total win prize-money £8765

Going (Turf): Sf: 0-9 GS: 1-7 **Gd: 3-11** GF: 0-11 Fm: 0-5
Distance: **5f/6f: 3-31** 7f-8f: 1-16 9f-13f: 0-0 14f+: 0-0
Track: **LH: 1-10** RH: 0-4 Tight: 0-3 Gall: 0-2
Aids: Bl: 0-0 **Vi: 2-18** Tstrap: 0-0
Best Rating: 47 8/01 Muss 1m gd-fm

All her wins have come in claiming or selling company at up to seven furlongs. Acts on good ground.

Patsy Stone

98 (41)**67**

5-y-o b m Jester-Third Dam (Slip Anchor)
M Kettle I Fraser & B Goldsmith

Placings:020304320/456364003460100/5011445320-050060 **(2485)**
2001: 7^{0}HY, 7^{5}G, 8^{0}GF, 8^{0}GF, 8^{6}G, 8^{0}HD

	Starts	1st	2nd	3rd	Win & Pl
Career Total (Turf)	37	3	3	5	20211
Career Total (AW)	3	0	0	0	0

69 6/00 Chep 7f16y E(0-70)H GD £2919
69 5/00 Leic 1m8y D(0-85)H SFT £7897
63 9/99 Yarm 1m3y F(0-60)H SFT £3589
Total win prize-money £14406

Going (Turf): **Sf: 2-7** GS: 0-5 Gd: 1-13 GF: 0-10 Fm: 0-2
Distance: 5f/6f: 0-6 7f-8f: 1-19 **9f-13f: 2-15** 14f+: 0-0
Track: LH: 0-8 RH: 0-10 Tight: 0-9 Gall: 0-3
Aids: Bl: 0-0 Vi: 0-0 Tstrap: 0-0
Best Rating: 67 5/01 Leic 7f9y good

Patsy's Double

108 **109**

3-y-o b c Emarati (USA)-Jungle Rose (Shirley Heights)
M Blanshard Mrs P Buckley

Placings:11153-500315200 **(5494)**
2001: 7^{5}GS, 8^{0}G, 7^{0}GF, 7^{3}GF, 5^{1}GS, 6^{5}GF, 7^{2}GF, 6^{0}G, 6^{0}HY

	Starts	1st	2nd	3rd	Win & Pl
Career Total (Turf)	14	4	1	2	47912

105 8/01 Leic 5f218y B(0-105)H G-S £9347
99 7/00 Newb 7f B G-F £11245
94 7/00 Sals 6f C GD £6583
84 5/00 Newb 6f8y D G-F £4576
Total win prize-money £31752

Going (Turf): Sf: 0-1 GS: 1-2 Gd: 1-4 **GF: 2-7** Fm: 0-0
Distance: 5f/6f: 2-4 7f-8f: 2-10 9f-13f: 0-0 14f+: 0-0
Track: LH: 0-2 RH: 0-0 Tight: 0-0 Gall: 0-2
Aids: Bl: 0-0 Vi: 0-0 Tstrap: 0-0
Best Rating: 109 9/01 Newb 7f64y gd-fm

Improved throughout 2000, winning his first three starts and running well at Group level later on. He has faced some stiff tasks this term, but got off the mark in a handicap over six at Leicester in August. Best at up to seven furlongs seems to handle any ground.

Paulas Pride

100 **66**

3-y-o ch f Pivotal-Sharp Top (Sharpo)
J R Best Thomas Tanton & Frederick French

Placings:006160-330625660 **(5082)**
2001: 9^{3}GF, 10^{3}GF, 10^{0}GF, 8^{6}S, 7^{2}F, 9^{5}G, 9^{6}GF, 7^{6}GF, 7^{0}S

	Starts	1st	2nd	3rd	Win & Pl
Career Total (Turf)	15	1	1	2	5926

52 9/00 Brig 7f214y F G-S £1767
Total win prize-money £1768

Going (Turf): Sf: 0-4 **GS: 1-1** Gd: 0-1 GF: 0-8 Fm: 0-1
Distance: 5f/6f: 0-2 **7f-8f: 1-7** 9f-13f: 0-6 14f+: 0-0
Track: **LH: 1-7** RH: 0-3 Tight: 0-2 Gall: 0-2
Aids: Bl: 0-1 Vi: 0-0 Tstrap: 0-0
Best Rating: 74 7/01 Pont 1m2f6y gd-fm

Pawn Broker

116 **112**

4-y-o ch c Selkirk (USA)-Dime Bag (High Line)
J L Dunlop Raymond Tooth

Placings:61/1220312-2333 **(2503)**
2001: 10^{2}S, 10^{3}S, 9^{3}GF, 10^{3}GF

	Starts	1st	2nd	3rd	Win & Pl
Career Total (Turf)	13	3	4	4	122187

114 9/00 Newb 1m3f5y A G-F £29000
106 4/00 NmkR 1m1f A G-S £13780
87 10/99 NmkJ 1m D GD £8545
Total win prize-money £51326

Going (Turf): Sf: 0-3 **GS: 1-2 Gd: 1-3 GF: 1-3** Fm: 0-1
Distance: 5f/6f: 0-0 7f-8f: 1-2 **9f-13f: 2-11** 14f+: 0-0
Track: **LH: 1-2** RH: 0-8 Tight: 0-1 **Gall: 1-5**
Aids: Bl: 0-2 Vi: 0-0 Tstrap: 0-0
Best Rating: 119 4/01 Kemp 1m2f soft

He looked a possible classic candidate early last season, winning a Listed event and finishing runner-up to Sakhee in the Thresher Classic Trial and the Dante. He disappointed in the French Derby, but was not at his best, and ended the season with victory in a Newbury Listed event and second in a Group Three at the same track. He was somewhat disappointing in Listed events in the first half of 2001 and was absent after June. Handles any ground. Has worn blinkers.

Pawn In Life (IRE)

(99) (55+)

3-y-o b g Midhish-Lady-Mumtaz (Martin John)
T D Barron Laurence O'Kane

Placings:040-10 (5051)
2001: 6^{1}SW, 6^{0}SD

	Starts	1st	2nd	3rd	Win & Pl
Career Total (Turf)	1	0	0	0	
Career Total (AW)	4	1	0	0	2254

55 2/01 Sthl 6f F(0-60)H SLW £2254
Total win prize-money £2254

Going (Turf): Sf: 0-1 GS: 0-0 Gd: 0-0 GF: 0-0 Fm: 0-0
Distance: **5f/6f: 1-5** 7f-8f: 0-0 9f-13f: 0-0 14f+: 0-0
Track : **LH: 1-3** RH: 0-0 Tight: 0-0 Gall: 0-0
Aids: Bl: 0-0 Vi: 0-0 Tstrap: 0-0
Best Rating: 55 2/01 Sthl 6f slow

Pax

102 62
4-y-o ch g Brief Truce (USA)-Child's Play (USA) (Sharpen Up)
J W Payne C Cotran

Placings:1/400-00005000 (5276)
2001: 6^{0}G, 7^{0}G, 8^{0}G, 8^{0}GF, 9^{5}G, 8^{0}GF, 7^{0}G, 8^{0}GS

	Starts	1st	2nd	3rd	Win & Pl
Career Total (Turf)	12	1	0	0	5242

79 10/99 NmkJ 6f D G-S £4695
Total win prize-money £4695

Going (Turf): Sf: 0-1 **GS: 1-3** Gd: 0-6 GF: 0-2 Fm: 0-0
Distance: **5f/6f: 1-5** 7f-8f: 0-4 9f-13f: 0-3 14f+: 0-0
Track : LH: 0-1 RH: 0-2 Tight: 0-1 Gall: 0-2
Aids: Bl: 0-6 Vi: 0-0 Tstrap: 0-0
Best Rating: 62 8/01 Newc 1m1f9y good

Pay The Silver

102(97) (68)76
3-y-o gr g Petong-Marjorie's Memory (IRE) (Fairy King (USA))
A P Jarvis Christopher Shankland

Placings:043554-62200510 (4952)
2001: 8^{6}SD, 9^{2}GF, 9^{2}GF, 8^{0}G, 9^{0}GF, 10^{5}S, 10^{1}G, 11^{0}G, 10^{0}SD

	Starts	1st	2nd	3rd	Win & Pl
Career Total (Turf)	13	1	2	1	8671
Career Total (AW)	1	0	0	0	0

72 9/01 Epsm 1m2f18y E(0-70)H GD £4855
Total win prize-money £4856

Going (Turf): Sf: 0-1 GS: 0-0 **Gd: 1-5** GF: 0-7 Fm: 0-0
Distance: 5f/6f: 0-3 7f-8f: 0-3 **9f-13f: 1-8** 14f+: 0-0
Track : **LH: 1-6** RH: 0-4 **Tight: 1-6** Gall: 0-0
Aids: Bl: 0-0 Vi: 0-0 Tstrap: 0-0
Best Rating: 76 6/01 Kemp 1m1f gd-fm

Ran well as a juvenile without getting his head in front, gradually getting the hang of things. Stepped up in trip to win an Epsom handicap in September. Appreciates a sound surface. Suited by hold-up tactics.

Pay To Play

(78) (27)
3-y-o br g Puissance-Times Of Times (IRE) (Distinctly North (USA))
Andrew Reid A S Reid

Placings:0 (0253)
2001: 5^{0}SW

	Starts	1st	2nd	3rd	Win & Pl
Career Total (Turf)	0	0	0	0	
Career Total (AW)	1	0	0	0	

Going (Turf): Sf: 0-0 GS: 0-0 Gd: 0-0 GF: 0-0 Fm: 0-0
Distance: 5f/6f: 0-1 7f-8f: 0-0 9f-13f: 0-0 14f+: 0-0
Track : LH: 0-1 RH: 0-0 Tight: 0-1 Gall: 0-0
Aids: Bl: 0-0 Vi: 0-0 Tstrap: 0-0
Best Rating: 25 2/01 Ling 5f slow

Pays D'Amour (IRE)

109 81
4-y-o b c Pursuit Of Love-Lady Of The Land (Wollow)
R Hannon Mrs M W Bird

Placings:05610/02001213023-62034000030 (5688)
2001: 7^{6}S, 6^{2}GS, 6^{0}GF, 7^{3}G, 6^{4}GF, 6^{0}G, 6^{0}G, 7^{0}GS, 6^{0}G, 6^{3}G, 7^{0}S

	Starts	1st	2nd	3rd	Win & Pl
Career Total (Turf)	27	3	4	4	35937

82 7/00 Epsm 7f D(0-80) G-F £7020
78 7/00 Hayd 6f C(0-100)H G-F £7085
61 9/99 Epsm 6f C(0-95)H GD £5771
Total win prize-money £19876

Going (Turf): Sf: 0-4 GS: 0-5 Gd: 1-8 **GF: 2-10** Fm: 0-0
Distance: **5f/6f: 2-14** 7f-8f: 1-13 9f-13f: 0-0 14f+: 0-0
Track : **LH: 2-4** RH: 0-3 **Tight: 2-3** Gall: 0-3
Aids: Bl: 0-0 Vi: 0-0 Tstrap: 0-0
Best Rating: 88 7/01 Newb 6f8y gd-fm

He looked a progressive sort in 2000, winning at Epsom and Haydock and running some fine races in decent handicaps otherwise. Some encouraging signs early this season, but was well beaten in the second half of the campaign. Probably best over seven furlongs now. Acts on fast ground.

Peace Band (IRE)

95(85) (44)67
3-y-o b c Desert Style (IRE)-Anita's Love (IRE) (Anita's Prince)
M H Tompkins Ian Lochhead

Placings:5430-54060 (4622)
2001: 6^{5}SD, 5^{4}GF, 6^{0}GF, 5^{6}GF, 6^{0}GF

	Starts	1st	2nd	3rd	Win & Pl
Career Total (Turf)	8	0	0	1	1144
Career Total (AW)	1	0	0	0	0

Going (Turf): Sf: 0-0 GS: 0-0 Gd: 0-1 GF: 0-7 Fm: 0-0
Distance: 5f/6f: 0-7 7f-8f: 0-2 9f-13f: 0-0 14f+: 0-0
Track : LH: 0-2 RH: 0-0 Tight: 0-0 Gall: 0-0
Aids: Bl: 0-1 Vi: 0-0 Tstrap: 0-0
Best Rating: 66 7/01 Bevl 5f gd-fm

Peace Within (IRE)

(91) (51)69
3-y-o b f Brief Truce (USA)-More Candy (Ballad Rock)
Edward Lynam (J Noseda 27/4) Mrs J M Ryan

Placings:63530 (5072a)
2001: 6^{6}SD, 7^{3}SD, 7^{5}G, 5^{3}GY, 7^{0}GF

	Starts	1st	2nd	3rd	Win & Pl
Career Total (Turf)	3	0	0	1	875
Career Total (AW)	2	0	0	1	257

Going (Turf): Sf: 0-0 GS: 0-0 Gd: 0-1 GF: 0-1 Fm: 0-0
Distance: 5f/6f: 0-2 7f-8f: 0-3 9f-13f: 0-0 14f+: 0-0
Track : LH: 0-2 RH: 0-0 Tight: 0-1 Gall: 0-0
Aids: Bl: 0-0 Vi: 0-0 Tstrap: 0-0
Best Rating: 69 8/01 Curr 5f gd-yld

Peaceful Paradise

106 101
3-y-o b f Turtle Island (IRE)-Megdale (IRE) (Waajib)
J W Hills Karen Scott Barrett(abbot Racing Ptnrs)

Placings:31513-0560343 (5271)
2001: 8^{0}G, 8^{5}GF, 8^{6}GF, 7^{0}G, 8^{3}G, 8^{4}HY, 8^{3}HY

	Starts	1st	2nd	3rd	Win & Pl
Career Total (Turf)	12	2	0	4	26872

98 8/00 NmkJ 7f A G-F £12470
76 6/00 Kemp 7f D G-F £4270
Total win prize-money £16741

Going (Turf): Sf: 0-2 GS: 0-1 Gd: 0-4 **GF: 2-5** Fm: 0-0
Distance: 5f/6f: 0-0 **7f-8f: 2-11** 9f-13f: 0-1 14f+: 0-0
Track : LH: 0-2 **RH: 1-5** Tight: 0-0 **Gall: 1-2**
Aids: Bl: 0-0 Vi: 0-0 Tstrap: 0-2
Best Rating: 101 9/01 Sand 1m14y good

She won twice over seven furlongs on fast ground at two, but faced some very stiff tasks this term and had shown little until faced with easier ground and fitted with a tongue tie. Has won on good to soft and good to firm. Yet to race beyond a mile.

Peacock Alley (IRE)

113 97
4-y-o gr f Salse (USA)-Tagiki (IRE) (Doyoun)
W J Haggas Mr & Mrs G Middlebrook

Placings:5023/51113623-0000 (2972)
2001: 7^{0}GF, 8^{0}GF, 8^{0}GF, 7^{0}G

	Starts	1st	2nd	3rd	Win & Pl
Career Total (Turf)	16	3	2	3	48919

92 6/00 Ayr 7f C(0-90)H GD £10400
83 6/00 Epsm 7f C(0-100)H G-S £22750
82 5/00 Wwck 6f168y D HVY £3818
Total win prize-money £36969

Going (Turf): Sf: 1-1 GS: 1-3 Gd: 1-7 GF: 0-4 Fm: 0-0
Distance: 5f/6f: 0-1 **7f-8f: 3-15** 9f-13f: 0-0 14f+: 0-0
Track : **LH: 3-5** RH: 0-3 **Tight: 1-3** Gall: 0-1
Aids: Bl: 0-0 Vi: 0-0 Tstrap: 0-0
Best Rating: 93 5/01 York 7f202y gd-fm

Improved to score a quick hat-trick in the early summer of 2000 and ran with credit off higher marks afterwards. Little form in 2001. Seems to handle most ground and is suited by seven furlongs and waiting tactics.

Peacock Theatre

77 37
3-y-o b c Red Rainbow-Fine Art (IRE) (Tate Gallery (USA))
A Streeter (J M Bradley 20/7) N Heath

Placings:00 (3205)
2001: 8^{0}GF, 7^{0}G

	Starts	1st	2nd	3rd	Win & Pl
Career Total (Turf)	2	0	0	0	

Going (Turf): Sf: 0-0 GS: 0-0 Gd: 0-1 GF: 0-1 Fm: 0-0
Distance: 5f/6f: 0-0 7f-8f: 0-1 9f-13f: 0-1 14f+: 0-0
Track : LH: 0-1 RH: 0-0 Tight: 0-0 Gall: 0-0
Aids: Bl: 0-0 Vi: 0-0 Tstrap: 0-0
Best Rating: 37 6/01 Nott 1m54y gd-fm

Peak Practice

48(81) (21)
3-y-o b f Saddlers' Hall (IRE)-High Habit (Slip Anchor)
J M P Eustace J C Smith

Placings:60 (1327)
2001: 11^{6}SD, 10^{0}G

	Starts	1st	2nd	3rd	Win & Pl
Career Total (Turf)	1	0	0	0	
Career Total (AW)	1	0	0	0	0

Going (Turf): Sf: 0-0 GS: 0-0 Gd: 0-1 GF: 0-0 Fm: 0-0
Distance: 5f/6f: 0-0 7f-8f: 0-0 9f-13f: 0-2 14f+: 0-0
Track : LH: 0-1 RH: 0-0 Tight: 0-1 Gall: 0-0
Aids: Bl: 0-0 Vi: 0-0 Tstrap: 0-0
Best Rating: 21 4/01 Sthl 1m3f stand

Pearly Brooks

99(89) (36)68
3-y-o b f Efisio-Elkie Brooks (Relkino)
T J Naughton R A Popely

Placings:53-40610 (4439)
2001: 5^{4}SW, 5^{0}F, 5^{6}GF, 6^{1}G, 6^{0}G

	Starts	1st	2nd	3rd	Win & Pl
Career Total (Turf)	6	1	0	1	4355
Career Total (AW)	1	0	0	0	0

68 8/01 Yarm 6f3y E(0-70)H GD £3753
Total win prize-money £3754

Going (Turf): Sf: 0-1 GS: 0-0 **Gd: 1-2** GF: 0-2 Fm: 0-1
Distance: 5f/6f: 0-4 **7f-8f: 1-3** 9f-13f: 0-0 14f+: 0-0
Track : LH: 0-3 RH: 0-0 Tight: 0-1 Gall: 0-1
Aids: Bl: 0-0 Vi: 0-0 Tstrap: 0-0
Best Rating: 68 8/01 Yarm 6f3y good

Pearly Gates (IRE)

111 **103**
3-y-o b f Night Shift (USA)-Pearl Shell (USA) (Bering)
B W Hills Mrs Drusilla Thomas

Placings:12054400 **(5679a)**
2001: 7^{1}GS, 7^{2}G, 7^{0}GF, 7^{5}GF, 6^{4}G, 6^{4}G, 7^{0}GS, 7^{0}S

	Starts	1st	2nd	3rd	Win & Pl
Career Total (Turf)	8	1	1	0	13496

91 4/01 Newb 7f D G-S £5362
Total win prize-money £5363

Going (Turf): Sf: 0-1 **GS: 1-2** Gd: 0-3 GF: 0-2 Fm: 0-0
Distance: 5f/6f: 0-1 **7f-8f: 1-7** 9f-13f: 0-0 14f+: 0-0
Track : LH: 0-1 RH: 0-2 Tight: 0-0 Gall: 0-1
Aids: Bl: 0-0 Vi: 0-0 Tstrap: 0-0
Best Rating: 103 10/01 NmkR 7f gd-sft

A 110,000gns daughter of a middle-distance winner. Looked a useful prospect when winning on her debut over seven furlongs in a newcomers' race at Newbury and took another step in the right direction with a neck second to Palace Affair in Listed event at Lingfield in May. Probably not helped by the draw when well beaten in the Jersey Stakes at Royal Ascot, and held since. Better over seven furlongs than shorter.

Peartree House (IRE)

110(90) (58)**90**
7-y-o b g Simply Majestic (USA)-Fashion Front (Habitat)
D Nicholls G Vettraino & Fayzad Thoroughbreds I

Placings:41416/21065034/00140**00**/0024000/00603124 40661000-0000000140060060 **(5005)**
2001: 8^{0}S, 7^{0}S, 8^{0}G, 8^{0}GF, 8^{0}GF, 8^{0}GF, 7^{0}GF, 7^{1}G, 7^{4}G, 7^{0}GF, 7^{0}G, 7^{6}G, 8^{0}G, 8^{0}G, 8^{6}GF, 7^{0}S

	Starts	1st	2nd	3rd	Win & Pl
Career Total (Turf)	56	7	3	2	87929
Career Total (AW)	3	0	0	0	

86 7/01 York 7f202y D(0-85)H GD £11797
96 8/00 York 7f202y B(0-105)H GD £27898
80 6/00 Ayr 1m D(0-80) GD £3731
92 5/98 Ling 7f140y C(0-90) GD £5711
97 5/97 Donc 1m C GD £4746
89 8/96 Catt 7f D G-F £3677
60 6/96 Ayr 6f F G-F £2775
Total win prize-money £60337

Going (Turf): Sf: 0-7 GS: 0-3 **Gd: 5-23** GF: 2-22 Fm: 0-0
Distance: 5f/6f: 1-2 **7f-8f: 6-48** 9f-13f: 0-9 14f+: 0-0
Track : **LH: 5-19** RH: 0-13 Tight: 1-10 **Gall: 3-9**
Aids: Bl: 0-0 Vi: 0-1 Tstrap: 0-0
Best Rating: 92 8/01 York 7f202y good

Often a front-runner, he put in a series of good efforts in 2000 including when landing the Bradford and Bingley at York, but was held subsequently until popping up back at York in July. Best over seven furlongs to a mile on a sound surface, but not particularly consistent.

Pease Blossom (IRE)

91 **76**
2-y-o b f Revoque (IRE)-Saneena (Kris)
C A Dwyer Roalco Limited

Placings:0040 **(4985)**
2001: 6^{0}GS, 7^{0}F, 7^{4}G, 6^{0}G

	Starts	1st	2nd	3rd	Win & Pl
Career Total (Turf)	4	0	0	0	333

Going (Turf): Sf: 0-0 GS: 0-1 Gd: 0-2 GF: 0-0 Fm: 0-1
Distance: 5f/6f: 0-1 7f-8f: 0-3 9f-13f: 0-0 14f+: 0-0
Track : LH: 0-1 RH: 0-0 Tight: 0-1 Gall: 0-0
Aids: Bl: 0-0 Vi: 0-0 Tstrap: 0-0
Best Rating: 76 9/01 Epsm 7f good

Pedro Jack (IRE)

100(101) (74)**68**
4-y-o b g Mujadil (USA)-Festival Of Light (High Top)
B J Meehan Michael F B Peart

Placings:0110/310603522066-06000342012 **(5612)**
2001: 6^{0}G, 6^{6}GF, 6^{0}GF, 6^{0}G, 6^{0}GF, 6^{3}F, 5^{4}GF, 5^{2}GF, 6^{0}G, 6^{1}SD, 6^{2}SD, 7^{0}SD

	Starts	1st	2nd	3rd	Win & Pl
Career Total (Turf)	25	3	3	3	20027
Career Total (AW)	2	1	1	0	3875

69 10/01 Wolv 6f F(0-65)H STD £2695
78 5/00 Wind 6f D(0-80)H G-F £4394
75 9/99 Nott 6f15y E(0-75)H G-F £3592
63 8/99 Nott 6f15y E G-F £3622
Total win prize-money £14305

Going (Turf): Sf: 0-2 GS: 0-0 Gd: 0-7 **GF: 3-14** Fm: 0-2
Distance: 5f/6f: 2-22 7f-8f: 2-5 9f-13f: 0-0 14f+: 0-0
Track : LH: 1-6 RH: 1-2 Tight: 1-3 Gall: 1-4
Aids: Bl: 0-4 Vi: 0-1 Tstrap: 0-0
Best Rating: 74 11/01 Wolv 6f stand

A useful sprinter. He scored on his All-Weather debut in October 2001. Suited by six furlongs and appreciates fast ground on turf.

Pedro Pete

104(98) (68)**80**
4-y-o ch g Fraam-Stride Home (Absalom)
N J Henderson Thurloe Thoroughbreds Vii

Placings:00/**41**433110501-013 **(2506)**
2001: 10^{0}GF, 11^{1}GF, 12^{3}GF

	Starts	1st	2nd	3rd	Win & Pl
Career Total (Turf)	13	4	0	3	30298
Career Total (AW)	3	1	0	0	2774

79 6/01 Wind 1m3f135yD(0-85)H G-F £4147
77 10/00 York 1m2f85y C(0-90)H SFT £7345
79 7/00 Asct 1m2f C(0-90)H G-F £8307
71 7/00 Ches 1m2f75y D(0-85)H SFT £8736
68 2/00 Ling 1m2f E(0-70)H STD £2563
Total win prize-money £31098

Going (Turf): Sf: 2-2 GS: 0-1 Gd: 0-5 **GF: 2-5** Fm: 0-0
Distance: 5f/6f: 0-0 7f-8f: 0-2 **9f-13f: 5-14** 14f+: 0-0
Track : **LH: 3-8** RH: 1-6 **Tight: 3-8** Gall: 2-3
Aids: Bl: 0-0 Vi: 0-0 Tstrap: 0-0
Best Rating: 80 6/01 Kemp 1m4f gd-fm

A useful hurdler and a decent handicapper on the Flat, he returned to form with a win on the level at Windsor in June. Handles all types of ground and is best over ten furlongs.

Peggy's Song

84(82) (40)**15**
3-y-o b f Mind Games-Miss Whittingham (IRE) (Fayruz)
D L Williams D L Williams

Placings:000004-600000 **(4610)**
2001: 5^{6}SD, 5^{0}SW, 5^{0}SD, 5^{0}GF, 5^{0}GF, 5^{0}F

	Starts	1st	2nd	3rd	Win & Pl
Career Total (Turf)	6	0	0	0	
Career Total (AW)	6	0	0	0	0

Going (Turf): Sf: 0-1 GS: 0-0 Gd: 0-0 GF: 0-4 Fm: 0-1
Distance: 5f/6f: 0-11 7f-8f: 0-1 9f-13f: 0-0 14f+: 0-0
Track : LH: 0-10 RH: 0-0 Tight: 0-5 Gall: 0-2
Aids: Bl: 0-2 Vi: 0-0 Tstrap: 0-0
Best Rating: 31 1/01 Ling 5f stand

Peggys Rose (IRE)

(80) (18)
4-y-o b f Shalford (IRE)-Afrique Noir (IRE) (Gallic League)
P D Evans F O'Brien

Placings:140020000-0 **(0462)**
2001: 6^{0}SD

	Starts	1st	2nd	3rd	Win & Pl
Career Total (Turf)	6	1	1	0	3467
Career Total (AW)	4	0	0	0	

70 4/00 Leic 5f218y G G-S £1991
Total win prize-money £1992

Going (Turf): Sf: 0-2 **GS: 1-2** Gd: 0-0 GF: 0-2 Fm: 0-0
Distance: **5f/6f: 1-6** 7f-8f: 0-3 9f-13f: 0-1 14f+: 0-0
Track : LH: 0-8 RH: 0-0 Tight: 0-6 Gall: 0-0
Aids: Bl: 0-1 Vi: 0-0 Tstrap: 0-0
Best Rating: 5 3/01 Wolv 6f stand

Pekan Heights (USA)

71 **66**
5-y-o br g Green Dancer (USA)-Battle Drum (USA) (Alydar (USA))
P D Evans Mrs Claire Massey

Placings:350/10400/1040-0 **(1566)**
2001: 9^{0}F

	Starts	1st	2nd	3rd	Win & Pl
Career Total (Turf)	13	2	0	1	8508

52 6/00 Ches 1m2f75y E G-F £3601
83 4/99 Nott 1m1f213yD(0-80)H G-S £4045
Total win prize-money £7646

Going (Turf): Sf: 0-0 **GS: 1-2** Gd: 0-5 **GF: 1-3** Fm: 0-3
Distance: 5f/6f: 0-0 7f-8f: 0-2 **9f-13f: 2-10** 14f+: 0-1
Track : **LH: 2-7** RH: 0-5 **Tight: 1-6** Gall: 0-1
Aids: Bl: 0-2 **Vi: 1-4** Tstrap: 0-0
Best Rating: 2 5/01 Brig 1m1f209y firm

Pekan Ku (USA)

78 **57**
2-y-o b c Kingmambo (USA)-Star Of Albion (Ajdal (USA))
M A Jarvis H R H Sultan Ahmad Shah

Placings:0 **(2880)**
2001: 7^{0}GS

	Starts	1st	2nd	3rd	Win & Pl
Career Total (Turf)	1	0	0	0	

Going (Turf): Sf: 0-0 GS: 0-1 Gd: 0-0 GF: 0-0 Fm: 0-0
Distance: 5f/6f: 0-0 7f-8f: 0-1 9f-13f: 0-0 14f+: 0-0
Track : LH: 0-0 RH: 0-0 Tight: 0-0 Gall: 0-0
Aids: Bl: 0-0 Vi: 0-0 Tstrap: 0-0
Best Rating: 57 7/01 NmkJ 7f gd-sft

Pekanese (IRE)

84 **47**
4-y-o b g Sri Pekan (USA)-Tootle (Main Reef)
R T Phillips Dozen Dreamers Partnership

Placings:6206-040 **(4048)**
2001: 12^{0}GF, 10^{4}S, 10^{0}F

	Starts	1st	2nd	3rd	Win & Pl
Career Total (Turf)	7	0	1	0	1210

Going (Turf): Sf: 0-3 GS: 0-2 Gd: 0-0 GF: 0-1 Fm: 0-1
Distance: 5f/6f: 0-0 7f-8f: 0-4 9f-13f: 0-3 14f+: 0-0
Track : LH: 0-3 RH: 0-1 Tight: 0-1 Gall: 0-1
Aids: Bl: 0-2 Vi: 0-0 Tstrap: 0-0
Best Rating: 35 8/01 Chep 1m2f36y soft

Pekanoora (IRE)

85 **24**

3-y-o b g Sri Pekan (USA)-Shanoora (IRE) (Don't Forget Me)

P W Harris J Cowan & Mrs P W Harris

Placings:050-00 **(5601)**

2001: 9^0S, 8^0GS

	Starts	1st	2nd	3rd	Win & Pl
Career Total (Turf)	5	0	0	0	0

Going (Turf): Sf: 0-2 GS: 0-2 Gd: 0-0 GF: 0-1 Fm: 0-0
Distance: 5f/6f: 0-0 7f-8f: 0-3 9f-13f: 0-2 14f+: 0-0
Track : LH: 0-2 RH: 0-0 Tight: 0-0 Gall: 0-0
Aids: Bl: 0-0 Vi: 0-0 Tstrap: 0-0
Best Rating: 24 11/01 NmkR 1m gd-sft

Pekay

97(73) (38)**47**

8-y-o b g Puissance-K-Sera (Lord Gayle (USA))

B Smart B Smart

Placings:3320/035132622004143/12/0035300-0433 **(5471)**

2001: 10^0HY, 9^4G, 12^3GS, 11^3S

	Starts	1st	2nd	3rd	Win & Pl
Career Total (Turf)	30	3	5	9	24765
Career Total (AW)	2	0	0	0	

66	6/98	Sals	1m4f	E(0-70)H	G-S	£3162
69	10/97	Ayr	1m2f192yD(0-80)H		SFT	£4055
64	6/97	Haml	1m1f36y	E(0-70)H	G-F	£3420

Total win prize-money £10637

Going (Turf): Sf: 1-6 GS: 1-5 Gd: 0-8 **GF: 1-9** Fm: 0-2
Distance: 5f/6f: 0-4 7f-8f: 0-1 **9f-13f: 3-25** 14f+: 0-2
Track : LH: 1-14 **RH: 2-14 Tight: 2-9** Gall: 0-4
Aids: **Bl: 1-6** Vi: 0-0 Tstrap: 0-0
Best Rating: 47 10/01 Brig 1m3f196y soft

Has not won for over two years, and has been well held since that last victory.

Pelagia (IRE)

(78) (12)**59**

3-y-o b f Lycius (USA)-Sahara Breeze (Ela-Mana-Mou)

R Hannon J Repard,G Doran,M Nicolson,C Witten

Placings:4-00000 **(5670)**

2001: 7^0GS, 8^0GS, 7^0GF, 7^0G, 8^0HY, 9^0SD

	Starts	1st	2nd	3rd	Win & Pl
Career Total (Turf)	6	0	0	0	387

Going (Turf): Sf: 0-1 GS: 0-2 Gd: 0-1 GF: 0-2 Fm: 0-0
Distance: 5f/6f: 0-0 7f-8f: 0-5 9f-13f: 0-1 14f+: 0-0
Track : LH: 0-0 RH: 0-2 Tight: 0-1 Gall: 0-1
Aids: Bl: 0-0 Vi: 0-0 Tstrap: 0-0
Best Rating: 59 6/01 Sals 1m gd-sft

Pelli

90(86) (38)**36**

3-y-o b f Saddlers' Hall (IRE)-Pellinora (USA) (King Pellinore (USA))

P Howling P A & M J Reditt

Placings:0030004-3030050 **(3963)**

2001: 10^3SD, 10^0SD, 8^3SW, 9^0SD, 7^0GF, 8^5G, 10^0G

	Starts	1st	2nd	3rd	Win & Pl
Career Total (Turf)	8	0	0	1	267
Career Total (AW)	6	0	0	2	581

Going (Turf): Sf: 0-0 GS: 0-1 Gd: 0-2 GF: 0-5 Fm: 0-0
Distance: 5f/6f: 0-1 7f-8f: 0-7 9f-13f: 0-6 14f+: 0-0
Track : LH: 0-7 RH: 0-0 Tight: 0-4 Gall: 0-0
Aids: Bl: 0-0 Vi: 0-0 Tstrap: 0-0
Best Rating: 37 2/01 Sthl 1m slow

Penalta

103(99) (49)**47**

5-y-o ch g Cosmonaut-Targuette (Targowice (USA))

M Wigham John Smallman

Placings:000310215-5242P0 **(1283)**

2001: 16^5SD, 16^2SD, 16^4SD, 16^2SD, 14^PS, 16^0G

	Starts	1st	2nd	3rd	Win & Pl
Career Total (Turf)	7	1	1	1	4023
Career Total (AW)	8	1	2	0	3398

48	11/00	Wolv	2m46y	F(0-60)H	STD	£2394
45	9/00	Brig	1m3f196yE(0-70)H		SFT	£2873

Total win prize-money £5267

Going (Turf): Sf: 1-3 GS: 0-0 Gd: 0-1 GF: 0-1 Fm: 0-2
Distance: 5f/6f: 0-0 7f-8f: 0-1 9f-13f: 1-5 14f+: 1-9
Track : **LH: 2-11** RH: 0-3 **Tight: 1-9** Gall: 0-0
Aids: Bl: 0-0 Vi: 0-3 Tstrap: 0-1
Best Rating: 49 2/01 Wolv 2m46y stand

Pendulum

103 **78+**

3-y-o ro f Pursuit Of Love-Brilliant Timing (USA) (The Minstrel (CAN))

W J Haggas Cheveley Park Stud

Placings:0-120 **(4705)**

2001: 7^1F, 7^2GF, 7^0G

	Starts	1st	2nd	3rd	Win & Pl
Career Total (Turf)	4	1	1	0	5610

73	7/01	Thsk	7f	D	FRM	£4280

Total win prize-money £4280

Going (Turf): Sf: 0-0 GS: 0-0 Gd: 0-1 GF: 0-2 **Fm: 1-1**
Distance: 5f/6f: 0-0 **7f-8f: 1-4** 9f-13f: 0-0 14f+: 0-0
Track : **LH: 1-2** RH: 0-0 **Tight: 1-2** Gall: 0-0
Aids: Bl: 0-0 Vi: 0-0 Tstrap: 0-0
Best Rating: 78 8/01 Ling 7f140y gd-fm

She overcame a break of ten months after her racecourse debut to land a Thirsk maiden in July and ran very well in a Lingfield handicap next time. Suited by seven furlongs and fast ground.

Peng (IRE)

71(92) (35)**32**

4-y-o ch g Case Law-Real Bold (Never So Bold)

R Bastiman Peter Beaton-Brown

Placings:000000000-000400 **(1637)**

2001: 7^0SD, 7^0SW, 6^0SD, 7^4SD, 7^0SD, 7^0F

	Starts	1st	2nd	3rd	Win & Pl
Career Total (Turf)	9	0	0	0	
Career Total (AW)	7	0	0	0	0

Going (Turf): Sf: 0-3 GS: 0-1 Gd: 0-2 GF: 0-1 Fm: 0-2
Distance: 5f/6f: 0-2 7f-8f: 0-11 9f-13f: 0-3 14f+: 0-0
Track : LH: 0-9 RH: 0-5 Tight: 0-5 Gall: 0-1
Aids: Bl: 0-0 Vi: 0-2 Tstrap: 0-6
Best Rating: 35 2/01 Sthl 7f stand

Penguin Bay

102 **51**

5-y-o b g Rock Hopper-Corn Lily (Aragon)

Mrs M Reveley Mrs Susan McDonald

Placings:5533050 **(4843)**

2001: 12^5G, 14^5GF, 12^3GF, 9^3F, 12^0G, 14^5GF, 16^0G

	Starts	1st	2nd	3rd	Win & Pl
Career Total (Turf)	7	0	0	2	1299

Going (Turf): Sf: 0-0 GS: 0-0 Gd: 0-3 GF: 0-3 Fm: 0-1
Distance: 5f/6f: 0-0 7f-8f: 0-0 9f-13f: 0-4 14f+: 0-3
Track : LH: 0-5 RH: 0-2 Tight: 0-4 Gall: 0-2
Aids: Bl: 0-0 Vi: 0-0 Tstrap: 0-0
Best Rating: 70 6/01 Rdcr 1m6f19y gd-fm

A fair maiden handicapper. Probably needs at least two miles. Has only raced on good and faster ground on the level.

Penne Dancer (IRE)

98 **77**

2-y-o gr c Pennekamp (USA)-Talama (FR) (Shakapour)

R Hannon Mrs Charles Sparrowhawk

Placings:44140 **(4716)**

2001: 6^4GF, 6^4GF, 7^1GF, 6^4GF, 7^0G

	Starts	1st	2nd	3rd	Win & Pl
Career Total (Turf)	5	1	0	0	4277

77	7/01	Ling	7f	E	G-F	£3122

Total win prize-money £3122

Going (Turf): Sf: 0-0 GS: 0-0 Gd: 0-1 **GF: 1-4** Fm: 0-0
Distance: 5f/6f: 0-2 **7f-8f: 1-3** 9f-13f: 0-0 14f+: 0-0
Track : LH: 0-1 RH: 0-0 Tight: 0-1 Gall: 0-0
Aids: Bl: 0-0 Vi: 0-0 Tstrap: 0-0
Best Rating: 77 8/01 Sals 6f212y gd-fm

Showed promise on his first two starts before winning nicely at Lingfield over seven. Ran well in a better race at Salisbury, and should stay a mile.

Pennechip

90 **75**

2-y-o ch f Pennekamp (USA)-Poker Chip (Bluebird (USA))

R Hannon J C Smith

Placings:064000 **(5078)**

2001: 6^0GF, 5^6GF, 6^4GF, 6^0GF, 6^0GF, 5^0S

	Starts	1st	2nd	3rd	Win & Pl
Career Total (Turf)	6	0	0	0	321

Going (Turf): Sf: 0-1 GS: 0-0 Gd: 0-0 GF: 0-5 Fm: 0-0
Distance: 5f/6f: 0-5 7f-8f: 0-1 9f-13f: 0-0 14f+: 0-0
Track : LH: 0-2 RH: 0-0 Tight: 0-0 Gall: 0-1
Aids: Bl: 0-0 Vi: 0-0 Tstrap: 0-0
Best Rating: 75 7/01 Nott 6f15y gd-fm

She hinted at some ability in maiden company, but was never competitive on her nursery debut.

Penneless Dancer

98(93) (70)**67**

2-y-o b c Pennekamp (USA)-Villella (Sadler's Wells (USA))

M Blanshard The Shell Seekers

Placings:6463560400 **(5467)**

2001: 5^6GS, 5^4GF, 6^6GF, 7^3F, 6^5GF, 5^6GS, 6^0GF, 6^4SD, 6^0HY, 6^0S

	Starts	1st	2nd	3rd	Win & Pl
Career Total (Turf)	9	0	0	1	802
Career Total (AW)	1	0	0	0	284

Going (Turf): Sf: 0-2 GS: 0-2 Gd: 0-0 GF: 0-4 Fm: 0-1
Distance: 5f/6f: 0-5 7f-8f: 0-3 9f-13f: 0-2 14f+: 0-0
Track : LH: 0-4 RH: 0-1 Tight: 0-2 Gall: 0-0
Aids: Bl: 0-0 Vi: 0-0 Tstrap: 0-0
Best Rating: 74 7/01 Ling 6f gd-fm

Pennine Lass (IRE)

6-y-o b m Archway (IRE)-Pennine Girl (IRE) (Pennine Walk)

L A Dace Ray Monaghan

Placings:0 **(0292)**

2001: 13^0SW

	Starts	1st	2nd	3rd	Win & Pl

Career Total (Turf)	0	0	0	0	
Career Total (AW)	1	0	0	0	

Going (Turf): Sf: 0-0 GS: 0-0 Gd: 0-0 GF: 0-0 Fm: 0-0
Distance: 5f/6f: 0-0 7f-8f: 0-0 9f-13f: 0-1 14f+: 0-0
Track : LH: 0-1 RH: 0-0 Tight: 0-1 Gall: 0-0
Aids: Bl: 0-0 Vi: 0-0 Tstrap: 0-0
Best Rating: 74 7/01 Ling 6f gd-fm

Penny Farthing

95 **60**

3-y-o b f Mind Games-Souveniers (Relko)
H Candy Mrs George Tricks

Placings:000-05000520 **(4906)**
2001: 8^{0}GS, 7^{5}GF, 7^{0}GF, 8^{0}GF, 9^{0}G, 13^{5}G, 11^{2}GF, 9^{0}G

	Starts	1st	2nd	3rd	Win & Pl
Career Total (Turf)	11	0	1	0	796

Going (Turf): Sf: 0-1 GS: 0-1 Gd: 0-3 GF: 0-6 Fm: 0-0
Distance: 5f/6f: 0-0 7f-8f: 0-7 9f-13f: 0-3 14f+: 0-1
Track : LH: 0-2 RH: 0-4 Tight: 0-1 Gall: 0-2
Aids: Bl: 0-0 Vi: 0-2 Tstrap: 0-0
Best Rating: 60 6/01 Kemp 7f gd-fm

Penny Ha'Penny

76 **58**

2-y-o b f Bishop Of Cashel-Madam Millie (Milford)
D W Barker P Asquith

Placings:60 **(5250)**
2001: 6^{6}GS, 6^{0}S

	Starts	1st	2nd	3rd	Win & Pl
Career Total (Turf)	2	0	0	0	0

Going (Turf): Sf: 0-1 GS: 0-1 Gd: 0-0 GF: 0-0 Fm: 0-0
Distance: 5f/6f: 0-2 7f-8f: 0-0 9f-13f: 0-0 14f+: 0-0
Track : LH: 0-0 RH: 0-0 Tight: 0-0 Gall: 0-0
Aids: Bl: 0-0 Vi: 0-0 Tstrap: 0-0
Best Rating: 58 10/01 Newc 6f gd-sft

Penny Pictures (IRE)

104 **84**

2-y-o b c Theatrical-Copper Creek (Habitat)
M Johnston J David Abell

Placings:43160 **(4678)**
2001: 6^{4}GF, 6^{3}F, 7^{1}GF, 6^{6}G, 8^{0}G

	Starts	1st	2nd	3rd	Win & Pl
Career Total (Turf)	5	1	0	1	4552

84 8/01 Catt 7f D G-F £3164
Total win prize-money £3164

Going (Turf): Sf: 0-0 GS: 0-0 Gd: 0-2 **GF: 1-2** Fm: 0-1
Distance: 5f/6f: 0-2 **7f-8f: 1-3** 9f-13f: 0-0 14f+: 0-0
Track : **LH: 1-2** RH: 0-0 **Tight: 1-1** Gall: 0-1
Aids: Bl: 0-0 Vi: 0-0 Tstrap: 0-0
Best Rating: 84 8/01 Catt 7f gd-fm

85,000gns half-brother to several decent performers, notably high-class juvenile/sprinter Tipsy Creek and useful six/seven furlong filly May Contessa. Well suited by a step up to seven furlongs when scoring at Catterick. Should stay further. Acts on fast ground.

Pennys From Heaven

103(100) (37)**44**

7-y-o gr g Generous (IRE)-Heavenly Cause (USA) (Grey Dawn Ii)
D Nicholls Paul And Glenys Kent

Placings:043/4435301260/034/0302412450464304044-0262066541620000300 **(5411)**
2001: 16^{0}SD, 16^{2}SD, 16^{6}SW, 12^{2}SW, 12^{0}SD, 16^{6}SD, 12^{6}GS, 16^{5}S, 12^{4}GF, 12^{1}G, 13^{6}G, 12^{2}GF, 16^{0}GF, 13^{0}GF, 16^{0}F, 9^{0}GF, 12^{3}F, 16^{0}GS, 14^{0}SD, 14^{0}SD

	Starts	1st	2nd	3rd	Win & Pl
Career Total (Turf)	44	3	4	7	22296
Career Total (AW)	10	0	2	0	1356

51 5/01 Ripn 1m4f60y D(0-85)H GD £4212
56 6/00 Ayr 1m2f192yE(0-60)H GD £3900
77 8/97 Bath 1m3f144yD(0-80)H GD £3670
Total win prize-money £11782

Going (Turf): Sf: 0-5 GS: 0-8 **Gd: 3-11** GF: 0-16 Fm: 0-4
Distance: 5f/6f: 0-0 7f-8f: 0-3 **9f-13f: 3-33** 14f+: 0-18
Track : **LH: 2-29** RH: 1-21 **Tight: 2-22** Gall: 0-6
Aids: Bl: 0-1 Vi: 0-0 Tstrap: 0-0
Best Rating: 56 5/01 Muss 1m4f gd-fm

Has ability but is not the most reliable type.

Pennys Pride (IRE)

103 **62**

6-y-o b m Pips Pride-Mursuma (Rarity)
Mrs M Reveley J Good

Placings:302303000-032320431010 **(5632)**
2001: 12^{0}GS, 8^{3}S, 9^{2}GF, 10^{3}F, 12^{2}GF, 8^{0}GF, 11^{4}GF, 12^{3}GF, 10^{1}G, 9^{0}GF, 10^{1}G, 10^{0}G

	Starts	1st	2nd	3rd	Win & Pl
Career Total (Turf)	21	2	3	6	19233

62 9/01 Ayr 1m2f C(0-90)H GD £7410
56 8/01 Rdcr 1m2f E(0-75)H GD £4290
Total win prize-money £11700

Going (Turf): Sf: 0-6 GS: 0-3 **Gd: 2-5** GF: 0-6 Fm: 0-1
Distance: 5f/6f: 0-0 7f-8f: 0-8 **9f-13f: 2-13** 14f+: 0-0
Track : **LH: 2-12** RH: 0-3 **Tight: 1-3** Gall: 0-3
Aids: Bl: 0-0 Vi: 0-1 Tstrap: 0-0
Best Rating: 62 9/01 Ayr 1m2f good

A half-sister to amongst others, Direct Route, started off life in bumpers, but was then switched to the Flat last season. A keen sort, she won in both August and September of 2001. Seems to act on any going. Stays ten furlongs.

Pension Fund

109(108) (73)**79**

7-y-o b g Emperor Fountain-Navarino Bay (Averof)
M W Easterby Stephen J Curtis

Placings:0501316/00002200212/00231004/106/30000-4623001102000 **(5529)**
2001: 8^{4}SW, 12^{6}SD, 9^{2}SW, 7^{3}SW, 8^{0}S, 9^{0}S, 10^{1}GF, 8^{1}G, 10^{0}G, 10^{2}GF, 10^{0}GF, 8^{0}GS, 8^{0}HY

	Starts	1st	2nd	3rd	Win & Pl
Career Total (Turf)	44	7	6	3	81665
Career Total (AW)	4	0	1	1	1031

79 6/01 York 1m205y B(0-105)H GD £17875
75 5/01 Ches 1m2f75y C(0-95)H G-F £10871
81 9/99 York 7f202y D(0-80)H G-F £8214
82 9/98 Ripn 1m2f C(0-90)H HVY £7165
70 8/97 Bevl 1m1f207yE(0-70)H GD £3977
72 8/96 York 6f214y C GD £11550
63 7/96 Rdcr 5f E G-F £3172
Total win prize-money £62825

Going (Turf): Sf: 1-7 GS: 0-4 **Gd: 3-15 GF: 3-16** Fm: 0-2
Distance: 5f/6f: 1-5 7f-8f: 2-12 **9f-13f: 4-31** 14f+: 0-0
Track : **LH: 4-30** RH: 2-9 Tight: 2-14 **Gall: 3-15**
Aids: Bl: 0-1 Vi: 0-0 Tstrap: 0-0
Best Rating: 79 8/01 Ripn 1m2f gd-fm

Fair handicapper who still retains plenty of ability, he is best at around ten furlongs these days. Recorded his first win for almost two years at Chester in May 2001, then followed up with another success at York in June and has a good record at that track. Acts on fast ground.

Pentecost

98 **90**

2-y-o ch c Tagula (IRE)-Boughtbyphone (Warning)
I A Balding Exors Of The Late Robert Hitchins

Placings:203221200 **(5364)**
2001: 5^{2}GF, 5^{0}GF, 6^{3}GF, 5^{2}GF, 5^{2}F, 6^{1}GF, 6^{2}GF, 6^{0}G, 6^{0}GS

	Starts	1st	2nd	3rd	Win & Pl
Career Total (Turf)	9	1	4	1	14075

78 8/01 Epsm 6f E G-F £3620
Total win prize-money £3621

Going (Turf): Sf: 0-0 GS: 0-1 Gd: 0-1 **GF: 1-6** Fm: 0-1
Distance: **5f/6f: 1-9** 7f-8f: 0-0 9f-13f: 0-0 14f+: 0-0
Track : **LH: 1-3** RH: 0-0 **Tight: 1-1** Gall: 0-1
Aids: Bl: 0-0 Vi: 0-1 Tstrap: 0-0
Best Rating: 90 10/01 Rdcr 6f good

Ran well on several occasions before getting off the mark at Epsom. Effective at five and six furlongs, and acts on fast ground. Consistent.

Pentland (JPN)

104 **82**

3-y-o br g Pentire-Lay Claim (USA) (Mr Prospector (USA))
G Wragg Mollers Racing

Placings:0500-01230 **(5249)**
2001: 10^{0}S, 9^{1}GF, 11^{2}F, 12^{3}G, 10^{0}S

	Starts	1st	2nd	3rd	Win & Pl
Career Total (Turf)	9	1	1	1	7267

75 6/01 Sals 1m1f198yD(0-75) G-F £3952
Total win prize-money £3952

Going (Turf): Sf: 0-2 GS: 0-1 Gd: 0-2 **GF: 1-3** Fm: 0-1
Distance: 5f/6f: 0-2 7f-8f: 0-2 **9f-13f: 1-5** 14f+: 0-0
Track : LH: 0-2 **RH: 1-2 Tight: 1-3** Gall: 0-1
Aids: Bl: 0-0 Vi: 0-0 Tstrap: 0-0
Best Rating: 82 7/01 Rdcr 1m3f firm

Penwell Hill (USA)

89 **68**

2-y-o b c Distant View (USA)-Avie's Jill (USA) (Lord Avie (USA))
T D Barron Mrs Liz Jones

Placings:460 **(5177)**
2001: 7^{4}GF, 7^{6}G, 6^{0}HY

	Starts	1st	2nd	3rd	Win & Pl
Career Total (Turf)	3	0	0	0	692

Going (Turf): Sf: 0-1 GS: 0-0 Gd: 0-1 GF: 0-1 Fm: 0-0
Distance: 5f/6f: 0-1 7f-8f: 0-2 9f-13f: 0-0 14f+: 0-0
Track : LH: 0-0 RH: 0-1 Tight: 0-0 Gall: 0-0
Aids: Bl: 0-0 Vi: 0-0 Tstrap: 0-0
Best Rating: 68 7/01 Sand 7f16y gd-fm

Pepper Ridge

95 **67**

2-y-o b f Bishop Of Cashel-Chief Celebrity (USA) (Chief's Crown (USA))
B A McMahon The Mavericks Racing Club

Placings:40 **(5274)**
2001: 7^{4}HY, 7^{0}GS

	Starts	1st	2nd	3rd	Win & Pl
Career Total (Turf)	2	0	0	0	334

Going (Turf): Sf: 0-1 GS: 0-1 Gd: 0-0 GF: 0-0 Fm: 0-0
Distance: 5f/6f: 0-0 7f-8f: 0-2 9f-13f: 0-0 14f+: 0-0
Track : LH: 0-1 RH: 0-0 Tight: 0-0 Gall: 0-0
Aids: Bl: 0-0 Vi: 0-0 Tstrap: 0-0
Best Rating: 67 9/01 Hayd 7f30y heavy

Pepper Road

92 **62**

2-y-o ch g Elmaamul (USA)-Floral Spark (Forzando)

R Bastiman B Selective Partnership

Placings:045630 **(4882)**

2001: 5^{0}GF, 5^{4}G, 5^{5}S, 5^{6}GF, 5^{3}G, 6^{0}GF

	Starts	1st	2nd	3rd	Win & Pl
Career Total (Turf)	6	0	0	1	829

Going (Turf): **Sf: 0-1 GS: 0-0 Gd: 0-2 GF: 0-3 Fm: 0-0**
Distance: 5f/6f: 0-5 7f-8f: 0-1 9f-13f: 0-0 14f+: 0-0
Track : LH: 0-0 RH: 0-0 Tight: 0-0 Gall: 0-0
Aids: Bl: 0-0 Vi: 0-0 Tstrap: 0-0
Best Rating: 62 9/01 Haml 6f5y gd-fm

Pepperdine (IRE)

97 **56**

5-y-o b g Indian Ridge-Rahwah (Northern Baby (CAN))

D Nicholls P D Savill

Placings:225061/2021002/35000-0000020P **(5384)**

2001: 5^{0}GS, 6^{0}S, 7^{0}GF, 7^{0}GF, 6^{0}G, 5^{2}GF, 7^{0}GF, 7^{P}S

	Starts	1st	2nd	3rd	Win & Pl
Career Total (Turf)	26	2	6	1	59503

93	6/99	York	6f	B(0-105)H	G-S	£38779
83	10/98	Wwck	7f	D(0-85)H	GD	£3550

Total win prize-money £42329

Going (Turf): Sf: 0-4 **GS: 1-4 Gd: 1-7** GF: 0-10 Fm: 0-0
Distance: 5f/6f: 1-18 7f-8f: 1-8 9f-13f: 0-0 14f+: 0-0
Track : **LH: 1-6** RH: 0-1 Tight: 0-3 Gall: 0-1
Aids: Bl: 0-1 Vi: 0-1 Tstrap: 0-2
Best Rating: 56 8/01 Catt 5f212y gd-fm

A one-time useful sprint handicapper, he has been on the downgrade in the last season or two. Suited by cut in the ground.

Pepperoni (IRE)

103(92) (71)**95**

2-y-o b g Nicolotte-Enchantica (Timeless Times (USA))

T D Easterby Mrs Janis Macpherson

Placings:44126611 **(4174)**

2001: 5^{4}GS, 6^{4}SD, 5^{1}GF, 5^{2}GF, 5^{6}GF, 6^{6}GS, 6^{1}G, 5^{1}G

	Starts	1st	2nd	3rd	Win & Pl
Career Total (Turf)	7	3	1	0	30542
Career Total (AW)	1	0	0	0	0

95	8/01	York	5f	A	GD	£17933
95	8/01	Ripn	6f	C	GD	£5707
85	6/01	Rdcr	5f	D	G-F	£3528

Total win prize-money £27169

Going (Turf): Sf: 0-0 GS: 0-2 **Gd: 2-2** GF: 1-3 Fm: 0-0
Distance: **5f/6f: 3-8** 7f-8f: 0-0 9f-13f: 0-0 14f+: 0-0
Track : LH: 0-2 RH: 0-0 Tight: 0-1 Gall: 0-0
Aids: Bl: 0-0 Vi: 0-0 Tstrap: 0-0
Best Rating: 95 8/01 York 5f good

Out of a five-furlong performer, won a maiden at Redcar and ran second at Chester, where he went down by only a short head, before a good effort in the Newbury Super Sprint. Scored a decent win at Ripon over six furlongs in August, and followed up back at five furlongs at York. Acts on fast ground, suited by making the running, genuine.

Peppiatt

103(88) (33)**44**

7-y-o ch g Efisio-Fleur Du Val (Valiyar)

N Bycroft Swinburne/moore Partnership

Placings:121/000404333321005/600560001500060605 0/03403500253500000-0002064050060 **(5535)**

2001: 7^{0}SD, 8^{0}S, 6^{0}GF, 7^{2}GF, 7^{0}GF, 6^{6}GS, 7^{4}G, 7^{0}GF, 6^{5}G, 6^{0}G, 6^{0}S, 6^{6}HY, 7^{0}S

	Starts	1st	2nd	3rd	Win & Pl
Career Total (Turf)	65	4	4	7	44601
Career Total (AW)	2	0	0	0	

70	7/99	Ayr	6f	C(0-90)H	SFT	£7067
77	9/98	Gdwd	6f	C(0-95)H	SFT	£11673
79	7/97	Ling	7f	C(0-90)H	G-F	£7700
75	4/97	Folk	6f	E	G-F	£3148

Total win prize-money £29589

Going (Turf): **Sf: 2-18** GS: 0-9 Gd: 0-21 **GF: 2-17** Fm: 0-0
Distance: **5f/6f: 3-39** 7f-8f: 1-27 9f-13f: 0-1 14f+: 0-0
Track : LH: 0-17 RH: 0-2 Tight: 0-5 Gall: 0-1
Aids: Bl: 0-4 Vi: 0-0 Tstrap: 0-0
Best Rating: 53 6/01 Bevl 7f100y gd-fm

He has changed stables a few times in his career and is a fair handicapper on his day. Six furlongs and cut in the ground look to be his ideal conditions, but has run well over seven. Has not won since July 1999.

Pequeno Mundo (IRE)

66(83) (7)**15**

4-y-o b/br g Marju (IRE)-Maryinsky (USA) (Northern Dancer)

A B Coogan A B Coogan

Placings:00 **(2649)**

2001: 8^{0}GF, 11^{0}SD

	Starts	1st	2nd	3rd	Win & Pl
Career Total (Turf)	1	0	0	0	
Career Total (AW)	1	0	0	0	

Going (Turf): **Sf: 0-0 GS: 0-0 Gd: 0-0 GF: 0-1 Fm: 0-0**
Distance: 5f/6f: 0-0 7f-8f: 0-0 9f-13f: 0-2 14f+: 0-0
Track : LH: 0-2 RH: 0-0 Tight: 0-0 Gall: 0-0
Aids: Bl: 0-0 Vi: 0-0 Tstrap: 0-0
Best Rating: 15 6/01 Nott 1m54y gd-fm

Perchance To Win

102 **60**

4-y-o b f Pelder (IRE)-French Plait (Thatching)

P J Makin Magno-Pulse Ltd

Placings:032000 **(5275)**

2001: 8^{0}GF, 7^{3}G, 7^{2}S, 8^{0}GF, 9^{0}G, 8^{0}GS

	Starts	1st	2nd	3rd	Win & Pl
Career Total (Turf)	6	0	1	1	1428

Going (Turf): **Sf: 0-1 GS: 0-1 Gd: 0-2 GF: 0-2 Fm: 0-0**
Distance: 5f/6f: 0-0 7f-8f: 0-3 9f-13f: 0-3 14f+: 0-0
Track : LH: 0-2 RH: 0-0 Tight: 0-1 Gall: 0-0
Aids: Bl: 0-0 Vi: 0-0 Tstrap: 0-0
Best Rating: 65 7/01 Chep 7f16y good

Lightly-raced filly. Probably best suited by a mile at present. Acts on soft ground.

Perchancer (IRE)

100(102) (61)**66**

5-y-o ch g Perugino (USA)-Irish Hope (Nishapour (FR))

P C Haslam N P Green

Placings:0030604/3230043120006/321100134403-46132031200U **(5407)**

2001: 8^{4}SD, 9^{6}SD, 11^{1}SD, 10^{3}S, 9^{2}G, 11^{0}SD, 10^{3}GF, 10^{1}F, 10^{2}G, 8^{0}SD, 9^{0}GF, 12^{U}SD, 11^{4}SD

	Starts	1st	2nd	3rd	Win & Pl
Career Total (Turf)	26	3	3	6	18081
Career Total (AW)	18	3	2	3	7297

66	6/01	Pont	1m2f6y	E(0-70)H	FRM	£3419
61	4/01	Sthl	1m3f	G(0-70)H	STD	£1393
61	4/00	Haml	1m1f36y	E(0-75)H	GD	£4543
61	2/00	Sthl	1m	F(0-65)H	STD	£2339
55	2/00	Wolv	1m100y	G(0-70)H	STD	£1542
53	7/99	Thsk	7f	E(0-70)H	FRM	£2689

Total win prize-money £15927

Going (Turf): Sf: 0-2 GS: 0-4 Gd: 1-8 GF: 0-10 **Fm: 2-2**
Distance: 5f/6f: 0-5 7f-8f: 2-9 **9f-13f: 4-30** 14f+: 0-0
Track : **LH: 5-30** RH: 1-10 **Tight: 3-23** Gall: 0-2
Aids: Bl: 0-2 Vi: 0-1 Tstrap: 0-0
Best Rating: 66 6/01 Pont 1m2f6y firm

Perchino

(80)

4-y-o b g Wolfhound (USA)-Last Request (Dancer's Image (USA))

Miss J Feilden Mrs M Slater

Placings:0-50 **(2584)**

2001: 12^{5}SW, 12^{0}SD

	Starts	1st	2nd	3rd	Win & Pl
Career Total (Turf)	0	0	0	0	
Career Total (AW)	3	0	0	0	0

Going (Turf): **Sf: 0-0 GS: 0-0 Gd: 0-0 GF: 0-0 Fm: 0-0**
Distance: 5f/6f: 0-0 7f-8f: 0-1 9f-13f: 0-2 14f+: 0-0
Track : LH: 0-3 RH: 0-0 Tight: 0-1 Gall: 0-0
Aids: Bl: 0-0 Vi: 0-0 Tstrap: 0-0

Perestroika (IRE)

103(81) (36)**76+**

3-y-o ch c Ashkalani (IRE)-Licentious (Reprimand)

E A L Dunlop Stars And Stripes Ii

Placings:0-404110 **(3035)**

2001: 10^{4}GS, 9^{0}SD, 11^{4}GF, 14^{1}G, 14^{1}GF, 15^{0}GF

	Starts	1st	2nd	3rd	Win & Pl
Career Total (Turf)	6	2	0	0	7490
Career Total (AW)	1	0	0	0	

76	7/01	Yarm	1m6f17y	E(0-75)H	G-F	£3688
73	6/01	Yarm	1m6f17y	E(0-75)H	GD	£3220

Total win prize-money £6909

Going (Turf): Sf: 0-0 GS: 0-1 **Gd: 1-2 GF: 1-3** Fm: 0-0
Distance: 5f/6f: 0-0 7f-8f: 0-1 9f-13f: 0-3 **14f+: 2-3**
Track : **LH: 2-5** RH: 0-1 **Tight: 2-5** Gall: 0-0
Aids: Bl: 0-0 Vi: 0-0 Tstrap: 0-0
Best Rating: 76 7/01 Yarm 1m6f17y gd-fm

Lightly raced. Appreciated longer trip when scoring twice over 14 furlongs on the bounce at Yarmouth in the summer of 2001. Has a decent turn of foot. Acts on fast ground.

Perfacto

66 **21**

2-y-o b g Factual (USA)-Hala (Persian Bold)

J S Moore Steve Murrell

Placings:00 **(5342)**

2001: 6^{0}HY, 7^{0}GS

	Starts	1st	2nd	3rd	Win & Pl
Career Total (Turf)	2	0	0	0	

Going (Turf): **Sf: 0-1 GS: 0-1 Gd: 0-0 GF: 0-0 Fm: 0-0**
Distance: 5f/6f: 0-1 7f-8f: 0-1 9f-13f: 0-0 14f+: 0-0
Track : LH: 0-0 RH: 0-0 Tight: 0-0 Gall: 0-0
Aids: Bl: 0-0 Vi: 0-0 Tstrap: 0-0
Best Rating: 21 10/01 NmkR 7f gd-sft

Perfect Fun

96 **73+**

2-y-o b f Marju (IRE)-Most Charming (FR) (Darshaan)

B W Hills Maktoum Al Maktoum

Placings:1 **(2332)**

2001: 6^{1}GF

	Starts	1st	2nd	3rd	Win & Pl
Career Total (Turf)	1	1	0	0	4394

73	6/01	Ripn	6f	D	G-F	£4394

Total win prize-money £4394

Going (Turf): Sf: 0-0 GS: 0-0 Gd: 0-0 **GF: 1-1** Fm: 0-0
Distance: **5f/6f: 1-1** 7f-8f: 0-0 9f-13f: 0-0 14f+: 0-0

Track : LH: 0-0 RH: 0-0 Tight: 0-0 Gall: 0-0
Aids: Bl: 0-0 Vi: 0-0 Tstrap: 0-0
Best Rating: 73 6/01 Ripn 6f gd-fm

Dam was a smart miler in France, and her third dam is the Cheveley Park Stakes and 1000 Guineas winner Ma Biche. Won in the style of a very useful horse on her only start at Ripon over six furlongs in June on fast ground.

Perfect Peach

113 **93**

6-y-o b m Lycius (USA)-Perfect Timing (Comedy Star (USA))
C W Fairhurst Mrs Ann Morris

Placings:62115/4630/040000200100/000434620640 6-006006420000 **(5365)**
2001: 5^0GS, 5^0GF, 6^6GF, 6^0GF, 6^0F, 6^6G, 6^4G, 6^2GF, 5^0GF, 6^0GF, 5^0S, 6^0GS

	Starts	1st	2nd	3rd	Win & Pl
Career Total (Turf)	**48**	**3**	**4**	**2**	**32515**

68	9/99	Muss	7f30y	D(0-85)H	GD	£5197
78	8/97	Bevl	5f	D	G-S	£3925
78	8/97	Thsk	5f	D	G-F	£4029

Total win prize-money £13152

Going (Turf): Sf: 0-4 **GS: 1-4 Gd: 1-10 GF: 1-25** Fm: 0-5
Distance: **5f/6f: 2-33** 7f-8f: 1-15 9f-13f: 0-0 14f+: 0-0
Track : LH: 0-11 **RH: 1-3 Tight: 1-6** Gall: 0-2
Aids: Bl: 0-1 Vi: 0-0 Tstrap: 0-0
Best Rating: 93 9/01 Ayr 6f gd-fm

Effective at between five and seven furlongs, he appreciates fast ground and is generally held up. Has a tendency to miss the break and is an in-and-out performer.

Perfect Pirouette (JPN)

105 **75**

3-y-o b f Warning-Prancing Ballerina (USA) (Nijinsky (CAN))
M L W Bell Richard C Colton Jr

Placings:2-0350 **(5591)**
2001: 10^0GF, 10^3GF, 10^5HY, 9^0GS

	Starts	1st	2nd	3rd	Win & Pl
Career Total (Turf)	**5**	**0**	**1**	**1**	**1676**

Going (Turf): Sf: 0-2 GS: 0-1 Gd: 0-0 GF: 0-2 Fm: 0-0
Distance: 5f/6f: 0-0 7f-8f: 0-0 9f-13f: 0-5 14f+: 0-0
Track : LH: 0-2 RH: 0-1 Tight: 0-0 Gall: 0-1
Aids: Bl: 0-0 Vi: 0-0 Tstrap: 0-0
Best Rating: 75 7/01 Kemp 1m2f gd-fm

She is a lightly-raced maiden, but has shown ability and may well improve when tackling 12 furlongs. Still has plenty of scope.

Perfect Storm

100 **81**

2-y-o b c Vettori (IRE)-Gorgeous Dancer (IRE) (Nordico (USA))
M Blanshard The Newchange Syndicate

Placings:3413 **(3031)**
2001: 5^3F, 6^4GF, 6^1GF, 6^3GF

	Starts	1st	2nd	3rd	Win & Pl
Career Total (Turf)	**4**	**1**	**0**	**2**	**6248**

78	7/01	Kemp	6f	D	G-F	£4251

Total win prize-money £4251

Going (Turf): Sf: 0-0 GS: 0-0 Gd: 0-0 **GF: 1-3** Fm: 0-1
Distance: **5f/6f: 1-3** 7f-8f: 0-1 9f-13f: 0-0 14f+: 0-0
Track : LH: 0-0 RH: 0-0 Tight: 0-0 Gall: 0-0
Aids: Bl: 0-0 Vi: 0-0 Tstrap: 0-0
Best Rating: 81 7/01 Asct 6f gd-fm

Perfect Sunday (USA)

109 **118**

3-y-o b c Quest For Fame-Sunday Bazaar (USA) (Nureyev (USA))
B W Hills K Abdulla

Placings:323-116202 **(4591)**
2001: 12^1GS, 11^1G, 12^6GF, 12^2G, 12^0GF, 12^2G

	Starts	1st	2nd	3rd	Win & Pl
Career Total (Turf)	**9**	**2**	**3**	**2**	**114119**

109	5/01	Ling	1m3f106yA		GD	£34800
100	4/01	NmkR	1m4f	D	G-S	£4680

Total win prize-money £39480

Going (Turf): Sf: 0-0 **GS: 1-1 Gd: 1-4** GF: 0-4 Fm: 0-0
Distance: 5f/6f: 0-0 7f-8f: 0-3 **9f-13f: 2-6** 14f+: 0-0
Track : LH: 1-2 RH: 1-3 Tight: 1-3 Gall: 1-1
Aids: Bl: 0-0 Vi: 0-0 Tstrap: 0-0
Best Rating: 118 7/01 StCl 1m4f good

Group-class middle-distance colt, he got off the mark in good style at Newmarket in April and followed up with a clear-cut victory in the Lingfield Derby Trial before running sixth behind Galileo in the Derby. Runner-up in the Grand Prix de Saint-Cloud and a Kempton Group Three, he disappointed in the Gordon Stakes and may not want the ground any faster than good.

Perfect Venue (IRE)

96 **42**

8-y-o b g Danehill (USA)-Welsh Fantasy (Welsh Pageant)
A J Wilson (N J Henderson 19/7) Mrs Barrie Gallop

Placings:52/42113/4 **(3187)**
2001: 11^4GS

	Starts	1st	2nd	3rd	Win & Pl
Career Total (Turf)	**8**	**2**	**2**	**1**	**10791**

89	10/97	Tipp	1m1f		SH	£4795
86	10/97	Thur	1m4f110y		YLD	£2226

Total win prize-money £7021

Going (Turf): Sf: 0-0 GS: 0-1 Gd: 0-3 GF: 0-0 Fm: 0-0
Distance: 5f/6f: 0-0 7f-8f: 0-0 **9f-13f: 2-8** 14f+: 0-0
Track : LH: 1-2 RH: 1-6 Tight: 0-0 Gall: 0-0
Aids: Bl: 0-0 Vi: 0-0 Tstrap: 0-0
Best Rating: 42 7/01 Leic 1m3f183y gd-sft

Perfectly Honest

93 **54**

3-y-o b f Charnwood Forest (IRE)-Carina Clare (Slip Anchor)
B Smart The Winfield Partnership

Placings:0-0400 **(5461)**
2001: 8^0GF, 9^4GF, 9^0GF, 8^0G

	Starts	1st	2nd	3rd	Win & Pl
Career Total (Turf)	**5**	**0**	**0**	**0**	**326**

Going (Turf): Sf: 0-1 GS: 0-0 Gd: 0-1 GF: 0-3 Fm: 0-0
Distance: 5f/6f: 0-0 7f-8f: 0-2 9f-13f: 0-3 14f+: 0-0
Track : LH: 0-1 RH: 0-3 Tight: 0-3 Gall: 0-0
Aids: Bl: 0-0 Vi: 0-0 Tstrap: 0-0
Best Rating: 54 6/01 Gdwd 1m1f gd-fm

Perfidious (USA)

103(103) (76+)**72d**

3-y-o b c Lear Fan (USA)-Perfolia (USA) (Nodouble (USA))
Sir Mark Prescott Eclipse Thoroughbreds - Osborne House Ii

Placings:006115-624550 **(4799)**
2001: 9^6SW, 10^2SW, 10^4GF, 10^5G, 11^5G, 10^0G

	Starts	1st	2nd	3rd	Win & Pl
Career Total (Turf)	**6**	**0**	**0**	**0**	**298**
Career Total (AW)	**6**	**2**	**1**	**0**	**6134**

76	12/00	Wolv	1m100y	E(0-85)	STD	£2688
58	12/00	Sthl	7f	E(0-75)	STD	£2198

Total win prize-money £4886

Going (Turf): Sf: 0-2 GS: 0-0 Gd: 0-3 GF: 0-1 Fm: 0-0
Distance: 5f/6f: 0-2 7f-8f: 1-3 9f-13f: 1-7 14f+: 0-0
Track : **LH: 2-10** RH: 0-0 **Tight: 1-6** Gall: 0-0
Aids: Bl: 0-0 Vi: 0-0 Tstrap: 0-0
Best Rating: 75 2/01 Ling 1m2f slow

Scored back-to-back victories on All-Weather at two over seven furlongs and a mile in the winter of 2000. Not quite so effective on turf. Tends to break slowly. Stays ten furlongs.

Perigeux (IRE)

97(107) (74)**44**

5-y-o b g Perugino (USA)-Rock On (IRE) (Ballad Rock)
Andrew Reid (K T Ivory 2/4) A S Reid

Placings:2511100/40632020200/55005100030040043 3-421020010050000 **(1544)**
2001: 5^4SD, 6^2SD, 5^1SD, 5^0SW, 5^2SW, 5^0SD, 5^0SW, 5^1SD, 5^0GS, 5^0HY, 5^5S, 5^0GS, 5^0GS, 5^0GF, 5^0GF

	Starts	1st	2nd	3rd	Win & Pl
Career Total (Turf)	**35**	**2**	**3**	**2**	**8081**
Career Total (AW)	**16**	**4**	**3**	**2**	**18865**

64	4/01	Ling	5f	F	STD	£2275
68	1/01	Ling	5f	E(0-75)H	STD	£2933
60	7/00	Brig	5f59y	F(0-60)H	SFT	£2383
86	7/98	Wolv	6f	B	STD	£6584
79	7/98	Ayr	6f	E H	GD	£2737
79	7/98	Sthl	6f	F	STD	£2532

Total win prize-money £19446

Going (Turf): **Sf: 1-10** GS: 0-6 **Gd: 1-9** GF: 0-9 Fm: 0-1
Distance: **5f/6f: 6-43** 7f-8f: 0-8 9f-13f: 0-0 14f+: 0-0
Track : **LH: 5-20** RH: 0-3 **Tight: 3-14** Gall: 0-4
Aids: **Bl: 3-24** Vi: 0-3 Tstrap: 0-0
Best Rating: 74 2/01 Ling 5f slow

Modest sprinter. Effective at five to six furlongs on the All-Weather and turf.

Perle D'Azur

103 **89**

2-y-o b f Mind Games-Pearls (Mon Tresor)
A Berry Chris & Antonia Deuters

Placings:20423112 **(3883)**
2001: 5^2GF, 5^0GF, 6^4GF, 7^2G, 7^3GF, 6^1GF, 6^1G, 6^2G

	Starts	1st	2nd	3rd	Win & Pl
Career Total (Turf)	**8**	**2**	**3**	**1**	**19376**

83	8/01	Gdwd	6f	C H	GD	£10920
71	7/01	Pont	6f	E	G-F	£4046

Total win prize-money £14966

Going (Turf): Sf: 0-0 GS: 0-0 **Gd: 1-3 GF: 1-5** Fm: 0-0
Distance: **5f/6f: 2-6** 7f-8f: 0-2 9f-13f: 0-0 14f+: 0-0
Track : **LH: 1-2** RH: 0-0 Tight: 0-0 Gall: 0-0
Aids: Bl: 0-0 Vi: 0-0 Tstrap: 0-0
Best Rating: 89 8/01 Wind 6f good

Very consistent, she got off the mark by narrowly beating a hotpot at Pontefract maiden auction event and showed that was no fluke by following up in a nursery at Glorious Goodwood. Suited by good/fast ground.

Perle De Sagesse

89(92) (43)**31**

4-y-o b f Namaqualand (USA)-Pearl Of Dubai (USA) (Red Ransom (USA))
Julian Poulton Russell Reed

Placings:330010521010/54530210000-6000000 **(4872)**
2001: 7^6SD, 7^0SD, 6^0G, 7^0GF, 6^0F, 6^0SW, 7^0G

	Starts	1st	2nd	3rd	Win & Pl
Career Total (Turf)	**16**	**2**	**0**	**3**	**6723**
Career Total (AW)	**14**	**2**	**2**	**0**	**5394**

57	6/00	Wind	6f	E(0-75)H	G-F	£3164
66	12/99	Ling	7f	F	STD	£2179
68	11/99	Ling	7f	G	STD	£1928
69	8/99	Wind	5f10y	F	GD	£2372

Total win prize-money £9645

Going (Turf): Sf: 0-3 GS: 0-0 **Gd: 1-6 GF: 1-4** Fm: 0-3
Distance: 5f/6f: 2-14 7f-8f: 2-16 9f-13f: 0-0 14f+: 0-0
Track : LH: 2-19 RH: 2-5 Tight: 2-13 Gall: 2-4
Aids: Bl: 0-0 Vi: 0-0 Tstrap: 0-0
Best Rating: 43 1/01 Ling 7f stand

Very moderate sprinter on turf and All-Weather.

Perlina (IRE)

80(73) (40)**61**
2-y-o ch f Woodborough (USA)-Kingdom Pearl (Statoblest)
B W Hills B W Hills

Placings:000 **(5163)**
2001: 5^{0}F, 6^{0}HY, 6^{0}SD

	Starts	1st	2nd	3rd	Win & Pl
Career Total (Turf)	2	0	0	0	
Career Total (AW)	1	0	0	0	

Going (Turf): Sf: 0-1 GS: 0-0 Gd: 0-0 GF: 0-0 Fm: 0-1
Distance: 5f/6f: 0-2 7f-8f: 0-1 9f-13f: 0-0 14f+: 0-0
Track : LH: 0-2 RH: 0-0 Tight: 0-1 Gall: 0-1
Aids: Bl: 0-0 Vi: 0-0 Tstrap: 0-0
Best Rating: 61 9/01 Bath 5f11y firm

Perpetuity

98 **70**
3-y-o ch g Timeless Times (USA)-Boadicea's Chariot (Commanche Run)
A Bailey Ray Bailey

Placings:304040 **(3309)**
2001: 6^{3}GS, 7^{0}G, 7^{4}GF, 7^{0}GF, 7^{4}S, 8^{0}GS

	Starts	1st	2nd	3rd	Win & Pl
Career Total (Turf)	6	0	0	1	1125

Going (Turf): Sf: 0-1 GS: 0-2 Gd: 0-1 GF: 0-2 Fm: 0-0
Distance: 5f/6f: 0-1 7f-8f: 0-5 9f-13f: 0-0 14f+: 0-0
Track : LH: 0-4 RH: 0-1 Tight: 0-0 Gall: 0-0
Aids: Bl: 0-1 Vi: 0-0 Tstrap: 0-0
Best Rating: 70 5/01 Pont 6f gd-sft

Still lightly raced, he looks as though he needs to be stepped up to middle distances in order to show his best.

Perpetuo

105 **71**
4-y-o b f Mtoto-Persian Fountain (IRE) (Persian Heights)
R A Fahey A N Barrett

Placings:3362100-0504144320 **(5661)**
2001: 12^{0}F, 12^{5}GF, 17^{0}GF, 13^{4}S, 11^{1}GF, 12^{4}G, 11^{4}GF, 12^{3}GF, 13^{2}GS, 16^{0}G

	Starts	1st	2nd	3rd	Win & Pl
Career Total (Turf)	17	2	2	3	15410

64	7/01	Bevl	1m3f216y	E(0-70)H	G-F	£4257
65	9/00	Bevl	1m3f216y	E(0-70)H	G-F	£3243

Total win prize-money £7502

Going (Turf): Sf: 0-3 GS: 0-2 Gd: 0-4 **GF: 2-7** Fm: 0-1
Distance: 5f/6f: 0-0 7f-8f: 0-0 **9f-13f: 2-12** 14f+: 0-5
Track : LH: 0-7 **RH: 2-10 Tight: 2-9** Gall: 0-3
Aids: Bl: 0-0 Vi: 0-0 Tstrap: 0-0
Best Rating: 71 10/01 York 1m5f194y gd-sft

She is not very big but is all heart. Has scored twice at Beverley over 12 furlongs on fast ground. Stays 14 furlongs, but is creeping up the handicap following a string of placed efforts.

Persian Bandit (IRE)

(83) (53)**72**
3-y-o b g Idris (IRE)-Ce Soir (Northern Baby (CAN))
M Quinn G Pinchen & R M Ellis

Placings:64322554-50 **(0075)**
2001: 8^{5}SD, 9^{0}SW

	Starts	1st	2nd	3rd	Win & Pl
Career Total (Turf)	7	0	2	1	2880
Career Total (AW)	3	0	0	0	0

Going (Turf): Sf: 0-1 GS: 0-0 Gd: 0-0 GF: 0-2 Fm: 0-1
Distance: 5f/6f: 0-6 7f-8f: 0-3 9f-13f: 0-1 14f+: 0-0
Track : LH: 0-3 RH: 0-3 Tight: 0-3 Gall: 0-0
Aids: Bl: 0-1 Vi: 0-0 Tstrap: 0-0
Best Rating: 24 1/01 Ling 1m stand

Persian Dollar (IRE)

69(81) (49)**35**
2-y-o b g Persian Bold-Dollar Magic (Fairy King (USA))
E J O'Neill M Donovan

Placings:000 **(4069)**
2001: 7^{0}GF, 6^{0}GS, 6^{0}SD

	Starts	1st	2nd	3rd	Win & Pl
Career Total (Turf)	2	0	0	0	
Career Total (AW)	1	0	0	0	

Going (Turf): Sf: 0-0 GS: 0-1 Gd: 0-0 GF: 0-1 Fm: 0-0
Distance: 5f/6f: 0-2 7f-8f: 0-1 9f-13f: 0-0 14f+: 0-0
Track : LH: 0-1 RH: 0-0 Tight: 0-1 Gall: 0-0
Aids: Bl: 0-0 Vi: 0-0 Tstrap: 0-2
Best Rating: 49 8/01 Wolv 6f stand

Persian Fact

(84) (63)
2-y-o b g Greensmith-Forest Song (Forzando)
K R Burke Mrs Elaine M Burke

Placings:50 **(5614)**
2001: 6^{5}SD, 6^{0}SD

	Starts	1st	2nd	3rd	Win & Pl
Career Total (Turf)	0	0	0	0	
Career Total (AW)	2	0	0	0	

Going (Turf): Sf: 0-0 GS: 0-0 Gd: 0-0 GF: 0-0 Fm: 0-0
Distance: 5f/6f: 0-2 7f-8f: 0-0 9f-13f: 0-0 14f+: 0-0
Track : LH: 0-2 RH: 0-0 Tight: 0-2 Gall: 0-0
Aids: Bl: 0-0 Vi: 0-0 Tstrap: 0-0
Best Rating: 63 10/01 Wolv 6f stand

Persian Fayre

104(74) (46)**57**
9-y-o b g Persian Heights-Dominion Fayre (Dominion)
A Berry Murray Grubb

Placings:3416454P/4105320650/62220314011/000240 22006/004155200030/01112000000/010002000-4021002500 **(5681)**
2001: 7^{4}GF, 7^{0}GF, 8^{2}GF, 8^{1}GF, 9^{0}GS, 7^{0}G, 9^{2}G, 8^{5}GF, 9^{0}G, 8^{0}S

	Starts	1st	2nd	3rd	Win & Pl
Career Total (Turf)	80	11	12	4	76901
Career Total (AW)	3	0	0	0	

62	6/01	Ayr	1m	G(0-60)H	G-F	£2233
65	6/00	Ayr	7f	D(0-80)H	G-F	£4485
80	5/99	Ayr	7f	D(0-80)H	GD	£4565
57	5/99	Carl	6f206y	F	FRM	£2458
66	4/99	Rdcr	7f	F	G-S	£2721
86	6/98	Hayd	7f30y	D(0-85)	GD	£6905
83	11/96	NmkR	7f	D(0-80)H	GD	£4788
78	10/96	York	6f214y	D(0-85)H	GD	£11034
77	8/96	Newc	7f	C(0-90)H	GD	£7100
73	5/95	Ayr	1m	F(0-65)	G-F	£2801
61	5/94	Ayr	5f	D	G-F	£3379

Total win prize-money £52470

Going (Turf): Sf: 0-12 GS: 1-7 **Gd: 5-28** GF: 4-26 Fm: 1-7
Distance: 5f/6f: 1-10 **7f-8f: 10-61** 9f-13f: 0-0 14f+: 0-0
Track : **LH: 6-37** RH: 1-16 Tight: 0-22 **Gall: 1-5**
Aids: Bl: 0-0 Vi: 0-0 Tstrap: 0-0
Best Rating: 62 6/01 Ayr 1m gd-fm

A veteran handicapper and a genuine front-runner, seven furlongs is his optimum trip but he stays a mile. Handles any ground. Likes Ayr.

Persian Flight

55 **62**
3-y-o ch f Catrail (USA)-Persian Victory (IRE) (Persian Bold)
Miss E C Lavelle Sir Gordon Brunton

Placings:0 **(4380)**
2001: 8^{0}GF

	Starts	1st	2nd	3rd	Win & Pl
Career Total (Turf)	1	0	0	0	

Going (Turf): Sf: 0-0 GS: 0-0 Gd: 0-0 GF: 0-1 Fm: 0-0
Distance: 5f/6f: 0-0 7f-8f: 0-1 9f-13f: 0-0 14f+: 0-0
Track : LH: 0-0 RH: 0-0 Tight: 0-0 Gall: 0-0
Aids: Bl: 0-0 Vi: 0-0 Tstrap: 0-0
Best Rating: 62 6/01 Ayr 1m gd-fm

Persian King (IRE)

89(88) (30)**81**
4-y-o ch g Persian Bold-Queen's Share (Main Reef)
J A B Old W E Sturt

Placings:05/06020016-00 **(0953)**
2001: 11^{0}SD, 12^{0}S

	Starts	1st	2nd	3rd	Win & Pl
Career Total (Turf)	11	1	1	0	13550
Career Total (AW)	1	0	0	0	

81	8/00	Cork	1m2f	(0-90)H	GD	£9750

Total win prize-money £9750

Going (Turf): Sf: 0-3 GS: 0-0 **Gd: 1-4** GF: 0-1 Fm: 0-0
Distance: 5f/6f: 0-1 7f-8f: 0-2 **9f-13f: 1-7** 14f+: 0-1
Track : LH: 0-6 **RH: 1-3** Tight: 0-1 Gall: 0-1
Aids: Bl: 0-0 Vi: 0-0 Tstrap: 0-1
Best Rating: 70 4/01 Epsm 1m4f10y soft

Persian Lightning (IRE)

93 **71**
2-y-o b c Sri Pekan (USA)-Persian Fantasy (Persian Bold)
J L Dunlop Windflower Overseas Holdings Inc

Placings:35650 **(5690)**
2001: 6^{3}GF, 7^{5}G, 8^{6}GS, 7^{5}GF, 7^{0}S

	Starts	1st	2nd	3rd	Win & Pl
Career Total (Turf)	5	0	0	1	740

Going (Turf): Sf: 0-1 GS: 0-1 Gd: 0-1 GF: 0-2 Fm: 0-0
Distance: 5f/6f: 0-1 7f-8f: 0-4 9f-13f: 0-0 14f+: 0-0
Track : LH: 0-1 RH: 0-0 Tight: 0-1 Gall: 0-0
Aids: Bl: 0-0 Vi: 0-0 Tstrap: 0-0
Best Rating: 71 8/01 Ling 7f gd-fm

A half-brother to stayer Height of Fantasy, he is likely to do better over further next year.

Persian Pearl

99 **70**
2-y-o b f Hurricane Sky (AUS)-Persian Fountain (IRE) (Persian Heights)
B A McMahon J D Graham

Placings:021 **(4325)**
2001: 6^{0}GS, 6^{2}G, 5^{1}GF

	Starts	1st	2nd	3rd	Win & Pl
Career Total (Turf)	3	1	1	0	4579

70 8/01 Ripn 5f F G-F £3444

Total win prize-money £3444

Going (Turf): Sf: 0-0 GS: 0-1 Gd: 0-1 **GF: 1-1** Fm: 0-0
Distance: **5f/6f: 1-2** 7f-8f: 0-1 9f-13f: 0-0 14f+: 0-0
Track : LH: 0-0 RH: 0-0 Tight: 0-0 Gall: 0-0
Aids: Bl: 0-0 Vi: 0-0 Tstrap: 0-0
Best Rating: 70 8/01 Ripn 5f gd-fm

Scored on her third start over the minimum trip at Ripon in August. Acts on fast ground.

Persian Pride (IRE)

109 **91**

3-y-o ch c Barathea (IRE)-Glenarff (USA) (Irish River (FR))
P W Harris Dr Jamal Ahmadzadeh

Placings:0420-100000 **(5669)**
2001: 10^{1}S, 12^{0}GF, 11^{0}G, 10^{0}G, 12^{0}GS, 10^{0}HY

	Starts	1st	2nd	3rd	Win & Pl
Career Total (Turf)	10	1	1	0	5894

76 7/01 Hayd 1m2f120yD SFT £4290

Total win prize-money £4290

Going (Turf): **Sf: 1-2** GS: 0-2 Gd: 0-3 GF: 0-3 Fm: 0-0
Distance: 5f/6f: 0-0 7f-8f: 0-4 **9f-13f: 1-6** 14f+: 0-0
Track : **LH: 1-2** RH: 0-3 Tight: 0-2 Gall: 0-3
Aids: Bl: 0-0 Vi: 0-0 Tstrap: 0-0
Best Rating: 91 8/01 Gdwd 1m4f gd-fm

Bolted up in a soft-ground Haydock maiden on his belated reappearance but disappointed later in the season. Suited by ten furlongs and cut in the ground, yet to prove he stays further.

Persian Punch (IRE)

112 **121**

8-y-o ch g Persian Heights-Rum Cay (USA) (Our Native (USA))
D R C Elsworth J C Smith

Placings:113133/011055223/131613/405401/20165132 1-4321143 **(5735a)**
2001: 16^{4}G, 16^{3}G, 20^{2}GF, 16^{1}G, 15^{1}G, 14^{4}GF, 16^{3}GS

	Starts	1st	2nd	3rd	Win & Pl
Career Total (Turf)	43	14	5	9	701153

121	8/01	York	1m7f195yA		GD	£58000
121	8/01	Gdwd	2m	A	GD	£52200
122	10/00	NmkR	2m	A	G-S	£29000
111	8/00	Deau	1m7f		G-S	£28818
114	5/00	Sand	2m78y	A	HVY	£24000
99	11/99	Donc	1m6f132yC		SFT	£6482
115	8/98	York	1m7f195yA		G-F	£32225
119	5/98	Sand	2m78y	A	GD	£25720
120	5/98	NmkR	2m45y	A	G-S	£19360
115	5/97	Sand	2m78y	A	G-F	£25240
116	5/97	Newb	1m5f61y	A	SFT	£11990
106	7/96	NmkJ	1m6f175yA		G-F	£10577
90	6/96	Sals	1m6f	C	GD	£4901
79	5/96	Wind	1m2f7y	E	G-F	£3095

Total win prize-money £331609

Going (Turf): Sf: 3-4 GS: 3-5 **Gd: 4-17 GF: 4-15** Fm: 0-1
Distance: 5f/6f: 0-0 7f-8f: 0-0 9f-13f: 1-4 **14f+: 13-39**
Track : LH: 4-12 **RH: 9-30** Tight: 3-6 **Gall: 7-24**
Aids: Bl: 0-0 Vi: 0-0 Tstrap: 0-0
Best Rating: 121 8/01 York 1m7f195y good

A huge individual who is a tough and genuine front-running stayer, he became the first horse to win Sandown's Group Three Henry II Stakes three times and was third in that race this year. Goes well for Richard Hughes, but Richard Quinn gave him a blinding ride when just touched off in the Ascot Gold Cup in 2001, a race in which he had looked a non-stayer in previous seasons. Best with cut in the ground nowadays, he is a tough nut to crack, and showed as much when gaining compensation for his Ascot defeat in the Goodwood Cup and Lonsdale Stakes. Ran a terrific race to be third in the Melbourne Cup for the second time in November.

Persian Spirit

87 **36**

3-y-o b f Persian Bold-Big Story (Cadeaux Genereux)
R Hannon R Gander

Placings:060-060 **(4609)**
2001: 9^{0}G, 6^{6}GF, 8^{0}F

	Starts	1st	2nd	3rd	Win & Pl
Career Total (Turf)	6	0	0	0	0

Going (Turf): Sf: 0-0 GS: 0-0 Gd: 0-2 GF: 0-3 Fm: 0-1
Distance: 5f/6f: 0-0 7f-8f: 0-4 9f-13f: 0-2 14f+: 0-0
Track : LH: 0-4 RH: 0-1 Tight: 0-3 Gall: 0-1
Aids: Bl: 0-0 Vi: 0-0 Tstrap: 0-0
Best Rating: 36 8/01 Folk 1m1f149y good

Persian Waters (IRE)

102 **74**

5-y-o b g Persian Bold-Emerald Waters (King's Lake (USA))
J R Fanshawe Paul & Jenny Green

Placings:40041/0300/12-13 **(2305)**
2001: 16^{1}GF, 20^{3}GF

	Starts	1st	2nd	3rd	Win & Pl
Career Total (Turf)	13	3	1	2	17560

73	5/01	Ripn	2m	E(0-75)H	G-F	£4582
68	9/00	Nott	2m9y	F(0-65)H	SFT	£2709
68	10/98	Pont	1m4y	E(0-75)H	SFT	£3692

Total win prize-money £10985

Going (Turf): **Sf: 2-5** GS: 0-0 Gd: 0-1 GF: 1-6 Fm: 0-1
Distance: 5f/6f: 0-0 7f-8f: 0-3 9f-13f: 1-4 **14f+: 2-6**
Track : **LH: 2-6** RH: 1-5 **Tight: 1-4** Gall: 0-3
Aids: Bl: 0-0 Vi: 0-0 Tstrap: 0-0
Best Rating: 74 6/01 Asct 2m4f gd-fm

A winner on soft ground at Pontefract at two, he has had a few trainers in his time and has been hurdling, but showed he still has what it takes on the level when winning at Nottingham in September.

Persiano

110 **102**

6-y-o ch g Efisio-Persiandale (Persian Bold)
J R Fanshawe Miss A Church

Placings:5044/4111/03053050/03132510-U02601330 **(5142)**
2001: 7^{U}S, 8^{0}GS, 8^{2}GF, 8^{6}G, 8^{0}G, 8^{1}G, 7^{3}GF, 7^{3}GF, 9^{0}G

	Starts	1st	2nd	3rd	Win & Pl
Career Total (Turf)	33	6	2	6	150266

102	8/01	Asct	1m	B(0-100)H	GD	£22550
102	8/00	Gdwd	1m	B H	GD	£65000
92	5/00	Gdwd	1m	C(0-100)H	GD	£10920
99	5/98	Donc	7f	C(0-100)H	G-F	£8616
89	5/98	Sals	6f212y	D(0-80)H	FRM	£4000
83	5/98	Wwck	7f	D(0-80)H	GD	£4207

Total win prize-money £115294

Going (Turf): Sf: 0-3 GS: 0-7 **Gd: 4-13** GF: 1-9 Fm: 1-1
Distance: 5f/6f: 0-3 **7f-8f: 6-27** 9f-13f: 0-3 14f+: 0-0
Track : LH: 1-4 **RH: 3-8** Tight: 0-1 **Gall: 1-4**
Aids: Bl: 0-0 Vi: 0-1 Tstrap: 0-0
Best Rating: 102 8/01 Asct 1m good

A useful handicapper when everything slots into pace as he showed by winning two valuable handicaps over a mile at Goodwood in 2000. Regained winning form at Ascot on Shergar Cup day despite looking high in the handicap and has been well held since. Probably best over a mile on a sound surface, he is game and genuine.

Perspicacious

73(70) (27)**32**

2-y-o b f Prince Daniel (USA)-Perspicacity (Petorius)
G M Moore Racing Reds Partnership

Placings:000 **(5049)**
2001: 7^{0}GF, 7^{0}G, 7^{0}SD

	Starts	1st	2nd	3rd	Win & Pl
Career Total (Turf)	2	0	0	0	
Career Total (AW)	1	0	0	0	

Going (Turf): Sf: 0-0 GS: 0-0 Gd: 0-1 GF: 0-1 Fm: 0-0
Distance: 5f/6f: 0-0 7f-8f: 0-3 9f-13f: 0-0 14f+: 0-0
Track : LH: 0-1 RH: 0-1 Tight: 0-0 Gall: 0-0
Aids: Bl: 0-0 Vi: 0-0 Tstrap: 0-0
Best Rating: 32 8/01 Rdcr 7f good

Persuade

103(104) (78)**81**

3-y-o ch c Lure (USA)-Shapely (USA) (Alleged (USA))
M Quinn Littleton Manor Racing

Placings:446-4213535302005304206 4 **(3371)**
2001: 10^{4}SD, 9^{2}SD, 10^{1}SW, 8^{3}SD, 10^{5}SW, 9^{3}SD, 10^{5}SD, 8^{3}S, 8^{0}GS, 7^{2}GF, 9^{0}GF, 8^{0}GF, 8^{5}F, 6^{3}GF, 7^{0}G, 6^{4}GF, 7^{2}GF, 6^{0}GS, 7^{6}GF, 7^{4}F

	Starts	1st	2nd	3rd	Win & Pl
Career Total (Turf)	16	0	2	2	11508
Career Total (AW)	7	1	1	2	7668

78 2/01 Ling 1m2f D(0-85)H SLW £4056

Total win prize-money £4056

Going (Turf): Sf: 0-1 GS: 0-2 Gd: 0-3 GF: 0-8 Fm: 0-2
Distance: 5f/6f: 0-3 7f-8f: 0-10 **9f-13f: 1-10** 14f+: 0-0
Track : **LH: 1-13** RH: 0-4 **Tight: 1-11** Gall: 0-0
Aids: Bl: 0-0 Vi: 0-0 Tstrap: 0-2
Best Rating: 87 3/01 Donc 1m soft

Joined Mick Quinn early in 2001 and soon won on the Lingfield Equitrack. He has since run consistently on turf and sand over a variety of trips without managing to get his head in front.

Pertemps Boycott (IRE)

93 **19**

3-y-o b g Indian Ridge-Coupe D'Hebe (Ile De Bourbon (USA))
H Alexander (N Tinkler 12/9) Alastair Baillie

Placings:000-000 **(4108)**
2001: 7^{0}G, 6^{0}F, 8^{0}S

	Starts	1st	2nd	3rd	Win & Pl
Career Total (Turf)	6	0	0	0	

Going (Turf): Sf: 0-3 GS: 0-0 Gd: 0-1 GF: 0-1 Fm: 0-1
Distance: 5f/6f: 0-3 7f-8f: 0-2 9f-13f: 0-1 14f+: 0-0
Track : LH: 0-2 RH: 0-1 Tight: 0-1 Gall: 0-0
Aids: Bl: 0-0 Vi: 0-0 Tstrap: 0-0
Best Rating: 19 8/01 Thsk 6f firm

Pertemps Fc

104(97) (42)**52**

4-y-o b g Prince Sabo-Top Mouse (High Top)
T D Easterby The Pertemps Professionals

Placings:4U012160/0000000-30030402102000560 **(5451)**
2001: 5^{3}SD, 6^{0}SD, 5^{0}GF, 5^{3}F, 5^{0}GF, 5^{4}GF, 5^{0}F, 5^{2}GS, 5^{1}GF, 5^{0}GF, 5^{2}G, 6^{0}G, 5^{0}GF, 5^{0}GF, 5^{5}S, 5^{6}GS, 5^{0}HY

	Starts	1st	2nd	3rd	Win & Pl
Career Total (Turf)	30	3	3	1	15361
Career Total (AW)	3	0	0	1	243

49	7/01	Muss	5f	F(0-60)H	G-F	£2674
67	8/99	Bevl	5f	C H	GD	£7165
62	7/99	Newc	6f	G	G-F	£1903

Total win prize-money £11742

Going (Turf): Sf: 0-3 GS: 0-5 Gd: 1-9 **GF: 2-10** Fm: 0-3

Distance: 5f/6f: 3-30 7f-8f: 0-3 9f-13f: 0-0 14f+: 0-0
Track : LH: 0-6 RH: 0-0 Tight: 0-5 Gall: 0-0
Aids: Bl: 0-1 Vi: 0-0 Tstrap: 0-4
Best Rating: 52 8/01 Pont 5f good

He is not very consistent, but can win modest events over the minimum trip and did so at Musselburgh in July. Suited by good/fast ground.

Pertemps Gill

98(81) (28)37

3-y-o b f Silca Blanka (IRE)-Royal Celerity (USA) (Riverman (USA))
A D Smith Pertemps Group Limited

Placings:0030540-03405005 (3700)
2001: 5⁰G, 5³F, 6⁴GF, 6⁰GF, 6⁵GF, 6⁰GF, 7⁰G, 5⁵GF

	Starts	1st	2nd	3rd	Win & Pl
Career Total (Turf)	13	0	0	1	322
Career Total (AW)	2	0	0	1	264

Going (Turf): Sf: 0-1 GS: 0-1 Gd: 0-3 GF: 0-6 Fm: 0-2
Distance: 5f/6f: 0-11 7f-8f: 0-4 9f-13f: 0-0 14f+: 0-0
Track : LH: 0-7 RH: 0-1 Tight: 0-2 Gall: 0-2
Aids: Bl: 0-0 Vi: 0-0 Tstrap: 0-0
Best Rating: 39 6/01 Wwck 6f21y gd-fm

Pertemps Jack

47(66) 11

3-y-o br g Silca Blanka (IRE)-Stella Royale (Astronef)
A D Smith Pertemps Group Limited

Placings:6630-00 (2726)
2001: 9⁰GF, 8⁰GF

	Starts	1st	2nd	3rd	Win & Pl
Career Total (Turf)	4	0	0	1	315
Career Total (AW)	2	0	0	0	0

Going (Turf): Sf: 0-0 GS: 0-0 Gd: 0-0 GF: 0-2 Fm: 0-2
Distance: 5f/6f: 0-2 7f-8f: 0-2 9f-13f: 0-2 14f+: 0-0
Track : LH: 0-4 RH: 0-1 Tight: 0-1 Gall: 0-0
Aids: Bl: 0-0 Vi: 0-0 Tstrap: 0-0
Best Rating: 39 6/01 Wwck 6f21y gd-fm

Pertemps Jardine (IRE)

99(89) (39)39

3-y-o b/br g General Monash (USA)-Indescent Blue (Bluebird (USA))
R A Fahey Pertemps Network Owners Syndicate

Placings:3450-000000000 (5288)
2001: 6⁰SD, 6⁰SD, 5⁰SD, 6⁰SD, 7⁰GS, 8⁰G, 5⁰G, 6⁰G, 6⁰HY

	Starts	1st	2nd	3rd	Win & Pl
Career Total (Turf)	9	0	0	1	764
Career Total (AW)	4	0	0	0	

Going (Turf): Sf: 0-1 GS: 0-3 Gd: 0-3 GF: 0-2 Fm: 0-0
Distance: 5f/6f: 0-11 7f-8f: 0-1 9f-13f: 0-1 14f+: 0-0
Track : LH: 0-6 RH: 0-0 Tight: 0-1 Gall: 0-0
Aids: Bl: 0-1 Vi: 0-1 Tstrap: 0-0
Best Rating: 50 7/01 Ayr 7f gd-sft

Pertemps Mission

65

7-y-o b g Safawan-Heresheis (Free State)
Mrs Lydia Pearce Michael C Whatley

Placings:060/000/0040301002612/23562/000 (2250)
2001: 16⁰SD, 16⁰G, 16⁰GF

	Starts	1st	2nd	3rd	Win & Pl
Career Total (Turf)	18	1	1	1	4736
Career Total (AW)	9	1	3	1	3591

49	12/98	Wolv	1m6f166yF(0-65)H	SLW	£1871
38	8/98	Catt	1m7f177yE(0-70)H	G-F	£2994

Total win prize-money £4866

Going (Turf): Sf: 0-2 GS: 0-3 Gd: 0-5 GF: 1-8 Fm: 0-0
Distance: 5f/6f: 0-0 7f-8f: 0-2 9f-13f: 0-3 14f+: 2-22
Track : LH: 2-17 RH: 0-9 Tight: 2-15 Gall: 0-3
Aids: Bl: 0-1 Vi: 2-15 Tstrap: 0-0
Best Rating: 38 8/98 Catt 1m7f177y GF

Pertemps Thatcher

94 60

3-y-o b f Petong-Nadema (Artaius (USA))
Michael Hourigan (S C Williams 30/5) Conor Clarkson

Placings:402-0004 (5714a)
2001: 7⁰S, 6⁰S, 6⁰GF, 8⁴S

	Starts	1st	2nd	3rd	Win & Pl
Career Total (Turf)	7	0	1	0	1277

Going (Turf): Sf: 0-3 GS: 0-1 Gd: 0-1 GF: 0-2 Fm: 0-0
Distance: 5f/6f: 0-3 7f-8f: 0-4 9f-13f: 0-0 14f+: 0-0
Track : LH: 0-0 RH: 0-1 Tight: 0-0 Gall: 0-0
Aids: Bl: 0-0 Vi: 0-0 Tstrap: 0-0
Best Rating: 59 11/01 Thur 1m soft

Peruvian Chief (IRE)

105(102) (90)87

4-y-o b g Foxhound (USA)-John's Ballad (IRE) (Ballad Rock)
N P Littmoden M C S D Racing Ltd

Placings:002113/052043360003-5603305003342000200 (5630)
2001: 5⁵SD, 6⁶SW, 7⁰S, 6³G, 6³GF, 6⁰GF, 6⁵GF, 6⁰GF, 6⁰F, 5³GF, 5³GS, 5⁴GF, 6²G, 6⁰G, 6⁰G, 5⁰HY, 6²G, 5⁰GS, 6⁰G

	Starts	1st	2nd	3rd	Win & Pl
Career Total (Turf)	30	0	3	6	29084
Career Total (AW)	7	2	1	2	7410

87	11/99	Ling	7f	E(0-85)H	STD	£2703
80	10/99	Wolv	6f	F	STD	£2511

Total win prize-money £5215

Going (Turf): Sf: 0-4 GS: 0-4 Gd: 0-8 GF: 0-11 Fm: 0-2
Distance: 5f/6f: 1-31 7f-8f: 1-6 9f-13f: 0-0 14f+: 0-0
Track : LH: 2-7 RH: 0-0 Tight: 2-6 Gall: 0-0
Aids: Bl: 0-2 Vi: 0-10 Tstrap: 0-0
Best Rating: 90 5/01 Thsk 6f gd-fm

He performed with credit this season and ran very well to finish runner-up at Newmarket in October, but is on a lengthy losing run. Effective at five to seven furlongs. Has run in blinkers or a visor for most of this term. Acts on sand and needs a sound surface on turf.

Peruvian Jade

98(94) (60)77

4-y-o gr f Petong-Rion River (IRE) (Taufan (USA))
N P Littmoden M C S D Racing Ltd

Placings:634211044/640-00 (0231)
2001: 6⁰SD, 6⁰SD

	Starts	1st	2nd	3rd	Win & Pl
Career Total (Turf)	8	2	0	0	13105
Career Total (AW)	6	0	1	1	7474

74	9/99	Leic	5f218y	E(0-75)H	GD	£3350
74	9/99	Gdwd	6f	D(0-85)H	G-F	£4182

Total win prize-money £7532

Going (Turf): Sf: 0-2 GS: 0-2 Gd: 1-3 GF: 1-1 Fm: 0-0
Distance: 5f/6f: 2-13 7f-8f: 0-1 9f-13f: 0-0 14f+: 0-0
Track : LH: 0-7 RH: 0-1 Tight: 0-5 Gall: 0-1
Aids: Bl: 0-0 Vi: 0-0 Tstrap: 0-0
Best Rating: 37 1/01 Sthl 6f stand

She had shown ability on Fibresand, but struck form on turf with wins at Goodwood and Leicester in September. She seemed to find the drop to the minimum trip against her at Newmarket.

Peruvian Wave (USA)

(98)101 (55+)50

3-y-o b/br g Alydeed (CAN)-Polish Devil (USA) (Devil's Bag (USA))
Mrs J R Ramsden Mrs J R Ramsden

Placings:00563005 (5349)
2001: 8⁰S, 9⁰GS, 8⁵HY, 7⁶GF, 6³G, 6⁰F, 5⁰HY, 5⁵SD

	Starts	1st	2nd	3rd	Win & Pl
Career Total (Turf)	7	0	0	1	470
Career Total (AW)	1	0	0	0	0

Going (Turf): Sf: 0-3 GS: 0-1 Gd: 0-1 GF: 0-1 Fm: 0-1
Distance: 5f/6f: 0-4 7f-8f: 0-2 9f-13f: 0-2 14f+: 0-0
Track : LH: 0-1 RH: 0-0 Tight: 0-0 Gall: 0-0
Aids: Bl: 0-0 Vi: 0-0 Tstrap: 0-0
Best Rating: 55 10/01 Sthl 5f stand

Who cost 50,000 gns as a two-year-old, has speed on his dam's side. He ran his best race when dropped to six furlongs at Ayr.

Perzian Cloud

67 9

3-y-o b c Ezzoud (IRE)-Persian Smoke (Persian Bold)
John Berry Jamie Donovan

Placings:0 (0774)
2001: 5⁰S

	Starts	1st	2nd	3rd	Win & Pl
Career Total (Turf)	1	0	0	0	

Going (Turf): Sf: 0-1 GS: 0-0 Gd: 0-0 GF: 0-0 Fm: 0-0
Distance: 5f/6f: 0-1 7f-8f: 0-0 9f-13f: 0-0 14f+: 0-0
Track : LH: 0-0 RH: 0-0 Tight: 0-0 Gall: 0-0
Aids: Bl: 0-0 Vi: 0-0 Tstrap: 0-0
Best Rating: 9 4/01 Nott 5f13y soft

Pet Express Flyer (IRE)

5-y-o b g Mukaddamah (USA)-Take The Option (USA) (Bold Bidder)
P C Haslam Middleham Park Racing Iii

Placings:3121310030/00/P (0005)
2001: 8ᴾSD

	Starts	1st	2nd	3rd	Win & Pl
Career Total (Turf)	12	3	1	3	11234
Career Total (AW)	1	0	0	0	

92	7/98	Ayr	7f	D H	GD	£3454
72	6/98	Muss	7f30y	E	G-F	£2737
78	6/98	Haml	6f5y	F	GD	£2318

Total win prize-money £8510

Going (Turf): Sf: 0-2 GS: 0-2 Gd: 2-5 GF: 1-3 Fm: 0-0
Distance: 5f/6f: 0-2 7f-8f: 3-9 9f-13f: 0-2 14f+: 0-0
Track : LH: 1-8 RH: 1-1 Tight: 1-2 Gall: 0-2
Aids: Bl: 0-0 Vi: 0-0 Tstrap: 0-0
Best Rating: 78 6/98 Haml 6f5y G

Petalite

95(99) (59)54

3-y-o gr f Petong-Veuve Hoornaert (IRE) (Standaan (FR))
M A Jarvis T G Warner

Placings:60-402065 (4302)
2001: 6⁴HY, 7⁰GF, 5²SD, 5⁰F, 6⁶G, 6⁵GF

	Starts	1st	2nd	3rd	Win & Pl
Career Total (Turf)	7	0	0	0	0
Career Total (AW)	1	0	1	0	678

Going (Turf): Sf: 0-1 GS: 0-0 Gd: 0-2 GF: 0-3 Fm: 0-1
Distance: 5f/6f: 0-6 7f-8f: 0-2 9f-13f: 0-0 14f+: 0-0
Track : LH: 0-1 RH: 0-1 Tight: 0-1 Gall: 0-0
Aids: Bl: 0-0 Vi: 0-0 Tstrap: 0-0
Best Rating: 59 7/01 Sthl 5f stand

Petara (IRE)

87 **34**

6-y-o ch g Petardia-Romangoddess (IRE) (Rhoman Rule (USA))

J S Wainwright Wisma Partnership

Placings:640305301350/400554260500/000100/5000-00P **(2868)**

2001: 9^{0}F, 8^{0}GF, 10^{P}GF

	Starts	1st	2nd	3rd	Win & Pl
Career Total (Turf)	**37**	**2**	**1**	**3**	**8872**

40 9/99 Ling 1m2f G(0-60)H FRM £2232
65 9/97 Catt 7f E(0-75) G-F £3564
Total win prize-money £5797

Going (Turf): Sf: 0-5 GS: 0-3 Gd: 0-11 **GF: 1-14 Fm: 1-4**
Distance: 5f/6f: 0-4 7f-8f: 1-16 9f-13f: 1-17 14f+: 0-0
Track : **LH: 2-24** RH: 0-7 **Tight: 2-12** Gall: 0-9
Aids: Bl: 0-1 **Vi: 2-25** Tstrap: 0-0
Best Rating: 34 5/01 Leic 1m1f218y firm

Petarga

101 **81**

6-y-o b m Petong-One Half Silver (CAN) (Plugged Nickle (USA))

J A R Toller Mrs R W Gore-Andrews

Placings:42100/30643/0300210300/0050110-04106400 **(4804)**

2001: 5^{0}G, 5^{4}GF, 5^{1}G, 5^{0}GF, 6^{6}GF, 6^{4}G, 5^{0}G, 6^{0}F

	Starts	1st	2nd	3rd	Win & Pl
Career Total (Turf)	**35**	**5**	**2**	**4**	**25925**

80 6/01 Bath 5f161y D(0-85)H GD £3815
76 9/00 Leic 5f2y D(0-80)H G-S £4147
78 9/00 Bath 5f161y D(0-80)H GD £4231
75 7/99 Folk 6f D(0-80)H G-F £3877
72 6/97 Bath 5f11y E G-F £2917
Total win prize-money £18991

Going (Turf): Sf: 0-1 GS: 1-1 **Gd: 2-13 GF: 2-18** Fm: 0-2
Distance: **5f/6f: 5-30** 7f-8f: 0-5 9f-13f: 0-0 14f+: 0-0
Track : **LH: 3-12** RH: 0-0 Tight: 0-0 **Gall: 3-11**
Aids: Bl: 0-0 Vi: 0-0 Tstrap: 0-0
Best Rating: 81 8/01 Ripn 6f good

A useful five-furlong handicapper with a good record at Bath, he returned to winning form at that track in June. Acts on anything except extremes of ground and comes with a strong late run.

Peter Perfect

(71) 84 (23d)

7-y-o gr g Chilibang-Misdevious (USA) (Alleged (USA))

Mrs S Lamyman P Lamyman

Placings:0003/00262200/00000/00/00-00 **(0215)**

2001: 8^{0}SD, 11^{0}SD

	Starts	1st	2nd	3rd	Win & Pl
Career Total (Turf)	**14**	**0**	**3**	**0**	**2750**
Career Total (AW)	**9**	**0**	**0**	**1**	**437**

Going (Turf): Sf: 0-2 GS: 0-4 Gd: 0-2 GF: 0-6 Fm: 0-0
Distance: 5f/6f: 0-7 7f-8f: 0-8 9f-13f: 0-7 14f+: 0-1
Track : LH: 0-14 RH: 0-5 Tight: 0-5 Gall: 0-0
Aids: Bl: 0-6 Vi: 0-5 Tstrap: 0-0
Best Rating: 81 8/01 Ripn 6f good

Peter The Great (IRE)

(92) 93 (72) **72**

2-y-o b c Hector Protector (USA)-Perfect Alibi (Law Society (USA))

R M Beckett Pedro Rosas

Placings:02 **(4947)**

2001: 6^{0}GF, 8^{2}G, 8^{4}SD

	Starts	1st	2nd	3rd	Win & Pl
Career Total (Turf)	**2**	**0**	**1**	**0**	**1324**

Going (Turf): Sf: 0-0 GS: 0-0 Gd: 0-1 GF: 0-1 Fm: 0-0
Distance: 5f/6f: 0-1 7f-8f: 0-1 9f-13f: 0-0 14f+: 0-0
Track : LH: 0-0 RH: 0-1 Tight: 0-0 Gall: 0-0
Aids: Bl: 0-0 Vi: 0-0 Tstrap: 0-0
Best Rating: 72 9/01 Gdwd 1m good

Peter's Imp (IRE)

104(91) (48)**50**

6-y-o b g Imp Society (USA)-Catherine Clare (Sallust)

A Berry Mr & Mrs Peter Foden

Placings:3341030/000312060/0121206050000/502530 11433600-00050000004000 **(5539)**

2001: 7^{0}GF, 8^{0}GF, 7^{0}F, 7^{5}GF, 7^{0}GF, 7^{0}GF, 8^{0}G, 7^{0}GF, 7^{0}GF, 7^{0}G, 8^{4}G, 7^{0}G, 7^{0}G, 8^{0}S

	Starts	1st	2nd	3rd	Win & Pl
Career Total (Turf)	**54**	**6**	**4**	**7**	**35400**
Career Total (AW)	**3**	**0**	**0**	**0**	**0**

78 7/00 Asct 7f D(0-85)H G-F £8580
63 7/00 Wwck 7f26y G(0-70)H G-F £1886
80 6/99 Rdcr 7f D(0-75) FRM £3847
67 5/99 Haml 6f5y F(0-65) G-F £2290
68 7/98 Hayd 7f30y D(0-75) G-F £3436
81 8/97 Newc 6f D G-F £3631
Total win prize-money £23671

Going (Turf): Sf: 0-10 GS: 0-3 Gd: 0-15 **GF: 5-22** Fm: 1-4
Distance: 5f/6f: 1-13 **7f-8f: 5-40** 9f-13f: 0-4 14f+: 0-0
Track : **LH: 2-26** RH: 0-5 Tight: 0-14 Gall: 0-4
Aids: **Bl: 1-9** Vi: 0-1 Tstrap: 0-0
Best Rating: 64 5/01 Ches 7f122y gd-fm

Petit Marquis (FR)

110(102) (87)**92+**

4-y-o b g Lost World (IRE)-Ephemeride (USA) (Al Nasr (FR))

J R Fanshawe Miss A Church

Placings:2/1200-310401 **(5137)**

2001: 7^{3}GF, 7^{1}GF, 8^{0}GF, 8^{4}G, 8^{0}S, 8^{1}G

	Starts	1st	2nd	3rd	Win & Pl
Career Total (Turf)	**10**	**2**	**2**	**1**	**17969**
Career Total (AW)	**1**	**1**	**0**	**0**	**2279**

92 10/01 NmkR 1m C(0-90) GD £7058
89 7/01 Hayd 7f30y C(0-95)H G-F £6449
87 3/00 Wolv 1m100y F STD £2278
Total win prize-money £15788

Going (Turf): Sf: 0-2 GS: 0-0 **Gd: 1-4 GF: 1-4** Fm: 0-0
Distance: 5f/6f: 0-1 **7f-8f: 2-6** 9f-13f: 1-4 14f+: 0-0
Track : **LH: 2-3** RH: 0-4 **Tight: 1-2** Gall: 0-1
Aids: Bl: 0-0 Vi: 0-0 Tstrap: 0-0
Best Rating: 92 10/01 NmkR 1m good

An All-Weather winner in 2000, he has improved for a drop to seven furlongs and fast ground this season. He is suited by waiting tactics.

Petite Danseuse

(107) (40d)**36**

7-y-o b m Aragon-Let Her Dance (USA) (Sovereign Dancer (USA))

D W Chapman David W Chapman

Placings:5114060332324200/3005512241055/5006403003400320456/006500354260/55001461160525460000-00 **(1588)**

2001: 6^{0}SD, 7^{0}SD

	Starts	1st	2nd	3rd	Win & Pl
Career Total (Turf)	**51**	**4**	**7**	**7**	**26004**
Career Total (AW)	**31**	**3**	**1**	**1**	**7427**

48 5/00 Sthl 6f F(0-60)H STD £2261
41 5/00 Wolv 6f F(0-65)H STD £2261
37 2/00 Sthl 6f G(0-60)H STD £1526
61 9/97 Leic 5f218y F G-F £3015
59 8/97 Leic 7f9y F GD £2847
75 5/96 Wind 5f10y C GD £4622
72 5/96 Bath 5f11y E G-F £3031
Total win prize-money £19564

Going (Turf): Sf: 0-5 GS: 0-7 **Gd: 2-17 GF: 2-20** Fm: 0-2
Distance: **5f/6f: 6-61** 7f-8f: 1-21 9f-13f: 0-0 14f+: 0-0
Track : **LH: 4-36** RH: 1-4 Tight: 1-11 **Gall: 2-5**
Aids: Bl: 0-1 Vi: 0-1 Tstrap: 0-0
Best Rating: 72 5/96 Bath 5f11y GF

Petite Futee

97 **66**

2-y-o b f Efisio-Q Factor (Tragic Role (USA))

D Haydn Jones The Lamorran Partnership

Placings:5553455 **(5690)**

2001: 7^{5}GF, 6^{5}GF, 5^{5}GF, 6^{3}G, 7^{4}GF, 7^{5}HY, 7^{5}S

	Starts	1st	2nd	3rd	Win & Pl
Career Total (Turf)	**7**	**0**	**0**	**1**	**1161**

Going (Turf): Sf: 0-2 GS: 0-0 Gd: 0-1 GF: 0-4 Fm: 0-0
Distance: 5f/6f: 0-1 7f-8f: 0-6 9f-13f: 0-0 14f+: 0-0
Track : LH: 0-3 RH: 0-1 Tight: 0-1 Gall: 0-1
Aids: Bl: 0-0 Vi: 0-0 Tstrap: 0-0
Best Rating: 66 7/01 Chep 6f16y gd-fm

Petite Galerie (IRE)

(86) (15)**27**

4-y-o b f Pips Pride-Tizzy (Formidable (USA))

J Larkin Mrs D McDowell

Placings:060-00 **(5303a)**

2001: 10^{0}S, 6^{0}G

	Starts	1st	2nd	3rd	Win & Pl
Career Total (Turf)	**3**	**0**	**0**	**0**	
Career Total (AW)	**2**	**0**	**0**	**0**	**0**

Going (Turf): Sf: 0-2 GS: 0-0 Gd: 0-1 GF: 0-0 Fm: 0-0
Distance: 5f/6f: 0-3 7f-8f: 0-1 9f-13f: 0-1 14f+: 0-0
Track : LH: 0-2 RH: 0-0 Tight: 0-2 Gall: 0-0
Aids: Bl: 0-0 Vi: 0-0 Tstrap: 0-2
Best Rating: 27 10/01 Fair 6f good

Petongski

104 **70**

3-y-o b g Petong-Madam Petoski (Petoski)

D W Barker P Asquith

Placings:21200-0000400605110 **(5449)**

2001: 6^{0}GF, 6^{0}GS, 5^{0}GF, 6^{0}GF, 5^{4}G, 6^{0}GF, 5^{0}G, 5^{0}GF, 5^{6}GF, 5^{0}GS, 5^{5}GS, 6^{1}HY, 6^{1}HY, 6^{0}HY

	Starts	1st	2nd	3rd	Win & Pl
Career Total (Turf)	**19**	**3**	**2**	**0**	**13617**

69 10/01 Ayr 6f E(0-70)H HVY £3318
63 10/01 Nott 6f15y F(0-60) HVY £2831
82 8/00 Newc 6f F GD £2709
Total win prize-money £8859

Going (Turf): Sf: 2-4 GS: 0-3 Gd: 1-5 GF: 0-7 Fm: 0-0
Distance: **5f/6f: 2-18** 7f-8f: 1-1 9f-13f: 0-0 14f+: 0-0
Track : LH: 0-1 RH: 0-0 Tight: 0-1 Gall: 0-0
Aids: Bl: 0-1 Vi: 0-1 Tstrap: 0-0
Best Rating: 74 6/01 Newc 6f gd-fm

Fair sprinter, suited by six furlongs and heavy ground.

Petra Nova

(81) (25)**37**

5-y-o ch m First Trump-Spinner (Blue Cashmere)

R M Whitaker R M Whitaker

Placings:2000/060000500/0060000-5 **(0143)**

2001: 6^{5}SW

	Starts	1st	2nd	3rd	Win & Pl
Career Total (Turf)	18	0	1	0	1493
Career Total (AW)	3	0	0	0	0

Going (Turf): Sf: 0-3 GS: 0-0 Gd: 0-6 GF: 0-8 Fm: 0-1
Distance: 5f/6f: 0-15 7f-8f: 0-6 9f-13f: 0-0 14f+: 0-0
Track : LH: 0-7 RH: 0-1 Tight: 0-5 Gall: 0-1
Aids: Bl: 0-4 Vi: 0-0 Tstrap: 0-0
Best Rating: 21 1/01 Sthl 6f slow

Petrail (IRE)

84 **60**

3-y-o b f Catrail (USA)-Smart Pet (Petong)
W R Muir N Phillips-Hill

Placings:004-6 (3050)
2001: 6^{6}GF

	Starts	1st	2nd	3rd	Win & Pl
Career Total (Turf)	4	0	0	0	0

Going (Turf): Sf: 0-0 GS: 0-1 Gd: 0-1 GF: 0-2 Fm: 0-0
Distance: 5f/6f: 0-4 7f-8f: 0-0 9f-13f: 0-0 14f+: 0-0
Track : LH: 0-0 RH: 0-0 Tight: 0-0 Gall: 0-0
Aids: Bl: 0-0 Vi: 0-0 Tstrap: 0-0
Best Rating: 46 7/01 Sals 6f gd-fm

Petrean

(75) 75 (35) **42**

2-y-o gr f Petong-Star (Most Welcome)
M A Jarvis T G Warner

Placings:000 (5415)
2001: 5^{0}GF, 5^{0}F, 6^{0}SD

	Starts	1st	2nd	3rd	Win & Pl
Career Total (Turf)	2	0	0	0	
Career Total (AW)	1	0	0	0	

Going (Turf): Sf: 0-0 GS: 0-0 Gd: 0-0 GF: 0-1 Fm: 0-1
Distance: 5f/6f: 0-3 7f-8f: 0-0 9f-13f: 0-0 14f+: 0-0
Track : LH: 0-2 RH: 0-0 Tight: 0-1 Gall: 0-0
Aids: Bl: 0-0 Vi: 0-0 Tstrap: 0-0
Best Rating: 42 9/01 Pont 5f firm

Petrie

76(76) (17) **12**

4-y-o ch g Fraam-Canadian Capers (Ballacashtal (CAN))
A J Chamberlain D N Carey

Placings:0554232256/035030006000-00000 (2991)
2001: 5^{0}G, 10^{0}GF, 7^{0}SD, 5^{0}HD, 8^{0}G

	Starts	1st	2nd	3rd	Win & Pl
Career Total (Turf)	20	0	1	2	1401
Career Total (AW)	7	0	2	1	1327

Going (Turf): Sf: 0-4 GS: 0-2 Gd: 0-4 GF: 0-4 Fm: 0-6
Distance: 5f/6f: 0-12 7f-8f: 0-11 9f-13f: 0-4 14f+: 0-0
Track : LH: 0-19 RH: 0-0 Tight: 0-5 Gall: 0-6
Aids: Bl: 0-0 Vi: 0-1 Tstrap: 0-0
Best Rating: 12 5/01 Bath 5f11y good

Petrov

101 **80**

3-y-o b c Cadeaux Genereux-Anna Petrovna (FR) (Wassl)
E A L Dunlop Maktoum Al Maktoum

Placings:040-6152335 (3471)
2001: 11^{6}GS, 9^{1}G, 11^{5}GF, 9^{2}GF, 12^{3}GF, 12^{3}GF, 12^{5}GF

	Starts	1st	2nd	3rd	Win & Pl
Career Total (Turf)	10	1	1	2	6849

75	5/01	Leic	1m1f218y	D(0-80)H	GD	£3887

Total win prize-money £3887

Going (Turf): Sf: 0-1 GS: 0-2 Gd: 1-1 GF: 0-6 Fm: 0-0
Distance: 5f/6f: 0-0 7f-8f: 0-2 9f-13f: 1-8 14f+: 0-0
Track : LH: 0-3 RH: 1-4 Tight: 0-2 Gall: 0-2
Aids: Bl: 0-1 Vi: 0-2 Tstrap: 0-0
Best Rating: 80 7/01 Sals 1m4f gd-fm

Petrula

98 **77**

2-y-o ch c Tagula (IRE)-Bouffant (High Top)
A Berry Mr & Mrs Peter Foden

Placings:002102 (5636)
2001: 6^{0}G, 6^{0}F, 7^{2}G, 6^{1}HY, 6^{0}GS, 5^{2}G

	Starts	1st	2nd	3rd	Win & Pl
Career Total (Turf)	6	1	2	0	6953

77	8/01	Hayd	6f	D	HVY	£4504

Total win prize-money £4505

Going (Turf): Sf: 1-1 GS: 0-1 Gd: 0-3 GF: 0-0 Fm: 0-1
Distance: 5f/6f: 1-5 7f-8f: 0-1 9f-13f: 0-0 14f+: 0-0
Track : LH: 0-2 RH: 0-0 Tight: 0-2 Gall: 0-0
Aids: Bl: 0-0 Vi: 0-0 Tstrap: 0-0
Best Rating: 77 11/01 Catt 5f212y good

Fair juvenile, has won on heavy but is suited by good ground and a sharp turning track.

Petrus (IRE)

(108) 103 (69) **75**

5-y-o b g Perugino (USA)-Love With Honey (USA) (Full Pocket (USA))
C E Brittain C E Brittain

Placings:6006/00103011660/0000500004-21401530050 (5055)
2001: 7^{2}SD, 6^{1}GF, 7^{4}G, 7^{0}GF, 7^{1}F, 7^{5}F, 7^{3}G, 8^{0}G, 7^{0}GF, 7^{5}GF, 10^{0}S, 8^{3}SD

	Starts	1st	2nd	3rd	Win & Pl
Career Total (Turf)	35	5	0	2	39814
Career Total (AW)	1	0	1	0	872

74	6/01	Ling	7f140y	E(0-70)H	FRM	£3388
73	5/01	Brig	6f209y	E(0-70)H	G-F	£2926
88	7/99	Gdwd	7f	C(0-100)H	FRM	£19300
80	7/99	Yarm	7f3y	C(0-100)H	G-F	£6677
73	5/99	Kemp	7f	D(0-85)H	G-F	£3842

Total win prize-money £36134

Going (Turf): Sf: 0-2 GS: 0-6 Gd: 0-11 GF: 3-13 Fm: 2-3
Distance: 5f/6f: 0-1 7f-8f: 5-32 9f-13f: 0-3 14f+: 0-0
Track : LH: 1-8 RH: 2-5 Tight: 0-6 Gall: 1-4
Aids: Bl: 0-0 Vi: 0-0 Tstrap: 0-5
Best Rating: 75 7/01 Yarm 7f3y good

Useful seven furlong handicapper, but not quite the force of old. Best on fast ground. Suited by an easy track.

Petrushka (IRE)

106 **121**

4-y-o ch f Unfuwain (USA)-Ballet Shoes (IRE) (Ela-Mana-Mou)
Sir Michael Stoute Highclere Thoroughbred Racing Ltd

Placings:1/1341115-5 (1974)
2001: 12^{5}GF

	Starts	1st	2nd	3rd	Win & Pl
Career Total (Turf)	9	5	0	1	390109

121	10/00	Lonc	1m2f		GD	£67243
122	8/00	York	1m3f195y	A	GD	£127600
122	7/00	Curr	1m4f		G-F	£112425
119	4/00	NmkR	7f	A	G-S	£20300
89	10/99	Leic	7f9y	D	G-S	£3785

Total win prize-money £331353

Going (Turf): Sf: 0-0 GS: 2-3 Gd: 2-3 GF: 1-2 Fm: 0-1
Distance: 5f/6f: 0-0 7f-8f: 2-3 9f-13f: 3-6 14f+: 0-0
Track : LH: 1-3 RH: 2-2 Tight: 0-2 Gall: 1-1
Aids: Bl: 0-0 Vi: 0-0 Tstrap: 0-0
Best Rating: 107 6/01 Epsm 1m4f10y gd-fm

The top middle-distance filly of 2000, gaining a fine victory in the Irish Oaks. She followed up in the Yorkshire Oaks when she beat the previous two Epsom Oaks winners, and completed the hat-trick in the Prix de l'Opera. Slightly below her best when only fifth in the Breeders Cup Fillies and Mares' Turf at Churchill Downs on her final start. Strained a tendon on her return and was retired to stud. Subsequently bought by Darley Stud.

Petuntse

102 (35) **50**

7-y-o b g Phountzi (USA)-Alipampa (IRE) (Glenstal (USA))
Mrs M Reveley Chicken Kiev Syndicate

Placings:06300/4621/6050/363101303 (5447)
2001: 11^{3}S, 12^{6}F, 10^{3}GF, 10^{1}F, 8^{0}F, 10^{1}G, 10^{3}HY, 10^{0}G, 10^{3}HY

	Starts	1st	2nd	3rd	Win & Pl
Career Total (Turf)	20	3	1	5	13501
Career Total (AW)	2	0	0	0	0

48	8/01	Hayd	1m2f120y	E(0-75)H	GD	£3850
43	7/01	Newc	1m2f32y	E(0-70)H	FRM	£4387
48	6/98	Yarm	1m3y	G(0-60)H	G-F	£2250

Total win prize-money £10488

Going (Turf): Sf: 0-3 GS: 0-1 Gd: 1-6 GF: 1-5 Fm: 1-5
Distance: 5f/6f: 0-1 7f-8f: 0-4 9f-13f: 3-17 14f+: 0-0
Track : LH: 2-15 RH: 0-2 Tight: 0-7 Gall: 1-2
Aids: Bl: 0-0 Vi: 0-0 Tstrap: 0-0
Best Rating: 50 8/01 Hayd 1m2f120y heavy

Suited by ten furlongs and fast ground.

Peyto Princess

104 **76**

3-y-o b/br f Bold Arrangement-Bo' Babbity (Strong Gale)
C W Fairhurst North Cheshire Trading & Storage Ltd

Placings:32243-5252610000 (5630)
2001: 5^{5}S, 5^{2}G, 5^{5}GF, 6^{2}F, 6^{6}G, 6^{1}GF, 5^{0}G, 6^{0}GF, 6^{0}GF, 6^{0}G

	Starts	1st	2nd	3rd	Win & Pl
Career Total (Turf)	15	1	4	2	10978

76	6/01	Pont	6f	D(0-80)	G-F	£5538

Total win prize-money £5538

Going (Turf): Sf: 0-2 GS: 0-0 Gd: 0-5 GF: 1-6 Fm: 0-2
Distance: 5f/6f: 1-14 7f-8f: 0-1 9f-13f: 0-0 14f+: 0-0
Track : LH: 1-1 RH: 0-0 Tight: 0-0 Gall: 0-0
Aids: Bl: 0-0 Vi: 0-0 Tstrap: 0-0
Best Rating: 78 5/01 Thsk 5f gd-fm

Fair sprinter. Got off the mark over six furlongs in June 2001 but has since struggled in better company.

Pfennig

91 **82**

2-y-o b c Petong-Petriece (Mummy's Pet)
D R Loder Sheikh Mohammed

Placings:60 (5248)
2001: 7^{6}G, 7^{0}S

	Starts	1st	2nd	3rd	Win & Pl
Career Total (Turf)	2	0	0	0	0

Going (Turf): Sf: 0-1 GS: 0-0 Gd: 0-1 GF: 0-0 Fm: 0-0
Distance: 5f/6f: 0-0 7f-8f: 0-2 9f-13f: 0-0 14f+: 0-0
Track : LH: 0-1 RH: 0-0 Tight: 0-0 Gall: 0-1
Aids: Bl: 0-0 Vi: 0-1 Tstrap: 0-0
Best Rating: 82 9/01 NmkR 7f good

Pharaoh Hatshepsut (IRE)

98(86) (37) **52**

3-y-o b f Definite Article-Maid Of Mourne (Fairy King (USA))
R A Fahey (J S Goldie 7/9) Mike Flynn

Placings:400045010-100040060000 (5490)
2001: 6^{1}G, 6^{0}F, 6^{0}GF, 5^{0}GF, 8^{4}GS, 7^{0}GS, 6^{0}G, 6^{6}G, 8^{0}HY, 6^{0}SD, 6^{0}HY, 7^{0}HY

	Starts	1st	2nd	3rd	Win & Pl
Career Total (Turf)	20	2	0	0	8182
Career Total (AW)	1	0	0	0	

62	5/01	Thsk	6f	E(0-70)	GD	£3854
53	10/00	Ayr	6f	D(0-85)	HVY	£3656

Total win prize-money £7511

Going (Turf): Sf: 1-5 GS: 0-4 **Gd: 1-5** GF: 0-3 Fm: 0-3
Distance: **5f/6f: 2-14** 7f-8f: 0-5 9f-13f: 0-2 14f+: 0-0
Track : LH: 0-5 RH: 0-2 Tight: 0-3 Gall: 0-1
Aids: Bl: 0-0 Vi: 0-0 Tstrap: 0-0
Best Rating: 62 5/01 Thsk 6f good

Moderate sprinter, best form over 6f. Made the most of a favourable draw when winning classified event at Thirsk on reappearance. Has shown her best form on good ground or slower to date.

Pharly Reef

81 (27) **22**
9-y-o b g Pharly (FR)-Hay Reef (Mill Reef (USA))
D Burchell Vivian Guy

Placings:0500600/55/0/540/000 (4892)
2001: 9^{0}GS, 10^{0}GF, 12^{0}GF

	Starts	1st	2nd	3rd	Win & Pl
Career Total (Turf)	10	0	0	0	261
Career Total (AW)	6	0	0	0	0

Going (Turf): Sf: 0-1 GS: 0-1 Gd: 0-4 GF: 0-4 Fm: 0-0
Distance: 5f/6f: 0-0 7f-8f: 0-3 9f-13f: 0-13 14f+: 0-0
Track : LH: 0-12 RH: 0-2 Tight: 0-10 Gall: 0-0
Aids: Bl: 0-0 Vi: 0-1 Tstrap: 0-0
Best Rating: 22 9/01 Kemp 1m4f gd-fm

Pharmacy's Pet (IRE)

95(47) **32**
3-y-o b f Petardia-Pharmacy (Mtoto)
H S Howe I Forster-Exe River Racing

Placings:00060-0000060 (4610)
2001: 5^{0}GF, 6^{0}GF, 6^{0}GF, 5^{0}GF, 5^{0}F, 7^{6}G, 5^{0}F

	Starts	1st	2nd	3rd	Win & Pl
Career Total (Turf)	11	0	0	0	162
Career Total (AW)	1	0	0	0	

Going (Turf): Sf: 0-1 GS: 0-1 Gd: 0-2 GF: 0-5 Fm: 0-2
Distance: 5f/6f: 0-8 7f-8f: 0-4 9f-13f: 0-0 14f+: 0-0
Track : LH: 0-4 RH: 0-1 Tight: 0-1 Gall: 0-3
Aids: Bl: 0-0 Vi: 0-0 Tstrap: 0-0
Best Rating: 32 8/01 Asct 7f good

Pharoah's Gold (IRE)

103 **91**
3-y-o b g Namaqualand (USA)-Queen Nefertiti (IRE) (Fairy King (USA))
W Jarvis Lone Star Racing Partnership

Placings:4410-2605 (5172)
2001: 6^{2}S, 8^{6}GF, 6^{0}G, 6^{5}GS

	Starts	1st	2nd	3rd	Win & Pl
Career Total (Turf)	8	1	1	0	5434

71	5/00	Nott	6f15y	E	GD	£2632

Total win prize-money £2632

Going (Turf): Sf: 0-1 GS: 0-2 **Gd: 1-3** GF: 0-1 Fm: 0-1
Distance: 5f/6f: 0-3 **7f-8f: 1-5** 9f-13f: 0-0 14f+: 0-0
Track : LH: 0-1 RH: 0-1 Tight: 0-0 Gall: 0-1
Aids: Bl: 0-0 Vi: 0-0 Tstrap: 0-0
Best Rating: 91 5/01 Newb 6f8y soft

Decent handicapper. Effective at six to eight furlongs. Handles any ground.

Phazed

93 **63**
2-y-o b f Zamindar (USA)-Ypha (USA) (Lyphard (USA))
B W Hills K Abdulla

Placings:3 (3557)
2001: 7^{3}GF

	Starts	1st	2nd	3rd	Win & Pl
Career Total (Turf)	1	0	0	1	672

Going (Turf): Sf: 0-0 GS: 0-0 Gd: 0-0 GF: 0-1 Fm: 0-0
Distance: 5f/6f: 0-0 7f-8f: 0-1 9f-13f: 0-0 14f+: 0-0
Track : LH: 0-0 RH: 0-1 Tight: 0-0 Gall: 0-1
Aids: Bl: 0-0 Vi: 0-0 Tstrap: 0-0
Best Rating: 63 8/01 Kemp 7f gd-fm

Pheckless

2-y-o ch g Be My Guest (USA)-Phlirty (Pharly (FR))
R F Johnson Houghton Mrs R F Johnson Houghton

Placings:0 (5177)
2001: 6^{0}HY

	Starts	1st	2nd	3rd	Win & Pl
Career Total (Turf)	1	0	0	0	

Going (Turf): Sf: 0-1 GS: 0-0 Gd: 0-0 GF: 0-0 Fm: 0-0
Distance: 5f/6f: 0-1 7f-8f: 0-0 9f-13f: 0-0 14f+: 0-0
Track : LH: 0-0 RH: 0-0 Tight: 0-0 Gall: 0-0
Aids: Bl: 0-0 Vi: 0-0 Tstrap: 0-0
Best Rating: 63 8/01 Kemp 7f gd-fm

Philagain

89 **25**
4-y-o b f Ardkinglass-Andalucia (Rheingold)
Miss L A Perratt C D Barber-Lomax

Placings:000/4016304003-0000000000 (3380)
2001: 9^{0}S, 8^{0}GS, 7^{0}F, 7^{0}GF, 8^{0}GF, 6^{0}GF, 7^{0}G, 8^{0}GF, 8^{0}F, 6^{0}G, 7^{0}GF

	Starts	1st	2nd	3rd	Win & Pl
Career Total (Turf)	24	1	0	2	3816

40	6/00	Muss	1m	F(0-65)H	FRM	£2744

Total win prize-money £2744

Going (Turf): Sf: 0-4 GS: 0-3 Gd: 0-4 GF: 0-9 **Fm: 1-3**
Distance: 5f/6f: 0-0 **7f-8f: 1-16** 9f-13f: 0-7 14f+: 0-0
Track : LH: 0-7 **RH: 1-9 Tight: 1-9** Gall: 0-0
Aids: Bl: 0-0 Vi: 0-0 Tstrap: 0-0
Best Rating: 28 6/01 Haml 6f5y gd-fm

Philatelic Lady (IRE)

89(99) (76)**87**
5-y-o ch m Pips Pride-Gold Stamp (Golden Act (USA))
M J Haynes G B Farmer

Placings:06215/1200421/53303145-0 (0956)
2001: 10^{0}S

	Starts	1st	2nd	3rd	Win & Pl
Career Total (Turf)	16	3	2	3	21447
Career Total (AW)	5	1	1	0	4221

81	8/00	Ling	1m1f	D(0-85)H	G-F	£4043
79	11/99	Wind	1m2f7y	D(0-80)H	G-S	£7620
73	6/99	Ling	1m2f	E(0-75)H	G-S	£2954
74	11/98	Ling	1m	D	STD	£2840

Total win prize-money £17457

Going (Turf): Sf: 0-5 **GS: 2-4** Gd: 0-3 GF: 1-4 Fm: 0-0
Distance: 5f/6f: 0-1 7f-8f: 1-5 **9f-13f: 3-15** 14f+: 0-0
Track : **LH: 3-11** RH: 0-3 **Tight: 4-17** Gall: 0-2
Aids: Bl: 0-0 Vi: 0-0 Tstrap: 0-0
Best Rating: 55 4/01 Epsm 1m2f18y soft

A useful handicapper at up to ten furlongs, she can act on any type of ground and is also effective on the All-Weather.

Philboy

90(67) (12)**58**
2-y-o b g Young Ern-Just Lady (Emarati (USA))
C W Fairhurst C D Barber-Lomax

Placings:00556305240 (5660)
2001: 5^{0}GS, 5^{0}S, 5^{5}GF, 5^{5}GF, 5^{6}SD, 5^{3}GF, 5^{0}F, 5^{5}GF, 5^{2}GS, 5^{4}S, 5^{0}G

	Starts	1st	2nd	3rd	Win & Pl
Career Total (Turf)	10	0	1	1	1362
Career Total (AW)	1	0	0	0	0

Going (Turf): Sf: 0-2 GS: 0-2 Gd: 0-1 GF: 0-4 Fm: 0-1
Distance: 5f/6f: 0-11 7f-8f: 0-0 9f-13f: 0-0 14f+: 0-0
Track : LH: 0-1 RH: 0-0 Tight: 0-1 Gall: 0-0
Aids: Bl: 0-1 Vi: 0-0 Tstrap: 0-6
Best Rating: 58 11/01 Muss 5f good

Philgirl

94 **65**
2-y-o ch f Bijou D'Inde-Ballagarrow Girl (North Stoke)
C W Fairhurst C D Barber-Lomax

Placings:6343052066560 (5536)
2001: 5^{6}GS, 5^{3}G, 6^{4}GF, 6^{3}GF, 7^{0}GF, 7^{5}F, 6^{2}GS, 6^{0}G, 6^{6}G, 6^{6}GF, 7^{5}GS, 6^{6}HY, 6^{0}S

	Starts	1st	2nd	3rd	Win & Pl
Career Total (Turf)	13	0	1	2	1944

Going (Turf): Sf: 0-2 GS: 0-3 Gd: 0-3 GF: 0-4 Fm: 0-1
Distance: 5f/6f: 0-6 7f-8f: 0-7 9f-13f: 0-0 14f+: 0-0
Track : LH: 0-2 RH: 0-0 Tight: 0-1 Gall: 0-0
Aids: Bl: 0-0 Vi: 0-0 Tstrap: 0-0
Best Rating: 65 9/01 Ayr 6f good

Philippi

87 **58d**
3-y-o b g Alzao (USA)-Lighted Glitter (FR) (Crystal Glitters (USA))
Mrs J R Ramsden Mrs J R Ramsden

Placings:0300-00 (1853)
2001: 8^{0}F, 10^{0}GF

	Starts	1st	2nd	3rd	Win & Pl
Career Total (Turf)	6	0	0	1	528

Going (Turf): Sf: 0-1 GS: 0-0 Gd: 0-0 GF: 0-3 Fm: 0-2
Distance: 5f/6f: 0-3 7f-8f: 0-2 9f-13f: 0-1 14f+: 0-0
Track : LH: 0-4 RH: 0-0 Tight: 0-0 Gall: 0-2
Aids: Bl: 0-3 Vi: 0-0 Tstrap: 0-0
Best Rating: 40 5/01 Newc 1m firm

Phoebe Buffay (IRE)

(102) (69)**58**
4-y-o b f Petardia-Art Duo (Artaius (USA))
C N Allen Newmarketconnections.Com

Placings:221200/000131-441215 (1271)
2001: 8^{4}SW, 9^{4}SD, 8^{1}SD, 7^{2}SD, 8^{1}SD, 10^{5}SD

	Starts	1st	2nd	3rd	Win & Pl
Career Total (Turf)	7	0	2	0	5444
Career Total (AW)	11	5	2	1	13364

69	4/01	Ling	1m	E(0-70)	STD	£2968
69	3/01	Sthl	1m	F(0-65)H	STD	£2303
64	12/00	Ling	1m2f	E(0-70)	STD	£2282
41	11/00	Sthl	1m	G	STD	£1414
72	7/99	Sthl	6f	F	STD	£2262

Total win prize-money £11229

Going (Turf): Sf: 0-1 GS: 0-1 Gd: 0-1 GF: 0-4 Fm: 0-0
Distance: 5f/6f: 1-4 **7f-8f: 3-10** 9f-13f: 1-4 14f+: 0-0
Track : **LH: 5-11** RH: 0-2 **Tight: 2-7** Gall: 0-0
Aids: Bl: 0-1 Vi: 0-0 Tstrap: 0-0
Best Rating: 69 4/01 Ling 1m stand

Improved handicapper on All-Weather, stays ten furlongs. Goes well for an inexperienced rider.

Phoebe Robinson (IRE)

100 **79**

3-y-o b f Alzao (USA)-Savelli (IRE) (Vision (USA))

G C Bravery Mrs Peter Robinson

Placings:032-3 **(1949)**

2001: 8³GF

	Starts	1st	2nd	3rd	Win & Pl
Career Total (Turf)	4	0	1	2	2258

Going (Turf): Sf: 0-3 GS: 0-0 Gd: 0-0 GF: 0-1 Fm: 0-0
Distance: 5f/6f: 0-0 7f-8f: 0-4 9f-13f: 0-0 14f+: 0-0
Track : LH: 0-1 RH: 0-1 Tight: 0-0 Gall: 0-1
Aids: Bl: 0-0 Vi: 0-0 Tstrap: 0-0
Best Rating: 79 6/01 Newb 1m gd-fm

Useful, lightly-raced miler. Acts on any ground.

Photo Flash (IRE)

94 **75**

2-y-o ch f Bahamian Bounty-Zoom Lens (IRE) (Caerleon (USA))

J L Dunlop Mrs P G M Jamison

Placings:0420 **(4962)**

2001: 7⁰GF, 7⁴GF, 6²F, 8⁰S

	Starts	1st	2nd	3rd	Win & Pl
Career Total (Turf)	4	0	1	0	818

Going (Turf): Sf: 0-1 GS: 0-0 Gd: 0-0 GF: 0-2 Fm: 0-1
Distance: 5f/6f: 0-0 7f-8f: 0-3 9f-13f: 0-1 14f+: 0-0
Track : LH: 0-2 RH: 0-1 Tight: 0-0 Gall: 0-0
Aids: Bl: 0-0 Vi: 0-0 Tstrap: 0-0
Best Rating: 75 8/01 Brig 6f209y firm

Photographer (USA)

104 **84**

3-y-o b/br g Mountain Cat (USA)-Clickety Click (USA) (Sovereign Dancer (USA))

Mrs N Smith (Sir Michael Stoute 26/6) Tony Hayward, Barry Fulton, Jamie Bruce

Placings:55130 **(5261)**

2001: 8⁵GF, 8⁵F, 8¹GF, 10³GF, 10⁰GS

	Starts	1st	2nd	3rd	Win & Pl
Career Total (Turf)	5	1	0	1	5188

80 6/01 Bevl 1m100y D G-F £4049

Total win prize-money £4050

Going (Turf): Sf: 0-0 GS: 0-1 Gd: 0-0 **GF: 1-3** Fm: 0-1
Distance: 5f/6f: 0-0 7f-8f: 0-2 **9f-13f: 1-3** 14f+: 0-0
Track : LH: 0-2 **RH: 1-3** Tight: 0-1 Gall: 0-2
Aids: Bl: 0-0 Vi: 0-0 Tstrap: 0-0
Best Rating: 84 8/01 Newb 1m2f6y gd-fm

Got off the mark on his third attempt in good style in a Beverley maiden, but has since looked well held for his new stable. Suited by a mile and acts on good to firm.

Phurtive

90 **30**

3-y-o b g Factual (USA)-Phlirty (Pharly (FR))

R F Johnson Houghton Mrs R F Johnson Houghton

Placings:000-0000 **(2057)**

2001: 8⁰S, 10⁰GS, 7⁰GF, 6⁰GF

	Starts	1st	2nd	3rd	Win & Pl
Career Total (Turf)	7	0	0	0	

Going (Turf): Sf: 0-3 GS: 0-1 Gd: 0-0 GF: 0-3 Fm: 0-0
Distance: 5f/6f: 0-1 7f-8f: 0-4 9f-13f: 0-2 14f+: 0-0
Track : LH: 0-5 RH: 0-0 Tight: 0-1 Gall: 0-1
Aids: Bl: 0-0 Vi: 0-0 Tstrap: 0-0
Best Rating: 30 5/01 Sthl 7f gd-fm

Physical Force

101(101) (52)**52**

3-y-o b g Casteddu-Kaiserlinde (GER) (Frontal)

J R Best S Lewis-Hamilton

Placings:0000-0060323255 **(5471)**

2001: 11⁰GS, 10⁰GS, 11⁶G, 14⁰F, 11³F, 12²GF, 10³S, 12²GS, 11⁵GS, 11⁵S, 13²SD, 14³SD

	Starts	1st	2nd	3rd	Win & Pl
Career Total (Turf)	14	0	2	2	3576

Going (Turf): Sf: 0-3 GS: 0-4 Gd: 0-3 GF: 0-1 Fm: 0-3
Distance: 5f/6f: 0-2 7f-8f: 0-2 9f-13f: 0-9 14f+: 0-1
Track : LH: 0-8 RH: 0-1 Tight: 0-8 Gall: 0-0
Aids: Bl: 0-1 Vi: 0-0 Tstrap: 0-0
Best Rating: 52 10/01 Pont 1m4f8y gd-sft

Physical Graffiti (USA)

(97) (58)**58**

4-y-o b g Mister Baileys-Gleaming Water (USA) (Pago Pago)

J A B Old Willie Robertson/nigel Dempster

Placings:240-4 **(0146)**

2001: 12⁴SW

	Starts	1st	2nd	3rd	Win & Pl
Career Total (Turf)	3	0	1	0	1300
Career Total (AW)	1	0	0	0	0

Going (Turf): Sf: 0-1 GS: 0-0 Gd: 0-0 GF: 0-0 Fm: 0-0
Distance: 5f/6f: 0-0 7f-8f: 0-0 9f-13f: 0-4 14f+: 0-0
Track : LH: 0-2 RH: 0-2 Tight: 0-0 Gall: 0-0
Aids: Bl: 0-0 Vi: 0-0 Tstrap: 0-0
Best Rating: 58 1/01 Sthl 1m4f slow

Piano Power

96 **50**

3-y-o b c Cool Jazz-Panayr (Faraway Times (USA))

Miss L A Perratt Miss Heather Galbraith

Placings:0-405 **(3160)**

2001: 5⁴GF, 6⁰GF, 5⁵G

	Starts	1st	2nd	3rd	Win & Pl
Career Total (Turf)	4	0	0	0	0

Going (Turf): Sf: 0-1 GS: 0-0 Gd: 0-1 GF: 0-2 Fm: 0-0
Distance: 5f/6f: 0-4 7f-8f: 0-0 9f-13f: 0-0 14f+: 0-0
Track : LH: 0-0 RH: 0-0 Tight: 0-0 Gall: 0-1
Aids: Bl: 0-0 Vi: 0-0 Tstrap: 0-0
Best Rating: 50 7/01 Newc 5f good

Pic Up Sticks

102 **97**

2-y-o gr c Piccolo-Between The Sticks (Pharly (FR))

M R Channon 1966 World Cup Winners Sporting Club

Placings:203213 **(5498)**

2001: 5²G, 6⁰GF, 6³GF, 5²GF, 6¹S, 6³HY

	Starts	1st	2nd	3rd	Win & Pl
Career Total (Turf)	6	1	2	2	20501

97 10/01 York 6f D SFT £7735

Total win prize-money £7735

Going (Turf): Sf: 1-2 GS: 0-0 Gd: 0-1 GF: 0-3 Fm: 0-0
Distance: 5f/6f: 1-5 7f-8f: 0-1 9f-13f: 0-0 14f+: 0-0
Track : LH: 0-0 RH: 0-0 Tight: 0-0 Gall: 0-0
Aids: Bl: 0-0 Vi: 0-0 Tstrap: 0-0
Best Rating: 97 10/01 York 6f soft

Bred for speed, he showed ability in maidens, including chasing home Dominica at Musselburgh, before getting off the mark when encountering soft ground for the first time at York in October.

Piccadilly

93

6-y-o ch m Belmez (USA)-Polly's Pear (USA) (Sassafras (FR))

Miss Kate Milligan S Ward

Placings:466/3306500600/1000/200465-0 **(2245)**

2001: 14⁰G

	Starts	1st	2nd	3rd	Win & Pl
Career Total (Turf)	24	1	1	2	5443

39 4/99 Ripn 1m4f60y F(0-60)H G-F £2368

Total win prize-money £2369

Going (Turf): Sf: 0-3 GS: 0-2 Gd: 0-7 **GF: 1-8** Fm: 0-4
Distance: 5f/6f: 0-0 7f-8f: 0-2 **9f-13f: 1-14** 14f+: 0-8
Track : LH: 0-11 **RH: 1-13 Tight: 1-15** Gall: 0-2
Aids: Bl: 0-2 Vi: 0-0 Tstrap: 0-0
Best Rating: 21 6/01 Muss 1m6f good

Piccalilli

81 **15**

4-y-o ch f Piccolo-Hat Hill (Roan Rocket)

S Woodman Mrs Sally Woodman

Placings:06060000-00000 **(4019)**

2001: 9⁰GF, 9⁰G, 11⁰F, 11⁰GF, 12⁰G

	Starts	1st	2nd	3rd	Win & Pl
Career Total (Turf)	13	0	0	0	0

Going (Turf): Sf: 0-1 GS: 0-1 Gd: 0-2 GF: 0-7 Fm: 0-2
Distance: 5f/6f: 0-1 7f-8f: 0-3 9f-13f: 0-9 14f+: 0-0
Track : LH: 0-7 RH: 0-2 Tight: 0-6 Gall: 0-0
Aids: Bl: 0-1 Vi: 0-0 Tstrap: 0-0
Best Rating: 15 6/01 Ling 1m3f106y firm

Piccled

71 **26**

3-y-o b g Piccolo-Creme De Menthe (IRE) (Green Desert (USA))

E J Alston The Pain And Heartache Partnership

Placings:610-0000 **(4944)**

2001: 7⁰S, 6⁰GF, 5⁰G, 5⁰S

	Starts	1st	2nd	3rd	Win & Pl
Career Total (Turf)	7	1	0	0	3884

65 6/00 Gdwd 5f E G-S £3883

Total win prize-money £3884

Going (Turf): Sf: 0-2 **GS: 1-2** Gd: 0-2 GF: 0-1 Fm: 0-0
Distance: 5f/6f: 1-6 7f-8f: 0-1 9f-13f: 0-0 14f+: 0-0
Track : LH: 0-2 RH: 0-0 Tight: 0-2 Gall: 0-0
Aids: Bl: 0-0 Vi: 0-0 Tstrap: 0-0
Best Rating: 26 9/01 Ches 5f16y good

Piccolitia

95 **51**

3-y-o ch f Piccolo-Miss Laetitia (IRE) (Entitled)

N A Graham T H Chadney

Placings:0-500002340 **(4459)**

2001: 6⁵HY, 6⁰HY, 6⁰S, 7⁰G, 6⁰GF, 8²GF, 8³GF, 7⁴F, 7⁰G

	Starts	1st	2nd	3rd	Win & Pl
Career Total (Turf)	10	0	1	1	1207

Going (Turf): Sf: 0-3 GS: 0-0 Gd: 0-3 GF: 0-3 Fm: 0-1
Distance: 5f/6f: 0-4 7f-8f: 0-4 9f-13f: 0-2 14f+: 0-0
Track : LH: 0-4 RH: 0-1 Tight: 0-0 Gall: 0-0
Aids: Bl: 0-0 Vi: 0-0 Tstrap: 0-0
Best Rating: 51 8/01 Leic 1m9y gd-fm

Piccolito

41

2-y-o b c Piccolo-Feather Glen (Glenstal (USA))
T J Naughton Mrs S Leech

Placings:0P (4246)
2001: 6^{0}GF, 6^{P}G

	Starts	1st	2nd	3rd	Win & Pl
Career Total (Turf)	2	0	0	0	

Going (Turf): Sf: 0-0 GS: 0-0 Gd: 0-1 GF: 0-1 Fm: 0-0
Distance: 5f/6f: 0-2 7f-8f: 0-0 9f-13f: 0-0 14f+: 0-0
Track : LH: 0-0 RH: 0-0 Tight: 0-0 Gall: 0-0
Aids: Bl: 0-0 Vi: 0-0 Tstrap: 0-0
Best Rating: 51 8/01 Leic 1m9y gd-fm

A half-brother to three winners. Pulled up on his second start at Goodwood when his jockey thought his mount had been struck into.

Piccolo Cativo

102(89) (25)**55**
6-y-o b m Komaite (USA)-Malcesine (IRE) (Auction Ring (USA))
Mrs G S Rees J W Gittins

Placings:16500/01406120420006400/15050002504500/10400020-460002131 (5288)
2001: 8^{4}S, 8^{6}G, 8^{0}F, 7^{0}SD, 7^{0}SD, 7^{2}GS, 6^{1}GS, 6^{3}G, 6^{1}HY

	Starts	1st	2nd	3rd	Win & Pl
Career Total (Turf)	43	6	5	1	25651
Career Total (AW)	10	1	0	0	2277

55	10/01	Ayr	6f	E(0-70)H	HVY	£3304
46	8/01	Haml	6f5y	E(0-70)H	G-S	£4550
49	5/00	Wwck	7f164y	G(0-60)H	SFT	£1911
58	4/99	Catt	5f212y	G(0-60)	SFT	£2066
64	6/98	Carl	5f	D(0-75)H	G-S	£5061
55	5/98	Haml	5f4y	F(0-70)H	GD	£2497
68	5/97	Sthl	5f	F	STD	£2277

Total win prize-money £21667

Going (Turf): Sf: 3-16 GS: 2-7 Gd: 1-9 GF: 0-8 Fm: 0-3
Distance: **5f/6f: 5-29** 7f-8f: 2-20 9f-13f: 0-4 14f+: 0-0
Track : **LH: 2-18** RH: 1-7 Tight: 1-10 Gall: 1-5
Aids: Bl: 0-0 Vi: 0-0 Tstrap: 0-0
Best Rating: 55 10/01 Ayr 6f heavy

Modest sprinter. Effective at six to seven furlongs plus. Suited by cut in the ground.

Piccolo Lady

85 **59**
2-y-o b f Piccolo-Tonic Chord (La Grange Music)
Mrs Lydia Pearce Mrs M Miller

Placings:300 (5022)
2001: 7^{3}GS, 6^{0}GF, 7^{0}S

	Starts	1st	2nd	3rd	Win & Pl
Career Total (Turf)	3	0	0	1	660

Going (Turf): Sf: 0-1 GS: 0-1 Gd: 0-0 GF: 0-1 Fm: 0-0
Distance: 5f/6f: 0-1 7f-8f: 0-2 9f-13f: 0-0 14f+: 0-0
Track : LH: 0-1 RH: 0-0 Tight: 0-0 Gall: 0-0
Aids: Bl: 0-0 Vi: 0-0 Tstrap: 0-0
Best Rating: 59 8/01 Leic 7f9y gd-sft

Piccolo Party

95(86) (71)**70**
2-y-o b c Piccolo-Silankka (Slip Anchor)
M R Channon Simon Legg, Terry Leigh & John White

Placings:315000304 (5458)
2001: 6^{3}G, 5^{1}F, 6^{5}GF, 6^{0}GF, 6^{0}GF, 6^{0}G, 8^{3}SD, 7^{0}GS, 5^{4}G

	Starts	1st	2nd	3rd	Win & Pl
Career Total (Turf)	8	1	0	1	4105
Career Total (AW)	1	0	0	1	530

80	7/01	Bath	5f161y	E	FRM	£2835

Total win prize-money £2835

Going (Turf): Sf: 0-0 GS: 0-1 Gd: 0-3 GF: 0-3 **Fm: 1-1**
Distance: **5f/6f: 1-6** 7f-8f: 0-3 9f-13f: 0-0 14f+: 0-0
Track : **LH: 1-3** RH: 0-0 Tight: 0-0 **Gall: 1-2**
Aids: Bl: 0-0 Vi: 0-0 Tstrap: 0-0
Best Rating: 80 7/01 Bath 5f161y firm

Landed a Bath maiden on his second start, but was held afterwards. Looks one paced and ran a better race when tried on Fibresand.

Pickens (USA)

(103) (56)
9-y-o b g Theatrical-Alchi (USA) (Alleged (USA))
Don Enrico Incisa Don Enrico Incisa

Placings:0/4522241210/0004150/0500104532/2111214 62/6014/00601460202-31222126613 (1470)
2001: 16^{3}SD, 16^{1}SD, 11^{2}SW, 16^{2}SD, 12^{2}SW, 16^{1}SD, 14^{2}SD, 16^{6}SD, 16^{6}SD, 12^{1}SD, 16^{3}SD

	Starts	1st	2nd	3rd	Win & Pl
Career Total (Turf)	23	4	4	0	14058
Career Total (AW)	40	9	10	3	25354

50	4/01	Sthl	1m4f	F	STD	£2373
53	2/01	Sthl	2m	F(0-60)H	STD	£1813
48	1/01	Sthl	2m	F	STD	£2142
46	5/00	Sthl	1m3f	F(0-60)	STD	£1848
62	2/99	Sthl	1m3f	G	STD	£1931
66	2/98	Sthl	1m4f	E(0-70)H	STD	£2788
52	2/98	Sthl	1m3f	G	STD	£1738
53	1/98	Sthl	1m3f	G	STD	£1738
55	1/98	Sthl	1m4f	G	STD	£2085
41	10/97	Rdcr	1m3f	F	G-F	£2598
52	7/96	Bevl	1m3f216y	G	G-F	£2302
	9/95	Fair	1m4f	(0-85)H	G-F	£3082
	8/95	Rosc	1m4f		G-F	£2911

Total win prize-money £29351

Going (Turf): Sf: 0-0 GS: 0-2 Gd: 0-3 **GF: 2-6** Fm: 0-1
Distance: 5f/6f: 0-0 7f-8f: 0-0 **9f-13f: 9-39** 14f+: 2-13
Track : **LH: 10-48** RH: 1-4 **Tight: 2-6** Gall: 0-4
Aids: Bl: 0-1 Vi: 0-0 Tstrap: 0-0
Best Rating: 56 5/01 Sthl 2m stand

Modest All-Weather stayer. All recent wins at Southwell.

Pickett Point

71
3-y-o b g Magic Ring (IRE)-Bay Runner (Bay Express)
J J Bridger Mrs Julie I Lankshear

Placings:000-00000 (5664)
2001: 9^{0}GF, 6^{0}F, 7^{0}GF, 10^{0}S, 8^{0}HY

	Starts	1st	2nd	3rd	Win & Pl
Career Total (Turf)	8	0	0	0	

Going (Turf): Sf: 0-3 GS: 0-0 Gd: 0-0 GF: 0-4 Fm: 0-1
Distance: 5f/6f: 0-2 7f-8f: 0-3 9f-13f: 0-3 14f+: 0-0
Track : LH: 0-2 RH: 0-3 Tight: 0-3 Gall: 0-1
Aids: Bl: 0-0 Vi: 0-0 Tstrap: 0-0

Pickwick Ayr

87 **66**
2-y-o b g Bijou D'Inde-Ayr Classic (Local Suitor (USA))
J S Goldie Tough Construction Ltd

Placings:500 (5268)
2001: 7^{5}G, 6^{0}G, 7^{0}HY

	Starts	1st	2nd	3rd	Win & Pl
Career Total (Turf)	3	0	0	0	0

Going (Turf): Sf: 0-1 GS: 0-0 Gd: 0-2 GF: 0-0 Fm: 0-0
Distance: 5f/6f: 0-1 7f-8f: 0-2 9f-13f: 0-0 14f+: 0-0
Track : LH: 0-0 RH: 0-0 Tight: 0-0 Gall: 0-0
Aids: Bl: 0-0 Vi: 0-0 Tstrap: 0-0
Best Rating: 66 9/01 Ayr 6f good

Pico

90 **62**
3-y-o ch f Piccolo-Chatterberry (Aragon)
C E Brittain Family Amusements Ltd

Placings:00-3 (1640)
2001: 6^{3}F

	Starts	1st	2nd	3rd	Win & Pl
Career Total (Turf)	3	0	0	1	413

Going (Turf): Sf: 0-2 GS: 0-0 Gd: 0-0 GF: 0-0 Fm: 0-1
Distance: 5f/6f: 0-2 7f-8f: 0-1 9f-13f: 0-0 14f+: 0-0
Track : LH: 0-0 RH: 0-0 Tight: 0-0 Gall: 0-0
Aids: Bl: 0-0 Vi: 0-0 Tstrap: 0-0
Best Rating: 62 5/01 Rdcr 6f firm

Picobella (IRE)

(77) (7)
3-y-o b f Piccolo-Chelsea Classic (IRE) (Classic Music (USA))
R J White Littleton Manor Racing

Placings:0 (5281)
2001: 7^{0}S

	Starts	1st	2nd	3rd	Win & Pl
Career Total (Turf)	1	0	0	0	

Going (Turf): Sf: 0-1 GS: 0-0 Gd: 0-0 GF: 0-0 Fm: 0-0
Distance: 5f/6f: 0-0 7f-8f: 0-1 9f-13f: 0-0 14f+: 0-0
Track : LH: 0-0 RH: 0-0 Tight: 0-0 Gall: 0-0
Aids: Bl: 0-0 Vi: 0-0 Tstrap: 0-0
Best Rating: 7 10/01 Leic 7f9y soft

Picture Mee

102(91) (51)**761**
3-y-o b f Aragon-Heemee (On Your Mark)
B S Rothwell The Three County Partnership

Placings:00000-416514100 (1994)
2001: 8^{4}SD, 9^{1}SW, 11^{6}SD, 11^{5}SW, 8^{1}HY, 8^{4}HY, 8^{1}S, 8^{0}HY, 8^{0}SD

	Starts	1st	2nd	3rd	Win & Pl
Career Total (Turf)	9	2	0	0	3945
Career Total (AW)	5	1	0	0	1820

61	4/01	Nott	1m54y	F(0-60)H	SFT	£2044
50	3/01	Nott	1m54y	G	HVY	£1901
51	1/01	Wolv	1m1f79y	G	SLW	£1820

Total win prize-money £5765

Going (Turf): Sf: 2-5 GS: 0-0 Gd: 0-0 GF: 0-4 Fm: 0-0
Distance: 5f/6f: 0-2 7f-8f: 0-4 **9f-13f: 3-8** 14f+: 0-0
Track : **LH: 3-10** RH: 0-1 **Tight: 1-1** Gall: 0-1
Aids: Bl: 0-0 Vi: 0-0 Tstrap: 0-0
Best Rating: 61 4/01 Nott 1m54y soft

He has won sellers on both Fibresand and turf this year and is suited by testing conditions. He stays up to 9f, but not much further.

Picture Palace

97(72) (28)**49**
3-y-o ch g Salse (USA)-Moviegoer (Pharly (FR))
T R George (Sir Mark Prescott 4/9) Mrs Victor Beeching

Placings:000-02521 (4478)
2001: 11^{0}F, 12^{2}GF, 16^{5}GF, 11^{2}GF, 16^{1}F

	Starts	1st	2nd	3rd	Win & Pl
Career Total (Turf)	6	1	2	0	4691
Career Total (AW)	2	0	0	0	

49	9/01	Muss	2m	F(0-65)H	FRM	£3206

Total win prize-money £3206

Going (Turf): Sf: 0-1 GS: 0-0 Gd: 0-0 GF: 0-3 **Fm: 1-2**
Distance: 5f/6f: 0-2 7f-8f: 0-0 9f-13f: 0-4 **14f+: 1-2**
Track : LH: 0-5 **RH: 1-2 Tight: 1-5** Gall: 0-0
Aids: **Bl: 1-5** Vi: 0-0 Tstrap: 0-0
Best Rating: 49 9/01 Muss 2m firm

A tricky ride, he was unsuccessful on the All-Weather, but managed to notch up a win in a plating-class event at Musselburgh on firm ground.

Pie High

91 **76**

2-y-o ch f Salse (USA)-Humble Pie (Known Fact (USA))
N P Littmoden Joy And Valentine Feerick

Placings:000 **(5689)**
2001: 8^{0}G, 7^{0}GS, 6^{0}S

	Starts	1st	2nd	3rd	Win & Pl
Career Total (Turf)	3	0	0	0	

Going (Turf): Sf: 0-1 GS: 0-1 Gd: 0-1 GF: 0-0 Fm: 0-0
Distance: 5f/6f: 0-1 7f-8f: 0-2 9f-13f: 0-0 14f+: 0-0
Track : LH: 0-0 RH: 0-0 Tight: 0-0 Gall: 0-0
Aids: Bl: 0-0 Vi: 0-0 Tstrap: 0-0
Best Rating: 76 11/01 NmkR 7f gd-sft

Pierdete (IRE)

(89) (46)

3-y-o br g Lahib (USA)-Distinct Element (IRE) (Doyoun)
T D Easterby Mrs Janis Macpherson

Placings:006500 **(1471)**
2001: 7^{0}SD, 8^{0}SD, 8^{6}SD, 8^{5}SD, 9^{0}S, 11^{0}SD

	Starts	1st	2nd	3rd	Win & Pl
Career Total (Turf)	1	0	0	0	
Career Total (AW)	5	0	0	0	0

Going (Turf): Sf: 0-1 GS: 0-0 Gd: 0-0 GF: 0-0 Fm: 0-0
Distance: 5f/6f: 0-0 7f-8f: 0-4 9f-13f: 0-2 14f+: 0-0
Track : LH: 0-6 RH: 0-0 Tight: 0-0 Gall: 0-0
Aids: Bl: 0-3 Vi: 0-0 Tstrap: 0-0
Best Rating: 46 2/01 Sthl 1m stand

Pierpoint (IRE)

99(104) (57)**65**

6-y-o ch g Archway (IRE)-Lavinia (Habitat)
D Shaw (D Nicholls 15/1) J H Knight

Placings:12134234/02020205000/00005061311000/00 01005300-**0402305303053200** **(3821)**
2001: 6^{0}SD, 6^{4}SD, 7^{0}SD, 6^{2}SD, 6^{3}SD, 6^{0}SD, 6^{5}SD, 5^{3}SD, 6^{0}SD, 6^{3}G, 6^{0}SD, 5^{5}GF, 5^{3}GF, 5^{2}GF, 6^{0}GF, 5^{0}SD

	Starts	1st	2nd	3rd	Win & Pl
Career Total (Turf)	46	5	6	5	26258
Career Total (AW)	13	1	1	3	4085

65	6/00	Pont	5f	E(0-65)	G-F	£2899
69	8/99	Pont	6f	E(0-70)H	GD	£3522
65	8/99	Rdcr	6f	F(0-60)H	FRM	£3506
64	6/99	Sthl	6f	F(0-60)H	STD	£2442
78	7/97	Haml	5f4y	D	G-F	£3653
69	6/97	Haml	5f4y	F	G-F	£2430

Total win prize-money £18452

Going (Turf): Sf: 0-3 GS: 0-8 Gd: 1-16 **GF: 3-16** Fm: 1-3
Distance: 5f/6f: 6-44 7f-8f: 0-15 9f-13f: 0-0 14f+: 0-0
Track : LH: 3-24 RH: 0-3 Tight: 0-9 Gall: 0-1
Aids: Bl: 3-22 Vi: 0-3 Tstrap: 0-0
Best Rating: 61 6/01 Ripn 5f gd-fm

Fair sprinter. He did well for David Nicholls a couple of seasons ago, but has not won for his current yard. Capable of decent form on fast ground, but not very consistent.

Pies Ar Us

97(88) (26)**25**

4-y-o b g Perpendicular-Jendor (Condorcet (FR))
C W Fairhurst H Taylor & Sons

Placings:4640-**0000003000** **(2440)**
2001: 11^{0}SD, 11^{0}SD, 8^{0}SD, 14^{0}HY, 10^{0}S, 9^{0}S, 11^{3}G, 9^{0}F, 13^{0}GF, 11^{0}GF

	Starts	1st	2nd	3rd	Win & Pl
Career Total (Turf)	11	0	0	1	957
Career Total (AW)	3	0	0	0	

Going (Turf): Sf: 0-3 GS: 0-1 Gd: 0-2 GF: 0-3 Fm: 0-2
Distance: 5f/6f: 0-0 7f-8f: 0-0 9f-13f: 0-11 14f+: 0-3
Track : LH: 0-9 RH: 0-5 Tight: 0-10 Gall: 0-0
Aids: Bl: 0-0 Vi: 0-4 Tstrap: 0-0
Best Rating: 30 5/01 Haml 1m3f16y good

Pieta (IRE)

84(101) (49)**43**

4-y-o b f Perugino (USA)-Auction Maid (IRE) (Auction Ring (USA))
K McAuliffe Brown, Czolak & Krosinsky

Placings:000500-**013040050** **(1998)**
2001: 5^{0}SD, 6^{1}SD, 6^{3}SD, 6^{0}SD, 6^{4}SD, 5^{0}G, 6^{0}SD, 7^{5}SD, 5^{0}SD

	Starts	1st	2nd	3rd	Win & Pl
Career Total (Turf)	6	0	0	0	0
Career Total (AW)	9	1	0	1	2496

41	3/01	Wolv	6f	G	STD	£1869

Total win prize-money £1869

Going (Turf): Sf: 0-0 GS: 0-2 Gd: 0-2 GF: 0-2 Fm: 0-0
Distance: 5f/6f: 1-13 7f-8f: 0-2 9f-13f: 0-0 14f+: 0-0
Track : LH: 1-9 RH: 0-0 **Tight: 1-5** Gall: 0-1
Aids: Bl: 0-0 Vi: 0-0 Tstrap: 0-0
Best Rating: 49 3/01 Wolv 6f stand

Pieter Brueghel (USA)

102 **94**

2-y-o b c Citidancer (USA)-Smart Tally (USA) (Smarten (USA))
P F I Cole Richard Green (fine Paintings)

Placings:4104166 **(5493)**
2001: 6^{4}GF, 5^{1}GF, 6^{0}GF, 5^{4}G, 6^{1}G, 6^{6}G, 7^{6}HY

	Starts	1st	2nd	3rd	Win & Pl
Career Total (Turf)	7	2	0	0	15395

91	9/01	Ches	6f18y	C	GD	£5729
91	5/01	Newb	5f34y	D	G-F	£4472

Total win prize-money £10202

Going (Turf): Sf: 0-1 GS: 0-0 **Gd: 1-3 GF: 1-3** Fm: 0-0
Distance: 5f/6f: 1-5 7f-8f: 1-2 9f-13f: 0-0 14f+: 0-0
Track : LH: 1-1 RH: 0-0 **Tight: 1-1** Gall: 0-0
Aids: Bl: 0-0 Vi: 0-0 Tstrap: 0-0
Best Rating: 94 10/01 Rdcr 6f good

He came on from his York debut to easily win a Newbury maiden over the minimum trip next time. He was held in Pattern company in his next two starts, but returned to winning form in a Chester conditions event. Ran well in the Betabet Two-Year-Old Trophy at Redcar and six furlongs looks his best trip.

Pietro Bembo (IRE)

86

7-y-o b g Midyan (USA)-Cut No Ice (Great Nephew)
Miss E C Lavelle (J Akehurst 27/7) Fraser Miller

Placings:6501/3002/0 **(3426)**
2001: 14^{0}GF

	Starts	1st	2nd	3rd	Win & Pl
Career Total (Turf)	9	1	1	1	5005

67	10/96	Rdcr	1m	E(0-70)	G-F	£3195

Total win prize-money £3196

Going (Turf): Sf: 0-1 GS: 0-0 Gd: 0-3 **GF: 1-3** Fm: 0-2
Distance: 5f/6f: 0-2 **7f-8f: 1-2** 9f-13f: 0-4 14f+: 0-1
Track : LH: 0-2 RH: 0-4 Tight: 0-3 Gall: 0-1
Aids: Bl: 0-1 Vi: 0-0 Tstrap: 0-0
Best Rating: 34 7/01 Sals 1m6f15y gd-fm

Pietro Siena (USA)

98 **80**

3-y-o b/br c Gone West (USA)-Via Borghese (USA) (Seattle Dancer (USA))
E A L Dunlop Maktoum Al Maktoum

Placings:4-31 **(5281)**
2001: 6^{3}GS, 7^{1}S

	Starts	1st	2nd	3rd	Win & Pl
Career Total (Turf)	3	1	0	1	4319

72	10/01	Leic	7f9y	D	SFT	£3230

Total win prize-money £3231

Going (Turf): Sf: 1-2 GS: 0-1 Gd: 0-0 GF: 0-0 Fm: 0-0
Distance: 5f/6f: 0-1 **7f-8f: 1-2** 9f-13f: 0-0 14f+: 0-0
Track : LH: 0-0 RH: 0-0 Tight: 0-0 Gall: 0-0
Aids: Bl: 0-0 Vi: 0-0 Tstrap: 0-0
Best Rating: 80 4/01 NmkR 6f gd-sft

Off the track since April, he stayed on to land a Leicester maiden at the backend.

Pigeon

98 **50**

6-y-o b m Casteddu-Wigeon (Divine Gift)
D W Barker D W Barker

Placings:1032/0002112523000030145/0000000200/0 40000 **(5189)**
2001: 5^{0}S, 5^{4}G, 6^{0}G, 6^{0}G, 5^{0}GS, 5^{0}GS

	Starts	1st	2nd	3rd	Win & Pl
Career Total (Turf)	38	4	5	3	21468
Career Total (AW)	2	0	0	0	

78	9/98	Ches	5f16y	D(0-85)H	GD	£3550
71	6/98	Catt	5f212y	E(0-70)H	G-S	£3099
71	5/98	Catt	5f212y	E(0-70)H	SFT	£3288
63	5/97	Catt	5f212y	G	G-F	£2244

Total win prize-money £12182

Going (Turf): Sf: 1-6 GS: 1-8 Gd: 1-16 GF: 1-7 Fm: 0-1
Distance: 5f/6f: 4-38 7f-8f: 0-2 9f-13f: 0-0 14f+: 0-0
Track : LH: 4-13 RH: 0-1 **Tight: 4-8** Gall: 0-1
Aids: Bl: 0-0 Vi: 0-0 Tstrap: 0-0
Best Rating: 50 8/01 Pont 5f good

A speedy front runner, she returned to the track in July after an absence of two years and has hinted at retaining some ability. Best on a sharp turning track with ease in the ground.

Pikestaff (USA)

95 **57**

3-y-o ch g Diesis-Navarene (USA) (Known Fact (USA))
T D Barron (Mme C Head-Maarek 30/6) Harrowgate Bloodstock Ltd

Placings:4663-00000 **(5171)**
2001: 6^{0}HY, 6^{0}S, 6^{0}G, 8^{0}G, 8^{0}GS

	Starts	1st	2nd	3rd	Win & Pl
Career Total (Turf)	9	0	0	1	3026

Going (Turf): Sf: 0-4 GS: 0-1 Gd: 0-2 GF: 0-0 Fm: 0-0
Distance: 5f/6f: 0-4 7f-8f: 0-1 9f-13f: 0-2 14f+: 0-0
Track : LH: 0-1 RH: 0-1 Tight: 0-0 Gall: 0-0
Aids: Bl: 0-0 Vi: 0-0 Tstrap: 0-0
Best Rating: 57 9/01 Bevl 1m100y good

Pilgrim Goose (IRE)

101(94) (41)**43**

3-y-o ch g Rainbows For Life (CAN)-Across The Ring (IRE) (Auction Ring (USA))
M H Tompkins M P Bowring

Placings:0000-**4654320400** **(5050)**
2001: 11^{4}GF, 9^{6}F, 10^{5}GF, 12^{4}SD, 11^{3}GF, 11^{2}GF, 15^{0}G, 12^{4}GF, 12^{0}G, 11^{0}SD

	Starts	1st	2nd	3rd	Win & Pl
Career Total (Turf)	12	0	1	1	1018
Career Total (AW)	2	0	0	0	0

Going (Turf): Sf: 0-1 GS: 0-0 Gd: 0-4 GF: 0-6 Fm: 0-1
Distance: 5f/6f: 0-1 7f-8f: 0-3 9f-13f: 0-9 14f+: 0-1
Track : LH: 0-8 RH: 0-3 Tight: 0-6 Gall: 0-1
Aids: Bl: 0-5 Vi: 0-0 Tstrap: 0-0
Best Rating: 43 8/01 Folk 1m4f gd-fm

Pilgrim Princess (IRE)

103(93) (45)**44**

3-y-o b f Flying Spur (AUS)-Hasaid Lady (IRE) (Shaadi (USA))
E J Alston Morris, Oliver, Pierce

Placings:0050-0002000165 **(3752)**
2001: 5^{0}SD, 6^{0}SW, 5^{0}GS, 7^{2}SD, 7^{0}G, 8^{0}GF, 7^{0}GS, 6^{1}GS, 7^{6}G, 7^{5}GS

	Starts	1st	2nd	3rd	Win & Pl
Career Total (Turf)	11	1	0	0	3705
Career Total (AW)	3	0	1	0	

44 7/01 Haml 6f5y E(0-70)H G-S £3705
Total win prize-money £3705

Going (Turf): Sf: 0-1 **GS: 1-4** Gd: 0-3 GF: 0-3 Fm: 0-0
Distance: 5f/6f: 0-7 **7f-8f: 1-7** 9f-13f: 0-0 14f+: 0-0
Track : LH: 0-7 RH: 0-1 Tight: 0-1 Gall: 0-2
Aids: Bl: 0-1 Vi: 0-0 Tstrap: 0-0
Best Rating: 45 4/01 Sthl 7f stand

Dropped back to six furlongs to score her first success at Hamilton in July 2001. Has struggled to stay seven furlongs so far on turf. Has won on good to soft ground.

Pillager

(93) (46)**67**

4-y-o b g Reprimand-Emerald Ring (Auction Ring (USA))
Mrs A J Bowlby J Shaw & Mrs Amanda Bowlby

Placings:0/60264505-000 **(0757)**
2001: 16^{0}SD, 16^{0}SD, 8^{0}SW

	Starts	1st	2nd	3rd	Win & Pl
Career Total (Turf)	9	0	1	0	938
Career Total (AW)	3	0	0	0	

Going (Turf): Sf: 0-1 GS: 0-3 Gd: 0-5 GF: 0-0 Fm: 0-0
Distance: 5f/6f: 0-1 7f-8f: 0-2 9f-13f: 0-7 14f+: 0-2
Track : LH: 0-10 RH: 0-0 Tight: 0-2 Gall: 0-1
Aids: Bl: 0-0 Vi: 0-0 Tstrap: 0-0
Best Rating: 46 2/01 Sthl 2m stand

Pilot's Harbour

94(60) **38**

5-y-o b g Distant Relative-Lillemor (Connaught)
F P Murtagh Clayton Bigley Partnership Ltd

Placings:352110/0500000/006-0 **(2245)**
2001: 14^{0}G

	Starts	1st	2nd	3rd	Win & Pl
Career Total (Turf)	15	2	1	1	11096
Career Total (AW)	2	0	0	0	

85 8/98 NmkJ 1m C GD £5825
80 7/98 Bevl 7f100y D G-F £3533
Total win prize-money £9360

Going (Turf): Sf: 0-0 GS: 0-0 **Gd: 1-10 GF: 1-5** Fm: 0-0
Distance: 5f/6f: 0-1 **7f-8f: 2-6** 9f-13f: 0-7 14f+: 0-3
Track : LH: 0-4 **RH: 1-9** Tight: 0-4 Gall: 0-1
Aids: Bl: 0-2 Vi: 0-0 Tstrap: 0-0
Best Rating: 38 6/01 Muss 1m6f good

Pina Colada

100 **79**

2-y-o ch f Sabrehill (USA)-Drei (USA) (Lyphard (USA))
R Hannon Team Valor

Placings:210 **(2306)**
2001: 5^{2}GS, 5^{1}F, 7^{0}GF

	Starts	1st	2nd	3rd	Win & Pl
Career Total (Turf)	3	1	1	0	3731

59 5/01 Brig 5f59y E FRM £2877
Total win prize-money £2877

Going (Turf): Sf: 0-0 GS: 0-1 Gd: 0-0 GF: 0-1 **Fm: 1-1**
Distance: **5f/6f: 1-2** 7f-8f: 0-1 9f-13f: 0-0 14f+: 0-0
Track : **LH: 1-2** RH: 0-0 Tight: 0-0 Gall: 0-0
Aids: Bl: 0-0 Vi: 0-0 Tstrap: 0-0
Best Rating: 79 6/01 Asct 7f gd-fm

A May foal, bred to appreciate a mile in due course. She was still showing greenness, but won quite well in the end, when beating La Perla by 1 1/2 lengths in maiden over an extended five furlongs at Brighton in May.

Pinball Wizard (IRE)

75 **45**

2-y-o b g College Chapel-Miss Bagatelle (Mummy's Pet)
J D Bethell Mrs R A Crossley

Placings:000000 **(5399)**
2001: 5^{0}S, 5^{0}S, 6^{0}G, 7^{0}HY, 5^{0}GS, 6^{0}S

	Starts	1st	2nd	3rd	Win & Pl
Career Total (Turf)	6	0	0	0	

Going (Turf): Sf: 0-4 GS: 0-1 Gd: 0-1 GF: 0-0 Fm: 0-0
Distance: 5f/6f: 0-5 7f-8f: 0-1 9f-13f: 0-0 14f+: 0-0
Track : LH: 0-2 RH: 0-0 Tight: 0-0 Gall: 0-0
Aids: Bl: 0-4 Vi: 0-0 Tstrap: 0-0
Best Rating: 45 10/01 Catt 5f gd-sft

Pinchaninch

107(84) (50)**67**

4-y-o ch g Inchinor-Wollow Maid (Wollow)
J G Portman A S B Portman

Placings:500/004212446-32500 **(5098)**
2001: 12^{3}S, 11^{2}G, 13^{5}GF, 12^{0}G, 14^{0}GS

	Starts	1st	2nd	3rd	Win & Pl
Career Total (Turf)	16	1	3	1	6405
Career Total (AW)	1	0	0	0	

60 6/00 Bath 1m3f144yE(0-65) G-F £2730
Total win prize-money £2730

Going (Turf): Sf: 0-5 GS: 0-1 Gd: 0-5 **GF: 1-5** Fm: 0-0
Distance: 5f/6f: 0-0 7f-8f: 0-1 **9f-13f: 1-13** 14f+: 0-3
Track : **LH: 1-6** RH: 0-5 **Tight: 1-11** Gall: 0-0
Aids: Bl: 0-2 Vi: 0-0 Tstrap: 0-0
Best Rating: 67 8/01 Wind 1m3f135y good

Has only won once and that was a Bath classified event. Acts with cut in the ground and is effective over 12 furlongs.

Pinchbeck

89 **68**

2-y-o b c Petong-Veuve Hoornaert (IRE) (Standaan (FR))
M A Jarvis T G Warner

Placings:00 **(5594)**
2001: 6^{0}GS, 6^{0}GS

	Starts	1st	2nd	3rd	Win & Pl
Career Total (Turf)	2	0	0	0	

Going (Turf): Sf: 0-0 GS: 0-2 Gd: 0-0 GF: 0-0 Fm: 0-0
Distance: 5f/6f: 0-2 7f-8f: 0-0 9f-13f: 0-0 14f+: 0-0
Track : LH: 0-0 RH: 0-0 Tight: 0-0 Gall: 0-0
Aids: Bl: 0-0 Vi: 0-0 Tstrap: 0-0
Best Rating: 68 11/01 NmkR 6f gd-sft

Pinchincha (FR)

110 (66)**88**

7-y-o b g Priolo (USA)-Western Heights (Shirley Heights)
D Morris T J Wells

Placings:012/23611413440200/64400/6500240422023/402343421533-45400222201 **(5558)**
2001: 8^{4}GS, 10^{5}F, 10^{4}G, 10^{0}GF, 10^{0}G, 10^{2}GF, 10^{2}G, 10^{2}G, 10^{2}S, 10^{0}S, 10^{1}S

	Starts	1st	2nd	3rd	Win & Pl
Career Total (Turf)	54	5	11	6	94038
Career Total (AW)	4	1	2	1	4583

79 10/01 Yarm 1m2f21y C(0-85) SFT £6955
81 8/00 NmkJ 1m2f C(0-90)H GD £8573
78 6/97 Pont 1m2f6y C(0-90)H G-F £6056
71 5/97 Donc 1m2f60y E G-S £2966
67 4/97 Folk 1m1f149yF(0-65)H G-F £2854
72 11/96 Sthl 1m G STD £1735
Total win prize-money £29141

Going (Turf): Sf: 1-9 GS: 1-9 Gd: 1-15 **GF: 2-18** Fm: 0-3
Distance: 5f/6f: 0-0 7f-8f: 1-4 **9f-13f: 5-54** 14f+: 0-0
Track : **LH: 4-40** RH: 2-12 Tight: 2-16 Gall: 2-24
Aids: Bl: 0-0 Vi: 0-3 Tstrap: 0-0
Best Rating: 88 10/01 NmkR 1m2f soft

He performs consistently and has run some decent races this season, but has a poor wins-to-runs ratio and gained only his second win since June 1997 in a classified event at Yarmouth in October. Best over ten furlongs and does not want the ground too fast.

Pinjarra

73 **56**

2-y-o b f Petong-Hoh Dancer (Indian Ridge)
J A R Toller Mrs R W Gore-Andrews

Placings:0 **(5139)**
2001: 6^{0}G

	Starts	1st	2nd	3rd	Win & Pl
Career Total (Turf)	1	0	0	0	

Going (Turf): Sf: 0-0 GS: 0-0 Gd: 0-1 GF: 0-0 Fm: 0-0
Distance: 5f/6f: 0-1 7f-8f: 0-0 9f-13f: 0-0 14f+: 0-0
Track : LH: 0-0 RH: 0-0 Tight: 0-0 Gall: 0-0
Aids: Bl: 0-0 Vi: 0-0 Tstrap: 0-0
Best Rating: 56 10/01 NmkR 6f good

Pink Champagne

90(95) (29)**24**

3-y-o ch f Cosmonaut-Riviere Rouge (Forzando)
S G Knight Richard Withers

Placings:06-0000 **(4950)**
2001: 5^{0}G, 5^{0}F, 5^{0}SD, 5^{0}G

	Starts	1st	2nd	3rd	Win & Pl
Career Total (Turf)	5	0	0	0	0
Career Total (AW)	1	0	0	0	

Going (Turf): Sf: 0-0 GS: 0-0 Gd: 0-2 **GF: 0-0** Fm: 0-3
Distance: 5f/6f: 0-6 7f-8f: 0-0 9f-13f: 0-0 14f+: 0-0
Track : LH: 0-5 RH: 0-0 Tight: 0-1 Gall: 0-3
Aids: Bl: 0-0 Vi: 0-0 Tstrap: 0-0
Best Rating: 33 7/01 Bath 5f161y good

Pinnacle Dolphin

64(73) (36)**35**

2-y-o b g Dolphin Street (FR)-Shifting Time (Night Shift (USA))
J L Eyre Pinnacle Dolphin Street Partnership

Placings:000 **(4771)**
2001: 7^{0}G, 8^{0}SW, 7^{0}G

	Starts	1st	2nd	3rd	Win & Pl
Career Total (Turf)	2	0	0	0	
Career Total (AW)	1	0	0	0	

Going (Turf): Sf: 0-0 GS: 0-0 Gd: 0-2 GF: 0-0 Fm: 0-0
Distance: 5f/6f: 0-0 7f-8f: 0-2 9f-13f: 0-1 14f+: 0-0
Track : LH: 0-1 RH: 0-1 Tight: 0-1 Gall: 0-0
Aids: Bl: 0-0 Vi: 0-0 Tstrap: 0-0

Best Rating: 36 9/01 Wolv 1m100y slow

Pinot Noir

102 **79**

3-y-o b c Saddlers' Hall (IRE)-Go For Red (IRE) (Thatching)

H Morrison Mr And Mrs John Wilson

Placings:062654 **(4946)**

2001: 10^{0}GF, 12^{6}GF, 12^{2}GF, 12^{6}GF, 11^{5}GF, 12^{4}G

	Starts	1st	2nd	3rd	Win & Pl
Career Total (Turf)	6	0	1	0	1600

Going (Turf): Sf: 0-0 GS: 0-0 Gd: 0-1 GF: 0-5 Fm: 0-0
Distance: 5f/6f: 0-0 7f-8f: 0-0 9f-13f: 0-6 14f+: 0-0
Track : LH: 0-2 RH: 0-4 Tight: 0-2 Gall: 0-2
Aids: Bl: 0-0 Vi: 0-0 Tstrap: 0-0
Best Rating: 79 7/01 Asct 1m4f gd-fm

Fair form at around a mile and a half on fast ground.

Pious

81(97) (73+)**77+**

2-y-o b f Bishop Of Cashel-La Cabrilla (Carwhite)

J R Fanshawe Cheveley Park Stud

Placings:31 **(5614)**

2001: 6^{3}HY, 6^{1}SD

	Starts	1st	2nd	3rd	Win & Pl
Career Total (Turf)	1	0	0	1	603
Career Total (AW)	1	1	0	0	2968

73	11/01	Wolv	6f	F	STD	£2968

Total win prize-money £2968

Going (Turf): Sf: 0-1 GS: 0-0 Gd: 0-0 GF: 0-0 Fm: 0-0
Distance: 5f/6f: 1-1 7f-8f: 0-1 9f-13f: 0-0 14f+: 0-0
Track : LH: 1-1 RH: 0-0 Tight: 1-1 Gall: 0-0
Aids: Bl: 0-0 Vi: 0-0 Tstrap: 0-0
Best Rating: 77 10/01 Nott 6f15y heavy

Not at all troubled to win a weak six-furlong maiden on the sand easily. She is bred to get much further in time.

Pipadash (IRE)

112(86) (53)**81**

4-y-o b f Pips Pride-Petite Maxine (Sharpo)

T D Easterby T H Bennett

Placings:112303150/200003000010-0030402400411623131 **(5630)**

2001: 6^{0}S, 7^{0}SD, 5^{3}S, 5^{0}S, 6^{4}G, 6^{0}GF, 5^{2}F, 6^{4}F, 6^{0}GF, 6^{0}GF, 6^{4}GS, 6^{1}G, 5^{1}HY, 5^{6}GS, 5^{2}G, 5^{3}HY, 6^{1}S, 6^{3}HY, 6^{1}G

	Starts	1st	2nd	3rd	Win & Pl
Career Total (Turf)	39	8	4	6	72748
Career Total (AW)	1	0	0	0	

81	11/01	Rdcr	6f	C(0-90)H	GD	£7865
65	10/01	York	6f	D(0-75)	SFT	£7637
76	9/01	Hayd	5f	C(0-95)H	HVY	£7767
68	9/01	Haml	6f5y	D(0-85)H	GD	£7280
59	10/00	Pont	6f	F	HVY	£2520
87	8/99	Asct	5f	B	GD	£7752
75	4/99	Pont	5f	D	G-S	£3858
73	4/99	Hayd	5f	E	SFT	£2827

Total win prize-money £47510

Going (Turf): Sf: 4-15 GS: 1-3 Gd: 3-9 GF: 0-10 Fm: 0-2
Distance: 5f/6f: 7-37 7f-8f: 1-2 9f-13f: 0-1 14f+: 0-0
Track : LH: 2-5 RH: 0-0 Tight: 0-0 Gall: 0-0
Aids: Bl: 1-5 Vi: 0-0 Tstrap: 0-0
Best Rating: 81 11/01 Rdcr 6f good

Useful sprinter. A drop in the handicap helped her score at Hamilton in September and she followed up at Haydock six days later. Ran a blinder from the wrong side at the Ayr Great Western meeting, she then won twice more a the back-end. Suited by cut in the ground.

Pipalong (IRE)

115 (77)**118**

5-y-o b m Pips Pride-Limpopo (Green Desert (USA))

T D Easterby T H Bennett

Placings:112241/4452424120521/112103313-001000043 **(5244a)**

2001: 6^{0}FT, 5^{0}G, 6^{1}GF, 6^{0}GF, 6^{0}G, 5^{0}G, 6^{0}HY, 6^{4}S, 5^{3}HO

	Starts	1st	2nd	3rd	Win & Pl
Career Total (Turf)	36	10	7	4	421698
Career Total (AW)	1	0	0	0	

118	5/01	York	6f	A	G-F	£36000
118	9/00	Hayd	6f	A	HVY	£87000
108	6/00	Hayd	6f	A	G-S	£15665
106	5/00	NmkR	5f	A	GD	£23200
108	4/00	Thsk	6f	C	G-S	£6539
99	11/99	Donc	6f	A	SFT	£15695
106	8/99	Ripn	6f	B(0-105)H	GD	£24125
100	10/98	Rdcr	6f	B	HVY	£80519
95	5/98	York	5f	D	GD	£7245
99	4/98	Ripn	5f	D	SFT	£3103

Total win prize-money £299091

Going (Turf): Sf: 4-6 GS: 2-5 Gd: 3-15 GF: 1-8 Fm: 0-1
Distance: 5f/6f: 10-34 7f-8f: 0-3 9f-13f: 0-0 14f+: 0-0
Track : LH: 0-3 RH: 0-0 Tight: 0-2 Gall: 0-0
Aids: Bl: 0-0 Vi: 0-0 Tstrap: 0-0
Best Rating: 118 9/01 Asct 6f soft

An admirably game, high-class sprinter, she won the Haydock Sprint Cup in 2000. She bounced back to her best when giving weight all round at York in May but, after a lean spell in the summer, returned to form with good efforts in the Diadem and Prix de l'Abbaye. Effective over five and six furlongs, she did not want the ground too fast. Retired to stud.

Pipe Dream

44(100) (40)**42**

5-y-o b g King's Signet (USA)-Rather Warm (Tribal Chief)

Jean-Rene Auvray The Simpsons Partnership

Placings:066304000000/336005043500-0 **(1630)**

2001: 9^{0}F

	Starts	1st	2nd	3rd	Win & Pl
Career Total (Turf)	15	0	0	2	1508
Career Total (AW)	10	0	0	2	810

Going (Turf): Sf: 0-1 GS: 0-2 Gd: 0-5 GF: 0-4 Fm: 0-1
Distance: 5f/6f: 0-1 7f-8f: 0-17 9f-13f: 0-7 14f+: 0-0
Track : LH: 0-14 RH: 0-7 Tight: 0-9 Gall: 0-3
Aids: Bl: 0-0 Vi: 0-0 Tstrap: 0-0
Best Rating: 118 9/01 Asct 6f soft

Pipe Music (IRE)

76(100) (35)**39**

6-y-o b g Mujadil (USA)-Sunset Cafe (IRE) (Red Sunset)

P C Haslam Middleham Park Racing Ii

Placings:0055/1400053245/23215600500236/3205002 21-0100 **(3966)**

2001: 16^{0}SD, 14^{1}SW, 14^{0}SD, 16^{0}GS, 14^{6}SD

	Starts	1st	2nd	3rd	Win & Pl
Career Total (Turf)	20	1	2	1	5753
Career Total (AW)	21	3	5	3	10716

35	1/01	Wolv	1m6f166yG		SLW	£1869
39	8/00	Carl	1m6f32y	F(0-60)H	GD	£2828
70	2/99	Sthl	2m	E(0-70)H	STD	£2698
71	2/98	Sthl	1m	F(0-60)H	STD	£1735

Total win prize-money £9131

Going (Turf): Sf: 0-3 GS: 0-4 Gd: 1-7 GF: 0-4 Fm: 0-2
Distance: 5f/6f: 0-3 7f-8f: 1-2 9f-13f: 0-9 14f+: 3-27
Track : LH: 3-29 RH: 1-10 Tight: 1-23 Gall: 0-1
Aids: Bl: 2-11 Vi: 2-11 Tstrap: 0-1
Best Rating: 35 1/01 Wolv 1m6f166y slow

A bit in-and-out and not an easy ride, but has enjoyed some success in modest staying events on sand.

Piped Aboard (IRE)

98(97) (43)**50**

6-y-o b g Pips Pride-Last Gunboat (Dominion)

R Brotherton (T D Barron 21/3) Binding Matters Ltd

Placings:566/1222246/00/3500606-040202305442 **(1529)**

2001: 9^{0}SD, 12^{4}SD, 8^{0}SD, 9^{2}SD, 8^{0}SD, 12^{2}SD, 10^{3}SW, 16^{0}SD, 12^{5}SD, 9^{4}GF, 9^{4}G, 11^{2}F

	Starts	1st	2nd	3rd	Win & Pl
Career Total (Turf)	22	1	5	1	9480
Career Total (AW)	9	0	2	1	1593

71	4/98	Thsk	7f	F	G-S	£2337

Total win prize-money £2338

Going (Turf): Sf: 0-2 GS: 1-5 Gd: 0-8 GF: 0-6 Fm: 0-1
Distance: 5f/6f: 0-1 7f-8f: 1-4 9f-13f: 0-24 14f+: 0-2
Track : LH: 1-23 RH: 0-4 Tight: 1-13 Gall: 0-2
Aids: Bl: 0-3 Vi: 0-6 Tstrap: 0-0
Best Rating: 52 2/01 Wolv 1m4f stand

Piper Dream

85(86) (35)**40**

3-y-o b g Contract Law (USA)-Good Fetch (Siberian Express (USA))

J Balding P O'Boyle

Placings:00505 **(2426)**

2001: 7^{0}SD, 7^{0}G, 11^{5}SD, 11^{0}SD, 8^{5}GF

	Starts	1st	2nd	3rd	Win & Pl
Career Total (Turf)	2	0	0	0	0
Career Total (AW)	3	0	0	0	0

Going (Turf): Sf: 0-0 GS: 0-0 Gd: 0-1 GF: 0-1 Fm: 0-0
Distance: 5f/6f: 0-0 7f-8f: 0-2 9f-13f: 0-3 14f+: 0-0
Track : LH: 0-4 RH: 0-0 Tight: 0-0 Gall: 0-0
Aids: Bl: 0-5 Vi: 0-0 Tstrap: 0-0
Best Rating: 40 5/01 Donc 7f good

Pipiji (IRE)

86(92) (30)**15**

6-y-o gr m Pips Pride-Blue Alicia (Wolver Hollow)

M Wellings Mrs S E Jordan

Placings:004000/42502/000400-600 **(3578)**

2001: 6^{6}SD, 8^{0}SD, 7^{0}GF

	Starts	1st	2nd	3rd	Win & Pl
Career Total (Turf)	15	0	2	0	2024
Career Total (AW)	5	0	0	0	0

Going (Turf): Sf: 0-2 GS: 0-1 Gd: 0-4 GF: 0-4 Fm: 0-4
Distance: 5f/6f: 0-2 7f-8f: 0-10 9f-13f: 0-7 14f+: 0-1
Track : LH: 0-14 RH: 0-4 Tight: 0-7 Gall: 0-1
Aids: Bl: 0-0 Vi: 0-0 Tstrap: 0-0
Best Rating: 30 6/01 Sthl 6f stand

Pippas Pride (IRE)

89(105) (35)**39**

6-y-o ch g Pips Pride-Al Shany (Burslem)

R Hollinshead (P S McEntee 20/2) Jolly Jockeycom

Placings:000/00660/140401/131154350030236000452-460030000 **(1727)**

2001: 6^{4}SW, 7^{6}SW, 6^{0}SD, 7^{0}SD, 7^{3}SD, 6^{0}G, 7^{0}SD, 6^{0}SD, 7^{0}GF

	Starts	1st	2nd	3rd	Win & Pl
Career Total (Turf)	13	0	0	1	368
Career Total (AW)	31	5	2	4	12848

66	2/00	Sthl	1m	E(0-75)H	STD	£2782
65	1/00	Sthl	1m	F	STD	£2005
60	1/00	Sthl	7f	F(0-60)	STD	£1743
53	12/99	Sthl	1m	F	STD	£1882
43	1/99	Ling	1m	F(0-65)H	STD	£1757

Total win prize-money £10170

Going (Turf): Sf: 0-2 GS: 0-1 Gd: 0-6 GF: 0-4 Fm: 0-0

Distance: 5f/6f: 0-8 **7f-8f: 5-29** 9f-13f: 0-7 14f+: 0-0
Track : **LH: 5-36** RH: 0-5 **Tight: 1-19** Gall: 0-4
Aids: Bl: 0-0 Vi: 0-0 Tstrap: 0-3
Best Rating: 47 1/01 Wolv 6f slow

Pips Magic (IRE)

109 **83**

5-y-o b g Pips Pride-Kentucky Starlet (USA) (Cox's Ridge (USA))
J S Goldie Frank Brady

Placings:0301100502440/000230100000/0000001001000000000-00430000361361000 **(4826)**
2001: 6^{0}S, 5^{0}S, 6^{4}G, 6^{3}GF, 5^{0}GF, 6^{0}GF, 5^{0}GF, 6^{0}G, 6^{3}GF, 6^{6}F, 6^{1}GF, 6^{3}G, 6^{6}GF, 6^{1}G, 6^{0}G, 6^{0}GF, 6^{0}G

				Starts	1st	2nd	3rd	Win & Pl
Career Total (Turf)				**62**	**7**	**2**	**5**	**59629**
83	8/01	Ripn	6f	C(0-95)H		GD	£6143	
76	7/01	Donc	6f	D(0-75)		G-F	£4270	
81	7/00	Newc	6f	D(0-85)H		GD	£3848	
80	7/00	Donc	6f	D(0-75)		GD	£4023	
94	6/99	Asct	5f	B(0-105)H		G-F	£14395	
84	5/98	Ayr	5f	D		G-F	£3072	
66	5/98	Ripn	6f	D		G-F	£4240	

Total win prize-money £39994

Going (Turf): Sf: 0-9 GS: 0-7 Gd: 2-20 **GF: 4-22** Fm: 0-3
Distance: **5f/6f: 6-59** 7f-8f: 0-2 9f-13f: 0-0 14f+: 0-0
Track : LH: 0-0 RH: 0-0 Tight: 0-0 Gall: 0-0
Aids: Bl: 0-0 Vi: 0-0 Tstrap: 0-0
Best Rating: 83 8/01 Ripn 6f good

Useful warm-weather sprinter. He won twice in July 2000 and put in some respectable efforts afterwards, but did not win again until Doncaster in July. Added a victory at Ripon in August, but has been held by the Handicapper since. Six furlongs is his trip and he appreciates fast ground.

Pips Song (IRE)

102(107) (78)**78**

6-y-o ch g Pips Pride-Friendly Song (Song)
Dr J D Scargill Mrs Susan Scargill

Placings:6/1046430/**0010**1306022**0**/**24**01030000-506000040 **(5449)**
2001: 6^{5}SD, 6^{0}SD, 6^{6}SD, 6^{0}SD, 6^{0}S, 7^{0}G, 7^{0}G, 6^{4}GS, 6^{0}HY

				Starts	1st	2nd	3rd	Win & Pl
Career Total (Turf)				**26**	**2**	**2**	**2**	**20283**
Career Total (AW)				**13**	**2**	**1**	**1**	**13624**
85	4/00	Pont	6f	C(0-90)H		HVY	£7572	
78	4/99	Leic	5f218y	D(0-85)H		HVY	£4308	
76	3/99	Wolv	6f	C(0-100)H		STD	£8364	
63	4/98	Wolv	6f	F		STD	£2322	

Total win prize-money £22568

Going (Turf): **Sf: 2-10** GS: 0-6 Gd: 0-5 GF: 0-5 Fm: 0-0
Distance: **5f/6f: 4-29** 7f-8f: 0-10 9f-13f: 0-0 14f+: 0-0
Track : **LH: 3-18** RH: 0-0 **Tight: 2-10** Gall: 0-0
Aids: Bl: 0-2 Vi: 0-0 Tstrap: 0-0
Best Rating: 78 10/01 Sals 6f gd-sft

A capable sprinter on Fibresand and turf. Best at six furlongs and suited by very soft ground.

Pips Way (IRE)

102 **50**

4-y-o ch f Pips Pride-Algonquin Park (High Line)
K R Burke Paul James McCaughey

Placings:16030040/60414315400-0005006 **(5013)**
2001: 9^{0}HY, 8^{0}HY, 8^{0}G, 10^{5}G, 7^{0}GF, 10^{0}S, 10^{6}HY

				Starts	1st	2nd	3rd	Win & Pl
Career Total (Turf)				**26**	**3**	**0**	**2**	**15631**
79	7/00	Kemp	1m1f	D(0-80)H		G-S	£4348	
77	6/00	Newc	1m	D(0-85)H		SFT	£3802	
67	5/99	Ripn	6f	D		G-S	£4533	

Total win prize-money £12685

Going (Turf): Sf: 1-9 **GS: 2-5** Gd: 0-9 GF: 0-3 Fm: 0-0
Distance: 5f/6f: 1-3 7f-8f: 1-9 9f-13f: 1-14 14f+: 0-0
Track : LH: 1-13 RH: 1-5 Tight: 0-8 **Gall: 1-3**
Aids: Bl: 0-0 Vi: 0-1 Tstrap: 0-0
Best Rating: 67 8/01 Ripn 1m2f good

Modest performer, she returned to form on soft ground in 2000, but has not reached that level of performance so far this season.

Pipssalio (SPA)

102(101) (65)**57**

4-y-o b c Pips Pride-Tesalia (SPA) (Finissimo (SPA))
Jamie Poulton Chris Steward & Christian Taylor

Placings:000/2140140-0000030003 **(5100)**
2001: 10^{0}S, 10^{0}S, 10^{0}G, 10^{0}GF, 10^{0}G, 9^{3}GF, 10^{0}G, 10^{0}G, 12^{0}G, 9^{3}GS, 12^{2}SD

				Starts	1st	2nd	3rd	Win & Pl
Career Total (Turf)				**20**	**2**	**1**	**2**	**25816**
85	5/00	Kemp	1m2f	C(0-90)H		SFT	£7475	
77	4/00	Sand	1m14y	C(0-100)H		HVY	£14950	

Total win prize-money £22425

Going (Turf): **Sf: 2-7** GS: 0-3 Gd: 0-6 GF: 0-4 Fm: 0-0
Distance: 5f/6f: 0-3 7f-8f: 0-0 **9f-13f: 2-17** 14f+: 0-0
Track : LH: 0-4 **RH: 2-12** Tight: 0-8 **Gall: 1-6**
Aids: Bl: 0-5 Vi: 0-0 Tstrap: 0-0
Best Rating: 70 4/01 Epsm 1m2f18y soft

Fair handicapper, suited by ten furlongs on a right-handed track, a mile looks on the short side nowadays. Needs soft ground.

Piquet

104(92) (55)**63**

3-y-o br f Mind Games-Petonellajill (Petong)
R Hannon Miss Jane Collier

Placings:045525-60016035410060 **(5497)**
2001: 6^{6}SD, 5^{0}GF, 7^{0}S, 6^{1}F, 6^{6}GF, 6^{0}GF, 6^{3}GF, 7^{5}GF, 6^{4}GF, 5^{1}GF, 7^{0}F, 5^{0}S, 6^{6}GS, 5^{0}HY

				Starts	1st	2nd	3rd	Win & Pl
Career Total (Turf)				**17**	**2**	**0**	**1**	**6797**
Career Total (AW)				**3**	**0**	**1**	**0**	**836**
66	8/01	Brig	5f213y	F(0-65)H		G-F	£3178	
63	6/01	Ling	6f	F(0-60)H		FRM	£2621	

Total win prize-money £5800

Going (Turf): Sf: 0-4 GS: 0-2 Gd: 0-1 **GF: 1-8 Fm: 1-2**
Distance: **5f/6f: 2-12** 7f-8f: 0-8 9f-13f: 0-0 14f+: 0-0
Track : **LH: 1-7** RH: 0-1 Tight: 0-3 Gall: 0-1
Aids: Bl: 0-0 Vi: 0-0 Tstrap: 0-0
Best Rating: 66 8/01 Brig 5f213y gd-fm

Not as fast as his namesake, but effective over six furlongs on fast ground and won twice under those conditions at Lingfield and Brighton this season.

Pirandello (IRE)

102 **65**

3-y-o ch g Shalford (IRE)-Scenic Villa (Top Ville)
Miss K B Boutflower Quicksilver Racing Partnership

Placings:4020 **(5463)**
2001: 11^{4}GF, 12^{0}GF, 10^{2}HY, 11^{0}G

	Starts	1st	2nd	3rd	Win & Pl
Career Total (Turf)	**4**	**0**	**1**	**0**	**0**

Going (Turf): **Sf: 0-1 GS: 0-0 Gd: 0-1 GF: 0-2 Fm: 0-0**
Distance: 5f/6f: 0-0 7f-8f: 0-0 9f-13f: 0-4 14f+: 0-0
Track : LH: 0-2 RH: 0-1 Tight: 0-3 Gall: 0-0
Aids: Bl: 0-0 Vi: 0-0 Tstrap: 0-0
Best Rating: 65 10/01 Wind 1m2f7y heavy

Is improving with racing and has run his best race over ten furlongs on heavy ground.

Pirro (IRE)

106 **79**

6-y-o ch g Persian Bold-Kindness Itself (IRE) (Ahonoora)
M H Tompkins P A & D G Sakal

Placings:1/0065606/-00415260 **(4592)**
2001: 10^{0}GF, 9^{0}GF, 11^{4}G, 12^{1}G, 12^{5}GF, 12^{2}G, 12^{6}GF, 10^{0}G

				Starts	1st	2nd	3rd	Win & Pl
Career Total (Turf)				**18**	**2**	**2**	**0**	**14697**
76	7/01	Donc	1m4f	D(0-80)H		GD	£4309	
101	6/98	Curr	1m			SFT	£5480	

Total win prize-money £9790

Going (Turf): **Sf: 1-2** GS: 0-0 **Gd: 1-8** GF: 0-6 Fm: 0-0
Distance: 5f/6f: 0-0 7f-8f: 1-5 9f-13f: 1-13 14f+: 0-0
Track : **LH: 1-8** RH: 0-5 Tight: 0-2 **Gall: 2-5**
Aids: Bl: 0-0 Vi: 0-0 Tstrap: 0-1
Best Rating: 79 8/01 Pont 1m4f8y good

Started his career in Ireland and ran some fair races in decent handicap company over there. Took time to find his way in Britain and eventually got off the mark at Doncaster over a mile and a half in July. Likes to front run.

Pivot D'Amour

83 **56**

2-y-o ch f Pivotal-Miss Loving (Northfields (USA))
J J Quinn B M Guerin

Placings:0300 **(4730)**
2001: 6^{0}GF, 5^{3}GS, 6^{0}GF, 5^{0}F

	Starts	1st	2nd	3rd	Win & Pl
Career Total (Turf)	**4**	**0**	**0**	**1**	**570**

Going (Turf): **Sf: 0-0 GS: 0-1 Gd: 0-0 GF: 0-2 Fm: 0-1**
Distance: 5f/6f: 0-4 7f-8f: 0-0 9f-13f: 0-0 14f+: 0-0
Track : LH: 0-0 RH: 0-0 Tight: 0-0 Gall: 0-0
Aids: Bl: 0-0 Vi: 0-0 Tstrap: 0-0
Best Rating: 56 8/01 Bevl 5f gd-sft

Pivotable

96(104) (76)**60**

3-y-o ch f Pivotal-Lady Dowery (USA) (Manila (USA))
K R Burke (M L W Bell 6/6) K Blackham, T Gould & E De Giles

Placings:32500-101005000 **(5612)**
2001: 6^{1}SD, 6^{0}S, 6^{1}SD, 6^{0}GF, 6^{0}G, 7^{5}GF, 8^{0}F, 6^{0}G, 6^{0}SD

				Starts	1st	2nd	3rd	Win & Pl
Career Total (Turf)				**11**	**0**	**1**	**1**	**1489**
Career Total (AW)				**3**	**2**	**0**	**0**	**6666**
75	5/01	Wolv	6f	D(0-85)H		STD	£3796	
76	2/01	Wolv	6f	D		STD	£2870	

Total win prize-money £6666

Going (Turf): **Sf: 0-3 GS: 0-1 Gd: 0-4 GF: 0-2 Fm: 0-1**
Distance: **5f/6f: 2-10** 7f-8f: 0-4 9f-13f: 0-0 14f+: 0-0
Track : **LH: 2-7** RH: 0-1 **Tight: 2-5** Gall: 0-3
Aids: Bl: 0-0 Vi: 0-0 Tstrap: 0-0
Best Rating: 76 2/01 Wolv 6f stand

Placate

101 **80**

3-y-o b f Rainbow Quest (USA)-Princess Borghese (USA) (Nijinsky (CAN))
J H M Gosden K Abdulla

Placings:430 **(3835)**
2001: 12^{4}GF, 10^{3}GF, 12^{0}G

	Starts	1st	2nd	3rd	Win & Pl
Career Total (Turf)	**3**	**0**	**0**	**1**	**1349**

Going (Turf): **Sf: 0-0 GS: 0-0 Gd: 0-1 GF: 0-2 Fm: 0-0**
Distance: 5f/6f: 0-0 7f-8f: 0-0 9f-13f: 0-3 14f+: 0-0
Track : LH: 0-1 RH: 0-2 Tight: 0-0 Gall: 0-3
Aids: Bl: 0-0 Vi: 0-0 Tstrap: 0-0

Best Rating: 80 7/01 Asct 1m2f gd-fm

Plain Chant

101 45

4-y-o b g Doyoun-Sing Softly (Luthier)
P W Harris Mrs P W Harris

Placings:000-653 (3156)
2001: 12^6GF, 14^5GF, 16^3GS

	Starts	1st	2nd	3rd	Win & Pl
Career Total (Turf)	6	0	0	1	460

Going (Turf): Sf: 0-1 GS: 0-1 Gd: 0-0 GF: 0-4 Fm: 0-0
Distance: 5f/6f: 0-0 7f-8f: 0-0 9f-13f: 0-4 14f+: 0-2
Track : LH. 0-3 RH. 0-2 Tight: 0-3 Gall: 0-0
Aids: Bl: 0-0 Vi: 0-0 Tstrap: 0-0
Best Rating: 45 6/01 Wwck 1m4f134y gd-fm

Plateau

94 90+

2-y-o b c Zamindar (USA)-Painted Desert (Green Desert (USA))
B W Hills K Abdulla

Placings:13 (3884)
2001: 6^1GS, 6^3G

	Starts	1st	2nd	3rd	Win & Pl
Career Total (Turf)	2	1	0	1	4835

90 7/01 Ayr 6f D G-S £3757
Total win prize-money £3757

Going (Turf): Sf: 0-0 **GS: 1-1** Gd: 0-1 GF: 0-0 Fm: 0-0
Distance: **5f/6f: 1-2** 7f-8f: 0-0 9f-13f: 0-0 14f+: 0-0
Track : LH: 0-0 RH: 0-0 Tight: 0-0 Gall: 0-0
Aids: Bl: 0-0 Vi: 0-0 Tstrap: 0-0
Best Rating: 90 7/01 Ayr 6f gd-sft

Has stamina and speed in his pedigree. An attractive scopey individual who was unimpressive to post on his debut and ran green but still managed to win. Had one more outing when third at Windsor in August but lacked experience. Has won on good to soft ground.

Platinum Duke

96 79

2-y-o br g Reprimand-Princess Alaska (Northern State (USA))
K A Ryan Platinum Racing Club Limited

Placings:2251266 (4309)
2001: 6^2GF, 6^2F, 7^5GF, 7^1F, 7^2GF, 7^6G, 8^6GF

	Starts	1st	2nd	3rd	Win & Pl
Career Total (Turf)	7	1	3	0	8522

77 7/01 Muss 7f30y F FRM £2618
Total win prize-money £2618

Going (Turf): Sf: 0-0 GS: 0-0 Gd: 0-1 GF: 0-4 **Fm: 1-2**
Distance: 5f/6f: 0-2 **7f-8f: 1-4** 9f-13f: 0-1 14f+: 0-0
Track : LH: 0-1 RH: 0-1 Tight: 0-0 Gall: 0-0
Aids: Bl: 0-0 Vi: 0-0 Tstrap: 0-0
Best Rating: 79 8/01 Newc 1m3y gd-fm

Bred to get a mile, and ran accordingly when beating Welsh Emperor in a seven-furlong maiden at Musselburgh in July. He had earlier run behind classy performers like Meshaheer and Leo's Luckyman. Has not had things go his way since. Needs fast ground.

Platonic

93 83

2-y-o b f Zafonic (USA)-Puce (Darshaan)
L M Cumani Fittocks Stud

Placings:46 (4871)
2001: 7^4GF, 8^6G

	Starts	1st	2nd	3rd	Win & Pl
Career Total (Turf)	2	0	0	0	382

Going (Turf): Sf: 0-0 GS: 0-0 Gd: 0-1 GF: 0-1 Fm: 0-0
Distance: 5f/6f: 0-0 7f-8f: 0-2 9f-13f: 0-0 14f+: 0-0
Track : LH: 0-0 RH: 0-0 Tight: 0-0 Gall: 0-0
Aids: Bl: 0-0 Vi: 0-0 Tstrap: 0-0
Best Rating: 83 9/01 NmkR 1m good

Play Games (USA)

(76) (16)

13-y-o ch g Nijinsky (CAN)-Playful Queen (USA) (Majestic Prince (USA))
R Lee Exors Of The Late J O Beavan

Placings:61046/0 (5044)
2001: 14^0SD

	Starts	1st	2nd	3rd	Win & Pl
Career Total (Turf)	5	1	0	0	2800
Career Total (AW)	1	0	0	0	

71 7/91 Bath 1m3f150yF G-F £2564
Total win prize-money £2565

Going (Turf): Sf: 0-0 GS: 0-0 Gd: 0-2 **GF: 1-1** Fm: 0-2
Distance: 5f/6f: 0-0 7f-8f: 0-0 **9f-13f: 1-4** 14f+: 0-2
Track : **LH: 1-4** RH: 0-2 **Tight: 1-3** Gall: 0-1
Aids: Bl: 0-0 Vi: 0-0 Tstrap: 0-1
Best Rating: 15 10/01 Sthl 1m6f stand

Play Misty (IRE)

98(85) (38)62

2-y-o b f Dr Devious (IRE)-Mystic Step (IRE) (Fairy King (USA))
John Berry A A Lyons

Placings:6463020 (5467)
2001: 5^6SD, 6^4GF, 5^6F, 5^3F, 6^0G, 5^2S, 6^0S, 6^0SD

	Starts	1st	2nd	3rd	Win & Pl
Career Total (Turf)	6	0	1	1	1010
Career Total (AW)	1	0	0	0	0

Going (Turf): Sf: 0-2 GS: 0-0 Gd: 0-1 GF: 0-1 Fm: 0-2
Distance: 5f/6f: 0-5 7f-8f: 0-2 9f-13f: 0-0 14f+: 0-0
Track : LH: 0-2 RH: 0-0 Tight: 0-0 Gall: 0-0
Aids: Bl: 0-3 Vi: 0-0 Tstrap: 0-0
Best Rating: 62 10/01 Brig 5f59y soft

Play Time

97 85+

3-y-o b f Unfuwain (USA)-Break Point (Reference Point)
D R C Elsworth Brian Cooper

Placings:00-6216 (2511)
2001: 10^6GS, 10^2G, 10^1GF, 12^6GF

	Starts	1st	2nd	3rd	Win & Pl
Career Total (Turf)	6	1	1	0	6791

81 6/01 NmkR 1m2f D G-F £5135
Total win prize-money £5135

Going (Turf): Sf: 0-2 GS: 0-1 Gd: 0-1 **GF: 1-2** Fm: 0-0
Distance: 5f/6f: 0-0 7f-8f: 0-1 **9f-13f: 1-5** 14f+: 0-0
Track : LH: 0-0 RH: 0-2 Tight: 0-2 Gall: 0-0
Aids: Bl: 0-0 Vi: 0-0 Tstrap: 0-0
Best Rating: 85 5/01 NmkR 1m2f good

Playapart (USA)

104 103

2-y-o b c Theatrical-Spotlight Dance (USA) (Miswaki (USA))
G A Butler Hesmonds Stud

Placings:32 (5260)
2001: 7^3GF, 7^2GS

	Starts	1st	2nd	3rd	Win & Pl
Career Total (Turf)	2	0	1	1	4207

Going (Turf): Sf: 0-0 GS: 0-1 Gd: 0-0 GF: 0-1 Fm: 0-0
Distance: 5f/6f: 0-0 7f-8f: 0-2 9f-13f: 0-0 14f+: 0-0
Track : LH: 0-0 RH: 0-0 Tight: 0-0 Gall: 0-0
Aids: Bl: 0-0 Vi: 0-0 Tstrap: 0-0
Best Rating: 103 10/01 Asct 7f gd-sft

He ran blinders in both of his starts at two and was unlucky not to win theHyperion at Ascot. Sure to win decent races at three.

Playback (IRE)

100 84

2-y-o b c Revoque (IRE)-Sound Tap (IRE) (Warning)
R Hannon Alessandro Gaucci

Placings:05432 (5590)
2001: 7^0G, 7^5G, 8^4GF, 10^3GS, 9^2GS

	Starts	1st	2nd	3rd	Win & Pl
Career Total (Turf)	5	0	1	1	2060

Going (Turf): Sf: 0-0 GS: 0-2 Gd: 0-2 GF: 0-1 Fm: 0-0
Distance: 5f/6f: 0-0 7f-8f: 0-3 9f-13f: 0-2 14f+: 0-0
Track : LH: 0-2 RH: 0-0 Tight: 0-0 Gall: 0-0
Aids: Bl: 0-0 Vi: 0-0 Tstrap: 0-0
Best Rating: 84 11/01 Brig 1m1f209y gd-sft

Playful Charlie

(45)

6-y-o b g Librate-Hayley's Lass (Royal Boxer)
J M Bradley Miss Diane Hill

Placings:0-0 (0061)
2001: 8^0SW

	Starts	1st	2nd	3rd	Win & Pl
Career Total (Turf)	0	0	0	0	
Career Total (AW)	2	0	0	0	

Going (Turf): Sf: 0-0 GS: 0-0 Gd: 0-0 GF: 0-0 Fm: 0-0
Distance: 5f/6f: 0-0 7f-8f: 0-0 9f-13f: 0-2 14f+: 0-0
Track : LH: 0-2 RH: 0-0 Tight: 0-2 Gall: 0-0
Aids: Bl: 0-0 Vi: 0-0 Tstrap: 0-0

Playful Spirit

94 91

2-y-o b f Mind Games-Kalimat (Be My Guest (USA))
P W Harris The Minders

Placings:1160 (3883)
2001: 6^1GF, 6^1GF, 7^6GF, 6^0G

	Starts	1st	2nd	3rd	Win & Pl
Career Total (Turf)	4	2	0	0	7600

91 7/01 Sals 6f F G-F £3388
70 6/01 Gdwd 6f E G-F £4212
Total win prize-money £7600

Going (Turf): Sf: 0-0 GS: 0-0 Gd: 0-1 **GF: 2-3** Fm: 0-0
Distance: **5f/6f: 2-3** 7f-8f: 0-1 9f-13f: 0-0 14f+: 0-0
Track : LH: 0-0 RH: 0-0 Tight: 0-0 Gall: 0-0
Aids: Bl: 0-0 Vi: 0-0 Tstrap: 0-0
Best Rating: 91 7/01 Sals 6f gd-fm

The first foal of a mile winner who is a half-sister to a Grade One winner in the States. She won readily on her debut and followed up at Goodwood. Met interference when upped in class next time. Suited by fast gruond.

Playgirl (IRE)

99 81

3-y-o b f Caerleon (USA)-Stage Struck (IRE) (Sadler's Wells (USA))
Sir Michael Stoute Lord Weinstock

Placings:224 (4434)
2001: 10^2GF, 10^2G, 8^4G

	Starts	1st	2nd	3rd	Win & Pl
Career Total (Turf)	3	0	2	0	2789

Going (Turf): Sf: 0-0 **GS: 0-0 Gd: 0-2 GF: 0-1 Fm: 0-0**
Distance: 5f/6f: 0-0 7f-8f: 0-0 9f-13f: 0-3 14f+: 0-0
Track: LH: 0-0 RH: 0-1 Tight: 0-2 Gall: 0-0
Aids: Bl: 0-0 Vi: 0-0 Tstrap: 0-0
Best Rating: 81 8/01 Wind 1m2f7y good

Playmaker

48
8-y-o b g Primo Dominie-Salacious (Sallust)
F P Murtagh Mrs Anna Kenny

Placings:15236/6506000050/060000/0-00 **(1000)**
2001: 17^{0}HY, 10^{0}S

	Starts	1st	2nd	3rd	Win & Pl
Career Total (Turf)	21	1	1	1	6768
Career Total (AW)	4	0	0	0	0

83 4/95 Ripn 5f D G-S £4240
Total win prize-money £4241

Going (Turf): Sf: 0-4 **GS: 1-3** Gd: 0-6 GF: 0-6 Fm: 0-2
Distance: **5f/6f: 1-19** 7f-8f: 0-4 9f-13f: 0-1 14f+: 0-1
Track: LH: 0-10 RH: 0-2 Tight: 0-4 Gall: 0-1
Aids: Bl: 0-7 Vi: 0-0 Tstrap: 0-0
Best Rating: 83 4/95 Ripn 5f GS

Plazzotta (IRE)

80(81) (19)**15**
4-y-o b g Sri Pekan (USA)-Porte Des Iles (IRE) (Kris)
M C Chapman Miss C T Hickford

Placings:0/6P0-06000000 **(3840)**
2001: 8^{0}SD, 6^{6}SW, 11^{0}SD, 12^{0}SW, 11^{0}SD, 5^{0}GF, 12^{0}SD, 7^{0}G

	Starts	1st	2nd	3rd	Win & Pl
Career Total (Turf)	5	0	0	0	0
Career Total (AW)	7	0	0	0	0

Going (Turf): Sf: 0-1 **GS: 0-1 Gd: 0-2 GF: 0-1 Fm: 0-0**
Distance: 5f/6f: 0-4 7f-8f: 0-3 9f-13f: 0-5 14f+: 0-0
Track: LH: 0-8 RH: 0-0 Tight: 0-0 Gall: 0-0
Aids: Bl: 0-0 Vi: 0-0 Tstrap: 0-0
Best Rating: 19 1/01 Sthl 6f slow

Pleading

98(102) (60)**59**
8-y-o b g Never So Bold-Ask Mama (Mummy's Pet)
M A Buckley Miss Kim Smith

Placings:04/1120/60004000/001006/**005**203043200301000/**2330050061000-50335U3000** **(5681)**
2001: 6^{5}SD, 7^{0}SD, 7^{3}GS, 7^{3}S, 7^{5}GF, 7^{U}G, 7^{3}G, 7^{0}GF, 8^{0}GS, 8^{0}S

	Starts	1st	2nd	3rd	Win & Pl
Career Total (Turf)	53	5	3	7	39735
Career Total (AW)	8	0	1	1	1748

60 8/00 NmkJ 7f E G-F £3562
73 9/99 Chep 7f16y F(0-65)H GD £2920
70 4/98 Pont 6f D(0-80)H G-S £7749
91 5/96 Leic 5f218y D(0-85)H G-S £3947
77 5/96 Sals 6f D GD £3078
Total win prize-money £21259

Going (Turf): Sf: 0-10 **GS: 2-15 Gd: 2-18** GF: 1-10 Fm: 0-0
Distance: **5f/6f: 3-23** 7f-8f: 2-35 9f-13f: 0-3 14f+: 0-0
Track: **LH: 1-15** RH: 0-5 Tight: 0-2 Gall: 0-2
Aids: Bl: 1-8 Vi: 1-10 Tstrap: 0-0
Best Rating: 64 4/01 Muss 7f30y gd-sft

Modest sprinter with a low strike rate. Not an easy ride and needs producing late. Seven furlongs is probably his best trip now.

Pleasant Mount

100(98) (65)**64d**
5-y-o b g First Trump-Alo Ez (Alzao (USA))
G M Moore Anmaf Partnership

Placings:00/033231112/01503023-050 **(4858)**
2001: 16^{0}S, 16^{5}GF, 15^{0}GF

	Starts	1st	2nd	3rd	Win & Pl
Career Total (Turf)	21	3	3	5	17494
Career Total (AW)	1	1	0	0	2338

65 4/00 Wolv 2m46y F(0-65)H STD £2338
60 8/99 Rdcr 1m6f19y E(0-70)H GD £4034
56 8/99 Thsk 2m F(0-60)H SFT £3252
53 7/99 Bevl 2m35y F(0-65)H G-F £2940
Total win prize-money £12566

Going (Turf): Sf: 1-5 GS: 0-3 **Gd: 1-6 GF: 1-6** Fm: 0-1
Distance: 5f/6f: 0-2 7f-8f: 0-1 9f-13f: 0-2 **14f+: 4-17**
Track: **LH: 3-15** RH: 1-5 **Tight: 4-13** Gall: 0-2
Aids: Bl: 0-0 Vi: 0-0 Tstrap: 0-0
Best Rating: 56 5/01 Thsk 2m gd-fm

Pleasure

90(102) (48)**55d**
6-y-o ch m Most Welcome-Peak Squaw (USA) (Icecapade (USA))
A Smith The Rufus Partnership

Placings:0/3000**150**/0001500/**5464100-360054050** **(4220)**
2001: 6^{3}SD, 5^{6}SD, 6^{0}HY, 6^{0}SD, 5^{5}SD, 6^{4}SD, 6^{0}SD, 5^{5}SD, 6^{0}G

	Starts	1st	2nd	3rd	Win & Pl
Career Total (Turf)	17	2	0	1	6544
Career Total (AW)	14	1	0	1	2555

48 6/00 Sthl 5f F(0-60)H STD £2296
56 6/99 Bevl 5f E(0-70)H SFT £3135
54 10/98 Donc 7f E(0-70)H SFT £3113
Total win prize-money £8545

Going (Turf): Sf: 2-8 GS: 0-2 Gd: 0-3 GF: 0-3 Fm: 0-1
Distance: **5f/6f: 2-21** 7f-8f: 1-10 9f-13f: 0-0 14f+: 0-0
Track: LH: 0-12 RH: 0-1 Tight: 0-4 Gall: 0-0
Aids: **Bl: 2-14** Vi: 0-0 Tstrap: 0-0
Best Rating: 47 3/01 Sthl 6f stand

Pleasure Dome

102(106) (64)**65**
3-y-o b f Most Welcome-Hickleton Lady (IRE) (Kala Shikari)
J M P Eustace Park Lane Racing

Placings:20-2450600110 **(5532)**
2001: 7^{2}SD, 7^{4}SD, 6^{5}GF, 6^{0}GF, 6^{6}G, 6^{0}GF, 5^{0}GF, 7^{1}S, 8^{1}GS, 9^{0}HY

	Starts	1st	2nd	3rd	Win & Pl
Career Total (Turf)	10	2	1	0	6248
Career Total (AW)	2	0	1	0	516

59 10/01 Leic 1m9y F(0-60) G-S £2691
63 10/01 Brig 7f214y E(0-65) SFT £2842
Total win prize-money £5534

Going (Turf): Sf: 1-3 GS: 1-1 Gd: 0-1 GF: 0-5 Fm: 0-0
Distance: 5f/6f: 0-5 7f-8f: 1-5 9f-13f: 1-2 14f+: 0-0
Track: **LH: 1-5** RH: 0-0 Tight: 0-1 Gall: 0-0
Aids: Bl: 0-1 Vi: 0-0 Tstrap: 0-0
Best Rating: 63 10/01 Brig 7f214y soft

She had shown bits and pieces of form early in her career, but did not get off the mark until stepped up to a mile for a classified event at Brighton in October. Followed up in a similar event at Leicester and landed a handicap on the Lingfield Polytrack. Best over a mile.

Pleasure Time

102(96) (54)**54**
8-y-o ch g Clantime-First Experience (Le Johnstan)
C Smith A E Needham

Placings:453150512200/3055435050/103020530/122001000/2100300/0600160-00000263 **(5350)**
2001: 5^{0}G, 5^{0}F, 5^{0}GS, 5^{0}G, 5^{0}G, 5^{2}GF, 5^{6}GF, 5^{3}SD

	Starts	1st	2nd	3rd	Win & Pl
Career Total (Turf)	60	7	7	6	33908
Career Total (AW)	2	0	0	1	334

66 8/00 Nott 5f13y E(0-65) G-F £3094
78 6/99 Bath 5f161y E(0-75) FRM £2612
70 8/98 Thsk 5f E(0-70)H G-F £3653
66 5/98 Nott 5f13y E(0-70)H G-F £3287
63 5/97 Nott 5f13y E(0-70)H GD £3252
67 8/95 Hayd 5f E G-F £3241
71 5/95 Rdcr 5f F FRM £2882
Total win prize-money £22022

Going (Turf): Sf: 0-4 GS: 0-6 Gd: 1-19 **GF: 4-26** Fm: 2-5
Distance: **5f/6f: 7-62** 7f-8f: 0-0 9f-13f: 0-0 14f+: 0-0
Track: **LH: 1-3** RH: 0-1 Tight: 0-2 **Gall: 1-2**
Aids: Bl: 2-14 **Vi: 4-34** Tstrap: 0-0
Best Rating: 54 10/01 Sthl 5f stand

Modest sprinter, he wins once in a while, but his overall profile is not inspiring. Suited by the minimum trip and fast ground.

Pleinmont Point (IRE)

97 **67d**
3-y-o b g Tagula (IRE)-Cree's Figurine (Creetown)
P D Evans Trevor Gallienne

Placings:460-2000 **(4736)**
2001: 7^{2}S, 6^{0}S, 6^{0}F, 6^{0}F

	Starts	1st	2nd	3rd	Win & Pl
Career Total (Turf)	7	0	1	0	1819

Going (Turf): Sf: 0-4 GS: 0-0 Gd: 0-1 GF: 0-0 Fm: 0-2
Distance: 5f/6f: 0-3 7f-8f: 0-4 9f-13f: 0-0 14f+: 0-0
Track: LH: 0-0 RH: 0-0 Tight: 0-0 Gall: 0-0
Aids: Bl: 0-0 Vi: 0-0 Tstrap: 0-1
Best Rating: 67 3/01 Donc 7f soft

Hinted at ability at two in a light campaign. Showed the benefit when running well on his return at Doncaster.

Plough Boy

97(83) (29)**49**
3-y-o br g Komaite (USA)-Plough Hill (North Briton)
D E Cantillon J W Orbell

Placings:066200144 **(4896)**
2001: 7^{0}SW, 7^{6}SD, 7^{6}SD, 7^{2}GF, 6^{0}GF, 7^{0}G, 8^{1}GS, 10^{4}G, 9^{4}GS

	Starts	1st	2nd	3rd	Win & Pl
Career Total (Turf)	6	1	1	0	3003
Career Total (AW)	3	0	0	0	0

49 8/01 Yarm 1m3y G(0-60)H G-S £2159
Total win prize-money £2160

Going (Turf): Sf: 0-0 **GS: 1-2** Gd: 0-2 GF: 0-2 Fm: 0-0
Distance: 5f/6f: 0-0 7f-8f: 0-6 **9f-13f: 1-3** 14f+: 0-0
Track: LH: 0-3 RH: 0-2 Tight: 0-3 Gall: 0-1
Aids: Bl: 0-0 Vi: 0-0 Tstrap: 0-0
Best Rating: 49 8/01 Yarm 1m3y gd-sft

Previously a front-runner, benefited from waiting tactics when getting off the mark on easy ground at Yarmouth in August.

Plum Beautiful

94 **54d**
3-y-o b f Wolfhound (USA)-Miss Haversham (Salse (USA))
C A Cyzer Mrs E A Cyzer

Placings:040460 **(4609)**
2001: 8^{0}GS, 8^{4}GF, 7^{0}GS, 8^{4}GF, 7^{6}GF, 8^{0}F

	Starts	1st	2nd	3rd	Win & Pl
Career Total (Turf)	6	0	0	0	276

Going (Turf): Sf: 0-0 GS: 0-2 Gd: 0-0 GF: 0-3 Fm: 0-1
Distance: 5f/6f: 0-0 7f-8f: 0-3 9f-13f: 0-3 14f+: 0-0
Track: LH: 0-1 RH: 0-1 Tight: 0-2 Gall: 0-0
Aids: Bl: 0-0 Vi: 0-0 Tstrap: 0-0

Best Rating: 54 8/01 NmkJ 7f gd-fm

Pluralist (IRE)

86(105) (70)**41**

5-y-o b g Mujadil (USA)-Encore Une Fois (IRE) (Shirley Heights)

Miss K M George Exterior Profiles Ltd

Placings:5220/04265621/24110043-60000 **(3404)**

2001: 16^{0}SD, 11^{0}SD, 15^{0}HY, 14^{0}GF, 16^{0}GF

	Starts	1st	2nd	3rd	Win & Pl
Career Total (Turf)	18	1	5	0	9378
Career Total (AW)	7	2	0	1	6595

72 6/00 Ling 1m4f D(0-85)H STD £3789
64 5/00 Wwck 1m2f110yF HVY £2436
47 12/99 Sthl 1m3f F STD £2116
Total win prize-money £8343

Going (Turf): Sf: **1-4** GS: 0-2 Gd: 0-3 GF: 0-8 Fm: 0-1
Distance: 5f/6f: 0-2 7f-8f: 0-2 **9f-13f: 3-16** 14f+: 0-5
Track : **LH: 3-15** RH: 0-8 **Tight: 1-11** Gall: 0-5
Aids: Bl: 0-0 Vi: 0-0 Tstrap: 0-2
Best Rating: 52 4/01 Sthl 1m3f stand

Plymsole (USA)

103 **75**

2-y-o ch f Diesis-Pump (USA) (Forli (ARG))

J L Dunlop Mrs Sonia Rogers

Placings:41 **(4234)**

2001: 7^{4}GS, 7^{1}GF

	Starts	1st	2nd	3rd	Win & Pl
Career Total (Turf)	2	1	0	0	4517

75 8/01 Bevl 7f100y D G-F £4199
Total win prize-money £4199

Going (Turf): Sf: 0-0 GS: 0-1 Gd: 0-0 **GF: 1-1** Fm: 0-0
Distance: 5f/6f: 0-0 **7f-8f: 1-2** 9f-13f: 0-0 14f+: 0-0
Track : LH: 0-0 **RH: 1-1** Tight: 0-0 Gall: 0-0
Aids: Bl: 0-0 Vi: 0-0 Tstrap: 0-0
Best Rating: 75 8/01 Bevl 7f100y gd-fm

Scored at her second attempt over an extended seven furlongs having previously shown ability on her debut. Acts on good to firm.

Pocket Style (IRE)

90 **65**

2-y-o b f Desert Style (IRE)-Practical (Ballymore)

C Grant C E Whiteley

Placings:4305000 **(5404)**

2001: 6^{4}GF, 5^{3}G, 6^{0}GS, 7^{5}G, 8^{0}HY, 7^{0}GS, 8^{0}S

	Starts	1st	2nd	3rd	Win & Pl
Career Total (Turf)	7	0	0	1	741

Going (Turf): Sf: 0-2 GS: 0-2 Gd: 0-2 GF: 0-1 Fm: 0-0
Distance: 5f/6f: 0-3 7f-8f: 0-2 9f-13f: 0-2 14f+: 0-0
Track : LH: 0-4 RH: 0-0 Tight: 0-1 Gall: 0-0
Aids: Bl: 0-0 Vi: 0-0 Tstrap: 0-0
Best Rating: 65 8/01 Newc 7f good

Point Of Dispute

110(99) (89+)**92**

6-y-o b g Cyrano De Bergerac-Opuntia (Rousillon (USA))

P J Makin Mrs B J Carrington

Placings:0100/0010001/441310-0432 **(5133)**

2001: 6^{0}GF, 6^{4}GF, 7^{3}GF, 7^{2}G, 8^{6}SD

	Starts	1st	2nd	3rd	Win & Pl
Career Total (Turf)	19	4	1	2	27510
Career Total (AW)	2	1	0	0	3705

89 11/00 Sthl 7f D(0-85)H STD £3705
84 8/00 NmkJ 6f C(0-90)H GD £7553
79 10/99 Nott 6f15y D(0-80)H FRM £5345
74 8/99 Ling 7f E(0-75)H GD £4272

82 5/98 Sals 6f D G-S £3143
Total win prize-money £24020

Going (Turf): Sf: 0-3 GS: 1-2 **Gd: 2-5** GF: 0-7 Fm: 1-2
Distance: 5f/6f: 2-13 **7f-8f: 3-8** 9f-13f: 0-0 14f+: 0-0
Track : **LH: 1-2** RH: 0-2 Tight: 0-1 Gall: 0-2
Aids: Bl: 0-0 **Vi: 4-15** Tstrap: 0-0
Best Rating: 92 9/01 Newb 7f gd-fm

Useful sprinter. Has reportedly had his share of training problems. He is not a straightforward character and usually wears a visor. Suited by Fibresand, and good or faster ground on turf.

Poker School (IRE)

(97) (59)

7-y-o b g Night Shift (USA)-Mosaique Bleue (Shirley Heights)

M R Bosley Mrs J L Brindley

Placings:3/42210000/**033**00000/1034500**33**/4053350 **(1315)**

2001: 12^{4}SD, 16^{0}SD, 12^{5}SD, 12^{3}SD, 12^{3}SD, 13^{5}SD, 14^{0}SD

	Starts	1st	2nd	3rd	Win & Pl
Career Total (Turf)	17	1	2	1	4370
Career Total (AW)	16	1	0	7	4160

64 1/99 Sthl 1m3f G(0-65)H STD £1522
75 5/97 Dund 1m1f GD £2740
Total win prize-money £4262

Going (Turf): Sf: 0-1 GS: 0-2 **Gd: 1-7** GF: 0-5 Fm: 0-0
Distance: 5f/6f: 0-0 7f-8f: 0-7 **9f-13f: 2-21** 14f+: 0-5
Track : **LH: 2-26** RH: 0-3 Tight: 0-9 Gall: 0-1
Aids: Bl: 0-4 Vi: 0-1 Tstrap: 0-1
Best Rating: 59 3/01 Wolv 1m4f stand

Polar Beauty (IRE)

98(67) **47**

4-y-o b f Distinctly North (USA)-How Gorgeous (Frimley Park)

B A McMahon The Nurthirst Farm Stud Partnership

Placings:06340 **(3014)**

2001: 6^{0}GS, 7^{6}GF, 5^{3}F, 5^{4}GF, 5^{0}SD

	Starts	1st	2nd	3rd	Win & Pl
Career Total (Turf)	4	0	0	1	438
Career Total (AW)	1	0	0	0	

Going (Turf): Sf: 0-0 GS: 0-1 Gd: 0-0 GF: 0-2 Fm: 0-1
Distance: 5f/6f: 0-4 7f-8f: 0-1 9f-13f: 0-0 14f+: 0-0
Track : LH: 0-3 RH: 0-0 Tight: 0-0 Gall: 0-1
Aids: Bl: 0-0 Vi: 0-0 Tstrap: 0-0
Best Rating: 47 6/01 Wwck 5f gd-fm

Polar Ben

96 **82+**

2-y-o b c Polar Falcon (USA)-Woodbeck (Terimon)

J R Fanshawe Simon Gibson

Placings:1 **(4320)**

2001: 7^{1}GF

	Starts	1st	2nd	3rd	Win & Pl
Career Total (Turf)	1	1	0	0	2643

82 8/01 Wwck 7f26y F G-F £2642
Total win prize-money £2643

Going (Turf): Sf: 0-0 GS: 0-0 Gd: 0-0 **GF: 1-1** Fm: 0-0
Distance: 5f/6f: 0-0 **7f-8f: 1-1** 9f-13f: 0-0 14f+: 0-0
Track : **LH: 1-1** RH: 0-0 Tight: 0-0 Gall: 0-0
Aids: Bl: 0-0 Vi: 0-0 Tstrap: 0-0
Best Rating: 82 8/01 Wwck 7f26y gd-fm

A 12,500 guinea yearling, is from the same family as French Oaks winner Madam Gay. Won on his sole start as a juvenile at Warwick in August over seven furlongs on a sound surface.

Polar Dance (USA)

84 **49**

3-y-o gr/ro c Nureyev (USA)-Arctic Swing (USA) (Swing Till Dawn (USA))

J W Hills Manchester United Racing Club

Placings:000 **(3882)**

2001: 7^{0}GF, 8^{0}GS, 8^{0}G

	Starts	1st	2nd	3rd	Win & Pl
Career Total (Turf)	3	0	0	0	

Going (Turf): Sf: 0-0 GS: 0-1 Gd: 0-1 GF: 0-1 Fm: 0-0
Distance: 5f/6f: 0-0 7f-8f: 0-1 9f-13f: 0-2 14f+: 0-0
Track : LH: 0-0 RH: 0-1 Tight: 0-1 Gall: 0-0
Aids: Bl: 0-0 Vi: 0-0 Tstrap: 0-0
Best Rating: 49 6/01 Newb 7f gd-fm

Polar Haze

96(99) (55)**49**

4-y-o ch g Polar Falcon (USA)-Sky Music (Absalom)

Miss S E Hall Mrs Joan Hodgson

Placings:2026/230360-000510 **(5451)**

2001: 6^{0}GF, 6^{0}F, 5^{0}GF, 5^{5}GF, 5^{1}SD, 5^{0}HY

	Starts	1st	2nd	3rd	Win & Pl
Career Total (Turf)	15	0	3	2	4259
Career Total (AW)	1	1	0	0	2338

55 10/01 Sthl 5f F(0-60)H STD £2338
Total win prize-money £2338

Going (Turf): Sf: 0-1 GS: 0-3 Gd: 0-2 GF: 0-6 Fm: 0-3
Distance: **5f/6f: 1-14** 7f-8f: 0-2 9f-13f: 0-0 14f+: 0-0
Track : LH: 0-3 RH: 0-1 Tight: 0-1 Gall: 0-0
Aids: Bl: 0-0 **Vi: 1-3** Tstrap: 0-0
Best Rating: 55 10/01 Sthl 5f stand

He took a long time in getting off the mark, but did so over the minimum trip on his sand debut at Southwell in October.

Polar Impact

97 **73**

2-y-o br c Polar Falcon (USA)-Boozy (Absalom)

A Berry Robert Heathcote

Placings:552326 **(5253)**

2001: 5^{5}GF, 5^{5}GF, 5^{2}G, 6^{3}GF, 5^{2}HY, 6^{6}S

	Starts	1st	2nd	3rd	Win & Pl
Career Total (Turf)	6	0	2	1	2988

Going (Turf): Sf: 0-2 GS: 0-0 Gd: 0-1 GF: 0-3 Fm: 0-0
Distance: 5f/6f: 0-5 7f-8f: 0-1 9f-13f: 0-0 14f+: 0-0
Track : LH: 0-0 RH: 0-0 Tight: 0-0 Gall: 0-0
Aids: Bl: 0-0 Vi: 0-0 Tstrap: 0-0
Best Rating: 73 10/01 Ling 5f heavy

Polar Kingdom

110 **92**

3-y-o b g Pivotal-Scarlet Lake (Reprimand)

J Noseda P G Goulandris

Placings:411355042 **(5266)**

2001: 6^{4}GS, 6^{1}GS, 6^{1}S, 6^{3}GS, 6^{5}GS, 7^{5}G, 7^{0}HY, 6^{4}G, 6^{2}GS

	Starts	1st	2nd	3rd	Win & Pl
Career Total (Turf)	9	2	1	1	27644

92 5/01 Newb 6f8y C(0-90)H SFT £7442
61 5/01 Sals 6f D G-S £3094
Total win prize-money £10537

Going (Turf): Sf: 1-2 GS: 1-5 Gd: 0-2 GF: 0-0 Fm: 0-0
Distance: 5f/6f: 1-6 7f-8f: 1-3 9f-13f: 0-0 14f+: 0-0
Track : LH: 0-1 RH: 0-1 Tight: 0-0 Gall: 0-0
Aids: Bl: 0-0 Vi: 0-1 Tstrap: 0-0
Best Rating: 92 5/01 Newb 6f8y soft

Unraced at two, he got off the mark on his second outing at Salisbury over six furlongs and followed up in a Newbury handicap. Far from disgraced in a hot handicap at York next time when not getting the best of runs and ran with credit in competitive handicaps afterwards. Best with cut in the ground. Has joined W. Haggas.

Polar Lady

(101) (65d)**66**

4-y-o ch f Polar Falcon (USA)-Soluce (Junius (USA))

D Morris Colin Davey

Placings:6/35042005421-06201635 **(1319)**

2001: 8^{0}SD, 7^{6}SD, 8^{2}SW, 8^{0}SD, 7^{1}SW, 8^{6}SD, 8^{3}SD, 7^{5}SD

	Starts	1st	2nd	3rd	Win & Pl
Career Total (Turf)	8	0	1	1	2133
Career Total (AW)	12	2	2	1	6804

59 2/01 Sthl 7f G SLW £1904
67 12/00 Sthl 1m E(0-70)H STD £2744
Total win prize-money £4648

Going (Turf): Sf: 0-2 GS: 0-1 Gd: 0-2 GF: 0-3 Fm: 0-0
Distance: 5f/6f: 0-7 **7f-8f: 2-13** 9f-13f: 0-0 14f+: 0-0
Track : **LH: 2-14** RH: 0-0 Tight: 0-1 Gall: 0-1
Aids: Bl: 0-0 Vi: 0-1 Tstrap: 0-0
Best Rating: 65 1/01 Sthl 1m slow

Polar Mist

93(103) (57)**56**

6-y-o b g Polar Falcon (USA)-Post Mistress (IRE) (Cyrano De Bergerac)

M Wigham Miss Arabella Smallman

Placings:2/31506020020/3125402131000522162000/0 0010602060**6030030-614204500** **(5497)**

2001: 5^{6}SD, 5^{1}SD, 5^{4}SW, 5^{2}SD, 5^{0}SD, 5^{4}SD, 5^{5}GS, 5^{0}G, 5^{0}HY

	Starts	1st	2nd	3rd	Win & Pl
Career Total (Turf)	22	2	1	2	8403
Career Total (AW)	39	5	9	3	20890

57 2/01 Wolv 5f F(0-60)H STD £1736
55 5/00 Gdwd 5f E(0-70)H SFT £3705
61 6/99 Wolv 5f D(0-80)H STD £3655
70 4/99 Folk 5f E(0-65) HVY £2856
56 3/99 Wolv 5f G STD £1871
64 1/99 Wolv 6f F STD £2107
73 1/98 Wolv 6f D STD £3452
Total win prize-money £19385

Going (Turf): Sf: 2-9 GS: 0-3 Gd: 0-4 GF: 0-6 Fm: 0-0
Distance: **5f/6f: 7-59** 7f-8f: 0-2 9f-13f: 0-0 14f+: 0-0
Track : **LH: 5-36** RH: 0-3 **Tight: 5-30** Gall: 0-6
Aids: Bl: 4-40 Vi: 2-9 **Tstrap: 6-47**
Best Rating: 57 2/01 Wolv 5f stand

He is an effective sort in Fibresand sprint handicaps, though he can win on soft ground on turf. He stays six furlongs, but is probably best over a stiff five. At his best when able to dominate.

Polar Red

113 **108**

4-y-o ch g Polar Falcon (USA)-Sharp Top (Sharpo)

M C Pipe Stanley W Clarke

Placings:64005123/312431110-05 **(5132)**

2001: 13^{0}G, 12^{5}G

	Starts	1st	2nd	3rd	Win & Pl
Career Total (Turf)	19	5	2	3	40905

108 9/00 Hayd 1m2f120yB(0-100)H HVY £9460
102 8/00 Hayd 1m2f120yC(0-95)H G-S £7377
95 7/00 Kemp 1m2f C(0-90)H G-F £7182
85 5/00 Hayd 1m2f120yC(0-95)H G-S £5896
73 10/99 Wind 1m67y E(0-75)H G-S £3046
Total win prize-money £32964

Going (Turf): Sf: 1-3 **GS: 3-5** Gd: 0-5 GF: 1-6 Fm: 0-0
Distance: 5f/6f: 0-1 7f-8f: 0-5 **9f-13f: 5-12** 14f+: 0-1
Track : **LH: 3-5** RH: 2-7 Tight: 1-3 Gall: 1-3
Aids: Bl: 0-3 Vi: 0-0 Tstrap: 0-0
Best Rating: 106 10/01 NmkR 1m4f good

A useful ten-furlong handicapper, he enjoyed a fine season in 2000, scoring five times. Best on an easy surface, he acts on most types of ground and performs well at Haydock. Not seen after October 2000 until finishing eighth in this season's Ebor, his first run for Martin Pipe.

Polar Rock

100 **66d**

3-y-o ch f Polar Falcon (USA)-South Rock (Rock City)

M L W Bell B H Farr

Placings:00-3653600 **(5082)**

2001: 6^{3}HY, 7^{6}G, 9^{5}GF, 8^{3}GF, 7^{6}F, 7^{0}GS, 7^{0}S

	Starts	1st	2nd	3rd	Win & Pl
Career Total (Turf)	9	0	0	2	1094

Going (Turf): Sf: 0-3 GS: 0-1 Gd: 0-1 GF: 0-3 Fm: 0-1
Distance: 5f/6f: 0-0 7f-8f: 0-6 9f-13f: 0-3 14f+: 0-0
Track : LH: 0-4 RH: 0-0 Tight: 0-0 Gall: 0-0
Aids: Bl: 0-0 Vi: 0-0 Tstrap: 0-0
Best Rating: 66 6/01 Nott 1m54y gd-fm

Polar Star

69(99) (57)**67**

4-y-o b g Polar Falcon (USA)-Glowing With Pride (Ile De Bourbon (USA))

M C Pipe Mr & Mrs Malcolm B Jones

Placings:02/04500-40 **(1236)**

2001: 12^{4}SW, 12^{0}GF

	Starts	1st	2nd	3rd	Win & Pl
Career Total (Turf)	8	0	1	0	1669
Career Total (AW)	1	0	0	0	0

Going (Turf): Sf: 0-3 GS: 0-1 Gd: 0-0 GF: 0-4 Fm: 0-0
Distance: 5f/6f: 0-2 7f-8f: 0-1 9f-13f: 0-6 14f+: 0-0
Track : LH: 0-4 RH: 0-2 Tight: 0-3 Gall: 0-2
Aids: Bl: 0-0 Vi: 0-0 Tstrap: 0-0
Best Rating: 57 3/01 Ling 1m4f slow

Polar Tryst

94 **67**

2-y-o ch f Polar Falcon (USA)-Lovers Tryst (Castle Keep)

Lady Herries Angmering Park Stud

Placings:05 **(5590)**

2001: 8^{0}S, 9^{5}GS

	Starts	1st	2nd	3rd	Win & Pl
Career Total (Turf)	2	0	0	0	0

Going (Turf): Sf: 0-1 GS: 0-1 Gd: 0-0 GF: 0-0 Fm: 0-0
Distance: 5f/6f: 0-0 7f-8f: 0-0 9f-13f: 0-2 14f+: 0-0
Track : LH: 0-1 RH: 0-0 Tight: 0-0 Gall: 0-0
Aids: Bl: 0-0 Vi: 0-0 Tstrap: 0-0
Best Rating: 67 11/01 Brig 1m1f209y gd-sft

Pole Star

112 **96**

3-y-o b/br c Polar Falcon (USA)-Ellie Ardensky (Slip Anchor)

J R Fanshawe D I Russell

Placings:32-13404 **(5057)**

2001: 8^{1}F, 9^{3}S, 10^{4}G, 12^{0}G, 12^{4}S

	Starts	1st	2nd	3rd	Win & Pl
Career Total (Turf)	7	1	1	2	8012

72 5/01 Leic 1m9y F FRM £2439
Total win prize-money £2440

Going (Turf): Sf: 0-3 GS: 0-0 Gd: 0-2 GF: 0-1 **Fm: 1-1**
Distance: 5f/6f: 0-0 7f-8f: 0-2 **9f-13f: 1-5** 14f+: 0-0
Track : LH: 0-0 RH: 0-4 Tight: 0-0 Gall: 0-2
Aids: Bl: 0-0 Vi: 0-0 Tstrap: 0-0
Best Rating: 96 7/01 NmkJ 1m2f good

A well bred colt whose dam is closely related to Circus Ring and Lady Shipley, showed plenty of promise in two outings as a juvenile. Duly got off the mark on his reappearance at three, over a mile at Leicester, and ran well in handicaps afterwards. Appreciates a fast surface and is suited by a mile.

Poli Knight

(99) (47)**76**

4-y-o b f Polish Precedent (USA)-River Spey (Mill Reef (USA))

J W Hills Mr Derek D & Mrs Jean P Clee

Placings:553605-4 **(0020)**

2001: 12^{4}SD

	Starts	1st	2nd	3rd	Win & Pl
Career Total (Turf)	5	0	0	1	633
Career Total (AW)	2	0	0	0	0

Going (Turf): Sf: 0-2 GS: 0-1 Gd: 0-0 GF: 0-2 Fm: 0-0
Distance: 5f/6f: 0-0 7f-8f: 0-0 9f-13f: 0-7 14f+: 0-0
Track : LH: 0-4 RH: 0-2 Tight: 0-3 Gall: 0-2
Aids: Bl: 0-0 Vi: 0-0 Tstrap: 0-1
Best Rating: 47 1/01 Ling 1m4f stand

Policastro

100(91) (52)**60**

3-y-o b c Anabaa (USA)-Belle Arrivee (Bustino)

J W Hills Roger Paul

Placings:0-000066 **(5407)**

2001: 8^{0}GF, 8^{0}GF, 10^{0}GF, 10^{0}G, 10^{6}HY, 12^{6}SD

	Starts	1st	2nd	3rd	Win & Pl
Career Total (Turf)	6	0	0	0	0
Career Total (AW)	1	0	0	0	0

Going (Turf): Sf: 0-1 GS: 0-0 Gd: 0-2 GF: 0-3 Fm: 0-0
Distance: 5f/6f: 0-1 7f-8f: 0-1 9f-13f: 0-5 14f+: 0-0
Track : LH: 0-3 RH: 0-1 Tight: 0-4 Gall: 0-0
Aids: Bl: 0-0 Vi: 0-0 Tstrap: 0-2
Best Rating: 60 10/01 Wind 1m2f7y heavy

Polish Baron (IRE)

102 **71**

4-y-o b g Barathea (IRE)-Polish Mission (Polish Precedent (USA))

P J Hobbs T A Curran

Placings:0/660304-1531 **(4210)**

2001: 11^{1}GF, 12^{5}GF, 11^{3}GF, 11^{1}GF

	Starts	1st	2nd	3rd	Win & Pl
Career Total (Turf)	11	2	0	2	6617

42 8/01 Bath 1m3f144yF G-F £2331
62 6/01 Hayd 1m3f200yE G-F £3066
Total win prize-money £5397

Going (Turf): Sf: 0-2 GS: 0-0 Gd: 0-0 **GF: 2-5** Fm: 0-1
Distance: 5f/6f: 0-0 7f-8f: 0-3 **9f-13f: 2-8** 14f+: 0-0
Track : **LH: 2-5** RH: 0-5 **Tight: 1-2** Gall: 0-1
Aids: Bl: 0-0 Vi: 0-0 Tstrap: 0-0
Best Rating: 70 6/01 Gdwd 1m4f gd-fm

A fair hurdler, he changed hands after winning a Bath seller in August. He is a useful sort in that grade.

Polish Corridor

83 **67**

2-y-o b g Danzig Connection (USA)-Possibility (Robellino (USA))

M Dods Russ Mould

Placings:040 **(4029)**

2001: 5^{0}GF, 6^{4}GF, 7^{0}G

	Starts	1st	2nd	3rd	Win & Pl
Career Total (Turf)	3	0	0	0	0

Going (Turf): Sf: 0-0 GS: 0-0 Gd: 0-1 GF: 0-2 Fm: 0-0

Distance: 5f/6f: 0-2 7f-8f: 0-1 9f-13f: 0-0 14f+: 0-0
Track : LH: 0-0 RH: 0-0 Tight: 0-0 Gall: 0-0
Aids: Bl: 0-0 Vi: 0-0 Tstrap: 0-0
Best Rating: 67 6/01 Ayr 6f gd-fm

Polish Falcon (IRE)

91(39) **39**

5-y-o b g Polish Patriot (USA)-Marie De Fresnaye (USA) (Dom Racine (FR))

Mrs N Smith K A Little

Placings:004/00000 **(5085)**

2001: 9^{0}HY, 11^{0}GS, 12^{0}GF, 10^{0}G, 11^{0}S

	Starts	1st	2nd	3rd	Win & Pl
Career Total (Turf)	6	0	0	0	
Career Total (AW)	2	0	0	0	197

Going (Turf): Sf: 0-3 GS: 0-1 Gd: 0-1 GF: 0-1 Fm: 0-0
Distance: 5f/6f: 0-0 7f-8f: 0-1 9f-13f: 0-7 14f+: 0-0
Track : LH: 0-7 RH: 0-1 Tight: 0-5 Gall: 0-1
Aids: Bl: 0-1 Vi: 0-0 Tstrap: 0-0
Best Rating: 39 5/01 Brlg 1m3f196y gd-sft

Polish Flame

95 **51**

3-y-o b g Blushing Flame (USA)-Lady Emm (Emarati (USA))

Mrs M Reveley Falcon Assets

Placings:3-462 **(5093)**

2001: 9^{4}GF, 8^{6}GF, 16^{2}GS

	Starts	1st	2nd	3rd	Win & Pl
Career Total (Turf)	4	0	1	1	1290

Going (Turf): Sf: 0-1 GS: 0-1 Gd: 0-0 GF: 0-2 Fm: 0-0
Distance: 5f/6f: 0-0 7f-8f: 0-0 9f-13f: 0-3 14f+: 0-1
Track : LH: 0-4 RH: 0-0 Tight: 0-1 Gall: 0-1
Aids: Bl: 0-0 Vi: 0-0 Tstrap: 0-0
Best Rating: 49 10/01 Newc 2m19y gd-sft

Ran well when runner-up in a staying handicap at Newcastle in October.

Polish Off

106 **78**

3-y-o b g Polish Precedent (USA)-Lovely Lyca (Night Shift (USA))

R M Beckett (B W Hills 28/9) Windsor House Thoroughbreds

Placings:443-3602104300 **(5681)**

2001: 8^{3}S, 10^{6}F, 10^{0}GF, 8^{2}GF, 8^{1}GS, 9^{0}G, 8^{4}G, 8^{3}F, 8^{0}G, 8^{0}S

	Starts	1st	2nd	3rd	Win & Pl
Career Total (Turf)	13	1	1	3	8941

81 7/01 Wwck 1m22y D G-S £4426
Total win prize-money £4427

Going (Turf): Sf: 0-2 **GS: 1-1** Gd: 0-5 GF: 0-3 Fm: 0-2
Distance: 5f/6f: 0-1 7f-8f: 0-6 **9f-13f: 1-6** 14f+: 0-0
Track : LH: 0-3 RH: 0-2 Tight: 0-3 Gall: 0-1
Aids: Bl: 0-0 Vi: 0-0 Tstrap: 0-0
Best Rating: 89 5/01 York 1m2f85y firm

Showed ability at two but lacked a turn of foot. He was tried in handicap company earlier in 2001 without success and had to revert to maiden company to get off the mark over a mile at Warwick in July. Harshly handicapped on what he has actually achieved.

Polish Paddy (IRE)

100(83) (54)**66**

3-y-o b g Priolo (USA)-Polish Widow (Polish Precedent (USA))

R Hannon Denis Barry

Placings:066446001-063020605 **(5198)**

2001: 8^{0}GS, 8^{6}HD, 8^{3}GF, 10^{0}G, 7^{2}GS, 6^{0}GF, 8^{6}GF, 7^{0}G, 9^{5}SD

	Starts	1st	2nd	3rd	Win & Pl
Career Total (Turf)	17	1	1	1	5730
Career Total (AW)	1	0	0	0	0

68 10/00 NmkR 1m E SFT £3575
Total win prize-money £3575

Going (Turf): Sf: 1-2 GS: 0-4 Gd: 0-5 GF: 0-4 Fm: 0-1
Distance: 5f/6f: 0-1 **7f-8f: 1-11** 9f-13f: 0-5 14f+: 0-0
Track : LH: 0-6 RH: 0-1 Tight: 0-5 Gall: 0-0
Aids: **Bl: 1-9** Vi: 0-0 Tstrap: 0-0
Best Rating: 66 8/01 Hayd 7f30y gd-sft

Polished Up

90 **46**

4-y-o b f Polish Precedent (USA)-Smarten Up (Sharpen Up)

R M Beckett Major & Mrs R B Kennard

Placings:0/6030-600 **(2362)**

2001: 9^{6}G, 8^{0}G, 6^{0}GF

	Starts	1st	2nd	3rd	Win & Pl
Career Total (Turf)	8	0	0	1	481

Going (Turf): Sf: 0-1 GS: 0-0 Gd: 0-3 GF: 0-4 Fm: 0-0
Distance: 5f/6f: 0-2 7f-8f: 0-2 9f-13f: 0-4 14f+: 0-0
Track : LH: 0-1 RH: 0-3 Tight: 0-1 Gall: 0-0
Aids: Bl: 0-0 Vi: 0-1 Tstrap: 0-0
Best Rating: 40 5/01 Bevl 1m1f207y good

Polly Flinders

97 **60**

3-y-o b f Polar Falcon (USA)-So True (So Blessed)

G B Balding Miss B Swire

Placings:00404 **(5532)**

2001: 7^{0}GS, 8^{0}G, 7^{4}HY, 8^{0}GS, 9^{4}HY

	Starts	1st	2nd	3rd	Win & Pl
Career Total (Turf)	5	0	0	0	348

Going (Turf): Sf: 0-2 GS: 0-2 Gd: 0-1 GF: 0-0 Fm: 0-0
Distance: 5f/6f: 0-0 7f-8f: 0-2 9f-13f: 0-3 14f+: 0-0
Track : LH: 0-2 RH: 0-1 Tight: 0-1 Gall: 0-0
Aids: Bl: 0-0 Vi: 0-0 Tstrap: 0-0
Best Rating: 60 10/01 Nott 1m1f213y heavy

Polly Golightly

103 (26)**71**

8-y-o ch m Weldnaas (USA)-Polly's Teahouse (Shack (USA))

M Blanshard David Sykes

Placings:145354031/04050434033000/0503211520040005214/04401102304500000/564640005160044/0022064000043011004-0000 **(2742)**

2001: 5^{0}GF, 5^{0}GF, 5^{0}G, 5^{0}GF

	Starts	1st	2nd	3rd	Win & Pl
Career Total (Turf)	96	10	6	8	71498
Career Total (AW)	1	0	0	0	

71	9/00	Hayd	5f	C(0-90)H	HVY	£9782
67	9/00	Ches	5f16y	D(0-85)H	SFT	£4043
68	8/99	Ches	5f16y	D(0-85)H	G-S	£5800
73	6/98	York	5f	C(0-100)H	G-S	£7635
76	6/98	Ches	5f16y	D(0-85)H	G-S	£4201
60	10/97	Catt	5f	D(0-85)H	SFT	£4003
64	6/97	Gdwd	5f	D(0-75)H	G-F	£3752
57	5/97	Ling	5f	E(0-70)H	G-F	£2862
80	11/95	Donc	5f	D(0-85)	G-F	£3882
60	5/95	Bath	5f11y	D	G-F	£3330

Total win prize-money £49295

Going (Turf): Sf: 3-16 GS: 3-17 Gd: 0-22 **GF: 4-35** Fm: 0-6
Distance: **5f/6f: 10-90** 7f-8f: 0-7 9f-13f: 0-0 14f+: 0-0
Track : **LH: 4-24** RH: 0-7 **Tight: 3-13** Gall: 1-12
Aids: **Bl: 9-81** Vi: 0-2 Tstrap: 0-0
Best Rating: 61 5/01 Hayd 5f gd-fm

She has won her share of sprint handicaps over the years, but can go a long time without a victory and is not totally consistent. Very versatile when it comes to ground, but recents wins have been on soft.

Polwhele

74(95) (40)**43d**

3-y-o ch g Mujtahid (USA)-Safayn (USA) (Lyphard (USA))

R M H Cowell Mr & Mrs D A Gamble

Placings:00046-060002 **(3015)**

2001: 6^{0}SD, 7^{6}SW, 8^{0}SD, 6^{0}GF, 7^{0}GF, 7^{2}SD

	Starts	1st	2nd	3rd	Win & Pl
Career Total (Turf)	5	0	0	0	
Career Total (AW)	6	0	1	0	652

Going (Turf): Sf: 0-0 GS: 0-0 Gd: 0-0 GF: 0-4 Fm: 0-0
Distance: 5f/6f: 0-2 7f-8f: 0-8 9f-13f: 0-0 14f+: 0-0
Track : LH: 0-8 RH: 0-0 Tight: 0-1 Gall: 0-0
Aids: Bl: 0-0 Vi: 0-5 Tstrap: 0-5
Best Rating: 40 1/01 Wolv 7f slow

Poly Amanshaa (IRE)

(90) (40)**58**

9-y-o b/br g Nashamaa-Mombones (Lord Gayle (USA))

W Jarvis M C Banks

Placings:64221646600640/0 **(0495)**

2001: 16^{0}SD

	Starts	1st	2nd	3rd	Win & Pl
Career Total (Turf)	14	1	2	0	23566
Career Total (AW)	1	0	0	0	

74 7/94 Ling 7f D GD £3659
Total win prize-money £3659

Going (Turf): Sf: 0-2 GS: 0-2 **Gd: 1-5** GF: 0-2 Fm: 0-3
Distance: 5f/6f: 0-2 **7f-8f: 1-11** 9f-13f: 0-1 14f+: 0-1
Track : LH: 0-6 RH: 0-1 Tight: 0-2 Gall: 0-2
Aids: Bl: 0-0 Vi: 0-0 Tstrap: 0-0
Best Rating: 40 3/01 Sthl 2m stand

Polyphonic

88 **28**

3-y-o b f Binary Star (USA)-Plainsong (Ballad Rock)

B S Rothwell (A B Mulholland 8/7) Mrs Helen Godfrey

Placings:065000-00000 **(4013)**

2001: 6^{0}GF, 5^{0}F, 8^{0}GF, 6^{0}F, 5^{0}G

	Starts	1st	2nd	3rd	Win & Pl
Career Total (Turf)	11	0	0	0	0

Going (Turf): Sf: 0-1 GS: 0-0 Gd: 0-5 GF: 0-3 Fm: 0-2
Distance: 5f/6f: 0-9 7f-8f: 0-1 9f-13f: 0-1 14f+: 0-0
Track : LH: 0-2 RH: 0-0 Tight: 0-0 Gall: 0-0
Aids: Bl: 0-0 Vi: 0-1 Tstrap: 0-0
Best Rating: 28 8/01 Catt 5f good

Pomfret Lad

106 **110**

3-y-o b g Cyrano De Bergerac-Lucky Flinders (Free State)

P J Makin Mrs Pauline Smith & Four Seasons Racing

Placings:0125-30 **(1819)**

2001: 6^{3}GF, 6^{0}GF

	Starts	1st	2nd	3rd	Win & Pl
Career Total (Turf)	6	1	1	1	21603

100 8/00 Kemp 6f E G-F £4446
Total win prize-money £4446

Going (Turf): Sf: 0-0 GS: 0-1 Gd: 0-1 **GF: 1-4** Fm: 0-0
Distance: **5f/6f: 1-5** 7f-8f: 0-1 9f-13f: 0-0 14f+: 0-0
Track : LH: 0-1 RH: 0-0 Tight: 0-0 Gall: 0-1
Aids: Bl: 0-0 Vi: 0-0 Tstrap: 0-0

Best Rating: 109 5/01 Gdwd 6f gd-fm

He won his maiden in 2000 by nine lengths in a fast time, and subsequently ran well in the Mill Reef, going down by the narrowest margin. Best on fast ground, he has raced only at six furlongs since his debut, but appears to have the pace for five. No excuse was offered for his poor effort at Windsor last time out in June.

Pomme D'Or

84(72) (6)**46**

3-y-o b f Celtic Swing-Glitter (FR) (Reliance Ii)

K O Cunningham-Brown A J Richards

Placings:0006 **(4877)**

2001: 10^{0}GF, 12^{0}GF, 12^{0}G, 14^{6}SD

	Starts	1st	2nd	3rd	Win & Pl
Career Total (Turf)	3	0	0	0	
Career Total (AW)	1	0	0	0	0

Going (Turf): Sf: 0-0 GS: 0-0 Gd: 0-1 GF: 0-2 Fm: 0-0
Distance: 5f/6f: 0-0 7f-8f: 0-0 9f-13f: 0-3 14f+: 0-1
Track : LH: 0-3 RH: 0-1 Tight: 0-2 Gall: 0-0
Aids: Bl: 0-0 Vi: 0-0 Tstrap: 0-0
Best Rating: 46 5/01 Ling 1m2f gd-fm

Pomme Swinger (FR)

91 **48**

3-y-o b f Celtic Swing-Tarte Aux Pommes (USA) (Local Talent (USA))

K O Cunningham-Brown A J Richards

Placings:050 **(5670)**

2001: 8^{0}G, 8^{5}S, 8^{0}HY

	Starts	1st	2nd	3rd	Win & Pl
Career Total (Turf)	3	0	0	0	264

Going (Turf): Sf: 0-2 GS: 0-0 Gd: 0-1 GF: 0-0 Fm: 0-0
Distance: 5f/6f: 0-0 7f-8f: 0-0 9f-13f: 0-3 14f+: 0-0
Track : LH: 0-1 RH: 0-1 Tight: 0-1 Gall: 0-0
Aids: Bl: 0-0 Vi: 0-0 Tstrap: 0-0
Best Rating: 48 10/01 Leic 1m9y soft

Pompeii (IRE)

103(83) (51)**61**

4-y-o b g Salse (USA)-Before Dawn (USA) (Raise A Cup (USA))

N Wilson (R T Phillips 12/5) J B Slatcher

Placings:620/211600-000550 **(5373)**

2001: 16^{0}GF, 8^{0}GS, 11^{0}GF, 11^{5}GF, 10^{5}S, 14^{0}G

	Starts	1st	2nd	3rd	Win & Pl
Career Total (Turf)	14	2	2	0	10715
Career Total (AW)	1	0	0	0	

81 5/00 Wwck 1m4f56y D(0-80)H SFT £4048
81 4/00 Leic 1m3f183yD G-S £3926
Total win prize-money £7975

Going (Turf): Sf: 1-3 GS: 1-2 Gd: 0-4 GF: 0-5 Fm: 0-0
Distance: 5f/6f: 0-0 7f-8f: 0-3 **9f-13f: 2-9** 14f+: 0-3
Track : LH: 1-10 RH: 1-3 Tight: 0-5 Gall: 0-4
Aids: Bl: 0-0 Vi: 0-0 Tstrap: 0-0
Best Rating: 61 8/01 Bevl 1m3f216y gd-fm

He won a Leicester maiden and a Warwick handicap in the spring of 2000, but has not shown much on the level since and has had a spell over hurdles.

Pop Shop

85 **57**

4-y-o b c Owington-Diamond Park (IRE) (Alzao (USA))

J W Payne Sir Simon Lycett Green

Placings:441662/0000000050-00 **(3672)**

2001: 6^{0}F, 5^{0}G

	Starts	1st	2nd	3rd	Win & Pl

	Starts	1st	2nd	3rd	Win & Pl
Career Total (Turf)	18	1	1	0	4254

68 6/99 Nott 5f13y E GD £3150
Total win prize-money £3150

Going (Turf): Sf: 0-1 GS: 0-1 **Gd: 1-5** GF: 0-10 Fm: 0-1
Distance: 5f/6f: 1-14 7f-8f: 0-4 9f-13f: 0-0 14f+: 0-0
Track : LH: 0-3 RH: 0-1 Tight: 0-2 Gall: 0-1
Aids: Bl: 0-3 Vi: 0-0 Tstrap: 0-1
Best Rating: 37 7/01 Ling 6f firm

Pop The Cork

104(82) (39)**72**

4-y-o ch g Clantime-Hyde Princess (Touch Paper)

R M Whitaker Country Lane Partnership

Placings:0/00300100-00003160051133 **(4676)**

2001: 5^{0}GS, 5^{0}G, 5^{0}F, 5^{0}GF, 5^{3}GF, 5^{1}GF, 5^{6}GF, 5^{0}GF, 5^{0}G, 5^{5}G, 5^{1}GF, 5^{1}GF, 5^{3}GF, 5^{3}G

	Starts	1st	2nd	3rd	Win & Pl
Career Total (Turf)	20	4	0	4	14289
Career Total (AW)	3	0	0	0	

72 8/01 Muss 5f F(0-65)H G-F £2817
62 8/01 Muss 5f D(0-80)H G-F £3913
57 6/01 Bevl 5f F(0-60)H G-F £2457
64 6/00 Muss 5f E(0-70)H FRM £2938
Total win prize-money £12126

Going (Turf): Sf: 0-0 GS: 0-2 Gd: 0-6 **GF: 3-10** Fm: 1-2
Distance: 5f/6f: 4-23 7f-8f: 0-0 9f-13f: 0-0 14f+: 0-0
Track : LH: 0-3 RH: 0-0 Tight: 0-1 Gall: 0-0
Aids: Bl: 0-0 Vi: 0-0 Tstrap: 0-0
Best Rating: 72 8/01 Muss 5f gd-fm

Fair fast-ground sprinter. Goes particularly well at Musselburgh.

Popocatepetl (FR)

92 **73**

2-y-o b/br f Nashwan (USA)-Dimakya (USA) (Dayjur (USA))

B W Hills Jeremy Gompertz

Placings:0 **(5603)**

2001: 7^{0}GS

	Starts	1st	2nd	3rd	Win & Pl
Career Total (Turf)	1	0	0	0	

Going (Turf): Sf: 0-0 GS: 0-1 Gd: 0-0 GF: 0-0 Fm: 0-0
Distance: 5f/6f: 0-0 7f-8f: 0-1 9f-13f: 0-0 14f+: 0-0
Track : LH: 0-0 RH: 0-0 Tight: 0-0 Gall: 0-0
Aids: Bl: 0-0 Vi: 0-0 Tstrap: 0-0
Best Rating: 73 11/01 NmkR 7f gd-sft

Poppaea (IRE)

90 **49**

3-y-o b f Definite Article-Classic Ring (IRE) (Auction Ring (USA))

R Hannon Thurloe Thoroughbreds V

Placings:4-5600050 **(5601)**

2001: 8^{5}GS, 8^{6}G, 7^{0}S, 7^{0}F, 5^{0}GF, 8^{5}G, 8^{0}GS

	Starts	1st	2nd	3rd	Win & Pl
Career Total (Turf)	8	0	0	0	297

Going (Turf): Sf: 0-1 GS: 0-2 Gd: 0-2 GF: 0-2 Fm: 0-1
Distance: 5f/6f: 0-2 7f-8f: 0-3 9f-13f: 0-3 14f+: 0-0
Track : LH: 0-2 RH: 0-2 Tight: 0-2 Gall: 0-1
Aids: Bl: 0-0 Vi: 0-0 Tstrap: 0-0
Best Rating: 61 5/01 Wwck 1m22y good

Porak (IRE)

107(98) (54)**70**

4-y-o ch g Perugino (USA)-Gayla Orchestra (Lord Gayle (USA))

G L Moore Allen, Manley, Pritchard, Russell

Placings:600-03051240060521 **(5293)**

2001: 7^{0}SW, 8^{3}SW, 10^{0}SD, 10^{5}SD, 9^{1}HY, 11^{2}GF, 10^{4}GF, 10^{0}GF, 9^{0}GF, 10^{6}G, 9^{0}G, 12^{5}G, 12^{2}G, 9^{1}S

	Starts	1st	2nd	3rd	Win & Pl
Career Total (Turf)	13	2	2	0	9410
Career Total (AW)	4	0	0	1	412

70 10/01 Leic 1m1f218yE(0-75)H SFT £3325
66 4/01 Folk 1m1f149yE(0-70)H HVY £3360
Total win prize-money £6685

Going (Turf): Sf: 2-4 GS: 0-0 Gd: 0-4 GF: 0-5 Fm: 0-0
Distance: 5f/6f: 0-0 7f-8f: 0-4 **9f-13f: 2-13** 14f+: 0-0
Track : LH: 0-9 **RH: 2-6 Tight: 1-8** Gall: 0-3
Aids: Bl: 0-0 Vi: 0-0 Tstrap: 0-0
Best Rating: 70 10/01 Leic 1m1f218y soft

Did not prove suited to Equitrack and scored when reverting to turf at Folkestone in April. He needs soft ground and did not have his conditions again until scoring at Leicester in October.

Port Moresby (IRE)

110(92) (71)**93**

3-y-o b g Tagula (IRE)-Santana Lady (IRE) (Blakeney)

N A Callaghan Martin Moore

Placings:0010001003-00310111000 **(5338)**

2001: 10^{0}S, 7^{0}GF, 9^{3}GF, 9^{1}F, 10^{0}GF, 10^{1}GF, 10^{1}GS, 10^{1}G, 10^{0}G, 9^{0}G, 12^{0}GS

	Starts	1st	2nd	3rd	Win & Pl
Career Total (Turf)	18	6	0	1	29332
Career Total (AW)	3	0	0	1	384

93 8/01 Pont 1m2f6y E(0-80)H GD £3526
81 8/01 NmkJ 1m2f C(0-90)H G-S £8346
75 7/01 NmkJ 1m2f E(0-75)H G-F £3640
72 6/01 Ling 1m1f C(0-90)H FRM £6922
77 10/00 Yarm 1m3y E(0-85) SFT £2926
72 8/00 Bevl 7f100y D GD £3263
Total win prize-money £28624

Going (Turf): Sf: 1-3 GS: 1-3 **Gd: 2-4** GF: 1-7 Fm: 1-1
Distance: 5f/6f: 0-1 7f-8f: 1-8 **9f-13f: 5-12** 14f+: 0-0
Track : LH: 2-8 **RH: 3-6** Tight: 1-5 **Gall: 2-5**
Aids: Bl: 0-3 Vi: 0-0 Tstrap: 0-2
Best Rating: 93 8/01 Pont 1m2f6y good

A winner twice at two, he has run well in some decent handicaps this term and scored over nine furlongs at Lingfield in June and over ten furlongs at Newmarket in July and August. He completed the hat-trick at Pontefract and ran with credit in the Cambridgeshire. Acts on any ground.

Port Of Call (IRE)

79(90) **20**

6-y-o ch g Arazi (USA)-Port Helene (Troy)

R F Marvin R A B Saville

Placings:560000-060 **(4552)**

2001: 6^{0}SD, 9^{6}GF, 14^{0}SW

	Starts	1st	2nd	3rd	Win & Pl
Career Total (Turf)	4	0	0	0	0
Career Total (AW)	5	0	0	0	0

Going (Turf): Sf: 0-0 GS: 0-2 Gd: 0-1 GF: 0-1 Fm: 0-0
Distance: 5f/6f: 0-3 7f-8f: 0-1 9f-13f: 0-4 14f+: 0-1
Track : LH: 0-8 RH: 0-1 Tight: 0-1 Gall: 0-1
Aids: Bl: 0-0 Vi: 0-0 Tstrap: 0-0
Best Rating: 17 8/01 Bevl 1m1f207y gd-fm

Port St Charles (IRE)

107 **65**

4-y-o b/br g Night Shift (USA)-Safe Haven (Blakeney)

N A Callaghan N A Callaghan

Placings:33/24506-023533150 **(5254)**

2001: 6^{0}HY, 5^{2}HY, 5^{3}GS, 5^{5}GF, 6^{3}G, 7^{3}G, 6^{1}GF, 7^{5}G, 6^{0}S

	Starts	1st	2nd	3rd	Win & Pl

Career Total (Turf) 16 1 2 5 8339
65 8/01 Folk 6f E(0-65) G-F £3024
Total win prize-money £3024

Going (Turf): Sf: 0-3 GS: 0-2 Gd: 0-6 **GF: 1-5** Fm: 0-0
Distance: **5f/6f: 1-11** 7f-8f: 0-5 9f-13f: 0-0 14f+: 0-0
Track : LH: 0-4 RH: 0-0 Tight: 0-1 Gall: 0-0
Aids: Bl: 0-0 Vi: 0-0 Tstrap: 0-0
Best Rating: 69 8/01 Brig 6f209y good

Got off the mark at the 14th attempt at Folkestone in August, where he goes well. Six furlongs and fast ground are his conditions, although he does handle softer.

Portacasa

83 **53**
2-y-o b f Robellino (USA)-Autumn Affair (Lugana Beach)
R A Fahey J G Porthouse

Placings:40 **(3878)**
2001: 6^{4}F, 7^{0}GS

	Starts	1st	2nd	3rd	Win & Pl
Career Total (Turf)	2	0	0	0	0

Going (Turf): Sf: 0-0 GS: 0-1 Gd: 0-0 GF: 0-0 Fm: 0-1
Distance: 5f/6f: 0-1 7f-8f: 0-1 9f-13f: 0-0 14f+: 0-0
Track : LH: 0-1 RH: 0-0 Tight: 0-1 Gall: 0-0
Aids: Bl: 0-0 Vi: 0-0 Tstrap: 0-0
Best Rating: 53 7/01 Rdcr 6f firm

Portrack Junction (IRE)

86(72) (25)**15**
4-y-o b g Common Grounds-Boldabsa (Persian Bold)
A B Mulholland Miss K Watson

Placings:0005/000000505-00000600 **(4805)**
2001: 10^{0}GF, 10^{0}GF, 10^{0}GF, 12^{0}F, 9^{0}F, 10^{6}GS, 16^{0}GF, 8^{0}F

	Starts	1st	2nd	3rd	Win & Pl
Career Total (Turf)	21	0	0	0	0
Career Total (AW)	1	0	0	0	

Going (Turf): Sf: 0-2 GS: 0-2 Gd: 0-3 GF: 0-9 Fm: 0-5
Distance: 5f/6f: 0-3 7f-8f: 0-4 9f-13f: 0-11 14f+: 0-4
Track : LH: 0-13 RH: 0-5 Tight: 0-8 Gall: 0-3
Aids: Bl: 0-2 Vi: 0-0 Tstrap: 0-1
Best Rating: 23 7/01 Newc 1m4f93y firm

Positive (IRE)

105(91) (75)**88?**
2-y-o ch g Fayruz-Interj (Salmon Leap (USA))
B J Meehan K R W Hawkins

Placings:0220255100 **(5496)**
2001: 5^{0}GF, 6^{2}SD, 6^{2}GF, 6^{0}SD, 7^{2}GF, 7^{5}SD, 8^{5}HY, 7^{1}G, 7^{0}HY, 7^{0}HY

	Starts	1st	2nd	3rd	Win & Pl
Career Total (Turf)	7	1	2	0	8630
Career Total (AW)	3	0	1	0	830

88 9/01 Gdwd 7f C GD £6786
Total win prize-money £6786

Going (Turf): Sf: 0-3 GS: 0-0 **Gd: 1-1** GF: 0-3 Fm: 0-0
Distance: 5f/6f: 0-4 **7f-8f: 1-5** 9f-13f: 0-1 14f+: 0-0
Track : LH: 0-4 **RH: 1-1** Tight: 0-2 Gall: 0-0
Aids: **Bl: 1-3** Vi: 0-0 Tstrap: 0-0
Best Rating: 88 9/01 Gdwd 7f good

Decent juvenile who appeared to run above himself when winning at Goodwood.

Positive Profile (IRE)

101(84) (34)**60**
3-y-o b g Definite Article-Leyete Gulf (IRE) (Slip Anchor)
P C Haslam (N A Graham 8/9) Chelgate Public Relations Ltd

Placings:006000010 **(5624)**
2001: 11^{0}S, 12^{0}GS, 8^{6}GF, 10^{0}G, 10^{0}GF, 14^{0}S, 8^{0}SD, 10^{1}S, 9^{0}GS

	Starts	1st	2nd	3rd	Win & Pl
Career Total (Turf)	8	1	0	0	4079
Career Total (AW)	1	0	0	0	

60 10/01 Pont 1m2f6y E(0-70)H SFT £4078
Total win prize-money £4079

Going (Turf): Sf: 1-3 GS: 0-2 Gd: 0-1 GF: 0-2 Fm: 0-0
Distance: 5f/6f: 0-0 7f-8f: 0-1 **9f-13f: 1-7** 14f+: 0-1
Track : **LH: 1-5** RH: 0-2 Tight: 0-4 Gall: 0-0
Aids: Bl: 0-0 Vi: 0-0 Tstrap: 0-0
Best Rating: 68 5/01 Kemp 1m gd-fm

Did not make much of an impression initially, but eventually got off the mark at Pontefract. Suited by ten furlongs and easy ground.

Post Box (USA)

109 **86**
3-y-o b c Quest For Fame-Crowning Ambition (USA) (Chief's Crown (USA))
R Charlton K Abdulla

Placings:25-24100046 **(5143)**
2001: 9^{2}GS, 12^{4}GF, 14^{1}GS, 14^{0}G, 13^{0}G, 14^{0}HY, 15^{4}S, 14^{6}G

	Starts	1st	2nd	3rd	Win & Pl
Career Total (Turf)	10	1	2	0	9690

83 6/01 Sals 1m6f15y C(0-95)H G-S £6666
Total win prize-money £6666

Going (Turf): Sf: 0-3 **GS: 1-3** Gd: 0-3 GF: 0-1 Fm: 0-0
Distance: 5f/6f: 0-0 7f-8f: 0-1 9f-13f: 0-3 **14f+: 1-6**
Track : LH: 0-6 **RH: 1-3 Tight: 1-5** Gall: 0-2
Aids: Bl: 0-0 Vi: 0-0 Tstrap: 0-0
Best Rating: 87 5/01 Ches 1m4f66y gd-fm

Suited by step up to 14 furlongs when scoring at Salisbury in June 2001, but has struggled in competitive handicaps since. Has won on good to soft.

Pot Of Gold (FR)

(94) (56)
3-y-o gr g Kendor (FR)-Golden Rainbow (FR) (Rainbow Quest (USA))
J G Fitzgerald J G Fitzgerald

Placings:04-4 **(0084)**
2001: 8^{4}SD

	Starts	1st	2nd	3rd	Win & Pl
Career Total (Turf)	0	0	0	0	
Career Total (AW)	3	0	0	0	0

Going (Turf): Sf: 0-0 GS: 0-0 Gd: 0-0 GF: 0-0 Fm: 0-0
Distance: 5f/6f: 0-0 7f-8f: 0-3 9f-13f: 0-0 14f+: 0-0
Track : LH: 0-3 RH: 0-0 Tight: 0-0 Gall: 0-0
Aids: Bl: 0-0 Vi: 0-0 Tstrap: 0-0
Best Rating: 56 1/01 Sthl 1m stand

Potemkin (IRE)

105 **108**
3-y-o ch c Ashkalani (IRE)-Ploy (Posse (USA))
R Hannon Michael Pescod

Placings:212130 **(4197a)**
2001: 8^{2}S, 8^{1}GS, 10^{2}GF, 10^{1}GF, 10^{3}GS, 10^{0}S

	Starts	1st	2nd	3rd	Win & Pl
Career Total (Turf)	6	2	2	1	34785

108 6/01 NmkR 1m2f A G-F £15254
94 5/01 Kemp 1m D G-S £4855
Total win prize-money £20110

Going (Turf): Sf: 0-2 **GS: 1-2** Gd: 0-0 **GF: 1-2** Fm: 0-0
Distance: 5f/6f: 0-0 7f-8f: 1-2 9f-13f: 1-4 14f+: 0-0
Track : LH: 0-1 **RH: 1-1** Tight: 0-0 Gall: 0-1
Aids: Bl: 0-0 Vi: 0-0 Tstrap: 0-0
Best Rating: 108 7/01 Deau 1m2f gd-sft

Tough and game, he made virtually all when beating Aldwych by a neck in Listed event at Newmarket in June. having just lost out to Musha Mer in a similar event at York. Ran a good third in a Deauville Group Two next time. He stays ten furlongs well, handles most surfaces, and is best suited by racing prominently.

Potsdam

98 **67**
3-y-o ch c Rainbow Quest (USA)-Danilova (USA) (Lyphard (USA))
J H M Gosden K Abdulla

Placings:05 **(4447)**
2001: 11^{0}G, 9^{5}G

	Starts	1st	2nd	3rd	Win & Pl
Career Total (Turf)	2	0	0	0	0

Going (Turf): Sf: 0-0 GS: 0-0 Gd: 0-2 GF: 0-0 Fm: 0-0
Distance: 5f/6f: 0-0 7f-8f: 0-0 9f-13f: 0-2 14f+: 0-0
Track : LH: 0-1 RH: 0-1 Tight: 0-1 Gall: 0-0
Aids: Bl: 0-0 Vi: 0-0 Tstrap: 0-1
Best Rating: 67 9/01 Sand 1m1f good

Potted Shrimp (USA)

84(85) (58)**46**
2-y-o ch c Prized (USA)-Mint Callee (USA) (Key To The Mint (USA))
A Berry Alan Berry

Placings:0000 **(4793)**
2001: 6^{0}GS, 6^{0}SD, 8^{0}HY, 8^{0}G

	Starts	1st	2nd	3rd	Win & Pl
Career Total (Turf)	3	0	0	0	
Career Total (AW)	1	0	0	0	

Going (Turf): Sf: 0-1 GS: 0-1 Gd: 0-1 GF: 0-0 Fm: 0-0
Distance: 5f/6f: 0-2 7f-8f: 0-1 9f-13f: 0-1 14f+: 0-0
Track : LH: 0-3 RH: 0-0 Tight: 0-1 Gall: 0-0
Aids: Bl: 0-0 Vi: 0-0 Tstrap: 0-0
Best Rating: 58 8/01 Wolv 6f stand

Pounce (IRE)

92(97) (44)**56**
3-y-o ch f Grand Lodge (USA)-Mary Ellen Best (IRE) (Danehill (USA))
J A Osborne Durkan Limited

Placings:4446-036 **(4906)**
2001: 7^{0}GF, 7^{3}GF, 9^{6}G

	Starts	1st	2nd	3rd	Win & Pl
Career Total (Turf)	7	0	0	1	5073

Going (Turf): Sf: 0-1 GS: 0-1 Gd: 0-2 GF: 0-3 Fm: 0-0
Distance: 5f/6f: 0-1 7f-8f: 0-5 9f-13f: 0-1 14f+: 0-0
Track : LH: 0-1 RH: 0-3 Tight: 0-0 Gall: 0-1
Aids: Bl: 0-0 Vi: 0-0 Tstrap: 0-0
Best Rating: 52 9/01 Bevl 1m1f207y good

Pour Nous

87 **24**
3-y-o gr g Petong-Pour Moi (Bay Express)
J J Quinn Mrs Karan Ridley

Placings:0000-0000 **(3308)**
2001: 6^{0}S, 8^{0}F, 6^{0}GF, 7^{0}GS

	Starts	1st	2nd	3rd	Win & Pl
Career Total (Turf)	8	0	0	0	

Going (Turf): Sf: 0-2 GS: 0-1 Gd: 0-1 GF: 0-3 Fm: 0-1
Distance: 5f/6f: 0-4 7f-8f: 0-4 9f-13f: 0-0 14f+: 0-0
Track : LH: 0-6 RH: 0-0 Tight: 0-2 Gall: 0-1

Aids: Bl: 0-0 Vi: 0-1 Tstrap: 0-0
Best Rating: 24 5/01 Newc 6f soft

Powder River

(70) (6)**61**
7-y-o b h Alzao (USA)-Nest (Sharpo)
A G Newcombe Online Racing Club

Placings:343155/11411/04/00310000501342/0-0 **(5419)**
2001: 12^{0}SD

	Starts	1st	2nd	3rd	Win & Pl
Career Total (Turf)	**23**	**6**	**1**	**3**	**22526**
Career Total (AW)	**6**	**1**	**0**	**1**	**7398**

58	8/99	Rdcr	1m3f	E(0-70)H	GD	£3920
67	3/99	Ling	1m2f	D(0-85)H	STD	£7165
	8/97	Karl	1m		FRM	£1309
	7/97	Prag	1m3f	H	GD	£1308
	6/97	Brat	1m2f		G-S	£4362
	4/97	Turf	7f		SFT	£1309
77	7/96	Epsm	6f	D	G-F	£3420

Total win prize-money £22793

Going (Turf): Sf: 0-3 GS: 0-0 **Gd: 1-4 GF: 1-9** Fm: 0-0
Distance: 5f/6f: 1-3 7f-8f: 0-5 **9f-13f: 2-14** 14f+: 0-0
Track : **LH: 3-13** RH: 0-5 **Tight: 3-11** Gall: 0-1
Aids: **Bl: 1-4** Vi: 0-0 Tstrap: 0-0
Best Rating: 6 10/01 Wolv 1m4f stand

Power And Demand

(95) (31)**31**
4-y-o b g Formidable (USA)-Mazurkanova (Song)
Miss M Bragg (D Shaw 20/2) Friends Of Rock Park

Placings:00604/02543000500-055 **(0333)**
2001: 5^{0}SD, 5^{5}SW, 5^{5}SD

	Starts	1st	2nd	3rd	Win & Pl
Career Total (Turf)	**7**	**0**	**0**	**0**	**0**
Career Total (AW)	**12**	**0**	**1**	**1**	**785**

Going (Turf): Sf: 0-2 GS: 0-2 Gd: 0-0 GF: 0-1 Fm: 0-2
Distance: 5f/6f: 0-18 7f-8f: 0-1 9f-13f: 0-0 14f+: 0-0
Track : LH: 0-13 RH: 0-0 Tight: 0-11 Gall: 0-0
Aids: Bl: 0-12 Vi: 0-0 Tstrap: 0-0
Best Rating: 31 2/01 Wolv 5f stand

Power Game

90 (16)
8-y-o b g Puissance-Play The Game (Mummy's Game)
D A Nolan Mrs J McFadyen-Murray

Placings:32553033/02302401301301301/45531100530/50000/0600000/040000-0000000000000 **(4881)**
2001: 6^{0}GF, 8^{0}GF, 8^{0}GF, 8^{0}G, 9^{0}G, 8^{0}F, 6^{0}GF, 12^{0}GS, 8^{0}F, 7^{0}GS, 10^{0}GS, 8^{0}GF, 7^{0}G, 6^{0}GF

	Starts	1st	2nd	3rd	Win & Pl
Career Total (Turf)	**66**	**6**	**3**	**9**	**25968**
Career Total (AW)	**1**	**0**	**0**	**0**	

59	5/97	Muss	1m	F(0-60)H	G-F	£3002
54	5/97	Muss	1m	G	G-S	£2234
66	10/96	Leic	1m8y	F	GD	£3166
64	9/96	Haml	1m65y	E	GD	£3050
59	9/96	Thsk	1m	G	G-F	£2670
58	8/96	Hayd	1m30y	F	G-F	£2675

Total win prize-money £16798

Going (Turf): Sf: 0-5 GS: 1-6 Gd: 2-21 **GF: 3-26** Fm: 0-8
Distance: 5f/6f: 0-8 7f-8f: 3-37 9f-13f: 3-22 14f+: 0-0
Track : LH: 2-17 **RH: 3-27 Tight: 4-24** Gall: 0-2
Aids: **Bl: 6-29** Vi: 0-11 Tstrap: 0-2
Best Rating: 21 7/01 Ayr 7f gd-sft

Poyle Jenny

81 **38**
2-y-o b f Piccolo-Poyle Amber (Sharrood (USA))
K T Ivory Miss Alison Wiggins

Placings:0 **(4157)**
2001: 5^{0}GF

	Starts	1st	2nd	3rd	Win & Pl
Career Total (Turf)	**1**	**0**	**0**	**0**	

Going (Turf): Sf: 0-0 GS: 0-0 Gd: 0-0 GF: 0-1 Fm: 0-0
Distance: 5f/6f: 0-1 7f-8f: 0-0 9f-13f: 0-0 14f+: 0-0
Track : LH: 0-0 RH: 0-0 Tight: 0-0 Gall: 0-0
Aids: Bl: 0-0 Vi: 0-0 Tstrap: 0-0
Best Rating: 38 8/01 Ling 5f gd-fm

Poyle Magic

97 **82**
2-y-o b g Magic Ring (IRE)-Poyle Fizz (Damister (USA))
W G M Turner Miss Alison Wiggins

Placings:31016 **(3498)**
2001: 5^{3}GS, 5^{1}GF, 6^{0}GF, 5^{1}GF, 5^{6}GF

	Starts	1st	2nd	3rd	Win & Pl
Career Total (Turf)	**5**	**2**	**0**	**1**	**8116**

82	6/01	Ches	5f16y	D	G-F	£3461
64	5/01	Ayr	5f	D	G-F	£4095

Total win prize-money £7556

Going (Turf): Sf: 0-0 GS: 0-1 Gd: 0-0 **GF: 2-4** Fm: 0-0
Distance: **5f/6f: 2-5** 7f-8f: 0-0 9f-13f: 0-0 14f+: 0-0
Track : **LH: 1-1** RH: 0-0 **Tight: 1-1** Gall: 0-0
Aids: Bl: 0-0 Vi: 0-0 Tstrap: 0-0
Best Rating: 82 6/01 Ches 5f16y gd-fm

Closely related to Lowther Stakes winner Jemima, was left at the start on his debut and did well to finish third. Won next time out at Ayr over the minimum trip and again at Chester in June. Likes to dominate. Acts on fast ground.

Poyle Pickle

84(84) (40)**44**
3-y-o b f Piccolo-Hithermoor Lass (Red Alert)
M S Saunders Cecil Wiggins

Placings:006-00 **(4785)**
2001: 6^{0}GF, 5^{0}G

	Starts	1st	2nd	3rd	Win & Pl
Career Total (Turf)	**4**	**0**	**0**	**0**	
Career Total (AW)	**1**	**0**	**0**	**0**	**0**

Going (Turf): Sf: 0-2 GS: 0-0 Gd: 0-1 GF: 0-1 Fm: 0-0
Distance: 5f/6f: 0-5 7f-8f: 0-0 9f-13f: 0-0 14f+: 0-0
Track : LH: 0-2 RH: 0-0 Tight: 0-1 Gall: 0-1
Aids: Bl: 0-0 Vi: 0-0 Tstrap: 0-0
Best Rating: 24 9/01 Gdwd 5f good

Practical Magic

77 **30**
2-y-o ch f Polar Falcon (USA)-Beneficiary (Jalmood (USA))
J D Bethell John E Lund

Placings:00 **(4595)**
2001: 5^{0}GF, 7^{0}GF

	Starts	1st	2nd	3rd	Win & Pl
Career Total (Turf)	**2**	**0**	**0**	**0**	

Going (Turf): Sf: 0-0 GS: 0-0 Gd: 0-0 GF: 0-2 Fm: 0-0
Distance: 5f/6f: 0-1 7f-8f: 0-1 9f-13f: 0-0 14f+: 0-0
Track : LH: 0-1 RH: 0-0 Tight: 0-1 Gall: 0-0
Aids: Bl: 0-0 Vi: 0-0 Tstrap: 0-0
Best Rating: 30 9/01 Thsk 7f gd-fm

Praetorian Force

70 **37**
2-y-o b g Atraf-Zaima (IRE) (Green Desert (USA))
K McAuliffe Highgrove Developments Limited

Placings:000 **(4838)**
2001: 6^{0}GF, 7^{0}GF, 6^{0}G

	Starts	1st	2nd	3rd	Win & Pl
Career Total (Turf)	**3**	**0**	**0**	**0**	

Going (Turf): Sf: 0-0 GS: 0-0 Gd: 0-1 GF: 0-2 Fm: 0-0
Distance: 5f/6f: 0-1 7f-8f: 0-2 9f-13f: 0-0 14f+: 0-0
Track : LH: 0-0 RH: 0-0 Tight: 0-0 Gall: 0-0
Aids: Bl: 0-1 Vi: 0-1 Tstrap: 0-0
Best Rating: 37 9/01 Nott 6f15y good

Prague

82 **42**
3-y-o b g Cyrano De Bergerac-Basenite (Mansingh (USA))
N Hamilton John Hopkins (t/a South Hatch Racing)

Placings:60 **(4893)**
2001: 9^{6}G, 12^{0}GF

	Starts	1st	2nd	3rd	Win & Pl
Career Total (Turf)	**2**	**0**	**0**	**0**	**0**

Going (Turf): Sf: 0-0 GS: 0-0 Gd: 0-1 GF: 0-1 Fm: 0-0
Distance: 5f/6f: 0-0 7f-8f: 0-0 9f-13f: 0-2 14f+: 0-0
Track : LH: 0-0 RH: 0-2 Tight: 0-0 Gall: 0-0
Aids: Bl: 0-0 Vi: 0-0 Tstrap: 0-0
Best Rating: 42 9/01 Kemp 1m4f gd-fm

Prague Express

83 **41**
2-y-o ch g Shaddad (USA)-Express Girl (Sylvan Express)
D Moffatt P G Airey, R R Whitton, F G Steel

Placings:400 **(2266)**
2001: 5^{4}GS, 6^{0}GF, 6^{0}G

	Starts	1st	2nd	3rd	Win & Pl
Career Total (Turf)	**3**	**0**	**0**	**0**	**326**

Going (Turf): Sf: 0-0 GS: 0-1 Gd: 0-1 GF: 0-1 Fm: 0-0
Distance: 5f/6f: 0-3 7f-8f: 0-0 9f-13f: 0-0 14f+: 0-0
Track : LH: 0-0 RH: 0-0 Tight: 0-0 Gall: 0-0
Aids: Bl: 0-0 Vi: 0-0 Tstrap: 0-0
Best Rating: 41 5/01 Haml 5f4y gd-sft

Prairie Falcon (IRE)

107 **83**
7-y-o b g Alzao (USA)-Sea Harrier (Grundy)
B W Hills Mrs B W Hills

Placings:35/2515000/00231100/24/604F060400165-0301060030104 **(5661)**
2001: 18^{0}S, 18^{3}GF, 14^{0}GF, 13^{1}G, 16^{0}F, 16^{6}G, 16^{0}GF, 13^{0}GF, 13^{3}GF, 14^{0}HY, 13^{1}GF, 13^{0}GS, 16^{4}G

	Starts	1st	2nd	3rd	Win & Pl
Career Total (Turf)	**45**	**6**	**3**	**4**	**64242**

80	9/01	Ayr	1m5f13y	C(0-95)H	G-F	£6254
83	6/01	York	1m5f194y	C(0-95)H	GD	£9430
85	9/00	Ches	1m7f195y	D(0-80)H	SFT	£7670
85	9/98	Gdwd	1m4f	E(0-85)H	G-F	£3533
80	9/98	Hayd	1m2f120y	E(0-85)H	GD	£2843
80	5/97	Chep	1m4f23y	D	GD	£3715

Total win prize-money £33449

Going (Turf): Sf: 1-7 GS: 0-3 **Gd: 3-17** GF: 2-17 Fm: 0-1
Distance: 5f/6f: 0-0 7f-8f: 0-2 9f-13f: 3-14 14f+: 3-29
Track : **LH: 5-24** RH: 1-21 **Tight: 2-13** Gall: 1-22
Aids: Bl: 0-0 Vi: 0-0 Tstrap: 0-0
Best Rating: 84 5/01 Ches 2m2f147y gd-fm

Useful staying handicapper. He won twice this season, most recently at Ayr over 13 furlongs on good to firm, although he is also effective on a soft surface. He goes well at Chester.

Prairie Wolf

112 (75)**92**

5-y-o ch g Wolfhound (USA)-Bay Queen (Damister (USA))
M L W Bell B J Warren

Placings:06/13131063210/3402002-032313 **(4706)**
2001: 10^{0}G, 9^{3}GF, 10^{2}GF, 9^{3}GF, 9^{1}GF, 10^{3}G

	Starts	1st	2nd	3rd	Win & Pl
Career Total (Turf)	25	4	4	7	66546
Career Total (AW)	1	1	0	0	2843

92	9/01	Gdwd	1m1f	C(0-100)H	G-F	£7865
93	8/99	Yarm	1m2f21y	C(0-90)	GD	£7013
85	5/99	Nott	1m54y	D(0-85)H	FRM	£8521
75	4/99	Ripn	1m	C(0-90)H	GD	£6594
75	3/99	Wolv	1m100y	D	STD	£2843

Total win prize-money £32838

Going (Turf): Sf: 0-2 GS: 0-1 **Gd: 2-10** GF: 1-10 Fm: 1-2
Distance: 5f/6f: 0-0 7f-8f: 1-8 **9f-13f: 4-18** 14f+: 0-0
Track : **LH: 3-8** RH: 2-11 **Tight: 4-11** Gall: 0-3
Aids: Bl: 0-0 Vi: 0-0 Tstrap: 0-0
Best Rating: 92 9/01 Gdwd 1m1f gd-fm

He had not won for two years before scoring at Goodwood in September. He acts on easy ground, but looks better on fast and stays ten furlongs.

Prayers For Rain (IRE)

92 **77**

2-y-o b f Darshaan-Whispered Melody (Primo Dominie)
M A Jarvis N R A Springer

Placings:4100 **(5609)**
2001: 6^{4}GF, 7^{1}GF, 7^{0}GS, 8^{0}GS

	Starts	1st	2nd	3rd	Win & Pl
Career Total (Turf)	4	1	0	0	4544

77	6/01	Kemp	7f	D	G-F	£4173

Total win prize-money £4173

Going (Turf): Sf: 0-0 GS: 0-2 Gd: 0-0 **GF: 1-2** Fm: 0-0
Distance: 5f/6f: 0-1 **7f-8f: 1-3** 9f-13f: 0-0 14f+: 0-0
Track : LH: 0-0 **RH: 1-1** Tight: 0-0 **Gall: 1-1**
Aids: Bl: 0-0 Vi: 0-0 Tstrap: 0-0
Best Rating: 77 8/01 Deau 7f gd-sft

Got off the mark on her second attempt at Kempton over seven furlongs having run well on her debut at Newmarket behind Silent Honor, she disappointed twice on soft ground afterwards.

Precedent (USA)

91 **68**

2-y-o b/br c El Prado (IRE)-Sheikh Fortysix (USA) (Sheikh Albadou)
Sir Michael Stoute Highclere Thoroughbred Racing Ltd

Placings:045 **(5168)**
2001: 7^{0}S, 8^{4}G, 10^{5}GS

	Starts	1st	2nd	3rd	Win & Pl
Career Total (Turf)	3	0	0	0	304

Going (Turf): Sf: 0-1 GS: 0-1 Gd: 0-1 GF: 0-0 Fm: 0-0
Distance: 5f/6f: 0-0 7f-8f: 0-1 9f-13f: 0-2 14f+: 0-0
Track : LH: 0-2 RH: 0-0 Tight: 0-0 Gall: 0-0
Aids: Bl: 0-0 Vi: 0-0 Tstrap: 0-0
Best Rating: 68 9/01 Nott 1m54y good

Precious

97 **71**

3-y-o b f Danehill (USA)-National Treasure (Shirley Heights)
W J Haggas Cheveley Park Stud

Placings:40 **(5286)**
2001: 7^{4}G, 10^{0}HY

	Starts	1st	2nd	3rd	Win & Pl
Career Total (Turf)	2	0	0	0	548

Going (Turf): Sf: 0-1 GS: 0-0 Gd: 0-1 GF: 0-0 Fm: 0-0
Distance: 5f/6f: 0-0 7f-8f: 0-1 9f-13f: 0-1 14f+: 0-0
Track : LH: 0-1 RH: 0-0 Tight: 0-0 Gall: 0-0
Aids: Bl: 0-0 Vi: 0-0 Tstrap: 0-0
Best Rating: 71 5/01 NmkR 7f good

Preciso (IRE)

101 **71**

3-y-o b g Definite Article-Symphony (IRE) (Cyrano De Bergerac)
Mrs A J Perrett John E Bodie

Placings:203-3000 **(5106)**
2001: 12^{3}GF, 14^{0}GF, 14^{0}G, 12^{0}GS

	Starts	1st	2nd	3rd	Win & Pl
Career Total (Turf)	7	0	1	2	1980

Going (Turf): Sf: 0-2 GS: 0-2 Gd: 0-1 GF: 0-2 Fm: 0-0
Distance: 5f/6f: 0-0 7f-8f: 0-2 9f-13f: 0-3 14f+: 0-2
Track : LH: 0-3 RH: 0-4 Tight: 0-1 Gall: 0-3
Aids: Bl: 0-0 Vi: 0-2 Tstrap: 0-0
Best Rating: 75 7/01 Newb 1m4f5y gd-fm

Preen

94 **71**

2-y-o b f Lion Cavern (USA)-Made Of Pearl (USA) (Nureyev (USA))
J R Fanshawe Cheveley Park Stud

Placings:3 **(5371)**
2001: 8^{3}G

	Starts	1st	2nd	3rd	Win & Pl
Career Total (Turf)	1	0	0	1	550

Going (Turf): Sf: 0-0 GS: 0-0 Gd: 0-1 GF: 0-0 Fm: 0-0
Distance: 5f/6f: 0-0 7f-8f: 0-1 9f-13f: 0-0 14f+: 0-0
Track : LH: 0-0 RH: 0-0 Tight: 0-0 Gall: 0-0
Aids: Bl: 0-0 Vi: 0-0 Tstrap: 0-0
Best Rating: 71 10/01 Rdcr 1m good

Made a good debut when third at Redcar in October, and should improve over the winter.

Preferred (IRE)

99 **78**

3-y-o b c Distant Relative-Fruhlingserwachen (USA) (Irish River (FR))
R Hannon R J Brennan & N J Hemmington

Placings:011300-00333 **(2512)**
2001: 8^{0}GS, 7^{0}GF, 8^{3}GF, 9^{3}GF, 9^{3}GF

	Starts	1st	2nd	3rd	Win & Pl
Career Total (Turf)	11	2	0	4	15727

85	7/00	Asct	6f	C	GD	£6825
70	6/00	Nott	5f13y	D	G-F	£3380

Total win prize-money £10205

Going (Turf): Sf: 0-1 GS: 0-1 **Gd: 1-2 GF: 1-7** Fm: 0-0
Distance: **5f/6f: 2-4** 7f-8f: 0-5 9f-13f: 0-2 14f+: 0-0
Track : LH: 0-1 RH: 0-3 Tight: 0-3 Gall: 0-0
Aids: Bl: 0-0 Vi: 0-1 Tstrap: 0-0
Best Rating: 76 6/01 Gdwd 1m1f192y gd-fm

Won twice in the summer as a juvenile. Struggling a little in handicaps this year, he appears to stay a ten furlongs and looks best on fast ground. Has worn a visor.

Premier Account

99(96) (66)**62**

3-y-o b g Mark Of Esteem (IRE)-Gemaasheh (Habitat)
R A Fahey C H Stevens

Placings:444600030 **(5146)**
2001: 8^{4}S, 7^{4}G, 9^{4}SD, 9^{6}GF, 10^{0}GF, 10^{0}G, 8^{0}G, 8^{3}G, 8^{0}G

	Starts	1st	2nd	3rd	Win & Pl
Career Total (Turf)	8	0	0	1	1108
Career Total (AW)	1	0	0	0	0

Going (Turf): Sf: 0-1 GS: 0-0 Gd: 0-5 GF: 0-2 Fm: 0-0
Distance: 5f/6f: 0-0 7f-8f: 0-4 9f-13f: 0-5 14f+: 0-0
Track : LH: 0-5 RH: 0-2 Tight: 0-4 Gall: 0-0
Aids: Bl: 0-0 Vi: 0-0 Tstrap: 0-0
Best Rating: 66 5/01 Wolv 1m1f79y stand

Premier Ambitions

98(79) (38)**51**

3-y-o b g Bin Ajwaad (IRE)-Good Thinking (USA) (Raja Baba (USA))
W J Haggas The First Division Partnership

Placings:000-05526 **(5681)**
2001: 9^{0}G, 12^{5}GF, 9^{5}HY, 8^{2}GS, 8^{6}S

	Starts	1st	2nd	3rd	Win & Pl
Career Total (Turf)	7	0	1	0	1138
Career Total (AW)	1	0	0	0	

Going (Turf): Sf: 0-2 GS: 0-1 Gd: 0-2 GF: 0-2 Fm: 0-0
Distance: 5f/6f: 0-1 7f-8f: 0-4 9f-13f: 0-3 14f+: 0-0
Track : LH: 0-4 RH: 0-1 Tight: 0-1 Gall: 0-1
Aids: Bl: 0-0 Vi: 0-0 Tstrap: 0-0
Best Rating: 51 10/01 Nott 1m1f213y heavy

Premier Baron

109 (63)**83**

6-y-o b g Primo Dominie-Anna Karietta (Precocious)
P S McEntee Miss T J Fitzgerald

Placings:634264030/253146220/14006444610004-4005600130546000401 **(5560)**
2001: 5^{4}S, 7^{0}S, 6^{0}G, 7^{5}G, 7^{6}GF, 7^{0}GF, 7^{0}S, 7^{1}GF, 7^{3}F, 5^{0}GF, 6^{5}GF, 6^{4}GS, 7^{6}G, 6^{0}G, 7^{0}GS, 7^{0}G, 6^{4}GS, 7^{0}GS, 7^{1}S

	Starts	1st	2nd	3rd	Win & Pl
Career Total (Turf)	47	5	4	2	71982
Career Total (AW)	4	0	0	2	871

83	10/01	Yarm	7f3y	D(0-80)H	SFT	£6058
84	6/01	NmkJ	7f	C(0-95)H	G-F	£7068
83	8/00	NmkJ	7f	B(0-105)H	G-F	£19500
85	3/00	Kemp	7f	C(0-95)H	GD	£14430
78	8/99	Sand	7f16y	C(0-90)H	G-S	£7457

Total win prize-money £54515

Going (Turf): Sf: 1-10 GS: 1-14 Gd: 1-14 **GF: 2-8** Fm: 0-1
Distance: 5f/6f: 0-13 **7f-8f: 5-37** 9f-13f: 0-1 14f+: 0-0
Track : LH: 0-10 **RH: 2-6** Tight: 0-3 **Gall: 1-5**
Aids: Bl: 0-1 Vi: 0-0 Tstrap: 0-0
Best Rating: 87 6/01 Newc 7f firm

A useful seven-furlong handicapper who usually pops up once or twice a year at rewarding odds, he took his time to find his best form this season, but a drop in the handicap and having the run of the race helped him do so at Newmarket in June and again at Yarmouth in October. Acts on easy ground, but looks best on fast and is suited by being held up for a late run.

Premier Boy (IRE)

76(72) (28)**43**

3-y-o b g Blues Traveller (IRE)-Little Min (Nebbiolo)
B S Rothwell Premier Protection Services Ltd

Placings:004065-00 **(4905)**
2001: 10^{0}G, 8^{0}G

	Starts	1st	2nd	3rd	Win & Pl
Career Total (Turf)	6	0	0	0	235
Career Total (AW)	2	0	0	0	0

Going (Turf): Sf: 0-1 GS: 0-0 Gd: 0-3 GF: 0-2 Fm: 0-0
Distance: 5f/6f: 0-2 7f-8f: 0-3 9f-13f: 0-3 14f+: 0-0
Track : LH: 0-2 RH: 0-3 Tight: 0-2 Gall: 0-0
Aids: Bl: 0-0 Vi: 0-1 Tstrap: 0-3
Best Rating: 15 8/01 Ripn 1m2f good

Premier Guest

94 **52**

3-y-o br c Primo Dominie-Song Of Hope (Chief Singer)

G G Margarson John Guest

Placings:50000 **(3300)**

2001: 7^{5}G, 7^{0}GF, 6^{0}GF, 7^{0}G, 5^{0}GF

	Starts	1st	2nd	3rd	Win & Pl
Career Total (Turf)	5	0	0	0	0

Going (Turf): **Sf: 0-0 GS: 0-0 Gd: 0-2 GF: 0-3 Fm: 0-0**
Distance: 5f/6f: 0-1 7f-8f: 0-4 9f-13f: 0-0 14f+: 0-0
Track : LH: 0-3 RH: 0-0 Tight: 0-1 Gall: 0-0
Aids: Bl: 0-2 Vi: 0-0 Tstrap: 0-0
Best Rating: 52 6/01 Sals 6f212y gd-fm

Premier Prize

111 **103**

4-y-o ch f Selkirk (USA)-Spot Prize (USA) (Seattle Dancer (USA))

D R C Elsworth J C Smith

Placings:61/630-0513356 **(5259)**

2001: 12^{0}GS, 9^{5}G, 9^{1}GF, 10^{3}GF, 9^{3}GF, 8^{5}G, 7^{6}GS

	Starts	1st	2nd	3rd	Win & Pl
Career Total (Turf)	12	2	0	3	33011

100	8/01	Sals	1m1f198yA		G-F	£15326
85	10/99	NmkJ	7f	D	SFT	£4477

Total win prize-money £19803

Going (Turf): **Sf: 1-2** GS: 0-4 Gd: 0-2 **GF: 1-4** Fm: 0-0
Distance: 5f/6f: 0-1 7f-8f: 1-4 9f-13f: 1-7 14f+: 0-0
Track : LH: 0-2 **RH: 1-4 Tight: 1-4** Gall: 0-2
Aids: Bl: 0-0 Vi: 0-0 Tstrap: 0-0
Best Rating: 103 10/01 NmkR 1m good

Lightly raced. She struggled in the early part of 2000, and was absent after an unplaced run in that season's Oaks. Well beaten twice in 2001 before causing an upset at Salisbury. Fair runs since. Best at ten furlongs

Premiere Foulee (FR)

94(100) (23)**34**

6-y-o ch m Sillery (USA)-Dee (Caerleon (USA))

F Jordan Warwick Davis

Placings:0022/4446020**0**/06066402-40300252050 **(4728)**

2001: 16^{4}SD, 16^{0}SW, 12^{3}SD, 16^{0}SD, 15^{0}HY, 16^{2}GF, 11^{5}GF, 14^{2}GF, 16^{0}GF, 16^{5}GF, 16^{0}GF

	Starts	1st	2nd	3rd	Win & Pl
Career Total (Turf)	20	0	4	0	5946
Career Total (AW)	11	0	2	1	1389

Going (Turf): **Sf: 0-3 GS: 0-1 Gd: 0-0 GF: 0-11 Fm: 0-1**
Distance: 5f/6f: 0-0 7f-8f: 0-0 9f-13f: 0-15 14f+: 0-12
Track : LH: 0-21 RH: 0-4 Tight: 0-14 Gall: 0-0
Aids: Bl: 0-2 Vi: 0-1 Tstrap: 0-0
Best Rating: 34 6/01 Nott 1m6f15y gd-fm

Premiere Valentino

90 **29**

4-y-o b g Tragic Role (USA)-Mirkan Honey (Ballymore)

D W P Arbuthnot Mrs W A Oram

Placings:0/5600-005 **(2704)**

2001: 12^{0}GF, 12^{0}GF, 11^{5}F

	Starts	1st	2nd	3rd	Win & Pl
Career Total (Turf)	8	0	0	0	0

Going (Turf): **Sf: 0-0 GS: 0-2 Gd: 0-2 GF: 0-2 Fm: 0-2**
Distance: 5f/6f: 0-1 7f-8f: 0-0 9f-13f: 0-6 14f+: 0-1
Track : LH: 0-4 RH: 0-4 Tight: 0-4 Gall: 0-1
Aids: Bl: 0-3 Vi: 0-1 Tstrap: 0-0

Best Rating: 29 6/01 Wwck 1m4f134y gd-fm

Premium Princess

100(85) (40)**58**

6-y-o b m Distant Relative-Solemn Occasion (USA) (Secreto (USA))

J J Quinn Derrick Bloy

Placings:00206223/04043402050/0140/00005533624 114410234-02000000 **(4439)**

2001: 5^{0}S, 5^{2}S, 5^{0}GF, 6^{0}F, 6^{0}G, 5^{0}GF, 5^{0}G, 6^{0}G

	Starts	1st	2nd	3rd	Win & Pl
Career Total (Turf)	49	4	7	6	36539
Career Total (AW)	3	0	0	0	0

70	9/00	Nott	6f15y	E(0-70)H	SFT	£3224
68	8/00	Pont	5f	F(0-65)H	G-F	£4641
57	8/00	Sand	5f6y	E(0-75)H	G-F	£4309
57	5/99	Newc	5f	E(0-75)H	FRM	£7360

Total win prize-money £19535

Going (Turf): Sf: 1-9 GS: 0-5 Gd: 0-13 **GF: 2-17** Fm: 1-4
Distance: **5f/6f: 3-33** 7f-8f: 1-16 9f-13f: 0-2 14f+: 0-0
Track : **LH: 1-14** RH: 0-1 Tight: 0-6 Gall: 0-0
Aids: Bl: 0-0 Vi: 0-0 Tstrap: 0-0
Best Rating: 72 5/01 Rdcr 5f soft

She had an awful wins-to-runs ratio until scoring three times in the second half of 2000, but she is devilishly difficult to predict. Best over five furlongs, but has won over six.

Present 'n Correct

105 (36)**43**

8-y-o ch g Cadeaux Genereux-Emerald Eagle (Sandy Creek)

J M Bradley J M Bradley

Placings:0/00301**0**00/50U0/5065423**1045/30**202545363 550/0310 **(5028)**

2001: 5^{0}G, 5^{3}G, 5^{1}GF, 5^{0}S

	Starts	1st	2nd	3rd	Win & Pl
Career Total (Turf)	33	2	3	5	10728
Career Total (AW)	9	1	0	1	2704

43	8/01	Brig	5f59y	E(0-75)H	G-F	£2772
42	11/98	Ling	7f	E(0-70)H	STD	£2502
45	9/96	Thsk	5f	F(0-60)H	G-F	£3142

Total win prize-money £8417

Going (Turf): Sf: 0-4 GS: 0-2 Gd: 0-11 **GF: 2-14** Fm: 0-2
Distance: **5f/6f: 2-32** 7f-8f: 1-9 9f-13f: 0-1 14f+: 0-0
Track : **LH: 2-20** RH: 0-3 **Tight: 1-8** Gall: 0-6
Aids: Bl: 0-0 Vi: 0-0 Tstrap: 0-0
Best Rating: 43 8/01 Brig 5f59y gd-fm

Moderate sprinter. Ended a losing run of almost three years when winning at Brighton in August. The Bradley magic works once again.

Present Chance

(98) (39)**56**

7-y-o ch g Cadeaux Genereux-Chance All (FR) (Glenstal (USA))

D Shaw Ian Guise & Celia M Guise

Placings:40/22205303434**0**/2434331500**0**/036015**34**/00 0000050556000-0550 **(0267)**

2001: 7^{0}SD, 6^{5}SW, 5^{5}SD, 6^{0}SW

	Starts	1st	2nd	3rd	Win & Pl
Career Total (Turf)	37	1	4	8	18841
Career Total (AW)	15	1	0	0	2486

65	6/99	Sthl	5f	F(0-65)H	STD	£2486
80	7/98	Gdwd	6f	D(0-80)	G-S	£7002

Total win prize-money £9489

Going (Turf): Sf: 0-8 **GS: 1-6** Gd: 0-13 GF: 0-8 Fm: 0-2
Distance: **5f/6f: 2-33** 7f-8f: 0-18 9f-13f: 0-1 14f+: 0-0
Track : LH: 0-25 RH: 0-1 Tight: 0-7 Gall: 0-7
Aids: **Bl: 1-17** Vi: 0-0 Tstrap: 0-2
Best Rating: 39 1/01 Sthl 5f stand

Modest sprinter, has shown no worthwhile form for a long time.

Presentation (IRE)

107 **64**

4-y-o b f Mujadil (USA)-Beechwood (USA) (Blushing Groom (FR))

R Hannon Dr A Haloute

Placings:1540633/2326605220-0060000 **(5138)**

2001: 6^{0}G, 6^{0}GF, 6^{6}GF, 6^{0}GF, 6^{0}G, 7^{0}GF, 6^{0}G

	Starts	1st	2nd	3rd	Win & Pl
Career Total (Turf)	24	1	4	3	47512

72	5/99	Wind	5f10y	D	GD	£5243

Total win prize-money £5243

Going (Turf): Sf: 0-3 GS: 0-3 **Gd: 1-8** GF: 0-10 Fm: 0-0
Distance: **5f/6f: 1-22** 7f-8f: 0-2 9f-13f: 0-0 14f+: 0-0
Track : LH: 0-1 **RH: 1-1** Tight: 0-1 **Gall: 1-1**
Aids: Bl: 0-0 Vi: 0-0 Tstrap: 0-0
Best Rating: 78 7/01 Asct 6f gd-fm

Fair handicapper who is equally effective at both five and six furlongs and seems to act on any ground. Below par in her races this season.

Pressionage

82 **46**

2-y-o b f Puissance-My Girl (Mon Tresor)

H S Howe Jonathan Leigh

Placings:0334000 **(5458)**

2001: 5^{0}GF, 5^{3}GS, 6^{3}GF, 6^{4}GF, 7^{0}GF, 6^{0}GS, 5^{0}G

	Starts	1st	2nd	3rd	Win & Pl
Career Total (Turf)	7	0	0	2	1605

Going (Turf): **Sf: 0-0 GS: 0-2 Gd: 0-1 GF: 0-4 Fm: 0-0**
Distance: 5f/6f: 0-4 7f-8f: 0-3 9f-13f: 0-0 14f+: 0-0
Track : LH: 0-2 RH: 0-1 Tight: 0-0 Gall: 0-3
Aids: Bl: 0-0 Vi: 0-0 Tstrap: 0-0
Best Rating: 46 7/01 Kemp 7f gd-fm

Presuming

91(87) (51)**59**

3-y-o b f Mtoto-D'Azy (Persian Bold)

J H M Gosden George Strawbridge

Placings:0-6 **(2878)**

2001: 8^{6}GF

	Starts	1st	2nd	3rd	Win & Pl
Career Total (Turf)	1	0	0	0	0
Career Total (AW)	1	0	0	0	

Going (Turf): **Sf: 0-0 GS: 0-0 Gd: 0-0 GF: 0-1 Fm: 0-0**
Distance: 5f/6f: 0-0 7f-8f: 0-1 9f-13f: 0-1 14f+: 0-0
Track : LH: 0-1 RH: 0-1 Tight: 0-2 Gall: 0-0
Aids: Bl: 0-0 Vi: 0-0 Tstrap: 0-0
Best Rating: 59 7/01 Wind 1m67y gd-fm

Pretending

94 **36**

4-y-o b g Primo Dominie-Red Salute (Soviet Star (USA))

J D Bethell Mrs John Lee

Placings:620060/0653600-00000 **(2356)**

2001: 8^{0}SD, 8^{0}GS, 7^{0}F, 8^{0}GF, 8^{0}GF

	Starts	1st	2nd	3rd	Win & Pl
Career Total (Turf)	17	0	1	1	1177
Career Total (AW)	1	0	0	0	

Going (Turf): **Sf: 0-4 GS: 0-3 Gd: 0-3 GF: 0-5 Fm: 0-2**
Distance: 5f/6f: 0-6 7f-8f: 0-7 9f-13f: 0-5 14f+: 0-0
Track : LH: 0-5 RH: 0-4 Tight: 0-0 Gall: 0-4
Aids: Bl: 0-0 Vi: 0-0 Tstrap: 0-0

Best Rating: 31 6/01 Ayr 1m gd-fm

Pretiosa (IRE)

87 **42**

3-y-o ch f Royal Abjar (USA)-Thatcherite (Final Straw)

N P Littmoden Joy And Valentine Feerick

Placings:46300 (5084)

2001: 9^{4}G, 9^{6}G, 10^{3}GF, 8^{0}G, 9^{0}S

	Starts	1st	2nd	3rd	Win & Pl
Career Total (Turf)	5	0	0	1	1343

Going (Turf): Sf: 0-1 GS: 0-0 Gd: 0-3 GF: 0-1 Fm: 0-0
Distance: 5f/6f: 0-0 7f-8f: 0-0 9f-13f: 0-5 14f+: 0-0
Track: LH: 0-3 RH: 0-1 Tight: 0-2 Gall: 0-1
Aids: Bl: 0-0 Vi: 0-0 Tstrap: 0-0
Best Rating: 43 6/01 Muss 1m1f good

Pretrail (IRE)

(110) (81+)**80**

4-y-o b g Catrail (USA)-Pretty Lady (High Top)

P W D'Arcy Terry Miller & Sandycove Partnership

Placings:02/02100230-0310 (0205)

2001: 8^{0}SD, 8^{3}SD, 8^{1}SW, 10^{0}SW, 8^{4}SD

	Starts	1st	2nd	3rd	Win & Pl
Career Total (Turf)	10	1	3	1	8404
Career Total (AW)	4	1	0	1	4146

81 1/01 Wolv 1m100y D(0-85)H SLW £3307
80 6/00 Ling 7f D G-S £3731
Total win prize-money £7039

Going (Turf): Sf: 0-1 GS: 1-3 Gd: 0-4 GF: 0-2 Fm: 0-0
Distance: 5f/6f: 0-2 7f-8f: 1-9 9f-13f: 1-3 14f+: 0-0
Track: LH: 1-4 RH: 0-3 Tight: 1-3 Gall: 0-2
Aids: Bl: 0-0 Vi: 0-0 Tstrap: 0-0
Best Rating: 81 1/01 Wolv 1m100y slow

Pretty Clear (USA)

100 **98?**

2-y-o b f Mr Prospector (USA)-Seven Springs (USA) (Irish River (FR))

H R A Cecil K Abdulla

Placings:222 (5139)

2001: 6^{2}GF, 6^{2}GF, 6^{2}G

	Starts	1st	2nd	3rd	Win & Pl
Career Total (Turf)	3	0	3	0	5214

Going (Turf): Sf: 0-0 GS: 0-0 Gd: 0-1 GF: 0-2 Fm: 0-0
Distance: 5f/6f: 0-1 7f-8f: 0-2 9f-13f: 0-0 14f+: 0-0
Track: LH: 0-0 RH: 0-0 Tight: 0-0 Gall: 0-0
Aids: Bl: 0-0 Vi: 0-0 Tstrap: 0-0
Best Rating: 98 9/01 Sals 6f212y gd-fm

Pretty Indulgent

95(91) (48)**35**

4-y-o b g Mistertopogigo (IRE)-American Beauty (Mill Reef (USA))

B Smart Miss N Jefford

Placings:00/5306 (3255)

2001: 9^{5}SD, 9^{3}SD, 8^{0}SD, 8^{6}GF

	Starts	1st	2nd	3rd	Win & Pl
Career Total (Turf)	3	0	0	0	0
Career Total (AW)	3	0	0	1	417

Going (Turf): Sf: 0-0 GS: 0-2 Gd: 0-0 GF: 0-1 Fm: 0-0
Distance: 5f/6f: 0-1 7f-8f: 0-3 9f-13f: 0-2 14f+: 0-0
Track: LH: 0-3 RH: 0-1 Tight: 0-2 Gall: 0-1
Aids: Bl: 0-0 Vi: 0-0 Tstrap: 0-0
Best Rating: 48 2/01 Wolv 1m1f79y stand

Pretty Obvious

83 **23**

5-y-o ch m Pursuit Of Love-Settlement (USA) (Irish River (FR))

Mrs M Reveley H Hurst

Placings:4602/004051611/00-00 (0708)

2001: 16^{0}HY, 17^{0}HY

	Starts	1st	2nd	3rd	Win & Pl
Career Total (Turf)	17	3	1	0	14303

61 10/99 Nott 2m9y D(0-80)H SFT £7295
55 9/99 Newc 2m19y E(0-75)H SFT £4037
43 8/99 Catt 1m7f177yG FRM £1842
Total win prize-money £13175

Going (Turf): Sf: 2-7 GS: 0-2 Gd: 0-4 GF: 0-2 Fm: 1-2
Distance: 5f/6f: 0-2 7f-8f: 0-2 9f-13f: 0-5 14f+: 3-8
Track: LH: 3-12 RH: 0-2 Tight: 1-6 Gall: 1-2
Aids: Bl: 0-1 Vi: 0-0 Tstrap: 0-0
Best Rating: 23 4/01 Nott 2m9y heavy

Priceless Second

(96) (44)**41**

4-y-o b g Lugana Beach-Early Gales (Precocious)

J A Glover J A Glover

Placings:060524/231432206400-50 (0081)

2001: 8^{5}SD, 11^{0}SD

	Starts	1st	2nd	3rd	Win & Pl
Career Total (Turf)	4	0	0	0	0
Career Total (AW)	16	1	4	2	4395

63 1/00 Sthl 7f G STD £1842
Total win prize-money £1842

Going (Turf): Sf: 0-0 GS: 0-1 Gd: 0-2 GF: 0-1 Fm: 0-0
Distance: 5f/6f: 0-7 7f-8f: 1-11 9f-13f: 0-2 14f+: 0-0
Track: LH: 1-17 RH: 0-0 Tight: 0-1 Gall: 0-0
Aids: Bl: 0-3 Vi: 0-8 Tstrap: 0-0
Best Rating: 34 1/01 Sthl 1m3f stand

Prickly Pear (USA)

(74) (5)

3-y-o b/br f Polar Falcon (USA)-Tootsiepop (USA) (Robellino (USA))

Sir Mark Prescott Faisal Salman

Placings:0 (0328)

2001: 6^{0}SD

	Starts	1st	2nd	3rd	Win & Pl
Career Total (Turf)	0	0	0	0	
Career Total (AW)	1	0	0	0	

Going (Turf): Sf: 0-0 GS: 0-0 Gd: 0-0 GF: 0-0 Fm: 0-0
Distance: 5f/6f: 0-1 7f-8f: 0-0 9f-13f: 0-0 14f+: 0-0
Track: LH: 0-1 RH: 0-0 Tight: 0-0 Gall: 0-0
Aids: Bl: 0-0 Vi: 0-0 Tstrap: 0-0
Best Rating: 5 2/01 Sthl 6f stand

Prickly Poppy

101 **73**

3-y-o b f Lear Fan (USA)-Prickwillow (USA) (Nureyev (USA))

M P Tregoning Sheikh Mohammed

Placings:5-525 (5180)

2001: 8^{5}G, 9^{2}G, 10^{5}HY

	Starts	1st	2nd	3rd	Win & Pl
Career Total (Turf)	4	0	1	0	1407

Going (Turf): Sf: 0-1 GS: 0-0 Gd: 0-2 GF: 0-1 Fm: 0-0
Distance: 5f/6f: 0-0 7f-8f: 0-1 9f-13f: 0-3 14f+: 0-0
Track: LH: 0-0 HH: 0-2 Tight: 0-2 Gall: 0-0
Aids: Bl: 0-0 Vi: 0-0 Tstrap: 0-0
Best Rating: 73 9/01 Gdwd 1m1f192y good

Priddy Fair

92 **25**

8-y-o b m North Briton-Rainbow Ring (Rainbow Quest (USA))

B Mactaggart Play Fair Partnership

Placings:640000/0/0/340-04 (3211)

2001: 12^{0}GF, 13^{4}G

	Starts	1st	2nd	3rd	Win & Pl
Career Total (Turf)	11	0	0	1	1295
Career Total (AW)	2	0	0	0	

Going (Turf): Sf: 0-0 GS: 0-1 Gd: 0-5 GF: 0-4 Fm: 0-1
Distance: 5f/6f: 0-3 7f-8f: 0-2 9f-13f: 0-4 14f+: 0-4
Track: LH: 0-4 RH: 0-6 Tight: 0-4 Gall: 0-1
Aids: Bl: 0-0 Vi: 0-0 Tstrap: 0-0
Best Rating: 25 7/01 Haml 1m5f9y good

Pride In Me

99(94) (46)**74**

3-y-o ch f Indian Ridge-Easy Option (IRE) (Prince Sabo)

E A L Dunlop Maktoum Al Maktoum

Placings:02-3120 (3633)

2001: 7^{3}SD, 6^{1}GF, 6^{2}GF, 5^{0}G

	Starts	1st	2nd	3rd	Win & Pl
Career Total (Turf)	5	1	2	0	6083
Career Total (AW)	1	0	0	1	464

65 5/01 Thsk 6f D G-F £3802
Total win prize-money £3803

Going (Turf): Sf: 0-1 GS: 0-1 Gd: 0-1 GF: 1-2 Fm: 0-0
Distance: 5f/6f: 1-5 7f-8f: 0-1 9f-13f: 0-0 14f+: 0-0
Track: LH: 0-1 RH: 0-0 Tight: 0-1 Gall: 0-0
Aids: Bl: 0-0 Vi: 0-0 Tstrap: 0-0
Best Rating: 74 6/01 Wind 6f gd-fm

Fair sprinter, winner at six furlongs has tried seven furlongs on Equitrack.

Pride Of Brixton

(110) (70)**46**

8-y-o b g Dominion-Caviar Blini (What A Guest)

Andrew Reid A S Reid

Placings:32/3201005002/00000000/104501050001311 0/5224050000000/11120000650-3646 (5414)

2001: 5^{3}SD, 5^{6}SD, 6^{4}SD, 6^{6}SD, 5^{2}SD

	Starts	1st	2nd	3rd	Win & Pl
Career Total (Turf)	30	2	4	2	14788
Career Total (AW)	34	7	2	2	19126

68 5/00 Wolv 5f D(0-85)H STD £3783
54 4/00 Wolv 5f F STD £2240
57 3/00 Wolv 5f G STD £1897
73 12/98 Wolv 5f G(0-85)H SLW £1903
68 12/98 Wolv 6f E(0-75)H STD £2305
62 11/98 Wolv 5f E(0-70)H STD £2815
65 8/98 Wolv 5f G STD £2057
64 5/98 Carl 5f F(0-60) G-S £2304
81 5/96 Ches 5f16y C(0-100)H GD £7304
Total win prize-money £26610

Going (Turf): Sf: 0-5 GS: 1-8 Gd: 1-9 GF: 0-8 Fm: 0-0
Distance: 5f/6f: 9-62 7f-8f: 0-2 9f-13f: 0-0 14f+: 0-0
Track: LH: 8-41 RH: 1-3 Tight: 8-38 Gall: 1-3
Aids: Bl: 0-0 Vi: 0-1 Tstrap: 0-0
Best Rating: 70 5/01 Wolv 5f stand

Pride Of Dubai (USA)

83 **41**

2-y-o b c Seeking The Gold (USA)-Bint Baladee (Nashwan (USA))

D R Loder Maktoum Al Maktoum

Placings:5 (5483)

2001: 7^{5}HY

	Starts	1st	2nd	3rd	Win & Pl
Career Total (Turf)	1	0	0	0	0

Going (Turf): Sf: 0-1 GS: 0-0 Gd: 0-0 GF: 0-0 Fm: 0-0
Distance: 5f/6f: 0-0 7f-8f: 0-1 9f-13f: 0-0 14f+: 0-0
Track : LH: 0-0 RH: 0-0 Tight: 0-0 Gall: 0-0
Aids: Bl: 0-0 Vi: 0-0 Tstrap: 0-0
Best Rating: 41 10/01 Donc 7f heavy

Pride Of India (IRE)

106 **78**
4-y-o b g Ezzoud (IRE)-Indian Queen (Electric)
J L Dunlop Sir Gordon Brunton

Placings:0/00-110206 **(3549)**
2001: 14^{1}HY, 16^{1}HY, 16^{0}S, 17^{2}F, 20^{0}GF, 21^{6}GF
Starts 1st 2nd 3rd Win & Pl
Career Total (Turf) 9 2 1 0 9130
75 4/01 Nott 2m9y D(0-80)H HVY £4654
68 3/01 Nott 1m6f15y E(0-70)H HVY £3108
Total win prize-money £7762

Going (Turf): Sf: 2-6 GS: 0-0 Gd: 0-0 GF: 0-2 Fm: 0-1
Distance: 5f/6f: 0-0 7f-8f: 0-1 9f-13f: 0-2 **14f+: 2-6**
Track : **LH: 2-4** RH: 0-3 Tight: 0-2 Gall: 0-1
Aids: Bl: 0-0 Vi: 0-2 Tstrap: 0-0
Best Rating: 78 6/01 Pont 2m1f22y firm

Fair stayer. Won twice in soft ground in the spring, but he has been held off higher marks, although he was a respectable seventh in the marathon Ascot Stakes.

Pride Of Peru (IRE)

96(98) (47)**38**
4-y-o b f Perugino (USA)-Nation's Game (Mummy's Game)
M Brittain Northgate Lodge Racing Club

Placings:400000/005505-**4**2**4**0 **(5374)**
2001: 7^{4}SW, 6^{2}SD, 5^{4}GF, 6^{0}G
Starts 1st 2nd 3rd Win & Pl
Career Total (Turf) 14 0 0 0 220
Career Total (AW) 2 0 1 0 832

Going (Turf): Sf: 0-1 GS: 0-2 Gd: 0-2 GF: 0-6 Fm: 0-3
Distance: 5f/6f: 0-12 7f-8f: 0-4 9f-13f: 0-0 14f+: 0-0
Track : LH: 0-3 RH: 0-3 Tight: 0-1 Gall: 0-2
Aids: Bl: 0-0 Vi: 0-0 Tstrap: 0-0
Best Rating: 47 2/01 Sthl 6f stand

Pride Of The Park (FR)

72(80) (49)**39**
2-y-o b g Marju (IRE)-Taj Victory (Final Straw)
P C Haslam Middleham Park Racing Iii

Placings:000 **(5610)**
2001: 6^{0}GF, 7^{0}G, 8^{0}SD
Starts 1st 2nd 3rd Win & Pl
Career Total (Turf) 2 0 0 0
Career Total (AW) 1 0 0 0

Going (Turf): Sf: 0-0 GS: 0-0 Gd: 0-1 GF: 0-1 Fm: 0-0
Distance: 5f/6f: 0-1 7f-8f: 0-1 9f-13f: 0-1 14f+: 0-0
Track : LH: 0-1 RH: 0-1 Tight: 0-1 Gall: 0-0
Aids: Bl: 0-0 Vi: 0-0 Tstrap: 0-0
Best Rating: 49 11/01 Wolv 1m100y stand

Prideway (IRE)

100(106) (60d)**24**
5-y-o b m Pips Pride-Up The Gates (Captain James)
W M Brisbourne K Bennett

Placings:05362406/160020200/**440613**065600060-26000004060 **(5592)**
2001: 8^{2}GF, 9^{6}GS, 8^{0}GF, 8^{0}SD, 8^{0}G, 8^{0}F, 8^{0}SD, 9^{4}HY, 8^{0}HY, 7^{6}HY, 6^{0}GS
Starts 1st 2nd 3rd Win & Pl
Career Total (Turf) 32 0 4 1 4546

Career Total (AW) 11 2 0 1 6335
67 5/00 Sthl 1m E(0-70)H STD £2814
80 2/99 Wolv 7f E(0-75)H STD £2658
Total win prize-money £5474

Going (Turf): Sf: 0-6 GS: 0-8 Gd: 0-6 GF: 0-10 Fm: 0-2
Distance: 5f/6f: 0-5 **7f-8f: 2-25** 9f-13f: 0-13 14f+: 0-0
Track : **LH: 2-28** RH: 0-5 **Tight: 1-20** Gall: 0-1
Aids: Bl: 0-5 Vi: 0-0 Tstrap: 0-0
Best Rating: 51 6/01 Ayr 1m gd-fm

Prima Stella

97 **68**
2-y-o br/gr f Primo Dominie-Raffelina (USA) (Carson City (USA))
B R Millman M A Mauro

Placings:066140020 **(5621)**
2001: 5^{0}S, 5^{6}F, 5^{6}GF, 5^{1}GF, 5^{4}GF, 5^{0}GF, 6^{0}G, 5^{2}GS, 5^{0}GS
Starts 1st 2nd 3rd Win & Pl
Career Total (Turf) 9 1 1 0 3585
51 7/01 Leic 5f2y G G-F £2226
Total win prize-money £2226

Going (Turf): Sf: 0-1 GS: 0-2 Gd: 0-1 **GF: 1-4** Fm: 0-1
Distance: **5f/6f: 1-8** 7f-8f: 0-1 9f-13f: 0-0 14f+: 0-0
Track : LH: 0-0 RH: 0-0 Tight: 0-0 Gall: 0-0
Aids: Bl: 0-0 Vi: 0-0 Tstrap: 0-0
Best Rating: 68 9/01 Leic 5f218y gd-sft

Winner of a poor seller at the fourth attempt, she has run well in nurseries. All her runs have been over five and six furlongs, and she seems to act on any type of ground.

Prima Venture

88(93) (41)**27**
3-y-o b f Pursuit Of Love-Prima Cominna (Unfuwain (USA))
M Dods Mrs B Riddell

Placings:4-0000300 **(3308)**
2001: 6^{0}HY, 7^{0}GS, 8^{0}GF, 8^{0}SD, 7^{3}SD, 6^{0}SD, 7^{0}GS
Starts 1st 2nd 3rd Win & Pl
Career Total (Turf) 5 0 0 0 277
Career Total (AW) 3 0 0 1 270

Going (Turf): Sf: 0-2 GS: 0-2 Gd: 0-0 GF: 0-1 Fm: 0-0
Distance: 5f/6f: 0-3 7f-8f: 0-5 9f-13f: 0-0 14f+: 0-0
Track : LH: 0-5 RH: 0-1 Tight: 0-1 Gall: 0-0
Aids: Bl: 0-1 Vi: 0-0 Tstrap: 0-0
Best Rating: 41 6/01 Sthl 7f stand

Primarosa

84(88) (55)**60**
2-y-o ch f Atraf-Prim Lass (Reprimand)
John A Harris (J L Harris 19/4) Mrs Susan Lee

Placings:00100000 **(5628)**
2001: 5^{0}S, 5^{0}SD, 5^{1}SD, 5^{0}S, 5^{0}GS, 7^{0}SD, 6^{0}HY, 8^{0}G
Starts 1st 2nd 3rd Win & Pl
Career Total (Turf) 5 0 0 0
Career Total (AW) 3 1 0 0 1827
55 4/01 Sthl 5f G STD £1827
Total win prize-money £1827

Going (Turf): Sf: 0-3 GS: 0-1 Gd: 0-1 GF: 0-0 Fm: 0-0
Distance: **5f/6f: 1-6** 7f-8f: 0-2 9f-13f: 0-1 14f+: 0-0
Track : LH: 0-1 RH: 0-0 Tight: 0-0 Gall: 0-0
Aids: Bl: 0-0 Vi: 0-0 Tstrap: 0-0
Best Rating: 60 10/01 Donc 6f heavy

Sprint bred, she is a leggy filly who won an All-Weather seller but found life somewhat tougher when reverting to the turf at Newmarket.

Prime Music

85(85) (19)**30**
4-y-o ch g Primo Dominie-Rose Music (Luthier)
R Wilman (Mrs H L Walton 22/6) Mrs Joanna Hughes

Placings:0000/**00000000** **(2379)**
2001: 7^{0}SW, 7^{0}SW, 6^{0}SW, 7^{0}SD, 6^{0}SD, 7^{0}SD, 7^{0}F, 8^{0}GF
Starts 1st 2nd 3rd Win & Pl
Career Total (Turf) 6 0 0 0
Career Total (AW) 6 0 0 0

Going (Turf): Sf: 0-1 GS: 0-1 Gd: 0-1 GF: 0-2 Fm: 0-1
Distance: 5f/6f: 0-5 7f-8f: 0-7 9f-13f: 0-0 14f+: 0-0
Track : LH: 0-8 RH: 0-1 Tight: 0-3 Gall: 0-1
Aids: Bl: 0-0 Vi: 0-0 Tstrap: 0-0
Best Rating: 33 1/01 Ling 7f slow

Prime Offer

98 **60**
5-y-o b g Primo Dominie-Single Bid (Auction Ring (USA))
D Morris Miss K A Bartlett

Placings:0/303410/50-2606040 **(4951)**
2001: 7^{2}GF, 7^{6}F, 6^{0}GF, 7^{6}G, 8^{0}G, 7^{4}GF, 8^{0}G
Starts 1st 2nd 3rd Win & Pl
Career Total (Turf) 16 1 1 2 5359
67 7/99 Haml 6f5y D FRM £3422
Total win prize-money £3423

Going (Turf): Sf: 0-3 GS: 0-0 Gd: 0-4 GF: 0-6 **Fm: 1-3**
Distance: 5f/6f: 0-6 **7f-8f: 1-9** 9f-13f: 0-1 14f+: 0-0
Track : LH: 0-1 RH: 0-1 Tight: 0-0 Gall: 0-0
Aids: Bl: 0-0 Vi: 0-0 Tstrap: 0-0
Best Rating: 63 5/01 Yarm 7f3y gd-fm

Prime Recreation

105(110) (76)**77**
4-y-o b g Primo Dominie-Night Transaction (Tina's Pet)
P S Felgate Moneyleague Ltd

Placings:003/000300000612-**42102300306105** **(5685)**
2001: 5^{4}SD, 5^{2}SD, 5^{1}SD, 6^{0}SD, 5^{2}SD, 5^{3}GF, 5^{0}SD, 5^{0}S, 5^{3}GS, 5^{0}G, 5^{6}HY, 5^{1}S, 5^{0}G, 5^{5}S
Starts 1st 2nd 3rd Win & Pl
Career Total (Turf) 23 2 1 4 18706
Career Total (AW) 6 1 2 0 4776
77 10/01 York 5f D(0-80)H SFT £7020
76 3/01 Sthl 5f E(0-70)H STD £2443
60 10/00 Ayr 5f E(0-70)H HVY £3087
Total win prize-money £12551

Going (Turf): Sf: 2-6 GS: 0-5 Gd: 0-9 GF: 0-3 Fm: 0-0
Distance: **5f/6f: 3-28** 7f-8f: 0-1 9f-13f: 0-0 14f+: 0-0
Track : LH: 0-5 RH: 0-3 Tight: 0-2 Gall: 0-3
Aids: Bl: 0-0 Vi: 0-0 Tstrap: 0-0
Best Rating: 77 10/01 York 5f soft

Fair sprinter.Has plenty of pace and took to Fibresand earlier in the year including a win at Southwell. Five furlongs is his trip and his is suited by very soft ground on turf.

Prime Trump

101 **76**
3-y-o b g First Trump-Maristax (Reprimand)
P W Harris The Full Deck

Placings:540-055220 **(4570)**
2001: 8^{0}G, 8^{5}F, 11^{5}G, 11^{2}F, 12^{2}GF, 11^{0}HY
Starts 1st 2nd 3rd Win & Pl
Career Total (Turf) 9 0 2 0 2678

Going (Turf): Sf: 0-1 GS: 0-0 Gd: 0-3 GF: 0-3 Fm: 0-2
Distance: 5f/6f: 0-0 7f-8f: 0-4 9f-13f: 0-5 14f+: 0-0
Track : LH: 0-4 RH: 0-1 Tight: 0-2 Gall: 0-0
Aids: Bl: 0-0 Vi: 0-0 Tstrap: 0-0
Best Rating: 73 6/01 Ling 1m3f106y firm

Prime Version

96 **72**

3-y-o b g Primo Dominie-Cashew (Sharrood (USA))
P F I Cole Richard Green (fine Paintings)

Placings:1-600060 **(4872)**
2001: 7^{6}GS, 8^{0}GF, 6^{0}GF, 8^{0}GF, 10^{6}GS, 7^{0}G

	Starts	1st	2nd	3rd	Win & Pl
Career Total (Turf)	7	1	0	0	5270

95 10/00 Newb 6f8y D HVY £5102
Total win prize-money £5103

Going (Turf): Sf: 1-1 GS: 0-2 Gd: 0-1 GF: 0-3 Fm: 0-0
Distance: 5f/6f: 0-1 **7f-8f: 1-5** 9f-13f: 0-1 14f+: 0-0
Track : LH: 0-1 RH: 0-0 Tight: 0-1 Gall: 0-0
Aids: Bl: 0-0 Vi: 0-0 Tstrap: 0-0
Best Rating: 85 4/01 NmkR 7f gd-sft

Primeflight (IRE)

62 **1**

2-y-o b f Primo Dominie-Auction Hall (Saddlers' Hall (IRE))
B A McMahon Stefan Upppstrom

Placings:0 **(4960)**
2001: 6^{0}S

	Starts	1st	2nd	3rd	Win & Pl
Career Total (Turf)	1	0	0	0	

Going (Turf): Sf: 0-1 GS: 0-0 Gd: 0-0 GF: 0-0 Fm: 0-0
Distance: 5f/6f: 0-1 7f-8f: 0-0 9f-13f: 0-0 14f+: 0-0
Track : LH: 0-1 RH: 0-0 Tight: 0-0 Gall: 0-0
Aids: Bl: 0-0 Vi: 0-0 Tstrap: 0-0
Best Rating: 1 9/01 Pont 6f soft

Primeval

89(82) (48d)**44**

7-y-o b g Primo Dominie-Class Adorns (Sadler's Wells (USA))
J C Fox S J V Construction

Placings:53/2/5000010/0-04 **(1076)**
2001: 12^{0}SD, 11^{4}GS

	Starts	1st	2nd	3rd	Win & Pl
Career Total (Turf)	5	0	0	1	545
Career Total (AW)	8	1	1	0	2992

49 7/99 Wolv 1m4f G STD £1871
Total win prize-money £1872

Going (Turf): Sf: 0-0 GS: 0-1 Gd: 0-1 GF: 0-3 Fm: 0-0
Distance: 5f/6f: 0-0 7f-8f: 0-2 **9f-13f: 1-9** 14f+: 0-2
Track : **LH: 1-10** RH: 0-1 **Tight: 1-8** Gall: 0-1
Aids: Bl: 0-0 Vi: 1-2 Tstrap: 1-2
Best Rating: 37 5/01 Brig 1m3f196y gd-sft

Primo Cariad (IRE)

54

2-y-o b f Primo Dominie-Croeso Cynnes (Most Welcome)
R Brotherton Davies And Bridgeman

Placings:00 **(3367)**
2001: 5^{0}GF, 7^{0}GF

	Starts	1st	2nd	3rd	Win & Pl
Career Total (Turf)	2	0	0	0	

Going (Turf): Sf: 0-0 GS: 0-0 Gd: 0-0 GF: 0-2 Fm: 0-0
Distance: 5f/6f: 0-1 7f-8f: 0-1 9f-13f: 0-0 14f+: 0-0
Track : LH: 0-1 RH: 0-0 Tight: 0-0 Gall: 0-1
Aids: Bl: 0-0 Vi: 0-0 Tstrap: 0-0

Primo Dancer

83 **45**

2-y-o b c Primo Dominie-Whittle Woods Girl (Emarati (USA))
C W Fairhurst Brian Cann

Placings:0560 **(4229)**
2001: 6^{0}GF, 7^{5}F, 7^{6}G, 7^{0}G

	Starts	1st	2nd	3rd	Win & Pl
Career Total (Turf)	4	0	0	0	0

Going (Turf): Sf: 0-0 GS: 0-0 Gd: 0-2 GF: 0-1 Fm: 0-1
Distance: 5f/6f: 0-1 7f-8f: 0-3 9f-13f: 0-0 14f+: 0-0
Track : LH: 0-2 RH: 0-0 Tight: 0-1 Gall: 0-0
Aids: Bl: 0-1 Vi: 0-0 Tstrap: 0-0
Best Rating: 45 8/01 Hayd 7f30y good

Primo Dawn

78(96) (75)**40**

2-y-o b c Primo Dominie-Sara Sprint (Formidable (USA))
N P Littmoden M C S D Racing Ltd

Placings:00 **(5604)**
2001: 6^{0}GS, 7^{0}GS, 7^{2}SD

	Starts	1st	2nd	3rd	Win & Pl
Career Total (Turf)	2	0	0	0	

Going (Turf): Sf: 0-0 GS: 0-2 Gd: 0-0 GF: 0-0 Fm: 0-0
Distance: 5f/6f: 0-1 7f-8f: 0-1 9f-13f: 0-0 14f+: 0-0
Track : LH: 0-0 RH: 0-0 Tight: 0-0 Gall: 0-0
Aids: Bl: 0-0 Vi: 0-0 Tstrap: 0-0
Best Rating: 40 11/01 NmkR 7f gd-sft

Primo Doria

76 **56**

2-y-o ch f Primo Dominie-Il Doria (IRE) (Mac's Imp (USA))
J H M Gosden Platt Promotions Ltd

Placings:4 **(4246)**
2001: 6^{4}G

	Starts	1st	2nd	3rd	Win & Pl
Career Total (Turf)	1	0	0	0	338

Going (Turf): Sf: 0-0 GS: 0-0 Gd: 0-1 GF: 0-0 Fm: 0-0
Distance: 5f/6f: 0-1 7f-8f: 0-0 9f-13f: 0-0 14f+: 0-0
Track : LH: 0-0 RH: 0-0 Tight: 0-0 Gall: 0-0
Aids: Bl: 0-0 Vi: 0-0 Tstrap: 0-0
Best Rating: 56 8/01 Gdwd 6f good

Primo Valentino (IRE)

110 **114**

4-y-o b c Primo Dominie-Dorothea Brooke (IRE) (Dancing Brave (USA))
P W Harris Primo Donnas

Placings:2411111/0640-100 **(2971)**
2001: 6^{1}GS, 6^{0}GF, 6^{0}G

	Starts	1st	2nd	3rd	Win & Pl
Career Total (Turf)	14	6	1	0	147283

114 4/01 NmkR 6f A G-S £14732
108 9/99 NmkJ 6f A G-S £68600
113 9/99 Newb 6f8y A G-F £32560
104 9/99 Kemp 6f A G-F £11698
85 6/99 Gdwd 6f D G-F £4890
83 6/99 Leic 5f218y E G-S £3113
Total win prize-money £135593

Going (Turf): Sf: 0-0 **GS: 3-5** Gd: 0-5 **GF: 3-4** Fm: 0-0
Distance: **5f/6f: 5-12** 7f-8f: 1-2 9f-13f: 0-0 14f+: 0-0
Track : LH: 0-0 RH: 0-1 Tight: 0-0 Gall: 0-1
Aids: Bl: 0-0 Vi: 0-0 Tstrap: 0-0
Best Rating: 114 4/01 NmkR 6f gd-sft

A top juvenile in 1999, he failed to stay a mile in the 2000 Guineas and found life tough against the top sprinters as a three-year-old. He made a successful return at Newmarket in April but, after a throat infection, has been well held in Group events since. He likes to make the running and has only ever won over six furlongs. Retired to stud.

Primo Venture

66(80) (35)

3-y-o b f Primo Dominie-Jade Venture (Never So Bold)
P Howling D C Patrick

Placings:6000-5000000 **(3963)**
2001: 7^{5}SD, 9^{0}SW, 8^{0}SW, 8^{0}GF, 7^{0}GF, 8^{0}GF, 10^{0}G

	Starts	1st	2nd	3rd	Win & Pl
Career Total (Turf)	7	0	0	0	0
Career Total (AW)	4	0	0	0	0

Going (Turf): Sf: 0-1 GS: 0-1 Gd: 0-1 GF: 0-3 Fm: 0-1
Distance: 5f/6f: 0-0 7f-8f: 0-7 9f-13f: 0-4 14f+: 0-0
Track : LH: 0-6 RH: 0-2 Tight: 0-3 Gall: 0-2
Aids: Bl: 0-0 Vi: 0-0 Tstrap: 0-0
Best Rating: 35 1/01 Sthl 7f stand

Primrose And Rose

91(89) (58)**68**

2-y-o b f Primo Dominie-Cointosser (IRE) (Nordico (USA))
J M P Eustace Blue Peter Racing

Placings:123600 **(5364)**
2001: 5^{1}SD, 5^{2}S, 5^{3}G, 6^{6}G, 6^{0}GF, 6^{0}GS

	Starts	1st	2nd	3rd	Win & Pl
Career Total (Turf)	5	0	1	1	1432
Career Total (AW)	1	1	0	0	2793

58 4/01 Sthl 5f E STD £2793
Total win prize-money £2793

Going (Turf): Sf: 0-1 GS: 0-1 Gd: 0-2 GF: 0-1 Fm: 0-0
Distance: **5f/6f: 1-6** 7f-8f: 0-0 9f-13f: 0-0 14f+: 0-0
Track : LH: 0-0 RH: 0-0 Tight: 0-0 Gall: 0-0
Aids: Bl: 0-0 Vi: 0-0 Tstrap: 0-0
Best Rating: 68 6/01 Wind 6f good

She won a maiden on the Southwell Fibresand on her debut over five, but looked short of pace in her runs on turf since.

Prince Albert

100(80) (31)**55d**

3-y-o ch g Rock City-Russell Creek (Sandy Creek)
J R Jenkins S A Barningham

Placings:600-005504 **(5131)**
2001: 7^{0}S, 8^{0}SD, 6^{5}GF, 8^{5}GF, 9^{0}GF, 7^{4}HY

	Starts	1st	2nd	3rd	Win & Pl
Career Total (Turf)	8	0	0	0	0
Career Total (AW)	1	0	0	0	

Going (Turf): Sf: 0-5 GS: 0-0 Gd: 0-0 GF: 0-3 Fm: 0-0
Distance: 5f/6f: 0-0 7f-8f: 0-8 9f-13f: 0-1 14f+: 0-0
Track : LH: 0-2 RH: 0-0 Tight: 0-0 Gall: 0-0
Aids: Bl: 0-0 Vi: 0-0 Tstrap: 0-0
Best Rating: 55 4/01 NmkR 7f soft

Prince Alex (IRE)

102 **102+**

7-y-o b g Night Shift (USA)-Finalist (Star Appeal)
Mrs A J Perrett M Dawson, K Mercer, A Jones

Placings:00013/011102/110-0 **(3056)**
2001: 10^{0}G

	Starts	1st	2nd	3rd	Win & Pl
Career Total (Turf)	15	6	1	1	63566

102 8/00 York 1m2f85y B(0-105)H GD £16882
94 7/00 NmkJ 1m2f C(0-95)H GD £17631
78 7/99 Asct 1m4f C(0-90)H G-F £10357
71 6/99 Kemp 1m4f E(0-75)H GD £4533
69 5/99 Kemp 1m4f D(0-80)H G-F £3810
68 8/97 NmkJ 1m4f E(0-70)H GD £4207
Total win prize-money £57422

Going (Turf): Sf: 0-0 GS: 0-2 **Gd: 4-7** GF: 2-6 Fm: 0-0
Distance: 5f/6f: 0-0 7f-8f: 0-0 **9f-13f: 6-14** 14f+: 0-1
Track : LH: 1-6 **RH: 5-8** Tight: 0-2 **Gall: 4-11**
Aids: Bl: 0-0 Vi: 0-0 **Tstrap: 5-10**
Best Rating: 93 7/01 York 1m2f85y good

His appearances have been limited in recent seasons, but he has a good wins-to-runs ratio. Scored a hat-trick in 1999 and won twice from just three starts in 2000, both of them valuable handicaps over ten furlongs. Stays 12 furlongs. Acts on fast ground.

Prince Among Men

96 **57**
4-y-o b g Robellino (USA)-Forelino (USA) (Trempolino (USA))
M Todhunter Jim Ennis

Placings:0633336/333322-0554036 **(5383)**
2001: 12^{0}G, 14^{5}GF, 13^{5}G, 11^{4}G, 11^{0}G, 12^{3}G, 13^{6}S

	Starts	1st	2nd	3rd	Win & Pl
Career Total (Turf)	20	0	2	9	9597

Going (Turf): Sf: 0-4 GS: 0-2 Gd: 0-7 GF: 0-4 Fm: 0-0
Distance: 5f/6f: 0-2 7f-8f: 0-5 9f-13f: 0-9 14f+: 0-4
Track : LH: 0-13 RH: 0-4 Tight: 0-5 Gall: 0-2
Aids: Bl: 0-1 Vi: 0-0 Tstrap: 0-0
Best Rating: 62 7/01 Hayd 1m6f gd-fm

He is a modest middle-distance handicapper. Stays 14 furlongs.

Prince Atraf

94 **83**
2-y-o b c Atraf-Forest Fantasy (Rambo Dancer (CAN))
B R Millman H Gooding

Placings:133506 **(5260)**
2001: 5^{1}S, 6^{3}GF, 7^{3}GF, 7^{5}G, 7^{0}HY, 7^{6}GS

	Starts	1st	2nd	3rd	Win & Pl
Career Total (Turf)	6	1	0	2	8238

67 4/01 Nott 5f13y D SFT £3477
Total win prize-money £3478

Going (Turf): Sf: 1-2 GS: 0-1 Gd: 0-1 GF: 0-2 Fm: 0-0
Distance: 5f/6f: 1-1 7f-8f: 0-5 9f-13f: 0-0 14f+: 0-0
Track : LH: 0-0 RH: 0-1 Tight: 0-0 Gall: 0-0
Aids: Bl: 0-1 Vi: 0-0 Tstrap: 0-0
Best Rating: 83 8/01 Asct 7f good

Made a winning debut in soft ground and has run well in better company. Seems to stay seven furlongs.

Prince Babar

92 **83**
10-y-o b g Fairy King (USA)-Bell Toll (High Line)
R A Fahey Giles W Pritchard-Gordon

Placings:012321/00/632323012/0206/0500012/600000/244501650-5 **(0517)**
2001: 8^{5}S

	Starts	1st	2nd	3rd	Win & Pl
Career Total (Turf)	44	5	8	4	282252

83 9/00 Hayd 7f30y C(0-90)H HVY £7540
92 10/98 NmkR 7f C(0-95)H GD £8760
83 10/96 Asct 1m E GD £4187
999 8/93 Deau 7f GD £179211
89 5/93 Newb 5f34y D GD £4175
Total win prize-money £203873

Going (Turf): Sf: 1-9 GS: 0-9 **Gd: 4-11** GF: 0-14 Fm: 0-1
Distance: 5f/6f: 1-6 **7f-8f: 4-28** 9f-13f: 0-10 14f+: 0-0
Track : **LH: 1-8** RH: 0-8 Tight: 0-1 Gall: 0-2
Aids: Bl: 0-0 Vi: 0-1 Tstrap: 0-0
Best Rating: 57 3/01 Donc 1m soft

Prince Caspian

83 **56**
4-y-o ch g Mystiko (USA)-Real Princess (Aragon)
Miss E C Lavelle Lady Sieff

Placings:14000-0 **(4569)**
2001: 7^{0}HY

	Starts	1st	2nd	3rd	Win & Pl
Career Total (Turf)	6	1	0	0	4531

70 6/00 Nott 1m54y D SFT £3981
Total win prize-money £3981

Going (Turf): Sf: 1-3 GS: 0-0 Gd: 0-1 GF: 0-1 Fm: 0-1
Distance: 5f/6f: 0-0 7f-8f: 0-5 **9f-13f: 1-1** 14f+: 0-0
Track : **LH: 1-4** RH: 0-0 Tight: 0-1 Gall: 0-1
Aids: Bl: 0-0 Vi: 0-0 Tstrap: 0-0
Best Rating: 51 9/01 Hayd 7f30y heavy

Prince Cyrano

106 **97**
2-y-o b g Cyrano De Bergerac-Odilese (Mummy's Pet)
S C Williams Judy And Rebecca Aston

Placings:02141240 **(5244a)**
2001: 7^{0}F, 7^{2}GF, 6^{1}G, 6^{4}G, 6^{1}G, 5^{2}S, 6^{4}GF, 5^{0}HO

	Starts	1st	2nd	3rd	Win & Pl
Career Total (Turf)	8	2	2	0	32630

90 9/01 Kemp 6f B GD £25000
75 8/01 Folk 6f F GD £2464
Total win prize-money £27464

Going (Turf): Sf: 0-1 GS: 0-0 **Gd: 2-3** GF: 0-2 Fm: 0-1
Distance: **5f/6f: 2-5** 7f-8f: 0-3 9f-13f: 0-0 14f+: 0-0
Track : LH: 0-0 RH: 0-0 Tight: 0-0 Gall: 0-0
Aids: Bl: 0-1 Vi: 0-0 Tstrap: 0-0
Best Rating: 97 10/01 Lonc 5f holding

A half-brother to three winners, including useful juveniles Tutu Sixtysix and Oriole. Well beaten when blinkered on his debut, he ran without them when defying his huge price to finish runner-up in a Newmarket maiden over seven in July. Went on to win a maiden auction event at Folkestone and a valuable Kempton sales race very easily and finished a close second in a Group Three in France a few days later. Out of his depth against older horses in the Prix de l'Abbaye. Acts on any ground, but suited by good. Has joined W. Musson.

Prince Dayjur (USA)

104 **94**
2-y-o b c Dayjur (USA)-Distinct Beauty (USA) (Phone Trick (USA))
R Hannon Major A M Everett

Placings:21320 **(4173)**
2001: 5^{2}GF, 6^{1}GF, 6^{3}G, 6^{2}GF, 6^{0}G

	Starts	1st	2nd	3rd	Win & Pl
Career Total (Turf)	5	1	2	1	31620

97 6/01 Sals 6f B G-F £9639
Total win prize-money £9640

Going (Turf): Sf: 0-0 GS: 0-0 Gd: 0-2 **GF: 1-3** Fm: 0-0
Distance: **5f/6f: 1-5** 7f-8f: 0-0 9f-13f: 0-0 14f+: 0-0
Track : LH: 0-0 RH: 0-0 Tight: 0-0 Gall: 0-0
Aids: Bl: 0-0 Vi: 0-0 Tstrap: 0-0
Best Rating: 97 6/01 Sals 6f gd-fm

Improved from his debut when running away with a valuable conditions event at Salisbury, but his limitations were exposed in Group company afterwards. Sold for 150,000 gns to race in Hong Kong.

Prince Dimitri

93 **63**
2-y-o ch c Desert King (IRE)-Pinta (IRE) (Ahonoora)
S P C Woods Lucayan Stud

Placings:030 **(4873)**
2001: 7^{0}GS, 8^{3}GF, 7^{0}G

	Starts	1st	2nd	3rd	Win & Pl
Career Total (Turf)	3	0	0	1	681

Going (Turf): Sf: 0-0 GS: 0-1 Gd: 0-1 GF: 0-1 Fm: 0-0
Distance: 5f/6f: 0-0 7f-8f: 0-3 9f-13f: 0-0 14f+: 0-0
Track : LH: 0-1 RH: 0-0 Tight: 0-1 Gall: 0-0
Aids: Bl: 0-0 Vi: 0-0 Tstrap: 0-0
Best Rating: 63 9/01 Thsk 1m gd-fm

Prince Domino

100 **82**
2-y-o b c Primo Dominie-Danzig Harbour (USA) (Private Account (USA))
R Hannon Mrs Charles Sparrowhawk

Placings:2120034 **(5291)**
2001: 7^{2}GF, 7^{1}GF, 7^{2}GF, 7^{0}G, 6^{0}G, 7^{3}GS, 7^{4}S

	Starts	1st	2nd	3rd	Win & Pl
Career Total (Turf)	7	1	2	1	9089

80 7/01 Epsm 7f E G-F £4309
Total win prize-money £4310

Going (Turf): Sf: 0-1 GS: 0-1 Gd: 0-2 **GF: 1-3** Fm: 0-0
Distance: 5f/6f: 0-1 **7f-8f: 1-6** 9f-13f: 0-0 14f+: 0-0
Track : **LH: 1-1** RH: 0-0 **Tight: 1-1** Gall: 0-0
Aids: Bl: 0-0 Vi: 0-0 Tstrap: 0-0
Best Rating: 82 9/01 Leic 7f9y gd-sft

Broke his maiden over seven furlongs at Epsom in July, despite struggling with the undulations. Acts on fast ground and seemed to struggle on easy going later in the season.

Prince Du Soleil (FR)

104 **59**
5-y-o b g Cardoun (FR)-Revelry (FR) (Blakeney)
J R Jenkins R Bradbury

Placings:01/501422/00000040-20004030 **(4489)**
2001: 8^{2}HY, 8^{0}S, 8^{0}GF, 8^{0}GF, 8^{4}G, 8^{0}GF, 7^{3}G, 8^{0}S

	Starts	1st	2nd	3rd	Win & Pl
Career Total (Turf)	24	2	3	1	24468

4/99 MsnL 1m HLD £7537
12/98 StCl 1m HVY £5555
Total win prize-money £13092

Going (Turf): Sf: 0-6 GS: 0-1 Gd: 0-5 GF: 0-4 Fm: 0-0
Distance: 5f/6f: 0-0 7f-8f: 0-7 9f-13f: 0-9 14f+: 0-0
Track : LH: 0-5 RH: 0-9 Tight: 0-3 Gall: 0-2
Aids: Bl: 0-0 Vi: 0-1 Tstrap: 0-0
Best Rating: 65 4/01 Nott 1m54y heavy

Prince Grigori (IRE)

90 **47**
3-y-o ch g Prince Of Birds (USA)-Zinovia (USA) (Ziggy's Boy (USA))
E J Alston Morris, Oliver, Pierce

Placings:0400-0000640 **(4226)**
2001: 6^{0}F, 7^{0}GS, 6^{0}GS, 6^{0}G, 8^{6}GS, 8^{4}HY, 7^{0}GF

	Starts	1st	2nd	3rd	Win & Pl
Career Total (Turf)	11	0	0	0	569

Going (Turf): Sf: 0-3 GS: 0-3 Gd: 0-2 GF: 0-1 Fm: 0-1
Distance: 5f/6f: 0-5 7f-8f: 0-3 9f-13f: 0-2 14f+: 0-0
Track : LH: 0-6 RH: 0-0 Tight: 0-1 Gall: 0-1
Aids: Bl: 0-5 Vi: 0-0 Tstrap: 0-6
Best Rating: 47 8/01 Hayd 1m30y heavy

Prince Hector

102 **87**
2-y-o ch c Hector Protector (USA)-Ceanothus (IRE) (Bluebird (USA))
Mrs A J Perrett Cheveley Park Stud

Placings:41 **(5604)**
2001: 7^{4}S, 7^{1}GS

	Starts	1st	2nd	3rd	Win & Pl

Career Total (Turf) 2 1 0 0 4694
87 11/01 NmkR 7f D G-S £4377
Total win prize money £1378

Going (Turf): Sf: 0-1 GS: 1-1 Gd: 0-0 GF: 0-0 Fm: 0-0
Distance: 5f/6f: 0-0 7f-8f: 1-2 9f-13f: 0-0 14f+: 0-0
Track : LH: 0-0 RH: 0-0 Tight: 0-0 Gall: 0-0
Aids: Bl: 0-0 Vi: 0-0 Tstrap: 0-0
Best Rating: 87 11/01 NmkR 7f gd-sft

Out of a Grade Two mile and a half winner in USA, he won a seven-furlong maiden on soft ground in the autumn. Will get further as a three-year-old.

Prince Jack

41
3-y-o b g Puissance-Sabo Song (Prince Sabo)
H A McWilliams James S Kennerley

Placings:0-00 **(2818)**
2001: 6^{0}GF, 5^{0}GF

	Starts	1st	2nd	3rd	Win & Pl
Career Total (Turf)	3	0	0	0	

Going (Turf): Sf: 0-1 GS: 0-0 Gd: 0-0 GF: 0-2 Fm: 0-0
Distance: 5f/6f: 0-3 7f-8f: 0-0 9f-13f: 0-0 14f+: 0-0
Track : LH: 0-0 RH: 0-0 Tight: 0-0 Gall: 0-0
Aids: Bl: 0-0 Vi: 0-0 Tstrap: 0-0

Prince Millennium

94(90) (59)44
3-y-o b c First Trump-Petit Point (IRE) (Petorius)
R Hannon Major A M Everett

Placings:56304054-0006240360 **(5469)**
2001: 9^{0}GS, 9^{0}GF, 7^{0}GF, 8^{6}GF, 6^{2}GF, 8^{4}GS, 7^{0}F, 9^{3}GS, 9^{6}GS, 9^{0}S

	Starts	1st	2nd	3rd	Win & Pl
Career Total (Turf)	16	0	1	2	1258
Career Total (AW)	2	0	0	0	0

Going (Turf): Sf: 0-2 GS: 0-4 Gd: 0-2 GF: 0-6 Fm: 0-2
Distance: 5f/6f: 0-2 7f-8f: 0-9 9f-13f: 0-7 14f+: 0-0
Track : LH: 0-7 RH: 0-4 Tight: 0-5 Gall: 0-0
Aids: Bl: 0-6 Vi: 0-1 Tstrap: 0-0
Best Rating: 55 5/01 Gdwd 1m1f gd-fm

Prince Minata (IRE)

103(97) (59)60
6-y-o b g Machiavellian (USA)-Aminata (Glenstal (USA))
P W Hiatt (Lindsay Woods 10/2) Miss Maria McKinney

Placings:0/34/00-1000053001042000 **(4667)**
2001: 8^{1}SD, 10^{0}SD, 7^{0}GS, 10^{0}GS, 8^{0}S, 7^{5}F, 8^{3}F, 9^{0}GF, 8^{0}G, 8^{1}F, 8^{0}GF, 8^{4}GF, 8^{2}F, 8^{0}G, 8^{0}F, 8^{0}GF

	Starts	1st	2nd	3rd	Win & Pl
Career Total (Turf)	19	1	1	2	5637
Career Total (AW)	2	1	0	0	2782

61 7/01 Muss 1m E(0-70)H FRM £3206
59 3/01 Wolv 1m100y D STD £2782
Total win prize-money £5988

Going (Turf): Sf: 0-4 GS: 0-2 Gd: 0-3 GF: 0-4 Fm: 1-5
Distance: 5f/6f: 0-2 7f-8f: 1-8 9f-13f: 1-11 14f+: 0-0
Track : LH: 1-10 RH: 1-7 Tight: 2-8 Gall: 0-1
Aids: Bl: 0-0 Vi: 0-0 Tstrap: 0-0
Best Rating: 61 7/01 Muss 1m firm

A moderate winning handicapper. Best at a mile, acts on Fibresand and fast ground.

Prince Nicholas

84 38
6-y-o ch g Midyan (USA)-Its My Turn (Palm Track)
K W Hogg Auldyn Stud Ltd

Placings:0060/22050/11/0224404060-0 **(5167)**
2001: 12^{0}GS

	Starts	1st	2nd	3rd	Win & Pl
Career Total (Turf)	22	2	4	0	10276

49 3/99 Haml 1m4f17y F(0-60)H HVY £2444
53 3/99 Donc 1m4f F(0-80)H GD £2500
Total win prize-money £4944

Going (Turf): Sf: 1-9 GS: 0-3 Gd: 1-5 GF: 0-5 Fm: 0-0
Distance: 5f/6f: 0-2 7f-8f: 0-2 9f-13f: 2-13 14f+: 0-5
Track : LH: 1-8 RH: 1-11 Tight: 1-14 Gall: 1-3
Aids: Bl: 0-0 Vi: 0-0 Tstrap: 0-0
Best Rating: 30 10/01 Pont 1m4f8y gd-sft

A half-brother to Silverdale Fox and Silverdale Knight, he won twice on the Flat in 1999, but has failed to add to that, although he has returned to a reasonable mark. Suited by cut in the ground, has been hurdling of late.

Prince Nico (IRE)

92(109) (72)47
4-y-o b g Nicolotte-Chummy's Friend (IRE) (Be My Guest (USA))
R Guest Michael Hills

Placings:000065411-1535106 **(1675)**
2001: 5^{1}SD, 6^{5}SW, 5^{3}SD, 5^{5}SW, 5^{1}SD, 5^{0}G, 5^{6}G

	Starts	1st	2nd	3rd	Win & Pl
Career Total (Turf)	5	0	0	0	0
Career Total (AW)	11	4	0	1	12715

72 5/01 Wolv 5f D(0-85)H STD £3796
69 1/01 Ling 5f E(0-75)H STD £2387
58 12/00 Ling 5f E(0-75)H STD £2772
47 12/00 Ling 6f D STD £2730
Total win prize-money £11685

Going (Turf): Sf: 0-0 GS: 0-2 Gd: 0-3 GF: 0-0 Fm: 0-0
Distance: 5f/6f: 4-16 7f-8f: 0-0 9f-13f: 0-0 14f+: 0-0
Track : LH: 4-11 RH: 0-0 Tight: 4-10 Gall: 0-0
Aids: Bl: 0-0 Vi: 0-0 Tstrap: 0-0
Best Rating: 72 5/01 Wolv 5f stand

Prince Of Blues (IRE)

100(100) (88)79
3-y-o b c Prince Of Birds (USA)-Reshift (Night Shift (USA))
N P Littmoden T Clarke

Placings:526500124-0602000000005020404 **(5629)**
2001: 7^{0}GS, 5^{6}GF, 6^{0}GF, 5^{2}GF, 5^{0}F, 5^{0}GF, 5^{0}GF, 5^{0}GF, 5^{0}G, 5^{0}GS, 5^{0}GF, 5^{5}GS, 5^{0}G, 5^{2}G, 5^{0}G, 5^{4}GS, 5^{0}GS, 5^{4}G

	Starts	1st	2nd	3rd	Win & Pl
Career Total (Turf)	25	1	3	0	8452
Career Total (AW)	2	0	1	0	1337

80 9/00 Ling 5f F GD £1974
Total win prize-money £1974

Going (Turf): Sf: 0-0 GS: 0-5 Gd: 1-9 GF: 0-9 Fm: 0-2
Distance: 5f/6f: 1-24 7f-8f: 0-3 9f-13f: 0-0 14f+: 0-0
Track : LH: 0-7 RH: 0-0 Tight: 0-7 Gall: 0-0
Aids: Bl: 0-5 Vi: 0-0 Tstrap: 0-0
Best Rating: 88 5/01 Thsk 5f gd-fm

Highly-tried as a juvenile before winning a maiden auction in autumn of 2000, then beaten twice on All-Weather surfaces. Seems best on a sound surface over five furlongs. On a fair mark but win-to-ratio not great.

Prince Of My Heart

99 80
8-y-o ch h Prince Daniel (USA)-Blue Room (Gorytus (USA))
J Neville (H R A Cecil 5/5) G J Hicks

Placings:003316/21304305/05100506/40003400/6/66-000 **(5669)**
2001: 10^{0}G, 9^{0}G, 10^{0}HY

	Starts	1st	2nd	3rd	Win & Pl
Career Total (Turf)	36	3	1	5	46802

108 5/97 Newb 1m1f B(0-105) SFT £7408
87 4/96 Catt 1m3f214yC GD £5177
85 10/95 York 7f202y E GD £6004
Total win prize-money £18590

Going (Turf): Sf: 1-6 GS: 0-3 Gd: 2-15 GF: 0-11 Fm: 0-1
Distance: 5f/6f: 0-0 7f-8f: 1-9 9f-13f: 2-27 14f+: 0-0
Track : LH: 3-17 RH: 0-7 Tight: 1-8 Gall: 2-11
Aids: Bl: 0-0 Vi: 0-1 Tstrap: 0-0
Best Rating: 80 5/01 NmkR 1m2f good

Useful handicapper on his day. Lightly raced in recent years.

Prince Of Mystery (IRE)

(93) (47)38
4-y-o b/br g Shalford (IRE)-Mary Kate Danagher (Petoski)
A B Coogan A B Coogan

Placings:630/00020-0 **(0171)**
2001: 12^{0}SD

	Starts	1st	2nd	3rd	Win & Pl
Career Total (Turf)	6	0	0	1	1025
Career Total (AW)	3	0	1	0	638

Going (Turf): Sf: 0-0 GS: 0-0 Gd: 0-3 GF: 0-2 Fm: 0-1
Distance: 5f/6f: 0-0 7f-8f: 0-4 9f-13f: 0-5 14f+: 0-0
Track : LH: 0-5 RH: 0-3 Tight: 0-4 Gall: 0-0
Aids: Bl: 0-1 Vi: 0-0 Tstrap: 0-0
Best Rating: 22 1/01 Sthl 1m4f stand

Prince Prospect

93(109) (70d)53
5-y-o b g Lycius (USA)-Princess Dechtra (IRE) (Bellypha)
Mrs L Stubbs Mrs L Stubbs

Placings:42233031/334004351364000/010220040000610-30003 **(4603)**
2001: 6^{3}SD, 5^{0}G, 6^{0}G, 6^{0}GF, 7^{3}SD

	Starts	1st	2nd	3rd	Win & Pl
Career Total (Turf)	29	1	3	4	11775
Career Total (AW)	13	3	1	5	17225

61 11/00 Ling 7f D(0-85) STD £3802
76 1/00 Ling 6f C STD £5890
76 7/99 Sand 5f6y D(0-80)H G-F £3777
81 12/98 Ling 6f D STD £2684
Total win prize-money £16156

Going (Turf): Sf: 0-3 GS: 0-2 Gd: 0-11 GF: 1-10 Fm: 0-3
Distance: 5f/6f: 3-34 7f-8f: 1-8 9f-13f: 0-0 14f+: 0-0
Track : LH: 3-16 RH: 0-1 Tight: 3-13 Gall: 0-3
Aids: Bl: 0-0 Vi: 0-1 Tstrap: 0-0
Best Rating: 55 1/01 Ling 6f stand

Prince Pyramus

101 63
3-y-o b g Pyramus (USA)-Rekindled Flame (IRE) (King's Lake (USA))
C Grant Havelock Racing

Placings:44122-5605000000 **(5535)**
2001: 6^{5}GF, 5^{6}F, 6^{0}GF, 6^{5}GS, 6^{0}G, 6^{0}G, 5^{0}GS, 6^{0}S, 7^{0}G, 7^{0}S

	Starts	1st	2nd	3rd	Win & Pl
Career Total (Turf)	15	1	2	0	13593

75 9/00 Bevl 5f D G-F £4091
Total win prize-money £4092

Going (Turf): Sf: 0-4 GS: 0-2 Gd: 0-3 GF: 1-5 Fm: 0-1
Distance: 5f/6f: 1-11 7f-8f: 0-4 9f-13f: 0-0 14f+: 0-0
Track : LH: 0-1 RH: 0-0 Tight: 0-1 Gall: 0-0
Aids: Bl: 0-1 Vi: 0-0 Tstrap: 0-0
Best Rating: 80 5/01 Ches 6f18y gd-fm

Prince Shaamaal

86(98) (74)66
3-y-o b c Shaamit (IRE)-Princess Alaska (Northern State (USA))
K Bell The Upshire Racing Partnership

Placings:1-500 **(4445)**

2001: 10^{5}S, 9^{0}GS, 8^{0}G, 12^{5}SD

	Starts	1st	2nd	3rd	Win & Pl
Career Total (Turf)	4	1	0	0	2321

81 10/00 Bath 1m5y E G-S £2320
Total win prize-money £2321

Going (Turf): Sf: 0-1 **GS: 1-2** Gd: 0-1 GF: 0-0 Fm: 0-0
Distance: 5f/6f: 0-0 7f-8f: 0-0 **9f-13f: 1-4** 14f+: 0-0
Track : **LH: 1-1** RH: 0-3 **Tight: 1-1** Gall: 0-1
Aids: Bl: 0-0 Vi: 0-0 Tstrap: 0-0
Best Rating: 66 4/01 Kemp 1m2f soft

Prince Slayer

102 **79d**
5-y-o b g Batshoof-Top Sovereign (High Top)
T P McGovern Ahmed Abdel-Khaleq

Placings:5/2352/0201000000-400 **(1322)**
2001: 10^{4}S, 10^{0}G, 10^{0}G

	Starts	1st	2nd	3rd	Win & Pl
Career Total (Turf)	18	1	3	1	27742

84 6/00 Epsm 1m114y C(0-100)H G-S £22750
Total win prize-money £22750

Going (Turf): Sf: 0-7 **GS: 1-3** Gd: 0-5 GF: 0-3 Fm: 0-0
Distance: 5f/6f: 0-0 7f-8f: 0-4 **9f-13f: 1-14** 14f+: 0-0
Track : **LH: 1-6** RH: 0-5 **Tight: 1-8** Gall: 0-1
Aids: Bl: 0-1 Vi: 0-0 Tstrap: 0-0
Best Rating: 72 4/01 Epsm 1m2f18y soft

Prince Tulum (USA)

96 **84**
2-y-o ch c Bien Bien (USA)-Eastsider (USA) (Diesis)
N P Littmoden P L Williams

Placings:36320500 **(5388)**
2001: 6^{3}GF, 6^{6}GF, 6^{3}GF, 7^{2}G, 6^{0}G, 7^{5}G, 6^{0}G, 7^{0}GS

	Starts	1st	2nd	3rd	Win & Pl
Career Total (Turf)	8	0	1	2	2612

Going (Turf): Sf: 0-0 GS: 0-1 Gd: 0-4 GF: 0-3 Fm: 0-0
Distance: 5f/6f: 0-3 7f-8f: 0-5 9f-13f: 0-0 14f+: 0-0
Track : LH: 0-1 RH: 0-1 Tight: 0-2 Gall: 0-0
Aids: Bl: 0-0 Vi: 0-0 Tstrap: 0-0
Best Rating: 84 9/01 NmkR 7f good

He has run some fair races on good ground or faster.

Prince's Passion

102 **78**
2-y-o b f Brief Truce (USA)-Green Bonnet (IRE) (Green Desert (USA))
D J Coakley Hurley Molossi Pattinson

Placings:354124500 **(4985)**
2001: 5^{3}G, 5^{5}GF, 6^{4}GF, 5^{1}HD, 6^{2}GF, 6^{4}GF, 6^{5}G, 6^{0}GF, 6^{0}G

	Starts	1st	2nd	3rd	Win & Pl
Career Total (Turf)	9	1	1	1	5706

69 6/01 Bath 5f161y E HRD £2898
Total win prize-money £2898

Going (Turf): Sf: 0-0 GS: 0-0 Gd: 0-3 GF: 0-5 **Fm: 1-1**
Distance: **5f/6f: 1-8** 7f-8f: 0-1 9f-13f: 0-0 14f+: 0-0
Track : **LH: 1-2** RH: 0-0 Tight: 0-0 **Gall: 1-2**
Aids: Bl: 0-0 Vi: 0-0 Tstrap: 0-0
Best Rating: 78 7/01 NmkJ 6f gd-fm

Her only win so far came in a modest Bath maiden auction event, but she has run well in some much better races since. Suited by six furlongs and fast ground.

Princely Venture (IRE)

99 **83**
2-y-o ch c Entrepreneur-Sun Princess (English Prince)
Sir Michael Stoute Lord Weinstock

Placings:5 **(5604)**
2001: 7^{5}GS

	Starts	1st	2nd	3rd	Win & Pl
Career Total (Turf)	1	0	0	0	0

Going (Turf): Sf: 0-0 GS: 0-1 Gd: 0-0 GF: 0-0 Fm: 0-0
Distance: 5f/6f: 0-0 7f-8f: 0-1 9f-13f: 0-0 14f+: 0-0
Track : LH: 0-0 RH: 0-0 Tight: 0-0 Gall: 0-0
Aids: Bl: 0-0 Vi: 0-0 Tstrap: 0-0
Best Rating: 83 11/01 NmkR 7f gd-sft

A half-brother to Prince of Dance, ran well on his debut and should improve over middle distances as a three-year-old.

Princes Street

102(95) (49)**63**
3-y-o b g Sri Pekan (USA)-Abbey Strand (USA) (Shadeed (USA))
G G Margarson (R Hannon 5/6) The Five Star Partnership

Placings:2-24330062210340 **(5593)**
2001: 7^{2}SW, 5^{4}SD, 6^{3}S, 7^{3}F, 8^{0}GF, 8^{0}GF, 7^{6}F, 6^{2}GF, 6^{2}GF, 6^{1}F, 6^{0}F, 5^{3}G, 5^{4}GS, 5^{0}GS

	Starts	1st	2nd	3rd	Win & Pl
Career Total (Turf)	13	1	3	3	7157
Career Total (AW)	2	0	1	0	818

60 9/01 Newc 6f F(0-65)H FRM £2443
Total win prize-money £2443

Going (Turf): Sf: 0-2 GS: 0-2 Gd: 0-1 GF: 0-4 **Fm: 1-4**
Distance: **5f/6f: 1-8** 7f-8f: 0-6 9f-13f: 0-1 14f+: 0-0
Track : LH: 0-4 RH: 0-1 Tight: 0-3 Gall: 0-0
Aids: Bl: 0-0 Vi: 0-0 **Tstrap: 1-10**
Best Rating: 63 9/01 Gdwd 5f good

An improving sprinter in the late summer of 2001, suited by fast ground and six furlongs. Wears a tongue tie and is usually held up for a late run.

Princes Theatre

100 **78d**
3-y-o b c Prince Sabo-Frisson (Slip Anchor)
I A Balding T J W Burton

Placings:44-3020200 **(5171)**
2001: 8^{3}GF, 8^{0}GF, 8^{2}GF, 10^{0}G, 8^{2}GF, 10^{0}GF, 8^{0}GS

	Starts	1st	2nd	3rd	Win & Pl
Career Total (Turf)	9	0	2	1	3564

Going (Turf): Sf: 0-0 GS: 0-1 Gd: 0-1 GF: 0-7 Fm: 0-0
Distance: 5f/6f: 0-0 7f-8f: 0-4 9f-13f: 0-5 14f+: 0-0
Track : LH: 0-3 RH: 0-2 Tight: 0-0 Gall: 0-2
Aids: Bl: 0-0 Vi: 0-0 Tstrap: 0-1
Best Rating: 78 8/01 Bevl 1m100y gd-fm

He has shown ability in varied company. Suited by a mile and fast ground and should still have some improvement in him.

Princess Almora

107 **85**
3-y-o b f Pivotal-Drama School (Young Generation)
I A Wood Exors Of The Late B P Macey

Placings:10522120015 **(5266)**
2001: 6^{1}G, 6^{0}GF, 6^{5}GF, 6^{2}GF, 7^{2}GF, 6^{1}GF, 7^{2}G, 6^{0}GF, 6^{0}G, 6^{1}GF, 6^{5}GS

	Starts	1st	2nd	3rd	Win & Pl
Career Total (Turf)	11	3	3	0	21025

85 9/01 Kemp 6f C(0-90)H G-F £7865
81 7/01 Wind 6f D(0-80)H G-F £4108
68 6/01 Wind 6f D GD £4361
Total win prize-money £16335

Going (Turf): Sf: 0-0 GS: 0-1 Gd: 1-3 **GF: 2-7** Fm: 0-0
Distance: **5f/6f: 3-8** 7f-8f: 0-3 9f-13f: 0-0 14f+: 0-0
Track : LH: 0-1 RH: 0-1 Tight: 0-0 Gall: 0-0
Aids: Bl: 0-0 Vi: 0-0 Tstrap: 0-0
Best Rating: 85 9/01 Kemp 6f gd-fm

Unraced at two, she made a winning debut at Windsor in June and ran well before scoring over the same course and distance in July. She showed she still had improvement in her when winning a decent handicap at Kempton in September. Handles fast ground and is best over six furlongs.

Princess Chloe

106 **74**
3-y-o br f Primo Dominie-Louise Moillon (Mansingh (USA))
M A Jarvis Mrs Christine Stevenson

Placings:01-004100 **(5181)**
2001: 6^{0}G, 6^{0}GF, 6^{4}GS, 6^{1}G, 6^{0}G, 6^{0}HY

	Starts	1st	2nd	3rd	Win & Pl
Career Total (Turf)	8	2	0	0	6750

74 8/01 Pont 6f E(0-70) GD £3526
69 10/00 Wind 6f D G-S £2908
Total win prize-money £6435

Going (Turf): Sf: 0-1 **GS: 1-2 Gd: 1-4** GF: 0-1 Fm: 0-0
Distance: **5f/6f: 2-8** 7f-8f: 0-0 9f-13f: 0-0 14f+: 0-0
Track : LH: 1-1 RH: 1-1 Tight: 0-0 **Gall: 1-1**
Aids: **Bl: 1-4** Vi: 0-0 Tstrap: 0-0
Best Rating: 74 8/01 Pont 6f good

She landed a Windsor maiden last season and returned to winning form in a classified event at Pontefract in August. Goes well in blinkers and needs cut in the ground.

Princess Claudia (IRE)

97 **51**
3-y-o b f Kahyasi-Shamarra (FR) (Zayyani)
Mrs H Dalton (T D Easterby 28/7) Peter E Clinton

Placings:0340-3354500 **(4858)**
2001: 12^{3}S, 14^{3}G, 16^{5}F, 16^{4}GF, 11^{5}F, 16^{0}GF, 15^{0}GF

	Starts	1st	2nd	3rd	Win & Pl
Career Total (Turf)	11	0	0	3	1816

Going (Turf): Sf: 0-1 GS: 0-1 Gd: 0-3 GF: 0-4 Fm: 0-2
Distance: 5f/6f: 0-0 7f-8f: 0-3 9f-13f: 0-3 14f+: 0-5
Track : LH: 0-7 RH: 0-3 Tight: 0-4 Gall: 0-2
Aids: Bl: 0-1 Vi: 0-0 Tstrap: 0-0
Best Rating: 54 7/01 Bevl 2m35y gd-fm

Princess Electra (IRE)

98 **63**
2-y-o b f Lake Coniston (IRE)-Elect (USA) (Vaguely Noble)
K A Ryan Mrs Angie Bailey

Placings:603165005260 **(5690)**
2001: 5^{6}GF, 5^{0}GF, 5^{3}G, 5^{1}GF, 5^{6}G, 6^{5}G, 6^{0}GF, 6^{0}GF, 6^{5}G, 7^{2}GS, 7^{6}HY, 7^{0}S

	Starts	1st	2nd	3rd	Win & Pl
Career Total (Turf)	12	1	1	1	6540

77 7/01 Donc 5f140y D G-F £4290
Total win prize-money £4290

Going (Turf): Sf: 0-2 GS: 0-1 Gd: 0-4 **GF: 1-5** Fm: 0-0
Distance: **5f/6f: 1-8** 7f-8f: 0-4 9f-13f: 0-0 14f+: 0-0
Track : LH: 0-2 RH: 0-0 Tight: 0-2 Gall: 0-0
Aids: Bl: 0-0 Vi: 0-0 Tstrap: 0-0
Best Rating: 77 7/01 Donc 5f140y gd-fm

She improved in each of her first four starts and got off the mark with a narrow victory at Doncaster in July, but mixed form afterwards.

Princess Emerald

76 **11**
3-y-o b f Mtoto-Diamond Princess (Horage)
D W P Arbuthnot Stephen Crown

Placings:00-000 **(3289)**
2001: 10^{0}GF, 12^{0}GF, 16^{0}GF

	Starts	1st	2nd	3rd	Win & Pl
Career Total (Turf)	5	0	0	0	

Going (Turf): Sf: 0-1 GS: 0-1 Gd: 0-0 GF: 0-3 Fm: 0-0

Distance: 5f/6f: 0-0 7f-8f: 0-2 9f-13f: 0-2 14f+: 0-1
Track : LH: 0-3 RH: 0-1 Tight: 0-2 Gall: 0-1
Aids: Bl: 0-0 Vi: 0-0 Tstrap: 0-0
Best Rating: 11 5/01 Newb 1m2f6y gd-fm

Princess Emily (IRE)

97 **45**

3-y-o b f Dolphin Street (FR)-Partita (Polish Precedent (USA))
B S Rothwell Ms Denise S Doyle

Placings:03150-002005040 **(4450)**
2001: 10^0S, 9^0GF, 8^2GF, 9^0GF, 8^0GF, 7^5GF, 8^0F, 7^4GF, 8^0GF

	Starts	1st	2nd	3rd	Win & Pl
Career Total (Turf)	14	1	1	1	7954

60 8/00 York 7f202y E GD £6698
Total win prize-money £6698

Going (Turf): Sf: 0-2 GS: 0-1 **Gd: 1-1** GF: 0-9 Fm: 0-1
Distance: 5f/6f: 0-0 **7f-8f: 1-9** 9f-13f: 0-5 14f+: 0-0
Track : **LH: 1-7** RH: 0-5 Tight: 0-3 **Gall: 1-3**
Aids: Bl: 0-0 Vi: 0-1 Tstrap: 0-0
Best Rating: 52 5/01 Ripn 1m gd-fm

Has shown her best form at around seven furlongs on decent ground.

Princess Grace

81 **54**

2-y-o b f Inchinor-Hardiprincess (Keen)
M L W Bell Mrs Anne Yearley

Placings:000 **(5526)**
2001: 6^0HY, 6^0G, 5^0S

	Starts	1st	2nd	3rd	Win & Pl
Career Total (Turf)	3	0	0	0	

Going (Turf): Sf: 0-2 GS: 0-0 Gd: 0-1 GF: 0-0 Fm: 0-0
Distance: 5f/6f: 0-3 7f-8f: 0-0 9f-13f: 0-0 14f+: 0-0
Track : LH: 0-0 RH: 0-0 Tight: 0-0 Gall: 0-0
Aids: Bl: 0-0 Vi: 0-0 Tstrap: 0-0
Best Rating: 54 10/01 Rdcr 6f good

Princess Lilli

82 **52**

2-y-o b f Vettori (IRE)-Move Darling (Rock City)
P S McEntee Miss Debbie Mountain

Placings:000 **(5684)**
2001: 7^0S, 7^0S, 8^0S

	Starts	1st	2nd	3rd	Win & Pl
Career Total (Turf)	3	0	0	0	

Going (Turf): Sf: 0-3 GS: 0-0 Gd: 0-0 GF: 0-0 Fm: 0-0
Distance: 5f/6f: 0-0 7f-8f: 0-3 9f-13f: 0-0 14f+: 0-0
Track : LH: 0-2 RH: 0-0 Tight: 0-0 Gall: 0-1
Aids: Bl: 0-0 Vi: 0-0 Tstrap: 0-0
Best Rating: 52 10/01 Brig 7f214y soft

Princess Miletrian (IRE)

100 **83**

2-y-o b f Danehill (USA)-Place Of Honour (Be My Guest (USA))
M R Channon Miletrian Plc

Placings:30 **(4022)**
2001: 6^3GF, 6^0GF

	Starts	1st	2nd	3rd	Win & Pl
Career Total (Turf)	2	0	0	1	1105

Going (Turf): Sf: 0-0 GS: 0-0 Gd: 0-0 GF: 0-2 Fm: 0-0
Distance: 5f/6f: 0-1 7f-8f: 0-1 9f-13f: 0-0 14f+: 0-0
Track : LH: 0-0 RH: 0-0 Tight: 0-0 Gall: 0-0
Aids: Bl: 0-0 Vi: 0-0 Tstrap: 0-0
Best Rating: 83 8/01 Gdwd 6f gd-fm

Princess Of Garda

101 **60**

3-y-o b f Komaite (USA)-Malcesine (IRE) (Auction Ring (USA))
Mrs G S Rees North West Racing Club - Owners Group

Placings:U43121454002-30606006005 **(5252)**
2001: 6^3S, 6^0GF, 5^6GF, 6^0GS, 5^6G, 5^0GF, 5^0G, 5^6G, 5^0HY, 5^0S, 5^5S

	Starts	1st	2nd	3rd	Win & Pl
Career Total (Turf)	23	2	2	2	11476

83 6/00 Ches 5f16y D G-F £3542
71 5/00 Hayd 5f E G-S £3024
Total win prize-money £6567

Going (Turf): Sf: 0-8 **GS: 1-5** Gd: 0-5 **GF: 1-4** Fm: 0-1
Distance: **5f/6f: 2-23** 7f-8f: 0-0 9f-13f: 0-0 14f+: 0-0
Track : **LH: 1-5** RH: 0-0 **Tight: 1-5** Gall: 0-0
Aids: Bl: 0-1 Vi: 0-1 Tstrap: 0-0
Best Rating: 82 5/01 Hayd 6f soft

Dual five-furlong juvenile scorer who stays six furlongs. Appreciates soft ground but acts on faster. Did not shown much this term and is steadily dropping in the handicap as a result.

Princess Of Persia (IRE)

83 **64**

2-y-o ch f Persian Bold-Kazimiera (IRE) (Polish Patriot (USA))
M R Channon Michael Hills

Placings:00 **(4608)**
2001: 7^0G, 5^0F

	Starts	1st	2nd	3rd	Win & Pl
Career Total (Turf)	2	0	0	0	

Going (Turf): Sf: 0-0 GS: 0-0 Gd: 0-1 GF: 0-0 Fm: 0-1
Distance: 5f/6f: 0-1 7f-8f: 0-1 9f-13f: 0-0 14f+: 0-0
Track : LH: 0-1 RH: 0-1 Tight: 0-0 Gall: 0-1
Aids: Bl: 0-0 Vi: 0-0 Tstrap: 0-0
Best Rating: 64 9/01 Bath 5f11y firm

Princess Petardia (IRE)

95 **76**

2-y-o b/br f Petardia-Coolrain Lady (IRE) (Common Grounds)
R Hannon Major A M Everett

Placings:3450210 **(4678)**
2001: 5^3G, 5^4G, 6^5GF, 5^0GF, 5^2GF, 6^1F, 8^0G

	Starts	1st	2nd	3rd	Win & Pl
Career Total (Turf)	7	1	1	1	6169

76 8/01 Brig 6f209y E FRM £2863
Total win prize-money £2863

Going (Turf): Sf: 0-0 GS: 0-0 Gd: 0-3 GF: 0-3 **Fm: 1-1**
Distance: 5f/6f: 0-5 **7f-8f: 1-2** 9f-13f: 0-0 14f+: 0-0
Track : **LH: 1-1** RH: 0-2 Tight: 0-0 Gall: 0-2
Aids: Bl: 0-0 Vi: 0-0 Tstrap: 0-0
Best Rating: 76 8/01 Brig 6f209y firm

Some ability in maiden company, but was out of her depth when tried in a Listed event and in the Weatherbys Super Sprint. A drop in class and a step up to seven furlongs worked the oracle in a median auction maiden at Brighton in August and that looks about as good as she is.

Princess Ria (IRE)

96(94) (44)**26**

4-y-o b f Petong-Walking Saint (Godswalk (USA))
M E Sowersby (N P Littmoden 6/7) Racing Ladies

Placings:13500/000000-036050 **(2808)**
2001: 12^0SD, 11^3SD, 9^6SD, 9^0S, 9^5G, 8^0GF

	Starts	1st	2nd	3rd	Win & Pl
Career Total (Turf)	11	1	0	1	4251
Career Total (AW)	6	0	0	1	196

61 7/99 Hayd 6f D G-S £3733
Total win prize-money £3734

Going (Turf): Sf: 0-4 **GS: 1-2** Gd: 0-2 GF: 0-3 Fm: 0-0
Distance: **5f/6f: 1-3** 7f-8f: 0-5 9f-13f: 0-8 14f+: 0-1
Track : LH: 0-9 RH: 0-1 Tight: 0-6 Gall: 0-0
Aids: Bl: 0-0 Vi: 0-0 Tstrap: 0-0
Best Rating: 44 2/01 Sthl 1m3f stand

Princess Royale (IRE)

89 **69**

2-y-o b f Royal Applause-On The Bank (IRE) (In The Wings)
G A Butler J Jones

Placings:663 **(4294)**
2001: 6^6G, 5^6GF, 7^3G

	Starts	1st	2nd	3rd	Win & Pl
Career Total (Turf)	3	0	0	1	642

Going (Turf): Sf: 0-0 GS: 0-0 Gd: 0-2 GF: 0-1 Fm: 0-0
Distance: 5f/6f: 0-2 7f-8f: 0-1 9f-13f: 0-0 14f+: 0-0
Track : LH: 0-1 RH: 0-0 Tight: 0-1 Gall: 0-0
Aids: Bl: 0-0 Vi: 0-0 Tstrap: 0-0
Best Rating: 69 7/01 Kemp 6f good

Princess Slane

4-y-o ch f Prince Daniel (USA)-Singing Slane (Cree Song)
C Grant J H Richardson

Placings:0 **(4085)**
2001: 8^0GF

	Starts	1st	2nd	3rd	Win & Pl
Career Total (Turf)	1	0	0	0	

Going (Turf): Sf: 0-0 GS: 0-0 Gd: 0-0 GF: 0-1 Fm: 0-0
Distance: 5f/6f: 0-0 7f-8f: 0-0 9f-13f: 0-1 14f+: 0-0
Track : LH: 0-1 RH: 0-0 Tight: 0-0 Gall: 0-0
Aids: Bl: 0-0 Vi: 0-0 Tstrap: 0-0

Princess Sofie

104 **86**

2-y-o b f Efisio-Dust (Green Desert (USA))
T D Easterby D H Brown

Placings:221120400 **(4316)**
2001: 5^2G, 5^2GF, 5^1GF, 5^1G, 5^2GF, 6^0GS, 5^4GF, 5^0GF, 6^0G

	Starts	1st	2nd	3rd	Win & Pl
Career Total (Turf)	9	2	3	0	20246

77 6/01 Wind 5f10y C GD £5423
77 6/01 Pont 5f F G-F £3575
Total win prize-money £8998

Going (Turf): Sf: 0-0 GS: 0-1 **Gd: 1-3 GF: 1-5** Fm: 0-0
Distance: **5f/6f: 2-9** 7f-8f: 0-0 9f-13f: 0-0 14f+: 0-0
Track : LH: 1-1 RH: 1-1 Tight: 0-0 **Gall: 1-1**
Aids: Bl: 0-1 Vi: 0-0 Tstrap: 0-0
Best Rating: 86 6/01 Donc 5f gd-fm

A February foal, she is not very big. A laid back sort, she managed to scramble home on fast ground at Pontefract before following up in a conditions event at Windsor. Out of her depth in Pattern company afterwards. Best on fast ground.

Princess Titania (IRE)

107 **95?**

3-y-o b f Fairy King (USA)-Chiquelina (FR) (Le Glorieux)
N A Callaghan Norcroft Park Stud

Placings:4023-024251104 **(4987)**
2001: 7^0S, 9^2F, 9^4GF, 10^2GF, 12^5GF, 10^1GS, 10^1HY, 12^0G, 10^4G

	Starts	1st	2nd	3rd	Win & Pl
Career Total (Turf)	13	2	3	1	18562

89 9/01 Hayd 1m2f120yB(0-100)H HVY £9368
80 7/01 NmkJ 1m2f D(0-80) G-S £4056
Total win prize-money £13424

Going (Turf): Sf: 1-3 GS: 1-1 Gd: 0-3 GF: 0-4 Fm: 0-2
Distance: 5f/6f: 0-0 7f-8f: 0-4 **9f-13f: 2-9** 14f+: 0-0
Track : **LH: 1-4** RH: 0-3 Tight: 0-3 Gall: 0-2
Aids: Bl: 0-0 Vi: 0-0 Tstrap: 0-0
Best Rating: 95 9/01 Asct 1m2f good

Took time to get off the mark, but finally did so at the tenth attempt when allowed her own way out in front in a Newmarket classified event in July. Followed up in a Haydock handicap and ran well at Ascot. Stays ten furlongs, acts on fast ground but goes particularly well on soft.

Princetown

67 **38**

2-y-o b g Cotation-The Prussian Queen (Dilum (USA))
C Smith A E Needham

Placings:00 **(5227)**
2001: 6^{0}G, 6^{0}S

	Starts	1st	2nd	3rd	Win & Pl
Career Total (Turf)	2	0	0	0	

Going (Turf): Sf: 0-1 GS: 0-0 Gd: 0-1 GF: 0-0 Fm: 0-0
Distance: 5f/6f: 0-1 7f-8f: 0-1 9f-13f: 0-0 14f+: 0-0
Track : LH: 0-1 RH: 0-0 Tight: 0-0 Gall: 0-1
Aids: Bl: 0-0 Vi: 0-0 Tstrap: 0-0
Best Rating: 38 9/01 Donc 6f good

Principal Boy (IRE)

96(98) (27)**40**

8-y-o br g Cyrano De Bergerac-Shenley Lass (Prince Tenderfoot (USA))
G M Moore Mrs S E Cooper

Placings:54050060/**2152053104040**4/**000**12213506066/**125040000/660304**33550050002050604653**04/60040**-503400 **(0592)**
2001: 8^{5}SD, 8^{0}SD, 11^{3}SD, 7^{4}SD, 7^{0}SD, 9^{0}S

	Starts	1st	2nd	3rd	Win & Pl
Career Total (Turf)	39	2	3	3	12673
Career Total (AW)	45	3	3	4	10477
40	1/98	Sthl	1m	F(0-60)H	STD £1745
47	6/97	Haml	1m1f36y	E(0-70)H	G-S £3485
45	5/97	Haml	1m65y	E(0-70)H	G-S £3468
52	5/96	Sthl	7f	E(0-70)H	STD £3343
45	2/96	Sthl	7f	F(0-60)H	STD £2278

Total win prize-money £14320

Going (Turf): Sf: 0-8 **GS: 2-6** Gd: 0-10 GF: 0-14 Fm: 0-1
Distance: 5f/6f: 0-22 **7f-8f: 3-42** 9f-13f: 2-20 14f+: 0-0
Track : **LH: 3-55** RH: 2-15 **Tight: 2-20** Gall: 0-3
Aids: Bl: 0-2 Vi: 0-1 Tstrap: 0-0
Best Rating: 31 3/01 Muss 1m1f soft

Pringipessa's Way

97 **78**

3-y-o b f Machiavellian (USA)-Miss Fancy That (USA) (The Minstrel (CAN))
P R Chamings Mrs Alexandra J Chandris

Placings:624 **(4784)**
2001: 9^{6}GF, 8^{2}G, 9^{4}G

	Starts	1st	2nd	3rd	Win & Pl
Career Total (Turf)	3	0	1	0	1552

Going (Turf): Sf: 0-0 GS: 0-0 Gd: 0-2 GF: 0-1 Fm: 0-0
Distance: 5f/6f: 0-0 7f-8f: 0-0 9f-13f: 0-3 14f+: 0-0
Track : LH: 0-0 RH: 0-3 Tight: 0-2 Gall: 0-0
Aids: Bl: 0-0 Vi: 0-0 Tstrap: 0-0
Best Rating: 78 9/01 Sand 1m14y good

Prinisha

(91) (47)**49**

4-y-o gr f Prince Sabo-Nisha (Nishapour (FR))
Mrs L Richards Wilwyn Racing (wwwwilwyncom)

Placings:02022000**0400-00** **(2342)**
2001: 8^{0}G, 7^{0}SD

	Starts	1st	2nd	3rd	Win & Pl
Career Total (Turf)	10	0	3	0	2613
Career Total (AW)	4	0	0	0	0

Going (Turf): Sf: 0-1 GS: 0-3 Gd: 0-1 GF: 0-5 Fm: 0-0
Distance: 5f/6f: 0-0 7f-8f: 0-8 9f-13f: 0-6 14f+: 0-0
Track : LH: 0-7 RH: 0-0 Tight: 0-6 Gall: 0-0
Aids: Bl: 0-0 Vi: 0-0 Tstrap: 0-0
Best Rating: 6 5/01 Wwck 1m22y good

Prins Willem (IRE)

85 **74**

2-y-o b c Alzao (USA)-American Gardens (USA) (Alleged (USA))
J R Fanshawe Chris Van Hoorn

Placings:040 **(5126)**
2001: 5^{0}G, 6^{4}G, 6^{0}HY

	Starts	1st	2nd	3rd	Win & Pl
Career Total (Turf)	3	0	0	0	284

Going (Turf): Sf: 0-1 GS: 0-0 Gd: 0-2 GF: 0-0 Fm: 0-0
Distance: 5f/6f: 0-2 7f-8f: 0-1 9f-13f: 0-0 14f+: 0-0
Track : LH: 0-0 RH: 0-0 Tight: 0-0 Gall: 0-0
Aids: Bl: 0-0 Vi: 0-0 Tstrap: 0-1
Best Rating: 74 8/01 Nott 6f15y good

Printsmith (IRE)

100(81) (32)**56**

4-y-o br f Petardia-Black And Blaze (Taufan (USA))
J R Norton Ecosse Racing

Placings:6010300/010603**0**01-00600 **(3864)**
2001: 7^{0}GF, 7^{0}F, 5^{6}G, 7^{0}GF, 7^{0}GF

	Starts	1st	2nd	3rd	Win & Pl
Career Total (Turf)	20	3	0	2	9266
Career Total (AW)	1	0	0	0	
56	10/00	Donc	7f	E(0-70)H	GD £3211
56	6/00	Wwck	6f168y	E(0-75)H	G-S £3198
61	7/99	Catt	5f	G	GD £2010

Total win prize-money £8419

Going (Turf): Sf: 0-1 GS: 1-1 **Gd: 2-7** GF: 0-9 Fm: 0-2
Distance: 5f/6f: 1-11 **7f-8f: 2-10** 9f-13f: 0-0 14f+: 0-0
Track : **LH: 1-5** RH: 0-1 Tight: 0-1 Gall: 0-1
Aids: Bl: 0-0 Vi: 0-0 Tstrap: 0-0
Best Rating: 50 6/01 Leic 5f218y good

Priors Lodge (IRE)

107 **110**

3-y-o br c Grand Lodge (USA)-Addaya (IRE) (Persian Bold)
R Hannon Lady Tennant

Placings:10-351102 **(5103)**
2001: 8^{3}GF, 7^{5}GF, 7^{1}G, 6^{1}G, 7^{0}GF, 8^{2}GS

	Starts	1st	2nd	3rd	Win & Pl
Career Total (Turf)	8	3	1	1	43952
105	8/01	York	6f214y	A	GD £23302
98	8/01	Gdwd	7f	B(0-95)	GD £8798
84	6/00	Sals	6f212y	D	G-F £3640

Total win prize-money £35742

Going (Turf): Sf: 0-1 GS: 0-1 **Gd: 2-2** GF: 1-4 Fm: 0-0
Distance: 5f/6f: 0-0 **7f-8f: 3-8** 9f-13f: 0-0 14f+: 0-0
Track : LH: 1-3 RH: 1-1 Tight: 0-0 **Gall: 1-3**
Aids: Bl: 0-0 Vi: 0-0 Tstrap: 0-0
Best Rating: 110 10/01 NmkR 1m gd-sft

He faced some stiff tasks after winning on his debut at Salisbury as a two-year-old, but also had a back problem. He made up for lost time by winning a valuable classified event at Glorious Goodwood and followed up in a York Listed race. Handled the step up to a mile when second in a Newmarket Listed race in the autumn.

Prisa (USA)

83(50) **51**

2-y-o b f Danehill (USA)-Cantonese (USA) (Easy Goer (USA))
J Noseda Sanford R Robertson

Placings:030 **(2321)**
2001: 5^{0}GS, 6^{3}GF, 6^{0}SD

	Starts	1st	2nd	3rd	Win & Pl
Career Total (Turf)	2	0	0	1	524
Career Total (AW)	1	0	0	0	

Going (Turf): Sf: 0-0 GS: 0-1 Gd: 0-0 GF: 0-1 Fm: 0-0
Distance: 5f/6f: 0-3 7f-8f: 0-0 9f-13f: 0-0 14f+: 0-0
Track : LH: 0-2 RH: 0-0 Tight: 0-1 Gall: 0-0
Aids: Bl: 0-0 Vi: 0-0 Tstrap: 0-0
Best Rating: 51 5/01 Sthl 6f gd-fm

Prism

104 **107**

2-y-o b g Spectrum (IRE)-Seal Indigo (IRE) (Glenstal (USA))
M P Tregoning M Calvert And Colin E Lewis

Placings:1241011 **(5264)**
2001: 5^{1}G, 6^{2}GF, 7^{4}GF, 6^{1}G, 6^{0}G, 6^{1}GS, 6^{1}GS

	Starts	1st	2nd	3rd	Win & Pl
Career Total (Turf)	7	4	1	0	39566
107	10/01	York	6f	A	G-S £12760
89	10/01	Sals	6f	C	G-S £6470
89	8/01	York	6f	C	GD £12324
69	6/01	Leic	5f218y	E	GD £3835

Total win prize-money £35390

Going (Turf): Sf: 0-0 **GS: 2-2 Gd: 2-3** GF: 0-2 Fm: 0-0
Distance: **5f/6f: 4-6** 7f-8f: 0-1 9f-13f: 0-0 14f+: 0-0
Track : LH: 0-0 RH: 0-0 Tight: 0-0 Gall: 0-0
Aids: Bl: 0-0 Vi: 0-0 Tstrap: 0-0
Best Rating: 107 10/01 York 6f gd-sft

Awarded the race on his Leicester debut and, gelded after running poorly at Ascot, bounced back to win a nursery at York. Picked up two races on easy ground, including a Listed race in the autumn. Suited by six furlongs and good ground, but handles softer. He has plenty of size and scope.

Private Kelly (IRE)

98 **65**

2-y-o b g General Monash (USA)-Flying Tribute (USA) (Fighting Fit (USA))
J R Best (K T Ivory 13/6) C Parker

Placings:0010500 **(3585)**
2001: 5^{0}G, 5^{0}F, 5^{1}F, 5^{0}GF, 5^{5}GF, 5^{0}GF, 5^{0}G

	Starts	1st	2nd	3rd	Win & Pl
Career Total (Turf)	7	1	0	0	1929
57	6/01	Ling	5f	G	FRM £1928

Total win prize-money £1929

Going (Turf): Sf: 0-0 GS: 0-0 Gd: 0-2 GF: 0-3 **Fm: 1-2**
Distance: **5f/6f: 1-7** 7f-8f: 0-0 9f-13f: 0-0 14f+: 0-0
Track : LH: 0-0 RH: 0-1 Tight: 0-0 Gall: 0-1
Aids: **Bl: 1-3** Vi: 0-0 Tstrap: 0-0
Best Rating: 65 7/01 Kemp 5f gd-fm

Winner of a seller at Lingfield over the minimum trip in June 2001. (DEAD)

Private Seal

98(98) (42)**22**

6-y-o b g King's Signet (USA)-Slender (Aragon)
Julian Poulton Russell Reed

Placings:3620516**332**/00550**4**/**430065000000**/**5660**040 05342-1000002245000 **(4462)**
2001: 8^{1}SD, 9^{0}SD, 9^{0}GF, 8^{0}SD, 8^{0}GF, 7^{0}GF, 11^{2}F, 10^{2}GF, 11^{4}GF, 11^{5}GF, 10^{0}F, 10^{0}GF, 9^{0}GS

	Starts	1st	2nd	3rd	Win & Pl
Career Total (Turf)	31	1	3	1	4325
Career Total (AW)	22	1	2	4	3759
42	1/01	Ling	1m	G	STD £1351
69	10/97	Brig	5f59y	G	FRM £1984

Total win prize-money £3336

Going (Turf): Sf: 0-2 GS: 0-1 Gd: 0-3 GF: 0-15 **Fm: 1-10**
Distance: 5f/6f: 1-11 7f-8f: 1-24 9f-13f: 0-18 14f+: 0-0
Track : **LH: 2-41** RH: 0-1 **Tight: 1-30** Gall: 0-0
Aids: Bl: 0-9 Vi: 0-0 **Tstrap: 1-36**
Best Rating: 42 7/01 Wind 1m3f135y gd-fm

Privilege (USA)

91 **69**

2-y-o b c Foxhound (USA)-Pretty Miswaki (USA) (Miswaki (USA))
J H M Gosden Sheikh Mohammed

Placings:04 **(4783)**
2001: 6^{0}GF, 8^{4}G

	Starts	1st	2nd	3rd	Win & Pl
Career Total (Turf)	2	0	0	0	343

Going (Turf): Sf: 0-0 GS: 0-0 Gd: 0-1 GF: 0-1 Fm: 0-0
Distance: 5f/6f: 0-0 7f-8f: 0-2 9f-13f: 0-0 14f+: 0-0
Track : LH: 0-0 RH: 0-1 Tight: 0-0 Gall: 0-0
Aids: Bl: 0-0 Vi: 0-1 Tstrap: 0-0
Best Rating: 69 9/01 Gdwd 1m good

Prix Star

107(92) (53)**74**

6-y-o ch g Superpower-Celestine (Skyliner)
C W Fairhurst M J Grace

Placings:2242146/330000/**000**0001020006024**55**/03204 00052230-20304051206114050 **(5638)**
2001: 6^{2}HY, 5^{0}SD, 6^{3}G, 6^{0}GF, 6^{4}GF, 6^{0}GF, 6^{5}GF, 6^{1}G, 6^{2}GF, 6^{0}G, 6^{6}GF, 6^{1}GF, 6^{1}G, 6^{4}G, 6^{0}GF, 6^{5}HY, 7^{0}G

	Starts	1st	2nd	3rd	Win & Pl
Career Total (Turf)	54	5	10	5	38868
Career Total (AW)	6	0	0	0	176

74	8/01	NmkJ	6f	D(0-85)H	GD	£4309
65	7/01	Newc	6f	D(0-85)H	G-F	£4260
62	6/01	Haml	6f5y	E(0-75)H	GD	£4329
61	6/99	Catt	5f212y	E(0-70)H	GD	£4156
76	7/97	Haml	5f4y	E	G-S	£3225

Total win prize-money £20281

Going (Turf): Sf: 0-9 GS: 1-7 **Gd: 3-13** GF: 1-19 Fm: 0-5
Distance: 5f/6f: 4-40 7f-8f: 1-19 9f-13f: 0-0 14f+: 0-0
Track : LH: 1-17 RH: 0-8 **Tight: 1-12** Gall: 0-6
Aids: Bl: 0-0 **Vi: 4-34** Tstrap: 0-0
Best Rating: 74 8/01 NmkJ 6f good

He had a good season in 2001, winning at Hamilton, Newcastle and Newmarket, but looks high in the handicap as a result. Suited by six furlongs and acts on good and fast ground.

Priya

105 **75**

3-y-o b f Primo Dominie-Promissory (Caerleon (USA))
C E Brittain B H Voak

Placings:462240-563000 **(5108)**
2001: 7^{5}GS, 7^{6}G, 7^{3}GF, 6^{0}GF, 6^{0}S, 5^{0}GS

	Starts	1st	2nd	3rd	Win & Pl
Career Total (Turf)	12	0	2	1	4900

Going (Turf): Sf: 0-1 GS: 0-4 Gd: 0-3 GF: 0-4 Fm: 0-0
Distance: 5f/6f: 0-7 7f-8f: 0-5 9f-13f: 0-0 14f+: 0-0
Track : LH: 0-1 RH: 0-2 Tight: 0-1 Gall: 0-1
Aids: Bl: 0-0 Vi: 0-0 Tstrap: 0-0
Best Rating: 89 4/01 Newb 7f gd-sft

Prize Dancer (FR)

107 **78**

3-y-o ch g Suave Dancer (USA)-Spot Prize (USA) (Seattle Dancer (USA))
D R C Elsworth J C Smith

Placings:0406-30616035 **(5039)**
2001: 10^{3}GF, 12^{0}GF, 9^{6}GF, 14^{1}GF, 14^{6}GF, 13^{0}G, 14^{3}G, 17^{5}G

	Starts	1st	2nd	3rd	Win & Pl
Career Total (Turf)	12	1	0	2	5780

73	7/01	Sals	1m6f15y	D	G-F	£3640

Total win prize-money £3640

Going (Turf): Sf: 0-1 GS: 0-1 Gd: 0-5 **GF: 1-5** Fm: 0-0
Distance: 5f/6f: 0-0 7f-8f: 0-4 9f-13f: 0-3 **14f+: 1-5**
Track : LH: 0-3 **RH: 1-6 Tight: 1-3** Gall: 0-2
Aids: Bl: 0-0 Vi: 0-0 Tstrap: 0-0
Best Rating: 78 7/01 Sand 1m6f gd-fm

A half-brother to the useful Premier Prize. Winner of a 14-furlong maiden at Salisbury, but limitations exposed in handicaps since. Suited by fast ground and waiting tactics.

Prize Winner

108 **106**

3-y-o b c Mtoto-Rose Show (Belmez (USA))
J Noseda Sir Gordon Brunton

Placings:13200030 **(4170)**
2001: 10^{1}S, 10^{3}S, 12^{2}G, 11^{0}G, 12^{0}G, 10^{0}G, 10^{3}GF, 10^{0}G

	Starts	1st	2nd	3rd	Win & Pl
Career Total (Turf)	8	1	1	2	10404

93	3/01	Donc	1m2f60y	D	SFT	£4231

Total win prize-money £4232

Going (Turf): Sf: 1-2 GS: 0-0 Gd: 0-5 GF: 0-1 Fm: 0-0
Distance: 5f/6f: 0-0 7f-8f: 0-0 **9f-13f: 1-8** 14f+: 0-0
Track : LH: 1-4 RH: 0-4 Tight: 0-1 **Gall: 1-7**
Aids: Bl: 0-0 Vi: 0-0 Tstrap: 0-0
Best Rating: 106 7/01 Asct 1m2f gd-fm

Unraced at two, he beat Mr Combustible in a maiden on his debut and ran with credit in better company afterwards. He stays a mile and a half and though he has won on soft ground, does act on a sound surface.

Prizeman (USA)

107 (90)**106**

3-y-o b c Prized (USA)-Shuttle (USA) (Conquistador Cielo (USA))
R Hannon Highclere Thoroughbred Racing Ltd

Placings:1142-05600 **(2943)**
2001: 9^{0}FT, 12^{5}GF, 11^{6}GF, 16^{0}GF, 14^{0}G

	Starts	1st	2nd	3rd	Win & Pl
Career Total (Turf)	8	2	1	0	34501
Career Total (AW)	1	0	0	0	0

102	8/00	Newb	7f	A	G-F	£12343
93	7/00	York	6f	E	GD	£7507

Total win prize-money £19852

Going (Turf): Sf: 0-2 GS: 0-0 **Gd: 1-2 GF: 1-4** Fm: 0-0
Distance: 5f/6f: 1-1 7f-8f: 1-3 9f-13f: 0-3 14f+: 0-2
Track : LH: 0-1 RH: 0-3 Tight: 0-1 Gall: 0-3
Aids: Bl: 0-0 Vi: 0-0 Tstrap: 0-0
Best Rating: 106 5/01 Gdwd 1m3f gd-fm

He made steady progress as a juvenile, beating Perfect Sunday in a Newbury Listed event and finishing placed in two Group races. Ran respectably in the UAE Derby on his return, but failed to fire on his return to Britain.

Procedure (USA)

99 **83**

5-y-o b/br g Strolling Along (USA)-Bold Courtesan (USA) (Bold Bidder)
J A B Old W E Sturt

Placings:63/6116/3000 **(5261)**
2001: 10^{3}GS, 12^{0}GS, 12^{0}S, 10^{0}GS

	Starts	1st	2nd	3rd	Win & Pl
Career Total (Turf)	10	2	0	2	16435

95	6/99	Sals	1m4f	C(0-95)H	G-F	£6937
84	5/99	Leic	1m1f218y	D(0-80)H	G-F	£7571

Total win prize-money £14509

Going (Turf): Sf: 0-3 GS: 0-3 Gd: 0-1 **GF: 2-2** Fm: 0-1
Distance: 5f/6f: 0-0 7f-8f: 0-2 **9f-13f: 2-7** 14f+: 0-1
Track : LH: 0-4 **RH: 2-4 Tight: 1-1** Gall: 0-4
Aids: Bl: 0-0 Vi: 0-0 Tstrap: 0-0
Best Rating: 83 4/01 Newb 1m2f6y gd-sft

Proceed With Care

111 **101**

3-y-o b g Danehill (USA)-Ultra Finesse (USA) (Rahy (USA))
M Johnston Maktoum Al Maktoum

Placings:51205-102060 **(4244)**
2001: 7^{1}GS, 6^{0}F, 8^{2}GF, 7^{0}GF, 8^{6}G, 7^{0}GF

	Starts	1st	2nd	3rd	Win & Pl
Career Total (Turf)	11	2	2	0	21273

100	4/01	NmkR	7f	C	G-S	£6472
86	6/00	Ripn	6f	D	G-F	£3601

Total win prize-money £10074

Going (Turf): Sf: 0-2 **GS: 1-1** Gd: 0-2 **GF: 1-5** Fm: 0-1
Distance: 5f/6f: 1-5 7f-8f: 1-6 9f-13f: 0-0 14f+: 0-0
Track : LH: 0-1 RH: 0-3 Tight: 0-0 Gall: 0-1
Aids: Bl: 0-1 Vi: 0-0 Tstrap: 0-0
Best Rating: 101 7/01 Gdwd 1m gd-fm

Made a winning reappearance at three in a seven-furlong Newmarket conditions stakes, but has been held in Listed company and top handicaps and is not easy to place. Prefers fast ground but has won on good to soft. Stays a mile.

Procession

95 **72**

2-y-o b f Zafonic (USA)-Applaud (USA) (Rahy (USA))
Sir Michael Stoute Faisal Salman

Placings:24 **(3843)**
2001: 7^{2}GF, 7^{4}G

	Starts	1st	2nd	3rd	Win & Pl
Career Total (Turf)	2	0	1	0	1344

Going (Turf): Sf: 0-0 GS: 0-0 Gd: 0-1 GF: 0-1 Fm: 0-0
Distance: 5f/6f: 0-0 7f-8f: 0-2 9f-13f: 0-0 14f+: 0-0
Track : LH: 0-0 RH: 0-1 Tight: 0-0 Gall: 0-1
Aids: Bl: 0-0 Vi: 0-0 Tstrap: 0-0
Best Rating: 72 8/01 Rdcr 7f good

Profile

96 **56**

3-y-o b g Spectrum (IRE)-Famosa (Dancing Brave (USA))
M L W Bell Highclere Thoroughbred Racing Ltd

Placings:0633450 **(4900)**
2001: 7^{0}GF, 8^{6}GF, 8^{3}GF, 10^{3}G, 10^{4}G, 12^{5}GF, 8^{0}GS

	Starts	1st	2nd	3rd	Win & Pl
Career Total (Turf)	7	0	0	2	1390

Going (Turf): Sf: 0-0 GS: 0-1 Gd: 0-2 GF: 0-4 Fm: 0-0
Distance: 5f/6f: 0-0 7f-8f: 0-1 9f-13f: 0-6 14f+: 0-0
Track : LH: 0-2 RH: 0-2 Tight: 0-3 Gall: 0-0
Aids: Bl: 0-0 Vi: 0-2 Tstrap: 0-0
Best Rating: 68 7/01 Chep 1m2f36y good

Profiteer (IRE)

100 **93**

2-y-o b c Entrepreneur-Champagne Girl (Robellino (USA))
D R Loder Sheikh Mohammed

Placings:66 **(4833)**
2001: 6^{6}G, 6^{6}GF

	Starts	1st	2nd	3rd	Win & Pl
Career Total (Turf)	2	0	0	0	750

Going (Turf): Sf: 0-0 GS: 0-0 Gd: 0-1 GF: 0-1 Fm: 0-0
Distance: 5f/6f: 0-1 7f-8f: 0-1 9f-13f: 0-0 14f+: 0-0
Track : LH: 0-1 RH: 0-0 Tight: 0-0 Gall: 0-0
Aids: Bl: 0-1 Vi: 0-0 Tstrap: 0-0
Best Rating: 93 9/01 Newb 6f8y gd-fm

Always behind on his debut and acted as pacemaker in the Mill Reef next time.

Proletariat

103 **90**

3-y-o gr g Petong-Primulette (Mummy's Pet)
H Candy Simon Broke And Partners

Placings:2420-41100 **(3273)**
2001: 6^{4}GS, 6^{1}G, 8^{1}F, 8^{0}GF, 8^{0}GF

	Starts	1st	2nd	3rd	Win & Pl
Career Total (Turf)	9	2	2	0	9667

90 6/01 Nott 1m54y D(0-85)H FRM £4108
76 5/01 Nott 6f15y E GD £2478
Total win prize-money £6586

Going (Turf): Sf: 0-1 GS: 0-1 **Gd: 1-2** GF: 0-3 **Fm: 1-2**
Distance: 5f/6f: 0-4 7f-8f: 1-4 9f-13f: 1-1 14f+: 0-0
Track : **LH: 1-1** RH: 0-1 Tight: 0-0 Gall: 0-0
Aids: **Bl: 1-1** Vi: 0-0 Tstrap: 0-0
Best Rating: 90 6/01 Nott 1m54y firm

Won twice during the summer of 2001 at six furlongs and a mile. Has won in blinkers and without. Acts on a sound surface. Has ability but is a bit of a character.

Promiscuous

(88) (45)

3-y-o ch g Pursuit Of Love-Sparkly Girl (IRE) (Danehill (USA))
P F I Cole Mrs V K Shaw

Placings:66 **(0487)**
2001: 8^{6}SD, 8^{6}SD

	Starts	1st	2nd	3rd	Win & Pl
Career Total (Turf)	0	0	0	0	
Career Total (AW)	2	0	0	0	0

Going (Turf): Sf: 0-0 GS: 0-0 Gd: 0-0 GF: 0-0 Fm: 0-0
Distance: 5f/6f: 0-0 7f-8f: 0-1 9f-13f: 0-1 14f+: 0-0
Track : LH: 0-2 RH: 0-0 Tight: 0-1 Gall: 0-0
Aids: Bl: 0-0 Vi: 0-0 Tstrap: 0-0
Best Rating: 45 3/01 Sthl 1m stand

Promised (IRE)

101 **88**

3-y-o b f Petardia-Where's The Money (Lochnager)
J A Glover Paul J Dixon

Placings:13000400-0005 **(1814)**
2001: 6^{0}S, 5^{0}GF, 6^{0}S, 6^{5}GF

	Starts	1st	2nd	3rd	Win & Pl
Career Total (Turf)	12	1	0	1	4580

75 5/00 Rdcr 5f E G-S £2522
Total win prize-money £2522

Going (Turf): Sf: 0-5 **GS: 1-3** Gd: 0-1 GF: 0-2 Fm: 0-0
Distance: **5f/6f: 1-11** 7f-8f: 0-1 9f-13f: 0-0 14f+: 0-0
Track : LH: 0-1 RH: 0-0 Tight: 0-1 Gall: 0-0
Aids: Bl: 0-0 Vi: 0-1 Tstrap: 0-0
Best Rating: 84 6/01 NmkR 6f gd-fm

Useful sprint handicapper.

Promising (FR)

70 **11**

3-y-o ch f Ashkalani (IRE)-Sea Thunder (Salse (USA))
M C Chapman John L Marriott

Placings:00 **(5281)**
2001: 8^{0}G, 7^{0}S

	Starts	1st	2nd	3rd	Win & Pl
Career Total (Turf)	2	0	0	0	

Going (Turf): Sf: 0-1 GS: 0-0 Gd: 0-1 GF: 0-0 Fm: 0-0
Distance: 5f/6f: 0-0 7f-8f: 0-1 9f-13f: 0-1 14f+: 0-0
Track : LH: 0-1 RH: 0-0 Tight: 0-0 Gall: 0-0
Aids: Bl: 0-0 Vi: 0-0 Tstrap: 0-0
Best Rating: 11 10/01 Leic 7f9y soft

Promote

76 **15**

5-y-o gr g Linamix (FR)-Rive (USA) (Riverman (USA))
Ms A E Embiricos The French Promotion

Placings:15/0 **(5625)**
2001: 8^{0}GS

	Starts	1st	2nd	3rd	Win & Pl
Career Total (Turf)	3	1	0	0	9091

9/98 Chan 1m SFT £9091
Total win prize-money £9091

Going (Turf): Sf: 0-0 GS: 0-1 Gd: 0-1 GF: 0-0 Fm: 0-0
Distance: 5f/6f: 0-0 7f-8f: 0-1 9f-13f: 0-1 14f+: 0-0
Track : LH: 0-1 RH: 0-1 Tight: 0-0 Gall: 0-0
Aids: Bl: 0-0 Vi: 0-0 Tstrap: 0-1
Best Rating: 15 11/01 Nott 1m54y gd-sft

Prompt Payment (IRE)

102 **81**

3-y-o b/br f In The Wings-Lady Lucre (IRE) (Last Tycoon)
J R Fanshawe Chris Van Hoorn

Placings:3154 **(5558)**
2001: 10^{3}G, 11^{1}GF, 10^{5}G, 10^{4}S

	Starts	1st	2nd	3rd	Win & Pl
Career Total (Turf)	4	1	0	1	5431

79 9/01 Ling 1m3f106yD G-F £4264
Total win prize-money £4264

Going (Turf): Sf: 0-1 GS: 0-0 Gd: 0-2 **GF: 1-1** Fm: 0-0
Distance: 5f/6f: 0-0 7f-8f: 0-0 **9f-13f: 1-4** 14f+: 0-0
Track : **LH: 1-2** RH: 0-0 **Tight: 1-3** Gall: 0-0
Aids: Bl: 0-0 Vi: 0-0 Tstrap: 0-0
Best Rating: 81 10/01 NmkR 1m2f good

Unraced at two, she got off the mark in a Lingfield maiden in her second start and ran well in better class afterwards. Stays 12 furlongs, acts on any ground.

Proper Squire (USA)

107(95) (66)**68**

4-y-o b g Bien Bien (USA)-La Cumbre (Sadler's Wells (USA))
B J Meehan Gallagher Equine Ltd

Placings:362/6200-301**3**40010 **(5492)**
2001: 15^{3}HY, 16^{0}G, **16**^{1}SD, **16**^{3}SD, 16^{4}GF, 14^{0}GF, 16^{0}GF, 16^{1}GS, 16^{0}HY

	Starts	1st	2nd	3rd	Win & Pl
Career Total (Turf)	14	1	2	2	7773
Career Total (AW)	2	1	0	1	2259

68 9/01 Gdwd 2m E(0-70)H G-S £3835
43 6/01 Wolv 2m46y F STD £1911
Total win prize-money £5746

Going (Turf): Sf: 0-3 **GS: 1-4** Gd: 0-2 GF: 0-5 Fm: 0-0
Distance: 5f/6f: 0-0 7f-8f: 0-0 9f-13f: 0-7 **14f+: 2-9**
Track : LH: 1-7 RH: 1-7 **Tight: 2-8** Gall: 0-3
Aids: **Bl: 1-5** Vi: 0-0 Tstrap: 0-0
Best Rating: 70 4/01 Folk 1m7f92y heavy

He was placed a few times in maiden and handicap company on turf, but did not get off the mark until landing a seller on the Wolverhampton Fibresand in June. Was given a good ride to win a race for jump jockeys at Goodwood in September. Stays very well.

Property Zone

96 **42**

3-y-o b g Cool Jazz-Prime Property (IRE) (Tirol)
M W Easterby Alan Black & Co

Placings:000-0406 **(4371)**
2001: 8^{0}GF, 11^{4}GF, 16^{0}GS, 11^{6}GF

	Starts	1st	2nd	3rd	Win & Pl
Career Total (Turf)	7	0	0	0	0

Going (Turf): Sf: 0-1 GS: 0-1 Gd: 0-1 GF: 0-3 Fm: 0-1
Distance: 5f/6f: 0-2 7f-8f: 0-1 9f-13f: 0-3 14f+: 0-1
Track : LH: 0-3 RH: 0-3 Tight: 0-4 Gall: 0-0
Aids: Bl: 0-0 Vi: 0-0 Tstrap: 0-0
Best Rating: 35 8/01 Catt 1m3f214y gd-fm

Proserpina

70 **21**

3-y-o b f Most Welcome-Hever Golf Lady (Dominion)
K R Burke L A Bolingbroke

Placings:006 **(4317)**
2001: 8^{0}GF, 9^{0}GF, 12^{6}G

	Starts	1st	2nd	3rd	Win & Pl
Career Total (Turf)	3	0	0	0	0

Going (Turf): Sf: 0-0 GS: 0-0 Gd: 0-1 GF: 0-2 Fm: 0-0
Distance: 5f/6f: 0-0 7f-8f: 0-1 9f-13f: 0-2 14f+: 0-0
Track : LH: 0-1 RH: 0-2 Tight: 0-2 Gall: 0-0
Aids: Bl: 0-0 Vi: 0-0 Tstrap: 0-0
Best Rating: 21 7/01 Nott 1m1f213y gd-fm

Proserpine

94 **95**

2-y-o b f Robellino (USA)-Hymne D'Amour (USA) (Dixieland Band (USA))
M P Tregoning The Earl Cadogan

Placings:5221 **(5282)**
2001: 6^{5}GF, 6^{2}GF, 8^{2}GS, 8^{1}HY

	Starts	1st	2nd	3rd	Win & Pl
Career Total (Turf)	4	1	2	0	6934

83 10/01 Ayr 1m D HVY £3786
Total win prize-money £3786

Going (Turf): Sf: 1-1 GS: 0-1 Gd: 0-0 GF: 0-2 Fm: 0-0
Distance: 5f/6f: 0-1 **7f-8f: 1-3** 9f-13f: 0-0 14f+: 0-0
Track : **LH: 1-1** RH: 0-0 Tight: 0-0 Gall: 0-0
Aids: Bl: 0-0 Vi: 0-0 Tstrap: 0-0
Best Rating: 95 10/01 Sals 1m gd-sft

Unlucky to be twice beaten a short head in Salisbury maidens in the autumn, but gained a deserved victory next time out in heavy ground at Ayr. Stays a mile, acts on any ground.

Prospector's Cove

100(99) (41)**37**

8-y-o b g Dowsing (USA)-Pearl Cove (Town And Country)
Mrs Lydia Pearce (J Pearce 22/2) Saracen Racing

Placings:1/100/0003650003/**53**005401400035**22512/563 2553**25**53**0023021601000/**3**0**0**000**0**10466236000**0**-**0050**003300505550**0**0600 **(5592)**
2001: **8**^{0}SW, **7**^{0}SD, **8**^{5}SD, **11**^{0}SD, 6^{0}F, 8^{0}G, 9^{3}F, 10^{3}GF, 10^{0}G, 10^{0}GF, 16^{5}GF, 8^{0}GS, 10^{5}GS, 7^{5}GF, 9^{5}GS, 8^{0}GF, 8^{0}GS, **11**^{0}SD, 11^{6}S, 9^{0}S, 6^{0}GS

	Starts	1st	2nd	3rd	Win & Pl
Career Total (Turf)	71	6	4	8	33543
Career Total (AW)	24	1	4	4	5726

68 5/00 Yarm 7f3y E(0-70)H GD £3107
74 9/99 Yarm 1m3y D(0-80)H G-S £5049
69 8/99 NmkJ 1m D(0-80)H GD £5400
61 12/98 Ling 1m2f F(0-60)H STD £1735
62 8/98 Brig 7f214y E(0-70)H FRM £2814
86 4/96 Kemp 1m2f C GD £4582
83 11/95 Muss 7f15y F SFT £2776
Total win prize-money £25464

Going (Turf): Sf: 1-11 GS: 1-10 **Gd: 3-25** GF: 0-20 Fm: 1-5
Distance: 5f/6f: 0-0 **7f-8f: 4-32** 9f-13f: 3-59 14f+: 0-4
Track : LH: 2-52 RH: 2-20 **Tight: 2-35** Gall: 1-6
Aids: Bl: 0-0 Vi: 0-4 Tstrap: 0-0
Best Rating: 59 6/01 Nott 1m1f213y firm

Prospectors Coral

89 **50**

2-y-o b f Primo Dominie-St Louis Lady (Absalom)
Mrs Lydia Pearce Saracen Racing

Placings:000U **(5165)**
2001: 5^{0}G, 5^{0}GF, 6^{0}GF, 5^{U}SD

	Starts	1st	2nd	3rd	Win & Pl
Career Total (Turf)	3	0	0	0	
Career Total (AW)	1	0	0	0	

Going (Turf): Sf: 0-0 GS: 0-0 Gd: 0-1 GF: 0-2 Fm: 0-0
Distance: 5f/6f: 0-4 7f-8f: 0-0 9f-13f: 0-0 14f+: 0-0
Track : LH: 0-1 RH: 0-0 Tight: 0-1 Gall: 0-0
Aids: Bl: 0-0 Vi: 0-0 Tstrap: 0-0
Best Rating: 50 8/01 Folk 5f good

Protagonist

97 **74**
3-y-o b/br c In The Wings-Fatah Flare (USA) (Alydar (USA))
M R Channon B E Nielsen

Placings:446 **(1332)**
2001: 11^{4}S, 10^{4}GS, 13^{6}F

	Starts	1st	2nd	3rd	Win & Pl
Career Total (Turf)	3	0	0	0	557

Going (Turf): Sf: 0-1 GS: 0-1 Gd: 0-0 GF: 0-0 Fm: 0-1
Distance: 5f/6f: 0-0 7f-8f: 0-0 9f-13f: 0-2 14f+: 0-1
Track : LH: 0-2 RH: 0-1 Tight: 0-1 Gall: 0-1
Aids: Bl: 0-0 Vi: 0-0 Tstrap: 0-0
Best Rating: 74 5/01 York 1m5f194y firm

Protectorate

100 **89?**
2-y-o ch f Hector Protector (USA)-Possessive Lady (Dara Monarch)
I A Wood John Purcell

Placings:12020 **(5609)**
2001: 5^{1}S, 7^{2}GS, 6^{0}G, 6^{2}GS, 8^{0}GS

	Starts	1st	2nd	3rd	Win & Pl
Career Total (Turf)	5	1	2	0	35374

72 8/01 Nott 5f13y E SFT £3024
Total win prize-money £3024

Going (Turf): Sf: **1-1** GS: 0-3 Gd: 0-1 GF: 0-0 Fm: 0-0
Distance: **5f/6f: 1-2** 7f-8f: 0-3 9f-13f: 0-0 14f+: 0-0
Track : LH: 0-0 RH: 0-1 Tight: 0-0 Gall: 0-0
Aids: Bl: 0-0 Vi: 0-0 Tstrap: 0-0
Best Rating: 89 8/01 Gdwd 7f gd-sft

A half-sister to a winner over middle distances, she made a successful debut in a soft-ground maiden at Nottingham in August and was not disgraced when second behind runaway winner Gossamer in a Goodwood Group Three next time. A very disappointing favourite in an Ascot sales race next time where she jumped the road and could never get back into contention. She showed that to be wrong when narrowly beaten in a similar race at Newmarket but was well beaten when stepped up to a mile on her last run. Goes well in soft ground.

Protectress

107 **96+**
2-y-o ch f Hector Protector (USA)-Quota (Rainbow Quest (USA))
H R A Cecil K Abdulla

Placings:1 **(5144)**
2001: 7^{1}G

	Starts	1st	2nd	3rd	Win & Pl
Career Total (Turf)	1	1	0	0	12760

96 10/01 NmkR 7f A GD £12760
Total win prize-money £12760

Going (Turf): Sf: 0-0 GS: 0-0 **Gd: 1-1** GF: 0-0 Fm: 0-0
Distance: 5f/6f: 0-0 **7f-8f: 1-1** 9f-13f: 0-0 14f+: 0-0
Track : LH: 0-0 RH: 0-0 Tight: 0-0 Gall: 0-0
Aids: Bl: 0-0 Vi: 0-0 Tstrap: 0-0
Best Rating: 96 10/01 NmkR 7f good

Out of a sister to Racing Post Trophy winner Armiger, she was well touted before justifying favouritism in the Listed Oh So Sharp Satkes on her debut. She is sure to get further than a mile in time but the 1000 Guineas looks the likely early-season target for her next year.

Protocol (IRE)

101(92) (29)**34**
7-y-o b g Taufan (USA)-Ukraine's Affair (USA) (The Minstrel (CAN))
Mrs S Lamyman P Lamyman

Placings:042/241400524/536503114600600/0000034 6643252510/00235504223103500-4642600004005500 **(5622)**
2001: **16**^{4}SD, **16**^{6}SW, 10^{4}HY, 14^{2}HY, 12^{6}S, 11^{0}F, 12^{0}GF, 10^{0}GF, 16^{0}GF, 11^{4}G, 17^{0}GF, 16^{0}GF, 10^{5}HY, 17^{5}F, 17^{0}S, 14^{0}GS

	Starts	1st	2nd	3rd	Win & Pl
Career Total (Turf)	64	5	7	5	26677
Career Total (AW)	14	0	2	2	2373

40 8/00 Pont 1m2f6y E(0-80)H G-F £2756
57 11/99 Nott 1m6f15y G(0-70) SFT £2150
83 4/98 Leic 1m1f218yD(0-80)H SFT £3915
78 3/98 Donc 1m4f F(0-80)H GD £2486
74 5/97 Sand 1m3f91y D(0-80)H G-F £3533
Total win prize-money £14841

Going (Turf): Sf: 2-12 GS: 0-10 Gd: 1-15 **GF: 2-22** Fm: 0-5
Distance: 5f/6f: 0-0 7f-8f: 0-3 **9f-13f: 4-48** 14f+: 1-27
Track : **LH: 3-53** RH: 2-21 Tight: 0-19 **Gall: 1-14**
Aids: Bl: 0-0 Vi: 0-1 **Tstrap: 2-48**
Best Rating: 47 5/01 Nott 1m6f15y heavy

Moderate handicapper. Ten furlongs and cut in the ground seem to suit him best, but he stays further.

Proud Boast

98 **92**
3-y-o b f Komaite (USA)-Red Rosein (Red Sunset)
Mrs G S Rees J W Gittins

Placings:10231526-2000 **(2205)**
2001: 5^{2}GF, 5^{0}GF, 6^{0}F, 6^{0}GS

	Starts	1st	2nd	3rd	Win & Pl
Career Total (Turf)	12	2	3	1	19352

90 8/00 Thsk 5f C G-F £7150
72 6/00 Ches 5f16y D G-S £3562
Total win prize-money £10712

Going (Turf): Sf: 0-1 **GS: 1-2** Gd: 0-1 **GF: 1-7** Fm: 0-1
Distance: **5f/6f: 2-12** 7f-8f: 0-0 9f-13f: 0-0 14f+: 0-0
Track : **LH: 1-3** RH: 0-0 **Tight: 1-2** Gall: 0-0
Aids: Bl: 0-0 Vi: 0-0 Tstrap: 0-0
Best Rating: 92 5/01 Ches 5f16y gd-fm

A daughter of a Wokingham winner, she was a speedy juvenile. Runner-up on her reappearance at Chester, she struggled afterwards. Acts on a fast surface.

Proud Cavalier

92(89) (33)**24**
5-y-o b g Pharly (FR)-Midnight Flit (Bold Lad (IRE))
K Bell S J Edwards

Placings:0/00/05004004-50300 **(3728)**
2001: 9^{5}F, 9^{0}G, 11^{3}F, 11^{0}G, 10^{0}GS

	Starts	1st	2nd	3rd	Win & Pl
Career Total (Turf)	12	0	0	1	337
Career Total (AW)	4	0	0	0	

Going (Turf): Sf: 0-2 GS: 0-1 Gd: 0-4 GF: 0-2 Fm: 0-3
Distance: 5f/6f: 0-0 7f-8f: 0-3 9f-13f: 0-13 14f+: 0-0
Track : LH: 0-14 RH: 0-1 Tight: 0-10 Gall: 0-0
Aids: Bl: 0-0 Vi: 0-0 Tstrap: 0-0
Best Rating: 24 7/01 Bath 1m3f144y firm

Proud Chief

108(80) (23)**58**
4-y-o ch g Be My Chief (USA)-Fleur De Foret (USA) (Green Forest (USA))
A P Jarvis Grant & Bowman Limited

Placings:010000/26000000-00000010 **(3370)**
2001: 7^{0}SD, 7^{0}SD, 7^{0}GS, 7^{0}GF, 6^{0}GF, 5^{0}F, 6^{1}GF, 6^{0}F

	Starts	1st	2nd	3rd	Win & Pl
Career Total (Turf)	20	2	1	0	9993
Career Total (AW)	2	0	0	0	

58 7/01 Epsm 6f D(0-80)H G-F £4251
87 6/99 Gdwd 6f D G-F £3550
Total win prize-money £7801

Going (Turf): Sf: 0-1 GS: 0-4 Gd: 0-4 **GF: 2-8** Fm: 0-3
Distance: **5f/6f: 2-10** 7f-8f: 0-11 9f-13f: 0-1 14f+: 0-0
Track : **LH: 1-7** RH: 0-5 **Tight: 1-3** Gall: 0-3
Aids: Bl: 0-0 Vi: 0-3 Tstrap: 0-0
Best Rating: 58 7/01 Epsm 6f gd-fm

Modest sprinter. Ended a long losing run at Epsom in July 2001. Best suited by a fast six furlongs. Acts on a sound surface.

Proud Monk

93(59) **36**
8-y-o gr g Aragon-Silent Sister (Kind Of Hush)
K Bell S J Edwards

Placings:4635633130/2204030540/004005/00000040 600350400/04444064044/06050 **(3187)**
2001: 11^{0}SD, 11^{6}GF, 10^{0}G, 10^{5}GF, 11^{0}GS

	Starts	1st	2nd	3rd	Win & Pl
Career Total (Turf)	54	1	2	6	15219
Career Total (AW)	6	0	0	0	0

82 10/95 Newb 7f64y D(0-85) G-S £4146
Total win prize-money £4146

Going (Turf): Sf: 0-7 **GS: 1-8** Gd: 0-16 GF: 0-20 Fm: 0-3
Distance: 5f/6f: 0-4 **7f-8f: 1-23** 9f-13f: 0-33 14f+: 0-0
Track : **LH: 1-34** RH: 0-9 Tight: 0-16 **Gall: 1-6**
Aids: Bl: 0-3 Vi: 0-7 Tstrap: 0-11
Best Rating: 37 6/01 Hayd 1m3f200y gd-fm

Proud Native (IRE)

107 **101**
7-y-o b g Imp Society (USA)-Karamana (Habitat)
D Nicholls P D Savill

Placings:11140215/0405100/100000010156/50115331 0/0022062230-0351350040 **(4902)**
2001: 5^{0}GS, 5^{3}G, 5^{5}GF, 5^{1}S, 5^{3}Y, 5^{5}G, 5^{0}GF, 5^{0}GF, 5^{4}GF, 5^{0}G

	Starts	1st	2nd	3rd	Win & Pl
Career Total (Turf)	56	12	5	5	299023

105 6/01 Sand 5f6y C SFT £6277
103 9/99 Taby 5f165y GD £31134
109 6/99 Leop 5f YLD £22750
109 5/99 Kemp 5f A G-F £12602
109 8/98 Nott 5f13y C G-F £5286
103 8/98 Hayd 5f C(0-100)H GD £14590
105 3/98 Donc 5f B(0-105)H GD £21495
101 8/97 Yarm 6f3y C G-F £4518
103 10/96 Rdcr 6f B G-F £71917
105 6/96 Epsm 6f A GD £13680
84 5/96 York 6f B G-F £6947
78 4/96 Ripn 5f D GD £3452
Total win prize-money £214650

Going (Turf): Sf: 1-4 GS: 0-6 **Gd: 5-25 GF: 5-18** Fm: 0-1
Distance: **5f/6f: 11-50** 7f-8f: 1-6 9f-13f: 0-0 14f+: 0-0
Track : **LH: 2-3** RH: 0-0 **Tight: 1-2** Gall: 0-0
Aids: Bl: 0-2 Vi: 0-0 Tstrap: 0-0
Best Rating: 105 6/01 Sand 5f6y soft

Very useful sprinter. He ran a string of solid races without winning in 2000 and remains dangerous in Listed events. Probably best over the minimum trip, he stays an easy six. Ran as if coming to hand at Epsom, and duly obliged in a small field at Sandown. Acts on any ground.

Proud Protector (IRE)

87 **67**
2-y-o ch c Hector Protector (USA)-Hooray Lady (Ahonoora)
T D Easterby Roger Dowsett

Placings:005 **(4838)**
2001: 6^{0}F, 8^{0}HY, 6^{5}G

	Starts	1st	2nd	3rd	Win & Pl
Career Total (Turf)	3	0	0	0	0

Going (Turf): Sf: 0-1 GS: 0-0 Gd: 0-1 GF: 0-0 Fm: 0-1
Distance: 5f/6f: 0-1 7f-8f: 0-1 9f-13f: 0-1 14f+: 0-0
Track : LH: 0-1 RH: 0-0 Tight: 0-0 Gall: 0-0
Aids: Bl: 0-0 Vi: 0-0 Tstrap: 0-0

Best Rating: 67 6/01 Newc 6f firm

Proud Reflection

88 **38**

3-y-o b c Petong-Fleur De Foret (USA) (Green Forest (USA))
J G Portman (A P Jarvis 24/8) Christopher Shankland

Placings:5-000 **(4900)**
2001: 6^0GF, 5^0GS, 8^0GS

	Starts	1st	2nd	3rd	Win & Pl
Career Total (Turf)	4	0	0	0	0

Going (Turf): Sf: 0-0 GS: 0-3 Gd: 0-0 GF: 0-1 Fm: 0-0
Distance: 5f/6f: 0-3 7f-8f: 0-0 9f-13f: 0-1 14f+: 0-0
Track : LH: 0-0 RH: 0-0 Tight: 0-0 Gall: 0-0
Aids: Bl: 0-0 Vi: 0-0 Tstrap: 0-0
Best Rating: 38 7/01 Sals 6f gd-fm

Proud Western (USA)

95 **51**

3-y-o b/br c Gone West (USA)-Proud Lou (USA) (Proud Clarion)
B Ellison (A Fabre 3/6) Spring Cottage Syndicate

Placings:343-045 **(5625)**
2001: 8^0G, 8^4G, 8^5GS

	Starts	1st	2nd	3rd	Win & Pl
Career Total (Turf)	6	0	0	2	7171

Going (Turf): Sf: 0-0 GS: 0-1 Gd: 0-2 GF: 0-0 Fm: 0-0
Distance: 5f/6f: 0-0 7f-8f: 0-2 9f-13f: 0-1 14f+: 0-0
Track : LH: 0-1 RH: 0-0 Tight: 0-0 Gall: 0-0
Aids: Bl: 0-0 Vi: 0-0 Tstrap: 0-0
Best Rating: 51 11/01 Nott 1m54y gd-sft

Proudwings (GER)

112 **122**

5-y-o b m Dashing Blade-Peraja (FR) (Kaiseradler)
R Suerland Hyperion Breeding

Placings:2210/321111211-310100 **(5006)**
2001: 8^3S, 8^1HY, 8^0G, 8^1G, 8^0GS, 8^0S

	Starts	1st	2nd	3rd	Win & Pl
Career Total (Turf)	19	9	4	2	142572

115 7/01 NmkJ 1m A GD £34800
116 5/01 StCl 1m HVY £29098
109 10/00 Siro 1m HVY £28185
10/00 Siro 1m HVY £22772
7/00 Duss 1m110y H GD £4742
6/00 Hanv 1m110y H GD £1677
5/00 Badn 1m H SFT £3871
5/00 Duss 1m110y H GD £2258
10/99 Neus 1m H SFT £1661
Total win prize-money £129064

Going (Turf): Sf: 5-9 GS: 0-1 **Gd: 3-4** GF: 0-0 Fm: 0-0
Distance: 5f/6f: 0-0 **7f-8f: 6-15** 9f-13f: 2-3 14f+: 0-0
Track : LH: 0-1 **RH: 1-2** Tight: 0-0 Gall: 0-1
Aids: Bl: 0-0 Vi: 0-0 Tstrap: 0-0
Best Rating: 122 8/01 Deau 1m gd-sft

A game and versatile German miler, won a Longchamp Group Two in May. She ran out a clear cut winner of the Falmouth Stakes at Newmarket in July. She was unlucky to be disqualified when taking the Jacques le Marois at Deauville. Goes well on heavy ground but handles good.

Proven (USA)

98 **92**

2-y-o br c Benny The Dip (USA)-Night Fax (USA) (Known Fact (USA))
J H M Gosden Sheikh Mohammed

Placings:1 **(5485)**
2001: 7^1HY

	Starts	1st	2nd	3rd	Win & Pl
Career Total (Turf)	1	1	0	0	4349

92 10/01 Donc 7f D HVY £4348
Total win prize-money £4349

Going (Turf): Sf: 1-1 GS: 0-0 Gd: 0-0 GF: 0-0 Fm: 0-0
Distance: 5f/6f: 0-0 **7f-8f: 1-1** 9f-13f: 0-0 14f+: 0-0
Track : LH: 0-0 RH: 0-0 Tight: 0-0 Gall: 0-0
Aids: Bl: 0-0 Vi: 0-0 Tstrap: 0-0
Best Rating: 92 10/01 Donc 7f heavy

A 150,000gns son of Benny The Dip, he won nicely on his debut in a back-end Doncaster maiden and looks to have a future.

Provender (IRE)

88 **65**

2-y-o b c Ashkalani (IRE)-Quiche (Formidable (USA))
Sir Mark Prescott Mr & Mrs Arthur Finn

Placings:520 **(4797)**
2001: 7^5GF, 6^2GF, 6^0G

	Starts	1st	2nd	3rd	Win & Pl
Career Total (Turf)	3	0	1	0	852

Going (Turf): Sf: 0-0 GS: 0-0 Gd: 0-1 GF: 0-2 Fm: 0-0
Distance: 5f/6f: 0-1 7f-8f: 0-2 9f-13f: 0-0 14f+: 0-0
Track : LH: 0-0 RH: 0-0 Tight: 0-0 Gall: 0-0
Aids: Bl: 0-0 Vi: 0-0 Tstrap: 0-0
Best Rating: 65 9/01 Ayr 6f good

Psalmist

87(65) **55**

4-y-o ch f Mystiko (USA)-Son Et Lumiere (Rainbow Quest (USA))
Noel T Chance R W And J R Fidler

Placings:300000-00 **(1719)**
2001: 8^0G, 13^0GF

	Starts	1st	2nd	3rd	Win & Pl
Career Total (Turf)	7	0	0	1	588
Career Total (AW)	1	0	0	0	

Going (Turf): Sf: 0-1 GS: 0-2 Gd: 0-2 GF: 0-2 Fm: 0-0
Distance: 5f/6f: 0-1 7f-8f: 0-2 9f-13f: 0-4 14f+: 0-1
Track : LH: 0-4 RH: 0-2 Tight: 0-1 Gall: 0-1
Aids: Bl: 0-0 Vi: 0-0 Tstrap: 0-0
Best Rating: 38 5/01 Wwck 1m22y good

Psychic (IRE)

92 **65**

2-y-o b f Alhaarth (IRE)-Mood Swings (IRE) (Shirley Heights)
M L W Bell The Hon Mrs J M Corbett

Placings:6 **(4637)**
2001: 7^6GF

	Starts	1st	2nd	3rd	Win & Pl
Career Total (Turf)	1	0	0	0	0

Going (Turf): Sf: 0-0 GS: 0-0 Gd: 0-0 GF: 0-1 Fm: 0-0
Distance: 5f/6f: 0-0 7f-8f: 0-1 9f-13f: 0-0 14f+: 0-0
Track : LH: 0-0 RH: 0-0 Tight: 0-0 Gall: 0-0
Aids: Bl: 0-0 Vi: 0-0 Tstrap: 0-0
Best Rating: 65 9/01 Ling 7f gd-fm

Ptah (IRE)

101(100) (40)**39**

4-y-o b g Petardia-Davenport Goddess (IRE) (Classic Secret (USA))
J L Eyre M Ford, M James & N Tritton

Placings:405000/0043230062044-001600500 **(5531)**
2001: 16^0SD, 16^0SW, 16^1S, 17^6HY, 13^0G, 16^0G, 15^5GF, 15^0GS, 16^0HY

	Starts	1st	2nd	3rd	Win & Pl
Career Total (Turf)	21	1	1	2	5907
Career Total (AW)	7	0	1	0	815

49 3/01 Muss 2m E(0-75)H SFT £3510
Total win prize-money £3510

Going (Turf): Sf: 1-6 GS: 0-6 Gd: 0-5 GF: 0-3 Fm: 0-1
Distance: 5f/6f: 0-4 7f-8f: 0-2 9f-13f: 0-5 **14f+: 1-17**
Track : LH: 0-19 **RH: 1-6 Tight: 1-15** Gall: 0-2
Aids: Bl: 0-1 Vi: 0-0 **Tstrap: 1-6**
Best Rating: 49 3/01 Muss 2m soft

Ptarmigan Ridge

107 **85**

5-y-o b h Sea Raven (IRE)-Panayr (Faraway Times (USA))
Miss L A Perratt Miss Heather Galbraith

Placings:1/02040000/10000-54410000010 **(5502)**
2001: 5^5G, 5^4S, 5^4GS, 5^1G, 6^0G, 5^0HY, 5^0G, 5^0HY, 5^0GS, 5^1S, 5^0HY

	Starts	1st	2nd	3rd	Win & Pl
Career Total (Turf)	25	4	1	0	34077

85 10/01 Catt 5f D(0-80)H SFT £4816
81 8/01 Hayd 5f C(0-100)H GD £15340
80 9/00 Ayr 5f D(0-85)H SFT £6500
80 10/98 Catt 5f D SFT £3626
Total win prize-money £30283

Going (Turf): Sf: 3-13 GS: 0-4 Gd: 1-7 GF: 0-1 Fm: 0-0
Distance: **5f/6f: 4-24** 7f-8f: 0-1 9f-13f: 0-0 14f+: 0-0
Track : LH: 0-1 RH: 0-0 Tight: 0-0 Gall: 0-0
Aids: Bl: 0-0 Vi: 0-0 Tstrap: 0-0
Best Rating: 85 10/01 Catt 5f soft

Useful sprinter. Returned from a layoff of a year when scoring at Ayr in September of 2000. Gradually found his form this season and got back to winning ways at Haydock in August and added to that at Catterick in the autumn. Suited by soft ground but has won on good. Has a habit of sweating up beforehand and has bags of early speed.

Puddle Duck

83 **44**

2-y-o b g First Trump-Aunt Jemima (Busted)
T D Easterby The Lincolnshire/yorkshire Partnership

Placings:00 **(4533)**
2001: 6^0GF, 7^0GF

	Starts	1st	2nd	3rd	Win & Pl
Career Total (Turf)	2	0	0	0	

Going (Turf): Sf: 0-0 GS: 0-0 Gd: 0-0 GF: 0-2 Fm: 0-0
Distance: 5f/6f: 0-1 7f-8f: 0-1 9f-13f: 0-0 14f+: 0-0
Track : LH: 0-1 RH: 0-0 Tight: 0-0 Gall: 0-1
Aids: Bl: 0-0 Vi: 0-0 Tstrap: 0-0
Best Rating: 44 5/01 Donc 6f gd-fm

Puffin

103 **81**

3-y-o b f Pennekamp (USA)-Spring (Sadler's Wells (USA))
J L Dunlop Lord Halifax

Placings:566-156600 **(5171)**
2001: 9^1S, 10^5GS, 8^6GF, 8^6G, 8^0G, 8^0GS

	Starts	1st	2nd	3rd	Win & Pl
Career Total (Turf)	9	1	0	0	4388

81 4/01 Kemp 1m1f D(0-85)H SFT £4387
Total win prize-money £4388

Going (Turf): Sf: 1-2 GS: 0-2 Gd: 0-2 GF: 0-3 Fm: 0-0
Distance: 5f/6f: 0-1 7f-8f: 0-6 **9f-13f: 1-3** 14f+: 0-0
Track : LH: 0-2 **RH: 1-2** Tight: 0-0 Gall: 0-0
Aids: Bl: 0-0 Vi: 0-0 Tstrap: 0-0
Best Rating: 81 8/01 NmkJ 1m good

Won over nine furlongs on soft ground on her handicap and seasonal debut in 2001. Has struggled off a higher mark since.

Pugin (IRE)

107 **116**

3-y-o b c Darshaan-Gothic Dream (IRE) (Nashwan (USA))
John M Oxx Lady Clague

Placings:121425 **(4711)**
2001: 10^1SH, 12^2G, 10^1G, 12^4Y, 14^2G, 14^5G

	Starts	1st	2nd	3rd	Win & Pl
Career Total (Turf)	6	2	2	0	78785

105 5/01 Curr 1m2f GD £30875

90	4/01	Navn	1m2f		SH	£6900

Total win prize-money £37775

Going (Turf): Sf: 0-0 GS: 0-0 **Gd: 1-4** GF: 0-0 Fm: 0-0
Distance: 5f/6f: 0-0 7f-8f: 0-0 **9f-13f: 2-4** 14f+: 0-2
Track : LH: 0-1 RH: 0-0 Tight: 0-0 Gall: 0-1
Aids: Bl: 0-0 Vi: 0-0 Tstrap: 0-0
Best Rating: 116 7/01 Curr 1m4f yield

A progressive colt, he stayed on well when beating Match King in a Listed event over ten furlongs at the Curragh in May and ran well to finish fourth to Galileo in the Irish Derby. Ran Vinnie Roe to a head at the Curragh before a fair effort in the St Leger. Likely to make a decent stayer next season.

Pulau Pinang (IRE)

103(101) (76)**85**

5-y-o ch m Dolphin Street (FR)-Inner Pearl (Gulf Pearl)
G A Butler Mrs A K H Ooi

Placings:310/221000-5011P0210 **(5338)**
2001: 12^{5}SD, 12^{0}SD, 10^{1}G, 9^{1}GF, 11^{P}GF, 9^{0}G, 10^{2}G, 12^{1}GF, 12^{0}GS

	Starts	1st	2nd	3rd	Win & Pl
Career Total (Turf)	15	5	2	1	31640
Career Total (AW)	3	0	1	0	776

85	9/01	Haml	1m4f17y	C(0-100)H	G-F	£14885
79	6/01	Beve	1m1f207y	D(0-80)H	G-F	£4696
79	5/01	Sand	1m2f7y	D(0-80)H	GD	£5505
76	5/00	Bath	1m5f22y	D(0-80)H	G-F	£3760
64	9/99	Ling	1m3f106yF		FRM	£2280

Total win prize-money £31128

Going (Turf): Sf: 0-1 GS: 0-3 Gd: 1-6 **GF: 3-4** Fm: 1-1
Distance: 5f/6f: 0-0 7f-8f: 0-0 **9f-13f: 4-14** 14f+: 1-4
Track : LH: 2-10 **RH: 3-7 Tight: 3-8** Gall: 0-3
Aids: Bl: 0-0 Vi: 0-0 **Tstrap: 4-12**
Best Rating: 85 9/01 Haml 1m4f17y gd-fm

Won over staying distances earlier in her career, but scored over ten furlongs twice this season at Sandown and Beverley. Was found to be suffering from a fibrillating heart after pulling up at Leicester in July. Returned to her best in September, winning a valuable 12 furlong Hamilton handicap. She bounced right back to form at Lingfield in November. Acts on fast ground and Polytrack.

Pulau Tioman

113 **108**

5-y-o b h Robellino (USA)-Ella Mon Amour (Ela-Mana-Mou)
M A Jarvis H R H Sultan Ahmad Shah

Placings:3415/220101500/2124120333-521104 **(4263)**
2001: 8^{5}S, 8^{2}GS, 8^{1}GS, 8^{1}GF, 8^{0}Y, 10^{4}GF

	Starts	1st	2nd	3rd	Win & Pl
Career Total (Turf)	29	7	6	4	157977

108	6/01	Epsm	1m114y	A	G-F	£43500
108	5/01	Kemp	1m	C	G-S	£6188
107	6/00	Hayd	7f30y	A	G-S	£15730
103	4/00	Kemp	1m	B(0-105)H	SFT	£22100
102	8/99	Sand	7f16y	C	G-S	£5885
98	7/99	Hayd	7f30y	C(0-95)H	G-S	£5790
82	8/98	Nott	1m54y	D	G-F	£3886

Total win prize-money £103080

Going (Turf): Sf: 1-4 **GS: 4-8** Gd: 0-9 GF: 2-6 Fm: 0-1
Distance: 5f/6f: 0-0 **7f-8f: 5-21** 9f-13f: 2-8 14f+: 0-0
Track : **LH: 4-10** RH: 3-13 Tight: 1-5 Gall: 1-8
Aids: Bl: 0-0 Vi: 0-0 Tstrap: 0-0
Best Rating: 108 6/01 Epsm 1m114y gd-fm

A very useful mile performer, he landed the Rosebery last season, but has graduated to pattern class since. Posted a career-best effort when snatching the Diomed Stakes on the line at Epsom but was below par in Ireland. He should continue to pay his way. Handles fast and easy ground.

Pulsaar

91(92) (57)**76d**

2-y-o br c Hamas (IRE)-Sure Victory (IRE) (Stalker)
R M Beckett Windsor House Racing

Placings:0430250 **(5079)**
2001: 6^{0}GF, 6^{4}GF, 5^{3}G, 5^{0}G, 5^{2}GF, 5^{5}G, 5^{0}S

	Starts	1st	2nd	3rd	Win & Pl
Career Total (Turf)	7	0	1	1	1119

Going (Turf): Sf: 0-1 GS: 0-0 Gd: 0-3 GF: 0-3 Fm: 0-0
Distance: 5f/6f: 0-6 7f-8f: 0-1 9f-13f: 0-0 14f+: 0-0
Track : LH: 0-1 RH: 0-1 Tight: 0-0 Gall: 0-1
Aids: Bl: 0-1 Vi: 0-0 Tstrap: 0-0
Best Rating: 82 7/01 Chep 6f16y gd-fm

Pulse

99(95) (56)**55**

3-y-o b c Salse (USA)-French Gift (Cadeaux Genereux)
R Hannon Raymond Tooth

Placings:0-000530 **(5392)**
2001: 8^{0}GF, 8^{0}GF, 7^{0}GF, 6^{5}F, 6^{3}SD, 6^{0}SD

	Starts	1st	2nd	3rd	Win & Pl
Career Total (Turf)	5	0	0	0	0
Career Total (AW)	2	0	0	1	353

Going (Turf): Sf: 0-0 GS: 0-0 Gd: 0-1 GF: 0-3 Fm: 0-1
Distance: 5f/6f: 0-3 7f-8f: 0-3 9f-13f: 0-1 14f+: 0-0
Track : LH: 0-2 RH: 0-2 Tight: 0-2 Gall: 0-0
Aids: Bl: 0-0 Vi: 0-0 Tstrap: 0-0
Best Rating: 56 10/01 Wolv 6f stand

Punctuality

(57) (56+)

3-y-o b f Chaddleworth (IRE)-Never Late (Never So Bold)
M R Ewer-Hoad Southdowns Partnership

Placings:06-0 **(0581)**
2001: 8^{0}HY

	Starts	1st	2nd	3rd	Win & Pl
Career Total (Turf)	1	0	0	0	
Career Total (AW)	2	0	0	0	0

Going (Turf): Sf: 0-1 GS: 0-0 Gd: 0-0 GF: 0-0 Fm: 0-0
Distance: 5f/6f: 0-1 7f-8f: 0-1 9f-13f: 0-1 14f+: 0-0
Track : LH: 0-3 RH: 0-0 Tight: 0-2 Gall: 0-0
Aids: Bl: 0-0 Vi: 0-0 Tstrap: 0-0

Punishment

106(110) (77)**67**

10-y-o b h Midyan (USA)-In The Shade (Bustino)
K O Cunningham-Brown A J Richards

Placings:54/3241016623/01215/42406600004/364104100/204062502001054/6363062004300306/2355000624600160-0344132420330 **(5570a)**
2001: 9^{0}SW, 12^{3}SW, 12^{4}SW, 10^{4}SW, 12^{1}SD, 13^{3}SD, 9^{2}F, 9^{4}GF, 10^{2}GS, 12^{0}GF, 10^{3}G, 9^{3}HY, 10^{0}VS, 10^{0}SD

	Starts	1st	2nd	3rd	Win & Pl
Career Total (Turf)	77	7	11	8	216465
Career Total (AW)	20	2	1	4	18149

49	3/01	Wolv	1m4f	D(0-75)	STD	£3191
78	11/00	Wolv	1m1f79y	E(0-75)H	STD	£4225
98	10/98	Leic	1m1f218y	B(0-105)H	SFT	£7746
	11/97	StCl	1m2f110y		HLD	£15713
	8/97	Deau	1m2f		GD	£6734
	6/95	Pari	1m4f		GD	£26347
	5/95	Lonc	1m2f	H	GD	£16168
	7/94	StCl	1m4f		GD	£20595
	6/94	StCl	1m2f	H	G-S	£6865

Total win prize-money £107586

Going (Turf): Sf: 1-13 GS: 0-5 Gd: 0-18 GF: 0-12 Fm: 0-1
Distance: 5f/6f: 0-0 7f-8f: 0-4 **9f-13f: 3-63** 14f+: 0-3
Track : **LH: 2-35** RH: 1-27 **Tight: 2-30** Gall: 0-18
Aids: Bl: 0-0 Vi: 0-1 **Tstrap: 2-43**
Best Rating: 77 2/01 Ling 1m2f slow

In the veteran stage of his career now, he is usually set stiff tasks and is difficult to win with but did manage to win a couple of races on the Wolverhampton Fibresand at the end of last season and at the start of this.

Pup's Pride

84(103) (55)**36**

4-y-o b g Efisio-Moogie (Young Generation)
R A Fahey Declan Kinahan

Placings:00600/500034001220-0103436023463 **(5406)**
2001: 6^{0}SD, 6^{1}SW, 7^{0}SD, 7^{3}SD, 7^{4}SD, 7^{3}SD, 7^{6}SD, 6^{0}GF, 6^{2}SD, 6^{3}SD, 7^{4}SD, 6^{6}SD, 8^{3}SD, 12^{0}SD

	Starts	1st	2nd	3rd	Win & Pl
Career Total (Turf)	12	0	0	0	0
Career Total (AW)	18	2	3	5	6934

58	1/01	Wolv	6f	F(0-60)H	SLW	£1729
53	10/00	Wolv	6f	F(0-60)H	STD	£1799

Total win prize-money £3528

Going (Turf): Sf: 0-4 GS: 0-2 Gd: 0-3 GF: 0-3 Fm: 0-0
Distance: **5f/6f: 2-16** 7f-8f: 0-11 9f-13f: 0-3 14f+: 0-0
Track : **LH: 2-20** RH: 0-3 **Tight: 2-11** Gall: 0-0
Aids: **Bl: 2-13** Vi: 0-4 Tstrap: 0-0
Best Rating: 58 1/01 Wolv 6f slow

Regularly makes the frame on Fibresand, but his only two wins have both come over six furlongs at Wolverhampton.

Puppet King

90 **69**

2-y-o b g Mistertopogigo (IRE)-Bold Gift (Persian Bold)
I A Balding Park House Partnership

Placings:0000 **(3620)**
2001: 6^{0}GF, 7^{0}GF, 6^{0}GF, 7^{0}F

	Starts	1st	2nd	3rd	Win & Pl
Career Total (Turf)	4	0	0	0	

Going (Turf): Sf: 0-0 GS: 0-0 Gd: 0-0 GF: 0-3 Fm: 0-1
Distance: 5f/6f: 0-1 7f-8f: 0-3 9f-13f: 0-0 14f+: 0-0
Track : LH: 0-3 RH: 0-0 Tight: 0-1 Gall: 0-0
Aids: Bl: 0-0 Vi: 0-0 Tstrap: 0-0
Best Rating: 69 7/01 Wwck 7f26y gd-fm

Puppet Play (IRE)

107(104) (71)**65**

6-y-o ch m Broken Hearted-Fantoccini (Taufan (USA))
E J Alston Mrs F D McAuley

Placings:42/0620006422/3342030413210210011120036300 **(4539)**
2001: 6^{1}SD, 6^{1}SD, 7^{2}SD, 6^{0}GF, 6^{0}F, 6^{3}GF, 7^{6}GF, 7^{3}GF, 6^{0}GF, 6^{0}GF

	Starts	1st	2nd	3rd	Win & Pl
Career Total (Turf)	23	2	3	4	13193
Career Total (AW)	17	4	5	2	14166

70	2/01	Sthl	6f	E(0-75)H	STD	£2912
63	2/01	Wolv	6f	E(0-70)H	STD	£2940
59	12/00	Wolv	6f	F(0-65)H	STD	£1788
53	10/00	Wolv	6f	F(0-60)H	STD	£1799
61	8/00	Rdcr	7f	D(0-80)H	FRM	£4771
52	7/00	Pont	1m4y	E(0-70)H	GD	£3068

Total win prize-money £17279

Going (Turf): Sf: 0-2 GS: 0-0 **Gd: 1-7** GF: 0-9 **Fm: 1-4**
Distance: **5f/6f: 4-8** 7f-8f: 1-21 9f-13f: 1-11 14f+: 0-0
Track : **LH: 5-25** RH: 0-8 **Tight: 3-12** Gall: 0-1
Aids: Bl: 0-4 Vi: 0-0 Tstrap: 0-0
Best Rating: 71 4/01 Sthl 7f stand

Pure Coincidence

107(105) (77)**78**

6-y-o b g Lugana Beach-Esilam (Frimley Park)
K R Burke Asterlane Ltd

Placings:51326120/0000034/004013600/300003033200100050 **(5685)**
2001: 5^{0}SD, 5^{1}GS, 5^{0}S, 5^{0}S, 6^{0}G, 5^{6}G, 5^{0}S

	Starts	1st	2nd	3rd	Win & Pl
Career Total (Turf)	34	3	2	6	68674
Career Total (AW)	8	1	1	1	4002

78	3/01	Donc	5f	B(0-105)H	G-S	£21450
78	8/99	Carl	5f	D(0-80)H	G-F	£7620

75 8/97 Rdcr 5f E FRM £2922
77 6/97 Sthl 5f F STD £2277
Total win prize-money £34270

Going (Turf): Sf: 0-11 **GS: 1-5** Gd: 0-10 **GF: 1-7 Fm: 1-1**
Distance: **5f/6f: 4-40** 7f-8f: 0-2 9f-13f: 0-0 14f+: 0-0
Track : LH: 0-9 **RH: 1-3** Tight: 0-8 **Gall: 1-4**
Aids: Bl: 0-3 Vi: 0-1 Tstrap: 0-0
Best Rating: 78 3/01 Donc 5f gd-sft

Fair handicapper, he did not reach the winner's enclosure until the start of the 2001 turf season at Doncaster. Likes to get his toe in these days.

Pure Elegancia

105(98) (49)**51**
5-y-o b m Lugana Beach-Esilam (Frimley Park)
K T Ivory Mrs Andry Muinos

Placings:6401516/024300-3000000400040 **(5497)**
2001: 5^{3}GS, 5^{0}GF, 5^{0}F, 5^{0}GF, 5^{0}GS, 5^{0}GF, 5^{0}GF, 5^{4}G, 5^{0}GF, 5^{0}G, 5^{0}G, 5^{4}SD, 5^{0}HY

	Starts	1st	2nd	3rd	Win & Pl
Career Total (Turf)	25	2	1	2	15331
Career Total (AW)	1	0	0	0	0

69 7/99 Gdwd 5f C(0-90)H G-F £8704
56 6/99 Catt 5f F(0-65)H GD £2416
Total win prize-money £11121

Going (Turf): Sf: 0-1 GS: 0-3 **Gd: 1-9 GF: 1-9** Fm: 0-3
Distance: **5f/6f: 2-26** 7f-8f: 0-0 9f-13f: 0-0 14f+: 0-0
Track : LH: 0-3 RH: 0-1 Tight: 0-1 Gall: 0-1
Aids: Bl: 0-1 Vi: 0-1 Tstrap: 0-0
Best Rating: 67 5/01 Ling 5f gd-sft

Pure Miracle

59 **4**
2-y-o b f Royal Applause-Deerlet (Darshaan)
I A Balding Beechgrove Stud

Placings:0 **(3613)**
2001: 5^{0}G

	Starts	1st	2nd	3rd	Win & Pl
Career Total (Turf)	1	0	0	0	

Going (Turf): Sf: 0-0 GS: 0-0 Gd: 0-1 GF: 0-0 Fm: 0-0
Distance: 5f/6f: 0-1 7f-8f: 0-0 9f-13f: 0-0 14f+: 0-0
Track : LH: 0-0 RH: 0-0 Tight: 0-0 Gall: 0-0
Aids: Bl: 0-0 Vi: 0-0 Tstrap: 0-0
Best Rating: 4 8/01 Nott 5f13y good

Pure Mischief (IRE)

94 **76**
2-y-o b c Alhaarth (IRE)-Bellissi (IRE) (Bluebird (USA))
E A L Dunlop Khalid Ali

Placings:042 **(5527)**
2001: 7^{0}GF, 7^{4}HY, 8^{2}HY

	Starts	1st	2nd	3rd	Win & Pl
Career Total (Turf)	3	0	1	0	1513

Going (Turf): Sf: 0-2 GS: 0-0 Gd: 0-0 GF: 0-1 Fm: 0-0
Distance: 5f/6f: 0-0 7f-8f: 0-2 9f-13f: 0-1 14f+: 0-0
Track : LH: 0-1 RH: 0-0 Tight: 0-0 Gall: 0-0
Aids: Bl: 0-0 Vi: 0-0 Tstrap: 0-0
Best Rating: 76 10/01 Nott 1m54y heavy

Purepleasureseeker (IRE)

87 **65**
2-y-o ch f Grand Lodge (USA)-Bianca Cappello (IRE) (Glenstal (USA))
P F I Cole C Wright & The Hon Mrs J M Corbett

Placings:000 **(4887)**
2001: 6^{0}GF, 7^{0}GF, 7^{0}GF

	Starts	1st	2nd	3rd	Win & Pl
Career Total (Turf)	3	0	0	0	

Going (Turf): Sf: 0-0 GS: 0-0 Gd: 0-0 GF: 0-3 Fm: 0-0
Distance: 5f/6f: 0-1 7f-8f: 0-2 9f-13f: 0-0 14f+: 0-0
Track : LH: 0-0 RH: 0-1 Tight: 0-0 Gall: 0-1
Aids: Bl: 0-0 Vi: 0-0 Tstrap: 0-0
Best Rating: 65 9/01 Kemp 7f gd-fm

Purple Flame (IRE)

96 **37**
5-y-o b m Thatching-Polistatic (Free State)
C A Horgan Mrs B Sumner

Placings:006500/00-50060 **(5469)**
2001: 11^{5}GF, 12^{0}GF, 11^{0}GF, 9^{6}GS, 9^{0}S

	Starts	1st	2nd	3rd	Win & Pl
Career Total (Turf)	13	0	0	0	0

Going (Turf): Sf: 0-1 GS: 0-2 Gd: 0-4 GF: 0-6 Fm: 0-0
Distance: 5f/6f: 0-0 7f-8f: 0-6 9f-13f: 0-7 14f+: 0-0
Track : LH: 0-3 RH: 0-7 Tight: 0-4 Gall: 0-2
Aids: Bl: 0-0 Vi: 0-0 Tstrap: 0-1
Best Rating: 37 6/01 Wwck 1m4f134y gd-fm

Purple Fling

(103) (55d)**50**
10-y-o ch g Music Boy-Divine Fling (Imperial Fling (USA))
Andrew Reid L R Gotch

Placings:621/346140000/55221201100/263455014/460110300/005505000/5460031316/00236304-0 **(0307)**
2001: 6^{0}SD

	Starts	1st	2nd	3rd	Win & Pl
Career Total (Turf)	49	7	5	4	34287
Career Total (AW)	20	3	1	3	9224

63 11/99 Wolv 6f F(0-60) STD £1892
58 9/99 Sthl 6f F(0-60)H STD £2010
76 7/97 Rdcr 7f G(0-75) G-S £2162
70 6/97 Sals 6f C(0-90)H G-F £5277
68 10/96 Folk 6f E(0-70) G-S £3343
76 7/95 Carl 6f206y E(0-70) FRM £3656
71 7/95 Donc 6f E(0-70) FRM £3273
67 6/95 Sthl 6f E(0-70) STD £3130
73 7/94 Carl 5f207y D FRM £3655
68 11/93 Bath 5f161y E GD £3006
Total win prize-money £31409

Going (Turf): Sf: 0-5 GS: 2-10 Gd: 1-13 GF: 1-15 **Fm: 3-6**
Distance: **5f/6f: 8-55** 7f-8f: 2-14 9f-13f: 0-0 14f+: 0-0
Track : **LH: 4-27** RH: 2-4 Tight: 1-15 **Gall: 2-8**
Aids: Bl: 0-0 Vi: 0-0 Tstrap: 0-0
Best Rating: 34 2/01 Sthl 6f stand

Purple Haze (IRE)

103 **87+**
2-y-o b f Spectrum (IRE)-Isticanna (USA) (Far North (CAN))
G A Butler Normandie Stud Ltd

Placings:15 **(5144)**
2001: 7^{1}GF, 7^{5}G

	Starts	1st	2nd	3rd	Win & Pl
Career Total (Turf)	2	1	0	0	5055

87 9/01 Kemp 7f D G-F £4504
Total win prize-money £4505

Going (Turf): Sf: 0-0 GS: 0-0 Gd: 0-1 **GF: 1-1** Fm: 0-0
Distance: 5f/6f: 0-0 **7f-8f: 1-2** 9f-13f: 0-0 14f+: 0-0
Track : LH: 0-0 **RH: 1-1** Tight: 0-0 **Gall: 1-1**
Aids: Bl: 0-0 Vi: 0-0 Tstrap: 0-0
Best Rating: 87 9/01 Kemp 7f gd-fm

A half-sister to Chancellor, she scored nicely on her Kempton debut in September and ran well in a Listed race next time after becoming upset beforehand.

Pursuit Of Dreams

97(103) (62)**51**
4-y-o ch g Pursuit Of Love-Follow The Stars (Sparkler)
P W Harris Backers Dozen

Placings:0005120-63050 **(5166)**
2001: 9^{6}G, 8^{3}SD, 11^{0}GF, 10^{5}F, 9^{0}SD

	Starts	1st	2nd	3rd	Win & Pl
Career Total (Turf)	7	0	0	0	0
Career Total (AW)	5	1	1	1	3579

62 11/00 Wolv 1m1f79y F(0-65)H STD £1960
Total win prize-money £1960

Going (Turf): Sf: 0-2 GS: 0-1 Gd: 0-1 GF: 0-2 Fm: 0-1
Distance: 5f/6f: 0-0 7f-8f: 0-2 **9f-13f: 1-10** 14f+: 0-0
Track : **LH: 1-9** RH: 0-0 **Tight: 1-8** Gall: 0-0
Aids: Bl: 0-0 Vi: 0-0 Tstrap: 0-0
Best Rating: 59 5/01 Wolv 1m100y stand

Pusey Sance

67 **21**
3-y-o br g Puissance-Pusey Street (Native Bazaar)
M R Bosley C R Marks (banbury)

Placings:0000 **(5382)**
2001: 8^{0}GF, 9^{0}GF, 8^{0}GF, 11^{0}S

	Starts	1st	2nd	3rd	Win & Pl
Career Total (Turf)	4	0	0	0	

Going (Turf): Sf: 0-1 GS: 0-0 Gd: 0-0 GF: 0-3 Fm: 0-0
Distance: 5f/6f: 0-0 7f-8f: 0-1 9f-13f: 0-3 14f+: 0-0
Track : LH: 0-1 RH: 0-1 Tight: 0-1 Gall: 0-0
Aids: Bl: 0-0 Vi: 0-0 Tstrap: 0-0
Best Rating: 21 8/01 Sals 1m gd-fm

Putra Pekan

110 **100**
3-y-o b c Grand Lodge (USA)-Mazarine Blue (Bellypha)
M A Jarvis H R H Sultan Ahmad Shah

Placings:0616-54010403 **(5607)**
2001: 7^{5}GS, 7^{4}G, 8^{0}G, 8^{1}GS, 7^{0}G, 7^{4}G, 9^{0}G, 8^{3}GS

	Starts	1st	2nd	3rd	Win & Pl
Career Total (Turf)	12	2	0	1	28247

100 7/01 NmkJ 1m B(0-100)H G-S £17400
89 8/00 Ches 7f2y D GD £3503
Total win prize-money £20904

Going (Turf): Sf: 0-0 **GS: 1-3 Gd: 1-7** GF: 0-2 Fm: 0-0
Distance: 5f/6f: 0-2 **7f-8f: 2-9** 9f-13f: 0-1 14f+: 0-0
Track : **LH: 1-2** RH: 0-1 **Tight: 1-1** Gall: 0-1
Aids: **Bl: 2-6** Vi: 0-0 Tstrap: 0-0
Best Rating: 100 7/01 NmkJ 1m gd-sft

Improved for step-up in trip and blinkers when scoring at Chester as a juvenile. Held at three until the blinkers were reapplied at Newmarket in July, they did not have the same effect after that, and he ran his best race after on the one occasion they where taken off. Suited by a mile and the ground no faster than good, and by a fast-run race as he is usually held up.

Putra Sandhurst (IRE)

107 **112**
3-y-o b c Royal Academy (USA)-Kharimata (IRE) (Kahyasi)
M A Jarvis H R H Sultan Ahmad Shah

Placings:5-20212 **(4241)**
2001: 11^{2}G, 12^{0}GF, 10^{2}G, 12^{1}GF, 14^{2}GF

	Starts	1st	2nd	3rd	Win & Pl
Career Total (Turf)	6	1	3	0	25488

83 7/01 NmkJ 1m4f D G-F £4347
Total win prize-money £4347

Going (Turf): Sf: 0-1 GS: 0-0 Gd: 0-2 **GF: 1-3** Fm: 0-0
Distance: 5f/6f: 0-0 7f-8f: 0-1 **9f-13f: 1-4** 14f+: 0-1
Track : LH: 0-2 **RH: 1-3** Tight: 0-3 **Gall: 1-2**
Aids: Bl: 0-0 Vi: 0-0 Tstrap: 0-0
Best Rating: 112 6/01 Epsm 1m4f10y gd-fm

He ran a good race considering it was only his second ever start to chase home Perfect Sunday in the Lingfield Derby Trial and was not disgraced when eighth in the Derby at Epsom, despite boiling over in the paddock. Ran into Alexius when trying to pick up a maiden at Newmarket, but made no mistake back at the same track two weeks later. Showed he stayed 14 furlongs when second in a Goodwood Listed race.

Puzzle

82 **44**

3-y-o b g First Trump-Eldoret (High Top)
Lady Herries Angmering Park Stud

Placings:00-00 **(5640)**
2001: 10^{0}G, 13^{0}G

	Starts	1st	2nd	3rd	Win & Pl
Career Total (Turf)	4	0	0	0	

Going (Turf): Sf: 0-2 GS: 0-0 **Gd: 0-2** GF: 0-0 Fm: 0-0
Distance: 5f/6f: 0-1 7f-8f: 0-0 9f-13f: 0-2 14f+: 0-1
Track : LH: 0-1 RH: 0-0 Tight: 0-2 Gall: 0-0
Aids: Bl: 0-0 Vi: 0-0 Tstrap: 0-2
Best Rating: 48 5/01 Wind 1m2f7y good

Puzzlement

90(105) (73)**72**

7-y-o gr g Mystiko (USA)-Abuzz (Absalom)
C E Brittain Mrs C E Brittain

Placings:6500500/**5115**2000**6113**/0000665**113**020/504 52645/**3333**10055065-2200 **(2369)**
2001: 12^{2}SD, 10^{2}SD, 12^{0}SW, 12^{0}GF

	Starts	1st	2nd	3rd	Win & Pl
Career Total (Turf)	35	3	3	1	23637
Career Total (AW)	21	4	2	5	25320

73 3/00 Leic 1m3f183yE(0-70)H GD £2856
71 8/98 Bevl 1m1f207yD(0-85)H G-F £7142
61 8/98 Bevl 1m1f207yC(0-90)H G-F £7025
73 11/97 Ling 1m E(0-70)H STD £2791
66 11/97 Ling 1m D(0-80)H STD £2981
60 2/97 Wolv 1m1f79y D(0-80)H STD £3387
59 2/97 Ling 1m E(0-70)H STD £2700
Total win prize-money £28883

Going (Turf): Sf: 0-5 GS: 0-5 Gd: 1-7 **GF: 2-18** Fm: 0-0
Distance: 5f/6f: 0-2 7f-8f: 3-13 **9f-13f: 4-41** 14f+: 0-0
Track : **LH: 4-34** RH: 3-13 **Tight: 4-24** Gall: 0-7
Aids: Bl: 0-0 Vi: 0-0 Tstrap: 0-0
Best Rating: 73 2/01 Ling 1m2f stand

Pyrrhic

80 **42**

2-y-o b c Salse (USA)-Bint Lariaaf (USA) (Diesis)
D R Loder Maktoum Al Maktoum

Placings:6 **(4960)**
2001: 6^{6}S

	Starts	1st	2nd	3rd	Win & Pl
Career Total (Turf)	1	0	0	0	0

Going (Turf): Sf: 0-1 GS: 0-0 Gd: 0-0 GF: 0-0 Fm: 0-0
Distance: 5f/6f: 0-1 7f-8f: 0-0 9f-13f: 0-0 14f+: 0-0
Track : LH: 0-1 RH: 0-0 Tight: 0-0 Gall: 0-0
Aids: Bl: 0-0 Vi: 0-0 Tstrap: 0-0
Best Rating: 42 9/01 Pont 6f soft

Pythagoras

97 **59**

4-y-o ch g Kris-Tricorne (Green Desert (USA))
M Sheppard (W R Muir 4/8) Mike Drake, Tim Doxsey, Ray Hitchin

Placings:40/600-00000 **(3013)**
2001: 10^{0}GS, 10^{0}G, 13^{0}GF, 7^{0}F, 10^{0}GF

	Starts	1st	2nd	3rd	Win & Pl
Career Total (Turf)	10	0	0	0	253

Going (Turf): Sf: 0-0 GS: 0-3 Gd: 0-1 GF: 0-4 Fm: 0-2
Distance: 5f/6f: 0-0 7f-8f: 0-5 9f-13f: 0-4 14f+: 0-1
Track : LH: 0-4 RH: 0-1 Tight: 0-2 Gall: 0-4
Aids: Bl: 0-1 Vi: 0-0 Tstrap: 0-0
Best Rating: 59 4/01 Newb 1m2f6y gd-sft

Qaatef (IRE)

112 **113**

3-y-o b c Darshaan-Solo De Lune (IRE) (Law Society (USA))
Sir Michael Stoute Hamdan Al Maktoum

Placings:13335 **(5237a)**
2001: 10^{1}GF, 11^{3}GF, 11^{3}S, 15^{3}G, 15^{5}VS

	Starts	1st	2nd	3rd	Win & Pl
Career Total (Turf)	5	1	0	3	21354

92 5/01 Sand 1m2f7y D G-F £4641
Total win prize-money £4641

Going (Turf): Sf: 0-1 GS: 0-0 Gd: 0-1 **GF: 1-2** Fm: 0-0
Distance: 5f/6f: 0-0 7f-8f: 0-0 **9f-13f: 1-3** 14f+: 0-2
Track : LH: 0-2 **RH: 1-2** Tight: 0-1 Gall: 0-1
Aids: Bl: 0-0 Vi: 0-2 Tstrap: 0-0
Best Rating: 113 8/01 York 1m7f195y good

Winner of what appeared a decent ten-furlong maiden at Sandown in May 2001 on his debut. Held in his next two runs, but he did not enjoy the fast-run race he needs. Tried at longer trips in the autumn, but pulled too hard on the second occasion. Has won on good to firm ground, but appears to handle softer.

Qandil (USA)

(101) (42)**42**

5-y-o ch g Riverman (USA)-Confirmed Affair (USA) (Affirmed (USA))
Miss J Feilden In The Know (1)

Placings:0/0/00/332-010630 **(0711)**
2001: 6^{0}SD, 7^{1}SW, 7^{0}SD, 6^{6}SD, 7^{3}SW, 7^{0}SD

	Starts	1st	2nd	3rd	Win & Pl
Career Total (Turf)	2	0	0	0	
Career Total (AW)	10	1	1	3	3127

42 1/01 Ling 7f F(0-60)H SLW £1708
Total win prize-money £1708

Going (Turf): Sf: 0-0 GS: 0-0 Gd: 0-2 GF: 0-0 Fm: 0-0
Distance: 5f/6f: 0-5 **7f-8f: 1-5** 9f-13f: 0-2 14f+: 0-0
Track : **LH: 1-10** RH: 0-0 **Tight: 1-9** Gall: 0-0
Aids: Bl: 0-1 **Vi: 1-5** Tstrap: 0-0
Best Rating: 42 1/01 Ling 7f slow

Qualitair Survivor

95(28) (26)**26**

6-y-o gr g Terimon-Comtec Princess (Gulf Pearl)
J Hetherton Qualitair Holdings Limited

Placings:40000**45**/0**4**6000040-00000 **(3187)**
2001: 10^{0}G, 9^{0}G, 8^{0}GF, 8^{0}GF, 11^{0}GS

	Starts	1st	2nd	3rd	Win & Pl
Career Total (Turf)	19	0	0	0	285
Career Total (AW)	2	0	0	0	0

Going (Turf): Sf: 0-1 GS: 0-1 Gd: 0-5 GF: 0-9 Fm: 0-3
Distance: 5f/6f: 0-1 7f-8f: 0-6 9f-13f: 0-13 14f+: 0-1
Track : LH: 0-8 RH: 0-9 Tight: 0-8 Gall: 0-1
Aids: Bl: 0-0 Vi: 0-5 Tstrap: 0-0
Best Rating: 26 6/01 Muss 1m1f good

Qualitair Wings

90 **68**

2-y-o b g Colonel Collins (USA)-Semperflorens (Don)
J Hetherton Qualitair Holdings Limited

Placings:003 **(5633)**
2001: 7^{0}S, 8^{0}S, 7^{3}G

	Starts	1st	2nd	3rd	Win & Pl
Career Total (Turf)	3	0	0	1	412

Going (Turf): Sf: 0-2 GS: 0-0 Gd: 0-1 GF: 0-0 Fm: 0-0
Distance: 5f/6f: 0-0 7f-8f: 0-2 9f-13f: 0-1 14f+: 0-0
Track : LH: 0-1 RH: 0-0 Tight: 0-1 Gall: 0-0
Aids: Bl: 0-0 Vi: 0-0 Tstrap: 0-0
Best Rating: 68 11/01 Catt 7f good

He was unsighted in two starts in the mud but appeared more at home on better ground on his third start.

Quality Sleep (IRE)

91 **60d**

2-y-o b f Mukaddamah (USA)-Blue Bell Lady (Dunphy)
S Dow The Champagno Quartet

Placings:055530 **(3703)**
2001: 5^{0}GS, 5^{5}F, 6^{5}G, 5^{5}GF, 5^{3}F, 5^{0}G

	Starts	1st	2nd	3rd	Win & Pl
Career Total (Turf)	6	0	0	1	260

Going (Turf): Sf: 0-0 GS: 0-1 Gd: 0-2 GF: 0-1 Fm: 0-2
Distance: 5f/6f: 0-6 7f-8f: 0-0 9f-13f: 0-0 14f+: 0-0
Track : LH: 0-3 RH: 0-0 Tight: 0-0 Gall: 0-1
Aids: Bl: 0-0 Vi: 0-0 Tstrap: 0-0
Best Rating: 60 6/01 Ling 5f firm

Quantica (IRE)

96(74) (41)**72+**

2-y-o b g Sri Pekan (USA)-Touche-A-Tout (IRE) (Royal Academy (USA))
N Tinkler Quantica Owners Group

Placings:600011 **(5621)**
2001: 7^{6}SD, 6^{0}G, 7^{0}GF, 7^{0}GF, 6^{1}S, 5^{1}GS

	Starts	1st	2nd	3rd	Win & Pl
Career Total (Turf)	5	2	0	0	6258
Career Total (AW)	1	0	0	0	0

72 11/01 Nott 5f13y E(0-75) G-S £3010
61 10/01 Rdcr 6f E(0-75) SFT £3248
Total win prize-money £6258

Going (Turf): Sf: 1-1 GS: 1-1 Gd: 0-1 GF: 0-2 Fm: 0-0
Distance: **5f/6f: 2-2** 7f-8f: 0-4 9f-13f: 0-0 14f+: 0-0
Track : LH: 0-2 RH: 0-0 Tight: 0-0 Gall: 0-1
Aids: Bl: 0-0 Vi: 0-0 **Tstrap: 2-2**
Best Rating: 72 11/01 Nott 5f13y gd-sft

He suddenly hit form right at the end of the season when encountering soft ground and wearing a tongue-tie, winning nurseries at Redcar and Nottingham.

Quantum Lady

94(95) (56)**70**

3-y-o b f Mujadil (USA)-Folly Finnesse (Joligeneration)
B R Millman N W Lake

Placings:41223641B-0000026604 **(5181)**
2001: 7^{0}GS, 5^{0}S, 6^{0}G, 7^{0}GF, 7^{0}SD, 6^{2}GF, 6^{6}GF, 6^{6}G, 7^{0}HY, 6^{4}HY

	Starts	1st	2nd	3rd	Win & Pl
Career Total (Turf)	18	2	3	1	9853
Career Total (AW)	1	0	0	0	

75 9/00 Nott 6f15y E(0-75) SFT £3289
62 5/00 Bath 5f11y E G-S £2772
Total win prize-money £6061

Going (Turf): Sf: 1-4 GS: 1-4 Gd: 0-4 GF: 0-6 Fm: 0-0
Distance: 5f/6f: 1-12 7f-8f: 1-7 9f-13f: 0-0 14f+: 0-0
Track : **LH: 1-4** RH: 0-2 Tight: 0-0 **Gall: 1-4**
Aids: Bl: 0-0 Vi: 0-0 Tstrap: 0-0
Best Rating: 70 7/01 Sals 6f gd-fm

A winner twice on soft ground as a juvenile, she seems to handle a quicker surface. Usually races prominently.

Quantum Leap

104 **70**

4-y-o b g Efisio-Prejudice (Young Generation)
S Dow Mrs M E O'Shea

Placings:451606400 **(5608)**
2001: 7^{4}GS, 7^{5}GF, 6^{1}F, 8^{6}GS, 8^{0}GF, 7^{6}G, 7^{4}G, 8^{0}GS, 7^{0}GS

	Starts	1st	2nd	3rd	Win & Pl
Career Total (Turf)	9	1	0	0	4575

54 6/01 Ling 6f D FRM £3672
Total win prize-money £3673

Going (Turf): Sf: 0-0 GS: 0-4 Gd: 0-2 GF: 0-2 **Fm: 1-1**
Distance: **5f/6f: 1-1** 7f-8f: 0-8 9f-13f: 0-0 14f+: 0-0
Track : LH: 0-0 RH: 0-0 Tight: 0-0 Gall: 0-0
Aids: Bl: 0-0 Vi: 0-0 Tstrap: 0-0
Best Rating: 79 5/01 Yarm 7f3y gd-fm

A half-brother to Al Moulouki and Hob Green, he was unraced at two and got off the mark in a fast-ground

Lingfield maiden on his third start. Has yet to establish himself in handicaps.

Quarter Masters (IRE)

76 **45**

2-y-o b c Mujadil (USA)-Kentucky Wildcat (Be My Guest (USA))
J L Eyre The Dowdstown Boy'S

Placings:0000 **(5370)**
2001: 6^{0}GF, 7^{0}G, 8^{0}GS, 7^{0}G

	Starts	1st	2nd	3rd	Win & Pl
Career Total (Turf)	4	0	0	0	

Going (Turf): Sf: 0-0 GS: 0-1 Gd: 0-2 GF: 0-1 Fm: 0-0
Distance: 5f/6f: 0-1 7f-8f: 0-3 9f-13f: 0-0 14f+: 0-0
Track : LH: 0-2 RH: 0-0 Tight: 0-1 Gall: 0-1
Aids: Bl: 0-0 Vi: 0-0 Tstrap: 0-1
Best Rating: 45 10/01 Rdcr 7f good

Quatredil (IRE)

(101) (65)

3-y-o b f Mujadil (USA)-Quatre Femme (Petorius)
R Hannon Deauville Daze Partnership

Placings:04060**1U512-1654**02016300**0**2 **(5418)**
2001: 7^{1}SD, 8^{6}SD, 7^{5}SW, 7^{4}SD, 7^{0}G, 5^{2}G, 7^{0}GF, 5^{1}GF, 6^{6}GF, 7^{3}G, 6^{0}G, 7^{0}GF, 5^{0}GS, 7^{2}SD, 7^{0}SD

	Starts	1st	2nd	3rd	Win & Pl
Career Total (Turf)	14	1	1	1	6013
Career Total (AW)	10	3	2	0	8861

64	7/01	Leic	5f218y	E(0-70)H	G-F	£3965
69	1/01	Ling	7f	F(0-65)H	STD	£2919
63	12/00	Wolv	7f	E(0-85)	STD	£2702
62	11/00	Ling	6f	G	STD	£1865

Total win prize-money £11452

Going (Turf): Sf: 0-1 GS: 0-2 Gd: 0-5 **GF: 1-6** Fm: 0-0
Distance: 5f/6f: 2-12 7f-8f: 2-11 9f-13f: 0-1 14f+: 0-0
Track : **LH: 3-12** RH: 0-0 **Tight: 3-10** Gall: 0-1
Aids: Bl: 0-0 Vi: 0-0 Tstrap: 0-0
Best Rating: 69 1/01 Ling 7f stand

She is an effective sort in modest company on turf and sand. Seven furlongs looks her best trip. Acts on a sound surface or turf.

Quazar (IRE)

104 **64**

3-y-o b c Inzar (USA)-Evictress (IRE) (Sharp Victor (USA))
J J O'Neill C D Carr

Placings:03050-42400 **(4535)**
2001: 8^{4}GS, 8^{2}F, 8^{4}G, 8^{0}G, 10^{0}GF

	Starts	1st	2nd	3rd	Win & Pl
Career Total (Turf)	10	0	1	1	1571

Going (Turf): Sf: 0-3 GS: 0-1 Gd: 0-3 GF: 0-2 Fm: 0-1
Distance: 5f/6f: 0-3 7f-8f: 0-1 9f-13f: 0-6 14f+: 0-0
Track : LH: 0-5 RH: 0-3 Tight: 0-3 Gall: 0-1
Aids: Bl: 0-0 Vi: 0-1 Tstrap: 0-0
Best Rating: 64 6/01 Hayd 1m30y good

Quebeck

107 **79**

3-y-o b c Rainbow Quest (USA)-Purbeck (IRE) (Polish Precedent (USA))
H R A Cecil Tprc Limited

Placings:2430 **(5279)**
2001: 12^{2}GF, 12^{4}G, 12^{3}G, 11^{0}S

	Starts	1st	2nd	3rd	Win & Pl
Career Total (Turf)	4	0	1	1	2205

Going (Turf): Sf: 0-1 GS: 0-0 Gd: 0-2 GF: 0-1 Fm: 0-0
Distance: 5f/6f: 0-0 7f-8f: 0-0 9f-13f: 0-4 14f+: 0-0
Track : LH: 0-1 RH: 0-3 Tight: 0-1 Gall: 0-1
Aids: Bl: 0-0 Vi: 0-0 Tstrap: 0-0
Best Rating: 79 8/01 Ripn 1m4f60y good

He has shown ability in maiden company over 12 furlongs, but looks rather one-paced.

Quecha (IRE)

93 **41**

3-y-o b f Indian Ridge-Spain Lane (USA) (Seeking The Gold (USA))
E A L Dunlop (Saeed Bin Suroor 24/8) Maktoum Al Maktoum

Placings:2-40 **(5528)**
2001: 7^{4}G, 8^{0}HY

	Starts	1st	2nd	3rd	Win & Pl
Career Total (Turf)	3	0	1	0	3458

Going (Turf): Sf: 0-1 GS: 0-0 Gd: 0-1 GF: 0-0 Fm: 0-0
Distance: 5f/6f: 0-0 7f-8f: 0-1 9f-13f: 0-1 14f+: 0-0
Track : LH: 0-1 RH: 0-0 Tight: 0-0 Gall: 0-0
Aids: Bl: 0-0 Vi: 0-0 Tstrap: 0-0
Best Rating: 41 8/01 Newc 7f good

Quedex

99(96) (56)**87**

5-y-o b h Deploy-Alwal (Pharly (FR))
E L James L Van Hijkoop

Placings:404004/2114/**60**201400100-40 **(1226)**
2001: 10^{4}GS, 18^{0}GF

	Starts	1st	2nd	3rd	Win & Pl
Career Total (Turf)	21	4	2	0	25349
Career Total (AW)	2	0	0	0	0

87	8/00	Kemp	2m	D(0-85)H	G-F	£6825
79	5/00	Hayd	1m6f	D(0-80)H	GD	£6922
68	6/99	Bath	1m3f144y	E(0-65)	GD	£2682
65	6/99	Gdwd	1m1f192y	D(0-80)H	G-S	£4017

Total win prize-money £20448

Going (Turf): Sf: 0-3 GS: 1-5 **Gd: 2-7** GF: 1-6 Fm: 0-0
Distance: 5f/6f: 0-1 7f-8f: 0-6 9f-13f: 2-8 14f+: 2-8
Track : LH: 2-14 RH: 2-7 **Tight: 2-8** Gall: 0-4
Aids: Bl: 0-0 Vi: 0-0 Tstrap: 0-0
Best Rating: 80 4/01 Newb 1m2f6y gd-sft

Developed into a decent stayer in 2000. Best on a sound surface. Lightly raced in 2001.

Queen Of Fashion (IRE)

99 **40**

5-y-o b m Barathea (IRE)-Valuewise (IRE) (Ahonoora)
J J Sheehan P J Sheehan

Placings:0430000-0500600 **(4523)**
2001: 12^{0}GS, 12^{5}GF, 16^{0}GF, 11^{0}GF, 12^{6}GF, 11^{0}GF, 16^{0}GF

	Starts	1st	2nd	3rd	Win & Pl
Career Total (Turf)	14	0	0	1	956

Going (Turf): Sf: 0-1 GS: 0-1 Gd: 0-3 GF: 0-8 Fm: 0-1
Distance: 5f/6f: 0-0 7f-8f: 0-0 9f-13f: 0-11 14f+: 0-3
Track : LH: 0-5 RH: 0-7 Tight: 0-11 Gall: 0-0
Aids: Bl: 0-0 Vi: 0-1 Tstrap: 0-0
Best Rating: 52 6/01 Wwck 1m4f134y gd-fm

Queen Of The May (IRE)

(96) (51)**80**

4-y-o b f Nicolotte-Varnish (Final Straw)
D Shaw J C Fretwell

Placings:10440441**3**/1654000605000**0340-400** **(0214)**
2001: 6^{4}SD, 5^{0}SD, 5^{0}SD

	Starts	1st	2nd	3rd	Win & Pl
Career Total (Turf)	19	2	0	0	8997
Career Total (AW)	9	1	0	2	2973

80	5/00	Wind	5f10y	D(0-80)H	G-S	£4101
73	11/99	Ling	6f	E(0-75)H	STD	£2278
66	5/99	Brig	5f59y	E	FRM	£3273

Total win prize-money £9654

Going (Turf): Sf: 0-6 **GS: 1-4** Gd: 0-3 GF: 0-3 **Fm: 1-3**
Distance: **5f/6f: 3-27** 7f-8f: 0-1 9f-13f: 0-0 14f+: 0-0
Track : **LH: 2-14** RH: 1-3 Tight: 1-6 Gall: 1-5
Aids: Bl: 0-3 Vi: 0-0 Tstrap: 0-0
Best Rating: 51 1/01 Sthl 6f stand

Queen's College (IRE)

96(84) (23)**45**

3-y-o b f College Chapel-Fairy Lore (IRE) (Fairy King (USA))
M L W Bell K W Green

Placings:0526-**0**00020 **(3961)**
2001: 6^{0}SD, 7^{0}GF, 6^{0}GF, 5^{0}GF, 5^{2}GF, 6^{0}G

	Starts	1st	2nd	3rd	Win & Pl
Career Total (Turf)	9	0	2	0	1547
Career Total (AW)	1	0	0	0	

Going (Turf): Sf: 0-0 GS: 0-0 Gd: 0-3 GF: 0-5 Fm: 0-1
Distance: 5f/6f: 0-7 7f-8f: 0-3 9f-13f: 0-0 14f+: 0-0
Track : LH: 0-5 RH: 0-3 Tight: 0-1 Gall: 0-3
Aids: Bl: 0-0 Vi: 0-0 Tstrap: 0-0
Best Rating: 45 6/01 Wwck 6f21y gd-fm

Queen's Logic (IRE)

114 **120+**

2-y-o ch f Grand Lodge (USA)-Lagrion (USA) (Diesis)
M R Channon Jaber Abdullah

Placings:1111 **(5054)**
2001: 5^{1}S, 5^{1}GF, 6^{1}G, 6^{1}S

	Starts	1st	2nd	3rd	Win & Pl
Career Total (Turf)	4	4	0	0	175696

120	10/01	NmkR	6f	A	SFT	£87000
102	8/01	York	6f	A	GD	£49300
98	6/01	Asct	5f	A	G-F	£33000
85	5/01	Newb	5f34y	C	SFT	£6396

Total win prize-money £175696

Going (Turf): Sf: 2-2 GS: 0-0 Gd: 1-1 GF: 1-1 Fm: 0-0
Distance: **5f/6f: 4-4** 7f-8f: 0-0 9f-13f: 0-0 14f+: 0-0
Track : LH: 0-0 RH: 0-0 Tight: 0-0 Gall: 0-0
Aids: Bl: 0-0 Vi: 0-0 Tstrap: 0-0
Best Rating: 120 10/01 NmkR 6f soft

A well-bred February foal out of a half-sister to Pure Genius, she is a half-sister to the ten-furlong winner Tulsa. Recovering from a slow start, she made a very favourable impression when winning a maiden over five furlongs at Newbury in May, and followed up by winning the Queen Mary at Royal Ascot. Handled the step up to six furlongs when a decisive winner of the Lowther, and annihilated her opponents in the Cheveley Park to claim the title of champion two-year-old filly. The 1000 Guineas is her target for 2002, when she will stay with Godolphin. Acts on fast but probably better suited by softer ground.

Queen's Pageant

103(43) (56)**75**

7-y-o ch m Risk Me (FR)-Mistral's Dancer (Shareef Dancer (USA))
J L Spearing Mrs Robert Heathcote

Placings:510/0005**3/20**0005100/10300005**0**/044651003 03260-64221060 **(5463)**
2001: 10^{6}G, 11^{4}GF, 10^{2}GF, 10^{2}GF, 11^{1}GF, 10^{0}G, 9^{6}S, 11^{0}G

	Starts	1st	2nd	3rd	Win & Pl
Career Total (Turf)	46	5	3	4	35541
Career Total (AW)	4	0	1	1	1756

73	7/01	Wind	1m3f135y	E(0-75)H	G-F	£3038
71	7/00	Wind	1m2f7y	E(0-70)H	G-F	£3318
75	4/99	Thsk	1m	D(0-80)H	GD	£3847
73	10/98	York	6f214y	D(0-85)H	GD	£11697
68	10/96	Hayd	5f	D	SFT	£3485

Total win prize-money £25385

Going (Turf): Sf: 1-16 GS: 0-6 **Gd: 2-15** GF: 1-8 Fm: 0-0
Distance: 5f/6f: 1-7 **7f-8f: 2-16** 9f-13f: 1-26 14f+: 0-0
Track : **LH: 2-22** RH: 0-6 **Tight: 2-17** Gall: 1-6
Aids: Bl: 0-1 Vi: 0-0 Tstrap: 0-0
Best Rating: 75 6/01 Wind 1m2f7y gd-fm

She takes a bit of knowing, but Michael Roberts gets on well with her and managed to get the right tune out of her at Windsor in July. Acts on most types of ground.

Queen's Song

98(65) **38**

3-y-o ch f King's Signet (USA)-Darakah (Doulab (USA))

R J Hodges Footsteps Flyers

Placings:036566-05002400 (4302)
2001: 5^{0}HY, 6^{5}G, 5^{0}F, 5^{0}G, 8^{2}GF, 6^{4}GF, 6^{0}GF, 6^{0}GF

	Starts	1st	2nd	3rd	Win & Pl
Career Total (Turf)	13	0	1	1	965
Career Total (AW)	1	0	0	0	

Going (Turf): Sf: 0-2 GS: 0-1 Gd: 0-2 GF: 0-7 Fm: 0-1
Distance: 5f/6f: 0-11 7f-8f: 0-2 9f-13f: 0-1 14f+: 0-0
Track : LH: 0-8 RH: 0-0 Tight: 0-1 Gall: 0-4
Aids: Bl: 0-0 Vi: 0-0 Tstrap: 0-0
Best Rating: 38 7/01 Chep 1m14y gd-fm

Queenboro Castle (FR)

66 **27**

2-y-o b f Night Shift (USA)-Magic Motion (USA) (Green Dancer (USA))
B J Meehan Mrs E A Lerpiniere

Placings:0 (5277)
2001: 7^{0}GS

	Starts	1st	2nd	3rd	Win & Pl
Career Total (Turf)	1	0	0	0	

Going (Turf): Sf: 0-0 GS: 0-1 Gd: 0-0 GF: 0-0 Fm: 0-0
Distance: 5f/6f: 0-0 7f-8f: 0-1 9f-13f: 0-0 14f+: 0-0
Track : LH: 0-0 RH: 0-0 Tight: 0-0 Gall: 0-0
Aids: Bl: 0-0 Vi: 0-0 Tstrap: 0-0
Best Rating: 27 10/01 Leic 7f9y gd-sft

Queenie

103 **73**

3-y-o b f Indian Ridge-Bint Zamayem (IRE) (Rainbow Quest (USA))
B W Hills Maurice Mogg

Placings:0-321200 (5638)
2001: 7^{3}S, 7^{2}GS, 7^{1}G, 8^{2}GS, 8^{0}G, 7^{0}G

	Starts	1st	2nd	3rd	Win & Pl
Career Total (Turf)	7	1	2	1	17185

65 7/01 Ches 7f122y D GD £4231
Total win prize-money £4232

Going (Turf): Sf: 0-1 GS: 0-3 Gd: 1-3 GF: 0-0 Fm: 0-0
Distance: 5f/6f: 0-0 7f-8f: 1-6 9f-13f: 0-1 14f+: 0-0
Track : LH: 1-3 RH: 0-1 Tight: 1-2 Gall: 0-1
Aids: Bl: 0-0 Vi: 0-0 Tstrap: 0-0
Best Rating: 86 4/01 NmkR 7f soft

Gradually improving and got off the mark at Chester in July despite not handling the track. Suited by a mile.

Queens Bench (IRE)

103(76) (9)**68d**

4-y-o ch f Wolfhound (USA)-Zafaaf (Kris)
P C Haslam Alex Gorrie Combi (uk)

Placings:423311/40506000-0004300 (5611)
2001: 5^{0}S, 6^{0}G, 7^{0}GF, 8^{4}G, 9^{3}GF, 9^{0}G, 8^{0}SD

	Starts	1st	2nd	3rd	Win & Pl
Career Total (Turf)	20	2	1	3	16212
Career Total (AW)	1	0	0	0	

85 8/99 Epsm 7f C H GD £6970
78 8/99 Bevl 5f D GD £3488
Total win prize-money £10458

Going (Turf): Sf: 0-3 GS: 0-4 Gd: 2-5 GF: 0-8 Fm: 0-0
Distance: 5f/6f: 1-8 7f-8f: 1-9 9f-13f: 0-4 14f+: 0-0
Track : LH: 1-6 RH: 0-3 Tight: 1-4 Gall: 0-4
Aids: Bl: 0-0 Vi: 0-0 Tstrap: 0-2
Best Rating: 60 6/01 Thsk 1m good

Held in a variety of races this term, slipping down the weights as a result. Ran perhaps her best race at a mile.

Queens Musician

96 **61d**

3-y-o b g Piccolo-Queens Welcome (Northfields (USA))
G A Swinbank (Mrs J R Ramsden 5/7) Alan Swinbank

Placings:3303-000005 (3844)
2001: 7^{0}S, 6^{0}G, 6^{0}GF, 5^{0}GF, 7^{0}GF, 10^{5}G

	Starts	1st	2nd	3rd	Win & Pl
Career Total (Turf)	10	0	0	3	1480

Going (Turf): Sf: 0-1 GS: 0-0 Gd: 0-4 GF: 0-4 Fm: 0-1
Distance: 5f/6f: 0-/ 7f-8f: 0-2 9f-13f: 0-1 14f+: 0-0
Track : LH: 0-2 RH: 0-0 Tight: 0-1 Gall: 0-0
Aids: Bl: 0-1 Vi: 0-0 Tstrap: 0-0
Best Rating: 48 8/01 Rdcr 1m2f good

Has shown ability in maidens on fast ground. Below form on soft, may be worth a try over further.

Queens Stroller (IRE)

88(96) (27)**22**

10-y-o b m Pennine Walk-Mount Isa (Miami Springs)
R E Peacock R E Peacock

Placings:00530211/351362006056224 2/11600420000 4/00000046/253241405020/4400050/0000-502006006 (4262)
2001: 9^{5}SD, 9^{0}SW, 9^{2}SW, 9^{0}SD, 7^{0}GF, 11^{6}G, 11^{0}F, 9^{0}GS, 11^{6}GF

	Starts	1st	2nd	3rd	Win & Pl
Career Total (Turf)	43	1	4	1	8191
Career Total (AW)	34	5	6	3	22669

38 5/97 Sthl 1m E(0-70)H STD £3174
57 3/95 Folk 1m1f149yE(0-70)H GD £3388
66 3/95 Wolv 1m1f79y E(0-70)H STD £2814
59 2/94 Sthl 7f D(0-80)H STD £3557
66 12/93 Sthl 7f D(0-75) STD £3494
61 12/93 Sthl 7f D(0-75) STD £3523
Total win prize-money £19952

Going (Turf): Sf: 0-2 GS: 0-6 Gd: 1-14 GF: 0-17 Fm: 0-4
Distance: 5f/6f: 0-3 7f-8f: 4-21 9f-13f: 2-53 14f+: 0-0
Track : LH: 5-54 RH: 1-11 Tight: 2-38 Gall: 0-2
Aids: Bl: 0-3 Vi: 0-1 Tstrap: 0-0
Best Rating: 27 1/01 Wolv 1m1f79y slow

Queensberry

66 **54**

2-y-o b c Up And At 'Em-Princess Poquito (Hard Fought)
A P Jarvis Jarvis Associates

Placings:00 (4794)
2001: 6^{0}GF, 7^{0}G

	Starts	1st	2nd	3rd	Win & Pl
Career Total (Turf)	2	0	0	0	

Going (Turf): Sf: 0-0 GS: 0-0 Gd: 0-1 GF: 0-1 Fm: 0-0
Distance: 5f/6f: 0-1 7f-8f: 0-1 9f-13f: 0-0 14f+: 0-0
Track : LH: 0-0 RH: 0-0 Tight: 0-0 Gall: 0-0
Aids: Bl: 0-0 Vi: 0-0 Tstrap: 0-0
Best Rating: 54 9/01 Ayr 7f50y good

Quest For Glory (IRE)

95(94) (85)**85**

2-y-o b c Fayruz-Moyhora (IRE) (Nashamaa)
G C Bravery Sawyer, Webb, Whatley

Placings:4310200101 (5194)
2001: 5^{1}SD, 5^{3}GS, 5^{1}F, 6^{0}GF, 6^{2}G, 5^{0}GS, 6^{0}GS, 5^{1}G, 6^{0}GF, 5^{1}SD

	Starts	1st	2nd	3rd	Win & Pl
Career Total (Turf)	8	2	1	1	7711
Career Total (AW)	2	1	0	0	3520

85 10/01 Wolv 5f D STD £3519
85 9/01 Haml 5f4y E GD £3416
67 5/01 Brig 5f213y E FRM £2884
Total win prize-money £9820

Going (Turf): Sf: 0-0 GS: 0-3 Gd: 1-2 GF: 0-2 Fm: 1-1
Distance: 5f/6f: 3-9 7f-8f: 0-1 9f-13f: 0-0 14f+: 0-0
Track : LH: 2-4 RH: 0-0 Tight: 1-3 Gall: 0-0
Aids: Bl: 0-0 Vi: 0-0 Tstrap: 0-0
Best Rating: 85 10/01 Wolv 5f stand

He managed to win three times this season, at Brighton and Hamilton and on sand at Wolverhampton. Suited by forcing tactics and though he has won over five furlongs, looks better over six.

Quest On Air

81 **47**

2-y-o b g Star Quest-Stormy Heights (Golden Heights)
J R Jenkins David Morris

Placings:0 (5604)
2001: 7^{0}GS

	Starts	1st	2nd	3rd	Win & Pl
Career Total (Turf)	1	0	0	0	

Going (Turf): Sf: 0-0 GS: 0-1 Gd: 0-0 GF: 0-0 Fm: 0-0
Distance: 5f/6f: 0-0 7f-8f: 0-1 9f-13f: 0-0 14f+: 0-0
Track : LH: 0-0 RH: 0-0 Tight: 0-0 Gall: 0-0
Aids: Bl: 0-0 Vi: 0-0 Tstrap: 0-0
Best Rating: 47 11/01 NmkR 7f gd-sft

Qui Warranto (IRE)

87 **38**

3-y-o ch g Spectrum (IRE)-Braneakins (Sallust)
J G Fitzgerald Marquesa De Moratalla

Placings:0400-0000 (3844)
2001: 8^{0}G, 9^{0}GF, 9^{0}GF, 10^{0}G

	Starts	1st	2nd	3rd	Win & Pl
Career Total (Turf)	8	0	0	0	316

Going (Turf): Sf: 0-0 GS: 0-2 Gd: 0-4 GF: 0-2 Fm: 0-0
Distance: 5f/6f: 0-1 7f-8f: 0-3 9f-13f: 0-4 14f+: 0-0
Track : LH: 0-4 RH: 0-3 Tight: 0-2 Gall: 0-1
Aids: Bl: 0-0 Vi: 0-0 Tstrap: 0-0
Best Rating: 38 7/01 Bevl 1m1f207y gd-fm

Quibble

98 **38**

4-y-o ch g Lammtarra (USA)-Blou Dan (USA) (Damascus (USA))
A Bailey Www.Mark-Kilner-Racing.Com (16)

Placings:646-0450 (4614)
2001: 10^{0}S, 12^{4}GF, 8^{5}GF, 13^{0}F

	Starts	1st	2nd	3rd	Win & Pl
Career Total (Turf)	7	0	0	0	1345

Going (Turf): Sf: 0-1 GS: 0-0 Gd: 0-0 GF: 0-2 Fm: 0-1
Distance: 5f/6f: 0-0 7f-8f: 0-0 9f-13f: 0-3 14f+: 0-1
Track : LH: 0-4 RH: 0-0 Tight: 0-1 Gall: 0-1
Aids: Bl: 0-2 Vi: 0-0 Tstrap: 0-0
Best Rating: 38 7/01 Newc 1m4f93y gd-fm

Quick To Please (USA)

106 **102+**

3-y-o b f Danzig (USA)-Razyana (USA) (His Majesty (USA))
H R A Cecil K Abdulla

Placings:1-30 (2382)
2001: 8^{3}GF, 10^{0}GF

	Starts	1st	2nd	3rd	Win & Pl
Career Total (Turf)	3	1	0	1	7046

89 10/00 Donc 1m D GD £4371
Total win prize-money £4371

Going (Turf): Sf: 0-0 GS: 0-0 Gd: 1-1 GF: 0-2 Fm: 0-0
Distance: 5f/6f: 0-0 7f-8f: 1-2 9f-13f: 0-1 14f+: 0-0
Track : LH: 1-1 RH: 0-2 Tight: 0-0 Gall: 1-2
Aids: Bl: 0-0 Vi: 0-0 Tstrap: 0-0
Best Rating: 102 5/01 Gdwd 1m gd-fm

Highly-touted filly. Won well on her only start at two in a maiden at Doncaster. Ran too freely in a Listed race at Goodwood in May and disappointed in a similar event at Ascot. Has gone to the USA.

Quicknap (USA)

87 **75**

2-y-o ch c Hennessy (USA)-Time Knap (USA) (Timeless Native (USA))
H Candy M L Al Bastl

Placings:355 (5126)
2001: 5^{3}F, 6^{5}GF, 6^{5}HY

	Starts	1st	2nd	3rd	Win & Pl
Career Total (Turf)	3	0	0	1	521

Going (Turf): Sf: 0-1 GS: 0-0 Gd: 0-0 GF: 0-1 Fm: 0-1
Distance: 5f/6f: 0-3 7f-8f: 0-0 9f-13f: 0-0 14f+: 0-0
Track : LH: 0-1 RH: 0-1 Tight: 0-0 Gall: 0-1
Aids: Bl: 0-0 Vi: 0-0 Tstrap: 0-0
Best Rating: 75 8/01 NmkJ 6f gd-fm

Quids Inn

(93) (41)**52**
4-y-o br g Timeless Times (USA)-Waltz On Air (Doc Marten)
M Quinn A Arton

Placings:650000/2006000265-00035 **(0343)**
2001: 8^0SD, 7^0SD, 7^0SW, 8^3SW, 8^5SW

	Starts	1st	2nd	3rd	Win & Pl
Career Total (Turf)	11	0	1	0	988
Career Total (AW)	10	0	1	1	649

Going (Turf): Sf: 0-1 GS: 0-3 Gd: 0-2 GF: 0-3 Fm: 0-2
Distance: 5f/6f: 0-4 7f-8f: 0-14 9f-13f: 0-3 14f+: 0-0
Track : LH: 0-13 RH: 0-2 Tight: 0-11 Gall: 0-1
Aids: Bl: 0-1 Vi: 0-0 Tstrap: 0-0
Best Rating: 41 2/01 Ling 1m slow

Quiet Reading (USA)

86(99) (59)**51d**
4-y-o b g Northern Flagship (USA)-Forlis Key (USA) (Forli (ARG))
M R Bosley Mrs Jean M O'Connor

Placings:003640526426-324500 **(2547)**
2001: 12^3SW, 12^2SD, 12^4SD, 12^5SD, 11^0SD, 9^0GF, 12^0SD

	Starts	1st	2nd	3rd	Win & Pl
Career Total (Turf)	6	0	0	1	672
Career Total (AW)	12	0	3	1	2356

Going (Turf): Sf: 0-2 GS: 0-0 Gd: 0-2 GF: 0-2 Fm: 0-0
Distance: 5f/6f: 0-0 7f-8f: 0-1 9f-13f: 0-14 14f+: 0-3
Track : LH: 0-13 RH: 0-3 Tight: 0-12 Gall: 0-1
Aids: Bl: 0-0 Vi: 0-0 Tstrap: 0-0
Best Rating: 59 1/01 Sthl 1m4f slow

Quiet Traveller (IRE)

104 **69**
3-y-o b g Blues Traveller (IRE)-Quietly Impressive (IRE) (Taufan (USA))
Miss L A Perratt Jamarac Construction Ltd

Placings:0000-014422211325356 **(5657)**
2001: 8^0S, 8^1F, 8^4F, 10^4GF, 8^2G, 9^2GF, 8^2GF, 9^1GF, 10^1F, 9^3G, 8^2GS, 8^5G, 8^3GS, 10^5HY, 8^6G

	Starts	1st	2nd	3rd	Win & Pl
Career Total (Turf)	19	3	4	2	19994

66	7/01	Rdcr	1m2f	E(0-75)H	FRM	£5255
66	7/01	Muss	1m1f	E(0-70)H	G-F	£4387
51	5/01	Haml	1m65y	E(0-70)H	FRM	£3486

Total win prize-money £13129

Going (Turf): Sf: 0-3 GS: 0-3 Gd: 0-5 GF: 1-5 **Fm: 2-3**
Distance: 5f/6f: 0-1 7f-8f: 0-8 **9f-13f: 3-10** 14f+: 0-0
Track : LH: 1-11 RH: 1-6 **Tight: 2-9** Gall: 0-4
Aids: Bl: 0-1 Vi: 0-0 Tstrap: 0-0
Best Rating: 69 8/01 Thsk 1m gd-sft

Fair handicapper, successful three times in 2001 between eight to ten furlongs. Suited by fast ground.

Quiet Venture

(103) (66)58
7-y-o b g Rainbow Quest (USA)-Jameelaty (USA) (Nureyev (USA))
J A Glover (B W Hills 15/1) David Jenkins

Placings:0430/000111010/023665/000041000**06410-500** **(5616)**
2001: 7^5SD, 6^0SD, 7^0SD

	Starts	1st	2nd	3rd	Win & Pl
Career Total (Turf)	25	4	1	2	17574
Career Total (AW)	11	2	0	0	5753

66	12/00	Wolv	6f	F	STD	£2268
59	8/00	Carl	6f206y	F(0-60)	FRM	£2299
88	11/98	Wolv	6f	D(0-85)H	STD	£3485
78	8/98	Newc	7f	C(0-90)H	G-F	£7067
74	8/98	Muss	7f30y	E(0-70)	G-F	£2784
65	8/98	Rdcr	1m	F(0-65)	FRM	£2346

Total win prize-money £20252

Going (Turf): Sf: 0-2 GS: 0-1 Gd: 0-10 **GF: 2-6 Fm: 2-6**
Distance: 5f/6f: 2-7 **7f-8f: 4-20** 9f-13f: 0-9 14f+: 0-0
Track : LH: 2-18 RH: 2-10 **Tight: 3-19** Gall: 0-2
Aids: Bl: 0-1 Vi: 2-9 Tstrap: 2-18
Best Rating: 66 1/01 Sthl 7f stand

He had shown little for quite a while, but bounced back to form with all-the-way wins at Redcar, Musselburgh and Newcastle in August 1998, and got off the mark on Fibresand with a brave performance at Wolverhampton in November. His first turf run this year was indifferent, and it is hard to assess the value of the form which saw him finish second in a four horse-race recently.

Quinta Lad

95(84) (62)**62**
3-y-o b g Alhijaz-Jersey Belle (Distant Relative)
J Balding J M Lacey

Placings:06-650 **(5490)**
2001: 8^6HY, 7^5G, 7^0HY

	Starts	1st	2nd	3rd	Win & Pl
Career Total (Turf)	4	0	0	0	0
Career Total (AW)	1	0	0	0	0

Going (Turf): Sf: 0-3 GS: 0-0 Gd: 0-1 GF: 0-0 Fm: 0-0
Distance: 5f/6f: 0-2 7f-8f: 0-2 9f-13f: 0-1 14f+: 0-0
Track : LH: 0-1 RH: 0-0 Tight: 0-0 Gall: 0-0
Aids: Bl: 0-0 Vi: 0-0 Tstrap: 0-1
Best Rating: 54 10/01 Rdcr 7f good

Quite A Night

79(98) (74)47
2-y-o b c Night Shift (USA)-Ellebanna (Tina's Pet)
J W Hills Lionel Godfrey

Placings:0 **(5099)**
2001: 6^0GS

	Starts	1st	2nd	3rd	Win & Pl
Career Total (Turf)	1	0	0	0	

Going (Turf): Sf: 0-0 GS: 0-1 Gd: 0-0 GF: 0-0 Fm: 0-0
Distance: 5f/6f: 0-0 7f-8f: 0-1 9f-13f: 0-0 14f+: 0-0
Track : LH: 0-0 RH: 0-0 Tight: 0-0 Gall: 0-0
Aids: Bl: 0-0 Vi: 0-0 Tstrap: 0-0
Best Rating: 47 10/01 Sals 6f212y gd-sft

Quite Frankly

81 **44**
3-y-o b g Environment Friend-Four-Legged Friend (Aragon)
Dr J D Scargill The Inn Crowd

Placings:00000 **(5601)**
2001: 8^0S, 8^0G, 8^0F, 12^0GS, 8^0GS

	Starts	1st	2nd	3rd	Win & Pl
Career Total (Turf)	5	0	0	0	

Going (Turf): Sf: 0-1 GS: 0-2 Gd: 0-1 GF: 0-0 Fm: 0-1
Distance: 5f/6f: 0-0 7f-8f: 0-3 9f-13f: 0-2 14f+: 0-0
Track : LH: 0-0 RH: 0-1 Tight: 0-0 Gall: 0-1
Aids: Bl: 0-0 Vi: 0-0 Tstrap: 0-0
Best Rating: 51 4/01 NmkR 1m soft

Quite Happy (IRE)

95(88) (38)**51**
6-y-o b m Statoblest-Four-Legged Friend (Aragon)
W J Musson Mrs Valerie Bennett

Placings:02/031030/020000031400/033353642222040-000 **(2718)**
2001: 5^0G, 5^0GF, 6^0GF

	Starts	1st	2nd	3rd	Win & Pl
Career Total (Turf)	37	2	6	7	14216
Career Total (AW)	1	0	0	0	

58	8/99	Catt	5f	F	GD	£2143
76	5/98	Folk	5f	E(0-70)H	G-F	£2950

Total win prize-money £5094

Going (Turf): Sf: 0-2 GS: 0-4 **Gd: 1-8 GF: 1-16** Fm: 0-7
Distance: **5f/6f: 2-38** 7f-8f: 0-0 9f-13f: 0-0 14f+: 0-0
Track : LH: 0-9 RH: 0-5 Tight: 0-1 Gall: 0-8
Aids: Bl: 0-1 Vi: 0-2 Tstrap: 0-0
Best Rating: 43 7/01 Kemp 6f gd-fm

Quite Remarkable

98(66) (17)**73**
2-y-o b g Danzig Connection (USA)-Kathy Fair (IRE) (Nicholas Bill)
W G M Turner Sporting Edge Partnership

Placings:35104 **(3480)**
2001: 5^3S, 5^5GS, 5^1GF, 5^0SD, 5^4GF

	Starts	1st	2nd	3rd	Win & Pl
Career Total (Turf)	4	1	0	1	4147
Career Total (AW)	1	0	0	0	

73	5/01	Thsk	5f	E	G-F	£3705

Total win prize-money £3705

Going (Turf): Sf: 0-1 GS: 0-1 Gd: 0-0 **GF: 1-2** Fm: 0-0
Distance: **5f/6f: 1-5** 7f-8f: 0-0 9f-13f: 0-0 14f+: 0-0
Track : LH: 0-2 RH: 0-0 Tight: 0-1 Gall: 0-0
Aids: Bl: 0-0 Vi: 0-0 Tstrap: 0-0
Best Rating: 73 5/01 Thsk 5f gd-fm

Out of a half-sister to Chester Cup winner Silence In Court. A bit of a nervous type,he got off the mark on his third outing at two in a Thirsk claimer on fast ground. Had one run on the All-Weather but did not handle the surface. Should stay further in time.

Quitte La France

105 **75**
3-y-o b f Saddlers' Hall (IRE)-Tafila (Adonijah)
J G Given (Mrs J R Ramsden 25/5) Mr & Mrs G Middlebrook/mr & Mrs P Brain

Placings:1-400U034 **(3753)**
2001: 8^4S, 8^0S, 8^0S, 8^UF, 12^0GF, 11^3S, 11^4GS

	Starts	1st	2nd	3rd	Win & Pl
Career Total (Turf)	8	1	0	1	5133

79	9/00	Rdcr	7f	D	SFT	£3146

Total win prize-money £3146

Going (Turf): Sf: 1-5 GS: 0-1 Gd: 0-0 GF: 0-1 Fm: 0-1
Distance: 5f/6f: 0-0 **7f-8f: 1-4** 9f-13f: 0-4 14f+: 0-0
Track : LH: 0-5 RH: 0-1 Tight: 0-1 Gall: 0-2
Aids: Bl: 0-1 Vi: 0-0 Tstrap: 0-0
Best Rating: 75 7/01 Hayd 1m3f200y soft

A late foal, she was a surprise winner on her only juvenile run. She has run some fair races over middle distances this term, but has also looked less than enthusiastic. Best on soft ground.

Quizzical

90 **44**
3-y-o ch g Indian Ridge-Mount Row (Alzao (USA))
A C Stewart Lord Hartington

Placings:0200 **(5400)**
2001: 8^0G, 10^2GF, 12^0GF, 10^0S

	Starts	1st	2nd	3rd	Win & Pl
Career Total (Turf)	4	0	1	0	2043

Going (Turf): Sf: 0-1 GS: 0-0 Gd: 0-1 GF: 0-2 Fm: 0-0
Distance: 5f/6f: 0-0 7f-8f: 0-1 9f-13f: 0-3 14f+: 0-0
Track : LH: 0-2 RH: 0-1 Tight: 0-0 Gall: 0-1
Aids: Bl: 0-0 Vi: 0-0 Tstrap: 0-0
Best Rating: 63 5/01 NmkR 1m good

Ra Ra Rasputin

77(97) (15)12

6-y-o b g Petong-Ra Ra Girl (Shack (USA))

B P J Baugh A J Deakin

Placings:0660100/00530400040 2/000060200300/1410 000000000-00060006 (3858)

2001: 7^{0}SD, 7^{0}SW, 8^{0}SW, 7^{6}SW, 9^{0}SD, 11^{0}SD, 10^{0}GF, 11^{6}GS

	Starts	1st	2nd	3rd	Win & Pl
Career Total (Turf)	27	0	1	1	2067
Career Total (AW)	26	3	1	1	22998
53 1/00 Wolv 7f		G		STD	£1536
54 1/00 Wolv 7f		G		STD	£1895
82 8/97 Wolv 6f		B		STD	£18555

Total win prize-money £21988

Going (Turf): Sf: 0-3 GS: 0-10 Gd: 0-4 GF: 0-9 Fm: 0-1
Distance: 5f/6f: 1-10 **7f-8f: 2-22** 9f-13f: 0-21 14f+: 0-0
Track: **LH: 3-40** RH: 0-1 **Tight: 3-25** Gall: 0-0
Aids: Bl: 0-7 Vi: 0-1 Tstrap: 0-0
Best Rating: 15 1/01 Wolv 7f slow

Scored a 50/1 shock win in the Weatherbys Dash at Wolverhampton in '97 and obviously likes Fibresand. A tight left-handed track suits, as he has run some of his best races on turf at Chester.

Ra-Boob (IRE)

90 57

2-y-o b f Alhaarth (IRE)-Harmless Albatross (Pas De Seul)

J L Dunlop Hamdan Al Maktoum

Placings:00 (5112)

2001: 7^{0}GF, 8^{0}HY

	Starts	1st	2nd	3rd	Win & Pl
Career Total (Turf)	2	0	0	0	

Going (Turf): Sf: 0-1 GS: 0-0 Gd: 0-0 GF: 0-1 Fm: 0-0
Distance: 5f/6f: 0-0 7f-8f: 0-1 9f-13f: 0-1 14f+: 0-0
Track: LH: 0-1 RH: 0-0 Tight: 0-0 Gall: 0-0
Aids: Bl: 0-0 Vi: 0-0 Tstrap: 0-0
Best Rating: 57 10/01 Nott 1m54y heavy

Raahyeh (USA)

66(92) (63)

3-y-o ch f Rahy (USA)-Queen's Gallery (USA) (Forty Niner (USA))

M R Channon Sheikh Ahmed Al Maktoum

Placings:43-300 (0640)

2001: 5^{3}SD, 6^{0}SW, 5^{0}S

	Starts	1st	2nd	3rd	Win & Pl
Career Total (Turf)	1	0	0	0	
Career Total (AW)	4	0	0	2	1038

Going (Turf): Sf: 0-1 GS: 0-0 Gd: 0-0 GF: 0-0 Fm: 0-0
Distance: 5f/6f: 0-5 7f-8f: 0-0 9f-13f: 0-0 14f+: 0-0
Track: LH: 0-4 RH: 0-0 Tight: 0-2 Gall: 0-0
Aids: Bl: 0-0 Vi: 0-0 Tstrap: 0-0
Best Rating: 58 1/01 Ling 5f stand

Raajiya (USA)

102 81+

3-y-o ch f Gulch (USA)-Elrafa Ah (USA) (Storm Cat (USA))

M P Tregoning Hamdan Al Maktoum

Placings:10 (3850)

2001: 7^{1}GF, 8^{0}G

	Starts	1st	2nd	3rd	Win & Pl
Career Total (Turf)	2	1	0	0	4232
81 5/01 Gdwd 7f		D		G-F	£4231

Total win prize-money £4232

Going (Turf): Sf: 0-0 GS: 0-0 Gd: 0-1 **GF: 1-1** Fm: 0-0
Distance: 5f/6f: 0-0 **7f-8f: 1-2** 9f-13f: 0-0 14f+: 0-0
Track: LH: 0-0 **RH: 1-2** Tight: 0-0 Gall: 0-1
Aids: Bl: 0-0 Vi: 0 0 Tstrap: 0-0
Best Rating: 81 5/01 Gdwd 7f gd-fm

A half-sister to Mujahid, she made a winning debut in a maiden at Goodwood in May which worked out very well, but ran poorly in an Ascot Listed event. Stays seven furlongs. Acts on fast ground.

Rabwah (USA)

77 73+

2-y-o ch f Gone West (USA)-Mamlakah (IRE) (Unfuwain (USA))

Sir Michael Stoute Hamdan Al Maktoum

Placings:6 (3960)

2001: 6^{6}G

	Starts	1st	2nd	3rd	Win & Pl
Career Total (Turf)	1	0	0	0	0

Going (Turf): Sf: 0-0 GS: 0-0 Gd: 0-1 GF: 0-0 Fm: 0-0
Distance: 5f/6f: 0-0 7f-8f: 0-1 9f-13f: 0-0 14f+: 0-0
Track: LH: 0-0 RH: 0-0 Tight: 0-0 Gall: 0-0
Aids: Bl: 0-0 Vi: 0-0 Tstrap: 0-0
Best Rating: 73 8/01 Yarm 6f3y good

Rachel Green (IRE)

89(78) (15)27

3-y-o b f Case Law-Alzeam (IRE) (Alzao (USA))

C N Allen Newmarketconnections.Com

Placings:604-00005 (5187)

2001: 5^{0}SW, 5^{0}SW, 5^{0}SD, 6^{0}SD, 5^{5}GS

	Starts	1st	2nd	3rd	Win & Pl
Career Total (Turf)	4	0	0	0	260
Career Total (AW)	4	0	0	0	

Going (Turf): Sf: 0-0 GS: 0-1 Gd: 0-0 GF: 0-2 Fm: 0-1
Distance: 5f/6f: 0-8 7f-8f: 0-0 9f-13f: 0-0 14f+: 0-0
Track: LH: 0-5 RH: 0-0 Tight: 0-4 Gall: 0-0
Aids: Bl: 0-0 Vi: 0-0 Tstrap: 0-0
Best Rating: 27 10/01 Catt 5f212y gd-sft

Racina

105 101

3-y-o ch f Bluebird (USA)-Swellegant (Midyan (USA))

W J Haggas I A Southcott

Placings:2130-04060 (4284)

2001: 5^{0}G, 6^{4}GF, 6^{0}GF, 5^{6}GF, 6^{0}G

	Starts	1st	2nd	3rd	Win & Pl
Career Total (Turf)	9	1	1	1	10110
79 8/00 Bevl 5f		D		G-F	£3727

Total win prize-money £3728

Going (Turf): Sf: 0-0 GS: 0-1 Gd: 0-4 **GF: 1-4** Fm: 0-0
Distance: **5f/6f: 1-8** 7f-8f: 0-1 9f-13f: 0-0 14f+: 0-0
Track: LH: 0-0 RH: 0-0 Tight: 0-0 Gall: 0-0
Aids: Bl: 0-0 Vi: 0-0 Tstrap: 0-0
Best Rating: 101 5/01 Hayd 6f gd-fm

She did not show much at Newmarket on her seasonal debut but appeared to appreciate the extra furlong back against her own age group at Haydock. Acts on fast ground. Six furlongs or further looks her trip now.

Racing Bailey's

98 93

2-y-o b c Zamindar (USA)-Sioux City (Simply Great (FR))

M Johnston G R Bailey Ltd (baileys Horse Feeds)

Placings:541010520 (5364)

2001: 5^{5}GS, 5^{4}S, 6^{1}GS, 7^{0}G, 6^{1}S, 6^{0}G, 6^{5}GF, 6^{2}G, 6^{0}GS

	Starts	1st	2nd	3rd	Win & Pl
Career Total (Turf)	9	2	1	0	9921
89 8/01 Haml 6f5y		D		SFT	£4153
92 7/01 Ayr 6f		E		G-S	£3237

Total win prize-money £7392

Going (Turf): Sf: 1-2 GS: 1-3 Gd: 0-3 GF: 0-1 Fm: 0-0
Distance: 5f/6f: 1-6 7f-8f: 1-3 9f-13f: 0-0 14f+: 0-0
Track: LH: 0-0 RH: 0-1 Tight: 0-0 Gall: 0-0
Aids: Bl: 0-0 Vi: 0-0 Tstrap: 0-0
Best Rating: 93 10/01 NmkR 6f good

Bred to stay. He gradually improved and got off the mark with a clear-cut victory at Ayr on his third start. Made all to score at Hamilton two outings later. Did not appear to stay seven furlongs in between. Touched off under top weight in a Newmarket nursery in October. Got squeezed out at the start in the Tattersalls Autumn Auction Stakes and that run should be ignored. Best on an easy surface.

Racingformclub Boy

93(85) (59?)67

2-y-o ch c Blushing Flame (USA)-Sonoco (Song)

P S McEntee Racingformclub.Com

Placings:00000460 (5342)

2001: 5^{0}S, 5^{0}G, 5^{0}G, 6^{0}SD, 8^{0}G, 6^{4}GF, 8^{6}SD, 7^{0}GS

	Starts	1st	2nd	3rd	Win & Pl
Career Total (Turf)	6	0	0	0	0
Career Total (AW)	2	0	0	0	0

Going (Turf): Sf: 0-1 GS: 0-1 Gd: 0-3 GF: 0-1 Fm: 0-0
Distance: 5f/6f: 0-4 7f-8f: 0-2 9f-13f: 0-2 14f+: 0-0
Track: LH: 0-3 RH: 0-0 Tight: 0-2 Gall: 0-0
Aids: Bl: 0-0 Vi: 0-1 Tstrap: 0-0
Best Rating: 67 8/01 Yarm 1m3y good

Racingforyou Lass

53(69) (20)12

3-y-o b f Moujeeb (USA)-Kentucky Mole Vii (Damsire Unregistered)

A Streeter Racing For You Limited

Placings:000-00 (2950)

2001: 12^{0}SD, 16^{0}GF

	Starts	1st	2nd	3rd	Win & Pl
Career Total (Turf)	3	0	0	0	
Career Total (AW)	2	0	0	0	

Going (Turf): Sf: 0-2 GS: 0-0 Gd: 0-0 GF: 0-1 Fm: 0-0
Distance: 5f/6f: 0-0 7f-8f: 0-3 9f-13f: 0-1 14f+: 0-1
Track: LH: 0-4 RH: 0-0 Tight: 0-1 Gall: 0-1
Aids: Bl: 0-0 Vi: 0-0 Tstrap: 0-0
Best Rating: 3 3/01 Sthl 1m4f stand

Racket (IRE)

73 38

2-y-o b f Great Commotion (USA)-Susie Sunshine (IRE) (Waajib)

D J S Cosgrove Prayer And A Song Syndicate

Placings:0000 (4261)

2001: 5^{0}G, 5^{0}GF, 5^{0}G, 5^{0}GF

	Starts	1st	2nd	3rd	Win & Pl
Career Total (Turf)	4	0	0	0	

Going (Turf): Sf: 0-0 GS: 0-0 Gd: 0-2 GF: 0-2 Fm: 0-0
Distance: 5f/6f: 0-4 7f-8f: 0-0 9f-13f: 0-0 14f+: 0-0
Track: LH: 0-1 RH: 0-2 Tight: 0-0 Gall: 0-2
Aids: Bl: 0-1 Vi: 0-0 Tstrap: 0-0
Best Rating: 38 5/01 Wind 5f10y good

Rada's Daughter

107 **98d**

5-y-o br m Robellino (USA)-Drama School (Young Generation)

I A Balding Mrs Richard Plummer

Placings:45/0113515610/000100204-34500505 **(4549)**

2001: 10^{3}G, 13^{4}S, 11^{5}G, 12^{0}GF, 11^{0}GS, 11^{5}GF, 13^{0}G, 14^{5}GF

	Starts	1st	2nd	3rd	Win & Pl
Career Total (Turf)	**29**	**5**	**1**	**2**	**75949**

96 7/00 Hayd 1m3f200yB(0-110)H G-F £36887
92 9/99 NmkJ 1m4f B(0-100)H G-S £9942
7/99 Asct 1m4f D(0-85)H FRM £7002
81 5/99 Wind 1m3f135yD(0-85)H GD £3811
74 4/99 Bath 1m2f46y E(0-75)H SFT £2780
Total win prize-money £60426

Going (Turf): Sf: 1-5 GS: 1-4 Gd: 1-8 GF: 1-10 Fm: 1-1
Distance: 5f/6f: 0-0 7f-8f: 0-1 **9f-13f: 5-22** 14f+: 0-6
Track : LH: 2-14 RH: 2-11 Tight: 2-9 Gall: 2-15
Aids: Bl: 0-0 Vi: 0-0 Tstrap: 0-0
Best Rating: 103 5/01 Newb 1m5f61y soft

A useful middle-distance performer on a sound surface, she won the Old Newton Cup last season and ran probably her best race when a close second in the Park Hill Stakes. She did not show her best this season.

Radanpour (IRE)

101 **48**

9-y-o b g Kahyasi-Rajpoura (Kashmir Ii)

Mrs M Reveley The Mary Reveley Racing Club

Placings:0640/13115 **(4169)**

2001: 16^{1}GF, 16^{3}GF, 16^{1}GF, 14^{1}G, 14^{5}GF

	Starts	1st	2nd	3rd	Win & Pl
Career Total (Turf)	**9**	**3**	**0**	**1**	**8965**

41 8/01 Rdcr 1m6f19y F GD £3136
42 7/01 Muss 2m E G-F £2982
43 6/01 Rdcr 2m4y F G-F £2317
Total win prize-money £8435

Going (Turf): Sf: 0-1 GS: 0-0 Gd: 1-2 **GF: 2-4** Fm: 0-0
Distance: 5f/6f: 0-0 7f-8f: 0-2 9f-13f: 0-1 **14f+: 3-6**
Track : **LH: 2-5** RH: 1-4 **Tight: 3-4** Gall: 0-0
Aids: **Bl: 3-5** Vi: 0-0 Tstrap: 0-0
Best Rating: 48 8/01 Muss 1m6f gd-fm

Radiant Sky (IRE)

100 **68**

3-y-o ch f Spectrum (IRE)-Shakey (IRE) (Caerleon (USA))

B W Hills Mrs D Joly

Placings:06000 **(4096)**

2001: 8^{0}S, 9^{6}GS, 9^{0}GF, 10^{0}F, 6^{0}G

	Starts	1st	2nd	3rd	Win & Pl
Career Total (Turf)	**5**	**0**	**0**	**0**	**0**

Going (Turf): Sf: 0-1 GS: 0-1 Gd: 0-1 GF: 0-1 Fm: 0-1
Distance: 5f/6f: 0-0 7f-8f: 0-2 9f-13f: 0-3 14f+: 0-0
Track : LH: 0-2 RH: 0-2 Tight: 0-3 Gall: 0-0
Aids: Bl: 0-1 Vi: 0-0 Tstrap: 0-0
Best Rating: 68 5/01 Sals 1m1f198y gd-sft

Radical Jack

73 **26**

4-y-o b g Presidium-Luckifosome (Smackover)

Denys Smith Lord Durham

Placings:R0000/00-000 **(2099)**

2001: 9^{0}S, 8^{0}F, 8^{0}GF

	Starts	1st	2nd	3rd	Win & Pl
Career Total (Turf)	**10**	**0**	**0**	**0**	

Going (Turf): Sf: 0-2 GS: 0-2 Gd: 0-0 GF: 0-3 Fm: 0-3
Distance: 5f/6f: 0-5 7f-8f: 0-3 9f-13f: 0-2 14f+: 0-0
Track : LH: 0-1 RH: 0-4 Tight: 0-3 Gall: 0-1
Aids: Bl: 0-1 Vi: 0-0 Tstrap: 0-0
Best Rating: 26 6/01 Thsk 1m firm

Raed

(99) (45)**38**

8-y-o b g Nashwan (USA)-Awayed (USA) (Sir Ivor)

Mrs A M Naughton David C Young

Placings:20/4404025/305050062**1**/**1120**2222/**062**21020 00**060**/**3605230-004** **(4165)**

2001: 8^{0}SD, 9^{0}GS, 12^{4}GF

	Starts	1st	2nd	3rd	Win & Pl
Career Total (Turf)	**33**	**1**	**8**	**1**	**14042**
Career Total (AW)	**17**	**3**	**4**	**2**	**12304**

61 8/99 Wind 1m2f7y E(0-80)H HVY £2780
72 2/98 Sthl 1m3f D(0-85)H STD £3741
65 2/98 Sthl 1m3f E(0-70)H STD £2879
62 12/97 Sthl 1m3f F(0-65)H STD £1944
Total win prize-money £11344

Going (Turf): Sf: 1-4 GS: 0-5 Gd: 0-7 GF: 0-10 Fm: 0-7
Distance: 5f/6f: 0-2 7f-8f: 0-11 **9f-13f: 4-35** 14f+: 0-2
Track : **LH: 3-32** RH: 0-10 **Tight: 1-14** Gall: 0-6
Aids: Bl: 0-0 Vi: 0-0 Tstrap: 0-0
Best Rating: 36 7/01 Sthl 1m stand

Rafferty (IRE)

102 **74**

2-y-o ch c Lion Cavern (USA)-Badawi (USA) (Diesis)

C E Brittain Sheikh Marwan Al Maktoum

Placings:3300 **(4678)**

2001: 6^{3}GF, 7^{3}GF, 7^{0}GF, 8^{0}G

	Starts	1st	2nd	3rd	Win & Pl
Career Total (Turf)	**4**	**0**	**0**	**2**	**1364**

Going (Turf): Sf: 0-0 GS: 0-0 Gd: 0-1 GF: 0-3 Fm: 0-0
Distance: 5f/6f: 0-1 7f-8f: 0-3 9f-13f: 0-0 14f+: 0-0
Track : LH: 0-0 RH: 0-1 Tight: 0-0 Gall: 0-0
Aids: Bl: 0-0 Vi: 0-0 Tstrap: 0-0
Best Rating: 74 7/01 Newb 7f gd-fm

Showed bags of promise on his Ripon debut and was a game third at Newbury next time. Was out of his depth in a Group Three at Goodwood.

Rafiya

110 **92**

3-y-o b f Halling (USA)-Nemesia (Mill Reef (USA))

C E Brittain Saeed Manana

Placings:252315600 **(5600)**

2001: 8^{2}GS, 10^{5}S, 9^{2}F, 10^{3}GF, 12^{1}G, 14^{5}GF, 12^{6}G, 12^{0}GS, 16^{0}GS

	Starts	1st	2nd	3rd	Win & Pl
Career Total (Turf)	**9**	**1**	**2**	**1**	**7607**

78 8/01 Ripn 1m4f60y D GD £3575
Total win prize-money £3575

Going (Turf): Sf: 0-1 GS: 0-3 **Gd: 1-2** GF: 0-2 Fm: 0-1
Distance: 5f/6f: 0-0 7f-8f: 0-1 **9f-13f: 1-6** 14f+: 0-2
Track : LH: 0-4 **RH: 1-5 Tight: 1-2** Gall: 0-5
Aids: Bl: 0-0 Vi: 0-0 Tstrap: 0-0
Best Rating: 92 9/01 Donc 1m6f132y gd-fm

Bred to stay at least ten furlongs, she showed ability before getting off the mark in a 12 furlong Ripon maiden. Found wanting in better company. Acts on good to soft and fast ground and stays a mile and half.

Rafters Music (IRE)

(109) (80)

6-y-o b g Thatching-Princess Dixieland (USA) (Dixieland Band (USA))

B W Hills Wilwyn Racing (wwwwilwyncom)

Placings:000/00051460460/**1216**0331304**35224**-**0341**105651120302600**25** **(5612)**

2001: **7**^{0}SW, **6**^{3}SD, **6**^{4}SD, **6**^{1}SW, 6^{1}HY, 5^{0}GS, 6^{5}G, 5^{6}G, 6^{5}GF, 6^{1}G, 6^{1}GF, 6^{2}GF, 6^{0}GF, 6^{3}GF, 6^{0}GS, 5^{2}G, 6^{6}G, 6^{0}G, 6^{0}GS, 6^{2}SD, **6**^{5}SD

	Starts	1st	2nd	3rd	Win & Pl
Career Total (Turf)	**35**	**5**	**2**	**4**	**26093**
Career Total (AW)	**16**	**3**	**4**	**2**	**14399**

76 6/01 Donc 6f D(0-80)H G-F £4426
66 6/01 Wind 6f D(0-80)H GD £7637
55 4/01 Folk 6f G(0-60)H HVY £1879
67 2/01 Sthl 6f E(0-75)H SLW £2408
55 5/00 Donc 7f F(0-70)H G-S £2278
65 1/00 Sthl 6f E(0-70)H STD £3188
60 1/00 Sthl 6f D(0-80)H STD £4173
52 7/99 Epsm 6f E G-F £2736
Total win prize-money £28730

Going (Turf): Sf: 1-2 GS: 1-7 Gd: 1-10 **GF: 2-13** Fm: 0-3
Distance: **5f/6f: 7-35** 7f-8f: 1-15 9f-13f: 0-1 14f+: 0-0
Track : **LH: 4-26** RH: 0-3 **Tight: 1-11** Gall: 0-3
Aids: Bl: 0-4 Vi: 0-0 **Tstrap: 1-10**
Best Rating: 80 10/01 Wolv 6f stand

Four times a winner so far this year of which one was on sand, he is best at six furlong and acts on any ground.

Ragamuffin

107 **77**

3-y-o ch g Prince Sabo-Valldemosa (Music Boy)

T D Easterby Mrs Jennifer E Pallister

Placings:4621-0020050000644 **(5630)**

2001: 5^{0}GF, 5^{0}GF, 5^{2}F, 6^{0}GS, 6^{0}G, 5^{5}GF, 6^{0}G, 5^{0}G, 6^{0}G, 6^{0}G, 6^{6}S, 5^{4}S, 6^{4}G

	Starts	1st	2nd	3rd	Win & Pl
Career Total (Turf)	**17**	**1**	**2**	**0**	**8446**

80 5/00 Rdcr 5f E G-S £2847
Total win prize-money £2847

Going (Turf): Sf: 0-3 **GS: 1-2** Gd: 0-8 GF: 0-3 Fm: 0-1
Distance: **5f/6f: 1-16** 7f-8f: 0-1 9f-13f: 0-0 14f+: 0-0
Track : LH: 0-3 RH: 0-0 Tight: 0-3 Gall: 0-0
Aids: Bl: 0-0 Vi: 0-0 Tstrap: 0-0
Best Rating: 86 5/01 Rdcr 5f firm

Scored as a juvenile at Redcar over the minimum trip and his best effort since then came at that track in May of this year. Has shown a tendency to hang in the past.

Ragasah

82(85) (35)**45**

3-y-o b f Glory Of Dancer-Slight Risk (Risk Me (FR))

Miss Gay Kelleway E Oertel

Placings:605 **(3817)**

2001: 6^{6}SD, 9^{0}GF, 9^{5}SD

	Starts	1st	2nd	3rd	Win & Pl
Career Total (Turf)	**1**	**0**	**0**	**0**	
Career Total (AW)	**2**	**0**	**0**	**0**	**0**

Going (Turf): Sf: 0-0 GS: 0-0 Gd: 0-0 GF: 0-1 Fm: 0-0
Distance: 5f/6f: 0-1 7f-8f: 0-0 9f-13f: 0-2 14f+: 0-0
Track : LH: 0-3 RH: 0-0 Tight: 0-2 Gall: 0-0
Aids: Bl: 0-0 Vi: 0-0 Tstrap: 0-0
Best Rating: 45 7/01 Nott 1m1f213y gd-fm

Ragdale Hall (USA)

106(102) (71)**83**

4-y-o b g Bien Bien (USA)-Gift Of Dance (USA) (Trempolino (USA))

J H M Gosden Ragdale Racing

Placings:510300-62033000 **(5463)**

2001: 11^{6}SW, 10^{2}GF, 10^{0}GF, 10^{3}GF, 10^{3}GF, 9^{0}G, 8^{0}GF, 11^{0}G

	Starts	1st	2nd	3rd	Win & Pl
Career Total (Turf)	13	1	1	3	9389
Career Total (AW)	1	0	0	0	0

77 6/00 Wind 1m2f7y E GD £2996

Total win prize-money £2996

Going (Turf): Sf: 0-0 GS: 0-1 **Gd: 1-4** GF: 0-8 Fm: 0-0
Distance: 5f/6f: 0-0 7f-8f: 0-1 **9f-13f: 1-13** 14f+: 0-0
Track : LH: 0-6 RH: 0-6 **Tight: 1-4** Gall: 0-5
Aids: Bl: 0-1 Vi: 0-2 Tstrap: 0-0
Best Rating: 83 7/01 Epsm 1m2f18y gd-fm

Unraced at two, he got off the mark on his second start as a three-year-old over ten furlongs. Suited by the application of visor when second in a Kempton handicap in spring of 2001. Acts on fast ground.

Raheibb (IRE)

111(96) (55)**93+**

3-y-o ch c Lion Cavern (USA)-Abeyr (Unfuwain (USA))
A C Stewart Sheikh Ahmed Al Maktoum

Placings:00-20110313 **(4053)**
2001: 7^{2}SD, 8^{0}GS, 7^{1}G, 7^{1}G, 8^{0}GF, 7^{3}GF, 7^{1}GF, 7^{3}GF

	Starts	1st	2nd	3rd	Win & Pl
Career Total (Turf)	9	3	0	2	23026
Career Total (AW)	1	0	1	0	927

93 7/01 Sand 7f16y C(0-90)H G-F £7247
85 5/01 Sand 7f16y D(0-80)H GD £5505
75 5/01 Wwck 7f26y D(0-80)H GD £4368

Total win prize-money £17122

Going (Turf): Sf: 0-1 GS: 0-1 **Gd: 2-3** GF: 1-4 Fm: 0-0
Distance: 5f/6f: 0-0 **7f-8f: 3-9** 9f-13f: 0-1 14f+: 0-0
Track : LH: 1-2 **RH: 2-4** Tight: 0-2 Gall: 0-0
Aids: Bl: 0-0 Vi: 0-0 Tstrap: 0-0
Best Rating: 93 8/01 Newb 7f gd-fm

He won a pair of handicaps at Warwick and Sandown in the spring before a respectable effort in the Britannia. Unlucky not to win a valuable handicap back at Sandown in July, but made no mistake with a smooth success at the same track next time. Suited by seven furlongs and the ground no softer than good.

Rahjel Sultan

95 **51**

3-y-o b c Puissance-Dalby Dancer (Bustiki)
B A McMahon G S D Imports Ltd

Placings:50 **(3882)**
2001: 8^{5}GF, 8^{0}G

	Starts	1st	2nd	3rd	Win & Pl
Career Total (Turf)	2	0	0	0	0

Going (Turf): Sf: 0-0 GS: 0-0 Gd: 0-1 GF: 0-1 Fm: 0-0
Distance: 5f/6f: 0-0 7f-8f: 0-0 9f-13f: 0-2 14f+: 0-0
Track : LH: 0-0 RH: 0-2 Tight: 0-2 Gall: 0-0
Aids: Bl: 0-0 Vi: 0-0 Tstrap: 0-0
Best Rating: 51 7/01 Wind 1m67y gd-fm

Rahlex (IRE)

92(88) (44)**50+**

3-y-o ch c Rahy (USA)-Lady Express (IRE) (Soviet Star (USA))
P F I Cole The Blandford Partnership

Placings:05004 **(4021)**
2001: 6^{0}SD, 6^{5}SD, 6^{0}G, 8^{0}GS, 5^{4}G

	Starts	1st	2nd	3rd	Win & Pl
Career Total (Turf)	3	0	0	0	0
Career Total (AW)	2	0	0	0	0

Going (Turf): Sf: 0-0 GS: 0-1 Gd: 0-2 GF: 0-0 Fm: 0-0
Distance: 5f/6f: 0-4 7f-8f: 0-0 9f-13f: 0-1 14f+: 0-0
Track : LH: 0-3 RH: 0-0 Tight: 0-1 Gall: 0-0
Aids: Bl: 0-0 Vi: 0-0 Tstrap: 0-0
Best Rating: 50 8/01 Folk 5f good

Rahwaan (IRE)

96 **78**

2-y-o b c Darshaan-Fawaakeh (USA) (Lyphard (USA))
J L Dunlop Hamdan Al Maktoum

Placings:34 **(5468)**
2001: 8^{3}G, 7^{4}S

	Starts	1st	2nd	3rd	Win & Pl
Career Total (Turf)	2	0	0	1	882

Going (Turf): Sf: 0-1 GS: 0-0 Gd: 0-1 GF: 0-0 Fm: 0-0
Distance: 5f/6f: 0-0 7f-8f: 0-1 9f-13f: 0-1 14f+: 0-0
Track : LH: 0-2 RH: 0-0 Tight: 0-0 Gall: 0-0
Aids: Bl: 0-0 Vi: 0-0 Tstrap: 0-0
Best Rating: 78 9/01 Nott 1m54y good

Railroader

106 **75**

4-y-o ch g Piccolo-Poyle Amber (Sharrood (USA))
G B Balding Peter Richardson

Placings:030340/61020000-0360 **(3405)**
2001: 6^{0}GF, 5^{3}GF, 6^{6}GF, 6^{0}GF

	Starts	1st	2nd	3rd	Win & Pl
Career Total (Turf)	18	1	1	3	27045

75 5/00 Ches 6f18y C(0-90)H GD £12506

Total win prize-money £12506

Going (Turf): Sf: 0-6 GS: 0-1 **Gd: 1-4** GF: 0-7 Fm: 0-0
Distance: 5f/6f: 0-15 **7f-8f: 1-3** 9f-13f: 0-0 14f+: 0-0
Track : **LH: 1-3** RH: 0-1 **Tight: 1-2** Gall: 0-1
Aids: Bl: 0-0 Vi: 0-0 Tstrap: 0-0
Best Rating: 75 6/01 Sals 5f gd-fm

He landed a gamble at Chester on his second start last season and ran well on his second start of this term. He is effective at five and six furlongs and is always worth watching out for in the market.

Rain Or Shine (IRE)

82(86) (42)**33**

3-y-o ch g Rainbow Quest (USA)-Fitnah (Kris)
E A L Dunlop Gainsborough Stud

Placings:0660 **(1649)**
2001: 8^{0}SD, 8^{6}SD, 8^{6}S, 11^{0}F

	Starts	1st	2nd	3rd	Win & Pl
Career Total (Turf)	2	0	0	0	0
Career Total (AW)	2	0	0	0	0

Going (Turf): Sf: 0-1 GS: 0-0 Gd: 0-0 GF: 0-0 Fm: 0-1
Distance: 5f/6f: 0-0 7f-8f: 0-3 9f-13f: 0-1 14f+: 0-0
Track : LH: 0-2 RH: 0-2 Tight: 0-2 Gall: 0-0
Aids: Bl: 0-0 Vi: 0-0 Tstrap: 0-4
Best Rating: 42 3/01 Sthl 1m stand

Rainbow Chase (IRE)

99 **72**

3-y-o b g Rainbow Quest (USA)-Fayrooz (USA) (Gulch (USA))
S Magnier (J L Dunlop 25/6) Fergus Jones

Placings:20540 **(5525)**
2001: 11^{2}GS, 12^{0}GS, 14^{5}G, 14^{4}G, 11^{0}HY

	Starts	1st	2nd	3rd	Win & Pl
Career Total (Turf)	5	0	1	0	1880

Going (Turf): Sf: 0-1 GS: 0-2 Gd: 0-2 GF: 0-0 Fm: 0-0
Distance: 5f/6f: 0-0 7f-8f: 0-0 9f-13f: 0-3 14f+: 0-2
Track : LH: 0-3 RH: 0-1 Tight: 0-3 Gall: 0-1
Aids: Bl: 0-1 Vi: 0-0 Tstrap: 0-0
Best Rating: 80 4/01 Newb 1m3f5y gd-sft

Rainbow D'Beaute

82 **55**

2-y-o ch f Rainbow Quest (USA)-Reine D'Beaute (Caerleon (USA))
M A Jarvis Sir Eric Parker

Placings:00 **(5295)**
2001: 7^{0}S, 8^{0}S

	Starts	1st	2nd	3rd	Win & Pl
Career Total (Turf)	2	0	0	0	

Going (Turf): Sf: 0-2 GS: 0-0 Gd: 0-0 GF: 0-0 Fm: 0-0
Distance: 5f/6f: 0-0 7f-8f: 0-1 9f-13f: 0-1 14f+: 0-0
Track : LH: 0-0 RH: 0-0 Tight: 0-0 Gall: 0-0
Aids: Bl: 0-0 Vi: 0-0 Tstrap: 0-0
Best Rating: 55 10/01 NmkR 7f soft

Rainbow High

112 **113**

6-y-o b h Rainbow Quest (USA)-Imaginary (IRE) (Dancing Brave (USA))
B W Hills K Abdulla

Placings:444/125524/1120321/54243-01003620 **(5385)**
2001: 12^{0}GS, 18^{1}GF, 16^{0}G, 20^{0}GF, 16^{3}G, 15^{6}G, 18^{2}G, 16^{0}GS

	Starts	1st	2nd	3rd	Win & Pl
Career Total (Turf)	29	5	6	3	238844

117 5/01 Ches 2m2f147yB H G-F £65000
114 10/99 NmkJ 2m24y A SFT £23150
107 5/99 Ches 2m2f147yB H G-F £48450
103 4/99 Newb 2m C(0-100)H G-F £6320
76 6/98 Ripn 1m4f60y D HVY £3517

Total win prize-money £146438

Going (Turf): Sf: 2-3 GS: 0-4 Gd: 0-14 **GF: 3-8** Fm: 0-0
Distance: 5f/6f: 0-0 7f-8f: 0-3 9f-13f: 1-6 **14f+: 4-20**
Track : **LH: 3-14** RH: 2-13 **Tight: 3-7** Gall: 1-16
Aids: Bl: 0-0 Vi: 0-0 Tstrap: 0-0
Best Rating: 117 5/01 Ches 2m2f147y gd-fm

He developed into a very useful stayer in 1999, winning the Chester Cup and the Jockey Club Cup, but he was held in 2000 and his attitude at times was questionable. Put up a record weight carrying performance to win his second Chester Cup in 2001, but has again tended to struggle in Group company since, although he ran well when second to Alleluia in the Doncaster Cup. Acts on fast ground.

Rainbow Hill

101 **50**

4-y-o b g Rainbow Quest (USA)-Hill Hopper (IRE) (Danehill (USA))
J J Quinn John Ward

Placings:210-000006300000304 **(4802)**
2001: 6^{0}S, 7^{0}G, 8^{0}G, 6^{0}GF, 8^{0}GF, 7^{6}G, 8^{3}GF, 10^{0}GF, 8^{0}GS, 7^{0}G, 6^{0}G, 9^{0}G, 9^{3}G, 8^{0}GF, 8^{4}F

	Starts	1st	2nd	3rd	Win & Pl
Career Total (Turf)	18	1	1	2	5532

76 6/00 Ripn 1m D G-F £3458

Total win prize-money £3458

Going (Turf): Sf: 0-1 GS: 0-1 Gd: 0-9 **GF: 1-6** Fm: 0-1
Distance: 5f/6f: 0-3 **7f-8f: 1-9** 9f-13f: 0-6 14f+: 0-0
Track : LH: 0-10 **RH: 1-4** **Tight: 1-7** Gall: 0-2
Aids: Bl: 0-0 Vi: 0-1 Tstrap: 0-0
Best Rating: 57 6/01 Newc 1m gd-fm

Rainbow Princess (IRE)

85(93) (46)**47**

3-y-o b f Spectrum (IRE)-Richly Deserved (IRE) (King's Lake (USA))
P W D'Arcy Terry And Gillian Miller

Placings:P-60000 (1613)
2001: 8^{6}SD, 8^{0}SD, 7^{0}S, 7^{0}SD, 10^{0}GF

	Starts	1st	2nd	3rd	Win & Pl
Career Total (Turf)	3	0	0	0	
Career Total (AW)	3	0	0	0	0

Going (Turf): Sf: 0-1 GS: 0-0 Gd: 0-0 GF: 0-2 Fm: 0-0
Distance: 5f/6f: 0-1 7f-8f: 0-3 9f-13f: 0-2 14f+: 0-0
Track : LH: 0-4 RH: 0-0 Tight: 0-2 Gall: 0-0
Aids: Bl: 0-0 Vi: 0-0 Tstrap: 0-0
Best Rating: 47 5/01 Ling 1m2f gd-fm

Rainbow Rain (USA)

103(105) (53)**58**
7-y-o b g Capote (USA)-Grana (USA) (Miswaki (USA))
S Dow P McCarthy

Placings:43052/06410500/00000600003256100**5402**/360020045101402**2305**/**3022**00020002U0-**5662**400020 (3150)
2001: 7^{5}SD, 7^{6}SD, 10^{6}SD, 9^{2}SD, 8^{4}SD, 9^{0}GF, 10^{0}F, 9^{0}GF, 10^{2}GF, 9^{0}G

	Starts	1st	2nd	3rd	Win & Pl
Career Total (Turf)	55	3	6	2	25445
Career Total (AW)	22	1	5	3	8917

62 7/99 Brig 5f213y F(0-60) FRM £2354
65 7/99 Brig 6f209y E(0-70)H FRM £3269
69 8/98 Ling 7f E(0-70)H STD £3235
75 6/97 Carl 7f214y D(0-80)H FRM £7490
Total win prize-money £16350

Going (Turf): Sf: 0-5 GS: 0-1 Gd: 0-20 GF: 0-23 **Fm: 3-6**
Distance: 5f/6f: 1-22 **7f-8f: 3-38** 9f-13f: 0-17 14f+: 0-0
Track : **LH: 3-43** RH: 1-8 **Tight: 1-31** Gall: 0-4
Aids: Bl: 0-0 Vi: 0-0 Tstrap: 0-3
Best Rating: 58 7/01 Epsm 1m2f18y gd-fm

He has shown his liking for Brighton by winning twice there so far this season, and again ran well on a downhill track when fourth to Royal Result in a hot Goodwood handicap in August.

Rainbow Raver (IRE)

90 (7)**25**
5-y-o ch m Rainbows For Life (CAN)-Foolish Passion (USA) (Secretariat (USA))
J L Eyre Alma & Stewart Pinner

Placings:5005600/0063022645/0000-00060 (3159)
2001: 16^{0}GF, 12^{0}GF, 12^{0}GF, 16^{6}GF, 12^{0}G

	Starts	1st	2nd	3rd	Win & Pl
Career Total (Turf)	25	0	2	1	2874
Career Total (AW)	1	0	0	0	

Going (Turf): Sf: 0-3 GS: 0-2 Gd: 0-4 GF: 0-12 Fm: 0-4
Distance: 5f/6f: 0-2 7f-8f: 0-5 9f-13f: 0-16 14f+: 0-3
Track : LH: 0-13 RH: 0-9 Tight: 0-10 Gall: 0-5
Aids: Bl: 0-0 Vi: 0-1 Tstrap: 0-1
Best Rating: 25 6/01 Newc 1m4f93y gd-fm

Rainbow River (IRE)

106(107) (65)**69**
3-y-o ch g Rainbows For Life (CAN)-Shrewd Girl (USA) (Sagace (FR))
M C Chapman (P C Haslam 29/1) Leo Fitzpatrick

Placings:005**333**-**5543414330303600** (4371)
2001: 8^{5}SD, 8^{5}SD, 8^{4}SD, 8^{3}SD, 12^{4}SD, 11^{1}SD, 12^{4}SW, 10^{3}GS, 9^{3}G, 7^{0}GF, 11^{3}GF, 9^{0}GF, 11^{3}GF, 11^{6}GF, 13^{0}G, 11^{0}GF

	Starts	1st	2nd	3rd	Win & Pl
Career Total (Turf)	13	0	0	5	3095
Career Total (AW)	9	1	0	3	4240

65 4/01 Sthl 1m3f F STD £2254
Total win prize-money £2254

Going (Turf): Sf: 0-0 GS: 0-2 Gd: 0-2 GF: 0-9 Fm: 0-0
Distance: 5f/6f: 0-2 7f-8f: 0-7 **9f-13f: 1-12** 14f+: 0-1
Track : **LH: 1-15** RH: 0-4 Tight: 0-6 Gall: 0-2
Aids: **Bl: 1-2** Vi: 0-1 Tstrap: 0-0
Best Rating: 70 5/01 Pont 1m2f6y gd-sft

He won his maiden on the All-Weather over 11 furlongs and has gone well on his three visits to Beverley. Stays a mile and a half and likes an end-to-end gallop.

Rainbow Spirit (IRE)

103(101) (62)**66**
4-y-o b g Rainbows For Life (CAN)-Merrie Moment (IRE) (Taufan (USA))
A P Jarvis Mrs Rebecca Caudle

Placings:0/503434233**302242**-**102030** (3866)
2001: 16^{1}SD, 16^{0}SD, 14^{2}GF, 20^{0}GF, 16^{3}GF, 16^{0}GF

	Starts	1st	2nd	3rd	Win & Pl
Career Total (Turf)	15	0	2	5	6292
Career Total (AW)	7	1	3	1	4240

61 2/01 Sthl 2m F(0-60)H STD £1806
Total win prize-money £1806

Going (Turf): Sf: 0-2 GS: 0-1 Gd: 0-2 GF: 0-9 Fm: 0-1
Distance: 5f/6f: 0-0 7f-8f: 0-1 9f-13f: 0-6 **14f+: 1-15**
Track : **LH: 1-17** RH: 0-5 Tight: 0-6 Gall: 0-4
Aids: Bl: 0-0 Vi: 0-1 Tstrap: 0-0
Best Rating: 66 6/01 Kemp 1m6f92y gd-fm

Rainbow View (IRE)

94 **45**
5-y-o b g Rainbows For Life (CAN)-L'Anno D'Oro (Habitat)
W M Brisbourne Miss Marjorie A Thompson

Placings:01000053/0-06600 (3282)
2001: 9^{0}F, 6^{6}GF, 6^{6}GF, 6^{0}GF, 8^{0}F

	Starts	1st	2nd	3rd	Win & Pl
Career Total (Turf)	14	1	0	1	3522

52 5/99 Rdcr 6f E G-F £3038
Total win prize-money £3038

Going (Turf): Sf: 0-3 GS: 0-0 Gd: 0-2 **GF: 1-5** Fm: 0-4
Distance: **5f/6f: 1-4** 7f-8f: 0-5 9f-13f: 0-5 14f+: 0-0
Track : LH: 0-4 RH: 0-3 Tight: 0-2 Gall: 0-0
Aids: Bl: 0-0 Vi: 0-0 Tstrap: 0-0
Best Rating: 45 6/01 Nott 6f15y gd-fm

Raining

96 **57**
3-y-o b f Mukaddamah (USA)-Piney River (Pharly (FR))
R Charlton Beckhampton Partnership

Placings:542 (2939)
2001: 5^{5}F, 5^{4}GF, 5^{2}GF

	Starts	1st	2nd	3rd	Win & Pl
Career Total (Turf)	3	0	1	0	757

Going (Turf): Sf: 0-0 GS: 0-0 Gd: 0-0 GF: 0-2 Fm: 0-1
Distance: 5f/6f: 0-3 7f-8f: 0-0 9f-13f: 0-0 14f+: 0-0
Track : LH: 0-0 RH: 0-0 Tight: 0-0 Gall: 0-0
Aids: Bl: 0-0 Vi: 0-0 Tstrap: 0-0
Best Rating: 57 6/01 Folk 5f gd-fm

Rainshine

103 **85**
3-y-o br f Rainbow Quest (USA)-El Opera (IRE) (Sadler's Wells (USA))
Sir Mark Prescott Faisal Salman

Placings:621360 (4310)
2001: 8^{6}GF, 10^{2}F, 10^{1}GF, 12^{3}GF, 12^{6}GF, 10^{0}GF

	Starts	1st	2nd	3rd	Win & Pl
Career Total (Turf)	6	1	1	1	5212

82 7/01 Chep 1m2f36y D G-F £2870
Total win prize-money £2870

Going (Turf): Sf: 0-0 GS: 0-0 Gd: 0-0 **GF: 1-5** Fm: 0-1
Distance: 5f/6f: 0-0 7f-8f: 0-1 **9f-13f: 1-5** 14f+: 0-0
Track : **LH: 1-4** RH: 0-2 Tight: 0-1 Gall: 0-3
Aids: Bl: 0-0 Vi: 0-0 Tstrap: 0-0
Best Rating: 85 7/01 Asct 1m4f gd-fm

Progressed steadily to win a Chepstow maiden on her third outing before being held on her handicap bow and in Listed company afterwards. Acts on fast ground. Had trouble with slow starts on her first two runs, but that may well be behind her now. Stays ten furlongs.

Rainstorm

103(90) (54)**48**
6-y-o b g Rainbow Quest (USA)-Katsina (USA) (Cox's Ridge (USA))
W M Brisbourne C M & S J Owen

Placings:605**214**/450000/03500000-**051660**301062520 (5055)
2001: 11^{0}SD, 9^{5}SD, 8^{1}SD, 8^{6}SD, 7^{6}SW, 8^{0}SD, 9^{3}GF, 9^{0}G, 9^{1}GF, 8^{0}S, 11^{6}GF, 9^{2}GS, 9^{5}SW, 10^{2}G, 10^{0}S

	Starts	1st	2nd	3rd	Win & Pl
Career Total (Turf)	20	1	2	2	6145
Career Total (AW)	15	2	1	0	5328

44 7/01 Bevl 1m1f207yE(0-75)H G-F £3659
54 1/01 Wolv 1m100y G(0-70)H STD £1344
64 12/98 Ling 7f D STD £2788
Total win prize-money £7792

Going (Turf): Sf: 0-3 GS: 0-2 Gd: 0-10 **GF: 1-3** Fm: 0-2
Distance: 5f/6f: 0-0 7f-8f: 1-10 **9f-13f: 2-25** 14f+: 0-0
Track : **LH: 2-24** RH: 1-7 **Tight: 2-16** Gall: 0-2
Aids: Bl: 0-0 Vi: 0-2 Tstrap: 0-0
Best Rating: 54 1/01 Wolv 1m100y stand

Moderate handicapper, suited by ten furlongs and positive tactics. Seems to handle most surfaces, including Fibresand, and goes well for an inexperienced rider.

Rainworth Lady

99(94) (38)**38**
4-y-o b f Governor General-Monongelia (Welsh Pageant)
P W Hiatt George Patching

Placings:0400/5000635P0-0060000200 (5617)
2001: 12^{0}GF, 10^{0}F, 8^{6}S, 10^{0}G, 8^{0}GF, 7^{0}GF, 10^{0}G, 10^{2}HY, 10^{0}HY, 8^{0}SD, 12^{6}SD

	Starts	1st	2nd	3rd	Win & Pl
Career Total (Turf)	18	0	1	1	1661
Career Total (AW)	5	0	0	0	0

Going (Turf): Sf: 0-4 GS: 0-1 Gd: 0-4 GF: 0-6 Fm: 0-2
Distance: 5f/6f: 0-1 7f-8f: 0-5 9f-13f: 0-16 14f+: 0-0
Track : LH: 0-13 RH: 0-4 Tight: 0-7 Gall: 0-1
Aids: Bl: 0-1 Vi: 0-0 Tstrap: 0-1
Best Rating: 38 10/01 Wind 1m2f7y heavy

Rainy River (IRE)

72(81) (24)**66**
3-y-o b f Irish River (FR)-Forest Storm (USA) (Woodman (USA))
B W Hills R A Scarborough

Placings:56-600 (2232)
2001: 6^{6}SD, 7^{0}S, 8^{0}GS

	Starts	1st	2nd	3rd	Win & Pl
Career Total (Turf)	3	0	0	0	0
Career Total (AW)	2	0	0	0	0

Going (Turf): Sf: 0-2 GS: 0-1 Gd: 0-0 GF: 0-0 Fm: 0-0
Distance: 5f/6f: 0-1 7f-8f: 0-4 9f-13f: 0-0 14f+: 0-0
Track : LH: 0-2 RH: 0-0 Tight: 0-0 Gall: 0-0

Aids: Bl: 0-0 Vi: 0-0 Tstrap: 0-0
Best Rating: 21 1/01 Sthl 6f stand

Raisa's Gold (IRE)

91(76) (21)**42**

3-y-o b f Goldmark (USA)-Princess Raisa (Indian King (USA))

B S Rothwell Brian Rothwell

Placings:500-60400 (2518)

2001: 7⁰SW, 8⁰SW, 11⁴GF, 10⁰GF, 16⁰F

	Starts	1st	2nd	3rd	Win & Pl
Career Total (Turf)	3	0	0	0	264
Career Total (AW)	5	0	0	0	0

Going (Turf): Sf: 0-0 GS: 0-0 Gd: 0-0 GF: 0-2 Fm: 0-1
Distance: 5f/6f: 0-3 7f-8f: 0-2 9f-13f: 0-2 14f+: 0-1
Track : LH: 0-6 RH: 0-1 Tight: 0-6 Gall: 0-0
Aids: Bl: 0-0 Vi: 0-0 Tstrap: 0-0
Best Rating: 42 6/01 Haml 1m3f16y gd-fm

Raise A Melody (IRE)

2-y-o ch f Hector Protector (USA)-Dumayla (Shernazar)

E Stanners Doubleprint

Placings:U (5095)

2001: 8ᵁGS

	Starts	1st	2nd	3rd	Win & Pl
Career Total (Turf)	1	0	0	0	

Going (Turf): Sf: 0-0 GS: 0-1 Gd: 0-0 GF: 0-0 Fm: 0-0
Distance: 5f/6f: 0-0 7f-8f: 0-1 9f-13f: 0-0 14f+: 0-0
Track : LH: 0-0 RH: 0-0 Tight: 0-0 Gall: 0-0
Aids: Bl: 0-0 Vi: 0-0 Tstrap: 0-0

Raise A Prince (FR)

100(93) (64)**91**

8-y-o b g Machiavellian (USA)-Enfant D'Amour (USA) (Lyphard (USA))

S P C Woods Mrs L Woods

Placings:5/4025424/0301114/1245401134/2130003033/56600253-004 (5557)

2001: 14⁰SD, 16⁰GS, 14⁴S, 14²SD

	Starts	1st	2nd	3rd	Win & Pl
Career Total (Turf)	42	6	5	6	104791
Career Total (AW)	4	1	0	1	4095

106	4/99	Nott	1m6f15y	C	SFT	£5542
92	9/98	Asct	1m4f	B H	SFT	£46300
92	9/98	Ayr	1m5f13y	C(0-95)H	G-S	£7505
89	4/98	NmkR	1m4f	C(0-95)H	SFT	£6680
82	11/97	Ling	1m4f	D	STD	£3306
81	10/97	Newb	1m4f5y	D	G-S	£3756
69	7/97	Nott	1m1f213y	E(0-70)H	SFT	£3694

Total win prize-money £76785

Going (Turf): Sf: 4-15 GS: 2-9 Gd: 0-11 GF: 0-5 Fm: 0-1
Distance: 5f/6f: 0-0 7f-8f: 0-2 9f-13f: 5-24 14f+: 2-20
Track : LH: 5-30 RH: 2-12 Tight: 1-8 Gall: 3-20
Aids: Bl: 0-0 Vi: 1-1 Tstrap: 1-20
Best Rating: 58 4/01 Newb 2m gd-sft

He was a very useful middle-distance handicapper a couple of seasons ago, bordering on Listed class, but those days are long gone.

Raised The Bar (USA)

95 **76**

2-y-o ch f Royal Academy (USA)-Barari (USA) (Blushing Groom (FR))

M Johnston Maktoum Al Maktoum

Placings:2240 (5052)

2001: 5²GF, 5²G, 5⁴GF, 7⁰S

	Starts	1st	2nd	3rd	Win & Pl
Career Total (Turf)	4	0	2	0	3010

Going (Turf): Sf: 0-1 GS: 0-0 Gd: 0-1 GF: 0-2 Fm: 0-0
Distance: 5f/6f: 0-3 7f-8f: 0-1 9f-13f: 0-0 14f+: 0-0
Track : LH: 0-0 RH: 0-0 Tight: 0-0 Gall: 0-0
Aids: Bl: 0-0 Vi: 0-0 Tstrap: 0-0
Best Rating: 76 6/01 York 5f good

A well-related filly, she passed the post first on her Ripon debut, but was demoted to second for hampering the runner-up. She looked in need of a step up in trip on her next start, but was disappointing at Doncaster on her third outing. Did not run badly after a three-month break in a Newmarket nursery.

Raison Garde (IRE)

102 **87**

2-y-o b f Ashkalani (IRE)-Didjala (USA) (Irish River (FR))

J G Fitzgerald Marquesa De Moratalla

Placings:616 (5401)

2001: 6⁰GF, 7¹G, 8⁰S

	Starts	1st	2nd	3rd	Win & Pl
Career Total (Turf)	3	1	0	0	4258

83	9/01	Bevl	7f100y	D	GD	£3838

Total win prize-money £3838

Going (Turf): Sf: 0-1 GS: 0-0 Gd: 1-1 GF: 0-1 Fm: 0-0
Distance: 5f/6f: 0-0 7f-8f: 1-2 9f-13f: 0-1 14f+: 0-0
Track : LH: 0-2 RH: 1-1 Tight: 0-0 Gall: 0-1
Aids: Bl: 0-0 Vi: 0-0 Tstrap: 0-0
Best Rating: 87 10/01 Pont 1m4y soft

Won a maiden at Beverley on her second outing, but the jump into Listed company has proved too much for her so far. Has won on good ground.

Rajab

96 **97+**

2-y-o br c Selkirk (USA)-Putout (Dowsing (USA))

M Johnston A Al-Rostamani

Placings:610 (5493)

2001: 6⁶G, 6¹GF, 7⁰HY

	Starts	1st	2nd	3rd	Win & Pl
Career Total (Turf)	3	1	0	0	4693

97	9/01	Gdwd	6f	D	G-F	£4693

Total win prize-money £4693

Going (Turf): Sf: 0-1 GS: 0-0 Gd: 0-1 GF: 1-1 Fm: 0-0
Distance: 5f/6f: 1-2 7f-8f: 0-1 9f-13f: 0-0 14f+: 0-0
Track : LH: 0-0 RH: 0-0 Tight: 0-0 Gall: 0-0
Aids: Bl: 0-0 Vi: 0-0 Tstrap: 0-0
Best Rating: 97 9/01 Gdwd 6f gd-fm

Showed ability in a very hot York maiden on his debut and went on to win a Goodwood maiden in good style. Should stay seven furlongs without a problem.

Rajah Eman (IRE)

76(106) (80)**61**

3-y-o b g Sri Pekan (USA)-Jungle Book (IRE) (Ballad Rock)

S P C Woods Arashan Ali

Placings:0216 (2012)

2001: 10⁰GS, 11²SD, 9¹SD, 11⁶GF

	Starts	1st	2nd	3rd	Win & Pl
Career Total (Turf)	2	0	0	0	237
Career Total (AW)	2	1	1	0	3943

80	5/01	Wolv	1m1f79y	D	STD	£2947

Total win prize-money £2947

Going (Turf): Sf: 0-0 GS: 0-1 Gd: 0-0 GF: 0-1 Fm: 0-0
Distance: 5f/6f: 0-0 7f-8f: 0-0 9f-13f: 1-4 14f+: 0-0
Track : LH: 1-3 RH: 0-0 Tight: 1-1 Gall: 0-0
Aids: Bl: 0-0 Vi: 0-0 Tstrap: 0-0
Best Rating: 80 5/01 Wolv 1m1f79y stand

Rajam

107 **95**

3-y-o b c Sadler's Wells (USA)-Rafif (USA) (Riverman (USA))

A C Stewart Hamdan Al Maktoum

Placings:22-21120 (4869)

2001: 10²G, 12¹GF, 12¹GF, 12²G, 14⁰G

	Starts	1st	2nd	3rd	Win & Pl
Career Total (Turf)	7	2	4	0	25505

92	8/01	Newb	1m4f5y	C(0-90)	G-F	£9002
77	6/01	Kemp	1m4f	D	G-F	£4446

Total win prize-money £13448

Going (Turf): Sf: 0-0 GS: 0-0 Gd: 0-3 GF: 2-2 Fm: 0-0
Distance: 5f/6f: 0-0 7f-8f: 0-0 9f-13f: 2-4 14f+: 0-1
Track : LH: 1-2 RH: 1-3 Tight: 0-1 Gall: 1-2
Aids: Bl: 0-0 Vi: 0-0 Tstrap: 0-0
Best Rating: 95 9/01 Kemp 1m4f good

Ex-French, he ended a sequence of three seconds when taking a Kempton maiden. Followed up in a Newbury classified event, again making all, and ran another good race back at Kempton. Looks to be improving.

Rake Hey

(93) (41)**47**

7-y-o gr g Petong-Dancing Daughter (Dance In Time (CAN))

D G Bridgwater D G Bridgwater

Placings:050026/645-0252 (0298)

2001: 16⁰SW, 14²SW, 13⁵SD, 12²SD

	Starts	1st	2nd	3rd	Win & Pl
Career Total (Turf)	7	0	1	0	959
Career Total (AW)	6	0	2	0	1138

Going (Turf): Sf: 0-1 GS: 0-1 Gd: 0-2 GF: 0-3 Fm: 0-0
Distance: 5f/6f: 0-3 7f-8f: 0-3 9f-13f: 0-5 14f+: 0-2
Track : LH: 0-9 RH: 0-1 Tight: 0-8 Gall: 0-0
Aids: Bl: 0-2 Vi: 0-2 Tstrap: 0-1
Best Rating: 41 2/01 Ling 1m5f stand

Rakeeb (USA)

89 **30**

6-y-o ch g Irish River (FR)-Ice House (Northfields (USA))

M W Easterby Major M Watson

Placings:033110/00006004/140-000P (4330)

2001: 16⁰SD, 12⁰GS, 16⁰GS, 16ᴾGF

	Starts	1st	2nd	3rd	Win & Pl
Career Total (Turf)	20	3	0	2	11536
Career Total (AW)	1	0	0	0	

66	3/00	Donc	1m4f	F(0-80)H	G-F	£3016
91	8/98	Hayd	1m3f200y	D(0-85)H	G-S	£3610
94	7/98	Ayr	1m2f	D	SFT	£3473

Total win prize-money £10100

Going (Turf): Sf: 1-4 GS: 1-4 Gd: 0-6 GF: 1-6 Fm: 0-0
Distance: 5f/6f: 0-0 7f-8f: 0-1 9f-13f: 3-14 14f+: 0-6
Track : LH: 3-15 RH: 0-5 Tight: 0-7 Gall: 1-6
Aids: Bl: 1-6 Vi: 0-0 Tstrap: 0-0
Best Rating: 30 3/01 Donc 1m4f gd-sft

Rallentando

82(68) (16)**32**

2-y-o b f Piccolo-Wrangbrook (Shirley Heights)

G M Moore John Lishman

Placings:0000 (4793)

2001: 5⁰SD, 5⁰GS, 7⁰G, 8⁰G

	Starts	1st	2nd	3rd	Win & Pl
Career Total (Turf)	3	0	0	0	
Career Total (AW)	1	0	0	0	

Going (Turf): Sf: 0-0 GS: 0-1 Gd: 0-2 GF: 0-0 Fm: 0-0
Distance: 5f/6f: 0-2 7f-8f: 0-2 9f-13f: 0-0 14f+: 0-0
Track : LH: 0-2 RH: 0-0 Tight: 0-1 Gall: 0-0
Aids: Bl: 0-0 Vi: 0-0 Tstrap: 0-0
Best Rating: 32 9/01 Ayr 1m good

Rambagh

100 **64**

3-y-o b f Polish Precedent (USA)-My Preference (Reference Point)
J L Dunlop The Rajmata Of Jaipur

Placings:4254-6443230**U**5 **(5082)**
2001: 9^{6}GS, 12^{4}GS, 10^{4}GF, 8^{3}G, 8^{2}GF, 8^{3}GF, 9^{0}GF, **8**^{U}SD, 7^{5}S

	Starts	1st	2nd	3rd	Win & Pl
Career Total (Turf)	12	0	2	2	4316
Career Total (AW)	1	0	0	0	

Going (Turf): Sf: 0-2 GS: 0-2 Gd: 0-1 GF: 0-6 Fm: 0-0
Distance: 5f/6f: 0-0 7f-8f: 0-5 9f-13f: 0-7 14f+: 0-0
Track : LH: 0-6 RH: 0-3 Tight: 0-3 Gall: 0-0
Aids: Bl: 0-1 Vi: 0-6 Tstrap: 0-0
Best Rating: 66 7/01 Leic 1m9y gd-fm

Ramblin' Man (IRE)

99(98) (53)**36**

3-y-o b c Blues Traveller (IRE)-Saborinie (Prince Sabo)
M Blanshard The First Timers

Placings:050300-**034**5424340200233 **(5081)**
2001: **7**^{0}SD, **7**^{3}SD, **8**^{4}SD, 8^{5}S, 8^{4}G, 10^{2}GF, 9^{4}GF, 9^{3}G, 10^{4}HD, 9^{0}GF, 11^{2}GF, 11^{0}GF, 12^{0}G, 11^{2}GF, 9^{3}GF, 9^{3}S

	Starts	1st	2nd	3rd	Win & Pl
Career Total (Turf)	19	0	3	4	3851
Career Total (AW)	3	0	0	1	581

Going (Turf): Sf: 0-2 GS: 0-0 Gd: 0-6 GF: 0-10 Fm: 0-1
Distance: 5f/6f: 0-5 7f-8f: 0-3 9f-13f: 0-14 14f+: 0-0
Track : LH: 0-11 RH: 0-4 Tight: 0-7 Gall: 0-3
Aids: Bl: 0-0 Vi: 0-0 Tstrap: 0-0
Best Rating: 56 6/01 Nott 1m1f213y good

He has been placed many times, but looks short of toe and always finds one or two to beat him.

Rambling Bear

101 **101**

8-y-o ch h Sharrood (USA)-Supreme Rose (Frimley Park)
M Blanshard Mrs Michael Hill

Placings:21214/611051300/66303003502/1660002506 0/1450F0350/330056300-005 **(3063)**
2001: 5^{0}G, 6^{0}GF, 5^{5}G

	Starts	1st	2nd	3rd	Win & Pl
Career Total (Turf)	57	7	4	8	129868

110	5/99	NmkJ	5f	A	G-F	£20000
109	5/98	Gdwd	6f	C	G-F	£4942
107	7/96	Gdwd	5f	A	G-F	£27680
114	6/96	Ling	6f	A	G-F	£12661
108	5/96	Newb	6f8y	B	G-F	£7570
92	9/95	Kemp	6f	A	GD	£10560
91	7/95	Wind	5f10y	D	G-F	£5572

Total win prize-money £88986

Going (Turf): Sf: 0-4 GS: 0-6 Gd: 1-16 **GF: 6-30** Fm: 0-1
Distance: **5f/6f: 6-52** 7f-8f: 1-5 9f-13f: 0-0 14f+: 0-0
Track : LH: 0-1 **RH: 1-1** Tight: 0-0 **Gall: 1-2**
Aids: Bl: 0-1 Vi: 0-0 Tstrap: 0-0
Best Rating: 86 5/01 NmkR 5f good

Invaraibaly looks well and is a very useful sprinter who goes well fresh. He ran third in the Palace House Stakes at Newmarket first time out in 2000, a race he won on his seasonal bow in 1999. However, he is not easy to win with, as he has to come with a late rattle. Acts on any ground. Retired.

Rambo Nine

40(88) (19)**19**

4-y-o b g Rambo Dancer (CAN)-Asmarina (Ascendant)
S R Bowring Mr J E Reed & Mr P M Sedgwick

Placings:0560/000-0000000 **(1079)**
2001: 6^{0}SW, 5^{0}SD, 7^{0}SD, 11^{0}SD, 8^{0}SW, 7^{0}SD, 7^{0}S

	Starts	1st	2nd	3rd	Win & Pl
Career Total (Turf)	5	0	0	0	0
Career Total (AW)	9	0	0	0	0

Going (Turf): Sf: 0-2 GS: 0-0 Gd: 0-2 GF: 0-1 Fm: 0-0
Distance: 5f/6f: 0-4 7f-8f: 0-5 9f-13f: 0-5 14f+: 0-0
Track : LH: 0-8 RH: 0-3 Tight: 0-3 Gall: 0-1
Aids: Bl: 0-2 Vi: 0-0 Tstrap: 0-0
Best Rating: 37 2/01 Sthl 7f stand

Rambo Waltzer

93(109) (61)**43**

9-y-o b g Rambo Dancer (CAN)-Vindictive Lady (USA) (Foolish Pleasure (USA))
Miss S J Wilton John Pointon And Sons

Placings:3611000/05564**034/15616**211100000000**05/ 1212221**1321565**3552/321263**210005**3**51**3/2**1010130000 00**141/1121261**13200**246032-11503334**000**0**000 **(4727)**
2001: **9**^{1}SD, **9**^{1}SW, **9**^{5}SD, **9**^{0}SD, **12**^{3}SD, **11**^{3}SD, **12**^{3}SD, 8^{4}G, 10^{0}F, 10^{0}GF, 8^{0}GF, **8**^{0}SD, 11^{0}G, 10^{0}GF

	Starts	1st	2nd	3rd	Win & Pl
Career Total (Turf)	55	6	4	4	26954
Career Total (AW)	61	21	12	10	80858

68	1/01	Wolv	1m1f79y	F	SLW	£2254
61	1/01	Wolv	1m1f79y	F	STD	£2114
69	3/00	Wolv	1m100y	F	STD	£2299
59	3/00	Sthl	7f	F	STD	£2310
59	2/00	Wolv	1m1f79y	F	STD	£2072
55	1/00	Wolv	7f	G	STD	£1518
63	1/00	Sthl	1m	G	STD	£2002
56	12/99	Sthl	1m	F	STD	£1871
56	11/99	Sthl	1m	G	STD	£1605
71	5/99	Sthl	7f	F	STD	£1924
69	4/99	Thsk	7f	E(0-70)H	GD	£3683
67	3/99	Catt	7f	D(0-80)H	G-S	£4887
73	12/98	Sthl	1m	F	STD	£1997
87	4/98	Sthl	1m	C(0-95)H	STD	£7107
78	1/98	Wolv	1m1f79y	D(0-80)H	STD	£3420
71	4/97	Haml	1m65y	E(0-70)H	G-S	£2682
78	3/97	Wolv	1m100y	B(0-105)H	STD	£14135
76	2/97	Sthl	1m	D(0-80)H	STD	£3566
70	1/97	Sthl	7f	G	STD	£2095
81	1/97	Sthl	1m	G	STD	£2085
68	4/96	Ripn	1m	E(0-70)H	GD	£3132
64	4/96	Thsk	1m	F(0-65)H	G-F	£3344
58	4/96	Haml	1m65y	E(0-70)H	G-S	£2790
78	1/96	Wolv	7f	F	STD	£2870
75	1/96	Sthl	1m	F	STD	£2222
75	7/94	Sthl	6f	D	STD	£3651
61	7/94	Sthl	7f	F	STD	£2779

Total win prize-money £86423

Going (Turf): Sf: 0-5 **GS: 3-11** Gd: 2-20 GF: 1-17 Fm: 0-2
Distance: 5f/6f: 1-3 **7f-8f: 18-64** 9f-13f: 8-49 14f+: 0-0
Track : **LH: 24-98** RH: 3-9 **Tight: 14-45** Gall: 0-11
Aids: Bl: 0-0 Vi: 0-1 Tstrap: 0-0
Best Rating: 68 1/01 Wolv 1m1f79y slow

He is a consistent performer, though most of his wins in recent seasons have been on Fibresand. A turning track suits him best and he seems to need at least a mile now.

Rampant (IRE)

105 **81**

3-y-o b c Pursuit Of Love-Flourishing (IRE) (Trojan Fen)
R M Beckett Mrs Richard Aykroyd

Placings:2-210504100 **(5693)**
2001: 8^{2}S, 8^{1}GS, 8^{0}GF, 9^{5}S, 10^{0}G, 10^{4}HY, 11^{1}S, 12^{0}HY, 12^{0}S

	Starts	1st	2nd	3rd	Win & Pl
Career Total (Turf)	10	2	2	0	14617

81	10/01	Leic	1m3f183y	C(0-90)H	SFT	£7306
75	5/01	Wind	1m67y	D	G-S	£4322

Total win prize-money £11629

Going (Turf): Sf: 1-7 GS: 1-1 Gd: 0-1 GF: 0-1 Fm: 0-0
Distance: 5f/6f: 0-0 7f-8f: 0-2 **9f-13f: 2-8** 14f+: 0-0
Track : LH: 0-5 **RH: 2-4 Tight: 1-2** Gall: 0-3
Aids: Bl: 0-0 Vi: 0-0 **Tstrap: 1-4**
Best Rating: 81 10/01 Leic 1m3f183y soft

Got off the mark on his second start at three at Windsor over a mile. Rather lost his way until winning at Leicester in soft ground over a mile and a half at the backend. Suited by cut.

Rampart

101(89) (36)**36**

4-y-o b g Kris-Balliasta (USA) (Lyphard (USA))
D Shaw The Whiteman Partnership

Placings:03/05**000**-000400 **(5617)**
2001: 7^{0}GF, 8^{0}F, 9^{0}GF, 8^{4}GS, 9^{0}GF, **8**^{0}SD, 6^{5}SD

	Starts	1st	2nd	3rd	Win & Pl
Career Total (Turf)	9	0	0	1	493
Career Total (AW)	4	0	0	0	

Going (Turf): Sf: 0-1 GS: 0-3 Gd: 0-0 GF: 0-4 Fm: 0-1
Distance: 5f/6f: 0-1 7f-8f: 0-5 9f-13f: 0-7 14f+: 0-0
Track : LH: 0-7 RH: 0-3 Tight: 0-5 Gall: 0-1
Aids: Bl: 0-3 Vi: 0-0 Tstrap: 0-0
Best Rating: 36 6/01 Bevl 1m1f207y gd-fm

Ramzain

94(99) (63)**65**

3-y-o b c Alzao (USA)-Romoosh (Formidable (USA))
P W D'Arcy Paul D'Arcy

Placings:210 **(1140)**
2001: **7**^{2}SD, **8**^{1}SW, 8^{0}G

	Starts	1st	2nd	3rd	Win & Pl
Career Total (Turf)	1	0	0	0	
Career Total (AW)	2	1	1	0	3485

63	4/01	Sthl	1m	D	SLW	£2779

Total win prize-money £2779

Going (Turf): Sf: 0-0 GS: 0-0 Gd: 0-1 GF: 0-0 Fm: 0-0
Distance: 5f/6f: 0-0 **7f-8f: 1-3** 9f-13f: 0-0 14f+: 0-0
Track : **LH: 1-2** RH: 0-0 Tight: 0-0 Gall: 0-0
Aids: Bl: 0-0 Vi: 0-0 Tstrap: 0-0
Best Rating: 65 5/01 NmkR 1m good

Random Kindness

88(99) (82d)**51**

8-y-o b g Alzao (USA)-Lady Tippins (USA) (Star De Naskra (USA))
R Ingram 949 Racing

Placings:03320/**52221**01**4**01201/**6**0**1**2312204000**134/0** 62442000/**400**-060 **(3426)**
2001: 11^{0}F, 14^{6}GF, 14^{0}GF

	Starts	1st	2nd	3rd	Win & Pl
Career Total (Turf)	32	2	7	3	14748
Career Total (AW)	17	5	3	1	25849

94	11/98	Ling	1m4f	D	STD	£3436
70	5/98	Brig	1m3f196y	E(0-70)	FRM	£2697
84	4/98	Ling	1m4f	D(0-85)	STD	£3622
82	11/97	Wolv	1m4f	D(0-85)H	STD	£3550
62	10/97	Ling	1m3f106y	F(0-65)	FRM	£2277
77	4/97	Wolv	1m6f166y	C(0-95)H	STD	£5732

77	3/97	Wolv	2m46y	E	STD	£2580

Total win prize-money £23895

Going (Turf): Sf: 0-0 GS: 0-2 Gd: 0-11 GF: 0-16 **Fm: 2-3**
Distance: 5f/6f: 0-0 7f-8f: 0-0 **9f-13f: 5-32** 14f+: 2-17
Track : **LH: 7-36** RH: 0-13 **Tight: 6-29** Gall: 0-5
Aids: Bl: 0-0 Vi: 0-0 Tstrap: 0-0
Best Rating: 51 7/01 Kemp 1m6f92y gd-fm

Random Quest

99 **90**

3-y-o b g Rainbow Quest (USA)-Anne Bonny (Ajdal (USA))
P F I Cole The Blandford Partnership

Placings:01-25 **(1748)**
2001: 12^{2}S, 12^{5}GF

	Starts	1st	2nd	3rd	Win & Pl
Career Total (Turf)	4	1	1	0	15889

80	10/00	Nott	1m54y	D	SFT	£5239

Total win prize-money £5239

Going (Turf): Sf: 1-2 GS: 0-1 Gd: 0-0 GF: 0-1 Fm: 0-0
Distance: 5f/6f: 0-0 7f-8f: 0-1 **9f-13f: 1-3** 14f+: 0-0
Track : **LH: 1-1** RH: 0-2 Tight: 0-2 Gall: 0-0
Aids: Bl: 0-0 Vi: 0-0 Tstrap: 0-0
Best Rating: 90 5/01 Sals 1m4f soft

Random Task (IRE)

79(100) (81) **73**

4-y-o b c Tirol-Minami (IRE) (Caerleon (USA))
D Shaw J C Fretwell

Placings:14/0610-0000 **(2255)**
2001: 6^{0}SD, 6^{0}SD, 7^{0}F, 6^{0}G

	Starts	1st	2nd	3rd	Win & Pl
Career Total (Turf)	6	1	0	0	8362
Career Total (AW)	4	1	0	0	2801

73	9/00	Kemp	6f	C(0-90)H	SFT	£7930
81	5/99	Wolv	6f	D	STD	£2801

Total win prize-money £10731

Going (Turf): Sf: 1-2 GS: 0-0 Gd: 0-2 GF: 0-1 Fm: 0-1
Distance: 5f/6f: 2-6 7f-8f: 0-4 9f-13f: 0-0 14f+: 0-0
Track : **LH: 1-5** RH: 0-0 **Tight: 1-3** Gall: 0-1
Aids: **Bl: 1-2** Vi: 0-1 Tstrap: 0-0
Best Rating: 70 3/01 Wolv 6f stand

Raneen Nashwan

90 **74**

5-y-o b g Nashwan (USA)-Raneen Alwatar (Sadler's Wells (USA))
M R Channon M Channon

Placings:6541/40/6-0 **(5692)**
2001: 16^{0}S

	Starts	1st	2nd	3rd	Win & Pl
Career Total (Turf)	8	1	0	0	4199

77	11/98	Muss	1m	D	SFT	£3512

Total win prize-money £3513

Going (Turf): Sf: 1-4 GS: 0-2 Gd: 0-0 GF: 0-2 Fm: 0-0
Distance: 5f/6f: 0-0 **7f-8f: 1-4** 9f-13f: 0-3 14f+: 0-1
Track : LH: 0-3 **RH: 1-2 Tight: 1-3** Gall: 0-1
Aids: Bl: 0-0 Vi: 0-0 Tstrap: 0-0
Best Rating: 52 11/01 Donc 2m110y soft

A winner of a mile maiden in soft ground back in 1998, he has been very lightly raced since and has clearly had his problems.

Range Trader (NZ)

94 **49**

7-y-o gr g Truly Vain (AUS)-Roopcotful (NZ) (Standaan (FR))
E J Alston (H D Daly 10/5) Trevor Hemmings

Placings:110/006252/010-42600 **(3798)**
2001: 8^{4}GF, 10^{2}GF, 6^{6}GF, 6^{0}GF, 8^{0}G

	Starts	1st	2nd	3rd	Win & Pl
Career Total (Turf)	17	3	3	0	12318

1/00	Tren	1m	H	FRM	£4777
10/98		6f55y		G-S	£1830
10/98	Otak	7f		G-S	£915

Total win prize-money £7522

Going (Turf): Sf: 0-2 **GS: 2-5** Gd: 0-1 GF: 0-4 Fm: 1-5
Distance: 5f/6f: 0-3 **7f-8f: 3-11** 9f-13f: 0-3 14f+: 0-0
Track : LH: 0-4 RH: 0-0 Tight: 0-0 Gall: 0-1
Aids: Bl: 0-0 Vi: 0-0 Tstrap: 0-0
Best Rating: 49 7/01 Hayd 6f gd-fm

A winner in New Zealand, possesses a little ability and might do better once handicapped. Stays a mile. Acts on fast ground.

Ranin

113 **107**

3-y-o b f Unfuwain (USA)-Nafhaat (USA) (Roberto (USA))
E A L Dunlop Hamdan Al Maktoum

Placings:352-21102154120 **(5257)**
2001: 8^{2}GS, 10^{1}GF, 10^{1}GF, 10^{0}GF, 11^{2}GS, 12^{1}GS, 13^{5}S, 11^{4}G, 14^{1}GF, 12^{2}VS, 12^{0}GS

	Starts	1st	2nd	3rd	Win & Pl
Career Total (Turf)	14	4	4	1	76702

100	9/01	Donc	1m6f132yA		G-F	£24000
103	7/01	NmkJ	1m4f	A	G-S	£14036
100	6/01	Newb	1m2f6y	C(0-90)H	G-F	£7163
79	5/01	Ling	1m2f	D	G-F	£3307

Total win prize-money £48507

Going (Turf): Sf: 0-2 GS: 1-4 Gd: 0-2 **GF: 3-5** Fm: 0-0
Distance: 5f/6f: 0-0 7f-8f: 0-2 **9f-13f: 3-10** 14f+: 1-2
Track : **LH: 3-5** RH: 0-4 Tight: 1-2 **Gall: 2-5**
Aids: Bl: 0-0 Vi: 0-0 Tstrap: 0-0
Best Rating: 107 10/01 Lonc 1m4f110y v soft

Rapid improvement this season, confirming earlier promise when second to Sacred Song in Lancashire Oaks at Haydock, before taking a Newmarket listed event. Has continued to run well, landing the Park Hill at Doncaster and finishing second in a Longchamp Group Two. Probably best over a mile and a half, handles fast and easy ground, and suited by waiting tactics.

Ranville

108 **95+**

3-y-o ch g Deploy-Kibitka (FR) (Baby Turk)
M A Jarvis K G Powter

Placings:00-002111110 **(5692)**
2001: 10^{0}G, 10^{0}GF, 14^{2}G, 14^{1}S, 14^{1}G, 15^{1}S, 16^{1}GS, 16^{1}HY, 16^{0}S

	Starts	1st	2nd	3rd	Win & Pl
Career Total (Turf)	11	5	1	0	29124

95	10/01	Newb	2m	C(0-90)H	HVY	£9022
83	10/01	Newc	2m19y	E(0-75)H	G-S	£2968
76	9/01	Ches	1m7f195y	D(0-80)H	SFT	£7507
68	8/01	Hayd	1m6f	D(0-85)H	GD	£4446
64	8/01	Nott	1m6f15y	E(0-70)H	SFT	£4240

Total win prize-money £28185

Going (Turf): Sf: 3-5 GS: 1-2 Gd: 1-3 GF: 0-1 Fm: 0-0
Distance: 5f/6f: 0-0 7f-8f: 0-1 9f-13f: 0-3 **14f+: 5-7**
Track : **LH: 5-7** RH: 0-0 Tight: 1-4 Gall: 1-2
Aids: Bl: 0-0 Vi: 0-0 Tstrap: 0-0
Best Rating: 95 10/01 Newb 2m heavy

A progressive stayer, he completed a brilliant five-timer in staying handicaps between August and October over trips from 14 to 16 furlongs, but looked to be feeling the effects of a tough campaign at Doncaster in November. He is suited by the ground good or softer and by positive tactics.

Rapadash (IRE)

91(97) (80)**86**

2-y-o ch c Doundary (USA)-Imelda (USA) (Manila (USA))
B J Meehan Mrs Susan Roy

Placings:4313 **(2794)**
2001: 5^{4}G, 6^{3}SD, 6^{1}SD, 6^{3}GF

	Starts	1st	2nd	3rd	Win & Pl
Career Total (Turf)	2	0	0	1	1092
Career Total (AW)	2	1	0	1	3373

80	6/01	Sthl	6f	D	STD	£2954

Total win prize-money £2954

Going (Turf): Sf: 0-0 GS: 0-0 Gd: 0-1 GF: 0-1 Fm: 0-0
Distance: 5f/6f: 1-3 7f-8f: 0-1 9f-13f: 0-0 14f+: 0-0
Track : **LH: 1-2** RH: 0-1 Tight: 0-0 Gall: 0-1
Aids: **Bl: 1-3** Vi: 0-0 Tstrap: 0-0
Best Rating: 86 7/01 Sals 6f212y gd-fm

He has shown ability on turf but his victory came in a maiden on the Southwell Fibresand.

Raphael (IRE)

101 **76**

2-y-o b f Perugino (USA)-Danny's Miracle (Superlative)
T D Easterby Mrs K Arton

Placings:352422110 **(5052)**
2001: 5^{3}S, 5^{5}S, 5^{2}F, 6^{4}GF, 7^{2}F, 7^{2}GS, 7^{1}G, 8^{1}GF, 7^{0}S

	Starts	1st	2nd	3rd	Win & Pl
Career Total (Turf)	9	2	3	1	12583

76	9/01	Ripn	1m	D(0-85)	G-F	£4426
69	8/01	Thsk	7f	E	GD	£3786

Total win prize-money £8213

Going (Turf): Sf: 0-3 GS: 0-1 **Gd: 1-1 GF: 1-2** Fm: 0-2
Distance: 5f/6f: 0-4 **7f-8f: 2-5** 9f-13f: 0-0 14f+: 0-0
Track : LH: 1-4 RH: 1-1 **Tight: 2-3** Gall: 0-0
Aids: Bl: 0-0 Vi: 0-0 Tstrap: 0-0
Best Rating: 76 9/01 Ripn 1m gd-fm

Very consistent, she showed plenty of ability in her early starts and improved as she went up in trip. Got off the mark in a Thirsk maiden in August and just lasted home over a mile at Ripon next time, making the running on both occasions. Seven furlongs may be her best trip.

Rapid Liner

(89) (4)**36**

8-y-o b g Skyliner-Stellaris (Star Appeal)
J Gallagher Mrs V W Jones

Placings:56040/0000/600/000/360-06 **(0350)**
2001: 16^{0}SD, 12^{8}SD

	Starts	1st	2nd	3rd	Win & Pl
Career Total (Turf)	13	0	0	0	207
Career Total (AW)	7	0	0	1	318

Going (Turf): Sf: 0-0 GS: 0-0 Gd: 0-6 GF: 0-5 Fm: 0-2
Distance: 5f/6f: 0-5 7f-8f: 0-4 9f-13f: 0-4 14f+: 0-7
Track : LH: 0-14 RH: 0-2 Tight: 0-10 Gall: 0-0
Aids: Bl: 0-2 Vi: 0-1 Tstrap: 0-0
Best Rating: 76 9/01 Ripn 1m gd-fm

Rapparee (USA)

105 **75**

3-y-o b f Red Ransom (USA)-Pixie Erin (Golden Fleece (USA))
J W Hills The Dan Abbott Racing Partnership

Placings:5315000 **(5463)**
2001: 8^{5}G, 9^{3}GF, 10^{1}G, 10^{5}GF, 10^{0}GF, 10^{0}GF, 11^{0}G

	Starts	1st	2nd	3rd	Win & Pl
Career Total (Turf)	7	1	0	1	7470

91	6/01	York	1m2f85y	D	GD	£6639

Total win prize-money £6640

Going (Turf): Sf: 0-0 GS: 0-0 Gd: 1-3 GF: 0-4 Fm: 0-0
Distance: 5f/6f: 0-0 7f-8f: 0-1 9f-13f: 1-6 14f+: 0-0
Track : LH: 1-5 RH: 0-1 Tight: 0-2 Gall: 1-4
Aids: Bl: 0-0 Vi: 0-0 Tstrap: 0-0
Best Rating: 91 6/01 York 1m2f85y good

Bred to stay, she got off the mark on her third outing in a York maiden over ten furlongs, but has looked held in handicap company since. Acts on fast ground.

Rapscallion (GER)

103 **103**

2-y-o b c Robellino (USA)-Rosy Outlook (USA) (Trempolino (USA))

J M P Eustace J C Smith

Placings:531111 **(5493)**

2001: 5^{5}GF, 6^{3}G, 6^{1}GF, 7^{1}HY, 7^{1}GS, 7^{1}HY

	Starts	1st	2nd	3rd	Win & Pl
Career Total (Turf)	6	4	0	1	47592

103	10/01	Newb	7f	A	HVY	£20300
103	10/01	Asct	7f	B	G-S	£8749
92	9/01	Asct	7f	B	HVY	£14332
78	8/01	Ling	6f	E	G-F	£3588

Total win prize-money £46970

Going (Turf): Sf: 2-2 GS: 1-1 Gd: 0-1 GF: 1-2 Fm: 0-0
Distance: 5f/6f: 1-2 7f-8f: 3-4 9f-13f: 0-0 14f+: 0-0
Track : LH: 0-0 RH: 0-0 Tight: 0-0 Gall: 0-0
Aids: Bl: 0-0 Vi: 0-0 Tstrap: 0-0
Best Rating: 103 10/01 Newb 7f heavy

Improving with racing and ran out the clear-cut winner of a Lingfield maiden on his third start. Got the seven furlongs really well when just getting up to win a valuable nursery on soft ground at Ascot in September and followed up in a valuable conditions race in similar style over the same course and distance. He earned deserved black type for yet another dour battling performance to win the Group Three Horris Hill Stakes at Newbury and must be one of the bravest horses in training.

Rapt (IRE)

98(97) (74)**67**

3-y-o b g Septieme Ciel (USA)-Dream Play (USA) (Blushing Groom (FR))

W Jarvis Stephen R Hobson

Placings:06-1203300 **(5375)**

2001: 6^{1}SD, 7^{2}SD, 7^{0}GS, 5^{3}F, 6^{3}GF, 7^{0}GF, 7^{0}G

	Starts	1st	2nd	3rd	Win & Pl
Career Total (Turf)	7	0	0	2	951
Career Total (AW)	2	1	1	0	4011

66	3/01	Sthl	6f	E	STD	£2730

Total win prize-money £2730

Going (Turf): Sf: 0-1 GS: 0-2 Gd: 0-1 GF: 0-2 Fm: 0-1
Distance: 5f/6f: 1-3 7f-8f: 0-6 9f-13f: 0-0 14f+: 0-0
Track : LH: 1-3 RH: 0-1 Tight: 0-1 Gall: 0-0
Aids: Bl: 0-0 Vi: 0-0 Tstrap: 0-0
Best Rating: 74 4/01 Sthl 7f stand

Unplaced in juvenile maidens before winning on Fibresand on his return, but beaten in a handicaps since then, and may well benefit from a return to the Fibresand. Usually races prominently.

Raptor (IRE)

95 **26**

3-y-o ch g Eagle Eyed (USA)-Ahakista (IRE) (Persian Bold)

S E Kettlewell The Tupgill Partnership

Placings:000-65060 **(4014)**

2001: 14^{6}GF, 11^{5}GF, 12^{0}GF, 11^{6}G, 15^{0}G

	Starts	1st	2nd	3rd	Win & Pl
Career Total (Turf)	8	0	0	0	0

Going (Turf): Sf: 0-1 GS: 0-0 Gd: 0-3 GF: 0-4 Fm: 0-0
Distance: 5f/6f: 0-1 7f-8f: 0-2 9f-13f: 0-3 14f+: 0-2
Track : LH: 0-4 RH: 0-2 Tight: 0-4 Gall: 0-1
Aids: Bl: 0-0 Vi: 0-2 Tstrap: 0-0
Best Rating: 42 6/01 Haml 1m3f16y gd-fm

Rare Genius (USA)

103 **66**

5-y-o ch g Beau Genius (CAN)-Aunt Nola (USA) (Olden Times)

Ian Williams The Heyfleet Partnership

Placings:0563052/23506-54 **(1987)**

2001: 16^{5}GF, 14^{4}G

	Starts	1st	2nd	3rd	Win & Pl
Career Total (Turf)	14	0	2	2	4314

Going (Turf): Sf: 0-1 GS: 0-0 Gd: 0-7 GF: 0-6 Fm: 0-0
Distance: 5f/6f: 0-0 7f-8f: 0-0 9f-13f: 0-9 14f+: 0-5
Track : LH: 0-8 RH: 0-4 Tight: 0-6 Gall: 0-1
Aids: Bl: 0-0 Vi: 0-0 Tstrap: 0-0
Best Rating: 65 6/01 Hayd 1m6f good

Rare Old Times (IRE)

98 **28**

3-y-o b f Inzar (USA)-Moona (USA) (Lear Fan (USA))

Mrs P N Dutfield Graham Brown

Placings:510600-606050000 **(5497)**

2001: 5^{6}GS, 5^{0}G, 6^{6}GF, 6^{0}GF, 5^{5}GF, 5^{0}G, 5^{0}HY, 6^{0}HY, 5^{0}HY

	Starts	1st	2nd	3rd	Win & Pl
Career Total (Turf)	15	1	0	0	7547

76	5/00	Wind	5f10y	B	G-S	£7308

Total win prize-money £7308

Going (Turf): Sf: 0-3 GS: 1-2 Gd: 0-4 GF: 0-6 Fm: 0-0
Distance: 5f/6f: 1-15 7f-8f: 0-0 9f-13f: 0-0 14f+: 0-0
Track : LH: 0-0 RH: 1-3 Tight: 0-0 Gall: 1-3
Aids: Bl: 0-4 Vi: 0-0 Tstrap: 0-0
Best Rating: 60 5/01 Wind 5f10y gd-sft

Rare Quality

54

3-y-o b f Chaddleworth (IRE)-Pink Mex (Tickled Pink)

P J Makin Magno-Pulse Ltd

Placings:0 **(5670)**

2001: 8^{0}HY

	Starts	1st	2nd	3rd	Win & Pl
Career Total (Turf)	1	0	0	0	

Going (Turf): Sf: 0-1 GS: 0-0 Gd: 0-0 GF: 0-0 Fm: 0-0
Distance: 5f/6f: 0-0 7f-8f: 0-0 9f-13f: 0-1 14f+: 0-0
Track : LH: 0-0 RH: 0-1 Tight: 0-1 Gall: 0-0
Aids: Bl: 0-0 Vi: 0-0 Tstrap: 0-0

Rare Talent

99 **65d**

7-y-o b g Mtoto-Bold As Love (Lomond (USA))

S Gollings John King, Bill Hobson, Graham King

Placings:63244501001000/301413040000/5060601212 62000/00303261522410-40500030 **(4009)**

2001: 12^{4}GF, 12^{0}F, 10^{5}GF, 11^{0}GS, 11^{0}GF, 9^{0}GF, 9^{3}GF, 11^{0}G

	Starts	1st	2nd	3rd	Win & Pl
Career Total (Turf)	63	8	7	6	46718

65	8/00	Epsm	1m4f10y	C(0-90)H	GD	£10432
59	7/00	Bevl	1m1f207y	E(0-70)H	G-F	£5304
58	8/99	Wind	1m3f135y	E(0-75)H	G-F	£2780
55	7/99	Bevl	1m1f207y	E(0-75)H	G-F	£3670
63	7/98	Ches	1m2f75y	D(0-80)H	G-F	£4328
59	6/98	Donc	1m2f60y	E(0-70)H	GD	£3517
60	9/97	Leic	1m1f218y	G	G-F	£2490
65	8/97	Ripn	1m2f	F(0-60)H	G-F	£2635

Total win prize-money £35158

Going (Turf): Sf: 0-2 GS: 0-5 Gd: 2-19 GF: 6-32 Fm: 0-5
Distance: 5f/6f: 0-0 7f-8f: 0-2 9f-13f: 8-61 14f+: 0-0
Track : LH: 3-35 RH: 4-24 Tight: 4-21 Gall: 1-13
Aids: Bl: 0-0 Vi: 0-1 Tstrap: 0-0
Best Rating: 65 5/01 Ches 1m4f66y gd-fm

A fair handicapper on his day, his best form has been over ten furlongs on good or faster ground. He ran well on his reappearance this term, but probably needs to drop a little in the handicap.

Rashik

93(104) (58)**58**

7-y-o ch h Cadeaux Genereux-Ghzaalh (USA) (Northern Dancer)

A Streeter Racing For You Limited

Placings:1/500-35204165 **(2649)**

2001: 8^{3}SD, 8^{5}SW, 12^{2}SD, 11^{0}SD, 12^{4}SD, 11^{1}SD, 12^{6}GF, 11^{5}SD, 14^{0}SD

	Starts	1st	2nd	3rd	Win & Pl
Career Total (Turf)	5	1	0	0	3701
Career Total (AW)	7	1	1	1	3308

58	5/01	Sthl	1m3f	F(0-60)	STD	£2359
97	4/97	Newb	1m	D	G-F	£3427

Total win prize-money £5787

Going (Turf): Sf: 0-0 GS: 0-0 Gd: 0-3 GF: 1-2 Fm: 0-0
Distance: 5f/6f: 0-0 7f-8f: 1-3 9f-13f: 1-9 14f+: 0-0
Track : LH: 1-9 RH: 0-2 Tight: 0-3 Gall: 0-1
Aids: Bl: 0-0 Vi: 0-0 Tstrap: 0-0
Best Rating: 58 5/01 Sthl 1m3f stand

Rasid (USA)

91 **90+**

3-y-o b c Bahri (USA)-Makadir (USA) (Woodman (USA))

E A L Dunlop Hamdan Al Maktoum

Placings:2 **(0791)**

2001: 10^{2}GS

	Starts	1st	2nd	3rd	Win & Pl
Career Total (Turf)	1	0	1	0	1544

Going (Turf): Sf: 0-0 GS: 0-1 Gd: 0-0 GF: 0-0 Fm: 0-0
Distance: 5f/6f: 0-0 7f-8f: 0-0 9f-13f: 0-1 14f+: 0-0
Track : LH: 0-0 RH: 0-0 Tight: 0-0 Gall: 0-0
Aids: Bl: 0-0 Vi: 0-0 Tstrap: 0-0
Best Rating: 90 4/01 NmkR 1m2f gd-sft

Rasmalai

13 **67**

4-y-o b f Sadler's Wells (USA)-Raymouna (IRE) (High Top)

R Hannon J A Lazzari

Placings:03020-00 **(1075)**

2001: 8^{0}S, 7^{0}GS

	Starts	1st	2nd	3rd	Win & Pl
Career Total (Turf)	7	0	1	1	1971

Going (Turf): Sf: 0-4 GS: 0-1 Gd: 0-1 GF: 0-1 Fm: 0-0
Distance: 5f/6f: 0-0 7f-8f: 0-2 9f-13f: 0-5 14f+: 0-0
Track : LH: 0-4 RH: 0-1 Tight: 0-4 Gall: 0-0
Aids: Bl: 0-0 Vi: 0-0 Tstrap: 0-0
Best Rating: 90 4/01 NmkR 1m2f gd-sft

Rasoum (USA)

107 **106**

3-y-o gr c Miswaki (USA)-Bel Ray (USA) (Restivo (USA))

E A L Dunlop Khalid Ali

Placings:313001-6400200 **(5105)**

2001: 7^{6}GS, 6^{4}G, 6^{0}GF, 6^{0}GS, 5^{2}GS, 6^{0}G, 5^{0}GS

	Starts	1st	2nd	3rd	Win & Pl
Career Total (Turf)	13	2	1	2	34787

110	10/00	Newb	6f8y	B	HVY	£22230
73	7/00	NmkJ	6f	D	GD	£4290

Total win prize-money £26520

Going (Turf): Sf: 1-2 GS: 0-4 **Gd: 1-5** GF: 0-2 Fm: 0-0
Distance: 5f/6f: 1-8 7f-8f: 1-5 9f-13f: 0-0 14f+: 0-0
Track : LH: 0-1 RH: 0-0 Tight: 0-0 Gall: 0-1
Aids: Bl: 0-1 Vi: 0-0 Tstrap: 0-0
Best Rating: 106 8/01 Leic 5f218y gd-sft

He took time to come to himself but ended his two-year-old campaign with a comfortable victory in a Newbury nursery in testing conditions. He has not proved easy to place at three but ran well at Leicester in August. Six furlongs is his optimum trip at present.

Rassendyll

86(92) (44)**53**
3-y-o b c Rudimentary (USA)-La Lutine (My Swallow)
A Bailey Skeltools Ltd

Placings:0-64000 **(4993)**
2001: 8^{6}G, 7^{4}S, 6^{0}G, 7^{0}SD, 7^{0}HY

	Starts	1st	2nd	3rd	Win & Pl
Career Total (Turf)	5	0	0	0	0
Career Total (AW)	1	0	0	0	0

Going (Turf): Sf: 0-2 GS: 0-0 Gd: 0-2 GF: 0-0 Fm: 0-1
Distance: 5f/6f: 0-1 7f-8f: 0-4 9f-13f: 0-1 14f+: 0-0
Track : LH: 0-3 RH: 0-0 Tight: 0-1 Gall: 0-0
Aids: Bl: 0-0 Vi: 0-0 Tstrap: 0-0
Best Rating: 53 8/01 Nott 1m54y good

Rateeba (IRE)

82 **43**
3-y-o b f Green Desert (USA)-Wathbat Mtoto (Mtoto)
A C Stewart Sheikh Ahmed Al Maktoum

Placings:00-0 **(1417)**
2001: 7^{0}GS

	Starts	1st	2nd	3rd	Win & Pl
Career Total (Turf)	3	0	0	0	

Going (Turf): Sf: 0-2 GS: 0-1 Gd: 0-0 GF: 0-0 Fm: 0-0
Distance: 5f/6f: 0-1 7f-8f: 0-2 9f-13f: 0-0 14f+: 0-0
Track : LH: 0-0 RH: 0-0 Tight: 0-0 Gall: 0-0
Aids: Bl: 0-0 Vi: 0-0 Tstrap: 0-0
Best Rating: 40 5/01 NmkR 7f gd-sft

Rathkenny (IRE)

100 **95**
3-y-o b c Standiford (USA)-Shine (Sharrood (USA))
J G Given Ray Monaghan

Placings:5641624-406106 **(3076)**
2001: 10^{4}S, 10^{0}GF, 8^{6}GF, 10^{1}F, 12^{0}GF, 10^{6}GS

	Starts	1st	2nd	3rd	Win & Pl
Career Total (Turf)	13	2	1	0	17441

95	6/01	Pont	1m2f6y	C(0-90)	FRM	£6792
59	9/00	Ayr	1m	E	SFT	£3250

Total win prize-money £10043

Going (Turf): Sf: 1-4 GS: 0-2 Gd: 0-1 GF: 0-5 **Fm: 1-1**
Distance: 5f/6f: 0-3 7f-8f: 1-2 9f-13f: 1-8 14f+: 0-0
Track : **LH: 2-8** RH: 0-1 Tight: 0-4 Gall: 0-1
Aids: Bl: 0-0 Vi: 0-0 Tstrap: 0-0
Best Rating: 95 6/01 Pont 1m2f6y firm

He has shown his best form since stepped up to a mile on soft ground. Creditable performances in Listed class but that would be his limit.

Ratified

89(100) (33)**39**
4-y-o b g Not In Doubt (USA)-Festival Of Magic (USA) (Clever Trick (USA))
M C Chapman Rasen Goes Racing

Placings:0000/2140526-0000000 **(3433)**
2001: 12^{0}GS, 11^{0}SD, 10^{0}HY, 12^{0}SD, 11^{0}SD, 14^{0}G, 16^{0}SD

	Starts	1st	2nd	3rd	Win & Pl
Career Total (Turf)	12	1	2	0	4163
Career Total (AW)	6	0	0	0	0

59	4/00	Nott	1m1f213yF(0-65)H		SFT	£2562

Total win prize-money £2562

Going (Turf): Sf: 1-4 GS: 0-3 Gd: 0-2 GF: 0-3 Fm: 0-0
Distance: 5f/6f: 0-0 7f-8f: 0-4 **9f-13f: 1-12** 14f+: 0-2
Track : **LH: 1-14** RH: 0-2 Tight: 0-4 Gall: 0-1
Aids: Bl: 0-0 Vi: 0-0 Tstrap: 0-0
Best Rating: 39 5/01 Yarm 1m6f17y good

Ratio

109 **107**
3-y-o ch c Pivotal-Owdbetts (IRE) (High Estate)
I A Balding Mrs John Davall

Placings:123426 **(4195)**
2001: 6^{1}GS, 7^{2}G, 7^{3}GF, 8^{4}GF, 8^{2}VS, 6^{6}G

	Starts	1st	2nd	3rd	Win & Pl
Career Total (Turf)	6	1	2	1	18591

81	5/01	Sals	6f	D	G-S	£3094

Total win prize-money £3094

Going (Turf): Sf: 0-0 **GS: 1-1** Gd: 0-2 GF: 0-2 Fm: 0-0
Distance: **5f/6f: 1-1** 7f-8f: 0-4 9f-13f: 0-1 14f+: 0-0
Track : LH: 0-1 RH: 0-1 Tight: 0-0 Gall: 0-1
Aids: Bl: 0-0 Vi: 0-0 Tstrap: 0-0
Best Rating: 107 6/01 Asct 7f gd-fm

Out of a mare who won over seven furlongs at two and three and ten furlongs at three and four, neeeded every yard of the stiff six at Salisbury on her debut at three. Stepped up to seven next time but ran too freely for her own good. Turned in a terrific performance, albeit from the best draw, to finish third in the Jersey Stakes at 100-1. Acts on a sound surface. Has won on good to soft.

Rattle

71
8-y-o b g Mazilier (USA)-Snake Song (Mansingh (USA))
D A Nolan Mrs J McFadyen-Murray

Placings:340540/5350243055/000000030/0/0-00 **(2121)**
2001: 8^{0}GF, 13^{0}GF

	Starts	1st	2nd	3rd	Win & Pl
Career Total (Turf)	27	0	1	4	2340
Career Total (AW)	2	0	0	0	

Going (Turf): Sf: 0-4 GS: 0-7 Gd: 0-6 GF: 0-7 Fm: 0-3
Distance: 5f/6f: 0-5 7f-8f: 0-6 9f-13f: 0-13 14f+: 0-5
Track : LH: 0-7 RH: 0-17 Tight: 0-18 Gall: 0-0
Aids: Bl: 0-6 Vi: 0-0 Tstrap: 0-1
Best Rating: 107 6/01 Asct 7f gd-fm

Rave On (ITY)

91 **83**
2-y-o b f Barathea (IRE)-Kalliopina (FR) (Arctic Tern (USA))
R Hannon A F Merritt

Placings:020 **(3554)**
2001: 6^{0}GF, 5^{2}G, 6^{0}GF

	Starts	1st	2nd	3rd	Win & Pl
Career Total (Turf)	3	0	1	0	1227

Going (Turf): Sf: 0-0 GS: 0-0 Gd: 0-1 GF: 0-2 Fm: 0-0
Distance: 5f/6f: 0-3 7f-8f: 0-0 9f-13f: 0-0 14f+: 0-0
Track : LH: 0-0 RH: 0-0 Tight: 0-0 Gall: 0-0
Aids: Bl: 0-0 Vi: 0-0 Tstrap: 0-0

Ravenglass (USA)

94 **70**
2-y-o b c Miswaki (USA)-Urus (USA) (Kris S (USA))
J H M Gosden Manton Racing Partnership

Placings:5 **(1431)**
2001: 6^{5}S

	Starts	1st	2nd	3rd	Win & Pl
Career Total (Turf)	1	0	0	0	0

Going (Turf): Sf: 0-1 GS: 0-0 Gd: 0-0 GF: 0-0 Fm: 0-0
Distance: 5f/6f: 0-0 7f-8f: 0-1 9f-13f: 0-0 14f+: 0-0
Track : LH: 0-0 RH: 0-0 Tight: 0-0 Gall: 0-0
Aids: Bl: 0-0 Vi: 0-0 Tstrap: 0-0
Best Rating: 70 5/01 Newb 6f8y soft

Ravenswood (IRE)

107 **96**
4-y-o b c Warning-Green Lucia (Green Dancer (USA))
M C Pipe D A Johnson

Placings:6100/421400-4520 **(5387)**
2001: 16^{4}F, 13^{5}G, 14^{2}GS, 18^{0}GS

	Starts	1st	2nd	3rd	Win & Pl
Career Total (Turf)	14	2	2	0	26515

86	6/00	Newb	1m5f61y	D(0-85)H	G-F	£4628
81	8/99	Brig	6f209y	E	FRM	£2879

Total win prize-money £7507

Going (Turf): Sf: 0-1 GS: 0-3 Gd: 0-4 **GF: 1-4 Fm: 1-2**
Distance: 5f/6f: 0-0 7f-8f: 1-4 9f-13f: 0-2 14f+: 1-8
Track : **LH: 2-6** RH: 0-5 Tight: 0-3 **Gall: 1-7**
Aids: Bl: 0-0 Vi: 0-0 **Tstrap: 1-11**
Best Rating: 96 9/01 Donc 1m6f132y gd-sft

Creditable fourth in 2000 Queens Vase. Wears a tongue tie. Probably needed his first outing of 2001 when fourth in the Northumberland Plate, and has run two good races since. Acts on a sound surface. Usually wears a tongue strap.

Ravishing (IRE)

106 **76**
4-y-o b f Bigstone (IRE)-Dazzling Maid (IRE) (Tate Gallery (USA))
W J Haggas G C Johnston

Placings:1/410000000-35210603225 **(4780)**
2001: 6^{3}GF, 6^{5}F, 6^{2}GF, 6^{1}GF, 6^{0}G, 6^{6}GS, 6^{0}GF, 5^{3}GF, 5^{2}G, 5^{2}GF, 6^{5}G

	Starts	1st	2nd	3rd	Win & Pl
Career Total (Turf)	21	3	3	2	22528

72	7/01	Yarm	6f3y	E(0-70)H	G-F	£3818
79	5/00	Newb	6f8y	C(0-90)H	G-F	£7312
77	10/99	Pont	6f	F	GD	£1955

Total win prize-money £13088

Going (Turf): Sf: 0-5 GS: 0-2 Gd: 1-4 **GF: 2-9** Fm: 0-1
Distance: 5f/6f: 1-15 **7f-8f: 2-6** 9f-13f: 0-0 14f+: 0-0
Track : **LH: 1-4** RH: 0-0 Tight: 0-0 Gall: 0-0
Aids: **Bl: 1-7** Vi: 0-0 Tstrap: 0-0
Best Rating: 76 9/01 Gdwd 6f good

She has fallen down the weights, but needed the application of blinkers to get her head back in front at Yarmouth in July 2001. Best over six furlongs and must have fast ground.

Raw Silk

85 **60d**
3-y-o b g Rudimentary (USA)-Misty Silks (Scottish Reel)
M J Ryan Paul Blows

Placings:0060-04000 **(5447)**

2001: 7^{0}GS, 8^{4}HY, 9^{0}G, 8^{0}F, 10^{0}HY

	Starts	1st	2nd	3rd	Win & Pl
Career Total (Turf)	9	0	0	0	0

Going (Turf): Sf: 0-2 GS: 0-2 Gd: 0-1 GF: 0-3 Fm: 0-1
Distance: 5f/6f: 0-3 7f-8f: 0-2 9f-13f: 0-4 14f+: 0-0
Track : LH: 0-3 RH: 0-1 Tight: 0-0 Gall: 0-2
Aids: Bl: 0-1 Vi: 0-0 Tstrap: 0-0
Best Rating: 60 4/01 Brig 7f214y gd-sft

Rawyaan

99 **97**

2-y-o b c Machiavellian (USA)-Raheefa (USA) (Riverman (USA))
J H M Gosden Hamdan Al Maktoum

Placings:51 **(5367)**
2001: 7^{5}GF, 8^{1}GS

	Starts	1st	2nd	3rd	Win & Pl
Career Total (Turf)	2	1	0	0	5655
97 10/01 NmkR 1m	D			G-S	£5655

Total win prize-money £5655

Going (Turf): Sf: 0-0 **GS: 1-1** Gd: 0-0 GF: 0-1 Fm: 0-0
Distance: 5f/6f: 0-0 **7f-8f: 1-2** 9f-13f: 0-0 14f+: 0-0
Track : LH: 0-0 RH: 0-0 Tight: 0-0 Gall: 0-0
Aids: Bl: 0-0 Vi: 0-0 Tstrap: 0-0
Best Rating: 97 10/01 NmkR 1m gd-sft

A staying-on fifth on his Newbury debut in September, he went one better in a Newmarket maiden over a mile the following month. Should stay further next term. Has won on good to soft.

Rayana (FR)

3-y-o b f Midyan (USA)-High Kash (FR) (Highest Honor (FR))
Ms A E Embiricos Mrs Jacquie Mikhailides

Placings:0-0 **(5296)**
2001: 8^{0}S

	Starts	1st	2nd	3rd	Win & Pl
Career Total (Turf)	2	0	0	0	

Going (Turf): Sf: 0-2 GS: 0-0 Gd: 0-0 GF: 0-0 Fm: 0-0
Distance: 5f/6f: 0-0 7f-8f: 0-1 9f-13f: 0-1 14f+: 0-0
Track : LH: 0-0 RH: 0-0 Tight: 0-0 Gall: 0-0
Aids: Bl: 0-0 Vi: 0-0 Tstrap: 0-0
Best Rating: 97 10/01 NmkR 1m gd-sft

Raybaan (IRE)

98 **78**

2-y-o b c Flying Spur (AUS)-Genetta (Green Desert (USA))
M H Tompkins Kenneth Macpherson

Placings:32210 **(4678)**
2001: 6^{3}GF, 6^{2}GS, 7^{2}GS, 8^{1}G, 8^{0}G

	Starts	1st	2nd	3rd	Win & Pl
Career Total (Turf)	5	1	2	1	6019
78 8/01 Yarm 1m3y	E			GD	£3542

Total win prize-money £3543

Going (Turf): Sf: 0-0 GS: 0-2 **Gd: 1-2** GF: 0-1 Fm: 0-0
Distance: 5f/6f: 0-2 7f-8f: 0-2 **9f-13f: 1-1** 14f+: 0-0
Track : LH: 0-0 RH: 0-1 Tight: 0-0 Gall: 0-0
Aids: Bl: 0-0 Vi: 0-0 Tstrap: 0-0
Best Rating: 78 8/01 Yarm 1m3y good

Improved for the step up in trip when scoring at Yarmouth.

Rayhan

91 **76**

2-y-o b f Unfuwain (USA)-Karawan (Kris)
J H M Gosden Hamdan Al Maktoum

Placings:34 **(5109)**
2001: 7^{3}GF, 6^{4}HY

	Starts	1st	2nd	3rd	Win & Pl
Career Total (Turf)	2	0	0	1	909

Going (Turf): Sf: 0-1 GS: 0-0 Gd: 0-0 GF: 0-1 Fm: 0-0
Distance: 5f/6f: 0-0 7f-8f: 0-2 9f-13f: 0-0 14f+: 0-0
Track : LH: 0-1 RH: 0-0 Tight: 0-0 Gall: 0-0
Aids: Bl: 0-0 Vi: 0-0 Tstrap: 0-0
Best Rating: 76 9/01 Wwck 7f26y gd-fm

Rayik

102(107) (53)**48**

6-y-o br g Marju (IRE)-Matila (IRE) (Persian Bold)
G L Moore Lancing Racing Syndicate

Placings:5/45361/26060000000060/121412001030500 53-23002600410350100 **(5407)**
2001: 12^{2}SD, 13^{3}SD, 12^{0}SD, 12^{0}SW, 12^{2}SW, 16^{6}SD, 12^{0}SD, 11^{0}GS, 9^{4}F, 11^{1}F, 12^{0}GF, 12^{3}GF, 12^{5}GF, 11^{0}F, 11^{1}G, 12^{0}GF, 12^{0}SD, 13^{3}SD

	Starts	1st	2nd	3rd	Win & Pl
Career Total (Turf)	27	3	0	2	9639
Career Total (AW)	27	4	5	3	30404

48	8/01	Wind	1m3f135y	E(0-70)H	GD	£3122
54	6/01	Brig	1m3f196y	F	FRM	£2534
56	8/00	Wind	1m3f135y	E(0-75)H	G-F	£2828
73	3/00	Ling	1m4f	E(0-75)H	STD	£3461
70	1/00	Ling	1m4f	C(0-95)H	STD	£6890
64	1/00	Ling	1m5f	E(0-70)H	STD	£3461
69	12/98	Ling	1m2f	D	STD	£2788

Total win prize-money £25084

Going (Turf): Sf: 0-4 GS: 0-3 **Gd: 1-3 GF: 1-12 Fm: 1-5**
Distance: 5f/6f: 0-0 7f-8f: 0-3 **9f-13f: 7-50** 14f+: 0-1
Track : **LH: 5-39** RH: 0-10 **Tight: 6-41** Gall: 0-2
Aids: Bl: 0-0 Vi: 0-2 Tstrap: 0-0
Best Rating: 63 2/01 Ling 1m4f slow

He looked much better on Equitrack than anything else and is suited by 12 furlongs.

Rayware Boy (IRE)

(103) (46)**40**

5-y-o b h Scenic-Amata (USA) (Nodouble (USA))
D Shaw Rayton Racing

Placings:0000/1142000000/0005452004033163-35300 **(0689)**
2001: 9^{3}SW, 12^{5}SD, 12^{3}SD, 12^{0}SW, 11^{0}SD

	Starts	1st	2nd	3rd	Win & Pl
Career Total (Turf)	14	0	1	0	980
Career Total (AW)	21	3	1	5	10326

46	11/00	Sthl	1m3f	F(0-60)H	STD	£1946
60	2/99	Sthl	1m	E(0-70)H	STD	£2775
57	1/99	Sthl	1m	E(0-70)H	STD	£2827

Total win prize-money £7548

Going (Turf): Sf: 0-1 GS: 0-1 Gd: 0-6 GF: 0-4 Fm: 0-1
Distance: 5f/6f: 0-2 **7f-8f: 2-7** 9f-13f: 1-24 14f+: 0-1
Track : **LH: 3-29** RH: 0-1 Tight: 0-18 Gall: 0-2
Aids: **Bl: 3-27** Vi: 0-3 Tstrap: 0-0
Best Rating: 46 2/01 Wolv 1m4f stand

Razkalla (USA)

100 **54++**

3-y-o b c Caerleon (USA)-Larrocha (IRE) (Sadler's Wells (USA))
D R Loder Maktoum Al Maktoum

Placings:1 **(4537)**
2001: 9^{1}GF

	Starts	1st	2nd	3rd	Win & Pl
Career Total (Turf)	1	1	0	0	4193
54 9/01 Rdcr 1m1f	D			G-F	£4192

Total win prize-money £4193

Going (Turf): Sf: 0-0 GS: 0-0 Gd: 0-0 **GF: 1-1** Fm: 0-0
Distance: 5f/6f: 0-0 7f-8f: 0-0 **9f-13f: 1-1** 14f+: 0-0
Track : **LH: 1-1** RH: 0-0 **Tight: 1-1** Gall: 0-0
Aids: Bl: 0-0 Vi: 0-0 Tstrap: 0-0
Best Rating: 54 9/01 Rdcr 1m1f gd-fm

Well bred, he scored comfortably on his belated debut over nine furlongs, giving the impression that there is more to come over further.

Razzle (IRE)

82 **59**

2-y-o b f Green Desert (USA)-Organza (High Top)
J L Dunlop Lordship Stud

Placings:0 **(5277)**
2001: 7^{0}GS

	Starts	1st	2nd	3rd	Win & Pl
Career Total (Turf)	1	0	0	0	

Going (Turf): Sf: 0-0 GS: 0-1 Gd: 0-0 GF: 0-0 Fm: 0-0
Distance: 5f/6f: 0-0 7f-8f: 0-1 9f-13f: 0-0 14f+: 0-0
Track : LH: 0-0 RH: 0-0 Tight: 0-0 Gall: 0-0
Aids: Bl: 0-0 Vi: 0-0 Tstrap: 0-0
Best Rating: 59 10/01 Leic 7f9y gd-sft

Reachforyourpocket (IRE)

104(103) (61)**44**

6-y-o b g Royal Academy (USA)-Gemaasheh (Habitat)
M D I Usher Bryan Fry

Placings:000P0006660/46120366000100025012 1-400533300350300000 **(4879)**
2001: 12^{4}SD, 10^{0}SD, 10^{0}SD, 10^{5}SD, 8^{3}SD, 8^{3}SW, 8^{3}SD, 10^{0}SD, 6^{0}GF, 6^{3}F, 6^{5}F, 7^{0}GF, 7^{3}G, 10^{0}GF, 9^{0}GF, 8^{0}SD, 9^{0}SW, 12^{0}SD

	Starts	1st	2nd	3rd	Win & Pl
Career Total (Turf)	32	1	1	3	4157
Career Total (AW)	18	3	2	3	9431

62	12/00	Ling	1m2f	F(0-60)H	STD	£1778
51	11/00	Ling	1m	E(0-75)H	STD	£2310
46	7/00	Brig	6f209y	F(0-60)H	FRM	£1925
40	2/00	Ling	7f	F(0-65)H	STD	£1907

Total win prize-money £7921

Going (Turf): Sf: 0-5 GS: 0-0 Gd: 0-8 GF: 0-14 **Fm: 1-5**
Distance: 5f/6f: 0-5 **7f-8f: 3-29** 9f-13f: 1-16 14f+: 0-0
Track : **LH: 4-34** RH: 0-7 **Tight: 3-22** Gall: 0-4
Aids: Bl: 0-2 Vi: 0-1 Tstrap: 0-4
Best Rating: 63 1/01 Ling 1m4f stand

Ready To Rock (IRE)

103(105) (61)**55**

5-y-o b g Up And At 'Em-Rocklands Rosie (Muscatite)
J S Moore J P Fitzgerald

Placings:5506000/0000030/00601224-5026125653300400 **(1675)**
2001: 5^{5}SD, 6^{0}SW, 5^{2}SD, 5^{6}SD, 5^{1}SW, 5^{2}SD, 5^{5}SD, 5^{6}SD, 5^{5}SD, 5^{3}SD, 5^{3}SD, 5^{0}SD, 5^{0}GS, 5^{4}GS, 5^{0}G, 5^{0}G

	Starts	1st	2nd	3rd	Win & Pl
Career Total (Turf)	16	0	0	0	675
Career Total (AW)	22	2	4	3	9183

56	2/01	Wolv	5f	E(0-70)H	SLW	£2401
49	2/00	Ling	5f	E(0-75)H	STD	£2769

Total win prize-money £5170

Going (Turf): Sf: 0-1 GS: 0-2 Gd: 0-5 GF: 0-1 Fm: 0-1
Distance: **5f/6f: 2-36** 7f-8f: 0-2 9f-13f: 0-0 14f+: 0-0
Track : **LH: 2-21** RH: 0-3 **Tight: 2-15** Gall: 0-1
Aids: **Bl: 2-27** Vi: 0-0 Tstrap: 0-0
Best Rating: 61 2/01 Wolv 5f stand

Real Ambition (IRE)

91(93) (78)**83**

2-y-o b g Fayruz-Mauradell (IRE) (Mujadil (USA))

B J Meehan Jim McCarthy

Placings:602325 **(5408)**

2001: 6^{6}GF, 6^{0}GS, 6^{2}GF, 6^{3}SD, 6^{2}SD, 6^{5}SD

	Starts	1st	2nd	3rd	Win & Pl
Career Total (Turf)	3	0	1	0	2194
Career Total (AW)	3	0	1	1	1287

Going (Turf): Sf: 0-0 GS: 0-1 Gd: 0-0 GF: 0-2 Fm: 0-0
Distance: 5f/6f: 0-5 7f-8f: 0-1 9f-13f: 0-0 14f+: 0-0
Track : LH: 0-3 RH: 0-0 Tight: 0-1 Gall: 0-0
Aids: Bl: 0-4 Vi: 0-0 Tstrap: 0-0
Best Rating: 83 9/01 Wwck 6f21y gd-fm

Real Delight (IRE)

81 **85**

2-y-o b f Nicolotte-Jumbo Delight (IRE) (Don't Forgot Me)

Patrick Carey Patrick Carey

Placings:20110034 **(5428a)**

2001: 6^{2}G, 5^{0}GF, 5^{1}GF, 5^{1}G, 6^{0}G, 5^{0}G, 5^{3}S, 5^{4}S

	Starts	1st	2nd	3rd	Win & Pl
Career Total (Turf)	8	2	1	1	28380

85 7/01 Curr 5f GD £13000
85 7/01 Bell 5f G-F £7935
Total win prize-money £20935

Going (Turf): Sf: 0-2 GS: 0-0 **Gd: 1-4 GF: 1-2** Fm: 0-0
Distance: 5f/6f: 2-8 7f-8f: 0-0 9f-13f: 0-0 14f+: 0-0
Track : LH: 0-1 RH: 0-0 Tight: 0-0 Gall: 0-0
Aids: Bl: 0-0 Vi: 0-0 Tstrap: 0-0
Best Rating: 85 10/01 Navn 5f soft

Won twice over the minimum trip in Ireland, but held since in Pattern company.

Reap

(93) (56)**48**

3-y-o b g Emperor Jones (USA)-Corn Futures (Nomination)

Mrs Lydia Pearce James Furlong

Placings:06450-400 **(5276)**

2001: 8^{4}GS, 9^{0}SD, 8^{0}GS

	Starts	1st	2nd	3rd	Win & Pl
Career Total (Turf)	4	0	0	0	0
Career Total (AW)	4	0	0	0	0

Going (Turf): Sf: 0-0 GS: 0-2 Gd: 0-1 GF: 0-1 Fm: 0-0
Distance: 5f/6f: 0-3 7f-8f: 0-2 9f-13f: 0-3 14f+: 0-0
Track : LH: 0-5 RH: 0-0 Tight: 0-5 Gall: 0-0
Aids: Bl: 0-0 Vi: 0-2 Tstrap: 0-0
Best Rating: 48 10/01 Leic 1m9y gd-sft

Rear Guard Action

74 **16**

5-y-o b g Almoojid-Belle Deirdrie (Mandamus)

P Butler G P Tresidder

Placings:0/03/0 **(4892)**

2001: 12^{0}GF

	Starts	1st	2nd	3rd	Win & Pl
Career Total (Turf)	3	0	0	1	600
Career Total (AW)	1	0	0	0	

Going (Turf): Sf: 0-0 GS: 0-0 Gd: 0-1 GF: 0-1 Fm: 0-1
Distance: 5f/6f: 0-0 7f-8f: 0-1 9f-13f: 0-3 14f+: 0-0
Track : LH: 0-2 RH: 0-2 Tight: 0-2 Gall: 0-0
Aids: Bl: 0-0 Vi: 0-0 Tstrap: 0-0
Best Rating: 15 9/01 Kemp 1m4f gd-fm

Rear Window

101(93) (27)**45**

7-y-o b g Night Shift (USA)-Last Clear Chance (USA) (Alleged (USA))

M J Ryan Dawn Build Ltd

Placings:05030/12212600/444550/030022 **(5663)**

2001: 11^{0}GS, 14^{3}G, 15^{0}GS, 14^{0}SD, 14^{2}S, 12^{2}G

	Starts	1st	2nd	3rd	Win & Pl
Career Total (Turf)	19	1	5	1	8430
Career Total (AW)	6	1	0	1	2666

60 5/98 Nott 1m1f213yF(0-60)H G-F £3036
61 3/98 Sthl 1m4f F(0-70)H STD £2368
Total win prize-money £5405

Going (Turf): Sf: 0-6 GS: 0-3 Gd: 0-6 **GF: 1-3** Fm: 0-1
Distance: 5f/6f: 0-0 7f-8f: 0-0 **9f-13f: 2-14** 14f+: 0-11
Track : **LH: 2-17** RH: 0-4 Tight: 0-10 Gall: 0-3
Aids: Bl: 0-1 Vi: 0-2 Tstrap: 0-3
Best Rating: 45 5/01 Yarm 1m6f17y good

Only plating class these days and has not won since May 1998. Ran some fair races towards the end of the season. Effective between twelve and fourteen furlongs and on the All-weather.

Reason (IRE)

105 **94**

3-y-o b c Sadler's Wells (USA)-Marseillaise (Artaius (USA))

H R A Cecil The Thoroughbred Corporation

Placings:410 **(2262)**

2001: 12^{4}G, 14^{1}G, 16^{0}GF

	Starts	1st	2nd	3rd	Win & Pl
Career Total (Turf)	3	1	0	0	4727

87 6/01 Hayd 1m6f D GD £4368
Total win prize-money £4368

Going (Turf): Sf: 0-0 GS: 0-0 **Gd: 1-2** GF: 0-1 Fm: 0-0
Distance: 5f/6f: 0-0 7f-8f: 0-0 9f-13f: 0-1 **14f+: 1-2**
Track : **LH: 1-1** RH: 0-2 Tight: 0-0 Gall: 0-2
Aids: Bl: 0-0 Vi: 0-1 Tstrap: 0-0
Best Rating: 94 6/01 Asct 2m45y gd-fm

Won a 14-furlong Haydock maiden on his second run, but may not quite have stayed in the Queen's Vase next time on fast ground.

Reasoning

97(86) (60)**64**

3-y-o ch f Selkirk (USA)-Attribute (Warning)

M L W Bell Highclere Thoroughbred Racing Ltd

Placings:0060023 **(5198)**

2001: 9^{0}GS, 10^{0}GF, 9^{6}GF, 8^{0}G, 7^{0}G, 8^{2}GF, 9^{3}SD

	Starts	1st	2nd	3rd	Win & Pl
Career Total (Turf)	6	0	1	0	1314
Career Total (AW)	1	0	0	1	342

Going (Turf): Sf: 0-0 GS: 0-1 Gd: 0-2 GF: 0-3 Fm: 0-0
Distance: 5f/6f: 0-0 7f-8f: 0-3 9f-13f: 0-4 14f+: 0-0
Track : LH: 0-4 RH: 0-2 Tight: 0-5 Gall: 0-1
Aids: Bl: 0-0 Vi: 0-0 Tstrap: 0-0
Best Rating: 64 8/01 Donc 1m gd-fm

Rebelle

69(65) (31)**31**

2-y-o b/br g Reprimand-Blushing Belle (Local Suitor (USA))

K Bell Christopher Shankland

Placings:000 **(5163)**

2001: 6^{0}F, 7^{0}GF, 6^{0}SD

	Starts	1st	2nd	3rd	Win & Pl
Career Total (Turf)	2	0	0	0	
Career Total (AW)	1	0	0	0	

Going (Turf): Sf: 0-0 GS: 0-0 Gd: 0-0 GF: 0-1 Fm: 0-1
Distance: 5f/6f: 0-1 7f-8f: 0-2 9f-13f: 0-0 14f+: 0-0
Track : LH: 0-1 RH: 0-0 Tight: 0-1 Gall: 0-0
Aids: Bl: 0-0 Vi: 0-0 Tstrap: 0-0
Best Rating: 31 10/01 Wolv 6f stand

Rebelline (IRE)

104 **111**

3-y-o b f Robellino (USA)-Fleeting Rainbow (Rainbow Quest (USA))

Kevin Prendergast Mrs C J O'Reilly

Placings:12-151030 **(5389)**

2001: 7^{1}S, 8^{5}G, 10^{1}Y, 12^{0}G, 10^{3}HO, 10^{0}GS

	Starts	1st	2nd	3rd	Win & Pl
Career Total (Turf)	8	3	1	1	120789

107 6/01 Curr 1m2f YLD £60000
111 4/01 Leop 7f SFT £26000
87 10/00 Navn 1m SH £9660
Total win prize-money £95660

Going (Turf): Sf: 1-2 GS: 0-1 Gd: 0-2 GF: 0-0 Fm: 0-0
Distance: 5f/6f: 0-0 **7f-8f: 2-3** 9f-13f: 1-5 14f+: 0-0
Track : **LH: 1-2** RH: 0-1 Tight: 0-0 Gall: 0-0
Aids: Bl: 0-0 Vi: 0-0 Tstrap: 0-0
Best Rating: 111 10/01 Lonc 1m2f holding

A Group-class Irish-trained filly, winner of the Group Two Pretty Polly Stakes at the Curragh in June and was not beaten far in the Group One Prix de l'Opera. Suited by ten furlongs and easy ground.

Reborn (IRE)

94 **39**

3-y-o b f Idris (IRE)-Tantum Ergo (Tanfirion)

E J O'Neill (T Keddy 22/9) Mrs Julie Mitchell

Placings:0000030 **(5659)**

2001: 7^{0}G, 10^{0}G, 7^{0}GS, 7^{0}GF, 7^{0}G, 8^{3}GS, 8^{0}G

	Starts	1st	2nd	3rd	Win & Pl
Career Total (Turf)	7	0	0	1	569

Going (Turf): Sf: 0-0 GS: 0-2 Gd: 0-4 GF: 0-1 Fm: 0-0
Distance: 5f/6f: 0-0 7f-8f: 0-6 9f-13f: 0-1 14f+: 0-0
Track : LH: 0-0 RH: 0-1 Tight: 0-2 Gall: 0-0
Aids: Bl: 0-0 Vi: 0-0 Tstrap: 0-0
Best Rating: 50 5/01 NmkR 7f good

Receivedwiththanx (IRE)

100 **82**

2-y-o b c Celtic Swing-Sabrata (IRE) (Zino)

A Dickman Mike Smallman

Placings:01100 **(4659)**

2001: 5^{0}GS, 7^{1}G, 7^{1}GF, 7^{0}GF, 6^{0}GF

	Starts	1st	2nd	3rd	Win & Pl
Career Total (Turf)	5	2	0	0	7732

82 7/01 Bevl 7f100y D G-F £4459
72 6/01 Thsk 7f F GD £3272
Total win prize-money £7732

Going (Turf): Sf: 0-0 GS: 0-1 **Gd: 1-1 GF: 1-3** Fm: 0-0
Distance: 5f/6f: 0-2 **7f-8f: 2-3** 9f-13f: 0-0 14f+: 0-0
Track : LH: 1-1 RH: 1-2 **Tight: 1-1** Gall: 0-0
Aids: Bl: 0-0 Vi: 0-0 Tstrap: 0-0
Best Rating: 82 7/01 Bevl 7f100y gd-fm

A genuine sort, he was well beaten in the Brocklesby but has recorded two decisive wins since over seven furlongs.

Reciprocal (IRE)

107 **80**

3-y-o gr f Night Shift (USA)-African Light (Kalaglow)

D R C Elsworth The Caledonian Racing Society

Placings:0040-5301130606 **(4717)**

2001: 9^{5}GS, 10^{3}GF, 10^{0}GF, 9^{1}GF, 9^{1}GF, 8^{3}GF, 9^{0}GF, 8^{6}F, 10^{0}G, 8^{6}G

	Starts	1st	2nd	3rd	Win & Pl
Career Total (Turf)	14	2	0	2	12983

83	7/01	Kemp	1m1f	C(0-90)H	G-F	£7020
80	6/01	Kemp	1m1f	D(0-80)H	G-F	£4329

Total win prize-money £11349

Going (Turf): Sf: 0-2 GS: 0-1 Gd: 0-2 **GF: 2-8** Fm: 0-1
Distance: 5f/6f: 0-1 7f-8f: 0-5 **9f-13f: 2-8** 14f+: 0-0
Track : LH: 0-2 **RH: 2-6** Tight: 0-4 Gall: 0-2
Aids: Bl: 0-0 Vi: 0-1 Tstrap: 0-0
Best Rating: 83 7/01 Kemp 1m1f gd-fm

Steadily improved during the summer and made all to win twice over nine furlongs at Kempton in the space of seven days, but struggled off a higher mark afterwards. Suited by fast ground.

Recoleta

(79) (7)**39**

4-y-o b f Ezzoud (IRE)-Hug Me (Shareef Dancer (USA))

Miss H M Irving A C Kemp

Placings:000/06-0 **(0691)**

2001: 16^{0}SD

	Starts	1st	2nd	3rd	Win & Pl
Career Total (Turf)	4	0	0	0	0
Career Total (AW)	2	0	0	0	

Going (Turf): Sf: 0-1 GS: 0-1 Gd: 0-1 GF: 0-1 Fm: 0-0
Distance: 5f/6f: 0-1 7f-8f: 0-2 9f-13f: 0-2 14f+: 0-1
Track : LH: 0-3 RH: 0-1 Tight: 0-2 Gall: 0-1
Aids: Bl: 0-1 Vi: 0-1 Tstrap: 0-0
Best Rating: 7 4/01 Sthl 2m stand

Red Briar (IRE)

97 **92**

2-y-o b c Desert King (IRE)-Rose Society (Caerleon (USA))

M L W Bell Terry Neill

Placings:3111 **(4204a)**

2001: 5^{3}F, 6^{1}GS, 6^{1}G, 7^{1}GS

	Starts	1st	2nd	3rd	Win & Pl
Career Total (Turf)	4	3	0	1	24080

92	8/01	Deau	7f		G-S	£13579
92	7/01	Donc	6f	C	GD	£6113
81	6/01	Haml	6f5y	D	G-S	£3867

Total win prize-money £23560

Going (Turf): Sf: 0-0 **GS: 2-2** Gd: 1-1 GF: 0-0 Fm: 0-1
Distance: 5f/6f: 1-2 **7f-8f: 2-2** 9f-13f: 0-0 14f+: 0-0
Track : LH: 0-0 RH: 0-0 Tight: 0-0 Gall: 0-0
Aids: Bl: 0-0 Vi: 0-0 Tstrap: 0-0
Best Rating: 92 8/01 Deau 7f gd-sft

He scored at Hamilton and Doncaster over six, and improved on that by taking a Listed event at Deauville. Tough and genuine, he is well suited by cut in the ground. Has been subsequently sold to race in America.

Red Cafe (IRE)

(102) (51)**44**

5-y-o ch m Perugino (USA)-Test Case (Busted)

P Howling (P D Evans 25/1) Paul Howling Racing Syndicate 2

Placings:4003/3600042400114314-4350 **(0288)**

2001: 11^{4}SD, 11^{3}SD, 12^{5}SD, 12^{0}SW

	Starts	1st	2nd	3rd	Win & Pl
Career Total (Turf)	15	2	1	2	6481
Career Total (AW)	9	1	0	2	3203

56	12/00	Wolv	1m4f	F(0-60)H	STD	£2331
44	10/00	Brig	1m1f209yF(0-60)H		SFT	£2394
32	10/00	Ayr	1m1f20y	F	HVY	£2478

Total win prize-money £7203

Going (Turf): Sf: 2-2 GS: 0-4 Gd: 0-3 GF: 0-4 Fm: 0-2
Distance: 5f/6f: 0-3 7f-8f: 0-5 **9f-13f: 3-16** 14f+: 0-0
Track : **LH: 3-19** RH: 0-3 **Tight: 1-9** Gall: 0-1
Aids: Bl: 0-3 Vi: 0-3 Tstrap: 0-0
Best Rating: 56 1/01 Sthl 1m3f stand

Red Canyon (IRE)

76 **63**

4-y-o b g Zieten (USA)-Bayazida (Bustino)

B I Case Lady Jane Grosvenor

Placings:06000/24412340400-0 **(3727)**

2001: 14^{0}GS

	Starts	1st	2nd	3rd	Win & Pl
Career Total (Turf)	17	1	2	1	7834

64	6/00	Ayr	1m2f192yD(0-80)H		G-F	£3757

Total win prize-money £3757

Going (Turf): Sf: 0-2 GS: 0-4 Gd: 0-2 **GF: 1-9** Fm: 0-0
Distance: 5f/6f: 0-4 7f-8f: 0-1 **9f-13f: 1-9** 14f+: 0-3
Track : **LH: 1-4** RH: 0-8 Tight: 0-7 Gall: 0-2
Aids: Bl: 0-0 Vi: 0-0 Tstrap: 0-0
Best Rating: 25 8/01 Yarm 1m6f17y gd-sft

Red Carnation (IRE)

107 **86**

3-y-o b f Polar Falcon (USA)-Red Bouquet (Reference Point)

M A Jarvis Red Carnation Partnership

Placings:33-551214 **(5693)**

2001: 7^{5}GF, 6^{5}GF, 8^{1}G, 8^{2}G, 10^{1}HY, 12^{4}S

	Starts	1st	2nd	3rd	Win & Pl
Career Total (Turf)	8	2	1	2	23172

84	9/01	Hayd	1m2f120yC(0-90)H		HVY	£11505
79	8/01	NmkJ	1m	D(0-80)H	GD	£4914

Total win prize-money £16419

Going (Turf): Sf: 1-3 GS: 0-0 **Gd: 1-3** GF: 0-2 Fm: 0-0
Distance: 5f/6f: 0-1 7f-8f: 1-4 9f-13f: 1-3 14f+: 0-0
Track : **LH: 1-2** RH: 0-2 Tight: 0-1 Gall: 0-1
Aids: Bl: 0-0 Vi: 0-0 Tstrap: 0-0
Best Rating: 86 11/01 Donc 1m4f soft

She showed ability in maiden company, but got off the mark on her handicap debut at Newmarket in August when stepped up to a mile, and has continued to run well, winning a Haydock handicap. Suited by cut in the ground, and acts well over a mile to ten furlongs.

Red Carpet

108 **117**

3-y-o ch c Pivotal-Fleur Rouge (Pharly (FR))

M L W Bell Cheveley Park Stud

Placings:25113-25 **(1119)**

2001: 8^{2}S, 8^{5}G

	Starts	1st	2nd	3rd	Win & Pl
Career Total (Turf)	7	2	2	1	54890

93	8/00	NmkJ	6f	B	G-F	£17745
78	7/00	Chep	6f16y	E	FRM	£2824

Total win prize-money £20570

Going (Turf): Sf: 0-1 GS: 0-0 Gd: 0-3 **GF: 1-2 Fm: 1-1**
Distance: 5f/6f: 1-2 7f-8f: 1-5 9f-13f: 0-0 14f+: 0-0
Track : LH: 0-1 RH: 0-0 Tight: 0-0 Gall: 0-1
Aids: Bl: 0-0 Vi: 0-0 Tstrap: 0-0
Best Rating: 117 4/01 NmkR 1m soft

A useful fast ground performer in his first season, he coped admirably with the step up to Group company on his last start at two, and showed he stayed a mile when a close second in the Craven. Stakes. Not seen out after finishing fifth in the 2000 Guineas.

Red Charger (IRE)

93 (45)**45**

5-y-o ch g Up And At 'Em-Smashing Pet (Mummy's Pet)

D Nicholls Gemini Upholstery/gr 1980 Ltd

Placings:3154135106/0002550001/000000-06 **(5451)**

2001: 6^{0}HY, 5^{6}HY

	Starts	1st	2nd	3rd	Win & Pl
Career Total (Turf)	26	4	1	2	22340
Career Total (AW)	2	0	0	0	0

62	8/99	Thsk	5f	D(0-80)H	SFT	£4370
79	8/98	York	6f	E	G-F	£11527
82	7/98	Catt	7f	F	FRM	£2220
67	5/98	Rdcr	5f	F	GD	£2407

Total win prize-money £20526

Going (Turf): Sf: 1-4 GS: 0-4 **Gd: 1-4 GF: 1-12 Fm: 1-2**
Distance: **5f/6f: 3-21** 7f-8f: 1-7 9f-13f: 0-0 14f+: 0-0
Track : **LH: 1-7** RH: 0-4 **Tight: 1-6** Gall: 0-2
Aids: **Bl: 1-1** Vi: 0-0 Tstrap: 0-0
Best Rating: 45 10/01 Newc 5f heavy

Red Cherry

88 **26**

4-y-o ch f Never So Bold-Romany Home (Gabitat)

J S Goldie J C McGee

Placings:00000000 **(5284)**

2001: 8^{0}S, 9^{0}GS, 11^{0}G, 8^{0}GF, 6^{0}G, 9^{0}G, 12^{0}GF, 9^{0}HY

	Starts	1st	2nd	3rd	Win & Pl
Career Total (Turf)	8	0	0	0	

Going (Turf): Sf: 0-2 GS: 0-1 Gd: 0-3 GF: 0-2 Fm: 0-0
Distance: 5f/6f: 0-1 7f-8f: 0-2 9f-13f: 0-5 14f+: 0-0
Track : LH: 0-0 RH: 0-2 Tight: 0-2 Gall: 0-0
Aids: Bl: 0-0 Vi: 0-0 Tstrap: 0-0
Best Rating: 31 8/01 Ayr 6f good

Red China

92(94) (68)**68**

2-y-o ch c Inchinor-Little Tramp (Trempolino (USA))

M Blanshard Mrs J Williams & Mrs G Wiseman

Placings:003535003 **(5562)**

2001: 6^{0}GF, 6^{0}GF, 6^{3}GS, 5^{5}GF, 5^{3}GS, 5^{5}GF, 5^{0}G, 6^{0}SD, 5^{3}S, 5^{3}SD

	Starts	1st	2nd	3rd	Win & Pl
Career Total (Turf)	8	0	0	3	1830
Career Total (AW)	1	0	0	0	

Going (Turf): Sf: 0-1 GS: 0-2 Gd: 0-1 GF: 0-4 Fm: 0-0
Distance: 5f/6f: 0-9 7f-8f: 0-0 9f-13f: 0-0 14f+: 0-0
Track : LH: 0-2 RH: 0-0 Tight: 0-0 Gall: 0-1
Aids: Bl: 0-0 Vi: 0-0 Tstrap: 0-0
Best Rating: 68 10/01 Yarm 5f43y soft

Red Conquest

95 **48**

3-y-o ch f Lycius (USA)-Crimson Conquest (USA) (Diesis)

C E Brittain Sheikh Marwan Al Maktoum

Placings:000002000 **(5659)**

2001: 10^{0}GS, 10^{0}G, 10^{0}GF, 10^{0}GF, 7^{0}F, 6^{2}GF, 7^{0}GF, 8^{0}GS, 8^{0}G

	Starts	1st	2nd	3rd	Win & Pl
Career Total (Turf)	9	0	1	0	650

Going (Turf): Sf: 0-0 GS: 0-2 Gd: 0-2 GF: 0-4 Fm: 0-1

Distance: 5f/6f: 0-0 7f-8f: 0-5 9f-13f: 0-4 14f+: 0-0
Track : LH: 0-5 RH: 0-2 Tight: 0-1 Gall: 0-3
Aids: Bl: 0-2 Vi: 0-3 Tstrap: 0-0
Best Rating: 71 5/01 NmkR 1m2f good

Red Crystal

(67)
3-y-o b f Presidium-Crystallography (Primitive Rising (USA))
J Norton Mrs V C Sugden

Placings:F0-0 **(0084)**
2001: 8^{0}SD

	Starts	1st	2nd	3rd	Win & Pl
Career Total (Turf)	1	0	0	0	
Career Total (AW)	2	0	0	0	

Going (Turf): Sf: 0-0 GS: 0-0 Gd: 0-1 GF: 0-0 Fm: 0-0
Distance: 5f/6f: 0-0 7f-8f: 0-3 9f-13f: 0-0 14f+: 0-0
Track : LH: 0-3 RH: 0-0 Tight: 0-0 Gall: 0-1
Aids: Bl: 0-0 Vi: 0-0 Tstrap: 0-0

Red Delirium

83(103) (63)**44**
5-y-o b g Robellino (USA)-Made Of Pearl (USA) (Nureyev (USA))
R Brotherton The Joiners Arms Racing Club Quarndon

Placings:61006205024/00000500/200000506003241-236032000000 **(5413)**
2001: 7^{2}SD, 7^{3}SW, 6^{6}SW, 7^{0}SD, 8^{3}SD, 8^{2}SW, 8^{0}G, 8^{0}GF, 11^{0}GF, 7^{0}G, 8^{0}SD, 8^{0}SD, 8^{0}SD

	Starts	1st	2nd	3rd	Win & Pl
Career Total (Turf)	36	1	3	0	7642
Career Total (AW)	12	1	3	3	5155

60 12/00 Wolv 6f F(0-65)H STD £1788
88 5/98 Gdwd 6f D G-F £4581
Total win prize-money £6370

Going (Turf): Sf: 0-3 GS: 0-5 Gd: 0-11 **GF: 1-15** Fm: 0-2
Distance: 5f/6f: 2-18 7f-8f: 0-23 9f-13f: 0-7 14f+: 0-0
Track : LH: 1-23 RH: 0-3 **Tight: 1-10** Gall: 0-8
Aids: Bl: 1-11 Vi: 0-1 Tstrap: 0-3
Best Rating: 63 4/01 Sthl 1m slow

Red Diamond

88 **70**
2-y-o b g Mind Games-Sandicroft Jewel (Grey Desire)
A Berry The Red Shirt Brigade Ltd

Placings:035 **(5633)**
2001: 5^{0}G, 6^{3}S, 7^{5}G

	Starts	1st	2nd	3rd	Win & Pl
Career Total (Turf)	3	0	0	1	550

Going (Turf): Sf: 0-1 GS: 0-0 Gd: 0-2 GF: 0-0 Fm: 0-0
Distance: 5f/6f: 0-2 7f-8f: 0-1 9f-13f: 0-0 14f+: 0-0
Track : LH: 0-2 RH: 0-0 Tight: 0-1 Gall: 0-0
Aids: Bl: 0-0 Vi: 0-0 Tstrap: 0-0
Best Rating: 70 10/01 Pont 6f soft

Little sign of ability on debut run but produced a marked improvement when third at Pontefract on his second start.

Red Eagle (IRE)

90(95) (66)**66?**
2-y-o b f Eagle Eyed (USA)-Dawn's Folly (IRE) (Bluebird (USA))
A Berry The Red Shirt Brigade Ltd

Placings:153641633 **(5660)**
2001: 5^{1}GS, 5^{5}GS, 5^{3}SD, 5^{6}GF, 5^{4}SD, 5^{1}SD, 5^{6}GS, 5^{3}SD, 5^{3}G, 5^{2}SD

	Starts	1st	2nd	3rd	Win & Pl
Career Total (Turf)	5	1	0	1	2702
Career Total (AW)	4	1	0	2	2430

58 7/01 Sthl 5f G STD £1820
57 4/01 Muss 5f F G-S £2702
Total win prize-money £4522

Going (Turf): Sf: 0-0 **GS: 1-3** Gd: 0-1 GF: 0-1 Fm: 0-0
Distance: 5f/6f: 2-9 7f-8f: 0-0 9f-13f: 0-0 14f+: 0-0
Track : LH: 0-2 RH: 0-0 Tight: 0-2 Gall: 0-0
Aids: Bl: 0-0 Vi: 0-0 Tstrap: 0-0
Best Rating: 66 11/01 Muss 5f good

Recovered from tardy start to win Musselburgh maiden on debut. Dropped to sellers afterwards, winning on the Southwell Fibresand. Suited by soft ground on turf.

Red Fanfare

88(87) (12)**53d**
3-y-o ch f First Trump-Corman-Style (Ahonoora)
S R Bowring (N Tinkler 22/1) Roland M Wheatley

Placings:0000250-00000000 **(2214)**
2001: 8^{0}SW, 8^{0}SW, 6^{0}SD, 12^{0}SD, 11^{0}SD, 7^{0}GF, 6^{0}SD, 5^{0}G

	Starts	1st	2nd	3rd	Win & Pl
Career Total (Turf)	6	0	0	0	
Career Total (AW)	9	0	1	0	563

Going (Turf): Sf: 0-0 GS: 0-0 Gd: 0-1 GF: 0-5 Fm: 0-0
Distance: 5f/6f: 0-6 7f-8f: 0-4 9f-13f: 0-5 14f+: 0-0
Track : LH: 0-10 RH: 0-0 Tight: 0-5 Gall: 0-0
Aids: Bl: 0-0 Vi: 0-0 Tstrap: 0-0
Best Rating: 29 6/01 Leic 5f218y good

Red Flyer (IRE)

91(84) (54)**67**
2-y-o br g Catrail (USA)-Marostica (ITY) (Stone)
P C Haslam J Potts & Peter Gosling

Placings:640 **(5614)**
2001: 7^{6}S, 7^{4}S, 6^{0}SD

	Starts	1st	2nd	3rd	Win & Pl
Career Total (Turf)	2	0	0	0	0
Career Total (AW)	1	0	0	0	

Going (Turf): Sf: 0-2 GS: 0-0 Gd: 0-0 GF: 0-0 Fm: 0-0
Distance: 5f/6f: 0-1 7f-8f: 0-2 9f-13f: 0-0 14f+: 0-0
Track : LH: 0-2 RH: 0-0 Tight: 0-2 Gall: 0-0
Aids: Bl: 0-0 Vi: 0-0 Tstrap: 0-0
Best Rating: 67 10/01 Rdcr 7f soft

Red Forest (IRE)

90(102) (86+)**76**
2-y-o b c Charnwood Forest (IRE)-High Atlas (Shirley Heights)
B W Hills Lee Jackson

Placings:322 **(5658)**
2001: 6^{3}S, 6^{2}SD, 7^{2}G, 7^{1}SD

	Starts	1st	2nd	3rd	Win & Pl
Career Total (Turf)	2	0	1	1	1502
Career Total (AW)	1	0	1	0	852

Going (Turf): Sf: 0-1 GS: 0-0 Gd: 0-1 GF: 0-0 Fm: 0-0
Distance: 5f/6f: 0-2 7f-8f: 0-1 9f-13f: 0-0 14f+: 0-0
Track : LH: 0-2 RH: 0-0 Tight: 0-0 Gall: 0-0
Aids: Bl: 0-0 Vi: 0-0 Tstrap: 0-0
Best Rating: 76 11/01 Muss 7f30y good

Effectove on turf and sand, he got off the mark at Wolverhampton on his fourth start. Consistent.

Red Halo

96 **79**
2-y-o b c Be My Guest (USA)-Pray (IRE) (Priolo (USA))
R Hannon Terry Neill

Placings:35 **(4548)**
2001: 7^{3}GF, 8^{5}GF

	Starts	1st	2nd	3rd	Win & Pl
Career Total (Turf)	2	0	0	1	886

Going (Turf): Sf: 0-0 GS: 0-0 Gd: 0-0 GF: 0-2 Fm: 0-0
Distance: 5f/6f: 0-0 7f-8f: 0-2 9f-13f: 0-0 14f+: 0-0
Track : LH: 0-0 RH: 0-1 Tight: 0-0 Gall: 0-1
Aids: Bl: 0-0 Vi: 0-0 Tstrap: 0-0
Best Rating: 79 9/01 Sals 1m gd-fm

A January foal from the family of Anshan, showed signs of greenness but also demonstrated good early speed on his Kempton debut in July.

Red Liason (IRE)

109 **93**
2-y-o ch f Selkirk (USA)-Red Affair (IRE) (Generous (IRE))
J L Dunlop Lady Clague

Placings:33121 **(5598)**
2001: 6^{3}GF, 6^{3}GF, 6^{1}GF, 7^{2}S, 6^{1}GS

	Starts	1st	2nd	3rd	Win & Pl
Career Total (Turf)	5	2	1	2	13799

93 11/01 NmkR 6f C G-S £6162
84 7/01 Nott 6f15y D G-F £4062
Total win prize-money £10225

Going (Turf): Sf: 0-1 **GS: 1-1** Gd: 0-0 **GF: 1-3** Fm: 0-0
Distance: 5f/6f: 1-2 7f-8f: 1-3 9f-13f: 0-0 14f+: 0-0
Track : LH: 0-0 RH: 0-0 Tight: 0-0 Gall: 0-0
Aids: Bl: 0-0 Vi: 0-0 Tstrap: 0-0
Best Rating: 93 11/01 NmkR 6f gd-sft

Got off the mark at the third attempt in a Nottingham maiden and was just touched off in a Leicester conditions event on his first encounter with soft ground. Returned to winning form in a Newmarket conditions event. Stays seven furlongs.

Red Lion

100 **65**
5-y-o ch g Lion Cavern (USA)-Fleur Rouge (Pharly (FR))
S Gollings (J W Payne 19/6) R G Gibney

Placings:141036/15001055000/000000-0000 **(4539)**
2001: 6^{0}G, 7^{0}F, 7^{0}G, 6^{0}GF

	Starts	1st	2nd	3rd	Win & Pl
Career Total (Turf)	27	4	0	1	21414

95 7/99 Yarm 6f3y C(0-95)H FRM £7505
101 6/99 Leic 5f218y C GD £5840
83 6/98 Wind 5f10y E GD £3176
89 5/98 Rdcr 5f E G-F £2862
Total win prize-money £19384

Going (Turf): Sf: 0-4 GS: 0-1 **Gd: 2-11** GF: 1-7 Fm: 1-4
Distance: 5f/6f: 3-19 7f-8f: 1-8 9f-13f: 0-0 14f+: 0-0
Track : LH: 0-2 **RH: 1-1** Tight: 0-1 **Gall: 1-1**
Aids: Bl: 0-2 Vi: 0-0 Tstrap: 0-0
Best Rating: 65 5/01 Donc 6f good

Red Lion (FR)

104 **65**
4-y-o ch g Lion Cavern (USA)-Mahogany River (Irish River (FR))
B J Meehan W H Ponsonby

Placings:000642-044 **(3810)**
2001: 12^{0}GF, 16^{4}GF, 16^{4}G

	Starts	1st	2nd	3rd	Win & Pl
Career Total (Turf)	9	0	1	0	2679

Going (Turf): Sf: 0-1 GS: 0-1 Gd: 0-4 GF: 0-3 Fm: 0-0
Distance: 5f/6f: 0-0 7f-8f: 0-1 9f-13f: 0-6 14f+: 0-2

Track : LH: 0-3 RH: 0-2 Tight: 0-4 Gall: 0-2
Aids: Bl: 0-0 Vi: 0-0 Tstrap: 0-0
Best Rating: 63 7/01 Newb 2m gd-fm

Red Magic (FR)

86 **99+**

3-y-o b/br c Grand Lodge (USA)-Ma Priere (FR) (Highest Honor (FR))
R Hannon Terry Neill

Placings:216-0 **(2301)**
2001: 7^{0}GF

	Starts	1st	2nd	3rd	Win & Pl
Career Total (Turf)	4	1	1	0	8675

99	7/00	Asct	7f	D	G-F	£6825

Total win prize-money £6825

Going (Turf): Sf: 0-0 GS: 0-1 Gd: 0-1 **GF: 1-2** Fm: 0-0
Distance: 5f/6f: 0-2 **7f-8f: 1-2** 9f-13f: 0-0 14f+: 0-0
Track : LH: 0-0 RH: 0-0 Tight: 0-0 Gall: 0-0
Aids: Bl: 0-0 Vi: 0-0 Tstrap: 0-0
Best Rating: 61 6/01 Asct 7f gd-fm

A useful juvenile, but well beaten in the Jersey Stakes on his only start at three.

Red Mail (USA)

87(88) (37)**60d**

3-y-o b g Red Ransom (USA)-Seattle Byline (USA) (Slew City Slew (USA))
T D McCarthy (M L W Bell 30/5) A D Spence

Placings:32000 **(4183)**
2001: 11^{3}SD, 16^{2}GF, 12^{0}GF, 16^{0}F, 16^{0}GF

	Starts	1st	2nd	3rd	Win & Pl
Career Total (Turf)	4	0	1	0	665
Career Total (AW)	1	0	0	1	318

Going (Turf): Sf: 0-0 GS: 0-0 Gd: 0-0 GF: 0-3 Fm: 0-1
Distance: 5f/6f: 0-0 7f-8f: 0-0 9f-13f: 0-2 14f+: 0-3
Track : LH: 0-3 RH: 0-2 Tight: 0-3 Gall: 0-0
Aids: Bl: 0-0 Vi: 0-0 Tstrap: 0-0
Best Rating: 60 6/01 Kemp 1m4f gd-fm

Red Millennium (IRE)

108 **101**

3-y-o b f Tagula (IRE)-Lovely Me (IRE) (Vision (USA))
A Berry The Red Shirt Brigade Ltd

Placings:1212113423-610005540 **(4861)**
2001: 5^{6}S, 5^{1}GS, 5^{0}GF, 5^{0}GF, 5^{0}Y, 5^{5}GF, 5^{5}GF, 5^{4}G, 5^{0}GF

	Starts	1st	2nd	3rd	Win & Pl
Career Total (Turf)	19	5	3	2	53735

100	5/01	Bath	5f11y	A	G-S	£13270
90	7/00	Ches	5f16y	B	SFT	£9135
90	7/00	Donc	5f	C	G-F	£6142
83	6/00	Nott	5f13y	F	SFT	£2457
66	4/00	Muss	5f	F	G-S	£2702

Total win prize-money £33707

Going (Turf): Sf: 2-5 GS: 2-3 Gd: 0-3 GF: 1-7 Fm: 0-0
Distance: 5f/6f: 5-19 7f-8f: 0-0 9f-13f: 0-0 14f+: 0-0
Track : LH: 2-3 RH: 0-0 Tight: 1-2 Gall: 1-1
Aids: Bl: 0-0 Vi: 0-0 Tstrap: 0-0
Best Rating: 101 8/01 York 5f good

A speedy filly, she held her form well through a busy juvenile campaign in 2000 and gained her first Listed prize at Bath in May. Best on an easy surface but effective on fast.

Red Mittens

99(79) (21)**30**

4-y-o ch f Wolfhound (USA)-Red Gloves (Red God)
R E Barr R E Barr

Placings:5600/006600-00000030000 **(5374)**
2001: 7^{0}GF, 7^{0}F, 10^{0}GF, 8^{0}GF, 6^{0}G, 8^{0}F, 9^{3}GF, 8^{0}GF, 9^{0}GF, 7^{0}GS, 6^{0}G, 8^{6}SD

	Starts	1st	2nd	3rd	Win & Pl
Career Total (Turf)	21	0	0	1	438

Going (Turf): Sf: 0-2 GS: 0-2 Gd: 0-7 GF: 0-7 Fm: 0-3
Distance: 5f/6f: 0-8 7f-8f: 0-10 9f-13f: 0-3 14f+: 0-0
Track : LH: 0-4 RH: 0-6 Tight: 0-6 Gall: 0-1
Aids: Bl: 0-0 Vi: 0-0 Tstrap: 0-0
Best Rating: 30 8/01 Muss 1m gd-fm

Maiden of moderate ability who's best chance will come in a seller.

Red N' Socks (USA)

110 **94**

4-y-o ch c Devil's Bag (USA)-Racing Blue (Reference Point)
J L Dunlop Mrs H Focke

Placings:44510/20010060-0102020200 **(5366)**
2001: 7^{0}S, 7^{1}GS, 8^{0}GF, 8^{2}GF, 8^{0}GF, 7^{2}GS, 7^{0}GF, 8^{2}G, 7^{0}G, 8^{0}GS

	Starts	1st	2nd	3rd	Win & Pl
Career Total (Turf)	23	3	4	0	34101

86	5/01	Ling	7f140y	C(0-90)	G-S	£7215
93	7/00	Ling	7f140y	C(0-90)	G-F	£5863
81	10/99	Yarm	1m3y	E(0-85)H	G-F	£3392

Total win prize-money £16471

Going (Turf): Sf: 0-2 GS: 1-3 Gd: 0-8 **GF: 2-10** Fm: 0-0
Distance: 5f/6f: 0-0 **7f-8f: 2-19** 9f-13f: 1-4 14f+: 0-0
Track : LH: 0-2 RH: 0-5 Tight: 0-1 Gall: 0-4
Aids: Bl: 0-0 Vi: 0-0 Tstrap: 0-0
Best Rating: 94 9/01 Donc 1m good

A winner at up to a mile, he acts on a firm surface but has looked especially well suited by Lingfield's extended seven furlongs with his only wins both last season and this coming over that course and distance. Has run well elsewhere without winning. Suited by most types of ground.

Red Ocarina

83 **7**

3-y-o ch f Piccolo-Morica (Moorestyle)
R N Bevis R J Bevis

Placings:00-00 **(3434)**
2001: 6^{0}GS, 8^{0}F

	Starts	1st	2nd	3rd	Win & Pl
Career Total (Turf)	4	0	0	0	

Going (Turf): Sf: 0-0 GS: 0-1 Gd: 0-0 GF: 0-1 Fm: 0-2
Distance: 5f/6f: 0-3 7f-8f: 0-1 9f-13f: 0-0 14f+: 0-0
Track : LH: 0-2 RH: 0-0 Tight: 0-1 Gall: 0-0
Aids: Bl: 0-0 Vi: 0-0 Tstrap: 0-0
Best Rating: 7 7/01 Thsk 1m firm

Red Opal (IRE)

97 **81**

2-y-o b f Flying Spur (AUS)-Tamaya (IRE) (Darshaan)
R Hannon Terry Neill

Placings:3023050 **(5150)**
2001: 5^{3}GF, 5^{0}GF, 6^{2}G, 6^{3}GF, 6^{0}GF, 5^{5}G, 6^{0}G

	Starts	1st	2nd	3rd	Win & Pl
Career Total (Turf)	7	0	1	2	2870

Going (Turf): Sf: 0-0 GS: 0-0 Gd: 0-3 GF: 0-4 Fm: 0-0
Distance: 5f/6f: 0-6 7f-8f: 0-1 9f-13f: 0-0 14f+: 0-0
Track : LH: 0-1 RH: 0-0 Tight: 0-0 Gall: 0-1
Aids: Bl: 0-0 Vi: 0-0 Tstrap: 0-0
Best Rating: 93 9/01 Sals 6f212y gd-fm

Still a maiden, but she has run well in the face of some very stiff tasks so far and certainly has the ability to win a race.

Red Oscar

98(78) (43)**58**

2-y-o b c Atraf-Late Matinee (Red Sunset)
S Kirk J S Threadwell

Placings:00240030050 **(5667)**
2001: 6^{0}G, 6^{0}GF, 7^{2}F, 7^{4}GF, 7^{0}SD, 7^{0}G, 7^{3}HY, 7^{0}GS, 8^{0}S, 8^{5}HY, 8^{0}HY

	Starts	1st	2nd	3rd	Win & Pl
Career Total (Turf)	10	0	1	1	1383
Career Total (AW)	1	0	0	0	

Going (Turf): Sf: 0-4 GS: 0-1 Gd: 0-2 GF: 0-2 Fm: 0-1
Distance: 5f/6f: 0-2 7f-8f: 0-6 9f-13f: 0-3 14f+: 0-0
Track : LH: 0-3 RH: 0-1 Tight: 0-2 Gall: 0-0
Aids: Bl: 0-1 Vi: 0-0 Tstrap: 0-0
Best Rating: 83 6/01 Ling 7f firm

Red Ramona

110 **79**

6-y-o b g Rudimentary (USA)-Apply (King's Lake (USA))
J Akehurst A D Spence

Placings:2156045/03000/00-43030 **(5692)**
2001: 14^{4}G, 14^{3}GF, 14^{0}HY, 16^{3}S, 16^{0}S

	Starts	1st	2nd	3rd	Win & Pl
Career Total (Turf)	19	1	1	3	12821

75	6/98	Folk	1m4f	F	GD	£2406

Total win prize-money £2406

Going (Turf): Sf: 0-9 GS: 0-1 **Gd: 1-6** GF: 0-3 Fm: 0-0
Distance: 5f/6f: 0-0 7f-8f: 0-0 **9f-13f: 1-9** 14f+: 0-10
Track : LH: 0-11 **RH: 1-8 Tight: 1-4** Gall: 0-12
Aids: Bl: 0-1 Vi: 0-0 Tstrap: 0-0
Best Rating: 79 8/01 NmkJ 1m6f175y gd-fm

Lightly raced in the last couple of seasons, he has been held in some competitive handicaps. Suited by hold-up tactics.

Red Revolution (USA)

88(111) (70)**67**

4-y-o ch g Explosive Red (CAN)-Braided Way (USA) (Mining (USA))
B Mactaggart B Mactaggart

Placings:32/16000-00 **(2224)**
2001: 5^{0}GF, 5^{0}G

	Starts	1st	2nd	3rd	Win & Pl
Career Total (Turf)	7	0	0	1	366
Career Total (AW)	2	1	1	0	3483

70	1/00	Ling	5f	D	STD	£2691

Total win prize-money £2691

Going (Turf): Sf: 0-0 GS: 0-0 Gd: 0-2 GF: 0-5 Fm: 0-0
Distance: 5f/6f: 1-9 7f-8f: 0-0 9f-13f: 0-0 14f+: 0-0
Track : LH: 1-1 RH: 0-0 **Tight: 1-1** Gall: 0-0
Aids: Bl: 0-0 Vi: 0-0 Tstrap: 0-0
Best Rating: 36 6/01 Muss 5f good

Red Rioja (IRE)

105 **95+**

2-y-o b f King's Theatre (IRE)-Foreign Relation (IRE) (Distant Relative)
E J O'Neill Dr Karen Sanderson

Placings:4114 **(5390)**
2001: 6^{4}F, 7^{1}GF, 7^{1}S, 7^{4}GS

	Starts	1st	2nd	3rd	Win & Pl
Career Total (Turf)	4	2	0	0	49255

95	10/01	Curr	7f		SFT	£42250
93	9/01	Kemp	7f	D	G-F	£4504

Total win prize-money £46755

Going (Turf): Sf: 1-1 GS: 0-1 Gd: 0-0 GF: 1-1 Fm: 0-1
Distance: 5f/6f: 0-1 7f-8f: 2-3 9f-13f: 0-0 14f+: 0-0
Track : LH: 0-0 RH: 1-1 Tight: 0-0 Gall: 1-1
Aids: Bl: 0-0 Vi: 0-0 Tstrap: 0-0
Best Rating: 95 10/01 Curr 7f soft

Showed plenty of promise on her debut and confirmed it with a fluent win in a Kempton maiden next time. Was well placed to take a Curragh Group Three next time and looks progressive.

Red River Rebel

101(88) (23)**65**

3-y-o b g Inchinor-Bidweaya (USA) (Lear Fan (USA))
J R Norton Jeff Slaney

Placings:600-05350011135 (5373)
2001: 8^{0}F, 10^{5}GF, 10^{3}GF, 12^{5}SD, 9^{0}GF, 9^{0}G, 12^{1}G, 12^{1}GF, 11^{1}G, 14^{3}G, 14^{5}G

	Starts	1st	2nd	3rd	Win & Pl
Career Total (Turf)	13	3	0	2	12082
Career Total (AW)	1	0	0	0	0

64 9/01 Bevl 1m3f216yE(0-70)H GD £4810
58 8/01 Newc 1m4f93y E(0-75)H G-F £3464
56 8/01 Newc 1m4f93y E(0-75)H GD £2975
Total win prize-money £11250

Going (Turf): Sf: 0-1 GS: 0-1 Gd: 2-6 GF: 1-4 Fm: 0-1
Distance: 5f/6f: 0-1 7f-8f: 0-3 9f-13f: 3-8 14f+: 0-2
Track : LH: 2-9 RH: 1-2 Tight: 1-4 Gall: 2-4
Aids: Bl: 0-0 Vi: 0-0 Tstrap: 0-0
Best Rating: 65 10/01 Rdcr 1m6f19y good

He had not shown a great deal of form before getting off the mark in August over 12 furlongs at Newcastle, he then followed up just ten days later, over the same course and distance before completing the hat trick with another win over 12 furlongs, this time at Beverley, but he is now higher in the weights as a result.

Red Rooney

82 **43**

2-y-o b g Astronef-Mica Male (ITY) (Law Society (USA))
P Butler Homewoodgate Racing Club

Placings:604000 (5128)
2001: 5^{6}G, 6^{0}G, 6^{4}GF, 7^{0}GF, 6^{0}GF, 6^{0}HY

	Starts	1st	2nd	3rd	Win & Pl
Career Total (Turf)	6	0	0	0	524

Going (Turf): Sf: 0-1 GS: 0-1 Gd: 0-2 GF: 0-2 Fm: 0-0
Distance: 5f/6f: 0-5 7f-8f: 0-1 9f-13f: 0-0 14f+: 0-0
Track : LH: 0-0 RH: 0-2 Tight: 0-0 Gall: 0-1
Aids: Bl: 0-0 Vi: 0-0 Tstrap: 0-0
Best Rating: 43 5/01 Wind 5f10y good

Red Roses (IRE)

79(68) **21**

5-y-o b m Mukaddamah (USA)-Roses Red (IRE) (Exhibitioner)
Don Enrico Incisa Don Enrico Incisa

Placings:0/200050036/00000400434-000 (1938)
2001: 11^{0}SD, 11^{0}SD, 11^{0}GF

	Starts	1st	2nd	3rd	Win & Pl
Career Total (Turf)	22	0	1	2	2205
Career Total (AW)	2	0	0	0	0

Going (Turf): Sf: 0-8 GS: 0-3 Gd: 0-4 GF: 0-5 Fm: 0-2
Distance: 5f/6f: 0-0 7f-8f: 0-2 9f-13f: 0-22 14f+: 0-0
Track : LH: 0-15 RH: 0-7 Tight: 0-11 Gall: 0-3
Aids: Bl: 0-2 Vi: 0-0 Tstrap: 0-1
Best Rating: 6 6/01 Hayd 1m3f200y gd-fm

Red Rosie (USA)

105 **85**

3-y-o b f Red Ransom (USA)-Do's Gent (CAN) (Vice Regent (CAN))
Mrs A J Perrett R C O'Hare

Placings:0-130 (3471)
2001: 10^{1}F, 9^{3}GF, 12^{0}GF

	Starts	1st	2nd	3rd	Win & Pl
Career Total (Turf)	4	1	0	1	4221

78 6/01 Bath 1m2f46y E FRM £2835
Total win prize-money £2835

Going (Turf): Sf: 0-1 GS: 0-0 Gd: 0-0 GF: 0-2 Fm: 1-1
Distance: 5f/6f: 0-0 7f-8f: 0-1 9f-13f: 1-3 14f+: 0-0
Track : LH: 1-1 RH: 0-2 Tight: 1-2 Gall: 0-1
Aids: Bl: 0-0 Vi: 0-0 Tstrap: 0-0
Best Rating: 85 6/01 Sals 1m1f198y gd-fm

A little disappointing since winning a Bath maiden.

Red Roulette (IRE)

79(51) **46**

2-y-o ch f Tagula (IRE)-Mini Project (IRE) (Project Manager)
A Berry The Red Shirt Brigade Ltd

Placings:40300 (5410)
2001: 5^{4}S, 5^{0}G, 6^{3}G, 8^{0}GF, 7^{0}SD

	Starts	1st	2nd	3rd	Win & Pl
Career Total (Turf)	4	0	0	1	685
Career Total (AW)	1	0	0	0	

Going (Turf): Sf: 0-1 GS: 0-0 Gd: 0-2 GF: 0-1 Fm: 0-0
Distance: 5f/6f: 0-3 7f-8f: 0-2 9f-13f: 0-0 14f+: 0-0
Track : LH: 0-1 RH: 0-1 Tight: 0-1 Gall: 0-0
Aids: Bl: 0-0 Vi: 0-0 Tstrap: 0-2
Best Rating: 46 8/01 Ripn 6f good

Red Ryding Hood

101(105) (77)**75**

3-y-o ch f Wolfhound (USA)-Downeaster Alexa (USA) (Red Ryder (USA))
C A Dwyer P Venner

Placings:634232054-1435001560026063 5 (4622)
2001: 5^{1}SD, 5^{4}SD, 6^{3}SD, 6^{5}G, 6^{0}S, 5^{0}F, 5^{1}GF, 5^{5}GF, 5^{6}GF, 6^{0}GF, 6^{0}GS, 5^{2}GF, 5^{6}G, 5^{0}G, 5^{6}G, 5^{3}GF, 6^{5}GF

	Starts	1st	2nd	3rd	Win & Pl
Career Total (Turf)	23	1	3	3	12730
Career Total (AW)	3	1	0	1	3822

78 6/01 Folk 5f D(0-85)H G-F £3815
63 3/01 Sthl 5f D STD £2940
Total win prize-money £6756

Going (Turf): Sf: 0-2 GS: 0-1 Gd: 0-7 GF: 1-11 Fm: 0-2
Distance: 5f/6f: 2-22 7f-8f: 0-4 9f-13f: 0-0 14f+: 0-0
Track : LH: 0-3 RH: 0-0 Tight: 0-2 Gall: 0-0
Aids: Bl: 0-1 Vi: 0-1 Tstrap: 0-0
Best Rating: 78 7/01 Sand 5f6y gd-fm

A speedy sort, she ran some fine races at two without winning. Made up for that when scoring on reappearance at three on the All-Weather and notched up another success at Folkestone in June. Appreciates being allowed to travel and not forced in her races. Best on a sound surface.

Red Satin (IRE)

73 **43**

2-y-o b c Mujadil (USA)-Satinette (Shirley Heights)
B A McMahon Mr A Stennett & Mrs J M Stennett

Placings:000 (5491)
2001: 7^{0}HY, 6^{0}S, 6^{0}HY

	Starts	1st	2nd	3rd	Win & Pl
Career Total (Turf)	3	0	0	0	

Going (Turf): Sf: 0-3 GS: 0-0 Gd: 0-0 GF: 0-0 Fm: 0-0
Distance: 5f/6f: 0-1 7f-8f: 0-2 9f-13f: 0-0 14f+: 0-0
Track : LH: 0-1 RH: 0-0 Tight: 0-0 Gall: 0-0
Aids: Bl: 0-0 Vi: 0-0 Tstrap: 0-0
Best Rating: 43 10/01 York 6f soft

Red September

102(69) **43**

4-y-o b g Presidium-Tangalooma (Hotfoot)
G M Moore Dr C I Emmerson

Placings:40665/0600-340 (4014)
2001: 12^{3}S, 16^{4}GF, 15^{0}G

	Starts	1st	2nd	3rd	Win & Pl
Career Total (Turf)	11	0	0	1	790
Career Total (AW)	1	0	0	0	

Going (Turf): Sf: 0-3 GS: 0-0 Gd: 0-5 GF: 0-3 Fm: 0-0
Distance: 5f/6f: 0-3 7f-8f: 0-3 9f-13f: 0-3 14f+: 0-3
Track : LH: 0-5 RH: 0-3 Tight: 0-2 Gall: 0-3
Aids: Bl: 0-2 Vi: 0-0 Tstrap: 0-0
Best Rating: 43 5/01 Newc 1m4f93y soft

Red Storm

91 **61**

2-y-o ch f Dancing Spree (USA)-Dam Certain (IRE) (Damister (USA))
R Ingram Brian McAtavey

Placings:00050 (5588)
2001: 6^{0}GF, 5^{0}F, 6^{0}HY, 6^{5}HY, 5^{0}GS

	Starts	1st	2nd	3rd	Win & Pl
Career Total (Turf)	5	0	0	0	

Going (Turf): Sf: 0-2 GS: 0-1 Gd: 0-0 GF: 0-1 Fm: 0-1
Distance: 5f/6f: 0-5 7f-8f: 0-0 9f-13f: 0-0 14f+: 0-0
Track : LH: 0-1 RH: 0-0 Tight: 0-0 Gall: 0-0
Aids: Bl: 0-0 Vi: 0-0 Tstrap: 0-0
Best Rating: 61 5/01 Gdwd 6f gd-fm

Red Sun

100(100) (49)**50**

4-y-o b g Foxhound (USA)-Superetta (Superlative)
A Streeter Bulls Head Racing Club

Placings:300660/21300 (4942)
2001: 11^{2}SD, 14^{1}SD, 14^{3}SD, 16^{0}SD, 15^{0}S

	Starts	1st	2nd	3rd	Win & Pl
Career Total (Turf)	7	0	0	1	446
Career Total (AW)	4	1	1	1	3132

47 5/01 Sthl 1m6f F(0-65)H STD £2387
Total win prize-money £2387

Going (Turf): Sf: 0-1 GS: 0-2 Gd: 0-1 GF: 0-3 Fm: 0-0
Distance: 5f/6f: 0-4 7f-8f: 0-2 9f-13f: 0-1 14f+: 1-4
Track : LH: 1-8 RH: 0-0 Tight: 0-3 Gall: 0-0
Aids: Bl: 0-0 Vi: 0-0 Tstrap: 0-0
Best Rating: 49 5/01 Sthl 1m6f stand

Suited by a stiff test of stamina. Won on the All-Weather in May 2001. Acts well on sand.

Red Sunrise

65(79) (41)**27**

2-y-o ch f Beveled (USA)-Sun In The Morning (Petardia)
A Berry The Red Shirt Brigade Ltd

Placings:24440 (1302)
2001: 5^{2}SD, 5^{4}SD, 5^{4}SD, 5^{4}S, 5^{0}GF

	Starts	1st	2nd	3rd	Win & Pl
Career Total (Turf)	2	0	0	0	0
Career Total (AW)	3	0	1	0	516

Going (Turf): Sf: 0-1 GS: 0-0 Gd: 0-0 GF: 0-1 Fm: 0-0
Distance: 5f/6f: 0-5 7f-8f: 0-0 9f-13f: 0-0 14f+: 0-0
Track : LH: 0-2 RH: 0-0 Tight: 0-2 Gall: 0-0
Aids: Bl: 0-0 Vi: 0-0 Tstrap: 0-0
Best Rating: 41 4/01 Ling 5f stand

Red Symphony

(86) (30)**47**

5-y-o b m Merdon Melody-Woodland Steps (Bold Owl)
M J Polglase The Lovatt Partnership

Placings:412134610/0003000030/50001000000-06 (0143)
2001: 5^{0}SD, 6^{0}SW

	Starts	1st	2nd	3rd	Win & Pl
Career Total (Turf)	26	3	1	3	9344
Career Total (AW)	6	1	0	0	1848

47	6/00	Newc	5f	G	SFT	£1981
72	9/98	Muss	5f	E(0-75)H	G-S	£3077
55	5/98	Muss	5f	F	G-S	£2220
48	4/98	Wolv	5f	G	STD	£1847

Total win prize-money £9126

Going (Turf): Sf: 1-8 **GS: 2-4** Gd: 0-8 GF: 0-3 Fm: 0-3
Distance: **5f/6f: 4-30** 7f-8f: 0-2 9f-13f: 0-0 14f+: 0-0
Track : **LH: 1-7** RH: 0-2 **Tight: 1-4** Gall: 0-2
Aids: Bl: 0-4 **Vi: 1-4** Tstrap: 0-0
Best Rating: 14 1/01 Sthl 6f slow

Red Tape

69 **21**

2-y-o ch g Danzig Connection (USA)-Jolizal (Good Times (ITY))
R Hollinshead G J Sargent

Placings:0 (4777)
2001: 5^{0}G

	Starts	1st	2nd	3rd	Win & Pl
Career Total (Turf)	1	0	0	0	

Going (Turf): Sf: 0-0 GS: 0-0 Gd: 0-1 GF: 0-0 Fm: 0-0
Distance: 5f/6f: 0-1 7f-8f: 0-0 9f-13f: 0-0 14f+: 0-0
Track : LH: 0-0 RH: 0-0 Tight: 0-0 Gall: 0-0
Aids: Bl: 0-0 Vi: 0-0 Tstrap: 0-0
Best Rating: 21 9/01 Bevl 5f good

Red Thatch

99(90) (14)**36**

4-y-o ch g Pelder (IRE)-Straw Castle (Final Straw)
A P Jones (M P Muggeridge 9/2) The Lambourn Racing Club

Placings:06/00-0664546004 (3870)
2001: 12^{0}SW, 8^{6}SD, 6^{6}HY, 5^{4}G, 7^{5}GF, 6^{4}GF, 6^{6}F, 8^{0}G, 5^{0}GF, 5^{4}G

	Starts	1st	2nd	3rd	Win & Pl
Career Total (Turf)	12	0	0	0	295
Career Total (AW)	2	0	0	0	0

Going (Turf): Sf: 0-2 GS: 0-1 Gd: 0-4 GF: 0-4 Fm: 0-1
Distance: 5f/6f: 0-4 7f-8f: 0-6 9f-13f: 0-4 14f+: 0-0
Track : LH: 0-6 RH: 0-4 Tight: 0-3 Gall: 0-2
Aids: Bl: 0-0 Vi: 0-0 Tstrap: 0-1
Best Rating: 36 5/01 Ling 7f gd-fm

Red To Violet

94 **70**

2-y-o b f Spectrum (IRE)-Khalsheva (Shirley Heights)
J A Glover Philip A Jarvis

Placings:051 (5399)
2001: 7^{0}GS, 6^{5}HY, 6^{1}S

	Starts	1st	2nd	3rd	Win & Pl
Career Total (Turf)	3	1	0	0	3591

70	10/01	Pont	6f	F	SFT	£3591

Total win prize-money £3591

Going (Turf): **Sf: 1-2** GS: 0-1 Gd: 0-0 GF: 0-0 Fm: 0-0
Distance: **5f/6f: 1-1** 7f-8f: 0-2 9f-13f: 0-0 14f+: 0-0
Track : **LH: 1-1** RH: 0-0 Tight: 0-0 Gall: 0-0
Aids: Bl: 0-0 Vi: 0-0 Tstrap: 0-0
Best Rating: 70 10/01 Pont 6f soft

Bred for middle distances, won a maiden auction in October over six furlongs, but looks to need a mile and a half next year. She likes to get her toe in.

Red Tower

88 **28**

6-y-o b g Damister (USA)-Tower Of Ivory (IRE) (Cyrano De Bergerac)
L Wells High As A Kite

Placings:02/0 (4471)
2001: 6^{0}GF

	Starts	1st	2nd	3rd	Win & Pl
Career Total (Turf)	3	0	1	0	812

Going (Turf): Sf: 0-0 GS: 0-0 Gd: 0-0 GF: 0-2 Fm: 0-1
Distance: 5f/6f: 0-0 7f-8f: 0-1 9f-13f: 0-2 14f+: 0-0
Track : LH: 0-2 RH: 0-1 Tight: 0-0 Gall: 0-0
Aids: Bl: 0-0 Vi: 0-0 Tstrap: 0-0
Best Rating: 28 9/01 Brig 6f209y gd-fm

Red Velvet

57 **6**

3-y-o ch f So Factual (USA)-Amber Fizz (USA) (Effervescing (USA))
K T Ivory Mrs Valerie Hubbard

Placings:0 (0841)
2001: 7^{0}GS

	Starts	1st	2nd	3rd	Win & Pl
Career Total (Turf)	1	0	0	0	

Going (Turf): Sf: 0-0 GS: 0-1 Gd: 0-0 GF: 0-0 Fm: 0-0
Distance: 5f/6f: 0-0 7f-8f: 0-1 9f-13f: 0-0 14f+: 0-0
Track : LH: 0-0 RH: 0-0 Tight: 0-0 Gall: 0-0
Aids: Bl: 0-0 Vi: 0-0 Tstrap: 0-0
Best Rating: 6 4/01 Newb 7f gd-sft

Red White And Blue

(90) (14)**30**

4-y-o b f Zafonic (USA)-Malham Tarn (Riverman (USA))
K O Cunningham-Brown A J Richards

Placings:00/000004-0 (0091)
2001: 7^{0}SD

	Starts	1st	2nd	3rd	Win & Pl
Career Total (Turf)	6	0	0	0	
Career Total (AW)	3	0	0	0	0

Going (Turf): Sf: 0-2 GS: 0-0 Gd: 0-0 GF: 0-2 Fm: 0-0
Distance: 5f/6f: 0-2 7f-8f: 0-3 9f-13f: 0-2 14f+: 0-0
Track : LH: 0-3 RH: 0-2 Tight: 0-4 Gall: 0-1
Aids: Bl: 0-0 Vi: 0-0 Tstrap: 0-0
Best Rating: 6 4/01 Newb 7f gd-sft

Red Wine

(87) (59)

2-y-o b g Hamas (IRE)-Red Bouquet (Reference Point)
J A Osborne Paul J Dixon

Placings:4 (5614)
2001: 6^{4}SD

	Starts	1st	2nd	3rd	Win & Pl
Career Total (Turf)	0	0	0	0	
Career Total (AW)	1	0	0	0	0

Going (Turf): Sf: 0-0 GS: 0-0 Gd: 0-0 GF: 0-0 Fm: 0-0
Distance: 5f/6f: 0-1 7f-8f: 0-0 9f-13f: 0-0 14f+: 0-0
Track : LH: 0-1 RH: 0-0 Tight: 0-1 Gall: 0-0
Aids: Bl: 0-0 Vi: 0-0 Tstrap: 0-0
Best Rating: 59 11/01 Wolv 6f stand

Redback

110 **108?**

2-y-o ch c Mark Of Esteem (IRE)-Patsy Western (Precocious)
R Hannon The Waney Racing Group Inc

Placings:2214410143 (5500)
2001: 5^{2}S, 5^{2}G, 5^{1}G, 6^{4}GF, 6^{4}Y, 7^{1}G, 7^{0}GF, 7^{1}G, 7^{4}G, 8^{3}HY

	Starts	1st	2nd	3rd	Win & Pl
Career Total (Turf)	10	3	2	1	71006

108	9/01	Sand	7f16y	A	GD	£18000
99	7/01	NmkJ	7f	A	GD	£12995
90	5/01	Wind	5f10y	B	GD	£7583

Total win prize-money £38578

Going (Turf): Sf: 0-2 GS: 0-0 **Gd: 3-5** GF: 0-2 Fm: 0-0
Distance: 5f/6f: 1-5 **7f-8f: 2-5** 9f-13f: 0-0 14f+: 0-0
Track : LH: 0-0 **RH: 2-3** Tight: 0-0 **Gall: 1-1**
Aids: Bl: 0-0 Vi: 0-0 Tstrap: 0-0
Best Rating: 108 9/01 Sand 7f16y good

A useful performer, he finished fourth in the Coventry at Ascot and the Railway Stakes, both Group Threes, before landing the Listed Superlative Stakes at Newmarket. Added to that with an easy win in the Solario, though he may have been flattered, and ran well in a Newmarket Group Three. He races keenly, stays seven and should get further. Suited by good ground.

Reddening

96 **77**

3-y-o b f Blushing Flame (USA)-Music In My Life (IRE) (Law Society (USA))
J R Fanshawe Cheveley Park Stud

Placings:014 (3478)
2001: 10^{0}G, 16^{1}GF, 14^{4}GF

	Starts	1st	2nd	3rd	Win & Pl
Career Total (Turf)	3	1	0	0	2871

35	7/01	Sthl	2m	F	G-F	£2348

Total win prize-money £2349

Going (Turf): Sf: 0-0 GS: 0-0 Gd: 0-1 **GF: 1-2** Fm: 0-0
Distance: 5f/6f: 0-0 7f-8f: 0-0 9f-13f: 0-1 **14f+: 1-2**
Track : **LH: 1-1** RH: 0-1 Tight: 0-1 Gall: 0-1
Aids: Bl: 0-0 Vi: 0-0 Tstrap: 0-0
Best Rating: 77 7/01 NmkJ 1m6f175y gd-fm

She got off the mark on her second start in a two-mile maiden on turf at Southwell when in foal to Pivotal.

Redhill

(79) (18)**56**

4-y-o b f Tragic Role (USA)-Indivisible (Remainder Man)
R Hollinshead R Hollinshead

Placings:0650000-00 (0233)
2001: 12^{0}SD, 14^{0}SD

	Starts	1st	2nd	3rd	Win & Pl
Career Total (Turf)	4	0	0	0	0
Career Total (AW)	5	0	0	0	

Going (Turf): Sf: 0-0 GS: 0-0 Gd: 0-1 GF: 0-3 Fm: 0-0
Distance: 5f/6f: 0-0 7f-8f: 0-2 9f-13f: 0-6 14f+: 0-1
Track : LH: 0-7 RH: 0-2 Tight: 0-3 Gall: 0-0
Aids: Bl: 0-0 Vi: 0-0 Tstrap: 0-0
Best Rating: 77 7/01 NmkJ 1m6f175y gd-fm

Redisham

91 **75**

2-y-o ch f Hector Protector (USA)-Barsham (De My Guest (USA))
J R Best (W J Haggas 18/10) Tony Stafford

Placings:20 **(5609)**
2001: 7^{2}GS, 8^{0}GS

	Starts	1st	2nd	3rd	Win & Pl
Career Total (Turf)	2	0	1	0	1788

Going (Turf): Sf: 0-0 GS: 0-2 Gd: 0-0 GF: 0-0 Fm: 0-0
Distance: 5f/6f: 0-0 7f-8f: 0-2 9f-13f: 0-0 14f+: 0-0
Track : LH: 0-0 RH: 0-0 Tight: 0-0 Gall: 0-0
Aids: Bl: 0-0 Vi: 0-0 Tstrap: 0-0
Best Rating: 75 11/01 NmkR 1m gd-sft

Made an eyecatching debut over seven furlongs at Newmarket, running on strongly. By Hector Protector, and out of a ten-furlong winner, she will eventually appreciate middle-distances.

Redouble

99(77) (51)**58**

5-y-o b g First Trump-Sunflower Seed (Mummy's Pet)
B R Millman The Dragisic Partnership

Placings:6366203005/24000354550/0223322-5416433400 **(4983)**
2001: 12^{5}SW, 11^{4}GS, 12^{1}GГ, 14^{6}GF, 12^{4}GF, 12^{3}GF, 12^{3}GF, 12^{4}GS, 12^{0}G, 12^{0}G

	Starts	1st	2nd	3rd	Win & Pl
Career Total (Turf)	34	1	6	7	9643
Career Total (AW)	4	0	0	0	0

Going (Turf): Sf: 0-4 GS: 0-4 Gd: 0-9 **GF: 1-16** Fm: 0-1
Distance: 5f/6f: 0-3 7f-8f: 0-7 **9f-13f: 1-22** 14f+: 0-6
Track : LH: 0-17 **RH: 1-12 Tight: 1-18** Gall: 0-3
Aids: Bl: 0-0 Vi: 0-0 Tstrap: 0-0
Best Rating: 58 7/01 Chep 1m4f23y gd-fm

Redoubtable (USA)

104(108) (76)**62**

10-y-o b h Grey Dawn Ii-Seattle Rockette (USA) (Seattle Slew (USA))
D W Chapman David W Chapman

Placings:11335/0224060/0001/1430003105100060620 00/00306262002201325405043063/6412143201000003 6004143050404335-1000011200020010000 **(5347)**
2001: 6^{1}SD, 7^{0}SD, 7^{0}SW, 7^{0}SD, 6^{0}SD, 6^{1}SD, 6^{1}SD, 8^{2}SD, 7^{0}SD, 6^{0}SD, 6^{0}GF, 7^{0}GF, 8^{2}GS, 6^{0}GF, 6^{0}F, 7^{1}G, 7^{0}GF, 6^{0}G, 6^{0}GF, 8^{0}SD

	Starts	1st	2nd	3rd	Win & Pl
Career Total (Turf)	76	8	8	8	97533
Career Total (AW)	39	7	4	5	36494

62	8/01	Newc	7f	D(0-85)H	GD	£4124
69	3/01	Sthl	6f	E(0-70)	STD	£2800
63	3/01	Wolv	6f	E(0-70)	STD	£2408
76	1/01	Ling	6f	D(0-75)	STD	£4046
47	7/00	Rdcr	7f	G(0-70)	G-F	£1974
84	5/00	Wwck	6f168y	D(0-80)	SFT	£3768
81	2/00	Ling	7f	D(0-80)H	STD	£4192
76	1/00	Sthl	6f	D(0-80)H	STD	£4706
79	5/99	Thsk	6f	C(0-95)H	G-S	£7532
77	6/98	Newc	7f	C(0-100)H	SFT	£10845
69	5/98	Ayr	7f	C(0-95)H	G-F	£6937
73	1/98	Ling	7f	D(0-85)H	STD	£4265
65	12/97	Wolv	6f	E(0-70)H	STD	£2388
97	6/93	Sand	5f6y	A	FRM	£8419
97	5/93	Ches	5f16y	D	G-F	£4825

Total win prize-money £73231

Going (Turf): Sf: 2-12 GS: 1-10 Gd: 1-19 **GF: 3-30** Fm: 1-5
Distance: **5f/6f: 8-49** 7f-8f: 7-63 9f-13f: 0-3 14f+: 0-0
Track : **LH: 10-60** RH: 0-2 **Tight: 6-33** Gall: 0-2
Aids: Bl: 0-3 Vi: 0-0 Tstrap: 0-0
Best Rating: 76 4/01 Ling 1m stand

He is an effective sort on turf and sand, but not altogether consistent and needs things his own way. A winner on Equitrack and Fibresand this year, he also scored on turf at Newcastle and is probably best suited by seven furlongs these days.

Redswan

103 (72)**67**

6-y-o ch g Risk Me (FR)-Bocas Rose (Jalmood (USA))
A W Carroll Graham Brown

Placings:00/5312/00653155401/0000020331506-003030 **(4951)**
2001: 6^{0}S, 8^{0}G, 7^{3}GF, 6^{0}GS, 8^{3}S, 8^{0}G

	Starts	1st	2nd	3rd	Win & Pl
Career Total (Turf)	35	4	2	5	28133
Career Total (AW)	1	0	0	1	401

64	9/00	NmkR	7f	F	SFT	£5541
71	9/99	Donc	7f	C(0-90)H	G-F	£7196
67	7/99	Leic	7f9y	D(0-80)H	G-F	£4077
67	6/98	NmkJ	1m	D	GD	£4045

Total win prize-money £20860

Going (Turf): Sf: 1-7 GS: 0-2 Gd: 1-10 **GF: 2-13** Fm: 0-2
Distance: 5f/6f: 0-3 **7f-8f: 4-27** 9f-13f: 0-5 14f+: 0-0
Track : LH: 0-4 RH: 0-5 Tight: 0-1 Gall: 0-1
Aids: Bl: 1-4 Vi: 0-0 **Tstrap: 3-20**
Best Rating: 67 7/01 Donc 7f gd-fm

Reduit

97 **107**

3-y-o ch c Lion Cavern (USA)-Soolaimon (IRE) (Shareef Dancer (USA))
G A Butler Five Horses Ltd

Placings:4412-64 **(1498)**
2001: 10^{6}G, 11^{4}GF

	Starts	1st	2nd	3rd	Win & Pl
Career Total (Turf)	6	1	1	0	22309

85	9/00	Chep	1m14y	E	G-S	£2775

Total win prize-money £2776

Going (Turf): Sf: 0-0 **GS: 1-1** Gd: 0-2 GF: 0-2 Fm: 0-0
Distance: 5f/6f: 0-0 7f-8f: 0-2 **9f-13f: 1-3** 14f+: 0-0
Track : LH: 0-1 RH: 0-1 Tight: 0-0 Gall: 0-1
Aids: Bl: 0-0 Vi: 0-0 Tstrap: 0-0
Best Rating: 107 5/01 Gdwd 1m3f gd-fm

Finished sixth to Rosi's Boy in steadily run Listed event at Newmarket on his reappearance, and stepped up on that effort to be fourth behind Asian Heights in the Predominate Stakes at Goodwood.

Redwood

75 **19**

3-y-o b g Kris-Pearl Venture (Salse (USA))
A W Carroll A Griffin,R Peachey,S Taylor,G Prestow

Placings:000 **(4455)**
2001: 8^{0}GF, 7^{0}GS, 10^{0}GF

	Starts	1st	2nd	3rd	Win & Pl
Career Total (Turf)	3	0	0	0	

Going (Turf): Sf: 0-0 GS: 0-1 Gd: 0-0 GF: 0-2 Fm: 0-0
Distance: 5f/6f: 0-0 7f-8f: 0-1 9f-13f: 0-2 14f+: 0-0
Track : LH: 0-1 RH: 0-1 Tight: 0-1 Gall: 0-1
Aids: Bl: 0-0 Vi: 0-0 Tstrap: 0-0
Best Rating: 19 9/01 York 1m2f85y gd-fm

Reeds Rains

92 **42**

3-y-o b f Mind Games-Me Spede (Valiyar)
T D Easterby Ron George

Placings:1440-0000060 **(3720)**
2001: 7^{0}S, 6^{0}GF, 7^{0}G, 7^{0}GF, 9^{0}GF, 10^{6}F, 8^{0}G

	Starts	1st	2nd	3rd	Win & Pl
Career Total (Turf)	11	1	0	0	4916

71	4/00	Thsk	5f	D	SFT	£4049

Total win prize-money £4050

Going (Turf): Sf: 1-2 GS: 0-0 Gd: 0-4 GF: 0-4 Fm: 0-1
Distance: **5f/6f: 1-5** 7f-8f: 0-3 9f-13f: 0-3 14f+: 0-0
Track : LH: 0-3 RH: 0-1 Tight: 0-1 Gall: 0-0
Aids: Bl: 0-4 Vi: 0-0 Tstrap: 0-0
Best Rating: 42 7/01 Rdcr 1m2f firm

Reef Diver

107 **107d**

3-y-o b c Pursuit Of Love-Triple Reef (Mill Reef (USA))
Mrs A J Perrett Hesmonds Stud

Placings:13030 **(5142)**
2001: 8^{1}G, 8^{3}GF, 8^{0}G, 9^{3}GF, 9^{0}G

	Starts	1st	2nd	3rd	Win & Pl
Career Total (Turf)	5	1	0	2	10872

90	5/01	NmkR	1m	D	GD	£6418

Total win prize-money £6419

Going (Turf): Sf: 0-0 GS: 0-0 **Gd: 1-3** GF: 0-2 Fm: 0-0
Distance: 5f/6f: 0-0 **7f-8f: 1-3** 9f-13f: 0-2 14f+: 0-0
Track : LH: 0-1 RH: 0-2 Tight: 0-0 Gall: 0-1
Aids: Bl: 0-0 Vi: 0-0 Tstrap: 0-0
Best Rating: 107 5/01 Kemp 1m gd-fm

Unraced at two, he displayed a fine turn of foot to win a slowly-run maiden at Newmarket on his debut and did not run badly when third in a Kempton Listed event next time. Disappointing after a break, however. Stays a mile. Acts on a sound surface. Sold to USA.

Reefs Sis

107 **87**

2-y-o ch f Muhtarram (USA)-Horseshoe Reef (Mill Reef (USA))
E J Alston Valley Paddocks Racing Limited

Placings:501523203 **(5598)**
2001: 5^{5}GF, 5^{0}GF, 6^{1}GF, 6^{5}GF, 7^{2}GF, 8^{3}G, 6^{2}GF, 8^{0}S, 6^{3}GS

	Starts	1st	2nd	3rd	Win & Pl
Career Total (Turf)	9	1	2	2	10193

68	6/01	Haml	6f5y	E	G-F	£3493

Total win prize-money £3494

Going (Turf): Sf: 0-1 GS: 0-1 Gd: 0-1 **GF: 1-6** Fm: 0-0
Distance: 5f/6f: 0-5 **7f-8f: 1-3** 9f-13f: 0-1 14f+: 0-0
Track : LH: 0-2 RH: 0-2 Tight: 0-1 Gall: 0-1
Aids: Bl: 0-0 Vi: 0-0 Tstrap: 0-0
Best Rating: 87 9/01 Donc 6f gd-fm

A half-sister to Warning Reef, she is only small but knuckled down well to win an ordinary race at Hamilton. Decent efforts since being stepped up in trip. Effective six furlongs to a mile she is suited by a strong pace, and good to firm.

Reel Buddy (USA)

111 **115**

3-y-o ch c Mr Greeley (USA)-Rosebud (Indian Ridge)
R Hannon Speedlith Group

Placings:620001120-311302566 **(4831)**
2001: 7^{3}S, 7^{1}G, 7^{1}GF, 7^{3}GF, 7^{0}GF, 7^{2}GF, 7^{5}G, 7^{6}GF, 7^{6}GF

	Starts	1st	2nd	3rd	Win & Pl
Career Total (Turf)	18	4	3	2	127712

112	5/01	Gdwd	7f	B(0-110)H	G-F	£32500
109	5/01	NmkR	7f	C(0-100)H	GD	£6987
97	8/00	Ripn	5f	C	GD	£5591
92	8/00	Bath	5f11y	D	GD	£4104

Total win prize-money £49184

Going (Turf): Sf: 0-3 GS: 0-0 **Gd: 3-6** GF: 1-8 Fm: 0-1
Distance: 5f/6f: 2-9 7f-8f: 2-9 9f-13f: 0-0 14f+: 0-0
Track : LH: 1-3 RH: 1-2 Tight: 0-0 **Gall: 1-3**
Aids: Bl: 0-0 Vi: 0-0 Tstrap: 0-0
Best Rating: 115 6/01 NmkJ 7f gd-fm

Very impressive when landing a decent Newmarket handicap on his second start, he followed up at Goodwood and had a luckless run when finishing third back at Headquarters. He did not have the luck of the draw in the Jersey Stakes, but ran much better to finish runner-up in the Criterion. Again unlucky at Goodwood, his style of running means he often finds trouble. Seven furlongs is his trip and he is best on a sound surface.

Refa'Ah (IRE)

87 **76**

2-y-o b f Lahib (USA)-Shurooq (USA) (Affirmed (USA))
E A L Dunlop Hamdan Al Maktoum

Placings:04 (5107)
2001: 6^{0}GF, 7^{4}GS

	Starts	1st	2nd	3rd	Win & Pl
Career Total (Turf)	2	0	0	0	450

Going (Turf): Sf: 0-0 GS: 0-1 Gd: 0-0 GF: 0-1 Fm: 0-0
Distance: 5f/6f: 0-0 7f-8f: 0-2 9f-13f: 0-0 14f+: 0-0
Track : LH: 0-0 RH: 0-0 Tight: 0-0 Gall: 0-0
Aids: Bl: 0-0 Vi: 0-0 Tstrap: 0-0
Best Rating: 76 10/01 NmkR 7f gd-sft

Referendum (IRE)

105(97) (67)**63**

7-y-o b g Common Grounds-Final Decision (Tap On Wood)
D Nicholls M A Scaife

Placings:32124/620/0205/446000/**0**000005266022300-**60**0042100000301003000 (4965)
2001: 5^{6}SD, 6^{0}SD, 5^{0}S, 5^{0}S, 5^{4}HY, 6^{2}G, 5^{1}G, 5^{0}GF, 5^{0}GF, 6^{0}GF, 6^{0}GF, 5^{0}F, 5^{3}F, 6^{0}G, 6^{1}G, 7^{0}GF, 5^{0}GF, 6^{3}G, 6^{0}GS, 5^{0}G, 5^{0}G, 5^{0}S

	Starts	1st	2nd	3rd	Win & Pl
Career Total (Turf)	53	3	8	4	82820
Career Total (AW)	3	0	0	0	0

66	7/01	Haml	6f5y	E(0-70)H	GD	£3178
65	5/01	Haml	5f4y	F(0-65)H	GD	£2579
94	8/96	Gdwd	6f	D	G-S	£4513

Total win prize-money £10272

Going (Turf): Sf: 0-7 GS: 1-9 **Gd: 2-17** GF: 0-15 Fm: 0-5
Distance: **5f/6f: 2-47** 7f-8f: 1-9 9f-13f: 0-0 14f+: 0-0
Track : LH: 0-7 RH: 0-1 Tight: 0-2 Gall: 0-0
Aids: Bl: 0-1 Vi: 0-0 Tstrap: 0-0
Best Rating: 67 1/01 Ling 5f stand

He has two ways of running these days. Capable when in the mood as he showed when winning at Hamilton in May and July, but more often than not has been finishing down the field. Currently well handicapped on his very best form, but is not one to trust.

Reflex Blue

104 **71**

4-y-o b g Ezzoud (IRE)-Briggsmaid (Elegant Air)
J W Hills The Jonathawn Q Partnership

Placings:2125/44236405-0010464 (4212)
2001: 12^{0}G, 12^{0}S, 14^{1}GF, 16^{0}GF, 14^{4}GF, 14^{6}GF, 13^{4}GF

	Starts	1st	2nd	3rd	Win & Pl
Career Total (Turf)	19	2	3	1	23045

71	6/01	Kemp	1m6f92y	D(0-80)H	G-F	£7117
82	7/99	NmkJ	7f	D	G-F	£4503

Total win prize-money £11621

Going (Turf): Sf: 0-1 GS: 0-2 Gd: 0-5 **GF: 2-11** Fm: 0-0
Distance: 5f/6f: 0-0 7f-8f: 1-2 9f-13f: 0-10 14f+: 1-7
Track : LH: 0-7 **RH: 1-10** Tight: 0-5 Gall: 0-9
Aids: **Bl: 1-5** Vi: 0-0 Tstrap: 0-0
Best Rating: 71 6/01 Kemp 1m6f92y gd-fm

Regal Air (IRE)

99(90) (36)**38**

3-y-o b f Distinctly North (USA)-Dignified Air (FR) (Wolver Hollow)
B I Case Just In Case Partnership

Placings:35303022-**00**00002000040 (5593)
2001: 6^{0}SD, 5^{0}SD, 7^{0}GF, 5^{0}GF, 5^{0}GF, 5^{0}G, 6^{2}S, 6^{0}G, 5^{0}GF, 6^{0}F, 7^{0}S, 6^{4}SD, 5^{0}GS

	Starts	1st	2nd	3rd	Win & Pl
Career Total (Turf)	16	0	3	1	2796
Career Total (AW)	5	0	0	2	651

Going (Turf): Sf: 0-3 GS: 0-1 Gd: 0-4 GF: 0-6 Fm: 0-2
Distance: 5f/6f: 0-15 7f-8f: 0-6 9f-13f: 0-0 14f+: 0-0
Track : LH: 0-7 RH: 0-1 Tight: 0-1 Gall: 0-2
Aids: Bl: 0-4 Vi: 0-6 Tstrap: 0-0
Best Rating: 58 8/01 Nott 6f15y soft

Regal Ali (IRE)

77 **30**

2-y-o ch g Ali-Royal (IRE)-Depeche (FR) (King's Lake (USA))
J S Wainwright Adrian Goodings

Placings:0060 (4536)
2001: 5^{0}S, 5^{0}GF, 7^{6}GF, 6^{0}GF

	Starts	1st	2nd	3rd	Win & Pl
Career Total (Turf)	4	0	0	0	0

Going (Turf): Sf: 0-1 GS: 0-0 Gd: 0-0 GF: 0-3 Fm: 0-0
Distance: 5f/6f: 0-3 7f-8f: 0-1 9f-13f: 0-0 14f+: 0-0
Track : LH: 0-0 RH: 0-1 Tight: 0-0 Gall: 0-0
Aids: Bl: 0-1 Vi: 0-0 Tstrap: 0-0
Best Rating: 30 5/01 Bevl 5f gd-fm

Regal Applause

71 **48**

2-y-o b f Royal Applause-Panchellita (USA) (Pancho Villa (USA))
G L Moore Bryan Pennick

Placings:000 (5665)
2001: 7^{0}GF, 6^{0}G, 6^{0}HY

	Starts	1st	2nd	3rd	Win & Pl
Career Total (Turf)	3	0	0	0	

Going (Turf): Sf: 0-1 GS: 0-0 Gd: 0-1 GF: 0-1 Fm: 0-0
Distance: 5f/6f: 0-2 7f-8f: 0-1 9f-13f: 0-0 14f+: 0-0
Track : LH: 0-0 RH: 0-0 Tight: 0-0 Gall: 0-0
Aids: Bl: 0-0 Vi: 0-0 Tstrap: 0-0
Best Rating: 48 10/01 NmkR 6f good

Regal Darcey (IRE)

96 **60**

3-y-o b f Darshaan-Royal Ballet (IRE) (Sadler's Wells (USA))
H Candy Mrs C M Poland

Placings:00 (2761)
2001: 10^{0}S, 12^{0}GF

	Starts	1st	2nd	3rd	Win & Pl
Career Total (Turf)	2	0	0	0	

Going (Turf): Sf: 0-1 GS: 0-0 Gd: 0-0 GF: 0-1 Fm: 0-0
Distance: 5f/6f: 0-0 7f-8f: 0-0 9f-13f: 0-2 14f+: 0-0
Track : LH: 0-1 RH: 0-1 Tight: 0-0 Gall: 0-1
Aids: Bl: 0-0 Vi: 0-0 Tstrap: 0-0
Best Rating: 60 7/01 Newb 1m4f5y gd-fm

Regal Gallery (IRE)

78 **37**

3-y-o b f Royal Academy (USA)-Polistatic (Free State)
C A Horgan Mrs B Sumner

Placings:0 (4380)
2001: 8^{0}GF

	Starts	1st	2nd	3rd	Win & Pl
Career Total (Turf)	1	0	0	0	

Going (Turf): Sf: 0-0 GS: 0-0 Gd: 0-0 GF: 0-1 Fm: 0-0
Distance: 5f/6f: 0-0 7f-8f: 0-1 9f-13f: 0-0 14f+: 0-0
Track : LH: 0-0 RH: 0-0 Tight: 0-0 Gall: 0-0
Aids: Bl: 0-0 Vi: 0-0 Tstrap: 0-0
Best Rating: 37 8/01 Sals 1m gd-fm

Regal Mistress

(82) (35)**23**

3-y-o b f Tragic Role (USA)-Regal Salute (Dara Monarch)
D Shaw D C G Cooper

Placings:50006-00 (0055)
2001: 7^{0}SD, 8^{0}SD

	Starts	1st	2nd	3rd	Win & Pl
Career Total (Turf)	2	0	0	0	0
Career Total (AW)	5	0	0	0	0

Going (Turf): Sf: 0-1 GS: 0-0 Gd: 0-1 GF: 0-0 Fm: 0-0
Distance: 5f/6f: 0-4 7f-8f: 0-3 9f-13f: 0-0 14f+: 0-0
Track : LH: 0-4 RH: 0-0 Tight: 0-1 Gall: 0-0
Aids: Bl: 0-2 Vi: 0-0 Tstrap: 0-0
Best Rating: 4 1/01 Ling 7f stand

Regal Song (IRE)

108(102) (50)**82**

5-y-o b g Anita's Prince-Song Beam (Song)
T J Etherington Mrs Y Brierley

Placings:050633/**00**431/**320**35**0**30102**0**-0110200**6**050042310 (5685)
2001: 5^{0}GS, 5^{1}S, 5^{1}S, 6^{0}S, 5^{2}GS, 5^{0}GS, 5^{0}GF, 5^{0}GF, 5^{6}SD, 5^{0}G, 5^{5}HY, 5^{0}G, 5^{0}HY, 5^{4}S, 5^{2}S, 5^{3}S, 5^{1}HY, 5^{0}S

	Starts	1st	2nd	3rd	Win & Pl
Career Total (Turf)	33	5	3	6	28550
Career Total (AW)	8	0	1	1	1192

82	10/01	Wind	5f10y	C(0-90)H	HVY	£7280
83	4/01	Muss	5f	D(0-85)H	SFT	£3932
81	3/01	Muss	5f	E(0-70)H	SFT	£3150
67	10/00	Newc	5f	E(0-70)H	HVY	£2999
67	6/99	Haml	5f4y	F	GD	£2220

Total win prize-money £19583

Going (Turf): **Sf: 4-17** GS: 0-5 Gd: 1-7 GF: 0-4 Fm: 0-0
Distance: **5f/6f: 5-37** 7f-8f: 0-4 9f-13f: 0-0 14f+: 0-0
Track : LH: 0-12 **RH: 1-3** Tight: 0-1 **Gall: 1-4**
Aids: **Bl: 4-27** Vi: 0-0 Tstrap: 0-0
Best Rating: 85 5/01 Thsk 5f gd-sft

Useful sprint handicapper, best over five furlongs on an easy surface. In great heart earlier this term, he found life harder on faster ground off marks in the eighties during the summer, but bounced back to winning form in heavy ground at Windsor in October.

Regal Splendour (CAN)

(93) (32)**34**

8-y-o ch g Vice Regent (CAN)-Seattle Princess (USA) (Seattle Slew (USA))
I W McInnes (J W Mullins 21/5) Ian McInnes

Placings:02020/**5**10600/0000000000/562660/00-00

(0458)
2001: 12^{0}SD, 8^{0}SD

	Starts	1st	2nd	3rd	Win & Pl
Career Total (Turf)	18	0	3	0	3100
Career Total (AW)	13	1	0	0	2427

62 2/97 Ling 1m E(0-70)H STD £2427
Total win prize-money £2427

Going (Turf): Sf: 0-2 GS: 0-0 Gd: 0-6 GF: 0-9 Fm: 0-1
Distance: 5f/6f: 0-0 **7f-8f: 1-15** 9f-13f: 0-15 14f+: 0-1
Track : **LH: 1-19** RH: 0-5 **Tight: 1-13** Gall: 0-2
Aids: Bl: 0-0 Vi: 0-0 Tstrap: 0-0
Best Rating: 62 2/97 Ling 1m SD

Regal Vision (IRE)

90 **46**
4-y-o b g Emperor Jones (USA)-Shining Eyes (USA) (Mr Prospector (USA))
C G Cox Axom

Placings:0005-000 **(2821)**
2001: 11^{0}GF, 16^{0}GF, 18^{0}GF

	Starts	1st	2nd	3rd	Win & Pl
Career Total (Turf)	7	0	0	0	0

Going (Turf): Sf: 0-1 GS: 0-0 Gd: 0-1 GF: 0-5 Fm: 0-0
Distance: 5f/6f: 0-0 7f-8f: 0-1 9f-13f: 0-4 14f+: 0-2
Track : LH: 0-5 RH: 0-1 Tight: 0-2 Gall: 0-0
Aids: Bl: 0-0 Vi: 0-0 Tstrap: 0-0
Best Rating: 39 7/01 Chep 2m2f gd-fm

Regal Wood (IRE)

20
2-y-o b f Ridgewood Ben-Regal Destiny (IRE) (Silver Kite (USA))
Paul Smith Double Jay Syndicate

Placings:0 **(5128)**
2001: 6^{0}HY

	Starts	1st	2nd	3rd	Win & Pl
Career Total (Turf)	1	0	0	0	

Going (Turf): Sf: 0-1 GS: 0-0 Gd: 0-0 GF: 0-0 Fm: 0-0
Distance: 5f/6f: 0-1 7f-8f: 0-0 9f-13f: 0-0 14f+: 0-0
Track : LH: 0-0 RH: 0-0 Tight: 0-0 Gall: 0-0
Aids: Bl: 0-0 Vi: 0-0 Tstrap: 0-0
Best Rating: 39 7/01 Chep 2m2f gd-fm

Regardez-Moi

88(90) (22)**20**
4-y-o b f Distinctly North (USA)-Tomard (Thatching)
A W Carroll Mrs Madeleine Gilles

Placings:00000366433/00630000000-00060000 **(3740)**
2001: 9^{0}SW, 7^{0}SW, 10^{0}SD, 12^{6}SW, 5^{0}GF, 5^{0}F, 7^{0}GF, 8^{0}S

	Starts	1st	2nd	3rd	Win & Pl
Career Total (Turf)	22	0	0	4	2969
Career Total (AW)	8	0	0	0	0

Going (Turf): Sf: 0-7 GS: 0-2 Gd: 0-6 GF: 0-5 Fm: 0-2
Distance: 5f/6f: 0-11 7f-8f: 0-12 9f-13f: 0-7 14f+: 0-0
Track : LH: 0-11 RH: 0-5 Tight: 0-6 Gall: 0-5
Aids: Bl: 0-2 Vi: 0-0 Tstrap: 0-0
Best Rating: 22 2/01 Ling 1m2f stand

Regatta Point (IRE)

110 **99**
3-y-o b c Goldmark (USA)-Flashing Raven (IRE) (Maelstrom Lake)
A P Jarvis Grant & Bowman Limited

Placings:02113-4253000 **(5338)**
2001: 10^{4}GS, 10^{2}GS, 12^{5}GF, 10^{3}GS, 12^{0}GF, 13^{0}G, 12^{0}GS

	Starts	1st	2nd	3rd	Win & Pl
Career Total (Turf)	12	2	2	2	19988

82 10/00 NmkR 1m D(0-95) SFT £5252
82 9/00 Sals 1m D SFT £4147
Total win prize-money £9399

Going (Turf): Sf: 2-3 GS: 0-4 Gd: 0-1 GF: 0-4 Fm: 0-0
Distance: 5f/6f: 0-0 **7f-8f: 2-3** 9f-13f: 0-8 14f+: 0-1
Track : LH: 0-3 RH: 0-4 Tight: 0-1 Gall: 0-6
Aids: Bl: 0-0 Vi: 0-0 Tstrap: 0-0
Best Rating: 99 7/01 NmkJ 1m2f gd-sft

Won twice over a mile last term and has put in a couple of decent efforts in middle-distance handicaps this season. Very much suited by soft ground, and may be most effective at ten furlongs now. Has joined Pat Hughes in Ireland.

Regency Red (IRE)

95(82) (36)**35**
3-y-o ch g Dolphin Street (FR)-Future Romance (Distant Relative)
S Mellor Mrs S C Haine

Placings:00-0060205 **(2639)**
2001: 7^{0}SD, 8^{0}SD, 8^{6}S, 7^{0}SD, 9^{2}F, 10^{0}GF, 12^{5}GF

	Starts	1st	2nd	3rd	Win & Pl
Career Total (Turf)	4	0	1	0	574
Career Total (AW)	5	0	0	0	

Going (Turf): Sf: 0-1 GS: 0-0 Gd: 0-0 GF: 0-2 Fm: 0-1
Distance: 5f/6f: 0-1 7f-8f: 0-4 9f-13f: 0-4 14f+: 0-0
Track : LH: 0-9 RH: 0-0 Tight: 0-4 Gall: 0-0
Aids: Bl: 0-0 Vi: 0-0 Tstrap: 0-0
Best Rating: 36 4/01 Sthl 7f stand

Regent Court (IRE)

105 **79**
3-y-o gr f Marju (IRE)-Silver Singing (USA) (Topsider (USA))
T D Easterby M P Burke

Placings:54530-1364 **(4828)**
2001: 8^{1}G, 10^{3}GF, 10^{6}GS, 10^{4}G

	Starts	1st	2nd	3rd	Win & Pl
Career Total (Turf)	9	1	0	2	7244

78 5/01 Ripn 1m D(0-75) GD £4231
Total win prize-money £4232

Going (Turf): Sf: 0-2 GS: 0-1 **Gd: 1-4** GF: 0-2 Fm: 0-0
Distance: 5f/6f: 0-0 **7f-8f: 1-6** 9f-13f: 0-3 14f+: 0-0
Track : LH: 0-7 **RH: 1-1 Tight: 1-3** Gall: 0-2
Aids: Bl: 0-0 Vi: 0-0 Tstrap: 0-0
Best Rating: 79 5/01 Hayd 1m2f120y gd-fm

Stayed a mile well when getting off the mark in a classified stakes at Ripon over a mile in May. Fair efforts over further since.

Reggie Buck (USA)

91 (55)**35**
7-y-o b/br g Alleged (USA)-Hello Memphis (USA) (Super Concorde (USA))
J Mackie Fools Who Dream

Placings:236/306000/000/60-00 **(3454)**
2001: 11^{0}GF, 14^{0}GF

	Starts	1st	2nd	3rd	Win & Pl
Career Total (Turf)	12	0	1	1	2024
Career Total (AW)	4	0	0	1	498

Going (Turf): Sf: 0-1 GS: 0-1 Gd: 0-5 GF: 0-5 Fm: 0-0
Distance: 5f/6f: 0-0 7f-8f: 0-2 9f-13f: 0-9 14f+: 0-5
Track : LH: 0-14 RH: 0-1 Tight: 0-5 Gall: 0-2
Aids: Bl: 0-1 Vi: 0-0 Tstrap: 0-0
Best Rating: 35 6/01 Hayd 1m3f200y gd-fm

Rehearsal Hall (USA)

96 **93**
2-y-o ch c Diesis-Performing Arts (The Minstrel (CAN))
J H M Gosden R E Sangster & A K Collins

Placings:1024 **(4548)**
2001: 5^{1}F, 6^{0}GF, 7^{2}S, 8^{4}GF

	Starts	1st	2nd	3rd	Win & Pl
Career Total (Turf)	4	1	1	0	6570

85 5/01 Leic 5f218y D FRM £3653
Total win prize-money £3653

Going (Turf): Sf: 0-1 GS: 0-0 Gd: 0-0 GF: 0-2 **Fm: 1-1**
Distance: **5f/6f: 1-2** 7f-8f: 0-2 9f-13f: 0-0 14f+: 0-0
Track : LH: 0-0 RH: 0-1 Tight: 0-0 Gall: 0-0
Aids: Bl: 0-0 Vi: 0-0 Tstrap: 0-0
Best Rating: 93 9/01 Sals 1m gd-fm

Looked good on his debut in a Leicester maiden, but got no run in the Coventry Stakes.

Reims (IRE)

90(79) (8)**50**
3-y-o b g Topanoora-Fairy Folk (IRE) (Fairy King (USA))
T D Easterby Elite Racing Club

Placings:000-0000 **(3289)**
2001: 11^{0}GF, 12^{0}GF, 12^{0}SD, 16^{0}GF

	Starts	1st	2nd	3rd	Win & Pl
Career Total (Turf)	6	0	0	0	
Career Total (AW)	1	0	0	0	

Going (Turf): Sf: 0-2 GS: 0-0 Gd: 0-0 GF: 0-4 Fm: 0-0
Distance: 5f/6f: 0-0 7f-8f: 0-3 9f-13f: 0-3 14f+: 0-1
Track : LH: 0-3 RH: 0-3 Tight: 0-4 Gall: 0-1
Aids: Bl: 0-1 Vi: 0-0 Tstrap: 0-0
Best Rating: 50 6/01 Ripn 1m4f60y gd-fm

Reine Indienne (IRE)

82 **69**
2-y-o b f College Chapel-Mystic Maid (IRE) (Mujtahid (USA))
H Akbary Mrs Elaine Holmes

Placings:300 **(5250)**
2001: 6^{3}GF, 6^{0}GF, 6^{0}S

	Starts	1st	2nd	3rd	Win & Pl
Career Total (Turf)	3	0	0	1	456

Going (Turf): Sf: 0-1 GS: 0-0 Gd: 0-0 GF: 0-2 Fm: 0-0
Distance: 5f/6f: 0-2 7f-8f: 0-1 9f-13f: 0-0 14f+: 0-0
Track : LH: 0-0 RH: 0-0 Tight: 0-0 Gall: 0-0
Aids: Bl: 0-0 Vi: 0-0 Tstrap: 0-0
Best Rating: 69 9/01 Ling 6f gd-fm

Relative Delight

95(76) (7)**38**
3-y-o b f Distant Relative-Pasja (IRE) (Posen (USA))
John A Harris (R Hollinshead 24/9) Ms S Queen

Placings:00-500006600006 **(5625)**
2001: 7^{5}SW, 11^{0}SD, 8^{0}S, 8^{0}G, 8^{0}SD, 8^{6}G, 11^{6}GF, 9^{0}SD, 9^{0}GS, 8^{0}S, 10^{0}S, 8^{6}GS

	Starts	1st	2nd	3rd	Win & Pl
Career Total (Turf)	10	0	0	0	167
Career Total (AW)	4	0	0	0	0

Going (Turf): Sf: 0-4 GS: 0-2 Gd: 0-2 GF: 0-2 Fm: 0-0
Distance: 5f/6f: 0-0 7f-8f: 0-3 9f-13f: 0-11 14f+: 0-0
Track : LH: 0-8 RH: 0-2 Tight: 0-5 Gall: 0-0
Aids: Bl: 0-0 Vi: 0-0 Tstrap: 0-0
Best Rating: 47 5/01 Wwck 1m22y good

Relish The Thought (IRE)

111 **112d**

3-y-o b f Sadler's Wells (USA)-Viz (USA) (Kris S (USA))
B W Hills Maktoum Al Maktoum

Placings:1-2305 (3657)
2001: 10^{2}F, 12^{3}GF, 12^{0}G, 12^{5}GF

	Starts	1st	2nd	3rd	Win & Pl
Career Total (Turf)	5	1	1	1	66020

102 10/00 Newb 7f A HVY £13520
Total win prize-money £13520

Going (Turf): Sf: 1-1 GS: 0-0 Gd: 0-1 GF: 0-2 Fm: 0-1
Distance: 5f/6f: 0-0 **7f-8f: 1-1** 9f-13f: 0-4 14f+: 0-0
Track : LH: 0-3 RH: 0-0 Tight: 0-1 Gall: 0-2
Aids: Bl: 0-0 Vi: 0-0 Tstrap: 0-0
Best Rating: 112 6/01 Epsm 1m4f10y gd-fm

A big rangy filly with bags of scope, she scored on her debut in a Newbury Listed event over seven furlongs at two. She ran well to finish runner-up in the Musidora on her return, and improved again to take third behind Imagine in the Oaks. Committed early, she was outrun close home, but battled on well to the line. Retired.

Rellim

91 **58**

2-y-o b f Rudimentary (USA)-Tycoon Girl (IRE) (Last Tycoon)
B J Meehan F C T Wilson

Placings:300 (5037)
2001: 5^{3}GF, 5^{0}GS, 5^{0}G

	Starts	1st	2nd	3rd	Win & Pl
Career Total (Turf)	3	0	0	1	566

Going (Turf): Sf: 0-0 GS: 0-1 Gd: 0-1 GF: 0-1 Fm: 0-0
Distance: 5f/6f: 0-3 7f-8f: 0-0 9f-13f: 0-0 14f+: 0-0
Track : LH: 0-1 RH: 0-1 Tight: 0-0 Gall: 0-2
Aids: Bl: 0-0 Vi: 0-0 Tstrap: 0-0
Best Rating: 58 10/01 Bath 5f161y good

Remains Of The Day

84 **44**

2-y-o ch g Prince Sabo-Pussy Foot (Red Sunset)
T D Barron Girls In Fashion

Placings:006 (5184)
2001: 5^{0}HY, 5^{0}G, 5^{6}GS

	Starts	1st	2nd	3rd	Win & Pl
Career Total (Turf)	3	0	0	0	0

Going (Turf): Sf: 0-1 GS: 0-1 Gd: 0-1 GF: 0-0 Fm: 0-0
Distance: 5f/6f: 0-3 7f-8f: 0-0 9f-13f: 0-0 14f+: 0-0
Track : LH: 0-0 RH: 0-0 Tight: 0-0 Gall: 0-0
Aids: Bl: 0-0 Vi: 0-0 Tstrap: 0-0
Best Rating: 44 10/01 Catt 5f gd-sft

Remarkable

94 **48d**

3-y-o ch f Wolfhound (USA)-Valika (Valiyar)
G Wragg The Romney Partnership

Placings:60-004600 (4290)
2001: 7^{0}G, 8^{0}GF, 10^{4}GF, 12^{6}GF, 12^{0}G, 16^{0}GF

	Starts	1st	2nd	3rd	Win & Pl
Career Total (Turf)	8	0	0	0	0

Going (Turf): Sf: 0-2 GS: 0-0 Gd: 0-2 GF: 0-4 Fm: 0-0
Distance: 5f/6f: 0-0 7f-8f: 0-3 9f-13f: 0-4 14f+: 0-1
Track : LH: 0-2 RH: 0-1 Tight: 0-2 Gall: 0-0
Aids: Bl: 0-2 Vi: 0-0 Tstrap: 0-0
Best Rating: 48 7/01 Muss 1m4f gd-fm

Remedy

96 **66**

2-y-o gr f Pivotal-Doctor Bid (USA) (Spectacular Bid (USA))
Sir Mark Prescott Cheveley Park Stud

Placings:004145 (5628)
2001: 8^{0}HY, 7^{0}G, 8^{4}GF, 8^{1}S, 6^{4}S, 8^{5}G

	Starts	1st	2nd	3rd	Win & Pl
Career Total (Turf)	6	1	0	0	4410

66 10/01 Pont 1m4y E(0-75) SFT £4143
Total win prize-money £4144

Going (Turf): Sf: 1-3 GS: 0-0 Gd: 0-2 GF: 0-1 Fm: 0-0
Distance: 5f/6f: 0-0 7f-8f: 0-3 **9f-13f: 1-3** 14f+: 0-0
Track : **LH: 1-4** RH: 0-1 Tight: 0-2 Gall: 0-0
Aids: **Bl: 1-3** Vi: 0-0 Tstrap: 0-0
Best Rating: 66 11/01 Rdcr 1m good

A half-sister to useful juveniles and the prolific stayer On Call. Had three quick runs in September 2001 to qualify for a handicap mark, and then scored at her first attempt in a handicap, but did not appear to have much left at the finish, she has since been a disappointing favourite on two occasions.

Remember Star

88(99) (34)**28**

8-y-o ch m Don't Forget Me-Star Girl Gay (Lord Gayle (USA))
A D Smith Duckhaven Stud

Placings:0000/00/432254-221550 (4728)
2001: 12^{2}SD, 12^{2}SD, 13^{1}SD, 16^{5}SD, 16^{5}SD, 16^{0}GF

	Starts	1st	2nd	3rd	Win & Pl
Career Total (Turf)	12	0	2	1	2019
Career Total (AW)	6	1	2	0	2739

34 2/01 Ling 1m5f G(0-60)H STD £1869
Total win prize-money £1869

Going (Turf): Sf: 0-2 GS: 0-1 Gd: 0-1 GF: 0-5 Fm: 0-2
Distance: 5f/6f: 0-0 7f-8f: 0-2 **9f-13f: 1-8** 14f+: 0-7
Track : **LH: 1-15** RH: 0-1 **Tight: 1-5** Gall: 0-1
Aids: Bl: 0-0 Vi: 0-0 Tstrap: 0-0
Best Rating: 34 2/01 Ling 1m5f stand

Reminiscent (IRE)

92 **77**

2-y-o b c Kahyasi-Eliza Orzeszkowa (IRE) (Polish Patriot (USA))
R F Johnson Houghton R F Johnson Houghton

Placings:0 (4056)
2001: 7^{0}GF

	Starts	1st	2nd	3rd	Win & Pl
Career Total (Turf)	1	0	0	0	

Going (Turf): Sf: 0-0 GS: 0-0 Gd: 0-0 GF: 0-1 Fm: 0-0
Distance: 5f/6f: 0-0 7f-8f: 0-1 9f-13f: 0-0 14f+: 0-0
Track : LH: 0-0 RH: 0-0 Tight: 0-0 Gall: 0-0
Aids: Bl: 0-0 Vi: 0-0 Tstrap: 0-0
Best Rating: 77 8/01 Newb 7f gd-fm

Ren's Magic

88 **59**

3-y-o gr g Petong-Bath (Runnett)
J R Jenkins D C Meek

Placings:0000 (4413)
2001: 6^{0}GF, 8^{0}GF, 6^{0}GF, 10^{0}S

	Starts	1st	2nd	3rd	Win & Pl
Career Total (Turf)	4	0	0	0	

Going (Turf): Sf: 0-1 GS: 0-0 Gd: 0-0 GF: 0-3 Fm: 0-0
Distance: 5f/6f: 0-0 7f-8f: 0-2 9f-13f: 0-2 14f+: 0-0
Track : LH: 0-1 RH: 0-2 Tight: 0-3 Gall: 0-0
Aids: Bl: 0-0 Vi: 0-0 Tstrap: 0-0
Best Rating: 59 6/01 Wind 1m67y gd-fm

Renaissance Lady (IRE)

107 **60**

5-y-o ch m Imp Society (USA)-Easter Morning (FR) (Nice Havrais (USA))
D W P Arbuthnot Alan A Wright

Placings:00/044616P200/0011125334-00101523200 (5661)
2001: 16^{0}G, 17^{0}GF, 16^{1}GF, 16^{0}GF, 16^{1}GF, 14^{5}GF, 14^{2}GS, 21^{3}GF, 16^{2}GF, 16^{0}G, 16^{0}G

	Starts	1st	2nd	3rd	Win & Pl
Career Total (Turf)	33	6	4	3	34086

55 6/01 Wwck 2m39y D(0-80)H G-F £3967
54 6/01 Folk 2m93y D(0-85)H G-F £3776
54 7/00 Wwck 1m6f135yE(0-70)H GD £3172
58 6/00 Wwck 1m7f181yD(0-80)H G-F £3883
49 6/00 Wwck 1m7f181yF(0-65)H G-F £3131
54 6/99 Brig 1m3f196yF G-F £2540
Total win prize-money £20473

Going (Turf): Sf: 0-2 GS: 0-2 Gd: 1-9 **GF: 5-18** Fm: 0-2
Distance: 5f/6f: 0-0 7f-8f: 0-3 9f-13f: 1-8 **14f+: 5-22**
Track : **LH: 5-16** RH: 1-11 **Tight: 1-9** Gall: 0-3
Aids: Bl: 0-0 Vi: 0-0 Tstrap: 0-0
Best Rating: 60 8/01 Wwck 2m39y gd-fm

A fair staying handicapper, she loves fast ground and performs well at Warwick. Suited by two miles and front-running tactics.

Renata's Prince (IRE)

101 **40**

8-y-o b g Prince Rupert (FR)-Maria Renata (Jaazeiro (USA))
M D I Usher P Sweeting

Placings:005/651400000/0523120/0020600 (4635)
2001: 9^{0}GF, 9^{0}GF, 7^{2}GF, 8^{0}GF, 9^{6}GF, 8^{0}G, 9^{0}GF

	Starts	1st	2nd	3rd	Win & Pl
Career Total (Turf)	24	2	3	1	9740
Career Total (AW)	2	0	0	0	

56 7/97 Sand 1m14y D(0-75)H G-S £3615
64 5/96 Tipp 1m1f (0-80)H GD £2740
Total win prize-money £6355

Going (Turf): Sf: 0-0 **GS: 1-3 Gd: 1-6** GF: 0-11 Fm: 0-0
Distance: 5f/6f: 0-0 7f-8f: 0-2 **9f-13f: 2-21** 14f+: 0-0
Track : LH: 1-12 RH: 1-9 Tight: 0-7 Gall: 0-1
Aids: Bl: 0-1 Vi: 0-0 Tstrap: 0-0
Best Rating: 40 7/01 Kemp 7f gd-fm

Rendita (IRE)

98(103) (56)**35**

5-y-o b m Waajib-Rend Rover (FR) (Monseigneur (USA))
D Haydn Jones Miss Gillian Byrne

Placings:34/061002000/0000534346166-420623242412400 (2057)
2001: 8^{4}SD, 9^{2}SW, 8^{0}SD, 9^{6}SD, 7^{2}SD, 9^{3}SD, 7^{2}SD, 8^{4}SD, 7^{2}SD, 8^{4}SD, 7^{1}SD, 7^{2}SD, 7^{4}GF, 7^{0}SD, 6^{0}GF

	Starts	1st	2nd	3rd	Win & Pl
Career Total (Turf)	11	0	1	0	998
Career Total (AW)	28	3	5	4	10877

52 5/01 Sthl 7f G STD £1925
39 11/00 Wolv 1m100y G STD £1939
59 4/99 Ling 7f E(0-70)H STD £2621
Total win prize-money £6485

Going (Turf): Sf: 0-1 GS: 0-2 Gd: 0-4 GF: 0-3 Fm: 0-1
Distance: 5f/6f: 0-2 **7f-8f: 2-24** 9f-13f: 1-13 14f+: 0-0
Track : **LH: 3-33** RH: 0-1 **Tight: 2-22** Gall: 0-1
Aids: Bl: 1-7 Vi: 1-14 Tstrap: 0-0
Best Rating: 56 5/01 Sthl 7f stand

Rendition

93 **91**

4-y-o b f Polish Precedent (USA)-Rensaler (USA) (Stop The Music (USA))

W J Haggas Pims Uk Limited

Placings:530/1130366-3 **(1269)**

2001: 7^{3}GS

	Starts	1st	2nd	3rd	Win & Pl
Career Total (Turf)	11	2	0	4	36659

91	5/00	York	6f214y	B(0-105)H	G-F	£22750
82	5/00	Brig	6f209y	D(0-75)	G-F	£3770

Total win prize-money £26520

Going (Turf): Sf: 0-0 GS: 0-4 Gd: 0-1 **GF: 2-6** Fm: 0-0
Distance: 5f/6f: 0-1 **7f-8f: 2-10** 9f-13f: 0-0 14f+: 0-0
Track : **LH: 2-2** RH: 0-2 Tight: 0-0 **Gall: 1-2**
Aids: Bl: 0-0 Vi: 0-0 Tstrap: 0-0
Best Rating: 78 5/01 Ling 7f140y gd-sft

She has ability, but ran just once this year.

Rene's Gold

65

2-y-o b f Pyramus (USA)-Balatina (Balidar)

G Brown Mrs K W Sneath

Placings:5 **(1196)**

2001: 5^{5}G

	Starts	1st	2nd	3rd	Win & Pl
Career Total (Turf)	1	0	0	0	0

Going (Turf): Sf: 0-0 GS: 0-0 Gd: 0-1 **GF: 0-0 Fm: 0-0**
Distance: 5f/6f: 0-1 7f-8f: 0-0 9f-13f: 0-0 14f+: 0-0
Track : LH: 0-0 RH: 0-0 Tight: 0-0 Gall: 0-0
Aids: Bl: 0-0 Vi: 0-0 Tstrap: 0-0
Best Rating: 78 5/01 Ling 7f140y gd sft

Renee

84 **46**

3-y-o b f Wolfhound (USA)-Montserrat (Aragon)

M L W Bell Mrs Anne Yearley

Placings:355060-00 **(5593)**

2001: 7^{0}G, 5^{0}GS

	Starts	1st	2nd	3rd	Win & Pl
Career Total (Turf)	8	0	0	1	494

Going (Turf): Sf: 0-1 GS: 0-1 Gd: 0-3 GF: 0-3 Fm: 0-0
Distance: 5f/6f: 0-7 7f-8f: 0-1 9f-13f: 0-0 14f+: 0-0
Track : LH: 0-2 RH: 0-0 Tight: 0-0 Gall: 0-1
Aids: Bl: 0-0 Vi: 0-0 Tstrap: 0-0
Best Rating: 28 11/01 Brig 5f213y gd-sft

Renzo (IRE)

99 **79**

8-y-o b g Alzao (USA)-Watership (USA) (Foolish Pleasure (USA))

John A Harris (J L Harris 16/6) Cleartherm Ltd

Placings:423231/0540213/5002501/04000000/1130120 30-010 **(3035)**

2001: 16^{0}GF, 14^{1}S, 15^{0}GF

	Starts	1st	2nd	3rd	Win & Pl
Career Total (Turf)	40	7	5	5	63572

76	6/01	Sand	1m6f	D(0-80)H	SFT	£4368
77	7/00	Sand	2m78y	C(0-90)H	GD	£14105
74	5/00	Thsk	2m	C(0-90)H	GD	£7046
62	4/00	Sand	2m78y	D(0-85)H	SFT	£7117
78	11/98	Donc	2m110y	C(0-95)H	SFT	£7700
86	9/97	Kemp	1m6f92y	D(0-85)H	G-F	£3631
83	11/96	Rdcr	1m3f	D(0-80)H	G-F	£3665

Total win prize-money £47633

Going (Turf): Sf: 3-6 GS: 0-5 Gd: 2-12 GF: 2-17 Fm: 0-0
Distance: 5f/6f: 0-0 7f-8f: 0-0 9f-13f: 1-7 **14f+: 6-33**
Track : LH: 3-11 **RH: 4-29 Tight: 2-10** Gall: 1-12
Aids: Bl: 0-2 Vi: 0-0 Tstrap: 0-0
Best Rating: 76 6/01 Sand 1m6f soft

Useful staying handicapper. Stays two miles. Acts on an easy surface. Has won three times at Sandown.

Repeat Performance (IRE)

88(88) (55)**62**

3-y-o b g Mujadil (USA)-Encore Une Fois (IRE) (Shirley Heights)

W G M Turner P A N Bailey

Placings:42444055005-6550 **(2639)**

2001: 12^{6}SD, 9^{5}F, 11^{5}F, 12^{0}GF

	Starts	1st	2nd	3rd	Win & Pl
Career Total (Turf)	12	0	1	0	1928
Career Total (AW)	3	0	0	0	0

Going (Turf): Sf: 0-0 GS: 0-3 Gd: 0-1 GF: 0-4 Fm: 0-4
Distance: 5f/6f: 0-5 7f-8f: 0-6 9f-13f: 0-4 14f+: 0-0
Track : LH: 0-11 RH: 0-0 Tight: 0-3 Gall: 0-1
Aids: Bl: 0-0 Vi: 0-0 Tstrap: 0-12
Best Rating: 62 5/01 Brig 1m1f209y firm

Repertory

110 **115**

8-y-o b g Anshan-Susie's Baby (Balidar)

M S Saunders M S Saunders

Placings:221/20000/14000030464/2022101423/405600 622543/0032350010010-3541043531 **(5584a)**

2001: 5^{3}GS, 5^{5}G, 5^{4}GF, 5^{1}Y, 5^{0}GF, 5^{4}G, 5^{3}G, 5^{5}HO, 5^{3}HY, 5^{1}HY

	Starts	1st	2nd	3rd	Win & Pl
Career Total (Turf)	64	8	10	8	281370

111	10/01	Lonc	5f		HVY	£21339
115	7/01	Curr	5f		YLD	£52000
105	10/00	Lonc	5f		HVY	£21134
104	8/00	Epsm	5f	B(0-105)H	GD	£19093
106	8/98	Epsm	5f	B(0-105)H	G-F	£17343
107	7/98	Curr	5f	(0-110)H	YLD	£30000
88	4/97	Newb	5f34y	B(0-100)	G-F	£8379
85	5/95	Sals	5f	D	GD	£3652

Total win prize-money £172943

Going (Turf): Sf: 2-11 GS: 0-8 **Gd: 2-24 GF: 2-16** Fm: 0-1
Distance: **5f/6f: 8-63** 7f-8f: 0-1 9f-13f: 0-0 14f+: 0-0
Track : LH: 0-5 RH: 0-1 Tight: 0-3 Gall: 0-2
Aids: Bl: 0-0 Vi: 0-0 Tstrap: 0-0
Best Rating: 115 7/01 Curr 5f yield

A real flying machine who looks as good as ever this term. He is a bit of a short runner who barely gets five furlongs. If enjoying an uncontested lead, he can be very difficult to overhaul. Goes particularly well at Epsom. Made all to win a Curragh Listed event in July 2001, but has found a few too good of late. Well suited by cut in the ground, he ran well in group races on the continent in the autumn and ended the season by winning a Longchamp Group Three.

Replacement Pet (IRE)

101(94) (46?)**36**

4-y-o b f Petardia-Richardstown Lass (IRE) (Muscatite)

H S Howe (M Kettle 25/10) Mrs Ruth Egan

Placings:40005645-4600006304 **(5664)**

2001: 8^{4}F, 8^{6}GF, 10^{0}F, 10^{0}GF, 8^{0}G, 8^{0}G, 10^{6}G, 10^{3}HY, 9^{0}S, 8^{4}HY

	Starts	1st	2nd	3rd	Win & Pl
Career Total (Turf)	13	0	0	1	740
Career Total (AW)	6	0	0	0	0

Going (Turf): Sf: 0-3 GS: 0-0 Gd: 0-3 GF: 0-5 Fm: 0-2
Distance: 5f/6f: 0-1 7f-8f: 0-4 9f-13f: 0-14 14f+: 0-0
Track : LH: 0-14 RH: 0-1 Tight: 0-9 Gall: 0-0
Aids: Bl: 0-1 Vi: 0-4 Tstrap: 0-3
Best Rating: 45 6/01 Nott 1m54y firm

Reprimand Rascal

50

3-y-o b g Reprimand-Summer Eve (Hotfoot)

A B Mulholland Miss K Watson

Placings:000 **(4084)**

2001: 8^{0}G, 8^{0}GS, 8^{0}GF

	Starts	1st	2nd	3rd	Win & Pl
Career Total (Turf)	3	0	0	0	

Going (Turf): Sf: 0-0 GS: 0-1 Gd: 0-1 GF: 0-1 Fm: 0-0
Distance: 5f/6f: 0-0 7f-8f: 0-1 9f-13f: 0-2 14f+: 0-0
Track : LH: 0-2 RH: 0-0 Tight: 0-0 Gall: 0-0
Aids: Bl: 0-0 Vi: 0-0 Tstrap: 0-0

Repton

103(99) (38)**43**

6-y-o ch g Rock City-Hasty Key (USA) (Key To The Mint (USA))

P T Dalton Mrs Julie Martin

Placings:060/01006333/013000600/00035-030110540 **(5531)**

2001: 12^{0}S, 18^{3}GF, 16^{0}GF, 16^{1}SD, 16^{1}GS, 16^{0}G, 15^{5}S, 17^{4}GS, 16^{0}HY

	Starts	1st	2nd	3rd	Win & Pl
Career Total (Turf)	25	2	0	4	8509
Career Total (AW)	9	2	0	2	4015

40	8/01	Thsk	2m	F(0-60)H	G-S	£3692
38	7/01	Sthl	2m	G(0-60)H	STD	£1883
52	3/99	Sthl	1m4f	F(0-70)H	STD	£1612
58	7/98	Rdcr	1m2f	E(0-70)H	G-S	£3162

Total win prize-money £10350

Going (Turf): Sf: 0-8 **GS: 2-6** Gd: 0-5 GF: 0-6 Fm: 0-0
Distance: 5f/6f: 0-2 7f-8f: 0-2 9f-13f: 2-19 14f+: 2-11
Track : **LH: 4-28** RH: 0-5 **Tight: 2-15** Gall: 0-1
Aids: Bl: 0-1 Vi: 0-0 Tstrap: 0-0
Best Rating: 43 9/01 Kemp 2m good

Has ability but has looked a bit of a funny customer. Looked suited to marathon trips when tackling two and a quarter miles for first time in summer of 2001, and won twice at two miles since. Acts on fast ground, but suited by an easy surface and Fibresand.

Repulse Bay (IRE)

103 **67**

3-y-o b c Barathea (IRE)-Bourbon Topsy (Ile De Bourbon (USA))

J S Goldie (M R Channon 3/7) John Breslin

Placings:4230-40305402000 **(5663)**

2001: 10^{4}S, 8^{0}G, 8^{3}GF, 9^{0}GF, 10^{5}GF, 8^{4}G, 8^{0}GF, 8^{2}GF, 10^{0}F, 10^{0}HY, 12^{0}G

	Starts	1st	2nd	3rd	Win & Pl
Career Total (Turf)	15	0	2	2	4681

Going (Turf): Sf: 0-4 GS: 0-0 Gd: 0-5 GF: 0-5 Fm: 0-1
Distance: 5f/6f: 0-0 7f-8f: 0-8 9f-13f: 0-7 14f+: 0-0
Track : LH: 0-4 RH: 0-6 Tight: 0-5 Gall: 0-2
Aids: Bl: 0-0 Vi: 0-1 Tstrap: 0-0
Best Rating: 87 4/01 Kemp 1m2f soft

Rescindo (IRE)

73 **25**

2-y-o b c Revoque (IRE)-Mystic Dispute (IRE) (Magical

Strike (USA))
N P Littmoden Paul Dixon, Joy And Valentine Feerick

Placings:000 **(5689)**
2001: 8^{0}G, 7^{0}HY, 6^{0}S

	Starts	1st	2nd	3rd	Win & Pl
Career Total (Turf)	3	0	0	0	

Going (Turf): Sf: 0-2 GS: 0-0 Gd: 0-1 GF: 0-0 Fm: 0-0
Distance: 5f/6f: 0-1 7f-8f: 0-1 9f-13f: 0-1 14f+: 0-0
Track : LH: 0-0 RH: 0-1 Tight: 0-1 Gall: 0-0
Aids: Bl: 0-0 Vi: 0-0 Tstrap: 0-0
Best Rating: 25 11/01 Donc 6f soft

Researched (IRE)

76 **48**
2-y-o b c Danehill (USA)-Sought Out (IRE) (Rainbow Quest (USA))
Sir Michael Stoute Lord Weinstock

Placings:0 **(5260)**
2001: 7^{0}GS

	Starts	1st	2nd	3rd	Win & Pl
Career Total (Turf)	1	0	0	0	

Going (Turf): Sf: 0-0 GS: 0-1 Gd: 0-0 GF: 0-0 Fm: 0-0
Distance: 5f/6f: 0-0 7f-8f: 0-1 9f-13f: 0-0 14f+: 0-0
Track : LH: 0-0 RH: 0-0 Tight: 0-0 Gall: 0-0
Aids: Bl: 0-0 Vi: 0-0 Tstrap: 0-0
Best Rating: 48 10/01 Asct 7f gd-sft

Researcher

93 **63**
2-y-o ch f Cosmonaut-Rest (Dance In Time (CAN))
R M Beckett R N Richmond-Watson

Placings:006 **(5527)**
2001: 8^{0}GS, 8^{0}HY, 8^{6}HY

	Starts	1st	2nd	3rd	Win & Pl
Career Total (Turf)	3	0	0	0	0

Going (Turf): Sf: 0-2 GS: 0-1 Gd: 0-0 GF: 0-0 Fm: 0-0
Distance: 5f/6f: 0-0 7f-8f: 0-1 9f-13f: 0-2 14f+: 0-0
Track : LH: 0-2 RH: 0-0 Tight: 0-0 Gall: 0-0
Aids: Bl: 0-0 Vi: 0-0 Tstrap: 0-0
Best Rating: 63 10/01 Nott 1m54y heavy

Resplendent Cee (IRE)

103 **98**
2-y-o ch c Polar Falcon (USA)-Western Friend (USA) (Gone West (USA))
P W Harris Resplendent Racing Limited

Placings:130110 **(5150)**
2001: 6^{1}G, 6^{3}GF, 6^{0}GF, 6^{1}G, 6^{1}G, 6^{0}G

	Starts	1st	2nd	3rd	Win & Pl
Career Total (Turf)	6	3	0	1	26837

98	8/01	Ripn	6f	A	GD	£13340
89	8/01	Wind	6f	C	GD	£5684
88	6/01	Wind	6f	E	GD	£3412

Total win prize-money £22437

Going (Turf): Sf: 0-0 GS: 0-0 **Gd: 3-4** GF: 0-2 Fm: 0-0
Distance: **5f/6f: 3-6** 7f-8f: 0-0 9f-13f: 0-0 14f+: 0-0
Track : LH: 0-1 RH: 0-0 Tight: 0-1 Gall: 0-0
Aids: Bl: 0-0 Vi: 0-0 Tstrap: 0-0
Best Rating: 98 8/01 Ripn 6f good

A winner three times this season, his latest win coming in Listed company at Ripon. He has plenty of speed, but he should stay further than six furlongs in time.

Resplendent Star (IRE)

102(111) (92)**78**

4-y-o b g Northern Baby (CAN)-Whitethroat (Artaius (USA))
P W Harris Resplendent Racing Limited

Placings:03210010/40035016-2212040 **(3148)**
2001: 10^{2}SW, 10^{2}SW, 10^{1}SW, 10^{2}SD, 10^{0}G, 9^{4}GF, 10^{0}G

	Starts	1st	2nd	3rd	Win & Pl
Career Total (Turf)	16	1	1	2	5756
Career Total (AW)	7	3	3	0	34818

88	2/01	Ling	1m2f	B	SLW	£12035
85	11/00	Ling	1m2f	G(0-85)H	STD	£1918
85	9/99	Sthl	1m	E	STD	£2927
85	8/99	Newc	7f	E H	FRM	£2885

Total win prize-money £19765

Going (Turf): Sf: 0-2 GS: 0-2 Gd: 0-4 GF: 0-6 **Fm: 1-2**
Distance: 5f/6f: 0-1 7f-8f: 2-9 9f-13f: 2-13 14f+: 0-0
Track : **LH: 3-14** RH: 0-4 **Tight: 2-9** Gall: 0-5
Aids: Bl: 0-3 **Vi: 3-13** Tstrap: 0-0
Best Rating: 92 3/01 Ling 1m2f stand

A formerly useful fast ground juvenile on turf, he was becoming disappointing but a switch to the All-Weather brought about a resurgance in form. Best at Lingfield over ten furlongs.

Retirement

89(93) (77)**70**
2-y-o b c Zilzal (USA)-Adeptation (USA) (Exceller (USA))
S P C Woods Ben Allen

Placings:015 **(5047)**
2001: 7^{0}G, 8^{1}SW, 8^{5}SD

	Starts	1st	2nd	3rd	Win & Pl
Career Total (Turf)	1	0	0	0	
Career Total (AW)	2	1	0	0	2282

77	9/01	Wolv	1m100y	F	SLW	£2282

Total win prize-money £2282

Going (Turf): Sf: 0-0 GS: 0-0 Gd: 0-1 GF: 0-0 Fm: 0-0
Distance: 5f/6f: 0-0 7f-8f: 0-2 **9f-13f: 1-1** 14f+: 0-0
Track : **LH: 1-2** RH: 0-0 **Tight: 1-1** Gall: 0-0
Aids: Bl: 0-0 Vi: 0-0 Tstrap: 0-0
Best Rating: 77 9/01 Wolv 1m100y slow

Showed signs of inexperience on his Newmarket debut over seven in decent company. Won next time out on the All-Weather at Wolverhampton over a mile again running green.

Retski

97(80) (24)**41**
4-y-o b g Gabitat-Born To Be (Never So Bold)
S Dow J A Redmond

Placings:00-000363345 **(4016)**
2001: 5^{0}SW, 5^{0}GS, 5^{0}GF, 5^{3}F, 5^{6}G, 6^{3}GF, 5^{3}GF, 5^{4}G, 7^{5}G

	Starts	1st	2nd	3rd	Win & Pl
Career Total (Turf)	10	0	0	3	1729
Career Total (AW)	1	0	0	0	

Going (Turf): Sf: 0-0 GS: 0-1 Gd: 0-4 GF: 0-4 Fm: 0-1
Distance: 5f/6f: 0-8 7f-8f: 0-3 9f-13f: 0-0 14f+: 0-0
Track : LH: 0-6 RH: 0-1 Tight: 0-1 Gall: 0-1
Aids: Bl: 0-0 Vi: 0-0 Tstrap: 0-0
Best Rating: 41 7/01 Yarm 6f3y gd-fm

Return (USA)

105 **90+**
4-y-o b f Sadler's Wells (USA)-Slightly Dangerous (USA) (Roberto (USA))
H R A Cecil K Abdulla

Placings:1-040 **(2261)**
2001: 10^{0}G, 12^{4}GF, 12^{0}G

	Starts	1st	2nd	3rd	Win & Pl
Career Total (Turf)	4	1	0	0	5030

84	9/00	Sand	1m2f7y	D	SFT	£4179

Total win prize-money £4180

Going (Turf): Sf: 1-1 GS: 0-0 Gd: 0-2 GF: 0-1 Fm: 0-0
Distance: 5f/6f: 0-0 7f-8f: 0-0 **9f-13f: 1-4** 14f+: 0-0
Track : LH: 0-0 **RH: 1-3** Tight: 0-1 Gall: 0-1
Aids: Bl: 0-0 Vi: 0-0 Tstrap: 0-0
Best Rating: 90 5/01 Gdwd 1m4f gd-fm

Very well bred filly. Sister to Dushyantor, closely related to Yashmak and Jibe, and half-sister to Commander In Chief and Warning. Favourite when winning Sandown maiden on only start at three, but did not make much impression this season.

Return Of Amin

93(92) (47)**48d**
7-y-o ch h Salse (USA)-Ghassanah (Pas De Seul)
D W Chapman Miss N F Thesiger

Placings:6030311/424651262002/606162200265/0555 00/000024000000-0006000600 **(4108)**
2001: 7^{0}G, 7^{0}F, 8^{0}GF, 7^{6}SD, 8^{0}SD, 8^{0}SD, 7^{0}SD, 9^{6}G, 8^{0}F, 8^{0}S

	Starts	1st	2nd	3rd	Win & Pl
Career Total (Turf)	49	3	8	1	79189
Career Total (AW)	10	1	0	1	3543

89	6/98	Pont	6f	C(0-90)H	HVY	£7830
78	6/97	York	6f	B(0-105)H	G-S	£35109
82	11/96	Sthl	7f	E(0-75)	STD	£2968
68	11/96	Folk	6f189y	E(0-75)	SFT	£3206

Total win prize-money £49114

Going (Turf): Sf: 2-13 GS: 1-8 Gd: 0-19 GF: 0-6 Fm: 0-2
Distance: 5f/6f: 2-28 7f-8f: 2-29 9f-13f: 0-2 14f+: 0-0
Track : **LH: 2-17** RH: 1-5 **Tight: 1-8** Gall: 0-2
Aids: Bl: 0-15 Vi: 0-1 Tstrap: 0-0
Best Rating: 48 5/01 Thsk 7f good

Revealing

94 **97+**
2-y-o ch f Halling (USA)-Rive (USA) (Riverman (USA))
H R A Cecil K Abdulla

Placings:1 **(4871)**
2001: 8^{1}G

	Starts	1st	2nd	3rd	Win & Pl
Career Total (Turf)	1	1	0	0	5577

97	9/01	NmkR	1m	D	GD	£5577

Total win prize-money £5577

Going (Turf): Sf: 0-0 GS: 0-0 **Gd: 1-1** GF: 0-0 Fm: 0-0
Distance: 5f/6f: 0-0 **7f-8f: 1-1** 9f-13f: 0-0 14f+: 0-0
Track : LH: 0-0 RH: 0-0 Tight: 0-0 Gall: 0-0
Aids: Bl: 0-0 Vi: 0-0 Tstrap: 0-0
Best Rating: 97 9/01 NmkR 1m good

A half-sister to Brevity, she was an impressive winner of a Newmarket maiden and looks a nice prospect.

Reveillez

85 **66**
2-y-o gr c First Trump-Amalancher (USA) (Alleged (USA))
J R Fanshawe Miss A Church

Placings:6 **(3867)**
2001: 7^{6}G

	Starts	1st	2nd	3rd	Win & Pl
Career Total (Turf)	1	0	0	0	0

Going (Turf): Sf: 0-0 GS: 0-0 Gd: 0-1 GF: 0-0 Fm: 0-0
Distance: 5f/6f: 0-0 7f-8f: 0-1 9f-13f: 0-0 14f+: 0-0
Track : LH: 0-0 RH: 0-0 Tight: 0-0 Gall: 0-0
Aids: Bl: 0-0 Vi: 0-0 Tstrap: 0-0
Best Rating: 66 8/01 Folk 7f good

Revelino (IRE)

100 **83**

2-y-o b c Revoque (IRE)-Forelino (USA) (Trempolino (USA))

E A L Dunlop Stars And Stripes Iii

Placings:52213 **(5589)**

2001: 7^{5}G, 8^{2}G, 7^{2}S, 7^{1}S, 7^{3}GS

	Starts	1st	2nd	3rd	Win & Pl
Career Total (Turf)	5	1	2	1	5518

74 10/01 Catt 7f E SFT £3108

Total win prize-money £3108

Going (Turf): Sf: 1-2 GS: 0-1 Gd: 0-2 GF: 0-0 Fm: 0-0
Distance: 5f/6f: 0-0 **7f-8f: 1-4** 9f-13f: 0-1 14f+: 0-0
Track : **LH: 1-3** RH: 0-0 **Tight: 1-1** Gall: 0-0
Aids: Bl: 0-0 Vi: 0-0 Tstrap: 0-0
Best Rating: 83 11/01 Brig 7f214y gd-sft

Revenge

73 **58**

5-y-o b g Saddlers' Hall (IRE)-Classic Heights (Shirley Heights)

C G Cox The Patient Dozen

Placings:04/0020-0 **(0879)**

2001: 21^{0}S

	Starts	1st	2nd	3rd	Win & Pl
Career Total (Turf)	7	0	1	0	1134

Going (Turf): Sf: 0-4 GS: 0-1 Gd: 0-1 GF: 0-1 Fm: 0-0
Distance: 5f/6f: 0-0 7f-8f: 0-0 9f-13f: 0-2 14f+: 0-5
Track : LH: 0-6 RH: 0-1 Tight: 0-2 Gall: 0-1
Aids: Bl: 0-4 Vi: 0-0 Tstrap: 0-0
Best Rating: 83 11/01 Brig 7f214y gd-sft

Reverie

101 **73+**

3-y-o b c Bishop Of Cashel-Space Travel (Dancing Dissident (USA))

R Hannon J A Lazzari

Placings:000-1610 **(5011)**

2001: 6^{1}GF, 6^{6}GF, 7^{1}G, 7^{0}HY

	Starts	1st	2nd	3rd	Win & Pl
Career Total (Turf)	7	2	0	0	9053

73 7/01 Epsm 7f E(0-70)H GD £5300
72 6/01 Rdcr 6f E(0-70)H G-F £3752

Total win prize-money £9053

Going (Turf): Sf: 0-2 GS: 0-0 **Gd: 1-2 GF: 1-2** Fm: 0-0
Distance: 5f/6f: 1-2 7f-8f: 1-4 9f-13f: 0-0 14f+: 0-0
Track : **LH: 1-2** RH: 0-1 **Tight: 1-1** Gall: 0-0
Aids: Bl: 0-0 Vi: 0-0 Tstrap: 0-0
Best Rating: 73 7/01 Epsm 7f good

Looked to have done well over the winter when taking a Redcar handicap on his return. May have found the race coming too soon when trying to follow up three days later, but won nicely when stepped up to seven at Epsom.

Reviewer (IRE)

104 **73**

3-y-o b g Sadler's Wells (USA)-Clandestina (USA) (Secretariat (USA))

M Meade Ladyswood Stud

Placings:60452-041660 **(5663)**

2001: 12^{0}GF, 11^{4}GF, 11^{1}GF, 12^{6}GF, 11^{6}GS, 12^{0}G

	Starts	1st	2nd	3rd	Win & Pl
Career Total (Turf)	11	1	1	0	4214

69 7/01 Bath 1m3f144yF(0-75)H G-F £3115

Total win prize-money £3115

Going (Turf): Sf: 0-3 GS: 0-1 Gd: 0-2 **GF: 1-5** Fm: 0-0
Distance: 5f/6f: 0-0 7f-8f: 0-1 **9f-13f: 1-10** 14f+: 0-0
Track : **LH: 1-6** RH: 0-1 **Tight: 1-4** Gall: 0-1
Aids: Bl: 0-3 Vi: 0-0 Tstrap: 0-0
Best Rating: 73 8/01 Gdwd 1m4f gd-fm

Landed an ordinary handicap at Bath in July.

Rex Is Okay

100(101) (51)**68**

5-y-o ch g Mazilier (USA)-Cocked Hat Girl (Ballacashtal (CAN))

S R Bowring Mark Belfitt, Debra Salt & S R Bowring

Placings:03553311/0000323330/**066640026000525306-03340051160050520** **(5449)**

2001: 6^{0}SD, 7^{3}SD, 8^{3}SD, 8^{4}SD, 7^{0}SD, 6^{0}HY, 8^{5}SW, 6^{1}G, 6^{1}SD, 7^{6}F, 7^{0}F, 6^{0}G, 6^{5}SD, 6^{0}SD, 7^{5}GF, 6^{2}G, 7^{2}S, 6^{0}HY

	Starts	1st	2nd	3rd	Win & Pl
Career Total (Turf)	36	3	5	7	24959
Career Total (AW)	18	1	0	3	3476

50 5/01 Sthl 6f F(0-60)H STD £2359
65 5/01 Nott 6f15y G(0-70)H GD £2121
77 11/98 Donc 7f D H SFT £4272
65 10/98 Leic 7f9y D(0-85)H SFT £7765

Total win prize-money £16518

Going (Turf): Sf: 2-18 GS: 0-3 **Gd: 1-10** GF: 0-3 Fm: 0-2
Distance: 5f/6f: 1-19 **7f-8f: 3-29** 9f-13f: 0-6 14f+: 0-0
Track : **LH: 1-27** RH: 0-3 Tight: 0-7 Gall: 0-2
Aids: **Bl: 2-29** Vi: 0-0 Tstrap: 0-0
Best Rating: 67 10/01 Catt 7f soft

An affable enough performer who notched up two wins in soft ground over seven furlongs towards the end of 1998, but then embarked on a long losing run until again winning back-to-back races at Nottingham and on the Southwell Fibresand in May. Suited by six and seven furlongs and soft ground or Fibresand.

Rhaetia (IRE)

92 **71**

2-y-o b f Priolo (USA)-Rainbow Mountain (Rainbow Quest (USA))

E A L Dunlop Hesmonds Stud

Placings:0300 **(5115)**

2001: 7^{0}GF, 6^{3}F, 8^{0}GF, 9^{0}HY

	Starts	1st	2nd	3rd	Win & Pl
Career Total (Turf)	4	0	0	1	409

Going (Turf): Sf: 0-1 GS: 0-0 Gd: 0-0 GF: 0-2 Fm: 0-1
Distance: 5f/6f: 0-0 7f-8f: 0-2 9f-13f: 0-2 14f+: 0-0
Track : LH: 0-2 RH: 0-0 Tight: 0-0 Gall: 0-0
Aids: Bl: 0-0 Vi: 0-0 Tstrap: 0-0
Best Rating: 71 8/01 Brig 6f209y firm

Rheinbold

(79) (7)**60**

7-y-o br g Never So Bold-Rheinbloom (Rheingold)

Ms A E Embiricos Chasers Iii

Placings:0/210200/0560633065/2035/**00** **(0345)**

2001: 12^{0}SW, 16^{0}SD

	Starts	1st	2nd	3rd	Win & Pl
Career Total (Turf)	19	1	2	3	7824
Career Total (AW)	4	0	1	0	527

64 5/97 Muss 1m4f F G-S £2617

Total win prize-money £2618

Going (Turf): Sf: 0-1 **GS: 1-4** Gd: 0-4 GF: 0-10 Fm: 0-0
Distance: 5f/6f: 0-0 7f-8f: 0-3 **9f-13f: 1-18** 14f+: 0-2
Track : LH: 0-13 **RH: 1-7 Tight: 1-15** Gall: 0-2
Aids: Bl: 0-0 Vi: 0-0 Tstrap: 0-0
Best Rating: 7 2/01 Wolv 2m46y stand

Rheinpark

101 **78**

2-y-o ch c Cadeaux Genereux-Marina Park (Local Suitor (USA))

M Johnston Around The World Partnership

Placings:54224 **(5029)**

2001: 6^{5}GF, 5^{4}GF, 5^{2}HY, 5^{2}GF, 5^{4}GF

	Starts	1st	2nd	3rd	Win & Pl
Career Total (Turf)	5	0	2	0	3353

Going (Turf): Sf: 0-1 GS: 0-0 Gd: 0-0 GF: 0-4 Fm: 0-0
Distance: 5f/6f: 0-5 7f-8f: 0-0 9f-13f: 0-0 14f+: 0-0
Track : LH: 0-2 RH: 0-0 Tight: 0-1 Gall: 0-0
Aids: Bl: 0-0 Vi: 0-0 Tstrap: 0-0
Best Rating: 78 9/01 Catt 5f212y gd-fm

Has shown enough ability in all starts to date to suggest he will win a race.

Rhetoric (IRE)

86 **49**

2-y-o b c Desert King (IRE)-Squaw Talk (USA) (Gulch (USA))

J H M Gosden Sheikh Mohammed

Placings:00 **(5627)**

2001: 7^{0}HY, 7^{0}G

	Starts	1st	2nd	3rd	Win & Pl
Career Total (Turf)	2	0	0	0	

Going (Turf): Sf: 0-1 GS: 0-0 Gd: 0-1 GF: 0-0 Fm: 0-0
Distance: 5f/6f: 0-0 7f-8f: 0-2 9f-13f: 0-0 14f+: 0-0
Track : LH: 0-0 RH: 0-0 Tight: 0-0 Gall: 0-0
Aids: Bl: 0-0 Vi: 0-0 Tstrap: 0-0
Best Rating: 49 11/01 Rdcr 7f good

Rhodamine (IRE)

100(97) (54)**60**

4-y-o b g Mukaddamah (USA)-Persian Empress (IRE) (Persian Bold)

J L Eyre M Gleason

Placings:00140354/**000426143404400-364001344** **(2566)**

2001: 11^{3}SD, 11^{6}SW, 12^{4}SD, 16^{0}SD, 10^{0}S, 9^{1}G, 10^{3}F, 10^{4}GF, 10^{4}GF

	Starts	1st	2nd	3rd	Win & Pl
Career Total (Turf)	26	3	1	3	22584
Career Total (AW)	6	0	0	1	208

57 5/01 Nott 1m1f213yF(0-60)H GD £2891
66 5/00 Rdcr 1m3f D(0-80)H G-S £4914
73 7/99 Newc 6f E G-F £3647

Total win prize-money £11453

Going (Turf): Sf: 0-5 **GS: 1-5 Gd: 1-5 GF: 1-9** Fm: 0-2
Distance: 5f/6f: 1-3 7f-8f: 0-4 **9f-13f: 2-24** 14f+: 0-1
Track : **LH: 2-23** RH: 0-5 **Tight: 1-9** Gall: 0-5
Aids: Bl: 0-0 Vi: 0-0 Tstrap: 0-0
Best Rating: 59 6/01 Pont 1m2f6y firm

Rhythm Of Life

90 **74+**

2-y-o ch f Dr Devious (IRE)-Nashville Blues (IRE) (Try My Best (USA))

J W Hills Freddy Bienstock And Martin Boase

Placings:6 **(2819)**

2001: 6^{6}GF

	Starts	1st	2nd	3rd	Win & Pl
Career Total (Turf)	1	0	0	0	0

Going (Turf): Sf: 0-0 GS: 0-0 Gd: 0-0 GF: 0-1 Fm: 0-0
Distance: 5f/6f: 0-0 7f-8f: 0-1 9f-13f: 0-0 14f+: 0-0
Track : LH: 0-0 RH: 0-0 Tight: 0-0 Gall: 0-0
Aids: Bl: 0-0 Vi: 0-0 Tstrap: 0-0
Best Rating: 74 7/01 Chep 6f16y gd-fm

Rhythmicall (IRE)

109 **90**

4-y-o b g In The Wings-Rhoman Ruby (IRE) (Rhoman Rule (USA))

Mrs A J Perrett Sunday School

Placings:016-020 **(4225)**

2001: 10^{0}G, 14^{2}G, 14^{0}GF

	Starts	1st	2nd	3rd	Win & Pl
Career Total (Turf)	6	1	1	0	5961

90	6/00	Bath	1m2f46y	D	G-S	£3750

Total win prize-money £3751

Going (Turf): Sf: 0-0 **GS: 1-1** Gd: 0-3 GF: 0-2 Fm: 0-0
Distance: 5f/6f: 0-0 7f-8f: 0-1 **9f-13f: 1-3** 14f+: 0-2
Track : **LH: 1-2** RH: 0-2 **Tight: 1-1** Gall: 0-1
Aids: Bl: 0-0 Vi: 0-0 Tstrap: 0-0
Best Rating: 89 8/01 Sand 1m6f good

Lightly raced, but showed ability this season without winning.

Ribbon Of Light

85 **53**

3-y-o b g Spectrum (IRE)-Brush Away (Ahonoora)

B W Hills J Hanson

Placings:0-0000 **(2114)**

2001: 8^{0}S, 8^{0}S, 10^{0}GF, 11^{0}F

	Starts	1st	2nd	3rd	Win & Pl
Career Total (Turf)	5	0	0	0	

Going (Turf): Sf: 0-2 GS: 0-0 Gd: 0-1 GF: 0-1 Fm: 0-1
Distance: 5f/6f: 0-0 7f-8f: 0-2 9f-13f: 0-3 14f+: 0-0
Track : LH: 0-3 RH: 0-0 Tight: 0-2 Gall: 0-1
Aids: Bl: 0-0 Vi: 0-0 Tstrap: 0-2
Best Rating: 53 5/01 Newb 1m soft

Ribeauville

91 **71**

2-y-o ch f Vettori (IRE)-Juvenilia (IRE) (Masterclass (USA))

J A R Toller G B Partnership

Placings:02 **(2573)**

2001: 5^{0}G, 6^{2}GF

	Starts	1st	2nd	3rd	Win & Pl
Career Total (Turf)	2	0	1	0	1464

Going (Turf): Sf: 0-0 GS: 0-0 Gd: 0-1 GF: 0-1 Fm: 0-0
Distance: 5f/6f: 0-2 7f-8f: 0-0 9f-13f: 0-0 14f+: 0-0
Track : LH: 0-0 RH: 0-0 Tight: 0-0 Gall: 0-0
Aids: Bl: 0-0 Vi: 0-0 Tstrap: 0-0
Best Rating: 71 6/01 NmkJ 6f gd-fm

Riberac

114 **109**

5-y-o b m Efisio-Ciboure (Norwick (USA))

M Johnston Mr & Mrs G Middlebrook

Placings:01356/0360/00200011011010-0461333110341 **(5605)**

2001: 10^{0}S, 8^{4}S, 8^{6}GS, 8^{1}GF, 8^{3}G, 10^{3}GF, 10^{3}GF, 8^{1}G, 8^{1}G, 8^{0}G, 8^{3}G, 10^{4}GS, 8^{1}GS, 8^{0}HY

	Starts	1st	2nd	3rd	Win & Pl
Career Total (Turf)	36	10	1	6	183972

98	11/01	NmkR	1m	A	G-S	£13862
109	8/01	Asct	1m	A	GD	£20150
105	8/01	Gdwd	1m	B H	GD	£65000
96	5/01	Bevl	1m100y	C(0-95)H	G-F	£6264
97	9/00	Asct	1m	A(0-105)H	G-S	£18560
95	9/00	Epsm	1m2f18y	D(0-80)	GD	£4446
90	8/00	Epsm	1m114y	C(0-90)H	GD	£8463
82	8/00	Ayr	1m	C(0-90)H	GD	£6857
84	8/00	Sand	1m14y	E(0-80)H	GD	£2785
74	7/98	Wind	5f10y	D	G-F	£3241

Total win prize-money £149629

Going (Turf): Sf: 0-4 GS: 2-8 **Gd: 6-14** GF: 2-9 Fm: 0-1
Distance: 5f/6f: 1-15 **7f-8f: 5-10** 9f-13f: 4-11 14f+: 0-0
Track : LH: 3-6 **RH: 5-12** Tight: 2-5 Gall: 2-5
Aids: Bl: 0-0 Vi: 0-0 Tstrap: 0-0
Best Rating: 109 8/01 Asct 1m good

She took off in the second half of 2000, winning five times at between a mile and ten furlongs, including an Ascot Listed handicap, and returned to winning form at Beverley on her fourth start of 2001. Ran particularly well in the summer, gaining an all-the-way win in the William Hill Mile at Goodwood and bolting up in a Listed race at Ascot, before finishing placed in a Newmarket Group Two in the autumn. Ended the season with victory in a Newmarket Listed event. Best over a mile, but has won over further. Acts on a sound surface, but also handles cut. Sometimes plays up at the start, and wears a Monty Roberts-style blanket these days.

Riccarton

86

8-y-o b g Nomination-Legendary Dancer (Shareef Dancer (USA))

D C Turner (J M Bradley 24/8) Mrs M E Turner

Placings:000533236/33456124/101431400/4645000/4-00 **(3301)**

2001: 8^{0}GF, 11^{0}GF

	Starts	1st	2nd	3rd	Win & Pl
Career Total (Turf)	36	4	2	6	18986

61	7/98	Donc	1m2f60y	D(0-85)H	G-F	£3525
57	6/98	Haml	1m1f36y	D(0-75)H	GD	£3517
55	4/98	Rdcr	1m3f	E(0-70)H	SFT	£3204
52	8/97	Bevl	1m1f207yF(0-60)H		GD	£2434

Total win prize-money £12682

Going (Turf): Sf: 1-3 GS: 0-5 **Gd: 2-11** GF: 1-14 Fm: 0-3
Distance: 5f/6f: 0-0 7f-8f: 0-7 **9f-13f: 4-29** 14f+: 0-0
Track : LH: 2-19 RH: 2-13 **Tight: 2-17** Gall: 1-2
Aids: Bl: 0-2 Vi: 0-0 Tstrap: 0-0
Best Rating: 35 7/01 Wwck 1m22y gd-fm

Rich Gift

110 **89**

3-y-o b f Cadeaux Genereux-Deep Divide (Nashwan (USA))

J D Bethell Mrs J E Vickers

Placings:51-22233500 **(5694)**

2001: 7^{2}GF, 7^{2}GF, 6^{2}G, 6^{3}GF, 6^{3}HY, 6^{5}G, 6^{0}GS, 6^{0}S

	Starts	1st	2nd	3rd	Win & Pl
Career Total (Turf)	10	1	3	2	14200

68	9/00	Pont	6f	D	G-S	£3347

Total win prize-money £3348

Going (Turf): Sf: 0-2 **GS: 1-3** Gd: 0-2 GF: 0-3 Fm: 0-0
Distance: **5f/6f: 1-7** 7f-8f: 0-3 9f-13f: 0-0 14f+: 0-0
Track : **LH: 1-2** RH: 0-1 Tight: 0-0 Gall: 0-0
Aids: Bl: 0-0 Vi: 0-0 Tstrap: 0-0
Best Rating: 89 9/01 Asct 6f good

Landed the second of two starts as a juvenile and has been placed on numerous occasions at three without quite managing to win, but despite that she continues to climb up the handicap. Effective at six or seven furlongs and on most types of ground.

Richest Vein (IRE)

98(94) (77+)**85**

2-y-o b c Ali-Royal (IRE)-Antapoura (IRE) (Bustino)

S P C Woods Arashan Ali

Placings:013241 **(3628)**

2001: 5^{0}G, 6^{1}SD, 6^{3}GF, 7^{2}GF, 7^{4}GF, 7^{1}G

	Starts	1st	2nd	3rd	Win & Pl
Career Total (Turf)	5	1	1	1	12919
Career Total (AW)	1	1	0	0	2933

85	8/01	Gdwd	7f	C H	GD	£11245
77	5/01	Sthl	6f	D	STD	£2933

Total win prize-money £14178

Going (Turf): Sf: 0-0 GS: 0-0 **Gd: 1-2** GF: 0-3 Fm: 0-0
Distance: 5f/6f: 1-2 7f-8f: 1-4 9f-13f: 0-0 14f+: 0-0
Track : LH: 1-2 RH: 1-2 Tight: 0-0 Gall: 0-0
Aids: Bl: 0-0 Vi: 0-0 Tstrap: 0-0
Best Rating: 85 8/01 Gdwd 7f good

He is the first foal of a useful stayer on the Flat who went on to be quite a smart long-distance hurdler. He scored on the sand on his second start and ended the season with victory in a Goodwood nursery.

Ride The Tiger (IRE)

97(102) (62)**42**

4-y-o ch g Imp Society (USA)-Krisdaline (USA) (Kris S (USA))

M D I Usher G A Summers

Placings:000/1362-00200040 **(3301)**

2001: 8^{0}G, 11^{0}F, 10^{2}GF, 8^{0}G, 8^{0}SD, 12^{0}GF, 9^{4}G, 11^{0}GF

	Starts	1st	2nd	3rd	Win & Pl
Career Total (Turf)	11	0	1	0	992
Career Total (AW)	4	1	1	1	3170

59	5/00	Wolv	1m100y	F	STD	£2219

Total win prize-money £2219

Going (Turf): Sf: 0-0 GS: 0-1 Gd: 0-5 GF: 0-4 Fm: 0-1
Distance: 5f/6f: 0-1 7f-8f: 0-4 **9f-13f: 1-10** 14f+: 0-0
Track : **LH: 1-7** RH: 0-1 **Tight: 1-4** Gall: 0-1
Aids: Bl: 0-0 Vi: 0-0 Tstrap: 0-0
Best Rating: 47 6/01 Newb 1m2f6y gd-fm

Ridge And Furrow (IRE)

88 **34**

3-y-o ch g Ridgewood Ben-Ryazana (IRE) (Fairy King (USA))

N Wilson (T P Tate 11/5) Mrs N C Wilson

Placings:040-0000 **(3503)**

2001: 14^{0}G, 10^{0}GF, 10^{0}GF, 11^{0}GF

	Starts	1st	2nd	3rd	Win & Pl
Career Total (Turf)	6	0	0	0	271
Career Total (AW)	1	0	0	0	

Going (Turf): Sf: 0-0 GS: 0-1 Gd: 0-2 GF: 0-3 Fm: 0-0
Distance: 5f/6f: 0-0 7f-8f: 0-2 9f-13f: 0-4 14f+: 0-1
Track : LH: 0-4 RH: 0-2 Tight: 0-3 Gall: 0-0
Aids: Bl: 0-0 Vi: 0-0 Tstrap: 0-0
Best Rating: 34 7/01 Pont 1m2f6y gd-fm

Ridge Manor (IRE)

80 **57**

2-y-o b c Charnwood Forest (IRE)-Tony's Ridge (Indian Ridge)

P W Harris Harrington Properties Ltd

Placings:0 **(5684)**

2001: 8^{0}S

	Starts	1st	2nd	3rd	Win & Pl
Career Total (Turf)	1	0	0	0	

Going (Turf): Sf: 0-1 GS: 0-0 Gd: 0-0 GF: 0-0 Fm: 0-0
Distance: 5f/6f: 0-0 7f-8f: 0-1 9f-13f: 0-0 14f+: 0-0
Track : LH: 0-0 RH: 0-0 Tight: 0-0 Gall: 0-0
Aids: Bl: 0-0 Vi: 0-0 Tstrap: 0-0
Best Rating: 57 11/01 Donc 1m soft

Ridgeway (IRE)

102 **80**

6-y-o b g Indian Ridge-Regal Promise (Pitskelly)

M W Easterby Mrs M E Curtis

Placings:00/124/4/000 **(1490)**
2001: 8^{0}S, 10^{0}S, 8^{0}GF

	Starts	1st	2nd	3rd	Win & Pl
Career Total (Turf)	9	1	1	0	10734

90	4/98	Nott	1m54y	D	SFT	£4337

Total win prize-money £4338

Going (Turf): Sf: 1-3 GS: 0-1 Gd: 0-2 GF: 0-3 Fm: 0-0
Distance: 5f/6f: 0-0 7f-8f: 0-4 **9f-13f: 1-5** 14f+: 0-0
Track : **LH: 1-4** RH: 0-2 Tight: 0-2 Gall: 0-1
Aids: Bl: 0-0 Vi: 0-0 Tstrap: 0-0
Best Rating: 80 5/01 Bevl 1m100y gd-fm

Formerly with Geoff Wragg, he has had his problems and is lightly-raced since.

Ridgeway Lad

100 **75**

3-y-o ch g Primo Dominie-Phyliel (USA) (Lyphard (USA))
T D Easterby David & Steven Dudley

Placings:3-46402230400 **(3841)**
2001: 6^{4}GS, 5^{6}G, 6^{4}F, 6^{0}GF, 7^{2}GF, 7^{2}F, 7^{3}GF, 6^{0}G, 7^{4}GF, 5^{0}GF, 6^{0}G

	Starts	1st	2nd	3rd	Win & Pl
Career Total (Turf)	12	0	2	2	4923

Going (Turf): Sf: 0-0 GS: 0-2 Gd: 0-3 GF: 0-5 Fm: 0-2
Distance: 5f/6f: 0-7 7f-8f: 0-5 9f-13f: 0-0 14f+: 0-0
Track : LH: 0-5 RH: 0-2 Tight: 0-1 Gall: 0-1
Aids: Bl: 0-0 Vi: 0-0 Tstrap: 0-0
Best Rating: 75 7/01 Hayd 7f30y gd-fm

He is still a maiden, but has run some fine races in both maiden and handicap company. Suited by seven furlongs and fast ground.

Ridgeway Sunset (IRE)

90 **73**

2-y-o b f Alhaarth (IRE)-Floralia (Auction Ring (USA))
M R Channon Ridgeway Downs Racing

Placings:0000 **(5115)**
2001: 7^{0}GF, 8^{0}GF, 6^{0}GF, 9^{0}HY

	Starts	1st	2nd	3rd	Win & Pl
Career Total (Turf)	4	0	0	0	

Going (Turf): Sf: 0-1 GS: 0-0 Gd: 0-0 GF: 0-3 Fm: 0-0
Distance: 5f/6f: 0-0 7f-8f: 0-2 9f-13f: 0-2 14f+: 0-0
Track : LH: 0-1 RH: 0-0 Tight: 0-0 Gall: 0-0
Aids: Bl: 0-0 Vi: 0-0 Tstrap: 0-0
Best Rating: 73 9/01 Sals 6f212y gd-fm

Ridgewood Bay (IRE)

65(99)

4-y-o b f Ridgewood Ben-Another Baileys (Deploy)
J C Fox Lord Mutton Racing Partnership

Placings:0006000/000010-0 **(2250)**
2001: 16^{0}GF

	Starts	1st	2nd	3rd	Win & Pl
Career Total (Turf)	13	0	0	0	88
Career Total (AW)	2	1	0	0	1845

32	7/00	Ling	1m5f	G	STD	£1844

Total win prize-money £1845

Going (Turf): Sf: 0-3 GS: 0-4 Gd: 0-4 GF: 0-2 Fm: 0-0
Distance: 5f/6f: 0-2 7f-8f: 0-3 **9f-13f: 1-8** 14f+: 0-2
Track : **LH: 1-7** RH: 0-3 **Tight: 1-5** Gall: 0-1
Aids: Bl: 0-0 Vi: 0-0 Tstrap: 0-0

Ridgewood Belle (IRE)

63

3-y-o b f Ridgewood Ben-Ring Dem Bells (Simply Great (FR))
B J Meehan O'Reilly Hyland & Pidgley Partnership

Placings:0-00 **(1718)**
2001: 8^{0}GS, 10^{0}GF

	Starts	1st	2nd	3rd	Win & Pl
Career Total (Turf)	3	0	0	0	

Going (Turf): Sf: 0-0 GS: 0-2 Gd: 0-0 GF: 0-1 Fm: 0-0
Distance: 5f/6f: 0-1 7f-8f: 0-0 9f-13f: 0-2 14f+: 0-0
Track : LH: 0-1 RH: 0-2 Tight: 0-1 Gall: 0-2
Aids: Bl: 0-2 Vi: 0-0 Tstrap: 0-0
Best Rating: 32 7/00 Ling 1m5f SD

Ridicule

78 **63**

2-y-o b c Piccolo-Mockingbird (Sharpo)
T D Easterby Byculla Thoroughbreds

Placings:0040 **(4841)**
2001: 5^{0}GS, 6^{0}G, 6^{4}GF, 6^{0}G

	Starts	1st	2nd	3rd	Win & Pl
Career Total (Turf)	4	0	0	0	300

Going (Turf): Sf: 0-0 GS: 0-1 Gd: 0-2 GF: 0-1 Fm: 0-0
Distance: 5f/6f: 0-3 7f-8f: 0-1 9f-13f: 0-0 14f+: 0-0
Track : LH: 0-0 RH: 0-0 Tight: 0-0 Gall: 0-0
Aids: Bl: 0-0 Vi: 0-0 Tstrap: 0-0
Best Rating: 63 9/01 Ripn 6f gd-fm

Ridley (IRE)

103 **94**

2-y-o ch c Grand Lodge (USA)-Richly Deserved (IRE) (King's Lake (USA))
B J Meehan Gallagher Equine Ltd

Placings:2222 **(5666)**
2001: 6^{2}HY, 7^{2}S, 6^{2}GS, 6^{2}HY

	Starts	1st	2nd	3rd	Win & Pl
Career Total (Turf)	4	0	4	0	5006

Going (Turf): Sf: 0-3 GS: 0-1 Gd: 0-0 GF: 0-0 Fm: 0-0
Distance: 5f/6f: 0-3 7f-8f: 0-1 9f-13f: 0-0 14f+: 0-0
Track : LH: 0-0 RH: 0-0 Tight: 0-0 Gall: 0-0
Aids: Bl: 0-0 Vi: 0-0 Tstrap: 0-0
Best Rating: 94 11/01 Wind 6f heavy

Second on all four runs.

Rififi

(104) (66)

8-y-o ch g Aragon-Bundled Up (USA) (Sharpen Up)
R Wilman (Mrs H L Walton 21/6) Mrs Joanna Hughes

Placings:50/0540/**115**050310110500/00000066114300 **014/0**20000/**0003**00000**500-25442300131300** **(5392)**
2001: 6^{2}SW, 6^{5}SD, 7^{4}SW, 6^{4}SD, 6^{2}SD, 6^{3}SD, 8^{0}SD, 6^{0}SD, 6^{1}SD, 6^{3}SD, 5^{1}SW, 6^{3}SD, 6^{0}SD, 6^{0}SD

	Starts	1st	2nd	3rd	Win & Pl
Career Total (Turf)	42	5	1	2	38480
Career Total (AW)	28	5	2	4	15695

61	9/01	Wolv	5f	F(0-60)H	SLW	£2359
50	7/01	Sthl	6f	G	STD	£1925
78	12/98	Ling	7f	E(0-75)H	STD	£2463
72	8/98	Sand	5f6y	D(0-80)H	G-F	£3680
72	8/98	Newb	6f8y	E(0-90)H	G-F	£3308
80	8/97	Gdwd	6f	C(0-95)H	G-F	£15045
71	8/97	NmkJ	6f	C(0-90)H	GD	£5872
61	6/97	Wind	5f217y	D(0-75)H	G-F	£5680
66	2/97	Ling	5f	F(0-70)H	STD	£2762
66	2/97	Ling	5f	D	STD	£3306

Total win prize-money £46391

Going (Turf): Sf: 0-2 GS: 0-5 Gd: 1-15 **GF: 4-16** Fm: 0-4
Distance: **5f/6f: 8-47** 7f-8f: 2-23 9f-13f: 0-0 14f+: 0-0
Track : **LH: 5-31** RH: 1-5 **Tight: 4-22** Gall: 1-3
Aids: Bl: 0-0 Vi: 0-2 Tstrap: 0-2
Best Rating: 66 9/01 Wolv 6f stand

Kept very busy, he has been a successful sprint handicapper on his day, but struggled last season after a promising first run on turf and has only shown average form on sand this year.

Rigadoon (IRE)

106 **49**

5-y-o b g Be My Chief (USA)-Loucoum (FR) (Iron Duke (FR))
M W Easterby C Buckton, K Mercer & A Ford

Placings:000/000613161/450462-003253653 **(4829)**
2001: 16^{0}GF, 16^{0}F, 17^{3}F, 17^{2}GF, 16^{5}GF, 16^{3}F, 16^{6}GF, 16^{5}G, 17^{3}G

	Starts	1st	2nd	3rd	Win & Pl
Career Total (Turf)	27	3	2	4	13651

55	9/99	Catt	1m7f177y	F(0-65)H	G-F	£2493
53	7/99	Nott	2m9y	F(0-65)H	G-F	£2457
45	6/99	Carl	2m1f52y	F(0-60)H	G-F	£2444

Total win prize-money £7394

Going (Turf): Sf: 0-2 GS: 0-1 Gd: 0-7 **GF: 3-13** Fm: 0-4
Distance: 5f/6f: 0-2 7f-8f: 0-3 9f-13f: 0-2 **14f+: 3-20**
Track : **LH: 2-16** RH: 1-8 Tight: 1-17 Gall: 1-2
Aids: **Bl: 3-20** Vi: 0-0 Tstrap: 0-0
Best Rating: 50 6/01 Pont 2m1f216y gd-fm

Right Approach

98 **96+**

2-y-o b c Machiavellian (USA)-Abbey Strand (USA) (Shadeed (USA))
Sir Michael Stoute The Queen

Placings:12 **(4589)**
2001: 7^{1}GS, 7^{2}G

	Starts	1st	2nd	3rd	Win & Pl
Career Total (Turf)	2	1	1	0	8682

96	8/01	NmkJ	7f	C	G-S	£6262

Total win prize-money £6262

Going (Turf): Sf: 0-0 **GS: 1-1** Gd: 0-1 GF: 0-0 Fm: 0-0
Distance: 5f/6f: 0-0 **7f-8f: 1-2** 9f-13f: 0-0 14f+: 0-0
Track : LH: 0-0 RH: 0-1 Tight: 0-0 Gall: 0-1
Aids: Bl: 0-0 Vi: 0-0 Tstrap: 0-0
Best Rating: 96 9/01 Kemp 7f good

A brother to the stayer Temple Way, he showed a turn of foot on easy ground to score on his debut and was beaten by the minimum margin next time. Should stay further and go on from that.

Right Wing (IRE)

119 **118**

7-y-o b h In The Wings-Nekhbet (Artaius (USA))
J L Dunlop The Earl Cadogan

Placings:3/0310310/3400316/1250301/312213212-115416 **(5605)**
2001: 8^{1}GS, 9^{1}S, 8^{5}S, 10^{4}GS, 9^{1}GS, 8^{6}GS

	Starts	1st	2nd	3rd	Win & Pl
Career Total (Turf)	37	11	5	8	249863

111	10/01	NmkR	1m1f	A	G-S	£15660
118	4/01	NmkR	1m1f	A	SFT	£20300
116	3/01	Donc	1m	A	G-S	£15015
110	10/00	Bord	1m1f110y		VS	£21134
114	8/00	York	1m205y	A	GD	£21645
110	4/00	Kemp	1m2f	A	SFT	£15015
101	11/99	Nott	1m54y	C	SFT	£6505
107	3/99	Donc	1m	B H	G-S	£43735
100	9/90	Donc	1m	B(0-105)H	GD	£15478
88	10/97	Ayr	1m	C	SFT	£4583
89	6/97	Asct	1m	C(0-90)	SFT	£6272

Total win prize-money £185344

Going (Turf): Sf: 5-12 GS: 3-9 Gd: 2-10 GF: 0-3 Fm: 0-0
Distance: 5f/6f: 0-0 7f-8f: 5-16 **9f-13f: 6-20** 14f+: 0-0
Track : **LH: 4-14** RH: 3-13 Tight: 0-4 **Gall: 4-12**
Aids: Bl: 1-2 **Vi: 8-21** Tstrap: 0-0

Best Rating: 118 4/01 NmkR 1m1f soft

The 1999 Lincoln winner, he has been very consistent in Pattern events since, the highlight being when coming with a late rattle to win the Earl of Sefton Stakes at Newmarket in April, and returned from a break to score over the same course and dist ance in the autumn. He usually wears blinkers or a visor, needs holding up until the last possible moment, and appreciates cut in the ground. Wins have come at eight to ten furlongs.

Righty Ho

104 (51)**43**

7-y-o b g Reprimand-Challanging (Mill Reef (USA))
W H Tinning W H Tinning

Placings:0040/05461361200**0**/63246603/00022125U-1000140 **(5225)**
2001: 10^{1}S, 16^{0}G, 11^{0}GF, 14^{0}GF, 11^{1}GF, 9^{4}G, 10^{0}S

	Starts	1st	2nd	3rd	Win & Pl
Career Total (Turf)	39	5	5	3	21436
Career Total (AW)	1	0	0	0	

43 8/01 Rdcr 1m3f E(0-70)H G-F £4241
45 4/01 Ripn 1m2f F SFT £2730
45 8/00 Carl 1m4f F GD £2278
66 8/97 Epsm 1m2f18y E(0-70)H GD £2830
62 6/97 Sals 1m F(0-70)H SFT £2798
Total win prize-money £14878

Going (Turf): Sf: 2-7 GS: 0-4 **Gd: 2-10** GF: 1-13 Fm: 0-5
Distance: 5f/6f: 0-1 7f-8f: 1-5 **9f-13f: 4-28** 14f+: 0-6
Track : LH: 2-27 RH: 2-11 **Tight: 3-13** Gall: 0-7
Aids: Bl: 0-0 **Vi: 1-6** Tstrap: 0-0
Best Rating: 45 4/01 Ripn 1m2f soft

Won a couple of very moderate events at Ripon and Redcar this season.

Rileys Rocket

83 **52**

2-y-o b f Makbul-Star Of Flanders (Puissance)
R Hollinshead D Lowe

Placings:0 **(4775)**
2001: 7^{0}G

	Starts	1st	2nd	3rd	Win & Pl
Career Total (Turf)	1	0	0	0	

Going (Turf): Sf: 0-0 GS: 0-0 Gd: 0-1 GF: 0-0 Fm: 0-0
Distance: 5f/6f: 0-0 7f-8f: 0-1 9f-13f: 0-0 14f+: 0-0
Track : LH: 0-0 RH: 0-1 Tight: 0-0 Gall: 0-0
Aids: Bl: 0-0 Vi: 0-0 Tstrap: 0-0
Best Rating: 52 9/01 Bevl 7f100y good

Rimatara

(102) (49)**32**

5-y-o ch g Selkirk (USA)-Humble Pie (Known Fact (USA))
M W Easterby J Fox

Placings:6/00000**036-1622513304000** **(5398)**
2001: 8^{1}SD, 9^{6}SW, 8^{2}SD, 8^{2}SD, 8^{5}SW, 7^{1}SD, 7^{3}SW, 8^{3}SD, 7^{0}SD, 7^{4}SD, 8^{0}SD, 7^{0}GF, 8^{0}SD

	Starts	1st	2nd	3rd	Win & Pl
Career Total (Turf)	7	0	0	0	0
Career Total (AW)	15	2	2	3	5594

50 2/01 Wolv 7f F(0-65)H STD £1729
42 1/01 Sthl 1m F(0-60)H STD £1778
Total win prize-money £3507

Going (Turf): Sf: 0-1 GS: 0-1 Gd: 0-2 GF: 0-3 Fm: 0-0
Distance: 5f/6f: 0-1 **7f-8f: 2-11** 9f-13f: 0-10 14f+: 0-0
Track : **LH: 2-19** RH: 0-1 **Tight: 1-7** Gall: 0-1
Aids: **Bl: 2-16** Vi: 0-0 Tstrap: 0-0
Best Rating: 54 3/01 Wolv 1m100y stand

Rimbaud (IRE)

100(93) (30)**38**

5-y-o b h College Chapel-Arcade (Rousillon (USA))
I A Wood Neardown Stables

Placings:0/52310/600003 **(5557)**
2001: 11^{6}GS, 11^{0}GF, 14^{0}G, 16^{0}G, 11^{0}S, 14^{3}S, **13**^{0}SD

	Starts	1st	2nd	3rd	Win & Pl
Career Total (Turf)	12	1	1	2	4564

86 9/99 Fair 1m1f G-Y £3036
Total win prize-money £3036

Going (Turf): Sf: 0-4 GS: 0-1 Gd: 0-5 GF: 0-1 Fm: 0-0
Distance: 5f/6f: 0-0 7f-8f: 0-3 **9f-13f: 1-6** 14f+: 0-3
Track : LH: 0-4 **RH: 1-5** Tight: 0-3 Gall: 0-1
Aids: Bl: 0-0 Vi: 0-0 **Tstrap: 1-2**
Best Rating: 41 7/01 Leic 1m3f183y gd-sft

A winner in Ireland, but has not shown a great deal in this country so far.

Rimfaxi

(70) (24)**29**

3-y-o ch g Risk Me (FR)-Legal Sound (Legal Eagle)
J M Jefferson (D Nicholls 5/1) J M Ranson

Placings:0-00 **(5032)**
2001: 7^{0}SD, 12^{0}GF

	Starts	1st	2nd	3rd	Win & Pl
Career Total (Turf)	2	0	0	0	
Career Total (AW)	1	0	0	0	

Going (Turf): Sf: 0-0 GS: 0-0 Gd: 0-0 GF: 0-1 Fm: 0-0
Distance: 5f/6f: 0-0 7f-8f: 0-1 9f-13f: 0-1 14f+: 0-0
Track : LH: 0-1 RH: 0-0 Tight: 0-0 Gall: 0-0
Aids: Bl: 0-0 Vi: 0-0 Tstrap: 0-0
Best Rating: 24 1/01 Sthl 7f stand

Ring Dancer

103(100) (62)**74**

6-y-o b g Polar Falcon (USA)-Ring Cycle (Auction Ring (USA))
Mrs L Stubbs Mrs L Stubbs

Placings:12/200430/00/00010**30-6**R0261122300**0** **(5161)**
2001: 6^{6}SD, 6^{R}GF, 6^{0}GF, 5^{2}GF, 5^{6}GF, 5^{1}G, 6^{1}GF, 5^{2}GF, 5^{2}F, 5^{3}GF, 5^{0}G, 5^{0}G, **6**^{0}SD

	Starts	1st	2nd	3rd	Win & Pl
Career Total (Turf)	26	4	5	2	20641
Career Total (AW)	4	0	0	1	434

56 6/01 Folk 6f F G-F £2369
61 6/01 Sand 5f6y E GD £3607
75 7/00 Bath 5f161y D(0-80)H FRM £3818
93 8/97 Ripn 6f E GD £3223
Total win prize-money £13021

Going (Turf): Sf: 0-3 GS: 0-0 **Gd: 2-7** GF: 1-14 Fm: 1-2
Distance: **5f/6f: 4-25** 7f-8f: 0-5 9f-13f: 0-0 14f+: 0-0
Track : **LH: 1-8** RH: 0-2 Tight: 0-3 **Gall: 1-5**
Aids: Bl: 0-0 Vi: 0-0 Tstrap: 0-0
Best Rating: 74 6/01 Yarm 5f43y gd-fm

Held in handicap company and both his wins this season came in claimers.

Ring Of Destiny

99 **68**

2-y-o b c Magic Ring (IRE)-Canna (Caerleon (USA))
P W Harris The Ringleaders

Placings:52 **(2963)**
2001: 6^{5}GF, 6^{2}GF

	Starts	1st	2nd	3rd	Win & Pl
Career Total (Turf)	2	0	1	0	722

Going (Turf): Sf: 0-0 GS: 0-0 Gd: 0-0 GF: 0-2 Fm: 0-0
Distance: 5f/6f: 0-0 7f-8f: 0-2 9f-13f: 0-0 14f+: 0-0
Track : LH: 0-0 RH: 0-1 Tight: 0-1 Gall: 0-0
Aids: Bl: 0-0 Vi: 0-0 Tstrap: 0-0
Best Rating: 68 7/01 Folk 6f189y gd-fm

Ring The Chief

(92) (30)**40**

9-y-o b g Chief Singer-Lomond Ring (Lomond (USA))
M D I Usher G A Summers

Placings:006/02**023060/05062533/0053313406610315 4403/04/12306/0440-40** **(0269)**
2001: 8^{4}SD, 7^{0}SW

	Starts	1st	2nd	3rd	Win & Pl
Career Total (Turf)	14	1	0	2	3617
Career Total (AW)	38	3	4	7	10553

42 1/99 Sthl 1m F(0-60)H STD £1657
42 8/97 Sals 6f212y G(0-70)H G-S £2193
39 6/97 Sthl 7f G(0-60)H STD £2007
34 2/97 Sthl 7f F(0-60)H STD £2083
Total win prize-money £7942

Going (Turf): Sf: 0-1 **GS: 1-1** Gd: 0-4 GF: 0-8 Fm: 0-0
Distance: 5f/6f: 0-14 **7f-8f: 4-26** 9f-13f: 0-12 14f+: 0-0
Track : **LH: 3-41** RH: 0-5 Tight: 0-25 Gall: 0-2
Aids: Bl: 0-0 Vi: 0-0 Tstrap: 0-0
Best Rating: 28 1/01 Sthl 1m stand

Ringmoor Down

95 **89+**

2-y-o b f Pivotal-Floppie (FR) (Law Society (USA))
P J Makin Prof C D Green

Placings:10 **(4985)**
2001: 6^{1}G, 6^{0}G

	Starts	1st	2nd	3rd	Win & Pl
Career Total (Turf)	2	1	0	0	4602

89 9/01 Kemp 6f D GD £4602
Total win prize-money £4602

Going (Turf): Sf: 0-0 GS: 0-0 **Gd: 1-2** GF: 0-0 Fm: 0-0
Distance: **5f/6f: 1-1** 7f-8f: 0-1 9f-13f: 0-0 14f+: 0-0
Track : LH: 0-0 RH: 0-0 Tight: 0-0 Gall: 0-0
Aids: Bl: 0-0 Vi: 0-0 Tstrap: 0-0
Best Rating: 89 9/01 Kemp 6f good

A half-sister to two six-furlong winners, she scored cosily on her Kempton debut, but was disappointing next time in an Ascot sales race.

Ringside Jack

106 **60**

5-y-o b g Batshoof-Celestine (Skyliner)
C W Fairhurst M J G Partnership

Placings:0013204/02000003050/1060400105-0042063200200004 **(5632)**
2001: 9^{0}HY, 10^{0}S, 11^{4}S, 10^{2}G, 10^{0}GF, 10^{6}G, 10^{3}GF, 10^{2}G, 10^{0}GF, 11^{0}GF, 10^{2}S, 10^{0}G, 10^{0}S, 10^{0}HY, 10^{0}S, 10^{4}G

	Starts	1st	2nd	3rd	Win & Pl
Career Total (Turf)	44	3	5	3	22215

69 9/00 Ches 1m2f75y E(0-70)H SFT £4459
66 4/00 Bevl 1m1f207yD(0-85)H HVY £3961
70 6/98 Rdcr 5f D G-S £3302
Total win prize-money £11724

Going (Turf): Sf: 2-12 GS: 1-6 Gd: 0-15 GF: 0-9 Fm: 0-2
Distance: 5f/6f: 1-3 7f-8f: 0-5 **9f-13f: 2-36** 14f+: 0-0
Track : LH: 1-25 RH: 1-12 **Tight: 1-17** Gall: 0-9
Aids: Bl: 0-0 **Vi: 1-22** Tstrap: 0-0
Best Rating: 70 6/01 Ripn 1m2f good

He wins from time to time, but is not particularly consistent. Best suited by ten furlongs and soft ground.

Ringwood (USA)

102(90) (59)**57**

3-y-o b g Foxhound (USA)-Tewksburygarden (USA) (Wolf Power (SAF))

C F Wall Jane Dobie & John Bridgo

Placings:644-4530300600 **(5187)**

2001: 8^{4}SW, 7^{5}SD, 5^{3}GS, 5^{0}G, 6^{3}GF, 6^{0}F, 6^{0}G, 7^{6}GF, 8^{0}S, 5^{0}GS, 8^{0}SD

	Starts	1st	2nd	3rd	Win & Pl
Career Total (Turf)	11	0	0	2	1563
Career Total (AW)	2	0	0	0	0

Going (Turf): Sf: 0-2 GS: 0-2 Gd: 0-3 GF: 0-3 Fm: 0-1
Distance: 5f/6f: 0-8 7f-8f: 0-4 9f-13f: 0-1 14f+: 0-0
Track : LH: 0-4 RH: 0-3 Tight: 0-2 Gall: 0-2
Aids: Bl: 0-0 Vi: 0-2 Tstrap: 0-0
Best Rating: 75 6/01 Kemp 6f gd-fm

Rio's Diamond

101(95) (46)**48**

4-y-o b f Formidable (USA)-Rio Piedras (Kala Shikari)

M J Ryan Mrs Sandie Ross

Placings:000030000/205134003005-00244020201605 **(5592)**

2001: 7^{0}SD, 7^{0}G, 6^{2}G, 7^{4}F, 6^{4}F, 7^{0}GF, 6^{2}F, 7^{0}GF, 6^{2}G, 7^{0}GF, 7^{1}G, 7^{6}S, 8^{0}G, 6^{5}GS, 8^{2}SD

	Starts	1st	2nd	3rd	Win & Pl
Career Total (Turf)	28	2	3	2	8479
Career Total (AW)	7	0	1	1	963

48	8/01	Brig	7f214y	E(0-70)H	GD	£2863
43	6/00	Wwck	6f168y	F(0-65)H	G-F	£2436

Total win prize-money £5299

Going (Turf): Sf: 0-6 GS: 0-2 **Gd: 1-6 GF: 1-9** Fm: 0-5
Distance: 5f/6f: 0-9 **7f-8f: 2-25** 9f-13f: 0-1 14f+: 0-0
Track : **LH: 2-20** RH: 0-4 Tight: 0-8 Gall: 0-3
Aids: Bl: 0-0 Vi: 0-1 Tstrap: 0-0
Best Rating: 48 8/01 Brig 7f214y good

Rioja

(98) (52)**54**

6-y-o ch g Anshan-Executive Flare (Executive Man)

M Wigham Tempranillo Partnership

Placings:23405/10000/00000-30 **(0352)**

2001: 7^{3}SD, 7^{0}SD

	Starts	1st	2nd	3rd	Win & Pl
Career Total (Turf)	14	1	1	1	9617
Career Total (AW)	3	0	0	1	251

77	4/98	NmkR	6f	C(0-90)H	SFT	£8220

Total win prize-money £8220

Going (Turf): Sf: 1-5 GS: 0-2 Gd: 0-4 GF: 0-2 Fm: 0-1
Distance: **5f/6f: 1-10** 7f-8f: 0-7 9f-13f: 0-0 14f+: 0-0
Track : LH: 0-7 RH: 0-0 Tight: 0-3 Gall: 0-1
Aids: Bl: 0-0 Vi: 0-0 Tstrap: 0-0
Best Rating: 52 2/01 Wolv 7f stand

He showed ability at two, and made the perfect start to his three-year-old season with a gutsy victory in very soft ground at Newmarket. Most disappointing since.

Ripcord (IRE)

95 **65**

3-y-o b g Diesis-Native Twine (Be My Native (USA))

J H M Gosden Lady Harrison

Placings:000-3000 **(3048)**

2001: 8^{3}GS, 10^{0}GF, 8^{0}G, 8^{0}GF

	Starts	1st	2nd	3rd	Win & Pl
Career Total (Turf)	7	0	0	1	486

Going (Turf): Sf: 0-1 GS: 0-2 Gd: 0-2 GF: 0-2 Fm: 0-0
Distance: 5f/6f: 0-1 7f-8f: 0-4 9f-13f: 0-2 14f+: 0-0
Track : LH: 0-1 RH: 0-1 Tight: 0-0 Gall: 0-0
Aids: Bl: 0-0 Vi: 0-0 Tstrap: 0-0
Best Rating: 65 5/01 Sals 1m gd-sft

Ripsnorter (IRE)

(69)

12-y-o ch h Rousillon (USA)-Formulate (Reform)

P D Purdy P D Purdy

Placings:052/005430100/120045200000/035012520/006000/0500/061360000000000/0/000-P0 **(2714)**

2001: 11^{P}SD, 9^{0}GF

	Starts	1st	2nd	3rd	Win & Pl
Career Total (Turf)	31	2	2	1	7072
Career Total (AW)	33	2	3	2	8019

36	2/98	Ling	1m	F(0-60)H	SLW	£1892
54	4/94	Ripn	1m	E(0-70)H	G-S	£3314
64	1/93	Sthl	1m	F(0-70)H	STD	£2511
73	7/92	Nott	1m54y	F(0-70)H	G-S	£1716

Total win prize-money £9434

Going (Turf): Sf: 0-6 **GS: 2-6** Gd: 0-11 GF: 0-6 Fm: 0-1
Distance: 5f/6f: 0-0 **7f-8f: 3-35** 9f-13f: 1-28 14f+: 0-0
Track : **LH: 3-44** RH: 1-11 **Tight: 2-23** Gall: 0-4
Aids: Bl: 0-1 Vi: 0-2 Tstrap: 0-0

Risalpur (IRE)

96 **67**

2-y-o b c Mukaddamah (USA)-Idrak (Young Generation)

Mrs L Stubbs Maurice Parker

Placings:50016 **(4254)**

2001: 5^{5}GF, 5^{0}GF, 5^{0}G, 5^{1}GF, 5^{6}GF

	Starts	1st	2nd	3rd	Win & Pl
Career Total (Turf)	5	1	0	0	3679

67	7/01	Wind	5f10y	D	G-F	£3679

Total win prize-money £3679

Going (Turf): Sf: 0-0 GS: 0-0 Gd: 0-1 **GF: 1-4** Fm: 0-0
Distance: **5f/6f: 1-5** 7f-8f: 0-0 9f-13f: 0-0 14f+: 0-0
Track : LH: 0-0 **RH: 1-1** Tight: 0-0 **Gall: 1-1**
Aids: Bl: 0-0 Vi: 0-0 Tstrap: 0-0
Best Rating: 67 7/01 Wind 5f10y gd-fm

Had shown little form before winning a Windsor maiden over the minimum trip in the summer. Acts on a sound surface.

Rise Above (IRE)

(54)

7-y-o b m Simply Great (FR)-La Tanque (USA) (Last Raise (USA))

Miss K M George R J Matthews

Placings:0/000/360 **(4552)**

2001: 16^{3}GF, 16^{6}GF, 14^{0}SW

	Starts	1st	2nd	3rd	Win & Pl
Career Total (Turf)	6	0	0	1	342
Career Total (AW)	1	0	0	0	

Going (Turf): Sf: 0-1 GS: 0-0 Gd: 0-1 GF: 0-3 Fm: 0-1
Distance: 5f/6f: 0-0 7f-8f: 0-0 9f-13f: 0-4 14f+: 0-3
Track : LH: 0-6 RH: 0-1 Tight: 0-2 Gall: 0-0
Aids: Bl: 0-0 Vi: 0-0 Tstrap: 0-0
Best Rating: 27 7/01 Chep 2m49y gd-fm

Rising Passion (IRE)

89(90) (17)**31**

3-y-o ch g General Monash (USA)-Brazilian Princess (Absalom)

D Nicholls David Waters

Placings:000-00000600 **(3434)**

2001: 8^{0}SD, 7^{0}SW, 6^{0}HY, 5^{0}SD, 6^{0}GF, 8^{6}GF, 7^{0}SD, 8^{0}F

	Starts	1st	2nd	3rd	Win & Pl
Career Total (Turf)	7	0	0	0	0
Career Total (AW)	4	0	0	0	

Going (Turf): Sf: 0-1 GS: 0-0 Gd: 0-1 GF: 0-3 Fm: 0-2
Distance: 5f/6f: 0-5 7f-8f: 0-6 9f-13f: 0-0 14f+: 0-0
Track : LH: 0-5 RH: 0-1 Tight: 0-3 Gall: 0-1
Aids: Bl: 0-2 Vi: 0-0 Tstrap: 0-0
Best Rating: 31 6/01 Rdcr 1m gd-fm

Rising Spray

100 **13**

10-y-o ch g Waajib-Rose Bouquet (General Assembly (USA))

Dr J R J Naylor Mrs Mary Heritage

Placings:060/05240/00063000330/503061122/1103304/456302/0206/0000600-00360600 **(4728)**

2001: 13^{0}GF, 12^{0}GF, 14^{3}GF, 14^{6}GF, 14^{0}GF, 14^{6}F, 12^{0}GF, 16^{0}GF

	Starts	1st	2nd	3rd	Win & Pl
Career Total (Turf)	60	4	5	8	24423

71	5/97	Sals	1m6f	C(0-90)H	G-F	£5407
66	4/97	Folk	1m4f	E(0-70)H	G-F	£3070
53	8/96	Folk	1m4f	E(0-70)H	G-F	£3343
52	8/96	Folk	1m4f	F(0-60)H	G-F	£2381

Total win prize-money £14201

Going (Turf): Sf: 0-3 GS: 0-6 Gd: 0-15 **GF: 4-35** Fm: 0-1
Distance: 5f/6f: 0-0 7f-8f: 0-6 **9f-13f: 3-36** 14f+: 1-18
Track : LH: 0-15 **RH: 4-40 Tight: 4-29** Gall: 0-9
Aids: Bl: 0-7 Vi: 0-1 Tstrap: 0-0
Best Rating: 42 6/01 Sals 1m6f15y gd-fm

Risk Free

102(108) (83)**63**

4-y-o ch g Risk Me (FR)-Princess Lily (Blakeney)

P D Evans (N P Littmoden 10/8) P Tarran

Placings:0102002/4214000023-501305500000401030006203 **(5612)**

2001: 6^{5}SW, 6^{0}SD, 8^{1}SD, 8^{3}SW, 10^{0}SW, 8^{5}SD, 8^{5}SD, 7^{0}SD, 7^{0}GF, 8^{0}GS, 8^{0}F, 7^{0}GF, 12^{4}SD, 8^{0}SD, 6^{1}SD, 9^{0}SD, 7^{3}G, 7^{0}GF, 7^{0}G, 5^{6}S, 7^{2}SD, 6^{0}SD, 6^{3}SD

	Starts	1st	2nd	3rd	Win & Pl
Career Total (Turf)	15	0	0	1	2838
Career Total (AW)	25	4	5	3	20491

58	8/01	Wolv	6f	G	STD	£1974
87	2/01	Ling	1m	D(0-80)H	STD	£5421
86	4/00	Wolv	1m100y	D(0-85)H	STD	£3887
78	5/99	Sthl	5f	F	STD	£2304

Total win prize-money £13586

Going (Turf): Sf: 0-2 GS: 0-2 Gd: 0-5 GF: 0-5 Fm: 0-1
Distance: **5f/6f: 2-13** 7f-8f: 1-17 9f-13f: 1-10 14f+: 0-0
Track : **LH: 3-29** RH: 0-0 **Tight: 3-24** Gall: 0-0
Aids: Bl: 0-9 **Vi: 1-5** Tstrap: 0-0
Best Rating: 87 2/01 Ling 1m slow

A busy performer on sand, he likes to race at or near the front and a mile is still probably his best trip, although he managed to win over six in August.

Risker (USA)

98 **82**

2-y-o b c Gone West (USA)-Trampoli (USA) (Trempolino (USA))

M Johnston Ali Saeed

Placings:5410 **(5031)**

2001: 7^{5}GS, 7^{4}G, 8^{1}GF, 8^{0}GF

	Starts	1st	2nd	3rd	Win & Pl
Career Total (Turf)	4	1	0	0	4987

73	9/01	Thsk	1m	D	G-F	£4426

Total win prize-money £4427

Going (Turf): Sf: 0-0 GS: 0-1 Gd: 0-1 **GF: 1-2** Fm: 0-0
Distance: 5f/6f: 0-0 **7f-8f: 1-4** 9f-13f: 0-0 14f+: 0-0
Track : **LH: 1-2** RH: 0-2 **Tight: 1-2** Gall: 0-0
Aids: Bl: 0-0 Vi: 0-0 Tstrap: 0-0
Best Rating: 82 8/01 Gdwd 7f good

Failed to progress on his Thirsk maiden win when never in contention at Musselburgh.

Risky Flight

(89) (23)**31**

7-y-o ch g Risk Me (FR)-Stairway To Heaven (IRE) (Godswalk (USA))
A Smith Mrs Sheila Oakes

Placings:06000/000000/0/**0-03004** **(1471)**
2001: 8⁰SD, 12³SD, 9⁰SD, 16⁰SD, 11⁴SD

	Starts	1st	2nd	3rd	Win & Pl
Career Total (Turf)	11	0	0	0	0
Career Total (AW)	7	0	0	1	238

Going (Turf): Sf: 0-0 GS: 0-1 Gd: 0-3 GF: 0-6 Fm: 0-1
Distance: 5f/6f: 0-9 7f-8f: 0-2 9f-13f: 0-6 14f+: 0-1
Track : LH: 0-7 RH: 0-2 Tight: 0-4 Gall: 0-0
Aids: Bl: 0-2 Vi: 0-0 Tstrap: 0-0
Best Rating: 23 1/01 Sthl 1m4f stand

Risky Girl

56

6-y-o gr m Risk Me (FR)-Jove's Voodoo (USA) (Northern Jove (CAN))
H J Manners H J Manners

Placings:10/00333/0 **(5178)**
2001: 11⁰HY

	Starts	1st	2nd	3rd	Win & Pl
Career Total (Turf)	7	1	0	2	4293
Career Total (AW)	1	0	0	1	268
66 6/97 Pont 6f	E			GD	£3347

Total win prize-money £3347

Going (Turf): Sf: 0-2 GS: 0-1 **Gd: 1-2** GF: 0-2 Fm: 0-0
Distance: **5f/6f: 1-2** 7f-8f: 0-0 9f-13f: 0-3 14f+: 0-3
Track : **LH: 1-5** RH: 0-2 Tight: 0-3 Gall: 0-1
Aids: Bl: 0-0 Vi: 0-2 Tstrap: 0-0

Risky Reef

102(106) (76)**62**

4-y-o ch g Risk Me (FR)-Pas De Reef (Pas De Seul)
I A Balding Park House Partnership

Placings:52/455040-**14416**000002 **(5503)**
2001: 7¹SD, 7⁴SW, 8⁴SD, 7¹SW, 8⁶SD, 6⁰G, 7⁰GF, 7⁰G, 6⁰G, 6⁰HY, 7²HY

	Starts	1st	2nd	3rd	Win & Pl
Career Total (Turf)	12	0	2	0	2012
Career Total (AW)	7	2	0	0	4677
76 2/01 Sthl 7f	G(0-75)H			SLW	£1351
69 1/01 Sthl 7f	E(0-70)H			STD	£2478

Total win prize-money £3829

Going (Turf): Sf: 0-5 GS: 0-1 Gd: 0-5 GF: 0-1 Fm: 0-0
Distance: 5f/6f: 0-9 **7f-8f: 2-9** 9f-13f: 0-1 14f+: 0-0
Track : **LH: 2-9** RH: 0-2 Tight: 0-3 Gall: 0-2
Aids: Bl: 0-0 **Vi: 1-7** Tstrap: 0-0
Best Rating: 76 2/01 Sthl 7f slow

Looks best on Fibresand.

Risky Reward

97 **50**

2-y-o b f First Trump-Baroness Gymcrak (Pharly (FR))
T D Easterby Ryedale Partnership No1

Placings:0320466 **(5636)**
2001: 5⁰GF, 6³G, 6²GF, 7⁰GF, 6⁴HY, 6⁶S, 5⁶G

	Starts	1st	2nd	3rd	Win & Pl
Career Total (Turf)	7	0	1	1	2258

Going (Turf): Sf: 0-2 GS: 0-0 Gd: 0-2 GF: 0-3 Fm: 0-0
Distance: 5f/6f: 0-6 7f-8f: 0-1 9f-13f: 0-0 14f+: 0-0
Track : LH: 0-1 RH: 0-0 Tight: 0-1 Gall: 0-0

Aids: Bl: 0-1 Vi: 0-0 Tstrap: 0-0
Best Rating: 66 6/01 Newc 6f gd-fm

Risotto (USA)

96 **73**

2-y-o b f Kris S (USA)-Routilante (Rousillon (USA))
I A Balding George Strawbridge

Placings:201 **(4703)**
2001: 6²GF, 6⁰GF, 7¹G

	Starts	1st	2nd	3rd	Win & Pl
Career Total (Turf)	3	1	1	0	5792
73 9/01 Epsm 7f	D			GD	£4153

Total win prize-money £4154

Going (Turf): Sf: 0-0 GS: 0-0 **Gd: 1-1** GF: 0-2 Fm: 0-0
Distance: 5f/6f: 0-1 **7f-8f: 1-2** 9f-13f: 0-0 14f+: 0-0
Track : **LH: 1-2** RH: 0-0 **Tight: 1-1** Gall: 0-0
Aids: Bl: 0-0 Vi: 0-0 Tstrap: 0-0
Best Rating: 73 9/01 Epsm 7f good

Fortunate Epsom maiden winner, just holding on from fast-finishing runner-up.

Risque Sermon

107 **66**

3-y-o b g Risk Me (FR)-Sunday Sport Star (Star Appeal)
Miss B Sanders R Lamb

Placings:010430-062405330 **(4251)**
2001: 6⁰G, 5⁶GF, 6²F, 6⁴GF, 6⁰GF, 5⁵GF, 6³GF, 6³GF, 7⁰GF

	Starts	1st	2nd	3rd	Win & Pl
Career Total (Turf)	15	1	1	3	8212
72 7/00 Ling 6f	D			G-F	£3601

Total win prize-money £3601

Going (Turf): Sf: 0-2 GS: 0-0 Gd: 0-2 **GF: 1-10** Fm: 0-1
Distance: **5f/6f: 1-14** 7f-8f: 0-1 9f-13f: 0-0 14f+: 0-0
Track : LH: 0-3 RH: 0-1 Tight: 0-3 Gall: 0-1
Aids: Bl: 0-0 Vi: 0-0 Tstrap: 0-11
Best Rating: 67 8/01 Epsm 6f gd-fm

Won a Lingfield maiden at two over six furlongs, but seems to lack an extra gear at the business end.

Ristra (USA)

100 **77**

2-y-o b f Kingmambo (USA)-Rhetorical Lass (USA) (Capote (USA))
J Noseda Sanford R Robertson

Placings:2100 **(5144)**
2001: 6²F, 6¹GF, 5⁰GF, 7⁰G

	Starts	1st	2nd	3rd	Win & Pl
Career Total (Turf)	4	1	1	0	6071
69 5/01 Ling 6f	D			G-F	£3941

Total win prize-money £3941

Going (Turf): Sf: 0-0 GS: 0-0 Gd: 0-1 **GF: 1-2** Fm: 0-1
Distance: **5f/6f: 1-3** 7f-8f: 0-1 9f-13f: 0-0 14f+: 0-0
Track : LH: 0-0 RH: 0-0 Tight: 0-0 Gall: 0-0
Aids: Bl: 0-0 Vi: 0-0 Tstrap: 0-0
Best Rating: 77 6/01 Asct 5f gd-fm

She showed a good turn of foot when running out a three length winner from Hufflepuff in maiden race over six furlongs at Lingfield in May.

Risucchio

87 **65**

2-y-o ch g Thatching-Skip To Somerfield (Shavian)
B S Rothwell Richard Blanchard

Placings:3000 **(4536)**
2001: 5³GF, 5⁰GF, 6⁰G, 6⁰GF

	Starts	1st	2nd	3rd	Win & Pl
Career Total (Turf)	4	0	0	1	387

Going (Turf): Sf: 0-0 GS: 0-0 Gd: 0-1 GF: 0-3 Fm: 0-0
Distance: 5f/6f: 0-4 7f-8f: 0-0 9f-13f: 0-0 14f+: 0-0
Track : LH: 0-1 RH: 0-0 Tight: 0-0 Gall: 0-0
Aids: Bl: 0-0 Vi: 0-0 Tstrap: 0-0
Best Rating: 65 6/01 Nott 5f13y gd-fm

Rita's Rock Ape

106(101) (67+)**83**

6-y-o b m Mon Tresor-Failand (Kala Shikari)
R Brotherton Mrs Janet Pearce

Placings:00422/30060323**354**/6**004111132130**/006001 002120-54016563206002 **(5349)**
2001: 5⁵G, 5⁴F, 5⁰F, 5¹GF, 5⁶GF, 5⁵GF, 5⁶GS, 5³GF, 5²GF, 5⁰G, 5⁶G, 5⁰G, 5⁰G, 5²SD

	Starts	1st	2nd	3rd	Win & Pl
Career Total (Turf)	49	8	7	6	41754
Career Total (AW)	6	0	1	1	1053
82 6/01 Sals 5f	D(0-85)H			G-F	£7475
73 8/00 Brig 5f59y	D(0-80)H			FRM	£3916
69 7/00 Chep 5f16y	E(0-70)H			FRM	£3013
79 9/99 Sals 5f	E(0-80)H			G-F	£2765
62 7/99 Brig 5f59y	F(0-60)			FRM	£2571
61 7/99 Ling 5f	E(0-70)H			G-F	£2791
65 7/99 Bath 5f11y	F(0-65)H			G-F	£2207
54 6/99 Brig 5f59y	F(0-60)H			GD	£2697

Total win prize-money £27440

Going (Turf): Sf: 0-1 GS: 0-3 Gd: 1-15 **GF: 4-23** Fm: 3-7
Distance: **5f/6f: 8-54** 7f-8f: 0-1 9f-13f: 0-0 14f+: 0-0
Track : **LH: 4-20** RH: 0-2 Tight: 0-5 **Gall: 1-9**
Aids: Bl: 0-0 Vi: 0-0 Tstrap: 0-0
Best Rating: 83 8/01 Bath 5f11y gd-fm

She has bags of pace, and continued to find races when allowed to lead, as at Salisbury in June 2001. A sharp five furlongs and fast ground are what she needs.

Rival (IRE)

95 **83**

2-y-o b c Desert Style (IRE)-Arab Scimetar (IRE) (Sure Blade (USA))
P F I Cole Highclere Thoroughbred Racing Ltd

Placings:32 **(4454)**
2001: 6³GF, 6²GF

	Starts	1st	2nd	3rd	Win & Pl
Career Total (Turf)	2	0	1	1	3280

Going (Turf): Sf: 0-0 GS: 0-0 Gd: 0-0 GF: 0-2 Fm: 0-0
Distance: 5f/6f: 0-1 7f-8f: 0-1 9f-13f: 0-0 14f+: 0-0
Track : LH: 0-0 RH: 0-0 Tight: 0-0 Gall: 0-0
Aids: Bl: 0-0 Vi: 0-0 Tstrap: 0-0
Best Rating: 83 9/01 York 6f gd-fm

Rivelli (IRE)

89 **76**

2-y-o b f Lure (USA)-Kama Tashoof (Mtoto)
P F I Cole Faisal Salman

Placings:55 **(5014)**
2001: 6⁵GF, 8⁵HY

	Starts	1st	2nd	3rd	Win & Pl
Career Total (Turf)	2	0	0	0	0

Going (Turf): Sf: 0-1 GS: 0-0 Gd: 0-0 GF: 0-1 Fm: 0-0
Distance: 5f/6f: 0-0 7f-8f: 0-1 9f-13f: 0-1 14f+: 0-0
Track : LH: 0-1 RH: 0-0 Tight: 0-0 Gall: 0-0
Aids: Bl: 0-0 Vi: 0-0 Tstrap: 0-0
Best Rating: 76 9/01 Sals 6f212y gd-fm

River Blest (IRE)

89(78) (24)**27**

5-y-o b g Unblest-Vaal Salmon (IRE) (Salmon Leap (USA))

Mrs A Duffield Turf 2000 Limited

Placings:00336/500203-0000000 **(5287)**
2001: 5^0S, 5^0GF, 5^0G, 7^0GF, 6^0GF, 5^0G, 6^0HY

	Starts	1st	2nd	3rd	Win & Pl
Career Total (Turf)	17	0	1	3	1879
Career Total (AW)	1	0	0	0	

Going (Turf): Sf: 0-3 GS: 0-2 Gd: 0-6 GF: 0-6 Fm: 0-0
Distance: 5f/6f: 0-10 7f-8f: 0-8 9f-13f: 0-0 14f+: 0-0
Track : LH: 0-3 RH: 0-2 Tight: 0-2 Gall: 0-0
Aids: Bl: 0-0 Vi: 0-0 Tstrap: 0-0
Best Rating: 36 5/01 Muss 5f gd-fm

River Boy (IRE)

5-y-o b g River Falls-Natty Gann (IRE) (Mister Majestic)
G Brown R C Blackman

Placings:04600/6520666/0 **(0120)**
2001: 14^0SW

	Starts	1st	2nd	3rd	Win & Pl
Career Total (Turf)	8	0	1	0	665
Career Total (AW)	5	0	0	0	0

Going (Turf): Sf: 0-0 GS: 0-1 Gd: 0-4 GF: 0-3 Fm: 0-0
Distance: 5f/6f: 0-0 7f-8f: 0-5 9f-13f: 0-7 14f+: 0-1
Track : LH: 0-7 RH: 0-1 Tight: 0-4 Gall: 0-1
Aids: Bl: 0-1 Vi: 0-2 Tstrap: 0-0

River Canyon (IRE)

100 **49**
5-y-o b g College Chapel-Na-Ammah (IRE) (Ela-Mana-Mou)
W Storey Tony Stafford

Placings:1/334/0-205 **(2337)**
2001: 9^2GS, 9^0G, 10^5GF

	Starts	1st	2nd	3rd	Win & Pl
Career Total (Turf)	8	1	1	2	11034

85	6/98	Tipp	7f	SH	£3767

Total win prize-money £3768

Going (Turf): Sf: 0-2 GS: 0-1 Gd: 0-2 GF: 0-1 Fm: 0-0
Distance: 5f/6f: 0-0 **7f-8f: 1-3** 9f-13f: 0-5 14f+: 0-0
Track : **LH: 1-2** RH: 0-4 Tight: 0-2 Gall: 0-1
Aids: Bl: 0-1 Vi: 0-0 Tstrap: 0-0
Best Rating: 49 5/01 Haml 1m1f36y gd-sft

River Ensign

101(103) (54d)**56**
8-y-o br m River God (ZIM)-Ensigns Kit (Saucy Kit)
W M Brisbourne Mrs Mary Brisbourne

Placings:00403451003354/1533420551002446500305 60/320205120002523410040621300416010360131005 -3266060 **(4558)**
2001: 9^3SD, 9^2HY, 12^6S, 9^6HY, 9^0HY, 12^6SD, 9^0SW

	Starts	1st	2nd	3rd	Win & Pl
Career Total (Turf)	32	5	1	4	19798
Career Total (AW)	55	5	8	8	22160

54	11/00	Wolv	1m1f79y	E(0-75)H	STD	£2884
56	5/00	Sthl	1m2f	E(0-75)H	HVY	£2926
49	4/00	Sthl	1m2f	F(0-65)H	G-S	£2415
48	2/00	Wolv	1m1f79y	E(0-70)H	STD	£2743
47	1/00	Wolv	1m1f79y	F	STD	£2289
50	9/99	Ches	1m2f75y	E(0-70)H	HVY	£3172
50	4/99	Wolv	6f	G	STD	£1553
44	4/98	Nott	6f15y	F(0-70)H	SFT	£3473
36	1/98	Sthl	6f	E(0-70)H	STD	£2749
41	8/97	Thsk	6f	E(0-70)H	G-F	£3874

Total win prize-money £28079

Going (Turf): Sf: 3-15 GS: 1-6 Gd: 0-5 GF: 1-6 Fm: 0-0
Distance: 5f/6f: 3-32 7f-8f: 1-20 **9f-13f: 6-35** 14f+: 0-0
Track : **LH: 6-67** RH: 0-3 **Tight: 5-48** Gall: 0-0

Aids: Bl: 0-0 Vi: 0-0 Tstrap: 0-0
Best Rating: 56 3/01 Nott 1m1f213y heavy

She has been a busy girl, but pays her way and is an effective sort when able to dominate. Suited by trips of around ten furlongs on Fibresand or soft turf.

River Kwai

60
4-y-o ch f Anshan-Brilliant (Never So Bold)
J J Bridger Mrs Julie Jenner

Placings:000 **(3425)**
2001: 9^0GS, 11^0GF, 9^0GF

	Starts	1st	2nd	3rd	Win & Pl
Career Total (Turf)	3	0	0	0	

Going (Turf): Sf: 0-0 GS: 0-1 Gd: 0-0 GF: 0-2 Fm: 0-0
Distance: 5f/6f: 0-0 7f-8f: 0-0 9f-13f: 0-3 14f+: 0-0
Track : LH: 0-0 RH: 0-2 Tight: 0-3 Gall: 0-0
Aids: Bl: 0-1 Vi: 0-0 Tstrap: 0-0

River Light (IRE)

94 **50**
3-y-o b c Bahri (USA)-Sister Troy (USA) (Far North (CAN))
G Wragg Mollers Racing

Placings:00600 **(4899)**
2001: 7^0S, 8^0GS, 8^6GF, 7^0GF, 8^0GS

	Starts	1st	2nd	3rd	Win & Pl
Career Total (Turf)	5	0	0	0	0

Going (Turf): Sf: 0-1 GS: 0-2 Gd: 0-0 GF: 0-2 Fm: 0-0
Distance: 5f/6f: 0-0 7f-8f: 0-3 9f-13f: 0-2 14f+: 0-0
Track : LH: 0-0 RH: 0-2 Tight: 0-1 Gall: 0-0
Aids: Bl: 0-0 Vi: 0-0 Tstrap: 0-0
Best Rating: 50 7/01 Wind 1m67y gd-fm

River Master

97 **70**
2-y-o b c Most Welcome-River Spey (Mill Reef (USA))
I A Balding Duncan R Lofts & David R Watson

Placings:004 **(5466)**
2001: 7^0GF, 8^0GS, 6^4S

	Starts	1st	2nd	3rd	Win & Pl
Career Total (Turf)	3	0	0	0	0

Going (Turf): Sf: 0-1 GS: 0-1 Gd: 0-0 GF: 0-1 Fm: 0-0
Distance: 5f/6f: 0-0 7f-8f: 0-3 9f-13f: 0-0 14f+: 0-0
Track : LH: 0-1 RH: 0-0 Tight: 0-0 Gall: 0-0
Aids: Bl: 0-0 Vi: 0-0 Tstrap: 0-0
Best Rating: 70 10/01 Brig 6f209y soft

River Nymph

103(64) (8)**68**
3-y-o ch f Cadeaux Genereux-La Riveraine (USA) (Riverman (USA))
Sir Michael Stoute J H Richmond-Watson

Placings:02350 **(5394)**
2001: 8^0GF, 6^2GF, 7^3F, 6^5G, 12^0SD

	Starts	1st	2nd	3rd	Win & Pl
Career Total (Turf)	4	0	1	1	1575
Career Total (AW)	1	0	0	0	

Going (Turf): Sf: 0-0 GS: 0-0 Gd: 0-1 GF: 0-2 Fm: 0-1
Distance: 5f/6f: 0-0 7f-8f: 0-4 9f-13f: 0-1 14f+: 0-0
Track : LH: 0-3 RH: 0-1 Tight: 0-3 Gall: 0-0
Aids: Bl: 0-0 Vi: 0-0 Tstrap: 0-0
Best Rating: 68 7/01 Thsk 7f firm

River Of Fire

95(81) (40)**61**
3-y-o ch g Dilum (USA)-Bracey Brook (Gay Fandango (USA))
J M P Eustace Park Lodge Racing

Placings:01150-0036450 **(3233)**
2001: 7^0SD, 10^0GS, 10^3GS, 10^6GF, 14^4GF, 12^5GF, 12^0SD

	Starts	1st	2nd	3rd	Win & Pl
Career Total (Turf)	9	2	0	1	4288
Career Total (AW)	3	0	0	0	

59	8/00	Leic	5f218y	G	G-F	£1991
53	7/00	Yarm	7f3y	G	G-F	£1865

Total win prize-money £3858

Going (Turf): Sf: 0-1 GS: 0-2 Gd: 0-0 **GF: 2-6** Fm: 0-0
Distance: 5f/6f: 1-2 7f-8f: 1-4 9f-13f: 0-5 14f+: 0-1
Track : LH: 0-6 RH: 0-1 Tight: 0-5 Gall: 0-1
Aids: Bl: 0-0 **Vi: 1-2** Tstrap: 0-0
Best Rating: 61 5/01 Bath 1m2f46y gd-sft

River Reine (IRE)

95 **80**
2-y-o br f Lahib (USA)-Talahari (IRE) (Roi Danzig (USA))
B W Hills Stephen Crown

Placings:5215 **(5368)**
2001: 6^5GF, 7^2GF, 7^1HY, 8^5GS

	Starts	1st	2nd	3rd	Win & Pl
Career Total (Turf)	4	1	1	0	5110

80	9/01	Hayd	7f30y	D	HVY	£4355

Total win prize-money £4355

Going (Turf): Sf: 1-1 GS: 0-1 Gd: 0-0 GF: 0-2 Fm: 0-0
Distance: 5f/6f: 0-0 **7f-8f: 1-4** 9f-13f: 0-0 14f+: 0-0
Track : **LH: 1-2** RH: 0-0 Tight: 0-0 Gall: 0-0
Aids: Bl: 0-0 Vi: 0-0 Tstrap: 0-0
Best Rating: 80 9/01 Hayd 7f30y heavy

Found the testing ground bringing her stamina into play when getting off the mark on her third outing at two over seven furlongs at Haydock.

River Tern

99(85) (38)**54**
8-y-o b g Puissance-Millaine (Formidable (USA))
J M Bradley Martyn James, Pete Smith, Neil Jenkins

Placings:034/520331000/20140315641600/030054230 6/313341002456045/6060003600000035-362000000 **(5349)**
2001: 5^3G, 5^6G, 5^2G, 5^0GF, 5^0GF, 5^0G, 5^0GS, 5^0G, 5^0SD

	Starts	1st	2nd	3rd	Win & Pl
Career Total (Turf)	74	6	5	12	40775
Career Total (AW)	2	0	0	0	0

68	7/99	York	5f	C(0-95)H	G-F	£7375
60	5/99	Thsk	5f	D(0-80)H	G-F	£4211
62	8/97	Catt	5f	F	G-F	£2616
64	7/97	Wwck	5f	E(0-70)H	G-F	£3018
65	5/97	Rdcr	6f	F	GD	£2810
59	9/96	Thsk	6f		G-F	£4367

Total win prize-money £24397

Going (Turf): Sf: 0-0 GS: 0-5 Gd: 1-26 **GF: 5-34** Fm: 0-9
Distance: **5f/6f: 6-72** 7f-8f: 0-4 9f-13f: 0-0 14f+: 0-0
Track : **LH: 1-12** RH: 0-3 Tight: 0-1 **Gall: 1-9**
Aids: Bl: 0-1 **Vi: 1-4** Tstrap: 0-0
Best Rating: 54 6/01 Bath 5f161y good

Has won over six furlongs but looks better on fast ground over five. He has run well in the last couple of seasons, but is currently on a long losing run.

River Trail

90(59) (1)**53**
3-y-o b g Catrail (USA)-River Maiden (USA) (Riverman (USA))
M Brittain Northgate October

Placings:40 (2979)
2001: 7^{4}G, 6^{0}SD

	Starts	1st	2nd	3rd	Win & Pl
Career Total (Turf)	1	0	0	0	325
Career Total (AW)	1	0	0	0	

Going (Turf): Sf: 0-0 GS: 0-0 Gd: 0-1 GF: 0-0 Fm: 0-0
Distance: 5f/6f: 0-1 7f-8f: 0-1 9f-13f: 0-0 14f+: 0-0
Track : LH: 0-2 RH: 0-0 Tight: 0-2 Gall: 0-0
Aids: Bl: 0-0 Vi: 0-0 Tstrap: 0-0
Best Rating: 53 6/01 Thsk 7f good

Riverblue (IRE)

106(102) (60)75
5-y-o b g Bluebird (USA)-La Riveraine (USA) (Riverman (USA))
D J Wintle Mrs Joan L Egan

Placings:342151/020500040/0051534046-5344416504000 (5293)
2001: 8^{5}SD, 11^{3}SW, 9^{4}SD, 8^{4}SD, 8^{4}S, 8^{1}HY, 10^{6}S, 10^{5}GS, 11^{0}SD, 9^{4}G, 10^{0}G, 10^{0}S, 9^{0}S

	Starts	1st	2nd	3rd	Win & Pl
Career Total (Turf)	24	3	2	1	30191
Career Total (AW)	14	1	0	2	2521

72 4/01 Nott 1m54y E(0-70)H HVY £3150
63 2/00 Wolv 1m1f79y F(0-60)H STD £1928
91 8/98 Thsk 6f D G-F £4341
76 8/98 Catt 7f D GD £3366
Total win prize-money £12786

Going (Turf): Sf: 1-8 GS: 0-3 Gd: 1-6 GF: 1-7 Fm: 0-0
Distance: 5f/6f: 1-3 7f-8f: 1-9 9f-13f: 2-26 14f+: 0-0
Track : LH: 3-27 RH: 0-7 Tight: 2-12 Gall: 0-6
Aids: Bl: 0-0 Vi: 0-2 Tstrap: 0-0
Best Rating: 75 9/01 Sand 1m1f good

Useful handicapper on turf, he has been busy on the All-Weather prior to finishing fourth in the Spring Mile at Doncaster and followed up with a success at Nottingham. Unlucky when returning from a break at Sandown in September. Best at around a mile in the mud.

Riverina (USA)

104(91) (60)82
3-y-o ch f Irish River (FR)-Pattimech (USA) (Nureyev (USA))
J L Dunlop Littleton Manor Racing

Placings:5110 (5486)
2001: 7^{5}GS, 7^{1}G, 8^{1}GS, 10^{0}HY, 10^{0}SD

	Starts	1st	2nd	3rd	Win & Pl
Career Total (Turf)	4	2	0	0	17459

82 10/01 York 1m205y D(0-80)H G-S £13741
75 5/01 Thsk 7f D GD £3718
Total win prize-money £17459

Going (Turf): Sf: 0-1 GS: 1-2 Gd: 1-1 GF: 0-0 Fm: 0-0
Distance: 5f/6f: 0-0 7f-8f: 1-2 9f-13f: 1-2 14f+: 0-0
Track : LH: 2-3 RH: 0-0 Tight: 1-1 Gall: 1-2
Aids: Bl: 0-0 Vi: 0-0 Tstrap: 0-0
Best Rating: 82 10/01 York 1m205y gd-sft

Won 7f good ground Thirsk maiden on her second start. and followed up in a York handicap.

Riversdale (IRE)

100(97) (46)43
5-y-o b g Elbio-Embustera (Sparkler)
J G Fitzgerald Mrs R A G Haggie

Placings:06/340020/06-2600 (5450)
2001: 8^{2}SW, 8^{6}S, 8^{0}GS, 8^{0}HY

	Starts	1st	2nd	3rd	Win & Pl
Career Total (Turf)	12	0	1	1	1901
Career Total (AW)	2	0	1	0	632

Going (Turf): Sf: 0-6 GS: 0-1 Gd: 0-5 GF: 0-0 Fm: 0-0
Distance: 5f/6f: 0-1 7f-8f: 0-5 9f-13f: 0-8 14f+: 0-0
Track : LH: 0-8 RH: 0-4 Tight: 0-6 Gall: 0-1
Aids: Bl: 0-0 Vi: 0-0 Tstrap: 0-0
Best Rating: 46 2/01 Sthl 1m slow

Riyadh

111(94) (63)87
3-y-o ch g Caerleon (USA)-Ausherra (USA) (Diesis)
P F I Cole Newgate Stud

Placings:02512220011 (5143)
2001: 8^{0}S, 8^{2}SD, 10^{5}GS, 11^{1}F, 14^{2}GS, 14^{2}G, 15^{2}GF, 14^{0}G, 13^{0}G, 16^{1}GF, 14^{1}G

	Starts	1st	2nd	3rd	Win & Pl
Career Total (Turf)	10	3	3	0	30005
Career Total (AW)	1	0	1	0	812

87 10/01 NmkR 1m6f C(0-95)H GD £13975
87 9/01 Gdwd 2m D(0-85)H G-F £5411
70 5/01 Leic 1m3f183yE(0-70)H FRM £3167
Total win prize-money £22554

Going (Turf): Sf: 0-1 GS: 0-2 Gd: 1-4 GF: 1-2 Fm: 1-1
Distance: 5f/6f: 0-0 7f-8f: 0-2 9f-13f: 1-2 14f+: 2-7
Track : LH: 0-4 RH: 3-5 Tight: 1-7 Gall: 1-2
Aids: Bl: 3-6 Vi: 0-1 Tstrap: 0-0
Best Rating: 87 10/01 NmkR 1m6f good

He held a Derby entry at one time, but failed to live up to those expectations and is a notoriously difficult ride. Got off mark when stepped up to a mile and a half at Leicester in May and successfully stepped up to two miles at Goodwood in September, before following up over 14 furlongs at Newmarket. Often blinkered and acts on good and fast ground. Has joined M. Pipe.

Rizerie (FR)

102 96
3-y-o gr f Highest Honor (FR)-Riziere (FR) (Groom Dancer (USA))
L M Cumani Robert H Smith

Placings:12030-0300 (5007)
2001: 7^{0}G, 10^{3}GF, 10^{0}F, 8^{0}S

	Starts	1st	2nd	3rd	Win & Pl
Career Total (Turf)	9	1	1	2	12656

69 6/00 Gdwd 7f D G-F £4231
Total win prize-money £4232

Going (Turf): Sf: 0-1 GS: 0-0 Gd: 0-3 GF: 1-4 Fm: 0-1
Distance: 5f/6f: 0-0 7f-8f: 1-7 9f-13f: 0-2 14f+: 0-0
Track : LH: 0-3 RH: 1-2 Tight: 0-0 Gall: 0-3
Aids: Bl: 0-0 Vi: 0-0 Tstrap: 0-0
Best Rating: 96 6/01 Newb 1m2f6y gd-fm

Won an ordinary maiden at Goodwood on her debut but has proved difficult to place since. Stays ten furlongs. Acts on fast ground.

Road To Justice

98 88
2-y-o ch c Danehill Dancer (IRE)-Hopesay (Warning)
J H M Gosden Mrs B V Sangster & Hugo Lascelles

Placings:26100 (5150)
2001: 6^{2}G, 6^{6}GF, 6^{1}GF, 6^{0}GF, 6^{0}G

	Starts	1st	2nd	3rd	Win & Pl
Career Total (Turf)	5	1	1	0	5120

86 9/01 Rdcr 6f F G-F £2579
Total win prize-money £2580

Going (Turf): Sf: 0-0 GS: 0-0 Gd: 0-2 GF: 1-3 Fm: 0-0
Distance: 5f/6f: 1-4 7f-8f: 0-1 9f-13f: 0-0 14f+: 0-0
Track : LH: 0-0 RH: 0-0 Tight: 0-0 Gall: 0-0
Aids: Bl: 0-0 Vi: 0-0 Tstrap: 0-0
Best Rating: 88 9/01 Newb 6f8y gd-fm

Easy winner of a modest Redcar maiden on his third start, he was anything but disgraced when beaten less than five lengths in the Mill Reef next time out.

Roaming Ronan (IRE)

72 51?
3-y-o b g Sri Pekan (USA)-Maradata (IRE) (Shardari)
J J O'Neill Mrs Jonjo O'Neill

Placings:04 (3829)
2001: 8^{0}GS, 11^{4}G

	Starts	1st	2nd	3rd	Win & Pl
Career Total (Turf)	2	0	0	0	339

Going (Turf): Sf: 0-0 GS: 0-1 Gd: 0-1 GF: 0-0 Fm: 0-0
Distance: 5f/6f: 0-0 7f-8f: 0-0 9f-13f: 0-2 14f+: 0-0
Track : LH: 0-1 RH: 0-0 Tight: 0-0 Gall: 0-0
Aids: Bl: 0-0 Vi: 0-0 Tstrap: 0-0
Best Rating: 51 8/01 Hayd 1m3f200y good

Roaring Twenties

105 80
3-y-o ch f Halling (USA)-Flower Girl (Pharly (FR))
M A Jarvis W J Gredley

Placings:2215 (5558)
2001: 7^{2}GS, 6^{2}G, 8^{1}G, 10^{5}S

	Starts	1st	2nd	3rd	Win & Pl
Career Total (Turf)	4	1	2	0	6468

80 9/01 Sand 1m14y D GD £3900
Total win prize-money £3900

Going (Turf): Sf: 0-1 GS: 0-1 Gd: 1-2 GF: 0-0 Fm: 0-0
Distance: 5f/6f: 0-1 7f-8f: 0-1 9f-13f: 1-2 14f+: 0-0
Track : LH: 0-1 RH: 1-1 Tight: 0-1 Gall: 0-0
Aids: Bl: 0-0 Vi: 0-0 Tstrap: 0-0
Best Rating: 80 9/01 Sand 1m14y good

Finished runner-up in her first two starts before getting off the mark with a hard-fought victory over a mile at Sandown in September. That trip looked about as far as she wanted to go.

Roassi (IRE)

89 62
2-y-o ch f Pennekamp (USA)-Virelai (Kris)
C E Brittain Saeed Manana

Placings:000 (4985)
2001: 7^{0}GF, 6^{0}GF, 6^{0}G

	Starts	1st	2nd	3rd	Win & Pl
Career Total (Turf)	3	0	0	0	

Going (Turf): Sf: 0-0 GS: 0-0 Gd: 0-1 GF: 0-2 Fm: 0-0
Distance: 5f/6f: 0-0 7f-8f: 0-3 9f-13f: 0-0 14f+: 0-0
Track : LH: 0-1 RH: 0-0 Tight: 0-0 Gall: 0-0
Aids: Bl: 0-0 Vi: 0-0 Tstrap: 0-0
Best Rating: 62 9/01 Brig 6f209y gd-fm

Rob Leach

107 80
4-y-o b g Robellino (USA)-Arc Empress Jane (IRE) (Rainbow Quest (USA))
G L Moore Richard Green (fine Paintings)

Placings:52655-3522 (4280)
2001: 12^{3}S, 12^{5}GS, 10^{2}G, 9^{2}GS

	Starts	1st	2nd	3rd	Win & Pl
Career Total (Turf)	9	0	3	1	5436

Going (Turf): Sf: 0-1 GS: 0-4 Gd: 0-3 GF: 0-1 Fm: 0-0
Distance: 5f/6f: 0-0 7f-8f: 0-2 9f-13f: 0-7 14f+: 0-0
Track : LH: 0-2 RH: 0-6 Tight: 0-5 Gall: 0-1
Aids: Bl: 0-0 Vi: 0-0 Tstrap: 0-0
Best Rating: 80 8/01 Gdwd 1m1f192y gd-sft

He has yet to win but has proved his effectiveness over ten as well as 12 furlongs. Best with some cut.

Robandela (USA)

107(109) (78)83

4-y-o b g Kingmambo (USA)-Yemanja (USA) (Alleged (USA))

M Johnston Robert Aird

Placings:0/11533014001050001010 1 (5669)

2001: 12¹SD, 12¹SD, 12⁵SD, 14³SW, 12³SD, 12⁰GS, 13¹S, 14⁰GS, 12⁰S, 12⁰GF, 12¹G, 12⁰S, 12⁵GF, 14⁰GF, 11⁰G, 13⁰GF, 9¹GF, 10⁰G, 12¹G, 10⁰HY, 10¹HY

	Starts	1st	2nd	3rd	Win & Pl
Career Total (Turf)	17	5	0	0	26243
Career Total (AW)	5	2	0	2	6891

83	11/01	Wind	1m2f7y	C(0-90)H	HVY	£7702
76	9/01	Gdwd	1m4f	D(0-75)	GD	£4602
79	9/01	Leic	1m1f218y	E(0-75)H	G-F	£3269
80	5/01	NmkR	1m4f	C(0-100)H	GD	£6293
78	4/01	Muss	1m5f	D(0-85)H	SFT	£4095
76	1/01	Wolv	1m4f	E(0-70)H	STD	£2912
56	1/01	Sthl	1m4f	D	STD	£2975

Total win prize-money £31849

Going (Turf): Sf: 2-5 GS: 0-2 **Gd: 2-4** GF: 1-6 Fm: 0-0
Distance: 5f/6f: 0-0 7f-8f: 0-1 **9f-13f: 7-17** 14f+: 0-4
Track: LH: 2-13 **RH: 4-7 Tight: 4-6** Gall: 1-9
Aids: **Bl: 5-15** Vi: 0-0 Tstrap: 0-0
Best Rating: 83 11/01 Wind 1m2f7y heavy

Won twice on the All-Weather in January and has added five more wins on turf. Not altogether consistent though. He is suited by 12 furlongs and goes well in blinkers.

Robber Red

92(92) (26)38

5-y-o b g Mon Tresor-Starisk (Risk Me (FR))

R M Flower The Secret Circle Ii

Placings:54202251202 5/50006205006 0/00000-00000 (2703)

2001: 7⁰F, 7⁰GF, 7⁰F, 6⁰F, 9⁰F

	Starts	1st	2nd	3rd	Win & Pl
Career Total (Turf)	31	1	6	0	7878
Career Total (AW)	3	0	0	0	

78	8/98	Ling	6f	F	FRM	£1972

Total win prize-money £1972

Going (Turf): Sf: 0-2 GS: 0-3 Gd: 0-6 GF: 0-10 **Fm: 1-10**
Distance: **5f/6f: 1-13** 7f-8f: 0-18 9f-13f: 0-3 14f+: 0-0
Track: LH: 0-15 RH: 0-2 Tight: 0-2 Gall: 0-1
Aids: Bl: 0-2 Vi: 0-0 Tstrap: 0-1
Best Rating: 38 5/01 Ling 7f gd-fm

Robbie Can Can

88 74

2-y-o b c Robellino (USA)-Can Can Lady (Anshan)

J G Given A W Robinson

Placings:5 (5250)

2001: 6⁵S

	Starts	1st	2nd	3rd	Win & Pl
Career Total (Turf)	1	0	0	0	0

Going (Turf): Sf: 0-1 GS: 0-0 Gd: 0-0 GF: 0-0 Fm: 0-0
Distance: 5f/6f: 0-1 7f-8f: 0-0 9f-13f: 0-0 14f+: 0-0
Track: LH: 0-0 RH: 0-0 Tight: 0-0 Gall: 0-0
Aids: Bl: 0-0 Vi: 0-0 Tstrap: 0-0
Best Rating: 74 10/01 York 6f soft

Robbies Dream (IRE)

(104) (58)41

5-y-o ch g Balla Cove-Royal Golden (IRE) (Digamist (USA))

R M H Cowell James Brown

Placings:0060/000/5001212304 0-00615100 (4071)

2001: 8⁰SD, 8⁰SW, 7⁶SD, 8¹SD, 8⁵SD, 8¹SD, 8⁰GS, 8⁰SD

	Starts	1st	2nd	3rd	Win & Pl
Career Total (Turf)	10	0	0	0	0
Career Total (AW)	16	4	2	1	12993

56	7/01	Sthl	1m	D(0-85)H	STD	£3900
50	7/01	Sthl	1m	F(0-60)H	STD	£2359
53	8/00	Wolv	1m100y	E(0-70)H	STD	£2779
43	7/00	Sthl	1m	F(0-60)H	STD	£1799

Total win prize-money £10837

Going (Turf): Sf: 0-1 GS: 0-2 Gd: 0-4 GF: 0-1 Fm: 0-2
Distance: 5f/6f: 0-3 **7f-8f: 3-15** 9f-13f: 1-8 14f+: 0-0
Track: **LH: 4-19** RH: 0-1 **Tight: 1-4** Gall: 0-0
Aids: Bl: 0-0 Vi: 0-1 **Tstrap: 4-16**
Best Rating: 56 7/01 Sthl 1m stand

Moderate handicapper, best on Fibresand, suited by a strongly-run race.

Robbo

102 (70)57

7-y-o b g Robellino (USA)-Basha (USA) (Chief's Crown (USA))

Mrs M Reveley The Scarth Racing Partnership

Placings:55602351061132/330/6/64-51 (5402)

2001: 15⁵GS, 17¹S

	Starts	1st	2nd	3rd	Win & Pl
Career Total (Turf)	12	1	1	4	6985
Career Total (AW)	10	3	1	0	6687

57	10/01	Pont	2m1f216y	E(0-70)H	SFT	£3656
70	10/97	Wolv	1m6f166y	G(0-60)H	STD	£1984
63	9/97	Wolv	1m6f166y	F(0-60)	STD	£2070
61	8/97	Sthl	1m6f	G(0-65)H	STD	£1984

Total win prize-money £9696

Going (Turf): Sf: 1-6 GS: 0-3 Gd: 0-3 GF: 0-0 Fm: 0-0
Distance: 5f/6f: 0-0 7f-8f: 0-3 9f-13f: 0-4 **14f+: 4-15**
Track: **LH: 4-19** RH: 0-3 **Tight: 2-11** Gall: 0-2
Aids: **Bl: 3-12** Vi: 0-0 Tstrap: 0-0
Best Rating: 57 10/01 Pont 2m1f216y soft

Rarely runs on the Flat these days and when he does it is usually just a pipe opener, but did win a moderate handicap at Pontefract over 2m2f.

Robe Chinoise

97 79

2-y-o b f Robellino (USA)-Kiliniski (Niniski (USA))

J L Dunlop Miss K Rausing

Placings:0020 (5589)

2001: 6⁰GF, 6⁰GF, 7²G, 7⁰GS

	Starts	1st	2nd	3rd	Win & Pl
Career Total (Turf)	4	0	1	0	1181

Going (Turf): Sf: 0-0 GS: 0-1 Gd: 0-1 GF: 0-2 Fm: 0-0
Distance: 5f/6f: 0-0 7f-8f: 0-4 9f-13f: 0-0 14f+: 0-0
Track: LH: 0-1 RH: 0-1 Tight: 0-0 Gall: 0-0
Aids: Bl: 0-0 Vi: 0-0 Tstrap: 0-0
Best Rating: 79 9/01 Bevl 7f100y good

Robellion

95(76) (55)56

10-y-o b g Robellino (USA)-Tickled Trout (Red Alert)

Miss E C Lavelle The Forty Ninth Partnership

Placings:13/0000320000/0432452104020000000044/13 13035002114004655 0/20223360006640051034 62/2213 151520630/100000/513000-400 (2173)

2001: 7⁴G, 8⁰GF, 7⁰SD

	Starts	1st	2nd	3rd	Win & Pl
Career Total (Turf)	72	7	6	6	35297
Career Total (AW)	31	5	6	6	20836

51	6/00	Ling	7f	F(0-75)H	G-S	£2324
58	5/99	Ling	7f	F(0-75)H	G-F	£2721
67	3/98	Sthl	7f	F(0-75)H	STD	£1871
62	2/98	Ling	1m	F(0-65)	SLW	£2169
62	1/98	Ling	1m	E	STD	£2832
53	10/97	Sals	6f	F(0-70)H	GD	£2721
69	8/96	NmkJ	6f	C(0-90)H	G-F	£6004
63	7/96	Chep	5f16y	E(0-70)H	G-F	£2953
62	2/96	Ling	1m2f	F(0-65)H	STD	£2695
55	1/96	Ling	1m	F(0-65)H	STD	£2811
69	7/95	Chep	5f16y	E(0-70)H	G-F	£3220
79	5/93	Bath	5f11y	F	FRM	£2833

Total win prize-money £35158

Going (Turf): Sf: 0-5 GS: 1-7 Gd: 1-17 **GF: 4-36** Fm: 1-7
Distance: 5f/6f: 5-45 **7f-8f: 6-47** 9f-13f: 1-11 14f+: 0-0
Track: **LH: 6-40** RH: 0-6 **Tight: 4-28** Gall: 1-9
Aids: Bl: 0-2 **Vi: 5-47** Tstrap: 0-0
Best Rating: 56 5/01 Ling 7f good

Robellita

70(92) (61)57d

7-y-o b g Robellino (USA)-Miellita (King Emperor (USA))

B G Powell Angels Racing Syndicate

Placings:000/2321126/000-0 (1076)

2001: 11⁰GS

	Starts	1st	2nd	3rd	Win & Pl
Career Total (Turf)	6	1	0	0	3199
Career Total (AW)	8	1	3	1	5916

57	3/99	Nott	1m6f15y	E(0-70)H	G-S	£3199
64	3/99	Sthl	1m4f	D	STD	£2815

Total win prize-money £6014

Going (Turf): Sf: 0-1 **GS: 1-4** Gd: 0-1 GF: 0-0 Fm: 0-0
Distance: 5f/6f: 0-0 7f-8f: 0-0 9f-13f: 1-11 14f+: 1-3
Track: **LH: 2-12** RH: 0-1 Tight: 0-6 Gall: 0-0
Aids: Bl: 0-0 Vi: 0-0 Tstrap: 0-0
Best Rating: 13 5/01 Brig 1m3f196y gd-sft

Robin Hood

99 31

4-y-o b g Komaite (USA)-Plough Hill (North Briton)

Miss L A Perratt Cree Lodge Racing Club

Placings:0/00444061020034-00000203300000 (5287)

2001: 5⁰GS, 5⁰GF, 5⁰GF, 5⁰G, 5⁰GF, 5²GF, 5⁰G, 6³GS, 6³G, 5⁰GF, 5⁰S, 5⁰GF, 5⁰G, 6⁰HY

	Starts	1st	2nd	3rd	Win & Pl
Career Total (Turf)	29	1	2	3	7115

48	8/00	Haml	5f4y	F(0-60)H	SFT	£2996

Total win prize-money £2996

Going (Turf): Sf: 1-8 GS: 0-4 Gd: 0-7 GF: 0-10 Fm: 0-0
Distance: **5f/6f: 1-23** 7f-8f: 0-4 9f-13f: 0-2 14f+: 0-0
Track: LH: 0-1 RH: 0-3 Tight: 0-2 Gall: 0-1
Aids: Bl: 0-0 Vi: 0-0 Tstrap: 0-0
Best Rating: 42 6/01 Haml 5f4y gd-fm

A quirky sort who finds little under pressure. Best with ease in the ground.

Robin Sharp

81(102) (74)73

3-y-o ch c First Trump-Mo Stopher (Sharpo)

W Jarvis Canisbay Bloodstock Ltd

Placings:5522-13020 (2216)

2001: 7¹SW, 6³SD, 7⁰S, 7²SD, 7⁰G, 7⁰SD

	Starts	1st	2nd	3rd	Win & Pl
Career Total (Turf)	3	0	0	0	0
Career Total (AW)	6	1	3	1	5205

63	1/01	Wolv	7f	D	SLW	£2366

Total win prize-money £2366

Going (Turf): Sf: 0-2 GS: 0-0 Gd: 0-1 GF: 0-0 Fm: 0-0
Distance: 5f/6f: 0-5 **7f-8f: 1-4** 9f-13f: 0-0 14f+: 0-0
Track: **LH: 1-6** RH: 0-0 **Tight: 1-3** Gall: 0-0
Aids: Bl: 0-0 Vi: 0-0 Tstrap: 0-0
Best Rating: 69 5/01 Wolv 7f stand

Has shown fair form over six and seven furlongs on Fibresand, but has yet to translate that to turf.

Roboastar (USA)

93 **67**

4-y-o b/br g Green Dancer (USA)-Sweet Alabastar (USA) (Gulch (USA))

P G Murphy Mrs John Spielman

Placings:033/50-560 **(3496)**

2001: 12^{5}GF, 12^{6}G, 11^{0}GF

	Starts	1st	2nd	3rd	Win & Pl
Career Total (Turf)	8	0	0	2	1113

Going (Turf): Sf: 0-1 GS: 0-0 Gd: 0-3 GF: 0-4 Fm: 0-0
Distance: 5f/6f: 0-0 7f-8f: 0-2 9f-13f: 0-6 14f+: 0-0
Track : LH: 0-4 RH: 0-3 Tight: 0-2 Gall: 0-1
Aids: Bl: 0-0 Vi: 0-0 Tstrap: 0-0
Best Rating: 67 6/01 Wwck 1m4f134y gd-fm

Robzelda

108(88) (44)**52**

5-y-o b g Robellino (USA)-Zelda (USA) (Sharpen Up)

K A Ryan Tony Fawcett

Placings:43632434/313/325644000-0430364340033005 **(5448)**

2001: 8^{0}SW, 9^{4}HY, 8^{3}HY, 10^{0}S, 9^{3}F, 8^{6}F, 10^{4}G, 12^{3}G, 14^{4}F, 15^{0}GF, 11^{0}GF, 12^{3}G, 10^{3}G, 14^{0}G, 11^{0}S, 10^{5}HY

	Starts	1st	2nd	3rd	Win & Pl
Career Total (Turf)	35	1	2	11	17306
Career Total (AW)	1	0	0	0	

79 8/99 Leop 6f GD £4140
Total win prize-money £4140

Going (Turf): Sf: 0-8 GS: 0-4 **Gd: 1-12** GF: 0-3 Fm: 0-3
Distance: 5f/6f: 1-6 7f-8f: 0-12 9f-13f: 0-15 14f+: 0-3
Track : LH: 0-22 RH: 0-7 Tight: 0-12 Gall: 0-4
Aids: Bl: 1-10 Vi: 0-0 Tstrap: 0-0
Best Rating: 64 5/01 Rdcr 1m1f firm

Trained in Ireland before 2000, he has not shown a great deal in this country. Slightly quirky. Stays a mile and a half, but may be better at shorter. Has only one win to his name.

Roccioso

65 **5**

4-y-o br g Pelder (IRE)-Priory Bay (Petong)

J C Fox Mrs J A Cleary

Placings:00/00-0 **(2057)**

2001: 6^{0}GF

	Starts	1st	2nd	3rd	Win & Pl
Career Total (Turf)	5	0	0	0	

Going (Turf): Sf: 0-1 GS: 0-1 Gd: 0-1 GF: 0-2 Fm: 0-0
Distance: 5f/6f: 0-2 7f-8f: 0-2 9f-13f: 0-1 14f+: 0-0
Track : LH: 0-1 RH: 0-1 Tight: 0-1 Gall: 0-1
Aids: Bl: 0-0 Vi: 0-0 Tstrap: 0-0

Rock Concert

90 **58**

3-y-o b f Bishop Of Cashel-Summer Pageant (Chief's Crown (USA))

H Candy W M Lidsey

Placings:0-005 **(2232)**

2001: 10^{0}GS, 10^{0}GF, 8^{5}GS

	Starts	1st	2nd	3rd	Win & Pl
Career Total (Turf)	4	0	0	0	0

Going (Turf): Sf: 0-1 GS: 0-2 Gd: 0-0 GF: 0-1 Fm: 0-0
Distance: 5f/6f: 0-0 7f-8f: 0-2 9f-13f: 0-2 14f+: 0-0
Track : LH: 0-2 RH: 0-0 Tight: 0-2 Gall: 0-0
Aids: Bl: 0-0 Vi: 0-0 Tstrap: 0-0
Best Rating: 58 5/01 Ling 1m2f gd-fm

Rock Of Gibraltar (IRE)

109 **113**

2-y-o b c Danehill (USA)-Offshore Boom (Be My Guest (USA))

A P O'Brien Sir Alex Ferguson & Mrs John Magnier

Placings:1611211 **(5388)**

2001: 5^{1}S, 6^{6}GF, 6^{1}Y, 6^{1}G, 7^{2}GS, 7^{1}HO, 7^{1}GS

	Starts	1st	2nd	3rd	Win & Pl
Career Total (Turf)	7	5	1	0	382142

109 10/01 NmkR 7f A G-S £116000
110 10/01 Lonc 7f HLD £121242
105 8/01 York 6f A GD £72500
108 7/01 Curr 6f YLD £39000
93 4/01 Curr 5f SFT £10400
Total win prize-money £359142

Going (Turf): Sf: 1-1 GS: 1-2 Gd: 1-1 GF: 0-1 Fm: 0-0
Distance: 5f/6f: 3-4 7f-8f: 2-3 9f-13f: 0-0 14f+: 0-0
Track : LH: 0-0 **RH: 1-1** Tight: 0-0 Gall: 0-0
Aids: Bl: 0-0 Vi: 0-0 Tstrap: 0-0
Best Rating: 113 9/01 Donc 7f gd-sft

A comfortable winner of a Curragh maiden over the minimum trip on soft ground in April, he was unlucky in running at Royal Ascot, but made amends with a comfortable win in the Railway Stakes at the Curragh the following month. Followed up in the Gimcrack but, despite beating the others well enough, was cut to pieces by Dubai Destination in the Champagne Stakes at Doncaster. He took the Grand Criterium on very soft ground in impressive fashion, but only just landed the odds in the Dewhurst. He looks a Guineas possibility, although the stable have other options for that race, and a return to France for the Poulains may be on the cards.

Rock Scene (IRE)

91(78) **37**

9-y-o b g Scenic-Rockeater (Roan Rocket)

A Streeter Mrs J Hughes

Placings:545/0/6001000/20655410060-6050 **(4319)**

2001: 10^{6}S, 9^{0}F, 10^{5}GF, 10^{0}GF

	Starts	1st	2nd	3rd	Win & Pl
Career Total (Turf)	22	2	1	0	6296
Career Total (AW)	4	0	0	0	

51 7/00 Ripn 1m2f F G-S £2275
49 7/98 Wwck 1m2f169yF(0-65)H GD £3036
Total win prize-money £5311

Going (Turf): Sf: 0-7 **GS: 1-4 Gd: 1-5** GF: 0-5 Fm: 0-1
Distance: 5f/6f: 0-0 7f-8f: 0-4 **9f-13f: 2-22** 14f+: 0-0
Track : LH: 1-18 RH: 1-8 **Tight: 1-10** Gall: 0-2
Aids: Bl: 0-0 Vi: 0-0 Tstrap: 0-0
Best Rating: 37 6/01 Ches 1m2f75y gd-fm

Rock Steady

92 **59**

2-y-o b f Puissance-Just A Gem (Superlative)

E J Alston The Burlington Partnership

Placings:3062 **(1908)**

2001: 5^{3}S, 5^{0}S, 5^{6}GF, 5^{2}GF

	Starts	1st	2nd	3rd	Win & Pl
Career Total (Turf)	4	0	1	1	1653

Going (Turf): Sf: 0-2 GS: 0-0 Gd: 0-0 GF: 0-2 Fm: 0-0
Distance: 5f/6f: 0-4 7f-8f: 0-0 9f-13f: 0-0 14f+: 0-0
Track : LH: 0-2 RH: 0-0 Tight: 0-2 Gall: 0-0
Aids: Bl: 0-1 Vi: 0-0 Tstrap: 0-0
Best Rating: 59 6/01 Ches 5f16y gd-fm

Rock'n Cold (IRE)

97(83) (18)**46**

3-y-o b g Bigstone (IRE)-Unalaska (IRE) (High Estate)

R M H Cowell C Akers

Placings:004006250546242 **(5469)**

2001: 8^{0}S, 8^{0}SD, 8^{4}S, 10^{0}GF, **12^{0}SD**, 9^{6}GF, 10^{2}G, 10^{5}G, 10^{0}G, 10^{5}GF, 10^{4}G, 9^{6}GS, 9^{2}S, 9^{4}GS, 9^{2}S

	Starts	1st	2nd	3rd	Win & Pl
Career Total (Turf)	13	0	3	0	2463
Career Total (AW)	2	0	0	0	

Going (Turf): Sf: 0-4 GS: 0-2 Gd: 0-4 GF: 0-3 Fm: 0-0
Distance: 5f/6f: 0-0 7f-8f: 0-3 9f-13f: 0-12 14f+: 0-0
Track : LH: 0-8 RH: 0-6 Tight: 0-5 Gall: 0-2
Aids: Bl: 0-2 Vi: 0-12 Tstrap: 0-0
Best Rating: 46 10/01 Brig 1m1f209y soft

She has shown bits and pieces of form, but looks very moderate.

Rockerlong

110 **109**

3-y-o b f Deploy-Dancing Rocks (Green Dancer (USA))

G Wragg A E Oppenheimer

Placings:220-5153300 **(5257)**

2001: 10^{5}GS, 11^{1}GF, 12^{5}GF, 12^{3}GS, 11^{3}G, 14^{0}GF, 12^{0}GS

	Starts	1st	2nd	3rd	Win & Pl
Career Total (Turf)	10	1	2	2	70490

97 5/01 Ches 1m3f79y A G-F £34612
Total win prize-money £34613

Going (Turf): Sf: 0-0 GS: 0-5 Gd: 0-1 **GF: 1-4** Fm: 0-0
Distance: 5f/6f: 0-0 7f-8f: 0-3 **9f-13f: 1-6** 14f+: 0-1
Track : LH: 1-4 RH: 0-2 **Tight: 1-1** Gall: 0-5
Aids: Bl: 0-0 Vi: 0-0 Tstrap: 0-0
Best Rating: 109 8/01 York 1m3f195y good

Runner-up to useful fillies on her first two juvenile starts, but disappointed on her three subsequent runs, before coming good in the Cheshire Oaks. Getting the run of the race, she kept on to hold Gay Heroine. Not beaten far in the Ribblesdale and was a good third in the Group One Yorkshire Oaks. Stays a mile and a half. Acts on good to firm to good to soft.

Rocking Ringo

44

2-y-o b c Mazaad-Dalgorian (IRE) (Lancastrian)

C N Kellett Mrs N Gidleywright

Placings:0 **(5667)**

2001: 8^{0}HY

	Starts	1st	2nd	3rd	Win & Pl
Career Total (Turf)	1	0	0	0	

Going (Turf): Sf: 0-1 GS: 0-0 Gd: 0-0 GF: 0-0 Fm: 0-0
Distance: 5f/6f: 0-0 7f-8f: 0-0 9f-13f: 0-1 14f+: 0-0
Track : LH: 0-0 RH: 0-1 Tight: 0-1 Gall: 0-0
Aids: Bl: 0-0 Vi: 0-0 Tstrap: 0-0

Rockon Arry

83(87) (47)**62**

2-y-o b g Aragon-Rockstine (IRE) (Ballad Rock)

K Bell North Farm Stud

Placings:004 **(5331)**

2001: 8^{0}SW, 6^{0}HY, 5^{4}HY, 6^{4}SD

	Starts	1st	2nd	3rd	Win & Pl
Career Total (Turf)	2	0	0	0	0
Career Total (AW)	1	0	0	0	

Going (Turf): Sf: 0-2 GS: 0-0 Gd: 0-0 GF: 0-0 Fm: 0-0
Distance: 5f/6f: 0-2 7f-8f: 0-0 9f-13f: 0-1 14f+: 0-0
Track : LH: 0-1 RH: 0-0 Tight: 0-1 Gall: 0-0
Aids: Bl: 0-0 Vi: 0-0 Tstrap: 0-0

Best Rating: 62 10/01 Ling 5f heavy

Rocky Island

100 **32**

4-y-o b g Rock Hopper-Queen's Eyot (Grundy)

Mrs M Reveley W G McHarg

Placings:000/0-50 **(1138)**

2001: 14^{5}HY, 13^{0}G

	Starts	1st	2nd	3rd	Win & Pl
Career Total (Turf)	6	0	0	0	0

Going (Turf): Sf: 0-2 GS: 0-1 Gd: 0-3 GF: 0-0 Fm: 0-0
Distance: 5f/6f: 0-3 7f-8f: 0-0 9f-13f: 0-0 14f+: 0-3
Track : LH: 0-2 RH: 0-1 Tight: 0-2 Gall: 0-0
Aids: Bl: 0-0 Vi: 0-0 Tstrap: 0-0
Best Rating: 32 3/01 Nott 1m6f15y heavy

Rodiak

85 **67**

2-y-o b g Distant Relative-Misty Silks (Scottish Reel)

Bob Jones The Rodiak Partnership

Placings:600 **(5682)**

2001: 6^{6}S, 7^{0}HY, 7^{0}S

	Starts	1st	2nd	3rd	Win & Pl
Career Total (Turf)	3	0	0	0	0

Going (Turf): Sf: 0-3 GS: 0-0 Gd: 0-0 GF: 0-0 Fm: 0-0
Distance: 5f/6f: 0-1 7f-8f: 0-2 9f-13f: 0-0 14f+: 0-0
Track : LH: 0-0 RH: 0-0 Tight: 0-0 Gall: 0-0
Aids: Bl: 0-0 Vi: 0-0 Tstrap: 0-0
Best Rating: 67 10/01 York 6f soft

Roffey Spinney (IRE)

89(76) (46)**47**

7-y-o ch g Masterclass (USA)-Crossed Line (Thatching)

C Drew John Huntridge

Placings:30/31130053**00/3300**0000120356010**20/160**
400**006**/002-00 **(4181)**

2001: 10^{0}G, 12^{0}GF

	Starts	1st	2nd	3rd	Win & Pl
Career Total (Turf)	23	2	2	3	7509
Career Total (AW)	23	3	1	4	9414

65	1/99	Wolv	1m1f79y	G	STD	£1505
67	10/98	Leic	7f9y	G(0-60)H	G-S	£2262
50	7/98	Folk	7f	F(0-55)	GD	£2119
69	2/97	Ling	5f	D(0-80)H	STD	£3322
63	2/97	Ling	6f	F	STD	£2394

Total win prize-money £11605

Going (Turf): Sf: 0-2 **GS: 1-5 Gd: 1-12** GF: 0-3 Fm: 0-1
Distance: 5f/6f: 2-14 7f-8f: 2-22 9f-13f: 1-10 14f+: 0-0
Track : **LH: 3-27** RH: 0-3 **Tight: 3-23** Gall: 0-1
Aids: Bl: 0-1 Vi: 0-1 Tstrap: 0-0
Best Rating: 25 8/01 Folk 1m4f gd-fm

Roger Ross

97(104) (43)**35**

6-y-o b g Touch Of Grey-Foggy Dew (Smoggy)

R M Flower K & D Computers Ltd

Placings:0/300621101203301**0/000000000060100/500**
00000-51500200000 **(5101)**

2001: 12^{5}SD, 11^{1}SW, 12^{5}SD, 11^{0}SD, 11^{0}SD, 11^{2}SD, 9^{0}GF, 8^{0}GF, 9^{0}G, 10^{0}GF, 9^{0}GS

	Starts	1st	2nd	3rd	Win & Pl
Career Total (Turf)	30	4	1	2	23928
Career Total (AW)	21	2	2	1	6001

43	1/01	Sthl	1m3f	E(0-70)H	SLW	£2191
54	11/99	Ling	1m2f	F(0-60)H	STD	£1850
75	10/98	Asct	1m	C(0-90)H	SFT	£8871
69	7/98	Sals	1m	D(0-85)H	FRM	£5862
64	6/98	Sand	1m14y	D(0-80)H	SFT	£3777
65	6/98	Sals	1m	E(0-70)H	SFT	£3352

Total win prize-money £25906

Going (Turf): Sf: 3-9 GS: 0-2 Gd: 0-10 GF: 0-8 Fm: 1-1
Distance: 5f/6f: 0-1 7f-8f: 3-24 9f-13f: 3-26 14f+: 0-0
Track : **LH: 2-28** RH: 1-10 **Tight: 1-22** Gall: 0-2
Aids: **Bl: 1-11** Vi: 0-0 Tstrap: 0-0
Best Rating: 43 1/01 Sthl 1m3f slow

Roghan Josh

(59) **8**

3-y-o b g Timeless Times (USA)-Macs Maharanee (Indian King (USA))

P S Felgate P S Felgate

Placings:00-00 **(1832)**

2001: 5^{0}SD, 6^{0}G

	Starts	1st	2nd	3rd	Win & Pl
Career Total (Turf)	3	0	0	0	
Career Total (AW)	1	0	0	0	

Going (Turf): Sf: 0-0 GS: 0-0 Gd: 0-1 GF: 0-2 Fm: 0-0
Distance: 5f/6f: 0-4 7f-8f: 0-0 9f-13f: 0-0 14f+: 0-0
Track : LH: 0-0 RH: 0-0 Tight: 0-0 Gall: 0-0
Aids: Bl: 0-0 Vi: 0-0 Tstrap: 0-0

Roi De Danse

83(106) (43)**18**

6-y-o ch g Komaite (USA)-Princess Lucy (Local Suitor (USA))

M Quinn Mrs S G Davies

Placings:005100/00050120**0664/4220000006006312/**
034225025000034-64152000400 **(3234)**

2001: 10^{6}SD, 8^{4}SD, 8^{1}SW, 10^{5}SD, 8^{2}SD, 9^{0}SD, 8^{0}SD, 6^{0}GS, 8^{4}SD, 8^{0}GF, 8^{0}SD

	Starts	1st	2nd	3rd	Win & Pl
Career Total (Turf)	25	2	1	0	8928
Career Total (AW)	36	2	7	3	11203

40	1/01	Wolv	1m100y	F	SLW	£2121
44	12/99	Ling	1m2f	F(0-60)H	STD	£1882
71	9/98	Brig	7f214y	F(0-65)	GD	£2347
72	8/97	Kemp	6f	E	GD	£3064

Total win prize-money £9415

Going (Turf): Sf: 0-2 GS: 0-6 **Gd: 2-10** GF: 0-7 Fm: 0-0
Distance: 5f/6f: 1-5 7f-8f: 1-27 **9f-13f: 2-29** 14f+: 0-0
Track : **LH: 3-44** RH: 0-7 **Tight: 2-30** Gall: 0-6
Aids: Bl: 0-0 Vi: 0-1 Tstrap: 0-0
Best Rating: 48 2/01 Wolv 1m100y stand

Roisin Splendour (IRE)

(91) (30)

6-y-o ch m Inchinor-Oriental Splendour (Runnett)

S Dow I P Blance

Placings:30/432410000**022/2515**06316050**000/000-060** **(0150)**

2001: 8^{0}SD, 6^{6}SD, 7^{0}SW

	Starts	1st	2nd	3rd	Win & Pl
Career Total (Turf)	21	2	1	3	9778
Career Total (AW)	14	1	3	0	6289

66	6/99	Gdwd	7f	E(0-80)H	G-F	£3533
72	2/99	Ling	7f	E(0-70)H	STD	£2696
77	7/98	Brig	6f209y	E	GD	£2762

Total win prize-money £8993

Going (Turf): Sf: 0-1 GS: 0-1 **Gd: 1-7 GF: 1-12** Fm: 0-0
Distance: 5f/6f: 0-4 **7f-8f: 3-30** 9f-13f: 0-1 14f+: 0-0
Track : **LH: 2-17** RH: 1-9 **Tight: 1-16** Gall: 0-2
Aids: Bl: 0-0 Vi: 0-3 Tstrap: 0-0
Best Rating: 23 1/01 Ling 6f stand

Roisterer

95(101) (29)**17**

5-y-o ch g Rudimentary (USA)-Raffle (Balidar)

D W Chapman Michael Hill

Placings:0000000-**0306**0002000600 **(4110)**

2001: 8^{0}SD, 5^{3}SD, 5^{0}SD, 5^{6}SD, 5^{0}GF, 8^{0}GF, 6^{0}F, 6^{2}SD, 5^{0}F, 6^{0}GF, 8^{0}F, 7^{6}F, 8^{0}GS, 5^{0}S

	Starts	1st	2nd	3rd	Win & Pl
Career Total (Turf)	13	0	0	0	0
Career Total (AW)	8	0	1	1	920

Going (Turf): Sf: 0-2 GS: 0-2 Gd: 0-1 GF: 0-3 Fm: 0-5
Distance: 5f/6f: 0-15 7f-8f: 0-5 9f-13f: 0-1 14f+: 0-0
Track : LH: 0-7 RH: 0-3 Tight: 0-6 Gall: 0-2
Aids: Bl: 0-7 Vi: 0-0 Tstrap: 0-0
Best Rating: 29 7/01 Sthl 6f stand

Rojabaa

75 **34**

2-y-o b g Anabaa (USA)-Slava (USA) (Diesis)

Mrs A Duffield Rojabaa Partnership

Placings:0650 **(2397)**

2001: 5^{0}S, 5^{6}GS, 5^{5}GF, 7^{0}GF

	Starts	1st	2nd	3rd	Win & Pl
Career Total (Turf)	4	0	0	0	0

Going (Turf): Sf: 0-1 GS: 0-1 Gd: 0-0 GF: 0-2 Fm: 0-0
Distance: 5f/6f: 0-3 7f-8f: 0-1 9f-13f: 0-0 14f+: 0-0
Track : LH: 0-1 RH: 0-0 Tight: 0-0 Gall: 0-0
Aids: Bl: 0-0 Vi: 0-0 Tstrap: 0-0
Best Rating: 34 6/01 Pont 5f gd-fm

Rokeby Bowl

97 **83**

9-y-o b g Salse (USA)-Rose Bowl (USA) (Habitat)

I A Balding Kingsclere Stud

Placings:2/402011242205/345/336061100/52211202/2
300/006 **(2877)**

2001: 12^{0}GF, 10^{0}GF, 11^{6}GF

	Starts	1st	2nd	3rd	Win & Pl
Career Total (Turf)	40	6	10	4	119754

96	8/98	York	1m3f195y	C(0-95)H	FRM	£20225
93	8/98	Epsm	1m4f10y	C(0-100)H	G-F	£14005
96	8/97	Newb	1m4f5y	C(0-90)	G-F	£6127
91	7/97	Sand	1m3f91y	C(0-90)	G-F	£6710
83	6/95	Sand	1m1f	C(0-95)H	GD	£7165
83	6/95	Pont	1m2f6y	C(0-90)H	GD	£6056

Total win prize-money £60288

Going (Turf): Sf: 0-3 GS: 0-1 Gd: 2-11 **GF: 3-23** Fm: 1-2
Distance: 5f/6f: 0-2 7f-8f: 0-3 **9f-13f: 6-33** 14f+: 0-2
Track : **LH: 4-15** RH: 2-21 Tight: 1-12 **Gall: 2-18**
Aids: Bl: 0-0 Vi: 0-0 Tstrap: 0-0
Best Rating: 83 6/01 Epsm 1m4f10y gd-fm

An admirable performer and multiple winner of middle-distance handicaps over the years. He was running for the first times in two years when reappearing at Epsom in June 2001. Acts on fast ground.

Roller

98(103) (52)**54**

5-y-o b g Bluebird (USA)-Tight Spin (High Top)

J M Bradley E A Hayward

Placings:43/015300005/32122040360630-300000505 **(5681)**

2001: 8^{3}SD, 7^{0}GS, 8^{0}S, 8^{0}GF, 8^{0}G, 8^{0}G, 9^{5}HY, 9^{0}SD, 8^{5}S

	Starts	1st	2nd	3rd	Win & Pl
Career Total (Turf)	31	2	3	4	15869
Career Total (AW)	3	0	0	2	830

81	4/00	Newc	1m	E(0-75)H	SFT	£3094
75	5/99	Wwck	6f168y	D	SFT	£3915

Total win prize-money £7009

Going (Turf): Sf: 2-13 GS: 0-6 Gd: 0-7 GF: 0-5 Fm: 0-0
Distance: 5f/6f: 0-2 **7f-8f: 2-15** 9f-13f: 0-17 14f+: 0-0
Track : **LH: 2-19** RH: 0-6 Tight: 0-10 **Gall: 1-4**

Aids: Bl: 1-7 Vi: 0-0 Tstrap: 0-0
Best Rating: 54 10/01 Nott 1m1f213y heavy

Rolly Polly (IRE)

110 **105**

3-y-o b f Mukaddamah (USA)-Rare Sound (Rarity)
H R A Cecil D Wildenstein

Placings:1140-10 **(1402a)**
2001: 7^{1}GS, 8^{0}G

	Starts	1st	2nd	3rd	Win & Pl
Career Total (Turf)	6	3	0	0	92484

98	4/01	Newb	7f	A	G-S	£23200
105	7/00	MsnL	5f110y		VS	£33622
	6/00	Siro	6f		G-F	£27977

Total win prize-money £84799

Going (Turf): Sf: 0-1 **GS: 1-2** Gd: 0-1 **GF: 1-1** Fm: 0-0
Distance: 5f/6f: 1-2 7f-8f: 1-3 9f-13f: 0-0 14f+: 0-0
Track: LH: 0-0 **RH: 1-2** Tight: 0-0 Gall: 0-0
Aids: Bl: 0-0 Vi: 0-0 Tstrap: 0-0
Best Rating: 104 5/01 Lonc 1m good

A speedy juvenile in Italy, and winner of the Prix Robert Papin, she joined Henry Cecil for the 2001 season and won the race formerly known as the Fred Darling on her British debut. Well beaten in the French 1000 Guineas, and subsequently joined Bobby Frankel in the USA.

Romaha (IRE)

87 **47**

5-y-o b g Storm Bird (CAN)-Eurobird (Ela-Mana-Mou)
S J Mahon James Gough

Placings:0 **(2355)**
2001: 22^{0}GF

	Starts	1st	2nd	3rd	Win & Pl
Career Total (Turf)	1	0	0	0	

Going (Turf): Sf: 0-0 GS: 0-0 Gd: 0-0 GF: 0-1 Fm: 0-0
Distance: 5f/6f: 0-0 7f-8f: 0-0 9f-13f: 0-0 14f+: 0-1
Track: LH: 0-0 RH: 0-1 Tight: 0-0 Gall: 0-1
Aids: Bl: 0-1 Vi: 0-0 Tstrap: 0-0
Best Rating: 47 6/01 Asct 2m6f34y gd-fm

Roman Candle (IRE)

80(97) (57)**20**

5-y-o b g Sabrehill (USA)-Penny Banger (IRE) (Pennine Walk)
G T Gaines Taylor Parker Associates

Placings:06521150/05-000 **(5226)**
2001: 12^{0}GF, 14^{0}GS, 11^{0}S

	Starts	1st	2nd	3rd	Win & Pl
Career Total (Turf)	11	2	1	0	8698
Career Total (AW)	2	0	0	0	0

71	7/99	Ripn	1m4f60y	D(0-80)H	GD	£5038
68	6/99	Wind	1m3f135y	E(0-75)H	G-F	£2827

Total win prize-money £7866

Going (Turf): Sf: 0-3 GS: 0-2 **Gd: 1-3 GF: 1-3** Fm: 0-0
Distance: 5f/6f: 0-0 7f-8f: 0-1 **9f-13f: 2-11** 14f+: 0-1
Track: LH: 0-4 **RH: 1-6 Tight: 2-8** Gall: 0-1
Aids: Bl: 0-0 Vi: 0-0 Tstrap: 0-0
Best Rating: 20 10/01 Sals 1m6f15y gd-sft

Roman Chief

75 **45**

2-y-o b c Forzando-Red Cloud (IRE) (Taufan (USA))
D Haydn Jones Kevan R Kynaston

Placings:600 **(2856)**
2001: 6^{6}GF, 6^{0}GF, 5^{0}GF

	Starts	1st	2nd	3rd	Win & Pl
Career Total (Turf)	3	0	0	0	0

Going (Turf): Sf: 0-0 GS: 0-0 Gd: 0-0 GF: 0-3 Fm: 0-0
Distance: 5f/6f: 0-3 7f-8f: 0-0 9f-13f: 0-0 14f+: 0-0
Track: LH: 0-2 RH: 0-0 Tight: 0-0 Gall: 0-1
Aids: Bl: 0-1 Vi: 0-0 Tstrap: 0-0
Best Rating: 45 7/01 Bath 5f11y gd-fm

Roman Hideaway (IRE)

102(108) (75+)**82**

3-y-o b c Hernando (FR)-Vaison La Romaine (Arctic Tern (USA))
Sir Mark Prescott Neil Greig - Osborne House

Placings:000-11112 **(4101)**
2001: 9^{1}SD, 12^{1}SD, 14^{1}GF, 16^{1}SD, 14^{2}G

	Starts	1st	2nd	3rd	Win & Pl
Career Total (Turf)	4	1	1	0	5719
Career Total (AW)	4	3	0	0	7889

75	7/01	Wolv	2m46y	F(0-65)H	STD	£2436
70	7/01	Hayd	1m6f	D(0-80)H	G-F	£4374
66	7/01	Sthl	1m4f	E(0-70)H	STD	£3094
60	6/01	Wolv	1m1f79y	F(0-65)H	STD	£2359

Total win prize-money £12264

Going (Turf): Sf: 0-2 GS: 0-0 Gd: 0-1 **GF: 1-1** Fm: 0-0
Distance: 5f/6f: 0-2 7f-8f: 0-1 9f-13f: 2-2 14f+: 2-3
Track: **LH: 4-6** RH: 0-0 **Tight: 2-2** Gall: 0-0
Aids: Bl: 0-0 Vi: 0-0 Tstrap: 0-0
Best Rating: 82 8/01 Nott 1m6f15y good

He had three runs for a handicap mark as a juvenile but, stepped up in trip this season, he completed a four-timer in the summer of which three were on Fibresand. Probably needs at least two miles now.

Roman King (IRE)

109 **89**

6-y-o b g Sadler's Wells (USA)-Romantic Feeling (Shirley Heights)
M Johnston D J & F A Jackson

Placings:541/60342-0160 **(2005)**
2001: 8^{0}S, 10^{1}S, 11^{6}F, 10^{0}GF

	Starts	1st	2nd	3rd	Win & Pl
Career Total (Turf)	12	2	1	1	23512

89	4/01	Epsm	1m2f18y	B(0-105)H	SFT	£14950
82	10/99	Hayd	1m3f200y	D	HVY	£4208

Total win prize-money £19158

Going (Turf): Sf: 2-4 GS: 0-0 Gd: 0-3 GF: 0-4 Fm: 0-1
Distance: 5f/6f: 0-0 7f-8f: 0-1 **9f-13f: 2-9** 14f+: 0-2
Track: **LH: 2-5** RH: 0-6 **Tight: 1-7** Gall: 0-2
Aids: Bl: 0-0 Vi: 0-0 Tstrap: 0-0
Best Rating: 89 4/01 Epsm 1m2f18y soft

He changed stables after his first two runs in 2000 and was steadily dropped back in trip. He bolted up in the City And Suburban Handicap on his second start of this season and goes particularly well in testing conditions. He was tried over longer and committed early when fading at York in May.

Romannie (BEL)

78 **43**

2-y-o b f Piccolo-Green Land (BEL) (Hero's Honor (USA))
S C Williams Mrs V Vilain

Placings:00 **(5342)**
2001: 7^{0}GS, 7^{0}GS

	Starts	1st	2nd	3rd	Win & Pl
Career Total (Turf)	2	0	0	0	

Going (Turf): Sf: 0-0 GS: 0-2 Gd: 0-0 GF: 0-0 Fm: 0-0
Distance: 5f/6f: 0-0 7f-8f: 0-2 9f-13f: 0-0 14f+: 0-0
Track: LH: 0-0 RH: 0-0 Tight: 0-0 Gall: 0-0
Aids: Bl: 0-0 Vi: 0-0 Tstrap: 0-0
Best Rating: 43 8/01 Leic 7f9y gd-sft

Romantic Affair (IRE)

108 **117**

4-y-o ch g Persian Bold-Broken Romance (IRE) (Ela-Mana-Mou)
J L Dunlop The Earl Cadogan

Placings:013/0211421213-32025 **(4112)**
2001: 16^{3}G, 16^{2}G, 20^{0}GF, 14^{2}HO, 15^{5}G

	Starts	1st	2nd	3rd	Win & Pl
Career Total (Turf)	18	5	5	3	102961

114	10/00	NmkR	2m	A(0-105)H	SFT	£13108
105	9/00	Donc	1m6f132y	B(0-105)H	G-F	£22035
94	7/00	Sals	1m4f	D(0-85)H	GD	£4062
81	6/00	Sand	1m3f91y	E(0-75)H	G-F	£4524
80	9/99	Newc	7f	F	SFT	£1819

Total win prize-money £45549

Going (Turf): Sf: 2-4 GS: 0-1 **Gd: 1-7 GF: 2-4** Fm: 0-0
Distance: 5f/6f: 0-0 7f-8f: 1-4 9f-13f: 2-5 14f+: 2-8
Track: LH: 1-4 **RH: 3-9** Tight: 1-2 **Gall: 2-8**
Aids: Bl: 0-0 Vi: 0-0 Tstrap: 0-0
Best Rating: 113 5/01 Sand 2m78y good

He progressed well after being stepped up in trip, and put in two good runs behind Solo Mio and behind Generic in France, this term. Best on soft and heavy, he stays two miles.

Romantic Myth

107 **102**

3-y-o b f Mind Games-My First Romance (Danehill (USA))
T D Easterby T G Holdcroft

Placings:1116450-05000 **(4193)**
2001: 5^{0}G, 6^{5}GF, 5^{0}GF, 6^{0}G, 5^{0}G

	Starts	1st	2nd	3rd	Win & Pl
Career Total (Turf)	12	3	0	0	51674

103	6/00	Asct	5f	A	G-F	£33000
98	5/00	Ches	5f16y	B	GD	£8613
79	4/00	Ripn	5f	D	SFT	£3523

Total win prize-money £45136

Going (Turf): Sf: 1-2 GS: 0-0 **Gd: 1-5 GF: 1-5** Fm: 0-0
Distance: **5f/6f: 3-12** 7f-8f: 0-0 9f-13f: 0-0 14f+: 0-0
Track: **LH: 1-1** RH: 0-0 **Tight: 1-1** Gall: 0-0
Aids: Bl: 0-0 Vi: 0-0 Tstrap: 0-0
Best Rating: 102 5/01 Hayd 6f gd-fm

Precocious as a juvenile, she lost her way in the second half of last season and her efforts this season appear to confirm that she did not train on.

Romantic Poet

74 **62**

3-y-o b g Cyrano De Bergerac-Lady Quinta (IRE) (Gallic League)
B R Millman Ray Gudge, Colin Lewis, Malcolm Calvert

Placings:35-00 **(1379)**
2001: 6^{0}GS, 8^{0}GS

	Starts	1st	2nd	3rd	Win & Pl
Career Total (Turf)	4	0	0	1	535

Going (Turf): Sf: 0-1 GS: 0-2 Gd: 0-1 GF: 0-0 Fm: 0-0
Distance: 5f/6f: 0-3 7f-8f: 0-1 9f-13f: 0-0 14f+: 0-0
Track: LH: 0-0 RH: 0-2 Tight: 0-0 Gall: 0-2
Aids: Bl: 0-0 Vi: 0-0 Tstrap: 0-1
Best Rating: 11 5/01 Sals 6f gd-sft

Romany Fair (IRE)

76 **43**

2-y-o b c Blues Traveller (IRE)-Fantasticus (IRE) (Lycius (USA))
M L W Bell Capt B W Bell

Placings:060 **(2806)**

2001: 6^{G}, 7^{GF}, 7^{GF}

	Starts	1st	2nd	3rd	Win & Pl
Career Total (Turf)	3	0	0	0	0

Going (Turf): Sf: 0-0 GS: 0-0 Gd: 0-1 GF: 0-2 Fm: 0-0
Distance: 5f/6f: 0-1 7f-8f: 0-2 9f-13f: 0-0 14f+: 0-0
Track : LH: 0-2 RH: 0-0 Tight: 0-0 Gall: 0-0
Aids: Bl: 0-0 Vi: 0-0 Tstrap: 0-0
Best Rating: 43 7/01 Wwck 7f26y gd-fm

Romanylei (IRE)

80 102
4-y-o gr f Blues Traveller (IRE)-Krayyalei (IRE) (Krayyan)
J G Burns Mrs J A Dene

Placings:11/6201-000 (3924a)
2001: 6^{GF}, 5^{Y}, 6^{Y}

	Starts	1st	2nd	3rd	Win & Pl
Career Total (Turf)	9	3	1	0	52220

102	8/00	Asct	6f	B(0-105)H	G-F	£25000
83	10/99	Naas	6f	H	Y-S	£17225
64	9/99	Cork	6f		G-F	£5175

Total win prize-money £47400

Going (Turf): Sf: 0-1 GS: 0-1 Gd: 0-1 GF: 2-3 Fm: 0-0
Distance: 5f/6f: 3-8 7f-8f: 0-1 9f-13f: 0-0 14f+: 0-0
Track : LH: 0-1 RH: 0-0 Tight: 0-0 Gall: 0-0
Aids: Bl: 0-0 Vi: 0-0 Tstrap: 0-0
Best Rating: 94 7/01 Curr 5f yield

Very useful Irish sprinter, winner of a race on Shergar Cup day last season, but no show this.

Romoh (IRE)

73(86) (55)55
3-y-o ch c Caerleon (USA)-Possessive (Posse (USA))
E A L Dunlop Ahmed Buhaleeba

Placings:60 (0791)
2001: 8^{6}SD, 10^{GS}

	Starts	1st	2nd	3rd	Win & Pl
Career Total (Turf)	1	0	0	0	
Career Total (AW)	1	0	0	0	0

Going (Turf): Sf: 0-0 GS: 0-1 Gd: 0-0 GF: 0-0 Fm: 0-0
Distance: 5f/6f: 0-0 7f-8f: 0-1 9f-13f: 0-1 14f+: 0-0
Track : LH: 0-1 RH: 0-0 Tight: 0-1 Gall: 0-0
Aids: Bl: 0-0 Vi: 0-0 Tstrap: 0-0
Best Rating: 55 4/01 NmkR 1m2f gd-sft

Romora Bay

82(55) 34
2-y-o b f Sri Pekan (USA)-Fighting Run (Runnett)
M D I Usher The Bays Racing Partnership

Placings:000000 (5342)
2001: 5^{G}, 6^{GF}, 5^{F}, 6^{G}, 7^{SD}, 7^{GS}

	Starts	1st	2nd	3rd	Win & Pl
Career Total (Turf)	5	0	0	0	
Career Total (AW)	1	0	0	0	

Going (Turf): Sf: 0-0 GS: 0-1 Gd: 0-2 GF: 0-1 Fm: 0-1
Distance: 5f/6f: 0-4 7f-8f: 0-2 9f-13f: 0-0 14f+: 0-0
Track : LH: 0-2 RH: 0-0 Tight: 0-0 Gall: 0-1
Aids: Bl: 0-0 Vi: 0-0 Tstrap: 0-0
Best Rating: 34 5/01 Ling 6f gd-fm

Romp In

76(85) (49)34
2-y-o b f Komaite (USA)-Sizzling Romp (Sizzling Melody)
C A Dwyer Cedar Lodge 2000 Syndicate

Placings:6406500 (2980)
2001: 5^{6}SD, 5^{4}G, 6^{0}G, 5^{6}GF, 5^{5}SD, 5^{0}SD, 5^{0}SD

	Starts	1st	2nd	3rd	Win & Pl
Career Total (Turf)	3	0	0	0	0
Career Total (AW)	4	0	0	0	0

Going (Turf): Sf: 0-0 GS: 0-0 Gd: 0-2 GF: 0-1 Fm: 0-0
Distance: 5f/6f: 0-6 7f-8f: 0-1 9f-13f: 0-0 14f+: 0-0
Track : LH: 0-1 RH: 0-0 Tight: 0-1 Gall: 0-0
Aids: Bl: 0-0 Vi: 0-1 Tstrap: 0-0
Best Rating: 49 6/01 Sthl 5f stand

Ron's Pet

101(105) (63)59
6-y-o ch g Ron's Victory (USA)-Penny Mint (Mummy's Game)
T D Barron Nigel Shields

Placings:22302120/00005505/14146000260/23322355 4000-23000212221623015 (5162)
2001: 8^{2}SD, 8^{3}SD, 7^{0}SD, 7^{0}SW, 8^{0}SW, 7^{2}SD, 7^{1}SD, 8^{2}SD, 7^{2}GF, 7^{2}GF, 7^{1}GF, 7^{6}G, 8^{2}SD, 8^{3}SD, 6^{0}GF, 7^{1}SD, 7^{5}SD

	Starts	1st	2nd	3rd	Win & Pl
Career Total (Turf)	25	2	6	1	13418
Career Total (AW)	31	4	8	5	21746

63	9/01	Wolv	7f	F	STD	£2558
58	5/01	Sthl	7f	F(0-60)	G-F	£2373
61	3/01	Sthl	7f	F	STD	£2303
74	3/99	Wolv	7f	D(0-85)H	STD	£4198
67	3/99	Wolv	7f	F	STD	£1665
79	8/07	Brig	6f200y	E	GD	£2992

Total win prize-money £16090

Going (Turf): Sf: 0-5 GS: 0-2 Gd: 1-7 GF: 1-10 Fm: 0-1
Distance: 5f/6f: 0-7 7f-8f: 6-44 9f-13f: 0-5 14f+: 0-0
Track : LH: 6-40 RH: 0-2 Tight: 3-26 Gall: 0-3
Aids: Bl: 3-26 Vi: 1-6 Tstrap: 2-21
Best Rating: 66 1/01 Sthl 1m stand

An effective sort in modest events on Fibresand. Best over seven furlongs.

Ron's Round

88(86) (34)38
7-y-o ch g Ron's Victory (USA)-Magical Spirit (Top Ville)
A B Coogan (Miss K M George 18/7) A B Coogan

Placings:0/000435224/3055323111422/540-06 (4366)
2001: 9^{0}SW, 9^{6}GF

	Starts	1st	2nd	3rd	Win & Pl
Career Total (Turf)	15	1	5	2	7386
Career Total (AW)	13	2	0	2	6038

46	7/98	Wolv	1m1f79y	F(0-65)H	STD	£2430
49	7/98	Sthl	1m3f	E(0-70)H	STD	£2899
56	6/98	Nott	1m1f213y	G(0-60)H	G-S	£2407

Total win prize-money £7737

Going (Turf): Sf: 0-0 GS: 1-3 Gd: 0-3 GF: 0-7 Fm: 0-2
Distance: 5f/6f: 0-2 7f-8f: 0-1 9f-13f: 3-25 14f+: 0-0
Track : LH: 3-22 RH: 0-4 Tight: 1-13 Gall: 0-1
Aids: Bl: 0-0 Vi: 0-0 Tstrap: 0-0
Best Rating: 38 8/01 Brig 1m1f209y gd-fm

Ronni Pancake

(74) (52)49
4-y-o b f Mujadil (USA)-Funny Choice (IRE) (Commanche Run)
J G Burns (J S Moore 3/2) Mrs T P Burns

Placings:020606/015060000-002 (5651a)
2001: 10^{0}GD, 9^{0}YS, 9^{0}HY

	Starts	1st	2nd	3rd	Win & Pl
Career Total (Turf)	17	1	2	0	4898
Career Total (AW)	3	0	0	0	0

56	5/00	Leic	1m8y	F	G-S	£2467

Total win prize-money £2468

Going (Turf): Sf: 0-3 GS: 1-1 Gd: 0-5 GF: 0-7 Fm: 0-0
Distance: 5f/6f: 0-3 7f-8f: 0-6 9f-13f: 1-11 14f+: 0-0
Track : LH: 0-10 RH: 0-2 Tight: 0-3 Gall: 0-2
Aids: Bl: 0-0 Vi: 0-0 Tstrap: 0-0
Best Rating: 49 10/01 Tipp 1m1f heavy

Ronquista D'Or

89(90) (21)24
7-y-o b g Ron's Victory (USA)-Gild The Lily (Ile De Bourbon (USA))
G A Ham Ms J C Hutley

Placings:00/3020562061/400051420001/32334253/604 006-000 (3454)
2001: 11^{0}SD, 11^{0}GF, 14^{0}GF

	Starts	1st	2nd	3rd	Win & Pl
Career Total (Turf)	20	1	3	2	4551
Career Total (AW)	21	2	2	3	7765

51	12/98	Wolv	1m4f	F(0-60)H	STD	£2102
52	7/98	Wwck	1m4f115y	G(0-60)H	G-F	£1725
56	1/98	Sthl	1m4f	E(0-70)H	STD	£2814

Total win prize-money £6642

Going (Turf): Sf: 0-2 GS: 0-2 Gd: 0-2 GF: 1-14 Fm: 0-0
Distance: 5f/6f: 0-0 7f-8f: 0-1 9f-13f: 3-28 14f+: 0-12
Track : LH: 3-32 RH: 0-6 Tight: 1-19 Gall: 0-1
Aids: Bl: 3-23 Vi: 0-2 Tstrap: 0-0
Best Rating: 24 7/01 Hayd 1m3f200y gd-fm

Roo

100 89
4-y-o b f Rudimentary (USA)-Shall We Run (Hotfoot)
R F Johnson Houghton Mrs H Johnson Houghton

Placings:1032621420/065322500-066 (2060)
2001: 6^{0}GF, 6^{6}GF, 6^{6}GF

	Starts	1st	2nd	3rd	Win & Pl
Career Total (Turf)	22	2	5	2	22826

86	8/99	Hayd	6f	D	SFT	£3629
82	4/99	Bath	5f11y	E	SFT	£3061

Total win prize-money £6691

Going (Turf): Sf: 2-5 GS: 0-3 Gd: 0-4 GF: 0-10 Fm: 0-0
Distance: 5f/6f: 2-17 7f-8f: 0-4 9f-13f: 0-1 14f+: 0-0
Track : LH: 1-5 RH: 0-3 Tight: 0-1 Gall: 1-6
Aids: Bl: 0-0 Vi: 0-0 Tstrap: 0-1
Best Rating: 85 5/01 Gdwd 6f gd-fm

Useful sprint juvenile in 1999, and ran well in decent handicaps in 2000, but just held in fair events this season.

Roofer (IRE)

100 71
3-y-o b f Barathea (IRE)-Castlerahan (IRE) (Thatching)
M R Channon Pine Crest Racing

Placings:542450-333430 (4828)
2001: 8^{3}GF, 8^{3}G, 8^{3}S, 9^{4}GS, 10^{3}G, 10^{0}G

	Starts	1st	2nd	3rd	Win & Pl
Career Total (Turf)	12	0	1	4	7342

Going (Turf): Sf: 0-3 GS: 0-2 Gd: 0-3 GF: 0-4 Fm: 0-0
Distance: 5f/6f: 0-2 7f-8f: 0-6 9f-13f: 0-4 14f+: 0-0
Track : LH: 0-4 RH: 0-3 Tight: 0-3 Gall: 0-1
Aids: Bl: 0-0 Vi: 0-0 Tstrap: 0-0
Best Rating: 72 8/01 Asct 1m good

She has shown plenty of ability and has been placed many times, but is still to win. A mile may be as far as she wants and she probably needs still more help from the Handicapper.

Rooftop

83(108) (56)31
5-y-o b g Thatching-Top Berry (High Top)
W Storey Gremlin Racing

Placings:00440/35200/65000004600-000 (5091)
2001: 8^{0}GF, 7^{0}G, 7^{0}GS

	Starts	1st	2nd	3rd	Win & Pl
Career Total (Turf)	21	0	1	1	2625
Career Total (AW)	3	0	0	0	0

Going (Turf): Sf: 0-3 GS: 0-2 Gd: 0-3 GF: 0-9 Fm: 0-0
Distance: 5f/6f: 0-0 7f-8f: 0-16 9f-13f: 0-7 14f+: 0-1
Track : LH: 0-7 RH: 0-13 Tight: 0-5 Gall: 0-5
Aids: Bl: 0-1 Vi: 0-6 Tstrap: 0-0
Best Rating: 20 10/01 Newc 7f gd-sft

Rooftop Romance

70 **49**

2-y-o ch f Pursuit Of Love-Singer On The Roof (Chief Singer)
I A Balding J C Smith

Placings:0 **(5139)**
2001: 6^{0}G

	Starts	1st	2nd	3rd	Win & Pl
Career Total (Turf)	1	0	0	0	

Going (Turf): Sf: 0-0 GS: 0-0 Gd: 0-1 GF: 0-0 Fm: 0-0
Distance: 5f/6f: 0-1 7f-8f: 0-0 9f-13f: 0-0 14f+: 0-0
Track : LH: 0-0 RH: 0-0 Tight: 0-0 Gall: 0-0
Aids: Bl: 0-0 Vi: 0-0 Tstrap: 0-0
Best Rating: 49 10/01 NmkR 6f good

Rookie

81(92) (27)**29**

5-y-o b g Magic Ring (IRE)-Shot At Love (IRE) (Last Tycoon)
M J Gingell (Ms A E Embiricos 29/1) H G T Partnership

Placings:0/22005020/04-00000 **(3019)**
2001: 10^{0}SD, 16^{0}SD, 8^{0}GF, 7^{0}GF, 12^{0}SD

	Starts	1st	2nd	3rd	Win & Pl
Career Total (Turf)	7	0	1	0	904
Career Total (AW)	9	0	2	0	1888

Going (Turf): Sf: 0-0 GS: 0-1 Gd: 0-2 GF: 0-3 Fm: 0-1
Distance: 5f/6f: 0-1 7f-8f: 0-4 9f-13f: 0-9 14f+: 0-2
Track : LH: 0-14 RH: 0-1 Tight: 0-8 Gall: 0-0
Aids: Bl: 0-1 Vi: 0-1 Tstrap: 0-1
Best Rating: 28 5/01 Gdwd 1m gd-fm

Room To Room Magic (IRE)

99(99) (38)**33**

4-y-o ch f Casteddu-Bellatrix (Persian Bold)
B Palling D Brennan

Placings:4560252034-4465550312 **(4553)**
2001: 14^{4}SD, 12^{4}SD, 14^{6}F, 12^{5}SD, 11^{5}GS, 11^{5}GF, 14^{0}GF, 11^{3}GF, 11^{1}GF, 14^{2}SW

	Starts	1st	2nd	3rd	Win & Pl
Career Total (Turf)	11	1	2	2	3714
Career Total (AW)	9	0	1	0	866

33 8/01 Ling 1m3f106yG G-F £1939
Total win prize-money £1939

Going (Turf): Sf: 0-2 GS: 0-1 Gd: 0-2 **GF: 1-5** Fm: 0-1
Distance: 5f/6f: 0-0 7f-8f: 0-1 **9f-13f: 1-15** 14f+: 0-4
Track : **LH: 1-16** RH: 0-1 **Tight: 1-12** Gall: 0-0
Aids: Bl: 0-0 Vi: 0-0 Tstrap: 0-0
Best Rating: 38 9/01 Wolv 1m6f166y slow

Rooster

94 **49**

6-y-o b g Roi Danzig (USA)-Jussoli (Don)
D E Cantillon Mrs Edward Cantillon

Placings:460/04/0026 **(2632)**
2001: 10^{0}G, 12^{0}GF, 16^{2}GF, 16^{6}F

	Starts	1st	2nd	3rd	Win & Pl
Career Total (Turf)	9	0	1	0	1365

Going (Turf): Sf: 0-0 GS: 0-1 Gd: 0-3 GF: 0-4 Fm: 0-1
Distance: 5f/6f: 0-0 7f-8f: 0-1 9f-13f: 0-6 14f+: 0-2
Track : LH: 0-4 RH: 0-4 Tight: 0-3 Gall: 0-3
Aids: Bl: 0-0 Vi: 0-0 Tstrap: 0-0
Best Rating: 49 6/01 Wwck 2m39y gd-fm

Rootle (FR)

96 **84**

2-y-o gr f Highest Honor (FR)-Delve (IRE) (Shernazar)
J L Dunlop Nigel & Carolyn Elwes

Placings:3 **(3225)**
2001: 7^{3}GS

	Starts	1st	2nd	3rd	Win & Pl
Career Total (Turf)	1	0	0	1	627

Going (Turf): Sf: 0-0 GS: 0-1 Gd: 0-0 GF: 0-0 Fm: 0-0
Distance: 5f/6f: 0-0 7f-8f: 0-1 9f-13f: 0-0 14f+: 0-0
Track : LH: 0-0 RH: 0-0 Tight: 0-0 Gall: 0-0
Aids: Bl: 0-0 Vi: 0-0 Tstrap: 0-0
Best Rating: 84 7/01 NmkJ 7f gd-sft

Roppongi Dancer

85 **34**

2-y-o b f Mtoto-Ice Chocolate (USA) (Icecapade (USA))
Mrs M Reveley J Shack

Placings:00000 **(5628)**
2001: 7^{0}F, 6^{0}GF, 5^{0}F, 6^{0}S, 8^{0}G

	Starts	1st	2nd	3rd	Win & Pl
Career Total (Turf)	5	0	0	0	

Going (Turf): Sf: 0-1 GS: 0-0 Gd: 0-1 GF: 0-1 Fm: 0-2
Distance: 5f/6f: 0-3 7f-8f: 0-2 9f-13f: 0-0 14f+: 0-0
Track : LH: 0-1 RH: 0-0 Tight: 0-0 Gall: 0-0
Aids: Bl: 0-0 Vi: 0-0 Tstrap: 0-0
Best Rating: 34 9/01 Rdcr 6f gd-fm

Rorkes Drift (IRE)

82 **48**

3-y-o ch f Royal Abjar (USA)-Scanno's Choice (IRE) (Pennine Walk)
T J Naughton Mrs L Archer

Placings:35-000 **(3577)**
2001: 7^{0}GS, 10^{0}GF, 8^{0}GF

	Starts	1st	2nd	3rd	Win & Pl
Career Total (Turf)	5	0	0	1	526

Going (Turf): Sf: 0-0 GS: 0-2 Gd: 0-0 GF: 0-3 Fm: 0-0
Distance: 5f/6f: 0-0 7f-8f: 0-3 9f-13f: 0-2 14f+: 0-0
Track : LH: 0-1 RH: 0-1 Tight: 0-1 Gall: 0-0
Aids: Bl: 0-0 Vi: 0-0 Tstrap: 0-0
Best Rating: 31 8/01 Wwck 1m22y gd-fm

Ros The Boss (IRE)

88 **41**

2-y-o b f Danehill (USA)-Bella Vitessa (IRE) (Thatching)
G A Butler Eastwind Racing Ltd

Placings:00 **(5682)**
2001: 5^{0}G, 7^{0}S

	Starts	1st	2nd	3rd	Win & Pl
Career Total (Turf)	2	0	0	0	

Going (Turf): Sf: 0-1 GS: 0-0 Gd: 0-1 GF: 0-0 Fm: 0-0
Distance: 5f/6f: 0-1 7f-8f: 0-1 9f-13f: 0-0 14f+: 0-0
Track : LH: 0-1 RH: 0-0 Tight: 0-0 Gall: 0-1
Aids: Bl: 0-0 Vi: 0-0 Tstrap: 0-0
Best Rating: 41 11/01 Donc 7f soft

Rosalia (USA)

(83) (56)**67**

3-y-o b f Red Ransom (USA)-Normandy Belle (USA) (Fit To Fight (USA))
J T Gorman Capt C M Ryan

Placings:463620-0 **(1709a)**
2001: 8^{0}G

	Starts	1st	2nd	3rd	Win & Pl
Career Total (Turf)	6	0	1	1	1883
Career Total (AW)	1	0	0	0	

Going (Turf): Sf: 0-2 GS: 0-0 Gd: 0-1 GF: 0-3 Fm: 0-0
Distance: 5f/6f: 0-4 7f-8f: 0-3 9f-13f: 0-0 14f+: 0-0
Track : LH: 0-1 RH: 0-1 Tight: 0-0 Gall: 0-0
Aids: Bl: 0-0 Vi: 0-0 Tstrap: 0-0

Rose D'Or (IRE)

80 **63+**

2-y-o b f Polish Precedent (USA)-Gold Rose (FR) (Noblequest (FR))
J L Dunlop Lordship Stud

Placings:0 **(5107)**
2001: 7^{0}GS

	Starts	1st	2nd	3rd	Win & Pl
Career Total (Turf)	1	0	0	0	

Going (Turf): Sf: 0-0 GS: 0-1 Gd: 0-0 GF: 0-0 Fm: 0-0
Distance: 5f/6f: 0-0 7f-8f: 0-1 9f-13f: 0-0 14f+: 0-0
Track : LH: 0-0 RH: 0-0 Tight: 0-0 Gall: 0-0
Aids: Bl: 0-0 Vi: 0-0 Tstrap: 0-0
Best Rating: 63 10/01 NmkR 7f gd-sft

Rose Gypsy

106 **117**

3-y-o b f Green Desert (USA)-Krisalya (Kris)
A P O'Brien Mrs John Magnier

Placings:31-22100 **(3129a)**
2001: 8^{2}S, 7^{2}G, 8^{1}G, 8^{0}GF, 12^{0}G

	Starts	1st	2nd	3rd	Win & Pl
Career Total (Turf)	7	2	2	1	122723

117 5/01 Lonc 1m GD £96993
88 10/00 Naas 6f YLD £10005
Total win prize-money £106998

Going (Turf): Sf: 0-1 GS: 0-0 **Gd: 1-4** GF: 0-1 Fm: 0-0
Distance: 5f/6f: 1-2 7f-8f: 1-4 9f-13f: 0-1 14f+: 0-0
Track : LH: 0-0 RH: 0-1 Tight: 0-0 Gall: 0-1
Aids: Bl: 0-0 Vi: 0-0 Tstrap: 0-0
Best Rating: 117 5/01 Lonc 1m good

Stepped up on her previous form to land the French 1000 Guineas, showing a nice turn of foot in the process. Has not built from that, well held on faster ground in the Coronation Stakes and failing to stay in the Irish Oaks.

Rose Hill

96 **53**

5-y-o b m Sabrehill (USA)-Petite Rosanna (Ile De Bourbon (USA))
W Clay G A Greaves

Placings:160/0/0 **(1578)**
2001: 10^{0}F

	Starts	1st	2nd	3rd	Win & Pl
Career Total (Turf)	5	1	0	0	2285

68 8/98 Wwck 7f F G-F £2203
Total win prize-money £2203

Going (Turf): Sf: 0-1 GS: 0-0 Gd: 0-2 **GF: 1-1** Fm: 0-1
Distance: 5f/6f: 0-0 **7f-8f: 1-2** 9f-13f: 0-3 14f+: 0-0
Track : **LH: 1-3** RH: 0-1 Tight: 0-1 Gall: 0-0

Aids: Bl: 0-0 Vi: 0-0 Tstrap: 0-0
Best Rating: 53 5/01 Pont 1m2f6y firm

Rose Of America

106 **75**

3-y-o ch f Brief Truce (USA)-Kilcoy (USA) (Secreto (USA))
Miss L A Perratt Gordon Cowan

Placings:5036-10321602 **(5657)**
2001: 7^{1}GF, 7^{0}GF, 7^{3}G, 8^{2}GF, 8^{1}F, 8^{6}GF, 10^{0}G, 8^{2}G

	Starts	1st	2nd	3rd	Win & Pl
Career Total (Turf)	12	2	2	2	10692

75	7/01	Newc	1m	E(0-75)H	FRM	£4270
64	5/01	Ayr	7f	D	G-F	£3900

Total win prize-money £8171

Going (Turf): Sf: 0-3 GS: 0-1 Gd: 0-3 **GF: 1-4 Fm: 1-1**
Distance: 5f/6f: 0-0 **7f-8f: 2-11** 9f-13f: 0-1 14f+: 0-0
Track : **LH: 2-5** RH: 0-4 Tight: 0-4 **Gall: 1-2**
Aids: Bl: 0-0 Vi: 0-0 Tstrap: 0-0
Best Rating: 75 7/01 Newc 1m firm

She has scored twice this term over seven furlongs at Ayr and a mile at Newcastle. Suited by a strongly-run race and acts on fast ground.

Rose Of Paradise (USA)

83 **49**

2-y-o b f Hansel (USA)-Vie En Rose (USA) (Blushing Groom (FR))
M Johnston Markus Graff

Placings:40P **(4880)**
2001: 6^{4}GF, 6^{0}GF, 8^{P}GF

	Starts	1st	2nd	3rd	Win & Pl
Career Total (Turf)	3	0	0	0	0

Going (Turf): Sf: 0-0 GS: 0-0 Gd: 0-0 GF: 0-3 Fm: 0-0
Distance: 5f/6f: 0-1 7f-8f: 0-1 9f-13f: 0-1 14f+: 0-0
Track : LH: 0-0 RH: 0-1 Tight: 0-1 Gall: 0-0
Aids: Bl: 0-0 Vi: 0-0 Tstrap: 0-0
Best Rating: 49 7/01 Haml 6f5y gd-fm

Rose Peel

99 **74**

3-y-o b f Danehill (USA)-Why So Silent (Mill Reef (USA))
P W Harris Mrs P W Harris

Placings:00-10 **(1205)**
2001: 8^{1}GS, 8^{0}GS

	Starts	1st	2nd	3rd	Win & Pl
Career Total (Turf)	4	1	0	0	3445

72	4/01	Wind	1m67y	D	G-S	£3445

Total win prize-money £3445

Going (Turf): Sf: 0-1 **GS: 1-2** Gd: 0-1 GF: 0-0 Fm: 0-0
Distance: 5f/6f: 0-0 7f-8f: 0-2 **9f-13f: 1-2** 14f+: 0-0
Track : LH: 0-2 **RH: 1-2 Tight: 1-2** Gall: 0-1
Aids: Bl: 0-0 Vi: 0-0 Tstrap: 0-0
Best Rating: 72 4/01 Wind 1m67y gd-sft

Rose Tinted

88 **78**

2-y-o b f Spectrum (IRE)-Marie La Rose (FR) (Night Shift (USA))
J H M Gosden Lady Bamford

Placings:00 **(4985)**
2001: 6^{0}GF, 6^{0}G

	Starts	1st	2nd	3rd	Win & Pl
Career Total (Turf)	2	0	0	0	

Going (Turf): Sf: 0-0 GS: 0-0 Gd: 0-1 GF: 0-1 Fm: 0-0
Distance: 5f/6f: 0-0 7f-8f: 0-2 9f-13f: 0-0 14f+: 0-0
Track : LH: 0-0 RH: 0-0 Tight: 0-0 Gall: 0-0

Aids: Bl: 0-0 Vi: 0-0 Tstrap: 0-0
Best Rating: 78 8/01 Newb 6f8y gd-fm

Roselyn

95(88) (56)**66**

3-y-o b f Efisio-Ciboure (Norwick (USA))
I A Balding Mr & Mrs G Middlebrook

Placings:64454-4000 **(1944)**
2001: 5^{4}S, 7^{0}SD, 7^{0}G, 7^{0}G

	Starts	1st	2nd	3rd	Win & Pl
Career Total (Turf)	8	0	0	0	818
Career Total (AW)	1	0	0	0	

Going (Turf): Sf: 0-1 GS: 0-1 Gd: 0-4 GF: 0-1 Fm: 0-1
Distance: 5f/6f: 0-5 7f-8f: 0-4 9f-13f: 0-0 14f+: 0-0
Track : LH: 0-3 RH: 0-1 Tight: 0-0 Gall: 0-1
Aids: Bl: 0-0 Vi: 0-0 Tstrap: 0-0
Best Rating: 59 4/01 Nott 5f13y soft

Rosemead Mary

85 **48**

2-y-o b f Keen-Arasong (Aragon)
M Dods R Howe

Placings:500 **(4793)**
2001: 6^{5}GF, 8^{0}G, 8^{0}G

	Starts	1st	2nd	3rd	Win & Pl
Career Total (Turf)	3	0	0	0	0

Going (Turf): Sf: 0-0 GS: 0-0 Gd: 0-2 GF: 0-1 Fm: 0-0
Distance: 5f/6f: 0-1 7f-8f: 0-2 9f-13f: 0-0 14f+: 0-0
Track : LH: 0-2 RH: 0-0 Tight: 0-0 Gall: 0-1
Aids: Bl: 0-0 Vi: 0-0 Tstrap: 0-0
Best Rating: 48 7/01 Newc 6f gd-fm

Roses Flutter

63(78) (32)

2-y-o b f Son Pardo-Silent Scream (IRE) (Lahib (USA))
A Smith Alfred Smith

Placings:0 **(5399)**
2001: 6^{0}S

	Starts	1st	2nd	3rd	Win & Pl
Career Total (Turf)	1	0	0	0	

Going (Turf): Sf: 0-1 GS: 0-0 Gd: 0-0 GF: 0-0 Fm: 0-0
Distance: 5f/6f: 0-1 7f-8f: 0-0 9f-13f: 0-0 14f+: 0-0
Track : LH: 0-1 RH: 0-0 Tight: 0-0 Gall: 0-0
Aids: Bl: 0-0 Vi: 0-0 Tstrap: 0-0

Roses Of Spring

106 **80**

3-y-o gr f Shareef Dancer (USA)-Couleur De Rose (Kalaglow)
R M H Cowell Bottisham Heath Stud

Placings:0521052222032 **(5108)**
2001: 7^{0}GS, 6^{5}G, 6^{2}F, 6^{1}GF, 7^{0}GF, 6^{5}GS, 6^{2}F, 6^{2}F, 6^{2}GF, 6^{2}GF, 5^{0}G, 6^{3}F, 5^{2}GS

	Starts	1st	2nd	3rd	Win & Pl
Career Total (Turf)	13	1	6	1	13422

54	6/01	Yarm	6f3y	E	G-F	£2968

Total win prize-money £2968

Going (Turf): Sf: 0-0 GS: 0-3 Gd: 0-2 **GF: 1-4** Fm: 0-4
Distance: 5f/6f: 0-10 **7f-8f: 1-3** 9f-13f: 0-0 14f+: 0-0
Track : LH: 0-3 RH: 0-1 Tight: 0-1 Gall: 0-0
Aids: Bl: 0-0 Vi: 0-1 Tstrap: 0-0
Best Rating: 80 10/01 NmkR 5f gd-sft

Unraced as a juvenile, she chased home the useful Summerhill Parkes at Pontefract on her third outing before making all at Yarmouth. Has failed to add to that despite some good efforts in handicaps since. She appears best suited by six furlongs and fast ground.

Rosetta

93 **36**

4-y-o b f Fraam-Starawak (Star Appeal)
R J Hodges Unity Farm Holiday Centre Ltd

Placings:064354550/000-50450 **(4303)**
2001: 5^{0}G, 8^{0}HD, 6^{4}GF, 5^{5}GF, 7^{0}GF

	Starts	1st	2nd	3rd	Win & Pl
Career Total (Turf)	17	0	0	1	906

Going (Turf): Sf: 0-1 GS: 0-2 Gd: 0-5 GF: 0-8 Fm: 0-1
Distance: 5f/6f: 0-7 7f-8f: 0-6 9f-13f: 0-4 14f+: 0-0
Track : LH: 0-8 RH: 0-1 Tight: 0-3 Gall: 0-3
Aids: Bl: 0-0 Vi: 0-0 Tstrap: 0-0
Best Rating: 36 7/01 Brig 5f213y gd-fm

Roseum

104 **64**

5-y-o b m Lahib (USA)-Rose Barton (Pas De Seul)
R Guest Mrs B Mills

Placings:0/1101/6040-002121 **(4013)**
2001: 6^{0}GS, 6^{0}GF, 6^{2}GF, 5^{1}GF, 7^{2}GS, 5^{1}G

	Starts	1st	2nd	3rd	Win & Pl
Career Total (Turf)	15	5	2	0	24488

54	8/01	Catt	5f	F	GD	£2506
64	7/01	Ling	5f	F	G-F	£2390
92	7/99	Hayd	6f	C(0-100)H	G-S	£6905
83	5/99	Newb	6f8y	C(0-90)H	SFT	£6580
68	4/99	Pont	6f	D	SFT	£3533

Total win prize-money £21916

Going (Turf): Sf: 2-5 GS: 1-4 Gd: 1-2 GF: 1-4 Fm: 0-0
Distance: **5f/6f: 4-11** 7f-8f: 1-4 9f-13f: 0-0 14f+: 0-0
Track : **LH: 1-3** RH: 0-0 Tight: 0-1 Gall: 0-0
Aids: Bl: 0-0 Vi: 0-0 Tstrap: 0-0
Best Rating: 64 7/01 Ling 5f gd-fm

Winner of three of her four starts at two in 1999, she was lightly-raced in 2000, and both her wins this season have been in claimers.

Rosewood Belle (USA)

98 **65**

3-y-o ch f Woodman (USA)-Supreme Excellence (USA) (Providential)
W R Muir M J Caddy

Placings:535 **(4673)**
2001: 9^{5}GF, 10^{3}GS, 12^{5}G

	Starts	1st	2nd	3rd	Win & Pl
Career Total (Turf)	3	0	0	1	678

Going (Turf): Sf: 0-0 GS: 0-1 Gd: 0-1 GF: 0-1 Fm: 0-0
Distance: 5f/6f: 0-0 7f-8f: 0-0 9f-13f: 0-3 14f+: 0-0
Track : LH: 0-3 RH: 0-0 Tight: 0-0 Gall: 0-0
Aids: Bl: 0-0 Vi: 0-0 Tstrap: 0-3
Best Rating: 65 8/01 Hayd 1m2f120y gd-sft

Rosheen Donn (IRE)

95(86) (41)**60d**

2-y-o b f Revoque (IRE)-Mashoura (Shareef Dancer (USA))
M Johnston Mcdowell Racing

Placings:245000 **(5660)**
2001: 5^{2}GS, 5^{4}GF, 5^{5}F, 6^{0}GS, 6^{0}GS, 5^{0}G, 6^{5}SD

	Starts	1st	2nd	3rd	Win & Pl
Career Total (Turf)	6	0	1	0	1627

Going (Turf): Sf: 0-0 GS: 0-3 Gd: 0-1 GF: 0-1 Fm: 0-1
Distance: 5f/6f: 0-6 7f-8f: 0-0 9f-13f: 0-0 14f+: 0-0
Track : LH: 0-1 RH: 0-0 Tight: 0-0 Gall: 0-0

Aids: Bl: 0-0 Vi: 0-0 Tstrap: 0-0
Best Rating: 60 6/01 Newc 5f firm

Good second on debut over five furlongs but has failed to progress since.

Rosi's Boy

106 **103**

3-y-o b c Caerleon (USA)-Come On Rosi (Valiyar)
J L Dunlop Wafic Said

Placings:214-1633044 **(5625)**
2001: 10^{1}G, 10^{6}GF, 8^{3}G, 8^{3}G, 8^{0}G, 9^{4}GS, 8^{4}GS

	Starts	1st	2nd	3rd	Win & Pl
Career Total (Turf)	10	2	1	2	35144

104 5/01 NmkR 1m2f A GD £15544
80 8/00 NmkJ 1m D G-F £4065
Total win prize-money £19610

Going (Turf): Sf: 0-1 GS: 0-3 **Gd: 1-4 GF: 1-2** Fm: 0-0
Distance: 5f/6f: 0-0 7f-8f: 1-6 9f-13f: 1-4 14f+: 0-0
Track : LH: 0-3 RH: 0-1 Tight: 0-0 Gall: 0-2
Aids: Bl: 0-0 Vi: 0-1 Tstrap: 0-0
Best Rating: 104 5/01 York 1m2f85y gd-fm

He is a half-brother to several talented but quirky sorts including Bin Rosie. Showed plenty of ability as a juvenile and put up a brave performance to win a Newmarket Listed event on his return in 2001, but found the company too hot in the Dante and lost a shoe when third in France. A mile looked a bit sharp for him at Goodwood in August and he looked outclassed at Doncaster in September. Stays ten furlongs. Has won on good ground and good to firm.

Rosie (FR)

95 **68**

3-y-o ch f Bering-Scarlet Plume (Warning)
J L Dunlop Nigel & Carolyn Elwes

Placings:550-400 **(2435)**
2001: 12^{4}S, 10^{0}GF, 14^{0}G

	Starts	1st	2nd	3rd	Win & Pl
Career Total (Turf)	6	0	0	0	373

Going (Turf): Sf: 0-4 GS: 0-0 Gd: 0-1 GF: 0-1 Fm: 0-0
Distance: 5f/6f: 0-0 7f-8f: 0-2 9f-13f: 0-3 14f+: 0-1
Track : LH: 0-1 RH: 0-2 Tight: 0-2 Gall: 0-0
Aids: Bl: 0-0 Vi: 0-0 Tstrap: 0-0
Best Rating: 60 6/01 Yarm 1m6f17y good

Rosie Starlight (IRE)

97 **62**

3-y-o b f Tagula (IRE)-Idrak (Young Generation)
D Nicholls Gemini Upholstery/gr 1980 Ltd

Placings:0430346 **(4236)**
2001: 6^{0}GF, 6^{4}GF, 5^{3}GF, 6^{0}GS, 5^{3}GF, 5^{4}G, 5^{6}GF

	Starts	1st	2nd	3rd	Win & Pl
Career Total (Turf)	7	0	0	2	1721

Going (Turf): Sf: 0-0 GS: 0-1 Gd: 0-1 GF: 0-5 Fm: 0-0
Distance: 5f/6f: 0-6 7f-8f: 0-1 9f-13f: 0-0 14f+: 0-0
Track : LH: 0-0 RH: 0-0 Tight: 0-0 Gall: 0-0
Aids: Bl: 0-0 Vi: 0-0 Tstrap: 0-0
Best Rating: 62 7/01 Bevl 5f gd-fm

Rosie's Posy

94 **85+**

2-y-o b f Suave Dancer (USA)-My Branch (Distant Relative)
B W Hills Wafic Said

Placings:15 **(5609)**
2001: 5^{1}G, 8^{5}GS

	Starts	1st	2nd	3rd	Win & Pl
Career Total (Turf)	2	1	0	0	4112

85 10/01 Bath 5f161y D GD £3571
Total win prize-money £3572

Going (Turf): Sf: 0-0 GS: 0-1 **Gd: 1-1** GF: 0-0 Fm: 0-0
Distance: 5f/6f: 1-1 7f-8f: 0-1 9f-13f: 0-0 14f+: 0-0
Track : **LH: 1-1** RH: 0-0 Tight: 0-0 **Gall: 1-1**
Aids: Bl: 0-0 Vi: 0-0 Tstrap: 0-0
Best Rating: 85 11/01 NmkR 1m gd-sft

Out of a useful racemare, she came with a strong late run to make a winning debut at Bath.

Rossel (USA)

102 **38d**

8-y-o b g Blushing John (USA)-Northern Aspen (USA) (Northern Dancer)
P Monteith Allan W Melville

Placings:05/00315400/0030/133022/4061/0004003550000 **(4165)**
2001: 16^{0}S, 13^{0}S, 14^{0}GS, 12^{4}GS, 12^{0}GF, 13^{0}GF, 9^{3}G, 12^{5}GF, 12^{5}G, 15^{0}GS, 12^{0}G, 9^{0}GS, 12^{0}GF

	Starts	1st	2nd	3rd	Win & Pl
Career Total (Turf)	37	3	2	5	19604

62 11/99 Muss 1m4f E(0-70)H GD £2957
62 4/98 Haml 1m5f9y D(0-85)H HVY £6775
63 7/96 Muss 1m4f31y F GD £2493
Total win prize-money £12225

Going (Turf): Sf: 1-11 GS: 0-7 **Gd: 2-7** GF: 0-9 Fm: 0-3
Distance: 5f/6f: 0-0 7f-8f: 0-2 **9f-13f: 2-21** 14f+: 1-14
Track : LH: 0-9 **RH: 3-22 Tight: 3-23** Gall: 0-2
Aids: Bl: 0-0 Vi: 0-1 Tstrap: 0-0
Best Rating: 42 7/01 Newc 1m4f93y good

Rosselli (USA)

107 **92**

5-y-o b g Puissance-Miss Rossi (Artaius (USA))
J A Glover T G Holdcroft

Placings:11130/0050/46002603100-0505050 **(5639)**
2001: 5^{0}S, 5^{5}G, 5^{0}GF, 5^{5}S, 5^{0}GF, 5^{5}G, 5^{0}G

	Starts	1st	2nd	3rd	Win & Pl
Career Total (Turf)	27	4	1	2	64008

100 9/00 Bevl 5f C HVY £5916
102 6/98 Asct 5f A SFT £29775
94 6/98 Bevl 5f B G-S £10081
78 5/98 Newc 5f D G-F £3061
Total win prize-money £48834

Going (Turf): Sf: 2-6 GS: 1-5 Gd: 0-7 GF: 1-8 Fm: 0-0
Distance: 5f/6f: 4-27 7f-8f: 0-0 9f-13f: 0-0 14f+: 0-0
Track : LH: 0-2 RH: 0-0 Tight: 0-2 Gall: 0-0
Aids: Bl: 1-6 Vi: 0-1 Tstrap: 0-2
Best Rating: 92 7/01 Ches 5f16y gd-fm

Very lightly raced in 1999, he failed to fulfil his juvenile promise and last win came in September 2000 with help of blinkers and stands rail. Might prefer six furlongs nowadays. Has run his best races on soft ground.

Rostropovich (IRE)

102 **110**

4-y-o gr g Sadler's Wells (USA)-Infamy (Shirley Heights)
M F Morris M A Kilduff

Placings:31350431-140 **(4758a)**
2001: 14^{1}G, 22^{4}GF, 14^{0}GF

	Starts	1st	2nd	3rd	Win & Pl
Career Total (Turf)	11	3	0	3	59469

110 5/01 Leop 1m6f GD £26000
97 10/00 Curr 1m4f Y-S £9750
85 8/00 Gway 1m4f GD £5520
Total win prize-money £41270

Going (Turf): Sf: 0-0 GS: 0-0 **Gd: 2-6** GF: 0-4 Fm: 0-0
Distance: 5f/6f: 0-0 7f-8f: 0-0 **9f-13f: 2-4** 14f+: 1-7
Track : LH: 0-4 **RH: 2-6** Tight: 0-0 Gall: 0-3
Aids: Bl: 0-0 Vi: 0-1 **Tstrap: 1-3**
Best Rating: 110 5/01 Leop 1m6f good

He has run some good races on the Flat, including when fourth in the Irish St Leger, and was a debut winner over flights, but each of his runs so far has been on soft ground and he will be seen to better effect on a sounder surface.

Rotuma (IRE)

85 **70**

2-y-o b c Tagula (IRE)-Cross Question (USA) (Alleged (USA))
I A Balding Robert Hitchins

Placings:4 **(1651)**
2001: 5^{4}F

	Starts	1st	2nd	3rd	Win & Pl
Career Total (Turf)	1	0	0	0	281

Going (Turf): Sf: 0-0 GS: 0-0 Gd: 0-0 GF: 0-0 Fm: 0-1
Distance: 5f/6f: 0-1 7f-8f: 0-0 9f-13f: 0-0 14f+: 0-0
Track : LH: 0-0 RH: 0-0 Tight: 0-0 Gall: 0-0
Aids: Bl: 0-0 Vi: 0-0 Tstrap: 0-0
Best Rating: 70 5/01 Leic 5f218y firm

Rouberia (IRE)

86 **58**

2-y-o ch f Alhaarth (IRE)-Robinia (USA) (Roberto (USA))
G A Butler Abdulla Al Khalifa

Placings:00 **(5682)**
2001: 6^{0}G, 7^{0}S

	Starts	1st	2nd	3rd	Win & Pl
Career Total (Turf)	2	0	0	0	

Going (Turf): Sf: 0-1 GS: 0-0 Gd: 0-1 GF: 0-0 Fm: 0-0
Distance: 5f/6f: 0-1 7f-8f: 0-1 9f-13f: 0-0 14f+: 0-0
Track : LH: 0-0 RH: 0-0 Tight: 0-0 Gall: 0-0
Aids: Bl: 0-0 Vi: 0-0 Tstrap: 0-0
Best Rating: 58 11/01 Donc 7f soft

Roue

94 **75+**

3-y-o b c Efisio-Ideal Home (Home Guard (USA))
Sir Michael Stoute Sir Evelyn De Rothschild

Placings:0-03401 **(2835)**
2001: 7^{0}S, 7^{3}G, 8^{4}F, 8^{0}GF, 8^{1}GF

	Starts	1st	2nd	3rd	Win & Pl
Career Total (Turf)	6	1	0	1	4323

75 7/01 Leic 1m9y E(0-70)H G-F £3377
Total win prize-money £3378

Going (Turf): Sf: 0-1 GS: 0-0 Gd: 0-2 **GF: 1-2** Fm: 0-1
Distance: 5f/6f: 0-0 7f-8f: 0-4 **9f-13f: 1-2** 14f+: 0-0
Track : LH: 0-3 RH: 0-0 Tight: 0-1 Gall: 0-1
Aids: Bl: 0-0 Vi: 0-0 **Tstrap: 1-4**
Best Rating: 75 7/01 Leic 1m9y gd-fm

Showed promise in maidens before winning a poor race at Leicester.

Rough Seas (IRE)

87 **64**

2-y-o b c Royal Applause-Hebrides (Gone West (USA))
B W Hills Mrs Belinda Harvey

Placings:030 **(2856)**
2001: 5^{0}G, 5^{3}GF, 5^{0}GF

	Starts	1st	2nd	3rd	Win & Pl
Career Total (Turf)	3	0	0	1	660

Going (Turf): Sf: 0-0 GS: 0-0 Gd: 0-1 GF: 0-2 Fm: 0-0
Distance: 5f/6f: 0-3 7f-8f: 0-0 9f-13f: 0-0 14f+: 0-0

Track : LH: 0-1 RH: 0-0 Tight: 0-0 Gall: 0-1
Aids: Bl: 0-0 Vi: 0-0 Tstrap: 0-0
Best Rating: 64 7/01 Donc 5f140y gd-fm

Roundtree (IRE)

104 **95**

2-y-o b f Night Shift (USA)-Island Desert (IRE) (Green Desert (USA))
R Hannon Fergus Jones

Placings:12336 **(4846)**
2001: 5^{1}G, 5^{2}GF, 5^{3}GF, 6^{3}Y, 6^{6}GF

	Starts	1st	2nd	3rd	Win & Pl
Career Total (Turf)	5	1	1	2	24260

78 5/01 Wind 5f10y D GD £4426
Total win prize-money £4427

Going (Turf): Sf: 0-0 GS: 0-0 **Gd: 1-1** GF: 0-3 Fm: 0-0
Distance: **5f/6f: 1-4** 7f-8f: 0-1 9f-13f: 0-0 14f+: 0-0
Track : LH: 0-0 **RH: 1-1** Tight: 0-0 **Gall: 1-1**
Aids: Bl: 0-0 Vi: 0-0 Tstrap: 0-0
Best Rating: 95 6/01 Asct 5f gd-fm

A scopey filly, she made a winning debut at Windsor before meeting trouble in running when going down by a neck to Good Girl in a Listed event at Beverley. Third twice since in warm company, she stays six furlongs.

Rousing Thunder

102 **60**

4-y-o b g Theatrical-Moss (USA) (Woodman (USA))
W J Musson In Partnership

Placings:336/02015-000000400 **(5447)**
2001: 10^{0}S, 10^{0}GF, 10^{0}GS, 9^{0}GS, 12^{0}G, 10^{0}GF, 12^{4}G, 13^{0}GS, 10^{0}HY

	Starts	1st	2nd	3rd	Win & Pl
Career Total (Turf)	17	1	1	2	6273

69 7/00 Pont 1m2f6y D G-F £3721
Total win prize-money £3721

Going (Turf): Sf: 0-2 GS: 0-4 Gd: 0-2 **GF: 1-9** Fm: 0-0
Distance: 5f/6f: 0-0 7f-8f: 0-3 **9f-13f: 1-13** 14f+: 0-1
Track : **LH: 1-6** RH: 0-8 Tight: 0-5 Gall: 0-5
Aids: Bl: 0-0 Vi: 0-1 Tstrap: 0-0
Best Rating: 60 9/01 Gdwd 1m4f good

Formerly with Ed Dunlop, he finally got off the mark with a hard-fought win in a ten-furlong Pontefract maiden in summer of 2000 after some creditable efforts. Lightly raced since, he has run poorly for his new yard on soft-ish ground this season, and needs it much faster.

Route Barree (FR)

104 **81**

3-y-o ch c Exit To Nowhere (USA)-Star Des Evees (FR) (Moulin)
S Dow Byerley Bloodstock

Placings:0-5422625 **(4047)**
2001: 9^{5}GS, 12^{4}GS, 11^{2}F, 12^{2}GF, 12^{6}G, 11^{2}GF, 14^{5}F

	Starts	1st	2nd	3rd	Win & Pl
Career Total (Turf)	8	0	3	0	3914

Going (Turf): Sf: 0-1 GS: 0-2 Gd: 0-1 GF: 0-2 Fm: 0-2
Distance: 5f/6f: 0-0 7f-8f: 0-0 9f-13f: 0-7 14f+: 0-1
Track : LH: 0-5 RH: 0-3 Tight: 0-2 Gall: 0-0
Aids: Bl: 0-0 Vi: 0-1 Tstrap: 0-0
Best Rating: 81 8/01 Brig 1m3f196y gd-fm

Route Sixty Six (IRE)

104 **57**

5-y-o b m Brief Truce (USA)-Lyphards Goddess (IRE) (Lyphard's Special (USA))
Jedd O'Keeffe Wetherby Racing Bureau 47

Placings:020661/01040050200/000232232-3600500

2001: 8^{3}HY, 8^{6}S, 9^{0}G, 10^{0}GF, 8^{5}GS, 8^{0}G, 8^{0}S **(5539)**

	Starts	1st	2nd	3rd	Win & Pl
Career Total (Turf)	34	2	6	3	30866

82 5/99 NmkJ 1m C(0-90)H G-F £15110
72 10/98 Brig 6f209y E(0-75)H G-S £3053
Total win prize-money £18163

Going (Turf): Sf: 0-9 **GS: 1-5** Gd: 0-8 **GF: 1-8** Fm: 0-4
Distance: 5f/6f: 0-1 **7f-8f: 2-21** 9f-13f: 0-12 14f+: 0-0
Track : **LH: 1-13** RH: 0-8 Tight: 0-1 Gall: 0-5
Aids: Bl: 0-1 Vi: 0-0 Tstrap: 0-0
Best Rating: 60 4/01 Nott 1m54y heavy

Roxanne Mill

104(103) (71)**71**

3-y-o b f Cyrano De Bergerac-It Must Be Millie (Reprimand)
M D I Usher The Goodracing Partnership

Placings:503463124-0000023432 **(4285)**
2001: 6^{0}SW, 5^{0}SD, 5^{0}GS, 6^{0}S, 5^{0}G, 5^{2}GF, 5^{3}GF, 5^{4}GF, 5^{3}G, 5^{2}G

	Starts	1st	2nd	3rd	Win & Pl
Career Total (Turf)	14	0	2	4	7185
Career Total (AW)	5	1	1	0	3000

71 10/00 Wolv 5f F STD £2226
Total win prize-money £2226

Going (Turf): Sf: 0-2 GS: 0-2 Gd: 0-4 GF: 0-5 Fm: 0-0
Distance: **5f/6f: 1-17** 7f-8f: 0-1 9f-13f: 0-0 14f+: 0-0
Track : **LH: 1-5** RH: 0-1 **Tight: 1-4** Gall: 0-2
Aids: Bl: 0-0 Vi: 0-0 Tstrap: 0-0
Best Rating: 64 8/01 Yarm 5f43y good

Roy

6-y-o ch g Keen-Billante (USA) (Graustark)
W Jenks P Russell

Placings:0/30506/P **(2323)**
2001: 16^{P}SD

	Starts	1st	2nd	3rd	Win & Pl
Career Total (Turf)	4	0	0	1	588
Career Total (AW)	3	0	0	0	0

Going (Turf): Sf: 0-0 GS: 0-0 Gd: 0-2 GF: 0-2 Fm: 0-0
Distance: 5f/6f: 0-0 7f-8f: 0-1 9f-13f: 0-1 14f+: 0-5
Track : LH: 0-5 RH: 0-2 Tight: 0-2 Gall: 0-3
Aids: Bl: 0-1 Vi: 0-0 Tstrap: 0-0

Roy McAvoy (IRE)

80 **42**

3-y-o b g Danehill (USA)-Decadence (Vaigly Great)
C A Cyzer Mrs E A Cyzer

Placings:0 **(1147)**
2001: 6^{0}GS

	Starts	1st	2nd	3rd	Win & Pl
Career Total (Turf)	1	0	0	0	

Going (Turf): Sf: 0-0 GS: 0-1 Gd: 0-0 GF: 0-0 Fm: 0-0
Distance: 5f/6f: 0-1 7f-8f: 0-0 9f-13f: 0-0 14f+: 0-0
Track : LH: 0-0 RH: 0-0 Tight: 0-0 Gall: 0-0
Aids: Bl: 0-0 Vi: 0-0 Tstrap: 0-0
Best Rating: 42 5/01 Sals 6f gd-sft

Royal Approval

91 **76**

2-y-o b c Royal Applause-Inimitable (Polish Precedent (USA))
J L Dunlop John Darby

Placings:401 **(4625)**
2001: 7^{4}GF, 7^{0}G, 8^{1}GF

	Starts	1st	2nd	3rd	Win & Pl
Career Total (Turf)	3	1	0	0	3248

76 9/01 Nott 1m54y E G-F £3248
Total win prize-money £3248

Going (Turf): Sf: 0-0 GS: 0-0 Gd: 0-1 **GF: 1-2** Fm: 0-0
Distance: 5f/6f: 0-0 7f-8f: 0-2 **9f-13f: 1-1** 14f+: 0-0
Track : **LH: 1-1** RH: 0-0 Tight: 0-0 Gall: 0-0
Aids: Bl: 0-0 Vi: 0-0 Tstrap: 0-0
Best Rating: 76 9/01 Nott 1m54y gd-fm

With both speed and stamina in his breeding, he was a winner of a maiden auction at Nottingham in September 2001.

Royal Artist

106(107) (78)**89d**

5-y-o b g Royal Academy (USA)-Council Rock (General Assembly (USA))
W J Haggas L K Piggott/a Hirschfeld/r Jenner

Placings:04231/21262110000-0620000 **(4872)**
2001: 6^{0}G, 7^{6}GF, 7^{2}GF, 7^{0}GF, 7^{0}G, 5^{0}G, 7^{0}G

	Starts	1st	2nd	3rd	Win & Pl
Career Total (Turf)	20	2	4	1	29256
Career Total (AW)	3	2	1	0	6441

89 7/00 Asct 6f C(0-95)H G-F £12261
87 7/00 Leic 7f9y D(0-80)H G-F £7514
78 4/00 Wolv 1m100y E(0-75)H STD £2814
52 11/99 Ling 7f D STD £2814
Total win prize-money £25404

Going (Turf): Sf: 0-1 GS: 0-2 Gd: 0-7 **GF: 2-8** Fm: 0-2
Distance: 5f/6f: 1-7 **7f-8f: 2-14** 9f-13f: 1-2 14f+: 0-0
Track : **LH: 2-4** RH: 0-2 **Tight: 2-4** Gall: 0-2
Aids: Bl: 0-4 Vi: 0-0 Tstrap: 0-0
Best Rating: 89 6/01 NmkJ 7f gd-fm

A fast-ground sprint handicapper over six and seven furlongs, he ran well in first-time blinkers at Newmarket in July. Tends to come from behind and as a consequence does find trouble in running.

Royal Axminster

98 **45**

6-y-o b g Alzao (USA)-Number One Spot (Reference Point)
Mrs P N Dutfield Axminster Carpets Ltd

Placings:0/005060/004003-425406 **(4614)**
2001: 11^{4}F, 12^{2}GF, 12^{5}GF, 12^{4}GF, 10^{0}G, 13^{6}F

	Starts	1st	2nd	3rd	Win & Pl
Career Total (Turf)	19	0	1	1	1817

Going (Turf): Sf: 0-1 GS: 0-2 Gd: 0-5 GF: 0-7 Fm: 0-3
Distance: 5f/6f: 0-0 7f-8f: 0-1 9f-13f: 0-12 14f+: 0-5
Track : LH: 0-7 RH: 0-8 Tight: 0-10 Gall: 0-2
Aids: Bl: 0-1 Vi: 0-0 Tstrap: 0-0
Best Rating: 45 6/01 NmkR 1m4f gd-fm

Royal Beau (IRE)

86(68) (24)**45**

2-y-o b f Fayruz-Castlelue (IRE) (Tremblant)
D Nicholls Dandy Nicholls Racing Club

Placings:04004 **(2397)**
2001: 5^{0}SD, 5^{4}GF, 6^{0}GF, 6^{0}G, 7^{4}GF

	Starts	1st	2nd	3rd	Win & Pl
Career Total (Turf)	4	0	0	0	285
Career Total (AW)	1	0	0	0	

Going (Turf): Sf: 0-0 GS: 0-0 Gd: 0-1 GF: 0-3 Fm: 0-0
Distance: 5f/6f: 0-4 7f-8f: 0-1 9f-13f: 0-0 14f+: 0-0
Track : LH: 0-0 RH: 0-0 Tight: 0-0 Gall: 0-0
Aids: Bl: 0-0 Vi: 0-0 Tstrap: 0-0
Best Rating: 45 5/01 Thsk 5f gd-fm

Royal Brighteyes

3-y-o b g Barbezieux-Royal Hanina (Royal Palace)
Ronald Thompson Mrs S Thrower

Placings:00 **(3142)**
2001: 8^{0}F, 8^{0}G

	Starts	1st	2nd	3rd	Win & Pl
Career Total (Turf)	2	0	0	0	

Going (Turf): Sf: 0-0 GS: 0-0 Gd: 0-1 GF: 0-0 Fm: 0-1
Distance: 5f/6f: 0-0 7f-8f: 0-1 9f-13f: 0-1 14f+: 0-0
Track : LH: 0-1 RH: 0-0 Tight: 0-0 Gall: 0-0
Aids: Bl: 0-0 Vi: 0-0 Tstrap: 0-0

Royal Cascade (IRE)

(103) (55)**41**
7-y-o b g River Falls-Relative Stranger (Cragador)
B A McMahon R L Bedding

Placings:62/1065056051411600250021/20111000350/063020201502634-44226410240034 (5613)
2001: 7^{4}SD, 7^{4}SW, 7^{2}SD, 8^{2}SW, 8^{6}SD, 7^{4}SD, 7^{1}SD, 7^{0}SD, 8^{2}SD, 8^{4}SD, 6^{0}SD, 7^{0}SD, 8^{3}SD, 9^{4}SD, 8^{0}SD

	Starts	1st	2nd	3rd	Win & Pl
Career Total (Turf)	11	0	1	0	542
Career Total (AW)	53	10	9	4	31140

57	4/01	Sthl	7f	F(0-60)	STD	£2611
58	8/00	Wolv	6f	G	STD	£2023
81	2/99	Sthl	7f	D(0-85)H	STD	£3701
71	2/99	Wolv	6f	D(0-80)H	STD	£3517
70	1/99	Sthl	7f	F(0-60)	STD	£1717
57	12/98	Wolv	6f	F	STD	£1934
65	3/98	Wolv	6f	F	STD	£1987
69	2/98	Sthl	6f	F	STD	£2085
53	1/98	Sthl	6f	G	STD	£1738
51	2/97	Wolv	6f	F	STD	£2580

Total win prize-money £23897

Going (Turf): Sf: 0-2 GS: 0-1 Gd: 0-4 GF: 0-3 Fm: 0-1
Distance: 5f/6f: 7-27 7f-8f: 3-30 9f-13f: 0-7 14f+: 0-0
Track : LH: 10-55 RH: 0-5 **Tight: 5-31** Gall: 0-3
Aids: Bl: 9-46 Vi: 0-0 Tstrap: 0-0
Best Rating: 57 4/01 Sthl 7f stand

A regular on the All-Weather, he has a powerful finishing kick, but is inclined to get behind and come on the scene too late. Has never won beyond seven furlongs. His turf form is indifferent.

Royal Castle (IRE)

76 **72**
7-y-o b g Caerleon (USA)-Sun Princess (English Prince)
M H Tompkins Mrs B Cross & Mr M Sakal

Placings:0/0510413/03450420/530/6500-0 **(5373)**
2001: 14^{0}G

	Starts	1st	2nd	3rd	Win & Pl
Career Total (Turf)	24	2	1	3	16281

80	10/97	Rdcr	1m6f19y	D(0-80)H	G-F	£3532
73	6/97	Pont	1m4f8y	D(0-80)H	G-F	£3720

Total win prize-money £7252

Going (Turf): Sf: 0-1 GS: 0-3 Gd: 0-4 **GF: 2-10** Fm: 0-1
Distance: 5f/6f: 0-0 7f-8f: 0-1 9f-13f: 1-5 14f+: 1-13
Track : LH: 2-11 RH: 0-7 **Tight: 1-7** Gall: 0-6
Aids: Bl: 0-0 Vi: 0-1 Tstrap: 0-0
Best Rating: 53 10/01 Rdcr 1m6f19y good

Royal Cavalier

108(101) (73)**79**
4-y-o b g Prince Of Birds (USA)-Gold Belt (IRE) (Bellypha)
R Hollinshead The Three R'S

Placings:43422/**0341**000620064054**0432-631025340333141** **(5693)**
2001: 8^{6}SD, 10^{3}G, 9^{1}F, 10^{0}GF, 9^{2}GF, 10^{5}GF, 10^{3}GF, 11^{4}G, 10^{0}GF, 9^{3}GS, 9^{3}GS, 11^{3}GF, 9^{1}GF, 8^{4}GS, 12^{1}S

	Starts	1st	2nd	3rd	Win & Pl
Career Total (Turf)	30	3	3	6	43861
Career Total (AW)	10	1	2	2	5267

79	11/01	Donc	1m4f	B H	SFT	£23400
73	9/01	Nott	1m1f213yE(0-70)		G-F	£3189
65	5/01	Leic	1m1f218yE(0-70)H		FRM	£3514
76	3/00	Wolv	1m1f79y D		STD	£2758

Total win prize-money £32861

Going (Turf): Sf: 1-7 GS: 0-6 Gd: 0-4 **GF: 1-12 Fm: 1-1**
Distance: 5f/6f: 0-1 7f-8f: 0-13 **9f-13f: 4-26** 14f+: 0-0
Track : LH: 3-28 RH: 1-8 Tight: 1-10 Gall: 1-6
Aids: Bl: 0-0 Vi: 0-0 Tstrap: 0-0
Best Rating: 79 11/01 Donc 1m4f soft

Fair handicapper at around ten furlongs, but stayed the mile and a half well when winning the November Handicap in 2001. Has scored once on the All-Weather. Has won on firm and with give underfoot.

Royal Eagle (GER)

95 **83**
2-y-o ch c Eagle Eyed (USA)-Royal Rivalry (USA) (Sir Ivor)
L M Cumani L Marinopoulos

Placings:23244 **(5459)**
2001: 7^{2}GF, 7^{3}GF, 7^{2}GF, 7^{4}S, 8^{4}G

	Starts	1st	2nd	3rd	Win & Pl
Career Total (Turf)	5	0	2	1	2718

Going (Turf): Sf: 0-1 GS: 0-0 Gd: 0-1 GF: 0-3 Fm: 0-0
Distance: 5f/6f: 0-0 7f-8f: 0-4 9f-13f: 0-1 14f+: 0-0
Track : LH: 0-2 RH: 0-0 Tight: 0-1 Gall: 0-1
Aids: Bl: 0-0 Vi: 0-0 Tstrap: 0-2
Best Rating: 83 8/01 Folk 7f gd-fm

Royal Eberspacher (IRE)

56
2-y-o b f Revoque (IRE)-Nicea (IRE) (Dominion)
Mrs P N Dutfield Royal Oak Racing Partnership

Placings:00 **(5040)**
2001: 6^{0}GF, 10^{0}G

	Starts	1st	2nd	3rd	Win & Pl
Career Total (Turf)	2	0	0	0	

Going (Turf): Sf: 0-0 GS: 0-0 Gd: 0-1 GF: 0-1 Fm: 0-0
Distance: 5f/6f: 0-0 7f-8f: 0-1 9f-13f: 0-1 14f+: 0-0
Track : LH: 0-1 RH: 0-0 Tight: 0-1 Gall: 0-0
Aids: Bl: 0-0 Vi: 0-0 Tstrap: 0-0

Royal Enclosure (IRE)

101(98) (49)**47**
3-y-o b g Royal Academy (USA)-Hi Bettina (Henbit (USA))
P D Evans (A T Murphy 22/1) Mike Nolan

Placings:000-**20642440**06**2**24**0**23244550 **(5532)**
2001: 9^{2}SW, 8^{0}SW, 8^{6}SD, 7^{4}SD, 8^{2}SD, 9^{4}SD, 8^{4}SD, 7^{0}SW, 7^{0}GF, 9^{6}F, 8^{2}SD, 8^{2}G, 8^{4}GF, 8^{0}SD, 8^{2}G, 8^{3}GF, 8^{2}GS, 10^{4}G, 8^{4}G, 10^{5}GF, 9^{5}G, 9^{0}HY

	Starts	1st	2nd	3rd	Win & Pl
Career Total (Turf)	15	0	3	1	2729
Career Total (AW)	10	0	3	0	1752

Going (Turf): Sf: 0-2 GS: 0-1 Gd: 0-5 GF: 0-6 Fm: 0-1
Distance: 5f/6f: 0-0 7f-8f: 0-12 9f-13f: 0-13 14f+: 0-0
Track : LH: 0-18 RH: 0-1 Tight: 0-8 Gall: 0-0
Aids: Bl: 0-2 Vi: 0-10 Tstrap: 0-12
Best Rating: 50 7/01 Nott 1m54y gd-fm

Royal Gent

87(51) **47**
3-y-o b g Presidium-Harem Queen (Prince Regent (FR))
L R James Mrs M Lingwood

Placings:0-55000 **(4164)**
2001: 11^{5}GF, 10^{5}G, 12^{0}GF, 12^{0}SD, 16^{0}GF

	Starts	1st	2nd	3rd	Win & Pl
Career Total (Turf)	5	0	0	0	0
Career Total (AW)	1	0	0	0	

Going (Turf): Sf: 0-0 GS: 0-0 Gd: 0-2 GF: 0-3 Fm: 0-0
Distance: 5f/6f: 0-0 7f-8f: 0-1 9f-13f: 0-4 14f+: 0-1
Track : LH: 0-4 RH: 0-2 Tight: 0-2 Gall: 0-2
Aids: Bl: 0-0 Vi: 0-1 Tstrap: 0-0
Best Rating: 47 5/01 Haml 1m3f16y gd-fm

Royal Glen (IRE)

87 **25**
3-y-o b f Royal Abjar (USA)-Sea Glen (IRE) (Glenstal (USA))
H A McWilliams James S Kennerley And Miss Jenny Hall

Placings:36-00000000500 **(5631)**
2001: 7^{0}G, 8^{0}F, 7^{0}G, 8^{0}GF, 8^{0}F, 8^{0}GS, 7^{0}F, 10^{0}S, 10^{5}HY, 11^{0}S, 10^{0}G

	Starts	1st	2nd	3rd	Win & Pl
Career Total (Turf)	13	0	0	1	530

Going (Turf): Sf: 0-3 GS: 0-1 Gd: 0-4 GF: 0-1 Fm: 0-3
Distance: 5f/6f: 0-1 7f-8f: 0-6 9f-13f: 0-5 14f+: 0-0
Track : LH: 0-7 RH: 0-0 Tight: 0-2 Gall: 0-3
Aids: Bl: 0-0 Vi: 0-0 Tstrap: 0-0
Best Rating: 47 5/01 Donc 7f good

Royal Insult

104(107) (79)**74**
4-y-o ch g Lion Cavern (USA)-Home Truth (Known Fact (USA))
K R Burke D R Kerr

Placings:21/00001-3002 **(3645)**
2001: 7^{3}GF, 7^{0}GF, 8^{0}GS, 8^{2}F

	Starts	1st	2nd	3rd	Win & Pl
Career Total (Turf)	10	1	2	1	8153
Career Total (AW)	1	1	0	0	7023

79	11/00	Ling	7f	C(0-95)H	STD	£7023
77	10/99	Rdcr	6f	D	GD	£3247

Total win prize-money £10271

Going (Turf): Sf: 0-2 GS: 0-2 **Gd: 1-3** GF: 0-2 Fm: 0-1
Distance: 5f/6f: 1-3 7f-8f: 1-8 9f-13f: 0-0 14f+: 0-0
Track : LH: 1-5 RH: 0-1 **Tight: 1-2** Gall: 0-1
Aids: Bl: 0-0 Vi: 0-1 Tstrap: 0-0
Best Rating: 74 8/01 Thsk 1m firm

Lightly raced, he is effective at up to a mile and has won on good ground and Equitrack. Took keen hold in first-time visor at Thirsk when stepped up to a mile.

Royal Ivy

104(104) (67d)**58**
4-y-o ch f Mujtahid (USA)-Royal Climber (King's Lake (USA))
J Akehurst The Goldmine Partnership

Placings:44454032/**2310**05420060**000**-00402454 **(5025)**
2001: 7^{0}GF, 7^{0}F, 7^{4}F, 7^{0}GF, 7^{2}GF, 6^{4}F, 7^{5}GF, 6^{4}S

	Starts	1st	2nd	3rd	Win & Pl
Career Total (Turf)	23	0	2	1	5147
Career Total (AW)	8	1	2	1	4783

55	1/00	Ling	7f	D	STD	£2808

Total win prize-money £2808

Going (Turf): Sf: 0-3 GS: 0-2 Gd: 0-5 GF: 0-10 Fm: 0-3
Distance: 5f/6f: 0-5 **7f-8f: 1-25** 9f-13f: 0-1 14f+: 0-0
Track : LH: 1-13 RH: 0-3 **Tight: 1-10** Gall: 0-1
Aids: Bl: 0-0 Vi: 0-0 Tstrap: 0-0

Best Rating: 58 8/01 Ling 7f gd-fm

Royal Kiss (IRE)

92 **56**

3-y-o b f Royal Academy (USA)-Hawajiss (Kris)

E A L Dunlop Gainsborough Stud

Placings:00-00535 **(2451)**

2001: 10^{0}GS, 11^{0}G, 14^{5}F, 11^{3}F, 11^{5}F

	Starts	1st	2nd	3rd	Win & Pl
Career Total (Turf)	7	0	0	1	405

Going (Turf): Sf: 0-1 GS: 0-1 Gd: 0-2 GF: 0-0 Fm: 0-3
Distance: 5f/6f: 0-0 7f-8f: 0-2 9f-13f: 0-4 14f+: 0-1
Track : LH: 0-4 RH: 0-0 Tight: 0-4 Gall: 0-1
Aids: Bl: 0-0 Vi: 0-0 Tstrap: 0-0
Best Rating: 56 6/01 Brig 1m3f196y firm

Royal Lady (IRE)

91 **76**

2-y-o b f Royal Academy (USA)-Shahoune (USA) (Blushing Groom (FR))

R Guest Mrs Jeanette Eng

Placings:00 **(5603)**

2001: 7^{0}GS, 7^{0}GS

	Starts	1st	2nd	3rd	Win & Pl
Career Total (Turf)	2	0	0	0	

Going (Turf): Sf: 0-0 GS: 0-2 Gd: 0-0 GF: 0-0 Fm: 0-0
Distance: 5f/6f: 0-0 7f-8f: 0-2 9f-13f: 0-0 14f+: 0-0
Track : LH: 0-0 RH: 0-0 Tight: 0-0 Gall: 0-0
Aids: Bl: 0-0 Vi: 0-0 Tstrap: 0-0
Best Rating: 76 10/01 Leic 7f9y gd-sft

Royal Measure

105 (38)**56**

5-y-o b g Inchinor-Sveltissima (Dunphy)

B R Millman The Royal Partnership

Placings:56450000/3000-2100 **(5098)**

2001: 14^{2}S, 14^{1}HY, 17^{0}GF, 14^{0}GS

	Starts	1st	2nd	3rd	Win & Pl
Career Total (Turf)	14	1	1	1	5053
Career Total (AW)	2	0	0	0	0

56	5/01	Nott	1m6f15y	E(0-70)H	HVY	£3388

Total win prize-money £3388

Going (Turf): Sf: 1-4 GS: 0-1 Gd: 0-5 GF: 0-4 Fm: 0-0
Distance: 5f/6f: 0-0 7f-8f: 0-0 9f-13f: 0-10 **14f+: 1-6**
Track : **LH: 1-8** RH: 0-7 Tight: 0-9 Gall: 0-0
Aids: Bl: 0-0 Vi: 0-0 Tstrap: 0-0
Best Rating: 56 5/01 Nott 1m6f15y heavy

Royal Millennium (IRE)

112 **93**

3-y-o b c Royal Academy (USA)-Galatrix (Be My Guest (USA))

M R Channon Jackie & George Smith

Placings:3212320 **(4195)**

2001: 8^{3}S, 7^{2}GF, 6^{1}GF, 7^{2}GF, 7^{3}GS, 7^{2}G, 6^{0}G

	Starts	1st	2nd	3rd	Win & Pl
Career Total (Turf)	7	1	3	2	24980

89	6/01	Sals	6f212y	D	G-F	£3640

Total win prize-money £3640

Going (Turf): Sf: 0-1 GS: 0-1 Gd: 0-2 **GF: 1-3** Fm: 0-0
Distance: 6f/6f: 0-0 **7f-8f: 1-7** 9f-13f: 0-0 14f+: 0-0
Track : LH: 0-1 RH: 0-3 Tight: 0-0 Gall: 0-1
Aids: Bl: 0-0 Vi: 0-0 Tstrap: 0-0
Best Rating: 93 8/01 Gdwd 7f good

He needed time and did not race at two, but won easily at Salisbury on his third start and only went down by the minimum margin in a very valuable handicap at Sandown in July. He needs fast ground and seven furlongs looks his trip.

Royal Minstrel (IRE)

109 **82**

4-y-o ch g Be My Guest (USA)-Shanntabariya (IRE) (Shernazar)

M H Tompkins P A & D G Sakal

Placings:664/3145200-065121105 **(5338)**

2001: 16^{0}S, 14^{6}GS, 14^{5}GS, 9^{1}GS, 10^{2}GF, 10^{1}GF, 11^{1}GF, 12^{0}HY, 12^{5}GS

	Starts	1st	2nd	3rd	Win & Pl
Career Total (Turf)	19	4	2	1	30287

82	9/01	York	1m3f195yD(0-85)H		G-F	£8830
78	8/01	Ripn	1m2f	C(0-90)H	G-F	£7202
73	8/01	Leic	1m1f218yD(0-85)H		G-S	£4566
87	4/00	Thsk	1m4f	D	SFT	£4445

Total win prize-money £25043

Going (Turf): Sf: 1-6 GS: 1-6 Gd: 0-2 **GF: 2-5** Fm: 0-0
Distance: 5f/6f: 0-0 7f-8f: 0-2 **9f-13f: 4-12** 14f+: 0-5
Track : LH: 2-8 RH: 2-7 **Tight: 2-5** Gall: 1-5
Aids: Bl: 0-1 Vi: 0-0 Tstrap: 0-0
Best Rating: 82 10/01 NmkR 1m4f gd-sft

Running over longer trips earlier in the season, but dropped back to middle distances in the summer and won at Leicester, Ripon and York. Effective at ten to 12 furlongs, he seems to handle any ground. Sometimes does not look a straightforward ride as he carries his head high and has a tendency to hang.

Royal Mirage (IRE)

90(88) (58)**61**

2-y-o ch f Lycius (USA)-Cariellor's Miss (FR) (Cariellor (FR))

M L W Bell William Archer

Placings:536 **(5610)**

2001: 7^{5}GS, 8^{3}SD, 8^{6}SD

	Starts	1st	2nd	3rd	Win & Pl
Career Total (Turf)	1	0	0	0	0
Career Total (AW)	2	0	0	1	414

Going (Turf): Sf: 0-0 GS: 0-1 Gd: 0-0 GF: 0-0 Fm: 0-0
Distance: 5f/6f: 0-0 7f-8f: 0-1 9f-13f: 0-2 14f+: 0-0
Track : LH: 0-2 RH: 0-0 Tight: 0-2 Gall: 0-0
Aids: Bl: 0-0 Vi: 0-0 Tstrap: 0-0
Best Rating: 61 10/01 Newc 7f gd-sft

Royal Musical

82(84) (17)**25**

3-y-o ch f Royal Abjar (USA)-Musical Sally (USA) (The Minstrel (CAN))

M Brittain Bob Abson Bjk Partnership

Placings:50000-50 **(3749)**

2001: 11^{5}SD, 8^{0}GS

	Starts	1st	2nd	3rd	Win & Pl
Career Total (Turf)	6	0	0	0	0
Career Total (AW)	1	0	0	0	0

Going (Turf): Sf: 0-1 GS: 0-2 Gd: 0-1 GF: 0-2 Fm: 0-0
Distance: 5f/6f: 0-3 7f-8f: 0-2 9f-13f: 0-2 14f+: 0-0
Track : LH: 0-4 RH: 0-1 Tight: 0-0 Gall: 0-0
Aids: Bl: 0-0 Vi: 0-0 Tstrap: 0-0
Best Rating: 17 7/01 Sthl 1m3f stand

Royal Partnership (IRE)

(105) (47)**59?**

5-y-o b g Royal Academy (USA)-Go Honey Go (General Assembly (USA))

D L Williams Reliance Car Hire Services Ltd

Placings:3/03000/P5140203051-20 **(0345)**

2001: 12^{2}SD, 16^{0}SD

	Starts	1st	2nd	3rd	Win & Pl
Career Total (Turf)	7	0	0	2	657
Career Total (AW)	12	2	2	1	4892

47	5/00	Sthl	1m3f	F(0-60)	STD	£1848
45	2/00	Sthl	1m3f	G	STD	£1892

Total win prize-money £3741

Going (Turf): Sf: 0-2 GS: 0-0 Gd: 0-2 GF: 0-1 Fm: 0-0
Distance: 5f/6f: 0-1 7f-8f: 0-7 **9f-13f: 2-10** 14f+: 0-1
Track : **LH: 2-13** RH: 0-5 Tight: 0-7 Gall: 0-1
Aids: Bl: 0-0 **Vi: 1-2** Tstrap: 0-0
Best Rating: 47 2/01 Wolv 1m4f stand

Royal Plum

99(92) (38)**24**

5-y-o ch g Inchinor-Miss Plum (Ardross)

Mrs M Reveley Lucayan Stud

Placings:00-500600 **(5170)**

2001: 12^{5}SW, 16^{0}SD, 16^{0}SD, 16^{6}GS, 16^{0}GF, 17^{0}GS

	Starts	1st	2nd	3rd	Win & Pl
Career Total (Turf)	4	0	0	0	0
Career Total (AW)	4	0	0	0	0

Going (Turf): Sf: 0-0 GS: 0-3 Gd: 0-0 GF: 0-1 Fm: 0-0
Distance: 5f/6f: 0-0 7f-8f: 0-0 9f-13f: 0-3 14f+: 0-5
Track : LH: 0-6 RH: 0-2 Tight: 0-3 Gall: 0-0
Aids: Bl: 0-3 Vi: 0-1 Tstrap: 0-0
Best Rating: 38 1/01 Sthl 1m4f slow

Royal Poppy

80 **28**

3-y-o b f Mind Games-Never So True (Never So Bold)

H A McWilliams James S Kennerley And Miss Jenny Hall

Placings:000 **(2534)**

2001: 6^{0}F, 7^{0}G, 6^{0}GF

	Starts	1st	2nd	3rd	Win & Pl
Career Total (Turf)	3	0	0	0	

Going (Turf): Sf: 0-0 GS: 0-0 Gd: 0-1 GF: 0-1 Fm: 0-1
Distance: 5f/6f: 0-2 7f-8f: 0-1 9f-13f: 0-0 14f+: 0-0
Track : LH: 0-1 RH: 0-0 Tight: 0-1 Gall: 0-0
Aids: Bl: 0-0 Vi: 0-0 Tstrap: 0-0
Best Rating: 28 6/01 Thsk 7f good

Royal Prodigy (USA)

92 **71**

2-y-o ch c Royal Academy (USA)-Prospector's Queen (USA) (Mr Prospector (USA))

J Noseda Crazy Radio Ltd

Placings:30 **(5604)**

2001: 7^{3}GS, 7^{0}GS

	Starts	1st	2nd	3rd	Win & Pl
Career Total (Turf)	2	0	0	1	1135

Going (Turf): Sf: 0-0 GS: 0-2 Gd: 0-0 GF: 0-0 Fm: 0-0
Distance: 5f/6f: 0-0 7f-8f: 0-2 9f-13f: 0-0 14f+: 0-0
Track : LH: 0-1 RH: 0-0 Tight: 0-0 Gall: 0-1
Aids: Bl: 0-0 Vi: 0-0 Tstrap: 0-0
Best Rating: 71 10/01 York 7f202y gd-sft

Royal Quarters (IRE)

104 **101+**

2-y-o ch c Common Grounds-Queen Canute (IRE) (Ahonoora)

B J Meehan Joe L Allbritton

Placings:421 **(5038)**

2001: 5^{4}G, 6^{2}GF, 5^{1}G

	Starts	1st	2nd	3rd	Win & Pl
Career Total (Turf)	3	1	1	0	5332

101	10/01	Bath	5f161y	D	GD	£3571

Total win prize-money £3572

Going (Turf): Sf: 0-0 GS: 0-0 **Gd: 1-2** GF: 0-1 Fm: 0-0
Distance: **5f/6f: 1-2** 7f-8f: 0-1 9f-13f: 0-0 14f+: 0-0
Track : **LH: 1-1** RH: 0-0 Tight: 0-0 **Gall: 1-1**
Aids: Bl: 0-0 Vi: 0-0 Tstrap: 0-0
Best Rating: 101 10/01 Bath 5f161y good

Ready winner on his third start at Bath. Suited by six furlongs and fast ground.

Royal Rebel

107 **116**

5-y-o b g Robellino (USA)-Greenvera (USA) (Riverman (USA))
M Johnston P D Savill

Placings:404/31230010/012211326-60160043 **(5385)**
2001: 13^{6}GF, 16^{0}G, 20^{1}GF, 16^{6}G, 15^{0}G, 18^{0}G, 20^{4}HO, 16^{3}GS

	Starts	1st	2nd	3rd	Win & Pl
Career Total (Turf)	**28**	**6**	**4**	**4**	**314243**

116	6/01	Asct	2m4f	A	G-F	£121800
119	8/00	York	1m7f195y	A	GD	£44625
119	8/00	Gdwd	2m	A	GD	£46400
103	5/00	Leop	1m6f		GD	£16250
103	8/99	Leop	1m6f		GD	£16250
82	4/99	Newc	1m	D	GD	£3631

Total win prize-money £248956

Going (Turf): Sf: 0-3 GS: 0-3 **Gd: 5-13** GF: 1-4 Fm: 0-2
Distance: 5f/6f: 0-0 7f-8f: 1-5 9f-13f: 0-5 **14f+: 5-18**
Track : **LH: 4-12** RH: 2-13 Tight: 1-4 **Gall: 3-11**
Aids: Bl: 2-10 Vi: 2-7 Tstrap: 0-0
Best Rating: 116 10/01 NmkR 2m gd-sft

A lazy individual, he responded well to blinkers and Mick Kinane's urgings when winning the Goodwood Cup and Lonsdale Stakes in 2000. Held in the early part of this year, but put up a fine battling performance to win the Ascot Gold Cup. He is a real stayer who is best on a sound surface. He has disappointed since Ascot, looking as if his heart is not in the right place, but ran better at Newmarket in October.

Royal Reprimand (IRE)

102 **48**

6-y-o b g Reprimand-Lake Ormond (King's Lake (USA))
R E Barr R E Barr

Placings:602/0660054545/000005243236-0204002400364060 **(5539)**
2001: 6^{0}F, 8^{2}F, 7^{0}GF, 7^{4}GF, 8^{0}F, 10^{0}F, 8^{2}F, 8^{4}F, 7^{0}G, 8^{0}GF, 7^{3}G, 9^{6}GF, 8^{4}F, 7^{0}GS, 7^{6}G, 8^{0}S

	Starts	1st	2nd	3rd	Win & Pl
Career Total (Turf)	**41**	**0**	**5**	**3**	**7746**

Going (Turf): **Sf: 0-6 GS: 0-3 Gd: 0-7 GF: 0-12 Fm: 0-13**
Distance: 5f/6f: 0-1 7f-8f: 0-28 9f-13f: 0-11 14f+: 0-1
Track : LH: 0-18 RH: 0-5 Tight: 0-16 Gall: 0-4
Aids: Bl: 0-0 Vi: 0-6 Tstrap: 0-0
Best Rating: 51 6/01 Thsk 1m firm

Royal Robbie

86 **43**

3-y-o b g Robellino (USA)-Moogie (Young Generation)
P Butler Mrs E Lucey-Butler

Placings:00 **(1614)**
2001: 8^{0}G, 11^{0}GF

	Starts	1st	2nd	3rd	Win & Pl
Career Total (Turf)	**2**	**0**	**0**	**0**	

Going (Turf): **Sf: 0-0 GS: 0-0 Gd: 0-1 GF: 0-1 Fm: 0-0**
Distance: 5f/6f: 0-0 7f-8f: 0-1 9f-13f: 0-1 14f+: 0-0
Track : LH: 0-1 RH: 0-0 Tight: 0-1 Gall: 0-0
Aids: Bl: 0-0 Vi: 0-0 Tstrap: 0-0
Best Rating: 43 5/01 NmkR 1m good

Royal Romeo

102(104) (69)**74**

4-y-o ch g Timeless Times (USA)-Farinara (Dragonara Palace (USA))
T D Easterby Peter C Bourke

Placings:60531/0163000503036**6-024250403** **(1159)**
2001: 7^{0}SD, 6^{2}SD, 6^{4}SW, 6^{2}SD, 6^{5}SW, 6^{0}S, 7^{4}SD, 7^{0}GS, 6^{3}G

	Starts	1st	2nd	3rd	Win & Pl
Career Total (Turf)	**19**	**2**	**0**	**4**	**10792**
Career Total (AW)	**9**	**0**	**2**	**1**	**3018**

74	6/00	Newc	6f	D(0-85)H	SFT	£3932
69	9/99	Bevl	5f	D	GD	£4056

Total win prize-money £7990

Going (Turf): **Sf: 1-7** GS: 0-2 **Gd: 1-8** GF: 0-2 Fm: 0-0
Distance: **5f/6f: 2-20** 7f-8f: 0-8 9f-13f: 0-0 14f+: 0-0
Track : LH: 0-12 RH: 0-1 Tight: 0-2 Gall: 0-1
Aids: Bl: 0-2 Vi: 0-0 Tstrap: 0-0
Best Rating: 69 2/01 Sthl 6f stand

Royal Satin (IRE)

82 **14**

3-y-o b g Royal Academy (USA)-Satinette (Shirley Heights)
N A Callaghan T Mohan

Placings:000-060 **(3734)**
2001: 11^{0}GF, 11^{6}GF, 11^{0}G

	Starts	1st	2nd	3rd	Win & Pl
Career Total (Turf)	**6**	**0**	**0**	**0**	**0**

Going (Turf): **Sf: 0-1 GS: 0-0 Gd: 0-2 GF: 0-3 Fm: 0-0**
Distance: 5f/6f: 0-0 7f-8f: 0-2 9f-13f: 0-4 14f+: 0-0
Track : LH: 0-3 RH: 0-0 Tight: 0-2 Gall: 0-0
Aids: Bl: 0-3 Vi: 0-0 Tstrap: 0-0
Best Rating: 14 7/01 Ling 1m3f106y gd-fm

Royal Storm (IRE)

85 **70**

2-y-o b c Royal Applause-Wakayi (Persian Bold)
Mrs A J Perrett The Cloran Family

Placings:000 **(5107)**
2001: 7^{0}G, 7^{0}GF, 7^{0}GS

	Starts	1st	2nd	3rd	Win & Pl
Career Total (Turf)	**3**	**0**	**0**	**0**	

Going (Turf): **Sf: 0-0 GS: 0-1 Gd: 0-1 GF: 0-1 Fm: 0-0**
Distance: 5f/6f: 0-0 7f-8f: 0-3 9f-13f: 0-0 14f+: 0-0
Track : LH: 0-0 RH: 0-0 Tight: 0-0 Gall: 0-0
Aids: Bl: 0-0 Vi: 0-0 Tstrap: 0-0
Best Rating: 70 10/01 NmkR 7f gd-sft

Royal Tarragon

98 (23)**39**

5-y-o b m Aragon-Lady Philippa (IRE) (Taufan (USA))
W De Best-Turner W De Best-Turner

Placings:000P40000/00000/000000-000300000500 **(5519)**
2001: 9^{0}F, 10^{0}GF, 9^{0}G, 7^{3}GF, 7^{0}GS, 7^{0}GS, 6^{0}F, 5^{0}GF, 6^{0}GF, 5^{5}S, 6^{0}G, 6^{0}HY

	Starts	1st	2nd	3rd	Win & Pl
Career Total (Turf)	**29**	**0**	**0**	**1**	**732**
Career Total (AW)	**3**	**0**	**0**	**0**	

Going (Turf): **Sf: 0-4 GS: 0-3 Gd: 0-9 GF: 0-9 Fm: 0-4**
Distance: 5f/6f: 0-14 7f-8f: 0-14 9f-13f: 0-4 14f+: 0-0
Track : LH: 0-10 RH: 0-4 Tight: 0-3 Gall: 0-6
Aids: Bl: 0-1 Vi: 0-5 Tstrap: 0-0
Best Rating: 39 9/01 Brig 5f213y soft

Royal Wanderer (IRE)

82(88) (37)**38**

3-y-o ch g Royal Abjar (USA)-Rose 'n Reason (IRE) (Reasonable (FR))
Mrs A Duffield Bill Martin

Placings:000-0400600 **(5046)**
2001: 12^{0}S, 10^{4}F, 8^{0}GF, 9^{0}G, 7^{6}F, 8^{0}F, 11^{0}SD

	Starts	1st	2nd	3rd	Win & Pl
Career Total (Turf)	**8**	**0**	**0**	**0**	**0**
Career Total (AW)	**2**	**0**	**0**	**0**	

Going (Turf): **Sf: 0-2 GS: 0-0 Gd: 0-2 GF: 0-1 Fm: 0-3**
Distance: 5f/6f: 0-2 7f-8f: 0-3 9f-13f: 0-5 14f+: 0-0
Track : LH: 0-5 RH: 0-0 Tight: 0-1 Gall: 0-3
Aids: Bl: 0-0 Vi: 0-0 Tstrap: 0-0
Best Rating: 43 5/01 Newc 1m2f32y firm

Royal Wave (IRE)

66(95) (29)**29**

5-y-o b/br g Polish Precedent (USA)-Mashmoon (USA) (Habitat)
J L Eyre D Hardy, B Cunningham, P Birchenough

Placings:5/100000/0300-0004000 **(5539)**
2001: 9^{0}SD, 8^{0}SW, 7^{0}SD, 7^{4}GF, 7^{0}SD, 8^{0}GF, 8^{0}S

	Starts	1st	2nd	3rd	Win & Pl
Career Total (Turf)	**11**	**1**	**0**	**0**	**2463**
Career Total (AW)	**7**	**0**	**0**	**1**	**281**

80	5/99	Pont	6f	D	GD	£2463

Total win prize-money £2463

Going (Turf): Sf: 0-4 GS: 0-3 **Gd: 1-1** GF: 0-2 Fm: 0-1
Distance: **5f/6f: 1-1** 7f-8f: 0-15 9f-13f: 0-2 14f+: 0-0
Track : **LH: 1-11** RH: 0-1 Tight: 0-3 Gall: 0-1
Aids: Bl: 0-0 Vi: 0-0 Tstrap: 0-1
Best Rating: 29 5/01 Muss 7f30y gd-fm

Royal Windmill (IRE)

90 **76**

2-y-o b g Ali-Royal (IRE)-Salarya (FR) (Darshaan)
J L Eyre Clayton Bigley Partnership Ltd

Placings:30230 **(5504)**
2001: 5^{3}GF, 6^{0}G, 5^{2}F, 5^{3}GF, 7^{0}HY

	Starts	1st	2nd	3rd	Win & Pl
Career Total (Turf)	**5**	**0**	**1**	**2**	**2227**

Going (Turf): **Sf: 0-1 GS: 0-0 Gd: 0-1 GF: 0-2 Fm: 0-1**
Distance: 5f/6f: 0-4 7f-8f: 0-1 9f-13f: 0-0 14f+: 0-0
Track : LH: 0-1 RH: 0-0 Tight: 0-0 Gall: 0-0
Aids: Bl: 0-0 Vi: 0-0 Tstrap: 0-0
Best Rating: 76 9/01 Pont 5f firm

Made a promising debut before being outclassed at Kempton. He has since run two good enough races in maiden company to suggest that there is a race to be won with him.

Roymillon (GER)

87(88) (74)**44**

7-y-o b g Milesius (USA)-Royal Slope (USA) (His Majesty (USA))
D J Wintle John W Egan/graham Brown

Placings:0/10502143621320/1346**0/102**001560**0401/15**1000-0 **(5387)**
2001: 18^{0}GS

	Starts	1st	2nd	3rd	Win & Pl
Career Total (Turf)	**30**	**5**	**3**	**3**	**16967**
Career Total (AW)	**10**	**4**	**1**	**0**	**22025**

2/00	Neus	1m1f110y	STD	£11290
1/00	Neus	1m1f110y H	STD	£4742
12/99	Neus	1m1f110y	STD	£3249
4/99	MAGD	1m2f	SFT	£3249
1/99	Dort	1m1f165y	STD	£1444

3/98	MAGD	1m2f	SFT	£3041
10/97	Dres	1m1f110y	GD	£1742
7/97	Hopp	1m2f	SFT	£1894
4/97	Dres	1m2f110y	SFT	£1894

Total win prize-money £32545

Going (Turf): Sf: 0-1 GS: 0-1 Gd: 0-3 GF: 0-0 Fm: 0-0
Distance: 5f/6f: 0-0 7f-8f: 0-1 9f-13f: 0-23 14f+: 0-2
Track : LH: 0-2 RH: 0-2 Tight: 0-2 Gall: 0-1
Aids: Bl: 0-0 Vi: 0-0 Tstrap: 0-0
Best Rating: 44 10/01 NmkR 2m2f gd-sft

Rozel (IRE)

109 **100?**

4-y-o ch f Wolfhound (USA)-Noirmant (Dominion)
R Guest Matthews Breeding And Racing

Placings:013432-450050 **(5584a)**
2001: 5^{4}G, 5^{5}GF, 5^{0}GF, 5^{0}G, 5^{5}HY, 5^{0}HY

	Starts	1st	2nd	3rd	Win & Pl
Career Total (Turf)	12	1	1	2	16202

79	5/00	Yarm	5f43y	D	GD	£3770

Total win prize-money £3770

Going (Turf): Sf: 0-3 GS: 0-0 **Gd: 1-5** GF: 0-4 Fm: 0-0
Distance: **5f/6f: 1-12** 7f-8f: 0-0 9f-13f: 0-0 14f+: 0-0
Track : LH: 0-0 RH: 0-0 Tight: 0-0 Gall: 0-0
Aids: Bl: 0-0 Vi: 0-0 Tstrap: 0-0
Best Rating: 100 8/01 York 5f good

She has struggled so far this season, but has faced some very difficult tasks.

Ruby Babe

87(44) **35**

3-y-o b f Aragon-Barrie Baby (Import)
J J Quinn Rosswood Racing

Placings:600-40000 **(4778)**
2001: 6^{4}HY, 6^{0}S, 5^{0}G, 5^{0}GF, 5^{0}G

	Starts	1st	2nd	3rd	Win & Pl
Career Total (Turf)	7	0	0	0	0
Career Total (AW)	1	0	0	0	0

Going (Turf): Sf: 0-3 GS: 0-0 Gd: 0-3 GF: 0-1 Fm: 0-0
Distance: 5f/6f: 0-7 7f-8f: 0-1 9f-13f: 0-0 14f+: 0-0
Track : LH: 0-1 RH: 0-0 Tight: 0-0 Gall: 0-0
Aids: Bl: 0-0 Vi: 0-0 Tstrap: 0-0
Best Rating: 35 6/01 Bevl 5f gd-fm

Ruby Legend

92 **37**

3-y-o b g Perpendicular-Singing High (Julio Mariner)
Mrs M Reveley Mrs J M Grimston

Placings:4300 **(5539)**
2001: 8^{4}F, 9^{3}GF, 7^{0}GF, 8^{0}S

	Starts	1st	2nd	3rd	Win & Pl
Career Total (Turf)	4	0	0	1	758

Going (Turf): Sf: 0-1 GS: 0-0 Gd: 0-0 GF: 0-2 Fm: 0-1
Distance: 5f/6f: 0-0 7f-8f: 0-3 9f-13f: 0-1 14f+: 0-0
Track : LH: 0-3 RH: 0-0 Tight: 0-2 Gall: 0-1
Aids: Bl: 0-0 Vi: 0-0 Tstrap: 0-0
Best Rating: 37 8/01 Rdcr 1m1f gd-fm

Ruby Rose

93 **57**

3-y-o b f Red Ransom (USA)-Rose De Reve (IRE) (Persian Heights)
J R Fanshawe Nigel & Carolyn Elwes

Placings:005 **(2705)**
2001: 10^{0}GF, 10^{0}S, 7^{5}F

	Starts	1st	2nd	3rd	Win & Pl
Career Total (Turf)	3	0	0	0	0

Going (Turf): Sf: 0-1 GS: 0-0 Gd: 0-0 GF: 0-1 Fm: 0-1
Distance: 5f/6f: 0-0 7f-8f: 0-1 9f-13f: 0-2 14f+: 0-0
Track : LH: 0-1 RH: 0-2 Tight: 0-1 Gall: 0-0
Aids: Bl: 0-0 Vi: 0-0 Tstrap: 0-0
Best Rating: 57 7/01 Brig 7f214y firm

Ruby Ruby

76 **4**

3-y-o ch f Binary Star (USA)-Runabay (Run The Gantlet (USA))
W G M Turner Hawks And Doves Racing Syndicate

Placings:000 **(4896)**
2001: 10^{0}GF, 10^{0}GF, 9^{0}GS

	Starts	1st	2nd	3rd	Win & Pl
Career Total (Turf)	3	0	0	0	

Going (Turf): Sf: 0-0 GS: 0-1 Gd: 0-0 GF: 0-2 Fm: 0-0
Distance: 5f/6f: 0-0 7f-8f: 0-0 9f-13f: 0-3 14f+: 0-0
Track : LH: 0-2 RH: 0-1 Tight: 0-0 Gall: 0-1
Aids: Bl: 0-0 Vi: 0-0 Tstrap: 0-0
Best Rating: 4 5/01 Nowb 1m2f6y gd-fm

Ruby Wedding

98 **60**

3-y-o b f Blushing Flame (USA)-First Sapphire (Simply Great (FR))
Mrs A J Perrett Ms E Reffo & B Cooper

Placings:6 **(5484)**
2001: 11^{6}G

	Starts	1st	2nd	3rd	Win & Pl
Career Total (Turf)	1	0	0	0	

Going (Turf): Sf: 0-0 GS: 0-0 Gd: 0-1 GF: 0-0 Fm: 0-0
Distance: 5f/6f: 0-0 7f-8f: 0-0 9f-13f: 0-1 14f+: 0-0
Track : LH: 0-1 RH: 0-0 Tight: 0-1 Gall: 0-0
Aids: Bl: 0-0 Vi: 0-0 Tstrap: 0-0
Best Rating: 60 10/01 Bath 1m3f144y good

Rudder

99 **70**

3-y-o ch g Deploy-Wave Dancer (Dance In Time (CAN))
B W Hills M H Dixon

Placings:2-2052240 **(5010)**
2001: 11^{2}S, 12^{0}G, 11^{5}GF, 12^{2}GF, 16^{2}GF, 11^{4}F, 14^{0}HY, 16^{0}SD

	Starts	1st	2nd	3rd	Win & Pl
Career Total (Turf)	8	0	4	0	5123

Going (Turf): Sf: 0-2 GS: 0-1 Gd: 0-1 GF: 0-3 Fm: 0-1
Distance: 5f/6f: 0-1 7f-8f: 0-0 9f-13f: 0-5 14f+: 0-2
Track : LH: 0-5 RH: 0-2 Tight: 0-1 Gall: 0-1
Aids: Bl: 0-1 Vi: 0-0 Tstrap: 0-0
Best Rating: 80 6/01 Pont 1m4f8y gd-fm

Rude Awakening

95(103) (61d)**49d**

7-y-o b g Rudimentary (USA)-Final Call (Town Crier)
C A Dwyer (C W Fairhurst 6/9) Mrs Shelley Dwyer

Placings:221640/00040400000/0130326545360520000/042000345506/4130310105204030-10065340000000 **(5619)**
2001: 6^{1}SD, 6^{0}SD, 6^{0}SW, 6^{6}SW, 5^{5}SD, 5^{3}SD, 6^{4}SD, 7^{0}GF, 5^{0}F, 5^{0}GF, 6^{0}F, 5^{0}G, 5^{0}SW, 6^{0}SD

	Starts	1st	2nd	3rd	Win & Pl
Career Total (Turf)	42	2	4	1	15253
Career Total (AW)	36	4	2	7	14989

58	1/01	Sthl	6f	F(0-60)	STD	£2201
46	7/00	Catt	5f	E(0-75)H	G-F	£3542
61	2/00	Ling	6f	F(0-70)H	STD	£2268
56	1/00	Ling	6f	E(0-70)H	STD	£2626
49	2/98	Sthl	6f	E(0-70)H	STD	£3146
94	4/96	Pont	5f	D	G-F	£4221

Total win prize-money £18065

Going (Turf): Sf: 0-2 GS: 0-3 Gd: 0-9 **GF: 2-24** Fm: 0-4
Distance: **5f/6f: 6-64** 7f-8f: 0-12 9f-13f: 0-2 14f+: 0-0
Track : **LH: 5-45** RH: 0-5 **Tight: 2-17** Gall: 0-2
Aids: Bl: 0-14 Vi: 0-4 Tstrap: 0-0
Best Rating: 58 1/01 Sthl 6f stand

Rudetski

101 **54**

4-y-o b g Rudimentary (USA)-Butosky (Busted)
M Dods A F & P Monk

Placings:0065612-661004300 **(4908)**
2001: 9^{6}GF, 10^{6}GF, 9^{1}G, 10^{0}GF, 8^{0}GF, 9^{4}G, 10^{3}G, 10^{0}G, 9^{0}G

	Starts	1st	2nd	3rd	Win & Pl
Career Total (Turf)	16	2	1	1	7559

54	6/01	Muss	1m1f	E(0-70)H	GD	£3234
56	8/00	Pont	1m4y	F(0-65)H	G-F	£2457

Total win prize-money £5691

Going (Turf): Sf: 0-3 GS: 0-1 **Gd: 1-6 GF: 1-6** Fm: 0-0
Distance: 5f/6f: 0-3 7f-8f: 0-1 **9f-13f: 2-12** 14f+: 0-0
Track : **LH: 1-8** RH: 0-5 Tight: 0-3 Gall: 0-1
Aids: Bl: 0-0 Vi: 0-0 Tstrap: 0-0
Best Rating: 54 8/01 Hayd 1m2f120y good

Suited by a fast pace over a mile to nine furlongs on a sound surface. Tends to race keenly.

Rudi's Pet (IRE)

110 **93d**

7-y-o ch g Don't Forget Me-Pink Fondant (Northfields (USA))
D Nicholls Dandy Nicholls Racing Club

Placings:461543165/300062051001/0056000000000/4410612116/103006-300205000 **(4634)**
2001: 5^{3}S, 5^{0}G, 5^{0}GF, 5^{2}GF, 5^{0}GF, 6^{5}GS, 5^{0}G, 5^{0}G, 5^{0}GF

	Starts	1st	2nd	3rd	Win & Pl
Career Total (Turf)	60	9	3	4	147808

120	6/00	Leop	5f		YLD	£22750
112	7/99	Gdwd	5f	A	G-F	£29600
109	7/99	Asct	5f	B(0-100)H	G-F	£15593
90	6/99	Newc	5f	B(0-105)H	GD	£17320
79	5/99	Thsk	5f	D(0-85)H	GD	£4302
97	10/97	Donc	5f	B(0-100)H	GD	£8266
88	8/97	Sand	5f6y	B(0-100)H	G-S	£6697
99	8/96	Sand	5f6y	D	GD	£3598
74	7/96	Wind	5f10y	D	GD	£3387

Total win prize-money £111515

Going (Turf): Sf: 0-7 GS: 1-9 **Gd: 5-23** GF: 2-18 Fm: 0-2
Distance: **5f/6f: 9-53** 7f-8f: 0-6 9f-13f: 0-1 14f+: 0-0
Track : LH: 0-4 **RH: 1-4** Tight: 0-3 **Gall: 1-3**
Aids: **Bl: 6-32** Vi: 0-3 Tstrap: 0-0
Best Rating: 94 7/01 Sand 5f6y gd-fm

Very fast, he usually likes to race up with the pace, acts on any ground, and seems well suited by Goodwood.

Rudik (USA)

105 **87**

4-y-o b g Nureyev (USA)-Nervous Baba (USA) (Raja Baba (USA))
D Nicholls Thoroughbred International

Placings:2313/500-00000000460 **(5266)**
2001: 5^{0}G, 6^{0}GF, 7^{0}F, 6^{0}G, 6^{0}GF, 6^{0}G, 6^{0}G, 7^{0}GS, 6^{4}G, 7^{6}G, 6^{0}GS

	Starts	1st	2nd	3rd	Win & Pl
Career Total (Turf)	18	1	1	2	8010

96	9/99	Newc	6f	D	SFT	£3598

Total win prize-money £3599

Going (Turf): **Sf: 1-2** GS: 0-4 Gd: 0-8 GF: 0-3 Fm: 0-1
Distance: **5f/6f: 1-13** 7f-8f: 0-5 9f-13f: 0-0 14f+: 0-0
Track : LH: 0-0 RH: 0-0 Tight: 0-0 Gall: 0-0
Aids: Bl: 0-0 Vi: 0-0 Tstrap: 0-5
Best Rating: 87 9/01 Ayr 6f good

Usually held up, he is a useful sprinter but had not been at his best this year until a good fourth in the Ayr Silver Cup. Appears to act on any ground.

Rufiji River

77 **65**

2-y-o b g Hernando (FR)-Jadirah (USA) (Deputy Minister (CAN))
J L Dunlop J L Dunlop

Placings:600 **(5623)**
2001: 8GS, 8G, 8GS

	Starts	1st	2nd	3rd	Win & Pl
Career Total (Turf)	3	0	0	0	0

Going (Turf): Sf: 0-0 GS: 0-2 Gd: 0-1 GF: 0-0 Fm: 0-0
Distance: 5f/6f: 0-0 7f-8f: 0-2 9f-13f: 0-1 14f+: 0-0
Track : LH: 0-1 RH: 0-0 Tight: 0-0 Gall: 0-0
Aids: Bl: 0-0 Vi: 0-0 Tstrap: 0-0
Best Rating: 65 10/01 Sals 1m gd-sft

Ruissec (USA)

80 **64**

2-y-o b/br f Woodman (USA)-Jadana (Pharly (FR))
J W Hills Wood Hall Stud Limited

Placings:00 **(4873)**
2001: 7G, 7G

	Starts	1st	2nd	3rd	Win & Pl
Career Total (Turf)	2	0	0	0	

Going (Turf): Sf: 0-0 GS: 0-0 Gd: 0-2 GF: 0-0 Fm: 0-0
Distance: 5f/6f: 0-0 7f-8f: 0-2 9f-13f: 0-0 14f+: 0-0
Track : LH: 0-0 RH: 0-1 Tight: 0-0 Gall: 0-1
Aids: Bl: 0-0 Vi: 0-0 Tstrap: 0-0
Best Rating: 64 9/01 Kemp 7f good

Rum Charger (IRE)

97 **95+**

2-y-o b f Spectrum (IRE)-Park Charger (Tirol)
D K Weld Bertram R Firestone

Placings:3251 **(4143a)**
2001: 5GF, 6Y, 7GF, 6S

	Starts	1st	2nd	3rd	Win & Pl
Career Total (Turf)	4	1	1	1	14880
95 8/01 Curr 6f				SFT	£10400

Total win prize-money £10400

Going (Turf): Sf: 1-1 GS: 0-0 Gd: 0-0 GF: 0-2 Fm: 0-0
Distance: 5f/6f: 1-3 7f-8f: 0-1 9f-13f: 0-0 14f+: 0-0
Track : LH: 0-0 RH: 0-0 Tight: 0-0 Gall: 0-0
Aids: Bl: 0-0 Vi: 0-0 Tstrap: 0-0
Best Rating: 95 8/01 Curr 6f soft

Unlucky in the Chesham on her third start, she then bolted up in a Curragh maiden.

Rum Destiny (IRE)

102 **92**

2-y-o b g Mujadil (USA)-Ruby River (Red God)
A Berry Chris & Antonia Deuters

Placings:013431013000 **(5150)**
2001: 5S, 5GF, 5G, 5GF, 5GF, 5GF, 5GF, 5G, 5G, 5G, 5G, 6G

	Starts	1st	2nd	3rd	Win & Pl
Career Total (Turf)	12	3	0	3	20605
90 8/01 Gdwd 5f	C H			GD	£7621
79 7/01 Bevl 5f	D			G-F	£3900
73 5/01 Muss 5f	F			G-F	£3010

Total win prize-money £14531

Going (Turf): Sf: 0-1 GS: 0-0 Gd: 1-6 **GF: 2-5** Fm: 0-0
Distance: 5f/6f: 3-12 7f-8f: 0-0 9f-13f: 0-0 14f+: 0-0
Track : LH: 0-1 RH: 0-1 Tight: 0-0 Gall: 0-2

Aids: Bl: 0-0 Vi: 0-0 Tstrap: 0-0
Best Rating: 92 8/01 York 5f good

Already a fully mature performer, he gained a well-deserved second win when beating Lone Chief in novice stakes over five furlongs at Beverley in July, and scored narrowly in a three-way-photo at Goodwood in August. Arguably his best effort was when third in a York Listed event. A tough individual. Acts on fast ground.

Rum Punch

98 **62**

4-y-o b c Shirley Heights-Gentle Persuasion (Bustino)
G M Moore Rum Bunch Syndicate

Placings:0/00200-00400 **(1963)**
2001: 8HY, 10S, 12G, 16F, 11GF

	Starts	1st	2nd	3rd	Win & Pl
Career Total (Turf)	11	0	1	0	2584

Going (Turf): Sf: 0-4 GS: 0-0 Gd: 0-3 GF: 0-3 Fm: 0-1
Distance: 5f/6f: 0-0 7f-8f: 0-3 9f-13f: 0-7 14f+: 0-1
Track : LH: 0-5 RH: 0-4 Tight: 0-3 Gall: 0-3
Aids: Bl: 0-0 Vi: 0-0 Tstrap: 0-2
Best Rating: 62 5/01 Newc 2m19y firm

Rumore Castagna (IRE)

78(72) (12)**41**

3-y-o ch g Great Commotion (USA)-False Spring (IRE) (Petorius)
S E Kettlewell Middleham Park Racing Xxiv

Placings:15302-00000 **(3706)**
2001: 8S, 6S, 6GF, 7SD, 7G

	Starts	1st	2nd	3rd	Win & Pl
Career Total (Turf)	9	1	1	1	18422
Career Total (AW)	1	0	0	0	
61 6/00 Newc 5f	D			SFT	£3493

Total win prize-money £3494

Going (Turf): Sf: 1-4 GS: 0-1 Gd: 0-2 GF: 0-2 Fm: 0-0
Distance: 5f/6f: 1-6 7f-8f: 0-4 9f-13f: 0-0 14f+: 0-0
Track : LH: 0-2 RH: 0-0 Tight: 0-1 Gall: 0-0
Aids: Bl: 0-0 Vi: 0-0 Tstrap: 0-0
Best Rating: 41 7/01 Ripn 6f gd-fm

Rumpold

102 **104+**

3-y-o ro c Mister Baileys-Southern Psychic (USA) (Alwasmi (USA))
Saeed Bin Suroor Godolphin

Placings:1-01 **(4700)**
2001: 8G, 8GS

	Starts	1st	2nd	3rd	Win & Pl
Career Total (Turf)	3	2	0	0	13211
101 9/01 Donc 1m	C			G-S	£6500
104 7/00 Asct 6f	D			G-F	£6711

Total win prize-money £13211

Going (Turf): Sf: 0-0 **GS: 1-1** Gd: 0-1 **GF: 1-1** Fm: 0-0
Distance: 5f/6f: 1-1 7f-8f: 1-2 9f-13f: 0-0 14f+: 0-0
Track : LH: 1-1 RH: 0-0 Tight: 0-0 **Gall: 1-1**
Aids: Bl: 0-0 Vi: 0-0 Tstrap: 0-0
Best Rating: 101 9/01 Donc 1m gd-sft

Looked a top class colt in the making when beating Minardi comprehensively in well above average maiden at Ascot on his only start at two and then went to Godolphin. Did not run again at two, but won slowly run private trial over a mile at Nad Al Sheba in April, making all to beat Devine Task and Tobougg in a close finish. Well beaten in the Guineas and was off for four months before winning a conditions event at Doncaster.

Run On

83(76) (26)**57**

3-y-o b c Runnett-Polar Storm (IRE) (Law Society (USA))
D G Bridgwater (B J Meehan 6/8) Miss V Howard Evans

Placings:420-0000 **(5497)**
2001: 6GF, 6SD, 8G, 5HY

	Starts	1st	2nd	3rd	Win & Pl
Career Total (Turf)	6	0	1	0	1377
Career Total (AW)	1	0	0	0	

Going (Turf): Sf: 0-1 GS: 0-1 Gd: 0-1 GF: 0-3 Fm: 0-0
Distance: 5f/6f: 0-5 7f-8f: 0-1 9f-13f: 0-1 14f+: 0-0
Track : LH: 0-2 RH: 0-1 Tight: 0-2 Gall: 0-1
Aids: Bl: 0-0 Vi: 0-0 Tstrap: 0-1
Best Rating: 33 7/01 Kemp 6f gd-fm

Runaway Bride

82(80) (31)**48**

3-y-o b f Bishop Of Cashel-Storm Nymph (USA) (Storm Bird (CAN))
C Smith David J Thompson

Placings:550006-000605 **(1844)**
2001: 8SD, 6SW, 7SW, 10GS, 7G, 7GF

	Starts	1st	2nd	3rd	Win & Pl
Career Total (Turf)	7	0	0	0	261
Career Total (AW)	5	0	0	0	0

Going (Turf): Sf: 0-1 GS: 0-1 Gd: 0-2 GF: 0-3 Fm: 0-0
Distance: 5f/6f: 0-4 7f-8f: 0-7 9f-13f: 0-1 14f+: 0-0
Track : LH: 0-5 RH: 0-1 Tight: 0-1 Gall: 0-0
Aids: Bl: 0-0 Vi: 0-2 Tstrap: 0-0
Best Rating: 48 5/01 NmkR 7f good

Runaway Star

107 **40**

4-y-o ch f Superlative-My Greatest Star (Great Nephew)
W J Musson Mrs N A Ward

Placings:6650060-00116 **(4721)**
2001: 8GF, 10GF, 12GF, 12G, 12G

	Starts	1st	2nd	3rd	Win & Pl
Career Total (Turf)	12	2	0	0	6868
38 8/01 Ripn 1m4f60y	E(0-70)H			GD	£3146
37 7/01 Pont 1m4f8y	E(0-70)H			G-F	£3721

Total win prize-money £6868

Going (Turf): Sf: 0-3 GS: 0-0 **Gd: 1-3 GF: 1-6** Fm: 0-0
Distance: 5f/6f: 0-0 7f-8f: 0-3 **9f-13f: 2-9** 14f+: 0-0
Track : LH: 1-5 RH: 1-4 **Tight: 1-4** Gall: 0-2
Aids: Bl: 0-0 Vi: 0-0 Tstrap: 0-0
Best Rating: 40 9/01 Epsm 1m4f10y good

Unplaced in nine starts before gaining back-to-back wins at Pontefract and Ripon. On the upgrade, she is suited by 12 furlongs and looks as though she would stay a bit further.

Running For Me (IRE)

87(96) (47d)**36**

3-y-o ch f Eagle Eyed (USA)-Running For You (FR) (Pampabird)
R Hollinshead R Hollinshead

Placings:610225103-1553461046600 **(5418)**
2001: 6SD, 6SW, 6SD, 7SD, 5SD, 6HY, 6SD, 6F, 6SD, 5GF, 6SD, 7SD, 7SD

	Starts	1st	2nd	3rd	Win & Pl
Career Total (Turf)	5	0	0	0	0
Career Total (AW)	17	4	2	2	9647
47 6/01 Sthl 6f	F			STD	£2275
60 1/01 Sthl 6f	F(0-60)			STD	£2121
58 7/00 Wolv 5f	G			STD	£1820
53 5/00 Sthl 5f	G			STD	£1813

Total win prize-money £8029

Going (Turf): Sf: 0-1 GS: 0-1 Gd: 0-1 GF: 0-1 Fm: 0-1
Distance: 5f/6f: 4-18 7f-8f: 0-4 9f-13f: 0-0 14f+: 0-0

Track : LH: 3-14 RH: 0-0 Tight: 1-8 Gall: 0-0
Aids: Bl: 0-0 Vi: 0-0 Tstrap: 0-0
Best Rating: 62 2/01 Wolv 6f stand

A plating-class winner on the All-Weather over five and six furlongs.

Running Red

65 **16**

2-y-o b c Tragic Role (USA)-Rose Mill (Puissance)
W A O'Gorman T Mohan

Placings:00 **(5047)**
2001: 7^{0}GS, 8^{0}SD

	Starts	1st	2nd	3rd	Win & Pl
Career Total (Turf)	1	0	0	0	
Career Total (AW)	1	0	0	0	

Going (Turf): Sf: 0-0 GS: 0-1 Gd: 0-0 GF: 0-0 Fm: 0-0
Distance: 5f/6f: 0-0 7f-8f: 0-2 9f-13f: 0-0 14f+: 0-0
Track : LH: 0-1 RH: 0-0 Tight: 0-0 Gall: 0-0
Aids: Bl: 0-0 Vi: 0-0 Tstrap: 0-0
Best Rating: 16 9/01 Leic 7f9y gd-sft

Running Times (USA)

108(90) (58)**64**

4-y-o b g Brocco (USA)-Concert Peace (USA) (Hold Your Peace (USA))
M C Pipe (T D Easterby 12/5) Neil J Edwards

Placings:34400/503543-002 **(1283)**
2001: 12^{0}SD, 11^{0}SD, 16^{2}G

	Starts	1st	2nd	3rd	Win & Pl
Career Total (Turf)	11	0	1	3	3717
Career Total (AW)	3	0	0	0	0

Going (Turf): Sf: 0-1 GS: 0-4 Gd: 0-3 GF: 0-2 Fm: 0-1
Distance: 5f/6f: 0-0 7f-8f: 0-5 9f-13f: 0-7 14f+: 0-2
Track : LH: 0-11 RH: 0-3 Tight: 0-7 Gall: 0-3
Aids: Bl: 0-1 Vi: 0-0 Tstrap: 0-0
Best Rating: 64 5/01 Bevl 2m35y good

Rupert Of Hentzau

83 **46**

2-y-o ch g Superpower-Walkonthemoon (Coquelin (USA))
G M McCourt (M Quinn 17/7) Astaire & Partners (holdings) Ltd

Placings:50500600 **(5667)**
2001: 5^{5}G, 5^{0}F, 6^{5}G, 7^{0}G, 5^{0}F, 6^{6}HY, 8^{0}G, 8^{0}HY

	Starts	1st	2nd	3rd	Win & Pl
Career Total (Turf)	8	0	0	0	0

Going (Turf): Sf: 0-2 GS: 0-0 Gd: 0-4 GF: 0-0 Fm: 0-2
Distance: 5f/6f: 0-4 7f-8f: 0-2 9f-13f: 0-2 14f+: 0-0
Track : LH: 0-3 RH: 0-1 Tight: 0-2 Gall: 0-1
Aids: Bl: 0-1 Vi: 0-0 Tstrap: 0-0
Best Rating: 46 7/01 Yarm 6f3y good

Rush About (IRE)

97 **78**

2-y-o ch c Kris-Rachrush (IRE) (Sadler's Wells (USA))
H R A Cecil Wafic Said

Placings:00 **(5604)**
2001: 8^{0}S, 7^{0}GS

	Starts	1st	2nd	3rd	Win & Pl
Career Total (Turf)	2	0	0	0	

Going (Turf): Sf: 0-1 GS: 0-1 Gd: 0-0 GF: 0-0 Fm: 0-0
Distance: 5f/6f: 0-0 7f-8f: 0-2 9f-13f: 0-0 14f+: 0-0
Track : LH: 0-0 RH: 0-0 Tight: 0-0 Gall: 0-0
Aids: Bl: 0-0 Vi: 0-0 Tstrap: 0-0
Best Rating: 78 11/01 NmkR 7f gd-sft

Rush Off

61

6-y-o b g Robellino (USA)-Arusha (IRE) (Dance Of Life (USA))
G H Yardley Deblins Green Racing Partnership

Placings:0/00/0 **(1620)**
2001: 16^{0}GF

	Starts	1st	2nd	3rd	Win & Pl
Career Total (Turf)	4	0	0	0	

Going (Turf): Sf: 0-0 GS: 0-2 Gd: 0-0 GF: 0-2 Fm: 0-0
Distance: 5f/6f: 0-1 7f-8f: 0-0 9f-13f: 0-2 14f+: 0-1
Track : LH: 0-2 RH: 0-0 Tight: 0-1 Gall: 0-0
Aids: Bl: 0-0 Vi: 0-0 Tstrap: 0-0

Rushby (IRE)

92 **64**

3-y-o b g Fayruz-Moira My Girl (Henbit (USA))
Mrs P N Dutfield The Rushby Partnership

Placings:636206-00020 **(4448)**
2001: 5^{0}F, 5^{0}GF, 5^{0}G, 5^{2}GF, 5^{0}G

	Starts	1st	2nd	3rd	Win & Pl
Career Total (Turf)	11	0	2	1	2419

Going (Turf): Sf: 0-1 GS: 0-1 Gd: 0-4 GF: 0-4 Fm: 0-1
Distance: 5f/6f: 0-11 7f-8f: 0-0 9f-13f: 0-0 14f+: 0-0
Track : LH: 0-2 RH: 0-1 Tight: 0-0 Gall: 0-1
Aids: Bl: 0-0 Vi: 0-0 Tstrap: 0-0
Best Rating: 64 8/01 Folk 5f gd-fm

Rushcutter Bay

116 (35)**106**

8-y-o br g Mon Tresor-Llwy Bren (Lidhame)
P L Gilligan Treasure Seekers Partnership

Placings:4136/60102534400/0040004/0150044/201055 050/2602100213-100000 **(5365)**
2001: 5^{1}G, 5^{0}GF, 5^{0}G, 5^{0}GF, 5^{0}HO, 6^{0}GS

	Starts	1st	2nd	3rd	Win & Pl
Career Total (Turf)	53	7	5	3	91152
Career Total (AW)	1	0	0	0	

115	5/01	NmkR	5f	A	GD	£23200
104	9/00	NmkR	5f	A	GD	£16066
80	8/00	NmkJ	6f	D(0-80)H	G-F	£4953
90	5/99	Wind	6f	C(0-90)	G-F	£6126
81	7/98	NmkJ	6f	C(0-90)H	GD	£6264
83	6/96	Nott	5f13y	D(0-80)H	G-F	£3817
63	7/95	Wind	5f10y	E	GD	£4484

Total win prize-money £64912

Going (Turf): Sf: 0-2 GS: 0-4 **Gd: 4-18** GF: 3-27 Fm: 0-1
Distance: **5f/6f: 7-51** 7f-8f: 0-3 9f-13f: 0-0 14f+: 0-0
Track : LH: 0-3 **RH: 2-5** Tight: 0-0 **Gall: 2-7**
Aids: Bl: 0-0 **Vi: 2-17** Tstrap: 0-0
Best Rating: 115 5/01 NmkR 5f good

Developed into decent sprinter in 2000. Ran his best races at Newmarket, progressing well to land a Listed event in October and improved again on his debut this season when a ready winner of the Group Three Palace House Stakes at Headquarters. His efforts since show that he is not quite so effective away from the Suffolk track.

Russian Dune (IRE)

91 **63**

2-y-o b c Danehill (USA)-Russian Ribbon (USA) (Nijinsky (CAN))
E A L Dunlop Ahmed Buhaleeba

Placings:6 **(5289)**
2001: 7^{0}S

	Starts	1st	2nd	3rd	Win & Pl
Career Total (Turf)	1	0	0	0	0

Going (Turf): Sf: 0-1 GS: 0-0 Gd: 0-0 GF: 0-0 Fm: 0-0
Distance: 5f/6f: 0-0 7f-8f: 0-1 9f-13f: 0-0 14f+: 0-0
Track : LH: 0-0 RH: 0-0 Tight: 0-0 Gall: 0-0
Aids: Bl: 0-0 Vi: 0-0 Tstrap: 0-0
Best Rating: 63 10/01 Leic 7f9y soft

Russian Fox (IRE)

104(97) (55)**57**

4-y-o ch g Foxhound (USA)-La Petruschka (Ballad Rock)
R Hannon Nicholas R Hodges

Placings:342341103201/00000000-04540020300000 **(5349)**
2001: 6^{0}SD, 8^{4}SW, 8^{5}SD, 7^{4}SD, 7^{0}SD, 6^{0}GF, 6^{2}GF, 6^{0}GF, 5^{3}F, 5^{0}G, 5^{0}G, 5^{0}GF, 5^{0}G, 5^{0}SD

	Starts	1st	2nd	3rd	Win & Pl
Career Total (Turf)	28	3	3	4	21935
Career Total (AW)	6	0	0	0	287

89	10/99	NmkJ	6f	C(0-95)H	GD	£7317
77	7/99	Ling	5f	D H	G-F	£3590
77	6/99	Ling	5f	D	G-F	£3590

Total win prize money £14497

Going (Turf): Sf: 0-4 GS: 0-2 Gd: 1-8 **GF: 2-12** Fm: 0-2
Distance: **5f/6f: 3-26** 7f-8f: 0-8 9f-13f: 0-0 14f+: 0-0
Track : LH: 0-12 RH: 0-3 Tight: 0-7 Gall: 0-4
Aids: Bl: 0-8 Vi: 0-0 Tstrap: 0-0
Best Rating: 61 2/01 Ling 1m slow

He has run with credit on many occasions and is very consistent. He gained back-to-back victories at Lingfield during the summer, and is well suited by fast ground and the minimum trip on a sharp track.

Russian Rhapsody

108 **97?**

4-y-o b f Cosmonaut-Hannah's Music (Music Boy)
M A Jarvis Magno-Pulse Ltd

Placings:5422215-50110201 **(5625)**
2001: 7^{5}HY, 7^{0}G, 7^{1}GF, 7^{1}G, 7^{0}G, 7^{2}GS, 7^{0}HY, 8^{1}GS

	Starts	1st	2nd	3rd	Win & Pl
Career Total (Turf)	15	4	4	0	28857

80	11/01	Nott	1m54y	C	G-S	£6438
88	7/01	Epsm	7f	D(0-80)	GD	£6890
76	6/01	Wwck	7f26y	D(0-80)	G-F	£3949
76	10/00	Yarm	7f3y	D	SFT	£3341

Total win prize-money £20618

Going (Turf): Sf: 1-6 GS: 1-2 Gd: 1-4 GF: 1-3 Fm: 0-0
Distance: 5f/6f: 0-1 **7f-8f: 3-12** 9f-13f: 1-2 14f+: 0-0
Track : **LH: 3-8** RH: 0-1 **Tight: 1-3** Gall: 0-0
Aids: Bl: 0-0 Vi: 0-0 Tstrap: 0-0
Best Rating: 97 8/01 Epsm 7f gd-sft

Bounced back to form at Warwick in June with front-running tactics paying off and followed up in good style in an Epsom classified stakes. She ran well in a Listed event at Epsom in August, and finished off the season by taking a Nottingham conditions event. Suited by seven to eight furlongs and racing prominently. Handles fast and easy ground.

Russian Romeo (IRE)

101(105) (71)**66**

6-y-o b g Soviet Lad (USA)-Aotearoa (IRE) (Flash Of Steel)
B A McMahon R L Bedding

Placings:06000445010 5102/402001R000000/1123030/6055223220023510240-1503 **(3188)**
2001: 6^{1}SD, 6^{5}SW, 6^{0}GF, 5^{3}GS

	Starts	1st	2nd	3rd	Win & Pl
Career Total (Turf)	24	2	3	3	10187
Career Total (AW)	34	5	6	2	18221

71	1/01	Sthl	6f	D(0-80)H	STD	£3191
70	9/00	Wolv	6f	E(0-70)H	STD	£3080
70	7/99	Sthl	6f	F(0-60)	STD	£2148
57	6/99	Wolv	6f	F(0-65)H	STD	£2284
72	6/98	Ches	6f18y	D	G-S	£3649
74	10/97	Wolv	6f	F	STD	£1932
74	0/97	Leic	5f210y	G	GD	£2595

Total win prize-money £18881

Going (Turf): Sf: 0-3 **GS: 1-6 Gd: 1-6** GF: 0-7 Fm: 0-2
Distance: **5f/6f: 6-52** 7f-8f: 1-6 9f-13f: 0-0 14f+: 0-0
Track : **LH: 6-43** RH: 0-3 **Tight: 4-22** Gall: 0-4
Aids: **Bl: 6-43** Vi: 1-5 Tstrap: 0-0
Best Rating: 71 1/01 Sthl 6f stand

Has shown his best form on Fibresand over six furlongs.

He is not so good on turf and last won on grass at Chester in 1998.

Russian Whispers (USA)

101(100) (88)**79**

3-y-o b g Red Ransom (USA)-Idle Gossip (USA) (Lyphard (USA))

B J Meehan Mrs Susan Roy

Placings:35061-003020205 **(4872)**

2001: 6^{0}S, 6^{0}GF, 5^{3}F, 6^{0}GF, 6^{2}G, 7^{0}GF, 7^{2}SD, 7^{0}G, 7^{5}G

	Starts	1st	2nd	3rd	Win & Pl
Career Total (Turf)	12	0	1	2	3167
Career Total (AW)	2	1	1	0	3526

93	11/00	Sthl	6f	D	STD	£2261

Total win prize-money £2261

Going (Turf): Sf: 0-3 GS: 0-0 Gd: 0-4 GF: 0-4 Fm: 0-1
Distance: **5f/6f: 1-6** 7f-8f: 0-8 9f-13f: 0-0 14f+: 0-0
Track: **LH: 1-5** RH: 0-2 Tight: 0-4 Gall: 0-2
Aids: Bl: 0-2 **Vi: 1-7** Tstrap: 0-0
Best Rating: 80 9/01 Wolv 7f stand

He has rather struggled in proper handicap company this season with his best efforts coming in classified and claiming events.

Rust En Vrede

91 **73**

2-y-o b c Royal Applause-Souveniers (Relko)

J L Eyre Alan Mann

Placings:064 **(5086)**

2001: 6^{0}GF, 6^{6}GF, 7^{4}GS

	Starts	1st	2nd	3rd	Win & Pl
Career Total (Turf)	3	0	0	0	0

Going (Turf): Sf: 0-0 GS: 0-1 Gd: 0-0 GF: 0-2 Fm: 0-0
Distance: 5f/6f: 0-1 7f-8f: 0-2 9f-13f: 0-0 14f+: 0-0
Track: LH: 0-0 RH: 0-0 Tight: 0-0 Gall: 0-0
Aids: Bl: 0-0 Vi: 0-0 Tstrap: 0-0
Best Rating: 73 10/01 Newc 7f gd-sft

Rutland Chantry (USA)

103(104) (74)**73**

7-y-o b g Dixieland Band (USA)-Christchurch (FR) (So Blessed)

S Gollings Richard Abbott & Mario Stavru

Placings:52421/1600/41022520000/2566053425-52002141200 **(5265)**

2001: 9^{5}G, 10^{2}S, 11^{0}GS, 10^{0}GF, 10^{2}G, 10^{1}G, 10^{4}HY, 12^{1}G, 10^{2}HY, 12^{0}G, 8^{0}GS

	Starts	1st	2nd	3rd	Win & Pl
Career Total (Turf)	37	5	7	1	39642
Career Total (AW)	4	0	3	0	3334

67	8/01	Epsm	1m4f10y	C(0-90)H	GD	£10676
66	8/01	NmkJ	1m2f	E(0-70)H	GD	£4745
75	6/99	Bevl	1m1f207y	D(0-80)H	SFT	£4484
72	4/98	Newb	1m2f6y	D(0-85)H	HVY	£6385
66	10/97	Pont	1m2f6y	E(0-70)H	G-S	£4207

Total win prize-money £30498

Going (Turf): Sf: 2-11 GS: 1-9 **Gd: 2-11** GF: 0-5 Fm: 0-1
Distance: 5f/6f: 0-0 7f-8f: 0-2 **9f-13f: 5-39** 14f+: 0-0
Track: **LH: 3-31** RH: 2-10 Tight: 1-14 **Gall: 2-13**
Aids: Bl: 0-1 Vi: 0-0 Tstrap: 0-0
Best Rating: 73 9/01 Hayd 1m2f120y heavy

Landed the 'Amateurs' Derby' at Epsom in August 2001. He likes to have his own way out in front. Stays a mile and a half. Acts on most types of ground.

Ruwaya (USA)

80 **62**

2-y-o b f Red Ransom (USA)-Upper Class Lady (USA) (Upper Nile (USA))

C E Brittain Saeed Manana

Placings:06 **(4485)**

2001: 6^{0}GF, 8^{6}S

	Starts	1st	2nd	3rd	Win & Pl
Career Total (Turf)	2	0	0	0	0

Going (Turf): Sf: 0-1 GS: 0-0 Gd: 0-0 GF: 0-1 Fm: 0-0
Distance: 5f/6f: 0-1 7f-8f: 0-0 9f-13f: 0-1 14f+: 0-0
Track: LH: 0-0 RH: 0-0 Tight: 0-0 Gall: 0-0
Aids: Bl: 0-0 Vi: 0-0 Tstrap: 0-0
Best Rating: 62 9/01 Yarm 1m3y soft

Ryan's Gold (IRE)

108 **72**

3-y-o b g Distant View (USA)-Kathleen's Dream (USA) (Last Tycoon)

Mrs A J Perrett John Connolly

Placings:0060-02000 **(4872)**

2001: 6^{0}GS, 8^{2}GF, 6^{0}GF, 8^{0}GF, 7^{0}G

	Starts	1st	2nd	3rd	Win & Pl
Career Total (Turf)	9	0	1	0	995

Going (Turf): Sf: 0-1 GS: 0-1 Gd: 0-3 GF: 0-4 Fm: 0-0
Distance: 5f/6f: 0-1 7f-8f: 0-7 9f-13f: 0-1 14f+: 0-0
Track: LH: 0-1 RH: 0-1 Tight: 0-1 Gall: 0-0
Aids: Bl: 0-1 Vi: 0-0 Tstrap: 0-0
Best Rating: 72 6/01 Wind 1m67y gd-fm

Ryan's Quest (IRE)

93 **66**

2-y-o b f Mukaddamah (USA)-Preponderance (IRE) (Cyrano De Bergerac)

K R Burke James Ryan

Placings:33250 **(5621)**

2001: 5^{3}G, 5^{3}GF, 5^{2}GF, 5^{5}GF, 5^{0}GS

	Starts	1st	2nd	3rd	Win & Pl
Career Total (Turf)	5	0	1	2	1927

Going (Turf): Sf: 0-0 GS: 0-1 Gd: 0-1 GF: 0-3 Fm: 0-0
Distance: 5f/6f: 0-5 7f-8f: 0-0 9f-13f: 0-0 14f+: 0-0
Track: LH: 0-0 RH: 0-0 Tight: 0-0 Gall: 0-0
Aids: Bl: 0-0 Vi: 0-0 Tstrap: 0-0
Best Rating: 66 7/01 Ripn 5f gd-fm

Ryders Storm (USA)

101 **89**

2-y-o b c Dynaformer (USA)-Justicara (Rusticaro (FR))

M Johnston Ryder Racing Ltd

Placings:3140 **(5255)**

2001: 6^{3}G, 7^{1}F, 8^{4}G, 8^{0}GS

	Starts	1st	2nd	3rd	Win & Pl
Career Total (Turf)	4	1	0	1	7986

83	7/01	Thsk	7f	C	FRM	£5860

Total win prize-money £5861

Going (Turf): Sf: 0-0 GS: 0-1 Gd: 0-2 GF: 0-0 **Fm: 1-1**
Distance: 5f/6f: 0-0 **7f-8f: 1-4** 9f-13f: 0-0 14f+: 0-0
Track: **LH: 1-2** RH: 0-2 **Tight: 1-1** Gall: 0-2
Aids: Bl: 0-0 Vi: 0-0 Tstrap: 0-0
Best Rating: 89 9/01 Gdwd 1m good

A half-brother to five winners, he got off the mark on his second outing over seven furlongs at Thirsk. Held in a Listed race next time. Best suited by strong pace. Acts on fast ground.

Ryefield

103 **67**

6-y-o b g Petong-Octavia (Sallust)

Miss L A Perratt Mrs Elaine Aird

Placings:22/43201000400/2005151000060/0R2142633 1660-2054104030020000 **(5630)**

2001: 7^{2}GF, 6^{0}G, 6^{5}F, 7^{4}GF, 6^{1}GF, 6^{0}G, 7^{4}GF, 7^{0}F, 6^{3}GS, 7^{0}GF, 8^{0}GF, 6^{2}G, 7^{0}GF, 6^{0}HY, 6^{0}HY, 6^{0}G

	Starts	1st	2nd	3rd	Win & Pl
Career Total (Turf)	55	6	8	4	45973

67	6/01	Ayr	6f	D(0-85)H	G-F	£4082
64	10/00	Ayr	6f	E(0-70)H	HVY	£3380
62	7/00	Ayr	7f	C(0-95)H	FRM	£6987
66	8/99	Ayr	1m	C(0-90)H	G-F	£7385
64	7/99	Newc	1m3y	C(0-90)H	G-F	£7002
76	7/98	Carl	6f206y	D	G-F	£3517

Total win prize-money £32357

Going (Turf): Sf: 1-11 GS: 0-7 Gd: 0-16 **GF: 4-15** Fm: 1-6
Distance: 5f/6f: 2-14 **7f-8f: 3-37** 9f-13f: 1-4 14f+: 0-0
Track: **LH: 2-13** RH: 1-13 Tight: 0-9 Gall: 0-2
Aids: Bl: 0-0 Vi: 0-0 Tstrap: 0-0
Best Rating: 67 8/01 Ayr 6f good

Comes to hand in the summer and he is very much suited by a strongly-run race over seven furlongs to a mile, but has won over six when the ground was testing. Comes with a late run and has won four times at Ayr.

Ryeland

90 **38**

5-y-o b m Presidium-Ewe Lamb (Free State)

Mrs P Sly Thorney Racing Club

Placings:00/3-00 **(3373)**

2001: 8^{0}G, 11^{0}F

	Starts	1st	2nd	3rd	Win & Pl
Career Total (Turf)	5	0	0	1	478

Going (Turf): Sf: 0-0 GS: 0-0 Gd: 0-3 GF: 0-1 Fm: 0-1
Distance: 5f/6f: 0-0 7f-8f: 0-2 9f-13f: 0-3 14f+: 0-0
Track: LH: 0-3 RH: 0-1 Tight: 0-2 Gall: 0-0
Aids: Bl: 0-0 Vi: 0-0 Tstrap: 0-0
Best Rating: 38 7/01 Ling 1m3f106y firm

Ryka

91 **48**

6-y-o ch g Deploy-Velda (Thatch (USA))

W Clay S Taberner

Placings:006-000 **(1138)**

2001: 9^{0}HY, 10^{0}S, 13^{0}G

	Starts	1st	2nd	3rd	Win & Pl
Career Total (Turf)	6	0	0	0	0

Going (Turf): Sf: 0-2 GS: 0-2 Gd: 0-2 GF: 0-0 Fm: 0-0
Distance: 5f/6f: 0-0 7f-8f: 0-0 9f-13f: 0-5 14f+: 0-1
Track: LH: 0-3 RH: 0-3 Tight: 0-2 Gall: 0-0
Aids: Bl: 0-0 Vi: 0-0 Tstrap: 0-0
Best Rating: 20 5/01 Haml 1m5f9y good

Rymer's Rascal

106(71) (36)**71**

9-y-o b g Rymer-City Sound (On Your Mark)

E J Alston Brian Chambers

Placings:06534426441/050230000/0/00502333061611 640/0554025330035001/002043513605050/56342530 3144-0050536210603 **(5535)**

2001: 8^{0}GF, 7^{0}F, 7^{5}GF, 8^{0}SD, 7^{5}GF, 8^{3}GF, 7^{6}G, 8^{2}GF, 7^{1}GF, 7^{0}GF, 7^{6}G, 8^{0}G, 7^{3}S

	Starts	1st	2nd	3rd	Win & Pl
Career Total (Turf)	91	8	7	15	70809
Career Total (AW)	4	0	0	0	0

67	8/01	Bevl	7f100y	E(0-70)H	G-F	£6448
66	9/00	Rdcr	1m	D(0-85)H	SFT	£6578
62	7/99	Ches	7f122y	C(0-90)H	G-F	£8949
61	10/98	Rdcr	7f	D(0-85)H	SFT	£7262
64	9/97	York	6f214y	D(0-75)H	SFT	£9520
61	8/97	Catt	7f	E(0-70)H	G-F	£3486
60	7/97	Bevl	7f100y	E(0-70)H	G-F	£4440
59	10/94	Pont	6f	F	G-S	£2641

Total win prize-money £49326

Going (Turf): Sf: 3-15 GS: 1-12 Gd: 0-18 **GF: 4-35** Fm: 0-11
Distance: 5f/6f: 1-19 **7f-8f: 7-73** 9f-13f: 0-3 14f+: 0-0
Track: **LH: 4-38** RH: 2-23 **Tight: 2-21** Gall: 1-11
Aids: Bl: 0-0 Vi: 0-0 Tstrap: 0-0
Best Rating: 71 9/01 York 7f202y gd-fm

He goes on any ground and is suited by seven furlongs to a mile. After a string of consistent efforts, he finally came good at Beverley in August and remains in good form.

S W Three

104 **82**

3-y-o b f Slip Anchor-Anna Karietta (Precocious)
M P Tregoning The Earl Cadogan

Placings:2-2 **(2486)**
2001: 11^{2}HD

	Starts	1st	2nd	3rd	Win & Pl
Career Total (Turf)	2	0	2	0	2228

Going (Turf): Sf: 0-0 GS: 0-0 Gd: 0-0 GF: 0-1 Fm: 0-1
Distance: 5f/6f: 0-0 7f-8f: 0-1 9f-13f: 0-1 14f+: 0-0
Track : LH: 0-1 RH: 0-0 Tight: 0-1 Gall: 0-0
Aids: Bl: 0-0 Vi: 0-0 Tstrap: 0-0
Best Rating: 82 6/01 Bath 1m3f144y hard

Saabirr

106 **84**

3-y-o b c Polish Precedent (USA)-Safa (Shirley Heights)
A C Stewart Sheikh Ahmed Al Maktoum

Placings:04252 **(2843)**
2001: 8^{0}G, 10^{4}GF, 11^{2}GF, 12^{5}GF, 10^{2}GF

	Starts	1st	2nd	3rd	Win & Pl
Career Total (Turf)	5	0	2	0	3434

Going (Turf): Sf: 0-0 GS: 0-0 Gd: 0-1 GF: 0-4 Fm: 0-0
Distance: 5f/6f: 0-0 7f-8f: 0-1 9f-13f: 0-4 14f+: 0-0
Track : LH: 0-2 RH: 0-2 Tight: 0-3 Gall: 0-0
Aids: Bl: 0-0 Vi: 0-0 Tstrap: 0-1
Best Rating: 84 7/01 Sand 1m2f7y gd-fm

Saafend Rocket (IRE)

96(104) (76) **67d**

3-y-o b/br g Distinctly North (USA)-Simple Annie (Simply Great (FR))
Andrew Reid A S Reid

Placings:550561-1155055300030400 **(4705)**
2001: 8^{1}SD, 8^{1}SW, 10^{5}SD, 8^{5}SD, 7^{0}SD, 8^{5}SD, 7^{5}G, 8^{3}SD, 9^{0}GF, 8^{0}G, 11^{0}GF, 7^{3}GF, 5^{0}GF, 8^{4}SD, 7^{0}GF, 7^{0}G

	Starts	1st	2nd	3rd	Win & Pl
Career Total (Turf)	11	0	0	1	464
Career Total (AW)	11	3	0	1	9760

76	1/01	Wolv	1m100y	E(0-70)H	SLW	£2954
76	1/01	Ling	1m	D(0-85)H	STD	£3757
63	12/00	Ling	1m	G	STD	£1876

Total win prize-money £8587

Going (Turf): Sf: 0-0 GS: 0-1 Gd: 0-3 GF: 0-7 Fm: 0-0
Distance: 5f/6f: 0-6 **7f-8f: 2-10** 9f-13f: 1-6 14f+: 0-0
Track : **LH: 3-14** RH: 0-2 **Tight: 3-12** Gall: 0-0
Aids: Bl: 0-1 Vi: 0-1 Tstrap: 0-0
Best Rating: 76 1/01 Wolv 1m100y slow

He completed a hat-trick on sand at the turn of the year, but has shown little since then.

Saanen (IRE)

98 **56**

4-y-o b g Port Lucaya-Ziffany (Taufan (USA))
Mrs A Duffield Miss Betty Duxbury

Placings:0400/3223-022000 **(3506)**
2001: 9^{0}S, 12^{2}G, 14^{2}F, 12^{0}GF, 14^{0}GF, 11^{0}GF

	Starts	1st	2nd	3rd	Win & Pl
Career Total (Turf)	14	0	4	2	4571

Going (Turf): Sf: 0-2 GS: 0-1 Gd: 0-3 GF: 0-5 Fm: 0-3
Distance: 5f/6f: 0-3 7f-8f: 0-1 9f-13f: 0-8 14f+: 0-2
Track : LH: 0-5 RH: 0-4 Tight: 0-7 Gall: 0-1
Aids: Bl: 0-0 Vi: 0-1 Tstrap: 0-0
Best Rating: 56 5/01 Rdcr 1m6f19y firm

Saaryeh

103 **77**

3-y-o b f Royal Academy (USA)-Belle Argentine (FR) (Fijar Tango (FR))
M P Tregoning Sheikh Ahmed Al Maktoum

Placings:03316 **(4674)**
2001: 7^{0}GS, 8^{3}GF, 8^{3}GF, 8^{1}GF, 10^{6}G

	Starts	1st	2nd	3rd	Win & Pl
Career Total (Turf)	5	1	0	2	6753

77	7/01	Asct	1m	D	G-F	£5395

Total win prize-money £5395

Going (Turf): Sf: 0-0 GS: 0-1 Gd: 0-1 **GF: 1-3** Fm: 0-0
Distance: 5f/6f: 0-0 **7f-8f: 1-3** 9f-13f: 0-2 14f+: 0-0
Track : LH: 0-1 **RH: 1-3** Tight: 0-1 **Gall: 1-1**
Aids: Bl: 0-0 Vi: 0-0 Tstrap: 0-0
Best Rating: 77 7/01 Asct 1m gd-fm

Gradually improving, she got off the mark in maiden at Ascot on her fourth start and won with more in hand than the narrow margin would suggest.

Sabana (IRE)

103 **74**

3-y-o b g Sri Pekan (USA)-Atyaaf (USA) (Irish River (FR))
N A Callaghan M Tabor

Placings:0250-00016365310 **(4489)**
2001: 7^{0}GS, 7^{0}G, 6^{0}S, 6^{1}GF, 7^{6}GF, 6^{3}F, 7^{6}GF, 7^{5}F, 6^{3}G, 7^{1}F, 8^{0}S

	Starts	1st	2nd	3rd	Win & Pl
Career Total (Turf)	15	2	1	2	8700

70	8/01	Brig	7f214y	E(0-70)	FRM	£2765
73	6/01	Yarm	6f3y	E(0-70)H	G-F	£3234

Total win prize-money £5999

Going (Turf): Sf: 0-2 GS: 0-1 Gd: 0-4 **GF: 1-5 Fm: 1-3**
Distance: 5f/6f: 0-3 **7f-8f: 2-11** 9f-13f: 0-1 14f+: 0-0
Track : **LH: 1-5** RH: 0-1 Tight: 0-2 Gall: 0-1
Aids: Bl: 0-1 Vi: 0-0 Tstrap: 0-0
Best Rating: 74 8/01 Pont 6f good

He got off the mark in a handicap over six furlongs at Yarmouth in June and got the mile well when winning at Brighton in August. Suited by fast ground.

Sabo Rose

108 **85**

3-y-o br f Prince Sabo-Crimson Rosella (Polar Falcon (USA))
W J Haggas Don Magnifico Partnership

Placings:3135-0012356624 **(5605)**
2001: 7^{0}G, 7^{0}GF, 7^{1}GF, 7^{2}GS, 8^{3}GS, 8^{5}GF, 6^{6}GF, 7^{6}G, 8^{2}GS, 8^{4}GS

	Starts	1st	2nd	3rd	Win & Pl
Career Total (Turf)	14	2	2	3	18583

82	6/01	NmkR	7f	D(0-85)H	G-F	£6938
73	9/00	Pont	6f	D	G-S	£3363

Total win prize-money £10303

Going (Turf): Sf: 0-2 **GS: 1-5** Gd: 0-2 **GF: 1-5** Fm: 0-0
Distance: 5f/6f: 1-2 7f-8f: 1-11 9f-13f: 0-1 14f+: 0-0
Track : **LH: 1-2** RH: 0-0 Tight: 0-0 Gall: 0-1
Aids: Bl: 0-0 Vi: 0-0 Tstrap: 0-0
Best Rating: 85 11/01 NmkR 1m gd-sft

Fair handicapper, effective at seven furlongs to a mile. Handles any ground, goes well at Newmarket.

Sabre Dance

83 **64**

2-y-o ch g Sabrehill (USA)-Anna Karietta (Precocious)
H Candy The Earl Cadogan

Placings:6 **(5684)**
2001: 8^{6}S

	Starts	1st	2nd	3rd	Win & Pl
Career Total (Turf)	1	0	0	0	0

Going (Turf): Sf: 0-1 GS: 0-0 Gd: 0-0 GF: 0-0 Fm: 0-0
Distance: 5f/6f: 0-0 7f-8f: 0-1 9f-13f: 0-0 14f+: 0-0
Track : LH: 0-0 RH: 0-0 Tight: 0-0 Gall: 0-0
Aids: Bl: 0-0 Vi: 0-0 Tstrap: 0-0
Best Rating: 64 11/01 Donc 1m soft

Sabre Lady

101 **37**

4-y-o ch f Sabrehill (USA)-Cal Norma's Lady (IRE) (Lyphard's Special (USA))
Miss L A Perratt David R Sutherland

Placings:1230/34000000-5650065060 **(4439)**
2001: 5^{5}F, 5^{6}GF, 5^{5}F, 6^{0}GF, 5^{0}G, 5^{6}G, 6^{5}GF, 6^{0}G, 5^{6}GF, 6^{0}G

	Starts	1st	2nd	3rd	Win & Pl
Career Total (Turf)	22	1	1	2	7592

60	7/99	Haml	5f4y	E	FRM	£3501

Total win prize-money £3501

Going (Turf): Sf: 0-4 GS: 0-1 Gd: 0-8 GF: 0-6 **Fm: 1-3**
Distance: **5f/6f: 1-16** 7f-8f: 0-6 9f-13f: 0-0 14f+: 0-0
Track : LH: 0-1 RH: 0-0 Tight: 0-1 Gall: 0-0
Aids: Bl: 0-1 Vi: 0-0 Tstrap: 0-0
Best Rating: 56 5/01 Thsk 5f gd-fm

Has not won since her racecourse debut at two. Best over five furlaongs on a sound surface.

Sabreeze

102 **72**

3-y-o ch g Sabrehill (USA)-Zipperti Do (Precocious)
P W Harris J M Beever

Placings:62403 **(4571)**
2001: 7^{6}G, 7^{2}GF, 6^{4}GF, 8^{0}GS, 8^{3}HY

	Starts	1st	2nd	3rd	Win & Pl
Career Total (Turf)	5	0	1	1	1484

Going (Turf): Sf: 0-1 GS: 0-1 Gd: 0-1 GF: 0-2 Fm: 0-0
Distance: 5f/6f: 0-0 7f-8f: 0-4 9f-13f: 0-1 14f+: 0-0
Track : LH: 0-3 RH: 0-0 Tight: 0-1 Gall: 0-0
Aids: Bl: 0-0 Vi: 0-0 Tstrap: 0-0
Best Rating: 72 5/01 Donc 7f good

Sabresong

81 **37**

3-y-o ch f Sabrehill (USA)-Winsong Melody (Music Maestro)
P R Rodford (C A Dwyer 22/6) Les Trott

Placings:00000 **(2372)**
2001: 7^{0}G, 7^{0}GS, 7^{0}GF, 10^{0}GF, 8^{0}GF

	Starts	1st	2nd	3rd	Win & Pl
Career Total (Turf)	5	0	0	0	

Going (Turf): Sf: 0-0 GS: 0-1 Gd: 0-1 GF: 0-3 Fm: 0-0
Distance: 5f/6f: 0-0 7f-8f: 0-4 9f-13f: 0-1 14f+: 0-0
Track : LH: 0-1 RH: 0-0 Tight: 0-1 Gall: 0-0
Aids: Bl: 0-0 Vi: 0-0 Tstrap: 0-0
Best Rating: 37 5/01 NmkR 7f gd-sft

Sachiko

(96) (46)

3-y-o b f Celtic Swing-Leap Of Faith (IRE) (Northiam (USA))
I A Wood John Purcell

Placings:630 **(0182)**
2001: 8^{6}SD, 7^{3}SW, 10^{0}SD

	Starts	1st	2nd	3rd	Win & Pl
Career Total (Turf)	0	0	0	0	
Career Total (AW)	3	0	0	1	338

Going (Turf): Sf: 0-0 GS: 0-0 Gd: 0-0 GF: 0-0 Fm: 0-0

Distance: 5f/6f: 0-0 7f-8f: 0-2 9f-13f: 0-1 14f+: 0-0
Track : LH: 0-3 RH: 0-0 Tight: 0-2 Gall: 0-0
Aids: Bl: 0-0 Vi: 0-0 Tstrap: 0-0
Best Rating: 46 1/01 Wolv 7f slow

Sacho (IRE)

84 **72**

8-y-o b g Sadler's Wells (USA)-Oh So Sharp (Kris)
J L Harris J H Henderson

Placings:2/2/16/2246/0-0 **(0522)**
2001: 12^0S

	Starts	1st	2nd	3rd	Win & Pl
Career Total (Turf)	10	1	4	0	22882

86 9/97 Leic 1m1f218yD G-F £4091
Total win prize-money £4092

Going (Turf): Sf: 0-2 GS: 0-0 Gd: 0-5 **GF: 1-3** Fm: 0-0
Distance: 5f/6f: 0-0 7f-8f: 0-1 **9f-13f: 1-7** 14f+: 0-2
Track : LH: 0-6 **RH: 1-2** Tight: 0-0 Gall: 0-5
Aids: Bl: 0-0 Vi: 0-0 Tstrap: 0-0
Best Rating: 35 3/01 Donc 1m4f soft

Beautifully bred, he has had his problems and has only been lightly raced as a consequence. His best form is with give in the ground but he was beaten a long way on his only start this year at Doncaster.

Sacred Song (USA)

113 **112**

4-y-o b f Diesis-Ruby Ransom (CAN) (Red Ransom (USA))
H R A Cecil Niarchos Family

Placings:1/121-3312 **(4171)**
2001: 13^3S, 11^3G, 11^1GS, 11^2G

	Starts	1st	2nd	3rd	Win & Pl
Career Total (Turf)	8	4	2	2	115718

111 7/01 Hayd 1m3f200yA G-S £24000
112 10/00 NmkR 1m4f A SFT £16200
99 6/00 Nott 1m54y C G-F £6110
79 7/99 Nott 6f15y D FRM £4207
Total win prize-money £50518

Going (Turf): Sf: 1-2 GS: 1-1 Gd: 0-2 **GF: 1-2 Fm: 1-1**
Distance: 5f/6f: 0-0 7f-8f: 1-1 **9f-13f: 3-6** 14f+: 0-1
Track : **LH: 2-5** RH: 1-2 Tight: 0-1 **Gall: 1-3**
Aids: Bl: 0-0 Vi: 0-0 Tstrap: 0-0
Best Rating: 112 8/01 York 1m3f195y good

Handled the soft ground well and ran out a two and a half length winner from Littlepacepaddocks in the Princess Royal Stakes at Newmarket (transferred from Ascot) in 2000. Third in a pair of Listed events in her first two starts of this season, she found her form at the right time when winning the Lancashire Oaks at Haydock in July, and was a close second in the Yorkshire equivalent. Retired to stud.

Sacrementum (IRE)

(100) (45)**50**

6-y-o b g Night Shift (USA)-Tantum Ergo (Tanfirion)
A W Carroll Dennis Deacon

Placings:00000/0453160600006/530200064/**64020**640 24424F**60440-4** **(0447)**
2001: 11^4SD

	Starts	1st	2nd	3rd	Win & Pl
Career Total (Turf)	36	1	3	2	11216
Career Total (AW)	11	0	1	0	798

77 7/98 Leop 6f (0-85)H G-F £5843
Total win prize-money £5844

Going (Turf): Sf: 0-6 GS: 0-1 Gd: 0-13 **GF: 1-6** Fm: 0-2
Distance: **5f/6f: 1-12** 7f-8f: 0-19 9f-13f: 0-16 14f+: 0-0
Track : LH: 0-22 RH: 0-6 Tight: 0-11 Gall: 0-4
Aids: Bl: 0-4 Vi: 0-0 Tstrap: 0-0
Best Rating: 30 3/01 Sthl 1m3f stand

Sad Mad Bad (USA)

93 **43**

7-y-o b g Sunny's Halo (CAN)-Quite Attractive (USA) (Well Decorated (USA))
Mrs M Reveley P D Savill

Placings:310/05200360**0**024/042/1/05 **(5402)**
2001: 17^0G, 17^5S

	Starts	1st	2nd	3rd	Win & Pl
Career Total (Turf)	19	2	3	2	10652
Career Total (AW)	1	0	0	0	

58 11/99 Catt 1m5f175yE(0-70)H SFT £3179
80 8/96 Ling 7f140y D G-S £3173
Total win prize-money £6353

Going (Turf): Sf: 1-4 GS: 1-3 Gd: 0-5 GF: 0-6 Fm: 0-1
Distance: 5f/6f: 0-1 7f-8f: 1-2 9f-13f: 0-2 14f+: 1-15
Track : **LH: 1-15** RH: 0-2 **Tight: 1-7** Gall: 0-1
Aids: Bl: 0-1 Vi: 0-0 Tstrap: 0-0
Best Rating: 43 10/01 Pont 2m1f216y soft

Saddad (USA)

111 **103+**

2-y-o ch c Gone West (USA)-Lite Light (USA) (Majestic Light (USA))
Sir Michael Stoute Hamdan Al Maktoum

Placings:151 **(4713)**
2001: 5^1G, 6^5G, 5^1G

	Starts	1st	2nd	3rd	Win & Pl
Career Total (Turf)	3	2	0	0	36733

103 9/01 Donc 5f A GD £30000
91 7/01 Yarm 5f43y D GD £3607
Total win prize-money £33608

Going (Turf): Sf: 0-0 GS: 0-0 **Gd: 2-3** GF: 0-0 Fm: 0-0
Distance: **5f/6f: 2-3** 7f-8f: 0-0 9f-13f: 0-0 14f+: 0-0
Track : LH: 0-0 RH: 0-0 Tight: 0-0 Gall: 0-0
Aids: Bl: 0-0 Vi: 0-0 Tstrap: 0-0
Best Rating: 103 9/01 Donc 5f good

A $400,000 yearling out of a Grade One winner, he was heavily backed on his Yarmouth debut and won easily. Pulled too hard in the Gimcrack, but was successfully dropped back to the minimum with a clear-cut victory in the Flying Childers. He settles better over the shorter trip.

Saddler's Creek (USA)

81 **84**

3-y-o b c Sadler's Wells (USA)-Gleeful (USA) (Seeking The Gold (USA))
A P O'Brien Mrs John Magnier & Mr M Tabor

Placings:310000 **(5247a)**
2001: 12^3GF, 13^1GY, 12^0GF, 11^0G, 14^0G, 12^0HO

	Starts	1st	2nd	3rd	Win & Pl
Career Total (Turf)	6	1	0	1	6290

84 7/01 Wxfd 1m5f G-Y £5520
Total win prize-money £5520

Going (Turf): Sf: 0-0 GS: 0-0 Gd: 0-2 GF: 0-2 Fm: 0-0
Distance: 5f/6f: 0-0 7f-8f: 0-0 **9f-13f: 1-5** 14f+: 0-1
Track : LH: 0-2 RH: 0-2 Tight: 0-1 Gall: 0-2
Aids: Bl: 0-0 Vi: 0-0 Tstrap: 0-0
Best Rating: 84 7/01 Wxfd 1m5f gd-yld

Made all in a Wexford maiden on his second start and may have found conditions on the fast side when well beaten in the Gordon Stakes. Subsequently used by Ballydoyle as a pacemaker for his more illustrious stable companions.

Saddler's Quest

109 **92**

4-y-o b c Saddlers' Hall (IRE)-Seren Quest (Rainbow Quest (USA))
G A Butler The Fairy Story Partnership

Placings:1/11-00044 **(5683)**
2001: 12^0GS, 16^0G, 14^0HY, 12^4GS, 14^4S

	Starts	1st	2nd	3rd	Win & Pl
Career Total (Turf)	8	3	0	0	46651

110 5/00 Ling 1m3f106yA G-S £34800
98 4/00 Kemp 1m2f C(0-90) SFT £6613
88 9/99 Bath 1m2f46y D G-S £3550
Total win prize-money £44964

Going (Turf): Sf: 1-3 **GS: 2-4** Gd: 0-1 GF: 0-0 Fm: 0-0
Distance: 5f/6f: 0-0 7f-8f: 0-0 **9f-13f: 3-5** 14f+: 0-3
Track : **LH: 2-5** RH: 1-3 **Tight: 2-2** Gall: 1-5
Aids: Bl: 0-0 Vi: 0-0 Tstrap: 0-0
Best Rating: 98 4/01 Newb 1m4f5y gd-sft

Sidelined through injury after winning the Lingfield Derby Trial in 2000, he came back in April of 2001, although he does not seem to be the horse he was. He is suited by cut in the ground.

Sadeebah

61

6-y-o b g Prince Sabo-Adeebah (USA) (Damascus (USA))
M Todhunter G C G Racing Partnership

Placings:000/00260044/0/0 **(3285)**
2001: 10^0GS

	Starts	1st	2nd	3rd	Win & Pl
Career Total (Turf)	12	0	1	0	625
Career Total (AW)	1	0	0	0	

Going (Turf): Sf: 0-1 GS: 0-3 Gd: 0-5 GF: 0-2 Fm: 0-1
Distance: 5f/6f: 0-1 7f-8f: 0-7 9f-13f: 0-5 14f+: 0-0
Track : LH: 0-7 RH: 0-4 Tight: 0-4 Gall: 0-0
Aids: Bl: 0-1 Vi: 0-0 Tstrap: 0-0

Sadie Sadie

(68) (42)**44**

2-y-o b f Primo Dominie-Ann's Pearl (IRE) (Cyrano De Bergerac)
P J Makin Mrs Paul Levinson

Placings:00 **(5346)**
2001: 6^0HY, 6^0SD

	Starts	1st	2nd	3rd	Win & Pl
Career Total (Turf)	1	0	0	0	
Career Total (AW)	1	0	0	0	

Going (Turf): Sf: 0-1 GS: 0-0 Gd: 0-0 GF: 0-0 Fm: 0-0
Distance: 5f/6f: 0-2 7f-8f: 0-0 9f-13f: 0-0 14f+: 0-0
Track : LH: 0-1 RH: 0-0 Tight: 0-0 Gall: 0-0
Aids: Bl: 0-0 Vi: 0-0 Tstrap: 0-0
Best Rating: 44 10/01 Wind 6f heavy

Sadlers Law (IRE)

67 **44**

2-y-o b c Sadler's Wells (USA)-Dathiyna (IRE) (Kris)
J W Hills George Tong & Partner

Placings:0 **(5094)**
2001: 8^0GS

	Starts	1st	2nd	3rd	Win & Pl
Career Total (Turf)	1	0	0	0	

Going (Turf): Sf: 0-0 GS: 0-1 Gd: 0-0 GF: 0-0 Fm: 0-0
Distance: 5f/6f: 0-0 7f-8f: 0-1 9f-13f: 0-0 14f+: 0-0
Track : LH: 0-0 RH: 0-0 Tight: 0-0 Gall: 0-0
Aids: Bl: 0-0 Vi: 0-0 Tstrap: 0-0
Best Rating: 44 10/01 Sals 1m gd-sft

Sadlers Swing (USA)

71 **44**

5-y-o b g Red Ransom (USA)-Noblissima (IRE) (Sadler's Wells (USA))
M R Channon Mrs Eileen Sheehan

Placings:0/00-00 (1483)
2001: 11^{0}GS, 17^{0}GF

	Starts	1st	2nd	3rd	Win & Pl
Career Total (Turf)	5	0	0	0	

Going (Turf): Sf: 0-1 GS: 0-2 Gd: 0-0 GF: 0-2 Fm: 0-0
Distance: 5f/6f: 0-0 7f-8f: 0-0 9f-13f: 0-4 14f+: 0-1
Track : LH: 0-3 RH: 0-2 Tight: 0-2 Gall: 0-0
Aids: Bl: 0-0 Vi: 0-0 Tstrap: 0-0
Best Rating: 15 5/01 Brig 1m3f196y gd-sft

Sadlers Waltz (IRE)

95(69) (7)**52**
4-y-o b g In The Wings-Fascination Waltz (Shy Groom (USA))
J J Sheehan (M R Channon 26/5) Mrs Christina Dowling

Placings:00-60400P (4580)
2001: 12^{6}GS, 12^{0}S, 16^{4}GF, 14^{0}S, 18^{0}GF, 16^{P}G

	Starts	1st	2nd	3rd	Win & Pl
Career Total (Turf)	7	0	0	0	0
Career Total (AW)	1	0	0	0	

Going (Turf): Sf: 0-2 GS: 0-2 Gd: 0-1 GF: 0-2 Fm: 0-0
Distance: 5f/6f: 0-0 7f-8f: 0-0 9f-13f: 0-4 14f+: 0-4
Track : LH: 0-5 RH: 0-3 Tight: 0-4 Gall: 0-0
Aids: Bl: 0-0 Vi: 0-0 Tstrap: 0-0
Best Rating: 66 5/01 Thsk 1m4f gd-sft

Did not show much in two runs as a three-year-old. Shaped a little better on first start for new stable in May. Stays two miles. Probably best suited by ease in the ground.

Safe Shot

77 **57**
2-y-o b c Salse (USA)-Optaria (Song)
D R C Elsworth J C Smith

Placings:040 (4671)
2001: 6^{0}GF, 6^{4}GF, 8^{0}G

	Starts	1st	2nd	3rd	Win & Pl
Career Total (Turf)	3	0	0	0	

Going (Turf): Sf: 0-0 GS: 0-0 Gd: 0-1 GF: 0-2 Fm: 0-0
Distance: 5f/6f: 0-0 7f-8f: 0-2 9f-13f: 0-1 14f+: 0-0
Track : LH: 0-0 RH: 0-0 Tight: 0-0 Gall: 0-0
Aids: Bl: 0-0 Vi: 0-0 Tstrap: 0-0
Best Rating: 57 8/01 Sals 6f212y gd-fm

Safe Trip

95 **78**
2-y-o b f Hector Protector (USA)-Green Charter (Green Desert (USA))
J L Dunlop Benny Andersson

Placings:454100 (4611)
2001: 5^{4}GS, 5^{5}F, 6^{4}GF, 6^{1}GF, 7^{0}GS, 8^{0}F

	Starts	1st	2nd	3rd	Win & Pl
Career Total (Turf)	6	1	0	0	4005

78 7/01 Brig 6f209y E G-F £3464
Total win prize-money £3465

Going (Turf): Sf: 0-0 GS: 0-2 Gd: 0-0 **GF: 1-2** Fm: 0-2
Distance: 5f/6f: 0-3 **7f-8f: 1-2** 9f-13f: 0-1 14f+: 0-0
Track : **LH: 1-4** RH: 0-1 Tight: 0-1 Gall: 0-1
Aids: Bl: 0-0 Vi: 0-0 Tstrap: 0-0
Best Rating: 78 7/01 Brig 6f209y gd-fm

From the family of Time Charter, she got off the mark at Brighton in July 2001 winning a seven-furlong nursery on good to firm ground, but failed to recapture this form when raised in class on her two subsequent starts.

Saffron

96(85) (22)**44**
5-y-o ch m Alhijaz-Silver Lodge (Homing)
D Shaw Ernest Bennett

Placings:32202551/004000/0000543640-6 (0738)
2001: 8^{6}GS

	Starts	1st	2nd	3rd	Win & Pl
Career Total (Turf)	23	1	3	2	7505
Career Total (AW)	2	0	0	0	675

74 9/98 Catt 7f E(0-75)H G-F £3246
Total win prize-money £3246

Going (Turf): Sf: 0-2 GS: 0-1 Gd: 0-8 **GF: 1-10** Fm: 0-2
Distance: 5f/6f: 0-8 **7f-8f: 1-14** 9f-13f: 0-3 14f+: 0-0
Track : **LH: 1-10** RH: 0-5 **Tight: 1-7** Gall: 0-1
Aids: Bl: 0-1 Vi: 0-0 Tstrap: 0-0
Best Rating: 26 4/01 Muss 1m gd-sft

Saffron Heights

87 **49**
3-y-o b f Shirley Heights-Persia (IRE) (Persian Bold)
C A Horgan Mrs B Sumner

Placings:0 (4784)
2001: 9^{0}G

	Starts	1st	2nd	3rd	Win & Pl
Career Total (Turf)	1	0	0	0	

Going (Turf): Sf: 0-0 GS: 0-0 Gd: 0-1 GF: 0-0 Fm: 0-0
Distance: 5f/6f: 0-0 7f-8f: 0-0 9f-13f: 0-1 14f+: 0-0
Track : LH: 0-0 RH: 0-1 Tight: 0-1 Gall: 0-0
Aids: Bl: 0-0 Vi: 0-0 Tstrap: 0-1
Best Rating: 49 9/01 Gdwd 1m1f192y good

Safi

85 (53)**26**
6-y-o b g Generous (IRE)-Jasarah (IRE) (Green Desert (USA))
D McCain D McCain

Placings:43500/605000002600/00 (2234)
2001: 10^{0}G, 7^{0}GF

	Starts	1st	2nd	3rd	Win & Pl
Career Total (Turf)	13	0	1	1	1853
Career Total (AW)	4	0	0	0	

Going (Turf): Sf: 0-1 GS: 0-2 Gd: 0-2 GF: 0-6 Fm: 0-2
Distance: 5f/6f: 0-1 7f-8f: 0-4 9f-13f: 0-11 14f+: 0-0
Track : LH: 0-13 RH: 0-3 Tight: 0-4 Gall: 0-0
Aids: Bl: 0-7 Vi: 0-0 Tstrap: 0-6
Best Rating: 26 6/01 Hayd 1m2f120y good

Safinaz

83(88) (38)**35**
3-y-o gr f Environment Friend-Safidar (Roan Rocket)
Mrs N Macauley (G Brown 1/5) Richard Underwood

Placings:06500-4000 (5174)
2001: 7^{4}SD, 9^{0}SD, 8^{0}HY, 8^{0}GS

	Starts	1st	2nd	3rd	Win & Pl
Career Total (Turf)	7	0	0	0	0
Career Total (AW)	2	0	0	0	0

Going (Turf): Sf: 0-2 GS: 0-2 Gd: 0-2 GF: 0-1 Fm: 0-0
Distance: 5f/6f: 0-3 7f-8f: 0-3 9f-13f: 0-3 14f+: 0-0
Track : LH: 0-5 RH: 0-0 Tight: 0-2 Gall: 0-0
Aids: Bl: 0-0 Vi: 0-0 Tstrap: 0-0
Best Rating: 38 3/01 Ling 7f stand

Safranine (IRE)

95(66) (38)**46**
4-y-o b f Dolphin Street (FR)-Webbiana (African Sky)
Miss A Stokell (J L Eyre 6/9) Mrs M McMahon

Placings:0120/00000-0000000 (5629)
2001: 6^{0}GF, 8^{0}GF, 9^{0}GF, 7^{0}G, 5^{0}G, 6^{0}GF, 5^{0}G, 6^{0}SD

	Starts	1st	2nd	3rd	Win & Pl
Career Total (Turf)	14	1	1	0	3844
Career Total (AW)	2	0	0	0	

92 7/99 Rdcr 6f E FRM £2994
Total win prize-money £2994

Going (Turf): Sf: 0-0 GS: 0-1 Gd: 0-3 GF: 0-9 **Fm: 1-1**
Distance: **5f/6f: 1-8** 7f-8f: 0-6 9f-13f: 0-2 14f+: 0-0
Track : LH: 0-6 RH: 0-0 Tight: 0-2 Gall: 0-2
Aids: Bl: 0-1 Vi: 0-1 Tstrap: 0-0
Best Rating: 50 7/01 Pont 1m4y gd-fm

Sage Dancer (USA)

96 **84**
4-y-o b g Green Dancer (USA)-Sophonisbe (Wollow)
D K Weld Michael W J Smurfit

Placings:4301042-004 (3790a)
2001: 12^{0}S, 20^{0}GF, 14^{4}GY

	Starts	1st	2nd	3rd	Win & Pl
Career Total (Turf)	10	1	1	1	9700

84 8/00 Gway 1m4f G-Y £5865
Total win prize-money £5865

Going (Turf): Sf: 0-1 GS: 0-0 Gd: 0-2 GF: 0-2 Fm: 0-0
Distance: 5f/6f: 0-0 7f-8f: 0-0 **9f-13f: 1-6** 14f+: 0-4
Track : LH: 0-3 **RH: 1-5** Tight: 0-0 Gall: 0-1
Aids: **Bl: 1-7** Vi: 0-0 Tstrap: 0-0
Best Rating: 79 6/01 Asct 2m4f gd-fm

Sagittarius

113 **116**
5-y-o b h Sadler's Wells (USA)-Ste. Nitouche (FR) (Riverman (USA))
Rune Haugen Stall Nor

Placings:5-1112122 (5016)
2001: 11^{1}HY, 12^{1}G, 13^{1}S, 12^{2}G, 12^{1}G, 12^{2}S, 12^{2}S

	Starts	1st	2nd	3rd	Win & Pl
Career Total (Turf)	8	4	3	0	59551

8/01 Taby 1m4f GD £3577
7/01 Taby 1m5f SFT £10730
6/01 Ovrl 1m4f H GD £1458
4/01 Kref 1m3f HVY £1303
Total win prize-money £17068

Going (Turf): Sf: 2-5 GS: 0-0 **Gd: 2-3** GF: 0-0 Fm: 0-0
Distance: 5f/6f: 0-0 7f-8f: 0-0 **9f-13f: 4-8** 14f+: 0-0
Track : **LH: 2-4** RH: 0-1 Tight: 0-0 Gall: 0-1
Aids: Bl: 0-0 Vi: 0-0 Tstrap: 0-0
Best Rating: 116 9/01 Asct 1m4f soft

Norwegian trained, he showed decent form in Scandinavia, but ran his best race when chasing home Nayef in the Cumberland Lodge.

Saguaro

93(105) (48)**38**
7-y-o b g Green Desert (USA)-Badawi (USA) (Diesis)
K A Morgan Rex Norton

Placings:2/0000/1140000/210310-604000600 (5023)
2001: 8^{6}SW, 8^{0}SD, 8^{4}SD, 7^{0}SD, 7^{0}SD, 10^{0}GF, 10^{6}GF, 8^{0}GS, 7^{0}S

	Starts	1st	2nd	3rd	Win & Pl
Career Total (Turf)	16	1	1	1	4742
Career Total (AW)	12	3	1	0	6719

49 11/00 Sthl 1m G STD £1414
46 5/00 Muss 7f30y F(0-65)H FRM £2842
75 3/99 Wolv 1m1f79y E(0-75)H SLW £2853
82 2/99 Sthl 1m F(0-70)H STD £1612
Total win prize-money £8721

Going (Turf): Sf: 0-3 GS: 0-2 Gd: 0-5 GF: 0-5 **Fm: 1-1**
Distance: 5f/6f: 0-1 **7f-8f: 3-18** 9f-13f: 1-9 14f+: 0-0
Track : **LH: 3-18** RH: 1-3 **Tight: 2-11** Gall: 0-0
Aids: Bl: 0-0 Vi: 0-2 Tstrap: 0-0
Best Rating: 48 1/01 Sthl 1m slow

Modest miler, he has shown little on turf or on sand this season, but remains a better horse on the artificial surface.

Sahara Rose

83 **39**

2-y-o b f Green Desert (USA)-Ruthless Rose (USA) (Conquistador Cielo (USA))

Sir Mark Prescott Cheveley Park Stud

Placings:0 **(5184)**

2001: 5^{0}GS

	Starts	1st	2nd	3rd	Win & Pl
Career Total (Turf)	1	0	0	0	

Going (Turf): Sf: 0-0 GS: 0-1 Gd: 0-0 GF: 0-0 Fm: 0-0
Distance: 5f/6f: 0-1 7f-8f: 0-0 9f-13f: 0-0 14f+: 0-0
Track : LH: 0-0 RH: 0-0 Tight: 0-0 Gall: 0-0
Aids: Bl: 0-0 Vi: 0-0 Tstrap: 0-0
Best Rating: 39 10/01 Catt 5f gd-sft

Sahara Slew (USA)

112 **104+**

3-y-o b f Seattle Slew (USA)-Sahara Sun (USA) (Alysheba (USA))

John M Oxx Mrs C J O'Reilly

Placings:311 **(2325)**

2001: 10^{3}GY, 12^{1}GY, 12^{1}GF

	Starts	1st	2nd	3rd	Win & Pl
Career Total (Turf)	3	2	0	1	89940

104	6/01	Asct	1m4f	A	G-F	£81000
89	6/01	Leop	1m4f		G-Y	£7590

Total win prize-money £88590

Going (Turf): Sf: 0-0 GS: 0-0 Gd: 0-0 **GF: 1-1** Fm: 0-0
Distance: 5f/6f: 0-0 7f-8f: 0-0 **9f-13f: 2-3** 14f+: 0-0
Track : LH: 0-0 **RH: 1-1** Tight: 0-0 **Gall: 1-1**
Aids: Bl: 0-0 Vi: 0-0 Tstrap: 0-0
Best Rating: 104 6/01 Asct 1m4f gd-fm

Short head winner of maiden over 12 furlongs at Leopardstown in June , she subsequently won the Ribblesdale Stakes at Royal Ascot appreciating every yard of the mile and a half.

Sahhar

77 **13**

8-y-o ch g Sayf El Arab (USA)-Native Magic (Be My Native (USA))

B D Leavy Mrs Margaret Underwood

Placings:032/66044/00/0-0 **(1000)**

2001: 10^{0}S

	Starts	1st	2nd	3rd	Win & Pl
Career Total (Turf)	6	0	0	0	0
Career Total (AW)	6	0	1	1	1209

Going (Turf): Sf: 0-1 GS: 0-2 Gd: 0-1 GF: 0-2 Fm: 0-0
Distance: 5f/6f: 0-1 7f-8f: 0-2 9f-13f: 0-8 14f+: 0-1
Track : LH: 0-9 RH: 0-2 Tight: 0-7 Gall: 0-0
Aids: Bl: 0-0 Vi: 0-0 Tstrap: 0-0
Best Rating: 8 4/01 Ripn 1m2f soft

Sailing Shoes (IRE)

105 **64**

5-y-o b g Lahib (USA)-Born To Glamour (Ajdal (USA))

D Nicholls Rupert Wace

Placings:414250/3240050/0006060-0001000 **(4965)**

2001: 5^{0}GS, 5^{0}G, 6^{0}G, 5^{1}GF, 5^{0}G, 5^{0}G, 5^{0}S

	Starts	1st	2nd	3rd	Win & Pl
Career Total (Turf)	27	2	2	1	43253

64	7/01	Sand	5f6y	D(0-80)H	G-F	£4348
85	6/98	Ches	5f16y	D	G-S	£3434

Total win prize-money £7784

Going (Turf): Sf: 0-6 **GS: 1-5** Gd: 0-10 **GF: 1-5** Fm: 0-1
Distance: **5f/6f: 2-24** 7f-8f: 0-3 9f-13f: 0-0 14f+: 0-0
Track : **LH: 1-4** RH: 0-2 **Tight: 1-2** Gall: 0-1
Aids: Bl: 0-3 Vi: 0-0 Tstrap: 0-1

Best Rating: 64 7/01 Sand 5f6y gd-fm

He found life tough off a stiff mark, but eventually enjoyed some mercy from the Handicapper and ended a very long losing run at Sandown in July 2001. Suited by fast ground and the minimum trip.

Sailor Jack (USA)

(81) (20)**39**

5-y-o b g Green Dancer (USA)-Chateaubrook (USA) (Alleged (USA))

D McCain Champ Chicken Co Ltd

Placings:04/005630406/00 **(0511)**

2001: 12^{0}SD, 12^{0}SD

	Starts	1st	2nd	3rd	Win & Pl
Career Total (Turf)	11	0	0	1	553
Career Total (AW)	2	0	0	0	

Going (Turf): Sf: 0-2 GS: 0-1 Gd: 0-3 GF: 0-5 Fm: 0-0
Distance: 5f/6f: 0-1 7f-8f: 0-1 9f-13f: 0-9 14f+: 0-2
Track : LH: 0-7 RH: 0-3 Tight: 0-6 Gall: 0-0
Aids: Bl: 0-2 Vi: 0-7 Tstrap: 0-0
Best Rating: 20 1/01 Sthl 1m4f stand

Saint Ciel (USA)

82 **10**

13-y-o b g Skywalker (USA)-Holy Tobin (USA) (J O Tobin (USA))

F Jordan Miss Laura Jordan

Placings:2/310315201/5003/630041454200/30030350/0/3/0 **(4728)**

2001: 16^{0}GF

	Starts	1st	2nd	3rd	Win & Pl
Career Total (Turf)	37	4	3	8	18187

69	6/93	Hayd	1m2f120yG(0-70)H		G-S	£2679
80	9/91	Hayd	1m2f120yE		G-S	£3094
75	6/91	Wind	1m2f22y	F	G-S	£0
84	4/91	Pont	1m2f	E	FRM	£3052

Total win prize-money £8825

Going (Turf): Sf: 0-9 **GS: 3-10** Gd: 0-7 GF: 0-8 Fm: 1-3
Distance: 5f/6f: 0-0 7f-8f: 0-2 **9f-13f: 4-34** 14f+: 0-1
Track : **LH: 3-27** RH: 0-8 **Tight: 1-4** Gall: 0-8
Aids: Bl: 0-2 Vi: 0-0 Tstrap: 0-1
Best Rating: 10 9/01 Wwck 2m39y gd-fm

Saint George (IRE)

65(97) (35)**34**

5-y-o b g Unblest-Jumana (Windjammer (USA))

Miss Z C Davison Mrs J Irvine

Placings:0060/00/0042400-00 **(2235)**

2001: 11^{0}GF, 9^{0}GF

	Starts	1st	2nd	3rd	Win & Pl
Career Total (Turf)	12	0	0	0	0
Career Total (AW)	3	0	1	0	551

Going (Turf): Sf: 0-0 GS: 0-1 Gd: 0-5 GF: 0-6 Fm: 0-0
Distance: 5f/6f: 0-6 7f-8f: 0-3 9f-13f: 0-6 14f+: 0-0
Track : LH: 0-7 RH: 0-1 Tight: 0-5 Gall: 0-2
Aids: Bl: 0-0 Vi: 0-0 Tstrap: 0-0
Best Rating: 5 6/01 Wind 1m3f135y gd-fm

Saint Johann (IRE)

82 **47**

2-y-o b g Ali-Royal (IRE)-Up To You (Sallust)

G M McCourt Derek Simester

Placings:0000 **(4644)**

2001: 5^{0}GS, 6^{0}GF, 5^{0}GF, 6^{0}GF

	Starts	1st	2nd	3rd	Win & Pl
Career Total (Turf)	4	0	0	0	

Going (Turf): Sf: 0-0 GS: 0-1 Gd: 0-0 GF: 0-3 Fm: 0-0
Distance: 5f/6f: 0-4 7f-8f: 0-0 9f-13f: 0-0 14f+: 0-0
Track : LH: 0-1 RH: 0-1 Tight: 0-0 Gall: 0-1
Aids: Bl: 0-0 Vi: 0-0 Tstrap: 0-0
Best Rating: 47 9/01 Ling 6f gd-fm

Sainte Just (IRE)

100 **78+**

2-y-o b g Polish Precedent (USA)-Charlotte Corday (Kris)

W J Musson (R Charlton 18/10) Broughton Thermal Insulation

Placings:615 **(5668)**

2001: 8^{6}GF, 7^{1}GS, 8^{5}HY

	Starts	1st	2nd	3rd	Win & Pl
Career Total (Turf)	3	1	0	0	5811

78	10/01	NmkR	7f	E	G-S	£5811

Total win prize-money £5811

Going (Turf): Sf: 0-1 **GS: 1-1** Gd: 0-0 GF: 0-1 Fm: 0-0
Distance: 5f/6f: 0-0 **7f-8f: 1-2** 9f-13f: 0-1 14f+: 0-0
Track : LH: 0-0 RH: 0-2 Tight: 0-1 Gall: 0-0
Aids: Bl: 0-0 Vi: 0-0 Tstrap: 0-0
Best Rating: 78 10/01 NmkR 7f gd-sft

Out of a half-sister to Glatisant and to the dam of Superstar Leo, was debuted at a mile, but dropped to seven furlongs when taking a Newmarket seller. Sold for 15,000gns after that race, and his stamina was tested to the limit over a mile on heavy next time.

Sakamoto

87(84) (19)**36**

3-y-o b g Celtic Swing-Possessive Lady (Dara Monarch)

R C Spicer (I A Wood 10/9) John Purcell

Placings:00504-0600000000 **(5601)**

2001: 7^{0}GS, 8^{6}HY, 8^{0}G, 9^{0}GF, 10^{0}GF, 7^{0}G, 11^{0}SD, 6^{0}GF, 6^{0}SD, 8^{0}GS

	Starts	1st	2nd	3rd	Win & Pl
Career Total (Turf)	11	0	0	0	326
Career Total (AW)	4	0	0	0	0

Going (Turf): Sf: 0-4 GS: 0-2 Gd: 0-2 GF: 0-3 Fm: 0-0
Distance: 5f/6f: 0-1 7f-8f: 0-8 9f-13f: 0-6 14f+: 0-0
Track : LH: 0-5 RH: 0-2 Tight: 0-1 Gall: 0-0
Aids: Bl: 0-3 Vi: 0-0 Tstrap: 0-3
Best Rating: 36 9/01 Nott 6f15y gd-fm

Sakhee (USA)

119 (129)**133+**

4-y-o b c Bahri (USA)-Thawakib (IRE) (Sadler's Wells (USA))

Saeed Bin Suroor Godolphin

Placings:411/1124-1112 **(5580a)**

2001: 10^{1}GF, 10^{1}G, 12^{1}HO, 10^{2}FT

	Starts	1st	2nd	3rd	Win & Pl
Career Total (Turf)	10	7	1	0	1240688
Career Total (AW)	1	0	1	0	533333

133	10/01	Lonc	1m4f		HLD	£581959
132	8/01	York	1m2f85y	A	GD	£261000
112	7/01	Newb	1m2f6y	A	G-F	£14428
118	5/00	York	1m2f85y	A	FRM	£86275
118	4/00	Sand	1m2f7y	A	HVY	£36000
101	10/99	Sand	1m14y	C	SFT	£6214
82	9/99	Nott	1m54y	D	G-F	£3785

Total win prize-money £989662

Going (Turf): Sf: 2-2 GS: 0-0 Gd: 1-3 **GF: 2-3** Fm: 1-1
Distance: 5f/6f: 0-0 7f-8f: 0-1 **9f-13f: 7-10** 14f+: 0-0
Track : LH: 3-5 RH: 3-4 Tight: 0-1 **Gall: 2-2**
Aids: Bl: 0-0 Vi: 0-0 Tstrap: 0-0
Best Rating: 133 10/01 Lonc 1m4f holding

An impressive-looking colt, he won the Dante and was a brave second in the Derby in 2000. Slightly disappointing in the Eclipse subsequently, he missed the rest of the year and had knee surgery in the winter. Now with Godolphin, he scored easily in a small race on his return, and followed up by running away with the Juddmonte International at York. Enjoyed his finest hour in the Prix de l'Arc de Triomphe, but arguably enhanced his reputation with a narrow defeat at the hands of Tiznow in the Breeders' Cup Classic on his first encounter with a dirt surface. He is effective at ten to 12 furlongs, races prominently and acts on any ground. At this stage the plan is for him to remain in training in 2002.

Sal's Gal

101(94) (56)**71**

3-y-o b f Efisio-Ann's Pearl (IRE) (Cyrano De Bergerac)

P J Makin Mrs Paul Levinson

Placings:34300 **(5352)**

2001: 6^{3}SD, 6^{4}GF, 6^{3}G, 6^{0}HY, 6^{0}SD

	Starts	1st	2nd	3rd	Win & Pl
Career Total (Turf)	3	0	0	1	928
Career Total (AW)	2	0	0	1	398

Going (Turf): **Sf: 0-1** GS: 0-0 **Gd: 0-1** **GF: 0-1** **Fm: 0-0**
Distance: 5f/6f: 0-5 7f-8f: 0-0 9f-13f: 0-0 14f+: 0-0
Track : LH: 0-2 RH: 0-0 Tight: 0-0 Gall: 0-0
Aids: Bl: 0-0 Vi: 0-0 Tstrap: 0-0
Best Rating: 71 8/01 NmkJ 6f good

Salerno

96 **85**

2-y-o ch c Mark Of Esteem (IRE)-Shamwari (USA) (Shahrastani (USA))

M P Tregoning Sheikh Mohammed

Placings:465 **(5491)**

2001: 7^{4}G, 6^{6}GF, 6^{5}HY

	Starts	1st	2nd	3rd	Win & Pl
Career Total (Turf)	3	0	0	0	329

Going (Turf): **Sf: 0-1** **GS: 0-0** **Gd: 0-1** **GF: 0-1** **Fm: 0-0**
Distance: 5f/6f: 0-0 7f-8f: 0-3 9f-13f: 0-0 14f+: 0-0
Track : LH: 0-0 RH: 0-1 Tight: 0-0 Gall: 0-0
Aids: Bl: 0-0 Vi: 0-0 Tstrap: 0-0
Best Rating: 85 9/01 Newb 6f8y gd-fm

Salford Express (IRE)

110 **107**

5-y-o ch h Be My Guest (USA)-Summer Fashion (Moorestyle)

D R C Elsworth A J Thompson

Placings:20/11050402/25 **(1098)**

2001: 12^{2}GS, 12^{5}G

	Starts	1st	2nd	3rd	Win & Pl
Career Total (Turf)	12	2	3	0	102526
115 5/99 York 1m2f85y A				SFT	£77250
86 4/99 Newb 1m3f5y D				G-F	£4760
				Total win prize-money	£82010

Going (Turf): **Sf: 1-3** GS: 0-2 Gd: 0-6 **GF: 1-1** Fm: 0-0
Distance: 5f/6f: 0-0 7f-8f: 0-2 **9f-13f: 2-10** 14f+: 0-0
Track : **LH: 2-7** RH: 0-4 Tight: 0-1 **Gall: 2-9**
Aids: Bl: 0-1 Vi: 0-0 Tstrap: 0-0
Best Rating: 107 4/01 Newb 1m4f5y gd-sft

The Dante winner in 1999, has had his problems but is a capable performer at Group level when things go his way. Goes well at Newbury and returned from an 18-month break to run well there again, finishing runner-up to the revitalised Lucido in the John Porter, but was well beaten in the Jockey Club Stakes next time. Has been tried in blinkers, but best form without.

Salford Flyer

103 (9)**80**

5-y-o b g Pharly (FR)-Edge Of Darkness (Vaigly Great)

D R C Elsworth A J Thompson

Placings:040402/06131144225/20-045405 **(2932)**

2001: 14^{0}GS, 13^{4}GF, 14^{5}GF, 14^{4}GF, 14^{0}S, 14^{5}GF

	Starts	1st	2nd	3rd	Win & Pl
Career Total (Turf)	24	3	4	1	18264
Career Total (AW)	1	0	0	0	
68 7/99 Sals 1m6f15y E(0-65)				G-S	£2822
68 6/99 Yarm 1m6f17y E(0-75)H				G-F	£2831
68 6/99 Hayd 1m3f200yE				G-S	£2696
				Total win prize-money	£8350

Going (Turf): Sf: 0-4 **GS: 2-6** Gd: 0-5 GF: 1-9 Fm: 0-0
Distance: 5f/6f: 0-0 7f-8f: 0-4 9f-13f: 1-6 **14f+: 2-15**
Track : **LH: 2-11** RH: 1-10 **Tight: 2-9** Gall: 0-3
Aids: Bl: 0-0 Vi: 0-0 Tstrap: 0-0
Best Rating: 80 5/01 York 1m5f194y gd-fm

A fair handicapper on the Flat, he stays 14 furlongs and is best on fast ground.

Salim

94(100) (59)**55**

4-y-o b g Salse (USA)-Moviegoer (Pharly (FR))

C A Dwyer David L Bowkett

Placings:0/140430-035156000010500000 **(4879)**

2001: 10^{0}SD, 8^{3}SW, 8^{5}SD, 8^{1}SD, 9^{5}SD, 8^{6}SD, 8^{0}SW, 9^{0}HY, 6^{0}GF, 8^{1}SD, 8^{0}G, 8^{5}GF, 8^{0}GF, 8^{0}SD, 9^{0}SW, 8^{0}G, 12^{0}SD

	Starts	1st	2nd	3rd	Win & Pl
Career Total (Turf)	13	1	0	1	6186
Career Total (AW)	11	2	0	1	4741
59 5/01 Wolv 1m100y F(0-60)H				STD	£2233
55 2/01 Wolv 1m100y F(0-60)				STD	£2205
86 5/00 Thsk 7f D				GD	£4306
				Total win prize-money	£8744

Going (Turf): Sf: 0-1 GS: 0-2 **Gd: 1-5** GF: 0-4 Fm: 0-1
Distance: 5f/6f: 0-1 7f-8f: 1-8 **9f-13f: 2-15** 14f+: 0-0
Track : **LH: 3-17** RH: 0-2 **Tight: 3-13** Gall: 0-2
Aids: Bl: 0-0 **Vi: 1-7** Tstrap: 0-0
Best Rating: 62 1/01 Wolv 1m100y stand

Salim Toto

105 **74**

3-y-o b f Mtoto-Villasanta (Corvaro (USA))

J G Smyth-Osbourne L A Garfield

Placings:023130 **(4946)**

2001: 8^{0}GS, 8^{2}G, 9^{3}F, 12^{1}F, 12^{3}GF, 12^{0}G

	Starts	1st	2nd	3rd	Win & Pl
Career Total (Turf)	6	1	1	2	6688
72 8/01 Thsk 1m4f E(0-70)H				FRM	£3633
				Total win prize-money	£3633

Going (Turf): Sf: 0-0 GS: 0-1 Gd: 0-2 GF: 0-1 **Fm: 1-2**
Distance: 5f/6f: 0-0 7f-8f: 0-0 **9f-13f: 1-6** 14f+: 0-0
Track : **LH: 1-4** RH: 0-2 **Tight: 1-5** Gall: 0-0
Aids: Bl: 0-0 Vi: 0-0 Tstrap: 0-0
Best Rating: 74 9/01 Thsk 1m4f gd-fm

Scored on her handicap debut at Thirsk. Stays a mile and a half. Acts on fast ground.

Salix Dancer

100(71) (11)**42**

4-y-o b g Shareef Dancer (USA)-Willowbank (Gay Fandango (USA))

Pat Mitchell The Hamilton Partnership

Placings:3060-00060000022 **(5531)**

2001: 7^{0}S, 10^{0}G, 7^{0}GF, 9^{6}G, 12^{0}GF, 14^{0}G, 15^{0}G, 16^{0}G, 17^{0}GS, 16^{2}HY, 16^{2}HY

	Starts	1st	2nd	3rd	Win & Pl
Career Total (Turf)	14	0	2	1	2234
Career Total (AW)	1	0	0	0	0

Going (Turf): **Sf: 0-5** **GS: 0-1** **Gd: 0-6** **GF: 0-2** **Fm: 0-0**
Distance: 5f/6f: 0-0 7f-8f: 0-4 9f-13f: 0-5 14f+: 0-6
Track : LH: 0-10 RH: 0-2 Tight: 0-4 Gall: 0-2
Aids: Bl: 0-0 Vi: 0-0 Tstrap: 0-0
Best Rating: 53 4/01 Kemp 7f soft

He ran well in a Kempton maiden on his debut last season, but showed nothing afterwards until finishing runner-up in a couple of two-mile handicaps on bottomless ground in October. He clearly relishes a test of stamina.

Sally Traffic

84 **46**

2-y-o b f River Falls-Yankeedoodledancer (Mashhor Dancer (USA))

R M Whitaker J Barry Pemberton

Placings:00000 **(5660)**

2001: 5^{0}GF, 6^{0}G, 5^{0}G, 5^{0}GF, 5^{0}G

	Starts	1st	2nd	3rd	Win & Pl
Career Total (Turf)	5	0	0	0	

Going (Turf): **Sf: 0-0** **GS: 0-0** **Gd: 0-3** **GF: 0-2** **Fm: 0-0**
Distance: 5f/6f: 0-5 7f-8f: 0-0 9f-13f: 0-0 14f+: 0-0
Track : LH: 0-1 RH: 0-0 Tight: 0-0 Gall: 0-0
Aids: Bl: 0-0 Vi: 0-0 Tstrap: 0-0
Best Rating: 46 11/01 Muss 5f good

Saloup

90 **48**

3-y-o b f Wolfhound (USA)-Sarcita (Primo Dominie)

M R Channon Raymond Tooth

Placings:0-050 **(2942)**

2001: 7^{0}S, 6^{5}GF, 7^{0}GF

	Starts	1st	2nd	3rd	Win & Pl
Career Total (Turf)	4	0	0	0	0

Going (Turf): **Sf: 0-1** **GS: 0-1** **Gd: 0-0** **GF: 0-2** **Fm: 0-0**
Distance: 5f/6f: 0-2 7f-8f: 0-2 9f-13f: 0-0 14f+: 0-0
Track : LH: 0-0 RH: 0-2 Tight: 0-0 Gall: 0-2
Aids: Bl: 0-0 Vi: 0-0 Tstrap: 0-0
Best Rating: 48 5/01 Thsk 6f gd-fm

Salsa

102(69) (3)**59**

3-y-o b g Salse (USA)-Lana Turrel (USA) (Trempolino (USA))

M Dods J A Wynn-Williams

Placings:53-0620006610 **(5375)**

2001: 7^{0}SD, 7^{6}GS, 7^{2}GF, 8^{0}F, 8^{0}GF, 6^{0}GF, 7^{6}GF, 7^{6}GS, 7^{1}GF, 7^{0}G

	Starts	1st	2nd	3rd	Win & Pl
Career Total (Turf)	11	1	1	1	5070
Career Total (AW)	1	0	0	0	
59 8/01 Muss 7f30y E(0-70)H				G-F	£3290
				Total win prize-money	£3290

Going (Turf): Sf: 0-0 GS: 0-3 Gd: 0-2 **GF: 1-5** Fm: 0-1
Distance: 5f/6f: 0-2 **7f-8f: 1-9** 9f-13f: 0-1 14f+: 0-0
Track : LH: 0-6 RH: 0-2 Tight: 0-1 Gall: 0-2
Aids: Bl: 0-0 Vi: 0-0 Tstrap: 0-0
Best Rating: 69 5/01 Ayr 7f gd-fm

His only win to date was due to the misfortune of the leader in a moderate Musselburgh handicap in August 2001.

Salsify

78 **24**

5-y-o b g Salse (USA)-Amaranthus (Shirley Heights)

G A Ham P A Dales

Placings:0/0/6-00 **(3741)**

2001: 9^{0}GF, 10^{0}S

	Starts	1st	2nd	3rd	Win & Pl
Career Total (Turf)	5	0	0	0	0

Going (Turf): **Sf: 0-1** **GS: 0-2** **Gd: 0-0** **GF: 0-2** **Fm: 0-0**
Distance: 5f/6f: 0-0 7f-8f: 0-1 9f-13f: 0-3 14f+: 0-1
Track : LH: 0-2 RH: 0-1 Tight: 0-2 Gall: 0-0
Aids: Bl: 0-0 Vi: 0-0 Tstrap: 0-0
Best Rating: 24 8/01 Chep 1m2f36y soft

Salska

99 (35)**41**

10-y-o b m Salse (USA)-Anzeige (GER) (Soderini)
P L Clinton P L Clinton

Placings:23/50404055**005/0**0402360510/520311/0015 01555020/112256/062106000/0054250660-0636000 **(4079)**

2001: 16^{0}F, 16^{6}GF, 16^{3}GF, 16^{6}F, 14^{0}GF, 18^{0}G, 17^{0}GF

	Starts	1st	2nd	3rd	Win & Pl
Career Total (Turf)	71	8	8	4	43380
Career Total (AW)	4	0	0	0	

64	7/99	Rdcr	2m4y	E(0-75)H	FRM	£4211
66	6/98	Newc	2m19y	E(0-70)H	GD	£3598
66	6/98	Nott	1m6f15y	F(0-70)H	GD	£2595
61	7/97	Rdcr	2m4y	D(0-75)H	G-F	£3769
61	6/97	Nott	1m6f15y	E(0-70)H	G-F	£3200
57	7/96	Rdcr	1m6f19y	F(0-65)H	FRM	£3218
54	7/96	Wwck	1m6f194y	E(0-70)H	G-F	£3370
50	9/95	Hayd	1m6f	E(0-70)H	GD	£3629

Total win prize-money £27593

Going (Turf): Sf: 0-2 GS: 0-7 **Gd: 3-23 GF: 3-31** Fm: 2-8
Distance: 5f/6f: 0-2 7f-8f: 0-5 9f-13f: 0-18 **14f+: 8-50**
Track : **LH: 8-57** RH: 0-13 **Tight: 3-28** Gall: 1-14
Aids: Bl: 0-0 Vi: 0-5 Tstrap: 0-0
Best Rating: 45 8/01 Ches 2m2f147y good

Saltrio

105 **96+**

3-y-o b c Slip Anchor-Hills' Presidium (Presidium)
J H M Gosden Dr Ornella Carlini Cozzi

Placings:6-114 **(5020)**

2001: 9^{1}GF, 10^{1}GF, 12^{4}HY

	Starts	1st	2nd	3rd	Win & Pl
Career Total (Turf)	4	2	0	0	14097

96	7/01	Newb	1m2f6y	C	G-F	£7021
94	6/01	Sals	1m1f198yD		G-F	£3575

Total win prize-money £10597

Going (Turf): Sf: 0-2 GS: 0-0 Gd: 0-0 **GF: 2-2** Fm: 0-0
Distance: 5f/6f: 0-0 7f-8f: 0-0 **9f-13f: 2-4** 14f+: 0-0
Track : LH: 1-2 RH: 1-2 Tight: 1-1 Gall: 1-2
Aids: Bl: 0-0 Vi: 0-0 Tstrap: 0-0
Best Rating: 96 7/01 Newb 1m2f6y gd-fm

Ran away with an ordinary maiden on his belated return to action, and followed up making all in a three-runner conditions stakes over ten furlongs at Newbury. He is not bred to get much further, but shapes lika a mile and a half performer.

Saltwood

73 **73**

3-y-o b f Mujtahid (USA)-Actualite (Polish Precedent (USA))
P Howling R J McCreery

Placings:04100-00 **(2023)**

2001: 10^{0}G, 7^{0}GF

	Starts	1st	2nd	3rd	Win & Pl
Career Total (Turf)	7	1	0	0	4815

79	9/00	Ayr	7f	D	SFT	£4426

Total win prize-money £4427

Going (Turf): Sf: 1-2 GS: 0-1 Gd: 0-1 GF: 0-3 Fm: 0-0
Distance: 5f/6f: 0-0 **7f-8f: 1-6** 9f-13f: 0-1 14f+: 0-0
Track : **LH: 1-1** RH: 0-0 Tight: 0-0 Gall: 0-0
Aids: Bl: 0-0 Vi: 0-0 Tstrap: 0-0
Best Rating: 11 6/01 NmkR 7f gd-fm

Got off the mark in an Ayr maiden on her third start when encountering soft ground for the first time. No show in two outings.

Salty Jack (IRE)

108(108) (84)**86**

7-y-o b h Salt Dome (USA)-Play The Queen (IRE) (King Of Clubs)
D R C Elsworth Salts Of The Earth

Placings:033133/005**412/0313**6402123110/004020002 01/**0213**000545130260-4001100000 **(5344)**

2001: 7^{4}SD, 8^{0}S, 8^{0}GS, 8^{1}GF, 8^{1}GF, 7^{0}G, 8^{0}GF, 8^{0}S, 9^{0}G, 8^{0}GS

	Starts	1st	2nd	3rd	Win & Pl
Career Total (Turf)	51	8	5	6	86233
Career Total (AW)	12	3	2	3	20054

86	7/01	Gdwd	1m	C(0-90)H	G-F	£15340
84	6/01	Kemp	1m	C(0-90)H	G-F	£7637
84	7/00	Asct	1m	C(0-90)H	G-F	£7085
84	2/00	Ling	1m	C(0-95)H	STD	£6435
77	12/99	Ling	7f	D(0-80)H	STD	£3929
90	10/98	NmkR	7f	B(0-100)H	GD	£8531
84	9/98	Donc	7f	C(0-90)H	GD	£6961
78	7/98	Epsm	7f	D(0-80)H	G-F	£5061
74	4/98	Folk	6f189y	E(0-70)	SFT	£2976
69	12/97	Ling	7f	D(0-80)H	STD	£3566
75	8/96	Sals	6f	E	G-F	£3262

Total win prize-money £70785

Going (Turf): Sf: 1-8 GS: 0-7 Gd: 2-16 **GF: 5-20** Fm: 0-0
Distance: 5f/6f: 1-5 **7f-8f: 10-56** 9f-13f: 0-2 14f+: 0-0
Track : **LH: 4-19** RH: 3-12 **Tight: 5-17** Gall: 0-4
Aids: Bl: 0-0 Vi: 0-0 Tstrap: 0-0
Best Rating: 86 7/01 Gdwd 1m gd-fm

Suited by being held up in a fast-run race, and things went just right for him when winning at Kempton and Goodwood during the summer. Best at around a mile and seems to have a preference for sounder surfaces.

Saluem

103 **74**

4-y-o b f Salse (USA)-Pat Or Else (Alzao (USA))
R Guest Matthews Breeding And Racing

Placings:32256-5201 **(5634)**

2001: 11^{5}G, 12^{2}G, 14^{0}G, 11^{1}G

	Starts	1st	2nd	3rd	Win & Pl
Career Total (Turf)	9	1	3	1	8282

60	11/01	Catt	1m3f214yD		GD	£2996

Total win prize-money £2996

Going (Turf): Sf: 0-2 GS: 0-0 **Gd: 1-7** GF: 0-0 Fm: 0-0
Distance: 5f/6f: 0-0 7f-8f: 0-0 **9f-13f: 1-6** 14f+: 0-3
Track : **LH: 1-4** RH: 0-5 **Tight: 1-3** Gall: 0-3
Aids: Bl: 0-0 Vi: 0-0 Tstrap: 0-0
Best Rating: 74 8/01 NmkJ 1m4f good

Put in some decent efforts in 2000 without winning and it was a similar story this season until he got off the mark in a weak back-end maiden. Does not have much in the way of a turn of foot.

Salute (IRE)

98 **86**

2-y-o b g Muhtarram (USA)-Alasib (Siberian Express (USA))
J M P Eustace Blue Peter Racing

Placings:142150 **(5364)**

2001: 6^{1}GF, 6^{4}GF, 7^{2}GF, 8^{1}GF, 8^{5}G, 6^{0}GS

	Starts	1st	2nd	3rd	Win & Pl
Career Total (Turf)	6	2	1	0	37254

86	8/01	Newc	1m3y	B H	G-F	£29250
82	6/01	Wind	6f	E	G-F	£4165

Total win prize-money £33415

Going (Turf): Sf: 0-0 GS: 0-1 Gd: 0-1 **GF: 2-4** Fm: 0-0
Distance: 5f/6f: 1-3 7f-8f: 0-2 9f-13f: 1-1 14f+: 0-0
Track : LH: 0-0 RH: 0-0 Tight: 0-0 Gall: 0-0
Aids: Bl: 0-0 Vi: 0-0 Tstrap: 0-0
Best Rating: 86 8/01 Newc 1m3y gd-fm

He did well to win from an unfavourable draw on his debut and looked to need seven based on his staying-on performance at Salisbury next time. He was unlucky not to be awarded the race after being hampered over that trip at Newmarket, but gained ample compensation when stepped up to a mile for the Blaydon nursery, and he was not beaten far in a similar event next time.

Salviano

71 **27**

3-y-o b g River Falls-Shiny Kay (Star Appeal)
N Tinkler Mrs Christine Cawley

Placings:00-00 **(2639)**

2001: 7^{0}GF, 12^{0}GF

	Starts	1st	2nd	3rd	Win & Pl
Career Total (Turf)	4	0	0	0	

Going (Turf): Sf: 0-1 GS: 0-0 Gd: 0-1 GF: 0-2 Fm: 0-0
Distance: 5f/6f: 0-0 7f-8f: 0-3 9f-13f: 0-1 14f+: 0-0
Track : LH: 0-4 RH: 0-0 Tight: 0-0 Gall: 0-2
Aids: Bl: 0-0 Vi: 0-0 Tstrap: 0-0
Best Rating: 9 6/01 Hayd 7f30y gd-fm

Salviati (USA)

108 **87**

4-y-o b g Lahib (USA)-Mother Courage (Busted)
J M Bradley J M Bradley

Placings:31/20-00002020061010 **(4658)**

2001: 7^{0}G, 6^{0}GF, 6^{0}GF, 6^{0}G, 6^{2}GF, 6^{0}F, 6^{2}G, 5^{0}GS, 6^{0}GF, 6^{6}G, 5^{1}G, 5^{0}G, 5^{1}G, 5^{0}GF

	Starts	1st	2nd	3rd	Win & Pl
Career Total (Turf)	18	3	3	1	25092

87	8/01	Bath	5f161y	C(0-90)H	GD	£6987
87	8/01	Asct	5f	D(0-80)H	GD	£5538
73	7/99	Folk	6f	D	G-F	£3687

Total win prize-money £16214

Going (Turf): Sf: 0-0 GS: 0-1 **Gd: 2-8** GF: 1-8 Fm: 0-1
Distance: **5f/6f: 3-15** 7f-8f: 0-3 9f-13f: 0-0 14f+: 0-0
Track : **LH: 1-2** RH: 0-0 Tight: 0-1 **Gall: 1-1**
Aids: Bl: 0-0 Vi: 0-0 Tstrap: 0-0
Best Rating: 87 8/01 Bath 5f161y good

He showed signs that he could be coming to hand this season when just touched off by stable-companion Juwwi at York. He did not show quite the same form afterwards, but returned to winning ways on his first try over the minimum trip at Ascot in August, and added to that in a decent Bath handicap.

Samadilla (IRE)

104 **77**

3-y-o b f Mujadil (USA)-Samnaun (USA) (Stop The Music (USA))
T D Easterby W T Whittle

Placings:1441043-62040646 **(5011)**

2001: 6^{6}S, 6^{2}S, 6^{0}GS, 6^{4}GS, 7^{0}GF, 6^{6}G, 7^{4}HY, 7^{6}HY

	Starts	1st	2nd	3rd	Win & Pl
Career Total (Turf)	15	2	1	1	12335

82	8/00	Ripn	6f	D	GD	£4212
67	7/00	Pont	5f	E	GD	£2925

Total win prize-money £7137

Going (Turf): Sf: 0-6 GS: 0-2 **Gd: 2-4** GF: 0-3 Fm: 0-0
Distance: **5f/6f: 2-11** 7f-8f: 0-4 9f-13f: 0-0 14f+: 0-0
Track : **LH: 1-3** RH: 0-1 Tight: 0-0 Gall: 0-0
Aids: Bl: 0-0 Vi: 0-0 Tstrap: 0-0
Best Rating: 83 5/01 Hayd 6f soft

A winner at Pontefract and Ripon as a juvenile, she needs ease in the ground to be seen to best effect and her best efforts of this season have come under those conditions.

Saman

74(87) (55)**30**

2-y-o ch c Samim (USA)-Redspet (Tina's Pet)
S R Bowring A H Ripley

Placings:003 (5410)
2001: 5^{0}G, 6^{0}SD, 7^{3}SD

	Starts	1st	2nd	3rd	Win & Pl
Career Total (Turf)	1	0	0	0	
Career Total (AW)	2	0	0	1	285

Going (Turf): Sf: 0-0 GS: 0-0 Gd: 0-1 GF: 0-0 Fm: 0-0
Distance: 5f/6f: 0-2 7f-8f: 0-1 9f-13f: 0-0 14f+: 0-0
Track : LH: 0-2 RH: 0-0 Tight: 0-1 Gall: 0-0
Aids: Bl: 0-3 Vi: 0-0 Tstrap: 0-0
Best Rating: 55 10/01 Sthl 7f stand

Samara Middle East (FR)

97 **95**
3-y-o b f Marju (IRE)-Modelliste (Machiavellian (USA))
M R Channon Jaber Abdullah

Placings:616-60 (4445)
2001: 9^{6}GF, 8^{0}G

	Starts	1st	2nd	3rd	Win & Pl
Career Total (Turf)	5	1	0	0	4254

86 10/00 Ayr 1m D HVY £3542
Total win prize-money £3543

Going (Turf): Sf: 1-1 GS: 0-1 Gd: 0-1 GF: 0-1 Fm: 0-0
Distance: 5f/6f: 0-0 **7f-8f: 1-2** 9f-13f: 0-2 14f+: 0-0
Track : **LH: 1-1** RH: 0-2 Tight: 0-1 Gall: 0-0
Aids: Bl: 0-0 Vi: 0-0 Tstrap: 0-0
Best Rating: 72 8/01 Sals 1m1f198y gd-fm

Samara Song

101(93) (45)**51**
8-y-o ch g Savahra Sound-Hosting (Thatching)
Ian Williams R J Turton

Placings:000/0654552006/02232423123/60452216304 0/00106201500000/005260040403-500060 (4256)
2001: 8^{5}GF, 7^{0}GF, 8^{0}GF, 8^{0}GF, 7^{6}GF, 8^{0}GF

	Starts	1st	2nd	3rd	Win & Pl
Career Total (Turf)	59	4	10	4	40246
Career Total (AW)	9	0	0	1	255

68 7/99 York 7f202y D(0-85)H G-F £10332
65 5/99 Sals 6f212y D(0-80)H G-F £4552
63 8/98 Sand 7f16y C(0-90)H GD £7002
54 9/97 Leic 7f9y E(0-70)H G-F £3951
Total win prize-money £25839

Going (Turf): Sf: 0-2 GS: 0-4 Gd: 1-15 **GF: 3-31** Fm: 0-7
Distance: 5f/6f: 0-3 **7f-8f: 4-47** 9f-13f: 0-18 14f+: 0-0
Track : LH: 1-28 RH: 1-15 Tight: 0-17 **Gall: 1-6**
Aids: Bl: 0-4 Vi: 0-1 Tstrap: 0-0
Best Rating: 51 5/01 Wwck 1m22y gd-fm

A fair handicapper at around a mile, he runs the occasional good race, but has failed to win since July 1999.

Samarardo

102(95) (42)**50**
4-y-o b g Son Pardo-Kinlet Vision (IRE) (Vision (USA))
N P Littmoden Trojan Racing

Placings:0005061203/54642140-005401400 (5531)
2001: 14^{0}S, 14^{0}HY, 16^{5}SD, 12^{4}GF, 12^{0}GF, 16^{1}GF, 17^{4}G, 15^{0}GF, 16^{0}HY

	Starts	1st	2nd	3rd	Win & Pl
Career Total (Turf)	20	2	1	0	7574
Career Total (AW)	7	1	1	1	2914

45 7/01 Folk 2m93y F(0-60)H G-F £2464
52 9/00 Gdwd 2m E(0-70)H SFT £3835
54 10/99 Wolv 1m100y G(0-65)H STD £2110
Total win prize-money £8409

Going (Turf): Sf: 1-6 GS: 0-0 Gd: 0-3 **GF: 1-11** Fm: 0-0
Distance: 5f/6f: 0-2 7f-8f: 0-6 9f-13f: 1-8 **14f+: 2-11**
Track : LH: 1-16 **RH: 2-8 Tight: 3-11** Gall: 0-5
Aids: Bl: 0-0 Vi: 0-1 Tstrap: 0-0
Best Rating: 45 7/01 Bath 2m1f34y good

Mosderate stayer, made all to win a two-mile handicap at Folkestone in July. Acts on any ground.

Samba Beat

70(73) (54)**28**
2-y-o ch f Efisio-Special Beat (Bustino)
J W Hills A D Shead

Placings:0005 (5346)
2001: 6^{0}G, 7^{0}GF, 6^{0}HY, 6^{5}SD

	Starts	1st	2nd	3rd	Win & Pl
Career Total (Turf)	3	0	0	0	
Career Total (AW)	1	0	0	0	0

Going (Turf): Sf: 0-1 GS: 0-0 Gd: 0-1 GF: 0-1 Fm: 0-0
Distance: 5f/6f: 0-3 7f-8f: 0-1 9f-13f: 0-0 14f+: 0-0
Track : LH: 0-1 RH: 0-0 Tight: 0-0 Gall: 0-0
Aids: Bl: 0-0 Vi: 0-0 Tstrap: 0-0
Best Rating: 54 10/01 Sthl 6f stand

Has yet to show much ability, and does not look like the keenest of types.

Samhari (USA)

98 **102**
2-y-o ch c Indian Ridge-Cambara (Dancing Brave (USA))
D R Loder Sheikh Ahmed Al Maktoum

Placings:31402 (5493)
2001: 8^{3}G, 7^{1}S, 6^{4}GF, 6^{0}G, 7^{2}HY

	Starts	1st	2nd	3rd	Win & Pl
Career Total (Turf)	5	1	1	1	14089

93 9/01 Yarm 7f3y D SFT £4316
Total win prize-money £4316

Going (Turf): Sf: 1-2 GS: 0-0 Gd: 0-2 GF: 0-1 Fm: 0-0
Distance: 5f/6f: 0-2 **7f-8f: 1-2** 9f-13f: 0-1 14f+: 0-0
Track : LH: 0-1 RH: 0-0 Tight: 0-0 Gall: 0-0
Aids: Bl: 0-0 Vi: 0-0 Tstrap: 0-0
Best Rating: 102 10/01 Newb 7f heavy

Apparently lazy at home, he came good on soft ground at Yarmouth at the second time of asking, but was then found out in a Curragh Listed event and the Redcar Two-Year-Old Trophy. Better effort in gruelling conditions when runner-up in the Horris Hill at Newbury.

Sammal (IRE)

82(84) (24)**34**
5-y-o b g Petardia-Prime Site (IRE) (Burslem)
D Nicholls Mrs Andrea M Mallinson

Placings:3120000/006043/005004620060-000 (4013)
2001: 5^{0}GF, 6^{0}F, 5^{0}G

	Starts	1st	2nd	3rd	Win & Pl
Career Total (Turf)	26	1	2	2	6293
Career Total (AW)	2	0	0	0	

74 4/98 Carl 5f D G-S £3195
Total win prize-money £3196

Going (Turf): Sf: 0-1 **GS: 1-2** Gd: 0-8 GF: 0-8 Fm: 0-7
Distance: **5f/6f: 1-26** 7f-8f: 0-2 9f-13f: 0-0 14f+: 0-0
Track : LH: 0-6 **RH: 1-5** Tight: 0-2 **Gall: 1-7**
Aids: Bl: 0-1 Vi: 0-2 Tstrap: 0-1
Best Rating: 15 8/01 Catt 5f good

Out of form for his new trainer this season.

Sammax (IRE)

88 **57**
2-y-o b/br g Mujadil (USA)-Run Bonnie (Runnett)
N Tinkler E C Gordon

Placings:00650030 (5660)
2001: 5^{0}GF, 5^{0}GF, 6^{6}GS, 6^{5}G, 6^{0}G, 5^{0}F, 5^{3}GS, 5^{0}G

	Starts	1st	2nd	3rd	Win & Pl
Career Total (Turf)	8	0	0	1	490

Going (Turf): Sf: 0-0 GS: 0-2 Gd: 0-3 GF: 0-2 Fm: 0-1
Distance: 5f/6f: 0-8 7f-8f: 0-0 9f-13f: 0-0 14f+: 0-0
Track : LH: 0-1 RH: 0-0 Tight: 0-1 Gall: 0-0
Aids: Bl: 0-0 Vi: 0-0 Tstrap: 0-4
Best Rating: 69 8/01 Ripn 6f good

Had shown little in the way of ability, until running in a Chepstow nursery where the penny seemed to drop, only beaten two and a quarter lengths, and progressed on that when third in a Catterick maiden.

Sammy

(63) (9)
4-y-o ch g Most Welcome-Miss Topville (FR) (Top Ville)
M A Jarvis T G Warner

Placings:6 (0535)
2001: 9^{6}SD

	Starts	1st	2nd	3rd	Win & Pl
Career Total (Turf)	0	0	0	0	
Career Total (AW)	1	0	0	0	0

Going (Turf): Sf: 0-0 GS: 0-0 Gd: 0-0 GF: 0-0 Fm: 0-0
Distance: 5f/6f: 0-0 7f-8f: 0-0 9f-13f: 0-1 14f+: 0-0
Track : LH: 0-1 RH: 0-0 Tight: 0-1 Gall: 0-0
Aids: Bl: 0-0 Vi: 0-0 Tstrap: 0-0
Best Rating: 9 3/01 Wolv 1m1f79y stand

Sammy's Shuffle

104(104) (59)**48**
6-y-o b g Touch Of Grey-Cabinet Shuffle (Thatching)
Jamie Poulton Mrs G M Temmerman

Placings:000/0606045124016l3/254060433251/50015 306402232123500-001 (4704)
2001: 9^{0}GS, 9^{0}GS, 8^{1}G

	Starts	1st	2nd	3rd	Win & Pl
Career Total (Turf)	27	4	5	2	20418
Career Total (AW)	26	3	2	4	12407

48 9/01 Epsm 1m114y E(0-75)H GD £5596
44 7/00 Epsm 1m2f18y E(0-75)H G-F £3474
59 2/00 Ling 1m2f D(0-85)H STD £3715
57 12/99 Ling 1m2f E(0-70)H STD £2391
47 12/98 Ling 1m2f E(0-70)H STD £2495
47 9/98 Brig 1m1f209yF(0-60)H GD £2410
35 7/98 Brig 1m1f209yF(0-60)H G-F £2739
Total win prize-money £22823

Going (Turf): Sf: 0-2 GS: 0-5 **Gd: 2-7 GF: 2-7** Fm: 0-6
Distance: 5f/6f: 0-0 7f-8f: 0-7 **9f-13f: 7-46** 14f+: 0-0
Track : **LH: 7-40** RH: 0-8 **Tight: 5-36** Gall: 0-1
Aids: **Bl: 7-49** Vi: 0-0 Tstrap: 0-0
Best Rating: 48 9/01 Epsm 1m114y good

He runs regularly and wins in his turn. Suited by a sharp left-handed track, he looks best suited by ten furlongs on turf and Equitrack. Bounced back to form when coming from off the pace in strongly-run extended mile handicap at Epsom in September.

Samsaam (IRE)

111 **112d**
4-y-o b h Sadler's Wells (USA)-Azyaa (Kris)
J L Dunlop Hamdan Al Maktoum

Placings:000/11132130-002205 (4991)
2001: 14^{0}HY, 16^{0}G, 13^{2}GF, 15^{2}GS, 13^{0}G, 14^{5}HY

	Starts	1st	2nd	3rd	Win & Pl
Career Total (Turf)	17	4	3	2	89263

105 7/00 Chan 1m7f SFT £21134
93 6/00 Hayd 1m6f D(0-85)H G-S £3867
88 5/00 Donc 1m6f132yD(0-80)H G-S £4290
72 4/00 Wind 1m3f135yE(0-70)H HVY £3066
Total win prize-money £32358

Going (Turf): Sf: 1-4 **GS: 2-4** Gd: 0-6 GF: 0-2 Fm: 0-0
Distance: 5f/6f: 0-0 7f-8f: 0-2 9f-13f: 1-2 **14f+: 2-12**
Track : **LH: 2-6** RH: 0-6 Tight: 1-3 Gall: 1-6
Aids: Bl: 0-0 Vi: 0-0 Tstrap: 0-0

Best Rating: 112 8/01 Deau 1m7f gd-sft

He improved thoughout the first half of last season, winning three handicaps early on before gaining his biggest victory to date in a Chantilly Group Three, but his form tailed off quite badly afterwards. Seemed suited by trips just short of two miles and soft ground, but ran his best race this season when a close second in the Yorkshire Cup on fast ground. Reappeared after a three-month absence to run Generic close in the Prix Kergorlay, but was subsequently disappointing
.

Samsara

94(86) (38)**65**

3-y-o ch g Pivotal-Fire Lily (Unfuwain (USA))
P F I Cole R A Instone

Placings:0536000 **(4602)**
2001: 11^{0}SD, 8^{5}SW, 6^{3}GF, 10^{6}HD, 8^{0}G, 14^{0}S, 8^{0}SD

	Starts	1st	2nd	3rd	Win & Pl
Career Total (Turf)	4	0	0	1	560
Career Total (AW)	3	0	0	0	0

Going (Turf): Sf: 0-1 GS: 0-0 Gd: 0-1 GF: 0-1 Fm: 0-1
Distance: 5f/6f: 0-0 7f-8f: 0-2 9f-13f: 0-4 14f+: 0-1
Track : LH: 0-6 RH: 0-0 Tight: 0-3 Gall: 0-0
Aids: Bl: 0-1 Vi: 0-0 Tstrap: 0-0
Best Rating: 65 6/01 Sals 6f212y gd-fm

Samwar

(106) (53)**49**

9-y-o b g Warning-Samaza (USA) (Arctic Tern (USA))
Mrs N Macauley Andy Peake

Placings:25/4461/60412200/00050000/04**0**400306500 302/**2**4436320325301535**11**00600**11501**/4062260632**01** 225632635P-0 **(5350)**
2001: 5^{0}SD

	Starts	1st	2nd	3rd	Win & Pl
Career Total (Turf)	39	1	3	2	34129
Career Total (AW)	51	8	10	8	29103

45	5/00	Wolv	5f	G	STD	£1848
75	12/99	Sthl	5f	F	SLW	£2158
73	12/99	Wolv	5f	E(0-70)H	STD	£2738
58	11/99	Sthl	5f	F	STD	£2232
68	8/99	Wolv	5f	F(0-65)H	STD	£2276
61	7/99	Sthl	5f	E(0-75)H	STD	£2836
57	6/99	Wolv	5f	G	STD	£1903
89	8/96	Ripn	6f	B(0-105)H	G-F	£19560
70	12/95	Ling	7f	D	STD	£3185

Total win prize-money £38737

Going (Turf): Sf: 0-8 GS: 0-3 Gd: 0-15 **GF: 1-12** Fm: 0-1
Distance: **5f/6f: 8-77** 7f-8f: 1-13 9f-13f: 0-10 14f+: 0-0
Track : **LH: 5-48** RH: 0-3 **Tight: 5-37** Gall: 0-6
Aids: Bl: 3-17 **Vi: 4-41** Tstrap: 0-0
Best Rating: 8 10/01 Sthl 5f stand

He is hardly the same horse he once was and runs mainly on Fibresand these days. Ended an extraordinarily long losing run when bolting up in a Wolverhampton seller in June, but has enjoyed further success in rather better races since. Looks best over the minimum trip now.

San Dimas (USA)

(91) (32)

4-y-o gr g Distant View (USA)-Chrystophard (USA) (Lypheor)
R Allan (Andrew Turnell 8/9) Mrs R P Aggio

Placings:00/00600-04 **(4606)**
2001: 8^{0}SD, 12^{4}SD

	Starts	1st	2nd	3rd	Win & Pl
Career Total (Turf)	7	0	0	0	0
Career Total (AW)	2	0	0	0	0

Going (Turf): Sf: 0-2 GS: 0-1 Gd: 0-2 GF: 0-1 Fm: 0-1
Distance: 5f/6f: 0-1 7f-8f: 0-2 9f-13f: 0-6 14f+: 0-0
Track : LH: 0-5 RH: 0-1 Tight: 0-3 Gall: 0-0

Aids: Bl: 0-1 Vi: 0-0 Tstrap: 0-0
Best Rating: 32 9/01 Wolv 1m4f stand

San Glamore Melody (FR)

(96) (38)

7-y-o b g Sanglamore (USA)-Lypharitissima (FR) (Lightning (FR))
Mrs P Ford K R Ford

Placings:043200/00600243230500**2**/033-0 **(0458)**
2001: 8^{0}SD

	Starts	1st	2nd	3rd	Win & Pl
Career Total (Turf)	18	0	3	2	4086
Career Total (AW)	7	0	1	3	1875

Going (Turf): Sf: 0-1 GS: 0-2 Gd: 0-10 GF: 0-5 Fm: 0-0
Distance: 5f/6f: 0-0 7f-8f: 0-3 9f-13f: 0-17 14f+: 0-5
Track : LH: 0-17 RH: 0-7 Tight: 0-15 Gall: 0-1
Aids: Bl: 0-0 Vi: 0-1 Tstrap: 0-0

San Michel (IRE)

96(92) (38)**32**

9-y-o b g Scenic-The Top Diesis (USA) (Diesis)
J L Eyre J L Eyre

Placings:6433400/015002434402404/04546031404002 0/0356520/032640403/**00**53000**0506305**/**0054**3030060-340560300 **(3666)**
2001: 7^{3}SW, 7^{4}SD, 6^{0}SD, 6^{5}SD, 7^{6}GF, 7^{0}SD, 6^{3}G, 6^{0}F, 8^{0}S

	Starts	1st	2nd	3rd	Win & Pl
Career Total (Turf)	67	2	5	11	18445
Career Total (AW)	20	0	0	2	522

58	7/96	Leop	5f	(0-85)H	GD	£3082
	6/95	Tral	5f		SFT	£2740

Total win prize-money £5823

Going (Turf): Sf: 0-10 GS: 0-2 **Gd: 1-11** GF: 0-5 Fm: 0-2
Distance: **5f/6f: 1-44** 7f-8f: 0-19 9f-13f: 0-2 14f+: 0-0
Track : LH: 0-34 RH: 0-4 Tight: 0-10 Gall: 0-1
Aids: **Bl: 1-50** Vi: 0-8 Tstrap: 0-3
Best Rating: 38 4/01 Sthl 6f stand

San Sebastian

109 **119**

7-y-o ch g Niniski (USA)-Top Of The League (High Top)
J L Dunlop Mrs Michael Watt

Placings:000/0411112/221130/0315442/4643612-24540340 **(5585a)**
2001: 16^{2}G, 20^{4}GF, 16^{5}G, 15^{4}G, 18^{0}G, 20^{3}HO, 16^{4}GS, 15^{0}HY

	Starts	1st	2nd	3rd	Win & Pl
Career Total (Turf)	38	8	6	4	231213

118	10/00	Lonc	2m4f		GD	£48031
98	6/99	Asct	2m6f34y	B	G-F	£20150
91	6/98	Asct	2m4f	C(0-95)H	G-S	£29700
99	5/98	Gowr	1m6f	(0-90)H	GD	£4795
72	10/97	Cork	1m4f	(0-70)H	YLD	£4110
72	8/97	Wxfd	1m5f	(0-75)H	Y-S	£3253
65	7/97	Wxfd	1m5f	(0-75)H	FRM	£2911
49	6/97	Slig	1m3f	(0-60)H	G-F	£3253

Total win prize-money £116205

Going (Turf): Sf: 0-7 GS: 1-3 **Gd: 2-13 GF: 2-8** Fm: 1-1
Distance: 5f/6f: 0-1 7f-8f: 0-2 9f-13f: 4-7 14f+: 4-28
Track : LH: 0-11 **RH: 8-26** Tight: 0-2 **Gall: 2-13**
Aids: **Bl: 8-31** Vi: 0-2 Tstrap: 0-0
Best Rating: 119 8/01 York 1m7f195y good

Landed the Queen Alexandra at Ascot in 1999 and the Prix du Cadran at Longchamp in 2000. Has run some good races this season wihtout reward. He is genuine and is suited by an extreme test of stamina, but is vulnerable to a rival with a little bit of toe. Normally runs in blinkers or a visor, seems to handle any ground.

Sanadja (IRE)

100 **82d**

3-y-o b f Slip Anchor-Sanamia (Top Ville)
Sir Michael Stoute H H Aga Khan

Placings:33260 **(5279)**
2001: 10^{3}G, 12^{3}GF, 11^{2}G, 14^{6}G, 11^{0}S

	Starts	1st	2nd	3rd	Win & Pl
Career Total (Turf)	5	0	1	2	2419

Going (Turf): Sf: 0-1 GS: 0-0 Gd: 0-3 GF: 0-1 Fm: 0-0
Distance: 5f/6f: 0-0 7f-8f: 0-0 9f-13f: 0-4 14f+: 0-1
Track : LH: 0-2 RH: 0-2 Tight: 0-3 Gall: 0-0
Aids: Bl: 0-0 Vi: 0-1 Tstrap: 0-0
Best Rating: 82 7/01 Yarm 1m3f101y good

Sanapta

93(76) (37)**51**

3-y-o b f Elmaamul (USA)-La Domaine (Dominion)
W R Muir Larksborough Stud Limited

Placings:00-00060 **(5106)**
2001: 8^{0}G, 8^{0}SD, 8^{0}GF, 9^{6}GF, 12^{0}GS

	Starts	1st	2nd	3rd	Win & Pl
Career Total (Turf)	5	0	0	0	0
Career Total (AW)	2	0	0	0	

Going (Turf): Sf: 0-0 GS: 0-1 Gd: 0-1 GF: 0-3 Fm: 0-0
Distance: 5f/6f: 0-0 7f-8f: 0-4 9f-13f: 0-3 14f+: 0-0
Track : LH: 0-5 RH: 0-1 Tight: 0-2 Gall: 0-1
Aids: Bl: 0-0 Vi: 0-0 Tstrap: 0-0
Best Rating: 51 5/01 Bath 1m5y good

Sand Hawk

85(109) (66)**53**

6-y-o ch g Polar Falcon (USA)-Ghassanah (Pas De Seul)
D Shaw Swann Racing Ltd

Placings:0030032**0**20/40206005000**4512**/**2**114235**0**041 0622**2**00-000**1**30**1**0060005 **(5616)**
2001: 7^{0}SD, 6^{0}SD, 7^{0}SD, 7^{1}SD, 7^{3}SD, 7^{0}SD, 7^{1}SD, 6^{0}SD, 7^{0}GF, 7^{6}SD, 6^{0}GS, 6^{0}SD, 7^{0}G, 7^{5}SD

	Starts	1st	2nd	3rd	Win & Pl
Career Total (Turf)	27	1	5	2	10548
Career Total (AW)	30	5	4	2	19277

63	3/01	Sthl	7f	E	STD	£2702
62	2/01	Wolv	7f	F(0-65)H	STD	£1729
44	8/00	Catt	7f	E(0-70)H	G-S	£3932
62	1/00	Wolv	7f	E(0-75)H	STD	£2873
58	1/00	Sthl	7f	D(0-85)H	STD	£3809
59	12/99	Wolv	7f	D	STD	£2654

Total win prize-money £17700

Going (Turf): Sf: 0-7 **GS: 1-7** Gd: 0-4 GF: 0-7 Fm: 0-2
Distance: 5f/6f: 0-13 **7f-8f: 6-37** 9f-13f: 0-7 14f+: 0-0
Track : **LH: 6-36** RH: 0-1 **Tight: 4-17** Gall: 0-0
Aids: Bl: 2-26 **Vi: 4-18** Tstrap: 0-0
Best Rating: 66 8/01 Wolv 7f stand

He took his time finding his form, but he has done well on Fibresand this year. Effective over seven furlongs.

Sandalwood (IRE)

86 **51**

3-y-o b f Charnwood Forest (IRE)-Miss Java (Persian Bold)
C F Wall Jill Kerr-Smiley & Geoffey Bovill

Placings:0000 **(3720)**
2001: 6^{0}GS, 7^{0}G, 8^{0}G, 8^{0}G

	Starts	1st	2nd	3rd	Win & Pl
Career Total (Turf)	4	0	0	0	

Going (Turf): Sf: 0-0 GS: 0-1 Gd: 0-3 GF: 0-0 Fm: 0-0
Distance: 5f/6f: 0-1 7f-8f: 0-1 9f-13f: 0-2 14f+: 0-0
Track : LH: 0-1 RH: 0-1 Tight: 0-1 Gall: 0-0
Aids: Bl: 0-0 Vi: 0-0 Tstrap: 0-0

Best Rating: 51 5/01 Wind 1m67y good

Sandbaggedagain

99 **54**

7-y-o b g Prince Daniel (USA)-Paircullis (Tower Walk)

M W Easterby Mrs Joan Burnett & Steve Hull

Placings:05323233/5310050/0003321131/0/0552040-0006P **(4620)**

2001: 12^{0}S, 16^{0}F, 17^{0}GF, 15^{6}G, 16^{P}F

				Starts	1st	2nd	3rd	Win & Pl
Career Total (Turf)				38	4	4	8	42571
76	9/98	Ches	1m7f195yD(0-80)H				GD	£8364
68	7/98	Asct	2m45y D(0-85)H				G-F	£10796
63	7/98	Catt	1m7f177yE(0-70)H				GD	£2847
76	6/97	York	1m3f195yE				G-S	£4386

Total win prize-money £26393

Going (Turf): Sf: 0-7 GS: 1-3 **Gd: 2-10** GF: 1-15 Fm: 0-3
Distance: 5f/6f: 0-2 7f-8f: 0-11 9f-13f: 1-11 **14f+: 3-14**
Track : **LH: 3-26** RH: 1-6 Tight: 2-12 Gall: 2-12
Aids: Bl: 0-2 Vi: 0-0 Tstrap: 0-0
Best Rating: 65 5/01 Newc 2m19y firm

A one-time useful staying handicapper, he has had his problems in recent seasons.

Sanderstead

89 **64**

2-y-o b c So Factual (USA)-Charnwood Queen (Cadeaux Genereux)

T D Easterby Chris & Antonia Deuters

Placings:56000 **(4587)**

2001: 6^{5}G, 5^{6}G, 6^{0}GS, 6^{0}G, 7^{0}HY

	Starts	1st	2nd	3rd	Win & Pl
Career Total (Turf)	5	0	0	0	0

Going (Turf): Sf: 0-1 GS: 0-1 Gd: 0-3 GF: 0-0 Fm: 0-0
Distance: 5f/6f: 0-4 7f-8f: 0-1 9f-13f: 0-0 14f+: 0-0
Track : LH: 0-1 RH: 0-0 Tight: 0-0 Gall: 0-0
Aids: Bl: 0-2 Vi: 0-0 Tstrap: 0-0
Best Rating: 64 6/01 Leic 5f218y good

Sandles

102(94) (65)**60**

3-y-o b g Komaite (USA)-Miss Calculate (Mummy's Game)

S C Williams Chris Wright

Placings:15440054-00542523356 **(5191)**

2001: 7^{0}GS, 8^{0}G, 9^{5}GF, 8^{4}GF, 8^{2}GF, 8^{5}GF, 9^{2}G, 9^{3}GS, 10^{3}G, 9^{5}S, 12^{6}SD

				Starts	1st	2nd	3rd	Win & Pl
Career Total (Turf)				17	0	2	2	6498
Career Total (AW)				2	1	0	0	2233
65	5/00	Wolv	5f	F			STD	£2233

Total win prize-money £2233

Going (Turf): Sf: 0-3 GS: 0-3 Gd: 0-4 GF: 0-7 Fm: 0-0
Distance: **5f/6f: 1-3** 7f-8f: 0-6 9f-13f: 0-10 14f+: 0-0
Track : **LH: 1-5** RH: 0-5 **Tight: 1-4** Gall: 0-0
Aids: Bl: 0-0 Vi: 0-0 Tstrap: 0-1
Best Rating: 61 7/01 Bevl 1m100y gd-fm

Winner on Fibresand on her debut, she has run well on both a fast and soft surface without reward.

Sandmason

114 **116**

4-y-o ch c Grand Lodge (USA)-Sandy Island (Mill Reef (USA))

H R A Cecil Plantation Stud

Placings:1/22-2210 **(2883)**

2001: 12^{2}G, 13^{2}S, 12^{1}GF, 12^{0}GS

					Starts	1st	2nd	3rd	Win & Pl
Career Total (Turf)					7	2	4	0	115030
116	6/01	Asct	1m4f	A				G-F	£81000
78	9/99	Kemp	1m	D				HVY	£3615

Total win prize-money £84615

Going (Turf): Sf: 1-2 GS: 0-1 Gd: 0-2 **GF: 1-1** Fm: 0-1
Distance: 5f/6f: 0-0 7f-8f: 1-1 9f-13f: 1-5 14f+: 0-1
Track : LH: 0-2 **RH: 2-4** Tight: 0-0 **Gall: 1-5**
Aids: Bl: 0-0 Vi: 0-0 Tstrap: 0-0
Best Rating: 116 6/01 Asct 1m4f gd-fm

Ran a couple of promising races in Listed company in the spring of 2000, but was not seen after May. He returned this season to finish a highly-creditable second to Millenary in the Jockey Club Stakes and filled the same position behind the progressive Water Jump at Newbury. Despite looking the stable's second string, he went on to run out a game winner of the Hardwicke at Royal Ascot. A winner on heavy as a juvenile, he appears to act on any ground. Retired to stud.

Sandorra

88 **51d**

3-y-o b f Emperor Jones (USA)-Oribi (Top Ville)

M Brittain Mel Brittain

Placings:0640-0040 **(3939)**

2001: 8^{0}G, 8^{0}F, 9^{4}GF, 9^{0}G

	Starts	1st	2nd	3rd	Win & Pl
Career Total (Turf)	8	0	0	0	670

Going (Turf): Sf: 0-2 GS: 0-0 Gd: 0-3 GF: 0-2 Fm: 0-1
Distance: 5f/6f: 0-2 7f-8f: 0-4 9f-13f: 0-2 14f+: 0-0
Track : LH: 0-2 RH: 0-3 Tight: 0-1 Gall: 0-2
Aids: Bl: 0-0 Vi: 0-0 Tstrap: 0-0
Best Rating: 43 5/01 Ripn 1m good

Sandown Aratino

89 **40**

3-y-o b g Aragon-Cigartino (Cigar)

J G Given Sandown Park Stud

Placings:0 **(5631)**

2001: 10^{0}G

	Starts	1st	2nd	3rd	Win & Pl
Career Total (Turf)	1	0	0	0	

Going (Turf): Sf: 0-0 GS: 0-0 Gd: 0-1 GF: 0-0 Fm: 0-0
Distance: 5f/6f: 0-0 7f-8f: 0-0 9f-13f: 0-1 14f+: 0-0
Track : LH: 0-1 RH: 0-0 Tight: 0-1 Gall: 0-0
Aids: Bl: 0-0 Vi: 0-0 Tstrap: 0-0
Best Rating: 40 11/01 Rdcr 1m2f good

Sandpoint

100(93) (25)**46**

5-y-o b m Lugana Beach-Instinction (Never So Bold)

J G Given (L G Cottrell 27/8) Maltby Sporting Club

Placings:0/00060/03000-4202520 **(4601)**

2001: 6^{4}SD, 5^{2}G, 5^{0}G, 5^{2}GF, 5^{5}GF, 5^{2}GF, 5^{0}GF

	Starts	1st	2nd	3rd	Win & Pl
Career Total (Turf)	17	0	3	1	2959
Career Total (AW)	1	0	0	0	0

Going (Turf): Sf: 0-2 GS: 0-2 Gd: 0-4 GF: 0-8 Fm: 0-1
Distance: 5f/6f: 0-18 7f-8f: 0-0 9f-13f: 0-0 14f+: 0-0
Track : LH: 0-8 RH: 0-2 Tight: 0-1 Gall: 0-7
Aids: Bl: 0-0 Vi: 0-1 Tstrap: 0-7
Best Rating: 46 7/01 Brig 5f213y gd-fm

Sandros Boy

(95) (32)**32**

4-y-o b g Alhijaz-Bearnaise (IRE) (Cyrano De Bergerac)

Mrs N Macauley Mrs N Macauley

Placings:3206005-626450 **(0444)**

2001: 9^{6}SD, 12^{2}SD, 16^{6}SD, 16^{4}SD, 12^{5}SD, 14^{0}SD

	Starts	1st	2nd	3rd	Win & Pl
Career Total (Turf)	4	0	1	1	1065
Career Total (AW)	9	0	1	0	396

Going (Turf): Sf: 0-1 GS: 0-1 Gd: 0-0 GF: 0-2 Fm: 0-0
Distance: 5f/6f: 0-0 7f-8f: 0-1 9f-13f: 0-6 14f+: 0-6
Track : LH: 0-12 RH: 0-1 Tight: 0-7 Gall: 0-0
Aids: Bl: 0-0 Vi: 0-9 Tstrap: 0-0
Best Rating: 32 2/01 Wolv 2m46y stand

Sandy Ground (FR)

98 **34**

6-y-o b m Cricket Ball (USA)-Song Of Tonga (FR) (Dancer's Image (USA))

J E Long (Julian Poulton 18/6) Mrs Elizabeth Reed

Placings:50206/0153/0400/000000005400 **(5042)**

2001: 6^{0}GS, 9^{0}GF, 9^{0}G, 7^{0}F, 7^{0}GF, 9^{0}GF, 9^{0}GF, 8^{0}GS, 9^{5}GF, 7^{4}GF, 7^{0}GF, 8^{0}G

				Starts	1st	2nd	3rd	Win & Pl
Career Total (Turf)				25	1	1	1	9353
8/98	Vich	1m2f					GD	£3535

Total win prize-money £3535

Going (Turf): Sf: 0-0 GS: 0-2 Gd: 0-2 GF: 0-7 Fm: 0-1
Distance: 5f/6f: 0-0 7f-8f: 0-6 9f-13f: 0-6 14f+: 0-0
Track : LH: 0-6 RH: 0-3 Tight: 0-3 Gall: 0-0
Aids: Bl: 0-1 Vi: 0-0 Tstrap: 0-0
Best Rating: 34 10/01 Bath 1m5y good

Sandy Lady (IRE)

99 **85**

2-y-o b f Desert King (IRE)-Mamma's Too (Skyliner)

R Hannon Thurloe Thoroughbreds Vii

Placings:52134230 **(5609)**

2001: 5^{5}G, 6^{2}GF, 6^{1}GS, 7^{3}G, 6^{4}G, 7^{2}HY, 7^{3}GS, 8^{0}GS

				Starts	1st	2nd	3rd	Win & Pl
Career Total (Turf)				8	1	2	2	13446
79	7/01	Hayd	6f	D			G-S	£3828

Total win prize-money £3829

Going (Turf): Sf: 0-1 **GS: 1-3** Gd: 0-3 GF: 0-1 Fm: 0-0
Distance: **5f/6f: 1-3** 7f-8f: 0-5 9f-13f: 0-0 14f+: 0-0
Track : LH: 0-2 RH: 0-2 Tight: 0-0 Gall: 0-2
Aids: Bl: 0-0 Vi: 0-0 Tstrap: 0-0
Best Rating: 85 11/01 NmkR 1m gd-sft

She came up against above-average maiden winners in her first two starts, and showed improvement to beat Hufflepuff by a short head over six furlongs at Haydock in July. Good efforts in nurseries since.

Sangiovese

90 **69**

2-y-o b c Piccolo-Kaprisky (IRE) (Red Sunset)

B R Millman Kentisbeare Quartet

Placings:05600 **(4638)**

2001: 6^{0}G, 7^{5}F, 7^{6}GF, 6^{0}GF, 7^{0}GF

	Starts	1st	2nd	3rd	Win & Pl
Career Total (Turf)	5	0	0	0	

Going (Turf): Sf: 0-0 GS: 0-0 Gd: 0-1 GF: 0-3 Fm: 0-1
Distance: 5f/6f: 0-2 7f-8f: 0-3 9f-13f: 0-0 14f+: 0-0
Track : LH: 0-1 RH: 0-0 Tight: 0-1 Gall: 0-0
Aids: Bl: 0-0 Vi: 0-0 Tstrap: 0-0
Best Rating: 69 8/01 Epsm 6f gd-fm

Sannaan

98 **66+**

3-y-o b c Robellino (USA)-Quest For The Best (Rainbow Quest (USA))

M P Tregoning Sheikh Ahmed Al Maktoum

Placings:0-35 **(1602)**

2001: 10^{3}G, 10^{5}GF

	Starts	1st	2nd	3rd	Win & Pl
Career Total (Turf)	3	0	0	1	620

Going (Turf): Sf: 0-0 GS: 0-0 Gd: 0-2 GF: 0-1 Fm: 0-0
Distance: 5f/6f: 0-0 7f-8f: 0-1 9f-13f: 0-2 14f+: 0-0
Track : LH: 0-2 RH: 0-1 Tight: 0-1 Gall: 0-0
Aids: Bl: 0-0 Vi: 0-0 Tstrap: 0-0
Best Rating: 66 5/01 Hayd 1m2f120y gd-fm

Santa Catalina (IRE)

91 **72**

2-y-o br f Tagula (IRE)-Bui-Doi (IRE) (Dance Of Life (USA))
I A Balding Exors Of The Late Robert Hitchins

Placings:000 **(4608)**
2001: 6^{0}F, 5^{0}G, 5^{0}F

	Starts	1st	2nd	3rd	Win & Pl
Career Total (Turf)	3	0	0	0	

Going (Turf): Sf: 0-0 GS: 0-0 Gd: 0-1 GF: 0-0 Fm: 0-2
Distance: 5f/6f: 0-2 7f-8f: 0-1 9f-13f: 0-0 14f+: 0-0
Track : LH: 0-1 RH: 0-0 Tight: 0-0 Gall: 0-1
Aids: Bl: 0-0 Vi: 0-0 Tstrap: 0-0
Best Rating: 72 9/01 Folk 5f good

Santa Isobel

99 **99d**

3-y-o ch f Nashwan (USA)-Atlantic Record (Slip Anchor)
I A Balding Exors Of The Late Robert Hitchins

Placings:33-21060 **(4310)**
2001: 8^{2}G, 10^{1}S, 12^{0}GF, 10^{6}F, 10^{0}GF

	Starts	1st	2nd	3rd	Win & Pl
Career Total (Turf)	7	1	1	2	17776

99	5/01	Newb	1m2f6y	A	SFT	£15145

Total win prize-money £15145

Going (Turf): Sf: 1-2 GS: 0-0 Gd: 0-1 GF: 0-3 Fm: 0-1
Distance: 5f/6f: 0-1 7f-8f: 0-1 **9f-13f: 1-5** 14f+: 0-0
Track : **LH: 1-4** RH: 0-0 Tight: 0-1 **Gall: 1-3**
Aids: Bl: 0-0 Vi: 0-0 Tstrap: 0-0
Best Rating: 99 5/01 Newb 1m2f6y soft

Bred to stay middle distances, she showed ability in her first three starts and got off the mark in a Newbury Listed event on her second start of 2001. Outclassed in the Oaks at Epsom. Has won on soft ground, acts on a sound surface. Stays ten furlongs.

Santa Lucia

97 (25)**45**

5-y-o b m Namaqualand (USA)-Villasanta (Corvaro (USA))
M Dods J A Wynn-Williams

Placings:666020/02601140-53024 **(2791)**
2001: 11^{5}S, 12^{3}GF, 10^{0}GF, 11^{2}GF, 11^{4}GF

	Starts	1st	2nd	3rd	Win & Pl
Career Total (Turf)	18	2	3	1	8353
Career Total (AW)	1	0	0	0	

48	7/00	Haml	1m3f16y	F(0-65)	G-F	£2712
53	7/00	Haml	1m3f16y	F(0-60)	G-F	£2240

Total win prize-money £4953

Going (Turf): Sf: 0-3 GS: 0-2 Gd: 0-2 **GF: 2-9** Fm: 0-1
Distance: 5f/6f: 0-0 7f-8f: 0-1 **9f-13f: 2-14** 14f+: 0-3
Track : LH: 0-12 **RH: 2-5 Tight: 2-8** Gall: 0-2
Aids: Bl: 0-0 Vi: 0-0 Tstrap: 0-0
Best Rating: 45 6/01 Newc 1m4f93y gd-fm

Santa Vida (USA)

103 **61**

3-y-o b f St Jovite (USA)-Castellina (USA) (Danzig Connection (USA))
B W Hills D J Deer

Placings:03006346 **(4290)**
2001: 8^{0}S, 8^{3}G, 10^{0}F, 10^{0}GF, 12^{6}G, 11^{3}GF, 12^{4}G, 16^{6}GF

	Starts	1st	2nd	3rd	Win & Pl
Career Total (Turf)	8	0	0	2	757

Going (Turf): Sf: 0-1 GS: 0-0 Gd: 0-3 GF: 0-3 Fm: 0-1
Distance: 5f/6f: 0-0 7f-8f: 0-1 9f-13f: 0-6 14f+: 0-1
Track : LH: 0-5 RH: 0-1 Tight: 0-5 Gall: 0-0
Aids: Bl: 0-0 Vi: 0-0 Tstrap: 0-0
Best Rating: 66 6/01 Bath 1m2f46y firm

Santana (IRE)

(78) (27)**51**

3-y-o b g Inzar (USA)-Annella (IRE) (Glenstal (USA))
M Wigham Mrs I Foley

Placings:00-000 **(0362)**
2001: 9^{0}SD, 6^{0}SD, 8^{0}SW

	Starts	1st	2nd	3rd	Win & Pl
Career Total (Turf)	2	0	0	0	
Career Total (AW)	3	0	0	0	

Going (Turf): Sf: 0-1 GS: 0-0 Gd: 0-0 GF: 0-0 Fm: 0-0
Distance: 5f/6f: 0-1 7f-8f: 0-2 9f-13f: 0-1 14f+: 0-0
Track : LH: 0-3 RH: 0-0 Tight: 0-2 Gall: 0-0
Aids: Bl: 0-0 Vi: 0-0 Tstrap: 0-0
Best Rating: 27 2/01 Ling 1m slow

Santandre

99(104) (70)**43**

5-y-o ch g Democratic (USA)-Smartie Lee (Dominion)
R Hollinshead Geoff Lloyd

Placings:44414602360/0305404510030453/006411500 0050630000140-11252000430056 **(5592)**
2001: 8^{1}SD, 8^{1}SW, 8^{2}SD, 9^{5}SD, 8^{2}SW, 8^{0}G, 7^{0}GF, 7^{0}GF, 8^{4}GF, 7^{3}F, 8^{0}GF, 8^{0}G, 7^{5}S, 6^{6}GS

	Starts	1st	2nd	3rd	Win & Pl
Career Total (Turf)	39	1	1	4	7327
Career Total (AW)	24	6	2	2	24084

51	1/01	Wolv	1m100y	G	SLW	£1981
64	1/01	Sthl	1m	G	STD	£1379
57	11/00	Wolv	7f	G	STD	£1480
67	3/00	Sthl	7f	C(0-95)H	STD	£10871
68	3/00	Wolv	7f	E(0-70)	STD	£2588
70	9/99	Wolv	6f	E(0-70)H	STD	£2897
75	7/98	Thsk	5f	D H	GD	£3647

Total win prize-money £24846

Going (Turf): Sf: 0-9 GS: 0-5 **Gd: 1-9** GF: 0-11 Fm: 0-5
Distance: 5f/6f: 2-19 **7f-8f: 4-36** 9f-13f: 1-8 14f+: 0-0
Track : **LH: 6-35** RH: 0-6 **Tight: 4-24** Gall: 0-3
Aids: Bl: 0-0 Vi: 0-0 Tstrap: 0-0
Best Rating: 70 2/01 Wolv 1m100y slow

He has only ever won once on turf and has had more success on Fibresand since then. A regular in sellers and claimers on that surface, he wins his share each winter. Suited by trips of around a mile.

Santandria

81(42)

3-y-o b f Desert Splendour-California Dreamin (Slip Anchor)
B N Doran A F Heselton

Placings:0-000 **(1771)**
2001: 6^{0}HY, 6^{0}S, 5^{0}F

	Starts	1st	2nd	3rd	Win & Pl
Career Total (Turf)	3	0	0	0	
Career Total (AW)	1	0	0	0	

Going (Turf): Sf: 0-2 GS: 0-0 Gd: 0-0 GF: 0-0 Fm: 0-1
Distance: 5f/6f: 0-2 7f-8f: 0-2 9f-13f: 0-0 14f+: 0-0
Track : LH: 0-2 RH: 0-0 Tight: 0-1 Gall: 0-1
Aids: Bl: 0-0 Vi: 0-0 Tstrap: 0-1

Santiburi Girl

103(84) (32)**68**

4-y-o b f Casteddu-Lake Mistassiu (Tina's Pet)
J R Best Alan Turner

Placings:30022134565400/06100230011240666-0030006 **(3157)**
2001: 12^{0}SD, 10^{0}G, 11^{3}GF, 12^{0}F, 16^{0}GF, 12^{0}GF, 10^{6}GS

	Starts	1st	2nd	3rd	Win & Pl
Career Total (Turf)	37	4	4	4	27477
Career Total (AW)	1	0	0	0	

71	8/00	Rdcr	1m3f	C(0-90)H	FRM	£7150
66	8/00	Newb	1m2f6y	D(0-85)H	G-F	£5005
73	5/00	Ling	7f	E(0-70)	G-S	£3094
80	7/99	Sals	6f212y	E	G-S	£3629

Total win prize-money £18879

Going (Turf): Sf: 0-2 **GS: 2-7** Gd: 0-8 GF: 1-17 Fm: 1-3
Distance: 5f/6f: 0-8 7f-8f: 2-14 9f-13f: 2-14 14f+: 0-2
Track : **LH: 2-9** RH: 0-7 Tight: 1-7 Gall: 1-5
Aids: Bl: 0-0 Vi: 0-0 Tstrap: 0-0
Best Rating: 68 6/01 Wind 1m3f135y gd-fm

She was kept busy last season and managed to win three times over trips ranging from seven to 11 furlongs, but is not very consistent. She has won on soft ground but looks better on fast. Only ran well once this season.

Santiburi Lad (IRE)

103(97) (70)**69**

4-y-o b g Namaqualand (USA)-Suggia (Alzao (USA))
A Berry E A Brook

Placings:1200-6010231146304 **(5347)**
2001: 8^{6}GF, 7^{0}GF, 8^{1}GF, 12^{0}GF, 8^{2}GF, 8^{3}GF, 8^{1}GS, 8^{1}GF, 9^{4}S, 7^{6}GF, 7^{3}F, 7^{0}SD, 8^{4}SD

	Starts	1st	2nd	3rd	Win & Pl
Career Total (Turf)	15	4	2	2	16192
Career Total (AW)	2	0	0	0	0

65	8/01	Rdcr	1m	E(0-65)	G-F	£3500
59	7/01	Haml	1m65y	F(0-60)	G-S	£3192
40	6/01	Ripn	1m	E	G-F	£3199
63	8/00	Ripn	5f	D	G-F	£3471

Total win prize-money £13362

Going (Turf): Sf: 0-3 GS: 1-1 Gd: 0-1 **GF: 3-9** Fm: 0-1
Distance: 5f/6f: 1-3 **7f-8f: 2-11** 9f-13f: 1-3 14f+: 0-0
Track : LH: 0-4 **RH: 2-6 Tight: 2-7** Gall: 0-1
Aids: Bl: 0-0 Vi: 0-0 Tstrap: 0-0
Best Rating: 70 10/01 Sthl 1m stand

Has won four times from five furlongs to a mile, the latest of which came in August, although he looks high enough in the handicap now.

Santisima Trinidad (IRE)

106 **74**

3-y-o b f Definite Article-Brazilia (Forzando)
T D Easterby Chris & Antonia Deuters

Placings:050-0511231126505 **(5535)**
2001: 8^{0}HY, 6^{5}F, 7^{1}GF, 7^{1}G, 7^{2}GF, 7^{3}GS, 7^{1}GF, 7^{1}GS, 8^{2}GF, 7^{6}G, 8^{5}GS, 6^{0}GS, 7^{5}S

	Starts	1st	2nd	3rd	Win & Pl
Career Total (Turf)	16	4	2	1	18853

72	8/01	Hayd	7f30y	E(0-70)H	G-S	£3472
70	7/01	Bevl	7f100y	E(0-70)H	G-F	£5616
58	6/01	Muss	7f30y	E(0-70)H	GD	£3640
55	6/01	Bevl	7f100y	G(0-60)	G-F	£1848

Total win prize-money £14576

Going (Turf): Sf: 0-4 GS: 1-5 Gd: 1-2 **GF: 2-4** Fm: 0-1
Distance: 5f/6f: 0-3 **7f-8f: 4-10** 9f-13f: 0-3 14f+: 0-0
Track : LH: 1-7 **RH: 2-3** Tight: 0-3 Gall: 0-1
Aids: Bl: 0-0 Vi: 0-0 Tstrap: 0-0
Best Rating: 74 9/01 Thsk 1m gd-fm

She improved a huge amount during the summer with wins at Musselburgh, Haydock and Beverley twice. Very much suited by seven furlongs, but should stay a mile on fast ground.

Santolina (USA)

102 **103**

3-y-o b f Boundary (USA)-Alamosa (Alydar (USA))
J H M Gosden H Lascelles, Indian Creek & A Stroud

Placings:12410-0 **(1142)**
2001: 8^{0}G

	Starts	1st	2nd	3rd	Win & Pl
Career Total (Turf)	6	2	1	0	22565

102 9/00 Kemp 6f A GD £12369
76 6/00 Leic 5f218y E G-F £3120
Total win prize-money £15490

Going (Turf): Sf: 0-0 GS: 0-1 **Gd: 1-2 GF: 1-3** Fm: 0-0
Distance: **5f/6f: 2-5** 7f-8f: 0-1 9f-13f: 0-0 14f+: 0-0
Track : LH: 0-0 RH: 0-0 Tight: 0-0 Gall: 0-0
Aids: Bl: 0-0 Vi: 0-0 Tstrap: 0-0
Best Rating: 103 5/01 NmkR 1m good

A winner of a Listed race as a juvenile, she finished eighth in the 1000 Guineas on her only start this year.

Saone Et Loire (FR)

(86) (22)

4-y-o b f Always Fair (USA)-Saone (USA) (Bering)
M C Pipe Yvonne Reynolds & Roger Stanley

Placings:06615006/60046002-0 **(0482)**
2001: 8^{0}SD

	Starts	1st	2nd	3rd	Win & Pl
Career Total (Turf)	16	1	1	0	11363
Career Total (AW)	1	0	0	0	

8/99 Deau 7f110y VS £7535
Total win prize-money £7535

Going (Turf): Sf: 0-1 GS: 0-0 Gd: 0-0 GF: 0-0 Fm: 0-0
Distance: 5f/6f: 0-0 7f-8f: 0-6 9f-13f: 0-0 14f+: 0-0
Track : LH: 0-1 RH: 0-2 Tight: 0-1 Gall: 0-0
Aids: Bl: 0-1 Vi: 0-0 Tstrap: 0-0
Best Rating: 22 3/01 Ling 1m stand

Saorsie

107 **58**

3-y-o b g Emperor Jones (USA)-Exclusive Lottery (Presidium)
J C Fox Lord Mutton Racing Partnership

Placings:000013-00301400500 **(5591)**
2001: 9^{0}G, 10^{0}GF, 8^{3}GF, 6^{0}GF, 8^{1}GS, 8^{4}GF, 8^{0}G, 7^{0}GS, 9^{5}GS, 11^{0}S, 9^{0}GS

	Starts	1st	2nd	3rd	Win & Pl
Career Total (Turf)	17	2	0	2	7090

61 6/01 Sals 1m E(0-70)H G-S £3017
55 10/00 Brig 6f209y E(0-75) SFT £3031
Total win prize-money £6048

Going (Turf): Sf: 1-3 GS: 1-5 Gd: 0-4 GF: 0-5 Fm: 0-0
Distance: 5f/6f: 0-3 **7f-8f: 2-6** 9f-13f: 0-8 14f+: 0-0
Track : **LH: 1-4** RH: 0-4 Tight: 0-2 Gall: 0-0
Aids: Bl: 0-0 Vi: 0-0 Tstrap: 0-0
Best Rating: 61 6/01 Sals 1m gd-sft

Modest miler suited by cut in the ground.

Saphir Indien

99 **88**

2-y-o b c Bijou D'Inde-Dark Kristal (IRE) (Gorytus (USA))
M Johnston J S Morrison

Placings:621605 **(5264)**
2001: 5^{6}GF, 5^{2}GF, 6^{1}GS, 6^{6}G, 6^{0}G, 6^{5}GS

	Starts	1st	2nd	3rd	Win & Pl
Career Total (Turf)	6	1	1	0	6104

94 8/01 Ayr 6f D G-S £3757
Total win prize-money £3757

Going (Turf): Sf: 0-0 **GS: 1-2** Gd: 0-2 GF: 0-2 Fm: 0-0
Distance: **5f/6f: 1-5** 7f-8f: 0-1 9f-13f: 0-0 14f+: 0-0
Track : LH: 0-1 RH: 0-0 Tight: 0-0 Gall: 0-1
Aids: Bl: 0-0 Vi: 0-0 Tstrap: 0-0
Best Rating: 94 8/01 Ayr 6f gd-sft

A very laid-back individual, he appreciated the more galloping track when scoring at Ayr on his third start. Held in Listed company afterwards, he should eventually be suited by seven furlongs.

Sarabande

80 **52**

2-y-o ch f Nashwan (USA)-Western Reel (USA) (Gone West (USA))
B W Hills Newgate Stud

Placings:0 **(5485)**
2001: 7^{0}HY

	Starts	1st	2nd	3rd	Win & Pl
Career Total (Turf)	1	0	0	0	

Going (Turf): Sf: 0-1 GS: 0-0 Gd: 0-0 GF: 0-0 Fm: 0-0
Distance: 5f/6f: 0-0 7f-8f: 0-1 9f-13f: 0-0 14f+: 0-0
Track : LH: 0-0 RH: 0-0 Tight: 0-0 Gall: 0-0
Aids: Bl: 0-0 Vi: 0-0 Tstrap: 0-0
Best Rating: 52 10/01 Donc 7f heavy

Saracen (IRE)

87 **69**

2-y-o br c Desert King (IRE)-Inanna (Persian Bold)
Sir Michael Stoute Sheikh Mohammed

Placings:3 **(3731)**
2001: 7^{3}GS

	Starts	1st	2nd	3rd	Win & Pl
Career Total (Turf)	1	0	0	1	636

Going (Turf): Sf: 0-0 GS: 0-1 Gd: 0-0 GF: 0-0 Fm: 0-0
Distance: 5f/6f: 0-0 7f-8f: 0-1 9f-13f: 0-0 14f+: 0-0
Track : LH: 0-0 RH: 0-0 Tight: 0-0 Gall: 0-0
Aids: Bl: 0-0 Vi: 0-0 Tstrap: 0-0
Best Rating: 69 8/01 Yarm 7f3y gd-sft

Sarangani

109 **89**

5-y-o b g Polish Precedent (USA)-Height Of Folly (Shirley Heights)
I A Balding Exors Of The Late Robert Hitchins

Placings:24212/400016331 **(3396)**
2001: 14^{4}HY, 16^{0}S, 12^{0}G, 12^{0}S, 10^{1}G, 10^{6}GF, 10^{3}GF, 11^{3}G, 10^{1}GF

	Starts	1st	2nd	3rd	Win & Pl
Career Total (Turf)	14	3	3	2	30178

89 7/01 Sand 1m2f7y C(0-90)H G-F £7150
88 5/01 Yarm 1m2f21y C(0-85) GD £6987
76 6/99 Gdwd 1m4f D G-F £3858
Total win prize-money £17997

Going (Turf): Sf: 0-5 GS: 0-0 Gd: 1-4 **GF: 2-5** Fm: 0-0
Distance: 5f/6f: 0-0 7f-8f: 0-0 **9f-13f: 3-12** 14f+: 0-2
Track : LH: 1-10 **RH: 2-4 Tight: 2-5** Gall: 0-5
Aids: Bl: 0-0 Vi: 0-0 **Tstrap: 2-7**
Best Rating: 89 7/01 Sand 1m2f7y gd-fm

He was given a canny ride when winning his maiden at Goodwood at three, but went missing after June 1999 until returning and running well at Nottingham on his reappearance in 2001. Well beaten in his next three starts, he suddenly bounced back to winning form when dropped back to ten furlongs at Yarmouth in May and added another victory over the same trip at Sandown in July. A fast-run race over that trip is ideal, but he needs to be produced late.

Saratov

106 **100**

3-y-o b c Rudimentary (USA)-Sarabah (IRE) (Ela-Mana-Mou)
M Johnston J David Abell

Placings:31130-106005 **(4532)**
2001: 10^{1}F, 10^{0}GF, 10^{6}GF, 9^{0}G, 10^{0}G, 11^{5}GF

	Starts	1st	2nd	3rd	Win & Pl
Career Total (Turf)	11	3	0	2	41711

104 5/01 York 1m2f85y B(0-100)H FRM £15399
92 7/00 Asct 7f B G-F £14495
89 7/00 York 6f214y D GD £7085
Total win prize-money £36979

Going (Turf): Sf: 0-1 GS: 0-0 **Gd: 1-4 GF: 1-5 Fm: 1-1**
Distance: 5f/6f: 0-1 **7f-8f: 2-4** 9f-13f: 1-6 14f+: 0-0
Track : **LH: 2-6** RH: 0-2 Tight: 0-1 **Gall: 2-7**
Aids: Bl: 0-1 Vi: 0-0 Tstrap: 0-0
Best Rating: 104 5/01 York 1m2f85y firm

A half-brother to Ice, he handles a quick surface and is a real battler once in front. He won at York and Ascot last term and regained winning ways back at York on his reappearance. Held in Listed companyand top handicaps since then, he seems to reserve his best for the Knavesmire.

Sarava (USA)

90 **74**

2-y-o br c Wild Again (USA)-Rhythm Of Life (USA) (Deputy Minister (CAN))
B J Meehan Mrs Susan Roy

Placings:440 **(4661)**
2001: 7^{4}S, 7^{4}GF, 8^{0}GF

	Starts	1st	2nd	3rd	Win & Pl
Career Total (Turf)	3	0	0	0	836

Going (Turf): Sf: 0-1 GS: 0-0 Gd: 0-0 GF: 0-2 Fm: 0-0
Distance: 5f/6f: 0-0 7f-8f: 0-3 9f-13f: 0-0 14f+: 0-0
Track : LH: 0-0 RH: 0-1 Tight: 0-0 Gall: 0-0
Aids: Bl: 0-0 Vi: 0-0 Tstrap: 0-0
Best Rating: 74 8/01 Sand 7f16y soft

Sardis (IRE)

82 **73**

2-y-o b c Priolo (USA)-Punta Gorda (IRE) (Roi Danzig (USA))
Mrs A J Perrett Mrs S L Whitehead

Placings:05 **(5460)**
2001: 8^{0}S, 8^{5}G

	Starts	1st	2nd	3rd	Win & Pl
Career Total (Turf)	2	0	0	0	0

Going (Turf): Sf: 0-1 GS: 0-0 Gd: 0-1 GF: 0-0 Fm: 0-0
Distance: 5f/6f: 0-0 7f-8f: 0-1 9f-13f: 0-1 14f+: 0-0
Track : LH: 0-1 RH: 0-0 Tight: 0-1 Gall: 0-0
Aids: Bl: 0-0 Vi: 0-0 Tstrap: 0-0
Best Rating: 73 10/01 Bath 1m5y good

Sareb (FR)

62 **25**

2-y-o b f Indian Ridge-Prends Ca (IRE) (Reprimand)
R Hannon B Bull

Placings:0 **(4211)**
2001: 5^{0}GF

	Starts	1st	2nd	3rd	Win & Pl
Career Total (Turf)	1	0	0	0	

Going (Turf): Sf: 0-0 GS: 0-0 Gd: 0-0 GF: 0-1 Fm: 0-0
Distance: 5f/6f: 0-1 7f-8f: 0-0 9f-13f: 0-0 14f+: 0-0
Track : LH: 0-1 RH: 0-0 Tight: 0-0 Gall: 0-1
Aids: Bl: 0-0 Vi: 0-0 Tstrap: 0-0
Best Rating: 25 8/01 Bath 5f11y gd-fm

Sarena Pride (IRE)

(102) (69)

4-y-o b f Persian Bold-Avidal Park (Horage)

R J O'Sullivan Sarena Mfg Ltd

Placings:0165120/0502430000**601-6340**10065333 **(4265)**

2001: **12**^{6}SD, **12**^{3}SW, **12**^{4}SD, **10**^{0}SD, 8^{1}GS, 10^{0}GF, 10^{0}GF, 9^{6}F, 9^{5}GF, 8^{3}GF, 10^{3}G, 8^{3}GF, **8**^{0}SD

	Starts	1st	2nd	3rd	Win & Pl
Career Total (Turf)	25	3	2	4	18816
Career Total (AW)	7	1	0	1	3142

70	5/01	Wind	1m67y	D(0-85)H	G-S	£4225
69	12/00	Ling	1m2f	E(0-70)	STD	£2268
75	8/99	Wwck	6f	E H	GD	£3164
78	6/99	Wind	6f	E	SFT	£3550

Total win prize-money £13207

Going (Turf): Sf: 1-4 GS: 1-2 Gd: 1-5 GF: 0-13 Fm: 0-1
Distance: 5f/6f: 2-9 7f-8f: 0-9 9f-13f: 2-14 14f+: 0-0
Track : LH: 2-14 RH: 2-11 **Tight: 2-15** Gall: 1-5
Aids: **Bl: 2-13** Vi: 0-0 Tstrap: 0-0
Best Rating: 70 5/01 Wind 1m67y gd-sft

Sarena Special

95(91) (45)**46**

4-y-o b c Lucky Guest-Lariston Gale (Pas De Seul)

R J O'Sullivan Sarena Mfg Ltd

Placings:02426/250304**005-000000** **(3146)**

2001: 7^{0}SW, 7^{0}SD, 5^{0}GS, 7^{0}F, 8^{0}GF, 6^{0}G

	Starts	1st	2nd	3rd	Win & Pl
Career Total (Turf)	16	0	3	1	5084
Career Total (AW)	4	0	0	0	0

Going (Turf): Sf: 0-3 GS: 0-2 Gd: 0-5 GF: 0-4 Fm: 0-1
Distance: 5f/6f: 0-5 7f-8f: 0-13 9f-13f: 0-1 14f+: 0-0
Track : LH: 0-7 RH: 0-4 Tight: 0-4 Gall: 0-2
Aids: Bl: 0-9 Vi: 0-0 Tstrap: 0-0
Best Rating: 46 5/01 Brig 7f214y firm

Sari (USA)

75 **51**

2-y-o gr f Cozzene (USA)-Yamuna (USA) (Forty Niner (USA))

Mrs A J Perrett K Abdulla

Placings:0 **(4573)**

2001: 6^{0}G

	Starts	1st	2nd	3rd	Win & Pl
Career Total (Turf)	1	0	0	0	

Going (Turf): Sf: 0-0 GS: 0-0 Gd: 0-1 GF: 0-0 Fm: 0-0
Distance: 5f/6f: 0-1 7f-8f: 0-0 9f-13f: 0-0 14f+: 0-0
Track : LH: 0-0 RH: 0-0 Tight: 0-0 Gall: 0-0
Aids: Bl: 0-0 Vi: 0-0 Tstrap: 0-0
Best Rating: 51 9/01 Kemp 6f good

Sarin

91 **64**

3-y-o b c Deploy-Secretilla (USA) (Secreto (USA))

L M Cumani Paolo Riccardi

Placings:0600 **(2257)**

2001: 9^{0}GF, 10^{6}G, 10^{0}GF, 10^{0}G

	Starts	1st	2nd	3rd	Win & Pl
Career Total (Turf)	4	0	0	0	0

Going (Turf): Sf: 0-0 GS: 0-0 Gd: 0-2 GF: 0-2 Fm: 0-0
Distance: 5f/6f: 0-0 7f-8f: 0-0 9f-13f: 0-4 14f+: 0-0
Track : LH: 0-0 RH: 0-0 Tight: 0-3 Gall: 0-0
Aids: Bl: 0-0 Vi: 0-0 Tstrap: 0-0
Best Rating: 64 5/01 Wind 1m2f7y good

Sarn

102(80) (45)**66**

2-y-o b c Atraf-Covent Garden Girl (Sizzling Melody)

A Bailey Willie McKay

Placings:0206010**0**10056155100 **(5690)**

2001: 5^{0}GF, 5^{2}G, 5^{0}GF, 6^{6}GF, 5^{0}GF, 7^{1}GF, 7^{0}G, **7**^{0}SD, 7^{1}G, 7^{0}GF, 8^{0}GF, 7^{5}GS, 7^{6}GF, 8^{1}G, 8^{5}G, 8^{5}GF, 8^{1}HY, 7^{0}S, 7^{0}S

Starts	1st	2nd	3rd	Win & Pl	
Career Total (Turf)	18	4	1	0	13541
Career Total (AW)	1	0	0	0	

66	10/01	Ayr	1m	D(0-85)H	HVY	£3851
65	9/01	Ayr	1m	E	GD	£3250
70	8/01	Catt	7f	G	GD	£1974
62	7/01	Muss	7f30y	D	G-F	£3493

Total win prize-money £12569

Going (Turf): Sf: 1-3 GS: 0-1 **Gd: 2-5** GF: 1-9 Fm: 0-0
Distance: 5f/6f: 0-5 **7f-8f: 4-13** 9f-13f: 0-1 14f+: 0-0
Track : **LH: 3-8** RH: 0-1 **Tight: 1-6** Gall: 0-0
Aids: Bl: 0-0 Vi: 0-0 Tstrap: 0-0
Best Rating: 70 8/01 Catt 7f good

Winner of four races this season, including a nursery at Ayr, he stays a mile, and acts on any ground. Likes to race prominently.

Sarrego

88 **81**

2-y-o b g Makbul-Simmie's Special (Precocious)

R Hollinshead M Pyle & Miss T Baulcombe

Placings:13 **(5378)**

2001: 5^{1}GF, 5^{3}S

	Starts	1st	2nd	3rd	Win & Pl
Career Total (Turf)	2	1	0	1	3164

81	9/01	Nott	5f13y	F	G-F	£2576

Total win prize-money £2576

Going (Turf): Sf: 0-1 GS: 0-0 Gd: 0-0 **GF: 1-1** Fm: 0-0
Distance: **5f/6f: 1-2** 7f-8f: 0-0 9f-13f: 0-0 14f+: 0-0
Track : LH: 0-0 RH: 0-0 Tight: 0-0 Gall: 0-0
Aids: Bl: 0-0 Vi: 0-0 Tstrap: 0-0
Best Rating: 81 9/01 Nott 5f13y gd-fm

Won his racecourse debut in a maiden auction at Nottingham in September 2001, but was found out by the ground and company on his subsequent run.

Sartorial (IRE)

111 (76)**112**

5-y-o b g Elbio-Madam Slaney (Prince Tenderfoot (USA))

P J Makin Mrs Greta Sarfaty Marchant

Placings:4/232/141000-311200 **(5365)**

2001: 6^{3}GF, 6^{1}G, 6^{1}GS, 6^{2}G, 6^{0}G, 6^{0}GS

	Starts	1st	2nd	3rd	Win & Pl
Career Total (Turf)	15	4	2	2	82079
Career Total (AW)	1	0	1	0	756

109	7/01	Deau	6f		G-S	£21339
104	6/01	York	6f	B(0-100)H	GD	£9239
101	5/00	NmkR	6f	C(0-95)H	GD	£26000
91	4/00	Hayd	5f	D	GD	£3295

Total win prize-money £59874

Going (Turf): Sf: 0-2 GS: 1-3 **Gd: 3-8** GF: 0-2 Fm: 0-0
Distance: **5f/6f: 4-16** 7f-8f: 0-0 9f-13f: 0-0 14f+: 0-0
Track : LH: 0-1 RH: 0-0 Tight: 0-1 Gall: 0-0
Aids: Bl: 0-0 Vi: 0-1 Tstrap: 0-0
Best Rating: 112 10/01 NmkR 6f gd-sft

Got off the mark on his second start of this term in a York handicap and followed up in a Deauville Group Three. Ran another fine race to finish runner-up in a Group Two at Baden-Baden. Effective over five, but best suited by six furlongs these days.

Sarwa

69 **11**

3-y-o ch f Timeless Times (USA)-Diebiedale (Dominion)

C F Wall T J Wells

Placings:0 **(4160)**

2001: 6^{0}GF

	Starts	1st	2nd	3rd	Win & Pl
Career Total (Turf)	1	0	0	0	

Going (Turf): Sf: 0-0 GS: 0-0 Gd: 0-0 GF: 0-1 Fm: 0-0
Distance: 5f/6f: 0-1 7f-8f: 0-0 9f-13f: 0-0 14f+: 0-0
Track : LH: 0-0 RH: 0-0 Tight: 0-0 Gall: 0-0
Aids: Bl: 0-0 Vi: 0-0 Tstrap: 0-0
Best Rating: 11 8/01 Ling 6f gd-fm

Sasaram (IRE)

83 **67**

2-y-o ch c Indian Ridge-Flaming June (USA) (Storm Bird (CAN))

M P Tregoning Sheikh Ahmed Al Maktoum

Placings:6 **(2196)**

2001: 7^{6}S

	Starts	1st	2nd	3rd	Win & Pl
Career Total (Turf)	1	0	0	0	0

Going (Turf): Sf: 0-1 GS: 0-0 Gd: 0-0 GF: 0-0 Fm: 0-0
Distance: 5f/6f: 0-0 7f-8f: 0-1 9f-13f: 0-0 14f+: 0-0
Track : LH: 0-0 RH: 0-1 Tight: 0-0 Gall: 0-0
Aids: Bl: 0-0 Vi: 0-0 Tstrap: 0-0
Best Rating: 67 6/01 Sand 7f16y soft

Sash (IRE)

(100) (35) **35**

4-y-o b f Sabrehill (USA)-Lady Nash (Nashwan (USA))

G M McCourt (S Dow 10/4) M Israr Ahmad

Placings:5050003032-063P6 **(1451)**

2001: 10^{0}SD, 13^{6}SD, 11^{3}SD, 11^{P}SD, 12^{6}SD

	Starts	1st	2nd	3rd	Win & Pl
Career Total (Turf)	5	0	0	0	0
Career Total (AW)	10	0	1	3	1595

Going (Turf): Sf: 0-1 GS: 0-1 Gd: 0-1 GF: 0-2 Fm: 0-0
Distance: 5f/6f: 0-0 7f-8f: 0-3 9f-13f: 0-12 14f+: 0-0
Track : LH: 0-11 RH: 0-3 Tight: 0-11 Gall: 0-1
Aids: Bl: 0-0 Vi: 0-0 Tstrap: 0-0
Best Rating: 50 2/01 Ling 1m5f stand

Sasha

97(94) (40)**39**

4-y-o ch g Factual (USA)-Twice In Bundoran (IRE) (Bold Arrangement)

A B Mulholland Miss K Watson

Placings:0/40040400-003440 **(4621)**

2001: 6^{0}HY, 6^{0}G, 7^{3}GF, 7^{4}GF, 7^{4}GS, 6^{0}F

	Starts	1st	2nd	3rd	Win & Pl
Career Total (Turf)	12	0	0	1	994
Career Total (AW)	3	0	0	0	208

Going (Turf): Sf: 0-2 GS: 0-1 Gd: 0-3 GF: 0-5 Fm: 0-1
Distance: 5f/6f: 0-11 7f-8f: 0-4 9f-13f: 0-0 14f+: 0-0
Track : LH: 0-6 RH: 0-1 Tight: 0-3 Gall: 0-0
Aids: Bl: 0-1 Vi: 0-0 Tstrap: 0-0
Best Rating: 39 6/01 Bevl 7f100y gd-fm

Sasha Star (IRE)

76(83) (32)**31**

3-y-o b g Namaqualand (USA)-Trojan Relation (Trojan Fen)

G Brown T Curry

Placings:06-50 **(1280)**

2001: 12^{5}SD, 14^{0}G

	Starts	1st	2nd	3rd	Win & Pl
Career Total (Turf)	3	0	0	0	0
Career Total (AW)	1	0	0	0	0

Going (Turf): Sf: 0-0 GS: 0-0 Gd: 0-1 GF: 0-1 Fm: 0-1
Distance: 5f/6f: 0-0 7f-8f: 0-2 9f-13f: 0-1 14f+: 0-1
Track : LH: 0-3 RH: 0-0 Tight: 0-2 Gall: 0-0
Aids: Bl: 0-0 Vi: 0-0 Tstrap: 0-0
Best Rating: 32 3/01 Wolv 1m4f stand

Sashay

99(101) (49)**37**
3-y-o b f Bishop Of Cashel-St James's Antigua (IRE) (Law Society (USA))
C G Cox E Young, J Hawkins, P Smyth, D Short

Placings:0-300062661 **(4066)**
2001: 7^{3}SD, 7^{0}SD, 7^{0}SD, 8^{0}GF, 11^{6}F, 10^{2}GF, 11^{6}GF, 9^{6}GF, 12^{1}SD, 13^{4}SD

	Starts	1st	2nd	3rd	Win & Pl
Career Total (Turf)	6	0	1	0	1066
Career Total (AW)	4	1	0	1	2229

49 8/01 Wolv 1m4f G(0-65)H STD £1820
Total win prize-money £1820

Going (Turf): Sf: 0-1 GS: 0-0 Gd: 0-0 GF: 0-4 Fm: 0-1
Distance: 5f/6f: 0-1 7f-8f: 0-3 **9f-13f: 1-6** 14f+: 0-0
Track : **LH: 1-7** RH: 0-2 **Tight: 1-5** Gall: 0-2
Aids: Bl: 0-0 Vi: 0-0 Tstrap: 0-0
Best Rating: 49 8/01 Wolv 1m4f stand

She is a very modest performer, but managed to grind out a victory in an apprentice maiden handicap on the Wolverhampton Fibresand in August.

Sastra (IRE)

84 **54**
2-y-o ch f Petardia-Come Dancing (Suave Dancer (USA))
J A Glover Paul J Dixon

Placings:600 **(5183)**
2001: 5^{6}GF, 5^{0}GF, 5^{0}GS

	Starts	1st	2nd	3rd	Win & Pl
Career Total (Turf)	3	0	0	0	0

Going (Turf): Sf: 0-0 GS: 0-1 Gd: 0-0 GF: 0-2 Fm: 0-0
Distance: 5f/6f: 0-3 7f-8f: 0-0 9f-13f: 0-0 14f+: 0-0
Track : LH: 0-0 RH: 0-0 Tight: 0-0 Gall: 0-0
Aids: Bl: 0-0 Vi: 0-0 Tstrap: 0-0
Best Rating: 54 7/01 Bevl 5f gd-fm

Sateen

103 **85**
4-y-o ch f Barathea (IRE)-Souk (IRE) (Ahonoora)
L M Cumani Fittocks Stud

Placings:5-1202000 **(5608)**
2001: 6^{1}GS, 9^{2}GF, 10^{0}G, 8^{2}G, 8^{0}G, 7^{0}G, 7^{0}GS

	Starts	1st	2nd	3rd	Win & Pl
Career Total (Turf)	8	1	2	0	5785

69 5/01 Pont 6f D G-S £2941
Total win prize-money £2941

Going (Turf): Sf: 0-1 **GS: 1-2** Gd: 0-4 GF: 0-1 Fm: 0-0
Distance: **5f/6f: 1-1** 7f-8f: 0-4 9f-13f: 0-3 14f+: 0-0
Track : **LH: 1-2** RH: 0-3 Tight: 0-0 Gall: 0-1
Aids: Bl: 0-0 Vi: 0-0 Tstrap: 0-0
Best Rating: 85 8/01 NmkJ 1m good

Lightly-raced, she got off the mark at Pontefract and ran well at Kempton next time. Started favourite at the same track next time but reportedly finished distressed. Lost nothing in defeat when second in a fillies handicap at Newmarket when dropped back to a mile. Has won on good to soft. Acts on good and good to firm.

Satire

98(88) (34)**33**
4-y-o br f Terimon-Salchow (Niniski (USA))
T J Etherington R V Hughes And Partners

Placings:0/500020-005040000 **(5447)**
2001: 8^{0}GS, 13^{0}G, 8^{5}GF, 12^{0}GS, 10^{4}GS, 14^{0}G, 10^{0}G, 10^{0}S, 10^{0}HY

	Starts	1st	2nd	3rd	Win & Pl
Career Total (Turf)	13	0	1	0	1166
Career Total (AW)	3	0	0	0	0

Going (Turf): Sf: 0-3 GS: 0-3 Gd: 0-5 GF: 0-2 Fm: 0-0
Distance: 5f/6f: 0-0 7f-8f: 0-4 9f-13f: 0-9 14f+: 0-3
Track : LH: 0-12 RH: 0-3 Tight: 0-4 Gall: 0-3
Aids: Bl: 0-2 Vi: 0-0 Tstrap: 0-0
Best Rating: 33 9/01 Pont 1m2f6y soft

A moderate individual. Still a maiden. Has been tried over a variety of trips.

Sattam

85 **68**
2-y-o b c Danehill (USA)-Mayaasa (USA) (Lyphard (USA))
D R Loder Hamdan Al Maktoum

Placings:0 **(5485)**
2001: 7^{0}HY

	Starts	1st	2nd	3rd	Win & Pl
Career Total (Turf)	1	0	0	0	

Going (Turf): Sf: 0-1 GS: 0-0 Gd: 0-0 GF: 0-0 Fm: 0-0
Distance: 5f/6f: 0-0 7f-8f: 0-1 9f-13f: 0-0 14f+: 0-0
Track : LH: 0-0 RH: 0-0 Tight: 0-0 Gall: 0-0
Aids: Bl: 0-0 Vi: 0-0 Tstrap: 0-0
Best Rating: 68 10/01 Donc 7f heavy

Satu Nusa

88 **81**
2-y-o b c So Factual (USA)-Tarry (Salse (USA))
G C Bravery Mohamad Razif Nazar

Placings:6420 **(5364)**
2001: 6^{6}GF, 7^{4}S, 7^{2}G, 6^{0}GS

	Starts	1st	2nd	3rd	Win & Pl
Career Total (Turf)	4	0	1	0	1252

Going (Turf): Sf: 0-1 GS: 0-1 Gd: 0-1 GF: 0-1 Fm: 0-0
Distance: 5f/6f: 0-2 7f-8f: 0-2 9f-13f: 0-0 14f+: 0-0
Track : LH: 0-0 RH: 0-1 Tight: 0-0 Gall: 0-0
Aids: Bl: 0-0 Vi: 0-0 Tstrap: 0-0
Best Rating: 81 9/01 Yarm 7f3y soft

Looks to have a bit of temperament about her. Has got upset in the stalls and hung badly right in the closing stages on her penultimate start at Beverley. Has only raced over six and seven furlongs.

Satwa Boulevard

97(96) (40?)**37**
6-y-o ch m Sabrehill (USA)-Winnie Reckless (Local Suitor (USA))
D Burchell D C White

Placings:00060**320/000000200030-00054560** **(0886)**
2001: 10^{0}SW, 7^{0}SD, 9^{0}SD, 6^{5}SD, 7^{4}SD, 8^{5}SD, 5^{6}S, 6^{0}GS

	Starts	1st	2nd	3rd	Win & Pl
Career Total (Turf)	15	0	1	1	1376
Career Total (AW)	13	0	1	1	1160

Going (Turf): Sf: 0-4 GS: 0-2 Gd: 0-2 GF: 0-3 Fm: 0-4
Distance: 5f/6f: 0-4 7f-8f: 0-15 9f-13f: 0-9 14f+: 0-0
Track : LH: 0-10 RH: 0-2 Tight: 0-14 Gall: 0-1
Aids: Bl: 0-0 Vi: 0-0 Tstrap: 0-5
Best Rating: 58 4/01 Nott 5f13y soft

Satyr

104 **70**
3-y-o b c Pursuit Of Love-Sardonic (Kris)
R Hannon Plantation Stud

Placings:0-63420254 **(5173)**
2001: 8^{6}GS, 7^{3}GS, 8^{4}GF, 7^{2}G, 8^{0}G, 8^{2}G, 8^{5}GF, 8^{4}GS

	Starts	1st	2nd	3rd	Win & Pl
Career Total (Turf)	9	0	2	1	3604

Going (Turf): Sf: 0-1 GS: 0-3 Gd: 0-3 GF: 0-2 Fm: 0-0
Distance: 5f/6f: 0-0 7f-8f: 0-6 9f-13f: 0-3 14f+: 0-0
Track : LH: 0-2 RH: 0-2 Tight: 0-3 Gall: 0-0
Aids: Bl: 0-0 Vi: 0-0 Tstrap: 0-0
Best Rating: 80 8/01 Wind 1m67y good

An exposed handicapper at present. Best over seven to eight furlongs on a sound surface.

Sauce Tartar

98 **85**
3-y-o ch f Salse (USA)-Filly Mignonne (IRE) (Nashwan (USA))
N A Callaghan Wafic Said

Placings:61003-003110 **(3515)**
2001: 8^{0}GF, 10^{0}GF, 8^{3}GF, 7^{1}GS, 7^{1}G, 8^{0}GF

	Starts	1st	2nd	3rd	Win & Pl
Career Total (Turf)	11	3	0	2	14603

85 7/01 Leic 7f9y D(0-80)H GD £4306
77 7/01 NmkJ 7f D(0-80)H G-S £4173
70 7/00 Folk 7f D G-F £4387
Total win prize-money £12867

Going (Turf): Sf: 0-0 **GS: 1-3 Gd: 1-1** GF: 0-6 Fm: 0-0
Distance: 5f/6f: 0-1 **7f-8f: 2-6** 9f-13f: 0-3 14f+: 0-0
Track : LH: 0-1 RH: 0-1 Tight: 0-1 Gall: 0-1
Aids: **Bl: 2-3** Vi: 0-0 Tstrap: 0-0
Best Rating: 85 7/01 Leic 7f9y good

Winner of a modest Folkestone maiden at two, she responded well to first-time blinkers when bolting up in a Newmarket handicap in July, and followed up four days later in a similar event. Suited by seven furlongs to a mile on most goings.

Saudia (USA)

101 **87**
3-y-o b f Gone West (USA)-Bint Pasha (USA) (Affirmed (USA))
P F I Cole H R H Prince Fahd Salman

Placings:1-000 **(1976)**
2001: 7^{0}GS, 10^{0}F, 7^{0}GF

	Starts	1st	2nd	3rd	Win & Pl
Career Total (Turf)	4	1	0	0	3640

78 6/00 Pont 6f D SFT £3640
Total win prize-money £3640

Going (Turf): Sf: 1-1 GS: 0-1 Gd: 0-0 GF: 0-1 Fm: 0-1
Distance: **5f/6f: 1-1** 7f-8f: 0-2 9f-13f: 0-1 14f+: 0-0
Track : **LH: 1-3** RH: 0-0 Tight: 0-1 Gall: 0-1
Aids: Bl: 0-1 Vi: 0-0 Tstrap: 0-0
Best Rating: 87 5/01 York 1m2f85y firm

A 540,000gns daughter of the Yorkshire Oaks and Prix Vermeille winner Bint Pasha, she was a comfortable winner of her only juvenile outing over six furlongs, but showed little in 2001

Sauterne

111 **99**
3-y-o ch f Rainbow Quest (USA)-Band (USA) (Northern Dancer)
H R A Cecil Lord Lloyd-Webber

Placings:412114 **(3956)**
2001: 8^{4}GF, 7^{1}GF, 8^{2}GF, 10^{1}GF, 10^{1}GF, 9^{4}GF

	Starts	1st	2nd	3rd	Win & Pl
Career Total (Turf)	6	3	1	0	28326

94 7/01 Chep 1m2f36y A G-F £13302
99 7/01 Donc 1m2f60y C(0-95)H G-F £7215
48 6/01 Bevl 7f100y D G-F £3796

Total win prize-money £24313

Going (Turf): Sf: 0-0 GS: 0-0 Gd: 0-0 **GF: 3-6** Fm: 0-0
Distance: 5f/6f: 0-0 7f-8f: 1-3 **9f-13f: 2-3** 14f+: 0-0
Track : **LH: 2-2** RH: 1-4 Tight: 0-2 **Gall: 1-1**
Aids: Bl: 0-0 Vi: 0-0 Tstrap: 0-0
Best Rating: 99 7/01 Donc 1m2f60y gd-fm

Got off the mark in a Beverley maiden over seven furlongs, but looked very much suited by the step up to ten furlongs when winning a decent Doncaster handicap and followed up in a Listed event at Chepstow.

Savannah Bay

102 **100**
2-y-o ch c In The Wings-High Savannah (Rousillon (USA))
B J Meehan Joe L Allbritton

Placings:6213 **(5134)**
2001: 7^{6}GS, 7^{2}GF, 7^{1}GF, 7^{3}G

	Starts	1st	2nd	3rd	Win & Pl
Career Total (Turf)	4	1	1	1	10020

92 8/01 NmkJ 7f D G-F £4862
Total win prize-money £4862

Going (Turf): Sf: 0-0 GS: 0-1 Gd: 0-1 **GF: 1-2** Fm: 0-0
Distance: 5f/6f: 0-0 **7f-8f: 1-4** 9f-13f: 0-0 14f+: 0-0
Track : LH: 0-0 RH: 0-1 Tight: 0-0 Gall: 0-0
Aids: Bl: 0-0 Vi: 0-0 Tstrap: 0-0
Best Rating: 100 10/01 NmkR 7f good

Progressed with racing to win a seven-furlong maiden at Newmarket in August, and stepped up on that when third in a Newmarket Group Three. Acts on fast ground.

Save The Planet

91(80) (26)**25**
4-y-o b f Environment Friend-Geoffreys Bird (Master Willie)
P Monteith Stan N Moffat

Placings:00000-00040 **(3951)**
2001: 8^{0}GF, 13^{0}GS, 13^{0}G, 16^{4}GF, 13^{0}GS

	Starts	1st	2nd	3rd	Win & Pl
Career Total (Turf)	9	0	0	0	0
Career Total (AW)	1	0	0	0	

Going (Turf): Sf: 0-2 GS: 0-2 Gd: 0-3 GF: 0-2 Fm: 0-0
Distance: 5f/6f: 0-0 7f-8f: 0-1 9f-13f: 0-5 14f+: 0-4
Track : LH: 0-3 RH: 0-6 Tight: 0-6 Gall: 0-0
Aids: Bl: 0-1 Vi: 0-1 Tstrap: 0-0
Best Rating: 25 7/01 Muss 2m gd-fm

Save The Pound (USA)

75 **32**
3-y-o br g Northern Flagship (USA)-Key Bid (USA) (Key To The Mint (USA))
T D Easterby C H Stevens

Placings:5006-600 **(1663)**
2001: 12^{6}S, 8^{0}F, 6^{0}F

	Starts	1st	2nd	3rd	Win & Pl
Career Total (Turf)	7	0	0	0	0

Going (Turf): Sf: 0-2 GS: 0-0 Gd: 0-1 GF: 0-0 Fm: 0-4
Distance: 5f/6f: 0-1 7f-8f: 0-5 9f-13f: 0-1 14f+: 0-0
Track : LH: 0-2 RH: 0-2 Tight: 0-1 Gall: 0-1
Aids: Bl: 0-1 Vi: 0-0 Tstrap: 0-0
Best Rating: 19 5/01 Rdcr 6f firm

Saved By The Belle

92 **22**
4-y-o b f Emarati (USA)-Belle Danseuse (Bellypha)
L A Dace L P Dace

Placings:5-00000 **(3871)**

2001: 7^{0}F, 7^{0}GS, 6^{0}GF, 7^{0}GF, 6^{0}G

	Starts	1st	2nd	3rd	Win & Pl
Career Total (Turf)	6	0	0	0	0

Going (Turf): Sf: 0-1 GS: 0-1 Gd: 0-1 GF: 0-2 Fm: 0-1
Distance: 5f/6f: 0-2 7f-8f: 0-4 9f-13f: 0-0 14f+: 0-0
Track : LH: 0-2 RH: 0-0 Tight: 0-0 Gall: 0-0
Aids: Bl: 0-0 Vi: 0-0 Tstrap: 0-0
Best Rating: 22 7/01 Brig 7f214y firm

Saving Lives Atsea (IRE)

(87) (47)**52**
3-y-o ch g Dolphin Street (FR)-Advantageous (Top Ville)
M H Tompkins Yours For A Day Limited

Placings:6006-0 **(0151)**
2001: 9^{0}SW

	Starts	1st	2nd	3rd	Win & Pl
Career Total (Turf)	3	0	0	0	189
Career Total (AW)	2	0	0	0	0

Going (Turf): Sf: 0-0 GS: 0-1 Gd: 0-1 GF: 0-1 Fm: 0-0
Distance: 5f/6f: 0-3 7f-8f: 0-1 9f-13f: 0-1 14f+: 0-0
Track : LH: 0-2 RH: 0-2 Tight: 0-1 Gall: 0-2
Aids: Bl: 0-0 Vi: 0-0 Tstrap: 0-0
Best Rating: 22 7/01 Brig 7f214y firm

Sayedah (IRE)

112 **104**
3-y-o b f Darshaan-Balaabel (USA) (Sadler's Wells (USA))
M P Tregoning Hamdan Al Maktoum

Placings:221-0423 **(5238a)**
2001: 8^{0}G, 12^{4}GF, 8^{2}G, 10^{3}VS

	Starts	1st	2nd	3rd	Win & Pl
Career Total (Turf)	7	1	3	1	45632

104 10/00 NmkR 7f A G-S £29000
Total win prize-money £29000

Going (Turf): Sf: 0-0 **GS: 1-1** Gd: 0-3 GF: 0-2 Fm: 0-0
Distance: 5f/6f: 0-0 **7f-8f: 1-4** 9f-13f: 0-3 14f+: 0-0
Track : LH: 0-1 RH: 0-3 Tight: 0-0 Gall: 0-1
Aids: Bl: 0-0 Vi: 0-0 Tstrap: 0-0
Best Rating: 104 10/01 Lonc 1m2f v soft

She finished runner-up in a couple of decent events on her first two starts at two and made all to land the Rockfel Stakes on her third outing. Unplaced in the 1000 Guineas on her reappearance, she was stepped up to a mile and a half next time but probably found the ground too fast for her. Dropped back to a mile at Sandown in September, she showed a good attitude in defeat. Showed her appreciation for cut in the ground when making all to take a ten-furlong Listed race at the Arc meeting, but was disqualified for interference.

Sayeh (IRE)

102 **65**
9-y-o b g Fool's Holme (USA)-Piffle (Shirley Heights)
P Bowen The Galloping Punters

Placings:12/353110/00/03/66 **(1428)**
2001: 12^{6}G, 12^{6}S

	Starts	1st	2nd	3rd	Win & Pl
Career Total (Turf)	14	3	1	3	27317

97 9/95 Epsm 1m2f18y B(0-105)H GD £7641
89 8/95 Yarm 1m2f21y D G-F £3935
69 9/94 Folk 6f E G-S £3273
Total win prize-money £14849

Going (Turf): Sf: 0-2 **GS: 1-2 Gd: 1-5 GF: 1-5** Fm: 0-0
Distance: 5f/6f: 1-1 7f-8f: 0-1 **9f-13f: 2-12** 14f+: 0-0
Track : **LH: 2-10** RH: 0-3 **Tight: 2-7** Gall: 0-5
Aids: Bl: 0-0 Vi: 0-0 Tstrap: 0-0
Best Rating: 65 5/01 Newb 1m4f5y soft

Good form on the Flat in the past, but is better known for hurdling nowadays.

Sayit

71(89) (55)**29**
2-y-o b c Sayaarr (USA)-Wigit (Safawan)
M D I Usher Mrs J Gawthorpe

Placings:0 **(4301)**
2001: 7^{0}GF

	Starts	1st	2nd	3rd	Win & Pl
Career Total (Turf)	1	0	0	0	

Going (Turf): Sf: 0-0 GS: 0-0 Gd: 0-0 GF: 0-1 Fm: 0-0
Distance: 5f/6f: 0-0 7f-8f: 0-1 9f-13f: 0-0 14f+: 0-0
Track : LH: 0-0 RH: 0-0 Tight: 0-0 Gall: 0-0
Aids: Bl: 0-0 Vi: 0-0 Tstrap: 0-0
Best Rating: 29 8/01 Folk 7f gd-fm

Sayso

(43)
5-y-o b m Anshan-Total Sa (IRE) (Gallic League)
Miss A Stokell T J Ford

Placings:0/0 **(0211)**
2001: 8^{0}SD

	Starts	1st	2nd	3rd	Win & Pl
Career Total (Turf)	1	0	0	0	
Career Total (AW)	1	0	0	0	

Going (Turf): Sf: 0-0 GS: 0-0 Gd: 0-0 GF: 0-1 Fm: 0-0
Distance: 5f/6f: 0-0 7f-8f: 0-0 9f-13f: 0-2 14f+: 0-0
Track : LH: 0-1 RH: 0-0 Tight: 0-2 Gall: 0-0
Aids: Bl: 0-0 Vi: 0-0 Tstrap: 0-1

Sayyidna

76 **39**
2-y-o b c Desert Style (IRE)-Anita's Love (IRE) (Anita's Prince)
R F Fisher Great Head House Estates Limited

Placings:00 **(3449)**
2001: 5^{0}GF, 6^{0}GF

	Starts	1st	2nd	3rd	Win & Pl
Career Total (Turf)	2	0	0	0	

Going (Turf): Sf: 0-0 GS: 0-0 Gd: 0-0 GF: 0-2 Fm: 0-0
Distance: 5f/6f: 0-2 7f-8f: 0-0 9f-13f: 0-0 14f+: 0-0
Track : LH: 0-0 RH: 0-0 Tight: 0-0 Gall: 0-0
Aids: Bl: 0-0 Vi: 0-0 Tstrap: 0-0
Best Rating: 39 7/01 Newc 6f gd-fm

Scafell

88(101) (54)**5**
4-y-o b g Puissance-One Half Silver (CAN) (Plugged Nickle (USA))
C Smith Mr & Mrs T I Gourley

Placings:62033250/0205310000-000000 **(4450)**
2001: 6^{0}GF, 5^{0}GF, 7^{0}G, 7^{0}GS, 11^{0}GF, 8^{0}GF

	Starts	1st	2nd	3rd	Win & Pl
Career Total (Turf)	23	1	2	3	6217
Career Total (AW)	1	0	1	0	844

61 6/00 Haml 5f4y F G-F £2401
Total win prize-money £2401

Going (Turf): Sf: 0-1 GS: 0-3 Gd: 0-6 **GF: 1-11** Fm: 0-2
Distance: **5f/6f: 1-14** 7f-8f: 0-8 9f-13f: 0-2 14f+: 0-0
Track : LH: 0-3 RH: 0-2 Tight: 0-2 Gall: 0-2
Aids: Bl: 0-1 **Vi: 1-7** Tstrap: 0-3
Best Rating: 68 6/01 Yarm 6f3y gd-fm

Scalado (USA)

85 (66)**67**
2-y-o ch c Mister Baileys-Lady Di Pomadora (USA) (Danzig Connection (USA))
R Charlton Hippodrome Racing

Placings:3 (4639)
2001: 6³GF

	Starts	1st	2nd	3rd	Win & Pl
Career Total (Turf)	1	0	0	1	458

Going (Turf): Sf: 0-0 GS: 0-0 Gd: 0-0 GF: 0-1 Fm: 0-0
Distance: 5f/6f: 0-1 7f-8f: 0-0 9f-13f: 0-0 14f+: 0-0
Track : LH: 0-0 RH: 0-0 Tight: 0-0 Gall: 0-0
Aids: Bl: 0-0 Vi: 0-0 Tstrap: 0-0
Best Rating: 67 9/01 Ling 6f gd-fm

Scarlet Ribbons

101 **92+**

2-y-o b f Anabaa (USA)-Scarlet Plume (Warning)
J L Dunlop Nigel & Carolyn Elwes

Placings:15 (5598)
2001: 6¹G, 6⁵GS

	Starts	1st	2nd	3rd	Win & Pl
Career Total (Turf)	2	1	0	0	5882
92 10/01 NmkR 6f	D			GD	£5616

Total win prize-money £5616

Going (Turf): Sf: 0-0 GS: 0-1 **Gd: 1-1** GF: 0-0 Fm: 0-0
Distance: **5f/6f: 1-2** 7f-8f: 0-0 9f-13f: 0-0 14f+: 0-0
Track : LH: 0-0 RH: 0-0 Tight: 0-0 Gall: 0-0
Aids: Bl: 0-0 Vi: 0-0 Tstrap: 0-0
Best Rating: 92 10/01 NmkR 6f good

Out of Oaks winner Circus Plume, she scored in style over six on her debut at Newmarket, beating an useful yardstick into second. She is likely to improve when stepped up in trip.

Scarlett Ribbon

(109) (90+)

4-y-o b f Most Welcome-Scarlett Holly (Red Sunset)
P J Makin R Angelini-Hurll

Placings:10/250-0030 (5259)
2001: 6⁰G, 6⁰G, 7³HY, 7⁰GS

	Starts	1st	2nd	3rd	Win & Pl
Career Total (Turf)	9	1	1	1	9757
96 11/99 Wind 6f	D			G-S	£3160

Total win prize money £3160

Going (Turf): Sf: 0-2 **GS: 1-3** Gd: 0-3 GF: 0-1 Fm: 0-0
Distance: **5f/6f: 1-6** 7f-8f: 0-3 9f-13f: 0-0 14f+: 0-0
Track : LH: 0-1 **RH: 1-1** Tight: 0-0 **Gall: 1-1**
Aids: Bl: 0-0 Vi: 0-0 Tstrap: 0-0
Best Rating: 85 9/01 Hayd 7f30y heavy

She has been lightly raced since making a winning debut at Windsor as a two-year-old and has mainly been out of her depth, though she did run with credit at haydock over seven. Best in testing conditions.

Scarpe Rosse (IRE)

108 **79**

3-y-o b f Sadler's Wells (USA)-Red Comes Up (USA) (Blushing Groom (FR))
C Collins (J L Dunlop 9/5) Mrs Sonia Rogers

Placings:56-100 (5556a)
2001: 10¹GS, 11⁰GF, 12⁰SH

	Starts	1st	2nd	3rd	Win & Pl
Career Total (Turf)	5	1	0	0	3215
79 5/01 Bath 1m2f46y D				G-S	£3052

Total win prize-money £3052

Going (Turf): Sf: 0-0 **GS: 1-1** Gd: 0-1 GF: 0-2 Fm: 0-0
Distance: 5f/6f: 0-0 7f-8f: 0-2 **9f-13f: 1-3** 14f+: 0-0
Track : **LH: 1-2** RH: 0-2 **Tight: 1-2** Gall: 0-1
Aids: Bl: 0-0 Vi: 0-0 Tstrap: 0-0
Best Rating: 79 5/01 Bath 1m2f46y gd-sft

A half-sister to four winners, got off the mark when stepped up to ten furlongs on her reappearance at three. Has acted on good to soft ground.

Scarrottoo

102(99) (55)**65**

3-y-o ch g Zilzal (USA)-Bold And Beautiful (Bold Lad (IRE))
S C Williams Michael Peacock

Placings:60-042316U112 (4736)
2001: 8⁰HY, 6⁴GF, 6²F, 6³GF, 6¹SD, 7⁶GF, 7ᵁGF, 6¹GF, 6¹GF, 6²F

				Starts	1st	2nd	3rd	Win & Pl
Career Total (Turf)				11	2	2	1	6865
Career Total (AW)				1	1	0	0	2989
54	8/01	Brig	6f209y	F(0-60)			G-F	£2275
61	8/01	Folk	6f	F(0-60)H			G-F	£2443
55	7/01	Wolv	6f	E(0-70)H			STD	£2989

Total win prize-money £7707

Going (Turf): Sf: 0-3 GS: 0-0 Gd: 0-0 **GF: 2-6** Fm: 0-2
Distance: **5f/6f: 2-5** 7f-8f: 1-6 9f-13f: 0-1 14f+: 0-0
Track : **LH: 2-4** RH: 0-0 **Tight: 1-1** Gall: 0-0
Aids: Bl: 0-0 Vi: 0-0 **Tstrap: 1-2**
Best Rating: 65 9/01 Chep 6f16y firm

Winner of a handicap on his All-Weather debut, he had a race at Musselburgh in August sewn up when his saddle slipped and he unseated his rider. Gained compensation at Folkestone and Brighton. Effective on fast ground and Fibresand, at six and seven furlongs.

Scarteen Sister (IRE)

94(100) (49)**52**

3-y-o ch f Eagle Eyed (USA)-Best Swinger (IRE) (Ela-Mana-Mou)
R M Beckett Pedro Rosas

Placings:30-0034 (5398)
2001: 6⁰HY, 8⁰GF, 8³SD, 8⁴SD, 9⁴SD

	Starts	1st	2nd	3rd	Win & Pl
Career Total (Turf)	4	0	0	1	554
Career Total (AW)	2	0	0	1	430

Going (Turf): Sf: 0-1 GS: 0-0 Gd: 0-0 GF: 0-3 Fm: 0-0
Distance: 5f/6f: 0-1 7f-8f: 0-2 9f-13f: 0-3 14f+: 0-0
Track : LH: 0-3 RH: 0-2 Tight: 0-4 Gall: 0-1
Aids: Bl: 0-0 Vi: 0-0 Tstrap: 0-0
Best Rating: 49 10/01 Wolv 1m100y stand

Lightly-raced maiden, stays an extended mile, handles fast ground on turf and Fibresand.

Scene (IRE)

104(104) (79)**66**

6-y-o b m Scenic-Avebury Ring (Auction Ring (USA))
J A Osborne (N P Littmoden 25/5) Paul J Dixon

Placings:4060003631/00101300P3042/0301423100000 41/0100000000004136664-000000400545 (5692)
2001: 9⁰SD, 8⁰S, 8⁰GS, 10⁰G, 10⁰S, 6⁰GF, 9⁴HY, 8⁰GS, 10⁰S, 12⁵GS, 9⁴GS, 16⁵S, 16⁰SD

				Starts	1st	2nd	3rd	Win & Pl
Career Total (Turf)				63	8	2	7	67120
Career Total (AW)				4	0	0	0	736
82	10/00	NmkR	1m	D(0-85)H			SFT	£6253
78	4/00	Leic	1m8y	D(0-80)H			G-S	£3945
72	11/99	Nott	1m1f213y	E(0-70)H			SFT	£3839
81	6/99	Epsm	1m114y	C(0-95)H			G-S	£17831
75	4/99	Asct	1m	D(0-80)H			GD	£7977
77	7/98	Hayd	1m30y	D(0-80)H			G-F	£3712
76	6/98	Thsk	1m	D(0-80)H			SFT	£3912
70	11/97	Donc	7f	D			SFT	£4370

Total win prize-money £51842

Going (Turf): Sf: 4-18 GS: 2-18 Gd: 1-13 GF: 1-14 Fm: 0-0
Distance: 5f/6f: 0-7 7f-8f: 4-28 9f-13f: 4-31 14f+: 0-1
Track : **LH: 4-37** RH: 0-5 **Tight: 2-15** Gall: 0-13
Aids: Bl: 0-2 Vi: 0-2 Tstrap: 0-0
Best Rating: 66 11/01 Donc 2m110y soft

A tough miler, he seemed to improve for a step up in trip in the autumn, firstly over a mile and a half at newmarket, then over two at Doncaster. Goes well in the mud, acts on the All-Weather.

Scenic Lady (IRE)

104(62) **54**

5-y-o b m Scenic-Tu Tu Maori (IRE) (King's Lake (USA))
L A Dace Eddie Davess

Placings:00/520500606/002540-2520112530 (5471)
2001: 9²F, 9⁵G, 11²GF, 14⁰GF, 11¹G, 10¹GF, 12²G, 9⁵G, 9³S, 11⁰S

				Starts	1st	2nd	3rd	Win & Pl
Career Total (Turf)				25	2	5	1	9959
Career Total (AW)				2	0	0	0	0
47	8/01	Ling	1m2f	F(0-65)H			G-F	£2807
41	8/01	Brig	1m3f196y	G(0-60)H			GD	£1904

Total win prize-money £4711

Going (Turf): Sf: 0-6 GS: 0-1 **Gd: 1-5 GF: 1-7** Fm: 0-6
Distance: 5f/6f: 0-0 7f-8f: 0-3 **9f-13f: 2-21** 14f+: 0-3
Track : **LH: 2-21** RH: 0-1 **Tight: 1-7** Gall: 0-0
Aids: Bl: 0-2 Vi: 0-0 Tstrap: 0-0
Best Rating: 54 9/01 Brig 1m1f209y soft

A fair plater, she got off the mark at the 23rd attempt in a seller at Brighton in August, but followed up in a better race at Lingfield. Stays 12 furlongs and goes well on fast ground.

Scent Ahead (USA)

83(84) (55)**55**

2-y-o b g Foxhound (USA)-Sonseri (Prince Tenderfoot (USA))
Mrs A J Bowlby The Rumble Racing Club

Placings:536000 (5165)
2001: 5⁵SD, 5³SD, 5⁶GF, 6⁰GF, 6⁰G, 5⁰SD

	Starts	1st	2nd	3rd	Win & Pl
Career Total (Turf)	3	0	0	0	0
Career Total (AW)	3	0	0	1	423

Going (Turf): Sf: 0-0 GS: 0-0 Gd: 0-1 GF: 0-2 Fm: 0-0
Distance: 5f/6f: 0-5 7f-8f: 0-1 9f-13f: 0-0 14f+: 0-0
Track : LH: 0-2 RH: 0-0 Tight: 0-1 Gall: 0-1
Aids: Bl: 0-1 Vi: 0-0 Tstrap: 0-1
Best Rating: 55 4/01 Sthl 5f stand

A half-brother to four winners including Glory Quest, walked out of the stalls on his Southwell debut but was sharper away next time. Has yet to make the frame on turf.

Scented Air

99(90) (43)**44**

4-y-o b f Lion Cavern (USA)-Jungle Rose (Shirley Heights)
Mrs J R Ramsden Manor Farm Stud (rutland)

Placings:050-0323044520 (5450)
2001: 7⁰GF, 8³GF, 8²GF, 8³GF, 10⁰GF, 8⁴F, 8⁴S, 8⁵GS, 8²GF, 8⁰HY

	Starts	1st	2nd	3rd	Win & Pl
Career Total (Turf)	12	0	2	2	3510
Career Total (AW)	1	0	0	0	

Going (Turf): Sf: 0-3 GS: 0-1 Gd: 0-0 GF: 0-7 Fm: 0-1
Distance: 5f/6f: 0-0 7f-8f: 0-6 9f-13f: 0-7 14f+: 0-0
Track : LH: 0-9 RH: 0-1 Tight: 0-3 Gall: 0-2
Aids: Bl: 0-0 Vi: 0-1 Tstrap: 0-0
Best Rating: 48 6/01 Pont 1m4y gd-fm

Moderate maiden who does not look the easiest of rides. Suited by a mile and fast ground.

Schatz

88 **50**

3-y-o b c General Monash (USA)-Mandalika (USA)

(Arctic Tern (USA))
L M Cumani Scuderia Rencati Srl

Placings:2-40 **(0961)**
2001: 5^{4}S, 6^{0}HY

	Starts	1st	2nd	3rd	Win & Pl
Career Total (Turf)	3	0	1	0	2863

Going (Turf): Sf: 0-2 GS: 0-0 Gd: 0-0 GF: 0-1 Fm: 0-0
Distance: 5f/6f: 0-2 7f-8f: 0-1 9f-13f: 0-0 14f+: 0-0
Track : LH: 0-0 RH: 0-1 Tight: 0-0 Gall: 0-0
Aids: Bl: 0-0 Vi: 0-0 Tstrap: 0-0
Best Rating: 50 4/01 Nott 5f13y soft

Schedule B

88(92) (54)**34**
3-y-o ch g Dancing Spree (USA)-Jolizal (Good Times (ITY))
R Hollinshead G J Sargent

Placings:3-40600 **(4631)**
2001: 7^{4}SW, 5^{0}G, 9^{6}SD, 10^{0}G, 9^{0}GF

	Starts	1st	2nd	3rd	Win & Pl
Career Total (Turf)	3	0	0	0	
Career Total (AW)	3	0	0	1	321

Going (Turf): Sf: 0-0 GS: 0-0 Gd: 0-2 GF: 0-1 Fm: 0-0
Distance: 5f/6f: 0-1 7f-8f: 0-2 9f-13f: 0-3 14f+: 0-0
Track : LH: 0-3 RH: 0-2 Tight: 0-4 Gall: 0-0
Aids: Bl: 0-0 Vi: 0-0 Tstrap: 0-0
Best Rating: 54 1/01 Wolv 7f slow

Scheherazade

100 **65**
3-y-o b f Sadler's Wells (USA)-Impatiente (USA) (Vaguely Noble)
L M Cumani Lindy Regis & Geoff Howard-Spink

Placings:0-05041 **(3298)**
2001: 8^{0}GS, 10^{5}GS, 10^{0}G, 14^{4}G, 11^{1}GF

	Starts	1st	2nd	3rd	Win & Pl
Career Total (Turf)	6	1	0	0	2947

65	7/01	Brig	1m3f196y	E(0-75)H	G-F	£2947

Total win prize-money £2947

Going (Turf): Sf: 0-0 GS: 0-2 Gd: 0-3 **GF: 1-1** Fm: 0-0
Distance: 5f/6f: 0-0 7f-8f: 0-2 **9f-13f: 1-3** 14f+: 0-1
Track : **LH: 1-4** RH: 0-0 Tight: 0-1 Gall: 0-1
Aids: Bl: 0-0 Vi: 0-0 Tstrap: 0-0
Best Rating: 65 7/01 Brig 1m3f196y gd-fm

Scheming

110 **93**
4-y-o br g Machiavellian (USA)-Alusha (Soviet Star (USA))
W M Brisbourne Christopher Chell

Placings:16001-00364131211 **(4250)**
2001: 10^{0}GS, 12^{0}S, 10^{3}F, 10^{6}G, 11^{4}GS, 9^{1}GF, 10^{3}GF, 10^{1}S, 10^{2}GF, 10^{1}G, 10^{1}GF

	Starts	1st	2nd	3rd	Win & Pl
Career Total (Turf)	16	6	1	2	62903

93	8/01	NmkJ	1m2f	C(0-95)H	G-F	£11049
87	8/01	Asct	1m2f	C(0-100)H	GD	£8287
83	7/01	Hayd	1m2f120y	C(0-90)H	SFT	£15486
79	6/01	Nott	1m1f213y	D(0-85)H	G-F	£7670
69	10/00	Donc	1m2f60y	D(0-80)H	GD	£5892
79	8/00	Hayd	1m3f200y	D	GD	£3926

Total win prize-money £52311

Going (Turf): Sf: 1-4 GS: 0-2 **Gd: 3-4** GF: 2-5 Fm: 0-1
Distance: 5f/6f: 0-0 7f-8f: 0-0 **9f-13f: 6-15** 14f+: 0-1
Track : **LH: 4-13** RH: 2-3 Tight: 0-3 **Gall: 3-9**
Aids: Bl: 0-0 Vi: 0-0 Tstrap: 0-0
Best Rating: 93 8/01 NmkJ 1m2f gd-fm

A progressive handicapper, he has enjoyed a fruitful campaign this season, winning at Nottingham, Haydock, Ascot and Newmarket. Usually held up, he stays 12 furlongs but has done most of his winning at ten. Seems to handle any ground.

Scholar Leo

88(93) (38)**50**
3-y-o b g Greensmith-Clary Sage (Sayf El Arab (USA))
C W Fairhurst M R Handy

Placings:00040406 **(2168)**
2001: 9^{0}SD, 8^{0}SD, 8^{0}S, 6^{4}SD, 6^{0}GF, 5^{4}GF, 5^{0}GF, 6^{6}SD

	Starts	1st	2nd	3rd	Win & Pl
Career Total (Turf)	4	0	0	0	273
Career Total (AW)	4	0	0	0	0

Going (Turf): Sf: 0-1 GS: 0-0 Gd: 0-0 GF: 0-3 Fm: 0-0
Distance: 5f/6f: 0-5 7f-8f: 0-1 9f-13f: 0-2 14f+: 0-0
Track : LH: 0-4 RH: 0-1 Tight: 0-3 Gall: 0-0
Aids: Bl: 0-1 Vi: 0-0 Tstrap: 0-0
Best Rating: 50 5/01 Donc 5f gd-fm

School Days

91 **87**
2-y-o b f Slip Anchor-Cradle Of Love (USA) (Roberto (USA))
M L W Bell Christopher Wright

Placings:30 **(5248)**
2001: 8^{3}G, 7^{0}S

	Starts	1st	2nd	3rd	Win & Pl
Career Total (Turf)	2	0	0	1	858

Going (Turf): Sf: 0-1 GS: 0-0 Gd: 0-1 GF: 0-0 Fm: 0-0
Distance: 5f/6f: 0-0 7f-8f: 0-2 9f-13f: 0-0 14f+: 0-0
Track : LH: 0-1 RH: 0-0 Tight: 0-0 Gall: 0-1
Aids: Bl: 0-0 Vi: 0-0 Tstrap: 0-0
Best Rating: 87 9/01 NmkR 1m good

A half-sister to Captain's Log and Ivory Dawn.

Schuschemiga

84(85) (41)**42**
2-y-o ch f Rock City-Bahrain Queen (IRE) (Caerleon (USA))
J G Given J Starbuck

Placings:4600 **(2583)**
2001: 5^{4}SD, 5^{6}GF, 6^{0}F, 7^{0}SD

	Starts	1st	2nd	3rd	Win & Pl
Career Total (Turf)	2	0	0	0	0
Career Total (AW)	2	0	0	0	0

Going (Turf): Sf: 0-0 GS: 0-0 Gd: 0-0 GF: 0-1 Fm: 0-1
Distance: 5f/6f: 0-3 7f-8f: 0-1 9f-13f: 0-0 14f+: 0-0
Track : LH: 0-1 RH: 0-0 Tight: 0-0 Gall: 0-0
Aids: Bl: 0-0 Vi: 0-0 Tstrap: 0-0
Best Rating: 42 6/01 Thsk 6f firm

Scippit

82 **68**
2-y-o ch g Unfuwain (USA)-Scierpan (USA) (Sharpen Up)
M R Channon Tim Corby

Placings:005 **(4184)**
2001: 7^{0}G, 6^{0}GF, 5^{5}GF

	Starts	1st	2nd	3rd	Win & Pl
Career Total (Turf)	3	0	0	0	0

Going (Turf): Sf: 0-0 GS: 0-0 Gd: 0-1 GF: 0-2 Fm: 0-0
Distance: 5f/6f: 0-2 7f-8f: 0-1 9f-13f: 0-0 14f+: 0-0
Track : LH: 0-0 RH: 0-0 Tight: 0-0 Gall: 0-0
Aids: Bl: 0-0 Vi: 0-0 Tstrap: 0-0
Best Rating: 68 8/01 Sals 6f gd-fm

Scissor Ridge

99(104) (55)**34**
9-y-o ch g Indian Ridge-Golden Scissors (Kalaglow)
J J Bridger J J Bridger

Placings:5256140050/644060043006200521/5206025143202224106114/2434500000352600440324/3643464502120000000006/004535300500005441304/324264023060505000252440-1400640500000 **(4733)**
2001: 7^{1}SD, 8^{4}SD, 7^{0}SD, 8^{0}SW, 7^{6}SD, 7^{4}GF, 6^{0}GF, 7^{5}F, 7^{0}GF, 10^{0}GF, 7^{0}G, 7^{0}S, 7^{0}F, 7^{0}SD

	Starts	1st	2nd	3rd	Win & Pl
Career Total (Turf)	86	3	12	3	27963
Career Total (AW)	66	6	7	9	36552

55	1/01	Ling	7f	B H	STD	£10140
57	11/99	Ling	7f	E(0-75)H	STD	£2515
56	7/98	Folk	6f	D(0-80)H	GD	£3785
65	12/96	Ling	5f	E(0-70)H	STD	£2913
65	11/96	Ling	6f	D(0-85)H	STD	£3598
60	9/96	Gdwd	5f	E(0-70)H	G-F	£4012
52	6/96	Gdwd	6f	D(0-75)H	GD	£4056
47	12/95	Ling	7f	F(0-60)H	STD	£2464
62	7/94	Wolv	7f	G	STD	£2174

Total win prize-money £35660

Going (Turf): Sf: 0-11 GS: 0-4 **Gd: 2-25** GF: 1-43 Fm: 0-3
Distance: **5f/6f: 5-61** 7f-8f: 4-83 9f-13f: 0-8 14f+: 0-0
Track : **LH: 6-71** RH: 0-13 **Tight: 6-70** Gall: 0-3
Aids: Bl: 0-2 Vi: 0-0 Tstrap: 0-0
Best Rating: 55 1/01 Ling 7f stand

Sconced (USA)

101(102) (43)**48**
6-y-o ch g Affirmed (USA)-Quaff (USA) (Raise A Cup (USA))
M J Polglase James S Kennerley And Miss Jenny Hall

Placings:045/314/600400533/00-06621523300214000400 **(5531)**
2001: 16^{0}SW, 16^{6}SD, 12^{6}SW, 16^{2}SD, 12^{1}SD, 16^{5}SD, 16^{2}HY, 14^{3}S, 14^{3}HY, 12^{0}S, 16^{0}GF, 11^{2}GF, 14^{1}G, 16^{4}GF, 12^{0}GF, 14^{0}GF, 15^{0}GF, 12^{4}SD, 14^{0}SD, 16^{0}HY

	Starts	1st	2nd	3rd	Win & Pl
Career Total (Turf)	24	2	2	3	12902
Career Total (AW)	13	1	1	2	3704

51	6/01	Muss	1m6f	D(0-80)H	GD	£4056
36	3/01	Sthl	1m4f	F(0-70)H	STD	£2233
73	9/98	Haml	1m1f36y	D	SFT	£3468

Total win prize-money £9758

Going (Turf): Sf: 1-6 GS: 0-2 **Gd: 1-6** GF: 0-9 Fm: 0-1
Distance: 5f/6f: 0-1 7f-8f: 0-2 **9f-13f: 2-12** 14f+: 1-22
Track : LH: 1-24 **RH: 2-10 Tight: 2-14** Gall: 0-2
Aids: Bl: 0-0 **Vi: 1-13** Tstrap: 0-0
Best Rating: 51 6/01 Muss 1m6f good

Moderate staying handicapper. 14 furlongs probably his optimum trip. Suited by a sound surface on turf, acts on Fibresand.

Scorned (GER)

108 **94**
6-y-o b g Selkirk (USA)-Spurned (USA) (Robellino (USA))
I A Balding Kingsclere Stud

Placings:01/112234210/602210 **(5693)**
2001: 14^{6}GF, 12^{0}G, 13^{2}GF, 12^{2}GS, 12^{1}HY, 12^{0}S

	Starts	1st	2nd	3rd	Win & Pl
Career Total (Turf)	17	5	5	1	117405

94	10/01	Donc	1m4f	C(0-100)H	HVY	£15015
113	9/98	Newb	1m3f5y	A	GD	£30635
106	4/98	Kemp	1m2f	C	HVY	£5168
106	3/98	Donc	1m	C	GD	£5744
88	11/97	Donc	7f	D	GD	£3494

Total win prize-money £60056

Going (Turf): Sf: 2-3 GS: 0-4 **Gd: 3-5** GF: 0-5 Fm: 0-0
Distance: 5f/6f: 0-0 7f-8f: 2-3 **9f-13f: 3-12** 14f+: 0-2
Track : **LH: 2-9** RH: 1-5 Tight: 0-2 **Gall: 3-8**
Aids: Bl: 0-0 Vi: 0-0 Tstrap: 0-0
Best Rating: 94 11/01 Donc 1m4f soft

Once a useful sort at up to Listed level, but was off the track for three years before reappearing in September. He put up an encouraging effort at Ayr when second in a handicap and improved on that effort when runner-up at Newmarket in October, before notching a deserved win at Doncaster. Acts well with cut in the ground, but handles faster. Suited by 12 furlongs plus.

Scotish Law (IRE)

105 **65**

3-y-o ch g Case Law-Scotia Rose (Tap On Wood)

P R Chamings G G N Productions Limited

Placings:2100-030043300 **(4735)**

2001: 8^{0}GS, 7^{3}G, 9^{0}GF, 8^{0}G, 8^{4}GF, 10^{3}GF, 8^{3}G, 7^{0}G, 10^{0}F

	Starts	1st	2nd	3rd	Win & Pl
Career Total (Turf)	13	1	1	3	7472

63 8/00 Epsm 6f E GD £3542

Total win prize-money £3543

Going (Turf): Sf: 0-1 GS: 0-1 **Gd: 1-5** GF: 0-4 Fm: 0-2
Distance: **5f/6f: 1-2** 7f-8f: 0-5 9f-13f: 0-6 14f+: 0-0
Track : **LH: 1-2** RH: 0-8 **Tight: 1-3** Gall: 0-1
Aids: Bl: 0-0 Vi: 0-0 Tstrap: 0-0
Best Rating: 69 5/01 Sand 7f16y good

He got off the mark at Epsom on his second start at two, but has shown little in the main since.

Scotmail Park

80(77) (41)**64**

2-y-o b c Presidium-Miss Tri Colour (Shavian)

G M Moore Gordon Brown/bert Watson

Placings:63000 **(4584)**

2001: 6^{6}GS, 6^{3}S, 6^{0}GS, 6^{0}SD, 8^{0}HY

	Starts	1st	2nd	3rd	Win & Pl
Career Total (Turf)	4	0	0	1	630
Career Total (AW)	1	0	0	0	

Going (Turf): Sf: 0-2 GS: 0-2 Gd: 0-0 GF: 0-0 Fm: 0-0
Distance: 5f/6f: 0-3 7f-8f: 0-1 9f-13f: 0-1 14f+: 0-0
Track : LH: 0-2 RH: 0-0 Tight: 0-1 Gall: 0-0
Aids: Bl: 0-0 Vi: 0-0 Tstrap: 0-0
Best Rating: 64 7/01 Hayd 6f soft

Scott's View

96 **69**

2-y-o b c Selkirk (USA)-Milly Of The Vally (Caerleon (USA))

M Johnston Great Escape Partnership

Placings:5626 **(5283)**

2001: 6^{5}GF, 7^{6}G, 8^{2}GF, 8^{6}HY

	Starts	1st	2nd	3rd	Win & Pl
Career Total (Turf)	4	0	1	0	1362

Going (Turf): Sf: 0-1 GS: 0-0 Gd: 0-1 GF: 0-2 Fm: 0-0
Distance: 5f/6f: 0-1 7f-8f: 0-3 9f-13f: 0-0 14f+: 0-0
Track : LH: 0-3 RH: 0-0 Tight: 0-2 Gall: 0-0
Aids: Bl: 0-0 Vi: 0-0 Tstrap: 0-0
Best Rating: 69 9/01 Thsk 1m gd-fm

By Selkirk, his best effort was a second in fast ground Thirsk maiden.

Scottish Knight

96(34) **63**

3-y-o b c Marju (IRE)-Scottish Eyes (USA) (Green Dancer (USA))

M R Bosley (Kevin Prendergast 24/6) Mrs Jean M O'Connor

Placings:0655000 **(5532)**

2001: 8^{0}GF, 7^{6}GF, 8^{5}GF, 10^{5}G, 9^{0}GS, 9^{0}SD, 9^{0}HY

	Starts	1st	2nd	3rd	Win & Pl
Career Total (Turf)	6	0	0	0	0
Career Total (AW)	1	0	0	0	

Going (Turf): Sf: 0-1 GS: 0-1 Gd: 0-1 GF: 0-3 Fm: 0-0
Distance: 5f/6f: 0-0 7f-8f: 0-3 9f-13f: 0-4 14f+: 0-0
Track : LH: 0-3 RH: 0-1 Tight: 0-3 Gall: 0-0
Aids: Bl: 0-0 Vi: 0-0 Tstrap: 0-0
Best Rating: 63 9/01 Gdwd 1m1f192y gd-sft

Scottish River (USA)

101 **98**

2-y-o b c Thunder Gulch (USA)-Overbrook (Storm Cat (USA))

M Johnston Jumeirah Racing

Placings:312400 **(5134)**

2001: 6^{3}GS, 6^{1}F, 6^{2}G, 7^{4}GF, 6^{0}G, 7^{0}G

	Starts	1st	2nd	3rd	Win & Pl
Career Total (Turf)	6	1	1	1	14258

92 6/01 Thsk 6f D FRM £3900

Total win prize-money £3900

Going (Turf): Sf: 0-0 GS: 0-1 Gd: 0-3 GF: 0-1 **Fm: 1-1**
Distance: **5f/6f: 1-3** 7f-8f: 0-3 9f-13f: 0-0 14f+: 0-0
Track : LH: 0-0 RH: 0-0 Tight: 0-0 Gall: 0-0
Aids: Bl: 0-0 Vi: 0-0 Tstrap: 0-0
Best Rating: 98 8/01 Newb 7f gd-fm

Left his debut effort behind when powering clear in the final furlong to win impressively at Thirsk over six furlongs in June and ran very well to finich runner-up in the Group Three July Stakes at Newmarket, but has since been very disappointing. Acts on fast ground.

Scottish Spice

107 **83**

4-y-o b f Selkirk (USA)-Dilwara (IRE) (Lashkari)

I A Balding J C Smith

Placings:6411/6005300203-062360100 **(5145)**

2001: 8^{0}HY, 8^{6}GS, 8^{2}G, 8^{3}GF, 9^{6}GF, 9^{0}GF, 8^{1}S, 8^{0}S, 7^{0}G

	Starts	1st	2nd	3rd	Win & Pl
Career Total (Turf)	23	3	2	3	34041

83 8/01 Sand 1m14y C(0-90)H SFT £11553
87 9/99 Newb 7f C(0-95)H G-F £6287
83 8/99 Folk 7f D G-S £4597

Total win prize money £22440

Going (Turf): Sf: 1-7 GS: 1-3 Gd: 0-6 **GF: 1-7** Fm: 0-0
Distance: 5f/6f: 0-0 **7f-8f: 2-8** 9f-13f: 1-15 14f+: 0-0
Track : LH: 0-5 **RH: 1-11** Tight: 0-8 Gall: 0-2
Aids: **Bl: 1-3** Vi: 0-0 Tstrap: 0-0
Best Rating: 85 6/01 Wind 1m67y good

She won twice at two, but not again until blinkered for the first time in soft ground at Sandown in August. Suited by a mile to a mile one and is best on an easy surface.

Scotty's Future (IRE)

111 **89**

3-y-o b c Namaqualand (USA)-Persian Empress (IRE) (Persian Bold)

A C Stewart Collins, Saunders, Kinge & McGuinness

Placings:000-2221134 **(4863)**

2001: 8^{2}G, 8^{2}F, 9^{2}G, 10^{1}GF, 10^{1}GF, 10^{3}GF, 10^{4}GF

	Starts	1st	2nd	3rd	Win & Pl
Career Total (Turf)	10	2	3	1	31815

85 8/01 Donc 1m2f60y D(0-85)H G-F £18408
76 7/01 Ripn 1m2f D(0-80)H G-F £4875

Total win prize-money £23283

Going (Turf): Sf: 0-3 GS: 0-0 Gd: 0-2 **GF: 2-4** Fm: 0-1
Distance: 5f/6f: 0-2 7f-8f: 0-2 **9f-13f: 2-6** 14f+: 0-0
Track : **LH: 1-4** RH: 0-1 Tight: 0-0 **Gall: 1-4**
Aids: Bl: 0-0 Vi: 0-0 Tstrap: 0-0
Best Rating: 89 9/01 Newb 1m2f60y gd-fm

Ran on testing ground over six furlongs as a juvenile. A step up to a mile on a sounder surface brought about improvement and he eventually got off the mark in a ten-furlong handicap at Ripon in July 2001, displaying a useful turn of foot. Followed up with another victory at Doncaster, and a good third at Newmarket, followed by another good effort this time at Newbury. Acts on fast ground.

Scramble (USA)

96 **71**

3-y-o ch c Gulch (USA)-Syzygy (ARG) (Big Play (USA))

J H M Gosden Stonerside Stables Llc

Placings:3-064 **(5113)**

2001: 8^{0}GF, 8^{6}GF, 8^{4}HY

	Starts	1st	2nd	3rd	Win & Pl
Career Total (Turf)	4	0	0	1	1789

Going (Turf): Sf: 0-2 GS: 0-0 Gd: 0-0 GF: 0-2 Fm: 0-0
Distance: 5f/6f: 0-0 7f-8f: 0-3 9f-13f: 0-1 14f+: 0-0
Track : LH: 0-1 RH: 0-1 Tight: 0-0 Gall: 0-0
Aids: Bl: 0-0 Vi: 0-0 Tstrap: 0-4
Best Rating: 71 6/01 NmkR 1m gd-fm

Scravels

88(73) (39)**64**

2-y-o ch g Elmaamul (USA)-Defined Feature (IRE) (Nabeel Dancer (USA))

Dr J D Scargill Derek W Johnson

Placings:000000 **(5667)**

2001: 6^{0}GF, 6^{0}GF, 8^{0}G, 8^{0}SD, 7^{0}GS, 8^{0}HY

	Starts	1st	2nd	3rd	Win & Pl
Career Total (Turf)	5	0	0	0	
Career Total (AW)	1	0	0	0	

Going (Turf): Sf: 0-1 GS: 0-1 Gd: 0-1 GF: 0-2 Fm: 0-0
Distance: 5f/6f: 0-0 7f-8f: 0-5 9f-13f: 0-1 14f+: 0-0
Track : LH: 0-1 RH: 0-4 Tight: 0-3 Gall: 0-0
Aids: Bl: 0-1 Vi: 0-0 Tstrap: 0-0
Best Rating: 64 9/01 Kemp 1m good

Has shown little ability in maiden events so far, should be better suited by nurseries.

Screamin' Georgina

101 **56**

3-y-o b f Muhtarram (USA)-Carrie Kool (Prince Sabo)

S C Williams The Lager Khan

Placings:0211050-0020540 **(4527)**

2001: 6^{0}G, 5^{0}GF, 5^{2}G, 5^{0}GF, 5^{5}GF, 5^{4}F, 6^{0}GF

	Starts	1st	2nd	3rd	Win & Pl
Career Total (Turf)	14	2	2	0	5748

61 7/00 Folk 5f F G-F £2194
56 7/00 Leic 5f2y G G-F £1907

Total win prize-money £4103

Going (Turf): Sf: 0-0 GS: 0-0 Gd: 0-4 **GF: 1-8** Fm: 0-1
Distance: **5f/6f: 1-12** 7f-8f: 0-1 9f-13f: 0-0 14f+: 0-0
Track : LH: 0-1 RH: 0-0 Tight: 0-0 Gall: 0-1
Aids: Bl: 0-0 Vi: 0-0 **Tstrap: 1-11**
Best Rating: 56 5/01 Ling 5f gd-fm

Screaming Eagle (IRE)

92 **76**

2-y-o b f Sadler's Wells (USA)-Ducking (Reprimand)

J L Dunlop Wood Hall Stud Limited

Placings:004 **(5520)**

2001: 7^{0}G, 8^{0}G, 8^{4}HY

	Starts	1st	2nd	3rd	Win & Pl
Career Total (Turf)	3	0	0	0	301

Going (Turf): Sf: 0-1 GS: 0-0 Gd: 0-2 GF: 0-0 Fm: 0-0
Distance: 5f/6f: 0-0 7f-8f: 0-2 9f-13f: 0-1 14f+: 0-0
Track : LH: 0-0 RH: 0-2 Tight: 0-1 Gall: 0-1

Aids: Bl: 0-0 Vi: 0-0 Tstrap: 0-0
Best Rating: 76 9/01 NmkR 1m good

Scurra

92 **75**

2-y-o b c Spectrum (IRE)-Tamnia (Green Desert (USA))
R Hollinshead (M J Polglase 1/8) D S Lovatt

Placings:032 **(5633)**
2001: 6^{0}GF, 7^{3}HY, 7^{2}G

	Starts	1st	2nd	3rd	Win & Pl
Career Total (Turf)	3	0	1	1	1494

Going (Turf): Sf: 0-1 GS: 0-0 Gd: 0-1 GF: 0-1 Fm: 0-0
Distance: 5f/6f: 0-0 7f-8f: 0-3 9f-13f: 0-0 14f+: 0-0
Track : LH: 0-2 RH: 0-0 Tight: 0-1 Gall: 0-0
Aids: Bl: 0-0 Vi: 0-0 Tstrap: 0-0
Best Rating: 75 11/01 Catt 7f good

Steadily improved runs in maiden company.

Sea Buzzard (IRE)

79 **41**

3-y-o b g Bluebird (USA)-Paloma Bay (IRE) (Alzao (USA))
M Blanshard G H S Bailey & N C D Hall

Placings:0000 **(1950)**
2001: 6^{0}HY, 7^{0}G, 10^{0}GF, 7^{0}GF

	Starts	1st	2nd	3rd	Win & Pl
Career Total (Turf)	4	0	0	0	

Going (Turf): Sf: 0-1 GS: 0-0 Gd: 0-1 GF: 0-2 Fm: 0-0
Distance: 5f/6f: 0-0 7f-8f: 0-3 9f-13f: 0-1 14f+: 0-0
Track : LH: 0-1 RH: 0-1 Tight: 0-2 Gall: 0-0
Aids: Bl: 0-0 Vi: 0-0 Tstrap: 0-0
Best Rating: 41 5/01 Leic 7f9y good

Sea Danzig

94(106) (70d)**51**

8-y-o ch g Roi Danzig (USA)-Tosara (Main Reef)
J J Bridger P Cook

Placings:046/2005006025054010643/03124046532000 650251430/411245016410532000/550632030204310005/0104221000000401050000-54 **(4019)**
2001: 16^{5}SD, 12^{4}G

	Starts	1st	2nd	3rd	Win & Pl
Career Total (Turf)	72	5	7	5	31206
Career Total (AW)	32	6	4	3	24316

50	7/00	Sals	1m6f15y	E(0-70)H	FRM	£3380
72	3/00	Ling	1m4f	E(0-70)	STD	£2716
67	1/00	Ling	1m2f	E(0-70)	STD	£2563
59	9/99	Epsm	1m2f18y	D(0-85)H	G-F	£5784
63	7/98	Folk	1m1f149y	F(0-65)	G-F	£2406
61	6/98	Gdwd	1m1f	E(0-70)H	GD	£4175
73	1/98	Ling	1m2f	D(0-85)H	STD	£3452
73	1/98	Ling	1m2f	F(0-70)H	STD	£2232
69	11/97	Ling	1m2f	F(0-80)H	STD	£2739
58	1/97	Ling	7f	E(0-70)H	STD	£2830
66	10/96	Ling	7f	E(0-70)H	GD	£3616

Total win prize-money £35894

Going (Turf): Sf: 0-8 GS: 0-8 **Gd: 2-16 GF: 2-32** Fm: 1-8
Distance: 5f/6f: 0-10 7f-8f: 2-24 **9f-13f: 8-64** 14f+: 1-6
Track : **LH: 7-53** RH: 3-27 **Tight: 10-58** Gall: 0-5
Aids: Bl: 0-5 Vi: 0-0 Tstrap: 0-0
Best Rating: 57 1/01 Ling 2m stand

Sea Fleur

82 **62**

2-y-o b f Botanic (USA)-Sea Fairy (Wollow)
R Guest Mrs A E V Wadman

Placings:0600 **(4627)**
2001: 5^{0}GF, 5^{6}S, 5^{0}G, 5^{0}GF

	Starts	1st	2nd	3rd	Win & Pl
Career Total (Turf)	4	0	0	0	0

Going (Turf): Sf: 0-1 GS: 0-0 Gd: 0-1 GF: 0-2 Fm: 0-0
Distance: 5f/6f: 0-4 7f-8f: 0-0 9f-13f: 0-0 14f+: 0-0
Track : LH: 0-1 RH: 0-1 Tight: 0-0 Gall: 0-2
Aids: Bl: 0-0 Vi: 0-0 Tstrap: 0-0
Best Rating: 62 8/01 Bath 5f11y good

Sea Fly

47

3-y-o ch f Presidium-Steelock (Lochnager)
M A Barnes R H Hall

Placings:0 **(3308)**
2001: 7^{0}GS

	Starts	1st	2nd	3rd	Win & Pl
Career Total (Turf)	1	0	0	0	

Going (Turf): Sf: 0-0 GS: 0-1 Gd: 0-0 GF: 0-0 Fm: 0-0
Distance: 5f/6f: 0-0 7f-8f: 0-1 9f-13f: 0-0 14f+: 0-0
Track : LH: 0-1 RH: 0-0 Tight: 0-0 Gall: 0-0
Aids: Bl: 0-0 Vi: 0-0 Tstrap: 0-1

Sea Haze

74(93) (46)**63d**

4-y-o ch g Emarati (USA)-Unveiled (Sayf El Arab (USA))
R J Baker P Slade

Placings:06015340/02000000-00 **(5398)**
2001: 5^{0}HD, 8^{0}SD

	Starts	1st	2nd	3rd	Win & Pl
Career Total (Turf)	16	1	1	1	4764
Career Total (AW)	2	0	0	0	

62	6/99	Bath	5f161y	E	FRM	£2808

Total win prize-money £2808

Going (Turf): Sf: 0-2 GS: 0-1 Gd: 0-3 GF: 0-7 **Fm: 1-3**
Distance: **5f/6f: 1-16** 7f-8f: 0-1 9f-13f: 0-1 14f+: 0-0
Track : **LH: 1-6** RH: 0-5 Tight: 0-2 **Gall: 1-8**
Aids: Bl: 0-1 Vi: 0-0 Tstrap: 0-0
Best Rating: 7 6/01 Bath 5f161y hard

Sea Isle

91(81) (39)**31**

5-y-o ch m Selkirk (USA)-Miss Blitz (Formidable (USA))
H Alexander (J Parkes 13/6) Miss A M Rees

Placings:56350/00-0000 **(2095)**
2001: 7^{0}S, 7^{0}GF, 6^{0}F, 5^{0}GF

	Starts	1st	2nd	3rd	Win & Pl
Career Total (Turf)	9	0	0	1	495
Career Total (AW)	2	0	0	0	

Going (Turf): Sf: 0-3 GS: 0-0 Gd: 0-3 GF: 0-2 Fm: 0-1
Distance: 5f/6f: 0-2 7f-8f: 0-7 9f-13f: 0-2 14f+: 0-0
Track : LH: 0-4 RH: 0-1 Tight: 0-3 Gall: 0-0
Aids: Bl: 0-1 Vi: 0-0 Tstrap: 0-0
Best Rating: 31 5/01 Rdcr 6f firm

Sea Jade (IRE)

84 **57**

2-y-o b f Mujadil (USA)-Mirabiliary (USA) (Crow (FR))
J W Payne T H Barma

Placings:000 **(3869)**
2001: 6^{0}G, 7^{0}GF, 5^{0}G

	Starts	1st	2nd	3rd	Win & Pl
Career Total (Turf)	3	0	0	0	

Going (Turf): Sf: 0-0 GS: 0-0 Gd: 0-2 GF: 0-1 Fm: 0-0
Distance: 5f/6f: 0-2 7f-8f: 0-1 9f-13f: 0-0 14f+: 0-0
Track : LH: 0-0 RH: 0-0 Tight: 0-0 Gall: 0-0
Aids: Bl: 0-0 Vi: 0-0 Tstrap: 0-0

Best Rating: 57 7/01 Kemp 6f good

Showed little on his debut.

Sea Mark

105 **85**

5-y-o ro g Warning-Mettlesome (Lomond (USA))
C Grant Akv Cladding Fabrications Ltd

Placings:02/1/01-0022250550 **(5142)**
2001: 8^{0}G, 10^{0}GF, 8^{2}GF, 8^{2}GF, 9^{2}GF, 8^{5}G, 8^{0}GF, 10^{5}GF, 7^{5}G, 9^{0}G

	Starts	1st	2nd	3rd	Win & Pl
Career Total (Turf)	15	2	4	0	19057

83	9/00	NmkR	7f	C(0-90)H	GD	£7631
67	10/99	Leic	7f9y	F	G-S	£2389

Total win prize-money £10021

Going (Turf): Sf: 0-0 **GS: 1-1 Gd: 1-8** GF: 0-6 Fm: 0-0
Distance: 5f/6f: 0-1 **7f-8f: 2-8** 9f-13f: 0-6 14f+: 0-0
Track : LH: 0-4 RH: 0-3 Tight: 0-2 Gall: 0-3
Aids: Bl: 0-0 Vi: 0-0 Tstrap: 0-0
Best Rating: 87 6/01 Hayd 1m30y gd-fm

A tough sort, stays a mile. Acts on fast ground, although both wins have come in the autumn. Does not have much in the way of a turn of foot though. Has been performing consistently for new stable this term.

Sea Minstrel

64(80) **16**

5-y-o b m Sea Raven (IRE)-Give Us A Treat (Cree Song)
J S Wainwright O R Dukes

Placings:5003400/00000P0/0-0 **(3865)**
2001: 8^{0}GF

	Starts	1st	2nd	3rd	Win & Pl
Career Total (Turf)	15	0	0	1	756
Career Total (AW)	1	0	0	0	

Going (Turf): Sf: 0-1 GS: 0-1 Gd: 0-3 GF: 0-4 Fm: 0-6
Distance: 5f/6f: 0-11 7f-8f: 0-3 9f-13f: 0-2 14f+: 0-0
Track : LH: 0-4 RH: 0-1 Tight: 0-3 Gall: 0-1
Aids: Bl: 0-0 Vi: 0-0 Tstrap: 0-1

Sea Plume

70 **34**

2-y-o b f Slip Anchor-Fine Quill (Unfuwain (USA))
Lady Herries Mrs E F Griffiths

Placings:0 **(5277)**
2001: 7^{0}GS

	Starts	1st	2nd	3rd	Win & Pl
Career Total (Turf)	1	0	0	0	

Going (Turf): Sf: 0-0 GS: 0-1 Gd: 0-0 GF: 0-0 Fm: 0-0
Distance: 5f/6f: 0-0 7f-8f: 0-1 9f-13f: 0-0 14f+: 0-0
Track : LH: 0-0 RH: 0-0 Tight: 0-0 Gall: 0-0
Aids: Bl: 0-0 Vi: 0-0 Tstrap: 0-0
Best Rating: 34 10/01 Leic 7f9y gd-sft

Sea Prince

76 **35**

2-y-o ch c Bering-Gersey (Generous (IRE))
I A Balding Holistic Racing Ltd

Placings:00 **(5053)**
2001: 7^{0}GF, 7^{0}S

	Starts	1st	2nd	3rd	Win & Pl
Career Total (Turf)	2	0	0	0	

Going (Turf): Sf: 0-1 GS: 0-0 Gd: 0-0 GF: 0-1 Fm: 0-0
Distance: 5f/6f: 0-0 7f-8f: 0-2 9f-13f: 0-0 14f+: 0-0
Track : LH: 0-0 RH: 0-0 Tight: 0-0 Gall: 0-0
Aids: Bl: 0-0 Vi: 0-1 Tstrap: 0-0

Best Rating: 35 10/01 NmkR 7f soft

From the same family as Jahafil and Mondschein, he looked very much in need of the experience on his Doncaster debut and should do much better in time.

Sea Star

105 **88**

3-y-o b c Distant Relative-Storm Card (Zalazl (USA))
H R A Cecil L Marinopoulos

Placings:3-10 **(5625)**
2001: 8^{1}GS, 8^{0}GS

	Starts	1st	2nd	3rd	Win & Pl
Career Total (Turf)	3	1	0	1	4248

88	10/01	Pont	1m4y	D	G-S	£3607

Total win prize-money £3608

Going (Turf): Sf: 0-1 **GS: 1-2** Gd: 0-0 GF: 0-0 Fm: 0-0
Distance: 5f/6f: 0-0 7f-8f: 0-1 **9f-13f: 1-2** 14f+: 0-0
Track : **LH: 1-2** RH: 0-0 Tight: 0-0 Gall: 0-0
Aids: Bl: 0-0 Vi: 0-0 Tstrap: 0-0
Best Rating: 88 10/01 Pont 1m4y gd-sft

Lightly-raced colt, chased home Halland on his only run as a juvenile, but had his problems and was off for nearly a year before winning at Pontefract. Bounced next time, but seems suited by a mile and easy ground.

Sea Storm (IRE)

104 **91**

3-y-o b g Dolphin Street (FR)-Prime Interest (IRE) (King's Lake (USA))
R F Fisher M W Chapman

Placings:00-4161126 **(4251)**
2001: 6^{4}GS, 7^{1}GF, 8^{6}GF, 7^{1}GF, 7^{1}GF, 7^{2}GF, 7^{6}GF

	Starts	1st	2nd	3rd	Win & Pl
Career Total (Turf)	9	3	1	0	18478

82	7/01	Bevl	7f100y	D(0-85)H	G-F	£8853
73	7/01	Sthl	7f	E(0-75)H	G-F	£3710
66	5/01	Sthl	7f	F	G-F	£2401

Total win prize-money £14964

Going (Turf): Sf: 0-0 GS: 0-2 Gd: 0-1 **GF: 3-6** Fm: 0-0
Distance: 5f/6f: 0-2 **7f-8f: 3-7** 9f-13f: 0-0 14f+: 0-0
Track : **LH: 2-5** RH: 1-1 Tight: 0-1 Gall: 0-0
Aids: Bl: 0-0 Vi: 0-0 Tstrap: 0-0
Best Rating: 91 7/01 Newc 7f gd-fm

A progressive sort, he has been enjoying a fruitful summer in handicap company with two wins on turf at Southwell and one at Beverley. Seven furlongs on fast ground are his conditions.

Sea Top

77(83) (49)**40**

2-y-o gr g Highest Honor (FR)-Anotheranniversary (Emarati (USA))
J J Bridger P Cook

Placings:005000 **(5331)**
2001: 5^{0}GS, 5^{0}GS, 6^{5}GF, 7^{0}F, 5^{0}SD, 5^{0}HY

	Starts	1st	2nd	3rd	Win & Pl
Career Total (Turf)	5	0	0	0	0
Career Total (AW)	1	0	0	0	

Going (Turf): Sf: 0-1 GS: 0-2 Gd: 0-0 GF: 0-1 Fm: 0-1
Distance: 5f/6f: 0-5 7f-8f: 0-1 9f-13f: 0-0 14f+: 0-0
Track : LH: 0-0 RH: 0-2 Tight: 0-0 Gall: 0-2
Aids: Bl: 0-0 Vi: 0-0 Tstrap: 0-0
Best Rating: 40 5/01 Gdwd 6f gd-fm

Sea Victor

(85) (29)

9-y-o b g Slip Anchor-Victoriana (USA) (Storm Bird (CAN))
J L Harris J L Harris

Placings:0/140006333121322/003011404216004520 2/465526000/0 **(0691)**
2001: 16^{0}SD

	Starts	1st	2nd	3rd	Win & Pl
Career Total (Turf)	39	5	4	5	46399
Career Total (AW)	6	1	3	0	8000

81	8/96	Ches	2m2f147y	C(0-95)H	G-F	£15230
80	6/96	Kemp	1m6f92y	D(0-75)	G-F	£3538
54	6/96	Sthl	2m	F	STD	£2381
80	10/95	Nott	2m9y	D(0-80)H	G-F	£4857
75	10/95	Catt	1m7f177y	D(0-80)H	G-F	£3915
87	3/95	Donc	1m2f60y	D	GD	£4171

Total win prize-money £34096

Going (Turf): Sf: 0-2 GS: 0-2 Gd: 1-15 **GF: 4-17** Fm: 0-3
Distance: 5f/6f: 0-0 7f-8f: 0-1 9f-13f: 1-11 **14f+: 5-33**
Track : **LH: 5-26** RH: 1-17 **Tight: 2-20** Gall: 1-12
Aids: Bl: 0-0 Vi: 0-4 Tstrap: 0-0
Best Rating: 29 4/01 Sthl 2m stand

Sea Vista (USA)

82 **55**

2-y-o gr/ro f Distant View (USA)-Sarba (USA) (Persepolis (FR))
I A Balding Robin F Scully

Placings:50 **(5468)**
2001: 6^{5}GF, 7^{0}S

	Starts	1st	2nd	3rd	Win & Pl
Career Total (Turf)	2	0	0	0	0

Going (Turf): Sf: 0-1 GS: 0-0 Gd: 0-0 GF: 0-1 Fm: 0-0
Distance: 5f/6f: 0-1 7f-8f: 0-1 9f-13f: 0-0 14f+: 0-0
Track : LH: 0-1 RH: 0-0 Tight: 0-0 Gall: 0-0
Aids: Bl: 0-0 Vi: 0-0 Tstrap: 0-1
Best Rating: 55 6/01 Asct 6f gd-fm

Sea Vixen

103(95) (84+)**68+**

3-y-o ch f Machiavellian (USA)-Hill Hopper (IRE) (Danehill (USA))
Sir Mark Prescott Cheveley Park Stud

Placings:1-1 **(5470)**
2001: 7^{1}S, 8^{0}SD

	Starts	1st	2nd	3rd	Win & Pl
Career Total (Turf)	1	1	0	0	3913
Career Total (AW)	1	1	0	0	2785

68	10/01	Brig	7f214y	D(0-80)	SFT	£3913
84	6/00	Sthl	6f	D	STD	£2785

Total win prize-money £6698

Going (Turf): Sf: 1-1 GS: 0-0 Gd: 0-0 GF: 0-0 Fm: 0-0
Distance: 5f/6f: 1-1 7f-8f: 1-1 9f-13f: 0-0 14f+: 0-0
Track : **LH: 2-2** RH: 0-0 Tight: 0-0 Gall: 0-0
Aids: Bl: 0-0 Vi: 0-0 Tstrap: 0-0
Best Rating: 68 10/01 Brig 7f214y soft

Scored on her debut over six furlongs on the Fibresand at Southwell, and followed up after over a year off to win at Brighton in October 2001.

Sea Ya Maite

103(105) (70)**35**

7-y-o b g Komaite (USA)-Marina Plata (Julio Mariner)
S R Bowring S R Bowring

Placings:004301303210 0/0301033000400/26060000500 21000/5315652165054230-5336034131301043 04023 **(5196)**
2001: 7^{5}SD, 8^{3}SD, 8^{3}SD, 8^{6}SD, 7^{0}SD, 9^{3}SD, 8^{4}SD, 7^{1}SD, 7^{3}SD, 8^{1}SD, 7^{3}SD, 11^{0}SD, 8^{1}SD, 8^{0}SD, 7^{4}GF, 8^{3}SD, 8^{0}GF, 8^{4}SD, 8^{0}SD, 8^{2}F, 8^{3}SD

	Starts	1st	2nd	3rd	Win & Pl
Career Total (Turf)	20	0	2	1	2822
Career Total (AW)	61	9	4	14	33091

70	4/01	Sthl	1m	E(0-65)	STD	£2779
60	3/01	Wolv	1m100y	F(0-60)	STD	£2261
60	3/01	Sthl	7f	F(0-60)	STD	£2212
66	2/00	Wolv	7f	F(0-65)H	STD	£1949
58	1/00	Sthl	1m	F(0-65)H	STD	£1970
54	11/99	Sthl	7f	D(0-85)H	STD	£3766
67	5/98	Sthl	1m	F(0-65)H	STD	£2070
65	10/97	Wolv	1m100y	F(0-60)H	STD	£2070
56	7/97	Sthl	6f	E(0-70)H	STD	£2810

Total win prize-money £21889

Going (Turf): Sf: 0-1 GS: 0-1 Gd: 0-12 GF: 0-5 Fm: 0-1
Distance: 5f/6f: 1-9 **7f-8f: 6-48** 9f-13f: 2-24 14f+: 0-0
Track : **LH: 9-63** RH: 0-7 **Tight: 3-20** Gall: 0-1
Aids: **Bl: 1-7** Vi: 0-0 Tstrap: 0-3
Best Rating: 70 6/01 Sthl 1m stand

He is a much better horse on Fibresand than on turf.

Sea-Deer

77 (72)**59**

12-y-o ch g Hadeer-Hi Tech Girl (Homeboy)
C A Dwyer M M Foulger

Placings:56443/0001U42216/511311U2/005040/**43543** **2322411112631032**10000/3255320100000**20**/064643301 04300005/400240430341100/0006005-00 **(3317)**
2001: 6^{0}GF, 7^{0}G

	Starts	1st	2nd	3rd	Win & Pl
Career Total (Turf)	101	15	10	12	89384
Career Total (AW)	9	1	2	2	5608

76	9/99	Yarm	7f3y	G(0-75)H	G-S	£1920
51	9/99	Yarm	7f3y	G	G-F	£2320
73	7/98	NmkJ	6f	C(0-90)H	G-F	£5796
87	6/97	Yarm	6f3y	C	GD	£5115
77	8/96	Wolv	6f	D(0-80)H	STD	£3264
96	7/96	NmkJ	5f	C	G-F	£5336
71	6/96	Yarm	6f3y	E(0-70)H	FRM	£3525
72	6/96	Yarm	6f3y	E(0-70)H	FRM	£2961
49	5/96	Catt	5f	F	GD	£2763
60	5/96	Newc	5f	G	GD	£2316
78	7/94	Gdwd	5f	D(0-80)H	G-F	£7050
75	7/94	NmkJ	5f	D(0-100)H	G-F	£6212
65	6/94	Nott	5f13y	D(0-80)H	G-F	£3289
64	5/94	Wind	5f217y	F(0-65)	SFT	£3052
58	8/93	Kemp	5f	E(0-70)H	GD	£3557
55	6/93	Newb	5f34y	D(0-80)H	GD	£4240

Total win prize-money £62718

Going (Turf): Sf: 1-9 GS: 1-8 Gd: 5-38 **GF: 6-38** Fm: 2-8
Distance: **5f/6f: 11-81** 7f-8f: 5-29 9f-13f: 0-0 14f+: 0-0
Track : LH: 1-17 RH: 1-5 Tight: 1-8 Gall: 1-7
Aids: Bl: 0-0 Vi: 0-0 Tstrap: 0-0
Best Rating: 17 7/01 Yarm 6f3y gd-fm

A useful sprinter in his prime, he is at the veteran stage of his career now.

Seaborne

90 **69**

2-y-o b f Slip Anchor-Jezebel Monroe (USA) (Lyphard (USA))
R Charlton Lady Rothschild

Placings:0 **(5603)**
2001: 7^{0}GS

	Starts	1st	2nd	3rd	Win & Pl
Career Total (Turf)	1	0	0	0	

Going (Turf): Sf: 0-0 GS: 0-1 Gd: 0-0 GF: 0-0 Fm: 0-0
Distance: 5f/6f: 0-0 7f-8f: 0-1 9f-13f: 0-0 14f+: 0-0
Track : LH: 0-0 RH: 0-0 Tight: 0-0 Gall: 0-0
Aids: Bl: 0-0 Vi: 0-0 Tstrap: 0-0
Best Rating: 69 11/01 NmkR 7f gd-sft

Seagull (IRE)

106 **103**

3-y-o ch g Polar Falcon (USA)-Bird Of Love (Ela-Mana-Mou)
D R C Elsworth & Mrs A J Dunn

Placings:11 **(2431)**
2001: 10^{1}S, 11^{1}GF

	Starts	1st	2nd	3rd	Win & Pl
Career Total (Turf)	2	2	0	0	11852

103 6/01 Wind 1m3f135yC G-F £6716
97 5/01 Newb 1m2f6y D SFT £5135
Total win prize-money £11852

Going (Turf): **Sf: 1-1** GS: 0-0 Gd: 0-0 **GF: 1-1** Fm: 0-0
Distance: 5f/6f: 0-0 7f-8f: 0-0 **9f-13f: 2-2** 14f+: 0-0
Track : **LH: 1-1** RH: 0-0 Tight: 1-1 Gall: 1-1
Aids: Bl: 0-0 Vi: 0-0 Tstrap: 0-0
Best Rating: 103 6/01 Wind 1m3f135y gd-fm

A long-priced winner on his debut, where he finished strongly he successfully stepped up in grade and trip at Windsor

Sealed By Fate (IRE)

102(96) (41)**52**
6-y-o b g Mac's Imp (USA)-Fairy Don (Don)
J S Wainwright J S Wainwright

Placings:06606**04**/**363**000024360/0302321260464260 000/**50**6604450200000**-00**0000005050006000600450000 **(5629)**
2001: 8^{0}SW, 6^{0}SD, 5^{0}S, 6^{0}S, 7^{0}G, 6^{0}GF, 7^{0}F, 5^{5}GF, 6^{0}GF, 6^{5}GF, 7^{0}GF, 6^{0}F, 6^{0}GF, 8^{6}GS, 5^{0}GF, 5^{0}G, 5^{0}S, 6^{0}HY, 5^{6}GF, 7^{0}G, 5^{4}G, 7^{5}GS, 5^{0}GS, 6^{0}S, 5^{0}G

	Starts	1st	2nd	3rd	Win & Pl
Career Total (Turf)	69	1	6	3	9964
Career Total (AW)	10	0	0	2	523

61 6/99 Carl 5f F(0-65)H G-F £2430
Total win prize-money £2430

Going (Turf): Sf: 0-11 GS: 0-7 Gd: 0-18 **GF: 1-25** Fm: 0-8
Distance: **5f/6f: 1-58** 7f-8f: 0-18 9f-13f: 0-3 14f+: 0-0
Track : LH: 0-16 **RH: 1-7** Tight: 0-7 **Gall: 1-7**
Aids: **Bl: 1-27** Vi: 0-36 Tstrap: 0-0
Best Rating: 52 10/01 Newc 7f gd-sft

On the downgrade, he has faced some impossible tasks of late, and is basically a plater. Has not won since June 1999.

Seamstress (IRE)

95 **74**
2-y-o b f Barathea (IRE)-Petite Epaulette (Night Shift (USA))
P W Harris G Godfrey, A Kirkland, S Slack

Placings:3140 **(5404)**
2001: 7^{3}F, 7^{1}G, 8^{4}HY, 8^{0}S

	Starts	1st	2nd	3rd	Win & Pl
Career Total (Turf)	4	1	0	1	3086

71 8/01 Muss 7f30y F GD £2628
Total win prize-money £2629

Going (Turf): Sf: 0-2 GS: 0-0 **Gd: 1-1** GF: 0-0 Fm: 0-1
Distance: 5f/6f: 0-0 **7f-8f: 1-2** 9f-13f: 0-2 14f+: 0-0
Track : LH: 0-1 RH: 0-1 Tight: 0-1 Gall: 0-0
Aids: Bl: 0-0 Vi: 0-0 Tstrap: 0-0
Best Rating: 74 6/01 Ling 7f firm

Showed promise on first three runs including a win at Musselburgh over seven furlongs on good ground, but she was a disappointing favourite at Pontefract in October.

Sean's Honor (IRE)

94(100) (57)**45**
3-y-o b f Mukaddamah (USA)-Great Land (USA) (Friend's Choice (USA))
Miss J F Craze (C N Kellett 17/4) Orange And Blue Partners

Placings:5440625**502533**-**5015520**010500000 **(5639)**
2001: 5^{5}SD, 5^{0}SD, 5^{1}SW, 5^{5}SW, 5^{5}SD, 5^{2}SD, 6^{0}SD, 6^{0}SD, 5^{1}F, 5^{0}F, 5^{5}G, 5^{0}G, 7^{0}GF, 6^{0}GS, 5^{0}SD, 5^{0}G

	Starts	1st	2nd	3rd	Win & Pl
Career Total (Turf)	14	1	1	0	1025
Career Total (AW)	15	1	2	2	3463

57 7/01 Muss 5f G FRM £1724
57 2/01 Ling 5f G SLW £1841
Total win prize-money £3565

Going (Turf): Sf: 0-1 GS: 0-3 Gd: 0-3 GF: 0-4 **Fm: 1-3**
Distance: **5f/6f: 2-28** 7f-8f: 0-1 9f-13f: 0-0 14f+: 0-0
Track : **LH: 1-13** RH: 0-0 **Tight: 1-8** Gall: 0-1
Aids: Bl: 0-0 **Vi: 2-19** Tstrap: 1-8
Best Rating: 57 7/01 Muss 5f firm

A winner of a five furlong seller on the All-Weather early in the season, she just got up for a dead-heat with Miss Equinox in a selling handicap over the same trip at Musselburgh in July.

Search And Destroy (USA)

104 **68+**
3-y-o b/br c Sky Classic (CAN)-Hunt The Thimble (USA) (Turn And Count (USA))
T R George (Sir Mark Prescott 4/8) Mrs R E R Rumboll

Placings:000-22116 **(3637)**
2001: 10^{2}GF, 13^{2}GF, 11^{1}F, 9^{1}GF, 12^{6}GS

	Starts	1st	2nd	3rd	Win & Pl
Career Total (Turf)	8	2	2	0	8392

68 7/01 Bevl 1m1f207yE(0-65) G-F £3304
66 7/01 Brig 1m3f196yE(0-75)H FRM £3523
Total win prize-money £6827

Going (Turf): Sf: 0-2 GS: 0-2 Gd: 0-0 **GF: 1-3 Fm: 1-1**
Distance: 5f/6f: 0-2 7f-8f: 0-1 **9f-13f: 2-4** 14f+: 0-1
Track : LH: 1-4 RH: 1-2 Tight: 0-1 Gall: 0-1
Aids: Bl: 0-0 Vi: 0-0 Tstrap: 0-0
Best Rating: 68 7/01 Bevl 1m1f207y gd-fm

Stepped up on his juvenile form when encountering a faster surface on reappearance at three. Scored over a mile and a half at Brighton in July, and followed up with another success at Beverley three weeks later when dropped back to ten furlongs. Acts on fast ground.

Search Party (FR)

91 **59**
2-y-o b g Efisio-Hunt The Thimble (FR) (Relkino)
T D Easterby M H Easterby

Placings:50000 **(4772)**
2001: 7^{5}GF, 7^{0}GF, 7^{0}G, 8^{0}GF, 7^{0}G

	Starts	1st	2nd	3rd	Win & Pl
Career Total (Turf)	5	0	0	0	0

Going (Turf): **Sf: 0-0 GS: 0-0 Gd: 0-2 GF: 0-3 Fm: 0-0**
Distance: 5f/6f: 0-0 7f-8f: 0-5 9f-13f: 0-0 14f+: 0-0
Track : LH: 0-1 RH: 0-4 Tight: 0-2 Gall: 0-0
Aids: Bl: 0-0 Vi: 0-0 Tstrap: 0-0
Best Rating: 67 7/01 Bevl 7f100y gd-fm

Seattle Alley (USA)

(90) (30)**37**
8-y-o b g Seattle Dancer (USA)-Alyanaabi (USA) (Roberto (USA))
D J Wintle Irish Racing Syndicate

Placings:0600/000411/35645/0/40 **(0258)**
2001: 11^{4}SD, 16^{0}SD

	Starts	1st	2nd	3rd	Win & Pl
Career Total (Turf)	14	2	0	0	8972
Career Total (AW)	4	0	0	1	425

68 6/96 Pont 1m2f6y D(0-75)H G-F £5526
63 6/96 Pont 1m2f6y E(0-70)H G-F £3158
Total win prize-money £8685

Going (Turf): Sf: 0-0 GS: 0-2 Gd: 0-7 **GF: 2-5** Fm: 0-0
Distance: 5f/6f: 0-1 7f-8f: 0-5 **9f-13f: 2-11** 14f+: 0-1
Track : **LH: 2-12** RH: 0-1 Tight: 0-6 Gall: 0-1
Aids: Bl: 0-0 Vi: 0-0 Tstrap: 0-0
Best Rating: 16 2/01 Wolv 2m46y stand

Seattle Prince (USA)

107 **78**
3-y-o gr c Cozzene (USA)-Chicken Slew (USA) (Seattle Slew (USA))
R Hannon Nicholas R Hodges

Placings:05360-601203015400 **(5373)**
2001: 10^{6}GF, 11^{0}G, 9^{1}GF, 10^{2}GF, 11^{0}GF, 14^{3}GF, 14^{0}G, 12^{1}GF, 14^{5}G, 16^{4}S, 14^{0}G, 14^{0}G

	Starts	1st	2nd	3rd	Win & Pl
Career Total (Turf)	17	2	1	2	11263

78 8/01 Sals 1m4f E(0-75)H G-F £3237
76 6/01 Sals 1m1f198yD(0-80)H G-F £4329
Total win prize-money £7567

Going (Turf): Sf: 0-3 GS: 0-0 Gd: 0-6 **GF: 2-8** Fm: 0-0
Distance: 5f/6f: 0-1 7f-8f: 0-1 **9f-13f: 2-9** 14f+: 0-6
Track : LH: 0-4 **RH: 2-9 Tight: 2-7** Gall: 0-2
Aids: Bl: 0-2 Vi: 0-2 Tstrap: 0-0
Best Rating: 78 9/01 Asct 2m45y soft

Got off the mark in a fast-run handicap at Salisbury in June and appreciated the mile and a half when scoring over that trip back at Salisbury in August. Best on fast ground.

Seba

101 **97**
2-y-o b f Alzao (USA)-Persian Secret (FR) (Persian Heights)
D R Loder Sheikh Mohammed

Placings:1105 **(4680)**
2001: 6^{1}GS, 7^{1}GF, 7^{0}GY, 8^{5}G

	Starts	1st	2nd	3rd	Win & Pl
Career Total (Turf)	4	2	0	0	30172

97 6/01 Asct 7f A G-F £24375
78 5/01 NmkR 6f D G-S £5447
Total win prize-money £29822

Going (Turf): Sf: 0-0 **GS: 1-1** Gd: 0-1 **GF: 1-1** Fm: 0-0
Distance: 5f/6f: 1-1 7f-8f: 1-3 9f-13f: 0-0 14f+: 0-0
Track : LH: 0-1 RH: 0-0 Tight: 0-0 Gall: 0-1
Aids: Bl: 0-0 Vi: 0-0 Tstrap: 0-0
Best Rating: 97 6/01 Asct 7f gd-fm

Won her Newmarket debut over six furlongs. A game winner of a Listed event over seven next time but subsequently disappointed in the Moyglare Stud Stakes. Has won on good to firm and good to soft.

Sebring

100 **72**
2-y-o ch c Hurricane Sky (AUS)-Carmenoura (IRE) (Carmelite House (USA))
N A Callaghan Brian Thrift

Placings:05044210 **(5668)**
2001: 5^{0}S, 5^{5}G, 6^{0}GF, 5^{4}F, 8^{4}GF, 8^{2}GF, 7^{1}GF, 8^{0}HY

	Starts	1st	2nd	3rd	Win & Pl
Career Total (Turf)	8	1	1	0	9521

72 9/01 Wwck 7f26y C(0-95)H G-F £7345
Total win prize-money £7345

Going (Turf): Sf: 0-2 GS: 0-0 Gd: 0-1 **GF: 1-4** Fm: 0-1
Distance: 5f/6f: 0-4 **7f-8f: 1-3** 9f-13f: 0-1 14f+: 0-0
Track : **LH: 1-2** RH: 0-3 Tight: 0-2 Gall: 0-1
Aids: Bl: 0-0 Vi: 0-0 Tstrap: 0-0
Best Rating: 72 9/01 Wwck 7f26y gd-fm

Is only small but showed ability in maidens before narrowly beaten in a nursery over a mile at Ripon. Went one better in a similar event over seven furlongs at Warwick, but is probably still better over the longer trip.

Sebulba (IRE)

(94) (70d)

3-y-o b/br g Dolphin Street (FR)-Twilight Calm (IRE) (Hatim (USA))
J G Given A Clarke

Placings:21605326-00 **(5616)**
2001: 8^{0}SD, 7^{0}SD, 8^{0}SD

	Starts	1st	2nd	3rd	Win & Pl
Career Total (Turf)	2	0	0	0	0
Career Total (AW)	8	1	2	1	4870
69 7/00 Sthl 6f F				STD	£2254

Total win prize-money £2254

Going (Turf): Sf: 0-0 GS: 0-1 Gd: 0-0 GF: 0-1 Fm: 0-0
Distance: 5f/6f: 1-4 7f-8f: 0-6 9f-13f: 0-0 14f+: 0-0
Track : LH: 1-8 RH: 0-1 Tight: 0-4 Gall: 0-0
Aids: Bl: 0-0 Vi: 0-0 Tstrap: 0-0
Best Rating: 59 10/01 Sthl 1m stand

Second Affair (IRE)

104 **78**

4-y-o b f Pursuit Of Love-Startino (Bustino)
Jedd O'Keeffe B McAllister

Placings:32422-22041 **(3858)**
2001: 9^{2}G, 9^{2}GF, 10^{0}S, 10^{4}GF, 11^{1}CS

	Starts	1st	2nd	3rd	Win & Pl
Career Total (Turf)	10	1	5	1	12548
76 8/01 Leic 1m3f183yD(0-75)				G-S	£4111

Total win prize-money £4111

Going (Turf): Sf: 0-3 **GS: 1-1** Gd: 0-2 GF: 0-4 Fm: 0-0
Distance: 5f/6f: 0-0 7f-8f: 0-0 **9f-13f: 1-10** 14f+: 0-0
Track : LH: 0-7 **RH: 1-3** Tight: 0-2 Gall. 0-3
Aids: Bl: 0-0 Vi: 0-0 Tstrap: 0-0
Best Rating: 78 6/01 Newc 1m1f9y gd-fm

A half-sister to Advance East. She got off the mark over 12 furlongs at Leicester. Acts on most ground, tends to make the running.

Second Burst (IRE)

62 **19**

2-y-o b f Sadler's Wells (USA)-Kanmary (FR) (Kenmare (FR))
J H M Gosden R E Sangster

Placings:0 **(5464)**
2001: 8^{0}HY

	Starts	1st	2nd	3rd	Win & Pl
Career Total (Turf)	1	0	0	0	

Going (Turf): Sf: 0-1 GS: 0-0 Gd: 0-0 GF: 0-0 Fm: 0-0
Distance: 5f/6f: 0-0 7f-8f: 0-1 9f-13f: 0-0 14f+: 0-0
Track : LH: 0-1 RH: 0-0 Tight: 0-0 Gall: 0-1
Aids: Bl: 0-0 Vi: 0-0 Tstrap: 0-0
Best Rating: 19 10/01 Donc 1m heavy

Second Generation (IRE)

94(89) (31)**45**

4-y-o ch g Cadeaux Genereux-Title Roll (IRE) (Tate Gallery (USA))
D R C Elsworth Graham Dalziel

Placings:05000006-0 **(1072)**
2001: 5^{0}GS

	Starts	1st	2nd	3rd	Win & Pl
Career Total (Turf)	7	0	0	0	0
Career Total (AW)	2	0	0	0	0

Going (Turf): Sf: 0-2 GS: 0-1 Gd: 0-3 GF: 0-0 Fm: 0-1
Distance: 5f/6f: 0-7 7f-8f: 0-2 9f-13f: 0-0 14f+; 0-0
Track : LH: 0-4 RH: 0-0 Tight: 0-2 Gall: 0-1
Aids: Bl: 0-2 Vi: 0-0 Tstrap: 0-0
Best Rating: 23 5/01 Brig 5f213y gd-sft

Second Minister

95 **75**

2-y-o ch c Lion Cavern (USA)-Crime Of Passion (Dragonara Palace (USA))
J M P Eustace R Carstairs

Placings:4520 **(4449)**
2001: 5^{4}GF, 6^{5}G, 5^{2}GF, 6^{0}GF

	Starts	1st	2nd	3rd	Win & Pl
Career Total (Turf)	4	0	1	0	1438

Going (Turf): Sf: 0-0 GS: 0-0 Gd: 0-1 GF: 0-3 Fm: 0-0
Distance: 5f/6f: 0-4 7f-8f: 0-0 9f-13f: 0-0 14f+: 0-0
Track : LH: 0-0 RH: 0-1 Tight: 0-0 Gall: 0-1
Aids: Bl: 0-0 Vi: 0-0 Tstrap: 0-0
Best Rating: 75 7/01 Sand 5f6y gd-fm

Second Paige (IRE)

103(83) (22)**69**

4-y-o b g Nicolotte-My First Paige (IRE) (Runnett)
N A Graham Coronation Partnership

Placings:000/40221150-50202460 **(5463)**
2001: 12^{5}G, 11^{0}GF, 14^{2}GF, 14^{0}GF, 14^{2}G, 14^{4}GS, 13^{6}GS, 11^{0}G

	Starts	1st	2nd	3rd	Win & Pl
Career Total (Turf)	17	2	4	0	10846
Career Total (AW)	2	0	0	0	
74 7/00 Wind 1m3f135yD(0-85)H				GD	£3887
71 6/00 Wind 1m3f135yE(0-75)H				G-F	£2940

Total win prize-money £6827

Going (Turf): Sf: 0-1 GS: 0-4 **Gd: 1-5 GF: 1-7** Fm: 0-0
Distance: 5f/6f: 0-0 7f-8f: 0-2 **9f-13f: 2-12** 14f+: 0-5
Track : LH: 0-7 RH: 0-6 **Tight: 2-13** Gall: 0-1
Aids: Bl: 0-4 Vi: 0-0 Tstrap: 0-0
Best Rating: 69 10/01 Sals 1m6f15y gd-sft

He won twice over the extended 11 furlongs at Windsor in the summer of 2000 and has run well since, though he has not always looked a straightforward ride. Best on fast ground.

Second Strike

93 **66**

3-y-o b g Kris-Honeyspike (IRE) (Chief's Crown (USA))
B Smart The Family Partnership

Placings:53-6050 **(4180)**
2001: 6^{6}GF, 10^{0}GF, 7^{5}F, 9^{0}GF

	Starts	1st	2nd	3rd	Win & Pl
Career Total (Turf)	6	0	0	1	1183

Going (Turf): Sf: 0-1 GS: 0-0 Gd: 0-1 GF: 0-3 Fm: 0-1
Distance: 5f/6f: 0-1 7f-8f: 0-3 9f-13f: 0-2 14f+: 0-0
Track : LH: 0-1 RH: 0-3 Tight: 0-3 Gall: 0-0
Aids: Bl: 0-0 Vi: 0-0 Tstrap: 0-0
Best Rating: 58 7/01 Wind 1m2f7y gd-fm

Second Time Around (IRE)

(87) (3)

4-y-o b f Mukaddamah (USA)-Up The Gates (Captain James)
M C Chapman Eric Knowles

Placings:00000030/0-00000 **(0304)**
2001: 11^{0}SD, 12^{0}SD, 8^{0}SD, 12^{0}SW, 16^{0}SD

	Starts	1st	2nd	3rd	Win & Pl
Career Total (Turf)	7	0	0	1	275
Career Total (AW)	7	0	0	0	

Going (Turf): Sf: 0-0 GS: 0-0 Gd: 0-3 GF: 0-3 Fm: 0-1
Distance: 5f/6f: 0-3 7f-8f: 0-7 9f-13f: 0-3 14f+: 0-1
Track : LH: 0-7 RH: 0-0 Tight: 0-0 Gall: 0-0
Aids: Bl: 0-0 Vi: 0-0 Tstrap: 0-0
Best Rating: 3 1/01 Sthl 1m stand

Second Venture (IRE)

101 **71**

3-y-o b c Petardia-Hilton Gateway (Hello Gorgeous (USA))
J R Weymes C I North Racing Club

Placings:032444-300 **(2216)**
2001: 6^{3}GS, 7^{0}G, 7^{0}G

	Starts	1st	2nd	3rd	Win & Pl
Career Total (Turf)	9	0	1	2	4555

Going (Turf): Sf: 0-2 GS: 0-2 Gd: 0-4 GF: 0-0 Fm: 0-1
Distance: 5f/6f: 0-5 7f-8f: 0-4 9f-13f: 0-0 14f+: 0-0
Track : LH: 0-4 RH: 0-0 Tight: 0-1 Gall: 0-0
Aids: Bl: 0-0 Vi: 0-0 Tstrap: 0-0
Best Rating: 56 5/01 Pont 6f gd-sft

Second Wind

98 **63**

6-y-o ch g Kris-Rimosa's Pet (Petingo)
I A Wood (C A Dwyer 16/4) John Purcell

Placings:1/55200600/00660110006304/1500124054-000050 **(3586)**
2001: 7^{0}S, 6^{0}G, 8^{0}GS, 6^{0}GF, 6^{5}G, 9^{0}G

	Starts	1st	2nd	3rd	Win & Pl
Career Total (Turf)	39	5	2	1	34734
84 6/00 NmkJ 7f C(0-95)H				G-F	£7865
79 4/00 Leic 7f9y D(0-85)H				G-S	£4160
70 7/99 Epsm 7f D(0-80)H				G-F	£4970
66 7/99 Brig 6f209y F				FRM	£2622
79 4/97 NmkR 5f C				G-F	£4213

Total win prize-money £23731

Going (Turf): Sf: 0-7 GS: 1-5 Gd: 0-8 **GF: 3-16** Fm: 1-3
Distance: 5f/6f: 1-13 **7f-8f: 4-20** 9f-13f: 0-6 14f+: 0-0
Track : **LH: 2-9** RH: 0-8 **Tight: 1-4** Gall: 0-8
Aids: Bl: 0-0 Vi: 0-0 **Tstrap: 3-14**
Best Rating: 63 6/01 Epsm 6f gd-fm

Best over seven furlongs, he won over that trip at both Leicester and Newmarket in 2000. Has won on soft ground, but looks better on a faster surface. Below par for new stable this term.

Secret Angel (USA)

68

3-y-o gr f Colonial Affair (USA)-Petong Secret (Petong)
G C H Chung H C Chung

Placings:50 **(5464)**
2001: 9^{5}F, 11^{0}G

	Starts	1st	2nd	3rd	Win & Pl
Career Total (Turf)	2	0	0	0	0

Going (Turf): Sf: 0-0 GS: 0-0 Gd: 0-1 GF: 0-0 Fm: 0-1
Distance: 5f/6f: 0-0 7f-8f: 0-0 9f-13f: 0-2 14f+: 0-0
Track : LH: 0-2 RH: 0-0 Tight: 0-1 Gall: 0-0
Aids: Bl: 0-0 Vi: 0-0 Tstrap: 0-0
Best Rating: 63 6/01 Epsm 6f gd-fm

Secret Conquest

105(78) (16)**51**

4-y-o b f Secret Appeal-Mohibbah (USA) (Conquistador Cielo (USA))
D W Barker Keith Nicholson

Placings:3001212100/00645000-0046431206040500 **(5406)**
2001: 8^{0}GS, 8^{0}GS, 7^{4}F, 7^{6}GF, 8^{4}GF, 7^{3}GF, 7^{1}GF, 7^{2}GF, 7^{0}GF, 7^{6}GF, 7^{0}C, 7^{4}CF, 0^{0}G, 7^{6}GF, 7^{0}G, 8^{0}SD

	Starts	1st	2nd	3rd	Win & Pl
Career Total (Turf)	34	4	3	2	21748
Career Total (AW)	1	0	0	0	
57 6/01 Donc 7f E(0-70)H				G-F	£4758
79 8/99 Catt 5f212y D H				G-F	£4575
69 7/99 Catt 7f D H				GD	£4614
65 7/99 Hayd 6f G				G-S	£1997

Total win prize-money £15945

Going (Turf): Sf: 0-2 GS: 1-6 Gd: 1-8 **GF: 2-15** Fm: 0-3
Distance: 5f/6f: 2-10 7f-8f: 2-23 9f-13f: 0-2 14f+: 0-0
Track : **LH: 2-12** RH: 0-6 **Tight: 2-7** Gall: 0-3
Aids: **Bl: 1-13** Vi: 0-0 Tstrap: 0-0
Best Rating: 57 6/01 Donc 7f gd-fm

She rather lost her form after winning three times as a juvenile, but a drop in the handicap has seen her running better and she returned to winning form at Doncaster in June. Has won on softish ground, but looks better on a faster surface.

Secret Flutter (IRE)

86 **72**

2-y-o b f Entrepreneur-Spend A Rubble (USA) (Spend A Buck (USA))
J G Portman Mrs Seamus Burns

Placings:40 **(5295)**
2001: 8^{4}HY, 8^{0}S

	Starts	1st	2nd	3rd	Win & Pl
Career Total (Turf)	2	0	0	0	356

Going (Turf): Sf: 0-2 GS: 0-0 Gd: 0-0 GF: 0-0 Fm: 0-0
Distance: 5f/6f: 0-0 7f-8f: 0-0 9f-13f: 0-2 14f+: 0-0
Track : LH: 0-1 RH: 0-0 Tight: 0-0 Gall: 0-0
Aids: Bl: 0-0 Vi: 0-0 Tstrap: 0-0
Best Rating: 72 9/01 Hayd 1m30y heavy

Secret Passion

(102) (52)

3-y-o gr f Petong-Jamarj (Tyrnavos)
P W D'Arcy Marinos Ioannou

Placings:664-0 **(5613)**
2001: 9^{0}SD

	Starts	1st	2nd	3rd	Win & Pl
Career Total (Turf)	2	0	0	0	0
Career Total (AW)	2	0	0	0	0

Going (Turf): Sf: 0-0 GS: 0-1 Gd: 0-0 GF: 0-1 Fm: 0-0
Distance: 5f/6f: 0-0 7f-8f: 0-2 9f-13f: 0-2 14f+: 0-0
Track : LH: 0-4 RH: 0-0 Tight: 0-2 Gall: 0-0
Aids: Bl: 0-0 Vi: 0-0 Tstrap: 0-0
Best Rating: 22 11/01 Wolv 1m1f79y stand

Secret Sentiment

89 **66**

3-y-o b f Mark Of Esteem (IRE)-Sahara Baladee (USA) (Shadeed (USA))
E A L Dunlop Maktoum Al Maktoum

Placings:0-0500 **(4844)**
2001: 8^{0}G, 11^{5}GF, 14^{0}F, 9^{0}G

	Starts	1st	2nd	3rd	Win & Pl
Career Total (Turf)	5	0	0	0	0

Going (Turf): Sf: 0-1 GS: 0-0 Gd: 0-2 GF: 0-1 Fm: 0-1
Distance: 5f/6f: 0-1 7f-8f: 0-0 9f-13f: 0-3 14f+: 0-1
Track : LH: 0-2 RH: 0-1 Tight: 0-1 Gall: 0-0
Aids: Bl: 0-0 Vi: 0-0 Tstrap: 0-0
Best Rating: 66 5/01 Hayd 1m3f200y gd-fm

Secret Spoof

99 **79**

2-y-o b c Mind Games-Silver Blessings (Statoblest)
T D Easterby David & Steven Dudley

Placings:045310050 **(5253)**
2001: 5^{0}GS, 5^{4}G, 5^{5}GF, 5^{3}G, 6^{1}GF, 6^{0}GF, 6^{0}GS, 5^{5}GS, 6^{0}S

	Starts	1st	2nd	3rd	Win & Pl
Career Total (Turf)	9	1	0	1	8244

79 8/01 Rdcr 6f C G-F £7605
Total win prize-money £7605

Going (Turf): Sf: 0-1 GS: 0-3 Gd: 0-2 GF: 1-3 Fm: 0-0
Distance: **5f/6f: 1-9** 7f-8f: 0-0 9f-13f: 0-0 14f+: 0-0
Track : LH: 0-1 RH: 0-0 Tight: 0-0 Gall: 0-0
Aids: Bl: 0-0 Vi: 0-0 Tstrap: 0-0
Best Rating: 79 10/01 NmkR 5f gd-sft

Gradually improved with racing and got off the mark on his first attempt at six furlongs in a Redcar nursery in August but has been disappointing in soft ground since. Suited by good to firm.

Secret Style

(82) (38) **74**

6-y-o b g Shirley Heights-Rosie Potts (Shareef Dancer (USA))
R Hollinshead Mrs B Ramsden

Placings:44/06004112/3-00 **(0049)**
2001: 16^{0}SD, 16^{0}SD

	Starts	1st	2nd	3rd	Win & Pl
Career Total (Turf)	11	2	1	1	6530
Career Total (AW)	2	0	0	0	

73 7/99 LES 1m7f H G-F £900
70 6/99 Nott 2m9y F GD £2427
Total win prize-money £3327

Going (Turf): Sf: 0-3 GS: 0-0 **Gd: 1-3 GF: 1-4** Fm: 0-0
Distance: 5f/6f: 0-0 7f-8f: 0-0 9f-13f: 0-2 **14f+: 2-10**
Track : **LH: 2-8** RH: 0-3 Tight: 0-3 Gall: 0-3
Aids: **Bl: 1-3** Vi: 0-0 Tstrap: 0-0
Best Rating: 38 1/01 Sthl 2m stand

Won a Nottingham claimer in 1999 before being sold to race in Jersey. Now with R. Hollinshead.

Secretario

91 (102) (24) **17**

4-y-o b f Efisio-Lucidity (Vision (USA))
J Hetherton C D Barber-Lomax

Placings:00/66000000500**00065-33440000** **(1138)**
2001: 12^{3}SW, 12^{3}SD, 12^{4}SD, 12^{4}SW, 16^{0}SD, 14^{0}SD, 11^{0}SD, 13^{0}G

	Starts	1st	2nd	3rd	Win & Pl
Career Total (Turf)	12	0	0	0	0
Career Total (AW)	14	0	0	2	636

Going (Turf): Sf: 0-2 GS: 0-1 Gd: 0-4 GF: 0-5 Fm: 0-0
Distance: 5f/6f: 0-1 7f-8f: 0-6 9f-13f: 0-15 14f+: 0-4
Track : LH: 0-17 RH: 0-5 Tight: 0-8 Gall: 0-0
Aids: Bl: 0-4 Vi: 0-1 Tstrap: 0-0
Best Rating: 41 1/01 Sthl 1m4f slow

Secrete Contract

89 **60**

3-y-o b c Contract Law (USA)-Secret Account (Blakeney)
G L Moore The Secrete Society Partnership

Placings:6-000 **(1480)**
2001: 11^{0}GS, 10^{0}GS, 11^{0}G

	Starts	1st	2nd	3rd	Win & Pl
Career Total (Turf)	4	0	0	0	0

Going (Turf): Sf: 0-1 GS: 0-2 Gd: 0-1 GF: 0-0 Fm: 0-0
Distance: 5f/6f: 0-0 7f-8f: 0-1 9f-13f: 0-3 14f+: 0-0
Track : LH: 0-2 RH: 0-1 Tight: 0-2 Gall: 0-1
Aids: Bl: 0-0 Vi: 0-0 Tstrap: 0-0
Best Rating: 33 5/01 Wind 1m3f135y good

Secreto Dreams (IRE)

91 **79**

2-y-o b c Distinctly North (USA)-Whittingham Girl (Primo Dominie)
S E Kettlewell Cable Media Consultancy Ltd

Placings:30402 **(5405)**
2001: 5^{3}G, 6^{0}GF, 5^{4}GS, 6^{0}S, 6^{2}S

	Starts	1st	2nd	3rd	Win & Pl
Career Total (Turf)	5	0	1	1	2174

Going (Turf): Sf: 0-2 GS: 0-1 Gd: 0-1 GF: 0-1 Fm: 0-0
Distance: 5f/6f: 0-5 7f-8f: 0-0 9f-13f: 0-0 14f+: 0-0
Track : LH: 0-1 RH: 0-0 Tight: 0-0 Gall: 0-0
Aids: Bl: 0-0 Vi: 0-0 Tstrap: 0-0
Best Rating: 79 10/01 Pont 6f soft

A half-brother to Inzacure who won over five and six furlongs as a juvenile. Showed ability on his debut but was slightly disappointing on good to firm ground in lesser company next time, but bounced right back to form at Pontefract when second to a nice sort. Might be better suited by an easier surface.

Securite (ARG)

97 (69)**99**

6-y-o ch h Southern Halo (USA)-Sesig (ARG) (Cinco Grande (USA))
Diego Lowther Buenos Aires Stallions H B

Placings:0161-C013150000 **(5004)**
2001: 5^{C}HY, 5^{0}HY, 6^{1}SD, 6^{3}FT, 6^{1}SD, 8^{5}S, 6^{0}G, 6^{0}SD, 5^{0}S, 6^{0}S

	Starts	1st	2nd	3rd	Win & Pl
Career Total (Turf)	8	0	0	0	1073
Career Total (AW)	6	4	0	1	20622

5/01 Taby 6f STD £3577
5/01 Jage 6f STD £3219
9/00 Jage 6f H STD £7310
8/00 Taby 6f165y STD £3655
Total win prize-money £17761

Going (Turf): Sf: 0-6 GS: 0-0 Gd: 0-2 GF: 0-0 Fm: 0-0
Distance: **5f/6f: 3-9** 7f-8f: 1-5 9f-13f: 0-0 14f+: 0-0
Track : LH: 0-2 RH: 0-0 Tight: 0-0 Gall: 0-0
Aids: Bl: 0-0 Vi: 0-0 Tstrap: 0-0
Best Rating: 99 7/01 Hopp 6f110y good

Winner on dirt in Sweden over six furlongs.

Security Council

81 **63**

3-y-o b c Polish Precedent (USA)-Set Fair (USA) (Alleged (USA))
B W Hills K Abdulla

Placings:5-0 **(1295)**
2001: 10^{0}G

	Starts	1st	2nd	3rd	Win & Pl
Career Total (Turf)	2	0	0	0	0

Going (Turf): Sf: 0-1 GS: 0-0 Gd: 0-1 GF: 0-0 Fm: 0-0
Distance: 5f/6f: 0-0 7f-8f: 0-1 9f-13f: 0-1 14f+: 0-0
Track : LH: 0-1 RH: 0-0 Tight: 0-1 Gall: 0-0
Aids: Bl: 0-0 Vi: 0-0 Tstrap: 0-0
Best Rating: 22 5/01 Ling 1m2f good

A February foal, is not very big and has a pronounced knee action. Saddle slipped on only outing this season.

Security Tag (USA)

95 **79**

2-y-o ch c Known Fact (USA)-Secret Angel (Halo (USA))
Mrs A J Perrett K Abdulla

Placings:46 **(4671)**
2001: 7^{4}GF, 8^{6}G

	Starts	1st	2nd	3rd	Win & Pl
Career Total (Turf)	2	0	0	0	327

Going (Turf): Sf: 0-0 GS: 0-0 Gd: 0-1 GF: 0-1 Fm: 0-0
Distance: 5f/6f: 0-0 7f-8f: 0-1 9f-13f: 0-1 14f+: 0-0
Track : LH: 0-0 RH: 0-1 Tight: 0-0 Gall: 0-0
Aids: Bl: 0-0 Vi: 0-0 Tstrap: 0-1
Best Rating: 79 9/01 Chep 1m14y good

Securon Dancer

96 47

3-y-o b f Emperor Jones (USA)-Gena Ivor (USA) (Sir Ivor)

R Rowe Mrs R A Proctor

Placings:40600-004000 (5100)

2001: 6^{0}GF, 6^{0}GF, 9^{4}GF, 10^{0}S, 7^{0}G, 9^{0}GS

	Starts	1st	2nd	3rd	Win & Pl
Career Total (Turf)	11	0	0	0	478

Going (Turf): Sf: 0-2 GS: 0-1 Gd: 0-2 GF: 0-5 Fm: 0-0
Distance: 5f/6f: 0-4 7f-8f: 0-3 9f-13f: 0-3 14f+: 0-0
Track : LH: 0-2 RH: 0-2 Tight: 0-3 Gall: 0-0
Aids: Bl: 0-0 Vi: 0-0 Tstrap: 0-0
Best Rating: 47 7/01 Folk 1m1f149y gd-fm

Seeing Reality (IRE)

81(83) (38)30

2-y-o b f Bin Ajwaad (IRE)-Visage (Vision (USA))

P D Evans P D Evans

Placings:0500 (1633)

2001: 5^{0}S, 5^{5}SD, 5^{0}GF, 5^{0}F

	Starts	1st	2nd	3rd	Win & Pl
Career Total (Turf)	3	0	0	0	
Career Total (AW)	1	0	0	0	0

Going (Turf): Sf: 0-1 GS: 0-0 Gd: 0-0 GF: 0-1 Fm: 0-1
Distance: 5f/6f: 0-4 7f-8f: 0-0 9f-13f: 0-0 14f+: 0-0
Track : LH: 0-0 RH: 0-0 Tight: 0-0 Gall: 0-0
Aids: Bl: 0-0 Vi: 0-2 Tstrap: 0-0
Best Rating: 38 4/01 Sthl 5f stand

Seek

93(89) (43)92

5-y-o br g Rainbow Quest (USA)-Souk (IRE) (Ahonoora)

J A B Old W E Sturt

Placings:21/2510-0000 (1377)

2001: 11^{0}SD, 12^{0}S, 12^{0}G, 13^{0}GF

	Starts	1st	2nd	3rd	Win & Pl
Career Total (Turf)	9	2	2	0	27584
Career Total (AW)	1	0	0	0	

92 8/00 York 1m3f195yC(0-95)H GD £19977
75 7/99 Pont 1m4f8y D G-S £3566
Total win prize-money £23544

Going (Turf): Sf: 0-2 **GS: 1-2 Gd: 1-3** GF: 0-2 Fm: 0-0
Distance: 5f/6f: 0-0 7f-8f: 0-0 **9f-13f: 2-8** 14f+: 0-2
Track : **LH: 2-6** RH: 0-4 Tight: 0-1 **Gall: 1-6**
Aids: Bl: 0-0 Vi: 0-0 Tstrap: 0-0
Best Rating: 82 5/01 NmkR 1m4f good

He landed a punt at York's Ebor Meeting in 2000, but failed to run up to that form for his new stable.

Seek The Light (USA)

87(102) (58)71

4-y-o b g Seeking The Gold (USA)-Jolypha (USA) (Lyphard (USA))

C J Gray (G L Moore 11/7) D J Staddon

Placings:64004-223400 (2941)

2001: 12^{2}SD, 10^{2}SD, 12^{3}SD, 10^{4}SW, 9^{0}F, 10^{0}GF

	Starts	1st	2nd	3rd	Win & Pl
Career Total (Turf)	5	0	0	0	335
Career Total (AW)	6	0	2	1	2297

Going (Turf): Sf: 0-1 GS: 0-0 Gd: 0-2 GF: 0-1 Fm: 0-1
Distance: 5f/6f: 0-0 7f-8f: 0-0 9f-13f: 0-11 14f+: 0-0
Track : LH: 0-9 RH: 0-1 Tight: 0-8 Gall: 0-0
Aids: Bl: 0-5 Vi: 0-0 Tstrap: 0-0
Best Rating: 58 1/01 Ling 1m2f stand

Seeking Sanctuary

(86) (21)42

4-y-o ch f Most Welcome-Tjakka (USA) (Little Missouri (USA))

Dr J D Scargill Mrs V Bayley

Placings:0/00450-0 (0115)

2001: 9^{0}SW

	Starts	1st	2nd	3rd	Win & Pl
Career Total (Turf)	5	0	0	0	279
Career Total (AW)	2	0	0	0	

Going (Turf): Sf: 0-0 GS: 0-1 Gd: 0-1 GF: 0-2 Fm: 0-1
Distance: 5f/6f: 0-0 7f-8f: 0-3 9f-13f: 0-4 14f+: 0-0
Track : LH: 0-3 RH: 0-1 Tight: 0-4 Gall: 0-0
Aids: Bl: 0-0 Vi: 0-0 Tstrap: 0-0
Best Rating: 21 1/01 Wolv 1m1f79y slow

Seeking The Sun (IRE)

97 85

2-y-o b/br c Petardia-Femme Savante (Glenstal (USA))

C F Wall The Boardroom Syndicate

Placings:6105 (5364)

2001: 5^{6}GF, 6^{1}GS, 7^{0}GF, 6^{5}GS

	Starts	1st	2nd	3rd	Win & Pl
Career Total (Turf)	4	1	0	0	8214

85 8/01 Hayd 6f E G-S £3584
Total win prize-money £3584

Going (Turf): Sf: 0-0 **GS: 1-2** Gd: 0-0 GF: 0-2 Fm: 0-0
Distance: **5f/6f: 1-3** 7f-8f: 0-1 9f-13f: 0-0 14f+: 0-0
Track : LH: 0-1 RH: 0-1 Tight: 0-0 Gall: 0-1
Aids: Bl: 0-0 Vi: 0-0 Tstrap: 0-0
Best Rating: 85 10/01 NmkR 6f gd-sft

Got off the mark with a clear-cut victory in a six furlong Haydock maiden auction event in August but was disappointing next time when up in grade. Did not get the run of the race when fifth in the Tattersalls Autumn Auction Stakes. Acts well with cut in the ground.

Seel Of Approval

88 65

2-y-o br c Polar Falcon (USA)-Petit Point (IRE) (Petoriuc)

M D I Usher A G Morgan

Placings:004 (4260)

2001: 5^{0}GF, 5^{0}G, 6^{4}GF

	Starts	1st	2nd	3rd	Win & Pl
Career Total (Turf)	3	0	0	0	303

Going (Turf): Sf: 0-0 GS: 0-0 Gd: 0-1 GF: 0-2 Fm: 0-0
Distance: 5f/6f: 0-3 7f-8f: 0-0 9f-13f: 0-0 14f+: 0-0
Track : LH: 0-0 RH: 0-1 Tight: 0-0 Gall: 0-1
Aids: Bl: 0-0 Vi: 0-0 Tstrap: 0-0
Best Rating: 65 6/01 Wind 5f10y good

Seems So Easy (USA)

73 18

2-y-o b f Palmister (USA)-I'm An Issue (USA) (Cox's Ridge (USA))

S Magnier Marcus Reeder

Placings:0 (5184)

2001: 5^{0}GS

	Starts	1st	2nd	3rd	Win & Pl
Career Total (Turf)	1	0	0	0	

Going (Turf): Sf: 0-0 GS: 0-1 Gd: 0-0 GF: 0-0 Fm: 0-0
Distance: 5f/6f: 0-1 7f-8f: 0-0 9f-13f: 0-0 14f+: 0-0
Track : LH: 0-0 RH: 0-0 Tight: 0-0 Gall: 0-0
Aids: Bl: 0-0 Vi: 0-0 Tstrap: 0-0
Best Rating: 18 10/01 Catt 5f gd-sft

Seeyouf (IRE)

96 72

3-y-o b c Danehill (USA)-Leipzig (Relkino)

E A L Dunlop Mohammed Jaber

Placings:033 (4446)

2001: 7^{0}GS, 7^{3}GS, 9^{3}G

	Starts	1st	2nd	3rd	Win & Pl
Career Total (Turf)	3	0	0	2	1290

Going (Turf): Sf: 0-0 GS: 0-2 Gd: 0-1 GF: 0-0 Fm: 0-0
Distance: 5f/6f: 0-0 7f-8f: 0-2 9f-13f: 0-1 14f+: 0-0
Track : LH: 0-0 RH: 0-1 Tight: 0-0 Gall: 0-0
Aids: Bl: 0-0 Vi: 0-0 Tstrap: 0-0
Best Rating: 72 7/01 NmkJ 7f gd-sft

Sefton Lodge

64 13

2-y-o b c Barathea (IRE)-Pine Needle (Kris)

J Noseda Lucayan Stud

Placings:0 (4864)

2001: 7^{0}GF

	Starts	1st	2nd	3rd	Win & Pl
Career Total (Turf)	1	0	0	0	

Going (Turf): Sf: 0-0 GS: 0-0 Gd: 0-0 GF: 0-1 Fm: 0-0
Distance: 5f/6f: 0-0 7f-8f: 0-1 9f-13f: 0-0 14f+: 0-0
Track : LH: 0-0 RH: 0-0 Tight: 0-0 Gall: 0-0
Aids: Bl: 0-0 Vi: 0-0 Tstrap: 0-0
Best Rating: 13 9/01 Newb 7f gd-fm

Seignosse (IRE)

103 73

3-y-o b g College Chapel-How Ya Been (IRE) (Last Tycoon)

I A Balding The Pink Hat Partnership

Placings:3130 (5252)

2001: 5^{3}F, 5^{1}G, 5^{3}GS, 5^{0}S

	Starts	1st	2nd	3rd	Win & Pl
Career Total (Turf)	4	1	0	2	5727

54 9/01 Bevi 5f D GD £4413
Total win prize-money £4414

Going (Turf): Sf: 0-1 GS: 0-1 **Gd: 1-1** GF: 0-0 Fm: 0-1
Distance: **5f/6f: 1-4** 7f-8f: 0-0 9f-13f: 0-0 14f+: 0-0
Track : LH: 0-1 RH: 0-0 Tight: 0-0 Gall: 0-1
Aids: Bl: 0-0 Vi: 0-0 Tstrap: 0-0
Best Rating: 73 10/01 NmkR 5f gd-sft

Seihali (IRE)

100 83

2-y-o b c Alzao (USA)-Edwina (IRE) (Caerleon (USA))

A C Stewart Sheikh Ahmed Al Maktoum

Placings:61 (5080)

2001: 6^{6}G, 6^{1}S

	Starts	1st	2nd	3rd	Win & Pl
Career Total (Turf)	2	1	0	0	3010

83 10/01 Brig 6f209y D SFT £3010
Total win prize-money £3010

Going (Turf): **Sf: 1-1** GS: 0-0 Gd: 0-1 GF: 0-0 Fm: 0-0
Distance: 5f/6f: 0-1 **7f-8f: 1-1** 9f-13f: 0-0 14f+: 0-0
Track : **LH: 1-1** RH: 0-0 Tight: 0-0 Gall: 0-0
Aids: Bl: 0-0 Vi: 0-0 Tstrap: 0-0
Best Rating: 83 10/01 Brig 6f209y soft

Caught the eye on his debut and improved from that to win a seven-furlong Brighton maiden next time. Should stay a mile.

Sel

95(87) (54)46

3-y-o b f Salse (USA)-Frog (Akarad (FR))

G L Moore John Hetherington

Placings:3512510560-205043645					(5524)

2001: 10^{2}SD, 10^{0}SD, 10^{5}GF, 9^{0}GF, 7^{4}G, 7^{3}GF, 9^{6}S, 9^{4}S, 10^{5}HY

	Starts	1st	2nd	3rd	Win & Pl
Career Total (Turf)	16	2	1	2	5286
Career Total (AW)	3	0	1	0	622

60 8/00 Brig 6f209y F FRM £2205
57 7/00 Brig 6f209y G G-S £1834
Total win prize-money £4039

Going (Turf): Sf: 0-6 **GS: 1-1** Gd: 0-2 GF: 0-4 **Fm: 1-3**
Distance: 5f/6f: 0-0 **7f-8f: 2-12** 9f-13f: 0-7 14f+: 0-0
Track : **LH: 2-14** RH: 0-2 Tight: 0-4 Gall: 0-1
Aids: **Bl: 2-17** Vi: 0-0 Tstrap: 0-0
Best Rating: 54 1/01 Ling 1m2f stand

Won twice in 2000 at Brighton over seven furlongs, but she has been well held since then. Acts on most types of ground.

Selective

98 **85**
2-y-o b c Selkirk (USA)-Portelet (Night Shift (USA))
A C Stewart Bruce Corman

Placings:02 (5089)
2001: 7^{0}GF, 8^{2}GS

	Starts	1st	2nd	3rd	Win & Pl
Career Total (Turf)	2	0	1	0	874

Going (Turf): Sf: 0-0 GS: 0-1 Gd: 0-0 GF: 0-1 Fm: 0-0
Distance: 5f/6f: 0-0 7f-8f: 0-2 9f-13f: 0-0 14f+: 0-0
Track : LH: 0-1 RH: 0-0 Tight: 0-0 Gall: 0-1
Aids: Bl: 0-0 Vi: 0-0 Tstrap: 0-0
Best Rating: 85 10/01 Newc 1m gd-sft

Good effort when runner-up in a backend Newcastle maiden.

Self Propelled (IRE)

87 **55**
3-y-o b f Caerleon (USA)-Self Assured (IRE) (Ahonoora)
C E Brittain Ali Saeed

Placings:46 (3458)
2001: 10^{4}GF, 9^{6}GF

	Starts	1st	2nd	3rd	Win & Pl
Career Total (Turf)	2	0	0	0	274

Going (Turf): Sf: 0-0 GS: 0-0 Gd: 0-0 GF: 0-2 Fm: 0-0
Distance: 5f/6f: 0-0 7f-8f: 0-0 9f-13f: 0-2 14f+: 0-0
Track : LH: 0-2 RH: 0-0 Tight: 0-0 Gall: 0-0
Aids: Bl: 0-0 Vi: 0-0 Tstrap: 0-0
Best Rating: 55 7/01 Nott 1m1f213y gd-fm

Seliana

113 **82**
5-y-o b m Unfuwain (USA)-Anafi (Slip Anchor)
G Wragg L Marinopoulos

Placings:0/3/2340223-100 (5387)
2001: 16^{1}GS, 16^{0}S, 18^{0}GS

	Starts	1st	2nd	3rd	Win & Pl
Career Total (Turf)	12	1	3	3	24983

82 4/01 Newb 2m C(0-100)H G-S £6955
Total win prize-money £6955

Going (Turf): Sf: 0-4 **GS: 1-4** Gd: 0-1 GF: 0-3 Fm: 0-0
Distance: 5f/6f: 0-0 7f-8f: 0-1 9f-13f: 0-3 **14f+: 1-8**
Track : **LH: 1-5** RH: 0-6 Tight: 0-4 Gall: 0-3
Aids: Bl: 0-0 Vi: 0-0 Tstrap: 0-0
Best Rating: 82 4/01 Newb 2m gd-sft

Finished runner-up in the Ascot and Goodwood Stakes in 2000. Won at Newbury first time out in April, but was then off the track for five months. Stays well, acts on fast ground, but her only win was with cut.

Sellinger's Round (IRE)

90(91) (27)**33**
5-y-o ch g Lucky Guest-Cellophane (Coquelin (USA))
Mrs L C Jewell The Likely Bunch

Placings:665/00363300000-0500 (3297)
2001: 6^{0}G, 11^{5}F, 9^{0}F, 6^{0}GF

	Starts	1st	2nd	3rd	Win & Pl
Career Total (Turf)	15	0	0	3	1085
Career Total (AW)	3	0	0	0	

Going (Turf): Sf: 0-1 GS: 0-0 Gd: 0-3 GF: 0-3 Fm: 0-5
Distance: 5f/6f: 0-1 7f-8f: 0-11 9f-13f: 0-5 14f+: 0-0
Track : LH: 0-12 RH: 0-3 Tight: 0-2 Gall: 0-0
Aids: Bl: 0-0 Vi: 0-4 Tstrap: 0-0
Best Rating: 33 6/01 Brig 1m1f209y firm

Selwan (USA)

97 **78**
2-y-o b f Mt. Livermore (USA)-Dubian (High Line)
D R Loder Sheikh Mohammed

Placings:3 (4775)
2001: 7^{3}G

	Starts	1st	2nd	3rd	Win & Pl
Career Total (Turf)	1	0	0	1	591

Going (Turf): Sf: 0-0 GS: 0-0 Gd: 0-1 GF: 0-0 Fm: 0-0
Distance: 5f/6f: 0-0 7f-8f: 0-1 9f-13f: 0-0 14f+: 0-0
Track : LH: 0-0 RH: 0-1 Tight: 0-0 Gall: 0-0
Aids: Bl: 0-0 Vi: 0-0 Tstrap: 0-0
Best Rating: 78 9/01 Bevl 7f100y good

Semiramis

(96) (62)**64**
4-y-o b f Darshaan-Sulitelma (USA) (The Minstrel (CAN))
Sir Mark Prescott Miss K Rausing

Placings:460040/500-1230 (0358)
2001: 9^{1}SD, 12^{2}SD, 12^{3}SW, 12^{0}SW

	Starts	1st	2nd	3rd	Win & Pl
Career Total (Turf)	4	0	0	0	208
Career Total (AW)	9	1	1	1	3991

61 2/01 Wolv 1m1f79y D STD £2912
Total win prize-money £2912

Going (Turf): Sf: 0-0 GS: 0-0 Gd: 0-1 GF: 0-3 Fm: 0-0
Distance: 5f/6f: 0-3 7f-8f: 0-2 **9f-13f: 1-8** 14f+: 0-0
Track : **LH: 1-10** RH: 0-0 **Tight: 1-7** Gall: 0-0
Aids: Bl: 1-4 Vi: 0-0 Tstrap: 1-4
Best Rating: 62 2/01 Wolv 1m4f stand

Semper Paratus (USA)

89 **70**
2-y-o b c Foxhound (USA)-Bletcha Lass (AUS) (Bletchingly (AUS))
G C Bravery Heavily Iced Partnership

Placings:0050 (5130)
2001: 6^{0}GF, 6^{0}GF, 7^{5}F, 7^{0}HY

	Starts	1st	2nd	3rd	Win & Pl
Career Total (Turf)	4	0	0	0	0

Going (Turf): Sf: 0-1 GS: 0-0 Gd: 0-0 GF: 0-2 Fm: 0-1
Distance: 5f/6f: 0-2 7f-8f: 0-2 9f-13f: 0-0 14f+: 0-0
Track : LH: 0-1 RH: 0-0 Tight: 0-1 Gall: 0-0
Aids: Bl: 0-0 Vi: 0-0 Tstrap: 0-0
Best Rating: 70 9/01 Chep 7f16y firm

Semper Sursum

(52)
5-y-o ch g Nicholas Bill-Queen Of The Celts (Celtic Cone)
B Palling (H D Daly 27/4) Celtic Racing

Placings:0 (4552)
2001: 14^{0}SW

	Starts	1st	2nd	3rd	Win & Pl
Career Total (Turf)	0	0	0	0	
Career Total (AW)	1	0	0	0	

Going (Turf): Sf: 0-0 GS: 0-0 Gd: 0-0 GF: 0-0 Fm: 0-0
Distance: 5f/6f: 0-0 7f-8f: 0-0 9f-13f: 0-0 14f+: 0-1
Track : LH: 0-1 RH: 0-0 Tight: 0-1 Gall: 0-0
Aids: Bl: 0-0 Vi: 0-0 Tstrap: 0-0

Senator's Alibi

106(98) (61)**74**
3-y-o b c Caerleon (USA)-Salul (Soviet Star (USA))
Sir Mark Prescott Barouche Stud Ltd

Placings:03-2614163 (5179)
2001: 6^{2}SD, 8^{6}GF, 8^{1}S, 8^{4}SD, 8^{1}HY, 8^{6}HY, 10^{3}HY

	Starts	1st	2nd	3rd	Win & Pl
Career Total (Turf)	6	2	0	1	6840
Career Total (AW)	3	0	1	1	1155

74 9/01 Hayd 1m30y E(0-70)H HVY £3626
61 8/01 Nott 1m54y F(0-60) SFT £2497
Total win prize-money £6124

Going (Turf): Sf: 2-5 GS: 0-0 Gd: 0-0 GF: 0-1 Fm: 0-0
Distance: 5f/6f: 0-1 7f-8f: 0-3 **9f-13f: 2-5** 14f+: 0-0
Track : **LH: 2-6** RH: 0-0 Tight: 0-3 Gall: 0-0
Aids: Bl: 0-0 Vi: 0-0 Tstrap: 0-0
Best Rating: 74 9/01 Hayd 1m30y heavy

Tough handicapper at around a mile in the mud. Lightly raced. In good form this term, but high enough in handicap now.

Send It To Penny (IRE)

67(95) (53)
4-y-o b f Marju (IRE)-Sparkish (IRE) (Persian Bold)
W Storey W Storey

Placings:0504/0020150010-000 (5189)
2001: 8^{0}GF, 8^{0}GF, 5^{0}GS

	Starts	1st	2nd	3rd	Win & Pl
Career Total (Turf)	15	1	1	0	3284
Career Total (AW)	2	1	0	0	2275

51 7/00 Thsk 1m F(0-60)H FRM £2632
53 6/00 Sthl 1m F(0-60)H STD £2275
Total win prize-money £4907

Going (Turf): Sf: 0-2 GS: 0-2 Gd: 0-3 GF: 0-5 **Fm: 1-3**
Distance: 5f/6f: 0-5 **7f-8f: 2-10** 9f-13f: 0-2 14f+: 0-0
Track : **LH: 2-8** RH: 0-6 **Tight: 1-4** Gall: 0-2
Aids: **Bl: 2-7** Vi: 0-0 Tstrap: 0-0
Best Rating: 53 6/00 Sthl 1m SD

Send Me An Angel (IRE)

92(83) (34)**30**
4-y-o ch f Lycius (USA)-Niamh Cinn Oir (IRE) (King Of Clubs)
M Mullineaux Miss Gill Quincey

Placings:0/442263150-00000000 (5407)
2001: 12^{0}GF, 15^{0}GF, 12^{0}GF, 11^{0}G, 11^{0}GF, 16^{0}F, 10^{0}G, 12^{0}SD

	Starts	1st	2nd	3rd	Win & Pl
Career Total (Turf)	17	1	2	1	6236
Career Total (AW)	1	0	0	0	

68 8/00 Yarm 1m6f17y E(0-75)H G-F £3542
Total win prize-money £3543

Going (Turf): Sf: 0-1 GS: 0-2 Gd: 0-4 **GF: 1-9** Fm: 0-1
Distance: 5f/6f: 0-0 7f-8f: 0-1 9f-13f: 0-9 **14f+: 1-8**
Track : **LH: 1-13** RH: 0-4 **Tight: 1-9** Gall: 0-1
Aids: Bl: 0-1 Vi: 0-0 Tstrap: 0-0
Best Rating: 50 7/01 Haml 1m4f17y gd-fm

She has plenty of stamina in her breeding. Scored over 14 furlongs in summer of 2000, suited by having less use made of her. Out of form this season. Acts on fast ground.

Senior Minister

109 **97**

3-y-o b c Lion Cavern (USA)-Crime Ofthecentury (Pharly (FR))

J M P Eustace R Carstairs

Placings:212-0 **(4861)**

2001: 5^{0}GF

	Starts	1st	2nd	3rd	Win & Pl
Career Total (Turf)	4	1	2	0	10456

83 8/00 Ling 5f D G-F £3750

Total win prize-money £3751

Going (Turf): Sf: 0-0 GS: 0-0 Gd: 0-1 **GF: 1-2** Fm: 0-0
Distance: **5f/6f: 1-3** 7f-8f: 0-0 9f-13f: 0-0 14f+: 0-0
Track : LH: 0-0 RH: 0-0 Tight: 0-0 Gall: 0-0
Aids: Bl: 0-0 Vi: 0-0 Tstrap: 0-0
Best Rating: 95 9/01 Newb 5f34y gd-fm

Ran into subsequent Group One winner Bad As I Wanna Be on his debut in 2000 and was workmanlike in victory next time. Stepped up on that form to take second in Listed event at York. Restricted to one outing this season, he might not want the ground too fast.

Sennen Cove

90 **76**

2-y-o ch c Bering-Dame Laura (IRE) (Royal Academy (USA))

H Morrison A J Morrison & Partners

Placings:000 **(5343)**

2001: 7^{0}GF, 6^{0}HY, 6^{0}GS

	Starts	1st	2nd	3rd	Win & Pl
Career Total (Turf)	3	0	0	0	

Going (Turf): Sf: 0-1 GS: 0-1 Gd: 0-0 GF: 0-1 Fm: 0-0
Distance: 5f/6f: 0-2 7f-8f: 0-1 9f-13f: 0-0 14f+: 0-0
Track : LH: 0-0 RH: 0-0 Tight: 0-0 Gall: 0-0
Aids: Bl: 0-0 Vi: 0-0 Tstrap: 0-0
Best Rating: 76 10/01 NmkR 6f gd-sft

Senor Manx Touch

81 **50**

2-y-o b c Magic Ring (IRE)-Inveraven (Alias Smith (USA))

C A Dwyer Mrs H M Lipscomb

Placings:00650 **(3499)**

2001: 6^{0}G, 6^{0}GF, 7^{6}F, 7^{5}GF, 6^{0}GF

	Starts	1st	2nd	3rd	Win & Pl
Career Total (Turf)	5	0	0	0	0

Going (Turf): Sf: 0-0 GS: 0-0 Gd: 0-1 GF: 0-3 Fm: 0-1
Distance: 5f/6f: 0-0 7f-8f: 0-5 9f-13f: 0-0 14f+: 0-0
Track : LH: 0-0 RH: 0-1 Tight: 0-0 Gall: 0-0
Aids: Bl: 0-0 Vi: 0-0 Tstrap: 0-0
Best Rating: 50 6/01 Ling 7f firm

Senor Miro

103 **72**

3-y-o b g Be My Guest (USA)-Classic Moonlight (IRE) (Machiavellian (USA))

R F Johnson Houghton C W Sumner

Placings:0540-302 **(3253)**

2001: 7^{3}GF, 8^{0}GF, 7^{2}GS

	Starts	1st	2nd	3rd	Win & Pl
Career Total (Turf)	7	0	1	1	2274

Going (Turf): Sf: 0-1 GS: 0-2 Gd: 0-1 GF: 0-3 Fm: 0-0
Distance: 5f/6f: 0-2 7f-8f: 0-4 9f-13f: 0-1 14f+: 0-0
Track : LH: 0-0 RH: 0-2 Tight: 0-1 Gall: 0-1
Aids: Bl: 0-0 Vi: 0-0 Tstrap: 0-1
Best Rating: 69 6/01 Kemp 7f gd-fm

Maiden handicapper, suited by seven furlongs and seems to be improving with experience.

Sensimelia (IRE)

104 **62**

3-y-o b f Inzar (USA)-In The Papers (Aragon)

G A Swinbank Leading Star Racing

Placings:53650-13251212 **(4859)**

2001: 8^{1}GF, 8^{3}GS, 8^{2}G, 8^{5}GF, 8^{1}GF, 8^{2}S, 8^{1}GF, 7^{2}GF

	Starts	1st	2nd	3rd	Win & Pl
Career Total (Turf)	13	3	3	2	14034

47 9/01 Thsk 1m F G-F £3010
58 7/01 Nott 1m54y F G-F £2891
62 5/01 Ripn 1m F G-F £2828

Total win prize-money £8729

Going (Turf): Sf: 0-1 GS: 0-3 Gd: 0-4 **GF: 3-5** Fm: 0-0
Distance: 5f/6f: 0-5 **7f-8f: 2-3** 9f-13f: 1-5 14f+: 0-0
Track : **LH: 2-4** RH: 1-4 **Tight: 2-6** Gall: 0-0
Aids: Bl: 0-0 Vi: 0-0 Tstrap: 0-0
Best Rating: 62 9/01 Catt 7f gd-fm

She did not run over further than six furlongs as a two-year-old, but she looked more comfortable when stepped up to a mile to take a Rippon claimer in May. She has since scored again twice at a similar level. Her wins have come over a mile on a sound surface.

Sentimental Value (USA)

94 **74**

2-y-o ch f Diesis-Stately Star (USA) (Deputy Minister (CAN))

H R A Cecil The Thoroughbred Corporation

Placings:4 **(5682)**

2001: 7^{4}S

	Starts	1st	2nd	3rd	Win & Pl
Career Total (Turf)	1	0	0	0	365

Going (Turf): Sf: 0-1 GS: 0-0 Gd: 0-0 GF: 0-0 Fm: 0-0
Distance: 5f/6f: 0-0 7f-8f: 0-1 9f-13f: 0-0 14f+: 0-0
Track : LH: 0-0 RH: 0-0 Tight: 0-0 Gall: 0-0
Aids: Bl: 0-0 Vi: 0-0 Tstrap: 0-0
Best Rating: 74 11/01 Donc 7f soft

Sept Etoiles (IRE)

72 **31**

2-y-o b c Machiavellian (USA)-Sueboog (IRE) (Darshaan)

D R Loder Sheikh Mohammed

Placings:0 **(5262)**

2001: 7^{0}GS

	Starts	1st	2nd	3rd	Win & Pl
Career Total (Turf)	1	0	0	0	

Going (Turf): Sf: 0-0 GS: 0-1 Gd: 0-0 GF: 0-0 Fm: 0-0
Distance: 5f/6f: 0-0 7f-8f: 0-1 9f-13f: 0-0 14f+: 0-0
Track : LH: 0-1 RH: 0-0 Tight: 0-0 Gall: 0-1
Aids: Bl: 0-0 Vi: 0-0 Tstrap: 0-0
Best Rating: 31 10/01 York 7f202y gd-sft

September Harvest (USA)

87 (104) (38) **22**

5-y-o ch g Mujtahid (USA)-Shawgatny (USA) (Danzig Connection (USA))

Mrs S Lamyman P Lamyman

Placings:005035003/006224651056400/**644**00000**0-**
31030500000 **(4901)**

2001: **8^{3}**SD, **8^{1}**SD, **11^{0}**SW, **8^{3}**SD, **8^{0}**SW, **9^{5}**SD, 8^{0}F, 10^{0}F, 8^{0}G, 8^{0}GF, 11^{0}G

	Starts	1st	2nd	3rd	Win & Pl
Career Total (Turf)	34	1	2	2	6927
Career Total (AW)	11	1	0	2	3234

36 1/01 Sthl 1m F(0-65)H STD £2401
56 8/99 Pont 1m4y F(0-65)H G-F £3730

Total win prize-money £6131

Going (Turf): Sf: 0-3 GS: 0-5 Gd: 0-12 **GF: 1-12** Fm: 0-2
Distance: 5f/6f: 0-3 7f-8f: 1-16 9f-13f: 1-25 14f+: 0-1
Track : **LH: 2-27** RH: 0-12 Tight: 0-8 Gall: 0-9
Aids: Bl: 0-7 Vi: 0-2 Tstrap: 0-0
Best Rating: 36 1/01 Sthl 1m stand

Sequin (IRE)

99 **77**

2-y-o b f Green Desert (USA)-Sans Escale (USA) (Diesis)

M A Jarvis Mohammed Bin Hendi

Placings:460130 **(5052)**

2001: 6^{4}GF, 5^{6}GF, 6^{0}GF, 7^{1}G, 7^{3}G, 7^{0}S

	Starts	1st	2nd	3rd	Win & Pl
Career Total (Turf)	6	1	0	1	4675

77 8/01 Folk 7f E GD £3248

Total win prize-money £3248

Going (Turf): Sf: 0-1 GS: 0-0 **Gd: 1-2** GF: 0-3 Fm: 0-0
Distance: 5f/6f: 0-3 **7f-8f: 1-3** 9f-13f: 0-0 14f+: 0-0
Track : LH: 0-1 RH: 0-0 Tight: 0-1 Gall: 0-0
Aids: Bl: 0-0 Vi: 0-0 Tstrap: 0-0
Best Rating: 77 8/01 Epsm 7f good

She improved for the step up to seven furlongs when getting off the mark at Folkestone in August and ran well at Epsom next time despite not looking totally happy on the track.

Sequoyah (IRE)

107 **111**

3-y-o b f Sadler's Wells (USA)-Brigid (USA) (Irish River (FR))

A P O'Brien Mrs John Magnier

Placings:31215-4040 **(3630)**

2001: 8^{4}G, 8^{0}GF, 12^{4}G, 9^{0}G

	Starts	1st	2nd	3rd	Win & Pl
Career Total (Turf)	9	2	1	1	131240

112 9/00 Curr 7f G-F £98250
90 7/00 Tipp 7f G-F £5865

Total win prize-money £104115

Going (Turf): Sf: 0-0 GS: 0-1 Gd: 0-5 **GF: 1-2** Fm: 0-0
Distance: 5f/6f: 0-2 **7f-8f: 1-4** 9f-13f: 0-2 14f+: 0-0
Track : LH: 0-0 RH: 0-2 Tight: 0-1 Gall: 0-1
Aids: Bl: 0-0 Vi: 0-0 Tstrap: 0-0
Best Rating: 111 7/01 Curr 1m4f good

A high-class filly, winner of the Moyglare Stud Stakes last term, she has finished fourth in both the Irish 1000 Guineas and Irish Oaks this year. Seemed to benefit from the step up in trip in the latter race.

Seren Teg

95 (102) (57) **36**

5-y-o ch m Timeless Times (USA)-Hill Of Fare (Brigadier Gerard)

R M Flower K & D Computers Ltd

Placings:535650**141**/**24**202353450000/**144**0006460**003**
42-0000055 **(4304)**

2001: 6^{0}G, 5^{0}F, 6^{0}GF, 5^{0}GF, 7^{0}G, 6^{5}F, 5^{5}GF

	Starts	1st	2nd	3rd	Win & Pl
Career Total (Turf)	32	0	2	3	5393
Career Total (AW)	13	3	2	1	9612

58 2/00 Ling 5f F STD £2009
73 12/98 Ling 6f F STD £2085
69 11/98 Wolv 6f F STD £1892

Total win prize-money £5987

Going (Turf): Sf: 0-2 GS: 0-4 Gd: 0-6 GF: 0-14 Fm: 0-5
Distance: **5f/6f: 3-34** 7f-8f: 0-10 9f-13f: 0-0 14f+: 0-0
Track : **LH: 3-21** RH: 0-5 **Tight: 3-13** Gall: 0-10
Aids: **Bl: 1-14** Vi: 0-0 Tstrap: 0-0
Best Rating: 40 7/01 Kemp 6f good

She is nothing special, but claiming races over sprint trips on sand are just about with in her reach.

Serengeti Bride (USA)

105 **83**

3-y-o ch f Lion Cavern (USA)-Island Wedding (USA) (Blushing Groom (FR))
E A L Dunlop Maktoum Al Maktoum

Placings:0-005411110 **(5143)**
2001: 7^{0}S, 7^{0}G, 8^{5}GF, 10^{4}G, 11^{1}G, 12^{1}GF, 12^{1}G, 12^{1}GF, 14^{0}G

	Starts	1st	2nd	3rd	Win & Pl
Career Total (Turf)	**10**	**4**	**0**	**0**	**32498**

83	9/01	Ripn	1m4f60y	D(0-85)H	G-F	£5534
81	8/01	Gdwd	1m4f	D(0-85)H	GD	£15275
73	8/01	Epsm	1m4f10y	D(0-85)H	G-F	£8346
69	8/01	Leic	1m3f183y	E(0-65)	GD	£3010

Total win prize-money £32166

Going (Turf): Sf: 0-2 GS: 0-0 **Gd: 2-5 GF: 2-3** Fm: 0-0
Distance: 5f/6f: 0-0 7f-8f: 0-3 **9f-13f: 4-6** 14f+: 0-1
Track : **LH: 1-1 RH: 3-4 Tight: 3-4** Gall: 0-1
Aids: Bl: 0-0 Vi: 0-0 Tstrap: 0-0
Best Rating: 83 9/01 Ripn 1m4f60y gd-fm

A well-bred filly, she is genuine and stays 12 furlongs well. Notched up four victories over a mile and a half from August to September on fast ground. Suited by a strong pace and has a good attitude.

Serenus (USA)

94 **74**

8-y-o b g Sunshine Forever (USA)-Curl And Set (USA) (Nijinsky (CAN))
D R C Elsworth (N J Henderson 25/4) W V M W & Mrs E S Robins

Placings:3324/10/5-4 **(0953)**
2001: 12^{4}S

	Starts	1st	2nd	3rd	Win & Pl
Career Total (Turf)	**8**	**1**	**1**	**2**	**11189**

72	5/99	Kemp	1m4f	C(0-90)H	GD	£7360

Total win prize-money £7360

Going (Turf): Sf: 0-2 GS: 0-0 **Gd: 1-2** GF: 0-4 Fm: 0-0
Distance: 5f/6f: 0-0 7f-8f: 0-0 **9f-13f: 1-6** 14f+: 0-2
Track : LH: 0-3 **RH: 1-5** Tight: 0-4 Gall: 0-1
Aids: Bl: 0-0 Vi: 0-0 Tstrap: 0-0
Best Rating: 70 4/01 Epsm 1m4f10y soft

Serge Lifar

109(102) (68)**99**

3-y-o b c Shirley Heights-Ballet (Sharrood (USA))
R Hannon Exors Of The Late Earl Of Carnavon

Placings:33-221312023 **(5057)**
2001: 12^{2}SD, 10^{2}GS, 9^{1}GS, 12^{3}S, 11^{1}GF, 10^{2}GF, 14^{0}GF, 14^{2}G, 12^{3}S

	Starts	1st	2nd	3rd	Win & Pl
Career Total (Turf)	**10**	**2**	**3**	**4**	**29762**
Career Total (AW)	**1**	**0**	**1**	**0**	**822**

99	7/01	Wind	1m3f135y	C(0-90)	G-F	£7029
89	5/01	Sals	1m1f198y	C(0-100)H	G-S	£8463

Total win prize-money £15493

Going (Turf): Sf: 0-3 **GS: 1-2** Gd: 0-2 **GF: 1-3** Fm: 0-0
Distance: 5f/6f: 0-0 7f-8f: 0-2 **9f-13f: 2-7** 14f+: 0-2
Track : LH: 0-2 **RH: 1-7 Tight: 2-6** Gall: 0-4
Aids: Bl: 0-0 Vi: 0-0 Tstrap: 0-0
Best Rating: 99 9/01 NmkR 1m6f good

Useful handicapper and a winner over ten furlongs at Salisbury in May 2001, he improved again to beat Isadora by a head over the extended 11 furlongs at Windsor in July, before chasing home an improving sort at Ascot. He continued to run well in competitive handicaps afterwards. Has performed with credit on good to firm and soft ground.

Sergeant Cecil

89 **70**

2-y-o ch g King's Signet (USA)-Jadidh (Touching Wood (USA))
J W Mullins Terry Cooper

Placings:00 **(5040)**
2001: 8^{0}GF, 10^{0}G

	Starts	1st	2nd	3rd	Win & Pl
Career Total (Turf)	**2**	**0**	**0**	**0**	

Going (Turf): Sf: 0-0 GS: 0-0 Gd: 0-1 GF: 0-1 Fm: 0-0
Distance: 5f/6f: 0-0 7f-8f: 0-1 9f-13f: 0-1 14f+: 0-0
Track : LH: 0-1 RH: 0-1 Tight: 0-1 Gall: 0-0
Aids: Bl: 0-0 Vi: 0-0 Tstrap: 0-0
Best Rating: 70 10/01 Bath 1m2f46y good

Sergeant Slipper

101(103) (49)**54**

4-y-o ch g Never So Bold-Pretty Scarce (Handsome Sailor)
C Smith C Smith

Placings:00652500401l/00100-000005420160200000 **(5497)**
2001: 5^{0}SD, 5^{0}SD, 6^{0}SW, 5^{0}SW, 5^{0}SD, 5^{5}SD, 5^{4}SD, 5^{2}SD, 6^{0}SD, 5^{1}S, 5^{6}HY, 5^{0}G, 5^{2}SD, 5^{0}SD, 7^{0}G, 6^{0}S, 5^{0}SD, 5^{0}HY

	Starts	1st	2nd	3rd	Win & Pl
Career Total (Turf)	**15**	**1**	**0**	**0**	**3052**
Career Total (AW)	**20**	**3**	**3**	**0**	**8258**

54	4/01	Ripn	5f	E	SFT	£3052
63	4/00	Sthl	5f	E(0-70)H	STD	£2884
62	12/99	Sthl	5f	G	SLW	£1850
60	12/99	Wolv	5f	G	STD	£1819

Total win prize-money £9606

Going (Turf): **Sf: 1-5** GS: 0-1 Gd: 0-6 GF: 0-2 Fm: 0-1
Distance: **5f/6f: 4-33** 7f-8f: 0-2 9f-13f: 0-1 14f+: 0-0
Track : **LH: 1-8** RH: 0-0 **Tight: 1-4** Gall: 0-0
Aids: Bl: 0-2 **Vi: 4-27** Tstrap: 0-0
Best Rating: 54 4/01 Ripn 5f soft

Sergeant York

(111) (93)**85**

5-y-o b g Be My Chief (USA)-Metaphysique (FR) (Law Society (USA))
T D Barron Nigel Shields

Placings:1030243/626506260300/05336045300-1016 **(1397a)**
2001: 8^{1}SW, 8^{0}SD, 10^{1}SD, 9^{6}FT

	Starts	1st	2nd	3rd	Win & Pl
Career Total (Turf)	**30**	**1**	**3**	**6**	**16925**
Career Total (AW)	**4**	**2**	**0**	**0**	**35716**

93	3/01	Ling	1m2f	A	STD	£31900
86	2/01	Sthl	1m	D(0-85)H	SLW	£3815
69	5/98	Haml	5f4y	E	SFT	£3436

Total win prize-money £39152

Going (Turf): **Sf: 1-3** GS: 0-6 Gd: 0-9 GF: 0-12 Fm: 0-0
Distance: 5f/6f: 1-4 7f-8f: 1-13 9f-13f: 1-17 14f+: 0-0
Track : **LH: 2-14** RH: 0-6 **Tight: 1-5** Gall: 0-9
Aids: Bl: 0-0 Vi: 0-4 Tstrap: 0-0
Best Rating: 93 3/01 Ling 1m2f stand

Useful performer on the All-Weather, winning the Winter derby in March 2001. He is now with Michael Dickinson in the USA.

Sergeant's Inn

95(70)

4-y-o b g Sabrehill (USA)-Pink Brief (IRE) (Ela-Mana-Mou)
G Brown (Andrew Reid 16/4) John W Barnard

Placings:00600 **(0762)**
2001: 12^{0}SD, 13^{0}SW, 12^{6}SW, 16^{0}SD, 8^{0}S

	Starts	1st	2nd	3rd	Win & Pl
Career Total (Turf)	**1**	**0**	**0**	**0**	
Career Total (AW)	**4**	**0**	**0**	**0**	**0**

Going (Turf): **Sf: 0-1 GS: 0-0 Gd: 0-0 GF: 0-0 Fm: 0-0**
Distance: 5f/6f: 0-0 7f-8f: 0-1 9f-13f: 0-3 14f+: 0-1
Track : LH: 0-4 RH: 0-1 Tight: 0-2 Gall: 0-0
Aids: Bl: 0-0 Vi: 0-0 Tstrap: 0-0
Best Rating: 65 4/01 Kemp 1m soft

Sergeevna (IRE)

75 **11**

3-y-o b f Barathea (IRE)-Sveltana (Soviet Star (USA))
J G Portman R C C Villers

Placings:00 **(5464)**
2001: 10^{0}GF, 11^{0}G

	Starts	1st	2nd	3rd	Win & Pl
Career Total (Turf)	**2**	**0**	**0**	**0**	

Going (Turf): **Sf: 0-0 GS: 0-0 Gd: 0-1 GF: 0-1 Fm: 0-0**
Distance: 5f/6f: 0-0 7f-8f: 0-0 9f-13f: 0-2 14f+: 0-0
Track : LH: 0-1 RH: 0-1 Tight: 0-1 Gall: 0-1
Aids: Bl: 0-0 Vi: 0-0 Tstrap: 0-0
Best Rating: 11 10/01 Bath 1m3f144y good

Serieux

99 **94**

2-y-o b c Cadeaux Genereux-Seranda (IRE) (Petoski)
B W Hills K Abdulla

Placings:215 **(4111)**
2001: 6^{2}GF, 6^{1}GF, 6^{5}G

	Starts	1st	2nd	3rd	Win & Pl
Career Total (Turf)	**3**	**1**	**1**	**0**	**13253**

87	7/01	Gdwd	6f	D	G-F	£11050

Total win prize-money £11050

Going (Turf): Sf: 0-0 GS: 0-0 Gd: 0-1 **GF: 1-2** Fm: 0-0
Distance: **5f/6f: 1-2** 7f-8f: 0-1 9f-13f: 0-0 14f+: 0-0
Track : LH: 0-1 RH: 0-0 Tight: 0-0 Gall: 0-1
Aids: Bl: 0-0 Vi: 0-0 Tstrap: 0-0
Best Rating: 94 8/01 York 6f214y good

Showed plenty of promise on his debut and got off the mark in good style at in Goodwood. His limitations were exposed subsequently in the Acomb Stakes at York. Acts on fast ground.

Serious Trust

97(81) (17)**19**

8-y-o b g Alzao (USA)-Mill Line (Mill Reef (USA))
Mrs L C Jewell Peter J Allen

Placings:50500/14330/200005010/00640/00060020U **(4523)**
2001: 16^{0}SW, 16^{0}SD, 13^{0}SW, 12^{6}SD, 14^{0}GF, 16^{0}GF, 16^{2}GF, 12^{0}GF, 16^{U}GF

	Starts	1st	2nd	3rd	Win & Pl
Career Total (Turf)	**27**	**2**	**2**	**2**	**9539**
Career Total (AW)	**6**	**0**	**0**	**0**	**0**

53	8/97	Sals	1m6f	E(0-70)H	G-F	£3366
55	5/96	Sals	1m4f	E(0-70)H	G-F	£3418

Total win prize-money £6784

Going (Turf): Sf: 0-2 GS: 0-1 Gd: 0-1 **GF: 2-21** Fm: 0-2
Distance: 5f/6f: 0-0 7f-8f: 0-5 9f-13f: 1-10 14f+: 1-18
Track : LH: 0-15 **RH: 2-18 Tight: 2-23** Gall: 0-0
Aids: Bl: 0-1 Vi: 0-3 Tstrap: 0-0
Best Rating: 19 7/01 Folk 2m93y gd-fm

Serotonin

91 **66+**

2-y-o b c Barathea (IRE)-Serotina (IRE) (Mtoto)
R Charlton Mountgrange Stud

Placings:0 **(5604)**
2001: 7^{0}GS

	Starts	1st	2nd	3rd	Win & Pl
Career Total (Turf)	1	0	0	0	

Going (Turf): Sf: 0-0 GS: 0-1 Gd: 0-0 GF: 0-0 Fm: 0-0
Distance: 5f/6f: 0-0 7f-8f: 0-1 9f-13f: 0-0 14f+: 0-0
Track : LH: 0-0 RH: 0-0 Tight: 0-0 Gall: 0-0
Aids: Bl: 0-0 Vi: 0-0 Tstrap: 0-0
Best Rating: 66 11/01 NmkR 7f gd-sft

Serra Negra

102 **76**
4-y-o b f Kris-Congress (IRE) (Dancing Brave (USA))
W J Haggas Cyril Humphris

Placings:0/162-044000 **(4283)**
2001: 7^{0}S, 7^{4}G, 7^{4}S, 6^{0}GF, 6^{0}G, 7^{0}G

	Starts	1st	2nd	3rd	Win & Pl
Career Total (Turf)	10	1	1	0	6508

83 5/00 Wwck 7f164y D SFT £2913
Total win prize-money £2914

Going (Turf): Sf: 1-5 GS: 0-0 Gd: 0-3 GF: 0-1 Fm: 0-1
Distance: 5f/6f: 0-2 **7f-8f: 1-8** 9f-13f: 0-0 14f+: 0-0
Track : **LH: 1-3** RH: 0-3 Tight: 0-0 Gall: 0-2
Aids: Bl: 0-1 Vi: 0-0 Tstrap: 0-0
Best Rating: 76 6/01 Sand 7f16y soft

Off the mark in a Warwick maiden on her reappearance in 2000 and ran with credit in handicap company in her two subsequent starts. She is suited by soft ground but has been below par so far this term.

Serviceable

108(81) (31)**70**
3-y-o ch f Pursuit Of Love-Absaloute Service (Absalom)
R M Whitaker G F Pemberton

Placings:31600-0001103P000 **(5611)**
2001: 6^{0}S, 8^{0}GF, 8^{0}GF, 8^{1}GF, 8^{1}GF, 8^{0}GF, 8^{3}GS, 10^{P}S, 7^{0}HY, 8^{0}GS, 8^{0}SD

	Starts	1st	2nd	3rd	Win & Pl
Career Total (Turf)	15	3	0	2	11283
Career Total (AW)	1	0	0	0	

73 7/01 Ripn 1m E(0-70)H G-F £3682
74 7/01 Haml 1m65y E(0-70) G-F £3080
74 4/00 Wwck 5f D HVY £3125
Total win prize-money £9887

Going (Turf): Sf: 1-6 GS: 0-2 Gd: 0-0 **GF: 2-7** Fm: 0-0
Distance: 5f/6f: 1-5 7f-8f: 1-5 9f-13f: 1-6 14f+: 0-0
Track : LH: 1-6 **RH: 2-3 Tight: 2-5** Gall: 1-1
Aids: Bl: 0-0 Vi: 0-0 Tstrap: 0-0
Best Rating: 74 7/01 Haml 1m65y gd-fm

Fair handicapper. A changeto forcing tactics brought about a dramatic change as she made all to win twice at Hamilton and Ripon in July 2001. Suited by a mile and fast ground.

Settle Down

86(84) (59)**55**
2-y-o b f Reprimand-Russell Creek (Sandy Creek)
M W Easterby Guy Reed

Placings:401650 **(4990)**
2001: 5^{4}S, 5^{0}SD, 5^{1}S, 7^{6}GF, 7^{5}SD, 6^{0}HY

	Starts	1st	2nd	3rd	Win & Pl
Career Total (Turf)	4	1	0	0	1851
Career Total (AW)	2	0	0	0	

55 4/01 Nott 5f13y G SFT £1850
Total win prize-money £1851

Going (Turf): Sf: 1-3 GS: 0-0 Gd: 0-0 GF: 0-1 Fm: 0-0
Distance: **5f/6f: 1-4** 7f-8f: 0-2 9f-13f: 0-0 14f+: 0-0
Track : LH: 0-1 RH: 0-0 Tight: 0-1 Gall: 0-0
Aids: Bl: 0-1 Vi: 0-0 Tstrap: 0-0
Best Rating: 59 9/01 Wolv 7f stand

Plating-class juvenile, bred to stay a mile.

Seven No Trumps

112 **94**
4-y-o ch g Pips Pride-Classic Ring (IRE) (Auction Ring (USA))
B W Hills Paul McNamara

Placings:0115520322/000300000-61135002031 **(5494)**
2001: 6^{6}S, 6^{1}G, 6^{1}GF, 6^{3}GF, 6^{5}GF, 6^{0}G, 6^{0}G, 5^{2}GF, 6^{0}GF, 6^{3}GS, 6^{1}HY

	Starts	1st	2nd	3rd	Win & Pl
Career Total (Turf)	31	5	4	4	64807

94 10/01 Newb 6f8y B(0-110)H HVY £10277
90 5/01 Gdwd 6f C(0-95)H G-F £7816
82 5/01 Donc 6f D(0-85)H GD £4680
78 5/99 Newc 5f D G-F £3022
77 5/99 Nott 6f15y E FRM £3626
Total win prize-money £29422

Going (Turf): Sf: 1-5 GS: 0-8 Gd: 1-7 **GF: 2-10** Fm: 1-1
Distance: **5f/6f: 3-26** 7f-8f: 2-5 9f-13f: 0-0 14f+: 0-0
Track : LH: 0-1 RH: 0-1 Tight: 0-1 Gall: 0-1
Aids: Bl: 0-1 Vi: 0-0 Tstrap: 0-0
Best Rating: 94 10/01 Newb 6f8y heavy

A useful juvenile, he lost his way in 2000 and came down the ratings to good effect, winning at Doncaster and Goodwood in the spring of 2001 and finishing a good third in the Wokingham. Back to form when runner-up in the Portland at Doncaster in September and made all to win in desperate ground at Newbury in October. Suited by six furlongs and any ground.

Seven Of Nine (IRE)

92 **64**
3-y-o b/br f Alzao (USA)-Sharakawa (IRE) (Darshaan)
W R Muir M J Caddy

Placings:4-56 **(1613)**
2001: 9^{5}S, 10^{6}GF

	Starts	1st	2nd	3rd	Win & Pl
Career Total (Turf)	3	0	0	0	425

Going (Turf): Sf: 0-2 GS: 0-0 Gd: 0-0 GF: 0-1 Fm: 0-0
Distance: 5f/6f: 0-0 7f-8f: 0-1 9f-13f: 0-2 14f+: 0-0
Track : LH: 0-1 RH: 0-1 Tight: 0-2 Gall: 0-0
Aids: Bl: 0-0 Vi: 0-0 Tstrap: 0-0
Best Rating: 64 5/01 Sals 1m1f198y soft

Seven Sing (USA)

95 **81**
3-y-o b f Machiavellian (USA)-Seven Springs (USA) (Irish River (FR))
B W Hills K Abdulla

Placings:310-0 **(2884)**
2001: 7^{0}GS

	Starts	1st	2nd	3rd	Win & Pl
Career Total (Turf)	4	1	0	1	4481

81 7/00 Thsk 6f D FRM £3591
Total win prize-money £3591

Going (Turf): Sf: 0-0 GS: 0-2 Gd: 0-0 GF: 0-1 **Fm: 1-1**
Distance: **5f/6f: 1-3** 7f-8f: 0-1 9f-13f: 0-0 14f+: 0-0
Track : LH: 0-0 RH: 0-0 Tight: 0-0 Gall: 0-0
Aids: Bl: 0-0 Vi: 0-0 Tstrap: 0-0
Best Rating: 75 7/01 NmkJ 7f gd-sft

Seven Springs (IRE)

89(103) (51)**33**
5-y-o b g Unblest-Zaydeen (Sassafras (FR))
R Hollinshead N Chapman

Placings:021/00000450000000/0062030000040-4313100000000 **(4013)**
2001: 6^{4}SD, 6^{3}SW, 5^{1}SD, 5^{3}SD, 6^{1}SW, 6^{0}G, 5^{0}SD, 5^{0}GF, 6^{0}SD, 5^{0}GS, 6^{0}SD, 6^{0}F, 5^{0}G

Starts 1st 2nd 3rd Win & Pl

	Starts	1st	2nd	3rd	Win & Pl
Career Total (Turf)	22	0	2	0	1563
Career Total (AW)	22	3	0	3	7771

51 2/01 Sthl 6f E(0-75)H SLW £2408
46 1/01 Sthl 5f E(0-70)H STD £2457
76 11/98 Wolv 6f F STD £1882
Total win prize-money £6747

Going (Turf): Sf: 0-4 GS: 0-2 Gd: 0-6 GF: 0-7 Fm: 0-3
Distance: **5f/6f: 3-30** 7f-8f: 0-14 9f-13f: 0-0 14f+: 0-0
Track : **LH: 2-25** RH: 0-2 **Tight: 1-12** Gall: 0-3
Aids: Bl: 0-0 Vi: 0-1 Tstrap: 0-0
Best Rating: 51 2/01 Sthl 6f slow

Moderate sprinter, best on the All-Weather.

Sewmuch Character

100 **89?**
2-y-o b g Magic Ring (IRE)-Diplomatist (Dominion)
M Blanshard Aykroyd And Sons Ltd

Placings:52220 **(5250)**
2001: 6^{5}GF, 6^{2}G, 7^{2}G, 7^{2}S, 6^{0}S

	Starts	1st	2nd	3rd	Win & Pl
Career Total (Turf)	5	0	3	0	3793

Going (Turf): Sf: 0-2 GS: 0-0 Gd: 0-2 GF: 0-1 Fm: 0-0
Distance: 5f/6f: 0-3 7f-8f: 0-2 9f-13f: 0-0 14f+: 0-0
Track : LH: 0-3 RH: 0-0 Tight: 0-2 Gall: 0-0
Aids: Bl: 0-0 Vi: 0-0 Tstrap: 0-0
Best Rating: 89 8/01 Pont 6f good

Runner-up three times in four runs, he seems genuine enough but lacks a change of pace. Handles any ground.

Seyooll (IRE)

96 **74**
3-y-o b f Danehill (USA)-Andromaque (USA) (Woodman (USA))
M R Channon Sheikh Ahmed Al Maktoum

Placings:43-333 **(4613)**
2001: 9^{3}GS, 10^{3}S, 11^{3}F

	Starts	1st	2nd	3rd	Win & Pl
Career Total (Turf)	5	0	0	4	2569

Going (Turf): Sf: 0-1 GS: 0-1 Gd: 0-0 GF: 0-2 Fm: 0-1
Distance: 5f/6f: 0-0 7f-8f: 0-0 9f-13f: 0-5 14f+: 0-0
Track : LH: 0-2 RH: 0-2 Tight: 0-2 Gall: 0-0
Aids: Bl: 0-0 Vi: 0-0 Tstrap: 0-0
Best Rating: 74 4/01 Ripn 1m2f soft

Shaam

80 **10**
3-y-o b g Charnwood Forest (IRE)-Badawi (USA) (Diesis)
C E Brittain Sheikh Marwan Al Maktoum

Placings:00 **(5024)**
2001: 9^{0}GF, 11^{0}S

	Starts	1st	2nd	3rd	Win & Pl
Career Total (Turf)	2	0	0	0	

Going (Turf): Sf: 0-1 GS: 0-0 Gd: 0-0 GF: 0-1 Fm: 0-0
Distance: 5f/6f: 0-0 7f-8f: 0-0 9f-13f: 0-2 14f+: 0-0
Track : LH: 0-1 RH: 0-1 Tight: 0-0 Gall: 0-0
Aids: Bl: 0-0 Vi: 0-0 Tstrap: 0-0
Best Rating: 10 9/01 Leic 1m1f218y gd-fm

Shaanara (IRE)

84 **71**
3-y-o b f Darshaan-Mochara (Last Fandango)
Andrew Turnell Dr John Hollowood

Placings:601-00 **(5265)**
2001: 10^{0}G, 8^{0}GS

Starts 1st 2nd 3rd Win & Pl

Career Total (Turf) 5 1 0 0 3315
71 10/00 Newc 7f D HVY £3315
Total win prize-money £3315

Going (Turf): Sf: 1-1 GS: 0-2 Gd: 0-1 GF: 0-1 Fm: 0-0
Distance: 5f/6f: 0-0 **7f-8f: 1-3** 9f-13f: 0-2 14f+: 0-0
Track : LH: 0-2 RH: 0-1 Tight: 0-0 Gall: 0-1
Aids: Bl: 0-0 Vi: 0-0 Tstrap: 0-0
Best Rating: 53 9/01 Ayr 1m2f good

Showed ability at two before winning a seven-furlong maiden at the back-end of 2000 in the mud. Lightly-raced in 2001.

Shaandar (IRE)

111 **100**
3-y-o br c Darshaan-Moon Parade (Welsh Pageant)
J L Dunlop Littleton Manor Racing

Placings:0-133 **(2943)**
2001: 11^{1}GS, 12^{3}G, 14^{3}G

	Starts	1st	2nd	3rd	Win & Pl
Career Total (Turf)	4	1	0	2	9145

94 4/01 Newb 1m3f5y D G-S £5102
Total win prize-money £5103

Going (Turf): Sf: 0-1 **GS: 1-1** Gd: 0-2 GF: 0-0 Fm: 0-0
Distance: 5f/6f: 0-0 7f-8f: 0-1 **9f-13f: 1-2** 14f+: 0-1
Track : **LH: 1-1** RH: 0-2 Tight: 0-0 **Gall: 1-3**
Aids: Bl: 0-0 Vi: 0-0 Tstrap: 0-0
Best Rating: 100 7/01 NmkJ 1m6f175y good

Lightly-raced half-brother to Rain Rider who won over fifteen furlongs. Easy winner of 1m3f Newbury maiden in April. Stays a mile and a half. Should get further. Has won on good to soft. Acts on good.

Shaanxi Romance (IRE)

77(106) (52)**22**
6-y-o b g Darshaan-Easy Romance (USA) (Northern Jove (CAN))
M J Polglase Mark Lewis

Placings:53/1200/00061400/250055436611234060000-00000 **(5450)**
2001: 7^{0}G, 8^{0}SD, 8^{0}G, 8^{0}HY, 8^{0}SD

	Starts	1st	2nd	3rd	Win & Pl
Career Total (Turf)	29	2	3	2	14551
Career Total (AW)	11	2	0	1	7483

46 8/00 Kemp 1m E(0-75)H G-F £4485
52 7/00 Sthl 1m D(0-85)H STD £3731
57 8/99 Carl 6f206y F(0-60) FRM £2304
67 3/98 Wolv 1m100y D STD £3273
Total win prize-money £13794

Going (Turf): Sf: 0-4 GS: 0-5 Gd: 0-10 **GF: 1-8 Fm: 1-2**
Distance: 5f/6f: 0-0 **7f-8f: 3-24** 9f-13f: 1-16 14f+: 0-0
Track : LH: 2-25 RH: 2-9 Tight: 1-16 Gall: 1-3
Aids: Bl: 0-0 **Vi: 3-29** Tstrap: 0-1
Best Rating: 31 6/01 Sthl 1m stand

A moderate handicapper, best over a mile. Acts on a sound surface, usually wears a visor.

Shaard (IRE)

95 **108**
3-y-o b c Anabaa (USA)-Braari (USA) (Gulch (USA))
B W Hills Hamdan Al Maktoum

Placings:1341-54 **(2666)**
2001: 7^{5}S, 7^{4}G

	Starts	1st	2nd	3rd	Win & Pl
Career Total (Turf)	6	2	0	1	23615

107 10/00 Donc 6f A SFT £12701
85 7/00 Bath 5f161y D G-S £3493
Total win prize-money £16195

Going (Turf): **Sf: 1-2 GS: 1-1** Gd: 0-2 GF: 0-1 Fm: 0-0
Distance: **5f/6f: 2-3** 7f-8f: 0-3 9f-13f: 0-0 14f+: 0-0
Track : **LH: 1-1** RH: 0-1 Tight: 0-0 **Gall: 1-1**
Aids: **Bl: 2-6** Vi: 0-0 Tstrap: 0-0

Best Rating: 96 4/01 NmkR 7f soft

Lightly-raced colt, always wears blinkers. Winner of a Listed event at Doncaster as a juvenile. Acts well on soft ground, but has started slowly and does not always look fully co-operative.

Shabaab

99 **71d**
3-y-o b c Unfuwain (USA)-Kronengold (USA) (Golden Act (USA))
M R Channon Sheikh Ahmed Al Maktoum

Placings:5435040 **(3669)**
2001: 12^{5}GS, 12^{4}GS, 11^{3}GF, 14^{5}GF, 14^{0}G, 11^{4}GF, 14^{0}S

	Starts	1st	2nd	3rd	Win & Pl
Career Total (Turf)	7	0	0	1	797

Going (Turf): Sf: 0-1 GS: 0-2 Gd: 0-1 GF: 0-3 Fm: 0-0
Distance: 5f/6f: 0-0 7f-8f: 0-0 9f-13f: 0-4 14f+: 0-3
Track : LH: 0-5 RH: 0-2 Tight: 0-5 Gall: 0-1
Aids: Bl: 0-0 Vi: 0-0 Tstrap: 0-0
Best Rating: 73 6/01 Yarm 1m3f101y gd-fm

Shadalhi

84 **54**
3-y-o ch f Alhijaz-Dangerous Shadow (Absalom)
K A Ryan The Shadowline Club Limited

Placings:05-6P **(2050)**
2001: 7^{6}GF, 6^{P}GF

	Starts	1st	2nd	3rd	Win & Pl
Career Total (Turf)	4	0	0	0	0

Going (Turf): Sf: 0-0 GS: 0-0 Gd: 0-0 GF: 0-3 Fm: 0-1
Distance: 5f/6f: 0-3 7f-8f: 0-1 9f-13f: 0-0 14f+: 0-0
Track : LH: 0-1 RH: 0-0 Tight: 0-0 Gall: 0-0
Aids: Bl: 0-0 Vi: 0-0 Tstrap: 0-0
Best Rating: 36 5/01 Sthl 7f gd-fm

Shadow Dancing

104 **93**
2-y-o b f Unfuwain (USA)-Salchow (Niniski (USA))
M P Tregoning Mrs Hugh Dalgety & Partners

Placings:313 **(4680)**
2001: 7^{3}G, 8^{1}S, 8^{3}G

	Starts	1st	2nd	3rd	Win & Pl
Career Total (Turf)	3	1	0	2	10591

88 8/01 Sand 1m14y D SFT £4348
Total win prize-money £4349

Going (Turf): **Sf: 1-1** GS: 0-0 Gd: 0-2 GF: 0-0 Fm: 0-0
Distance: 5f/6f: 0-0 7f-8f: 0-2 **9f-13f: 1-1** 14f+: 0-0
Track : LH: 0-1 **RH: 1-2** Tight: 0-0 Gall: 0-1
Aids: Bl: 0-0 Vi: 0-0 Tstrap: 0-0
Best Rating: 93 9/01 Donc 1m good

She showed ability on her Goodwood debut and bolted up in soft ground at Sandown on her second start. A useful prospect. Stays a mile. Has won on soft ground.

Shadow Roll (IRE)

94 **77**
2-y-o ch f Mark Of Esteem (IRE)-Warning Shadows (IRE) (Cadeaux Genereux)
C E Brittain Sheikh Marwan Al Maktoum

Placings:633650 **(5052)**
2001: 6^{6}GF, 6^{3}GF, 7^{3}G, 6^{6}GS, 7^{5}GF, 7^{0}S

	Starts	1st	2nd	3rd	Win & Pl
Career Total (Turf)	6	0	0	2	4190

Going (Turf): Sf: 0-1 GS: 0-1 Gd: 0-1 GF: 0-3 Fm: 0-0
Distance: 5f/6f: 0-2 7f-8f: 0-4 9f-13f: 0-0 14f+: 0-0
Track : LH: 0-1 RH: 0-0 Tight: 0-1 Gall: 0-0

Aids: Bl: 0-0 Vi: 0-0 Tstrap: 0-0
Best Rating: 77 9/01 Newb 7f gd-fm

Dam won Group Two Sun Chariot Stakes. She has been taking on some decent fillies in her career to date and has not quite been good enough, but should be able to find an ordinary race.

Shadowblaster (IRE)

105 **67**
4-y-o b g Wolfhound (USA)-Swame (USA) (Jade Hunter (USA))
B Hanbury J Vettriano

Placings:52204-0515556600 **(4541)**
2001: 10^{0}G, 12^{5}S, 14^{1}GF, 16^{5}GF, 12^{5}GF, 14^{5}GF, 13^{6}GF, 12^{6}GS, 12^{0}GF, 14^{0}GF

	Starts	1st	2nd	3rd	Win & Pl
Career Total (Turf)	15	1	2	0	7133

79 5/01 Hayd 1m6f D(0-80)H G-F £4426
Total win prize-money £4427

Going (Turf): Sf: 0-2 GS: 0-1 Gd: 0-3 **GF: 1-9** Fm: 0-0
Distance: 5f/6f: 0-0 7f-8f: 0-2 9f-13f: 0-8 **14f+: 1-5**
Track : **LH: 1-6** RH: 0-6 Tight: 0-5 Gall: 0-4
Aids: Bl: 0-0 Vi: 0-0 Tstrap: 0-1
Best Rating: 79 6/01 NmkJ 1m4f gd-fm

Scored his first success in May 2001 over 14 furlongs on fast ground. Does not do anything quickly. Had yet to prove he stays two miles.

Shady Deal

101(99) (25)**49**
5-y-o b g No Big Deal-Taskalady (Touching Wood (USA))
Simon Earle (M D I Usher 21/3) A Wills, Y Dallal, G Macgregor, A Galvin

Placings:0005/44220306000000/040030022134000-0000000352003 **(5639)**
2001: 6^{0}SD, 5^{0}SD, 5^{0}SW, 6^{0}SW, 6^{0}SD, 5^{0}SD, 5^{0}G, 6^{3}GF, 5^{5}GF, 5^{2}GF, 5^{0}G, 5^{0}G, 5^{3}G

	Starts	1st	2nd	3rd	Win & Pl
Career Total (Turf)	27	1	3	4	6705
Career Total (AW)	20	0	2	1	2244

49 7/00 Bath 5f11y F(0-65)H G-S £2215
Total win prize-money £2216

Going (Turf): Sf: 0-3 **GS: 1-3** Gd: 0-8 GF: 0-13 Fm: 0-0
Distance: **5f/6f: 1-34** 7f-8f: 0-12 9f-13f: 0-1 14f+: 0-0
Track : **LH: 1-22** RH: 0-4 Tight: 0-17 **Gall: 1-6**
Aids: Bl: 0-0 Vi: 0-0 Tstrap: 0-0
Best Rating: 49 7/01 Chep 5f16y gd-fm

He has just the one win to his name, but has run one or two decent races in defeat over five furlongs on fast ground. Acts on Equitrack.

Shady Suspect (USA)

(70) (3)
6-y-o b g Shadeed (USA)-Ann Alleged (USA) (Alleged (USA))
M D Hammond Www.Mark-Kilner-Racing.Com (14)

Placings:0 **(0563)**
2001: 12^{0}SD

	Starts	1st	2nd	3rd	Win & Pl
Career Total (Turf)	0	0	0	0	
Career Total (AW)	1	0	0	0	

Going (Turf): Sf: 0-0 GS: 0-0 Gd: 0-0 GF: 0-0 Fm: 0-0
Distance: 5f/6f: 0-0 7f-8f: 0-0 9f-13f: 0-1 14f+: 0-0
Track : LH: 0-1 RH: 0-0 Tight: 0-1 Gall: 0-0
Aids: Bl: 0-0 Vi: 0-0 Tstrap: 0-0
Best Rating: 3 3/01 Wolv 1m4f stand

Shafeeq (FR)

97 **82**

2-y-o ch c Halling (USA)-Ta Awun (USA) (Housebuster (USA))

A C Stewart Hamdan Al Maktoum

Placings:334 **(5295)**

2001: 7[3]GF, 8[3]GF, 8[4]S

	Starts	1st	2nd	3rd	Win & Pl
Career Total (Turf)	3	0	0	2	1654

Going (Turf): Sf: 0-1 GS: 0-0 Gd: 0-0 GF: 0-2 Fm: 0-0
Distance: 5f/6f: 0-0 7f-8f: 0-2 9f-13f: 0-1 14f+: 0-0
Track : LH: 0-0 RH: 0-1 Tight: 0-0 Gall: 0-0
Aids: Bl: 0-0 Vi: 0-0 Tstrap: 0-0
Best Rating: 82 9/01 Kemp 1m gd-fm

Shaffishayes

104 (66)**43**

9-y-o ch g Clantime-Mischievous Miss (Niniski (USA))

Mrs M Reveley P Davidson-Brown

Placings:1300/13406**220**/3231216520/510405532102/23305014455/06546530600-04300000 **(3797)**

2001: 12[0]S, 12[4]GF, 11[3]GF, 12[0]GF, 12[0]GF, 11[0]GS, 12[0]G, 11[0]G

	Starts	1st	2nd	3rd	Win & Pl
Career Total (Turf)	61	7	7	8	43568
Career Total (AW)	3	0	1	1	882

67	8/99	Ripn	1m4f60y	D(0-85)H	GD	£5405
73	9/98	Nott	1m1f213yF(0-65)		GD	£2952
73	4/98	Thsk	1m4f	E(0-70)	G-S	£2834
70	6/97	NmkJ	1m4f	D(0-80)I I	SFT	£7197
69	5/97	Newc	1m4f93y	D(0-80)H	G-S	£3420
66	4/96	Pont	1m4y	F(0-60)	G-F	£2920
45	4/95	Muss	7f15y	F	GD	£2624

Total win prize-money £27354

Going (Turf): Sf: 1-11 GS: 2-10 **Gd: 3-22** GF: 1-18 Fm: 0-0
Distance: 5f/6f: 0-0 7f-8f: 1-4 **9f-13f: 6-53** 14f+: 0-7
Track : **LH: 4-47** RH: 3-14 **Tight: 3-27** Gall: 2-14
Aids: Bl: 0-0 Vi: 0-0 Tstrap: 0-0
Best Rating: 49 6/01 Bevl 1m3f216y gd-fm

Shagraan

90 **73**

2-y-o b c Darshaan-L'Ideale (USA) (Alysheba (USA))

J L Dunlop The Thoroughbrod Corporation

Placings:000 **(5367)**

2001: 7[0]GF, 8[0]GS, 8[0]GS

	Starts	1st	2nd	3rd	Win & Pl
Career Total (Turf)	3	0	0	0	

Going (Turf): Sf: 0-0 GS: 0-2 Gd: 0-0 GF: 0-1 Fm: 0-0
Distance: 5f/6f: 0-0 7f-8f: 0-3 9f-13f: 0-0 14f+: 0-0
Track : LH: 0-0 RH: 0-0 Tight: 0-0 Gall: 0-0
Aids: Bl: 0-0 Vi: 0-0 Tstrap: 0-0
Best Rating: 73 10/01 NmkR 1m gd-sft

500,000gns half-brother to Aegean Dream. Promise on his debut but disappointed on soft ground subsequently.

Shah Jehan (USA)

103 **99**

2-y-o b c Mr Prospector (USA)-Voodoo Lily (USA) (Baldski (USA))

A P O'Brien M Tabor & Mrs John Magnier

Placings:1240 **(5388)**

2001: 6[1]G, 7[2]GF, 7[4]HO, 7[0]GS

	Starts	1st	2nd	3rd	Win & Pl
Career Total (Turf)	4	1	1	0	31074

87	6/01	Leop	6f	GD	£10400

Total win prize-money £10400

Going (Turf): Sf: 0-0 GS: 0-1 **Gd: 1-1** GF: 0-1 Fm: 0-0
Distance: **5f/6f: 1-1** 7f-8f: 0-3 9f-13f: 0-0 14f+: 0-0
Track : LH: 0-0 RH: 0-1 Tight: 0-0 Gall: 0-0
Aids: Bl: 0-0 Vi: 0-0 Tstrap: 0-0
Best Rating: 99 10/01 NmkR 7f gd-sft

He made a winning debut in a Leopardstown maiden and was narrowly beaten in a Listed event at the Curragh next time. Out of his depth in the Grand Criterium in October.

Shahirah (USA)

101 **89**

3-y-o b f Diesis-Shemaq (USA) (Blushing John (USA))

M P Tregoning Hamdan Al Maktoum

Placings:100-40 **(4310)**

2001: 9[4]GF, 10[0]GF

	Starts	1st	2nd	3rd	Win & Pl
Career Total (Turf)	5	1	0	0	5213

81	8/00	Kemp	7f	D	G-F	£4368

Total win prize-money £4368

Going (Turf): Sf: 0-1 GS: 0-1 Gd: 0-0 **GF: 1-3** Fm: 0-0
Distance: 5f/6f: 0-0 **7f-8f: 1-3** 9f-13f: 0-2 14f+: 0-0
Track : LH: 0-1 **RH: 1-3** Tight: 0-1 **Gall: 1-3**
Aids: Bl: 0-0 Vi: 0-0 Tstrap: 0-0
Best Rating: 89 8/01 Gdwd 1m1f gd-fm

Ready winner on her debut, she finished last in the Group One Fillies' Mile after being hampered, and probably did not handle the heavy ground on her only other run. Had to overcome a ten-month lay-off on reappearance at three and ran with credit to finish fourth. Has won over seven furlongs. Acts on fast ground.

Shahm (IRE)

99 **75**

2-y-o b c Marju (IRE)-Istibshar (USA) (Mr Prospector (USA))

J H M Gosden Hamdan Al Maktoum

Placings:5025300 **(5283)**

2001: 6[5]GF, 5[0]G, 6[2]GF, 6[5]G, 7[3]GS, 8[0]GS, 8[0]HY

	Starts	1st	2nd	3rd	Win & Pl
Career Total (Turf)	7	0	1	1	2386

Going (Turf): Sf: 0-1 GS: 0-2 Gd: 0-2 GF: 0-2 Fm: 0-0
Distance: 5f/6f: 0-4 7f-8f: 0-3 9f-13f: 0-0 14f+: 0-0
Track : LH: 0-2 RH: 0-2 Tight: 0-1 Gall: 0-0
Aids: Bl: 0-1 Vi: 0-1 Tstrap: 0-5
Best Rating: 75 8/01 Gdwd 7f gd-sft

He has shown ability but has not really progressed, and disappointed when tried in a visor.

Shahzan House (IRE)

91 **75**

2-y-o b c Sri Pekan (USA)-Nsx (Roi Danzig (USA))

M A Jarvis H R H Sultan Ahmad Shah

Placings:00 **(5289)**

2001: 7[0]G, 7[0]S

	Starts	1st	2nd	3rd	Win & Pl
Career Total (Turf)	2	0	0	0	

Going (Turf): Sf: 0-1 GS: 0-0 Gd: 0-1 GF: 0-0 Fm: 0-0
Distance: 5f/6f: 0-0 7f-8f: 0-2 9f-13f: 0-0 14f+: 0-0
Track : LH: 0-0 RH: 0-1 Tight: 0-0 Gall: 0-1
Aids: Bl: 0-0 Vi: 0-0 Tstrap: 0-0
Best Rating: 75 9/01 Kemp 7f good

Shakakhan

102(101) (77)**79**

3-y-o ch f Night Shift (USA)-Sea Wedding (Groom Dancer (USA))

B W Hills Peter M Law

Placings:531-0340210 **(4994)**

2001: 8[0]S, 10[3]G, 10[4]GF, 8[0]G, 9[2]GS, 8[1]G, 8[0]HY, 8[5]SD

	Starts	1st	2nd	3rd	Win & Pl
Career Total (Turf)	9	1	1	2	6683
Career Total (AW)	1	1	0	0	3136

79	8/01	Ayr	1m	D(0-80)H	GD	£4283
77	11/00	Wolv	1m1f79y	D	STD	£3135

Total win prize-money £7420

Going (Turf): Sf: 0-3 GS: 0-2 **Gd: 1-3** GF: 0-1 Fm: 0-0
Distance: 5f/6f: 0-2 7f-8f: 1-2 9f-13f: 1-6 14f+: 0-0
Track : **LH: 2-6** RH: 0-1 **Tight: 1-3** Gall: 0-0
Aids: Bl: 0-0 Vi: 0-0 Tstrap: 0-0
Best Rating: 79 8/01 Ayr 1m good

She got off the mark in a maiden on the Wolverhampton Fibresand on her third and final start at two and added to that in an Ayr handicap in August. Suited by some cut on turf.

Shakran

84 **79+**

2-y-o ch c Zafonic (USA)-Myself (Nashwan (USA))

Sir Michael Stoute Hamdan Al Maktoum

Placings:3 **(3446)**

2001: 6[3]GF

	Starts	1st	2nd	3rd	Win & Pl
Career Total (Turf)	1	0	0	1	1033

Going (Turf): Sf: 0-0 GS: 0-0 Gd: 0-0 GF: 0-1 Fm: 0-0
Distance: 5f/6f: 0-1 7f-8f: 0-0 9f-13f: 0-0 14f+: 0-0
Track : LH: 0-0 RH: 0-0 Tight: 0-0 Gall: 0-0
Aids: Bl: 0 0 Vi: 0-0 Tstrap: 0-0
Best Rating: 79 7/01 Asct 6f gd-fm

Shalamantika (IRE)

90 **75+**

2-y-o b f Nashwan (USA)-Sharamana (IRE) (Darshaan)

Sir Michael Stoute H H Aga Khan

Placings:0 **(5277)**

2001: 7[0]GS

	Starts	1st	2nd	3rd	Win & Pl
Career Total (Turf)	1	0	0	0	

Going (Turf): Sf: 0-0 GS: 0-1 Gd: 0-0 GF: 0-0 Fm: 0-0
Distance: 5f/6f: 0-0 7f-8f: 0-1 9f-13f: 0-0 14f+: 0-0
Track : LH: 0-0 RH: 0 0 Tight: 0-0 Gall: 0-0
Aids: Bl: 0-0 Vi: 0-0 Tstrap: 0-0
Best Rating: 75 10/01 Leic 7f9y gd-sft

Shalbeblue (IRE)

98(101) (61)**49**

4-y-o b g Shalford (IRE)-Alberjas (IRE) (Sure Blade (USA))

B Ellison P M Schofield & S Kimberley

Placings:350004042-1604 **(4855)**

2001: 11[1]GD, 10[6]3, 10[0]GF, 11[4]GF

	Starts	1st	2nd	3rd	Win & Pl
Career Total (Turf)	11	0	0	1	994
Career Total (AW)	2	1	1	0	3024

55	1/01	Sthl	1m3f	F	STD	£2149

Total win prize-money £2149

Going (Turf): Sf: 0-3 GS: 0-1 Gd: 0-2 GF: 0-3 Fm: 0-2
Distance: 5f/6f: 0-0 7f-8f: 0-3 **9f-13f: 1-10** 14f+: 0-0
Track : **LH: 1-8** RH: 0-3 Tight: 0-4 Gall: 0-3
Aids: **Bl: 1-1** Vi: 0-4 Tstrap: 0-0
Best Rating: 55 1/01 Sthl 1m3f stand

Did not show a lot last season on turf and ran slightly better on the All-Weather. Runs in headgear now but that could be losing its effect.

Shallat (IRE)

104 **49**

3-y-o b f Pennekamp (USA)-Zivania (IRE) (Shernazar)

M R Channon Sheikh Ahmed Al Maktoum

Placings:034 (1447)
2001: 8^{0}GS, 11^{3}G, 12^{4}GF

	Starts	1st	2nd	3rd	Win & Pl
Career Total (Turf)	3	0	0	1	884

Going (Turf): Sf: 0-0 GS: 0-1 Gd: 0-1 GF: 0-1 Fm: 0-0
Distance: 5f/6f: 0-0 7f-8f: 0-1 9f-13f: 0-2 14f+: 0-0
Track : LH: 0-1 RH: 0-1 Tight: 0-2 Gall: 0-0
Aids: Bl: 0-0 Vi: 0-0 Tstrap: 0-0
Best Rating: 49 5/01 Thsk 1m4f gd-fm

Shallus

79(90) (54)**44**
2-y-o b c Zamindar (USA)-Wild Truffes (IRE) (Danehill (USA))
W G M Turner A Wilkinson

Placings:4330 **(4623)**
2001: 5^{4}S, 5^{3}SD, 5^{3}SD, 5^{0}GF

	Starts	1st	2nd	3rd	Win & Pl
Career Total (Turf)	2	0	0	0	289
Career Total (AW)	2	0	0	2	732

Going (Turf): Sf: 0-1 GS: 0-0 Gd: 0-0 GF: 0-1 Fm: 0-0
Distance: 5f/6f: 0-4 7f-8f: 0-0 9f-13f: 0-0 14f+: 0-0
Track : LH: 0-1 RH: 0-0 Tight: 0-1 Gall: 0-0
Aids: Bl: 0-0 Vi: 0-0 Tstrap: 0-0
Best Rating: 60 5/01 Wolv 5f stand

He has shown bags of pace on both starts but was not suited by the ground first time and hung badly to his left under pressure on his subsequent sand debut.

Shamaiel (IRE)

113 **106**
4-y-o b f Lycius (USA)-Pearl Kite (USA) (Silver Hawk (USA))
G A Butler Abdulla Al Khalifa

Placings:440430100-2351100 **(4660)**
2001: 10^{2}G, 14^{3}GF, 12^{5}GS, 11^{1}GF, 14^{1}GF, 13^{0}G, 14^{0}GF

	Starts	1st	2nd	3rd	Win & Pl
Career Total (Turf)	16	3	1	2	45933

106 8/01 Gdwd 1m6f A G-F £15877
106 8/01 Newb 1m3f5y B(0-100)H G-F £9122
86 9/00 Bath 1m3f144yD GD £3916
Total win prize-money £28915

Going (Turf): Sf: 0-1 GS: 0-1 Gd: 1-4 **GF: 2-10** Fm: 0-0
Distance: 5f/6f: 0-0 7f-8f: 0-0 **9f-13f: 2-12** 14f+: 1-4
Track : **LH: 2-7** RH: 1-5 **Tight: 2-6** Gall: 1-6
Aids: Bl: 0-0 Vi: 0-0 Tstrap: 0-0
Best Rating: 106 8/01 Gdwd 1m6f gd-fm

A useful staying filly, she won a maiden at Bath by seven lengths last year and was also fourth in a Listed event at Ascot. She made an encouraging start to the new season when going down narrowly to the race-fit Moon Solitaire over ten furlongs at Newmarket in May, and ran a blinder to finish third behind Akbar when stepped up to 14 furlongs at Goodwood. Ran a sound race in a Listed event at Newmarket before running out an easy winner of a Newbury handicap, and capped that with her first Pattern victory at Goodwood. Stays 14 furlongs, appears to act on fast and easy ground.

Shaman

103(98) (65)**58**
4-y-o b g Fraam-Magic Maggie (Beveled (USA))
G L Moore Mrs S M Redjep

Placings:62241030**041**/**21**0132200-0**000**2603310 **(5624)**
2001: 12^{0}SW, 10^{0}SW, 9^{0}HY, 9^{0}G, 9^{2}GF, 10^{6}GF, 9^{0}G, 9^{3}GF, 9^{3}GF, 9^{1}GS, 9^{0}GS

	Starts	1st	2nd	3rd	Win & Pl
Career Total (Turf)	23	3	5	3	12778
Career Total (AW)	8	2	1	1	4810

58 10/01 Sals 1m1f198yE(0-70)H G-S £3209
64 6/00 Brig 1m1f209yF(0-60) FRM £2331
65 4/00 Ling 1m2f G STD £1834
60 12/99 Ling 1m G STD £1889
68 8/99 Folk 7f F G-S £2635
Total win prize-money £11899

Going (Turf): Sf: 0-3 **GS: 2-3** Gd: 0-4 GF: 0-7 Fm: 1-6
Distance: 5f/6f: 0-2 7f-8f: 2-10 **9f-13f: 3-19** 14f+: 0-0
Track : **LH: 3-18** RH: 1-3 **Tight: 3-13** Gall: 0-0
Aids: Bl: 0-0 Vi: 0-0 Tstrap: 0-0
Best Rating: 58 10/01 Sals 1m1f198y gd-sft

Consistent sort who won twice in 2000 and twice in 1999, and has won once this season. Acts on most types of ground and is effective at ten furlongs plus.

Shamarco (IRE)

89 **71**
2-y-o b f Common Grounds-Fanciful (IRE) (Mujtahid (USA))
P W Harris Bowstead, Holmes, Mansfield & Rice

Placings:000 **(3145)**
2001: 6^{0}GF, 6^{0}GF, 6^{0}G

	Starts	1st	2nd	3rd	Win & Pl
Career Total (Turf)	3	0	0	0	

Going (Turf): Sf: 0-0 GS: 0-0 Gd: 0-1 GF: 0-2 Fm: 0-0
Distance: 5f/6f: 0-1 7f-8f: 0-2 9f-13f: 0-0 14f+: 0-0
Track : LH: 0-0 RH: 0-0 Tight: 0-0 Gall: 0-0
Aids: Bl: 0-0 Vi: 0-0 Tstrap: 0-1
Best Rating: 71 7/01 Chep 6f16y gd-fm

Shamokin

(89) (21)**16d**
9-y-o b g Green Desert (USA)-Shajan (Kris)
F Watson F Watson

Placings:0/655000/5000630/**030**000/243056060/50-00 **(0370)**
2001: 8^{0}SW, 8^{0}SW

	Starts	1st	2nd	3rd	Win & Pl
Career Total (Turf)	22	0	0	1	368
Career Total (AW)	11	0	1	2	1088

Going (Turf): Sf: 0-1 GS: 0-0 Gd: 0-8 GF: 0-9 Fm: 0-4
Distance: 5f/6f: 0-0 7f-8f: 0-19 9f-13f: 0-14 14f+: 0-0
Track : LH: 0-24 RH: 0-6 Tight: 0-7 Gall: 0-4
Aids: Bl: 0-0 Vi: 0-1 Tstrap: 0-0
Best Rating: 10 2/01 Sthl 1m slow

Shampooed (IRE)

92 **47**
7-y-o b m Law Society (USA)-White Cap'S (Shirley Heights)
R Dickin Warwick Members Racing Club

Placings:0/001306/055120/32-6 **(1620)**
2001: 16^{6}GF

	Starts	1st	2nd	3rd	Win & Pl
Career Total (Turf)	16	2	2	2	8049

72 6/98 Thur 2m GD £2568
63 6/97 Tral 1m3f (0-65)H FRM £2740
Total win prize-money £5309

Going (Turf): Sf: 0-3 GS: 0-2 **Gd: 1-3** GF: 0-4 **Fm: 1-2**
Distance: 5f/6f: 0-0 7f-8f: 0-2 9f-13f: 1-7 14f+: 1-7
Track : LH: 1-9 RH: 1-6 Tight: 0-1 Gall: 0-1
Aids: Bl: 0-1 Vi: 0-0 Tstrap: 0-0
Best Rating: 44 5/01 Wwck 2m39y gd-fm

Shamsan (IRE)

98(99) (68)**68**
4-y-o ch c Night Shift (USA)-Awayil (USA) (Woodman (USA))
P J Hobbs Jack Joseph

Placings:064/1032052230**34**-5 **(2406)**
2001: 10^{5}F

	Starts	1st	2nd	3rd	Win & Pl
Career Total (Turf)	10	0	2	2	2814
Career Total (AW)	6	1	1	1	5666

68 1/00 Ling 1m D(0-85)H STD £4056
Total win prize-money £4056

Going (Turf): Sf: 0-2 GS: 0-0 Gd: 0-3 GF: 0-2 Fm: 0-3
Distance: 5f/6f: 0-3 **7f-8f: 1-5** 9f-13f: 0-8 14f+: 0-0
Track : **LH: 1-13** RH: 0-1 **Tight: 1-8** Gall: 0-1
Aids: Bl: 0-2 Vi: 0-0 Tstrap: 0-1
Best Rating: 61 6/01 Ling 1m2f firm

Shane

90 **40**
3-y-o ch g Aragon-Angel Fire (Nashwan (USA))
C W Thornton Guy Reed

Placings:0060 **(4905)**
2001: 6^{0}G, 5^{0}G, 6^{6}G, 8^{0}G

	Starts	1st	2nd	3rd	Win & Pl
Career Total (Turf)	4	0	0	0	0

Going (Turf): Sf: 0-0 GS: 0-0 Gd: 0-4 GF: 0-0 Fm: 0-0
Distance: 5f/6f: 0-3 7f-8f: 0-0 9f-13f: 0-1 14f+: 0-0
Track : LH: 0-0 RH: 0-1 Tight: 0-0 Gall: 0-0
Aids: Bl: 0-0 Vi: 0-0 Tstrap: 0-0
Best Rating: 40 8/01 Ayr 6f good

Shanghai Crab (USA)

(97) (61d)
5-y-o b g Manila (USA)-Saraa Ree (USA) (Caro)
J G Given A Clarke

Placings:1430420505/0-0066 **(0229)**
2001: 8^{0}SD, 8^{0}SD, 11^{6}SW, 12^{6}SD

	Starts	1st	2nd	3rd	Win & Pl
Career Total (Turf)	8	0	1	1	2306
Career Total (AW)	7	1	0	0	2773

74 3/99 Sthl 1m D STD £2773
Total win prize-money £2773

Going (Turf): Sf: 0-1 GS: 0-1 Gd: 0-0 GF: 0-6 Fm: 0-0
Distance: 5f/6f: 0-0 **7f-8f: 1-5** 9f-13f: 0-10 14f+: 0-0
Track : **LH: 1-10** RH: 0-4 Tight: 0-4 Gall: 0-1
Aids: Bl: 0-0 Vi: 0-0 Tstrap: 0-0
Best Rating: 55 1/01 Sthl 1m stand

Shanghai Lady

99(42) **45**
5-y-o b m Sabrehill (USA)-Session (Reform)
G A Butler Pacific Hawk (hk) Limited

Placings:0/04100/00-000 **(5419)**
2001: 9^{0}G, 14^{0}GS, 12^{0}SD

	Starts	1st	2nd	3rd	Win & Pl
Career Total (Turf)	10	1	0	0	3633
Career Total (AW)	1	0	0	0	

68 9/99 Brig 7f214y D SFT £3382
Total win prize-money £3383

Going (Turf): **Sf: 1-4** GS: 0-2 Gd: 0-3 GF: 0-0 Fm: 0-1
Distance: 5f/6f: 0-0 **7f-8f: 1-5** 9f-13f: 0-5 14f+: 0-1
Track : **LH: 1-5** RH: 0-2 Tight: 0-3 Gall: 0-0
Aids: Bl: 0-0 Vi: 0-0 **Tstrap: 1-5**
Best Rating: 45 10/01 Sals 1m6f15y gd-sft

Shannon Flyer (USA)

100 **65**
3-y-o br c Irish River (FR)-Stormeor (CAN) (Lypheor)
J W Hills Freddy Bienstock And Martin Boase

Placings:0-052160 **(4016)**
2001: 7^{0}G, 7^{5}GF, 6^{2}GF, 6^{1}GF, 7^{6}GF, 7^{0}G

	Starts	1st	2nd	3rd	Win & Pl
Career Total (Turf)	7	1	1	0	4957

65 7/01 Wwck 6f21y D G-F £3558
Total win prize-money £3559

Going (Turf): Sf: 0-1 GS: 0-0 Gd: 0-2 **GF: 1-4** Fm: 0-0
Distance: 5f/6f: 0-1 **7f-8f: 1-6** 9f-13f: 0-0 14f+: 0-0
Track : LH: 0-1 RH: 0-1 Tight: 0-1 Gall: 0-1
Aids: Bl: 0-0 Vi: 0-0 Tstrap: 0-0
Best Rating: 65 7/01 Wwck 6f21y gd-fm

Has progressed this season, winning over six furlongs, but looked in need of further on that occasion. Handles fast ground.

Shannon's Dream

(81) (24)**37**
5-y-o gr m Anshan-Jenny's Call (Petong)
Mrs Barbara Waring Hugh J Shapter

Placings:00/0000-00 (0796)
2001: 11⁰SD, 6⁰SD

	Starts	1st	2nd	3rd	Win & Pl
Career Total (Turf)	4	0	0	0	
Career Total (AW)	4	0	0	0	

Going (Turf): Sf: 0-1 GS: 0-0 Gd: 0-1 GF: 0-1 Fm: 0-0
Distance: 5f/6f: 0-1 7f-8f: 0-3 9f-13f: 0-3 14f+: 0-0
Track : LH: 0-4 RH: 0-1 Tight: 0-1 Gall: 0-0
Aids: Bl: 0-0 Vi: 0-0 Tstrap: 0-0

Shanook

82+
2-y-o ch c Rainbow Quest (USA)-Twafeaj (USA) (Topsider (USA))
M Johnston Abdulla Buhaleeba

Placings:3 (5268)
2001: 7³HY

	Starts	1st	2nd	3rd	Win & Pl
Career Total (Turf)	1	0	0	1	585

Going (Turf): Sf: 0-1 GS: 0-0 Gd: 0-0 GF: 0-0 Fm: 0-0
Distance: 5f/6f: 0-0 7f-8f: 0-1 9f-13f: 0-0 14f+: 0-0
Track : LH: 0-0 RH: 0-0 Tight: 0-0 Gall: 0-0
Aids: Bl: 0-0 Vi: 0-0 Tstrap: 0-0
Best Rating: 82 10/01 Ayr 7f50y heavy

Bred to stay, put in a fine debut performance at Ayr over seven furlongs in the mud.

Shanty

95 **95**
2-y-o b f Selkirk (USA)-Pippas Song (Reference Point)
B W Hills Mrs Belinda Harvey

Placings:01 (5094)
2001: 6⁰GF, 8¹GS

	Starts	1st	2nd	3rd	Win & Pl
Career Total (Turf)	2	1	0	0	4544

95 10/01 Sals 1m D G-S £4543
Total win prize-money £4544

Going (Turf): Sf: 0-0 **GS: 1-1** Gd: 0-0 GF: 0-1 Fm: 0-0
Distance: 5f/6f: 0-0 **7f-8f: 1-2** 9f-13f: 0-0 14f+: 0-0
Track : LH: 0-0 RH: 0-0 Tight: 0-0 Gall: 0-0
Aids: Bl: 0-0 Vi: 0-0 Tstrap: 0-0
Best Rating: 95 10/01 Sals 1m gd-sft

A half-sister to Nightbird, benefited from her debut to score narrowly at Salisbury in October. Stays a mile, acts on easy ground, and likely to go on from that.

Shara (IRE)

105 **76**
3-y-o b f Kahyasi-Sharamana (IRE) (Darshaan)
Sir Michael Stoute H H Aga Khan

Placings:4230 (5178)
2001: 10⁴G, 11²G, 12³G, 11⁰HY

	Starts	1st	2nd	3rd	Win & Pl
Career Total (Turf)	4	0	1	1	1803

Going (Turf): Sf: 0-1 GS: 0-0 Gd: 0-3 GF: 0-0 Fm: 0-0
Distance: 5f/6f: 0-0 7f-8f: 0-0 9f-13f: 0-4 14f+: 0-0
Track : LH: 0-2 RH: 0-0 Tight: 0-3 Gall: 0-0
Aids: Bl: 0-0 Vi: 0-0 Tstrap: 0-0
Best Rating: 76 8/01 Bath 1m3f144y good

Sharaf (IRE)

100(96) (47)**47**
8-y-o b g Sadler's Wells (USA)-Marie De Flandre (FR) (Crystal Palace (FR))
Mrs A J Perrett Mrs A E Chapman

Placings:052/2134040400/50550/543521324206/20030 45/P4230440266-25300 (5039)
2001: 18²GF, 21⁵GF, 16³G, 16⁰G, 17⁰G

	Starts	1st	2nd	3rd	Win & Pl
Career Total (Turf)	47	2	9	5	20033
Career Total (AW)	6	0	0	1	267

51 7/98 Bath 2m1f34y E(0-70)H GD £2892
80 4/96 Folk 1m4f D G-F £4026
Total win prize-money £6918

Going (Turf): Sf: 0-9 GS: 0-11 **Gd: 1-11 GF: 1-16** Fm: 0-0
Distance: 5f/6f: 0-0 7f-8f: 0-1 9f-13f: 1-7 14f+: 1-45
Track : LH: 1-32 RH: 1-18 **Tight: 2-18** Gall: 0-5
Aids: Bl: 0-2 Vi: 0-1 Tstrap: 0-0
Best Rating: 52 8/01 Gdwd 2m5f gd-fm

Ran quite well on his belated reappearance and first run for his new yard, and was not disgraced on a couple of other occasions..

Shararah

93 **69**
2-y-o br f Machiavellian (USA)-Raknah (IRE) (Night Shift (USA))
E A L Dunlop Mohammed Jaber

Placings:5 (5594)
2001: 6⁵GS

	Starts	1st	2nd	3rd	Win & Pl
Career Total (Turf)	1	0	0	0	0

Going (Turf): Sf: 0-0 GS: 0-1 Gd: 0-0 GF: 0-0 Fm: 0-0
Distance: 5f/6f: 0-1 7f-8f: 0-0 9f-13f: 0-0 14f+: 0-0
Track : LH: 0-0 RH: 0-0 Tight: 0-0 Gall: 0-0
Aids: Bl: 0-0 Vi: 0-0 Tstrap: 0-0
Best Rating: 69 11/01 NmkR 6f gd-sft

Sharazan (IRE)

102 (47)**59**
8-y-o b g Akarad (FR)-Sharaniya (USA) (Alleged (USA))
O O'Neill Merry Fellows

Placings:4212/62134/00/06060/0300-53 (0879)
2001: 18⁵S, 21³S

	Starts	1st	2nd	3rd	Win & Pl
Career Total (Turf)	20	2	3	3	17562
Career Total (AW)	2	0	0	0	0

109 7/97 Curr 2m (0-95) GD £6850
70 5/96 Leop 1m4f GD £4110
Total win prize-money £10960

Going (Turf): Sf: 0-4 GS: 0-1 **Gd: 2-8** GF: 0-3 Fm: 0-0
Distance: 5f/6f: 0-0 7f-8f: 0-1 9f-13f: 1-8 14f+: 1-13
Track : LH: 1-12 RH: 1-10 Tight: 0-4 Gall: 0-4
Aids: Bl: 0-6 Vi: 0-1 Tstrap: 0-0
Best Rating: 52 4/01 Pont 2m5f122y soft

An ex-Irish gelding, he is a thorough stayer. Runs under both codes but is not easy to win with.

Shared Harmony (IRE)

91 **46**
3-y-o b g Common Grounds-Harmer (IRE) (Alzao (USA))
P W Harris The Charmers

Placings:60-200000 (5129)
2001: 6²F, 6⁰GS, 5⁰GF, 6⁰GF, 8⁰F, 7⁰HY

	Starts	1st	2nd	3rd	Win & Pl
Career Total (Turf)	8	0	1	0	1130

Going (Turf): Sf: 0-1 GS: 0-1 Gd: 0-2 GF: 0-2 Fm: 0-2
Distance: 5f/6f: 0-6 7f-8f: 0-2 9f-13f: 0-0 14f+: 0-0
Track : LH: 0-2 RH: 0-1 Tight: 0-2 Gall: 0-0
Aids: Bl: 0-0 Vi: 0-0 Tstrap: 0-0
Best Rating: 60 6/01 Ling 6f firm

Shark (IRE)

77(59)
8-y-o b g Tirol-Gay Appeal (Star Appeal)
K A Morgan M J Harmer

Placings:0/003310/056/0000 (3966)
2001: 11⁰SD, 10⁰GF, 11⁰GS, 16⁰GS

	Starts	1st	2nd	3rd	Win & Pl
Career Total (Turf)	12	1	0	2	4575
Career Total (AW)	2	0	0	0	

49 9/97 Yarm 1m3y F(0-60)H FRM £3886
Total win prize-money £3886

Going (Turf): Sf: 0-1 GS: 0-4 Gd: 0-0 GF: 0-5 **Fm: 1-2**
Distance: 5f/6f: 0-1 7f-8f: 0-4 **9f-13f: 1-0** 14f+: 0-1
Track : LH: 0-3 RH: 0-8 Tight: 0-6 Gall: 0-2
Aids: Bl: 0-0 Vi: 0-0 Tstrap: 0-0

Shark Games

81 **50**
3-y-o b f Mind Games-Sinking (Midyan (USA))
R Hannon Loucas Poutziouri

Placings:040 (1415)
2001: 7⁰GS, 7⁴G, 8⁰S

	Starts	1st	2nd	3rd	Win & Pl
Career Total (Turf)	3	0	0	0	305

Going (Turf): Sf: 0-1 GS: 0-1 Gd: 0-1 GF: 0-0 Fm: 0-0
Distance: 5f/6f: 0-0 7f-8f: 0-3 9f-13f: 0-0 14f+: 0-0
Track : LH: 0-0 RH: 0-0 Tight: 0-0 Gall: 0-0
Aids: Bl: 0-0 Vi: 0-0 Tstrap: 0-0
Best Rating: 50 5/01 Newb 1m soft

Sharks Eyes (IRE)

2-y-o br f Marju (IRE)-Dwingeloo (IRE) (Dancing Dissident (USA))
T D Easterby North Riding Aqua Lung Club

Placings:P0 (2052)
2001: 5ᴾGS, 6⁰GF

	Starts	1st	2nd	3rd	Win & Pl
Career Total (Turf)	2	0	0	0	

Going (Turf): Sf: 0-0 GS: 0-1 Gd: 0-0 GF: 0-1 Fm: 0-0
Distance: 5f/6f: 0-2 7f-8f: 0-0 9f-13f: 0-0 14f+: 0-0
Track : LH: 0-1 RH: 0-0 Tight: 0-0 Gall: 0-0
Aids: Bl: 0-0 Vi: 0-0 Tstrap: 0-0

Sharmy (IRE)

95 **100**
5-y-o b g Caerleon (USA)-Petticoat Lane (Ela-Mana-Mou)
Ian Williams T J And Mrs H Parrott

Placings:12/145-0 (4710)
2001: 8⁰G

	Starts	1st	2nd	3rd	Win & Pl
Career Total (Turf)	6	2	1	0	15256

99	5/00	Asct	1m	C	G-S	£7203
82	8/99	Sand	1m14y	D	G-S	£3858

Total win prize-money £11063

Going (Turf): Sf: 0-1 **GS: 2-2** Gd: 0-2 GF: 0-0 Fm: 0-1
Distance: 5f/6f: 0-0 7f-8f: 1-2 9f-13f: 1-4 14f+: 0-0
Track : LH: 0-2 **RH: 2-3** Tight: 0-1 **Gall: 1-2**
Aids: Bl: 0-0 Vi: 0-0 Tstrap: 0-0
Best Rating: 69 9/01 Donc 1m good

He won at Sandown first time out at two and at Ascot on his reappearance at three. He is lightly-raced, but obviously goes well fresh. Acts on easy ground.

Sharoura

104(97) (60)**61**

5-y-o ch m Inchinor-Kinkajoo (Precocious)
J M Bradley (D Nicholls 27/7) Manor House Partnership

Placings:2/1660050100/0002000300-000050001552 **(5619)**
2001: 6^{0}HY, 8^{0}GF, 5^{0}F, 6^{0}GF, 5^{0}G, 5^{5}GS, 6^{0}GS, 6^{0}F, 5^{0}G, 6^{1}F, 6^{5}SD, 5^{5}G, 6^{2}SD

	Starts	1st	2nd	3rd	Win & Pl
Career Total (Turf)	32	3	2	1	23040
Career Total (AW)	2	0	1	0	680

61	9/01	Pont	6f	D(0-85)H	FRM	£7865
79	9/99	Yarm	5f43y	C(0-90)H	G-F	£7613
83	3/99	Donc	6f	D	G-S	£4013

Total win prize-money £19491

Going (Turf): Sf: 0-7 **GS: 1-3** Gd: 0-11 **GF: 1-7 Fm: 1-4**
Distance: **5f/6f: 3-28** 7f-8f: 0-6 9f-13f: 0-14 14f+: 0-0
Track : **LH: 1-8** RH: 0-2 Tight: 0-2 Gall: 0-2
Aids: Bl: 0-0 Vi: 0-3 Tstrap: 0-1
Best Rating: 61 9/01 Pont 6f firm

Fair sprinter, she benefited from having plummeted down the weights when scoring at Pontefract in the autumn. Effective at five or six furlongs on fast ground, although has won on an easy surface. Handles Fibresand.

Sharp Belline (IRE)

108(103) (55d)**50**

4-y-o b g Robellino (USA)-Moon Watch (Night Shift (USA))
John A Harris (J L Harris 26/5) Townville C C Racing Club

Placings:4340426226440-040 **(1548)**
2001: 12^{0}SD, 16^{4}G, 16^{0}F

	Starts	1st	2nd	3rd	Win & Pl
Career Total (Turf)	8	0	0	1	1115
Career Total (AW)	8	0	3	0	2555

Going (Turf): **Sf: 0-1 GS: 0-0 Gd: 0-3 GF: 0-2 Fm: 0-2**
Distance: 5f/6f: 0-0 7f-8f: 0-0 9f-13f: 0-13 14f+: 0-3
Track : LH: 0-11 RH: 0-5 Tight: 0-5 Gall: 0-3
Aids: Bl: 0-1 Vi: 0-1 Tstrap: 0-0
Best Rating: 47 5/01 Newc 2m19y firm

Sharp City

78 **60**

2-y-o b g Rock City-Mary Miller (Sharpo)
A C Whillans I Campbell

Placings:004 **(5030)**
2001: 6^{0}G, 7^{0}GF, 5^{4}GF

	Starts	1st	2nd	3rd	Win & Pl
Career Total (Turf)	3	0	0	0	323

Going (Turf): **Sf: 0-0 GS: 0-0** Gd: 0-1 **GF: 0-2 Fm: 0-0**
Distance: 5f/6f: 0-2 7f-8f: 0-1 9f-13f: 0-0 14f+: 0-0
Track : LH: 0-0 RH: 0-0 Tight: 0-0 Gall: 0-0
Aids: Bl: 0-0 Vi: 0-0 Tstrap: 0-0
Best Rating: 60 9/01 Muss 5f gd-fm

Sharp Command

8-y-o ch g Sharpo-Bluish (USA) (Alleged (USA))
R M Stronge (S Mellor 29/1) A P Holland

Placings:60004055421**0P**/560/4/0 **(0074)**
2001: 16^{0}SW

	Starts	1st	2nd	3rd	Win & Pl
Career Total (Turf)	7	0	0	0	0
Career Total (AW)	11	1	1	0	2718

48	11/96	Wolv	1m6f166yF(0-65)H	STD	£2085

Total win prize-money £2085

Going (Turf): **Sf: 0-0 GS: 0-2 Gd: 0-2 GF: 0-3 Fm: 0-0**
Distance: 5f/6f: 0-0 7f-8f: 0-2 9f-13f: 0-8 **14f+: 1-8**
Track : **LH: 1-14** RH: 0-4 **Tight: 1-12** Gall: 0-0
Aids: Bl: 0-1 Vi: 0-0 Tstrap: 0-0
Best Rating: 48 11/96 Wolv 1m6f166y SD

Sharp Decision

94(75) (29)**67**

2-y-o ch f Greensmith-Nihaayib (Kris)
Miss D A McHale S W James

Placings:3330 **(5408)**
2001: 5^{3}GF, 5^{3}G, 5^{3}GS, 6^{0}SD

	Starts	1st	2nd	3rd	Win & Pl
Career Total (Turf)	3	0	0	3	1510
Career Total (AW)	1	0	0	0	

Going (Turf): **Sf: 0-0 GS: 0-1 Gd: 0-1 GF: 0-1 Fm: 0-0**
Distance: 5f/6f: 0-4 7f-8f: 0-0 9f-13f: 0-0 14f+: 0-0
Track : LH: 0-1 RH: 0-0 Tight: 0-0 Gall: 0-0
Aids: Bl: 0-0 Vi: 0-0 Tstrap: 0-0
Best Rating: 67 10/01 Catt 5f gd-sft

Fair form in sprint maidens on varying ground.

Sharp Edge Boy

93(93) (36)**33**

5-y-o gr g Mystiko (USA)-Leap Castle (Never So Bold)
J M Bradley Terry Reffell

Placings:0005630/**05**1023160354000/**00**0000020000**00** -000040 **(3889)**
2001: 5^{0}GS, 5^{0}F, 7^{0}GF, 5^{0}G, 5^{4}GF, 6^{0}F

	Starts	1st	2nd	3rd	Win & Pl
Career Total (Turf)	36	2	2	3	9234
Career Total (AW)	6	0	0	0	0

66	6/99	Hayd	7f30y	E(0-70)H	G-S	£2934
59	3/99	Haml	6f5y	E(0-70)H	HVY	£2814

Total win prize-money £5748

Going (Turf): **Sf: 1-11 GS: 1-5** Gd: 0-9 GF: 0-9 Fm: 0-2
Distance: 5f/6f: 0-27 **7f-8f: 2-15** 9f-13f: 0-0 14f+: 0-0
Track : **LH: 1-23** RH: 0-1 Tight: 0-8 Gall: 0-3
Aids: Bl: 0-1 Vi: 0-2 Tstrap: 0-3
Best Rating: 33 8/01 Bath 5f161y gd-fm

Sharp Gossip (IRE)

(101) (66)**61+**

5-y-o b g College Chapel-Idle Gossip (Runnett)
J A R Toller Buckingham Thoroughbreds

Placings:0/004203622/000002211**3-45** **(2341)**
2001: 8^{4}SD, 8^{5}SD

	Starts	1st	2nd	3rd	Win & Pl
Career Total (Turf)	18	1	5	1	13006
Career Total (AW)	4	1	0	1	2454

61	10/00	Yarm	7f3y	D(0-80)H	SFT	£7637
62	10/00	Sthl	1m	G(0-75)H	STD	£1967

Total win prize-money £9605

Going (Turf): **Sf: 1-8** GS: 0-2 Gd: 0-1 GF: 0-4 Fm: 0-0
Distance: 5f/6f: 0-6 **7f-8f: 2-13** 9f-13f: 0-3 14f+: 0-0
Track : **LH: 1-9** RH: 0-3 Tight: 0-2 Gall: 0-2
Aids: Bl: 0-5 Vi: 0-0 Tstrap: 0-0
Best Rating: 59 6/01 Sthl 1m stand

Sharp Hat

107(112) (65)**84**

7-y-o b g Shavian-Madam Trilby (Grundy)
D W Chapman Miss N F Thesiger

Placings:0201120/5413406200/0006300000/60000000 **01300/34244**0205261163023030**0563-1314**550100000110043021040 **(5612)**
2001: 5^{1}SD, 5^{3}SW, 5^{1}SD, 5^{4}GS, 5^{5}GF, 5^{5}GF, 5^{0}GF, 5^{1}F, 6^{0}G, 5^{0}GF, 5^{0}GF, 5^{0}F, 5^{0}S, 5^{1}GF, 5^{1}GF, 5^{0}G, 5^{0}G, 5^{4}HY, 5^{3}GS, 5^{0}G, 6^{2}G, 5^{1}GS, 6^{0}GS, 5^{4}HY, 6^{0}SD

	Starts	1st	2nd	3rd	Win & Pl
Career Total (Turf)	73	9	6	7	77889
Career Total (AW)	18	3	2	4	11945

84	10/01	Newc	5f	D(0-85)H	G-S	£4225
76	8/01	Leic	5f218y	E(0-70)	G-F	£2936
73	7/01	Bevl	5f	E(0-70)	G-F	£3052
73	6/01	Thsk	5f	D(0-80)H	FRM	£4426
65	4/01	Ling	5f	E(0-65)	STD	£2754
63	1/01	Ling	5f	E(0-75)H	STD	£2387
69	7/00	Ayr	5f	C(0-90)H	G-F	£7020
67	7/00	Newc	5f	E(0-75)H	G-F	£7202
58	11/99	Ling	5f	E(0-75)H	STD	£2788
90	5/97	Newb	6f8y	C(0-90)H	SFT	£5637
83	9/96	Donc	6f	D(0-85)	G-F	£5010
67	8/96	Wwck	6f	E	GD	£3261

Total win prize-money £50702

Going (Turf): Sf: 1-10 GS: 1-12 Gd: 1-21 **GF: 5-26** Fm: 1-4
Distance: **5f/6f: 11-83** 7f-8f: 1-8 9f-13f: 0-0 14f+: 0-0
Track : **LH: 4-22** RH: 0-2 **Tight: 3-13** Gall: 0-3
Aids: Bl: 0-1 Vi: 0-0 Tstrap: 0-0
Best Rating: 84 10/01 Newc 5f gd-sft

He has been around a bit and is capable in modest sprint handicaps on turf or sand. In good heart this year, winning six times including two on sand and was also second in the Ayr Silver Cup. A fast-ground five furlongs suits him best, but he has won over six and shown form on soft.

Sharp Play

110 **98**

6-y-o b g Robellino (USA)-Child's Play (USA) (Sharpen Up)
M Johnston Mrs I Bird

Placings:1240/141163/1042041006-4505000 **(3583)**
2001: 10^{4}F, 10^{5}G, 10^{0}GF, 10^{5}GF, 10^{0}G, 9^{0}GF, 8^{0}G

	Starts	1st	2nd	3rd	Win & Pl
Career Total (Turf)	27	6	2	1	86900

101	8/00	Gdwd	1m1f192yB H		G-F	£32500
62	5/00	Pont	1m4y	F	GD	£2530
109	5/98	Thsk	1m	B	G-F	£8270
85	5/98	Diel	1m		G-S	£7967
93	4/98	Ripn	1m1f	C	SFT	£5286
80	7/97	York	6f214y	D	GD	£6316

Total win prize-money £62871

Going (Turf): Sf: 1-1 GS: 1-3 **Gd: 2-11 GF: 2-9** Fm: 0-2
Distance: 5f/6f: 0-0 7f-8f: 3-11 9f-13f: 3-16 14f+: 0-0
Track : **LH: 4-14** RH: 2-11 **Tight: 3-8** Gall: 1-11
Aids: Bl: 0-1 Vi: 0-0 Tstrap: 0-0
Best Rating: 103 5/01 Rdcr 1m2f firm

Enjoyed a good season in 2000, winning a valuable handicap over ten furlongs at goodwood in August. Has won on soft ground, but is best on a sound surface. requires a fast-run race over ten furlongs.

Sharp Rebuff

43(90) (40)**24**

10-y-o b h Reprimand-Kukri (Kris)
Mrs L Stubbs Mrs L Stubbs

Placings:05/001/3222153**00**/54521/031630/4014**20**/054 2350/003-0 **(1595)**
2001: 7^{0}GF

	Starts	1st	2nd	3rd	Win & Pl

Career Total (Turf)	39	5	6	5	40294
Career Total (AW)	3	0	0	1	202

90	6/98	Sand	7f16y	C(0-90)H	G-S	£7197
83	6/97	Wwck	1m	D(0-80)H	GD	£3741
81	7/96	Kemp	1m	D(0-80)H	G-F	£3694
73	6/95	Wwck	1m	E(0-70)H	GD	£3523
64	7/94	Ayr	7f	F(0-60)H	GD	£3355

Total win prize-money £21513

Going (Turf): Sf: 0-9 GS: 1-9 **Gd: 3-13** GF: 1-8 Fm: 0-0
Distance: 5f/6f: 0-1 **7f-8f: 5-34** 9f-13f: 0-7 14f+: 0-0
Track : **LH: 3-13** RH: 2-13 Tight: 0-5 Gall: 0-4
Aids: Bl: 0-0 Vi: 0-2 Tstrap: 0-0
Best Rating: 64 7/94 Ayr 7f G

Sharp Shuffle (IRE)

99(100) (39)**45**

8-y-o ch g Exactly Sharp (USA)-Style (Homing)
Ian Williams G A Gilbert

Placings:50252/032220153/3162315300005/5502302 1130022/04020110/20240023210 0-000500620 **(4672)**
2001: 8^{0}SD, 8^{0}SD, 8^{0}SD, 8^{0}F, 8^{5}GF, 7^{0}GF, 8^{0}HD, 8^{6}GF, 7^{F}, 8^{0}G

	Starts	1st	2nd	3rd	Win & Pl
Career Total (Turf)	54	6	12	8	42350
Career Total (AW)	18	2	4	0	5471

56	8/00	Chep	7f16y	F	G-F	£2303
47	12/99	Wolv	1m100y	G	STD	£1574
53	11/99	Wolv	7f	G	STD	£1595
71	8/98	NmkJ	7f	E	G-F	£3882
61	7/98	NmkJ	1m	E	GD	£3817
78	6/97	Gdwd	1m	C(0-90)H	G-F	£5628
74	4/97	Brig	7f214y	D(0-75)	FRM	£3550
74	9/96	Kemp	7f	E(0-70)H	GD	£3355

Total win prize-money £25707

Going (Turf): Sf: 0-5 GS: 0-5 Gd: 2-13 **GF: 3-25** Fm: 1-6
Distance: 5f/6f: 0-3 **7f-8f: 7-37** 9f-13f: 1-32 14f+: 0-0
Track : **LH: 3-39** RH: 2-10 **Tight: 2-24** Gall: 0-3
Aids: Bl: 0-0 Vi: 0-0 Tstrap: 0-0
Best Rating: 55 6/01 Wwck 7f26y gd-fm

Sharp Soprano

85 **65**

2-y-o b f Mon Tresor-Gentle Star (Comedy Star (USA))
B R Millman Mrs Izabel Palmer

Placings:066 **(4608)**
2001: 6^{0}GF, 6^{6}GF, 5^{6}F

	Starts	1st	2nd	3rd	Win & Pl
Career Total (Turf)	3	0	0	0	0

Going (Turf): Sf: 0-0 GS: 0-0 Gd: 0-0 GF: 0-2 Fm: 0-1
Distance: 5f/6f: 0-1 7f-8f: 0-2 9f-13f: 0-0 14f+: 0-0
Track : LH: 0-1 RH: 0-0 Tight: 0-0 Gall: 0-1
Aids: Bl: 0-0 Vi: 0-0 Tstrap: 0-0
Best Rating: 65 9/01 Bath 5f11y firm

Sharp Spice

103(91) (39)**59**

5-y-o b m Lugana Beach-Ewar Empress (IRE) (Persian Bold)
D J Coakley The Nags Head Racing Syndicate

Placings:050/60005014334/44452553031403-33454 **(5599)**
2001: 12^{3}GF, 11^{3}GF, 12^{4}G, 13^{5}GS, 12^{4}GS, 12^{6}SD

	Starts	1st	2nd	3rd	Win & Pl
Career Total (Turf)	31	2	1	7	19526
Career Total (AW)	2	0	0	0	

59	9/00	Epsm	1m4f10y	E(0-75)H	GD	£4524
58	8/99	Gdwd	1m1f192y	E(0-70)H	GD	£4200

Total win prize-money £8724

Going (Turf): Sf: 0-7 GS: 0-7 **Gd: 2-7** GF: 0-7 Fm: 0-3
Distance: 5f/6f: 0-1 7f-8f: 0-6 **9f-13f: 2-25** 14f+: 0-1
Track : LH: 1-21 RH: 1-6 **Tight: 2-12** Gall: 0-7
Aids: Bl: 0-0 Vi: 0-1 Tstrap: 0-0

Best Rating: 59 9/01 York 1m3f195y gd-fm

A fair handicapper over a mile and a half. Lightly raced in 2001. Has only won on good ground.

Sharp Steel

96(108) (54d)**27**

6-y-o ch g Beveled (USA)-Shift Over (USA) (Night Shift (USA))
Miss S J Wilton John Pointon And Sons

Placings:600/2515/35002/5621253200-120040500500 **(4672)**
2001: 8^{1}SD, 8^{2}SD, 8^{0}SD, 8^{0}SD, 8^{4}SW, 8^{0}SD, 7^{5}GF, 8^{0}SD, 8^{0}SD, 8^{5}SD, 10^{0}GF, 8^{0}G, 8^{0}SD

	Starts	1st	2nd	3rd	Win & Pl
Career Total (Turf)	7	0	0	0	0
Career Total (AW)	27	3	6	2	9488

58	1/01	Sthl	1m	G	STD	£1379
60	5/00	Sthl	1m	G	STD	£1946
61	3/98	Sthl	7f	G	STD	£1922

Total win prize-money £5248

Going (Turf): Sf: 0-0 GS: 0-1 Gd: 0-3 GF: 0-3 Fm: 0-0
Distance: 5f/6f: 0-3 **7f-8f: 3-25** 9f-13f: 0-6 14f+: 0-0
Track : **LH: 3-30** RH: 0-0 Tight: 0-9 Gall: 0-0
Aids: Bl: 0-0 Vi: 0-1 Tstrap: 0-0
Best Rating: 61 1/01 Sthl 1m stand

Sharpe's Lady

68 **5**

3-y-o b f Prince Des Coeurs (USA)-To The Point (Sharpen Up)
Nick Williams Mrs Sarah Fox

Placings:000 **(4610)**
2001: 7^{0}S, 6^{0}F, 5^{0}F

	Starts	1st	2nd	3rd	Win & Pl
Career Total (Turf)	3	0	0	0	

Going (Turf): Sf: 0-1 GS: 0-0 Gd: 0-0 GF: 0-0 Fm: 0-2
Distance: 5f/6f: 0-1 7f-8f: 0-2 9f-13f: 0-0 14f+: 0-0
Track : LH: 0-1 RH: 0-0 Tight: 0-0 Gall: 0-1
Aids: Bl: 0-0 Vi: 0-0 Tstrap: 0-0
Best Rating: 5 8/01 Chep 7f16y soft

Sharpinch

98(105) (76)**64**

3-y-o b c Beveled (USA)-Giant Nipper (Nashwan (USA))
P R Chamings Mrs Ann Jenkins

Placings:6-200220001 **(5131)**
2001: 7^{2}SD, 6^{0}G, 7^{0}F, 8^{2}SD, 7^{2}GF, 8^{0}G, 7^{0}F, 8^{0}F, 7^{1}HY, 7^{2}SD

	Starts	1st	2nd	3rd	Win & Pl
Career Total (Turf)	8	1	1	0	5006
Career Total (AW)	2	0	2	0	1360

63	10/01	Ling	7f	E(0-70)H	HVY	£4077

Total win prize-money £4078

Going (Turf): Sf: 1-2 GS: 0-0 Gd: 0-2 GF: 0-1 Fm: 0-3
Distance: 5f/6f: 0-1 **7f-8f: 1-7** 9f-13f: 0-2 14f+: 0-0
Track : LH: 0-4 RH: 1-4 Tight: 0-1 Gall: 0-0
Aids: Bl: 0-0 Vi: 0-0 Tstrap: 0-0
Best Rating: 76 6/01 Sthl 1m stand

Has shown ability on Fibresand and turf. He relished the testing conditions when making almost all the running to land a seven-furlong handicap at Lingfield in October

Sharvie

104(104) (52)**42**

4-y-o b g Rock Hopper-Heresheis (Free State)
Mrs Lydia Pearce (J Pearce 22/2) Mrs Jennifer Marsh

Placings:0/00603223-23124000 **(5170)**
2001: 16^{2}SD, 16^{3}SW, 16^{1}SD, 16^{2}SD, 16^{4}SD, 16^{0}GF, 16^{0}G, 17^{0}GS, 16^{6}SD

	Starts	1st	2nd	3rd	Win & Pl
Career Total (Turf)	8	0	0	0	0
Career Total (AW)	9	1	4	3	5121

51	2/01	Wolv	2m46y	F(0-65)H	STD	£2289

Total win prize-money £2289

Going (Turf): Sf: 0-0 GS: 0-2 Gd: 0-3 GF: 0-3 Fm: 0-0
Distance: 5f/6f: 0-0 7f-8f: 0-1 9f-13f: 0-1 **14f+: 1-15**
Track : **LH: 1-15** RH: 0-1 **Tight: 1-8** Gall: 0-0
Aids: Bl: 0-0 Vi: 0-0 Tstrap: 0-0
Best Rating: 52 2/01 Wolv 2m46y stand

Shasta

83 **48**

2-y-o b f Shareef Dancer (USA)-Themeda (Sure Blade (USA))
W R Muir Larksborough Stud Limited

Placings:0 **(4637)**
2001: 7^{0}GF

	Starts	1st	2nd	3rd	Win & Pl
Career Total (Turf)	1	0	0	0	

Going (Turf): Sf: 0-0 GS: 0-0 Gd: 0-0 GF: 0-1 Fm: 0-0
Distance: 5f/6f: 0-0 7f-8f: 0-1 9f-13f: 0-0 14f+: 0-0
Track : LH: 0-0 RH: 0-0 Tight: 0-0 Gall: 0-0
Aids: Bl: 0-0 Vi: 0-0 Tstrap: 0-0
Best Rating: 48 9/01 Ling 7f gd-fm

Shatarah

94 **92+**

2-y-o ch f Gulch (USA)-Arjuzah (IRE) (Ahonoora)
J H M Gosden Hamdan Al Maktoum

Placings:3 **(4384)**
2001: 0^{3}GF

	Starts	1st	2nd	3rd	Win & Pl
Career Total (Turf)	1	0	0	1	720

Going (Turf): Sf: 0-0 GS: 0-0 Gd: 0-0 GF: 0-1 Fm: 0-0
Distance: 5f/6f: 0-0 7f-8f: 0-1 9f-13f: 0-0 14f+: 0-0
Track : LH: 0-0 RH: 0-0 Tight: 0-0 Gall: 0-0
Aids: Bl: 0-0 Vi: 0-0 Tstrap: 0-0
Best Rating: 92 8/01 Sals 6f212y gd-fm

Shatin Beauty

97 **24**

4-y-o b f Mistertopogigo (IRE)-Starisk (Risk Me (FR))
Miss L A Perratt Shatin Racing Group

Placings:124440/0000000-050260000500 **(4466)**
2001: 5^{0}S, 5^{5}GF, 5^{0}G, 5^{2}GF, 5^{6}F, 5^{0}GF, 5^{0}F, 5^{0}GF, 6^{0}G, 5^{5}GF, 5^{0}G, 5^{0}G

	Starts	1st	2nd	3rd	Win & Pl
Career Total (Turf)	25	1	2	0	4747

69	7/99	Haml	5f4y	F	FRM	£2737

Total win prize-money £2738

Going (Turf): Sf: 0-5 GS: 0-1 Gd: 0-8 GF: 0-8 **Fm: 1-3**
Distance: **5f/6f: 1-22** 7f-8f: 0-3 9f-13f: 0-0 14f+: 0-0
Track : LH: 0-0 RH: 0-1 Tight: 0-0 Gall: 0-1
Aids: Bl: 0-0 Vi: 0-0 Tstrap: 0-0
Best Rating: 36 5/01 Muss 5f gd-fm

Shatin Dollybird (IRE)

86 **69**

3-y-o ch f Up And At 'Em-Pumpona (USA) (Sharpen Up)
Miss L A Perratt Shatin Racing Group

Placings:223310340-00 **(1725)**
2001: 5^{0}GF, 6^{0}GF

	Starts	1st	2nd	3rd	Win & Pl
Career Total (Turf)	11	1	2	3	6398

73	7/00	Haml	5f4y	F	G-F	£2843

Total win prize-money £2844

Going (Turf): Sf: 0-0 GS: 0-0 Gd: 0-3 **GF: 1-6** Fm: 0-2
Distance: **5f/6f: 1-10** 7f-8f: 0-1 9f-13f: 0-0 14f+: 0-0

Track : LH: 0-0 RH: 0-0 Tight: 0-0 Gall: 0-0
Aids: Bl: 0-0 Vi: 0-0 Tstrap: 0-0
Best Rating: **49** 5/01 Ayr 5f gd-fm

Shatin Lad

76 **12**
4-y-o b g Timeless Times (USA)-Fauve (Dominion)
Miss L A Perratt Shatin Racing Group

Placings:0/0 **(4400)**
2001: 6^{0}G

	Starts	1st	2nd	3rd	Win & Pl
Career Total (Turf)	2	0	0	0	

Going (Turf): Sf: 0-0 GS: 0-0 Gd: 0-2 GF: 0-0 Fm: 0-0
Distance: 5f/6f: 0-2 7f-8f: 0-0 9f-13f: 0-0 14f+: 0-0
Track : LH: 0-0 RH: 0-0 Tight: 0-0 Gall: 0-0
Aids: Bl: 0-0 Vi: 0-0 Tstrap: 0-0
Best Rating: **12** 8/01 Ayr 6f good

Shatin Princess (IRE)

96 **55**
2-y-o b f Darnay-Lady Conchita (IRE) (Whistling Deer)
Miss L A Perratt Shatin Racing Group

Placings:06440303000 **(5660)**
2001: 5^{0}G, 6^{6}GF, 6^{4}GF, 5^{4}G, 6^{0}GF, 7^{3}GF, 5^{0}G, 6^{3}GF, 6^{0}HY, 6^{0}S, 5^{0}G

	Starts	1st	2nd	3rd	Win & Pl
Career Total (Turf)	11	0	0	2	2961

Going (Turf): Sf: 0-2 GS: 0-0 Gd: 0-4 GF: 0-5 Fm: 0-0
Distance: 5f/6f: 0-8 7f-8f: 0-3 9f-13f: 0-0 14f+: 0-0
Track : LH: 0-0 RH: 0-0 Tight: 0-0 Gall: 0-0
Aids: Bl: 0-0 Vi: 0-0 Tstrap: 0-0
Best Rating: **76** 6/01 Ayr 6f gd-fm

Shatin Venture (IRE)

102 **60**
4-y-o b g Lake Coniston (IRE)-Justitia (Dunbeath (USA))
Miss L A Perratt Shatin Racing Group

Placings:1424/3000501-00050053000 **(5288)**
2001: 6^{0}G, 6^{0}GF, 6^{0}G, 7^{5}GF, 7^{0}F, 6^{0}S, 7^{5}GS, 7^{3}GS, 7^{0}HY, 7^{0}GF, 6^{0}HY

	Starts	1st	2nd	3rd	Win & Pl		
Career Total (Turf)	22	2	1	2	16987		
61	9/00	Hayd	6f	C(0-90)		SFT	£7058
91	5/99	Ayr	5f	D		GD	£3072

Total win prize-money £10131

Going (Turf): Sf: 1-4 GS: 0-2 **Gd: 1-8** GF: 0-7 Fm: 0-1
Distance: **5f/6f: 2-11** 7f-8f: 0-11 9f-13f: 0-0 14f+: 0-0
Track : LH: 0-6 RH: 0-1 Tight: 0-1 Gall: 0-1
Aids: Bl: 0-0 Vi: 0-0 Tstrap: 0-0
Best Rating: **78** 6/01 Ayr 7f gd-fm

He was too high in the handicap for quite a while and his only win since his racecourse debut came in a Haydock classified event at the end of 2000. He has dropped to a fair mark nowadays and is running a bit better as a result. Has yet to win beyond six furlongs, but does stay seven.

Shaven Rock

(91) (33)
4-y-o b g Rock City-So Bold (Never So Bold)
K R Burke M J Wilson And Mrs Elaine Burke

Placings:0-540 **(0263)**
2001: 11^{5}SD, 9^{4}SW, 8^{0}SW

	Starts	1st	2nd	3rd	Win & Pl
Career Total (Turf)	0	0	0	0	
Career Total (AW)	4	0	0	0	0

Going (Turf): Sf: 0-0 GS: 0-0 Gd: 0-0 GF: 0-0 Fm: 0-0
Distance: 5f/6f: 0-0 7f-8f: 0-1 9f-13f: 0-3 14f+: 0-0
Track : LH: 0-4 RH: 0-0 Tight: 0-1 Gall: 0-0
Aids: Bl: 0-0 Vi: 0-0 Tstrap: 0-0
Best Rating: **33** 1/01 Sthl 1m3f stand

Shaw Venture

84(74) (30)**36**
4-y-o ch g Whittingham (IRE)-Al Shany (Burslem)
B Palling Mrs M M Palling

Placings:054516060/**6**0605630-0 **(1367)**
2001: 9^{0}G

	Starts	1st	2nd	3rd	Win & Pl		
Career Total (Turf)	16	1	0	1	3154		
Career Total (AW)	2	0	0	0	0		
73	7/99	Wind	5f10y	E		G-F	£2827

Total win prize-money £2827

Going (Turf): Sf: 0-2 GS: 0-2 Gd: 0-3 **GF: 1-8** Fm: 0-1
Distance: **5f/6f: 1-11** 7f-8f: 0-1 9f-13f: 0-6 14f+: 0-0
Track : LH: 0-6 **RH: 1-2** Tight: 0-4 **Gall: 1-2**
Aids: Bl: 0-2 Vi: 0-0 Tstrap: 0-0
Best Rating: **3** 5/01 Brig 1m1f209y good

Shayadi (IRE)

105 **91**
4-y-o b g Kahyasi-Shayrdia (IRE) (Storm Bird (CAN))
M Johnston Bill Wilson

Placings:2421-100020 **(4172)**
2001: 10^{1}HY, 10^{0}S, 10^{0}G, 10^{0}GF, 15^{2}GF, 13^{0}G

	Starts	1st	2nd	3rd	Win & Pl		
Career Total (Turf)	10	2	3	0	17398		
91	4/01	Pont	1m2f6y	C(0-90)		HVY	£7377
89	8/00	Rosc	1m2f			FRM	£3450

Total win prize-money £10828

Going (Turf): Sf: 1-2 GS: 0-0 Gd: 0-3 GF: 0-3 **Fm: 1-1**
Distance: 5f/6f: 0-0 7f-8f: 0-1 **9f-13f: 2-7** 14f+: 0-2
Track : LH: 1-7 RH: 1-3 Tight: 0-0 Gall: 0-4
Aids: Bl: 0-0 Vi: 0-0 Tstrap: 0-0
Best Rating: **91** 4/01 Pont 1m2f6y heavy

Lightly raced, he was trained in 2000 by John Oxx, he won a Roscommon maiden on fast ground and acted as Sinndar's pacemaker on one occasion. He loved the testing conditions at Pontefract where he won on his first start for Mark Johnston over ten furlongs. Also ran well over 15 furlongs in the summer.

Shayzara (IRE)

92 **57**
4-y-o b f Turtle Island (IRE)-Shayraz (Darshaan)
N J Henderson Peter E Clinton

Placings:0 **(1126)**
2001: 12^{0}GS

	Starts	1st	2nd	3rd	Win & Pl
Career Total (Turf)	1	0	0	0	

Going (Turf): Sf: 0-0 GS: 0-1 Gd: 0-0 GF: 0-0 Fm: 0-0
Distance: 5f/6f: 0-0 7f-8f: 0-0 9f-13f: 0-1 14f+: 0-0
Track : LH: 0-1 RH: 0-0 Tight: 0-1 Gall: 0-0
Aids: Bl: 0-0 Vi: 0-0 Tstrap: 0-0
Best Rating: **57** 5/01 Thsk 1m4f gd-sft

She Wadi Wadi

101 **58**
3-y-o b f Green Desert (USA)-Great Inquest (Shernazar)
A C Stewart Lord Dalmeny

Placings:00-0032000 **(4773)**
2001: 7^{0}GS, 8^{0}GF, 8^{3}GF, 7^{2}G, 8^{0}G, 7^{0}GF, 8^{0}G

	Starts	1st	2nd	3rd	Win & Pl
Career Total (Turf)	9	0	1	1	1679

Going (Turf): Sf: 0-1 GS: 0-1 Gd: 0-4 GF: 0-3 Fm: 0-0
Distance: 5f/6f: 0-0 7f-8f: 0-6 9f-13f: 0-3 14f+: 0-0
Track : LH: 0-2 RH: 0-3 Tight: 0-2 Gall: 0-0
Aids: Bl: 0-0 Vi: 0-0 Tstrap: 0-0
Best Rating: **58** 7/01 Leic 7f9y good

Modest handicapper, she gets a mile and acts on fast ground.

She's Bonnie (IRE)

4-y-o b f Mtoto-Clyde Goddess (IRE) (Scottish Reel)
W De Best-Turner W De Best-Turner

Placings:00 **(2593)**
2001: 11^{0}G, 10^{0}GF

	Starts	1st	2nd	3rd	Win & Pl
Career Total (Turf)	2	0	0	0	

Going (Turf): Sf: 0-0 GS: 0-0 Gd: 0-1 GF: 0-1 Fm: 0-0
Distance: 5f/6f: 0-0 7f-8f: 0-0 9f-13f: 0-2 14f+: 0-0
Track : LH: 0-1 RH: 0-1 Tight: 0-0 Gall: 0-1
Aids: Bl: 0-0 Vi: 0-0 Tstrap: 0-0

She's Flash (IRE)

87(88) (59)**50**
2-y-o b f Woodborough (USA)-Beechwood Quest (IRE) (River Falls)
G A Swinbank (B S Rothwell 13/6) B Valentine

Placings:403630 **(4772)**
2001: 5^{4}F, 5^{0}GF, 5^{3}GF, 7^{6}G, 8^{3}SW, 7^{0}G

	Starts	1st	2nd	3rd	Win & Pl
Career Total (Turf)	5	0	0	1	314
Career Total (AW)	1	0	0	1	326

Going (Turf): Sf: 0-0 GS: 0-0 Gd: 0-2 GF: 0-2 Fm: 0-1
Distance: 5f/6f: 0-3 7f-8f: 0-2 9f-13f: 0-1 14f+: 0-0
Track : LH: 0-2 RH: 0-1 Tight: 0-2 Gall: 0-0
Aids: Bl: 0-0 Vi: 0-0 Tstrap: 0-0
Best Rating: **59** 9/01 Wolv 1m100y slow

She's Smokin

95(82) (19)**27**
3-y-o b f Cigar-Beau Dada (IRE) (Pine Circle (USA))
J Cullinan Turf 2000 Limited

Placings:00000 **(3961)**
2001: 7^{0}SW, 6^{0}SD, 5^{0}SD, 5^{0}GF, 6^{0}G, 6^{0}SD

	Starts	1st	2nd	3rd	Win & Pl
Career Total (Turf)	2	0	0	0	
Career Total (AW)	3	0	0	0	

Going (Turf): Sf: 0-0 GS: 0-0 Gd: 0-1 GF: 0-1 Fm: 0-0
Distance: 5f/6f: 0-3 7f-8f: 0-2 9f-13f: 0-0 14f+: 0-0
Track : LH: 0-2 RH: 0-0 Tight: 0-1 Gall: 0-0
Aids: Bl: 0-0 Vi: 0-0 Tstrap: 0-0
Best Rating: **27** 7/01 Leic 5f218y gd-fm

Shearwater

(79) (17)
4-y-o b f Shareef Dancer (USA)-Sea Ballad (USA) (Bering)
G L Moore Leydens Farm Stud

Placings:0-66 **(0249)**
2001: 12^{6}SD, 13^{6}SW

	Starts	1st	2nd	3rd	Win & Pl
Career Total (Turf)	0	0	0	0	
Career Total (AW)	3	0	0	0	0

Going (Turf): Sf: 0-0 GS: 0-0 Gd: 0-0 GF: 0-0 Fm: 0-0
Distance: 5f/6f: 0-0 7f-8f: 0-0 9f-13f: 0-3 14f+: 0-0
Track : LH: 0-3 RH: 0-0 Tight: 0-3 Gall: 0-0
Aids: Bl: 0-0 Vi: 0-0 Tstrap: 0-0

Best Rating: 17 2/01 Ling 1m4f stand

Sheer Bliss (IRE)

103 **81+**

2-y-o b f Sadler's Wells (USA)-Sheer Audacity (Troy)
Sir Mark Prescott Mrs Max Morris

Placings:10 **(5569a)**
2001: 8^{1}HY, 8^{0}HO

	Starts	1st	2nd	3rd	Win & Pl
Career Total (Turf)	2	1	0	0	4371

81 10/01 Nott 1m54y D HVY £4371
Total win prize-money £4371

Going (Turf): Sf: 1-1 GS: 0-0 Gd: 0-0 GF: 0-0 Fm: 0-0
Distance: 5f/6f: 0-0 7f-8f: 0-1 **9f-13f: 1-1** 14f+: 0-0
Track : LH: 1-1 RH: 0-1 Tight: 0-0 Gall: 0-0
Aids: Bl: 0-0 Vi: 0-0 Tstrap: 0-0
Best Rating: 81 10/01 Nott 1m54y heavy

A half-sister to Derby winner Oath, she quickened up well in the heavy ground when winning her debut at Nottingham. Ran too free in a Deauville Group Three subsequently.

Sheer Devious (IRE)

47(82) (34)**4**

3-y-o ch g Dr Devious (IRE)-Peruke (IRE) (Thatching)
B W Hills Mrs B W Hills

Placings:000 **(1415)**
2001: 8^{6}SD, 8^{0}SD, 8^{0}S

	Starts	1st	2nd	3rd	Win & Pl
Career Total (Turf)	1	0	0	0	
Career Total (AW)	2	0	0	0	0

Going (Turf): Sf: 0-1 **GS: 0-0 Gd: 0-0 GF: 0-0 Fm: 0-0**
Distance: 5f/6f: 0-0 7f-8f: 0-2 9f-13f: 0-1 14f+: 0-0
Track : LH: 0-2 RH: 0-0 Tight: 0-1 Gall: 0-0
Aids: Bl: 0-0 Vi: 0-0 Tstrap: 0-0
Best Rating: 34 1/01 Sthl 1m stand

Sheer Face

102(100) (55)**54**

7-y-o b g Midyan (USA)-Rock Face (Ballad Rock)
W R Muir M J Caddy

Placings:6512143/002003420350/0010500**2**000/34606 3440/**5654**0133501225-05602300 **(4635)**
2001: 9^{0}F, 11^{5}F, 10^{6}GF, 9^{0}G, 9^{2}G, 10^{3}GF, 9^{0}GF, 9^{0}GF

	Starts	1st	2nd	3rd	Win & Pl
Career Total (Turf)	56	5	7	8	36346
Career Total (AW)	5	0	0	0	0

59 8/00 Brig 1m1f209yF(0-60)H GD £2208
46 5/00 Brig 1m1f209yF(0-60) FRM £2425
74 6/98 Gdwd 1m D(0-85)H G-F £6067
90 9/96 Bath 1m5y C G-F £5307
81 8/96 Brig 6f209y E FRM £3261
Total win prize-money £19272

Going (Turf): Sf: 0-3 GS: 0-5 Gd: 1-12 **GF: 2-27 Fm: 2-9**
Distance: 5f/6f: 0-0 7f-8f: 2-21 **9f-13f: 3-40** 14f+: 0-0
Track : LH: 4-36 RH: 1-18 **Tight: 1-20** Gall: 0-7
Aids: Bl: 0-2 Vi: 0-0 Tstrap: 0-0
Best Rating: 54 8/01 Chep 1m2f36y gd-fm

Modest mile handicapper, suited by a sharp track and fast ground.

Sheer Focus (IRE)

102(95) (67)**56**

3-y-o b g Eagle Eyed (USA)-Persian Danser (IRE) (Persian Bold)
E J Alston Whitehills Racing Syndicate

Placings:0506015-**4656**6061100050 **(5539)**
2001: 8^{4}SW, 6^{6}SW, 8^{5}SD, 9^{6}GF, 8^{6}G, 7^{0}GF, 7^{6}GF, 8^{1}GF, 8^{1}GF, 8^{0}G, 8^{0}GF, 8^{0}HY, 8^{5}G, 8^{0}S, 8^{4}SD

	Starts	1st	2nd	3rd	Win & Pl
Career Total (Turf)	16	2	0	0	6780
Career Total (AW)	5	1	0	0	1932

63 8/01 Wwck 1m22y F(0-60)H G-F £2766
60 7/01 Pont 1m4y E(0-70)H G-F £4013
62 9/00 Sthl 7f G STD £1932
Total win prize-money £8712

Going (Turf): Sf: 0-2 GS: 0-1 Gd: 0-4 **GF: 2-7** Fm: 0-2
Distance: 5f/6f: 0-5 7f-8f: 1-7 **9f-13f: 2-9** 14f+: 0-0
Track : LH: 2-13 RH: 0-2 Tight: 0-4 Gall: 0-2
Aids: Bl: 0-0 Vi: 0-0 **Tstrap: 1-4**
Best Rating: 63 8/01 Wwck 1m22y gd-fm

Moderate handicapper, suited by a mile on a sound surface.

Sheer Passion

85(75) (35)**51**

3-y-o b c Distant Relative-Yldizlar (Star Appeal)
R Brotherton (B W Hills 25/1) J Laughton

Placings:000-**0000000** **(4672)**
2001: 7^{0}SD, 8^{0}SD, 6^{0}GF, 7^{0}G, 8^{0}GF, 9^{0}G, 8^{0}G

	Starts	1st	2nd	3rd	Win & Pl
Career Total (Turf)	8	0	0	0	
Career Total (AW)	2	0	0	0	

Going (Turf): Sf: 0-0 GS: 0-0 Gd: 0-5 GF: 0-3 Fm: 0-0
Distance: 5f/6f: 0-3 7f-8f: 0-3 9f-13f: 0-4 14f+: 0-0
Track : LH: 0 4 RH: 0-0 Tight: 0-1 Gall: 0-0
Aids: Bl: 0-0 Vi: 0-2 Tstrap: 0-0
Best Rating: 51 6/01 Hayd 7f30y good

Sheik'n Swing

(58) (6)

2-y-o b f Celtic Swing-Elegantissima (Polish Precedent (USA))
W G M Turner Gongolfin

Placings:0 **(3432)**
2001: 7^{0}SD

	Starts	1st	2nd	3rd	Win & Pl
Career Total (Turf)	0	0	0	0	
Career Total (AW)	1	0	0	0	

Going (Turf): Sf: 0-0 GS: 0-0 Gd: 0-0 GF: 0-0 Fm: 0-0
Distance: 5f/6f: 0-0 7f-8f: 0-1 9f-13f: 0-0 14f+: 0-0
Track : LH: 0-1 RH: 0-0 Tight: 0-0 Gall: 0-0
Aids: Bl: 0-0 Vi: 0-0 Tstrap: 0-0
Best Rating: 6 7/01 Sthl 7f stand

Sheila Blige

100 **81**

2-y-o ch f Zamindar (USA)-Stripanoora (Ahonoora)
A Berry Mrs Julie Mitchell

Placings:100600 **(4659)**
2001: 5^{1}G, 5^{0}GF, 5^{0}GF, 5^{6}GF, 6^{0}G, 6^{0}GF

	Starts	1st	2nd	3rd	Win & Pl
Career Total (Turf)	6	1	0	0	3738

63 5/01 Wwck 5f D GD £3737
Total win prize-money £3738

Going (Turf): Sf: 0-0 GS: 0-0 **Gd: 1-2** GF: 0-4 Fm: 0-0
Distance: 5f/6f: 1-6 7f-8f: 0-0 9f-13f: 0-0 14f+: 0-0
Track : LH: 1-1 RH: 0-0 Tight: 0-0 **Gall: 1-1**
Aids: Bl: 0-0 Vi: 0-0 Tstrap: 0-0
Best Rating: 81 8/01 Gdwd 5f gd-fm

A half-sister to five winners, all of whom were successful as juveniles, she showed good pace when winning a five-furlong maiden at Warwick in May, but was well exposed in better company.

Sheilas Fantasy

(80) (51)**64**

2-y-o b c So Factual (USA)-Aspen (IRE) (Scenic)
P M Mooney (Mrs L C Jewell 18/6) Sean F Gallagher

Placings:06466 **(2897a)**
2001: 5^{0}SH, 5^{6}G, 6^{4}SD, 6^{6}G, 5^{6}GF

	Starts	1st	2nd	3rd	Win & Pl
Career Total (Turf)	4	0	0	0	0
Career Total (AW)	1	0	0	0	0

Going (Turf): Sf: 0-0 GS: 0-0 Gd: 0-2 GF: 0-1 Fm: 0-0
Distance: 5f/6f: 0-5 7f-8f: 0-0 9f-13f: 0-0 14f+: 0-0
Track : LH: 0-1 RH: 0-0 Tight: 0-0 Gall: 0-0
Aids: Bl: 0-1 Vi: 0-2 Tstrap: 0-0
Best Rating: 64 5/01 Curr 5f good

Shell-B-Cosmic

78(57) (1)**40**

2-y-o ch f Cosmonaut-Shelley Marie (Gunner B)
J G Given Mrs E P Smith

Placings:0060 **(3316)**
2001: 5^{0}GF, 6^{0}SD, 6^{6}G, 7^{0}G

	Starts	1st	2nd	3rd	Win & Pl
Career Total (Turf)	3	0	0	0	0
Career Total (AW)	1	0	0	0	

Going (Turf): Sf: 0-0 GS: 0-0 Gd: 0-2 GF: 0-1 Fm: 0-0
Distance: 5f/6f: 0-2 7f-8f: 0-2 9f-13f: 0-0 14f+: 0-0
Track : LH: 0-1 RH: 0-0 Tight: 0-0 Gall: 0-0
Aids: Bl: 0-0 Vi: 0-0 Tstrap: 0-0
Best Rating: 40 7/01 Yarm 6f3y good

Shepherds Rest (IRE)

(89)

9-y-o b g Accordion-Mandy's Last (Krayyan)
S Mellor The Odd Dozen

Placings:0004055/3/3/22320/0-00 **(1470)**
2001: 14^{0}SD, 16^{0}SD

	Starts	1st	2nd	3rd	Win & Pl
Career Total (Turf)	9	0	1	1	1422
Career Total (AW)	8	0	2	2	1759

Going (Turf): Sf: 0-1 GS: 0-2 Gd: 0-0 GF: 0-6 Fm: 0-0
Distance: 5f/6f: 0-0 7f-8f: 0-0 9f-13f: 0-10 14f+: 0-7
Track : LH: 0-13 RH: 0-3 Tight: 0-4 Gall: 0-0
Aids: Bl: 0-0 Vi: 0-3 Tstrap: 0-0
Best Rating: 24 5/01 Sthl 2m stand

Sheppard's Watch

109 **105**

3-y-o b f Night Shift (USA)-Sheppard's Cross (Soviet Star (USA))
M P Tregoning Lael Stable

Placings:4110-0411624
2001: 7^{0}GS, 7^{4}G, 8^{1}GF, 8^{1}GF, 8^{6}G, 7^{2}GF, 9^{4}F

	Starts	1st	2nd	3rd	Win & Pl
Career Total (Turf)	11	4	1	0	66364

104 6/01 Epsm 1m114y A G-F £22750
103 5/01 Gdwd 1m A G-F £17387
94 8/00 Hayd 6f D GD £3679
85 8/00 Gdwd 6f D G-F £7052
Total win prize-money £50870

Going (Turf): Sf: 0-0 GS: 0-1 Gd: 1-4 **GF: 3-5** Fm: 0-1
Distance: 5f/6f: 2-4 7f-8f: 1-5 9f-13f: 1-2 14f+: 0-0
Track : LH: 1-1 RH: 1-2 **Tight: 1-1** Gall: 0-0
Aids: Bl: 0-0 Vi: 0-0 Tstrap: 0-0
Best Rating: 105 7/01 NmkJ 1m good

She looked good when winning twice over six furlongs in August 2000, but always gave the impression she would be better over further and duly scored twice over a mile in Listed events at Goodwood and Epsom this season. Acts on a sound surface.

Sherazade

79 **64**

2-y-o ch f Beveled (USA)-Miss Ritz (Robellino (USA))

G L Moore Barry Prichard & Wayne Russell

Placings:506 **(5665)**

2001: 6^{5}HY, 6^{0}HY, 6^{6}HY

	Starts	1st	2nd	3rd	Win & Pl
Career Total (Turf)	3	0	0	0	0

Going (Turf): Sf: 0-3 GS: 0-0 Gd: 0-0 GF: 0-0 Fm: 0-0
Distance: 5f/6f: 0-3 7f-8f: 0-0 9f-13f: 0-0 14f+: 0-0
Track : LH: 0-0 RH: 0-0 Tight: 0-0 Gall: 0-0
Aids: Bl: 0-0 Vi: 0-0 Tstrap: 0-0
Best Rating: 64 10/01 Donc 6f heavy

Fair form in maidens on heavy ground, could do better in handicaps.

Sherekiya (IRE)

79 **69**

3-y-o b f Lycius (USA)-Sheriya (USA) (Green Dancer (USA))

Sir Michael Stoute H H Aga Khan

Placings:55-0 **(4085)**

2001: 8^{0}GF

	Starts	1st	2nd	3rd	Win & Pl
Career Total (Turf)	3	0	0	0	0

Going (Turf): Sf: 0-2 GS: 0-0 Gd: 0-0 GF: 0-1 Fm: 0-0
Distance: 5f/6f: 0-0 7f-8f: 0-2 9f-13f: 0-1 14f+: 0-0
Track : LH: 0-2 RH: 0-1 Tight: 0-0 Gall: 0-1
Aids: Bl: 0-0 Vi: 0-0 Tstrap: 0-0
Best Rating: 29 8/01 Pont 1m4y gd-fm

Sheriff

100(81) (63d)**45**

10-y-o b g Midyan (USA)-Daisy Warwick (USA) (Sir Gaylord)

J W Hills The Sheriff Partnership

Placings:02004162/330500/03/1254/005/1114/24/0202 1034110-000050 **(5402)**

2001: 17^{0}GF, 17^{0}G, 18^{0}GF, 16^{0}SD, 16^{5}G, 17^{0}S

	Starts	1st	2nd	3rd	Win & Pl
Career Total (Turf)	38	4	5	4	21052
Career Total (AW)	8	4	1	0	11818

61	10/00	Pont	2m1f216y	E(0-70)H	HVY	£2834
53	9/00	Bath	2m1f34y	D(0-80)H	SFT	£4124
47	6/00	Bath	2m1f34y	D(0-80)H	G-F	£3740
76	2/98	Ling	2m	D(0-75)H	SLW	£3371
75	2/98	Ling	2m	E(0-70)H	SLW	£2792
59	1/98	Ling	2m	F(0-65)H	STD	£2242
56	2/96	Ling	2m	F(0-65)H	STD	£2202
69	8/93	Sand	7f16y	E H	G-F	£2900

Total win prize-money £24208

Going (Turf): Sf: 2-5 GS: 0-2 Gd: 0-12 **GF: 2-17** Fm: 0-2
Distance: 5f/6f: 0-2 7f-8f: 1-7 9f-13f: 0-7 **14f+: 7-30**
Track : **LH: 7-29** RH: 1-10 **Tight: 6-21** Gall: 0-2
Aids: Bl: 0-1 Vi: 0-0 Tstrap: 0-0
Best Rating: 45 9/01 Kemp 2m good

Sheriff Song

101(84) (60)**53**

3-y-o br g Hernando (FR)-Zippy Zoe (Rousillon (USA))

M W Easterby Yorkshire Racing Club Iii

Placings:000-006656 **(3429)**

2001: 9^{0}GF, 10^{0}GF, 10^{6}GF, 10^{6}GF, 9^{5}GF, 11^{6}SD

	Starts	1st	2nd	3rd	Win & Pl
Career Total (Turf)	7	0	0	0	0
Career Total (AW)	2	0	0	0	0

Going (Turf): Sf: 0-1 GS: 0-1 Gd: 0-0 GF: 0-5 Fm: 0-0
Distance: 5f/6f: 0-3 7f-8f: 0-0 9f-13f: 0-6 14f+: 0-0
Track : LH: 0-6 RH: 0-1 Tight: 0-2 Gall: 0-1
Aids: Bl: 0-0 Vi: 0-0 Tstrap: 0-0
Best Rating: 53 6/01 Rdcr 1m2f gd-fm

Sheringham (USA)

68(99) (75+)**65**

4-y-o b f Robin Des Pins (USA)-Kimberley (URU) (Paradise Bay)

P J Makin Mrs P J Makin

Placings:15-0 **(1715)**

2001: 7^{0}GF

	Starts	1st	2nd	3rd	Win & Pl
Career Total (Turf)	2	0	0	0	274
Career Total (AW)	1	1	0	0	1701

75	10/00	Sthl	6f	F	STD	£1701

Total win prize-money £1701

Going (Turf): Sf: 0-1 GS: 0-0 Gd: 0-0 GF: 0-1 Fm: 0-0
Distance: 5f/6f: 1-2 7f-8f: 0-1 9f-13f: 0-0 14f+: 0-0
Track : LH: 1-1 RH: 0-0 Tight: 0-0 Gall: 0-0
Aids: Bl: 0-0 Vi: 0-0 Tstrap: 0-0
Best Rating: 3 5/01 Newb 7f gd-fm

Shervana

80 **33**

5-y-o b m Cigar-Marsdale (Royal Palace)

C Drew Mrs M F White

Placings:000-0 **(1674)**

2001: 8^{0}G

	Starts	1st	2nd	3rd	Win & Pl
Career Total (Turf)	4	0	0	0	

Going (Turf): Sf: 0-0 GS: 0-0 Gd: 0-1 GF: 0-3 Fm: 0-0
Distance: 5f/6f: 0-0 7f-8f: 0-0 9f-13f: 0-4 14f+: 0-0
Track : LH: 0-0 RH: 0-2 Tight: 0-2 Gall: 0-0
Aids: Bl: 0-0 Vi: 0-0 Tstrap: 0-0
Best Rating: 4 5/01 Yarm 1m3y good

Sherzabad (IRE)

102(82) (37)**52**

4-y-o b/br g Doyoun-Sheriya (USA) (Green Dancer (USA))

H J Collingridge C V Lines

Placings:00/00000-650021350 **(4735)**

2001: 10^{6}S, 11^{5}F, 12^{0}GF, 12^{0}GF, 9^{2}GF, 11^{1}GF, 12^{3}GF, 11^{5}GF, 10^{0}F

	Starts	1st	2nd	3rd	Win & Pl
Career Total (Turf)	15	1	1	1	4676
Career Total (AW)	1	0	0	0	

47	8/01	Ling	1m3f106yE(0-75)H	G-F	£3164

Total win prize-money £3164

Going (Turf): Sf: 0-3 GS: 0-1 Gd: 0-2 **GF: 1-7** Fm: 0-2
Distance: 5f/6f: 0-0 7f-8f: 0-3 **9f-13f: 1-13** 14f+: 0-0
Track : LH: 1-9 RH: 0-4 **Tight: 1-5** Gall: 0-3
Aids: Bl: 0-0 **Vi: 1-6** Tstrap: 0-1
Best Rating: 52 9/01 York 1m3f195y gd-fm

A fair handicapper at around a mile and a half. Scored at Lingfield in August 2001. Acts on fast ground.

Shibboleth (USA)

113 **118**

4-y-o b h Danzig (USA)-Razyana (USA) (His Majesty (USA))

H R A Cecil K Abdulla

Placings:114-1015 **(2971)**

2001: 7^{1}G, 8^{0}G, 7^{1}GF, 6^{5}G

	Starts	1st	2nd	3rd	Win & Pl
Career Total (Turf)	7	4	0	0	66978

118	6/01	NmkJ	7f	A	G-F	£20300
112	5/01	NmkR	7f	C	GD	£7429
112	6/00	NmkR	7f	A	G-F	£14616
102	4/00	NmkR	7f	D	G-S	£5382

Total win prize-money £47728

Going (Turf): Sf: 0-0 GS: 1-1 Gd: 1-3 **GF: 2-3** Fm: 0-0
Distance: 5f/6f: 0-1 **7f-8f: 4-6** 9f-13f: 0-0 14f+: 0-0
Track : LH: 0-0 RH: 0-1 Tight: 0-0 Gall: 0-1
Aids: Bl: 0-0 Vi: 0-0 **Tstrap: 2-4**
Best Rating: 118 6/01 NmkJ 7f gd-fm

Injured on the gallops after finishing fourth in the St James's Palace Stakes in 2000, he returned to action with a fluent win at Newmarket and looked ready to make up for lost time. However, sent off favourite for the Queen Anne, he ran a bit free and patently failed to see out the mile. Had the tongue tie back on for his success in the Criterion Stakes, and ran well when dropped to six furlongs in the July Cup. Reportedly sent to race in America.

Shifty

98 **86**

2-y-o b c Night Shift (USA)-Crodelle (IRE) (Formidable (USA))

L M Cumani M J Dawson

Placings:21200 **(5053)**

2001: 6^{2}GF, 7^{1}GF, 7^{2}GF, 8^{0}G, 7^{0}S

	Starts	1st	2nd	3rd	Win & Pl
Career Total (Turf)	5	1	2	0	5488

78	7/01	Ling	7f	E	G-F	£3122

Total win prize-money £3122

Going (Turf): Sf: 0-1 GS: 0-0 Gd: 0-1 **GF: 1-3** Fm: 0-0
Distance: 5f/6f: 0-1 **7f-8f: 1-4** 9f-13f: 0-0 14f+: 0-0
Track : LH: 0-0 RH: 0-0 Tight: 0-0 Gall: 0-0
Aids: Bl: 0-0 Vi: 0-0 Tstrap: 0-0
Best Rating: 86 8/01 Ling 7f gd-fm

A half-brother to the smart middle-distance filly Ela Athena, he made an encouraging debut when runner-up in a six-furlong maiden at Salisbury in July and went on to win over an extra furlong at Lingfield next time. He has not really gone on from there and seemed to find a mile too far for him when tried over it at Doncaster. Likes to race prominently.

Shii-Take's Girl

102 **77**

3-y-o ch f Deploy-Super Sally (Superlative)

Mrs A J Perrett Clive Batt & Mrs Elaine Batt

Placings:305-34310066 **(5179)**

2001: 9^{3}GS, 12^{4}GS, 9^{3}GF, 10^{1}GF, 9^{0}GS, 10^{0}G, 11^{6}G, 10^{6}HY

	Starts	1st	2nd	3rd	Win & Pl
Career Total (Turf)	11	1	0	3	6870

77	7/01	Newb	1m2f6y	D(0-80)H	G-F	£4576

Total win prize-money £4576

Going (Turf): Sf: 0-2 GS: 0-3 Gd: 0-2 **GF: 1-4** Fm: 0-0
Distance: 5f/6f: 0-0 7f-8f: 0-2 **9f-13f: 1-9** 14f+: 0-0
Track : LH: 1-3 RH: 0-5 Tight: 0-4 **Gall: 1-2**
Aids: Bl: 1-4 Vi: 0-0 Tstrap: 0-0
Best Rating: 77 7/01 Newb 1m2f6y gd-fm

She finished in the frame a few times before a change to front-running tactics helped her get off the mark in a handicap at Newbury in July. Suited by ten furlongs and fast ground.

Shimla (IRE)

(85) (48)**57**

3-y-o b f Rudimentary (USA)-Olivia Jane (IRE) (Ela-Mana-Mou)

Edward Lynam Gerald W Jennings

Placings:005020-0 **(4499a)**

2001: 8^{0}GF

	Starts	1st	2nd	3rd	Win & Pl
Career Total (Turf)	6	0	1	0	984
Career Total (AW)	1	0	0	0	

Going (Turf): Sf: 0-2 GS: 0-1 Gd: 0-0 GF: 0-3 Fm: 0-0
Distance: 5f/6f: 0-1 7f-8f: 0-4 9f-13f: 0-2 14f+: 0-0

Track : LH: 0-3 RH: 0-1 Tight: 0-2 Gall: 0-1
Aids: Bl: 0-0 Vi: 0-0 Tstrap: 0-1
Best Rating: 36 8/01 Tral 1m gd-fm

Shinbone Alley

74(88) (33)71d

4-y-o b g Lake Coniston (IRE)-Villota (Top Ville)
D W Chapman T S Redman

Placings:20205/5100000-00 **(5685)**
2001: 5^{0}S, 5^{0}S

	Starts	1st	2nd	3rd	Win & Pl
Career Total (Turf)	12	1	2	0	6360
Career Total (AW)	2	0	0	0	

77 6/00 Donc 5f D G-F £4309
Total win prize-money £4310

Going (Turf): Sf: 0-3 GS: 0-0 Gd: 0-2 **GF: 1-5** Fm: 0-2
Distance: **5f/6f: 1-13** 7f-8f: 0-1 9f-13f: 0-0 14f+: 0-0
Track : LH: 0-2 RH: 0-0 Tight: 0-2 Gall: 0-0
Aids: Bl: 0-0 Vi: 0-0 Tstrap: 0-0
Best Rating: 77 6/00 Donc 5f GF

Shining Oasis (IRE)

98(81) (37)52

3-y-o b f Mujtahid (USA)-Desert Maiden (Green Desert (USA))
P F I Cole Elite Racing Club

Placings:43512-05460600 **(5198)**
2001: 8^{0}GS, 8^{5}G, 10^{4}GF, 10^{6}G, 8^{0}GF, 9^{6}SW, 12^{0}GS, 9^{0}SD

	Starts	1st	2nd	3rd	Win & Pl
Career Total (Turf)	11	1	1	1	6399
Career Total (AW)	2	0	0	0	0

71 8/00 Folk 7f E G-F £2856
Total win prize-money £2856

Going (Turf): Sf: 0-0 GS: 0-2 Gd: 0-3 **GF: 1-5** Fm: 0-1
Distance: 5f/6f: 0-2 **7f-8f: 1-3** 9f-13f: 0-8 14f+: 0-0
Track : LH: 0-3 RH: 0-5 Tight: 0-5 Gall: 0-3
Aids: Bl: 0-2 Vi: 0-0 Tstrap: 0-0
Best Rating: 71 7/01 Chep 1m14y good

Shinner

96(87) (50)52

3-y-o b f Charnwood Forest (IRE)-Trick (IRE) (Shirley Heights)
T D Easterby Sandal Racing

Placings:421400-0300040 **(5292)**
2001: 7^{0}G, 8^{3}GS, 8^{0}GF, 7^{0}GF, 6^{0}G, 6^{4}GS, 7^{0}S

	Starts	1st	2nd	3rd	Win & Pl
Career Total (Turf)	11	1	1	1	5226
Career Total (AW)	2	0	0	0	0

62 6/00 Pont 6f E G-F £3737
Total win prize-money £3738

Going (Turf): Sf: 0-1 GS: 0-4 Gd: 0-2 **GF: 1-4** Fm: 0-0
Distance: **5f/6f: 1-6** 7f-8f: 0-4 9f-13f: 0-3 14f+: 0-0
Track : **LH: 1-7** RH: 0-1 Tight: 0-1 Gall: 0-0
Aids: Bl: 0-0 Vi: 0-0 Tstrap: 0-0
Best Rating: 52 7/01 Hayd 1m30y gd-sft

Shiny

102 86

2-y-o b f Shambo-Abuzz (Absalom)
C E Brittain Mrs C E Brittain

Placings:5105 **(2882)**
2001: 6^{5}F, 5^{1}GF, 5^{0}GF, 6^{5}GS

	Starts	1st	2nd	3rd	Win & Pl
Career Total (Turf)	4	1	0	0	13652

86 5/01 Sand 5f6y A G-F £12402
Total win prize-money £12402

Going (Turf): Sf: 0-0 GS: 0-1 Gd: 0-0 **GF: 1-2** Fm: 0-1
Distance: **5f/6f: 1-4** 7f-8f: 0-0 9f-13f: 0-0 14f+: 0-0
Track : LH: 0-0 RH: 0-0 Tight: 0-0 Gall: 0-0
Aids: Bl: 0-0 Vi: 0-0 Tstrap: 0-0
Best Rating: 86 5/01 Sand 5f6y gd-fm

From the family of Revoque, she is related to three winners from five to 12 furlongs and made a good start to her career. Running a bit green, she had to find her way between horses when landing the National Stakes at Sandown in May, but was a well held in group races.

Shipton Wood

106 73

3-y-o b c Caerleon (USA)-Bolas (Unfuwain (USA))
H R A Cecil K Abdulla

Placings:6422 **(3051)**
2001: 11^{6}GS, 11^{4}GF, 14^{2}GF, 14^{2}GF

	Starts	1st	2nd	3rd	Win & Pl
Career Total (Turf)	4	0	2	0	2429

Going (Turf): Sf: 0-0 GS: 0-1 Gd: 0-0 GF: 0-3 Fm: 0-0
Distance: 5f/6f: 0-0 7f-8f: 0-0 9f-13f: 0-2 14f+: 0-2
Track : LH: 0-2 RH: 0-2 Tight: 0-2 Gall: 0-1
Aids: Bl: 0-0 Vi: 0-0 Tstrap: 0-0
Best Rating: 73 7/01 Sals 1m6f15y gd-fm

A son of an Irish Oaks winner, has looked short of pace.

Shirazi

104 77

3-y-o b c Mtoto-Al Shadeedah (USA) (Nureyev (USA))
J W Hills K Berry & D Kerr

Placings:5630-34210100 **(5179)**
2001: 9^{3}GS, 10^{4}GF, 9^{2}GF, 9^{1}GF, 9^{0}G, 10^{1}GF, 10^{0}G, 10^{0}HY

	Starts	1st	2nd	3rd	Win & Pl
Career Total (Turf)	12	2	1	2	10787

77 8/01 Epsm 1m2f18y D(0-75) G-F £4231
69 7/01 Ripn 1m1f E G-F £3108
Total win prize-money £7340

Going (Turf): Sf: 0-1 GS: 0-1 Gd: 0-3 **GF: 2-6** Fm: 0-1
Distance: 5f/6f: 0-1 7f-8f: 0-2 **9f-13f: 2-9** 14f+: 0-0
Track : **LH: 1-4** RH: 0-3 **Tight: 1-7** Gall: 0-0
Aids: Bl: 0-0 Vi: 0-0 Tstrap: 0-0
Best Rating: 77 8/01 Epsm 1m2f18y gd-fm

Won five runner maiden over nine furlongs on fast ground in July 2001, and added to that over ten at Epsom, but was disappointing after that. Suited by good to firm ground.

Shirley Collins

89 73

2-y-o b f Robellino (USA)-Kisumu (Damister (USA))
M L W Bell Dgh Partnership

Placings:50600 **(5467)**
2001: 6^{5}G, 6^{0}G, 7^{6}G, 5^{0}GS, 6^{0}S

	Starts	1st	2nd	3rd	Win & Pl
Career Total (Turf)	5	0	0	0	0

Going (Turf): Sf: 0-1 GS: 0-1 Gd: 0-3 GF: 0-0 Fm: 0-0
Distance: 5f/6f: 0-3 7f-8f: 0-2 9f-13f: 0-0 14f+: 0-0
Track : LH: 0-2 RH: 0-0 Tight: 0-1 Gall: 0-0
Aids: Bl: 0-0 Vi: 0-0 Tstrap: 0-0
Best Rating: 73 9/01 Epsm 7f good

Shirley Fong (IRE)

95 62

3-y-o b f Bluebird (USA)-Decrescendo (IRE) (Polish Precedent (USA))
C F Wall Mrs Julie Mitchell

Placings:0600-00 **(2429)**
2001: 8^{0}GF, 10^{0}GF

	Starts	1st	2nd	3rd	Win & Pl
Career Total (Turf)	6	0	0	0	0

Going (Turf): Sf: 0-2 GS: 0-1 Gd: 0-0 GF: 0-3 Fm: 0-0
Distance: 5f/6f: 0-2 7f-8f: 0-3 9f-13f: 0-1 14f+: 0-0
Track : LH: 0-0 RH: 0-3 Tight: 0-2 Gall: 0-2
Aids: Bl: 0-0 Vi: 0-0 Tstrap: 0-0
Best Rating: 55 6/01 Wind 1m2f7y gd-fm

Shirley Not

104 (51)65

5-y-o gr g Paris House-Hollia (Touch Boy)
S Gollings P Whinham-P Brown-J Stelling

Placings:1225102/064223000/03104055000-344055443450 **(4904)**
2001: 5^{3}G, 5^{4}GF, 5^{4}G, 5^{0}GF, 5^{5}GF, 5^{5}GS, 5^{4}GF, 5^{4}G, 5^{3}G, 5^{4}G, 5^{5}GF, 7^{0}G

	Starts	1st	2nd	3rd	Win & Pl
Career Total (Turf)	38	2	5	4	20086
Career Total (AW)	1	1	0	0	1970

65 5/00 Bevl 5f E(0-70)H G-F £4836
73 8/98 Ches 5f16y D H G-S £3420
51 4/98 Sthl 5f G STD £1970
Total win prize-money £10226

Going (Turf): Sf: 0-5 **GS: 1-4** Gd: 0-13 **GF: 1-15** Fm: 0-1
Distance: **5f/6f: 3-38** 7f-8f: 0-1 9f-13f: 0-0 14f+: 0-0
Track : **LH: 1-8** RH: 0-2 **Tight: 1-4** Gall: 0-1
Aids: Bl: 0-4 Vi: 0-1 Tstrap: 0-0
Best Rating: 65 7/01 Pont 5f gd-fm

Has run some good races, but has been unfortunate enough to come up against some in-form sprinters this term and is not receiving much leniency from the Handicapper. Likes the minimum trip on fast ground.

Shirley's Shine (IRE)

83 59

2-y-o b f Sri Pekan (USA)-Encore Une Fois (IRE) (Shirley Heights)
S C Williams Christopher E Rohde

Placings:00 **(4271)**
2001: 7^{0}G, 8^{0}GF

	Starts	1st	2nd	3rd	Win & Pl
Career Total (Turf)	2	0	0	0	

Going (Turf): Sf: 0-0 GS: 0-0 Gd: 0-1 GF: 0-1 Fm: 0-0
Distance: 5f/6f: 0-0 7f-8f: 0-1 9f-13f: 0-1 14f+: 0-0
Track : LH: 0-0 RH: 0-1 Tight: 0-0 Gall: 0-0
Aids: Bl: 0-0 Vi: 0-0 Tstrap: 0-0
Best Rating: 59 7/01 Leic 7f9y good

Shockland (IRE)

92 69?

2-y-o b c Zamindar (USA)-Eurythmic (Pharly (FR))
A Berry Alan Berry

Placings:52000406446 **(4435)**
2001: 5^{5}GF, 6^{2}F, 6^{0}GF, 6^{0}Y, 7^{0}GS, 7^{4}F, 7^{0}G, 6^{6}G, 7^{4}G, 6^{4}G, 5^{6}G

	Starts	1st	2nd	3rd	Win & Pl
Career Total (Turf)	11	0	1	0	3456

Going (Turf): Sf: 0-0 GS: 0-1 Gd: 0-5 GF: 0-2 Fm: 0-2
Distance: 5f/6f: 0-5 7f-8f: 0-6 9f-13f: 0-0 14f+: 0-0
Track : LH: 0-6 RH: 0-0 Tight: 0-4 Gall: 0-0
Aids: Bl: 0-1 Vi: 0-0 Tstrap: 0-0
Best Rating: 83 5/01 Pont 6f firm

Shoeshine Boy (IRE)

106 89

3-y-o b g Prince Sabo-Susie Sunshine (IRE) (Waajib)
B J Meehan Oneoneone Racing

Placings:2111000-46310000005 **(5523)**
2001: 5^{4}S, 5^{6}S, 5^{3}GF, 5^{1}GF, 5^{0}GF, 5^{0}GF, 5^{0}G, 5^{0}G, 6^{0}G, 5^{0}S, 5^{5}HY

	Starts	1st	2nd	3rd	Win & Pl
Career Total (Turf)	18	4	1	1	29229

103	5/01	Thsk	5f	C(0-100)H	G-F	£7319
94	5/00	Asct	5f	B	G-S	£9001
90	4/00	NmkR	5f	C	SFT	£5712
78	4/00	Wwck	5f	E	SFT	£2949

Total win prize-money £24982

Going (Turf): Sf: 2-6 GS: 1-1 Gd: 0-4 GF: 1-7 Fm: 0-0
Distance: **5f/6f: 4-18** 7f-8f: 0-0 9f-13f: 0-0 14f+: 0-0
Track : **LH: 1-2** RH: 0-2 Tight: 0-1 **Gall: 1-3**
Aids: Bl: 0-1 Vi: 0-0 Tstrap: 0-0
Best Rating: 103 5/01 Thsk 5f gd-fm

Useful juvenile, he scored three times over the minimum trip this term. Unlucky in running at Sandown and Chester, he gained compensation at Thirsk, but has been held off higher marks since. Acts on all bar extremes of going.

Shoetime Shadow

88(74) (22)**65**
2-y-o ch g Timeless Times (USA)-Willrack Farrier (Lugana Beach)
C N Allen Shadowfax Racing

Placings:055000 **(5331)**
2001: 5^{0}SD, 5^{5}GF, 5^{5}GF, 6^{0}GF, 5^{0}S, 5^{0}HY

	Starts	1st	2nd	3rd	Win & Pl
Career Total (Turf)	5	0	0	0	236
Career Total (AW)	1	0	0	0	

Going (Turf): Sf: 0-2 GS: 0-0 Gd: 0-0 GF: 0-3 Fm: 0-0
Distance: 5f/6f: 0-6 7f-8f: 0-0 9f-13f: 0-0 14f+: 0-0
Track : LH: 0-2 RH: 0-1 Tight: 0-1 Gall: 0-1
Aids: Bl: 0-0 Vi: 0-0 Tstrap: 0-0
Best Rating: 65 8/01 Wind 5f10y gd-fm

Sholay (IRE)

97 **80**
2-y-o b c Bluebird (USA)-Splicing (Sharpo)
G A Butler Mrs S Trikha

Placings:321 **(5627)**
2001: 5^{3}G, 7^{2}S, 7^{1}G

	Starts	1st	2nd	3rd	Win & Pl
Career Total (Turf)	3	1	1	1	5270

71	11/01	Rdcr	7f	D	GD	£3752

Total win prize-money £3752

Going (Turf): Sf: 0-1 GS: 0-0 **Gd: 1-2** GF: 0-0 Fm: 0-0
Distance: 5f/6f: 0-1 **7f-8f: 1-2** 9f-13f: 0-0 14f+: 0-0
Track : LH: 0-1 RH: 0-0 Tight: 0-0 Gall: 0-1
Aids: Bl: 0-0 Vi: 0-0 Tstrap: 0-0
Best Rating: 80 10/01 Rdcr 7f soft

Got off the mark on his third attempt, having shown good promise on his two previous starts. Acts on good ground, and is effective over seven furlongs.

Sholto

102(88) (39)**53**
3-y-o b g Tragic Role (USA)-Rose Mill (Puissance)
J O'Reilly Burntwood Sports Ltd

Placings:006-01206 **(5350)**
2001: 7^{0}GF, 6^{1}S, 6^{2}GF, 6^{0}F, 5^{6}SD

	Starts	1st	2nd	3rd	Win & Pl
Career Total (Turf)	7	1	1	0	3439
Career Total (AW)	1	0	0	0	0

53	8/01	Nott	6f15y	F(0-60)H	SFT	£2699

Total win prize-money £2699

Going (Turf): Sf: 1-1 GS: 0-0 Gd: 0-0 GF: 0-5 Fm: 0-1
Distance: 5f/6f: 0-6 **7f-8f: 1-2** 9f-13f: 0-0 14f+: 0-0
Track : LH: 0-1 RH: 0-0 Tight: 0-0 Gall: 0-0
Aids: **Bl: 1-6** Vi: 0-0 Tstrap: 0-0
Best Rating: 53 8/01 Nott 6f15y soft

Plating-class sprinter. Acts on any ground, has worn blinkers.

Shontaine

(102) (27)**29**
8-y-o b g Pharly (FR)-Hinari Televideo (Caerleon (USA))
Mrs L Stubbs Mrs L Stubbs

Placings:31010200/46003621300533003166/40010600 42106360451002160533545/2121500000/00436045000 214320630002000/5166333000000045006-40P **(0124)**
2001: 8^{4}SD, 8^{0}SD, 8^{P}SW

	Starts	1st	2nd	3rd	Win & Pl
Career Total (Turf)	65	7	6	7	28080
Career Total (AW)	51	5	3	8	17095

40	1/00	Sthl	1m	F(0-60)H	STD	£1641
44	6/99	Ayr	1m	G(0-60)H	GD	£2332
63	2/98	Sthl	1m	D(0-75)H	STD	£3881
56	1/98	Sthl	1m	F(0-65)H	STD	£1735
59	9/97	Haml	1m65y	F(0-60)H	GD	£2416
57	8/97	Thsk	1m	F(0-60)H	G-F	£3099
56	5/97	Carl	6f206y	E(0-70)H	FRM	£3038
52	3/97	Ling	6f	F	STD	£2484
67	11/96	Sthl	7f	F(0-60)H	STD	£2048
64	7/96	Catt	7f	G(0-60)H	G-F	£2388
78	7/95	Newc	6f	E	G-F	£3009
74	7/95	Donc	6f	D	G-F	£3452

Total win prize-money £31526

Going (Turf): Sf: 0-8 GS: 0-10 Gd: 2-16 **GF: 4-27** Fm: 1-4
Distance: 5f/6f: 3-18 **7f-8f: 8-75** 9f-13f: 1-23 14f+: 0-0
Track : **LH: 8-72** RH: 2-22 **Tight: 4-53** Gall: 0-4
Aids: Bl: 0-11 Vi: 0-0 Tstrap: 0-0
Best Rating: 37 1/01 Sthl 1m stand

Shoof (USA)

91 **76**
2-y-o b f Dayjur (USA)-Shemaq (USA) (Blushing John (USA))
A C Stewart Hamdan Al Maktoum

Placings:6 **(5277)**
2001: 7^{6}GS

	Starts	1st	2nd	3rd	Win & Pl
Career Total (Turf)	1	0	0	0	0

Going (Turf): Sf: 0-0 GS: 0-1 Gd: 0-0 GF: 0-0 Fm: 0-0
Distance: 5f/6f: 0-0 7f-8f: 0-1 9f-13f: 0-0 14f+: 0-0
Track : LH: 0-0 RH: 0-0 Tight: 0-0 Gall: 0-0
Aids: Bl: 0-0 Vi: 0-0 Tstrap: 0-0
Best Rating: 76 10/01 Leic 7f9y gd-sft

Shoot Away

84(87) (45)**19**
3-y-o b f Polar Falcon (USA)-Cut Clear (Kris)
R M H Cowell Bottisham Heath Stud

Placings:00-30400 **(1994)**
2001: 8^{3}SW, 8^{0}SD, 8^{4}SD, 9^{0}F, 8^{0}SD

	Starts	1st	2nd	3rd	Win & Pl
Career Total (Turf)	2	0	0	0	
Career Total (AW)	5	0	0	1	264

Going (Turf): Sf: 0-1 GS: 0-0 Gd: 0-0 GF: 0-0 Fm: 0-1
Distance: 5f/6f: 0-0 7f-8f: 0-4 9f-13f: 0-3 14f+: 0-0
Track : LH: 0-6 RH: 0-1 Tight: 0-4 Gall: 0-0
Aids: Bl: 0-0 Vi: 0-0 Tstrap: 0-0
Best Rating: 45 1/01 Wolv 1m100y slow

Shore Vision

98 **78**
3-y-o b c Efisio-South Shore (Caerleon (USA))
P W Harris Beach Combers

Placings:0-0336 **(2163)**
2001: 7^{0}G, 7^{3}GF, 8^{3}GF, 8^{6}G

	Starts	1st	2nd	3rd	Win & Pl
Career Total (Turf)	5	0	0	2	1726

Going (Turf): Sf: 0-1 GS: 0-0 Gd: 0-2 GF: 0-2 Fm: 0-0
Distance: 5f/6f: 0-1 7f-8f: 0-3 9f-13f: 0-1 14f+: 0-0
Track : LH: 0-1 RH: 0-1 Tight: 0-0 Gall: 0-0
Aids: Bl: 0-0 Vi: 0-0 Tstrap: 0-0
Best Rating: 78 6/01 Sand 1m14y good

Short Change (IRE)

98 **70**
2-y-o b c Revoque (IRE)-Maafi Esm (Polish Precedent (USA))
B J Meehan R A Bernard

Placings:0220340 **(5021)**
2001: 7^{0}S, 6^{2}GF, 6^{2}GF, 6^{0}GF, 7^{3}GF, 8^{4}G, 7^{0}HY

	Starts	1st	2nd	3rd	Win & Pl
Career Total (Turf)	7	0	2	1	4007

Going (Turf): Sf: 0-2 GS: 0-0 Gd: 0-1 GF: 0-4 Fm: 0-0
Distance: 5f/6f: 0-1 7f-8f: 0-6 9f-13f: 0-0 14f+: 0-0
Track : LH: 0-1 RH: 0-1 Tight: 0-1 Gall: 0-0
Aids: Bl: 0-1 Vi: 0-0 Tstrap: 0-0
Best Rating: 85 7/01 Chep 6f16y gd-fm

A half-brother to seven-furlong juvenile winner Sawbo Lad, he very nearly landed a gamble on his third start, but has since disappointed in maidens and nurserys. Tried from six to seven furlongs.

Short Reign (IRE)

89(99) (52)**56**
2-y-o b f Mujadil (USA)-Echoing (Formidable (USA))
C A Dwyer Miss Lilo Blum

Placings:32220606 **(5660)**
2001: 5^{3}SD, 5^{2}SD, 5^{2}GF, 5^{2}SD, 5^{0}GF, 5^{6}G, 5^{0}G, 5^{6}G, 5^{0}SD

	Starts	1st	2nd	3rd	Win & Pl
Career Total (Turf)	5	0	1	0	656
Career Total (AW)	3	0	2	1	1663

Going (Turf): Sf: 0-0 GS: 0-0 Gd: 0-3 GF: 0-2 Fm: 0-0
Distance: 5f/6f: 0-8 7f-8f: 0-0 9f-13f: 0-0 14f+: 0-0
Track : LH: 0-1 RH: 0-0 Tight: 0-1 Gall: 0-0
Aids: Bl: 0-0 Vi: 0-0 Tstrap: 0-0
Best Rating: 56 11/01 Muss 5f good

Speedily bred. Placed form on the All-Weather at Southwell. Runner-up at Yarmouth on her first start on Turf. Has only raced over five furlongs on a sound surface.

Short Respite

98 **84**
2-y-o b f Brief Truce (USA)-Kingdom Princess (Forzando)
M L W Bell T S Redman

Placings:01 **(5087)**
2001: 6^{0}GF, 7^{1}GS

	Starts	1st	2nd	3rd	Win & Pl
Career Total (Turf)	2	1	0	0	2436

84	10/01	Newc	7f	F	G-S	£2436

Total win prize-money £2436

Going (Turf): Sf: 0-0 **GS: 1-1** Gd: 0-0 GF: 0-1 Fm: 0-0
Distance: 5f/6f: 0-0 **7f-8f: 1-2** 9f-13f: 0-0 14f+: 0-0
Track : LH: 0-0 RH: 0-0 Tight: 0-0 Gall: 0-0
Aids: Bl: 0-0 Vi: 0-0 Tstrap: 0-0
Best Rating: 84 10/01 Newc 7f gd-sft

A Brief Truce daughter of a dual All-Weather winner, she stayed on to land a Newcastle maiden on her second start.

Shorts

93(86) (57)**54**
2-y-o b f Primo Dominie-Gentle Irony (Mazilier (USA))

P D Evans (Andrew Reid 6/10) P D Evans

Placings:64052034 (5636)

2001: 6^{6}GF, 6^{4}F, 6^{0}GF, 5^{5}F, 5^{2}SD, 5^{0}G, 6^{3}S, 5^{4}G

	Starts	1st	2nd	3rd	Win & Pl
Career Total (Turf)	7	0	0	1	1187
Career Total (AW)	1	0	1	0	568

Going (Turf): Sf: 0-1 GS: 0-0 Gd: 0-2 GF: 0-2 Fm: 0-2
Distance: 5f/6f: 0-8 7f-8f: 0-0 9f-13f: 0-0 14f+: 0-0
Track : LH: 0-4 RH: 0-0 Tight: 0-2 Gall: 0-2
Aids: Bl: 0-0 Vi: 0-0 Tstrap: 0-0
Best Rating: 65 9/01 Bath 5f11y firm

Showed some ability on turf before running second in a seller on Fibresand debut from a poor draw. Claimed by David Evans after that race

Shot To Fame (USA)

103 98+

2-y-o b c Quest For Fame-Exocet (USA) (Deposit Ticket (USA))
P W Harris The Conquistadors

Placings:13 (5495)

2001: 7^{1}S, 8^{3}HY

	Starts	1st	2nd	3rd	Win & Pl
Career Total (Turf)	2	1	0	1	9850

98 10/01 York 7f202y E SFT £8417
Total win prize-money £8418

Going (Turf): Sf: 1-2 GS: 0-0 Gd: 0-0 GF: 0-0 Fm: 0-0
Distance: 5f/6f: 0-0 **7f-8f: 1-2** 9f-13f: 0-0 14f+: 0-0
Track : **LH: 1-1** RH: 0-0 Tight: 0-0 **Gall: 1-1**
Aids: Bl: 0-0 Vi: 0-0 Tstrap: 0-0
Best Rating: 98 10/01 York 7f202y soft

He was impressive when getting off the mark on his debut at York in October, but was last of three at odds-on at Newbury next time. He can possibly be excused on the grounds that conditions were terrible that day.

Shotacross The Bow (IRE)

89(105) (67)36

4-y-o b g Warning-Nordica (Northfields (USA))
M Blanshard The Wardroom Boys

Placings:041/0003230300-0002 (5613)

2001: 8^{0}GF, 12^{0}GF, 10^{0}GF, 9^{2}SD, 8^{0}SD

	Starts	1st	2nd	3rd	Win & Pl
Career Total (Turf)	14	1	1	2	5823
Career Total (AW)	3	0	1	1	1130

78 9/99 Epsm 6f D G-F £3468
Total win prize-money £3469

Going (Turf): Sf: 0-1 GS: 0-3 Gd: 0-2 **GF: 1-8** Fm: 0-0
Distance: **5f/6f: 1-3** 7f-8f: 0-3 9f-13f: 0-11 14f+: 0-0
Track : **LH: 1-9** RH: 0-3 **Tight: 1-9** Gall: 0-0
Aids: Bl: 0-0 Vi: 0-0 Tstrap: 0-0
Best Rating: 64 11/01 Wolv 1m1f79y stand

Handles Fibresand. Went hurdling in autumn of 2001.

Shotley Dancer

94 69

2-y-o ch f Danehill Dancer (IRE)-Hayhurst (Sandhurst Prince)
N Bycroft J A Swinburne

Placings:3543040 (4595)

2001: 5^{3}F, 5^{5}G, 7^{4}GF, 7^{3}GF, 6^{0}GF, 8^{4}G, 7^{0}GF

	Starts	1st	2nd	3rd	Win & Pl
Career Total (Turf)	7	0	0	2	1176

Going (Turf): Sf: 0-0 GS: 0-0 Gd: 0-2 GF: 0-4 Fm: 0-1
Distance: 5f/6f: 0-3 7f-8f: 0-3 9f-13f: 0-1 14f+: 0-0
Track : LH: 0-1 RH: 0-1 Tight: 0-1 Gall: 0-0
Aids: Bl: 0-0 Vi: 0-0 Tstrap: 0-0
Best Rating: 69 7/01 Newc 7f gd-fm

A half-sister to a multiple winner in Italy. Stays seven furlongs. Acts on a sound surface.

Shotstoppa (IRE)

85(70) (27)47

3-y-o ch g Beveled (USA)-From The Rooftops (IRE) (Thatching)
J L Eyre Dean Kiely & The Lloyd Organisation

Placings:0600 (3075)

2001: 8^{0}GF, 7^{0}GF, 8^{0}SD, 7^{0}GS

	Starts	1st	2nd	3rd	Win & Pl
Career Total (Turf)	3	0	0	0	0
Career Total (AW)	1	0	0	0	

Going (Turf): Sf: 0-0 GS: 0-1 Gd: 0-0 GF: 0-2 Fm: 0-0
Distance: 5f/6f: 0-0 7f-8f: 0-4 9f-13f: 0-0 14f+: 0-0
Track : LH: 0-4 RH: 0-0 Tight: 0-1 Gall: 0-0
Aids: Bl: 0-0 Vi: 0-0 Tstrap: 0-0
Best Rating: 47 5/01 Hayd 7f30y gd-fm

Shouf Al Badou (USA)

103(104) (77)56

4-y-o b g Sheikh Albadou-Millfit (USA) (Blushing Groom (FR))
Mrs J R Ramsden (D Nicholls 20/6) Sammy Doo Racing

Placings:34111/000650601-046004600650 (5414)

2001: 5^{0}GS, 7^{4}SD, 6^{6}G, 7^{0}GF, 6^{0}GF, 5^{4}SD, 8^{6}GF, 6^{0}GF, 6^{0}F, 6^{6}HY, 6^{5}HY, 6^{0}SD

	Starts	1st	2nd	3rd	Win & Pl
Career Total (Turf)	19	1	0	1	6616
Career Total (AW)	7	3	0	0	9295

77 10/00 Wolv 6f E(0-75)H STD £3038
90 11/99 Donc 1m C SFT £5414
90 10/99 Wolv 6f D STD £3415
72 10/99 Wolv 6f F STD £2253
Total win prize-money £14120

Going (Turf): Sf: 1-4 GS: 0-2 Gd: 0-2 GF: 0-10 Fm: 0-1
Distance: **5f/6f: 3-10** 7f-8f: 1-14 9f-13f: 0-2 14f+: 0-0
Track : **LH: 3-12** RH: 0-2 **Tight: 3-7** Gall: 0-2
Aids: Bl: 0-3 Vi: 0-0 Tstrap: 0-0
Best Rating: 70 5/01 Haml 6f5y good

His sire won the Breeders' Cup Sprint and he has a good record on the Fibresand at Wolverhampton. Not so good on turf but should continue to pay his way when racing on sand.

Shove Ha'Penny (IRE)

100(84) (57)85

2-y-o b c Night Shift (USA)-Penny Fan (Nomination)
N A Callaghan John Livock

Placings:0324042340523 (5590)

2001: 5^{0}S, 5^{3}GS, 5^{2}GF, 6^{4}SD, 6^{0}GF, 6^{4}GF, 7^{2}GS, 6^{3}G, 7^{4}G, 8^{0}G, 10^{5}G, 7^{2}S, 9^{3}GS

	Starts	1st	2nd	3rd	Win & Pl
Career Total (Turf)	12	0	3	3	6724
Career Total (AW)	1	0	0	0	0

Going (Turf): Sf: 0-2 GS: 0-3 Gd: 0-4 GF: 0-3 Fm: 0-0
Distance: 5f/6f: 0-6 7f-8f: 0-5 9f-13f: 0-2 14f+: 0-0
Track : LH: 0-8 RH: 0-1 Tight: 0-2 Gall: 0-1
Aids: Bl: 0-1 Vi: 0-0 Tstrap: 0-0
Best Rating: 85 10/01 Drig 7f214y soft

A late foal, has speed on his dam's side. Runs well at Brighton.

Show The Way

96(83) (36)43

3-y-o ch g Hernando (FR)-Severine (USA) (Trempolino (USA))
J R Jenkins (A P Jarvis 19/8) Uk Packaging Supplies Ltd

Placings:0-0046060 (4079)

2001: 11^{0}SD, 11^{0}GS, 11^{4}F, 14^{6}GF, 14^{0}G, 14^{6}S, 17^{0}GF

	Starts	1st	2nd	3rd	Win & Pl
Career Total (Turf)	7	0	0	0	0
Career Total (AW)	1	0	0	0	

Going (Turf): Sf: 0-2 GS: 0-1 Gd: 0-1 GF: 0-2 Fm: 0-1
Distance: 5f/6f: 0-0 7f-8f: 0-0 9f-13f: 0-4 14f+: 0-4
Track : LH: 0-5 RH: 0-2 Tight: 0-2 Gall: 0-1
Aids: Bl: 0-0 Vi: 0-0 Tstrap: 0-0
Best Rating: 43 6/01 Gdwd 1m6f gd-fm

Showdown

82 66

2-y-o gr f Darshaan-Last Second (IRE) (Alzao (USA))
Sir Mark Prescott Faisal Salman

Placings:3 (3479)

2001: 7^{3}GF

	Starts	1st	2nd	3rd	Win & Pl
Career Total (Turf)	1	0	0	1	654

Going (Turf): Sf: 0-0 GS: 0-0 Gd: 0-0 GF: 0-1 Fm: 0-0
Distance: 5f/6f: 0-0 7f-8f: 0-1 9f-13f: 0-0 14f+: 0-0
Track : LH: 0-0 RH: 0-0 Tight: 0-0 Gall: 0-0
Aids: Bl. 0-0 Vi: 0-0 Tstrap: 0-0
Best Rating: 66 7/01 Folk 7f gd-fm

Showering

72 53

2-y-o b f Danehill (USA)-Bright Spells (USA) (Alleged (USA))
J H M Gosden K Abdulla

Placings:0 (5561)

2001: 7^{0}S

	Starts	1st	2nd	3rd	Win & Pl
Career Total (Turf)	1	0	0	0	

Going (Turf): Sf: 0-1 GS: 0-0 Gd: 0-0 GF: 0-0 Fm: 0-0
Distance: 5f/6f: 0-0 7f-8f: 0-1 9f-13f: 0-0 14f+: 0-0
Track : LH: 0-0 RH: 0-0 Tight: 0-0 Gall: 0-0
Aids: Bl: 0-0 Vi: 0-0 Tstrap: 0-0
Best Rating: 53 10/01 Yarm 7f3y soft

Showing

96(88) (43)55

4-y-o b g Owington-Sharanella (Shareef Dancer (USA))
B R Johnson (W M Brisbourne 25/1) Mrs Mary B Woolterton

Placings:00/0060000-00000600 (4641)

2001: 6^{0}SW, 6^{0}SD, 8^{0}S, 6^{0}F, 6^{0}GF, 5^{6}F, 6^{0}GF, 7^{0}GF

	Starts	1st	2nd	3rd	Win & Pl
Career Total (Turf)	13	0	0	0	0
Career Total (AW)	4	0	0	0	

Going (Turf): Sf: 0-2 GS: 0-2 Gd: 0-1 GF: 0-5 Fm: 0-2
Distance: 5f/6f: 0-8 7f-8f: 0-6 9f-13f: 0-2 14f+: 0-0
Track : LH: 0-7 RH: 0-0 Tight: 0-4 Gall: 0-0
Aids: Bl: 0-1 Vi: 0-0 Tstrap: 0-5
Best Rating: 55 9/01 Ling 7f gd-fm

Showpiece

100 71

3-y-o b c Selkirk (USA)-Hawayah (IRE) (Shareef Dancer (USA))
Sir Michael Stoute Highclere Thoroughbred Racing Ltd

Placings:0025 (5464)

2001: 8^{0}S, 10^{0}GS, 10^{2}HY, 11^{5}G

	Starts	1st	2nd	3rd	Win & Pl
Career Total (Turf)	4	0	1	0	1255

Going (Turf): Sf: 0-2 GS: 0-1 Gd: 0-1 GF: 0-0 Fm: 0-0
Distance: 5f/6f: 0-0 7f-8f: 0-1 9f-13f: 0-3 14f+: 0-0
Track : LH: 0-3 RH: 0-0 Tight: 0-2 Gall: 0-0
Aids: Bl: 0-0 Vi: 0-0 Tstrap: 0-0
Best Rating: 71 4/01 NmkR 1m soft

Showtime Shirley

94(82) (26)**48**

3-y-o ch f First Trump-Wollow Maid (Wollow)
A Bailey Showtime Ice Cream Concessionaire

Placings:06001500 **(4469)**
2001: 8^{0}SD, 8^{6}SD, 8^{0}SD, 10^{0}GF, 12^{1}GF, 12^{5}GF, 12^{0}G, 12^{0}G

	Starts	1st	2nd	3rd	Win & Pl
Career Total (Turf)	5	1	0	0	2723
Career Total (AW)	3	0	0	0	0

48 6/01 Muss 1m4f F(0-65)H G-F £2723
Total win prize-money £2723

Going (Turf): Sf: 0-0 GS: 0-0 Gd: 0-2 **GF: 1-3** Fm: 0-0
Distance: 5f/6f: 0-0 7f-8f: 0-3 **9f-13f: 1-5** 14f+: 0-0
Track : LH: 0-5 RH: 0-1 Tight: 0-2 Gall: 0-0
Aids: Bl: 0-0 Vi: 0-0 Tstrap: 0-0
Best Rating: 48 6/01 Muss 1m4f gd-fm

Lightly raced. A surprise winner when stepped up to a mile and a half in summer of 2001, when out of the handicap. Acts on fast ground.

Shrivar (IRE)

94 **80**

4-y-o b g Sri Pekan (USA)-Kriva (Reference Point)
M R Channon (Mrs M Reveley 20/1) P D Savill

Placings:605/0552464140421100-40 **(3510)**
2001: 11^{4}G, 9^{0}GF

	Starts	1st	2nd	3rd	Win & Pl
Career Total (Turf)	21	3	2	0	17799

80 9/00 NmkR 1m2f C(0-100)H GD £8918
80 9/00 Pont 1m2f6y E(0-70) G-S £3068
69 7/00 Wwck 1m2f110yF(0-65)H GD £2751
Total win prize-money £14737

Going (Turf): Sf: 0-3 GS: 1-7 **Gd: 2-5** GF: 0-6 Fm: 0-0
Distance: 5f/6f: 0-0 7f-8f: 0-5 **9f-13f: 3-14** 14f+: 0-2
Track : **LH: 2-13** RH: 0-3 Tight: 0-7 Gall: 0-1
Aids: Bl: 0-0 **Vi: 2-6** Tstrap: 0-0
Best Rating: 76 7/01 Bath 1m3f144y good

Improved when a visor was fitted in the autumn of 2000. Won over hurdles for Mary Reveley during the winter. Little to write home about on turf this season.

Shudder

103 **69**

6-y-o b g Distant Relative-Oublier L'Ennui (FR) (Bellman (FR))
R J Hodges Footsteps Flyers

Placings:1233/6/5150000/43031630-201302143201 **(5671)**
2001: 6^{2}GS, 6^{0}HY, 6^{1}G, 7^{3}GF, 6^{0}GF, 6^{2}GF, 5^{1}GF, 6^{4}GF, 5^{3}F, 6^{2}HY, 5^{0}G, 6^{1}HY

	Starts	1st	2nd	3rd	Win & Pl
Career Total (Turf)	32	6	4	7	43353

69 11/01 Wind 6f E(0-70)H HVY £3052
59 8/01 Bath 5f161y E G-F £2989
59 5/01 Wind 6f F GD £2569
59 6/00 Folk 6f F FRM £1939
80 8/99 Hayd 6f F G-S £2295
85 8/97 Gdwd 6f D G-F £3590
Total win prize-money £16434

Going (Turf): Sf: 1-6 GS: 1-3 Gd: 1-9 **GF: 2-11** Fm: 1-2
Distance: **5f/6f: 6-22** 7f-8f: 0-9 9f-13f: 0-0 14f+: 0-0
Track : **LH: 1-9** RH: 0-0 Tight: 0-1 **Gall: 1-5**
Aids: Bl: 0-0 **Vi: 1-4** Tstrap: 0-0
Best Rating: 69 11/01 Wind 6f heavy

Claiming-class sprinter, suited by six furlongs, but managed to win his first ever handicap in heavy ground at Windsor in November.

Shuffle

(85) (17)

4-y-o b c First Trump-Secret Dance (Sadler's Wells (USA))
Mrs N Macauley Mrs N Macauley

Placings:065-60000 **(1471)**
2001: 12^{6}SD, 7^{0}SW, 8^{0}SW, 12^{0}SD, 11^{0}SD

	Starts	1st	2nd	3rd	Win & Pl
Career Total (Turf)	1	0	0	0	
Career Total (AW)	7	0	0	0	0

Going (Turf): Sf: 0-0 GS: 0-1 Gd: 0-0 GF: 0-0 Fm: 0-0
Distance: 5f/6f: 0-0 7f-8f: 0-3 9f-13f: 0-5 14f+: 0-0
Track : LH: 0-7 RH: 0-0 Tight: 0-0 Gall: 0-0
Aids: Bl: 0-2 Vi: 0-3 Tstrap: 0-0
Best Rating: 17 2/01 Sthl 7f slow

Shuffling Kid

101 **90**

2-y-o ch g Rock City-Clashfern (Smackover)
B A McMahon J D Graham

Placings:126055065 **(5498)**
2001: 5^{1}GS, 5^{2}GF, 5^{6}GF, 5^{0}GF, 5^{5}G, 5^{5}G, 5^{0}G, 6^{6}GS, 6^{5}HY

	Starts	1st	2nd	3rd	Win & Pl
Career Total (Turf)	9	1	1	0	10251

83 3/01 Donc 5f D G-S £5850
Total win prize-money £5850

Going (Turf): Sf: 0-1 **GS: 1-2** Gd: 0-3 GF: 0-3 Fm: 0-0
Distance: **5f/6f: 1-9** 7f-8f: 0-0 9f-13f: 0-0 14f+: 0-0
Track : LH: 0-2 RH: 0-0 Tight: 0-2 Gall: 0-0
Aids: Bl: 0-0 Vi: 0-0 Tstrap: 0-0
Best Rating: 90 8/01 York 5f good

A late foal with plenty of scope, he ran straight and true to score in the Brocklesby but has found life tough since then. Suited by cut in the ground.

Shukran

96 **85**

2-y-o b f Hamas (IRE)-Ajeebah (IRE) (Mujtahid (USA))
R Hannon Ms Liza Judd

Placings:1246 **(4546)**
2001: 5^{1}GF, 6^{2}GF, 6^{4}GS, 6^{6}GF

	Starts	1st	2nd	3rd	Win & Pl
Career Total (Turf)	4	1	1	0	7934

79 6/01 Kemp 5f E G-F £3526
Total win prize-money £3526

Going (Turf): Sf: 0-0 GS: 0-1 Gd: 0-0 **GF: 1-3** Fm: 0-0
Distance: **5f/6f: 1-4** 7f-8f: 0-0 9f-13f: 0-0 14f+: 0-0
Track : LH: 0-0 RH: 0-0 Tight: 0-0 Gall: 0-0
Aids: Bl: 0-0 Vi: 0-0 Tstrap: 0-0
Best Rating: 85 7/01 NmkJ 6f gd-sft

She made a winning debut at Kempton, but still looked green when beaten under her penalty in an Ascot novice event next time. Gave the impression the soft ground was against her when a close fourth in the Cherry Hinton. Likely to improve over further.

Shush

110(88) (62)**77**

3-y-o b g Shambo-Abuzz (Absalom)
C E Brittain Mrs C E Brittain

Placings:15601005-000000444304103 **(5293)**
2001: 7^{0}SD, 5^{0}SD, 7^{0}SD, 8^{0}G, 6^{0}F, 10^{4}GF, 10^{4}GF, 12^{4}GF, 10^{3}GF, 12^{0}GF, 10^{4}GS, 10^{1}G, 8^{0}S, 9^{3}S

	Starts	1st	2nd	3rd	Win & Pl
Career Total (Turf)	19	3	0	2	15773
Career Total (AW)	3	0	0	0	

70 9/01 Chep 1m2f36y D(0-80)H GD £4069
83 7/00 Leic 5f218y E G-F £3698
79 4/00 Kemp 5f D SFT £3575
Total win prize-money £11343

Going (Turf): Sf: 1-4 GS: 0-2 **Gd: 1-5 GF: 1-7** Fm: 0-1
Distance: **5f/6f: 2-6** 7f-8f: 0-8 9f-13f: 1-8 14f+: 0-0
Track : **LH: 1-9** RH: 0-5 Tight: 0-5 Gall: 0-2
Aids: Bl: 0-0 Vi: 0-0 Tstrap: 0-0
Best Rating: 83 6/01 Ripn 1m4f60y gd-fm

Ended a long losing run when scoring at Chepstow in September having previously run well in some competitive handicaps. Suited by ten to 12 furlongs, but not particularly consistent.

Shuwaib

101 **108**

4-y-o b c Polish Precedent (USA)-Ajab Alzamaan (Rainbow Quest (USA))
M R Channon Sheikh Ahmed Al Maktoum

Placings:13143-00 **(2010)**
2001: 15^{0}HY, 12^{0}GF

	Starts	1st	2nd	3rd	Win & Pl
Career Total (Turf)	7	2	0	2	30119

103 8/00 Deau 1m7f G-F £13449
75 6/00 Gdwd 1m4f D G-F £3900
Total win prize-money £17349

Going (Turf): Sf: 0-3 GS: 0-0 Gd: 0-1 **GF: 2-3** Fm: 0-0
Distance: 5f/6f: 0-0 7f-8f: 0-0 9f-13f: 1-2 14f+: 1-5
Track : LH: 0-1 **RH: 2-5 Tight: 1-2** Gall: 0-1
Aids: Bl: 0-0 Vi: 0-0 Tstrap: 0-0
Best Rating: 96 6/01 Epsm 1m4f10y gd-fm

Does much of his racing on the continent and landed a Deauville Listed race last season. Well beaten in heavy ground on his reappearance. Lost all chance leaving the stalls at Epsom.

Sidbury Girl

91 **39**

4-y-o b f Presidium-Busted Love (Busted)
Miss E C Lavelle Cornelius Lysaght

Placings:30000 **(5330)**
2001: 12^{3}HY, 10^{0}G, 11^{0}GF, 12^{0}GF, 16^{0}HY

	Starts	1st	2nd	3rd	Win & Pl
Career Total (Turf)	5	0	0	1	414

Going (Turf): Sf: 0-2 GS: 0-0 Gd: 0-1 GF: 0-2 Fm: 0-0
Distance: 5f/6f: 0-0 7f-8f: 0-0 9f-13f: 0-4 14f+: 0-1
Track : LH: 0-3 RH: 0-1 Tight: 0-4 Gall: 0-0
Aids: Bl: 0-0 Vi: 0-0 Tstrap: 0-0
Best Rating: 52 4/01 Folk 1m4f heavy

Siena Star (IRE)

100(96) (53)**59**

3-y-o b g Brief Truce (USA)-Gooseberry Pie (Green Desert (USA))
J L Eyre R Peel, J H A Hopkinson, J M H Binney

Placings:0044322104-56645641432 **(4896)**
2001: 8^{5}GF, 8^{6}GF, 8^{6}GF, 10^{4}GF, 8^{5}F, 8^{6}G, 8^{4}G, 9^{1}GF, 8^{4}GF, 8^{3}F, 9^{2}GS

	Starts	1st	2nd	3rd	Win & Pl
Career Total (Turf)	20	2	3	2	14506
Career Total (AW)	1	0	0	0	208

57 8/01 Muss 1m1f E G-F £3066
74 8/00 NmkJ 1m C G-F £6240
Total win prize-money £9306

Going (Turf): Sf: 0-2 GS: 0-2 Gd: 0-3 **GF: 2-9** Fm: 0-4
Distance: 5f/6f: 0-3 7f-8f: 1-12 9f-13f: 1-6 14f+: 0-0
Track : LH: 0-10 RH: 0-7 Tight: 0-6 Gall: 0-3
Aids: Bl: 0-0 Vi: 0-0 Tstrap: 0-0

Best Rating: 73 5/01 Thsk 1m gd-fm

Scored as a juvenile when stepped up to a mile on a fast surface, and took advantage of a drop in the weights to score at Musselburgh this term.

Sienna Sunset (IRE)

89 **51**

2-y-o ch f Spectrum (IRE)-Wasabi (IRE) (Polar Falcon (USA))

Mrs H Dalton Ray Bailey

Placings:4 **(5627)**

2001: 7^{4}G

	Starts	1st	2nd	3rd	Win & Pl
Career Total (Turf)	1	0	0	0	0

Going (Turf): Sf: 0-0 GS: 0-0 Gd: 0-1 GF: 0-0 Fm: 0-0
Distance: 5f/6f: 0-0 7f-8f: 0-1 9f-13f: 0-0 14f+: 0-0
Track : LH: 0-0 RH: 0-0 Tight: 0-0 Gall: 0-0
Aids: Bl: 0-0 Vi: 0-0 Tstrap: 0-0
Best Rating: 51 11/01 Rdcr 7f good

Made a good debut at Redcar in November 2001.

Sifat

105 **65**

6-y-o b m Marju (IRE)-Reine Maid (USA) (Mr Prospector (USA))

J R Jenkins Mr C N & Mrs J C Wright

Placings:4635513/0005040/511230-524554 **(3965)**

2001: 11^{5}G, 11^{2}GF, 10^{4}F, 10^{5}GF, 10^{5}GF, 10^{4}G

	Starts	1st	2nd	3rd	Win & Pl
Career Total (Turf)	26	3	2	3	12028

65	6/00	Yarm	1m2f21y	F(0-70)H	GD	£2163
58	5/00	Yarm	1m2f21y	F(0-60)H	GD	£2204
76	10/98	Pont	1m4y	D	G-S	£3647

Total win prize-money £8076

Going (Turf): Sf: 0-3 GS: 1-3 **Gd: 2-9** GF: 0-9 Fm: 0-2
Distance: 5f/6f: 0-0 7f-8f: 0-2 **9f-13f: 3-24** 14f+: 0-0
Track : **LH: 3-13** RH: 0-8 **Tight: 2-10** Gall: 0-2
Aids: Bl: 0-4 **Vi: 2-13** Tstrap: 0-0
Best Rating: 65 5/01 Yarm 1m3f101y gd-fm

Ten-furlong handicapper, fairly consistent without winning in 2001.

Sighting (IRE)

101 **82**

2-y-o b c Eagle Eyed (USA)-Sandystones (Selkirk (USA))

R F Johnson Houghton Anthony Pye-Jeary And Michael Smith

Placings:5042241200 **(4668)**

2001: 6^{5}GF, 6^{0}G, 6^{4}GF, 5^{2}GF, 5^{2}GF, 6^{4}G, 5^{1}GS, 5^{2}G, 6^{0}GY, 6^{0}GF

	Starts	1st	2nd	3rd	Win & Pl
Career Total (Turf)	10	1	3	0	8476

82	8/01	Hayd	5f	E	G-S	£3164

Total win prize-money £3164

Going (Turf): Sf: 0-0 **GS: 1-1** Gd: 0-3 GF: 0-5 Fm: 0-0
Distance: **5f/6f: 1-9** 7f-8f: 0-1 9f-13f: 0-0 14f+: 0-0
Track : LH: 0-1 RH: 0-0 Tight: 0-1 Gall: 0-0
Aids: **Bl: 1-8** Vi: 0-0 Tstrap: 0-0
Best Rating: 82 8/01 Hayd 5f gd-sft

Got off the mark at Haydock in August but was a beaten favourite next time. He has been well held since. Suited by most types of ground and acts well over five furlongs.

Sign Of The Dragon

104 **46**

4-y-o b g Sri Pekan (USA)-Tartique Twist (USA) (Arctic Tern (USA))

Miss L A Perratt (I Semple 9/7) Shatin Racing Group

Placings:453-402640610050 **(5535)**

2001: 8^{4}S, 8^{0}GS, 7^{2}GF, 6^{6}GF, 8^{4}GF, 8^{0}GF, 6^{6}G, 7^{1}G, 7^{0}G, 6^{0}GS, 8^{5}GF, 7^{0}S

	Starts	1st	2nd	3rd	Win & Pl
Career Total (Turf)	15	1	1	1	4651

46	8/01	Muss	7f30y	F(0-60)H	GD	£2828

Total win prize-money £2828

Going (Turf): Sf: 0-4 GS: 0-2 **Gd: 1-4** GF: 0-5 Fm: 0-0
Distance: 5f/6f: 0-0 **7f-8f: 1-12** 9f-13f: 0-3 14f+: 0-0
Track : LH: 0-6 RH: 0-4 Tight: 0-6 Gall: 0-0
Aids: Bl: 0-0 Vi: 0-0 Tstrap: 0-0
Best Rating: 46 9/01 Haml 1m65y gd-fm

Sign Of The Tiger

80(106) (34)**34**

4-y-o b g Beveled (USA)-Me Spede (Valiyar)

P C Haslam Mrs B Hawkins

Placings:00043/1144231000-000 **(4603)**

2001: 8^{0}SD, 10^{0}G, 7^{0}SD

	Starts	1st	2nd	3rd	Win & Pl
Career Total (Turf)	10	1	1	1	5184
Career Total (AW)	8	2	0	1	7606

72	5/00	Newc	1m3y	E(0-70)H	GD	£3120
76	2/00	Wolv	7f	E(0-70)H	STD	£2613
64	1/00	Sthl	7f	D(0-85)H	STD	£4251

Total win prize-money £9985

Going (Turf): Sf: 0-0 GS: 0-2 **Gd: 1-5** GF: 0-2 Fm: 0-1
Distance: 5f/6f: 0 3 **7f-8f: 2-12** 9f-13f: 1-3 14f+. 0-0
Track : **LH: 2-12** RH: 0-2 **Tight: 1-5** Gall: 0-2
Aids: Bl: 0-0 Vi: 0-0 Tstrap: 0-0
Best Rating: 32 9/01 Wolv 7f stand

Signed And Dated (USA)

91 **61**

2-y-o b c Red Ransom (USA)-Libeccio (NZ) (Danzatore (CAN))

P F I Cole Richard Green (fine Paintings)

Placings:40000 **(5404)**

2001: 8^{4}G, 7^{0}G, 7^{0}GF, 9^{0}HY, 8^{0}S

	Starts	1st	2nd	3rd	Win & Pl
Career Total (Turf)	5	0	0	0	286

Going (Turf): Sf: 0-2 GS: 0-0 Gd: 0-2 GF: 0-1 Fm: 0-0
Distance: 5f/6f: 0-0 7f-8f: 0-2 9f-13f: 0-3 14f+: 0-0
Track : LH: 0-4 RH: 0-0 Tight: 0-1 Gall: 0-0
Aids: Bl: 0-0 Vi: 0-0 Tstrap: 0-0
Best Rating: 61 8/01 Nott 1m54y good

Sigy Sam

86 **58**

2-y-o ch f King's Signet (USA)-Hosting (Thatching)

R J Baker S F Turton

Placings:003505 **(4211)**

2001: 5^{0}GF, 5^{0}GF, 5^{3}GF, 6^{5}GF, 5^{0}S, 5^{5}GF

	Starts	1st	2nd	3rd	Win & Pl
Career Total (Turf)	6	0	0	1	526

Going (Turf): Sf: 0-1 GS: 0-0 Gd: 0-0 GF: 0-5 Fm: 0-0
Distance: 5f/6f: 0-6 7f-8f: 0-0 9f-13f: 0-0 14f+: 0-0
Track : LH: 0-3 RH: 0-0 Tight: 0-0 Gall: 0-3
Aids: Bl: 0-0 Vi: 0-0 Tstrap: 0-0
Best Rating: 58 8/01 Bath 5f11y gd-fm

Sihafi (USA)

105 (83)**71**

8-y-o ch g Elmaamul (USA)-Kit's Double (USA) (Spring Double)

D Nicholls John Gilbertson

Placings:02/45242000**0012**/**51**0005000**005**/**100**003121 1114126352000110**020205**/00503356000000/04302361 0432450100-00514400440 **(3555)**

2001: 5^{0}S, 5^{0}S, 5^{5}GF, 5^{1}F, 5^{4}GF, 5^{4}F, 5^{0}F, 5^{0}GF, 5^{4}F, 5^{4}F, 5^{0}GF

	Starts	1st	2nd	3rd	Win & Pl
Career Total (Turf)	82	10	8	7	55915
Career Total (AW)	18	4	3	0	13618

63	5/01	Haml	5f4y	E(0-65)	FRM	£3374
68	8/00	Muss	5f	F(0-65)H	G-F	£2828
57	7/00	Ling	5f	E(0-75)H	G-F	£2786
77	10/98	Wolv	6f	D(0-85)H	STD	£4012
71	9/98	Hayd	5f	C(0-90)H	G-F	£11381
70	7/98	Sand	5f6y	D(0-80)H	G-F	£3533
64	7/98	Sals	5f	F(0-70)H	GD	£2237
53	7/98	Ling	5f	E(0-70)H	G-F	£3080
51	7/98	Folk	5f	D(0-80)H	G-F	£3752
61	7/98	Bath	5f11y	F(0-65)H	GD	£2193
54	6/98	Wind	6f	D(0-80)H	GD	£3590
64	1/98	Ling	6f	E(0-70)H	STD	£2805
57	2/97	Ling	6f	F(0-60)H	STD	£2495
51	12/96	Ling	6f	F(0-60)H	STD	£2238

Total win prize-money £50310

Going (Turf): Sf: 0-7 GS: 0-7 Gd: 3-21 **GF: 6-35** Fm: 1-12
Distance: **5f/6f: 14-92** 7f-8f: 0-8 9f-13f: 0-0 14f+: 0-0
Track : **LH: 5-29** RH: 1-7 **Tight: 4-20** Gall: 2-9
Aids: Bl: 0-1 Vi: 0-0 Tstrap: 0-0
Best Rating: 71 6/01 Newc 5f firm

Won over five furlongs in May 2001 but needs things to go his way. Acts on fast ground.

Sikasso (USA)

108 **80**

5-y-o b/br g Silver Hawk (USA)-Silken Doll (USA) (Chieftain Ii)

G A Swinbank Gee & Jay Partnership

Placings:25113552 **(3950)**

2001: 12^{2}S, 9^{5}GS, 11^{1}G, 13^{1}G, 14^{3}G, 13^{5}S, 12^{5}GF, 11^{2}GS

	Starts	1st	2nd	3rd	Win & Pl
Career Total (Turf)	8	2	2	1	10074

80	5/01	Haml	1m5f9y	E(0-75)H	GD	£3570
53	5/01	Haml	1m3f16y	D	GD	£3568

Total win prize-money £7139

Going (Turf): Sf: 0-2 GS: 0-2 **Gd: 2-3** GF: 0-1 Fm: 0-0
Distance: 5f/6f: 0-0 7f-8f: 0-0 9f-13f: 1-5 14f+: 1-3
Track : LH: 0-1 **RH: 2-4 Tight: 2-4** Gall: 0-0
Aids: Bl: 0-0 Vi: 0-0 Tstrap: 0 0
Best Rating: 80 6/01 Hayd 1m6f good

Won a weak maiden at Hamilton over 11 furlongs then followed up at same course over 13 furlongs. Has won on good ground but seems to acts on most surfaces.

Silca Blanka (IRE)

100(95) (83)**73**

9-y-o b h Law Society (USA)-Reality (Known Fact (USA))

A G Newcombe Duckhaven Stud

Placings:1104450/005102/0645060/03300041020020/1 002202100440000/11103206035-000 **(5025)**

2001: 7^{0}GS, 7^{0}G, 6^{0}S

	Starts	1st	2nd	3rd	Win & Pl
Career Total (Turf)	57	8	5	4	117752
Career Total (AW)	8	1	2	0	9327

93	6/00	Ches	7f2y	C(0-95)H	G-S	£11066
85	5/00	Ches	7f122y	C(0-90)H	GD	£9028
79	4/00	Brig	7f214y	C(0-90)H	G-S	£6922
87	6/99	Epsm	7f	D(0-85)H	GD	£7100
83	1/99	Ling	7f	C(0-95)H	STD	£6331
86	7/98	Wwck	7f	D(0-85)	G-F	£6815
98	6/95	Epsm	7f	B	FRM	£12752
100	6/94	Epsm	6f	A	GD	£10625
69	4/94	NmkR	5f	D	SFT	£4425

Total win prize-money £75067

Going (Turf): Sf: 1-10 GS: 2-9 **Gd: 3-22** GF: 1-13 Fm: 1-2
Distance: 5f/6f: 2-8 **7f-8f: 7-51** 9f-13f: 0-5 14f+: 0-0

Track : LH: **8-37** RH: 0-8 **Tight: 6-22** Gall: 0-6
Aids: Bl: 0-0 Vi: 0-0 Tstrap: 0-0
Best Rating: 73 8/01 Ches 7f2y gd-sft

Now back in training in this country after a spell at stud, he is a somewhat moody individual, but is a fair handicapper on turf and Equitrack. A sharp left-handed seven furlongs is absolutely ideal.

Silcabee

83 **37**

3-y-o b f Silca Blanka (IRE)-Shamrock Dancer (IRE) (Dance Of Life (USA))
A D Smith Miss K Smith

Placings:000 **(5024)**
2001: 9^{0}G, 8^{0}GF, 11^{0}S

	Starts	1st	2nd	3rd	Win & Pl
Career Total (Turf)	3	0	0	0	

Going (Turf): Sf: 0-1 GS: 0-0 Gd: 0-1 GF: 0-1 Fm: 0-0
Distance: 5f/6f: 0-0 7f-8f: 0-0 9f-13f: 0-3 14f+: 0-0
Track : LH: 0-1 RH: 0-1 Tight: 0-0 Gall: 0-0
Aids: Bl: 0-0 Vi: 0-0 Tstrap: 0-0
Best Rating: 37 9/01 Wwck 1m22y gd-fm

Silence And Rage

97 **60**

2-y-o b c Green Desert (USA)-Shot At Love (IRE) (Last Tycoon)
C A Cyzer Mrs E A Cyzer

Placings:0001 **(5467)**
2001: 6^{0}G, 6^{0}GF, 7^{0}GS, 6^{1}S

	Starts	1st	2nd	3rd	Win & Pl
Career Total (Turf)	4	1	0	0	3038

60 10/01 Brig 6f209y E(0-75) SFT £3038
Total win prize-money £3038

Going (Turf): Sf: 1-1 GS: 0-1 Gd: 0-1 GF: 0-1 Fm: 0-0
Distance: 5f/6f: 0-2 **7f-8f: 1-2** 9f-13f: 0-0 14f+: 0-0
Track : **LH: 1-1** RH: 0-0 Tight: 0-0 Gall: 0-0
Aids: Bl: 0-0 Vi: 0-0 Tstrap: 0-0
Best Rating: 60 10/01 Brig 6f209y soft

Won a nursery on soft ground when bottom of the weights at Brighton, under an enterprising ride.

Silence Is Golden

96 **77**

2-y-o ch f Danehill Dancer (IRE)-Silent Girl (Krayyan)
B J Meehan Miss J Semple

Placings:43031410 **(5052)**
2001: 5^{4}GS, 6^{3}GF, 6^{0}GF, 6^{3}GF, 7^{1}GF, 7^{4}G, 8^{1}GF, 7^{0}S

	Starts	1st	2nd	3rd	Win & Pl
Career Total (Turf)	8	2	0	2	11361

77 8/01 NmkJ 1m C G-F £6305
75 7/01 Ling 7f F G-F £2702
Total win prize-money £9007

Going (Turf): Sf: 0-1 GS: 0-1 Gd: 0-1 **GF: 2-5** Fm: 0-0
Distance: 5f/6f: 0-4 **7f-8f: 2-4** 9f-13f: 0-0 14f+: 0-0
Track : LH: 0-0 RH: 0-1 Tight: 0-0 Gall: 0-0
Aids: Bl: 0-1 Vi: 0-0 Tstrap: 0-0
Best Rating: 77 8/01 NmkJ 1m gd-fm

She showed some ability in her early starts and got off the mark on her first attempt over seven furlongs at Lingfield in July. Did not get the best of runs at Goodwood next time, but made no mistake at Newmarket in August when relishing the step up to a mile. Still on the upgrade.

Silent Gift

98 **72d**

2-y-o b f Brief Truce (USA)-Goodwood Lass (IRE) (Alzao (USA))

P L Gilligan B S Chatwal

Placings:00516000 **(5589)**
2001: 5^{0}G, 5^{0}GF, 6^{5}GF, 7^{1}GF, 7^{6}GF, 7^{0}GF, 6^{0}GS, 7^{0}GS

	Starts	1st	2nd	3rd	Win & Pl
Career Total (Turf)	8	1	0	0	2993

72 6/01 Bevl 7f100y E G-F £2992
Total win prize-money £2993

Going (Turf): Sf: 0-0 GS: 0-2 Gd: 0-1 **GF: 1-5** Fm: 0-0
Distance: 5f/6f: 0-4 **7f-8f: 1-4** 9f-13f: 0-0 14f+: 0-0
Track : LH: 0-2 **RH: 1-2** Tight: 0-0 Gall: 0-1
Aids: Bl: 0-0 Vi: 0-0 Tstrap: 0-0
Best Rating: 72 6/01 Bevl 7f100y gd-fm

Is only small but appreciated a step up to seven and a half furlongs at Beverley in the summer. Has been held since.

Silent Honor (IRE)

107 **98**

2-y-o ch f Sunday Silence (USA)-Wood Vine (USA) (Woodman (USA))
D R Loder Sheikh Mohammed

Placings:113 **(4191)**
2001: 6^{1}GF, 6^{1}GS, 6^{3}G

	Starts	1st	2nd	3rd	Win & Pl
Career Total (Turf)	3	2	0	1	43173

88 7/01 NmkJ 6f A G-S £29000
95 6/01 NmkR 6f D G-F £4823
Total win prize-money £33823

Going (Turf): Sf: 0-0 **GS: 1-1** Gd: 0-1 **GF: 1-1** Fm: 0-0
Distance: **5f/6f: 2-3** 7f-8f: 0-0 9f-13f: 0-0 14f+: 0-0
Track : LH: 0-0 RH: 0-0 Tight: 0-0 Gall: 0-0
Aids: Bl: 0-0 Vi: 0-0 Tstrap: 0-0
Best Rating: 98 8/01 York 6f good

From the same female line as Miesque, she looked top-class prospect when hacking up at Newmarket over six furlongs on her racecourse debut, and justified short odds in the Cherry Hinton when scrambling home by a short head on unsuitably soft ground. She appeared to be beaten fair and square when third in the Lowther. Tends to race freely and wore a cross noseband at York.

Silent Sea

78(77) (23) **14**

2-y-o b f Mistertopogigo (IRE)-Whispering Sea (Bustino)
J L Spearing Kinnersley Racing Club

Placings:000056 **(2857)**
2001: 5^{0}SD, 5^{0}SD, 5^{0}F, 5^{0}F, 5^{5}SD, 5^{6}GF

	Starts	1st	2nd	3rd	Win & Pl
Career Total (Turf)	3	0	0	0	0
Career Total (AW)	3	0	0	0	0

Going (Turf): Sf: 0-0 GS: 0-0 Gd: 0-0 GF: 0-1 Fm: 0-2
Distance: 5f/6f: 0-6 7f-8f: 0-0 9f-13f: 0-0 14f+: 0-0
Track : LH: 0-3 RH: 0-0 Tight: 0-2 Gall: 0-1
Aids: Bl: 0-0 Vi: 0-0 Tstrap: 0-0
Best Rating: 29 5/01 Wolv 5f stand

Silent Sound (IRE)

98(80) (14)**51**

5-y-o b g Be My Guest (USA)-Whist Awhile (Caerleon (USA))
Mrs A J Perrett G Harwood

Placings:5560/040023166020/040025340-00000 **(4366)**
2001: 10^{0}GS, 9^{0}GF, 11^{0}G, 12^{0}GF, 9^{0}GF

	Starts	1st	2nd	3rd	Win & Pl
Career Total (Turf)	29	1	3	2	7853
Career Total (AW)	1	0	0	0	

53 8/99 Rdcr 1m2f E(0-75)H FRM £4289
Total win prize-money £4289

Going (Turf): Sf: 0-2 GS: 0-2 Gd: 0-12 GF: 0-9 **Fm: 1-4**
Distance: 5f/6f: 0-0 7f-8f: 0-2 **9f-13f: 1-25** 14f+: 0-3
Track : **LH: 1-16** RH: 0-10 **Tight: 1-20** Gall: 0-3

Aids: **Bl: 1-8** Vi: 0-0 Tstrap: 0-0
Best Rating: 49 8/01 Wind 1m3f135y good

Silistra

86 **60**

2-y-o gr c Sadler's Wells (USA)-Dundel (IRE) (Machiavellian (USA))
Sir Michael Stoute Ahmed Buhaleeba

Placings:3 **(5527)**
2001: 8^{3}HY

	Starts	1st	2nd	3rd	Win & Pl
Career Total (Turf)	1	0	0	1	610

Going (Turf): Sf: 0-1 GS: 0-0 Gd: 0-0 GF: 0-0 Fm: 0-0
Distance: 5f/6f: 0-0 7f-8f: 0-0 9f-13f: 0-1 14f+: 0-0
Track : LH: 0-1 RH: 0-0 Tight: 0-0 Gall: 0-0
Aids: Bl: 0-0 Vi: 0-0 Tstrap: 0-0
Best Rating: 60 10/01 Nott 1m54y heavy

Silk Law (IRE)

100(92) (59)**80d**

3-y-o ch f Barathea (IRE)-Jural (Kris)
A Berry Kangaroo Courtiers

Placings:11230-302205460 **(4605)**
2001: 7^{3}GF, 8^{0}GF, 8^{2}GF, 7^{2}G, 8^{0}GF, 7^{5}F, 8^{4}GF, 7^{6}GF, 7^{0}SD

	Starts	1st	2nd	3rd	Win & Pl
Career Total (Turf)	13	2	3	2	16030
Career Total (AW)	1	0	0	0	

77 6/00 Wwck 6f168y E G-F £2917
66 6/00 Nott 6f15y E G-F £2980
Total win prize-money £5899

Going (Turf): Sf: 0-0 GS: 0-0 Gd: 0-3 **GF: 2-9** Fm: 0-1
Distance: 5f/6f: 0-1 **7f-8f: 2-12** 9f-13f: 0-1 14f+: 0-0
Track : **LH: 1-6** RH: 0-2 Tight: 0-4 Gall: 0-1
Aids: Bl: 0-0 Vi: 0-0 Tstrap: 0-0
Best Rating: 80 6/01 Sand 7f16y good

Silk On Song (USA)

89(99) (63)**39**

3-y-o b g Hazaam (USA)-Wazeerah (USA) (The Minstrel (CAN))
B Smart Paul Darling & Michael Broke

Placings:0-454220540 **(3816)**
2001: 7^{4}SD, 8^{5}SD, 8^{4}SW, 11^{2}SD, 12^{2}SD, 11^{0}F, 12^{5}SD, 12^{4}SD, 14^{0}SD

	Starts	1st	2nd	3rd	Win & Pl
Career Total (Turf)	1	0	0	0	
Career Total (AW)	9	0	2	0	1318

Going (Turf): Sf: 0-0 GS: 0-0 Gd: 0-0 GF: 0-0 Fm: 0-1
Distance: 5f/6f: 0-0 7f-8f: 0-3 9f-13f: 0-6 14f+: 0-1
Track : LH: 0-10 RH: 0-0 Tight: 0-6 Gall: 0-0
Aids: Bl: 0-0 Vi: 0-0 Tstrap: 0-1
Best Rating: 63 5/01 Wolv 1m4f stand

Silk St John

106(84) (64)**72**

7-y-o b g Damister (USA)-Silk St James (Pas De Seul)
M J Ryan C R S Partners

Placings:65022/3134200**30**/**64**0012131600122 05/001 0440204164340300/006513164000500-0000505064520640 5651 **(5659)**
2001: 8^{0}SD, 9^{0}SD, 8^{0}SD, 8^{0}GS, 8^{5}F, 8^{0}GF, 8^{5}GF, 8^{0}GF, 8^{6}G, 8^{4}GS, 8^{5}GS, 8^{2}GS, 8^{0}S, 9^{6}G, 10^{4}G, 8^{0}S, 8^{5}GS, 8^{6}S, 9^{5}GS, 8^{1}G

	Starts	1st	2nd	3rd	Win & Pl
Career Total (Turf)	79	10	8	6	98542
Career Total (AW)	7	0	0	1	477

70	11/01	Muss	1m	E(0-70)H	GD	£3066
90	6/00	Hayd	1m30y	C(0-95)H	G-S	£7182
88	5/00	Hayd	1m30y	C(0-90)H	G-S	£7377
93	7/99	Newb	1m	C(0-100)H	G-F	£7262
95	4/99	Sand	1m14y	C(0-95)H	G-S	£6179

90	8/98	Wind	1m67y	C(0-90)H	G-F	£4956
87	7/98	Newb	1m	C(0-95)H	GD	£7230
83	6/98	Wind	1m67y	D(0-80)	GD	£3590
83	5/98	Chep	1m14y	D(0-75)	G-F	£3403
78	8/97	NmkJ	1m	D(0-80)H	GD	£4698

Total win prize-money £54948

Going (Turf): Sf: 0-18 GS: 3-15 **Gd: 4-22** GF: 3-23 Fm: 0-1
Distance: 5f/6f: 0-1 7f-8f: 4-51 **9f-13f: 6-34** 14f+: 0-0
Track : LH: 2-21 **RH: 4-23 Tight: 3-7** Gall: 0-13
Aids: Bl: 0-0 Vi: 0-0 Tstrap: 0-0
Best Rating: 78 7/01 NmkJ 1m gd-sft

A useful handicapper over a mile on his day, he won twice at Haydock during the summer of 2000. Ended a long losing run at Musselburgh in November. He is best on easy ground and has a useful turn of foot.

Silken Brief (IRE)

99 **86**

2-y-o b f Ali-Royal (IRE)-Tiffany's Case (IRE) (Thatching)
S P C Woods John Kelsey-Fry

Placings:2 **(5603)**
2001: 7^{2}GS

	Starts	1st	2nd	3rd	Win & Pl
Career Total (Turf)	1	0	1	0	1296

Going (Turf): Sf: 0-0 GS: 0-1 Gd: 0-0 GF: 0-0 Fm: 0-0
Distance: 5f/6f: 0-0 7f-8f: 0-1 9f-13f: 0-0 14f+: 0-0
Track : LH: 0-0 RH: 0-0 Tight: 0-0 Gall: 0-0
Aids: Bl: 0-0 Vi: 0-0 Tstrap: 0-0
Best Rating: 86 11/01 NmkR 7f gd-sft

Silken Lady

85(96) (28)**23**

5-y-o br m Rock Hopper-Silk St James (Pas De Seul)
M J Ryan Sez Les Partnership

Placings:000/000360505500-540 **(4319)**
2001: 16^{5}SD, 10^{4}G, 10^{0}GF

	Starts	1st	2nd	3rd	Win & Pl
Career Total (Turf)	15	0	0	1	670
Career Total (AW)	3	0	0	0	0

Going (Turf): Sf: 0-4 GS: 0-1 Gd: 0-4 GF: 0-6 Fm: 0-0
Distance: 5f/6f: 0-0 7f-8f: 0-1 9f-13f: 0-13 14f+: 0-4
Track : LH: 0-11 RH: 0-4 Tight: 0-10 Gall: 0-0
Aids: Bl: 0-0 Vi: 0-0 Tstrap: 0-0
Best Rating: 23 8/01 Yarm 1m2f21y good

Silken Touch

74 **52d**

3-y-o b f Pivotal-Prima Silk (Primo Dominie)
M J Ryan William Dixon

Placings:26-0 **(1736)**
2001: 7^{0}GF

	Starts	1st	2nd	3rd	Win & Pl
Career Total (Turf)	3	0	1	0	812

Going (Turf): Sf: 0-1 GS: 0-0 Gd: 0-1 GF: 0-1 Fm: 0-0
Distance: 5f/6f: 0-2 7f-8f: 0-1 9f-13f: 0-0 14f+: 0-0
Track : LH: 0-0 RH: 0-0 Tight: 0-0 Gall: 0-0
Aids: Bl: 0-0 Vi: 0-0 Tstrap: 0-0
Best Rating: 17 5/01 Yarm 7f3y gd-fm

Silken Wings (IRE)

96(98) (66)**67**

3-y-o b f Brief Truce (USA)-Winged Victory (IRE) (Dancing Brave (USA))
I A Balding The C H F Partnership

Placings:32200-4231000 **(3390)**
2001: 7^{4}SD, 6^{2}SD, 5^{3}G, 6^{1}GF, 6^{0}GF, 6^{0}SD, 5^{0}F

	Starts	1st	2nd	3rd	Win & Pl
Career Total (Turf)	9	1	2	2	5673
Career Total (AW)	3	0	1	0	1168

67	6/01	Wind	6f	E(0-75)H	G-F	£3066

Total win prize-money £3066

Going (Turf): Sf: 0-1 GS: 0-0 Gd: 0-4 **GF: 1-2** Fm: 0-2
Distance: **5f/6f: 1-8** 7f-8f: 0-4 9f-13f: 0-0 14f+: 0-0
Track : LH: 0-6 RH: 0-1 Tight: 0-2 Gall: 0-3
Aids: Bl: 0-0 Vi: 0-0 Tstrap: 0-0
Best Rating: 67 6/01 Wind 6f gd-fm

Modest performer whose only win to date was a fair Windsor handicap in June 2001. Suited to a firm surface.

Silky Dawn (IRE)

109 **85**

3-y-o b f Night Shift (USA)-Bluffing (IRE) (Darshaan)
H R A Cecil Wafic Said

Placings:35-031230 **(5529)**
2001: 7^{0}S, 8^{3}G, 8^{1}GS, 8^{2}G, 8^{3}S, 8^{0}HY

	Starts	1st	2nd	3rd	Win & Pl
Career Total (Turf)	8	1	1	3	10438

85	6/01	Sals	1m	D	G-S	£3913

Total win prize-money £3913

Going (Turf): Sf: 0-3 **GS: 1-2** Gd: 0-3 GF: 0-0 Fm: 0-0
Distance: 5f/6f: 0-0 **7f-8f: 1-5** 9f-13f: 0-3 14f+: 0-0
Track : LH: 0-2 RH: 0-0 Tight: 0-0 Gall: 0-0
Aids: Bl: 0-0 Vi: 0-0 Tstrap: 0-3
Best Rating: 85 6/01 Sals 1m gd-sft

Had a big home reputation before making her debut, but was beginning to look disappointing until comfortably winning a Salisbury maiden in June. Fair effort on her next run in October, but was below par on soft ground afterwards.

Silla (USA)

102 **95**

3-y-o br f Gone West (USA)-Silver Fling (USA) (The Minstrel (CAN))
I A Balding George Strawbridge

Placings:0311200-6000 **(2806)**
2001: 5^{6}GS, 6^{0}G, 6^{0}GF, 6^{0}F

	Starts	1st	2nd	3rd	Win & Pl
Career Total (Turf)	11	2	1	1	14047

82	7/00	Kemp	5f	D	G-F	£5512
74	7/00	Sand	5f6y	D	GD	£4290

Total win prize-money £9802

Going (Turf): Sf: 0-1 GS: 0-2 **Gd: 1-3 GF: 1-4** Fm: 0-1
Distance: **5f/6f: 2-11** 7f-8f: 0-0 9f-13f: 0-0 14f+: 0-0
Track : LH: 0-2 RH: 0-0 Tight: 0-0 Gall: 0-2
Aids: Bl: 0-0 Vi: 0-0 Tstrap: 0-0
Best Rating: 92 6/01 NmkR 6f gd-fm

She ran some good races on fast ground over five furlongs last summer, but found life tougher when stepped up in class on softer ground in the autumn. She has been difficult to place this season.

Silly Goose (IRE)

103 **77**

3-y-o b f Sadler's Wells (USA)-Ducking (Reprimand)
J L Dunlop Wafic Said

Placings:62-56320215 **(5178)**
2001: 10^{5}S, 14^{6}GF, 11^{3}GF, 10^{2}F, 9^{0}GF, 10^{2}G, 11^{1}S, 11^{5}HY

	Starts	1st	2nd	3rd	Win & Pl
Career Total (Turf)	10	1	3	1	8438

62	9/01	Brig	1m3f196yD	SFT	£3062

Total win prize-money £3063

Going (Turf): Sf: 1-4 GS: 0-0 Gd: 0-1 GF: 0-4 Fm: 0-1
Distance: 5f/6f: 0-0 7f-8f: 0-1 **9f-13f: 1-8** 14f+: 0-1
Track : **LH: 1-6** RH: 0-2 Tight: 0-4 Gall: 0-0
Aids: Bl: 0-0 Vi: 0-0 Tstrap: 0-0
Best Rating: 77 7/01 Rdcr 1m2f firm

She looked one-paced, but eventually got off the mark in a soft-ground backend maiden.

Silogue (IRE)

97(84) (18)**36**

4-y-o b/br g Distinctly North (USA)-African Bloom (African Sky)
O Brennan O Brennan

Placings:0060-05202 **(4319)**
2001: 8^{0}SD, 14^{5}GF, 15^{2}G, 16^{0}GS, 10^{2}GF

	Starts	1st	2nd	3rd	Win & Pl
Career Total (Turf)	8	0	2	0	1140
Career Total (AW)	1	0	0	0	

Going (Turf): Sf: 0-0 GS: 0-1 Gd: 0-1 GF: 0-6 Fm: 0-0
Distance: 5f/6f: 0-1 7f-8f: 0-2 9f-13f: 0-3 14f+: 0-3
Track : LH: 0-6 RH: 0-1 Tight: 0-3 Gall: 0-0
Aids: Bl: 0-0 Vi: 0-0 Tstrap: 0-0
Best Rating: 36 7/01 Nott 1m6f15y gd-fm

Silvaani (USA)

86 **44**

3-y-o gr c Dumaani (USA)-Ruby Silver (USA) (Silver Hawk (USA))
Miss Gay Kelleway Lingfield Breakfast Club

Placings:4-0000 **(2117)**
2001: 8^{0}G, 10^{0}G, 10^{0}GF, 11^{0}F

	Starts	1st	2nd	3rd	Win & Pl
Career Total (Turf)	5	0	0	0	273

Going (Turf): Sf: 0-1 GS: 0-0 Gd: 0-2 GF: 0-1 Fm: 0-1
Distance: 5f/6f: 0-0 7f-8f: 0-2 9f-13f: 0-3 14f+: 0-0
Track : LH: 0-2 RH: 0-0 Tight: 0-2 Gall: 0-0
Aids: Bl: 0-1 Vi: 0-2 Tstrap: 0-0
Best Rating: 44 5/01 NmkR 1m good

Silver Band

104 **67**

2-y-o ch f Zilzal (USA)-Silver Braid (USA) (Miswaki (USA))
T D Easterby Giles W Pritchard-Gordon

Placings:6042120 **(4657)**
2001: 6^{6}G, 7^{0}GF, 6^{4}GF, 7^{2}GS, 5^{1}G, 6^{2}GF, 6^{0}GF

	Starts	1st	2nd	3rd	Win & Pl
Career Total (Turf)	7	1	2	0	6923

66	8/01	Catt	5f212y	D	GD	£4693

Total win prize-money £4693

Going (Turf): Sf: 0-0 GS: 0-1 **Gd: 1-2** GF: 0-4 Fm: 0-0
Distance: **5f/6f: 1-5** 7f-8f: 0-2 9f-13f: 0-0 14f+: 0-0
Track : **LH: 1-2** RH: 0-1 **Tight: 1-1** Gall: 0-0
Aids: **Bl: 1-5** Vi: 0-0 Tstrap: 0-0
Best Rating: 67 8/01 Ripn 6f gd-fm

She showed ability before getting off the mark in a six-furlong Catterick nursery. Suited by fast ground.

Silver Bomber

59 **22**

2-y-o gr f Persian Bold-Rich Lass (Broxted)
A Berry The Blackburn Seven

Placings:00 **(4801)**
2001: 7^{0}G, 5^{0}F

	Starts	1st	2nd	3rd	Win & Pl
Career Total (Turf)	2	0	0	0	

Going (Turf): Sf: 0-0 GS: 0-0 Gd: 0-1 GF: 0-0 Fm: 0-1
Distance: 5f/6f: 0-1 7f-8f: 0-1 9f-13f: 0-0 14f+: 0-0
Track : LH: 0-1 RH: 0-0 Tight: 0-0 Gall: 0-0
Aids: Bl: 0-0 Vi: 0-0 Tstrap: 0-0
Best Rating: 22 8/01 Ayr 7f50y good

Silver Bracelet

103(100) (89)**83**

3-y-o b/br f Machiavellian (USA)-Love Of Silver (USA) (Arctic Tern (USA))

C E Brittain Ali Saeed

Placings:5230250100520 **(5499)**

2001: 7^{5}SD, 10^{2}SW, 8^{3}S, 10^{0}F, 9^{2}GF, 8^{5}GF, 8^{0}G, 8^{1}G, 8^{0}G, 7^{0}G, 7^{5}G, 8^{2}S, 7^{0}HY

	Starts	1st	2nd	3rd	Win & Pl
Career Total (Turf)	11	1	2	1	10433
Career Total (AW)	2	0	1	0	826

73 8/01 Wind 1m67y D GD £4225

Total win prize-money £4225

Going (Turf): Sf: 0-3 GS: 0-0 **Gd: 1-5** GF: 0-2 Fm: 0-1
Distance: 5f/6f: 0-0 7f-8f: 0-7 **9f-13f: 1-6** 14f+: 0-0
Track : LH: 0-3 **RH: 1-5 Tight: 1-4** Gall: 0-2
Aids: Bl: 0-0 Vi: 0-0 Tstrap: 0-0
Best Rating: 94 7/01 NmkJ 1m good

A well-bred filly, she looked much better on turf than sand when third in a Kempton Listed event. Was disappointing at various levels before getting off the mark at Windsor in August 2001, and came close to adding to that when touched off at Leicester. Inconsistent. Stays a mile and acts on any ground.

Silver Charmer

96 **70**

2-y-o b f Charmer-Sea Dart (Air Trooper)

H S Howe John Bull

Placings:40404 **(5333)**

2001: 6^{4}S, 6^{0}GF, 6^{4}G, 5^{0}GS, 6^{4}HY

	Starts	1st	2nd	3rd	Win & Pl
Career Total (Turf)	5	0	0	0	1103

Going (Turf): Sf: 0-2 GS: 0-1 Gd: 0-1 GF: 0-1 Fm: 0-0
Distance: 5f/6f: 0-4 7f-8f: 0-1 9f-13f: 0-0 14f+: 0-0
Track : LH: 0-0 RH: 0-0 Tight: 0-0 Gall: 0-0
Aids: Bl: 0-0 Vi: 0-0 Tstrap: 0-0
Best Rating: 70 5/01 Newb 6f8y soft

A lightly-built filly, yet to win a race, tested only over five and six furlongs but has not really gone on from her promising Newbury debut.

Silver Charter (USA)

92 **76**

2-y-o b c Silver Hawk (USA)-Pride Of Darby (USA) (Danzig (USA))

G B Balding Argent Racing

Placings:160 **(5368)**

2001: 7^{1}GF, 8^{6}G, 8^{0}GS

	Starts	1st	2nd	3rd	Win & Pl
Career Total (Turf)	3	1	0	0	4176

76 7/01 Kemp 7f D G-F £4176

Total win prize-money £4176

Going (Turf): Sf: 0-0 GS: 0-1 Gd: 0-1 **GF: 1-1** Fm: 0-0
Distance: 5f/6f: 0-0 **7f-8f: 1-3** 9f-13f: 0-0 14f+: 0-0
Track : LH: 0-0 **RH: 1-2** Tight: 0-0 **Gall: 1-1**
Aids: Bl: 0-0 Vi: 0-0 Tstrap: 0-0
Best Rating: 76 7/01 Kemp 7f gd-fm

From the family of the Derby winner Secreto and the outstanding Champion Hurdler Istabraq, he scored at Kempton on his racecourse debut in a moderate maiden in July, but did not benefit form being run in a Listed race at Goodwood a couple of months later. His pedigree suggests he would be seen to better effect over a mile.

Silver Chevalier (IRE)

89(75) (5)**5**

3-y-o gr g Petong-Princess Eurolink (Be My Guest (USA))

C N Allen Green Square Racing

Placings:0-00000000 **(5601)**

2001: 10^{0}GS, 12^{0}GF, 7^{0}GF, 8^{0}GF, 8^{0}GF, 10^{0}G, 9^{0}GS, 8^{0}GS, 12^{0}SD

	Starts	1st	2nd	3rd	Win & Pl
Career Total (Turf)	9	0	0	0	

Going (Turf): Sf: 0-1 GS: 0-3 Gd: 0-1 GF: 0-4 Fm: 0-0
Distance: 5f/6f: 0-0 7f-8f: 0-4 9f-13f: 0-5 14f+: 0-0
Track : LH: 0-3 RH: 0-1 Tight: 0-3 Gall: 0-0
Aids: Bl: 0-3 Vi: 0-2 Tstrap: 0-0
Best Rating: 33 6/01 Newb 7f gd-fm

Silver Cloud

90 **12**

3-y-o gr f Petong-Pepeke (Mummy's Pet)

R E Barr M O'Connor

Placings:000-00000050 **(4266)**

2001: 8^{0}S, 6^{0}G, 8^{0}F, 7^{0}GF, 8^{0}F, 5^{0}F, 9^{5}GF, 7^{0}GF

	Starts	1st	2nd	3rd	Win & Pl
Career Total (Turf)	11	0	0	0	0

Going (Turf): Sf: 0-1 GS: 0-1 Gd: 0-2 GF: 0-4 Fm: 0-3
Distance: 5f/6f: 0-5 7f-8f: 0-5 9f-13f: 0-1 14f+: 0-0
Track : LH: 0-3 RH: 0-5 Tight: 0-2 Gall: 0-4
Aids: Bl: 0-1 Vi: 0-1 Tstrap: 0-0
Best Rating: 32 4/01 Ripn 1m soft

Silver Grey Lady (IRE)

100 **102**

3-y-o gr f Saddlers' Hall (IRE)-Early Rising (USA) (Grey Dawn Ii)

J L Dunlop Mrs Philippa Cooper

Placings:30-12060 **(4984)**

2001: 10^{1}GS, 11^{2}G, 12^{0}GF, 11^{6}GS, 12^{0}G

	Starts	1st	2nd	3rd	Win & Pl
Career Total (Turf)	7	1	1	1	12618

96 4/01 Newb 1m2f6y D G-S £5167

Total win prize-money £5168

Going (Turf): Sf: 0-1 **GS: 1-2** Gd: 0-3 GF: 0-1 Fm: 0-0
Distance: 5f/6f: 0-0 7f-8f: 0-2 **9f-13f: 1-5** 14f+: 0-0
Track : **LH: 1-5** RH: 0-1 Tight: 0-2 **Gall: 1-3**
Aids: Bl: 0-0 Vi: 0-0 Tstrap: 0-0
Best Rating: 102 5/01 Ling 1m3f106y good

A sister to Silver Patriarch, she left her juvenile form behind with an awesome performance on her reappearance in a ten-furlong maiden at Newbury. She was then awarded the Lingfield Oaks Trial by the local stewards after some argy-bargy with Double Crossed, but lost the race again when the connections of that filly appealed. She seemed ill at ease on the track when eighth in the Oask and has not progressed subsequently. Suited by good and good to soft.

Silver Instinct (IRE)

79(64) (18)**48**

2-y-o gr g Petardia-Aussie Aisle (IRE) (Godswalk (USA))

J L Eyre The Maynooth Men

Placings:050 **(5049)**

2001: 7^{0}GS, 7^{5}HY, 7^{0}SD

	Starts	1st	2nd	3rd	Win & Pl
Career Total (Turf)	2	0	0	0	0
Career Total (AW)	1	0	0	0	

Going (Turf): Sf: 0-1 GS: 0-1 Gd: 0-0 GF: 0-0 Fm: 0-0
Distance: 5f/6f: 0-0 7f-8f: 0-3 9f-13f: 0-0 14f+: 0-0
Track : LH: 0-3 RH: 0-0 Tight: 0-1 Gall: 0-0
Aids: Bl: 0-0 Vi: 0-1 Tstrap: 0-0
Best Rating: 48 9/01 Hayd 7f30y heavy

Silver Mascot

89(90) (57)**81**

2-y-o gr g Mukaddamah (USA)-Always Lucky (Absalom)

R Hollinshead Mrs Christine Painting

Placings:45305050 **(5690)**

2001: 5^{4}SD, 5^{5}SD, 5^{3}SD, 6^{0}GF, 6^{5}GF, 5^{0}F, 6^{5}HY, 7^{0}S

	Starts	1st	2nd	3rd	Win & Pl
Career Total (Turf)	5	0	0	0	983
Career Total (AW)	3	0	0	1	334

Going (Turf): Sf: 0-2 GS: 0-0 Gd: 0-0 GF: 0-2 Fm: 0-1
Distance: 5f/6f: 0-7 7f-8f: 0-1 9f-13f: 0-0 14f+: 0-0
Track : LH: 0-1 RH: 0-0 Tight: 0-1 Gall: 0-0
Aids: Bl: 0-0 Vi: 0-0 Tstrap: 0-0
Best Rating: 81 10/01 Donc 6f heavy

Fair form so far, although he was a little disappointing at Doncaster in November.

Silver Prophet (IRE)

90 **69**

2-y-o gr c Idris (IRE)-Silver Heart (Yankee Gold)

K McAuliffe Paul Blows

Placings:34500 **(5040)**

2001: 6^{3}GF, 8^{4}S, 7^{5}G, 8^{0}G, 10^{0}G

	Starts	1st	2nd	3rd	Win & Pl
Career Total (Turf)	5	0	0	1	989

Going (Turf): Sf: 0-1 GS: 0-0 Gd: 0-3 GF: 0-1 Fm: 0-0
Distance: 5f/6f: 0-0 7f-8f: 0-2 9f-13f: 0-3 14f+: 0-0
Track : LH: 0-2 RH: 0-2 Tight: 0-2 Gall: 0-0
Aids: Bl: 0-0 Vi: 0-1 Tstrap: 0-0
Best Rating: 69 10/01 Bath 1m2f46y good

Silver Secret

94 **31**

7-y-o ro g Absalom-Secret Dance (Sadler's Wells (USA))

S Gollings Mrs Jayne M Gollings

Placings:0035/0040100/640040/030441640463/051606 0555-00054300 **(4901)**

2001: 8^{0}F, 10^{0}G, 12^{0}GF, 10^{5}GF, 9^{4}GF, 8^{3}GS, 10^{0}HY, 11^{0}G

	Starts	1st	2nd	3rd	Win & Pl
Career Total (Turf)	47	3	0	4	12409

44 6/00 Hayd 1m2f120yG(0-70)H G-S £2023
43 7/99 NmkJ 1m E(0-75)H G-F £3817
60 8/97 Folk 6f F G-F £2277

Total win prize-money £8118

Going (Turf): Sf: 0-3 GS: 1-3 Gd: 0-12 **GF: 2-24** Fm: 0-5
Distance: 5f/6f: 1-3 7f-8f: 1-18 9f-13f: 1-26 14f+: 0-0
Track : **LH: 1-12** RH: 0-17 Tight: 0-6 Gall: 0-9
Aids: Bl: 0-2 Vi: 0-1 Tstrap: 0-0
Best Rating: 44 8/01 Bevl 1m100y gd-sft

Silver Shoes

96(89) (59)**51**

2-y-o b f Woodborough (USA)-Emerald Dream (IRE) (Vision (USA))

J L Eyre Howard Jackson

Placings:0633354020 **(4772)**

2001: 6^{0}F, 5^{6}GF, 7^{3}GF, 7^{3}SD, 7^{3}GF, 7^{5}F, 7^{4}G, 7^{0}G, 8^{2}SW, 7^{0}G

	Starts	1st	2nd	3rd	Win & Pl
Career Total (Turf)	8	0	0	2	530
Career Total (AW)	2	0	1	1	921

Going (Turf): Sf: 0-0 GS: 0-0 Gd: 0-3 GF: 0-3 Fm: 0-2
Distance: 5f/6f: 0-2 7f-8f: 0-7 9f-13f: 0-1 14f+: 0-0
Track : LH: 0-3 RH: 0-1 Tight: 0-2 Gall: 0-0
Aids: Bl: 0-0 Vi: 0-1 Tstrap: 0-0
Best Rating: 59 9/01 Wolv 1m100y slow

Silver Socks

89(111) (65)**63**

4-y-o gr g Petong-Tasmim (Be My Guest (USA))

M W Easterby Mrs Angela K Geraghty

Placings:5000/0062-**1111213260**060 **(4855)**

2001: 11^{1}SD, 12^{1}SW, 12^{1}SD, 12^{1}SW, 11^{2}SW, 12^{1}SD, 12^{3}SD, 10^{2}S, 11^{6}SD, 11^{0}SD, 12^{0}F, 10^{6}GF, 11^{0}GF

	Starts	1st	2nd	3rd	Win & Pl
Career Total (Turf)	12	0	2	0	1571
Career Total (AW)	9	5	1	1	12149

65	2/01	Wolv	1m4f	G(0-60)H	STD	£1386
65	2/01	Sthl	1m4f	E(0-75)H	SLW	£2940
57	2/01	Wolv	1m4f	F(0-80)H	STD	£2142
50	2/01	Wolv	1m4f	F(0-60)H	SLW	£1757
47	2/01	Sthl	1m3f	E(0-70)H	STD	£2443

Total win prize-money £10668

Going (Turf): Sf: 0-2 GS: 0-0 Gd: 0-3 GF: 0-3 Fm: 0-4
Distance: 5f/6f: 0-5 7f-8f: 0-1 **9f-13f: 5-15** 14f+: 0-0
Track : **LH: 5-13** RH: 0-3 **Tight: 3-5** Gall: 0-1
Aids: **Bl: 5-13** Vi: 0-0 Tstrap: 0-0
Best Rating: 65 3/01 Sthl 1m4f stand

Has been in fine form on the All-Weather since being fitted with blinkers. Ran well on his return to turf at Doncaster. A much improved individual, he is at his best at around ten furlongs and is suited by cut in the ground on turf.

Silver Tango (IRE)

97 **96?**

2-y-o gr c Danehill Dancer (IRE)-Lightning Bug (Prince Bee)

S Kirk Park Walk Racing Ii

Placings:614033 **(5291)**

2001: 5^{6}S, 5^{1}GS, 6^{4}G, 6^{0}GS, 6^{3}GS, 7^{3}S

	Starts	1st	2nd	3rd	Win & Pl
Career Total (Turf)	6	1	0	2	4792
71 5/01 Bath 5f11y	E			G-S	£2422

Total win prize-money £2422

Going (Turf): Sf: 0-2 **GS: 1-3** Gd: 0-1 GF: 0-0 Fm: 0-0
Distance: **5f/6f: 1-5** 7f-8f: 0-1 9f-13f: 0-0 14f+: 0-0
Track : **LH: 1-2** RH: 0-0 Tight: 0-1 **Gall: 1-1**
Aids: Bl: 0-0 Vi: 0-0 Tstrap: 0-0
Best Rating: 96 9/01 Gdwd 6f gd-sft

He got off the mark at Bath on his second start, but has been held since. Should stay a mile.

Silver Tongued

(91) (27)**30**

5-y-o b g Green Desert (USA)-Love Of Silver (USA) (Arctic Tern (USA))

J M Bradley N Savage

Placings:00500/000604**005**-054000 **(0214)**

2001: 6^{0}SD, 5^{5}SD, 7^{4}SW, 7^{0}SD, 7^{0}SD, 5^{0}SD

	Starts	1st	2nd	3rd	Win & Pl
Career Total (Turf)	12	0	0	0	318
Career Total (AW)	8	0	0	0	0

Going (Turf): Sf: 0-1 GS: 0-0 Gd: 0-5 GF: 0-3 Fm: 0-3
Distance: 5f/6f: 0-5 7f-8f: 0-10 9f-13f: 0-5 14f+: 0-0
Track : LH: 0-10 RH: 0-3 Tight: 0-7 Gall: 0-0
Aids: Bl: 0-1 Vi: 0-0 Tstrap: 0-0
Best Rating: 34 1/01 Sthl 5f stand

Silvernus

90 **37**

3-y-o b f Machiavellian (USA)-Agnus (IRE) (In The Wings)

S R Bowring (H R A Cecil 14/7) Clark Industrial Services Partnership

Placings:560 **(5174)**

2001: 11^{5}G, 9^{6}GF, 8^{0}GS

	Starts	1st	2nd	3rd	Win & Pl
Career Total (Turf)	3	0	0	0	0

Going (Turf): Sf: 0-0 GS: 0-1 Gd: 0-1 GF: 0-1 Fm: 0-0
Distance: 5f/6f: 0-0 7f-8f: 0-0 9f-13f: 0-3 14f+: 0-0
Track : LH: 0-2 RH: 0-1 Tight: 0-0 Gall: 0-1
Aids: Bl: 0-0 Vi: 0-0 Tstrap: 0-0
Best Rating: 37 10/01 Pont 1m4y gd-sft

Silverware (IRE)

92 **86**

5-y-o b g Mukaddamah (USA)-Diabola (USA) (Devil's Bag (USA))

P Hughes P Hughes

Placings:4560605/341145630/0003604106-350600300000 **(4761a)**

2001: 7^{3}S, 8^{5}S, 8^{0}GY, 7^{6}GF, 8^{0}GF, 8^{0}Y, 8^{3}G, 9^{0}G, 8^{0}GY, 8^{0}G, 8^{0}GY, 10^{0}GF

	Starts	1st	2nd	3rd	Win & Pl
Career Total (Turf)	38	3	0	5	37434

78	9/00	Curr	1m	H	G-F	£21000
76	6/99	Curr	1m	(0-80)H	G-F	£6875
65	6/99	Rosc	7f	(0-65)H	G-F	£3781

Total win prize-money £31656

Going (Turf): Sf: 0-5 GS: 0-0 Gd: 0-13 **GF: 3-8** Fm: 0-0
Distance: 5f/6f: 0-1 **7f-8f: 3-26** 9f-13f: 0-10 14f+: 0-0
Track : LH: 0-8 **RH: 1-13** Tight: 0-0 **Gall: 2-3**
Aids: **Bl: 1-14** Vi: 0-0 Tstrap: 0-0
Best Rating: 86 4/01 Curr 1m soft

Useful handicapper. Won 2000 Irish Cambridgeshire. Appreciates fast ground and a mile.

Sima's Gold (IRE)

87(88) (53)**36**

3-y-o b f Goldmark (USA)-Mujadil Princess (IRE) (Mujadil (USA))

W R Muir D J Kerwood

Placings:61-00000 **(4422)**

2001: 6^{0}GF, 8^{0}GF, 9^{0}GF, 8^{0}GF, 10^{0}GF

	Starts	1st	2nd	3rd	Win & Pl
Career Total (Turf)	6	0	0	0	0
Career Total (AW)	1	1	0	0	1827
53 7/00 Sthl 5f	G			STD	£1827

Total win prize-money £1827

Going (Turf): Sf: 0-0 GS: 0-0 Gd: 0-0 GF: 0-6 Fm: 0-0
Distance: **5f/6f: 1-2** 7f-8f: 0-2 9f-13f: 0-3 14f+: 0-0
Track : LH: 0-2 RH: 0-1 Tight: 0-1 Gall: 0-1
Aids: Bl: 0-1 Vi: 0-0 Tstrap: 0-0
Best Rating: 47 6/01 Wwck 6f21y gd-fm

Simeon

103 **90**

2-y-o b c Lammtarra (USA)-Noble Lily (USA) (Vaguely Noble)

M Johnston Jumeirah Racing

Placings:2211 **(5687)**

2001: 8^{2}S, 6^{2}GF, 8^{1}G, 8^{1}S

	Starts	1st	2nd	3rd	Win & Pl
Career Total (Turf)	4	2	2	0	14084

90	11/01	Donc	1m	C	SFT	£6489
82	9/01	Gdwd	1m	D	GD	£4455

Total win prize-money £10945

Going (Turf): Sf: 1-2 GS: 0-0 **Gd: 1-1** GF: 0-1 Fm: 0-0
Distance: 5f/6f: 0-0 **7f-8f: 2-3** 9f-13f: 0-1 14f+: 0-0
Track : LH: 0-1 **RH: 1-2** Tight: 0-1 Gall: 0-1
Aids: Bl: 0-0 Vi: 0-0 Tstrap: 0-0
Best Rating: 90 11/01 Donc 1m soft

Half-brother to smart middle-distance filly Noble Rose, he built on his promising, albeit green, perfomances at Hamilton and York to score over a mile at Goodwood in September 2001. Had an easy task on his final turf start of the season in a three-runner affair at Doncaster.

Simianna

101 **95**

2-y-o b f Bluegrass Prince (IRE)-Lowrianna (IRE) (Cyrano De Bergerac)

A Berry The Monkey Partnership

Placings:12114546 **(4023)**

2001: 5^{1}S, 5^{2}S, 5^{1}S, 5^{1}GF, 5^{4}GF, 5^{5}G, 5^{4}GF, 5^{6}GF

	Starts	1st	2nd	3rd	Win & Pl
Career Total (Turf)	8	3	1	0	20798

81	5/01	Ches	5f16y	B	G-F	£9700
64	4/01	Ripn	5f	E	SFT	£3052
58	3/01	Muss	5f	F	SFT	£2576

Total win prize-money £15328

Going (Turf): Sf: 2-3 GS: 0-0 Gd: 0-1 GF: 1-4 Fm: 0-0
Distance: **5f/6f: 3-8** 7f-8f: 0-0 9f-13f: 0-0 14f+: 0-0
Track : **LH: 1-1** RH: 0-0 **Tight: 1-1** Gall: 0-0
Aids: Bl: 0-1 Vi: 0-0 Tstrap: 0-0
Best Rating: 95 6/01 Asct 5f gd-fm

A speed filly, she won three of her first four starts including a decent event at Chester. Ran well in the Windsor Castle and again at Goodwood. Has won on soft and good to firm going.

Simiola

74 **42**

2-y-o b f Shaamit (IRE)-Brave Vanessa (USA) (Private Account (USA))

I A Wood John Purcell

Placings:0 **(5602)**

2001: 7^{0}GS

	Starts	1st	2nd	3rd	Win & Pl
Career Total (Turf)	1	0	0	0	

Going (Turf): Sf: 0-0 GS: 0-1 Gd: 0-0 GF: 0-0 Fm: 0-0
Distance: 5f/6f: 0-0 7f-8f: 0-1 9f-13f: 0-0 14f+: 0-0
Track : LH: 0-0 RH: 0-0 Tight: 0-0 Gall: 0-0
Aids: Bl: 0-0 Vi: 0-0 Tstrap: 0-0
Best Rating: 42 11/01 NmkR 7f gd-sft

Simla Bibi

98 **55**

3-y-o ch f Indian Ridge-Scandalette (Niniski (USA))

B J Meehan Miss K Rausing

Placings:33-0000550 **(4413)**

2001: 9^{0}GS, 8^{0}GS, 8^{0}F, 7^{0}GF, 10^{5}GF, 9^{5}GF, 10^{0}S

	Starts	1st	2nd	3rd	Win & Pl
Career Total (Turf)	9	0	0	2	1624

Going (Turf): Sf: 0-2 GS: 0-2 Gd: 0-0 GF: 0-4 Fm: 0-1
Distance: 5f/6f: 0-0 7f-8f: 0-3 9f-13f: 0-6 14f+: 0-0
Track : LH: 0-6 RH: 0-1 Tight: 0-2 Gall: 0-2
Aids: Bl: 0-1 Vi: 0-0 Tstrap: 0-0
Best Rating: 55 6/01 Nott 1m54y firm

Simlet

89(83) (49)**59**

6-y-o b g Forzando-Besito (Wassl)

E W Tuer E Tuer

Placings:66022/13233005520/0-40 **(3086)**

2001: 16^{4}GF, 16^{0}GF

	Starts	1st	2nd	3rd	Win & Pl
Career Total (Turf)	16	0	4	2	5128
Career Total (AW)	3	1	0	1	2880
57 2/98 Ling 1m	F			SLW	£2169

Total win prize-money £2169

Going (Turf): Sf: 0-2 GS: 0-1 Gd: 0-6 GF: 0-5 Fm: 0-2
Distance: 5f/6f: 0-0 **7f-8f: 1-8** 9f-13f: 0-9 14f+: 0-2
Track : **LH: 1-11** RH: 0-5 **Tight: 1-6** Gall: 0-1
Aids: Bl: 0-6 Vi: 0-1 Tstrap: 0-0
Best Rating: 59 7/01 Sthl 2m gd-fm

Simon The Poacher

55

2-y-o br g Chaddleworth (IRE)-Lady Crusty (Golden Dipper)

L P Grassick Postlip Racing

Placings:50 **(5291)**

2001: 7^{5}S, 7^{0}S

	Starts	1st	2nd	3rd	Win & Pl
Career Total (Turf)	2	0	0	0	524

Going (Turf): Sf: 0-2 GS: 0-0 Gd: 0-0 GF: 0-0 Fm: 0-0

Distance: 5f/6f: 0-0 7f-8f: 0-2 9f-13f: 0-0 14f+: 0-0

Track : LH: 0-0 RH: 0-0 Tight: 0-0 Gall: 0-0

Aids: Bl: 0-0 Vi: 0-0 Tstrap: 0-0

Simpatich (FR)

103 **73**

3-y-o ch c First Trump-Arc Empress Jane (IRE) (Rainbow Quest (USA))

L M Cumani Scuderia Rencati Srl

Placings:436311-00065 **(4952)**

2001: 7^{0}GS, 8^{0}G, 10^{0}GF, 11^{6}S, 11^{5}G

	Starts	1st	2nd	3rd	Win & Pl
Career Total (Turf)	11	2	0	2	16210

83 10/00 Siro 7f110y HVY £8133

78 9/00 Siro 7f110y GD £6506

Total win prize-money £14639

Going (Turf): Sf: 1-2 GS: 0-1 **Gd: 1-5** GF: 0-3 Fm: 0-0

Distance: 5f/6f: 0-1 **7f-8f: 2-7** 9f-13f: 0-3 14f+: 0-0

Track : LH: 0-2 **RH: 2-5** Tight: 0-1 Gall: 0-0

Aids: Bl: 0-1 Vi: 0-0 Tstrap: 0-0

Best Rating: 73 7/01 Hayd 1m3f200y soft

Produced ordinary maiden form in Britain as a juvenile in 2000, before scoring twice over seven furlongs at the back-end in Italy. Generally held up, he has shown little this term over further.

Simple Ideals (USA)

103(96) (33)**52**

7-y-o b/br g Woodman (USA)-Comfort And Style (Be My Guest (USA))

Don Enrico Incisa Don Enrico Incisa

Placings:3/43004/500000005/500444423631124463133/0205565425246-**0**060006255450344316 **(5640)**

2001: 14^{0}SD, 14^{0}S, 14^{6}S, 12^{0}S, 13^{0}GF, 14^{0}GF, 14^{6}GF, 14^{2}GF, 16^{5}GF, 15^{5}GS, 14^{4}G, 14^{5}G, 14^{0}GF, 16^{3}F, 16^{4}G, 14^{4}HY, 15^{3}GS, 14^{1}G, 13^{6}G

	Starts	1st	2nd	3rd	Win & Pl
Career Total (Turf)	67	4	6	9	32438
Career Total (AW)	1	0	0	0	

49 10/01 Rdcr 1m6f19y E(0-75)H GD £4758

46 10/99 Rdcr 1m6f19y E(0-75)H GD £4987

41 8/99 Ayr 1m7f E(0-70)H G-F £2804

39 8/99 Hayd 1m3f200yF(0-60)H G-S £2652

Total win prize-money £15202

Going (Turf): Sf: 0-14 GS: 1-9 **Gd: 2-12** GF: 1-23 Fm: 0-3

Distance: 5f/6f: 0-0 7f-8f: 0-1 9f-13f: 1-31 **14f+: 3-36**

Track : **LH: 4-51** RH: 0-17 **Tight: 2-31** Gall: 0-13

Aids: Bl: 0-2 Vi: 0-0 Tstrap: 0-0

Best Rating: 54 5/01 York 1m5f194y gd-fm

A three-time winner in the second half of 1999, at 11 to 15 furlongs, on ground ranging from good to soft, to good to firm, but he did not win again until October of 2001, although he went close on several occasions. His losing run came to an end at Redcar. Stays two miles, and suited by a good pace.

Simply Broke

57

3-y-o br g Simply Great (FR)-Empty Purse (Pennine Walk)

P C Haslam Mrs J Trotter/marquess Of Downshire

Placings:00-0 **(2873)**

2001: 8^{0}GF

	Starts	1st	2nd	3rd	Win & Pl
Career Total (Turf)	3	0	0	0	

Going (Turf): Sf: 0-0 GS: 0-0 Gd: 0-1 GF: 0-1 Fm: 0-1

Distance: 5f/6f: 0-2 7f-8f: 0-1 9f-13f: 0-0 14f+: 0-0

Track : LH: 0-0 RH: 0-1 Tight: 0-1 Gall: 0-0

Aids: Bl: 0-0 Vi: 0-0 Tstrap: 0-0

Simply Eric (IRE)

100 **55**

3-y-o b c Simply Great (FR)-Sanjana (GER) (Priamos (GER))

J L Eyre Pinnacle Great Partnership

Placings:244-4504000 **(3844)**

2001: 8^{4}S, 8^{5}S, 10^{0}GF, 10^{4}GF, 8^{0}GF, 9^{0}GS, 10^{0}G

	Starts	1st	2nd	3rd	Win & Pl
Career Total (Turf)	10	0	1	0	1705

Going (Turf): Sf: 0-4 GS: 0-1 Gd: 0-2 GF: 0-3 Fm: 0-0

Distance: 5f/6f: 0-1 7f-8f: 0-2 9f-13f: 0-7 14f+: 0-0

Track : LH: 0-6 RH: 0-3 Tight: 0-3 Gall: 0-2

Aids: Bl: 0-1 Vi: 0-0 Tstrap: 0-0

Best Rating: 57 3/01 Muss 1m soft

Some form in varied company, but is still a maiden and does not look to be progressing.

Simply Noble

85(99) (52)**69d**

5-y-o b g Noble Patriarch-Simply Candy (IRE) (Simply Great (FR))

W M Brisbourne (M Johnston 26/2) Christopher Chell

Placings:001/502630/000-**05025603** **(1471)**

2001: 8^{0}SD, **11**^{5}SD, **16**^{0}SD, **12**^{2}SW, **12**^{5}SD, **11**^{6}SW, 10^{0}GF, 11^{3}SD

	Starts	1st	2nd	3rd	Win & Pl
Career Total (Turf)	13	1	1	1	5978
Career Total (AW)	7	0	1	1	841

81 9/98 Haml 1m65y E SFT £2738

Total win prize-money £2738

Going (Turf): Sf: 1-1 GS: 0-3 Gd: 0-4 GF: 0-5 Fm: 0-0

Distance: 5f/6f: 0-0 7f-8f: 0-3 **9f-13f: 1-15** 14f+: 0-2

Track : LH: 0-14 **RH: 1-3 Tight: 1-7** Gall: 0-5

Aids: Bl: 0-0 Vi: 0-0 Tstrap: 0-0

Best Rating: 52 2/01 Wolv 1m4f slow

Simply Remy

102(97) (37)**48**

3-y-o ch g Chaddleworth (IRE)-Exemplaire (FR) (Polish Precedent (USA))

John Berry Simply 2000

Placings:000-0**30**325654 **(4800)**

2001: 8^{0}S, **11**^{3}SD, **12**^{0}SD, 12^{3}GF, 12^{2}GS, 12^{5}G, 12^{6}GF, 10^{5}GF, 10^{4}F

	Starts	1st	2nd	3rd	Win & Pl
Career Total (Turf)	10	0	1	1	1978
Career Total (AW)	2	0	0	1	327

Going (Turf): Sf: 0-2 GS: 0-1 Gd: 0-2 GF: 0-4 Fm: 0-1

Distance: 5f/6f: 0-2 7f-8f: 0-1 9f-13f: 0-9 14f+: 0-0

Track : LH: 0-5 RH: 0-4 Tight: 0-4 Gall: 0-1

Aids: Bl: 0-0 Vi: 0-0 Tstrap: 0-0

Best Rating: 48 8/01 Folk 1m4f good

Has shown improvement since upped in trip. Acts on Fibresand and turf, battles well if short of pace.

Simply Sensational (IRE)

105(95) (50)**72**

4-y-o ch c Cadeaux Genereux-Monaiya (Shareef Dancer (USA))

P F I Cole M Arbib

Placings:44342-401 **(1414)**

2001: 12^{4}SD, 8^{0}SD, 10^{1}S

	Starts	1st	2nd	3rd	Win & Pl
Career Total (Turf)	5	1	0	1	6342
Career Total (AW)	3	0	1	0	694

71 5/01 Newb 1m2f6y D(0-80)H SFT £4862

Total win prize-money £4862

Going (Turf): Sf: 1-4 GS: 0-1 Gd: 0-0 GF: 0-0 Fm: 0-0

Distance: 5f/6f: 0-0 7f-8f: 0-2 **9f-13f: 1-6** 14f+: 0-0

Track : **LH: 1-7** RH: 0-0 Tight: 0-2 **Gall: 1-2**

Aids: Bl: 0-1 Vi: 0-0 Tstrap: 0-0

Best Rating: 71 5/01 Newb 1m2f6y soft

Simply The Guest (IRE)

95(94) (69)**69**

2-y-o b c Mujadil (USA)-Ned's Contessa (IRE) (Persian Heights)

M R Channon John Guest

Placings:00344242660**13** **(5393)**

2001: 5^{0}GS, 5^{0}S, 5^{3}F, 5^{4}GF, 5^{4}GF, 5^{2}GF, 6^{4}GF, 5^{2}GF, 6^{6}GF, 6^{6}GS, 5^{0}GF, **6**^{1}SD, **6**^{3}SD

	Starts	1st	2nd	3rd	Win & Pl
Career Total (Turf)	11	0	2	1	3559
Career Total (AW)	2	1	0	1	2659

69 10/01 Wolv 6f F STD £2317

Total win prize-money £2317

Going (Turf): Sf: 0-1 GS: 0-2 Gd: 0-0 GF: 0-7 Fm: 0-1

Distance: **5f/6f: 1-13** 7f-8f: 0-0 9f-13f: 0-0 14f+: 0-0

Track : **LH: 1-4** RH: 0-1 **Tight: 1-4** Gall: 0-1

Aids: Bl: 0-0 Vi: 0-0 Tstrap: 0-0

Best Rating: 74 6/01 Ling 5f gd-fm

He showed some form on sand, but looked exposed until the switch to sand paid dividends in a claimer at Wolverhampton in October.

Sinamatella

97 **71**

2-y-o ch f Lion Cavern (USA)-Regent's Folly (IRE) (Touching Wood (USA))

C G Cox The Cox's Orange Pippins

Placings:540 **(4985)**

2001: 7^{5}G, 7^{4}F, 6^{0}G

	Starts	1st	2nd	3rd	Win & Pl
Career Total (Turf)	3	0	0	0	0

Going (Turf): Sf: 0-0 GS: 0-0 Gd: 0-2 GF: 0-0 Fm: 0-1

Distance: 5f/6f: 0-0 7f-8f: 0-3 9f-13f: 0-0 14f+: 0-0

Track : LH: 0-0 RH: 0-0 Tight: 0-0 Gall: 0-0

Aids: Bl: 0-0 Vi: 0-0 Tstrap: 0-0

Best Rating: 71 8/01 NmkJ 7f good

Has run moderately in maidens.

Sincerity

(94) (61)**81**

4-y-o b f Selkirk (USA)-Integrity (Reform)

J R Fanshawe Mrs Mary Watt

Placings:0230433-0 **(0242)**

2001: 8^{0}SD

	Starts	1st	2nd	3rd	Win & Pl
Career Total (Turf)	5	0	1	1	1759
Career Total (AW)	3	0	0	2	785

Going (Turf): Sf: 0-2 GS: 0-0 Gd: 0-3 GF: 0-0 Fm: 0-0

Distance: 5f/6f: 0-0 7f-8f: 0-6 9f-13f: 0-2 14f+: 0-0

Track : LH: 0-4 RH: 0-1 Tight: 0-1 Gall: 0-1

Aids: Bl: 0-0 Vi: 0-1 Tstrap: 0-0

Best Rating: 18 2/01 Wolv 1m100y stand

Sing A Song (IRE)

(92) (52)

3-y-o b f Blues Travellor (IRE)-Raja Moulana (Raja Baba (USA))

R Hannon Lady Davis

Placings:13-000004 (5671)

2001: 7^{0}GS, 6^{0}S, 7^{0}G, 6^{0}GF, 6^{0}SD, 6^{4}HY, 7^{0}SD

	Starts	1st	2nd	3rd	Win & Pl
Career Total (Turf)	7	1	0	1	4124
Career Total (AW)	1	0	0	0	

70 7/00 Wind 5f10y D SFT £2938

Total win prize-money £2938

Going (Turf): Sf: **1-4** GS: 0-1 Gd: 0-1 GF: 0-1 Fm: 0-0
Distance: **5f/6f: 1-5** 7f-8f: 0-3 9f-13f: 0-0 14f+: 0-0
Track : LH: 0-1 **RH: 1-1** Tight: 0-1 **Gall: 1-1**
Aids: Bl: 0-0 Vi: 0-0 Tstrap: 0-0
Best Rating: 76 5/01 Newb 6f8y soft

Won on her juvenile debut on soft ground, and ran well next time. Has struggled in 2001.

Sing And Dance

103 **48**

8-y-o b m Rambo Dancer (CAN)-Musical Princess (Cavo Doro)

J R Weymes Mrs N Napier

Placings:00/02300005/200364356144000/4034312164 4015/4145363031202/2553205-026454023446310 (5663)

2001: 13^{0}S, 12^{2}GS, 12^{6}GF, 12^{4}GF, 12^{5}F, 12^{4}GF, 13^{0}GF, 12^{2}GF, 12^{3}GF, 12^{4}GF, 12^{4}F, 14^{4}GF, 12^{6}G, 10^{3}F, 11^{1}GF, 12^{0}G

	Starts	1st	2nd	3rd	Win & Pl
Career Total (Turf)	75	7	9	11	42027

47 9/01 Catt 1m3f214yD(0-80)H G-F £4946
52 8/99 Haml 1m4f17y F(0-60)H G-F £2542
52 5/99 Muss 1m4f31y F(0-65)H G-F £4474
50 10/98 Catt 1m3f214yD(0-75)H G-S £3964
46 7/98 Newc 1m4f93y D(0-80)H G-F £3355
42 6/98 Muss 1m4f F(0-65)H G-F £2584
44 8/97 Rdcr 1m2f D(0-75)H G-F £3652

Total win prize-money £25519

Going (Turf): Sf: 0-7 GS: 1-10 Gd: 0-17 **GF: 6-33** Fm: 0-8
Distance: 5f/6f: 0-0 7f-8f: 0-4 **9f-13f: 7-63** 14f+: 0-8
Track : **LH: 4-34** RH: 3-32 **Tight: 6-40** Gall: 1-7
Aids: Bl: 0-2 Vi: 0-2 Tstrap: 0-0
Best Rating: 49 5/01 Muss 1m4f gd-fm

Sing For Fame (USA)

99 **87**

3-y-o b f Quest For Fame-Singing (USA) (The Minstrel (CAN))

Mrs A J Perrett K Abdulla

Placings:1200 (5135)

2001: 9^{1}F, 11^{2}G, 12^{0}GF, 10^{0}G

	Starts	1st	2nd	3rd	Win & Pl
Career Total (Turf)	4	1	1	0	3634

73 6/01 Ling 1m1f F FRM £2478

Total win prize-money £2478

Going (Turf): Sf: 0-0 GS: 0-0 Gd: 0-2 GF: 0-1 **Fm: 1-1**
Distance: 5f/6f: 0-0 7f-8f: 0-0 **9f-13f: 1-4** 14f+: 0-0
Track : **LH: 1-2** RH: 0-1 **Tight: 1-3** Gall: 0-0
Aids: Bl: 0-0 Vi: 0-0 Tstrap: 0-0
Best Rating: 87 7/01 Bath 1m3f144y good

Made a winning debut at Lingfield but was just worn down by Elsaamri next time out at Bath when upped in trip. Pulled too hard at Goodwood. Has won on fast ground. Acts on good.

Sing For Me (IRE)

(97) (32)**32**

6-y-o b/br m Songlines (FR)-Running For You (FR) (Pampabird)

R Hollinshead Miss Sarah Hollinshead

Placings:003404560**460/0314602**50036005**050/050650** 50005666005**0000/0040424506**006506-523600666 (0564)

2001: 7^{5}SW, 5^{2}SW, 6^{3}SD, 6^{6}SD, 5^{0}SD, 5^{0}SD, 6^{6}SD, 6^{6}SD, 5^{6}SD

	Starts	1st	2nd	3rd	Win & Pl
Career Total (Turf)	26	0	1	2	1301
Career Total (AW)	50	1	2	2	3238

53 2/98 Wolv 5f G STD £1738

Total win prize-money £1738

Going (Turf): Sf: 0-4 GS: 0-2 Gd: 0-9 GF: 0-10 Fm: 0-1
Distance: **5f/6f: 1-53** 7f-8f: 0-21 9f-13f: 0-2 14f+: 0-0
Track : **LH: 1-58** RH: 0-2 **Tight: 1-31** Gall: 0-4
Aids: Bl: 0-0 Vi: 0-1 Tstrap: 0-0
Best Rating: 42 1/01 Wolv 6f stand

Single Currency

85(69) **17**

5-y-o b h Barathea (IRE)-Kithanga (IRE) (Darshaan)

P Butler Christopher W Wilson

Placings:3/006-000000 (2386)

2001: 13^{0}SD, 11^{0}GS, 11^{0}GS, 11^{0}F, 12^{0}GF, 16^{0}GF

	Starts	1st	2nd	3rd	Win & Pl
Career Total (Turf)	9	0	0	1	625
Career Total (AW)	1	0	0	0	

Going (Turf): Sf: 0-2 GS: 0-4 Gd: 0-0 GF: 0-2 Fm: 0-1
Distance: 5f/6f: 0-0 7f-8f: 0-0 9f-13f: 0-9 14f+: 0-1
Track : LH: 0-7 RH: 0-3 Tight: 0-3 Gall: 0-1
Aids: Bl: 0-0 Vi: 0-1 Tstrap: 0 1
Best Rating: 17 6/01 Sals 1m4f gd-fm

Single Honour

104 **86**

3-y-o b f Mark Of Esteem (IRE)-Once Upon A Time (Teenoso (USA))

R Hannon The Queen

Placings:5226-03612 (5591)

2001: 8^{0}GF, 10^{3}F, 8^{6}GS, 8^{1}GF, 9^{2}GS

	Starts	1st	2nd	3rd	Win & Pl
Career Total (Turf)	9	1	3	1	8169

63 7/01 Wind 1m67y D G-F £4322

Total win prize-money £4323

Going (Turf): Sf: 0-0 GS: 0-3 Gd: 0-0 **GF: 1-5** Fm: 0-1
Distance: 5f/6f: 0-1 7f-8f: 0-4 **9f-13f: 1-4** 14f+: 0-0
Track : LH: 0-4 **RH: 1-2 Tight: 1-2** Gall: 0-2
Aids: Bl: 0-0 Vi: 0-0 Tstrap: 0-0
Best Rating: 93 5/01 Gdwd 1m gd-fm

A lightly-made filly, she showed plenty of ability in her early starts and even tried Pattern company, but she did not win until landing a mile maiden at Windsor in July. Acts on fast ground, but has raced keenly in the past.

Single Track Mind

103(97) (82)**66**

3-y-o b c Mind Games-Compact Disc (IRE) (Royal Academy (USA))

N Hamilton John Hopkins (t/a South Hatch Racing)

Placings:05215-0625200000 (5025)

2001: 6^{0}G, 6^{6}GF, 6^{2}GF, 6^{5}GF, 6^{2}GF, 6^{0}GF, 6^{0}G, 6^{0}GF, 6^{0}GF, 6^{0}G

	Starts	1st	2nd	3rd	Win & Pl
Career Total (Turf)	13	0	3	0	4148
Career Total (AW)	2	1	0	0	2261

82 11/00 Sthl 6f D STD £2261

Total win prize-money £2261

Going (Turf): Sf: 0-3 GS: 0-0 Gd: 0-2 GF: 0-7 Fm: 0-0
Distance: **5f/6f: 1-12** 7f-8f: 0-2 9f-13f: 0-0 14f+: 0-0
Track : **LH: 1-6** RH: 0-0 Tight: 0-2 Gall: 0-0
Aids: Bl: 0-0 Vi: 0-1 Tstrap: 0-0
Best Rating: 79 6/01 Pont 6f gd-fm

His only win came in an All-Weather maiden at two over six furlongs. Has run some fine races in defeat during the first half of the season. Probably needs to drop in the handicap before he scores again. Acts on fast ground.

Singsong

97(91) (65)**57d**

4-y-o b g Paris House-Miss Whittingham (IRE) (Fayruz)

A Berry G L Tanner

Placings:13401520/430330006-**000000** (3209)

2001: 5^{0}SD, 6^{0}SW, 5^{0}GS, 5^{0}S, 6^{0}G, 6^{0}G

	Starts	1st	2nd	3rd	Win & Pl
Career Total (Turf)	21	2	1	4	16148
Career Total (AW)	2	0	0	0	

87 6/99 Ripn 5f E G-F £2710
80 3/99 Donc 5f E G-S £3745

Total win prize-money £6455

Going (Turf): Sf: 0-4 **GS: 1-2** Gd: 0-9 **GF: 1-5** Fm: 0-1
Distance: **5f/6f: 2-22** 7f-8f: 0-1 9f-13f: 0-0 14f+: 0-0
Track : LH: 0-2 RH: 0-0 Tight: 0-1 Gall: 0-0
Aids: Bl: 0-0 Vi: 0-0 Tstrap: 0-0
Best Rating: 67 3/01 Donc 5f gd-sft

Too high in the handicap now, he has been well beaten in claimers and seller this term.

Sinjaree

94 **69**

3-y-o b c Mark Of Esteem (IRE)-Forthwith (Midyan (USA))

E A L Dunlop Mohammed Jaber

Placings:05-00 (2191)

2001: 8^{0}GF, 9^{0}G

	Starts	1st	2nd	3rd	Win & Pl
Career Total (Turf)	4	0	0	0	0

Going (Turf): Sf: 0-1 GS: 0-0 Gd: 0-1 GF: 0-2 Fm: 0-0
Distance: 5f/6f: 0-0 7f-8f: 0-3 9f-13f: 0-1 14f+: 0-0
Track : LH: 0-3 RH: 0-0 Tight: 0-1 Gall: 0-0
Aids: Bl: 0-0 Vi: 0-0 Tstrap: 0-0
Best Rating: 56 6/01 Nott 1m1f213y good

Siouxsie Sioux

89 **64**

2-y-o b f Pivotal-Tres Sage (Reprimand)

J G Given A Clarke

Placings:3 (1988)

2001: 6^{3}G

	Starts	1st	2nd	3rd	Win & Pl
Career Total (Turf)	1	0	0	1	687

Going (Turf): Sf: 0-0 GS: 0-0 Gd: 0-1 GF: 0-0 Fm: 0-0
Distance: 5f/6f: 0-1 7f-8f: 0-0 9f-13f: 0-0 14f+: 0-0
Track : LH: 0-0 RH: 0-0 Tight: 0-0 Gall: 0-0
Aids: Bl: 0-0 Vi: 0-0 Tstrap: 0-0
Best Rating: 64 6/01 Hayd 6f good

Sir Alfred

88 **71**

2-y-o b g Royal Academy (USA)-Magnificent Star (USA) (Silver Hawk (USA))

B R Millman (Sir Mark Prescott 15/8) W A Harrison-Allan

Placings:430 (5289)

2001: 6^{4}GS, 6^{3}GF, 7^{0}S

	Starts	1st	2nd	3rd	Win & Pl
Career Total (Turf)	3	0	0	1	725

Going (Turf): Sf: 0-1 GS: 0-1 Gd: 0-0 GF: 0-1 Fm: 0-0
Distance: 5f/6f: 0-1 7f-8f: 0-2 9f-13f: 0-0 14f+: 0-0
Track : LH: 0-0 RH: 0-0 Tight: 0-0 Gall: 0-0
Aids: Bl: 0-0 Vi: 0-0 Tstrap: 0-0
Best Rating: 71 8/01 Sals 6f212y gd-fm

Sir Azzaro (IRE)

99 76

2-y-o b c Charnwood Forest (IRE)-Supreme Crown (USA) (Chief's Crown (USA))
Franck Mourier Cameron Express Inc

Placings:3301000 **(4202a)**
2001: 4^{3}FT, 4^{3}FT, 6^{0}Y, 8^{1}GF, 6^{0}GY, 5^{0}GF, 8^{0}GS

	Starts	1st	2nd	3rd	Win & Pl
Career Total (Turf)	5	1	0	0	7590
Career Total (AW)	2	0	0	2	2340

7/01 Bell 1m G-F £7590
Total win prize-money £7590

Going (Turf): Sf: 0-0 GS: 0-1 Gd: 0-0 **GF: 1-2** Fm: 0-0
Distance: 5f/6f: 0-1 **7f-8f: 1-4** 9f-13f: 0-0 14f+: 0-0
Track : LH: 0-0 RH: 0-0 Tight: 0-0 Gall: 0-0
Aids: Bl: 0-0 Vi: 0-0 Tstrap: 0-0
Best Rating: 76 7/01 Newb 5f34y gd-fm

Ex-American performer, placed in his two starts in the US. Ran green when winning a mile maiden at Bellewstown in July, but was found wanting behind Johannesburg in Group Three over six furlongs at The Curragh in July.

Sir Brastias

91 65

2-y-o b c Shaamit (IRE)-Premier Night (Old Vic)
S Dow Mr & Mrs D G Churston & S Dow

Placings:0 **(5604)**
2001: 7^{0}GS

	Starts	1st	2nd	3rd	Win & Pl
Career Total (Turf)	1	0	0	0	

Going (Turf): Sf: 0-0 GS: 0-1 Gd: 0-0 GF: 0-0 Fm: 0-0
Distance: 5f/6f: 0-0 7f-8f: 0-1 9f-13f: 0-0 14f+: 0-0
Track : LH: 0-0 RH: 0-0 Tight: 0-0 Gall: 0-0
Aids: Bl: 0-0 Vi: 0-0 Tstrap: 0-0
Best Rating: 65 11/01 NmkR 7f gd-sft

Sir Desmond

106 77

3-y-o gr g Petong-I'm Your Lady (Risk Me (FR))
R Guest The Quintessentials

Placings:00-036113243003042 **(5523)**
2001: 6^{0}G, 5^{3}GF, 6^{6}F, 5^{1}F, 5^{1}G, 5^{3}GF, 5^{2}GF, 5^{4}F, 5^{3}G, 5^{0}G, 6^{0}GF, 5^{3}GS, 5^{0}GS, 5^{4}GS, 5^{2}HY

	Starts	1st	2nd	3rd	Win & Pl
Career Total (Turf)	17	2	2	4	15617

70 6/01 Muss 5f E(0-70)H GD £3164
53 6/01 Nott 5f13y E FRM £3066
Total win prize-money £6230

Going (Turf): Sf: 0-1 GS: 0-4 **Gd: 1-4** GF: 0-5 **Fm: 1-3**
Distance: **5f/6f: 2-14** 7f-8f: 0-3 9f-13f: 0-0 14f+: 0-0
Track : LH: 0-1 RH: 0-1 Tight: 0-0 Gall: 0-2
Aids: Bl: 0-0 Vi: 0-0 Tstrap: 0-0
Best Rating: 77 10/01 Wind 5f10y heavy

Able five-furlong handicapper who has shown his best form on a sound surface.

Sir Don (IRE)

93 73

2-y-o b c Lake Coniston (IRE)-New Sensitive (Wattlefield)
J M P Eustace Michael Scott

Placings:322 **(4627)**

2001: 5^{3}GF, 5^{2}GS, 5^{2}GF

	Starts	1st	2nd	3rd	Win & Pl
Career Total (Turf)	3	0	2	1	2361

Going (Turf): Sf: 0-0 GS: 0-1 Gd: 0-0 GF: 0-2 Fm: 0-0
Distance: 5f/6f: 0-3 7f-8f: 0-0 9f-13f: 0-0 14f+: 0-0
Track : LH: 0-0 RH: 0-0 Tight: 0-0 Gall: 0-0
Aids: Bl: 0-0 Vi: 0-0 Tstrap: 0-0
Best Rating: 73 9/01 Nott 5f13y gd-fm

Sir Edward Burrow (IRE)

96(90) (42)43

3-y-o b g Distinctly North (USA)-Alalja (IRE) (Entitled)
R F Fisher Mrs D Miller

Placings:04000360-0604306000 **(5383)**
2001: 10^{0}GF, 12^{6}GF, 8^{0}GF, 13^{4}GF, 16^{3}F, 14^{0}SD, 16^{6}GF, 16^{0}F, 13^{0}GF, 13^{0}S

	Starts	1st	2nd	3rd	Win & Pl
Career Total (Turf)	16	0	0	2	1198
Career Total (AW)	2	0	0	0	

Going (Turf): Sf: 0-2 GS: 0-0 Gd: 0-2 GF: 0-9 Fm: 0-3
Distance: 5f/6f: 0-2 7f-8f: 0-4 9f-13f: 0-5 14f+: 0-7
Track : LH: 0-8 RH: 0-6 Tight: 0-9 Gall: 0-2
Aids: Bl: 0-0 Vi: 0-0 Tstrap: 0-0
Best Rating: 47 6/01 Newc 1m4f93y gd-fm

Sir Effendi (IRE)

106 99

5-y-o ch h Nashwan (USA)-Jeema (Thatch (USA))
M P Tregoning Hamdan Al Maktoum

Placings:012/2010-03 **(1986)**
2001: 7^{0}G, 7^{3}G

	Starts	1st	2nd	3rd	Win & Pl
Career Total (Turf)	9	2	2	1	16841

101 8/00 Chep 7f16y C G-F £6032
88 7/99 Ling 7f140y D G-F £4129
Total win prize-money £10161

Going (Turf): Sf: 0-1 GS: 0-0 Gd: 0-4 **GF: 2-4** Fm: 0-0
Distance: 5f/6f: 0-0 **7f-8f: 2-6** 9f-13f: 0-3 14f+: 0-0
Track : LH: 0-3 RH: 0-2 Tight: 0-2 Gall: 0-1
Aids: Bl: 0-0 Vi: 0-0 Tstrap: 0-0
Best Rating: 81 5/01 Ling 7f good

Winning form around seven furlongson fast ground, he has been lightly-raced this term. stays a mile plus.

Sir Ferbet (IRE)

104(115) (100)88

4-y-o b c Mujadil (USA)-Mirabiliary (USA) (Crow (FR))
B W Hills R J C Upton & International Plywood Plc

Placings:43/**2**1001004250020**24**-200010 **(5344)**
2001: 7^{2}GF, 8^{0}G, 8^{0}GF, 8^{0}S, 7^{1}SD, 8^{0}GS

	Starts	1st	2nd	3rd	Win & Pl
Career Total (Turf)	17	1	2	1	13631
Career Total (AW)	5	2	2	0	8574

80 10/01 Wolv 7f F STD £2506
88 6/00 NmkR 1m C(0-95)H G-F £7377
81 4/00 Wolv 1m100y D STD £2828
Total win prize-money £12712

Going (Turf): Sf: 0-4 GS: 0-3 Gd: 0-2 **GF: 1-7** Fm: 0-1
Distance: 5f/6f: 0-2 **7f-8f: 2-12** 9f-13f: 1-8 14f+: 0-0
Track : **LH: 2-9** RH: 0-3 **Tight: 2-7** Gall: 0-2
Aids: Bl: 0-0 Vi: 0-0 Tstrap: 0-0
Best Rating: 88 5/01 Ches 7f122y gd-fm

He scored on the All-Weather at three and fast ground at Newmarket over a mile. Has a good record at Wolverhampton. Best when ridden up with the pace over a mile on a sound surface. Did not have to beat his best to take a claimer at Dunstall Park in October.

Sir Francis (IRE)

94 70

3-y-o b g Common Grounds-Red Note (Rusticaro (FR))
J Noseda L P Calvente

Placings:521061321-0000 **(5685)**
2001: 5^{0}S, 6^{0}HY, 5^{0}GS, 5^{0}S

	Starts	1st	2nd	3rd	Win & Pl
Career Total (Turf)	13	3	2	1	14966

94 10/00 Yarm 6f3y C SFT £5779
88 8/00 Brig 5f213y D G-F £3461
79 4/00 Brig 5f59y D G-S £3181
Total win prize-money £12422

Going (Turf): **Sf: 1-6 GS: 1-3** Gd: 0-1 **GF: 1-3** Fm: 0-0
Distance: **5f/6f: 2-11** 7f-8f: 1-2 9f-13f: 0-0 14f+: 0-0
Track : **LH: 2-5** RH: 0-0 Tight: 0-1 Gall: 0-1
Aids: Bl: 0-0 Vi: 0-1 Tstrap: 0-0
Best Rating: 70 10/01 NmkR 5f gd-sft

He has not always looked an easy ride, but handled a busy 2000 season well and seems to act on any surface. Best when ridden positively, he has been difficult to place this term.

Sir George Turner

102 98

2-y-o ch c Nashwan (USA)-Ingozi (Warning)
M Johnston Paul Dean

Placings:3121 **(5053)**
2001: 7^{3}GF, 7^{1}G, 7^{2}G, 7^{1}S

	Starts	1st	2nd	3rd	Win & Pl
Career Total (Turf)	4	2	1	1	211810

98 10/01 NmkR 7f B SFT £200000
97 7/01 Leic 7f9y E GD £3251
Total win prize-money £203252

Going (Turf): **Sf: 1-1** GS: 0-0 **Gd: 1-2** GF: 0-1 Fm: 0-0
Distance: 5f/6f: 0-0 **7f-8f: 2-4** 9f-13f: 0-0 14f+: 0-0
Track : LH: 0-0 RH: 0-0 Tight: 0-0 Gall: 0-0
Aids: Bl: 0-0 Vi: 0-0 Tstrap: 0-0
Best Rating: 98 10/01 NmkR 7f soft

A half-brother to the useful juvenile Tissifer, he showed promise on his Ascot debut and went on to score at Leicester next time. He finished runner-up in a valuable event back at Ascot on Shergar Cup day, but was still very green there. Earned a big payday when taking a Newmarket sales race in October. Open to improvement, his trainer sees him as a possible Derby candidate.

Sir Hamelin (IRE)

69(98) (60)33

4-y-o b g Hernando (FR)-Georgia Stephens (USA) (The Minstrel (CAN))
M C Pipe A S Helaissi

Placings:010/06300043006031-40 **(2133)**
2001: 10^{4}SD, 10^{0}GF

	Starts	1st	2nd	3rd	Win & Pl
Career Total (Turf)	18	2	0	3	17843
Career Total (AW)	1	0	0	0	0

10/00 MsnL 1m2f110y VS £4803
11/99 MsnL 1m1f HVY £6459
Total win prize-money £11262

Going (Turf): Sf: 0-1 GS: 0-0 Gd: 0-2 GF: 0-1 Fm: 0-0
Distance: 5f/6f: 0-0 7f-8f: 0-1 9f-13f: 0-10 14f+: 0-1
Track : LH: 0-4 RH: 0-1 Tight: 0-1 Gall: 0-1
Aids: Bl: 0-0 Vi: 0-2 Tstrap: 0-1
Best Rating: 60 3/01 Ling 1m2f stand

Sir Netbetsports (IRE)

78(83) (58)34

2-y-o b g Dolphin Street (FR)-Bid High (IRE) (High Estate)
B S Rothwell Full Time Whistle Limited

Placings:0061000 **(5049)**

2001: 5^{0}S, 5^{0}GS, 5^{6}SD, 6^{1}SD, 7^{0}HY, 7^{0}G, 7^{0}SD

	Starts	1st	2nd	3rd	Win & Pl
Career Total (Turf)	4	0	0	0	
Career Total (AW)	3	1	0	0	1813

58 5/01 Sthl 6f G STD £1813
Total win prize-money £1813

Going (Turf): Sf: 0-2 GS: 0-1 Gd: 0-1 GF: 0-0 Fm: 0-0
Distance: 5f/6f: 1-4 7f-8f: 0-3 9f-13f: 0-0 14f+: 0-0
Track : LH: 1-4 RH: 0-1 Tight: 0-0 Gall: 0-0
Aids: Bl: 1-4 Vi: 0-0 Tstrap: 0-0
Best Rating: 58 5/01 Sthl 6f stand

His personal best was a win in six-furlong seller at Southwell in May 2001.

Sir Ninja (IRE)

109 **87**
4-y-o b g Turtle Island (IRE)-The Poachers Lady (IRE) (Salmon Leap (USA))
D J S Ffrench Davis Hargood Limited

Placings:462120210/56260060-00050030203 **(5669)**
2001: 8^{0}SD, 8^{0}S, 7^{0}GS, 10^{5}S, 10^{0}GF, 11^{0}G, 8^{3}HY, 8^{0}G, 7^{2}S, 8^{0}HY, 10^{3}HY

	Starts	1st	2nd	3rd	Win & Pl
Career Total (Turf)	27	2	5	2	26898
Career Total (AW)	1	0	0	0	

104 10/99 Asct 7f B G-S £9186
87 8/99 Thsk 7f E SFT £3740
Total win prize-money £12927

Going (Turf): Sf: 1-10 GS: 1-5 Gd: 0-9 GF: 0-2 Fm: 0-0
Distance: 5f/6f: 0-0 7f-8f: 2-16 9f-13f: 0-11 14f+: 0-0
Track : LH: 1-16 RH: 0-3 Tight: 1-10 Gall: 0-5
Aids: Bl: 0-0 Vi: 0-1 Tstrap: 0-0
Best Rating: 88 4/01 Epsm 1m2f18y soft

Suited by plenty of give underfoot, he regularly ran in Listed company last season due to being too high in the handicap. He was generally well beaten at that level, but has dropped back down to a more realistic level this season.

Sir Northerndancer (IRE)

103 **83**
2-y-o b c Danehill Dancer (IRE)-Lady At War (Warning)
R Hannon John Michael

Placings:6652215052 **(5521)**
2001: 5^{6}GF, 6^{6}G, 5^{5}G, 6^{2}GF, 7^{2}G, 7^{1}GS, 7^{5}G, 7^{0}HY, 6^{5}S, 6^{2}HY

	Starts	1st	2nd	3rd	Win & Pl
Career Total (Turf)	10	1	3	0	9648

79 8/01 Ches 7f2y C G-S £6318
Total win prize-money £6318

Going (Turf): Sf: 0-3 GS: 1-1 Gd: 0-4 GF: 0-2 Fm: 0-0
Distance: 5f/6f: 0-4 7f-8f: 1-6 9f-13f: 0-0 14f+: 0-0
Track : LH: 1-3 RH: 0-0 Tight: 1-2 Gall: 0-0
Aids: Bl: 0-0 Vi: 0-0 Tstrap: 0-0
Best Rating: 83 10/01 Wind 6f heavy

Well suited by a sharp track and seven furlongs. He won a nursery at Chester in August, but has looked held since. Acts on fast and easy ground, likes to race prominently.

Sir Perse

(75) (6)
5-y-o b g Precocious-Anne's Bank (IRE) (Burslem)
Jamie Poulton Robert Townsend

Placings:00602/040000/00 **(0479)**
2001: 11^{0}SD, 7^{0}SD

	Starts	1st	2nd	3rd	Win & Pl
Career Total (Turf)	8	0	0	0	0
Career Total (AW)	5	0	1	0	761

Going (Turf): Sf: 0-1 GS: 0-2 Gd: 0-2 GF: 0-2 Fm: 0-1
Distance: 5f/6f: 0-3 7f-8f: 0-7 9f-13f: 0-3 14f+: 0-0
Track : LH: 0-8 RH: 0-1 Tight: 0-6 Gall: 0-0
Aids: Bl: 0-1 Vi: 0-0 Tstrap: 0-0
Best Rating: 6 3/01 Ling 7f stand

Sir Sandrovitch (IRE)

109(107) (68)**78**
5-y-o b g Polish Patriot (USA)-Old Downie (Be My Guest (USA))
R A Fahey W G Moore & G Winton

Placings:6/010024600/0004105-0532006041330613000300 **(4796)**
2001: 5^{0}SW, 5^{5}SD, 5^{3}SD, 6^{2}SD, 6^{0}S, 5^{0}S, 5^{6}SD, 5^{0}GF, 5^{4}GF, 5^{1}GF, 5^{3}G, 5^{3}GF, 5^{0}GF, 6^{6}G, 5^{1}GF, 5^{3}GF, 6^{0}G, 5^{0}G, 5^{0}GF, 5^{3}G, 5^{0}GS, 5^{0}G

	Starts	1st	2nd	3rd	Win & Pl
Career Total (Turf)	34	4	1	4	23412
Career Total (AW)	5	0	1	1	1399

78 7/01 Pont 5f D(0-80)H G-F £7410
70 6/01 Bevl 5f E(0-70)H G-F £3835
72 6/00 Ayr 5f E(0-70)H G-F £3010
70 5/99 Muss 5f D FRM £2710
Total win prize-money £16965

Going (Turf): Sf: 0-5 GS: 0-1 Gd: 0-12 GF: 3-13 Fm: 1-3
Distance: 5f/6f: 4-38 7f-8f: 0-1 9f-13f: 0-0 14f+: 0-0
Track : LH: 1-10 RH: 0-0 Tight: 0-9 Gall: 0-0
Aids: Bl: 0-0 Vi: 0-0 Tstrap: 0-0
Best Rating: 78 7/01 Pont 5f gd-fm

Not an easy ride, he is a fair sprint handicapper and all of his wins to date have come over five furlongs on fast ground. Likes to come from off the pace and needs luck in running.

Sir Walter (IRE)

104(84) (22)**31**
8-y-o b g The Dart (USA)-Glenbalda (Kambalda)
A G Hobbs (D Burchell 24/8) J Parfitt

Placings:50401055/043206344 00600/6-2 **(3204)**
2001: 7^{2}G

	Starts	1st	2nd	3rd	Win & Pl
Career Total (Turf)	9	1	1	0	3842
Career Total (AW)	15	0	1	2	997

49 8/98 Tram 1m1f (0-50)H G-F £2750
Total win prize-money £2750

Going (Turf): Sf: 0-1 GS: 0-0 Gd: 0-3 GF: 1-4 Fm: 0-0
Distance: 5f/6f: 0-0 7f-8f: 0-2 9f-13f: 1-21 14f+: 0-1
Track : LH: 0-19 RH: 1-4 Tight: 0-15 Gall: 0-0
Aids: Bl: 0-3 Vi: 0-0 Tstrap: 0-2
Best Rating: 31 7/01 Chep 7f16y good

Sisal (IRE)

101(95) (78+)**82**
2-y-o b f Danehill (USA)-Ship's Twine (IRE) (Slip Anchor)
M A Jarvis Saif Ali

Placings:01223 **(3883)**
2001: 6^{0}GF, 6^{1}SD, 6^{2}GF, 5^{2}GS, 6^{3}G

	Starts	1st	2nd	3rd	Win & Pl
Career Total (Turf)	4	0	2	1	2992
Career Total (AW)	1	1	0	0	2905

78 6/01 Wolv 6f D STD £2905
Total win prize-money £2905

Going (Turf): Sf: 0-0 GS: 0-1 Gd: 0-1 GF: 0-2 Fm: 0-0
Distance: 5f/6f: 1-5 7f-8f: 0-0 9f-13f: 0-0 14f+: 0-0
Track : LH: 1-1 RH: 0-0 Tight: 1-1 Gall: 0-0
Aids: Bl: 0-0 Vi: 0-0 Tstrap: 0-0
Best Rating: 82 8/01 Wind 6f good

She is a half-sister to smart miler Restructure and came good at the second time of asking in a maiden on the Fibresand at Wolverhampton. Always going well, she won as she liked. She should stay seven furlongs.

Sister In Law (FR)

89 **77**
2-y-o b f Distant Relative-Despina (Waajib)
H Candy The Earl Cadogan

Placings:24 **(5125)**
2001: 5^{2}GF, 5^{4}HY

	Starts	1st	2nd	3rd	Win & Pl
Career Total (Turf)	2	0	1	0	1393

Going (Turf): Sf: 0-1 GS: 0-0 Gd: 0-0 GF: 0-1 Fm: 0-0
Distance: 5f/6f: 0-2 7f-8f: 0-0 9f-13f: 0-0 14f+: 0-0
Track : LH: 0-1 RH: 0-0 Tight: 0-0 Gall: 0-1
Aids: Bl: 0-0 Vi: 0-0 Tstrap: 0-0
Best Rating: 77 8/01 Bath 5f11y gd-fm

Sita (IRE)

87 **47**
3-y-o gr f Indian Ridge-Moon Festival (Be My Guest (USA))
J R Fanshawe (Kevin Prendergast 29/4) Lael Stable

Placings:3-1100 **(5686)**
2001: 8^{1}S, 10^{1}SH, 12^{0}G, 10^{0}S

	Starts	1st	2nd	3rd	Win & Pl
Career Total (Turf)	5	2	0	1	23125

91 4/01 Navn 1m2f SH £11700
86 4/01 Leop 1m SFT £10075
Total win prize-money £21775

Going (Turf): Sf: 1-2 GS: 0-0 Gd: 0-1 GF: 0-0 Fm: 0-0
Distance: 5f/6f: 0-0 7f-8f: 1-1 9f-13f: 1-3 14f+: 0-0
Track : LH: 0-1 RH: 0-1 Tight: 0-0 Gall: 0-2
Aids: Bl: 0-0 Vi: 0-0 Tstrap: 0-0
Best Rating: 91 4/01 Navn 1m2f sft-hvy

Potentially top class. Beat the subsequent Listed winner Cool Clarity on her reappearance, before scooting up by nine lengths over ten furlongs at Navan (both runs in April). Has since joined James Fanshawe, but has disappointed on both starts for him.

Sitara

104 **69**
3-y-o ch f Salse (USA)-Souk (IRE) (Ahonoora)
L M Cumani Fittocks Stud

Placings:000-21035 **(5663)**
2001: 12^{2}GF, 12^{1}F, 14^{0}HY, 11^{3}G, 12^{5}G

	Starts	1st	2nd	3rd	Win & Pl
Career Total (Turf)	8	1	1	1	4456

60 9/01 Muss 1m4f E(0-65) FRM £3010
Total win prize-money £3010

Going (Turf): Sf: 0-4 GS: 0-0 Gd: 0-2 GF: 0-1 Fm: 1-1
Distance: 5f/6f: 0-0 7f-8f: 0-2 9f-13f: 1-5 14f+: 0-1
Track : LH: 0-2 RH: 0-2 Tight: 0-3 Gall: 0-0
Aids: Bl: 0-0 Vi: 0-0 Tstrap: 0-0
Best Rating: 69 8/01 Folk 1m4f gd-fm

Showed improved form when stepped up to 12 furlongs and just managed to win a bad race at Musselburgh in September. Suited by fast ground, does not want it soft.

Sittin Bull

74 **39**
2-y-o b c Revoque (IRE)-Taiga (Northfields (USA))
L M Cumani Eurolink Group Plc

Placings:00 **(5620)**
2001: 7^{0}S, 8^{0}GS

	Starts	1st	2nd	3rd	Win & Pl
Career Total (Turf)	2	0	0	0	

Going (Turf): Sf: 0-1 GS: 0-1 Gd: 0-0 GF: 0-0 Fm: 0-0
Distance: 5f/6f: 0-0 7f-8f: 0-1 9f-13f: 0-1 14f+: 0-0
Track : LH: 0-1 RH: 0-0 Tight: 0-0 Gall: 0-0
Aids: Bl: 0-0 Vi: 0-0 Tstrap: 0-0
Best Rating: 39 11/01 Nott 1m54y gd-sft

Six Bells

(52)
5-y-o b m Gildoran-Strikealightlady (Lighter)
R H Buckler G E Amey

Placings:0 (0223)
2001: 12⁰SD, 12⁰SD

	Starts	1st	2nd	3rd	Win & Pl
Career Total (Turf)	0	0	0	0	
Career Total (AW)	1	0	0	0	

Going (Turf): Sf: 0-0 GS: 0-0 Gd: 0-0 GF: 0-0 Fm: 0-0
Distance: 5f/6f: 0-0 7f-8f: 0-0 9f-13f: 0-1 14f+: 0-0
Track : LH: 0-1 RH: 0-0 Tight: 0-1 Gall: 0-0
Aids: Bl: 0-0 Vi: 0-0 Tstrap: 0-0

Six Hitter (USA)

93 **86+**
2-y-o ch c Boundary (USA)-Granny Kelly (USA) (Irish River (FR))
P F I Cole W J Smith And M D Dudley

Placings:2131 (4564a)
2001: 6²GF, 6¹GF, 7³HY, 7¹G

	Starts	1st	2nd	3rd	Win & Pl
Career Total (Turf)	4	2	1	1	37008
86 9/01 Casc 7f110y				GD	£23000
83 7/01 Pont 6f C				G-F	£6336

Total win prize-money £29337

Going (Turf): Sf: 0-1 GS: 0-0 **Gd: 1-1 GF: 1-2** Fm: 0-0
Distance: 5f/6f: 1-1 7f-8f: 1-3 9f-13f: 0-0 14f+: 0-0
Track : **LH: 1-1** RH: 0-0 Tight: 0-0 Gall: 0-0
Aids: Bl: 0-0 Vi: 0-0 Tstrap: 0-0
Best Rating: 86 9/01 Casc 7f110y good

Touched off by Lake Verdi on his debut, he had a hard race when getting off the mark at Pontefract, but then found a weak Listed race in Italy. Should stay a mile.

Six Pack (IRE)

97 **51**
3-y-o ch g Royal Abjar (USA)-Regal Entrance (Be My Guest (USA))
Andrew Turnell Mrs Claire Hollowood

Placings:040062 (5131)
2001: 8⁰S, 10⁴GF, 10⁰S, 10⁰GS, 7⁶G, 7²HY

	Starts	1st	2nd	3rd	Win & Pl
Career Total (Turf)	6	0	1	0	1165

Going (Turf): Sf: 0-3 GS: 0-1 Gd: 0-1 GF: 0-1 Fm: 0-0
Distance: 5f/6f: 0-0 7f-8f: 0-3 9f-13f: 0-3 14f+: 0-0
Track : LH: 0-2 RH: 0-2 Tight: 0-2 Gall: 0-0
Aids: Bl: 0-0 Vi: 0-0 Tstrap: 0-0
Best Rating: 51 10/01 Ling 7f heavy

Lightly-raced, has yet to show much in races up to ten furlongs.

Sixty Seconds (IRE)

108 **100**
3-y-o b c Definite Article-Damemill (IRE) (Danehill (USA))
J H M Gosden The Smoking/brady Partnership

Placings:210-444404 (4025)
2001: 10⁴G, 10⁴F, 11⁴GF, 10⁴GF, 8⁰GS, 11⁴GF

	Starts	1st	2nd	3rd	Win & Pl
Career Total (Turf)	9	1	1	0	11553
99 9/00 Leic 7f9y D				G-F	£4069

Total win prize-money £4069

Going (Turf): Sf: 0-0 GS: 0-1 Gd: 0-2 **GF: 1-5** Fm: 0-1
Distance: 5f/6f: 0-0 **7f-8f: 1-4** 9f-13f: 0-5 14f+: 0-0
Track : LH: 0-3 RH: 0-1 Tight: 0-0 Gall: 0-3

Aids: Bl: 0-0 Vi: 0-3 Tstrap: 0-0
Best Rating: 100 5/01 York 1m2f85y firm

Has been stepped up in trip this season, but has looked a non-stayer. Wore a visor on a couple of occasions, without any obvious effect. Acts on fast ground.

Size Doesnt Matter

80(75) (29)**35**
3-y-o b g Greensmith-Singing Rock (IRE) (Ballad Rock)
J R Best Mercato Limited

Placings:0300-00 (0469)
2001: 11⁰SD, 7⁰SD

	Starts	1st	2nd	3rd	Win & Pl
Career Total (Turf)	3	0	0	0	
Career Total (AW)	3	0	0	1	493

Going (Turf): Sf: 0-1 GS: 0-0 Gd: 0-0 GF: 0-2 Fm: 0-0
Distance: 5f/6f: 0-3 7f-8f: 0-2 9f-13f: 0-1 14f+: 0-0
Track : LH: 0-4 RH: 0-0 Tight: 0-2 Gall: 0-1
Aids: Bl: 0-0 Vi: 0-0 Tstrap: 0-0

Skenfrith

87(64) (27)**64**
2-y-o b g Atraf-Hobbs Choice (Superpower)
A Berry Chris & Antonia Deuters

Placings:603500 (5163)
2001: 5⁶GF, 5⁰S, 6³S, 6⁵G, 6⁰G, 6⁰SD

	Starts	1st	2nd	3rd	Win & Pl
Career Total (Turf)	5	0	0	1	639
Career Total (AW)	1	0	0	0	

Going (Turf): Sf: 0-2 GS: 0-0 Gd: 0-2 GF: 0-1 Fm: 0-0
Distance: 5f/6f: 0-4 7f-8f: 0-2 9f-13f: 0-0 14f+: 0-0
Track : LH: 0-2 RH: 0-0 Tight: 0-1 Gall: 0-1
Aids: Bl: 0-3 Vi: 0-0 Tstrap: 0-0
Best Rating: 64 8/01 Chep 5f16y soft

Ski For Me (IRE)

98 **83**
2-y-o ch f Barathea (IRE)-Ski For Gold (Shirley Heights)
J L Dunlop Windflower Overseas Holdings Inc

Placings:41 (5520)
2001: 7⁴GS, 8¹HY

	Starts	1st	2nd	3rd	Win & Pl
Career Total (Turf)	2	1	0	0	4229
83 10/01 Wind 1m67y D				HVY	£3916

Total win prize-money £3916

Going (Turf): Sf: 1-1 GS: 0-1 Gd: 0-0 GF: 0-0 Fm: 0-0
Distance: 5f/6f: 0-0 7f-8f: 0-1 **9f-13f: 1-1** 14f+: 0-0
Track : LH: 0-0 **RH: 1-1 Tight: 1-1** Gall: 0-0
Aids: Bl: 0-0 Vi: 0-0 Tstrap: 0-0
Best Rating: 83 10/01 Wind 1m67y heavy

She showed a lot of promise on her Leicester debut and duly obliged at the second time of asking in heavy ground at Windsor. She should stay further than a mile.

Ski Run

103 **101**
5-y-o b m Petoski-Cut And Run (Slip Anchor)
G A Butler T D Holland-Martin

Placings:001/01330-600 (3055)
2001: 10⁶GF, 16⁰G, 13⁰G

	Starts	1st	2nd	3rd	Win & Pl
Career Total (Turf)	11	2	0	2	29588
84 7/00 Asct 2m45y D(0-85)H				G-F	£12155
74 10/99 Bath 1m3f144yD				SFT	£4110

Total win prize-money £16266

Going (Turf): Sf: 1-4 GS: 0-0 Gd: 0-4 **GF: 1-3** Fm: 0-0
Distance: 5f/6f: 0-0 7f-8f: 0-0 9f-13f: 1-6 14f+: 1-5

Track : LH: 1-6 RH: 1-4 Tight: 1-2 Gall: 1-6
Aids: Bl: 0-0 Vi: 0-0 Tstrap: 0-0
Best Rating: 101 5/01 Sand 2m78y good

She looked an improved stayer in 2000, winning a decent Ascot handicap before filling the minor berth in the Lonsdale Stakes when she suffered a slipping saddle. She went on to fill the same position in the Park Hill. Below that form in 2001, looks to need 14 furlongs plus.

Skies Are Blue

90 **63**
2-y-o b f Unfuwain (USA)-Blue Birds Fly (Rainbow Quest (USA))
I A Balding T D Rootes

Placings:33 (4087)
2001: 7³GF, 8³S

	Starts	1st	2nd	3rd	Win & Pl
Career Total (Turf)	2	0	0	2	1311

Going (Turf): Sf: 0-1 GS: 0-0 Gd: 0-0 GF: 0-1 Fm: 0-0
Distance: 5f/6f: 0-0 7f-8f: 0-1 9f-13f: 0-1 14f+: 0-0
Track : LH: 0-0 RH: 0-2 Tight: 0-0 Gall: 0-1
Aids: Bl: 0-0 Vi: 0-0 Tstrap: 0-0
Best Rating: 63 6/01 Kemp 7f gd-fm

Skiffle Man

(82) (14)
5-y-o b g Alhijaz-Laundry Maid (Forzando)
B I Case Mrs M Howlett

Placings:300/00 (0261)
2001: 12⁰SD, 16⁰SD

	Starts	1st	2nd	3rd	Win & Pl
Career Total (Turf)	1	0	0	0	
Career Total (AW)	4	0	0	1	394

Going (Turf): Sf: 0-0 GS: 0-0 Gd: 0-1 GF: 0-0 Fm: 0-0
Distance: 5f/6f: 0-0 7f-8f: 0-0 9f-13f: 0-4 14f+: 0-1
Track : LH: 0-4 RH: 0-1 Tight: 0-4 Gall: 0-0
Aids: Bl: 0-0 Vi: 0-0 Tstrap: 0-0
Best Rating: 14 1/01 Wolv 1m4f stand

Skinflint

74(77) (33)**26**
2-y-o b f Emperor Fountain-Bad Payer (Tanfirion)
C W Thornton Mrs C Wilson

Placings:00 (5345)
2001: 5⁰G, 6⁰SD, 7⁰SD

	Starts	1st	2nd	3rd	Win & Pl
Career Total (Turf)	1	0	0	0	
Career Total (AW)	1	0	0	0	

Going (Turf): Sf: 0-0 GS: 0-0 Gd: 0-1 GF: 0-0 Fm: 0-0
Distance: 5f/6f: 0-2 7f-8f: 0-0 9f-13f: 0-0 14f+: 0-0
Track : LH: 0-1 RH: 0-0 Tight: 0-0 Gall: 0-0
Aids: Bl: 0-0 Vi: 0-0 Tstrap: 0-0
Best Rating: 28 10/01 Sthl 6f stand

Skippy Mac

84 **59**
2-y-o ch c Presidium-Ski Path (Celtic Cone)
N Bycroft N Bycroft

Placings:060400 (4538)
2001: 5⁰GF, 5⁶GF, 6⁰GF, 7⁴F, 8⁰GF, 7⁰GF

	Starts	1st	2nd	3rd	Win & Pl
Career Total (Turf)	6	0	0	0	313

Going (Turf): Sf: 0-0 GS: 0-0 Gd: 0-0 GF: 0-5 Fm: 0-1
Distance: 5f/6f: 0-3 7f-8f: 0-2 9f-13f: 0-1 14f+: 0-0
Track : LH: 0-1 RH: 0-1 Tight: 0-0 Gall: 0-0
Aids: Bl: 0-0 Vi: 0-0 Tstrap: 0-0

Best Rating: 59 8/01 Bevl 1m100y gd-fm

Skukusa

(100) (58)**41**

3-y-o b f Emarati (USA)-Glensara (Petoski)

R Guest The Bricklayers Partnership

Placings:0-62412 **(0316)**

2001: 7^{6}SD, 6^{2}SD, 6^{4}SD, 7^{1}SD, 7^{2}SW

	Starts	1st	2nd	3rd	Win & Pl
Career Total (Turf)	1	0	0	0	
Career Total (AW)	5	1	2	0	3511

57	2/01	Ling	7f	F(0-60)	STD	£2065

Total win prize-money £2065

Going (Turf): Sf: 0-0 GS: 0-0 Gd: 0-0 GF: 0-1 Fm: 0-0
Distance: 5f/6f: 0-2 **7f-8f: 1-4** 9f-13f: 0-0 14f+: 0-0
Track : **LH: 1-5** RH: 0-0 **Tight: 1-4** Gall: 0-0
Aids: Bl: 0-0 Vi: 0-0 Tstrap: 0-0
Best Rating: 58 2/01 Ling 7f slow

Despite showing signs of ability in fair handicap company, her best effort to date was landing a Lingfield claimer in January 2001.

Sky Dome (IRE)

105(104) (52)**65**

8-y-o ch g Bluebird (USA)-God Speed Her (Pas De Seul)

M H Tompkins Www.Raceworld.Co.Uk

Placings:614/160011005/05000/2600004400/3221060/060230325456-3400021625 **(5376)**

2001: 8^{3}GF, 9^{4}GF, 8^{0}GF, 9^{0}G, 9^{0}G, 7^{2}G, 7^{1}GF, 8^{6}GF, 8^{2}GF, 9^{5}G, 8^{0}SD

	Starts	1st	2nd	3rd	Win & Pl
Career Total (Turf)	56	6	7	4	55425

63	9/01	Ling	7f140y	E(0-65)	G-F	£3192
77	5/99	NmkJ	1m	E(0-75)H	GD	£4240
89	8/96	Gdwd	1m	C(0-90)H	GD	£14785
86	8/96	NmkJ	1m	D(0-80)H	G-F	£4581
80	4/96	NmkR	7f	C(0-95)H	G-F	£6212
74	4/95	Carl	5f	D	GD	£3469

Total win prize-money £36479

Going (Turf): Sf: 0-4 GS: 0-8 **Gd: 3-19 GF: 3-24** Fm: 0-1
Distance: 5f/6f: 1-3 **7f-8f: 5-39** 9f-13f: 0-14 14f+: 0-0
Track : LH: 0-12 **RH: 2-19** Tight: 0-8 **Gall: 1-7**
Aids: **Bl: 1-5** Vi: 0-0 Tstrap: 0-0
Best Rating: 69 6/01 Kemp 1m1f gd-fm

He has plummeted in the weights this term and has been revitalised by the reapplication of blinkers, as he showed when winning at Lingfield in September, although the blinkers have not had quite the same effect since then. He has won on both good and good to firm, and he is suited by seven furlongs.

Skye Blue (IRE)

97 (22)**54**

4-y-o b g Blues Traveller (IRE)-Hitopah (Bustino)

D W P Arbuthnot (N J Henderson 8/5) W H Ponsonby

Placings:50/530232056542-30300 **(4330)**

2001: 16^{3}HY, 11^{0}GS, 18^{3}GF, 14^{0}G, 16^{0}GF

	Starts	1st	2nd	3rd	Win & Pl
Career Total (Turf)	18	0	3	4	5473
Career Total (AW)	1	0	0	0	

Going (Turf): Sf: 0-5 GS: 0-2 Gd: 0-9 GF: 0-2 Fm: 0-0
Distance: 5f/6f: 0-1 7f-8f: 0-1 9f-13f: 0-11 14f+: 0-6
Track : LH: 0-10 RH: 0-3 Tight: 0-8 Gall: 0-3
Aids: Bl: 0-0 Vi: 0-0 Tstrap: 0-0
Best Rating: 55 4/01 Nott 2m9y heavy

Skyers A Kite

93(95) (36)**60**

6-y-o b m Deploy-Milady Jade (IRE) (Drumalis)

Ronald Thompson G A W Racing Partnership

Placings:00/032102513/006360130/206531521561005-0 **(0500)**

2001: 12^{0}GS

	Starts	1st	2nd	3rd	Win & Pl
Career Total (Turf)	31	6	4	5	26128
Career Total (AW)	5	0	0	0	0

60	10/00	York	1m2f85y	D	SFT	£7020
51	8/00	Haml	1m5f9y	E(0-70)H	SFT	£2973
49	6/00	Bevl	1m3f216y	F	G-F	£2296
43	9/99	Bevl	1m1f207y	F(0-60)H	SFT	£2355
45	10/98	Catt	1m3f214y	E(0-70)H	GD	£4666
45	7/98	Bevl	1m3f216y	G(0-60)H	G-F	£2075

Total win prize-money £21386

Going (Turf): Sf: 3-9 GS: 0-6 Gd: 1-8 GF: 2-6 Fm: 0-2
Distance: 5f/6f: 0-0 7f-8f: 0-3 **9f-13f: 5-25** 14f+: 1-8
Track : LH: 2-21 **RH: 4-15 Tight: 4-18** Gall: 1-4
Aids: Bl: 0-0 Vi: 0-0 Tstrap: 0-0
Best Rating: 39 3/01 Donc 1m4f gd-sft

A tough mare, she has recorded six wins on turf at up to a mile and five and usually pays her way through the season. Better on grass than on sand.

Skyers Flyer (IRE)

(87) (32)**34**

7-y-o b/br m Magical Wonder (USA)-Siwana (IRE) (Dom Racine (FR))

Ronald Thompson A Bell

Placings:641334243150050/2010322631/3250300460000060/00512004503/0000000602-0 **(0091)**

2001: 7^{0}SD

	Starts	1st	2nd	3rd	Win & Pl
Career Total (Turf)	58	5	7	8	25376
Career Total (AW)	5	0	0	0	

46	7/99	Carl	5f207y	F(0-60)H	GD	£3074
48	8/97	Newc	6f	G	G-F	£2211
68	4/97	Nott	6f15y	G	GD	£1984
72	8/96	Brig	5f59y	D H	FRM	£3498
47	5/96	Bevl	5f	F	G-F	£2651

Total win prize-money £13420

Going (Turf): Sf: 0-5 GS: 0-9 **Gd: 2-17 GF: 2-21** Fm: 1-6
Distance: **5f/6f: 4-39** 7f-8f: 1-24 9f-13f: 0-0 14f+: 0-0
Track : LH: 1-15 RH: 1-11 Tight: 0-13 **Gall: 1-4**
Aids: Bl: 0-0 Vi: 0-0 Tstrap: 0-0
Best Rating: 31 1/01 Ling 7f stand

Ran well in modest company in 1997, winning a brace of sellers. Mixed efforts in '98. She reportedly has problems with her joints and prefers good ground.

Skylark

103(36) (35)**51**

4-y-o ch f Polar Falcon (USA)-Boozy (Absalom)

J L Spearing Robert Heathcote

Placings:233000/4653000-66242605220000 **(5671)**

2001: 5^{6}F, 5^{6}GF, 5^{2}GF, 5^{4}GF, 5^{2}G, 5^{6}G, 6^{0}G, 5^{5}G, 5^{2}F, 5^{2}G, 6^{0}G, 5^{0}GS, 5^{0}G, 6^{0}HY

	Starts	1st	2nd	3rd	Win & Pl
Career Total (Turf)	26	0	5	3	7174
Career Total (AW)	1	0	0	0	

Going (Turf): Sf: 0-1 GS: 0-5 Gd: 0-7 GF: 0-11 Fm: 0-2
Distance: 5f/6f: 0-23 7f-8f: 0-4 9f-13f: 0-0 14f+: 0-0
Track : LH: 0-5 RH: 0-4 Tight: 0-1 Gall: 0-7
Aids: Bl: 0-0 Vi: 0-0 Tstrap: 0-0
Best Rating: 65 9/01 Chep 5f16y good

She has been placed often but is still a maiden. She tends to give herself a lot to do before finishing with a real rattle, but her style of running means that she runs into traffic problems. One of these days she will get it right.

Skylarker (USA)

108 **83**

3-y-o b g Sky Classic (CAN)-O My Darling (USA) (Mr Prospector (USA))

C F Wall Peter R Pritchard

Placings:0136 **(4532)**

2001: 8^{0}S, 10^{1}GF, 11^{3}GF, 11^{6}GF

	Starts	1st	2nd	3rd	Win & Pl
Career Total (Turf)	4	1	0	1	5731

79	6/01	NmkJ	1m2f	D	G-F	£4212

Total win prize-money £4212

Going (Turf): Sf: 0-1 GS: 0-0 Gd: 0-0 **GF: 1-3** Fm: 0-0
Distance: 5f/6f: 0-0 7f-8f: 0-1 **9f-13f: 1-3** 14f+: 0-0
Track : LH: 0-1 **RH: 1-1** Tight: 0-1 **Gall: 1-2**
Aids: Bl: 0-0 Vi: 0-0 Tstrap: 0-0
Best Rating: 83 9/01 York 1m3f195y gd-fm

Won a Newmarket maiden in June, but was held in a conditions event two months later and might not be easy to place.

Slam Bid

92(86) (36d)**25**

4-y-o b g First Trump-Nadema (Artaius (USA))

R E Barr Middleham Park Racing Xxvi

Placings:00/5630000000-050600 **(4326)**

2001: 10^{0}GF, 11^{5}GF, 10^{0}GF, 9^{6}GF, 8^{0}GS, 8^{0}GF

	Starts	1st	2nd	3rd	Win & Pl
Career Total (Turf)	13	0	0	1	356
Career Total (AW)	5	0	0	0	0

Going (Turf): Sf: 0-0 GS: 0-5 Gd: 0-1 GF: 0-7 Fm: 0-0
Distance: 5f/6f: 0-3 7f-8f: 0-3 9f-13f: 0-11 14f+: 0-1
Track : LH: 0-8 RH: 0-7 Tight: 0-10 Gall: 0-2
Aids: Bl: 0-1 Vi: 0-0 Tstrap: 0-0
Best Rating: 25 8/01 Rdcr 1m1f gd-fm

Poor plater, no recent form.

Slaneyside (IRE)

91(94) (52)**54**

4-y-o ch g Project Manager-Erneside (Lomond (USA))

I Semple Gordon McDowall

Placings:436005/36001000600-360 **(2121)**

2001: 12^{3}GF, 11^{6}GF, 13^{0}GF

	Starts	1st	2nd	3rd	Win & Pl
Career Total (Turf)	18	1	0	3	4820
Career Total (AW)	2	0	0	0	0

68	8/00	Muss	1m4f	E(0-65)	G-F	£2954

Total win prize-money £2954

Going (Turf): Sf: 0-5 GS: 0-1 Gd: 0-1 **GF: 1-6** Fm: 0-0
Distance: 5f/6f: 0-1 7f-8f: 0-4 **9f-13f: 1-12** 14f+: 0-3
Track : LH: 0-6 **RH: 1-12 Tight: 1-8** Gall: 0-0
Aids: Bl: 0-1 Vi: 0-4 Tstrap: 0-0
Best Rating: 54 5/01 Muss 1m4f gd-fm

Slapy Dam

92(73) (1)**24**

9-y-o b g Deploy-Key To The River (USA) (Irish River (FR))

D Burchell Three Acres Racing

Placings:00/5521000344116/6000064500/000450/0/42110050/000-2000500 **(5294)**

2001: 9^{2}GF, 11^{0}F, 18^{0}GF, 8^{0}G, 10^{5}S, 11^{0}G, 11^{0}G

	Starts	1st	2nd	3rd	Win & Pl
Career Total (Turf)	45	5	3	1	19877
Career Total (AW)	5	0	0	0	0

56	8/99	Chep	1m4f23y	F	G-S	£2374
47	8/99	Brig	1m3f196y	E	SFT	£2762
60	10/95	Leic	1m3f183y	D(0-85)H	GD	£4509
59	9/95	Folk	1m4f	E(0-70)H	SFT	£3817
53	4/95	Muss	1m3f32y	E(0-70)H	GD	£2944

Total win prize-money £16407

Going (Turf): Sf: 2-8 GS: 1-5 **Gd: 2-15** GF: 0-15 Fm: 0-2
Distance: 5f/6f: 0-0 7f-8f: 0-4 **9f-13f: 5-41** 14f+: 0-5
Track : LH: 2-30 **RH: 3-15 Tight: 2-14** Gall: 0-6
Aids: Bl: 0-0 Vi: 0-7 Tstrap: 0-0
Best Rating: 38 5/01 Brig 1m1f209y gd-fm

Slasher Jack (IRE)

75 (32)**47**
10-y-o b g Alzao (USA)-Sherkraine (Shergar)
Mrs D Thomson The Boozers Brigade

Placings:0100/141515656/00615233/000052/02044501/2/0-6 **(3286)**
2001: 13^{6}GS

	Starts	1st	2nd	3rd	Win & Pl
Career Total (Turf)	37	6	4	2	50344
Career Total (AW)	1	0	0	0	

59	7/98	Hayd	1m3f200yE(0-70)		GD	£2740
87	5/95	Hayd	1m3f200yC(0-90)H		G-F	£5368
86	7/94	York	1m3f195yB(0-100)H		GD	£7075
73	6/94	Pont	1m4f8y	D(0-80)H	FRM	£3318
65	4/94	Muss	1m3f32y	E(0-70)H	GD	£1903
72	6/93	Kemp	6f	F	GD	£3626

Total win prize-money £24032

Going (Turf): Sf: 0-4 GS: 0-6 **Gd: 4-13** GF: 1-13 Fm: 1-1
Distance: 5f/6f: 1-2 7f-8f: 0-1 **9f-13f: 5-27** 14f+: 0-8
Track : **LH: 4-25** RH: 1-10 Tight: 1-12 Gall: 1-9
Aids: Bl: 0-4 Vi: 0-0 Tstrap: 0-0
Best Rating: 37 7/01 Ayr 1m5f13y gd-sft

Sleeting

88 **25**
8-y-o ch g Lycius (USA)-Pluvial (Habat)
J Gallagher Horses Away Racing Club

Placings:00 **(4019)**
2001: 10^{0}S, 12^{0}G

	Starts	1st	2nd	3rd	Win & Pl
Career Total (Turf)	2	0	0	0	

Going (Turf): Sf: 0-1 GS: 0-0 Gd: 0-1 GF: 0-0 Fm: 0-0
Distance: 5f/6f: 0-0 7f-8f: 0-0 9f-13f: 0-2 14f+: 0-0
Track : LH: 0-1 RH: 0-1 Tight: 0-1 Gall: 0-0
Aids: Bl: 0-0 Vi: 0-0 Tstrap: 0-0
Best Rating: 25 8/01 Folk 1m4f good

Slickly (FR)

114 **123**
5-y-o gr h Linamix (FR)-Slipstream Queen (USA) (Conquistador Cielo (USA))
Saeed Bin Suroor Godolphin

Placings:11/14125/1010-6111 **(5357a)**
2001: 8^{6}G, 9^{1}G, 8^{1}GS, 8^{1}GS

	Starts	1st	2nd	3rd	Win & Pl
Career Total (Turf)	15	9	1	0	513440

123	10/01	Siro	1m		G-S	£67447
123	9/01	Lonc	1m		G-S	£87294
104	8/01	Sand	1m1f	C	GD	£6485
121	9/00	Lonc	1m1f165y		GD	£28818
116	6/00	Lonc	1m2f		GD	£21134
121	6/99	Lonc	1m2f		GD	£129171
104	4/99	Lonc	1m3f		SFT	£46152
107	9/98	Chan	1m		GD	£22222
	8/98	Deau	7f110y		GD	£8081

Total win prize-money £416805

Going (Turf): Sf: 1-2 GS: 2-3 **Gd: 5-7** GF: 0-0 Fm: 0-0
Distance: 5f/6f: 0-0 7f-8f: 3-5 **9f-13f: 5-9** 14f+: 0-0
Track : LH: 0-1 **RH: 8-11** Tight: 0-0 Gall: 0-0
Aids: Bl: 0-0 Vi: 0-0 Tstrap: 0-0
Best Rating: 123 10/01 Siro 1m gd-sft

Switched to Godolphin in 2000 and landed two Group events at Longchamp. Decent effort in Dubai on his first run of this term. Landed a five-runner conditions event at Sandown in August, but then ran away with two Group Ones, the Prix du Moulin and the Premio Vittorio di Capua in the autumn. Effective at a mile to ten furlongs on good ground or softer.

Slieve Bloom (IRE)

(84) (24)**56d**
4-y-o b g Dancing Dissident (USA)-Full Of Sparkle (IRE) (Persian Heights)
T G Mills Mrs Stephanie Merrydew

Placings:60500306-6 **(0059)**
2001: 9^{6}SW

	Starts	1st	2nd	3rd	Win & Pl
Career Total (Turf)	5	0	0	1	332
Career Total (AW)	4	0	0	0	0

Going (Turf): Sf: 0-2 GS: 0-1 Gd: 0-0 GF: 0-2 Fm: 0-0
Distance: 5f/6f: 0-0 7f-8f: 0-3 9f-13f: 0-6 14f+: 0-0
Track : LH: 0-6 RH: 0-0 Tight: 0-4 Gall: 0-0
Aids: Bl: 0-0 Vi: 0-0 Tstrap: 0-0
Best Rating: 17 1/01 Wolv 1m1f79y slow

Slip Killick

100(97) (49)**34**
4-y-o b f Cosmonaut-Killick (Slip Anchor)
M Mullineaux Esprit De Corps Racing

Placings:540/60-**0403030**2000000300 **(5026)**
2001: 8^{0}SD, 9^{4}SD, 9^{0}SD, 8^{3}SW, 7^{0}SD, 8^{3}SD, 11^{0}SD, 5^{2}GS, 5^{0}GS, 5^{0}GF, 5^{0}GS, 6^{0}GF, 7^{0}F, 7^{0}G, 8^{3}G, 10^{0}G, 9^{0}S

	Starts	1st	2nd	3rd	Win & Pl
Career Total (Turf)	15	0	1	1	1659
Career Total (AW)	7	0	0	2	645

Going (Turf): Sf: 0-2 GS: 0-3 Gd: 0-6 GF: 0-2 Fm: 0-2
Distance: 5f/6f: 0-6 7f-8f: 0-10 9f-13f: 0-6 14f+: 0-0
Track : LH: 0-12 RH: 0-2 Tight: 0-6 Gall: 0-0
Aids: Bl: 0-0 Vi: 0-2 Tstrap: 0-0
Best Rating: 49 2/01 Sthl 1m slow

Slipper Rose

70(94) (46)**36**
3-y-o ch f Democratic (USA)-Brown Taw (Whistlefield)
R Hollinshead Mrs D A Hodson

Placings:430600000**5065231-0545005**0 **(1088)**
2001: 8^{0}SD, 8^{5}SW, 8^{4}SW, 7^{5}SD, 8^{0}SW, 7^{0}SD, 12^{5}S, 9^{0}SD

	Starts	1st	2nd	3rd	Win & Pl
Career Total (Turf)	11	0	0	1	723
Career Total (AW)	13	1	1	1	2745

55	12/00	Sthl	1m	G	STD	£1939

Total win prize-money £1939

Going (Turf): Sf: 0-2 GS: 0-1 Gd: 0-2 GF: 0-6 Fm: 0-0
Distance: 5f/6f: 0-11 **7f-8f: 1-8** 9f-13f: 0-5 14f+: 0-0
Track : **LH: 1-14** RH: 0-1 Tight: 0-5 Gall: 0-0
Aids: Bl: 0-0 Vi: 0-0 Tstrap: 0-0
Best Rating: 46 1/01 Sthl 1m slow

Sloane

105 **86**
5-y-o ch g Machiavellian (USA)-Gussy Marlowe (Final Straw)
M L W Bell Mrs John Van Geest

Placings:4620/21-2023310 **(3837)**
2001: 7^{2}G, 6^{0}S, 7^{2}F, 7^{3}GF, 8^{3}GF, 7^{1}GF, 7^{0}G

	Starts	1st	2nd	3rd	Win & Pl
Career Total (Turf)	13	2	4	2	21418

86	7/01	Newc	7f	D(0-85)H	G-F	£10686
55	8/00	Newc	7f	D	G-F	£3662

Total win prize-money £14349

Going (Turf): Sf: 0-1 GS: 0-0 Gd: 0-4 **GF: 2-7** Fm: 0-1
Distance: 5f/6f: 0-0 **7f-8f: 2-9** 9f-13f: 0-4 14f+: 0-0
Track : LH: 0-6 RH: 0-1 Tight: 0-2 Gall: 0-1
Aids: Bl: 0-0 Vi: 0-0 Tstrap: 0-0
Best Rating: 86 7/01 Newc 7f gd-fm

Capable of fairly useful form around a mile but took a long time to break his maiden. Has recorded his best form on fast ground and has run well on that surface during the summer. Both his victories have been over seven furlongs at Newcastle.

Slumbering (IRE)

106(93) (54)**80**
5-y-o b g Thatching-Bedspread (USA) (Seattle Dancer (USA))
B A Pearce Mrs Christine Painting

Placings:04155/006/400000634005110**0-0310604260** **(5607)**
2001: 9^{0}SD, 8^{3}S, 7^{1}S, 7^{0}G, 7^{6}GS, 7^{0}GF, 7^{4}GS, 6^{2}GS, 8^{6}GS, 8^{0}GS

	Starts	1st	2nd	3rd	Win & Pl
Career Total (Turf)	32	4	1	2	33503
Career Total (AW)	2	0	0	0	

83	4/01	Kemp	7f	C(0-95)H	SFT	£7150
72	10/00	Nott	6f15y	D(0-80)H	SFT	£4452
68	9/00	Sand	7f16y	D(0-80)H	SFT	£6344
84	10/98	York	6f	D	GD	£6914

Total win prize-money £24861

Going (Turf): Sf: 3-8 GS: 0-8 Gd: 1-10 GF: 0-6 Fm: 0-0
Distance: 5f/6f: 1-7 **7f-8f: 3-23** 9f-13f: 0-4 14f+: 0-0
Track : LH: 0-8 **RH: 2-7** Tight: 0-6 **Gall: 1-5**
Aids: Bl: 0-7 Vi: 0-0 Tstrap: 0-0
Best Rating: 83 4/01 Kemp 7f soft

He was successful in a couple of handicaps at six and seven furlongs towards the end of 2000, and returned to winning form at Kempton in April. Very much suited by soft ground, he has struggled off higher marks since.

Slupia (IRE)

99 **89+**
2-y-o b f Indian Ridge-Ustka (Lomond (USA))
J H M Gosden James Wigan

Placings:3 **(5372)**
2001: 6^{3}G

	Starts	1st	2nd	3rd	Win & Pl
Career Total (Turf)	1	0	0	1	560

Going (Turf): Sf: 0-0 GS: 0-0 Gd: 0-1 GF: 0-0 Fm: 0-0
Distance: 5f/6f: 0-1 7f-8f: 0-0 9f-13f: 0-0 14f+: 0-0
Track : LH: 0-0 RH: 0-0 Tight: 0-0 Gall: 0-0
Aids: Bl: 0-0 Vi: 0-0 Tstrap: 0-0
Best Rating: 89 10/01 Rdcr 6f good

Made a good debut when third at Redcar in October, and should be better next year.

Small Fry (IRE)

90(81) (4)**45**
3-y-o b f Tagula (IRE)-Alaroos (IRE) (Persian Bold)
H A McWilliams Peter McWilliams

Placings:3-6000 **(3875)**
2001: 6^{6}GF, 6^{0}SD, 5^{0}F, 8^{0}GS

	Starts	1st	2nd	3rd	Win & Pl
Career Total (Turf)	3	0	0	0	0
Career Total (AW)	2	0	0	1	315

Going (Turf): Sf: 0-0 GS: 0-1 Gd: 0-0 GF: 0-1 Fm: 0-1
Distance: 5f/6f: 0-4 7f-8f: 0-1 9f-13f: 0-0 14f+: 0-0
Track : LH: 0-2 RH: 0-0 Tight: 0-2 Gall: 0-0
Aids: Bl: 0-0 Vi: 0-0 Tstrap: 0-0
Best Rating: 45 6/01 Newc 6f gd-fm

Small Print

88 **37?**

3-y-o b g Saddlers' Hall (IRE)-A Nymph Too Far (IRE) (Precocious)
Dr J D Scargill Robert A Gladdis

Placings:00065 **(5278)**
2001: 9^{0}GS, 10^{0}GF, 10^{0}G, 11^{6}S, 9^{5}GS

	Starts	1st	2nd	3rd	Win & Pl
Career Total (Turf)	5	0	0	0	0

Going (Turf): Sf: 0-1 GS: 0-2 Gd: 0-1 GF: 0-1 Fm: 0-0
Distance: 5f/6f: 0-0 7f-8f: 0-0 9f-13f: 0-5 14f+: 0-0
Track : LH: 0-2 RH: 0-3 Tight: 0-1 Gall: 0-1
Aids: Bl: 0-2 Vi: 0-0 Tstrap: 0-0
Best Rating: 37 9/01 Brig 1m3f196y soft

Smart Dancer (IRE)

99(77) (22)80

3-y-o b g Spectrum (IRE)-Plessaya (USA) (Nureyev (USA))
T D Easterby Bernard Hathaway

Placings:504410-0026 **(3017)**
2001: 8^{0}GF, 7^{0}G, 8^{2}GF, 7^{6}SD

	Starts	1st	2nd	3rd	Win & Pl
Career Total (Turf)	9	1	1	0	5400
Career Total (AW)	1	0	0	0	0

80	8/00	Thsk	7f	E	G-F	£3851

Total win prize-money £3851

Going (Turf): Sf: 0-0 GS: 0-0 Gd: 0-3 **GF: 1-4** Fm: 0-1
Distance: 5f/6f: 0-2 **7f-8f: 1-7** 9f-13f: 0-0 14f+: 0-0
Track : **LH: 1-4** RH: 0-1 **Tight: 1-2** Gall: 0-2
Aids: Bl: 0-0 Vi: 0-0 Tstrap: 0-0
Best Rating: 57 5/01 Thsk 1m gd-fm

Smart Hostess

86 51

2-y-o b f Most Welcome-She's Smart (Absalom)
J J Quinn B Shaw

Placings:03 **(5445)**
2001: 5^{0}G, 6^{3}HY

	Starts	1st	2nd	3rd	Win & Pl
Career Total (Turf)	2	0	0	1	426

Going (Turf): Sf: 0-1 GS: 0-0 Gd: 0-1 GF: 0-0 Fm: 0-0
Distance: 5f/6f: 0-2 7f-8f: 0-0 9f-13f: 0-0 14f+: 0-0
Track : LH: 0-0 RH: 0-0 Tight: 0-0 Gall: 0-0
Aids: Bl: 0-0 Vi: 0-0 Tstrap: 0-0
Best Rating: 51 9/01 Bevl 5f good

Smart Predator

113 106

5-y-o gr g Polar Falcon (USA)-She's Smart (Absalom)
J J Quinn B Shaw

Placings:4420221006/0030310520301325-50100100261312 **(5502)**
2001: 6^{5}S, 6^{0}G, 5^{1}GF, 5^{0}GF, 6^{0}GF, 5^{1}GF, 5^{0}G, 6^{0}G, 5^{2}G, 5^{6}GF, 5^{1}G, 5^{3}S, 5^{1}GS, 5^{2}HY

	Starts	1st	2nd	3rd	Win & Pl
Career Total (Turf)	40	7	7	5	94714

105	10/01	NmkR	5f	B(0-105)H	G-S	£9094
60	9/01	Bevl	5f	C	GD	£6368
92	7/01	Donc	5f	B(0-100)H	G-F	£10539
91	5/01	York	5f	B(0-110)H	G-F	£19012
82	8/00	Yarm	5f43y	C(0-90)H	G-F	£5887
74	5/00	Rdcr	7f	E(0-70)	G-S	£2899
81	9/99	York	7f202y	D	G-F	£6758

Total win prize-money £60559

Going (Turf): Sf: 0-8 GS: 2-5 Gd: 1-11 **GF: 4-15** Fm: 0-1
Distance: **5f/6f: 5-25** 7f-8f: 2-13 9f-13f: 0-2 14f+: 0-0
Track : **LH: 1-9** RH: 0-2 Tight: 0-1 **Gall: 1-3**
Aids: Bl: 0-0 Vi: 0-0 Tstrap: 0-0
Best Rating: 106 10/01 Donc 5f heavy

He is versatile and has won at up to a mile in the past, but he has plied his trade in sprints lately. Made all over the minimum trip at York in May and at Doncaster in July, and showed plenty of dash in the Stewards' Cup before his stamina gave in. Finished runner-up at Epsom in August despite his stall opening late and added further victories at Beverley and Newmarket. Best over five furlongs on fast ground, although has won on good to soft.

Smart Ridge

109 97

4-y-o ch c Indian Ridge-Guanhumara (Caerleon (USA))
Jamie Poulton Achilles International

Placings:0215506110/5020234050-6056262060 **(5366)**
2001: 7^{6}S, 8^{0}GS, 7^{5}G, 6^{6}GF, 7^{2}S, 7^{6}GF, 8^{2}G, 9^{0}GF, 8^{6}G, 8^{0}GS

	Starts	1st	2nd	3rd	Win & Pl
Career Total (Turf)	30	3	5	1	47663

86	8/99	Brig	5f59y	D H	G-F	£4045
86	7/99	Haml	6f5y	D H	G-F	£4299
79	5/99	Brig	5f59y	D	FRM	£3810

Total win prize-money £12155

Going (Turf): Sf: 0-6 GS: 0-4 Gd: 0-6 **GF: 2-13** Fm: 1-1
Distance: **5f/6f: 2-10** 7f-8f: 1-15 9f-13f: 0-5 14f+: 0-0
Track : **LH: 2-8** RH: 0-8 Tight: 0-2 Gall: 0-6
Aids: Bl: 0-0 Vi: 0-0 Tstrap: 0-0
Best Rating: 101 6/01 Wind 6f gd-fm

Classy handicapper, best around six/seven furlongs on any ground. On a long losing run but has run some decent races this term.

Smart Savannah

85 87

5-y-o b g Primo Dominie-High Savannah (Rousillon (USA))
E Stanners George Ward

Placings:310/600010500/0-0 **(1164)**
2001: 8^{0}GS

	Starts	1st	2nd	3rd	Win & Pl
Career Total (Turf)	14	2	0	1	12164

99	8/99	Asct	1m	C(0-100)H	SFT	£7490
88	9/98	Sand	7f16y	D	GD	£3533

Total win prize-money £11024

Going (Turf): Sf: 1-3 GS: 0-2 **Gd: 1-5** GF: 0-4 Fm: 0-0
Distance: 5f/6f: 0-0 **7f-8f: 2-11** 9f-13f: 0-3 14f+: 0-0
Track : LH: 0-2 **RH: 1-7** Tight: 0-0 Gall: 0-5
Aids: Bl: 0-0 Vi: 0-0 **Tstrap: 1-5**
Best Rating: 39 5/01 Kemp 1m gd-sft

Smart Scot

91 62

2-y-o ch g Selkirk (USA)-Amazing Bay (Mazilier (USA))
J G Given Mr & Mrs D J Smart

Placings:0400 **(4856)**
2001: 7^{0}G, 7^{4}GF, 6^{0}G, 7^{0}GF

	Starts	1st	2nd	3rd	Win & Pl
Career Total (Turf)	4	0	0	0	353

Going (Turf): Sf: 0-0 GS: 0-0 Gd: 0-2 GF: 0-2 Fm: 0-0
Distance: 5f/6f: 0-0 7f-8f: 0-4 9f-13f: 0-0 14f+: 0-0
Track : LH: 0-1 RH: 0-0 Tight: 0-1 Gall: 0-0
Aids: Bl: 0-0 Vi: 0-0 Tstrap: 0-0
Best Rating: 62 8/01 Nott 6f15y good

Second foal of a smart sprint juvenile performer, made 30,000gns as a two-year-old.

Smarter Charter

102 (28)48

8-y-o br g Master Willie-Irene's Charter (Persian Bold)
Mrs L Stubbs O J Williams

Placings:00/041226300154/003300000420/2110006/03 0410505034042463/123223256300450-564261B660001000060 **(5663)**
2001: 12^{5}GS, 10^{6}HY, 9^{4}HY, 11^{2}S, 9^{6}F, 10^{1}G, 10^{8}GF, 10^{6}GF, 9^{6}GF, 12^{0}GF, 10^{0}G, 12^{0}GF, 14^{1}GF, 16^{0}G, 10^{0}S, 12^{0}GS, 14^{0}G, 10^{6}HY, 12^{0}G

	Starts	1st	2nd	3rd	Win & Pl
Career Total (Turf)	85	8	10	9	42861
Career Total (AW)	1	0	0	0	

43	9/01	Rdcr	1m6f19y	E(0-70)H	G-F	£3794
44	6/01	Yarm	1m2f21y	E(0-75)H	GD	£3108
55	4/00	Pont	1m2f6y	F(0-70)H	G-S	£2205
54	6/99	Muss	1m1f	E(0-70)H	GD	£2788
65	7/98	Bevl	7f100y	E(0-70)H	G-F	£3670
57	7/98	Kemp	1m	D(0-80)H	G-F	£3793
75	7/96	Bevl	1m100y	D(0-80)H	G-F	£3998
61	5/96	Bevl	7f100y	E(0-70)H	G-F	£4056

Total win prize-money £27414

Going (Turf): Sf: 0-16 GS: 1-9 Gd: 2-19 **GF: 5-34** Fm: 0-7
Distance: 5f/6f: 0-2 7f-8f: 3-23 **9f-13f: 4-58** 14f+: 1-3
Track : LH: 3-40 **RH: 5-34 Tight: 3-20** Gall: 0-10
Aids: Bl: 0-0 Vi: 0-0 Tstrap: 0-0
Best Rating: 50 6/01 Nott 1m1f213y firm

Benefited from the longer trip when scoring at Redcar in September. He is usually apprentice ridden and does need things to go his own way.

Smashing Time (USA)

99 73

3-y-o b f Smart Strike (CAN)-Broken Peace (USA) (Devil's Bag (USA))
Mrs A J Perrett Lady Harrison & Sir Eric Parker

Placings:00-00400 **(4959)**
2001: 8^{0}G, 9^{0}GF, 8^{4}GF, 8^{0}G, 7^{0}GS

	Starts	1st	2nd	3rd	Win & Pl
Career Total (Turf)	7	0	0	0	415

Going (Turf): Sf: 0-1 GS: 0-1 Gd: 0-3 GF: 0-2 Fm: 0-0
Distance: 5f/6f: 0-0 7f-8f: 0-4 9f-13f: 0-3 14f+: 0-0
Track : LH: 0-0 RH: 0-4 Tight: 0-2 Gall: 0-1
Aids: Bl: 0-0 Vi: 0-0 Tstrap: 0-0
Best Rating: 73 5/01 NmkR 1m good

Smiling Applause

75 47

2-y-o b c Royal Applause-Smilingatstrangers (Macmillion)
Mrs Barbara Waring Eddys A Team

Placings:00 **(5623)**
2001: 8^{0}S, 8^{0}GS

	Starts	1st	2nd	3rd	Win & Pl
Career Total (Turf)	2	0	0	0	

Going (Turf): Sf: 0-1 GS: 0-1 Gd: 0-0 GF: 0-0 Fm: 0-0
Distance: 5f/6f: 0-0 7f-8f: 0-0 9f-13f: 0-2 14f+: 0-0
Track : LH: 0-1 RH: 0-0 Tight: 0-0 Gall: 0-0
Aids: Bl: 0-0 Vi: 0-0 Tstrap: 0-0
Best Rating: 47 11/01 Nott 1m54y gd-sft

Smirfys Night

80 51

2-y-o b c Tina's Pet-Nightmare Lady (Celestial Storm (USA))
B A McMahon Mrs Dian Plant

Placings:00 **(4961)**
2001: 5^{0}HY, 6^{0}S

	Starts	1st	2nd	3rd	Win & Pl
Career Total (Turf)	2	0	0	0	

Going (Turf): Sf: 0-2 GS: 0-0 Gd: 0-0 GF: 0-0 Fm: 0-0
Distance: 5f/6f: 0-2 7f-8f: 0-0 9f-13f: 0-0 14f+: 0-0
Track : LH: 0-1 RH: 0-0 Tight: 0-0 Gall: 0 0
Aids: Bl: 0-0 Vi: 0-0 Tstrap: 0-0
Best Rating: 51 9/01 Pont 6f soft

Smirfys Party

103(98) (80)75

3-y-o ch c Clantime-Party Scenes (Most Welcome)

B A McMahon Mrs Dian Plant

Placings:625533-22610600 **(5267)**

2001: 6^{2}G, 5^{2}GF, 5^{6}GF, 6^{1}GS, 5^{0}GS, 7^{6}SD, 6^{0}S, 6^{0}GS

	Starts	1st	2nd	3rd	Win & Pl
Career Total (Turf)	11	1	3	0	10695
Career Total (AW)	3	0	0	2	662

75 7/01 Hayd 6f C(0-100)H G-S £7312

Total win prize-money £7313

Going (Turf): Sf: 0-2 **GS: 1-4** Gd: 0-1 GF: 0-4 Fm: 0-0
Distance: **5f/6f: 1-9** 7f-8f: 0-5 9f-13f: 0-0 14f+: 0-0
Track : LH: 0-10 RH: 0-0 Tight: 0-8 Gall: 0-1
Aids: Bl: 0-0 Vi: 0-0 Tstrap: 0-0
Best Rating: 75 7/01 Hayd 6f gd-sft

He won a decent handicap over six furlongs on easy ground at Haydock in July, but was made to pay for it by the Handicapper.

Smirk

113 102

3-y-o ch c Selkirk (USA)-Elfin Laughter (Alzao (USA))

D R C Elsworth M Tabor

Placings:602-1012422 **(5605)**

2001: 7^{1}S, 6^{0}F, 8^{1}G, 7^{2}G, 9^{4}G, 9^{2}GS, 8^{2}GS

	Starts	1st	2nd	3rd	Win & Pl
Career Total (Turf)	10	2	4	0	45468

92 7/01 NmkJ 1m C(0-95)H GD £8482
83 4/01 NmkR 7f D SFT £4940

Total win prize-money £13423

Going (Turf): Sf: 1-3 GS: 0-2 **Gd: 1-3** GF: 0-1 Fm: 0-1
Distance: 5f/6f: 0-1 **7f-8f: 2-7** 9f-13f: 0-2 14f+: 0-0
Track : LH: 0-2 RH: 0-0 Tight: 0-0 Gall: 0-2
Aids: Bl: 0-0 Vi: 0-0 Tstrap: 0-0
Best Rating: 102 10/01 NmkR 1m1f gd-sft

Progressed with racing as a three-year-old, winning a Newmarket maiden in good style on his return over seven furlongs before winning a decent mile handicap at the Newmarket July meeting. Twice second in Listed company in the autumn of 2001, he should win races at that level in time. Has won on soft ground and goes well on both Newmarket courses.

Smith N Allan Oils

92 66

2-y-o b g Bahamian Bounty-Grand Splendour (Shirley Heights)

M Dods Smith & Allan Racing

Placings:5366 **(5087)**

2001: 6^{5}GF, 6^{3}GS, 7^{6}GS, 7^{6}GS

	Starts	1st	2nd	3rd	Win & Pl
Career Total (Turf)	4	0	0	1	460

Going (Turf): Sf: 0-0 GS: 0-3 Gd: 0-0 GF: 0-1 Fm: 0-0
Distance: 5f/6f: 0-1 7f-8f: 0-3 9f-13f: 0-0 14f+: 0-0
Track : LH: 0-1 RH: 0-0 Tight: 0-1 Gall: 0-0
Aids: Bl: 0-0 Vi: 0-0 Tstrap: 0-0
Best Rating: 66 6/01 Rdcr 6f gd-fm

Smoker's Folly

82 70

2-y-o b f Puissance-Fair Attempt (IRE) (Try My Best (USA))

N Tinkler The Non Smokers

Placings:2005 **(5446)**

2001: 6^{2}G, 7^{0}G, 7^{0}G, 7^{5}HY

	Starts	1st	2nd	3rd	Win & Pl
Career Total (Turf)	4	0	1	0	768

Going (Turf): Sf: 0-1 GS: 0-0 Gd: 0-3 GF: 0-0 Fm: 0-0
Distance: 5f/6f: 0-1 7f-8f: 0-3 9f-13f: 0-0 14f+: 0-0
Track : LH: 0-1 RH: 0-1 Tight: 0-1 Gall: 0-0
Aids: Bl: 0-0 Vi: 0-0 Tstrap: 0-0
Best Rating: 70 8/01 Newc 6f good

Smokey From Caplaw

105(79) (6)48

7-y-o b g Sizzling Melody-Mary From Dunlow (Nicholas Bill)

J S Goldie J S Goldie

Placings:01020/001166640P0100/0600322010/0500000/05-0114000 **(4884)**

2001: 7^{0}SD, 8^{1}GF, 7^{1}GF, 8^{4}F, 6^{0}G, 6^{0}F, 8^{0}GF

	Starts	1st	2nd	3rd	Win & Pl
Career Total (Turf)	44	7	3	1	28832
Career Total (AW)	1	0	0	0	

48	7/01	Donc	7f	E(0-75)H	G-F	£4797
44	6/01	Ayr	1m	F(0-65)H	G-F	£2464
69	7/98	Carl	6f206y	E(0-70)H	G-F	£2931
67	10/97	Rdcr	7f	E(0-70)H	G-F	£3190
70	5/97	Thsk	6f	D(0-75)H	GD	£4523
64	5/97	Newc	6f	E(0-70)H	GD	£3615
66	5/96	Haml	6f5y	F	G-F	£2521

Total win prize-money £24042

Going (Turf): Sf: 0-5 GS: 0-3 Gd: 2-15 **GF: 5-16** Fm: 0-5
Distance: 5f/6f: 2-13 **7f-8f: 5-28** 9f-13f: 0-4 14f+: 0-0
Track : LH: 1-13 RH: 1-10 Tight: 0-12 Gall: 0-2
Aids: Bl: 0-1 Vi: 0-0 Tstrap: 0-0
Best Rating: 48 7/01 Donc 7f gd-fm

Very much suited by fast ground, he is equally effective over seven furlongs or a mile and has been in fine form this summer with victories at Ayr and Doncaster.

Smokin Beau

112(116) (86+)108

4-y-o b g Cigar-Beau Dada (IRE) (Pine Circle (USA))

J Cullinan Turf 2000 Limited

Placings:043315/3200200036110000-10024010012132 **(5105)**

2001: 5^{1}SD, 5^{0}GS, 5^{0}S, 5^{2}GF, 5^{4}GF, 5^{0}GF, 5^{1}GF, 6^{0}G, 5^{0}GF, 6^{1}G, 5^{2}G, 5^{1}GF, 6^{3}GF, 5^{2}GS

	Starts	1st	2nd	3rd	Win & Pl
Career Total (Turf)	29	5	4	3	144980
Career Total (AW)	7	2	1	2	9201

102	9/01	Donc	5f140y	B(0-110)H	G-F	£30290
96	8/01	Gdwd	6f	C(0-95)H	GD	£23107
93	7/01	Asct	5f	B H	G-F	£46400
86	3/01	Wolv	5f	D(0-85)H	STD	£3796
81	8/00	Newb	5f34y	C(0-95)H	G-F	£6604
75	8/00	Gdwd	5f	C(0-90)H	GD	£9262
67	11/99	Sthl	5f	D	STD	£2822

Total win prize-money £122283

Going (Turf): Sf: 0-7 GS: 0-5 Gd: 2-7 **GF: 3-10** Fm: 0-0
Distance: **5f/6f: 7-36** 7f-8f: 0-0 9f-13f: 0-0 14f+: 0-0
Track : **LH: 1-7** RH: 0-3 **Tight: 1-6** Gall: 0-3
Aids: Bl: 0-0 Vi: 0-2 Tstrap: 0-0
Best Rating: 108 10/01 NmkR 5f gd-sft

He has plenty of early pace and showed that to good effect when winning a very valuable handicap over the minimum trip at Ascot in July. Got the easy lead he needs when taking a six-furlong handicap at Goodwood in August, and then scored at Doncaster in the very hot Portland Handicap. Lost no caste in defeat when a close third in the Ayr Gold Cup and ran another fine race at Newmarket. Though preferring a sound surface on turf, he does act on soft. He also goes particularly well on Fibresand.

Smooth Passage

77 52

2-y-o b c Suave Dancer (USA)-Flagship (Rainbow Quest (USA))

M P Tregoning Exors Of The Late R D Hollingsworth

Placings:000 (4670)

2001: 6^{0}GF, 6^{0}G, 7^{0}G

	Starts	1st	2nd	3rd	Win & Pl
Career Total (Turf)	3	0	0	0	

Going (Turf): Sf: 0-0 GS: 0-0 Gd: 0-2 GF: 0-1 Fm: 0-0
Distance: 5f/6f: 0-1 7f-8f: 0-2 9f-13f: 0-0 14f+: 0-0
Track : LH: 0-0 RH: 0-0 Tight: 0-0 Gall: 0-0
Aids: Bl: 0-0 Vi: 0-0 Tstrap: 0-0
Best Rating: 52 9/01 Chep 7f16y good

Smooth Sailing

106 (28)77

6-y-o gr g Beveled (USA)-Sea Farer Lake (Gairloch)

K McAuliffe A R Parrish

Placings:51225034060/00060521304R0220/030200000020/040051000-00345000 **(5265)**

2001: 8^{0}GS, 10^{0}G, 9^{3}G, 9^{4}G, 9^{5}GS, 9^{0}GS, 8^{0}HY, 8^{0}GS

	Starts	1st	2nd	3rd	Win & Pl
Career Total (Turf)	54	3	7	4	34133
Career Total (AW)	2	0	0	0	

82	8/00	NmkJ	1m	D(0-80)H	GD	£4582
80	6/98	Leic	7f9y	D(0-80)H	SFT	£4207
78	4/97	Sand	5f6y	D	G-F	£3571

Total win prize-money £12362

Going (Turf): Sf: 1-9 GS: 0-12 **Gd: 1-20 GF: 1-12** Fm: 0-1
Distance: 5f/6f: 1-11 **7f-8f: 2-33** 9f-13f: 0-12 14f+: 0-0
Track : LH: 0-17 RH: 0-16 Tight: 0-8 Gall: 0-8
Aids: Bl: 0-2 Vi: 0-1 Tstrap: 0-0
Best Rating: 77 8/01 Leic 1m1f218y gd-sft

He only showed bits and pieces of formthis season, but his win rate is poor. Stays a mile. Acts on a sound surface.

Smoothie (IRE)

103(101) (68)79

3-y-o gr c Definite Article-Limpopo (Green Desert (USA))

P F I Cole Ben Arbib

Placings:30540-141245 **(2512)**

2001: 7^{1}SD, 7^{4}G, 10^{1}GF, 10^{2}GF, 10^{4}GF, 9^{5}GF

	Starts	1st	2nd	3rd	Win & Pl
Career Total (Turf)	10	1	1	1	10215
Career Total (AW)	1	1	0	0	2797

71	5/01	Bath	1m2f46y	C(0-90)H	G-F	£6678
68	3/01	Ling	7f	E(0-70)H	STD	£2796

Total win prize-money £9476

Going (Turf): Sf: 0-3 GS: 0-0 Gd: 0-1 **GF: 1-6** Fm: 0-0
Distance: 5f/6f: 0-2 7f-8f: 1-4 9f-13f: 1-5 14f+: 0-0
Track : **LH: 2-5** RH: 0-1 **Tight: 2-4** Gall: 0-0
Aids: Bl: 0-0 Vi: 0-0 Tstrap: 0-0
Best Rating: 79 6/01 Wind 1m2f7y gd-fm

Smuggler's Song (IRE)

94 92

2-y-o b g Dr Devious (IRE)-Liberty Song (IRE) (Last Tycoon)

Charles O'Brien J P McManus

Placings:210 **(2306)**

2001: 7^{2}GF, 7^{1}GY, 7^{0}GF

	Starts	1st	2nd	3rd	Win & Pl
Career Total (Turf)	3	1	1	0	9660

92 6/01 Naas 7f G-Y £9660

Total win prize-money £9660

Going (Turf): Sf: 0-0 GS: 0-0 Gd: 0-0 GF: 0-2 Fm: 0-0
Distance: 5f/6f: 0-0 **7f-8f: 1-3** 9f-13f: 0-0 14f+: 0-0
Track : LH: 0-0 RH: 0-0 Tight: 0-0 Gall: 0-0
Aids: Bl: 0-0 Vi: 0-0 Tstrap: 0-0
Best Rating: 92 6/01 Naas 7f gd-yld

Smyslov

106 **78**

3-y-o b c Rainbow Quest (USA)-Vlaanderen (IRE) (In The Wings)

J L Dunlop Benny Andersson

Placings:04414-030040 **(5463)**

2001: 10^{0}GS, 11^{3}G, 11^{0}HY, 11^{0}G, 10^{4}G, 11^{0}G

	Starts	1st	2nd	3rd	Win & Pl
Career Total (Turf)	11	1	0	1	6130

62 8/00 Haml 1m65y D SFT £3867

Total win prize-money £3868

Going (Turf): Sf: 1-3 GS: 0-1 Gd: 0-5 GF: 0-2 Fm: 0-0
Distance: 5f/6f: 0-0 7f-8f: 0-4 **9f-13f: 1-7** 14f+: 0-0
Track : LH: 0-6 **RH: 1-2 Tight: 1-4** Gall: 0-1
Aids: Bl: 0-0 Vi: 0-0 Tstrap: 0-0
Best Rating: 78 5/01 Leic 1m3f183y good

He won a soft-ground Hamilton maiden last season and put a poor reappearance at Doncaster behind him with a better effort at Leicester over a mile and a half behind Zanzibar but has looked in the grasp of the Handicapper all season. Has won on soft. Acts on good.

Snails Castle (IRE)

87(95) (68+)**62**

2-y-o b c Danehill (USA)-Bean Island (USA) (Afleet (CAN))

N A Callaghan M Tabor

Placings:00 **(4037)**

2001: 7^{0}GS, 8^{0}G, 8^{4}SD

	Starts	1st	2nd	3rd	Win & Pl
Career Total (Turf)	2	0	0	0	

Going (Turf): Sf: 0-0 GS: 0-1 Gd: 0-1 GF: 0-0 Fm: 0-0
Distance: 5f/6f: 0-0 7f-8f: 0-2 9f-13f: 0-0 14f+: 0-0
Track : LH: 0-0 RH: 0-0 Tight: 0-0 Gall: 0-0
Aids: Bl: 0-0 Vi: 0-0 Tstrap: 0-0
Best Rating: 62 8/01 NmkJ 1m good

18,000gns second foal whose dam won over a mile in America and has produced several winners including the high-class middle-distance performer Johan Cuff. Little form in maidens so far.

Snake Goddess

96 **50**

3-y-o b f Primo Dominie-Shoshone (Be My Chief (USA))

H Morrison Angela McAlpine And Partners

Placings:0-00403 **(5024)**

2001: 8^{0}GS, 8^{0}G, 11^{4}GF, 14^{0}GF, 11^{3}S

	Starts	1st	2nd	3rd	Win & Pl
Career Total (Turf)	6	0	0	1	797

Going (Turf): Sf: 0-2 GS: 0-1 Gd: 0-1 GF: 0-2 Fm: 0-0
Distance: 5f/6f: 0-0 7f-8f: 0-1 9f-13f: 0-4 14f+: 0-1
Track : LH: 0-2 RH: 0-2 Tight: 0-3 Gall: 0-0
Aids: Bl: 0-0 Vi: 0-0 Tstrap: 0-0
Best Rating: 50 9/01 Brig 1m3f196y soft

Snappy

86(87) (61)**49**

2-y-o ch f First Trump-Better Still (IRE) (Glenstal (USA))

M W Easterby Mrs Jean Turpin

Placings:035 **(0877)**

2001: 5^{0}GS, 5^{3}SD, 5^{5}S

	Starts	1st	2nd	3rd	Win & Pl
Career Total (Turf)	2	0	0	0	0
Career Total (AW)	1	0	0	1	329

Going (Turf): Sf: 0-1 GS: 0-1 Gd: 0-0 GF: 0-0 Fm: 0-0
Distance: 5f/6f: 0-3 7f-8f: 0-0 9f-13f: 0-0 14f+: 0-0
Track : LH: 0-1 RH: 0-0 Tight: 0-0 Gall: 0-0
Aids: Bl: 0-0 Vi: 0-0 Tstrap: 0-0
Best Rating: 61 3/01 Sthl 5f stand

Snatch

(98) (41)**49**

4-y-o b f Elmaamul (USA)-Tarkhana (IRE) (Dancing Brave (USA))

M Quinn (M L W Bell 9/1) Corey M Gardner

Placings:64001**234**-200 **(0285)**

2001: 12^{2}SW, 12^{0}SW, 9^{0}SW

	Starts	1st	2nd	3rd	Win & Pl
Career Total (Turf)	5	1	0	0	2226
Career Total (AW)	6	0	2	1	1788

49 9/00 Yarm 1m3y F(0-60)H G-F £2226

Total win prize-money £2226

Going (Turf): Sf: 0-0 GS: 0-0 Gd: 0-1 **GF: 1-4** Fm: 0-0
Distance: 5f/6f: 0-0 7f-8f: 0-0 **9f-13f: 1-11** 14f+: 0-0
Track : LH: 0-6 RH: 0-2 Tight: 0-7 Gall: 0-0
Aids: Bl: 0-0 Vi: 0-0 Tstrap: 0-0
Best Rating: 40 1/01 Wolv 1m4f slow

Sneck Lifter

97 **60d**

2-y-o b f Zilzal (USA)-Linpac North Moor (Moorestyle)

J G Given D Maloney

Placings:53063300 **(4630)**

2001: 5^{5}GS, 5^{3}S, 5^{0}GF, 5^{6}GF, 7^{3}GS, 8^{3}GF, 8^{0}GF, 8^{0}GF

	Starts	1st	2nd	3rd	Win & Pl
Career Total (Turf)	8	0	0	3	2037

Going (Turf): Sf: 0-1 GS: 0-2 Gd: 0-0 GF: 0-5 Fm: 0-0
Distance: 5f/6f: 0-4 7f-8f: 0-3 9f-13f: 0-1 14f+: 0-0
Track : LH: 0-1 RH: 0-2 Tight: 0-2 Gall: 0-0
Aids: Bl: 0-0 Vi: 0-0 Tstrap: 0-4
Best Rating: 60 8/01 Bevl 7f100y gd-sft

A half-sister to two winners, is out of a mare who won at up to ten furlongs.

Snip Snap

99 **81**

2-y-o b f Revoque (IRE)-Snap Crackle Pop (IRE) (Statoblest)

Sir Mark Prescott W E A Fox & S Frisby

Placings:2210 **(4668)**

2001: 5^{2}GF, 5^{2}G, 5^{1}GF, 6^{0}GF

	Starts	1st	2nd	3rd	Win & Pl
Career Total (Turf)	4	1	2	0	5159

81 8/01 Brig 5f213y D G-F £3461

Total win prize-money £3461

Going (Turf): Sf: 0-0 GS: 0-0 Gd: 0-1 **GF: 1-3** Fm: 0-0
Distance: **5f/6f: 1-4** 7f-8f: 0-0 9f-13f: 0-0 14f+: 0-0
Track : **LH: 1-3** RH: 0-0 Tight: 0-0 Gall: 0-2
Aids: Bl: 0-0 Vi: 0-0 Tstrap: 0-0
Best Rating: 81 8/01 Brig 5f213y gd-fm

Showed ability in her first two starts and ran out the convincing winner of a Brighton maiden on her third outing. She should have no difficulty staying seven furlongs.

Snizort (USA)

96 **55**

3-y-o b c Bahri (USA)-Ava Singstheblues (USA) (Dixieland Band (USA))

J D Bethell M J Dawson

Placings:40 666 **(2028)**

2001: 10^{6}S, 11^{6}F, 12^{6}GF

	Starts	1st	2nd	3rd	Win & Pl
Career Total (Turf)	5	0	0	0	327

Going (Turf): Sf: 0-2 GS: 0-0 Gd: 0-1 GF: 0-1 Fm: 0-1
Distance: 5f/6f: 0-0 7f-8f: 0-2 9f-13f: 0-3 14f+: 0-0
Track : LH: 0-1 RH: 0-2 Tight: 0-1 Gall: 0-1
Aids: Bl: 0-1 Vi: 0-0 Tstrap: 0-0
Best Rating: 55 5/01 Leic 1m3f183y firm

Snow Bunting

93(84) (33)**49**

3-y-o ch g Polar Falcon (USA)-Marl (Lycius (USA))

Jedd O'Keeffe (R Charlton 30/3) Andrew Clarke

Placings:3-500100 **(5490)**

2001: 7^{5}SD, 8^{0}GF, 6^{0}G, 6^{1}G, 7^{0}G, 7^{0}HY

	Starts	1st	2nd	3rd	Win & Pl
Career Total (Turf)	6	1	0	1	3728
Career Total (AW)	1	0	0	0	0

45 8/01 Ayr 6f E GD £3024

Total win prize-money £3024

Going (Turf): Sf: 0-1 GS: 0-0 **Gd: 1-3** GF: 0-2 Fm: 0-0
Distance: **5f/6f: 1-2** 7f-8f: 0-4 9f-13f: 0-1 14f+: 0-0
Track : LH: 0-2 RH: 0-0 Tight: 0-0 Gall: 0-0
Aids: Bl: 0-0 Vi: 0-0 Tstrap: 0-0
Best Rating: 49 10/01 Rdcr 7f good

Showed some ability in his early starts for Roger Charlton and eventually managed to get off the mark for his new yard in a modest Ayr maiden in August, but was well down the field next time in a Redcar handicap.

Snow Leopard (IRE)

100 **86**

2-y-o gr c Highest Honor (FR)-Leopardess (IRE) (Ela-Mana-Mou)

J L Dunlop Miss Susan Struthers (susan Abbott Racing)

Placings:03210 **(5229)**

2001: 0^{0}GF, 7^{0}G, 6^{2}F, 8^{1}G, 7^{0}S

	Starts	1st	2nd	3rd	Win & Pl
Career Total (Turf)	5	1	1	1	5182

86 9/01 Chep 1m14y E GD £2912

Total win prize-money £2912

Going (Turf): Sf: 0-1 GS: 0-0 **Gd: 1-2** GF: 0-1 Fm: 0-1
Distance: 5f/6f: 0-0 7f-8f: 0-4 **9f-13f: 1-1** 14f+: 0-0
Track : LH: 0-1 RH: 0-1 Tight: 0-0 Gall: 0-1
Aids: Bl: 0-0 Vi: 0-0 Tstrap: 0-0
Best Rating: 86 9/01 Chep 1m14y good

Scored at Chepstow in an auction maiden when stepped up to a mile in September. His pedigree oozes stamina and he will be seen to best effect over middle distances next season. He is suited to a sound surface.

Snow Partridge (USA)

89 **22**

7-y-o ch g Arctic Tern (USA)-Lady Sharp (FR) (Sharpman)

N E Berry T Chamberlain

Placings:23/635230/004030622010/06/0 **(1568)**

2001: 9^{0}F

	Starts	1st	2nd	3rd	Win & Pl
Career Total (Turf)	23	1	4	4	11349

50 9/98 Brig 1m3f196yE(0-70)H GD £3011

Total win prize-money £3011

Going (Turf): Sf: 0-0 GS: 0-2 **Gd: 1-9** GF: 0-11 Fm: 0-1
Distance: 5f/6f: 0-0 7f-8f: 0-3 **9f-13f: 1-17** 14f+: 0-3
Track : **LH: 1-12** RH: 0-6 Tight: 0-12 Gall: 0-2
Aids: Bl: 0-2 Vi: 0-0 Tstrap: 0-2
Best Rating: 22 5/01 Brig 1m1f209y firm

Snow Shoes

97 **79**

2-y-o b f Sri Pekan (USA)-Tundra (IRE) (Common Grounds)

D J S Cosgrove Mrs Mette Campbell

Placings:26610 **(5140)**

2001: 6^{2}GF, 6^{6}GF, 7^{6}GF, 5^{1}GS, 6^{0}G

	Starts	1st	2nd	3rd	Win & Pl
Career Total (Turf)	**5**	**1**	**1**	**0**	**4200**

79 9/01 Leic 5f218y E(0-75) G-S £3251
Total win prize-money £3252

Going (Turf): Sf: 0-0 **GS: 1-1** Gd: 0-1 GF: 0-3 Fm: 0-0
Distance: **5f/6f: 1-4** 7f-8f: 0-1 9f-13f: 0-0 14f+: 0-0
Track : LH: 0-0 RH: 0-0 Tight: 0-0 Gall: 0-0
Aids: Bl: 0-0 Vi: 0-0 Tstrap: 0-0
Best Rating: 79 9/01 Leic 5f218y gd-sft

Appreciated the easier ground when landing a Leicester nursery. Stays six furlongs.

Snowfire

106 **96**

2-y-o b f Machiavellian (USA)-Hill Of Snow (Reference Point)
J L Dunlop L Neil Jones

Placings:2212 **(5144)**
2001: 7^{2}GS, 7^{2}GF, 7^{1}GF, 7^{2}G

	Starts	1st	2nd	3rd	Win & Pl
Career Total (Turf)	**4**	**1**	**3**	**0**	**12359**

87 9/01 Ling 7f D G-F £4719
Total win prize-money £4719

Going (Turf): Sf: 0-0 GS: 0-1 Gd: 0-1 **GF: 1-2** Fm: 0-0
Distance: 5f/6f: 0-0 **7f-8f: 1-4** 9f-13f: 0-0 14f+: 0-0
Track : LH: 0-0 RH: 0-0 Tight: 0-0 Gall: 0-0
Aids: Bl: 0-0 Vi: 0-0 Tstrap: 0-0
Best Rating: 96 10/01 NmkR 7f good

She finished runner-up on her first two starts before narrowly getting off the mark in what may have been a decent Lingfield maiden.

Snowflake (IRE)

110 **112**

3-y-o b f Caerleon (USA)-Ivyanna (IRE) (Reference Point)
A P O'Brien Mrs John Magnier

Placings:324-02400202 **(4515a)**
2001: 8^{0}G, 10^{2}GY, 12^{4}GF, 10^{0}Y, 12^{0}G, 9^{2}G, 11^{0}G, 10^{2}GY

	Starts	1st	2nd	3rd	Win & Pl
Career Total (Turf)	**11**	**0**	**4**	**1**	**47105**

Going (Turf): Sf: 0-1 GS: 0-0 Gd: 0-5 GF: 0-1 Fm: 0-0
Distance: 5f/6f: 0-0 7f-8f: 0-3 9f-13f: 0-7 14f+: 0-0
Track : LH: 0-1 RH: 0-3 Tight: 0-1 Gall: 0-2
Aids: Bl: 0-0 Vi: 0-0 Tstrap: 0-0
Best Rating: 112 8/01 Gdwd 1m1f192y good

She has shown ability and must be one of the highest rated maidens in Europe. Ran a blinder in the Nassau stakes, going off in front and only just being caught. Stays ten furlongs.

Snowstorm

110 **108**

3-y-o gr c Environment Friend-Choral Sundown (Night Shift (USA))
M L W Bell Lord Blyth

Placings:261210-2324036 **(5132)**
2001: 12^{2}GF, 11^{3}GF, 12^{2}GF, 12^{4}GF, 10^{0}Y, 8^{3}GF, 12^{6}G

	Starts	1st	2nd	3rd	Win & Pl
Career Total (Turf)	**13**	**2**	**4**	**2**	**75137**

93 9/00 Donc 1m B G-F £15015
80 7/00 Ayr 7f D FRM £3542
Total win prize-money £18558

Going (Turf): Sf: 0-1 GS: 0-0 Gd: 0-2 **GF: 1-8 Fm: 1-1**
Distance: 5f/6f: 0-1 **7f-8f: 2-4** 9f-13f: 0-8 14f+: 0-0
Track : **LH: 1-5** RH: 0-3 Tight: 0-2 Gall: 0-4
Aids: Bl: 0-0 Vi: 0-0 Tstrap: 0-0
Best Rating: 114 6/01 Asct 1m4f gd-fm

Running well, in the frame in the Chester Vase, the Predominate Stakes and the King Edward VII Stakes. Not disgraced in a Grade One at Arlington Park, and was a good third in Listed company on his return to England. He is probably best on fast ground and he races from the front.

So Divine

96 **65**

3-y-o br f So Factual (USA)-Divina Mia (Dowsing (USA))
M Johnston The 5th Middleham Partnership

Placings:415-000 **(3948)**
2001: 6^{0}GF, 5^{0}G, 6^{0}GS

	Starts	1st	2nd	3rd	Win & Pl
Career Total (Turf)	**6**	**1**	**0**	**0**	**3053**

65 7/00 Ripn 5f F G-S £2824
Total win prize-money £2824

Going (Turf): Sf: 0-0 **GS: 1-2** Gd: 0-1 GF: 0-3 Fm: 0-0
Distance: **5f/6f: 1-5** 7f-8f: 0-1 9f-13f: 0-0 14f+: 0-0
Track : LH: 0-0 RH: 0-1 Tight: 0-0 Gall: 0-1
Aids: Bl: 0-0 Vi: 0-0 Tstrap: 0-0
Best Rating: 57 8/01 Gdwd 5f good

Lightly-raced as a juvenile, winning on easy ground at Ripon. Has only raced at five so far, but should get a little further.

So It Is

88(70) (13)**55**

2-y-o b f So Factual (USA)-Big Story (Cadeaux Genereux)
K R Burke Threemustavbeers

Placings:00060000 **(5396)**
2001: 5^{0}G, 6^{0}GF, 5^{0}G, 5^{6}F, 6^{0}G, 6^{0}S, 6^{0}SD, 8^{0}SD

	Starts	1st	2nd	3rd	Win & Pl
Career Total (Turf)	**6**	**0**	**0**	**0**	**0**
Career Total (AW)	**2**	**0**	**0**	**0**	

Going (Turf): Sf: 0-1 GS: 0-0 Gd: 0-3 GF: 0-1 Fm: 0-1
Distance: 5f/6f: 0-6 7f-8f: 0-1 9f-13f: 0-1 14f+: 0-0
Track : LH: 0-4 RH: 0-1 Tight: 0-2 Gall: 0-1
Aids: Bl: 0-0 Vi: 0-0 Tstrap: 0-0
Best Rating: 55 7/01 Brig 5f213y firm

So Precious (IRE)

93 **57**

4-y-o b f Batshoof-Golden Form (Formidable (USA))
Ian Williams (N P Littmoden 2/6) M Murphy

Placings:61/400000-00000U0 **(5622)**
2001: 10^{0}S, 12^{0}G, 10^{0}HY, 12^{0}G, 12^{0}G, 11^{U}S, 14^{0}GS

	Starts	1st	2nd	3rd	Win & Pl
Career Total (Turf)	**15**	**1**	**0**	**0**	**4230**

68 9/99 Kemp 7f D HVY £3078
Total win prize-money £3079

Going (Turf): Sf: 1-5 GS: 0-4 Gd: 0-3 GF: 0-3 Fm: 0-0
Distance: 5f/6f: 0-1 **7f-8f: 1-3** 9f-13f: 0-10 14f+: 0-1
Track : LH: 0-6 **RH: 1-7** Tight: 0-2 Gall: 0-5
Aids: Bl: 0-0 Vi: 0-2 Tstrap: 0-0
Best Rating: 66 5/01 NmkR 1m4f good

She ran in Group company early in 2000, including the Oaks, but was way short of that class. A drop to handicap company later in the season did not result in an improvement in her fortunes, and she has shown nothing this season.

So Royal (USA)

81(90) (70)**96**

2-y-o ch f Royal Academy (USA)-Exactly So (Caro)
M Johnston R W Huggins

Placings:220 **(5609)**
2001: 8^{2}GF, 8^{2}HY, 8^{0}GS, 9^{4}SD

	Starts	1st	2nd	3rd	Win & Pl
Career Total (Turf)	**3**	**0**	**2**	**0**	**2230**

Going (Turf): Sf: 0-1 GS: 0-1 Gd: 0-0 GF: 0-1 Fm: 0-0
Distance: 5f/6f: 0-0 7f-8f: 0-2 9f-13f: 0-1 14f+: 0-0
Track : LH: 0-1 RH: 0-1 Tight: 0-1 Gall: 0-0
Aids: Bl: 0-0 Vi: 0-0 Tstrap: 0-0
Best Rating: 81 10/01 Ayr 1m heavy

A $50,000 half-sister to a Prix Lupin winner among others, she has done enough so far to suggest she can win races and will appreciate middle distances in time.

So Sober (IRE)

103(106) (78)**78**

3-y-o b g Common Grounds-Femme Savante (Glenstal (USA))
C F Wall The Boardroom Syndicate

Placings:5420620-**21106516000** **(5352)**
2001: 6^{2}SD, **6**^{1}SD, **6**^{1}SD, **6**^{0}SW, 6^{6}GF, 5^{5}G, **6**^{1}SD, 5^{6}GF, 5^{0}GF, 6^{0}GF, **6**^{0}SD

	Starts	1st	2nd	3rd	Win & Pl
Career Total (Turf)	**12**	**0**	**2**	**0**	**2372**
Career Total (AW)	**6**	**3**	**1**	**0**	**8782**

67 6/01 Sthl 6f F STD £2275
78 4/01 Ling 6f E(0-75)H STD £2754
70 3/01 Sthl 6f D STD £2912
Total win prize-money £7942

Going (Turf): Sf: 0-4 GS: 0-1 Gd: 0-2 GF: 0-5 Fm: 0-0
Distance: **5f/6f: 3-16** 7f-8f: 0-2 9f-13f: 0-0 14f+: 0-0
Track : **LH: 3-7** RH: 0-2 **Tight: 1-2** Gall: 0-2
Aids: Bl: 0-0 Vi: 0-0 Tstrap: 0-0
Best Rating: 78 5/01 Wind 5f10y good

Having shown little over five furlongs, he came into his own when moved to the sand and stepped up an extra furlong in the spring of 2001, with back-to-back wins in a maiden and a handicap. Bar a claiming victory, he has gone off the boil since then.

So Tempting

103(96) (77)**74**

3-y-o b g So Factual (USA)-Persuasion (Batshoof)
J R Fanshawe Countess Of Lonsdale

Placings:32-106203 **(5486)**
2001: **8**^{1}SD, 8^{0}GS, 7^{6}G, 9^{2}G, 10^{0}G, 10^{3}HY

	Starts	1st	2nd	3rd	Win & Pl
Career Total (Turf)	**7**	**0**	**2**	**2**	**2795**
Career Total (AW)	**1**	**1**	**0**	**0**	**2961**

77 6/01 Sthl 1m E STD £2961
Total win prize-money £2961

Going (Turf): Sf: 0-2 GS: 0-2 Gd: 0-3 GF: 0-0 Fm: 0-0
Distance: 5f/6f: 0-0 **7f-8f: 1-5** 9f-13f: 0-3 14f+: 0-0
Track : **LH: 1-3** RH: 0-2 Tight: 0-3 Gall: 0-1
Aids: Bl: 0-0 Vi: 0-0 Tstrap: 0-0
Best Rating: 77 6/01 Sthl 1m stand

He showed promise in a couple of turf maidens last season, but got off the mark on the Southwell Fibresand on his belated reappearance. He looks suited by testing conditions.

Soaked

103(100) (60)**70**

8-y-o b g Dowsing (USA)-Water Well (Sadler's Wells (USA))
D W Chapman David W Chapman

Placings:06040/**62056**04003065/**245103**0412111**1**0010 **4002114601/343**005604/**00000**0L21133402-000**3**3021214000000220300 **(5403)**
2001: 5^{0}GF, 5^{0}G, 5^{0}GF, **5**^{3}SD, 5^{3}GF, 5^{0}GS, 5^{2}GF, 5^{1}GS, 5^{2}GF, 5^{1}G, 5^{4}G, 5^{0}G, 5^{0}GF, 5^{0}GF, 5^{0}G, 5^{0}G, 5^{2}GS, 5^{2}S, 5^{0}GS, 5^{3}G, 5^{0}S, 5^{0}S

	Starts	1st	2nd	3rd	Win & Pl
Career Total (Turf)	**59**	**8**	**7**	**5**	**45635**
Career Total (AW)	**33**	**6**	**3**	**4**	**23782**

70	8/01	Nott	5f13y	E(0-65)	GD	£3248
60	7/01	Wwck	5f110y	D(0-85)H	G-S	£8710
60	8/00	Bath	5f11y	D(0-85)H	G-F	£3789
55	8/00	Wind	5f10y	E(0-70)H	G-F	£2926
84	1/99	Ling	5f	D(0-85)H	STD	£4507
82	11/98	Ling	6f	D(0-85)H	STD	£3582
75	11/98	Ling	5f	D(0-80)H	STD	£3452
63	9/98	Pont	5f	E(0-70)H	G-F	£3472
67	6/98	Sthl	5f	E(0-70)H	STD	£2950
63	6/98	Sthl	5f	F(0-65)H	STD	£2637
56	6/98	Haml	6f5y	F(0-65)H	GD	£2836
57	5/98	Muss	5f	D(0-75)H	G-S	£4224
44	5/98	Muss	5f	F(0-65)H	GD	£2916
49	3/98	Sthl	6f	G(0-60)H	STD	£1530

Total win prize-money £50784

Going (Turf): Sf: 0-6 GS: 2-10 **Gd: 3-18 GF: 3-22** Fm: 0-3
Distance: **5f/6f: 13-80** 7f-8f: 1-10 9f-13f: 0-2 14f+: 0-0
Track : **LH: 6-38** RH: 1-7 **Tight: 3-19** Gall: 2-7
Aids: **Bl: 6-47** Vi: 0-1 Tstrap: 0-0
Best Rating: 70 9/01 Pont 5f soft

A real speedster from the stalls, he is effective on turf, Equitrack and Fibresand. He bounced back to his best when winning a handicap at Warwick in July and has since won again at Nottingham. He had looked held in the handicap after that until putting in three good efforts at the end of September, early October, twice beaten by Bond Boy.

Soaring Phoenix (USA)

94(106) (73)**62**
3-y-o b/br c St Jovite (USA)-Pamzig (USA) (Danzig (USA))
B W Hills Deln Ltd

Placings:0-02502 **(2648)**
2001: 7^{0}G, 8^{2}SD, 9^{5}GF, 10^{0}GF, 12^{0}SD

	Starts	1st	2nd	3rd	Win & Pl
Career Total (Turf)	4	0	0	0	0
Career Total (AW)	2	0	2	0	1738

Going (Turf): Sf: 0-2 GS: 0-0 Gd: 0-0 GF: 0-2 Fm: 0-0
Distance: 5f/6f: 0-0 7f-8f: 0-3 9f-13f: 0-3 14f+: 0-0
Track : LH: 0-3 RH: 0-1 Tight: 0-0 Gall: 0-0
Aids: Bl: 0-0 Vi: 0-0 Tstrap: 0-0
Best Rating: 73 7/01 Sthl 1m4f stand

Soba Jones

109(89) (40)**70**
4-y-o b g Emperor Jones (USA)-Soba (Most Secret)
T D Easterby Mrs M Hills

Placings:3/6602343153350-100250150020 **(5629)**
2001: 5^{1}G, 5^{0}GF, 5^{0}GF, 5^{2}S, 5^{5}G, 5^{0}GF, 5^{1}GF, 5^{5}G, 5^{0}GS, 5^{0}S, 5^{2}S, 5^{0}G

	Starts	1st	2nd	3rd	Win & Pl
Career Total (Turf)	24	3	3	5	20926
Career Total (AW)	2	0	0	0	0

67	8/01	Catt	5f212y	E(0-70)	G-F	£3332
65	6/01	Hayd	5f	D(0-80)H	GD	£4394
56	7/00	Newc	5f	D	GD	£3328

Total win prize-money £11054

Going (Turf): Sf: 0-4 GS: 0-2 **Gd: 1-7 GF: 1-8** Fm: 0-2
Distance: **5f/6f: 2-21** 7f-8f: 0-4 9f-13f: 0-0 14f+: 0-0
Track : **LH: 1-6** RH: 0-2 **Tight: 1-3** Gall: 0-1
Aids: **Bl: 1-12** Vi: 0-0 Tstrap: 0-0
Best Rating: 70 10/01 Pont 5f soft

Returned to form in winning style at Haydock in June after a nine-month break and with the blinkers left off. Best over five furlongs and sound surface.

Sober As A Judge

90(93) (37)**37**
4-y-o b g Mon Tresor-Flicker Toa Flame (USA) (Empery (USA))
C A Dwyer (J Pearce 1/1) M M Foulger

Placings:500/00030000002635-4004000 **(4872)**
2001: 8^{4}SD, 8^{0}GF, 7^{0}GF, 6^{4}F, 7^{0}GF, 6^{0}SW, 7^{0}G

	Starts	1st	2nd	3rd	Win & Pl
Career Total (Turf)	17	0	0	1	277
Career Total (AW)	7	0	1	1	684

Going (Turf): Sf: 0-2 GS: 0-2 Gd: 0-2 GF: 0-8 Fm: 0-3
Distance: 5f/6f: 0-2 7f-8f: 0-17 9f-13f: 0-5 14f+: 0-0
Track : LH: 0-12 RH: 0-0 Tight: 0-4 Gall: 0-0
Aids: Bl: 0-0 Vi: 0-4 Tstrap: 0-0
Best Rating: 37 9/01 NmkR 7f good

Sober Hill

77(93) (45)**15**
3-y-o b g Komaite (USA)-Mamoda (Good Times (ITY))
D Shaw M Wainman

Placings:040-044350 **(5412)**
2001: 7^{0}SW, 6^{4}SW, 7^{4}SD, 6^{3}SD, 6^{5}HY, 6^{0}SD

	Starts	1st	2nd	3rd	Win & Pl
Career Total (Turf)	1	0	0	0	0
Career Total (AW)	8	0	0	1	323

Going (Turf): Sf: 0-1 GS: 0-0 Gd: 0-0 GF: 0-0 Fm: 0-0
Distance: 5f/6f: 0-5 7f-8f: 0-4 9f-13f: 0-0 14f+: 0-0
Track : LH: 0-8 RH: 0-0 Tight: 0-5 Gall: 0-0
Aids: Bl: 0-6 Vi: 0-0 Tstrap: 0-0
Best Rating: 45 2/01 Wolv 7f stand

Soca

87 **59**
2-y-o ch f So Factual (USA)-Calypso Lady (IRE) (Priolo (USA))
R Hannon Mrs D M Wight

Placings:0300 **(5667)**
2001: 5^{0}GF, 6^{3}GF, 7^{0}GF, 8^{0}HY

	Starts	1st	2nd	3rd	Win & Pl
Career Total (Turf)	4	0	0	1	291

Going (Turf): Sf: 0-1 GS: 0-0 Gd: 0-0 GF: 0-3 Fm: 0-0
Distance: 5f/6f: 0-2 7f-8f: 0-1 9f-13f: 0-1 14f+: 0-0
Track : LH: 0-0 RH: 0-2 Tight: 0-1 Gall: 0-1
Aids: Bl: 0-0 Vi: 0-0 Tstrap: 0-0
Best Rating: 59 8/01 Ling 6f gd-fm

Sociable

86 **81**
2-y-o b f Danehill (USA)-Society Rose (Saddlers' Hall (IRE))
W J Haggas Cheveley Park Stud

Placings:03 **(5561)**
2001: 6^{0}G, 7^{3}S

	Starts	1st	2nd	3rd	Win & Pl
Career Total (Turf)	2	0	0	1	699

Going (Turf): Sf: 0-1 GS: 0-0 Gd: 0-1 GF: 0-0 Fm: 0-0
Distance: 5f/6f: 0-1 7f-8f: 0-1 9f-13f: 0-0 14f+: 0-0
Track : LH: 0-0 RH: 0-0 Tight: 0-0 Gall: 0-0
Aids: Bl: 0-0 Vi: 0-0 Tstrap: 0-0
Best Rating: 81 10/01 Yarm 7f3y soft

She has shown some ability in maiden company.

Social Contract

106(110) (83)**77**
4-y-o b g Emarati (USA)-Just Buy Baileys (Formidable (USA))
S Kirk J G Lambton

Placings:3301410/0013401-031000000 **(4433)**
2001: 7^{0}SD, 7^{3}SW, 7^{1}SD, 7^{0}SD, 8^{0}GS, 7^{0}G, 7^{0}GF, 7^{0}GF, 7^{0}G

	Starts	1st	2nd	3rd	Win & Pl
Career Total (Turf)	18	3	0	3	17138
Career Total (AW)	5	2	0	1	11332

83	2/01	Ling	7f	C(0-90)H	STD	£8190
84	10/00	NmkR	7f	C(0-100)H	G-S	£7748
78	6/00	Leic	7f9y	E(0-75)H	G-F	£3263
75	8/99	Ling	7f	E H	GD	£3063
80	7/99	Sthl	6f	G	STD	£1882

Total win prize-money £24147

Going (Turf): Sf: 0-2 **GS: 1-3 Gd: 1-5 GF: 1-8** Fm: 0-0
Distance: 5f/6f: 1-5 **7f-8f: 4-18** 9f-13f: 0-0 14f+: 0-0
Track : **LH: 2-6** RH: 0-6 **Tight: 1-2** Gall: 0-1
Aids: **Bl: 2-7** Vi: 0-0 Tstrap: 0-0
Best Rating: 83 2/01 Ling 7f stand

A fair handicapper, he has picked up his share of races each season, and whilst he stays a mile, has never won beyond seven furlongs. Best blinkered nowadays, out of form on turf recently.

Social Order (IRE)

97 **73**
3-y-o b c Sadler's Wells (USA)-Aunt Pearl (USA) (Seattle Slew (USA))
J H M Gosden R E Sangster & A K Collins

Placings:06 **(5286)**
2001: 12^{0}GF, 10^{6}HY

	Starts	1st	2nd	3rd	Win & Pl
Career Total (Turf)	2	0	0	0	0

Going (Turf): Sf: 0-1 GS: 0-0 Gd: 0-0 GF: 0-1 Fm: 0-0
Distance: 5f/6f: 0-0 7f-8f: 0-0 9f-13f: 0-2 14f+: 0-0
Track : LH: 0-1 RH: 0-1 Tight: 0-0 Gall: 0-0
Aids: Bl: 0-0 Vi: 0-0 Tstrap: 0-0
Best Rating: 73 9/01 Kemp 1m4f gd-fm

Socialist (USA)

(94) (33)
5-y-o b g Hermitage (USA)-Social Missy (USA) (Raised Socially (USA))
G Brown Mrs Carol Ann Brown

Placings:630004 0 **(0074)**
2001: 16^{0}SW

	Starts	1st	2nd	3rd	Win & Pl
Career Total (Turf)	3	0	0	1	318
Career Total (AW)	4	0	0	0	0

Going (Turf): Sf: 0-1 GS: 0-1 Gd: 0-0 GF: 0-1 Fm: 0-0
Distance: 5f/6f: 0-0 7f-8f: 0-0 9f-13f: 0-5 14f+: 0-2
Track : LH: 0-7 RH: 0-0 Tight: 0-2 Gall: 0-0
Aids: Bl: 0-1 Vi: 0-0 Tstrap: 0-1

Societe Generale

51
2-y-o b g Eagle Eyed (USA)-Canlubang (Mujtahid (USA))
A Bailey Willie McKay

Placings:0O **(1132)**
2001: 5^{0}GS, 5^{0}GS

	Starts	1st	2nd	3rd	Win & Pl
Career Total (Turf)	2	0	0	0	

Going (Turf): Sf: 0-0 GS: 0-2 Gd: 0-0 GF: 0-0 Fm: 0-0
Distance: 5f/6f: 0-2 7f-8f: 0-0 9f-13f: 0-0 14f+: 0-0
Track : LH: 0-0 RH: 0-0 Tight: 0-0 Gall: 0-0
Aids: Bl: 0-1 Vi: 0-0 Tstrap: 0-0

Society King (IRE)

(96) (44)
6-y-o b g Fairy King (USA)-Volga (USA) (Riverman (USA))
K R Burke Lifestyle Bloodstock (uk) Ltd

Placings:0/3000/**0000**/00R-**42600** (0711)
2001: 8^4SW, 8^2SD, 7^6SD, 8^0SD, 7^0SD

	Starts	1st	2nd	3rd	Win & Pl
Career Total (Turf)	7	0	0	1	450
Career Total (AW)	10	0	1	0	622

Going (Turf): **Sf: 0-4 GS: 0-2 Gd: 0-1 GF: 0-0 Fm: 0-0**
Distance: 5f/6f: 0-1 7f-8f: 0-10 9f-13f: 0-6 14f+: 0-0
Track : LH: 0-11 RH: 0-0 Tight: 0-3 Gall: 0-0
Aids: Bl: 0-0 Vi: 0-1 Tstrap: 0-0
Best Rating: 44 2/01 Wolv 1m100y stand

Society Pet

84 **64**

2-y-o b f Runnett-Polar Storm (IRE) (Law Society (USA))
B J Meehan Miss V Howard Evans

Placings:040 (3952)
2001: 6^0GF, 5^4F, 6^0GF

	Starts	1st	2nd	3rd	Win & Pl
Career Total (Turf)	3	0	0	0	261

Going (Turf): **Sf: 0-0 GS: 0-0 Gd: 0-0 GF: 0-2 Fm: 0-1**
Distance: 5f/6f: 0-2 7f-8f: 0-1 9f-13f: 0-0 14f+: 0-0
Track : LH: 0-1 RH: 0-0 Tight: 0-0 Gall: 0-1
Aids: Bl: 0-0 Vi: 0-0 Tstrap: 0-0
Best Rating: 64 7/01 Nott 6f15y gd-fm

Society Times (USA)

(83) (20)

8-y-o b g Imp Society (USA)-Mauna Loa (USA) (Hawaii)
A Bailey Sandybrow Stables Ltd

Placings:606/500-**4500** (0350)
2001: 7^4SD, 8^5SW, 9^0SD, 12^0SD

	Starts	1st	2nd	3rd	Win & Pl
Career Total (Turf)	5	0	0	0	0
Career Total (AW)	5	0	0	0	0

Going (Turf): **Sf: 0-0 GS: 0-1 Gd: 0-2 GF: 0-1 Fm: 0-1**
Distance: 5f/6f: 0-0 7f-8f: 0-3 9f-13f: 0-7 14f+: 0-0
Track : LH: 0-7 RH: 0-3 Tight: 0-5 Gall: 0-1
Aids: Bl: 0-0 Vi: 0-0 Tstrap: 0-0
Best Rating: 20 1/01 Wolv 1m100y slow

Socks

(73) (15)

2-y-o b f Sabrehill (USA)-Pink Brief (IRE) (Ela-Mana-Mou)
Andrew Reid A S Reid

Placings:0 (1083)
2001: 5^0SD

	Starts	1st	2nd	3rd	Win & Pl
Career Total (Turf)	0	0	0	0	
Career Total (AW)	1	0	0	0	

Going (Turf): **Sf: 0-0 GS: 0-0 Gd: 0-0 GF: 0-0 Fm: 0-0**
Distance: 5f/6f: 0-1 7f-8f: 0-0 9f-13f: 0-0 14f+: 0-0
Track : LH: 0-1 RH: 0-0 Tight: 0-1 Gall: 0-0
Aids: Bl: 0-0 Vi: 0-0 Tstrap: 0-0
Best Rating: 21 5/01 Wolv 5f stand

Sofisio

(106) (61)

4-y-o ch g Efisio-Legal Embrace (CAN) (Legal Bid (USA))
Miss S J Wilton John Pointon And Sons

Placings:0402144/03245006210-**02405500** (5166)
2001: 11^0SD, 9^2SD, 8^4SD, 9^0SD, 8^5SD, 11^5SD, 8^0GF, 9^0SD, 11^6SD

	Starts	1st	2nd	3rd	Win & Pl
Career Total (Turf)	10	0	1	0	1657
Career Total (AW)	16	2	3	1	7122
69 11/00 Ling 1m	F			STD	£1809
77 11/99 Ling 7f	F			STD	£2127

Total win prize-money £3937

Going (Turf): **Sf: 0-2 GS: 0-1 Gd: 0-1 GF: 0-5 Fm: 0-1**
Distance: 5f/6f: 0-0 **7f-8f: 2-16** 9f-13f: 0-10 14f+: 0-0
Track : **LH: 2-17** RH: 0-1 **Tight: 2-11** Gall: 0-1
Aids: **Bl: 1-11** Vi: 0-0 Tstrap: 0-10
Best Rating: 68 3/01 Wolv 1m1f79y stand

Soft Breeze

107 **95**

3-y-o ch f Zafonic (USA)-Tropical (Green Desert (USA))
E A L Dunlop Maktoum Al Maktoum

Placings:3-433165100300 (5339)
2001: 7^4S, 7^3G, 7^3GF, 7^1GF, 7^6GS, 8^5GF, 8^1G, 7^0G, 9^0GF, 10^3GF, 9^0G, 10^0GS

	Starts	1st	2nd	3rd	Win & Pl
Career Total (Turf)	13	2	0	4	28099
90 8/01 Asct 1m	C(0-100)H			GD	£8307
55 6/01 Ayr 7f	D			G-F	£3640

Total win prize-money £11947

Going (Turf): Sf: 0-1 GS: 0-2 **Gd: 1-4 GF: 1-6** Fm: 0-0
Distance: 5f/6f: 0-1 **7f-8f: 2-8** 9f-13f: 0-4 14f+: 0-0
Track : **LH: 1-3** RH: 0-3 Tight: 0-1 Gall: 0-2
Aids: Bl: 0-0 Vi: 0-0 Tstrap: 0-0
Best Rating: 95 9/01 Newb 1m2f6y gd-fm

A half-sister to Coronation Stakes winner Shake The Yoke. Third in a Goodwood handicap prior to breaking her duck in a moderate maiden at Ayr over seven furlongs in summer of 2001. Ran an eye-catching race at Glorious Goodwood on her first run over a mile and confirmed the promise with an impressive win over that trip at Ascot. Another step up in trip to ten furlongs at Newbury in September saw her finish an unlucky third, and further progress is likely at that trip. Has won on good and good to firm.

Softly (IRE)

102 **83**

2-y-o ch f Grand Lodge (USA)-Decrescendo (IRE) (Polish Precedent (USA))
M L W Bell E D Kessly

Placings:03300 (5589)
2001: 5^0S, 7^3GF, 6^3F, 8^0GF, 7^0GS

	Starts	1st	2nd	3rd	Win & Pl
Career Total (Turf)	5	0	0	2	1265

Going (Turf): **Sf: 0-1 GS: 0-1 Gd: 0-0 GF: 0-2 Fm: 0-1**
Distance: 5f/6f: 0-1 7f-8f: 0-3 9f-13f: 0-1 14f+: 0-0
Track : LH: 0-1 RH: 0-0 Tight: 0-0 Gall: 0-0
Aids: Bl: 0-0 Vi: 0-0 Tstrap: 0-0
Best Rating: 83 8/01 Sals 6f212y firm

Stayed on well on her second and third runs and should get a mile. Acts on fast ground.

Softly Tread (IRE)

112 **108**

3-y-o b f Tirol-Second Guess (Ela-Mana-Mou)
J R Fanshawe (C Collins 27/5) Lael Stable

Placings:11-10224 (5141)
2001: 7^1HY, 8^0G, 7^2GF, 7^2G, 8^4G

	Starts	1st	2nd	3rd	Win & Pl
Career Total (Turf)	7	3	2	0	66196
100 4/01 Curr 7f				HVY	£35750
83 7/00 Curr 7f				G-F	£16250
83 5/00 Cork 6f				GD	£6900

Total win prize-money £58900

Going (Turf): **Sf: 1-1** GS: 0-0 **Gd: 1-4** GF: 0-1 Fm: 0-0
Distance: 5f/6f: 1-1 7f-8f: 1-5 9f-13f: 0-0 14f+: 0-0
Track : LH: 0-0 RH: 0-1 Tight: 0-0 Gall: 0-0
Aids: Bl: 0-0 Vi: 0-0 Tstrap: 0-0
Best Rating: 108 8/01 Gdwd 7f gd-fm

Ex-Irish, she was unlucky on her first run for connections at Goodwood and ran good races at Doncaster and Newmarket. Seems to stay a mile although may be best at seven. Acts on any ground.

Sohaib (USA)

103 **94**

2-y-o b c Kingmambo (USA)-Fancy Ruler (USA) (Half A Year (USA))
B W Hills Hamdan Al Maktoum

Placings:2156 (5134)
2001: 7^2GS, 7^1GF, 7^5GS, 7^6G

	Starts	1st	2nd	3rd	Win & Pl
Career Total (Turf)	4	1	1	0	9038
94 7/01 Asct 7f	D			G-F	£6825

Total win prize-money £6825

Going (Turf): Sf: 0-0 GS: 0-2 Gd: 0-1 **GF: 1-1** Fm: 0-0
Distance: 5f/6f: 0-0 **7f-8f: 1-4** 9f-13f: 0-0 14f+: 0-0
Track : LH: 0-0 RH: 0-0 Tight: 0-0 Gall: 0-0
Aids: Bl: 0-0 Vi: 0-0 Tstrap: 0-0
Best Rating: 94 10/01 NmkR 7f good

A $425,000 yearling, closely related to a couple of top-class American juveniles, ran well at Newmarket on his debut before taking an Ascot maiden and was not disgraced in Group company afterwards.

Solanza

73 **40**

2-y-o ch f Bahamian Bounty-Son Et Lumiere (Rainbow Quest (USA))
Noel T Chance R W And J R Fidler

Placings:0 (5602)
2001: 7^0GS

	Starts	1st	2nd	3rd	Win & Pl
Career Total (Turf)	1	0	0	0	

Going (Turf): **Sf: 0-0 GS: 0-1 Gd: 0-0 GF: 0-0 Fm: 0-0**
Distance: 5f/6f: 0-0 7f-8f: 0-1 9f-13f: 0-0 14f+: 0-0
Track : LH: 0-0 RH: 0-0 Tight: 0-0 Gall: 0-0
Aids: Bl: 0-0 Vi: 0-0 Tstrap: 0-0
Best Rating: 40 11/01 NmkR 7f gd-sft

Solar Colours

90 **60**

3-y-o ch g Spectrum (IRE)-Instant Desire (USA) (Northern Dancer)
M Johnston Buckram Oak Holdings

Placings:6060P (2821)
2001: 10^6GF, 9^0GF, 12^6G, 14^0F, 18^PGF

	Starts	1st	2nd	3rd	Win & Pl
Career Total (Turf)	5	0	0	0	0

Going (Turf): **Sf: 0-0 GS: 0-0 Gd: 0-1 GF: 0-3 Fm: 0-1**
Distance: 5f/6f: 0-0 7f-8f: 0-0 9f-13f: 0-3 14f+: 0-2
Track : LH: 0-1 RH: 0-4 Tight: 0-4 Gall: 0-0
Aids: Bl: 0-1 Vi: 0-0 Tstrap: 0-0
Best Rating: 60 6/01 Ripn 1m4f60y good

Soldier Point

106(95) (49)**81d**

3-y-o ch g Sabrehill (USA)-Reel Foyle (USA) (Irish River (FR))
P C Haslam Mrs B Hawkins & S A B Dinsmore

Placings:02-3626353 (5535)
2001: 8^3S, 7^6G, 7^2GF, 8^6F, 7^3GF, 6^5GS, 7^3S, 7^6SD

	Starts	1st	2nd	3rd	Win & Pl
Career Total (Turf)	9	0	2	3	3490

Going (Turf): Sf: 0-2 GS: 0-1 Gd: 0-1 GF: 0-4 Fm: 0-1
Distance: 5f/6f: 0-2 7f-8f: 0-6 9f-13f: 0-1 14f+: 0-0
Track : LH: 0-4 RH: 0-2 Tight: 0-2 Gall: 0-1
Aids: Bl: 0-0 Vi: 0-0 Tstrap: 0-0
Best Rating: 81 5/01 Bevl 7f100y gd-fm

He has yet to win, but has made the frame a few times in maiden company. Stays a mile, but looks best over seven furlongs on fast ground.

Solitary

105 **58**
4-y-o b g Sanglamore (USA)-Set Fair (USA) (Alleged (USA))
J G Given Mrs Jo Hardy

Placings:4/22105-02004500 **(4942)**
2001: 16^{0}S, 16^{2}S, 18^{0}GF, 16^{0}GF, 16^{4}G, 15^{5}G, 14^{0}HY, 15^{0}S

	Starts	1st	2nd	3rd	Win & Pl
Career Total (Turf)	14	1	3	0	9845

80 8/00 Ripn 1m4f60y D GD £4173
Total win prize-money £4173

Going (Turf): Sf: 0-6 GS: 0-2 **Gd: 1-4** GF: 0-2 Fm: 0-0
Distance: 5f/6f: 0-0 7f-8f: 0-1 **9f-13f: 1-4** 14f+: 0-9
Track : LH: 0-6 **RH: 1-7 Tight: 1-7** Gall: 0-2
Aids: **Bl: 1-4** Vi: 0-0 Tstrap: 0-0
Best Rating: 83 4/01 Ripn 2m soft

Has only the one win to his name in a Ripon maiden when fitted with blinkers. Has been held in handicap company since. Effective when forcing the issue. Acts on ground and soft ground. Likes to dominate.

Soller Bay

105(90) (64+)**83**
4-y-o b g Contract Law (USA)-Bichette (Lidhame)
K R Burke Mrs Melba Bryce

Placings:2/131010-023004510 **(5681)**
2001: 10^{0}S, 10^{2}GS, 9^{3}S, 12^{0}G, 10^{0}G, 10^{4}HY, 8^{5}HY, 8^{1}GS, 8^{0}S

	Starts	1st	2nd	3rd	Win & Pl
Career Total (Turf)	14	3	2	1	29398
Career Total (AW)	2	1	0	1	3415

83 11/01 NmkR 1m C(0-100)H G-S £17400
83 6/00 Ayr 1m1f20y D(0-80)H GD £3848
77 4/00 Wind 1m67y D(0-85)H HVY £4355
64 1/00 Wolv 1m1f79y D STD £2782
Total win prize-money £28385

Going (Turf): Sf: 1-6 GS: 1-2 Gd: 1-5 GF: 0-1 Fm: 0-0
Distance: 5f/6f: 0-0 7f-8f: 1-3 **9f-13f: 3-13** 14f+: 0-0
Track : **LH: 2-8** RH: 1-5 **Tight: 2-6** Gall: 0-0
Aids: Bl: 0-0 Vi: 0-0 Tstrap: 0-0
Best Rating: 83 11/01 NmkR 1m gd-sft

Lightly raced, he scored three times in 2000 over a mile and nine furlongs and has run well in defeat this season. Goes on sand and looks best with some cut on turf.

Solly's Pal

80(104) (59)**42**
6-y-o gr g Petong-Petriece (Mummy's Pet)
P J Makin Mrs Paul Levinson

Placings:00/004/5310322-0413000 **(3840)**
2001: 7^{0}SD, 7^{4}SD, 7^{1}SD, 7^{3}SD, 7^{0}G, 7^{0}GF, 7^{0}G

	Starts	1st	2nd	3rd	Win & Pl
Career Total (Turf)	8	0	0	1	267
Career Total (AW)	11	2	2	2	6528

59 3/01 Wolv 7f F(0-60)H STD £2317
48 6/00 Sthl 7f F(0-65)H STD £2359
Total win prize-money £4676

Going (Turf): Sf: 0-1 GS: 0-2 Gd: 0-2 GF: 0-3 Fm: 0-0
Distance: 5f/6f: 0-4 **7f-8f: 2-15** 9f-13f: 0-0 14f+: 0-3
Track : **LH: 2-12** RH: 0-3 **Tight: 1-4** Gall: 0-3
Aids: Bl: 0-0 **Vi: 2-11** Tstrap: 0-0
Best Rating: 59 3/01 Wolv 7f stand

He has a questionable attitude under pressure and should be treated with caution.

Solo Dancer

94 **40**
3-y-o ch f Sayaarr (USA)-Oiseval (National Trust)
Jane Southcombe (W G M Turner 17/5) Mrs H M Bridges

Placings:00 **(5180)**
2001: 9^{0}S, 10^{0}HY

	Starts	1st	2nd	3rd	Win & Pl
Career Total (Turf)	2	0	0	0	

Going (Turf): Sf: 0-2 GS: 0-0 Gd: 0-0 GF: 0-0 Fm: 0-0
Distance: 5f/6f: 0-0 7f-8f: 0-0 9f-13f: 0-2 14f+: 0-0
Track : LH: 0-0 RH: 0-1 Tight: 0-2 Gall: 0-0
Aids: Bl: 0-0 Vi: 0-0 Tstrap: 0-0
Best Rating: 40 10/01 Wind 1m2f7y heavy

Solo Flight

109 **92**
4-y-o gr g Mtoto-Silver Singer (Pharly (FR))
B W Hills Lady Hardy

Placings:45/21004-421600000 **(5338)**
2001: 12^{4}S, 12^{2}GF, 12^{1}F, 12^{6}G, 11^{0}GS, 13^{0}G, 14^{0}GS, 12^{0}S, 12^{0}GS

	Starts	1st	2nd	3rd	Win & Pl
Career Total (Turf)	16	2	2	0	18213

90 6/01 Donc 1m4f D(0-85)H FRM £11358
87 5/00 Brig 1m1f209yF SFT £2247
Total win prize-money £13606

Going (Turf): Sf: 1-5 GS: 0-4 Gd: 0-3 GF: 0-3 **Fm: 1-1**
Distance: 5f/6f: 0-0 7f-8f: 0-2 **9f-13f: 2-12** 14f+: 0-2
Track : **LH: 2-7** RH: 0-5 Tight: 0-3 **Gall: 1-8**
Aids: Bl: 0-0 Vi: 0-0 Tstrap: 0-0
Best Rating: 96 6/01 Asct 1m4f good

He got off the mark in a Brighton maiden in May 2000, but did not score again until winning on the bridle at Doncaster in June 2001. Likes to come from off the pace and endured a terrible run at both Royal Ascot and York, but his style of running does make traffic problems a possibility. Capable of winning a decent handicap when things do fall his way. Suited by 12 furlongs and a good or fast surface.

Solo Mio (IRE)

110 **117**
7-y-o b h Sadler's Wells (USA)-Marie De Flandre (FR) (Crystal Palace (FR))
Mrs A J Perrett (A King 6/4) Cheveley Park Stud

Placings:020/21500013/33132/6106/114 **(3582)**
2001: 16^{1}G, 16^{1}G, 16^{4}G

	Starts	1st	2nd	3rd	Win & Pl
Career Total (Turf)	23	6	3	4	137011

117 5/01 Sand 2m78y A GD £24000
114 5/01 NmkR 2m A GD £18000
109 5/99 Badn 2m GD £27076
109 5/98 Badn 2m GD £25338
98 9/97 NmkR 1m4f B(0-100)H G-F £8064
85 5/97 Bath 1m2f46y D G-S £3101
Total win prize-money £105580

Going (Turf): Sf: 0-2 GS: 1-2 **Gd: 4-10** GF: 1-5 Fm: 0-0
Distance: 5f/6f: 0-0 7f-8f: 0-3 9f-13f: 2-8 **14f+: 4-11**
Track : LH: 3-9 RH: 3-12 Tight: 1-4 **Gall: 2-9**
Aids: Bl: 0-1 Vi: 0-0 Tstrap: 0-0
Best Rating: 117 5/01 Sand 2m78y good

He has been around a bit in his career, including a spell in France and has enjoyed some success over hurdles, but has looked better than ever on the Flat this term. He won the Sagaro Stakes at Newmarket first time out and followed up in the Henry II. Suited by two miles and goes on any ground.

Solomon's Mine (USA)

93(95) (66)**54**
2-y-o b c Rahy (USA)-Shes A Sheba (USA) (Alysheba (USA))
M J Polglase (Sir Mark Prescott 18/10) Paul J Dixon

Placings:6604310 **(5606)**
2001: 6^{6}GF, 7^{6}GF, 6^{0}GF, 7^{4}SD, 7^{3}HY, 8^{1}SD, 10^{0}GS, 7^{0}SD

	Starts	1st	2nd	3rd	Win & Pl
Career Total (Turf)	5	0	0	1	470
Career Total (AW)	2	1	0	0	1974

66 10/01 Sthl 1m G STD £1974
Total win prize-money £1974

Going (Turf): Sf: 0-1 GS: 0-1 Gd: 0-0 GF: 0-3 Fm: 0-0
Distance: 5f/6f: 0-2 **7f-8f: 1-4** 9f-13f: 0-1 14f+: 0-0
Track : **LH: 1-2** RH: 0-0 Tight: 0-1 Gall: 0-0
Aids: Bl: 0-0 Vi: 0-0 Tstrap: 0-0
Best Rating: 66 10/01 Sthl 1m stand

He was progressing slowly before easily winning a seller on the Southwell Fibresand in October and is a bit better than that.

Soltaat

78 **37**
2-y-o b c Royal Applause-About Face (Midyan (USA))
A C Stewart Sheikh Ahmed Al Maktoum

Placings:000 **(5289)**
2001: 7^{0}S, 7^{0}GF, 7^{0}S

	Starts	1st	2nd	3rd	Win & Pl
Career Total (Turf)	3	0	0	0	

Going (Turf): Sf: 0-2 GS: 0-0 Gd: 0-0 GF: 0-1 Fm: 0-0
Distance: 5f/6f: 0-0 7f-8f: 0-3 9f-13f: 0-0 14f+: 0-0
Track : LH: 0-1 RH: 0-0 Tight: 0-0 Gall: 0-0
Aids: Bl: 0-0 Vi: 0-0 Tstrap: 0-0
Best Rating: 37 10/01 Leic 7f9y soft

Somayya

102(103) (89+)**68++**
3-y-o b f Polar Falcon (USA)-Moonshine Lake (Kris)
M P Tregoning Sheikh Ahmed Al Maktoum

Placings:2110 **(5348)**
2001: 8^{2}G, 11^{1}GF, 12^{1}SD, 12^{0}SD

	Starts	1st	2nd	3rd	Win & Pl
Career Total (Turf)	2	1	1	0	3387
Career Total (AW)	2	1	0	0	3465

89 10/01 Wolv 1m4f E(0-75)H STD £3465
68 9/01 Ling 1m3f106yF G-F £2516
Total win prize-money £5982

Going (Turf): Sf: 0-0 GS: 0-0 Gd: 0-1 **GF: 1-1** Fm: 0-0
Distance: 5f/6f: 0-0 7f-8f: 0-0 **9f-13f: 2-4** 14f+: 0-0
Track : **LH: 2-3** RH: 0-0 **Tight: 2-2** Gall: 0-0
Aids: Bl: 0-0 Vi: 0-0 Tstrap: 0-0
Best Rating: 89 10/01 Wolv 1m4f stand

She appreciated the longer trip when winning an 11-furlong Lingfield maiden on her second start and had no problem with the surface when bolting up on the Wolverhampton Fibresand next time, although she was never traveling when disappointing at Southwell.

Some Dust

(98) (56)**51**
3-y-o ch g King's Signet (USA)-Some Dream (Vitiges (FR))
Andrew Reid A S Reid

Placings:U021255-6330225000 **(5619)**
2001: 5^{6}SD, 5^{3}SW, 5^{3}SD, 6^{0}SD, 6^{2}SD, 6^{2}SD, 5^{5}SD, 5^{0}SD, 6^{0}SD, 6^{0}SD, 7^{0}SD

	Starts	1st	2nd	3rd	Win & Pl
Career Total (Turf)	2	1	0	0	1834

	Starts	1st	2nd	3rd	Win & Pl
Career Total (AW)	15	0	4	2	3178

51 6/00 Yarm 5f43y G FRM £1834
Total win prize-money £1834

Going (Turf): Sf: 0-0 GS: 0-0 Gd: 0-1 GF: 0-0 **Fm: 1-1**
Distance: **5f/6f: 1-17** 7f-8f: 0-0 9f-13f: 0-0 14f+: 0-0
Track : LH: 0-13 RH: 0-0 Tight: 0-12 Gall: 0-0
Aids: Bl: 0-0 Vi: 0-11 Tstrap: 0-0
Best Rating: 56 3/01 Wolv 6f stand

Some Will

101(89) (43)**70**
3-y-o b g Handsome Sailor-Bollin Sophie (Efisio)
T D Easterby Bill Toner

Placings:040-011460000 **(5352)**
2001: 6^{0}SD, 6^{1}S, 6^{1}GF, 7^{4}G, 6^{6}G, 7^{0}GS, 6^{0}G, 5^{0}S, 6^{0}SD

	Starts	1st	2nd	3rd	Win & Pl
Career Total (Turf)	10	2	0	0	7628
Career Total (AW)	2	0	0	0	

70 5/01 Hayd 6f E(0-70)H G-F £3514
64 5/01 Newc 6f E(0-70)H SFT £3045
Total win prize-money £6559

Going (Turf): Sf: 1-2 GS: 0-1 Gd: 0-4 **GF: 1-3** Fm: 0-0
Distance: **5f/6f: 2-8** 7f-8f: 0-4 9f-13f: 0-0 14f+: 0-0
Track : LH: 0-4 RH: 0-0 Tight: 0-1 Gall: 0-0
Aids: Bl: 0-0 Vi: 0-0 Tstrap: 0-0
Best Rating: 70 5/01 Hayd 6f gd-fm

Fair handicap sprinter, twice a winner in the spring, on fast and easy ground, when held up.

Somers Heath (IRE)

97 **37**
3-y-o b f Definite Article-Glen Of Imaal (IRE) (Common Grounds)
T D Easterby Mrs P E Needham

Placings:001056-000044000 **(4898)**
2001: 8^{0}G, 7^{0}GF, 5^{0}GF, 6^{0}GF, 7^{4}GF, 7^{4}GS, 5^{0}G, 6^{0}F, 5^{0}GS

	Starts	1st	2nd	3rd	Win & Pl
Career Total (Turf)	15	1	0	0	7410

63 6/00 York 6f E GD £7410
Total win prize-money £7410

Going (Turf): Sf: 0-1 GS: 0-2 **Gd: 1-6** GF: 0-5 Fm: 0-1
Distance: **5f/6f: 1-7** 7f-8f: 0-7 9f-13f: 0-1 14f+: 0-0
Track : LH: 0-3 RH: 0-2 Tight: 0-1 Gall: 0-0
Aids: Bl: 0-1 Vi: 0-0 Tstrap: 0-0
Best Rating: 43 6/01 Rdcr 7f gd-fm

Somesession

103(95) (48)**44**
4-y-o b g Prince Sabo-Session (Reform)
R A Fahey R A Fahey

Placings:040/001000000-34424404024005 **(4556)**
2001: 6^{3}HY, 5^{4}S, 6^{4}SD, 5^{2}F, 5^{4}G, 5^{4}GF, 5^{0}GF, 5^{4}GS, 5^{0}GF, 5^{2}GF, 5^{4}GF, 5^{0}G, 5^{0}GF, 5^{5}SW

	Starts	1st	2nd	3rd	Win & Pl
Career Total (Turf)	21	1	2	1	9169
Career Total (AW)	5	0	0	0	0

53 7/00 Curr 5f (0-90)H G-F £6900
Total win prize-money £6900

Going (Turf): Sf: 0-3 GS: 0-1 Gd: 0-5 GF: 0-9 Fm: 0-1
Distance: 5f/6f: 0-23 7f-8f: 0-2 9f-13f: 0-0 14f+: 0-0
Track : LH: 0-9 RH: 0-0 Tight: 0-3 Gall: 0-0
Aids: Bl: 0-14 Vi: 0-2 Tstrap: 0-0
Best Rating: 59 5/01 Haml 5f4y firm

Something Special

72 **38**
3-y-o b g Petong-My Dear Watson (Chilibang)
H E Haynes Miss Sally R Haynes

Placings:0P0000 **(5622)**
2001: 11^{0}G, 10^{P}S, 8^{0}GF, 9^{0}GS, 11^{0}G, 14^{0}GS

	Starts	1st	2nd	3rd	Win & Pl
Career Total (Turf)	6	0	0	0	

Going (Turf): Sf: 0-1 GS: 0-2 Gd: 0-2 GF: 0-1 Fm: 0-0
Distance: 5f/6f: 0-0 7f-8f: 0-0 9f-13f: 0-5 14f+: 0-1
Track : LH: 0-4 RH: 0-1 Tight: 0-3 Gall: 0-0
Aids: Bl: 0-0 Vi: 0-0 Tstrap: 0-0
Best Rating: 38 9/01 Wwck 1m22y gd-fm

Somethingabout-mary (IRE)

66 **37**
3-y-o b f Fayruz-Cut It Fine (USA) (Big Spruce (USA))
J S Wainwright R C Bond

Placings:0003-0 **(1493)**
2001: 9^{0}GF

	Starts	1st	2nd	3rd	Win & Pl
Career Total (Turf)	5	0	0	1	405

Going (Turf): Sf: 0-1 GS: 0-1 Gd: 0-0 GF: 0-3 Fm: 0-0
Distance: 5f/6f: 0-3 7f-8f: 0-1 9f-13f: 0-1 14f+: 0-0
Track : LH: 0-1 RH: 0-2 Tight: 0-0 Gall: 0-0
Aids: Bl: 0-0 Vi: 0-0 Tstrap: 0-0
Best Rating: 38 9/01 Wwck 1m22y gd-fm

Son Of A Gun

100 **74**
7-y-o b g Gunner B-Sola Mia (Tolomeo)
J Neville Mrs P A Barratt

Placings:423-000 **(5692)**
2001: 13^{0}GS, 18^{0}GS, 16^{0}S

	Starts	1st	2nd	3rd	Win & Pl
Career Total (Turf)	6	0	1	1	2083

Going (Turf): Sf: 0-1 GS: 0-4 Gd: 0-1 GF: 0-0 Fm: 0-0
Distance: 5f/6f: 0-0 7f-8f: 0-0 9f-13f: 0-1 14f+: 0-5
Track : LH: 0-4 RH: 0-2 Tight: 0-1 Gall: 0-3
Aids: Bl: 0-0 Vi: 0-0 Tstrap: 0-0
Best Rating: 74 10/01 York 1m5f194y gd-sft

Started his career in National Hunt Flat races where he was succesful once, before trying his hand on the Flat where he has shown enough ability to suggest that he can win a race. Did not shape badly on his belated reappearance in 2001 and ran a cracker in the Cesarewitch.

Son Of Flighty

79 **31**
3-y-o b g Then Again-Record Flight (Record Token)
R J Hodges Frank E Crumpler

Placings:06 **(4047)**
2001: 8^{0}GF, 14^{6}F

	Starts	1st	2nd	3rd	Win & Pl
Career Total (Turf)	2	0	0	0	0

Going (Turf): Sf: 0-0 GS: 0-0 Gd: 0-0 GF: 0-1 Fm: 0-1
Distance: 5f/6f: 0-0 7f-8f: 0-0 9f-13f: 0-1 14f+: 0-1
Track : LH: 0-1 RH: 0-1 Tight: 0-2 Gall: 0-0
Aids: Bl: 0-0 Vi: 0-0 Tstrap: 0-0
Best Rating: 31 8/01 Ling 1m6f firm

Son Of Snurge (FR)

94 (69)**58**
5-y-o b g Snurge-Swift Spring (FR) (Bluebird (USA))
T P Tate Mohare Racing

Placings:265/02050011203/04043-00000 **(3693)**
2001: 16^{0}GF, 12^{0}F, 12^{0}F, 17^{0}GF, 13^{0}G

	Starts	1st	2nd	3rd	Win & Pl
Career Total (Turf)	23	2	2	2	14171
Career Total (AW)	1	0	1	0	718

72 7/99 Sand 1m6f D(0-85)H G-F £4221
65 7/99 Brig 1m3f196yF(0-60) FRM £2592
Total win prize-money £6814

Going (Turf): Sf: 0-1 GS: 0-2 Gd: 0-8 **GF: 1-7 Fm: 1-5**
Distance: 5f/6f: 0-0 7f-8f: 0-2 9f-13f: 1-10 14f+: 1-12
Track : LH: 1-14 RH: 1-9 Tight: 0-7 Gall: 0-7
Aids: **Bl: 2-8** Vi: 0-0 Tstrap: 0-0
Best Rating: 58 5/01 Pont 1m4f8y firm

Sonatina

107 **97**
3-y-o b f Distant Relative-Son Et Lumiere (Rainbow Quest (USA))
J W Payne Mrs R A C Vigors

Placings:11-3425 **(5007)**
2001: 8^{3}GF, 8^{4}GF, 8^{2}G, 8^{5}S

	Starts	1st	2nd	3rd	Win & Pl
Career Total (Turf)	6	2	1	1	18239

83 9/00 Yarm 6f3y C G-F £5713
81 8/00 Folk 6f F G-F £2499
Total win prize-money £8212

Going (Turf): Sf: 0-1 GS: 0-0 Gd: 0-1 **GF: 2-4** Fm: 0-0
Distance: 5f/6f: 1-1 7f-8f: 1-5 9f-13f: 0-0 14f+: 0-0
Track : LH: 0-1 RH: 0-1 Tight: 0-1 Gall: 0-0
Aids: Bl: 0-0 Vi: 0-0 Tstrap: 0-0
Best Rating: 97 8/01 Gdwd 1m good

She won both of her starts at two over six furlongs and did not enjoy the clearest of runs when stepped up to a mile at Thirsk on her reappearance. Not at all disgraced in Listed events at Ascot and Goodwood and may still be capable of better. Stays a mile, acts on fast ground.

Soneau (IRE)

(101) (70)
3-y-o b c Ela-Mana-Mou-Acquilata (USA) (Irish River (FR))
P F I Cole M Arbib

Placings:2 **(0657)**
2001: 11^{2}SD

	Starts	1st	2nd	3rd	Win & Pl
Career Total (Turf)	0	0	0	0	
Career Total (AW)	1	0	1	0	972

Going (Turf): Sf: 0-0 GS: 0-0 Gd: 0-0 GF: 0-0 Fm: 0-0
Distance: 5f/6f: 0-0 7f-8f: 0-0 9f-13f: 0-1 14f+: 0-0
Track : LH: 0-1 RH: 0-0 Tight: 0-0 Gall: 0-0
Aids: Bl: 0-0 Vi: 0-0 Tstrap: 0-0
Best Rating: 70 4/01 Sthl 1m3f stand

Song 'n Dance

99(95) (52)**43**
3-y-o br f Dancing Spree (USA)-Don't Smile (Sizzling Melody)
M D I Usher The Magic And Dance Partnership

Placings:056040055-2100646 **(3627)**
2001: 5^{2}SW, 6^{1}SW, 5^{0}G, 6^{0}GF, 5^{6}GF, 5^{4}F, 5^{6}GF

	Starts	1st	2nd	3rd	Win & Pl
Career Total (Turf)	10	0	0	0	0
Career Total (AW)	6	1	1	0	2353

45 2/01 Ling 6f G SLW £1827
Total win prize-money £1827

Going (Turf): Sf: 0-0 GS: 0-1 Gd: 0-3 GF: 0-4 Fm: 0-2
Distance: **5f/6f: 1-16** 7f-8f: 0-0 9f-13f: 0-0 14f+: 0-0
Track : **LH: 1-10** RH: 0-0 **Tight: 1-6** Gall: 0-3
Aids: Bl: 0-0 Vi: 0-1 Tstrap: 0-0
Best Rating: 47 2/01 Ling 5f slow

Bar winning a seller on the All-Weather in February 2001, she has shown little to write home about.

Sonique

75 **7**

3-y-o b f Shaamit (IRE)-Dolly Bevan (Another Realm)
R C Spicer (I A Wood 8/1) John Purcell

Placings:0-00 **(5625)**
2001: 8^{0}S, 8^{0}GS

	Starts	1st	2nd	3rd	Win & Pl
Career Total (Turf)	3	0	0	0	

Going (Turf): Sf: 0-2 GS: 0-1 Gd: 0-0 GF: 0-0 Fm: 0-0
Distance: 5f/6f: 0-0 7f-8f: 0-1 9f-13f: 0-2 14f+: 0-0
Track : LH: 0-1 RH: 0-0 Tight: 0-0 Gall: 0-0
Aids: Bl: 0-0 Vi: 0-0 Tstrap: 0-0
Best Rating: 7 11/01 Nott 1m54y gd-sft

Sonny Jim

97 **51d**
3-y-o b g Timeless Times (USA)-Allesca (Alleging (USA))
M D I Usher Miss D G Kerr

Placings:004000300 **(4707)**
2001: 7^{0}G, 8^{0}G, 8^{4}F, 8^{0}G, 8^{0}GF, 9^{0}G, 12^{3}GF, 12^{0}GF, 10^{0}G

	Starts	1st	2nd	3rd	Win & Pl
Career Total (Turf)	9	0	0	1	777

Going (Turf): Sf: 0-0 GS: 0-0 Gd: 0-5 GF: 0-3 Fm: 0-1
Distance: 5f/6f: 0-0 7f-8f: 0-1 9f-13f: 0-7 14f+: 0-0
Track : LH: 0-3 RH: 0-3 Tight: 0-4 Gall: 0-0
Aids: Bl: 0-0 Vi: 0-0 Tstrap: 0-0
Best Rating: 57 5/01 Leic 1m9y firm

Soon Or Late

94(82) (32)**43**
3-y-o ch g Kris-Silky Heights (IRE) (Head For Heights)
Miss J A Camacho Bernard Bloom

Placings:0056 **(3163)**
2001: 7^{0}SD, 8^{0}SW, 10^{5}S, 12^{6}G

	Starts	1st	2nd	3rd	Win & Pl
Career Total (Turf)	2	0	0	0	0
Career Total (AW)	2	0	0	0	

Going (Turf): Sf: 0-1 GS: 0-0 Gd: 0-1 GF: 0-0 Fm: 0-0
Distance: 5f/6f: 0 0 7f-8f: 0-2 9f-13f: 0-2 14f+: 0-0
Track : LH: 0-4 RH: 0-0 Tight: 0-0 Gall: 0-2
Aids: Bl: 0-0 Vi: 0-0 Tstrap: 0-0
Best Rating: 43 5/01 Newc 1m2f32y soft

Soona

95(91) (52)**40**
3-y-o ch f Royal Abjar (USA)-Presently (Cadeaux Genereux)
Ronald Thompson A Bell

Placings:05552240-45050550506 **(5174)**
2001: 9^{4}SD, 8^{5}SW, 8^{0}S, 10^{5}S, 8^{0}GF, 9^{5}GF, 10^{5}GF, 8^{0}F, 8^{5}GF, 9^{0}GF, 8^{6}GS

	Starts	1st	2nd	3rd	Win & Pl
Career Total (Turf)	16	0	2	0	1730
Career Total (AW)	3	0	0	0	0

Going (Turf): Sf: 0-3 GS: 0-1 Gd: 0-3 GF: 0-7 Fm: 0-2
Distance: 5f/6f: 0-3 7f-8f: 0-9 9f-13f: 0-7 14f+: 0-0
Track : LH: 0-7 RH: 0-6 Tight: 0-6 Gall: 0-1
Aids: Bl: 0-0 Vi: 0-0 Tstrap: 0-0
Best Rating: 52 6/01 Rdcr 1m2f gd-fm

Sooty Time

94(95) (59)**49d**
3-y-o ch g Timeless Times (USA)-Gymcrak Gem (IRE) (Don't Forget Me)
J S Moore A D Crook

Placings:63066234036152-0020400000 **(5418)**
2001: 6^{0}SD, 7^{0}SD, 6^{2}S, 7^{0}GF, 8^{4}GS, 7^{0}GS, 7^{0}G, 6^{0}GF, 5^{0}GS, 7^{0}SD

	Starts	1st	2nd	3rd	Win & Pl
Career Total (Turf)	13	0	2	2	2072
Career Total (AW)	11	1	1	1	2798

65 11/00 Ling 7f G STD £1841
Total win prize-money £1841

Going (Turf): Sf: 0-1 GS: 0-4 Gd: 0-1 GF: 0-5 Fm: 0-1
Distance: 5f/6f: 0-12 **7f-8f: 1-11** 9f-13f: 0-0 14f+: 0-0
Track : **LH: 1-13** RH: 0-1 **Tight: 1-9** Gall: 0-2
Aids: Bl: 0-0 Vi: 0-0 Tstrap: 0-0
Best Rating: 49 6/01 Sals 1m gd-sft

Sophala

104 **63**
4-y-o b f Magical Wonder (USA)-Fujaiyrah (In Fijar (USA))
C F Wall T J Wells

Placings:0/3001340-450 **(5230)**
2001: 8^{4}G, 10^{5}G, 11^{0}S

	Starts	1st	2nd	3rd	Win & Pl
Career Total (Turf)	11	1	0	2	4104

65 9/00 Brig 1m1f209yF(0-60)H SFT £2695
Total win prize-money £2695

Going (Turf): Sf: 1-6 GS: 0-1 Gd: 0-2 GF: 0-2 Fm: 0-0
Distance: 5f/6f: 0-0 7f-8f: 0-1 **9f-13f: 1-10** 14f+: 0-0
Track : **LH: 1-5** RH: 0-3 Tight: 0-4 Gall: 0-2
Aids: Bl: 0-0 Vi: 0-0 Tstrap: 0-0
Best Rating: 63 8/01 Ripn 1m2f good

Lightly-raced handicapper, has tried various distances but only win was over ten furlongs on soft ground.

Sophielu

80+
3-y-o ch f Rudimentary (USA)-Aquaglow (Caerleon (USA))
M Johnston Hertford Offset Limited

Placings:24-1 **(0900)**
2001: 7^{1}GS

	Starts	1st	2nd	3rd	Win & Pl
Career Total (Turf)	3	1	1	0	4552

76 4/01 Muss 7f30y D G-S £3607
Total win prize-money £3608

Going (Turf): Sf: 0-2 **GS: 1-1** Gd: 0-0 GF: 0-0 Fm: 0-0
Distance: 5f/6f: 0-2 **7f-8f: 1-1** 9f-13f: 0-0 14f+: 0-0
Track : LH: 0-0 RH: 0-0 Tight: 0-0 Gall: 0-0
Aids: Bl: 0-0 Vi: 0-0 Tstrap: 0-0
Best Rating: 76 4/01 Muss 7f30y gd-sft

Sophies Symphony

99 **83**
2-y-o b f Merdon Melody-Gracious Imp (USA) (Imp Society (USA))
K R Burke M J Wilson

Placings:321240 **(5504)**
2001: 6^{3}G, 5^{2}G, 6^{1}GF, 6^{2}GF, 7^{4}S, 7^{0}HY

	Starts	1st	2nd	3rd	Win & Pl
Career Total (Turf)	6	1	2	1	15895

73 9/01 York 6f E G-F £8450
Total win prize-money £8450

Going (Turf): Sf: 0-2 GS: 0-0 Gd: 0-2 **GF: 1-2** Fm: 0-0
Distance: **5f/6f: 1-2** 7f-8f: 0-4 9f-13f: 0-0 14f+: 0-0
Track : LH: 0-0 RH: 0-0 Tight: 0-0 Gall: 0-0
Aids: Bl: 0-0 Vi: 0-0 Tstrap: 0-0
Best Rating: 83 9/01 Haml 6f5y gd-fm

Showed promise in her first two starts before just winning a York maiden auction event from a big field in September and was only just beaten in a valuable Hamilton nursery next time. Suited by six furlongs and fast ground.

Sophisticat (USA)

109 (101)**101**
2-y-o b/br f Storm Cat (USA)-Serena's Song (USA) (Rahy (USA))
A P O'Brien Mrs John Magnier & Mr M Tabor

Placings:21222325 **(5574a)**
2001: 5^{2}GF, 6^{1}G, 5^{2}GF, 6^{2}G, 6^{2}G, 7^{3}GY, 6^{2}S, 8^{5}FT

	Starts	1st	2nd	3rd	Win & Pl
Career Total (Turf)	7	1	5	1	106615
Career Total (AW)	1	0	0	0	13333

96 6/01 Naas 6f GD £10075
Total win prize-money £10075

Going (Turf): Sf: 0-1 GS: 0-0 **Gd: 1-3** GF: 0-2 Fm: 0-0
Distance: **5f/6f: 1-6** 7f-8f: 0-1 9f-13f: 0-1 14f+: 0-0
Track : LH: 0-1 RH: 0-0 Tight: 0-0 Gall: 0-0
Aids: Bl: 0-0 Vi: 0-1 Tstrap: 0-0
Best Rating: 101 10/01 Belm 1m110y fast

A $3.4 million yearling whose dam won the Breeders' Cup Juvenile Fillies and Breeders' Cup Distaff. She was second to the subsequent Listed winner High Society on her debut, she won her maiden easily at Naas and ran very well when going down narrowly in the Queen Mary. She also chased home Queen's Logic in the Lowther and the Cheveley Park, and ran a close third when stepped up to seven in the Moyglare Stud Stakes. Ran creditably in the Breeders' Cup Juvenile Fillies on dirt. She seems to handle any ground, and has been tried in a visor. She deserves to find a Pattern race.

Sophorific (IRE)

103 **89**
2-y-o b f Danehill (USA)-Saucy Maid (IRE) (Sure Blade (USA))
M W Easterby M P Burke

Placings:3212364 **(5401)**
2001: 6^{3}GF, 6^{2}F, 6^{1}S, 7^{2}GF, 8^{3}GF, 7^{6}G, 8^{4}S, 9^{5}HO

	Starts	1st	2nd	3rd	Win & Pl
Career Total (Turf)	7	1	2	2	13707

80 7/01 Hayd 6f D SFT £4095
Total win prize-money £4095

Going (Turf): Sf: 1-2 GS: 0-0 Gd: 0-1 GF: 0-3 Fm: 0-1
Distance: **5f/6f: 1-3** 7f-8f: 0-3 9f-13f: 0-1 14f+: 0-0
Track : LH: 0-3 RH: 0-1 Tight: 0-0 Gall: 0-0
Aids: Bl: 0-0 Vi: 0-0 Tstrap: 0-0
Best Rating: 89 10/01 Pont 1m4y soft

By Danehill, showed ability before getting off the mark in a soft-ground six-furlong Haydock maiden on her third start. Has failed to score in Listed company. Should stay further. Has won on soft ground.

Sorbonne

87 **62**
2-y-o b g College Chapel-French Mist (Mystiko (USA))
B Hanbury Mrs A M Upsdell

Placings:0 **(4888)**
2001: 8^{0}GF

	Starts	1st	2nd	3rd	Win & Pl
Career Total (Turf)	1	0	0	0	

Going (Turf): Sf: 0-0 GS: 0-0 Gd: 0-0 GF: 0-1 Fm: 0-0
Distance: 5f/6f: 0-0 7f-8f: 0-1 9f-13f: 0-0 14f+: 0-0
Track : LH: 0-0 RH: 0-1 Tight: 0-0 Gall: 0-0
Aids: Bl: 0-0 Vi: 0-0 Tstrap: 0-1
Best Rating: 62 9/01 Kemp 1m gd-fm

Sorrento King

95(79) (5)**36**
4-y-o ch g First Trump-Star Face (African Sky)
Mrs M Reveley (M W Easterby 5/8) B Padgett, K Bennett & A Davies

Placings:000400/000236-0606 **(2643)**
2001: 11^{0}SD, 14^{6}F, 11^{0}GF, 10^{6}GF

	Starts	1st	2nd	3rd	Win & Pl
Career Total (Turf)	15	0	1	1	1725
Career Total (AW)	1	0	0	0	

Going (Turf): Sf: 0-3 GS: 0-2 Gd: 0-1 GF: 0-7 Fm: 0-2
Distance: 5f/6f: 0-1 7f-8f: 0-5 9f-13f: 0-8 14f+: 0-2
Track : LH: 0-10 RH: 0-4 Tight: 0-8 Gall: 0-2
Aids: Bl: 0-12 Vi: 0-0 Tstrap: 0-0
Best Rating: 36 6/01 Bevl 1m3f216y gd-fm

Sosumi

100 **93**
2-y-o b f Be My Chief (USA)-Princess Deya (Be My Guest (USA))
M H Tompkins P A & D G Sakal

Placings:411540 **(4680)**
2001: 5^{4}GF, 5^{1}S, 5^{1}G, 6^{5}GF, 7^{4}GS, 8^{0}G

	Starts	1st	2nd	3rd	Win & Pl
Career Total (Turf)	6	2	0	0	17017

83	7/01	Ches	5f16y	B	GD	£9326
70	6/01	Sand	5f6y	D	SFT	£3477

Total win prize-money £12805

Going (Turf): Sf: 1-1 GS: 0-1 **Gd: 1-2** GF: 0-2 Fm: 0-0
Distance: 5f/6f: 2-4 7f-8f: 0-2 9f-13f: 0-0 14f+: 0-0
Track : LH: 1-2 RH: 0-0 **Tight: 1-1** Gall: 0-1
Aids: Bl: 0-0 Vi: 0-0 Tstrap: 0-0
Best Rating: 93 8/01 Deau 7f gd-sft

She got off the mark in soft ground at Sandown on her second start and followed-up at Chester despite giving the field a huge start. Has won on good and soft ground.

Sotonian (HOL)

97(108) (63)**58**
8-y-o br g Statoblest-Visage (Vision (USA))
P S Felgate Tim Dean

Placings:0000003/1100052503435504500/5000336123 30403/2211131001066306200/0500306634536510040544-1301650602100 **(4950)**
2001: 5^{1}SD, 5^{3}SD, 5^{0}SW, 5^{1}SW, 5^{6}G, 5^{5}G, 5^{0}SD, 5^{6}SD, 5^{0}GF, 5^{2}GF, 5^{1}G, 5^{0}GF, 5^{0}G

	Starts	1st	2nd	3rd	Win & Pl
Career Total (Turf)	45	3	4	7	19642
Career Total (AW)	49	9	2	7	27511

58	8/01	Catt	5f	F(0-65)H	GD	£2632
63	2/01	Wolv	5f	E(0-70)H	SLW	£2394
60	1/01	Wolv	5f	F(0-60)H	STD	£2121
56	8/00	Wolv	5f	F(0-65)H	STD	£2275
65	5/99	Catt	5f	D(0-85)H	G-F	£5117
62	4/99	Wwck	5f	E(0-70)H	GD	£3052
62	2/99	Ling	5f	E(0-70)H	STD	£2646
58	2/99	Ling	5f	E(0-70)H	STD	£2558
52	1/99	Wolv	5f	F(0-65)H	STD	£2220
46	8/98	Wolv	5f	F(0-65)H	STD	£2553
44	1/97	Wolv	5f	F(0-65)H	STD	£2484
44	1/97	Wolv	5f	D(0-75)H	STD	£3420

Total win prize-money £33474

Going (Turf): Sf: 0-1 GS: 0-5 **Gd: 2-17** GF: 1-19 Fm: 0-3
Distance: 5f/6f: 12-91 7f-8f: 0-2 9f-13f: 0-1 14f+: 0-0
Track : LH: 10-53 RH: 0-4 **Tight: 9-46** Gall: 1-8
Aids: Bl: 0-2 Vi: 0-0 Tstrap: 0-0
Best Rating: 63 2/01 Wolv 5f slow

A speedy sprinter on his day, most of his recent wins have been on the All-Weather, but he is capable on turf. Needs fast ground on grass.

Souhaite (FR)

(102) (50)**45**
5-y-o ch h Salse (USA)-Parannda (Bold Lad (IRE))
J Rossi J Bernstein

Placings:0061303/0010001016-0
2001: 8^{0}S

	Starts	1st	2nd	3rd	Win & Pl
Career Total (Turf)	10	2	0	0	4739
Career Total (AW)	8	2	0	2	4299

50	10/00	Wolv	1m100y	F(0-60)H	STD	£1785
45	9/00	Chep	7f16y	F(0-65)H	G-S	£2240
41	6/00	Leic	1m8y	F(0-65)H	G-F	£2499
46	11/99	Sthl	1m4f	F(0-60)H	STD	£2008

Total win prize-money £8532

Going (Turf): Sf: 0-3 **GS: 1-1** Gd: 0-3 **GF: 1-2** Fm: 0-1
Distance: 5f/6f: 0-0 7f-8f: 1-6 **9f-13f: 3-11** 14f+: 0-1
Track : LH: 2-10 RH: 0-2 **Tight: 1-5** Gall: 0-1
Aids: Bl: 0-0 Vi: 0-0 Tstrap: 0-1
Best Rating: 46 11/99 Sthl 1m4f SD

Sound Of Cheers

71(68) **5**
4-y-o br g Zilzal (USA)-Martha Stevens (USA) (Super Concorde (USA))
P W D'Arcy Paul D'Arcy

Placings:60 **(1200)**
2001: 12^{6}SD, 7^{0}G

	Starts	1st	2nd	3rd	Win & Pl
Career Total (Turf)	1	0	0	0	
Career Total (AW)	1	0	0	0	0

Going (Turf): Sf: 0-0 GS: 0-0 Gd: 0-1 GF: 0-0 Fm: 0-0
Distance: 5f/6f: 0-0 7f-8f: 0-1 9f-13f: 0-1 14f+: 0-0
Track : LH: 0-1 RH: 0-0 Tight: 0-1 Gall: 0-0
Aids: Bl: 0-0 Vi: 0-0 Tstrap: 0-1
Best Rating: 5 5/01 Leic 7f9y good

Sound Sense

81 **41**
3-y-o br g So Factual (USA)-Sight'n Sound (Chief Singer)
D R C Elsworth Fintloch Stud

Placings:000 **(4381)**
2001: 8^{0}GF, 9^{0}GF, 8^{0}GF

	Starts	1st	2nd	3rd	Win & Pl
Career Total (Turf)	3	0	0	0	

Going (Turf): Sf: 0-0 GS: 0-0 Gd: 0-0 GF: 0-3 Fm: 0-0
Distance: 5f/6f: 0-0 7f-8f: 0-2 9f-13f: 0-1 14f+: 0-0
Track : LH: 0-1 RH: 0-1 Tight: 0-0 Gall: 0-1
Aids: Bl: 0-0 Vi: 0-0 Tstrap: 0-0
Best Rating: 41 7/01 Kemp 1m gd-fm

Sound The Trumpet (IRE)

(96) (37)**37**
9-y-o b g Fayruz-Red Note (Rusticaro (FR))
R C Spicer Mrs J A Nichols

Placings:3323265/666000/5205052406/0006465462000/15000/44030600504413 0/060000600006005-50 **(0179)**
2001: 8^{5}SD, 7^{0}SD

	Starts	1st	2nd	3rd	Win & Pl
Career Total (Turf)	41	1	4	4	10492
Career Total (AW)	34	2	1	1	6461

54	11/99	Ling	1m	E(0-75)H	STD	£2437
50	1/98	Ling	5f	E(0-70)H	STD	£2778
64	3/94	Newc	5f	D	GD	£3026

Total win prize-money £8242

Going (Turf): Sf: 0-3 GS: 0-5 **Gd: 1-11** GF: 0-16 Fm: 0-6
Distance: 5f/6f: 2-44 7f-8f: 1-27 9f-13f: 0-4 14f+: 0-0
Track : LH: 2-39 RH: 0-2 **Tight: 2-28** Gall: 0-2
Aids: Bl: 0-5 Vi: 0-6 **Tstrap: 1-32**
Best Rating: 35 1/01 Ling 1m stand

Sound's Ace

(93) (26)**46**
5-y-o ch m Savahra Sound-Ace Girl (Stanford)
D Shaw Paul J Dixon

Placings:051316/00006/060303000060065050-0 **(0033)**
2001: 5^{0}SD

	Starts	1st	2nd	3rd	Win & Pl
Career Total (Turf)	24	2	0	3	8186
Career Total (AW)	6	0	0	0	0

67	10/98	NmkR	5f	D H	G-S	£4503
64	8/98	Bevl	5f	G	G-F	£2080

Total win prize-money £6583

Going (Turf): Sf: 0-3 **GS: 1-5** Gd: 0-4 **GF: 1-11** Fm: 0-1
Distance: 5f/6f: 2-29 7f-8f: 0-1 9f-13f: 0-0 14f+: 0-0
Track : LH: 0-7 RH: 0-0 Tight: 0-3 Gall: 0-1
Aids: Bl: 1-18 Vi: 0-0 Tstrap: 0-0
Best Rating: 13 1/01 Sthl 5f stand

Sounds Lucky

95(100) (39)**49**
5-y-o b g Savahra Sound-Sweet And Lucky (Lucky Wednesday)
N P Littmoden Paul J Dixon

Placings:5600/602115001004045006/04416050000-4000453551010 **(2138)**
2001: 6^{4}SD, 5^{0}SD, 5^{0}SD, 6^{0}SW, 5^{4}SD, 6^{5}SD, 5^{3}SD, 7^{5}SD, 6^{5}SD, 6^{1}SD, 6^{0}SD, 7^{1}GF, 6^{0}GF

	Starts	1st	2nd	3rd	Win & Pl
Career Total (Turf)	17	2	0	0	5261
Career Total (AW)	29	4	1	1	9465

49	5/01	Yarm	7f3y	F(0-70)H	G-F	£2450
39	5/01	Wolv	6f	G	STD	£1365
54	2/00	Wolv	5f	F(0-60)H	STD	£1855
62	5/99	Ling	6f	F(0-65)H	G-F	£2540
59	3/99	Wolv	6f	E(0-75)H	SLW	£3550
59	3/99	Wolv	5f	G(0-60)H	STD	£1855

Total win prize-money £13617

Going (Turf): Sf: 0-2 GS: 0-1 Gd: 0-4 **GF: 2-8** Fm: 0-1
Distance: 5f/6f: 5-40 7f-8f: 1-6 9f-13f: 0-0 14f+: 0-0
Track : LH: 4-32 RH: 0-1 **Tight: 4-19** Gall: 0-2
Aids: Bl: 0-4 **Vi: 1-9** Tstrap: 0-0
Best Rating: 49 5/01 Yarm 7f3y gd-fm

South Lane

71
4-y-o br g Rock City-Steppey Lane (Tachypous)
Don Enrico Incisa (N Tinkler 18/5) Don Enrico Incisa

Placings:00/50-000 **(1852)**
2001: 10^{0}S, 11^{0}G, 12^{0}GF

	Starts	1st	2nd	3rd	Win & Pl
Career Total (Turf)	7	0	0	0	0

Going (Turf): Sf: 0-1 GS: 0-2 Gd: 0-3 GF: 0-1 Fm: 0-0
Distance: 5f/6f: 0-2 7f-8f: 0-1 9f-13f: 0-4 14f+: 0-0
Track : LH: 0-1 RH: 0-2 Tight: 0-2 Gall: 0-1
Aids: Bl: 0-0 Vi: 0-0 Tstrap: 0-0

South Sea Pearl (IRE)

93(91) (47)**51**
3-y-o ch f Mujtahid (USA)-Rainstone (Rainbow Quest (USA))
B J Meehan R L Harding

Placings:060505 **(5398)**
2001: 7^{0}GF, 8^{6}GF, 8^{0}GF, 7^{5}GF, 10^{0}G, 8^{5}SD, 9^{0}SD

	Starts	1st	2nd	3rd	Win & Pl
Career Total (Turf)	5	0	0	0	0
Career Total (AW)	1	0	0	0	0

Going (Turf): Sf: 0-0 GS: 0-0 Gd: 0-1 GF: 0-4 Fm: 0-0
Distance: 5f/6f: 0-0 7f-8f: 0-3 9f-13f: 0-3 14f+: 0-0
Track : LH: 0-3 RH: 0-1 Tight: 0-2 Gall: 0-0
Aids: Bl: 0-1 Vi: 0-0 Tstrap: 0-0
Best Rating: 59 6/01 Newb 7f gd-fm

Southern Dancer

89(75) (36)**61**
3-y-o b g Makbul-Bye-Bye (Superlative)

R Hollinshead Attymon Syndicate

Placings:000-404 **(3264)**
2001: 9^{4}GF, 10^{0}GF, 10^{4}GS

	Starts	1st	2nd	3rd	Win & Pl
Career Total (Turf)	5	0	0	0	650
Career Total (AW)	1	0	0	0	

Going (Turf): Sf: 0-1 GS: 0-1 Gd: 0-1 GF: 0-2 Fm: 0-0
Distance: 5f/6f: 0-1 7f-8f: 0-1 9f-13f: 0-4 14f+: 0-0
Track : LH: 0-3 RH: 0-1 Tight: 0-1 Gall: 0-0
Aids: Bl: 0-0 Vi: 0-0 Tstrap: 0-0
Best Rating: 61 6/01 Ripn 1m1f gd-fm

Southern Dominion

96(104) (51)**34**
9-y-o ch g Dominion-Southern Sky (Comedy Star (USA))
Miss J F Craze Mrs Angela Wilson

Placings:0030606535/512030224544402031352/45200000500/030500100453200442141 30/00040615651000022/000400503020002204/31000-001006560000600 **(5639)**
2001: 5^{0}SD, 5^{0}SD, 5^{1}SD, 5^{0}SD, 5^{0}SD, 6^{6}SD, 5^{5}SD, 5^{6}F, 5^{0}G, 6^{0}SD, 5^{0}G, 5^{0}G, 5^{6}G, 5^{0}G, 5^{0}G

	Starts	1st	2nd	3rd	Win & Pl
Career Total (Turf)	72	6	6	4	29167
Career Total (AW)	48	3	7	6	14470

47	3/01	Wolv	5f	G	STD	£1855
60	1/00	Ling	5f	F(0-60)H	STD	£1865
61	8/98	Muss	5f	F(0-65)H	GD	£2915
51	7/98	Muss	5f	F(0-60)H	GD	£4172
56	11/97	Donc	5f	D(0-80)H	GD	£4240
54	10/97	Ayr	5f	E(0-70)H	SFT	£3112
40	5/97	Muss	5f	F(0-65)H	G-F	£2670
50	11/95	Ling	6f	D(0-85)H	STD	£3203
57	5/95	Bath	5f11y	G	G-F	£2619

Total win prize-money £26653

Going (Turf): Sf: 1-8 GS: 0-6 **Gd: 3-29** GF: 2-22 Fm: 0-7
Distance: **5f/6f: 9-110** 7f-8f: 0-10 9f-13f: 0-0 14f+: 0-0
Track : **LH: 4-44** RH: 0-4 **Tight: 3-36** Gall: 1-6
Aids: **Bl: 5-56** Vi: 1-9 Tstrap: 0-0
Best Rating: 51 1/01 Sthl 5f stand

Usually blazes from the stalls and it is just a question of whether he can hold on. Best suited by an easy five, he can act on sand as well.

Southern Dunes

(57)
5-y-o b g Ardkinglass-Leprechaun Lady (Royal Blend)
G Fierro G Fierro

Placings:0/0505/0 **(2172)**
2001: 11^{0}SD

	Starts	1st	2nd	3rd	Win & Pl
Career Total (Turf)	5	0	0	0	0
Career Total (AW)	1	0	0	0	

Going (Turf): **Sf: 0-0 GS: 0-1 Gd: 0-3 GF: 0-0 Fm: 0-1**
Distance: 5f/6f: 0-1 7f-8f: 0-1 9f-13f: 0-4 14f+: 0-0
Track : LH: 0-3 RH: 0-2 Tight: 0-2 Gall: 0-0
Aids: Bl: 0-2 Vi: 0-0 Tstrap: 0-0

Sovereign State (IRE)

96 **46**
4-y-o b g Soviet Lad (USA)-Portree (Slip Anchor)
Miss S E Hall Miss S E Hall

Placings:0514/010546000-000040 **(4799)**
2001: 8^{0}F, 7^{0}GF, 7^{0}G, 8^{0}GF, 9^{4}G, 10^{0}G

	Starts	1st	2nd	3rd	Win & Pl
Career Total (Turf)	19	2	0	0	9789

80	5/00	Thsk	1m	D(0-80)H	GD	£4758
79	9/99	Thsk	1m	D	FRM	£3899

Total win prize-money £8657

Going (Turf): Sf: 0-2 GS: 0-2 **Gd: 1-6** GF: 0-6 **Fm: 1-3**
Distance: 5f/6f: 0-0 **7f-8f: 2-11** 9f-13f: 0-8 14f+: 0-0
Track : **LH: 2-11** RH: 0-2 **Tight: 2-7** Gall: 0-0
Aids: Bl: 0-0 Vi: 0-2 Tstrap: 0-0
Best Rating: 47 6/01 Thsk 7f good

Soviet Flash (IRE)

118 **109**
4-y-o b h Warning-Mrs Moonlight (Ajdal (USA))
E A L Dunlop Khalifa Sultan

Placings:41/246-1300 **(3583)**
2001: 7^{1}GF, 8^{3}GF, 8^{0}GF, 8^{0}G

	Starts	1st	2nd	3rd	Win & Pl
Career Total (Turf)	9	2	1	1	34509

109	5/01	York	7f202y	A(0-110)H	G-F	£18896
83	8/99	Leic	7f9y	D	G-F	£3241

Total win prize-money £22137

Going (Turf): Sf: 0-1 GS: 0-0 Gd: 0-2 **GF: 2-6** Fm: 0-0
Distance: 5f/6f: 0-0 **7f-8f: 2-7** 9f-13f: 0-2 14f+: 0-0
Track : **LH: 1-4** RH: 0-1 Tight: 0-1 **Gall: 1-3**
Aids: Bl: 0-0 Vi: 0-0 Tstrap: 0-0
Best Rating: 109 5/01 York 7f202y gd-fm

Won a Leicester maiden on his second and final run at two, but did not reappear until the end of 2000 and did not manage to win in three starts. He was very impressive in winning a York Listed handicap on his reappearance in 2001 though and showed he had a future at pattern level when placed in the Diomed Stakes at Espom on Derby Day.

Soviet Hero (IRE)

79(58) **40**
4-y-o br g Soviet Lad (USA)-Tajanama (IRE) (Gorytus (USA))
Miss Gay Kelleway A P Griffin

Placings:06000 **(4070)**
2001: 5^{0}F, 8^{6}GF, 8^{0}GF, 8^{0}GS, 9^{0}SD

	Starts	1st	2nd	3rd	Win & Pl
Career Total (Turf)	4	0	0	0	0
Career Total (AW)	1	0	0	0	

Going (Turf): **Sf: 0-0 GS: 0-1 Gd: 0-0 GF: 0-2 Fm: 0-1**
Distance: 5f/6f: 0-1 7f-8f: 0-0 9f-13f: 0-4 14f+: 0-0
Track : LH: 0-2 RH: 0-0 Tight: 0-1 Gall: 0-0
Aids: Bl: 0-1 Vi: 0-0 Tstrap: 0-0
Best Rating: 40 6/01 Nott 1m54y gd-fm

Spa Gulch (USA)

87(91) (44)**16**
3-y-o ch g Gulch (USA)-Carezza (USA) (Caro)
M E Sowersby (S C Williams 12/7) The Southwold Set

Placings:000-302646400250 **(5149)**
2001: 8^{3}SW, 8^{0}SD, 11^{2}SD, 12^{6}SD, 9^{4}SD, 11^{6}GF, 16^{4}GF, 9^{0}F, 8^{0}GF, 9^{2}SD, 11^{5}GF, 7^{0}G

	Starts	1st	2nd	3rd	Win & Pl
Career Total (Turf)	8	0	0	0	0
Career Total (AW)	7	0	2	1	1560

Going (Turf): **Sf: 0-1 GS: 0-0 Gd: 0-1 GF: 0-5 Fm: 0-1**
Distance: 5f/6f: 0-2 7f-8f: 0-4 9f-13f: 0-8 14f+: 0-1
Track : LH: 0-10 RH: 0-1 Tight: 0-7 Gall: 0-0
Aids: Bl: 0-1 Vi: 0-1 Tstrap: 0-9
Best Rating: 44 2/01 Sthl 1m3f stand

He is a very modest performer on turf and sand.

Spa Lane

108(92) (42d)**29**
8-y-o ch g Presidium-Sleekit (Blakeney)
Mrs S Lamyman Sotby Farming Company Limited

Placings:0000/21431/00402000006/13246222035004412040014220000/5143325005000-030P010000 **(5170)**
2001: 21^{0}S, 16^{3}G, 14^{0}GF, 16^{P}GF, 13^{0}G, 16^{1}GS, 17^{0}GF, 16^{0}GF, 11^{0}G, 17^{0}GS

	Starts	1st	2nd	3rd	Win & Pl
Career Total (Turf)	62	6	9	6	32355
Career Total (AW)	11	1	1	0	2708

41	8/01	Bevl	2m35y	F(0-60)H	G-S	£2576
39	5/00	Bevl	2m35y	E(0-75)H	G-F	£3087
41	5/99	Pont	1m4f8y	E(0-70)H	G-F	£3158
38	1/99	Sthl	2m	F(0-60)H	STD	£1892
40	5/98	Bevl	2m35y	E(0-70)H	GD	£3096
58	8/96	Nott	1m6f15y	F(0-55)	G-S	£2410
54	6/96	Nott	1m1f213yF		G-F	£3351

Total win prize-money £19574

Going (Turf): Sf: 0-7 GS: 2-8 Gd: 1-18 **GF: 3-26** Fm: 0-3
Distance: 5f/6f: 0-2 7f-8f: 0-1 9f-13f: 2-18 **14f+: 5-52**
Track : **LH: 4-47** RH: 3-24 **Tight: 3-29** Gall: 0-5
Aids: Bl: 0-0 Vi: 0-0 Tstrap: 0-0
Best Rating: 41 8/01 Bevl 2m35y gd-sft

Spanish Bells

77 **46**
2-y-o b c Robellino (USA)-Legend Of Aragon (Aragon)
H Candy M L Al Basti

Placings:0 **(3423)**
2001: 6^{0}GF

	Starts	1st	2nd	3rd	Win & Pl
Career Total (Turf)	1	0	0	0	

Going (Turf): **Sf: 0-0 GS: 0-0 Gd: 0-0 GF: 0-1 Fm: 0-0**
Distance: 5f/6f: 0-1 7f-8f: 0-0 9f-13f: 0-0 14f+: 0-0
Track : LH: 0-0 RH: 0-0 Tight: 0-0 Gall: 0-0
Aids: Bl: 0-0 Vi: 0-0 Tstrap: 0-0
Best Rating: 46 7/01 Sals 6f gd-fm

Spanish Buccaneer

69 **26**
2-y-o b g Forzando-Spanish Heart (King Of Spain)
J W Hills The Farleigh Court Racing Partnership

Placings:0 **(5342)**
2001: 7^{0}GS

	Starts	1st	2nd	3rd	Win & Pl
Career Total (Turf)	1	0	0	0	

Going (Turf): **Sf: 0-0 GS: 0-1 Gd: 0-0 GF: 0-0 Fm: 0-0**
Distance: 5f/6f: 0-0 7f-8f: 0-1 9f-13f: 0-0 14f+: 0-0
Track : LH: 0-0 RH: 0-0 Tight: 0-0 Gall: 0-0
Aids: Bl: 0-1 Vi: 0-0 Tstrap: 0-0
Best Rating: 26 10/01 NmkR 7f gd-sft

Spanish John (USA)

96 **90+**
2-y-o b/br c Dynaformer (USA)-Esprit D'Escalier (USA) (Diesis)
P F I Cole Anthony Speelman

Placings:116 **(4982a)**
2001: 6^{1}GF, 7^{1}G, 8^{6}HY

	Starts	1st	2nd	3rd	Win & Pl
Career Total (Turf)	3	2	0	0	28742

90	7/01	Siro	7f110y		GD	£23000
77	5/01	Kemp	6f	C	G-F	£5742

Total win prize-money £28742

Going (Turf): Sf: 0-1 GS: 0-0 **Gd: 1-1 GF: 1-1** Fm: 0-0
Distance: 5f/6f: 1-1 7f-8f: 1-2 9f-13f: 0-0 14f+: 0-0
Track : LH: 0-0 RH: 0-1 Tight: 0-0 Gall: 0-0
Aids: Bl: 0-0 Vi: 0-0 Tstrap: 0-0
Best Rating: 90 7/01 Siro 7f110y good

He overcame his inexperience to gain a narrow verdict at Kempton on his debut in May 2001 and built on this form with a win in Listed company in Italy next time. A combination of the heavy ground and the step up to a mile found him out on his only other run, again in Italy.

Spanish Spur

103 **96**

3-y-o b c Indian Ridge-Las Flores (IRE) (Sadler's Wells (USA))

J H M Gosden George Strawbridge

Placings:254-04100 **(2970)**

2001: 7^{0}GS, 10^{4}G, 8^{1}GF, 8^{0}GF, 8^{0}G

	Starts	1st	2nd	3rd	Win & Pl
Career Total (Turf)	8	1	1	0	6320

96 6/01 Newb 1m D(0-80) G-F £4446

Total win prize-money £4446

Going (Turf): Sf: 0-1 GS: 0-1 Gd: 0-4 **GF: 1-2** Fm: 0-0
Distance: 5f/6f: 0-0 **7f-8f: 1-7** 9f-13f: 0-1 14f+: 0-0
Track : LH: 0-1 RH: 0-1 Tight: 0-1 Gall: 0-0
Aids: Bl: 0-0 Vi: 0-0 Tstrap: 0-0
Best Rating: 96 6/01 Newb 1m gd-fm

Made a good start as a juvenile, but appeared to race on the unfavoured side in two subsequent runs. Scored over a mile on third outing at three. Needs a strongly-run race. Acts on good to firm.

Spanish Star

102(108) (64d)**46**

4-y-o b g Hernando (FR)-Desert Girl (Green Desert (USA))

Mrs N Macauley (T D Barron 19/2) Mrs N Macauley

Placings:43/513606010500-242106605000054100 **(5681)**

2001: 11^{2}SD, 11^{4}SD, 11^{2}SW, 12^{1}SD, 11^{0}SW, 11^{6}SD, 12^{6}SW, 8^{0}SD, 11^{5}SD, 9^{0}F, 12^{0}SD, 12^{0}GF, 8^{0}SD, 10^{5}G, 9^{4}GF, 8^{1}S, 9^{0}G, 8^{0}S

	Starts	1st	2nd	3rd	Win & Pl
Career Total (Turf)	13	1	0	1	3886
Career Total (AW)	19	3	2	1	9507

46 8/01 Nott 1m54y E(0-70)H SFT £3066
66 2/01 Sthl 1m4f F STD £2212
66 9/00 Sthl 1m3f F(0-60) STD £1830
66 2/00 Wolv 1m4f D STD £2782

Total win prize-money £9891

Going (Turf): Sf: 1-3 GS: 0-0 Gd: 0-6 GF: 0-3 Fm: 0-1
Distance: 5f/6f: 0-0 7f-8f: 0-5 **9f-13f: 4-26** 14f+: 0-1
Track : **LH: 4-24** RH: 0-4 **Tight: 1-8** Gall: 0-4
Aids: Bl: 0-0 Vi: 0-2 Tstrap: 0-0
Best Rating: 66 2/01 Sthl 1m4f stand

Spankinfrankie

81(66) (19)**37**

2-y-o ch f Alhijaz-Rose Ciel (IRE) (Red Sunset)

R A Fahey Lets Go Racing 1

Placings:500 **(1995)**

2001: 5^{5}S, 6^{0}F, 6^{0}SD

	Starts	1st	2nd	3rd	Win & Pl
Career Total (Turf)	2	0	0	0	0
Career Total (AW)	1	0	0	0	

Going (Turf): Sf: 0-1 GS: 0-0 Gd: 0-0 GF: 0-0 Fm: 0-1
Distance: 5f/6f: 0-3 7f-8f: 0-0 9f-13f: 0-0 14f+: 0-0
Track : LH: 0-1 RH: 0-0 Tight: 0-0 Gall: 0-0
Aids: Bl: 0-0 Vi: 0-0 Tstrap: 0-0
Best Rating: 37 6/01 Thsk 6f firm

Spark Of Life

102 **55**

4-y-o b f Rainbows For Life (CAN)-Sparkly Girl (IRE) (Danehill (USA))

T D McCarthy A D Spence

Placings:060/03231130-000213000 **(4463)**

2001: 9^{0}G, 10^{0}GF, 11^{0}GF, 10^{2}GF, 10^{1}F, 11^{3}GF, 11^{0}F, 10^{0}GF, 9^{0}GS

	Starts	1st	2nd	3rd	Win & Pl
Career Total (Turf)	20	3	2	4	11850

53 6/01 Ling 1m2f E(0-70)H FRM £3472
59 8/00 Kemp 1m1f E(0-70)H G-F £2749
47 7/00 Brig 7f214y G FRM £1926

Total win prize-money £8148

Going (Turf): Sf: 0-3 GS: 0-1 Gd: 0-2 GF: 1-11 **Fm: 2-3**
Distance: 5f/6f: 0-0 7f-8f: 1-5 **9f-13f: 2-15** 14f+: 0-0
Track : **LH: 2-11** RH: 1-4 **Tight: 1-9** Gall: 0-0
Aids: **Bl: 3-19** Vi: 0-0 Tstrap: 0-0
Best Rating: 55 7/01 Ling 1m3f106y gd-fm

Sparkling Dove

85(66) **17**

8-y-o ch m Lighter-Nimble Dove (Starch Reduced)

C J Price Cecil J Price And Mr P Crawford

Placings:0000-60 **(0708)**

2001: 16^{6}HY, 17^{0}HY

	Starts	1st	2nd	3rd	Win & Pl
Career Total (Turf)	4	0	0	0	0
Career Total (AW)	2	0	0	0	

Going (Turf): Sf: 0-3 GS: 0-0 Gd: 0-1 GF: 0-0 Fm: 0-0
Distance: 5f/6f: 0-0 7f-8f: 0-1 9f-13f: 0-2 14f+: 0-3
Track : LH: 0-5 RH: 0-0 Tight: 0-2 Gall: 0-0
Aids: Bl: 0-5 Vi: 0-0 Tstrap: 0-0
Best Rating: 17 4/01 Nott 2m9y heavy

Sparkling Water (USA)

107 **100**

2-y-o b/br c Woodman (USA)-Shirley Valentine (Shirley Heights)

H R A Cecil K Abdulla

Placings:2122 **(4781)**

2001: 7^{2}S, 7^{1}GF, 8^{2}G, 8^{2}G

	Starts	1st	2nd	3rd	Win & Pl
Career Total (Turf)	4	1	3	0	10402

95 7/01 Bevl 7f100y D G-F £3766

Total win prize-money £3766

Going (Turf): Sf: 0-1 GS: 0-0 Gd: 0-2 **GF: 1-1** Fm: 0-0
Distance: 5f/6f: 0-0 **7f-8f: 1-3** 9f-13f: 0-1 14f+: 0-0
Track : LH: 0-1 **RH: 1-3** Tight: 0-0 Gall: 0-0
Aids: Bl: 0-0 Vi: 0-0 Tstrap: 0-0
Best Rating: 100 9/01 Gdwd 1m good

Bred to stay. Beaten in soft ground on his debut. Scored on a sounder surface next time in a Beverley maiden. Put in a decent effort next when second to Assaaf, giving that rival plenty of weight. Second to Henri Labasque in a Listed event in September.

Sparky Glenn

96 **48**

3-y-o b c Shareef Dancer (USA)-Warthill Girl (Anfield)

J Cullinan (N P Littmoden 6/5) Mrs H F Mahr

Placings:005003 **(4463)**

2001: 10^{0}GS, 8^{0}G, 9^{5}GF, 10^{0}GF, 9^{0}G, 9^{3}GS

	Starts	1st	2nd	3rd	Win & Pl
Career Total (Turf)	6	0	0	1	342

Going (Turf): Sf: 0-0 GS: 0-2 Gd: 0-2 GF: 0-2 Fm: 0-0
Distance: 5f/6f: 0-0 7f-8f: 0-1 9f-13f: 0-5 14f+: 0-0
Track : LH: 0-0 RH: 0-3 Tight: 0-3 Gall: 0-0
Aids: Bl: 0-0 Vi: 0-0 Tstrap: 0-0
Best Rating: 48 6/01 Sals 1m1f198y gd-fm

Spartak (IRE)

(101) (64)

3-y-o b c Charnwood Forest (IRE)-Pretext (Polish Precedent (USA))

M R Channon Sheikh Ahmed Al Maktoum

Placings:1 **(0185)**

2001: 7^{1}SD

	Starts	1st	2nd	3rd	Win & Pl
Career Total (Turf)	0	0	0	0	
Career Total (AW)	1	1	0	0	3010

64 1/01 Ling 7f D STD £3010

Total win prize-money £3010

Going (Turf): Sf: 0-0 GS: 0-0 Gd: 0-0 GF: 0-0 Fm: 0-0
Distance: 5f/6f: 0-0 **7f-8f: 1-1** 9f-13f: 0-0 14f+: 0-0
Track : **LH: 1-1** RH: 0-0 **Tight: 1-1** Gall: 0-0
Aids: Bl: 0-0 Vi: 0-0 Tstrap: 0-0
Best Rating: 64 1/01 Ling 7f stand

Spartan Fair

69 **15**

3-y-o ch g Spartan Monarch-Fair Atlanta (Tachypous)

J R Best Broomdown Racing 1

Placings:400 **(5024)**

2001: 9^{4}G, 9^{0}GF, 11^{0}S

	Starts	1st	2nd	3rd	Win & Pl
Career Total (Turf)	3	0	0	0	317

Going (Turf): Sf: 0-1 GS: 0-0 Gd: 0-1 GF: 0-1 Fm: 0-0
Distance: 5f/6f: 0-0 7f-8f: 0-0 9f-13f: 0-3 14f+: 0-0
Track : LH: 0-1 RH: 0-2 Tight: 0-1 Gall: 0-0
Aids: Bl: 0-0 Vi: 0-0 Tstrap: 0-0
Best Rating: 15 8/01 Sand 1m1f good

Spartan Sailor

45

3-y-o b g Handsome Sailor-Spartan Native (Native Bazaar)

A Senior G B Maher

Placings:0-00 **(5528)**

2001: 7^{0}HY, 8^{0}HY

	Starts	1st	2nd	3rd	Win & Pl
Career Total (Turf)	3	0	0	0	

Going (Turf): Sf: 0-3 GS: 0-0 Gd: 0-0 GF: 0-0 Fm: 0-0
Distance: 5f/6f: 0-0 7f-8f: 0-2 9f-13f: 0-1 14f+: 0-0
Track : LH: 0-3 RH: 0-0 Tight: 0-1 Gall: 0-0
Aids: Bl: 0-0 Vi: 0-0 Tstrap: 0-0

Spearhead (IRE)

12

2-y-o b g Elbio-Lake Flyer (USA) (Lomond (USA))

M L W Bell Raymond Tooth

Placings:0 **(5666)**

2001: 6^{0}HY

	Starts	1st	2nd	3rd	Win & Pl
Career Total (Turf)	1	0	0	0	

Going (Turf): Sf: 0-1 GS: 0-0 Gd: 0-0 GF: 0-0 Fm: 0-0
Distance: 5f/6f: 0-1 7f-8f: 0-0 9f-13f: 0-0 14f+: 0-0
Track : LH: 0-0 RH: 0-0 Tight: 0-0 Gall: 0-0
Aids: Bl: 0-0 Vi: 0-0 Tstrap: 0-0
Best Rating: 12 11/01 Wind 6f heavy

Special

107 **83**

3-y-o b f Polar Falcon (USA)-Shore Line (High Line)

Sir Michael Stoute Cheveley Park Stud

Placings:0-4322115 **(4697)**

2001: 10^{4}F, 12^{3}GF, 12^{2}GF, 12^{2}F, 14^{1}G, 14^{1}GF, 14^{5}GS

	Starts	1st	2nd	3rd	Win & Pl
Career Total (Turf)	8	2	2	1	15312

81 8/01 Newc 1m6f97y D(0-80)H G-F £5109
79 8/01 Sand 1m6f C(0-90)H GD £7182

Total win prize-money £12292

Going (Turf): Sf: 0-0 GS: 0-2 **Gd: 1-1 GF: 1-3** Fm: 0-2
Distance: 5f/6f: 0-1 7f-8f: 0-0 9f-13f: 0-4 **14f+: 2-3**
Track : LH: 1-6 RH: 1-2 Tight: 0-2 **Gall: 1-3**

Aids: Bl: 0-0 Vi: 0-0 Tstrap: 0-0
Best Rating: 83 9/01 Donc 1m6f132y gd-sft

Improved as she has gone up in trip. She got off the mark with a dour staying performance to win a 14-furlong handicap at Sandown in August and followed up over the same trip at Newcastle. She should stay further. Acts on fast ground.

Special Hero (IRE)

95 **79+**

2-y-o b c Spectrum (IRE)-Royal Heroine (Lypheor)
K A Ryan The Gloria Darley Racing Partnership

Placings:1 **(4797)**
2001: 6^{1}G

	Starts	1st	2nd	3rd	Win & Pl
Career Total (Turf)	1	1	0	0	3991

79 9/01 Ayr 6f E GD £3991
Total win prize-money £3991

Going (Turf): Sf: 0-0 GS: 0-0 Gd: 1-1 GF: 0-0 Fm: 0-0
Distance: **5f/6f: 1-1** 7f-8f: 0-0 9f-13f: 0-0 14f+: 0-0
Track : LH: 0-0 RH: 0-0 Tight: 0-0 Gall: 0-0
Aids: Bl: 0-0 Vi: 0-0 Tstrap: 0-0
Best Rating: 79 9/01 Ayr 6f good

Made a winning debut at Ayr in September and should go on to better things.

Special Promise (IRE)

104(101) (37)**36**

4-y-o ch g Anjiz (USA)-Woodonitbenice (USA) (Nasty And Bold (USA))
I Semple (P C Haslam 19/8) Mrs D Santonocito

Placings:66005/11110000-064605240030 **(5411)**
2001: 11^{0}SD, 16^{6}SD, 12^{4}SD, 16^{6}S, 13^{0}G, 16^{5}GF, 17^{2}GF, 14^{4}G, 12^{0}GS, 17^{0}GF, 15^{3}GF, 14^{0}SD

	Starts	1st	2nd	3rd	Win & Pl
Career Total (Turf)	14	0	1	1	1529
Career Total (AW)	11	4	0	0	12017

79 2/00 Wolv 1m100y D(0-85)H STD £3906
78 2/00 Sthl 1m E(0-70)H STD £2821
62 1/00 Wolv 1m1f79y E(0-75)H STD £2689
58 1/00 Ling 1m2f F(0-65)H STD £2310
Total win prize-money £11727

Going (Turf): Sf: 0-4 GS: 0-2 Gd: 0-3 GF: 0-5 Fm: 0-0
Distance: 5f/6f: 0-3 **7f-8f: 1-4 9f-13f: 3-9** 14f+: 0-9
Track : **LH: 4-15** RH: 0-6 **Tight: 3-12** Gall: 0-0
Aids: Bl: 0-0 Vi: 0-2 Tstrap: 0-0
Best Rating: 59 3/01 Sthl 1m4f stand

He improved out of all recognition at the start of 2000, reeling off a fine four-timer on sand. Ten furlongs looks to be his trip.

Spectina

110 **83**

3-y-o b f Spectrum (IRE)-Catina (Nureyev (USA))
J R Fanshawe Chris Machin

Placings:0-22422 **(4381)**
2001: 8^{2}GF, 8^{2}G, 8^{4}GF, 7^{2}G, 8^{2}GF

	Starts	1st	2nd	3rd	Win & Pl
Career Total (Turf)	6	0	4	0	5788

Going (Turf): Sf: 0-1 GS: 0-0 Gd: 0-2 GF: 0-3 Fm: 0-0
Distance: 5f/6f: 0-0 7f-8f: 0-4 9f-13f: 0-2 14f+: 0-0
Track : LH: 0-1 RH: 0-1 Tight: 0-0 Gall: 0-0
Aids: Bl: 0-0 Vi: 0-0 Tstrap: 0-0
Best Rating: 83 8/01 Yarm 7f3y good

Regularly placed but might lack resolution.

Spectre Brown

11-y-o b g Respect-My Goddess (Palm Track)
D A Nolan Mrs J McFadyen-Murray

Placings:00-0 **(1136)**
2001: 11^{0}G

	Starts	1st	2nd	3rd	Win & Pl
Career Total (Turf)	3	0	0	0	

Going (Turf): Sf: 0-0 GS: 0-1 Gd: 0-1 GF: 0-1 Fm: 0-0
Distance: 5f/6f: 0-1 7f-8f: 0-0 9f-13f: 0-3 14f+: 0-0
Track : LH: 0-0 RH: 0-3 Tight: 0-3 Gall: 0-0
Aids: Bl: 0-0 Vi: 0-0 Tstrap: 0-0

Spectroscope (IRE)

89 **70**

2-y-o b c Spectrum (IRE)-Paloma Bay (IRE) (Alzao (USA))
J J O'Neill Mrs G Smith

Placings:0 **(3813)**
2001: 7^{0}G

	Starts	1st	2nd	3rd	Win & Pl
Career Total (Turf)	1	0	0	0	

Going (Turf): Sf: 0-0 GS: 0-0 Gd: 0-1 GF: 0-0 Fm: 0-0
Distance: 5f/6f: 0-0 7f-8f: 0-1 9f-13f: 0-0 14f+: 0-0
Track : LH: 0-0 RH: 0-0 Tight: 0-0 Gall: 0-0
Aids: Bl: 0-0 Vi: 0-0 Tstrap: 0-0
Best Rating: 70 8/01 NmkJ 7f good

Speed Of Light (IRE)

103(100) (74)**72**

3-y-o b g Spectrum (IRE)-Phylella (Persian Bold)
W R Muir A J De V Patrick

Placings:4-3206554 **(4626)**
2001: 7^{3}G, 9^{2}SD, 8^{0}GF, 7^{6}S, 10^{5}GF, 10^{5}GS, 9^{4}GF

	Starts	1st	2nd	3rd	Win & Pl
Career Total (Turf)	7	0	0	1	1263
Career Total (AW)	1	0	1	0	842

Going (Turf): Sf: 0-2 GS: 0-1 Gd: 0-1 GF: 0-3 Fm: 0-0
Distance: 5f/6f: 0-0 7f-8f: 0-4 9f-13f: 0-4 14f+: 0-0
Track : LH: 0-3 RH: 0-2 Tight: 0-1 Gall: 0-2
Aids: Bl: 0-1 Vi: 0-0 Tstrap: 0-0
Best Rating: 76 5/01 Leic 7f9y good

Lightly raced maiden, effective on turf and Fibresand. Stays nine furlongs.

Speed On

104 **60**

8-y-o b g Sharpo-Pretty Poppy (Song)
H Candy Henry Candy

Placings:212360/506033/10000605O/16510660/063050 4600-00060020 **(4897)**
2001: 5^{0}GS, 5^{0}GF, 5^{0}GF, 5^{6}GS, 5^{0}GF, 5^{0}G, 5^{2}G, 5^{0}GS

	Starts	1st	2nd	3rd	Win & Pl
Career Total (Turf)	47	4	3	4	35836

88 6/99 Chep 5f16y C(0-100)H G-F £6775
89 4/99 Newb 5f34y B(0-100)H G-F £8913
97 4/98 Bath 5f11y C SFT £6243
83 5/96 Bevl 5f D G-F £3977
Total win prize-money £25908

Going (Turf): Sf: 1-8 GS: 0-9 Gd: 0-15 **GF: 3-14** Fm: 0-1
Distance: **5f/6f: 4-47** 7f-8f: 0-0 9f-13f: 0-0 14f+: 0-0
Track : **LH: 1-10** RH: 0-2 Tight: 0-2 **Gall: 1-9**
Aids: Bl: 0-0 Vi: 0-4 Tstrap: 0-0
Best Rating: 60 9/01 Sand 5f6y good

He is a pacey sort well capable of winning sprint handicaps. Does not like big fields or trips in the excess of the minimum according to his trainer.

Speed Queen (IRE)

71 **38**

2-y-o b f Goldmark (USA)-Blues Queen (Lahib (USA))
A P Jarvis Jarvis Associates

Placings:0 **(4608)**
2001: 5^{0}F

	Starts	1st	2nd	3rd	Win & Pl
Career Total (Turf)	1	0	0	0	

Going (Turf): Sf: 0-0 GS: 0-0 Gd: 0-0 GF: 0-0 Fm: 0-1
Distance: 5f/6f: 0-1 7f-8f: 0-0 9f-13f: 0-0 14f+: 0-0
Track : LH: 0-1 RH: 0-0 Tight: 0-0 Gall: 0-1
Aids: Bl: 0-0 Vi: 0-0 Tstrap: 0-0
Best Rating: 38 9/01 Bath 5f11y firm

Speed Venture

107(85) (41)**67**

4-y-o b g Owington-Jade Venture (Never So Bold)
J Mackie Wall Racing Partners

Placings:422550404-0140600 **(5463)**
2001: 14^{0}SD, 9^{1}HY, 8^{4}HY, 10^{0}G, 10^{6}GF, 9^{0}S, 11^{0}G

	Starts	1st	2nd	3rd	Win & Pl
Career Total (Turf)	14	1	2	0	6931
Career Total (AW)	2	0	0	0	0

66 4/01 Nott 1m1f213yE(0-70) HVY £2996
Total win prize-money £2996

Going (Turf): Sf: 1-4 GS: 0-3 Gd: 0-3 GF: 0-4 Fm: 0-0
Distance: 5f/6f: 0-0 7f-8f: 0-1 **9f-13f: 1-14** 14f+: 0-1
Track : **LH: 1-9** RH: 0-6 Tight: 0-7 Gall: 0-3
Aids: Bl: 0-0 Vi: 0-0 **Tstrap: 1-7**
Best Rating: 67 5/01 Donc 1m2f60y good

Speedfit Free (IRE)

103(98) (54) **58**

4-y-o b g Night Shift (USA)-Dedicated Lady (IRE) (Pennine Walk)
E J Alston Papermates Racing

Placings:0010604/00504413640-1600430430000 **(4403)**
2001: 6^{1}SD, 7^{6}SD, 7^{0}SD, 5^{0}F, 6^{4}GF, 5^{3}GF, 5^{U}GF, 6^{4}GF, 6^{3}GF, 5^{0}S, 5^{0}G, 6^{U}G, 6^{0}G, 6^{4}SD

	Starts	1st	2nd	3rd	Win & Pl
Career Total (Turf)	28	2	0	3	9768
Career Total (AW)	3	1	0	0	1813

54 3/01 Sthl 6f F(0-65)H STD £1813
48 7/00 Nott 1m54y F G-F £2727
75 5/99 Yarm 6f3y D FRM £3557
Total win prize-money £8098

Going (Turf): Sf: 0-2 GS: 0-0 Gd: 0-8 **GF: 1-13 Fm: 1-5**
Distance: 5f/6f: 1-17 7f-8f: 1-11 9f-13f: 1-3 14f+: 0-0
Track : **LH: 2-10** RH: 0-6 Tight: 0-5 Gall: 0-0
Aids: Bl: 0-2 Vi: 0-0 Tstrap: 0-0
Best Rating: 58 7/01 Pont 6f gd-fm

An able sprint handicapper. Best over six furlongs on fast ground.

Speedy Gee (IRE)

95 **91d**

3-y-o b g Petardia-Champagne Girl (Robellino (USA))
M R Channon John Guest

Placings:3610560463-00000 **(3857)**
2001: 5^{0}S, 7^{0}GF, 7^{0}GF, 7^{0}G, 5^{0}GS

	Starts	1st	2nd	3rd	Win & Pl
Career Total (Turf)	15	1	0	2	6135

69 6/00 Sand 5f6y D G-F £3412
Total win prize-money £3413

Going (Turf): Sf: 0-2 GS: 0-1 Gd: 0-7 **GF: 1-5** Fm: 0-0
Distance: **5f/6f: 1-11** 7f-8f: 0-4 9f-13f: 0-0 14f+: 0-0
Track : LH: 0-1 RH: 0-4 Tight: 0-1 Gall: 0-2
Aids: Bl: 0-0 Vi: 0-1 Tstrap: 0-0
Best Rating: 84 5/01 Ches 7f122y gd-fm

A half-brother to Halmahera, he scored over the minimum trip at Sandown on his third start at two, but was then found out in Pattern company and has not fared much better in high-class handicaps. Too high in the weights just now and is still to convince that he stays seven furlongs.

Speedy James (IRE)

102(81) (39)55

5-y-o ch g Fayruz-Haraabah (USA) (Topsider (USA))

D Nicholls H E Lhendup Dorji

Placings:1120300/360/6000-046000000 **(5090)**

2001: 6[0]SD, 5[4]GS, 6[6]F, 5[0]F, 5[0]GF, 5[0]G, 5[0]G, 5[0]GS, 5[0]GS

	Starts	1st	2nd	3rd	Win & Pl
Career Total (Turf)	22	2	1	2	16968
Career Total (AW)	1	0	0	0	

98	4/98	NmkR	5f	C	SFT	£5108
84	3/98	Newc	5f	D	GD	£3048

Total win prize-money £8156

Going (Turf): Sf: 1-3 GS: 0-6 **Gd: 1-6** GF: 0-4 Fm: 0-3
Distance: **5f/6f: 2-22** 7f-8f: 0-1 9f-13f: 0-0 14f+: 0-0
Track : LH: 0-2 RH: 0-0 Tight: 0-1 Gall: 0-0
Aids: Bl: 0-0 Vi: 0-1 Tstrap: 0-0
Best Rating: 70 5/01 Thsk 5f gd-sft

He looked useful early on in his career, but went the wrong way and endured a fruitless 2000 for David Nicholls finishing last on all four starts. Shaped with considerable promise on turf this term and may be capable of winning soon. Versatile as regards ground, best over five furlongs

Spencers Wood (IRE)

107 107

4-y-o b g Pips Pride-Ascoli (Skyliner)

P J Makin Four Seasons Racing Ltd

Placings:1/14365-0602411 **(5319a)**

2001: 7[0]G, 7[6]G, 7[0]GF, 7[2]G, 7[4]GF, 6[1]GF, 6[1]S, 6[0]VS

	Starts	1st	2nd	3rd	Win & Pl
Career Total (Turf)	13	4	1	1	57102

102	10/01	Curr	6f		SFT	£26000
66	9/01	Haml	6f5y	C	G-F	£6609
101	5/00	NmkR	7f	B(0-95)	GD	£10286
79	10/99	Wind	6f	D	G-S	£3387

Total win prize-money £46283

Going (Turf): Sf: 1-1 GS: 1-1 Gd: 1-6 GF: 1-5 Fm: 0-0
Distance: 5f/6f: 2-2 7f-8f: 2-9 9f-13f: 0-2 14f+: 0-0
Track : LH: 0-3 **RH: 1-5** Tight: 0-0 **Gall: 1-4**
Aids: Bl: 0-0 Vi: 0-0 Tstrap: 0-0
Best Rating: 107 5/01 NmkR 7f good

Effective at seven furlongs or a mile, he ran two good races in August after being gelded and gained his reward when dropped to six at Hamilton in September. Ran away with a Curragh Listed event next time on easy ground. Seems to handle any going, but possibly best with cut.

Spettro (IRE)

100 109

3-y-o b c Spectrum (IRE)-Overruled (IRE) (Last Tycoon)

P F I Cole Alessandro Gaucci

Placings:511130-0 **(1231)**

2001: 10[0]GF, 10[0]HY

	Starts	1st	2nd	3rd	Win & Pl
Career Total (Turf)	7	3	0	1	33224

102	9/00	Hayd	1m30y	B	HVY	£8122
92	8/00	Nott	1m54y	D	GD	£3493
80	8/00	Catt	7f	D	G-F	£2951

Total win prize-money £14567

Going (Turf): Sf: 1-2 GS: 0-0 **Gd: 1-2 GF: 1-2** Fm: 0-0
Distance: 5f/6f: 0-1 7f-8f: 1-2 **9f-13f: 2-3** 14f+: 0-0
Track : **LH: 3-4** RH: 0-1 **Tight: 1-2** Gall: 0-0
Aids: Bl: 0-0 Vi: 0-0 Tstrap: 0-0
Best Rating: 90 5/01 Ches 1m2f75y gd-fm

Well beaten in a Listed race on his only start.

Spice Island

94 66

3-y-o b f Reprimand-Little Emmeline (Emarati (USA))

J A Glover Mrs R Morley

Placings:530010-20 **(1433)**

2001: 8[2]HY, 7[0]S

	Starts	1st	2nd	3rd	Win & Pl
Career Total (Turf)	8	1	1	1	4551

66	10/00	Pont	6f	E(0-75)	HVY	£3263

Total win prize-money £3263

Going (Turf): Sf: 1-4 GS: 0-1 Gd: 0-1 GF: 0-2 Fm: 0-0
Distance: **5f/6f: 1-6** 7f-8f: 0-1 9f-13f: 0-1 14f+: 0-0
Track : **LH: 1-2** RH: 0-0 Tight: 0-0 Gall: 0-0
Aids: Bl: 0-0 Vi: 0-0 Tstrap: 0-0
Best Rating: 63 5/01 Nott 1m54y heavy

Spice Of Life

60

3-y-o b g Tagula (IRE)-Lloc (Absalom)

M L W Bell Billy Maguire

Placings:0 **(4600)**

2001: 6[0]GF

	Starts	1st	2nd	3rd	Win & Pl
Career Total (Turf)	1	0	0	0	

Going (Turf): Sf: 0-0 GS: 0-0 Gd: 0-0 GF: 0-1 Fm: 0-0
Distance: 5f/6f: 0-1 7f-8f: 0-0 9f-13f: 0-0 14f+: 0-0
Track : LH: 0-0 RH: 0-0 Tight: 0-0 Gall: 0-0
Aids: Bl: 0-0 Vi: 0-0 Tstrap: 0-0

Spin A Yarn

92 47

4-y-o b g Wolfhound (USA)-Green Flower (USA) (Fappiano (USA))

J G Given Mrs Jo Hardy

Placings:04441/005545-00000 **(4108)**

2001: 7[0]GF, 8[0]GF, 10[0]GF, 11[0]GF, 8[0]S

	Starts	1st	2nd	3rd	Win & Pl
Career Total (Turf)	16	1	0	0	7564

76	8/99	Newb	7f64y	C H	GD	£6190

Total win prize-money £6190

Going (Turf): Sf: 0-1 GS: 0-1 **Gd: 1-5** GF: 0-7 Fm: 0-2
Distance: 5f/6f: 0-1 **7f-8f: 1-9** 9f-13f: 0-6 14f+: 0-0
Track : **LH: 1-8** RH: 0-3 Tight: 0-5 **Gall: 1-4**
Aids: Bl: 0-0 Vi: 0-0 Tstrap: 0-0
Best Rating: 51 6/01 Wwck 7f26y gd-fm

An able sort but looks to have his own ideas about the game. Stays a mile. Acts on a sound surface.

Spinamix

91 72

2-y-o gr f Spinning World (USA)-Vadsagreya (FR) (Linamix (FR))

H R A Cecil Tigerland Ltd

Placings:4000 **(4962)**

2001: 7[4]GF, 7[0]GF, 7[0]S, 8[0]S

	Starts	1st	2nd	3rd	Win & Pl
Career Total (Turf)	4	0	0	0	321

Going (Turf): Sf: 0-2 GS: 0-0 Gd: 0-0 GF: 0-2 Fm: 0-0
Distance: 5f/6f: 0-0 7f-8f: 0-3 9f-13f: 0-1 14f+: 0-0
Track : LH: 0-1 RH: 0-1 Tight: 0-0 Gall: 0-0
Aids: Bl: 0-0 Vi: 0-0 Tstrap: 0-0
Best Rating: 72 8/01 NmkJ 7f gd-fm

Spindara (IRE)

86 72

2-y-o ch f Spinning World (USA)-Lydara (USA) (Alydar (USA))

P F I Cole M Arbib

Placings:0000 **(5176)**

2001: 6[0]GF, 7[0]GF, 6[0]G, 8[0]HY

	Starts	1st	2nd	3rd	Win & Pl
Career Total (Turf)	4	0	0	0	

Going (Turf): Sf: 0-1 GS: 0-0 Gd: 0-1 GF: 0-2 Fm: 0-0
Distance: 5f/6f: 0-2 7f-8f: 0-1 9f-13f: 0-1 14f+: 0-0
Track : LH: 0-0 RH: 0-1 Tight: 0-1 Gall: 0-0
Aids: Bl: 0-0 Vi: 0-0 Tstrap: 0-0
Best Rating: 72 9/01 Kemp 6f good

Spinetail Rufous (IRE)

(100) (71)

3-y-o b c Prince Of Birds (USA)-Miss Kinabalu (Shirley Heights)

D W P Arbuthnot Noel Cronin

Placings:000452-30112 **(0420)**

2001: 6[3]SW, 5[0]SD, 5[1]SW, 5[1]SW, 5[2]SD

	Starts	1st	2nd	3rd	Win & Pl
Career Total (Turf)	3	0	0	0	
Career Total (AW)	8	2	2	1	8001

70	2/01	Ling	5f	E(0-70)H	SLW	£2884
59	2/01	Ling	5f	D	SLW	£2884

Total win prize-money £5768

Going (Turf): Sf: 0-0 GS: 0-1 Gd: 0-1 GF: 0-1 Fm: 0-0
Distance: **5f/6f: 2-10** 7f-8f: 0-1 9f-13f: 0-0 14f+: 0-0
Track : **LH: 2-8** RH: 0-1 **Tight: 2-6** Gall: 0-1
Aids: Bl: 0-0 Vi: 0-0 **Tstrap: 2-6**
Best Rating: 71 3/01 Ling 5f stand

Spiney Norman

90 36

3-y-o gr g Petong-Fairy Ballerina (Fairy King (USA))

Jamie Poulton Robert Townsend

Placings:000000 **(5084)**

2001: 7[0]GS, 8[0]GF, 6[0]GF, 8[0]GF, 7[0]G, 9[0]S

	Starts	1st	2nd	3rd	Win & Pl
Career Total (Turf)	6	0	0	0	

Going (Turf): Sf: 0-1 GS: 0-1 Gd: 0-1 GF: 0-3 Fm: 0-0
Distance: 5f/6f: 0-0 7f-8f: 0-5 9f-13f: 0-1 14f+: 0-0
Track : LH: 0-2 RH: 0-1 Tight: 0-1 Gall: 0-0
Aids: Bl: 0-0 Vi: 0-0 Tstrap: 0-0
Best Rating: 55 6/01 Sals 6f212y gd-fm

Spinner Toy

73 15

6-y-o ch g Seven Hearts-Priory Bay (Petong)

J C Fox Ground Force

Placings:0/0/0-00 **(2057)**

2001: 10[0]GF, 6[0]GF

	Starts	1st	2nd	3rd	Win & Pl
Career Total (Turf)	4	0	0	0	
Career Total (AW)	1	0	0	0	

Going (Turf): Sf: 0-0 GS: 0-0 Gd: 0-1 GF: 0-3 Fm: 0-0
Distance: 5f/6f: 0-0 7f-8f: 0-2 9f-13f: 0-2 14f+: 0-1
Track : LH: 0-1 RH: 0-2 Tight: 0-2 Gall: 0-0
Aids: Bl: 0-0 Vi: 0-0 Tstrap: 0-0
Best Rating: 15 5/01 Sand 1m2f7y gd-fm

Spinnette (IRE)

95 92

2-y-o b/br f Spinning World (USA)-Net Worth (USA) (Forty Niner (USA))

J Noseda Dr T A Ryan

Placings:2 (5609)
2001: 8²GS

	Starts	1st	2nd	3rd	Win & Pl
Career Total (Turf)	1	0	1	0	4752

Going (Turf): Sf: 0-0 GS: 0-1 Gd: 0-0 GF: 0-0 Fm: 0-0
Distance: 5f/6f: 0-0 7f-8f: 0-1 9f-13f: 0-0 14f+: 0-0
Track : LH: 0-0 RH: 0-0 Tight: 0-0 Gall: 0-0
Aids: Bl: 0-0 Vi: 0-0 Tstrap: 0-0
Best Rating: 92 11/01 NmkR 1m gd-sft

American bred, dam a winner in America at three years.

Spiptunia

58
3-y-o ch f Blushing Flame (USA)-Comhail (USA) (Nodouble (USA))
Miss J Feilden Miss D Gates

Placings:0 (1277)
2001: 8⁰G

	Starts	1st	2nd	3rd	Win & Pl
Career Total (Turf)	1	0	0	0	

Going (Turf): Sf: 0-0 GS: 0-0 Gd: 0-1 GF: 0-0 Fm: 0-0
Distance: 5f/6f: 0-0 7f-8f: 0-0 9f-13f: 0-1 14f+: 0-0
Track : LH: 0-1 RH: 0-0 Tight: 0-0 Gall: 0-0
Aids: Bl: 0-0 Vi: 0-0 Tstrap: 0-0

Spirit House (USA)

91 **85d**
3-y-o b c Hansel (USA)-Ashwood Angel (USA) (Well Decorated (USA))
M Johnston J David Abell

Placings:20-00 (4312)
2001: 11⁰G, 14⁰GF

	Starts	1st	2nd	3rd	Win & Pl
Career Total (Turf)	4	0	1	0	2836

Going (Turf): Sf: 0-0 GS: 0-0 Gd: 0-2 GF: 0-2 Fm: 0-0
Distance: 5f/6f: 0-0 7f-8f: 0-2 9f-13f: 0-1 14f+: 0-1
Track : LH: 0-1 RH: 0-3 Tight: 0-1 Gall: 0-2
Aids: Bl: 0-0 Vi: 0-0 Tstrap: 0-0
Best Rating: 50 8/01 Newc 1m6f97y gd-fm

Spirit Of Light (IRE)

51(85) (35)**64**
4-y-o b g Unblest-Light Thatch (Thatch (USA))
B R Johnson Mrs Beryl Williams

Placings:0205/0023000500-000 (0897)
2001: 8⁰SW, 8⁰SW, 9⁰HY

	Starts	1st	2nd	3rd	Win & Pl
Career Total (Turf)	14	0	2	1	2991
Career Total (AW)	3	0	0	0	

Going (Turf): Sf: 0-4 GS: 0-2 Gd: 0-4 GF: 0-3 Fm: 0-1
Distance: 5f/6f: 0-0 7f-8f: 0-9 9f-13f: 0-8 14f+: 0-0
Track : LH: 0-9 RH: 0-7 Tight: 0-8 Gall: 0-1
Aids: Bl: 0-1 Vi: 0-2 Tstrap: 0-0
Best Rating: 35 2/01 Ling 1m slow

Spirit Of Love (USA)

98(103) (79)**68**
6-y-o ch g Trempolino (USA)-Dream Mary (USA) (Marfa (USA))
J G Given (Andrew Reid 6/9) Mrs Jo Hardy

Placings:00/1323114131/40001/03032403016-2600600140 (5531)
2001: 16²SW, 16⁶SD, 16⁰G, 16⁰GF, 18⁶G, 16⁰G, 14⁰G, 14¹SW, 17⁴G, 16⁰HY, 16⁰SD

	Starts	1st	2nd	3rd	Win & Pl
Career Total (Turf)	28	5	1	4	132108
Career Total (AW)	10	3	2	2	10832

43	9/01	Wolv	1m6f166yF		SLW	£2289
41	11/00	Wolv	1m6f166yF		STD	£2226
84	11/99	Mulh	2m2f		VS	£7220
112	10/98	NmkR	2m2f	B H	GD	£70750
99	9/98	Donc	1m6f132yB(0-105)H		GD	£18925
90	8/98	Asct	2m45y	C(0-90)H	G-F	£8169
81	5/98	Donc	1m6f132yD(0-80)H		GD	£3525
70	1/98	Sthl	1m3f	D	STD	£3436

Total win prize-money £116540

Going (Turf): Sf: 0-3 GS: 0-1 **Gd: 3-13** GF: 1-9 Fm: 0-1
Distance: 5f/6f: 0-0 7f-8f: 0-0 9f-13f: 1-7 **14f+: 7-31**
Track : **LH: 5-23** RH: 2-13 Tight: 2-9 **Gall: 4-15**
Aids: **Bl: 1-4** Vi: 0-1 Tstrap: 0-0
Best Rating: 90 1/01 Wolv 2m46y slow

A high-class stayer at his best when with Mark Johnston, he is not the force of old. Plies his trade on Fibresand these days.

Spirit Of Song (IRE)

100 **50**
3-y-o b f Selkirk (USA)-Roxy Music (IRE) (Song)
M R Channon Michael Hills

Placings:440-000 (5082)
2001: 5⁰F, 7⁰GS, 7⁰S

	Starts	1st	2nd	3rd	Win & Pl
Career Total (Turf)	6	0	0	0	757

Going (Turf): Sf: 0-1 GS: 0-2 Gd: 0-1 GF: 0-1 Fm: 0-1
Distance: 5f/6f: 0-3 7f-8f: 0-3 9f-13f: 0-0 14f+: 0-0
Track : LH: 0-3 RH: 0-1 Tight: 0-0 Gall: 0-2
Aids: Bl: 0-0 Vi: 0-0 Tstrap: 0-0
Best Rating: 50 9/01 Gdwd 7f gd-sft

Spirit Of Texas (IRE)

92(99) (50)**58**
3-y-o b g Namaqualand (USA)-Have A Flutter (Auction Ring (USA))
K McAuliffe The Tri Nations Syndicate

Placings:0000**162**-**1534**500 (5348)
2001: 11¹SD, 12⁵SD, 11³GS, 12⁴SD, 14⁵SD, 11⁰GS, 12⁰SD

	Starts	1st	2nd	3rd	Win & Pl
Career Total (Turf)	8	1	0	1	2425
Career Total (AW)	7	1	1	0	2223

60	2/01	Sthl	1m3f	F(0-60)H	STD	£1687
68	10/00	Nott	1m54y	G	SFT	£1985

Total win prize-money £3672

Going (Turf): Sf: 1-2 GS: 0-3 Gd: 0-0 GF: 0-3 Fm: 0-0
Distance: 5f/6f: 0-3 7f-8f: 0-2 **9f-13f: 2-9** 14f+: 0-1
Track : **LH: 2-10** RH: 0-1 Tight: 0-6 Gall: 0-1
Aids: Bl: 0-2 Vi: 0-1 **Tstrap: 1-10**
Best Rating: 60 2/01 Sthl 1m3f stand

A Nottingham seller in October 2000 and a modest handicap on the sand the following February are all he has managed so far. A half-brother to four juvenile winners, including two Listed performers, connections must be hoping he has been saving up his talent for the future.

Spirit's Awakening

82 **61**
2-y-o b c Danzig Connection (USA)-Mo Stopher (Sharpo)
J Akehurst Canisbay Bloodstock Ltd

Placings:0503 (5521)
2001: 5⁰GS, 5⁵GF, 8⁰GS, 6³HY

	Starts	1st	2nd	3rd	Win & Pl
Career Total (Turf)	4	0	0	1	590

Going (Turf): Sf: 0-1 GS: 0-2 Gd: 0-0 GF: 0-1 Fm: 0-0
Distance: 5f/6f: 0-3 7f-8f: 0-1 9f-13f: 0-0 14f+: 0-0
Track : LH: 0-0 RH: 0-1 Tight: 0-0 Gall: 0-1
Aids: Bl: 0-0 Vi: 0-0 Tstrap: 0-0
Best Rating: 61 5/01 Newb 5f34y gd-fm

Still a maiden, but has shown enough ability to suggest there is a race to be won with him.

Splash Out Again

98 **64**
3-y-o b g River Falls-Kajetana (FR) (Caro)
R J O'Sullivan M T Bevan

Placings:0000023 (5591)
2001: 10⁰GF, 8⁰GF, 8⁰GF, 12⁰GS, 9⁰GF, 11²G, 9³GS

	Starts	1st	2nd	3rd	Win & Pl
Career Total (Turf)	7	0	1	1	2179

Going (Turf): Sf: 0-0 GS: 0-2 Gd: 0-1 GF: 0-4 Fm: 0-0
Distance: 5f/6f: 0-0 7f-8f: 0-1 9f-13f: 0-6 14f+: 0-0
Track : LH: 0-1 RH: 0-3 Tight: 0-3 Gall: 0-1
Aids: Bl: 0-0 Vi: 0-0 Tstrap: 0-0
Best Rating: 66 6/01 Wind 1m2f7y gd-fm

Yet to win a race, suited by good ground and 11 furlongs.

Splendid Rose

99 **78**
2-y-o b f Prince Sabo-Little Emmeline (Emarati (USA))
R M Beckett Pedro Rosas

Placings:0223210 (3883)
2001: 5⁰G, 6²GF, 5²GF, 5³G, 5²F, 6¹F, 6⁰G

	Starts	1st	2nd	3rd	Win & Pl
Career Total (Turf)	7	1	3	1	6198

67	7/01	Rdcr	6f	E	FRM	£2922

Total win prize-money £2923

Going (Turf): Sf: 0-0 GS: 0-0 Gd: 0-3 GF: 0-2 **Fm: 1-2**
Distance: **5f/6f: 1-7** 7f-8f: 0-0 9f-13f: 0-0 14f+: 0-0
Track : LH: 0-2 RH: 0-1 Tight: 0-0 Gall: 0-2
Aids: Bl: 0-0 Vi: 0-0 Tstrap: 0-0
Best Rating: 78 7/01 Brig 5f213y firm

Bred for speed, she broke her duck at the sixth time of asking in a six-furlong maiden auction at Redcar in July 2001 on firm ground.

Split The Aces (IRE)

75 (10)**6**
5-y-o gr g Balla Cove-Hazy Lady (Habitat)
R J Hodges R J Hodges

Placings:4000/203100000/00550000-00 (4182)
2001: 5⁰GF, 6⁰GF

	Starts	1st	2nd	3rd	Win & Pl
Career Total (Turf)	22	1	1	1	3439
Career Total (AW)	1	0	0	0	

61	5/99	Bath	5f11y	F	GD	£2332

Total win prize-money £2332

Going (Turf): Sf: 0-5 GS: 0-3 **Gd: 1-2** GF: 0-8 Fm: 0-4
Distance: **5f/6f: 1-15** 7f-8f: 0-7 9f-13f: 0-1 14f+: 0-0
Track : **LH: 1-13** RH: 0-0 Tight: 0-2 **Gall: 1-9**
Aids: Bl: 0-2 Vi: 0-0 Tstrap: 0-0
Best Rating: 61 5/99 Bath 5f11y G

Splodger Mac (IRE)

72 **29**
2-y-o b c Lahib (USA)-Little Love (Warrshan (USA))
N Bycroft N Bycroft

Placings:0 (5227)
2001: 6⁰S

	Starts	1st	2nd	3rd	Win & Pl
Career Total (Turf)	1	0	0	0	

Going (Turf): Sf: 0-1 GS: 0-0 Gd: 0-0 GF: 0-0 Fm: 0-0

Distance: 5f/6f: 0-0 7f-8f: 0-1 9f-13f: 0-0 14f+: 0-0
Track : LH: 0-1 RH: 0-0 Tight: 0-0 Gall: 0-1
Aids: Bl: 0-0 Vi: 0-0 Tstrap: 0-0
Best Rating: 29 10/01 York 6f214y soft

Sporting Gesture

109 **76**
4-y-o ch g Safawan-Polly Packer (Reform)
M W Easterby Steve Hull

Placings:0566010/000161000-0000011143005 **(5632)**
2001: 9^0HY, 8^0HY, 10^0S, 8^0GF, 10^0GF, 9^1GF, 12^1F, 12^1GF, 11^4G, 12^3G, 12^0GF, 10^0G, 10^5G

	Starts	1st	2nd	3rd	Win & Pl
Career Total (Turf)	29	6	0	1	40719

66	8/01	Pont	1m4f8y	C(0-100)H	G-F	£7117
56	8/01	Thsk	1m4f	D(0-80)H	FRM	£4264
57	7/01	Nott	1m1f213y	E(0-70)H	G-F	£3682
73	8/00	Ches	1m2f75y	C(0-90)H	GD	£7085
69	7/00	York	7f202y	D(0-85)H	GD	£11017
73	9/99	Catt	7f	E(0-75)H	G-F	£3072

Total win prize-money £36240

Going (Turf): Sf: 0-5 GS: 0-2 Gd: 2-10 **GF: 3-10** Fm: 1-2
Distance: 5f/6f: 0-4 7f-8f: 2-7 **9f-13f: 4-18** 14f+: 0-0
Track : **LH: 6-20** RH: 0-6 **Tight: 3-9** Gall: 1-8
Aids: Bl: 0-0 Vi: 0-0 Tstrap: 0-0
Best Rating: 76 9/01 Donc 1m4f good

A fair handicapper, he scored twice in 2000 and had fallen down the handicap before winning at Nottingham in July. Went on to complete the hat trick at Thirsk and Pontefract and has continued to run well despite climbing back up the ratings. Suited by fast ground and middle distances.

Sporting Ladder (USA)

(104) (76)**79**
4-y-o b f Danzig (USA)-Lydara (USA) (Alydar (USA))
P F I Cole M Arbib

Placings:4040-11 **(0658)**
2001: 7^1SD, 7^1SD

	Starts	1st	2nd	3rd	Win & Pl
Career Total (Turf)	3	0	0	0	268
Career Total (AW)	3	2	0	0	6539

76	4/01	Sthl	7f	E(0-75)H	STD	£2772
68	3/01	Sthl	7f	D(0-80)H	STD	£3766

Total win prize-money £6539

Going (Turf): Sf: 0-1 GS: 0-1 Gd: 0-0 **GF: 0-1 Fm: 0-0**
Distance: 5f/6f: 0-1 **7f-8f: 2-2** 9f-13f: 0-3 14f+: 0-0
Track : **LH: 2-5** RH: 0-1 Tight: 0-1 Gall: 0-0
Aids: Bl: 0-0 Vi: 0-0 Tstrap: 0-0
Best Rating: 76 4/01 Sthl 7f stand

Sports Express

102(87) (51)**51**
3-y-o ch f Then Again-Lady St Lawrence (USA) (Bering)
G A Swinbank (W W Haigh 22/1) Tim Hawkins

Placings:44554-040 **(2639)**
2001: 8^0SW, 9^4G, 12^0GF

	Starts	1st	2nd	3rd	Win & Pl
Career Total (Turf)	5	0	0	0	0
Career Total (AW)	3	0	0	0	0

Going (Turf): Sf: 0-0 GS: 0-0 Gd: 0-1 **GF: 0-4 Fm: 0-0**
Distance: 5f/6f: 0-1 7f-8f: 0-5 9f-13f: 0-2 14f+: 0-0
Track : LH: 0-6 RH: 0-1 Tight: 0-3 Gall: 0-0
Aids: Bl: 0-0 Vi: 0-0 Tstrap: 0-0
Best Rating: 36 6/01 Haml 1m1f36y good

Sportsdaysstroller (IRE)

86(78) (18)**36**
3-y-o b f Definite Article-Morning Stroll (Tower Walk)
C N Allen Sportsdays.Co.Uk

Placings:000 **(5395)**
2001: 7^0GF, 5^0F, 7^0SD

	Starts	1st	2nd	3rd	Win & Pl
Career Total (Turf)	2	0	0	0	
Career Total (AW)	1	0	0	0	

Going (Turf): Sf: 0-0 GS: 0-0 Gd: 0-0 GF: 0-1 Fm: 0-1
Distance: 5f/6f: 0-1 7f-8f: 0-2 9f-13f: 0-0 14f+: 0-0
Track : LH: 0-2 RH: 0-0 Tight: 0-1 Gall: 0-1
Aids: Bl: 0-0 Vi: 0-0 Tstrap: 0-0
Best Rating: 36 8/01 NmkJ 7f gd-fm

Spot

93(98) (34)**38**
4-y-o gr f Inchinor-Billie Grey (Chilibang)
Andrew Reid A S Reid

Placings:034000-004000600040 **(5625)**
2001: 6^0SD, 8^0SD, 8^4SD, 9^0SD, 8^0SD, 6^0G, 5^6GF, 5^0F, 5^0GF, 8^0GS, 6^4G, 8^0GS

	Starts	1st	2nd	3rd	Win & Pl
Career Total (Turf)	10	0	0	1	565
Career Total (AW)	8	0	0	0	745

Going (Turf): Sf: 0-0 GS: 0-2 Gd: 0-3 GF: 0-3 Fm: 0-2
Distance: 5f/6f: 0-6 7f-8f: 0-6 9f-13f: 0-6 14f+: 0-0
Track : LH: 0-14 RH: 0-0 Tight: 0-8 Gall: 0-0
Aids: Bl: 0-0 Vi: 0-1 Tstrap: 0-3
Best Rating: 52 2/01 Wolv 1m100y stand

Spree Dance

78 **63**
2-y-o ch f Dancing Spree (USA)-Irene's Charter (Persian Bold)
J G Given D Bass

Placings:060 **(5606)**
2001: 8^0G, 8^6HY, 10^0GS

	Starts	1st	2nd	3rd	Win & Pl
Career Total (Turf)	3	0	0	0	0

Going (Turf): Sf: 0-1 GS: 0-1 Gd: 0-1 GF: 0-0 Fm: 0-0
Distance: 5f/6f: 0-0 7f-8f: 0-1 9f-13f: 0-2 14f+: 0-0
Track : LH: 0-1 RH: 0-1 Tight: 0-0 Gall: 0-0
Aids: Bl: 0-0 Vi: 0-0 Tstrap: 0-0
Best Rating: 63 9/01 NmkR 1m good

A half-sister to Smarter Charter, has shown a little ability in maidens.

Spree Love

94(89) (59)**46**
3-y-o b f Dancing Spree (USA)-Locorotondo (IRE) (Broken Hearted)
A G Newcombe D Bass

Placings:2450-00460 **(3749)**
2001: 8^0SW, 7^0GF, 7^4GF, 8^6F, 8^0GS

	Starts	1st	2nd	3rd	Win & Pl
Career Total (Turf)	6	0	0	0	840
Career Total (AW)	3	0	1	0	644

Going (Turf): Sf: 0-0 GS: 0-1 Gd: 0-1 GF: 0-3 Fm: 0-1
Distance: 5f/6f: 0-2 7f-8f: 0-6 9f-13f: 0-1 14f+: 0-0
Track : LH: 0-5 RH: 0-2 Tight: 0-2 Gall: 0-0
Aids: Bl: 0-0 Vi: 0-0 Tstrap: 0-0
Best Rating: 46 6/01 Gdwd 7f gd-fm

Spree Vision

105 **52**
5-y-o b g Suave Dancer (USA)-Regent's Folly (IRE) (Touching Wood (USA))
P Monteith I Bell

Placings:041/602056000/0004516500230-0440043112033 **(5448)**
2001: 12^0GS, 13^4G, 12^4F, 13^0G, 10^0GF, 12^4GF, 10^3GS, 9^1GS, 11^1GS, 9^2G, 10^0G, 10^3HY, 10^3HY

	Starts	1st	2nd	3rd	Win & Pl
Career Total (Turf)	38	4	3	4	21827

52	8/01	Haml	1m3f16y	D(0-80)H	G-S	£4309
46	8/01	Ayr	1m1f20y	E(0-70)H	G-S	£3622
55	6/00	Haml	1m4f17y	E(0-75)H	GD	£5447
82	10/98	Newc	1m3y	E	SFT	£2717

Total win prize-money £16097

Going (Turf): Sf: 1-9 **GS: 2-11** Gd: 1-10 GF: 0-6 Fm: 0-2
Distance: 5f/6f: 0-0 7f-8f: 0-2 **9f-13f: 4-29** 14f+: 0-7
Track : LH: 0-18 **RH: 2-16 Tight: 2-14** Gall: 0-9
Aids: Bl: 0-0 Vi: 0-2 Tstrap: 0-0
Best Rating: 54 5/01 Haml 1m5f9y good

A fair handicapper at around ten furlongs. Acts on an easy surface.

Spring Pursuit

106(92) (62)**66**
5-y-o b g Rudimentary (USA)-Pursuit Of Truth (USA) (Irish River (FR))
R J Price E G Bevan

Placings:0100/0034500302011162/60213005000330-631330040000250 **(5692)**
2001: 14^6HY, 12^3S, 12^1S, 12^3GS, 12^3S, 14^0GF, 14^0G, 12^4GF, 12^0G, 12^0G, 12^0G, 11^0S, 11^2S, 12^5HY, 16^0S

	Starts	1st	2nd	3rd	Win & Pl
Career Total (Turf)	49	7	4	8	68877
Career Total (AW)	1	0	0	0	157

84	4/01	Epsm	1m4f10y	C(0-95)H	SFT	£11505
87	4/00	Hayd	1m3f200y	C(0-100)H	HVY	£7442
75	10/99	Ling	1m2f	E(0-75)H	G-F	£7262
73	10/99	Wind	1m2f7y	D(0-80)H	G-S	£4364
65	10/99	York	1m205y	D(0-80)H	SFT	£16035
59	9/99	Brig	1m1f209y	F(0-60)H	SFT	£2505
85	6/98	Wwck	6f	E	GD	£3330

Total win prize-money £52446

Going (Turf): Sf: 4-16 GS: 1-8 Gd: 1-13 GF: 1-10 Fm: 0-2
Distance: 5f/6f: 1-2 7f-8f: 0-9 **9f-13f: 6-33** 14f+: 0-6
Track : **LH: 6-29** RH: 0-11 **Tight: 3-8** Gall: 1-15
Aids: Bl: 0-1 Vi: 0-0 Tstrap: 0-0
Best Rating: 84 5/01 Newb 1m4f5y soft

He is a very able handicapper with give underfoot and was successful in Epsom's Great Metropolitan in April, but had shown little until finishing second at Brighton in October. Nothing like so good on fast ground, he is best over 12 furlongs.

Spring Song

75 **41**
4-y-o b f Petong-Naturally Fresh (Thatching)
M E Sowersby Mrs Jean W Robinson

Placings:05050500/0 **(4268)**
2001: 9^0GF

	Starts	1st	2nd	3rd	Win & Pl
Career Total (Turf)	9	0	0	0	0

Going (Turf): Sf: 0-1 GS: 0-1 Gd: 0-3 GF: 0-4 Fm: 0-0
Distance: 5f/6f: 0-3 7f-8f: 0-3 9f-13f: 0-3 14f+: 0-0
Track : LH: 0-2 RH: 0-4 Tight: 0-2 Gall: 0-0
Aids: Bl: 0-0 Vi: 0-2 Tstrap: 0-0
Best Rating: 3 8/01 Bevl 1m1f207y gd-fm

Spring Symphony (IRE)

104 **88+**
3-y-o b f Darshaan-Well Head (IRE) (Sadler's Wells (USA))
Sir Michael Stoute Lord Weinstock

Placings:0-12 **(2028)**
2001: 11^1GF, 12^2GF

	Starts	1st	2nd	3rd	Win & Pl
Career Total (Turf)	3	1	1	0	5899

80	5/01	Hayd	1m3f200yD		G-F	£4173

Total win prize-money £4173

Going (Turf): Sf: 0-0 GS: 0-0 Gd: 0-1 **GF: 1-2** Fm: 0-0
Distance: 5f/6f: 0-0 7f-8f: 0-1 **9f-13f: 1-2** 14f+: 0-0
Track : **LH: 1-2** RH: 0-1 Tight: 0-1 Gall: 0-1
Aids: Bl: 0-0 Vi: 0-0 Tstrap: 0-0
Best Rating: 88 6/01 Ripn 1m4f60y gd-fm

Springtime Lady

94(102) (52)**59**

5-y-o ch m Desert Dirham (USA)-Affaire De Coeur (Imperial Fling (USA))
J G M O'Shea Graham Brown

Placings:002500405**220**/**223**036-006 **(1368)**
2001: 7^0SD, 11^0GS, 11^6G

	Starts	1st	2nd	3rd	Win & Pl
Career Total (Turf)	13	0	1	1	1991
Career Total (AW)	8	0	4	1	3533

Going (Turf): Sf: 0-0 GS: 0-1 Gd: 0-7 GF: 0-4 Fm: 0-1
Distance: 5f/6f: 0-3 7f-8f: 0-10 9f-13f: 0-8 14f+: 0-0
Track : LH: 0-11 RH: 0-3 Tight: 0-11 Gall: 0-0
Aids: Bl: 0-0 Vi: 0-0 Tstrap: 0-0
Best Rating: 46 5/01 Bath 1m3f144y gd-sft

Springtime Sunray (IRE)

82 **53**

2-y-o ch f Gulch (USA)-Youm Jadeed (IRE) (Sadler's Wells (USA))
E A L Dunlop Maktoum Al Maktoum

Placings:30 **(5559)**
2001: 7^3GS, 8^0S

	Starts	1st	2nd	3rd	Win & Pl
Career Total (Turf)	2	0	0	1	0

Going (Turf): Sf: 0-1 GS: 0-1 Gd: 0-0 GF: 0-0 Fm: 0-0
Distance: 5f/6f: 0-0 7f-8f: 0-1 9f-13f: 0-1 14f+: 0-0
Track : LH: 0-0 RH: 0-0 Tight: 0-0 Gall: 0-0
Aids: Bl: 0-0 Vi: 0-0 Tstrap: 0-0
Best Rating: 53 10/01 Yarm 1m3y soft

Bred to stay, she could only stay on at the one pace when the leading pair kicked away in the final couple of furlongs on her debut in the Newmarket Challenge Cup. Has only raced on good to soft ground.

Springwood Jasmin (IRE)

77(80) (9)**39**

3-y-o b f Midhish-White Jasmin (Jalmood (USA))
D W Chapman The Springwood Syndicate

Placings:05600-00000 **(2054)**
2001: 5^0SD, 7^0SD, 8^0SD, 7^0F, 10^0GF

	Starts	1st	2nd	3rd	Win & Pl
Career Total (Turf)	7	0	0	0	0
Career Total (AW)	3	0	0	0	

Going (Turf): Sf: 0-1 GS: 0-1 Gd: 0-1 GF: 0-2 Fm: 0-2
Distance: 5f/6f: 0-3 7f-8f: 0-6 9f-13f: 0-1 14f+: 0-0
Track : LH: 0-4 RH: 0-0 Tight: 0-2 Gall: 0-0
Aids: Bl: 0-1 Vi: 0-0 Tstrap: 0-5
Best Rating: 14 5/01 Rdcr 7f firm

Spritzeria

96(90) (52)**80**

2-y-o b f Bigstone (IRE)-Clincher Club (Polish Patriot (USA))
W J Haggas Jolly Farmers Racing

Placings:120302 **(5467)**
2001: 6^1GF, 7^2GF, 7^0GF, 5^3GS, 6^0G, 6^2S, 7^0SD

	Starts	1st	2nd	3rd	Win & Pl
Career Total (Turf)	6	1	2	1	5821

84	6/01	Pont	6f	E	G-F	£3640

Total win prize-money £3640

Going (Turf): Sf: 0-1 GS: 0-1 Gd: 0-1 **GF: 1-3** Fm: 0-0
Distance: **5f/6f: 1-3** 7f-8f: 0-3 9f-13f: 0-0 14f+: 0-0
Track : **LH: 1-2** RH: 0-0 Tight: 0-0 Gall: 0-0
Aids: Bl: 0-0 Vi: 0-0 Tstrap: 0-0
Best Rating: 84 6/01 Pont 6f gd-fm

Made a winning debut at Pontefract, but her form deteriorated until a good run at Brighton in October. There are races to be won with her.

Spunkie

86 **70**

8-y-o ch g Jupiter Island-Super Sol (Rolfe (USA))
R F Johnson Houghton Jim Short

Placings:15613/500210/5-00 **(5387)**
2001: 16^0S, 18^0GS

	Starts	1st	2nd	3rd	Win & Pl		
Career Total (Turf)	14	3	1	1	45601		
87	9/99	Newb	2m	B(0-105)H		G-S	£10690
76	9/98	Asct	2m45y	C(0-95)H		GD	£14590
73	7/98	Sals	1m6f15y	D		GD	£3649

Total win prize-money £28929

Going (Turf): Sf: 0-2 GS: 1-2 **Gd: 2-7** GF: 0-3 Fm: 0-0
Distance: 5f/6f: 0-0 7f-8f: 0-0 9f-13f: 0-2 **14f+: 3-12**
Track : LH: 1-5 **RH: 2-9** Tight: 1-2 Gall: 1-9
Aids: Bl: 0-0 Vi: 0-0 Tstrap: 0-0
Best Rating: 58 9/01 Asct 2m45y soft

He was a fair stayer a couple of seasons ago, but has more recently been campaigned over hurdles.

Spur Of Gold (IRE)

72 **24**

3-y-o b f Flying Spur (AUS)-Tony's Ridge (Indian Ridge)
J S Wainwright Mrs Kay Harrison

Placings:660-00000 **(5271)**
2001: 9^0GS, 6^0F, 8^0GF, 6^0GF, 8^0HY

	Starts	1st	2nd	3rd	Win & Pl
Career Total (Turf)	8	0	0	0	0

Going (Turf): Sf: 0-2 GS: 0-2 Gd: 0-0 GF: 0-2 Fm: 0-2
Distance: 5f/6f: 0-4 7f-8f: 0-2 9f-13f: 0-2 14f+: 0-0
Track : LH: 0-2 RH: 0-1 Tight: 0-0 Gall: 0-1
Aids: Bl: 0-0 Vi: 0-0 Tstrap: 0-0
Best Rating: 24 5/01 Rdcr 6f firm

Spy Knoll

96 **53**

7-y-o b g Shirley Heights-Garden Pink (FR) (Bellypha)
Jamie Poulton M K George

Placings:64/03332401/200/5-06 **(5492)**
2001: 13^0GS, 16^0HY

	Starts	1st	2nd	3rd	Win & Pl		
Career Total (Turf)	16	1	2	3	10536		
83	9/97	Ches	1m5f89y	D		GD	£3798

Total win prize-money £3799

Going (Turf): Sf: 0-3 GS: 0-3 **Gd: 1-3** GF: 0-7 Fm: 0-0
Distance: 5f/6f: 0-1 7f-8f: 0-1 9f-13f: 0-5 **14f+: 1-10**
Track : **LH: 1-6** RH: 0-8 **Tight: 1-7** Gall: 0-4
Aids: Bl: 0-0 Vi: 0-1 Tstrap: 0-0
Best Rating: 53 10/01 Newb 2m heavy

Spy Master

88 **53**

3-y-o b c Green Desert (USA)-Obsessive (USA) (Seeking The Gold (USA))
Miss J F Craze (M Brittain 24/3) K Silvester And Mr B Silvester

Placings:023413-00000 **(4965)**

2001: 7^0S, 6^0G, 6^0G, 5^0GS, 5^0S

	Starts	1st	2nd	3rd	Win & Pl		
Career Total (Turf)	11	1	1	2	9080		
72	9/00	Catt	5f212y	D		SFT	£3068

Total win prize-money £3068

Going (Turf): **Sf: 1-4** GS: 0-1 Gd: 0-4 GF: 0-2 Fm: 0-0
Distance: **5f/6f: 1-6** 7f-8f: 0-5 9f-13f: 0-0 14f+: 0-0
Track : **LH: 1-5** RH: 0-0 **Tight: 1-3** Gall: 0-0
Aids: Bl: 0-3 **Vi: 1-4** Tstrap: 0-1
Best Rating: 53 8/01 Ripn 6f good

Square Dancer

102(97) (67)**54**

5-y-o b g Then Again-Cubist (IRE) (Tate Gallery (USA))
M Dods A Mallen

Placings:54000/0435212200100/000054026055060135 0-030004000 **(4159)**
2001: 6^0G, 6^3F, 6^0F, 6^0GS, 6^0GF, 6^4G, 6^0GF, 6^0G, 6^0GF

	Starts	1st	2nd	3rd	Win & Pl		
Career Total (Turf)	43	3	4	2	14318		
Career Total (AW)	3	0	0	1	362		
58	10/00	Wind	6f	F(0-60)H		G-S	£1869
70	8/99	Brig	5f213y	E(0-70)		SFT	£2684
71	6/99	Carl	5f207y	E		G-F	£2885

Total win prize-money £7438

Going (Turf): **Sf: 1-3 GS: 1-4** Gd: 0-11 **GF: 1-19** Fm: 0-6
Distance: **5f/6f: 3-28** 7f-8f: 0-17 9f-13f: 0-1 14f+: 0-0
Track : LH: 1-16 **RH: 2-6** Tight: 0-3 **Gall: 2-6**
Aids: Bl: 0-0 Vi: 0-1 Tstrap: 0-0
Best Rating: 63 5/01 Brig 6f209y firm

He has ability, but also has a poor wins-to-runs ratio. Best over six furlongs and needs everything to go right.

Squibnocket (IRE)

87 **46**

2-y-o b c Charnwood Forest (IRE)-Serenad Dancer (FR) (Antheus (USA))
T D Easterby D J Power

Placings:0 **(2264)**
2001: 7^0C

	Starts	1st	2nd	3rd	Win & Pl
Career Total (Turf)	1	0	0	0	

Going (Turf): Sf: 0-0 GS: 0-0 Gd: 0-1 GF: 0-0 Fm: 0-0
Distance: 5f/6f: 0-0 7f-8f: 0-1 9f-13f: 0-0 14f+: 0-0
Track : LH: 0-1 RH: 0-0 Tight: 0-1 Gall: 0-0
Aids: Bl: 0-0 Vi: 0-0 Tstrap: 0-0
Best Rating: 46 6/01 Thsk 7f good

Squire Tat (IRE)

92 **38**

3-y-o b g Lake Coniston (IRE)-Classic Dilemma (Sandhurst Prince)
B S Rothwell (R A Fahey 24/4) J H Tattersall

Placings:50-00000 **(3752)**
2001: 5^0GS, 9^0G, 8^0GF, 6^0GF, 7^0GS

	Starts	1st	2nd	3rd	Win & Pl
Career Total (Turf)	7	0	0	0	0

Going (Turf): Sf: 0-0 GS: 0-2 Gd: 0-2 GF: 0-2 Fm: 0-1
Distance: 5f/6f: 0-4 7f-8f: 0-2 9f-13f: 0-1 14f+: 0-0
Track : LH: 0-3 RH: 0-0 Tight: 0-0 Gall: 0-1
Aids: Bl: 0-0 Vi: 0-0 Tstrap: 0-0
Best Rating: 38 6/01 Newc 1m gd-fm

Squirrel Nutkin (IRE)

96(105) (54d)**49**

3-y-o gr g Bluebird (USA)-Saltoki (Ballad Rock)
Jedd O'Keeffe (B W Hills 26/2) The Squirrel Fanclub Partnership

Placings:224-24300006000 (4466)
2001: 6^{2}SD, 7^{4}SD, 6^{3}SD, 5^{0}SW, 5^{0}GF, 6^{0}GF, 5^{0}GF, 6^{6}GF, 7^{0}G, 7^{0}GF, 5^{0}G

	Starts	1st	2nd	3rd	Win & Pl
Career Total (Turf)	10	0	2	0	2235
Career Total (AW)	4	0	1	1	1236

Going (Turf): Sf: 0-1 GS: 0-0 Gd: 0-4 GF: 0-5 Fm: 0-0
Distance: 5f/6f: 0-11 7f-8f: 0-3 9f-13f: 0-0 14f+: 0-0
Track : LH: 0-3 RH: 0-0 Tight: 0-3 Gall: 0-0
Aids: Bl: 0-2 Vi: 0-0 Tstrap: 0-0
Best Rating: 66 1/01 Wolv 6f stand

Sri Ganesha (IRE)

93(86) (55)**41**
2-y-o b f Sri Pekan (USA)-Sarabi (Alzao (USA))
P Mitchell Mrs Carol Williamson

Placings:0450 (4411)
2001: 5^{0}G, 5^{4}SD, 6^{5}SD, 6^{0}GS

	Starts	1st	2nd	3rd	Win & Pl
Career Total (Turf)	2	0	0	0	
Career Total (AW)	2	0	0	0	825

Going (Turf): Sf: 0-0 GS: 0-1 Gd: 0-1 GF: 0-0 Fm: 0-0
Distance: 5f/6f: 0-4 7f-8f: 0-0 9f-13f: 0-0 14f+: 0-0
Track : LH: 0-3 RH: 0-0 Tight: 0-2 Gall: 0-1
Aids: Bl: 0-0 Vi: 0-0 Tstrap: 0-0
Best Rating: 55 8/01 Wolv 6f stand

St Expedit

113 **117**
4-y-o b c Sadler's Wells (USA)-Miss Rinjani (Shirley Heights)
G Wragg J L C Pearce

Placings:3/20120306-4120 (2883)
2001: 12^{4}GS, 13^{1}GF, 12^{2}G, 12^{0}GS

	Starts	1st	2nd	3rd	Win & Pl		
Career Total (Turf)	13	2	3	2	79039		
112	5/01	Ches	1m5f89y	A		G-F	£45000
89	5/00	Pont	1m2f6y	D		SFT	£7085

Total win prize-money £52085

Going (Turf): Sf: 1-1 GS: 0-5 Gd: 0-4 **GF: 1-3** Fm: 0-0
Distance: 5f/6f: 0-0 7f-8f: 0-1 9f-13f: 1-11 14f+: 1-1
Track : **LH: 2-6** RH: 0-4 **Tight: 1-4** Gall: 0-2
Aids: Bl: 0-0 Vi: 0-0 Tstrap: 0-0
Best Rating: 117 6/01 Chan 1m4f good

Effective at a mile and a half, he was an useful three-year-old, if overfaced at times. Ran respectably, despite pulling hard, on his return at Newbury, but bolted up in the Ormonde Stakes at Chester next time when allowed his own way out in front. Fine effort subsequently when only narrowly beaten by Egyptband in the Grand Prix de Chantilly. Below par at Newmarket on his next start. Seems to handle soft and fast ground and should stay 14 furlongs.

St George's Boy

88(85) (24)**18**
4-y-o b g Inchinor-Deanta In Eirinn (Red Sunset)
M A Barnes (H Morrison 27/6) Thirdtimelucky

Placings:000/6002450-000 (2518)
2001: 11^{0}GS, 11^{0}GF, 16^{0}F

	Starts	1st	2nd	3rd	Win & Pl
Career Total (Turf)	9	0	1	0	675
Career Total (AW)	4	0	0	0	0

Going (Turf): Sf: 0-1 GS: 0-2 Gd: 0-1 GF: 0-2 Fm: 0-3
Distance: 5f/6f: 0-0 7f-8f: 0-4 9f-13f: 0-6 14f+: 0-3
Track : LH: 0-9 RH: 0-1 Tight: 0-7 Gall: 0-0
Aids: Bl: 0-0 Vi: 0-2 Tstrap: 0-0
Best Rating: 15 5/01 Brig 1m3f196y gd-sft

St Helensfield

97(95) (61)**69**
6-y-o ch g Kris-On Credit (FR) (No Pass No Sale)
M C Pipe Paul Dean

Placings:123/4/06103004/03032201102-00 (5387)
2001: 12^{0}G, 18^{0}GS

	Starts	1st	2nd	3rd	Win & Pl		
Career Total (Turf)	24	4	4	4	32661		
Career Total (AW)	1	0	0	0			
92	7/00	Newc	1m6f97y	D(0-85)H		FRM	£4532
85	7/00	Ripn	1m4f60y	D(0-85)H		G-F	£6786
86	7/99	Newc	1m2f32y	D(0-85)H		FRM	£3793
86	9/97	Bath	1m2f46y	D		G-F	£3291

Total win prize-money £18404

Going (Turf): Sf: 0-3 GS: 0-6 Gd: 0-4 **GF: 2-9 Fm: 2-2**
Distance: 5f/6f: 0-0 7f-8f: 0-0 **9f-13f: 3-20** 14f+: 1-5
Track : **LH: 3-11** RH: 1-13 Tight: 2-9 Gall: 2-10
Aids: Bl: 0-0 Vi: 0-1 Tstrap: 0-0
Best Rating: 69 10/01 NmkR 2m2f gd-sft

A winner twice on fast ground in 2000, he was ultimately well held on his belated return in September.

St Kristopher

80 **57**
2-y-o ch g Kris-Enlisted (IRE) (Sadler's Wells (USA))
W J Musson The Verulam Partnership

Placings:00 (5684)
2001: 7^{0}GS, 8^{0}S

	Starts	1st	2nd	3rd	Win & Pl
Career Total (Turf)	2	0	0	0	

Going (Turf): Sf: 0-1 GS: 0-1 Gd: 0-0 GF: 0-0 Fm: 0-0
Distance: 5f/6f: 0-0 7f-8f: 0-2 9f-13f: 0-0 14f+: 0-0
Track : LH: 0-0 RH: 0-0 Tight: 0-0 Gall: 0-0
Aids: Bl: 0-0 Vi: 0-0 Tstrap: 0-0
Best Rating: 57 11/01 Donc 1m soft

St Matthew (USA)

103 **79**
3-y-o b c Lear Fan (USA)-Social Crown (USA) (Chief's Crown (USA))
J W Hills George Tong

Placings:0-1040304 (5114)
2001: 8^{1}S, 10^{0}GF, 12^{4}GF, 14^{0}G, 14^{3}G, 15^{0}G, 16^{4}HY

	Starts	1st	2nd	3rd	Win & Pl		
Career Total (Turf)	8	1	0	1	4860		
68	4/01	Nott	1m54y	D		SFT	£3510

Total win prize-money £3510

Going (Turf): Sf: 1-3 GS: 0-0 Gd: 0-3 GF: 0-2 Fm: 0-0
Distance: 5f/6f: 0-0 7f-8f: 0-1 **9f-13f: 1-3** 14f+: 0-4
Track : **LH: 1-5** RH: 0-2 Tight: 0-1 Gall: 0-1
Aids: Bl: 0-0 Vi: 0-0 Tstrap: 0-0
Best Rating: 79 8/01 Nott 1m6f15y good

Won on reappearance at three over a mile. Ran well over fourteen furlongs in August 2001 but was beaten by some speedier rivals. Has won on soft ground. Handles fast ground.

St Nicholas

71(86) (25)**46**
3-y-o b g Komaite (USA)-Nikoola Eve (Roscoe Blake)
D Shaw D C G Cooper

Placings:00050-040 (2324)
2001: 6^{0}GF, 8^{4}SD, 9^{0}SD

	Starts	1st	2nd	3rd	Win & Pl
Career Total (Turf)	5	0	0	0	0
Career Total (AW)	3	0	0	0	0

Going (Turf): Sf: 0-1 GS: 0-0 Gd: 0-2 GF: 0-1 Fm: 0-0
Distance: 5f/6f: 0-3 7f-8f: 0-3 9f-13f: 0-1 14f+: 0-0
Track : LH: 0-5 RH: 0-0 Tight: 0-2 Gall: 0-1
Aids: Bl: 0-0 Vi: 0-2 Tstrap: 0-0
Best Rating: 25 6/01 Sthl 1m stand

St Pacokise (IRE)

100(70) **44**
4-y-o b f Brief Truce (USA)-Classic Opera (Lomond (USA))
R J Smith Silent Running Syndicate

Placings:504/0050-330040 (3805)
2001: 7^{3}GF, 7^{3}GF, 8^{0}SD, 8^{0}F, 7^{4}GF, 7^{0}GF

	Starts	1st	2nd	3rd	Win & Pl
Career Total (Turf)	12	0	0	2	1045
Career Total (AW)	1	0	0	0	

Going (Turf): Sf: 0-1 GS: 0-0 Gd: 0-2 GF: 0-7 Fm: 0-2
Distance: 5f/6f: 0-2 7f-8f: 0-9 9f-13f: 0-2 14f+: 0-0
Track : LH: 0-7 RH: 0-1 Tight: 0-2 Gall: 0-0
Aids: Bl: 0-0 Vi: 0-0 Tstrap: 0-0
Best Rating: 44 8/01 Wwck 7f26y gd-fm

St Palais

63 **16**
2-y-o b f Timeless Times (USA)-Crambella (IRE) (Red Sunset)
A Smith Mrs Sheila Oakes

Placings:000 (5168)
2001: 6^{0}G, 5^{0}GF, 10^{0}GS

	Starts	1st	2nd	3rd	Win & Pl
Career Total (Turf)	3	0	0	0	

Going (Turf): Sf: 0-0 GS: 0-1 Gd: 0-1 GF: 0-1 Fm: 0-0
Distance: 5f/6f: 0-2 7f-8f: 0-0 9f-13f: 0-1 14f+: 0-0
Track : LH: 0-2 RH: 0-0 Tight: 0-0 Gall: 0-0
Aids: Bl: 0-0 Vi: 0-0 Tstrap: 0-0
Best Rating: 16 8/01 Newc 6f good

St Rose Of Lima

93(90) (64)**54**
2-y-o ch f Dr Devious (IRE)-Mayfair (Green Desert (USA))
M R Channon M Channon

Placings:0 (5666)
2001: 6^{0}HY, 8^{6}SD

	Starts	1st	2nd	3rd	Win & Pl
Career Total (Turf)	1	0	0	0	

Going (Turf): Sf: 0-1 GS: 0-0 Gd: 0-0 GF: 0-0 Fm: 0-0
Distance: 5f/6f: 0-1 7f-8f: 0-0 9f-13f: 0-0 14f+: 0-0
Track : LH: 0-0 RH: 0-0 Tight: 0-0 Gall: 0-0
Aids: Bl: 0-0 Vi: 0-0 Tstrap: 0-0
Best Rating: 54 11/01 Wind 6f heavy

Moderate ability shown so far.

Stafford King (IRE)

(95) (44)
4-y-o b c Nicolotte-Opening Day (Day Is Done)
J G M O'Shea The Stafford Syndicate

Placings:00/0420006400-40306000 (5617)
2001: 13^{4}SW, 11^{0}SD, 12^{3}SD, 14^{0}S, 11^{6}GF, 11^{0}GF, 12^{0}S, 8^{0}SD, 12^{0}SD

	Starts	1st	2nd	3rd	Win & Pl
Career Total (Turf)	16	0	1	0	1190
Career Total (AW)	4	0	0	1	470

Going (Turf): Sf: 0-5 GS: 0-3 Gd: 0-4 GF: 0-4 Fm: 0-0
Distance: 5f/6f: 0-1 7f-8f: 0-2 9f-13f: 0-16 14f+: 0-1
Track : LH: 0-11 RH: 0-4 Tight: 0-10 Gall: 0-1
Aids: Bl: 0-0 Vi: 0-2 Tstrap: 0-0

Best Rating: 44 2/01 Ling 1m5f slow

Stafford Prince

(68) (6)
4-y-o br c Bin Ajwaad (IRE)-Petonellajill (Petong)
J G M O'Shea The Stafford Syndicate

Placings:00600/000-0 **(4210)**
2001: 11^{0}GF

	Starts	1st	2nd	3rd	Win & Pl
Career Total (Turf)	7	0	0	0	0
Career Total (AW)	2	0	0	0	

Going (Turf): Sf: 0-0 GS: 0-2 Gd: 0-0 GF: 0-5 Fm: 0-0
Distance: 5f/6f: 0-2 7f-8f: 0-3 9f-13f: 0-4 14f+: 0-0
Track : LH: 0-6 RH: 0-1 Tight: 0-4 Gall: 0-3
Aids: Bl: 0-0 Vi: 0-2 Tstrap: 0-0

Well bred, he made a promising debut at Yarmouth and will appreciate middle distances at three.

Stage By Stage (USA)

98 97
2-y-o ch c In The Wings-Lady Thynn (FR) (Crystal Glitters (USA))
M L W Bell Mrs Evelyn Hankinson

Placings:2215 **(5478a)**
2001: 7^{2}GS, 8^{2}G, 10^{1}G, 9^{5}HY

	Starts	1st	2nd	3rd	Win & Pl
Career Total (Turf)	4	1	2	0	8025

87 10/01 Bath 1m2f46y D GD £3513
Total win prize-money £3513

Going (Turf): Sf: 0-1 GS: 0-1 **Gd: 1-2** GF: 0-0 Fm: 0-0
Distance: 5f/6f: 0-0 7f-8f: 0-1 **9f-13f: 1-3** 14f+: 0-0
Track : **LH: 1-1** RH: 0-2 **Tight: 1-2** Gall: 0-0
Aids: Bl: 0-0 Vi: 0-0 Tstrap: 0-0
Best Rating: 97 10/01 Lonc 1m1f heavy

Impressive winner of a ten-furlong maiden at Bath.

Stage Presence (IRE)

105(100) (81)82
3-y-o ch f Selkirk (USA)-Park Charger (Tirol)
B W Hills R E Sangster

Placings:00-421640 **(5608)**
2001: 7^{4}GF, 7^{2}G, 6^{1}G, 7^{6}G, 7^{4}GS, 7^{0}GS, 10^{6}SD

	Starts	1st	2nd	3rd	Win & Pl
Career Total (Turf)	8	1	1	0	6717

68 8/01 Brig 6f209y D GD £2884
Total win prize-money £2884

Going (Turf): Sf: 0-0 GS: 0-3 **Gd: 1-3** GF: 0-2 Fm: 0-0
Distance: 5f/6f: 0-0 **7f-8f: 1-8** 9f-13f: 0-0 14f+: 0-0
Track : **LH: 1-2** RH: 0-0 Tight: 0-1 Gall: 0-0
Aids: Bl: 0-0 Vi: 0-0 Tstrap: 0-0
Best Rating: 82 10/01 Asct 7f gd-sft

She took time in getting off the mark and had a throat operation before getting off the mark in a weak maiden at Brighton in August. Ran her best race when fourth in a sub-standard Ascot listed race in October. Suited by seven furlongs, but has been known to spoil her chance by pulling hard.

Staging Post (USA)

109 99
3-y-o b c Pleasant Colony (USA)-Interim (Sadler's Wells (USA))
H R A Cecil K Abdulla

Placings:32-21221 **(4532)**
2001: 10^{2}S, 10^{1}GF, 10^{2}GS, 12^{2}GF, 11^{1}GF

	Starts	1st	2nd	3rd	Win & Pl
Career Total (Turf)	7	2	4	1	27794

99 9/01 York 1m3f195yB(0-105)H G-F £13972
80 6/01 Wind 1m2f7y D G-F £4634
Total win prize-money £18607

Going (Turf): Sf: 0-2 GS: 0-2 Gd: 0-0 **GF: 2-3** Fm: 0-0
Distance: 5f/6f: 0-0 7f-8f: 0-1 **9f-13f: 2-6** 14f+: 0-0
Track : **LH: 1-4** RH: 0-1 Tight: 1-1 Gall: 1-3
Aids: Bl: 0-0 Vi: 0-0 Tstrap: 0-0
Best Rating: 99 9/01 York 1m3f195y gd-fm

Improved for the step up to ten furlongs when second at Newbury, and broke his duck next time out on fast ground. Showed a tendency to carry his head at an awkward angle at Newmarket.

Stairwell

94 66
3-y-o b f Hernando (FR)-Sliprail (USA) (Our Native (USA))
H Candy Major M G Wyatt

Placings:5040 **(5464)**
2001: 10^{5}GF, 10^{0}G, 11^{4}G, 11^{0}G

	Starts	1st	2nd	3rd	Win & Pl
Career Total (Turf)	4	0	0	0	267

Going (Turf): Sf: 0-0 GS: 0-0 Gd: 0-3 GF: 0-1 Fm: 0-0
Distance: 5f/6f: 0-0 7f-8f: 0-0 9f-13f: 0-4 14f+: 0-0
Track : LH: 0-2 RH: 0-0 Tight: 0-4 Gall: 0-0
Aids: Bl: 0-0 Vi: 0-0 Tstrap: 0-0
Best Rating: 66 7/01 Wind 1m2f7y gd-fm

Stalky

85(85) (51)56
2-y-o ch f Bahamian Bounty-La Noisette (Rock Hopper)
J A Osborne The Woolfie And Tom Partnership

Placings:4006 **(3804)**
2001: 5^{4}SD, 7^{0}GF, 6^{0}GF, 6^{6}GF, 5^{5}SD

	Starts	1st	2nd	3rd	Win & Pl
Career Total (Turf)	3	0	0	0	0
Career Total (AW)	1	0	0	0	0

Going (Turf): Sf: 0-0 GS: 0-0 Gd: 0-0 GF: 0-3 Fm: 0-0
Distance: 5f/6f: 0-3 7f-8f: 0-1 9f-13f: 0-0 14f+: 0-0
Track : LH: 0-0 RH: 0-0 Tight: 0-0 Gall: 0-0
Aids: Bl: 0-0 Vi: 0-0 Tstrap: 0-0
Best Rating: 56 7/01 Ling 7f gd-fm

Stallone

104 75
4-y-o ch g Brief Truce (USA)-Bering Honneur (USA) (Bering)
D Nicholls Lucayan Stud

Placings:4551113-0050030050 **(5249)**
2001: 8^{0}HY, 10^{0}S, 8^{5}GF, 10^{0}GF, 10^{0}GF, 10^{3}GF, 10^{0}GF, 10^{0}GF, 9^{5}GF, 10^{5}S

	Starts	1st	2nd	3rd	Win & Pl
Career Total (Turf)	17	3	0	2	16276

81 7/00 Rdcr 1m2f D(0-80)H G-F £5027
79 7/00 Newc 1m E(0-75)H G-F £5343
74 6/00 Rdcr 1m1f E(0-75)H FRM £2968
Total win prize-money £13339

Going (Turf): Sf: 0-4 GS: 0-1 Gd: 0-2 **GF: 2-9** Fm: 1-1
Distance: 5f/6f: 0-0 7f-8f: 1-3 **9f-13f: 2-14** 14f+: 0-0
Track : **LH: 3-11** RH: 0-4 **Tight: 2-9** Gall: 1-4
Aids: Bl: 0-0 Vi: 0-0 Tstrap: 0-0
Best Rating: 78 6/01 Epsm 1m2f18y gd-fm

Improved considerably for encountering fast ground and handicap company in the middle of 2000, completing a hat-trick. Well beaten on unsuitably soft ground at the start of this season, has run better since the ground firmed up. Suited by at least a mile, and now back to a winning mark.

Stamford Hill

95 12
6-y-o ch g Jendali (USA)-Laxay (Laxton)
G P Kelly (M E Sowersby 6/7) A M McArdle

Placings:000560050000-0040005000000000 **(5683)**
2001: 10^{0}GF, 10^{0}GF, 10^{4}GF, 11^{0}GF, 10^{0}S, 10^{0}GF, 6^{5}GF, 8^{0}GF, 17^{0}GF, 11^{0}GF, 6^{0}HY, 10^{0}GF, 17^{0}F, 6^{0}GF, 11^{0}G, 14^{0}HY, 11^{0}S, 14^{0}S

	Starts	1st	2nd	3rd	Win & Pl
Career Total (Turf)	31	0	0	0	906

Going (Turf): Sf: 0-9 GS: 0-1 Gd: 0-2 GF: 0-16 Fm: 0-3
Distance: 5f/6f: 0-2 7f-8f: 0-5 9f-13f: 0-19 14f+: 0-5
Track : LH: 0-18 RH: 0-7 Tight: 0-8 Gall: 0-7
Aids: Bl: 0-0 Vi: 0-0 Tstrap: 0-0
Best Rating: 28 9/01 Donc 1m2f60y gd-fm

Poor middle-distance maiden on the Flat.

Stance

84 60
2-y-o b c Salse (USA)-De Stael (USA) (Nijinsky (CAN))
H R A Cecil K Abdulla

Placings:6 **(5620)**
2001: 8^{6}GS

	Starts	1st	2nd	3rd	Win & Pl
Career Total (Turf)	1	0	0	0	0

Going (Turf): Sf: 0-0 GS: 0-1 Gd: 0-0 GF: 0-0 Fm: 0-0
Distance: 5f/6f: 0-0 7f-8f: 0-0 9f-13f: 0-1 14f+: 0-0
Track : LH: 0-1 RH: 0-0 Tight: 0-0 Gall: 0-0
Aids: Bl: 0-0 Vi: 0-0 Tstrap: 0-0
Best Rating: 60 11/01 Nott 1m54y gd-sft

Stand And Stare (IRE)

87 48
2-y-o b g Vettori (IRE)-Premium Gift (Most Welcome)
M H Tompkins Www.Raceworld.Co.Uk

Placings:000530 **(5331)**
2001: 6^{0}GF, 7^{0}G, 7^{0}G, 6^{5}S, 6^{3}HY, 5^{0}HY

	Starts	1st	2nd	3rd	Win & Pl
Career Total (Turf)	6	0	0	1	426

Going (Turf): Sf: 0-3 GS: 0-0 Gd: 0-2 GF: 0-1 Fm: 0-0
Distance: 5f/6f: 0-3 7f-8f: 0-3 9f-13f: 0-0 14f+: 0-0
Track : LH: 0-0 RH: 0-0 Tight: 0-0 Gall: 0-0
Aids: Bl: 0-3 Vi: 0-0 Tstrap: 0-0
Best Rating: 48 10/01 Ling 6f heavy

Standiford Girl (IRE)

(98) (41)36
4-y-o b f Standiford (USA)-Pennine Girl (IRE) (Pennine Walk)
L A Dace Noel Monaghan

Placings:620003240-0 **(5046)**
2001: 11^{0}SD

	Starts	1st	2nd	3rd	Win & Pl
Career Total (Turf)	4	0	0	0	0
Career Total (AW)	6	0	2	1	1336

Going (Turf): Sf: 0-1 GS: 0-1 Gd: 0-0 GF: 0-2 Fm: 0-0
Distance: 5f/6f: 0-0 7f-8f: 0-4 9f-13f: 0-6 14f+: 0-0
Track : LH: 0-8 RH: 0-2 Tight: 0-3 Gall: 0-0
Aids: Bl: 0-0 Vi: 0-0 Tstrap: 0-0
Best Rating: 0 10/01 Sthl 1m3f stand

Stands To Reason (USA)

82 86
2-y-o b f Gulch (USA)-Sheer Reason (USA) (Danzig (USA))
B W Hills Maktoum Al Maktoum

Placings:2 (5110)
2001: 6^{2}HY

	Starts	1st	2nd	3rd	Win & Pl
Career Total (Turf)	1	0	1	0	1200

Going (Turf): Sf: 0-1 GS: 0-0 Gd: 0-0 GF: 0-0 Fm: 0-0
Distance: 5f/6f: 0-0 7f-8f: 0-1 9f-13f: 0-0 14f+: 0-0
Track : LH: 0-0 RH: 0-0 Tight: 0-0 Gall: 0-0
Aids: Bl: 0-0 Vi: 0-0 Tstrap: 0-0
Best Rating: 86 10/01 Nott 6f15y heavy

Stands To Reason

111 **81**
3-y-o gr g Hernando (FR)-Reason To Dance (Damister (USA))
L G Cottrell Mrs D Joly

Placings:4-46130 (3471)
2001: 8^{4}GS, 10^{6}S, 9^{1}S, 10^{3}GF, 12^{0}GF

	Starts	1st	2nd	3rd	Win & Pl
Career Total (Turf)	6	1	0	1	8875

78 6/01 Sand 1m1f C(0-95)H SFT £6987
Total win prize-money £6988

Going (Turf): Sf: 1-3 GS: 0-1 Gd: 0-0 GF: 0-2 Fm: 0-0
Distance: 5f/6f: 0-0 7f-8f: 0-2 **9f-13f: 1-4** 14f+: 0-0
Track : LH: 0-1 **RH: 1-3** Tight: 0-0 Gall: 0-2
Aids: Bl: 0-0 Vi: 0-0 Tstrap: 0-0
Best Rating: 81 7/01 Sand 1m2f7y gd-fm

Fourth to the Greenham winner Munir on his only run as a juvenile, ran with credit on his reappearance at three over a mile at Newbury before landing a handicap at Sandown. Likes soft ground.

Stanza (USA)

105(93) (48)**58**
3-y-o ch f Opening Verse (USA)-Raweyah (USA) (Our Native (USA))
M Johnston A Foustok

Placings:54013504004 (5657)
2001: 9^{5}SW, 8^{4}S, 7^{0}S, 8^{1}GF, 9^{3}GF, 10^{5}GF, 10^{0}GF, 8^{4}GF, 9^{0}GF, 9^{0}G, 8^{4}G

	Starts	1st	2nd	3rd	Win & Pl
Career Total (Turf)	10	1	0	1	4214
Career Total (AW)	1	0	0	0	0

64 5/01 Muss 1m F(0-65)H G-F £2940
Total win prize-money £2940

Going (Turf): Sf: 0-2 GS: 0-0 Gd: 0-2 **GF: 1-6** Fm: 0-0
Distance: 5f/6f: 0-0 **7f-8f: 1-3** 9f-13f: 0-8 14f+: 0-0
Track : LH: 0-6 **RH: 1-4 Tight: 1-6** Gall: 0-0
Aids: Bl: 0-3 Vi: 0-0 Tstrap: 0-0
Best Rating: 64 5/01 Muss 1m gd-fm

Scored her first success in her first season in May over a mile. Should stay a mile and a half. Acts on fast ground.

Staploy

105 **64**
3-y-o b f Deploy-Balliasta (USA) (Lyphard (USA))
B W Hills K Abdulla

Placings:3-2036 (4806)
2001: 11^{2}G, 9^{0}GS, 11^{3}GF, 10^{6}F

	Starts	1st	2nd	3rd	Win & Pl
Career Total (Turf)	5	0	1	2	2101

Going (Turf): Sf: 0-1 GS: 0-1 Gd: 0-1 GF: 0-1 Fm: 0-1
Distance: 5f/6f: 0-0 7f-8f: 0-1 9f-13f: 0-4 14f+: 0-0
Track : LH: 0-3 RH: 0-1 Tight: 0-2 Gall: 0-0
Aids: Bl: 0-0 Vi: 0-0 Tstrap: 0-0
Best Rating: 85 7/01 Yarm 1m3f101y good

Star Attraction

25
4-y-o b f Rambo Dancer (CAN)-Flying Fascination (Flying Tyke)
Derrick Morris Bright Sparks Racing

Placings:40500-00 (0117)
2001: 16^{0}SD, 9^{0}SW

	Starts	1st	2nd	3rd	Win & Pl
Career Total (Turf)	4	0	0	0	301
Career Total (AW)	3	0	0	0	

Going (Turf): Sf: 0-0 GS: 0-0 Gd: 0-0 GF: 0-3 Fm: 0-1
Distance: 5f/6f: 0-0 7f-8f: 0-0 9f-13f: 0-5 14f+: 0-2
Track : LH: 0-7 RH: 0-0 Tight: 0-3 Gall: 0-0
Aids: Bl: 0-0 Vi: 0-2 Tstrap: 0-0

Star Cast (IRE)

106 **75**
4-y-o ch f In The Wings-Thank One's Stars (Alzao (USA))
R F Johnson Houghton Mrs G C Maxwell

Placings:0500/113-452530 (5178)
2001: 11^{4}GS, 12^{5}S, 14^{2}GF, 12^{5}GF, 12^{3}G, 11^{0}HY

	Starts	1st	2nd	3rd	Win & Pl
Career Total (Turf)	13	2	1	2	16723

75 6/00 Gdwd 1m4f C(0-95)H GD £8346
75 5/00 Wind 1m3f135yD(0-85)H G-S £4004
Total win prize-money £12350

Going (Turf): Sf: 0-2 **GS: 1-2 Gd: 1-3** GF: 0-6 Fm: 0-0
Distance: 5f/6f: 0-0 7f-8f: 0-4 **9f-13f: 2-8** 14f+: 0-1
Track : LH: 0-3 **RH: 1-6 Tight: 2-5** Gall: 0-4
Aids: Bl: 0-0 Vi: 0-0 Tstrap: 0-0
Best Rating: 76 5/01 Bath 1m3f144y gd-sft

Won two races in 2000 but has since found it difficult to get back to winning ways, although has continued to perform well off higher marks. Suited by hold-up tactics, seems to handle any ground.

Star Cross (IRE)

95 **80+**
2-y-o b g Ashkalani (IRE)-Solar Star (USA) (Lear Fan (USA))
J L Dunlop Mrs M E Slade

Placings:41 (5620)
2001: 7^{4}HY, 8^{1}GS

	Starts	1st	2nd	3rd	Win & Pl
Career Total (Turf)	2	1	0	0	4056

80 11/01 Nott 1m54y D G-S £3721
Total win prize-money £3721

Going (Turf): Sf: 0-1 **GS: 1-1** Gd: 0-0 GF: 0-0 Fm: 0-0
Distance: 5f/6f: 0-0 7f-8f: 0-1 **9f-13f: 1-1** 14f+: 0-0
Track : **LH: 1-1** RH: 0-0 Tight: 0-0 Gall: 0-0
Aids: Bl: 0-0 Vi: 0-0 Tstrap: 0-0
Best Rating: 80 11/01 Nott 1m54y gd-sft

Showed promise on his debut and ran out the clear winner of a Nottingham maiden next time. He should make up into an effective middle-distance performer at three.

Star Dynasty (IRE)

90 **88**
4-y-o b g Bering-Siwaayib (Green Desert (USA))
E A L Dunlop Maktoum Al Maktoum

Placings:4/322-5 (3313)
2001: 11^{5}G

	Starts	1st	2nd	3rd	Win & Pl
Career Total (Turf)	5	0	2	1	6434

Going (Turf): Sf: 0-1 GS: 0-2 Gd: 0-2 GF: 0-0 Fm: 0-0
Distance: 5f/6f: 0-0 7f-8f: 0-1 9f-13f: 0-4 14f+: 0-0
Track : LH: 0-3 RH: 0-0 Tight: 0-2 Gall: 0-0
Aids: Bl: 0-0 Vi: 0-0 Tstrap: 0-0
Best Rating: 77 7/01 Yarm 1m3f101y good

Showed plenty of ability at three but incurred a knee injury and was not seen out again until reappearing at Yarmouth in July 2001. Stays ten furlongs. Probably best with cut in the ground.

Star Express

100 **82**
2-y-o b f Sadler's Wells (USA)-Vaigly Star (Star Appeal)
D R Loder Maktoum Al Maktoum

Placings:4 (4637)
2001: 7^{4}GF

	Starts	1st	2nd	3rd	Win & Pl
Career Total (Turf)	1	0	0	0	363

Going (Turf): Sf: 0-0 GS: 0-0 Gd: 0-0 GF: 0-1 Fm: 0-0
Distance: 5f/6f: 0-0 7f-8f: 0-1 9f-13f: 0-0 14f+: 0-0
Track : LH: 0-0 RH: 0-0 Tight: 0-0 Gall: 0-0
Aids: Bl: 0-0 Vi: 0-0 Tstrap: 0-0
Best Rating: 82 9/01 Ling 7f gd-fm

Star Glade

82 **21**
3-y-o b f Charnwood Forest (IRE)-Movieland (USA) (Nureyev (USA))
G Brown Mrs Carol Ann Brown

Placings:00-000 (2187)
2001: 8^{0}GS, 11^{0}G, 8^{0}GF

	Starts	1st	2nd	3rd	Win & Pl
Career Total (Turf)	5	0	0	0	

Going (Turf): Sf: 0-1 GS: 0-1 Gd: 0-1 GF: 0-2 Fm: 0-0
Distance: 5f/6f: 0-0 7f-8f: 0-3 9f-13f: 0-2 14f+: 0-0
Track : LH: 0-2 RH: 0-0 Tight: 0-1 Gall: 0-0
Aids: Bl: 0-0 Vi: 0-0 Tstrap: 0-0
Best Rating: 11 6/01 Nott 1m54y gd-fm

Star Guest (IRE)

77 **41**
2-y-o b f Alhaarth (IRE)-Lady's Vision (IRE) (Vision (USA))
G G Margarson John Guest

Placings:005 (5377)
2001: 7^{0}GF, 7^{0}G, 7^{5}S

	Starts	1st	2nd	3rd	Win & Pl
Career Total (Turf)	3	0	0	0	0

Going (Turf): Sf: 0-1 GS: 0-0 Gd: 0-1 GF: 0-1 Fm: 0-0
Distance: 5f/6f: 0-0 7f-8f: 0-3 9f-13f: 0-0 14f+: 0-0
Track : LH: 0-1 RH: 0-1 Tight: 0-1 Gall: 0-0
Aids: Bl: 0-0 Vi: 0-0 Tstrap: 0-0
Best Rating: 41 9/01 Leic 7f9y gd-fm

Star Of Normandie (USA)

96 **81**
2-y-o b f Gulch (USA)-Depaze (USA) (Deputy Minister (CAN))
J Noseda Mrs Julie Mitchell

Placings:54 (5603)
2001: 6^{5}G, 7^{4}GS

	Starts	1st	2nd	3rd	Win & Pl
Career Total (Turf)	2	0	0	0	324

Going (Turf): Sf: 0-0 GS: 0-1 Gd: 0-1 GF: 0-0 Fm: 0-0
Distance: 5f/6f: 0-1 7f-8f: 0-1 9f-13f: 0-0 14f+: 0-0
Track : LH: 0-0 RH: 0-0 Tight: 0-0 Gall: 0-0
Aids: Bl: 0-0 Vi: 0-0 Tstrap: 0-0
Best Rating: 81 11/01 NmkR 7f gd-sft

Out of a half sister to Fast Topaze, she showed enough promise on her debut to suggest she can win races.

Star Of Pakistan

77 **32**

2-y-o b f Lugana Beach-Annabel's Baby (IRE) (Alzao (USA))

G M McCourt M Israr Ahmad

Placings:0 **(4524)**

2001: 6^{0}GF

	Starts	1st	2nd	3rd	Win & Pl
Career Total (Turf)	1	0	0	0	

Going (Turf): Sf: 0-0 GS: 0-0 Gd: 0-0 GF: 0-1 Fm: 0-0
Distance: 5f/6f: 0-1 7f-8f: 0-0 9f-13f: 0-0 14f+: 0-0
Track : LH: 0-0 RH: 0-0 Tight: 0-0 Gall: 0-0
Aids: Bl: 0-0 Vi: 0-0 Tstrap: 0-0
Best Rating: 32 9/01 Ling 6f gd-fm

Star Of Wonder

95 **50**

3-y-o b f Celtic Swing-Meant To Be (Morston (FR))

Lady Herries Lady Mary Mumford

Placings:00-0050 **(3874)**

2001: 10^{0}GF, 11^{0}G, 11^{5}GF, 12^{0}G

	Starts	1st	2nd	3rd	Win & Pl
Career Total (Turf)	6	0	0	0	0

Going (Turf): Sf: 0-2 GS: 0-0 Gd: 0-2 GF: 0-2 Fm: 0-0
Distance: 5f/6f: 0-0 7f-8f: 0-1 9f-13f: 0-5 14f+: 0-0
Track : LH: 0-2 RH: 0-3 Tight: 0-4 Gall: 0-0
Aids: Bl: 0-0 Vi: 0-0 Tstrap: 0-0
Best Rating: 50 5/01 Bath 1m2f46y gd-fm

Star Ovation (IRE)

71 **16**

4-y-o ch g Fourstars Allstar (USA)-Standing Ovation (Godswalk (USA))

Paul Smith R Vanslembrouck

Placings:000 **(3313)**

2001: 10^{0}G, 9^{0}GS, 11^{0}G

	Starts	1st	2nd	3rd	Win & Pl
Career Total (Turf)	3	0	0	0	

Going (Turf): Sf: 0-0 GS: 0-1 Gd: 0-2 GF: 0-0 Fm: 0-0
Distance: 5f/6f: 0-0 7f-8f: 0-0 9f-13f: 0-3 14f+: 0-0
Track : LH: 0-1 RH: 0-1 Tight: 0-2 Gall: 0-0
Aids: Bl: 0-0 Vi: 0-0 Tstrap: 0-0
Best Rating: 16 7/01 Yarm 1m3f101y good

Star Princess

101 **53**

4-y-o b f Up And At 'Em-Princess Sharpenup (Lochnager)

K T Ivory The Star Princess Partnership

Placings:0324/64224253305-302060 **(3555)**

2001: 5^{3}G, 5^{0}F, 5^{2}F, 5^{0}F, 6^{6}GF, 5^{0}GF

	Starts	1st	2nd	3rd	Win & Pl
Career Total (Turf)	21	0	5	4	10400

Going (Turf): Sf: 0-6 GS: 0-0 Gd: 0-6 GF: 0-6 Fm: 0-3
Distance: 5f/6f: 0-18 7f-8f: 0-3 9f-13f: 0-0 14f+: 0-0
Track : LH: 0-4 RH: 0-0 Tight: 0-2 Gall: 0-0
Aids: Bl: 0-6 Vi: 0-3 Tstrap: 0-0
Best Rating: 54 6/01 Brig 5f59y firm

Star Protector (FR)

89 **75**

2-y-o b c Hector Protector (USA)-Frustration (Salse (USA))

J W Hills George Tong

Placings:023 **(4794)**

2001: 7^{0}GF, 7^{2}G, 7^{3}G

	Starts	1st	2nd	3rd	Win & Pl
Career Total (Turf)	3	0	1	1	1583

Going (Turf): Sf: 0-0 GS: 0-0 Gd: 0-2 GF: 0-1 Fm: 0-0
Distance: 5f/6f: 0-0 7f-8f: 0-3 9f-13f: 0-0 14f+: 0-0
Track : LH: 0-0 RH: 0-0 Tight: 0-0 Gall: 0-0
Aids: Bl: 0-0 Vi: 0-0 Tstrap: 0-0
Best Rating: 75 9/01 Ayr 7f50y good

Star Rage (IRE)

104 (83)**78**

11-y-o b g Horage-Star Bound (Crowned Prince (USA))

M Johnston J David Abell

Placings:000/0/4211123112332112102123436062/500 05115021044430/**2**/**23**0410230400/**5**106225/**15**0165321 131/60F22554210-60400132440 **(4829)**

2001: 16^{6}GF, 16^{0}F, 16^{4}GF, 16^{0}GF, 16^{0}GF, 16^{1}GF, 16^{3}F, 16^{2}G, 16^{4}G, 16^{4}F, 17^{0}G

	Starts	1st	2nd	3rd	Win & Pl
Career Total (Turf)	91	17	16	10	109365
Career Total (AW)	12	4	3	1	17699

78	7/01	Sthl	2m	E(0-75)H	G-F	£3965
78	8/00	Thsk	2m	D(0-85)H	G-F	£4101
85	9/99	Gdwd	2m	C(0-90)H	G-F	£7205
80	8/99	Bevl	2m35y	D(0-80)H	GD	£4276
77	7/99	Rdcr	2m4y	D(0-85)H	FRM	£5312
77	5/99	Bevl	2m35y	E(0-75)H	GD	£3077
83	2/99	Ling	2m	D(0-85)H	STD	£3555
80	4/98	Wolv	1m6f166y	D(0-85)H	STD	£3590
77	8/97	Rdcr	2m4y	D(0-75)H	FRM	£3501
84	8/95	Newc	2m19y	R H	GD	£10745
80	8/95	Bevl	2m35y	D(0-80)H	G-F	£4147
79	8/95	Newc	2m19y	E(0-70)H	FRM	£3052
75	8/94	Bevl	2m35y	D(0-80)H	G-F	£4926
70	7/94	Bevl	2m35y	D(0-75)H	G-F	£3439
66	7/94	Muss	1m7f16y	E(0-70)H	G-F	£2710
66	6/94	Wwck	2m20y	E(0-70)H	G-F	£2976
56	6/94	Donc	2m110y	E(0-70)H	G-F	£3132
58	5/94	Wolv	1m4f	D(0-80)H	STD	£3231
53	5/94	Sthl	1m3f	F(0-65)H	STD	£3209
49	5/94	Bevl	1m3f216y	E(0-70)H	G-F	£3054
43	5/94	Muss	1m4f31y	F(0-60)H	G-F	£2460

Total win prize-money £88669

Going (Turf): Sf: 0-2 GS: 0-7 Gd: 3-27 **GF: 11-43** Fm: 3-12
Distance: 5f/6f: 0-0 7f-8f: 0-2 9f-13f: 4-14 **14f+: 17-87**
Track : **LH: 12-65** RH: 9-38 **Tight: 15-54** Gall: 3-25
Aids: Bl: 0-0 Vi: 0-0 Tstrap: 0-0
Best Rating: 80 5/01 Newc 2m19y firm

Not getting any younger, but he retains ability and still pays his way each season. Suited by top of the ground and coming off a fast pace. He stays two miles and is a credit to connections.

Star Seventeen

98(100) (55)**69**

3-y-o ch f Rock City-Westminster Waltz (Dance In Time (CAN))

P W D'Arcy Keith Harrison & Terry Miller

Placings:622660241 **(4844)**

2001: 8^{6}SW, 8^{2}SD, 8^{2}SW, 9^{6}GS, 9^{6}GF, 11^{0}G, 9^{2}G, 10^{4}S, 9^{1}G

	Starts	1st	2nd	3rd	Win & Pl
Career Total (Turf)	6	1	1	0	5079
Career Total (AW)	3	0	2	0	1650

55	9/01	Nott	1m1f213y	E(0-65)	GD	£3176

Total win prize-money £3177

Going (Turf): Sf: 0-1 GS: 0-1 **Gd: 1-3** GF: 0-1 Fm: 0-0
Distance: 5f/6f: 0-0 7f-8f: 0-2 **9f-13f: 1-7** 14f+: 0-0
Track : **LH: 1-5** RH: 0-4 Tight: 0-4 Gall: 0-0
Aids: Bl: 0-0 Vi: 0-0 Tstrap: 0-0
Best Rating: 69 5/01 Gdwd 1m1f gd-fm

Her best effort to date was victory in a modest Nottingham event over a mile and two furlongs on good ground last September.

Star Trecker (IRE)

75 **37**

2-y-o b c Spectrum (IRE)-Night Patrol (IRE) (Night Shift (USA))

K McAuliffe Jim McCarthy

Placings:0 **(5262)**

2001: 7^{0}GS

	Starts	1st	2nd	3rd	Win & Pl
Career Total (Turf)	1	0	0	0	

Going (Turf): Sf: 0-0 GS: 0-1 Gd: 0-0 GF: 0-0 Fm: 0-0
Distance: 5f/6f: 0-0 7f-8f: 0-1 9f-13f: 0-0 14f+: 0-0
Track : LH: 0-1 RH: 0-0 Tight: 0-0 Gall: 0-1
Aids: Bl: 0-0 Vi: 0-0 Tstrap: 0-0
Best Rating: 37 10/01 York 7f202y gd-sft

Star Turn (IRE)

103 (55?)**59**

7-y-o ch g Night Shift (USA)-Ringtail (Auction Ring (USA))

R M Flower K & D Computers Ltd

Placings:050/342043525/**4525**00**4**/**10**10/10-0033 **(3957)**

2001: 9^{0}G, 9^{0}G, 10^{3}G, 9^{3}GF

	Starts	1st	2nd	3rd	Win & Pl
Career Total (Turf)	21	2	2	3	16854
Career Total (AW)	8	1	1	1	2791

71	5/00	NmkR	1m2f	D(0-85)H	GD	£7826
56	8/99	NmkJ	1m2f	F(0-65)H	GD	£4856
55	1/99	Ling	1m2f	F(0-65)H	STD	£1717

Total win prize-money £14400

Going (Turf): Sf: 0-4 GS: 0-1 **Gd: 2-10** GF: 0-5 Fm: 0-1
Distance: 5f/6f: 0-2 7f-8f: 0-8 **9f-13f: 3-19** 14f+: 0-0
Track : LH: 1-17 RH: 1-9 Tight: 1-13 Gall: 1-5
Aids: Bl: 0-0 Vi: 0-0 Tstrap: 0-0
Best Rating: 59 8/01 Sals 1m1f198y gd-fm

Got off the mark at the 20th attempt when winning over ten furlongs on the Lingfield Equitrack in January 1999, and came back from a seven-month break to win a lady amateur riders' race at Newmarket over ten furlongs. Scored again at the same course in 2000. Off the track for over a year before reappearing at Kempton in July 2001 and is steadily running himself back into form.

Starbeck (IRE)

103 **83**

3-y-o b f Spectrum (IRE)-Tide Of Fortune (Soviet Star (USA))

J D Bethell Wwwclarendon Racingcom

Placings:410-0602060 **(4117)**

2001: 6^{0}F, 6^{6}GS, 6^{0}F, 6^{2}GS, 6^{0}GF, 5^{6}GS, 6^{0}G

	Starts	1st	2nd	3rd	Win & Pl
Career Total (Turf)	10	1	1	0	10659

80	10/00	York	6f	D	SFT	£6581

Total win prize-money £6581

Going (Turf): Sf: 1-2 GS: 0-3 Gd: 0-1 GF: 0-2 Fm: 0-2
Distance: **5f/6f: 1-9** 7f-8f: 0-1 9f-13f: 0-0 14f+: 0-0
Track : LH: 0-1 RH: 0-0 Tight: 0-0 Gall: 0-1
Aids: Bl: 0-0 Vi: 0-0 Tstrap: 0-0
Best Rating: 83 7/01 NmkJ 6f gd-sft

She got off the mark on her second start at two by the minimum margin at York with the rest well beaten and ran her best race since when just touched off in a rated stakes at the Newmarket July meeting this year. Suited by six furlongs and soft ground, she sometimes misses the break.

Stardara (USA)

72 **56**

3-y-o b f Theatrical-Lydara (USA) (Alydar (USA))
P F I Cole M Arbib

Placings:65-00 (4245)
2001: 8^{0}GS, 12^{0}GF

	Starts	1st	2nd	3rd	Win & Pl
Career Total (Turf)	4	0	0	0	0

Going (Turf): Sf: 0-1 GS: 0-1 Gd: 0-0 GF: 0-2 Fm: 0-0
Distance: 5f/6f: 0-0 7f-8f: 0-1 9f-13f: 0-3 14f+: 0-0
Track : LH: 0-0 RH: 0-2 Tight: 0-2 Gall: 0-0
Aids: Bl: 0-0 Vi: 0-0 Tstrap: 0-0
Best Rating: 21 4/01 Wind 1m67y gd-sft

Starfan (USA)

102 **89**
2-y-o b f Lear Fan (USA)-Willstar (USA) (Nureyev (USA))
J H M Gosden K Abdulla

Placings:24 (5245a)
2001: 7^{2}GF, 8^{4}HO

	Starts	1st	2nd	3rd	Win & Pl
Career Total (Turf)	2	0	1	0	9211

Going (Turf): Sf: 0-0 GS: 0-0 Gd: 0-0 GF: 0-1 Fm: 0-0
Distance: 5f/6f: 0-0 7f-8f: 0-2 9f-13f: 0-0 14f+: 0-0
Track : LH: 0-0 RH: 0-1 Tight: 0-0 Gall: 0-0
Aids: Bl: 0-0 Vi: 0-0 Tstrap: 0-0
Best Rating: 89 10/01 Lonc 1m holding

Narrowly beaten on her debut, she ran well to be fourth in the Marcel Boussac next time, and should have no difficulty winning races.

Starfleet

91(80) (39)**51**
3-y-o ch f Inchinor-Sunfleet (Red Sunset)
Mrs P N Dutfield (P F I Cole 29/6) Simon Dutfield

Placings:50-45004 (5101)
2001: 7^{4}GF, 6^{5}SD, 7^{0}GF, 7^{0}F, 9^{4}GS

	Starts	1st	2nd	3rd	Win & Pl
Career Total (Turf)	6	0	0	0	274
Career Total (AW)	1	0	0	0	0

Going (Turf): Sf: 0-0 GS: 0-1 Gd: 0-1 GF: 0-3 Fm: 0-1
Distance: 5f/6f: 0-3 7f-8f: 0-3 9f-13f: 0-1 14f+: 0-0
Track : LH: 0-1 RH: 0-2 Tight: 0-1 Gall: 0-1
Aids: Bl: 0-0 Vi: 0-0 Tstrap: 0-0
Best Rating: 78 6/01 Yarm 7f3y gd-fm

Still a maiden and improvement needed to win a race.

Starlight Dancer (IRE)

72(62) (4)**24**
3-y-o b f Muhtarram (USA)-Tintomara (IRE) (Niniski (USA))
J G Portman T M Curtis

Placings:00 (2171)
2001: 10^{0}G, 8^{0}SD

	Starts	1st	2nd	3rd	Win & Pl
Career Total (Turf)	1	0	0	0	
Career Total (AW)	1	0	0	0	

Going (Turf): Sf: 0-0 GS: 0-0 Gd: 0-1 GF: 0-0 Fm: 0-0
Distance: 5f/6f: 0-0 7f-8f: 0-1 9f-13f: 0-1 14f+: 0-0
Track : LH: 0-1 RH: 0-0 Tight: 0-1 Gall: 0-0
Aids: Bl: 0-0 Vi: 0-0 Tstrap: 0-0
Best Rating: 24 5/01 Wind 1m2f7y good

Starry Mary

104(74) (16)**56**
3-y-o b f Deploy-Darling Splodge (Elegant Air)

E L James The Westenholz Family

Placings:04003-64035140 (5471)
2001: 10^{6}GS, 11^{4}GS, 11^{0}GF, 12^{3}G, 14^{5}G, 9^{1}S, 10^{4}HY, 11^{0}S

	Starts	1st	2nd	3rd	Win & Pl
Career Total (Turf)	12	1	0	2	5229
Career Total (AW)	1	0	0	0	

54 9/01 Brig 1m1f209yE(0-75)H SFT £4290
Total win prize-money £4290

Going (Turf): Sf: 1-3 GS: 0-4 Gd: 0-3 GF: 0-2 Fm: 0-0
Distance: 5f/6f: 0-2 7f-8f: 0-3 **9f-13f: 1-7** 14f+: 0-1
Track : **LH: 1-8** RH: 0-0 Tight: 0-5 Gall: 0-2
Aids: Bl: 0-0 Vi: 0-0 Tstrap: 0-0
Best Rating: 57 4/01 Wind 1m3f135y gd-sft

Stars In Her Eyes (IRE)

97 **76**
2-y-o b f Woodman (USA)-Wind In Her Hair (IRE) (Alzao (USA))
J W Hills Mrs David Nagle & Mrs John Magnier

Placings:4033 (4668)
2001: 6^{4}GF, 6^{0}GF, 5^{3}GF, 6^{3}GF

	Starts	1st	2nd	3rd	Win & Pl
Career Total (Turf)	4	0	0	2	1426

Going (Turf): Sf: 0-0 GS: 0-0 Gd: 0-0 GF: 0-4 Fm: 0-0
Distance: 5f/6f: 0-3 7f-8f: 0-1 9f-13f: 0-0 14f+: 0-0
Track : LH: 0-1 RH: 0-0 Tight: 0-0 Gall: 0-0
Aids: Bl: 0-0 Vi: 0-0 Tstrap: 0-1
Best Rating: 76 9/01 Gdwd 6f gd-fm

Dam top class ten to twelve furlong filly. Half-sister to Veil of Avalon.

Start Over (IRE)

91 **57**
2-y-o b c Barathea (IRE)-Carnelly (IRE) (Priolo (USA))
E J O'Neill Mrs Ying Shen

Placings:043 (5627)
2001: 7^{0}GF, 7^{4}HY, 7^{3}G

	Starts	1st	2nd	3rd	Win & Pl
Career Total (Turf)	3	0	0	1	871

Going (Turf): Sf: 0-1 GS: 0-0 Gd: 0-1 GF: 0-1 Fm: 0-0
Distance: 5f/6f: 0-0 7f-8f: 0-3 9f-13f: 0-0 14f+: 0-0
Track : LH: 0-0 RH: 0-0 Tight: 0-0 Gall: 0-0
Aids: Bl: 0-0 Vi: 0-0 Tstrap: 0-0
Best Rating: 57 11/01 Rdcr 7f good

Has shown promise on all starts so far, but is best watched until tackling handicaps. Tested only at seven furlongs.

Starzaan (IRE)

89 **83**
2-y-o b c Darshaan-Stellina (IRE) (Caerleon (USA))
P F I Cole M Arbib

Placings:00 (5367)
2001: 8^{0}GS, 8^{0}GS

	Starts	1st	2nd	3rd	Win & Pl
Career Total (Turf)	2	0	0	0	

Going (Turf): Sf: 0-0 GS: 0-2 Gd: 0-0 GF: 0-0 Fm: 0-0
Distance: 5f/6f: 0-0 7f-8f: 0-2 9f-13f: 0-0 14f+: 0-0
Track : LH: 0-0 RH: 0-0 Tight: 0-0 Gall: 0-0
Aids: Bl: 0-0 Vi: 0-0 Tstrap: 0-0
Best Rating: 83 10/01 NmkR 1m gd-sft

A 220,000gns half-brother to French Derby third Sestino, showed ability on his Salisbury debut.

State Of Confusion (IRE)

77(67) (22)**45**
2-y-o ch g Great Commotion (USA)-Burina (Burslem)
R M Beckett Willie McKay

Placings:000 (5197)
2001: 5^{0}SD, 7^{0}GF, 8^{0}SD

	Starts	1st	2nd	3rd	Win & Pl
Career Total (Turf)	1	0	0	0	
Career Total (AW)	2	0	0	0	

Going (Turf): Sf: 0-0 GS: 0-0 Gd: 0-0 GF: 0-1 Fm: 0-0
Distance: 5f/6f: 0-1 7f-8f: 0-1 9f-13f: 0-1 14f+: 0-0
Track : LH: 0-1 RH: 0-0 Tight: 0-1 Gall: 0-0
Aids: Bl: 0-0 Vi: 0-0 Tstrap: 0-0
Best Rating: 45 7/01 Ling 7f gd-fm

State Opening

95 **28**
4-y-o ch f Absalom-Lightning Legend (Lord Gayle (USA))
Miss Z C Davison Highly Charged Partnership

Placings:0-000000 (5664)
2001: 7^{0}GF, 6^{0}F, 7^{0}GF, 7^{0}G, 7^{0}S, 8^{0}HY

	Starts	1st	2nd	3rd	Win & Pl
Career Total (Turf)	7	0	0	0	

Going (Turf): Sf: 0-2 GS: 0-1 Gd: 0-1 GF: 0-2 Fm: 0-1
Distance: 5f/6f: 0-1 7f-8f: 0-4 9f-13f: 0-2 14f+: 0-0
Track : LH: 0-3 RH: 0-2 Tight: 0-2 Gall: 0-1
Aids: Bl: 0-0 Vi: 0-0 Tstrap: 0-0
Best Rating: 28 7/01 Kemp 7f gd-fm

Stateroom (USA)

99 **87+**
3-y-o ch c Affirmed (USA)-Sleet (USA) (Summer Squall (USA))
J A R Toller Lady Sophia Topley

Placings:0-4010 (4053)
2001: 8^{4}G, 7^{0}GS, 8^{1}GF, 7^{0}GF

	Starts	1st	2nd	3rd	Win & Pl
Career Total (Turf)	5	1	0	0	4913

76 7/01 Kemp 1m D G-F £4420
Total win prize-money £4420

Going (Turf): Sf: 0-1 GS: 0-1 Gd: 0-1 **GF: 1-2** Fm: 0-0
Distance: 5f/6f: 0-0 **7f-8f: 1-5** 9f-13f: 0-0 14f+: 0-0
Track : LH: 0-0 **RH: 1-1** Tight: 0-0 Gall: 0-0
Aids: Bl: 0-0 Vi: 0-0 **Tstrap: 1-2**
Best Rating: 87 5/01 NmkR 1m good

Performed with credit in the Newmarket maiden won by Mugharreb on his reappearance and got off the mark over a mile at Kempton in July. Stays a mile and acts on fast ground.

Statim

90 **85**
2-y-o b f Marju (IRE)-Rapid Repeat (IRE) (Exactly Sharp (USA))
L M Cumani Lord Hartington

Placings:002 (5460)
2001: 7^{0}G, 8^{0}HY, 8^{2}G

	Starts	1st	2nd	3rd	Win & Pl
Career Total (Turf)	3	0	1	0	856

Going (Turf): Sf: 0-1 GS: 0-0 Gd: 0-2 GF: 0-0 Fm: 0-0
Distance: 5f/6f: 0-0 7f-8f: 0-1 9f-13f: 0-2 14f+: 0-0
Track : LH: 0-2 RH: 0-1 Tight: 0-1 Gall: 0-0
Aids: Bl: 0-0 Vi: 0-0 Tstrap: 0-0
Best Rating: 85 10/01 Bath 1m5y good

Statosilver

(89) (21)**31**
3-y-o b g Puissance-Silver Blessings (Statoblest)

Mrs A Duffield T Shaw & S Smith

Placings:50-00 **(2579)**
2001: 8^{0}SD, 6^{0}SD

	Starts	1st	2nd	3rd	Win & Pl
Career Total (Turf)	2	0	0	0	0
Career Total (AW)	2	0	0	0	

Going (Turf): Sf: 0-2 GS: 0-0 Gd: 0-0 GF: 0-0 Fm: 0-0
Distance: 5f/6f: 0-3 7f-8f: 0-1 9f-13f: 0-0 14f+: 0-0
Track : LH: 0-2 RH: 0-0 Tight: 0-0 Gall: 0-0
Aids: Bl: 0-0 Vi: 0-0 Tstrap: 0-0
Best Rating: 21 6/01 Sthl 6f stand

Statoyork

98(87) (46)**49**
8-y-o b g Statoblest-Ultimate Dream (Kafu)
D Shaw Century Racing

Placings:56/5010000/402050000/**06633406302256620165630/05011033210006040040000/005000002141500 0-00000405000** **(5451)**
2001: 6^{0}SD, 5^{0}SD, 5^{0}G, 5^{0}GF, 5^{0}GF, 5^{0}S, 5^{4}G, 5^{0}GS, 5^{5}G, 5^{0}S, 5^{0}G, 5^{0}HY

	Starts	1st	2nd	3rd	Win & Pl
Career Total (Turf)	79	7	6	5	45418
Career Total (AW)	12	0	0	1	315

64 9/00 Hayd 5f C(0-95)H HVY £7507
58 8/00 Carl 5f D(0-80)H GD £4738
69 6/99 Ripn 5f D(0-80)H G-F £4299
61 5/99 Ripn 5f C(0-90)H G-S £7197
59 5/99 Carl 5f F(0-60) FRM £2388
57 8/98 Pont 5f F(0-65)H G-F £4591
48 6/96 Ayr 7f D G-F £3598
Total win prize-money £34323

Going (Turf): Sf: 1-11 GS: 1-10 Gd: 1-22 **GF: 3-28** Fm: 1-8
Distance: **5f/6f: 6-74** 7f-8f: 1-17 9f-13f: 0-0 14f+: 0-0
Track : LH: 2-25 RH: 2-8 Tight: 0-10 **Gall: 2-6**
Aids: Bl: 0-1 Vi: 0-7 Tstrap: 0-0
Best Rating: 53 7/01 Donc 5f good

He appears to travel well through his races, but finds little off the bridle and needs to be held up for a late run. Gradually dropping down the handicap and is the sort likely to pop up at a massive price one day. Has been known to break blood vessels.

Statue Gallery (IRE)

102 **82**
3-y-o ch c Cadeaux Genereux-Kinlochewe (Old Vic)
J A R Toller Duke Of Devonshire

Placings:5216-41000 **(2885)**
2001: 6^{4}S, 6^{1}GF, 6^{0}S, 6^{0}GF, 6^{0}GS

	Starts	1st	2nd	3rd	Win & Pl
Career Total (Turf)	9	2	1	0	16147

82 5/01 Ches 6f18y C(0-90)H G-F £11066
66 8/00 Brig 5f213y D FRM £3432
Total win prize-money £14498

Going (Turf): Sf: 0-3 GS: 0-1 Gd: 0-1 **GF: 1-3 Fm: 1-1**
Distance: 5f/6f: 1-6 7f-8f: 1-3 9f-13f: 0-0 14f+: 0-0
Track : **LH: 2-3** RH: 0-0 **Tight: 1-1** Gall: 0-0
Aids: Bl: 0-0 Vi: 0-0 Tstrap: 0-0
Best Rating: 82 5/01 Ches 6f18y gd-fm

Winner of a small maiden as a juvenile on fast ground, did not appear to act on soft on final outing. Appears best when racing prominently.

Stay Behind

105 **94**
3-y-o ch f Elmaamul (USA)-I Will Lead (USA) (Seattle Slew (USA))
Mrs A J Perrett K Abdulla

Placings:3-411200 **(5339)**
2001: 10^{4}G, 9^{1}GF, 10^{1}GF, 10^{2}GF, 11^{0}G, 10^{0}GS

	Starts	1st	2nd	3rd	Win & Pl
Career Total (Turf)	7	2	1	1	17034

49 6/01 Pont 1m2f6y C(0-90) G-F £8463
71 6/01 Folk 1m1f149yD G-F £2856
Total win prize-money £11319

Going (Turf): Sf: 0-0 GS: 0-1 Gd: 0-3 **GF: 2-3** Fm: 0-0
Distance: 5f/6f: 0-0 7f-8f: 0-1 **9f-13f: 2-6** 14f+: 0-0
Track : LH: 1-3 RH: 1-2 **Tight: 1-2** Gall: 0-2
Aids: Bl: 0-0 Vi: 0-0 Tstrap: 0-0
Best Rating: 94 7/01 Chep 1m2f36y gd-fm

Fulfilled some of the early promise when running out quite an easy winner of a maiden at Folkestone in June and followed up with a comfortable win in a Pontefract classified event. Narrowly beaten in a Listed event at Chepstow, she should stay 12 furlongs. Acts on fast ground.

Steadfast And True (USA)

94 **79+**
2-y-o b c Danzig (USA)-Always Loyal (USA) (Zilzal (USA))
D R Loder Maktoum Al Maktoum

Placings:2 **(1738)**
2001: 6^{2}GF

	Starts	1st	2nd	3rd	Win & Pl
Career Total (Turf)	1	0	1	0	1020

Going (Turf): Sf: 0-0 GS: 0-0 Gd: 0-0 GF: 0-1 Fm: 0-0
Distance: 5f/6f: 0-0 7f-8f: 0-1 9f-13f: 0-0 14f+: 0-0
Track : LH: 0-0 RH: 0-0 Tight: 0-0 Gall: 0-0
Aids: Bl: 0-0 Vi: 0-0 Tstrap: 0-0
Best Rating: 79 5/01 Yarm 6f3y gd-fm

Stealthy Times

97(86) (60)**53**
4-y-o ch f Timeless Times (USA)-Stealthy (Kind Of Hush)
W M Brisbourne G D Kendrick

Placings:1/00005540000-603660 **(3847)**
2001: 6^{6}F, 5^{0}GF, 7^{3}GF, 6^{6}GF, 7^{6}GF, 6^{0}G

	Starts	1st	2nd	3rd	Win & Pl
Career Total (Turf)	17	1	0	1	4017
Career Total (AW)	1	0	0	0	

86 7/99 Nott 6f15y E G-F £3202
Total win prize-money £3202

Going (Turf): Sf: 0-2 GS: 0-2 Gd: 0-3 **GF: 1-9** Fm: 0-1
Distance: 5f/6f: 0-7 **7f-8f: 1-11** 9f-13f: 0-0 14f+: 0-0
Track : LH: 0-7 RH: 0-0 Tight: 0-2 Gall: 0-3
Aids: Bl: 0-0 Vi: 0-0 Tstrap: 0-0
Best Rating: 53 7/01 Hayd 7f30y gd-fm

Steaming Home (USA)

102 **101**
2-y-o b f Salt Lake (USA)-County Fair (USA) (Mr Prospector (USA))
D K Weld K L Ramsey

Placings:22110 **(5054)**
2001: 5^{2}GF, 5^{2}GF, 6^{1}GY, 6^{1}GY, 6^{0}S

	Starts	1st	2nd	3rd	Win & Pl
Career Total (Turf)	5	2	2	0	49590

101 9/01 Curr 6f G-Y £29250
94 7/01 Curr 6f G-Y £10400
Total win prize-money £39650

Going (Turf): Sf: 0-1 GS: 0-0 Gd: 0-0 GF: 0-2 Fm: 0-0
Distance: **5f/6f: 2-5** 7f-8f: 0-0 9f-13f: 0-0 14f+: 0-0
Track : LH: 0-0 RH: 0-0 Tight: 0-0 Gall: 0-0
Aids: Bl: 0-0 Vi: 0-0 Tstrap: 0-0
Best Rating: 101 9/01 Curr 6f gd-yld

A January foal, she is out of a half-sister to the US Grade One winner Corporate Report. She almost got up to win the Windsor Castle on her second start, but did manage to get off the mark at the Curragh next time and won a Listed race at the same track in September. Disappointed in the Cheveley Park. Suited by six furlongs and cut in the ground, but acts on fast going.

Steamroller Stanly

(104) (25)
8-y-o b g Shirley Heights-Miss Demure (Shy Groom (USA))
D W Chapman David W Chapman

Placings:03/61463501/**121043/1150030/303513312036 64333/52460004122003-54505** **(1992)**
2001: 16^{5}SD, 16^{4}SD, 16^{5}SD, 16^{0}SD, 14^{5}SD

	Starts	1st	2nd	3rd	Win & Pl
Career Total (Turf)	18	1	0	3	7098
Career Total (AW)	41	8	5	10	39844

50 6/00 Sthl 1m6f E(0-70) STD £2705
84 6/99 Sthl 2m F STD £2109
85 4/99 Wolv 1m6f166yC(0-95)H STD £6092
93 2/98 Ling 1m2f C SLW £5226
91 2/98 Ling 1m2f D SLW £3371
90 2/97 Ling 1m2f D STD £3306
90 1/97 Ling 1m4f D(0-80)H STD £3371
84 11/96 Ling 1m4f D STD £3485
69 6/96 Newb 1m5f61y D(0-80)H G-F £4370
Total win prize-money £34039

Going (Turf): Sf: 0-2 GS: 0-1 Gd: 0-4 **GF: 1-9** Fm: 0-1
Distance: 5f/6f: 0-1 7f-8f: 0-2 **9f-13f: 5-28** 14f+: 4-28
Track : **LH: 9-51** RH: 0-7 **Tight: 6-32** Gall: 1-6
Aids: Bl: 0-4 Vi: 0-3 Tstrap: 0-0
Best Rating: 36 2/01 Sthl 2m stand

Formerly smart on the Flat and especially on Equitrack, he can still win staying events on sand when able to dominate, but he has also been beaten at very short prices and may not be completely trustworthy these days.

Steel Band

111 **88**
3-y-o b c Kris-Quaver (USA) (The Minstrel (CAN))
H Candy Girsonfield Ltd

Placings:312-0042400 **(4712)**
2001: 7^{0}GS, 9^{0}GF, 9^{4}GF, 11^{2}GS, 12^{4}GS, 11^{0}G, 10^{0}G

	Starts	1st	2nd	3rd	Win & Pl
Career Total (Turf)	10	1	2	1	18003

87 8/00 Chep 1m14y D G-F £3493
Total win prize-money £3494

Going (Turf): Sf: 0-0 GS: 0-4 Gd: 0-2 **GF: 1-4** Fm: 0-0
Distance: 5f/6f: 0-0 7f-8f: 0-3 **9f-13f: 1-7** 14f+: 0-0
Track : LH: 0-3 RH: 0-3 Tight: 0-2 Gall: 0-3
Aids: Bl: 0-0 Vi: 0-0 Tstrap: 0-0
Best Rating: 88 7/01 Hayd 1m3f200y gd-sft

Won over a mile on fast ground as a juvenile, but was well beaten on his first two starts this season. Much better efforts during the summer and looks capable of winning a handicap at ten or twelve furlongs. Best form so far on good to firm ground.

Steely Dan

92(90) (71)**78**
2-y-o b c Danzig Connection (USA)-No Comebacks (Last Tycoon)
J R Best Mercato Limited

Placings:01615050000 **(5408)**
2001: 5^{0}GS, 5^{1}SD, 5^{6}S, 5^{1}S, 5^{5}GF, 8^{0}GF, 6^{5}G, 6^{0}GF, 7^{0}G, 7^{0}S, 6^{0}SD

	Starts	1st	2nd	3rd	Win & Pl
Career Total (Turf)	9	1	0	0	5777
Career Total (AW)	2	1	0	0	2303

60 4/01 NmkR 5f C SFT £5776
71 3/01 Sthl 5f F STD £2303
Total win prize-money £8080

Going (Turf): Sf: 1-3 GS: 0-1 Gd: 0-2 GF: 0-3 Fm: 0-0

Distance: 5f/6f: 2-7 7f-8f: 0-3 9f-13f: 0-1 14f+: 0-0
Track : LH: 0-4 RH: 0-1 Tight: 0-4 Gall: 0-0
Aids: Bl: 0-0 Vi: 0-0 Tstrap: 0-0
Best Rating: 78 9/01 Folk 6f189y good

A precocious sort, he scored on Southwell's All-Weather track and in a Newmarket conditions stakes in the spring. He has raced with his head rather high but battles on gamely. His wins have been over five furlongs, and he has failed when tried over longer trips. Has won on soft ground, yet to prove he handles fast ground.

Steenberg (IRE)

99 **93+**

2-y-o ch c Flying Spur (AUS)-Kip's Sister (Cawston's Clown)
M H Tompkins Kenneth Macpherson

Placings:421 **(3824)**
2001: 6^{4}GS, 6^{2}GF, 7^{1}G

	Starts	1st	2nd	3rd	Win & Pl
Career Total (Turf)	3	1	1	0	23918

93 8/01 Asct 7f B GD £22550
Total win prize-money £22550

Going (Turf): Sf: 0-0 GS: 0-1 **Gd: 1-1** GF: 0-1 Fm: 0-0
Distance: 5f/6f: 0-0 **7f-8f: 1-3** 9f-13f: 0-0 14f+: 0-0
Track : LH: 0-0 RH: 0-0 Tight: 0-0 Gall: 0-0
Aids: Bl: 0-0 Vi: 0-0 Tstrap: 0-0
Best Rating: 93 8/01 Asct 7f good

Improving fast, he bolted up on his third start in a valuable race at Ascot on Shergar Cup day despite still looking green. A useful prospect.

Steinitz

101 **83**

3-y-o ch c Nashwan (USA)-Circe's Isle (Be My Guest (USA))
J L Dunlop Benny Andersson

Placings:20-424114 **(3845)**
2001: 10^{4}S, 11^{2}GF, 11^{4}G, 12^{1}F, 12^{1}GF, 11^{4}G

	Starts	1st	2nd	3rd	Win & Pl
Career Total (Turf)	8	2	2	0	16013

83 7/01 Ripn 1m4f60y D(0-85)H G-F £7150
49 7/01 Newc 1m4f93y D(0-80) FRM £4163
Total win prize-money £11313

Going (Turf): Sf: 0-1 GS: 0-0 Gd: 0-4 **GF: 1-2 Fm: 1-1**
Distance: 5f/6f: 0-0 7f-8f: 0-2 **9f-13f: 2-6** 14f+: 0-0
Track : **LH: 1-4** RH: 0-3 Tight: 0-2 **Gall: 1-2**
Aids: Bl: 0-0 Vi: 0-0 Tstrap: 0-0
Best Rating: 83 7/01 Ripn 1m4f60y gd-fm

He was beginning to look disappointing after being beaten in maiden and classified evetns, but managed to find a very modest event at Newcastle in July and his confidence just have been helped by that.

Step Back (IRE)

101 (38)**89**

8-y-o ch g Salt Dome (USA)-Hazy Lady (Habitat)
Gerard Keane Francis Duffy

Placings:0006030625-0410410511130 **(5502)**
2001: 9^{0}F, 6^{4}SD, 5^{1}F, 6^{0}G, 5^{4}GF, 5^{1}F, 6^{0}GY, 6^{5}S, 5^{1}GF, 5^{1}GY, 5^{1}G, 5^{3}S, 5^{0}HY

	Starts	1st	2nd	3rd	Win & Pl
Career Total (Turf)	22	5	1	2	61275
Career Total (AW)	1	0	0	0	280

76 9/01 Curr 5f H GD £26000
71 9/01 Curr 5f (0-95)H G-Y £16250
68 8/01 Tral 5f (0-80)H G-F £5865
66 7/01 DRoy 5f (0-60)H FRM £4830
66 6/01 DRoy 5f (0-60)H FRM £4830
Total win prize-money £57775

Going (Turf): Sf: 0-6 GS: 0-0 Gd: 1-3 GF: 1-6 **Fm: 2-3**
Distance: **5f/6f: 5-12** 7f-8f: 0-6 9f-13f: 0-5 14f+: 0-0
Track : LH: 0-3 RH: 0-6 Tight: 0-0 Gall: 0-0
Aids: Bl: 0-0 Vi: 0-0 Tstrap: 0-0
Best Rating: 89 10/01 Curr 5f soft

Step On Degas

95 (55)**47**

8-y-o b m Superpower-Vivid Impression (Cure The Blues (USA))
Mrs A L M King Mrs Pennie Muir

Placings:5032/1500020252/103004512000/016250060 00/030543620302200/000-40 **(1567)**
2001: 6^{4}G, 7^{0}F

	Starts	1st	2nd	3rd	Win & Pl
Career Total (Turf)	44	3	6	3	12463
Career Total (AW)	13	1	3	2	5163

58 5/98 Brig 5f213y E(0-70)H FRM £2905
54 8/97 Brig 6f209y F(0-55) G-F £2277
63 1/97 Ling 7f E(0-70)H STD £2401
Total win prize-money £7583

Going (Turf): Sf: 0-4 GS: 0-4 Gd: 0-12 GF: 1-18 **Fm: 2-6**
Distance: 5f/6f: 2-22 7f-8f: 2-33 9f-13f: 0-2 14f+: 0-0
Track : **LH: 4-32** RH: 0-11 Tight: 1-16 Gall: 1-7
Aids: Bl: 0-0 Vi: 0-2 Tstrap: 0-0
Best Rating: 44 5/01 Brig 6f209y good

On a lengthy losing run since scoring at Brighton in May '98.

Stepastray

98 **41**

4-y-o gr g Alhijaz-Wandering Stranger (Petong)
R E Barr D Thomson

Placings:000/00363300-004400200044006 **(5032)**
2001: 11^{0}S, 12^{0}GF, 14^{4}F, 11^{4}GF, 12^{0}G, 14^{0}GF, 9^{2}GF, 9^{0}GF, 10^{0}GF, 10^{0}G, 11^{4}G, 11^{4}GF, 9^{0}GF, 11^{0}GF, 12^{6}GF

	Starts	1st	2nd	3rd	Win & Pl
Career Total (Turf)	26	0	1	3	3044

Going (Turf): Sf: 0-1 GS: 0-1 Gd: 0-5 GF: 0-15 Fm: 0-4
Distance: 5f/6f: 0-0 7f-8f: 0-3 9f-13f: 0-21 14f+: 0-2
Track : LH: 0-18 RH: 0-3 Tight: 0-16 Gall: 0-2
Aids: Bl: 0-1 Vi: 0-4 Tstrap: 0-0
Best Rating: 46 7/01 Bevl 1m1f207y gd-fm

Sterling High (IRE)

81 (103) (40)**34**

6-y-o b g Mujadil (USA)-Verusa (IRE) (Petorius)
J L Eyre Peter J Watson

Placings:00600/000036145360/000001105/040354000 0006-00 **(1824)**
2001: 10^{0}GF, 10^{0}GF

	Starts	1st	2nd	3rd	Win & Pl
Career Total (Turf)	34	3	0	2	8465
Career Total (AW)	7	0	0	1	360

51 9/99 Tram 1m1f (0-70)H G-Y £3001
47 9/99 Dund 1m1f (0-70)H FRM £2415
71 8/98 Rosc 7f (0-60)H G-Y £2234
Total win prize-money £7650

Going (Turf): Sf: 0-6 GS: 0-0 Gd: 0-9 GF: 0-6 **Fm: 1-1**
Distance: 5f/6f: 0-7 7f-8f: 1-17 **9f-13f: 2-17** 14f+: 0-0
Track : LH: 1-26 **RH: 2-8** Tight: 0-3 Gall: 0-2
Aids: Bl: 0-3 Vi: 0-0 **Tstrap: 2-21**
Best Rating: 20 6/01 Pont 1m2f6y gd-fm

Stickwithsterling (USA)

97 (92) (78)**78**

2-y-o b c Silver Hawk (USA)-Chesa Plana (Niniski (USA))
P F I Cole M Arbib

Placings:34 **(5590)**
2001: 8^{3}GS, 9^{4}GS, 9^{2}SD

	Starts	1st	2nd	3rd	Win & Pl
Career Total (Turf)	2	0	0	1	696

Going (Turf): Sf: 0-0 GS: 0-2 Gd: 0-0 GF: 0-0 Fm: 0-0
Distance: 5f/6f: 0-0 7f-8f: 0-1 9f-13f: 0-1 14f+: 0-0
Track : LH: 0-1 RH: 0-0 Tight: 0-0 Gall: 0-0
Aids: Bl: 0-0 Vi: 0-0 Tstrap: 0-0
Best Rating: 78 11/01 Brig 1m1f209y gd-sft

A $100,000 yearling out of a half-sister to Noushkey, ran with promise on his Salisbury debut.

Stiletto (IRE)

102 (98) (55)**73**

3-y-o b c Danehill (USA)-Pinta (IRE) (Ahonoora)
J Noseda Lucayan Stud

Placings:0312635 **(3736)**
2001: 8^{0}SD, 5^{3}SD, 5^{1}G, 5^{2}F, 5^{6}HD, 7^{3}G, 5^{5}G

	Starts	1st	2nd	3rd	Win & Pl
Career Total (Turf)	5	1	1	1	5481
Career Total (AW)	2	0	0	1	424

49 5/01 Brig 5f213y D GD £3835
Total win prize-money £3835

Going (Turf): Sf: 0-0 GS: 0-0 **Gd: 1-3** GF: 0-0 Fm: 0-2
Distance: **5f/6f: 1-5** 7f-8f: 0-1 9f-13f: 0-1 14f+: 0-0
Track : **LH: 1-7** RH: 0-0 Tight: 0-3 Gall: 0-1
Aids: Bl: 0-0 Vi: 0-0 Tstrap: 0-1
Best Rating: 73 7/01 Epsm 7f good

A Brighton maiden winner over six, he never showed a real turn of foot and looked a horse that needed further. He was unsuited by the hard ground at Bath.

Still Waters

82 (102) (50)**11**

6-y-o b g Rainbow Quest (USA)-Krill (Kris)
B A Pearce (I A Wood 1/1) A Leg Each Partnership

Placings:0/0200/1000/060031343-30000 **(5023)**
2001: 8^{3}SD, 7^{0}F, 11^{0}F, 10^{0}GF, 7^{0}S

	Starts	1st	2nd	3rd	Win & Pl
Career Total (Turf)	10	0	1	0	990
Career Total (AW)	13	2	0	4	5008

49 6/00 Sthl 7f G(0-65)H STD £1918
68 1/99 Sthl 1m F(0-65)H STD £2008
Total win prize-money £3926

Going (Turf): Sf: 0-1 GS: 0-1 Gd: 0-3 GF: 0-2 Fm: 0-3
Distance: 5f/6f: 0-0 **7f-8f: 2-14** 9f-13f: 0-9 14f+: 0-0
Track : **LH: 2-18** RH: 0-3 Tight: 0-5 Gall: 0-0
Aids: Bl: 0-0 Vi: 0-0 Tstrap: 0-0
Best Rating: 40 1/01 Sthl 1m stand

Stilmemaite

89 (78) (15)**30**

3-y-o b f Komaite (USA)-Stilvella (Camden Town)
N Bycroft J A Swinburne

Placings:350040-000000000 **(4400)**
2001: 6^{0}SW, 5^{0}SW, 5^{0}S, 5^{0}S, 6^{0}S, 6^{0}GF, 7^{0}SD, 7^{0}G, 6^{0}G

	Starts	1st	2nd	3rd	Win & Pl
Career Total (Turf)	11	0	0	1	1193
Career Total (AW)	4	0	0	0	

Going (Turf): Sf: 0-5 GS: 0-0 Gd: 0-4 GF: 0-2 Fm: 0-0
Distance: 5f/6f: 0-13 7f-8f: 0-2 9f-13f: 0-0 14f+: 0-0
Track : LH: 0-3 RH: 0-0 Tight: 0-0 Gall: 0-0
Aids: Bl: 0-2 Vi: 0-0 Tstrap: 0-0
Best Rating: 30 8/01 Ayr 6f good

Sting Like A Bee (IRE)

97 **91**

2-y-o b c Ali-Royal (IRE)-Hidden Agenda (FR) (Machiavellian (USA))
H R A Cecil Greenbay Stables Ltd

Placings:22 **(5485)**
2001: 8^{2}S, 7^{2}HY

	Starts	1st	2nd	3rd	Win & Pl
Career Total (Turf)	2	0	2	0	3082

Going (Turf): Sf: 0-2 GS: 0-0 Gd: 0-0 GF: 0-0 Fm: 0-0
Distance: 5f/6f: 0-0 7f-8f: 0-2 9f-13f: 0-0 14f+: 0-0
Track : LH: 0-0 RH: 0-0 Tight: 0-0 Gall: 0-0
Aids: Bl: 0-0 Vi: 0-0 Tstrap: 0-0
Best Rating: 91 10/01 Donc 7f heavy

Ran a very promising race to finish runner-up on his Newmarket debut and will be winning before too long.

Stirred Not Shaken (IRE)

56 **9**
2-y-o b g Revoque (IRE)-Shakey (IRE) (Caerleon (USA))
Miss L C Siddall Mrs Ann Morgan

Placings:0 (5485)
2001: 7^{0}HY

	Starts	1st	2nd	3rd	Win & Pl
Career Total (Turf)	1	0	0	0	

Going (Turf): Sf: 0-1 GS: 0-0 Gd: 0-0 GF: 0-0 Fm: 0-0
Distance: 5f/6f: 0-0 7f-8f: 0-1 9f-13f: 0-0 14f+: 0-0
Track : LH: 0-0 RH: 0-0 Tight: 0-0 Gall: 0-0
Aids: Bl: 0-0 Vi: 0-0 Tstrap: 0-0
Best Rating: 9 10/01 Donc 7f heavy

Stitch In Time

105(106) (66)**52**
5-y-o ch g Inchinor-Late Matinee (Red Sunset)
G C Bravery H P Carrington

Placings:0000000/2233020543332**35113323-0310221012534306** (5400)
2001: 10^{0}S, 12^{3}SD, **11^{1}SD**, 11^{0}GS, 9^{2}F, 10^{2}GF, 10^{1}GF, 10^{0}GF, 10^{1}GF, 10^{2}GF, 9^{5}GF, 9^{3}G, 10^{4}GS, 9^{3}GS, 10^{0}G, 10^{6}S, **11^{0}SD**

	Starts	1st	2nd	3rd	Win & Pl
Career Total (Turf)	32	2	6	6	12836
Career Total (AW)	12	3	2	6	9286

45	7/01	Ling	1m2f	E(0-70)H	G-F	£3220
45	7/01	Pont	1m2f6y	F(0-70)H	G-F	£2600
62	4/01	Sthl	1m3f	G(0-70)H	STD	£1393
55	11/00	Sthl	1m3f	F(0-60)H	STD	£1960
50	11/00	Sthl	1m4f	F(0-60)H	STD	£2044

Total win prize-money £11218

Going (Turf): Sf: 0-5 GS: 0-4 Gd: 0-5 **GF: 2-14** Fm: 0-4
Distance: 5f/6f: 0-0 7f-8f: 0-6 **9f-13f: 5-37** 14f+: 0-1
Track : **LH: 5-31** RH: 0-10 **Tight: 1-17** Gall: 0-3
Aids: Bl: 0-0 Vi: 0-3 Tstrap: 0-0
Best Rating: 62 4/01 Sthl 1m3f stand

A three-time winner on Southwell's Fibresand, he got off the mark on turf at Pontefract in July 2001. Stays 12 furlongs, and is at his best when ridden prominently.

Stokesie

92 **70d**
3-y-o gr g Fumo Di Londra (IRE)-Lesley's Fashion (Dominion)
J M Bradley (Edward Lynam 28/7) Byron J Stokes

Placings:0416-000000 (5252)
2001: 7^{0}GF, 6^{0}G, 6^{0}GF, 5^{0}GF, 5^{0}GS, 5^{0}S

	Starts	1st	2nd	3rd	Win & Pl
Career Total (Turf)	10	1	0	0	4885

81	7/00	Bell	5f		GD	£4485

Total win prize-money £4485

Going (Turf): Sf: 0-1 GS: 0-1 **Gd: 1-3** GF: 0-4 Fm: 0-0
Distance: **5f/6f: 1-9** 7f-8f: 0-1 9f-13f: 0-0 14f+: 0-0
Track : LH: 0-0 RH: 0-0 Tight: 0-0 Gall: 0-0
Aids: Bl: 0-0 Vi: 0 0 Tstrap: 0-0
Best Rating: 59 7/01 Curr 5f gd-fm

Stolen Hat

89 **79d**
2-y-o b c Robellino (USA)-Madam Trilby (Grundy)
R Hannon J C Smith

Placings:563505 (5128)
2001: 6^{5}GF, 7^{6}G, 6^{3}GF, 7^{5}G, 7^{0}GF, 6^{5}HY

	Starts	1st	2nd	3rd	Win & Pl
Career Total (Turf)	6	0	0	1	655

Going (Turf): Sf: 0-1 GS: 0-0 Gd: 0-2 GF: 0-3 Fm: 0-0
Distance: 5f/6f: 0-2 7f-8f: 0-4 9f-13f: 0-0 14f+: 0-0
Track : LH: 0-1 RH: 0-1 Tight: 0-1 Gall: 0-0
Aids: Bl: 0-0 Vi: 0-0 Tstrap: 0-0
Best Rating: 79 8/01 Sals 6f gd-fm

Stoli (IRE)

97 **71**
3-y-o ch g Spectrum (IRE)-Crystal City (Kris)
P J Makin Brian Brackpool

Placings:06-05010 (4988)
2001: 7^{0}S, 7^{5}GS, 8^{0}GF, 8^{1}F, 8^{0}G

	Starts	1st	2nd	3rd	Win & Pl
Career Total (Turf)	7	1	0	0	3024

71	9/01	Chep	1m14y	E(0-75)H	FRM	£3024

Total win prize-money £3024

Going (Turf): Sf: 0-2 GS: 0-1 Gd: 0-1 GF: 0-2 **Fm: 1-1**
Distance: 5f/6f: 0-0 7f-8f: 0-6 **9f-13f: 1-1** 14f+: 0-0
Track : LH: 0-1 RH: 0-1 Tight: 0-0 Gall: 0-1
Aids: Bl: 0-0 Vi: 0-0 Tstrap: 0-0
Best Rating: 71 9/01 Chep 1m14y firm

Showed ability in maidens as a juvenile, but struggled this season and was dropped in the weights to a handy mark before winning at Chepstow, although ran very badly at Ascot. Acts on firm ground and fas won over a mile.

Stone Crest (IRE)

88 **45**
3-y-o b f Bigstone (IRE)-Hillcrest (IRE) (Thatching)
R A Fahey Harvey Ashworth

Placings:660 (5173)
2001: 7^{6}G, 0^{6}GF, 8^{0}GS

	Starts	1st	2nd	3rd	Win & Pl
Career Total (Turf)	3	0	0	0	0

Going (Turf): Sf: 0-0 GS: 0-1 Gd: 0-1 GF: 0-1 Fm: 0-0
Distance: 5f/6f: 0-0 7f-8f: 0-1 9f-13f: 0-2 14f+: 0-0
Track : LH: 0-2 RH: 0-1 Tight: 0-1 Gall: 0-0
Aids: Bl: 0-0 Vi: 0-0 Tstrap: 0-0
Best Rating: 45 6/01 Thsk 7f good

Stone Dock

91(86) (20)**56**
4-y-o b g Bigstone (IRE)-Docklands (USA) (Theatrical)
P Mitchell Dungolfin (jdrp)

Placings:50000 (5469)
2001: 12^{5}SD, 10^{0}G, 10^{0}G, 16^{0}GS, 9^{0}S

	Starts	1st	2nd	3rd	Win & Pl
Career Total (Turf)	4	0	0	0	
Career Total (AW)	1	0	0	0	0

Going (Turf): Sf: 0-1 GS: 0-1 Gd: 0-2 GF: 0-0 Fm: 0-0
Distance: 5f/6f: 0-0 7f-8f: 0-0 9f-13f: 0-4 14f+: 0-1
Track : LH: 0-4 RH: 0-1 Tight: 0-4 Gall: 0-0
Aids: Bl: 0-0 Vi: 0-0 Tstrap: 0-0
Best Rating: 56 9/01 Epsm 1m2f18y good

Stoney Garnett

90(94) (44)**50d**
4-y-o b f Emarati (USA)-Etourdie (USA) (Arctic Tern (USA))
J D Czerpak (M S Saunders 16/6) K C Payne

Placings:00233U30/126000-**443040** (2185)
2001: 7^{4}SW, 7^{4}SD, 6^{3}SD, 6^{0}GS, 5^{4}F, 5^{0}G

	Starts	1st	2nd	3rd	Win & Pl
Career Total (Turf)	16	1	2	3	5487
Career Total (AW)	4	0	0	1	319

69	5/00	Brig	5f59y	E(0-70)H	SFT	£2731

Total win prize-money £2731

Going (Turf): Sf: 1-2 GS: 0-1 Gd: 0-6 GF: 0-4 Fm: 0-3
Distance: **5f/6f: 1-16** 7f-8f: 0-4 9f-13f: 0-0 14f+: 0-0
Track : **LH: 1-14** RH: 0-0 Tight: 0-4 Gall: 0-6
Aids: Bl: 0-4 Vi: 0-0 Tstrap: 0-0
Best Rating: 44 2/01 Ling 7f slow

Stop The Traffic (IRE)

(102) (49)**61**
4-y-o b f College Chapel-Miss Bagatelle (Mummy's Pet)
P Howling Mrs A K Petersen

Placings:0330/**42522055000055600020O-0** (0136)
2001: 9^{0}SW

	Starts	1st	2nd	3rd	Win & Pl
Career Total (Turf)	12	0	0	2	1394
Career Total (AW)	14	0	4	0	4139

Going (Turf): Sf: 0-1 GS: 0-2 Gd: 0-0 GF: 0-7 Fm: 0-2
Distance: 5f/6f: 0-13 7f-8f: 0-11 9f-13f: 0-2 14f+: 0-0
Track : LH: 0-17 RH: 0-1 Tight: 0-11 Gall: 0-2
Aids: Bl: 0-0 Vi: 0-1 Tstrap: 0 5

Stoppes Brow

109(101) (79)**71**
9-y-o b g Primo Dominie-So Bold (Never So Bold)
G L Moore Bryan Pennick

Placings:43000**112/1131**0064414320/**02**04031300342/066624004**23/404262**025160523602600/**61**1561423310 0/400652563440-620061421320 (4664)
2001: 9^{6}SD, 7^{2}GS, 8^{0}S, 8^{0}GF, 8^{6}GF, 8^{1}GF, 9^{4}GF, 9^{2}G, 8^{1}GF, 7^{3}GF, 7^{2}GF, 9^{0}GF

	Starts	1st	2nd	3rd	Win & Pl
Career Total (Turf)	75	7	10	10	59521
Career Total (AW)	29	7	6	2	34083

69	8/01	Epsm	1m114y	E	G-F	£3672
70	6/01	Gdwd	1m	D(0-85)H	G-F	£5300
80	8/99	Epsm	1m114y	C(0-90)H	GD	£7002
71	6/99	Kemp	1m	D(0-80)H	GD	£4630
75	4/99	Ling	7f	E(0-75)H	STD	£2558
74	4/99	Ling	1m	F(0-65)H	STD	£2165
72	5/98	Gdwd	1m	D(0-80)H	G-F	£5970
71	5/96	Newb	6f8y	D(0-80)H	SFT	£4185
66	8/95	Gdwd	7f	D(0-75)H	G-F	£4020
81	2/95	Ling	6f	C(0-90)H	STD	£5446
77	1/95	Ling	6f	D(0-80)H	STD	£3538
71	1/95	Ling	5f	D(0-80)H	STD	£3572
76	11/94	Ling	5f	D(0-85)	STD	£2710
68	11/94	Ling	5f	E(0-75)	STD	£2301

Total win prize-money £57076

Going (Turf): Sf: 1-11 GS: 0-10 Gd: 2-23 **GF: 4-29** Fm: 0-2
Distance: 5f/6f: 5-25 **7f-8f: 7-59** 9f-13f: 2-20 14f+: 0-0
Track : **LH: 9-55** RH: 4-27 **Tight: 9-52** Gall: 0-4
Aids: Bl: 6-51 Vi: 6-32 Tstrap: 0-0
Best Rating: 71 8/01 Gdwd 1m1f good

He has been around for a while, but is a capable handicapper when things go right on both turf and Equitrack. Goes well on an undulating course.

Stopwatch (IRE)

(87) (19)
6-y-o b g Lead On Time (USA)-Rose Bonbon (FR) (High Top)
Mrs L C Jewell The Stopwatch Partnership

Placings:63/01055246/**6**000/**0**0-0 (0204)
2001: 12^{0}SW

	Starts	1st	2nd	3rd	Win & Pl
Career Total (Turf)	13	1	1	1	5791
Career Total (AW)	4	0	0	0	0

90 4/98 Cork 1m SFT £3767
Total win prize-money £3768

Going (Turf): Sf: 1-5 GS: 0-1 Gd: 0-3 GF: 0-0 Fm: 0-1
Distance: 5f/6f: 0-0 **7f-8f: 1-9** 9f-13f: 0-7 14f+: 0-1
Track : LH: 0-8 **RH: 1-8** Tight: 0-4 Gall: 0-2
Aids: Bl: 0-1 Vi: 0-0 Tstrap: 0-0
Best Rating: 4 1/01 Ling 1m4f slow

Storm Clear (IRE)

92 **86**
2-y-o b c Mujadil (USA)-Escape Path (Wolver Hollow)
R Hannon D Boocock

Placings:644 (4957)
2001: 6^{6}GF, 6^{4}GF, 6^{4}GS

	Starts	1st	2nd	3rd	Win & Pl
Career Total (Turf)	3	0	0	0	676

Going (Turf): Sf: 0-0 GS: 0-1 Gd: 0-0 GF: 0-2 Fm: 0-0
Distance: 5f/6f: 0-3 7f-8f: 0-0 9f-13f: 0-0 14f+: 0-0
Track : LH: 0-0 RH: 0-0 Tight: 0-0 Gall: 0-0
Aids: Bl: 0-0 Vi: 0-0 Tstrap: 0-0
Best Rating: 86 9/01 Gdwd 6f gd-sft

A half-brother to the smart sprinter Andreyev. Gave away ground at the start on his Ascot debut over six furlongs. Should stay further. Has put in his best performances on good to firm so far.

Storm Cry (USA)

83(83) (41)**31**
6-y-o b g Hermitage (USA)-Doonesbury Lady (USA) (Doonesbury (USA))
M S Saunders B McFadzean

Placings:02/1530/4000540610**0**/**00**000-0 (4073)
2001: 8^{0}G

	Starts	1st	2nd	3rd	Win & Pl
Career Total (Turf)	21	2	1	1	8850
Career Total (AW)	2	0	0	0	

65 9/99 Ling 7f E(0-70)H HVY £3567
64 5/98 Bath 1m5y F FRM £2444
Total win prize-money £6012

Going (Turf): Sf: 1-5 GS: 0-4 Gd: 0-7 GF: 0-2 **Fm: 1-3**
Distance: 5f/6f: 0-1 7f-8f: 1-16 9f-13f: 1-6 14f+: 0-0
Track : **LH: 1-6** RH: 0-7 **Tight: 1-5** Gall: 0-3
Aids: Bl: 0-1 Vi: 0-0 **Tstrap: 1-9**
Best Rating: 21 8/01 Bath 1m5y good

Storm From Heaven (IRE)

92(80) (53)**26**
3-y-o b/br g Mujadil (USA)-Lady Of Man (So Blessed)
P C Haslam T S Palin

Placings:400-60060 (3503)
2001: 8^{6}SW, 7^{0}S, 8^{0}SD, 12^{6}GF, 11^{0}GF

	Starts	1st	2nd	3rd	Win & Pl
Career Total (Turf)	3	0	0	0	0
Career Total (AW)	5	0	0	0	0

Going (Turf): Sf: 0-1 GS: 0-0 Gd: 0-0 GF: 0-2 Fm: 0-0
Distance: 5f/6f: 0-3 7f-8f: 0-2 9f-13f: 0-3 14f+: 0-0
Track : LH: 0-6 RH: 0-1 Tight: 0-4 Gall: 0-0
Aids: Bl: 0-0 Vi: 0-0 Tstrap: 0-0
Best Rating: 31 1/01 Wolv 1m100y slow

Storm Fromthe East

(84) (20)**40**
6-y-o b g Formidable (USA)-Callas Star (Chief Singer)
Edward C Sexton (R Hannon 1/1) Edward C Sexton

Placings:022244/501/0502000/0000000**0**-0000000
(3901a)
2001: 8^{0}SD, 7^{0}S, 8^{0}HY, 7^{0}G, 7^{0}G, 7^{0}GF, 7^{0}Y

	Starts	1st	2nd	3rd	Win & Pl
Career Total (Turf)	29	1	4	0	8208
Career Total (AW)	2	0	0	0	

81 6/98 Gdwd 7f E GD £3720
Total win prize-money £3720

Going (Turf): Sf: 0-4 GS: 0-0 **Gd: 1-7** GF: 0-9 Fm: 0-0
Distance: 5f/6f: 0-7 **7f-8f: 1-17** 9f-13f: 0-5 14f+: 0-0
Track : LH: 0-9 **RH: 1-5** Tight: 0-1 Gall: 0-0
Aids: Bl: 0-4 Vi: 0-0 Tstrap: 0-2
Best Rating: 37 7/01 Tipp 7f gd-fm

Storm King (IRE)

(61) **52**
3-y-o b c Mukaddamah (USA)-Busker (Bustino)
J A Osborne Andy Miller

Placings:005-0 (0452)
2001: 12^{0}SD

	Starts	1st	2nd	3rd	Win & Pl
Career Total (Turf)	3	0	0	0	0
Career Total (AW)	1	0	0	0	

Going (Turf): Sf: 0-0 GS: 0-1 Gd: 0-0 GF: 0-1 Fm: 0-1
Distance: 5f/6f: 0-3 7f-8f: 0-0 9f-13f: 0-1 14f+: 0-0
Track : LH: 0-1 RH: 0-0 Tight: 0-1 Gall: 0-0
Aids: Bl: 0-0 Vi: 0-0 Tstrap: 0-0

Storm Seeker

83 **75+**
2-y-o b c Rainbow Quest (USA)-Siwaayib (Green Desert (USA))
B W Hills Maktoum Al Maktoum

Placings:0 (5107)
2001: 7^{0}GS

	Starts	1st	2nd	3rd	Win & Pl
Career Total (Turf)	1	0	0	0	

Going (Turf): Sf: 0-0 GS: 0-1 Gd: 0-0 GF: 0-0 Fm: 0-0
Distance: 5f/6f: 0-0 7f-8f: 0-1 9f-13f: 0-0 14f+: 0-0
Track : LH: 0-0 RH: 0-0 Tight: 0-0 Gall: 0-0
Aids: Bl: 0-0 Vi: 0-0 Tstrap: 0-0
Best Rating: 75 10/01 NmkR 7f gd-sft

Storm Shower (IRE)

74 **20**
3-y-o b g Catrail (USA)-Crimson Shower (Dowsing (USA))
E Stanners Doubleprint

Placings:0 (2271)
2001: 7^{0}G

	Starts	1st	2nd	3rd	Win & Pl
Career Total (Turf)	1	0	0	0	

Going (Turf): Sf: 0-0 GS: 0-0 Gd: 0-1 GF: 0-0 Fm: 0-0
Distance: 5f/6f: 0-0 7f-8f: 0-1 9f-13f: 0-0 14f+: 0-0
Track : LH: 0-1 RH: 0-0 Tight: 0-1 Gall: 0-0
Aids: Bl: 0-0 Vi: 0-0 Tstrap: 0-0
Best Rating: 20 6/01 Thsk 7f good

Stormdancer (IRE)

13
4-y-o ch g Bluebird (USA)-Unspoiled (Tina's Pet)
G T Gaines Largesse Racing

Placings:000/0-50 (3859)
2001: 8^{5}GF, 9^{0}GS

	Starts	1st	2nd	3rd	Win & Pl
Career Total (Turf)	6	0	0	0	0

Going (Turf): Sf: 0-1 GS: 0-2 Gd: 0-1 GF: 0-2 Fm: 0-0
Distance: 5f/6f: 0-0 7f-8f: 0-2 9f-13f: 0-4 14f+: 0-0
Track : LH: 0-4 RH: 0-1 Tight: 0-1 Gall: 0-0
Aids: Bl: 0-0 Vi: 0-0 Tstrap: 0-0
Best Rating: 20 6/01 Thsk 7f good

Stormey Wonder (IRE)

66 **15**
2-y-o b f Darnay-Polaregina (FR) (Rex Magna (FR))
J S Moore Bruno Brookes

Placings:0 (5342)
2001: 7^{0}GS

	Starts	1st	2nd	3rd	Win & Pl
Career Total (Turf)	1	0	0	0	

Going (Turf): Sf: 0-0 GS: 0-1 Gd: 0-0 GF: 0-0 Fm: 0-0
Distance: 5f/6f: 0-0 7f-8f: 0-1 9f-13f: 0-0 14f+: 0-0
Track : LH: 0-0 RH: 0-0 Tight: 0-0 Gall: 0-0
Aids: Bl: 0-0 Vi: 0-0 Tstrap: 0-0
Best Rating: 15 10/01 NmkR 7f gd-sft

Storming Foley

87 **63**
3-y-o b g Makbul-Cute Dancer (Remainder Man)
W M Brisbourne Foley Steelstock

Placings:4250-00 (3880)
2001: 5^{0}GF, 5^{0}GS

	Starts	1st	2nd	3rd	Win & Pl
Career Total (Turf)	6	0	1	0	913

Going (Turf): Sf: 0-1 GS: 0-2 Gd: 0-0 GF: 0-2 Fm: 0-1
Distance: 5f/6f: 0-6 7f-8f: 0-0 9f-13f: 0-0 14f+: 0-0
Track : LH: 0-2 RH: 0-1 Tight: 0-0 Gall: 0-1
Aids: Bl: 0-0 Vi: 0-0 Tstrap: 0-0
Best Rating: 36 8/01 Thsk 5f gd-sft

Storming Home

117 **126**
3-y-o b c Machiavellian (USA)-Try To Catch Me (USA) (Shareef Dancer (USA))
B W Hills Maktoum Al Maktoum

Placings:0120-1351420 (4820a)
2001: 10^{1}S, 10^{3}GF, 12^{5}GF, 12^{1}GF, 12^{4}GF, 11^{2}G, 12^{0}G

	Starts	1st	2nd	3rd	Win & Pl
Career Total (Turf)	11	3	2	1	215992

116 6/01 Asct 1m4f A G-F £81000
111 4/01 Epsm 1m2f18y B SFT £12390
91 8/00 NmkJ 7f D GD £4251
Total win prize-money £97642

Going (Turf): Sf: 1-1 GS: 0-0 **Gd: 1-5 GF: 1-5** Fm: 0-0
Distance: 5f/6f: 0-0 **7f-8f: 1-4 9f-13f: 2-7** 14f+: 0-0
Track : LH: 1-4 RH: 1-5 Tight: 1-2 Gall: 1-5
Aids: Bl: 0-0 Vi: 0-0 Tstrap: 0-0
Best Rating: 126 7/01 Asct 1m4f gd-fm

He showed fair form as a juvenile in 2000, but stepped up to middle distances this season, he landed an Epsom conditons event in good style on his return. Improved again to be third behind Dilshaan in the Dante Stakes at York and ran to a similar level when fifth behind Galileo in the Derby. He got it right when landing his first group victory in the King Edward VII at Royal Ascot, but arguably ran his best race when fourth in the King George. He was unable to confirm Royal Ascot form with subsequent St Leger winner Milan in the Great Voltigeur, and then ran flat in the Prix Niel. Suited by fast ground and a good pace, he has some decent performances on his record. With normal improvement he should be among the top older middle-distance performers in 2002.

Stormswell

102 **29**

4-y-o ch f Persian Bold-Stormswept (USA) (Storm Bird (CAN))
J Hetherton Exors Of The Late M J Paver

Placings:0060/003153040400-0405000 **(4800)**
2001: 8^{0}G, 9^{4}F, 8^{0}F, 9^{5}GF, 8^{0}F, 9^{0}GF, 10^{0}F

	Starts	1st	2nd	3rd	Win & Pl
Career Total (Turf)	23	1	0	2	4659

51 6/00 Haml 1m65y F(0-65)H GD £3835
Total win prize-money £3835

Going (Turf): Sf: 0-6 GS: 0-1 **Gd: 1-3** GF: 0-6 Fm: 0-7
Distance: 5f/6f: 0-4 7f-8f: 0-6 **9f-13f: 1-13** 14f+: 0-0
Track : LH: 0-10 **RH: 1-8 Tight: 1-10** Gall: 0-0
Aids: Bl: 0-0 Vi: 0-0 Tstrap: 0-0
Best Rating: 44 5/01 Rdcr 1m1f firm

Stormville (IRE)

102 **54**

4-y-o b g Catrail (USA)-Haut Volee (Top Ville)
M Brittain Northgate Gold

Placings:6355/6400260-0602460 **(5535)**
2001: 8^{0}GF, 8^{6}GF, 7^{0}GF, 7^{2}G, 8^{4}GF, 7^{6}G, 7^{0}S

	Starts	1st	2nd	3rd	Win & Pl
Career Total (Turf)	18	0	2	1	7411

Going (Turf): Sf: 0-3 GS: 0-1 Gd: 0-7 GF: 0-6 Fm: 0-1
Distance: 5f/6f: 0-1 7f-8f: 0-12 9f-13f: 0-5 14f+: 0-0
Track : LH: 0-7 RH: 0-6 Tight: 0-3 Gall: 0-2
Aids: Bl: 0-0 Vi: 0-0 Tstrap: 0-0
Best Rating: 54 8/01 Newc 7f good

He has shown some ability in varied company, but is still a maiden.

Stormy Crest (IRE)

103 **69**

3-y-o b g Catrail (USA)-Broken Wave (Bustino)
John Berry J McCarthy

Placings:00-03120520 **(4402)**
2001: 7^{0}GS, 8^{3}GF, 9^{1}GF, 9^{2}GF, 8^{0}GF, 10^{5}GS, 8^{2}GF, 8^{0}G

	Starts	1st	2nd	3rd	Win & Pl
Career Total (Turf)	10	1	2	1	6176

69 5/01 Ayr 1m1f20y E(0-70) G-F £2996
Total win prize-money £2996

Going (Turf): Sf: 0-1 GS: 0-3 Gd: 0-1 **GF: 1-5** Fm: 0-0
Distance: 5f/6f: 0-1 7f-8f: 0-4 **9f-13f: 1-5** 14f+: 0-0
Track : LH: 0-3 RH: 0-4 Tight: 0-5 Gall: 0-0
Aids: Bl: 0-0 Vi: 0-0 Tstrap: 0-0
Best Rating: 69 8/01 Epsm 1m114y gd-fm

Scored over nine furlongs on third start at three. Tends to race keenly. Acts on fast ground.

Stormy Parkes

2-y-o ch f Zamindar (USA)-Lucky Parkes (Full Extent (USA))
A Berry Joseph Heler

Placings:U **(1113)**
2001: 5^{U}S

	Starts	1st	2nd	3rd	Win & Pl
Career Total (Turf)	1	0	0	0	

Going (Turf): Sf: 0-1 GS: 0-0 Gd: 0-0 GF: 0-0 Fm: 0-0
Distance: 5f/6f: 0-1 7f-8f: 0-0 9f-13f: 0-0 14f+: 0-0
Track : LH: 0-0 RH: 0-0 Tight: 0-0 Gall: 0-0
Aids: Bl: 0-0 Vi: 0-0 Tstrap: 0-0
Best Rating: 69 8/01 Epsm 1m114y gd-fm

Stormy Rainbow

99(97) (69)**68**

4-y-o b c Red Rainbow-Stormy Heights (Golden Heights)
M Blanshard Michael Hancock

Placings:0/2250-0010000 **(3686)**
2001: 7^{0}HY, 7^{0}F, 8^{1}G, 8^{0}GF, 7^{0}G, 7^{0}GS, 8^{0}GF

	Starts	1st	2nd	3rd	Win & Pl
Career Total (Turf)	9	1	0	0	3835
Career Total (AW)	3	0	2	0	1510

68 6/01 Leic 1m9y F(0-65)H GD £3835
Total win prize-money £3835

Going (Turf): Sf: 0-2 GS: 0-1 **Gd: 1-3** GF: 0-2 Fm: 0-1
Distance: 5f/6f: 0-0 7f-8f: 0-10 **9f-13f: 1-2** 14f+: 0-0
Track : LH: 0-6 RH: 0-1 Tight: 0-3 Gall: 0-1
Aids: Bl: 0-0 Vi: 0-0 Tstrap: 0-0
Best Rating: 68 6/01 Leic 1m9y good

A fair handicapper, he scored his first success for new connections at Leicester in June. Stays a mile and is suited by a good ground.

Stormy Skye (IRE)

97(91) (43)**69**

5-y-o b g Bluebird (USA)-Canna (Caerleon (USA))
G L Moore Mrs J Moore,Mrs J Agnew,T Pollock

Placings:5035/442/32460-0201 **(5622)**
2001: 16^{0}S, 11^{2}S, 18^{0}GS, 14^{1}GS

	Starts	1st	2nd	3rd	Win & Pl
Career Total (Turf)	15	1	3	2	8572
Career Total (AW)	1	0	0	0	0

69 11/01 Nott 1m6f15y G(0-70) G-S £2117
Total win prize-money £2118

Going (Turf): Sf: 0-5 **GS: 1-3** Gd: 0-3 GF: 0-3 Fm: 0-1
Distance: 5f/6f: 0-0 7f-8f: 0-4 9f-13f: 0-5 **14f+: 1-7**
Track : **LH: 1-8** RH: 0-8 Tight: 0-2 Gall: 0-4
Aids: Bl: 1-9 Vi: 0-0 Tstrap: 1-9
Best Rating: 69 11/01 Nott 1m6f15y gd-sft

He finally won his first race on the Flat in an amateur riders' event at Nottingham in November. Needs a test of stamina and is regularly fitted with blinkers and a tongue strap.

Stormy Voyage

95(100) (68)**50**

3-y-o b g Storm Bird (CAN)-Vividimagination (USA) (Raise A Man (USA))
K R Burke Mrs Elaine M Burke

Placings:40-014500660 **(2618)**
2001: 8^{0}SW, 7^{1}SD, 7^{4}SD, 7^{5}SD, 6^{0}S, 8^{0}GF, 7^{6}GF, 8^{6}GF, 7^{0}GF

	Starts	1st	2nd	3rd	Win & Pl
Career Total (Turf)	7	0	0	0	275
Career Total (AW)	4	1	0	0	2744

68 3/01 Ling 7f E(0-75)H STD £2744
Total win prize-money £2744

Going (Turf): Sf: 0-1 GS: 0-0 Gd: 0-1 GF: 0-5 Fm: 0-0
Distance: 5f/6f: 0-1 **7f-8f: 1-9** 9f-13f: 0-1 14f+: 0-0
Track : **LH: 1-5** RH: 0-2 **Tight: 1-3** Gall: 0-0
Aids: Bl: 0-0 Vi: 0-2 Tstrap: 0-0
Best Rating: 68 3/01 Ling 7f stand

Winner of a three-year-old seven-furlong handicap at Lingfield in March 2001, has shown little else since then.

Stornoway

(96) (48)

3-y-o b f Catrail (USA)-Heavenly Waters (Celestial Storm (USA))
G C Bravery Orange Racing

Placings:2-2 **(0190)**
2001: 7^{2}SD

	Starts	1st	2nd	3rd	Win & Pl
Career Total (Turf)	1	0	1	0	822
Career Total (AW)	1	0	1	0	638

Going (Turf): Sf: 0-1 GS: 0-0 Gd: 0-0 GF: 0-0 Fm: 0-0
Distance: 5f/6f: 0-0 7f-8f: 0-2 9f-13f: 0-0 14f+: 0-0
Track : LH: 0-1 RH: 0-0 Tight: 0-0 Gall: 0-0
Aids: Bl: 0-0 Vi: 0-0 Tstrap: 0-0
Best Rating: 48 1/01 Sthl 7f stand

Storyteller (IRE)

102 **72**

7-y-o b g Thatching-Please Believe Me (Try My Best (USA))
M Dods Mrs Karen S Pratt

Placings:56454130060/622214111212502/00411244/0004305-0000001000 **(4588)**
2001: 5^{0}GS, 6^{0}G, 5^{0}GF, 5^{0}GF, 5^{0}GF, 6^{0}GS, 5^{1}G, 5^{0}GF, 5^{0}G, 5^{0}HY

	Starts	1st	2nd	3rd	Win & Pl
Career Total (Turf)	51	9	7	2	56709

63	8/01	Pont	5f	E(0-70)H	GD	£3721
83	6/99	Sals	5f	D(0-85)H	GD	£7165
79	5/99	Donc	6f	D(0-80)	G-F	£5602
84	7/98	Pont	5f	D(0-80)H	G-F	£5162
76	7/98	Bevl	5f	D(0-80)H	GD	£3782
67	7/98	Hayd	5f	E(0-70)H	G-S	£2950
62	6/98	Ayr	5f	D(0-85)H	GD	£3522
61	6/98	Carl	5f	F(0-65)H	G-S	£2598
54	7/97	Donc	5f	E(0-70)H	GD	£3348

Total win prize-money £37851

Going (Turf): Sf: 0-3 GS: 2-7 **Gd: 5-24** GF: 2-16 Fm: 0-1
Distance: **5f/6f: 9-46** 7f-8f: 0-5 9f-13f: 0-0 14f+: 0-0
Track : **LH: 2-8** RH: 1-4 Tight: 0-2 **Gall: 1-2**
Aids: Bl: 0-0 **Vi: 9-42** Tstrap: 0-0
Best Rating: 63 8/01 Pont 5f good

He was terrific form in the summer of '98, winning a string of races at five furlongs and won twice the following season. He has not surprisingly been unable to repeat that level of success, but a big drop in the handicap ultimately saw him return to winning form at Pontefract in August.

Straight And True

93 **70**

2-y-o b f Lake Coniston (IRE)-Play The Game (Mummy's Game)
A Berry J Hanson & A Patrick

Placings:45 **(3708)**
2001: 5^{4}G, 6^{5}G

	Starts	1st	2nd	3rd	Win & Pl
Career Total (Turf)	2	0	0	0	366

Going (Turf): Sf: 0-0 GS: 0-0 Gd: 0-2 GF: 0-0 Fm: 0-0
Distance: 5f/6f: 0-2 7f-8f: 0-0 9f-13f: 0-0 14f+: 0-0
Track : LH: 0-0 RH: 0-0 Tight: 0-0 Gall: 0-0
Aids: Bl: 0-0 Vi: 0-0 Tstrap: 0-0
Best Rating: 70 7/01 Donc 5f good

Straight Eight

82 **55**

2-y-o b c Octagonal (NZ)-Kalymnia (GER) (Mondrian (GER))
T D Easterby Giles W Pritchard-Gordon

Placings:000 **(4939)**
2001: 7^{0}HY, 7^{0}G, 7^{0}S

	Starts	1st	2nd	3rd	Win & Pl
Career Total (Turf)	3	0	0	0	

Going (Turf): Sf: 0-2 GS: 0-0 Gd: 0-1 GF: 0-0 Fm: 0-0
Distance: 5f/6f: 0-0 7f-8f: 0-3 9f-13f: 0-0 14f+: 0-0
Track : LH: 0-2 RH: 0-1 Tight: 0-1 Gall: 0-0
Aids: Bl: 0-0 Vi: 0-0 Tstrap: 0-0
Best Rating: 55 9/01 Bevl 7f100y good

Strait Talking (FR)

95 **66**

3-y-o b c Bering-Servia (Le Marmot (FR))
S Dow Byerley Bloodstock

Placings:0005010 **(4550)**
2001: 8^{0}S, 8^{0}GS, 8^{0}GF, 9^{5}GF, 8^{0}GF, 7^{1}G, 8^{0}GF

	Starts	1st	2nd	3rd	Win & Pl
Career Total (Turf)	7	1	0	0	3318

66 8/01 Brig 7f214y E(0-75)H GD £3318
Total win prize-money £3318

Going (Turf): Sf: 0-1 GS: 0-1 **Gd: 1-1** GF: 0-4 Fm: 0-0
Distance: 5f/6f: 0-0 **7f-8f: 1-5** 9f-13f: 0-2 14f+: 0-0
Track : **LH: 1-1** RH: 0-3 Tight: 0-1 Gall: 0-0
Aids: Bl: 0-0 Vi: 0-0 Tstrap: 0-0
Best Rating: 70 5/01 Kemp 1m gd-sft

Strand Of Gold

(78) (32)**70**
4-y-o b g Lugana Beach-Miss Display (Touch Paper)
B S Rothwell Mrs Marie Tinkler

Placings:0204/5505000030-00 **(0171)**
2001: 11^{0}SD, 12^{0}SD

	Starts	1st	2nd	3rd	Win & Pl
Career Total (Turf)	13	0	1	1	1728
Career Total (AW)	3	0	0	0	

Going (Turf): Sf: 0-4 GS: 0-3 Gd: 0-4 GF: 0-1 Fm: 0-1
Distance: 5f/6f: 0-4 7f-8f: 0-10 9f-13f: 0-2 14f+: 0-0
Track : LH: 0-10 RH: 0-0 Tight: 0-1 Gall: 0-0
Aids: Bl: 0-5 Vi: 0-1 Tstrap: 0-1
Best Rating: 25 1/01 Sthl 1m4f stand

Strand Onthe Green (IRE)

98(55) **69**
3-y-o b c Ela-Mana-Mou-Fleuretta (USA) (The Minstrel (CAN))
T G Mills Ian Hutchins

Placings:0450 **(5348)**
2001: 8^{0}GF, 8^{4}GF, 9^{5}GS, 12^{0}SD

	Starts	1st	2nd	3rd	Win & Pl
Career Total (Turf)	3	0	0	0	282
Career Total (AW)	1	0	0	0	

Going (Turf): Sf: 0-0 GS: 0-1 Gd: 0-0 GF: 0-2 Fm: 0-0
Distance: 5f/6f: 0-0 7f-8f: 0-2 9f-13f: 0-2 14f+: 0-0
Track : LH: 0-1 RH: 0-1 Tight: 0-1 Gall: 0-0
Aids: Bl: 0-0 Vi: 0-0 Tstrap: 0-0
Best Rating: 69 8/01 Sals 1m gd-fm

Strandiam (IRE)

86(91) (51)**61**
2-y-o b/br g Darnay-Jack-N-Jilly (IRE) (Anita's Prince)
J S Moore Alan J Speyer

Placings:0501411 **(2397)**
2001: 5^{0}GS, 5^{5}SD, 5^{0}SD, 5^{1}G, 5^{4}F, 7^{1}GF, 7^{1}GF

	Starts	1st	2nd	3rd	Win & Pl
Career Total (Turf)	5	3	0	0	7126
Career Total (AW)	2	0	0	0	0

61 6/01 Rdcr 7f G G-F £1869
57 6/01 Yarm 7f3y G G-F £1855
57 5/01 Haml 5f4y E GD £3402
Total win prize-money £7126

Going (Turf): Sf: 0-0 GS: 0-1 Gd: 1-1 **GF: 2-2** Fm: 0-1
Distance: 5f/6f: 1-5 **7f-8f: 2-2** 9f-13f: 0-0 14f+: 0-0
Track : LH: 0-1 RH: 0-0 Tight: 0-1 Gall: 0-0
Aids: Bl: 0-0 Vi: 0-1 Tstrap: 0-0
Best Rating: 61 6/01 Rdcr 7f gd-fm

He landed three low-grade wins in the summer of 2001, where he was seen to best effect over seven furlongs on a sound surface, and was subsequently sent to race in Sweden.

Strasbourg (USA)

95(75) (27)**54**
4-y-o ch g Dehere (USA)-Pixie Erin (Golden Fleece (USA))
N Tinkler Mr James Marshall & Mrs Susan Marshall

Placings:120/0022000060-00055000 **(4907)**
2001: 8^{0}SD, 8^{0}G, 7^{0}F, 8^{5}S, 8^{5}GS, 9^{0}G, 7^{0}G, 7^{0}G

	Starts	1st	2nd	3rd	Win & Pl
Career Total (Turf)	20	1	3	0	9841
Career Total (AW)	1	0	0	0	

82 9/99 Chep 7f16y D GD £3192
Total win prize-money £3193

Going (Turf): Sf: 0-3 GS: 0-3 **Gd: 1-8** GF: 0-4 Fm: 0-2
Distance: 5f/6f: 0-0 **7f-8f: 1-14** 9f-13f: 0-7 14f+: 0-0
Track : LH: 0-10 RH: 0-5 Tight: 0-3 Gall: 0-6
Aids: Bl: 0-1 Vi: 0-0 Tstrap: 0-1
Best Rating: 54 8/01 Bevl 1m100y gd-sft

Strat's Quest

97(94) (27)**31**
7-y-o b m Nicholas (USA)-Eagle's Quest (Legal Eagle)
D W P Arbuthnot Philip Banfield

Placings:645400100/010000060/0036005000050/42126 0045/65001005005000-50300400060000 **(5592)**
2001: 7^{5}SD, 7^{0}SW, 8^{3}SW, 12^{0}SD, 8^{0}SD, 6^{4}GS, 6^{0}HY, 8^{0}GS, 7^{0}SD, 7^{6}SD, 5^{0}G, 5^{0}HY, 6^{0}GS, 8^{0}SD

	Starts	1st	2nd	3rd	Win & Pl
Career Total (Turf)	43	3	1	1	12452
Career Total (AW)	23	1	1	1	2253

49 4/00 Wwck 6f168y F SFT £2520
48 3/99 Sthl 6f G(0-60)H STD £1514
58 5/97 Wind 5f217y D(0-80)H SFT £3935
64 10/96 Chep 6f16y E(0-75)H SFT £3129
Total win prize-money £11098

Going (Turf): Sf: 3-15 GS: 0-11 Gd: 0-8 GF: 0-8 Fm: 0-1
Distance: 5f/6f: 2-30 7f-8f: 2-34 9f-13f: 0-2 14f+: 0-0
Track : **LH: 2-37** RH: 1-8 Tight: 0-12 **Gall: 1-11**
Aids: Bl: 0-0 **Vi: 1-19** Tstrap: 0-0
Best Rating: 34 4/01 Brig 6f209y gd-sft

Strath Fillan

91 **37**
3-y-o b f Dolphin Street (FR)-Adarama (IRE) (Persian Bold)
W J Musson Mrs P A Linton

Placings:0005-000500 **(4422)**
2001: 8^{0}S, 9^{0}GF, 12^{0}GS, 9^{5}G, 9^{0}GF, 10^{0}GF

	Starts	1st	2nd	3rd	Win & Pl
Career Total (Turf)	10	0	0	0	0

Going (Turf): Sf: 0-1 GS: 0-1 Gd: 0-1 GF: 0-7 Fm: 0-0
Distance: 5f/6f: 0-1 7f-8f: 0-2 9f-13f: 0-7 14f+: 0-0
Track : LH: 0-4 RH: 0-4 Tight: 0-1 Gall: 0-1
Aids: Bl: 0-0 Vi: 0-0 Tstrap: 0-0
Best Rating: 37 8/01 Bevl 1m1f207y good

Has not shown much in races up to ten furlongs, mainly on fast ground.

Strathspey

87 **58**
2-y-o ch f Dancing Spree (USA)-Diebiedale (Dominion)
C F Wall T J Wells

Placings:0 **(5594)**
2001: 6^{0}GS

	Starts	1st	2nd	3rd	Win & Pl
Career Total (Turf)	1	0	0	0	

Going (Turf): Sf: 0-0 GS: 0-1 Gd: 0-0 GF: 0-0 Fm: 0-0
Distance: 5f/6f: 0-1 7f-8f: 0-0 9f-13f: 0-0 14f+: 0-0
Track : LH: 0-0 RH: 0-0 Tight: 0-0 Gall: 0-0
Aids: Bl: 0-0 Vi: 0-0 Tstrap: 0-0
Best Rating: 58 11/01 NmkR 6f gd-sft

Stratton (IRE)

111(105) (74)**104+**
4-y-o b g Fairy King (USA)-Golden Bloom (Main Reef)
D E Cantillon Mrs E M Clarke

Placings:6/40304-2111645001141114 **(5391)**
2001: 8^{2}SD, 7^{1}SD, 7^{1}SD, 7^{1}SD, 7^{6}SD, 7^{4}F, 9^{5}F, 7^{0}GF, 6^{0}GF, 7^{1}GS, 7^{1}G, 7^{4}G, 7^{1}GF, 7^{1}GF, 7^{1}G, 7^{4}GS

	Starts	1st	2nd	3rd	Win & Pl
Career Total (Turf)	16	5	0	1	35388
Career Total (AW)	6	3	1	0	6491

100 10/01 NmkR 7f C(0-90)H GD £7588
91 9/01 Newb 7f C(0-95)H G-F £8092
87 9/01 Ling 7f140y D(0-80)H G-F £7962
76 8/01 Yarm 7f3y D(0-80)H GD £5518
71 8/01 Yarm 7f3y D(0-80)H G-S £4563
74 1/01 Ling 7f E(0-70)H STD £2443
69 1/01 Ling 7f F(0-60) STD £2296
63 1/01 Sthl 7f G STD £1358
Total win prize-money £39824

Going (Turf): Sf: 0-2 GS: 1-2 **Gd: 2-5 GF: 2-5** Fm: 0-2
Distance: 5f/6f: 0-3 **7f-8f: 8-16** 9f-13f: 0-3 14f+: 0-0
Track : **LH: 3-10** RH: 0-1 **Tight: 2-3** Gall: 0-0
Aids: Bl: 0-0 Vi: 0-0 Tstrap: 0-0
Best Rating: 104 10/01 NmkR 7f gd-sft

A triple winner on sand at the start of this year, he has since shown he can handle turf with five wins despite a 26lb rise in the weights and has improved out of all recognition. Best over seven furlongs, he travels well in his races, but needs a decent gallop. Does not want the ground too soft. Sold for 110,000 gns to race in the USA.

Stravrole

(85) (48?)
3-y-o b g Tragic Role (USA)-La Stravaganza (Slip Anchor)
R Hollinshead E Bennion

Placings:20P **(2767)**
2001: 12^{2}SD, 11^{0}SD, 16^{P}GF

	Starts	1st	2nd	3rd	Win & Pl
Career Total (Turf)	1	0	0	0	
Career Total (AW)	2	0	1	0	834

Going (Turf): Sf: 0-0 GS: 0-0 Gd: 0-0 GF: 0-1 Fm: 0-0
Distance: 5f/6f: 0-0 7f-8f: 0-0 9f-13f: 0-2 14f+: 0-1
Track : LH: 0-3 RH: 0-0 Tight: 0-1 Gall: 0-0
Aids: Bl: 0-0 Vi: 0-0 Tstrap: 0-0
Best Rating: 48 2/01 Wolv 1m4f stand

Stravsea

(105) (58)
6-y-o b m Handsome Sailor-La Stravaganza (Slip Anchor)
R Hollinshead E Bennion

Placings:00200/2252230300/04330022201006001/03 511635042000-00360000012231045230000 **(5413)**
2001: 6^{0}SD, 8^{0}SD, 8^{3}SW, 8^{6}SD, 8^{0}SW, 8^{0}SD, 7^{0}SD, 8^{0}SD, 8^{0}SW, 7^{1}SD, 8^{2}SD, 8^{2}SD, 8^{3}SD, 7^{1}SD, 7^{0}SD, 8^{4}SD, 8^{5}SD, 8^{2}SD, 8^{3}SD, 9^{0}SD, 7^{0}SD

	Starts	1st	2nd	3rd	Win & Pl
Career Total (Turf)	9	0	1	0	712
Career Total (AW)	60	6	11	9	27603

58 5/01 Sthl 7f F(0-65)H STD £2352
48 4/01 Sthl 7f D(0-80)H STD £3932
60 1/00 Sthl 1m E(0-75)H STD £2769
53 1/00 Sthl 1m E(0-70)H STD £2769
46 12/99 Sthl 1m F(0-60)H STD £1882
49 7/99 Sthl 1m F(0-65)H STD £2416
Total win prize-money £16121

Going (Turf): Sf: 0-0 GS: 0-1 Gd: 0-3 GF: 0-5 Fm: 0-0
Distance: 5f/6f: 0-11 **7f-8f: 6-51** 9f-13f: 0-7 14f+: 0-0
Track : **LH: 6-62** RH: 0-0 Tight: 0-10 Gall: 0-0
Aids: Bl: 0-0 Vi: 0-0 Tstrap: 0-0
Best Rating: 58 7/01 Sthl 1m stand

A regular on the Southwell Fibresand, she pops up now and again, but her wins to runs ratio is very moderate these days.

Strawberry Bank

(54) **38**

2-y-o ch g Shaddad (USA)-Precious Girl (Precious Metal)

D Moffatt P G Airey & R R Whitton

Placings:000 **(2762)**

2001: 5^{0}GF, 6^{0}G, 5^{0}SD

	Starts	1st	2nd	3rd	Win & Pl
Career Total (Turf)	2	0	0	0	
Career Total (AW)	1	0	0	0	

Going (Turf): Sf: 0-0 GS: 0-0 Gd: 0-1 GF: 0-1 Fm: 0-0
Distance: 5f/6f: 0-3 7f-8f: 0-0 9f-13f: 0-0 14f+: 0-0
Track : LH: 0-0 RH: 0-0 Tight: 0-0 Gall: 0-0
Aids: Bl: 0-0 Vi: 0-0 Tstrap: 0-0
Best Rating: 38 6/01 Thsk 6f good

Strawberry Dawn

47

3-y-o gr f Fayruz-Alasib (Siberian Express (USA))

N Hamilton John Hopkins (t/a South Hatch Racing)

Placings:45-0 **(4842)**

2001: 8^{0}G

	Starts	1st	2nd	3rd	Win & Pl
Career Total (Turf)	3	0	0	0	280

Going (Turf): Sf: 0-0 GS: 0-0 Gd: 0-1 GF: 0-1 Fm: 0-1
Distance: 5f/6f: 0-2 7f-8f: 0-0 9f-13f: 0-1 14f+: 0-0
Track : LH: 0-2 RH: 0-0 Tight: 0-0 Gall: 0-0
Aids: Bl: 0-0 Vi: 0-0 Tstrap: 0-0
Best Rating: 38 6/01 Thsk 6f good

Strawberry Patch (IRE)

99 **82**

2-y-o b c Woodborough (USA)-Okino (USA) (Strawberry Road (AUS))

Miss L A Perratt T P Finch

Placings:03150120 **(4479)**

2001: 5^{0}GF, 5^{3}GF, 5^{1}G, 6^{5}G, 5^{0}G, 5^{1}G, 5^{2}GF, 5^{0}F

	Starts	1st	2nd	3rd	Win & Pl
Career Total (Turf)	8	2	1	1	8714

76 8/01 Muss 5f D GD £4153
72 6/01 Muss 5f E GD £3290
Total win prize-money £7444

Going (Turf): Sf: 0-0 GS: 0-0 **Gd: 2-4** GF: 0-3 Fm: 0-1
Distance: 5f/6f: 2-7 7f-8f: 0-1 9f-13f: 0-0 14f+: 0-0
Track : LH: 0-0 RH: 0-0 Tight: 0-0 Gall: 0-0
Aids: Bl: 0-0 Vi: 0-0 Tstrap: 0-0
Best Rating: 82 8/01 Rdcr 5f gd-fm

He confirmed the ability he showed in a modest Musselburgh in June 2001 with a tidy win in a nursery, over course and distance in August. He is a strong sort with plenty of scope for improvement over his favoured five-furlong trip.

Strawberry Sands

96 **80**

2-y-o b f Lugana Beach-Strawberry Song (Final Straw)

J G Portman Fourever Hopeful

Placings:03051256 **(4730)**

2001: 5^{0}G, 5^{3}G, 5^{0}GF, 5^{5}GS, 5^{1}G, 5^{2}GF, 5^{5}GF, 5^{6}F

	Starts	1st	2nd	3rd	Win & Pl
Career Total (Turf)	8	1	1	1	4664

80 8/01 Bath 5f11y E GD £2982
Total win prize-money £2982

Going (Turf): Sf: 0-0 GS: 0-1 **Gd: 1-3** GF: 0-3 Fm: 0-1
Distance: 5f/6f: 1-8 7f-8f: 0-0 9f-13f: 0-0 14f+: 0-0
Track : **LH: 1-1** RH: 0-1 Tight: 0-0 **Gall: 1-2**
Aids: Bl: 0-0 Vi: 0-0 Tstrap: 0-0
Best Rating: 80 8/01 Bath 5f11y good

Strawman

79(93) (40)**52d**

4-y-o b g Ela-Mana-Mou-Oatfield (Great Nephew)

J G Given J E Titley

Placings:00650-05200 **(1635)**

2001: 14^{0}HY, 11^{5}SD, 12^{2}SD, 11^{0}SD, 11^{0}F

	Starts	1st	2nd	3rd	Win & Pl
Career Total (Turf)	7	0	0	0	0
Career Total (AW)	3	0	1	0	523

Going (Turf): Sf: 0-5 GS: 0-0 Gd: 0-0 GF: 0-1 Fm: 0-1
Distance: 5f/6f: 0-0 7f-8f: 0-1 9f-13f: 0-8 14f+: 0-1
Track : LH: 0-7 RH: 0-2 Tight: 0-0 Gall: 0-0
Aids: Bl: 0-4 Vi: 0-0 Tstrap: 0-0
Best Rating: 40 4/01 Sthl 1m3f stand

Street Index (IRE)

80 **60**

2-y-o br f Dolphin Street (FR)-Casaveha (IRE) (Persian Bold)

Mrs P N Dutfield The Index Racing Partnership

Placings:0 **(4249)**

2001: 6^{0}GF

	Starts	1st	2nd	3rd	Win & Pl
Career Total (Turf)	1	0	0	0	

Going (Turf): Sf: 0-0 GS: 0-0 Gd: 0-0 GF: 0-1 Fm: 0-0
Distance: 5f/6f: 0-1 7f-8f: 0-0 9f-13f: 0-0 14f+: 0-0
Track : LH: 0-0 RH: 0-0 Tight: 0-0 Gall. 0-0
Aids: Bl: 0-0 Vi: 0-0 Tstrap: 0-0
Best Rating: 60 8/01 NmkJ 6f gd-fm

A half-sister to useful juvenile Harrier.

Street Life (IRE)

109 **70+**

3-y-o ch g Dolphin Street (FR)-Wolf Cleugh (IRE) (Last Tycoon)

W J Musson Howard Spooner & Partners (i)

Placings:004-003612 **(5532)**

2001: 8^{0}G, 7^{0}GF, 8^{3}GF, 8^{6}G, 10^{1}HY, 9^{2}HY

	Starts	1st	2nd	3rd	Win & Pl
Career Total (Turf)	9	1	1	1	6162

67 10/01 Wind 1m2f7y D(0-80)H HVY £4654
Total win prize-money £4654

Going (Turf): Sf: 1-5 GS: 0-0 Gd: 0-2 GF: 0-2 Fm: 0-0
Distance: 5f/6f: 0-2 7f-8f: 0-4 **9f-13f: 1-3** 14f+: 0-0
Track : LH: 0-2 RH: 0-0 **Tight: 1-1** Gall: 0-0
Aids: Bl: 0-0 Vi: 0-0 Tstrap: 0-0
Best Rating: 70 10/01 Nott 1m1f213y heavy

Fairly lightly-raced. Has raced keenly in the past. Got off the mark at eighth attempt in a ten-furlong Windsor handicap on heavy ground. Acts on a fast surface aswell.

Street Walker (IRE)

91 **43**

5-y-o b m Dolphin Street (FR)-Foolish Dame (USA) (Foolish Pleasure (USA))

W Storey D O Cremin

Placings:0/60024252/400640-00 **(2313)**

2001: 7^{0}F, 8^{0}G

	Starts	1st	2nd	3rd	Win & Pl
Career Total (Turf)	17	0	3	0	2814

Going (Turf): Sf: 0-3 GS: 0-1 Gd: 0-6 GF: 0-6 Fm: 0-1
Distance: 5f/6f: 0-0 7f-8f: 0-4 9f-13f: 0-9 14f+: 0-4
Track : LH: 0-7 RH: 0-5 Tight: 0-7 Gall: 0-1
Aids: Bl: 0-0 Vi: 0-1 Tstrap: 0-0
Best Rating: 24 6/01 Ripn 1m good

Strensall

101 **45**

4-y-o b g Beveled (USA)-Payvashooz (Ballacashtal (CAN))

R E Barr R E Barr

Placings:00/0-034506020502006 **(5629)**

2001: 9^{0}GS, 5^{3}GF, 5^{4}F, 5^{5}G, 6^{0}GF, 5^{6}F, 5^{0}GF, 5^{2}GF, 5^{0}G, 5^{5}G, 5^{0}GF, 5^{2}F, 5^{0}G, 5^{0}G, 5^{6}G

	Starts	1st	2nd	3rd	Win & Pl
Career Total (Turf)	18	0	2	1	2188

Going (Turf): Sf: 0-1 GS: 0-1 Gd: 0-7 GF: 0-6 Fm: 0-3
Distance: 5f/6f: 0-16 7f-8f: 0-1 9f-13f: 0-1 14f+: 0-0
Track : LH: 0-0 RH: 0-1 Tight: 0-1 Gall: 0-0
Aids: Bl: 0-0 Vi: 0-0 Tstrap: 0-0
Best Rating: 52 8/01 Ripn 5f good

Moderate sprinter, suited by five furlongs and fast ground. Runs well at Newcastle.

Stretton (IRE)

109(83) (59)**84**

3-y-o br c Doyoun-Awayil (USA) (Woodman (USA))

J D Bethell M J Dawson

Placings:032006-23011016306 **(5249)**

2001: 10^{2}VS, 10^{3}S, 10^{0}GS, 7^{1}GF, 9^{1}GF, 8^{0}GF, 10^{1}G, 10^{6}GF, 10^{3}GS, 10^{0}G, 10^{6}S

	Starts	1st	2nd	3rd	Win & Pl
Career Total (Turf)	16	3	2	3	28117
Career Total (AW)	1	0	0	0	0

83 7/01 Ches 1m2f75y D(0-85)H GD £8658
80 5/01 Gdwd 1m1f D(0-80)H G-F £4602
79 5/01 York 7f202y C(0-95)H G-F £7767
Total win prize-money £21028

Going (Turf): Sf: 0-2 GS: 0-2 Gd: 1-5 **GF: 2-5** Fm: 0-1
Distance: 5f/6f: 0-4 7f-8f: 1-4 **9f-13f: 2-9** 14f+: 0-0
Track : **LH: 2-8** RH: 1-2 **Tight: 2-3** Gall: 1-6
Aids: Bl: 0-0 Vi: 0-0 Tstrap: 0-0
Best Rating: 84 9/01 Donc 1m2f60y good

A progressive colt, he won three times last season at York, Goodwood and Chester. Suited by trips of around ten furlongs and fast ground.

Strictly Speaking (IRE)

98(99) (66)**56**

4-y-o b g Sri Pekan (USA)-Gaijin (Caerleon (USA))

P F I Cole P F I Cole Ltd

Placings:6345/0660123-65006320 **(3409)**

2001: 14^{6}SD, 11^{5}GS, 8^{0}GF, 12^{0}GF, 10^{6}GF, 12^{3}GF, 12^{2}G, 12^{0}GF

	Starts	1st	2nd	3rd	Win & Pl
Career Total (Turf)	17	0	2	3	4040
Career Total (AW)	2	1	0	0	1810

66 8/00 Wolv 1m4f G(0-65)H STD £1809
Total win prize-money £1810

Going (Turf): Sf: 0-5 GS: 0-4 Gd: 0-1 GF: 0-7 Fm: 0-0
Distance: 5f/6f: 0-1 7f-8f: 0-1 **9f-13f: 1-16** 14f+: 0-1
Track : **LH: 1-11** RH: 0-4 **Tight: 1-9** Gall: 0-1
Aids: Bl: 0-3 Vi: 0-0 Tstrap: 0-0
Best Rating: 56 7/01 Fpsm 1m4f10y good

Strike Accord (IRE)

52

7-y-o br g Accordion-Ritual Girl (Ballad Rock)

I A Wood A Rybak

Placings:0 (0580)
2001: 8^0HY

	Starts	1st	2nd	3rd	Win & Pl
Career Total (Turf)	1	0	0	0	

Going (Turf): Sf: 0-1 GS: 0-0 Gd: 0-0 GF: 0-0 Fm: 0-0
Distance: 5f/6f: 0-0 7f-8f: 0-0 9f-13f: 0-1 14f+: 0-0
Track : LH: 0-1 RH: 0-0 Tight: 0-0 Gall: 0-0
Aids: Bl: 0-0 Vi: 0-0 Tstrap: 0-0

Strike Midnight (USA)

76 **55**
2-y-o b c Silver Hawk (USA)-Fleur De Nuit (USA) (Woodman (USA))
D R C Elsworth W V M W & Mrs E S Robins

Placings:6 (1945)
2001: 5^6GF

	Starts	1st	2nd	3rd	Win & Pl
Career Total (Turf)	1	0	0	0	0

Going (Turf): Sf: 0-0 GS: 0-0 Gd: 0-0 GF: 0-1 Fm: 0-0
Distance: 5f/6f: 0-1 7f-8f: 0-0 9f-13f: 0-0 14f+: 0-0
Track : LH: 0-0 RH: 0-0 Tight: 0-0 Gall: 0-0
Aids: Bl: 0-0 Vi: 0-0 Tstrap: 0-0
Best Rating: 55 6/01 Newb 5f34y gd-fm

Strike The Green (USA)

90(104) (77)**59**
3-y-o b/br c Smart Strike (CAN)-Durrah Green (Green Desert (USA))
B J Meehan Peter Wetzel

Placings:0010-2000 (1323)
2001: 5^2SD, 6^0S, 6^0GF, 6^0G

	Starts	1st	2nd	3rd	Win & Pl
Career Total (Turf)	4	0	0	0	
Career Total (AW)	4	1	1	0	4283
69 12/00 Wolv 6f D					STD £3090
					Total win prize-money £3091

Going (Turf): Sf: 0-1 GS: 0-0 Gd: 0-1 GF: 0-1 Fm: 0-0
Distance: **5f/6f: 1-6** 7f-8f: 0-2 9f-13f: 0-0 14f+: 0-0
Track : **LH: 1-5** RH: 0-0 **Tight: 1-4** Gall: 0-0
Aids: Bl: 0-2 Vi: 0-0 Tstrap: 0-0
Best Rating: 77 4/01 Ling 5f stand

An ex-Irish individual, he showed fair speed to land his first race on the All-Weather over six furlongs.

Strip Search

(69)
5-y-o b m Bluebird (USA)-Swift Pursuit (Posse (USA))
J G Smyth-Osbourne J G Smyth-Osbourne

Placings:6000/60000/0 (0540)
2001: 16^0SD

	Starts	1st	2nd	3rd	Win & Pl
Career Total (Turf)	7	0	0	0	0
Career Total (AW)	3	0	0	0	0

Going (Turf): Sf: 0-0 GS: 0-1 Gd: 0-2 GF: 0-4 Fm: 0-0
Distance: 5f/6f: 0-2 7f-8f: 0-4 9f-13f: 0-3 14f+: 0-1
Track : LH: 0-3 RH: 0-3 Tight: 0-4 Gall: 0-1
Aids: Bl: 0-1 Vi: 0-0 Tstrap: 0-0

Stroke Of Six (IRE)

94 **76**
2-y-o b f Woodborough (USA)-Angelus Chimes (Northfields (USA))
R Hannon N Hayes

Placings:01445625 (5176)
2001: 5^0F, 6^1GF, 6^4GF, 7^4G, 6^5G, 6^6G, 8^2S, 8^5HY

	Starts	1st	2nd	3rd	Win & Pl
Career Total (Turf)	8	1	1	0	5173
65 6/01 Sals 6f F					G-F £3318
					Total win prize-money £3318

Going (Turf): Sf: 0-2 GS: 0-0 Gd: 0-3 **GF: 1-2** Fm: 0-1
Distance: **5f/6f: 1-4** 7f-8f: 0-2 9f-13f: 0-2 14f+: 0-0
Track : LH: 0-1 RH: 0-2 Tight: 0-2 Gall: 0-0
Aids: Bl: 0-0 Vi: 0-0 Tstrap: 0-0
Best Rating: 76 9/01 Pont 1m4y soft

Got off the mark on her second run at Salisbury, looking as if seven furlongs would suit.

Stromsholm (IRE)

106(92) (61)**73**
5-y-o ch g Indian Ridge-Upward Trend (Salmon Leap (USA))
R Ingram (J R Fanshawe 9/1) The Stargazers

Placings:02/406324230-10015003020 (4891)
2001: 8^1SW, 8^0SD, 8^0S, 8^1GF, 8^5GF, 9^0G, 8^0GF, 8^3G, 8^0S, 8^2GF, 8^0GF, 10^0SD

	Starts	1st	2nd	3rd	Win & Pl
Career Total (Turf)	19	1	4	3	10958
Career Total (AW)	3	1	0	0	3159
71 7/01 Wind 1m67y E(0-70)H					G-F £3465
47 1/01 Wolv 1m100y D					SLW £2940
					Total win prize-money £6405

Going (Turf): Sf: 0-3 GS: 0-3 Gd: 0-4 **GF: 1-8** Fm: 0-1
Distance: 5f/6f: 0-1 7f-8f: 0-6 **9f-13f: 2-15** 14f+: 0-0
Track : LH: 1-9 RH: 1-8 **Tight: 2-10** Gall: 0-0
Aids: Bl: 0-0 Vi: 0-0 Tstrap: 0-0
Best Rating: 73 9/01 Sals 1m gd-fm

He had looked pretty moderate when with James Franshawe, but was found to be a bleeder and judging by his victory at Windsor in July 2001, that problem may have been sorted. Stays a mile. Acts on fast ground.

Strudel Ruse (IRE)

90 **63**
2-y-o b f Fayruz-Sweet Disorder (IRE) (Never So Bold)
P W Harris The Disorderlies

Placings:360 (5038)
2001: 5^3G, 6^6GF, 5^0G

	Starts	1st	2nd	3rd	Win & Pl
Career Total (Turf)	3	0	0	1	322

Going (Turf): Sf: 0-0 GS: 0-0 Gd: 0-2 GF: 0-1 Fm: 0-0
Distance: 5f/6f: 0-3 7f-8f: 0-0 9f-13f: 0-0 14f+: 0-0
Track : LH: 0-2 RH: 0-0 Tight: 0-0 Gall: 0-1
Aids: Bl: 0-0 Vi: 0-0 Tstrap: 0-0
Best Rating: 63 8/01 Brig 5f213y good

Strumpet

99(96) (75d)**55**
3-y-o gr f Tragic Role (USA)-Fee (Mandamus)
P W D'Arcy Sandycove Partnership

Placings:2016300602-644460550130 (5278)
2001: 7^6SD, 8^4SD, 8^4SD, 8^4S, 9^6G, 6^0F, 8^5F, 8^5GF, 7^0GF, 8^1G, 8^3GF, 9^0GS

	Starts	1st	2nd	3rd	Win & Pl
Career Total (Turf)	18	2	1	2	9963
Career Total (AW)	4	0	1	0	1068
55 7/01 Leic 1m9y G					GD £1960
68 6/00 Sals 5f D					G-F £3354
					Total win prize-money £5314

Going (Turf): Sf: 0-4 GS: 0-2 **Gd: 1-3 GF: 1-7** Fm: 0-2
Distance: 5f/6f: 1-6 7f-8f: 0-9 9f-13f: 1-7 14f+: 0-0
Track : LH: 0-9 RH: 0-2 Tight: 0-2 Gall: 0-0
Aids: Bl: 0-0 Vi: 0-0 Tstrap: 0-0
Best Rating: 65 4/01 Sthl 1m stand

Half-sister to several winners including a couple of juvenile milers, she lost her way after winning a Salisbury maiden in June 2000, until landing an uncompetitive seller at Leicester a year later on the lowest handicap mark of her career. She is suited to a sound surface and stays a mile.

Studio Time (USA)

67 **68+**
2-y-o b c Gone West (USA)-Ratings (USA) (Caveat (USA))
J H M Gosden George Strawbridge

Placings:1 (5369)
2001: 7^1GS

	Starts	1st	2nd	3rd	Win & Pl
Career Total (Turf)	1	1	0	0	0
68 10/01 NmkR 7f G					G-S £0

Going (Turf): Sf: 0-0 **GS: 1-1** Gd: 0-0 GF: 0-0 Fm: 0-0
Distance: 5f/6f: 0-0 **7f-8f: 1-1** 9f-13f: 0-0 14f+: 0-0
Track : LH: 0-0 RH: 0-0 Tight: 0-0 Gall: 0-0
Aids: Bl: 0-0 Vi: 0-0 Tstrap: 0-0
Best Rating: 68 10/01 NmkR 7f gd-sft

An American-bred colt, made all the running but had to be kept up to his work to score on his debut in the Newmarket Challenge Cup. Dettori later reported that the colt had been distracted by the headlamps of the cars leaving the course. Has only raced on good to soft ground.

Stunning (USA)

102 **105**
3-y-o b f Nureyev (USA)-Gorgeous (USA) (Slew O'Gold (USA))
Mme C Head-Maarek Robert N Clay

Placings:22132-105200
2001: 7^1HY, 8^0G, 10^5G, 7^2GS, 8^0S, 7^0S

	Starts	1st	2nd	3rd	Win & Pl
Career Total (Turf)	11	2	4	1	54282
100 4/01 Lonc 7f					HVY £13579
9/00 Chan 6f					SFT £8646
					Total win prize-money £22225

Going (Turf): **Sf: 1-4** GS: 0-2 Gd: 0-2 GF: 0-0 Fm: 0-0
Distance: 5f/6f: 0-0 **7f-8f: 1-7** 9f-13f: 0-1 14f+: 0-0
Track : LH: 0-1 RH: 0-1 Tight: 0-0 Gall: 0-0
Aids: Bl: 0-0 Vi: 0-0 Tstrap: 0-0
Best Rating: 105 7/01 Deau 7f gd-sft

She showed consistent form at two and showed she had trained on with victory in the Prix Imprudence at Longchamp on her return. Seventh in the 1000 Guineas but did not go on from that.

Stunning Force (IRE)

98 **82**
2-y-o b c Ezzoud (IRE)-New Wind (GER) (Windwurf (GER))
M Johnston Maktoum Al Maktoum

Placings:2210 (5021)
2001: 7^2G, 8^2GF, 8^1G, 7^0HY

	Starts	1st	2nd	3rd	Win & Pl
Career Total (Turf)	4	1	2	0	6355
82 9/01 Epsm 1m114y D					GD £4348
					Total win prize-money £4349

Going (Turf): Sf: 0-1 GS: 0-0 **Gd: 1-2** GF: 0-1 Fm: 0-0
Distance: 5f/6f: 0-0 7f-8f: 0-2 **9f-13f: 1-2** 14f+: 0-0
Track : **LH: 1-1** RH: 0-1 **Tight: 1-1** Gall: 0-0
Aids: Bl: 0-0 Vi: 0-0 Tstrap: 0-0
Best Rating: 82 9/01 Epsm 1m114y good

Got off the mark at the third attempt after two promising runs previous to that. Suited by seven furlongs to an extended mile. Acts well on good ground.

Sturgeon (IRE)

(77) **67**
7-y-o ch g Caerleon (USA)-Ridge The Times (USA)

(Riva Ridge (USA))
G Brown J Cleeve

Placings:022/053/304466/014000/0 **(0461)**
2001: 12^{0}SD

	Starts	1st	2nd	3rd	Win & Pl
Career Total (Turf)	18	1	2	2	8349
Career Total (AW)	1	0	0	0	

68	6/99	Ripn	1m2f	D(0-85)H	G-F	£4201

Total win prize-money £4202

Going (Turf): Sf: 0-2 GS: 0-0 Gd: 0-10 **GF: 1-6** Fm: 0-0
Distance: 5f/6f: 0-0 7f-8f: 0-5 **9f-13f: 1-14** 14f+: 0-0
Track : LH: 0-6 **RH: 1-8 Tight: 1-8** Gall: 0-1
Aids: Bl: 0-0 Vi: 0-1 Tstrap: 0-1
Best Rating: 68 6/99 Ripn 1m2f GF

He took a very long time in getting off the mark, but took a ten-furlong Ripon handicap in June.

Stutter

96 **60**
3-y-o ch c Polish Precedent (USA)-Bright Spells (Salse (USA))
W J Haggas B Haggas & Wentworth Racing (pty) Ltd

Placings:55-40 **(5374)**
2001: 7^{4}GF, 6^{0}G

	Starts	1st	2nd	3rd	Win & Pl
Career Total (Turf)	4	0	0	0	0

Going (Turf): Sf: 0-1 GS: 0-0 Gd: 0-1 GF: 0-2 Fm: 0-0
Distance: 5f/6f: 0-3 7f-8f: 0-1 9f-13f: 0-0 14f+: 0-0
Track : LH: 0-1 RH: 0-0 Tight: 0-1 Gall: 0-0
Aids: Bl: 0-0 Vi: 0-0 Tstrap: 0-0
Best Rating: 60 9/01 Catt 7f gd-fm

Good fifth to Rumpold, on his debut, he has not quite progressed from there, including when beaten favourite at Redcar.

Style Dancer (IRE)

109(72) (63)**69**
7-y-o b g Dancing Dissident (USA)-Showing Style (Pas De Seul)
T D Easterby (R M Whitaker 13/10) Mrs C A Hodgotto

Placings:00043201/30030203233000/001605506/0005 064154003344000**0330**/54040110031020-040363610200600 **(5638)**
2001: 7^{0}G, 7^{4}GF, 8^{0}GS, 8^{3}GF, 8^{6}GF, 7^{3}GF, 7^{6}GF, 8^{1}GF, 6^{0}G, 8^{2}GF, 9^{0}G, 9^{0}GS, 7^{6}GF, 7^{0}HY, 6^{0}GS, 7^{0}G

	Starts	1st	2nd	3rd	Win & Pl
Career Total (Turf)	80	7	5	11	72611
Career Total (AW)	4	0	0	2	973

75	7/01	Bevl	1m100y	D(0-85)H	G-F	£7969
72	9/00	York	6f214y	E(0-75)H	GD	£8901
66	7/00	Bevl	1m100y	D(0-85)H	GD	£6851
64	7/00	Donc	1m	D(0-80)H	GD	£7767
61	7/99	Hayd	7f30y	E(0-70)H	G-S	£3074
73	7/98	York	6f214y	C(0-90)H	FRM	£7570
72	10/96	Rdcr	6f	E(0-75)	G-F	£3172

Total win prize-money £45307

Going (Turf): Sf: 0-8 GS: 1-11 **Gd: 3-26** GF: 2-33 Fm: 1-2
Distance: 5f/6f: 1-20 **7f-8f: 4-54** 9f-13f: 2-10 14f+: 0-0
Track : **LH: 4-36** RH: 2-15 Tight: 0-18 **Gall: 3-12**
Aids: Bl: 0-1 **Vi: 4-33** Tstrap: 0-0
Best Rating: 77 7/01 Gdwd 1m gd-fm

Has a poor strike rate, but won the same race at Beverley for the second year running in July and obviously likes that track. A mile looks his best trip these days.

Stylish Clare (IRE)

100 **75**
3-y-o b f Desert Style (IRE)-Brockley Hill Lass (IRE) (Alzao (USA))
J W Payne Oremsa Partnership

Placings:5001000 **(4890)**
2001: 7^{5}GF, 7^{0}GF, 8^{0}GF, 6^{1}GF, 6^{0}G, 5^{0}G, 6^{0}GF

	Starts	1st	2nd	3rd	Win & Pl
Career Total (Turf)	7	1	0	0	3276

75	7/01	Wind	6f	E(0-75)H	G-F	£3276

Total win prize-money £3276

Going (Turf): Sf: 0-0 GS: 0-0 Gd: 0-2 **GF: 1-5** Fm: 0-0
Distance: **5f/6f: 1-4** 7f-8f: 0-2 9f-13f: 0-1 14f+: 0-0
Track : LH: 0-1 RH: 0-1 Tight: 0-1 Gall: 0-0
Aids: Bl: 0-0 Vi: 0-0 Tstrap: 0-0
Best Rating: 75 7/01 Wind 6f gd-fm

She made a successful handicap debut when dropped to six furlongs at Windsor in July, but was well drawn and had the run of the race.

Stylish Fella (USA)

70 **45**
3-y-o b g Irish River (FR)-Dariela (USA) (Manila (USA))
Ian Williams Horses For Courses Partnership

Placings:0066-000 **(4240)**
2001: 11^{0}GF, 12^{0}G, 9^{0}GF

	Starts	1st	2nd	3rd	Win & Pl
Career Total (Turf)	7	0	0	0	0

Going (Turf): Sf: 0-0 GS: 0-0 Gd: 0-2 GF: 0-4 Fm: 0-0
Distance: 5f/6f: 0-1 7f-8f: 0-1 9f-13f: 0-4 14f+: 0-0
Track : LH: 0-1 RH: 0-2 Tight: 0-2 Gall: 0-0
Aids: Bl: 0-1 Vi: 0-1 Tstrap: 0-0
Best Rating: 15 8/01 Folk 1m4f good

Showed a little ability in plating company as a juvenile in 2000.

Stylish Ways (IRE)

84(94) (51)**33**
9-y-o b g Thatching-Style Of Life (USA) (The Minstrel (CAN))
Mrs Lydia Pearce (J Pearce 6/2) Ian Hall

Placings:413/13350/44000000/500030/332230210156/4530600020000050/06253000**0-644**000 **(5181)**
2001: 8^{6}SD, 8^{4}SD, 8^{4}SD, 6^{0}GF, 6^{0}HY, 6^{0}HY

	Starts	1st	2nd	3rd	Win & Pl
Career Total (Turf)	60	4	5	9	47789
Career Total (AW)	4	0	0	0	0

76	10/98	Hayd	6f	D(0-80)H	SFT	£8075
69	8/98	NmkJ	6f	E(0-80)H	GD	£3582
93	5/95	Leic	5f218y	C	GD	£5256
89	9/94	Nott	6f15y	D	SFT	£3792

Total win prize-money £20707

Going (Turf): Sf: 2-12 GS: 0-9 **Gd: 2-22** GF: 0-14 Fm: 0-3
Distance: **5f/6f: 3-42** 7f-8f: 1-20 9f-13f: 0-2 14f+: 0-0
Track : LH: 0-12 RH: 0-4 Tight: 0-6 Gall: 0-7
Aids: Bl: 0-0 Vi: 0-1 Tstrap: 0-0
Best Rating: 51 1/01 Wolv 1m100y stand

Best when held up, he is suited by six furlongs. Having his first run since February when well down the field at York in September.

Sualamar (IRE)

88 **61**
5-y-o b g Magical Strike (USA)-Annagh Trust (Jester)
G M Moore Mrs Mary And Miss Susan Hatfield

Placings:4340 **(4328)**
2001: 8^{4}GF, 8^{3}F, 8^{4}G, 10^{0}GF

	Starts	1st	2nd	3rd	Win & Pl
Career Total (Turf)	4	0	0	1	1183

Going (Turf): Sf: 0-0 GS: 0-0 Gd: 0-1 GF: 0-2 Fm: 0-1
Distance: 5f/6f: 0-0 7f-8f: 0-2 9f-13f: 0-2 14f+: 0-0
Track : LH: 0-2 RH: 0-2 Tight: 0-3 Gall: 0-0
Aids: Bl: 0-0 Vi: 0-0 Tstrap: 0-0
Best Rating: 61 8/01 Pont 1m4y good

Sualda (IRE)

97 **75**
2-y-o b c Idris (IRE)-Winning Heart (Horage)
K McAuliffe The Beach Men

Placings:44023000 **(5668)**
2001: 6^{4}G, 7^{4}GF, 6^{0}F, 8^{2}GF, 7^{3}S, 7^{0}S, 8^{0}G, 8^{0}HY

	Starts	1st	2nd	3rd	Win & Pl
Career Total (Turf)	8	0	1	1	1644

Going (Turf): Sf: 0-3 GS: 0-0 Gd: 0-2 GF: 0-2 Fm: 0-1
Distance: 5f/6f: 0-1 7f-8f: 0-4 9f-13f: 0-3 14f+: 0-0
Track : LH: 0-5 RH: 0-1 Tight: 0-3 Gall: 0-1
Aids: Bl: 0-0 Vi: 0-0 Tstrap: 0-5
Best Rating: 75 9/01 Nott 1m54y gd-fm

Ordinary placed form in maiden auctions.

Sualtach (IRE)

100(103) (60)**49**
8-y-o b h Marju (IRE)-Astra Adastra (Mount Hagen (FR))
Andrew Reid (R Hollinshead 27/3) A S Reid

Placings:3421040/**0**1024**01**55020000/400402304015/2 **103615610**6205**2**2024**1**40010**222/416530**00**0**00**4**65000/ **0-32031423203363**0**5**26000**016** **(5166)**
2001: 9^{3}SW, 9^{2}SD, 9^{0}SD, 8^{3}SW, 9^{1}SW, 9^{1}SD, 8^{2}SD, 9^{0}SD, 8^{2}SD, 11^{0}SD, 8^{3}SW, 8^{3}SD, 8^{6}SD, 10^{3}GS, 9^{0}G, 8^{5}SD, 9^{2}F, 9^{6}GF, 9^{0}GF, 8^{0}GF, 9^{0}G, 10^{0}GF, 9^{1}SW

	Starts	1st	2nd	3rd	Win & Pl
Career Total (Turf)	60	4	8	3	31740
Career Total (AW)	44	8	8	7	35629

60	9/01	Wolv	1m1f79y	F(0-65)H	SLW	£2345
57	2/01	Wolv	1m1f79y	E(0-75)H	SLW	£2933
82	1/99	Wolv	1m1f79y	D(0-80)H	STD	£3747
72	9/98	Hayd	1m30y	D(0-85)H	G-F	£3745
76	7/98	Wolv	1m100y	F	STD	£1996
78	4/98	Wolv	1m100y	D(0-80)H	STD	£3460
71	2/98	Wolv	1m100y	D(0-85)H	STD	£3403
71	1/98	Wolv	1m1f70y	D(0-85)H	STD	£3403
74	10/97	Rdcr	1m	D(0-75)H	G-F	£4091
81	5/96	Wolv	7f	E(0-70)H	STD	£3406
83	3/96	Donc	7f	D(0-85)H	G-S	£4854
87	6/95	Nott	6f15y	D	G-F	£4012

Total win prize-money £41399

Going (Turf): Sf: 0-5 GS: 1-11 Gd: 0-15 **GF: 3-26** Fm: 0-3
Distance: 5f/6f: 0-5 7f-8f: 4-37 **9f-13f: 8-62** 14f+: 0-0
Track : **LH: 9-75** RH: 0-11 **Tight: 8-48** Gall: 0-8
Aids: Bl: 0-0 Vi: 0-1 Tstrap: 0-0
Best Rating: 60 9/01 Wolv 1m1f79y slow

Suave Frankie

(84) (16)
5-y-o ch g Suave Dancer (USA)-Francia (Legend Of France (USA))
I W McInnes (A Smith 21/5) I W McInnes

Placings:000/204200/00-000000 **(1471)**
2001: 16^{0}SD, 16^{0}SD, 12^{0}SD, 7^{0}SD, 11^{0}SD, 11^{0}SD

	Starts	1st	2nd	3rd	Win & Pl
Career Total (Turf)	9	0	2	0	1724
Career Total (AW)	8	0	0	0	

Going (Turf): Sf: 0-2 GS: 0-2 Gd: 0-1 GF: 0-2 Fm: 0-2
Distance: 5f/6f: 0-1 7f-8f: 0-4 9f-13f: 0-7 14f+: 0-5
Track : LH: 0-12 RH: 0-1 Tight: 0-6 Gall: 0-0
Aids: Bl: 0-4 Vi: 0-0 Tstrap: 0-0
Best Rating: 16 4/01 Sthl 1m3f stand

Suave Native (USA)

96 **88**

3-y-o ch c Shuailaan (USA)-Courtly Courier (USA) (Raise A Native)

A C Stewart Roy Clemons

Placings:1-400 **(5391)**

2001: 7^{4}GF, 7^{0}G, 7^{0}GS

	Starts	1st	2nd	3rd	Win & Pl
Career Total (Turf)	4	1	0	0	4815

98	10/00	Yarm	6f3y	D		HVY	£4225

Total win prize-money £4225

Going (Turf): Sf: 1-1 GS: 0-1 Gd: 0-1 GF: 0-1 Fm: 0-0
Distance: 5f/6f: 0-0 **7f-8f: 1-4** 9f-13f: 0-0 14f+: 0-0
Track : LH: 0-0 RH: 0-1 Tight: 0-0 Gall: 0-0
Aids: Bl: 0-0 Vi: 0-0 Tstrap: 0-0
Best Rating: 88 9/01 Gdwd 7f gd-fm

Suave Performer

101(93) (45d)**54**

4-y-o b g Suave Dancer (USA)-Francia (Legend Of France (USA))

S C Williams D A Shekells

Placings:04542445-0020215663010 **(5230)**

2001: 8^{0}SD, 12^{0}SD, 9^{2}SD, 12^{0}SD, 9^{2}HY, 9^{1}S, 10^{5}GS, 12^{6}GF, 9^{6}GF, 10^{3}G, 12^{0}GF, 9^{1}G, 11^{0}S

	Starts	1st	2nd	3rd	Win & Pl
Career Total (Turf)	14	2	2	1	8259
Career Total (AW)	7	0	1	0	1044

53	9/01	Bevl	1m1f207yF(0-60)H		GD	£3097
52	5/01	Rdcr	1m1f	G(0-65)H	SFT	£1900

Total win prize-money £4999

Going (Turf): Sf: 1-4 GS: 0-3 **Gd: 1-3** GF: 0-3 Fm: 0-1
Distance: 5f/6f: 0-2 7f-8f: 0-2 **9f-13f: 2-17** 14f+: 0-0
Track : LH: 1-11 RH: 1-8 **Tight: 1-13** Gall: 0-2
Aids: Bl: 0-0 Vi: 0-0 Tstrap: 0-0
Best Rating: 53 9/01 Bevl 1m1f207y good

Subadar Major

101(88) (22)**7**

4-y-o b g Komaite (USA)-Rather Gorgeous (Billion (USA))

Mrs G S Rees Major P Bailey

Placings:0/006-0041600 **(5538)**

2001: 13^{0}G, 14^{0}F, 14^{4}F, 13^{1}GF, 16^{6}SD, 12^{0}G, 10^{0}S

	Starts	1st	2nd	3rd	Win & Pl
Career Total (Turf)	6	1	0	0	3024
Career Total (AW)	5	0	0	0	0

33	6/01	Ayr	1m5f13y	E(0-70)H	G-F	£3024

Total win prize-money £3024

Going (Turf): Sf: 0-1 GS: 0-0 Gd: 0-2 **GF: 1-1** Fm: 0-2
Distance: 5f/6f: 0-0 7f-8f: 0-2 9f-13f: 0-4 **14f+: 1-5**
Track : **LH: 1-9** RH: 0-2 Tight: 0-7 Gall: 0-0
Aids: Bl: 0-0 Vi: 0-0 Tstrap: 0-0
Best Rating: 33 6/01 Ayr 1m5f13y gd-fm

Sudden Flight (IRE)

103 **79**

4-y-o b g In The Wings-Ma Petite Cherie (USA) (Caro)

E A L Dunlop Maktoum Al Maktoum

Placings:500130/130252126-0063300 **(5178)**

2001: 16^{0}S, 18^{0}GF, 14^{6}G, 12^{3}GF, 14^{3}G, 14^{0}HY, 11^{0}HY

	Starts	1st	2nd	3rd	Win & Pl
Career Total (Turf)	22	3	3	4	24418

84	8/00	Hayd	1m6f	D(0-85)H	GD	£3984
78	4/00	Thsk	1m4f	E(0-70)	G-S	£3614
67	9/99	Yarm	1m3y	E(0-75)H	SFT	£3314

Total win prize-money £10913

Going (Turf): Sf: 1-8 GS: 1-3 Gd: 1-6 GF: 0-5 Fm: 0-0
Distance: 5f/6f: 0-0 7f-8f: 0-3 **9f-13f: 2-10** 14f+: 1-9
Track : **LH: 2-12** RH: 0-6 **Tight: 1-5** Gall: 0-3
Aids: Bl: 0-0 Vi: 0-1 Tstrap: 0-0
Best Rating: 81 5/01 Ches 2m2f147y gd-fm

A half-brother to a number of winners on the Flat and over hurdles, he is a winning staying handicapper. Acts on good and heavy ground. Needs strong handling. Has won at up to fourteen furlongs.

Sudra

103 **65**

4-y-o b g Indian Ridge-Bunting (Shaadi (USA))

T D Barron East West Partnership

Placings:310/0000-20310600600 **(5638)**

2001: 7^{2}GS, 7^{0}G, 8^{3}GF, 7^{1}GF, 8^{0}F, 7^{6}F, 8^{0}GS, 7^{0}GF, 7^{6}GF, 7^{0}S, 7^{0}G

	Starts	1st	2nd	3rd	Win & Pl
Career Total (Turf)	18	2	1	2	7048

68	6/01	Beve	7f110y	E(0-70)H	G-F	£2637
94	8/99	Thsk	6f	D	G-F	£4391

Total win prize-money £7028

Going (Turf): Sf: 0-2 GS: 0-3 Gd: 0-5 **GF: 2-5** Fm: 0-3
Distance: 5f/6f: 1-4 7f-8f: 1-12 9f-13f: 0-2 14f+: 0-0
Track : LH: 0-5 **RH: 1-4** Tight: 0-6 Gall: 0-0
Aids: Bl: 0-0 Vi: 0-0 Tstrap: 0-0
Best Rating: 71 6/01 Newc 7f firm

A useful juvenile for Ed Dunlop, but rather lost his way last term. Better efforts for his new yard in handicaps at around a mile this season, including when dead heating at Beverley in June.

Sue Me (IRE)

95(102) (47)**56**

9-y-o b/br g Contract Law (USA)-Pink Fondant (Northfields (USA))

D Nicholls T G Meynell

Placings:64321035/20502000**0**/00006000460/5033500 20/43110040156641025000120**4**/1340030301000**6**/001 06-20310440050 **(4796)**

2001: 6^{2}SD, 6^{0}SW, 6^{3}SW, 5^{1}SD, 6^{0}HY, 5^{4}GF, 6^{4}GF, 5^{0}SD, 6^{0}G, 5^{5}G, 5^{0}G

	Starts	1st	2nd	3rd	Win & Pl
Career Total (Turf)	60	5	4	5	28514
Career Total (AW)	31	5	3	4	17175

47	3/01	Sthl	5f	F(0-65)H	STD	£1778
57	5/00	Muss	5f	F	FRM	£2758
59	9/99	Ayr	5f	D(0-85)H	G-S	£6440
67	1/99	Sthl	6f	F	STD	£2087
58	9/98	Sthl	6f	F(0-60)H	STD	£2161
68	7/98	Donc	5f	F(0-65)H	G-F	£2358
62	4/98	Pont	5f	F(0-70)H	G-S	£2161
49	2/98	Sthl	6f	D(0-80)H	STD	£4484
45	1/98	Sthl	6f	E(0-70)H	STD	£3165
75	10/94	York	6f	C	SFT	£6004

Total win prize-money £33397

Going (Turf): Sf: 1-12 **GS: 2-14** Gd: 0-18 GF: 1-14 Fm: 1-2
Distance: **5f/6f: 10-75** 7f-8f: 0-15 9f-13f: 0-1 14f+: 0-0
Track : **LH: 5-37** RH: 0-4 Tight: 0-12 Gall: 0-5
Aids: **Bl: 2-15** Vi: 0-0 Tstrap: 0-0
Best Rating: 56 5/01 Muss 5f gd-fm

Sugar Cube Treat

100(92) (30)**45**

5-y-o b m Lugana Beach-Fair Eleanor (Saritamer (USA))

M Mullineaux Abbey Racing

Placings:0445300/053356001 0/000350000-60060 **(4568)**

2001: 6^{6}SD, 6^{0}GF, 6^{0}G, 6^{6}G, 6^{0}HY

	Starts	1st	2nd	3rd	Win & Pl
Career Total (Turf)	30	1	0	4	6000
Career Total (AW)	1	0	0	0	0

55	10/99	Ayr	6f	E(0-70)H	SFT	£3369

Total win prize-money £3370

Going (Turf): Sf: 1-6 GS: 0-4 Gd: 0-9 GF: 0-9 Fm: 0-2
Distance: **5f/6f: 1-23** 7f-8f: 0-8 9f-13f: 0-0 14f+: 0-0
Track : LH: 0-15 RH: 0-2 Tight: 0-4 Gall: 0-2
Aids: Bl: 0-0 Vi: 0-0 Tstrap: 0-0
Best Rating: 45 7/01 Pont 6f gd-fm

Has just one win to her name, as a juvenile. Well beaten this term.

Sugar Rolo

(84) (39)

3-y-o b f Bin Ajwaad (IRE)-Spriolo (Priolo (USA))

D Morris W J Palmer

Placings:65403040-00 **(0192)**

2001: 8^{0}SW, 8^{0}SD

	Starts	1st	2nd	3rd	Win & Pl
Career Total (Turf)	6	0	0	0	275
Career Total (AW)	4	0	0	1	276

Going (Turf): Sf: 0-2 GS: 0-0 Gd: 0-0 GF: 0-4 Fm: 0-0
Distance: 5f/6f: 0-0 7f-8f: 0-9 9f-13f: 0-1 14f+: 0-0
Track : LH: 0-4 RH: 0-0 Tight: 0-0 Gall: 0-0
Aids: Bl: 0-1 Vi: 0-0 Tstrap: 0-0
Best Rating: 22 1/01 Sthl 1m slow

Sugarfoot

111 (96)**116**

7-y-o ch h Thatching-Norpella (Northfields (USA))

N Tinkler Mrs D Wright

Placings:1/34020/0024215121/316301125/1551005336 0-40200 **(2304)**

2001: 9^{4}FT, 8^{0}FT, 7^{2}G, 8^{0}S, 8^{0}GF

	Starts	1st	2nd	3rd	Win & Pl
Career Total (Turf)	39	9	6	5	255640
Career Total (AW)	2	0	0	0	3188

114	7/00	Asct	1m	A	GD	£33800
116	4/00	Donc	7f		G-S	£20300
117	9/99	Donc	1m	A	G-F	£20700
116	8/99	York	7f202y	B(0-105)H	GD	£29481
106	5/99	York	7f202y	A(0-110)H	SFT	£16367
104	10/98	York	7f202y	B(0-100)H	GD	£10185
97	8/98	York	7f202y	B(0-105)H	FRM	£27996
92	7/98	Asct	1m	B(0-105)H	G-F	£14135
82	7/96	Ayr	6f	D	G-F	£3517

Total win prize-money £176485

Going (Turf): Sf: 1-7 GS: 1-3 **Gd: 3-15 GF: 3-13** Fm: 1-1
Distance: 5f/6f: 1-1 **7f-8f: 8-36** 9f-13f: 0-4 14f+: 0-0
Track : **LH: 5-8** RH: 1-9 Tight: 0-0 **Gall: 6-11**
Aids: Bl: 0-0 Vi: 0-0 Tstrap: 0-0
Best Rating: 113 5/01 NmkR 7f good

A genuine Pattern-class miler, he has been globe-trotting for much of the last year. He has a tremendous record over a mile at York, winning four times in all. He ran up to his best when runner-up to Warningford in Group 3 at Newmarket in May. He has been retired.

Suggestive

109 **98+**

3-y-o b g Reprimand-Pleasuring (Good Times (ITY))

W J Haggas Mrs Barbara Bassett

Placings:11 **(1673)**

2001: 7^{1}GS, 7^{1}G

	Starts	1st	2nd	3rd	Win & Pl
Career Total (Turf)	2	2	0	0	11122

98	5/01	Yarm	7f3y	C(0-85)	GD	£6955
79	5/01	Ling	7f	D	G-S	£4166

Total win prize-money £11122

Going (Turf): Sf: 0-0 **GS: 1-1 Gd: 1-1** GF: 0-0 Fm: 0-0
Distance: 5f/6f: 0-0 **7f-8f: 2-2** 9f-13f: 0-0 14f+: 0-0
Track : LH: 0-0 RH: 0-0 Tight: 0-0 Gall: 0-0
Aids: Bl: 0-0 Vi: 0-0 Tstrap: 0-0
Best Rating: 98 5/01 Yarm 7f3y good

Looked a very useful prospect but injured a tendon. One to follow if returning sound.

Suhail (IRE)

78 (14)**14**

5-y-o b g Wolfhound (USA)-Sharayif (IRE) (Green Desert (USA))
Jane Southcombe Mark Savill

Placings:00/**2**0000/0-000 **(3746)**
2001: 5^{0}GF, 17^{0}G, 7^{0}S

	Starts	1st	2nd	3rd	Win & Pl
Career Total (Turf)	9	0	0	0	
Career Total (AW)	2	0	1	0	806

Going (Turf): Sf: 0-3 GS: 0-1 Gd: 0-2 GF: 0-3 Fm: 0-0
Distance: 5f/6f: 0-1 7f-8f: 0-7 9f-13f: 0-2 14f+: 0-1
Track : LH: 0-4 RH: 0-1 Tight: 0-1 Gall: 0-0
Aids: Bl: 0-0 Vi: 0-0 Tstrap: 0-2
Best Rating: 14 6/01 Leic 5f218y gd-fm

Sulk (IRE)

95 **96**

2-y-o ch f Selkirk (USA)-Masskana (IRE) (Darshaan)
J H M Gosden James Wigan

Placings:4511 **(5245a)**
2001: 7^{4}GS, 7^{5}GF, 6^{1}GF, 8^{1}HO

	Starts	1st	2nd	3rd	Win & Pl
Career Total (Turf)	4	2	0	0	83596

96	10/01	Lonc	1m		HLD	£77595
96	9/01	Sals	6f212y	D	G-F	£5687

Total win prize-money £83283

Going (Turf): Sf: 0-0 GS: 0-1 Gd: 0-0 **GF: 1-2** Fm: 0-0
Distance: 5f/6f: 0-0 **7f-8f: 2-4** 9f-13f: 0-0 14f+: 0-0
Track : LH: 0-0 **RH: 1-1** Tight: 0-0 Gall: 0-0
Aids: Bl: 0-0 **Vi: 1-1** Tstrap: 0-0
Best Rating: 96 10/01 Lonc 1m holding

A half-sister to Wallace, she improved with experience to win her maiden at Salisbury. Left that form well behind when taking the Prix Marcel Boussac in a first-time visor. Stays a mile and seems to handle any ground.

Sultan Gamal

99 **82**

3-y-o b c Mind Games-Jobiska (Dunbeath (USA))
B A McMahon G S D Imports Ltd

Placings:1-50 **(1099)**
2001: 7^{5}GS, 7^{0}G

	Starts	1st	2nd	3rd	Win & Pl
Career Total (Turf)	3	1	0	0	3254

75	4/00	Hayd	5f	E	HVY	£2975

Total win prize-money £2975

Going (Turf): Sf: 1-1 GS: 0-1 Gd: 0-1 GF: 0-0 Fm: 0-0
Distance: 5f/6f: 1-1 7f-8f: 0-2 9f-13f: 0-0 14f+: 0-0
Track : LH: 0-0 RH: 0-0 Tight: 0-0 Gall: 0-0
Aids: Bl: 0-0 Vi: 0-0 Tstrap: 0-0
Best Rating: 82 4/01 NmkR 7f gd-sft

Sulu (IRE)

100 **45**

5-y-o b g Elbio-Foxy Fairy (IRE) (Fairy King (USA))
M W Easterby Mr Cowling,Mr Hutchinson & Mr Winton

Placings:4/356233/00010000-0000000 **(4621)**
2001: 6^{0}HY, 5^{0}S, 6^{0}GF, 5^{0}GF, 8^{0}GF, 6^{0}F, 6^{0}F

	Starts	1st	2nd	3rd	Win & Pl
Career Total (Turf)	22	1	1	3	7489

70	5/00	Thsk	5f	D(0-85)H	GD	£4862

Total win prize-money £4862

Going (Turf): Sf: 0-7 GS: 0-1 **Gd: 1-4** GF: 0-8 Fm: 0-2
Distance: 5f/6f: 1-14 7f-8f: 0-7 9f-13f: 0-1 14f+: 0-0
Track : LH: 0-5 RH: 0-0 Tight: 0-0 Gall: 0-3
Aids: Bl: 0-1 Vi: 0-0 Tstrap: 0-0
Best Rating: 45 7/01 Pont 1m4y gd-fm

Sum Baby (IRE)

58 **25**

2-y-o b g Royal Abjar (USA)-Matsuri (IRE) (Darshaan)
D Nicholls Tony Ashwell

Placings:0 **(4423)**
2001: 6^{0}GF

	Starts	1st	2nd	3rd	Win & Pl
Career Total (Turf)	1	0	0	0	

Going (Turf): Sf: 0-0 GS: 0-0 Gd: 0-0 GF: 0-1 Fm: 0-0
Distance: 5f/6f: 0-1 7f-8f: 0-0 9f-13f: 0-0 14f+: 0-0
Track : LH: 0-0 RH: 0-0 Tight: 0-0 Gall: 0-0
Aids: Bl: 0-0 Vi: 0-0 Tstrap: 0-0
Best Rating: 25 9/01 Ripn 6f gd-fm

Summer Bounty

98(99) (49d)**45**

5-y-o b g Lugana Beach-Tender Moment (IRE) (Caerleon (USA))
F Jordan Mrs S J Le Gros

Placings:035/1443602/**06002**000-040310100000 **(4727)**
2001: 11^{0}GS, 9^{4}F, 9^{0}F, 9^{3}F, 8^{1}GF, 10^{0}GF, 11^{1}F, 11^{0}G, 9^{0}SD, 9^{0}GF, 10^{0}GF, 10^{0}GF

	Starts	1st	2nd	3rd	Win & Pl
Career Total (Turf)	22	2	1	3	9313
Career Total (AW)	8	1	1	0	3679

45	7/01	Bath	1m3f144yF		FRM	£2359
52	7/01	Wwck	1m22y	G(0-60)H	G-F	£2279
71	2/99	Ling	1m2f	D	STD	£3021

Total win prize-money £7660

Going (Turf): Sf: 0-1 GS: 0-4 Gd: 0-5 **GF: 1-8 Fm: 1-4**
Distance: 5f/6f: 0-0 7f-8f: 0-3 **9f-13f: 3-27** 14f+: 0-0
Track : **LH: 2-23** RH: 0-4 **Tight: 2-17** Gall: 0-2
Aids: Bl: 0-1 Vi: 0-0 Tstrap: 0-1
Best Rating: 52 7/01 Wwck 1m22y gd-fm

Fairly useful plater, successful at Warwick and Bath in the Summer.

Summer Break (IRE)

91(92) (44)**69**

4-y-o ch f Foxhound (USA)-Out In The Sun (USA) (It's Freezing (USA))
S Dow (C M Kinane 27/1) Paul G Jacobs & Keith A Cosby

Placings:6453421/000541525-0000 **(1204)**
2001: 10^{0}SD, 11^{0}SD, 12^{0}S, 11^{0}GS

	Starts	1st	2nd	3rd	Win & Pl
Career Total (Turf)	18	2	2	1	13688
Career Total (AW)	2	0	0	0	

72	9/00	Clon	1m2f		GD	£4140
76	10/99	Tipp	1m1f	H	SH	£4485

Total win prize-money £8625

Going (Turf): Sf: 0-3 GS: 0-1 **Gd: 1-6** GF: 0-1 Fm: 0-0
Distance: 5f/6f: 0-0 7f-8f: 0-5 **9f-13f: 2-15** 14f+: 0-0
Track : LH: 1-8 RH: 1-11 Tight: 0-2 Gall: 0-0
Aids: Bl: 0-0 Vi: 0-0 Tstrap: 0-0
Best Rating: 44 3/01 Ling 1m2f stand

Summer Cherry (USA)

100(107) (49)**53**

4-y-o b g Summer Squall (USA)-Cherryrob (USA) (Roberto (USA))
Jamie Poulton Jamie Poulton

Placings:00/44636000**6-0205145**230600 **(4366)**
2001: 12^{0}SD, 8^{2}SD, 10^{0}SD, 7^{5}SW, 10^{1}SD, 8^{4}SD, 8^{5}SW, 10^{2}SD, 9^{3}F, 10^{0}G, 10^{6}F, 8^{0}GF, 9^{0}GF

	Starts	1st	2nd	3rd	Win & Pl
Career Total (Turf)	14	0	0	2	1175
Career Total (AW)	10	1	2	0	4081

46	2/01	Ling	1m2f	E(0-70)H	STD	£2415

Total win prize-money £2415

Going (Turf): Sf: 0-2 GS: 0-2 Gd: 0-3 GF: 0-5 Fm: 0-2
Distance: 5f/6f: 0-0 7f-8f: 0-9 **9f-13f: 1-15** 14f+: 0-0
Track : **LH: 1-17** RH: 0-4 **Tight: 1-13** Gall: 0-2
Aids: Bl: 0-0 Vi: 0-0 **Tstrap: 1-15**
Best Rating: 53 5/01 Brig 1m1f209y firm

Summer Jazz

91(96) (56+)**37**

4-y-o b f Alhijaz-Salvezza (IRE) (Superpower)
P J Makin D A Poole

Placings:52-000400 **(3263)**
2001: 11^{0}SD, 10^{0}GS, 11^{0}GF, 11^{4}F, 11^{0}GF, 12^{0}GS

	Starts	1st	2nd	3rd	Win & Pl
Career Total (Turf)	6	0	0	0	0
Career Total (AW)	2	0	1	0	892

Going (Turf): Sf: 0-1 GS: 0-2 Gd: 0-0 GF: 0-2 Fm: 0-1
Distance: 5f/6f: 0-0 7f-8f: 0-1 9f-13f: 0-7 14f+: 0-0
Track : LH: 0-3 RH: 0-0 Tight: 0-5 Gall: 0-0
Aids: Bl: 0-2 Vi: 0-0 Tstrap: 0-0
Best Rating: 40 4/01 Sthl 1m3f stand

Summer Key (IRE)

87(75) (13)**625**

3-y-o b f Doyoun-Summer Silence (USA) (Stop The Music (USA))
R Guest Mrs Jane Poulter

Placings:000 00000 **(2728)**
2001: 8^{0}GS, 10^{0}GF, 7^{0}GF, 6^{0}GF, 7^{0}GF, 8^{0}SD

	Starts	1st	2nd	3rd	Win & Pl
Career Total (Turf)	8	0	0	0	

Going (Turf): Sf: 0-1 GS: 0-1 Gd: 0-1 GF: 0-5 Fm: 0-0
Distance: 5f/6f: 0-1 7f-8f: 0-5 9f-13f: 0-2 14f+: 0-0
Track : LH: 0-3 RH: 0-2 Tight: 0-1 Gall: 0-1
Aids: Bl: 0-1 Vi: 0-0 Tstrap: 0-0
Best Rating: 25 6/01 Bevl 7f100y gd-fm

Summer Shades

94 **45**

3-y-o b f Green Desert (USA)-Sally Slade (Dowsing (USA))
C A Cyzer Mrs E A Cyzer

Placings:364-600030000 **(4609)**
2001: 7^{6}GS, 5^{0}GS, 6^{0}S, 9^{0}F, 6^{3}GF, 6^{0}GS, 5^{0}GF, 6^{0}G, 8^{0}F

	Starts	1st	2nd	3rd	Win & Pl
Career Total (Turf)	12	0	0	2	1252

Going (Turf): Sf: 0-1 GS: 0-3 Gd: 0-2 GF: 0-4 Fm: 0-2
Distance: 5f/6f: 0-7 7f-8f: 0-3 9f-13f: 0-2 14f+: 0-0
Track : LH: 0-4 RH: 0-2 Tight: 0-1 Gall: 0-2
Aids: Bl: 0-4 Vi: 0-0 Tstrap: 0-0
Best Rating: 59 4/01 Brig 7f214y gd-sft

Summer Symphony (IRE)

99 **111**

3-y-o gr f Caerleon (USA)-Summer Sonnet (Baillamont (USA))
L M Cumani Gerald W Leigh - Cancer Bacup

Placings:122-0 **(5141)**
2001: 8^{0}G

	Starts	1st	2nd	3rd	Win & Pl
Career Total (Turf)	4	1	2	0	58364

87	7/00	NmkJ	7f	D	GD	£5164

Total win prize-money £5164

Going (Turf): Sf: 0-0 GS: 0-1 **Gd: 1-3** GF: 0-0 Fm: 0-0
Distance: 5f/6f: 0-0 **7f-8f: 1-4** 9f-13f: 0-0 14f+: 0-0
Track : LH: 0-0 RH: 0-2 Tight: 0-0 Gall: 0-1
Aids: Bl: 0-0 Vi: 0-0 Tstrap: 0-0
Best Rating: 90 10/01 NmkR 1m good

High-class at two, she was just collared at Goodwood on her second start before finishing runner-up to Crystal Music in the Ascot Fillies' Mile. A setback kept her out of action in 2001 until October.

Summer View (USA)

108 **115**

4-y-o ch h Distant View (USA)-Miss Summer (Luthier)
R Charlton K Abdulla

Placings:1132-251 **(2033)**
2001: 8^{2}G, 10^{5}GF, 8^{1}F

			Starts	1st	2nd	3rd	Win & Pl
Career Total (Turf)			7	3	2	1	30181
42 6/01	Nott	1m54y	C			FRM	£7001
99 8/00	Sals	1m	C(0-90)			G-F	£7185
87 7/00	Kemp	1m	D			G-F	£4306

Total win prize-money £18494

Going (Turf): Sf: 0-1 GS: 0-0 Gd: 0-1 **GF: 2-4** Fm: 1-1
Distance: 5f/6f: 0-0 **7f-8f: 2-3** 9f-13f: 1-4 14f+: 0-0
Track : LH: 1-2 RH: 1-3 Tight: 0-1 **Gall: 1-2**
Aids: Bl: 0-0 Vi: 0-0 **Tstrap: 1-1**
Best Rating: 101 5/01 Wind 1m67y good

Progressed well at three, and made a promising return at Windsor, but he looked out of his depth in the Group One Lockinge Stakes next time. His win came in a non-event.

Summer Wine

96 **87+**

2-y-o b f Desert King (IRE)-Generous Lady (Generous (IRE))
C F Wall S Fustok

Placings:3 **(5602)**
2001: 7^{3}GS

	Starts	1st	2nd	3rd	Win & Pl
Career Total (Turf)	1	0	0	1	650

Going (Turf): Sf: 0-0 GS: 0-1 Gd: 0-0 GF: 0-0 Fm: 0-0
Distance: 5f/6f: 0-0 7f-8f: 0-1 9f-13f: 0-0 14f+: 0-0
Track : LH: 0-0 RH: 0-0 Tight: 0-0 Gall: 0-0
Aids: Bl: 0-0 Vi: 0-0 Tstrap: 0-0
Best Rating: 87 11/01 NmkR 7f gd-sft

Summerhill Parkes

103 **108d**

3-y-o b f Zafonic (USA)-Summerhill Spruce (Windjammer (USA))
M A Jarvis Joseph Heler

Placings:3-1100 **(5105)**
2001: 6^{1}F, 6^{1}GF, 6^{0}GF, 5^{0}GS

			Starts	1st	2nd	3rd	Win & Pl
Career Total (Turf)			5	2	0	1	21596
108 6/01	Hayd	6f	A			G-F	£17095
84 5/01	Pont	6f	D			FRM	£3948

Total win prize-money £21044

Going (Turf): Sf: 0-0 GS: 0-1 Gd: 0-0 **GF: 1-2 Fm: 1-2**
Distance: 5f/6f: 2-5 7f-8f: 0-0 9f-13f: 0-0 14f+: 0-0
Track : LH: 1-1 RH: 0-0 Tight: 0-0 Gall: 0-0
Aids: Bl: 0-0 Vi: 0-0 Tstrap: 0-0
Best Rating: 108 6/01 Hayd 6f gd-fm

Once raced as a juvenile, she got off the mark in a Pontefract maiden on her reappearance and had no problem with the huge climb into Listed company by winning well at Haydock in June. Withdrawn at Pontefract in August after breaking out of the stalls and ran very disappointingly in the Ayr Gold Cup. She can improve even further.

Summoner

119 **121?**

4-y-o b c Inchinor-Sumoto (Mtoto)
Saeed Bin Suroor Godolphin

Placings:61/10412-121 **(5006)**
2001: 10^{1}F, 8^{2}GF, 8^{1}S

			Starts	1st	2nd	3rd	Win & Pl
Career Total (Turf)			10	5	2	0	226557
121 9/01	Asct	1m	A			SFT	£188500
58 6/01	Donc	1m2f60y	C			FRM	£6955
115 7/00	Donc	1m	C			G-F	£7215
106 3/00	Donc	1m	C			GD	£7052
82 11/99	Donc	1m	E			SFT	£3208

Total win prize-money £212932

Going (Turf): Sf: 2-2 GS: 0-0 Gd: 1-4 GF: 1-3 Fm: 1-1
Distance: 5f/6f: 0-0 **7f-8f: 4-7** 9f-13f: 1-3 14f+: 0-0
Track : LH: 1-2 RH: 1-3 Tight: 0-0 **Gall: 2-3**
Aids: Bl: 0-0 Vi: 0-0 Tstrap: 0-0
Best Rating: 121 9/01 Asct 1m soft

Lightly raced colt, half-brother to the Eclipse winner Compton Admiral. He won three times at Doncaster as a three-year-old, when he was also ninth in the 2000 Guineas, and ran a fine second to Adilabad in Listed event over a mile at Goodwood. Has won a conditions event this term over ten furlongs at Doncaster, but was beaten back at a mile next time. Stole the Queen Elizabeth II Stakes thanks to a fine tactical ride from Richard Hills, but will find life tougher next year with a Group One penalty. Has won on a variety of surfaces, but handles soft ground particularly well.

Sumthinelse

94(101) (60) **52**

4-y-o ch g Magic Ring (IRE)-Minne Love (Homeric)
N P Littmoden Hanibel Racing Partnership

Placings:53340/5402146030**0-043000000505** **(5397)**
2001: 7^{0}SD, 6^{4}SD, 7^{3}SD, 7^{0}SD, 7^{0}GF, 7^{0}G, 7^{0}GF, 6^{0}F, 6^{0}F, 6^{5}SW, 7^{0}G, 8^{5}SD

			Starts	1st	2nd	3rd	Win & Pl
Career Total (Turf)			20	1	1	2	8087
Career Total (AW)			8	0	0	2	1218
75 6/00	Ches	7f2y	D(0-80)H			G-F	£4101

Total win prize-money £4102

Going (Turf): Sf: 0-1 GS: 0-2 Gd: 0-5 **GF: 1-10** Fm: 0-2
Distance: 5f/6f: 0-13 **7f-8f: 1-14** 9f-13f: 0-1 14f+: 0-0
Track : LH: 1-15 RH: 0-0 **Tight: 1-11** Gall: 0-0
Aids: Bl: 0-0 Vi: 0-1 Tstrap: 0-0
Best Rating: 68 3/01 Wolv 6f stand

Sun Bird (IRE)

104(67) (36) **75**

3-y-o ch g Prince Of Birds (USA)-Summer Fashion (Moorestyle)
R Allan Mrs R P Aggio

Placings:505005-422211416 **(4883)**
2001: 11^{4}GF, 10^{2}GF, 8^{2}GF, 9^{2}G, 12^{1}GF, 11^{1}G, 12^{4}G, 10^{1}GS, 12^{6}GF

			Starts	1st	2nd	3rd	Win & Pl
Career Total (Turf)			14	3	3	0	23403
Career Total (AW)			1	0	0	0	0
74 8/01	Ches	1m2f75y	C(0-90)H			G-S	£7182
69 8/01	Rdcr	1m3f	C(0-90)H			GD	£6890
67 7/01	Ripn	1m4f60y	D(0-80)H			G-F	£5037

Total win prize-money £19111

Going (Turf): Sf: 0-2 **GS: 1-2 Gd: 1-4 GF: 1-5** Fm: 0-0
Distance: 5f/6f: 0-3 7f-8f: 0-0 **9f-13f: 3-11** 14f+: 0-0
Track : LH: 2-5 RH: 1-5 **Tight: 3-8** Gall: 0-0
Aids: Bl: 0-2 **Vi: 1-5** Tstrap: 0-0
Best Rating: 75 9/01 Haml 1m4f17y gd-fm

Improved in the summer of 2001, winning three times, although possibly helped by the removal of the visor on the first two occasions. Effective ten to 12 furlongs, suited by good ground or faster, less at home on soft.

Sundari (IRE)

96 **86+**

2-y-o b f Danehill (USA)-My Ballerina (USA) (Sir Ivor)
J H M Gosden Lady Bamford

Placings:5131 **(4444)**
2001: 6^{5}GF, 6^{1}GF, 6^{3}GS, 8^{1}G

			Starts	1st	2nd	3rd	Win & Pl
Career Total (Turf)			4	2	0	1	17327
86 9/01	Sand	1m14y	C			GD	£7068
72 6/01	NmkJ	6f	D			G-F	£4758

Total win prize-money £11827

Going (Turf): Sf: 0-0 GS: 0-1 **Gd: 1-1 GF: 1-2** Fm: 0-0
Distance: 5f/6f: 1-3 7f-8f: 0-0 9f-13f: 1-1 14f+: 0-0
Track : LH: 0-0 **RH: 1-1** Tight: 0-0 Gall: 0-0
Aids: Bl: 0-0 Vi: 0-0 Tstrap: 0-0
Best Rating: 86 9/01 Sand 1m14y good

She had to fight hard to land the odds in a Newmarket maiden on her second start and was beaten less than a length into third in the Cherry Hinton, and a comfortable winner when stepped up to a mile at Sandown. Her dam won twice at middle distances, and she has improvement in her.

Sunday Rain (USA)

91 **67**

4-y-o b g Summer Squall (USA)-Oxava (FR) (Antheus (USA))
Miss Lucinda V Russell (J J O'Neill 10/5) Peter K Dale Ltd

Placings:40440/42245-00 **(1236)**
2001: 18^{0}S, 12^{0}GF

	Starts	1st	2nd	3rd	Win & Pl
Career Total (Turf)	12	0	2	0	3137

Going (Turf): Sf: 0-3 GS: 0-3 Gd: 0-1 GF: 0-5 Fm: 0-0
Distance: 5f/6f: 0-0 7f-8f: 0-3 9f-13f: 0-6 14f+: 0-3
Track : LH: 0-8 RH: 0-3 Tight: 0-4 Gall: 0-3
Aids: Bl: 0-3 Vi: 0-0 Tstrap: 0-0
Best Rating: 50 5/01 Ches 1m4f66y gd-fm

Sunday Sport (USA)

100 **89?**

2-y-o b f Honour And Glory (USA)-Gold Rule (USA) (Forty Niner (USA))
B J Meehan Roldvale Limited

Placings:4640 **(3581)**
2001: 5^{4}GF, 5^{6}GF, 6^{4}GF, 5^{0}GF

	Starts	1st	2nd	3rd	Win & Pl
Career Total (Turf)	4	0	0	0	744

Going (Turf): Sf: 0-0 GS: 0-0 Gd: 0-0 GF: 0-4 Fm: 0-0
Distance: 5f/6f: 0-4 7f-8f: 0-0 9f-13f: 0-0 14f+: 0-0
Track : LH: 0-0 RH: 0-0 Tight: 0-0 Gall: 0-0
Aids: Bl: 0-0 Vi: 0-0 Tstrap: 0-0
Best Rating: 89 6/01 Asct 5f gd-fm

A well bred filly, from the family of Contredance (Grade One winner over a mile at two), she did best of the newcomers on her Haydock debut and ran well in the Windsor Castle, but did not seem suited by making the running at Windsor on her third start.

Sundays Sarah

3-y-o b f Sea Raven (IRE)-Sundays Off (Dubassoff (USA))
Jedd O'Keeffe R W Tunstall

Placings:0 **(0380)**
2001: 8^{0}SD

	Starts	1st	2nd	3rd	Win & Pl
Career Total (Turf)	0	0	0	0	
Career Total (AW)	1	0	0	0	

Going (Turf): Sf: 0-0 GS: 0-0 Gd: 0-0 GF: 0-0 Fm: 0-0
Distance: 5f/6f: 0-0 7f-8f: 0-0 9f-13f: 0-1 14f+: 0-0
Track : LH: 0-1 RH: 0-0 Tight: 0-1 Gall: 0-0
Aids: Bl: 0-0 Vi: 0-0 Tstrap: 0-0

Sundial

83 61

2-y-o ch f Cadeaux Genereux-Ruby Setting (Gorytus (USA))
B W Hills Mrs Belinda Harvey

Placings:6 (3584)
2001: 7^6G

	Starts	1st	2nd	3rd	Win & Pl
Career Total (Turf)	1	0	0	0	0

Going (Turf): Sf: 0-0 GS: 0-0 Gd: 0-1 GF: 0-0 Fm: 0-0
Distance: 5f/6f: 0-0 7f-8f: 0-1 9f-13f: 0-0 14f+: 0-0
Track : LH: 0-0 RH: 0-1 Tight: 0-0 Gall: 0-0
Aids: Bl: 0-0 Vi: 0-0 Tstrap: 0-0
Best Rating: 61 8/01 Gdwd 7f good

Sundown

98(79) (22)62

3-y-o b f Polish Precedent (USA)-Ruby Setting (Gorytus (USA))
M P Tregoning R J McCreery

Placings:03-405060 (5611)
2001: 7^4GF, 8^0GF, 10^5GF, 8^0GF, 7^6GF, 8^0SD

	Starts	1st	2nd	3rd	Win & Pl
Career Total (Turf)	7	0	0	1	894
Career Total (AW)	1	0	0	0	

Going (Turf): Sf: 0-0 GS: 0-1 Gd: 0-0 GF: 0-6 Fm: 0-0
Distance: 5f/6f: 0-1 7f-8f: 0-4 9f-13f: 0-3 14f+: 0-0
Track : LH: 0-2 RH: 0-3 Tight: 0-3 Gall: 0-1
Aids: Bl: 0-1 Vi: 0-0 Tstrap: 0-0
Best Rating: 73 5/01 Gdwd 7f gd-fm

Sundrenched (IRE)

98 97+

2-y-o ch f Desert King (IRE)-Utr (USA) (Mr Prospector (USA))
W J Haggas Lael Stable

Placings:21 (5609)
2001: 8^2G, 8^1GS

	Starts	1st	2nd	3rd	Win & Pl
Career Total (Turf)	2	1	1	0	14244

97 11/01 NmkR 1m A G-S £12528
Total win prize-money £12528

Going (Turf): Sf: 0-0 GS: 1-1 Gd: 0-1 GF: 0-0 Fm: 0-0
Distance: 5f/6f: 0-0 7f-8f: 1-2 9f-13f: 0-0 14f+: 0-0
Track : LH: 0-0 RH: 0-0 Tight: 0-0 Gall: 0-0
Aids: Bl: 0-0 Vi: 0-0 Tstrap: 0-0
Best Rating: 97 11/01 NmkR 1m gd-sft

A half-sister to Andromedes and Bonnard, she made a very promising debut behind a potentially very smart filly at Newmarket in September despite running green. Got off the mark over course and distance and should win more races.

Sundried Tomato

77 39

2-y-o b c Lugana Beach-Little Scarlett (Mazilier (USA))
P W Hiatt Jeremy Arnold

Placings:00 (2428)
2001: 5^0G, 6^0GF

	Starts	1st	2nd	3rd	Win & Pl
Career Total (Turf)	2	0	0	0	

Going (Turf): Sf: 0-0 GS: 0-0 Gd: 0-1 GF: 0-1 Fm: 0-0
Distance: 5f/6f: 0-2 7f-8f: 0-0 9f-13f: 0-0 14f+: 0-0
Track : LH: 0-0 RH: 0-1 Tight: 0-0 Gall: 0-1
Aids: Bl: 0-0 Vi: 0-0 Tstrap: 0-0
Best Rating: 39 6/01 Wind 6f gd-fm

Sungio

103 66

3-y-o b g Halling (USA)-Time Or Never (FR) (Dowsing (USA))
B G Powell (L M Cumani 17/9) Mrs Rachel A Powell

Placings:6062-00236452 (4727)
2001: 9^0GS, 8^0HY, 10^2G, 11^3GF, 12^6S, 12^4GF, 11^5GF, 10^2GF

	Starts	1st	2nd	3rd	Win & Pl
Career Total (Turf)	12	0	3	1	3651

Going (Turf): Sf: 0-4 GS: 0-2 Gd: 0-2 GF: 0-4 Fm: 0-0
Distance: 5f/6f: 0-0 7f-8f: 0-4 9f-13f: 0-8 14f+: 0-0
Track : LH: 0-7 RH: 0-3 Tight: 0-3 Gall: 0-0
Aids: Bl: 0-3 Vi: 0-0 Tstrap: 0-0
Best Rating: 66 7/01 Wind 1m3f135y gd-fm

Sunley Scent

106(94) (64)75

3-y-o ch f Wolfhound (USA)-Brown Velvet (Mansingh (USA))
M R Channon John B Sunley

Placings:004-02413220 (4705)
2001: 7^0G, 6^2GF, 6^4S, 6^1G, 6^3GF, 7^2GF, 6^2GF, 7^0G

	Starts	1st	2nd	3rd	Win & Pl
Career Total (Turf)	10	1	3	1	6669
Career Total (AW)	1	0	0	0	0

68 8/01 Folk 6f F(0-65)H GD £2723
Total win prize-money £2723

Going (Turf): Sf: 0-2 GS: 0-1 Gd: 1-3 GF: 0-4 Fm: 0-0
Distance: 5f/6f: 1-5 7f-8f: 0-6 9f-13f: 0-0 14f+: 0-0
Track : LH: 0-3 RH: 0-1 Tight: 0-3 Gall: 0-1
Aids: Bl: 0-0 Vi: 0-0 Tstrap: 0-0
Best Rating: 75 9/01 Nott 6f15y gd-fm

Sunley Sense

106 86

5-y-o b g Komaite (USA)-Brown Velvet (Mansingh (USA))
M R Channon John B Sunley

Placings:52552321125/00600/00220020066465-02440501000 (4718)
2001: 5^0GF, 5^2GF, 5^4GF, 6^4GF, 5^0G, 5^5GF, 5^0G, 5^1S, 5^0G, 5^0G, 5^0G

	Starts	1st	2nd	3rd	Win & Pl
Career Total (Turf)	41	3	8	1	45870

86 8/01 Sand 5f6y D(0-80)H SFT £6188
91 9/98 Newb 5f34y C H GD £5192
80 9/98 Sand 5f6y D H G-S £3566
Total win prize-money £14947

Going (Turf): Sf: 1-4 GS: 1-3 Gd: 1-19 GF: 0-14 Fm: 0-1
Distance: 5f/6f: 3-41 7f-8f: 0-0 9f-13f: 0-0 14f+: 0-0
Track : LH: 0-4 RH: 0-3 Tight: 0-2 Gall: 0-4
Aids: Bl: 0-0 Vi: 0-1 Tstrap: 0-0
Best Rating: 86 8/01 Sand 5f6y soft

He finally ended a long losing run when making all and winning easily on soft ground at Sandown in August 2001. Likes to front run and best over five furlongs. Equally effective on soft and fast ground.

Sunningdale (IRE)

95 66

3-y-o gr f Indian Ridge-Hayati (Hotfoot)
M A Jarvis Mr & Mrs John Poynton

Placings:06 (1417)
2001: 7^0GS, 7^6GS

	Starts	1st	2nd	3rd	Win & Pl
Career Total (Turf)	2	0	0	0	0

Going (Turf): Sf: 0-0 GS: 0-2 Gd: 0-0 GF: 0-0 Fm: 0-0
Distance: 5f/6f: 0-0 7f-8f: 0-2 9f-13f: 0-0 14f+: 0-0
Track : LH: 0-0 RH: 0-0 Tight: 0-0 Gall: 0-0
Aids: Bl: 0-0 Vi: 0-0 Tstrap: 0-0
Best Rating: 66 5/01 NmkR 7f gd-sft

Sunny Glenn

104 111

3-y-o ch c Rock Hopper-La Ballerine (Lafontaine (USA))
N P Littmoden Mrs H F Mahr

Placings:051-2600 (2883)
2001: 9^2S, 11^6G, 12^0GF, 12^0GS

	Starts	1st	2nd	3rd	Win & Pl
Career Total (Turf)	7	1	1	0	9682

78 9/00 Llng 6f D SFT £3461
Total win prize-money £3461

Going (Turf): Sf: 1-4 GS: 0-1 Gd: 0-1 GF: 0-1 Fm: 0-0
Distance: 5f/6f: 1-1 7f-8f: 0-2 9f-13f: 0-4 14f+: 0-0
Track : LH: 0-4 RH: 0-1 Tight: 0-3 Gall: 0-1
Aids: Bl: 0-0 Vi: 0-0 Tstrap: 0-0
Best Rating: 111 6/01 Epsm 1m4f10y gd-fm

Stepped up on his juvenile form when going down by the minimum margin in a Listed race at Newmarket in April, but was well beaten behind Perfect Sunday in the Lingfield Derby Trial next time. Ran much better when ninth in the Espom Derby and deserves to win a decent event this term.

Sunnyside Royale (IRE)

86 53

2-y-o b g Ali-Royal (IRE)-Kuwah (IRE) (Be My Guest (USA))
M W Easterby S Durkin, P Earnshaw & J Groonan

Placings:000 (4771)
2001: 7^0G, 7^0GF, 7^0G

	Starts	1st	2nd	3rd	Win & Pl
Career Total (Turf)	3	0	0	0	

Going (Turf): Sf: 0-0 GS: 0-0 Gd: 0-2 GF: 0-1 Fm: 0-0
Distance: 5f/6f: 0-0 7f-8f: 0-3 9f-13f: 0-0 14f+: 0-0
Track : LH: 0-2 RH: 0-1 Tight: 0-1 Gall: 0-1
Aids: Bl: 0-0 Vi: 0-0 Tstrap: 0-2
Best Rating: 53 8/01 Thsk 7f good

Sunray Superstar

99 96+

2-y-o b f Nashwan (USA)-Nazoo (IRE) (Nijinsky (CAN))
Sir Michael Stoute Maktoum Al Maktoum

Placings:2 (5274)
2001: 7^2GS

	Starts	1st	2nd	3rd	Win & Pl
Career Total (Turf)	1	0	1	0	1252

Going (Turf): Sf: 0-0 GS: 0-1 Gd: 0-0 GF: 0-0 Fm: 0-0
Distance: 5f/6f: 0-0 7f-8f: 0-1 9f-13f: 0-0 14f+: 0-0
Track : LH: 0-0 RH: 0-0 Tight: 0-0 Gall: 0-0
Aids: Bl: 0-0 Vi: 0-0 Tstrap: 0-0
Best Rating: 96 10/01 Leic 7f9y gd-sft

Sister to the French Group One winner Nadia, ran green on her first outing and is bred to require a longer trip.

Sunridge Fairy (IRE)

85(91) (49)**49**

2-y-o b f Definite Article-Foxy Fairy (IRE) (Fairy King (USA))

P C Haslam R Young

Placings:55006 **(5351)**

2001: 5^{5}S, 5^{5}GF, 7^{0}F, 7^{0}GF, 8^{6}SD, 8^{3}SD

	Starts	1st	2nd	3rd	Win & Pl
Career Total (Turf)	4	0	0	0	0
Career Total (AW)	1	0	0	0	0

Going (Turf): Sf: 0-1 GS: 0-0 Gd: 0-0 GF: 0-2 Fm: 0-1

Distance: 5f/6f: 0-2 7f-8f: 0-3 9f-13f: 0-0 14f+: 0-0

Track : LH: 0-2 RH: 0-0 Tight: 0-1 Gall: 0-0

Aids: Bl: 0-0 Vi: 0-0 Tstrap: 0-0

Best Rating: 49 8/01 Thsk 7f firm

Sunridge Rose

99(98) (46)**57**

3-y-o b f Piccolo-Floral Spark (Forzando)

Andrew Reid (Mrs N Macauley 16/3) A S Reid

Placings:360-32650140010544040 **(5593)**

2001: 7^{3}SW, 7^{2}SD, 9^{6}SD, 8^{5}SW, 7^{0}SW, 7^{1}SD, 8^{4}SD, 7^{0}SD, 7^{0}SW, 5^{1}HY, 6^{0}SD, 6^{5}GF, 6^{4}S, 7^{4}SD, 7^{0}F, 7^{4}SD, 5^{0}GS

	Starts	1st	2nd	3rd	Win & Pl
Career Total (Turf)	6	1	0	1	2758
Career Total (AW)	14	1	1	1	2675

49 4/01 Folk 5f F HVY £2338

49 3/01 Sthl 7f G STD £1869

Total win prize-money £4207

Going (Turf): Sf: 1-2 GS: 0-1 Gd: 0-1 GF: 0-1 Fm: 0-1

Distance: 5f/6f: 1-6 7f-8f: 1-13 9f-13f: 0-1 14f+: 0-0

Track : LH: 1-17 RH: 0-0 Tight: 0-6 Gall: 0-0

Aids: Bl: 0-0 **Vi: 1-4** Tstrap: 0-0

Best Rating: 57 5/01 Brig 6f209y gd-fm

Winner of a seller in a first-time visor on the sand, she was subsequently claimed but had to be dropped back two furlongs to win again at a similar level in heavy ground.

Sunrise Girl

102(80) (11)**49**

4-y-o ch f King's Signet (USA)-Dawn Ditty (Song)

Mrs P N Dutfield Unity Farm Holiday Centre Ltd

Placings:06000-202252450 **(4950)**

2001: 6^{2}G, 6^{0}G, 5^{2}G, 5^{2}GF, 5^{5}F, 5^{2}G, 5^{4}GF, 5^{5}G, 5^{0}G

	Starts	1st	2nd	3rd	Win & Pl
Career Total (Turf)	12	0	4	0	3224
Career Total (AW)	2	0	0	0	0

Going (Turf): Sf: 0-0 GS: 0-2 Gd: 0-6 GF: 0-3 Fm: 0-1

Distance: 5f/6f: 0-14 7f-8f: 0-0 9f-13f: 0-0 14f+: 0-0

Track : LH: 0-8 RH: 0-0 Tight: 0-2 Gall: 0-5

Aids: Bl: 0-0 Vi: 0-0 Tstrap: 0-0

Best Rating: 49 8/01 Folk 5f good

Sunset (IRE)

(76) (20)

3-y-o b f Polish Precedent (USA)-Up Anchor (IRE) (Slip Anchor)

P F I Cole H R H Prince Fahd Salman

Placings:0 **(0378)**

2001: 9^{0}SD

	Starts	1st	2nd	3rd	Win & Pl
Career Total (Turf)	0	0	0	0	
Career Total (AW)	1	0	0	0	

Going (Turf): Sf: 0-0 GS: 0-0 Gd: 0-0 GF: 0-0 Fm: 0-0

Distance: 5f/6f: 0-0 7f-8f: 0-0 9f-13f: 0-1 14f+: 0-0

Track : LH: 0-1 RH: 0-0 Tight: 0-1 Gall: 0-0

Aids: Bl: 0-0 Vi: 0-0 Tstrap: 0-0

Best Rating: 20 2/01 Wolv 1m1f79y stand

Sunset Glow

60(105) (73)**50**

4-y-o gr c Rainbow Quest (USA)-Oscura (USA) (Caro)

J Noseda (J Pearce 2/2) Miss Sarah Diane Warren

Placings:4/3-21040 **(5471)**

2001: 12^{2}SD, 12^{1}SW, 12^{0}SD, 12^{4}SD, 11^{0}S

	Starts	1st	2nd	3rd	Win & Pl
Career Total (Turf)	3	0	0	1	957
Career Total (AW)	4	1	1	0	3769

73 1/01 Sthl 1m4f D SLW £2919

Total win prize-money £2919

Going (Turf): Sf: 0-1 GS: 0-1 Gd: 0-0 GF: 0-1 Fm: 0-0

Distance: 5f/6f: 0-0 7f-8f: 0-1 **9f-13f: 1-6** 14f+: 0-0

Track : **LH: 1-5** RH: 0-1 Tight: 0-2 Gall: 0-0

Aids: Bl: 0-0 Vi: 0-0 Tstrap: 0-0

Best Rating: 73 1/01 Sthl 1m4f slow

Sunset Harbour (IRE)

(102) (50)

8-y-o br m Prince Sabo-City Link Pet (Tina's Pet)

J M Bradley N Savage

Placings:655430/**2353250**00030**1**430/005**31**6360002**6**/**56010130163220**/**464**000000/241636056060000000**1043** 0-30361646 **(0377)**

2001: 5^{3}SD, 5^{0}SD, 5^{3}SD, 5^{6}SD, 5^{1}SD, 5^{6}SW, 5^{4}SD, 5^{6}SD

	Starts	1st	2nd	3rd	Win & Pl
Career Total (Turf)	55	5	2	8	21584
Career Total (AW)	33	3	4	5	11180

50	2/01	Wolv	5f	F(0-60)H	STD	£1736
45	11/00	Sthl	5f	E(0-70)H	STD	£2226
47	6/00	Brig	5f59y	F(0-65)H	FRM	£3419
50	8/98	Catt	5f	F(0-65)H	GD	£2486
44	5/98	Newc	5f	D(0-75)H	G-F	£3452
40	4/98	Wolv	5f	F(0-65)H	STD	£2070
41	6/97	Bevl	5f	E(0-70)H	G-F	£3153
45	7/96.	Rdcr	5f	G(0-60)H	FRM	£2469

Total win prize-money £21012

Going (Turf): Sf: 0-3 GS: 0-9 Gd: 1-12 **GF: 2-20 Fm: 2-11**

Distance: **5f/6f: 8-85** 7f-8f: 0-3 9f-13f: 0-0 14f+: 0-0

Track : **LH: 3-37** RH: 0-4 **Tight: 2-24** Gall: 0-11

Aids: Bl: 0-4 Vi: 0-1 Tstrap: 0-0

Best Rating: 50 2/01 Wolv 5f stand

She is no world beater, but has done quite well this term, winning three handicaps, one of which was on Fibresand.

Sunsetter (USA)

103 **97**

3-y-o ch f Diesis-Hushi (USA) (Riverman (USA))

G A Butler Des Swan

Placings:0-6 **(0787)**

2001: 7^{6}GS

	Starts	1st	2nd	3rd	Win & Pl
Career Total (Turf)	2	0	0	0	525

Going (Turf): Sf: 0-0 GS: 0-2 Gd: 0-0 GF: 0-0 Fm: 0-0

Distance: 5f/6f: 0-1 7f-8f: 0-1 9f-13f: 0-0 14f+: 0-0

Track : LH: 0-0 RH: 0-0 Tight: 0-0 Gall: 0-0

Aids: Bl: 0-0 Vi: 0-0 Tstrap: 0-0

Best Rating: 92 4/01 NmkR 7f gd-sft

A light-framed filly, she showed a choppy action on her only outing at two in a Group one event.

Sunshine Boy

(93) (52)

5-y-o b g Cadeaux Genereux-Sahara Baladee (USA) (Shadeed (USA))

G M McCourt D M Huglin

Placings:3621504230/30 **(2981)**

2001: 12^{3}SD, 16^{0}SD

	Starts	1st	2nd	3rd	Win & Pl
Career Total (Turf)	10	1	2	2	6912
Career Total (AW)	2	0	0	1	330

72 6/99 Leic 1m1f218yE(0-70)H GD £3029

Total win prize-money £3029

Going (Turf): Sf: 0-0 GS: 0-4 **Gd: 1-3** GF: 0-3 Fm: 0-0

Distance: 5f/6f: 0-0 7f-8f: 0-1 **9f-13f: 1-10** 14f+: 0-1

Track : LH: 0-6 **RH: 1-6** Tight: 0-4 Gall: 0-2

Aids: Bl: 0-0 Vi: 0-3 Tstrap: 0-0

Best Rating: 52 6/01 Sthl 1m4f stand

Sunshine N'Showers

88 **69d**

3-y-o b f Spectrum (IRE)-Mainly Dry (The Brianstan)

A Berry Mrs David Brown

Placings:35-0000 **(2414)**

2001: 6^{0}GS, 6^{0}F, 8^{0}F, 8^{0}GF

	Starts	1st	2nd	3rd	Win & Pl
Career Total (Turf)	6	0	0	1	558

Going (Turf): Sf: 0-0 GS: 0-1 Gd: 0-1 GF: 0-2 Fm: 0-2

Distance: 5f/6f: 0-3 7f-8f: 0-1 9f-13f: 0-2 14f+: 0-0

Track : LH: 0-4 RH: 0-0 Tight: 0-0 Gall: 0-0

Aids: Bl: 0-1 Vi: 0-0 Tstrap: 0-0

Best Rating: 47 6/01 Nott 1m54y firm

Sunspeckled

100(85) (26)**50**

3-y-o ch f Salse (USA)-Western Horizon (USA) (Gone West (USA))

S Kirk Wyck Hall Stud

Placings:03400 **(4210)**

2001: 11^{0}F, 14^{3}GF, 16^{4}GF, 14^{0}SD, 11^{0}GF

	Starts	1st	2nd	3rd	Win & Pl
Career Total (Turf)	4	0	0	1	636
Career Total (AW)	1	0	0	0	

Going (Turf): Sf: 0-0 GS: 0-0 Gd: 0-0 GF: 0-3 Fm: 0-1

Distance: 5f/6f: 0-0 7f-8f: 0-0 9f-13f: 0-2 14f+: 0-3

Track : LH: 0-4 RH: 0-1 Tight: 0-2 Gall: 0-0

Aids: Bl: 0-1 Vi: 0-0 Tstrap: 0-0

Best Rating: 50 7/01 Sand 1m6f gd-fm

Sunstone

107 **107d**

3-y-o b f Caerleon (USA)-Chita Rivera (Chief Singer)

M R Channon Mrs M J Vincent

Placings:0-203500 **(2827)**

2001: 10^{2}GS, 10^{0}F, 12^{3}GF, 12^{5}GF, 12^{0}GF, 11^{0}GS, 12^{0}HY

	Starts	1st	2nd	3rd	Win & Pl
Career Total (Turf)	7	0	1	1	11892

Going (Turf): Sf: 0-0 GS: 0-2 Gd: 0-1 GF: 0-3 Fm: 0-1

Distance: 5f/6f: 0-0 7f-8f: 0-1 9f-13f: 0-6 14f+: 0-0

Track : LH: 0-6 RH: 0-1 Tight: 0-1 Gall: 0-4

Aids: Bl: 0-0 Vi: 0-0 Tstrap: 0-0

Best Rating: 107 6/01 Epsm 1m4f10y gd-fm

Useful filly, who has faced some stiff tasks in her career to date. Ran by far her best race when fifth in the Oaks, beaten four lengths behind Imagine. Probably one of the best maiden fillies in Europe.

Super Canyon

103 **52+**
3-y-o ch g Gulch (USA)-Marina Park (Local Suitor (USA))
P W Harris Mrs G A Godfrey

Placings:601 **(4619)**
2001: 6^{6}GS, 6^{0}GF, 5^{1}F

	Starts	1st	2nd	3rd	Win & Pl
Career Total (Turf)	3	1	0	0	2856

50 9/01 Newc 5f D FRM £2856
Total win prize-money £2856

Going (Turf): Sf: 0-0 GS: 0-1 Gd: 0-0 GF: 0-1 **Fm: 1-1**
Distance: **5f/6f: 1-3** 7f-8f: 0-0 9f-13f: 0-0 14f+: 0-0
Track : LH: 0-0 RH: 0-0 Tight: 0-0 Gall: 0-0
Aids: Bl: 0-0 Vi: 0-0 Tstrap: 0-0
Best Rating: 52 7/01 NmkJ 6f gd-sft

Got off the mark at the third attempt in an five-furlong maiden at Newcastle. Won well and looks sure to improve.

Super Decision

70 **21**
2-y-o ch f Superlative-Kiveton Komet (Precocious)
J J Quinn Mrs S Quinn

Placings:0 **(1823)**
2001: 5^{0}GF

	Starts	1st	2nd	3rd	Win & Pl
Career Total (Turf)	1	0	0	0	

Going (Turf): Sf: 0-0 GS: 0-0 Gd: 0-0 GF: 0-1 Fm: 0-0
Distance: 5f/6f: 0-1 7f-8f: 0-0 9f-13f: 0-0 14f+: 0-0
Track : LH: 0-1 RH: 0-0 Tight: 0-0 Gall: 0-0
Aids: Bl: 0-0 Vi: 0-0 Tstrap: 0-0
Best Rating: 21 6/01 Pont 5f gd-fm

Super Dolphin

86 **53**
2-y-o ch g Dolphin Street (FR)-Supergreen (Superlative)
T P Tate T P Tate

Placings:5 **(4880)**
2001: 8^{5}GF

	Starts	1st	2nd	3rd	Win & Pl
Career Total (Turf)	1	0	0	0	0

Going (Turf): Sf: 0-0 GS: 0-0 Gd: 0-0 GF: 0-1 Fm: 0-0
Distance: 5f/6f: 0-0 7f-8f: 0-0 9f-13f: 0-1 14f+: 0-0
Track : LH: 0-0 RH: 0-1 Tight: 0-1 Gall: 0-0
Aids: Bl: 0-0 Vi: 0-0 Tstrap: 0-0
Best Rating: 53 9/01 Haml 1m65y gd-fm

Super Dominion

104(96) (49)**63**
4-y-o ch c Superpower-Smartie Lee (Dominion)
R Hollinshead Mrs Norman Hill

Placings:433600**555100-045**00112000201 **(5626)**
2001: 9^{0}SW, 7^{4}SD, 8^{5}SD, 8^{0}G, 10^{0}GF, 5^{1}GS, 8^{1}G, 7^{2}GF, 6^{0}GF, 7^{0}GF, 6^{0}S, 8^{2}GS, 8^{0}S, 8^{1}GS

	Starts	1st	2nd	3rd	Win & Pl
Career Total (Turf)	17	3	2	2	13483
Career Total (AW)	9	1	0	0	2724

63 11/01 Nott 1m54y F(0-60)H G-S £2711
49 8/01 Bevl 1m100y E GD £3132
49 7/01 Leic 5f218y E(0-70)H G-S £3304
50 11/00 Wolv 1m1f79y D STD £2723
Total win prize-money £11873

Going (Turf): Sf: 0-4 **GS: 2-3** Gd: 1-3 GF: 0-5 Fm: 0-2
Distance: 5f/6f: 1-2 7f-8f: 0-12 **9f-13f: 3-12** 14f+: 0-0
Track : **LH: 2-16** RH: 1-4 **Tight: 1-8** Gall: 0-1
Aids: Bl: 0-0 Vi: 0-0 **Tstrap: 4-16**
Best Rating: 63 11/01 Nott 1m54y gd-sft

Broke his duck at the tenth attempt in a fair maiden on the All-Weather in 2000 and has been successful in modest handicaps since, seemingly improved by the fitting of a tongue tie. He is effective between six furlongs and a mile, and likes to get his toe in.

Super Sonic Sonia (IRE)

75(67) **9**
6-y-o b m Tirol-Lunulae (Tumble Wind (USA))
K A Morgan John Sheridan

Placings:60134/500/00 **(3505)**
2001: 7^{0}SD, 9^{0}GF

	Starts	1st	2nd	3rd	Win & Pl
Career Total (Turf)	9	1	0	1	6570
Career Total (AW)	1	0	0	0	

82 10/97 Cork 7f SFT £4795
Total win prize-money £4795

Going (Turf): Sf: 1-3 GS: 0-0 Gd: 0-1 GF: 0-2 Fm: 0-0
Distance: 5f/6f: 0-0 **7f-8f: 1-6** 9f-13f: 0-4 14f+: 0-0
Track : LH: 0-4 **RH: 1-6** Tight: 0-0 Gall: 0-1
Aids: Bl: 0-0 Vi: 0-0 Tstrap: 0-0
Best Rating: 9 7/01 Bevl 1m1f207y gd-fm

Super Tassa (IRE)

106 **113**
5-y-o ch m Lahib (USA)-Center Moriches (IRE) (Magical Wonder (USA))
V Valiani V Valiani

Placings:112/2014602/411300-2213631 **(4171)**
2001: 12^{2}HY, 10^{2}HO, 14^{1}GF, 12^{3}G, 12^{6}G, 13^{3}S, 11^{1}G

	Starts	1st	2nd	3rd	Win & Pl
Career Total (Turf)	23	7	5	3	369643

113 8/01 York 1m3f195yA GD £145000
103 5/01 Capa 1m6f G-F £68736
105 5/00 StCl 1m2f110y GD £21134
4/00 Siro 1m2f HLD £22772
5/99 Siro 1m2f G-F £16403
9/98 Siro 1m SFT £8596
9/98 Casc 6f110y VS £4298
Total win prize-money £286939

Going (Turf): Sf: 0-5 GS: 0-0 **Gd: 2-6** GF: 1-3 Fm: 0-0
Distance: 5f/6f: 0-0 7f-8f: 0-5 **9f-13f: 2-12** 14f+: 1-2
Track : **LH: 2-2** RH: 0-10 Tight: 0-0 **Gall: 1-1**
Aids: Bl: 0-0 Vi: 0-0 Tstrap: 0-0
Best Rating: 113 8/01 York 1m3f195y good

She won three times in Group class, including when causing a surprise in the Yorkshire Oaks, and has been placed a number of times. Has won at up to 14 furlongs. Has been retired.

Superapparos

100(100) (37)**34**
7-y-o b g Superpower-Ayodessa (Lochnager)
S R Bowring S R Bowring

Placings:600000003044/0/6/40602240243506534400 **(5629)**
2001: 6^{4}SD, 7^{0}SW, 5^{6}SD, 5^{0}SD, 5^{2}SD, 5^{2}SD, 5^{4}SD, 6^{0}SD, 7^{2}SD, 6^{4}SD, 5^{3}SD, 7^{5}SD, 7^{0}SD, 6^{6}F, 7^{5}SD, 6^{3}SD, 6^{4}F, 6^{4}F, 5^{0}G, 5^{0}G

	Starts	1st	2nd	3rd	Win & Pl
Career Total (Turf)	9	0	0	0	336
Career Total (AW)	25	0	3	3	2733

Going (Turf): Sf: 0-1 GS: 0-0 Gd: 0-3 GF: 0-2 Fm: 0-3
Distance: 5f/6f: 0-22 7f-8f: 0-11 9f-13f: 0-1 14f+: 0-0
Track : LH: 0-22 RH: 0-0 Tight: 0-4 Gall: 0-0
Aids: Bl: 0-14 Vi: 0-0 Tstrap: 0-0
Best Rating: 41 4/01 Sthl 7f stand

Finished a very flattering third at Wolverhampton in October, but is basically very moderate.

Superbit

101(84) (49)**55**
9-y-o b g Superpower-On A Bit (Mummy's Pet)
T Wall Neville H Smith

Placings:00404/**53230000**01304600**463/00**023130501**35**/413300400304/03004610005024/3040**2**00**3**1/061**0**0-0300003 **(4322)**
2001: 5^{0}GF, 6^{3}GF, 6^{0}GF, 5^{0}GS, 5^{0}F, 6^{0}GF, 5^{3}GF

	Starts	1st	2nd	3rd	Win & Pl
Career Total (Turf)	67	7	2	10	23413
Career Total (AW)	18	0	2	5	3374

48 7/00 Nott 6f15y G G-F £2052
56 10/99 Nott 6f15y F(0-60) SFT £2849
54 8/98 Ripn 5f F(0-60)H GD £2452
64 6/97 Nott 6f15y F(0-60)H GD £3224
60 10/96 Nott 5f13y F(0-65) GD £2381
58 6/95 Bath 5f11y F GD £3020
Total win prize-money £15979

Going (Turf): Sf: 1-5 GS: 0-8 **Gd: 5-18** GF: 1-31 Fm: 0-5
Distance: **5f/6f: 4-71** 7f-8f: 3-14 9f-13f: 0-0 14f+: 0-0
Track : **LH: 1-38** RH: 0-1 Tight: 0-13 **Gall: 1-15**
Aids: Bl: 0-4 Vi: 0-1 Tstrap: 0-0
Best Rating: 55 6/01 Nott 6f15y gd-fm

He has a poor wins to runs ratio, his only victory in recent seasons coming in selling company. A good second on the All-Weather last time out to Samwar.

Superchief

97(102) (70)**49**
6-y-o b g Precocious-Rome Express (Siberian Express (USA))
Miss B Sanders Copy Xpress Ltd

Placings:0/6000060/00**003034/421115000**0**23541121-040**000260 **(4528)**
2001: 7^{0}SD, 10^{4}SD, 8^{0}SD, 8^{0}SW, 10^{0}GF, 8^{0}GF, 7^{2}G, 7^{6}G, 7^{0}GF, 8^{0}SD

	Starts	1st	2nd	3rd	Win & Pl
Career Total (Turf)	17	0	1	0	940
Career Total (AW)	26	6	3	3	17633

70 12/00 Ling 7f E(0-70)H STD £2340
64 12/00 Ling 7f D(0-80)H STD £3217
56 11/00 Ling 1m E(0-75)H STD £2310
58 2/00 Ling 1m E(0-75)H STD £2276
48 2/00 Ling 7f F(0-70)H STD £1806
53 2/00 Ling 7f F(0-65)H STD £1907
Total win prize-money £13858

Going (Turf): Sf: 0-0 GS: 0-1 Gd: 0-5 GF: 0-9 Fm: 0-2
Distance: 5f/6f: 0-6 **7f-8f: 6-26** 9f-13f: 0-11 14f+: 0-0
Track : **LH: 6-32** RH: 0-1 **Tight: 6-31** Gall: 0-0
Aids: Bl: 6-26 Vi: 0-4 Tstrap: 6-33
Best Rating: 67 1/01 Ling 1m2f stand

Superfrills

98(101) (36)**36**
8-y-o b m Superpower-Pod's Daughter (IRE) (Tender King)
Miss L C Siddall Podso Racing

Placings:00363000/4002500/604306450/00002130014 01**02**/062600006/**02**0**004**00502-**034**200100000 **(5288)**
2001: 5^{0}SD, 6^{3}SW, 6^{4}SD, 6^{2}HY, 5^{0}S, 5^{0}G, 6^{1}SD, 5^{0}GS, 6^{0}GS, 5^{0}S, 5^{0}G, 6^{0}HY

	Starts	1st	2nd	3rd	Win & Pl
Career Total (Turf)	55	3	5	4	14868
Career Total (AW)	16	1	2	1	4089

36 7/01 Sthl 6f F(0-60)H STD £2359
47 10/98 Newc 5f E(0-70)H SFT £3053
47 8/98 Haml 5f4y F(0-60)H SFT £2500
40 6/98 Haml 5f4y F(0-65)H G-S £2346
Total win prize-money £10258

Going (Turf): Sf: 2-12 GS: 1-10 Gd: 0-14 GF: 0-15 Fm: 0-4
Distance: **5f/6f: 4-70** 7f-8f: 0-1 9f-13f: 0-0 14f+: 0-0

Track : LH: 1-13 RH: 0-1 Tight: 0-3 Gall: 0-1
Aids: Bl: 0-0 Vi: 0-0 Tstrap: 0-0
Best Rating: 36 7/01 Leic 5f218y gd-sft

Moderate handicapper, she had not won for over two and a half years before scoring at Southwell on the All-Weather over six furlongs. Appreciates heavy ground on turf.

Superior Premium

108 **119**

7-y-o br h Forzando-Devils Dirge (Song)
R A Fahey J C Parsons

Placings:122662155/103604/0200311150/2014006011 0/000161-30605 **(3652)**
2001: 6^{3}GS, 6^{0}F, 6^{6}GF, 6^{0}G, 6^{5}G

	Starts	1st	2nd	3rd	Win & Pl
Career Total (Turf)	47	11	5	3	253794

119	6/00	Asct	6f	A	G-F	£72000
111	5/00	Gdwd	6f	C	G-S	£6148
110	10/99	Newb	6f8y	B(0-110)H	G-S	£9655
108	10/99	Asct	5f	B(0-110)H	G-S	£18481
102	6/99	Taby	5f165y		FRM	£22239
105	8/98	Gdwd	6f	B H	GD	£51500
95	7/98	Hayd	6f	C	GD	£5261
98	6/98	Ches	6f18y	B(0-100)H	G-S	£9458
100	3/97	Hayd	5f	A	SFT	£12136
90	10/96	Hayd	5f	C	SFT	£4484
79	4/96	Nott	5f13y	F	G-S	£2381

Total win prize-money £213745

Going (Turf): Sf: 2-7 **GS: 5-13** Gd: 2-15 GF: 1-9 Fm: 1-2
Distance: **5f/6f: 9-44** 7f-8f: 2-3 9f-13f: 0-0 14f+: 0-0
Track : **LH: 2-4** RH: 0-0 **Tight: 1-3** Gall: 0-0
Aids: Bl: 0-1 Vi: 0-0 Tstrap: 0-4
Best Rating: 119 4/01 NmkR 6f gd-sft

He has been a great servant to connections and enjoyed another solid campaign in 2000. Third in Listed event over six furlongs at Newmarket in April. He stayed six furlongs well, seemed to act on any ground and had a fine record in competitive handicaps. Has been retired to stud.

Superlola

4-y-o ch f Superpower-Polola (Aragon)
Mrs P Townsley Alan Walder

Placings:0 **(0343)**
2001: 8^{0}SW

	Starts	1st	2nd	3rd	Win & Pl
Career Total (Turf)	0	0	0	0	
Career Total (AW)	1	0	0	0	

Going (Turf): Sf: 0-0 GS: 0-0 Gd: 0-0 GF: 0-0 Fm: 0-0
Distance: 5f/6f: 0-0 7f-8f: 0-1 9f-13f: 0-0 14f+: 0-0
Track : LH: 0-1 RH: 0-0 Tight: 0-1 Gall: 0-0
Aids: Bl: 0-0 Vi: 0-0 Tstrap: 0-0

Superstar Leo (IRE)

113 **106**

3-y-o b f College Chapel-Council Rock (General Assembly (USA))
W J Haggas Lael Stable

Placings:21111212-60240 **(3514)**
2001: 5^{6}GF, 5^{0}G, 5^{2}GF, 6^{4}GF, 5^{0}GF

	Starts	1st	2nd	3rd	Win & Pl
Career Total (Turf)	13	5	4	0	201676

108	9/00	Donc	5f	A	G-F	£27000
108	7/00	Newb	5f34y	B	G-F	£72500
103	6/00	Asct	5f	A	G-F	£33000
87	6/00	Catt	5f	D	G-S	£3705
68	6/00	Catt	5f	F	GD	£2310

Total win prize-money £138515

Going (Turf): Sf: 0-0 GS: 1-2 Gd: 1-4 **GF: 3-7** Fm: 0-0
Distance: **5f/6f: 5-12** 7f-8f: 0-1 9f-13f: 0-0 14f+: 0-0
Track : LH: 0-1 RH: 0-1 Tight: 0-1 Gall: 0-1
Aids: Bl: 0-0 Vi: 0-0 Tstrap: 0-0
Best Rating: 106 7/01 Ches 5f16y gd-fm

Stamped herself a useful juvenile with decisive wins in both the Norfolk and Weatherbys Super Sprint. Ran well when stepped up to six in the Heinz 57 Phoenix Stakes and ended the 2000 season with a fine effort against older sprinters in the Prix de L'Abbaye. She showed that she has trained on when displaying plenty of speed against her elders at Sandown on her reappearance, and when runner-up to Danehurst in Listed event at Chester in July . Had the draw against her at Royal Ascot in between. Acts on fast ground. Has been retired.

Supreme Angel

99(107) (68)**67**

6-y-o b m Beveled (USA)-Blue Angel (Lord Gayle (USA))
E A Wheeler (M P Muggeridge 23/4) Least Moved Partners

Placings:0142261/30100000/0000000/**3**104013500000 0-54030013104400 **(5414)**
2001: 5^{5}SD, 6^{4}GS, 5^{0}GS, 5^{3}G, 6^{0}GF, 5^{0}GF, 6^{1}GF, 5^{3}GF, 6^{1}SW, 5^{0}HY, 6^{4}G, 7^{4}SD, 6^{0}HY, 6^{0}SD

	Starts	1st	2nd	3rd	Win & Pl
Career Total (Turf)	42	5	2	4	30742
Career Total (AW)	8	2	0	1	5454

68	9/01	Wolv	6f	E(0-65)	SLW	£2842
67	8/01	Newb	6f8y	E(0-75)H	G-F	£3927
62	5/00	Ling	5f	D(0-85)H	G-S	£7410
61	3/00	Sthl	5f	E(0-70)H	STD	£2296
84	5/98	Kemp	6f	C(0-90)H	GD	£7002
81	10/97	Hayd	5f	D	HVY	£3550
69	4/97	Newb	5f34y	D	G-F	£3817

Total win prize-money £30846

Going (Turf): Sf: 1-10 GS: 1-8 Gd: 1-16 **GF: 2-8** Fm: 0-0
Distance: **5f/6f: 6-41** 7f-8f: 1-9 9f-13f: 0-0 14f+: 0-0
Track : **LH: 1-11** RH: 0-4 **Tight: 1-7** Gall: 0-6
Aids: **Bl: 3-19** Vi: 0-0 Tstrap: 0-0
Best Rating: 68 9/01 Wolv 6f slow

Ended a 15-month losing sequence in a Newbury apprentice handicap in August, and added to that on the Wolverhampton Fibresand. Suited by five furlongs and handles any ground.

Supreme Salutation

104(102) (71)**71**

5-y-o ch g Most Welcome-Cardinal Press (Sharrood (USA))
T D Barron J Baggott

Placings:0650322121/60620603553420-5602354523300 **(5638)**
2001: 7^{5}GS, 7^{6}G, 6^{0}GF, 7^{2}F, 8^{3}GF, 7^{5}GF, 6^{4}GS, 8^{5}G, 8^{2}G, 8^{3}GF, 8^{3}G, 8^{0}GS, 7^{0}G, 7^{2}SD

	Starts	1st	2nd	3rd	Win & Pl
Career Total (Turf)	35	2	7	6	28365
Career Total (AW)	2	0	0	0	0

79	8/99	Thsk	1m	D(0-80)H	SFT	£4402
72	7/99	Catt	7f	E(0-75)H	GD	£4263

Total win prize-money £8666

Going (Turf): Sf: 1-5 GS: 0-4 **Gd: 1-11** GF: 0-9 Fm: 0-6
Distance: 5f/6f: 0-3 **7f-8f: 2-28** 9f-13f: 0-6 14f+: 0-0
Track : **LH: 2-18** RH: 0-5 **Tight: 2-13** Gall: 0-2
Aids: Bl: 0-0 Vi: 0-0 Tstrap: 0-0
Best Rating: 73 5/01 Thsk 7f good

Fairly useful 7f/1m handicapper who often finds trouble in running. Finds winning difficult but capable enough when things fall his way. Acts on most types of ground.

Supreme Silence (IRE)

57(101) (56+)**53d**

4-y-o b g Bluebird (USA)-Why So Silent (Mill Reef (USA))
Jedd O'Keeffe Wetherby Racing Bureau 50

Placings:0000001-0 **(5152)**
2001: 14^{0}G

	Starts	1st	2nd	3rd	Win & Pl
Career Total (Turf)	7	0	0	0	
Career Total (AW)	1	1	0	0	2321

56	10/00	Ling	2m	F(0-65)H	STD	£2320

Total win prize-money £2321

Going (Turf): Sf: 0-1 GS: 0-1 Gd: 0-1 GF: 0-4 Fm: 0-0
Distance: 5f/6f: 0-0 7f-8f: 0-1 9f-13f: 0-4 **14f+: 1-3**
Track : **LH: 1-4** RH: 0-4 **Tight: 1-3** Gall: 0-1
Aids: Bl: 0-0 Vi: 0-0 Tstrap: 0-0
Best Rating: 56 10/00 Ling 2m SD

Supreme Travel

94 **42**

3-y-o b c Piccolo-Salinas (Bay Express)
Mrs Lydia Pearce Bridge Veasey Whatley Partnership

Placings:000-00 **(5375)**
2001: 7^{0}GF, 7^{0}G

	Starts	1st	2nd	3rd	Win & Pl
Career Total (Turf)	5	0	0	0	

Going (Turf): Sf: 0-0 GS: 0-1 Gd: 0-1 GF: 0-3 Fm: 0-0
Distance: 5f/6f: 0-1 7f-8f: 0-4 9f-13f: 0-0 14f+: 0-0
Track : LH: 0-2 RH: 0-0 Tight: 0-0 Gall: 0-0
Aids: Bl: 0-0 Vi: 0-0 Tstrap: 0-0
Best Rating: 42 10/01 Rdcr 7f good

Surakarta

99 **65**

3-y-o b f Bin Ajwaad (IRE)-Lady Of Jakarta (USA) (Procida (USA))
J W Hills D J Deer

Placings:50 **(2740)**
2001: 8^{5}GS, 10^{0}GF

	Starts	1st	2nd	3rd	Win & Pl
Career Total (Turf)	2	0	0	0	0

Going (Turf): Sf: 0-0 GS: 0-1 Gd: 0-0 GF: 0-1 Fm: 0-0
Distance: 5f/6f: 0-0 7f-8f: 0-1 9f-13f: 0-1 14f+: 0-0
Track : LH: 0-1 RH: 0-0 Tight: 0-0 Gall: 0-0
Aids: Bl: 0-0 Vi: 0-0 Tstrap: 0-0
Best Rating: 65 6/01 Sals 1m gd-sft

Sure Quest

105(100) (61)**58**

6-y-o b m Sure Blade (USA)-Eagle's Quest (Legal Eagle)
D W P Arbuthnot Miss P E Decker

Placings:65/5033164/0000/**2341**1122234233-002050005310 **(5599)**
2001: 11^{0}SD, 11^{0}GS, 12^{2}S, 11^{0}GF, 10^{5}GF, 11^{0}GF, 11^{0}GF, 11^{0}G, 11^{5}G, 10^{3}HY, 12^{1}SD, 12^{0}GS

	Starts	1st	2nd	3rd	Win & Pl
Career Total (Turf)	29	3	3	4	23735
Career Total (AW)	9	2	2	3	7485

61	10/01	Wolv	1m4f	F(0-60)H	STD	£2436
59	5/00	Bath	1m3f144y	D(0-80)H	G-S	£6711
50	4/00	Wind	1m3f135y	D(0-80)H	GD	£3926
46	3/00	Wolv	1m4f	G	STD	£1859
61	8/98	Folk	1m1f149y	E(0-70)H	G-F	£3158

Total win prize-money £18090

Going (Turf): Sf: 0-5 **GS: 1-3 Gd: 1-7 GF: 1-13** Fm: 0-1
Distance: 5f/6f: 0-0 7f-8f: 0-2 **9f-13f: 5-36** 14f+: 0-0
Track : **LH: 3-21** RH: 1-6 **Tight: 5-21** Gall: 0-3
Aids: Bl: 0-0 Vi: 0-1 Tstrap: 0-0
Best Rating: 61 10/01 Wolv 1m4f stand

She completed a hat-trick in the spring of 2000, one of which was on sand, but has had a long losing run on the turf since. She returned to sand with success at Wolverhampton when stepped up in trip. Suited by cut in the ground.

Surprise Encounter

108 **108**

5-y-o ch g Cadeaux Genereux-Scandalette (Niniski (USA))
E A L Dunlop Ahmed Buhaleeba

Placings:00/156/005421-110310 **(5386)**
2001: 7^{1}GF, 8^{1}GF, 7^{0}G, 8^{3}F, 7^{1}GF, 7^{0}GS

	Starts	1st	2nd	3rd	Win & Pl
Career Total (Turf)	17	5	1	1	96214

105	9/01	Gdwd	7f	C	G-F	£7316
108	6/01	Asct	1m	B H	G-F	£69600
102	5/01	Donc	7f	C(0-100)H	G-F	£7805
86	8/00	Ling	7f	D(0-85)H	G-F	£4062
81	4/99	Kemp	7f	D	G-F	£3208

Total win prize-money £91793

Going (Turf): Sf: 0-1 GS: 0-3 Gd: 0-4 **GF: 5-8** Fm: 0-1
Distance: 5f/6f: 0-0 **7f-8f: 5-17** 9f-13f: 0-0 14f+: 0-0
Track : LH: 0-2 **RH: 2-5** Tight: 0-0 **Gall: 1-4**
Aids: Bl: 0-0 Vi: 0-0 Tstrap: 0-0
Best Rating: 108 6/01 Asct 1m gd-fm

He has returned better than ever this season and after winning at Doncaster, put up a tremendous performance to win the Royal Hunt Cup. Disappointed when stepped up in class at Goodwood and Salisbury, but came back to form in a conditions event back at Goodwood. Suited by seven furlongs or a mile and fast ground.

Surprise Selection

85(73) (35)**42**

2-y-o b f Be My Chief (USA)-Shamaka (Kris)
S R Bowring Sconce Furniture Racing Syndicate

Placings:0060 **(5346)**
2001: 7^{0}GF, 8^{0}GF, 8^{6}SD, 6^{0}SD

	Starts	1st	2nd	3rd	Win & Pl
Career Total (Turf)	2	0	0	0	
Career Total (AW)	2	0	0	0	0

Going (Turf): Sf: 0-0 GS: 0-0 Gd: 0-0 GF: 0-2 Fm: 0-0
Distance: 5f/6f: 0-1 7f-8f: 0-2 9f-13f: 0-1 14f+: 0-0
Track : LH: 0-2 RH: 0-1 Tight: 0-0 Gall: 0-0
Aids: Bl: 0-0 Vi: 0-0 Tstrap: 0-0
Best Rating: 42 8/01 Bevl 7f100y gd-fm

No signs of ability on all starts so far.

Surprised

108 **88**

6-y-o b g Superpower-Indigo (Primo Dominie)
R A Fahey D R Brotherton

Placings:042/0060/21352520/001544134-01440 **(3445)**
2001: 6^{0}S, 6^{1}F, 6^{4}F, 6^{4}GF, 7^{0}GF

	Starts	1st	2nd	3rd	Win & Pl
Career Total (Turf)	29	4	4	2	48043

83	5/01	Haml	6f5y	D(0-80)H	FRM	£7150
75	8/00	Gdwd	6f	C(0-95)H	GD	£22717
68	6/00	Haml	6f5y	E(0-70)	GD	£3607
66	6/99	Pont	6f	E(0-70)H	GD	£3392

Total win prize-money £36868

Going (Turf): Sf: 0-4 GS: 0-4 **Gd: 3-8** GF: 0-9 Fm: 1-4
Distance: 5f/6f: 2-21 7f-8f: 2-8 9f-13f: 0-0 14f+: 0-0
Track : **LH: 1-5** RH: 0-1 Tight: 0-0 Gall: 0-1
Aids: Bl: 0-1 **Vi: 2-8** Tstrap: 0-0
Best Rating: 88 7/01 Gdwd 6f gd-fm

A sprint-bred half-brother to the owner's Surprise Mission and Bishops Court, he has plenty of ability but has not always looked straightforward. Best at six furlongs on good ground. Has been running well in a visor.

Susan's Dowry

101(101) (49)**47**

5-y-o b m Efisio-Adjusting (IRE) (Busted)
Andrew Turnell Mrs Claire Hollowood

Placings:64164/0/00040325-1252220020 **(5447)**
2001: 11^{1}SD, 12^{2}SD, 12^{5}SD, 11^{2}SD, 11^{2}SD, 10^{2}HY, 8^{0}SD, 10^{0}GS, 9^{2}G, 10^{0}HY

	Starts	1st	2nd	3rd	Win & Pl
Career Total (Turf)	16	1	2	1	5877
Career Total (AW)	8	1	4	0	3591

45	1/01	Sthl	1m3f	G(0-65)H	STD	£1449
76	6/98	Pont	6f	E	SFT	£3615

Total win prize-money £5064

Going (Turf): Sf: 1-7 GS: 0-4 Gd: 0-3 GF: 0-2 Fm: 0-0
Distance: 5f/6f: 1-4 7f-8f: 0-3 9f-13f: 0-5 14f+: 0-0
Track : **LH: 2-15** RH: 0-5 Tight: 0-5 Gall: 0-4
Aids: Bl: 0-0 Vi: 0-0 Tstrap: 0-0
Best Rating: 49 3/01 Sthl 1m3f stand

Susie The Floosie (IRE)

80(77) (22)**16**

3-y-o b f General Monarch (USA)-Cala-Holme (IRE) (Fool's Holme (USA))
R D Wylie E A Draper

Placings:00000-0000 **(4420)**
2001: 7^{0}GF, 11^{0}GF, 10^{0}G, 15^{0}G

	Starts	1st	2nd	3rd	Win & Pl
Career Total (Turf)	7	0	0	0	
Career Total (AW)	2	0	0	0	

Going (Turf): Sf: 0-0 GS: 0-1 Gd: 0-4 GF: 0-2 Fm: 0-0
Distance: 5f/6f: 0-1 7f-8f: 0-3 9f-13f: 0-4 14f+: 0-1
Track : LH: 0-6 RH: 0-1 Tight: 0-5 Gall: 0-0
Aids: Bl: 0-1 Vi: 0-0 Tstrap: 0-0
Best Rating: 16 8/01 Hayd 1m2f120y good

Susie's Flyer (IRE)

99(81) (31)**55**

4-y-o br f Frimaire-Wisdom To Know (Bay Express)
A Berry Mrs U O'Reilly

Placings:25115/5006-0000400 **(3695)**
2001: 5^{0}S, 6^{0}SD, 5^{0}SD, 5^{0}GS, 5^{4}GF, 6^{0}F, 5^{0}G

	Starts	1st	2nd	3rd	Win & Pl
Career Total (Turf)	14	2	1	0	11070
Career Total (AW)	2	0	0	0	

90	9/99	Newb	5f34y	C(0-95)H	GD	£6222
72	8/99	Ling	5f	D	GD	£3817

Total win prize-money £10041

Going (Turf): Sf: 0-4 GS: 0-1 **Gd: 2-5** GF: 0-2 Fm: 0-2
Distance: **5f/6f: 2-15** 7f-8f: 0-1 9f-13f: 0-0 14f+: 0-0
Track : LH: 0-3 RH: 0-0 Tight: 0-2 Gall: 0-0
Aids: Bl: 0-0 Vi: 0-0 Tstrap: 0-0
Best Rating: 55 7/01 Bevl 5f gd-fm

Sussex Lad

105(90) (58)**70**

4-y-o b g Prince Sabo-Pea Green (Try My Best (USA))
P R Chamings (Mrs A J Perrett 25/10) Twenty Twenty Research

Placings:60/04064616006-0501060030 **(5671)**
2001: 6^{0}GF, 7^{5}S, 6^{0}G, 6^{1}F, 6^{0}GF, 5^{6}GF, 5^{0}GS, 6^{0}HY, 5^{3}G, 6^{0}HY

	Starts	1st	2nd	3rd	Win & Pl
Career Total (Turf)	21	2	0	1	6496
Career Total (AW)	2	0	0	0	0

70	8/01	Sals	6f	E(0-80)H	FRM	£3031
77	8/00	Sals	6f	E(0-80)H	G-F	£2782

Total win prize-money £5813

Going (Turf): Sf: 0-5 GS: 0-3 Gd: 0-3 **GF: 1-8 Fm: 1-2**
Distance: **5f/6f: 2-19** 7f-8f: 0-4 9f-13f: 0-0 14f+: 0-0
Track : LH: 0-4 RH: 0-2 Tight: 0-2 Gall: 0-3
Aids: Bl: 0-0 Vi: 0-0 Tstrap: 0-0
Best Rating: 70 8/01 Sals 6f firm

He won an apprentice handicap on fast ground at Salisbury last season and his only other victory was in the same race this year. Seems to need fast ground.

Sutton Common (IRE)

100(88) (46)**60d**

4-y-o b g Common Grounds-Fadaki Hawaki (USA) (Vice Regent (CAN))
K A Ryan The North Broomhill Racing Syndicate

Placings:04/2021000-05400600 **(5146)**
2001: 8^{0}S, 8^{5}G, 7^{4}GF, 7^{0}SD, 7^{0}GF, 8^{6}G, 7^{0}G, 8^{0}G

	Starts	1st	2nd	3rd	Win & Pl
Career Total (Turf)	15	1	2	0	6696
Career Total (AW)	2	0	0	0	

76	6/00	Bevl	7f100y	D	G-S	£3477

Total win prize-money £3478

Going (Turf): Sf: 0-4 **GS: 1-1** Gd: 0-7 GF: 0-3 Fm: 0-0
Distance: 5f/6f: 0-2 **7f-8f: 1-13** 9f-13f: 0-2 14f+: 0-0
Track : LH: 0-4 **RH: 1-6** Tight: 0-1 Gall: 0-1
Aids: Bl: 0-0 Vi: 0-0 Tstrap: 0-0
Best Rating: 70 5/01 Donc 7f gd-fm

He has slipped down the ratings, following a string of moderate efforts. His best form has been shown around a mile on softer ground.

Suvretta (USA)

56 **6**

2-y-o b f Nureyev (USA)-Naughty Nana (USA) (Houston (USA))
J H M Gosden Blue Blood And Wentworth Racing

Placings:0 **(4278)**
2001: 6^{0}GS

	Starts	1st	2nd	3rd	Win & Pl
Career Total (Turf)	1	0	0	0	

Going (Turf): Sf: 0-0 GS: 0-1 Gd: 0-0 GF: 0-0 Fm: 0-0
Distance: 5f/6f: 0-1 7f-8f: 0-0 9f-13f: 0-0 14f+: 0-0
Track : LH: 0-0 RH: 0-0 Tight: 0-0 Gall: 0-0
Aids: Bl: 0-0 Vi: 0-0 Tstrap: 0-0
Best Rating: 6 8/01 Gdwd 6f gd-sft

Swallow Flight (IRE)

122 **119**

5-y-o b h Bluebird (USA)-Mirage (Red Sunset)
G Wragg Mollers Racing

Placings:0232/5313325124/21131345-0213220 **(5103)**
2001: 8^{0}G, 8^{2}S, 8^{1}G, 8^{3}S, 8^{2}G, 8^{2}GF, 8^{0}GS

	Starts	1st	2nd	3rd	Win & Pl
Career Total (Turf)	**29**	**6**	**8**	**7**	**240318**

112 5/01 Wind 1m67y A GD £15145
123 7/00 Gdwd 1m A GD £24687
111 5/00 Sand 1m14y B(0-105)H HVY £16269
96 5/00 Wind 1m67y A G-F £14885
101 9/99 Donc 1m C G-F £5967
96 5/99 York 6f214y B(0-105)H G-S £23750
Total win prize-money £100704

Going (Turf): Sf: 1-5 GS: 1-3 **Gd: 2-10 GF: 2-10** Fm: 0-0
Distance: 5f/6f: 0-2 7f-8f: 3-19 9f-13f: 3-8 14f+: 0-0
Track : LH: 2-7 **RH: 4-9** Tight: 2-2 Gall: 2-6
Aids: Bl: 0-0 Vi: 0-0 Tstrap: 0-0
Best Rating: 119 6/01 Asct 1m good

Smart miler. Second in a Group Three at Sandown, he followed up to win Listed race at Windsor. Just held behind Medicean in the Group One Lockinge Stakes at Newbury, he again lost out to the same horse in the Queen Anne at Royal Ascot, but was outbattled by Cape Town in a Listed event at the same track. Seems to act on any surface.

Swallow Magic (IRE)

42

3-y-o b g Magic Ring (IRE)-Scylla (Rock City)
P S Felgate Foreneish Racing

Placings:0-0 **(1274)**
2001: 6^{0}G

	Starts	1st	2nd	3rd	Win & Pl
Career Total (Turf)	**2**	**0**	**0**	**0**	

Going (Turf): Sf: 0-0 GS: 0-1 Gd: 0-1 GF: 0-0 Fm: 0-0
Distance: 5f/6f: 0-1 7f-8f: 0-1 9f-13f: 0-0 14f+: 0-0
Track : LH: 0-0 RH: 0-0 Tight: 0-0 Gall: 0-0
Aids: Bl: 0-0 Vi: 0-0 Tstrap: 0-0

Swan Knight (USA)

104(95) (73)**95**

5-y-o b/br g Sadler's Wells (USA)-Shannkara (IRE) (Akarad (FR))
B Moreno (R J White 14/7) Figaro Syndicate

Placings:10/4002601003000-60520000
2001: 8^{6}S, 10^{0}GF, 12^{5}S, 11^{2}G, 8^{0}G, 8^{0}GF, 12^{0}G, 12^{0}S

	Starts	1st	2nd	3rd	Win & Pl
Career Total (Turf)	**19**	**2**	**2**	**1**	**18720**
Career Total (AW)	**4**	**0**	**0**	**0**	

82 9/00 Bath 1m5y C SFT £6104
77 4/99 NmkJ 1m D GD £4565
Total win prize-money £10669

Going (Turf): Sf: 1-7 GS: 0-0 **Gd: 1-7** GF: 0-3 Fm: 0-0
Distance: 5f/6f: 0-0 7f-8f: 1-9 9f-13f: 1-11 14f+: 0-0
Track : **LH: 1-7** RH: 0-3 **Tight: 1-3** Gall: 0-6
Aids: Bl: 0-0 Vi: 0-0 Tstrap: 0-0
Best Rating: 89 5/01 York 1m2f85y gd-fm

Smart handicapper at around a mile on soft ground.

Swan Lake (FR)

(81) (17)

5-y-o b m Lyphard (USA)-Dame Au Faucon (USA) (Silver Hawk (USA))
K O Cunningham-Brown A J Richards

Placings:0005/006605600/000-00 **(0233)**
2001: 12^{0}SD, 14^{0}SD

	Starts	1st	2nd	3rd	Win & Pl
Career Total (Turf)	**10**	**0**	**0**	**0**	**0**
Career Total (AW)	**8**	**0**	**0**	**0**	**0**

Going (Turf): Sf: 0-2 GS: 0-1 Gd: 0-1 GF: 0-3 Fm: 0-1
Distance: 5f/6f: 0-0 7f-8f: 0-3 9f-13f: 0-12 14f+: 0-1
Track : LH: 0-10 RH: 0-4 Tight: 0-10 Gall: 0-0
Aids: Bl: 0-0 Vi: 0-0 Tstrap: 0-0

Swandale Flyer

82 (34)**28**

9-y-o ch g Weldnaas (USA)-Misfire (Gunner B)
N Bycroft Barrie Abbott

Placings:04/00500/0640665060/4020P0/0000300/050/0050210-0 **(2440)**
2001: 11^{0}GF

	Starts	1st	2nd	3rd	Win & Pl
Career Total (Turf)	**30**	**1**	**1**	**1**	**3873**
Career Total (AW)	**11**	**0**	**1**	**0**	**644**

28 8/00 Carl 2m1f52y F(0-60)H GD £2247
Total win prize-money £2247

Going (Turf): Sf: 0-2 GS: 0-4 **Gd: 1-13** GF: 0-8 Fm: 0-2
Distance: 5f/6f: 0-0 7f-8f: 0-6 9f-13f: 0-22 **14f+: 1-12**
Track : LH: 0-25 **RH: 1-13** Tight: 0-11 **Gall: 1-4**
Aids: Bl: 0-0 Vi: 0-0 Tstrap: 0-0
Best Rating: 4 6/01 Bevl 1m3f216y gd-fm

Swanmore Delight

85(71) (18)**16**

3-y-o b f Aragon-St Louis Lady (Absalom)
J J Bridger A G Axton

Placings:600-000 **(2878)**
2001: 6^{0}GF, 6^{0}GF, 8^{0}GF

	Starts	1st	2nd	3rd	Win & Pl
Career Total (Turf)	**3**	**0**	**0**	**0**	
Career Total (AW)	**3**	**0**	**0**	**0**	**0**

Going (Turf): Sf: 0-0 GS: 0-0 Gd: 0-0 GF: 0-3 Fm: 0-0
Distance: 5f/6f: 0-1 7f-8f: 0-4 9f-13f: 0-1 14f+: 0-0
Track : LH: 0-3 RH: 0-1 Tight: 0-4 Gall: 0-0
Aids: Bl: 0-0 Vi: 0-0 Tstrap: 0-0
Best Rating: 16 6/01 Sals 6f gd-fm

Swanton Abbot (IRE)

92 **55**

3-y-o b g Charnwood Forest (IRE)-Shaping Up (USA) (Storm Bird (CAN))
M H Tompkins M H Tompkins

Placings:0050-006500 **(3706)**
2001: 6^{0}GS, 8^{0}G, 6^{6}GF, 6^{5}GF, 5^{0}GF, 7^{0}G

	Starts	1st	2nd	3rd	Win & Pl
Career Total (Turf)	**10**	**0**	**0**	**0**	**0**

Going (Turf): Sf: 0-0 GS: 0-2 Gd: 0-2 GF: 0-6 Fm: 0-0
Distance: 5f/6f: 0-4 7f-8f: 0-5 9f-13f: 0-1 14f+: 0-0
Track : LH: 0-4 RH: 0-0 Tight: 0-0 Gall: 0-0
Aids: Bl: 0-0 Vi: 0-0 Tstrap: 0-0
Best Rating: 55 6/01 Brig 6f209y gd-fm

Sweet Angeline

105 **70**

4-y-o b f Deploy-Fiveofive (IRE) (Fairy King (USA))
G G Margarson Mrs T A Foreman

Placings:0444030/005431230-43024046 **(4844)**
2001: 11^{4}GF, 12^{3}F, 12^{0}GF, 10^{2}GF, 12^{4}GF, 12^{0}G, 12^{4}GS, 9^{6}G

	Starts	1st	2nd	3rd	Win & Pl
Career Total (Turf)	**24**	**1**	**2**	**4**	**10513**

64 8/00 Thsk 1m4f E(0-70)H GD £3373
Total win prize-money £3374

Going (Turf): Sf: 0-0 GS: 0-5 **Gd: 1-8** GF: 0-7 Fm: 0-4
Distance: 5f/6f: 0-0 7f-8f: 0-6 **9f-13f: 1-18** 14f+: 0-0
Track : **LH: 1-12** RH: 0-6 **Tight: 1-15** Gall: 0-2
Aids: Bl: 0-0 Vi: 0-0 Tstrap: 0-1
Best Rating: 70 7/01 Yarm 1m2f21y gd-fm

Sweet Applause

83 **56**

2-y-o b f Royal Applause-Silver Cape (Kris)
A P Jarvis Eurostrait Ltd

Placings:00 **(4625)**
2001: 7^{0}GS, 8^{0}GF

	Starts	1st	2nd	3rd	Win & Pl
Career Total (Turf)	**2**	**0**	**0**	**0**	

Going (Turf): Sf: 0-0 GS: 0-1 Gd: 0-0 GF: 0-1 Fm: 0-0
Distance: 5f/6f: 0-0 7f-8f: 0-1 9f-13f: 0-1 14f+: 0-0
Track : LH: 0-1 RH: 0-0 Tight: 0-0 Gall: 0-0
Aids: Bl: 0-0 Vi: 0-0 Tstrap: 0-0
Best Rating: 56 9/01 Nott 1m54y gd-fm

Sweet Band (USA)

97 **93+**

2-y-o b/br c Dixieland Band (USA)-Sweetheart (USA) (Mr Prospector (USA))
E A L Dunlop Abdulla Buhaleeba

Placings:31 **(3602)**
2001: 7^{3}GS, 7^{1}G

	Starts	1st	2nd	3rd	Win & Pl
Career Total (Turf)	**2**	**1**	**0**	**1**	**8124**

93 8/01 Gdwd 7f D GD £7280
Total win prize-money £7280

Going (Turf): Sf: 0-0 GS: 0-1 **Gd: 1-1** GF: 0-0 Fm: 0-0
Distance: 5f/6f: 0-0 **7f-8f: 1-2** 9f-13f: 0-0 14f+: 0-0
Track : LH: 0-0 **RH: 1-1** Tight: 0-0 Gall: 0-0
Aids: Bl: 0-0 Vi: 0-0 Tstrap: 0-0
Best Rating: 93 8/01 Gdwd 7f good

Third in a very hot Newmarket maiden on his debut, he got off the mark in fine style at Goodwood next time and should continue to improve.

Sweet Briar

78 **57**

2-y-o b f Common Grounds-Pervenche (Latest Model)
H Candy Girsonfield Ltd

Placings:00 **(4573)**
2001: 6^{0}G, 6^{0}G

	Starts	1st	2nd	3rd	Win & Pl
Career Total (Turf)	**2**	**0**	**0**	**0**	

Going (Turf): Sf: 0-0 GS: 0-0 Gd: 0-2 GF: 0-0 Fm: 0-0
Distance: 5f/6f: 0-2 7f-8f: 0-0 9f-13f: 0-0 14f+: 0-0
Track : LH: 0-0 RH: 0-0 Tight: 0-0 Gall: 0-0
Aids: Bl: 0-0 Vi: 0-0 Tstrap: 0-0
Best Rating: 57 9/01 Kemp 6f good

Sweet Chat (IRE)

93 **56**

3-y-o b f Common Grounds-Kaskazi (Dancing Brave (USA))

W Jarvis Raymond N R Auld

Placings:00 **(4989)**

2001: 8^{0}GF, 8^{0}HY

	Starts	1st	2nd	3rd	Win & Pl
Career Total (Turf)	2	0	0	0	

Going (Turf): Sf: 0-1 GS: 0-0 Gd: 0-0 GF: 0-1 Fm: 0-0
Distance: 5f/6f: 0-0 7f-8f: 0-1 9f-13f: 0-1 14f+: 0-0
Track : LH: 0-1 RH: 0-0 Tight: 0-0 Gall: 0-0
Aids: Bl: 0-0 Vi: 0-0 Tstrap: 0-0
Best Rating: 56 8/01 NmkJ 1m gd-fm

Sweet Deimos

100 **93**

2-y-o b f Green Desert (USA)-Bint Zamayem (IRE) (Rainbow Quest (USA))

M J Grassick J Higgins

Placings:21365 **(5054)**

2001: 6^{2}GY, 6^{1}G, 7^{3}S, 7^{6}GY, 6^{5}S

	Starts	1st	2nd	3rd	Win & Pl
Career Total (Turf)	5	1	1	1	25190
91 7/01 Curr 6f			GD		£10400

Total win prize-money £10400

Going (Turf): Sf: 0-2 GS: 0-0 **Gd: 1-1** GF: 0-0 Fm: 0-0
Distance: **5f/6f: 1-3** 7f-8f: 0-2 9f-13f: 0-0 14f+: 0-0
Track : LH: 0-0 RH: 0-0 Tight: 0-0 Gall: 0-0
Aids: Bl: 0-0 Vi: 0-0 Tstrap: 0-0
Best Rating: 93 10/01 NmkR 6f soft

Second to Steaming Home on her debut, after winning a six-furlong Curragh maiden next time, she has taken on some useful sorts, and was not beaten far in the Moyglare Stud Stakes, and ran a reasonable race in the Cheveley Park. She looks likely to improve with time, and has yet to encounter ground faster than good.

Sweet Egyptian (FR)

88 **57**

2-y-o b f Snurge-Egyptale (Crystal Glitters (USA))

P F I Cole M Arbib

Placings:0000 **(5667)**

2001: 8^{0}GF, 7^{0}GF, 7^{0}S, 8^{0}HY

	Starts	1st	2nd	3rd	Win & Pl
Career Total (Turf)	4	0	0	0	

Going (Turf): Sf: 0-2 GS: 0-0 Gd: 0-0 GF: 0-2 Fm: 0-0
Distance: 5f/6f: 0-0 7f-8f: 0-2 9f-13f: 0-2 14f+: 0-0
Track : LH: 0-1 RH: 0-2 Tight: 0-1 Gall: 0-2
Aids: Bl: 0-1 Vi: 0-0 Tstrap: 0-0
Best Rating: 57 9/01 Kemp 7f gd-fm

Sweet Environment

86 **9**

4-y-o gr f Environment Friend-Sweets (IRE) (Persian Heights)

D G Bridgwater R W Neale

Placings:0-00 **(5664)**

2001: 10^{0}G, 8^{0}HY

	Starts	1st	2nd	3rd	Win & Pl
Career Total (Turf)	3	0	0	0	

Going (Turf): Sf: 0-1 GS: 0-0 Gd: 0-1 GF: 0-1 Fm: 0-0
Distance: 5f/6f: 0-0 7f-8f: 0-0 9f-13f: 0-3 14f+: 0-0
Track : LH: 0-2 RH: 0-1 Tight: 0-2 Gall: 0-0
Aids: Bl: 0-0 Vi: 0-0 Tstrap: 0-0
Best Rating: 9 11/01 Wind 1m67y heavy

Sweet Georgia (IRE)

79(64) (13)**28**

2-y-o ch f Forzando-Woodbury Princess (Never So Bold)

L A Dace Noel Monaghan

Placings:000000 **(5049)**

2001: 5^{0}SD, 5^{0}F, 5^{0}F, 6^{0}G, 6^{0}S, 7^{0}SD

	Starts	1st	2nd	3rd	Win & Pl
Career Total (Turf)	4	0	0	0	
Career Total (AW)	2	0	0	0	

Going (Turf): Sf: 0-1 GS: 0-0 Gd: 0-1 GF: 0-0 Fm: 0-2
Distance: 5f/6f: 0-4 7f-8f: 0-2 9f-13f: 0-0 14f+: 0-0
Track : LH: 0-1 RH: 0-0 Tight: 0-0 Gall: 0-0
Aids: Bl: 0-0 Vi: 0-0 Tstrap: 0-0
Best Rating: 28 9/01 Yarm 6f3y soft

Sweet Haven

(96) (22)

4-y-o b f Lugana Beach-Sweet Enough (Caerleon (USA))

C G Cox P G Horrocks

Placings:0100600/0000200020-600 **(0322)**

2001: 9^{6}SW, 9^{0}SD, 9^{0}SD

	Starts	1st	2nd	3rd	Win & Pl
Career Total (Turf)	14	1	1	0	3093
Career Total (AW)	6	0	1	0	554
72 4/99 Bevl 5f E			G-F		£2372

Total win prize-money £2373

Going (Turf): Sf: 0-4 GS: 0-2 Gd: 0-3 **GF: 1-5** Fm: 0-0
Distance: **5f/6f: 1-7** 7f-8f: 0-3 9f-13f: 0-10 14f+: 0-0
Track : LH: 0-10 RH: 0-2 Tight: 0-6 Gall: 0-0
Aids: Bl: 0-0 Vi: 0-9 Tstrap: 0-0
Best Rating: 13 1/01 Wolv 1m1f79y slow

Sweet Kristeen (USA)

88 **69**

2-y-o ch f Candy Stripes (USA)-Aneesati (Kris)

J R Fanshawe Nigel & Carolyn Elwes

Placings:43 **(5380)**

2001: 6^{4}GF, 7^{3}S

	Starts	1st	2nd	3rd	Win & Pl
Career Total (Turf)	2	0	0	1	444

Going (Turf): Sf: 0-1 GS: 0-0 Gd: 0-0 GF: 0-1 Fm: 0-0
Distance: 5f/6f: 0-1 7f-8f: 0-1 9f-13f: 0-0 14f+: 0-0
Track : LH: 0-1 RH: 0-0 Tight: 0-1 Gall: 0-0
Aids: Bl: 0-0 Vi: 0-0 Tstrap: 0-0
Best Rating: 69 9/01 Ling 6f gd-fm

Sweet Prospect

104 **96**

3-y-o b f Shareef Dancer (USA)-Vayavaig (Damister (USA))

C F Wall The Silver And Blue Horse Racing Club

Placings:01455-34044103 **(5572a)**

2001: 10^{3}F, 10^{4}GS, 8^{0}GF, 8^{4}F, 8^{4}GF, 8^{1}G, 8^{0}S, 8^{3}F

	Starts	1st	2nd	3rd	Win & Pl
Career Total (Turf)	13	2	0	2	38285
95 9/01 Epsm 1m114y C(0-90)H			GD		£10871
73 7/00 Kemp 6f E			G-F		£3591

Total win prize-money £14462

Going (Turf): Sf: 0-1 GS: 0-1 **Gd: 1-4 GF: 1-4** Fm: 0-3
Distance: 5f/6f: 1-4 7f-8f: 0-4 9f-13f: 1-5 14f+: 0-0
Track : **LH: 1-5** RH: 0-0 **Tight: 1-2** Gall: 0-2
Aids: Bl: 0-0 Vi: 0-0 Tstrap: 0-0
Best Rating: 96 10/01 Belm 1m110y firm

Scored at Kempton on her second start at two, but was too high in the handicap for much of this season prior to her return to the winner's enclosure at Epsom in September. The extended mile proved right up her street on that occasion.

Sweet Reward

104 **74d**

6-y-o ch g Beveled (USA)-Sweet Revival (Claude Monet (USA))

J G Smyth-Osbourne Mrs Andria Dorler & Partners

Placings:6315/306335000/220330/44035331-1060000 **(5293)**

2001: 10^{1}GS, 8^{0}GS, 11^{6}GF, 11^{0}GS, 10^{0}G, 9^{0}GS, 9^{0}S

	Starts	1st	2nd	3rd	Win & Pl
Career Total (Turf)	34	3	2	9	28492
75 4/01 Newb 1m2f6y C(0-90)H			G-S		£7767
71 9/00 Kemp 1m D(0-80)H			SFT		£4836
72 6/97 Leic 5f218y D			GD		£3392

Total win prize-money £15996

Going (Turf): Sf: 1-13 GS: 1-5 Gd: 1-13 GF: 0-3 Fm: 0-0
Distance: 5f/6f: 1-4 7f-8f: 1-8 9f-13f: 1-22 14f+: 0-0
Track : LH: 1-8 RH: 1-16 Tight: 0-5 **Gall: 2-6**
Aids: Bl: 0-0 Vi: 0-0 Tstrap: 0-0
Best Rating: 75 4/01 Newb 1m2f6y gd-sft

Won a competitive handicap at Newbury in April 2001 with plenty in hand, but has failed to run up to that form since. Obviously goes well after a break. Suited by ten furlongs and soft ground.

Sweet Singer

85(89) (68+)**37**

2-y-o b f Hector Protector (USA)-Sweet Contralto (Danehill (USA))

Sir Mark Prescott S R Frisby & W E A Fox

Placings:01 **(3432)**

2001: 7^{0}G, 7^{1}SD

	Starts	1st	2nd	3rd	Win & Pl
Career Total (Turf)	1	0	0	0	
Career Total (AW)	1	1	0	0	1897
68 7/01 Sthl 7f G			STD		£1897

Total win prize-money £1897

Going (Turf): Sf: 0-0 GS: 0-0 Gd: 0-1 GF: 0-0 Fm: 0-0
Distance: 5f/6f: 0-0 **7f-8f: 1-2** 9f-13f: 0-0 14f+: 0-0
Track : **LH: 1-1** RH: 0-0 Tight: 0-0 Gall: 0-0
Aids: Bl: 0-0 Vi: 0-0 Tstrap: 0-0
Best Rating: 68 7/01 Sthl 7f stand

Winner of a seven-furlong seller on the sand on her second outing, she subsequently went to race in Sweden then Spain.

Sweet Supposin (IRE)

(65)

10-y-o b g Posen (USA)-Go Honey Go (General Assembly (USA))

C A Dwyer G Middlemiss

Placings:0066000123/52113303011010012/05211610

124064500/3105415363365524/3435050/0 (0574)
2001: 12^{0}SW

	Starts	1st	2nd	3rd	Win & Pl
Career Total (Turf)	14	0	0	1	367
Career Total (AW)	55	13	6	9	46363

64	3/97	Ling	1m2f	D(0-80)H	STD	£4269
62	2/97	Ling	1m2f	D(0-80)H	STD	£3436
65	5/96	Wolv	1m1f79y	F	STD	£2381
77	3/96	Ling	1m4f	F	STD	£2690
77	2/96	Ling	1m2f	E	STD	£2859
77	2/96	Ling	1m2f	E	STD	£3022
59	11/95	Wolv	1m1f79y	F	STD	£2187
81	8/95	Wolv	7f	F	STD	£2519
74	7/95	Wolv	7f	F	STD	£2519
78	6/95	Wolv	1m100y	F	STD	£2519
68	2/95	Ling	7f	F	STD	£2688
68	2/95	Ling	7f	F	STD	£2700
64	12/94	Ling	1m	E(0-70)H	STD	£2788

Total win prize-money £36579

Going (Turf): Sf: 0-0 GS: 0-1 Gd: 0-4 GF: 0-2 Fm: 0-0
Distance: 5f/6f: 0-2 7f-8f: 5-22 **9f-13f: 8-38** 14f+: 0-0
Track : **LH: 13-58** RH: 0-2 **Tight: 13-51** Gall: 0-0
Aids: Bl: 5-14 **Vi: 7-38** Tstrap: 0-0

Sweet Touch

71(84) (50)**26**
2-y-o b f Definite Article-Shirley's Touch (Touching Wood (USA))
M D I Usher Andrew Elliott

Placings:046 **(4878)**
2001: 7^{0}G, 8^{4}SW, 7^{6}SD

	Starts	1st	2nd	3rd	Win & Pl
Career Total (Turf)	1	0	0	0	
Career Total (AW)	2	0	0	0	0

Going (Turf): Sf: 0-0 GS: 0-0 Gd: 0-1 GF: 0-0 Fm: 0-0
Distance: 5f/6f: 0-0 7f-8f: 0-2 9f-13f: 0-1 14f+: 0-0
Track : LH: 0-2 RH: 0-1 Tight: 0-2 Gall: 0-0
Aids: Bl: 0-0 Vi: 0-0 Tstrap: 0-0
Best Rating: 50 9/01 Wolv 1m100y slow

Sweet Veleta

88(81) (39)**33**
3-y-o b f Cosmonaut-Redgrave Design (Nebbiolo)
R M Whitaker R M Whitaker

Placings:24400-0000000 **(5278)**
2001: 8^{0}SW, 6^{0}G, 8^{0}G, 8^{0}GF, 8^{0}GF, 10^{0}GF, 7^{0}GF, 9^{0}GS

	Starts	1st	2nd	3rd	Win & Pl
Career Total (Turf)	7	0	0	0	
Career Total (AW)	6	0	1	0	524

Going (Turf): Sf: 0-0 GS: 0-1 Gd: 0-2 GF: 0-4 Fm: 0-0
Distance: 5f/6f: 0-3 7f-8f: 0-6 9f-13f: 0-4 14f+: 0-0
Track : LH: 0-7 RH: 0-5 Tight: 0-4 Gall: 0-0
Aids: Bl: 0-0 Vi: 0-0 Tstrap: 0-0
Best Rating: 41 5/01 Ripn 1m good

Sweetstock

91 **42**
3-y-o b f Anshan-Stockline (Capricorn Line)
G A Butler Mrs M Fairbairn

Placings:000 **(5041)**
2001: 8^{0}GF, 12^{0}G, 10^{0}G

	Starts	1st	2nd	3rd	Win & Pl
Career Total (Turf)	3	0	0	0	

Going (Turf): Sf: 0-0 GS: 0-0 Gd: 0-2 GF: 0-1 Fm: 0-0

Distance: 5f/6f: 0-0 7f-8f: 0-0 9f-13f: 0-3 14f+: 0-0
Track : LH: 0-2 RH: 0-1 Tight: 0-2 Gall: 0-0
Aids: Bl: 0-0 Vi: 0-0 Tstrap: 0-0
Best Rating: 42 9/01 Chep 1m4f23y good

Swemby

94 **27**
4-y-o ch f Mizoram (USA)-Equilibrium (Statoblest)
K Bell North Farm Stud

Placings:000-0 **(2940)**
2001: 11^{0}GF

	Starts	1st	2nd	3rd	Win & Pl
Career Total (Turf)	4	0	0	0	

Going (Turf): Sf: 0-0 GS: 0-2 Gd: 0-1 GF: 0-1 Fm: 0-0
Distance: 5f/6f: 0-0 7f-8f: 0-0 9f-13f: 0-4 14f+: 0-0
Track : LH: 0-4 RH: 0-0 Tight: 0-3 Gall: 0-0
Aids: Bl: 0-0 Vi: 0-0 Tstrap: 0-0
Best Rating: 27 7/01 Ling 1m3f106y gd-fm

Swift

96(96) (63)**44**
7-y-o ch g Sharpo-Three Terns (USA) (Arctic Tern (USA))
M J Polglase General Sir Geoffrey Howlett

Placings:006106/**231**0330101566206**5460**/**4302**066630 20504205004400/**45325211**011460100050**0**/**006**00-064P **(5106)**
2001: 11^{0}G, 11^{6}GF, 11^{4}SD, 12^{P}GS

	Starts	1st	2nd	3rd	Win & Pl
Career Total (Turf)	58	6	3	2	34703
Career Total (AW)	24	3	4	4	15268

68	5/99	York	1m5f194y	C(0-90)H	SFT	£8155
76	4/99	Wwck	1m2f169y	D(0-80)H	GD	£4240
67	3/99	Nott	1m1f213y	D(0-85)H	G-S	£4184
77	3/99	Sthl	1m4f	D(0-85)H	STD	£4045
65	3/99	Sthl	1m4f	F(0-65)H	STD	£1903
66	6/97	Rdcr	7f	D(0-80)H	GD	£3886
63	5/97	Ripn	6f	E(0-70)H	G-F	£2934
61	3/97	Wolv	1m100y	F	STD	£2363
61	10/96	Catt	5f	D	GD	£3281

Total win prize-money £34993

Going (Turf): Sf: 1-12 GS: 1-7 **Gd: 3-23** GF: 1-16 Fm: 0-0
Distance: 5f/6f: 2-10 7f-8f: 1-32 **9f-13f: 5-34** 14f+: 1-6
Track : **LH: 6-47** RH: 0-13 Tight: 1-20 Gall: 1-10
Aids: Bl: 0-0 Vi: 0-0 Tstrap: 0-0
Best Rating: 48 10/01 Sthl 1m3f stand

He was a successful middle-distance performer on turf and Fibresand a few years ago, but looks a light of other days.

Swift Appraisal

72 **57**
2-y-o gr g Slip Anchor-Minsden's Image (Dancer's Image (USA))
S C Williams Mrs Marion E Southcott

Placings:0 **(5561)**
2001: 7^{0}S

	Starts	1st	2nd	3rd	Win & Pl
Career Total (Turf)	1	0	0	0	

Going (Turf): Sf: 0-1 GS: 0-0 Gd: 0-0 GF: 0-0 Fm: 0-0
Distance: 5f/6f: 0-0 7f-8f: 0-1 9f-13f: 0-0 14f+: 0-0
Track : LH: 0-0 RH: 0-0 Tight: 0-0 Gall: 0-0
Aids: Bl: 0-0 Vi: 0-0 Tstrap: 0-0
Best Rating: 57 10/01 Yarm 7f3y soft

Swift Dispersal

108(75) (23)**83?**
4-y-o gr f Shareef Dancer (USA)-Minsden's Image (Dancer's Image (USA))
S C Williams Mrs Marion E Southcott

Placings:001023-00100000030 **(5678a)**
2001: 8^{0}S, 6^{0}G, 7^{1}G, 8^{0}GF, 8^{0}GF, 8^{0}G, 8^{0}GF, 7^{0}GF, 8^{0}G, 8^{3}S, 8^{0}HO

	Starts	1st	2nd	3rd	Win & Pl
Career Total (Turf)	15	2	1	2	20689
Career Total (AW)	2	0	0	0	

84	5/01	Sand	7f16y	C(0-90)H	GD	£7182
71	4/00	Pont	6f	D	G-S	£3542

Total win prize-money £10726

Going (Turf): Sf: 0-3 **GS: 1-2 Gd: 1-4** GF: 0-5 Fm: 0-0
Distance: 5f/6f: 1-3 7f-8f: 1-11 9f-13f: 0-3 14f+: 0-0
Track : LH: 1-5 RH: 1-5 Tight: 0-2 Gall: 0-0
Aids: Bl: 0-1 Vi: 0-0 Tstrap: 0-0
Best Rating: 84 5/01 Sand 7f16y good

Returned to form this season on her third outing over seven furlongs at Sandown, but has struggled off a higher mark since. Needs to come late off a fast pace and is best over seven furlongs. Acts on most goings.

Swiftly

(93) (69)
2-y-o ch f Cadeaux Genereux-Run Faster (IRE) (Commanche Run)
M A Jarvis Saif Ali

Placings:41300 **(5194)**
2001: 6^{4}GF, 5^{1}SD, 5^{3}GF, 6^{0}G, 5^{0}SD

	Starts	1st	2nd	3rd	Win & Pl
Career Total (Turf)	3	0	0	1	533
Career Total (AW)	2	1	0	0	2919

69	6/01	Sthl	5f	E	STD	£2919

Total win prize-money £2919

Going (Turf): Sf: 0-0 GS: 0-0 Gd: 0-1 GF: 0-2 Fm: 0-0
Distance: **5f/6f: 1-4** 7f-8f: 0-1 9f-13f: 0-0 14f+: 0-0
Track : LH: 0-2 RH: 0-0 Tight: 0-2 Gall: 0-0
Aids: Bl: 0-0 Vi: 0-0 Tstrap: 0-0
Best Rating: 69 6/01 Sthl 5f stand

Highly regarded at home, she is bred for speed and, although the maiden she won on the sand at Southwell was not hotly contested, she won it well, and has since run well in a more competitive event. Suited by five furlongs, and handles Fibresand and acts on good to firm.

Swiftmar

96(76) (22)**61**
3-y-o b f Marju (IRE)-Swift Spring (FR) (Bluebird (USA))
P F I Cole M Arbib

Placings:36-60330200 **(5398)**
2001: 6^{6}HY, 7^{0}GF, 8^{3}GF, 8^{3}S, 8^{0}GF, 7^{2}GF, 8^{0}G, 8^{0}SD

	Starts	1st	2nd	3rd	Win & Pl
Career Total (Turf)	9	0	1	3	1991
Career Total (AW)	1	0	0	0	

Going (Turf): Sf: 0-4 GS: 0-0 Gd: 0-1 GF: 0-4 Fm: 0-0
Distance: 5f/6f: 0-0 7f-8f: 0-6 9f-13f: 0-4 14f+: 0-0
Track : LH: 0-4 RH: 0-3 Tight: 0-3 Gall: 0-0
Aids: Bl: 0-0 Vi: 0-0 Tstrap: 0-0
Best Rating: 61 8/01 Wwck 1m22y gd-fm

Swiftway

79 **39**

7-y-o ch g Anshan-Solemn Occasion (USA) (Secreto (USA))

K W Hogg Anthony White

Placings:63P/506520303/60514U/34/150-0 **(5170)**

2001: 17^{0}GS

	Starts	1st	2nd	3rd	Win & Pl
Career Total (Turf)	24	2	1	4	9495

47	3/00	Newc	2m19y	E(0-70)H	G-S	£2853
49	7/98	Bevl	2m35y	E(0-70)H	G-F	£3036

Total win prize-money £5890

Going (Turf): Sf: 0-1 **GS: 1-4** Gd: 0-7 **GF: 1-11** Fm: 0-1
Distance: 5f/6f: 0-0 7f-8f: 0-1 9f-13f: 0-8 **14f+: 2-15**
Track : LH: 1-11 RH: 1-13 Tight: 1-13 Gall: 1-4
Aids: Bl: 0-0 Vi: 0-0 Tstrap: 0-0
Best Rating: 49 7/98 Bevl 2m35y GF

Swing Along

(97) (54)

6-y-o ch m Alhijaz-So It Goes (Free State)

A B Coogan A B Coogan

Placings:2/20/35005305316/241005333400200-00 **(0163)**

2001: 11^{0}SD, 9^{0}SD

	Starts	1st	2nd	3rd	Win & Pl
Career Total (Turf)	16	0	3	3	6033
Career Total (AW)	15	2	1	3	5057

65	1/00	Wolv	1m1f79y	G(0-65)H	STD	£1636
65	11/99	Wolv	7f	F(0-65)H	STD	£2263

Total win prize-money £3901

Going (Turf): Sf: 0-3 GS: 0-5 Gd: 0-3 GF: 0-5 Fm: 0-0
Distance: 5f/6f: 0-3 7f-8f: 1-15 9f-13f: 1-13 14f+: 0-0
Track : LH: 2-18 RH: 0-1 **Tight: 2-8** Gall: 0-1
Aids: Bl: 0-0 Vi: 0-0 Tstrap: 0-0
Best Rating: 28 1/01 Sthl 1m3f stand

Swing Band

102 **94**

3-y-o b g Celtic Swing-Inchkeith (Reference Point)

G B Balding The Swingers

Placings:1245-400 **(2838)**

2001: 10^{4}GS, 9^{0}GF, 7^{0}GF

	Starts	1st	2nd	3rd	Win & Pl
Career Total (Turf)	7	1	1	0	11809

84	7/00	Newb	7f	D	G-F	£5356

Total win prize money £5356

Going (Turf): Sf: 0-1 GS: 0-1 Gd: 0-0 **GF: 1-5** Fm: 0-0
Distance: 5f/6f: 0-0 **7f-8f: 1-4** 9f-13f: 0-3 14f+: 0-0
Track : LH: 0-1 RH: 0-3 Tight: 0-2 Gall: 0-0
Aids: Bl: 0-0 Vi: 0-1 Tstrap: 0-0
Best Rating: 94 5/01 Bath 1m2f46y gd-sft

Showed useful form at two, but has not recaptured his best this term. Probably best at a mile.

Swing Bar

99 **41**

8-y-o b m Sadeem (USA)-Murex (Royalty)

J M Bradley Miss S Howell

Placings:04624100/0000004-02626 **(3298)**

2001: 9^{0}F, 9^{2}GF, 11^{6}GF, 9^{2}GF, 11^{6}GF

	Starts	1st	2nd	3rd	Win & Pl
Career Total (Turf)	20	1	3	0	5191

51	8/99	Bevl	1m1f207yF(0-60)H		GD	£2210

Total win prize-money £2211

Going (Turf): Sf: 0-2 GS: 0-0 **Gd: 1-3** GF: 0-11 Fm: 0-4
Distance: 5f/6f: 0-0 7f-8f: 0-3 **9f-13f: 1-17** 14f+: 0-0
Track : LH: 0-10 **RH: 1-9** Tight: 0-8 Gall: 0-0
Aids: Bl: 0-0 Vi: 0-0 Tstrap: 0-0
Best Rating: 41 7/01 Folk 1m1f149y gd-fm

Swing Job

(97) (29)

5-y-o b m Ezzoud (IRE)-Leave Her Be (USA) (Known Fact (USA))

P S McEntee Shipman Racing

Placings:56660/0060/0350645-65440 **(0323)**

2001: 16^{6}SD, 13^{5}SD, 12^{4}SW, 12^{4}SW, 12^{0}SD

	Starts	1st	2nd	3rd	Win & Pl
Career Total (Turf)	7	0	0	1	590
Career Total (AW)	14	0	0	0	288

Going (Turf): Sf: 0-0 GS: 0-2 Gd: 0-1 GF: 0-3 Fm: 0-1
Distance: 5f/6f: 0-1 7f-8f: 0-8 9f-13f: 0-10 14f+: 0-2
Track : LH: 0-18 RH: 0-1 Tight: 0-15 Gall: 0-0
Aids: Bl: 0-2 Vi: 0-0 Tstrap: 0-0
Best Rating: 31 1/01 Ling 1m5f stand

Swing Of The Tide

109(85) (25)**47**

4-y-o b f Sri Pekan (USA)-Rawya (USA) (Woodman (USA))

A Berry Chris & Antonia Deuters

Placings:240/0005112330000600 **(5225)**

2001: 6^{0}SD, 7^{0}SD, 6^{0}SD, 6^{5}HY, 9^{1}GF, 8^{1}G, 10^{2}F, 10^{3}GF, 9^{3}GF, 9^{0}GS, 9^{0}GF, 9^{0}GF, 10^{0}G, 9^{6}G, 10^{0}G, 10^{0}S

	Starts	1st	2nd	3rd	Win & Pl
Career Total (Turf)	16	2	2	2	14658
Career Total (AW)	3	0	0	0	

66	5/01	Haml	1m65y	E(0-75)H	GD	£3900
61	5/01	Haml	1m1f36y	D(0-85)H	G-F	£6812

Total win prize-money £10712

Going (Turf): Sf: 0-3 GS: 0-1 **Gd: 1-5 GF: 1-6** Fm: 0-1
Distance: 5f/6f: 0-5 7f-8f: 0-2 **9f-13f: 2-12** 14f+: 0-0
Track : LH: 0-9 **RH: 2-7 Tight: 2-8** Gall: 0-4
Aids: Bl: 0-0 Vi: 0-0 Tstrap: 0-1
Best Rating: 67 6/01 Ches 1m2f75y gd-fm

Twice a winner at Hamilton over eight and nine furlongs in the spring of 2001. Goes well on fast ground, has missed the break on occasions.

Swing Wing

102(95) (76)**109**

2-y-o b c In The Wings-Swift Spring (FR) (Bluebird (USA))

P F I Cole M Arbib

Placings:2242112 **(5480a)**

2001: 6^{2}SD, 6^{2}SD, 7^{4}SD, 7^{2}G, 8^{1}S, 8^{1}F, 8^{2}HY, 10^{0}HY

	Starts	1st	2nd	3rd	Win & Pl
Career Total (Turf)	4	2	2	0	66812
Career Total (AW)	3	0	2	0	1682

89	9/01	Bath	1m5y	C(0-90)	FRM	£6922
83	8/01	Haml	1m65y	D	SFT	£3591

Total win prize-money £10514

Going (Turf): Sf: 1-2 GS: 0-0 Gd: 0-1 GF: 0-0 **Fm: 1-1**
Distance: 5f/6f: 0-2 7f-8f: 0-3 **9f-13f: 2-2** 14f+: 0-0
Track : LH: 1-4 RH: 1-3 **Tight: 2-2** Gall: 0-0
Aids: Bl: 0-0 Vi: 0-0 Tstrap: 0-0
Best Rating: 101 10/01 Siro 1m heavy

He acts on both Fibresand and turf and stays particularly well. Got off the mark over a mile at Hamilton, and followed up at Bath. Ran his best race when second to Sholokhov in an Italian Group One. He is bred to come into his own over much further as a three-year-old.

Swinging The Blues (IRE)

101(100) (46)**44**

7-y-o b g Bluebird (USA)-Winsong Melody (Music Maestro)

C A Dwyer S B Components (international) Ltd

Placings:00/40050/302133210/0006004012/001000036 4-52233000500 **(2669)**

2001: 11^{5}SD, 12^{2}SD, 12^{2}SD, 12^{3}SD, 12^{3}SD, 10^{0}S, 10^{0}G, 9^{0}G, 10^{5}GF, 12^{0}GF, 10^{0}G

	Starts	1st	2nd	3rd	Win & Pl
Career Total (Turf)	39	4	3	4	18532
Career Total (AW)	8	0	2	2	1334

56	6/00	Yarm	1m2f21y	E(0-75)H	FRM	£2951
54	10/99	Rdcr	1m1f	F(0-65)H	GD	£2862
66	10/98	Rdcr	1m1f	E(0-70)H	G-S	£3267
56	7/98	Nott	1m54y	E(0-70)H	G-F	£3314

Total win prize-money £12395

Going (Turf): Sf: 0-5 **GS: 1-6 Gd: 1-14 GF: 1-12 Fm: 1-2**
Distance: 5f/6f: 0-1 7f-8f: 0-9 **9f-13f: 4-37** 14f+: 0-0
Track : LH: 4-25 RH: 0-13 **Tight: 3-18** Gall: 0-6
Aids: Bl: 0-1 **Vi: 2-18** Tstrap: 0-3
Best Rating: 49 5/01 NmkR 1m2f good

Swino

106(94) (52)**31**

7-y-o b g Forzando-St Helena (Monsanto (FR))

W M Brisbourne (P D Evans 25/6) Swinnerton Transport Ltd

Placings:3222622210/440620003060664105OO/521601 4540000200O/00206003500054034002/4600446000002 00000-100000 **(4675)**

2001: 5^{1}GS, 5^{0}GS, 6^{0}G, 6^{0}GF, 6^{0}GF, 7^{0}G

	Starts	1st	2nd	3rd	Win & Pl
Career Total (Turf)	83	5	11	4	47403
Career Total (AW)	8	0	1	0	1189

47	4/01	Brig	5f59y	E(0-75)H	G-S	£2912
84	5/98	Hayd	6f	C(0-95)H	GD	£12741
84	4/98	Thsk	5f	C(0-90)H	G-S	£7772
66	10/97	Rdcr	5f	E(0-70)	G-F	£2917
85	8/96	Carl	5f	E	FRM	£2845

Total win prize-money £29189

Going (Turf): Sf: 0-16 **GS: 2-19** Gd: 1-19 GF: 1-22 Fm: 1-7
Distance: 5f/6f: 5-72 7f-8f: 0-19 9f-13f: 0-0 14f+: 0-0
Track : LH: 1-34 RH: 1-5 Tight: 0-16 **Gall: 1-7**
Aids: Bl: 0-11 **Vi: 3-48** Tstrap: 0-0
Best Rating: 47 4/01 Brig 5f59y gd-sft

Swiss Lake (USA)

108 **92**

2-y-o b/br f Indian Ridge-Blue Iris (Petong)

G A Butler The Thoroughbred Corporation

Placings:1612 **(4713)**

2001: 5^{1}G, 6^{6}GF, 5^{1}GF, 5^{2}G

	Starts	1st	2nd	3rd	Win & Pl
Career Total (Turf)	4	2	1	0	27101

91	8/01	Newb	5f34y	A	G-F	£11327
89	7/01	Sand	5f6y	D	GD	£4273

Total win prize-money £15601

Going (Turf): Sf: 0-0 GS: 0-0 **Gd: 1-2 GF: 1-2** Fm: 0-0
Distance: 5f/6f: 2-4 7f-8f: 0-0 9f-13f: 0-0 14f+: 0-0
Track : LH: 0-0 RH: 0-0 Tight: 0-0 Gall: 0-0

Aids: Bl: 0-0 Vi: 0-0 Tstrap: 0-0
Best Rating: 92 9/01 Donc 5f good

She created a big impression when making a winning debut at Sandown in July, but went too fast in the Princess Margaret over six furlongs. Back to form when dropped to five at Newbury in August, but found one too good in the Flying Childers at Doncaster. Very speedy, has won on good and fast ground.

Swordplay

103(66) (15)**67**

3-y-o ch c Kris-Throw Away Line (USA) (Assert)
G A Butler T D Holland-Martin

Placings:06052121000 **(5525)**
2001: 10^{0}GS, 10^{6}G, 8^{0}GF, 12^{5}GF, 11^{2}GF, 12^{1}G, 13^{2}GS, 11^{1}G, 10^{0}G, 12^{0}SD, 11^{0}HY

	Starts	1st	2nd	3rd	Win & Pl
Career Total (Turf)	10	2	2	0	10668
Career Total (AW)	1	0	0	0	

76	9/01	Gdwd	1m3f	D(0-80)H	GD	£5157
58	7/01	Ches	1m4f66y	E(0-70)	GD	£3750

Total win prize-money £8909

Going (Turf): Sf: 0-1 GS: 0-2 **Gd: 2-4** GF: 0-3 Fm: 0-0
Distance: 5f/6f: 0-0 7f-8f: 0-1 **9f-13f: 2-9** 14f+: 0-1
Track : **LH: 1-7** RH: 0-1 **Tight: 1-5** Gall: 0-1
Aids: Bl: 0-0 Vi: 0-0 Tstrap: 0-0
Best Rating: 76 9/01 Gdwd 1m3f good

He is gradually progressing and got off the mark in a Chester classified event in July, before adding to that at Goodwood in September. Suited by 11 to 13 furlongs and most types of ground.

Swynford Dream

102(83) (29)**53**

8-y-o b g Statoblest-Qualitair Dream (Dreams To Reality (USA))
J Hetherton Qualitair Holdings Limited

Placings:11210/020000621030/06606000300**0**/**00**000 0642001600/10**0**2002600600**0**/52042600050-06060020230**0** **(5350)**
2001: 5^{0}GF, 5^{6}GF, 5^{0}GF, 5^{6}GF, 5^{0}F, 5^{0}GF, 5^{2}GF, 5^{0}GF, 5^{2}GF, 5^{3}G, 6^{0}F, 5^{0}SD

	Starts	1st	2nd	3rd	Win & Pl
Career Total (Turf)	77	6	10	3	43631
Career Total (AW)	6	0	0	0	

60	4/99	Muss	5f	E(0-70)H	GD	£2866
57	7/98	Catt	5f	D(0-85)H	GD	£6710
82	10/96	NmkR	5f	D(0-80)H	G-F	£4620
84	10/95	Catt	5f	D(0-85)	G-F	£4272
73	9/95	Rdcr	5f	E(0-75)	GD	£3575
67	9/95	Ayr	5f	E	GD	£4142

Total win prize-money £26188

Going (Turf): Sf: 0-2 GS: 0-6 **Gd: 4-28** GF: 2-35 Fm: 0-6
Distance: **5f/6f: 6-83** 7f-8f: 0-0 9f-13f: 0-0 14f+: 0-0
Track : LH: 0-6 RH: 0-0 Tight: 0-5 Gall: 0-0
Aids: Bl: 0-1 Vi: 0-0 Tstrap: 0-0
Best Rating: 53 8/01 Catt 5f gd-fm

A fair sprint handicapper, he wins in his turn but is not the most consistent of sorts. Acts on fast ground.

Swynford Elegance

101 (37)**47**

4-y-o ch f Charmer-Qualitairess (Kampala)
J Hetherton Qualitair Holdings Limited

Placings:0605**0**/0200002400-0042340320141000 **(5659)**

2001: 8^{0}GS, 8^{0}GF, 8^{4}GF, 10^{2}GF, 8^{3}GF, 8^{4}GF, 11^{0}S, 8^{3}GS, 7^{2}G, 8^{0}S, 8^{1}F, 8^{4}GF, 8^{1}GF, 10^{0}HY, 8^{0}S, 8^{0}G

	Starts	1st	2nd	3rd	Win & Pl
Career Total (Turf)	29	2	4	2	11675
Career Total (AW)	2	0	0	0	0

47	9/01	Haml	1m65y	E(0-70)H	G-F	£3809
43	9/01	Muss	1m	F(0-60)H	FRM	£2544

Total win prize-money £6354

Going (Turf): Sf: 0-8 GS: 0-4 Gd: 0-6 **GF: 1-9 Fm: 1-2**
Distance: 5f/6f: 0-5 7f-8f: 1-12 9f-13f: 1-14 14f+: 0-0
Track : LH: 0-13 **RH: 2-8 Tight: 2-10** Gall: 0-2
Aids: Bl: 0-0 Vi: 0-0 Tstrap: 0-0
Best Rating: 47 9/01 Haml 1m65y gd-fm

She had run some fair races in ordinary company, but did not get off the mark until the 26th attempt in a modest handicap at Musselburgh in September 2001, but was able to add to that at Hamilton later in the month. Suited by a mile and fast ground.

Swynford Pleasure

109(45) (29)**63**

5-y-o b m Reprimand-Pleasuring (Good Times (ITY))
J Hetherton Qualitair Holdings Limited

Placings:42200/502503000**0**/44013253343003044-35012611321663350200 5 **(5657)**
2001: 9^{3}GF, 8^{5}G, 10^{0}F, 8^{1}GF, 7^{2}GF, 8^{6}GF, 8^{1}GF, 10^{1}GF, 8^{3}GF, 10^{2}GF, 8^{1}GF, 10^{6}GS, 8^{6}GS, 8^{3}S, 7^{3}GF, 9^{5}G, 7^{0}G, 8^{2}GS, 8^{0}GS, 8^{0}S, 8^{5}G

	Starts	1st	2nd	3rd	Win & Pl
Career Total (Turf)	52	5	7	10	41438
Career Total (AW)	1	0	0	0	

65	7/01	Bevl	1m100y	D(0-80)H	G-F	£7358
57	6/01	Newc	1m2f32y	E(0-75)H	G-F	£3493
58	6/01	NmkJ	1m	E(0-70)H	G-F	£3766
50	6/01	NmkR	1m	E(0-70)H	G-F	£5161
38	6/00	Haml	1m1f36y	E(0-75)H	GD	£3542

Total win prize-money £23323

Going (Turf): Sf: 0-7 GS: 0-7 Gd: 1-13 **GF: 4-21** Fm: 0-4
Distance: 5f/6f: 0-0 7f-8f: 2-18 **9f-13f: 3-35** 14f+: 0-0
Track : LH: 1-12 **RH: 2-24** Tight: 1-16 Gall: 1-6
Aids: Bl: 0-3 Vi: 0-0 Tstrap: 0-0
Best Rating: 65 7/01 Bevl 1m100y gd-fm

A bit inconsistent, she won four times in the summer of 2001, twice over a mile at Newmarket and once at Beverley, and stayed the extra two furlongs well when winning at Newcastle, and she has run some good races since then without winning. Best on fast ground and suited by a mile to ten furlongs.

Swynford Welcome

109(91) (36)**69**

5-y-o b m Most Welcome-Qualitair Dream (Dreams To Reality (USA))
I A Wood Qualitair Holdings Limited

Placings:24213000/00000001**0000**/00000100000-**0**4010161422211200045 0 **(5688)**
2001: 7^{0}SD, 5^{4}F, 6^{0}GF, 6^{1}G, 7^{0}G, 5^{1}G, 8^{6}GS, 5^{1}G, 5^{4}GF, 7^{2}GF, 8^{2}GF, 6^{2}F, 6^{1}S, 6^{1}G, 7^{2}G, 8^{0}GS, 7^{0}GS, 6^{0}HY, 7^{4}S, 7^{5}G, 7^{0}S, 7^{0}SD

	Starts	1st	2nd	3rd	Win & Pl
Career Total (Turf)	47	8	6	1	41353
Career Total (AW)	5	0	0	0	

72	10/01	NmkR	6f	D(0-85)H	GD	£4670
69	9/01	Brig	6f209y	D(0-85)H	SFT	£4407
54	8/01	Brig	5f59y	E(0-75)H	GD	£2709
49	8/01	Brig	5f213y	E(0-75)H	GD	£4797
44	7/01	Brig	6f209y	F(0-60)H	GD	£2639
46	7/00	Hayd	7f30y	E(0-70)H	G-F	£3276
51	10/99	Brig	5f213y	F(0-65)H	G-S	£2934
76	7/98	Rdcr	6f	E	G-F	£2973

Total win prize-money £28405

Going (Turf): Sf: 1-6 GS: 1-8 **Gd: 4-15** GF: 2-14 Fm: 0-4
Distance: **5f/6f: 5-27** 7f-8f: 3-23 9f-13f: 0-2 14f+: 0-0
Track : **LH: 6-20** RH: 0-5 Tight: 0-8a Gall: 0-2
Aids: Bl: 0-2 Vi: 0-0 Tstrap: 0-0
Best Rating: 72 10/01 NmkR 6f good

She goes very well at Brighton having won five times there, four of them this season. Ran well on successive days at Newmarket in October, winning the first and finishing second in the other, she has run well since then, failing to get a clear run back at Newmarket, although she does look a little high in the handicap. Seems to handle most surfaces, although does not look at home on sand and is suited by trips from five to seven furlongs.

Sycamore Lodge (IRE)

95 (37)**39**

10-y-o ch g Thatching-Bell Tower (Lyphard's Wish (FR))
K A Ryan Platinum Racing Club Limited

Placings:053244333530/362262245/23344**4**2535616/00 **00**/**0**505235235/405101165000/00034060300-60360 **(3932)**
2001: 6^{6}G, 7^{0}F, 7^{3}G, 7^{6}GF, 8^{0}G

	Starts	1st	2nd	3rd	Win & Pl
Career Total (Turf)	72	4	9	14	25347
Career Total (AW)	3	0	0	0	0

66	7/99	Catt	7f	F(0-65)H	GD	£2084
57	7/99	Catt	5f212y	G	FRM	£1940
54	5/99	Catt	5f212y	F	G-F	£2402
67	6/96	Donc	6f	E(0-70)H	GD	£3470

Total win prize-money £9897

Going (Turf): Sf: 0-3 GS: 0-8 **Gd: 2-21** GF: 1-20 Fm: 1-8
Distance: **5f/6f: 3-17** 7f-8f: 1-40 9f-13f: 0-6 14f+: 0-0
Track : **LH: 3-23** RH: 0-10 **Tight: 3-15** Gall: 0-5
Aids: Bl: 0-1 Vi: 0-0 Tstrap: 0-0
Best Rating: 39 6/01 Muss 7f30y good

Sydenham (USA)

109 **110**

3-y-o b c A.P. Indy (USA)-Crystal Shard (USA) (Mr Prospector (USA))
J H M Gosden Sheikh Mohammed

Placings:201054 **(4696)**
2001: 10^{2}GF, 12^{0}G, 12^{1}G, 12^{0}GF, 13^{5}GF, 10^{4}GS

	Starts	1st	2nd	3rd	Win & Pl
Career Total (Turf)	6	1	1	0	7952

80	6/01	Ripn	1m4f60y	D	GD	£4371

Total win prize-money £4371

Going (Turf): Sf: 0-0 GS: 0-1 **Gd: 1-2** GF: 0-3 Fm: 0-0
Distance: 5f/6f: 0-0 7f-8f: 0-0 **9f-13f: 1-5** 14f+: 0-1
Track : LH: 0-3 **RH: 1-2 Tight: 1-3** Gall: 0-2
Aids: Bl: 0-0 Vi: 0-1 Tstrap: 0-0
Best Rating: 115 6/01 Chan 1m4f good

Cost $525,000 as a yearling and, although beaten at Bath on his debut, ran next in a slowly-run Prix du Jockey-Club, where he produced a creditable performance for one so inexperienced. Got off the mark in a Ripon maiden but ran below expectations subsequently. Has won on good ground. Stays a mile and a half.

Sylcan Express

97 **36**

8-y-o br g Sylvan Express-Dercanny (Derek H)
C N Kellett Vince, Ady, Bob And Rich

Placings:0300 (3846)
2001: 10^{0}GF, 11^{3}GS, 12^{0}GF, 14^{0}G

	Starts	1st	2nd	3rd	Win & Pl
Career Total (Turf)	4	0	0	1	361

Going (Turf): Sf: 0-0 GS: 0-1 Gd: 0-1 GF: 0-2 Fm: 0-0
Distance: 5f/6f: 0-0 7f-8f: 0-0 9f-13f: 0-3 14f+: 0-1
Track : LH: 0-2 RH: 0-2 Tight: 0-2 Gall: 0-1
Aids: Bl: 0-0 Vi: 0-2 Tstrap: 0-0
Best Rating: 36 7/01 Leic 1m3f183y gd-sft

Sylv

84 **55**
3-y-o b f Ridgewood Ben-High Commotion (IRE) (Taufan (USA))
J G Portman Miss R Wakeford

Placings:0600 (5043)
2001: 9^{0}GF, 8^{6}S, 8^{0}G, 8^{0}G

	Starts	1st	2nd	3rd	Win & Pl
Career Total (Turf)	4	0	0	0	0

Going (Turf): Sf: 0-1 GS: 0-0 Gd: 0-2 GF: 0-1 Fm: 0-0
Distance: 5f/6f: 0-0 7f-8f: 0-0 9f-13f: 0-4 14f+: 0-0
Track : LH: 0-2 RH: 0-2 Tight: 0-1 Gall: 0-1
Aids: Bl: 0-0 Vi: 0-0 Tstrap: 0-0
Best Rating: 55 8/01 Newb 1m1f gd-fm

Sylva Bounty

89 **54**
2-y-o br c Bahamian Bounty-Spriolo (Priolo (USA))
C E Brittain Eddy Grimstead Honda

Placings:66 (1905)
2001: 5^{6}GS, 5^{6}GF

	Starts	1st	2nd	3rd	Win & Pl
Career Total (Turf)	2	0	0	0	256

Going (Turf): Sf: 0-0 GS: 0-1 Gd: 0-0 GF: 0-1 Fm: 0-0
Distance: 5f/6f: 0-2 7f-8f: 0-0 9f-13f: 0-0 14f+: 0-0
Track : LH: 0-0 RH: 0-1 Tight: 0-0 Gall: 0-1
Aids: Bl: 0-0 Vi: 0-0 Tstrap: 0-0
Best Rating: 54 6/01 Bevl 5f gd-fm

Sylva Legend (USA)

99(106) (57)**66**
5-y-o b g Lear Fan (USA)-Likeashot (CAN) (Gun Shot)
R J Baker M A Swift, A J Chapman And T Warden

Placings:06/2300603364/56033000-640 (3886)
2001: 9^{6}G, 12^{4}GF, 11^{0}G

	Starts	1st	2nd	3rd	Win & Pl
Career Total (Turf)	20	0	1	5	9530
Career Total (AW)	3	0	0	0	0

Going (Turf): Sf: 0-1 GS: 0-3 Gd: 0-9 GF: 0-6 Fm: 0-1
Distance: 5f/6f: 0-1 7f-8f: 0-7 9f-13f: 0-15 14f+: 0-0
Track : LH: 0-11 RH: 0-5 Tight: 0-9 Gall: 0-3
Aids: Bl: 0-0 Vi: 0-5 Tstrap: 0-5
Best Rating: 61 8/01 Kemp 1m4f gd-fm

Fair maiden, but has been tried in handicap company and has been found wanting.

Sylva Paradise (IRE)

103 **68**
8-y-o b g Dancing Dissident (USA)-Brentsville (USA) (Arctic Tern (USA))
C E Brittain Eddy Grimstead Honda

Placings:6641/024321202P4/3066000000/0033400344 0/346302453500/045030100-205000 (4363)
2001: 5^{2}GS, 5^{0}GS, 5^{5}GF, 5^{0}GF, 5^{0}GF, 5^{0}GF

	Starts	1st	2nd	3rd	Win & Pl	
Career Total (Turf)	63	3	6	9	130407	

71	8/00	Brig	5f59y	D(0-80)H	FRM	£6909
93	7/96	Yarm	6f3y	C(0-95)H	FRM	£5796
77	9/95	Folk	6f	D	SFT	£4664

Total win prize-money £17370

Going (Turf): Sf: 1-2 GS: 0-11 Gd: 0-15 GF: 0-29 **Fm: 2-5**
Distance: **5f/6f: 2-54** 7f-8f: 1-9 9f-13f: 0-0 14f+: 0-0
Track : **LH: 1-10** RH: 0-3 Tight: 0-2 Gall: 0-0
Aids: Bl: 0-7 **Vi: 1-23** Tstrap: 0-0
Best Rating: 71 4/01 Brig 5f59y gd-sft

He wins infrequently though he often makes the frame.

Sylva Storm (USA)

101(103) (81)**71**
3-y-o ch c Miswaki (USA)-Sudden Storm Bird (USA) (Storm Bird (CAN))
C E Brittain Peter Head Racing Limited

Placings:4-13006050 (3475)
2001: 8^{1}SD, 10^{3}SW, 9^{0}S, 9^{0}GS, 9^{6}GF, 8^{0}GF, 8^{5}GF, 8^{0}GF

	Starts	1st	2nd	3rd	Win & Pl
Career Total (Turf)	7	0	0	0	349
Career Total (AW)	2	1	0	1	5265

65	1/01	Sthl	1m	D	STD	£2982

Total win prize-money £2982

Going (Turf): Sf: 0-1 GS: 0-1 Gd: 0-0 GF: 0-5 Fm: 0-0
Distance: 5f/6f: 0-0 **7f-8f: 1-5** 9f-13f: 0-4 14f+: 0-0
Track : **LH: 1-2** RH: 0-4 Tight: 0-2 Gall: 0-1
Aids: Bl: 0-1 Vi: 0-0 Tstrap: 0-0
Best Rating: 81 2/01 Ling 1m2f slow

He won a maiden over a mile on the sand in February 2001 and was subsequently upped in class and trip at Lingfield. He by no means disgraced himself in the company but has lost his way slightly since then.

Sylvan Girl (IRE)

(99) (73)**68**
3-y-o ch f Case Law-Nordic Living (IRE) (Nordico (USA))
C N Allen Shadowfax Racing.Com

Placings:3253040052222123-21 (0189)
2001: 8^{2}SD, 6^{1}SD

	Starts	1st	2nd	3rd	Win & Pl
Career Total (Turf)	8	0	1	2	6139
Career Total (AW)	10	2	6	1	9338

69	1/01	Sthl	6f	F	STD	£2184
71	12/00	Ling	7f	F	STD	£2226

Total win prize-money £4410

Going (Turf): Sf: 0-0 GS: 0-1 Gd: 0-4 GF: 0-2 Fm: 0-1
Distance: 5f/6f: 1-9 7f-8f: 1-9 9f-13f: 0-0 14f+: 0-0
Track : **LH: 2-11** RH: 0-0 **Tight: 1-8** Gall: 0-0
Aids: Bl: 0-0 Vi: 0-0 Tstrap: 0-0
Best Rating: 73 1/01 Ling 1m stand

A full sister to a couple of sprint winners, she did not cut much ice in nurseries in 2000, and had to be dropped in class to land two claimers at the turn of that year on the All-Weather. Has been runner-up numerous times over six and seven furlongs and even a mile, although this did not look to be her trip.

Synergie (IRE)

82 **32**
3-y-o ch f Exit To Nowhere (USA)-Keepers Dawn (IRE) (Alzao (USA))
E J Alston The Syngergie Partnership

Placings:005 (2724)
2001: 6^{0}GF, 7^{0}G, 6^{5}GF

	Starts	1st	2nd	3rd	Win & Pl
Career Total (Turf)	3	0	0	0	0

Going (Turf): Sf: 0-0 GS: 0-0 Gd: 0-1 GF: 0-2 Fm: 0-0
Distance: 5f/6f: 0-2 7f-8f: 0-1 9f-13f: 0-0 14f+: 0-0
Track : LH: 0-2 RH: 0-0 Tight: 0-1 Gall: 0-0
Aids: Bl: 0-0 Vi: 0-0 Tstrap: 0-0
Best Rating: 32 6/01 Thsk 7f good

Syrah

90(70) (47?)**29?**
5-y-o b m Minshaanshu Amad (USA)-La Domaine (Dominion)
W Storey Steve Howard And Tony Peters

Placings:045/0000/6002-00 (1548)
2001: 13^{0}G, 16^{0}F

	Starts	1st	2nd	3rd	Win & Pl
Career Total (Turf)	9	0	1	0	516
Career Total (AW)	4	0	0	0	0

Going (Turf): Sf: 0-1 GS: 0-1 Gd: 0-2 GF: 0-3 Fm: 0-2
Distance: 5f/6f: 0-0 7f-8f: 0-2 9f-13f: 0-8 14f+: 0-3
Track : LH: 0-9 RH: 0-2 Tight: 0-6 Gall: 0-1
Aids: Bl: 0-0 Vi: 0-0 Tstrap: 0-0
Best Rating: 21 5/01 Haml 1m5f9y good

Syrian Flutist

86 **65**
3-y-o ch f Shaamit (IRE)-Brave Vanessa (USA) (Private Account (USA))
H Akbary Khalifa Dasmal

Placings:005 (3623)
2001: 10^{0}G, 11^{0}G, 12^{5}GF

	Starts	1st	2nd	3rd	Win & Pl
Career Total (Turf)	3	0	0	0	0

Going (Turf): Sf: 0-0 GS: 0-0 Gd: 0-2 GF: 0-1 Fm: 0-0
Distance: 5f/6f: 0-0 7f-8f: 0-0 9f-13f: 0-3 14f+: 0-0
Track : LH: 0-2 RH: 0-0 Tight: 0-2 Gall: 0-1
Aids: Bl: 0-0 Vi: 0-0 Tstrap: 0-3
Best Rating: 65 7/01 Yarm 1m3f101y good

Systematic

89 **76t**
2-y-o b c Rainbow Quest (USA)-Sensation (Soviet Star (USA))
M Johnston Maktoum Al Maktoum

Placings:23 (5089)
2001: 8^{2}S, 8^{3}GS

	Starts	1st	2nd	3rd	Win & Pl
Career Total (Turf)	2	0	1	1	1697

Going (Turf): Sf: 0-1 GS: 0-1 Gd: 0-0 GF: 0-0 Fm: 0-0
Distance: 5f/6f: 0-0 7f-8f: 0-1 9f-13f: 0-1 14f+: 0-0
Track : LH: 0-2 RH: 0-0 Tight: 0-0 Gall: 0-1
Aids: Bl: 0-0 Vi: 0-0 Tstrap: 0-0
Best Rating: 76 9/01 Pont 1m4y soft

Made a promising debut but was a little disappointing six days later.

T K O Gym

88 **67**

2-y-o b g Atraf-Pearl Pet (Mummy's Pet)
D Nicholls Dandy Nicholls Racing Club

Placings:55530 **(4269)**
2001: 5^{5}GF, 5^{5}GF, 6^{5}GF, 5^{3}GF, 5^{0}GF

	Starts	1st	2nd	3rd	Win & Pl
Career Total (Turf)	5	0	0	1	558

Going (Turf): Sf: 0-0 GS: 0-0 Gd: 0-0 GF: 0-5 Fm: 0-0
Distance: 5f/6f: 0-5 7f-8f: 0-0 9f-13f: 0-0 14f+: 0-0
Track : LH: 0-1 RH: 0-0 Tight: 0-0 Gall: 0-0
Aids: Bl: 0-0 Vi: 0-0 Tstrap: 0-0
Best Rating: 67 7/01 Muss 5f gd-fm

Taabeer

76 **96d**

3-y-o b c Caerleon (USA)-Himmah (USA) (Habitat)
E A L Dunlop Hamdan Al Maktoum

Placings:022-0 **(5528)**
2001: 8^{0}HY

	Starts	1st	2nd	3rd	Win & Pl
Career Total (Turf)	4	0	2	0	2503

Going (Turf): Sf: 0-1 GS: 0-0 Gd: 0-0 GF: 0-3 Fm: 0-0
Distance: 5f/6f: 0-0 7f-8f: 0-3 9f-13f: 0-1 14f+: 0-0
Track : LH: 0-1 RH: 0-0 Tight: 0-0 Gall: 0-0
Aids: Bl: 0-0 Vi: 0-0 Tstrap: 0-0
Best Rating: 31 10/01 Nott 1m54y heavy

Tabbetinna Blue

89(83) (23)**19**

4-y-o b f Interrex (CAN)-True Is Blue (Gabitat)
J C McConnochie Mrs E Lake

Placings:0/002060-00000 **(3805)**
2001: 8^{0}G, 6^{0}GF, 7^{0}GF, 10^{0}GF, 7^{0}GF

	Starts	1st	2nd	3rd	Win & Pl
Career Total (Turf)	9	0	1	0	550
Career Total (AW)	3	0	0	0	0

Going (Turf): Sf: 0-0 GS: 0-1 Gd: 0-3 GF: 0-5 Fm: 0-0
Distance: 5f/6f: 0-4 7f-8f: 0-6 9f-13f: 0-2 14f+: 0-0
Track : LH: 0-6 RH: 0-0 Tight: 0-2 Gall: 0-0
Aids: Bl: 0-0 Vi: 0-0 Tstrap: 0-0
Best Rating: 19 8/01 Ling 7f gd-fm

Taboor (IRE)

100(94) (66)**71**

3-y-o b g Mujadil (USA)-Christoph's Girl (Efisio)
J W Payne G Jabre

Placings:24331002 **(5352)**
2001: 5^{2}GS, 5^{4}G, 6^{3}G, 6^{3}GS, 5^{1}G, 5^{0}GS, 5^{0}S, 6^{2}SD

	Starts	1st	2nd	3rd	Win & Pl
Career Total (Turf)	7	1	1	2	5278
Career Total (AW)	1	0	1	0	1087

71	7/01	Leic	5f2y	F	GD	£2450

Total win prize-money £2450

Going (Turf): Sf: 0-1 GS: 0-3 **Gd: 1-3** GF: 0-0 Fm: 0-0
Distance: **5f/6f: 1-8** 7f-8f: 0-0 9f-13f: 0-0 14f+: 0-0
Track : LH: 0-1 RH: 0-0 Tight: 0-0 Gall: 0-0
Aids: Bl: 0-0 Vi: 0-0 Tstrap: 0-0
Best Rating: 71 7/01 Leic 5f2y good

Sprint-bred but unraced as a juvenile, he got off the mark over the minimum trip at Leicester in July. Tough tasks in handicap since but did show some ability when tried on Fibresand.

Tachometer (IRE)

74 **32**

7-y-o b m Jurado (USA)-Tacheo (Tachypous)
H S Howe Richard Garrard

Placings:404-000 **(5330)**
2001: 12^{0}G, 14^{0}GS, 16^{0}HY

	Starts	1st	2nd	3rd	Win & Pl
Career Total (Turf)	6	0	0	0	631

Going (Turf): Sf: 0-1 GS: 0-2 Gd: 0-1 GF: 0-2 Fm: 0-0
Distance: 5f/6f: 0-0 7f-8f: 0-0 9f-13f: 0-4 14f+: 0-2
Track : LH: 0-2 RH: 0-3 Tight: 0-5 Gall: 0-0
Aids: Bl: 0-0 Vi: 0-0 Tstrap: 0-0
Best Rating: 6 9/01 Gdwd 1m4f good

Tachyon

59(62) **3**

3-y-o b c Tachyon Park-Raisa Point (Raised Socially (USA))
P Howling J J Amass

Placings:000 **(5412)**
2001: 6^{0}G, 5^{0}GF, 6^{0}SD

	Starts	1st	2nd	3rd	Win & Pl
Career Total (Turf)	2	0	0	0	
Career Total (AW)	1	0	0	0	

Going (Turf): Sf: 0-0 GS: 0-0 Gd: 0-1 GF: 0-1 Fm: 0-0
Distance: 5f/6f: 0-3 7f-8f: 0-0 9f-13f: 0-0 14f+: 0-0
Track : LH: 0-1 RH: 0-0 Tight: 0-0 Gall: 0-0
Aids: Bl: 0-0 Vi: 0-0 Tstrap: 0-0
Best Rating: 3 6/01 Wind 6f good

Tactful Remark (USA)

100 **70**

5-y-o ch h Lord At War (ARG)-Right Word (USA) (Verbatim (USA))
J A Osborne Dr D B A & Mrs Heather Silk

Placings:000/134103/05403000-0505 **(4624)**
2001: 9^{0}GF, 10^{5}GF, 8^{0}GF, 8^{5}GF

	Starts	1st	2nd	3rd	Win & Pl
Career Total (Turf)	21	2	0	3	16363

90	7/99	Newb	1m1f	C(0-90)H	G-F	£6905
80	4/99	Kemp	1m1f	D(0-85)H	GD	£3826

Total win prize-money £10731

Going (Turf): Sf: 0-3 GS: 0-1 **Gd: 1-6 GF: 1-9** Fm: 0-2
Distance: 5f/6f: 0-0 7f-8f: 0-4 **9f-13f: 2-17** 14f+: 0-0
Track : **LH: 1-11 RH: 1-6** Tight: 0-3 **Gall: 1-7**
Aids: Bl: 0-0 Vi: 0-0 Tstrap: 0-0
Best Rating: 70 8/01 Bath 1m5y gd-fm

Tadeo

107 **86**

8-y-o ch g Primo Dominie-Royal Passion (Ahonoora)
J M Bradley Mrs A M Johnson

Placings:4212256325341/3005200001105/0250013041000100/4130000136/206064/03000350-0011362050553300 **(4718)**
2001: 5^{0}GS, 6^{0}GF, 5^{1}GF, 5^{1}GF, 5^{3}GF, 6^{6}GF, 5^{2}G, 5^{0}GF, 5^{5}GF, 5^{0}G, 5^{5}GS, 5^{5}GF, 5^{3}GF, 5^{3}G, 5^{0}G, 5^{0}G

	Starts	1st	2nd	3rd	Win & Pl
Career Total (Turf)	82	11	8	11	133163

79	5/01	Bath	5f11y	D(0-85)H	G-F	£4095
77	5/01	Thsk	5f	D(0-80)H	G-F	£4634
102	8/98	Fair	6f		G-F	£9712
105	5/98	Hayd	5f	B(0-105)H	G-F	£8302
95	9/97	Nott	5f13y	C	GD	£5186
101	8/97	Ripn	6f	B(0-105)H	G-F	£20470
93	7/97	NmkJ	5f	C(0-100)H	GD	£5531
95	10/96	Asct	5f	B(0-110)H	GD	£18237
93	10/96	Hayd	5f	C	SFT	£4727
95	10/95	Ling	5f	C	GD	£4971
62	5/95	Carl	5f	D	FRM	£4084

Total win prize-money £89954

Going (Turf): Sf: 1-7 GS: 0-6 Gd: 4-30 **GF: 5-34** Fm: 1-5
Distance: **5f/6f: 11-80** 7f-8f: 0-2 9f-13f: 0-0 14f+: 0-0
Track : LH: 1-15 **RH: 2-2** Tight: 0-7 **Gall: 2-5**
Aids: Bl: 0-0 Vi: 0-0 Tstrap: 0-0
Best Rating: 86 6/01 York 5f good

Decent sprint handicapper at the minimum trip. Suited by fast ground, he retains plenty of enthusiasm despite his years. Scored twice in the space of four days in May and ran well at York in June, but he remains on a fair mark based on his best form from two years ago.

Taffrail

108(73) (29)**95**

3-y-o b g Slip Anchor-Tizona (Pharly (FR))
J L Dunlop The Hon Sir David Sieff

Placings:000-0121110 **(5387)**
2001: 9^{0}S, 14^{1}G, 14^{2}GF, 16^{1}GF, 16^{1}GF, 16^{1}G, 18^{0}GS

	Starts	1st	2nd	3rd	Win & Pl
Career Total (Turf)	9	4	1	0	25382
Career Total (AW)	1	0	0	0	

95	8/01	Bevl	2m35y	D(0-85)H	GD	£4563
83	7/01	Asct	2m45y	D(0-85)H	G-F	£12610
76	7/01	Bevl	2m35y	E(0-70)H	G-F	£4303
55	5/01	Nott	1m6f15y	E(0-70)H	GD	£2982

Total win prize-money £24458

Going (Turf): Sf: 0-2 GS: 0-1 **Gd: 2-3 GF: 2-3** Fm: 0-0
Distance: 5f/6f: 0-0 7f-8f: 0-2 9f-13f: 0-2 **14f+: 4-6**
Track : LH: 1-4 **RH: 3-4 Tight: 2-4** Gall: 1-2
Aids: Bl: 0-0 Vi: 0-0 Tstrap: 0-0
Best Rating: 95 8/01 Bevl 2m35y good

Progressed from two to three and scored four times over staying distances in handicap company this season. Stays two miles and acts on a sound surface, and is still improving.

Taffs Well

107 **74d**

8-y-o b g Dowsing (USA)-Zahiah (So Blessed)
B Ellison Ashley Carr

Placings:024203/0525606000002/0011210130000606/404260000000-014100503560 **(5092)**
2001: 6^{0}HY, 7^{1}GF, 8^{4}GF, 8^{1}GF, 7^{0}GF, 8^{0}GF, 8^{5}GF, 8^{0}GS, 7^{3}GF, 7^{5}G, 9^{6}G, 8^{0}GS

	Starts	1st	2nd	3rd	Win & Pl
Career Total (Turf)	59	6	6	3	52916

76	5/01	Hayd	1m30y	C(0-90)H	G-F	£7800
73	5/01	Muss	7f30y	F(0-65)H	G-F	£2324
78	6/99	Newc	1m	C(0-90)H	GD	£8497
76	5/99	Hayd	1m30y	C(0-90)H	GD	£7392
69	5/99	Ches	7f122y	C(0-90)H	G-F	£9504
63	4/99	Muss	7f30y	F(0-65)H	G-F	£2388

Total win prize-money £37908

Going (Turf): Sf: 0-9 GS: 0-9 Gd: 2-18 **GF: 4-22** Fm: 0-1
Distance: 5f/6f: 0-6 **7f-8f: 4-37** 9f-13f: 2-16 14f+: 0-0
Track : **LH: 4-30** RH: 1-6 **Tight: 2-11** Gall: 1-11
Aids: Bl: 0-0 Vi: 0-0 Tstrap: 0-0
Best Rating: 76 5/01 Hayd 1m30y gd-fm

A decent handicapper who excels on sharp tracks, he is best over seven furlongs and a mile. Acts on fast ground and is suited by coming from behind off a fast pace.

Taffy Dancer

83 **56**

3-y-o b g Emperor Jones (USA)-Ballerina Bay (Myjinski (USA))
H Morrison Rosemary Jenks & Partners

Placings:500 **(3313)**
2001: 10^{5}F, 14^{0}G, 11^{0}G

	Starts	1st	2nd	3rd	Win & Pl
Career Total (Turf)	3	0	0	0	0

Going (Turf): Sf: 0-0 GS: 0-0 Gd: 0-2 GF: 0-0 Fm: 0-1
Distance: 5f/6f: 0-0 7f-8f: 0-0 9f-13f: 0-2 14f+: 0-1
Track : LH: 0-3 RH: 0-0 Tight: 0-1 Gall: 0-1

Aids: Bl: 0-0 Vi: 0-0 Tstrap: 0-0
Best Rating: 56 6/01 Hayd 1m6f good

Taggerty (IRE)

89(67) (12)**62**

3-y-o b f Definite Article-Kewaashi (USA) (Storm Bird (CAN))
J A Gilbert C L Jennison, M D Bromley, N S A Dragone

Placings:0300600 **(5145)**
2001: 8^{0}S, 8^{3}GS, 7^{0}G, 10^{0}GF, 9^{6}G, 8^{0}SD, 7^{0}G

	Starts	1st	2nd	3rd	Win & Pl
Career Total (Turf)	6	0	0	1	1150
Career Total (AW)	1	0	0	0	

Going (Turf): Sf: 0-1 GS: 0-1 Gd: 0-3 GF: 0-1 Fm: 0-0
Distance: 5f/6f: 0-0 7f-8f: 0-4 9f-13f: 0-3 14f+: 0-0
Track : LH: 0-2 RH: 0-2 Tight: 0-1 Gall: 0-0
Aids: Bl: 0-1 Vi: 0-0 Tstrap: 0-0
Best Rating: 68 7/01 Chep 1m2f36y gd-fm

Tahini

88 **75**

2-y-o b f Mtoto-Sesame (Derrylin)
J L Dunlop J Morley

Placings:00 **(4871)**
2001: 6^{0}GF, 8^{0}G

	Starts	1st	2nd	3rd	Win & Pl
Career Total (Turf)	2	0	0	0	

Going (Turf): Sf: 0-0 GS: 0-0 Gd: 0-1 GF: 0-1 Fm: 0-0
Distance: 5f/6f: 0-0 7f-8f: 0-2 9f-13f: 0-0 14f+: 0-0
Track : LH: 0-0 RH: 0-0 Tight: 0-0 Gall: 0-0
Aids: Bl: 0-0 Vi: 0-0 Tstrap: 0-0
Best Rating: 75 9/01 NmkR 1m good

Tahitian Storm (IRE)

102 **96**

2-y-o b c Catrail (USA)-Razana (IRE) (Kahyasi)
M H Tompkins P A & D G Sakal

Placings:02211 **(4587)**
2001: 6^{0}GF, 6^{2}GF, 6^{2}GF, 6^{1}G, 7^{1}HY

	Starts	1st	2nd	3rd	Win & Pl
Career Total (Turf)	5	2	2	0	15655

91	9/01	Hayd	7f30y	C(0-95)	HVY	£9776
94	8/01	Yarm	6f3y	D	GD	£4043

Total win prize-money £13819

Going (Turf): Sf: 1-1 GS: 0-0 **Gd: 1-1** GF: 0-3 Fm: 0-0
Distance: 5f/6f: 0-3 **7f-8f: 2-2** 9f-13f: 0-0 14f+: 0-0
Track : **LH: 1-1** RH: 0-0 Tight: 0-0 Gall: 0-0
Aids: Bl: 0-0 Vi: 0-0 Tstrap: 0-0
Best Rating: 96 6/01 Ayr 6f gd-fm

A half-brother to Ovambo, he appreciated the easier ground when scoring at the fourth attempt in a Yarmouth maiden. Followed up in heavy ground at Haydock when stepped up to seven furlongs and should have little difficulty staying a mile.

Tahlil

84 **37**

2-y-o ch f Cadeaux Genereux-Amaniy (USA) (Dayjur (USA))
E A L Dunlop Hamdan Al Maktoum

Placings:0 **(1611)**
2001: 6^{0}GF

	Starts	1st	2nd	3rd	Win & Pl
Career Total (Turf)	1	0	0	0	

Going (Turf): Sf: 0-0 GS: 0-0 Gd: 0-0 GF: 0-1 Fm: 0-0
Distance: 5f/6f: 0-1 7f-8f: 0-0 9f-13f: 0-0 14f+: 0-0
Track : LH: 0-0 RH: 0-0 Tight: 0-0 Gall: 0-0

Aids: Bl: 0-0 Vi: 0-0 Tstrap: 0-0
Best Rating: 37 5/01 Ling 6f gd-fm

Tai Simsek

89 **48?**

3-y-o b f Minshaanshu Amad (USA)-Bedswerver (IRE) (Doulab (USA))
P L Gilligan Ian Neville Marks

Placings:0550 **(4535)**
2001: 8^{0}GF, 9^{5}GF, 8^{5}GF, 10^{0}GF

	Starts	1st	2nd	3rd	Win & Pl
Career Total (Turf)	4	0	0	0	0

Going (Turf): Sf: 0-0 GS: 0-0 Gd: 0-0 GF: 0-4 Fm: 0-0
Distance: 5f/6f: 0-0 7f-8f: 0-0 9f-13f: 0-4 14f+: 0-0
Track : LH: 0-3 RH: 0-1 Tight: 0-2 Gall: 0-1
Aids: Bl: 0-0 Vi: 0-0 Tstrap: 0-0
Best Rating: 48 8/01 Pont 1m4y gd-fm

Tajar (USA)

100(97) (41)**30**

9-y-o b g Slew O'Gold (USA)-Mashaarif (USA) (Mr Prospector (USA))
T Keddy The Veg Chef Partnership

Placings:320/0604305/05001203400**6**/0301001300/020103506030/6000310300**2500-00**000404022050 **(4728)**
2001: 12^{0}SD, 12^{0}SD, 11^{0}GS, 11^{0}GS, 10^{0}G, 11^{4}F, 12^{0}GF, 13^{4}GF, 16^{0}GF, 12^{2}GF, 14^{2}GF, 14^{0}GS, 12^{6}GF, 16^{0}GF, 14^{3}SD

	Starts	1st	2nd	3rd	Win & Pl
Career Total (Turf)	64	5	5	9	23247
Career Total (AW)	8	0	1	0	576

36	6/00	Ripn	1m4f60y	E(0-70)H	G-F	£2804
50	5/99	Wind	1m3f135yF(0-60)H		G-F	£2752
52	8/98	Wwck	1m2f169yF(0-60)		G-F	£2595
45	7/98	Pont	1m2f6y	F(0-60)H	G-F	£3106
35	7/97	Chep	1m4f23y	G(0-70)H	G-F	£2612

Total win prize-money £13870

Going (Turf): Sf: 0-4 GS: 0-5 Gd: 0-22 **GF: 5-27** Fm: 0-6
Distance: 5f/6f: 0-0 7f-8f: 0-6 **9f-13f: 5-59** 14f+: 0-7
Track : **LH: 3-46** RH: 1-19 **Tight: 2-19** Gall: 0-12
Aids: Bl: 0-2 Vi: 0-0 Tstrap: 0-3
Best Rating: 37 7/01 Chep 1m4f23y gd-fm

Takamaka Bay (IRE)

112 **98+**

4-y-o ch c Unfuwain (USA)-Stay Sharpe (USA) (Sharpen Up)
M Johnston The Chaps Partnership

Placings:221-1110 **(2828)**
2001: 10^{1}G, 9^{1}G, 12^{1}G, 11^{0}GS

	Starts	1st	2nd	3rd	Win & Pl
Career Total (Turf)	7	4	2	0	53755

98	6/01	Asct	1m4f	B(0-105)H	GD	£35750
67	6/01	Leic	1m1f218yD(0 80)		GD	£4257
90	6/01	Hayd	1m2f120yC(0-95)H		GD	£7280
65	10/00	Ayr	1m2f	D	HVY	£3997

Total win prize-money £51286

Going (Turf): Sf: 1-1 GS: 0-2 **Gd: 3-3** GF: 0-1 Fm: 0-0
Distance: 5f/6f: 0-0 7f-8f: 0-0 **9f-13f: 4-7** 14f+: 0-0
Track : LH: 2-4 RH: 2-3 Tight: 0-1 **Gall: 1-1**
Aids: Bl: 0-0 Vi: 0-0 Tstrap: 0-0
Best Rating: 98 6/01 Asct 1m4f good

Got off the mark on his third outing at three over ten furlongs in heavy ground at Ayr. Won ordinary races at Haydock and Leicester before a game victory over stable companion Akbar in the Duke Of Edinburgh Handicap at Royal Ascot. Stays 12 furlongs well and is improving fast.

Takaroa

104 **75**

3-y-o b c Tagula (IRE)-Mountain Harvest (FR) (Shirley Heights)
I A Balding Exors Of The Late Robert Hitchins

Placings:3310150-0000021 **(4905)**
2001: 8^{0}GF, 10^{0}GF, 10^{0}GF, 8^{0}G, 7^{0}G, 7^{2}G, 8^{1}G

	Starts	1st	2nd	3rd	Win & Pl
Career Total (Turf)	14	3	1	2	14549

68	9/01	Bevl	1m100y	E(0-70)H	GD	£3850
87	9/00	Sals	6f212y	D	SFT	£4004
87	8/00	Thsk	6f	D	G-F	£4257

Total win prize-money £12112

Going (Turf): Sf: 1-3 GS: 0-0 **Gd: 1-7 GF: 1-4** Fm: 0-0
Distance: 5f/6f: 1-2 7f-8f: 1-9 9f-13f: 1-3 14f+: 0-0
Track : LH: 0-3 **RH: 1-4** Tight: 0-1 Gall: 0-3
Aids: Bl: 0-0 **Vi: 1-2** Tstrap: 0-0
Best Rating: 75 7/01 Asct 1m2f gd-fm

Won twice as a juvenile in 2000 on varying ground. No show earlier this season, but found his form in the autumn after dropping in the handicap, running well at Epsom before winning in good style at Beverley.

Take A Turn

(85) (50)**47**

6-y-o br g Forzando-Honeychurch (USA) (Bering)
M J Wilkinson The Dann, Gomersall & Pullan Partnership

Placings:30220551000/3025606145350/00000/60-4 **(0194)**
2001: 8^{4}SD

	Starts	1st	2nd	3rd	Win & Pl
Career Total (Turf)	27	2	3	2	13062
Career Total (AW)	5	0	0	1	743

75	7/98	Sals	1m	E(0-70)H	G-F	£3127
79	8/97	Ches	7f2y	C	SFT	£5605

Total win prize-money £8733

Going (Turf): Sf: 1-6 GS: 0-2 Gd: 0-8 **GF: 1-9** Fm: 0-1
Distance: 5f/6f: 0-6 **7f-8f: 2-9** 9f-13f: 0-17 14f+: 0-0
Track : **LH: 1-13** RH: 0-9 **Tight: 1-17** Gall: 0-1
Aids: Bl: 0-6 **Vi: 2-10** Tstrap: 0-0
Best Rating: 50 1/01 Wolv 1m100y stand

Take Flite

106(94) (62)**66**

4-y-o b g Cadeaux Genereux-Green Seed (IRE) (Lead On Time (USA))
W R Muir The Wheet Partnership

Placings:53034/20031600-2566044034 **(5406)**
2001: 6^{2}S, 7^{5}GF, 7^{6}GF, 8^{6}GF, 7^{0}G, 7^{4}GF, 7^{4}GF, 7^{0}GF, 6^{3}S, 8^{4}SD

	Starts	1st	2nd	3rd	Win & Pl
Career Total (Turf)	22	1	2	4	8984
Career Total (AW)	1	0	0	0	0

78	7/00	Folk	7f	D	GD	£2769

Total win prize-money £2769

Going (Turf): Sf: 0-6 GS: 0-1 **Gd: 1-5** GF: 0-10 Fm: 0-0
Distance: 5f/6f: 0-5 **7f-8f: 1-17** 9f-13f: 0-1 14f+: 0-0
Track : LH: 0-3 RH: 0-5 Tight: 0-0 Gall: 0-0
Aids: Bl: 0-0 Vi: 0-0 Tstrap: 0-0
Best Rating: 77 5/01 Sals 6f212y soft

Fair handicapper, best over six/seven furlongs and versatile with regard to underfoot conditions. Looks as good as ever this term.

Take To Task (USA)

97 **85d**

3-y-o b/br c Conquistador Cielo (USA)-Tash (USA) (Never Bend)
M Johnston F Gillespie

Placings:222-06 **(5225)**
2001: 7^{0}GF, 10^{6}S

	Starts	1st	2nd	3rd	Win & Pl
Career Total (Turf)	5	0	3	0	3778

Going (Turf): Sf: 0-1 GS: 0-0 Gd: 0-2 GF: 0-2 Fm: 0-0
Distance: 5f/6f: 0-0 7f-8f: 0-4 9f-13f: 0-1 14f+: 0-0
Track : LH: 0-3 RH: 0-0 Tight: 0-0 Gall: 0-1
Aids: Bl: 0-0 Vi: 0-0 Tstrap: 0-0
Best Rating: 49 10/01 York 1m2f85y soft

Takeonjon

71(74) (36)**48**
2-y-o ch c Factual (USA)-Society Girl (Shavian)
J L Spearing Kinnersley Racing Club

Placings:000 **(5415)**
2001: 7^{0}F, 6^{0}HY, 6^{0}SD

	Starts	1st	2nd	3rd	Win & Pl
Career Total (Turf)	2	0	0	0	
Career Total (AW)	1	0	0	0	

Going (Turf): Sf: 0-1 GS: 0-0 Gd: 0-0 GF: 0-0 Fm: 0-1
Distance: 5f/6f: 0-2 7f-8f: 0-1 9f-13f: 0-0 14f+: 0-0
Track : LH: 0-1 RH: 0-0 Tight: 0-1 Gall: 0-0
Aids: Bl: 0-0 Vi: 0-0 Tstrap: 0-0
Best Rating: 48 9/01 Chep 7f16y firm

Takes Tutu (USA)

96(103) (78)**78**
2-y-o b c Afternoon Deelites (USA)-Lady Affirmed (USA) (Affirmed (USA))
M Johnston C M , B J & R F Batterham li

Placings:633503 **(5408)**
2001: 6^{6}GF, 6^{3}GF, 6^{3}GF, 8^{5}GS, 6^{0}S, 6^{3}SD, 7^{2}SD

	Starts	1st	2nd	3rd	Win & Pl
Career Total (Turf)	5	0	0	2	1032
Career Total (AW)	1	0	0	1	564

Going (Turf): Sf: 0-1 GS: 0-1 Gd: 0-0 GF: 0-3 Fm: 0-0
Distance: 5f/6f: 0-5 7f-8f: 0-1 9f-13f: 0-0 14f+: 0-0
Track : LH: 0-1 RH: 0-1 Tight: 0-0 Gall: 0-0
Aids: Bl: 0-0 Vi: 0-0 Tstrap: 0-0
Best Rating: 78 6/01 Ayr 6f gd-fm

He has yet to win, but has run with credit in varied company on turf and sand and should win a race or two on either surface. Seven furlongs may turn out to be his best trip.

Takhlid (USA)

(102) (61)**58**
10-y-o b h Nureyev (USA)-Savonnerie (USA) (Irish River (FR))
D W Chapman S B Clark

Placings:3323511/0000/401014023560006100003 40/4 0036214143036300000/2611144101011141002 3116/40 2253665013313-6020 **(0240)**
2001: 6^{6}SD, 7^{0}SD, 7^{2}SD, 6^{0}SD

	Starts	1st	2nd	3rd	Win & Pl
Career Total (Turf)	40	4	3	8	30347
Career Total (AW)	56	16	5	6	41992

54	6/00	Ling	7f	E	STD	£2391
66	5/00	Wolv	6f	G	STD	£1512
75	12/99	Wolv	7f	F	STD	£2305
86	12/99	Wolv	6f	F	STD	£1808
68	10/99	Wolv	7f	F	STD	£2305
72	7/99	Wolv	1m100y	F	STD	£1966
80	7/99	Sthl	7f	F	STD	£1840
80	6/99	Wolv	7f	F	STD	£2225
82	5/99	Sthl	7f	F	STD	£1924
76	4/99	Wolv	6f	G	STD	£1542
79	2/99	Ling	1m	E(0-75)H	STD	£2220
71	1/99	Ling	7f	E(0-70)	STD	£2583
70	1/99	Sthl	1m	E(0-70)H	STD	£2918
72	6/98	Haml	1m65y	D(0-85)H	SFT	£7002
62	6/98	Thsk	1m	E(0-70)H	GD	£3176
73	9/97	Wolv	6f	E(0-70)H	STD	£3262
69	4/97	Sthl	1m	G(0-70)H	STD	£2070
59	3/97	Wolv	6f	G(0-70)H	STD	£1648
84	9/95	Epsm	1m114y	B(0-100)H	SFT	£7765
79	8/95	Brig	6f209y	D(0-80)H	FRM	£3698

Total win prize-money £56169

Going (Turf): Sf: 2-8 GS: 0-4 **Gd: 1-10** GF: 0-14 **Fm: 1-4**
Distance: 5f/6f: 5-28 **7f-8f: 12-53** 9f-13f: 3-15 14f+: 0-0
Track : **LH: 19-72** RH: 1-12 **Tight: 15-41** Gall: 0-8
Aids: Bl: 0-0 Vi: 0-0 Tstrap: 0-0
Best Rating: 57 2/01 Wolv 7f stand

Talaash (IRE)

105 **102**
4-y-o b c Darshaan-Royal Ballet (IRE) (Sadler's Wells (USA))
M R Channon Sheikh Ahmed Al Maktoum

Placings:136106-06050 (2949)
2001: 12^{0}GS, 16^{6}G, 16^{0}G, 22^{5}GF, 16^{0}G

	Starts	1st	2nd	3rd	Win & Pl
Career Total (Turf)	11	2	0	1	19317

107	8/00	Claf	1m4f		HLD	£12488
91	6/00	Gdwd	1m4f	D	GD	£4134

Total win prize-money £16622

Going (Turf): Sf: 0-0 GS: 0-1 **Gd: 1-6** GF: 0-3 Fm: 0-0
Distance: 5f/6f: 0-0 7f-8f: 0-0 **9f-13f: 2-5** 14f+: 0-6
Track : LH: 0-3 **RH: 2-7 Tight: 1-2** Gall: 0-6
Aids: Bl: 0-0 Vi: 0-0 Tstrap: 0-0
Best Rating: 102 5/01 NmkR 2m good

A Listed winner in the French provinces at three, he has tackled further in warm company since without flourishing. Best on a sound surface.

Talaria (IRE)

100(98) (49)**60**
5-y-o ch m Petardia-Million At Dawn (IRE) (Fayruz)
W J Musson (M Quinn 4/6) Mrs Valerie Bennett

Placings:46/5014000/6010040561100-05062033050000 **(5497)**
2001: 6^{0}SD, 6^{5}SD, 7^{0}SW, 5^{6}GS, 6^{2}HY, 5^{0}G, 5^{3}GF, 5^{3}G, 6^{0}GS, 6^{5}GF, 7^{0}GF, 7^{0}G, 6^{0}SD, 5^{0}HY

	Starts	1st	2nd	3rd	Win & Pl
Career Total (Turf)	29	3	1	2	12315
Career Total (AW)	7	1	0	0	1778

43	10/00	Ling	7f	F	STD	£1778
56	9/00	Leic	5f218y	F	G-S	£2429
67	5/00	Nott	6f15y	E(0-70)H	G-S	£3043
80	7/99	NmkJ	6f	D	G-F	£4175

Total win prize-money £11426

Going (Turf): Sf: 0-4 **GS: 2-6** Gd: 0-8 GF: 1-9 Fm: 0-2
Distance: 5f/6f: 2-24 7f-8f: 2-11 9f-13f: 0-1 14f+: 0-0
Track : **LH: 1-11** RH: 0-1 **Tight: 1-6** Gall: 0-1
Aids: Bl: 0-0 Vi: 0-1 **Tstrap: 2-14**
Best Rating: 60 6/01 Leic 5f218y good

Talat

101 **58**
3-y-o b f Missed Flight-Tawnais (Artaius (USA))
M J Ryan M J Ryan

Placings:060-31510 **(4462)**
2001: 8^{3}GF, 9^{1}GF, 10^{5}GF, 10^{1}G, 9^{0}GS

	Starts	1st	2nd	3rd	Win & Pl
Career Total (Turf)	8	2	0	1	7002

37	8/01	NmkJ	1m2f	E	GD	£3445
58	6/01	Kemp	1m1f	E(0-70)H	G-F	£3073

Total win prize-money £6518

Going (Turf): Sf: 0-0 GS: 0-1 **Gd: 1-2 GF: 1-5** Fm: 0-0
Distance: 5f/6f: 0-1 7f-8f: 0-2 **9f-13f: 2-5** 14f+: 0-0
Track : LH: 0-1 **RH: 2-3** Tight: 0-2 **Gall: 1-1**
Aids: Bl: 0-0 Vi: 0-0 Tstrap: 0-0
Best Rating: 58 6/01 Kemp 1m1f gd-fm

A half-sister to a seven-furlong winner by Persian Heights and a ten furlong winner by Bairn, she is a lightly-raced plating-class filly, who stays ten furlongs on fast ground.

Talbot Avenue

102 **76**
3-y-o b c Puissance-Dancing Daughter (Dance In Time (CAN))
M Mullineaux Mrs C S Wilson

Placings:4430-05341602 **(4785)**
2001: 6^{0}GF, 5^{5}GF, 6^{3}GF, 5^{4}G, 5^{1}GF, 5^{6}G, 6^{0}GF, 5^{2}G

	Starts	1st	2nd	3rd	Win & Pl
Career Total (Turf)	12	1	1	2	8887

74	7/01	Sand	5f6y	D(0-80)H	G-F	£4621

Total win prize-money £4622

Going (Turf): Sf: 0-1 GS: 0-0 Gd: 0-4 **GF: 1-7** Fm: 0-0
Distance: **5f/6f: 1-10** 7f-8f: 0-2 9f-13f: 0-0 14f+: 0-0
Track : LH: 0-5 RH: 0-1 Tight: 0-4 Gall: 0-1
Aids: Bl: 0-0 Vi: 0-0 Tstrap: 0-0
Best Rating: 76 9/01 Gdwd 5f good

A half-brother to four winners, is at his best over five or six furlongs on a sound surface. Ran well at Chester and Haydock before scoring an overdue success at Sandown over five. Fast ground suits.

Taleca Son (IRE)

98(96) (36)**30**
6-y-o b g Conquering Hero (USA)-Lady Taleca (IRE) (Exhibitioner)
Mrs L Williamson Miss Judy Eaton

Placings:0060506020 0/040055005020 0300/003004400 6305**0434/225400**065405-65 **(2868)**
2001: 12^{6}SD, 10^{5}GF

	Starts	1st	2nd	3rd	Win & Pl
Career Total (Turf)	44	0	2	3	2721
Career Total (AW)	14	0	2	1	1339

Going (Turf): Sf: 0-2 GS: 0-0 Gd: 0-12 GF: 0-12 Fm: 0-1
Distance: 5f/6f: 0-2 7f-8f: 0-24 9f-13f: 0-32 14f+: 0-0
Track : LH: 0-35 RH: 0-17 Tight: 0-5 Gall: 0-2
Aids: Bl: 0-15 Vi: 0-2 Tstrap: 0-2
Best Rating: 30 7/01 Ripn 1m2f gd-fm

Talent Star

103 **51**
4-y-o b g Mizoram (USA)-Bells Of Longwick (Myjinski (USA))
A W Carroll Talent Entertainment

Placings:0460-46050 **(4677)**
2001: 6^{4}GF, 7^{6}GF, 7^{0}GF, 6^{5}GF, 7^{0}G

	Starts	1st	2nd	3rd	Win & Pl
Career Total (Turf)	9	0	0	0	683

Going (Turf): Sf: 0-0 GS: 0-0 Gd: 0-2 GF: 0-7 Fm: 0-0
Distance: 5f/6f: 0-2 7f-8f: 0-5 9f-13f: 0-2 14f+: 0-0
Track : LH: 0-2 RH: 0-1 Tight: 0-0 Gall: 0-2
Aids: Bl: 0-0 Vi: 0-0 Tstrap: 0-0
Best Rating: 51 5/01 Gdwd 6f gd-fm

Talents Little Gem

99(93) (30)**41**
4-y-o b f Democratic (USA)-Le Saule D'Or (Sonnen Gold)
A W Carroll Group 1 Racing (1994) Ltd

Placings:600300/450500-055100645 **(5026)**
2001: 7^{0}SD, 12^{5}SD, 9^{5}F, 10^{1}GF, 10^{0}F, 12^{0}S, 11^{6}GF, 8^{4}F, 9^{5}S

	Starts	1st	2nd	3rd	Win & Pl
Career Total (Turf)	16	1	0	1	7379
Career Total (AW)	5	0	0	0	0

46	7/01	Bath	1m2f46y	D(0-80)H	G-F	£6841

Total win prize-money £6841

Going (Turf): Sf: 0-3 GS: 0-1 Gd: 0-1 **GF: 1-5** Fm: 0-6
Distance: 5f/6f: 0-5 7f-8f: 0-6 **9f-13f: 1-10** 14f+: 0-0

Track : LH: 1-17 RH: 0-1 Tight: 1-8 Gall: 0-1
Aids: Bl: 0-2 Vi: 0-0 Tstrap: 0-0
Best Rating: 46 7/01 Bath 1m2f46y gd-fm

Taliban (IRE)

(74) **41**

5-y-o b g Bigstone (IRE)-Aunt Hester (IRE) (Caerleon (USA))
M W Easterby J W P Curtis

Placings:600-00 **(0688)**
2001: 12^{0}GS, 11^{0}SD

	Starts	1st	2nd	3rd	Win & Pl
Career Total (Turf)	4	0	0	0	0
Career Total (AW)	1	0	0	0	

Going (Turf): Sf: 0-1 GS: 0-1 Gd: 0-2 GF: 0-0 Fm: 0-0
Distance: 5f/6f: 0-0 7f-8f: 0-2 9f-13f: 0-3 14f+: 0-0
Track : LH: 0-4 RH: 0-0 Tight: 0-1 Gall: 0-1
Aids: Bl: 0-0 Vi: 0-0 Tstrap: 0-0

Talisker Bay

65 **46**

3-y-o b c Clantime-Fabulous Rina (FR) (Fabulous Dancer (USA))
C Smith Mrs N Stewart

Placings:05536-000 **(1593)**
2001: 5^{0}S, 5^{0}G, 5^{0}GF

	Starts	1st	2nd	3rd	Win & Pl
Career Total (Turf)	8	0	0	1	806

Going (Turf): Sf: 0-2 GS: 0-1 Gd: 0-2 GF: 0-3 Fm: 0-0
Distance: 5f/6f: 0-8 7f-8f: 0-0 9f-13f: 0-0 14f+: 0-0
Track : LH: 0-0 RH: 0-0 Tight: 0-0 Gall: 0-0
Aids: Bl: 0-0 Vi: 0-1 Tstrap: 0-0
Best Rating: 12 4/01 Nott 5f13y soft

Talldark'N'Andsome

95(90) (63)**76**

2-y-o b c Efisio-Fleur Du Val (Valiyar)
N P Littmoden Mrs Gillian Curley

Placings:503434 **(5420)**
2001: 5^{5}GF, 5^{0}G, 7^{3}G, 7^{4}GF, 7^{3}GS, 7^{4}SD

	Starts	1st	2nd	3rd	Win & Pl
Career Total (Turf)	5	0	0	2	1218
Career Total (AW)	1	0	0	0	0

Going (Turf): Sf: 0-0 GS: 0-1 Gd: 0-2 GF: 0-2 Fm: 0-0
Distance: 5f/6f: 0-2 7f-8f: 0-4 9f-13f: 0-0 14f+: 0-0
Track : LH: 0-3 RH: 0-0 Tight: 0-2 Gall: 0-0
Aids: Bl: 0-0 Vi: 0-0 Tstrap: 0-0
Best Rating: 76 9/01 Ches 7f2y good

In the frame in ordinary maidens.

Tam O'Shanter

97(90) (23)**35**

7-y-o gr g Persian Bold-No More Rosies (Warpath)
J G M O'Shea (A P James 13/6) Gary Roberts

Placings:000200/6-0005 **(3064)**
2001: 17^{0}GF, 18^{0}GF, 18^{0}GF, 17^{5}G

	Starts	1st	2nd	3rd	Win & Pl
Career Total (Turf)	8	0	1	0	748
Career Total (AW)	3	0	0	0	0

Going (Turf): Sf: 0-1 GS: 0-2 Gd: 0-2 GF: 0-3 Fm: 0-0
Distance: 5f/6f: 0-0 7f-8f: 0-1 9f-13f: 0-2 14f+: 0-8
Track : LH: 0-8 RH: 0-3 Tight: 0-5 Gall: 0-0
Aids: Bl: 0-0 Vi: 0-0 Tstrap: 0-0
Best Rating: 35 7/01 Bath 2m1f34y good

Tama (IRE)

94 **59**

2-y-o ch f Indian Ridge-Web Of Intrigue (Machiavellian (USA))
Andrew Turnell Paradime Ltd

Placings:666 **(4234)**
2001: 6^{6}GF, 5^{6}GF, 7^{6}GF

	Starts	1st	2nd	3rd	Win & Pl
Career Total (Turf)	3	0	0	0	0

Going (Turf): Sf: 0-0 GS: 0-0 Gd: 0-0 GF: 0-3 Fm: 0-0
Distance: 5f/6f: 0-2 7f-8f: 0-1 9f-13f: 0-0 14f+: 0-0
Track : LH: 0-0 RH: 0-1 Tight: 0-0 Gall: 0-0
Aids: Bl: 0-0 Vi: 0-0 Tstrap: 0-0
Best Rating: 59 8/01 Bevl 7f100y gd-fm

Tamarisk (IRE)

110 **109**

6-y-o b h Green Desert (USA)-Sine Labe (USA) (Vaguely Noble)
R Charlton G Hofmeister

Placings:1112/01210/500-426020 **(5365)**
2001: 6^{4}GF, 6^{2}GF, 5^{6}G, 6^{0}GS, 6^{2}GF, 6^{0}GS

	Starts	1st	2nd	3rd	Win & Pl
Career Total (Turf)	17	5	4	0	203437
Career Total (AW)	1	0	0	0	

122	9/98	Hayd	6f	A	GD	£73900
112	5/98	Llng	6f	A	GD	£11606
106	9/97	NmkR	7f	B	G-F	£18634
103	9/97	Kemp	7f	C	GD	£4454
86	8/97	Gdwd	6f	D	G-F	£7067

Total win prize-money £115663

Going (Turf): Sf: 0-1 GS: 0-3 **Gd: 3-5** GF: 2-5 Fm: 0-3
Distance: **5f/6f: 3-11** 7f-8f: 2-5 9f-13f: 0-1 14f+: 0-0
Track : LH: 0-0 **RH: 1-1** Tight: 0-0 **Gall: 1-1**
Aids: Bl: 0-1 Vi: 0-0 Tstrap: 0-0
Best Rating: 113 6/01 Wind 6f gd-fm

Formerly a top-class sprinter, he was retired to Coolmore Stud in 1998 but was unsuccessful there and went to America afterwards, but he did not take to racing on the other side of the Atlantic. He ran well at Windsor on his second run back in 2001 and again performed well from an unfavourable draw at Royal Ascot. Ran too bad to be true when only seventh in a Group Three at Deauville in July and was comfortably beaten in a Doncaster conditions event.

Tamburlaine (IRE)

117 **118**

3-y-o b c Royal Academy (USA)-Well Bought (IRE) (Auction Ring (USA))
R Hannon Jeffen Racing

Placings:2212-12502246 **(5006)**
2001: 7^{4}GS, 8^{2}G, 8^{5}GY, 8^{0}G, 7^{2}GF, 8^{2}GF, 8^{4}G, 8^{6}S

	Starts	1st	2nd	3rd	Win & Pl
Career Total (Turf)	12	1	6	0	157248

97	9/00	NmkR	1m	D	G-S	£5707

Total win prize-money £5707

Going (Turf): Sf: 0-2 **GS: 1-2** Gd: 0-4 GF: 0-3 Fm: 0-0
Distance: 5f/6f: 0-0 **7f-8f: 1-12** 9f-13f: 0-0 14f+: 0-0
Track : LH: 0-3 RH: 0-4 Tight: 0-0 Gall: 0-5
Aids: Bl: 0-0 Vi: 0-0 Tstrap: 0-0
Best Rating: 120 5/01 NmkR 1m good

Runner-up in the Racing Post Trophy at two, he was only fourth in the Greenham on his reappearance, but left that running behind when second to Golan in the Guineas. Disappointed in the Irish version, but was not beaten far when seventh in the St James's Palace. Ran better when dropped to a Group Three at Newbury and in the Celebration Mile. He may stay further than a mile and acts on any ground.

Tamdali (IRE)

84 **55**

2-y-o b c Be My Chief (USA)-Tamarzana (IRE) (Lear Fan (USA))
Sir Michael Stoute H H Aga Khan

Placings:0 **(4722)**
2001: 7^{0}GF

	Starts	1st	2nd	3rd	Win & Pl
Career Total (Turf)	1	0	0	0	

Going (Turf): Sf: 0-0 GS: 0-0 Gd: 0-0 GF: 0-1 Fm: 0-0
Distance: 5f/6f: 0-0 7f-8f: 0-1 9f-13f: 0-0 14f+: 0-0
Track : LH: 0-1 RH: 0-0 Tight: 0-0 Gall: 0-0
Aids: Bl: 0-0 Vi: 0-0 Tstrap: 0-0
Best Rating: 55 9/01 Wwck 7f26y gd-fm

Tamiami Trail (IRE)

110 **100**

3-y-o ch c Indian Ridge-Eurobird (Ela-Mana-Mou)
B J Meehan Mrs Susan Roy

Placings:0052-12405 **(2943)**
2001: 10^{1}GS, 10^{2}S, 13^{4}F, 16^{0}GF, 14^{5}G

	Starts	1st	2nd	3rd	Win & Pl
Career Total (Turf)	9	1	2	0	11452

94	3/01	Donc	1m2f60y	D(0-85)H	G-S	£4368

Total win prize-money £4368

Going (Turf): Sf: 0-2 **GS: 1-1** Gd: 0-2 GF: 0-3 Fm: 0-1
Distance: 5f/6f: 0-1 7f-8f: 0-2 **9f-13f: 1-3** 14f+: 0-3
Track : **LH: 1-4** RH: 0-4 Tight: 0-2 **Gall: 1-5**
Aids: Bl: 0-0 Vi: 0-0 Tstrap: 0-0
Best Rating: 100 7/01 NmkJ 1m6f175y good

A decent middle-distance stayer, but the sort who will not be easy to place.

Tamilia (IRE)

77(85) (50)**19**

3-y-o b f Ridgewood Ben-Nellie's Away (IRE) (Magical Strike (USA))
Mrs L C Jewell (D W P Arbuthnot 28/3) Mrs Linda Jewell

Placings:00040-406400 **(1872)**
2001: 7^{4}SW, 8^{0}SD, 8^{6}SW, 8^{4}HY, 7^{0}GF, 7^{0}F

	Starts	1st	2nd	3rd	Win & Pl
Career Total (Turf)	7	0	0	0	0
Career Total (AW)	4	0	0	0	0

Going (Turf): Sf: 0-2 GS: 0-1 Gd: 0-1 GF: 0-2 Fm: 0-1
Distance: 5f/6f: 0-2 7f-8f: 0-7 9f-13f: 0-2 14f+: 0-0
Track : LH: 0-7 RH: 0-1 Tight: 0-3 Gall: 0-1
Aids: Bl: 0-0 Vi: 0-0 Tstrap: 0-0
Best Rating: 50 1/01 Wolv 7f slow

Tammam (IRE)

95(85) (47)**63**

5-y-o b g Priolo (USA)-Bristle (Thatch (USA))
Mrs L Stubbs Maurice Parker

Placings:2333/1534/00534466000-000 **(1739)**
2001: 10^{0}GF, 10^{0}G, 11^{0}GF

	Starts	1st	2nd	3rd	Win & Pl
Career Total (Turf)	22	1	1	5	14279
Career Total (AW)	1	0	0	0	

88	5/99	Ches	1m2f75y	D	G-F	£8367

Total win prize-money £8367

Going (Turf): Sf: 0-1 GS: 0-3 Gd: 0-8 **GF: 1-9** Fm: 0-1
Distance: 5f/6f: 0-1 7f-8f: 0-10 **9f-13f: 1-12** 14f+: 0-0
Track : **LH: 1-9** RH: 0-6 **Tight: 1-10** Gall: 0-3
Aids: Bl: 0-2 Vi: 0-0 Tstrap: 0-0
Best Rating: 60 5/01 Ches 1m2f75y gd-fm

Tan Hill Fair (IRE)

92 **67**

2-y-o b f Woodborough (USA)-Ron's Secret (Efisio)
R Hannon Tweenhills Racing (may Hill Syndicate)

Placings:050000 **(5342)**
2001: 6^{0}GF, 6^{5}F, 7^{0}GF, 7^{0}GF, 8^{0}S, 7^{0}GS

	Starts	1st	2nd	3rd	Win & Pl
Career Total (Turf)	6	0	0	0	0

Going (Turf): Sf: 0-1 GS: 0-1 Gd: 0-0 GF: 0-3 Fm: 0-1
Distance: 5f/6f: 0-0 7f-8f: 0-5 9f-13f: 0-1 14f+: 0-0
Track : LH: 0-3 RH: 0-0 Tight: 0-0 Gall: 0-0
Aids: Bl: 0-0 Vi: 0-0 Tstrap: 0-0
Best Rating: 67 8/01 Folk 7f gd-fm

Tana Mana (IRE)

86 **60**

2-y-o b f Alzao (USA)-Belle Bijou (Midyan (USA))
R A Fahey Capt C M Ryan

Placings:000 **(3620)**
2001: 5^{0}GF, 7^{0}GS, 7^{0}F

	Starts	1st	2nd	3rd	Win & Pl
Career Total (Turf)	3	0	0	0	

Going (Turf): Sf: 0-0 GS: 0-1 Gd: 0-0 GF: 0-1 Fm: 0-1
Distance: 5f/6f: 0-1 7f-8f: 0-2 9f-13f: 0-0 14f+: 0-0
Track : LH: 0-1 RH: 0-0 Tight: 0-1 Gall: 0-0
Aids: Bl: 0-0 Vi: 0-0 Tstrap: 0-0
Best Rating: 60 7/01 Wwck 7f26y gd-sft

Tanaji

88 **87**

2-y-o b f Marju (IRE)-Hamsaat (IRE) (Sadler's Wells (USA))
B Hanbury Hamdan Al Maktoum

Placings:4 **(4871)**
2001: 8^{4}G

	Starts	1st	2nd	3rd	Win & Pl
Career Total (Turf)	1	0	0	0	429

Going (Turf): Sf: 0-0 GS: 0-0 Gd: 0-1 GF: 0-0 Fm: 0-0
Distance: 5f/6f: 0-0 7f-8f: 0-1 9f-13f: 0-0 14f+: 0-0
Track : LH: 0-0 RH: 0-0 Tight: 0-0 Gall: 0-0
Aids: Bl: 0-0 Vi: 0-0 Tstrap: 0-0
Best Rating: 87 9/01 NmkR 1m good

Tancholo

70 **32**

3-y-o br f So Factual (USA)-Tiszta Sharok (Song)
L G Cottrell Tedwood Bloodstock Limited

Placings:0 **(0841)**
2001: 7^{0}GS

	Starts	1st	2nd	3rd	Win & Pl
Career Total (Turf)	1	0	0	0	

Going (Turf): Sf: 0-0 GS: 0-1 Gd: 0-0 GF: 0-0 Fm: 0-0
Distance: 5f/6f: 0-0 7f-8f: 0-1 9f-13f: 0-0 14f+: 0-0
Track : LH: 0-0 RH: 0-0 Tight: 0-0 Gall: 0-0
Aids: Bl: 0-0 Vi: 0-0 Tstrap: 0-0
Best Rating: 32 4/01 Newb 7f gd-sft

Tancred Arms

96(98) (40)**39**

5-y-o b m Clantime-Mischievous Miss (Niniski (USA))
D W Barker Miss A Clift

Placings:6002660226/**03**020500005100000/**0**223000302030044-**01000340**U **(2784)**
2001: 6^{0}SD, 7^{1}SD, 7^{0}SD, 7^{0}S, 7^{0}SD, 8^{3}GF, 7^{4}G, 8^{0}SD, 7^{U}GF

	Starts	1st	2nd	3rd	Win & Pl
Career Total (Turf)	42	1	7	4	11381
Career Total (AW)	9	1	0	1	2122

40	4/01	Sthl	7f	F(0-60)H	STD	£1841
68	7/99	Catt	5f212y	E(0-70)H	GD	£3629

Total win prize-money £5471

Going (Turf): Sf: 0-6 GS: 0-6 **Gd: 1-9** GF: 0-17 Fm: 0-4
Distance: 5f/6f: 1-35 7f-8f: 1-16 9f-13f: 0-0 14f+: 0-0
Track : LH: 2-16 RH: 0-7 **Tight: 1-6** Gall: 0-4
Aids: Bl: 0-0 **Vi: 1-11** Tstrap: 0-0
Best Rating: 40 4/01 Sthl 7f stand

Tancred Miss

86(89) (65)**50**

2-y-o b f Presidium-Mischievous Miss (Niniski (USA))
D W Barker Mrs S J Barker

Placings:0200 **(5536)**
2001: 6^{0}GF, 6^{2}SD, 7^{0}GF, 6^{0}S, 6^{0}SD

	Starts	1st	2nd	3rd	Win & Pl
Career Total (Turf)	3	0	0	0	
Career Total (AW)	1	0	1	0	684

Going (Turf): Sf: 0-1 GS: 0-0 Gd: 0-0 GF: 0-2 Fm: 0-0
Distance: 5f/6f: 0-3 7f-8f: 0-1 9f-13f: 0-0 14f+: 0-0
Track : LH: 0-2 RH: 0-0 Tight: 0-1 Gall: 0-0
Aids: Bl: 0-0 Vi: 0-0 Tstrap: 0-0
Best Rating: 65 7/01 Sthl 6f stand

Tancred Times

104(107) (63)**65**

6-y-o ch m Clantime-Mischievous Miss (Niniski (USA))
D W Barker D W Barker

Placings:0113005/004340512500303**405**/**400**000000226502**6**/**003**505324115526062055-**5211**50510**11**5021304050135000 **(5252)**
2001: 6^{5}SW, 5^{5}SD, 5^{2}SD, 5^{1}SD, 5^{1}SD, 5^{5}S, 5^{0}GF, 6^{5}GF, 5^{1}F, 5^{0}GF, 5^{1}SD, 5^{1}SD, 5^{5}GF, 5^{0}F, 5^{2}GF, 5^{1}F, 6^{3}F, 5^{0}GF, 5^{4}G, 5^{0}G, 5^{5}GF, 5^{0}G, 5^{1}G, 6^{3}GF, 5^{5}GS

	Starts	1st	2nd	3rd	Win & Pl
Career Total (Turf)	69	8	7	6	39510
Career Total (AW)	20	4	2	2	13090

66	9/01	Haml	5f4y	F(0-70)H	GD	£2954
64	7/01	Newc	5f	E(0-75)H	FRM	£4377
63	6/01	Sthl	5f	E(0-70)H	STD	£3003
57	6/01	Sthl	5f	F(0-60)H	STD	£2394
57	5/01	Newc	5f	E(0-75)H	FRM	£2982
54	4/01	Sthl	5f	F(0-60)H	STD	£2359
45	3/01	Wolv	5f	E(0-75)H	STD	£2877
50	7/00	Haml	5f4y	D(0-80)H	G-F	£6857
46	6/00	Haml	5f4y	F	G-F	£2324
62	8/98	Carl	5f207y	F(0-60)H	G-S	£2920
68	7/97	Catt	7f	D	G-F	£3847
64	6/97	Thsk	6f	G	GD	£2442

Total win prize-money £39339

Going (Turf): Sf: 0-10 GS: 1-8 Gd: 2-14 **GF: 3-28** Fm: 2-9
Distance: 5f/6f: 11-75 7f-8f: 1-13 9f-13f: 0-1 14f+: 0-0
Track : LH: 2-26 RH: 1-6 **Tight: 2-14** Gall: 1-4
Aids: Bl: 0-1 Vi: 0-0 Tstrap: 0-0
Best Rating: 66 9/01 Haml 5f4y good

She has been a revelation this season, winning seven times including four on Fibresand. Suited by five furlongs and fast ground and likes to dominate from the front.

Tancred Walk

100 **35**

3-y-o b f Clantime-Mischievous Miss (Niniski (USA))
D W Barker Red Card Racing Partnership

Placings:060-66004005 **(4233)**
2001: 5^{6}GS, 6^{6}S, 6^{0}GF, 5^{0}G, 5^{4}GS, 6^{0}GS, 5^{0}G, 5^{5}G

	Starts	1st	2nd	3rd	Win & Pl
Career Total (Turf)	11	0	0	0	0

Going (Turf): Sf: 0-1 GS: 0-3 Gd: 0-4 GF: 0-2 Fm: 0-1
Distance: 5f/6f: 0-10 7f-8f: 0-1 9f-13f: 0-0 14f+: 0-0
Track : LH: 0-0 RH: 0-1 Tight: 0-0 Gall: 0-1
Aids: Bl: 0-0 Vi: 0-0 Tstrap: 0-0
Best Rating: 35 7/01 Hayd 5f gd-sft

Tandava (IRE)

88 **87+**

3-y-o ch c Indian Ridge-Kashka (USA) (The Minstrel (CAN))
Sir Michael Stoute Lady Clague

Placings:1 **(2889)**
2001: 10^{1}GF

	Starts	1st	2nd	3rd	Win & Pl
Career Total (Turf)	1	1	0	0	3559

87	7/01	Pont	1m2f6y	D		G-F	£3558

Total win prize-money £3559

Going (Turf): Sf: 0-0 GS: 0-0 Gd: 0-0 **GF: 1-1** Fm: 0-0
Distance: 5f/6f: 0-0 7f-8f: 0-0 **9f-13f: 1-1** 14f+: 0-0
Track : LH: 1-1 RH: 0-0 Tight: 0-0 Gall: 0-0
Aids: Bl: 0-0 Vi: 0-0 Tstrap: 0-0
Best Rating: 87 7/01 Pont 1m2f6y gd-fm

Tantric

90(92) (66)**67**

2-y-o br c Greensmith-Petunia (GER) (Chief Singer)
J O'Reilly (S P C Woods 18/10) J Saul

Placings:0225233120 **(5410)**
2001: 6^{0}SD, 6^{2}G, 5^{2}F, 7^{5}G, 6^{2}GF, 5^{3}G, 6^{3}S, 7^{1}SD, 8^{2}SD, 7^{0}SD

	Starts	1st	2nd	3rd	Win & Pl
Career Total (Turf)	6	0	3	2	2207
Career Total (AW)	4	1	1	0	2510

66	10/01	Sthl	7f	G	STD	£1946

Total win prize-money £1946

Going (Turf): Sf: 0-1 GS: 0-0 Gd: 0-3 GF: 0-1 Fm: 0-1
Distance: 5f/6f: 0-3 **7f-8f: 1-7** 9f-13f: 0-0 14f+: 0-0
Track : LH: 1-5 RH: 0-0 Tight: 0-1 Gall: 0-0
Aids: Bl: 0-0 Vi: 0-0 Tstrap: 0-0
Best Rating: 67 7/01 Yarm 6f3y gd-fm

Genuine plater, handles any ground on turf and stays a mile. Often races prominently, but held up when scoring in a seller at Southwell in October.

Tap

90(97) (72)**37**

4-y-o b g Emarati (USA)-Pubby (Doctor Wall)
Mrs A J Perrett G Harwood

Placings:2/1605600-00005 **(5469)**
2001: 7^{0}G, 7^{0}GF, 9^{0}GS, 8^{0}G, 9^{5}S

	Starts	1st	2nd	3rd	Win & Pl
Career Total (Turf)	12	1	1	0	3746
Career Total (AW)	1	0	0	0	0

91	4/00	Folk	7f	D	SFT	£2646

Total win prize-money £2646

Going (Turf): Sf: 1-5 GS: 0-2 Gd: 0-4 GF: 0-1 Fm: 0-0
Distance: 5f/6f: 0-0 **7f-8f: 1-9** 9f-13f: 0-4 14f+: 0-0
Track : LH: 0-4 RH: 0-2 Tight: 0-2 Gall: 0-1
Aids: Bl: 0-1 Vi: 0-0 Tstrap: 0-0
Best Rating: 43 5/01 Ling 7f good

Tap The Stone (IRE)

85(78) (50)**63**

2-y-o b g Bigstone (IRE)-Wadeyaa (Green Desert (USA))
J S Wainwright Barry J Ross

Placings:5056006 **(5370)**
2001: 5^{5}F, 6^{0}SD, 6^{5}S, 6^{6}G, 6^{0}G, 7^{0}HY, 7^{6}G

	Starts	1st	2nd	3rd	Win & Pl
Career Total (Turf)	6	0	0	0	0
Career Total (AW)	1	0	0	0	

Going (Turf): Sf: 0-2 GS: 0-0 Gd: 0-3 GF: 0-0 Fm: 0-1
Distance: 5f/6f: 0-3 7f-8f: 0-4 9f-13f: 0-0 14f+: 0-0
Track : LH: 0-2 RH: 0-0 Tight: 0-1 Gall: 0-0
Aids: Bl: 0-0 Vi: 0-1 Tstrap: 0-0
Best Rating: 63 8/01 Nott 6f15y good

Little obvious ability in all starts to date.

Tapage (IRE)

98(108) (62)**60**

5-y-o b g Great Commotion (USA)-Irena (Bold Lad (IRE))
Mrs N Macauley (Andrew Reid 21/2) West Indies Capital Company Limited

Placings:012/52520000030/11116215014-111500500060000 **(5406)**
2001: 7^{1}SW, 7^{1}SW, 7^{1}SW, 8^{5}SD, 7^{0}SW, 7^{0}SD, 7^{5}G, 8^{0}G, 8^{0}F, 8^{0}GF, 8^{6}GF, 7^{0}GF, 9^{0}SD, 8^{0}SD, 8^{0}SD, 7^{0}SD

	Starts	1st	2nd	3rd	Win & Pl
Career Total (Turf)	19	3	3	0	14174
Career Total (AW)	21	7	1	1	21312

80	2/01	Ling	7f	E	SLW	£2884
67	2/01	Ling	7f	D(0-80)H	SLW	£3727
68	2/01	Ling	7f	F(0-70)H	SLW	£2226
64	10/00	Ling	1m	E(0-75)H	STD	£2299
65	8/00	Wind	1m67y	D(0-80)H	GD	£3945
63	7/00	Brig	7f214y	D(0-80)H	FRM	£3835
51	6/00	Ling	1m	E(0-70)H	STD	£2828
53	5/00	Bath	1m5y	E(0-70)H	G-F	£2947
47	5/00	Ling	1m	D(0-80)H	STD	£3957
77	11/98	Ling	7f	F	STD	£2085

Total win prize-money £30736

Going (Turf): Sf: 0-1 GS: 0-0 **Gd: 1-6 GF: 1-7 Fm: 1-5**
Distance: 5f/6f: 0-0 **7f-8f: 8-20** 9f-13f: 2-20 14f+: 0-0
Track : **LH: 9-34** RH: 1-2 **Tight: 9-27** Gall: 0-0
Aids: Bl: 0-1 Vi: 0-1 Tstrap: 0-0
Best Rating: 80 2/01 Ling 7f slow

Not at his best in 2001.

Tapau (IRE)

106(98) (73)**77**

3-y-o b f Nicolotte-Urtica (IRE) (Cyrano De Bergerac)
D R C Elsworth Gary B Watts

Placings:01-4015140 **(5259)**
2001: 8^{4}SD, 7^{0}G, 6^{1}G, 6^{5}GF, 6^{1}GF, 6^{4}F, 7^{0}GS

	Starts	1st	2nd	3rd	Win & Pl
Career Total (Turf)	6	2	0	0	7276
Career Total (AW)	3	1	0	0	3110

72	9/01	Ling	6f	E(0-70)H	G-F	£3416
68	8/01	Brig	6f209y	E(0-70)	GD	£3255
73	12/00	Ling	7f	D	STD	£2821

Total win prize-money £9492

Going (Turf): Sf: 0-0 GS: 0-1 **Gd: 1-2 GF: 1-2** Fm: 0-1
Distance: 5f/6f: 1-4 **7f-8f: 2-5** 9f-13f: 0-0 14f+: 0-0
Track : **LH: 2-5** RH: 0-1 **Tight: 1-2** Gall: 0-1
Aids: Bl: 0-0 Vi: 0-0 Tstrap: 0-0
Best Rating: 77 10/01 Asct 7f gd-sft

Progressive, she is suited by seven furlongs, although she is effective over six, and likes to race prominently.

Tapis Fille (IRE)

88(82) (34)**68**

2-y-o b f Fayruz-Trubbach (Vitiges (FR))
R Ford D F Price

Placings:55000000 **(5351)**
2001: 5^{5}GF, 6^{5}GF, 6^{0}GS, 6^{0}G, 6^{0}SW, 7^{0}SD, 8^{0}SD, 8^{0}SD

	Starts	1st	2nd	3rd	Win & Pl
Career Total (Turf)	4	0	0	0	0
Career Total (AW)	4	0	0	0	

Going (Turf): Sf: 0-0 GS: 0-1 Gd: 0-1 GF: 0-2 Fm: 0-0
Distance: 5f/6f: 0-4 7f-8f: 0-3 9f-13f: 0-1 14f+: 0-0
Track : LH: 0-5 RH: 0-0 Tight: 0-2 Gall: 0-0
Aids: Bl: 0-0 Vi: 0-0 Tstrap: 0-0
Best Rating: 68 7/01 Ling 6f gd-fm

Tappit (IRE)

94 **70**

2-y-o b c Mujadil (USA)-Green Life (Green Desert (USA))
M R Channon Tim Corby

Placings:053160060 **(4714)**
2001: 5^{0}GS, 5^{5}S, 5^{3}F, 5^{1}F, 6^{6}GF, 6^{0}GF, 6^{0}GF, 5^{6}F, 7^{0}G

	Starts	1st	2nd	3rd	Win & Pl
Career Total (Turf)	9	1	0	1	3916

59	6/01	Brig	5f213y	E	FRM	£2905

Total win prize-money £2905

Going (Turf): Sf: 0-1 GS: 0-1 Gd: 0-1 GF: 0-3 **Fm: 1-3**
Distance: **5f/6f: 1-7** 7f-8f: 0-2 9f-13f: 0-0 14f+: 0-0
Track : **LH: 1-5** RH: 0-0 Tight: 0-1 Gall: 0-0
Aids: Bl: 0-0 Vi: 0-0 Tstrap: 0-0
Best Rating: 74 6/01 Epsm 6f gd-fm

He showed promise over the minimum trip, but eventually got off the mark over an extra furlong at Brighton in June. Not much from him since though he has faced some very stiff tasks.

Tar Fih (USA)

94 **77**

3-y-o b f Gone West (USA)-Najiya (Nashwan (USA))
J L Dunlop Hamdan Al Maktoum

Placings:434-26 **(2034)**
2001: 8^{2}HY, 8^{6}F

	Starts	1st	2nd	3rd	Win & Pl
Career Total (Turf)	5	0	1	1	2496

Going (Turf): Sf: 0-1 GS: 0-0 Gd: 0-1 GF: 0-2 Fm: 0-1
Distance: 5f/6f: 0-2 7f-8f: 0-1 9f-13f: 0-2 14f+: 0-0
Track : LH: 0-2 RH: 0-0 Tight: 0-0 Gall: 0-0
Aids: Bl: 0-0 Vi: 0-0 Tstrap: 0-0
Best Rating: 74 4/01 Wwck 1m22y heavy

Tara Gold (IRE)

104 **77**

3-y-o b f Royal Academy (USA)-Soha (USA) (Dancing Brave (USA))
R Hannon Tom Gaffney

Placings:4340-55612240 **(4860)**
2001: 8^{5}G, 10^{5}GF, 10^{6}G, 10^{1}GF, 10^{2}GF, 12^{2}GF, 12^{4}G, 13^{0}GF

	Starts	1st	2nd	3rd	Win & Pl
Career Total (Turf)	12	1	2	1	9466

66	7/01	Epsm	1m2f18y	D	G-F	£4153

Total win prize-money £4154

Going (Turf): Sf: 0-0 GS: 0-1 Gd: 0-4 **GF: 1-7** Fm: 0-0
Distance: 5f/6f: 0-1 7f-8f: 0-3 **9f-13f: 1-7** 14f+: 0-1
Track : **LH: 1-4** RH: 0-4 **Tight: 1-6** Gall: 0-2
Aids: Bl: 0-0 Vi: 0-0 Tstrap: 0-0
Best Rating: 77 8/01 Gdwd 1m4f good

Scored with a little in hand when getting her head in front in a weakly-contested maiden over ten furlongs in July. Has since been far from disgraced in handicap company, and seemed to stay 12 furlongs well at Salisbury, but may have found 13 furlongs a bit too far. Suited by a strong pace.

Taranaki

106(96) (61)**79**

3-y-o b c Delta Dancer-Miss Ticklepenny (Distant Relative)
P D Cundell E D Evers

Placings:63120300000**10** **(5347)**
2001: 9^{6}SD, 9^{3}SD, 8^{1}SD, 7^{2}GS, 8^{0}GS, 6^{3}GS, 6^{0}F, 6^{0}G, 6^{0}G, 5^{0}G, 6^{0}G, 7^{1}F, 8^{0}SD, 7^{0}SD

	Starts	1st	2nd	3rd	Win & Pl
Career Total (Turf)	9	1	1	1	6970
Career Total (AW)	4	1	0	1	3234

69	9/01	Chep	7f16y	E(0-70)	FRM	£2912
58	4/01	Sthl	1m	E	STD	£2821

Total win prize-money £5733

Going (Turf): Sf: 0-0 GS: 0-3 Gd: 0-4 GF: 0-0 **Fm: 1-2**
Distance: 5f/6f: 0-5 **7f-8f: 2-5** 9f-13f: 0-3 14f+: 0-0
Track : **LH: 1-6** RH: 0-1 Tight: 0-3 Gall: 0-2
Aids: Bl: 0-0 Vi: 0-0 Tstrap: 0-0
Best Rating: 83 4/01 NmkR 7f gd-sft

Unraced at two, he got off the mark at 33/1 in a maiden on the Southwell Fibresand in April and has run well on turf since then, including a win at Chepstow. Suited by testing conditions and is effective between six furlongs and a mile.

Taranog

81 **60**

2-y-o b c Perpendicular-Onemoretime (Timeless Times (USA))
B Palling Nigel Thomas

Placings:006 **(5623)**
2001: 10^{0}G, 8^{0}G, 8^{6}GS

	Starts	1st	2nd	3rd	Win & Pl
Career Total (Turf)	3	0	0	0	0

Going (Turf): Sf: 0-0 GS: 0-1 Gd: 0-2 GF: 0-0 Fm: 0-0
Distance: 5f/6f: 0-0 7f-8f: 0-0 9f-13f: 0-3 14f+: 0-0
Track : LH. 0-3 RH: 0-0 Tight: 0-2 Gall: 0 0
Aids: Bl: 0-1 Vi: 0-0 Tstrap: 0-0
Best Rating: 60 11/01 Nott 1m54y gd-sft

Taras Emperor (IRE)

109 **69**

3-y-o b g Common Grounds-Strike It Rich (FR) (Rheingold)
J J Quinn Tara Leisure

Placings:414105000-000000001120 **(5685)**
2001: 6^{0}GS, 5^{0}GF, 5^{0}GF, 6^{0}GS, 7^{0}GF, 7^{0}GF, 7^{0}GF, 5^{0}G, 5^{1}HY, 5^{1}HY, 5^{2}GS, 5^{0}S

	Starts	1st	2nd	3rd	Win & Pl
Career Total (Turf)	21	4	1	0	23600

67	10/01	Newc	5f	E(0-70)H	HVY	£3150
59	10/01	Ayr	5f	E(0-70)H	HVY	£3395
102	5/00	Sand	5f6y	A	HVY	£11927
76	4/00	Newc	5f	D	SFT	£3406

Total win prize-money £21879

Going (Turf): Sf: 4-7 GS: 0-4 Gd: 0-3 GF: 0-7 Fm: 0-0
Distance: **5f/6f: 4-18** 7f-8f: 0-3 9f-13f: 0-0 14f+: 0-0
Track : LH: 0-1 RH: 0-1 Tight: 0-0 Gall: 0-0
Aids: Bl: 0-0 Vi: 0-0 Tstrap: 0-0
Best Rating: 68 11/01 Brig 5f213y gd-sft

Scored twice over five furlongs as a juvenile including once in Listed company at Sandown, but spent the rest of the campaign being well beaten in Group races. He has been running in competitive handicaps this season and returned to winning ways in a Class E handicap on heavy ground in October.

Tarashani (IRE)

88 **46**

3-y-o ch c Primo Dominie-Tarakana (USA) (Shahrastani (USA))
B Ellison (Sir Michael Stoute 10/6) Eddie Kirtland/r W L Bowden

Placings:60660 **(4707)**
2001: 8^{6}S, 9^{0}GF, 8^{6}G, 12^{6}GF, 10^{0}G

	Starts	1st	2nd	3rd	Win & Pl
Career Total (Turf)	5	0	0	0	0

Going (Turf): Sf: 0-1 GS: 0-0 Gd: 0-2 GF: 0-2 Fm: 0-0

Distance: 5f/6f: 0-0 7f-8f: 0-0 9f-13f: 0-5 14f+: 0-0
Track : LH: 0-4 RH: 0-1 Tight: 0-2 Gall: 0-1
Aids: Bl: 0-0 Vi: 0-2 Tstrap: 0-0
Best Rating: 46 6/01 Ripn 1m1f gd-fm

Tarawan

104(84) (35)**74**
5-y-o ch g Nashwan (USA)-Soluce (Junius (USA))
I A Balding Exors Of The Late Robert Hitchins

Placings:002/2562423221210/00005000-00310264420 **(4983)**
2001: 10^0GS, 8^0G, 8^3G, 10^1F, 10^0GF, 9^2GF, 10^6GF, 10^4GF, 10^4HY, 10^2F, 12^0G

	Starts	1st	2nd	3rd	Win & Pl
Career Total (Turf)	34	3	9	2	34149
Career Total (AW)	1	0	0	0	

69 6/01 Bath 1m2f46y F(0-70)H FRM £2436
90 10/99 Sand 1m14y C(0-90)H SFT £11186
81 8/99 Newc 1m D GD £3875
Total win prize-money £17497

Going (Turf): Sf: 1-5 GS: 0-2 **Gd: 1-14** GF: 0-11 **Fm: 1-2**
Distance: 5f/6f: 0-0 7f-8f: 1-8 **9f-13f: 2-27** 14f+: 0-0
Track : **LH: 2-15** RH: 1-10 Tight: 1-14 Gall: 1-7
Aids: Bl: 0-2 **Vi: 3-18** Tstrap: 0-0
Best Rating: 74 6/01 Gdwd 1m1f gd-fm

Not easy to win with, a mile looks to be his best trip and he seems to appreciate easy ground.

Tarazonic

91(82) (23)**39**
3-y-o ch f Zafonic (USA)-Tarasova (USA) (Green Forest (USA))
J Balding (C F Wall 2/7) J E Abbey

Placings:054600 **(5532)**
2001: 10^0GF, 10^5GF, 10^4GF, 12^6SD, 8^0SD, 9^0HY

	Starts	1st	2nd	3rd	Win & Pl
Career Total (Turf)	4	0	0	0	511
Career Total (AW)	2	0	0	0	0

Going (Turf): Sf: 0-1 GS: 0-0 Gd: 0-0 GF: 0-3 Fm: 0-0
Distance: 5f/6f: 0-0 7f-8f: 0-0 9f-13f: 0-6 14f+: 0-0
Track : LH: 0-5 RH: 0-1 Tight: 0-2 Gall: 0-2
Aids: Bl: 0-3 Vi: 0-0 Tstrap: 0-0
Best Rating: 60 7/01 Pont 1m2f6y gd-fm

Tarboush

107(93) (80)**86**
4-y-o b c Polish Precedent (USA)-Barboukh (Night Shift (USA))
H R A Cecil Wafic Said

Placings:031-004620 **(3477)**
2001: 10^0G, 10^0GF, 8^4G, 8^6GF, 10^2G, 10^0GF, 10^5SD

	Starts	1st	2nd	3rd	Win & Pl
Career Total (Turf)	9	1	1	1	8208

78 6/00 Sand 1m2f7y D G-F £4270
Total win prize-money £4271

Going (Turf): Sf: 0-0 GS: 0-1 Gd: 0-3 **GF: 1-5** Fm: 0-0
Distance: 5f/6f: 0-0 7f-8f: 0-1 **9f-13f: 1-8** 14f+: 0-0
Track : LH: 0-1 **RH: 1-4** Tight: 0-1 Gall: 0-3
Aids: Bl: 0-0 Vi: 0-0 Tstrap: 0-0
Best Rating: 86 6/01 Wind 1m67y good

Made all to get off the mark on his third outing of 2000 at Sandown, after a promising effort at Newmarket the time before. Good effort when dropped back to a mile in summer of 2001, he has looked held since then. Acts on fast ground. Stays ten furlongs.

Tarcoola

93(100) (47)**19**
4-y-o ch g Pursuit Of Love-Miswaki Belle (USA) (Miswaki (USA))
Mrs A M Naughton (M Johnston 16/3) J P Hames

Placings:04/0F000-**00306**0000 **(5382)**
2001: 9^0SD, 11^0SW, 11^3SD, 8^0SW, 12^6SD, 7^0GF, 12^0GS, 10^0G, 11^0S

	Starts	1st	2nd	3rd	Win & Pl
Career Total (Turf)	11	0	0	0	325
Career Total (AW)	5	0	0	1	253

Going (Turf): Sf: 0-2 GS: 0-2 Gd: 0-2 GF: 0-5 Fm: 0-0
Distance: 5f/6f: 0-0 7f-8f: 0-5 9f-13f: 0-11 14f+: 0-0
Track : LH: 0-9 RH: 0-3 Tight: 0-6 Gall: 0-0
Aids: Bl: 0-3 Vi: 0-1 Tstrap: 0-1
Best Rating: 47 2/01 Sthl 1m3f stand

Tarfshi

108 **102**
3-y-o b f Mtoto-Pass The Peace (Alzao (USA))
M A Jarvis Sheikh Ahmed Al Maktoum

Placings:131-020130 **(5243a)**
2001: 8^0S, 10^2G, 12^0GF, 10^1F, 10^3GF, 10^0HO

	Starts	1st	2nd	3rd	Win & Pl
Career Total (Turf)	9	3	1	2	40310

95 6/01 Newc 1m2f32y A FRM £15109
85 9/00 Sand 1m14y C SFT £6351
84 8/00 Donc 7f D G-F £3770
Total win prize-money £25230

Going (Turf): Sf: 1-2 GS: 0-0 Gd: 0-2 **GF: 1-3 Fm: 1-1**
Distance: 5f/6f: 0-0 7f-8f: 1-3 **9f-13f: 2-6** 14f+: 0-0
Track : LH: 1-2 RH: 1-5 Tight: 0-1 **Gall: 1-2**
Aids: Bl: 0-0 Vi: 0-0 Tstrap: 0-0
Best Rating: 102 9/01 Curr 1m2f gd-fm

A winner at Doncaster and Sandown as a juvenile, she was well beaten in a Kempton Listed event on her return, but showed that running to be all wrong when going down by a short-head to Mot Juste in the Pretty Polly Stakes at Newmarket in May. Well beaten in the Oaks. Dropped back to ten furlongs to score at Newcastle in a Listed event. Stays ten furlongs. Acts on a sound surface, but has won on soft.

Tarradale

97(95) (36)**33**
7-y-o br g Interrex (CAN)-Encore L'Amour (USA) (Monteverdi)
C B B Booth J A Porteous

Placings:0/600006550/04126502**305**/**06**20023030230/0000-**360**0630405000 **(4966)**
2001: 8^3SD, 9^6SD, 9^0SD, 8^0S, 8^6GS, 9^3F, 8^0GF, 10^4GF, 10^0GF, 9^5GF, 9^0GS, 11^0GF, 10^0S

	Starts	1st	2nd	3rd	Win & Pl
Career Total (Turf)	43	1	5	4	9362
Career Total (AW)	8	0	0	2	462

35 6/98 Haml 1m65y F(0-65)H G-S £2983
Total win prize-money £2983

Going (Turf): Sf: 0-12 **GS: 1-8** Gd: 0-6 GF: 0-14 Fm: 0-3
Distance: 5f/6f: 0-2 7f-8f: 0-19 **9f-13f: 1-30** 14f+: 0-0
Track : LH: 0-25 **RH: 1-12 Tight: 1-20** Gall: 0-5
Aids: Bl: 0-0 Vi: 0-0 Tstrap: 0-0
Best Rating: 41 5/01 Leic 1m1f218y firm

Tarragona (IRE)

90(85) (50)**55**
2-y-o b f Charnwood Forest (IRE)-Limerick Princess (IRE) (Polish Patriot (USA))
A Berry Chris & Antonia Deuters

Placings:000565000 **(4856)**
2001: 5^0SW, 5^0GF, 6^0GF, 5^5G, 5^6GF, 5^5G, 5^0GF, 8^0G, 7^0GF

	Starts	1st	2nd	3rd	Win & Pl
Career Total (Turf)	8	0	0	0	0
Career Total (AW)	1	0	0	0	

Going (Turf): Sf: 0-0 GS: 0-0 Gd: 0-3 GF: 0-5 Fm: 0-0
Distance: 5f/6f: 0-7 7f-8f: 0-1 9f-13f: 0-1 14f+: 0-0
Track : LH: 0-4 RH: 0-1 Tight: 0-3 Gall: 0-1
Aids: Bl: 0-0 Vi: 0-0 Tstrap: 0-0
Best Rating: 67 7/01 Bath 5f161y good

Tarski

100(63) **43**
7-y-o ch g Polish Precedent (USA)-Illusory (King's Lake (USA))
W S Kittow Midd Shire Racing

Placings:14/25/0600000/0621203650/00335460-2243364 **(4377)**
2001: 9^2F, 10^2F, 10^4F, 9^3G, 11^3GF, 13^6G, 11^4GF

	Starts	1st	2nd	3rd	Win & Pl
Career Total (Turf)	35	2	5	5	21688
Career Total (AW)	1	0	0	0	

54 6/99 Gdwd 1m1f192yD(0-80)H G-F £7741
92 7/96 Sand 7f16y D G-F £4240
Total win prize-money £11982

Going (Turf): Sf: 0-4 GS: 0-4 Gd: 0-10 **GF: 2-13** Fm: 0-4
Distance: 5f/6f: 0-0 7f-8f: 1-7 9f-13f: 1-28 14f+: 0-1
Track : LH: 0-17 **RH: 2-11 Tight: 1-24** Gall: 0-3
Aids: Bl: 0-1 Vi: 0-3 Tstrap: 0-0
Best Rating: 43 7/01 Wind 1m3f135y gd-fm

Tarxien

97 **83**
7-y-o b g Kendor (FR)-Tanz (IRE) (Sadler's Wells (USA))
M C Pipe (Mrs Merrita Jones 12/5) B A Kilpatrick

Placings:00622116342/33114105004/40/0-0 **(5387)**
2001: 18^0GS

	Starts	1st	2nd	3rd	Win & Pl
Career Total (Turf)	26	5	3	3	25802

88 6/98 Gdwd 1m6f C(0-90)H G-F £5840
86 5/98 Newb 1m5f61y D(0-80)H GD £3444
77 5/98 Hayd 1m6f D(0-80)H G-F £3468
68 9/97 Pont 1m4f8y F G-S £2378
68 8/97 Hayd 1m3f200yF(0-80)H G-F £2416
Total win prize-money £17548

Going (Turf): Sf: 0-3 GS: 1-6 Gd: 1-7 **GF: 3-10** Fm: 0-0
Distance: 5f/6f: 0-0 7f-8f: 0-1 9f-13f: 2-12 **14f+: 3-13**
Track : **LH: 4-15** RH: 1-10 Tight: 1-6 Gall: 1-6
Aids: Bl: 0-0 Vi: 0-0 Tstrap: 0-1
Best Rating: 65 10/01 NmkR 2m2f gd-sft

In good form in 1998, but has been lightly raced on the Flat since. However, he has been in fine form over hurdles in the summer of 2001 since being equipped with a tongue strap.

Tashawak (IRE)

103 **99+**
2-y-o b f Night Shift (USA)-Dedicated Lady (IRE) (Pennine Walk)
J L Dunlop Hamdan Al Maktoum

Placings:311 **(4546)**
2001: 6^3G, 6^1GF, 6^1GF

	Starts	1st	2nd	3rd	Win & Pl
Career Total (Turf)	3	2	0	1	16961

99 9/01 Sals 6f B G-F £9106
88 8/01 Gdwd 6f D G-F £7182
Total win prize-money £16289

Going (Turf): Sf: 0-0 GS: 0-0 Gd: 0-1 **GF: 2-2** Fm: 0-0
Distance: **5f/6f: 2-3** 7f-8f: 0-0 9f-13f: 0-0 14f+: 0-0
Track : LH: 0-0 RH: 0-0 Tight: 0-0 Gall: 0-0
Aids: Bl: 0-0 Vi: 0-0 Tstrap: 0-0
Best Rating: 99 9/01 Sals 6f gd-fm

Confirmed the promise of her Kempton debut with a narrow win at Goodwood. Followed up with another gutsty effort by pipping the owner's first-string in the closing stages at Salisbury. She is likely to get further in time.

Tass Heel (IRE)

94 **67**

2-y-o b c Danehill (USA)-Mamouna (USA) (Vaguely Noble)

M R Channon Jumeirah Racing

Placings:4050 **(4954)**

2001: 7^{4}GF, 7^{0}G, 8^{5}GF, 8^{0}GS

	Starts	1st	2nd	3rd	Win & Pl
Career Total (Turf)	4	0	0	0	379

Going (Turf): Sf: 0-0 GS: 0-1 Gd: 0-1 GF: 0-2 Fm: 0-0
Distance: 5f/6f: 0-0 7f-8f: 0-4 9f-13f: 0-0 14f+: 0-0
Track : LH: 0-1 RH: 0-1 Tight: 0-1 Gall: 0-0
Aids: Bl: 0-0 Vi: 0-0 Tstrap: 0-0
Best Rating: 67 8/01 NmkJ 7f good

Tasso Dancer

95(82) **37**

5-y-o gr m Dilum (USA)-Dancing Diana (Raga Navarro (ITY))

M R Bosley Mrs J Tredwell

Placings:0/P0050-0500 **(2379)**

2001: 11^{0}SD, 10^{5}F, 6^{0}F, 8^{0}GF

	Starts	1st	2nd	3rd	Win & Pl
Career Total (Turf)	9	0	0	0	0
Career Total (AW)	1	0	0	0	

Going (Turf): Sf: 0-2 GS: 0-1 Gd: 0-0 GF: 0-2 Fm: 0-4
Distance: 5f/6f: 0-0 7f-8f: 0-3 9f-13f: 0-6 14f+: 0-1
Track : LH: 0-5 RH: 0-2 Tight: 0-4 Gall: 0-0
Aids: Bl: 0-0 Vi: 0-0 Tstrap: 0-0
Best Rating: 30 6/01 Bath 1m2f46y firm

Tatante (IRE)

91

3-y-o gr f Highest Honor (FR)-Tamnia (Green Desert (USA))

Sir Mark Prescott S Frisby

Placings:03-3L **(3369)**

2001: 6^{3}S, 7^{L}GF

	Starts	1st	2nd	3rd	Win & Pl
Career Total (Turf)	4	0	0	2	995

Going (Turf): Sf: 0-1 GS: 0-2 Gd: 0-0 GF: 0-1 Fm: 0-0
Distance: 5f/6f: 0-2 7f-8f: 0-2 9f-13f: 0-0 14f+: 0-0
Track : LH: 0-0 RH: 0-1 Tight: 0-0 Gall: 0-1
Aids: Bl: 0-2 Vi: 0-0 Tstrap: 0-0
Best Rating: 46 7/01 Haml 6f5y soft

Tatty The Tank

94(67) (17)**66**

3-y-o b g Tragic Role (USA)-Springfield Girl (Royal Vulcan)

M C Pipe Sandicroft Stud Syndicate

Placings:020-3 **(2941)**

2001: 10^{3}GF

	Starts	1st	2nd	3rd	Win & Pl
Career Total (Turf)	2	0	1	1	864
Career Total (AW)	2	0	0	0	

Going (Turf): Sf: 0-1 GS: 0-0 Gd: 0-0 GF: 0-1 Fm: 0-0
Distance: 5f/6f: 0-0 7f-8f: 0-1 9f-13f: 0-3 14f+: 0-0
Track : LH: 0-4 RH: 0-0 Tight: 0-2 Gall: 0-0
Aids: Bl: 0-0 Vi: 0-0 Tstrap: 0-0
Best Rating: 34 7/01 Ling 1m2f gd-fm

Taw Park

97 **40**

7-y-o b g Inca Chief (USA)-Parklands Belle (Stanford)

R J Baker R P Maddock

Placings:566-300000 **(4900)**

2001: 10^{3}F, 10^{0}GF, 9^{0}GF, 9^{0}GF, 8^{0}G, 8^{0}GS

	Starts	1st	2nd	3rd	Win & Pl
Career Total (Turf)	9	0	0	1	348

Going (Turf): Sf: 0-0 GS: 0-1 Gd: 0-1 GF: 0-6 Fm: 0-1
Distance: 5f/6f: 0-0 7f-8f: 0-1 9f-13f: 0-8 14f+: 0-0
Track : LH: 0-4 RH: 0-3 Tight: 0-4 Gall: 0-2
Aids: Bl: 0-0 Vi: 0-0 Tstrap: 0-0
Best Rating: 59 6/01 Bath 1m2f46y firm

Taxi-For-Robbo (IRE)

86(62) **12**

4-y-o b f Shalford (IRE)-Miromaid (Simply Great (FR))

B W Murray B Murray

Placings:0360/0**P-0**00000000 **(5226)**

2001: 8^{0}SW, 5^{0}GF, 8^{0}GF, 6^{0}GF, 8^{0}F, 5^{0}G, 5^{0}GF, 7^{0}G, 11^{0}S

	Starts	1st	2nd	3rd	Win & Pl
Career Total (Turf)	13	0	0	1	270
Career Total (AW)	2	0	0	0	

Going (Turf): Sf: 0-2 GS: 0-0 Gd: 0-4 GF: 0-5 Fm: 0-2
Distance: 5f/6f: 0-7 7f-8f: 0-5 9f-13f: 0-3 14f+: 0-0
Track : LH: 0-5 RH: 0-0 Tight: 0-0 Gall: 0-1
Aids: Bl: 0-0 Vi: 0-0 Tstrap: 0-0
Best Rating: 27 7/01 Donc 6f gd-fm

Tayif

106 **91**

5-y-o gr g Taufan (USA)-Rich Lass (Broxted)

D Nicholls J Herrington, P Forster, J Hames

Placings:2/131510/00000-0300104041 **(4826)**

2001: 6^{0}S, 5^{3}S, 6^{0}G, 5^{0}GF, 6^{1}G, 7^{0}F, 6^{4}S, 6^{0}G, 7^{4}GS, 6^{1}G

	Starts	1st	2nd	3rd	Win & Pl
Career Total (Turf)	22	5	1	2	40497

91	9/01	Ayr	6f	B H	GD	£11635
87	6/01	York	6f	D(0-80)H	GD	£7865
94	8/99	Newc	7f	C(0-90)H	GD	£6581
89	7/99	Sand	7f16y	C(0-90)H	G-F	£7035
92	4/99	Nott	5f13y	E	G-S	£2805

Total win prize-money £35922

Going (Turf): Sf: 0-3 GS: **1-6** Gd: **3-9** GF: 1-3 Fm: 0-1
Distance: **5f/6f: 3-9** 7f-8f: 2-13 9f-13f: 0-0 14f+: 0-0
Track : LH: 0-0 **RH: 1-3** Tight: 0-0 Gall: 0-1
Aids: Bl: 0-0 Vi: 0-0 **Tstrap: 3-9**
Best Rating: 91 9/01 Ayr 6f good

Sold out of Pip Payne's yard in October 2000 for 7,000gns, he is now with Dandy Nicholls and has been gelded. After not showing a lot for a couple of seasons, he slipped down the ratings and bounced back to form for new connections in June with a surprise victory over six furlongs at York with his tongue tied. Landed the Ayr Silver Cup on his final start. Best on an easier surface these days and probably does not want it any faster than good.

Te Anau

(80) (32)**16**

4-y-o b f Reprimand-Neenah (Bold Lad (IRE))

W J Musson W J Musson

Placings:0300/00000-0 **(0356)**

2001: 8^{0}SW

	Starts	1st	2nd	3rd	Win & Pl
Career Total (Turf)	5	0	0	0	
Career Total (AW)	5	0	0	1	264

Going (Turf): Sf: 0-2 GS: 0-0 Gd: 0-2 GF: 0-0 Fm: 0-1
Distance: 5f/6f: 0-1 7f-8f: 0-6 9f-13f: 0-3 14f+: 0-0
Track : LH: 0-7 RH: 0-1 Tight: 0-3 Gall: 0-0
Aids: Bl: 0-0 Vi: 0-0 Tstrap: 0-0
Best Rating: 91 9/01 Ayr 6f good

Te Quiero

100 **73**

3-y-o gr c Bering-Ma Lumiere (FR) (Niniski (USA))

Miss Gay Kelleway A P Griffin

Placings:0-6226 **(4720)**

2001: 9^{6}GF, 10^{2}G, 9^{2}GF, 10^{6}G

	Starts	1st	2nd	3rd	Win & Pl
Career Total (Turf)	5	0	2	0	2059

Going (Turf): Sf: 0-1 GS: 0-0 Gd: 0-2 GF: 0-2 Fm: 0-0
Distance: 5f/6f: 0-0 7f-8f: 0-1 9f-13f: 0-4 14f+: 0-0
Track : LH: 0-3 RH: 0-1 Tight: 0-3 Gall: 0-1
Aids: Bl: 0-0 Vi: 0-0 Tstrap: 0-0
Best Rating: 73 8/01 Folk 1m1f149y gd-fm

Te Quiero (FR)

101(95) (48)**49**

5-y-o gr g Turgeon (USA)-Passerene (FR) (Persepolis (FR))

P Mitchell J Morton

Placings:04/3312200/010364000-000 **(1918)**

2001: 12^{0}S, 11^{0}GS, 14^{0}GF

	Starts	1st	2nd	3rd	Win & Pl
Career Total (Turf)	20	2	2	3	19085
Career Total (AW)	1	0	0	0	

5/00	Stra	1m3f165y	SFT	£4803
7/99	Vitt	1m4f	GD	£4306

Total win prize-money £9109

Going (Turf): **Sf: 1-4** GS: 0-2 **Gd: 1-3** GF: 0-1 Fm: 0-0
Distance: 5f/6f: 0-0 7f-8f: 0-2 **9f-13f: 2-17** 14f+: 0-1
Track : LH: 0-2 RH: 0-1 Tight: 0-3 Gall: 0-0
Aids: Bl: 0-0 Vi: 0-0 Tstrap: 0-0
Best Rating: 49 6/01 Kemp 1m6f92y gd-fm

Tea For Texas

102(95) (48)**37**

4-y-o ch f Weldnaas (USA)-Polly's Teahouse (Shack (USA))

P L Clinton The Buckers

Placings:4/352016000430-00000030105 **(4168)**

2001: 6^{0}G, 7^{0}GF, 8^{0}F, 5^{0}G, 7^{0}GF, 8^{0}GF, 7^{3}GF, 8^{0}F, 7^{1}GF, 7^{0}GF, 8^{5}GF

	Starts	1st	2nd	3rd	Win & Pl
Career Total (Turf)	19	2	0	2	6082
Career Total (AW)	5	0	1	1	948

37	7/01	Chep	7f16y	E(0-70)H	G-F	£2968
55	5/00	Brig	6f209y	F	FRM	£2284

Total win prize-money £5253

Going (Turf): Sf: 0-2 GS: 0-1 Gd: 0-3 **GF: 1-9 Fm: 1-4**
Distance: 5f/6f: 0-7 **7f-8f: 2-15** 9f-13f: 0-2 14f+: 0-0
Track : **LH: 1-14** RH: 0-2 Tight: 0-9 Gall: 0-0
Aids: Bl: 0-0 Vi: 0-1 Tstrap: 0-1
Best Rating: 37 8/01 Muss 1m gd-fm

Team-Mate (IRE)

101 **82**

3-y-o b g Nashwan (USA)-Ustka (Lomond (USA))

J R Fanshawe Peter And Noreen Hodgson

Placings:02424 **(5279)**

2001: 8^{0}G, 9^{2}GF, 10^{4}G, 12^{2}GF, 11^{4}S

	Starts	1st	2nd	3rd	Win & Pl
Career Total (Turf)	5	0	2	0	3543

Going (Turf): Sf: 0-1 GS: 0-0 Gd: 0-2 GF: 0-2 Fm: 0-0
Distance: 5f/6f: 0-0 7f-8f: 0-1 9f-13f: 0-4 14f+: 0-0
Track : LH: 0-0 RH: 0-4 Tight: 0-1 Gall: 0-0
Aids: Bl: 0-0 Vi: 0-0 Tstrap: 0-2
Best Rating: 82 9/01 Kemp 1m4f gd-fm

A half-brother to Travelmate, has shown ability in fast-ground maidens. Stays 12 furlongs and may get further.

Tears In Heaven (IRE)

86 **55**

2-y-o ch f Spectrum (IRE)-Dai E Dai (USA) (Seattle Dancer (USA))

M L W Bell Christopher Wright

Placings:306 **(3620)**

2001: 7^{3}G, 7^{0}G, 7^{6}F

	Starts	1st	2nd	3rd	Win & Pl
Career Total (Turf)	3	0	0	1	1577

Going (Turf): Sf: 0-0 GS: 0-0 Gd: 0-2 GF: 0-0 Fm: 0-1
Distance: 5f/6f: 0-0 7f-8f: 0-3 9f-13f: 0-0 14f+: 0-0
Track : LH: 0-1 RH: 0-0 Tight: 0-1 Gall: 0-0
Aids: Bl: 0-0 Vi: 0-0 Tstrap: 0-0
Best Rating: 55 8/01 Thsk 7f firm

Technician (IRE)

107(103) (64)**90**

6-y-o ch g Archway (IRE)-How It Works (Commanche Run)

E J Alston All Saints Racing

Placings:000**5/2032**42004225335200/**3**62230630200302030/**00**520012322200**05361-35**0121422100 **(5133)**

2001: 7^{3}SD, **7**^{5}SD, 7^{0}HY, 6^{1}GF, 6^{2}GF, 6^{1}F, 6^{4}G, 6^{2}F, 6^{2}GF, 6^{1}G, 6^{0}GF, 7^{0}G

	Starts	1st	2nd	3rd	Win & Pl
Career Total (Turf)	56	4	16	6	69203
Career Total (AW)	15	1	2	5	5086

90	8/01	York	6f	C(0-100)H	GD	£20819
76	6/01	Pont	6f	C(0-95)H	FRM	£7670
69	5/01	Thsk	6f	E(0-75)H	G-F	£8762
64	12/00	Wolv	7f	F(0-60)H	STD	£1750
53	6/00	Carl	5f207y	E(0-70)H	FRM	£4030

Total win prize-money £43032

Going (Turf): Sf: 0-9 GS: 0-10 Gd: 1-15 GF: 1-15 **Fm: 2-6**
Distance: **5f/6f: 4-24** 7f-8f: 1-43 9f-13f: 0-3 14f+: 0-0
Track : **LH: 2-35** RH: 1-13 Tight: 1-25 Gall: 1-5
Aids: **Bl: 5-53** Vi: 0-3 Tstrap: 0-0
Best Rating: 90 8/01 York 6f good

Not the most consistent of individuals, but he has hit form this summer with three wins including one at the York Ebor meeting and he was not beaten as far as his finishing position suggests in the Ayr Gold Cup. Six furlongs on fast ground is ideal for him. Races prominently.

Ted's Boy

59(56) **18**

2-y-o b g Reprimand-Sylvan Rime (Weldnaas (USA))

J R Norton Exors Of The Late E Morrell

Placings:000 **(5351)**

2001: 7^{0}HY, 8^{0}G, 8^{0}SD

	Starts	1st	2nd	3rd	Win & Pl
Career Total (Turf)	2	0	0	0	
Career Total (AW)	1	0	0	0	

Going (Turf): Sf: 0-1 GS: 0-0 Gd: 0-1 GF: 0-0 Fm: 0-0
Distance: 5f/6f: 0-0 7f-8f: 0-2 9f-13f: 0-1 14f+: 0-0
Track : LH: 0-3 RH: 0-0 Tight: 0-0 Gall: 0-0
Aids: Bl: 0-0 Vi: 0-0 Tstrap: 0-0
Best Rating: 18 9/01 Hayd 7f30y heavy

Tedburrow

111 (61)**112**

9-y-o b g Dowsing (USA)-Gwiffina (Welsh Saint)

E J Alston Mrs Irene Davies & Peter Davies

Placings:01560/301111660/04242130040054/1106165010/3150016122/10001110/000013024-**0**442010304000 **(5494)**

2001: **6**^{0}FT, 6^{4}GS, 5^{4}G, 6^{2}GF, 6^{0}GF, 6^{1}GF, 5^{0}GF, 6^{3}G, 6^{0}HY, 5^{4}GS, 6^{0}S, 6^{0}GS, 6^{0}HY

	Starts	1st	2nd	3rd	Win & Pl
Career Total (Turf)	77	19	6	5	304519
Career Total (AW)	1	0	0	0	

103	7/01	Hayd	6f	C	G-F	£6496
113	7/00	Newc	6f	A	FRM	£21576
113	9/99	Leop	5f		Y-S	£32500
98	7/99	Ches	6f18y	A	G-F	£13124
105	7/99	Ches	5f16y	A	G-F	£20140
113	3/99	Donc	6f	A	G-S	£13875
110	9/98	Leop	5f		SFT	£22750
110	7/98	Ches	5f16y	A	G-F	£18381
110	4/98	NmkR	6f	A	G-S	£11267
108	9/97	Asct	5f	B(0-105)H	G-F	£15680
100	7/97	Ches	5f16y	B	G-F	£15535
98	6/97	York	6f	B(0-100)	G-S	£9472
94	5/97	Hayd	5f	C(0-90)H	G-S	£5322
91	7/96	NmkJ	5f	C(0-100)H	G-F	£6056
82	7/95	Donc	6f	D(0-85)H	FRM	£4737
75	7/95	Sand	5f6y	D(0-80)H	G-F	£4201
67	7/95	Sand	5f6y	E(0-70)H	GD	£3785
56	6/95	Ayr	5f	D(0-80)H	FRM	£3647
63	6/94	Muss	5f	F	FRM	£2348

Total win prize-money £230898

Going (Turf): Sf: 1-7 GS: 4-14 Gd: 1-25 **GF: 8-24** Fm: 4-6
Distance: **5f/6f: 18-73** 7f-8f: 1-5 9f-13f: 0-0 14f+: 0-0
Track : **LH: 4-8** RH: 0-1 **Tight: 4-8** Gall: 0-0
Aids: Bl: 0-0 Vi: 0-0 Tstrap: 0-0
Best Rating: 112 5/01 York 6f gd-fm

Effective at five and six furlongs, he can sweat up beforehand but is tremendously game. Usually ridden with restraint, he has a brilliant record at Chester. Best on a sound surface, he is now a veteran but is still running well in Pattern company and won a conditions stakes at Haydock in July.

Tedjen

74 **54**

2-y-o br g Overbury (IRE)-Plum Bold (Be My Guest (USA))

P J Makin The Highly Sociable Syndicate

Placings:0 **(4731)**

2001: 7^{0}F

	Starts	1st	2nd	3rd	Win & Pl
Career Total (Turf)	1	0	0	0	

Going (Turf): Sf: 0-0 GS: 0-0 Gd: 0-0 GF: 0-0 Fm: 0-1
Distance: 5f/6f: 0-0 7f-8f: 0-1 9f-13f: 0-0 14f+: 0-0
Track : LH: 0-0 RH: 0-0 Tight: 0-0 Gall: 0-0
Aids: Bl: 0-0 Vi: 0-0 Tstrap: 0-0
Best Rating: 54 9/01 Chep 7f16y firm

Tedsdale Mac

87 **70**

2-y-o ch c Presidium-Stilvella (Camden Town)

N Bycroft N Bycroft

Placings:0555360 **(5253)**

2001: 6^{0}GF, 7^{5}F, 6^{5}G, 6^{5}G, 6^{3}GF, 5^{6}G, 6^{0}S

	Starts	1st	2nd	3rd	Win & Pl
Career Total (Turf)	7	0	0	1	1130

Going (Turf): Sf: 0-1 GS: 0-0 Gd: 0-3 GF: 0-2 Fm: 0-1
Distance: 5f/6f: 0-6 7f-8f: 0-1 9f-13f: 0-0 14f+: 0-0
Track : LH: 0-1 RH: 0-0 Tight: 0-1 Gall: 0-0
Aids: Bl: 0-0 Vi: 0-0 Tstrap: 0-0
Best Rating: 70 9/01 Rdcr 6f gd-fm

A half-brother to five-furlong juvenile scorer Pathaze. Has not shown much so far but does not help his cause by rearing at the start.

Tedstale (USA)

104 **79**

3-y-o ch c Irish River (FR)-Carefree Kate (USA) (Lyphard (USA))

T D Easterby M J Dawson

Placings:044350-03351053010 **(5607)**

2001: 10^{0}GS, 12^{3}GF, 11^{3}F, 12^{5}GF, 8^{1}GF, 8^{0}GF, 9^{5}G, 8^{3}GF, 6^{0}GF, 8^{1}GS, 8^{0}GS

	Starts	1st	2nd	3rd	Win & Pl
Career Total (Turf)	17	2	0	4	18487

79	10/01	Pont	1m4y	D(0-80)H	G-S	£7995
75	7/01	Bevl	1m100y	D(0-85)H	G-F	£6467

Total win prize-money £14463

Going (Turf): Sf: 0-2 **GS: 1-4** Gd: 0-2 **GF: 1-8** Fm: 0-1
Distance: 5f/6f: 0-0 7f-8f: 0-8 **9f-13f: 2-9** 14f+: 0-0
Track : LH: 1-8 RH: 1-4 Tight: 0-4 Gall: 0-1
Aids: **Bl: 2-7** Vi: 0-0 Tstrap: 0-0
Best Rating: 79 10/01 Pont 1m4y gd-sft

A bit inconsistent, but he is in good form at the moment winning at Pontefract in October. Best over a mile. Improved for fitting of blinkers this summer.

Teehee (IRE)

96 **80**

3-y-o b c Anita's Prince-Regal Charmer (Royal And Regal (USA))

B Palling Celtic Racing

Placings:5533-210000 **(5638)**

2001: 8^{2}S, 8^{1}HY, 8^{0}F, 8^{0}G, 8^{0}G, 7^{0}G

	Starts	1st	2nd	3rd	Win & Pl
Career Total (Turf)	10	1	1	2	6085

80	5/01	Nott	1m54y	D	HVY	£3818

Total win prize-money £3819

Going (Turf): **Sf: 1-3** GS: 0-2 Gd: 0-3 GF: 0-1 Fm: 0-1
Distance: 5f/6f: 0-0 7f-8f: 0-5 **9f-13f: 1-5** 14f+: 0-0
Track : **LH: 1-4** RH: 0-0 Tight: 0-1 Gall: 0-0
Aids: Bl: 0-0 Vi: 0-1 Tstrap: 0-0
Best Rating: 80 5/01 Nott 1m54y heavy

A heavy-ground maiden winner in May, he has been held since on a faster surface.

Teejay'N'Aitch (IRE)

87(78) **29**

9-y-o b g Maelstrom Lake-Middle Verde (USA) (Sham (USA))

J S Goldie Mrs Alice S Goldie

Placings:600/66420306500630/6033600/0400/06/00-00 **(1137)**

2001: 16^{0}SD, 11^{0}G

	Starts	1st	2nd	3rd	Win & Pl
Career Total (Turf)	32	0	1	4	3484
Career Total (AW)	2	0	0	0	

Going (Turf): Sf: 0-0 GS: 0-5 Gd: 0-12 GF: 0-9 Fm: 0-6
Distance: 5f/6f: 0-3 7f-8f: 0-15 9f-13f: 0-10 14f+: 0-6
Track : LH: 0-13 RH: 0-15 Tight: 0-15 Gall: 0-3
Aids: Bl: 0-3 Vi: 0-2 Tstrap: 0-1
Best Rating: 12 5/01 Haml 1m3f16y good

Teenawon (IRE)

72 **48d**

3-y-o ch f Polar Falcon (USA)-Oasis (Valiyar)

G G Margarson Haydn D Kelly

Placings:320-00 **(2728)**

2001: 6^{0}GF, 7^{0}GF

	Starts	1st	2nd	3rd	Win & Pl
Career Total (Turf)	5	0	1	1	809

Going (Turf): Sf: 0-0 GS: 0-0 Gd: 0-0 GF: 0-4 Fm: 0-0
Distance: 5f/6f: 0-1 7f-8f: 0-3 9f-13f: 0-0 14f+: 0-0
Track : LH: 0-0 RH: 0-0 Tight: 0-0 Gall: 0-0
Aids: Bl: 0-0 Vi: 0-0 Tstrap: 0-0
Best Rating: 1 6/01 Sals 6f212y gd-fm

Tefi

89(89) (35)**33**

3-y-o ch g Efisio-Masuri Kabisa (USA) (Ascot Knight (CAN))
T D Easterby T E F Freight (scarborough) Ltd

Placings:5322306-0000000 (4778)
2001: 8⁰GF, 6⁰G, 7⁰GF, 8⁰F, 7⁰G, 7⁰GF, 5⁰G, 7⁴SD

	Starts	1st	2nd	3rd	Win & Pl
Career Total (Turf)	14	0	2	2	2762

Going (Turf): Sf: 0-1 GS: 0-1 Gd: 0-5 GF: 0-3 Fm: 0-4
Distance: 5f/6f: 0-7 7f-8f: 0-7 9f-13f: 0-0 14f+: 0-0
Track : LH: 0-5 RH: 0-4 Tight: 0-4 Gall: 0-2
Aids: Bl: 0-3 Vi: 0-0 Tstrap: 0-0
Best Rating: 51 6/01 Thsk 6f good

Teg

45

3-y-o b f Petong-Felinwen (White Mill)
S C Williams Tyrnest Ltd

Placings:0 (4226)
2001: 7⁰GF

	Starts	1st	2nd	3rd	Win & Pl
Career Total (Turf)	1	0	0	0	

Going (Turf): Sf: 0-0 GS: 0-0 Gd: 0-0 GF: 0-1 Fm: 0-0
Distance: 5f/6f: 0-0 7f-8f: 0-1 9f-13f: 0-0 14f+: 0-0
Track : LH: 0-0 RH: 0-0 Tight: 0-0 Gall: 0-0
Aids: Bl: 0-0 Vi: 0-0 Tstrap: 0-0

Telecaster (IRE)

(100) (75)**35+**

5-y-o ch g Indian Ridge-Monashee (USA) (Sovereign Dancer (USA))
C R Egerton Casting Partners B

Placings:000/3112115203-00 (0259)
2001: 6⁰SW, 5⁰SD

	Starts	1st	2nd	3rd	Win & Pl		
Career Total (Turf)	2	0	0	0			
Career Total (AW)	13	4	2	2	16797		
70	3/00	Wolv	6f	E(0-70)H		STD	£2912
62	2/00	Sthl	6f	D(0-80)H		STD	£4309
58	1/00	Sthl	6f	D(0-80)H		STD	£4706
48	1/00	Wolv	6f	F(0-60)H		STD	£1928

Total win prize-money £13857

Going (Turf): Sf: 0-1 GS: 0-1 Gd: 0-0 GF: 0-0 Fm: 0-0
Distance: 5f/6f: 4-12 7f-8f: 0-1 9f-13f: 0-2 14f+: 0-0
Track : LH: 4-13 RH: 0-2 Tight: 2-9 Gall: 0-1
Aids: Bl: 3-11 Vi: 0-0 Tstrap: 0-0
Best Rating: 49 1/01 Wolv 6f slow

Improved beyond all recognition in 2001, winning four times on Fibresand and taking a hike up the handicap as a result. Suited by six furlongs, he also has a commendable attitude in a battle.

Telegram Girl

76(95) (64)**47**

2-y-o b f Magic Ring (IRE)-Lucky Message (USA) (Phone Trick (USA))
J G Smyth-Osbourne D Llewelyn

Placings:000001 (5410)
2001: 5⁰GF, 5⁰F, 7⁰GF, 6⁰G, 8⁰SD, 7¹SD

	Starts	1st	2nd	3rd	Win & Pl	
Career Total (Turf)	4	0	0	0		
Career Total (AW)	2	1	0	0	1995	
64 10/01 Sthl	7f	G			STD	£1995

Total win prize-money £1995

Going (Turf): Sf: 0-0 GS: 0-0 Gd: 0-1 GF: 0-2 Fm: 0-1
Distance: 5f/6f: 0-3 7f-8f: 1-2 9f-13f: 0-1 14f+: 0-0
Track : LH: 1-3 RH: 0-0 Tight: 0-1 Gall: 0-1
Aids: Bl: 0-0 Vi: 1-1 Tstrap: 0-0
Best Rating: 64 10/01 Sthl 7f stand

Got off the mark in a seller on the Southwell Fibresand in October and may be a bit better than that.

Telesto (USA)

92 **92**

2-y-o b c Mr Prospector (USA)-Aviance (Northfields (USA))
Sir Michael Stoute Niarchos Family

Placings:53 (4708)
2001: 6⁵G, 6³G

	Starts	1st	2nd	3rd	Win & Pl
Career Total (Turf)	2	0	0	1	1338

Going (Turf): Sf: 0-0 GS: 0-0 Gd: 0-2 GF: 0-0 Fm: 0-0
Distance: 5f/6f: 0-2 7f-8f: 0-0 9f-13f: 0-0 14f+: 0-0
Track : LH: 0-0 RH: 0-0 Tight: 0-0 Gall: 0-0
Aids: Bl: 0-0 Vi: 0-0 Tstrap: 0-0
Best Rating: 92 9/01 Donc 6f good

Well regarded half-brother to Chimes Of Freedom, held in warm maidens.

Tellion

(84) (26)

7-y-o b g Mystiko (USA)-Salchow (Niniski (USA))
J R Jenkins Mrs Jean Hale

Placings:4465430/6360/00/30-6 (1997)
2001: 14⁰SD

	Starts	1st	2nd	3rd	Win & Pl
Career Total (Turf)	10	0	0	2	1317
Career Total (AW)	6	0	0	1	503

Going (Turf): Sf: 0-3 GS: 0-1 Gd: 0-3 GF: 0-3 Fm: 0-0
Distance: 5f/6f: 0-0 7f-8f: 0-2 9f-13f: 0-11 14f+: 0-3
Track : LH: 0-12 RH: 0-3 Tight: 0-5 Gall: 0-0
Aids: Bl: 0-0 Vi: 0-4 Tstrap: 0-0
Best Rating: 92 9/01 Donc 6f good

Telori

87 **42**

3-y-o ch f Muhtarram (USA)-Elita (Sharpo)
S C Williams Tyrnest Ltd

Placings:4300 (5131)
2001: 7⁴S, 7³F, 5⁰G, 7⁰HY

	Starts	1st	2nd	3rd	Win & Pl
Career Total (Turf)	4	0	0	1	379

Going (Turf): Sf: 0-2 GS: 0-0 Gd: 0-1 GF: 0-0 Fm: 0-1
Distance: 5f/6f: 0-1 7f-8f: 0-3 9f-13f: 0-0 14f+: 0-0
Track : LH: 0-0 RH: 0-0 Tight: 0-0 Gall: 0-0
Aids: Bl: 0-0 Vi: 0-0 Tstrap: 0-0
Best Rating: 42 9/01 Muss 7f30y firm

Temeraire (USA)

(110) (87d)**82d**

6-y-o b g Dayjur (USA)-Key Dancer (USA) (Nijinsky (CAN))
D J S Cosgrove G G Grayson

Placings:0/211000/602000005210510/020042300000 01-3 (0205)
2001: 10³SW

	Starts	1st	2nd	3rd	Win & Pl		
Career Total (Turf)	29	3	5	1	31659		
Career Total (AW)	9	2	0	1	8784		
59	12/00	Ling	1m	D(0-85)		STD	£3786
87	11/99	Ling	7f	D(0-85)		STD	£3747
85	9/99	Newb	7f64y	C(0-95)H		GD	£7766
93	7/98	Ling	7f140y	C(0-90)		G-F	£6791
84	6/98	Wind	1m67y	D		G-F	£3902

Total win prize-money £25993

Going (Turf): Sf: 0-2 GS: 0-6 Gd: 1-11 GF: 2-10 Fm: 0-0
Distance: 5f/6f: 0-3 7f-8f: 4-31 9f-13f: 1-4 14f+: 0-0
Track : LH: 3-10 RH: 1-9 Tight: 3-10 Gall: 1-4
Aids: Bl: 0-0 Vi: 0-2 Tstrap: 0-0
Best Rating: 83 1/01 Ling 1m2f slow

Temper Tantrum

(95) (66)

3-y-o b g Pursuit Of Love-Queenbird (Warning)
Andrew Reid A S Reid

Placings:010-000 (5416)
2001: 7⁰GF, 10⁰S, 9⁰SD

	Starts	1st	2nd	3rd	Win & Pl		
Career Total (Turf)	2	0	0	0			
Career Total (AW)	4	1	0	0	2247		
66	11/00	Sthl	1m	F		STD	£2247

Total win prize-money £2247

Going (Turf): Sf: 0-1 GS: 0-0 Gd: 0-0 GF: 0-1 Fm: 0-0
Distance: 5f/6f: 0-0 7f-8f: 1-4 9f-13f: 0-2 14f+: 0-0
Track : LH: 1-6 RH: 0-0 Tight: 0-3 Gall: 0-1
Aids: Bl: 0-0 Vi: 0-0 Tstrap: 0-0
Best Rating: 53 9/01 York 7f202y gd-fm

Tempest

96 **114**

3-y-o b c Zafonic (USA)-Pidona (Baillamont (USA))
Sir Michael Stoute Cheveley Park Stud

Placings:41263-0 (1119)
2001: 8⁰G

	Starts	1st	2nd	3rd	Win & Pl		
Career Total (Turf)	6	1	1	1	31108		
86	8/00	Newb	7f	D		G-F	£4446

Total win prize-money £4446

Going (Turf): Sf: 0-0 GS: 0-1 Gd: 0-4 GF: 1-1 Fm: 0-0
Distance: 5f/6f: 0-0 7f-8f: 1-6 9f-13f: 0-0 14f+: 0-0
Track : LH: 0-0 RH: 0-0 Tight: 0-0 Gall: 0-0
Aids: Bl: 0-0 Vi: 0-0 Tstrap: 0-0
Best Rating: 90 5/01 NmkR 1m good

A useful two-year-old, he was down the field in the Guineas in his only run at three and is now in America.

Temple Way

109 **95**

5-y-o b g Shirley Heights-Abbey Strand (USA) (Shadeed (USA))
R Charlton The Queen

Placings:034415420/0222105-5000 (4225)
2001: 14⁵GF, 20⁰GF, 16⁰G, 14⁰GF

	Starts	1st	2nd	3rd	Win & Pl		
Career Total (Turf)	20	2	4	1	73894		
93	8/00	Gdwd	1m6f	B(0-105)H		G-F	£32500
75	7/99	Chep	2m49y	D(0-80)H		G-F	£3798

Total win prize-money £36299

Going (Turf): Sf: 0-0 GS: 0-1 Gd: 0-5 GF: 2-13 Fm: 0-1
Distance: 5f/6f: 0-0 7f-8f: 0-0 9f-13f: 0-4 14f+: 2-16
Track : LH: 1-6 RH: 1-13 Tight: 1-9 Gall: 0-10
Aids: Bl: 1-6 Vi: 1-4 Tstrap: 0-0
Best Rating: 95 5/01 Gdwd 1m6f gd-fm

A useful stayer at up to two miles, he had a good season in 2000 but has not been as effective this year. He acts on fast ground and sometimes wears a visor.

Temples Time (IRE)

99(96) (62)**57**

3-y-o b f Distinctly North (USA)-Midnight Patrol (Ashmore (FR))
R Brotherton (R Hannon 8/5) Mrs S Arcourt-Rippingale

Placings:436105-04354044633566 (5532)
2001: 7⁰SD, 8⁴SD, 6³GF, 10⁵G, 10⁴GF, 9⁰GF, 11⁴F, 12⁴SD,

10^{6}G, 11^{3}SD, 10^{3}GF, 11^{5}GF, 7^{6}GF, 9^{6}HY

	Starts	1st	2nd	3rd	Win & Pl
Career Total (Turf)	16	1	0	3	4035
Career Total (AW)	4	0	0	1	723

69 9/00 Brig 7f214y F G-S £1767

Total win prize-money £1768

Going (Turf): Sf: 0-3 **GS: 1-3** Gd: 0-2 GF: 0-7 Fm: 0-1
Distance: 5f/6f: 0-2 **7f-8f: 1-7** 9f-13f: 0-11 14f+: 0-0
Track : **LH: 1-15** RH: 0-1 Tight: 0-5 Gall: 0-0
Aids: Bl: 0-0 Vi: 0-0 Tstrap: 0-0
Best Rating: 64 5/01 Wwck 1m2f188y gd-fm

Tempramental (IRE)

59(100) (27)**46**

5-y-o ch m Midhish-Musical Horn (Music Boy)
Dr P Pritchard Dominic Ryan

Placings:04503566105/050034000553**0/225333141500**00-0 **(2185)**
2001: 5^{0}G

	Starts	1st	2nd	3rd	Win & Pl
Career Total (Turf)	27	3	0	5	12929
Career Total (AW)	12	0	2	1	1329

53 6/00 Rdcr 1m E(0-70)H GD £3981
49 5/00 Pont 1m2f6y E(0-70)H GD £3029
60 8/98 Chep 5f16y D H G-F £3257

Total win prize-money £10268

Going (Turf): Sf: 0-3 GS: 0-2 **Gd: 2-17** GF: 1-5 Fm: 0-0
Distance: 5f/6f: 1-15 7f-8f: 1-11 9f-13f: 1-12 14f+: 0-1
Track : **LH: 1-21** RH: 0-2 Tight: 0-7 Gall: 0-3
Aids: Bl: 0-6 **Vi: 1-4** Tstrap: 0-0
Best Rating: 60 8/98 Chep 5f16y GF

Tempting Fate (IRE)

111 (93)**115**

3-y-o b f Persian Bold-West Of Eden (Crofter (USA))
Saeed Bin Suroor Godolphin

Placings:2114-3436 **(3762a)**
2001: 8^{3}FT, 8^{4}G, 8^{3}GF, 8^{6}S

	Starts	1st	2nd	3rd	Win & Pl
Career Total (Turf)	7	2	1	1	58424
Career Total (AW)	1	0	0	1	13333

94 8/00 Sals 6f B G-F £9252
84 8/00 Newb 6f8y D G-F £5102

Total win prize-money £14355

Going (Turf): Sf: 0-1 GS: 0-1 Gd: 0-1 **GF: 2-4** Fm: 0-0
Distance: 5f/6f: 1-2 7f-8f: 1-6 9f-13f: 0-0 14f+: 0-0
Track : LH: 0-0 RH: 0-1 Tight: 0-0 Gall: 0-1
Aids: Bl: 0-0 Vi: 0-0 Tstrap: 0-1
Best Rating: 115 6/01 Asct 1m gd-fm

Interesting filly, ran fourth to Rose Gypsy in Poule d'Essai des Pouliches at Lonchamp in May, after having been well beaten in fillies' race at Nad Al Sheba in February. A good third in the Group One Coronation Stakes next time, a mile looks as far as she wants.

Tempus Fugit

97(99) (42)**35**

6-y-o ch m Timeless Times (USA)-Kabella (Kabour)
B R Millman Seasons Holidays

Placings:0122360/0000/0/306055005 **(4322)**
2001: 5^{3}SD, 5^{0}SD, 5^{6}GF, 5^{0}G, 6^{5}F, 5^{5}GF, 5^{0}F, 5^{0}GF, 5^{5}GF

	Starts	1st	2nd	3rd	Win & Pl
Career Total (Turf)	17	1	2	1	5523
Career Total (AW)	4	0	0	1	349

77 6/97 Nott 5f13y E GD £3148

Total win prize-money £3148

Going (Turf): Sf: 0-2 GS: 0-3 **Gd: 1-2** GF: 0-7 Fm: 0-3
Distance: **5f/6f: 1-19** 7f-8f: 0-2 9f-13f: 0-0 14f+: 0-0
Track : LH: 0-6 RH: 0-2 Tight: 0-2 Gall: 0-6
Aids: Bl: 0-0 Vi: 0-1 Tstrap: 0-0
Best Rating: 42 3/01 Sthl 5f stand

Ten Past Six

(92) (18)

9-y-o ch g Kris-Tashinsky (USA) (Nijinsky (CAN))
M J Polglase James S Kennerley

Placings:42/1020/225460050/65100/50**1**0012221050/50/**056**0000-6 **(5683)**
2001: 14^{6}S, 14^{0}SD

	Starts	1st	2nd	3rd	Win & Pl
Career Total (Turf)	38	4	7	0	23264
Career Total (AW)	5	1	0	0	1720

57 8/98 Carl 1m4f F G-S £2290
56 6/98 Haml 1m3f16y F(0-55) G-S £2346
64 5/98 Sthl 1m3f F(0-55) STD £1720
59 4/97 Ripn 1m2f F GD £2790
76 5/95 Hayd 7f30y D G-F £3993

Total win prize-money £13140

Going (Turf): Sf: 0-10 **GS: 2-7** Gd: 1-8 GF: 1-11 Fm: 0-2
Distance: 5f/6f: 0-0 7f-8f: 1-6 **9f-13f: 4-33** 14f+: 0-4
Track : LH: 2-20 **RH: 3-19 Tight: 2-20** Gall: 0-10
Aids: Bl: 0-3 **Vi: 2-13** Tstrap: 0-0
Best Rating: 14 11/01 Donc 1m6f132y soft

Tenaja Trail (USA)

73 **47**

2-y-o ch c Irish River (FR)-Buckeye Gal (USA) (Good Counsel (USA))
W J Haggas Gary E Biszantz

Placings:0 **(5056)**
2001: 8^{0}S

	Starts	1st	2nd	3rd	Win & Pl
Career Total (Turf)	1	0	0	0	

Going (Turf): Sf: 0-1 GS: 0-0 Gd: 0-0 GF: 0-0 Fm: 0-0
Distance: 5f/6f: 0-0 7f-8f: 0-1 9f-13f: 0-0 14f+: 0-0
Track : LH: 0-0 RH: 0-0 Tight: 0-0 Gall: 0-0
Aids: Bl: 0-0 Vi: 0-0 Tstrap: 0-0
Best Rating: 47 10/01 NmkR 1m soft

Tender Trap (IRE)

102 **81**

3-y-o b c Sadler's Wells (USA)-Shamiyda (USA) (Sir Ivor)
T G Mills T G Mills

Placings:5-562223 **(4414)**
2001: 10^{5}S, 12^{6}GS, 9^{2}GF, 10^{2}GF, 10^{2}GF, 10^{3}S

	Starts	1st	2nd	3rd	Win & Pl
Career Total (Turf)	7	0	3	1	4459

Going (Turf): Sf: 0-3 GS: 0-1 Gd: 0-0 GF: 0-3 Fm: 0-0
Distance: 5f/6f: 0-0 7f-8f: 0-0 9f-13f: 0-7 14f+: 0-0
Track : LH: 0-5 RH: 0-2 Tight: 0-3 Gall: 0-2
Aids: Bl: 0-0 Vi: 0-0 Tstrap: 0-0
Best Rating: 81 7/01 Pont 1m2f6y gd-fm

A late foal bred to stay middle distances, he was regularly in the frame in maidens.

Tenderfoot

95(86) (48)**54d**

3-y-o b f Be My Chief (USA)-Kelimutu (Top Ville)
Mrs Lydia Pearce James Furlong

Placings:65-0203100 **(4776)**
2001: 11^{0}GF, 12^{2}GF, 12^{0}GS, 12^{3}G, 14^{1}GF, 14^{0}S, 11^{0}G

	Starts	1st	2nd	3rd	Win & Pl
Career Total (Turf)	8	1	1	1	5052
Career Total (AW)	1	0	0	0	0

54 8/01 Rdcr 1m6f19y E(0-70)H G-F £3688

Total win prize-money £3689

Going (Turf): Sf: 0-2 GS: 0-1 Gd: 0-2 **GF: 1-3** Fm: 0-0
Distance: 5f/6f: 0-0 7f-8f: 0-1 9f-13f: 0-6 **14f+: 1-2**
Track : **LH: 1-5** RH: 0-4 **Tight: 1-6** Gall: 0-1
Aids: Bl: 0-0 Vi: 0-0 Tstrap: 0-0
Best Rating: 54 8/01 Rdcr 1m6f19y gd-fm

A free-running sort, was just touched off in a Folkestone handicap. Acts on fast ground, and suited by front-running tactics.

Tendulkar (USA)

108 **108+**

2-y-o b c Spinning World (USA)-Romanette (USA) (Alleged (USA))
A P O'Brien Mrs J Magnier, M Tabor, Mrs D Nagle

Placings:13 **(5388)**
2001: 5^{1}G, 7^{3}GS

	Starts	1st	2nd	3rd	Win & Pl
Career Total (Turf)	2	1	0	1	30625

97 5/01 Curr 5f GD £8625

Total win prize-money £8625

Going (Turf): Sf: 0-0 GS: 0-1 **Gd: 1-1** GF: 0-0 Fm: 0-0
Distance: **5f/6f: 1-1** 7f-8f: 0-1 9f-13f: 0-0 14f+: 0-0
Track : LH: 0-0 RH: 0-0 Tight: 0-0 Gall: 0-0
Aids: Bl: 0-0 Vi: 0-0 Tstrap: 0-0
Best Rating: 108 10/01 NmkR 7f gd-sft

Odds-on winner of a Curragh maiden in May, subsequently absent after injuring his pelvis, he ran a cracker when third to two stable companions in the Dewhurst. Looks a useful prospect for next year.

Tenerife Flyer

79(45) **54d**

3-y-o ch f Rock City-Nobleata (Dunbeath (USA))
J R Norton K Swift

Placings:60460440-000 **(2409)**
2001: 9^{0}G, 11^{0}GF, 10^{0}GF

	Starts	1st	2nd	3rd	Win & Pl
Career Total (Turf)	10	0	0	0	236
Career Total (AW)	1	0	0	0	

Going (Turf): Sf: 0-4 GS: 0-1 Gd: 0-2 GF: 0-3 Fm: 0-0
Distance: 5f/6f: 0-2 7f-8f: 0-3 9f-13f: 0-6 14f+: 0-0
Track : LH: 0-4 RH: 0-4 Tight: 0-2 Gall: 0-1
Aids: Bl: 0-0 Vi: 0-0 Tstrap: 0-0
Best Rating: 31 5/01 Leic 1m1f218y good

Tennessee (IRE)

73(85) **73**

4-y-o b g Blues Traveller (IRE)-Valiant Friend (USA) (Shahrastani (USA))
S P C Woods B Allen/r Hine/r Dawson/a Duke

Placings:534/000-000 **(2235)**
2001: 12^{0}SD, 8^{0}G, 9^{0}GF

	Starts	1st	2nd	3rd	Win & Pl
Career Total (Turf)	5	0	0	1	545
Career Total (AW)	4	0	0	0	

Going (Turf): Sf: 0-0 GS: 0-1 Gd: 0-1 GF: 0-3 Fm: 0-0
Distance: 5f/6f: 0-0 7f-8f: 0-2 9f-13f: 0-7 14f+: 0-0
Track : LH: 0-6 RH: 0-1 Tight: 0-3 Gall: 0-0
Aids: Bl: 0-2 Vi: 0-0 Tstrap: 0-0
Best Rating: 24 1/01 Ling 1m4f stand

Tennessee Moon

106 **73**

3-y-o b f Darshaan-Mrs Moonlight (Ajdal (USA))
G Wragg Bloomsbury Stud

Placings:00030 **(3609)**
2001: 7^{0}G, 8^{0}G, 10^{0}GF, 10^{3}GF, 12^{0}GS

	Starts	1st	2nd	3rd	Win & Pl
Career Total (Turf)	5	0	0	1	687

Going (Turf): Sf: 0-0 GS: 0-1 Gd: 0-2 GF: 0-2 Fm: 0-0
Distance: 5f/6f: 0-0 7f-8f: 0-1 9f-13f: 0-4 14f+: 0-0
Track : LH: 0-0 RH: 0-3 Tight: 0-1 Gall: 0-2
Aids: Bl: 0-0 Vi: 0-0 Tstrap: 0-0
Best Rating: 73 6/01 Kemp 1m2f gd-fm

Tennessee Waltz

92 **53**

3-y-o b f Caerleon (USA)-Military Tune (IRE) (Nashwan (USA))
E A L Dunlop Geoff Howard-Spink & Lindy Regis

Placings:000-3600 **(4162)**
2001: 9^{3}F, 10^{6}GF, 9^{0}G, 10^{0}GF

	Starts	1st	2nd	3rd	Win & Pl
Career Total (Turf)	7	0	0	1	524

Going (Turf): Sf: 0-1 GS: 0-0 Gd: 0-2 GF: 0-3 Fm: 0-1
Distance: 5f/6f: 0-0 7f-8f: 0-3 9f-13f: 0-4 14f+: 0-0
Track : LH: 0-5 RH: 0-0 Tight: 0-2 Gall: 0-1
Aids: Bl: 0-0 Vi: 0-0 Tstrap: 0-0
Best Rating: 53 6/01 Brig 1m1f209y firm

Tensile (IRE)

109 **77**

6-y-o b g Tenby-Bonnie Isle (Pitcairn)
P J Hobbs (M C Pipe 7/6) D Charlesworth

Placings:04200/150250/02530/60043350-05500 **(5492)**
2001: 18^{0}S, 16^{6}GS, 10^{6}GF, 10^{0}G, 10^{0}HY

	Starts	1st	2nd	3rd	Win & Pl
Career Total (Turf)	29	1	3	3	17547
87 4/98 Bevl 1m1f207yD(0-85)H				G-S	£3938

Total win prize-money £3938

Going (Turf): Sf: 0-4 **GS: 1-9** Gd: 0-8 GF: 0-8 Fm: 0-0
Distance: 5f/6f: 0-0 7f-8f: 0-4 **9f-13f: 1-7** 14f+: 0-18
Track : LH: 0-12 **RH: 1-12** Tight: 0-6 Gall: 0-9
Aids: Bl: 0-0 Vi: 0-1 Tstrap: 0-0
Best Rating: 79 4/01 Newb 2m gd-sft

Useful handicapper for Luca Cumani in '98, then with Martin Pipe, before going to Philip Hobbs. He runs under both codes but is rather in the Handicapper's grip just now. Always seems to run well without winning and stays all day.

Teofilio (IRE)

(104) (68)**67**

7-y-o ch h Night Shift (USA)-Rivoltade (USA) (Sir Ivor)
Andrew Reid (Miss Venetia Williams 15/9) L R Gotch

Placings:22/1300/00600**500**/**421**52113260/1600002300 4540222-03 **(5616)**
2001: 8^{0}SD, 7^{3}SD, 8^{4}SD

	Starts	1st	2nd	3rd	Win & Pl
Career Total (Turf)	30	3	5	3	40625
Career Total (AW)	14	2	4	1	7926
67 2/00 Ling 1m E(0-75)H				STD	£2276
72 6/99 NmkJ 7f C(0-95)H				G-F	£6781
75 6/99 Sand 7f16y C(0-100)H				GD	£14046
59 2/99 Ling 1m F(0-60)				STD	£2038
74 4/97 Bevl 1m100y D				G-F	£3860

Total win prize-money £29001

Going (Turf): Sf: 0-3 GS: 0-0 Gd: 1-10 **GF: 2-17** Fm: 0-0
Distance: 5f/6f: 0-4 **7f-8f: 4-31** 9f-13f: 1-9 14f+: 0-0
Track : LH: 2-20 RH: 2-9 **Tight: 2-18** Gall: 0-6
Aids: Bl: 4-27 Vi: 0-0 Tstrap: 0-0
Best Rating: 58 11/01 Wolv 7f stand

Best over seven furlongs to a mile, he prefers fast ground on turf, and also acts on the All-Weather. However, he has not won since February 2000.

Tequila

6-y-o b g Mystiko (USA)-Black Ivor (USA) (Sir Ivor)
W Clay H Clewlow

Placings:4316602/P **(3798)**
2001: 8^{P}G

	Starts	1st	2nd	3rd	Win & Pl
Career Total (Turf)	8	1	1	1	6536
78 6/98 Gdwd 1m E				GD	£3817

Total win prize-money £3818

Going (Turf): Sf: 0-1 GS: 0-1 **Gd: 1-3** GF: 0-2 Fm: 0-1
Distance: 5f/6f: 0-0 **7f-8f: 1-4** 9f-13f: 0-4 14f+: 0-0
Track : LH: 0-2 **RH: 1-5** Tight: 0-2 Gall: 0-1
Aids: Bl: 0-0 Vi: 0-0 Tstrap: 0-0

Teresa Balbi

100 **93**

2-y-o ch f Master Willie-Pondicherry (USA) (Sir Wimborne (USA))
S P C Woods Dwayne Woods

Placings:16 **(5609)**
2001: 8^{1}HY, 8^{6}GS

	Starts	1st	2nd	3rd	Win & Pl
Career Total (Turf)	2	1	0	0	5024
93 10/01 Donc 1m D				HVY	£4699

Total win prize-money £4700

Going (Turf): Sf: 1-1 GS: 0-1 Gd: 0-0 GF: 0-0 Fm: 0-0
Distance: 5f/6f: 0-0 **7f-8f: 1-2** 9f-13f: 0-0 14f+: 0-0
Track : LH: 1-1 RH: 0-0 Tight: 0-0 **Gall: 1-1**
Aids: Bl: 0-0 Vi: 0-0 Tstrap: 0-0
Best Rating: 93 10/01 Donc 1m heavy

A half sister to the sprint winner Kirsch, she made an encouraging start when showing the right attitude to win a backend Doncaster maiden on heavy ground.

Terfel

98 **91**

2-y-o ch c Lion Cavern (USA)-Montserrat (Aragon)
M L W Bell Mrs Anne Yearley

Placings:123143 **(5227)**
2001: 6^{1}GF, 7^{2}G, 7^{3}GS, 7^{1}GF, 8^{4}HY, 6^{3}S

	Starts	1st	2nd	3rd	Win & Pl
Career Total (Turf)	6	2	1	2	19283
91 8/01 Rdcr 7f E				G-F	£3575
76 6/01 Yarm 6f3y E				G-F	£3465

Total win prize-money £7040

Going (Turf): Sf: 0-2 GS: 0-1 Gd: 0-1 **GF: 2-2** Fm: 0-0
Distance: 5f/6f: 0-0 **7f-8f: 2-6** 9f-13f: 0-0 14f+: 0-0
Track : LH: 0-1 RH: 0-1 Tight: 0-0 Gall: 0-1
Aids: Bl: 0-0 Vi: 0-0 Tstrap: 0-0
Best Rating: 91 9/01 Siro 1m heavy

Fairly useful prospect who made an impressive debut when winning over six furlongs at Yarmouth in June, despite giving away ground at the start. Beaten in better company afterwards on easier ground, he returned to winning ways at Redcar in August. Stays seven furlongs and seems best suited by fast going.

Tern Intern (IRE)

83 **64**

2-y-o b/br g Dr Devious (IRE)-Arctic Bird (USA) (Storm Bird (CAN))
Miss J Feilden Ms Anne Dawson

Placings:00 **(4282)**
2001: 7^{0}GF, 8^{0}G

	Starts	1st	2nd	3rd	Win & Pl
Career Total (Turf)	2	0	0	0	

Going (Turf): Sf: 0-0 GS: 0-0 Gd: 0-1 GF: 0-1 Fm: 0-0
Distance: 5f/6f: 0-0 7f-8f: 0-1 9f-13f: 0-1 14f+: 0-0
Track : LH: 0-0 RH: 0-0 Tight: 0-0 Gall: 0-0
Aids: Bl: 0-0 Vi: 0-0 Tstrap: 0-0
Best Rating: 64 7/01 Yarm 7f3y gd-fm

Terrapin (IRE)

91 **66**

2-y-o b f Turtle Island (IRE)-Lady Taufan (IRE) (Taufan (USA))
Mrs A Duffield P J & C H Watson

Placings:500 **(4615)**
2001: 6^{5}G, 6^{0}GF, 6^{0}F

	Starts	1st	2nd	3rd	Win & Pl
Career Total (Turf)	3	0	0	0	0

Going (Turf): Sf: 0-0 GS: 0-0 Gd: 0-1 GF: 0-1 Fm: 0-1
Distance: 5f/6f: 0-3 7f-8f: 0-0 9f-13f: 0-0 14f+: 0-0
Track : LH: 0-1 RH: 0-0 Tight: 0-0 Gall: 0-0
Aids: Bl: 0-0 Vi: 0-0 Tstrap: 0-0
Best Rating: 66 8/01 Pont 6f good

Terrestrial (USA)

107 **104+**

3-y-o ch c Theatrical-Stellaria (USA) (Roberto (USA))
J H M Gosden K Abdulla

Placings:1-51 **(1116)**
2001: 9^{5}S, 12^{1}G

	Starts	1st	2nd	3rd	Win & Pl
Career Total (Turf)	3	2	0	0	14381
104 5/01 NmkR 1m4f C				GD	£6003
86 10/00 NmkR 1m D				SFT	£7800

Total win prize-money £13803

Going (Turf): Sf: 1-2 GS: 0-0 **Gd: 1-1** GF: 0-0 Fm: 0-0
Distance: 5f/6f: 0-0 7f-8f: 1-1 9f-13f: 1-2 14f+: 0-0
Track : LH: 0-0 **RH: 1-1** Tight: 0-0 **Gall: 1-1**
Aids: Bl: 0-0 Vi: 0-0 Tstrap: 0-0
Best Rating: 104 5/01 NmkR 1m4f good

A half-brother to Group one winner Observatory, made a winning debut on his only start at two, from a field that has produced several subsequent winners. He was disappointing on his reappearance in the Fielden Stakes, but won nicely next time before being badly injured on the gallops.

Tertullian (IRE)

96 **70**

2-y-o b c Petorius-Fiddes (IRE) (Alzao (USA))
R Hannon Louis Stadler

Placings:5130 **(5668)**
2001: 6^{5}F, 7^{1}GF, 8^{3}GS, 8^{0}HY

	Starts	1st	2nd	3rd	Win & Pl
Career Total (Turf)	4	1	0	1	8848
67 9/01 York 7f202y E				G-F	£8060

Total win prize-money £8060

Going (Turf): Sf: 0-1 GS: 0-1 Gd: 0-0 **GF: 1-1** Fm: 0-1
Distance: 5f/6f: 0-0 **7f-8f: 1-3** 9f-13f: 0-1 14f+: 0-0
Track : LH: 1-1 RH: 0-1 Tight: 0-1 **Gall: 1-1**
Aids: Bl: 0-0 Vi: 0-0 Tstrap: 0-0
Best Rating: 70 10/01 NmkR 1m gd-sft

A May foal, he is bred to stay. He lost a shoe on his debut but still performed with credit, staying on well at the finish over seven furlongs. He subsequently won a moderate maiden over a mile at York in September and was just found out by stiff mile when third at Newmarket the following month.

Test The Water (IRE)

98(98) (40)**49**

7-y-o ch g Maelstrom Lake-Baliana (CAN) (Riverman (USA))
P Howling Bvi Partnership

Placings:022231/605300/0600301204/050062/0000-000354402 **(5450)**
2001: 11^{0}SW, 9^{0}SD, 11^{0}SD, 9^{3}SD, 8^{5}HY, 8^{4}S, 10^{4}GS, 11^{0}S, 8^{2}HY

	Starts	1st	2nd	3rd	Win & Pl
Career Total (Turf)	34	2	6	3	20787
Career Total (AW)	7	0	0	1	251

74	7/98	Sand	1m14y	E	G-F	£2866
90	10/96	Asct	7f	C	GD	£8754

Total win prize-money £11620

Going (Turf): Sf: 0-10 GS: 0-5 **Gd: 1-10 GF: 1-9** Fm: 0-0
Distance: 5f/6f: 0-5 7f-8f: 1-15 9f-13f: 1-21 14f+: 0-0
Track : LH: 0-22 **RH: 1-5** Tight: 0-11 Gall: 0-6
Aids: Bl: 0-4 Vi: 0-1 Tstrap: 0-0
Best Rating: 49 4/01 Pont 1m4y soft

Has plenty of ability, but is by no means consistent. His best form is on fast ground.

Texannie

89(82) (22)**36**

4-y-o b f Inchinor-Texanne (BEL) (Efisio)
S C Williams Stuart C Williams

Placings:00000-**0**00000 **(2188)**
2001: 8^{0}SD, 8^{0}SW, 10^{0}HY, 8^{0}GS, 12^{0}GF, 14^{0}GF

	Starts	1st	2nd	3rd	Win & Pl
Career Total (Turf)	9	0	0	0	
Career Total (AW)	2	0	0	0	

Going (Turf): Sf: 0-2 GS: 0-2 Gd: 0-0 GF: 0-2 Fm: 0-0
Distance: 5f/6f: 0-0 7f-8f: 0-2 9f-13f: 0-5 14f+: 0-1
Track : LH: 0-5 RH: 0-1 Tight: 0-0 Gall: 0-1
Aids: Bl: 0-0 Vi: 0-0 Tstrap: 0-0
Best Rating: 60 6/01 NmkR 1m4f gd-fm

Texas Ranger

102 **51**

3-y-o b c Mtoto-Favorable Exchange (USA) (Exceller (USA))
J W Hills T Milsom, T Morning, J Hawkes

Placings:00303633 **(5531)**
2001: 10^{0}GF, 11^{0}GF, 10^{3}GF, 14^{0}G, 16^{3}GF, 12^{6}GS, 16^{3}HY, 16^{3}HY

	Starts	1st	2nd	3rd	Win & Pl
Career Total (Turf)	8	0	0	4	1644

Going (Turf): Sf: 0-2 GS: 0-1 Gd: 0-1 GF: 0-4 Fm: 0-0
Distance: 5f/6f: 0-0 7f-8f: 0-0 9f-13f: 0-4 14f+: 0-4
Track : LH: 0-5 RH: 0-2 Tight: 0-3 Gall: 0-3
Aids: Bl: 0-0 Vi: 0-0 Tstrap: 0-0
Best Rating: 51 10/01 Nott 2m9y heavy

He has made the frame a few times in modest events and looks a stayer, but was treated harshly by the Handicapper after finishing sixth in a Newmarket claimer in October.

Teyaar

104(112) (79)**62**

5-y-o b g Polar Falcon (USA)-Music In My Life (IRE) (Law Society (USA))
D Shaw Justin R Aaron

Placings:502002/**5**1011252**22**000-0332252300100000000**6** **(5612)**
2001: 5^{0}SD, 6^{3}SD, 5^{3}SW, 6^{2}SD, 6^{2}SW, 6^{5}SD, 5^{2}SD, 6^{3}S, 7^{0}HY, 6^{0}SD, 6^{1}G, 5^{0}G, 6^{0}G, 5^{0}GS, 5^{0}G, 6^{0}S, 6^{0}G, 6^{0}S, 5^{0}S, 6^{6}SD, 6^{6}SD

	Starts	1st	2nd	3rd	Win & Pl
Career Total (Turf)	22	1	4	1	16738
Career Total (AW)	17	3	5	2	16833

78	5/01	Haml	6f5y	C(0-90)H	GD	£8970
71	4/00	Wolv	6f	E(0-70)H	STD	£2870
65	3/00	Sthl	6f	E(0-70)	STD	£2716
65	2/00	Sthl	6f	D	STD	£2795

Total win prize-money £17351

Going (Turf): Sf: 0-7 GS: 0-2 **Gd: 1-9** GF: 0-4 Fm: 0-0
Distance: **5f/6f: 3-30** 7f-8f: 1-9 9f-13f: 0-0 14f+: 0-0
Track : **LH: 3-19** RH: 0-4 **Tight: 1-10** Gall: 0-2
Aids: Bl: 0-1 Vi: 0-0 Tstrap: 0-0
Best Rating: 79 3/01 Wolv 5f stand

Performs well on turf and the All-Weather but normally finds a few too good. Came good at Hamilton to score for the first time on turf in May but has been disappointing since. Best with cut in the ground.

Thaayer

(102) (67)**47**

6-y-o b g Wolfhound (USA)-Hamaya (USA) (Mr Prospector (USA))
I A Wood Mrs Joyce Wood

Placings:0600**635**/**1**2000**3014**/602-4006**5342152** **(5616)**
2001: 6^{4}SD, 6^{0}SW, 5^{0}SD, 6^{6}SD, 6^{5}GF, 6^{3}SD, 6^{4}SD, 6^{2}SD, 6^{1}SD, 6^{5}SD, 7^{2}SD, 6^{2}SD

	Starts	1st	2nd	3rd	Win & Pl
Career Total (Turf)	7	0	0	0	0
Career Total (AW)	23	3	4	3	11272

67	10/01	Sthl	6f	F(0-60)H	STD	£2464
63	12/99	Sthl	6f	E(0-75)H	SLW	£2374
61	1/99	Sthl	6f	F(0-60)	STD	£2274

Total win prize-money £7112

Going (Turf): Sf: 0-1 GS: 0-2 Gd: 0-0 GF: 0-3 Fm: 0-1
Distance: 5f/6f: 3-25 7f-8f: 0-5 9f-13f: 0-0 14f+: 0-0
Track : LH: 3-21 RH: 0-0 Tight: 0-9 Gall: 0-0
Aids: Bl: 0-1 Vi: 0-0 Tstrap: 0-0
Best Rating: 67 11/01 Wolv 7f stand

Fibresand handicapper, suited by six furlongs at Southwell. Best held up just off the pace.

Thanks Max (IRE)

103(82) (61)**69**

3-y-o b g Goldmark (USA)-Almost A Lady (IRE) (Entitled)
Miss L A Perratt T P Finch

Placings:05100-603364100 **(5273)**
2001: 8^{6}GF, 6^{0}GF, 5^{3}GS, 5^{3}GF, 6^{6}GF, 7^{4}GS, 6^{1}GF, 7^{0}GF, 5^{0}HY

	Starts	1st	2nd	3rd	Win & Pl
Career Total (Turf)	13	2	0	2	11817
Career Total (AW)	1	0	0	0	

69	7/01	Newc	6f	C(0-90)H	G-F	£7003
69	9/00	Haml	5f4y	E	SFT	£3094

Total win prize-money £10098

Going (Turf): Sf: 1-3 GS: 0-2 Gd: 0-0 **GF: 1-8** Fm: 0-0
Distance: 5f/6f: 2-7 7f-8f: 0-7 9f-13f: 0-0 14f+: 0-0
Track : LH: 0-4 RH: 0-2 Tight: 0-2 Gall: 0-0
Aids: Bl: 0-0 Vi: 0-0 Tstrap: 0-0
Best Rating: 69 7/01 Newc 6f gd-fm

He got off the mark on soft ground over the minimum trip at two, but then struggled until some leniency by the Handicapper enabled him to win over six furlongs on fast ground at Newcastle in July. Effective at five to seven furlongs, handles fast ground but goes well when there is cut.

Thaqib (IRE)

80 **69**

2-y-o b c Sadler's Wells (USA)-Temple (Shirley Heights)
J L Dunlop Hamdan Al Maktoum

Placings:0 **(5107)**
2001: 7^{0}GS

	Starts	1st	2nd	3rd	Win & Pl
Career Total (Turf)	1	0	0	0	

Going (Turf): Sf: 0-0 GS: 0-1 Gd: 0-0 GF: 0-0 Fm: 0-0
Distance: 5f/6f: 0-0 7f-8f: 0-1 9f-13f: 0-0 14f+: 0-0
Track : LH: 0-0 RH: 0-0 Tight: 0-0 Gall: 0-0
Aids: Bl: 0-0 Vi: 0-0 Tstrap: 0-0
Best Rating: 69 10/01 NmkR 7f gd-sft

Thari (USA)

112 **99**

4-y-o b/br g Silver Hawk (USA)-Magic Slipper (Habitat)
B Hanbury Hamdan Al Maktoum

Placings:2136/06310-42004 **(5338)**
2001: 10^{4}G, 11^{2}GF, 14^{0}GS, 12^{0}HY, 12^{4}GS

	Starts	1st	2nd	3rd	Win & Pl
Career Total (Turf)	14	2	2	2	27024

101	9/00	NmkR	1m6f	C(0-95)H	GD	£14046
79	9/99	Chep	7f16y	D	GD	£3176

Total win prize-money £17223

Going (Turf): Sf: 0-3 GS: 0-2 **Gd: 2-5** GF: 0-4 Fm: 0-0
Distance: 5f/6f: 0-0 7f-8f: 1-4 9f-13f: 0-7 14f+: 1-3
Track : LH: 0-4 **RH: 1-5** Tight: 0-2 **Gall: 1-8**
Aids: Bl: 0-1 Vi: 0-0 Tstrap: 0-0
Best Rating: 99 10/01 NmkR 1m4f gd-sft

He proved a shade disappointing after winning his maiden in 1999 and did not prove easy to place, but returned to winning form when stepped up to 14 furlongs for the first time at Newmarket in 2000. Showed promise over inadequate trips on his belated return in 2001, but struggled on soft ground. Acts on a sound surface.

That Man Again

107(103) (73)**71**

9-y-o ch g Prince Sabo-Milne's Way (The Noble Player (USA))
S C Williams J T Duffy & R E Duffy

Placings:04031620124/**5**64553111403/400406000/440 2260305**605**/**33**0001400140/06261146660/0000100430 0531**332**-050016103000 **(4285)**
2001: 5^{0}GS, 5^{5}GS, 5^{0}GF, 5^{0}G, 5^{1}GS, 5^{6}GF, 5^{1}GF, 5^{0}GS, 5^{3}GF, 5^{0}GF, 5^{0}GF, 5^{0}G

	Starts	1st	2nd	3rd	Win & Pl
Career Total (Turf)	88	13	5	7	96025
Career Total (AW)	9	0	1	4	3020

70	7/01	Sand	5f6y	C(0-95)H	G-F	£11115
66	6/01	Sals	5f	D(0-85)H	G-S	£7312
57	9/00	Sand	5f6y	E	G-F	£2951
73	6/00	Sals	5f	D(0-85)H	G-F	£7475
79	7/99	NmkJ	5f	D(0-85)H	GD	£5231
69	7/99	Sand	5f6y	C(0-95)H	GD	£7035
65	8/98	Ling	5f	E	G-F	£3080
77	6/98	Folk	5f	D(0-80)H	G-F	£3557
96	8/95	Hayd	5f	C(0-100)H	G-F	£10755
92	7/95	Bath	5f11y	C(0-90)H	FRM	£5609
88	7/95	Sand	5f6y	C(0-95)H	G-F	£5784
84	10/94	Catt	5f	D(0-85)	G-F	£3987
69	8/94	Brig	5f59y	E	FRM	£2924

Total win prize-money £76819

Going (Turf): Sf: 0-5 GS: 1-11 Gd: 2-26 **GF: 8-39** Fm: 2-7
Distance: 5f/6f: 13-97 7f-8f: 0-0 9f-13f: 0-0 14f+: 0-0
Track : LH: 2-21 RH: 0-5 Tight: 0-10 **Gall: 1-11**
Aids: Bl: 12-70 Vi: 0-1 Tstrap: 0-0
Best Rating: 70 7/01 Sand 5f6y gd-fm

In fine form in the summer of 2000, he returned to winning ways at Salisbury in June 2001, and won over the same trip at Sandown in July (after breaking by far the best). Five furlongs and fast ground are his ideal conditions. He has only once finished out of the first four in ten starts at Sandown.

That's Jazz

105(93) (52)**66**

3-y-o b f Cool Jazz-Miss Mercy (IRE) (Law Society (USA))
M L W Bell Billy Maguire

Placings:0220-**222**403410004 **(4898)**
2001: 8^{2}SW, 7^{2}SD, 7^{2}SD, 6^{4}SD, 7^{0}S, 7^{3}GF, 7^{4}G, 6^{1}GF, 6^{0}GF, 6^{0}GF, 6^{0}GF, 5^{4}GS

	Starts	1st	2nd	3rd	Win & Pl
Career Total (Turf)	12	1	2	1	6510
Career Total (AW)	4	0	3	0	2282

66	7/01	Chep	6f16y	E(0-70)H	G-F	£2877

Total win prize-money £2877

Going (Turf): Sf: 0-2 GS: 0-1 Gd: 0-3 **GF: 1-6** Fm: 0-0
Distance: 5f/6f: 0-8 **7f-8f: 1-8** 9f-13f: 0-0 14f+: 0-0
Track : LH: 0-4 RH: 0-1 Tight: 0-3 Gall: 0-1
Aids: Bl: 0-0 Vi: 0-0 Tstrap: 0-0
Best Rating: 66 7/01 Chep 6f16y gd-fm

Had been runner-up on several occasions on turf and All-Weather before getting off the mark on fast ground when dropping back in trip. Favoured by being held up.

Thatcham (IRE)

96(101) (47)**61**
5-y-o ch g Thatching-Calaloo Sioux (USA) (Our Native (USA))
Mrs Lydia Pearce A J Thompson

Placings:054000/**320041234006P**-6P **(2730)**
2001: 6^{6}GF, 6^{P}GF

	Starts	1st	2nd	3rd	Win & Pl
Career Total (Turf)	13	1	1	1	5288
Career Total (AW)	8	0	1	1	1118

56	6/00	Yarm	6f3y	E(0-70)H	G-F	£2938

Total win prize-money £2938

Going (Turf): Sf: 0-1 GS: 0-2 Gd: 0-4 **GF: 1-6** Fm: 0-0
Distance: 5f/6f: 0-2 **7f-8f: 1-14** 9f-13f: 0-5 14f+: 0-0
Track : LH: 0-9 RH: 0-3 Tight: 0-6 Gall: 0-2
Aids: **Bl: 1-6** Vi: 0-2 Tstrap: 0-0
Best Rating: 45 6/01 Yarm 6f3y gd-fm

Thatched (IRE)

101 **42**
11-y-o b g Thatching-Shadia (USA) (Naskra (USA))
R E Barr R E Barr

Placings:640066066/622331553160450/613665314441 20045/006353315324100010/0100440045400004 0/016 05022000/500330246/506056302400-006644600060 **(4450)**
2001: 9^{0}F, 8^{0}G, 7^{6}GF, 9^{6}F, 8^{4}GF, 9^{4}F, 10^{6}GF, 8^{0}GF, 8^{0}GS, 11^{0}GF, 8^{6}GF, 8^{0}GF

	Starts	1st	2nd	3rd	Win & Pl
Career Total (Turf)	118	10	8	12	54607
Career Total (AW)	2	0	0	0	

44	5/98	Rdcr	1m1f	F(0-70)H	G-F	£3183
56	4/97	Carl	7f214y	D(0-85)H	FRM	£3551
52	10/96	Rdcr	1m	D(0-75)H	G-F	£3951
43	9/96	Bevl	1m100y	F(0-65)H	G-F	£3210
46	7/96	Bevl	7f100y	E(0-70)H	G-F	£3522
64	8/95	Carl	7f214y	D(0-80)H	HRD	£3606
51	7/95	Muss	1m16y	D(0-80)H	G-F	£5602
44	4/95	Newc	1m	F(0-70)H	G-F	£2620
47	7/94	Rdcr	1m	E(0-70)H	G-F	£3322
38	6/94	Muss	1m16y	F(0-60)H	G-F	£2885

Total win prize-money £35452

Going (Turf): Sf: 0-2 GS: 0-7 Gd: 0-26 **GF: 8-56** Fm: 2-27
Distance: 5f/6f: 0-0 **7f-8f: 6-70** 9f-13f: 4-50 14f+: 0-0
Track : LH: 2-39 **RH: 6-62 Tight: 3-48** Gall: 1-12
Aids: Bl: 0-3 Vi: 0-9 Tstrap: 0-0
Best Rating: 42 7/01 Newc 1m2f32y gd-fm

Veteran mile handicapper, has not won since 1998.

Thatched Cottage

49
3-y-o b f Thatching-Attaproffitt (Batshoof)
B Palling Merthyr Motor Auctions

Placings:6-0 **(3564)**
2001: 8^{0}GF

	Starts	1st	2nd	3rd	Win & Pl
Career Total (Turf)	2	0	0	0	0

Going (Turf): Sf: 0-0 GS: 0-0 Gd: 0-1 GF: 0-1 Fm: 0-0
Distance: 5f/6f: 0-1 7f-8f: 0-0 9f-13f: 0-1 14f+: 0-0
Track : LH: 0-1 RH: 0-0 Tight: 0-0 Gall: 0-1
Aids: Bl: 0-0 Vi: 0-0 Tstrap: 0-0
Best Rating: 20 8/01 Leic 1m9y gd-fm

Thatchmaster (IRE)

94 **37**
10-y-o b g Thatching-Key Maneuver (USA) (Key To Content (USA))
C A Horgan Mrs B Sumner

Placings:006/00400040/66221213/430140/5001515230 /0030144/00200-00400 **(3678)**
2001: 10^{0}GF, 12^{0}GF, 10^{4}GF, 11^{0}GF, 11^{0}G

	Starts	1st	2nd	3rd	Win & Pl
Career Total (Turf)	52	6	5	4	31025

65	8/99	Gdwd	1m1f	E(0-85)H	GD	£3663
67	7/98	Wind	1m3f135y	E(0-70)H	G-F	£2981
62	6/98	Wind	1m3f135y	D(0-75)H	GD	£3571
67	8/97	Gdwd	1m2f	E(0-70)H	G-F	£4142
58	8/96	Gdwd	1m2f	E(0-70)H	GD	£4370
51	7/96	Sand	1m14y	E(0-60)H	G-F	£4005

Total win prize-money £22734

Going (Turf): Sf: 0-5 GS: 0-1 **Gd: 3-18 GF: 3-26** Fm: 0-2
Distance: 5f/6f: 0-0 7f-8f: 0-14 **9f-13f: 6-37** 14f+: 0-1
Track : LH: 0-8 **RH: 4-32 Tight: 5-22** Gall: 0-6
Aids: Bl: 0-0 Vi: 0-1 **Tstrap: 1-16**
Best Rating: 45 6/01 Newb 1m2f6y gd-fm

A fine old servant to the game, who goes particularly well in the Autumn and on right-handed tracks.

Thats All Jazz

105 **53**
3-y-o b f Prince Sabo-Gate Of Heaven (Starry Night (USA))
I A Wood (R C Spicer 26/5) John Purcell

Placings:00600-006001204010 **(5129)**
2001: 8^{0}HY, 5^{0}GF, 5^{6}GF, 6^{0}GF, 5^{0}GF, 7^{1}G, 7^{2}GF, 8^{0}S, 6^{4}GF, 7^{0}S, 5^{1}S, 7^{0}HY

	Starts	1st	2nd	3rd	Win & Pl
Career Total (Turf)	17	2	1	0	6998

53	9/01	Brig	5f213y	E(0-75)H	SFT	£2985
39	7/01	Chep	7f16y	E(0-70)H	GD	£3164

Total win prize-money £6150

Going (Turf): Sf: 1-6 GS: 0-0 **Gd: 1-4** GF: 0-7 Fm: 0-0
Distance: 5f/6f: 1-11 7f-8f: 1-4 9f-13f: 0-2 14f+: 0-0
Track : **LH: 1-6** RH: 0-0 Tight: 0-1 Gall: 0-1
Aids: Bl: 0-0 Vi: 0-2 Tstrap: 0-0
Best Rating: 53 9/01 Brig 5f213y soft

Effective at six or seven furlongs in easy ground.

The Bargate Fox

(97) (55)**51**
5-y-o b g Magic Ring (IRE)-Hithermoor Lass (Red Alert)
R Brotherton The Joiners Arms Racing Club Quarndon

Placings:00051041/3403000300-00 **(1076)**
2001: 11^{0}SD, 11^{0}GS

	Starts	1st	2nd	3rd	Win & Pl
Career Total (Turf)	7	0	0	1	453
Career Total (AW)	13	2	0	2	4766

54	12/99	Wolv	1m100y	F(0-60)H	STD	£1976
50	11/99	Wolv	1m1f79y	F(0-65)H	STD	£1945

Total win prize-money £3922

Going (Turf): Sf: 0-1 GS: 0-1 Gd: 0-3 GF: 0-2 Fm: 0-0
Distance: 5f/6f: 0-0 7f-8f: 0-7 **9f-13f: 2-13** 14f+: 0-0
Track : **LH: 2-18** RH: 0-1 **Tight: 2-9** Gall: 0-0
Aids: Bl: 0-0 Vi: 0-0 Tstrap: 0-1
Best Rating: 50 11/99 Wolv 1m1f79y SD

The Best Yet

(90) (63)
3-y-o ch c King's Signet (USA)-Miss Klew (Never So Bold)
A G Newcombe Wetherby Racing Bureau 45

Placings:564-00 **(5619)**
2001: 8^{0}SD, 6^{0}SD

	Starts	1st	2nd	3rd	Win & Pl
Career Total (Turf)	0	0	0	0	
Career Total (AW)	5	0	0	0	0

Going (Turf): Sf: 0-0 GS: 0-0 Gd: 0-0 GF: 0-0 Fm: 0-0
Distance: 5f/6f: 0-2 7f-8f: 0-2 9f-13f: 0-1 14f+: 0-0
Track : LH: 0-5 RH: 0-0 Tight: 0-4 Gall: 0-0
Aids: Bl: 0-0 Vi: 0-0 Tstrap: 0-0
Best Rating: 6 9/01 Wolv 1m100y stand

The Bolter

92 **66**
2-y-o b g Puissance-Miami Dolphin (Derrylin)
D Moffatt J W Barrett

Placings:00003200 **(4990)**
2001: 5^{0}S, 5^{0}GF, 5^{0}G, 6^{0}GF, 5^{3}GF, 5^{2}GS, 5^{0}G, 6^{0}HY

	Starts	1st	2nd	3rd	Win & Pl
Career Total (Turf)	8	0	1	1	1272

Going (Turf): Sf: 0-2 GS: 0-1 Gd: 0-2 GF: 0-3 Fm: 0-0
Distance: 5f/6f: 0-7 7f-8f: 0-1 9f-13f: 0-0 14f+: 0-0
Track : LH: 0-0 RH: 0-0 Tight: 0-0 Gall: 0-0
Aids: Bl: 0-0 Vi: 0-0 Tstrap: 0-0
Best Rating: 66 8/01 Hayd 5f gd-sft

The Broker (IRE)

(83) (30)**47**
3-y-o br g Rainbows For Life (CAN)-Roberts Pride (Roberto (USA))
M Blanshard Mrs C J Ward

Placings:0-5 **(0690)**
2001: 11^{5}SD

	Starts	1st	2nd	3rd	Win & Pl
Career Total (Turf)	1	0	0	0	
Career Total (AW)	1	0	0	0	0

Going (Turf): Sf: 0-0 GS: 0-1 Gd: 0-0 GF: 0-0 Fm: 0-0
Distance: 5f/6f: 0-0 7f-8f: 0-0 9f-13f: 0-2 14f+: 0-0
Track : LH: 0-1 RH: 0-0 Tight: 0-0 Gall: 0-0
Aids: Bl: 0-0 Vi: 0-0 Tstrap: 0-0
Best Rating: 30 4/01 Sthl 1m3f stand

The Bull Macabe

39(100) (64)**64**
4-y-o ch c Efisio-Tranquillity (Night Shift (USA))
Andrew Reid A S Reid

Placings:6013/200-44300 **(5451)**
2001: 5^{4}SD, 5^{4}SD, 5^{3}SD, 5^{0}SW, 5^{0}HY, 6^{6}SD

	Starts	1st	2nd	3rd	Win & Pl
Career Total (Turf)	4	1	0	0	4240
Career Total (AW)	8	0	1	2	1814

73	10/99	Nott	5f13y	D	GD	£4240

Total win prize-money £4240

Going (Turf): Sf: 0-1 GS: 0-1 **Gd: 1-2** GF: 0-0 Fm: 0-0
Distance: **5f/6f: 1-9** 7f-8f: 0-3 9f-13f: 0-0 14f+: 0-0
Track : LH: 0-8 RH: 0-0 Tight: 0-7 Gall: 0-1
Aids: Bl: 0-0 Vi: 0-0 Tstrap: 0-5
Best Rating: 64 1/01 Sthl 5f stand

The Butterwick Kid

107(109) (74)**69**
8-y-o ch g Interrex (CAN)-Ville Air (Town Crier)
R A Fahey Mr Robert Chambers & Mrs M W Kenyon

Placings:2100/0004503140/121126004/1333130/120/0460-21300 **(1993)**
2001: 12^{2}GS, 14^{1}SD, 12^{3}SW, 12^{0}S, 12^{0}SD

	Starts	1st	2nd	3rd	Win & Pl
Career Total (Turf)	38	7	5	5	41224
Career Total (AW)	4	2	0	1	7262

74	4/01	Sthl	1m6f	D(0-85)H	STD	£3883
72	3/99	Haml	1m3f16y	D(0-80)H	HVY	£6872
66	5/98	Rdcr	1m6f19y	E(0-70)H	G-F	£2862
60	1/98	Sthl	1m3f	E(0-70)H	STD	£2788
57	5/97	Muss	1m4f	F(0-65)H	G-S	£2827
59	5/97	Ches	1m4f66y	D(0-80)H	HVY	£7340
49	4/97	Nott	1m6f15y	D(0-80)H	G-F	£3900
45	9/96	Haml	1m4f17y	E(0-70)H	GD	£3317
69	7/95	Bevl	5f	F	GD	£2838

Total win prize-money £36632

Going (Turf): Sf: 2-9 GS: 1-6 **Gd: 2-11 GF: 2-8** Fm: 0-4
Distance: 5f/6f: 1-6 7f-8f: 0-4 **9f-13f: 5-14** 14f+: 3-18
Track : **LH: 5-22** RH: 3-14 **Tight: 5-18** Gall: 0-4
Aids: Bl: 0-3 **Vi: 1-4** Tstrap: 0-0
Best Rating: 74 4/01 Sthl 1m6f stand

Mixing Flat racing with jumping in recent seasons, he last won on turf in 1999. He was just touched off at Doncaster on the first day of the 2001 season, wearing blinkers for the first time for two years. He loves Hamilton and testing ground

The Bystander (IRE)

103 **93?**

3-y-o b f Bin Ajwaad (IRE)-Dilwara (IRE) (Lashkari)
N P Littmoden Mrs D E Sharp

Placings:012-5006 **(4487)**
2001: 7^{5}GS, 10^{0}G, 10^{0}F, 7^{6}S

	Starts	1st	2nd	3rd	Win & Pl
Career Total (Turf)	7	1	1	0	15998

76	10/00	York	7f202y	E	SFT	£7400

Total win prize-money £7400

Going (Turf): Sf: 1-3 GS: 0-1 Gd: 0-2 GF: 0-0 Fm: 0-1
Distance: 5f/6f: 0-1 **7f-8f: 1-3** 9f-13f: 0-3 14f+: 0-0
Track : **LH: 1-3** RH: 0-0 Tight: 0-0 **Gall: 1-2**
Aids: Bl: 0-0 Vi: 0-0 Tstrap: 0-0
Best Rating: 93 4/01 NmkR 7f gd-sft

She showed useful form in her early starts at two, but has found life tough so far this season and evidence suggests she does not stay ten furlongs.

The Castigator

89(58) **13**

4-y-o b g Reprimand-Summer Eve (Hotfoot)
R Bastiman Peter Julian

Placings:004/60000000050000-**000**00000000000066000000000000000 **(5625)**
2001: **8**^{0}SW, **10**^{0}SW, **12**^{0}SD, 12^{0}S, 5^{0}S, 10^{0}HY, 6^{0}HY, 7^{0}G, 7^{0}F, 7^{0}F, 7^{0}G, 10^{0}GF, 7^{0}GF, 10^{6}GF, 12^{6}GF, 12^{0}F, 6^{0}GF, 8^{0}F, 6^{0}GF, 9^{0}GF, 8^{0}GF, 9^{0}GF, 8^{0}F, 6^{0}S, 7^{0}G, 11^{0}S, 7^{0}HY, 8^{0}GS

	Starts	1st	2nd	3rd	Win & Pl
Career Total (Turf)	42	0	0	0	444
Career Total (AW)	3	0	0	0	

Going (Turf): Sf: 0-14 GS: 0-3 Gd: 0-6 GF: 0-12 Fm: 0-7
Distance: 5f/6f: 0-5 7f-8f: 0-20 9f-13f: 0-19 14f+: 0-1
Track : LH: 0-23 RH: 0-6 Tight: 0-11 Gall: 0-8
Aids: Bl: 0-1 Vi: 0-0 Tstrap: 0-0
Best Rating: 35 5/01 NmkR 7f good

Moderate maiden who has been tried over a variety of distances, and has earnt his keep in 'appearance money' races.

The Chaplain (IRE)

93 **57**

2-y-o ch c College Chapel-Danzig Craft (IRE) (Roi Danzig (USA))
R Hannon J C Smith

Placings:366040 **(4730)**
2001: 5^{3}GF, 5^{6}G, 6^{6}GS, 5^{0}G, 5^{4}GF, 5^{0}F

	Starts	1st	2nd	3rd	Win & Pl
Career Total (Turf)	6	0	0	1	903

Going (Turf): Sf: 0-0 GS: 0-1 Gd: 0-2 GF: 0-2 Fm: 0-1
Distance: 5f/6f: 0-6 7f-8f: 0-0 9f-13f: 0-0 14f+: 0-0
Track : LH: 0-0 RH: 0-1 Tight: 0-0 Gall: 0-1
Aids: Bl: 0-0 Vi: 0-0 Tstrap: 0-0
Best Rating: 77 6/01 Wind 5f10y gd-fm

The Chocolatier (IRE)

101(93) (67)**70**

3-y-o b f Inzar (USA)-Clover Honey (King Of Clubs)
P L Gilligan Treasure Seekers 2000

Placings:6505-0412040414 **(5591)**
2001: 8^{0}F, 8^{4}GF, 8^{1}GF, 7^{2}GF, 8^{0}GF, 8^{4}GF, 9^{0}G, 8^{4}G, 9^{1}GS, 9^{4}GS, **10**^{0}SD

	Starts	1st	2nd	3rd	Win & Pl
Career Total (Turf)	13	2	1	0	8824
Career Total (AW)	1	0	0	0	0

68	10/01	Sals	1m1f198y	E(0-70)H	G-S	£3209
68	7/01	Sals	1m	E(0-70)H	G-F	£3262

Total win prize-money £6472

Going (Turf): Sf: 0-0 **GS: 1-2** Gd: 0-4 **GF: 1-6** Fm: 0-1
Distance: 5f/6f: 0-2 7f-8f: 1-8 9f-13f: 1-4 14f+: 0-0
Track : LH: 0-5 **RH: 1-1 Tight: 1-1** Gall: 0-2
Aids: Bl: 0-0 Vi: 0-0 Tstrap: 0-0
Best Rating: 70 11/01 Brig 1m1f209y gd-sft

Fair handicapper, won an apprentice handicap over a mile at Salisbury in July 2001, and followed up with another success at the same track in October under the same rider. Stays ten furlongs, suited by fast ground but handles cut.

The Come Back Kid

80 **11**

4-y-o b g Shareef Dancer (USA)-Clockwatch (USA) (Alleged (USA))
B Ellison B Batey

Placings:006/0500 **(4009)**
2001: 8^{0}SD, 8^{5}F, 8^{0}F, 11^{0}G

	Starts	1st	2nd	3rd	Win & Pl
Career Total (Turf)	6	0	0	0	0
Career Total (AW)	1	0	0	0	

Going (Turf): Sf: 0-1 GS: 0-2 Gd: 0-1 GF: 0-0 Fm: 0-2
Distance: 5f/6f: 0-0 7f-8f: 0-5 9f-13f: 0-2 14f+: 0-0
Track : LH: 0-3 RH: 0-0 Tight: 0-1 Gall: 0-1
Aids: Bl: 0-0 Vi: 0-0 Tstrap: 0-1
Best Rating: 30 6/01 Newc 1m firm

The Cottonwool Kid

(99) (28)

9-y-o b g Blakeney-Relatively Smart (Great Nephew)
Mrs Merrita Jones Stephen Appelbee

Placings:3000/00530/0/0/**06**000000/1323-06 **(0345)**
2001: 16^{0}SW, 16^{6}SD

	Starts	1st	2nd	3rd	Win & Pl
Career Total (Turf)	11	0	0	1	319
Career Total (AW)	14	1	1	3	2859

31	2/00	Wolv	2m46y	G(0-60)H	STD	£1527

Total win prize-money £1527

Going (Turf): Sf: 0-1 GS: 0-1 Gd: 0-3 GF: 0-4 Fm: 0-2
Distance: 5f/6f: 0-2 7f-8f: 0-3 9f-13f: 0-8 **14f+: 1-12**
Track : **LH: 1-19** RH: 0-5 **Tight: 1-14** Gall: 0-1
Aids: **Bl: 1-6** Vi: 0-6 Tstrap: 0-0
Best Rating: 11 2/01 Wolv 2m46y stand

The Count (FR)

88 **67**

2-y-o b g Sillery (USA)-Dear Countess (FR) (Fabulous Dancer (USA))
Mrs J R Ramsden Swisspartners

Placings:6 **(2782)**
2001: 5^{6}GF

	Starts	1st	2nd	3rd	Win & Pl
Career Total (Turf)	1	0	0	0	0

Going (Turf): Sf: 0-0 GS: 0-0 Gd: 0-0 GF: 0-1 Fm: 0-0
Distance: 5f/6f: 0-1 7f-8f: 0-0 9f-13f: 0-0 14f+: 0-0
Track : LH: 0-0 RH: 0-0 Tight: 0-0 Gall: 0-0
Aids: Bl: 0-0 Vi: 0-0 Tstrap: 0-0
Best Rating: 67 7/01 Bevl 5f gd-fm

The Dark Lady

(80) (24)**38**

3-y-o b f Definite Article-Nuthatch (IRE) (Thatching)
M D I Usher P Sweeting

Placings:000-**000** **(0422)**
2001: 7^{0}SW, **6**^{0}SW, 7^{0}SD

	Starts	1st	2nd	3rd	Win & Pl
Career Total (Turf)	2	0	0	0	
Career Total (AW)	4	0	0	0	

Going (Turf): Sf: 0-1 GS: 0-1 Gd: 0-0 GF: 0-0 Fm: 0-0
Distance: 5f/6f: 0-4 7f-8f: 0-2 9f-13f: 0-0 14f+: 0-0
Track : LH: 0-6 RH: 0-0 Tight: 0-4 Gall: 0-2
Aids: Bl: 0-0 Vi: 0-0 Tstrap: 0-0
Best Rating: 24 2/01 Ling 7f slow

The Doctor (IRE)

(61) **59**

3-y-o b c Dr Devious (IRE)-Night Spell (IRE) (Fairy King (USA))
P F I Cole Alessandro Gaucci

Placings:000-0 **(0797)**
2001: 12^{0}SD

	Starts	1st	2nd	3rd	Win & Pl
Career Total (Turf)	3	0	0	0	
Career Total (AW)	1	0	0	0	

Going (Turf): Sf: 0-2 GS: 0-1 Gd: 0-0 GF: 0-0 Fm: 0-0
Distance: 5f/6f: 0-0 7f-8f: 0-2 9f-13f: 0-2 14f+: 0-0
Track : LH: 0-2 RH: 0-0 Tight: 0-1 Gall: 0-0
Aids: Bl: 0-0 Vi: 0-0 Tstrap: 0-0

The Dolphin (IRE)

90 **45**

2-y-o b f Dolphin Street (FR)-Saintly Guest (What A Guest)
J G Portman Edward Benson

Placings:05 **(4287)**
2001: 6^{0}F, 8^{5}GF

	Starts	1st	2nd	3rd	Win & Pl
Career Total (Turf)	2	0	0	0	0

Going (Turf): Sf: 0-0 GS: 0-0 Gd: 0-0 GF: 0-1 Fm: 0-1
Distance: 5f/6f: 0-0 7f-8f: 0-1 9f-13f: 0-1 14f+: 0-0
Track : LH: 0-0 RH: 0-0 Tight: 0-0 Gall: 0-0
Aids: Bl: 0-0 Vi: 0-0 Tstrap: 0-0
Best Rating: 45 8/01 Chep 1m14y gd-fm

The Fairy Flag (IRE)

103(96) (41)**54**

3-y-o ch f Inchinor-Good Reference (IRE) (Reference Point)
A Bailey (J Hetherton 15/10) Sandybrow Stables Ltd

Placings:05**60**-01554053002203**1**3 **(5532)**
2001: 9^{0}GS, 8^{1}F, 8^{5}GF, 8^{5}GS, 9^{4}GF, 9^{0}GF, 11^{5}GS, 9^{3}G, 12^{0}S, 10^{0}G, 11^{2}G, 10^{2}GF, 10^{0}G, **11**^{3}SD, 10^{1}HY, 9^{3}HY

	Starts	1st	2nd	3rd	Win & Pl

	Starts	1st	2nd	3rd	Win & Pl
Career Total (Turf)	17	2	2	2	8808
Career Total (AW)	3	0	0	1	335

50 10/01 Ayr 1m2f192yE HVY £3038
50 5/01 Leic 1m9y F FRM £2502
Total win prize-money £5541

Going (Turf): Sf: 1-3 GS: 0-4 Gd: 0-4 GF: 0-5 **Fm: 1-1**
Distance: 5f/6f: 0-1 7f-8f: 0-3 **9f-13f: 2-16** 14f+: 0-0
Track : **LH: 1-11** RH: 0-7 Tight: 0-10 Gall: 0-0
Aids: Bl: 0-0 Vi: 0-0 Tstrap: 0-0
Best Rating: 56 6/01 Haml 1m65y gd-sft

Scored on fast ground over a mile at Leicester in May and on heavy ground over ten furlongs at Ayr in October where she was subsequently claimed by Alan Bailey for £5,000. Suited by middle distances.

The Fancy Man (IRE)

85 **30**
3-y-o ch g Definite Article-Fanciful (IRE) (Mujtahid (USA))
N Tinkler W F Burton

Placings:4060100-00000 **(5269)**
2001: 10^{0}F, 11^{0}G, 8^{0}G, 10^{0}S, 10^{0}HY

	Starts	1st	2nd	3rd	Win & Pl
Career Total (Turf)	12	1	0	0	2836

62 9/00 Bevl 7f100y F(0-65) G-F £2492
Total win prize-money £2492

Going (Turf): Sf: 0-3 GS: 0-2 Gd: 0-4 **GF: 1-2** Fm: 0-1
Distance: 5f/6f: 0-3 **7f-8f: 1-2** 9f-13f: 0-7 14f+: 0-0
Track : LH: 0-4 **RH: 1-3** Tight: 0-2 Gall: 0-2
Aids: Bl: 0-1 **Vi: 1-6** Tstrap: 0-1
Best Rating: 30 9/01 Bevl 1m100y good

The Flyer (IRE)

70(89) **67**
4-y-o b g Blues Traveller (IRE)-National Ballet (Shareef Dancer (USA))
Miss S J Wilton John Pointon And Sons

Placings:6/602000-0 **(4945)**
2001: 10^{0}S

	Starts	1st	2nd	3rd	Win & Pl
Career Total (Turf)	7	0	1	0	705
Career Total (AW)	1	0	0	0	0

Going (Turf): Sf: 0-2 GS: 0-2 Gd: 0-0 GF: 0-1 Fm: 0-2
Distance: 5f/6f: 0-0 7f-8f: 0-1 9f-13f: 0-7 14f+: 0-0
Track : LH: 0-4 RH: 0-1 Tight: 0-2 Gall: 0-0
Aids: Bl: 0-1 Vi: 0-0 Tstrap: 0-0
Best Rating: 5 9/01 Ches 1m2f75y soft

The Frisky Farmer

(77) (16)
8-y-o b g Emarati (USA)-Farceuse (Comedy Star (USA))
Ian Williams The Four Musketeers

Placings:1220200/**6020**2512**0**3355**004**/**350304**4400451 6/**6620**3506**0400**/6 **(0171)**
2001: 12^{6}SD

	Starts	1st	2nd	3rd	Win & Pl
Career Total (Turf)	29	3	3	3	13183
Career Total (AW)	21	0	4	2	3059

58 8/97 Brig 5f213y G G-F £1984
67 3/96 Leic 5f218y G SFT £2238
62 4/95 Bevl 5f F G-F £2861
Total win prize-money £7084

Going (Turf): Sf: 1-2 GS: 0-3 Gd: 0-8 **GF: 2-13** Fm: 0-3
Distance: 5f/6f: 3-39 7f-8f: 0-10 9f-13f: 0-1 14f+: 0-0
Track : LH: 1-38 RH: 0-1 Tight: 0-22 Gall: 0-2
Aids: Bl: 0-1 Vi: 0-2 Tstrap: 0-0
Best Rating: 16 1/01 Sthl 1m4f stand

The Gaikwar (IRE)

84 **51**

2-y-o b c Indian Ridge-Broadmara (IRE) (Thatching)
Mrs A J Perrett John E Bodie

Placings:0 **(5604)**
2001: 7^{0}GS

	Starts	1st	2nd	3rd	Win & Pl
Career Total (Turf)	1	0	0	0	

Going (Turf): Sf: 0-0 GS: 0-1 Gd: 0-0 GF: 0-0 Fm: 0-0
Distance: 5f/6f: 0-0 7f-8f: 0-1 9f-13f: 0-0 14f+: 0-0
Track : LH: 0-0 RH: 0-0 Tight: 0-0 Gall: 0-0
Aids: Bl: 0-0 Vi: 0-0 Tstrap: 0-0
Best Rating: 51 11/01 NmkR 7f gd-sft

The Gay Fox

99(97) (60)**50**
7-y-o gr g Never So Bold-School Concert (Music Boy)
B G Powell (M Quinn 7/8) Mrs Rachel A Powell

Placings:3242500/64100410100402/301030665000000 25/040060354445050/53024100466-063030000062350500003 **(5592)**
2001: 6^{0}SD, 7^{6}SD, 6^{3}SD, 6^{0}S, 6^{3}SD, 7^{0}SD, 6^{0}GS, 5^{0}G, 6^{0}GF, 7^{6}F, 6^{2}GF, 6^{3}SD, 5^{5}HD, 6^{0}GF, 6^{5}SD, 6^{0}F, 7^{0}GF, 5^{0}GF, 5^{0}HY, 6^{3}GS

	Starts	1st	2nd	3rd	Win & Pl
Career Total (Turf)	77	5	6	6	59343
Career Total (AW)	7	0	0	3	1234

72 7/00 York 6f C(0-90)H GD £11895
90 4/98 Sand 5f6y C(0-90)H HVY £5836
83 7/97 Ches 5f16y C(0-95)H G-F £5894
76 6/97 NmkJ 5f D(0-85)H SFT £4503
70 5/97 Wwck 7f D(0-80)H FRM £4218
Total win prize-money £32347

Going (Turf): Sf: 2-17 GS: 0-16 Gd: 1-15 GF: 1-23 Fm: 1-6
Distance: 5f/6f: 4-69 7f-8f: 1-15 9f-13f: 0-0 14f+: 0-0
Track : LH: 2-23 RH: 0-0 **Tight: 1-12** Gall: 0-5
Aids: Bl: 1-20 Vi: 0-4 Tstrap: 1-34
Best Rating: 60 6/01 Haml 6f5y gd-fm

He is quite a useful sprint handicapper on his day, and his best performances in recent seasons have been with plenty of cut in the ground.

The Generals Lady (IRE)

71 **33**
3-y-o gr f General Monash (USA)-Brooks Masquerade (Absalom)
B S Rothwell Brian Rothwell

Placings:00-00 **(4236)**
2001: 6^{0}G, 5^{0}GF

	Starts	1st	2nd	3rd	Win & Pl
Career Total (Turf)	4	0	0	0	

Going (Turf): Sf: 0-0 GS: 0-0 Gd: 0-2 GF: 0-2 Fm: 0-0
Distance: 5f/6f: 0-3 7f-8f: 0-1 9f-13f: 0-0 14f+: 0-0
Track : LH: 0-0 RH: 0-0 Tight: 0-0 Gall: 0-0
Aids: Bl: 0-0 Vi: 0-0 Tstrap: 0-0
Best Rating: 15 5/01 Nott 6f15y good

The Girls' Filly

(96) (53)**51**
4-y-o b f Emperor Jones (USA)-Sioux City (Simply Great (FR))
Miss B Sanders T J Blake

Placings:3400/23000260-000 **(0224)**
2001: 10^{0}SD, 13^{0}SD, 13^{0}SD

	Starts	1st	2nd	3rd	Win & Pl
Career Total (Turf)	7	0	0	1	894
Career Total (AW)	8	0	2	1	2118

Going (Turf): Sf: 0-0 GS: 0-1 Gd: 0-0 GF: 0-5 Fm: 0-1
Distance: 5f/6f: 0-2 7f-8f: 0-4 9f-13f: 0-9 14f+: 0-0
Track : LH: 0-10 RH: 0-2 Tight: 0-9 Gall: 0-1
Aids: Bl: 0-1 Vi: 0-0 Tstrap: 0-1
Best Rating: 11 1/01 Ling 1m2f stand

The Glen

109 **88**
3-y-o gr c Mtoto-Silver Singer (Pharly (FR))
B W Hills John C Grant

Placings:0-05221026 **(4409)**
2001: 10^{0}GS, 10^{5}GF, 10^{2}G, 10^{2}GF, 10^{1}GS, 12^{0}GF, 11^{2}GF, 10^{6}GS

	Starts	1st	2nd	3rd	Win & Pl
Career Total (Turf)	9	1	3	0	10810

35 7/01 Ayr 1m2f D G-S £4010
Total win prize-money £4011

Going (Turf): Sf: 0-1 **GS: 1-3** Gd: 0-1 GF: 0-4 Fm: 0-0
Distance: 5f/6f: 0-0 7f-8f: 0-1 **9f-13f: 1-8** 14f+: 0-0
Track : LH: 1-6 RH: 0-1 Tight: 0-3 Gall: 0-3
Aids: Bl: 0-0 Vi: 0-0 Tstrap: 0-0
Best Rating: 103 5/01 Ches 1m2f75y gd-fm

A close fifth in the Listed Dee Stakes at Chester on his second start of this season, he was runner-up in a couple of maidens before winning one at odds of 1/25 at Ayr. Chased Shamaiel home over 11 furlongs at Ayr and should stay a mile and a half.

The Gooch (IRE)

2 y o br c Idris (IRE)-Malpractice (IRE) (Maledetto (IRE))
Miss Lucinda V Russell Peter J S Russell

Placings:0 **(5268)**
2001: 7^{0}HY

	Starts	1st	2nd	3rd	Win & Pl
Career Total (Turf)	1	0	0	0	

Going (Turf): Sf: 0-1 GS: 0-0 Gd: 0-0 GF: 0-0 Fm: 0-0
Distance: 5f/6f: 0-0 7f-8f: 0-1 9f-13f: 0-0 14f+: 0-0
Track : LH: 0-0 RH: 0-0 Tight: 0-0 Gall: 0-0
Aids: Bl: 0-0 Vi: 0-0 Tstrap: 0-0

The Green Grey

102(110) (88)**67**
7-y-o gr g Environment Friend-Pea Green (Try My Best (USA))
L Montague Hall J Daniels

Placings:600/5000021**060**/0011211**531**/**2200**/00610015 25431**110**-**6436**0000002400 **(4983)**
2001: 12^{6}SD, 12^{4}SD, 12^{3}SW, 10^{6}SW, 12^{0}SW, 10^{0}GS, 12^{0}GS, 10^{0}GF, 9^{0}G, 12^{0}GF, 12^{2}G, 14^{4}G, 12^{0}G, 12^{0}G

	Starts	1st	2nd	3rd	Win & Pl
Career Total (Turf)	41	7	4	1	34472
Career Total (AW)	16	4	2	2	23833

90 11/00 Ling 1m4f C(0-95)H STD £6672
79 10/00 Ling 1m4f D(0-80)H STD £7312
68 9/00 Ling 1m4f E(0-70) STD £3080
70 7/00 Wind 1m2f7y D(0-80)H G-F £4309
68 6/00 Wind 1m2f7y D(0-85)H G-F £4101
60 11/98 Ling 1m E(0-75)H STD £2502
70 9/98 Kemp 1m D(0-80)H GD £7490
68 9/98 Brig 7f214y F FRM £2368
61 8/98 Bath 1m5y F FRM £2444
49 8/98 Yarm 1m3y G(0-60)H G-F £2232
51 9/97 Bath 1m5y F(0-60)H G-F £2708
Total win prize-money £45223

Going (Turf): Sf: 0-0 GS: 0-6 Gd: 1-13 **GF: 4-18** Fm: 2-4
Distance: 5f/6f: 0-2 7f-8f: 3-14 **9f-13f: 8-39** 14f+: 0-2
Track : LH: 7-33 RH: 1-16 **Tight: 8-30** Gall: 0-6
Aids: Bl: 0-0 Vi: 0-1 Tstrap: 0-0
Best Rating: 88 1/01 Ling 1m4f stand

Much better on the All-Weather than he is on turf, he won five races in 2000, three over a mile and a half on sand, and two over ten furlongs on turf at Windsor. Signs of a return to form in the late summer. Needs fast ground on turf.

The Hunter (IRE)

93 **69**

2-y-o b c Grand Lodge (USA)-Ring Side (IRE) (Alzao (USA))

G C Bravery M I L Racing

Placings:0 (4864)

2001: 7^{0}GF

	Starts	1st	2nd	3rd	Win & Pl
Career Total (Turf)	1	0	0	0	

Going (Turf): Sf: 0-0 GS: 0-0 Gd: 0-0 GF: 0-1 Fm: 0-0
Distance: 5f/6f: 0-0 7f-8f: 0-1 9f-13f: 0-0 14f+: 0-0
Track : LH: 0-0 RH: 0-0 Tight: 0-0 Gall: 0-0
Aids: Bl: 0-0 Vi: 0-0 Tstrap: 0-0
Best Rating: 69 9/01 Newb 7f gd-fm

The Imposter (IRE)

(96) (40)**43**

6-y-o ch g Imp Society (USA)-Phoenix Dancer (IRE) (Gorytus (USA))

Miss S J Wilton John Pointon And Sons

Placings:634/506305620/142/100005000-0 (2341)

2001: 8^{0}SD

	Starts	1st	2nd	3rd	Win & Pl
Career Total (Turf)	9	0	0	1	260
Career Total (AW)	16	2	2	1	5749

63 3/00 Wolv 1m100y F(0-60) STD £2278
56 5/99 Wolv 1m100y G STD £1955
Total win prize-money £4235

Going (Turf): Sf: 0-1 GS: 0-2 Gd: 0-1 GF: 0-5 Fm: 0-0
Distance: 5f/6f: 0-2 7f-8f: 0-10 **9f-13f: 2-13** 14f+: 0-0
Track : **LH: 2-22** RH: 0-0 **Tight: 2-12** Gall: 0-0
Aids: Bl: 0-0 Vi: 0-1 Tstrap: 0-0
Best Rating: 56 5/99 Wolv 1m100y SD

Acts on Fibresand, with the extended mile at Wolverhampton looking his optimum conditions.

The Judge

102 **82**

3-y-o b c Polish Precedent (USA)-Just Speculation (IRE) (Ahonoora)

P F I Cole The Hon Mrs J M Corbett & Mr C Wright

Placings:0-313 (5265)

2001: 7^{3}GF, 9^{1}GF, 8^{3}GS

	Starts	1st	2nd	3rd	Win & Pl
Career Total (Turf)	4	1	0	2	6397

80 9/01 Haml 1m1f36y D G-F £3607
Total win prize-money £3608

Going (Turf): Sf: 0-1 GS: 0-1 Gd: 0-0 **GF: 1-2** Fm: 0-0
Distance: 5f/6f: 0-0 7f-8f: 0-2 **9f-13f: 1-2** 14f+: 0-0
Track : LH: 0-2 **RH: 1-1 Tight: 1-1** Gall: 0-1
Aids: Bl: 0-0 Vi: 0-0 Tstrap: 0-0
Best Rating: 82 10/01 York 1m205y gd-sft

Lightly-raced, showed the benefit of his first run in a year when scoring at Hamilton in September 2001. Has won on fast ground. Stays nine furlongs.

The Knapp

2-y-o b f Zamindar (USA)-Fernlea (USA) (Sir Ivor)

C Smith Anne Lady Scott

Placings:0P (1848)

2001: 5^{0}F, 5^{P}GF

	Starts	1st	2nd	3rd	Win & Pl
Career Total (Turf)	2	0	0	0	

Going (Turf): Sf: 0-0 GS: 0-0 Gd: 0-0 GF: 0-1 Fm: 0-1
Distance: 5f/6f: 0-2 7f-8f: 0-0 9f-13f: 0-0 14f+: 0-0
Track : LH: 0-0 RH: 0-0 Tight: 0-0 Gall: 0-0
Aids: Bl: 0-0 Vi: 0-0 Tstrap: 0-0

The Lady Would (IRE)

78 **46**

2-y-o ch f Woodborough (USA)-Kealbra Lady (Petong)

M Quinn The East Manton Partnership

Placings:0006 (3685)

2001: 5^{0}HD, 6^{0}GF, 5^{0}F, 5^{6}GF

	Starts	1st	2nd	3rd	Win & Pl
Career Total (Turf)	4	0	0	0	0

Going (Turf): Sf: 0-0 GS: 0-0 Gd: 0-0 GF: 0-2 Fm: 0-2
Distance: 5f/6f: 0-4 7f-8f: 0-0 9f-13f: 0-0 14f+: 0-0
Track : LH: 0-3 RH: 0-0 Tight: 0-0 Gall: 0-3
Aids: Bl: 0-0 Vi: 0-0 Tstrap: 0-0
Best Rating: 46 7/01 Ling 6f gd-fm

The Last Cast

93 **75**

2-y-o ch c Prince Of Birds (USA)-Atan's Gem (USA) (Sharpen Up)

C R Egerton D P Barrie

Placings:52 (5665)

2001: 7^{5}S, 6^{2}HY

	Starts	1st	2nd	3rd	Win & Pl
Career Total (Turf)	2	0	1	0	1155

Going (Turf): Sf: 0-2 GS: 0-0 Gd: 0-0 GF: 0-0 Fm: 0-0
Distance: 5f/6f: 0-1 7f-8f: 0-1 9f-13f: 0-0 14f+: 0-0
Track : LH: 0-0 RH: 0-0 Tight: 0-0 Gall: 0-0
Aids: Bl: 0-0 Vi: 0-0 Tstrap: 0-0
Best Rating: 75 11/01 Wind 6f heavy

Fair maiden who has shown promise on all runs to date, and is suited by six furlongs plus.

The Last Mohican

79 **55**

2-y-o b c Common Grounds-Arndilly (Robellino (USA))

P Howling Kentavr (uk) Ltd

Placings:00 (5290)

2001: 8^{0}GF, 7^{0}S

	Starts	1st	2nd	3rd	Win & Pl
Career Total (Turf)	2	0	0	0	

Going (Turf): Sf: 0-1 GS: 0-0 Gd: 0-0 GF: 0-1 Fm: 0-0
Distance: 5f/6f: 0-0 7f-8f: 0-2 9f-13f: 0-0 14f+: 0-0
Track : LH: 0-0 RH: 0-1 Tight: 0-0 Gall: 0-0
Aids: Bl: 0-0 Vi: 0-0 Tstrap: 0-0
Best Rating: 55 9/01 Kemp 1m gd-fm

The Last Word

89(103) (40)**37**

5-y-o b g Cosmonaut-Jolizal (Good Times (ITY))

R Hollinshead Pkr Partnership

Placings:00052/2135244032/606-502020362P (4606)

2001: 9^{5}SW, 11^{0}SW, 12^{2}SD, 12^{0}SD, 11^{2}SD, 14^{0}SD, 14^{3}SD, 12^{6}SD, 11^{2}F, 12^{P}SD

	Starts	1st	2nd	3rd	Win & Pl
Career Total (Turf)	4	0	1	0	674
Career Total (AW)	24	1	6	3	7543

52 2/99 Sthl 1m F(0-60)H STD £2295
Total win prize-money £2295

Going (Turf): Sf: 0-2 GS: 0-1 Gd: 0-0 GF: 0-0 Fm: 0-1
Distance: 5f/6f: 0-3 **7f-8f: 1-5** 9f-13f: 0-18 14f+: 0-2
Track : **LH: 1-27** RH: 0-0 Tight: 0-15 Gall: 0-1
Aids: Bl: 0-0 Vi: 0-0 Tstrap: 0-0
Best Rating: 40 1/01 Wolv 1m4f stand

The Leather Wedge (IRE)

97 **80**

2-y-o b c Hamas (IRE)-Wallflower (Polar Falcon (USA))

A Berry J L Young

Placings:22213000 (4623)

2001: 5^{2}GS, 5^{2}F, 5^{2}GF, 5^{1}GF, 5^{3}G, 5^{0}F, 5^{0}G, 5^{0}GF

	Starts	1st	2nd	3rd	Win & Pl
Career Total (Turf)	8	1	3	1	7406

76 7/01 Muss 5f E G-F £2912
Total win prize-money £2912

Going (Turf): Sf: 0-0 GS: 0-1 Gd: 0-2 **GF: 1-3** Fm: 0-2
Distance: **5f/6f: 1-8** 7f-8f: 0-0 9f-13f: 0-0 14f+: 0-0
Track : LH: 0-1 RH: 0-0 Tight: 0-1 Gall: 0-0
Aids: Bl: 0-0 Vi: 0-0 Tstrap: 0-0
Best Rating: 80 7/01 Ches 5f16y good

A close relative to top-class sprinter Pivotal. A beaten favourite on his first three starts, he finally got off the mark at Musselburgh in July over the minimum trip. Lost of early pace but is vulnerable to a fast-finisher. Acts on fast ground.

The Links

85(64) (19)**62**

2-y-o b g Mind Games-Zihuatanejo (Efisio)

D W Chapman (T D Easterby 7/9) David W Chapman

Placings:00000000 (5351)

2001: 6^{0}G, 6^{0}GF, 6^{0}G, 6^{0}G, 6^{0}G, 7^{0}HY, 6^{0}SD, 8^{0}SD

	Starts	1st	2nd	3rd	Win & Pl
Career Total (Turf)	6	0	0	0	
Career Total (AW)	2	0	0	0	

Going (Turf): Sf: 0-1 GS: 0-0 Gd: 0-4 GF: 0-1 Fm: 0-0
Distance: 5f/6f: 0-5 7f-8f: 0-3 9f-13f: 0-0 14f+: 0-0
Track : LH: 0-4 RH: 0-0 Tight: 0-1 Gall: 0-0
Aids: Bl: 0-3 Vi: 0-0 Tstrap: 0-1
Best Rating: 62 7/01 York 6f good

The Loose Screw (IRE)

95(71) (28)**45**

3-y-o b g Bigstone (IRE)-Princess Of Dance (IRE) (Dancing Dissident (USA))

J L Eyre Sykes Distribution Lad

Placings:6000-00630 (5287)

2001: 5^{0}GF, 5^{0}HY, 5^{6}G, 5^{3}GS, 6^{0}HY

	Starts	1st	2nd	3rd	Win & Pl
Career Total (Turf)	8	0	0	1	330
Career Total (AW)	1	0	0	0	

Going (Turf): Sf: 0-3 GS: 0-2 Gd: 0-1 GF: 0-1 Fm: 0-1
Distance: 5f/6f: 0-8 7f-8f: 0-1 9f-13f: 0-0 14f+: 0-0
Track : LH: 0-4 RH: 0-0 Tight: 0-2 Gall: 0-0
Aids: Bl: 0-0 Vi: 0-0 Tstrap: 0-0
Best Rating: 45 8/01 Pont 5f gd-fm

Not very flattered by his name and yet to show much on the track.

The Manx Touch (IRE)

(86) (34)**56?**

5-y-o gr m Petardia-Chapter And Verse (Dancer's Image (USA))

R Ford Nick Shutts

Placings:000/06544011/4 (0215)

2001: 11^{4}SD

	Starts	1st	2nd	3rd	Win & Pl
Career Total (Turf)	11	2	0	0	5296
Career Total (AW)	1	0	0	0	

56 10/99 Leic 7f9y G(0-60)H GD £2290
50 9/99 Bath 1m5y F(0-60)H G-S £2594
Total win prize-money £4884

Going (Turf): Sf: 0-1 GS: 1-4 Gd: 1-4 GF: 0-2 Fm: 0-0
Distance: 5f/6f: 0-1 7f-8f: 1-6 9f-13f: 1-5 14f+: 0-0
Track : LH: 1-6 RH: 0-1 Tight: 1-2 Gall: 0-0
Aids: Bl: 0-0 Vi: 0-0 Tstrap: 0-0
Best Rating: 34 2/01 Sthl 1m3f stand

The Merry Widow (IRE)

94(88) (23)37
3-y-o ch f Brief Truce (USA)-Classic Opera (Lomond (USA))
B S Rothwell Brian Rothwell

Placings:00000030-31000000400 (4266)
2001: 7^{3}SD, 7^{1}SD, 8^{0}SD, 8^{0}SD, 7^{0}SD, 6^{0}S, 8^{0}GF, 7^{0}GF, 6^{4}GF, 7^{0}SD, 7^{0}GF

	Starts	1st	2nd	3rd	Win & Pl
Career Total (Turf)	8	0	0	0	0
Career Total (AW)	11	1	0	2	2433

50 1/01 Sthl 7f G STD £1890
Total win prize-money £1890

Going (Turf): Sf: 0-1 GS: 0-0 Gd: 0-1 GF: 0-6 Fm: 0-0
Distance: 5f/6f: 0-4 7f-8f: 1-13 9f-13f: 0-2 14f+: 0-0
Track : LH: 1-15 RH: 0-2 Tight: 0-3 Gall: 0-0
Aids: Bl: 0-0 Vi: 1-12 Tstrap: 0-2
Best Rating: 50 1/01 Sthl 7f stand

Put to use on the All-Weather and the turf, she has not cut much ice in plating-class company and her best effort to date was winning a Southwell seller over seven furlongs. She often races in a visor and more recently a tongue-tie.

The Mog

78 (47)43
2-y-o b g Atraf-Safe Secret (Seclude (USA))
M R Channon Ross Jones

Placings:00600 (4178)
2001: 5^{0}GS, 5^{0}GF, 5^{6}F, 7^{0}G, 7^{0}GF, 6^{0}SD

	Starts	1st	2nd	3rd	Win & Pl
Career Total (Turf)	5	0	0	0	0

Going (Turf): Sf: 0-0 GS: 0-1 Gd: 0-1 GF: 0-2 Fm: 0-1
Distance: 5f/6f: 0-3 7f-8f: 0-2 9f-13f: 0-0 14f+: 0-0
Track : LH: 0-2 RH: 0-1 Tight: 0-0 Gall: 0-2
Aids: Bl: 0-0 Vi: 0-0 Tstrap: 0-0
Best Rating: 43 6/01 Pont 5f firm

The Names Bond

102 57
3-y-o b g Tragic Role (USA)-Artistic Licence (High Top)
Andrew Turnell Mrs Claire Hollowood

Placings:3140000-056354 (3044)
2001: 7^{0}S, 9^{5}S, 11^{6}GF, 11^{3}GF, 11^{5}GF, 9^{4}GF

	Starts	1st	2nd	3rd	Win & Pl
Career Total (Turf)	13	1	0	2	5659

70 5/00 Carl 5f D FRM £3737
Total win prize-money £3738

Going (Turf): Sf: 0-3 GS: 0-3 Gd: 0-0 GF: 0-5 Fm: 1-2
Distance: 5f/6f: 1-4 7f-8f: 0-3 9f-13f: 0-6 14f+: 0-0
Track : LH: 0-3 RH: 1-3 Tight: 0-4 Gall: 1-1
Aids: Bl: 0-0 Vi: 0-0 Tstrap: 0-0
Best Rating: 57 6/01 Bevl 1m3f216y gd-fm

Made all to win a fast-ground maiden at Carlisle as a juvenile, but has not progressed since.

The Nobleman (USA)

(95)
5-y-o b g Quiet American (USA)-Furajet (USA) (The Minstrel (CAN))
T J Etherington Mrs J E Todd

Placings:0/053300-400 (0356)
2001: 16^{4}SD, 11^{0}SW, 8^{0}SW

	Starts	1st	2nd	3rd	Win & Pl
Career Total (Turf)	2	0	0	0	
Career Total (AW)	8	0	0	2	537

Going (Turf): Sf: 0-0 GS: 0-0 Gd: 0-1 GF: 0-1 Fm: 0-0
Distance: 5f/6f: 0-0 7f-8f: 0-4 9f-13f: 0-5 14f+: 0-1
Track : LH: 0-8 RH: 0-0 Tight: 0-0 Gall: 0-0
Aids: Bl: 0-1 Vi: 0-0 Tstrap: 0-1
Best Rating: 18 2/01 Sthl 1m slow

The Old Soldier

100 52
3-y-o b g Magic Ring (IRE)-Grecian Belle (Ilium)
A Dickman A D Simmons

Placings:000-0043 (4601)
2001: 7^{0}F, 8^{0}GF, 6^{4}GF, 5^{3}GF

	Starts	1st	2nd	3rd	Win & Pl
Career Total (Turf)	7	0	0	1	503

Going (Turf): Sf: 0-1 GS: 0-1 Gd: 0-1 GF: 0-3 Fm: 0-1
Distance: 5f/6f: 0-3 7f-8f: 0-3 9f-13f: 0-1 14f+: 0-0
Track : LH: 0-3 RH: 0-0 Tight: 0-0 Gall: 0-2
Aids: Bl: 0-0 Vi: 0-0 Tstrap: 0-0
Best Rating: 48 9/01 Thsk 5f gd-fm

The President

100 45
6-y-o b g Yaheeb (USA)-When The Saints (Bay Express)
Mrs M Reveley North Racing Partnership

Placings:64650/0U40/033063 (4014)
2001: 11^{0}S, 13^{3}G, 16^{3}GF, 13^{0}GF, 16^{6}F, 15^{3}G

	Starts	1st	2nd	3rd	Win & Pl
Career Total (Turf)	15	0	0	3	2160

Going (Turf): Sf: 0-3 GS: 0-1 Gd: 0-5 GF: 0-3 Fm: 0-3
Distance: 5f/6f: 0-0 7f-8f: 0-0 9f-13f: 0-8 14f+: 0-7
Track : LH: 0-8 RH: 0-7 Tight: 0-13 Gall: 0-1
Aids: Bl: 0-0 Vi: 0-0 Tstrap: 0-1
Best Rating: 45 5/01 Ripn 2m gd-fm

The Priest

(92) (37)
4-y-o b g College Chapel-Pharazini (Pharly (FR))
J A Osborne The Woolfie And Tom Partnership

Placings:0-00654 (0981)
2001: 6^{0}SD, 6^{0}SD, 7^{6}SD, 6^{5}SD, 5^{4}SD

	Starts	1st	2nd	3rd	Win & Pl
Career Total (Turf)	1	0	0	0	
Career Total (AW)	5	0	0	0	0

Going (Turf): Sf: 0-1 GS: 0-0 Gd: 0-0 GF: 0-0 Fm: 0-0
Distance: 5f/6f: 0-5 7f-8f: 0-1 9f-13f: 0-0 14f+: 0-0
Track : LH: 0-5 RH: 0-0 Tight: 0-5 Gall: 0-0
Aids: Bl: 0-0 Vi: 0-0 Tstrap: 0-0
Best Rating: 37 1/01 Wolv 6f stand

The Prince

(109) (96)89
7-y-o b g Machiavellian (USA)-Mohican Girl (Dancing Brave (USA))
Ian Williams Patrick Kelly

Placings:421546/210600021303/10560-430 (0477)
2001: 8^{4}SD, 8^{3}SD, 10^{0}SD

	Starts	1st	2nd	3rd	Win & Pl
Career Total (Turf)	22	3	3	2	30357
Career Total (AW)	4	1	0	1	38120

94 3/00 Wolv 1m100y B(0-105)H STD £32500
90 9/99 Haml 1m65y C(0-90)H G-F £7490
92 5/99 Ling 7f140y C(0-90) G-F £6286
82 5/97 NmkR 1m D G-F £4163
Total win prize-money £50441

Going (Turf): Sf: 0-1 GS: 0-2 Gd: 0-10 GF: 3-8 Fm: 0-1
Distance: 5f/6f: 0-0 7f-8f: 2-13 9f-13f: 2-13 14f+: 0-0
Track : LH: 1-10 RH: 1-8 Tight: 2-8 Gall: 0-7
Aids: Bl: 0-1 Vi: 1-5 Tstrap: 3-19
Best Rating: 96 3/01 Wolv 1m100y stand

The Prosecutor

84(102) (68)60
4-y-o b c Contract Law (USA)-Elsocko (Swing Easy (USA))
B A McMahon Whiston Management Ltd

Placings:2260301/6150014400000-050 (1176)
2001: 6^{0}SD, 6^{5}SW, 7^{0}G

	Starts	1st	2nd	3rd	Win & Pl
Career Total (Turf)	12	1	1	0	4150
Career Total (AW)	11	2	1	1	9240

65 5/00 Hayd 6f E(0-70)H G-S £3290
82 3/00 Sthl 6f D(0-85)H STD £5408
70 11/99 Wolv 6f D STD £2866
Total win prize-money £11564

Going (Turf): Sf: 0-4 GS: 1-4 Gd: 0-4 GF: 0-0 Fm: 0-0
Distance: 5f/6f: 3-13 7f-8f: 0-9 9f-13f: 0-1 14f+: 0-0
Track : LH: 2-17 RH: 0-1 Tight: 1-5 Gall: 0-0
Aids: Bl: 0-0 Vi: 0-0 Tstrap: 0-0
Best Rating: 53 2/01 Sthl 6f slow

The Robster (USA)

(94) (47)64
4-y-o ch g Woodman (USA)-Country Cruise (USA) (Riverman (USA))
B J Meehan R L Harding

Placings:00/02005-60 (1319)
2001: 7^{6}SD, 7^{0}SD

	Starts	1st	2nd	3rd	Win & Pl
Career Total (Turf)	7	0	1	0	1175
Career Total (AW)	2	0	0	0	0

Going (Turf): Sf: 0-2 GS: 0-0 Gd: 0-2 GF: 0-1 Fm: 0-2
Distance: 5f/6f: 0-0 7f-8f: 0-7 9f-13f: 0-2 14f+: 0-0
Track : LH: 0-4 RH: 0-1 Tight: 0-1 Gall: 0-0
Aids: Bl: 0-1 Vi: 0-0 Tstrap: 0-0
Best Rating: 47 4/01 Sthl 7f stand

The Roxburgh (USA)

96 58
4-y-o b/br c Known Fact (USA)-Musical Precedent (USA) (Seattle Song (USA))
J A R Toller Duke Of Devonshire

Placings:4-645 (4368)
2001: 5^{6}GS, 5^{4}GF, 5^{5}GF

	Starts	1st	2nd	3rd	Win & Pl
Career Total (Turf)	4	0	0	0	249

Going (Turf): Sf: 0-0 GS: 0-1 Gd: 0-0 GF: 0-3 Fm: 0-0
Distance: 5f/6f: 0-4 7f-8f: 0-0 9f-13f: 0-0 14f+: 0-0
Track : LH: 0-1 RH: 0-0 Tight: 0-1 Gall: 0-0
Aids: Bl: 0-0 Vi: 0-0 Tstrap: 0-0
Best Rating: 58 8/01 Folk 5f gd-fm

The Scaffolder

97(100) (53)46
3-y-o b g Tachyon Park-Fallal (IRE) (Fayruz)
Mrs N Macauley West Indies Capital Company Limited

Placings:6542-52424024560233200033 (5412)
2001: 7^{5}SD, 6^{2}SD, 6^{4}SD, 6^{2}SD, 5^{4}SD, 5^{0}SD, 5^{2}S, 5^{4}GF, 6^{5}GF, 5^{6}F, 7^{0}G, 6^{2}SD, 6^{3}GF, 6^{3}SD, 6^{2}SD, 5^{0}G, 6^{0}GF, 6^{0}SD, 7^{3}SD, 6^{3}SD

	Starts	1st	2nd	3rd	Win & Pl
Career Total (Turf)	10	0	1	1	1242
Career Total (AW)	14	0	5	3	5014

Going (Turf): Sf: 0-2 GS: 0-1 Gd: 0-2 GF: 0-4 Fm: 0-1
Distance: 5f/6f: 0-19 7f-8f: 0-5 9f-13f: 0-0 14f+: 0-0
Track : LH: 0-14 RH: 0-0 Tight: 0-4 Gall: 0-1
Aids: Bl: 0-0 Vi: 0-2 Tstrap: 0-0
Best Rating: 67 5/01 Bath 5f11y gd-fm

Consistently placed on the All-Weather but seems to have his own ideas about the game.

The Student Prince

99 **61**

3-y-o b c Piccolo-Affaire De Coeur (Imperial Fling (USA))
S Dow D R Hunnisett

Placings:000003 **(3890)**
2001: 8^{0}GF, 10^{0}G, 8^{0}GF, 8^{0}G, 9^{0}GF, 7^{3}F

	Starts	1st	2nd	3rd	Win & Pl
Career Total (Turf)	6	0	0	1	424

Going (Turf): Sf: 0-0 GS: 0-0 Gd: 0-2 GF: 0-3 Fm: 0-1
Distance: 5f/6f: 0-0 7f-8f: 0-2 9f-13f: 0-4 14f+: 0-0
Track : LH: 0-3 RH: 0-2 Tight: 0-3 Gall: 0-0
Aids: Bl: 0-0 Vi: 0-0 Tstrap: 0-0
Best Rating: 61 6/01 Wind 1m67y gd-fm

The Tatling (IRE)

107 **94**

4-y-o b/br g Perugino (USA)-Aunty Eileen (Ahonoora)
D Nicholls (M L W Bell 20/4) The Gardening Partnership

Placings:364121262/0300-020 **(4849)**
2001: 5^{0}GS, 6^{2}G, 6^{0}GF

	Starts	1st	2nd	3rd	Win & Pl
Career Total (Turf)	16	2	4	2	49756

95	8/99	Brig	5f59y	E	SFT	£2749
87	7/99	Yarm	5f43y	D	G-F	£3557

Total win prize-money £6307

Going (Turf): Sf: **1-2** GS: 0-2 Gd: 0-5 **GF: 1-6** Fm: 0-0
Distance: **5f/6f: 2-15** 7f-8f: 0-1 9f-13f: 0-0 14f+: 0-0
Track : **LH: 1-2** RH: 0-0 Tight: 0-0 Gall: 0-0
Aids: Bl: 0-0 Vi: 0-0 Tstrap: 0-1
Best Rating: 94 9/01 Ayr 6f gd-fm

Lightly raced at three, he struggled to make an impact against some top sprinters. Much better run at Epsom in September, his first outing since the spring, he looks sure to win races for his new connections.

The Thief

46

3-y-o b g Robellino (USA)-Lady Bankes (IRE) (Alzao (USA))
D W Barker P Asquith

Placings:2 **(2359)**
2001: 7^{2}GF, 7^{P}SD

	Starts	1st	2nd	3rd	Win & Pl
Career Total (Turf)	1	0	1	0	1120

Going (Turf): Sf: 0-0 GS: 0-0 Gd: 0-0 GF: 0-1 Fm: 0-0
Distance: 5f/6f: 0-0 7f-8f: 0-1 9f-13f: 0-0 14f+: 0-0
Track : LH: 0-1 RH: 0-0 Tight: 0-0 Gall: 0-0
Aids: Bl: 0-0 Vi: 0-0 Tstrap: 0-0
Best Rating: 46 6/01 Ayr 7f gd-fm

The Third Curate (IRE)

(103) (46)**47**

6-y-o b g Fairy King (USA)-Lassalia (Sallust)
B J Curley P Byrne

Placings:64/0010000000/001100-0 **(0245)**
2001: 7^{0}SD

	Starts	1st	2nd	3rd	Win & Pl
Career Total (Turf)	15	2	0	0	7602
Career Total (AW)	5	1	0	0	1806

47	7/00	Brig	6f209y	F(0-60)H	FRM	£1914
46	7/00	Sthl	1m	F(0-60)H	STD	£1806
63	6/99	Curr	7f	(0-70)H	GD	£5500

Total win prize-money £9221

Going (Turf): Sf: 0-6 GS: 0-2 **Gd: 1-2** GF: 0-2 **Fm: 1-2**
Distance: 5f/6f: 0-3 **7f-8f: 3-11** 9f-13f: 0-5 14f+: 0-1
Track : **LH: 2-10** RH: 0-5 Tight: 0-5 Gall: 0-4
Aids: **Bl: 2-5** Vi: 0-0 Tstrap: 0-0
Best Rating: 33 2/01 Wolv 7f stand

Winner of a seven-furlong event at the Curragh for Dermot Weld, he is now with Barney Curley, and has been well beaten on his English starts so far.

The Trader (IRE)

117 **111**

3-y-o ch g Selkirk (USA)-Snowing (Tate Gallery (USA))
M Blanshard Mrs C J Ward

Placings:332211340-2400601031613 **(5105)**
2001: 5^{2}S, 6^{4}S, 6^{0}S, 6^{0}GF, 5^{6}GS, 7^{0}G, 5^{1}GF, 5^{0}G, 5^{3}G, 5^{1}GF, 5^{6}GS, 5^{1}GF, 5^{3}GS

	Starts	1st	2nd	3rd	Win & Pl
Career Total (Turf)	22	5	3	5	57786

111	9/01	Newb	5f34y	A	G-F	£23200
72	9/01	Leic	5f2y	C	G-F	£6264
101	8/01	Newb	5f34y	C(0-95)H	G-F	£7514
88	8/00	Folk	5f	D	G-F	£2847
72	8/00	Nott	5f13y	D	G-F	£3835

Total win prize-money £43660

Going (Turf): Sf: 0-5 GS: 0-4 Gd: 0-4 **GF: 5-8** Fm: 0-1
Distance: **5f/6f: 5-20** 7f-8f: 0-2 9f-13f: 0-0 14f+: 0-0
Track : LH: 0-2 RH: 0-1 Tight: 0-0 Gall: 0-2
Aids: **Bl: 3-7** Vi: 0-0 Tstrap: 0-0
Best Rating: 111 9/01 Newb 5f34y gd-fm

A useful sprinter, he shown some useful form at two and has won three times so far this season, two of them at Newbury. He gained his first win in Listed company on the second occasion and is a much better horse over the minimum trip on fast ground.

The Tube (IRE)

88(85) (35)**36**

3-y-o b f Royal Abjar (USA)-Grandeur And Grace (USA) (Septieme Ciel (USA))
Andrew Reid A S Reid

Placings:0-56035004000 **(5395)**
2001: 9^{5}SW, 7^{6}SW, 8^{0}S, 7^{3}SD, 11^{5}GF, 8^{0}SD, 7^{0}F, 9^{4}F, 7^{0}G, 11^{0}HY, 7^{0}SD

	Starts	1st	2nd	3rd	Win & Pl
Career Total (Turf)	6	0	0	0	0
Career Total (AW)	6	0	0	1	258

Going (Turf): **Sf: 0-2 GS: 0-0 Gd: 0-1 GF: 0-1 Fm: 0-2**
Distance: 5f/6f: 0-1 7f-8f: 0-6 9f-13f: 0-5 14f+: 0-0
Track : LH: 0-9 RH: 0-0 Tight: 0-6 Gall: 0-0
Aids: Bl: 0-0 Vi: 0-0 Tstrap: 0-0
Best Rating: 36 8/01 Brig 1m1f209y firm

The Wall

98(87) (37)**40**

3-y-o b f Mistertopogigo (IRE)-Lady Pennington (Blue Cashmere)
J A Gilbert The Black And White Partnership

Placings:05000000000-0500060664000 **(4610)**
2001: 6^{0}SD, 6^{5}SD, 5^{0}SD, 8^{0}G, 7^{0}GS, 9^{6}F, 5^{0}F, 5^{6}G, 6^{6}F, 5^{4}GF, 5^{0}F, 5^{0}G, 5^{0}F

	Starts	1st	2nd	3rd	Win & Pl
Career Total (Turf)	17	0	0	0	0
Career Total (AW)	7	0	0	0	0

Going (Turf): **Sf: 0-2 GS: 0-2 Gd: 0-6 GF: 0-2 Fm: 0-5**
Distance: 5f/6f: 0-18 7f-8f: 0-5 9f-13f: 0-1 14f+: 0-0
Track : LH: 0-11 RH: 0-2 Tight: 0-5 Gall: 0-6
Aids: Bl: 0-0 Vi: 0-0 Tstrap: 0-0
Best Rating: 41 5/01 Ling 7f140y gd-sft

The Walrus (IRE)

(94) (32)**58d**

4-y-o b g Sri Pekan (USA)-Cathy Garcia (IRE) (Be My Guest (USA))
J Neville Miss Derien Edwards

Placings:03300552-0 **(0256)**
2001: 12^{0}SD

	Starts	1st	2nd	3rd	Win & Pl
Career Total (Turf)	5	0	0	2	715
Career Total (AW)	4	0	1	0	522

Going (Turf): **Sf: 0-0 GS: 0-0 Gd: 0-3 GF: 0-1 Fm: 0-1**
Distance: 5f/6f: 0-0 7f-8f: 0-0 9f-13f: 0-9 14f+: 0-0
Track : LH: 0-7 RH: 0-1 Tight: 0-7 Gall: 0-0
Aids: Bl: 0-0 Vi: 0-0 Tstrap: 0-0
Best Rating: 20 2/01 Wolv 1m4f stand

The Whistling Teal

114(102) (89)**108**

5-y-o b g Rudimentary (USA)-Lonely Shore (Blakeney)
G Wragg Mrs F A Veasey

Placings:66/3102512320/003000-152151 **(4170)**
2001: 8^{1}HY, 8^{5}GS, 10^{2}GF, 10^{1}F, 10^{5}GF, 10^{1}G

	Starts	1st	2nd	3rd	Win & Pl
Career Total (Turf)	21	4	3	3	69954
Career Total (AW)	3	1	1	0	5151

108	8/01	York	1m2f85y	B(0-105)H	GD	£20558
95	5/01	Rdcr	1m2f	B(0-105)H	FRM	£18281
86	4/01	Pont	1m4y	D(0-85)H	HVY	£7865
89	8/99	Wolv	1m100y	D(0-85)H	STD	£3954
76	4/99	Wind	1m67y	D(0-85)H	G-F	£5485

Total win prize-money £56144

Going (Turf): **Sf: 1-7** GS: 0-3 **Gd: 1-5 GF: 1-5 Fm: 1-1**
Distance: 5f/6f: 0-0 7f-8f: 0-7 **9f-13f: 5-17** 14f+: 0-0
Track : **LH: 4-10** RH: 1-6 **Tight: 3-7** Gall: 1-3
Aids: Bl: 0-0 Vi: 0-0 Tstrap: 0-0
Best Rating: 108 8/01 York 1m2f85y good

Able on turf and sand, he has done well since joining Geoff Wragg before this season having been gelded in the meantime, winning at Pontefract and the Zetland Gold Cup at Redcar and at York. Effective from a mile to an extended ten furlongs.

The Wife

105(54) **68**

4-y-o b f Efisio-Great Steps (Vaigly Great)
T D Easterby Jonathan Gill

Placings:03122100/00355-00032005024100 **(5384)**
2001: 8^{0}G, 8^{0}G, 8^{0}GF, 8^{3}GF, 8^{2}G, 8^{0}F, 7^{0}G, 10^{5}GF, 8^{0}G, 8^{2}GF, 8^{4}G, 7^{1}G, 7^{0}SD, 7^{0}S

	Starts	1st	2nd	3rd	Win & Pl
Career Total (Turf)	26	3	4	3	23807
Career Total (AW)	1	0	0	0	

68	9/01	Bevl	7f100y	E(0-70)H	GD	£3535
89	9/99	York	7f202y	C H	G-F	£8610
75	6/99	Bevl	7f100y	E	G-F	£2740

Total win prize-money £14885

Going (Turf): Sf: 0-1 GS: 0-3 Gd: 1-11 **GF: 2-8** Fm: 0-3
Distance: 5f/6f: 0-2 **7f-8f: 3-18** 9f-13f: 0-7 14f+: 0-0
Track : LH: 1-15 **RH: 2-9** Tight: 0-7 **Gall: 1-7**
Aids: Bl: 0-0 Vi: 0-0 **Tstrap: 1-5**
Best Rating: 75 6/01 Thsk 1m good

She scored twice as a two-year-old and has run some decent races since, but did not add to her score until landing a handicap at Beverley in September. Suited by forcing tactics.

Theatre Lady (IRE)

100 **51**

3-y-o b f King's Theatre (IRE)-Littlepace (Indian King (USA))

P D Evans (M Johnston 18/7) Waterline Racing Club

Placings:43-46030200423640 **(5532)**

2001: 11^{4}G, 8^{6}GF, 7^{0}GF, 9^{3}GF, 8^{0}GF, 12^{2}G, 8^{0}GF, 9^{0}G, 6^{4}GF, 8^{2}G, 8^{3}F, 8^{6}G, 8^{4}G, 9^{0}HY

	Starts	1st	2nd	3rd	Win & Pl
Career Total (Turf)	16	0	2	3	3549

Going (Turf): Sf: 0-3 GS: 0-0 Gd: 0-6 GF: 0-6 Fm: 0-1
Distance: 5f/6f: 0-0 7f-8f: 0-7 9f-13f: 0-9 14f+: 0-0
Track : LH: 0-8 RH: 0-2 Tight: 0-3 Gall: 0-2
Aids: Bl: 0-0 Vi: 0-1 Tstrap: 0-0
Best Rating: 68 6/01 Ayr 1m1f20y gd-fm

Ran well last term on heavy ground, has not appealed on a faster surface this time though. Has been tried over a variety of distances but is probably going to need at least a mile.

Theatre Of Life (IRE)

87(58) (13)**67**

2-y-o b g King's Theatre (IRE)-Miss Ironwood (Junius (USA))

B J Meehan The Ladys Partnership

Placings:0 **(5468)**

2001: 7^{0}S, 9^{0}SD

	Starts	1st	2nd	3rd	Win & Pl
Career Total (Turf)	1	0	0	0	

Going (Turf): Sf: 0-1 GS: 0-0 Gd: 0-0 GF: 0-0 Fm: 0-0
Distance: 5f/6f: 0-0 7f-8f: 0-1 9f-13f: 0-0 14f+: 0-0
Track : LH: 0-1 RH: 0-0 Tight: 0-0 Gall: 0-0
Aids: Bl: 0-0 Vi: 0-0 Tstrap: 0-0
Best Rating: 67 10/01 Brig 7f214y soft

Theatre Script (USA)

106 **113**

3-y-o ch c Theatrical-Gossiping (USA) (Chati (USA))

J H M Gosden R E Sangster & A K Collins

Placings:1-030 **(4114)**

2001: 10^{0}G, 12^{3}GF, 11^{0}G

	Starts	1st	2nd	3rd	Win & Pl
Career Total (Turf)	4	1	0	1	19776

85 9/00 Donc 1m D GD £4251
Total win prize-money £4251

Going (Turf): Sf: 0-0 GS: 0-0 **Gd: 1-3** GF: 0-1 Fm: 0-0
Distance: 5f/6f: 0-0 **7f-8f: 1-1** 9f-13f: 0-3 14f+: 0-0
Track : LH: 0-1 RH: 0-1 Tight: 0-0 Gall: 0-2
Aids: Bl: 0-0 Vi: 0-0 Tstrap: 0-0
Best Rating: 113 6/01 Asct 1m4f gd-fm

Made a winning debut at Doncaster despite running as green as grass. Ran respectably on his reappearance before a cracking effort when third in the King Edward VII at Ascot. Ran as if something was amiss in the Great Voltigeur.

Theatrical Waltz

78 **56**

2-y-o b f Barathea (IRE)-Fascination Waltz (Shy Groom (USA))

J J Sheehan Mrs Christina Dowling

Placings:0000 **(5127)**

2001: 6^{0}GF, 6^{0}G, 6^{0}GF, 7^{0}HY

	Starts	1st	2nd	3rd	Win & Pl
Career Total (Turf)	4	0	0	0	

Going (Turf): Sf: 0-1 GS: 0-0 Gd: 0-1 GF: 0-2 Fm: 0-0
Distance: 5f/6f: 0-2 7f-8f: 0-2 9f-13f: 0-0 14f+: 0-0
Track : LH: 0-0 RH: 0-0 Tight: 0-0 Gall: 0-0
Aids: Bl: 0-0 Vi: 0-0 Tstrap: 0-0
Best Rating: 56 9/01 Kemp 6f good

Theban (IRE)

97(89) (59)**65**

3-y-o b g Inzar (USA)-Phoenix Forli (USA) (Forli (ARG))

D Nicholls Neil Smith

Placings:5434-0500 **(1965)**

2001: 7^{0}SD, 8^{5}GF, 8^{0}GF, 7^{0}GF

	Starts	1st	2nd	3rd	Win & Pl
Career Total (Turf)	6	0	0	1	678
Career Total (AW)	2	0	0	0	0

Going (Turf): Sf: 0-0 GS: 0-0 Gd: 0-2 GF: 0-4 Fm: 0-0
Distance: 5f/6f: 0-2 7f-8f: 0-5 9f-13f: 0-1 14f+: 0-0
Track : LH: 0-4 RH: 0-3 Tight: 0-3 Gall: 0-0
Aids: Bl: 0-0 Vi: 0-0 Tstrap: 0-0
Best Rating: 53 5/01 Muss 1m gd-fm

Theme Time (USA)

86(95) (33)**23**

5-y-o b g Stop The Music (USA)-Ranales (USA) (Majestic Light (USA))

H J Collingridge R Nunn

Placings:05/0030 **(3221)**

2001: 10^{0}G, 8^{0}F, 8^{3}SD, 8^{0}GS

	Starts	1st	2nd	3rd	Win & Pl
Career Total (Turf)	5	0	0	0	0
Career Total (AW)	1	0	0	1	337

Going (Turf): Sf: 0-0 GS: 0-1 Gd: 0-2 GF: 0-0 Fm: 0-2
Distance: 5f/6f: 0-0 7f-8f: 0-2 9f-13f: 0-4 14f+: 0-0
Track : LH: 0-4 RH: 0-1 Tight: 0-1 Gall: 0-0
Aids: Bl: 0-0 Vi: 0-0 Tstrap: 0-2
Best Rating: 33 7/01 Sthl 1m stand

There With Me (USA)

(96) (43)**65**

4-y-o b f Distant View (USA)-Breeze Lass (USA) (It's Freezing (USA))

G G Margarson Peter McCutcheon

Placings:33-30515 **(0327)**

2001: 7^{3}SD, 8^{0}SD, 8^{5}SD, 6^{1}SD, 6^{5}SD

	Starts	1st	2nd	3rd	Win & Pl
Career Total (Turf)	2	0	0	2	907
Career Total (AW)	5	1	0	1	3266

41 2/01 Wolv 6f D STD £2891
Total win prize-money £2891

Going (Turf): Sf: 0-2 GS: 0-0 Gd: 0-0 GF: 0-0 Fm: 0-0
Distance: 5f/6f: 1-2 7f-8f: 0-4 9f-13f: 0-1 14f+: 0-0
Track : LH: 1-5 RH: 0-1 **Tight: 1-5** Gall: 0-0
Aids: Bl: 1-2 Vi: 0-0 Tstrap: 0-0
Best Rating: 43 1/01 Wolv 7f stand

Theresa Green (IRE)

95 **67d**

3-y-o b f Charnwood Forest (IRE)-In Your Dreams (IRE) (Suave Dancer (USA))

Mrs P N Dutfield Mrs Margaret Sinanan

Placings:0030140-056 **(2510)**

2001: 6^{0}GF, 7^{5}GF, 6^{6}GF

	Starts	1st	2nd	3rd	Win & Pl
Career Total (Turf)	10	1	0	1	4968

67 8/00 Kemp 6f D G-F £4231
Total win prize-money £4232

Going (Turf): Sf: 0-1 GS: 0-1 Gd: 0-3 **GF: 1-5** Fm: 0-0
Distance: 5f/6f: 1-7 7f-8f: 0-3 9f-13f: 0-0 14f+: 0-0
Track : LH: 0-1 RH: 0-0 Tight: 0-0 Gall: 0-1
Aids: Bl: 0-0 Vi: 0-0 Tstrap: 0-0
Best Rating: 59 6/01 Newb 7f gd-fm

Theroseofloughrea (IRE)

87 **56**

4-y-o b f Lake Coniston (IRE)-Fabulous Pet (Somethingfabulous (USA))

N Tinkler J P Hardiman

Placings:56650-00 **(1731)**

2001: 9^{0}S, 7^{0}GF

	Starts	1st	2nd	3rd	Win & Pl
Career Total (Turf)	7	0	0	0	

Going (Turf): Sf: 0-1 GS: 0-0 Gd: 0-2 GF: 0-2 Fm: 0-0
Distance: 5f/6f: 0-0 7f-8f: 0-2 9f-13f: 0-5 14f+: 0-0
Track : LH: 0-2 RH: 0-4 Tight: 0-1 Gall: 0-0
Aids: Bl: 0-0 Vi: 0-0 Tstrap: 0-0
Best Rating: 33 5/01 Sthl 7f gd-fm

Thesaurus

99 **66?**

2-y-o gr g Most Welcome-Red Embers (Saddlers' Hall (IRE))

I A Wood John Purcell

Placings:006500 **(5668)**

2001: 5^{0}GF, 6^{0}GF, 7^{6}G, 7^{5}S, 6^{0}GS, 8^{0}HY

	Starts	1st	2nd	3rd	Win & Pl
Career Total (Turf)	6	0	0	0	2491

Going (Turf): Sf: 0-2 GS: 0-1 Gd: 0-1 GF: 0-2 Fm: 0-0
Distance: 5f/6f: 0-2 7f-8f: 0-3 9f-13f: 0-1 14f+: 0-0
Track : LH: 0-1 RH: 0-2 Tight: 0-1 Gall: 0-1
Aids: Bl: 0-0 Vi: 0-0 Tstrap: 0-0
Best Rating: 66 10/01 NmkR 6f gd-sft

Gradually getting the hang of things but did not improve for a step up to a mile.

Thesis (IRE)

108 **86+**

3-y-o ch c Definite Article-Chouette (Try My Best (USA))

J A Osborne Martyn Booth & Andy Miller

Placings:21235 **(5344)**

2001: 8^{2}G, 8^{1}F, 10^{2}GF, 10^{3}GF, 8^{5}GS

	Starts	1st	2nd	3rd	Win & Pl
Career Total (Turf)	5	1	2	1	8460

65 5/01 Leic 1m9y F FRM £2450
Total win prize-money £2450

Going (Turf): Sf: 0-0 GS: 0-1 Gd: 0-1 GF: 0-2 **Fm: 1-1**
Distance: 5f/6f: 0-0 7f-8f: 0-1 **9f-13f: 1-4** 14f+: 0-0
Track : LH: 0-2 RH: 0-1 Tight: 0-1 Gall: 0-2
Aids: Bl: 0-0 Vi: 0-0 Tstrap: 0-0
Best Rating: 86 8/01 NmkJ 1m2f gd-fm

From the same female line as Sayyedati, he did not race at two and ran a good second at Bath on his debut. Confirmed the promise with a smooth win over a mile at Leicester next time, and lost no caste in defeat in handicaps at Newmarket and Doncaster. Acts on fast ground.

Thewhirlingdervish (IRE)

100 **69**

3-y-o ch g Definite Article-Nomadic Dancer (IRE) (Nabeel Dancer (USA))

T D Easterby Major I C Straker

Placings:003200-46222 **(2754)**

2001: 8^{4}F, 10^{0}GF, 11^{2}GF, 11^{2}GF, 14^{2}GF

	Starts	1st	2nd	3rd	Win & Pl
Career Total (Turf)	11	0	4	1	5635

Going (Turf): Sf: 0-1 GS: 0-1 Gd: 0-1 GF: 0-7 Fm: 0-1
Distance: 5f/6f: 0-2 7f-8f: 0-4 9f-13f: 0-4 14f+: 0-1
Track : LH: 0-5 RH: 0-2 Tight: 0-2 Gall: 0-3
Aids: Bl: 0-0 Vi: 0-0 Tstrap: 0-0

Best Rating: 69 7/01 Hayd 1m6f gd-fm

Theyab (USA)

88 **56**

3-y-o b/br c Bahri (USA)-Dish Dash (Bustino)
N A Graham Hamdan Al Maktoum

Placings:6 **(0857)**
2001: 8^{6}GS

	Starts	1st	2nd	3rd	Win & Pl
Career Total (Turf)	1	0	0	0	0

Going (Turf): Sf: 0-0 GS: 0-1 Gd: 0-0 GF: 0-0 Fm: 0-0
Distance: 5f/6f: 0-0 7f-8f: 0-1 9f-13f: 0-0 14f+: 0-0
Track : LH: 0-0 RH: 0-0 Tight: 0-0 Gall: 0-0
Aids: Bl: 0-0 Vi: 0-0 Tstrap: 0-0
Best Rating: 56 4/01 Newb 1m gd-sft

Thieving

(49)

3-y-o b g Common Grounds-Ethical (USA) (Mt. Livermore (USA))
J A Osborne The Woolfie And Tom Partnership

Placings:00 **(0310)**
2001: 6^{0}SW, 7^{0}SD

	Starts	1st	2nd	3rd	Win & Pl
Career Total (Turf)	0	0	0	0	
Career Total (AW)	2	0	0	0	

Going (Turf): Sf: 0-0 GS: 0-0 Gd: 0-0 GF: 0-0 Fm: 0-0
Distance: 5f/6f: 0-1 7f-8f: 0-1 9f-13f: 0-0 14f+: 0-0
Track : LH: 0-2 RH: 0-0 Tight: 0-1 Gall: 0-0
Aids: Bl: 0-0 Vi: 0-0 Tstrap: 0-0

Thihn (IRE)

111 **93**

6-y-o ch g Machiavellian (USA)-Hasana (USA) (Private Account (USA))
J L Spearing The Square Milers

Placings:00/630522/20360023122052-62112321230645522 **(5607)**
2001: 9^{6}HY, 9^{2}S, 8^{1}GS, 8^{1}S, 8^{2}G, 8^{3}G, 8^{2}GF, 8^{1}GF, 8^{2}G, 8^{3}GF, 8^{0}G, 8^{6}G, 9^{4}GF, 8^{5}S, 9^{5}G, 8^{2}GS, 8^{2}GS

	Starts	1st	2nd	3rd	Win & Pl
Career Total (Turf)	39	4	13	5	63877

84	6/01	Wind	1m67y	D(0-80)	G-F	£3948
75	4/01	Epsm	1m114y	E(0-70)	SFT	£4738
74	4/01	Muss	1m	E(0-75)H	G-S	£3220
62	9/00	Bevl	1m100y	F(0-65)H	G-F	£3594

Total win prize-money £15503

Going (Turf): Sf: 1-9 GS: 1-7 Gd: 0-13 **GF: 2-10** Fm: 0-0
Distance: 5f/6f: 0-0 7f-8f: 1-12 **9f-13f: 3-27** 14f+: 0-0
Track : LH: 1-14 **RH: 3-15 Tight: 3-18** Gall: 0-0
Aids: Bl: 0-0 Vi: 0-0 Tstrap: 0-0
Best Rating: 93 11/01 NmkR 1m gd-sft

A consistent handicapper, better than ever this year, scoring three times. Best around a mile and seems effective on most ground. Suited by a strong pace and waiting tactics.

Thin Client (USA)

103 **90**

2-y-o ch c Atticus (USA)-Aliata (USA) (Mr Prospector (USA))
P F I Cole W J Smith And M D Dudley

Placings:3321 **(4196)**
2001: 6^{3}GF, 6^{3}GS, 7^{2}GF, 6^{1}G

	Starts	1st	2nd	3rd	Win & Pl
Career Total (Turf)	4	1	1	2	13719

90	8/01	York	6f214y	C H	GD	£11635

Total win prize-money £11635

Going (Turf): Sf: 0-0 GS: 0-1 **Gd: 1-1** GF: 0-2 Fm: 0-0
Distance: 5f/6f: 0-2 **7f-8f: 1-2** 9f-13f: 0-0 14f+: 0-0
Track : **LH: 1-2** RH: 0-0 Tight: 0-1 **Gall: 1-1**
Aids: Bl: 0-0 Vi: 0-0 Tstrap: 0-0
Best Rating: 90 8/01 York 6f214y good

Ran well in maidens before winning a valuable York nursery.

Thirn

91 **73**

2-y-o b c Piccolo-Midnight Owl (FR) (Ardross)
J D Bethell Www.Clarendon Racing.Oc.Uk

Placings:505 **(4797)**
2001: 6^{5}G, 7^{0}GF, 6^{5}G

	Starts	1st	2nd	3rd	Win & Pl
Career Total (Turf)	3	0	0	0	0

Going (Turf): Sf: 0-0 GS: 0-0 Gd: 0-2 GF: 0-1 Fm: 0-0
Distance: 5f/6f: 0-2 7f-8f: 0-1 9f-13f: 0-0 14f+: 0-0
Track : LH: 0-0 RH: 0-0 Tight: 0-0 Gall: 0-0
Aids: Bl: 0-0 Vi: 0-0 Tstrap: 0-0
Best Rating: 73 9/01 Ayr 6f good

Tholjanah (IRE)

110 **103**

2-y-o b c Darshaan-Alkaffeyeh (IRE) (Sadler's Wells (USA))
M P Tregoning Hamdan Al Maktoum

Placings:122 **(5002)**
2001: 7^{1}GF, 7^{2}G, 8^{2}S

	Starts	1st	2nd	3rd	Win & Pl
Career Total (Turf)	3	1	2	0	38676

83	7/01	Kemp	7f	D	G-F	£4176

Total win prize-money £4176

Going (Turf): Sf: 0-1 GS: 0-0 Gd: 0-1 **GF: 1-1** Fm: 0-0
Distance: 5f/6f: 0-0 **7f-8f: 1-3** 9f-13f: 0-0 14f+: 0-0
Track : LH: 0-0 **RH: 1-3** Tight: 0-0 **Gall: 1-2**
Aids: Bl: 0-0 Vi: 0-0 Tstrap: 0-0
Best Rating: 103 9/01 Asct 1m soft

A half-brother to Mudaa-Eb and Ta-Lim, he is bred to get middle distances at least. Made a winning debut at Kempton and stayed on nicely when second in the Solario next time. Sent off co-favourite when runner-up in the Royal Lodge, and should go on to better things.

Thomas Henry (IRE)

(96) (30d)**47**

5-y-o br g Petardia-Hitopah (Bustino)
J S Moore J S Moore

Placings:004040/6134404160/06605500350364635100-0040 **(0417)**
2001: 12^{0}SD, 13^{0}SD, 13^{4}SW, 16^{0}SD

	Starts	1st	2nd	3rd	Win & Pl
Career Total (Turf)	20	1	0	1	3055
Career Total (AW)	20	2	0	3	6196

47	10/00	Yarm	1m3f101y	G(0-60)H	SFT	£2012
58	11/99	Ling	1m2f	G	STD	£1532
59	1/99	Ling	7f	D	STD	£3572

Total win prize-money £7118

Going (Turf): Sf: 1-4 GS: 0-1 Gd: 0-6 GF: 0-8 Fm: 0-1
Distance: 5f/6f: 0-2 7f-8f: 1-10 **9f-13f: 2-27** 14f+: 0-1
Track : **LH: 3-29** RH: 0-5 **Tight: 3-24** Gall: 0-2
Aids: Bl: 0-0 Vi: 0-2 Tstrap: 0-0
Best Rating: 27 2/01 Ling 1m5f stand

Thoralby

67 **19**

2-y-o b g Son Pardo-Polish Lady (IRE) (Posen (USA))
C W Fairhurst David Hawes

Placings:00 **(5537)**
2001: 8^{0}G, 7^{0}S

	Starts	1st	2nd	3rd	Win & Pl
Career Total (Turf)	2	0	0	0	

Going (Turf): Sf: 0-1 GS: 0-0 Gd: 0-1 GF: 0-0 Fm: 0-0
Distance: 5f/6f: 0-0 7f-8f: 0-2 9f-13f: 0-0 14f+: 0-0
Track : LH: 0-0 RH: 0-0 Tight: 0-0 Gall: 0-0
Aids: Bl: 0-0 Vi: 0-0 Tstrap: 0-0
Best Rating: 19 10/01 Rdcr 7f soft

Thornaby Girl (IRE)

87 (63d)**18**

5-y-o b m Fayruz-Anita's Love (IRE) (Anita's Prince)
Mrs L B Normile L B N Racing Club

Placings:132/60200/0 **(4403)**
2001: 6^{0}G

	Starts	1st	2nd	3rd	Win & Pl
Career Total (Turf)	5	1	0	1	3152
Career Total (AW)	4	0	2	0	1290

61	5/98	Muss	5f	E	GD	£2784

Total win prize-money £2785

Going (Turf): Sf: 0-0 GS: 0-0 **Gd: 1-3** GF: 0-2 Fm: 0-0
Distance: **5f/6f: 1-9** 7f-8f: 0-0 9f-13f: 0-0 14f+: 0-0
Track : LH: 0-3 RH: 0-0 Tight: 0-3 Gall: 0-0
Aids: Bl: 0-0 Vi: 0-0 Tstrap: 0-0
Best Rating: 18 8/01 Ayr 6f good

Thorntoun Connect

92 **35**

2-y-o b f Danzig Connection (USA)-Furry Friend (USA) (Bold Bidder)
J S Goldie W M Johnstone

Placings:00435360000 **(5270)**
2001: 5^{0}S, 5^{0}GS, 6^{4}F, 5^{3}GF, 5^{5}GF, 6^{3}GF, 7^{6}GS, 6^{0}GS, 7^{0}G, 8^{0}G, 6^{0}HY

	Starts	1st	2nd	3rd	Win & Pl
Career Total (Turf)	11	0	0	2	1620

Going (Turf): Sf: 0-2 GS: 0-3 Gd: 0-2 GF: 0-3 Fm: 0-1
Distance: 5f/6f: 0-8 7f-8f: 0-3 9f-13f: 0-0 14f+: 0-0
Track : LH: 0-2 RH: 0-0 Tight: 0-0 Gall: 0-1
Aids: Bl: 0-0 Vi: 0-0 Tstrap: 0-0
Best Rating: 57 6/01 Newc 6f gd-fm

Thorntoun Dancer

97 **23**

3-y-o b f Unfuwain (USA)-Westry (Gone West (USA))
J S Goldie W M Johnstone

Placings:00563023-00050323040000 **(4187)**
2001: 10^{0}GS, 8^{0}S, 9^{0}S, 8^{5}F, 8^{0}F, 10^{3}GF, 11^{2}GF, 12^{3}GF, 16^{0}F, 12^{4}GS, 15^{0}GS, 8^{0}G, 9^{0}GS, 9^{0}GF

	Starts	1st	2nd	3rd	Win & Pl
Career Total (Turf)	22	0	2	4	4259

Going (Turf): Sf: 0-6 GS: 0-4 Gd: 0-2 GF: 0-5 Fm: 0-5
Distance: 5f/6f: 0-3 7f-8f: 0-5 9f-13f: 0-12 14f+: 0-2
Track : LH: 0-10 RH: 0-8 Tight: 0-7 Gall: 0-3
Aids: Bl: 0-2 Vi: 0-2 Tstrap: 0-0
Best Rating: 50 6/01 Haml 1m3f16y gd-fm

Thorntoun Diva

100 **41**

3-y-o ch f Wolfhound (USA)-Al Guswa (Shernazar)
J S Goldie W M Johnstone

Placings:3020060-0034033000550650000 **(5287)**
2001: 7^{0}S, 8^{0}S, 6^{3}S, 5^{4}GF, 6^{0}GF, 6^{3}GF, 6^{3}F, 7^{0}G, 5^{0}G, 6^{0}GF, 7^{5}GS, 7^{5}GS, 7^{0}GF, 7^{6}GS, 8^{5}GS, 8^{0}G, 10^{0}G, 5^{0}HY, 6^{0}HY

	Starts	1st	2nd	3rd	Win & Pl
Career Total (Turf)	26	0	1	4	3200

Going (Turf): Sf: 0-9 GS: 0-4 Gd: 0-6 GF: 0-6 Fm: 0-1

Distance: 5f/6f: 0-16 7f-8f: 0-7 9f-13f: 0-3 14f+: 0-0
Track : LH: 0-7 RH: 0-0 Tight: 0-0 Gall: 0-0
Aids: Bl: 0-2 Vi: 0-1 Tstrap: 0-1
Best Rating: 56 5/01 Ripn 6f gd-fm

Thorntoun Gold (IRE)

100(90) (22)38
5-y-o ch m Lycius (USA)-Gold Braisim (IRE) (Jareer (USA))
I A Wood Tough Construction Ltd

Placings:540400/000441203000/4010023552000-6022634500 (4463)
2001: 10^6GF, 7^0SD, 7^2GF, 10^2GF, 8^6GF, 10^3GF, 10^4F, 8^5S, 10^0GF, 9^0GS

	Starts	1st	2nd	3rd	Win & Pl
Career Total (Turf)	40	2	5	3	13602
Career Total (AW)	1	0	0	0	

46 6/00 Pont 1m4y E(0-75)H G-F £4251
44 7/99 Thsk 1m F(0-60)H FRM £3107
Total win prize-money £7359

Going (Turf): Sf: 0-6 GS: 0-6 Gd: 0-10 GF: 1-11 Fm: 1-7
Distance: 5f/6f: 0-0 7f-8f: 1-18 9f-13f: 1-23 14f+: 0-0
Track : LH: 2-28 RH: 0-6 Tight: 1-12 Gall: 0-1
Aids: Bl: 0-3 Vi: 0-0 Tstrap: 0-0
Best Rating: 46 7/01 Bath 1m2f46y firm

Thorpeness (IRE)

65 61
2-y-o b c Barathea (IRE)-Brisighella (IRE) (Al Hareb (USA))
C F Wall P H Betts

Placings:000 (5559)
2001: 7^0S, 8^0S, 8^0S

	Starts	1st	2nd	3rd	Win & Pl
Career Total (Turf)	3	0	0	0	

Going (Turf): Sf: 0-3 GS: 0-0 Gd: 0-0 GF: 0-0 Fm: 0-0
Distance: 5f/6f: 0-0 7f-8f: 0-1 9f-13f: 0-2 14f+: 0-0
Track : LH: 0-0 RH: 0-0 Tight: 0-0 Gall: 0-0
Aids: Bl: 0-0 Vi: 0-0 Tstrap: 0-0
Best Rating: 61 10/01 Leic 1m9y soft

Thrasher

104 85
2-y-o b f Hector Protector (USA)-Thracian (Green Desert (USA))
J H M Gosden Hesmonds Stud

Placings:2551 (5466)
2001: 7^2GF, 8^5G, 8^5HY, 6^1S

	Starts	1st	2nd	3rd	Win & Pl
Career Total (Turf)	4	1	1	0	4217

78 10/01 Brig 6f209y E SFT £2933
Total win prize-money £2933

Going (Turf): Sf: 1-2 GS: 0-0 Gd: 0-1 GF: 0-1 Fm: 0-0
Distance: 5f/6f: 0-0 7f-8f: 1-3 9f-13f: 0-1 14f+: 0-0
Track : LH: 1-2 RH: 0-1 Tight: 1-2 Gall: 0-0
Aids: Bl: 0-0 Vi: 0-0 Tstrap: 0-0
Best Rating: 85 9/01 NmkR 1m good

From a high-class family, sealed the promise of her debut in an auction maiden at Brighton over seven furlongs. Her pedigree suggests she will stay middle distances next year.

Threat

103(102) (64)62
5-y-o br g Zafonic (USA)-Prophecy (IRE) (Warning)
S C Williams Pertemps Flexipeople Owners Syndicate

Placings:13/0402/000060005135034-000035460303540000 (5497)
2001: 6^0S, 6^0G, 5^0F, 6^0GF, 5^0GF, 5^3GF, 5^5GS, 6^4GF, 7^6GS, 6^0G, 5^3S, 5^0GF, 5^3G, 5^5GF, 5^4G, 5^0GS, 5^0S, 5^0HY

	Starts	1st	2nd	3rd	Win & Pl
Career Total (Turf)	39	2	1	6	20890
Career Total (AW)	1	0	0	0	0

70 9/00 Donc 5f D(0-80)H G-F £3900
97 7/98 Gdwd 6f D G-S £6872
Total win prize-money £10773

Going (Turf): Sf: 0-8 GS: 1-8 Gd: 0-10 GF: 1-11 Fm: 0-2
Distance: 5f/6f: 2-35 7f-8f: 0-5 9f-13f: 0-0 14f+: 0-0
Track : LH: 0-5 RH: 0-3 Tight: 0-3 Gall: 0-2
Aids: Bl: 0-1 Vi: 0-1 Tstrap: 1-28
Best Rating: 70 7/01 Folk 5f gd-fm

Dropped dramatically in the ratings before returning to winning form at the end of 2000 at Doncaster. Acts on fast ground over the minimum trip.

Three Angels (IRE)

104 63
6-y-o b g Houmayoun (FR)-Mullaghroe (Tarboosh (USA))
A W Carroll (M H Tompkins 5/6) R T C Racing

Placings:623/00115323463/0420202302060/25000-013253 (4528)
2001: 7^0GF, 7^1F, 7^3GF, 6^2G, 8^5GF, 7^3GF

	Starts	1st	2nd	3rd	Win & Pl
Career Total (Turf)	38	3	8	7	23237

53 6/01 Ling 7f E FRM £2899
75 6/98 Hayd 7f30y E(0-70)H GD £3053
70 5/98 Folk 7f F G-F £2595
Total win prize-money £8547

Going (Turf): Sf: 0-0 GS: 0-5 Gd: 1-11 GF: 1-17 Fm: 1-5
Distance: 5f/6f: 0-2 7f-8f: 3-32 9f-13f: 0-4 14f+: 0-0
Track : LH: 1-7 RH: 0-12 Tight: 0-9 Gall: 0-1
Aids: Bl: 1-5 Vi: 0-5 Tstrap: 0-0
Best Rating: 63 9/01 Ling 7f gd-fm

Three Black Dales (IRE)

87(83) (51)55
2-y-o b f Alhaarth (IRE)-Annsfield Lady (Red Sunset)
M Johnston R N Pennell

Placings:0666 (4551)
2001: 6^0G, 6^6GF, 7^6GF, 8^6SW

	Starts	1st	2nd	3rd	Win & Pl
Career Total (Turf)	3	0	0	0	0
Career Total (AW)	1	0	0	0	0

Going (Turf): Sf: 0-0 GS: 0-0 Gd: 0-1 GF: 0-2 Fm: 0-0
Distance: 5f/6f: 0-1 7f-8f: 0-2 9f-13f: 0-1 14f+: 0-0
Track : LH: 0-2 RH: 0-0 Tight: 0-1 Gall: 0-0
Aids: Bl: 0-0 Vi: 0-0 Tstrap: 0-0
Best Rating: 55 7/01 Newc 7f gd-fm

Three Cherries

97(83) (1)28
5-y-o ch m Formidable (USA)-Mistral's Dancer (Shareef Dancer (USA))
R E Barr P Cartmell

Placings:0050/40000004564500-000426044500 (4165)
2001: 8^0SW, 11^0SD, 16^0SD, 10^4GF, 11^2GF, 11^6GF, 12^0GF, 12^4G, 12^4G, 14^5G, 16^0GS, 12^0GF

	Starts	1st	2nd	3rd	Win & Pl
Career Total (Turf)	27	0	1	0	1088
Career Total (AW)	3	0	0	0	0

Going (Turf): Sf: 0-3 GS: 0-1 Gd: 0-9 GF: 0-11 Fm: 0-3
Distance: 5f/6f: 0-3 7f-8f: 0-6 9f-13f: 0-18 14f+: 0-3
Track : LH: 0-14 RH: 0-10 Tight: 0-12 Gall: 0-4
Aids: Bl: 0-0 Vi: 0-0 Tstrap: 0-0
Best Rating: 30 6/01 Bevl 1m3f216y gd-fm

Three Clouds

83 35
4-y-o b g Rainbow Quest (USA)-Three Tails (Blakeney)
G L Moore Rodger Sargent

Placings:34-0000 (5471)
2001: 7^0G, 7^0S, 10^0HY, 11^0S

	Starts	1st	2nd	3rd	Win & Pl
Career Total (Turf)	6	0	0	1	1040

Going (Turf): Sf: 0-3 GS: 0-0 Gd: 0-2 GF: 0-0 Fm: 0-0
Distance: 5f/6f: 0-0 7f-8f: 0-2 9f-13f: 0-4 14f+: 0-0
Track : LH: 0-2 RH: 0-2 Tight: 0-1 Gall: 0-0
Aids: Bl: 0-1 Vi: 0-0 Tstrap: 0-0
Best Rating: 35 10/01 Brig 7f214y soft

Three Days In May

75 30
2-y-o b f Cadeaux Genereux-Corn Futures (Nomination)
W J Haggas East Anglian Floral Society

Placings:0 (5125)
2001: 5^0HY

	Starts	1st	2nd	3rd	Win & Pl
Career Total (Turf)	1	0	0	0	

Going (Turf): Sf: 0-1 GS: 0-0 Gd: 0-0 GF: 0-0 Fm: 0-0
Distance: 5f/6f: 0-1 7f-8f: 0-0 9f-13f: 0-0 14f+: 0-0
Track : LH: 0-0 RH: 0-0 Tight: 0-0 Gall: 0-0
Aids: Bl: 0-0 Vi: 0-0 Tstrap: 0-0
Best Rating: 30 10/01 Ling 5f heavy

Three Eagles (USA)

103(65) 42
4-y-o ch g Eagle Eyed (USA)-Tertiary (USA) (Vaguely Noble)
A Bailey Granite By Design Ltd

Placings:3-000150000 (3836)
2001: 8^0SD, 12^0S, 10^0S, 16^1GF, 17^5F, 17^0G, 14^0G, 16^0GF, 10^0G

	Starts	1st	2nd	3rd	Win & Pl
Career Total (Turf)	9	1	0	1	4265
Career Total (AW)	1	0	0	0	

40 5/01 Wwck 2m39y E(0-70)H G-F £3112
Total win prize-money £3112

Going (Turf): Sf: 0-3 GS: 0-0 Gd: 0-3 GF: 1-2 Fm: 0-1
Distance: 5f/6f: 0-0 7f-8f: 0-1 9f-13f: 0-4 14f+: 1-5
Track : LH: 1-5 RH: 0-3 Tight: 0-4 Gall: 0-2
Aids: Bl: 1-6 Vi: 0-0 Tstrap: 0-0
Best Rating: 42 6/01 Pont 2m1f22y firm

Had been disappointing since coming over from France until scoring for the first time over two miles on fast ground in May in blinkers. Needs decent pace.

Three Leaders (IRE)

92(85) (13)30
5-y-o ch g Up And At 'Em-Wolviston (Wolverlife)
W Storey R J H Limited & Heath Private & Commerci

Placings:000/032015600505/06000400405-00000 (2866)
2001: 8^0GF, 9^0G, 8^0G, 10^0GF, 16^0GF

	Starts	1st	2nd	3rd	Win & Pl
Career Total (Turf)	28	1	1	1	3730
Career Total (AW)	3	0	0	0	0

56 6/99 Bevl 5f F(0-70)H G-F £2189
Total win prize-money £2190

Going (Turf): Sf: 0-2 GS: 0-3 Gd: 0-8 GF: 1-14 Fm: 0-1
Distance: 5f/6f: 1-15 7f-8f: 0-8 9f-13f: 0-7 14f+: 0-1
Track : LH: 0-11 RH: 0-7 Tight: 0-7 Gall: 0-5
Aids: Bl: 0-4 Vi: 0-2 Tstrap: 0-0
Best Rating: 30 6/01 Newc 1m2f32y gd-fm

Three Lions

105(94) (68)**71**
4-y-o ch g Jupiter Island-Super Sol (Rolfe (USA))
R F Johnson Houghton Jim Short

Placings:040/0164101-0040401 **(5640)**
2001: 10^{0}GF, 13^{0}GF, 14^{4}GS, 14^{0}HY, 16^{4}GF, 16^{0}HY, 13^{1}G, 14^{1}SD

	Starts	1st	2nd	3rd	Win & Pl
Career Total (Turf)	17	4	0	0	16260

67 11/01 Catt 1m5f175yE(0-70)H GD £3262
79 10/00 Wind 1m3f135yD(0-80)H HVY £3848
75 9/00 Kemp 1m6f92y E(0-75)H GD £4524
68 7/00 Bevl 1m1f207yE(0-65) G-F £2873
Total win prize-money £14507

Going (Turf): Sf: 1-3 GS: 0-4 **Gd: 2-6** GF: 1-4 Fm: 0-0
Distance: 5f/6f: 0-3 7f-8f: 0-0 9f-13f: 2-5 14f+: 2-9
Track : LH: 1-7 **RH: 2-8 Tight: 2-2** Gall: 0-6
Aids: Bl: 0-0 Vi: 0-0 Tstrap: 0-0
Best Rating: 71 7/01 NmkJ 1m6f175y gd-sft

Did well in 2000 and came good in the last week of the turf season when successful at Catterick. Stays well and acts on any type of ground, but prefers a sound surface.

Three Points

114 (85)**116**
4-y-o b h Bering-Trazl (IRE) (Zalazl (USA))
Saeed Bin Suroor Godolphin

Placings:113/3244121-0224205 **(5386)**
2001: 6^{0}FT, 7^{2}G, 6^{2}GF, 6^{4}G, 6^{2}S, 6^{0}HY, 7^{5}GS

	Starts	1st	2nd	3rd	Win & Pl
Career Total (Turf)	16	4	5	2	137516
Career Total (AW)	1	0	0	0	

115 8/00 Deau 6f G-S £21134
114 7/00 Newb 7f B G-F £9674
95 8/99 Nott 1m54y D G-F £3947
79 8/99 Kemp 7f D G-F £3615
Total win prize-money £38371

Going (Turf): Sf: 0-2 GS: 1-3 Gd: 0-4 **GF: 3-6** Fm: 0-0
Distance: 5f/6f: 1-5 **7f-8f: 2-8** 9f-13f: 1-4 14f+: 0-0
Track : LH: 1-2 RH: 1-4 Tight: 0-1 **Gall: 1-1**
Aids: Bl: 0-0 Vi: 0-0 Tstrap: 0-3
Best Rating: 116 8/01 Deau 6f110y soft

Running really well this term, finishing in the frame in the Cork and Orrery, July Cup and Prix Maurice de Gheest, but below par in heavy ground in the Haydock Sprint Cup. He likes to run from the front and six furlongs is his trip.

Threezedzz

104 **71**
3-y-o ch g Emarati (USA)-Exotic Forest (Dominion)
J G Portman Steve Evans

Placings:1263402-20506300 **(4849)**
2001: 6^{2}S, 5^{0}S, 6^{5}G, 6^{0}GF, 7^{6}G, 5^{3}GF, 6^{0}G, 6^{0}GF

	Starts	1st	2nd	3rd	Win & Pl
Career Total (Turf)	15	1	3	2	12635

70 4/00 Wind 5f10y E GD £2926
Total win prize-money £2926

Going (Turf): Sf: 0-2 GS: 0-0 **Gd: 1-7** GF: 0-6 Fm: 0-0
Distance: **5f/6f: 1-14** 7f-8f: 0-1 9f-13f: 0-0 14f+: 0-0
Track : LH: 0-0 **RH: 1-4** Tight: 0-0 **Gall: 1-3**
Aids: Bl: 0-1 Vi: 0-0 Tstrap: 0-0
Best Rating: 97 5/01 Ling 6f good

Ran well on soft ground on his Newmarket reappearance, but although he has not run up to that form since, has not always had luck on his side.

Through The Rye

101 **68**
5-y-o ch g Sabrehill (USA)-Baharlilys (Green Dancer (USA))
W J Haggas W J Gredley

Placings:45/340104/0-6204 **(2726)**
2001: 10^{6}G, 11^{2}GF, 10^{0}GF, 8^{4}GF

	Starts	1st	2nd	3rd	Win & Pl
Career Total (Turf)	13	1	1	1	10487

69 6/99 Newc 1m3y D GD £5277
Total win prize-money £5277

Going (Turf): Sf: 0-2 GS: 0-3 **Gd: 1-3** GF: 0-5 Fm: 0-0
Distance: 5f/6f: 0-0 7f-8f: 0-3 **9f-13f: 1-10** 14f+: 0-0
Track : LH: 0-6 RH: 0-2 Tight: 0-4 Gall: 0-1
Aids: Bl: 0-0 Vi: 0-0 Tstrap: 0-2
Best Rating: 68 5/01 Yarm 1m2f21y good

Thrower

59(94) (42)
10-y-o b g Thowra (FR)-Atlantic Line (Capricorn Line)
W M Brisbourne C M & S J Owen

Placings:005/402500032/4/4/11/145003-00 **(5531)**
2001: 17^{0}S, 16^{0}HY, 14^{0}SD

	Starts	1st	2nd	3rd	Win & Pl
Career Total (Turf)	20	2	2	2	9628
Career Total (AW)	4	1	0	0	2567

55 2/00 Sthl 2m F(0-80)H STD £2299
50 4/99 Nott 1m1f213yF(0-75)H SFT £2700
46 4/99 Leic 1m3f183yE(0-70)H G-S £3008
Total win prize-money £8008

Going (Turf): Sf: 1-7 GS: 1-3 Gd: 0-2 GF: 0-8 Fm: 0-0
Distance: 5f/6f: 0-0 7f-8f: 0-1 **9f-13f: 2-13** 14f+: 1-10
Track : **LH: 2-18** RH: 1-5 Tight: 0-6 Gall: 0-3
Aids: Bl: 0-0 Vi: 0-0 Tstrap: 0-0
Best Rating: 46 4/99 Leic 1m3f183y GS

He had a very successful time on the Flat and over hurdles a few years back, but went missing after September 2000. He has won over two miles on sand, but looks best suited by shorter.

Thrust

95(92) **36**
5-y-o br g Prince Sabo-La Piaf (FR) (Fabulous Dancer (USA))
W R Muir J Bernstein

Placings:202/506000 **(5560)**
2001: 7^{5}S, 7^{0}G, 8^{6}SD, 8^{0}HY, 8^{0}GS, 7^{0}S

	Starts	1st	2nd	3rd	Win & Pl
Career Total (Turf)	7	0	2	0	2598
Career Total (AW)	2	0	0	0	0

Going (Turf): Sf: 0-3 GS: 0-2 Gd: 0-2 GF: 0-0 Fm: 0-0
Distance: 5f/6f: 0-2 7f-8f: 0-5 9f-13f: 0-2 14f+: 0-0
Track : LH: 0-4 RH: 0-1 Tight: 0-1 Gall: 0-2
Aids: Bl: 0-0 Vi: 0-0 Tstrap: 0-0
Best Rating: 71 4/01 Kemp 7f soft

He showed ability in both of his turf starts at two. Off the track for over two years subsequently. Showed he retained his ability on reappearance in April 2001 but has been a bit disappointing since.

Thumamah (IRE)

89 **72**
2-y-o b f Charnwood Forest (IRE)-Anam (Persian Bold)
B Hanbury Hamdan Al Maktoum

Placings:403 **(4801)**
2001: 6^{4}GS, 6^{0}G, 5^{3}F

	Starts	1st	2nd	3rd	Win & Pl
Career Total (Turf)	3	0	0	1	956

Going (Turf): Sf: 0-0 GS: 0-1 Gd: 0-1 GF: 0-0 Fm: 0-1
Distance: 5f/6f: 0-3 7f-8f: 0-0 9f-13f: 0-0 14f+: 0-0
Track : LH: 0-1 RH: 0-0 Tight: 0-0 Gall: 0-0
Aids: Bl: 0-0 Vi: 0-0 Tstrap: 0-0
Best Rating: 72 9/01 Kemp 6f good

Thumper (IRE)

91 **78**
3-y-o b c Grand Lodge (USA)-Parkeen Princess (He Loves Me)
R Hannon The South-Western Partnership Ii

Placings:000P **(5664)**
2001: 8^{0}S, 8^{0}GF, 7^{0}GS, 8^{P}HY

	Starts	1st	2nd	3rd	Win & Pl
Career Total (Turf)	4	0	0	0	

Going (Turf): Sf: 0-2 GS: 0-1 Gd: 0-0 GF: 0-1 Fm: 0-0
Distance: 5f/6f: 0-0 7f-8f: 0-3 9f-13f: 0-1 14f+: 0-0
Track : LH: 0-0 RH: 0-2 Tight: 0-1 Gall: 0-0
Aids: Bl: 0-0 Vi: 0-0 Tstrap: 0-0
Best Rating: 78 4/01 NmkR 1m soft

Maiden who ran well in the spring, but has disappointed last twice, including when pulling up at Windsor in November 2001.

Thunder Canyon (USA)

88 **76**
2-y-o b/br c Gulch (USA)-Naazeq (Nashwan (USA))
M Johnston The Knavesmire Partnership

Placings:560 **(5483)**
2001: 8^{5}S, 6^{6}S, 7^{0}HY

	Starts	1st	2nd	3rd	Win & Pl
Career Total (Turf)	3	0	0	0	211

Going (Turf): Sf: 0-3 GS: 0-0 Gd: 0-0 GF: 0-0 Fm: 0-0
Distance: 5f/6f: 0-0 7f-8f: 0-3 9f-13f: 0-0 14f+: 0-0
Track : LH: 0-1 RH: 0-0 Tight: 0-0 Gall: 0-1
Aids: Bl: 0-0 Vi: 0-0 Tstrap: 0-0
Best Rating: 76 10/01 NmkR 1m soft

Thunder King (USA)

78 **63**
2-y-o b c Thunder Gulch (USA)-Savannah's Honor (USA) (Storm Bird (CAN))
M Johnston Markus Graff

Placings:45 **(4423)**
2001: 6^{4}S, 6^{5}GF

	Starts	1st	2nd	3rd	Win & Pl
Career Total (Turf)	2	0	0	0	315

Going (Turf): Sf: 0-1 GS: 0-0 Gd: 0-0 GF: 0-1 Fm: 0-0
Distance: 5f/6f: 0-2 7f-8f: 0-0 9f-13f: 0-0 14f+: 0-0
Track : LH: 0-0 RH: 0-0 Tight: 0-0 Gall: 0-0
Aids: Bl: 0-0 Vi: 0-0 Tstrap: 0-0
Best Rating: 63 9/01 Ripn 6f gd-fm

A half-brother to two winners in the States out of a dam who was a Group Three winner as a juvenile,showed up well on his debut at Haydock over six furlongs on soft ground. Might prefer a sounder surface.

Thunder Sky

105(107) (40)**48**
5-y-o b g Zafonic (USA)-Overcast (IRE) (Caerleon (USA))
D W Chapman (N P Littmoden 19/7) Michael Hill

Placings:5540/04510050-026015040002014100205000000 **(5613)**
2001: 7^{0}SW, 10^{2}SD, 10^{6}SW, 10^{0}SW, 8^{1}SD, 8^{5}SD, 7^{0}SD, 8^{4}SD, 10^{0}GF, 7^{0}GF, 8^{0}GF, 11^{2}F, 12^{0}GF, 10^{1}GF, 9^{4}F, 9^{1}GS, 8^{0}SD, 9^{0}G, 9^{2}GS, 12^{0}S, 9^{5}G, 8^{0}G, 8^{0}F, 7^{0}SD

	Starts	1st	2nd	3rd	Win & Pl
Career Total (Turf)	25	3	2	0	14514
Career Total (AW)	13	1	1	0	3557

54 7/01 Haml 1m1f36y F(0-65) G-S £2730
41 6/01 Rdcr 1m2f F G-F £2495
72 3/01 Wolv 1m100y E(0-70)H STD £2401

75 6/00 Folk 7f D FRM £2996
Total win prize-money £10623

Going (Turf): Sf: 0-1 **GS: 1-3** Gd: 0-8 **GF: 1-8 Fm: 1-5**
Distance: 5f/6f: 0-0 7f-8f: 1-14 **9f-13f: 3-24** 14f+: 0-0
Track : **LH: 2-21** RH: 1-8 **Tight: 3-19** Gall: 0-1
Aids: Bl: 0-9 **Vi: 4-19** Tstrap: 0-0
Best Rating: 72 3/01 Wolv 1m100y stand

Thunderbird Legend (IRE)

89(85) (42)**30**
2-y-o ch f Common Grounds-Alaroos (IRE) (Persian Bold)
T D Easterby The Four Ball Partnership

Placings:040400 **(4215)**
2001: 5^{0}G, 5^{4}SD, 5^{0}GF, 5^{4}G, 7^{0}G, 8^{0}G

	Starts	1st	2nd	3rd	Win & Pl
Career Total (Turf)	5	0	0	0	0
Career Total (AW)	1	0	0	0	0

Going (Turf): Sf: 0-0 GS: 0-0 Gd: 0-4 GF: 0-1 Fm: 0-0
Distance: 5f/6f: 0-4 7f-8f: 0-2 9f-13f: 0-0 14f+: 0-0
Track : LH: 0-2 RH: 0-0 Tight: 0-1 Gall: 0-1
Aids: Bl: 0-2 Vi: 0-0 Tstrap: 0-0
Best Rating: 42 7/01 Sthl 5f stand

Thunderclap

99 **85+**
2-y-o b c Royal Applause-Gloriana (Formidable (USA))
J W Hills The Dan Abbott Racing Partnership

Placings:3010 **(4659)**
2001: 6^{3}GF, 6^{0}G, 6^{1}GF, 6^{0}GF

	Starts	1st	2nd	3rd	Win & Pl
Career Total (Turf)	4	1	0	1	3440
85 9/01 Brig	6f209y	E		G-F	£2786

Total win prize-money £2786

Going (Turf): Sf: 0-0 GS: 0-0 Gd: 0-1 **GF: 1-3** Fm: 0-0
Distance: 5f/6f: 0-3 **7f-8f: 1-1** 9f-13f: 0-0 14f+: 0-0
Track : **LH: 1-1** RH: 0-0 Tight: 0-0 Gall: 0-0
Aids: Bl: 0-0 Vi: 0-0 Tstrap: 0-0
Best Rating: 85 9/01 Brig 6f209y gd-fm

Comfortable winner of a Brighton maiden on his third start. Stays seven furlongs, acts on fast ground.

Thundered (USA)

99(75) (24)**53**
3-y-o gr g Thunder Gulch (USA)-Lady Lianga (USA) (Secretariat (USA))
G A Swinbank (Mrs J R Ramsden 11/6) Scotnorth Racing Ltd

Placings:00-0034246 **(3308)**
2001: 8^{0}HY, 12^{0}SD, 8^{3}F, 7^{4}G, 8^{2}GF, 9^{4}S, 7^{6}GS

	Starts	1st	2nd	3rd	Win & Pl
Career Total (Turf)	8	0	1	1	1243
Career Total (AW)	1	0	0	0	

Going (Turf): Sf: 0-3 GS: 0-1 Gd: 0-1 GF: 0-2 Fm: 0-1
Distance: 5f/6f: 0-0 7f-8f: 0-5 9f-13f: 0-4 14f+: 0-0
Track : LH: 0-7 RH: 0-2 Tight: 0-3 Gall: 0-2
Aids: Bl: 0-3 Vi: 0-0 Tstrap: 0-0
Best Rating: 57 5/01 Newc 1m firm

Thundergod

91 **68**
2-y-o b c Torrential (USA)-Reach The Wind (USA) (Relaunch (USA))
I A Balding Miss A V Hill

Placings:003000 **(4954)**
2001: 6^{0}GF, 6^{0}GF, 7^{3}GF, 6^{0}G, 8^{0}F, 8^{0}GS
Starts 1st 2nd 3rd Win & Pl

	Starts	1st	2nd	3rd	Win & Pl
Career Total (Turf)	6	0	0	1	446

Going (Turf): Sf: 0-0 GS: 0-1 Gd: 0-1 GF: 0-3 Fm: 0-1
Distance: 5f/6f: 0-0 7f-8f: 0-5 9f-13f: 0-1 14f+: 0-0
Track : LH: 0-2 RH: 0-1 Tight: 0-1 Gall: 0-1
Aids: Bl: 0-0 Vi: 0-0 Tstrap: 0-0
Best Rating: 68 7/01 Ling 7f gd-fm

Thundering Surf

110 **94**
4-y-o b c Lugana Beach-Thunder Bug (USA) (Secreto (USA))
J R Jenkins Mr C N & Mrs J C Wright

Placings:5/00135432-42426131360 **(5693)**
2001: 10^{4}G, 10^{2}G, 10^{4}GF, 10^{2}GF, 12^{6}GF, 12^{1}G, 12^{3}GF, 12^{1}G, 12^{3}HY, 12^{6}GS, 12^{0}S

	Starts	1st	2nd	3rd	Win & Pl
Career Total (Turf)	20	3	3	4	80827

94 9/01 Kemp 1m4f C(0-100)H GD £8931
91 8/01 Asct 1m4f B(0-100)H GD £22550
81 7/00 Sand 1m2f7y D(0-85)H GD £7507
Total win prize-money £38989

Going (Turf): Sf: 0-4 GS: 0-2 **Gd: 3-8** GF: 0-6 Fm: 0-0
Distance: 5f/6f: 0-0 7f-8f: 0-1 **9f-13f: 3-19** 14f+: 0-0
Track : LH: 0-6 **RH: 3-9** Tight: 0-3 **Gall: 1-9**
Aids: Bl: 0-0 Vi: 0-0 Tstrap: 0-0
Best Rating: 94 9/01 Asct 1m4f heavy

Made a winning debut in handicap company at Sandown in the summer of 2000 ovor ton furlongc and was unlucky not to score on several occasions afterwards. He finally got it right on his second attempt over 12 furlongs on Shergar Cup day at Ascot 2001 in August and added to that at Kempton the following month, before running well in a competitive event at Ascot on ground that may not have been to his liking. Suited by a sound surface and a good gallop.

Thundermill (USA)

105(98) (72)**71**
3-y-o ch g Thunder Gulch (USA)-Specifically (USA) (Sky Classic (CAN))
T G Mills Resplendent Racing Limited

Placings:536021-0045100 **(4704)**
2001: 10^{0}SW, 9^{0}G, 8^{4}GF, 12^{5}GF, 9^{1}GF, 10^{0}G, 8^{0}G

	Starts	1st	2nd	3rd	Win & Pl
Career Total (Turf)	10	1	0	1	5203
Career Total (AW)	3	1	1	0	3572

71 8/01 Folk 1m1f149yD(0-80)H G-F £4143
72 11/00 Ling 1m2f D STD £2856
Total win prize-money £7000

Going (Turf): Sf: 0-1 GS: 0-0 Gd: 0-5 **GF: 1-4** Fm: 0-0
Distance: 5f/6f: 0-0 7f-8f: 0-6 **9f-13f: 2-7** 14f+: 0-0
Track : LH: 1-5 RH: 1-7 **Tight: 2-6** Gall: 0-2
Aids: Bl: 0-0 Vi: 0-1 Tstrap: 0-0
Best Rating: 71 8/01 Folk 1m1f149y gd-fm

Has ability but is far from consistent. Suited by ten furlongs and fast ground. Likes to dominate. Won well at Folkestone in August 2001.

Thwaab

99 (19)**58**
9-y-o b g Dominion-Velvet Habit (Habitat)
F Watson F Watson

Placings:0000/536046/020505131210240/0623003030 0/00012000400/000/061110-000501 **(4550)**
2001: 9^{0}F, 8^{0}GF, 8^{0}GF, 8^{5}GF, 8^{0}GF, 8^{1}GF

	Starts	1st	2nd	3rd	Win & Pl
Career Total (Turf)	59	8	5	5	41293
Career Total (AW)	3	0	0	0	

54 9/01 Sals 1m E(0-70)H G-F £3444
55 8/00 Rdcr 1m D(0-85)H FRM £5170
52 7/00 Rdcr 1m G(0-60)H G-F £2261
49 7/00 Carl 6f206y E(0-70)H FRM £3042
58 7/98 Donc 7f D(0-75)H FRM £3980
61 8/96 Rdcr 6f F(0-60)H G-F £2994
56 7/96 Ayr 6f D(0-85)H G-F £4318
50 6/96 Ayr 6f F(0-85)H G-F £2918
Total win prize-money £28129

Going (Turf): Sf: 0-1 GS: 0-5 Gd: 0-16 **GF: 5-26** Fm: 3-11
Distance: 5f/6f: 3-22 **7f-8f: 5-37** 9f-13f: 0-3 14f+: 0-0
Track : LH: 0-16 **RH: 1-8** Tight: 0-8 Gall: 0-4
Aids: Bl: 2-11 **Vi: 4-19** Tstrap: 0-0
Best Rating: 54 9/01 Sals 1m gd-fm

A bit inconsistent, but a decent handicapper when in form. He completed a hat-trick during the summer of 2000 and returned to winning form this season at Salisbury in September. Suited by a mile and fast ground.

Thwaites Smoothie

88(75) (30)**50**
2-y-o b f River Falls-Chilibang Bang (Chilibang)
A Berry Thwaites Brewery

Placings:5600000 **(5618)**
2001: 6^{5}GF, 5^{6}GF, 5^{0}GF, 5^{0}GS, 7^{0}GS, 8^{0}HY, 8^{0}SD

	Starts	1st	2nd	3rd	Win & Pl
Career Total (Turf)	6	0	0	0	0
Career Total (AW)	1	0	0	0	

Going (Turf): Sf: 0-1 GS: 0-2 Gd: 0-0 GF: 0-3 Fm: 0-0
Distance: 5f/6f: 0-4 7f-8f: 0-1 9f-13f: 0-2 14f+: 0-0
Track : LH: 0-4 RH: 0-0 Tight: 0-2 Gall: 0-0
Aids: Bl: 0-0 Vi: 0-0 Tstrap: 0-0
Best Rating: 50 7/01 Sthl 6f gd-fm

Thwaites Star (IRE)

97(73) (23)**55**
2-y-o b f Petardia-Monterana (Sallust)
A Berry Thwaites Brewery

Placings:30530000 **(5660)**
2001: 5^{3}GF, 6^{0}GF, 6^{5}F, 5^{3}HY, 5^{0}G, 6^{0}HY, 6^{0}SD, 5^{0}G

	Starts	1st	2nd	3rd	Win & Pl
Career Total (Turf)	7	0	0	2	1118
Career Total (AW)	1	0	0	0	

Going (Turf): Sf: 0-2 GS: 0-0 Gd: 0-2 GF: 0-2 Fm: 0-1
Distance: 5f/6f: 0-7 7f-8f: 0-1 9f-13f: 0-0 14f+: 0-0
Track : LH: 0-2 RH: 0-0 Tight: 0-1 Gall: 0-1
Aids: Bl: 0-0 Vi: 0-0 Tstrap: 0-0
Best Rating: 68 6/01 Wwck 5f gd-fm

Tibbie

100(89) (27)**54**
3-y-o b f Slip Anchor-Circe (Main Reef)
R M Beckett A D G Oldrey

Placings:05-00502555 **(4478)**
2001: 8^{0}GS, 11^{0}G, 11^{5}GF, 14^{0}G, 12^{2}GF, 14^{5}F, 16^{5}GF, 16^{5}F, 13^{0}SD

	Starts	1st	2nd	3rd	Win & Pl
Career Total (Turf)	10	0	1	0	1145

Going (Turf): Sf: 0-0 GS: 0-2 Gd: 0-3 GF: 0-3 Fm: 0-2
Distance: 5f/6f: 0-1 7f-8f: 0-0 9f-13f: 0-5 14f+: 0-4
Track : LH: 0-4 RH: 0-4 Tight: 0-7 Gall: 0-0
Aids: Bl: 0-0 Vi: 0-0 Tstrap: 0-0
Best Rating: 54 7/01 Pont 1m4f8y gd-fm

Ticcatoo (IRE)

(99) (63)**62**
3 y o br f Dolphin Street (FR)-Accountancy Jewel (IRE) (Pennine Walk)
R Hollinshead John L Marriott

Placings:100020040422-434 (0187)
2001: 6^4SD, 5^3SW, 5^4SD

	Starts	1st	2nd	3rd	Win & Pl
Career Total (Turf)	7	0	1	0	900
Career Total (AW)	9	1	2	1	4202

62 4/00 Sthl 5f F STD £2299
Total win prize-money £2300

Going (Turf): Sf: 0-3 GS: 0-2 Gd: 0-1 GF: 0-1 Fm: 0-0
Distance: **5f/6f: 1-14** 7f-8f: 0-2 9f-13f: 0-0 14f+: 0-0
Track : LH: 0-6 RH: 0-0 Tight: 0-4 Gall: 0-0
Aids: Bl: 0-0 Vi: 0-0 Tstrap: 0-0
Best Rating: 57 1/01 Sthl 5f slow

Tick Tock

105(78) (8)**58**
4-y-o ch f Timeless Times (USA)-Aquiletta (Bairn (USA))
M Mullineaux Michael Mullineaux

Placings:50020/0022000400630-0006000041142503 (5629)
2001: 5^0GF, 5^0G, 6^0F, 5^0GF, 5^6GF, 6^0GF, 6^0SD, 5^0GF, 5^0G, 5^4GF, 5^1GF, 5^1G, 5^4S, 5^2S, 5^5G, 5^0HY, 5^3G

	Starts	1st	2nd	3rd	Win & Pl
Career Total (Turf)	34	2	4	2	14852
Career Total (AW)	1	0	0	0	

58 9/01 Ayr 5f D(0-85)H GD £6500
51 9/01 Thsk 5f F(0-60)H G-F £3517
Total win prize-money £10018

Going (Turf): Sf: 0-9 GS: 0-3 **Gd: 1-8 GF: 1-12** Fm: 0-2
Distance: **5f/6f: 2-33** 7f-8f: 0-2 9f-13f: 0-0 14f+: 0-0
Track : LH: 0-10 RH: 0-1 Tight: 0-3 Gall: 0-2
Aids: Bl: 0-0 Vi: 0-10 Tstrap: 0-0
Best Rating: 68 5/01 Ches 5f16y gd-fm

She went 28 starts without winning, but then suddenly took off in September with consecutive wins in big-field handicaps at Thirsk and Ayr, but has since looked to be high enough in the handicap. Suited by the minimum trip and fast ground.

Ticker

104 **69**
3-y-o b g Timeless Times (USA)-Lady Day (FR) (Lightning (FR))
Denys Smith Evelyn Duchess Of Sutherland

Placings:36-01523664360 (5272)
2001: 9^0GS, 10^1S, 10^5GF, 10^2GF, 9^3GF, 10^6GF, 8^6GS, 11^4GS, 9^3G, 8^6GS, 10^0HY

	Starts	1st	2nd	3rd	Win & Pl
Career Total (Turf)	13	1	1	3	7411

69 5/01 Newc 1m2f32y D SFT £3435
Total win prize-money £3435

Going (Turf): Sf: 1-2 GS: 0-4 Gd: 0-1 GF: 0-5 Fm: 0-1
Distance: 5f/6f: 0-2 7f-8f: 0-1 **9f-13f: 1-10** 14f+: 0-0
Track : **LH: 1-7** RH: 0-2 Tight: 0-3 **Gall: 1-1**
Aids: Bl: 0-0 Vi: 0-0 Tstrap: 0-0
Best Rating: 74 6/01 Rdcr 1m1f gd-fm

He got off the mark in a fair Newcastle maiden over ten furlongs in May 2001 and has been in the minor placings regularly since then. He has run well on fast ground but can be seen to best effect on an easier surface. He is currently running close to the mark he won off.

Ticket To Dance (IRE)

92 **77+**
2-y-o b f Sadler's Wells (USA)-River Missy (USA) (Riverman (USA))
J H M Gosden R E Sangster

Placings:0 (5602)
2001: 7^0GS

	Starts	1st	2nd	3rd	Win & Pl
Career Total (Turf)	1	0	0	0	

Going (Turf): Sf: 0-0 GS: 0-1 Gd: 0-0 GF: 0-0 Fm: 0-0
Distance: 5f/6f: 0-0 7f-8f: 0-1 9f-13f: 0-0 14f+: 0-0
Track : LH: 0-0 RH: 0-0 Tight: 0-0 Gall: 0-0
Aids: Bl: 0-0 Vi: 0-0 Tstrap: 0-0
Best Rating: 77 11/01 NmkR 7f gd-sft

Tickit (IRE)

92 **53**
2-y-o b c Alhaarth (IRE)-Pericolo (IRE) (Kris)
M R Channon Tim Corby

Placings:004600 (4856)
2001: 8^0GF, 6^0GF, 6^4GF, 7^0GF, 8^0GF, 7^0GF

	Starts	1st	2nd	3rd	Win & Pl
Career Total (Turf)	6	0	0	0	289

Going (Turf): Sf: 0-0 GS: 0-0 Gd: 0-0 GF: 0-6 Fm: 0-0
Distance: 5f/6f: 0-2 7f-8f: 0-3 9f-13f: 0-1 14f+: 0-0
Track : LH: 0-1 RH: 0-0 Tight: 0-1 Gall: 0-0
Aids: Bl: 0-0 Vi: 0-0 Tstrap: 0-0
Best Rating: 59 7/01 Sals 6f gd-fm

Tickle

91(87) (50)**79**
3-y-o b f Primo Dominie-Funny Choice (IRE) (Commanche Run)
P J Makin Mrs Derek Strauss

Placings:02211-003 (3253)
2001: 6^0GF, 7^0SD, 7^3GS

	Starts	1st	2nd	3rd	Win & Pl
Career Total (Turf)	7	2	2	1	12341
Career Total (AW)	1	0	0	0	

79 10/00 Ling 6f D(0-85) SFT £4010
64 9/00 York 6f E GD £5239
Total win prize-money £9250

Going (Turf): Sf: 1-1 GS: 0-1 **Gd: 1-3** GF: 0-2 Fm: 0-0
Distance: **5f/6f: 2-6** 7f-8f: 0-2 9f-13f: 0-0 14f+: 0-0
Track : LH: 0-2 RH: 0-1 Tight: 0-0 Gall: 0-2
Aids: Bl: 0-0 Vi: 0-0 Tstrap: 0-0
Best Rating: 75 7/01 NmkJ 7f gd-sft

Tickover

75 **42**
2-y-o b c Overbury (IRE)-Celtic Chimes (Celtic Cone)
G P Enright Chris Wall

Placings:00 (4574)
2001: 7^0G, 8^0G

	Starts	1st	2nd	3rd	Win & Pl
Career Total (Turf)	2	0	0	0	

Going (Turf): Sf: 0-0 GS: 0-0 Gd: 0-2 GF: 0-0 Fm: 0-0
Distance: 5f/6f: 0-0 7f-8f: 0-2 9f-13f: 0-0 14f+: 0-0
Track : LH: 0-0 RH: 0-1 Tight: 0-0 Gall: 0-0
Aids: Bl: 0-0 Vi: 0-0 Tstrap: 0-0
Best Rating: 42 9/01 Kemp 1m good

Tidal Beach

87 **61**
2-y-o b c Lugana Beach-Efficacy (Efisio)
C W Thornton Brookes, Brown, Busbey & Moses

Placings:03 (3485)
2001: 6^0G, 6^3GF

	Starts	1st	2nd	3rd	Win & Pl
Career Total (Turf)	2	0	0	1	436

Going (Turf): Sf: 0-0 GS: 0-0 Gd: 0-1 GF: 0-1 Fm: 0-0
Distance: 5f/6f: 0-2 7f-8f: 0-0 9f-13f: 0-0 14f+: 0-0
Track : LH: 0-0 RH: 0-0 Tight: 0-0 Gall: 0-0
Aids: Bl: 0-0 Vi: 0-0 Tstrap: 0-0
Best Rating: 61 7/01 Newc 6f gd-fm

Tie Break (IRE)

92(82) (11)**35**
6-y-o ch g Second Set (IRE)-Karayasha (Posse (USA))
R J O'Sullivan Jack Joseph

Placings:03/0500311/03 (1529)
2001: 12^0SD, 11^3F

	Starts	1st	2nd	3rd	Win & Pl
Career Total (Turf)	9	2	0	2	5748
Career Total (AW)	2	0	0	1	314

52 8/98 Muss 1m4f E(0-70) GD £2745
55 8/98 Leic 1m1f218yF GD £2406
Total win prize-money £5152

Going (Turf): Sf: 0-1 GS: 0-1 **Gd: 2-4** GF: 0-2 Fm: 0-1
Distance: 5f/6f: 0-3 7f-8f: 0-0 **9f-13f: 2-8** 14f+: 0-0
Track : LH: 0-6 **RH: 2-3 Tight: 1-2** Gall: 0-1
Aids: **Bl: 2-4** Vi: 0-0 Tstrap: 0-0
Best Rating: 35 5/01 Brig 1m3f196y firm

Tiger Feet

98(97) (82)**76**
2-y-o b c Petong-Selvi (Mummy's Pet)
A Berry Norman Jackson

Placings:3442100 (5408)
2001: 5^3GF, 5^4SD, 5^4F, 6^2SD, 5^1GF, 6^0GF, 6^0SD

	Starts	1st	2nd	3rd	Win & Pl
Career Total (Turf)	4	1	0	1	8169
Career Total (AW)	3	0	1	0	7260

76 8/01 Bevl 5f C G-F £7280
Total win prize-money £7280

Going (Turf): Sf: 0-0 GS: 0-0 Gd: 0-0 **GF: 1-3** Fm: 0-1
Distance: **5f/6f: 1-7** 7f-8f: 0-0 9f-13f: 0-0 14f+: 0-0
Track : LH: 0-3 RH: 0-0 Tight: 0-1 Gall: 0-0
Aids: Bl: 0-0 Vi: 0-0 Tstrap: 0-0
Best Rating: 82 8/01 Wolv 6f stand

Winner of a decent Beverley nursery over five furlongs in the summer of 2001, he looks to have the ample amount of speed his pedigree suggests he should have and it will not be long before he scores again over his favoured five-furlong trip.

Tiger Grass (IRE)

(94) (47)**58d**
5-y-o gr g Ezzoud (IRE)-Rustic Lawn (Rusticaro (FR))
W R Muir M J Caddy

Placings:024/00000240/06-20 (0311)
2001: 16^2SD, 16^0SD

	Starts	1st	2nd	3rd	Win & Pl
Career Total (Turf)	13	0	2	0	2727
Career Total (AW)	2	0	1	0	694

Going (Turf): Sf: 0-2 GS: 0-2 Gd: 0-4 GF: 0-5 Fm: 0-0
Distance: 5f/6f: 0-0 7f-8f: 0-4 9f-13f: 0-8 14f+: 0-3
Track : LH: 0-7 RH: 0-1 Tight: 0-4 Gall: 0-0
Aids: Bl: 0-1 Vi: 0-0 Tstrap: 0-0
Best Rating: 47 1/01 Sthl 2m stand

Tiger Princess

46(55)
4-y-o b f Bin Ajwaad (IRE)-Penny Dip (Cadeaux Genereux)
C N Kellett Willwewontwe Club

Placings:0-000 (3187)
2001: 6^0GS, 8^0GF, 11^0GS

	Starts	1st	2nd	3rd	Win & Pl
Career Total (Turf)	3	0	0	0	
Career Total (AW)	1	0	0	0	

Going (Turf): Sf: 0-0 GS: 0-2 Gd: 0-0 GF: 0-1 Fm: 0-0
Distance: 5f/6f: 0-1 7f-8f: 0-2 9f-13f: 0-1 14f+: 0-0
Track : LH: 0-1 RH: 0-2 Tight: 0-1 Gall: 0-0
Aids: Bl: 0-0 Vi: 0-0 Tstrap: 0-1
Best Rating: 47 1/01 Sthl 2m stand

Tiger Royal (IRE)

104 **101**

5-y-o gr g Royal Academy (USA)-Lady Redford (Bold Lad (IRE))
D K Weld (D Nicholls 1/7) Peter Jones

Placings:5401023/266443321323-000002302 **(5549a)**
2001: 5^{0}G, 6^{0}GF, 6^{0}GF, 6^{0}GF, 6^{0}Y, 5^{2}GY, 5^{3}G, 5^{0}S, 6^{2}YS, 7^{2}S

	Starts	1st	2nd	3rd	Win & Pl
Career Total (Turf)	**28**	**2**	**6**	**6**	**50045**

93 9/00 Curr 5f (0-105)H Y-S £9750
87 8/99 Curr 5f G-Y £4485
Total win prize-money £14235

Going (Turf): Sf: 0-6 GS: 0-0 Gd: 0-7 GF: 0-4 Fm: 0-1
Distance: **5f/6f: 2-22** 7f-8f: 0-4 9f-13f: 0-0 14f+: 0-0
Track : LH: 0-2 RH: 0-1 Tight: 0-0 Gall: 0-0
Aids: **Bl: 2-22** Vi: 0-0 Tstrap: 0-0
Best Rating: 101 10/01 Leop 6f yld-sft

Twice a winner over five furlongs at the Curragh when trained by Dermot Weld, he was poorly drawn on his British debut at Beverley and ran much better at York. He appeared to be in need of some ease in the handicap and when he got it he ran into some good place form. Soft ground suits.

Tiger Talk

76 **36**

5-y-o ch g Sabrehill (USA)-Tebre (USA) (Sir Ivor)
M E Sowersby M E Sowersby

Placings:00022/110000/0000050-0 **(1004)**
2001: 12^{0}S

	Starts	1st	2nd	3rd	Win & Pl
Career Total (Turf)	**19**	**2**	**2**	**0**	**13049**

89 4/99 Sand 1m14y B(0-105)H SFT £8926
89 3/99 Folk 7f F SFT £2408
Total win prize-money £11334

Going (Turf): Sf: 2-9 GS: 0-0 Gd: 0-5 GF: 0-3 Fm: 0-1
Distance: 5f/6f: 0-0 7f-8f: 1-10 9f-13f: 1-9 14f+: 0-0
Track : LH: 0-4 **RH: 1-6** Tight: 0-7 Gall: 0-1
Aids: Bl. 0-1 Vi. 0-2 Tstrap. 0-0
Best Rating: 17 4/01 Ripn 1m4f60y soft

Tight Squeeze

103(92) (32)**49**

4-y-o br f Petoski-Snowline (Bay Express)
P W Hiatt Anthony Harrison

Placings:0003-5005005024 **(4162)**
2001: 12^{5}SD, 12^{0}SW, 10^{0}GF, 9^{5}GF, 9^{0}G, 12^{0}GF, 9^{5}GS, 11^{0}G, 9^{2}GF, 10^{4}GF

	Starts	1st	2nd	3rd	Win & Pl
Career Total (Turf)	**8**	**0**	**1**	**0**	**980**
Career Total (AW)	**6**	**0**	**0**	**1**	**321**

Going (Turf): Sf: 0-0 GS: 0-1 Gd: 0-2 GF: 0-5 Fm: 0-0
Distance: 5f/6f: 0-0 7f-8f: 0-1 9f-13f: 0-13 14f+: 0-0
Track : LH: 0-10 RH: 0-4 Tight: 0-5 Gall: 0-0
Aids: Bl: 0-0 Vi: 0-0 Tstrap: 0-0
Best Rating: 57 6/01 Folk 1m1f149y gd-fm

Tightrope

101(112) (69)**43**

6-y-o b g Alzao (USA)-Circus Act (Shirley Heights)
J Balding (J A Osborne 6/8) J E Abbey

Placings:0044216/500/10220246/30010000-1306205023460 **(5406)**
2001: 8^{1}SD, 10^{3}SD, 10^{0}SW, 8^{6}SW, 8^{2}SD, 8^{0}HY, 8^{5}HD, 8^{0}GF, 8^{2}SD, 8^{3}S, 9^{4}SD, 8^{6}SD, 8^{0}SD, 8^{0}SD

	Starts	1st	2nd	3rd	Win & Pl
Career Total (Turf)	**18**	**2**	**2**	**1**	**8482**
Career Total (AW)	**21**	**2**	**4**	**2**	**15279**

69 1/01 Ling 1m G STD £1358
69 3/00 Ling 1m2f C(0-95)H STD £8385
51 9/99 Yarm 1m2f21y G G-S £2162
79 10/97 Leic 1m8y E(0-75) G-F £3956
Total win prize-money £15862

Going (Turf): Sf: 0-6 **GS: 1-2** Gd: 0-5 **GF: 1-4** Fm: 0-1
Distance: 5f/6f: 0-4 7f-8f: 1-8 **9f-13f: 3-27** 14f+: 0-0
Track : **LH: 3-29** RH: 0-4 **Tight: 3-21** Gall: 0-2
Aids: Bl: 0-0 Vi: 0-1 Tstrap: 0-0
Best Rating: 69 10/01 Wolv 1m1f79y stand

Has won four times from a mile to ten furlongs, although he looks held in the handicap at the moment.

Tigne

95(76) (44)**74+**

2-y-o b g Magic Ring (IRE)-Elkie (Most Welcome)
N P Littmoden (M Johnston 30/7) Richard Green (fine Paintings)

Placings:621 **(3499)**
2001: 5^{6}SD, 5^{2}GF, 6^{1}GF

	Starts	1st	2nd	3rd	Win & Pl
Career Total (Turf)	**2**	**1**	**1**	**0**	**2747**
Career Total (AW)	**1**	**0**	**0**	**0**	**0**

74 7/01 Yarm 6f3y G G-F £1886
Total win prize-money £1887

Going (Turf): Sf: 0-0 GS: 0-0 Gd: 0-0 **GF: 1-2** Fm: 0-0
Distance: 5f/6f: 0-2 **7f-8f: 1-1** 9f-13f: 0-0 14f+: 0-0
Track : LH: 0-0 RH: 0-0 Tight: 0-0 Gall: 0-0
Aids: Bl. 0-0 Vi. 0-0 Tstrap. 0-0
Best Rating: 74 7/01 Yarm 6f3y gd-fm

Won a seller in good style at Yarmouth and was sold for 11,000gns afterwards.

Tigre Bois

95 **42**

4-y-o b g Mon Tresor-Gentle Star (Comedy Star (USA))
B R Millman Victor G Palmer

Placings:00/00566604 **(4048)**
2001: 7^{0}S, 9^{0}F, 6^{5}GF, 9^{6}GF, 8^{6}G, 8^{6}GF, 9^{0}G, 10^{4}F

	Starts	1st	2nd	3rd	Win & Pl
Career Total (Turf)	**10**	**0**	**0**	**0**	**0**

Going (Turf): Sf: 0-1 GS: 0-1 Gd: 0-3 GF: 0-3 Fm: 0-2
Distance: 5f/6f: 0-0 7f-8f: 0-4 9f-13f: 0-6 14f+: 0-0
Track : LH: 0-2 RH: 0-4 Tight: 0-2 Gall: 0-1
Aids: Bl: 0-0 Vi: 0-0 Tstrap: 0-0
Best Rating: 42 7/01 Sand 1m14y gd-fm

Tigrello

97 **48**

7-y-o ch g Efisio-Prejudice (Young Generation)
J M Bradley T G Williams

Placings:526/2510460/0/0001/00404500 **(3151)**
2001: 8^{0}G, 8^{0}GF, 7^{4}GF, 8^{0}G, 8^{4}G, 8^{5}GF, 8^{0}G, 7^{0}GS

	Starts	1st	2nd	3rd	Win & Pl
Career Total (Turf)	**23**	**2**	**2**	**0**	**10161**

54 7/99 Brig 7f214y F FRM £2316
85 5/97 Wwck 1m D FRM £3349
Total win prize-money £5666

Going (Turf): Sf: 0-1 GS: 0-2 Gd: 0-12 GF: 0-6 **Fm: 2-2**
Distance: 5f/6f: 0-3 **7f-8f: 2-14** 9f-13f: 0-6 14f+: 0-0
Track : **LH: 2-9** RH: 0-2 Tight: 0-2 Gall: 0-5
Aids: Bl: 0-0 Vi: 0-0 Tstrap: 0-0
Best Rating: 53 5/01 Wwck 1m22y gd-fm

Tigress (IRE)

97(97) (74)**59**

2-y-o b f Desert Style (IRE)-Ervedya (IRE) (Doyoun)
P D Evans (B J Meehan 6/10) Men Behaving Badly

Placings:316140403145 **(5621)**
2001: 5^{3}G, 5^{1}SD, 5^{6}GF, 5^{1}SD, 6^{4}GF, 6^{0}GY, 6^{4}GS, 6^{0}SW, 5^{3}S, 5^{1}SD, 5^{4}S, 5^{5}GS, 6^{3}SD, 5^{1}SD

	Starts	1st	2nd	3rd	Win & Pl
Career Total (Turf)	**8**	**0**	**0**	**2**	**2017**
Career Total (AW)	**4**	**3**	**0**	**0**	**6643**

74 10/01 Wolv 5f G STD £1988
65 6/01 Wolv 5f F STD £2268
65 5/01 Sthl 5f E STD £2387
Total win prize-money £6643

Going (Turf): Sf: 0-2 GS: 0-2 Gd: 0-1 GF: 0-2 Fm: 0-0
Distance: **5f/6f: 3-12** 7f-8f: 0-0 9f-13f: 0-0 14f+: 0-0
Track : **LH: 2-7** RH: 0-0 **Tight: 2-4** Gall: 0-2
Aids: **Bl: 1-3** Vi: 0-0 Tstrap: 0-0
Best Rating: 74 10/01 Wolv 5f stand

Basically a plater and has gained all three of her wins over the minimum trip on Fibresand, but she seemed to stay six furlongs when third at Southwell in November.

Tikkun (IRE)

96 **99+**

2-y-o ch c Grand Lodge (USA)-Moon Festival (Be My Guest (USA))
R Charlton Mountgrange Stud

Placings:21 **(4458)**
2001: 6^{2}GF, 6^{1}G

	Starts	1st	2nd	3rd	Win & Pl
Career Total (Turf)	**2**	**1**	**1**	**0**	**4068**

99 9/01 Folk 6f D GD £2814
Total win prize-money £2814

Going (Turf): Sf: 0-0 GS: 0-0 **Gd: 1-1** GF: 0-1 Fm: 0-0
Distance: **5f/6f: 1-2** 7f-8f: 0-0 9f-13f: 0-0 14f+: 0-0
Track : LH: 0-0 RH: 0-0 Tight: 0-0 Gall: 0-0
Aids: Bl: 0-0 Vi: 0-0 Tstrap: 0-0
Best Rating: 99 9/01 Folk 6f good

Slammed some modest opposition at Folkestone in September.

Tikopia

98 (7)**44**

7-y-o b g Saddlers' Hall (IRE)-Shesadelight (Shirley Heights)
M E Sowersby A Milner

Placings:32426513/30600405/0400P **(1581)**
2001: 17^{0}HY, 14^{4}S, 12^{0}S, 12^{0}S, 12^{P}F

	Starts	1st	2nd	3rd	Win & Pl
Career Total (Turf)	**20**	**1**	**2**	**3**	**8229**
Career Total (AW)	**1**	**0**	**0**	**0**	

72 9/97 Bath 1m3f144yD GD £4011
Total win prize-money £4011

Going (Turf): Sf: 0-6 GS: 0-2 **Gd: 1-6** GF: 0-4 Fm: 0-2
Distance: 5f/6f: 0-0 7f-8f: 0-0 **9f-13f: 1-15** 14f+: 0-6
Track : **LH: 1-13** RH: 0-8 **Tight: 1-9** Gall: 0-2
Aids: Bl: 0-4 Vi: 0-2 Tstrap: 0-0
Best Rating: 44 4/01 Nott 1m6f15y soft

Tikram

103 **88**

4-y-o ch g Lycius (USA)-Black Fighter (USA) (Secretariat (USA))
G L Moore Mike Charlton And Rodger Sargent

Placings:031-625 **(5693)**
2001: 10^{6}GS, 10^{2}S, 12^{5}S

	Starts	1st	2nd	3rd	Win & Pl
Career Total (Turf)	**6**	**1**	**1**	**1**	**6580**

88 10/00 Nott 1m1f213yD SFT £3445
Total win prize-money £3445

Going (Turf): Sf: 1-4 GS: 0-1 Gd: 0-0 GF: 0-1 Fm: 0-0
Distance: 5f/6f: 0-0 7f-8f: 0-0 **9f-13f: 1-6** 14f+: 0-0
Track : **LH: 1-3** RH: 0-2 Tight: 0-2 Gall: 0-2
Aids: Bl: 0-0 Vi: 0-0 Tstrap: 0-0
Best Rating: 84 11/01 Donc 1m4f soft

He has ability on the Flat and won a soft-ground maiden

at Nottingham towards the end of 2000. Successful over hurdles since. Lightly raced on turf this season, he has performed with credit, and is at his best with give.

Tillerman

115 **114**

5-y-o b h In The Wings-Autumn Tint (USA) (Roberto (USA))
Mrs A J Perrett K Abdulla

Placings:11/35016-4034 **(4054)**
2001: 6^4GF, 6^0G, 7^3GF, 7^4GF

	Starts	1st	2nd	3rd	Win & Pl
Career Total (Turf)	11	3	0	2	125741

114 7/00 Asct 7f B H G-F £87000
99 10/99 NmkJ 1m C(0-90) G-S £7048
84 8/99 Ling 1m1f F G-F £2476
Total win prize-money £96526

Going (Turf): Sf: 0-0 GS: 1-3 Gd: 0-1 **GF: 2-7** Fm: 0-0
Distance: 5f/6f: 0-2 **7f-8f: 2-8** 9f-13f: 1-1 14f+: 0-0
Track : **LH: 1-3** RH: 0-1 **Tight: 1-1** Gall: 0-3
Aids: Bl: 0-0 Vi: 0-0 Tstrap: 0-0
Best Rating: 114 7/01 Asct 7f gd-fm

A very useful handicapper at three, winner of the Tote International at Ascot, he ran well on his first try at six furlongs in the Cork and Orrery when short of room more than once, and ran a blinder to finish third in this year's Tote International. A fair fourth in a Group Three next time, he needs fast ground to be at his best.

Timber Lodge (IRE)

88 **62**

2-y-o ch g Woodborough (USA)-Ornette (IRE) (Bluebird (USA))
I A Balding D H Caslon

Placings:040 **(1482)**
2001: 5^0GS, 5^4GS, 5^0GF

	Starts	1st	2nd	3rd	Win & Pl
Career Total (Turf)	3	0	0	0	0

Going (Turf): Sf: 0-0 GS: 0-2 Gd: 0-0 GF: 0-1 Fm: 0-0
Distance: 5f/6f: 0-3 7f-8f: 0-0 9f-13f: 0-0 14f+: 0-0
Track : LH: 0-2 RH: 0-1 Tight: 0-0 Gall: 0-3
Aids: Bl: 0-0 Vi: 0-0 Tstrap: 0-0
Best Rating: 62 5/01 Wind 5f10y gd-sft

Time Away (IRE)

111 **115**

3-y-o b f Darshaan-Not Before Time (IRE) (Polish Precedent (USA))
J L Dunlop R Barnett

Placings:21-5313630 **(4113)**
2001: 8^5S, 10^3G, 10^1F, 10^3G, 12^6G, 9^3G, 10^0G

	Starts	1st	2nd	3rd	Win & Pl
Career Total (Turf)	9	2	1	3	88378

111 5/01 York 1m2f85y A FRM £29000
73 9/00 Sand 1m14y D G-F £4231
Total win prize-money £33232

Going (Turf): Sf: 0-1 GS: 0-0 Gd: 0-5 **GF: 1-2 Fm: 1-1**
Distance: 5f/6f: 0-0 7f-8f: 0-2 **9f-13f: 2-7** 14f+: 0-0
Track : LH: 1-2 RH: 1-3 Tight: 0-1 **Gall: 1-2**
Aids: Bl: 0-0 Vi: 0-0 Tstrap: 0-0
Best Rating: 115 6/01 Chan 1m2f110y good

A smart filly from a good middle-distance family, her dam being a half-sister to Time Charter. She gave a good account when stepped up to ten furlongs in the Pretty Polly, and ran out a convincing winner of the Musidora Stakes at York, beating Relish The Thought. She came up against a pair of very smart French fillies when third in the Prix de Diane Hermes at Chantilly in June, but did not seem to stay in the Irish Oaks. Returned to form back at ten furlongs in the Nassau. Suited by fast ground. Retired to stud.

Time Bomb

87(89) (37)**38**

4-y-o b f Great Commotion (USA)-Play For Time (Comedy Star (USA))
B R Millman Wild Beef Racing

Placings:0/4006000002-0051 **(5522)**
2001: 6^0GF, 5^0S, 7^5S, 6^1HY, 7^0SD

	Starts	1st	2nd	3rd	Win & Pl
Career Total (Turf)	15	1	1	0	4257

50 10/01 Wind 6f D HVY £3038
Total win prize-money £3038

Going (Turf): Sf: 1-6 GS: 0-1 Gd: 0-1 GF: 0-7 Fm: 0-0
Distance: **5f/6f: 1-8** 7f-8f: 0-6 9f-13f: 0-1 14f+: 0-0
Track : LH: 0-7 RH: 0-1 Tight: 0-2 Gall: 0-3
Aids: Bl: 0-0 Vi: 0-0 Tstrap: 0-0
Best Rating: 50 10/01 Wind 6f heavy

Got off the mark in a poor end-of-season maiden at Windsor. Goes well in the mud.

Time Can Tell

96(101) (41)**38**

7-y-o ch g Sylvan Express-Stellaris (Star Appeal)
A G Juckes A C W Price

Placings:00462144/**432544**5243550330**054/21324363**4/**042441260**6**450/55134**20**302-3534U005**30**540 (3816)**
2001: **16**^{3}SD, **16**^{5}SW, **16**^{3}SD, **16**^{4}SD, **16**^{U}SD, **16**^{0}SD, **16**^{0}SD, **14**^{5}SD, 16^{3}GF, 16^{0}GF, **16**^{5}SD, **16**^{4}SD, **14**^{0}SD

	Starts	1st	2nd	3rd	Win & Pl
Career Total (Turf)	24	1	2	4	6743
Career Total (AW)	48	3	7	8	16431

46 3/00 Sthl 2m F(0-60)H STD £2394
63 4/99 Wolv 2m46y F(0-65)H STD £2332
69 1/98 Ling 1m5f E STD £2739
62 10/96 Nott 1m54y G GD £2070
Total win prize-money £9535

Going (Turf): Sf: 0-0 GS: 0-3 **Gd: 1-6** GF: 0-14 Fm: 0-1
Distance: 5f/6f: 0-2 7f-8f: 0-5 9f-13f: 2-29 14f+: 2-36
Track : **LH: 4-58** RH: 0-6 **Tight: 2-35** Gall: 0-3
Aids: Bl: 0-3 Vi: 0-2 Tstrap: 0-0
Best Rating: 48 2/01 Sthl 2m stand

He pops up from time to time in staying events on sand, but his strike rate is moderate and he may not be one to place too much faith in.

Time For Music (IRE)

105(97) (56)**69**

4-y-o b g Mukaddamah (USA)-Shrewd Girl (USA) (Sagace (FR))
T G Mills M A Shipman

Placings:52261/0000**000**-0126300 **(4016)**
2001: 6^0GF, 6^1F, 6^2F, 6^6GF, 7^3GF, 7^0G, 7^0G

	Starts	1st	2nd	3rd	Win & Pl
Career Total (Turf)	16	2	3	1	9547
Career Total (AW)	3	0	0	0	

63 5/01 Brig 6f209y E(0-65) FRM £3052
80 8/99 Nott 6f15y E H G-F £2988
Total win prize-money £6040

Going (Turf): Sf: 0-1 GS: 0-0 Gd: 0-5 **GF: 1-8 Fm: 1-2**
Distance: 5f/6f: 0-4 **7f-8f: 2-13** 9f-13f: 0-2 14f+: 0-0
Track : **LH: 1-9** RH: 0-2 Tight: 0-5 Gall: 0-2
Aids: Bl: 0-1 Vi: 0-0 Tstrap: 0-0
Best Rating: 69 6/01 Brig 6f209y firm

A nursery winner at two, she was off the track in 2000 until August and has been found wanting in handicaps.

Time For One More

72 **22**

2-y-o ch f Timeless Times (USA)-Croft Original (Crofthall)
M J Haynes David M Butler

Placings:006 **(3972)**
2001: 5^0GS, 5^0GF, 7^6GF

	Starts	1st	2nd	3rd	Win & Pl
Career Total (Turf)	3	0	0	0	0

Going (Turf): Sf: 0-0 GS: 0-1 Gd: 0-0 GF: 0-2 Fm: 0-0
Distance: 5f/6f: 0-2 7f-8f: 0-1 9f-13f: 0-0 14f+: 0-0
Track : LH: 0-1 RH: 0-2 Tight: 0-1 Gall: 0-2
Aids: Bl: 0-0 Vi: 0-0 Tstrap: 0-0
Best Rating: 22 7/01 Wind 5f10y gd-fm

Time For The Clan

95(74) (13)

4-y-o ch g Clantime-Fyas (Sayf El Arab (USA))
R Bastiman Mrs C B Bastiman

Placings:0000400/000000605000000000-**0000**00000000000000005000000000000000 **(5625)**
2001: **6**^{0}SD, **8**^{0}SW, **10**^{0}SW, **12**^{0}SD, 12^{0}S, 5^{0}S, 10^{0}HY, 6^{0}HY, 6^{0}S, 9^{0}G, 7^{0}G, 8^{0}GF, 6^{0}GF, 7^{0}F, 7^{0}G, 6^{0}GF, 7^{0}GF, 10^{0}GF, 10^{5}GF, 12^{0}F, 6^{0}GF, 8^{0}F, 6^{0}GF, 9^{0}GF, 8^{0}GF, 8^{0}G, 10^{0}GF, 9^{0}G, 10^{0}GF, 8^{0}F, 6^{0}S, 7^{0}G, 11^{0}S, 7^{0}HY, 8^{0}GS

	Starts	1st	2nd	3rd	Win & Pl
Career Total (Turf)	54	0	0	0	0
Career Total (AW)	5	0	0	0	

Going (Turf): Sf: 0-13 GS: 0-3 Gd: 0-11 GF: 0-22 Fm: 0-5
Distance: 5f/6f: 0-19 7f-8f: 0-17 9f-13f: 0-23 14f+: 0-0
Track : LH: 0-27 RH: 0-5 Tight: 0-12 Gall: 0-7
Aids: Bl: 0-1 Vi: 0-2 Tstrap: 0-0
Best Rating: 60 5/01 Hayd 6f soft

A very moderate individual. Tried at various trips, and an 'appearance money' regular.

Time Maite

89(87) (50)**78**

3-y-o b g Komaite (USA)-Martini Time (Ardoon)
M W Easterby Tom Beston & Bernard Bargh

Placings:4313531301-000 **(3880)**
2001: 6^0S, 5^0GS, 5^0GS

	Starts	1st	2nd	3rd	Win & Pl
Career Total (Turf)	12	3	0	3	11767
Career Total (AW)	1	0	0	1	313

78 10/00 Newc 5f E(0-75) HVY £2751
68 8/00 Hayd 5f D G-S £4023
53 5/00 Newc 6f F GD £2733
Total win prize-money £9509

Going (Turf): Sf: 1-6 GS: 1-3 Gd: 1-3 GF: 0-0 Fm: 0-0
Distance: **5f/6f: 3-13** 7f-8f: 0-0 9f-13f: 0-0 14f+: 0-0
Track : LH: 0-0 RH: 0-0 Tight: 0-0 Gall: 0-0
Aids: Bl: 0-0 Vi: 0-0 Tstrap: 0-0
Best Rating: 56 8/01 Thsk 5f gd-sft

Time Marches On

96(85) (26)**33**

3-y-o b g Timeless Times (USA)-Tees Gazette Girl (Kalaglow)
Mrs M Reveley Mrs M B Thwaites

Placings:00-063616 **(2055)**
2001: 6^0SW, 11^6SD, 11^3SD, 8^6S, 9^1F, 10^6GF

	Starts	1st	2nd	3rd	Win & Pl
Career Total (Turf)	4	1	0	0	2010
Career Total (AW)	4	0	0	1	257

33 6/01 Nott 1m1f213yG(0-60)H FRM £2010
Total win prize-money £2010

Going (Turf): Sf: 0-2 GS: 0-0 Gd: 0-0 GF: 0-1 **Fm: 1-1**
Distance: 5f/6f: 0-2 7f-8f: 0-1 **9f-13f: 1-5** 14f+: 0-0
Track : **LH: 1-7** RH: 0-0 Tight: 0-1 Gall: 0-0
Aids: Bl: 0-0 Vi: 0-0 Tstrap: 0-0
Best Rating: 33 6/01 Nott 1m1f213y firm

Time N Time Again

103 **90**

3-y-o b g Timeless Times (USA)-Primum Tempus (Primo Dominie)

E J Alston Springs Equestrian Ltd

Placings:10000-1463000 **(4588)**

2001: 5^{1}GF, 5^{4}GF, 5^{6}GF, 5^{3}G, 5^{0}G, 6^{0}HY, 5^{0}HY

	Starts	1st	2nd	3rd	Win & Pl
Career Total (Turf)	12	2	0	1	20073

84 5/01 Ches 5f16y C(0-100)H G-F £14625
74 4/00 Haml 5f4y D GD £3558
Total win prize-money £18184

Going (Turf): Sf: 0-3 GS: 0-1 **Gd: 1-3 GF: 1-5** Fm: 0-0
Distance: **5f/6f: 2-12** 7f-8f: 0-0 9f-13f: 0-0 14f+: 0-0
Track : **LH: 1-3** RH: 0-0 **Tight: 1-3** Gall: 0-0
Aids: Bl: 0-0 Vi: 0-0 Tstrap: 0-0
Best Rating: 85 7/01 Ches 5f16y good

Goes well fresh and, having won on his juvenile debut, repeated the feat as a three-year-old. Appreciates the minimum trip and fast ground.

Time Proof

(72) (1) **49**

3-y-o b g Clantime-Off Camera (Efisio)

R A Fahey Mrs J Hazell

Placings:000-0 **(0711)**

2001: 7^{0}SD

	Starts	1st	2nd	3rd	Win & Pl
Career Total (Turf)	3	0	0	0	
Career Total (AW)	1	0	0	0	

Going (Turf): Sf: 0-0 GS: 0-1 Gd: 0-1 GF: 0-1 Fm: 0-0
Distance: 5f/6f: 0-1 7f-8f: 0-3 9f-13f: 0-0 14f+: 0-0
Track : LH: 0-4 RH: 0-0 Tight: 0-2 Gall: 0-0
Aids: Bl: 0-0 Vi: 0-0 Tstrap: 0-0
Best Rating: 1 4/01 Sthl 7f stand

Time Royal

95 **80**

2-y-o b c Timeless Times (USA)-Royal Girl (Kafu)

B A McMahon J D Graham

Placings:110040 **(5150)**

2001: 5^{1}S, 5^{1}GS, 5^{0}GF, 5^{0}GF, 6^{4}G, 6^{0}G

	Starts	1st	2nd	3rd	Win & Pl
Career Total (Turf)	6	2	0	0	9361

80 4/01 Newb 5f34y D G-S £5070
70 3/01 Donc 5f E SFT £3753
Total win prize-money £8824

Going (Turf): Sf: 1-1 GS: 1-1 Gd: 0-2 GF: 0-2 Fm: 0-0
Distance: **5f/6f: 2-6** 7f-8f: 0-0 9f-13f: 0-0 14f+: 0-0
Track : LH: 0-0 RH: 0-0 Tight: 0-0 Gall: 0-0
Aids: Bl: 0-0 Vi: 0-0 Tstrap: 0-0
Best Rating: 80 4/01 Newb 5f34y gd-sft

He scored with something in hand on his debut and handled the testing conditions well, followed up at Newbury over the minimum trip. Creditable seventh, five and a half lengths behind Johannesburg, in the Norfolk Stakes at Royal Ascot. Should stay further. Has shown his best form with give.

Time Temptress

94 (85) (19) **25**

5-y-o b m Timeless Times (USA)-Tangalooma (Hotfoot)

I W McInnes (A Crook 1/8) I W McInnes

Placings:05044024/143030506/000**2**2-00300 **(3570)**

2001: 10^{0}F, 8^{0}GF, 11^{3}GF, 12^{0}G, 12^{0}G

	Starts	1st	2nd	3rd	Win & Pl
Career Total (Turf)	24	1	3	3	8228
Career Total (AW)	3	0	0	0	

64 5/99 Newc 1m3y D(0-80)H G-F £3956
Total win prize-money £3956

Going (Turf): Sf: 0-3 GS: 0-3 Gd: 0-3 **GF: 1-11** Fm: 0-4
Distance: 5f/6f: 0-5 7f-8f: 0-10 **9f-13f: 1-12** 14f+: 0-0
Track : LH: 0-14 RH: 0-5 Tight: 0-7 Gall: 0-5
Aids: Bl: 0-2 Vi: 0-1 Tstrap: 0-0
Best Rating: 25 6/01 Bevl 1m3f216y gd-fm

Time To Burn

87 (75) (39) **53**

2-y-o b f Atraf-Into The Fire (Dominion)

W G M Turner Paul Thorman

Placings:303 **(0717)**

2001: 5^{3}S, 5^{0}S, 5^{3}SD

	Starts	1st	2nd	3rd	Win & Pl
Career Total (Turf)	2	0	0	1	426
Career Total (AW)	1	0	0	1	324

Going (Turf): Sf: 0-2 GS: 0-0 Gd: 0-0 GF: 0-0 Fm: 0-0
Distance: 5f/6f: 0-3 7f-8f: 0-0 9f-13f: 0-0 14f+: 0-0
Track : LH: 0-1 RH: 0-0 Tight: 0-1 Gall: 0-0
Aids: Bl: 0-0 Vi: 0-1 Tstrap: 0-0
Best Rating: 53 3/01 Donc 5f soft

Time To Fly

93 (84) (62) **8**

8-y-o b g Timeless Times (USA)-Dauntless Flight (Golden Mallard)

B W Murray B Murray

Placings:5035302/500**6**000/0**6**5105123052/111224000/540**1**000203**0**/005040060000**0**-500000000000 **(5629)**

2001: 6^{5}SD, 6^{0}SD, 5^{0}S, 5^{0}G, 6^{0}GF, 7^{0}F, 5^{0}F, 6^{0}GF, 7^{0}GF, 6^{0}HY, 5^{0}G, 7^{0}GS, 5^{0}G

	Starts	1st	2nd	3rd	Win & Pl
Career Total (Turf)	44	0	2	3	3659
Career Total (AW)	29	6	4	1	19942

66 4/99 Ling 6f D(0-80)H STD £3606
72 1/98 Ling 6f E(0-70)H STD £2832
70 1/98 Wolv 5f E(0-70)H STD £2372
61 1/90 Wolv 6f G(0-70)H STD £1388
46 6/97 Sthl 6f F(0-60)H STD £2277
43 4/97 Wolv 5f F(0-60)H STD £2277
Total win prize-money £14752

Going (Turf): Sf: 0-6 GS: 0-2 Gd: 0-10 GF: 0-15 Fm: 0-11
Distance: **5f/6f: 6-64** 7f-8f: 0-9 9f-13f: 0-0 14f+: 0-0
Track : **LH: 6-32** RH: 0-2 **Tight: 5-21** Gall: 0-2
Aids: **Bl: 6-47** Vi: 0-0 Tstrap: 0-0
Best Rating: 52 4/01 Nott 5f13y soft

Time To Remember (IRE)

109 **80**

3-y-o b g Pennekamp (USA)-Bequeath (USA) (Lyphard (USA))

T D Easterby Reg Griffin And Jim McGrath

Placings:3146-001 **(3864)**

2001: 7^{0}GF, 6^{0}GF, 7^{1}GF

	Starts	1st	2nd	3rd	Win & Pl
Career Total (Turf)	7	2	0	1	10731

79 8/01 Rdcr 7f D(0-80)H G-F £5102
74 8/00 Pont 6f D G-F £3575
Total win prize-money £8678

Going (Turf): Sf: 0-0 GS: 0-0 Gd: 0-3 **GF: 2-4** Fm: 0-0
Distance: 5f/6f: 1-4 7f-8f: 1-3 9f-13f: 0-0 14f+: 0-0
Track : **LH: 1-4** RH: 0-0 Tight: 0-0 Gall: 0-2
Aids: Bl: 0-0 Vi: 0-0 Tstrap: 0-0
Best Rating: 79 8/01 Rdcr 7f gd-fm

He faced some stiff tasks after winning at Pontefract on his second start at two, but appreciated the step down in class at Redcar in August. Not a straightforward ride.

Time To Travel (USA)

96 **85+**

2-y-o b c Lear Fan (USA)-Split Sentence (USA) (Northjet)

P F I Cole J S Gutkin

Placings:001 **(5380)**

2001: 8^{0}GF, 8^{0}S, 7^{1}S

	Starts	1st	2nd	3rd	Win & Pl
Career Total (Turf)	3	1	0	0	3108

85 10/01 Catt 7f E SFT £3108
Total win prize-money £3108

Going (Turf): Sf: 1-2 GS: 0-0 Gd: 0-0 GF: 0-1 Fm: 0-0
Distance: 5f/6f: 0-0 **7f-8f: 1-3** 9f-13f: 0-0 14f+: 0-0
Track : **LH: 1-1** RH: 0-0 **Tight: 1-1** Gall: 0-0
Aids: Bl: 0-0 Vi: 0-0 Tstrap: 0-0
Best Rating: 85 10/01 Catt 7f soft

Dropped in class to win a maiden auction at the third attempt in the autumn.

Time To Wyn

103 (68) **3**

5-y-o b g Timeless Times (USA)-Wyn-Bank (Green God)

J G Fitzgerald Mike Browne

Placings:0606130/0312P00000/00562-5021U00 **(5448)**

2001: 9^{5}S, 8^{0}S, 8^{2}GS, 8^{1}G, 10^{U}GF, 8^{0}F, 10^{0}HY

	Starts	1st	2nd	3rd	Win & Pl
Career Total (Turf)	27	3	3	2	10903
Career Total (AW)	2	0	0	0	0

44 6/01 Ripn 1m F(0-60)H GD £2737
63 6/99 Carl 7f214y F(0-60) G-F £2500
57 9/98 Bevl 7f100y F(0-65)H G-F £2530
Total win prize-money £7767

Going (Turf): Sf: 0-9 GS: 0-3 Gd: 1-8 **GF: 2-5** Fm: 0-2
Distance: 5f/6f: 0-1 **7f-8f: 3-12** 9f-13f: 0-16 14f+: 0-0
Track : LH: 0-16 **RH: 3-10 Tight: 1-5** Gall: 0-2
Aids: **Bl: 1-4** Vi: 0-1 Tstrap: 0-0
Best Rating: 44 6/01 Ripn 1m good

Time Vally

105 **34**

4-y-o ch f Timeless Times (USA)-Fort Vally (Belfort (FR))

J J Quinn Mrs M Lingwood

Placings:006/01055400-000030000 **(4859)**

2001: 7^{0}GF, 8^{0}GF, 7^{0}GF, 7^{0}GF, 8^{3}G, 8^{0}GS, 7^{0}GF, 8^{0}GF, 7^{0}GF

	Starts	1st	2nd	3rd	Win & Pl
Career Total (Turf)	20	1	0	1	8224

73 6/00 NmkR 7f D(0-85)H G-F £7182
Total win prize-money £7183

Going (Turf): Sf: 0-3 GS: 0-2 Gd: 0-3 **GF: 1-12** Fm: 0-0
Distance: 5f/6f: 0-0 **7f-8f: 1-17** 9f-13f: 0-3 14f+: 0-0
Track : LH: 0-5 RH: 0-3 Tight: 0-3 Gall: 0-1
Aids: Bl: 0-0 Vi: 0-1 Tstrap: 0-0
Best Rating: 61 7/01 Donc 1m good

She won a handicap at Newmarket last summer, but has failed to make the frame in most of her other starts. Suited by seven furlongs or a mile on a straight track.

Timecini

76 **34**

2-y-o ch f Timeless Times (USA)-Veracini (Whittingham (IRE))

B S Rothwell Mrs C A Brown

Placings:000 **(5184)**

2001: 6^{0}GF, 6^{0}F, 5^{0}GS

	Starts	1st	2nd	3rd	Win & Pl
Career Total (Turf)	3	0	0	0	

Going (Turf): Sf: 0-0 GS: 0-1 Gd: 0-0 GF: 0-1 Fm: 0-1
Distance: 5f/6f: 0-3 7f-8f: 0-0 9f-13f: 0-0 14f+: 0-0

Track : LH: 0-0 RH: 0-0 Tight: 0-0 Gall: 0-0
Aids: Bl: 0-0 Vi: 0-0 Tstrap: 0-0
Best Rating: 34 9/01 York 6f gd-fm

Timeless Charm

81 **64**

2-y-o b c Timeless Times (USA)-Whittle Rock (Rock City)
N Tinkler Raymond Gomersall

Placings:60 **(2178)**
2001: 5^6^S, 6^0^G

	Starts	1st	2nd	3rd	Win & Pl
Career Total (Turf)	2	0	0	0	0

Going (Turf): Sf: 0-1 GS: 0-0 Gd: 0-1 GF: 0-0 Fm: 0-0
Distance: 5f/6f: 0-2 7f-8f: 0-0 9f-13f: 0-0 14f+: 0-0
Track : LH: 0-0 RH: 0-0 Tight: 0-0 Gall: 0-0
Aids: Bl: 0-0 Vi: 0-0 Tstrap: 0-0
Best Rating: 64 6/01 York 5f good

Timeless Chick

100(93) (37)**39**

4-y-o ch f Timeless Times (USA)-Be My Bird (Be My Chief (USA))
J L Spearing (B A McMahon 29/6) Be Luckies

Placings:06660/0043051060050-0554000054106 **(5023)**
2001: 6^0^SD, 7^5^SD, 7^5^SW, 7^4^SD, 8^0^GS, 7^0^SD, 8^0^G, 8^0^SD, 7^5^G, 7^4^GF, 8^1^G, 10^0^GF, 7^6^S

	Starts	1st	2nd	3rd	Win & Pl	
Career Total (Turf)	18	2	0	1	4982	
Career Total (AW)	13	0	0	0	0	
39 9/01	Chep	1m14y	F		GD	£2555
51 7/00	Wwck	7f164y	G(0-60)H		G-F	£2144

Total win prize-money £4700

Going (Turf): Sf: 0-1 GS: 0-2 **Gd: 1-6 GF: 1-8** Fm: 0-1
Distance: 5f/6f: 0-4 7f-8f: 1-18 9f-13f: 1-9 14f+: 0-0
Track : **LH: 1-23** RH: 0-1 Tight: 0-6 Gall: 0-0
Aids: Bl: 0-5 **Vi: 1-10** Tstrap: 0-0
Best Rating: 39 9/01 Chep 1m14y good

Timeless Farrier

91(98) (77)**61**

3-y-o b g Timeless Times (USA)-Willrack Farrier (Lugana Beach)
B Smart Willrackers

Placings:6600452-212506 **(3509)**
2001: 6^2^SD, 6^1^SD, 6^2^SW, 6^5^SW, 5^0^GF, 5^6^GF

	Starts	1st	2nd	3rd	Win & Pl	
Career Total (Turf)	6	0	0	0	0	
Career Total (AW)	7	1	3	0	5688	
75 1/01	Ling	6f	D		STD	£2891

Total win prize-money £2891

Going (Turf): Sf: 0-0 GS: 0-0 Gd: 0-1 GF: 0-4 Fm: 0-1
Distance: **5f/6f: 1-13** 7f-8f: 0-0 9f-13f: 0-0 14f+: 0-0
Track : **LH: 1-8** RH: 0-0 **Tight: 1-5** Gall: 0-0
Aids: **Bl: 1-5** Vi: 0-1 Tstrap: 0-1
Best Rating: 77 1/01 Ling 6f slow

His attempts over five furlongs have been fruitless, but he took well to the Equitrack to win a fair maiden at the beginning of 2001 over six furlongs. He appreciates front-running tactics and has previously been fitted with blinkers/visor.

Timeless Quest

(78) (27)**38**

4-y-o ch f Timeless Times (USA)-Animate (IRE) (Tate Gallery (USA))
J J Quinn Mrs M Lingwood

Placings:04020/000-00 **(0240)**
2001: 6^0^SW, 6^0^SD

	Starts	1st	2nd	3rd	Win & Pl
Career Total (Turf)	5	0	0	0	
Career Total (AW)	5	0	1	0	590

Going (Turf): Sf: 0-1 GS: 0-2 Gd: 0-1 GF: 0-1 Fm: 0-0
Distance: 5f/6f: 0-3 7f-8f: 0-6 9f-13f: 0-1 14f+: 0-0
Track : LH: 0-7 RH: 0-1 Tight: 0-2 Gall: 0-0
Aids: Bl: 0-2 Vi: 0-1 Tstrap: 0-0
Best Rating: 13 2/01 Sthl 6f stand

Timeless Question

80(74) (42)**51**

2-y-o ch f Timeless Times (USA)-Tarda (Absalom)
R M Whitaker Mrs Dorothy Horner

Placings:5 **(5533)**
2001: 5^5^S, 6^0^SD

	Starts	1st	2nd	3rd	Win & Pl
Career Total (Turf)	1	0	0	0	0

Going (Turf): Sf: 0-1 GS: 0-0 Gd: 0-0 GF: 0-0 Fm: 0-0
Distance: 5f/6f: 0-1 7f-8f: 0-0 9f-13f: 0-0 14f+: 0-0
Track : LH: 0-0 RH: 0-0 Tight: 0-0 Gall: 0-0
Aids: Bl: 0-0 Vi: 0-0 Tstrap: 0-0
Best Rating: 51 10/01 Rdcr 5f soft

Timeless Treasure

82(75) (29)**53**

2-y-o ch c Timeless Times (USA)-Treasure Hunt (Hadeer)
Miss S E Hall Miss S E Hall

Placings:050 **(4078)**
2001: 5^0^GF, 5^5^SD, 5^0^GF

	Starts	1st	2nd	3rd	Win & Pl
Career Total (Turf)	2	0	0	0	
Career Total (AW)	1	0	0	0	0

Going (Turf): Sf: 0-0 GS: 0-0 Gd: 0-0 GF: 0-2 Fm: 0-0
Distance: 5f/6f: 0-3 7f-8f: 0-0 9f-13f: 0-0 14f+: 0-0
Track : LH: 0-1 RH: 0-0 Tight: 0-0 Gall: 0-0
Aids: Bl: 0-0 Vi: 0-0 Tstrap: 0-0
Best Rating: 53 6/01 Rdcr 5f gd-fm

Timing

95 **67**

2-y-o b f Alhaarth (IRE)-Pretty Davis (USA) (Trempolino (USA))
T D Easterby Times Of Wigan

Placings:54 **(5399)**
2001: 7^5^HY, 6^4^S

	Starts	1st	2nd	3rd	Win & Pl
Career Total (Turf)	2	0	0	0	276

Going (Turf): Sf: 0-2 GS: 0-0 Gd: 0-0 GF: 0-0 Fm: 0-0
Distance: 5f/6f: 0-1 7f-8f: 0-1 9f-13f: 0-0 14f+: 0-0
Track : LH: 0-2 RH: 0-0 Tight: 0-0 Gall: 0-0
Aids: Bl: 0-0 Vi: 0-0 Tstrap: 0-0
Best Rating: 67 9/01 Hayd 7f30y heavy

Half-sister to the useful one-to-two miler Fait Le Jojo, ran a promisingrace in soft ground on her second outing.

Timoko

80 **34**

3-y-o b f Dancing Spree (USA)-Encore M'Lady (IRE) (Dancing Dissident (USA))
A Berry T G Holdcroft

Placings:000 **(1845)**
2001: 7^0^S, 6^0^F, 5^0^GF

	Starts	1st	2nd	3rd	Win & Pl
Career Total (Turf)	3	0	0	0	

Going (Turf): Sf: 0-1 GS: 0-0 Gd: 0-0 GF: 0-1 Fm: 0-1
Distance: 5f/6f: 0-2 7f-8f: 0-1 9f-13f: 0-0 14f+: 0-0
Track : LH: 0-1 RH: 0-0 Tight: 0-0 Gall: 0-0
Aids: Bl: 0-0 Vi: 0-0 Tstrap: 0-0
Best Rating: 34 5/01 Rdcr 7f soft

Tina Ballerina

80(67) (14)**10**

2-y-o ch f Komaite (USA)-Very Bold (Never So Bold)
W M Brisbourne John E Oldknow

Placings:565 **(5445)**
2001: 5^5^S, 5^6^SD, 6^5^HY

	Starts	1st	2nd	3rd	Win & Pl
Career Total (Turf)	2	0	0	0	0
Career Total (AW)	1	0	0	0	0

Going (Turf): Sf: 0-2 GS: 0-0 Gd: 0-0 GF: 0-0 Fm: 0-0
Distance: 5f/6f: 0-3 7f-8f: 0-0 9f-13f: 0-0 14f+: 0-0
Track : LH: 0-0 RH: 0-0 Tight: 0-0 Gall: 0-0
Aids: Bl: 0-0 Vi: 0-0 Tstrap: 0-0
Best Rating: 14 5/01 Sthl 5f stand

A half-sister to Italian winner Rainbow King who won over seven to eleven furlongs. Raced keenly on her debut on turf and switched to the All-Weather next time and eased when soon beaten.

Ting (IRE)

103(103) (61)**61**

4-y-o b g Magical Wonder (USA)-Rozmiyn (Caerleon (USA))
M J Polglase (P C Haslam 16/3) Paul J Dixon

Placings:0055/4605-2213006150241 0 **(5146)**
2001: 8^2^SD, 8^2^S, 8^1^SD, 8^3^G, 10^0^F, 9^0^G, 8^6^SD, 8^1^SD, 8^5^SD, 8^0^SD, 8^2^S, 9^4^GS, 8^1^GS, 8^0^G

	Starts	1st	2nd	3rd	Win & Pl	
Career Total (Turf)	11	1	2	1	5089	
Career Total (AW)	11	2	1	0	5144	
59 9/01	Leic	1m9y	F(0-60)		G-S	£3167
61 7/01	Sthl	1m	F(0-60)H		STD	£2352
52 4/01	Sthl	1m	G(0-60)H		STD	£1932

Total win prize-money £7452

Going (Turf): Sf: 0-2 **GS: 1-3** Gd: 0-4 GF: 0-1 Fm: 0-1
Distance: 5f/6f: 0-4 **7f-8f: 2-10** 9f-13f: 1-8 14f+: 0-0
Track : **LH: 2-14** RH: 0-1 Tight: 0-5 Gall: 0-0
Aids: Bl: 0-0 Vi: 0-0 Tstrap: 0-0
Best Rating: 61 7/01 Sthl 1m stand

Fair handicapper, best around a mile. Prior to September, all his wins had been on the All-Weather but, having won at Leicester on softish ground, there should be more to come on turf, given ease in the ground. Best when held up.

Tinian

95(60) **74**

3-y-o b g Mtoto-Housefull (Habitat)
I A Balding Exors Of The Late Robert Hitchins

Placings:34000 **(5348)**
2001: 10^3^S, 10^4^HY, 10^0^GS, 11^0^G, 12^0^SD

	Starts	1st	2nd	3rd	Win & Pl
Career Total (Turf)	4	0	0	1	651
Career Total (AW)	1	0	0	0	

Going (Turf): Sf: 0-2 GS: 0-1 Gd: 0-1 GF: 0-0 Fm: 0-0
Distance: 5f/6f: 0-0 7f-8f: 0-0 9f-13f: 0-5 14f+: 0-0
Track : LH: 0-4 RH: 0-0 Tight: 0-0 Gall: 0-1
Aids: Bl: 0-0 Vi: 0-1 Tstrap: 0-0
Best Rating: 74 3/01 Donc 1m2f60y soft

Tink's Man

73(88) (66)**28**

2-y-o b c Puissance-Expectation (IRE) (Night Shift (USA))

Mrs A Duffield The Hon Mrs Heimann

Placings:006 (5194)
2001: 6^0G, 5^0HY, 5^6SD

	Starts	1st	2nd	3rd	Win & Pl
Career Total (Turf)	2	0	0	0	
Career Total (AW)	1	0	0	0	0

Going (Turf): Sf: 0-1 GS: 0-0 Gd: 0-1 GF: 0-0 Fm: 0-0
Distance: 5f/6f: 0-3 7f-8f: 0-0 9f-13f: 0-0 14f+: 0-0
Track : LH: 0-1 RH: 0-0 Tight: 0-1 Gall: 0-0
Aids: Bl: 0-0 Vi: 0-0 Tstrap: 0-0
Best Rating: 66 10/01 Wolv 5f stand

Tinsel Moon (IRE)

90 (10)68
4-y-o b f River Falls-Fordes Cross (Ya Zaman (USA))
G B Balding Thurloe Coolinn

Placings:642225-00 (5686)
2001: 10^0GS, 10^0S, 8^0SD

	Starts	1st	2nd	3rd	Win & Pl
Career Total (Turf)	8	0	3	0	4035

Going (Turf): Sf: 0-1 GS: 0-1 Gd: 0-0 GF: 0-1 Fm: 0-1
Distance: 5f/6f: 0-0 7f-8f: 0-0 9f-13f: 0-8 14f+: 0-0
Track : LH: 0-3 RH: 0-5 Tight: 0-0 Gall: 0-2
Aids: Bl: 0-0 Vi: 0-0 Tstrap: 0-0
Best Rating: 68 4/01 Newb 1m2f6y gd-sft

Tinsel Whistle

(90) (35)
4-y-o b g Piccolo-Pewter Lass (Dowsing (USA))
B R Johnson Miss Julie Reeves

Placings:6030101426/0660-050 (0565)
2001: 6^0SD, 7^5SD, 7^0SD

	Starts	1st	2nd	3rd	Win & Pl
Career Total (Turf)	14	2	1	1	5472
Career Total (AW)	3	0	0	0	0

74	7/99	Yarm	6f3y	G	G-F	£2040
72	6/99	Yarm	5f43y	G	G-F	£1900

Total win prize-money £3940

Going (Turf): Sf: 0-0 GS: 0-0 Gd: 0-2 **GF: 2-11** Fm: 0-1
Distance: 5f/6f: 1-14 7f-8f: 1-3 9f-13f: 0-0 14f+: 0-0
Track : LH: 0-4 RH: 0-3 Tight: 0-3 Gall: 0-3
Aids: Bl: 0-2 Vi: 0-0 Tstrap: 0-0
Best Rating: 35 3/01 Wolv 7f stand

Both of his wins to date have been in fast-ground Yarmouth sellers.

Tinstre (IRE)

96(84) (26)41
3-y-o ch c Dolphin Street (FR)-Satin Poppy (Satin Wood)
P W Hiatt (Miss Jacqueline S Doyle 23/4) P W Hiatt

Placings:0-0450005000020 (2836)
2001: 8^0SD, 7^4SW, 8^5SD, 8^0S, 10^0GS, 6^0GS, 9^5G, 10^0GF, 9^0GF, 11^0F, 9^0G, 10^2GF, 9^0GF

	Starts	1st	2nd	3rd	Win & Pl
Career Total (Turf)	10	0	1	0	531
Career Total (AW)	4	0	0	0	0

Going (Turf): Sf: 0-1 GS: 0-2 Gd: 0-2 GF: 0-4 Fm: 0-1
Distance: 5f/6f: 0-0 7f-8f: 0-5 9f-13f: 0-9 14f+: 0-0
Track : LH: 0-10 RH: 0-3 Tight: 0-5 Gall: 0-0
Aids: Bl: 0-0 Vi: 0-0 Tstrap: 0-4
Best Rating: 54 5/01 Nott 1m1f213y good

Tiny Tim (IRE)

93(63) (2)43
3-y-o b g Brief Truce (USA)-Nonnita (Welsh Saint)
I A Balding I A Balding

Placings:6400-0000003 (3087)
2001: 7^0SW, 6^0G, 8^0F, 6^0GF, 7^0GF, 7^0GF, 7^3GF

	Starts	1st	2nd	3rd	Win & Pl
Career Total (Turf)	10	0	0	1	455
Career Total (AW)	1	0	0	0	

Going (Turf): Sf: 0-1 GS: 0-0 Gd: 0-3 GF: 0-4 Fm: 0-2
Distance: 5f/6f: 0-1 7f-8f: 0-9 9f-13f: 0-1 14f+: 0-0
Track : LH: 0-4 RH: 0-2 Tight: 0-1 Gall: 0-2
Aids: Bl: 0-0 Vi: 0-0 Tstrap: 0-0
Best Rating: 43 7/01 Bevl 7f100y gd-fm

Tioga Gold (IRE)

72 66
2-y-o b g Goldmark (USA)-Coffee Bean (Doulab (USA))
B J Meehan Mrs Sheila Tucker

Placings:000 (2948)
2001: 6^0S, 6^0G, 7^0G

	Starts	1st	2nd	3rd	Win & Pl
Career Total (Turf)	3	0	0	0	

Going (Turf): Sf: 0-1 GS: 0-0 Gd: 0-2 GF: 0-0 Fm: 0-0
Distance: 5f/6f: 0-1 7f-8f: 0-2 9f-13f: 0-0 14f+: 0-0
Track : LH: 0-0 RH: 0-0 Tight: 0-0 Gall: 0-0
Aids: Bl: 0-0 Vi: 0-0 Tstrap: 0-0
Best Rating: 66 6/01 Wind 6f good

Tip It Over

83 53
2-y-o b c Revoque (IRE)-On Tiptoes (Shareef Dancer (USA))
J G Given J W Rowles

Placings:050 (5290)
2001: 6^0F, 7^5HY, 7^0S

	Starts	1st	2nd	3rd	Win & Pl
Career Total (Turf)	3	0	0	0	0

Going (Turf): Sf: 0-2 GS: 0-0 Gd: 0-0 GF: 0-0 Fm: 0-1
Distance: 5f/6f: 0-1 7f-8f: 0-2 9f-13f: 0-0 14f+: 0-0
Track : LH: 0-1 RH: 0-0 Tight: 0-0 Gall: 0-0
Aids: Bl: 0 0 Vi: 0-0 Tstrap: 0-0
Best Rating: 53 9/01 Hayd 7f30y heavy

Tip The Scales

90 36
3-y-o b g Dancing Spree (USA)-Keen Melody (USA) (Sharpen Up)
R M Whitaker G F Pemberton

Placings:0502-0000500 (4422)
2001: 11^0GF, 10^0GF, 12^0GF, 16^0GF, 15^5G, 18^0GS, 10^0GF

	Starts	1st	2nd	3rd	Win & Pl
Career Total (Turf)	11	0	1	0	1060

Going (Turf): Sf: 0-0 GS: 0-2 Gd: 0-3 GF: 0-6 Fm: 0-0
Distance: 5f/6f: 0-1 7f-8f: 0-3 9f-13f: 0-4 14f+: 0-3
Track : LH: 0-5 RH: 0-4 Tight: 0-6 Gall: 0-1
Aids: Bl: 0-4 Vi: 0-3 Tstrap: 0-0
Best Rating: 47 6/01 Newc 1m2f32y gd-fm

Tip Top

64 16
2-y-o b f Mistertopogigo (IRE)-Strawberry Pink (Absalom)
T D Easterby Mrs Anne Henson

Placings:0 (1656)
2001: 6^0F

	Starts	1st	2nd	3rd	Win & Pl
Career Total (Turf)	1	0	0	0	

Going (Turf): Sf: 0-0 GS: 0-0 Gd: 0-0 GF: 0-0 Fm: 0-1
Distance: 5f/6f: 0-1 7f-8f: 0-0 9f-13f: 0-0 14f+: 0-0
Track : LH: 0-0 RH: 0-0 Tight: 0-0 Gall: 0-0
Aids: Bl: 0-0 Vi: 0-0 Tstrap: 0-0
Best Rating: 16 5/01 Rdcr 6f firm

Tipperary Sunset (IRE)

105 (18)65
7-y-o gr g Red Sunset-Chapter And Verse (Dancer's Image (USA))
D Shaw Harold Bray

Placings:6/30501102311/00504102503330/301440002 30025/002366541400-060100 (4452)
2001: 8^0HY, 7^6HY, 7^0G, 8^1G, 8^0S, 7^0GF

	Starts	1st	2nd	3rd	Win & Pl
Career Total (Turf)	56	8	5	8	46252
Career Total (AW)	2	0	0	0	

65	5/01	Bevl	1m100y	D(0-85)H	GD	£6194
62	8/00	Bevl	7f100y	E(0-70)H	G-F	£4992
64	6/99	Bevl	7f100y	E(0-70)H	GD	£3572
55	8/98	Haml	1m65y	D(0-75)H	SFT	£3728
64	11/97	Donc	1m	E(0-80)H	G-S	£4272
58	10/97	NmkR	1m1f	E(0-70)H	G-F	£3655
48	8/97	Ripn	1m2f	E(0-70)H	G-F	£3093
44	8/97	Pont	1m4y	F(0-65)H	G-F	£2805

Total win prize-money £32316

Going (Turf): Sf: 1-20 GS: 1-6 Gd: 2-15 **GF: 4-14** Fm: 0-1
Distance: 5f/6f: 0-1 7f-8f: 3-28 **9f-13f: 5-29** 14f+: 0-0
Track : LH: 1-16 **RH: 5-25 Tight: 2-11** Gall: 0-4
Aids: **Bl: 2-7** Vi: 0-0 Tstrap: 0-0
Best Rating: 65 5/01 Bevl 1m100y good

Wins in his turn, but is not particularly consistent. Won at Beverley in June beating subsequent winner Tropical Beach, coming late which is the way to ride him.

Tirana (IRE)

94(97) (58)56
3-y-o b g Brief Truce (USA)-Cloche Du Roi (FR) (Fairy King (USA))
D Shaw J C Fretwell

Placings:00043-0013300064 (5801)
2001: 8^0SD, 8^0SD, 7^1SW, 7^3SD, 8^3G, 8^0HY, 8^0G, 8^0SD, 7^6G, 8^4GS

	Starts	1st	2nd	3rd	Win & Pl
Career Total (Turf)	8	0	0	1	649
Career Total (AW)	7	1	0	2	2744

58	4/01	Sthl	7f	F(0-65)H	SLW	£2338

Total win prize-money £2338

Going (Turf): Sf: 0-2 GS: 0-2 Gd: 0-4 GF: 0-0 Fm: 0-0
Distance: 5f/6f: 0-2 **7f-8f: 1-8** 9f-13f: 0-5 14f+: 0-0
Track : **LH: 1-9** RH: 0-1 Tight: 0-2 Gall: 0-0
Aids: Bl: 0-0 Vi: 0-0 **Tstrap: 1-7**
Best Rating: 58 4/01 Sthl 7f slow

Won an uncompetitive seven-furlong handicap at Southwell in April of 2001, but has been well beaten since then on both turf and sand.

Tirari (IRE)

84 62
2-y-o b f Charnwood Forest (IRE)-Desert Victory (Green Desert (USA))
C F Wall Zubieta Limited

Placings:040 (5086)
2001: 6^0G, 6^4GF, 7^0GS

	Starts	1st	2nd	3rd	Win & Pl
Career Total (Turf)	3	0	0	0	0

Going (Turf): Sf: 0-0 GS: 0-1 Gd: 0-1 GF: 0-1 Fm: 0-0
Distance: 5f/6f: 0-1 7f-8f: 0-2 9f-13f: 0-0 14f+: 0-0
Track : LH: 0-0 RH: 0-0 Tight: 0-0 Gall: 0-0
Aids: Bl: 0-0 Vi: 0-0 Tstrap: 0-0
Best Rating: 62 9/01 Wwck 6f21y gd-fm

Tiree

61 **2**

2-y-o ch f Be My Chief (USA)-Madam Zando (Forzando)
J Balding Mrs Gillian A R Jones

Placings:00 (4839)
2001: 5^{0}GF, 6^{0}G

	Starts	1st	2nd	3rd	Win & Pl
Career Total (Turf)	2	0	0	0	

Going (Turf): Sf: 0-0 GS: 0-0 Gd: 0-1 GF: 0-1 Fm: 0-0
Distance: 5f/6f: 0-1 7f-8f: 0-1 9f-13f: 0-0 14f+: 0-0
Track : LH: 0-0 RH: 0-0 Tight: 0-0 Gall: 0-0
Aids: Bl: 0-0 Vi: 0-0 Tstrap: 0-0
Best Rating: 2 9/01 Nott 6f15y good

Tishomingo

92(83) (48)**62**

2-y-o ch c Alhijaz-Enchanted Guest (IRE) (Be My Guest (USA))
G M Moore A W Sergeant

Placings:06010405 (5351)
2001: 6^{0}SD, 5^{6}GF, 6^{0}G, 8^{1}G, 7^{0}HY, 8^{4}G, 8^{0}GF, 8^{5}SD

	Starts	1st	2nd	3rd	Win & Pl
Career Total (Turf)	6	1	0	0	2714
Career Total (AW)	2	0	0	0	0

62 8/01 Newc 1m F GD £2464
Total win prize-money £2464

Going (Turf): Sf: 0-1 GS: 0-0 **Gd: 1-3** GF: 0-2 Fm: 0-0
Distance: 5f/6f: 0-3 **7f-8f: 1-5** 9f-13f: 0-0 14f+: 0-0
Track : **LH: 1-5** RH: 0-1 Tight: 0-1 **Gall: 1-1**
Aids: Bl: 0-0 Vi: 0-0 Tstrap: 0-0
Best Rating: 62 9/01 Ayr 1m good

He has run his best races to date over a mile in weak company including a win in a claimer at Newcastle in the summer of 2001 on good ground.

Tissaly

94 **80**

3-y-o b f Pennekamp (USA)-Island Ruler (Ile De Bourbon (USA))
C E Brittain Saeed Manana

Placings:236-6 (1673)
2001: 7^{6}G

	Starts	1st	2nd	3rd	Win & Pl
Career Total (Turf)	4	0	1	1	2726

Going (Turf): Sf: 0-0 GS: 0-0 Gd: 0-2 GF: 0-1 Fm: 0-0
Distance: 5f/6f: 0-0 7f-8f: 0-3 9f-13f: 0-0 14f+: 0-0
Track : LH: 0-0 RH: 0-0 Tight: 0-0 Gall: 0-0
Aids: Bl: 0-0 Vi: 0-0 Tstrap: 0-0
Best Rating: 64 5/01 Yarm 7f3y good

Has yet to win a race but has done enough to suggest that a victory is not far away.

Tissifer

107 **97**

5-y-o b g Polish Precedent (USA)-Ingozi (Warning)
M C Pipe (M Johnston 4/10) Richard Abbott & Mario Stavrou li

Placings:115/10220/220040330-21 (5106)
2001: 10^{2}G, 12^{1}GS

	Starts	1st	2nd	3rd	Win & Pl
Career Total (Turf)	19	4	5	2	45228

57 10/01 NmkR 1m4f E G-S £5330
112 4/99 Thsk 1m B GD £10050
82 9/98 Kemp 7f C SFT £4474
81 8/98 Epsm 6f D G-F £3436
Total win prize-money £23290

Going (Turf): Sf: 1-3 GS: 1-3 Gd: 1-5 GF: 1-7 Fm: 0-0
Distance: 5f/6f: 1-1 **7f-8f: 2-7** 9f-13f: 1-11 14f+: 0-0
Track : LH: 2-9 RH: 2-8 Tight: 2-2 Gall: 2-12
Aids: Bl: 0-3 Vi: 0-0 Tstrap: 0-0
Best Rating: 97 9/01 Asct 1m2f good

He ran well in the face of some stiff tasks in 2000, notably when failing by three lengths to concede the St Leger winner Mutafaweq nine pounds at Doncaster in May. His best effort after that was when second to the Champion Stakes third Indian Creek at Ascot in September, before winning a hot claimer, being claimed by Martin Pipe in the process.

Titan

52(87) (30)**38**

6-y-o b g Lion Cavern (USA)-Sutosky (Great Nephew)
J S Moore (M P Muggeridge 23/4) Brian A Lewendon & Mrs Carol Lewendon

Placings:020125/003000/0000502050060/0005005-000 (1870)
2001: 6^{0}GS, 9^{0}F, 7^{0}F

	Starts	1st	2nd	3rd	Win & Pl
Career Total (Turf)	30	1	3	1	8603
Career Total (AW)	5	0	0	0	0

76 9/97 Gdwd 7f D H GD £4110
Total win prize-money £4110

Going (Turf): Sf: 0-5 GS: 0-5 **Gd: 1-9** GF: 0-9 Fm: 0-2
Distance: 5f/6f: 0-3 **7f-8f: 1-28** 9f-13f: 0-4 14f+: 0-0
Track : LH: 0-14 **RH: 1-11** Tight: 0-7 Gall: 0-0
Aids: Bl: 0-0 Vi: 0-0 Tstrap: 0-0
Best Rating: 11 4/01 Wind 6f gd-sft

Titchfield (USA)

98 **86**

2-y-o b/br c Mt. Livermore (USA)-Morning Colors (USA) (Raise A Native)
P F I Cole Sir George Meyrick

Placings:26 (4661)
2001: 7^{2}GF, 8^{6}GF

	Starts	1st	2nd	3rd	Win & Pl
Career Total (Turf)	2	0	1	0	2100

Going (Turf): Sf: 0-0 GS: 0-0 Gd: 0-0 GF: 0-2 Fm: 0-0
Distance: 5f/6f: 0-0 7f-8f: 0-2 9f-13f: 0-0 14f+: 0-0
Track : LH: 0-0 RH: 0-1 Tight: 0-0 Gall: 0-0
Aids: Bl: 0-0 Vi: 0-0 Tstrap: 0-0
Best Rating: 86 7/01 Sand 7f16y gd-fm

A interesting colt, who made an encouraging debut when beaten half a length by Kriskova at Sandown in July. He is a half-brother to four US winners, dam very closely related to top-class filly Prospectors Delite and half-sister to several high-class performers, including the Premio Presidente Della Repubblica winner Flagbird.

Titian Angel (IRE)

109 **52**

4-y-o ch f Brief Truce (USA)-Kuwah (IRE) (Be My Guest (USA))
A B Coogan A B Coogan

Placings:2/604-00465325400040 (5599)
2001: 12^{0}HY, 8^{0}G, 9^{4}GF, 10^{6}F, 12^{5}GF, 10^{3}GF, 9^{2}G, 11^{5}G, 14^{4}GF, 10^{0}HY, 12^{0}G, 12^{0}G, 11^{4}S, 12^{0}GS

	Starts	1st	2nd	3rd	Win & Pl
Career Total (Turf)	18	0	2	1	3704

Going (Turf): Sf: 0-4 GS: 0-2 Gd: 0-7 GF: 0-4 Fm: 0-1
Distance: 5f/6f: 0-0 7f-8f: 0-0 9f-13f: 0-17 14f+: 0-1
Track : LH: 0-6 RH: 0-9 Tight: 0-5 Gall: 0-4
Aids: Bl: 0-1 Vi: 0-0 Tstrap: 0-0
Best Rating: 66 8/01 NmkJ 1m6f175y gd-fm

Still a maiden, but stayed the fourteen furlongs well when upped in trip in summer 2001. Should stay further. Has dropped in the handicap. Acts on fast ground.

Titus Bramble

84(77) (9)**43**

4-y-o b g Puissance-Norska (Northfields (USA))
P C Ritchens Mrs B D Adams

Placings:00500/000601415-0 (1074)
2001: 11^{0}GS

	Starts	1st	2nd	3rd	Win & Pl
Career Total (Turf)	14	2	0	0	3989
Career Total (AW)	1	0	0	0	

43 8/00 Wind 1m3f135yG GD £1886
42 7/00 Yarm 1m2f21y C GD £1886
Total win prize-money £3774

Going (Turf): Sf: 0-1 GS: 0-3 **Gd: 2-4** GF: 0-4 Fm: 0-2
Distance: 5f/6f: 0-2 7f-8f: 0-3 **9f-13f: 2-10** 14f+: 0-0
Track : **LH: 1-6** RH: 0-1 **Tight: 2-9** Gall: 0-0
Aids: Bl: 0-1 Vi: 0-0 Tstrap: 0-0
Best Rating: 31 5/01 Brig 1m3f196y gd-sft

Tiye

(72) (1)**27**

6-y-o b m Salse (USA)-Kiya (USA) (Dominion)
D L Williams P F Moore

Placings:05/562306/00-0 (0577)
2001: 10^{0}SW

	Starts	1st	2nd	3rd	Win & Pl
Career Total (Turf)	8	0	1	1	1491
Career Total (AW)	3	0	0	0	0

Going (Turf): Sf: 0-1 GS: 0-1 Gd: 0-1 GF: 0-4 Fm: 0-1
Distance: 5f/6f: 0-0 7f-8f: 0-3 9f-13f: 0-6 14f+: 0-2
Track : LH: 0-6 RH: 0-2 Tight: 0-5 Gall: 0-1
Aids: Bl: 0-1 Vi: 0-2 Tstrap: 0-0
Best Rating: 31 5/01 Brig 1m3f196y gd-sft

Tiyoun (IRE)

105 **90**

3-y-o b g Kahyasi-Taysala (IRE) (Akarad (FR))
D W Barker Miss Sharon Long

Placings:3214-00011004322140 (5135)
2001: 10^{0}HY, 12^{0}GF, 10^{0}F, 11^{1}F, 12^{1}GF, 12^{0}GF, 11^{0}S, 12^{4}GF, 12^{3}G, 12^{2}G, 12^{2}GF, 12^{1}GF, 12^{4}GF, 10^{0}G

	Starts	1st	2nd	3rd	Win & Pl
Career Total (Turf)	18	4	3	2	30881

88 9/01 Thsk 1m4f C(0-90)H G-F £7540
86 6/01 Ripn 1m4f60y D(0-85)H G-F £5609
82 5/01 Rdcr 1m3f D(0-80)H FRM £5057
80 9/00 Pont 1m4y D G-S £3965
Total win prize-money £22172

Going (Turf): Sf: 0-3 GS: 1-2 Gd: 0-3 **GF: 2-8** Fm: 1-2
Distance: 5f/6f: 0-0 7f-8f: 0-1 **9f-13f: 4-17** 14f+: 0-0
Track : **LH: 3-10** RH: 1-5 **Tight: 3-7** Gall: 0-3
Aids: Bl: 0-0 Vi: 0-0 Tstrap: 0-0
Best Rating: 90 9/01 Haml 1m4f17y gd-fm

Took a drop in class to score over 11 furlongs at Redcar in 2001 and followed up over a mile and a half at Ripon. Has run some fair races since including a victory at Thirsk. Acts on fast ground.

Tjinouska (USA)

101 **85+**

3-y-o gr/ro f Cozzene (USA)-Ocean Jewel (USA) (Alleged (USA))
J H M Gosden I M S Racing

Placings:310 (3251)
2001: 12^{3}G, 12^{1}GF, 12^{0}GS

	Starts	1st	2nd	3rd	Win & Pl
Career Total (Turf)	3	1	0	1	4982

85 7/01 Gdwd 1m4f D G-F £4309
Total win prize-money £4310

Going (Turf): Sf: 0-0 GS: 0-1 Gd: 0-1 **GF: 1-1** Fm: 0-0
Distance: 5f/6f: 0-0 7f-8f: 0-0 **9f-13f: 1-3** 14f+: 0-0
Track : LH: 0-0 **RH: 1-2 Tight: 1-2** Gall: 0-0
Aids: Bl: 0-0 Vi: 0-0 Tstrap: 0-0
Best Rating: 85 7/01 Gdwd 1m4f gd-fm

Improved from her debut to win an ordinary Goodwood maiden, and looks likely to get further than 12 furlongs.

To The Last Man

95(86) (47)**32**

5-y-o b g Warrshan (USA)-Shirley's Touch (Touching Wood (USA))
T D Barron (G M Moore 2/2) N B Atkinson

Placings:2642004/4005154404310506/00000-0640 **(5284)**
2001: 8^{0}SD, 8^{6}S, 8^{4}F, 9^{0}HY

	Starts	1st	2nd	3rd	Win & Pl
Career Total (Turf)	28	2	1	1	8291
Career Total (AW)	4	0	1	0	510

60	8/99	Brig	7f214y	F(0-60)	G-S	£2840
62	6/99	Sals	1m	E(0-70)H	GD	£2864

Total win prize-money £5704

Going (Turf): Sf: 0-9 **GS: 1-2 Gd: 1-5** GF: 0-7 Fm: 0-5
Distance: 5f/6f: 0-2 **7f-8f: 2-17** 9f-13f: 0-13 14f+: 0-0
Track : **LH: 1-18** RH: 0-5 Tight: 0-6 Gall: 0-6
Aids: Bl: 0-3 Vi: 0-1 Tstrap: 0-0
Best Rating: 32 9/01 Muss 1m firm

To The Woods (IRE)

97 **74**

2-y-o ch f Woodborough (USA)-Iktidar (Green Desert (USA))
N P Littmoden Mrs Linda Francis

Placings:341060 **(3838)**
2001: 5^{3}S, 5^{4}HY, 5^{1}GF, 6^{0}GF, 6^{6}GS, 7^{0}G

	Starts	1st	2nd	3rd	Win & Pl
Career Total (Turf)	6	1	0	1	5809

74	5/01	Hayd	5f	D	G-F	£4329

Total win prize-money £4329

Going (Turf): Sf: 0-2 GS: 0-1 Gd: 0-1 **GF: 1-2** Fm: 0-0
Distance: **5f/6f: 1-5** 7f-8f: 0-1 9f-13f: 0-0 14f+: 0-0
Track : LH: 0-2 RH: 0-0 Tight: 0-1 Gall: 0-1
Aids: Bl: 0-0 Vi: 0-0 Tstrap: 0-0
Best Rating: 74 7/01 NmkJ 6f gd-sft

She put her previous experience to good use when making all to win a Haydock maiden in May, her first attempt on fast ground, but was well beaten when tried in better company afterwards.

Tobougg (IRE)

114 **122**

3-y-o b c Barathea (IRE)-Lacovia (USA) (Majestic Light (USA))
Saeed Bin Suroor Godolphin

Placings:111-0342 **(5389)**
2001: 8^{0}G, 12^{3}GF, 10^{4}GF, 10^{2}GS

	Starts	1st	2nd	3rd	Win & Pl
Career Total (Turf)	7	3	1	1	395429

117	10/00	NmkR	7f	A	G-S	£124700
116	9/00	Lonc	7f		G-S	£38425
92	8/00	York	6f214y	D	GD	£6493

Total win prize-money £169619

Going (Turf): Sf: 0-0 **GS: 2-3** Gd: 1-2 GF: 0-2 Fm: 0-0
Distance: 5f/6f: 0-0 **7f-8f: 3-4** 9f-13f: 0-3 14f+: 0-0
Track : LH: 1-2 RH: 1-2 Tight: 0-1 **Gall: 1-1**
Aids: Bl: 0-0 Vi: 0-0 Tstrap: 0-0
Best Rating: 122 10/01 NmkR 1m2f gd-sft

Successful twice in Group One company at two when winning the Prix de la Salamandre and the Dewhurst, although neither was a vintage renewal. Moved to Godolphin afterwards, he finished a rather disappointing ninth in the Guineas, but put up his lifetime best when stepped up in distance in the Derby, staying on to finish third just a neck behind the runner-up Golan. He seemed to find the trip on the sharp side when fourth in the Eclipse, but ran well over ten furlongs when going down narrowly to Nayef in the Champion Stakes.

Toccata Aria

100 **63**

3-y-o b f Unfuwain (USA)-Distant Music (Darshaan)
J M Bradley (S G Knight 19/6) Richard Withers

Placings:005 **(5041)**
2001: 14^{0}G, 16^{0}GF, 10^{5}G

	Starts	1st	2nd	3rd	Win & Pl
Career Total (Turf)	3	0	0	0	0

Going (Turf): Sf: 0-0 GS: 0-0 Gd: 0-2 GF: 0-1 Fm: 0-0
Distance: 5f/6f: 0-0 7f-8f: 0-0 9f-13f: 0-1 14f+: 0-2
Track : LH: 0-2 RH: 0-1 Tight: 0-1 Gall: 0-1
Aids: Bl: 0-0 Vi: 0-0 Tstrap: 0-0
Best Rating: 52 6/01 Asct 2m45y gd-fm

Toejam

102 **49**

8-y-o ch g Move Off-Cheeky Pigeon (Brave Invader (USA))
R E Barr Mrs R E Barr

Placings:065040/00150460-035053303021000 **(5657)**
2001: 7^{0}F, 7^{3}GF, 8^{5}G, 8^{0}F, 8^{5}F, 8^{3}F, 9^{3}G, 8^{0}GF, 9^{3}GS, 10^{0}GF, 8^{2}GF, 8^{1}F, 8^{0}GS, 8^{0}S, 8^{0}G

	Starts	1st	2nd	3rd	Win & Pl
Career Total (Turf)	29	2	1	4	8666

49	9/01	Pont	1m4y	F(0-60)H	FRM	£3528
42	6/00	Rdcr	1m	G(0-70)H	FRM	£1848

Total win prize-money £5376

Going (Turf): Sf: 0-2 GS: 0-3 Gd: 0-6 GF: 0-8 **Fm: 2-10**
Distance: 5f/6f: 0-0 7f-8f: 1-15 9f-13f: 1-11 14f+: 0-3
Track : **LH: 1-13** RH: 0-8 Tight: 0-13 Gall: 0-2
Aids: Bl: 0-0 **Vi: 1-4** Tstrap: 0-0
Best Rating: 49 9/01 Pont 1m4y firm

He gained due reward for a string of consistent efforts when dropped into selling grade at Pontefract in September. Best at a mile on fast ground.

Toffee Nosed

110 **91**

3-y-o ch f Selkirk (USA)-Ever Welcome (Be My Guest (USA))
B W Hills W J Gredley

Placings:42-35222101 **(5259)**
2001: 7^{3}GS, 10^{5}F, 8^{2}F, 8^{2}F, 7^{2}G, 7^{1}GF, 6^{0}G, 7^{1}GS, 8^{0}HY

	Starts	1st	2nd	3rd	Win & Pl
Career Total (Turf)	10	2	4	1	34449

91	10/01	Asct	7f	A	G-S	£17810
60	8/01	Wwck	7f26y	D	G-F	£4208

Total win prize-money £22019

Going (Turf): Sf: 0-1 **GS: 1-2** Gd: 0-3 **GF: 1-1** Fm: 0-3
Distance: 5f/6f: 0-1 **7f-8f: 2-7** 9f-13f: 0-2 14f+: 0-0
Track : **LH: 1-4** RH: 0-0 Tight: 0-1 Gall: 0-2
Aids: Bl: 0-0 Vi: 0-0 Tstrap: 0-0
Best Rating: 100 5/01 York 1m2f85y firm

A well-bred filly who is a half-sister to two winners, she ran well in decent company at the start of the season, but became a habitual loser and was beaten at some very short odds. Finally broke her maiden at Warwick and gained a very unlikely win in an Ascot Listed event, but is a very enigmatic filly. Best at seven furlongs, she seems to act on any ground.

Tojoneski

100(84) (52)**76**

2-y-o b c Emperor Jones (USA)-Sampower Lady (Rock City)
P J Makin Racingclubcouk

Placings:011 **(4051)**
2001: 6^{0}GF, 5^{1}G, 5^{1}F, 7^{0}SD

	Starts	1st	2nd	3rd	Win & Pl
Career Total (Turf)	3	2	0	0	6188

76	8/01	Ling	5f	E	FRM	£3178
75	7/01	Chep	5f16y	E	GD	£3010

Total win prize-money £6188

Going (Turf): Sf: 0-0 GS: 0-0 **Gd: 1-1** GF: 0-1 **Fm: 1-1**
Distance: **5f/6f: 2-3** 7f-8f: 0-0 9f-13f: 0-0 14f+: 0-0
Track : LH: 0-0 RH: 0-0 Tight: 0-0 Gall: 0-0
Aids: Bl: 0-0 Vi: 0-0 Tstrap: 0-0
Best Rating: 76 8/01 Ling 5f firm

He was ridden too hard by Seb Sanders, according to the Stewards, when scraping home to win a Chepstow maiden in July 2001. He made it two in a row when enduring the unsuitable early pace in a nursery at Lincoln under a different pilot, he snatched the race at the post. He is suited to five furlongs on a sound surface.

Toking N' Joken (IRE)

63 **24**

2-y-o b f Mukaddamah (USA)-We'Re Joken (Statoblest)
W G M Turner Miss S A Ryder

Placings:40 **(4627)**
2001: 5^{4}GF, 5^{0}GF

	Starts	1st	2nd	3rd	Win & Pl
Career Total (Turf)	2	0	0	0	0

Going (Turf): Sf: 0-0 GS: 0-0 Gd: 0-0 GF: 0-2 Fm: 0-0
Distance: 5f/6f: 0-2 7f-8f: 0-0 9f-13f: 0-0 14f+: 0-0
Track : LH: 0-1 RH: 0-0 Tight: 0-0 Gall: 0-0
Aids: Bl: 0-0 Vi: 0-0 Tstrap: 0-0
Best Rating: 24 9/01 Nott 5f13y gd-fm

Tolcea (IRE)

82 **70**

2-y-o ch c Barathea (IRE)-Mosaique Bleue (Shirley Heights)
E A L Dunlop Mohammed Ali

Placings:000 **(5367)**
2001: 7^{0}S, 8^{0}G, 8^{0}GS

	Starts	1st	2nd	3rd	Win & Pl
Career Total (Turf)	3	0	0	0	

Going (Turf): Sf: 0-1 GS: 0-1 Gd: 0-1 GF: 0-0 Fm: 0-0
Distance: 5f/6f: 0-0 7f-8f: 0-2 9f-13f: 0-1 14f+: 0-0
Track : LH: 0-1 RH: 0-0 Tight: 0-0 Gall: 0-0
Aids: Bl: 0-0 Vi: 0-0 Tstrap: 0-0
Best Rating: 70 10/01 NmkR 1m gd-sft

Toldya

104(101) (66)**68**

4-y-o b f Beveled (USA)-Run Amber Run (Run The Gantlet (USA))
M Kettle Benham Racing

Placings:00022/4321324165-5645005130 **(5671)**
2001: 6^{5}SD, 5^{6}G, 5^{4}G, 5^{5}G, 6^{0}GF, 5^{0}G, 6^{5}G, 6^{1}SD, 5^{3}HY, 6^{0}HY

	Starts	1st	2nd	3rd	Win & Pl
Career Total (Turf)	15	1	1	1	5117
Career Total (AW)	10	2	3	2	8366

66	10/01	Wolv	6f	F(0-65)H	STD	£2471
68	10/00	Ling	6f	E(0-75)H	SFT	£3377
60	2/00	Ling	5f	E(0-70)H	STD	£2730

Total win prize-money £8579

Going (Turf): **Sf: 1-4** GS: 0-1 Gd: 0-6 GF: 0-4 Fm: 0-0
Distance: **5f/6f: 3-23** 7f-8f: 0-2 9f-13f: 0-0 14f+: 0-0
Track : **LH: 2-12** RH: 0-2 **Tight: 2-10** Gall: 0-3
Aids: **Bl: 1-6** Vi: 0-0 Tstrap: 0-0
Best Rating: 68 6/01 Leic 5f218y good

Won her first race in 12 months when successful in a

six-furlong handicap on the Fibresand at Wolverhampton. Best at six furlongs.

Toledo Star

81 **67**

2-y-o br c Petong-Shafir (IRE) (Shaadi (USA))
D Nicholls Mrs C C Regaldo-Gonzalez

Placings:0 **(4708)**
2001: 6^{0}G

	Starts	1st	2nd	3rd	Win & Pl
Career Total (Turf)	1	0	0	0	

Going (Turf): Sf: 0-0 GS: 0-0 Gd: 0-1 GF: 0-0 Fm: 0-0
Distance: 5f/6f: 0-1 7f-8f: 0-0 9f-13f: 0-0 14f+: 0-0
Track : LH: 0-0 RH: 0-0 Tight: 0-0 Gall: 0-0
Aids: Bl: 0-0 Vi: 0-0 Tstrap: 0-1
Best Rating: 67 9/01 Donc 6f good

Toleration

99(80) (31)**73**

4-y-o b f Petong-Dancing Chimes (London Bells (CAN))
K O Cunningham-Brown C Leafe

Placings:41/000-05000 **(4607)**
2001: 6^{0}GS, 5^{5}G, 7^{0}GF, 6^{0}G, 6^{0}SD

	Starts	1st	2nd	3rd	Win & Pl
Career Total (Turf)	9	1	0	0	3754
Career Total (AW)	1	0	0	0	

81	10/99	Wind	6f	D	G-S	£3403

Total win prize-money £3404

Going (Turf): Sf: 0-1 **GS: 1-2** Gd: 0-2 GF: 0-4 Fm: 0-0
Distance: **5f/6f: 1-8** 7f-8f: 0-2 9f-13f: 0-0 14f+: 0-0
Track : LH: 0-2 **RH: 1-1** Tight: 0-1 **Gall: 1-2**
Aids: Bl: 0-0 Vi: 0-0 Tstrap: 0-0
Best Rating: 73 4/01 NmkR 6f gd-sft

A full sister to Palacegate Touch, she ran well as a juvenile but has shown little since. She is best with cut in the ground.

Tollgate Melody

67 **10**

3-y-o b f Sabrehill (USA)-Breed Reference (Reference Point)
R Rowe Mrs P V Crocker

Placings:00 **(4958)**
2001: 7^{0}GF, 9^{0}GS

	Starts	1st	2nd	3rd	Win & Pl
Career Total (Turf)	2	0	0	0	

Going (Turf): Sf: 0-0 GS: 0-1 Gd: 0-0 GF: 0-1 Fm: 0-0
Distance: 5f/6f: 0-0 7f-8f: 0-1 9f-13f: 0-1 14f+: 0-0
Track : LH: 0-0 RH: 0-1 Tight: 0-1 Gall: 0-0
Aids: Bl: 0-0 Vi: 0-0 Tstrap: 0-0
Best Rating: 0 9/01 Gdwd 1m1f192y gd-sft

Tom Dougal

102 (56)**61**

6-y-o b g Ron's Victory (USA)-Fabulous Rina (FR) (Fabulous Dancer (USA))
C Smith Mrs N Stewart

Placings:0556402/301130000/0512045000/005000-640000 **(5626)**
2001: 8^{6}S, 8^{4}GF, 8^{0}G, 8^{0}G, 8^{0}GS, 8^{0}GS

	Starts	1st	2nd	3rd	Win & Pl
Career Total (Turf)	37	3	2	2	43124
Career Total (AW)	1	0	0	0	334

86	5/99	Ayr	1m	C(0-85)	GD	£7593
90	5/98	York	7f202y	C(0-95)H	GD	£8285
86	5/98	NmkR	1m	C(0-90)H	GD	£15760

Total win prize-money £31639

Going (Turf): Sf: 0-6 GS: 0-9 **Gd: 3-13** GF: 0-8 Fm: 0-1
Distance: 5f/6f: 0-5 **7f-8f: 3-21** 9f-13f: 0-12 14f+: 0-0
Track : **LH: 2-17** RH: 0-4 Tight: 0-6 **Gall: 1-6**
Aids: Bl: 0-0 Vi: 0-0 Tstrap: 0-0
Best Rating: 61 5/01 Muss 1m gd-fm

Tom Tun

106(114) (83)**85**

6-y-o b g Bold Arrangement-B Grade (Lucky Wednesday)
Miss J F Craze Mrs O Tunstall

Placings:00015510610/1131314645124230026/523005 0011000-361212100500006 **(5630)**
2001: 5^{3}SD, 6^{6}SW, 5^{1}SD, 5^{2}SD, 5^{1}SD, 6^{2}S, 6^{1}S, 5^{0}GF, 6^{0}F, 6^{5}G, 6^{0}G, 5^{0}HY, 5^{0}G, 6^{0}GS, 6^{6}G, 6^{3}SD

	Starts	1st	2nd	3rd	Win & Pl
Career Total (Turf)	40	7	3	3	43210
Career Total (AW)	18	6	3	2	37355

90	4/01	Pont	6f	C(0-90)H	SFT	£7442
83	3/01	Wolv	5f	C(0-100)H	STD	£6695
78	2/01	Wolv	5f	D(0-85)H	STD	£3786
74	8/00	Haml	6f5y	E(0-70)H	SFT	£3916
65	8/00	Leic	5f218y	E(0-70)	G-F	£2778
77	7/99	Donc	6f	E(0-75)	G-F	£2723
73	5/99	Donc	6f	D(0-85)H	G-F	£3967
61	3/99	Newc	5f	D(0-85)H	G-S	£7002
74	2/99	Sthl	6f	B H	STD	£9849
65	1/99	Sthl	6f	D(0-80)H	STD	£3712
58	11/98	Ling	5f	F(0-60)H	STD	£2085
50	9/98	Newc	6f	F(0-65)H	GD	£2515
44	7/98	Sthl	6f	E(0-70)H	STD	£3236

Total win prize-money £59712

Going (Turf): Sf: 2-11 GS: 1-5 Gd: 1-12 **GF: 3-10** Fm: 0-2
Distance: **5f/6f: 12-53** 7f-8f: 1-5 9f-13f: 0-0 14f+: 0-0
Track : **LH: 7-20** RH: 0-1 **Tight: 3-7** Gall: 0-2
Aids: Bl: 0-0 Vi: 0-0 **Tstrap: 5-20**
Best Rating: 90 4/01 Pont 6f soft

A pretty decent sprinter on turf and sand, he is equally effective over five and six furlongs. Ran a fine race to finish runner-up on his turf reappearance at Doncaster and went one better at Pontefract next time, but held since off a higher mark. Acts on any ground.

Tom Tygrys

76 **52**

2-y-o b c Danzig Connection (USA)-Strath Kitten (Scottish Reel)
P S McEntee Ms Clare Sharp

Placings:000 **(4873)**
2001: 7^{0}S, 7^{0}G, 7^{0}G

	Starts	1st	2nd	3rd	Win & Pl
Career Total (Turf)	3	0	0	0	

Going (Turf): Sf: 0-1 GS: 0-0 Gd: 0-2 GF: 0-0 Fm: 0-0
Distance: 5f/6f: 0-0 7f-8f: 0-3 9f-13f: 0-0 14f+: 0-0
Track : LH: 0-0 RH: 0-2 Tight: 0-0 Gall: 0-1
Aids: Bl: 0-0 Vi: 0-0 Tstrap: 0-0
Best Rating: 52 8/01 Sand 7f16y soft

Faced a stiff task when last of seven in a Sandown conditions event on his debut.

Tomamie

(66) **30**

3-y-o b f Tina's Pet-Springhead (Komaite (USA))
J R Norton G A Hancock & A Parsonage

Placings:000000-00 **(3361)**
2001: 6^{0}SD, 8^{0}G

	Starts	1st	2nd	3rd	Win & Pl
Career Total (Turf)	6	0	0	0	
Career Total (AW)	2	0	0	0	

Going (Turf): Sf: 0-1 GS: 0-1 Gd: 0-4 GF: 0-0 Fm: 0-0
Distance: 5f/6f: 0-5 7f-8f: 0-2 9f-13f: 0-1 14f+: 0-0
Track : LH: 0-4 RH: 0-0 Tight: 0-2 Gall: 0-1
Aids: Bl: 0-0 Vi: 0-0 Tstrap: 0-0
Best Rating: 52 8/01 Sand 7f16y soft

Tomanivi

3-y-o b f Caerleon (USA)-Balleta (USA) (Lyphard (USA))
H R A Cecil K Abdulla

Placings:6 **(3964)**
2001: 10^{6}G

	Starts	1st	2nd	3rd	Win & Pl
Career Total (Turf)	1	0	0	0	0

Going (Turf): Sf: 0-0 GS: 0-0 Gd: 0-1 GF: 0-0 Fm: 0-0
Distance: 5f/6f: 0-0 7f-8f: 0-0 9f-13f: 0-1 14f+: 0-0
Track : LH: 0-1 RH: 0-0 Tight: 0-1 Gall: 0-0
Aids: Bl: 0-0 Vi: 0-0 Tstrap: 0-0

Tomasino

114 **104**

3-y-o br c Celtic Swing-Bustinetta (Bustino)
M Johnston P D Savill

Placings:461-12323 **(3552)**
2001: 12^{1}S, 12^{2}GF, 12^{3}S, 12^{2}GF, 12^{3}GF

	Starts	1st	2nd	3rd	Win & Pl
Career Total (Turf)	8	2	2	2	31457

91	4/01	Ripn	1m4f60y	D(0-85)H	SFT	£4842
72	10/00	Newc	1m	D	HVY	£3435

Total win prize-money £8278

Going (Turf): Sf: 2-5 GS: 0-0 Gd: 0-0 GF: 0-3 Fm: 0-0
Distance: 5f/6f: 0-0 7f-8f: 1-3 9f-13f: 1-5 14f+: 0-0
Track : LH: 1-5 RH: 1-3 Tight: 1-3 Gall: 1-4
Aids: Bl: 0-0 Vi: 0-0 Tstrap: 0-0
Best Rating: 104 8/01 Gdwd 1m4f gd-fm

Scored on his last start as a juvenile at Newcastle over a mile and won on his reappearance at three over a mile and a half at Ripon. Just caught at Chester, but ran very badly when last of three at Newbury. Showed that running to be all wrong when just beaten in the King George V Handicap at Royal Ascot, but fractured a cannonbone at Goodwood. He has won on soft and heavy ground but acts on fast.

Tomenoso

87(61) **43**

3-y-o b g Teenoso (USA)-Guarded Expression (Siberian Express (USA))
W G M Turner D & J Racing

Placings:00-60 **(5269)**
2001: 7^{6}S, 10^{0}HY

	Starts	1st	2nd	3rd	Win & Pl
Career Total (Turf)	3	0	0	0	0
Career Total (AW)	1	0	0	0	

Going (Turf): Sf: 0-2 GS: 0-0 Gd: 0-1 GF: 0-0 Fm: 0-0
Distance: 5f/6f: 0-1 7f-8f: 0-2 9f-13f: 0-1 14f+: 0-0
Track : LH: 0-4 RH: 0-0 Tight: 0-1 Gall: 0-0
Aids: Bl: 0-0 Vi: 0-0 Tstrap: 0-0
Best Rating: 43 10/01 Brig 7f214y soft

Tomillie

90 **61**

2-y-o ch c Ventiquattrofogli (IRE)-Royal Comedian (Jester)
A Berry Gary Flitcroft

Placings:22 **(5399)**
2001: 6^{2}S, 6^{2}S

	Starts	1st	2nd	3rd	Win & Pl
Career Total (Turf)	2	0	2	0	2345

Going (Turf): Sf: 0-2 GS: 0-0 Gd: 0-0 GF: 0-0 Fm: 0-0
Distance: 5f/6f: 0-2 7f-8f: 0-0 9f-13f: 0-0 14f+: 0-0
Track : LH: 0-2 RH: 0-0 Tight: 0-0 Gall: 0-0
Aids: Bl: 0-0 Vi: 0-0 Tstrap: 0-0
Best Rating: 61 10/01 Pont 6f soft

Two near-misses over the same course, distance and ground to his name so far. There is a race in him.

Tommy Carson

94

6-y-o b g Last Tycoon-Ivory Palm (USA) (Sir Ivor)
Jamie Poulton J Logan

Placings:03/042332/625040600-020 **(4377)**
2001: 11^{0}GS, 9^{2}G, 11^{0}GF

	Starts	1st	2nd	3rd	Win & Pl
Career Total (Turf)	20	0	4	3	4546

Going (Turf): Sf: 0-4 GS: 0-1 Gd: 0-6 GF: 0-8 Fm: 0-1
Distance: 5f/6f: 0-0 7f-8f: 0-0 9f-13f: 0-15 14f+: 0-5
Track : LH: 0-8 RH: 0-11 Tight: 0-13 Gall: 0-1
Aids: Bl: 0-11 Vi: 0-0 Tstrap: 0-0
Best Rating: 40 8/01 Brig 1m1f209y good

Tommy Dod

86 **64**

2-y-o ch c Keen-Wyse Folly (Colmore Row)
M Johnston Tommy Dod Syndicate

Placings:000 **(5460)**
2001: 5^{0}F, 7^{0}S, 8^{0}G

	Starts	1st	2nd	3rd	Win & Pl
Career Total (Turf)	3	0	0	0	

Going (Turf): Sf: 0-1 GS: 0-0 Gd: 0-1 GF: 0-0 Fm: 0-1
Distance: 5f/6f: 0-1 7f-8f: 0-1 9f-13f: 0-1 14f+: 0-0
Track : LH: 0-3 RH: 0-0 Tight: 0-1 Gall: 0-1
Aids: Bl: 0-0 Vi: 0-0 Tstrap: 0-0
Best Rating: 64 10/01 York 7f202y soft

Tommy Lorne

96 **52**

3-y-o b c Inchinor-Actress (Known Fact (USA))
J L Dunlop J L Dunlop

Placings:630-0000 **(5400)**
2001: 8^{0}G, 9^{0}G, 10^{0}S, 10^{0}S

	Starts	1st	2nd	3rd	Win & Pl
Career Total (Turf)	7	0	0	1	600

Going (Turf): Sf: 0-3 GS: 0-1 Gd: 0-2 GF: 0-1 Fm: 0-0
Distance: 5f/6f: 0-0 7f-8f: 0-2 9f-13f: 0-5 14f+: 0-0
Track : LH: 0-3 RH: 0-1 Tight: 0-0 Gall: 0-0
Aids: Bl: 0-0 Vi: 0-0 Tstrap: 0-0
Best Rating: 52 8/01 Nott 1m54y good

Tommy Smith

108 **69**

3-y-o ch g Timeless Times (USA)-Superstream (Superpower)
J S Wainwright T W Heseltine

Placings:004116500-60242000100100 **(4965)**
2001: 6^{6}HY, 6^{0}S, 5^{2}GF, 5^{4}GF, 5^{2}G, 5^{0}GF, 5^{0}GF, 5^{0}GF, 5^{1}F, 6^{0}S, 5^{0}GF, 5^{1}GF, 6^{0}GF, 5^{0}S

				Starts	1st	2nd	3rd	Win & Pl
Career Total (Turf)				23	4	2	0	16802
69	8/01	Bevl	5f	F(0-75)H		GF		£7995
61	7/01	Rdcr	5f	F(0-60)H		FRM		£2548
60	7/00	Haml	6f5y	F		G-F		£2163
56	6/00	Muss	5f	F		FRM		£2604

Total win prize-money £15310

Going (Turf): Sf: 0-5 GS: 0-1 Gd: 0-3 **GF: 2-12 Fm: 2-2**
Distance: **5f/6f: 3-21** 7f-8f: 1-2 9f-13f: 0-0 14f+: 0-0
Track : LH: 0-3 RH: 0-0 Tight: 0-0 Gall: 0-0
Aids: Bl: 0-1 **Vi: 2-6** Tstrap: 0-0
Best Rating: 69 8/01 Bevl 5f gd-fm

Loves the minimum trip and fast ground and all of his wins to date have come under those conditions. He has on occasions spoilt his chances with a slow start.

Tomthevic

99 **59**

3-y-o ch g Emarati (USA)-Madame Bovary (Ile De Bourbon (USA))
J J Quinn Derrick Bloy

Placings:4032101-0000060325430060 **(4965)**
2001: 6^{0}S, 5^{0}GS, 5^{0}GF, 6^{0}F, 5^{0}F, 5^{6}GF, 5^{0}GS, 5^{3}G, 5^{2}GF, 5^{5}G, 5^{4}GS, 5^{3}GF, 5^{0}GF, 6^{0}F, 6^{6}F, 5^{0}S

				Starts	1st	2nd	3rd	Win & Pl
Career Total (Turf)				23	2	2	3	11718
78	8/00	Rdcr	5f	E		FRM		£2828
80	8/00	Thsk	5f	D		G-F		£4179

Total win prize-money £7008

Going (Turf): Sf: 0-3 GS: 0-3 Gd: 0-3 **GF: 1-8 Fm: 1-6**
Distance: **5f/6f: 2-22** 7f-8f: 0-1 9f-13f: 0-0 14f+: 0-0
Track : LH: 0-6 RH: 0-0 Tight: 0-1 Gall: 0-0
Aids: Bl: 0-0 Vi: 0-1 **Tstrap: 2-7**
Best Rating: 59 8/01 Thsk 5f gd-sft

A winner twice over the minimum trip on fast ground in August 2000, has dropped in the handicap and has been showing signs of a return to form lately.

Tong Ice

78 **35**

2-y-o gr c Petong-Efficacious (IRE) (Efisio)
I Semple (Miss L A Porratt 2/9) Jamaic Plant Hire Limited

Placings:006000 **(5662)**
2001: 6^{0}GF, 5^{0}GF, 5^{6}G, 5^{0}GS, 5^{0}G, 8^{0}G

	Starts	1st	2nd	3rd	Win & Pl
Career Total (Turf)	6	0	0	0	0

Going (Turf): Sf: 0-0 GS: 0-1 Gd: 0-3 GF: 0-2 Fm: 0-0
Distance: 5f/6f: 0-5 7f-8f: 0-1 9f-13f: 0-0 14f+: 0-0
Track : LH: 0-0 RH: 0-1 Tight: 0-1 Gall: 0-0
Aids: Bl: 0-0 Vi: 0-0 Tstrap: 0-0
Best Rating: 35 6/01 Haml 5f4y gd-fm

Tong Road

96(76) (19)**35**

5-y-o gr g Petong-Wayzgoose (USA) (Diesis)
D W Chapman J B Wilcox

Placings:000/000060**0/0**00020-00U0000350400 **(4110)**
2001: 5^{0}G, 6^{0}F, 6^{U}GF, 6^{0}SD, 5^{0}F, 5^{0}F, 5^{0}GF, 6^{3}GF, 8^{5}F, 6^{0}F, 5^{4}G, 6^{0}GS, 5^{0}S

	Starts	1st	2nd	3rd	Win & Pl
Career Total (Turf)	25	0	1	1	1485
Career Total (AW)	4	0	0	0	

Going (Turf): Sf: 0-5 GS: 0-3 Gd: 0-5 GF: 0-7 Fm: 0-5
Distance: 5f/6f: 0-24 7f-8f: 0-5 9f-13f: 0-0 14f+: 0-0
Track : LH: 0-6 RH: 0-1 Tight: 0-2 Gall: 0-2
Aids: Bl: 0-2 Vi: 0-0 Tstrap: 0-0
Best Rating: 35 7/01 Ripn 6f gd-fm

Toni Alcala

98(83) (51)**63**

2-y-o b g Ezzoud (IRE)-Etourdie (USA) (Arctic Tern (USA))
R F Fisher Alan Willoughby

Placings:60220536046 **(4793)**
2001: 5^{6}S, 5^{0}GS, 5^{2}S, 6^{2}GF, 5^{0}GF, 6^{5}GF, 7^{3}F, 7^{6}G, 7^{0}SD, 8^{4}F, 8^{6}G

	Starts	1st	2nd	3rd	Win & Pl
Career Total (Turf)	10	0	2	1	2168
Career Total (AW)	1	0	0	0	

Going (Turf): Sf: 0-2 GS: 0-1 Gd: 0-2 GF: 0-3 Fm: 0-2
Distance: 5f/6f: 0-6 7f-8f: 0-5 9f-13f: 0-0 14f+: 0-0
Track : LH: 0-4 RH: 0-1 Tight: 0-2 Gall: 0-0
Aids: Bl: 0-0 Vi: 0-0 Tstrap: 0-0
Best Rating: 63 9/01 Muss 1m firm

Tonight At Mamma's

67(75) (21)**3**

2-y-o b f Timeless Times (USA)-Henpot (IRE) (Alzao (USA))
A Berry J K Brown & Partners

Placings:600 **(2646)**
2001: 5^{6}SD, 5^{0}GF, 5^{0}SD

	Starts	1st	2nd	3rd	Win & Pl
Career Total (Turf)	1	0	0	0	
Career Total (AW)	2	0	0	0	0

Going (Turf): Sf: 0-0 GS: 0-0 Gd: 0-0 GF: 0-1 Fm: 0-0
Distance: 5f/6f: 0-3 7f-8f: 0-0 9f-13f: 0-0 14f+: 0-0
Track : LH: 0-0 RH: 0-0 Tight: 0-0 Gall: 0-0
Aids: Bl: 0-0 Vi: 0-0 Tstrap: 0-0
Best Rating: 21 4/01 Sthl 5f stand

Tonight's Prize (IRE)

99 **61**

7-y-o b g Night Shift (USA)-Bestow (Shirley Heights)
C F Wall Hintlesham Thoroughbreds

Placings:0522221/003515300/600200035/14600 0000 **(2577)**
2001: 10^{0}G, 10^{0}GF, 9^{0}GF, 12^{0}GF

				Starts	1st	2nd	3rd	Win & Pl
Career Total (Turf)				34	3	5	3	26302
79	5/00	Wind	1m2f7y	D(0-75)		G-F		£3926
87	8/98	Pont	1m4y	C(0-90)H		G-F		£7652
72	10/97	Pont	1m4y	D		G-F		£3550

Total win prize-money £15129

Going (Turf): Sf: 0-0 GS: 0-2 Gd: 0-14 **GF: 3-18** Fm: 0-0
Distance: 5f/6f: 0-0 7f-8f: 0-5 **9f-13f: 3-29** 14f+: 0-0
Track : **LH: 2-11** RH: 0-15 **Tight: 1-9** Gall: 0-7
Aids: Bl: 0-0 Vi: 0-0 Tstrap: 0-0
Best Rating: 61 6/01 Wind 1m2f7y gd-fm

He won at Pontefract on his final start last season, and returned to winning form on the same track in July. He ideally needs ten furlongs or a very stiff mile to be seen at his best.

Tonto O'Reilly

93(67) (27)**59**

3-y-o gr c Mind Games-Most Uppitty (Absalom)
B Smart Mrs Julie Martin And David R Martin

Placings:0000-50000 **(3259)**
2001: 6^{5}HY, 6^{0}GS, 5^{0}GF, 7^{0}F, 6^{0}GF

	Starts	1st	2nd	3rd	Win & Pl
Career Total (Turf)	8	0	0	0	0
Career Total (AW)	1	0	0	0	

Going (Turf): Sf: 0-4 GS: 0-1 Gd: 0-0 GF: 0-2 Fm: 0-1
Distance: 5f/6f: 0-6 7f-8f: 0-3 9f-13f: 0-0 14f+: 0-0
Track : LH: 0-3 RH: 0-0 Tight: 0-0 Gall: 0-0
Aids: Bl: 0-0 Vi: 0-0 Tstrap: 0-3
Best Rating: 57 4/01 Wwck 6f21y heavy

Tony

92(83) (25)**24**

3-y-o b g Marju (IRE)-Present Imperfect (Cadeaux Genereux)
M W Easterby Guy Reed

Placings:0000-64600 (2055)
2001: 8^{6}S, 8^{4}S, 12^{6}SD, 10^{0}GF, 10^{0}GF

	Starts	1st	2nd	3rd	Win & Pl
Career Total (Turf)	8	0	0	0	0
Career Total (AW)	1	0	0	0	0

Going (Turf): Sf: 0-3 GS: 0-1 Gd: 0-0 GF: 0-3 Fm: 0-1
Distance: 5f/6f: 0-3 7f-8f: 0-1 9f-13f: 0-5 14f+: 0-0
Track : LH: 0-5 RH: 0-1 Tight: 0-3 Gall: 0-1
Aids: Bl: 0-1 Vi: 0-0 Tstrap: 0-0
Best Rating: 25 5/01 Wolv 1m4f stand

Tony Tie

107(60) (51)**88**
5-y-o b g Ardkinglass-Queen Of The Quorn (Governor General)
J S Goldie Frank Brady

Placings:1043106/00000210/6223102021222000300-000004154323210300 (5688)
2001: 8^{0}GS, 8^{0}G, 10^{0}GF, 10^{0}GF, 8^{0}GF, 8^{4}G, 8^{1}GF, 7^{5}GF, 7^{4}G, 7^{3}GF, 7^{2}G, 8^{3}G, 8^{2}S, 8^{1}G, 8^{0}S, 8^{3}GS, 8^{0}GS, 7^{0}S

	Starts	1st	2nd	3rd	Win & Pl
Career Total (Turf)	51	7	10	6	88348
Career Total (AW)	1	0	0	0	

84	9/01	Haml	1m65y	C(0-90)H	GD	£8807
77	6/01	Newc	1m	C(0-90)H	G-F	£6955
87	7/00	Newc	7f	C(0-90)H	G-F	£10400
85	6/00	Ayr	1m2f	C(0-95)H	G-F	£6773
81	11/99	Donc	1m	E(0-80)H	SFT	£4689
89	8/98	Ches	7f2y	C	G-S	£5345
79	5/98	Sals	5f	C	G-S	£4420

Total win prize-money £47390

Going (Turf): Sf: 1-12 GS: 2-9 Gd: 1-15 **GF: 3-13** Fm: 0-2
Distance: 5f/6f: 1-3 **7f-8f: 4-32** 9f-13f: 2-17 14f+: 0-0
Track : **LH: 3-28** RH: 1-6 **Tight: 2-10** Gall: 1-11
Aids: Bl: 0-0 Vi: 0-1 Tstrap: 0-0
Best Rating: 85 10/01 NmkR 1m gd-sft

A decent sort, he was given a chance by the Handicapper and took it at Newcastle in June. Effective from seven to 10 furlongs, he continued to run well before scoring at Hamilton in September. Met trouble in running in a showcase handicap at Newmarket in October but still dead-heated for third, although he has struggled since then. Genuine and consistent.

Tootorial (IRE)

(89) (37)
4-y-o b c College Chapel-Touche-A-Tout (IRE) (Royal Academy (USA))
Mrs L Stubbs Maurice Parker

Placings:40-030 (0579)
2001: 7^{0}SW, 7^{3}SD, 8^{0}SW

	Starts	1st	2nd	3rd	Win & Pl
Career Total (Turf)	0	0	0	0	
Career Total (AW)	5	0	0	1	385

Going (Turf): Sf: 0-0 GS: 0-0 Gd: 0-0 GF: 0-0 Fm: 0-0
Distance: 5f/6f: 0-2 7f-8f: 0-3 9f-13f: 0-0 14f+: 0-0
Track : LH: 0-5 RH: 0-0 Tight: 0-3 Gall: 0-0
Aids: Bl: 0-0 Vi: 0-0 Tstrap: 0-2
Best Rating: 37 3/01 Ling 7f stand

Top Act

76
5-y-o b g Inchinor-Actress (Known Fact (USA))
J S Wainwright Mrs D Drewery

Placings:6000/00000/00000 (2337)
2001: 10^{0}HY, 12^{0}S, 10^{0}F, 7^{0}GF, 10^{0}GF

	Starts	1st	2nd	3rd	Win & Pl
Career Total (Turf)	14	0	0	0	0

Going (Turf): Sf: 0-3 GS: 0-0 Gd: 0-4 GF: 0-5 Fm: 0-2
Distance: 5f/6f: 0-2 7f-8f: 0-5 9f-13f: 0-7 14f+: 0-0
Track : LH: 0-6 RH: 0-5 Tight: 0-3 Gall: 0-2
Aids: Bl: 0-0 Vi: 0-2 Tstrap: 0-0
Best Rating: 31 4/01 Pont 1m2f6y heavy

Top Crystal (IRE)

90 **55**
3-y-o b f Sadler's Wells (USA)-State Crystal (IRE) (High Estate)
H R A Cecil Michael Poland

Placings:0 (4893)
2001: 12^{0}GF

	Starts	1st	2nd	3rd	Win & Pl
Career Total (Turf)	1	0	0	0	

Going (Turf): Sf: 0-0 GS: 0-0 Gd: 0-0 GF: 0-1 Fm: 0-0
Distance: 5f/6f: 0-0 7f-8f: 0-0 9f-13f: 0-1 14f+: 0-0
Track : LH: 0-0 RH: 0-1 Tight: 0-0 Gall: 0-0
Aids: Bl: 0-0 Vi: 0-0 Tstrap: 0-0
Best Rating: 55 9/01 Kemp 1m4f gd-fm

Top Dirham

107 **94**
3-y-o ch c Night Shift (USA)-Miller's Melody (Chief Singer)
Sir Michael Stoute Saeed Suhail

Placings:0115 (2330)
2001: 7^{0}S, 7^{1}GF, 7^{1}GF, 8^{5}GF

	Starts	1st	2nd	3rd	Win & Pl
Career Total (Turf)	4	2	0	0	23790

93	6/01	Epsm	7f	C(0-100)H	G-F	£19500
84	5/01	Bevl	7f100y	D	G-F	£4290

Total win prize-money £23790

Going (Turf): Sf: 0-1 GS: 0-0 Gd: 0-0 **GF: 2-3** Fm: 0-0
Distance: 5f/6f: 0-0 **7f-8f: 2-4** 9f-13f: 0-0 14f+: 0-0
Track : LH: 1-1 RH: 1-1 **Tight: 1-1** Gall: 0-0
Aids: Bl: 0-0 Vi: 0-0 Tstrap: 0-0
Best Rating: 94 6/01 Asct 1m gd-fm

Made a promising start to his career with back-to-back wins in a Beverley maiden and a valuable handicap at Epsom in the summer of 2001. The step up to a mile next time out clearly did not suit him, as he failed to show the turn of foot with which he impressed at Epsom, consequently contradicting his heavy market support. He is at home on a sound surface.

Top Flight Queen

90 **64**
2-y-o b f Mark Of Esteem (IRE)-Blessed Event (King's Lake (USA))
Mrs G S Rees P Bamford

Placings:44050 (5379)
2001: 5^{4}GF, 5^{4}GF, 7^{0}HY, 6^{5}GS, 7^{0}S

	Starts	1st	2nd	3rd	Win & Pl
Career Total (Turf)	5	0	0	0	290

Going (Turf): Sf: 0-2 GS: 0-1 Gd: 0-0 GF: 0-2 Fm: 0-0
Distance: 5f/6f: 0-3 7f-8f: 0-2 9f-13f: 0-0 14f+: 0-0
Track : LH: 0-4 RH: 0-0 Tight: 0-1 Gall: 0-0
Aids: Bl: 0-0 Vi: 0-0 Tstrap: 0-0
Best Rating: 64 7/01 Bevl 5f gd-fm

Top Nolans (IRE)

92(96) (51)**55**
3-y-o ch g Topanoora-Lauretta Blue (IRE) (Bluebird (USA))
M H Tompkins Flint Fairyhouse Partnership

Placings:0333040-00602 (5292)
2001: 9^{0}GF, 8^{0}G, 7^{6}GF, 5^{0}S, 7^{2}S, 7^{0}SD

	Starts	1st	2nd	3rd	Win & Pl
Career Total (Turf)	12	0	1	3	2312

Going (Turf): Sf: 0-2 GS: 0-1 Gd: 0-4 GF: 0-3 Fm: 0-2
Distance: 5f/6f: 0-7 7f-8f: 0-3 9f-13f: 0-2 14f+: 0-0
Track : LH: 0-4 RH: 0-3 Tight: 0-3 Gall: 0-1
Aids: Bl: 0-0 Vi: 0-1 Tstrap: 0-0
Best Rating: 55 10/01 Leic 7f9y soft

Still a maiden, but looks capable of winning a modest event.

Top Of The Charts

(88) (26)**38**
5-y-o b g Salse (USA)-Celebrity (Troy)
D L Williams Wentworths Racing Group

Placings:000/4044/501040-006 (0161)
2001: 12^{0}SD, 14^{0}SW, 16^{6}SD

	Starts	1st	2nd	3rd	Win & Pl
Career Total (Turf)	12	1	0	0	3302
Career Total (AW)	4	0	0	0	0

37	8/00	Muss	2m	F(0-60)H	GD	£3103

Total win prize-money £3104

Going (Turf): Sf: 0-4 GS: 0-0 **Gd: 1-4** GF: 0-3 Fm: 0-1
Distance: 5f/6f: 0-0 7f-8f: 0-3 9f-13f: 0-4 **14f+: 1-9**
Track : LH: 0-9 **RH: 1-4 Tight: 1-7** Gall: 0-2
Aids: **Bl: 1-5** Vi: 0-2 Tstrap: 0-0
Best Rating: 20 1/01 Ling 1m4f stand

Top Of The Class (IRE)

98(92) (33)**36**
4-y-o b f Rudimentary (USA)-School Mum (Reprimand)
P D Evans P D Evans

Placings:35503543160/00030000-03050100 (4404)
2001: 10^{0}F, 10^{3}GF, 8^{0}GF, 10^{5}GS, 9^{0}GS, 9^{1}SD, 7^{0}G, 12^{0}GS

	Starts	1st	2nd	3rd	Win & Pl
Career Total (Turf)	26	1	0	5	10593
Career Total (AW)	1	1	0	0	1932

33	8/01	Wolv	1m1f79y	G	STD	£1932
67	9/99	Ayr	6f	C(0-95)H	G-S	£7766

Total win prize-money £9698

Going (Turf): Sf: 0-5 **GS: 1-6** Gd: 0-10 GF: 0-3 Fm: 0-2
Distance: 5f/6f: 1-11 7f-8f: 0-8 9f-13f: 1-8 14f+: 0-0
Track : **LH: 1-7** RH: 0-4 **Tight: 1-5** Gall: 0-1
Aids: Bl: 0-1 Vi: 0-1 Tstrap: 0-0
Best Rating: 43 6/01 Ling 1m2f firm

She won an Ayr nursery as a juvenile, but was winning her first race since when landing a seller on the Wolverhampton Fibresand in August.

Top Of The Parkes

(99) (37)**62**
4-y-o b f Mistertopogigo (IRE)-Bella Parkes (Tina's Pet)
N P Littmoden Tim Godkin

Placings:350/302030000-565 (0336)
2001: 7^{5}SD, 6^{6}SD, 7^{5}SD

	Starts	1st	2nd	3rd	Win & Pl
Career Total (Turf)	6	0	1	2	1964
Career Total (AW)	9	0	0	1	426

Going (Turf): Sf: 0-1 GS: 0-0 Gd: 0-1 GF: 0-3 Fm: 0-1
Distance: 5f/6f: 0-13 7f-8f: 0-2 9f-13f: 0-0 14f+: 0-0
Track : LH: 0-10 RH: 0-0 Tight: 0-8 Gall: 0-1
Aids: Bl: 0-1 Vi: 0-0 Tstrap: 0-0
Best Rating: 37 1/01 Wolv 6f stand

Top Quality

100 **47**
3-y-o br f Simply Great (FR)-Qurrat Al Ain (Wolver Hollow)
T D Easterby T H Bennett

Placings:500-54500 **(4469)**
2001: 12^{5}GF, 12^{4}G, 12^{5}F, 16^{0}G, 12^{0}G

	Starts	1st	2nd	3rd	Win & Pl
Career Total (Turf)	8	0	0	0	283

Going (Turf): Sf: 0-2 GS: 0-0 Gd: 0-3 GF: 0-1 Fm: 0-2
Distance: 5f/6f: 0-0 7f-8f: 0-3 9f-13f: 0-4 14f+: 0-1
Track : LH: 0-5 RH: 0-1 Tight: 0-2 Gall: 0-3
Aids: Bl: 0-0 Vi: 0-0 Tstrap: 0-0
Best Rating: 48 6/01 Newc 1m4f93y gd-fm

Top Trees

90(99) (71)**65**
3-y-o b g Charnwood Forest (IRE)-Low Line (High Line)
J A Osborne The Tree Tops

Placings:3P06000 **(4609)**
2001: 9^{3}SD, 11^{P}GF, 11^{0}GF, 8^{6}GS, 9^{0}GF, 10^{0}G, 8^{0}F

	Starts	1st	2nd	3rd	Win & Pl
Career Total (Turf)	6	0	0	0	0
Career Total (AW)	1	0	0	1	421

Going (Turf): Sf: 0-0 GS: 0-1 Gd: 0-1 GF: 0-3 Fm: 0-1
Distance: 5f/6f: 0-0 7f-8f: 0-0 9f-13f: 0-7 14f+: 0-0
Track : LH: 0-3 RH: 0-2 Tight: 0-4 Gall: 0-0
Aids: Bl: 0-0 Vi: 0-0 Tstrap: 0-0
Best Rating: 71 5/01 Wolv 1m1f79y stand

Topaz

89(93) (34)**31**
6-y-o b g Alhijaz-Daisy Topper (Top Ville)
H J Collingridge The Topaz Partnership

Placings:0/6060000/00000/**040026000-600** **(3727)**
2001: 12^{6}SD, 10^{0}GF, 14^{0}GS

	Starts	1st	2nd	3rd	Win & Pl
Career Total (Turf)	17	0	0	0	0
Career Total (AW)	8	0	1	0	517

Going (Turf): Sf: 0-4 GS: 0-4 Gd: 0-3 GF: 0-5 Fm: 0-1
Distance: 5f/6f: 0-0 7f-8f: 0-2 9f-13f: 0-19 14f+: 0-4
Track : LH: 0-17 RH: 0-5 Tight: 0-13 Gall: 0-2
Aids: Bl: 0-0 Vi: 0-0 Tstrap: 0-0
Best Rating: 31 0/01 Yarm 1m6f17y gd-sft

Topless In Tuscany

(95) (38)**39**
4-y-o b f Lugana Beach-Little Scarlett (Mazilier (USA))
P W Hiatt Jeremy Arnold

Placings:03600400**00-40020004006** **(0421)**
2001: 6^{4}SD, 6^{0}SD, 6^{0}SW, 7^{2}SW, 6^{0}SD, 7^{0}SD, 7^{0}SW, 6^{4}SD, 6^{0}SD, 7^{0}SW, 6^{6}SD

	Starts	1st	2nd	3rd	Win & Pl
Career Total (Turf)	7	0	0	1	845
Career Total (AW)	14	0	1	0	638

Going (Turf): Sf: 0-0 GS: 0-0 Gd: 0-3 GF: 0-3 Fm: 0-1
Distance: 5f/6f: 0-12 7f-8f: 0-8 9f-13f: 0-1 14f+: 0-0
Track : LH: 0-17 RH: 0-0 Tight: 0-9 Gall: 0-0
Aids: Bl: 0-0 Vi: 0-0 Tstrap: 0-0
Best Rating: 46 1/01 Sthl 7f slow

Topman

74(43)
4-y-o ch g Komaite (USA)-Top Yard (Teekay)
A P Jones George W Smith

Placings:0/0500-000 **(1187)**
2001: 12^{0}SD, 15^{0}HY, 11^{0}GF

	Starts	1st	2nd	3rd	Win & Pl
Career Total (Turf)	6	0	0	0	0
Career Total (AW)	2	0	0	0	

Going (Turf): Sf: 0-1 GS: 0-1 Gd: 0-1 GF: 0-3 Fm: 0-0
Distance: 5f/6f: 0-1 7f-8f: 0-0 9f-13f: 0-5 14f+: 0-2
Track : LH: 0-6 RH: 0-1 Tight: 0-5 Gall: 0-0
Aids: Bl: 0-0 Vi: 0-0 Tstrap: 0-2

Topo's Guest

91(77) (17)**42**
3-y-o b f Mistertopogigo (IRE)-Arctic Guest (IRE) (Arctic Tern (USA))
J G Given John Starbuck And Swallow Homes

Placings:540-000650 **(5534)**
2001: 8^{0}GF, 11^{0}SD, 16^{0}G, 10^{6}GF, 13^{5}GF, 11^{0}S

	Starts	1st	2nd	3rd	Win & Pl
Career Total (Turf)	8	0	0	0	403
Career Total (AW)	1	0	0	0	

Going (Turf): Sf: 0-1 GS: 0-0 Gd: 0-3 GF: 0-4 Fm: 0-0
Distance: 5f/6f: 0-3 7f-8f: 0-0 9f-13f: 0-4 14f+: 0-2
Track : LH: 0-4 RH: 0-2 Tight: 0-3 Gall: 0-0
Aids: Bl: 0-2 Vi: 0-2 Tstrap: 0-0
Best Rating: 42 9/01 Ripn 1m2f gd-fm

Toppling

104 **89**
3-y-o b c Cadeaux Genereux-Topicality (USA) (Topsider (USA))
Mrs A J Perrett K Abdulla

Placings:4100 **(5344)**
2001: 7^{4}GF, 8^{1}GF, 7^{0}GS, 8^{0}GS

	Starts	1st	2nd	3rd	Win & Pl
Career Total (Turf)	4	1	0	0	4653
89 6/01 Wind 1m67y D				G-F	£4303

Total win prize-money £4303

Going (Turf): Sf: 0-0 GS: 0-2 Gd: 0-0 **GF: 1-2** Fm: 0-0
Distance: 5f/6f: 0-0 7f-8f: 0-3 **9f-13f: 1-1** 14f+: 0-0
Track : LH: 0-1 **RH: 1-1 Tight: 1-1** Gall: 0-0
Aids: Bl: 0-0 Vi: 0-0 Tstrap: 0-0
Best Rating: 89 6/01 Wind 1m67y gd-fm

Got off the mark a the second time of asking in a Windsor maiden on good to firm over a mile, although was disappointing after that.

Topton (IRE)

106(106) (94d)**78**
7-y-o b g Royal Academy (USA)-Circo (High Top)
P Howling Liam Sheridan

Placings:43424221/002615630000000**21314442/01326 0600031034141030000232/4261300**200500235106004 02**034-4434**000210000020500 **(5344)**
2001: 8^{4}SW, 8^{4}FT, 7^{3}FT, 6^{4}FT, 6^{0}G, 7^{0}G, 8^{0}GS, 7^{2}GF, 7^{1}F, 7^{0}GF, 8^{0}GF, 8^{0}GF, 8^{0}GS, 7^{0}GF, 8^{2}GS, 7^{0}GS, 7^{5}G, 7^{0}G, 7^{0}G, 8^{0}GS

	Starts	1st	2nd	3rd	Win & Pl
Career Total (Turf)	74	7	10	6	55216
Career Total (AW)	31	4	5	6	33925

80	6/01	Donc	7f	D(0-80)H	FRM	£8255
74	7/00	Yarm	7f3y	E(0-75)H	G-F	£2782
94	2/00	Ling	1m	D(0-85)H	STD	£3838
78	8/99	Yarm	7f3y	D(0-80)H	FRM	£3913
70	7/99	Donc	7f	E(0-75)H	G-F	£4455
67	6/99	Donc	7f	D(0-80)H	GD	£4455
83	1/99	Ling	7f	D(0-80)H	STD	£3613
73	11/98	Ling	7f	E(0-70)H	STD	£2515
69	11/98	Sthl	7f	F(0-65)H	STD	£1987
74	6/98	Donc	7f	D(0-75)H	GD	£4402
74	10/97	Folk	6f	E(0-70)	G-S	£3226

Total win prize-money £43443

Going (Turf): Sf: 0-8 GS: 1-13 **Gd: 2-21 GF: 2-28 Fm: 2-4**
Distance: 5f/6f: 1-6 **7f-8f: 10-90** 9f-13f: 0-9 14f+: 0-0
Track : **LH: 4-37** RH: 0-5 **Tight: 3-27** Gall: 0-3
Aids: **Bl: 10-94** Vi: 1-5 Tstrap: 0-0
Best Rating: 84 2/01 Ling 1m slow

He has been kept incredibly busy in the last couple of seasons, but keeps his form remarkably well, winning regularly on turf and sand. He has won over a mile, but is really a true seven-furlong specialist who is suited by coming late off a strong pace.

Torcello (IRE)

109 **106**
3-y-o b c Royal Academy (USA)-Vanya (Busted)
G Wragg Mollers Racing

Placings:53414055 **(5597)**
2001: 10^{5}GS, 10^{3}GF, 10^{4}S, 10^{1}S, 11^{4}S, 12^{0}GF, 10^{5}GS, 10^{5}GS

	Starts	1st	2nd	3rd	Win & Pl
Career Total (Turf)	8	1	0	1	12227
81 6/01 Sand 1m2f7y D				SFT	£4602

Total win prize-money £4602

Going (Turf): Sf: 1-3 GS: 0-3 Gd: 0-0 GF: 0-2 Fm: 0-0
Distance: 5f/6f: 0-0 7f-8f: 0-0 **9f-13f: 1-8** 14f+: 0-0
Track : LH: 0-4 **RH: 1-2** Tight: 0-2 Gall: 0-2
Aids: Bl: 0-0 Vi: 0-0 Tstrap: 0-0
Best Rating: 106 9/01 Donc 1m2f60y gd-sft

Unraced at two, he ran well in the Dee Stakes before getting off the mark at Sandown over ten furlongs on soft ground. Disappointed on his first attempt at twelve furlongs on good to firm, but the trip may not have been the reason.

Toreador (IRE)

101 **98**
2-y-o b c Danehill (USA)-Purchasepaperchase (Young Generation)
A P O'Brien Michael Tabor

Placings:22301 **(5058a)**
2001: 7^{2}G, 6^{2}F, 6^{3}G, 5^{0}G, 6^{1}GF

	Starts	1st	2nd	3rd	Win & Pl
Career Total (Turf)	5	1	2	1	18977
88 9/01 List 6f				G-F	£9750

Total win prize-money £9750

Going (Turf): Sf: 0-0 GS: 0-0 Gd: 0-3 **GF: 1-1** Fm: 0-1
Distance: **5f/6f: 1-3** 7f-8f: 0-2 9f-13f: 0-0 14f+: 0-0
Track : LH: 0-1 RH: 0-0 Tight: 0-0 Gall: 0-1
Aids: Bl: 0-0 Vi: 0-0 Tstrap: 0-0
Best Rating: 98 8/01 York 6f214y good

He finished second on his first two starts at Leopardstown and Cork and did not run badly when third in the Acomb. Disappointed when dropped back to the minimum trip in the Flying Childers, but finally broke his duck when stepped back up to six at Listowel.

Torigo (USA)

99(95) (74)**74**
2-y-o b c Distant View (USA)-Our Way (USA) (His Majesty (USA))
P Mitchell The Torigo Partners

Placings:554552 **(5253)**
2001: 6^{5}GS, 5^{5}GF, 7^{4}GF, 6^{5}G, 6^{5}GF, 6^{2}S, 7^{3}SD

	Starts	1st	2nd	3rd	Win & Pl
Career Total (Turf)	6	0	1	0	2534

Going (Turf): Sf: 0-1 GS: 0-1 Gd: 0-1 GF: 0-3 Fm: 0-0
Distance: 5f/6f: 0-5 7f-8f: 0-1 9f-13f: 0-0 14f+: 0-0
Track : LH: 0-1 RH: 0-1 Tight: 0-1 Gall: 0-1
Aids: Bl: 0-0 Vi: 0-0 Tstrap: 0-0
Best Rating: 74 10/01 York 6f soft

Still a maiden but has run with credit on all starts to date, and it should not be long before he gets off the mark. Acts well over six furlongs.

Tormentoso

70(89) (35)**31**

4-y-o b g Catrail (USA)-Chita Rivera (Chief Singer)
D N Carey (A J Chamberlain 12/9) D N Carey

Placings:050/4605050-000000 **(3740)**
2001: 8^{0}SD, 12^{0}SW, 10^{0}SD, 8^{0}SD, 10^{0}SD, 8^{0}S

	Starts	1st	2nd	3rd	Win & Pl
Career Total (Turf)	9	0	0	0	260
Career Total (AW)	7	0	0	0	215

Going (Turf): Sf: 0-2 GS: 0-1 Gd: 0-4 GF: 0-2 Fm: 0-0
Distance: 5f/6f: 0-0 7f-8f: 0-4 9f-13f: 0-10 14f+: 0-2
Track : LH: 0-10 RH: 0-1 Tight: 0-11 Gall: 0-0
Aids: Bl: 0-0 Vi: 0-1 Tstrap: 0-0
Best Rating: 35 4/01 Ling 1m stand

Tornado Prince (IRE)

104 (48)**56**
6-y-o ch g Caerleon (USA)-Welsh Flame (Welsh Pageant)
K A Ryan (Mrs J R Ramsden 30/9) Wooster Partnership

Placings:500/00136/0600403642010005011000/01442 0100-005002000000P **(5681)**
2001: 7^{0}S, 8^{0}G, 7^{5}GF, 7^{0}F, 8^{0}GF, 6^{2}G, 7^{0}GF, 10^{0}G, 8^{0}GS, 8^{0}GF, 8^{0}S, 7^{0}G, 8^{P}S

	Starts	1st	2nd	3rd	Win & Pl
Career Total (Turf)	49	6	3	2	53935
Career Total (AW)	3	0	0	0	0

91	9/00	Asct	1m	B H	SFT	£29000
67	6/00	Thsk	7f	E(0-70)H	FRM	£3646
63	9/99	Pont	1m4y	F(0-60)H	G-F	£3015
56	9/99	Thsk	1m	F	FRM	£3125
56	7/99	Ripn	1m	E	G-F	£2495
69	7/98	Folk	1m1f149y	D(0-80)H	G-F	£3492

Total win prize-money £44775

Going (Turf): Sf: 1-7 GS: 0-5 Gd: 0-14 **GF: 3-17** Fm: 2-6
Distance: 5f/6f: 0-3 **7f-8f: 4-36** 9f-13f: 2-13 14f+: 0-0
Track : **LH: 3-23** RH: 2-9 **Tight: 4-18** Gall: 0-3
Aids: Bl: 0-0 Vi: 0-0 Tstrap: 0-0
Best Rating: 75 7/01 York 6f214y good

Enjoyed a fine season in 2000, including a facile win in the Mail On Sunday Series Final at Ascot. He was hammered by the Handicapper for that and struggled as a result, but has been steadily falling again and ran his best race of this season when just beaten in a big field at York in July. Goes on any ground and is suited by coming off a strong pace.

Toroca (USA)

113 **110**
3-y-o ch f Nureyev (USA)-Grand Falls (USA) (Ogygian (USA))
A P O'Brien Mrs E M Stockwell

Placings:362-1336532225261 **(5479a)**
2001: 6^{1}S, 8^{3}G, 8^{3}G, 8^{6}GF, 10^{5}Y, 8^{3}G, 6^{2}G, 8^{2}GY, 6^{2}G, 6^{5}S, 7^{2}S, 6^{6}S, 8^{1}HY

	Starts	1st	2nd	3rd	Win & Pl
Career Total (Turf)	16	2	5	4	179953

104	10/01	Siro	1m		HVY	£35288
100	4/01	Curr	6f		SFT	£8625

Total win prize-money £43913

Going (Turf): Sf: 2-6 GS: 0-1 Gd: 0-5 GF: 0-1 Fm: 0-0
Distance: 5f/6f: 1-6 7f-8f: 1-9 9f-13f: 0-1 14f+: 0-0
Track : LH: 0-2 **RH: 1-3** Tight: 0-0 Gall: 0-2
Aids: Bl: 0-0 Vi: 0-0 Tstrap: 0-0
Best Rating: 115 5/01 NmkR 1m good

Runner-up in the Cheveley Park in 2000, she was third in both the English and Irish 1000 Guineas in 2001. However, it was not until scoring in a San Siro Group Three in October that she added to her maiden win. Stays a mile, appreciates soft ground..

Torosay Spring

111 **92+**
3-y-o ch f First Trump-Spring Sixpence (Dowsing (USA))
J R Fanshawe C I T Racing Ltd

Placings:13112 **(4986)**
2001: 5^{1}GF, 5^{3}GF, 6^{1}GF, 6^{1}G, 6^{2}G

	Starts	1st	2nd	3rd	Win & Pl
Career Total (Turf)	5	3	1	1	33652

90	9/01	Kemp	6f	C(0-95)H	GD	£15795
86	8/01	Ling	6f	D(0-80)H	G-F	£7150
63	5/01	Donc	5f	E	G-F	£3549

Total win prize-money £26494

Going (Turf): Sf: 0-0 GS: 0-0 Gd: 1-2 GF: 2-3 Fm: 0-0
Distance: **5f/6f: 3-5** 7f-8f: 0-0 9f-13f: 0-0 14f+: 0-0
Track : LH: 0-0 RH: 0-1 Tight: 0-0 Gall: 0-1
Aids: Bl: 0-0 Vi: 0-0 Tstrap: 0-0
Best Rating: 92 9/01 Asct 6f good

She did not race at two, but won three of her first four starts this term, a Doncaster maiden and decent handicaps at Lingfield, and a Kempton handicap. Suited by fast ground and good, and probably still has improvement in her.

Torrealta

106 **97**
5-y-o b m In The Wings-Sea Ring (FR) (Bering)
J Lesbordes J Fairley

Placings:503423/2100006020-023360002 **(5676a)**
2001: 12^{0}, 12^{2}HY, 12^{3}HY, 15^{3}HY, 15^{6}HO, 10^{0}GS, 14^{0}GF, 12^{0}HO, 15^{2}HO, 12^{0}HY

	Starts	1st	2nd	3rd	Win & Pl
Career Total (Turf)	25	1	5	4	49406

	4/00	StCl	1m4f	H	HLD	£13449

Total win prize-money £13449

Going (Turf): Sf: 0-4 GS: 0-1 Gd: 0-1 GF: 0-1 Fm: 0-0
Distance: 5f/6f: 0-0 7f-8f: 0-0 9f-13f: 0-9 14f+: 0-4
Track : LH: 0-1 RH: 0-3 Tight: 0-0 Gall: 0-1
Aids: Bl: 0-0 Vi: 0-0 Tstrap: 0-0
Best Rating: 97 11/01 MsnL 1m7f110y holding

Useful French staying handicapper. Has only scored once over a mile and a half. Races on a soft surface.

Torrecilla

92(84) (57)**73**
2-y-o b f General Monash (USA)-Mystical Heights (IRE) (High Estate)
R M Beckett Zubieta Limited

Placings:326150P **(4730)**
2001: 5^{3}GF, 5^{2}F, 6^{6}GF, 6^{1}GF, 6^{5}SD, 6^{0}GF, 5^{P}F

	Starts	1st	2nd	3rd	Win & Pl
Career Total (Turf)	6	1	1	1	4529
Career Total (AW)	1	0	0	0	0

73	7/01	Ling	6f	E	G-F	£2968

Total win prize-money £2968

Going (Turf): Sf: 0-0 GS: 0-0 Gd: 0-0 **GF: 1-4** Fm: 0-2
Distance: **5f/6f: 1-6** 7f-8f: 0-1 9f-13f: 0-0 14f+: 0-0
Track : LH: 0-3 RH: 0-0 Tight: 0-0 Gall: 0-2
Aids: Bl: 0-0 Vi: 0-0 Tstrap: 0-0
Best Rating: 73 7/01 Ling 6f gd-fm

She is a bit of a madam, but did everything right when winning at Lingfield on her fourth start. Did not appear to take to racing on sand.

Torrent

102(103) (68)**58**
6-y-o ch g Prince Sabo-Maiden Pool (Sharpen Up)
D W Chapman Mrs J Hazell

Placings:6340/16106000/0300004106403202232113/3 65530444463331335103000623- 420052033022040365432052 **(5639)**
2001: 5^{4}SD, 5^{2}SD, 5^{0}SD, 5^{0}SW, 5^{5}SD, 5^{2}S, 5^{0}GS, 5^{3}F, 5^{3}GF, 5^{0}GF, 5^{2}GF, 5^{2}SD, 5^{0}GF, 6^{4}GF, 5^{0}G, 6^{3}G, 5^{6}GF, 6^{5}GF, 5^{4}S, 6^{3}HY, 5^{2}G, 6^{0}HY, 5^{5}S, 5^{2}G

	Starts	1st	2nd	3rd	Win & Pl
Career Total (Turf)	67	5	6	14	35130
Career Total (AW)	19	2	5	4	10398

73	9/00	Pont	5f	E(0-70)H	G-S	£3185
60	8/00	Brig	5f59y	F(0-60)	FRM	£2431
69	12/99	Ling	5f	E(0-70)H	STD	£2640
64	12/99	Ling	6f	F(0-60)H	STD	£1840
68	7/99	Bevl	5f	E(0-70)	G-F	£2726
83	5/98	Thsk	5f	C(0-100)H	G-F	£7564
79	4/98	Catt	5f212y	D	GD	£3548

Total win prize-money £23936

Going (Turf): Sf: 0-16 GS: 1-6 Gd: 1-19 **GF: 2-23** Fm: 1-3
Distance: **5f/6f: 7-81** 7f-8f: 0-5 9f-13f: 0-0 14f+: 0-0
Track : **LH: 5-32** RH: 0-0 **Tight: 3-21** Gall: 0-0
Aids: **Bl: 4-59** Vi: 0-0 Tstrap: 0-1
Best Rating: 68 6/01 Wolv 5f stand

Without a win since September 2000, he has gone close on a few occasions, and is now dropping to a decent mark. A slightly weak finisher, he acts on most ground types.

Torrential Storm (USA)

106 **85**
3-y-o b g Torrential (USA)-Lady Nitro (USA) (Oh Say (USA))
M A Jarvis The C H F Partnership

Placings:14001 **(5225)**
2001: 10^{1}GS, 10^{4}GF, 12^{0}G, 12^{0}GS, 10^{1}S

	Starts	1st	2nd	3rd	Win & Pl
Career Total (Turf)	5	2	0	0	11278

65	10/01	York	1m2f85y	D	SFT	£7049
65	5/01	Pont	1m2f6y	D	G-S	£3688

Total win prize-money £10738

Going (Turf): Sf: 1-1 GS: 1-2 Gd: 0-1 GF: 0-1 Fm: 0-0
Distance: 5f/6f: 0-0 7f-8f: 0-0 **9f-13f: 2-5** 14f+: 0-0
Track : **LH: 2-3** RH: 0-2 Tight: 0-1 **Gall: 1-2**
Aids: Bl: 0-0 Vi: 0-0 Tstrap: 0-0
Best Rating: 85 7/01 Epsm 1m2f18y gd-fm

Came from off the pace to score quite nicely on this debut at Pontefract over ten furlongs, but has since been well beaten. Suited by ten to 12 furlongs. Acts on good to soft.

Torrid Kentavr (USA)

108(102) (88)**87**
4-y-o b g Trempolino (USA)-Torrid Tango (USA) (Green Dancer (USA))
B Ellison (T G Mills 8/7) Henry Rix

Placings:4/33100512650-0056114650 **(4863)**
2001: 10^{0}S, 10^{0}S, 10^{5}GF, 12^{6}GF, 12^{1}GF, 11^{1}G, 9^{4}GF, 11^{6}GF, 12^{5}GF, 10^{0}GF

	Starts	1st	2nd	3rd	Win & Pl
Career Total (Turf)	17	3	0	2	18231
Career Total (AW)	5	1	1	0	5265

84	7/01	Sand	1m3f91y	D(0-80)H	GD	£4998
79	6/01	Kemp	1m4f	D(0-85)H	G-F	£4309
88	9/00	Wolv	1m4f	D(0-85)H	STD	£4140
73	7/00	Bath	1m3f144y	D	FRM	£3770

Total win prize-money £17220

Going (Turf): Sf: 0-2 GS: 0-0 **Gd: 1-2 GF: 1-11 Fm: 1-1**
Distance: 5f/6f: 0-0 7f-8f: 0-0 **9f-13f: 4-22** 14f+: 0-0
Track : LH: 2-13 RH: 2-8 **Tight: 2-11** Gall: 0-5
Aids: Bl: 0-2 Vi: 0-0 Tstrap: 0-0
Best Rating: 87 7/01 Gdwd 1m1f192y gd-fm

Effective on turf and sand, he scored twice in the space of 12 days at Kempton and Sandown during the summer, but has since appeared high enough in the handicap. Suited by fast ground on turf, he likes to come from behind off a strong pace. Needs 11 furlongs plus to be seen at his best.

Tory Boy

99(97) (48)**48**

6-y-o b g Deploy-Mukhayyalah (Dancing Brave (USA))

Ian Williams Mary Ann Properties Ltd

Placings:01504/20326**04**3/4-06 **(2524)**

2001: 16^{0}GF, 16^{6}GF

	Starts	1st	2nd	3rd	Win & Pl
Career Total (Turf)	11	1	1	0	4369
Career Total (AW)	5	0	1	2	1450

76 6/98 Wwck 1m2f169yE SFT £3235

Total win prize-money £3236

Going (Turf): Sf: 1-3 GS: 0-0 Gd: 0-3 GF: 0-5 Fm: 0-0
Distance: 5f/6f: 0-0 7f-8f: 0-0 **9f-13f: 1-3** 14f+: 0-13
Track : **LH: 1-13** RH: 0-2 Tight: 0-4 Gall: 0-1
Aids: Bl: 0-4 Vi: 0-0 Tstrap: 0-0
Best Rating: 45 6/01 Wwck 2m39y gd-fm

Toshiba Times

83(90) (7)**7**

5-y-o b g Persian Bold-Kirkby Belle (Bay Express)

B Ellison B Batey

Placings:0/00000/000-60 **(2379)**

2001: 7^{6}SD, 8^{0}GF

	Starts	1st	2nd	3rd	Win & Pl
Career Total (Turf)	10	0	0	0	
Career Total (AW)	1	0	0	0	0

Going (Turf): Sf: 0-1 GS: 0-3 Gd: 0-3 GF: 0-2 Fm: 0-1
Distance: 5f/6f: 0-1 7f-8f: 0-7 9f-13f: 0-3 14f+: 0-0
Track : LH: 0-3 RH: 0-4 Tight: 0-4 Gall: 0-0
Aids: Bl: 0-0 Vi: 0-1 Tstrap: 0-0
Best Rating: 35 3/01 Sthl 7f stand

Toskano

9-y-o b g Salse (USA)-Kukri (Kris)

D L Williams Berkshire Commercial Components Ltd

Placings:00/5430/0/0 **(0321)**

2001: 16^{0}SD

	Starts	1st	2nd	3rd	Win & Pl
Career Total (Turf)	6	0	0	1	592
Career Total (AW)	2	0	0	0	

Going (Turf): Sf: 0-1 GS: 0-1 Gd: 0-2 GF: 0-2 Fm: 0-0
Distance: 5f/6f: 0-0 7f-8f: 0-1 9f-13f: 0-6 14f+: 0-1
Track : LH: 0-6 RH: 0-1 Tight: 0-4 Gall: 0-1
Aids: Bl: 0-0 Vi: 0-0 Tstrap: 0-0

Total Care

103(104) (62)**76d**

4-y-o br c Caerleon (USA)-Totality (Dancing Brave (USA))

S C Williams Alex Gorrie Combi (uk)

Placings:2221**000-0040660** **(4860)**

2001: 11^{0}SD, 12^{0}SD, 9^{4}SW, 10^{0}S, 10^{6}GF, 12^{6}G, 13^{0}GF

	Starts	1st	2nd	3rd	Win & Pl
Career Total (Turf)	9	1	3	0	8411
Career Total (AW)	5	0	0	0	0

83 6/00 Kemp 1m4f D G-F £4192

Total win prize-money £4193

Going (Turf): Sf: 0-2 GS: 0-0 Gd: 0-3 **GF: 1-4** Fm: 0-0
Distance: 5f/6f: 0-0 7f-8f: 0-0 **9f-13f: 1-13** 14f+: 0-1
Track : LH: 0-10 **RH: 1-3** Tight: 0-6 Gall: 0-3
Aids: Bl: 0-0 Vi: 0-0 Tstrap: 0-7
Best Rating: 68 0/01 Ling 1m2f gd-fm

Has only won once from 14 starts, that was over one mile four furlongs on good to firm, but has since struggled at a number of different trips.

Total Delight

106(101) (75)

5-y-o b g Mtoto-Shesadelight (Shirley Heights)

P R Webber D Heath

Placings:5/320/1004**1200040-30P** **(3478)**

2001: 11^{3}G, 15^{0}GF, 14^{P}GF

	Starts	1st	2nd	3rd	Win & Pl
Career Total (Turf)	17	2	2	2	13142
Career Total (AW)	1	0	0	0	292

81 6/00 Sand 1m6f D(0-80)H G-F £4231
79 3/00 Leic 1m1f218yD(0-80)H GD £4043

Total win prize-money £8275

Going (Turf): Sf: 0-1 GS: 0-3 **Gd: 1-5 GF: 1-7** Fm: 0-1
Distance: 5f/6f: 0-0 7f-8f: 0-1 9f-13f: 1-11 14f+: 1-6
Track : LH: 0-5 **RH: 2-12** Tight: 0-8 Gall: 0-3
Aids: Bl: 0-0 Vi: 0-2 **Tstrap: 2-8**
Best Rating: 72 7/01 Sand 1m3f91y good

Useful staying handicapper. Needs to dominate to be seen to best effect. Has worn a tongue-strap and a visor on occasions. Has won over a mile and six furlongs.

Total Love

105 **78**

4-y-o ch f Cadeaux Genereux-Favorable Exchange (USA) (Exceller (USA))

G A Butler John Brown & Megan Dennis

Placings:210360233/0253400-03600006 **(5686)**

2001: 6^{0}GS, 5^{3}GS, 5^{6}GF, 6^{0}GF, 6^{0}G, 5^{0}G, 6^{0}S, 10^{6}S

	Starts	1st	2nd	3rd	Win & Pl
Career Total (Turf)	24	1	3	5	34464

80 5/99 Leic 5f218y D GD £3457

Total win prize-money £3457

Going (Turf): Sf: 0-4 GS: 0-7 **Gd: 1-5** GF: 0-7 Fm: 0-1
Distance: **5f/6f: 1-12** 7f-8f: 0-9 9f-13f: 0-3 14f+: 0-0
Track : LH: 0-5 RH: 0-3 Tight: 0-1 Gall: 0-7
Aids: Bl: 0-0 Vi: 0-0 Tstrap: 0-1
Best Rating: 97 5/01 Bath 5f11y gd-sft

A useful performer, she was beaten ten lengths when fifth to Crimplene in last year's Coronation Stakes at Royal Ascot. Now running in sprints, she was third to Red Millennium in a five-furlong Listed event at Bath in May, but has disappointed since.

Total Magic

94(82) (47)**47**

3-y-o ch c Pivotal-Inherent Magic (IRE) (Magical Wonder (USA))

I A Balding N H Harris / D F Allport / A Tuckerman

Placings:0-460360 **(4734)**

2001: 6^{4}SD, 7^{6}G, 6^{0}F, 6^{3}GF, 7^{6}G, 8^{0}F

	Starts	1st	2nd	3rd	Win & Pl
Career Total (Turf)	6	0	0	1	0
Career Total (AW)	1	0	0	0	0

Going (Turf): Sf: 0-0 GS: 0-1 Gd: 0-2 GF: 0-1 Fm: 0-2
Distance: 5f/6f: 0-4 7f-8f: 0-2 9f-13f: 0-1 14f+: 0-0
Track : LH: 0-2 RH: 0-0 Tight: 0-1 Gall: 0-1
Aids: Bl: 0-0 Vi: 0-0 Tstrap: 0-0
Best Rating: 47 8/01 Folk 6f gd-fm

Total Turtle (IRE)

88(90) (70)**78**

2-y-o b c Turtle Island (IRE)-Chagrin D'Amour (IRE) (Last Tycoon)

P F I Cole W J Smith And M D Dudley

Placings:43100 **(5229)**

2001: 5^{4}G, 6^{3}SD, 6^{1}SD, 7^{0}G, 7^{0}S

	Starts	1st	2nd	3rd	Win & Pl
Career Total (Turf)	3	0	0	0	295
Career Total (AW)	2	1	0	1	2809

70 7/01 Sthl 6f F STD £2394

Total win prize-money £2394

Going (Turf): Sf: 0-1 GS: 0-0 Gd: 0-2 GF: 0-0 Fm: 0-0
Distance: **5f/6f: 1-3** 7f-8f: 0-2 9f-13f: 0-0 14f+: 0-0
Track : **LH: 1-4** RH: 0-0 Tight: 0-1 Gall: 0-2
Aids: Bl: 0-0 Vi: 0-0 Tstrap: 0-0
Best Rating: 78 9/01 Donc 7f good

He was helped to victory in an auction maiden by the long straight at Southwell in July 2001, but this six-furlong trip still looked on the short side for him. His breeding suggests he will stay further as a three-year-old.

Totally Scottish

92 **38**

5-y-o b g Mtoto-Glenfinlass (Lomond (USA))

Mrs M Reveley The Phoenix Racing C O

Placings:004/056500-00 **(3280)**

2001: 11^{0}GF, 9^{0}F

	Starts	1st	2nd	3rd	Win & Pl
Career Total (Turf)	11	0	0	0	197

Going (Turf): Sf: 0-2 GS: 0-1 Gd: 0-4 GF: 0-2 Fm: 0-2
Distance: 5f/6f: 0-0 7f-8f: 0-0 9f-13f: 0-6 14f+: 0-5
Track : LH: 0-7 RH: 0-4 Tight: 0-5 Gall: 0-1
Aids: Bl: 0-1 Vi: 0-0 Tstrap: 0-1
Best Rating: 21 7/01 Rdcr 1m1f firm

Staying maiden who has shown his best form over hurdles.

Totem Dancer

107(88) (34)**49**

8-y-o b m Mtoto-Ballad Opera (Sadler's Wells (USA))

J L Eyre Graham Lloyd & Dean Kiely

Placings:334224221/060**51**0/43542312246/**0**50004320 0/**000**010242063003-0053361222064000 **(5383)**

2001: 14^{0}HY, 13^{0}GF, 14^{5}GF, 14^{3}GF, 14^{3}GF, 13^{6}S, 15^{1}GS, 16^{2}GF, 17^{2}GF, 16^{2}G, 15^{0}G, 16^{6}G, 16^{4}GF, 14^{0}HY, 17^{0}GS, 13^{0}S

	Starts	1st	2nd	3rd	Win & Pl
Career Total (Turf)	62	5	13	9	47646
Career Total (AW)	5	0	0	0	0

48 7/01 Ayr 1m7f F(0-65)H G-S £3272
54 5/00 Nott 1m0f15y F(0-60)H G-S £2530
79 8/98 Ches 1m4f66y E(0-80)H GD £3062
76 9/97 Haml 1m4f17y D(0-85)H GD £4838
76 10/96 Nott 1m6f15y D GD £4175

Total win prize-money £17881

Going (Turf): Sf: 0-17 GS: 2-8 **Gd: 3-15** GF: 0-18 Fm: 0-4
Distance: 5f/6f: 0-0 7f-8f: 0-0 9f-13f: 2-22 **14f+: 3-45**
Track : **LH: 4-48** RH: 1-19 **Tight: 2-26** Gall: 0-19
Aids: Bl: 0-0 Vi: 0-4 **Tstrap: 1-10**
Best Rating: 51 8/01 Thsk 2m good

She does not win that often and was ending another long losing run when winning at Ayr in July. Suited by a test of stamina and soft ground.

Totem Pole

86 **69**

2-y-o ch c Pivotal-Taza (Persian Bold)

B W Hills Guy Reed

Placings:00 **(5343)**

2001: 6^{0}GF, 6^{0}GS

	Starts	1st	2nd	3rd	Win & Pl
Career Total (Turf)	2	0	0	0	

Going (Turf): Sf: 0-0 GS: 0-1 Gd: 0-0 GF: 0-1 Fm: 0-0
Distance: 5f/6f: 0-1 7f-8f: 0-1 9f-13f: 0-0 14f+: 0-0
Track : LH: 0-0 RH: 0-0 Tight: 0-0 Gall: 0-0
Aids: Bl: 0-0 Vi: 0-0 Tstrap: 0-0
Best Rating: 69 10/01 NmkR 6f gd-sft

Touch Of Ebony (IRE)

82 **41**

2-y-o b c Darshaan-Cormorant Wood (Home Guard (USA))
B W Hills Maktoum Al Maktoum

Placings:60 **(4633)**
2001: 7^{6}GF, 7^{0}GF

	Starts	1st	2nd	3rd	Win & Pl
Career Total (Turf)	2	0	0	0	0

Going (Turf): Sf: 0-0 GS: 0-0 Gd: 0-0 GF: 0-2 Fm: 0-0
Distance: 5f/6f: 0-0 7f-8f: 0-2 9f-13f: 0-0 14f+: 0-0
Track : LH: 0-0 RH: 0-0 Tight: 0-0 Gall: 0-0
Aids: Bl: 0-0 Vi: 0-0 Tstrap: 0-0
Best Rating: 41 7/01 NmkJ 7f gd-fm

Touch Of Fairy (IRE)

94 **72**

5-y-o b h Fairy King (USA)-Decadence (Vaigly Great)
J M Bradley Marinos Ioannou

Placings:2/0400-000 **(5685)**
2001: 6^{0}GS, 6^{0}G, 5^{0}S

	Starts	1st	2nd	3rd	Win & Pl
Career Total (Turf)	8	0	1	0	1138

Going (Turf): Sf: 0-3 GS: 0-1 Gd: 0-4 GF: 0-0 Fm: 0-0
Distance: 5f/6f: 0-7 7f-8f: 0-1 9f-13f: 0-0 14f+: 0-0
Track : LH: 0-0 RH: 0-2 Tight: 0-0 Gall: 0-2
Aids: Bl: 0-0 Vi: 0-0 Tstrap: 0-1
Best Rating: 66 10/01 Sals 6f gd-sft

Unraced at two, he showed ability on his only start at three, but has not produced a great deal in an abbreviated career since and has obviously had his problems.

Touch Of Spirit

74(81) (47)**37**

2-y-o b f Dancing Spree (USA)-Soft Touch (GER) (Horst-Herbert)
J G Given Kingsland Bloodstock

Placings:500 **(3432)**
2001: 6^{5}SD, 6^{0}GF, 7^{0}SD

	Starts	1st	2nd	3rd	Win & Pl
Career Total (Turf)	1	0	0	0	
Career Total (AW)	2	0	0	0	0

Going (Turf): Sf: 0-0 GS: 0-0 Gd: 0-0 GF: 0-1 Fm: 0-0
Distance: 5f/6f: 0-2 7f-8f: 0-1 9f-13f: 0-0 14f+: 0-0
Track : LH: 0-3 RH: 0-0 Tight: 0-0 Gall: 0-0
Aids: Bl: 0-0 Vi: 0-0 Tstrap: 0-0
Best Rating: 47 5/01 Sthl 6f stand

Touch'N'Go

77 **19**

7-y-o b g Rainbow Quest (USA)-Mary Martin (Be My Guest (USA))
A B Mulholland Andrew Lloyd

Placings:60/411203/03/5/0000 **(1315)**
2001: 14^{0}HY, 10^{0}HY, 12^{0}S, 14^{0}SD

	Starts	1st	2nd	3rd	Win & Pl
Career Total (Turf)	6	0	0	1	368
Career Total (AW)	9	2	1	1	6444

70 3/97 Ling 1m2f E(0-70)H STD £2752
55 2/97 Sthl 1m F(0-60)H STD £2294
Total win prize-money £5046

Going (Turf): Sf: 0-3 GS: 0-1 Gd: 0-1 GF: 0-0 Fm: 0-1
Distance: 5f/6f: 0-0 7f-8f: 1-1 9f-13f: 1-10 14f+: 0-4
Track : **LH: 2-13** RH: 0-2 **Tight: 1-8** Gall: 0-0
Aids: Bl: 0-0 Vi: 0-0 Tstrap: 0-2
Best Rating: 19 4/01 Ripn 1m4f60y soft

Touchy Feelings (IRE)

96 **63**

3-y-o b f Ashkalani (IRE)-Adjalisa (IRE) (Darshaan)
R Hannon Teviot Stud

Placings:30-3 **(3853)**
2001: 7^{3}G

	Starts	1st	2nd	3rd	Win & Pl
Career Total (Turf)	3	0	0	2	1487

Going (Turf): Sf: 0-0 GS: 0-0 Gd: 0-1 GF: 0-2 Fm: 0-0
Distance: 5f/6f: 0-0 7f-8f: 0-3 9f-13f: 0-0 14f+: 0-0
Track : LH: 0-0 RH: 0-1 Tight: 0-0 Gall: 0-1
Aids: Bl: 0-0 Vi: 0-0 Tstrap: 0-0
Best Rating: 60 8/01 Asct 7f good

Tough Leader

103 **70**

7-y-o b g Lead On Time (USA)-Al Guswa (Shernazar)
D J S Cosgrove G G Grayson

Placings:24413/50/**0141**3134162340/0310425/201-0060000 **(5692)**
2001: 12^{0}F, 11^{0}G, 11^{6}G, 10^{0}G, 12^{0}G, 16^{0}GF, 16^{0}S

	Starts	1st	2nd	3rd	Win & Pl
Career Total (Turf)	34	5	4	5	88131
Career Total (AW)	4	2	0	0	7161

9/00 Belm 1m3f SFT £17926
97 6/99 Epsm 1m4f10y B(0-105)H GD £24879
95 7/98 York 1m3f195y B(0-100)H G-F £9420
82 5/98 Sand 1m2f7y D(0-80)H GD £3761
80 3/98 Sthl 1m4f D(0-85)H STD £3468
77 2/98 Wolv 1m1f79y D(0-85)H STD £3452
66 6/96 Thsk 7f F FRM £2915
Total win prize-money £65823

Going (Turf): Sf: 1-2 GS: 0-3 **Gd: 2-11** GF: 1-13 Fm: 1-4
Distance: 5f/6f: 0-3 7f-8f: 1-5 **9f-13f: 6-24** 14f+: 0-5
Track : **LH: 5-18** RH: 1-13 **Tight: 3-13** Gall: 1-9
Aids: Bl: 0-1 Vi: 0-0 **Tstrap: 1-8**
Best Rating: 90 6/01 DRoy 1m4f68y firm

A tough and likeable handicapper over a mile and a half, he was sent to America and won for Michael Dickinson over there. He returned from the US to finish seventh in the Ulster Derby in June 2001, ran too freely in blinkers and has since had them removed. He has looked well held since returning from America. Effective on any ground but probably at his best on fast. Stays a mile and a half. Has worn a tongue tie recently.

Tough Love

96 **83d**

2-y-o ch c Pursuit Of Love-Food Of Love (Music Boy)
T D Easterby The Gordon Partnership

Placings:3312000 **(5253)**
2001: 6^{3}G, 6^{3}GS, 6^{1}GF, 6^{2}G, 6^{0}GF, 6^{0}HY, 6^{0}S

	Starts	1st	2nd	3rd	Win & Pl
Career Total (Turf)	7	1	1	2	5870

83 7/01 Newc 6f E G-F £3052
Total win prize-money £3052

Going (Turf): Sf: 0-2 GS: 0-1 Gd: 0-2 **GF: 1-2** Fm: 0-0
Distance: **5f/6f: 1-7** 7f-8f: 0-0 9f-13f: 0-0 14f+: 0-0
Track : LH: 0-0 RH: 0-0 Tight: 0-0 Gall: 0-0
Aids: Bl: 0-0 Vi: 0-0 Tstrap: 0-0
Best Rating: 83 7/01 Newc 6f gd-fm

Showed ability before scoring at Newcastle over six furlongs in July.Acts on fast ground.

Tough Speed (USA)

117 **122+**

4-y-o b h Miswaki (USA)-Nature's Magic (USA) (Nijinsky (CAN))
Sir Michael Stoute Saeed Suhail

Placings:214/5-20110 **(5386)**
2001: 7^{2}GF, 8^{0}GF, 7^{1}G, 8^{1}G, 7^{0}GS

	Starts	1st	2nd	3rd	Win & Pl
Career Total (Turf)	9	3	2	0	78436

122 9/01 Donc 1m A GD £24000
114 8/01 York 7f202y B(0-105)H GD £35003
95 9/99 Donc 7f C G-F £6035
Total win prize-money £65039

Going (Turf): Sf: 0-0 GS: 0-2 **Gd: 2-3** GF: 1-4 Fm: 0-0
Distance: 5f/6f: 0-1 **7f-8f: 3-8** 9f-13f: 0-0 14f+: 0-0
Track : **LH: 2-3** RH: 0-0 Tight: 0-0 **Gall: 2-3**
Aids: Bl: 0-0 Vi: 0-0 Tstrap: 0-0
Best Rating: 122 9/01 Donc 1m good

He ran just once in 2000, and went into many a notebook when second on his return in York, where he would have won granted luck in running. He reappeared to run second behind Soviet Flash at York , where he was unlucky in running, but was disappointing when favouite for the Royal Hunt Cup. A ready winner of a decent York handicap in August under top weight, he had no problem with the step into Group Three company next time at Doncaster. Stays a mile. Has won on good and good to firm ground.

Toujours Riviera

95(97) (60)**51**

11-y-o ch g Rainbow Quest (USA)-Miss Beaulieu (Northfields (USA))
Mrs Lydia Pearce The Fantasy Fellowship

Placings:4234/03104351011O/01046400**3/0**006020460002/30442461315**53/1023**003402400**02**/001512**62**-**0**14000 **(3875)**
2001: **12**^{0}SD, 10^{1}GF, 8^{4}GF, 9^{0}G, 11^{0}GF, 8^{0}GS

	Starts	1st	2nd	3rd	Win & Pl
Career Total (Turf)	67	10	6	6	78076
Career Total (AW)	13	1	3	3	10615

45 6/01 Pont 1m2f6y E G-F £3802
56 9/00 Thsk 1m F GD £2992
37 8/00 NmkJ 1m E GD £3913
77 1/98 Ling 1m4f D(0-80)H STD £5370
81 9/97 Brig 7f214y D(0-75)H FRM £4947
74 8/97 Haml 1m65y D(0-75)H G-F £3436
89 7/95 Yarm 1m3y D(0-85)H G-F £7570
82 10/94 NmkR 1m D(0-85)H G-F £5946
77 10/94 Asct 1m C(0-90)H G-F £13402
70 8/94 Sand 1m14y D(0-80)H GD £4357
61 6/94 Folk 6f189y F(0-70) GD £2735
Total win prize-money £58475

Going (Turf): Sf: 0-6 GS: 0-3 Gd: 4-24 **GF: 5-32** Fm: 1-2
Distance: 5f/6f: 0-0 **7f-8f: 6-40** 9f-13f: 5-40 14f+: 0-0
Track : LH: 4-31 RH: 4-20 **Tight: 4-33** Gall: 1-5
Aids: Bl: 0-0 Vi: 0-0 Tstrap: 0-0
Best Rating: 45 6/01 Pont 1m2f6y gd-fm

Tourvel

67 **26**

2-y-o b c Bahamian Bounty-Cominna (Dominion)
N P Littmoden Joy And Valentine Feerick

Placings:0 **(5526)**
2001: 5^{0}S

	Starts	1st	2nd	3rd	Win & Pl
Career Total (Turf)	1	0	0	0	

Going (Turf): Sf: 0-1 GS: 0-0 Gd: 0-0 GF: 0-0 Fm: 0-0
Distance: 5f/6f: 0-1 7f-8f: 0-0 9f-13f: 0-0 14f+: 0-0
Track : LH: 0-0 RH: 0-0 Tight: 0-0 Gall: 0-0
Aids: Bl: 0-0 Vi: 0-0 Tstrap: 0-0
Best Rating: 26 10/01 Nott 5f13y soft

Tower Of Song (IRE)

(92) (9)**60**

4-y-o ch g Perugino (USA)-New Rochelle (IRE) (Lafontaine (USA))
D W Chapman K Nicholls

Placings:2053501420/54235040000000-00 **(0059)**
2001: 6^{0}SD, 9^{0}SW

	Starts	1st	2nd	3rd	Win & Pl
Career Total (Turf)	8	0	1	1	1034
Career Total (AW)	18	1	2	1	4541

68 11/99 Sthl 1m G STD £2029
Total win prize-money £2029

Going (Turf): Sf: 0-3 GS: 0-0 Gd: 0-3 GF: 0-1 Fm: 0-1
Distance: 5f/6f: 0-1 **7f-8f: 1-14** 9f-13f: 0-11 14f+: 0-0
Track : LH: 1-22 RH: 0-1 Tight: 0-9 Gall: 0-0
Aids: Bl: 0-3 Vi: 0-0 Tstrap: 0-0
Best Rating: 9 1/01 Sthl 6f stand

Town Gossip (IRE)

91(101) (60)52
4-y-o ch f Indian Ridge-Only Gossip (USA) (Trempolino (USA))
J L Eyre Sunpak Potatoes

Placings:0/05003**1**240-0000 (2755)
2001: 14^{0}SD, 11^{0}GF, 12^{0}G, 11^{0}GF

	Starts	1st	2nd	3rd	Win & Pl
Career Total (Turf)	8	0	0	0	0
Career Total (AW)	6	1	1	1	3788

59 10/00 Wolv 1m4f E(0-75)H STD £2723
Total win prize-money £2724

Going (Turf): Sf: 0-0 GS: 0-2 Gd: 0-2 GF: 0-4 Fm: 0-0
Distance: 5f/6f: 0-0 7f-8f: 0-2 **9f-13f: 1-9** 14f+: 0-3
Track : **LH: 1-11** RH: 0-1 **Tight: 1-6** Gall: 0-0
Aids: Bl: 0-0 Vi: 0-0 Tstrap: 0-0
Best Rating: 46 6/01 Bevl 1m3f216y gd-fm

Trace Clip

112 89+
3-y-o b c Zafonic (USA)-Illusory (King's Lake (USA))
B W Hills K Abdulla

Placings:031542233 (5341)
2001: 6^{6}GS, 6^{3}F, 5^{1}F, 6^{5}G, 6^{4}GF, 6^{2}GF, 5^{2}G, 6^{3}G, 5^{3}GS

	Starts	1st	2nd	3rd	Win & Pl
Career Total (Turf)	9	1	2	3	21343

64 6/01 Donc 5f D FRM £4387
Total win prize-money £4388

Going (Turf): Sf: 0-0 GS: 0-2 Gd: 0-3 GF: 0-2 **Fm: 1-2**
Distance: **5f/6f: 1-9** 7f-8f: 0-0 9f-13f: 0-0 14f+: 0-0
Track : LH: 0-1 RH: 0-0 Tight: 0-0 Gall: 0-0
Aids: Bl: 0-0 Vi: 0-0 **Tstrap: 1-9**
Best Rating: 89 9/01 Asct 6f good

He was unraced as a juvenile and got off the mark in a Doncaster maiden in June. Not at all disgraced in decent handicap company since and looks suited by fast ground. Stays six furlongs although possibly slightly better at five, he regularly wears a tongue strap.

Traikey (IRE)

83(94) (32)23
9-y-o b g Scenic-Swordlestown Miss (USA) (Apalachee (USA))
Mrs S Lamyman P Lamyman

Placings:1/3/000000/0005-5000 (1824)
2001: 8^{5}SD, 11^{0}SD, 8^{0}F, 10^{0}GF

	Starts	1st	2nd	3rd	Win & Pl
Career Total (Turf)	12	1	0	1	6762
Career Total (AW)	4	0	0	0	0

91 10/94 Yarm 1m3y D GD £5250
Total win prize-money £5250

Going (Turf): Sf: 0-2 GS: 0-3 **Gd: 1-2** GF: 0-4 Fm: 0-1
Distance: 5f/6f: 0-3 7f-8f: 0-7 **9f-13f: 1-6** 14f+: 0-0
Track : LH: 0-8 RH: 0-4 Tight: 0-1 Gall: 0-3
Aids: Bl: 0-0 Vi: 0-0 Tstrap: 0-0
Best Rating: 32 1/01 Sthl 1m stand

Came back from more than four years off in 1999, but has shown only the odd indication that he retains his ability.

Trained Bythe Best

94 61
3-y-o b f Alderbrook-Princess Moodyshoe (Jalmood (USA))
M C Pipe Mrs Allison C Farrant

Placings:0550 (5085)
2001: 7^{0}GF, 8^{5}GF, 7^{5}GF, 11^{0}S

	Starts	1st	2nd	3rd	Win & Pl
Career Total (Turf)	4	0	0	0	0

Going (Turf): Sf: 0-1 GS: 0-0 Gd: 0-0 GF: 0-3 Fm: 0-0
Distance: 5f/6f: 0-0 7f-8f: 0-3 9f-13f: 0-1 14f+: 0-0
Track : LH: 0-1 RH: 0-0 Tight: 0-0 Gall: 0-0
Aids: Bl: 0-0 Vi: 0-0 Tstrap: 0-0
Best Rating: 61 8/01 Sals 1m gd-fm

Tramline

93 (52)50
8-y-o b g Shirley Heights-Trampship (High Line)
M Blanshard Mrs P Buckley

Placings:0551400/00030/00211261200/0-00 (3219)
2001: 14^{0}GF, 16^{0}GF

	Starts	1st	2nd	3rd	Win & Pl
Career Total (Turf)	25	4	3	1	22832
Career Total (AW)	2	0	0	0	

66 8/99 Sand 2m78y E(0-70)H GD £3615
58 6/99 Donc 1m6f132yD(0-80)H G-F £4201
54 6/99 Sand 1m6f D(0-80)H GD £4299
82 6/97 NmkJ 1m0f175yD G-S £3557
Total win prize-money £15674

Going (Turf): Sf: 0-7 GS: 1-6 **Gd: 2-4** GF: 1-8 Fm: 0-0
Distance: 5f/6f: 0-0 7f-8f: 0-1 9f-13f: 0-6 **14f+: 4-20**
Track : LH: 1-14 **RH: 3-12** Tight: 0-5 **Gall: 2-6**
Aids: Bl: 0-0 Vi: 0-0 Tstrap: 0-0
Best Rating: 50 7/01 Kemp 1m6f92y gd-fm

Tramonto

100 80
2-y-o b f Sri Pekan (USA)-Manhattan Sunset (USA) (El Gran Senor (USA))
M P Tregoning R C C Villers

Placings:0411 (5291)
2001: 6^{0}G, 7^{4}G, 7^{1}GF, 7^{1}S

	Starts	1st	2nd	3rd	Win & Pl
Career Total (Turf)	4	2	0	0	9180

80 10/01 Leic 7f9y C SFT £5800
80 8/01 Ling 7f140y F G-F £2558
Total win prize-money £8359

Going (Turf): **Sf: 1-1** GS: 0-0 Gd: 0-2 **GF: 1-1** Fm: 0-0
Distance: 5f/6f: 0-1 **7f-8f: 2-3** 9f-13f: 0-0 14f+: 0-0
Track : LH: 0-0 RH: 0-1 Tight: 0-0 Gall: 0-0
Aids: Bl: 0-0 Vi: 0-0 Tstrap: 0-0
Best Rating: 80 10/01 Leic 7f9y soft

Improved with each run and got off the mark with an easy victory in a Lingfield maiden in August. Followed up with a narrow victory in a Leicester conditions event on much softer ground and should stay a mile without any problem.

Tramway

105 106
3-y-o ch c Lycius (USA)-Black Fighter (USA) (Secretariat (USA))
H R A Cecil Buckram Oak Holdings

Placings:2-1422 (3067)
2001: 10^{1}F, 10^{4}GF, 11^{2}GF, 11^{2}S

	Starts	1st	2nd	3rd	Win & Pl
Career Total (Turf)	5	1	3	0	12717

53 5/01 Newc 1m2f32y E FRM £2786
Total win prize-money £2786

Going (Turf): Sf: 0-1 GS: 0-0 Gd: 0-1 GF: 0-2 **Fm: 1-1**
Distance: 5f/6f: 0-0 7f-8f: 0-1 **9f-13f: 1-4** 14f+: 0-0
Track : **LH: 1-2** RH: 0-0 Tight: 0-1 **Gall: 1-1**
Aids: Bl: 0-0 Vi: 0-0 Tstrap: 0-0
Best Rating: 106 6/01 NmkR 1m2f gd-fm

Scored his first success onhis reappearance at Newcastle over ten furlongs. Good efforts over twelve since, looking a relentless galloper.

Tranquil Moon

78(75) (3)
3-y-o ch f Deploy-Bright Landing (Sun Prince)
D W P Arbuthnot C G Rowles Nicholson

Placings:00 (5182)
2001: 10^{0}SW, 10^{0}HY

	Starts	1st	2nd	3rd	Win & Pl
Career Total (Turf)	1	0	0	0	
Career Total (AW)	1	0	0	0	

Going (Turf): Sf: 0-1 GS: 0-0 Gd: 0-0 GF: 0-0 Fm: 0-0
Distance: 5f/6f: 0-0 7f-8f: 0-0 9f-13f: 0-2 14f+: 0-0
Track : LH: 0-1 RH: 0-0 Tight: 0-2 Gall: 0-0
Aids: Bl: 0-0 Vi: 0-0 Tstrap: 0-0
Best Rating: 3 3/01 Ling 1m2f slow

Transatlantic (USA)

108 95+
3-y-o gr c Dumaani (USA)-Viendra (USA) (Raise A Native)
R F Johnson Houghton Major D N Chappell

Placings:5461410 (5142)
2001: 7^{5}GS, 7^{4}GF, 8^{6}GF, 9^{1}G, 10^{4}GF, 8^{1}G, 9^{0}G

	Starts	1st	2nd	3rd	Win & Pl
Career Total (Turf)	7	2	0	0	16829

95 9/01 Sand 1m14y C(0-95)H GD £11163
84 7/01 Kemp 1m1f E(0-75)H GD £4699
Total win prize-money £15864

Going (Turf): Sf: 0-0 GS: 0-1 **Gd: 2-3** GF: 0-3 Fm: 0-0
Distance: 5f/6f: 0-0 7f-8f: 0-3 **9f-13f: 2-4** 14f+: 0-0
Track : LH: 0-0 **RH: 2-5** Tight: 0-0 Gall: 0-1
Aids: Bl: 0-0 Vi: 0-0 Tstrap: 0-0
Best Rating: 95 9/01 Sand 1m14y good

Related to decent winners at up to nine furlongs in Germany and the United States. Won well on his handicap debut, but looked to find the ground too fast at Ascot next time, and back on good ground at Sandown he duly obliged. Seems suited by cut in the ground.

Transcendantale (FR)

96 62
3-y-o b/br f Apple Tree (FR)-Kataba (FR) (Shardari)
J H M Gosden Mrs J Wood, Mrs N Cowan, Ms Rachel Hood

Placings:363600 (4643)
2001: 10^{3}GF, 10^{6}GF, 9^{3}GF, 10^{6}G, 12^{0}GF, 11^{0}GF

	Starts	1st	2nd	3rd	Win & Pl
Career Total (Turf)	6	0	0	2	1111

Going (Turf): Sf: 0-0 GS: 0-0 Gd: 0-1 GF: 0-5 Fm: 0-0
Distance: 5f/6f: 0-0 7f-8f: 0-0 9f-13f: 0-6 14f+: 0-0
Track : LH: 0-4 RH: 0-2 Tight: 0-4 Gall: 0-0
Aids: Bl: 0-0 Vi: 0-0 Tstrap: 0-0
Best Rating: 62 7/01 Chep 1m2f36y gd-fm

Transit

96 66
2-y-o b c Lion Cavern (USA)-Black Fighter (USA) (Secretariat (USA))
H R A Cecil Buckram Oak Holdings

Placings:3 (5483)

2001: 7^{3}HY

	Starts	1st	2nd	3rd	Win & Pl
Career Total (Turf)	1	0	0	1	669

Going (Turf): Sf: 0-1 GS: 0-0 Gd: 0-0 GF: 0-0 Fm: 0-0
Distance: 5f/6f: 0-0 7f-8f: 0-1 9f-13f: 0-0 14f+: 0-0
Track : LH: 0-0 RH: 0-0 Tight: 0-0 Gall: 0-0
Aids: Bl: 0-0 Vi: 0-0 Tstrap: 0-0
Best Rating: 66 10/01 Donc 7f heavy

Trapio

70 **13**

3-y-o ch c Mark Of Esteem (IRE)-Pernilla (IRE) (Tate Gallery (USA))
D Morris Cuadra Africa

Placings:0 **(3841)**
2001: 6^{0}G

	Starts	1st	2nd	3rd	Win & Pl
Career Total (Turf)	1	0	0	0	

Going (Turf): Sf: 0-0 GS: 0-0 Gd: 0-1 GF: 0-0 Fm: 0-0
Distance: 5f/6f: 0-1 7f-8f: 0-0 9f-13f: 0-0 14f+: 0-0
Track : LH: 0-0 RH: 0-0 Tight: 0-0 Gall: 0-0
Aids: Bl: 0-0 Vi: 0-0 Tstrap: 0-0
Best Rating: 13 8/01 NmkJ 6f good

Trapper Norman

89(91) (9)**24**

9-y-o b g Mazilier (USA)-Free Skip (Free State)
R Wilman (C Smith 12/2) H G Norman

Placings:0/06000000/0/4/63233/0000000-000000 **(5113)**
2001: 11^{0}SD, 7^{0}SW, 7^{0}SW, 7^{0}GF, 7^{0}GS, 8^{0}HY

	Starts	1st	2nd	3rd	Win & Pl
Career Total (Turf)	17	0	1	3	1867
Career Total (AW)	12	0	0	0	

Going (Turf): Sf: 0-1 GS: 0-2 Gd: 0-0 GF: 0-9 Fm: 0-5
Distance: 5f/6f: 0-5 7f-8f: 0-15 9f-13f: 0-7 14f+: 0-2
Track : LH: 0-18 RH: 0-4 Tight: 0-7 Gall: 0-2
Aids: Bl: 0-1 Vi: 0-0 Tstrap: 0-0
Best Rating: 34 7/01 Leic 7f9y gd-fm

Travel Tardia (IRE)

91(99) (86+)**78**

3-y-o br c Petardia-Annie's Travels (IRE) (Mac's Imp (USA))
I A Wood Neardown Stables

Placings:0214-00 **(2381)**
2001: 6^{0}GS, 5^{0}GF

	Starts	1st	2nd	3rd	Win & Pl
Career Total (Turf)	4	0	1	0	520
Career Total (AW)	2	1	0	0	2529

86 10/00 Wolv 6f F STD £2261
Total win prize-money £2261

Going (Turf): Sf: 0-2 GS: 0-1 Gd: 0-0 GF: 0-1 Fm: 0-0
Distance: **5f/6f: 1-4** 7f-8f: 0-2 9f-13f: 0-0 14f+: 0-0
Track : **LH: 1-3** RH: 0-0 **Tight: 1-1** Gall: 0-0
Aids: Bl: 0-0 Vi: 0-0 Tstrap: 0-0
Best Rating: 63 6/01 Asct 5f gd-fm

Ran with promise on second start at two then switched to the Fibresand to get off the mark over six furlongs. Tends to race keenly. Has run well on heavy ground.

Traveller's Tale

90 **65**

2-y-o b g Selkirk (USA)-Chere Amie (USA) (Mr Prospector (USA))
P W Harris Mr & Mrs George Willett

Placings:406 **(4533)**

2001: 7^{4}F, 7^{0}G, 7^{6}GF

	Starts	1st	2nd	3rd	Win & Pl
Career Total (Turf)	3	0	0	0	0

Going (Turf): Sf: 0-0 GS: 0-0 Gd: 0-1 GF: 0-1 Fm: 0-1
Distance: 5f/6f: 0-0 7f-8f: 0-3 9f-13f: 0-0 14f+: 0-0
Track : LH: 0-1 RH: 0-0 Tight: 0-0 Gall: 0-1
Aids: Bl: 0-0 Vi: 0-0 Tstrap: 0-0
Best Rating: 65 7/01 Muss 7f30y firm

His dam won over ten furlongs in France, and is a half-sister to Grade Two winners Esteemed Friend and Badouizm.

Travellers Rest

89(92) (48)**25**

4-y-o b g Nomadic Way (USA)-Rest (Dance In Time (CAN))
J S Moore (J G Smyth-Osbourne 6/7) Ernest H Moore

Placings:0500-000000 **(2808)**
2001: 11^{0}SD, 12^{0}SD, 10^{0}GS, 9^{0}F, 6^{0}F, 8^{0}GF

	Starts	1st	2nd	3rd	Win & Pl
Career Total (Turf)	8	0	0	0	0
Career Total (AW)	2	0	0	0	

Going (Turf): Sf: 0-1 GS: 0-3 Gd: 0-0 GF: 0-2 Fm: 0-2
Distance: 5f/6f: 0-1 7f-8f: 0-0 9f-13f: 0-8 14f+: 0-1
Track : LH: 0-3 RH: 0-3 Tight: 0-3 Gall: 0-0
Aids: Bl: 0-0 Vi: 0-0 Tstrap: 0-0
Best Rating: 48 4/01 Sthl 1m3f stand

Travelling Times

96(93) (64)**79**

2-y-o ch c Timeless Times (USA)-Bollin Sophie (Efisio)
T D Easterby Ian Morgan

Placings:01403110 **(4823)**
2001: 5^{0}GS, 5^{1}SD, 5^{4}G, 6^{0}GS, 6^{3}GF, 6^{1}GF, 6^{1}GF, 6^{0}G

	Starts	1st	2nd	3rd	Win & Pl
Career Total (Turf)	7	2	0	1	14511
Career Total (AW)	1	1	0	0	2338

79 9/01 York 6f C G-F £8580
71 8/01 Ripn 6f D G-F £4338
64 5/01 Sthl 5f F STD £2338
Total win prize-money £15257

Going (Turf): Sf: 0-0 GS: 0-2 Gd: 0-2 **GF: 2-3** Fm: 0-0
Distance: **5f/6f: 3-8** 7f-8f: 0-0 9f-13f: 0-0 14f+: 0-0
Track : LH: 0-2 RH: 0-0 Tight: 0-1 Gall: 0-0
Aids: **Bl: 2-4** Vi: 0-0 Tstrap: 0-0
Best Rating: 79 9/01 York 6f gd-fm

Despite being steered by a different person in every race he has run in, his form has remained consistent. Prior to his surprisingly bad run at Ayr, he was an improving horse in blinkers over six furlongs, winning a decent York nursery in September 2001. He is best suited to a sound surface.

Travelmate

97 **89**

7-y-o b g Persian Bold-Ustka (Lomond (USA))
J R Fanshawe Barford Bloodstock Ii

Placings:0/00121/516161/2225/0-20 **(4172)**
2001: 10^{2}G, 13^{0}G

	Starts	1st	2nd	3rd	Win & Pl
Career Total (Turf)	19	5	5	0	124234

93 9/98 NmkR 1m4f B(0-100)H GD £8357
84 8/98 NmkJ 1m6f175yC(0-95)H GD £6056
79 6/98 NmkJ 1m4f C(0-90)H GD £5744
74 6/97 NmkJ 1m4f C(0-90)H G-S £5900
74 5/97 Nott 1m1f213yE(0-70)H GD £3486
Total win prize-money £29543

Going (Turf): Sf: 0-0 GS: 1-3 **Gd: 4-13** GF: 0-2 Fm: 0-1
Distance: 5f/6f: 0-0 7f-8f: 0-2 **9f-13f: 4-10** 14f+: 1-7
Track : LH: 1-9 **RH: 4-9** Tight: 0-0 **Gall: 4-13**
Aids: Bl: 0-0 Vi: 0-0 Tstrap: 0-0
Best Rating: 89 8/01 York 1m5f194y good

Short-headed by Far Cry after an epic battle in the Northumberland Plate, he again filled the runner's-up spot in the Ebor in 1999. Prepared for the Melbourne Cup, he finished a fine fifth, showing enough for the legendary Aussie trainer Bart Cummings to offer big money for him, although the deal fell through. Only raced once in 2000 when unsuited by soft ground at Ascot. Ran well on reappearance in 2001 at Newmarket over a trip short of his best, but was injured in the Ebor and his career is in doubt.

Travesty Of Law (IRE)

99(92) (62)**78**

4-y-o ch g Case Law-Bold As Love (Lomond (USA))
S Kirk Stephen W Molloy

Placings:541250104050/000003255400-402050 **(4543)**
2001: 5^{4}G, 5^{0}G, 5^{2}GF, 5^{0}G, 5^{5}GF, 5^{0}GF, 5^{0}SD

	Starts	1st	2nd	3rd	Win & Pl
Career Total (Turf)	30	2	3	1	15146

93 6/99 Wind 5f10y E G-F £3192
86 5/99 Sals 5f D G-F £3322
Total win prize-money £6516

Going (Turf): Sf: 0-3 GS: 0-1 Gd: 0-9 **GF: 2-16** Fm: 0-0
Distance: **5f/6f: 2-29** 7f-8f: 0-1 9f-13f: 0-0 14f+: 0-0
Track : LH: 0-2 **RH: 1-2** Tight: 0-0 **Gall: 1-3**
Aids: Bl: 0-4 Vi: 0-0 Tstrap: 0-0
Best Rating: 78 6/01 Gdwd 5f gd-fm

Has plenty of speed, and benefited from fast ground to win at Salisbury and Windsor as a juvenile in 1999. He put up some sound efforts when conditions were in his favour last term but was unable to get his head in front.

Tre Colline

89 **67**

2-y-o b c Efisio-Triple Joy (Most Welcome)
S P C Woods Tweenhills Racing (may Hill Syndicate)

Placings:04 **(5009)**
2001: 7^{0}G, 7^{4}HY

	Starts	1st	2nd	3rd	Win & Pl
Career Total (Turf)	2	0	0	0	335

Going (Turf): Sf: 0-1 GS: 0-0 Gd: 0-1 GF: 0-0 Fm: 0-0
Distance: 5f/6f: 0-0 7f-8f: 0-2 9f-13f: 0-0 14f+: 0-0
Track : LH: 0-1 RH: 0-1 Tight: 0-0 Gall: 0-0
Aids: Bl: 0-0 Vi: 0-0 Tstrap: 0-0
Best Rating: 67 9/01 Sand 7f16y good

Treasure Chest (IRE)

106 **65**

6-y-o b g Last Tycoon-Sought Out (IRE) (Rainbow Quest (USA))
M C Pipe S A Helaissi

Placings:653/530226/035250/000405060P-123 **(3404)**
2001: 16^{1}GF, 16^{2}GF, 16^{3}GF

	Starts	1st	2nd	3rd	Win & Pl
Career Total (Turf)	27	1	4	4	18184
Career Total (AW)	1	0	0	0	

52 6/01 Asct 2m45y D(0-80)H G-F £7182
Total win prize-money £7183

Going (Turf): Sf: 0-4 GS: 0-3 Gd: 0-6 **GF: 1-14** Fm: 0-0
Distance: 5f/6f: 0-0 7f-8f: 0-1 9f-13f: 0-3 **14f+: 1-24**
Track : LH: 0-13 **RH: 1-15** Tight: 0-7 **Gall: 1-11**
Aids: Bl: 0-0 Vi: 0-18 Tstrap: 0-6
Best Rating: 57 7/01 Asct 2m45y gd-fm

Better known as a modest staying hurdler these days, but managed to win on the Flat over two miles at Ascot in June. It was not a great race for the track though.

Treasure Touch (IRE)

93(96) (39)**39**

7-y-o b g Treasure Kay-Bally Pourri (IRE) (Law Society (USA))

P D Evans David Oxley

Placings:4306/321111510300000/00000600/4020/00011 30131301240400513615 40-6500000000003006 **(3801)**

2001: 7^{6}SW, 7^{5}SD, 7^{0}GS, 5^{0}S, 5^{0}GS, 6^{0}GF, 5^{0}G, 6^{0}F, 7^{0}GF, 7^{0}GF, 6^{3}G, 7^{0}G, 7^{0}GS, 6^{6}G, 8^{0}SD

	Starts	1st	2nd	3rd	Win & Pl
Career Total (Turf)	57	10	2	7	45754
Career Total (AW)	14	2	1	1	5472

59	11/00	Sthl	7f	F(0-60)H	STD	£2016
71	10/00	Rdcr	7f	D(0-85)H	SFT	£4680
68	8/00	Carl	5f207y	F	FRM	£2394
69	7/00	Leic	5f218y	E(0-70)H	G-F	£3266
50	6/00	Carl	5f207y	F	G-F	£2446
59	6/00	Catt	5f212y	E(0-70)H	G-S	£3900
51	6/00	Catt	5f212y	F	GD	£1897
85	5/97	Thsk	5f	C(0-100)H	GD	£7200
86	4/97	NmkR	6f	C(0-90)H	G-F	£6360
78	4/97	Nott	6f15y	E(0-70)H	G-F	£3356
71	3/97	Nott	6f15y	E(0-70)H	G-F	£3174
69	2/97	Sthl	6f	F	STD	£2294

Total win prize-money £42984

Going (Turf): Sf: 1-10 GS: 1-10 Gd: 2-15 **GF: 5-19** Fm: 1-3
Distance: **5f/6f: 8-45** 7f-8f: 4-26 9f-13f: 0-0 14f+: 0-0
Track : **LH: 4-27** RH: 2-3 Tight: 2-10 Gall: 2-6
Aids: Bl: 0-1 Vi: 0-0 Tstrap: 0-2
Best Rating: 60 5/01 Bath 5f11y gd-sft

Won seven times in 2000 but failed to fire last term. Six furlongs is probably his best trip though he stays seven. Yet to fire this season.

Treasure Trail

90 **68**

2-y-o b c Millkom-Forever Shineing (Glint Of Gold)

S Kirk T Neill & Mrs John Lee

Placings:600 **(5289)**

2001: 6^{6}GF, 8^{0}GF, 7^{0}S

	Starts	1st	2nd	3rd	Win & Pl
Career Total (Turf)	3	0	0	0	0

Going (Turf): Sf: 0-1 GS: 0-0 Gd: 0-0 GF: 0-2 Fm: 0-0
Distance: 5f/6f: 0-0 7f-8f: 0-3 9f-13f: 0-0 14f+: 0-0
Track : LH: 0-1 RH: 0-1 Tight: 0-0 Gall: 0-0
Aids: Bl: 0-0 Vi: 0-0 Tstrap: 0-0
Best Rating: 68 9/01 Brig 6f209y gd-fm

Treasured Coin

3-y-o b g Overbury (IRE)-Slip A Coin (Slip Anchor)

D Burchell Eamonn O'Malley

Placings:0 **(5464)**

2001: 11^{0}G

	Starts	1st	2nd	3rd	Win & Pl
Career Total (Turf)	1	0	0	0	

Going (Turf): Sf: 0-0 GS: 0-0 Gd: 0-1 GF: 0-0 Fm: 0-0
Distance: 5f/6f: 0-0 7f-8f: 0-0 9f-13f: 0-1 14f+: 0-0
Track : LH: 0-1 RH: 0-0 Tight: 0-1 Gall: 0-0
Aids: Bl: 0-0 Vi: 0-0 Tstrap: 0-0

Treasured Guest

98 **55+**

3-y-o b g Rainbow Quest (USA)-Free Guest (Be My Guest (USA))

L M Cumani Fittocks Stud

Placings:006106 **(4399)**

2001: 7^{0}S, 6^{0}HY, 8^{6}HY, 10^{1}GF, 10^{0}GF, 10^{6}G

	Starts	1st	2nd	3rd	Win & Pl
Career Total (Turf)	6	1	0	0	3304
55	6/01 Newc 1m2f32y E(0-70)H			G-F	£3304

Total win prize-money £3304

Going (Turf): Sf: 0-3 GS: 0-0 Gd: 0-1 **GF: 1-2** Fm: 0-0
Distance: 5f/6f: 0-0 7f-8f: 0-2 **9f-13f: 1-4** 14f+: 0-0
Track : **LH: 1-3** RH: 0-3 Tight: 0-1 **Gall: 1-3**
Aids: Bl: 0-0 Vi: 0-0 Tstrap: 0-0
Best Rating: 55 6/01 Newc 1m2f32y gd-fm

Tree Pipit (USA)

88 **58**

2-y-o ch f Woodman (USA)-Skimble (USA) (Lyphard (USA))

B W Hills K Abdulla

Placings:4 **(5262)**

2001: 7^{4}GS

	Starts	1st	2nd	3rd	Win & Pl
Career Total (Turf)	1	0	0	0	568

Going (Turf): Sf: 0-0 GS: 0-1 Gd: 0-0 GF: 0-0 Fm: 0-0
Distance: 5f/6f: 0-0 7f-8f: 0-1 9f-13f: 0-0 14f+: 0-0
Track : LH: 0-1 RH: 0-0 Tight: 0-0 Gall: 0-1
Aids: Bl: 0-0 Vi: 0-0 Tstrap: 0-0
Best Rating: 58 10/01 York 7f202y gd-sft

Tree Roofer

83 **63**

2-y-o b g King's Signet (USA)-Armaiti (Sayf El Arab (USA))

Dr J R J Naylor K Cooper

Placings:060 **(5126)**

2001: 6^{0}F, 7^{6}G, 6^{0}HY

	Starts	1st	2nd	3rd	Win & Pl
Career Total (Turf)	3	0	0	0	0

Going (Turf): Sf: 0-1 GS: 0-0 Gd: 0-1 GF: 0-0 Fm: 0-1
Distance: 5f/6f: 0-1 7f-8f: 0-2 9f-13f: 0-0 14f+: 0-0
Track : LH: 0-0 RH: 0-0 Tight: 0-0 Gall: 0-0
Aids: Bl: 0-0 Vi: 0-0 Tstrap: 0-0
Best Rating: 63 9/01 Chep 7f16y good

Treetops Hotel (IRE)

97 **95?**

2-y-o ch c Grand Lodge (USA)-Rousinette (Rousillon (USA))

Mrs A J Perrett Seymour Cohn

Placings:532613 **(5333)**

2001: 6^{5}GF, 6^{3}GF, 6^{2}GS, 7^{6}G, 6^{1}GS, 6^{3}HY

	Starts	1st	2nd	3rd	Win & Pl
Career Total (Turf)	6	1	1	2	6592
95	9/01 Gdwd 6f D			G-S	£4098

Total win prize-money £4098

Going (Turf): Sf: 0-1 **GS: 1-2** Gd: 0-1 GF: 0-2 Fm: 0-0
Distance: **5f/6f: 1-5** 7f-8f: 0-1 9f-13f: 0-0 14f+: 0-0
Track : LH: 0-0 RH: 0-1 Tight: 0-0 Gall: 0-0
Aids: Bl: 0-0 Vi: 0-0 Tstrap: 0-0
Best Rating: 95 9/01 Gdwd 6f gd-sft

He showed ability early on, but had look exposed until winning a four-runner novice event at Goodwood in September.

Trembley

95(87) (30)**57d**

4-y-o b c Komaite (USA)-Cold Blow (Posse (USA))

J L Eyre Billy Parker

Placings:524/0050040 **(5451)**

2001: 6^{0}GF, 6^{0}GF, 6^{5}GF, 7^{0}GF, 7^{0}G, 6^{4}HY, 5^{0}HY, 6^{0}SD

	Starts	1st	2nd	3rd	Win & Pl
Career Total (Turf)	10	0	1	0	2206

Going (Turf): Sf: 0-2 GS: 0-0 Gd: 0-2 GF: 0-6 Fm: 0-0
Distance: 5f/6f: 0-7 7f-8f: 0-3 9f-13f: 0-0 14f+: 0-0
Track : LH: 0-4 RH: 0-0 Tight: 0-0 Gall: 0-1
Aids: Bl: 0-0 Vi: 0-0 Tstrap: 0-3
Best Rating: 57 7/01 Pont 6f gd-fm

Tremezzo

89 **41**

3-y-o b g Mind Games-Rosa Van Fleet (Sallust)

B R Millman G Battocchi

Placings:30-00406 **(3701)**

2001: 5^{0}GF, 7^{0}GF, 6^{4}GF, 6^{0}GF, 6^{6}GF

	Starts	1st	2nd	3rd	Win & Pl
Career Total (Turf)	7	0	0	1	645

Going (Turf): Sf: 0-2 GS: 0-0 Gd: 0-0 GF: 0-5 Fm: 0-0
Distance: 5f/6f: 0-4 7f-8f: 0-3 9f-13f: 0-0 14f+: 0-0
Track : LH: 0-3 RH: 0-0 Tight: 0-0 Gall: 0-2
Aids: Bl: 0-1 Vi: 0-0 Tstrap: 0-0
Best Rating: 51 5/01 Bath 5f11y gd-fm

Tremor

94(90) (35)**50**

3-y-o ch c Zilzal (USA)-Happydrome (Ahonoora)

W R Muir Mrs J M Muir

Placings:0046-245022310 **(1902)**

2001: 8^{2}SW, 8^{4}SD, 9^{5}SD, 7^{0}SD, 11^{2}SD, 9^{2}SD, 9^{3}G, 11^{1}GF, 11^{0}GF

	Starts	1st	2nd	3rd	Win & Pl
Career Total (Turf)	4	1	0	1	2298
Career Total (AW)	9	0	3	0	1578
47	5/01 Ling 1m3f106yG			G-F	£1907

Total win prize-money £1908

Going (Turf): Sf: 0-1 GS: 0-0 Gd: 0-1 **GF: 1-2** Fm: 0-0
Distance: 5f/6f: 0-0 7f-8f: 0-5 **9f-13f: 1-8** 14f+: 0-0
Track : **LH: 1-10** RH: 0-2 **Tight: 1-7** Gall: 0-0
Aids: Bl: 0-0 Vi: 0-0 Tstrap: 0-0
Best Rating: 56 1/01 Wolv 1m100y slow

Trevors Spree

93 **65**

2-y-o ch g Dancing Spree (USA)-Trevorsninepoints (Jester)

Mrs Lydia Pearce T S Child

Placings:54000 **(5342)**

2001: 5^{5}GF, 5^{4}G, 6^{0}G, 6^{0}G, 7^{0}GS

	Starts	1st	2nd	3rd	Win & Pl
Career Total (Turf)	5	0	0	0	308

Going (Turf): Sf: 0-0 GS: 0-1 Gd: 0-3 GF: 0-1 Fm: 0-0
Distance: 5f/6f: 0-2 7f-8f: 0-3 9f-13f: 0-0 14f+: 0-0
Track : LH: 0-0 RH: 0-1 Tight: 0-0 Gall: 0-1
Aids: Bl: 0-0 Vi: 0-0 Tstrap: 0-0
Best Rating: 65 8/01 Leic 5f218y good

Tribal Prince

101 **75**

4-y-o b g Prince Sabo-Tshusick (Dancing Brave (USA))

P W Harris The Tribe

Placings:25025/00134200-630400 **(5608)**

2001: 7^{6}G, 8^{3}GF, 8^{0}G, 8^{4}G, 6^{0}GS, 7^{0}GS

	Starts	1st	2nd	3rd	Win & Pl
Career Total (Turf)	19	1	3	2	10045
75	8/00 Folk 7f E(0-75)H			G-F	£3024

Total win prize-money £3024

Going (Turf): Sf: 0-5 GS: 0-2 Gd: 0-6 **GF: 1-6** Fm: 0-0
Distance: 5f/6f: 0-4 **7f-8f: 1-12** 9f-13f: 0-3 14f+: 0-0
Track : LH: 0-5 RH: 0-3 Tight: 0-0 Gall: 0-4
Aids: Bl: 0-0 Vi: 0-1 Tstrap: 0-0
Best Rating: 74 10/01 Rdcr 1m good

A seven-furlong handicap winner at Folkestone in the summer of 2000, he has run well in better grade since.

Has shown form on soft and fast ground. Best form over seven furlongs but does stay a mile.

Tricks (IRE)

(91) (30)**51**

5-y-o b m First Trump-Party Line (Never So Bold)
D J Coakley Chris Van Hoorn

Placings:0321/00060/56-402 (0322)
2001: 10^{4}SD, 12^{0}SW, 9^{2}SD

	Starts	1st	2nd	3rd	Win & Pl
Career Total (Turf)	7	0	0	0	0
Career Total (AW)	7	1	2	1	4458

73 12/98 Ling 7f D STD £2814
Total win prize-money £2814

Going (Turf): Sf: 0-1 GS: 0-2 Gd: 0-3 GF: 0-1 Fm: 0-0
Distance: 5f/6f: 0-2 7f-8f: 1-6 9f-13f: 0-6 14f+: 0-0
Track : LH: 1-8 RH: 0-3 Tight: 1-8 Gall: 0-1
Aids: Bl: 0-1 Vi: 0-0 Tstrap: 0-0
Best Rating: 43 1/01 Ling 1m2f stand

Tricksy (IRE)

69(95) (48?)

3-y-o b f Dr Devious (IRE)-Shoof Althahab (Sadler's Wells (USA))
Mrs M Reveley J Shack

Placings:0-02000 (4422)
2001: 8^{0}SW, 11^{2}SW, 11^{0}SD, 11^{0}GF, 10^{0}GF

	Starts	1st	2nd	3rd	Win & Pl
Career Total (Turf)	3	0	0	0	
Career Total (AW)	3	0	1	0	746

Going (Turf): Sf: 0-0 GS: 0-0 Gd: 0-0 GF: 0-3 Fm: 0-0
Distance: 5f/6f: 0-0 7f-8f: 0-2 9f-13f: 0-4 14f+: 0-0
Track : LH: 0-4 RH: 0-1 Tight: 0-2 Gall: 0-0
Aids: Bl: 0-0 Vi: 0-0 Tstrap: 0-1
Best Rating: 48 2/01 Sthl 1m3f slow

Tricky Lady (IRE)

83 **61**

2-y-o b f Persian Bold-Tropicana (IRE) (Imperial Frontier (USA))
M Johnston R Fabrizius

Placings:005 (5088)
2001: 8^{0}HY, 7^{0}G, 6^{5}GS

	Starts	1st	2nd	3rd	Win & Pl
Career Total (Turf)	3	0	0	0	0

Going (Turf): Sf: 0-1 GS: 0-1 Gd: 0-1 GF: 0-0 Fm: 0-0
Distance: 5f/6f: 0-1 7f-8f: 0-1 9f-13f: 0-1 14f+: 0-0
Track : LH: 0-1 RH: 0-1 Tight: 0-0 Gall: 0-0
Aids: Bl: 0-0 Vi: 0-0 Tstrap: 0-0
Best Rating: 61 9/01 Hayd 1m30y heavy

Trillie

95 **62**

3-y-o b f Never So Bold-Trull (Lomond (USA))
C F Wall Sir Stanley And Lady Grinstead

Placings:116020-60000 (5097)
2001: 6^{6}S, 6^{0}GF, 6^{0}G, 8^{0}GS, 6^{0}GS

	Starts	1st	2nd	3rd	Win & Pl
Career Total (Turf)	11	2	1	0	9848

88 8/00 Sals 6f212y D GD £3484
70 7/00 Sals 6f D FRM £4172
Total win prize-money £7656

Going (Turf): Sf: 0-3 GS: 0-3 Gd: 1-3 GF: 0-1 Fm: 1-1
Distance: 5f/6f: 1-4 7f-8f: 1-6 9f-13f: 0-1 14f+: 0-0
Track : LH: 0-0 RH: 0-1 Tight: 0-0 Gall: 0-0
Aids: Bl: 0-0 Vi: 0-0 Tstrap: 0-0
Best Rating: 83 5/01 Newb 6f8y soft

Won both of her first two races at Salisbury, but found the step up to Group Three company too much for her at Goodwood. Well held in 2001.

Trillionaire

94(40) **60**

3-y-o ch g Dilum (USA)-Madam Trilby (Grundy)
D W Chapman (D Nicholls 7/6) Miss N F Thesiger

Placings:0640-0000600 (4874)
2001: 8^{0}GF, 5^{0}GF, 7^{0}G, 7^{0}GF, 7^{6}G, 8^{0}GS, 8^{0}SD

	Starts	1st	2nd	3rd	Win & Pl
Career Total (Turf)	10	0	0	0	330
Career Total (AW)	1	0	0	0	

Going (Turf): Sf: 0-1 GS: 0-1 Gd: 0-3 GF: 0-5 Fm: 0-0
Distance: 5f/6f: 0-1 7f-8f: 0-9 9f-13f: 0-1 14f+: 0-0
Track : LH: 0-6 RH: 0-0 Tight: 0-5 Gall: 0-0
Aids: Bl: 0-0 Vi: 0-0 Tstrap: 0-0
Best Rating: 52 8/01 Catt 7f good

Trilogy

102 **90**

2-y-o ch c Grand Lodge (USA)-Three More (USA) (Sanglamore (USA))
J H M Gosden K Abdulla

Placings:031400 (5134)
2001: 6^{0}GF, 6^{3}GF, 6^{1}GF, 6^{4}GF, 7^{0}G, 7^{0}G

	Starts	1st	2nd	3rd	Win & Pl
Career Total (Turf)	6	1	0	1	8586

90 7/01 Sals 6f212y D G-F £4251
Total win prize-money £4251

Going (Turf): Sf: 0-0 GS: 0-0 Gd: 0-2 GF: 1-4 Fm: 0-0
Distance: 5f/6f: 0-1 7f-8f: 1-5 9f-13f: 0-0 14f+: 0-0
Track : LH: 0-0 RH: 0-1 Tight: 0-0 Gall: 0-0
Aids: Bl: 0-0 Vi: 0-0 Tstrap: 0-0
Best Rating: 90 7/01 Sals 6f212y gd-fm

He got off the mark with an easy all-the-way win at Salisbury in July, but looked out of his depth in the Richmond Stakes at Goodwood and the Solario. Acts on fast ground.

Trimontium (USA)

97 **78**

2-y-o b/br c Mt. Livermore (USA)-Sailing Minstrel (USA) (The Minstrel (CAN))
J R Fanshawe Eildon Racing Partnership

Placings:3334 (5368)
2001: 6^{3}GF, 6^{3}G, 6^{3}S, 8^{4}GS

	Starts	1st	2nd	3rd	Win & Pl
Career Total (Turf)	4	0	0	3	1999

Going (Turf): Sf: 0-1 GS: 0-1 Gd: 0-1 GF: 0-1 Fm: 0-0
Distance: 5f/6f: 0-1 7f-8f: 0-3 9f-13f: 0-0 14f+: 0-0
Track : LH: 0-1 RH: 0-0 Tight: 0-0 Gall: 0-0
Aids: Bl: 0-0 Vi: 0-0 Tstrap: 0-0
Best Rating: 78 10/01 Brig 6f209y soft

Placed in his first three starts at two, but looks short of a turn of foot.

Trimstone

(84) (34)**23**

4-y-o br g Bandmaster (USA)-Klairover (Smackover)
R J Hodges R J Hodges

Placings:0 (5522)
2001: 6^{0}HY, 8^{2}SD

	Starts	1st	2nd	3rd	Win & Pl
Career Total (Turf)	1	0	0	0	

Going (Turf): Sf: 0-1 GS: 0-0 Gd: 0-0 GF: 0-0 Fm: 0-0
Distance: 5f/6f: 0-1 7f-8f: 0-0 9f-13f: 0-0 14f+: 0-0
Track : LH: 0-0 RH: 0-0 Tight: 0-0 Gall: 0-0
Aids: Bl: 0-0 Vi: 0-0 Tstrap: 0-0
Best Rating: 23 10/01 Wind 6f heavy

Trinity (IRE)

102 **57**

5-y-o b h College Chapel-Kaskazi (Dancing Brave (USA))
M Brittain Miss Debi J Woods

Placings:462532204/100050000/0064000-0600410 (5111)
2001: 5^{0}GS, 6^{6}G, 5^{0}G, 6^{0}G, 6^{4}G, 6^{1}G, 6^{0}HY

	Starts	1st	2nd	3rd	Win & Pl
Career Total (Turf)	32	2	3	1	16876

57 8/01 Newc 6f F(0-65)H GD £2716
84 5/99 Donc 5f E G-F £2853
Total win prize-money £5569

Going (Turf): Sf: 0-4 GS: 0-4 Gd: 1-11 GF: 1-12 Fm: 0-0
Distance: 5f/6f: 2-29 7f-8f: 0-2 9f-13f: 0-0 14f+: 0-0
Track : LH: 0-1 RH: 0-0 Tight: 0-0 Gall: 0-0
Aids: Bl: 0-0 Vi: 0-0 Tstrap: 0-1
Best Rating: 57 8/01 Newc 6f good

He showed promise at two and got off the mark at Doncaster on his reappearance at three. Scored for the first time since at Newcastle in August.

Trio

96

5-y-o b g Cyrano De Bergerac-May Light (Midyan (USA))
N Hamilton City Industrial Supplies Ltd

Placings:35603143/5446000000/060R0 (5469)
2001: 8^{0}GF, 11^{6}F, 10^{0}GF, 11^{R}F, 9^{0}S

	Starts	1st	2nd	3rd	Win & Pl
Career Total (Turf)	23	1	0	3	26152

78 9/98 Donc 1m B H GD £19737
Total win prize-money £19738

Going (Turf): Sf: 0-4 GS: 0-3 Gd: 1-9 GF: 0-5 Fm: 0-2
Distance: 5f/6f: 0-2 7f-8f: 1-7 9f-13f: 0-14 14f+: 0-0
Track : LH: 0-8 RH: 0-8 Tight: 0-10 Gall: 0-1
Aids: Bl: 0-0 Vi: 0-0 Tstrap: 0-0
Best Rating: 55 6/01 Ling 1m3f106y firm

Trip The Switch (IRE)

86 **41**

3-y-o b f Imperial Frontier (USA)-Brite Mist (IRE) (Shy Groom (USA))
B S Rothwell Jim Browne

Placings:000 (5286)
2001: 7^{0}G, 8^{0}HY, 10^{0}GF

	Starts	1st	2nd	3rd	Win & Pl
Career Total (Turf)	3	0	0	0	

Going (Turf): Sf: 0-2 GS: 0-0 Gd: 0-1 GF: 0-0 Fm: 0-0
Distance: 5f/6f: 0-0 7f-8f: 0-1 9f-13f: 0-2 14f+: 0-0
Track : LH: 0-2 RH: 0-0 Tight: 0-0 Gall: 0-0
Aids: Bl: 0-0 Vi: 0-0 Tstrap: 0-0
Best Rating: 41 10/01 Nott 1m54y heavy

Triphenia (IRE)

105(108) (76+)**84**

3-y-o b g Ashkalani (IRE)-Atsuko (IRE) (Mtoto)
M L W Bell Mrs Caroline Parker

Placings:3140 (2329)
2001: 8^{3}GS, 11^{1}SD, 8^{4}GF, 12^{0}GF

	Starts	1st	2nd	3rd	Win & Pl
Career Total (Turf)	3	0	0	1	1250
Career Total (AW)	1	1	0	0	3486

76 4/01 Sthl 1m3f D STD £3486
Total win prize-money £3486

Going (Turf): Sf: 0-0 GS: 0-1 Gd: 0-0 GF: 0-2 Fm: 0-0

Distance: 5f/6f: 0-0 7f-8f: 0-1 **9f-13f: 1-3** 14f+: 0-0
Track : **LH: 1-1** RH: 0-2 Tight: 0-0 Gall: 0-1
Aids: Bl: 0-0 Vi: 0-0 Tstrap: 0-0
Best Rating: 84 5/01 Bevl 1m100y gd-fm

Triple Blue (IRE)

101 **99**

3-y-o ch c Bluebird (USA)-Persian Tapestry (Tap On Wood)
R Hannon J C Smith

Placings:11352453406-000500 **(5133)**
2001: 6^{0}G, 6^{0}GF, 8^{0}G, 6^{5}GF, 7^{0}G, 7^{0}G

	Starts	1st	2nd	3rd	Win & Pl
Career Total (Turf)	17	2	1	2	26038

93	5/00	Kemp	6f	C	SFT	£6130
76	5/00	Ling	5f	D	G-S	£3493

Total win prize-money £9625

Going (Turf): Sf: 1-2 GS: 1-1 Gd: 0-9 GF: 0-5 Fm: 0-0
Distance: **5f/6f: 2-9** 7f-8f: 0-7 9f-13f: 0-1 14f+: 0-0
Track : LH: 0-1 RH: 0-2 Tight: 0-1 Gall: 0-0
Aids: Bl: 0-0 Vi: 0-0 Tstrap: 0-0
Best Rating: 99 5/01 Ling 6f good

Ran creditably in Listed and Group company after winning twice in the spring of 2000 but falls a bit short of that level. Acts with cut in the ground.

Triple Concerto

(79) (3)**56**

4-y-o ch f Grand Lodge (USA)-On The Bank (IRE) (In The Wings)
B S Rothwell Brian Rothwell

Placings:0/00 **(0099)**
2001: 12^{0}SD, 12^{0}SD

	Starts	1st	2nd	3rd	Win & Pl
Career Total (Turf)	1	0	0	0	
Career Total (AW)	2	0	0	0	

Going (Turf): Sf: 0-0 GS: 0-0 Gd: 0-1 GF: 0-0 Fm: 0-0
Distance: 5f/6f: 0-0 7f-8f: 0-1 9f-13f: 0-2 14f+: 0-0
Track : LH: 0-2 RH: 0-0 Tight: 0-0 Gall: 0-0
Aids: Bl: 0-1 Vi: 0-0 Tstrap: 0-0
Best Rating: 3 1/01 Sthl 1m4f stand

Triple Decision (USA)

80 **52**

3-y-o b f Torrential (USA)-Triple Kiss (Shareef Dancer (USA))
B Hanbury Hilal Salem

Placings:0 **(0841)**
2001: 7^{0}GS

	Starts	1st	2nd	3rd	Win & Pl
Career Total (Turf)	1	0	0	0	

Going (Turf): Sf: 0-0 GS: 0-1 Gd: 0-0 GF: 0-0 Fm: 0-0
Distance: 5f/6f: 0-0 7f-8f: 0-1 9f-13f: 0-0 14f+: 0-0
Track : LH: 0-0 RH: 0-0 Tight: 0-0 Gall: 0-0
Aids: Bl: 0-0 Vi: 0-0 Tstrap: 0-0
Best Rating: 52 4/01 Newb 7f gd-sft

Triple Glory (IRE)

97 **70**

2-y-o b f Goldmark (USA)-Trebles (IRE) (Kenmare (FR))
Mrs P N Dutfield Mrs Pat Scott

Placings:00 **(3980)**
2001: 7^{0}GF, 6^{0}F

	Starts	1st	2nd	3rd	Win & Pl
Career Total (Turf)	2	0	0	0	

Going (Turf): Sf: 0-0 GS: 0-0 Gd: 0-0 GF: 0-1 Fm: 0-1
Distance: 5f/6f: 0-0 7f-8f: 0-2 9f-13f: 0-0 14f+: 0-0
Track : LH: 0-0 RH: 0-0 Tight: 0-0 Gall: 0-0
Aids: Bl: 0-0 Vi: 0-0 Tstrap: 0-0
Best Rating: 70 8/01 Sals 6f212y firm

Triple Play (IRE)

101 **78**

2-y-o br g Tagula (IRE)-Shiyra (Darshaan)
B J Meehan Matham Investments

Placings:413063000 **(5140)**
2001: 5^{4}S, 5^{1}G, 5^{3}GF, 6^{0}GF, 5^{6}G, 6^{3}G, 6^{0}GF, 6^{0}GF, 6^{0}G

	Starts	1st	2nd	3rd	Win & Pl
Career Total (Turf)	9	1	0	2	6503

62	5/01	Leic	5f2y	E	GD	£3286

Total win prize-money £3287

Going (Turf): Sf: 0-1 GS: 0-0 **Gd: 1-4** GF: 0-4 Fm: 0-0
Distance: **5f/6f: 1-9** 7f-8f: 0-0 9f-13f: 0-0 14f+: 0-0
Track : LH: 0-0 RH: 0-0 Tight: 0-0 Gall: 0-0
Aids: Bl: 0-2 Vi: 0-0 Tstrap: 0-0
Best Rating: 84 5/01 Sand 5f6y gd-fm

Broke his maiden at Leicester over five furlongs in May and has faced some stiff tasks since. Effective at five or six furlongs.

Triplemoon (USA)

92 **74**

2-y-o ch f Trempolino (USA)-Placer Queen (Habitat)
P W Harris Dream Chasers

Placings:4054430 **(5115)**
2001: 6^{4}GF, 6^{0}GF, 5^{5}GF, 7^{4}GF, 7^{4}GF, 8^{3}S, 9^{0}HY

	Starts	1st	2nd	3rd	Win & Pl
Career Total (Turf)	7	0	0	1	948

Going (Turf): Sf: 0-2 GS: 0-0 Gd: 0-0 GF: 0-5 Fm: 0-0
Distance: 5f/6f: 0-1 7f-8f: 0-4 9f-13f: 0-2 14f+: 0-0
Track : LH: 0-2 RH: 0-2 Tight: 0-2 Gall: 0-0
Aids: Bl: 0-0 Vi: 0-0 Tstrap: 0-0
Best Rating: 74 9/01 Pont 1m4y soft

Tripper (USA)

95 **79**

2-y-o b f Kingmambo (USA)-Summer Trip (USA) (L'Emigrant (USA))
J L Dunlop Robin F Scully

Placings:06 **(5603)**
2001: 7^{0}G, 7^{6}GS

	Starts	1st	2nd	3rd	Win & Pl
Career Total (Turf)	2	0	0	0	

Going (Turf): Sf: 0-0 GS: 0-1 Gd: 0-1 GF: 0-0 Fm: 0-0
Distance: 5f/6f: 0-0 7f-8f: 0-2 9f-13f: 0-0 14f+: 0-0
Track : LH: 0-0 RH: 0-0 Tight: 0-0 Gall: 0-0
Aids: Bl: 0-0 Vi: 0-0 Tstrap: 0-0
Best Rating: 79 11/01 NmkR 7f gd-sft

Trippitaka

90 **45**

4-y-o b f Ezzoud (IRE)-Bluish (USA) (Alleged (USA))
N A Graham W J De Ruiter

Placings:003-0050 **(2250)**
2001: 14^{0}S, 12^{0}S, 14^{5}G, 16^{0}GF

	Starts	1st	2nd	3rd	Win & Pl
Career Total (Turf)	7	0	0	1	673

Going (Turf): Sf: 0-3 GS: 0-0 Gd: 0-2 GF: 0-2 Fm: 0-0
Distance: 5f/6f: 0-0 7f-8f: 0-0 9f-13f: 0-4 14f+: 0-3
Track : LH: 0-6 RH: 0-1 Tight: 0-1 Gall: 0-3
Aids: Bl: 0-2 Vi: 0-0 Tstrap: 0-0
Best Rating: 45 5/01 Yarm 1m6f17y good

Triumphant Return (NZ)

106 **91**

6-y-o br g Asti Bay (NZ)-Vaniteux (AUS) (Vain (AUS))
P Busuttin Mrs B D Busuttin

Placings:1/5222111132-050 **(4861)**
2001: 6^{0}G, 6^{5}G, 5^{0}GF

	Starts	1st	2nd	3rd	Win & Pl
Career Total (Turf)	14	5	4	1	90848

4/00	Kran	6f	H	GD	£22037
4/00	Kran	6f	H	GD	£16528
3/00	Kran	6f	H	GD	£12120
3/00	Kran	7f	H	GD	£8225
12/99	Kran	6f	H	GD	£6747

Total win prize-money £65657

Going (Turf): Sf: 0-0 GS: 0-0 **Gd: 5-11** GF: 0-1 Fm: 0-2
Distance: **5f/6f: 4-13** 7f-8f: 1-1 9f-13f: 0-0 14f+: 0-0
Track : LH: 0-0 RH: 0-0 Tight: 0-0 Gall: 0-0
Aids: Bl: 0-0 Vi: 0-0 Tstrap: 0-1
Best Rating: 91 9/01 Newb 5f34y gd-fm

A New Zealand-bred winner of handicaps in Singapore.

Trojan (IRE)

89 **73**

2-y-o ch c Up And At 'Em-Fantasise (FR) (General Assembly (USA))
S P C Woods B Allen/R Hine/R Dawson/A Duke

Placings:3 **(3868)**
2001: 7^{3}G

	Starts	1st	2nd	3rd	Win & Pl
Career Total (Turf)	1	0	0	1	423

Going (Turf): Sf: 0-0 GS: 0-0 Gd: 0-1 GF: 0-0 Fm: 0-0
Distance: 5f/6f: 0-0 7f-8f: 0-1 9f-13f: 0-0 14f+: 0-0
Track : LH: 0-0 RH: 0-0 Tight: 0-0 Gall: 0-0
Aids: Bl: 0-0 Vi: 0-0 Tstrap: 0-0
Best Rating: 73 8/01 Folk 7f good

Trojan Girl (IRE)

81(81) (9)**6**

5-y-o b m Up And At 'Em-Lady-Mumtaz (Martin John)
Miss S J Wilton John Pointon And Sons

Placings:224063023012/141123106030/0000 **(2173)**
2001: 6^{0}SD, 5^{0}SD, 7^{0}GF, 7^{0}SD

	Starts	1st	2nd	3rd	Win & Pl
Career Total (Turf)	4	0	0	0	0
Career Total (AW)	24	5	5	4	18699

77	4/99	Wolv	5f	F	STD	£2318
77	2/99	Wolv	5f	D(0-80)H	STD	£3710
71	2/99	Wolv	5f	F	STD	£2015
75	1/99	Wolv	5f	E(0-70)H	STD	£2775
58	12/98	Wolv	5f	G	SLW	£1882

Total win prize-money £12701

Going (Turf): Sf: 0-1 GS: 0-0 Gd: 0-1 GF: 0-1 Fm: 0-1
Distance: **5f/6f: 5-26** 7f-8f: 0-2 9f-13f: 0-0 14f+: 0-0
Track : **LH: 5-24** RH: 0-0 **Tight: 5-20** Gall: 0-1
Aids: Bl: 0-0 Vi: 0-0 Tstrap: 0-0
Best Rating: 9 5/01 Wolv 5f stand

Trojan Prince (USA)

82 **57**

3-y-o b/br g Known Fact (USA)-Helen V (USA) (Slewacide (USA))
B W Hills Stephen Crown

Placings:0025604-0P **(2238)**
2001: 6^{0}F, 6^{P}GF

	Starts	1st	2nd	3rd	Win & Pl
Career Total (Turf)	9	0	1	0	1095

Going (Turf): Sf: 0-0 GS: 0-1 Gd: 0-5 GF: 0-2 Fm: 0-1
Distance: 5f/6f: 0-6 7f-8f: 0-3 9f-13f: 0-0 14f+: 0-0
Track : LH: 0-2 RH: 0-0 Tight: 0-0 Gall: 0-1
Aids: Bl: 0-0 Vi: 0-0 Tstrap: 0-0

Best Rating: 32 6/01 Newc 6f firm

Trojan Princess

100 **87**

2-y-o b f Hector Protector (USA)-Robellino Miss (USA) (Robellino (USA))

G Wragg The Eclipse Partnership - 2

Placings:631 **(5277)**

2001: 7^{6}GF, 7^{3}GF, 7^{1}GS

	Starts	1st	2nd	3rd	Win & Pl
Career Total (Turf)	3	1	0	1	4795

87	10/01	Leic	7f9y	D	G-S	£4069

Total win prize-money £4069

Going (Turf): Sf: 0-0 **GS: 1-1** Gd: 0-0 GF: 0-2 Fm: 0-0
Distance: 5f/6f: 0-0 **7f-8f: 1-3** 9f-13f: 0-0 14f+: 0-0
Track : LH: 0-0 RH: 0-0 Tight: 0-0 Gall: 0-0
Aids: Bl: 0-0 Vi: 0-0 Tstrap: 0-0
Best Rating: 87 10/01 Leic 7f9y gd-sft

Showed promise before narrowly getting off the mark in a Leicester maiden in October and should make a decent three-year-old.

Trojan Wolf

103(103) (57)**46**

6-y-o ch g Wolfhound (USA)-Trojan Lady (USA) (Irish River (FR))

P Howling Max Pocock

Placings:0/0464444/050024205**11**/14530000006150-65306021300 **(5615)**

2001: 8^{6}SW, 7^{5}SD, 8^{3}GS, 8^{0}SD, 8^{6}GF, 8^{0}G, 8^{2}SD, 8^{1}SD, 8^{3}SD, 8^{0}F, 12^{0}SD, 8^{0}SD, 8^{1}SD

	Starts	1st	2nd	3rd	Win & Pl
Career Total (Turf)	24	0	1	1	3264
Career Total (AW)	20	5	2	2	12363

57	7/01	Sthl	1m	F(0-65)	STD	£2303
64	7/00	Sthl	1m	F(0-65)	STD	£2254
72	1/00	Wolv	1m100y	F(0-75)H	STD	£1939
72	11/99	Sthl	1m3f	F(0-60)H	STD	£1871
67	11/99	Sthl	1m	G(0-60)H	STD	£1616

Total win prize-money £9984

Going (Turf): Sf: 0-1 **GS: 0-4 Gd: 0-8 GF: 0-7 Fm: 0-4**
Distance: 5f/6f: 0-1 **7f-8f: 3-25** 9f-13f: 2-18 14f+: 0-0
Track : **LH: 5-31** RH: 0-5 **Tight: 1-11** Gall: 0-2
Aids: Bl: 0-0 Vi: 0-1 Tstrap: 0-4
Best Rating: 57 7/01 Sthl 1m stand

He goes well on Fibresand, having won four times at Southwell. Effective from a mile to 11 furlongs, he is suited by forcing tactics and goes well for an inexperienced rider.

Trooper Collins (IRE)

96(74) (37)**66**

3-y-o b c Dolphin Street (FR)-Born To Fly (IRE) (Last Tycoon)

J J O'Neill Mrs J Carrington

Placings:54040 **(5198)**

2001: 8^{5}GS, 7^{4}G, 8^{0}GF, 8^{4}F, 9^{0}SD

	Starts	1st	2nd	3rd	Win & Pl
Career Total (Turf)	4	0	0	0	415
Career Total (AW)	1	0	0	0	

Going (Turf): Sf: 0-0 GS: 0-1 Gd: 0-1 GF: 0-1 Fm: 0-1
Distance: 5f/6f: 0-0 7f-8f: 0-1 9f-13f: 0-4 14f+: 0-0
Track : LH: 0-2 RH: 0-0 Tight: 0-1 Gall: 0-0
Aids: Bl: 0-0 Vi: 0-0 Tstrap: 0-0
Best Rating: 66 7/01 Wwck 1m22y gd-sft

Trop Chere (IRE)

87(72) (31)**54**

2-y-o b f Distinctly North (USA)-Break For Tee (IRE) (Executive Perk)

A P Jarvis Christopher Shankland

Placings:00024 **(2135)**

2001: 5^{0}SD, 5^{0}S, 6^{0}GF, 6^{2}GF, 7^{4}GF

	Starts	1st	2nd	3rd	Win & Pl
Career Total (Turf)	4	0	1	0	1075
Career Total (AW)	1	0	0	0	

Going (Turf): Sf: 0-1 GS: 0-0 Gd: 0-0 GF: 0-3 Fm: 0-0
Distance: 5f/6f: 0-4 7f-8f: 0-1 9f-13f: 0-0 14f+: 0-0
Track : LH: 0-0 RH: 0-0 Tight: 0-0 Gall: 0-0
Aids: Bl: 0-0 Vi: 0-0 Tstrap: 0-0
Best Rating: 54 5/01 Gdwd 6f gd-fm

Tropical River (IRE)

55

3-y-o b g Lahib (USA)-Tropical Dance (USA) (Thorn Dance (USA))

E Stanners George Ward

Placings:6000-0 **(1476)**

2001: 6^{0}G

	Starts	1st	2nd	3rd	Win & Pl
Career Total (Turf)	4	0	0	0	0
Career Total (AW)	1	0	0	0	

Going (Turf): Sf: 0-1 GS: 0-1 Gd: 0-1 GF: 0-1 Fm: 0-0
Distance: 5f/6f: 0-3 7f-8f: 0-2 9f-13f: 0-0 14f+: 0-0
Track : LH: 0-1 RH: 0-0 Tight: 0-1 Gall: 0-0
Aids: Bl: 0-0 Vi: 0-0 Tstrap: 0-0
Best Rating: 8 5/01 Wind 6f good

Trotter's Future

107(77) (12)**64**

3-y-o b c Emperor Jones (USA)-Miss Up N Go (Gorytus (USA))

M W Easterby (A C Stewart 21/9) M W Easterby

Placings:00-40411342135 **(4843)**

2001: 7^{4}SD, 11^{0}GS, 14^{4}G, 14^{1}F, 14^{1}GF, 14^{3}G, 16^{4}GF, 16^{2}G, 16^{1}GF, 16^{3}GF, 16^{5}G

	Starts	1st	2nd	3rd	Win & Pl
Career Total (Turf)	12	3	1	2	10047
Career Total (AW)	1	0	0	0	0

59	8/01	Folk	2m93y	F(0-70)H	G-F	£2338
54	6/01	Yarm	1m6f17y	E(0-70)H	G-F	£3234
41	5/01	Rdcr	1m6f19y	F(0-60)H	FRM	£2464

Total win prize-money £8036

Going (Turf): Sf: 0-2 GS: 0-1 Gd: 0-4 **GF: 2-4** Fm: 1-1
Distance: 5f/6f: 0-0 7f-8f: 0-3 9f-13f: 0-1 **14f+: 3-9**
Track : **LH: 2-7** RH: 1-3 **Tight: 3-9** Gall: 0-0
Aids: Bl: 0-0 Vi: 0-0 Tstrap: 0-0
Best Rating: 64 9/01 Ling 2m gd-fm

Improved considerably when stepped up to staying distances. Has won three times on fast ground in the 2001 season. Best when ridden close to the pace.

Trouble

(94) (55)**55d**

5-y-o b g Kris-Ringlet (USA) (Secreto (USA))

P W Hiatt Red Lion (chipping Norton) Partnership

Placings:6006/005-043 **(0217)**

2001: 9^{0}SW, 8^{4}SD, 8^{3}SD

	Starts	1st	2nd	3rd	Win & Pl
Career Total (Turf)	4	0	0	0	0
Career Total (AW)	6	0	0	1	301

Going (Turf): Sf: 0-0 GS: 0-0 Gd: 0-2 GF: 0-2 Fm: 0-0
Distance: 5f/6f: 0-0 7f-8f: 0-4 9f-13f: 0-6 14f+: 0-0
Track : LH: 0-7 RH: 0-2 Tight: 0-4 Gall: 0-2
Aids: Bl: 0-0 Vi: 0-0 Tstrap: 0-0
Best Rating: 46 1/01 Wolv 1m100y stand

Trouble Mountain (USA)

103 **73**

4-y-o br g Mt. Livermore (USA)-Trouble Free (USA) (Nodouble (USA))

M W Easterby Mrs Jean Turpin

Placings:1132/650006-00000000104020 **(5624)**

2001: 6^{0}HY, 7^{0}G, 10^{0}GF, 8^{0}GF, 6^{0}G, 6^{0}G, 7^{0}GF, 9^{0}G, 10^{1}GF, 12^{0}G, 10^{4}S, 8^{0}GS, 8^{2}S, 9^{0}GS

	Starts	1st	2nd	3rd	Win & Pl
Career Total (Turf)	24	3	2	1	32694

73	9/01	York	1m2f85y	E(0-70)H	G-F	£6838
95	7/99	Donc	7f	C	G-F	£6360
92	7/99	Hayd	6f	D	FRM	£3663

Total win prize-money £16863

Going (Turf): Sf: 0-4 GS: 0-4 Gd: 0-5 **GF: 2-9** Fm: 1-2
Distance: 5f/6f: 1-2 7f-8f: 1-13 9f-13f: 1-9 14f+: 0-0
Track : **LH: 1-11** RH: 0-1 Tight: 0-3 **Gall: 1-8**
Aids: Bl: 0-0 Vi: 0-0 Tstrap: 0-0
Best Rating: 75 5/01 York 1m2f85y gd-fm

Very useful on his day for Barry Hills earlier in his career, he lost his way before joining Mick Easterby and a massive drop in the handicap finally paid dividends at York in September. Stays ten furlongs and quite capable of adding to his score.

Trouble Next Door (IRE)

92(83) (42)**37**

3-y-o b g Persian Bold-Adjacent (IRE) (Doulab (USA))

N P Littmoden Mrs Linda Francis

Placings:06-664500 **(4614)**

2001: 8^{6}SD, 9^{6}SW, 9^{4}G, 9^{5}GF, 11^{0}GF, 13^{0}F

	Starts	1st	2nd	3rd	Win & Pl
Career Total (Turf)	5	0	0	0	390
Career Total (AW)	3	0	0	0	0

Going (Turf): Sf: 0-1 GS: 0-0 Gd: 0-1 GF: 0-2 Fm: 0-1
Distance: 5f/6f: 0-0 7f-8f: 0-3 9f-13f: 0-4 14f+: 0-1
Track : LH: 0-5 RH: 0-2 Tight: 0-4 Gall: 0-0
Aids: Bl: 0-0 Vi: 0-0 Tstrap: 0-0
Best Rating: 39 8/01 Bevl 1m1f207y good

Lightly-raced maiden, has missed the break on occasions.

Troubleshooter

78 **49**

3-y-o b g Ezzoud (IRE)-Oublier L'Ennui (FR) (Bellman (FR))

M Dods Harry Whitton

Placings:60202062630-0000 **(5538)**

2001: 8^{0}S, 8^{0}GS, 7^{0}G, 10^{0}S

	Starts	1st	2nd	3rd	Win & Pl
Career Total (Turf)	15	0	3	1	3743

Going (Turf): Sf: 0-3 GS: 0-1 Gd: 0-5 GF: 0-6 Fm: 0-0
Distance: 5f/6f: 0-8 7f-8f: 0-5 9f-13f: 0-2 14f+: 0-0
Track : LH: 0-2 RH: 0-1 Tight: 0-2 Gall: 0-0
Aids: Bl: 0-5 Vi: 0-0 Tstrap: 0-0
Best Rating: 21 10/01 Rdcr 7f good

Troys Guest (IRE)

88(65) **47**

3-y-o gr f Be My Guest (USA)-Troja (Troy)

E J Alston Trevor Hemmings

Placings:53360-0000 **(2099)**

2001: 11^{0}SD, 11^{0}GF, 10^{0}GF, 8^{0}GF

	Starts	1st	2nd	3rd	Win & Pl
Career Total (Turf)	8	0	0	2	1089
Career Total (AW)	1	0	0	0	

Going (Turf): Sf: 0-2 GS: 0-0 Gd: 0-1 GF: 0-5 Fm: 0-0
Distance: 5f/6f: 0-3 7f-8f: 0-2 9f-13f: 0-4 14f+: 0-0
Track : LH: 0-4 RH: 0-2 Tight: 0-3 Gall: 0-0

Aids: Bl: 0-0 Vi: 0-0 Tstrap: 0-0
Best Rating: 47 5/01 Bevl 1m3f216y gd-fm

Trudie

99(86) (42)**40**

3-y-o b f Komaite (USA)-Irish Limerick (Try My Best (USA))
Mrs A M Naughton (Miss J F Craze 6/2) Mrs S E Cooper

Placings:6030-0004021 (5409)
2001: 5^{0}SW, 6^{0}SD, 6^{0}G, 5^{4}G, 5^{0}GF, 5^{2}GS, 6^{1}SD

	Starts	1st	2nd	3rd	Win & Pl
Career Total (Turf)	7	0	1	1	1374
Career Total (AW)	4	1	0	0	2254
42 10/01 Sthl 6f F				STD	£2254

Total win prize-money £2254

Going (Turf): Sf: 0-2 GS: 0-1 Gd: 0-2 GF: 0-2 Fm: 0-0
Distance: 5f/6f: 1-11 7f-8f: 0-0 9f-13f: 0-0 14f+: 0-0
Track: LH: 1-3 RH: 0-0 Tight: 0-2 Gall: 0-0
Aids: Bl: 0-1 Vi: 0-0 Tstrap: 0-0
Best Rating: 42 10/01 Sthl 6f stand

Got off the mark by the minimum margin on the Southwell Fibresand in October.

True Blade

93 **40**

3-y-o ch f Sabrehill (USA)-Certain Story (Known Fact (USA))
P F I Cole (G A Butler 4/7) The Fairy Story Partnership

Placings:33060500 (5292)
2001: 8^{3}G, 8^{3}F, 8^{0}GS, 7^{6}F, 6^{0}G, 6^{5}GF, 5^{0}GF, 7^{0}S

	Starts	1st	2nd	3rd	Win & Pl
Career Total (Turf)	8	0	0	2	785

Going (Turf): Sf: 0-1 GS: 0-1 Gd: 0-2 GF: 0-2 Fm: 0-2
Distance: 5f/6f: 0-1 7f-8f: 0-5 9f-13f: 0-2 14f+: 0-0
Track: LH: 0-2 RH: 0-0 Tight: 0-0 Gall: 0-0
Aids: Bl: 0-0 Vi: 0-0 Tstrap: 0-1
Best Rating: 63 5/01 Wwck 1m22y good

True Courage

87 **75**

2-y-o b c Machiavellian (USA)-Try To Catch Me (USA) (Shareef Dancer (USA))
B W Hills Maktoum Al Maktoum

Placings:06 (5056)
2001: 6^{0}G, 8^{6}S

	Starts	1st	2nd	3rd	Win & Pl
Career Total (Turf)	2	0	0	0	0

Going (Turf): Sf: 0-1 GS: 0-0 Gd: 0-1 GF: 0-0 Fm: 0-0
Distance: 5f/6f: 0-0 7f-8f: 0-2 9f-13f: 0-0 14f+: 0-0
Track: LH: 0-1 RH: 0-0 Tight: 0-0 Gall: 0-1
Aids: Bl: 0-0 Vi: 0-0 Tstrap: 0-0
Best Rating: 75 10/01 NmkR 1m soft

True Fantasy (USA)

82 **46**

3-y-o b f Seeking The Gold (USA)-Jood (USA) (Nijinsky (CAN))
Sir Michael Stoute Maktoum Al Maktoum

Placings:0 (0810)
2001: 7^{0}S

	Starts	1st	2nd	3rd	Win & Pl
Career Total (Turf)	1	0	0	0	

Going (Turf): Sf: 0-1 GS: 0-0 Gd: 0-0 GF: 0-0 Fm: 0-0
Distance: 5f/6f: 0-0 7f-8f: 0-1 9f-13f: 0-0 14f+: 0-0
Track: LH: 0-0 RH: 0-0 Tight: 0-0 Gall: 0-0
Aids: Bl: 0-0 Vi: 0-0 Tstrap: 0-0

Best Rating: 46 4/01 NmkR 7f soft

True Night

109 **87**

4-y-o b g Night Shift (USA)-Dead Certain (Absalom)
H Candy The Hon Mrs M A Marten

Placings:41-000421313000060 (5142)
2001: 6^{0}S, 7^{0}GF, 7^{0}GF, 8^{4}GF, 7^{2}F, 8^{1}GF, 8^{3}G, 7^{1}GS, 8^{3}GF, 7^{0}GF, 7^{0}G, 7^{0}GF, 7^{0}GS, 7^{6}GF, 9^{0}G

	Starts	1st	2nd	3rd	Win & Pl
Career Total (Turf)	17	3	1	2	26276
90 7/01 Leic 7f9y D(0-80)H				G-S	£7332
83 6/01 Sals 1m C(0-100)H				G-F	£7215
73 8/00 Ling 6f D				G-F	£3016

Total win prize-money £17563

Going (Turf): Sf: 0-1 GS: 1-2 Gd: 0-3 GF: 2-9 Fm: 0-2
Distance: 5f/6f: 1-2 7f-8f: 2-13 9f-13f: 0-2 14f+: 0-0
Track: LH: 0-1 RH: 0-2 Tight: 0-1 Gall: 0-0
Aids: Bl: 0-0 Vi: 0-0 Tstrap: 0-0
Best Rating: 90 7/01 Leic 7f9y gd-sft

A come-from-behind handicapper, he has won at Salisbury and Leicester this season but lost his way after wards. He tends to find trouble in running, but that seems to be how he likes it. Suited by seven furlongs and a mile.

True Note

98(91) (35)**12**

3-y-o b g So Factual (USA)-Singer On The Roof (Chief Singer)
J Hetherton Eureka Racing

Placings:00-005005000000 (5269)
2001: 7^{0}SD, 7^{0}SD, 6^{5}SW, 6^{0}SD, 8^{0}F, 8^{5}F, 9^{0}GF, 8^{0}G, 7^{0}F, 5^{0}G, 11^{0}SD, 10^{0}HY

	Starts	1st	2nd	3rd	Win & Pl
Career Total (Turf)	8	0	0	0	0
Career Total (AW)	6	0	0	0	0

Going (Turf): Sf: 0-2 GS: 0-0 Gd: 0-2 GF: 0-1 Fm: 0-3
Distance: 5f/6f: 0-4 7f-8f: 0-5 9f-13f: 0-5 14f+: 0-0
Track: LH: 0-10 RH: 0-2 Tight: 0-3 Gall: 0-1
Aids: Bl: 0-0 Vi: 0-0 Tstrap: 0-1
Best Rating: 47 5/01 Newc 1m firm

Trump Appeal

90 **48**

3-y-o b g First Trump-Appelania (Star Appeal)
J G Portman Simon Skinner

Placings:060 (3659)
2001: 10^{0}G, 9^{6}GS, 9^{0}GF

	Starts	1st	2nd	3rd	Win & Pl
Career Total (Turf)	3	0	0	0	0

Going (Turf): Sf: 0-0 GS: 0-1 Gd: 0-1 GF: 0-1 Fm: 0-0
Distance: 5f/6f: 0-0 7f-8f: 0-0 9f-13f: 0-3 14f+: 0-0
Track: LH: 0-1 RH: 0-2 Tight: 0-0 Gall: 0-1
Aids: Bl: 0-0 Vi: 0-0 Tstrap: 0-0
Best Rating: 48 8/01 Newb 1m1f gd-fm

Trumpet Major

91 **68**

2-y-o b c First Trump-Trundley Wood (Wassl)
P Mitchell W R Mann

Placings:060 (4301)
2001: 7^{0}GF, 7^{6}GF, 7^{0}GF

	Starts	1st	2nd	3rd	Win & Pl
Career Total (Turf)	3	0	0	0	0

Going (Turf): Sf: 0-0 GS: 0-0 Gd: 0-0 GF: 0-3 Fm: 0-0
Distance: 5f/6f: 0-0 7f-8f: 0-3 9f-13f: 0-0 14f+: 0-0
Track: LH: 0-0 RH: 0-1 Tight: 0-0 Gall: 0-1
Aids: Bl: 0-0 Vi: 0-0 Tstrap: 0-0

Best Rating: 68 7/01 Kemp 7f gd-fm

Trumpington

104(99) (65)**74**

3-y-o ch f First Trump-Brockton Flame (Emarati (USA))
J A R Toller Buckingham Thoroughbreds

Placings:0310401-05605 (5411)
2001: 12^{0}GF, 14^{5}GF, 16^{6}HY, 14^{0}G, 14^{5}SD

	Starts	1st	2nd	3rd	Win & Pl
Career Total (Turf)	11	2	0	1	8005
Career Total (AW)	1	0	0	0	0
74 10/00 Wind 1m2f7y E(0-75)				G-S	£2786
63 7/00 Newb 7f E				G-F	£4446

Total win prize-money £7232

Going (Turf): Sf: 0-1 GS: 1-1 Gd: 0-1 GF: 1-8 Fm: 0-0
Distance: 5f/6f: 0-1 7f-8f: 1-5 9f-13f: 1-2 14f+: 0-4
Track: LH: 0-4 RH: 0-4 Tight: 1-1 Gall: 0-3
Aids: Bl: 0-0 Vi: 0-0 Tstrap: 0-0
Best Rating: 74 7/01 Sand 1m6f gd-fm

A lightly-raced stayer, she is rather a keen sort.

Trushan

91 **58**

3-y-o ch f Anshan-Home Truth (Known Fact (USA))
B W Hills D J Deer

Placings:05 (1494)
2001: 7^{0}GS, 7^{5}GF

	Starts	1st	2nd	3rd	Win & Pl
Career Total (Turf)	2	0	0	0	0

Going (Turf): Sf: 0-0 GS: 0-1 Gd: 0-0 GF: 0-1 Fm: 0-0
Distance: 5f/6f: 0-0 7f-8f: 0-2 9f-13f: 0-0 14f+: 0-0
Track: LH: 0-0 RH: 0-1 Tight: 0-0 Gall: 0-0
Aids: Bl: 0-0 Vi: 0-0 Tstrap: 0-0
Best Rating: 58 5/01 Bevl 7f100y gd-fm

Trust In Paula (USA)

93(79) (29)**45**

3-y-o b f Arazi (USA)-Trust In Dixie (USA) (Dixieland Band (USA))
D Haydn Jones S Hunter

Placings:000-000604 (5081)
2001: 6^{0}SD, 7^{0}SD, 10^{0}GF, 8^{6}GF, 8^{0}GF, 9^{4}S

	Starts	1st	2nd	3rd	Win & Pl
Career Total (Turf)	7	0	0	0	0
Career Total (AW)	2	0	0	0	

Going (Turf): Sf: 0-1 GS: 0-1 Gd: 0-0 GF: 0-5 Fm: 0-0
Distance: 5f/6f: 0-2 7f-8f: 0-3 9f-13f: 0-4 14f+: 0-0
Track: LH: 0-4 RH: 0-1 Tight: 0-3 Gall: 0-1
Aids: Bl: 0-0 Vi: 0-0 Tstrap: 0-0
Best Rating: 45 7/01 Leic 1m9y gd-fm

Trusted Mole (IRE)

103(87) (40)**57**

3-y-o b g Eagle Eyed (USA)-Orient Air (Prince Sabo)
S Kirk (J A Osborne 29/6) Mrs T M Moriarty

Placings:66304400-001240113300400 (5348)
2001: 9^{0}GS, 8^{0}G, 9^{1}G, 10^{2}GF, 10^{4}GF, 10^{0}GF, 10^{1}GF, 9^{1}GF, 9^{3}GF, 9^{3}GF, 12^{0}S, 9^{0}GS, 10^{4}GF, 9^{0}GS, 12^{0}SD

	Starts	1st	2nd	3rd	Win & Pl
Career Total (Turf)	20	3	1	3	11878
Career Total (AW)	3	0	0	0	
64 7/01 Leic 1m1f218yF				G-F	£2968
43 6/01 NmkJ 1m2f E				G-F	£3464
58 5/01 Bevl 1m1f207yF				GD	£2730

Total win prize-money £9163

Going (Turf): Sf: 0-1 GS: 0-3 Gd: 1-5 GF: 2-11 Fm: 0-0
Distance: 5f/6f: 0-3 7f-8f: 0-4 9f-13f: 3-16 14f+: 0-0
Track: LH: 0-12 RH: 3-6 Tight: 0-5 Gall: 1-2

Aids: **Bl: 3-14** Vi: 0-0 Tstrap: 0-0
Best Rating: 64 7/01 Nott 1m1f213y gd-fm

Three times a winner over ten furlongs in sellers and claimers this term, he wears blinkers and acts on fast ground.

Trustthunder

98(102) (63)**67**
3-y-o ch f Selkirk (USA)-Royal Cat (Royal Academy (USA))
N P Littmoden Tallulah Racing

Placings:022010-00035050 **(4736)**
2001: 7^{0}GS, 6^{0}GF, 6^{0}F, 7^{3}F, 7^{5}GS, 6^{0}GF, 7^{5}SD, 6^{0}F, 7^{2}SD

	Starts	1st	2nd	3rd	Win & Pl
Career Total (Turf)	13	1	2	1	8485
Career Total (AW)	1	0	0	0	0

74 9/00 Ling 6f D SFT £3484
Total win prize-money £3484

Going (Turf): Sf: 1-2 GS: 0-2 Gd: 0-0 GF: 0-6 Fm: 0-3
Distance: **5f/6f: 1-4** 7f-8f: 0-10 9f-13f: 0-0 14f+: 0-0
Track : LH: 0-3 RH: 0-1 Tight: 0-2 Gall: 0-1
Aids: Bl: 0-0 Vi: 0-0 Tstrap: 0-0
Best Rating: 67 7/01 Ling 7f firm

Try Paris (IRE)

84(84) (34)**17**
5-y-o b g Paris House-Try My Rosie (Try My Best (USA))
Mrs L C Jewell (H J Collingridge 30/5) The Headquarters Partnership Ii

Placings:6060/000060/000440-000000 **(4472)**
2001: 12^{0}SD, 11^{0}GF, 9^{0}G, 10^{0}GF, 9^{0}GF, 9^{0}GF

	Starts	1st	2nd	3rd	Win & Pl
Career Total (Turf)	19	0	0	0	0
Career Total (AW)	3	0	0	0	0

Going (Turf): Sf: 0-3 GS: 0-1 Gd: 0-4 GF: 0-7 Fm: 0-1
Distance: 5f/6f: 0-8 7f-8f: 0-1 9f-13f: 0-13 14f+: 0-0
Track : LH: 0-13 RH: 0-2 Tight: 0-4 Gall: 0-2
Aids: Bl: 0-0 Vi: 0-14 Tstrap: 0-0
Best Rating: 17 8/01 Brig 1m1f209y gd-fm

Tryfan

87(73) (30)**67**
2-y-o b c Distant Relative-Sister Sal (Bairn (USA))
A Bailey C M Martin

Placings:40 **(5086)**
2001: 8^{4}GF, 7^{0}GS, 7^{0}SD

	Starts	1st	2nd	3rd	Win & Pl
Career Total (Turf)	2	0	0	0	332

Going (Turf): Sf: 0-0 GS: 0-1 Gd: 0-0 GF: 0-1 Fm: 0-0
Distance: 5f/6f: 0-0 7f-8f: 0-2 9f-13f: 0-0 14f+: 0-0
Track : LH: 0-1 RH: 0-0 Tight: 0-0 Gall: 0-0
Aids: Bl: 0-0 Vi: 0-0 Tstrap: 0-0
Best Rating: 67 9/01 Ayr 1m gd-fm

Trysull Dream (IRE)

70 **37**
2-y-o b f Mujadil (USA)-Emma's Whisper (Kind Of Hush)
C A Dwyer Glynn Darrall & I Dodd

Placings:050 **(2215)**
2001: 6^{0}GS, 5^{5}GF, 5^{0}G

	Starts	1st	2nd	3rd	Win & Pl
Career Total (Turf)	3	0	0	0	0

Going (Turf): Sf: 0-0 GS: 0-1 Gd: 0-1 GF: 0-1 Fm: 0-0
Distance: 5f/6f: 0-3 7f-8f: 0-0 9f-13f: 0-0 14f+: 0-0
Track : LH: 0-0 RH: 0-0 Tight: 0-0 Gall: 0-0
Aids: Bl: 0-0 Vi: 0-0 Tstrap: 0-0
Best Rating: 37 6/01 Yarm 5f43y gd-fm

Tsunami

(102)
5-y-o b m Beveled (USA)-Alvecote Lady (Touching Wood (USA))
B D Leavy (P D Evans 20/6) K J Condliffe

Placings:0004/436660464/0660305-6 **(0080)**
2001: 11^{6}SD

	Starts	1st	2nd	3rd	Win & Pl
Career Total (Turf)	14	0	0	1	1831
Career Total (AW)	7	0	0	1	433

Going (Turf): Sf: 0-4 GS: 0-1 Gd: 0-7 GF: 0-1 Fm: 0-1
Distance: 5f/6f: 0-0 7f-8f: 0-13 9f-13f: 0-7 14f+: 0-1
Track : LH: 0-10 RH: 0-5 Tight: 0-4 Gall: 0-3
Aids: Bl: 0-0 Vi: 0-0 Tstrap: 0-0
Best Rating: 25 1/01 Sthl 1m3f stand

Tswalu

(79) (15)**57**
4-y-o b f Cosmonaut-Madam Taylor (Free State)
M Mullineaux Michael Mullineaux

Placings:306/0-00 **(0255)**
2001: 12^{0}SD, 12^{0}SD

	Starts	1st	2nd	3rd	Win & Pl
Career Total (Turf)	4	0	0	1	518
Career Total (AW)	2	0	0	0	

Going (Turf): Sf: 0-3 GS: 0-0 Gd: 0-1 GF: 0-0 Fm: 0-0
Distance: 5f/6f: 0-0 7f-8f: 0-2 9f-13f: 0-4 14f+: 0-0
Track : LH: 0-5 RH: 0-1 Tight: 0-2 Gall: 0-0
Aids: Bl: 0-0 Vi: 0-0 Tstrap: 0-0
Best Rating: 15 2/01 Wolv 1m4f stand

Tucker Fence

101(96) (73)**72**
2-y-o br g So Factual (USA)-Daisy Topper (Top Ville)
A Berry Men Behaving Badly

Placings:00321061240**2**000 **(5193)**
2001: 5^{0}GF, 5^{0}GF, 5^{3}GF, 7^{2}GF, 6^{1}GF, 6^{0}GF, 6^{6}GF, 6^{1}G, 6^{2}GF, 5^{4}G, 6^{0}G, 6^{2}SW, 6^{0}G, 7^{0}S, 6^{0}SD

	Starts	1st	2nd	3rd	Win & Pl
Career Total (Turf)	13	2	2	1	12351
Career Total (AW)	2	0	1	0	804

69 8/01 Ches 6f18y D H GD £3623
73 6/01 Newc 6f E G-F £5148
Total win prize-money £8772

Going (Turf): Sf: 0-1 GS: 0-0 **Gd: 1-4 GF: 1-8** Fm: 0-0
Distance: 5f/6f: 1-12 7f-8f: 1-3 9f-13f: 0-0 14f+: 0-0
Track : **LH: 1-7** RH: 0-0 **Tight: 1-6** Gall: 0-0
Aids: Bl: 0-1 **Vi: 1-3** Tstrap: 0-0
Best Rating: 73 9/01 Wolv 6f slow

A 6,000 gns yearling, has won a Newcastle seller and had visor removed for his victory in a Chester nursery. Best over six furlongs on a sound surface.

Tudor Wood

99 **94?**
2-y-o b c Royal Applause-Silent Indulgence (USA) (Woodman (USA))
D J S Cosgrove Paul V Jackson

Placings:2050 **(5343)**
2001: 5^{2}F, 5^{0}G, 7^{5}G, 6^{0}GS

	Starts	1st	2nd	3rd	Win & Pl
Career Total (Turf)	4	0	1	0	1999

Going (Turf): Sf: 0-0 GS: 0-1 Gd: 0-2 GF: 0-0 Fm: 0-1
Distance: 5f/6f: 0-3 7f-8f: 0-1 9f-13f: 0-0 14f+: 0-0
Track : LH: 0-0 RH: 0-0 Tight: 0-0 Gall: 0-0
Aids: Bl: 0-0 Vi: 0-0 Tstrap: 0-0
Best Rating: 94 10/01 NmkR 7f good

A half-brother to the six-furlong two-year-old Listed winner In The Woods, made a promising debut, but hurt his back next time when disappointing in a similar event. Showed ability in Listed company before failing in a maiden on easy ground.

Tufamore (USA)

77(102) (49)**38**
5-y-o ch g Mt. Livermore (USA)-Tufa (Warning)
E W Tuer E Tuer

Placings:44453005/421053350-00 **(1997)**
2001: 14^{0}GF, 14^{0}SD

	Starts	1st	2nd	3rd	Win & Pl
Career Total (Turf)	8	0	0	1	618
Career Total (AW)	11	1	1	2	4403

54 1/00 Wolv 1m100y E(0-70)H STD £2802
Total win prize-money £2803

Going (Turf): Sf: 0-0 GS: 0-1 Gd: 0-1 GF: 0-6 Fm: 0-0
Distance: 5f/6f: 0-1 7f-8f: 0-3 **9f-13f: 1-13** 14f+: 0-2
Track : **LH: 1-14** RH: 0-4 **Tight: 1-16** Gall: 0-0
Aids: Bl: 0-3 **Vi: 1-8** Tstrap: 0-0
Best Rating: 28 5/01 Muss 1m6f gd-fm

Tufty Hopper

100(104) (58)**53**
4-y-o b g Rock Hopper-Melancolia (Legend Of France (USA))
P Howling Michael Tufts

Placings:0/**644224**33220453326**623412-44123**000500436 **(5188)**
2001: 13^{4}SD, 12^{4}SD, 12^{1}SD, 12^{2}SW, 12^{3}SD, 14^{0}GF, 10^{0}GF, 11^{0}GF, 14^{5}GS, 11^{0}G, 14^{0}G, 12^{4}SD, 14^{3}SD, 15^{6}GS

	Starts	1st	2nd	3rd	Win & Pl
Career Total (Turf)	22	0	4	4	7237
Career Total (AW)	17	2	5	3	9410

58 2/01 Wolv 1m4f F(0-60)H STD £2331
56 12/00 Wolv 1m4f D STD £2695
Total win prize-money £5026

Going (Turf): Sf: 0-1 GS: 0-3 Gd: 0-7 GF: 0-9 Fm: 0-2
Distance: 5f/6f: 0-0 7f-8f: 0-0 **9f-13f: 2-26** 14f+: 0-13
Track : **LH: 2-33** RH: 0-4 **Tight: 2-31** Gall: 0-2
Aids: Bl: 0-1 Vi: 0-1 Tstrap: 0-0
Best Rating: 58 2/01 Wolv 1m4f slow

He is slow and tends to run on past beaten horses at the end of his races. Twelve furlongs on Fibresand look his ideal conditions.

Tui

98
6-y-o b m Tina's Pet-Curious Feeling (Nishapour (FR))
P Bowen Dragon Racing

Placings:0060/0003221551560000/00006000/515403-05 **(3409)**
2001: 14^{0}GF, 12^{5}GF

	Starts	1st	2nd	3rd	Win & Pl
Career Total (Turf)	29	3	2	2	13080
Career Total (AW)	6	0	0	0	

34 5/00 Brig 1m3f196yE(0-70)H FRM £2766
56 8/98 NmkJ 1m4f E(0-70)H G-F £4854
47 7/98 Bevl 1m1f207yE(0-70)H GD £2901
Total win prize-money £10522

Going (Turf): Sf: 0-2 GS: 0-6 **Gd: 1-7 GF: 1-12 Fm: 1-2**
Distance: 5f/6f: 0-4 7f-8f: 0-2 **9f-13f: 3-25** 14f+: 0-4
Track : LH: 1-16 **RH: 2-11** Tight: 0-11 **Gall: 1-4**
Aids: Bl: 0-0 Vi: 0-0 Tstrap: 0-0
Best Rating: 32 7/01 Chep 1m4f23y gd-fm

Tuigamala

(102) (38)
10-y-o b g Welsh Captain-Nelliellamay (Super Splash (USA))
R Ingram Roger Ingram

Placings:00006060/00100**010/445414400/03200**006/0/0563-35412504 **(0719)**

2001: 8^{3}SD, 10^{5}SD, 8^{4}SD, 9^{1}SD, 10^{2}SD, 10^{5}SW, 10^{0}SD, 10^{4}SD

	Starts	1st	2nd	3rd	Win & Pl
Career Total (Turf)	18	1	0	0	3124
Career Total (AW)	28	3	2	3	9818

38	2/01	Wolv	1m1f79y	F(0-60)H	STD	£1757
58	2/96	Ling	1m	F(0-65)H	STD	£2683
57	11/95	Ling	7f	F(0-55)	STD	£2338
31	8/95	Brig	6f209y	F(0-60)H	FRM	£3123

Total win prize-money £9903

Going (Turf): Sf: 0-1 GS: 0-1 Gd: 0-7 GF: 0-2 **Fm: 1-7**
Distance: 5f/6f: 0-1 **7f-8f: 3-22** 9f-13f: 1-23 14f+: 0-0
Track : **LH: 4-35** RH: 0-9 **Tight: 3-34** Gall: 0-0
Aids: Bl: 0-0 Vi: 0-0 Tstrap: 0-0
Best Rating: 38 2/01 Wolv 1m1f79y stand

Tumbleweed Charm (IRE)

97 **86**

2-y-o b c Zafonic (USA)-Vienna Charm (IRE) (Sadler's Wells (USA))
B J Meehan The Eighth Tumbleweed Partnership

Placings:6100 **(4656)**
2001: 6^{6}GF, 6^{1}GF, 6^{0}GS, 7^{0}GF

	Starts	1st	2nd	3rd	Win & Pl
Career Total (Turf)	4	1	0	0	4420
83 7/01 Newb 6f8y	D			G-F	£4420

Total win prize-money £4420

Going (Turf): Sf: 0-0 GS: 0-1 Gd: 0-0 **GF: 1-3** Fm: 0-0
Distance: 5f/6f: 0-1 **7f-8f: 1-3** 9f-13f: 0-0 14f+: 0-0
Track : LH: 0-0 RH: 0-0 Tight: 0-0 Gall: 0-0
Aids: Bl: 0-0 Vi: 0-0 Tstrap: 0-0
Best Rating: 86 9/01 Donc 7f gd-fm

Created a good impression when winning at Newbury on his second start, but was down the field in the Prix Morny and may not have handled the softer ground.

Tumbleweed Ridge

105 (74)**102**

8-y-o ch h Indian Ridge-Billie Blue (Ballad Rock)
B J Meehan The Tumbleweed Partnership

Placings:241221/50003/360220130040/16100004/0321 15210/231304P-03445130 **(4831)**
2001: 7^{0}G, 7^{3}G, 7^{4}G, 7^{4}GF, 7^{5}GF, 7^{1}GF, 7^{3}GS, 7^{0}GF

	Starts	1st	2nd	3rd	Win & Pl
Career Total (Turf)	54	10	8	8	256591
Career Total (AW)	1	0	0	0	0

66	8/01	Chep	7f16y	C	G-F	£6046
113	6/00	Leop	7f		GD	£22750
118	9/99	Epsm	7f	A	GD	£14330
113	6/99	Lonc	7f		GD	£23681
111	6/99	Leop	7f		GD	£22750
109	6/98	Leop	7f		Y-S	£19500
106	4/98	NmkR	7f	B(0-105)H	SFT	£9010
101	7/97	NmkJ	7f	B(0-105)H	G-F	£23200
103	10/95	Newb	7f64y	A	G-S	£21840
84	7/95	Ling	5f	D	G-F	£3682

Total win prize-money £166789

Going (Turf): Sf: 1-2 GS: 1-6 **Gd: 4-23** GF: 3-20 Fm: 0-1
Distance: 5f/6f: 1-8 **7f-8f: 9-47** 9f-13f: 0-0 14f+: 0-0
Track : **LH: 5-17** RH: 1-6 Tight: 1-3 Gall: 1-8
Aids: Bl: 4-30 Vi: 0-0 Tstrap: 4-19
Best Rating: 106 5/01 NmkR 7f good

A somewhat quirky character, he is a solid Group Three performer and a seven-furlong specialist. Often blinkered and tongue-tied, he likes to make the running, and goes particularly well at Leopardstown, where he has won the Ballycorus Stakes three times. His win at Chepstow in August was his first for 15 months.

Tumbleweed River (IRE)

(94) (56)**76**

5-y-o ch g Thatching-Daphne Indica (IRE) (Ballad Rock)
B J Meehan The Fourth Tumbleweed Partnership

Placings:2/4105/000200-0P **(0959)**
2001: 7^{0}SD, 7^{P}HY

	Starts	1st	2nd	3rd	Win & Pl
Career Total (Turf)	12	1	2	0	6816
Career Total (AW)	1	0	0	0	
77 9/99 Hayd 7f30y	D			SFT	£4188

Total win prize-money £4189

Going (Turf): Sf: 1-6 GS: 0-3 Gd: 0-1 GF: 0-2 Fm: 0-0
Distance: 5f/6f: 0-1 **7f-8f: 1-11** 9f-13f: 0-1 14f+: 0-0
Track : **LH: 1-6** RH: 0-2 Tight: 0-1 Gall: 0-2
Aids: Bl: 0-1 Vi: 0-0 Tstrap: 0-0
Best Rating: 56 4/01 Ling 7f stand

Tumbleweed Tenor (IRE)

(95) (80)**70**

3-y-o b g Mujadil (USA)-Princess Carmen (IRE) (Arokar (FR))
B J Meehan The Seventh Tumbleweed Partnership

Placings:52031-0 **(0755)**
2001: 6^{0}SW

	Starts	1st	2nd	3rd	Win & Pl
Career Total (Turf)	4	0	1	1	1444
Career Total (AW)	2	1	0	0	1750
80 10/00 Wolv 6f	F			STD	£1750

Total win prize-money £1750

Going (Turf): Sf: 0-0 GS: 0-1 Gd: 0-1 GF: 0-1 Fm: 0-1
Distance: **5f/6f: 1-5** 7f-8f: 0-1 9f-13f: 0-0 14f+: 0-0
Track : **LH: 1-3** RH: 0-1 **Tight: 1-1** Gall: 0-1
Aids: Bl: 0-0 Vi: 0-0 Tstrap: 0-0
Best Rating: 26 4/01 Sthl 6f slow

Tunnel Of Love

94 **54**

3-y-o ch f Mark Of Esteem (IRE)-La Dama Bonita (USA) (El Gran Senor (USA))
D W P Arbuthnot Christopher Wright

Placings:5 **(4842)**
2001: 8^{5}G

	Starts	1st	2nd	3rd	Win & Pl
Career Total (Turf)	1	0	0	0	0

Going (Turf): Sf: 0-0 GS: 0-0 Gd: 0-1 GF: 0-0 Fm: 0-0
Distance: 5f/6f: 0-0 7f-8f: 0-0 9f-13f: 0-1 14f+: 0-0
Track : LH: 0-1 RH: 0-0 Tight: 0-0 Gall: 0-0
Aids: Bl: 0-0 Vi: 0-0 Tstrap: 0-0
Best Rating: 54 9/01 Nott 1m54y good

Tunstall (USA)

96 **78**

2-y-o b c Bahri (USA)-Princess West (GER) (Gone West (USA))
L M Cumani M J Dawson

Placings:5400 **(5368)**
2001: 7^{5}GS, 8^{4}G, 7^{0}G, 8^{0}GS

	Starts	1st	2nd	3rd	Win & Pl
Career Total (Turf)	4	0	0	0	579

Going (Turf): Sf: 0-0 GS: 0-2 Gd: 0-2 GF: 0-0 Fm: 0-0
Distance: 5f/6f: 0-0 7f-8f: 0-4 9f-13f: 0-0 14f+: 0-0
Track : LH: 0-0 RH: 0-0 Tight: 0-0 Gall: 0-0
Aids: Bl: 0-0 Vi: 0-0 Tstrap: 0-0
Best Rating: 78 8/01 NmkJ 1m good

Tupgill Centurion

86(58) **36**

3-y-o b g Emperor Jones (USA)-Elisa War (Warning)
S E Kettlewell The Tupgill Partnership

Placings:450-000 **(3461)**
2001: 10^{0}GF, 8^{0}F, 11^{0}F

	Starts	1st	2nd	3rd	Win & Pl
Career Total (Turf)	5	0	0	0	264
Career Total (AW)	1	0	0	0	

Going (Turf): Sf: 0-0 GS: 0-0 Gd: 0-0 GF: 0-3 Fm: 0-2
Distance: 5f/6f: 0-0 7f-8f: 0-4 9f-13f: 0-2 14f+: 0-0
Track : LH: 0-3 RH: 0-3 Tight: 0-2 Gall: 0-2
Aids: Bl: 0-0 Vi: 0-0 Tstrap: 0-0
Best Rating: 24 7/01 Newc 1m firm

Tupgill Flight (IRE)

70(76) (26)**37**

3-y-o b f Be My Chief (USA)-Wing Partner (IRE) (In The Wings)
S E Kettlewell The Tupgill Partnership

Placings:00005-0 **(2055)**
2001: 10^{0}GF

	Starts	1st	2nd	3rd	Win & Pl
Career Total (Turf)	5	0	0	0	
Career Total (AW)	1	0	0	0	0

Going (Turf): Sf: 0-1 GS: 0-1 Gd: 0-1 GF: 0-2 Fm: 0-0
Distance: 5f/6f: 0-2 7f-8f: 0-3 9f-13f: 0-1 14f+: 0-0
Track : LH: 0-4 RH: 0-1 Tight: 0-2 Gall: 0-0
Aids: Bl: 0-0 Vi: 0-0 Tstrap: 0-0
Best Rating: 24 7/01 Newc 1m firm

Tupgill Tipple

(85) (19)**35**

3-y-o b f Emperor Jones (USA)-Highest Baby (FR) (Highest Honor (FR))
Patrick Carey (S E Kettlewell 16/1) David Hogan

Placings:2340050-00000000 **(5655a)**
2001: 7^{0}SD, 8^{0}SD, 8^{0}SW, 12^{0}GY, 9^{0}GF, 6^{0}GF, 9^{0}G, 10^{0}YS

	Starts	1st	2nd	3rd	Win & Pl
Career Total (Turf)	9	0	0	1	352
Career Total (AW)	6	0	1	0	646

Going (Turf): Sf: 0-0 GS: 0-1 Gd: 0-2 GF: 0-4 Fm: 0-0
Distance: 5f/6f: 0-8 7f-8f: 0-2 9f-13f: 0-5 14f+: 0-0
Track : LH: 0-4 RH: 0-0 Tight: 0-2 Gall: 0-0
Aids: Bl: 0-0 Vi: 0-2 Tstrap: 0-0
Best Rating: 35 9/01 Gowr 1m1f100y gd-fm

Tupgill Turbo

85 **52d**

3-y-o ch g Rudimentary (USA)-Persian Alexandra (Persian Bold)
S E Kettlewell The Tupgill Partnership

Placings:35-0000 **(2845)**
2001: 7^{0}S, 8^{0}F, 8^{0}GF, 8^{0}F

	Starts	1st	2nd	3rd	Win & Pl
Career Total (Turf)	6	0	0	1	1741

Going (Turf): Sf: 0-1 GS: 0-0 Gd: 0-1 GF: 0-1 Fm: 0-2
Distance: 5f/6f: 0-0 7f-8f: 0-5 9f-13f: 0-0 14f+: 0-0
Track : LH: 0-3 RH: 0-1 Tight: 0-1 Gall: 0-3
Aids: Bl: 0-0 Vi: 0-0 Tstrap: 0-0
Best Rating: 23 7/01 Newc 1m firm

Tuppence Ha'Penny

68 **62**

2-y-o gr f Never So Bold-Mummy's Chick (Mummy's Pet)
G G Margarson Mrs Patricia J Williams

Placings:00 **(5666)**
2001: 7^{0}GS, 6^{0}HY

	Starts	1st	2nd	3rd	Win & Pl
Career Total (Turf)	2	0	0	0	

Going (Turf): Sf: 0-1 GS: 0-1 Gd: 0-0 GF: 0-0 Fm: 0-0
Distance: 5f/6f: 0-1 7f-8f: 0-1 9f-13f: 0-0 14f+: 0-0
Track : LH: 0-0 RH: 0-0 Tight: 0-0 Gall: 0-0
Aids: Bl: 0-0 Vi: 0-0 Tstrap: 0-0
Best Rating: 62 11/01 Wind 6f heavy

Turaath (IRE)

82(94) (63)**88**

5-y-o b g Sadler's Wells (USA)-Diamond Field (USA) (Mr Prospector (USA))
G M McCourt Mrs Kathy Stuart

Placings:43/1/0020-00 (1144)
2001: 9^{0}SD, 12^{0}G

	Starts	1st	2nd	3rd	Win & Pl
Career Total (Turf)	8	1	1	1	8834
Career Total (AW)	1	0	0	0	

84 3/99 Donc 1m2f60y D G-S £4201
Total win prize-money £4202

Going (Turf): Sf: 0-2 **GS: 1-2** Gd: 0-4 GF: 0-0 Fm: 0-0
Distance: 5f/6f: 0-0 7f-8f: 0-2 **9f-13f: 1-7** 14f+: 0-0
Track : **LH: 1-4** RH: 0-3 Tight: 0-2 **Gall: 1-5**
Aids: Bl: 0-0 Vi: 0-0 Tstrap: 0-0
Best Rating: 63 3/01 Wolv 1m1f79y stand

Bolted up in a Doncaster maiden in March of 1999, but lightly-raced subsequently. Seems suited by soft ground and front-running tactics.

Turbo (IRE)

102 **80**

2-y-o b c Piccolo-By Arrangement (IRE) (Bold Arrangement)
G B Balding Peter Richardson

Placings:0231403360 (5496)
2001: 5^{0}GF, 6^{2}G, 6^{3}GF, 7^{1}GS, 7^{4}GF, 6^{0}G, 7^{3}HY, 7^{3}S, 7^{6}S, 7^{0}HY

	Starts	1st	2nd	3rd	Win & Pl
Career Total (Turf)	10	1	1	3	7470

92 7/01 Wwck 7f26y E G-S £2891
Total win prize-money £2891

Going (Turf): Sf: 0-4 **GS: 1-1** Gd: 0-2 GF: 0-3 Fm: 0-0
Distance: 5f/6f: 0-3 **7f-8f: 1-7** 9f-13f: 0-0 14f+: 0-0
Track : LH: 0-5 RH: 0-0 Tight: 0-2 Gall: 0-2
Aids: Bl: 0-0 **Vi: 1-3** Tstrap: 0-0
Best Rating: 92 7/01 Wwck 7f26y gd-sft

Finally got off the mark on his fourth attempt in a poor event at Warwick. Has shown a tendency to hang left-handed, and was visored for the first time at Warwick.

Turibius

100 **70**

2-y-o b g Puissance-Compact Disc (IRE) (Royal Academy (USA))
T E Powell (B J Meehan 18/6) Vogue Development Company (kent) Ltd

Placings:01200440 (4668)
2001: 6^{0}GF, 6^{1}G, 5^{2}GF, 5^{0}GF, 5^{0}G, 5^{4}F, 5^{4}G, 6^{0}GF

	Starts	1st	2nd	3rd	Win & Pl
Career Total (Turf)	8	1	1	0	3427

56 6/01 Wind 6f G GD £1949
Total win prize-money £1950

Going (Turf): Sf: 0-0 GS: 0-0 **Gd: 1-3** GF: 0-4 Fm: 0-1
Distance: **5f/6f: 1-8** 7f-8f: 0-0 9f-13f: 0-0 14f+: 0-0
Track : LH: 0-0 RH: 0-1 Tight: 0-0 Gall: 0-1
Aids: Bl: 0-0 Vi: 0-3 Tstrap: 0-0
Best Rating: 78 7/01 Wind 5f10y gd-fm

Dam won over seven furlongs at two, and is out of a half-sister to high-class juvenile Greenland Park and Red Sunset. Flashed tail under pressure when winning seller at Windsor in June, but looked game went going down by half a length to Anima Mundi at the same course in July.

Turku

106 **89**

3-y-o b c Polar Falcon (USA)-Princess Zepoli (Persepolis (FR))
M Johnston J R Good

Placings:132-01040202000 (5366)
2001: 8^{0}GF, 8^{1}GF, 7^{0}F, 7^{4}G, 8^{0}GS, 8^{2}G, 9^{0}GS, 8^{2}G, 8^{0}G, 8^{0}GF, 8^{0}GS

	Starts	1st	2nd	3rd	Win & Pl
Career Total (Turf)	14	2	3	1	21313

92 6/01 Ripn 1m C(0-90)H G-F £7572
80 9/00 Hayd 7f30y D HVY £4013
Total win prize-money £11587

Going (Turf): Sf: 1-3 GS: 0-3 Gd: 0-4 **GF: 1-3** Fm: 0-1
Distance: 5f/6f: 0-0 **7f-8f: 2-10** 9f-13f: 0-4 14f+: 0-0
Track : LH: 1-7 RH: 1-3 **Tight: 1-3** Gall: 0-2
Aids: Bl: 0-0 Vi: 0-0 Tstrap: 0-0
Best Rating: 92 6/01 Ripn 1m gd-fm

A winner on good to firm at Ripon over a mile in June. Fair efforts in defeat since. Usually races prominently.

Turn Of A Century

106 **77+**

3-y-o b f Halling (USA)-Colorspin (FR) (High Top)
L M Cumani Helena Springfield Ltd

Placings:210 (5226)
2001: 10^{2}S, 12^{1}G, 11^{0}S

	Starts	1st	2nd	3rd	Win & Pl
Career Total (Turf)	3	1	1	0	6117

77 8/01 NmkJ 1m4f D GD £4797
Total win prize-money £4797

Going (Turf): Sf: 0-2 GS: 0-0 **Gd: 1-1** GF: 0-0 Fm: 0-0
Distance: 5f/6f: 0-0 7f-8f: 0-0 **9f-13f: 1-3** 14f+: 0-0
Track : LH: 0-2 **RH: 1-1** Tight: 0-0 **Gall: 1-2**
Aids: Bl: 0-0 Vi: 0-0 Tstrap: 0-0
Best Rating: 77 8/01 NmkJ 1m4f good

Landed a Newmarket maiden on her second start. She stays well and appreciates cut in the ground.

Turn To Blue

82 **43**

2-y-o b c Bluegrass Prince (IRE)-Alvecote Lady (Touching Wood (USA))
J C Fox Lord Mutton Racing Partnership

Placings:0 (2541)
2001: 6^{0}GF

	Starts	1st	2nd	3rd	Win & Pl
Career Total (Turf)	1	0	0	0	

Going (Turf): Sf: 0-0 GS: 0-0 Gd: 0-0 GF: 0-1 Fm: 0-0
Distance: 5f/6f: 0-0 7f-8f: 0-1 9f-13f: 0-0 14f+: 0-0
Track : LH: 0-0 RH: 0-0 Tight: 0-0 Gall: 0-0
Aids: Bl: 0-0 Vi: 0-0 Tstrap: 0-0
Best Rating: 43 6/01 Sals 6f212y gd-fm

Turned Out Well

80(99) (41)**49**

4-y-o b g Robellino (USA)-In The Shade (Bustino)
P C Haslam Middleham Park Racing Xviii

Placings:000/55134-012 (1585)
2001: 17^{0}HY, 16^{1}G, 14^{2}SD

	Starts	1st	2nd	3rd	Win & Pl
Career Total (Turf)	8	2	0	1	7394
Career Total (AW)	3	0	1	0	694

45 5/01 Bevl 2m35y E(0-75)H GD £3885
44 7/00 Bevl 2m35y F(0-65)H G-F £3107
Total win prize-money £6992

Going (Turf): Sf: 0-1 GS: 0-3 **Gd: 1-2 GF: 1-2** Fm: 0-0
Distance: 5f/6f: 0-2 7f-8f: 0-2 9f-13f: 0-1 **14f+: 2-6**
Track : LH: 0-8 **RH: 2-2 Tight: 2-3** Gall: 0-0
Aids: Bl: 0-0 Vi: 0-0 Tstrap: 0-0
Best Rating: 45 5/01 Bevl 2m35y good

Turning The Tide

69(39) **44**

2-y-o b c Lugana Beach-Robert's Daughter (Robellino (USA))
J M Bradley Mrs A M Johnson

Placings:050 (4729)
2001: 5^{0}SW, 5^{5}F, 6^{0}GF

	Starts	1st	2nd	3rd	Win & Pl
Career Total (Turf)	2	0	0	0	0
Career Total (AW)	1	0	0	0	

Going (Turf): Sf: 0-0 GS: 0-0 Gd: 0-0 GF: 0-1 Fm: 0-1
Distance: 5f/6f: 0-2 7f-8f: 0-1 9f-13f: 0-0 14f+: 0-0
Track : LH: 0-0 RH: 0-0 Tight: 0-0 Gall: 0-0
Aids: Bl: 0-0 Vi: 0-0 Tstrap: 0-0
Best Rating: 44 9/01 Wwck 6f21y gd-fm

Turnpole (IRE)

109 **80**

10-y-o br g Satco (FR)-Mountain Chase (Mount Hagen (FR))
Mrs M Reveley Mr & Mrs W J Williams

Placings:505212/50/1212021/1204/0641400-21010 (5263)
2001: 13^{2}GF, 16^{1}G, 16^{0}G, 17^{1}F, 13^{0}GS

	Starts	1st	2nd	3rd	Win & Pl
Career Total (Turf)	31	8	7	0	138853

28 9/01 Pont 2m1f216yC FRM £6148
80 6/01 Hayd 2m45y C(0-100)H GD £7182
78 7/00 NmkJ 2m24y C(0-95)H GD £7046
87 3/98 Donc 2m2f C(0-90)H GD £7570
82 10/97 NmkR 2m2f B H GD £73350
78 5/97 York 1m5f194yC(0-90)H GD £7830
69 4/97 Haml 1m4f17y F G-S £2458
66 8/95 Rdcr 1m3f E(0-70)H FRM £3579
Total win prize-money £115164

Going (Turf): Sf: 0-1 GS: 1-9 **Gd: 5-12** GF: 0-6 Fm: 2-3
Distance: 5f/6f: 0-0 7f-8f: 0-0 9f-13f: 2-7 **14f+: 6-24**
Track : **LH: 5-22** RH: 3-9 Tight: 2-6 **Gall: 4-18**
Aids: Bl: 0-0 Vi: 0-0 Tstrap: 0-0
Best Rating: 80 6/01 Hayd 2m45y good

Despite getting on in years, he still retains his enthusiasm for the game, as he showed at Pontefract in September when landing his second win of the year. Needs two miles on a sound surface these days.

Turtle Love (IRE)

93(87) (60)**58**

2-y-o b f Turtle Island (IRE)-A Little Loving (He Loves Me)
Miss V Haigh Tune Pack Produce Ltd

Placings:0301202 (4010)
2001: 6^{0}F, 6^{3}SD, 7^{0}GF, 7^{1}SD, 7^{2}SD, 7^{0}SD, 7^{2}G

	Starts	1st	2nd	3rd	Win & Pl
Career Total (Turf)	3	0	1	0	564
Career Total (AW)	4	1	1	1	2698

60 6/01 Sthl 7f G STD £1883
Total win prize-money £1883

Going (Turf): Sf: 0-0 GS: 0-0 Gd: 0-1 GF: 0-1 Fm: 0-1
Distance: 5f/6f: 0-2 **7f-8f: 1-5** 9f-13f: 0-0 14f+: 0-0
Track : **LH: 1-5** RH: 0-0 Tight: 0-2 Gall: 0-0
Aids: Bl: 0-0 Vi: 0-0 Tstrap: 0-0
Best Rating: 60 7/01 Sthl 7f stand

A plating-class All-Weather regular, her best effort to date was landing a seller at Southwell in June 2001 over seven furlongs.

Turtle Recall (IRE)

75 **37**

2-y-o b c Turtle Island (IRE)-Nora Yo Ya (Ahonoora)

P W Harris Circle Of Good Fortune

Placings:00 **(5262)**

2001: 8^{0}G, 7^{0}GS

	Starts	1st	2nd	3rd	Win & Pl
Career Total (Turf)	2	0	0	0	

Going (Turf): Sf: 0-0 GS: 0-1 Gd: 0-1 GF: 0-0 Fm: 0-0
Distance: 5f/6f: 0-0 7f-8f: 0-1 9f-13f: 0-1 14f+: 0-0
Track : LH: 0-2 RH: 0-0 Tight: 0-0 Gall: 0-1
Aids: Bl: 0-0 Vi: 0-0 Tstrap: 0-0
Best Rating: 37 9/01 Nott 1m54y good

Turtle Valley (IRE)

110(92) (82)**93d**

5-y-o b g Turtle Island (IRE)-Primrose Valley (Mill Reef (USA))

S Dow Cazanove Clear Height Racing

Placings:062064/5026211100540/00023-160052 **(5683)**

2001: 14^{1}HY, 16^{6}S, 16^{0}GS, 18^{0}GS, 16^{5}GS, 14^{2}S

	Starts	1st	2nd	3rd	Win & Pl
Career Total (Turf)	28	4	5	1	43848
Career Total (AW)	2	0	0	0	0

90	4/01	Nott	1m6f15y	C	HVY	£6438
92	6/99	Sals	1m6f15y	C(0-95)H	GD	£6112
91	5/99	Newb	1m4f5y	C(0-95)H	SFT	£9528
87	5/99	York	1m5f194yB		G-S	£9507

Total win prize-money £31585

Going (Turf): Sf: 2-9 GS: 1-6 Gd: 1-7 GF: 0-5 Fm: 0-0
Distance: 5f/6f: 0-1 7f-8f: 0-6 9f-13f: 1-7 **14f+: 3-16**
Track : LH: 3-12 RH: 1-13 Tight: 1-7 **Gall: 2-6**
Aids: Bl: 0-1 Vi: 0-0 Tstrap: 0-0
Best Rating: 93 4/01 Kemp 2m soft

Picked up a hat-trick of wins in 1999, but it was April 2001 before he scored on the Flat again. He enjoyed a couple of wins over hurdles in 2000. Suited by a soft surface and 14 furlongs.

Tuscan (IRE)

90(103) (66)**32**

3-y-o b f Charnwood Forest (IRE)-Madam Loving (Vaigly Great)

B G Powell Mrs John M Weld

Placings:46024010-20440000 **(4736)**

2001: 5^{2}SD, 6^{0}SW, 5^{4}SW, 5^{4}SW, 7^{0}GF, 6^{0}GF, 6^{0}GF, 6^{0}F

	Starts	1st	2nd	3rd	Win & Pl
Career Total (Turf)	9	0	1	0	981
Career Total (AW)	7	1	1	0	3580

66	11/00	Ling	6f	E(0-85)	STD	£2758

Total win prize-money £2758

Going (Turf): Sf: 0-0 GS: 0-0 Gd: 0-1 GF: 0-7 Fm: 0-1
Distance: 5f/6f: 1-11 7f-8f: 0-5 9f-13f: 0-0 14f+: 0-0
Track : LH: 1-9 RH: 0-0 **Tight: 1-7** Gall: 0-1
Aids: Bl: 0-0 Vi: 0-1 Tstrap: 0-0
Best Rating: 66 1/01 Ling 5f stand

Tuscan Dream

104(96) (64)**79**

6-y-o b g Clantime-Excavator Lady (Most Secret)

A Berry Chris & Antonia Deuters

Placings:2302600/0301143122014/0051240353-0030002236U0 **(4718)**

2001: 5^{0}S, 5^{0}SD, 5^{3}GF, 5^{0}G, 5^{0}GF, 5^{0}GF, 5^{2}GF, 5^{2}GF, 5^{3}GF, 5^{6}GF, 5^{U}G, 5^{0}G, 5^{5}SD

	Starts	1st	2nd	3rd	Win & Pl
Career Total (Turf)	35	4	6	6	36824
Career Total (AW)	7	1	1	1	3230

71	6/00	Ripn	5f	D(0-80)H	G-F	£4208
71	9/99	Epsm	5f	C(0-90)H	GD	£10845
63	6/99	Ling	5f	E(0-75)H	G-F	£2880
61	5/99	Wolv	5f	F	STD	£2109
43	5/99	Muss	5f	F	G-F	£2304

Total win prize-money £22349

Going (Turf): Sf: 0-1 GS: 0-2 Gd: 1-9 **GF: 3-20** Fm: 0-3
Distance: 5f/6f: 5-42 7f-8f: 0-0 9f-13f: 0-0 14f+: 0-0
Track : LH: 1-13 RH: 0-0 **Tight: 1-9** Gall: 0-3
Aids: Bl: 0-1 Vi: 0-0 Tstrap: 0-0
Best Rating: 80 5/01 Ches 5f16y gd-fm

He is a very speedy sprinter who needs fast ground and the minimum trip to show his best. Likes to dominate. Got rather upset in the stalls at Epsom in August and had to pass a stalls test .

Tuscan Flyer

100(72) (19)**69**

3-y-o b g Clantime-Excavator Lady (Most Secret)

A Berry Chris & Antonia Deuters

Placings:0500-02103463454 **(4785)**

2001: 6^{0}SD, 5^{2}GF, 5^{1}GF, 5^{0}G, 5^{3}G, 5^{4}GF, 5^{6}GF, 5^{3}GF, 5^{4}GF, 5^{5}G, 5^{4}G

	Starts	1st	2nd	3rd	Win & Pl
Career Total (Turf)	14	1	1	2	6815
Career Total (AW)	1	0	0	0	

65	5/01	Ayr	5f	D(0-85)H	G-F	£4127

Total win prize-money £4128

Going (Turf): Sf: 0-1 GS: 0-2 Gd: 0-4 **GF: 1-7** Fm: 0-0
Distance: 5f/6f: 1-15 7f-8f: 0-0 9f-13f: 0-0 14f+: 0-0
Track : LH: 0-2 RH: 0-2 Tight: 0-2 Gall: 0-2
Aids: Bl: 0-1 Vi: 0-0 Tstrap: 0-0
Best Rating: 69 6/01 Muss 5f good

Took his time to get off the mark, but did so when carrying overweight in a decent handicap at Ayr in May 2001. The rest of that season saw him knocking at the door but always finding one or two too good. He likes to dominate and favours five furlongs on a sound surface.

Tuscan Tempo

85 **67**

2-y-o ch c Perugino (USA)-Fact Of Time (Known Fact (USA))

R Hannon D J Walker

Placings:005 **(4670)**

2001: 6^{0}GF, 7^{0}GF, 7^{5}G

	Starts	1st	2nd	3rd	Win & Pl
Career Total (Turf)	3	0	0	0	0

Going (Turf): Sf: 0-0 GS: 0-0 Gd: 0-1 GF: 0-2 Fm: 0-0
Distance: 5f/6f: 0-1 7f-8f: 0-2 9f-13f: 0-0 14f+: 0-0
Track : LH: 0-0 RH: 0-0 Tight: 0-0 Gall: 0-0
Aids: Bl: 0-0 Vi: 0-0 Tstrap: 0-0
Best Rating: 67 9/01 Chep 7f16y good

Tuscarora (IRE)

91 **68**

2-y-o b f Revoque (IRE)-Fresh Look (IRE) (Alzao (USA))

P C Haslam J Roundtree

Placings:50330 **(4856)**

2001: 5^{5}G, 7^{0}G, 7^{3}F, 7^{3}GF, 7^{0}GF

	Starts	1st	2nd	3rd	Win & Pl
Career Total (Turf)	5	0	0	2	1256

Going (Turf): Sf: 0-0 GS: 0-0 Gd: 0-2 GF: 0-2 Fm: 0-1
Distance: 5f/6f: 0-1 7f-8f: 0-4 9f-13f: 0-0 14f+: 0-0
Track : LH: 0-3 RH: 0-0 Tight: 0-3 Gall: 0-0
Aids: Bl: 0-0 Vi: 0-0 Tstrap: 0-0
Best Rating: 68 8/01 Muss 7f30y gd-fm

Tweed

77(96) (50)**57**

4-y-o ch g Barathea (IRE)-In Perpetuity (Great Nephew)

Jedd O'Keeffe Richard Johnson

Placings:050/0042-00 **(0882)**

2001: 13^{0}S, 10^{0}S

	Starts	1st	2nd	3rd	Win & Pl
Career Total (Turf)	8	0	1	0	0
Career Total (AW)	1	0	0	0	0

Going (Turf): Sf: 0-5 GS: 0-2 Gd: 0-0 GF: 0-1 Fm: 0-0
Distance: 5f/6f: 0-0 7f-8f: 0-2 9f-13f: 0-7 14f+: 0-0
Track : LH: 0-3 RH: 0-3 Tight: 0-4 Gall: 0-0
Aids: Bl: 0-1 Vi: 0-1 Tstrap: 0-0
Best Rating: 7 4/01 Pont 1m2f6y soft

Twenty Seven (IRE)

99 **77**

2-y-o b f Efisio-Naked Poser (IRE) (Night Shift (USA))

J A R Toller P J Smith

Placings:42160 **(4657)**

2001: 5^{4}G, 5^{2}G, 5^{1}G, 6^{6}GF, 6^{0}GF

	Starts	1st	2nd	3rd	Win & Pl
Career Total (Turf)	5	1	1	0	5443

74	8/01	Leic	5f218y	E	GD	£4004

Total win prize-money £4004

Going (Turf): Sf: 0-0 GS: 0-0 **Gd: 1-3** GF: 0-2 Fm: 0-0
Distance: 5f/6f: 1-5 7f-8f: 0-0 9f-13f: 0-0 14f+: 0-0
Track : LH: 0-0 RH: 0-0 Tight: 0-0 Gall: 0-0
Aids: Bl: 0-0 Vi: 0-0 Tstrap: 0-0
Best Rating: 77 7/01 Yarm 5f43y good

She ran well behind some useful sorts in her first two starts and got off the mark with a comfortable victory in a Leicester maiden, but was slightly disappointing on her nursery debut at Newmarket, and even more so next time at Doncaster in a similar event. Acts well over six furongs, and is suited by good ground.

Twentyfoureve

69 **29**

2-y-o b f Emperor Jones (USA)-Topwinder (USA) (Topsider (USA))

G C H Chung Alan Lee

Placings:000 **(5361)**

2001: 7^{0}GF, 8^{0}HY, 8^{0}GS

	Starts	1st	2nd	3rd	Win & Pl
Career Total (Turf)	3	0	0	0	

Going (Turf): Sf: 0-1 GS: 0-1 Gd: 0-0 GF: 0-1 Fm: 0-0
Distance: 5f/6f: 0-0 7f-8f: 0-2 9f-13f: 0-1 14f+: 0-0
Track : LH: 0-1 RH: 0-0 Tight: 0-0 Gall: 0-0
Aids: Bl: 0-0 Vi: 0-0 Tstrap: 0-0
Best Rating: 29 10/01 NmkR 1m gd-sft

Twice

(104) (72)**60d**

5-y-o b g Rainbow Quest (USA)-Bolas (Unfuwain (USA))

G L Moore Trotters Independent Racing

Placings:440/0053511-2 **(0181)**

2001: 16^{2}SD

	Starts	1st	2nd	3rd	Win & Pl
Career Total (Turf)	6	0	0	0	648
Career Total (AW)	5	2	1	1	4752

70	12/00	Sthl	1m6f	F(0-65)H	STD	£1764
60	11/00	Ling	2m	F(0-65)H	STD	£1736

Total win prize-money £3500

Going (Turf): Sf: 0-1 GS: 0-2 Gd: 0-1 GF: 0-1 Fm: 0-1
Distance: 5f/6f: 0-0 7f-8f: 0-0 9f-13f: 0-8 **14f+: 2-3**
Track : LH: 2-9 RH: 0-1 **Tight: 1-7** Gall: 0-1
Aids: Bl: 0-0 Vi: 0-0 **Tstrap: 2-7**
Best Rating: 72 1/01 Ling 2m stand

Twice Blessed (IRE)

99(67) **58**

4-y-o ch c Thatching-Fairy Blesse (IRE) (Fairy King (USA))

R Hannon J C Smith

Placings:0021/0-000 **(1664)**

2001: 8^{0}SD, 6^{0}S, 8^{0}GF

	Starts	1st	2nd	3rd	Win & Pl
Career Total (Turf)	5	0	0	0	
Career Total (AW)	3	1	1	0	3572
72 12/99 Ling 7f	D			STD	£2703

Total win prize-money £2704

Going (Turf): Sf: 0-3 GS: 0-1 Gd: 0-0 GF: 0-1 Fm: 0-0
Distance: 5f/6f: 0-2 **7f-8f: 1-4** 9f-13f: 0-2 14f+: 0-0
Track : **LH: 1-3** RH: 0-3 **Tight: 1-3** Gall: 0-1
Aids: Bl: 0-0 Vi: 0-0 Tstrap: 0-0
Best Rating: 58 5/01 Sals 6f212y soft

Twice Bright

73 **4**

5-y-o br g Precocious-Sweet Helen (No Mercy)

C Drew C Drew

Placings:00 **(4268)**

2001: 10^{0}G, 9^{0}GF

	Starts	1st	2nd	3rd	Win & Pl
Career Total (Turf)	2	0	0	0	

Going (Turf): Sf: 0-0 GS: 0-0 Gd: 0-1 GF: 0-1 Fm: 0-0
Distance: 5f/6f: 0-0 7f-8f: 0-0 9f-13f: 0-2 14f+: 0-0
Track : LH: 0-1 RH: 0-1 Tight: 0-1 Gall: 0-0
Aids: Bl: 0-0 Vi: 0-0 Tstrap: 0-0
Best Rating: 4 8/01 Bevl 1m1f207y gd-fm

Twice Upon A Time

90 **67**

2-y-o ch f Primo Dominie-Opuntia (Rousillon (USA))

B Smart John W Ford

Placings:244023 **(5621)**

2001: 6^{2}G, 6^{4}GF, 6^{4}G, 6^{0}G, 5^{2}GS, 5^{3}GS

	Starts	1st	2nd	3rd	Win & Pl
Career Total (Turf)	6	0	2	1	3041

Going (Turf): Sf: 0-0 GS: 0-2 Gd: 0-3 GF: 0-1 Fm: 0-0
Distance: 5f/6f: 0-5 7f-8f: 0-1 9f-13f: 0-0 14f+: 0-0
Track : LH: 0-0 RH: 0-0 Tight: 0-0 Gall: 0-0
Aids: Bl: 0-0 Vi: 0-0 Tstrap: 0-0
Best Rating: 71 8/01 NmkJ 6f gd-fm

She has shown ability in maiden and nursery company without winning and may be better suited by six furlongs than five.

Twig N' Berries

64

5-y-o b g Rock City-Mardessa (Ardross)

M Mullineaux F H Lee

Placings:0 **(1409)**

2001: 12^{0}G

	Starts	1st	2nd	3rd	Win & Pl
Career Total (Turf)	1	0	0	0	

Going (Turf): Sf: 0-0 GS: 0-0 Gd: 0-1 GF: 0-0 Fm: 0-0
Distance: 5f/6f: 0-0 7f-8f: 0-0 9f-13f: 0-1 14f+: 0-0
Track : LH: 0-0 RH: 0-1 Tight: 0-1 Gall: 0-0
Aids: Bl: 0-0 Vi: 0-0 Tstrap: 0-0

Twilight Blues (IRE)

102 **95**

2-y-o ch c Bluebird (USA)-Pretty Sharp (Interrex (CAN))

B J Meehan Mrs Susan Roy

Placings:105323U **(5493)**

2001: 5^{1}GF, 6^{0}GF, 6^{5}Y, 6^{3}G, 6^{2}G, 6^{3}GF, 7^{U}HY

	Starts	1st	2nd	3rd	Win & Pl
Career Total (Turf)	7	1	1	2	32731
85 6/01 Newb 5f34y	D			G-F	£4251

Total win prize-money £4251

Going (Turf): Sf: 0-1 GS: 0-0 Gd: 0-2 **GF: 1-3** Fm: 0-0
Distance: **5f/6f: 1-5** 7f-8f: 0-2 9f-13f: 0-0 14f+: 0-0
Track : LH: 0-0 RH: 0-0 Tight: 0-0 Gall: 0-0
Aids: Bl: 0-0 Vi: 0-0 Tstrap: 0-0
Best Rating: 95 9/01 Newb 6f8y gd-fm

Well regarded, he scored on his debut at Newbury over the minimum trip before having his limitations exposed in Pattern company, but has put in decent efforts in both the Gimcrack and Sirenia Stakes. Acts on fast ground.

Twilight Dancer (IRE)

95(81) (36)**50**

3-y-o b f Sri Pekan (USA)-Manhattan Sunset (USA) (El Gran Senor (USA))

P W Harris The Manhattan Club

Placings:650-006504 **(5084)**

2001: 9^{0}GS, 10^{0}F, 12^{6}G, 11^{5}GF, 10^{0}G, 9^{4}S

	Starts	1st	2nd	3rd	Win & Pl
Career Total (Turf)	8	0	0	0	0
Career Total (AW)	1	0	0	0	0

Going (Turf): Sf: 0-2 GS: 0-2 Gd: 0-2 GF: 0-1 Fm: 0-1
Distance: 5f/6f: 0-0 7f-8f: 0-0 9f-13f: 0-9 14f+: 0-0
Track : LH: 0-7 RH: 0-1 Tight: 0-5 Gall: 0-0
Aids: Bl: 0-0 Vi: 0-0 Tstrap: 0-0
Best Rating: 50 8/01 Folk 1m4f good

Twilight Haze

105(104) (70)**75**

3-y-o b c Darshaan-Hiwaayati (Shadeed (USA))

E A L Dunlop Maktoum Al Maktoum

Placings:02-13200 **(2855)**

2001: 12^{1}SD, 12^{3}S, 14^{2}G, 12^{0}G, 11^{0}G

	Starts	1st	2nd	3rd	Win & Pl
Career Total (Turf)	5	0	1	1	2011
Career Total (AW)	2	1	1	0	3642
70 3/01 Wolv 1m4f	D			STD	£2926

Total win prize-money £2926

Going (Turf): Sf: 0-2 GS: 0-0 Gd: 0-3 GF: 0-0 Fm: 0-0
Distance: 5f/6f: 0-0 7f-8f: 0-2 **9f-13f: 1-4** 14f+: 0-1
Track : **LH: 1-3** RH: 0-2 **Tight: 1-3** Gall: 0-1
Aids: Bl: 0-0 Vi: 0-0 Tstrap: 0-0
Best Rating: 75 5/01 Donc 1m6f132y good

Twilight Mistress

103 **77**

3-y-o b f Bin Ajwaad (IRE)-By Candlelight (IRE) (Roi Danzig (USA))

D W P Arbuthnot The Twilight Team

Placings:00430-1402 **(4421)**

2001: 5^{1}GF, 5^{4}G, 5^{0}G, 5^{2}G

	Starts	1st	2nd	3rd	Win & Pl
Career Total (Turf)	9	1	1	1	6195
73 6/01 Wwck 5f	E(0-70)H			G-F	£3125

Total win prize-money £3126

Going (Turf): Sf: 0-0 GS: 0-1 Gd: 0-4 **GF: 1-4** Fm: 0-0
Distance: **5f/6f: 1-8** 7f-8f: 0-1 9f-13f: 0-0 14f+: 0-0
Track : **LH: 1-3** RH: 0-1 Tight: 0-1 **Gall: 1-3**
Aids: Bl: 0-0 Vi: 0-0 Tstrap: 0-0
Best Rating: 77 9/01 Ches 5f16y good

She improved on her two-year-old form with a win in a Warwick handicap over five on her seasonal reappearance, in which she carried 9st 10lb to victory. She deserves a step up in grade and may well improve over six furlongs.

Twilight Sonnet

101 **85+**

2-y-o b f Exit To Nowhere (USA)-Shawanni (Shareef Dancer (USA))

E A L Dunlop Maktoum Al Maktoum

Placings:3221014 **(4269)**

2001: 6^{3}GF, 5^{2}GF, 5^{2}G, 5^{1}GF, 6^{0}GS, 5^{1}G, 5^{4}GF

	Starts	1st	2nd	3rd	Win & Pl
Career Total (Turf)	7	2	2	1	11001
78 8/01 Bevl 5f	D			GD	£3792
78 7/01 Bevl 5f	D			G-F	£4017

Total win prize-money £7810

Going (Turf): Sf: 0-0 GS: 0-1 **Gd: 1-2 GF: 1-4** Fm: 0-0
Distance: **5f/6f: 2-7** 7f-8f: 0-0 9f-13f: 0-0 14f+: 0-0
Track : LH: 0-0 RH: 0-0 Tight: 0-0 Gall: 0-0
Aids: Bl: 0-0 Vi: 0-0 Tstrap: 0-0
Best Rating: 85 8/01 Bevl 5f gd-fm

Showed plenty of ability before getting off the mark in a weak Beverley maiden over five furlongs. Returned to that track for her first handicap victory in August. Has shown signs of temperament in the past. Has won on good and good to firm.

Twin Time

106(84) (36)**70**

7-y-o b m Syrtos-Carramba (CZE) (Tumble Wind (USA))

J S King Dajam Ltd

Placings:3250246/35256100/14313500/42314340-1262 **(3578)**

2001: 8^{1}G, 7^{2}GF, 10^{6}GF, 7^{2}GF

	Starts	1st	2nd	3rd	Win & Pl
Career Total (Turf)	32	5	6	5	23728
Career Total (AW)	3	0	0	1	409
67 5/01 Bath 1m5y	E(0-70)H			GD	£2884
64 6/00 Gdwd 7f	E(0-80)H			G-F	£3623
64 5/99 Bath 1m5y	E(0-70)H			GD	£3067
60 8/98 Bath 1m2f46y	E(0-80)H			GD	£2739

Total win prize-money £12315

Going (Turf): Sf: 0-2 GS: 0-3 **Gd: 3-10** GF: 1-13 Fm: 1-4
Distance: 5f/6f: 0-0 7f-8f: 1-7 **9f-13f: 4-28** 14f+: 0-0
Track : **LH: 4-23** RH: 1-8 **Tight: 4-17** Gall: 0-0
Aids: Bl: 0-0 Vi: 0-0 **Tstrap: 1-1**
Best Rating: 70 8/01 Wwck 7f26y gd-fm

Twist

98(95) (38)**46**

4-y-o b g Suave Dancer (USA)-Reason To Dance (Damister (USA))

W R Muir John O'Mulloy

Placings:064/05050250-00023301 **(4642)**

2001: 10^{0}SD, 11^{0}GS, 9^{0}G, 9^{2}F, 9^{3}F, 10^{3}F, 11^{0}GF, 10^{1}GF

	Starts	1st	2nd	3rd	Win & Pl
Career Total (Turf)	18	1	2	2	4645
Career Total (AW)	1	0	0	0	
42 9/01 Ling 1m2f	G(0-60)H			G-F	£2093

Total win prize-money £2093

Going (Turf): Sf: 0-1 GS: 0-1 Gd: 0-2 **GF: 1-9** Fm: 0-5
Distance: 5f/6f: 0-1 7f-8f: 0-3 **9f-13f: 1-15** 14f+: 0-0
Track : **LH: 1-14** RH: 0-3 **Tight: 1-11** Gall: 0-1
Aids: Bl: 0-1 Vi: 0-1 Tstrap: 0-0
Best Rating: 46 6/01 Brig 1m1f209y firm

He had looked held in selling company before winning one over ten furlongs at Lingfield in September.

Two Jacks (IRE)

93(71) **38**

4-y-o b g Fayruz-Kaya (GER) (Young Generation)

W S Cunningham Mrs Ann Bell

Placings:00/0000-000560 **(5374)**

2001: 9^{0}F, 7^{0}SD, 8^{0}F, 7^{5}G, 6^{6}GF, 6^{0}G

	Starts	1st	2nd	3rd	Win & Pl
Career Total (Turf)	11	0	0	0	0
Career Total (AW)	1	0	0	0	

Going (Turf): Sf: 0-1 GS: 0-1 Gd: 0-5 GF: 0-2 Fm: 0-2
Distance: 5f/6f: 0-8 7f-8f: 0-3 9f-13f: 0-1 14f+: 0-0
Track : LH: 0-2 RH: 0-0 Tight: 0-1 Gall: 0-0
Aids: Bl: 0-0 Vi: 0-0 Tstrap: 0-1
Best Rating: 38 8/01 Newc 7f good

Two Marks (USA)

82 **68**

2-y-o ch f Woodman (USA)-Munnaya (USA) (Nijinsky (CAN))
Sir Michael Stoute Maktoum Al Maktoum

Placings:0 (4593)
2001: 7^{0}G

	Starts	1st	2nd	3rd	Win & Pl
Career Total (Turf)	1	0	0	0	

Going (Turf): Sf: 0-0 GS: 0-0 Gd: 0-1 GF: 0-0 Fm: 0-0
Distance: 5f/6f: 0-0 7f 8f: 0-1 9f-13f: 0-0 14f+: 0-0
Track : LH: 0-0 RH: 0-1 Tight: 0-0 Gall: 0-1
Aids: Bl: 0-0 Vi: 0-0 Tstrap: 0-0
Best Rating: 68 9/01 Kemp 7f good

Two Rainbows (IRE)

76 **25**

3-y-o b f Spectrum (IRE)-Titulata (GER) (Danehill (USA))
B A McMahon Miss Elizabeth George

Placings:0 (1600)
2001: 7^{0}GF

	Starts	1st	2nd	3rd	Win & Pl
Career Total (Turf)	1	0	0	0	

Going (Turf): Sf: 0-0 GS: 0-0 Gd: 0-0 GF: 0-1 Fm: 0-0
Distance: 5f/6f: 0-0 7f-8f: 0-1 9f-13f: 0-0 14f+: 0-0
Track : LH: 0-1 RH: 0-0 Tight: 0-0 Gall: 0-0
Aids: Bl: 0-0 Vi: 0-0 Tstrap: 0-0
Best Rating: 25 5/01 Hayd 7f30y gd-fm

Two Socks

100 (50)**61**

8-y-o ch g Phountzi (USA)-Mrs Feathers (Pyjama Hunt)
J S King Mrs Satu Marks

Placings:0000432500/0654221000/542262/132/616536000/61410200-001100 (3556)
2001: 12^{0}S, 13^{0}GF, 10^{1}F, 12^{1}GF, 10^{0}G, 12^{0}GF

	Starts	1st	2nd	3rd	Win & Pl
Career Total (Turf)	46	7	7	2	32542
Career Total (AW)	6	0	1	1	1460

58	7/01	Epsm	1m4f10y	E(0-70)H	G-F	£4485
61	6/01	Ling	1m2f	G(0-60)H	FRM	£2170
65	6/00	Kemp	1m4f	E(0-75)H	G-F	£4387
60	5/00	Brig	1m3f196y	E(0-70)H	FRM	£2915
67	6/99	Kemp	1m4f	D(0-85)H	G-F	£3793
67	6/98	Wwck	1m2f169y	D(0-80)H	G-S	£3720
59	7/96	Ling	1m3f106y	E(0-70)H	FRM	£3124

Total win prize-money £24598

Going (Turf): Sf: 0-6 GS: 1-8 Gd: 0-11 GF: 3-16 Fm: 3-5
Distance: 5f/6f: 0-4 7f-8f: 0-5 9f-13f: 7-40 14f+: 0-3
Track : LH: 5-32 RH: 2-18 Tight: 3-23 Gall: 0-8
Aids: Bl: 0-1 Vi: 0-0 Tstrap: 0-0
Best Rating: 61 6/01 Ling 1m2f firm

A fair handicapper, he landed a double in the summer of 2001, but has since gone off the boil again. He is seen to best effect over 12 furlongs on a firm surface, though he has won on easy ground.

Two Step

103(105) (55)**51**

5-y-o b m Mujtahid (USA)-Polka Dancer (Dancing Brave (USA))
R M H Cowell Bottisham Heath Stud

Placings:060/001050325302-4124340240 (1453)
2001: 8^{4}SD, 7^{1}SD, 6^{2}SD, 7^{4}SW, 6^{3}SD, 6^{4}SD, 6^{0}HY, 5^{2}G, 5^{4}GF, 6^{0}SD

	Starts	1st	2nd	3rd	Win & Pl
Career Total (Turf)	9	0	2	1	2362
Career Total (AW)	16	2	2	2	7843

55	1/01	Ling	7f	E(0-70)H	STD	£2443
35	7/00	Sthl	5f	F(0-65)H	STD	£2261

Total win prize-money £4704

Going (Turf): Sf: 0-1 GS: 0-1 Gd: 0-1 GF: 0-4 Fm: 0-1
Distance: 5f/6f: 1-14 7f-8f: 1-7 9f-13f: 0-3 14f+: 0-0
Track : LH: 1-17 RH: 0-0 Tight: 1-13 Gall: 0-0
Aids: Bl: 0-0 Vi: 0-3 Tstrap: 2-21
Best Rating: 55 3/01 Ling 6f stand

Two Steps To Go (USA)

99 **76**

2-y-o b g Rhythm (USA)-Lyonushka (CAN) (Private Account (USA))
T D Barron J Baggott

Placings:4362035260 (5169)
2001: 5^{4}S, 5^{3}GF, 7^{6}G, 6^{2}GF, 6^{0}GF, 7^{3}G, 8^{5}F, 7^{2}GF, 7^{6}G, 6^{0}GS

	Starts	1st	2nd	3rd	Win & Pl
Career Total (Turf)	10	0	2	2	3190

Going (Turf): Sf: 0-1 GS: 0-1 Gd: 0-3 GF: 0-4 Fm: 0-1
Distance: 5f/6f: 0-5 7f-8f: 0-5 9f-13f: 0-0 14f+: 0-0
Track : LH: 0-5 RH: 0-2 Tight: 0-4 Gall: 0-0
Aids: Bl: 0-1 Vi: 0-0 Tstrap: 0-0
Best Rating: 77 7/01 Pont 6f gd-fm

Bred to stay. Showed improvement to finish second on handicap debut over six furlongs. Acts on fast ground.

Twoforten

98(93) (30)**35**

6-y-o b g Robellino (USA)-Grown At Rowan (Gabitat)
P Butler P Butler

Placings:660/00050300/432403305/066000365000603 0055-0000010650050000 (4525)
2001: 12^{0}SD, 16^{0}SD, 13^{0}SD, 10^{0}G, 12^{0}GF, 7^{1}GF, 8^{0}GF, 7^{6}GF, 7^{5}GF, 10^{0}F, 9^{0}GF, 7^{5}GS, 10^{0}GF, 7^{0}GF, 9^{0}GF, 7^{0}GF

	Starts	1st	2nd	3rd	Win & Pl
Career Total (Turf)	47	1	1	6	6788
Career Total (AW)	8	0	0	0	0

42	5/01	Ling	7f	E(0-75)H	G-F	£3304

Total win prize-money £3304

Going (Turf): Sf: 0-4 GS: 0-2 Gd: 0-14 GF: 1-21 Fm: 0-6
Distance: 5f/6f: 0-4 7f-8f: 1-12 9f-13f: 0-37 14f+: 0-2
Track : LH: 0-24 RH: 0-16 Tight: 0-20 Gall: 0-2
Aids: Bl: 0-8 Vi: 0-10 Tstrap: 0-0
Best Rating: 71 5/01 NmkR 1m2f good

Tyballa (IRE)

73 **7**

3-y-o b f Blues Traveller (IRE)-Mary Mary Mouse (USA) (Valdez (USA))
M H Tompkins Ben Turner Racing

Placings:00 (5173)
2001: 8^{0}G, 8^{0}GS

	Starts	1st	2nd	3rd	Win & Pl
Career Total (Turf)	2	0	0	0	

Going (Turf): Sf: 0-0 GS: 0-1 Gd: 0-1 GF: 0-0 Fm: 0-0
Distance: 5f/6f: 0-0 7f-8f: 0-0 9f-13f: 0-2 14f+: 0-0
Track : LH: 0-2 RH: 0-0 Tight: 0-0 Gall: 0-0
Aids: Bl: 0-0 Vi: 0-0 Tstrap: 0-0
Best Rating: 7 9/01 Nott 1m54y good

Tycoon's Last

105(92) (35)**58**

4-y-o b f Nalchik (USA)-Royal Tycoon (Tycoon II)
W M Brisbourne L R Owen

Placings:6604000/3500435304106-10005326102050 5 (5686)
2001: 12^{1}S, 11^{0}GS, 10^{0}GF, 14^{0}GF, 12^{5}GS, 11^{3}GF, 12^{2}G, 11^{6}GS, 11^{1}G, 11^{0}G, 10^{2}HY, 11^{0}S, 13^{5}S, 12^{0}GS, 10^{5}S

	Starts	1st	2nd	3rd	Win & Pl
Career Total (Turf)	34	3	2	4	25829
Career Total (AW)	1	0	0	0	

55	8/01	Hayd	1m3f200y	F(0-60)H	GD	£3069
63	4/01	Kemp	1m4f	D(0-85)H	SFT	£4777
56	9/00	Hayd	1m2f120y	C(0-90)H	HVY	£11017

Total win prize-money £18866

Going (Turf): Sf: 2-10 GS: 0-5 Gd: 1-9 GF: 0-8 Fm: 0-2
Distance: 5f/6f: 0-6 7f-8f: 0-1 9f-13f: 3-23 14f+: 0-5
Track : LH: 2-22 RH: 1-7 Tight: 0-13 Gall: 0-6
Aids: Bl: 0-0 Vi: 0-0 Tstrap: 0-0
Best Rating: 63 4/01 Kemp 1m4f soft

Best at a mile and a half, she had only won in the mud prior to her victory at Haydock in August, but is still a much better horse with cut in the ground. Suited by 12 furlongs.

Tyler's Toast

(109) (84+)**74d**

5-y-o ch g Grand Lodge (USA)-Catawba (Mill Reef (USA))
S Dow S Dow

Placings:3/6640/2111050-21 (0210)
2001: 9^{2}SW, 9^{1}SD

	Starts	1st	2nd	3rd	Win & Pl
Career Total (Turf)	7	0	0	1	775
Career Total (AW)	7	4	2	0	13928

84	2/01	Wolv	1m1f79y	D(0-80)H	STD	£3883
72	3/00	Wolv	1m1f79y	E(0-75)H	STD	£2834
66	2/00	Wolv	1m1f79y	E(0-75)H	STD	£2689
66	2/00	Wolv	1m1f79y	D	STD	£2743

Total win prize-money £12150

Going (Turf): Sf: 0-1 GS: 0-1 Gd: 0-2 GF: 0-3 Fm: 0-0
Distance: 5f/6f: 0-0 7f-8f: 0-1 9f-13f: 4-13 14f+: 0-0
Track : LH: 4-8 RH: 0-4 Tight: 4-10 Gall: 0-2
Aids: Bl: 0-0 Vi: 0-0 Tstrap: 0-0
Best Rating: 84 2/01 Wolv 1m1f79y stand

Type One (IRE)

103 **86**

3-y-o b g Bigstone (IRE)-Isca (Caerleon (USA))
T G Mills Mrs A K Petersen

Placings:034-61120 (2205)
2001: 5^{6}S, 5^{1}GS, 6^{1}G, 6^{2}GF, 6^{0}GS

	Starts	1st	2nd	3rd	Win & Pl
Career Total (Turf)	8	2	1	1	18881

83	5/01	Wind	6f	D(0-80)H	GD	£4186
81	5/01	Wind	5f10y	D(0-80)H	G-S	£4147

Total win prize-money £8333

Going (Turf): Sf: 0-1 GS: 1-2 Gd: 1-2 GF: 0-2 Fm: 0-1
Distance: 5f/6f: 2-8 7f-8f: 0-0 9f-13f: 0-0 14f+: 0-0
Track : LH: 0-0 RH: 1-2 Tight: 0-0 Gall: 1-2
Aids: Bl: 0-0 Vi: 0-0 Tstrap: 0-0
Best Rating: 86 6/01 NmkR 6f gd-fm

Ran with promise on two starts as a juvenile, but was rather keen. Now gelded, he got off the mark on his second outing at three, then followed up with another success over six furlongs. Should stay a mile. Has won on good and good to soft.

Typhoon Eight (IRE)

84 (29)**37**

9-y-o b g High Estate-Dance Date (IRE) (Sadler's Wells (USA))
I Semple Mrs D Santonocito

Placings:06/06540/00200010/33404/66000/**000**20505/000 **(1134)**
2001: 13^{0}S, 8^{0}GS, 9^{0}GS

	Starts	1st	2nd	3rd	Win & Pl
Career Total (Turf)	33	1	2	2	9478
Career Total (AW)	3	0	0	0	0

71 10/96 Catt 1m3f214yD(0-75)H GD £4662
Total win prize-money £4663

Going (Turf): Sf: 0-4 GS: 0-9 **Gd: 1-7** GF: 0-13 Fm: 0-0
Distance: 5f/6f: 0-0 7f-8f: 0-7 **9f-13f: 1-25** 14f+: 0-4
Track : **LH: 1-16** RH: 0-18 **Tight: 1-16** Gall: 0-5
Aids: Bl: 0-9 Vi: 0-0 Tstrap: 0-6
Best Rating: 9 4/01 Muss 1m gd-sft

Typhoon Ginger (IRE)

107(82) (39)**75**
6-y-o ch m Archway (IRE)-Pallas Viking (Viking (USA))
A B Mulholland Andrew Lloyd

Placings:26403/00345243/662053630-0026311502 **(5265)**
2001: 8^{0}GF, 8^{0}GF, 10^{2}GF, 10^{6}GF, 8^{3}GF, 8^{1}GF, 7^{1}GF, 7^{5}G, 8^{0}GS, 8^{2}GS

	Starts	1st	2nd	3rd	Win & Pl
Career Total (Turf)	31	2	5	6	31951
Career Total (AW)	1	0	0	0	

70 9/01 York 7f202y D(0-80)H G-F £12431
66 8/01 Rdcr 1m D(0-80)H G-F £5551
Total win prize-money £17982

Going (Turf): Sf: 0-5 GS: 0-4 Gd: 0-7 **GF: 2-15** Fm: 0-0
Distance: 5f/6f: 0-4 **7f-8f: 2-11** 9f-13f: 0-17 14f+: 0-0
Track : **LH: 1-12** RH: 0-5 Tight: 0-2 **Gall: 1-9**
Aids: Bl: 0-0 Vi: 0-0 Tstrap: 0-0
Best Rating: 75 10/01 York 1m205y gd-sft

It took her 28 starts before she finally got off the mark at Redcar in August and then followed up in a competitive handicap at York. Suited by a mile on fast ground and a strongly run race.

Typhoon Tilly

102 **67d**
4-y-o b g Hernando (FR)-Meavy (Kalaglow)
C R Egerton Mrs Evelyn Hankinson

Placings:000/311126-340000 **(4594)**
2001: 12^{3}GF, 14^{4}GF, 20^{0}GF, 12^{0}GF, 16^{0}GF, 14^{0}G

	Starts	1st	2nd	3rd	Win & Pl
Career Total (Turf)	15	3	1	2	12985

71 7/00 Nott 1m6f15y E(0-75)H G-F £2955
68 7/00 Yarm 1m6f17y E(0-75)H G-F £3591
65 6/00 Yarm 1m6f17y E(0-75)H FRM £2821
Total win prize-money £9367

Going (Turf): Sf: 0-1 GS: 0-2 Gd: 0-3 **GF: 2-8** Fm: 1-1
Distance: 5f/6f: 0-0 7f-8f: 0-1 9f-13f: 0-5 **14f+: 3-9**
Track : **LH: 3-6** RH: 0-6 **Tight: 2-6** Gall: 0-1
Aids: Bl: 0-2 Vi: 0-0 Tstrap: 0-0
Best Rating: 72 5/01 Sand 1m6f gd-fm

He completed a hat-trick over staying distances in modest handicap company in the middle of the 2000 season. Suited by 14 furlongs and fast ground.

Typhoon Todd (IRE)

92 **78**
2-y-o ch c Entrepreneur-Petite Liqueurelle (IRE) (Shernazar)
R Hannon Lucayan Stud

Placings:00430 **(3655)**
2001: 5^{0}GF, 7^{0}S, 7^{4}GF, 6^{3}GF, 7^{0}GF

	Starts	1st	2nd	3rd	Win & Pl
Career Total (Turf)	5	0	0	1	904

Going (Turf): Sf: 0-1 GS: 0-0 Gd: 0-0 GF: 0-4 Fm: 0-0
Distance: 5f/6f: 0-1 7f-8f: 0-4 9f-13f: 0-0 14f+: 0-0
Track : LH: 0-1 RH: 0-1 Tight: 0-0 Gall: 0-0
Aids: Bl: 0-0 Vi: 0-0 Tstrap: 0-0
Best Rating: 78 7/01 Brig 6f209y gd-fm

A couple of promising runs over seven furlongs, but more needed in order to lose maiden tag.

Tzar

101(90) (70)**70**
2-y-o b g Makbul-Tzarina (USA) (Gallant Romeo (USA))
J R Best (B A McMahon 1/10) Tendorra

Placings:35521402223 **(5467)**
2001: 5^{3}GF, 5^{5}GF, 6^{5}SD, 6^{2}SD, 5^{1}HY, 6^{4}GF, 7^{0}HY, 7^{2}SD, 6^{2}SD, 6^{2}SD, 6^{3}S, 6^{0}SD

	Starts	1st	2nd	3rd	Win & Pl
Career Total (Turf)	6	1	0	2	5387
Career Total (AW)	5	0	4	0	2695

70 8/01 Hayd 5f D HVY £4082
Total win prize-money £4082

Going (Turf): Sf: 1-3 GS: 0-0 Gd: 0-0 GF: 0-3 Fm: 0-0
Distance: **5f/6f: 1-8** 7f-8f: 0-3 9f-13f: 0-0 14f+: 0-0
Track : LH: 0-8 RH: 0-0 Tight: 0-3 Gall: 0-0
Aids: Bl: 0-0 Vi: 0-0 Tstrap: 0-0
Best Rating: 70 10/01 Brig 6f209y soft

Fair juvenile, acts on any ground. Tends to chase leaders. Stays seven furlongs, has been runner-up four times in five runs on Fibresand.

Uhoomagoo

101(96) (66)**78**
3-y-o b g Namaqualand (USA)-Point Of Law (Law Society (USA))
K A Ryan (D Nicholls 26/1) Platinum Racing Club Limited

Placings:21131345-**640030066404133113000** **(5681)**
2001: 6^{6}SD, 5^{4}SW, 7^{0}SD, 7^{0}SD, 8^{3}SD, 6^{0}SD, 7^{0}S, 8^{6}SD, 7^{6}SW, 6^{4}GF, 6^{0}G, 7^{4}GF, 7^{1}GF, 7^{3}GS, 7^{3}GS, 7^{1}GF, 6^{1}GF, 7^{3}HY, 6^{0}GS, 7^{0}HY, 8^{0}S

	Starts	1st	2nd	3rd	Win & Pl
Career Total (Turf)	20	5	1	5	26083
Career Total (AW)	9	1	0	1	3072

78 9/01 Nott 6f15y D(0-80)H G-F £4647
51 8/01 Bevl 7f100y E G-F £3272
60 7/01 Bevl 7f100y E G-F £3185
79 8/00 Catt 5f212y D G-S £4251
65 5/00 Sthl 5f F STD £2191
64 4/00 Thsk 5f E G-S £3266
Total win prize-money £20814

Going (Turf): Sf: 0-4 GS: 2-5 Gd: 0-4 **GF: 3-7** Fm: 0-0
Distance: 5f/6f: 3-9 7f-8f: 3-19 9f-13f: 0-1 14f+: 0-0
Track : LH: 1-14 **RH: 2-3 Tight: 1-7** Gall: 0-1
Aids: **Bl: 2-9** Vi: 0-0 Tstrap: 0-0
Best Rating: 78 9/01 Nott 6f15y gd-fm

A fair juvenile who was placed to win three times in ordinary company, he went through a quiet spell, but dropped in the handicap and has been in good form this season with two wins in claimers at Beverley and another victory in a Nottingham handicap. Suited by six and seven furlongs.

Ulshaw

104(100) (44)**49**
4-y-o ch g Salse (USA)-Kintail (Kris)
B J Llewellyn Vivian Guy

Placings:05/0300044-**114434130** **(4942)**
2001: 16^{1}SD, 16^{1}SD, 16^{4}HY, 14^{4}S, 16^{3}GF, 17^{4}GF, 16^{1}GS, 15^{3}G, 15^{0}S

	Starts	1st	2nd	3rd	Win & Pl
Career Total (Turf)	16	1	0	3	6182
Career Total (AW)	2	2	0	0	3073

45 7/01 Llng 2m E(0-75)H G-S £3220
44 2/01 Wolv 2m46y F(0-60)H STD £1701
35 2/01 Wolv 2m46y G(0-60)H STD £1372
Total win prize-money £6293

Going (Turf): Sf: 0-3 **GS: 1-1** Gd: 0-4 GF: 0-5 Fm: 0-3
Distance: 5f/6f: 0-0 7f-8f: 0-2 9f-13f: 0-1 **14f+: 3-15**
Track : **LH: 3-14** RH: 0-4 **Tight: 3-11** Gall: 0-1
Aids: Bl: 0-0 Vi: 0-3 Tstrap: 0-0
Best Rating: 49 9/01 Ches 1m7f195y good

A fair staying handicapper, his first two wins were both over the extended two miles on the Wolverhampton Fibresand, but he used his stamina to good effect when winning on turf at Lingfield in July.

Ultimajur (USA)

99(85) (58d)**41**
3-y-o br c Dayjur (USA)-Crystal Lady (CAN) (Stop The Music (USA))
M D I Usher (J W Hills 23/1) M D I Usher

Placings:000-0060 **(4543)**
2001: 6^{0}SW, 5^{0}SD, 5^{6}F, 5^{0}GF

	Starts	1st	2nd	3rd	Win & Pl
Career Total (Turf)	3	0	0	0	0
Career Total (AW)	4	0	0	0	

Going (Turf): Sf: 0-1 GS: 0-0 Gd: 0-0 GF: 0-1 Fm: 0-1
Distance: 5f/6f: 0-5 7f-8f: 0-2 9f-13f: 0-0 14f+: 0-0
Track : LH: 0-4 RH: 0-0 Tight: 0-2 Gall: 0-1
Aids: Bl: 0-1 Vi: 0-0 Tstrap: 0-0
Best Rating: 41 6/01 Bath 5f11y firm

Ultimate Choice

95(86) (61)**47**
3-y-o b g Petong-Jay Gee Ell (Vaigly Great)
W J Haggas A A Goodman

Placings:056-000014540 **(5129)**
2001: 5^{0}G, 5^{0}GF, 5^{0}GF, 6^{0}F, 7^{1}G, 7^{4}GF, 7^{5}GF, 7^{4}G, 7^{0}HY

	Starts	1st	2nd	3rd	Win & Pl
Career Total (Turf)	10	1	0	0	2534
Career Total (AW)	2	0	0	0	0

47 8/01 Leic 7f9y F GD £2534
Total win prize-money £2534

Going (Turf): Sf: 0-2 GS: 0-0 **Gd: 1-3** GF: 0-4 Fm: 0-1
Distance: 5f/6f: 0-6 **7f-8f: 1-6** 9f-13f: 0-0 14f+: 0-0
Track : LH: 0-4 RH: 0-0 Tight: 0-2 Gall: 0-0
Aids: Bl: 0-0 Vi: 0-1 Tstrap: 0-1
Best Rating: 47 8/01 Muss 7f30y gd-fm

Ultra Calm (IRE)

(101) (46)**29**
5-y-o ch g Doubletour (USA)-Shyonn (IRE) (Shy Groom (USA))
Miss K M George Stableline

Placings:0004/41201126500/300600220-00 **(0284)**
2001: 12^{0}SD, 9^{0}SW

	Starts	1st	2nd	3rd	Win & Pl
Career Total (Turf)	10	1	1	0	3894
Career Total (AW)	16	2	3	1	6844

61 4/99 Ripn 1m2f E(0-70)H G-F £2996
63 3/99 Wolv 1m100y F(0-60) SLW £2200
54 1/99 Wolv 1m1f79y F(0-65) STD £1999
Total win prize-money £7196

Going (Turf): Sf: 0-4 GS: 0-0 Gd: 0-2 **GF: 1-3** Fm: 0-1
Distance: 5f/6f: 0-3 7f-8f: 0-3 **9f-13f: 3-20** 14f+: 0-0
Track : **LH: 2-21** RH: 1-2 **Tight: 3-16** Gall: 0-0
Aids: Bl: 0-2 Vi: 0-2 Tstrap: 0-2
Best Rating: 22 2/01 Wolv 1m1f79y slow

He is a fairly effective sort in modest company on Fibresand. Trips of around a mile seem to suit.

Ulundi

111(103) (86)**109**

6-y-o b g Rainbow Quest (USA)-Flit (USA) (Lyphard (USA))

P R Webber D Heath

Placings:113300252I0-611 **(2801)**

2001: 12^{6}SD, 12^{1}GF, 10^{1}GF

	Starts	1st	2nd	3rd	Win & Pl
Career Total (Turf)	12	4	2	2	90432
Career Total (AW)	2	1	0	0	2418

109	7/01	Sand	1m2f7y	B H	G-F	£58000
102	5/01	Gdwd	1m4f	B	G-F	£9860
100	9/00	Kemp	1m4f	C(0-100)H	GD	£10773
87	3/00	Wind	1m2f7y	D(0-80)	G-F	£3770
77	3/00	Wolv	1m100y	D	STD	£2418

Total win prize-money £84822

Going (Turf): Sf: 0-1 GS: 0-1 Gd: 1-3 **GF: 3-6** Fm: 0-1
Distance: 5f/6f: 0-0 7f-8f: 0-0 **9f-13f: 5-14** 14f+: 0-0
Track : LH: 1-4 **RH: 3-9 Tight: 3-4** Gall: 0-3
Aids: Bl: 0-0 Vi: 0-0 Tstrap: 0-0
Best Rating: 109 7/01 Sand 1m2f7y gd-fm

A very effective performer both on the Flat and over hurdles, he won the Scottish Champion Hurdle in April and underlined his versatility by following up in a conditions event at Goodwood and a valuable handicap at Sandown. Suited by ten or twelve furlongs and a sound surface.

Ulysses Daughter (IRE)

90(83) (33)**63**

4-y-o ch f College Chapel-Trysinger (IRE) (Try My Best (USA))

G A Butler The Travellers

Placings:4215420-0600 **(5392)**

2001: 5^{0}GF, 5^{6}GF, 6^{0}G, 6^{0}SD

	Starts	1st	2nd	3rd	Win & Pl
Career Total (Turf)	10	1	2	0	6766
Career Total (AW)	1	0	0	0	

71	9/00	Bath	5f161y	D	GD	£3799

Total win prize-money £3799

Going (Turf): Sf: 0-2 GS: 0-1 **Gd: 1-4** GF: 0-3 Fm: 0-0
Distance: **5f/6f: 1-9** 7f-8f: 0-2 9f-13f: 0-0 14f+: 0-0
Track : **LH: 1-3** RH: 0-0 Tight: 0-1 **Gall: 1-2**
Aids: Bl: 0-1 Vi: 0-0 **Tstrap: 1-9**
Best Rating: 63 8/01 Folk 5f gd-fm

She has not shown much in a light campaign in 2000. Usually tongue tied and is often slowly away.

Umbopa (USA)

95(105) (65)**57**

3-y-o b g Gilded Time (USA)-How Fortunate (CAN) (What Luck (USA))

K R Burke Tendorra

Placings:00-35**205** **(5407)**

2001: 8^{3}S, 10^{5}GF, 8^{2}SD, 9^{0}SD, 12^{5}SD, 11^{2}SD, 12^{1}SD

	Starts	1st	2nd	3rd	Win & Pl
Career Total (Turf)	4	0	0	1	550
Career Total (AW)	3	0	1	0	713

Going (Turf): **Sf: 0-2 GS: 0-1 Gd: 0-0 GF: 0-1 Fm: 0-0**
Distance: 5f/6f: 0-0 7f-8f: 0-1 9f-13f: 0-6 14f+: 0-0
Track : LH: 0-6 RH: 0-1 Tight: 0-3 Gall: 0-0
Aids: Bl: 0-0 Vi: 0-0 Tstrap: 0-0
Best Rating: 57 5/01 Ayr 1m2f192y gd-fm

Has shown ability on Fibresand and ran his best race in first-time blinkers over eleven furlongs at Southwell in November.

Umista (IRE)

76 **40**

2-y-o b f Tagula (IRE)-Nishiki (USA) (Brogan (USA))

M Quinn M Quinn

Placings:00000 **(3654)**

2001: 5^{0}GF, 6^{0}GF, 6^{0}GF, 5^{0}G, 5^{0}GF

	Starts	1st	2nd	3rd	Win & Pl
Career Total (Turf)	5	0	0	0	

Going (Turf): **Sf: 0-0 GS: 0-0 Gd: 0-1 GF: 0-4 Fm: 0-0**
Distance: 5f/6f: 0-5 7f-8f: 0-0 9f-13f: 0-0 14f+: 0-0
Track : LH: 0-2 RH: 0-0 Tight: 0-0 Gall: 0-1
Aids: Bl: 0-0 Vi: 0-1 Tstrap: 0-0
Best Rating: 40 6/01 Pont 6f gd-fm

Umistim

109 **116**

4-y-o ch h Inchinor-Simply Sooty (Absalom)

R Hannon Mrs S Joint

Placings:31151/16520201-5055110 **(4679)**

2001: 9^{5}S, 8^{0}S, 8^{5}S, 8^{5}G, 7^{1}GF, 8^{1}F, 8^{0}G

	Starts	1st	2nd	3rd	Win & Pl
Career Total (Turf)	20	7	2	1	122183

110	8/01	Sals	1m	A	FRM	£13937
107	7/01	Newb	7f64y	B	G-F	£9952
95	10/00	Donc	7f	B	SFT	£11163
118	4/00	NmkR	1m	A	G-S	£20300
104	10/99	Newb	7f64y	A	G-S	£21040
94	8/99	Wind	6f	C	HVY	£5300
85	7/99	Newb	7f64y	D	G-F	£5732

Total win prize-money £87427

Going (Turf): **Sf: 2-7 GS: 2-3** Gd: 0-4 **GF: 2-5** Fm: 1-1
Distance: 5f/6f: 1-2 **7f-8f: 6-15** 9f-13f: 0-3 14f+: 0-0
Track : **LH: 3-7** RH: 1-3 Tight: 0-0 **Gall: 4-9**
Aids: Bl: 0-0 Vi: 0-0 Tstrap: 0-0
Best Rating: 116 6/01 Asct 1m good

A promising juvenile in 1999, he beat the eventual 2000 Guineas winner King's Best in the Craven in the spring of 2000. Well beaten in the Classic, he subsequently proved a little disappointing, and has found his level in Listed company. Best suited by racing prominently. Had been considered an easy ground performer, but his two wins in 2001 were on fast ground.

Un Autre Espere

2-y-o b g Golden Heights-Drummer's Dream (IRE) (Drumalis)

A Streeter Snax Catering Services

Placings:0 **(5620)**

2001: 8^{0}GS

	Starts	1st	2nd	3rd	Win & Pl
Career Total (Turf)	1	0	0	0	

Going (Turf): **Sf: 0-0 GS: 0-1 Gd: 0-0 GF: 0-0 Fm: 0-0**
Distance: 5f/6f: 0-0 7f-8f: 0-0 9f-13f: 0-1 14f+: 0-0
Track : LH: 0-1 RH: 0-0 Tight: 0-0 Gall: 0-0
Aids: Bl: 0-0 Vi: 0-0 Tstrap: 0-0

Unchain My Heart

99(100) (49)**52d**

5-y-o b m Pursuit Of Love-Addicted To Love (Touching Wood (USA))

W G M Turner Mascalls Stud

Placings:003/330303422420**130**/**163**0014110-666 **(4471)**

2001: 7^{6}G, 6^{6}GF, 6^{6}GF

	Starts	1st	2nd	3rd	Win & Pl
Career Total (Turf)	24	3	3	5	11435
Career Total (AW)	7	2	0	2	5269

59	9/00	Leic	7f9y	E(0-70)H	G-F	£2912
57	8/00	Kemp	7f	E(0-70)H	G-F	£3770
49	3/00	Ling	7f	F	STD	£2150
57	11/99	Ling	1m	D	STD	£2411

Total win prize-money £11243

Going (Turf): Sf: 0-4 GS: 0-3 Gd: 0-3 **GF: 3-7** Fm: 0-7
Distance: 5f/6f: 0-2 **7f-8f: 5-23** 9f-13f: 0-6 14f+: 0-0
Track : **LH: 2-19** RH: 1-1 **Tight: 2-9** Gall: 1-1
Aids: **Bl: 3-16** Vi: 2-4 Tstrap: 0-0
Best Rating: 52 7/01 Chep 7f16y good

Uncle Clockwise

78 **38**

4-y-o gr c Absalom-Summer Flower (Nomination)

Miss Z C Davison Highly Charged Partnership

Placings:050 **(1268)**

2001: 7^{0}S, 6^{5}HY, 7^{0}GS

	Starts	1st	2nd	3rd	Win & Pl
Career Total (Turf)	3	0	0	0	0

Going (Turf): **Sf: 0-2 GS: 0-1 Gd: 0-0 GF: 0-0 Fm: 0-0**
Distance: 5f/6f: 0-0 7f-8f: 0-3 9f-13f: 0-0 14f+: 0-0
Track : LH: 0-0 RH: 0-2 Tight: 0-1 Gall: 0-1
Aids: Bl: 0-0 Vi: 0-0 Tstrap: 0-0
Best Rating: 38 4/01 Kemp 7f soft

Uncle Folding (IRE)

84 **21**

3-y-o b g Danehill (USA)-Bubbling Danseuse (USA) (Arctic Tern (USA))

Mrs D Thomson Paul Byrne

Placings:6000-0L **(3005)**

2001: 8^{0}F, 9^{L}S

	Starts	1st	2nd	3rd	Win & Pl
Career Total (Turf)	6	0	0	0	0

Going (Turf): **Sf: 0-1 GS: 0-0 Gd: 0-2 GF: 0-2 Fm: 0-1**
Distance: 5f/6f: 0-1 7f-8f: 0-3 9f-13f: 0-2 14f+: 0-0
Track : LH: 0-1 RH: 0-2 Tight: 0-1 Gall: 0-1
Aids: Bl: 0-1 Vi: 0-0 Tstrap: 0-1
Best Rating: 21 7/01 Newc 1m firm

Uncle Oberon

82(78) (21)**18**

5-y-o b g Distant Relative-Fairy Story (IRE) (Persian Bold)

H J Manners H J Manners

Placings:00/50/**604**00-**000**0000 **(3155)**

2001: 11^{0}SD, 8^{0}SW, 7^{0}SW, 11^{0}F, 9^{0}F, 8^{0}GF, 7^{0}GS

	Starts	1st	2nd	3rd	Win & Pl
Career Total (Turf)	11	0	0	0	0
Career Total (AW)	5	0	0	0	0

Going (Turf): **Sf: 0-1 GS: 0-3 Gd: 0-2 GF: 0-3 Fm: 0-2**
Distance: 5f/6f: 0-1 7f-8f: 0-10 9f-13f: 0-5 14f+: 0-0
Track : LH: 0-9 RH: 0-0 Tight: 0-3 Gall: 0-0
Aids: Bl: 0-0 Vi: 0-2 Tstrap: 0-1
Best Rating: 18 7/01 Ling 7f140y gd-sft

Uncle Sam

45(62) (4)

2-y-o ch c Superpower-Treasure Time (IRE) (Treasure Kay)

P D Evans Miss E Saunders

Placings:00 **(1458)**

2001: 5^{0}SD, 5^{0}G

	Starts	1st	2nd	3rd	Win & Pl
Career Total (Turf)	1	0	0	0	
Career Total (AW)	1	0	0	0	

Going (Turf): **Sf: 0-0 GS: 0-0 Gd: 0-1 GF: 0-0 Fm: 0-0**
Distance: 5f/6f: 0-2 7f-8f: 0-0 9f-13f: 0-0 14f+: 0-0
Track : LH: 0-1 RH: 0-0 Tight: 0-0 Gall: 0-1
Aids: Bl: 0-0 Vi: 0-0 Tstrap: 0-0
Best Rating: 4 5/01 Sthl 5f stand

Undeniable

105(87) (62)**67**
3-y-o b g Unfuwain (USA)-Shefoog (Kefaah (USA))
J L Dunlop J L Dunlop

Placings:000-1620 **(4483)**
2001: 14^{1}GF, 14^{6}GF, 16^{2}GF, 14^{0}S

	Starts	1st	2nd	3rd	Win & Pl
Career Total (Turf)	6	1	1	0	4778
Career Total (AW)	1	0	0	0	

66 6/01 Gdwd 1m6f E(0-75)H G-F £4777
Total win prize-money £4778

Going (Turf): Sf: 0-3 GS: 0-0 Gd: 0-0 **GF: 1-3** Fm: 0-0
Distance: 5f/6f: 0-0 7f-8f: 0-2 9f-13f: 0-1 **14f+: 1-4**
Track : LH: 0-5 **RH: 1-1 Tight: 1-5** Gall: 0-0
Aids: Bl: 0-0 Vi: 0-0 Tstrap: 0-0
Best Rating: 67 7/01 Yarm 2m gd-fm

Under Construction (IRE)

104(99) (53)**69**
3-y-o b g Pennekamp (USA)-Madame Nureyev (USA) (Nureyev (USA))
M Johnston Guildford Construction (york) Ltd

Placings:22400 **(5400)**
2001: 8^{2}GF, 8^{2}GF, 9^{4}GF, 8^{0}GS, 10^{0}S, 8^{5}SD

	Starts	1st	2nd	3rd	Win & Pl
Career Total (Turf)	5	0	2	0	3176

Going (Turf): Sf: 0-1 GS: 0-1 Gd: 0-0 GF: 0-3 Fm: 0-0
Distance: 5f/6f: 0-0 7f-8f: 0-1 9f-13f: 0-4 14f+: 0-0
Track : LH: 0-4 RH: 0-1 Tight: 0-1 Gall: 0-1
Aids: Bl: 0-0 Vi: 0-0 Tstrap: 0-0
Best Rating: 69 9/01 Haml 1m1f36y gd-fm

Undercover Girl (IRE)

91(88) (41)**49d**
3-y-o b f Barathea (IRE)-Les Trois Lamas (IRE) (Machiavellian (USA))
W R Muir M J Caddy

Placings:5000-04000 **(3874)**
2001: 10^{0}GF, 9^{4}SD, 11^{0}F, 16^{0}GF, 12^{0}G

	Starts	1st	2nd	3rd	Win & Pl
Career Total (Turf)	8	0	0	0	0
Career Total (AW)	1	0	0	0	0

Going (Turf): Sf: 0-2 GS: 0-1 Gd: 0-1 GF: 0-3 Fm: 0-1
Distance: 5f/6f: 0-0 7f-8f: 0-4 9f-13f: 0-4 14f+: 0-1
Track : LH: 0-3 RH: 0-6 Tight: 0-4 Gall: 0-2
Aids: Bl: 0-0 Vi: 0-0 Tstrap: 0-0
Best Rating: 42 7/01 Folk 2m93y gd-fm

Undeterred

114 **88**
5-y-o ch g Zafonic (USA)-Mint Crisp (IRE) (Green Desert (USA))
D Nicholls P D Savill

Placings:4141/43400/0364100-060213000000 **(5133)**
2001: 6^{0}S, 5^{6}GS, 5^{0}GF, 6^{2}GF, 6^{1}F, 6^{3}G, 6^{0}G, 6^{0}G, 7^{0}G, 6^{0}GF, 7^{0}S, 7^{0}G

	Starts	1st	2nd	3rd	Win & Pl
Career Total (Turf)	28	4	1	3	63140

90 6/01 Newc 6f C(0-95)H FRM £19500
88 7/00 Chep 6f16y C(0-90) G-F £7818
99 10/98 York 6f A GD £11421
Total win prize-money £38739

Going (Turf): Sf: 0-2 GS: 0-7 Gd: 1-12 GF: 1-5 **Fm: 2-2**
Distance: 5f/6f: 2-16 7f-8f: 2-12 9f-13f: 0-0 14f+: 0-0
Track : LH: 0-3 RH: 0-0 Tight: 0-1 Gall: 0-0
Aids: Bl: 0-1 **Vi: 1-7** Tstrap: 0-0
Best Rating: 93 8/01 Gdwd 6f good

Successful in Listed company as a juvenile in 1998, he is a useful handicapper nowadays. He has run well in a visor this term and scored at Newcastle in June before an unlucky run when favourite for the Stewards' Cup. Only beaten four lengths in the Ayr Gold Cup, but was well beaten next time at Ascot when probably not at home in the soft ground. Best over six furlongs in a fast-run race, he acts on fast ground.

Unfaithful Thought

97 **88+**
2-y-o b/br f Mind Games-Fleeting Affair (Hotfoot)
P W Harris The Quick-Wits

Placings:2 **(5602)**
2001: 7^{2}GS

	Starts	1st	2nd	3rd	Win & Pl
Career Total (Turf)	1	0	1	0	1299

Going (Turf): Sf: 0-0 GS: 0-1 Gd: 0-0 GF: 0-0 Fm: 0-0
Distance: 5f/6f: 0-0 7f-8f: 0-1 9f-13f: 0-0 14f+: 0-0
Track : LH: 0-0 RH: 0-0 Tight: 0-0 Gall: 0-0
Aids: Bl: 0-0 Vi: 0-0 Tstrap: 0-0
Best Rating: 88 11/01 NmkR 7f gd-sft

Unfortunate

(93) (28)**52**
4-y-o ch f Komaite (USA)-Honour And Glory (Hotfoot)
Miss J F Craze P Walton

Placings:00600214/65306001440U-04 **(0150)**
2001: 6^{0}SD, 7^{4}SW

	Starts	1st	2nd	3rd	Win & Pl
Career Total (Turf)	9	1	0	0	2669
Career Total (AW)	13	1	1	1	2610

45 6/00 Leic 5f218y G(0-60)H G-S £2170
45 12/99 Sthl 6f G STD £1840
Total win prize-money £4010

Going (Turf): Sf: 0-1 **GS: 1-3** Gd: 0-1 GF: 0-3 Fm: 0-1
Distance: **5f/6f: 2-15** 7f-8f: 0-7 9f-13f: 0-0 14f+: 0-0
Track : **LH: 1-14** RH: 0-1 Tight: 0-6 Gall: 0-1
Aids: **Bl: 1-7** Vi: 0-0 Tstrap: 0-0
Best Rating: 24 1/01 Wolv 7f slow

Unicorn Star (IRE)

93 (30)**28**
4-y-o b g Persian Bold-Highland Warning (Warning)
J S Wainwright Ms Julie French

Placings:040/43625230-004050500 **(5637)**
2001: 11^{0}F, 17^{0}GF, 12^{4}GF, 16^{0}F, 11^{5}GF, 11^{0}G, 9^{5}GF, 10^{0}GF, 11^{0}G

	Starts	1st	2nd	3rd	Win & Pl
Career Total (Turf)	19	0	2	2	2550
Career Total (AW)	1	0	0	0	

Going (Turf): Sf: 0-0 GS: 0-2 Gd: 0-7 GF: 0-8 Fm: 0-2
Distance: 5f/6f: 0-0 7f-8f: 0-3 9f-13f: 0-13 14f+: 0-4
Track : LH: 0-8 RH: 0-11 Tight: 0-10 Gall: 0-3
Aids: Bl: 0-1 Vi: 0-5 Tstrap: 0-0
Best Rating: 41 7/01 Donc 1m4f gd-fm

Universal Star

99 **79**
3-y-o b f Unfuwain (USA)-Shirley Superstar (Shirley Heights)
H R A Cecil Helena Springfield Ltd

Placings:626 **(4893)**
2001: 12^{6}G, 11^{2}GF, 12^{6}GF

	Starts	1st	2nd	3rd	Win & Pl
Career Total (Turf)	3	0	1	0	1312

Going (Turf): Sf: 0-0 GS: 0-0 Gd: 0-1 GF: 0-2 Fm: 0-0
Distance: 5f/6f: 0-0 7f-8f: 0-0 9f-13f: 0-3 14f+: 0-0
Track : LH: 0-1 RH: 0-2 Tight: 0-1 Gall: 0-1
Aids: Bl: 0-0 Vi: 0-0 Tstrap: 0-0
Best Rating: 79 9/01 Ling 1m3f106y gd-fm

A half-sister to Lady Carla, ran well at Lingfield on her second start, but disappointed next time.

Unleash (USA)

97(100) (82)**75**
2-y-o ch c Benny The Dip (USA)-Lemhi Go (USA) (Lemhi Gold (USA))
Sir Mark Prescott Cheveley Park Stud

Placings:4441 **(4875)**
2001: 7^{4}G, 8^{4}S, 7^{4}G, 8^{1}SD

	Starts	1st	2nd	3rd	Win & Pl
Career Total (Turf)	3	0	0	0	895
Career Total (AW)	1	1	0	0	3689

82 9/01 Wolv 1m100y D STD £3688
Total win prize-money £3689

Going (Turf): Sf: 0-1 GS: 0-0 Gd: 0-2 GF: 0-0 Fm: 0-0
Distance: 5f/6f: 0-0 7f-8f: 0-2 **9f-13f: 1-2** 14f+: 0-0
Track : **LH: 1-3** RH: 0-1 **Tight: 1-3** Gall: 0-0
Aids: Bl: 0-0 Vi: 0-0 Tstrap: 0-0
Best Rating: 82 9/01 Wolv 1m100y stand

By Derby-winner Benny The Dip, he broke his duck at the fourth time of asking on his sand debut over a mile at Wolverhampton in September 2001.

Unmasked

75(70) (11)**36**
5-y-o ch m Safawan-Unveiled (Sayf El Arab (USA))
A Scott R McClelland

Placings:40/0/000000333000-0400 **(5637)**
2001: 11^{0}G, 12^{4}GF, 8^{0}SD, 11^{0}G

	Starts	1st	2nd	3rd	Win & Pl
Career Total (Turf)	17	0	0	3	1344
Career Total (AW)	2	0	0	0	

Going (Turf): Sf: 0-2 GS: 0-3 Gd: 0-4 GF: 0-6 Fm: 0-2
Distance: 5f/6f: 0-6 7f-8f: 0-5 9f-13f: 0-8 14f+: 0-0
Track : LH: 0-6 RH: 0-7 Tight: 0-9 Gall: 0-1
Aids: Bl: 0-1 Vi: 0-0 Tstrap: 0-0
Best Rating: 36 9/01 Muss 1m4f gd-fm

Moderate maiden plater at a mile plus.

Uno Mente

87 **67**
2-y-o b f Mind Games-One Half Silver (CAN) (Plugged Nickle (USA))
Mrs P N Dutfield D Bevan

Placings:54 **(4099)**
2001: 6^{5}GF, 6^{4}G

	Starts	1st	2nd	3rd	Win & Pl
Career Total (Turf)	2	0	0	0	284

Going (Turf): Sf: 0-0 GS: 0-0 Gd: 0-1 GF: 0-1 Fm: 0-0
Distance: 5f/6f: 0-1 7f-8f: 0-1 9f-13f: 0-0 14f+: 0-0
Track : LH: 0-0 RH: 0-0 Tight: 0-0 Gall: 0-0
Aids: Bl: 0-0 Vi: 0-0 Tstrap: 0-0
Best Rating: 67 8/01 Nott 6f15y good

Has shown ability in auction events, especially from a bad draw at Nottingham.

Unparalleled

86(96) (62)**65**
3-y-o b f Primo Dominie-Sharp Chief (Chief Singer)
G L Moore Raymond Gross, Ms Adrienne Gross

Placings:2200004-24000 **(5593)**
2001: 7^{2}SD, 6^{4}SD, 7^{0}SW, 6^{0}GF, 5^{0}GS

	Starts	1st	2nd	3rd	Win & Pl

	Starts	1st	2nd	3rd	Win & Pl
Career Total (Turf)	6	0	2	0	2366
Career Total (AW)	6	0	1	0	1096

Going (Turf): Sf: 0-1 GS: 0-1 Gd: 0-1 GF: 0-2 Fm: 0-0
Distance: 5f/6f: 0-5 7f-8f: 0-6 9f-13f: 0-0 14f+: 0-0
Track : LH: 0-9 RH: 0-0 Tight: 0-6 Gall: 0-0
Aids: Bl: 0-4 Vi: 0-0 Tstrap: 0-0
Best Rating: 62 1/01 Ling 7f stand

Unshakable (IRE)

94 **86**
2-y-o b c Eagle Eyed (USA)-Pepper And Salt (IRE) (Double Schwartz)
Bob Jones Unshakable Partnership

Placings:52 **(5684)**
2001: 7^{5}S, 8^{2}S

	Starts	1st	2nd	3rd	Win & Pl
Career Total (Turf)	2	0	1	0	1440

Going (Turf): Sf: 0-2 GS: 0-0 Gd: 0-0 GF: 0-0 Fm: 0-0
Distance: 5f/6f: 0-0 7f-8f: 0-2 9f-13f: 0-0 14f+: 0-0
Track : LH: 0-1 RH: 0-0 Tight: 0-0 Gall: 0-1
Aids: Bl: 0-0 Vi: 0-0 Tstrap: 0-0
Best Rating: 86 11/01 Donc 1m soft

He improved on his debut when finishing runner-up in a back-end maiden at Doncaster, and will surely make his mark next year.

Unshaken

75(100) (59d)**75**
7-y-o b h Environment Friend-Reel Foyle (USA) (Irish River (FR))
E J Alston G C Sanderson & A J Picton

Placings:015/00560000/**33**5213612302**50**/**33**21010041050004300/0240000000010500**0-6033**01126004306 **(5196)**
2001: 7^{6}SD, **6**^{0}SD, **7**^{3}SD, 7^{3}SD, 6^{0}G, 7^{1}GF, 8^{1}F, 8^{2}GF, 7^{6}GF, 8^{0}GF, 8^{0}G, 7^{4}G, 8^{3}G, 8^{0}S, **8**^{6}SD

	Starts	1st	2nd	3rd	Win & Pl
Career Total (Turf)	65	9	6	4	75042
Career Total (AW)	10	0	0	6	2523

69	6/01	Thok	1m	E(0-70)H	FRM	£4342
65	5/01	Newb	7f	D(0-85)H	G-F	£4940
66	8/00	Carl	6f206y	E(0-65)	GD	£2873
81	6/99	Newc	6f	C(0-95)H	GD	£18562
80	5/99	Haml	6f5y	C(0-90)H	GD	£8325
73	4/99	Haml	6f5y	D(0-85)H	HVY	£5914
67	6/98	Haml	6f5y	F(0-60)	G-S	£2346
56	5/98	Carl	5f207y	E(0-70)H	G-S	£3074
86	10/96	Folk	5f	F	G-S	£2381

Total win prize-money £52758

Going (Turf): Sf: 1-18 **GS: 3-13 Gd: 3-19** GF: 1-13 Fm: 1-2
Distance: 5f/6f: 3-43 **7f-8f: 6-28** 9f-13f: 0-4 14f+: 0-0
Track : LH: 1-25 **RH: 2-5** Tight: 1-12 Gall: 1-4
Aids: Bl: 0-1 Vi: 0-3 Tstrap: 0-0
Best Rating: 75 7/01 Donc 1m gd-fm

Decent handicapper over seven furlongs and a mile, winning over both trips in the spring of 2001. Acts on fast ground. Come-from-behind performer.

Unsigned (USA)

101 **73**
3-y-o b/br g Cozzene (USA)-Striata (USA) (Gone West (USA))
J R Fanshawe Great Cumberland Pals

Placings:043-6420500 **(5106)**
2001: 9^{6}GF, 12^{4}GF, 12^{2}GF, 12^{0}GF, 16^{5}GF, 14^{0}G, 12^{0}GS

	Starts	1st	2nd	3rd	Win & Pl
Career Total (Turf)	10	0	1	1	3154

Going (Turf): Sf: 0-2 GS: 0-1 Gd: 0-2 GF: 0-5 Fm: 0-0
Distance: 5f/6f: 0-0 7f-8f: 0-3 9f-13f: 0-5 14f+: 0-2
Track : LH: 0-1 RH: 0-8 Tight: 0-2 Gall: 0-2
Aids: Bl: 0-0 Vi: 0-0 Tstrap: 0-0
Best Rating: 79 7/01 Ripn 1m4f60y gd-fm

Untidy Son

97 **73**
2-y-o b c Efisio-Reel Foyle (USA) (Irish River (FR))
R Hannon W J Gredley

Placings:000 **(2947)**
2001: 5^{0}S, 5^{0}GF, 6^{0}G

	Starts	1st	2nd	3rd	Win & Pl
Career Total (Turf)	3	0	0	0	

Going (Turf): Sf: 0-1 GS: 0-0 Gd: 0-1 GF: 0-1 Fm: 0-0
Distance: 5f/6f: 0-3 7f-8f: 0-0 9f-13f: 0-0 14f+: 0-0
Track : LH: 0-0 RH: 0-0 Tight: 0-0 Gall: 0-0
Aids: Bl: 0-0 Vi: 0-0 Tstrap: 0-2
Best Rating: 73 6/01 Hayd 5f gd-fm

Unveil

92(92) (48)**44**
3-y-o b f Rudimentary (USA)-Magical Veil (Majestic Light (USA))
G M McCourt Graham McCourt

Placings:4466503404-0020 **(3701)**
2001: 10^{0}GS, 6^{0}G, 7^{2}F, 6^{0}GF

	Starts	1st	2nd	3rd	Win & Pl
Career Total (Turf)	11	0	1	1	1168
Career Total (AW)	3	0	0	0	0

Going (Turf): Sf: 0-1 GS: 0-2 Gd: 0-2 GF: 0-4 Fm: 0-1
Distance: 5f/6f: 0-8 7f-8f: 0-3 9f-13f: 0-2 14f+: 0-0
Track : LH: 0-7 RH: 0-1 Tight: 0-3 Gall: 0-3
Aids: Bl: 0-0 Vi: 0-0 Tstrap: 0-0
Best Rating: 27 8/01 Brig 6f209y gd-fm

Up Front (IRE)

99(77) (44)**64**
2-y-o b f Up And At 'Em-Sable Lake (Thatching)
A Berry Paul J Dixon

Placings:04045010216 **(5621)**
2001: **5**^{0}SD, 5^{4}GF, 5^{0}GS, **7**^{4}SD, 5^{5}G, 7^{0}GF, 6^{1}S, 7^{0}SD, 6^{2}HY, 5^{1}G, 5^{6}GS

	Starts	1st	2nd	3rd	Win & Pl
Career Total (Turf)	8	2	1	0	5574
Career Total (AW)	3	0	0	0	0

63	10/01	Bath	5f161y	F	GD	£2359
64	9/01	Yarm	6f3y	G(0-65)	SFT	£2362

Total win prize-money £4722

Going (Turf): Sf: 1-2 GS: 0-2 **Gd: 1-2** GF: 0-2 Fm: 0-0
Distance: 5f/6f: 1-7 7f-8f: 1-4 9f-13f: 0-0 14f+: 0-0
Track : **LH: 1-5** RH: 0-0 Tight: 0-1 **Gall: 1-2**
Aids: Bl: 0-0 Vi: 0-0 Tstrap: 0-0
Best Rating: 64 9/01 Yarm 6f3y soft

Has won a couple of sellers at Bath and Yarmouth over five and a half furlongs and six. Best with cut in the ground.

Up In Flames (IRE)

105(89) (18)**39**
10-y-o b g Nashamaa-Bella Lucia (Camden Town)
Mrs G S Rees Www.Mark-Kilner-Racing.Com (17)

Placings:0424/00032/051130/00065006206/**06**0600003U1**0512/415**00260**043060/0/0000**203563**00**-60005230200 **(5632)**
2001: 11^{6}G, 10^{0}GF, 8^{0}GF, 8^{0}GF, 9^{5}GS, 8^{2}S, 10^{3}G, 9^{0}GS, 10^{2}S, 10^{0}S, 10^{0}G

	Starts	1st	2nd	3rd	Win & Pl
Career Total (Turf)	57	3	7	6	32945
Career Total (AW)	22	2	1	1	4960

55	1/98	Sthl	1m	F(0-65)H	STD	£1735
46	12/97	Wolv	1m1f79y	F(0-65)H	STD	£1944
46	11/97	Nott	1m54y	F(0-60)H	GD	£1927
75	6/95	Epsm	1m114y	C(0-90)H	G-F	£14265
71	5/95	Hayd	1m30y	C(0-90)H	GD	£5654

Total win prize-money £25525

Going (Turf): Sf: 0-8 GS: 0-8 **Gd: 2-19** GF: 1-19 Fm: 0-3
Distance: 5f/6f: 0-2 7f-8f: 1-32 **9f-13f: 4-44** 14f+: 0-0
Track : **LH: 5-51** RH: 0-20 **Tight: 2-29** Gall: 0-9
Aids: Bl: 0-1 Vi: 0-0 Tstrap: 0-21
Best Rating: 55 10/01 York 1m2f85y soft

Up On Points

89 **62**
3-y-o ch f Royal Academy (USA)-Champagne 'n Roses (Chief Singer)
R Hannon Vernon Carl Matalon

Placings:21-00000 **(5145)**
2001: 6^{0}GF, 8^{0}GF, 7^{0}GS, 6^{0}GF, 7^{0}G

	Starts	1st	2nd	3rd	Win & Pl
Career Total (Turf)	7	1	1	0	5925

85	8/00	Sals	6f212y	D	G-F	£5024

Total win prize-money £5025

Going (Turf): Sf: 0-0 GS: 0-1 Gd: 0-1 **GF: 1-5** Fm: 0-0
Distance: 5f/6f: 0-1 **7f-8f: 1-6** 9f-13f: 0-0 14f+: 0-0
Track : LH: 0-0 RH: 0-0 Tight: 0-0 Gall: 0-0
Aids: Bl: 0-0 Vi: 0-0 Tstrap: 0-0
Best Rating: 65 6/01 Asct 1m gd-fm

Showed herself to be a useful juvenile in two outings on fast ground in 2000, but was beaten a long way in a Haydock Listed race on her belated reappearance and has shown little since. Acts on fast ground.

Up Tempo (IRE)

107 **97**
3-y-o b c Flying Spur (AUS)-Musical Essence (Song)
T D Easterby T H Bennett

Placings:2132232-066454020 **(4062)**
2001: 6^{0}S, 7^{6}GF, 6^{6}F, 8^{4}GF, 7^{5}G, 6^{4}GS, 6^{0}G, 6^{2}G, 6^{0}G

	Starts	1st	2nd	3rd	Win & Pl
Career Total (Turf)	16	1	5	2	18745

66	5/00	Muss	5f	F	FRM	£2814

Total win prize-money £2814

Going (Turf): Sf: 0-2 GS: 0-2 Gd: 0-6 GF: 0-4 **Fm: 1-2**
Distance: **5f/6f: 1-12** 7f-8f: 0-3 9f-13f: 0-1 14f+: 0-0
Track : LH: 0-4 RH: 0-0 Tight: 0-1 Gall: 0-1
Aids: Bl: 0-2 Vi: 0-0 Tstrap: 0-0
Best Rating: 93 5/01 Hayd 1m30y gd-fm

A tough customer, he has run a series of good races this season without getting his head in front, especially when fourth in the William Hill Trophy. Probably best over six to seven furlongs.

Up The Clarets (IRE)

58
6-y-o b g Petardia-Madeira Lady (On Your Mark)
E J Alston Valley Paddocks Racing Limited

Placings:665054305/036060/0 **(5447)**
2001: 10^{0}HY

	Starts	1st	2nd	3rd	Win & Pl
Career Total (Turf)	15	0	0	2	738
Career Total (AW)	1	0	0	0	0

Going (Turf): Sf: 0-2 GS: 0-2 Gd: 0-4 GF: 0-5 Fm: 0-2
Distance: 5f/6f: 0-3 7f-8f: 0-10 9f-13f: 0-3 14f+: 0-0
Track : LH: 0-6 RH: 0-5 Tight: 0-4 Gall: 0-3
Aids: Bl: 0-1 Vi: 0-0 Tstrap: 0-0

Up The Kyber

101 **48**
4-y-o b g Missed Flight-Najariya (Northfields (USA))

A Crook The Adbrokes Partnership

Placings:00/300-2000 **(3573)**
2001: 11^{2}G, 12^{0}GF, 11^{0}S, 7^{0}G

	Starts	1st	2nd	3rd	Win & Pl
Career Total (Turf)	9	0	1	1	1712

Going (Turf): Sf: 0-4 GS: 0-0 Gd: 0-3 GF: 0-2 Fm: 0-0
Distance: 5f/6f: 0-0 7f-8f: 0-5 9f-13f: 0-4 14f+: 0-0
Track : LH: 0-3 RH: 0-2 Tight: 0-3 Gall: 0-0
Aids: Bl: 0-0 Vi: 0-1 Tstrap: 0-0
Best Rating: 48 5/01 Haml 1m3f16y good

Upheaval (IRE)

89(87) (52)**50**
2-y-o b g Great Commotion (USA)-Magic Green (Magic Mirror)
M W Easterby B Bargh,Tswain,J Walsh,K Wreglesworth

Placings:0560062345 **(3747)**
2001: 5^{0}SD, 5^{5}SD, 5^{6}GF, 5^{0}GF, 6^{0}F, 6^{6}G, 5^{2}SD, 5^{3}G, 5^{4}G, 5^{5}GS

	Starts	1st	2nd	3rd	Win & Pl
Career Total (Turf)	7	0	0	1	756
Career Total (AW)	3	0	1	0	520

Going (Turf): Sf: 0-0 GS: 0-1 Gd: 0-3 GF: 0-2 Fm: 0-1
Distance: 5f/6f: 0-10 7f-8f: 0-0 9f-13f: 0-0 14f+: 0-0
Track : LH: 0-0 RH: 0-0 Tight: 0-0 Gall: 0-0
Aids: Bl: 0-5 Vi: 0-0 Tstrap: 0-0
Best Rating: 52 7/01 Sthl 5f stand

Upper Bullens

(69) (31)
4-y-o ch g Rock City-Monstrosa (Monsanto (FR))
A Bailey R Farrington

Placings:644/000-0P **(2360)**
2001: 12^{0}GF, 10^{P}GF

	Starts	1st	2nd	3rd	Win & Pl
Career Total (Turf)	7	0	0	0	522
Career Total (AW)	1	0	0	0	

Going (Turf):Sf: 0-2 GS: 0-1 Gd: 0-0 GF: 0-4 Fm: 0-0
Distance: 5f/6f: 0-0 7f-8f: 0-3 9f-13f: 0-5 14f+: 0-0
Track : LH: 0-5 RH: 0-2 Tight: 0-2 Gall: 0-0
Aids: Bl: 0-0 Vi: 0-0 Tstrap: 0-0

Upper Chamber

97(101) (37)**28**
5-y-o b g Presidium-Vanishing Trick (Silly Season)
J G Fitzgerald J G Fitzgerald

Placings:346620/205056000/00005100001-066100F0 **(4618)**
2001: 5^{0}GS, 5^{6}GF, 5^{6}G, 6^{1}F, 5^{0}G, 6^{0}G, 5^{F}GF, 6^{0}F

	Starts	1st	2nd	3rd	Win & Pl
Career Total (Turf)	29	2	2	1	10063
Career Total (AW)	5	1	0	0	1743

44	8/01	Thsk	6f	F(0-60)H	FRM	£4459
37	12/00	Sthl	5f	F(0-65)H	STD	£1743
36	9/00	Thsk	5f	F(0-60)H	GD	£3201

Total win prize-money £9403

Going (Turf): Sf: 0-1 GS: 0-5 **Gd: 1-9** GF: 0-10 **Fm: 1-4**
Distance: **5f/6f: 3-33** 7f-8f: 0-1 9f-13f: 0-0 14f+: 0-0
Track : LH: 0-6 RH: 0-1 Tight: 0-2 Gall: 0-1
Aids: **Bl: 2-9** Vi: 0-3 Tstrap: 0-0
Best Rating: 44 8/01 Thsk 6f firm

Uppity

(75) (10)**23**
6-y-o ch m Great Commotion (USA)-Nuit D'Ete (USA) (Super Concorde (USA))
S J Mahon (Edward C Sexton 1/2) H Platt

Placings:6050/00000/0-0060 **(3107a)**
2001: 7^{0}SD, 9^{0}F, 8^{6}GF, 12^{0}F

	Starts	1st	2nd	3rd	Win & Pl
Career Total (Turf)	13	0	0	0	
Career Total (AW)	1	0	0	0	

Going (Turf): Sf: 0-0 GS: 0-0 Gd: 0-1 GF: 0-4 Fm: 0-2
Distance: 5f/6f: 0-3 7f-8f: 0-7 9f-13f: 0-3 14f+: 0-0
Track : LH: 0-3 RH: 0-5 Tight: 0-1 Gall: 0-0
Aids: Bl: 0-3 Vi: 0-0 Tstrap: 0-0
Best Rating: 17 7/01 Dund 1m4f firm

Uproar

99(91) (71)**77**
2-y-o b g Piccolo-Kittycatoo Katango (USA) (Verbatim (USA))
R M Beckett Julie Dolphin & Friends

Placings:022002 **(5415)**
2001: 7^{0}SD, 5^{2}G, 5^{2}GF, 6^{0}G, 6^{0}G, 6^{2}SD

	Starts	1st	2nd	3rd	Win & Pl
Career Total (Turf)	4	0	2	0	1428
Career Total (AW)	2	0	1	0	868

Going (Turf): Sf: 0-0 GS: 0-0 Gd: 0-3 GF: 0-1 Fm: 0-0
Distance: 5f/6f: 0-4 7f-8f: 0-2 9f-13f: 0-0 14f+: 0-0
Track : LH: 0-2 RH: 0-0 Tight: 0-1 Gall: 0-0
Aids: Bl: 0-0 Vi: 0-0 Tstrap: 0-0
Best Rating: 77 8/01 Catt 5f gd-fm

A speedy sort who was well beaten on his All-Weather debut, put in a decent effort next time when dropped back to the minimum trip at Folkestone. Acts on a sound surface.

Upstage

97 **52**
3-y-o b f Quest For Fame-Pedestal (High Line)
G C Bravery Bloomsbury Stud

Placings:646050 **(5376)**
2001: 8^{6}G, 10^{4}GF, 10^{6}GF, 11^{0}GF, 8^{5}GF, 9^{0}G

	Starts	1st	2nd	3rd	Win & Pl
Career Total (Turf)	6	0	0	0	357

Going (Turf): Sf: 0-0 GS: 0-0 Gd: 0-2 GF: 0-4 Fm: 0-0
Distance: 5f/6f: 0-0 7f-8f: 0-0 9f-13f: 0-6 14f+: 0-0
Track : LH: 0-3 RH: 0-0 Tight: 0-3 Gall: 0-0
Aids: Bl: 0-0 Vi: 0-0 Tstrap: 0-2
Best Rating: 66 6/01 Wind 1m2f7y gd-fm

She comes from a good family, but has shown only modest form.

Upstream

102 **79**
3-y-o b/br f Prince Sabo-Rivers Rhapsody (Dominion)
R F Johnson Houghton Major P G Pusinelli

Placings:4430-42150001 **(4785)**
2001: 5^{4}GS, 5^{2}F, 5^{1}GF, 5^{5}G, 5^{0}GS, 5^{0}GF, 5^{0}G, 5^{1}G

	Starts	1st	2nd	3rd	Win & Pl
Career Total (Turf)	12	2	1	1	9278

76	9/01	Gdwd	5f	E(0-75)H	GD	£4062
79	6/01	Folk	5f	D	G-F	£3010

Total win prize-money £7073

Going (Turf): Sf: 0-1 GS: 0-3 **Gd: 1-3 GF: 1-4** Fm: 0-1
Distance: **5f/6f: 2-11** 7f-8f: 0-1 9f-13f: 0-0 14f+: 0-0
Track : LH: 0-2 RH: 0-2 Tight: 0-1 Gall: 0-2
Aids: Bl: 0-0 Vi: 0-0 Tstrap: 0-0
Best Rating: 79 6/01 Folk 5f gd-fm

Showed ability as a juvenile for since-retired David Chappell as a juvenile without winning. She duly won her maiden in summer of 2001 and landed a five-furlong Goodwood handicap in September.Acts on fast ground, best over minimum trip.

Uptown Lad (IRE)

70(79) (56)**48**
2-y-o b c Definite Article-Shoka (FR) (Kaldoun (FR))
Mrs A Duffield Uptown Girls

Placings:00 **(5378)**
2001: 6^{0}GS, 5^{0}S, 6^{4}SD

	Starts	1st	2nd	3rd	Win & Pl
Career Total (Turf)	2	0	0	0	

Going (Turf): Sf: 0-1 GS: 0-1 Gd: 0-0 GF: 0-0 Fm: 0-0
Distance: 5f/6f: 0-2 7f-8f: 0-0 9f-13f: 0-0 14f+: 0-0
Track : LH: 0-0 RH: 0-0 Tight: 0-0 Gall: 0-0
Aids: Bl: 0-0 Vi: 0-0 Tstrap: 0-0
Best Rating: 48 10/01 Newc 6f gd-sft

Urban Myth

96(101) (63)**69d**
3-y-o b c Shaamit (IRE)-Nashville Blues (IRE) (Try My Best (USA))
J W Unett (J W Hills 30/7) T Morning

Placings:0-0044032 **(5198)**
2001: 10^{0}G, 10^{0}GF, 10^{4}GF, 12^{4}G, 11^{0}GF, 9^{3}SW, 9^{2}SD

	Starts	1st	2nd	3rd	Win & Pl
Career Total (Turf)	6	0	0	0	682
Career Total (AW)	2	0	1	1	1018

Going (Turf): Sf: 0-0 GS: 0-1 Gd: 0-2 GF: 0-3 Fm: 0-0
Distance: 5f/6f: 0-0 7f-8f: 0-0 9f-13f: 0-8 14f+: 0-0
Track : LH: 0-5 RH: 0-0 Tight: 0-7 Gall: 0-1
Aids: Bl: 0-0 Vi: 0-0 Tstrap: 0-3
Best Rating: 63 9/01 Wolv 1m1f79y slow

Urgent Reply (USA)

62 **15**
8-y-o b g Green Dancer (USA)-Bowl Of Honey (USA) (Lyphard (USA))
B W Murray B Murray

Placings:40500001122000/65011106000/0060510400/00066260-004 **(4237)**
2001: 12^{0}F, 16^{0}GF, 11^{4}GF

	Starts	1st	2nd	3rd	Win & Pl
Career Total (Turf)	44	6	3	0	19510
Career Total (AW)	2	0	0	0	

42	6/99	Wwck	2m20y	E(0-70)H	HVY	£3101
51	7/98	Chep	1m4f23y	F(0-70)H	GD	£2402
49	6/98	Muss	2m	F(0-60)H	G-S	£2154
44	6/98	Haml	1m5f9y	F(0-70)H	SFT	£2570
51	8/97	Catt	1m3f214yF		G-F	£2532
52	7/97	Haml	1m4f17y	D	G-F	£3403

Total win prize-money £16164

Going (Turf): Sf: 2-10 GS: 1-9 Gd: 1-10 **GF: 2-7** Fm: 0-7
Distance: 5f/6f: 0-0 7f-8f: 0-0 9f-13f: 3-23 14f+: 3-22
Track : LH: 3-21 RH: 3-24 **Tight: 4-26** Gall: 0-2
Aids: Bl: 0-0 Vi: 0-1 **Tstrap: 1-6**
Best Rating: 52 7/97 Haml 1m4f17y GF

In fine form in June 1998, completing a quick hat-trick, but has not won since scoring at Warwick in the middle of 1999 and is a shadow of his former self.

Urgent Swift

102(103) (52)**60**
8-y-o ch g Beveled (USA)-Good Natured (Troy)
A P Jarvis A P Jarvis

Placings:5402005/5022310/3020320/0050/3013030163 0050523/514401012405005-30310445122200 **(5152)**
2001: 16^{3}SD, 16^{0}SD, 12^{3}SW, 14^{1}SD, 12^{0}GS, 13^{4}GF, 14^{4}G, 13^{5}GF, 12^{1}GF, 14^{2}GF, 12^{2}GF, 14^{2}F, 14^{0}G, 14^{0}G

	Starts	1st	2nd	3rd	Win & Pl
Career Total (Turf)	61	5	10	7	40160

Career Total (AW)	10	3	0	3		8154
55	7/01	Epsm	1m4f10y	E(0-75)H	G-F	£3454
52	3/01	Sthl	1m6f	F(0-60)	STD	£2114
66	6/00	Gdwd	1m6f	D(0-85)H	G-F	£3900
68	5/00	Sthl	1m6f	F(0-65)H	STD	£2261
65	2/00	Sthl	1m4f	E(0-70)H	STD	£2782
76	7/99	Hayd	1m6f	D(0-85)H	G-S	£4013
66	5/99	Sals	1m4f	D(0-80)H	G-F	£4065
71	9/96	Rdcr	1m2f	D(0-80)H	FRM	£4159

Total win prize-money £26749

Going (Turf): Sf: 0-4 GS: 1-6 Gd: 0-15 **GF: 3-30** Fm: 1-6
Distance: 5f/6f: 0-1 7f-8f: 0-6 9f-13f: 4-24 14f+: 4-40
Track : **LH: 6-49** RH: 2-22 **Tight: 4-23** Gall: 0-14
Aids: Bl: 0-1 Vi: 0-0 Tstrap: 0-0
Best Rating: 60 8/01 Sals 1m6f15y firm

Somewhat in-and-out, he has been running on the All-Weather during the winter, winning at Southwell over a mile and six. Scored at Epsom in July. Despite his years he still retains his enthusiasm for the game. Best suited by small fields. Acts on a sound surface.

Ursa Major

87(112) (81) **48**
7-y-o b g Warning-Double Entendre (Dominion)
C N Allen Newmarketconnections.Com

Placings:5621/000000**001**/4111440003336/000204604100040/212116030531-4504000 **(4667)**
2001: 12^{4}SD, 12^{5}SD, 10^{0}SW, 11^{4}SW, 7^{0}GF, 10^{0}GF, 8^{0}GF, 8^{5}SD

	Starts	1st	2nd	3rd	Win & Pl		
Career Total (Turf)	25	1	2	0	13218		
Career Total (AW)	35	9	2	5	49750		
81	12/00	Ling	1m4f	C(0-100)H		STD	£6613
81	2/00	Ling	1m4f	C(0-95)H		STD	£6500
80	2/00	Ling	1m4f	C(0-100)H		STD	£8268
67	1/00	Ling	1m2f	C(0-100)H		STD	£6467
59	9/99	York	6f214y	E(0-75)H		G-F	£10430
87	2/98	Ling	1m	D(0-85)H		SLW	£3403
87	1/98	Ling	1m	E(0-70)H		STD	£2818
82	1/98	Sthl	1m	G		STD	£2433
69	1/98	Sthl	1m	F		STD	£1735
70	12/96	Ling	6f	D		STD	£3318

Total win prize-money £51990

Going (Turf): Sf: 0-1 GS: 0-4 Gd: 0-7 **GF: 1-12** Fm: 0-1
Distance: 5f/6f: 1-8 **7f-8f: 5-28** 9f-13f: 4-24 14f+: 0-0
Track : **LH: 10-43** RH: 0-5 **Tight: 7-36** Gall: 1-3
Aids: **Bl: 1-7** Vi: 0-0 Tstrap: 0-0
Best Rating: 77 1/01 Ling 1m4f stand

He is a winner on turf, but is a much better performer on Equitrack and has won three races this winter in fine style. Suited by forcing tactics, he has shown that he gets twelve furlongs really well and a very effective front runner.

Usloob (IRE)

94 **64**
3-y-o ch c Elmaamul (USA)-Rawaabe (USA) (Nureyev (USA))
J Cullinan (B W Hills 6/7) Chris Marsh

Placings:3542000 **(5519)**
2001: 7^{3}GF, 7^{5}GF, 6^{4}GF, 6^{2}GF, 7^{0}GF, 8^{0}GS, 6^{0}HY

	Starts	1st	2nd	3rd	Win & Pl
Career Total (Turf)	7	0	1	1	1755

Going (Turf): Sf: 0-1 GS: 0-1 Gd: 0-0 GF: 0-5 Fm: 0-0
Distance: 5f/6f: 0-2 7f-8f: 0-4 9f-13f: 0-1 14f+: 0-0
Track : LH: 0-0 RH: 0-1 Tight: 0-0 Gall: 0-0
Aids: Bl: 0-0 Vi: 0-0 Tstrap: 0-0
Best Rating: 69 6/01 Newb 7f gd-fm

Utah (IRE)

(97) (29) **28**
7-y-o b g High Estate-Easy Romance (USA) (Northern Jove (CAN))
A G Juckes Itzabuzz Racing Club

Placings:05/60/0/52000/0432000-000 **(0319)**
2001: 8^{0}SD, 8^{0}SW, 8^{0}SD

	Starts	1st	2nd	3rd	Win & Pl
Career Total (Turf)	6	0	0	0	0
Career Total (AW)	14	0	2	1	1657

Going (Turf): Sf: 0-2 GS: 0-3 Gd: 0-0 GF: 0-1 Fm: 0-0
Distance: 5f/6f: 0-0 7f-8f: 0-9 9f-13f: 0-11 14f+: 0-0
Track : LH: 0-17 RH: 0-1 Tight: 0-13 Gall: 0-1
Aids: Bl: 0-8 Vi: 0-0 Tstrap: 0-0
Best Rating: 20 1/01 Sthl 1m stand

Uther Pendragon (IRE)

82 (30) **18**
6-y-o b g Petardia-Mountain Stage (IRE) (Pennine Walk)
M Bradstock Miss J C Blackwell

Placings:00/000/0/0 **(4471)**
2001: 6^{0}GF

	Starts	1st	2nd	3rd	Win & Pl
Career Total (Turf)	4	0	0	0	
Career Total (AW)	3	0	0	0	

Going (Turf): Sf: 0-0 GS: 0-0 Gd: 0-2 GF: 0-1 Fm: 0-1
Distance: 5f/6f: 0-2 7f-8f: 0-4 9f-13f: 0-1 14f+: 0-0
Track : LH: 0-5 RH: 0-0 Tight: 0-3 Gall: 0-0
Aids: Bl: 0-1 Vi: 0-0 Tstrap: 0-0
Best Rating: 18 9/01 Brig 6f209y gd-fm

Utmost (IRE)

86(86) (28) **23**
3-y-o ch f Most Welcome-Bint Alhabib (Nashwan (USA))
P D Evans Mrs H Raw

Placings:0000-0630030000 **(4483)**
2001: 8^{0}SD, 9^{6}SW, 9^{3}SD, 8^{0}SW, 10^{0}SW, 11^{3}SW, 11^{0}SD, 12^{0}G, 11^{0}GF, 14^{0}S

	Starts	1st	2nd	3rd	Win & Pl
Career Total (Turf)	6	0	0	0	
Career Total (AW)	8	0	0	2	642

Going (Turf): Sf: 0-1 GS: 0-1 Gd: 0-1 GF: 0-3 Fm: 0-0
Distance: 5f/6f: 0-2 7f-8f: 0-4 9f-13f: 0-7 14f+: 0-1
Track : LH: 0-12 RH: 0-2 Tight: 0-7 Gall: 0-2
Aids: Bl: 0-2 Vi: 0-6 Tstrap: 0-0
Best Rating: 29 2/01 Wolv 1m1f79y stand

Uzy

84(95) (26) **30**
5-y-o ch g Common Grounds-Loch Clair (IRE) (Lomond (USA))
M J Polglase Mike Bromley

Placings:02/4030020600/000000-0000460000 (2578)
2001: 8^{0}SD, 7^{0}SW, 7^{0}SD, 12^{0}SW, 5^{4}SD, 6^{6}GF, 6^{0}GF, 6^{0}GF, 7^{0}GF, 6^{0}SD

	Starts	1st	2nd	3rd	Win & Pl
Career Total (Turf)	20	0	2	1	2577
Career Total (AW)	8	0	0	0	0

Going (Turf): Sf: 0-4 GS: 0-0 Gd: 0-4 GF: 0-9 Fm: 0-3
Distance: 5f/6f: 0-11 7f-8f: 0-13 9f-13f: 0-4 14f+: 0-0
Track : LH: 0-13 RH: 0-4 Tight: 0-3 Gall: 0-3
Aids: Bl: 0-9 Vi: 0-3 Tstrap: 0-3
Best Rating: 40 5/01 Donc 6f gd-fm

Vahorimix (FR)

113 **122**
3-y-o gr c Linamix (FR)-Vadsa Honor (FR) (Highest Honor (FR))
A Fabre J-L Lagardere

Placings:612-114165 **(5006)**
2001: 9^{1}HY, 8^{1}G, 8^{4}G, 8^{1}GS, 8^{6}GS, 8^{5}S

	Starts	1st	2nd	3rd	Win & Pl	
Career Total (Turf)	9	4	1	0	293057	
122	8/01	Deau	1m		G-S	£145490
119	5/01	Lonc	1m		GD	£96993
	4/01	Chan	1m1f		HVY	£13579
	8/00	Lonc	1m		G-S	£7685

Total win prize-money £263747

Going (Turf): Sf: 1-3 GS: 1-2 Gd: 1-2 GF: 0-0 Fm: 0-0
Distance: 5f/6f: 0-0 **7f-8f: 2-6** 9f-13f: 1-1 14f+: 0-0
Track : LH: 0-0 RH: 0-4 Tight: 0-0 Gall: 0-2
Aids: Bl: 0-0 Vi: 0-0 Tstrap: 0-0
Best Rating: 122 8/01 Deau 1m gd-sft

Smart French miler who was unlucky when narrowly defeated in the French 2000 Guineas in May, but was subsequently awarded the race when Noverre was disqualified. Had won in Listed company prior to that and does not look too far behind with the best British milers. Gained another fortunate Group One victory when awarded the Jacques le Marois at the expense of Proudwings, before failing in the Moulin. Has been retired.

Valdasho

74 **36**
2-y-o b f Classic Cliche (IRE)-Ma Rivale (Last Tycoon)
G G Margarson Sho Racing

Placings:00 **(5620)**
2001: 6^{0}S, 8^{0}GS

	Starts	1st	2nd	3rd	Win & Pl
Career Total (Turf)	2	0	0	0	

Going (Turf): Sf: 0-1 GS: 0-1 Gd: 0-0 GF: 0-0 Fm: 0-0
Distance: 5f/6f: 0-1 7f-8f: 0-0 9f-13f: 0-1 14f+: 0-0
Track : LH: 0-2 RH: 0-0 Tight: 0-0 Gall: 0-0
Aids: Bl: 0-0 Vi: 0-0 Tstrap: 0-0
Best Rating: 36 11/01 Nott 1m54y gd-sft

Valdero

88(90) (37) **37**
4-y-o ch g Arazi (USA)-Vale Of Truth (USA) (Lyphard's Wish (FR))
W R Muir J Haim

Placings:04000-00000 **(2868)**
2001: 11^{0}SD, 11^{0}GF, 11^{0}GF, 11^{0}F, 10^{0}GF

	Starts	1st	2nd	3rd	Win & Pl
Career Total (Turf)	9	0	0	0	349
Career Total (AW)	1	0	0	0	

Going (Turf): Sf: 0-1 GS: 0-2 Gd: 0-1 GF: 0-4 Fm: 0-1
Distance: 5f/6f: 0-0 7f-8f: 0-1 9f-13f: 0-9 14f+: 0-0
Track : LH: 0-2 RH: 0-4 Tight: 0-7 Gall: 0-0
Aids: Bl: 0-0 Vi: 0-0 Tstrap: 0-0
Best Rating: 37 6/01 Wind 1m3f135y gd-fm

Valdesco (IRE)

98 **74**
3-y-o ch c Bluebird (USA)-Allegheny River (USA) (Lear Fan (USA))
Mrs M Reveley Ian D Rosenberg

Placings:34104-030300 **(5172)**
2001: 5^{0}F, 6^{3}GF, 6^{0}GF, 7^{3}GF, 8^{0}F, 6^{0}GS

	Starts	1st	2nd	3rd	Win & Pl	
Career Total (Turf)	11	1	0	3	5822	
67	7/00	Brig	5f213y	D	FRM	£3380

Total win prize-money £3380

Going (Turf): Sf: 0-1 GS: 0-1 Gd: 0-2 GF: 0-4 **Fm: 1-3**
Distance: **5f/6f: 1-7** 7f-8f: 0-4 9f-13f: 0-0 14f+: 0-0
Track : **LH: 1-3** RH: 0-2 Tight: 0-0 Gall: 0-2
Aids: Bl: 0-2 Vi: 0-1 Tstrap: 0-0
Best Rating: 74 6/01 Rdcr 7f gd-fm

Vale Of Leven (IRE)

(88) (16)
5-y-o b g Fayruz-Speedy Action (Horage)
R Williams (W G M Turner 2/2) R Williams

Placings:0004211**6/060000000000/0305** **(0220)**
2001: 8^{0}SD, 12^{3}SW, 12^{0}SD, 11^{5}SD

	Starts	1st	2nd	3rd	Win & Pl
Career Total (Turf)	13	1	0	0	3141
Career Total (AW)	12	1	1	1	3738

61 11/98 Sthl 7f E(0-85)H STD £2853
56 10/98 Rdcr 6f E(0-75)H SFT £3141
Total win prize-money £5994

Going (Turf): Sf: 1-2 GS: 0-3 Gd: 0-5 GF: 0-3 Fm: 0-0
Distance: 5f/6f: 1-7 7f-8f: 1-13 9f-13f: 0-5 14f+: 0-0
Track : **LH: 1-16** RH: 0-0 Tight: 0-5 Gall: 0-0
Aids: Bl: 0-0 Vi: 0-1 Tstrap: 0-3
Best Rating: 16 1/01 Wolv 1m4f slow

Valentine Band (USA)

107 **98**
4-y-o b f Dixieland Band (USA)-Shirley Valentine (Shirley Heights)
R Charlton K Abdulla

Placings:6/1-230 **(3251)**
2001: 10^{2}GF, 10^{3}F, 12^{0}GS

	Starts	1st	2nd	3rd	Win & Pl
Career Total (Turf)	5	1	1	1	13472

97 7/00 Pont 1m2f6y D GD £3542
Total win prize-money £3543

Going (Turf): Sf: 0-1 GS: 0-1 **Gd: 1-1** GF: 0-1 Fm: 0-1
Distance: 5f/6f: 0-0 7f-8f: 0-1 **9f-13f: 1-4** 14f+: 0-0
Track : **LH: 1-3** RH: 0-0 Tight: 0-0 Gall: 0-2
Aids: Bl: 0-0 Vi: 0-0 Tstrap: 0-0
Best Rating: 98 5/01 York 1m2f85y gd-fm

She only ran once in each of her two and three-year-old campaigns and got off the mark in a four-runner Pontefract maiden last season. She subsequently suffered a stress fracture but came back to run Moselle to two lengths in a Listed event at York. Bred to stay a mile and a half. Acts on a sound surface.

Valentines Vision

(98) (53)
4-y-o b g Distinctly North (USA)-Sharp Anne (Belfort (FR))
Mrs S Lamyman David Fravigar And Nigel Underwood

Placings:650/03416200-0000 **(5503)**
2001: 7^{0}SD, 8^{0}HY, 6^{0}SD, 7^{0}HY, 6^{0}SD

	Starts	1st	2nd	3rd	Win & Pl
Career Total (Turf)	6	0	0	1	313
Career Total (AW)	9	1	1	0	2371

54 10/00 Wolv 7f G STD £1939
Total win prize-money £1939

Going (Turf): Sf: 0-2 GS: 0-0 Gd: 0-1 GF: 0-3 Fm: 0-0
Distance: 5f/6f: 0-3 **7f-8f: 1-9** 9f-13f: 0-3 14f+: 0-0
Track : **LH: 1-12** RH: 0-0 **Tight: 1-5** Gall: 0-1
Aids: Bl: 0-0 Vi: 0-3 Tstrap: 0-0
Best Rating: 26 3/01 Wolv 7f stand

Valentino

111 **114d**
4-y-o ch h Nureyev (USA)-Divine Danse (FR) (Kris)
J H M Gosden A E Oppenheimer

Placings:14/32020-14343 **(4831)**
2001: 7^{1}F, 8^{4}G, 7^{3}GF, 7^{4}G, 7^{3}GF

	Starts	1st	2nd	3rd	Win & Pl
Career Total (Turf)	12	2	2	3	122067

76 5/01 Leic 7f9y C FRM £6496
80 7/99 Asct 6f D G-F £7002
Total win prize-money £13499

Going (Turf): Sf: 0-0 GS: 0-1 Gd: 0-2 **GF: 1-6 Fm: 1-1**
Distance: 5f/6f: 1-1 7f-8f: 1-11 9f-13f: 0-0 14f+: 0-0
Track : LH: 0-2 RH: 0-6 Tight: 0-0 Gall: 0-4
Aids: Bl: 0-0 Vi: 0-0 **Tstrap: 2-10**
Best Rating: 116 6/01 Asct 1m good

He was a useful three-year-old, runner-up in the St James' Palace Stakes, but he did not impress as the heartiest of battlers. Showed a nice turn of foot to win on his reappearance at Leicester but has found less than anticipated when in the frame in Group races since. It appears that he needs things to fall just right.

Valeureux

105 **89d**
3-y-o ch g Cadeaux Genereux-La Strada (Niniski (USA))
J Hetherton Eureka Racing

Placings:0-150 **(5251)**
2001: 8^{1}HY, 10^{5}GF, 7^{0}S

	Starts	1st	2nd	3rd	Win & Pl
Career Total (Turf)	4	1	0	0	4646

78 3/01 Nott 1m54y D HVY £3851
Total win prize-money £3851

Going (Turf): Sf: 1-3 GS: 0-0 Gd: 0-0 GF: 0-1 Fm: 0-0
Distance: 5f/6f: 0-0 7f-8f: 0-2 **9f-13f: 1-2** 14f+: 0-0
Track : **LH: 1-3** RH: 0-0 Tight: 0-0 Gall: 0-2
Aids: Bl: 0-0 Vi: 0-0 Tstrap: 0-0
Best Rating: 89 5/01 York 1m2f85y gd-fm

He caused a real surprise when wining a Nottingham maiden at 100/1 on his reappearance and obviously handles testing conditions well but he was well held at York after that. Acts well over a mile.

Valfonic

101 **75**
3-y-o b c Zafonic (USA)-Valbra (Dancing Brave (USA))
Mrs A J Perrett K Abdulla

Placings:310 **(5179)**
2001: 9^{3}GF, 9^{1}GF, 10^{0}HY

	Starts	1st	2nd	3rd	Win & Pl
Career Total (Turf)	3	1	0	1	4164

75 8/01 Folk 1m1f149yD G-F £3234
Total win prize-money £3234

Going (Turf): Sf: 0-1 GS: 0-0 Gd: 0-0 **GF: 1-2** Fm: 0-0
Distance: 5f/6f: 0-0 7f-8f: 0-0 **9f-13f: 1-3** 14f+: 0-0
Track : LH: 0-1 **RH: 1-1 Tight: 1-2** Gall: 0-1
Aids: Bl: 0-0 Vi: 0-0 Tstrap: 0-0
Best Rating: 75 8/01 Folk 1m1f149y gd-fm

Improved for his belated debut when winning a Folkestone maiden. May have found the track too sharp, and may be capable of improving on that effort.

Valjean (IRE)

(65) (6)**51**
5-y-o b g Alzao (USA)-Escape Path (Wolver Hollow)
R J Price (D J Wintle 18/1) John Richards

Placings:00/050/400-0 **(0117)**
2001: 9^{0}SW

	Starts	1st	2nd	3rd	Win & Pl
Career Total (Turf)	8	0	0	0	240
Career Total (AW)	1	0	0	0	

Going (Turf): Sf: 0-1 GS: 0-0 Gd: 0-3 GF: 0-1 Fm: 0-0
Distance: 5f/6f: 0-1 7f-8f: 0-3 9f-13f: 0-5 14f+: 0-0
Track : LH: 0-5 RH: 0-3 Tight: 0-1 Gall: 0-0
Aids: Bl: 0-1 Vi: 0-0 Tstrap: 0-0
Best Rating: 6 1/01 Wolv 1m1f79y slow

Valley Of Dreams (IRE)

77 **59**
3-y-o b f Fairy King (USA)-Capegulch (USA) (Gulch (USA))
P Howling Liam Sheridan

Placings:0-0 **(2136)**
2001: 7^{0}GF

	Starts	1st	2nd	3rd	Win & Pl
Career Total (Turf)	2	0	0	0	

Going (Turf): Sf: 0-0 GS: 0-0 Gd: 0-0 GF: 0-2 Fm: 0-0
Distance: 5f/6f: 0-0 7f-8f: 0-2 9f-13f: 0-0 14f+: 0-0
Track : LH: 0-0 RH: 0-0 Tight: 0-0 Gall: 0-0
Aids: Bl: 0-0 Vi: 0-0 Tstrap: 0-0
Best Rating: 59 6/01 Yarm 7f3y gd-fm

Valley Of Song

104 **74**
3-y-o ch f Caerleon (USA)-Hill Of Snow (Reference Point)
J L Dunlop L Neil Jones

Placings:1 **(4958)**
2001: 9^{1}GS

	Starts	1st	2nd	3rd	Win & Pl
Career Total (Turf)	1	1	0	0	4807

74 9/01 Gdwd 1m1f192yD G-S £4806
Total win prize-money £4807

Going (Turf): Sf: 0-0 **GS: 1-1** Gd: 0-0 GF: 0-0 Fm: 0-0
Distance: 5f/6f: 0-0 7f-8f: 0-0 **9f-13f: 1-1** 14f+: 0-0
Track : LH: 0-0 **RH: 1-1 Tight: 1-1** Gall: 0-0
Aids: Bl: 0-0 Vi: 0-0 Tstrap: 0-0
Best Rating: 74 9/01 Gdwd 1m1f192y gd-sft

She did not race at two and made a winning debut at Goodwood in September. Should go on to better things.

Vals Ring

98(82) (36)**50**
3-y-o ch g King's Signet (USA)-Factuelle (Known Fact (USA))
J Gallagher Horses Away Racing Club

Placings:0-00050050 **(3670)**
2001: 7^{0}S, 6^{0}GS, 5^{0}F, 5^{5}F, 6^{0}GF, 6^{0}SD, 6^{5}SD, 8^{0}S

	Starts	1st	2nd	3rd	Win & Pl
Career Total (Turf)	6	0	0	0	0
Career Total (AW)	3	0	0	0	0

Going (Turf): Sf: 0-2 GS: 0-1 Gd: 0-0 GF: 0-1 Fm: 0-2
Distance: 5f/6f: 0-7 7f-8f: 0-1 9f-13f: 0-1 14f+: 0-0
Track : LH: 0-6 RH: 0-1 Tight: 0-1 Gall: 0-1
Aids: Bl: 0-0 Vi: 0-0 Tstrap: 0-1
Best Rating: 74 5/01 Leic 5f218y firm

Valuable Gift

94 **58**
4-y-o ch g Cadeaux Genereux-Valbra (Dancing Brave (USA))
T D Barron London Gold (fanway Limited)

Placings:05000 **(4110)**
2001: 8^{0}S, 5^{5}GS, 6^{0}GF, 6^{0}GF, 5^{0}S

	Starts	1st	2nd	3rd	Win & Pl
Career Total (Turf)	5	0	0	0	0

Going (Turf): Sf: 0-2 GS: 0-1 Gd: 0-0 GF: 0-2 Fm: 0-0
Distance: 5f/6f: 0-4 7f-8f: 0-1 9f-13f: 0-0 14f+: 0-0
Track : LH: 0-0 RH: 0-1 Tight: 0-1 Gall: 0-0
Aids: Bl: 0-0 Vi: 0-0 Tstrap: 0-0
Best Rating: 58 4/01 Muss 5f gd-sft

Van De Velde

91 **78**
2-y-o ch g Alhijaz-Lucky Flinders (Free State)
P F I Cole Richard Green (fine Paintings)

Placings:23 (4852)
2001: 6²GF, 5³GF

	Starts	1st	2nd	3rd	Win & Pl
Career Total (Turf)	2	0	1	1	1430

Going (Turf): Sf: 0-0 GS: 0-0 Gd: 0-0 GF: 0-2 Fm: 0-0
Distance: 5f/6f: 0-2 7f-8f: 0-0 9f-13f: 0-0 14f+: 0-0
Track : LH: 0-1 RH: 0-0 Tight: 0-1 Gall: 0-0
Aids: Bl: 0-0 Vi: 0-0 Tstrap: 0-0
Best Rating: 78 9/01 Ling 6f gd-fm

Vandenberghe

82(84) (38)58
2-y-o b c Millkom-Child Star (FR) (Bellypha)
Mrs Merrita Jones (D Marks 14/6) D Marks

Placings:00000 (5127)
2001: 6⁰GF, 7⁰GF, 8⁰S, 8⁰GF, 7⁰HY, 7⁰SD

	Starts	1st	2nd	3rd	Win & Pl
Career Total (Turf)	5	0	0	0	

Going (Turf): Sf: 0-2 GS: 0-0 Gd: 0-0 GF: 0-3 Fm: 0-0
Distance: 5f/6f: 0-0 7f-8f: 0-4 9f-13f: 0-1 14f+: 0-0
Track : LH: 0-0 RH: 0-2 Tight: 0-0 Gall: 0-1
Aids: Bl: 0-0 Vi: 0-0 Tstrap: 0-0
Best Rating: 58 9/01 Newb 1m gd-fm

Cut no ice in his initial runs.

Vanderlin

102 88
2-y-o ch c Halling (USA)-Massorah (FR) (Habitat)
I A Balding Exors Of The Late Robert Hitchins

Placings:202 (3227)
2001: 5²GF, 7⁰GF, 6²GF

	Starts	1st	2nd	3rd	Win & Pl
Career Total (Turf)	3	0	2	0	2621

Going (Turf): Sf: 0-0 GS: 0-0 Gd: 0-0 GF: 0-3 Fm: 0-0
Distance: 5f/6f: 0-2 7f-8f: 0-1 9f-13f: 0-0 14f+: 0-0
Track : LH: 0-1 RH: 0-0 Tight: 0-0 Gall: 0-0
Aids: Bl: 0-0 Vi: 0-0 Tstrap: 0-0
Best Rating: 88 6/01 Asct 7f gd-fm

Vanity (IRE)

103 64
4-y-o b f Thatching-Penny Fan (Nomination)
G B Balding Theo Waddington

Placings:6-222404 (5522)
2001: 6²GS, 5²F, 5²GF, 6⁴GS, 6⁰GS, 6⁴HY

	Starts	1st	2nd	3rd	Win & Pl
Career Total (Turf)	7	0	3	0	3476

Going (Turf): Sf: 0-2 GS: 0-3 Gd: 0-0 GF: 0-1 Fm: 0-1
Distance: 5f/6f: 0-7 7f-8f: 0-0 9f-13f: 0-0 14f+: 0-0
Track : LH: 0-0 RH: 0-1 Tight: 0-0 Gall: 0-1
Aids: Bl: 0-0 Vi: 0-0 Tstrap: 0-0
Best Rating: 75 5/01 Sals 6f gd-sft

Lightly raced for a four-year-old, she has run well in maiden company but is becoming a something of a bridesmaid.

Vantage Point

90(101) (35)24
5-y-o b g Casteddu-Rosie Dickins (Blue Cashmere)
K McAuliffe The Hare And Hounds Partnership

Placings:0000/24244313403322/0451-06035006 (5531)
2001: 16⁰SW, 16⁶SD, 16⁰SD, 16³SD, 15⁵HY, 14⁰SD, 11⁰S, 16⁶HY

	Starts	1st	2nd	3rd	Win & Pl
Career Total (Turf)	17	1	2	2	8300
Career Total (AW)	13	1	2	3	3815

41	12/00	Wolv	2m46y	F(0-60)H		STD	£1778
49	8/99	Folk	1m4f	E(0-70)H		G-S	£4659

Total win prize-money £6438

Going (Turf): Sf: 0-6 GS: 1-1 Gd: 0-3 GF: 0-5 Fm: 0-2
Distance: 5f/6f: 0-0 7f-8f: 0-3 9f-13f: 1-13 14f+: 1-14
Track : LH: 1-22 RH: 1-6 Tight: 2-17 Gall: 0-1
Aids: Bl: 0-0 Vi: 0-0 Tstrap: 0-0
Best Rating: 35 3/01 Sthl 2m stand

Vasari (IRE)

96(105) (56)43
7-y-o ch g Imperial Frontier (USA)-Why Not Glow (IRE) (Glow (USA))
P Howling (Jamie Poulton 31/3) Bvi Partnership

Placings:210353/500/6646034/34600000060/606-62060000000 (3317)
2001: 7⁶SD, 8²SD, 9⁰SW, 8⁶SW, 10⁰SD, 5⁰F, 8⁰G, 7⁰GF, 6⁰GF, 5⁰GF, 7⁰G

	Starts	1st	2nd	3rd	Win & Pl
Career Total (Turf)	31	1	1	3	13747
Career Total (AW)	10	0	1	1	2277

83	5/96	Ches	5f16y	D	GD	£7112

Total win prize-money £7113

Going (Turf): Sf: 0-5 GS: 0-4 Gd: 1-13 GF: 0-8 Fm: 0-1
Distance: 5f/6f: 1-23 7f-8f: 0-15 9f-13f: 0-3 14f+: 0-0
Track : LH: 1-15 RH: 0-1 Tight: 1-12 Gall: 0 2
Aids: Bl: 0-1 Vi: 0-0 Tstrap: 0-1
Best Rating: 56 2/01 Ling 1m stand

Veda's Rainbow (IRE)

92 71
2-y-o b/br f Petardia-Sama Veda (IRE) (Rainbow Quest (USA))
S Kirk Ascot Brew Racing

Placings:0000000 (5340)
2001: 6⁰S, 6⁰GF, 6⁰GF, 7⁰GF, 6⁰GF, 7⁰GF, 6⁰GS

	Starts	1st	2nd	3rd	Win & Pl
Career Total (Turf)	7	0	0	0	

Going (Turf): Sf: 0-1 GS: 0-1 Gd: 0-0 GF: 0-5 Fm: 0-0
Distance: 5f/6f: 0-2 7f-8f: 0-5 9f-13f: 0-0 14f+: 0-0
Track : LH: 0-0 RH: 0-2 Tight: 0-1 Gall: 0-1
Aids: Bl: 0-3 Vi: 0-0 Tstrap: 0-0
Best Rating: 87 9/01 Sals 6f212y gd-fm

Modest form to date. Has raced in blinkers to little effect.

Velvet Glade (USA)

107 97
3-y-o b f Kris S (USA)-Vailmont (USA) (Diesis)
I A Balding George Strawbridge

Placings:316-01050 (4682)
2001: 7⁰G, 7¹GS, 7⁰GF, 7⁵GS, 7⁰G

	Starts	1st	2nd	3rd	Win & Pl
Career Total (Turf)	8	2	0	1	16358

97	7/01	NmkJ	7f	B(0-100)H	G-S	£9071
83	9/00	Ling	7f	D	G-F	£3038

Total win prize-money £12110

Going (Turf): Sf: 0-0 GS: 1-3 Gd: 0-2 GF: 1-3 Fm: 0-0
Distance: 5f/6f: 0-1 7f-8f: 2-7 9f-13f: 0-0 14f+: 0-0
Track : LH: 0-1 RH: 0-1 Tight: 0-1 Gall: 0-1
Aids: Bl: 0-0 Vi: 0-0 Tstrap: 0-0
Best Rating: 97 7/01 NmkJ 7f gd-sft

Third behind Regal Rose in a useful race on her juvenile debut, she won readily at Lingfield on her second outing but found Group company a different ball game on her final start. She returned to winning ways in a fillies' rated stakes on her second start of 2001 season at the Newmarket July meeting.

Velvet Island (IRE)

98(102) (69)69
3-y-o b f Turtle Island (IRE)-Double Grange (IRE) (Double Schwartz)
W J Haggas Phil Davis

Placings:4-263100301 (5611)
2001: 6²G, 5⁶GF, 6³GF, 6¹SD, 7⁰GS, 6⁰G, 7³SD, 7⁰HY, 8¹SD, 10⁰SD

	Starts	1st	2nd	3rd	Win & Pl
Career Total (Turf)	6	0	1	1	1146
Career Total (AW)	4	2	0	1	6204

69	11/01	Wolv	1m100y	E(0-75)H	STD	£2898
64	6/01	Sthl	6f	D	STD	£2786

Total win prize-money £5684

Going (Turf): Sf: 0-1 GS: 0-1 Gd: 0-2 GF: 0-2 Fm: 0-0
Distance: 5f/6f: 1-4 7f-8f: 0-5 9f-13f: 1-1 14f+: 0-0
Track : LH: 2-5 RH: 0-0 Tight: 1-1 Gall: 0-1
Aids: Bl: 0-1 Vi: 0-0 Tstrap: 0-0
Best Rating: 69 11/01 Wolv 1m100y stand

Landed a Southwell maiden in June and won a handicap at Wolverhampton in November. Her action suggests she would not appreciate firm ground on turf.

Velvet Jones

86 (38)34
8-y-o gr g Sharrood (USA)-Cradle Of Love (USA) (Roberto (USA))
G F H Charles-Jones Mrs Jessica Charles-Jones

Placings:0226234060/02344553630/4050600000/0506400/5650/0-0000 (4181)
2001: 6⁰GF, 7⁰F, 8⁰GF, 12⁰GF

	Starts	1st	2nd	3rd	Win & Pl
Career Total (Turf)	42	0	3	4	4487
Career Total (AW)	5	0	1	0	618

Going (Turf): Sf: 0-0 GS: 0-1 Gd: 0-9 GF: 0-21 Fm: 0-11
Distance: 5f/6f: 0-12 7f-8f: 0-22 9f-13f: 0-13 14f+: 0-0
Track : LH: 0-26 RH: 0-9 Tight: 0-11 Gall: 0-2
Aids: Bl: 0-1 Vi: 0-0 Tstrap: 0-0
Best Rating: 34 7/01 Sals 6f gd-fm

Velvet Slipper

97(92) (46)50
3-y-o b f Muhtafal (USA)-Magic Slipper (Habitat)
G C Bravery D B Clark

Placings:5502050 (5131)
2001: 8⁵SD, 7⁵SD, 8⁰SW, 7²GF, 6⁰GF, 7⁵G, 7⁰HY

	Starts	1st	2nd	3rd	Win & Pl
Career Total (Turf)	4	0	1	0	1311
Career Total (AW)	3	0	0	0	0

Going (Turf): Sf: 0-1 GS: 0-0 Gd: 0-1 GF: 0-2 Fm: 0-0
Distance: 5f/6f: 0-1 7f-8f: 0-6 9f-13f: 0-0 14f+: 0-0
Track : LH: 0-3 RH: 0-0 Tight: 0-2 Gall: 0-0
Aids: Bl: 0-0 Vi: 0-0 Tstrap: 0-0
Best Rating: 50 6/01 NmkJ 7f gd-fm

Vendome (IRE)

103 79
3-y-o b g General Monash (USA)-Kealbra Lady (Petong)
J A Osborne John Livock

Placings:0003312230-003005 (4214)
2001: 5⁰S, 5⁰GF, 6³GF, 5⁰G, 5⁰GF, 5⁵GF

	Starts	1st	2nd	3rd	Win & Pl
Career Total (Turf)	16	1	2	4	14075

77	8/00	Bevl	5f	C	G-F	£7289

Total win prize-money £7290

Going (Turf): Sf: 0-2 GS: 0-1 Gd: 0-3 GF: 1-9 Fm: 0-1

Distance: 5f/6f: 1-15 7f-8f: 0-1 9f-13f: 0-0 14f+: 0-0
Track : LH: 0-2 RH: 0-1 Tight: 0-1 Gall: 0-2
Aids: Bl: 0-0 Vi: 0-0 Tstrap: 0-0
Best Rating: 79 5/01 Thsk 5f gd-fm

Venika Vitesse

85(95) (44)**44**
5-y-o b g Puissance-Vilanika (FR) (Top Ville)
T D Barron Kevin Shaw

Placings:00/10031310/00000005-**0605000000** **(4481)**
2001: 6^{0}SD, 6^{6}SD, 5^{0}SD, 6^{5}SD, 5^{0}GF, 7^{0}SD, 6^{0}GF, 6^{0}GF, 6^{0}F, 8^{0}F

	Starts	1st	2nd	3rd	Win & Pl
Career Total (Turf)	20	2	0	2	8461
Career Total (AW)	8	1	0	0	2087

69	8/99	Nott	6f15y	E(0-75)H	G-F	£3643
66	6/99	Carl	5f207y	E(0-70)H	G-F	£3875
73	1/99	Ling	5f	F	STD	£2087

Total win prize-money £9605

Going (Turf): Sf: 0-1 GS: 0-3 Gd: 0-0 **GF: 2-11** Fm: 0-4
Distance: **5f/6f: 2-21** 7f-8f: 1-6 9f-13f: 0-0 14f+: 0-0
Track : LH: 1-8 RH: 1-2 Tight: 1-4 Gall: 1-1
Aids: Bl: 0-1 Vi: 0-0 Tstrap: 0-0
Best Rating: 45 6/01 Haml 6f5y gd-fm

Venosa (IRE)

95(76) (36)**63**
2-y-o b f Presidium-Breakfast Creek (Hallgate)
D Haydn Jones Mrs E M Haydn Jones

Placings:000500 **(5393)**
2001: 5^{0}SD, 6^{0}SD, 5^{0}SD, 5^{5}G, 6^{0}G, 6^{0}SD

	Starts	1st	2nd	3rd	Win & Pl
Career Total (Turf)	2	0	0	0	0
Career Total (AW)	4	0	0	0	

Going (Turf): Sf: 0-0 GS: 0-0 Gd: 0-2 GF: 0-0 Fm: 0-0
Distance: 5f/6f: 0-5 7f-8f: 0-1 9f-13f: 0-0 14f+: 0-0
Track : LH: 0-2 RH: 0-0 Tight: 0-1 Gall: 0-0
Aids: Bl: 0-0 Vi: 0-0 Tstrap: 0-0
Best Rating: 63 8/01 Folk 5f good

Vento Del Oreno (FR)

(84) (41)**67**
4-y-o ch f Lando (GER)-Very Sweet (Bellypha)
Mrs D Haine H Thomson Jones

Placings:656004250-50 **(0347)**
2001: 12^{5}SW, 9^{0}SD

	Starts	1st	2nd	3rd	Win & Pl
Career Total (Turf)	9	0	1	0	819
Career Total (AW)	2	0	0	0	0

Going (Turf): Sf: 0-3 GS: 0-1 Gd: 0-3 GF: 0-1 Fm: 0-0
Distance: 5f/6f: 0-0 7f-8f: 0-4 9f-13f: 0-6 14f+: 0-0
Track : LH: 0-4 RH: 0-4 Tight: 0-4 Gall: 0-0
Aids: Bl: 0-0 Vi: 0-0 Tstrap: 0-0
Best Rating: 41 2/01 Sthl 1m4f slow

Venturer (USA)

104 **97**
3-y-o b c Gone West (USA)-Angel In My Heart (FR) (Rainbow Quest (USA))
J H M Gosden Sheikh Mohammed

Placings:1130100 **(4782)**
2001: 8^{1}G, 8^{1}GF, 8^{3}GF, 7^{0}GF, 7^{1}G, 8^{0}G, 7^{0}G

	Starts	1st	2nd	3rd	Win & Pl
Career Total (Turf)	7	3	0	1	36956

97	8/01	Gdwd	7f	C(0-100)H	GD	£29250
85	5/01	Gdwd	1m	D	G-F	£6045
	5/01	NmkR	1m	G	GD	£0

Total win prize-money £35295

Going (Turf): Sf: 0-0 GS: 0-0 **Gd: 2-4** GF: 1-3 Fm: 0-0
Distance: 5f/6f: 0-0 **7f-8f: 3-7** 9f-13f: 0-0 14f+: 0-0
Track : LH: 0-1 **RH: 2-4** Tight: 0-0 Gall: 0-2
Aids: Bl: 0-0 Vi: 0-0 Tstrap: 0-0
Best Rating: 97 8/01 Gdwd 7f good

Winner of a match on his debut, he beat a subsequent winner when following up at Goodwood, but was well beaten in conditions events in his next two starts. Back in handicap company, he returned to winning form in a very valuable handicap at Glorious Goodwood. Stays a mile and acts on fast ground.

Vera Two

82 **37**
3-y-o ch f King's Signet (USA)-Vera's First (IRE) (Exodal (USA))
G L Moore The Laurels Stud Farm

Placings:000 **(2939)**
2001: 6^{0}GF, 6^{0}GF, 5^{0}GF

	Starts	1st	2nd	3rd	Win & Pl
Career Total (Turf)	3	0	0	0	

Going (Turf): Sf: 0-0 GS: 0-0 Gd: 0-0 GF: 0-3 Fm: 0-0
Distance: 5f/6f: 0-1 7f-8f: 0-2 9f-13f: 0-0 14f+: 0-0
Track : LH: 0-0 RH: 0-0 Tight: 0-0 Gall: 0-0
Aids: Bl: 0-0 Vi: 0-0 Tstrap: 0-0
Best Rating: 37 6/01 Sals 6f212y gd-fm

Vergil's Venture

91 **77**
2-y-o b g Alhijaz-Quick Profit (Formidable (USA))
G C H Chung A Cramphorn

Placings:53220 **(3638)**
2001: 6^{5}GF, 7^{3}GF, 7^{2}GF, 7^{2}GF, 6^{0}GS

	Starts	1st	2nd	3rd	Win & Pl
Career Total (Turf)	5	0	2	1	2855

Going (Turf): Sf: 0-0 GS: 0-1 Gd: 0-0 GF: 0-4 Fm: 0-0
Distance: 5f/6f: 0-2 7f-8f: 0-3 9f-13f: 0-0 14f+: 0-0
Track : LH: 0-1 RH: 0-0 Tight: 0-0 Gall: 0-0
Aids: Bl: 0-0 Vi: 0-0 Tstrap: 0-0
Best Rating: 77 6/01 Ayr 7f gd-fm

Half-brother to a couple of juvenile winners, promising fifth, albeit not acheiving too much, in a big field over six furlongs on debut. Has since run well without winning, giving the impression that he needs a mile already. Acts on fast ground.

Veridian

101 **88**
8-y-o b g Green Desert (USA)-Alik (FR) (Targowice (USA))
N J Henderson Thurloe Thoroughbreds Iii

Placings:450621/0001512462/1342-004 **(3447)**
2001: 12^{0}S, 12^{0}GF, 12^{4}GF

	Starts	1st	2nd	3rd	Win & Pl
Career Total (Turf)	23	4	4	1	41623

78	5/00	Ches	1m4f66y	D(0-80)H	GD	£7475
80	7/97	Ches	1m4f66y	C(0-90)H	G-F	£6089
78	5/97	Donc	1m4f	D(0-85)H	G-F	£4386
75	8/96	Ling	1m3f106y	D(0-80)H	G-S	£4324

Total win prize-money £22275

Going (Turf): Sf: 0-5 GS: 1-2 Gd: 1-7 **GF: 2-9** Fm: 0-0
Distance: 5f/6f: 0-0 7f-8f: 0-2 **9f-13f: 4-20** 14f+: 0-1
Track : **LH: 4-11** RH: 0-10 **Tight: 3-11** Gall: 1-10
Aids: Bl: 0-1 Vi: 0-0 Tstrap: 0-0
Best Rating: 80 6/01 Gdwd 1m4f gd-fm

Vermilion Creek

93(63) (5)**70**
2-y-o b f Makbul-Cloudy Reef (Cragador)
R Hollinshead M Johnson

Placings:0553500 **(5169)**
2001: 5^{0}SW, 5^{5}F, 6^{5}GF, 6^{3}GF, 6^{5}GF, 6^{0}G, 6^{0}GS

	Starts	1st	2nd	3rd	Win & Pl
Career Total (Turf)	6	0	0	1	478
Career Total (AW)	1	0	0	0	

Going (Turf): Sf: 0-0 GS: 0-1 Gd: 0-1 GF: 0-3 Fm: 0-1
Distance: 5f/6f: 0-6 7f-8f: 0-1 9f-13f: 0-0 14f+: 0-0
Track : LH: 0-2 RH: 0-0 Tight: 0-0 Gall: 0-0
Aids: Bl: 0-0 Vi: 0-0 Tstrap: 0-0
Best Rating: 70 7/01 Sthl 6f gd-fm

Vetority

(74) (2)**71**
4-y-o b f Vettori (IRE)-Celerite (USA) (Riverman (USA))
M Alonso L Alvarez Cervera

Placings:3530400-1
2001: 15^{1}HO

	Starts	1st	2nd	3rd	Win & Pl
Career Total (Turf)	7	1	0	2	5686
Career Total (AW)	1	0	0	0	

11/01	MsnL	1m7f110y		HLD	£4365

Total win prize-money £4365

Going (Turf): Sf: 0-1 GS: 0-1 Gd: 0-0 GF: 0-4 Fm: 0-0
Distance: 5f/6f: 0-0 7f-8f: 0-0 9f-13f: 0-7 **14f+: 1-1**
Track : LH: 0-4 **RH: 1-4** Tight: 0-3 Gall: 0-1
Aids: Bl: 0-0 Vi: 0-1 Tstrap: 0-0
Best Rating: 11/01 MsnL 1m7f110y HO

Vice Presidential

(104) (42)
6-y-o ch g Presidium-Steelock (Lochnager)
J A Glover (J Balding 16/2) J A Glover

Placings:1306450/0501135050000/00000010/2500450 4000-1400050 **(1475)**
2001: 6^{1}SD, 5^{4}SD, 6^{0}SD, 5^{0}S, 6^{0}SD, 6^{5}G, 6^{0}SD, 6^{0}SD

	Starts	1st	2nd	3rd	Win & Pl
Career Total (Turf)	27	3	0	1	8720
Career Total (AW)	19	2	1	1	4937

58	2/01	Sthl	6f	F	STD	£2261
55	11/99	Sthl	6f	F	STD	£1850
62	6/98	Muss	7f30y	F	SFT	£2285
77	6/98	Wwck	7f	F	SFT	£2847
93	5/97	Haml	5f4y	E	SFT	£2752

Total win prize-money £11996

Going (Turf): Sf: 3-11 GS: 0-5 Gd: 0-9 GF: 0-1 Fm: 0-1
Distance: **5f/6f: 3-30** 7f-8f: 2-16 9f-13f: 0-0 14f+: 0-0
Track : **LH: 3-23** RH: 1-5 **Tight: 1-6** Gall: 0-2
Aids: Bl: 0-0 Vi: 0-0 Tstrap: 0-0
Best Rating: 58 2/01 Sthl 6f stand

Vicious Circle

108
7-y-o b g Lahib (USA)-Tight Spin (High Top)
L M Cumani D Metcalf

Placings:3/4210/1211/44-2P **(2327)**
2001: 16^{2}G, 20^{P}GF

	Starts	1st	2nd	3rd	Win & Pl
Career Total (Turf)	13	4	3	1	185580

106	9/99	Asct	1m4f	B H	HVY	£46300
97	8/99	York	1m5f194y	B H	GD	£109350
87	6/99	Newc	1m2f32y	C(0-90)	GD	£7777
97	10/98	Ayr	1m2f	D	HVY	£3496

Total win prize-money £166923

Going (Turf): Sf: 2-3 GS: 0-1 **Gd: 2-4** GF: 0-5 Fm: 0-0
Distance: 5f/6f: 0-0 7f-8f: 0-0 **9f-13f: 3-9** 14f+: 1-4
Track : **LH: 3-5** RH: 1-7 Tight: 0-3 **Gall: 3-6**
Aids: Bl: 0-0 Vi: 0-0 Tstrap: 0-0
Best Rating: 97 10/98 Ayr 1m2f HY

He scored three times in '99 including the Ebor at York and a valuable Ascot handicap but has been lightly raced since. Ran well in a valuable handicap in Dubai in Apri, but was fatally injured in the Ascot Gold Cup

(DEAD).

Vicious Dancer

105 **100**

3-y-o b g Timeless Times (USA)-Yankeedoodledancer (Mashhor Dancer (USA))

R M Whitaker Mr & Mrs J Samuel

Placings:06110-1060405000 **(5266)**

2001: 6^{1}G, 6^{0}GF, 7^{6}GF, 6^{0}GF, 6^{4}GF, 6^{0}G, 5^{5}G, 5^{0}G, 5^{0}GS, 6^{0}GS

	Starts	1st	2nd	3rd	Win & Pl
Career Total (Turf)	15	3	0	0	49783

104 5/01 Ling 6f B(0-105)H GD £32500
95 9/00 Ayr 5f A SFT £11484
84 9/00 York 6f E GD £5239
Total win prize-money £49223

Going (Turf): Sf: 1-2 GS: 0-2 **Gd: 2-6** GF: 0-5 Fm: 0-0
Distance: **5f/6f: 3-14** 7f-8f: 0-1 9f-13f: 0-0 14f+: 0-0
Track : LH: 0-1 RH: 0-0 Tight: 0-1 Gall: 0-0
Aids: Bl: 0-0 Vi: 0-0 Tstrap: 0-0
Best Rating: 104 5/01 Ling 6f good

He made a winning reappearance this season in a Lingfield handicap over his best trip of six furlongs, but has found life a bit tougher since being asked to take on older horses. Has won on good and soft ground.

Vicious Hero

45

2-y-o b g Timeless Times (USA)-Syke Lane (Clantime)

R M Whitaker Mr & Mrs J Samuel

Placings:0 **(2189)**

2001: 5^{0}GF

	Starts	1st	2nd	3rd	Win & Pl
Career Total (Turf)	1	0	0	0	

Going (Turf): Sf: 0-0 GS: 0-0 Gd: 0-0 GF: 0-1 Fm: 0-0
Distance: 5f/6f: 0-1 7f-8f: 0-0 9f-13f: 0-0 14f+: 0-0
Track : LH: 0-0 RH: 0-0 Tight: 0-0 Gall: 0-0
Aids: Bl: 0-0 Vi: 0-0 Tstrap: 0-0
Best Rating: 104 5/01 Ling 6f good

Vicious Knight

103 **107**

3-y-o b c Night Shift (USA)-Myth (Troy)

L M Cumani D Metcalf

Placings:6126-01 **(2802)**

2001: 10^{0}G, 8^{1}GF

	Starts	1st	2nd	3rd	Win & Pl
Career Total (Turf)	6	2	1	0	20881

105 7/01 Sand 1m14y C G-F £7746
93 7/00 Bevl 7f100y D G-F £4134
Total win prize-money £11881

Going (Turf): Sf: 0-0 GS: 0-0 Gd: 0-2 **GF: 2-4** Fm: 0-0
Distance: 5f/6f: 0-0 7f-8f: 1-4 9f-13f: 1-2 14f+: 0-0
Track : LH: 0-0 **RH: 2-4** Tight: 0-0 Gall: 0-1
Aids: Bl: 0-0 Vi: 0-0 Tstrap: 0-0
Best Rating: 105 7/01 Sand 1m14y gd-fm

An interesting colt, beat Carnival Dancer by half a length in conditions stakes over a mile at Sandown in July (after a two-month break). He raced a bit freely, wearing a cross noseband, and led two out. Looks up to Listed class.

Vicious Lover

102 **61**

2-y-o ch g Rudimentary (USA)-Parfait Amour (Clantime)

R M Whitaker Mr & Mrs J Samuel

Placings:000100 **(5589)**

2001: 6^{0}GF, 7^{0}G, 6^{0}GF, 8^{1}GF, 7^{0}S, 7^{0}GS

	Starts	1st	2nd	3rd	Win & Pl
Career Total (Turf)	6	1	0	0	5483

61 9/01 Muss 1m D(0-80) G-F £5482
Total win prize-money £5483

Going (Turf): Sf: 0-1 GS: 0-1 Gd: 0-1 **GF: 1-3** Fm: 0-0
Distance: 5f/6f: 0-2 **7f-8f: 1-4** 9f-13f: 0-0 14f+: 0-0
Track : LH: 0-3 **RH: 1-1 Tight: 1-2** Gall: 0-1
Aids: Bl: 0-0 Vi: 0-0 Tstrap: 0-0
Best Rating: 61 9/01 Muss 1m gd-fm

No sign of ability before scoring at Musselburgh in a nursery over a mile on good to firm.

Vicious Prince (IRE)

90 **74**

2-y-o b c Sadler's Wells (USA)-Sunny Flower (FR) (Dom Racine (FR))

R M Whitaker R M Whitaker

Placings:050 **(5053)**

2001: 6^{0}G, 8^{5}GF, 7^{0}S

	Starts	1st	2nd	3rd	Win & Pl
Career Total (Turf)	3	0	0	0	0

Going (Turf): Sf: 0-1 GS: 0-0 Gd: 0-1 GF: 0-1 Fm: 0-0
Distance: 5f/6f: 0-0 7f-8f: 0-3 9f-13f: 0-0 14f+: 0-0
Track : LH: 0-2 RH: 0-0 Tight: 0-0 Gall: 0-1
Aids: Bl: 0-0 Vi: 0-0 Tstrap: 0-0
Best Rating: 74 10/01 NmkR 7f soft

He finished down the field in a York Listed event on his racecourse debut and was a well-beaten last of five in an Ayr conditions event next time. His sights need lowering a bit.

Vicious Warrior

93 **73**

2-y-o b g Elmaamul (USA)-Ling Lane (Slip Anchor)

R M Whitaker Mr & Mrs J Samuel

Placings:4503 **(5662)**

2001: 7^{4}G, 7^{5}GF, 6^{0}GF, 8^{3}G

	Starts	1st	2nd	3rd	Win & Pl
Career Total (Turf)	4	0	0	1	669

Going (Turf): Sf: 0-0 GS: 0-0 Gd: 0-2 GF: 0-2 Fm: 0-0
Distance: 5f/6f: 0-0 7f-8f: 0-4 9f-13f: 0-0 14f+: 0-0
Track : LH: 0-1 RH: 0-1 Tight: 0-1 Gall: 0-1
Aids: Bl: 0-0 Vi: 0-0 Tstrap: 0-0
Best Rating: 73 11/01 Muss 1m good

Showed enough in maidens as a juvenile to suggest he can win races.

Vicky Scarlett

64 **10**

4-y-o gr f Missed Flight-Just Greenwich (Chilibang)

P A Pritchard P A Pritchard

Placings:00-00 **(3204)**

2001: 8^{0}GF, 7^{0}G

	Starts	1st	2nd	3rd	Win & Pl
Career Total (Turf)	4	0	0	0	

Going (Turf): Sf: 0-0 GS: 0-1 Gd: 0-1 GF: 0-2 Fm: 0-0
Distance: 5f/6f: 0-0 7f-8f: 0-2 9f-13f: 0-2 14f+: 0-0
Track : LH: 0-2 RH: 0-1 Tight: 0-0 Gall: 0-0
Aids: Bl: 0-0 Vi: 0-0 Tstrap: 0-0
Best Rating: 73 11/01 Muss 1m good

Victeddu

98 **77**

3-y-o b f Casteddu-Glint Of Victory (Glint Of Gold)

M G Quinlan Roy Matthews

Placings:60-60 **(1071)**

2001: 7^{6}S, 6^{0}GS

	Starts	1st	2nd	3rd	Win & Pl
Career Total (Turf)	4	0	0	0	0

Going (Turf): Sf: 0-2 GS: 0-1 Gd: 0-0 GF: 0-1 Fm: 0-0
Distance: 5f/6f: 0-1 7f-8f: 0-3 9f-13f: 0-0 14f+: 0-0
Track : LH: 0-1 RH: 0-0 Tight: 0-0 Gall: 0-0
Aids: Bl: 0-0 Vi: 0-0 Tstrap: 0-0
Best Rating: 77 4/01 NmkR 7f soft

Victor Valentine (IRE)

63(88) (72)**56**

2-y-o ch c Ridgewood Ben-Tarliya (IRE) (Doyoun)

E A Wheeler Mrs Jane Tuhill

Placings:0003 **(5415)**

2001: 7^{0}GF, 8^{0}G, 6^{0}HY, 6^{3}SD, 6^{2}SD

	Starts	1st	2nd	3rd	Win & Pl
Career Total (Turf)	3	0	0	0	
Career Total (AW)	1	0	0	1	434

Going (Turf): Sf: 0-1 GS: 0-0 Gd: 0-1 GF: 0-1 Fm: 0-0
Distance: 5f/6f: 0-2 7f-8f: 0-2 9f-13f: 0-0 14f+: 0-0
Track : LH: 0-1 RH: 0-2 Tight: 0-1 Gall: 0-1
Aids: Bl: 0-0 Vi: 0-0 Tstrap: 0-0
Best Rating: 64 10/01 Wolv 6f stand

He shows plenty of speed but is not getting home in his races. Looks worth a try over the minimum trip.

Victor's Crown (IRE)

100 **52**

4-y-o b g Desert Style (IRE)-Royal Wolff (Prince Tenderfoot (USA))

M H Tompkins Mrs Brian Grice

Placings:6200/06000-2405602 **(4159)**

2001: 5^{2}GF, 5^{4}F, 6^{0}GF, 6^{5}GF, 6^{6}G, 8^{0}S, 6^{2}GF

	Starts	1st	2nd	3rd	Win & Pl
Career Total (Turf)	16	0	3	0	2426

Going (Turf): Sf: 0-1 GS: 0-1 Gd: 0-6 GF: 0-7 Fm: 0-1
Distance: 5f/6f: 0-10 7f-8f: 0-4 9f-13f: 0-2 14f+: 0-0
Track : LH: 0-3 RH: 0-0 Tight: 0-0 Gall: 0-0
Aids: Bl: 0-1 Vi: 0-0 Tstrap: 0-0
Best Rating: 52 8/01 Ling 6f gd-fm

Victoria Cross (IRE)

107 **101**

3-y-o b f Mark Of Esteem (IRE)-Glowing With Pride (Ile De Bourbon (USA))

G Wragg A E Oppenheimer

Placings:0-10443 **(5118a)**

2001: 7^{1}S, 8^{0}G, 8^{4}G, 10^{4}GF, 8^{3}S

	Starts	1st	2nd	3rd	Win & Pl
Career Total (Turf)	6	1	0	1	11462

89 4/01 NmkR 7f D SFT £5096
Total win prize-money £5096

Going (Turf): Sf: 1-3 GS: 0-0 Gd: 0-2 GF: 0-1 Fm: 0-0
Distance: 5f/6f: 0-1 **7f-8f: 1-4** 9f-13f: 0-1 14f+: 0-0
Track : LH: 0-2 RH: 0-1 Tight: 0-0 Gall: 0-2
Aids: Bl: 0-0 Vi: 0-0 Tstrap: 0-0
Best Rating: 101 5/01 Lonc 1m good

Fulfilled the promise of her solitary juvenile outing when taking a Newmarket maiden in style. Ran no sort of race from a poor draw in the French Guineas. Beaten in Listed company since. Acts on soft ground. Has won over seven furlongs. Reportedly going to race in the USA.

Victorian Lady

93(87) (7)**26**

4-y-o b f Old Vic-Semperflorens (Don)

R M H Cowell Bottisham Heath Stud

Placings:0040-006 **(3666)**
2001: 11^{0}SD, 12^{0}SD, 8^{6}S

	Starts	1st	2nd	3rd	Win & Pl
Career Total (Turf)	5	0	0	0	296
Career Total (AW)	2	0	0	0	

Going (Turf): Sf: 0-2 GS: 0-0 Gd: 0-0 GF: 0-2 Fm: 0-1
Distance: 5f/6f: 0-0 7f-8f: 0-0 9f-13f: 0-6 14f+: 0-1
Track : LH: 0-6 RH: 0-0 Tight: 0-2 Gall: 0-0
Aids: Bl: 0-0 Vi: 0-1 Tstrap: 0-0
Best Rating: 24 8/01 Nott 1m54y soft

Victoriet

99(91) (37)**31**
4-y-o ch f Hamas (IRE)-Wedgewood (USA) (Woodman (USA))
N Hamilton Mr & Mrs Peter Foden

Placings:0400000/550444404-6000 **(4642)**
2001: 8^{6}SW, 9^{0}F, 8^{0}GF, 10^{0}GF

	Starts	1st	2nd	3rd	Win & Pl
Career Total (Turf)	18	0	0	0	1504
Career Total (AW)	2	0	0	0	0

Going (Turf): Sf: 0-1 GS: 0-0 Gd: 0-4 GF: 0-12 Fm: 0-1
Distance: 5f/6f: 0-5 7f-8f: 0-5 9f-13f: 0-10 14f+: 0-0
Track : LH: 0-11 RH: 0-1 Tight: 0-7 Gall: 0-1
Aids: Bl: 0-2 Vi: 0-0 Tstrap: 0-0
Best Rating: 37 3/01 Ling 1m slow

Victorious

(108) (65)
5-y-o ch g Formidable (USA)-Careful Dancer (Gorytus (USA))
R A Fahey Tommy Staunton

Placings:004/00100050/11005003450-111 **(0278)**
2001: 7^{1}SW, 7^{1}SD, 7^{1}SW

	Starts	1st	2nd	3rd	Win & Pl
Career Total (Turf)	17	2	0	0	7176
Career Total (AW)	8	4	0	1	9059

55	2/01	Sthl	7f	F	SLW	£2275
65	2/01	Wolv	7f	G	STD	£1904
46	1/01	Wolv	7f	G	SLW	£1372
59	4/00	Thsk	7f	E(0-70)H	SFT	£3932
68	3/00	Wolv	7f	E(0-70)H	STD	£2842
66	8/99	Hayd	7f30y	E(0-70)H	G-S	£3032

Total win prize-money £15358

Going (Turf): Sf: 1-6 GS: 1-4 Gd: 0-3 GF: 0-3 Fm: 0-1
Distance: 5f/6f: 0-2 **7f-8f: 6-21** 9f-13f: 0-2 14f+: 0-0
Track : **LH: 6-14** RH: 0-2 **Tight: 4-6** Gall: 0-0
Aids: Bl: 0-0 Vi: 0-0 Tstrap: 0-2
Best Rating: 65 2/01 Wolv 7f stand

View The Facts

95 **61**
2-y-o b f So Factual (USA)-Scenic View (IRE) (Scenic)
P L Gilligan Patrick L Gilligan

Placings:000 **(5603)**
2001: 7^{0}GS, 6^{0}S, 7^{0}GS

	Starts	1st	2nd	3rd	Win & Pl
Career Total (Turf)	3	0	0	0	

Going (Turf): Sf: 0-1 GS: 0-2 Gd: 0-0 GF: 0-0 Fm: 0-0
Distance: 5f/6f: 0-0 7f-8f: 0-3 9f-13f: 0-0 14f+: 0-0
Track : LH: 0-1 RH: 0-0 Tight: 0-0 Gall: 0-0
Aids: Bl: 0-0 Vi: 0-0 Tstrap: 0-0
Best Rating: 61 10/01 Brig 6f209y soft

Viewforth

98 **57**
3-y-o b g Emarati (USA)-Miriam (Forzando)

Miss L A Perratt Alex Penman Builders Ltd

Placings:4300-303150604600 **(4796)**
2001: 5^{3}GS, 6^{0}G, 5^{3}GF, 5^{1}GF, 5^{5}G, 5^{0}GF, 5^{6}GS, 5^{0}G, 5^{4}GF, 5^{6}GS, 5^{0}G, 5^{0}G

	Starts	1st	2nd	3rd	Win & Pl
Career Total (Turf)	16	1	0	3	5676

54	6/01	Muss	5f	D	G-F	£3432

Total win prize-money £3432

Going (Turf): Sf: 0-3 GS: 0-3 Gd: 0-6 **GF: 1-4** Fm: 0-0
Distance: **5f/6f: 1-15** 7f-8f: 0-1 9f-13f: 0-0 14f+: 0-0
Track : LH: 0-0 RH: 0-1 Tight: 0-0 Gall: 0-1
Aids: Bl: 0-0 Vi: 0-0 Tstrap: 0-0
Best Rating: 67 5/01 Ayr 5f gd-fm

Front-running sprinter, acts on fast and easy ground, best at the minimum trip.

Viking Prince

(54) (29)
4-y-o b g Chilibang-Fire Sprite (Mummy's Game)
Jamie Poulton Glendale Partnership Ltd

Placings:50000/00000-0 **(0028)**
2001: 7^{0}SD

	Starts	1st	2nd	3rd	Win & Pl
Career Total (Turf)	8	0	0	0	0
Career Total (AW)	3	0	0	0	

Going (Turf): Sf: 0-0 GS: 0-1 Gd: 0-2 GF: 0-4 Fm: 0-1
Distance: 5f/6f: 0-7 7f-8f: 0-4 9f-13f: 0-0 14f+: 0-0
Track : LH: 0-4 RH: 0-0 Tight: 0-2 Gall: 0-0
Aids: Bl: 0-0 Vi: 0-0 Tstrap: 0-0

Villa Carlotta

104 **106**
3-y-o ch f Rainbow Quest (USA)-Subya (Night Shift (USA))
J L Dunlop Prince A A Faisal

Placings:303-31132221 **(5680a)**
2001: 10^{3}S, 12^{1}GS, 12^{1}S, 11^{3}GF, 11^{2}S, 10^{2}GS, 10^{2}GS, 12^{1}S

	Starts	1st	2nd	3rd	Win & Pl
Career Total (Turf)	11	3	3	4	52256

106	11/01	Siro	1m4f		SFT	£23000
92	5/01	Newb	1m4f5y	B(0-100)H	SFT	£10301
78	5/01	Thsk	1m4f	D	G-S	£4608

Total win prize-money £37910

Going (Turf): Sf: 2-7 GS: 1-3 Gd: 0-0 GF: 0-1 Fm: 0-0
Distance: 5f/6f: 0-0 7f-8f: 0-3 **9f-13f: 3-8** 14f+: 0-0
Track : **LH: 2-5** RH: 1-1 Tight: 1-1 Gall: 1-1
Aids: Bl: 0-0 Vi: 0-0 Tstrap: 0-0
Best Rating: 106 11/01 Siro 1m4f soft

Showed promise at two. Got off the mark over a mile and a half at Thirsk on her second outing at three then hacked up in a three-runner affair at Newbury. Decent efforts since, including in listed company. Best on an easy surface. Effective at ten furlongs, but stays a mile and a half.

Villa Del Sol

105(86) (46)**86**
2-y-o br f Tagula (IRE)-Admonish (Warning)
A Bailey Willie McKay

Placings:22312315112040000 **(4823)**
2001: 5^{2}S, 5^{2}S, 5^{3}S, 5^{1}S, 5^{2}F, 5^{3}F, 6^{1}G, 6^{5}GF, 5^{1}G, 5^{1}GS, 6^{2}GS, 5^{0}GF, 6^{4}G, 6^{0}G, 6^{0}GS, 7^{0}GF, 6^{0}G, 7^{0}SD

	Starts	1st	2nd	3rd	Win & Pl
Career Total (Turf)	17	4	4	2	24955

79	7/01	Leic	5f218y	E	G-S	£3653
68	7/01	Ches	5f16y	D	GD	£5486
68	6/01	York	6f	E	GD	£7475
	5/01	Hayd	5f	D	SFT	£3815

Total win prize-money £20430

Going (Turf): Sf: 1-4 GS: 1-3 **Gd: 2-5** GF: 0-3 Fm: 0-2
Distance: **5f/6f: 4-14** 7f-8f: 0-3 9f-13f: 0-0 14f+: 0-0
Track : **LH: 1-4** RH: 0-0 **Tight: 1-3** Gall: 0-0
Aids: Bl: 0-0 Vi: 0-0 Tstrap: 0-0
Best Rating: 88 7/01 Ayr 6f gd-sft

She is very consistent and has managed four victories in varied company, a Haydock maiden, a very valuable York seller and nurseries at Chester and Leicester. She is equally effective over five or six furlongs, although she has looked in the Handicapper's grasp of late. She looks to need the ground no faster than good.

Villa Romana

87(97) (41)**38**
4-y-o b f Komaite (USA)-Keep Quiet (Reprimand)
P Cluskey (W M Brisbourne 9/6) P Cluskey

Placings:63204043415**0**/06**5**0330-00000 **(5427a)**
2001: 7^{0}SD, 7^{0}GF, 5^{0}GF, 6^{0}F, 5^{0}S

	Starts	1st	2nd	3rd	Win & Pl
Career Total (Turf)	17	1	1	2	5711
Career Total (AW)	7	0	0	2	489

73	10/99	Brig	6f209y	E(0-75)H	G-F	£3165

Total win prize-money £3165

Going (Turf): Sf: 0-3 GS: 0-1 Gd: 0-3 **GF: 1-8** Fm: 0-2
Distance: 5f/6f: 0-12 **7f-8f: 1-12** 9f-13f: 0-0 14f+: 0-0
Track : **LH: 1-14** RH: 0-2 Tight: 0-9 Gall: 0-1
Aids: Bl: 0-1 Vi: 0-0 Tstrap: 0-2
Best Rating: 38 10/01 Navn 5f182y soft

Villa Via (IRE)

(78) (19)**74**
4-y-o b f Night Shift (USA)-Joma Kaanem (Double Form)
Miss J F Craze Peter Onslow

Placings:53221000-000 **(0449)**
2001: 6^{0}SD, 5^{0}SD, 6^{0}SD

	Starts	1st	2nd	3rd	Win & Pl
Career Total (Turf)	8	1	2	1	6564
Career Total (AW)	3	0	0	0	

54	8/00	Bevl	5f	D	G-F	£3893

Total win prize-money £3894

Going (Turf): Sf: 0-1 GS: 0-1 Gd: 0-4 **GF: 1-2** Fm: 0-0
Distance: **5f/6f: 1-11** 7f-8f: 0-0 9f-13f: 0-0 14f+: 0-0
Track : LH: 0-2 RH: 0-0 Tight: 0-1 Gall: 0-0
Aids: Bl: 0-0 Vi: 0-0 Tstrap: 0-1
Best Rating: 19 1/01 Sthl 5f stand

Village Native (FR)

90(98) (36)**32**
8-y-o ch g Village Star (FR)-Zedative (FR) (Zeddaan)
K O Cunningham-Brown A J Richards

Placings:0235510/0606/4600401240**550136/3546**00**0**50 10016**501020/0552**400261/**00000**000620000**031**-**050460**00506 **(3888)**
2001: 10^{0}SD, 8^{5}SD, 8^{0}SD, 9^{4}SW, 8^{6}SW, 8^{0}SW, 10^{0}SD, 6^{0}GF, 6^{5}GF, 8^{0}GF, 7^{6}F

	Starts	1st	2nd	3rd	Win & Pl
Career Total (Turf)	44	4	4	1	15721
Career Total (AW)	40	4	2	3	10842

46	12/00	Ling	1m	G	STD	£1428
66	6/99	Sals	1m	F	G-F	£1987
59	9/98	Wolv	6f	E(0-70)H	STD	£3236
61	7/98	Bath	5f11y	F	GD	£2332
52	5/98	Sand	1m14y	E	G-S	£2788
57	11/97	Wolv	5f	F(0-60)H	STD	£2085
59	8/97	Wolv	5f	F(0-65)H	STD	£2277
76	11/95	Folk	6f	E	G-F	£3817

Total win prize-money £19952

Going (Turf): Sf: 0-4 GS: 1-5 Gd: 1-13 **GF: 2-16** Fm: 0-6
Distance: **5f/6f: 5-43** 7f-8f: 2-29 9f-13f: 1-12 14f+: 0-0
Track : **LH: 5-48** RH: 2-14 **Tight: 5-42** Gall: 1-9
Aids: **Bl: 7-61** Vi: 0-3 Tstrap: 0-0
Best Rating: 39 1/01 Ling 1m stand

Ville De Paris (IRE)

94 **77**

2-y-o b c Common Grounds-Muqaddima (FR) (Kaldoun (FR))
R F Johnson Houghton Gary Stevens & Henry Ponsonby

Placings:060 **(4533)**
2001: 5^{0}G, 7^{6}GF, 7^{0}GF

	Starts	1st	2nd	3rd	Win & Pl
Career Total (Turf)	3	0	0	0	0

Going (Turf): Sf: 0-0 GS: 0-0 Gd: 0-1 GF: 0-2 Fm: 0-0
Distance: 5f/6f: 0-1 7f-8f: 0-2 9f-13f: 0-0 14f+: 0-0
Track : LH: 0-1 RH: 0-0 Tight: 0-0 Gall: 0-1
Aids: Bl: 0-0 Vi: 0-0 Tstrap: 0-0
Best Rating: 77 8/01 Folk 7f gd-fm

Vinca

63(70) (18)**16**

2-y-o b f Aragon-Zamarra (Clantime)
A Berry (H S Howe 25/5) Peter E Clinton

Placings:0 **(5533)**
2001: 5^{0}S, 5^{0}SD

	Starts	1st	2nd	3rd	Win & Pl
Career Total (Turf)	1	0	0	0	

Going (Turf): Sf: 0-1 GS: 0-0 Gd: 0-0 GF: 0-0 Fm: 0-0
Distance: 5f/6f: 0-1 7f-8f: 0-0 9f-13f: 0-0 14f+: 0-0
Track : LH: 0-0 RH: 0-0 Tight: 0-0 Gall: 0-0
Aids: Bl: 0-0 Vi: 0-0 Tstrap: 0-0
Best Rating: 16 10/01 Rdcr 5f soft

Vincent

(103) (57d)**41**

6-y-o b g Anshan-Top-Anna (IRE) (Ela-Mana-Mou)
John A Harris (J L Harris 8/6) Exors Of The Late J L Harris

Placings:46/52000/516404000304143344/10134411524 1-0000022 **(3433)**
2001: 14^{0}SW, 16^{0}SD, 14^{0}SD, 12^{0}SW, 16^{0}SD, 14^{2}SD, 16^{2}SD

	Starts	1st	2nd	3rd	Win & Pl
Career Total (Turf)	14	0	0	0	1063
Career Total (AW)	29	7	4	3	18779

64 11/00 Sthl 2m E(0-75)H STD £2789
61 9/00 Sthl 2m G(0-65)H STD £2117
56 9/00 Wolv 1m6f166y F(0-60) STD £2324
52 7/00 Wolv 2m46y F(0-65)H STD £2303
51 5/00 Sthl 2m F(0-65)H STD £2240
50 7/99 Wolv 2m46y G(0-60)H STD £1836
55 1/99 Sthl 1m4f G(0-60)H STD £1530
Total win prize-money £15142

Going (Turf): Sf: 0-2 GS: 0-3 Gd: 0-2 GF: 0-7 Fm: 0-0
Distance: 5f/6f: 0-0 7f-8f: 0-1 9f-13f: 1-16 **14f+: 6-26**
Track : **LH: 7-33** RH: 0-8 **Tight: 3-13** Gall: 0-1
Aids: Bl: 0-1 Vi: 0-2 Tstrap: 0-0
Best Rating: 48 7/01 Sthl 2m stand

He is extremely inconsistent, but can win modest events on Fibresand when he wants to.

Vincentia

96(94) (42)**58**

3-y-o ch f Komaite (USA)-Vatersay (USA) (Far North (CAN))
C Smith The Brave Few

Placings:0443-03300032 **(5519)**
2001: 7^{0}GS, 7^{3}S, 7^{3}GF, 7^{0}GF, 6^{0}GF, 7^{0}GF, 7^{3}S, 6^{2}HY, 7^{3}SD

	Starts	1st	2nd	3rd	Win & Pl
Career Total (Turf)	12	0	1	4	3094

Going (Turf): Sf: 0-4 GS: 0-2 Gd: 0-0 GF: 0-6 Fm: 0-0
Distance: 5f/6f: 0-2 7f-8f: 0-10 9f-13f: 0-0 14f+: 0-0
Track : LH: 0-4 RH: 0-1 Tight: 0-2 Gall: 0-1
Aids: Bl: 0-0 Vi: 0-0 Tstrap: 0-0
Best Rating: 67 4/01 NmkR 7f gd-sft

Still a maiden, she has made the frame a number of times but keeps meeting one or two too good. Best at seven furlongs.

Vintage Premium

114(107) (104)**101**

4-y-o b g Forzando-Julia Domna (Dominion)
R A Fahey J C Parsons

Placings:2210/214022160230-40355000430 **(5142)**
2001: 8^{4}SD, 8^{0}S, 8^{3}GS, 7^{5}GF, 10^{5}GF, 8^{0}GF, 10^{0}GF, 10^{0}G, 10^{4}G, 10^{3}G, 9^{0}G

	Starts	1st	2nd	3rd	Win & Pl
Career Total (Turf)	26	3	6	3	58754
Career Total (AW)	1	0	0	0	2500

101 7/00 Donc 1m2f60y C GD £6955
89 4/00 Newb 1m7y B(0-100)H SFT £9092
84 9/99 Bevl 7f100y E GD £4193
Total win prize-money £20240

Going (Turf): Sf: 1-6 GS: 0-3 **Gd: 2-11** GF: 0-6 Fm: 0-0
Distance: 5f/6f: 0-2 7f-8f: 1-6 **9f-13f: 2-19** 14f+: 0-0
Track : **LH: 2-15** RH: 1-5 Tight: 0-2 **Gall: 2-12**
Aids: Bl: 0-0 Vi: 0-1 Tstrap: 0-0
Best Rating: 104 4/01 Newb 1m gd-sft

Effective in a fast-run mile, he stays further. Caught the eye when finishing well on his seasonal debut at Wolverhampton and ran well at Newbury in April, but the Handicapper looks to have him in his grip at present. Can make the running or come from behind.

Vintage Rock

71 **29**

4-y-o b g Rock City-Classical Vintage (Stradavinsky)
R Hannon Mrs S Joint

Placings:0 **(2545)**
2001. 9^{0}GF

	Starts	1st	2nd	3rd	Win & Pl
Career Total (Turf)	1	0	0	0	

Going (Turf): Sf: 0-0 GS: 0-0 Gd: 0-0 GF: 0-1 Fm: 0-0
Distance: 5f/6f: 0-0 7f-8f: 0-0 9f-13f: 0-1 14f+: 0-0
Track : LH: 0-0 RH: 0-1 Tight: 0-1 Gall: 0-0
Aids: Bl: 0-0 Vi: 0-0 Tstrap: 0-0
Best Rating: 29 6/01 Sals 1m1f198y gd-fm

Vintage Style

94(93) (69)**61**

2-y-o ch g Piccolo-Gibaltarik (IRE) (Jareer (USA))
R Hannon N A Woodcock

Placings:05006500 **(5521)**
2001: 5^{0}GS, 5^{5}GS, 6^{0}G, 6^{0}GF, 6^{6}G, 7^{5}HY, 6^{0}GS, 6^{0}HY, 7^{4}SD

	Starts	1st	2nd	3rd	Win & Pl
Career Total (Turf)	8	0	0	0	0

Going (Turf): Sf: 0-2 GS: 0-3 Gd: 0-2 GF: 0-1 Fm: 0-0
Distance: 5f/6f: 0-6 7f-8f: 0-2 9f-13f: 0-0 14f+: 0-0
Track : LH: 0-0 RH: 0-1 Tight: 0-0 Gall: 0-1
Aids: Bl: 0-0 Vi: 0-0 Tstrap: 0-0
Best Rating: 61 9/01 Nott 6f15y good

A 16,500gns half-brother to a useful juvenile five-furlong winner, weak in the market and showed little on debut, and has shown little progression since.

Violent

95(97) (53)**48**

3-y-o b f Deploy-Gentle Irony (Mazilier (USA))
Jamie Poulton (Andrew Reid 8/5) Chris Steward

Placings:000212040336-40631006120600 **(5470)**
2001: 7^{4}SD, 8^{0}SD, 10^{6}SD, 8^{3}SD, 8^{1}SD, 8^{0}SD, 8^{0}SD, 7^{6}SD, 6^{1}HY, 6^{2}GF, 7^{0}GF, 5^{6}S, 7^{0}HY, 7^{0}S

	Starts	1st	2nd	3rd	Win & Pl
Career Total (Turf)	14	2	3	0	7388
Career Total (AW)	12	1	0	3	3701

44 5/01 Nott 6f15y G HVY £1985
53 3/01 Wolv 1m100y F STD £2310
60 7/00 Brig 6f209y F FRM £2236
Total win prize-money £6532

Going (Turf): Sf: 1-4 GS: 0-0 Gd: 0-2 GF: 0-6 **Fm: 1-2**
Distance: 5f/6f: 0-4 **7f-8f: 2-18** 9f-13f: 1-4 14f+: 0-0
Track : **LH: 2-18** RH: 0-0 **Tight: 1-10** Gall: 0-0
Aids: Bl: 0-0 **Vi: 1-8** Tstrap: 0-0
Best Rating: 53 3/01 Wolv 1m100y stand

A selling-class filly, she has won on heavy and firm ground on the turf, the former of which was her last win in May 2001. She has lost her way amongst better company since then and is on a regressive handicap mark.

Virbius (IRE)

66(97) (42)

5-y-o ch g Wolfhound (USA)-Virelai (Kris)
R D E Woodhouse R D E Woodhouse

Placings:60/6000000/00 **(0879)**
2001: 12^{0}SW, 21^{0}S

	Starts	1st	2nd	3rd	Win & Pl
Career Total (Turf)	8	0	0	0	0
Career Total (AW)	3	0	0	0	0

Going (Turf): Sf: 0-1 GS: 0-2 Gd: 0-4 GF: 0-1 Fm: 0-0
Distance: 5f/6f: 0-0 7f-8f: 0-5 9f-13f: 0-5 14f+: 0-1
Track : LH: 0-5 RH: 0-4 Tight: 0-3 Gall: 0-1
Aids: Bl: 0-1 Vi: 0-0 Tstrap: 0-0
Best Rating: 42 4/01 Sthl 1m4f slow

Virgin Soldier (IRE)

105(85) (89+)**92**

5-y-o ch g Waajib-Never Been Chaste (Posse (USA))
M Johnston J David Abell

Placings:036/63000021111112/102421330-001004040 **(3826)**
2001: 12^{0}S, 11^{0}F, 16^{1}GF, 13^{0}G, 16^{0}F, 13^{4}G, 14^{0}GF, 18^{4}G, 16^{0}G

	Starts	1st	2nd	3rd	Win & Pl
Career Total (Turf)	29	4	3	4	61758
Career Total (AW)	6	5	1	0	13290

94 5/01 Kemp 2m C(0-95)H G-F £7377
90 8/00 NmkJ 2m24y C(0-90)H G-F £6760
83 5/00 Newc 2m19y D(0-80)H GD £3916
89 11/99 Sthl 1m6f E(0-75)H STD £2696
76 11/99 Wolv 2m46y F(0-60)H STD £2358
68 11/99 Sthl 1m6f G(0-80)H STD £1976
63 11/99 Ling 2m E(0-70)H STD £2854
58 11/99 Muss 2m E(0-75)H GD £7360
55 10/99 Ling 1m4f E(0-70)H STD £2847
Total win prize-money £38147

Going (Turf): Sf: 0-3 GS: 0-1 **Gd: 2-12 GF: 2-10** Fm: 0-3
Distance: 5f/6f: 0-1 7f-8f: 0-1 9f-13f: 1-11 **14f+: 8-22**
Track : **LH: 6-21** RH: 3-13 **Tight: 4-14** Gall: 2-13
Aids: Bl: 0-1 Vi: 0-1 Tstrap: 0-0
Best Rating: 94 5/01 Kemp 2m gd-fm

A useful stayer, he has won at up to two miles on fact ground. Proved very successful on sand a couple of seasons ago. Successful at Kempton in May, he has been off the boil since.

Virginian (FR)

92(98) (45)**30**

5-y-o b g Al Nasr (FR)-Violet Dancer (FR) (Fabulous Dancer (USA))
A Crook (M D Hammond 20/1) A G Chappell

Placings:043100/40**5000** (3712)
2001: 16^{4}GF, 16^{0}GF, **12^{5}SD**, **16^{0}SD**, **16^{0}SD**, 14^{0}G

	Starts	1st	2nd	3rd	Win & Pl
Career Total (Turf)	9	1	0	1	9155
Career Total (AW)	3	0	0	0	0

8/99 Claf 1m6f110y H HLD £5764
Total win prize-money £5764

Going (Turf): Sf: 0-0 GS: 0-0 Gd: 0-1 GF: 0-2 Fm: 0-0
Distance: 5f/6f: 0-0 7f-8f: 0-0 9f-13f: 0-2 **14f+: 1-6**
Track : LH: 0-5 RH: 0-2 Tight: 0-3 Gall: 0-1
Aids: **Bl: 1-2** Vi: 0-4 Tstrap: 0-0
Best Rating: 45 6/01 Sthl 1m4f stand

Virgos Bambino (IRE)

(33)
4-y-o ch f Perugino (USA)-Deep In September (IRE) (Common Grounds)
R J Price R J Price

Placings:0000/0 **(1084)**
2001: 6^{0}SD

	Starts	1st	2nd	3rd	Win & Pl
Career Total (Turf)	4	0	0	0	
Career Total (AW)	1	0	0	0	

Going (Turf): Sf: 0-0 GS: 0-1 Gd: 0-0 GF: 0-2 Fm: 0-1
Distance: 5f/6f: 0-3 7f-8f: 0-1 9f-13f: 0-1 14f+: 0-0
Track : LH: 0-1 RH: 0-1 Tight: 0-1 Gall: 0-1
Aids: Bl: 0-0 Vi: 0-0 Tstrap: 0-0

Virtual Reality

99(98) (41)**64**
10-y-o b g Diamond Shoal-Warning Bell (Bustino)
J A R Toller Mrs J Toller

Placings:0/031212B00/22560300/20240F0/160120/305 1230/05516-05066 **(3735)**
2001: 7^{0}G, 8^{5}GF, 9^{0}GF, 8^{6}GF, 6^{6}G

	Starts	1st	2nd	3rd	Win & Pl
Career Total (Turf)	49	6	8	4	56875
Career Total (AW)	1	0	0	0	0

74 8/00 Brig 7f214y E FRM £2301
85 7/99 Wwck 7f164y C(0-85) G-F £6996
84 8/98 Sals 1m D(0-80)H G-F £3532
78 5/98 Bath 1m5y C(0-95)H GD £7295
72 6/94 NmkJ 1m2f (0-90)H G-F £7180
59 5/94 Brig 1m1f209yF(0-60) G-F £2249
Total win prize-money £29553

Going (Turf): Sf: 0-1 GS: 0-6 Gd: 1-17 **GF: 4-23** Fm: 1-2
Distance: 5f/6f: 0-0 7f-8f: 3-17 9f-13f: 3-33 14f+: 0-0
Track : **LH: 4-26** RH: 1-11 Tight: 1-15 Gall: 1-13
Aids: Bl: 0-0 Vi: 0-1 Tstrap: 0-0
Best Rating: 72 5/01 NmkR 7f good

Vision Of Night

118 **111**
5-y-o b h Night Shift (USA)-Dreamawhile (Known Fact (USA))
J L Dunlop Hesmonds Stud

Placings:2113/5135410/30110-0524011 **(4561a)**
2001: 6^{0}GS, 6^{5}GF, 5^{2}GF, 5^{4}G, 6^{0}G, 6^{1}GF, 6^{1}G

	Starts	1st	2nd	3rd	Win & Pl
Career Total (Turf)	23	8	2	3	168717

111 8/01 Badn 6f GD £40717
99 8/01 Donc 6f C G-F £8502
112 8/00 NmkJ 6f A G-F £13398
101 8/00 Yarm 6f3y C GD £5950
109 8/99 Deau 6f GD £23681
111 5/99 Newb 6f8y B GD £8736
93 9/98 Donc 6f C GD £5796
89 8/98 Ripn 6f D G-F £3671
Total win prize-money £110452

Going (Turf): Sf: 0-2 GS: 0-1 **Gd: 5-9** GF: 3-8 Fm: 0-0
Distance: **5f/6f: 6-17** 7f-8f: 2-4 9f-13f: 0-0 14f+: 0-0
Track : LH: 0-0 RH: 0-0 Tight: 0-0 Gall: 0-0
Aids: Bl: 0-0 Vi: 0-0 Tstrap: 0-0
Best Rating: 111 8/01 Badn 6f good

He proved disappointing in America and rejoined former trainer John Dunlop. Successful in the summer of 2000, he is not suited by heavy conditions. Best at around six furlongs, he just falls shy of top class but is capable of paying his way. Has been running well over a stiff five furlongs this term in Group company, and gained a confidence booster over six at Doncaster in August and was a narrow winner of a Group Two at Baden-Baden later in the month.

Visitation

(85) (47)**40**
3-y-o b f Bishop Of Cashel-Golden Envoy (USA) (Dayjur (USA))
K A Ryan Tony Fawcett

Placings:01200-040000 **(4905)**
2001: 7^{0}SD, 8^{4}SW, 7^{0}SD, 10^{0}G, 6^{0}G, 8^{0}G, 8^{0}SD

	Starts	1st	2nd	3rd	Win & Pl
Career Total (Turf)	7	0	1	0	735
Career Total (AW)	4	1	0	0	1862

47 7/00 Sthl 7f G STD £1862
Total win prize-money £1862

Going (Turf): Sf: 0-0 GS: 0-0 Gd: 0-5 GF: 0-2 Fm: 0-0
Distance: 5f/6f: 0-0 **7f-8f: 1-9** 9f-13f: 0-2 14f+: 0-0
Track : **LH: 1-6** RH: 0-2 Tight: 0-2 Gall: 0-1
Aids: Bl: 0-0 Vi: 0-0 Tstrap: 0-0
Best Rating: 41 2/01 Sthl 1m slow

Vislink (IRE)

(72) (23)**62**
3-y-o br g Shalford (IRE)-Wide Outside (IRE) (Don't Forget Me)
K A Ryan Mrs K E Fletcher

Placings:000020-05 **(0310)**
2001: 7^{0}SD, 7^{5}SD

	Starts	1st	2nd	3rd	Win & Pl
Career Total (Turf)	5	0	1	0	1090
Career Total (AW)	3	0	0	0	0

Going (Turf): Sf: 0-0 GS: 0-1 Gd: 0-2 GF: 0-2 Fm: 0-0
Distance: 5f/6f: 0-3 7f-8f: 0-5 9f-13f: 0-0 14f+: 0-0
Track : LH: 0-6 RH: 0-0 Tight: 0-2 Gall: 0-0
Aids: Bl: 0-1 Vi: 0-0 Tstrap: 0-0
Best Rating: 23 2/01 Sthl 7f stand

Vista Chino (IRE)

86 **49**
2-y-o b f Perugino (USA)-La Fille De Cirque (Cadeaux Genereux)
D Haydn Jones Mrs Marlene Kynaston

Placings:60 **(3684)**
2001: 5^{6}F, 5^{0}GF

	Starts	1st	2nd	3rd	Win & Pl
Career Total (Turf)	2	0	0	0	0

Going (Turf): Sf: 0-0 GS: 0-0 Gd: 0-0 GF: 0-1 Fm: 0-1
Distance: 5f/6f: 0-2 7f-8f: 0-0 9f-13f: 0-0 14f+: 0-0
Track : LH: 0-2 RH: 0-0 Tight: 0-0 Gall: 0-2
Aids: Bl: 0-0 Vi: 0-0 Tstrap: 0-0
Best Rating: 49 7/01 Bath 5f161y firm

Showed signs of ability in the first of two runs at Bath.

Vita Spericolata (IRE)

114 **101**
4-y-o b f Prince Sabo-Ahonita (Ahonoora)
J S Wainwright The Blue Check Partnership

Placings:125135060/2403304250-20431104040 **(5584a)**

2001: 5^{2}G, 5^{0}GF, 6^{4}GF, 6^{3}G, 5^{1}GF, 6^{1}G, 6^{0}G, 5^{4}GF, 5^{0}S, 5^{4}GS, 5^{0}HY

	Starts	1st	2nd	3rd	Win & Pl
Career Total (Turf)	30	4	4	4	71878

105 8/01 Ches 6f18y A GD £14210
62 7/01 NmkJ 5f C G-F £6148
88 7/99 Sand 5f6y A GD £11793
60 5/99 Muss 5f F FRM £2262
Total win prize-money £34414

Going (Turf): Sf: 0-5 GS: 0-3 **Gd: 2-11** GF: 1-10 Fm: 1-1
Distance: **5f/6f: 3-27** 7f-8f: 1-3 9f-13f: 0-0 14f+: 0-0
Track : **LH: 1-2** RH: 0-0 **Tight: 1-1** Gall: 0-1
Aids: Bl: 0-0 **Vi: 2-8** Tstrap: 0-0
Best Rating: 105 8/01 Ches 6f18y good

A useful sprinter, she was on a long losing run until scoring at Newmarket in July and followed up at Chester, although disappointed next time when last of 10 after banging her head in the stalls and racing too freely. Thoroughly consistent, she is fully effective on good to firm/soft over five-six furlongs.

Vitelucy

88 **65**
2-y-o b f Vettori (IRE)-Classic Line (Last Tycoon)
I A Balding Mrs Jerrard Williamson

Placings:05 **(5520)**
2001: 8^{0}GS, 8^{5}HY

	Starts	1st	2nd	3rd	Win & Pl
Career Total (Turf)	2	0	0	0	0

Going (Turf): Sf: 0-1 GS: 0-1 Gd: 0-0 GF: 0-0 Fm: 0-0
Distance: 5f/6f: 0-0 7f-8f: 0-1 9f-13f: 0-1 14f+: 0-0
Track : LH: 0-0 RH: 0-1 Tight: 0-1 Gall: 0-0
Aids: Bl: 0-0 Vi: 0-0 Tstrap: 0-0
Best Rating: 65 10/01 Wind 1m67y heavy

Vitesse (IRE)

82(75) **62**
3-y-o b f Royal Academy (USA)-Brentsville (USA) (Arctic Tern (USA))
Mrs Lydia Pearce Paul Sandy

Placings:00-0100 **(5171)**
2001: 10^{0}GF, 8^{1}HY, 8^{0}HY, 8^{0}GS, 11^{0}SD

	Starts	1st	2nd	3rd	Win & Pl
Career Total (Turf)	6	1	0	0	3991

52 8/01 Hayd 1m30y D HVY £3991
Total win prize-money £3991

Going (Turf): **Sf: 1-3** GS: 0-1 Gd: 0-0 GF: 0-2 Fm: 0-0
Distance: 5f/6f: 0-2 7f-8f: 0-0 **9f-13f: 1-4** 14f+: 0-0
Track : **LH: 1-3** RH: 0-1 Tight: 0-0 Gall: 0-1
Aids: Bl: 0-0 Vi: 0-0 Tstrap: 0-0
Best Rating: 52 8/01 Hayd 1m30y heavy

She won a four-runner maiden on heavy ground at Hamilton in August, but the rest of her form is modest.

Vitus Bering (USA)

99 **75**
4-y-o b g Bering-Most Precious (USA) (Nureyev (USA))
S Kirk Colin G R Booth

Placings:0-2300 **(5670)**
2001: 7^{2}S, 7^{3}GF, 8^{0}GF, 8^{0}HY

	Starts	1st	2nd	3rd	Win & Pl
Career Total (Turf)	5	0	1	1	1454

Going (Turf): Sf: 0-2 GS: 0-0 Gd: 0-0 GF: 0-3 Fm: 0-0
Distance: 5f/6f: 0-0 7f-8f: 0-3 9f-13f: 0-2 14f+: 0-0
Track : LH: 0-2 RH: 0-2 Tight: 0-1 Gall: 0-0
Aids: Bl: 0-0 Vi: 0-0 Tstrap: 0-1
Best Rating: 75 8/01 Chep 7f16y soft

Viva Maria (FR)

92 **87**
2-y-o gr f Kendor (FR)-Tambura (FR) (Kaldoun (FR))
J H M Gosden Dr Ornella Carlini Cozzi

Placings:41 **(5110)**
2001: 6^{4}G, 6^{1}HY

	Starts	1st	2nd	3rd	Win & Pl
Career Total (Turf)	2	1	0	0	4236

87 10/01 Nott 6f15y D HVY £3900
Total win prize-money £3900

Going (Turf): Sf: 1-1 GS: 0-0 Gd: 0-1 GF: 0-0 Fm: 0-0
Distance: 5f/6f: 0-1 **7f-8f: 1-1** 9f-13f: 0-0 14f+: 0-0
Track : LH: 0-0 RH: 0-0 Tight: 0-0 Gall: 0-0
Aids: Bl: 0-0 Vi: 0-0 Tstrap: 0-0
Best Rating: 87 10/01 Nott 6f15y heavy

Handled the heavy ground well when winning a backend Nottingham maiden.

Vodka (IRE)

96(100) (62)**58+**
3-y-o b g Inzar (USA)-Clearglade (Vitiges (FR))
J R Best (P C Haslam 23/2) Tendorra

Placings:560-21213010 **(2343)**
2001: 11^{2}SD, 11^{1}SW, 12^{2}SD, 12^{1}S, 12^{3}SD, 12^{0}SD, 11^{1}SD, 12^{0}SD

	Starts	1st	2nd	3rd	Win & Pl
Career Total (Turf)	4	1	0	0	2548
Career Total (AW)	7	2	2	1	7064

64 5/01 Sthl 1m3f F STD £2226
58 3/01 Muss 1m4f F(0-60) SFT £2548
58 2/01 Sthl 1m3f E SLW £2611
Total win prize-money £7385

Going (Turf): Sf: 1-1 GS: 0-1 Gd: 0-1 GF: 0-1 Fm: 0-0
Distance: 5f/6f: 0-3 7f-8f: 0-0 **9f-13f: 3-8** 14f+: 0-0
Track : **LH: 2-7** RH: 0-0 Tight: 0-2 Gall: 0-0
Aids: Bl: 0-0 Vi: 0-0 Tstrap: 0-0
Best Rating: 62 3/01 Sthl 1m4f stand

He confirmed the promise he showed in a handicap on his sand debut with two wins over course and distance. His only win on the turf was on soft ground over 12 furlongs.

Voice Mail

82 **54**
2-y-o b c So Factual (USA)-Wizardry (Shirley Heights)
I A Balding Roger Parry

Placings:000 **(5126)**
2001: 6^{0}G, 7^{0}HY, 6^{0}HY

	Starts	1st	2nd	3rd	Win & Pl
Career Total (Turf)	3	0	0	0	

Going (Turf): Sf: 0-2 GS: 0-0 Gd: 0-1 GF: 0-0 Fm: 0-0
Distance: 5f/6f: 0-2 7f-8f: 0-1 9f-13f: 0-0 14f+: 0-0
Track : LH: 0-1 RH: 0-0 Tight: 0-0 Gall: 0-0
Aids: Bl: 0-0 Vi: 0-0 Tstrap: 0-0
Best Rating: 54 10/01 Ling 6f heavy

Volali (IRE)

(65) **62**
2-y-o b c Ali-Royal (IRE)-Vol De Reve (IRE) (Nordico (USA))
Mrs A Duffield Paul J Dixon

Placings:03060 **(4577)**
2001: 6^{0}GF, 5^{3}G, 5^{0}GF, 5^{6}G, 6^{0}G, 7^{0}SD

	Starts	1st	2nd	3rd	Win & Pl
Career Total (Turf)	5	0	0	1	470

Going (Turf): Sf: 0-0 GS: 0-0 Gd: 0-3 GF: 0-2 Fm: 0-0
Distance: 5f/6f: 0-5 7f-8f: 0-0 9f-13f: 0-0 14f+: 0-0
Track : LH: 0-1 RH: 0-0 Tight: 0-0 Gall: 0-0
Aids: Bl: 0-1 Vi: 0-0 Tstrap: 0-0
Best Rating: 62 6/01 Muss 5f good

Volata (IRE)

112 **114+**
3-y-o b c Flying Spur (AUS)-Musianica (Music Boy)
M H Tompkins J Ellis

Placings:10-01106 **(3828)**
2001: 8^{0}G, 6^{1}GF, 6^{1}F, 6^{0}G, 6^{6}G

	Starts	1st	2nd	3rd	Win & Pl
Career Total (Turf)	7	3	0	0	44934

111 6/01 Newc 6f A FRM £20300
114 5/01 Hayd 6f A(0-110)H G-F £15381
89 6/00 NmkR 6f D G-F £5252
Total win prize-money £40934

Going (Turf): Sf: 0-0 GS: 0-1 Gd: 0-3 **GF: 2-2** Fm: 1-1
Distance: **5f/6f: 3-5** 7f-8f: 0-2 9f-13f: 0-0 14f+: 0-0
Track : LH: 0-0 RH: 0-0 Tight: 0-0 Gall: 0-0
Aids: Bl: 0-0 Vi: 0-0 Tstrap: 0-0
Best Rating: 114 5/01 Hayd 6f gd-fm

Scored on his juvenile debut at Newmarket, but failed to build on that when well beaten in Dewhurst Stakes. Eleventh in the 2,000 Guineas on his reappearance, he showed good early speed and got off the mark next time when stepping back to six furlongs and followed up with another success at Newcastle. May have found the easing ground against him in the July Cup. Lightly-raced, he is best suited by six furlongs and fast ground. An improving type.

Volontiers (FR)

110(80) (82d)**101**
6-y-o b g Common Grounds-Senlis (USA) (Sensitive Prince (USA))
P W Harris The Commoners

Placings:2/421100030/3000025/0416022002034-2100 **(2972)**
2001: 7^{2}GF, 8^{1}GF, 7^{0}GF, 7^{0}G

	Starts	1st	2nd	3rd	Win & Pl
Career Total (Turf)	32	4	6	3	64512
Career Total (AW)	2	0	1	0	1145

97 6/01 Newb 1m B(0-100)H G-F £9456
81 5/00 Thsk 1m C(0-95)H GD £11700
101 6/98 Epsm 7f A GD £21444
95 5/98 Hayd 7f30y D G-F £3468
Total win prize-money £46070

Going (Turf): Sf: 0-3 GS: 0-3 **Gd: 2-12 GF: 2-13** Fm: 0-1
Distance: 5f/6f: 0-1 **7f-8f: 4-31** 9f-13f: 0-2 14f+: 0-0
Track : **LH: 3-10** RH: 0-9 **Tight: 2-4** Gall: 0-4
Aids: Bl: 0-0 Vi: 0-0 Tstrap: 0-0
Best Rating: 97 6/01 Newb 1m gd-fm

A useful handicapper at his best, he has run well since making a belated reappearance this season, winning well at Newbury on his second start and getting no sort of run next time. Suited by a mile on fast ground and by coming late off a strong pace.

Volte Face

90(94) (38)**43**
3-y-o ch f Polar Falcon (USA)-Krameria (Kris)
S Kirk Lord Roborough

Placings:0-50 **(5519)**
2001: 6^{5}G, 6^{0}HY, 6^{5}SD

	Starts	1st	2nd	3rd	Win & Pl
Career Total (Turf)	3	0	0	0	0

Going (Turf): Sf: 0-2 GS: 0-0 Gd: 0-1 GF: 0-0 Fm: 0-0
Distance: 5f/6f: 0-3 7f-8f: 0-0 9f-13f: 0-0 14f+: 0-0
Track : LH: 0-0 RH: 0-0 Tight: 0-0 Gall: 0-0
Aids: Bl: 0-0 Vi: 0-0 Tstrap: 0-0
Best Rating: 43 10/01 Rdcr 6f good

She would probably have finished third but for losing her action in the Dip on her Newmarket debut over six furlongs in October of 2000, when trained by Richard Hannon, and she was not seen out again for over a year. She returned at Redcar in October of 2001, for Sylvester Kirk, and was a fair fifth.

Voucher

89 **79**
2-y-o ch f Polish Precedent (USA)-Superstore (USA) (Blushing Groom (FR))
B W Hills K Abdulla

Placings:05 **(4573)**
2001: 7^{0}GF, 6^{5}G

	Starts	1st	2nd	3rd	Win & Pl
Career Total (Turf)	2	0	0	0	0

Going (Turf): Sf: 0-0 GS: 0-0 Gd: 0-1 GF: 0-1 Fm: 0-0
Distance: 5f/6f: 0-1 7f-8f: 0-1 9f-13f: 0-0 14f+: 0-0
Track : LH: 0-0 RH: 0-0 Tight: 0-0 Gall: 0-0
Aids: Bl: 0-0 Vi: 0-0 Tstrap: 0-0
Best Rating: 79 9/01 Kemp 6f good

Vrubel (IRE)

89(87) (68)**68**
2-y-o ch c Entrepreneur-Renzola (Dragonara Palace (USA))
N A Callaghan M Tabor

Placings:3400 **(5588)**
2001: 6^{3}GF, 6^{4}SD, 6^{0}S, 5^{0}GS

	Starts	1st	2nd	3rd	Win & Pl
Career Total (Turf)	3	0	0	1	510
Career Total (AW)	1	0	0	0	0

Going (Turf): Sf: 0-1 GS: 0-1 Gd: 0-0 GF: 0-1 Fm: 0-0
Distance: 5f/6f: 0-3 7f-8f: 0-1 9f-13f: 0-0 14f+: 0-0
Track : LH: 0-2 RH: 0-0 Tight: 0-1 Gall: 0-0
Aids: Bl: 0-0 Vi: 0-0 Tstrap: 0-0
Best Rating: 68 6/01 Wolv 6f stand

Vuela-Mana-Mou (IRE)

87 **47**
3-y-o b g Goldmark (USA)-Carnival Fugue (High Top)
G A Butler Mrs Andry Muinos

Placings:00 **(5182)**
2001: 11^{0}F, 10^{0}HY

	Starts	1st	2nd	3rd	Win & Pl
Career Total (Turf)	2	0	0	0	

Going (Turf): Sf: 0-1 GS: 0-0 Gd: 0-0 GF: 0-0 Fm: 0-1
Distance: 5f/6f: 0-0 7f-8f: 0-0 9f-13f: 0-2 14f+: 0-0
Track : LH: 0-1 RH: 0-0 Tight: 0-2 Gall: 0-0
Aids: Bl: 0-0 Vi: 0-0 Tstrap: 0-0
Best Rating: 47 9/01 Bath 1m3f144y firm

Wa-Naam

102 **76**
3-y-o ch g Cadeaux Genereux-Na-Ayim (IRE) (Shirley Heights)
I Semple (E A L Dunlop 18/5) J And J Hunter

Placings:0-423 **(5631)**
2001: 7^{4}GS, 9^{2}GF, 10^{3}G

	Starts	1st	2nd	3rd	Win & Pl
Career Total (Turf)	4	0	1	1	1995

Going (Turf): Sf: 0-1 GS: 0-1 Gd: 0-1 GF: 0-1 Fm: 0-0
Distance: 5f/6f: 0-1 7f-8f: 0-1 9f-13f: 0-2 14f+: 0-0
Track : LH: 0-1 RH: 0-1 Tight: 0-2 Gall: 0-0
Aids: Bl: 0-0 Vi: 0-0 Tstrap: 0-0
Best Rating: 77 5/01 NmkR 7f gd-sft

A Maktoum cast-off who cost current connections 16,000gns. Returned from a break to run well in a

Hamilton maiden in September, and then he ran a good third in a similar event at Redcar in November, and should be capable of winning a similar event.

Waafiah

102 **56**

3-y-o b f Anabaa (USA)-First Waltz (FR) (Green Dancer (USA))

M Johnston Ziad A Galadari

Placings:2 **(3646)**

2001: 7^{2}F

	Starts	1st	2nd	3rd	Win & Pl
Career Total (Turf)	1	0	1	0	1306

Going (Turf): Sf: 0-0 GS: 0-0 Gd: 0-0 GF: 0-0 Fm: 0-1
Distance: 5f/6f: 0-0 7f-8f: 0-1 9f-13f: 0-0 14f+: 0-0
Track : LH: 0-1 RH: 0-0 Tight: 0-1 Gall: 0-0
Aids: Bl: 0-0 Vi: 0-0 Tstrap: 0-0
Best Rating: 56 8/01 Thsk 7f firm

Wadenhoe (IRE)

91 **25**

4-y-o b f Persian Bold-Frill (Henbit (USA))

M S Saunders Mrs Margaret Hall

Placings:0210000/600000-000000 **(4526)**

2001: 8^{0}GS, 7^{0}F, 7^{0}GF, 8^{0}HD, 6^{0}F, 7^{0}GF

	Starts	1st	2nd	3rd	Win & Pl
Career Total (Turf)	19	1	1	0	4824

81 6/99 Ayr 7f D G-S £3522
Total win prize-money £3522

Going (Turf): Sf: 0-2 GS: 1-5 Gd: 0-4 GF: 0-5 Fm: 0-3
Distance: 5f/6f: 0-1 7f-8f: 1-10 9f-13f: 0-7 14f+: 0-1
Track : LH: 1-12 RH: 0-3 Tight: 0-7 Gall: 0-2
Aids: Bl: 0-1 Vi: 0-0 Tstrap: 0-0
Best Rating: 35 5/01 Brig 7f214y firm

Improved form when upped to seven furlongs, winning nicely at Ayr in June.

Wadi

101 (63)**62**

6-y-o b g Green Desert (USA)-Eternal (Kris)

Dr J R J Naylor Robert House

Placings:33/016/03262441100/060410143-000100000 **(4721)**

2001: 12^{0}GF, 12^{0}GF, 10^{0}GF, 11^{1}F, 12^{0}S, 13^{0}G, 10^{0}GF, 9^{0}GS, 12^{0}G

	Starts	1st	2nd	3rd	Win & Pl
Career Total (Turf)	31	6	2	3	20670
Career Total (AW)	3	0	0	1	262

62 7/01 Ling 1m3f106yF(0-60)H FRM £3108
65 7/00 Haml 1m3f16y E(0-70)H G-F £3510
59 6/00 Folk 1m4f F(0-65)H FRM £2604
68 7/99 Sals 1m1f198yF FRM £2332
59 7/99 Wwck 1m4f56y G(0-60)H G-F £2092
79 7/98 Pont 1m2f6y D G-F £3631
Total win prize-money £17278

Going (Turf): Sf: 0-3 GS: 0-2 Gd: 0-7 GF: 3-12 Fm: 3-6
Distance: 5f/6f: 0-0 7f-8f: 0-0 9f-13f: 6-32 14f+: 0-1
Track : LH: 3-15 RH: 3-16 Tight: 4-18 Gall: 0-4
Aids: Bl: 0-2 Vi: 0-0 Tstrap: 0-2
Best Rating: 62 7/01 Ling 1m3f106y firm

Wadsworth (NZ)

91 **33**

8-y-o br g Kirmann-Guard The Gold (NZ) (Imperial Guard)

B P J Baugh (S A Brookshaw 27/2) M W & A N Harris

Placings:0/30 **(2375)**

2001: 10^{3}F, 10^{0}GF

	Starts	1st	2nd	3rd	Win & Pl
Career Total (Turf)	3	0	0	1	1070

Going (Turf): Sf: 0-0 GS: 0-0 Gd: 0-0 GF: 0-1 Fm: 0-1
Distance: 5f/6f: 0-0 7f-8f: 0-0 9f-13f: 0-2 14f+: 0-0
Track : LH: 0-2 RH: 0-0 Tight: 0-1 Gall: 0-1
Aids: Bl: 0-0 Vi: 0-0 Tstrap: 0-0
Best Rating: 33 6/01 Donc 1m2f60y firm

Waff's Folly

102(92) (44)**55**

6-y-o b m Handsome Sailor-Shirl (Shirley Heights)

D J S Ffrench Davis P H Wafford

Placings:00/106006/30353034/003532440-502506 **(5462)**

2001: 6^{5}SD, 6^{0}F, 5^{2}G, 5^{5}G, 5^{0}G, 5^{6}G

	Starts	1st	2nd	3rd	Win & Pl
Career Total (Turf)	29	1	2	6	6561
Career Total (AW)	2	0	0	0	0

65 4/98 Folk 6f F GD £2070
Total win prize-money £2070

Going (Turf): Sf: 0-6 GS: 0-6 Gd: 1-7 GF: 0-6 Fm: 0-4
Distance: 5f/6f: 1-22 7f-8f: 0-9 9f-13f: 0-0 14f+: 0-0
Track : LH: 0-4 RH: 0-4 Tight: 0-2 Gall: 0-5
Aids: Bl: 0-0 Vi: 0-0 Tstrap: 0-0
Best Rating: 55 8/01 Wind 5f10y good

Last won in 1998, although has suffered some narrow defeats. Effective five to six furlongs, handles any ground.

Waffles Of Amin

96(92) (52)**43**

4-y-o b g Owington-Alzianah (Alzao (USA))

S Kirk S Kirk

Placings:5262316/0040050-060000060006 **(5469)**

2001: 8^{0}SD, 6^{6}SD, 7^{0}SD, 7^{0}SD, 7^{0}SD, 6^{0}F, 9^{0}F, 10^{6}GF, 10^{0}GF, 10^{0}F, 10^{0}GF, 9^{6}S

	Starts	1st	2nd	3rd	Win & Pl
Career Total (Turf)	19	0	2	1	2885
Career Total (AW)	7	1	0	0	2788

78 11/99 Wolv 5f D STD £2788
Total win prize-money £2788

Going (Turf): Sf: 0-2 GS: 0-2 Gd: 0-2 GF: 0-10 Fm: 0-3
Distance: 5f/6f: 1-12 7f-8f: 0-8 9f-13f: 0-6 14f+: 0-0
Track : LH: 1-15 RH: 0-2 Tight: 1-11 Gall: 0-1
Aids: Bl: 0-1 Vi: 0-0 Tstrap: 0-0
Best Rating: 57 1/01 Sthl 1m stand

Wahchi (IRE)

93 **95+**

2-y-o ch c Nashwan (USA)-Nafhaat (USA) (Roberto (USA))

E A L Dunlop Hamdan Al Maktoum

Placings:01 **(4661)**

2001: 6^{0}G, 8^{1}GF

	Starts	1st	2nd	3rd	Win & Pl
Career Total (Turf)	2	1	0	0	7508

95 9/01 Donc 1m D G-F £7507
Total win prize-money £7508

Going (Turf): Sf: 0-0 GS: 0-0 Gd: 0-1 GF: 1-1 Fm: 0-0
Distance: 5f/6f: 0-0 7f-8f: 1-2 9f-13f: 0-0 14f+: 0-0
Track : LH: 0-1 RH: 0-0 Tight: 0-0 Gall: 0-1
Aids: Bl: 0-0 Vi: 0-0 Tstrap: 0-0
Best Rating: 95 9/01 Donc 1m gd-fm

A close relation to the 2001 Lancashire Oaks runner-up Ranin and four other useful performers, he won an ordinary maiden on his second outing when stepped up to a mile on a firm surface.

Wahj (IRE)

113(108) (103)**101**

6-y-o ch g Indian Ridge-Sabaah (USA) (Nureyev (USA))

C A Dwyer S B Components (international) Ltd

Placings:11/03040/0112010-240051036 **(5228)**

2001: 8^{2}SD, 8^{4}GS, 8^{0}GF, 8^{0}GF, 7^{5}GF, 7^{1}GS, 7^{0}G, 7^{3}G, 6^{6}S

	Starts	1st	2nd	3rd	Win & Pl
Career Total (Turf)	22	6	1	2	47158
Career Total (AW)	1	0	1	0	10000

101 8/01 Ches 7f2y B(0-100)H G-S £9657
100 8/00 Newb 7f C(0-95)H G-F £6760
93 7/00 Hayd 7f30y C(0-95)H G-F £6246
89 6/00 Hayd 7f30y C(0-90) G-S £7477
103 8/98 Chep 7f16y C G-F £5416
82 8/98 Wind 1m67y D G-F £3746
Total win prize-money £39304

Going (Turf): Sf: 0-1 GS: 2-7 Gd: 0-4 GF: 4-10 Fm: 0-0
Distance: 5f/6f: 0-1 7f-8f: 5-19 9f-13f: 1-3 14f+: 0-0
Track : LH: 3-8 RH: 1-3 Tight: 2-3 Gall: 0-2
Aids: Bl: 0-0 Vi: 0-0 Tstrap: 0-1
Best Rating: 103 3/01 Wolv 1m100y stand

Tough front-running seven furlong handicapper who is very capable on his day in decent company. Won three races after joining present connections in 2000 and had been racing over too long a trip this term, but the drop back to seven furlongs saw him return to winning ways at Chester in August. Looked outclassed in Ireland next time. Suited by most types of ground.

Waikiki Beach (USA)

74(94) (35)**36**

10-y-o ch g Fighting Fit (USA)-Running Melody (Rheingold)

G L Moore Mrs J Moore

Placings:06214210/000003005/2143414021/50205200/351002030000010/5441003533303401/000400620603-000 **(3740)**

2001: 11^{0}GS, 8^{0}SD, 8^{0}S

	Starts	1st	2nd	3rd	Win & Pl
Career Total (Turf)	36	2	4	2	24327
Career Total (AW)	43	7	4	7	20780

56 12/99 Wolv 1m100y G STD £1574
65 3/99 Ling 1m F(0-60)H STD £1708
60 11/98 Ling 1m2f G STD £1550
61 4/98 Sthl 1m G(0-70)H STD £1725
69 12/96 Ling 1m2f F STD £2528
80 6/96 Ling 1m E(0-70) STD £3179
65 4/96 Wolv 1m100y F(0-60) STD £2381
92 8/94 Badn 1m GD £15564
74 7/94 Chep 7f16y D FRM £3414
Total win prize-money £33626

Going (Turf): Sf: 0-4 GS: 0-5 Gd: 1-10 GF: 0-14 Fm: 1-3
Distance: 5f/6f: 0-3 7f-8f: 5-43 9f-13f: 4-33 14f+: 0-0
Track : LH: 8-53 RH: 0-11 Tight: 6-41 Gall: 0-0
Aids: Bl: 3-27 Vi: 0-2 Tstrap: 0-0
Best Rating: 30 6/01 Sthl 1m stand

He has won on Fibresand, but looks better on Equitrack. Good ride for an amateur.

Waikiki Dancer (IRE)

94(85) (44)**52**

3-y-o br f General Monash (USA)-Waikiki (GER) (Zampano (GER))

B Palling B Reynolds

Placings:0006-066030 **(3706)**

2001: 8^{0}SD, 8^{6}G, 7^{6}GF, 8^{0}GF, 6^{3}SD, 7^{0}G

	Starts	1st	2nd	3rd	Win & Pl
Career Total (Turf)	7	0	0	0	0
Career Total (AW)	3	0	0	1	329

Going (Turf): Sf: 0-1 GS: 0-0 Gd: 0-2 GF: 0-4 Fm: 0-0
Distance: 5f/6f: 0-3 7f-8f: 0-5 9f-13f: 0-2 14f+: 0-0
Track : LH: 0-6 RH: 0-0 Tight: 0-2 Gall: 0-0
Aids: Bl: 0-0 Vi: 0-0 Tstrap: 0-0
Best Rating: 52 5/01 Bath 1m5y good

Wainak (USA)

94(95) (64)**56**

3-y-o b g Silver Hawk (USA)-Cask (Be My Chief (USA))

M H Tompkins P A & D G Sakal

Placings:02232-00404 **(5348)**

2001: 7^{0}GF, 8^{0}G, 10^{4}F, 11^{0}GS, 12^{4}SD

	Starts	1st	2nd	3rd	Win & Pl
Career Total (Turf)	9	0	3	1	4376
Career Total (AW)	1	0	0	0	273

Going (Turf): **Sf: 0-0 GS: 0-1 Gd: 0-4 GF: 0-3 Fm: 0-1**
Distance: 5f/6f: 0-0 7f-8f: 0-6 9f-13f: 0-4 14f+: 0-0
Track : LH: 0-5 RH: 0-2 Tight: 0-3 Gall: 0-0
Aids: Bl: 0-1 Vi: 0-0 Tstrap: 0-0
Best Rating: 64 10/01 Sthl 1m4f stand

Showed useful form at two, being placed four times from five runs. Should stay further than a mile. Looked a bit reluctant to put his best foot forward on his last outing of 2000, and has continued to show poor form in 2001, so improvement needed to win a race. Acts on good and good to firm ground.

Wait For The Will (USA)

104 **75**

5-y-o ch g Seeking The Gold (USA)-You'd Be Surprised (USA) (Blushing Groom (FR))

G L Moore Richard Green (fine Paintings)

Placings:55/613060/001223130-00000650 **(4779)**

2001: 12^{0}G, 12^{0}GF, 12^{0}GF, 12^{0}GF, 12^{0}GF, 14^{6}GF, 12^{5}G, 12^{0}G

			Starts	1st	2nd	3rd	Win & Pl
Career Total (Turf)			25	3	2	3	26145
87	7/00	Asct	1m4f	C(0-95)H		G-F	£8006
76	5/00	Sals	1m4f	D(0-80)H		GD	£4218
78	7/99	Sals	1m4f	F(0-75)H		G-F	£2430

Total win prize-money £15645

Going (Turf): Sf: 0-0 GS: 0-4 Gd: 1-8 **GF: 2-12** Fm: 0-1
Distance: 5f/6f: 0-0 7f-8f: 0-0 **9f-13f: 3-19** 14f+: 0-6
Track : LH: 0-7 **RH: 3-18 Tight: 2-9** Gall: 1-12
Aids: **Bl: 1-10** Vi: 0-1 Tstrap: 0-1
Best Rating: 77 5/01 Donc 1m4f gd-fm

Suited by 12 furlongs but stays further. Appreciates fast ground, and seems suited by coming late and between rivals. Has worn blinkers.

Waki Music (USA)

108 **100**

3-y-o b f Miswaki (USA)-Light Music (USA) (Nijinsky (CAN))

R Charlton K Abdulla

Placings:135-3530 **(3634)**

2001: 10^{3}GF, 10^{5}GF, 8^{3}G, 7^{0}G

			Starts	1st	2nd	3rd	Win & Pl
Career Total (Turf)			7	1	0	3	12607
85	8/00	Kemp	7f	D		G-F	£4524

Total win prize-money £4524

Going (Turf): Sf: 0-0 GS: 0-0 Gd: 0-3 **GF: 1-4** Fm: 0-0
Distance: 5f/6f: 0-0 **7f-8f: 1-5** 9f-13f: 0-2 14f+: 0-0
Track : LH: 0-3 **RH: 1-3** Tight: 0-0 **Gall: 1-4**
Aids: Bl: 0-0 Vi: 0-0 Tstrap: 0-0
Best Rating: 96 5/01 Donc 1m2f60y gd-fm

Looked a filly for the future when scoring on her debut at Kempton last season and she ran with credit in Group company subsequently, but has not shown much this season and still has to convince that she stays beyond a mile.

Waldenburg (USA)

101 **102+**

2-y-o b c Miswaki (USA)-Erandel (USA) (Danzig (USA))

J H M Gosden Sheikh Mohammed

Placings:14 **(4173)**

2001: 6^{1}GF, 6^{4}G

			Starts	1st	2nd	3rd	Win & Pl
Career Total (Turf)			2	1	0	0	10930
102	6/01	Newb	6f8y	D		G-F	£4680

Total win prize-money £4680

Going (Turf): Sf: 0-0 GS: 0-0 Gd: 0-1 **GF: 1-1** Fm: 0-0
Distance: 5f/6f: 0-1 **7f-8f: 1-1** 9f-13f: 0-0 14f+: 0-0
Track : LH: 0-0 RH: 0-0 Tight: 0-0 Gall: 0-0
Aids: Bl: 0-0 Vi: 0-0 Tstrap: 0-0
Best Rating: 102 6/01 Newb 6f8y gd-fm

Turned over the favourite on his Newbury debut and pulled out just enough to hold on. Will only come on for that and should be suited by a mile in time. Acts on fast ground.

Waltzing Wizard

84 **66**

2-y-o b c Magic Ring (IRE)-Legendary Dancer (Shareef Dancer (USA))

A Berry Paul J Dixon

Placings:31560 **(4577)**

2001: 5^{3}GF, 5^{1}S, 5^{5}G, 6^{6}G, 6^{0}G

			Starts	1st	2nd	3rd	Win & Pl
Career Total (Turf)			5	1	0	1	4604
61	7/01	Haml	5f4y	D		SFT	£4046

Total win prize-money £4046

Going (Turf): **Sf: 1-1** GS: 0-0 Gd: 0-3 GF: 0-1 Fm: 0-0
Distance: **5f/6f: 1-5** 7f-8f: 0-0 9f-13f: 0-0 14f+: 0-0
Track : LH: 0-0 RH: 0-0 Tight: 0-0 Gall: 0-0
Aids: Bl: 0-0 Vi: 0-0 Tstrap: 0-1
Best Rating: 66 6/01 Ayr 5f gd-fm

A half-brother to three winner including Legend of Aragon who won over five furlongs as a juvenile. Proved well suited by soft ground when winning a Hamilton maiden over the minimum trip.

Walworth Star

96(77) (38)**44**

3-y-o ch g Clantime-Walworth Lady (Belfort (FR))

M Dods Vernon Spinks

Placings:30005300650060 **(5538)**

2001: 8^{3}S, 8^{0}S, 10^{0}S, 6^{0}F, 6^{5}F, 7^{3}GF, 6^{0}F, 7^{0}GF, 6^{6}GS, 5^{5}GF, 6^{0}G, 6^{0}G, 6^{6}SD, 10^{0}S

	Starts	1st	2nd	3rd	Win & Pl
Career Total (Turf)	13	0	0	2	964
Career Total (AW)	1	0	0	0	0

Going (Turf): **Sf: 0-4 GS: 0-1 Gd: 0-2 GF: 0-3 Fm: 0-3**
Distance: 5f/6f: 0-7 7f-8f: 0-5 9f-13f: 0-2 14f+: 0-0
Track : LH: 0-5 RH: 0-2 Tight: 0-3 Gall: 0-1
Aids: Bl: 0-0 Vi: 0-1 Tstrap: 0-5
Best Rating: 46 6/01 Ayr 7f gd-fm

Wanna Shout

98(98) (71d)**49**

3-y-o b f Missed Flight-Lulu (Polar Falcon (USA))

R Dickin E R Clifford Beech

Placings:552010-0000004005 **(5497)**

2001: 6^{0}SD, 6^{0}SW, 6^{0}SD, 7^{0}GF, 7^{0}G, 5^{0}GF, 6^{4}GF, 6^{0}GF, 6^{0}F, 5^{5}HY

			Starts	1st	2nd	3rd	Win & Pl
Career Total (Turf)			10	0	1	0	660
Career Total (AW)			6	1	0	0	2772
71	11/00	Wolv	6f	E(0-75)		STD	£2772

Total win prize-money £2772

Going (Turf): **Sf: 0-3 GS: 0-0 Gd: 0-2 GF: 0-4 Fm: 0-1**
Distance: **5f/6f: 1-12** 7f-8f: 0-4 9f-13f: 0-0 14f+: 0-0
Track : **LH: 1-8** RH: 0-0 **Tight: 1-4** Gall: 0-2
Aids: Bl: 0-2 Vi: 0-1 Tstrap: 0-2
Best Rating: 49 8/01 Newb 6f8y gd-fm

Wannabe Around

110(101) (68)**108**

3-y-o b c Primo Dominie-Noble Peregrine (Lomond (USA))

T G Mills T G Mills

Placings:6324-23121541240 **(4679)**

2001: 7^{2}SD, 7^{3}S, 8^{1}S, 9^{2}GS, 9^{1}GF, 10^{5}GF, 8^{4}GF, 8^{1}GF, 8^{2}G, 9^{4}S, 8^{0}G

			Starts	1st	2nd	3rd	Win & Pl
Career Total (Turf)			14	3	3	2	79826
Career Total (AW)			1	0	1	0	704
101	7/01	Sals	1m	B(0-95)		G-F	£9008
91	5/01	Gdwd	1m1f	B(0-105)H		G-F	£32500
74	4/01	Epsm	1m114y	D		SFT	£4309

Total win prize-money £45818

Going (Turf): Sf: 1-5 GS: 0-1 Gd: 0-2 **GF: 2-6** Fm: 0-0
Distance: 5f/6f: 0-0 7f-8f: 1-10 **9f-13f: 2-5** 14f+: 0-0
Track : LH: 1-4 RH: 1-4 **Tight: 2-3** Gall: 0-2
Aids: Bl: 0-0 Vi: 0-0 Tstrap: 0-0
Best Rating: 108 8/01 Gdwd 1m good

Remarkably game and durable miler. Received 9lb from Bourgainville when making all to beat him by two lengths in valuable handicap at Goodwood in May and was giving 3lb to the same opponent at Salisbury in July, but again came out a clear number one. Ran a creditable races at Epsom and Royal Ascot in between. Far from disgraced in a Group Three at Ovrevoll at the end of August. Has won on fast and soft ground.

Wansford Lady

95 **35**

5-y-o b m Michelozzo (USA)-Marnie's Girl (Crooner)

A W Carroll Mrs J Webster

Placings:0/0/00 **(2656)**

2001: 11^{0}GF, 11^{0}GF

	Starts	1st	2nd	3rd	Win & Pl
Career Total (Turf)	4	0	0	0	

Going (Turf): **Sf: 0-1 GS: 0-0 Gd: 0-0 GF: 0-3 Fm: 0-0**
Distance: 5f/6f: 0-0 7f-8f: 0-0 9f-13f: 0-4 14f+: 0-0
Track : LH: 0-2 RH: 0-0 Tight: 0-2 Gall: 0-0
Aids: Bl: 0-0 Vi: 0-0 Tstrap: 0-0
Best Rating: 35 7/01 Wind 1m3f135y gd-fm

War Tune

39

5-y-o b g Warrshan (USA)-Keen Melody (USA) (Sharpen Up)

G F Edwards (R M Whitaker 7/4) G F Edwards

Placings:5 **(0684)**

2001: 12^{5}G

	Starts	1st	2nd	3rd	Win & Pl
Career Total (Turf)	1	0	0	0	0

Going (Turf): **Sf: 0-1 GS: 0-0 Gd: 0-0 GF: 0-0 Fm: 0-0**
Distance: 5f/6f: 0-0 7f-8f: 0-0 9f-13f: 0-1 14f+: 0-0
Track : LH: 0-0 RH: 0-0 Tight: 0-0 Gall: 0-0
Aids: Bl: 0-0 Vi: 0-0 Tstrap: 0-0
Best Rating: 39 4/01 Muss 1m4f soft

War Valor (USA)

92 **90**

2-y-o b c Royal Academy (USA)-Western Music (USA) (Lord At War (ARG))

J Nicol Team Valor

Placings:43 **(5491)**

2001: 7^{4}G, 6^{3}HY

	Starts	1st	2nd	3rd	Win & Pl
Career Total (Turf)	2	0	0	1	1292

Going (Turf): Sf: 0-1 GS: 0-0 Gd: 0-1 GF: 0-0 Fm: 0-0
Distance: 5f/6f: 0-0 7f-8f: 0-2 9f-13f: 0-0 14f+: 0-0
Track : LH: 0-0 RH: 0-0 Tight: 0-0 Gall: 0-0
Aids: Bl: 0-0 Vi: 0-0 Tstrap: 0-0
Best Rating: 90 10/01 Newb 6f8y heavy

He showed ability in both of his first two starts and there is a race or two in him.

Waraqa (USA)

92 **79**

2-y-o b f Red Ransom (USA)-Jafn (Sharpo)
B Hanbury Hamdan Al Maktoum

Placings:5523 **(3613)**
2001: 5^{5}S, 6^{5}GF, 6^{2}GF, 5^{3}G

	Starts	1st	2nd	3rd	Win & Pl
Career Total (Turf)	4	0	1	1	1840

Going (Turf): Sf: 0-1 GS: 0-0 Gd: 0-1 GF: 0-2 Fm: 0-0
Distance: 5f/6f: 0-3 7f-8f: 0-1 9f-13f: 0-0 14f+: 0-0
Track : LH: 0-0 RH: 0-0 Tight: 0-0 Gall: 0-0
Aids: Bl: 0-0 Vi: 0-0 Tstrap: 0-2
Best Rating: 79 7/01 Nott 6f15y gd-fm

Warden Belle

91 **51**

3-y-o b f Emperor Jones (USA)-Sing A Rainbow (IRE) (Rainbow Quest (USA))
J R Fanshawe Park Farm Racing

Placings:0600 **(5461)**
2001: 8^{0}G, 8^{6}GF, 7^{0}G, 8^{0}G

	Starts	1st	2nd	3rd	Win & Pl
Career Total (Turf)	4	0	0	0	0

Going (Turf): Sf: 0-0 GS: 0-0 Gd: 0-3 GF: 0-1 Fm: 0-0
Distance: 5f/6f: 0-0 7f-8f: 0-1 9f-13f: 0-3 14f+: 0-0
Track : LH: 0-1 RH: 0-1 Tight: 0-1 Gall: 0-0
Aids: Bl: 0-0 Vi: 0-0 Tstrap: 0-3
Best Rating: 51 9/01 Wwck 1m22y gd-fm

Warden Warren

103 **75**

3-y-o b c Petong-Silver Spell (Aragon)
M A Jarvis John E Sims

Placings:01265-000100 **(4872)**
2001: 6^{0}S, 6^{0}GF, 6^{0}G, 7^{1}GF, 6^{0}G, 7^{0}G

	Starts	1st	2nd	3rd	Win & Pl
Career Total (Turf)	11	2	1	0	10535

75	8/01	NmkJ	7f	E	G-F	£3630
85	6/00	NmkJ	6f	D	G-F	£4891

Total win prize-money £8521

Going (Turf): Sf: 0-1 GS: 0-0 Gd: 0-5 **GF: 2-5** Fm: 0-0
Distance: 5f/6f: 1-9 7f-8f: 1-2 9f-13f: 0-0 14f+: 0-0
Track : LH: 0-1 RH: 0-1 Tight: 0-1 Gall: 0-1
Aids: **Bl: 1-3** Vi: 0-0 Tstrap: 0-0
Best Rating: 75 8/01 NmkJ 7f gd-fm

Had to drop into a claimer to score.

Wareed (IRE)

104 **112**

3-y-o b c Sadler's Wells (USA)-Truly Special (Caerleon (USA))
Saeed Bin Suroor Godolphin

Placings:1-2610 **(5585a)**
2001: 11^{2}GF, 12^{6}GF, 15^{1}VS, 15^{0}HY

	Starts	1st	2nd	3rd	Win & Pl
Career Total (Turf)	5	2	1	0	45424

112	10/01	Lonc	1m7f	VS	£29028
	10/00	Lonc	1m1f	SFT	£8646

Total win prize-money £37674

Going (Turf): Sf: 0-1 GS: 0-0 Gd: 0-0 GF: 0-2 Fm: 0-0
Distance: 5f/6f: 0-0 7f-8f: 0-0 9f-13f: 0-2 **14f+: 1-2**
Track : LH: 0-0 **RH: 1-3** Tight: 0-1 Gall: 0-0
Aids: Bl: 0-0 **Vi: 1-4** Tstrap: 0-0
Best Rating: 112 10/01 Lonc 1m7f v soft

Out of a mare who won the Prix de Royaumont and a half-brother to the smart middle-distance filly Truly A Dream, he was an impressive six-length winner of a newcomers' race at Longchamp as a juvenile when trained by David Loder. He beat Musha Merr by a short head in a strongly-run private trial over a mile at Nad Al Sheba in April, but was comprehensively beaten by Asian Heights in the Predominate and was well behind in the Gordon Stakes, both at Goodwood on fast ground. Looked much happier on soft ground when making all to win a Group Two at Longchamp in October. Wears blinkers, stays 15 furlongs.

Warlingham (IRE)

79(94) (65)**67**

3-y-o b g Catrail (USA)-Tadjnama (USA) (Exceller (USA))
Miss Gay Kelleway Martin Butler

Placings:463621430-000 **(2448)**
2001: 6^{0}G, 6^{0}GF, 7^{0}F

	Starts	1st	2nd	3rd	Win & Pl
Career Total (Turf)	11	1	1	2	5815
Career Total (AW)	1	0	0	0	1650

74	7/00	Yarm	5f43y	D	GD	£3428

Total win prize-money £3429

Going (Turf): Sf: 0-0 GS: 0-2 **Gd: 1-3** GF: 0-5 Fm: 0-1
Distance: **5f/6f: 1-11** 7f-8f: 0-1 9f-13f: 0-0 14f+: 0-0
Track : LH: 0-1 RH: 0-0 Tight: 0-1 Gall: 0-0
Aids: Bl: 0-1 Vi: 0-0 Tstrap: 0-0
Best Rating: 52 5/01 Wind 6f good

Warning Reef

109 (51)**56**

8-y-o b g Warning-Horseshoe Reef (Mill Reef (USA))
E J Alston Valley Paddocks Racing Limited

Placings:5204/43630022/06606000/520632112125330/00235533324040/456533312142400-403003620050 **(5632)**
2001: 10^{4}GF, 12^{0}GF, 12^{3}F, 11^{0}G, 12^{0}GF, 10^{3}GF, 12^{6}G, 11^{2}G, 12^{0}G, 12^{0}GF, 12^{5}GS, 10^{0}G

	Starts	1st	2nd	3rd	Win & Pl
Career Total (Turf)	73	5	11	14	90174
Career Total (AW)	3	0	1	0	880

66	8/00	NmkJ	1m4f	C(0-90)H	G-F	£6760
57	7/00	Kemp	1m4f	D(0-80)H	G-F	£7182
60	8/98	Asct	1m4f	D(0-85)H	G-F	£7035
54	7/98	Sand	1m3f91y	D(0-85)H	GD	£3870
51	6/98	Carl	1m4f	D(0-80)H	G-S	£14915

Total win prize-money £39763

Going (Turf): Sf: 0-8 GS: 1-9 Gd: 1-23 **GF: 3-29** Fm: 0-4
Distance: 5f/6f: 0-0 7f-8f: 0-5 **9f-13f: 5-65** 14f+: 0-6
Track : LH: 0-49 **RH: 5-26** Tight: 0-25 **Gall: 2-27**
Aids: Bl: 0-0 Vi: 0-0 Tstrap: 0-0
Best Rating: 68 8/01 York 1m3f195y good

Fair handicapper. Despite running well to make the frame on a couple of occasions, is not proving particularly consistent. Best suited by coming off a fast pace, he stays a mile and a half and is suited by fast ground.

Warningford

116 **118**

7-y-o b h Warning-Barford Lady (Stanford)
J R Fanshawe Barford Bloodstock

Placings:54106/0260251061030/11212206/242531503-0123433 **(5386)**
2001: 6^{0}GS, 7^{1}G, 8^{2}S, 7^{3}GF, 8^{4}GS, 7^{3}VS, 7^{3}GS

	Starts	1st	2nd	3rd	Win & Pl
Career Total (Turf)	42	8	8	6	222642

113	5/01	NmkR	7f	A	GD	£17400
113	9/00	Newb	7f64y	A	G-F	£23200
104	6/99	Hayd	7f30y	A	G-S	£13615
110	4/99	Leic	7f9y	A	HVY	£18360
104	4/99	Wwck	7f	C	GD	£5634
104	9/98	Gdwd	7f	B(0-105)H	SFT	£9486
99	7/98	Yarm	7f3y	B(0-100)H	G-F	£7386
90	6/97	Sand	7f16y	D	G-F	£3403

Total win prize-money £98486

Going (Turf): Sf: 2-9 GS: 1-10 Gd: 2-17 **GF: 3-5** Fm: 0-0
Distance: 5f/6f: 0-6 **7f-8f: 8-34** 9f-13f: 0-2 14f+: 0-0
Track : **LH: 3-12** RH: 2-9 Tight: 0-3 **Gall: 1-7**
Aids: Bl: 0-0 **Vi: 2-9** Tstrap: 0-0
Best Rating: 118 10/01 Lonc 7f v soft

Very useful performer. Came back to form on his second run this year, when beating Sugarfoot in Group Three at Newmarket, and then ran a blinder to be second in the Lockinge Stakes. Off the track three months afterwards, he has run well since, reaching the frame in two Longchamp Group Ones. Effective at six furlongs to a mile, he has gained all his wins at seven furlongs. Usually held up, he goes well on easy ground and is a genuine sort.

Warring

100 (25)**38**

7-y-o b g Warrshan (USA)-Emerald Ring (Auction Ring (USA))
M S Saunders Chris Scott

Placings:0000/40260000/052142104000/02020540/50300341300-0000 **(3686)**
2001: 8^{0}HD, 8^{0}GF, 8^{0}GF, 8^{0}GF

	Starts	1st	2nd	3rd	Win & Pl
Career Total (Turf)	45	3	5	3	24829
Career Total (AW)	3	0	0	0	

45	8/00	Bath	1m5y	D(0-80)H	GD	£4095
60	8/98	Wind	1m67y	D(0-80)H	G-F	£7360
54	7/98	Wind	1m67y	E(0-70)H	GD	£3192

Total win prize-money £14648

Going (Turf): Sf: 0-6 GS: 0-6 **Gd: 2-13** GF: 1-16 Fm: 0-4
Distance: 5f/6f: 0-0 7f-8f: 0-20 **9f-13f: 3-28** 14f+: 0-0
Track : LH: 1-25 **RH: 2-12 Tight: 3-27** Gall: 0-1
Aids: Bl: 0-0 Vi: 0-0 Tstrap: 0-1
Best Rating: 38 7/01 Wind 1m67y gd-fm

Warriors Path (IRE)

2-y-o b c Namaqualand (USA)-Azinter (IRE) (Magical Strike (USA))
B G Powell Mrs John M Weld

Placings:0 **(5665)**
2001: 6^{0}HY

	Starts	1st	2nd	3rd	Win & Pl
Career Total (Turf)	1	0	0	0	

Going (Turf): Sf: 0-1 GS: 0-0 Gd: 0-0 GF: 0-0 Fm: 0-0
Distance: 5f/6f: 0-1 7f-8f: 0-0 9f-13f: 0-0 14f+: 0-0
Track : LH: 0-0 RH: 0-0 Tight: 0-0 Gall: 0-0
Aids: Bl: 0-0 Vi: 0-0 Tstrap: 0-0

Warrsan (IRE)

107 **82**

3-y-o b c Caerleon (USA)-Lucayan Princess (High Line)
C E Brittain Saeed Manana

Placings:545162 **(4860)**
2001: 10^{5}G, 11^{4}GF, 12^{5}GF, 14^{1}GF, 13^{6}G, 13^{2}GF

	Starts	1st	2nd	3rd	Win & Pl
Career Total (Turf)	6	1	1	0	10284

81	7/01	Sand	1m6f	D(0-85)H	G-F	£5164

Total win prize-money £5164

Going (Turf): Sf: 0-0 GS: 0-0 Gd: 0-2 **GF: 1-4** Fm: 0-0
Distance: 5f/6f: 0-0 7f-8f: 0-0 9f-13f: 0-3 **14f+: 1-3**
Track : LH: 0-5 **RH: 1-1** Tight: 0-2 Gall: 0-3
Aids: Bl: 0-0 Vi: 0-0 Tstrap: 0-0

Best Rating: 82 9/01 Newb 1m5f61y gd-fm

A half-brother to Luso and Needle Gun, he appreciated the step up to 14 furlongs when winning on his handicap debut in July 2001, and has since run well in much more competitive handicaps. Should be able to win more races at that level, and is likely to improve with experience. Acts on fast ground.

Waseyla (IRE)

107(100) (48)**58**

4-y-o b f Sri Pekan (USA)-Lady Windley (Baillamont (USA))

Miss E C Lavelle (Julian Poulton 1/5) Tony Taylor

Placings:054/00**335-3060**0030103160 **(5624)**

2001: **12**^{3}SD, **13**^{0}SD, **12**^{6}SW, **16**^{0}SW, 12^{0}S, 11^{0}GS, 12^{3}GF, 14^{0}GF, 10^{1}GF, 9^{0}GF, 9^{3}G, 9^{1}GS, 10^{6}F, 9^{0}GS

	Starts	1st	2nd	3rd	Win & Pl
Career Total (Turf)	15	2	0	2	6767
Career Total (AW)	7	0	0	3	1160

58 9/01 Folk 1m1f149yF(0-60)H G-S £2394
50 7/01 Wind 1m2f7y E(0-70)H G-F £3276
Total win prize-money £5670

Going (Turf): Sf: 0-3 **GS: 1-3** Gd: 0-3 **GF: 1-5** Fm: 0-1
Distance: 5f/6f: 0-0 7f-8f: 0-3 **9f-13f: 2-17** 14f+: 0-2
Track : LH: 0-15 **RH: 1-3 Tight: 2-12** Gall: 0-1
Aids: Bl: 0-1 Vi: 0-1 Tstrap: 0-0
Best Rating: 58 9/01 Folk 1m1f149y gd-sft

Washington Pink (IRE)

100 **73**

2-y-o b c Tagula (IRE)-Little Red Rose (Precocious)

M R Channon Glass Associates

Placings:02505330454 **(5668)**

2001: 6^{0}GF, 7^{2}G, 8^{5}GS, 8^{0}GF, 8^{5}F, 8^{3}GF, 8^{3}HY, 7^{0}S, 8^{4}S, 7^{5}GS, 8^{4}HY

	Starts	1st	2nd	3rd	Win & Pl
Career Total (Turf)	11	0	1	2	3424

Going (Turf): Sf: 0-4 GS: 0-2 Gd: 0-1 GF: 0-3 Fm: 0-1
Distance: 5f/6f: 0-1 7f-8f: 0-6 9f-13f: 0-4 14f+: 0-0
Track : LH: 0-5 RH: 0-3 Tight: 0-5 Gall: 0-1
Aids: Bl: 0-0 Vi: 0-0 Tstrap: 0-0
Best Rating: 73 10/01 Pont 1m4y soft

Still a maiden, he has run with credit over seven furlongs and a mile so far but looks to need further.

Wasp Ranger (USA)

96(89) (61)**79**

7-y-o b g Red Ransom (USA)-Lady Climber (USA) (Mount Hagen (FR))

G L Moore Mike Charlton And Rodger Sargent

Placings:352/01206406/0404100200/0223162204-00 **(1918)**

2001: 12^{0}GS, 14^{0}GF

	Starts	1st	2nd	3rd	Win & Pl
Career Total (Turf)	32	3	7	2	43790
Career Total (AW)	1	0	0	0	281

77 7/00 Sand 1m3f91y D(0-85)H GD £7312
72 7/99 Kemp 1m2f C(0-90)H G-F £7100
78 5/97 Gdwd 1m D G-S £4889
Total win prize-money £19303

Going (Turf): Sf: 0-1 **GS: 1-4 Gd: 1-11 GF: 1-15** Fm: 0-1
Distance: 5f/6f: 0-1 7f-8f: 1-11 **9f-13f: 2-20** 14f+: 0-1
Track : LH: 0-12 **RH: 3-16** Tight: 0-7 **Gall: 1-9**
Aids: **Bl: 1-5** Vi: 0-0 Tstrap: 0-0
Best Rating: 61 5/01 Kemp 1m4f gd-sft

Watching

107 **103**

4-y-o ch h Indian Ridge-Sweeping (Indian King (USA))

R Hannon Mrs Dare Wigan

Placings:313225423/2122014450-00003002 **(5499)**

2001: 5^{0}G, 5^{0}G, 5^{0}Y, 6^{0}S, 5^{3}S, 5^{0}GS, 6^{0}GS, 7^{2}HY

	Starts	1st	2nd	3rd	Win & Pl
Career Total (Turf)	27	3	7	4	104353

110 7/00 Sand 5f6y A GD £19500
108 4/00 Hayd 5f A HVY £16445
83 6/99 Ches 5f16y D SFT £3415
Total win prize-money £39360

Going (Turf): Sf: 2-5 GS: 0-5 Gd: 1-8 GF: 0-6 Fm: 0-0
Distance: **5f/6f: 3-23** 7f-8f: 0-4 9f-13f: 0-0 14f+: 0-0
Track : **LH: 1-2** RH: 0-2 **Tight: 1-1** Gall: 0-0
Aids: Bl: 0-0 Vi: 0-0 Tstrap: 0-0
Best Rating: 103 8/01 Deau 6f110y soft

A pacey individual, he was always prominent when winning Listed races at Haydock and Sandown in 2000. He has disappointed this year, failing to win a race, although he did show signs of a return to form in Sweden in September. Suited by soft ground and is best over five furlongs. Sold for 82,000 gns in the autumn and has joined David Nicholls.

Watchkeeper (IRE)

104 **85**

3-y-o b f Rudimentary (USA)-Third Watch (Slip Anchor)

J L Dunlop Hesmonds Stud

Placings:4 604331120 **(5135)**

2001: 7^{6}G, 8^{0}G, 7^{4}GF, 10^{3}GF, 9^{3}GS, 10^{1}GF, 10^{1}GF, 8^{2}G, 10^{0}G

	Starts	1st	2nd	3rd	Win & Pl
Career Total (Turf)	10	2	1	2	10909

83 8/01 Ling 1m2f E(0-75)H G-F £3374
70 8/01 Ling 1m2f E(0-70) G-F £3150
Total win prize-money £6524

Going (Turf): Sf: 0-0 GS: 0-1 Gd: 0-4 **GF: 2-5** Fm: 0-0
Distance: 5f/6f: 0-0 7f-8f: 0-3 **9f-13f: 2-7** 14f+: 0-0
Track : **LH: 2-4** RH: 0-1 **Tight: 2-5** Gall: 0-0
Aids: Bl: 0-0 Vi: 0-0 Tstrap: 0-0
Best Rating: 85 9/01 Epsm 1m114y good

She gradually found her form and got off the mark in a classified event over ten furlongs at Lingfield in August. Followed up in a handicap over the same course and distance later that month, and ran another good race when up in grade at Epsom and finishing second. Suited by fast ground and forcing tactics.

Watchword

99 **70**

2-y-o ch f Polish Precedent (USA)-Step Aloft (Shirley Heights)

R Charlton The Queen

Placings:05420 **(4954)**

2001: 6^{0}GF, 7^{5}GF, 8^{4}GF, 7^{2}GF, 8^{0}GS

	Starts	1st	2nd	3rd	Win & Pl
Career Total (Turf)	5	0	1	0	1287

Going (Turf): Sf: 0-0 GS: 0-1 Gd: 0-0 GF: 0-4 Fm: 0-0
Distance: 5f/6f: 0-0 7f-8f: 0-4 9f-13f: 0-1 14f+: 0-0
Track : LH: 0-0 RH: 0-2 Tight: 0-0 Gall: 0-1
Aids: Bl: 0-0 Vi: 0-0 Tstrap: 0-0
Best Rating: 70 9/01 Ling 7f gd-fm

Water Baby (IRE)

86(92) (68) **68**

2-y-o b g Tagula (IRE)-Flooding (USA) (Irish River (FR))

T D Barron Mrs J Hazell

Placings:041 **(3236)**

2001: 5^{0}GF, 5^{4}GF, 5^{1}SD

	Starts	1st	2nd	3rd	Win & Pl
Career Total (Turf)	2	0	0	0	0
Career Total (AW)	1	1	0	0	2240

68 7/01 Sthl 5f F STD £2240
Total win prize-money £2240

Going (Turf): Sf: 0-0 GS: 0-0 Gd: 0-0 GF: 0-2 Fm: 0-0
Distance: **5f/6f: 1-3** 7f-8f: 0-0 9f-13f: 0-0 14f+: 0-0
Track : LH: 0-0 RH: 0-0 Tight: 0-0 Gall: 0-0
Aids: Bl: 0-0 Vi: 0-0 Tstrap: 0-0
Best Rating: 68 7/01 Sthl 5f stand

Well backed on his debut, he ran green on his first two starts. Got off the mark on her All-Weather debut, and likely to improve with experience.

Water Jump (IRE)

114 **119+**

4-y-o b h Suave Dancer (USA)-Jolies Eaux (Shirley Heights)

J L Dunlop The Earl Cadogan

Placings:221/123-5111 **(1834)**

2001: 10^{5}S, 12^{1}S, 13^{1}S, 11^{1}G

	Starts	1st	2nd	3rd	Win & Pl
Career Total (Turf)	10	5	3	1	66510

119 6/01 Wind 1m3f135yA GD £17420
116 5/01 Newb 1m5f61y A SFT £14220
91 4/01 Ripn 1m4f60y C SFT £6269
93 5/00 Sals 1m1f198yC(0-100)H G-F £6890
74 9/99 Haml 1m65y E SFT £3322
Total win prize-money £48124

Going (Turf): Sf: 3-4 GS: 0-0 Gd: 1-3 GF: 1-3 Fm: 0-0
Distance: 5f/6f: 0-0 7f-8f: 0-1 **9f-13f: 4-8** 14f+: 1-1
Track : LH: 1-1 **RH: 3-6 Tight: 4-5** Gall: 1-3
Aids: Bl: 0-0 Vi: 0-0 Tstrap: 0-0
Best Rating: 119 6/01 Wind 1m3f135y good

He won twice last season, but has looked a very progressive performer this season, completing a hat trick in the spring with victories at Ripon and Listed races at Newbury (beating subsequent Royal Ascot winner Sandmason) and Windsor. Stays 13 furlongs.

Water King (USA)

87 **81+**

2-y-o b c Irish River (FR)-Brookshield Baby (IRE) (Sadler's Wells (USA))

E A L Dunlop Khalid Ali

Placings:056 **(5483)**

2001: 7^{0}G, 7^{5}GS, 7^{6}HY

	Starts	1st	2nd	3rd	Win & Pl
Career Total (Turf)	3	0	0	0	0

Going (Turf): Sf: 0-1 GS: 0-1 Gd: 0-1 GF: 0-0 Fm: 0-0
Distance: 5f/6f: 0-0 7f-8f: 0-3 9f-13f: 0-0 14f+: 0-0
Track : LH: 0-1 RH: 0-0 Tight: 0-0 Gall: 0-1
Aids: Bl: 0-0 Vi: 0-0 Tstrap: 0-0
Best Rating: 81 9/01 NmkR 7f good

Water Of Life (IRE)

98 **78**

2-y-o b f Dr Devious (IRE)-Simulcast (Generous (IRE))

J W Hills Campbell Ross & Partners

Placings:05402 **(5052)**

2001: 7^{0}GF, 6^{5}GF, 7^{4}GS, 6^{0}GF, 7^{2}S

	Starts	1st	2nd	3rd	Win & Pl
Career Total (Turf)	5	0	1	0	6321

Going (Turf): Sf: 0-1 GS: 0-1 Gd: 0-0 GF: 0-3 Fm: 0-0
Distance: 5f/6f: 0-2 7f-8f: 0-3 9f-13f: 0-0 14f+: 0-0
Track : LH: 0-2 RH: 0-0 Tight: 0-2 Gall: 0-0
Aids: Bl: 0-0 Vi: 0-0 Tstrap: 0-4
Best Rating: 78 10/01 NmkR 7f soft

The first foal of an unraced dam, she improved steadily with racing, putting up her best performance in a Newmarket nursery in October. Suited by cut in the ground, she will appreciate middle distances next season.

Waterford Spirit (IRE)

103(100) (55)**50**

5-y-o ch g Shalford (IRE)-Rebecca's Girl (IRE) (Nashamaa)

D Nicholls Pubs And Clubs Syndicate

Placings:5522/60041040/0000000000-20200102000036 **(4110)**

2001: 6^2SD, 6^0SD, 5^2SD, 5^0SD, 6^0SD, 6^1SD, 5^0SD, 5^2G, 6^0SD, 6^0SD, 5^0GF, 6^0F, 6^3GS, 5^6S

	Starts	1st	2nd	3rd	Win & Pl
Career Total (Turf)	27	1	3	1	11788
Career Total (AW)	9	1	2	0	3211

55 3/01 Sthl 6f F(0-65)H STD £1813
74 5/99 Thsk 5f C(0-100)H G-S £7064
Total win prize-money £8877

Going (Turf): Sf: 0-6 **GS: 1-5** Gd: 0-11 GF: 0-4 Fm: 0-1
Distance: **5f/6f: 2-33** 7f-8f: 0-3 9f-13f: 0-0 14f+: 0-0
Track : **LH: 1-7** RH: 0-1 Tight: 0-0 Gall: 0-1
Aids: Bl: 0-1 Vi: 0-0 Tstrap: 0-1
Best Rating: 55 3/01 Sthl 6f stand

He has a moderate strike rate and looks marginally better on sand than on turf.

Waterfront (IRE)

91(81) (19)**17**

5-y-o b g Turtle Island (IRE)-Rising Tide (Red Alert)

G P Kelly G P Kelly

Placings:0/5200500000/000-0000000000000000000000600040000000 **(5499)**

2001: 8^0SD, 7^0SD, 9^0SD, 6^0SD, 12^0SD, 12^0S, 5^0S, 10^0HY, 6^0S, 9^0G, 5^0G, 8^0GF, 6^0GF, 7^0F, 8^0GF, 10^0GF, 7^0GF, 10^0GF, 10^0F, 6^0GF, 7^0S, 8^0G, 7^0GF, 6^6GF, 5^0G, 7^0GF

	Starts	1st	2nd	3rd	Win & Pl
Career Total (Turf)	41	0	1	0	1385
Career Total (AW)	8	0	0	0	

Going (Turf): **Sf: 0-9 GS: 0-2 Gd: 0-9 GF: 0-18 Fm: 0-3**
Distance: 5f/6f: 0-14 7f-8f: 0-18 9f-13f: 0-16 14f+: 0-1
Track : LH: 0-23 RH: 0-6 Tight: 0-13 Gall: 0-4
Aids: Bl: 0-4 Vi: 0-1 Tstrap: 0-13
Best Rating: 40 7/01 Donc 6f gd-fm

A moderate individual, he showed promise early on at three, but his form soon tailed off and he has earned his keep running regularly in 'appearance money' events.

Waterliner

86(79) (32)**51**

2-y-o b f Merdon Melody-Double Touch (FR) (Nonoalco (USA))

P D Evans Waterline Racing Club

Placings:0004000 **(4488)**

2001: 5^0F, 5^0G, 5^0SD, 5^4SD, 7^0G, 7^0GF, 6^0S

	Starts	1st	2nd	3rd	Win & Pl
Career Total (Turf)	5	0	0	0	
Career Total (AW)	2	0	0	0	0

Going (Turf): **Sf: 0-1 GS: 0-0 Gd: 0-2 GF: 0-1 Fm: 0-1**
Distance: 5f/6f: 0-4 7f-8f: 0-3 9f-13f: 0-0 14f+: 0-0
Track : LH: 0-1 RH: 0-0 Tight: 0-1 Gall: 0-0
Aids: Bl: 0-1 Vi: 0-1 Tstrap: 0-0
Best Rating: 51 8/01 Ling 7f gd-fm

Waterpark

91(84) (31)**42**

3-y-o b f Namaqualand (USA)-Willisa (Polar Falcon (USA))

M Dods Russ Mould

Placings:632110-00000000 **(5375)**

2001: 6^0G, 7^0GF, 5^0SD, 5^0SD, 6^0G, 6^0HY, 6^0GS, 7^0G, 6^0SD

	Starts	1st	2nd	3rd	Win & Pl
Career Total (Turf)	11	2	1	1	7254
Career Total (AW)	3	0	0	0	0

70 6/00 Ayr 6f D G-F £3474
58 5/00 Hayd 5f F G-S £2352
Total win prize-money £5826

Going (Turf): Sf: 0-1 **GS: 1-3** Gd: 0-5 **GF: 1-2** Fm: 0-0
Distance: **5f/6f: 2-11** 7f-8f: 0-3 9f-13f: 0-0 14f+: 0-0
Track : LH: 0-3 RH: 0-0 Tight: 0-1 Gall: 0-0
Aids: Bl: 0-0 Vi: 0-0 Tstrap: 0-0
Best Rating: 50 5/01 Wind 6f good

Waterside (IRE)

94 **90**

2-y-o b c Lake Coniston (IRE)-Classic Ring (IRE) (Auction Ring (USA))

J W Hills J W Robb

Placings:43220 **(4713)**

2001: 5^4GF, 5^3GF, 5^2GF, 5^2GF, 5^0G

	Starts	1st	2nd	3rd	Win & Pl
Career Total (Turf)	5	0	2	1	14156

Going (Turf): **Sf: 0-0 GS: 0-0 Gd: 0-1 GF: 0-4 Fm: 0-0**
Distance: 5f/6f: 0-5 7f-8f: 0-0 9f-13f: 0-0 14f+: 0-0
Track : LH: 0-1 RH: 0-0 Tight: 0-0 Gall: 0-1
Aids: Bl: 0-0 Vi: 0-0 Tstrap: 0-0
Best Rating: 90 6/01 Asct 5f gd-fm

A half-brother to useful sprinter Seven No Trumps, showed good speed on his debut and put in another creditable effort at Newbury next time. After a good second to Johannesburg at Royal Ascot, he was beaten in a maiden auction, albeit by a useful filly, at Bath. Has only ever run on a fast surface. Suited by a strong pace.

Watkins

(99) (41)

6-y-o ch g King's Signet (USA)-Windbound Lass (Crofter (USA))

Miss D Cole (A T Murphy 6/2) R W Savery

Placings:54600/200060/005/3400 **(0247)**

2001: 16^3SW, 16^4SW, 16^0SD, 16^0SD

	Starts	1st	2nd	3rd	Win & Pl
Career Total (Turf)	12	0	0	0	242
Career Total (AW)	6	0	1	1	856

Going (Turf): **Sf: 0-1 GS: 0-1 Gd: 0-4 GF: 0-5 Fm: 0-1**
Distance: 5f/6f: 0-0 7f-8f: 0-8 9f-13f: 0-4 14f+: 0-6
Track : LH: 0-13 RH: 0-1 Tight: 0-8 Gall: 0-1
Aids: Bl: 0-1 Vi: 0-0 Tstrap: 0-5
Best Rating: 41 1/01 Wolv 2m46y slow

Wattno Eljohn (IRE)

106(98) (66)**51**

3-y-o b c Namaqualand (USA)-Caroline Connors (Fairy King (USA))

D W P Arbuthnot Essandess Partners

Placings:00016353442-2630030600 **(5681)**

2001: 8^2SW, 7^6SD, 10^3GS, 9^0GS, 8^0HY, 8^3G, 8^0G, 7^6HY, 8^0GS, 8^0S

	Starts	1st	2nd	3rd	Win & Pl
Career Total (Turf)	17	1	0	4	5637
Career Total (AW)	4	0	2	0	1616

57 7/00 Bath 5f11y F G-S £2163
Total win prize-money £2163

Going (Turf): Sf: 0-7 **GS: 1-4** Gd: 0-3 GF: 0-2 Fm: 0-1
Distance: **5f/6f: 1-5** 7f-8f: 0-12 9f-13f: 0-4 14f+: 0-0
Track : **LH: 1-10** RH: 0-2 Tight: 0-2 **Gall: 1-3**
Aids: Bl: 0-0 Vi: 0-0 Tstrap: 0-0
Best Rating: 66 9/01 Kemp 1m good

Had a handful of runs on the All-Weather during the winter and has yet to prove that he really stays beyond a mile on turf. Suited by cut and seemed to run an improved race on his return from a break in September.

Wave Of Optimism

106 **94**

6-y-o ch g Elmaamul (USA)-Ballerina Bay (Myjinski (USA))

Mrs Lydia Pearce Wave Of Optimism Partnership

Placings:3221/0130/01100026-3610 **(5387)**

2001: 16^3S, 16^6G, 16^1S, 18^0GS

	Starts	1st	2nd	3rd	Win & Pl
Career Total (Turf)	20	5	3	3	68561

93 9/01 Asct 2m45y C(0-95)H SFT £14072
83 5/00 Kemp 2m C(0-95)H SFT £7215
77 4/00 Donc 2m110y C(0-90)H G-S £6838
75 4/99 Sand 2m78y D(0-85)H G-S £5576
80 10/98 Nott 1m6f15y D SFT £4045
Total win prize-money £37747

Going (Turf): **Sf: 3-4** GS: 2-10 Gd: 0-4 GF: 0-2 Fm: 0-0
Distance: 5f/6f: 0-0 7f-8f: 0-0 9f-13f: 0-5 **14f+: 5-15**
Track : LH: 2-7 **RH: 3-13** Tight: 0-5 **Gall: 2-10**
Aids: Bl: 0-0 Vi: 0-0 Tstrap: 0-0
Best Rating: 94 4/01 Kemp 2m soft

An effective staying handicapper, he scored at Doncaster and Kempton early on last season, and was a fine runner-up in the Cesarewitch later in the season. Needs plenty of cut in the ground and holding up in his races. Produced a fine performance under a big weight to score at Ascot in September.

Waverley (IRE)

96 **78**

2-y-o b c Catrail (USA)-Marble Halls (IRE) (Ballad Rock)

H Morrison Lord Margadale

Placings:43264 **(5460)**

2001: 6^4GF, 7^3GF, 7^2G, 7^6S, 8^4G

	Starts	1st	2nd	3rd	Win & Pl
Career Total (Turf)	5	0	1	1	1819

Going (Turf): **Sf: 0-1 GS: 0-0 Gd: 0-2 GF: 0-2 Fm: 0-0**
Distance: 5f/6f: 0-1 7f-8f: 0-3 9f-13f: 0-1 14f+: 0-0
Track : LH: 0-2 RH: 0-1 Tight: 0-1 Gall: 0-1
Aids: Bl: 0-0 Vi: 0-0 Tstrap: 0-0
Best Rating: 78 10/01 Bath 1m5y good

Waverley Road

106(98) (60)**66**

4-y-o ch g Pelder (IRE)-Lillicara (FR) (Caracolero (USA))

A P Jarvis All Four Corners

Placings:4/50650262512-0642061032 **(5230)**

2001: 8^0SW, 8^6GF, 10^4GF, 9^2GF, 8^0GF, 9^6G, 9^1G, 7^0GF, 10^3S, 11^2S

	Starts	1st	2nd	3rd	Win & Pl
Career Total (Turf)	18	1	4	1	17352
Career Total (AW)	4	1	1	0	2328

62 8/01 Gdwd 1m1f D(0-80)H GD £9964
60 11/00 Ling 1m2f F(0-60)H STD £1820
Total win prize-money £11785

Going (Turf): Sf: 0-2 GS: 0-4 **Gd: 1-3** GF: 0-7 Fm: 0-1
Distance: 5f/6f: 0-0 7f-8f: 0-5 **9f-13f: 2-16** 14f+: 0-0
Track : LH: 1-9 RH: 1-6 **Tight: 2-6** Gall: 0-2
Aids: Bl: 0-0 Vi: 0-0 Tstrap: 0-0
Best Rating: 66 10/01 York 1m3f195y soft

He is all that consistent, but is capable of decent form on a going day as when winning at Goodwood in August. Suited by nine to ten furlongs and acts on sand.

Wax Lyrical

101 **63**

5-y-o b m Safawan-Hannah's Music (Music Boy)

P J Makin Magno-Pulse Ltd

Placings:10/00000-2000 **(5560)**

2001: 6^{2}GF, 6^{0}G, 6^{0}GF, 7^{0}S

	Starts	1st	2nd	3rd	Win & Pl
Career Total (Turf)	11	1	1	0	5579

84 5/99 Sals 6f D G-F £3208
Total win prize-money £3209

Going (Turf): Sf: 0-2 GS: 0-1 Gd: 0-3 **GF: 1-5** Fm: 0-0
Distance: **5f/6f: 1-7** 7f-8f: 0-4 9f-13f: 0-0 14f+: 0-0
Track : LH: 0-1 RH: 0-2 Tight: 0-1 Gall: 0-1
Aids: Bl: 0-1 Vi: 0-0 Tstrap: 0-0
Best Rating: 63 5/01 Newb 6f8y gd-fm

Unraced at two, she won a Salisbury maiden in good style on her debut in 2000, but has not added to her score since. Has gone well fresh.

Waxwing

100(94) (66)62
2-y-o b f Efisio-Mountain Bluebird (USA) (Clever Trick (USA))
N P Littmoden (R Hannon 7/7) Richard Green (fine Paintings)

Placings:04121320 **(4538)**
2001: 6^{0}GF, 6^{4}G, 7^{1}GF, 6^{2}GF, 7^{1}F, 7^{3}GF, 7^{2}SD, 7^{0}GF

	Starts	1st	2nd	3rd	Win & Pl
Career Total (Turf)	7	2	1	1	9409
Career Total (AW)	1	0	1	0	806

62 7/01 Rdcr 7f D H FRM £4771
66 7/01 Bevl 7f100y F G-F £2422
Total win prize-money £7193

Going (Turf): Sf: 0-0 GS: 0-0 Gd: 0-1 **GF: 1-5 Fm: 1-1**
Distance: 5f/6f: 0-2 **7f-8f: 2-6** 9f-13f: 0-0 14f+: 0-0
Track : LH: 0-2 **RH: 1-1** Tight: 0-1 Gall: 0-0
Aids: Bl: 0-0 Vi: 0-0 Tstrap: 0-0
Best Rating: 66 8/01 Wolv 7f stand

A winner of a Beverley seller and a Redcar nursery so far, seven furlongs is about as far as she wants.

Waylaah

93 61
2-y-o b f Common Grounds-Inonder (Belfort (FR))
J L Dunlop Kuwait Racing Syndicate Iii

Placings:033460 **(5467)**
2001: 5^{0}G, 6^{3}GF, 6^{3}F, 6^{4}G, 5^{6}S, 6^{0}S

	Starts	1st	2nd	3rd	Win & Pl
Career Total (Turf)	6	0	0	2	836

Going (Turf): Sf: 0-2 GS: 0-0 Gd: 0-2 GF: 0-1 Fm: 0-1
Distance: 5f/6f: 0-3 7f-8f: 0-3 9f-13f: 0-0 14f+: 0-0
Track : LH: 0-2 RH: 0-0 Tight: 0-0 Gall: 0-0
Aids: Bl: 0-0 Vi: 0-1 Tstrap: 0-0
Best Rating: 79 7/01 Chep 6f16y gd-fm

Wayyak (USA)

88 67
2-y-o ch c Gold Fever (USA)-My Testarossa (USA) (Black Tie Affair)
J W Payne C Cotran

Placings:403005 **(5562)**
2001: 5^{4}F, 5^{0}GF, 6^{3}GF, 5^{0}GF, 5^{0}GF, 5^{5}S

	Starts	1st	2nd	3rd	Win & Pl
Career Total (Turf)	6	0	0	1	599

Going (Turf): Sf: 0-1 GS: 0-0 Gd: 0-0 GF: 0-4 Fm: 0-1
Distance: 5f/6f: 0-6 7f-8f: 0-0 9f-13f: 0-0 14f+: 0-0
Track : LH: 0-1 RH: 0-0 Tight: 0-0 Gall: 0-0
Aids: Bl: 0-0 Vi: 0-0 Tstrap: 0-0
Best Rating: 67 7/01 Wind 6f gd-fm

Some hint of ability in maiden company, but may need further than six furlongs.

We'll Make It (IRE)

102(97) (64)71
3-y-o b g Spectrum (IRE)-Walliser (Niniski (USA))
G L Moore Mrs Charles Sparrowhawk

Placings:60003-25045 **(5279)**
2001: 9^{2}GS, 11^{5}G, 10^{0}GF, 10^{4}GF, 11^{5}S

	Starts	1st	2nd	3rd	Win & Pl
Career Total (Turf)	9	0	1	0	2930
Career Total (AW)	1	0	0	1	406

Going (Turf): Sf: 0-2 GS: 0-1 Gd: 0-3 GF: 0-3 Fm: 0-0
Distance: 5f/6f: 0-1 7f-8f: 0-4 9f-13f: 0-5 14f+: 0-0
Track : LH: 0-2 RH: 0-6 Tight: 0-4 Gall: 0-1
Aids: Bl: 0-3 Vi: 0-0 Tstrap: 0-0
Best Rating: 76 5/01 Wind 1m3f135y good

We're Not Joken

89(92) (18)43
4-y-o b f Foxhound (USA)-We'Re Joken (Statoblest)
Mrs N Macauley John Wardle

Placings:06600/0000-0003600 **(4159)**
2001: 5^{0}SD, 7^{0}SW, 5^{0}SD, 5^{3}SD, 5^{6}GF, 5^{0}SD, 6^{0}GF

	Starts	1st	2nd	3rd	Win & Pl
Career Total (Turf)	9	0	0	0	0
Career Total (AW)	7	0	0	1	256

Going (Turf): Sf: 0-0 GS: 0-1 Gd: 0-1 GF: 0-6 Fm: 0-1
Distance: 5f/6f: 0-13 7f-8f: 0-3 9f-13f: 0-0 14f+: 0-0
Track : LH: 0-5 RH: 0-1 Tight: 0-3 Gall: 0-1
Aids: Bl: 0-0 Vi: 0-3 Tstrap: 0-0
Best Rating: 18 6/01 Leic 5f218y gd-fm

Wealthy Star (IRE)

64(78) (9)36
6-y-o b g Soviet Star (USA)-Catalonda (African Sky)
N Tinkler Harrogate Lady Golfers Club

Placings:61/4000/0550-00000 **(4167)**
2001: 8^{0}G, 8^{0}SD, 8^{0}SD, 6^{0}SD, 7^{0}GF

	Starts	1st	2nd	3rd	Win & Pl
Career Total (Turf)	12	1	0	0	5388
Career Total (AW)	3	0	0	0	

92 6/98 Nott 1m54y D GD £4467
Total win prize-money £4468

Going (Turf): Sf: 0-1 GS: 0-5 **Gd: 1-4** GF: 0-2 Fm: 0-0
Distance: 5f/6f: 0-1 7f-8f: 0-12 **9f-13f: 1-2** 14f+: 0-0
Track : **LH: 1-6** RH: 0-2 Tight: 0-1 Gall: 0-3
Aids: Bl: 0-0 Vi: 0-1 Tstrap: 0-8
Best Rating: 36 8/01 Muss 7f30y gd-fm

Useful mile handicapper for Ben Hanbury, but has not been at his best in the last couple of seasons. Changed stables before this season and has yet to show any improvement and has been withdrawn three times because of soft ground.

Weaver Sam

65 4
6-y-o ch g Ron's Victory (USA)-Grove Star (Upper Case (USA))
Ferdy Murphy (P S McEntee 18/7) J Wightman

Placings:55500/00 **(1773)**
2001: 16^{0}GF, 11^{0}F

	Starts	1st	2nd	3rd	Win & Pl
Career Total (Turf)	7	0	0	0	0

Going (Turf): Sf: 0-1 GS: 0-0 Gd: 0-1 GF: 0-3 Fm: 0-2
Distance: 5f/6f: 0-0 7f-8f: 0-0 9f-13f: 0-4 14f+: 0-3
Track : LH: 0-6 RH: 0-1 Tight: 0-1 Gall: 0-2
Aids: Bl: 0-0 Vi: 0-0 Tstrap: 0-0
Best Rating: 4 6/01 Brig 1m3f196y firm

Wee Nel

80 37
3-y-o ch f Imp Society (USA)-Eskimo Nel (IRE) (Shy Groom (USA))
N P Littmoden First Chance Racing

Placings:0006 **(5448)**
2001: 9^{0}GF, 11^{0}GF, 9^{0}GF, 10^{6}HY

	Starts	1st	2nd	3rd	Win & Pl
Career Total (Turf)	4	0	0	0	0

Going (Turf): Sf: 0-1 GS: 0-0 Gd: 0-0 GF: 0-3 Fm: 0-0
Distance: 5f/6f: 0-0 7f-8f: 0-0 9f-13f: 0-4 14f+: 0-0
Track : LH: 0-2 RH: 0-2 Tight: 0-3 Gall: 0-1
Aids: Bl: 0-0 Vi: 0-0 Tstrap: 0-0
Best Rating: 37 9/01 Haml 1m1f36y gd-fm

Weecandoo (IRE)

105 82
3-y-o b f Turtle Island (IRE)-Romantic Air (He Loves Me)
C N Allen Sportsdays.Co.Uk

Placings:4245 **(5174)**
2001: 8^{4}S, 9^{2}G, 9^{4}G, 8^{5}GS

	Starts	1st	2nd	3rd	Win & Pl
Career Total (Turf)	4	0	1	0	2974

Going (Turf): Sf: 0-1 GS: 0-1 Gd: 0-2 GF: 0-0 Fm: 0-0
Distance: 5f/6f: 0-0 7f-8f: 0-0 9f-13f: 0-4 14f+: 0-0
Track : LH: 0-1 RH: 0-3 Tight: 0-1 Gall: 0-0
Aids: Bl: 0-0 Vi: 0-0 Tstrap: 0-0
Best Rating: 82 9/01 Gdwd 1m1f192y good

Weet A Round

96(88) (70)86
2-y-o ch c Whittingham (IRE)-Hollia (Touch Boy)
N P Littmoden Ed Weetman (haulage & Storage) Ltd

Placings:4506305353 **(5690)**
2001: 5^{4}S, 5^{5}GF, 5^{0}SD, 6^{6}GF, 7^{3}G, 7^{0}G, 6^{5}GS, 7^{3}SD, 7^{5}HY, 7^{3}S

	Starts	1st	2nd	3rd	Win & Pl
Career Total (Turf)	8	0	0	2	2988
Career Total (AW)	2	0	0	1	415

Going (Turf): Sf: 0-3 GS: 0-1 Gd: 0-2 GF: 0-2 Fm: 0-0
Distance: 5f/6f: 0-5 7f-8f: 0-5 9f-13f: 0-0 14f+: 0-0
Track : LH: 0-2 RH: 0-1 Tight: 0-2 Gall: 0-0
Aids: Bl: 0-0 Vi: 0-0 Tstrap: 0-0
Best Rating: 86 9/01 Donc 6f gd-sft

A maiden who has had plenty of chances before now, although he did run well at Doncaster in November.

Weet A While (IRE)

74(86) (44)61
3-y-o b g Lahib (USA)-Takeshi (IRE) (Cadeaux Genereux)
R Hollinshead Ed Weetman (haulage & Storage) Ltd

Placings:005000005-00 **(2590)**
2001: 7^{0}SD, 7^{0}GF

	Starts	1st	2nd	3rd	Win & Pl
Career Total (Turf)	7	0	0	0	0
Career Total (AW)	4	0	0	0	0

Going (Turf): Sf: 0-2 GS: 0-1 Gd: 0-2 GF: 0-2 Fm: 0-0
Distance: 5f/6f: 0-4 7f-8f: 0-7 9f-13f: 0-0 14f+: 0-0
Track : LH: 0-7 RH: 0-0 Tight: 0-2 Gall: 0-0
Aids: Bl: 0-0 Vi: 0-0 Tstrap: 0-0
Best Rating: 34 6/01 Ches 7f122y gd-fm

Weet And See

74(50) 18
7-y-o b g Lochnager-Simply Style (Bairn (USA))

T Wall Ed Weetman (haulage & Storage) Ltd

Placings:63621646000/00/0-0 **(0643)**
2001: 9^{0}HY

	Starts	1st	2nd	3rd	Win & Pl
Career Total (Turf)	4	0	0	0	252
Career Total (AW)	11	1	1	1	3626

64	3/97	Wolv	1m100y	F(0-65)H	STD	£2277

Total win prize-money £2277

Going (Turf): Sf: 0-1 GS: 0-0 Gd: 0-1 GF: 0-1 Fm: 0-1
Distance: 5f/6f: 0-0 7f-8f: 0-4 9f-13f: 1-11 14f+: 0-0
Track : LH: 1-14 RH: 0-1 Tight: 1-9 Gall: 0-0
Aids: Bl: 0-0 Vi: 0-0 Tstrap: 0-0
Best Rating: 18 4/01 Nott 1m1f213y heavy

Weet For Me

106(118) (95+)**90**
5-y-o b h Warning-Naswara (USA) (Al Nasr (FR))
R Hollinshead Ed Weetman (haulage & Storage) Ltd

Placings:422/601404402/003016300**121**-**1**00631103 **(5683)**
2001: 11^{1}SD, 13^{0}GF, 14^{0}GF, 16^{6}G, 13^{3}G, 14^{1}GF, 16^{1}F, 13^{0}G, 14^{3}S, 12^{3}SD

	Starts	1st	2nd	3rd	Win & Pl
Career Total (Turf)	29	4	3	4	28137
Career Total (AW)	4	3	1	0	19379

84	7/01	Rdcr	2m4y	D(0-85)H	FRM	£4800
90	7/01	Hayd	1m6f	D(0-85)H	G-F	£4199
95	1/01	Sthl	1m3f	C(0-95)H	STD	£8248
89	12/00	Sthl	1m4f	C(0-95)H	STD	£6337
84	11/00	Wolv	2m46y	D(0-85)H	STD	£3662
77	7/00	Donc	1m6f132y	D(0-80)H	G-F	£4212
81	7/99	Hayd	1m2f120y	D	FRM	£3993

Total win prize-money £35455

Going (Turf): Sf: 0-9 GS: 0-2 Gd: 0-8 **GF: 2-7 Fm: 2-3**
Distance: 5f/6f: 0-0 7f-8f: 0-1 9f-13f: 3-11 **14f+: 4-21**
Track : **LH: 7-26** RH: 0-4 **Tight: 2-3** Gall: 1-11
Aids: Bl: 0-0 Vi: 0-0 Tstrap: 0-0
Best Rating: 95 1/01 Sthl 1m3f stand

A fair handicapper, he returned to form when making all to win at Haydock in July, followed up at Redcar when stepped up to two miles. He stays well and is best on fast ground, but proved very effective over middle distances on sand during the winter, winning two very decent events on Fibresand in fine style.

Weet U There (IRE)

82 (36)**36**
5-y-o b g Forest Wind (USA)-Lady Aladdin (Persian Bold)
T Wall Ed Weetman (haulage & Storage) Ltd

Placings:605530001/43510026410603400/0 **(0643)**
2001: 9^{0}HY

	Starts	1st	2nd	3rd	Win & Pl
Career Total (Turf)	10	0	0	1	539
Career Total (AW)	17	3	1	2	7990

57	4/99	Wolv	1m1f79y	G	STD	£1861
63	2/99	Wolv	6f	G	STD	£1822
61	12/98	Wolv	7f	E H	SLW	£2857

Total win prize-money £6540

Going (Turf): Sf: 0-3 GS: 0-3 Gd: 0-3 GF: 0-1 Fm: 0-0
Distance: 5f/6f: 1-5 7f-8f: 1-10 9f-13f: 1-11 14f+: 0-1
Track : **LH: 3-23** RH: 0-2 **Tight: 3-14** Gall: 0-3
Aids: Bl: 0-2 Vi: 0-0 Tstrap: 0-0
Best Rating: 35 4/01 Nott 1m1f213y heavy

He has only ever won at Wolverhampnton, but is plating class and none-too-consistent.

Weetman's Weigh (IRE)

101(104) (54)**60**
8-y-o b h Archway (IRE)-Indian Sand (Indian King (USA))
R Hollinshead Ed Weetman (haulage & Storage) Ltd

Placings:352241620/1221133/05411154320200/10460 003150261032/112602420000543422**2**/4640000564065 01611-42212316014564500560 **(5613)**
2001: 9^{4}SD, 7^{2}SD, 8^{2}SW, 8^{1}SD, 7^{2}SW, 8^{3}SW, 7^{1}SD, 11^{6}SD, 7^{0}GF, 8^{1}F, 8^{4}GF, 7^{5}GF, 10^{6}GF, 7^{4}GF, 7^{5}GS, 8^{0}SD, 8^{0}GF, 8^{5}SD, 8^{6}SD, 9^{0}SD, 8^{3}SD

	Starts	1st	2nd	3rd	Win & Pl
Career Total (Turf)	67	9	9	5	60336
Career Total (AW)	37	9	9	3	46362

51	5/01	Pont	1m4y	F	FRM	£2870
51	3/01	Wolv	7f	F	STD	£2240
59	2/01	Sthl	1m	F	STD	£2107
63	12/00	Sthl	1m	F	STD	£1757
54	11/00	Wolv	7f	F	STD	£1750
68	10/00	NmkR	7f	D(0-85)H	SFT	£5837
94	2/99	Wolv	1m100y	C(0-90)H	STD	£6302
91	1/99	Sthl	7f	D(0-85)H	STD	£3728
77	10/98	NmkR	7f	D(0-80)H	SFT	£5478
72	8/98	Newc	7f	D(0-85)H	GD	£3420
84	2/98	Wolv	7f	C(0-95)H	STD	£5498
81	6/97	Thsk	7f	D	G-F	£3470
81	5/97	Rdcr	7f	D	G-F	£3431
76	5/97	Thsk	7f	C(0-90)H	G-F	£5605
75	3/96	Leic	5f218y	C(0-90)H	SFT	£5341
74	1/96	Wolv	6f	C(0-90)H	STD	£5255
65	1/96	Sthl	6f	D(0-75)H	STD	£3726
66	7/95	Carl	5f	E	FRM	£3023

Total win prize-money £70841

Going (Turf): **Sf: 3-8** GS: 0-4 Gd: 1-22 **GF: 3-29** Fm: 2-4
Distance: 5f/6f: 4-15 **7f-8f: 12-67** 9f-13f: 2-22 14f+: 0-0
Track : **LH: 12-60** RH: 1-6 **Tight: 7-34** Gall: 1-2
Aids: Bl: 0-0 Vi: 0-0 Tstrap: 0-0
Best Rating: 68 1/01 Sthl 7f stand

His last taste of glory was in a Pontefract claimer in May 2001, his first attempt over eight furlongs. Since then, he has just been out of the frame. He has won over five to 12 furlongs, but is suited by seven on firm ground.

Welch's Dream (IRE)

81(81) (71)**58**
4-y-o b f Brief Truce (USA)-Swift Chorus (Music Boy)
E J Alston David Hall

Placings:2014434424/5600600-00 **(4372)**
2001: 6^{0}GF, 5^{0}GF

	Starts	1st	2nd	3rd	Win & Pl
Career Total (Turf)	14	1	1	1	5838
Career Total (AW)	5	0	1	0	615

66	5/99	Ripn	5f	D	G-F	£3126

Total win prize-money £3126

Going (Turf): Sf: 0-1 GS: 0-0 Gd: 0-5 **GF: 1-8** Fm: 0-0
Distance: **5f/6f: 1-19** 7f-8f: 0-0 9f-13f: 0-0 14f+: 0-0
Track : LH: 0-9 RH: 0-1 Tight: 0-8 Gall: 0-1
Aids: Bl: 0-1 Vi: 0-0 Tstrap: 0-0
Best Rating: 17 8/01 Catt 5f gd-fm

Welcome Exchange

25
2-y-o b f Most Welcome-Santarem (USA) (El Gran Senor (USA))
J J Bridger Saddle Up Partnership

Placings:0 **(3045)**
2001: 6^{0}GF

	Starts	1st	2nd	3rd	Win & Pl
Career Total (Turf)	1	0	0	0	

Going (Turf): Sf: 0-0 GS: 0-0 Gd: 0-0 GF: 0-1 Fm: 0-0
Distance: 5f/6f: 0-0 7f-8f: 0-1 9f-13f: 0-0 14f+: 0-0
Track : LH: 0-0 RH: 0-0 Tight: 0-0 Gall: 0-0
Aids: Bl: 0-0 Vi: 0-0 Tstrap: 0-0

Welcome Friend (USA)

111 **111**
4-y-o b h Kingmambo (USA)-Kingscote (King's Lake (USA))
R Charlton K Abdulla

Placings:122-10261210 **(5365)**
2001: 7^{1}S, 7^{0}G, 7^{2}F, 7^{6}GF, 6^{1}GS, 6^{2}GF, 7^{1}GF, 6^{0}GS

	Starts	1st	2nd	3rd	Win & Pl
Career Total (Turf)	11	4	4	0	55374

111	9/01	Newb	7f64y	A	G-F	£23200
107	8/01	Yarm	6f3y	C	G-S	£6264
107	4/01	NmkR	7f	B(0-105)H	SFT	£10048
83	5/00	Sals	6f	D	G-F	£3233

Total win prize-money £42746

Going (Turf): Sf: 1-1 GS: 1-2 Gd: 0-2 **GF: 2-5** Fm: 0-1
Distance: 5f/6f: 1-3 **7f-8f: 3-8** 9f-13f: 0-0 14f+: 0-0
Track : **LH: 1-2** RH: 0-1 Tight: 0-0 **Gall: 1-1**
Aids: Bl: 0-0 Vi: 0-0 Tstrap: 0-0
Best Rating: 111 9/01 Newb 7f64y gd-fm

A half-brother to Rainbow Corner, he has won three times over six and seven furlongs this season on varying ground including a Newbury Listed contest. He is best when held up as he can race freely.

Welcome Gift

(101) (53)**61**
5-y-o b g Prince Sabo-Ausonia (Beldale Flutter (USA))
Mrs L Stubbs O J Williams

Placings:2/22160-0002300 **(5392)**
2001: 6^{0}SD, 6^{0}SW, 6^{0}SW, 6^{2}SD, 6^{3}SD, 6^{0}SD, 6^{0}SD

	Starts	1st	2nd	3rd	Win & Pl
Career Total (Turf)	2	0	0	0	0
Career Total (AW)	11	1	4	1	6137

66	2/00	Wolv	6f	D	STD	£2730

Total win prize-money £2730

Going (Turf): **Sf: 0-1 GS: 0-1** Gd: 0-0 **GF: 0-0 Fm: 0-0**
Distance: **5f/6f: 1-8** 7f-8f: 0-5 9f-13f: 0-0 14f+: 0-0
Track : **LH: 1-11** RH: 0-1 **Tight: 1-7** Gall: 0-0
Aids: Bl: 0-1 Vi: 0-0 Tstrap: 0-0
Best Rating: 56 9/01 Wolv 6f stand

Welcome Heights

72 (47)**40d**
7-y-o b g Most Welcome-Mount Ida (USA) (Conquistador Cielo (USA))
R C Spicer Sean Michael Toynton

Placings:000/0023131420**21**/**36**1000356000/00060520 0/0-00 **(4046)**
2001: 7^{0}G, 10^{0}HY

	Starts	1st	2nd	3rd	Win & Pl
Career Total (Turf)	32	3	2	3	15201
Career Total (AW)	7	1	2	1	4175

64	5/98	Leic	1m8y	D(0-85)H	GD	£5071
60	12/97	Ling	1m2f	E(0-70)H	STD	£2518
55	7/97	Donc	7f	E(0-70)H	GD	£3703
44	7/97	Chep	6f16y	F(0-65)H	G-S	£2862

Total win prize-money £14156

Going (Turf): Sf: 0-6 GS: 1-6 **Gd: 2-13** GF: 0-7 Fm: 0-0
Distance: 5f/6f: 0-1 7f-8f: 2-17 9f-13f: 2-21 14f+: 0-0
Track : **LH: 1-21** RH: 0-6 **Tight: 1-12** Gall: 0-5
Aids: Bl: 0-1 Vi: 0-0 Tstrap: 0-0
Best Rating: 2 8/01 NmkJ 7f good

Bolted up at Leicester in May of last year, and put some modest efforts behind him when third on a faster surface at Newbury in July, but has not shown a great deal since.

Welcome Rose

79(87) (57)**45**
2-y-o ch f Most Welcome-Bonica (Rousillon (USA))
P C Haslam Mrs J Trotter, S Freeland, J Metcalf

Placings:000020 **(5618)**
2001: 6^{0}GF, 5^{0}GF, 7^{0}G, 6^{0}SW, 8^{2}SD, 8^{0}SD

	Starts	1st	2nd	3rd	Win & Pl
Career Total (Turf)	3	0	0	0	
Career Total (AW)	3	0	1	0	558

Going (Turf): Sf: 0-0 GS: 0-0 Gd: 0-1 GF: 0-2 Fm: 0-0
Distance: 5f/6f: 0-3 7f-8f: 0-1 9f-13f: 0-2 14f+: 0-0
Track: LH: 0-3 RH: 0-0 Tight: 0-3 Gall: 0-0
Aids: Bl: 0-0 Vi: 0-0 Tstrap: 0-0
Best Rating: 57 10/01 Wolv 1m100y stand

Dropped in grade to finish runner-up in a mile Wolverhampton seller in October.

Welcome Shade

(86) (38)**61**
4-y-o gr g Green Desert (USA)-Grey Angel (Kenmare (FR))
L A Dace M C S D Racing Ltd

Placings:00014/200000-0 (0089)
2001: 10^{0}SD

	Starts	1st	2nd	3rd	Win & Pl
Career Total (Turf)	7	0	1	0	653
Career Total (AW)	5	1	0	0	2291

62 11/99 Ling 6f E(0-75)H STD £2290
Total win prize-money £2291

Going (Turf): Sf: 0-1 GS: 0-0 Gd: 0-2 GF: 0-3 Fm: 0-1
Distance: 5f/6f: 1-2 7f-8f: 0-5 9f-13f: 0-5 14f+: 0-0
Track: LH: 1-8 RH: 0-1 Tight: 1-7 Gall: 0-0
Aids: Bl: 0-1 Vi: 0-0 Tstrap: 0-0
Best Rating: 62 11/99 Ling 6f SD

Welcome To Due's (USA)

(75) (20)
4-y-o gr g Cozzene (USA)-Etoile D'Amore (USA) (The Minstrel (CAN))
G M Moore J & M Leisure / Unos Restaurant

Placings:06 (2891)
2001: 12^{0}SD, 12^{6}GF

	Starts	1st	2nd	3rd	Win & Pl
Career Total (Turf)	1	0	0	0	0
Career Total (AW)	1	0	0	0	0

Going (Turf): Sf: 0-0 GS: 0-0 Gd: 0-0 GF: 0-1 Fm: 0-0
Distance: 5f/6f: 0-0 7f-8f: 0-0 9f-13f: 0-2 14f+: 0-0
Track: LH: 0-2 RH: 0-0 Tight: 0-0 Gall: 0-0
Aids: Bl: 0-0 Vi: 0-0 Tstrap: 0-0
Best Rating: 20 6/01 Sthl 1m4f stand

Welenska

(95) (81)
2-y-o b c Danzig Connection (USA)-Fairy Story (IRE) (Persian Bold)
P F I Cole The Fairy Story Partnership

Placings:131 (5047)
2001: 7^{1}G, 7^{3}G, 8^{1}SD

	Starts	1st	2nd	3rd	Win & Pl
Career Total (Turf)	2	1	0	1	4171
Career Total (AW)	1	1	0	0	3432

81 10/01 Sthl 1m E STD £3432
84 8/01 Folk 7f E GD £2961
Total win prize-money £6393

Going (Turf): Sf: 0-0 GS: 0-0 Gd: 1-2 GF: 0-0 Fm: 0-0
Distance: 5f/6f: 0-0 7f-8f: 2-3 9f-13f: 0-0 14f+: 0-0
Track: LH: 1-1 RH: 0-1 Tight: 0-0 Gall: 0-1
Aids: Bl: 0-0 Vi: 0-0 Tstrap: 0-0
Best Rating: 87 9/01 Kemp 7f good

Won a Folkestone maiden very easily on his debut and stepped up on that when third in a decent conditions event next time. He got back to winning form in a novice event on the Southwell Fibresand, but made hard work of it.

Well Chosen

85 **77+**
2-y-o b c Sadler's Wells (USA)-Hawajiss (Kris)
E A L Dunlop Maktoum Al Maktoum

Placings:6 (4484)
2001: 7^{6}S

	Starts	1st	2nd	3rd	Win & Pl
Career Total (Turf)	1	0	0	0	0

Going (Turf): Sf: 0-1 GS: 0-0 Gd: 0-0 GF: 0-0 Fm: 0-0
Distance: 5f/6f: 0-0 7f-8f: 0-1 9f-13f: 0-0 14f+: 0-0
Track: LH: 0-0 RH: 0-0 Tight: 0-0 Gall: 0-0
Aids: Bl: 0-0 Vi: 0-0 Tstrap: 0-0
Best Rating: 77 9/01 Yarm 7f3y soft

Well Heeled (IRE)

77 **36**
2-y-o b f Woodborough (USA)-Doumayna (Kouban (FR))
R M Beckett Mrs Richard Aykroyd

Placings:0 (1175)
2001: 5^{0}G

	Starts	1st	2nd	3rd	Win & Pl
Career Total (Turf)	1	0	0	0	

Going (Turf): Sf: 0-0 GS: 0-0 Gd: 0-1 GF: 0-0 Fm: 0-0
Distance: 5f/6f: 0-1 7f-8f: 0-0 9f-13f: 0-0 14f+: 0-0
Track: LH: 0-1 RH: 0-0 Tight: 0-0 Gall: 0-1
Aids: Bl: 0-0 Vi: 0-0 Tstrap: 0-0
Best Rating: 36 5/01 Wwck 5f good

Well Spotted (IRE)

76(52) **34**
3-y-o ch f Eagle Eyed (USA)-Sand Grouse (USA) (Arctic Tern (USA))
J G Portman Madhatter Racing

Placings:00000 (4471)
2001: 10^{0}GF, 9^{0}GS, 9^{0}SD, 11^{0}GF, 6^{0}GF

	Starts	1st	2nd	3rd	Win & Pl
Career Total (Turf)	4	0	0	0	
Career Total (AW)	1	0	0	0	

Going (Turf): Sf: 0-0 GS: 0-1 Gd: 0-0 GF: 0-3 Fm: 0-0
Distance: 5f/6f: 0-0 7f-8f: 0-1 9f-13f: 0-4 14f+: 0-0
Track: LH: 0-4 RH: 0-1 Tight: 0-2 Gall: 0-0
Aids: Bl: 0-0 Vi: 0-0 Tstrap: 0-0
Best Rating: 34 7/01 Chep 1m2f36y gd-fm

Wellbeing

112 **124**
4-y-o b h Sadler's Wells (USA)-Charming Life (NZ) (Sir Tristram)
H R A Cecil Plantation Stud

Placings:3/11511-425 (2351)
2001: 12^{4}G, 12^{2}GF, 12^{5}GF

	Starts	1st	2nd	3rd	Win & Pl
Career Total (Turf)	9	4	1	1	135776

118 10/00 Newb 1m4f5y A HVY £21000
116 9/00 NmkR 1m4f A GD £15834
100 5/00 NmkR 1m4f C GD £6391
92 4/00 NmkR 1m4f D G-S £4836
Total win prize-money £48062

Going (Turf): Sf: 1-2 GS: 1-1 Gd: 2-4 GF: 0-2 Fm: 0-0
Distance: 5f/6f: 0-0 7f-8f: 0-1 9f-13f: 4-8 14f+: 0-0
Track: LH: 1-3 RH: 3-5 Tight: 0-2 Gall: 4-6
Aids: Bl: 0-0 Vi: 0-0 Tstrap: 0-0
Best Rating: 124 6/01 Epsm 1m4f10y gd-fm

He progressed really well in 2000, winning his first two starts at Newmarket before finishing fifth to Sinndar in the Derby, and overcame a three month lay off to win a Listed event at Newmarket and a Group Three at Newbury. He was a bit disappointing when only fourth in the Jockey Club Stakes on his return, but his stable was not firing at the time and he ran a cracker when touched off in the Coronation Cup. Disappointed at Royal Ascot, however.

Wellcome Inn

(103) (30)**28**
7-y-o ch g Most Welcome-Mimining (Tower Walk)
J O'Reilly Burntwood Sports Ltd

Placings:0/5023010000/00020500/022334140-6000 (2580)
2001: 12^{6}SD, 12^{0}SD, 12^{0}SD, 12^{0}SD

	Starts	1st	2nd	3rd	Win & Pl
Career Total (Turf)	18	1	2	1	4506
Career Total (AW)	14	1	2	2	3897

38 3/00 Wolv 1m1f79y F(0-65)H STD £2331
64 8/97 Bevl 1m3f216yF(0-60) G-S £2495
Total win prize-money £4826

Going (Turf): Sf: 0-5 GS: 1-5 Gd: 0-2 GF: 0-4 Fm: 0-2
Distance: 5f/6f: 0-0 7f-8f: 0-3 9f-13f: 2-23 14f+: 0-6
Track: LH: 1-21 RH: 1-10 Tight: 2-14 Gall: 0-0
Aids: Bl: 0-0 Vi: 0-0 Tstrap: 1-13
Best Rating: 30 3/01 Wolv 1m4f stand

Welody

69(100) (43)
5-y-o ch g Weldnaas (USA)-The Boozy News (USA) (L'Emigrant (USA))
G Prodromou George Prodromou

Placings:0/540/421004000000003-00030F0 (5023)
2001: 8^{0}SD, 12^{0}SD, 8^{0}SD, 8^{3}SD, 8^{0}SD, 8^{F}GF, 7^{0}3

	Starts	1st	2nd	3rd	Win & Pl
Career Total (Turf)	15	0	0	0	536
Career Total (AW)	11	1	1	2	3916

69 3/00 Wolv 1m100y D STD £2418
Total win prize-money £2418

Going (Turf): Sf: 0-4 GS: 0-0 Gd: 0-3 GF: 0-7 Fm: 0-0
Distance: 5f/6f: 0-0 7f-8f: 0-13 9f-13f: 1-12 14f+: 0-0
Track: LH: 1-17 RH: 0-3 Tight: 1-9 Gall: 0-2
Aids: Bl: 1-9 Vi: 0-5 Tstrap: 0-0
Best Rating: 43 2/01 Wolv 1m100y stand

Welsh Border

102 **98**
3-y-o ch c Zafonic (USA)-Welsh Daylight (Welsh Pageant)
H R A Cecil K Abdulla

Placings:11-200 (4991)
2001: 10^{2}GS, 10^{0}G, 14^{0}HY

	Starts	1st	2nd	3rd	Win & Pl
Career Total (Turf)	5	2	1	0	13039

92 10/00 NmkR 1m C SFT £5707
75 9/00 Nott 1m54y D G-S £3900
Total win prize-money £9607

Going (Turf): Sf: 1-2 GS: 1-2 Gd: 0-1 GF: 0-0 Fm: 0-0
Distance: 5f/6f: 0-0 7f-8f: 1-1 9f-13f: 1-3 14f+: 0-1
Track: LH: 1-3 RH: 0-0 Tight: 0-0 Gall: 0-1
Aids: Bl: 0-0 Vi: 0-0 Tstrap: 0-0
Best Rating: 98 4/01 Newb 1m2f6y gd-sft

A strongly-made colt, he won a Nottingham maiden at two before following up at Newmarket. He ran well at Newbury on his return, but badly in a Newmarket Listed event next time.

Welsh Charger (IRE)

87(84) (50)**50**
2-y-o b g Up And At 'Em-Timissara (USA) (Shahrastani (USA))
J J Quinn Tormented Taffys

Placings:0003543300 (4313)
2001: 5^{0}S, 5^{0}S, 5^{0}GF, 5^{3}GF, 6^{5}G, 7^{4}SD, 5^{3}SD, 5^{3}GS, 5^{0}G, 6^{0}G

	Starts	1st	2nd	3rd	Win & Pl
Career Total (Turf)	8	0	0	2	652
Career Total (AW)	2	0	0	1	260

Going (Turf): Sf: 0-2 GS: 0-1 Gd: 0-3 GF: 0-2 Fm: 0-0
Distance: 5f/6f: 0-9 7f-8f: 0-1 9f-13f: 0-0 14f+: 0-0
Track : LH: 0-1 RH: 0-0 Tight: 0-0 Gall: 0-0
Aids: Bl: 0-0 Vi: 0-0 Tstrap: 0-0
Best Rating: 50 7/01 Leic 5f2y gd-sft

Welsh Diva

90 **71**

2-y-o b f Selkirk (USA)-Khubza (Green Desert (USA))
Mrs A J Perrett Usk Valley Stud

Placings:0 **(5361)**
2001: 8^{0}GS

	Starts	1st	2nd	3rd	Win & Pl
Career Total (Turf)	1	0	0	0	

Going (Turf): Sf: 0-0 GS: 0-1 Gd: 0-0 GF: 0-0 Fm: 0-0
Distance: 5f/6f: 0-0 7f-8f: 0-1 9f-13f: 0-0 14f+: 0-0
Track : LH: 0-0 RH: 0-0 Tight: 0-0 Gall: 0-0
Aids: Bl: 0-0 Vi: 0-0 Tstrap: 0-0
Best Rating: 71 10/01 NmkR 1m gd-sft

A full-sister to Trans Island, she ran green on her Newmarket debut in October.

Welsh Dream

101(99) (49)**59d**

4-y-o b g Mtoto-Morgannwg (IRE) (Simply Great (FR))
P C Haslam Mrs B M Hawkins & S A B Dinsmore

Placings:000/112-00500 **(4469)**
2001: 8^{0}S, 13^{0}GS, 12^{5}F, 13^{0}GS, 12^{0}G, 16^{3}SD

	Starts	1st	2nd	3rd	Win & Pl
Career Total (Turf)	11	2	1	0	9074

71 8/00 Brig 1m3f196yE(0-70)H FRM £2740
63 8/00 NmkJ 1m4f E(0-70)H GD £5408
Total win prize-money £8148

Going (Turf): Sf: 0-4 GS: 0-1 **Gd: 1-4** GF: 0-0 **Fm: 1-2**
Distance: 5f/6f: 0-0 7f-8f: 0-3 **9f-13f: 2-6** 14f+: 0-2
Track : LH: 1-4 RH: 1-5 Tight: 0-6 **Gall: 1-1**
Aids: Bl: 0-0 Vi: 0-0 Tstrap: 0-0
Best Rating: 59 8/01 Thsk 1m4f firm

Welsh Emperor (IRE)

100 **100?**

2-y-o b g Emperor Jones (USA)-Simply Times (USA) (Dodge (USA))
T P Tate Mrs Sylvia Clegg

Placings:3322130201 **(5378)**
2001: 5^{3}GS, 5^{3}F, 7^{2}G, 7^{2}F, 6^{1}GS, 6^{3}G, 6^{0}G, 6^{2}G, 6^{0}GF, 5^{1}S

	Starts	1st	2nd	3rd	Win & Pl
Career Total (Turf)	10	2	3	3	11713

100 10/01 Catt 5f D SFT £3818
71 7/01 Haml 6f5y E G-S £3220
Total win prize-money £7039

Going (Turf): Sf: 1-1 GS: 1-2 Gd: 0-4 GF: 0-1 Fm: 0-2
Distance: 5f/6f: 1-4 7f-8f: 1-6 9f-13f: 0-0 14f+: 0-0
Track : LH: 0-3 RH: 0-0 Tight: 0-2 Gall: 0-0
Aids: Bl: 2-7 Vi: 0-0 Tstrap: 0-0
Best Rating: 100 10/01 Catt 5f soft

A free-running half-brother to Forever Times (won over five furlongs at two, later won over seven). Seemed to have stamina stretched when runner-up in seven-furlong maiden at Musselburgh in July, and won when dropped back to six on easy ground at Hamilton, and has run fair races in similar company since.

Welsh Holly (IRE)

85 **62**

2-y-o br f Idris (IRE)-Jane Avril (IRE) (Danehill (USA))
M H Tompkins P Heath

Placings:64 **(4536)**
2001: 5^{6}F, 6^{4}GF

	Starts	1st	2nd	3rd	Win & Pl
Career Total (Turf)	2	0	0	0	0

Going (Turf): Sf: 0-0 GS: 0-0 Gd: 0-0 GF: 0-1 Fm: 0-1
Distance: 5f/6f: 0-2 7f-8f: 0-0 9f-13f: 0-0 14f+: 0-0
Track : LH: 0-0 RH: 0-0 Tight: 0-0 Gall: 0-0
Aids: Bl: 0-0 Vi: 0-0 Tstrap: 0-0
Best Rating: 62 9/01 Rdcr 6f gd-fm

Welsh Lady

(78) (40)**56**

2-y-o b f Magic Ring (IRE)-Little Unknown (Known Fact (USA))
P D Evans E A R Morgans

Placings:060 **(5666)**
2001: 6^{0}SD, 6^{6}SD, 6^{0}HY

	Starts	1st	2nd	3rd	Win & Pl
Career Total (Turf)	1	0	0	0	
Career Total (AW)	2	0	0	0	0

Going (Turf): Sf: 0-1 GS: 0-0 Gd: 0-0 GF: 0-0 Fm: 0-0
Distance: 5f/6f: 0-3 7f-8f: 0-0 9f-13f: 0-0 14f+: 0-0
Track : LH: 0-2 RH: 0-0 Tight: 0-1 Gall: 0-0
Aids: Bl: 0-0 Vi: 0-0 Tstrap: 0-0
Best Rating: 56 11/01 Wind 6f heavy

Welsh Main

98 **106**

4-y-o br c Zafonic (USA)-Welsh Daylight (Welsh Pageant)
H R A Cecil K Abdulla

Placings:11-0 **(1123)**
2001: 10^{0}G

	Starts	1st	2nd	3rd	Win & Pl
Career Total (Turf)	3	2	0	0	11006

98 8/00 Yarm 1m2f21y C(0-90) G-F £7041
82 7/00 Wind 1m2f7y D G-F £3965
Total win prize-money £11006

Going (Turf): Sf: 0-0 GS: 0-0 Gd: 0-1 **GF: 2-2** Fm: 0-0
Distance: 5f/6f: 0-0 7f-8f: 0-0 **9f-13f: 2-3** 14f+: 0-0
Track : LH: 1-1 RH: 0-0 **Tight: 2-2** Gall: 0-0
Aids: Bl: 0-0 Vi: 0-0 Tstrap: 0-0
Best Rating: 106 5/01 NmkR 1m2f good

Very interesting colt, from a good family. Won both his races in 2000, maiden at Windsor and minor event at Yarmouth (after a troubled run). He reappeeared to finish a repectable seventh to Zindabad in conditions stakes at Newmarket in May.

Welsh Ploy

85(103) (56d)**35**

4-y-o b f Deploy-Safe House (Lyphard (USA))
K McAuliffe G E Amey

Placings:03250512/00003040-54233256 **(2323)**
2001: 8^{5}SW, 12^{4}SD, 12^{2}SD, 12^{3}SD, 12^{3}SD, 12^{2}SD, 12^{5}S, 16^{6}SD

	Starts	1st	2nd	3rd	Win & Pl
Career Total (Turf)	10	0	1	1	2590
Career Total (AW)	14	1	3	3	7266

81 12/99 Ling 1m E(0-85)H STD £2640
Total win prize-money £2641

Going (Turf): Sf: 0-7 GS: 0-1 Gd: 0-1 GF: 0-1 Fm: 0-0
Distance: 5f/6f: 0-1 **7f-8f: 1-10** 9f-13f: 0-12 14f+: 0-1
Track : LH: 1-16 RH: 0-5 **Tight: 1-13** Gall: 0-2
Aids: Bl: 0-1 Vi: 0-1 Tstrap: 0-0
Best Rating: 59 4/01 Ling 1m4f stand

Short of pace, and her only victory to date came on Equitrack.

Welsh Wind (IRE)

108(100) (72)**84**

5-y-o b g Tenby-Bavaria (Top Ville)
M Wigham (B G Powell 20/9) D Hassan

Placings:55133000/22042230-03300632210 **(5607)**
2001: 10^{0}SD, 7^{3}GS, 8^{3}GS, 8^{0}GF, 9^{0}F, 9^{6}GF, 8^{3}G, 8^{2}GF, 8^{2}F, 6^{1}GS, 8^{0}GS

	Starts	1st	2nd	3rd	Win & Pl
Career Total (Turf)	26	2	6	6	35497
Career Total (AW)	1	0	0	0	

84 10/01 York 6f214y D(0-85)H G-S £10507
87 7/99 Leop 1m2f G-F £3781
Total win prize-money £14288

Going (Turf): Sf: 0-2 **GS: 1-6** Gd: 0-6 **GF: 1-6** Fm: 0-2
Distance: 5f/6f: 0-0 7f-8f: 1-7 9f-13f: 1-20 14f+: 0-0
Track : LH: 2-13 RH: 0-10 Tight: 0-7 **Gall: 1-2**
Aids: Bl: 0-0 Vi: 0-0 Tstrap: 0-1
Best Rating: 91 4/01 Brig 7f214y gd-sft

He has made the frame on numerous occasions in the last couple of seasons, and at last got his head back in front at York on first run for current trainer in October. Suited by seven furlongs plus, he acts on most ground.

Welton Arsenal

99(101) (57)**59**

9-y-o b g Statoblest-Miller's Gait (Mill Reef (USA))
K Bishop Slabs And Lucan

Placings:60323134/52404200/014560240/4106000/006 23400/000/02000 **(5626)**
2001: 7^{0}HY, 7^{2}G, 7^{0}GF, 10^{0}G, 8^{0}GS, 7^{4}SD

	Starts	1st	2nd	3rd	Win & Pl
Career Total (Turf)	48	3	6	4	39196

93 5/97 NmkR 7f B(0-100) GD £7349
91 4/96 Wwck 7f C GD £4934
79 7/94 Sals 6f C FRM £4787
Total win prize-money £17070

Going (Turf): Sf: 0-6 GS: 0-7 **Gd: 2-19** GF: 0-14 Fm: 1-2
Distance: 5f/6f: 1-12 **7f-8f: 2-30** 9f-13f: 0-6 14f+: 0-0
Track : LH: 1-14 RH: 0-7 Tight: 0-4 Gall: 0-9
Aids: Bl: 0-0 Vi: 0-1 Tstrap: 0-0
Best Rating: 59 5/01 Ling 7f good

He has ability, but refuses to exert himself and cannot be trusted.

Wendi'Ouse

71 **6**

3-y-o b f Mind Games-Brown's Cay (Formidable (USA))
M Mullineaux Mega Micks Racing Partnership

Placings:0000 **(5187)**
2001: 5^{0}S, 10^{0}S, 5^{0}GF, 5^{0}GS

	Starts	1st	2nd	3rd	Win & Pl
Career Total (Turf)	4	0	0	0	

Going (Turf): Sf: 0-2 GS: 0-1 Gd: 0-0 GF: 0-1 Fm: 0-0
Distance: 5f/6f: 0-3 7f-8f: 0-0 9f-13f: 0-1 14f+: 0-0
Track : LH: 0-2 RH: 0-1 Tight: 0-3 Gall: 0-0
Aids: Bl: 0-0 Vi: 0-1 Tstrap: 0-0
Best Rating: 6 8/01 Catt 5f212y gd-fm

Wensley Blue (IRE)

83 **58+**

2-y-o b g Blues Traveller (IRE)-Almasa (Faustus (USA))
P C Haslam Mrs B M Hawkins & R Young

Placings:005 **(5087)**
2001: 6^{0}G, 6^{0}S, 7^{5}GS

	Starts	1st	2nd	3rd	Win & Pl
Career Total (Turf)	3	0	0	0	0

Going (Turf): Sf: 0-1 GS: 0-1 Gd: 0-1 GF: 0-0 Fm: 0-0
Distance: 5f/6f: 0-2 7f-8f: 0-1 9f-13f: 0-0 14f+: 0-0
Track : LH: 0-1 RH: 0-0 Tight: 0-0 Gall: 0-0

Aids: Bl: 0-0 Vi: 0-0 Tstrap: 0-0
Best Rating: 58 10/01 Newc 7f gd-sft

Were Not Stoppin

98(85) (29)47
6-y-o b g Mystiko (USA)-Power Take Off (Aragon)
R Bastiman I B Barker

Placings:0000/**00505**11141360-60000230 (3797)
2001: 9^{6}HY, 8^{0}S, 7^{0}F, 8^{0}GF, 10^{0}GF, 9^{2}GF, 9^{3}G, 11^{0}G

	Starts	1st	2nd	3rd	Win & Pl
Career Total (Turf)	20	4	1	2	14769
Career Total (AW)	5	0	0	0	0

58	7/00	Pont	1m2f6y	F(0-60)H	GD	£3120
52	5/00	Rdcr	1m1f	E(0-70)H	G-S	£3198
45	5/00	Rdcr	1m	F(0-65)H	G-F	£3211
34	4/00	Bevl	1m100y	G	HVY	£2184

Total win prize-money £11713

Going (Turf): Sf: 1-4 GS: 1-2 Gd: 1-6 GF: 1-7 Fm: 0-1
Distance: 5f/6f: 0-0 7f-8f: 1-5 **9f-13f: 3-20** 14f+: 0-0
Track : **LH: 2-16** RH: 1-7 **Tight: 1-9** Gall: 0-3
Aids: Bl: 0-0 Vi: 0-0 Tstrap: 0-0
Best Rating: 47 8/01 Hayd 1m3f200y good

West Order (USA)

102 85+
3-y-o ch c Gone West (USA)-Irish Order (USA) (Irish River (FR))
Saeed Bin Suroor Godolphin

Placings:11-03 (5149)
2001: 7^{0}GF, 7^{3}G

	Starts	1st	2nd	3rd	Win & Pl
Career Total (Turf)	4	2	0	1	14276

85	10/00	NmkR	7f	B	SFT	£7569
85	9/00	Newb	7f	D	G-F	£5414

Total win prize-money £12984

Going (Turf): Sf: 1-1 GS: 0-0 Gd: 0-1 **GF: 1-2** Fm: 0-0
Distance: 5f/6f: 0-0 **7f-8f: 2-4** 9f-13f: 0-0 14f+: 0-0
Track : LH: 0-0 RH: 0-0 Tight: 0-0 Gall: 0-0
Aids: Bl: 0-0 Vi: 0-0 Tstrap: 0-0
Best Rating: 63 10/01 Hdcr 7f good

From the family of Entrepreneur, he won both his starts at two for Richard Hannon before joining Godolphin. Fifth in a trial in Dubai in the spring, something appeared amiss when he finished last in the Jersey at Royal Ascot, but he put in an improved effort next time in a Redcar conditions event when third. Best over seven furlongs.

Westbound Road (USA)

73+(108) (73++)
4-y-o b c Gone West (USA)-Jood (USA) (Nijinsky (CAN))
D R Loder Maktoum Al Maktoum

Placings:23-1 (0573)
2001: 10^{1}SW

	Starts	1st	2nd	3rd	Win & Pl
Career Total (Turf)	2	0	1	1	6052
Career Total (AW)	1	1	0	0	2884

73	3/01	Ling	1m2f	D	SLW	£2884

Total win prize-money £2884

Going (Turf): Sf: 0-0 GS: 0-0 Gd: 0-0 GF: 0-0 Fm: 0-0
Distance: 5f/6f: 0-0 7f-8f: 0-0 **9f-13f: 1-1** 14f+: 0-0
Track : **LH: 1-1** RH: 0-0 **Tight: 1-1** Gall: 0-0
Aids: Bl: 0-0 Vi: 0-0 Tstrap: 0-0
Best Rating: 73 3/01 Ling 1m2f slow

Westcoast

10-y-o b g Handsome Sailor-Pichon (Formidable (USA))
M Tate M Tate

Placings:06300030/00/0 (4728)
2001: 16^{0}GF

	Starts	1st	2nd	3rd	Win & Pl
Career Total (Turf)	10	0	0	2	879
Career Total (AW)	1	0	0	0	

Going (Turf): Sf: 0-0 GS: 0-5 Gd: 0-2 GF: 0-2 Fm: 0-1
Distance: 5f/6f: 0-6 7f-8f: 0-3 9f-13f: 0-1 14f+: 0-1
Track : LH: 0-6 RH: 0-1 Tight: 0-4 Gall: 0-1
Aids: Bl: 0-3 Vi: 0-0 Tstrap: 0-0

Westcourt Magic

90(92) (32)37
8-y-o b g Emarati (USA)-Magic Milly (Simply Great (FR))
M W Easterby Mr K Hodgson & Mrs J Hodgson

Placings:0001111212/130050/4605020001000/51010 6400401000000/02020000 6100/000006-**00000** (5451)
2001: 5^{0}SW, 5^{0}SD, 5^{0}S, 5^{0}GS, 5^{0}HY

	Starts	1st	2nd	3rd	Win & Pl
Career Total (Turf)	69	11	5	1	95586
Career Total (AW)	2	0	0	0	

75	9/99	Ches	5f16y	D(0-85)H	HVY	£4091
87	8/98	Ches	5f16y	D(0-85)H	G-S	£6417
89	5/98	Ches	5f16y	B(0-100)H	G-F	£9046
85	3/98	Newc	5f	D(0-85)H	GD	£7100
88	8/97	Ches	5f16y	D(0-85)H	SFT	£6690
103	4/96	Hayd	5f	A	GD	£12136
104	9/95	Ayr	5f	A	GD	£10290
88	8/95	Thsk	6f	D	G-F	£4017
88	8/95	Sand	5f6y	D	G-F	£4221
68	8/95	Bevl	5f	D	G-F	£4352
63	7/95	Newc	5f	F	G-F	£2675

Total win prize-money £71039

Going (Turf): Sf: 2-12 GS: 1-13 Gd: 3-19 **GF: 5-22** Fm: 0-2
Distance: **5f/6f: 11-68** 7f-8f: 0-2 9f-13f: 0-0 14f+: 0-0
Track : **LH: 4-14** RH: 0-0 **Tight: 4-13** Gall: 0-0
Aids: Bl: 0-1 Vi: 0-0 Tstrap: 0-0
Best Rating: 32 2/01 Wolv 5f stand

Westcourt Pearl

(82) (39)
2-y-o b f Emarati (USA)-Carolside (Music Maestro)
M W Easterby Mr K Hodgson & Mrs J Hodgson

Placings:00 (0792)
2001: 5^{0}SD, 5^{0}SD

	Starts	1st	2nd	3rd	Win & Pl
Career Total (Turf)	0	0	0	0	
Career Total (AW)	2	0	0	0	

Going (Turf): Sf: 0-0 GS: 0-0 Gd: 0-0 GF: 0-0 Fm: 0-0
Distance: 5f/6f: 0-2 7f-8f: 0-0 9f-13f: 0-0 14f+: 0-0
Track : LH: 0-0 RH: 0-0 Tight: 0-0 Gall: 0-0
Aids: Bl: 0-0 Vi: 0-0 Tstrap: 0-0
Best Rating: 39 4/01 Sthl 5f stand

Westender (FR)

109 99
5-y-o b g In The Wings-Trude (GER) (Windwurf (GER))
M C Pipe Matt Archer & Miss Jean Broadhurst

Placings:0/12213/2250210-06 (2828)
2001: 12^{0}G, 11^{6}GS

	Starts	1st	2nd	3rd	Win & Pl
Career Total (Turf)	15	3	5	1	38403

99	8/00	Newb	1m3f5y	B(0-100)H	G-F	£9309
87	8/99	Ripn	1m2f	C(0-90)H	GD	£7295
75	7/99	Yarm	7f3y	D	G-F	£3984

Total win prize-money £20589

Going (Turf): Sf: 0-1 GS: 0-2 Gd: 1-5 **GF: 2-5** Fm: 0-2
Distance: 5f/6f: 0-0 7f-8f: 1-3 **9f-13f: 2-12** 14f+: 0-0
Track : LH: 1-6 RH: 1-6 Tight: 1-2 Gall: 1-8
Aids: Bl: 0-0 Vi: 0-2 Tstrap: 0-0
Best Rating: 94 7/01 Hayd 1m3f200y gd-sft

Now a very useful hurdler.

Western Applause

84 78+
2-y-o b f Royal Applause-Western Sal (Salse (USA))
J Noseda B McAllister

Placings:40 (5343)
2001: 6^{4}G, 6^{0}GS

	Starts	1st	2nd	3rd	Win & Pl
Career Total (Turf)	2	0	0	0	432

Going (Turf): Sf: 0-0 GS: 0-1 Gd: 0-1 GF: 0-0 Fm: 0-0
Distance: 5f/6f: 0-2 7f-8f: 0-0 9f-13f: 0-0 14f+: 0-0
Track : LH: 0-0 RH: 0-0 Tight: 0-0 Gall: 0-0
Aids: Bl: 0-0 Vi: 0-0 Tstrap: 0-0
Best Rating: 78 10/01 NmkR 6f good

Western Belle

102(85) (40)57
2-y-o b f Magic Ring (IRE)-Western Horizon (USA) (Gone West (USA))
D Morris Wyck Hall Stud

Placings:53060053 (5458)
2001: 6^{5}GF, 5^{3}GF, 5^{0}GF, 5^{6}G, 7^{0}G, 5^{0}GS, 5^{5}HY, 5^{3}G, 6^{0}SD

	Starts	1st	2nd	3rd	Win & Pl
Career Total (Turf)	8	0	0	2	698

Going (Turf): Sf: 0-1 GS: 0-1 Gd: 0-3 GF: 0-3 Fm: 0-0
Distance: 5f/6f: 0-6 7f-8f: 0-2 9f-13f: 0-0 14f+: 0-0
Track : LH: 0-2 RH: 0-1 Tight: 0-0 Gall: 0-1
Aids: Bl: 0-0 Vi: 0-0 Tstrap: 0-0
Best Rating: 62 8/01 Folk 5f good

Has been dropped to selling class to run her best races over five and six furlongs.

Western Bluebird (IRE)

102(100) (53)57
3-y-o b g Bluebird (USA)-Arrastra (Bustino)
H Morrison Hugh Scott-Barrett And Partners

Placings:0600012340644 (5411)
2001: 8^{0}S, 7^{6}SD, 7^{0}S, 10^{0}GS, 8^{0}F, 10^{1}GF, 11^{2}GF, 11^{3}GF, 14^{4}GF, 9^{0}G, 14^{6}GS, 11^{4}S, 14^{4}SD

	Starts	1st	2nd	3rd	Win & Pl
Career Total (Turf)	11	1	1	1	5539
Career Total (AW)	2	0	0	0	0

54	5/01	Newb	1m2f6y	E	G-F	£3304

Total win prize-money £3304

Going (Turf): Sf: 0-3 GS: 0-2 Gd: 0-1 **GF: 1-4** Fm: 0-1
Distance: 5f/6f: 0-0 7f-8f: 0-4 **9f-13f: 1-6** 14f+: 0-3
Track : **LH: 1-6** RH: 0-5 Tight: 0-4 **Gall: 1-3**
Aids: Bl: 0-0 Vi: 0-1 Tstrap: 0-0
Best Rating: 58 6/01 Wind 1m3f135y gd-fm

Half-brother to a seven-furlong winner, is out of a winner over one mile six furlongs. Got off the mark in Newbury claimer.

Western Chief (IRE)

(90)
7-y-o b h Caerleon (USA)-Go Honey Go (General Assembly (USA))
D L Williams Miss B W Palmer

Placings:53416410240/003/66 (0346)
2001: 12^{6}SD, 16^{6}SD

	Starts	1st	2nd	3rd	Win & Pl
Career Total (Turf)	13	2	1	2	16363
Career Total (AW)	3	0	0	0	0

94	8/97	Tral	1m4f	(0-100)H	G-Y	£6850
94	7/97	Gway	1m4f	(0-85)H	GD	£4110

Total win prize-money £10960

Going (Turf): Sf: 0-2 GS: 0-0 **Gd: 1-2** GF: 0-3 Fm: 0-0
Distance: 5f/6f: 0-0 7f-8f: 0-0 **9f-13f: 2-12** 14f+: 0-3
Track : LH: 1-7 RH: 1-8 Tight: 0-4 Gall: 0-1

Aids: Bl: 2-7 Vi: 0-0 Tstrap: 0-3
Best Rating: 46 2/01 Wolv 1m4f stand

Western Command (GER)

(112) (59d)**46d**
5-y-o b g Saddlers' Hall (IRE)-Western Friend (USA) (Gone West (USA))
Mrs N Macauley Andy Peake

Placings:52/331103005460242062 21/45033621603464 51062060353103006 2-53131546464000035 (5044)
2001: 11^{5}SD, 9^{3}SW, 9^{1}SW, 9^{3}SD, 9^{1}SD, 9^{5}SW, 9^{4}SD, 12^{6}SD, 9^{4}SD, 8^{6}SD, 11^{4}SD, 11^{0}SD, 11^{0}SD, 14^{0}SD, 12^{0}SD, 9^{3}SW, 14^{5}SD

	Starts	1st	2nd	3rd	Win & Pl
Career Total (Turf)	8	0	1	1	2158
Career Total (AW)	63	8	7	11	29100

73	2/01	Wolv	1m1f79y	E(0-70)H	STD	£2744
66	1/01	Wolv	1m1f79y	E(0-70)H	SLW	£2464
61	11/00	Sthl	1m3f	F(0-60)	STD	£2331
64	5/00	Sthl	1m6f	F(0-60)H	STD	£2254
66	2/00	Sthl	1m3f	F(0-65)H	STD	£1960
66	12/99	Wolv	1m4f	F(0-60)H	STD	£2389
73	3/99	Sthl	1m4f	F(0-70)H	STD	£1612
70	3/99	Sthl	1m3f	E(0-70)H	SLW	£2271

Total win prize-money £18026

Going (Turf): Sf: 0-2 GS: 0-0 Gd: 0-2 GF: 0-2 Fm: 0-2
Distance: 5f/6f: 0-0 7f-8f: 0-3 **9f-13f: 7-55** 14f+: 1-13
Track : **LH: 8-70** RH: 0-1 **Tight: 3-35** Gall: 0-1
Aids: Bl: 0-3 Vi: 0-2 Tstrap: 0-0
Best Rating: 73 2/01 Wolv 1m1f79y stand

Western Flame (USA)

106 **65**
3-y-o b f Zafonic (USA)-Samya's Flame (Artaius (USA))
R Guest Matthews Breeding And Racing

Placings:5200-00212000 **(5273)**
2001: 6^{0}G, 5^{0}G, 6^{2}GF, 6^{1}F, 5^{2}G, 5^{0}G, 5^{0}GF, 5^{0}HY

	Starts	1st	2nd	3rd	Win & Pl
Career Total (Turf)	12	1	3	0	6389

56	6/01	Ling	6f	D	FRM	£3672

Total win prize-money £3673

Going (Turf): Sf: 0-4 GS: 0-0 Gd: 0-5 GF: 0-2 **Fm: 1-1**
Distance: **5f/6f: 1-10** 7f-8f: 0-2 9f-13f: 0-0 14f+: 0-0
Track : LH: 0-3 RH: 0-1 Tight: 0-1 Gall: 0-1
Aids: Bl: 0-2 Vi: 0-0 Tstrap: 0-0
Best Rating: 65 7/01 Chep 5f16y good

By the top-class two-year-old miler Zafonic, she got off the mark at the eighth time of asking in a poor Lingfield maiden on firm ground. She has been tried over five furlongs but with no success and is occasionally fitted with blinkers.

Western Ridge (FR)

95(98) (61)**61**
4-y-o b g Darshaan-Helvellyn (USA) (Gone West (USA))
P Mitchell Mrs Barbara Gerber & Mr Richard J Cohen

Placings:45/0-**2550**000 **(4461)**
2001: 9^{2}SD, 8^{5}SW, 9^{5}SD, 8^{0}SD, 10^{0}GF, 10^{0}G, 12^{0}GS

	Starts	1st	2nd	3rd	Win & Pl
Career Total (Turf)	6	0	0	0	815
Career Total (AW)	4	0	1	0	836

Going (Turf): Sf: 0-1 GS: 0-2 Gd: 0-2 GF: 0-1 Fm: 0-0
Distance: 5f/6f: 0-0 7f-8f: 0-4 9f-13f: 0-6 14f+: 0-0
Track : LH: 0-6 RH: 0-3 Tight: 0-6 Gall: 0-2
Aids: Bl: 0-0 Vi: 0-0 Tstrap: 0-0
Best Rating: 61 7/01 Epsm 1m2f18y gd-fm

Ran with credit in a couple of Listed events as a juvenile. Started off running well on the All-Weather at the beginning of 2001 but became disappointing and ran as if needing in excess of ten furlongs. Has run well in the past on an easy surface.

Western Verse (USA)

97 **100+**
2-y-o b c Gone West (USA)-Reams Of Verse (USA) (Nureyev (USA))
H R A Cecil K Abdulla

Placings:10 **(2263)**
2001: 6^{1}GF, 6^{0}GF

	Starts	1st	2nd	3rd	Win & Pl
Career Total (Turf)	2	1	0	0	7150

100	5/01	York	6f	D	G-F	£7150

Total win prize-money £7150

Going (Turf): Sf: 0-0 GS: 0-0 Gd: 0-0 **GF: 1-2** Fm: 0-0
Distance: **5f/6f: 1-2** 7f-8f: 0-0 9f-13f: 0-0 14f+: 0-0
Track : LH: 0-0 RH: 0-0 Tight: 0-0 Gall: 0-0
Aids: Bl: 0-0 Vi: 0-0 Tstrap: 0-0
Best Rating: 100 5/01 York 6f gd-fm

Out of the Oaks winner Reams Of Verse, he travelled with supremity to take his racecourse debut in style and looked to be an exciting prospect for the Coventry. However, the likes of Landseer, Rock Of Gibraltar and Redback proved too much for him and, having faded in the closing stages, he was nowhere near the money.

Westernmost

100(96) (59)**49**
3-y-o b g Most Welcome-Dakota Girl (Northern State (USA))
T D Barron Mrs J Hazell

Placings:006-**022442**023 **(4371)**
2001: **8^{0}SD**, 12^{2}S, **12^{2}SD**, 12^{4}F, 14^{4}F, **12^{2}SD**, 16^{0}F, 12^{2}G, 11^{3}GF

	Starts	1st	2nd	3rd	Win & Pl
Career Total (Turf)	9	0	2	1	2210
Career Total (AW)	3	0	2	0	1340

Going (Turf): Sf: 0-2 GS: 0-0 Gd: 0-2 GF: 0-2 Fm: 0-3
Distance: 5f/6f: 0-2 7f-8f: 0-1 9f-13f: 0-7 14f+: 0-2
Track : LH: 0-9 RH: 0-2 Tight: 0-5 Gall: 0-1
Aids: Bl: 0-0 Vi: 0-0 Tstrap: 0-0
Best Rating: 59 6/01 Sthl 1m4f stand

Westfield Star (IRE)

105(104) (60)**65**
4-y-o b g Fourstars Allstar (USA)-Mokaite (Komaite (USA))
T D Barron Richard Riorden

Placings:66006203-**562201**6102 **(4012)**
2001: **6^{5}SD**, **6^{6}SD**, **7^{2}SD**, **6^{2}SD**, **6^{0}SD**, **6^{1}SD**, 6^{6}GF, 7^{1}G, 7^{0}F, 7^{2}G

	Starts	1st	2nd	3rd	Win & Pl
Career Total (Turf)	12	1	2	1	7485
Career Total (AW)	6	1	2	0	3583

65	6/01	Thsk	7f	E(0-70)H	GD	£3854
59	4/01	Sthl	6f	F(0-60)	STD	£2303

Total win prize-money £6158

Going (Turf): Sf: 0-2 GS: 0-0 **Gd: 1-2** GF: 0-3 Fm: 0-1
Distance: 5f/6f: 1-9 7f-8f: 1-7 9f-13f: 0-1 14f+: 0-0
Track : **LH: 2-14** RH: 0-3 **Tight: 1-4** Gall: 0-0
Aids: Bl: 0-1 Vi: 0-0 Tstrap: 0-0
Best Rating: 65 8/01 Catt 7f good

A fair performer in Ireland in 2000, he has found his level in ordinary handicaps in this country. He has won over six on Fibresand and seven on turf this season. Suited by good ground on turf, races prominently and goes well for Lynsey Hanna.

Westgate Flame (IRE)

50
2-y-o ch g Priolo (USA)-Hawksbill Special (IRE) (Taufan (USA))
R A Fahey G H Leatham

Placings:0 **(5248)**
2001: 7^{0}S

	Starts	1st	2nd	3rd	Win & Pl
Career Total (Turf)	1	0	0	0	

Going (Turf): Sf: 0-1 GS: 0-0 Gd: 0-0 GF: 0-0 Fm: 0-0
Distance: 5f/6f: 0-0 7f-8f: 0-1 9f-13f: 0-0 14f+: 0-0
Track : LH: 0-1 RH: 0-0 Tight: 0-0 Gall: 0-1
Aids: Bl: 0-0 Vi: 0-0 Tstrap: 0-0

Westgate Run

98 **48**
4-y-o b f Emperor Jones (USA)-Glowing Reference (Reference Point)
R A Fahey Mark A Leatham

Placings:6364240000/01133112100-00025000 **(4535)**
2001: 11^{0}F, 10^{0}GF, 11^{0}GS, 12^{2}GF, 10^{5}GS, 10^{0}GF, 10^{0}G, 10^{0}GF

	Starts	1st	2nd	3rd	Win & Pl
Career Total (Turf)	29	5	3	3	20311

71	8/00	Ayr	1m2f192yE(0-70)H	G-F	£2941
71	7/00	Nott	1m1f213yE(0-70)H	G-F	£4192
63	7/00	Brig	1m3f196yF(0-60)	FRM	£2310
60	6/00	Haml	1m1f36y E(0-75)H	G-F	£3558
62	6/00	Wwck	1m2f110yG(0-60)H	G-F	£2279

Total win prize-money £15282

Going (Turf): Sf: 0-2 GS: 0-3 Gd: 0-7 **GF: 4-13** Fm: 1-4
Distance: 5f/6f: 0-7 7f-8f: 0-4 **9f-13f: 5-18** 14f+: 0-0
Track : **LH: 4-15** RH: 1-6 **Tight: 1-7** Gall: 0-7
Aids: Bl: 0-0 Vi: 0-1 Tstrap: 0-0
Best Rating: 66 7/01 Muss 1m4f gd-fm

She enjoyed a fine time in 2000, winning five times from nine to 12 furlongs on fast ground. Has struggled off a higher mark this term, but now back to a winning mark.

Westlife (IRE)

(72) (26)
3-y-o b f Mind Games-Enchantica (Timeless Times (USA))
H J Collingridge D Burke

Placings:066-0 **(0180)**
2001: 8^{0}SD

	Starts	1st	2nd	3rd	Win & Pl
Career Total (Turf)	1	0	0	0	
Career Total (AW)	3	0	0	0	0

Going (Turf): Sf: 0-0 GS: 0-1 Gd: 0-0 GF: 0-0 Fm: 0-0
Distance: 5f/6f: 0-3 7f-8f: 0-1 9f-13f: 0-0 14f+: 0-0
Track : LH: 0-3 RH: 0-0 Tight: 0-1 Gall: 0-1
Aids: Bl: 0-0 Vi: 0-0 Tstrap: 0-0

Westmead Empress

95 **71**
2-y-o br f Emperor Jones (USA)-Glossary (Reference Point)
S C Williams Westmead

Placings:053 **(4703)**
2001: 7^{0}G, 7^{5}GF, 7^{3}G

	Starts	1st	2nd	3rd	Win & Pl
Career Total (Turf)	3	0	0	1	639

Going (Turf): Sf: 0-0 GS: 0-0 Gd: 0-2 GF: 0-1 Fm: 0-0
Distance: 5f/6f: 0-0 7f-8f: 0-3 9f-13f: 0-0 14f+: 0-0
Track : LH: 0-1 RH: 0-0 Tight: 0-1 Gall: 0-0
Aids: Bl: 0-0 Vi: 0-0 Tstrap: 0-0
Best Rating: 71 9/01 Epsm 7f good

Westminster City (USA)

101(113) (64)**37**
5-y-o b g Alleged (USA)-Promanade Fan (USA) (Timeless Moment (USA))

B J Llewellyn (Ian Williams 11/9) Miss S Rudge

Placings:1030/0505000**500**/**3212**U0440405**3221-456**030200 **(4642)**
2001: 11^{4}SD, 12^{5}SW, 16^{0}SD, 10^{0}S, 9^{3}HY, 11^{0}GS, 9^{2}G, 10^{0}G, 10^{0}GF

	Starts	1st	2nd	3rd	Win & Pl
Career Total (Turf)	25	1	2	2	6594
Career Total (AW)	14	2	3	2	7530

62	12/00	Wolv	1m4f	F(0-60)H		STD	£1764
55	1/00	Wolv	1m100y	G		STD	£1981
76	5/98	Ling	5f	D		GD	£3187

Total win prize-money £6933

Going (Turf): Sf: 0-6 GS: 0-4 **Gd: 1-4** GF: 0-10 Fm: 0-1
Distance: 5f/6f: 1-2 7f-8f: 0-4 **9f-13f: 2-31** 14f+: 0-2
Track : **LH: 2-26** RH: 0-4 **Tight: 2-23** Gall: 0-2
Aids: Bl: 0-5 **Vi: 1-8** Tstrap: 0-0
Best Rating: 64 1/01 Sthl 1m4f slow

Moderate handicapper, effective ten to 12 furlongs on Turf and All-Weather.

Wethaab (USA)

89(90) (33)**44d**

4-y-o b g Pleasant Colony (USA)-Binntastic (USA) (Lyphard's Wish (FR))
Mrs A M Naughton (G M Moore 27/8) Mrs S E Cooper

Placings:0/0401600-5500050 **(3255)**
2001: 13^{5}S, 12^{5}GF, 12^{0}G, 14^{0}SD, 11^{0}SD, 12^{5}SD, 8^{0}GF

	Starts	1st	2nd	3rd	Win & Pl
Career Total (Turf)	12	1	0	0	2960
Career Total (AW)	3	0	0	0	0

55	6/00	Wwck	1m4f56y	F(0-60)H		G-F	£2415

Total win prize-money £2415

Going (Turf): Sf: 0-2 GS: 0-2 Gd: 0-3 **GF: 1-4** Fm: 0-1
Distance: 5f/6f: 0-0 7f-8f: 0-3 **9f-13f: 1-10** 14f+: 0-2
Track : **LH: 1-8** RH: 0-4 Tight: 0-6 Gall: 0-0
Aids: **Bl: 1-5** Vi: 0-1 Tstrap: 0-0
Best Rating: 44 5/01 Muss 1m4f gd-fm

Whalah (USA)

104 **71**

3-y-o ch f Dixieland Band (USA)-Firm Stance (USA) (Affirmed (USA))
C E Brittain Prince Abdul Aziz Bin Saud

Placings:0-64113 **(5686)**
2001: 8^{6}GF, 10^{4}S, 9^{1}HY, 9^{1}GS, 10^{3}S

	Starts	1st	2nd	3rd	Win & Pl
Career Total (Turf)	6	2	0	1	7940

71	11/01	Brig	1m1f209yD(0-85)H		G-S	£3848
65	10/01	Nott	1m1f213yF(0-65)H		HVY	£2684

Total win prize-money £6533

Going (Turf): **Sf: 1-3 GS: 1-1** Gd: 0-0 GF: 0-2 Fm: 0-0
Distance: 5f/6f: 0-0 7f-8f: 0-1 **9f-13f: 2-5** 14f+: 0-0
Track : **LH: 2-4** RH: 0-1 Tight: 0-1 Gall: 0-1
Aids: Bl: 0-0 Vi: 0-0 Tstrap: 0-0
Best Rating: 71 11/01 Brig 1m1f209y gd-sft

Made a successful debut in handicap company and followed up three days later under a penalty. Stays ten furlongs well, should get a mile and a half. Acts well with cut in the ground. On paper she put up a vastly improved display when third on her final turf start of the season.

Whale Beach (USA)

110 **89**

3-y-o b c Known Fact (USA)-Zulu Dance (USA) (Danzatore (CAN))
B W Hills C Wright & The Hon Mrs J M Corbett

Placings:0123-000302400 **(5005)**
2001: 7^{0}GS, 7^{0}G, 6^{0}F, 7^{3}GF, 8^{0}G, 7^{2}GF, 7^{4}GS, 8^{0}GF, 7^{0}S

	Starts	1st	2nd	3rd	Win & Pl
Career Total (Turf)	13	1	2	2	13530

73	8/00	Wind	6f	E		GD	£3705

Total win prize-money £3705

Going (Turf): Sf: 0-2 GS: 0-2 **Gd: 1-4** GF: 0-4 Fm: 0-1
Distance: **5f/6f: 1-2** 7f-8f: 0-11 9f-13f: 0-0 14f+: 0-0
Track : LH: 0-5 **RH: 1-1** Tight: 0-3 **Gall: 1-2**
Aids: Bl: 0-0 Vi: 0-0 Tstrap: 0-0
Best Rating: 89 8/01 Epsm 7f gd-fm

He got off the mark over six furlongs on his second start at two and has run some fine races over trips up to a mile since then without winning. Usually held up for a late run and sometimes takes a keen hold. Runs well at Epsom.

Whaleef

(104) (91+)**85+**

3-y-o br c Darshaan-Wilayif (USA) (Danzig (USA))
Saeed Bin Suroor Godolphin

Placings:1 **(1980)**
2001: 11^{1}GF

	Starts	1st	2nd	3rd	Win & Pl
Career Total (Turf)	1	1	0	0	4427

85	6/01	Gdwd	1m3f	D		G-F	£4426

Total win prize-money £4427

Going (Turf): Sf: 0-0 GS: 0-0 Gd: 0-0 **GF: 1-1** Fm: 0-0
Distance: 5f/6f: 0-0 7f-8f: 0-0 **9f-13f: 1-1** 14f+: 0-0
Track : LH: 0-0 RH: 0-0 Tight: 0-0 Gall: 0-0
Aids: Bl: 0-0 Vi: 0-0 Tstrap: 0-0
Best Rating: 85 6/01 Gdwd 1m3f gd-fm

He was well beaten in one of the Godolphin trials at the start of the season and made a winning debut in a conventional race over 11 furlongs at Goodwood in June. Swished his tail a lot that day and might have a touch of temperament.

Wharfedale Cygnet

82 **36**

3-y-o b f King's Signet (USA)-Your Care (FR) (Caerwent)
B G Powell W T Kemp

Placings:640-4 **(2739)**
2001: 8^{4}GF

	Starts	1st	2nd	3rd	Win & Pl
Career Total (Turf)	4	0	0	0	215

Going (Turf): **Sf: 0-0 GS: 0-0 Gd: 0-2 GF: 0-1 Fm: 0-1**
Distance: 5f/6f: 0-3 7f-8f: 0-0 9f-13f: 0-1 14f+: 0-0
Track : LH: 0-0 RH: 0-0 Tight: 0-0 Gall: 0-0
Aids: Bl: 0-0 Vi: 0-0 Tstrap: 0-0
Best Rating: 23 7/01 Chep 1m14y gd-fm

Whass Urrp (IRE)

86 **62**

2-y-o b c Desert King (IRE)-Blue Burgee (USA) (Lyphard's Wish (FR))
R Hannon M Mulholland

Placings:60 **(3980)**
2001: 6^{6}GF, 6^{0}F

	Starts	1st	2nd	3rd	Win & Pl
Career Total (Turf)	2	0	0	0	147

Going (Turf): **Sf: 0-0 GS: 0-0 Gd: 0-0 GF: 0-1 Fm: 0-1**
Distance: 5f/6f: 0-0 7f-8f: 0-2 9f-13f: 0-0 14f+: 0-0
Track : LH: 0-0 RH: 0-0 Tight: 0-0 Gall: 0-0
Aids: Bl: 0-0 Vi: 0-0 Tstrap: 0-0
Best Rating: 62 6/01 Newb 6f8y gd-fm

What A Cracker

68(71) (10)**15**

4-y-o b f Bustino-Moon Spin (Night Shift (USA))
Miss H M Irving The Nap Hand Partnership

Placings:000/6000-00 **(2379)**
2001: 11^{0}F, 8^{0}GF

	Starts	1st	2nd	3rd	Win & Pl
Career Total (Turf)	8	0	0	0	0
Career Total (AW)	1	0	0	0	

Going (Turf): **Sf: 0-2 GS: 0-0 Gd: 0-1 GF: 0-3 Fm: 0-2**
Distance: 5f/6f: 0-1 7f-8f: 0-2 9f-13f: 0-4 14f+: 0-2
Track : LH: 0-5 RH: 0-1 Tight: 0-5 Gall: 0-0
Aids: Bl: 0-0 Vi: 0-0 Tstrap: 0-0
Best Rating: 15 6/01 Brig 1m3f196y firm

What A View

85 **75**

2-y-o b c Sadler's Wells (USA)-Ocean View (USA) (Gone West (USA))
J L Dunlop The Thoroughbred Corporation

Placings:03 **(4575)**
2001: 7^{0}G, 8^{3}G

	Starts	1st	2nd	3rd	Win & Pl
Career Total (Turf)	2	0	0	1	666

Going (Turf): **Sf: 0-0 GS: 0-0 Gd: 0-2 GF: 0-0 Fm: 0-0**
Distance: 5f/6f: 0-0 7f-8f: 0-2 9f-13f: 0-0 14f+: 0-0
Track : LH: 0-0 RH: 0-1 Tight: 0-0 Gall: 0-0
Aids: Bl: 0-0 Vi: 0-0 Tstrap: 0-0
Best Rating: 75 9/01 Kemp 1m good

What's The Count

91(88) (38)**41**

5-y-o gr g Theatrical Charmer-Yankee Silver (Yankee Gold)
B R Johnson The Twenty Five Club

Placings:00 **(1295)**
2001: 12^{0}SD, 10^{0}G

	Starts	1st	2nd	3rd	Win & Pl
Career Total (Turf)	1	0	0	0	
Career Total (AW)	1	0	0	0	

Going (Turf): **Sf: 0-0 GS: 0-0 Gd: 0-1 GF: 0-0 Fm: 0-0**
Distance: 5f/6f: 0-0 7f-8f: 0-0 9f-13f: 0-2 14f+: 0-0
Track : LH: 0-2 RH: 0-0 Tight: 0-2 Gall: 0-0
Aids: Bl: 0-0 Vi: 0-0 Tstrap: 0-1
Best Rating: 41 5/01 Ling 1m2f good

What-A-Dancer (IRE)

107 **79+**

4-y-o b g Dancing Dissident (USA)-Cool Gales (Lord Gayle (USA))
G A Swinbank Tom Chambers

Placings:026-51432166 **(5146)**
2001: 8^{5}F, 8^{1}GF, 9^{4}GS, 7^{3}GF, 8^{2}GF, 6^{1}GF, 8^{6}F, 8^{6}G

	Starts	1st	2nd	3rd	Win & Pl
Career Total (Turf)	11	2	2	1	17216

79	9/01	York	6f214y	E(0-75)H		G-F	£9295
66	6/01	Haml	1m65y	F(0-65)H		G-F	£4127

Total win prize-money £13423

Going (Turf): Sf: 0-0 GS: 0-1 Gd: 0-1 **GF: 2-6** Fm: 0-3
Distance: 5f/6f: 0-0 7f-8f: 1-6 9f-13f: 1-5 14f+: 0-0
Track : LH: 1-4 RH: 1-4 Tight: 1-5 Gall: 1-1
Aids: Bl: 0-0 Vi: 0-0 Tstrap: 0-0
Best Rating: 79 10/01 Rdcr 1m good

Twice a winner this season over seven furlongs and a mile, he is at his best on fast ground, but he has shot up the handicap and looked in need of a break when running below par at Pontefract.

Whatsitsname

97(83) (19)**22**

5-y-o br g Tragic Role (USA)-Princessyasmin (USA) (Le Fabuleux)
J L Eyre T S Ely

Placings:0/050/00-000 **(2312)**
2001: 9^{0}GS, 9^{0}F, 13^{0}GS

	Starts	1st	2nd	3rd	Win & Pl
Career Total (Turf)	3	0	0	0	

	Starts	1st	2nd	3rd	Win & Pl
Career Total (AW)	6	0	0	0	0

Going (Turf): Sf: 0-0 GS: 0-2 Gd: 0-0 GF: 0-0 Fm: 0-1
Distance: 5f/6f: 0-1 7f-8f: 0-1 9f-13f: 0-6 14f+: 0-1
Track : LH: 0-7 RH: 0-2 Tight: 0-7 Gall: 0-0
Aids: Bl: 0-0 Vi: 0-0 Tstrap: 0-0
Best Rating: 22 5/01 Rdcr 1m1f firm

Wheathill

96 **76**
2-y-o ch f Magic Ring (IRE)-Hanglands (Bustino)
M P Tregoning Sarah, Lady Allendale & Mrs Vivian Wallis

Placings:5133000 **(5270)**
2001: 6^{5}GF, 5^{1}GF, 6^{3}GF, 5^{3}S, 5^{0}G, 6^{0}GF, 6^{0}HY

	Starts	1st	2nd	3rd	Win & Pl
Career Total (Turf)	7	1	0	2	5704
71 6/01 Ling 5f	D			G-F	£4153

Total win prize-money £4154

Going (Turf): Sf: 0-2 GS: 0-0 Gd: 0-1 **GF: 1-4** Fm: 0-0
Distance: **5f/6f: 1-7** 7f-8f: 0-0 9f-13f: 0-0 14f+: 0-0
Track : LH: 0-0 RH: 0-0 Tight: 0-0 Gall: 0-0
Aids: Bl: 0-1 Vi: 0-1 Tstrap: 0-0
Best Rating: 76 8/01 Sand 5f6y soft

A half-sister to five winners, including the useful two-year-old Zuno Warrior, he has cut little ice in nurseries since winning an ordinary Lingfield maiden over five furlongs in June 2001, despite being tried in blinkers and a visor.

When In Rome

110 **112**
3-y-o b c Saddlers' Hall (IRE)-Seasonal Splendour (IRE) (Prince Rupert (FR))
C A Cyzer Mrs E A Cyzer

Placings:636-3232105546 **(5122a)**
2001: 10^{3}HY, 10^{2}GS, 11^{3}G, 16^{2}GF, 14^{1}GF, 14^{0}G, 12^{5}GF, 14^{5}GF, 14^{4}G, 14^{6}S

	Starts	1st	2nd	3rd	Win & Pl
Career Total (Turf)	13	1	2	3	51077
66 7/01 Sand 1m6f	D			G-F	£4452

Total win prize-money £4452

Going (Turf): Sf: 0-3 GS: 0-2 Gd: 0-3 **GF: 1-5** Fm: 0-0
Distance: 5f/6f: 0-0 7f-8f: 0-2 9f-13f: 0-5 **14f+: 1-6**
Track : LH: 0-4 **RH: 1-7** Tight: 0-4 Gall: 0-4
Aids: Bl: 0-0 Vi: 0-0 Tstrap: 0-0
Best Rating: 112 9/01 Donc 1m6f132y good

A staying colt, he went down by only a neck to And Beyond in the Queen's Vase and followed up with an easy victory in three-runner maiden at Sandown. Ran a good race to be fourth in the St Leger, but may have found the soft ground against him in the German equivalent two weeks later.

Whenwilliemetharry

95(91) (29)**48**
4-y-o b f Sabrehill (USA)-William's Bird (USA) (Master Willie)
M E Sowersby (A Bailey 20/7) M E Sowersby

Placings:004500/606050-0000 **(5382)**
2001: 8^{0}GF, 8^{0}GF, 6^{0}G, 11^{0}S

	Starts	1st	2nd	3rd	Win & Pl
Career Total (Turf)	12	0	0	0	260
Career Total (AW)	4	0	0	0	0

Going (Turf): Sf: 0-1 GS: 0-3 Gd: 0-3 GF: 0-4 Fm: 0-1
Distance: 5f/6f: 0-3 7f-8f: 0-7 9f-13f: 0-6 14f+: 0-0
Track : LH: 0-8 RH: 0-3 Tight: 0-5 Gall: 0-0
Aids: Bl: 0-0 Vi: 0-0 Tstrap: 0-0
Best Rating: 48 6/01 Ayr 1m gd-fm

Where Are You

96 **61**
3-y-o b f Green Desert (USA)-Dafinah (USA) (Graustark)
Sir Michael Stoute Mitaab Abdullah

Placings:4224 **(4641)**
2001: 8^{4}GF, 6^{2}F, 7^{2}GF, 7^{4}GF

	Starts	1st	2nd	3rd	Win & Pl
Career Total (Turf)	4	0	2	0	3051

Going (Turf): Sf: 0-0 GS: 0-0 Gd: 0-0 GF: 0-3 Fm: 0-1
Distance: 5f/6f: 0-0 7f-8f: 0-3 9f-13f: 0-1 14f+: 0-0
Track : LH: 0-1 RH: 0-0 Tight: 0-0 Gall: 0-0
Aids: Bl: 0-0 Vi: 0-0 Tstrap: 0-0
Best Rating: 61 8/01 Sals 6f212y firm

Where Eagles Dare (USA)

95 **48**
4-y-o b g Eagle Eyed (USA)-Velveteen (USA) (Pirateer (USA))
J A Osborne Godiva

Placings:000/4 **(3454)**
2001: 14^{4}GF

	Starts	1st	2nd	3rd	Win & Pl
Career Total (Turf)	4	0	0	0	0

Going (Turf): Sf: 0-1 GS: 0-0 Gd: 0-0 GF: 0-3 Fm: 0-0
Distance: 5f/6f: 0-0 7f-8f: 0-3 9f-13f: 0-0 14f+: 0-1
Track : LH: 0-3 RH: 0-0 Tight: 0-1 Gall: 0-0
Aids: Bl: 0-0 Vi: 0-0 Tstrap: 0-0
Best Rating: 48 7/01 Nott 1m6f15y gd-fm

Where Or When (IRE)

107 **105**
2-y-o ch c Danehill Dancer (IRE)-Future Past (USA) (Super Concorde (USA))
T G Mills John Humphreys (turf Accountants) Ltd

Placings:101414 **(5388)**
2001: 7^{1}GF, 7^{0}GF, 6^{1}GF, 7^{4}G, 7^{1}G, 7^{4}GS

	Starts	1st	2nd	3rd	Win & Pl
Career Total (Turf)	6	3	0	0	43000
104 10/01 NmkR 7f	A			GD	£20300
97 8/01 Sals 6f212y	D			G-F	£4290
75 7/01 Asct 7f	D			G-F	£6760

Total win prize-money £31350

Going (Turf): Sf: 0-0 GS: 0-1 Gd: 1-2 **GF: 2-3** Fm: 0-0
Distance: 5f/6f: 0-0 **7f-8f: 3-6** 9f-13f: 0-0 14f+: 0-0
Track : LH: 0-0 RH: 0-2 Tight: 0-0 Gall: 0-0
Aids: Bl: 0-0 Vi: 0-0 Tstrap: 0-0
Best Rating: 105 10/01 NmkR 7f gd-sft

A half-brother to All The Way and Just In Time, he nearly came down on his debut, before recovering well and quickening up impressively. He disappointed in a Group Three at Goodwood, but put that performance behind him in ordinary company at Salisbury and with a decent effort in a Sandown Group Three. Landed the Group Three Somerville Tattersall Stakes at Newmarket in October in decent style and ran well in the Dewhurst.

Where The Heart Is

108 **84**
3-y-o ch g Efisio-Luminary (Kalaglow)
M H Tompkins Www.Raceworld.Co.Uk

Placings:3540-324 **(2358)**
2001: 7^{3}GF, 8^{2}GF, 8^{4}GF

	Starts	1st	2nd	3rd	Win & Pl
Career Total (Turf)	7	0	1	2	3600

Going (Turf): Sf: 0-2 GS: 0-0 Gd: 0-1 GF: 0-4 Fm: 0-0
Distance: 5f/6f: 0-0 7f-8f: 0-7 9f-13f: 0-0 14f+: 0-0
Track : LH: 0-5 RH: 0-0 Tight: 0-0 Gall: 0-3
Aids: Bl: 0-0 Vi: 0-0 Tstrap: 0-0
Best Rating: 84 6/01 Newc 1m gd-fm

Looked short on speed as a juvenile. Made a promising reappearance at three over seven furlongs and again ran with credit over a mile subsequently. Looks sure to need at least ten furlongs. Acts on a fast surface.

Where's Jasper (IRE)

100 **80**
3-y-o ch g Common Grounds-Stifen (Burslem)
K A Ryan Jimm Racing

Placings:2120105-3000000 **(5011)**
2001: 6^{3}S, 6^{0}GF, 6^{0}GS, 5^{0}GF, 5^{0}G, 5^{0}HY, 7^{0}HY

	Starts	1st	2nd	3rd	Win & Pl
Career Total (Turf)	14	2	2	1	18703
87 8/00 Hayd 6f	C			GD	£6069
73 6/00 Hayd 6f	D			G-S	£4465

Total win prize-money £10535

Going (Turf): Sf: 0-4 **GS: 1-3 Gd: 1-4** GF: 0-3 Fm: 0-0
Distance: **5f/6f: 2-13** 7f-8f: 0-1 9f-13f: 0-0 14f+: 0-0
Track : LH: 0-1 RH: 0-0 Tight: 0-0 Gall: 0-0
Aids: Bl: 0-3 Vi: 0-0 Tstrap: 0-0
Best Rating: 90 4/01 NmkR 6f soft

A dual juvenile winner, he ran a respectable race on his reappearance in a Newmarket handicap in April, but has not gone on from that despite dropping in the handicap.

Which Witch (IRE)

77
3-y-o b f Alzao (USA)-First Fastnet (Ahonoora)
M Johnston The Low Flyers (thoroughbreds) Ltd

Placings:40 **(4619)**
2001: 8^{4}GF, 5^{0}F

	Starts	1st	2nd	3rd	Win & Pl
Career Total (Turf)	2	0	0	0	393

Going (Turf): Sf: 0-0 GS: 0-0 Gd: 0-0 GF: 0-1 Fm: 0-1
Distance: 5f/6f: 0-1 7f-8f: 0-1 9f-13f: 0-0 14f+: 0-0
Track : LH: 0-1 RH: 0-0 Tight: 0-0 Gall: 0-1
Aids: Bl: 0-0 Vi: 0-0 Tstrap: 0-0
Best Rating: 90 4/01 NmkR 6f soft

Whiskaway

82 **29**
3-y-o ch f Alhijaz-Whirling Words (Sparkler)
P J Makin Mrs P J Makin

Placings:030 **(4896)**
2001: 8^{0}GS, 8^{3}GF, 9^{0}GS

	Starts	1st	2nd	3rd	Win & Pl
Career Total (Turf)	3	0	0	1	328

Going (Turf): Sf: 0-0 GS: 0-2 Gd: 0-0 GF: 0-1 Fm: 0-0
Distance: 5f/6f: 0-0 7f-8f: 0-1 9f-13f: 0-2 14f+: 0-0
Track : LH: 0-0 RH: 0-1 Tight: 0-0 Gall: 0-0
Aids: Bl: 0-0 Vi: 0-0 Tstrap: 0-0
Best Rating: 29 6/01 Sals 1m gd-sft

Whisky Echo

39(58)
2-y-o ch c Dancing Spree (USA)-Stock Pile (Galveston)
J G Given Mrs P M Daniel

Placings:00 **(5530)**
2001: 8^{0}SD, 8^{0}HY

	Starts	1st	2nd	3rd	Win & Pl
Career Total (Turf)	1	0	0	0	
Career Total (AW)	1	0	0	0	

Going (Turf): Sf: 0-1 GS: 0-0 Gd: 0-0 GF: 0-0 Fm: 0-0
Distance: 5f/6f: 0-0 7f-8f: 0-1 9f-13f: 0-1 14f+: 0-0
Track : LH: 0-2 RH: 0-0 Tight: 0-0 Gall: 0-0
Aids: Bl: 0-0 Vi: 0-0 Tstrap: 0-0

Whisky Nine

106 — 78

3-y-o b c Makbul-Indivisible (Remainder Man)
W J Haggas (M A Jarvis 11/5) Wentworth Racing (pty) Ltd

Placings:0-1245 (4034)
2001: 6^{1}G, 6^{2}GF, 6^{4}G, 6^{5}G

	Starts	1st	2nd	3rd	Win & Pl
Career Total (Turf)	5	1	1	0	4674

78	5/01	Nott	6f15y	E	GD	£2492

Total win prize-money £2492

Going (Turf): Sf: 0-1 GS: 0-0 **Gd: 1-3** GF: 0-1 Fm: 0-0
Distance: 5f/6f: 0-3 **7f-8f: 1-2** 9f-13f: 0-0 14f+: 0-0
Track : LH: 0-0 RH: 0-0 Tight: 0-0 Gall: 0-0
Aids: Bl: 0-0 Vi: 0-0 Tstrap: 0-0
Best Rating: 78 7/01 Donc 6f gd-fm

Lightly-raced sprinter, he took a Nottingham maiden in style on his return. He changed stables before finishing second on his handicap debut at Doncaster when he did not get the best of runs. Looked as if a longer trip might help when short of pace next time.

Whispering Rain

(73) (29)

2-y-o ch c Young Ern-Bay Meadows Star (Sharpo)
A G Newcombe A G Newcombe

Placings:0 (5393)
2001: 6^{0}SD, 7^{0}SD

	Starts	1st	2nd	3rd	Win & Pl
Career Total (Turf)	0	0	0	0	
Career Total (AW)	1	0	0	0	

Going (Turf): Sf: 0-0 GS: 0-0 Gd: 0-0 GF: 0-0 Fm: 0-0
Distance: 5f/6f: 0-1 7f-8f: 0-0 9f-13f: 0-0 14f+: 0-0
Track : LH: 0-1 RH: 0-0 Tight: 0-1 Gall: 0-0
Aids: Bl: 0-0 Vi: 0-0 Tstrap: 0-0
Best Rating: 23 10/01 Wolv 6f stand

Whistfilly

87 — 55

3-y-o b f First Trump-Zinzi (Song)
D R C Elsworth C J Harper

Placings:00000 (4162)
2001: 8^{0}G, 8^{0}GF, 6^{0}GF, 9^{0}G, 10^{0}GF

	Starts	1st	2nd	3rd	Win & Pl
Career Total (Turf)	5	0	0	0	

Going (Turf): Sf: 0-0 GS: 0-0 Gd: 0-2 GF: 0-3 Fm: 0-0
Distance: 5f/6f: 0-0 7f-8f: 0-2 9f-13f: 0-3 14f+: 0-0
Track : LH: 0-2 RH: 0-2 Tight: 0-2 Gall: 0-0
Aids: Bl: 0-0 Vi: 0-0 Tstrap: 0-0
Best Rating: 55 6/01 Gdwd 1m gd-fm

Whistler

105 — 79

4-y-o ch g Selkirk (USA)-French Gift (Cadeaux Genereux)
R Hannon Raymond Tooth

Placings:4203/2412153-0400000006 (5685)
2001: 5^{0}GS, 5^{4}GF, 5^{0}GF, 5^{0}GF, 6^{0}GF, 5^{0}GS, 5^{0}GF, 6^{0}G, 5^{0}HY, 5^{6}S

	Starts	1st	2nd	3rd	Win & Pl
Career Total (Turf)	21	2	3	2	17715

82	9/00	NmkR	5f	D(0-80)H	GD	£5248
76	7/00	Sals	6f	D	FRM	£3737

Total win prize-money £8987

Going (Turf): Sf: 0-4 GS: 0-4 **Gd: 1-3** GF: 0-8 **Fm: 1-2**
Distance: **5f/6f: 2-21** 7f-8f: 0-0 9f-13f: 0-0 14f+: 0-0
Track : LH: 0-2 RH: 0-2 Tight: 0-1 Gall: 0-3
Aids: Bl: 0-1 Vi: 0-0 Tstrap: 0-0
Best Rating: 85 5/01 Ches 5f16y gd-fm

Progressive sprint handicapper, he beat a big field in a Newmarket handicap in September 2000. He ran better than his finishing position would suggest on his first two starts of this season and was reported to have finished lame when down the field at Salisbury, but has not really done any better since then.

Whistling Dixie (IRE)

102(105) — (36)64

5-y-o ch g Forest Wind (USA)-Camdens Gift (Camden Town)
Mrs M Reveley P D Savill

Placings:04020/30606024465600/2601415306-111303 (5383)
2001: 12^{1}GF, 13^{1}S, 12^{1}S, 12^{3}G, 12^{0}GF, 13^{3}S

	Starts	1st	2nd	3rd	Win & Pl
Career Total (Turf)	32	5	2	4	24992
Career Total (AW)	3	0	1	0	654

64	8/01	Haml	1m4f17y	F(0-60)H	SFT	£2870
55	7/01	Haml	1m5f9y	D(0-80)H	SFT	£6831
52	7/01	Sthl	1m4f	E(0-75)H	G-F	£3472
47	7/00	Ling	1m2f	E(0-70)H	GD	£3027
44	7/00	Pont	1m2f6y	F(0-70)H	GD	£2173

Total win prize-money £18376

Going (Turf): Sf: 2-7 GS: 0-0 **Gd: 2-13** GF: 1-8 Fm: 0-4
Distance: 5f/6f: 0-3 7f-8f: 0-5 **9f-13f: 4-17** 14f+: 1-10
Track : **LH: 3-23** RH: 2-7 **Tight: 3-12** Gall: 0-6
Aids: Bl: 0-3 Vi: 0-0 Tstrap: 0-0
Best Rating: 64 8/01 Haml 1m4f17y soft

An improved performer over hurdles in the winter, he won a 12-furlong handicap at Southwell in July, his first run on the Flat since October 2000. He has since won twice in soft ground at Hamilton and is suited by trips of around 12 furlongs.

Whitbarrow (IRE)

105 — 101

2-y-o b c Royal Abjar (USA)-Danccini (IRE) (Dancing Dissident (USA))
B R Millman Seasons Holidays

Placings:011101004 (5493)
2001: 5^{0}GS, 5^{1}GS, 5^{1}G, 6^{1}GF, 5^{0}GF, 5^{1}GF, 6^{0}GS, 5^{0}G, 7^{4}HY

	Starts	1st	2nd	3rd	Win & Pl
Career Total (Turf)	9	4	0	0	63182

101	8/01	Gdwd	5f	A	G-F	£27000
98	6/01	Epsm	6f	A	G-F	£23200
82	5/01	Wind	5f10y	B	GD	£7624
72	5/01	Ling	5f	D	G-S	£3607

Total win prize-money £61432

Going (Turf): Sf: 0-1 GS: 1-3 Gd: 1-2 **GF: 2-3** Fm: 0-0
Distance: **5f/6f: 4-8** 7f-8f: 0-1 9f-13f: 0-0 14f+: 0-0
Track : LH: 1-2 RH: 1-1 Tight: 1-1 Gall: 1-2
Aids: **Bl: 1-4** Vi: 0-0 Tstrap: 0-0
Best Rating: 101 8/01 Gdwd 5f gd-fm

He got off the mark in a Lingfield maiden on his second start and followed up in good style in a Windsor conditions event. Scored the hat-trick in the Woodcote Stakes at Epsom when stepped up to six furlongs. A poor performance in the Weatherbys Super Sprint was followed by a fine win in the Molecomb at Goodwood, but was out of his depth in both the Prix Morny and Flying Childers. Failed to stay seven furlongs in heavy ground on his final start.

White Amit

74(60) — 42

3-y-o b f Shaamit (IRE)-White African (Carwhite)
J A Gilbert James A Gilbert

Placings:00-000 (3470)
2001: 7^{0}GS, 8^{0}F, 8^{0}GF

	Starts	1st	2nd	3rd	Win & Pl
Career Total (Turf)	4	0	0	0	
Career Total (AW)	1	0	0	0	

Going (Turf): Sf: 0-0 GS: 0-1 Gd: 0-1 GF: 0-1 Fm: 0-1
Distance: 5f/6f: 0-0 7f-8f: 0-4 9f-13f: 0-1 14f+: 0-0
Track : LH: 0-1 RH: 0-2 Tight: 0-1 Gall: 0-2
Aids: Bl: 0-0 Vi: 0-0 Tstrap: 0-1
Best Rating: 27 4/01 NmkR 7f gd-sft

White Bridle (IRE)

89 — 69

2-y-o ch f Singspiel (IRE)-Samira (Rainbow Quest (USA))
J L Dunlop The Thoroughbred Corporation

Placings:35 (3225)
2001: 7^{3}GF, 7^{5}GS

	Starts	1st	2nd	3rd	Win & Pl
Career Total (Turf)	2	0	0	1	639

Going (Turf): Sf: 0-0 GS: 0-1 Gd: 0-0 GF: 0-1 Fm: 0-0
Distance: 5f/6f: 0-0 7f-8f: 0-2 9f-13f: 0-0 14f+: 0-0
Track : LH: 0-0 RH: 0-0 Tight: 0-0 Gall: 0-0
Aids: Bl: 0-0 Vi: 0-0 Tstrap: 0-0
Best Rating: 69 7/01 NmkJ 7f gd-sft

White Cliffs

92 — 75

2-y-o ch c Bluebird (USA)-Preening (Persian Bold)
W J Haggas Ailsa Daniels & Guy Reed

Placings:002 (5526)
2001: 6^{0}S, 6^{0}HY, 5^{2}S

	Starts	1st	2nd	3rd	Win & Pl
Career Total (Turf)	3	0	1	0	1150

Going (Turf): Sf: 0-3 GS: 0-0 Gd: 0-0 GF: 0-0 Fm: 0-0
Distance: 5f/6f: 0-3 7f-8f: 0-0 9f-13f: 0-0 14f+: 0-0
Track : LH: 0-1 RH: 0-0 Tight: 0-0 Gall: 0-0
Aids: Bl: 0-0 Vi: 0-0 Tstrap: 0-2
Best Rating: 75 10/01 Nott 5f13y soft

White Dove (FR)

92 — 57

3-y-o b f Beaudelaire (USA)-Hermine And Pearls (FR) (Shirley Heights)
R Dickin M Al Gaoud

Placings:00005 (5114)
2001: 10^{0}GS, 8^{0}GS, 8^{0}G, 10^{0}G, 16^{5}HY

	Starts	1st	2nd	3rd	Win & Pl
Career Total (Turf)	5	0	0	0	0

Going (Turf): Sf: 0-1 GS: 0-2 Gd: 0-2 GF: 0-0 Fm: 0-0
Distance: 5f/6f: 0-0 7f-8f: 0-0 9f-13f: 0-4 14f+: 0-1
Track : LH: 0-1 RH: 0-2 Tight: 0-4 Gall: 0-0
Aids: Bl: 0-0 Vi: 0-0 Tstrap: 0-0
Best Rating: 57 5/01 Wind 1m67y good

White Emir

107(54) — (55)71

8-y-o b g Emarati (USA)-White African (Carwhite)
L G Cottrell Miss D M Stafford

Placings:01262103/05545223020/0005201100020000/22000633036/330000304000/321401-6125000 (5592)
2001: 7^{6}GF, 7^{1}GF, 7^{2}GF, 7^{5}GF, 7^{0}G, 7^{0}GF, 6^{0}GS

	Starts	1st	2nd	3rd	Win & Pl
Career Total (Turf)	71	7	11	9	66190
Career Total (AW)	1	0	0	0	

69	6/01	Kemp	7f	D(0-85)H	G-F	£4290
66	9/00	Brig	6f209y	D(0-85)H	SFT	£4543
64	7/00	Kemp	7f	E(0-70)H	G-F	£4036
80	6/97	Sals	5f	D(0-85)H	G-S	£3743
80	6/97	Sand	5f6y	F	G-F	£2788
80	9/95	Sand	5f6y	D	GD	£4201
60	5/95	Rdcr	5f	E	G-F	£3276

Total win prize-money £27680

Going (Turf): Sf: 1-10 GS: 1-8 Gd: 1-20 **GF: 4-30** Fm: 0-3
Distance: **5f/6f: 4-57** 7f-8f: 3-15 9f-13f: 0-10 14f+: 0-0

Track : LH: 1-14 **RH: 2-7** Tight: 0-6 **Gall: 2-11**
Aids: **Bl: 2-24** Vi: 0-0 Tstrap: 0-0
Best Rating: 73 7/01 Newb 7f gd-fm

White Ledger (IRE)

88(79) (59)**75**

2-y-o ch c Ali-Royal (IRE)-Boranwood (IRE) (Exhibitioner)

T G Mills Mr C Stephens

Placings:066 **(5163)**

2001: 6^{0}GF, 6^{6}G, 6^{6}SD

	Starts	1st	2nd	3rd	Win & Pl
Career Total (Turf)	2	0	0	0	0
Career Total (AW)	1	0	0	0	0

Going (Turf): Sf: 0-0 GS: 0-0 Gd: 0-1 GF: 0-1 Fm: 0-0
Distance: 5f/6f: 0-2 7f-8f: 0-1 9f-13f: 0-0 14f+: 0-0
Track : LH: 0-1 RH: 0-0 Tight: 0-1 Gall: 0-0
Aids: Bl: 0-0 Vi: 0-0 Tstrap: 0-0
Best Rating: 75 9/01 Gdwd 6f gd-fm

White Plains (IRE)

(115) (78)**45**

8-y-o b g Nordico (USA)-Flying Diva (Chief Singer)

T D Barron Nigel Shields

Placings:051/33552314410110/10602100050**02113/212650520/61534**0004336605**43311/40333500050-**22013501206 **(1993)**

2001: 11^{2}SD, 12^{2}SD, 12^{0}SD, 10^{1}SW, 12^{3}SD, 9^{5}SD, 12^{0}SD, 11^{1}SD, 12^{2}SW, 12^{0}GF, 12^{6}SD

	Starts	1st	2nd	3rd	Win & Pl
Career Total (Turf)	36	7	2	4	30303
Career Total (AW)	48	8	7	9	67948

75	4/01	Sthl	1m3f	F	STD	£2380
78	2/01	Ling	1m2f	C(0-100)H	SLW	£10842
90	1/00	Ling	1m2f	C(0-95)H	STD	£10676
85	12/99	Ling	1m4f	C(0-100)H	STD	£6318
89	2/99	Ling	1m2f	C	STD	£5462
84	2/98	Sthl	1m4f	D	STD	£4026
90	12/97	Ling	1m2f	G(0-80)H	STD	£1998
75	12/97	Ling	1m2f	E(0-70)H	STD	£2505
81	7/97	Haml	1m1f36y	D	G-S	£3696
80	4/97	Nott	1m1f213y	D(0-80)H	G-F	£4123
74	9/96	Ling	1m2f	D(0-75)H	FRM	£4556
75	9/96	Leic	1m1f218y	E(0-75)H	FRM	£3118
72	8/96	Newc	1m1f9y	E(0-70)	FRM	£2814
74	6/96	Ling	1m2f	F(0-70)H	FRM	£2557
70	11/95	Folk	6f	E	G-F	£3817

Total win prize-money £68894

Going (Turf): Sf: 0-2 GS: 1-2 Gd: 0-11 GF: 2-17 **Fm: 4-4**
Distance: 5f/6f: 1-3 7f-8f: 0-8 **9f-13f: 14-73** 14f+: 0-0
Track : **LH: 12-61** RH: 2-15 **Tight: 9-55** Gall: 1-7
Aids: Bl: 0-0 Vi: 0-0 **Tstrap: 5-35**
Best Rating: 78 2/01 Ling 1m2f slow

A smart performer on sand on his day, especially Equitrack, he remains capable of winning races on that surface, but is not altogether consistent and struggles against the better sand performers.

White Rabbit

104 **90**

2-y-o b f Zilzal (USA)-Trick (IRE) (Shirley Heights)

T D Easterby Lord Halifax

Placings:12033 **(5401)**

2001: 6^{1}G, 6^{2}GS, 8^{0}G, 6^{3}GS, 8^{3}S

	Starts	1st	2nd	3rd	Win & Pl
Career Total (Turf)	5	1	1	2	13209

86	8/01	Pont	6f	D	GD	£4095

Total win prize-money £4095

Going (Turf): Sf: 0-1 GS: 0-2 **Gd: 1-2** GF: 0-0 Fm: 0-0
Distance: **5f/6f: 1-2** 7f-8f: 0-2 9f-13f: 0-1 14f+: 0-0
Track : **LH: 1-4** RH: 0-0 Tight: 0-1 Gall: 0-1
Aids: Bl: 0-0 Vi: 0-0 Tstrap: 0-0
Best Rating: 90 10/01 Pont 1m4y soft

Showed a good attitude to win a Pontefract maiden on her debut and ran well at Chester next time, but success in Group company has eluded her. Acts on good ground.

White Settler

99 (2)**50**

8-y-o b g Polish Patriot (USA)-Oasis (Valiyar)

Miss S J Wilton John Pointon And Sons

Placings:530/0031230/046553000/1023**0**021/00/3100-6300 **(4672)**

2001: 8^{6}GF, 7^{3}GF, 8^{0}GS, 8^{0}G

	Starts	1st	2nd	3rd	Win & Pl
Career Total (Turf)	36	4	3	7	16562
Career Total (AW)	1	0	0	0	

49	9/00	Yarm	7f3y	G	G-F	£2191
56	9/98	Chep	1m14y	F	G-S	£2626
63	4/98	Leic	7f9y	G	SFT	£2679
67	7/96	Chep	7f16y	E(0-70)H	G-F	£3343

Total win prize-money £10840

Going (Turf): Sf: 1-4 GS: 1-4 Gd: 0-9 **GF: 2-19** Fm: 0-0
Distance: 5f/6f: 0-6 **7f-8f: 3-23** 9f-13f: 1-8 14f+: 0-0
Track : LH: 0-8 RH: 0-2 Tight: 0-4 Gall: 0-2
Aids: Bl: 0-1 Vi: 0-0 Tstrap: 0-0
Best Rating: 50 5/01 Wwck 1m22y gd-fm

White Stag

43

2-y-o b g King's Signet (USA)-Hibernica (IRE) (Law Society (USA))

G B Balding Theo Waddington

Placings:0 **(5665)**

2001: 6^{0}HY

	Starts	1st	2nd	3rd	Win & Pl
Career Total (Turf)	1	0	0	0	

Going (Turf): Sf: 0-1 GS: 0-0 Gd: 0-0 GF: 0-0 Fm: 0-0
Distance: 5f/6f: 0-1 7f-8f: 0-0 9f-13f: 0-0 14f+: 0-0
Track : LH: 0-0 RH: 0-0 Tight: 0-0 Gall: 0-0
Aids: Bl: 0-0 Vi: 0-0 Tstrap: 0-0
Best Rating: 43 11/01 Wind 6f heavy

White Star Lady

108(90) (30)**40**

3-y-o ch f So Factual (USA)-Cottonwood (Teenoso (USA))

J R Weymes White Star Racing

Placings:5050130-0000**4**005100 **(4599)**

2001: 6^{0}G, 6^{0}GF, 7^{0}G, 7^{0}GF, 7^{4}SD, 8^{0}GF, 6^{0}F, 6^{5}SD, 7^{1}GF, 6^{0}GF, 8^{0}GF, 8^{0}SD

	Starts	1st	2nd	3rd	Win & Pl
Career Total (Turf)	15	2	0	1	6449
Career Total (AW)	3	0	0	0	0

40	8/01	Bevl	7f100y	E	G-F	£3272
58	8/00	Muss	5f	F	G-F	£2716

Total win prize-money £5989

Going (Turf): Sf: 0-0 GS: 0-2 Gd: 0-4 **GF: 2-7** Fm: 0-2
Distance: 5f/6f: 1-11 7f-8f: 1-7 9f-13f: 0-0 14f+: 0-0
Track : LH: 0-4 **RH: 1-2** Tight: 0-2 Gall: 0-1
Aids: Bl: 0-0 Vi: 0-1 Tstrap: 0-0
Best Rating: 40 8/01 Bevl 7f100y gd-fm

Bar winning a Beverley claimer in August 2001, she has run poorly since her selling win at Musselburgh a year before.

Whitefoot

105 **93**

4-y-o b f Be My Chief (USA)-Kelimutu (Top Ville)

G A Butler Gary A Tanaka

Placings:013/4105-05650 **(3826)**

2001: 12^{0}S, 13^{5}GF, 22^{6}GF, 18^{5}G, 16^{0}G

	Starts	1st	2nd	3rd	Win & Pl
Career Total (Turf)	12	2	0	1	25218

106	5/00	Newb	1m2f6y	A	G-F	£15275
90	9/99	Sand	1m14y	D	GD	£3468

Total win prize-money £18744

Going (Turf): Sf: 0-3 GS: 0-1 **Gd: 1-4 GF: 1-4** Fm: 0-0
Distance: 5f/6f: 0-0 7f-8f: 0-1 **9f-13f: 2-7** 14f+: 0-4
Track : LH: 1-5 RH: 1-6 Tight: 0-3 **Gall: 1-6**
Aids: Bl: 0-0 Vi: 0-0 Tstrap: 0-0
Best Rating: 93 8/01 Asct 2m45y good

Successful in Listed company last season, she was subsequently outclassed in the Oaks and Ribblesdale Stakes. She ran better than her final placing would suggest in the Ormonde Stakes this season, but has been well beaten otherwise and probably needs a drop in class. Acts on fast ground.

Whiteney

2-y-o b f Whittingham (IRE)-Polgwynne (Forzando)

E J O'Neill W Clifford

Placings:F **(1324)**

2001: 5^{F}G

	Starts	1st	2nd	3rd	Win & Pl
Career Total (Turf)	1	0	0	0	

Going (Turf): Sf: 0-0 GS: 0-0 Gd: 0-1 GF: 0-0 Fm: 0-0
Distance: 5f/6f: 0-1 7f-8f: 0-0 9f-13f: 0-0 14f+: 0-0
Track : LH: 0-0 RH: 0-1 Tight: 0-0 Gall: 0-1
Aids: Bl: 0-0 Vi: 0-0 Tstrap: 0-0

Whitgift Rose

96 **74**

4-y-o b/br f Polar Falcon (USA)-Celtic Wing (Midyan (USA))

Lady Herries Whitgift Racing Limited

Placings:042-0 **(1096)**

2001: 10^{0}G

	Starts	1st	2nd	3rd	Win & Pl
Career Total (Turf)	4	0	1	0	1658

Going (Turf): Sf: 0-0 GS: 0-0 Gd: 0-2 GF: 0-2 Fm: 0-0
Distance: 5f/6f: 0-0 7f-8f: 0-2 9f-13f: 0-2 14f+: 0-0
Track : LH: 0-0 RH: 0-3 Tight: 0-0 Gall: 0-2
Aids: Bl: 0-0 Vi: 0-0 Tstrap: 0-0
Best Rating: 58 5/01 NmkR 1m2f good

Whitleygrange Girl

(78) (10)**19**

4-y-o b f Rudimentary (USA)-Choir's Image (Lochnager)

J L Eyre Mrs Carole Sykes

Placings:60506-00 **(0124)**

2001: 7^{0}SD, 8^{0}SW

	Starts	1st	2nd	3rd	Win & Pl
Career Total (Turf)	2	0	0	0	0
Career Total (AW)	5	0	0	0	0

Going (Turf): Sf: 0-2 GS: 0-0 Gd: 0-0 GF: 0-0 Fm: 0-0
Distance: 5f/6f: 0-1 7f-8f: 0-6 9f-13f: 0-0 14f+: 0-0
Track : LH: 0-7 RH: 0-0 Tight: 0-4 Gall: 0-0
Aids: Bl: 0-0 Vi: 0-0 Tstrap: 0-0
Best Rating: 58 5/01 NmkR 1m2f good

Whizz

92(93) (44)**60**

4-y-o b f Salse (USA)-Cut Ahead (Kalaglow)

R Charlton Lady Rothschild

Placings:6-630 **(2230)**

2001: 12^{6}SD, 10^{3}GF, 12^{0}GS

	Starts	1st	2nd	3rd	Win & Pl
Career Total (Turf)	3	0	0	1	678
Career Total (AW)	1	0	0	0	0

Going (Turf): Sf: 0-1 GS: 0-1 Gd: 0-0 GF: 0-1 Fm: 0-0
Distance: 5f/6f: 0-0 7f-8f: 0-0 9f-13f: 0-4 14f+: 0-0
Track : LH: 0-2 RH: 0-2 Tight: 0-3 Gall: 0-1
Aids: Bl: 0-0 Vi: 0-0 Tstrap: 0-0
Best Rating: 60 5/01 Ripn 1m2f gd-fm

Whizz Kid

100(102) (53+)**52**
7-y-o b m Puissance-Panienka (POL) (Dom Racine (FR))
J M Bradley B Paling

Placings:6251340004**4/440**5640346000306000**/5**1104 1550001005030100/005123126010000005026004**0100**-014000600005 **(5629)**
2001: 5^{0}S, 5^{1}GS, 5^{4}G, 5^{0}GF, 5^{0}GF, 5^{0}F, 5^{6}F, 5^{0}SD, 5^{0}G, 6^{0}HY, 5^{0}G, 5^{5}G

	Starts	1st	2nd	3rd	Win & Pl
Career Total (Turf)	73	9	3	5	44198
Career Total (AW)	19	2	1	0	5327

66	5/01	Bath	5f11y	E(0-70)H	G-S	£3017
53	12/00	Sthl	5f	F(0-65)H	STD	£1743
69	7/00	Chep	5f16y	C(0-100)H	G-F	£6727
43	5/00	Wolv	6f	E(0-70)H	STD	£2775
61	4/00	Wwck	5f	E(0-70)H	HVY	£2993
58	10/99	Newc	5f	E(0-70)H	G-S	£3025
59	7/99	Ayr	5f	C(0-90)H	GD	£7304
59	5/99	Chep	5f16y	D(0-85)H	G-S	£3792
47	4/99	Rdcr	5f	D(0-80)H	G-S	£5247
43	4/99	Ripn	5f	E(0-70)H	G-S	£2532
67	6/96	Wind	5f10y	G	G-F	£2318

Total win prize-money £41477

Going (Turf): Sf: 1-15 **GS: 5-14** Gd: 1-11 GF: 2-23 Fm: 0-9
Distance: **5f/6f: 11-86** 7f-8f: 0-5 9f-13f: 0-0 14f+: 0-0
Track : **LH: 3-23** RH: 1-9 Tight: 1-14 **Gall: 3-13**
Aids: Bl: 0-3 Vi: 0-0 Tstrap: 0-0
Best Rating: 66 5/01 Bath 5f11y gd-sft

Won at Bath in the summer on good to soft , but she has struggled since. Best over sprint trips.

Who Cares Wins

104 **73**
5-y-o ch g Kris-Anne Bonny (Ajdal (USA))
J R Jenkins The B C W Partnership

Placings:033120/000340-40000 **(3043)**
2001: 16^{4}S, 18^{0}GF, 20^{0}GF, 16^{0}GF, 14^{0}GF

	Starts	1st	2nd	3rd	Win & Pl
Career Total (Turf)	17	1	1	3	14271

69	6/99	Ches	1m5f89y	D	G-F	£3616

Total win prize-money £3617

Going (Turf): Sf: 0-1 GS: 0-1 Gd: 0-5 **GF: 1-9** Fm: 0-1
Distance: 5f/6f: 0-0 7f-8f: 0-1 9f-13f: 0-5 **14f+: 1-11**
Track : **LH: 1-9** RH: 0-7 **Tight: 1-3** Gall: 0-7
Aids: Bl: 0-1 Vi: 0-1 Tstrap: 0-0
Best Rating: 73 4/01 Kemp 2m soft

Failed to progress after shaping well as a three-year-old. Two miles is probably stretching him and he is probably best at up to fourteen furlongs. Best on a sound surface. He is a winning hurdler.

Who Goes There

103(86) (27)**55**
5-y-o ch m Wolfhound (USA)-Challanging (Mill Reef (USA))
T M Jones The Rest Hill Partnership

Placings:000/**0**00202354250/**5**0002003016100-05000035561500 **(4951)**
2001: 8^{0}S, 8^{5}GS, 7^{0}G, 6^{0}GF, 7^{0}F, 10^{0}F, 8^{3}GF, 7^{5}G, 7^{5}GF, 8^{6}GF, 7^{1}GF, 7^{5}G, 7^{0}G, 8^{0}G

	Starts	1st	2nd	3rd	Win & Pl
Career Total (Turf)	40	3	4	3	12838
Career Total (AW)	4	0	0	0	0

54	8/01	Ling	7f	F(0-65)H	G-F	£2520
56	8/00	Ling	7f	F(0-65)H	G-F	£2660
50	7/00	Chep	7f16y	E(0-70)H	FRM	£3055

Total win prize-money £8236

Going (Turf): Sf: 0-4 GS: 0-3 Gd: 0-10 **GF: 2-19** Fm: 1-4
Distance: 5f/6f: 0-3 **7f-8f: 3-25** 9f-13f: 0-16 14f+: 0-0
Track : LH: 0-13 RH: 0-12 Tight: 0-13 Gall: 0-3
Aids: Bl: 0-0 Vi: 0-0 Tstrap: 0-0
Best Rating: 55 8/01 NmkJ 7f good

She has the ability to win races, but is just about the slowest starter in training and that handicap is making life very difficult for her. Suited by fast ground, her wins have come over seven furlongs but she does stay a mile.

Who's On First (IRE)

88(81) (53)**66**
2-y-o ch c Common Grounds-Telemania (IRE) (Mujtahid (USA))
J A Osborne Torrance Racing 2

Placings:445 **(5345)**
2001: 5^{4}G, 6^{4}HY, 6^{5}SD

	Starts	1st	2nd	3rd	Win & Pl
Career Total (Turf)	2	0	0	0	672
Career Total (AW)	1	0	0	0	0

Going (Turf): Sf: 0-1 GS: 0-0 Gd: 0-1 GF: 0-0 Fm: 0-0
Distance: 5f/6f: 0-3 7f-8f: 0-0 9f-13f: 0-0 14f+: 0-0
Track : LH: 0-1 RH: 0-0 Tight: 0-0 Gall: 0-0
Aids: Bl: 0-0 Vi: 0-0 Tstrap: 0-0
Best Rating: 66 10/01 Ling 6f heavy

Ran well on his first two starts, although he was a little disappointing next time at Southwell.

Why Alys

94 **55**
2-y-o b f Lugana Beach-Classic Times (Dominion)
A W Carroll Wellesbourne Property Ltd

Placings:224641 **(4730)**
2001: 5^{2}F, 5^{2}F, 5^{4}GF, 5^{6}GS, 5^{4}GF, 5^{1}F

	Starts	1st	2nd	3rd	Win & Pl
Career Total (Turf)	6	1	2	0	4174

55	9/01	Chep	5f16y	E(0-75)	FRM	£2905

Total win prize-money £2905

Going (Turf): Sf: 0-0 GS: 0-1 Gd: 0-0 GF: 0-2 **Fm: 1-3**
Distance: **5f/6f: 1-6** 7f-8f: 0-0 9f-13f: 0-0 14f+: 0-0
Track : LH: 0-1 RH: 0-0 Tight: 0-0 Gall: 0-1
Aids: **Bl: 1-1** Vi: 0-0 Tstrap: 0-0
Best Rating: 55 9/01 Chep 5f16y firm

She suffered from sore shins after finishing second on her first two starts and needed blinkers to put her in a winning frame of mind in a Chepstow seller over five furlongs in September 2001.

Wicked Uncle

94 **81**
2-y-o b c Distant Relative-The Kings Daughter (Indian King (USA))
R M Beckett Dangerous Liasons Partnership

Placings:0031320 **(4348a)**
2001: 5^{0}S, 5^{0}G, 5^{3}GF, 5^{1}GF, 5^{3}G, 6^{2}GF, 6^{0}GY

	Starts	1st	2nd	3rd	Win & Pl
Career Total (Turf)	7	1	1	2	7036

73	7/01	Donc	5f	D	G-F	£4251

Total win prize-money £4251

Going (Turf): Sf: 0-1 GS: 0-0 Gd: 0-2 **GF: 1-3** Fm: 0-0
Distance: **5f/6f: 1-7** 7f-8f: 0-0 9f-13f: 0-0 14f+: 0-0
Track : LH: 0-1 RH: 0-0 Tight: 0-1 Gall: 0-0
Aids: Bl: 0-0 Vi: 0-0 Tstrap: 0-0
Best Rating: 81 8/01 Kemp 6f gd-fm

Showed a good attitude to score over the minimum trip at Doncaster in July and has run well in similar events since, but she was outclassed in Ireland in October. Acts on good to firm and is suited by five furlongs.

Wigman Lady (IRE)

96(83) (35)**36**
4-y-o b f Tenby-Height Of Elegance (Shirley Heights)
T J Etherington Mr & Mrs J M Swinglehurst & Partners

Placings:3/50-035000000 **(5407)**
2001: 13^{0}S, 9^{3}S, 9^{5}G, 12^{0}GF, 16^{0}GF, 11^{0}GF, 12^{0}GF, 10^{0}S, 12^{0}SD, 16^{5}SD

	Starts	1st	2nd	3rd	Win & Pl
Career Total (Turf)	11	0	0	2	519
Career Total (AW)	1	0	0	0	

Going (Turf): Sf: 0-4 GS: 0-1 Gd: 0-2 GF: 0-4 Fm: 0-0
Distance: 5f/6f: 0-0 7f-8f: 0-2 9f-13f: 0-9 14f+: 0-1
Track : LH: 0-6 RH: 0-3 Tight: 0-3 Gall: 0-0
Aids: Bl: 0-0 Vi: 0-0 Tstrap: 0-0
Best Rating: 47 5/01 Nott 1m1f213y good

She is plating class and has yet to win.

Wigmo Princess

89(88) (52)**55**
2-y-o ch f Factual (USA)-Queen Of Shannon (IRE) (Nordico (USA))
A W Carroll J Wigmore Racing Partnership

Placings:600420 **(5690)**
2001: 5^{6}GS, 6^{0}G, 6^{0}GF, 6^{4}SD, 5^{2}G, 7^{0}S

	Starts	1st	2nd	3rd	Win & Pl
Career Total (Turf)	5	0	1	0	674
Career Total (AW)	1	0	0	0	0

Going (Turf): Sf: 0-1 GS: 0-1 Gd: 0-2 GF: 0-1 Fm: 0-0
Distance: 5f/6f: 0-5 7f-8f: 0-1 9f-13f: 0-0 14f+: 0-0
Track : LH: 0-2 RH: 0-1 Tight: 0-1 Gall: 0-2
Aids: Bl: 0-0 Vi: 0-0 Tstrap: 0-0
Best Rating: 55 10/01 Bath 5f161y good

Plating class. Placed at up to six furlongs. Has raced on Wolverhampton's Fibresand and good to soft ground.

Wild Mushroom

61(70)
3-y-o ro g Norton Challenger-Wild Strawborry (Ballacashtal (CAN))
Miss B Sanders Copy Xpress Ltd

Placings:0 **(5182)**
2001: 10^{0}HY, 12^{0}SD

	Starts	1st	2nd	3rd	Win & Pl
Career Total (Turf)	1	0	0	0	

Going (Turf): Sf: 0-1 GS: 0-0 Gd: 0-0 GF: 0-0 Fm: 0-0
Distance: 5f/6f: 0-0 7f-8f: 0-0 9f-13f: 0-1 14f+: 0-0
Track : LH: 0-0 RH: 0-0 Tight: 0-1 Gall: 0-0
Aids: Bl: 0-0 Vi: 0-0 Tstrap: 0-0
Best Rating: 70 8/94 Leic 1m8y GF

Wild Water (FR)

83 **49**
3-y-o b c Salse (USA)-Dashing Water (Dashing Blade)
I A Balding J C Smith

Placings:00 **(1032)**
2001: 11^{0}S, 10^{0}GS

	Starts	1st	2nd	3rd	Win & Pl
Career Total (Turf)	2	0	0	0	

Going (Turf): Sf: 0-1 GS: 0-1 Gd: 0-0 GF: 0-0 Fm: 0-0
Distance: 5f/6f: 0-0 7f-8f: 0-0 9f-13f: 0-2 14f+: 0-0
Track : LH: 0-1 RH: 0-1 Tight: 0-1 Gall: 0-0
Aids: Bl: 0-0 Vi: 0-0 Tstrap: 0-0
Best Rating: 49 4/01 Kemp 1m3f30y soft

Wilderbrook Lahri

90 **56**

2-y-o b c Lahib (USA)-Wilsonic (Damister (USA))

Mrs J R Ramsden Mrs J E Morton

Placings:0300 **(4538)**

2001: 5^{0}GF, 6^{3}GF, 6^{0}GS, 7^{0}GF

	Starts	1st	2nd	3rd	Win & Pl
Career Total (Turf)	4	0	0	1	623

Going (Turf): Sf: 0-0 GS: 0-1 Gd: 0-0 GF: 0-3 Fm: 0-0
Distance: 5f/6f: 0-3 7f-8f: 0-1 9f-13f: 0-0 14f+: 0-0
Track : LH: 0-1 RH: 0-0 Tight: 0-0 Gall: 0-0
Aids: Bl: 0-0 Vi: 0-0 Tstrap: 0-0
Best Rating: 56 8/01 Hayd 6f gd-sft

Wilemmgeo

88(91) (53)**65d**

4-y-o b f Emarati (USA)-Floral Spark (Forzando)

P D Evans R J Hayward

Placings:0423**010/2121**050**5**0001141102-**500**000010000 **(2112)**

2001: **9**^{5}SD, **12**^{0}SD, **12**^{0}SD, 12^{0}GS, 9^{0}S, 10^{0}HY, 9^{0}HY, 8^{1}G, 7^{0}GF, 8^{0}F, 10^{0}F, 7^{0}F

	Starts	1st	2nd	3rd	Win & Pl
Career Total (Turf)	25	5	2	1	21713
Career Total (AW)	12	3	2	0	6321

56	5/01	Wwck	1m22y	G(0-60)H	GD	£1932
63	10/00	Pont	1m4y	D(0-80)H	HVY	£7800
56	9/00	Sand	1m2f7y	E(0-70)H	SFT	£2925
50	7/00	Bevl	7f100y	E(0-70)H	G-F	£4524
47	7/00	Bevl	1m100y	F(0-65)H	G-F	£2478
53	2/00	Sthl	1m	G	STD	£1842
48	1/00	Wolv	1m1f79y	G	STD	£1505
55	11/99	Wolv	1m100y	G	STD	£1924

Total win prize-money £24930

Going (Turf): Sf: 2-7 GS: 0-3 Gd: 1-5 **GF: 2-7** Fm: 0-3
Distance: 5f/6f: 0-2 7f-8f: 2-11 **9f-13f: 6-24** 14f+: 0-0
Track : **LH: 4-21** RH: 3-6 **Tight: 2-13** Gall: 0-2
Aids: Bl: 0-1 **Vi: 2-3** Tstrap: 0-0
Best Rating: 56 5/01 Wwck 1m22y good

Wilfram

102(87) (41)**59**

4-y-o b g Fraam-Ming Blue (Primo Dominie)

J M Bradley R D Willis

Placings:040/00031632451-0005565006010 **(5465)**

2001: 8^{0}S, 8^{0}GF, 8^{0}G, 10^{5}GF, 12^{5}GF, 12^{6}G, 10^{5}GF, 8^{0}GF, 9^{0}G, 8^{6}G, 8^{0}G, 9^{1}G, 10^{0}G, **8**^{6}SD

	Starts	1st	2nd	3rd	Win & Pl
Career Total (Turf)	27	3	1	2	11732

59	10/01	Rdcr	1m1f	F(0-65)H	GD	£2747
63	9/00	Leic	1m8y	F(0-60)	G-S	£2466
54	7/00	Chep	6f16y	E(0-70)H	G-F	£2860

Total win prize-money £8075

Going (Turf): Sf: 0-3 **GS: 1-4 Gd: 1-8 GF: 1-11** Fm: 0-1
Distance: 5f/6f: 0-3 7f-8f: 1-6 **9f-13f: 2-18** 14f+: 0-0
Track : **LH: 1-12** RH: 0-9 **Tight: 1-9** Gall: 0-3
Aids: **Bl: 1-5** Vi: 0-0 Tstrap: 0-0
Best Rating: 59 10/01 Rdcr 1m1f good

A fair handicapper at around a mile, he gained his third career success in October at Redcar over nine furlongs, but was disappointing next time with no obvious excuse. He tends to run in blinkers. Best on a sound surface,

William George (IRE)

96 **74**

2-y-o b g Turtle Island (IRE)-Lady's Dream (Mazilier (USA))

K A Ryan Mrs Margaret Forsyth

Placings:004006300 **(5283)**

2001: 5^{0}GF, 6^{0}G, 7^{4}G, 7^{0}G, 7^{0}G, 8^{6}HY, 7^{3}HY, 7^{0}S, 8^{0}HY

	Starts	1st	2nd	3rd	Win & Pl
Career Total (Turf)	9	0	0	1	1002

Going (Turf): Sf: 0-4 GS: 0-0 Gd: 0-4 GF: 0-1 Fm: 0-0
Distance: 5f/6f: 0-2 7f-8f: 0-6 9f-13f: 0-1 14f+: 0-0
Track : LH: 0-6 RH: 0-0 Tight: 0-1 Gall: 0-1
Aids: Bl: 0-0 Vi: 0-0 Tstrap: 0-0
Best Rating: 74 9/01 Hayd 7f30y heavy

William's Well

96 (46)**79**

7-y-o ch g Superpower-Catherines Well (Junius (USA))

M W Easterby Mr K Hodgson & Mrs J Hodgson

Placings:00003034/000511226642630000/4533045042 3/301122625004/0601436552221160000-0000 **(1306)**

2001: 6^{0}S, 6^{0}S, 5^{0}GS, 6^{0}GF

	Starts	1st	2nd	3rd	Win & Pl
Career Total (Turf)	70	7	10	8	59184
Career Total (AW)	1	0	0	0	0

79	8/00	Ripn	6f	B(0-105)H	G-F	£24375
77	8/00	Pont	5f	E(0-70)H	G-F	£3802
63	5/00	Nott	5f13y	E(0-70)H	GD	£3055
60	7/99	Catt	5f	E(0-75)H	FRM	£3454
54	7/99	Carl	5f	E(0-70)H	GD	£2944
53	6/97	Muss	5f	E(0-70)H	GD	£3148
44	6/97	Catt	5f	F(0-65)H	G-F	£2635

Total win prize-money £43415

Going (Turf): Sf: 0-9 GS: 0-7 **Gd: 3-26 GF: 3-24** Fm: 1-4
Distance: **5f/6f: 7-69** 7f-8f: 0-2 9f-13f: 0-0 14f+: 0-0
Track : LH: 1-10 RH: 1-3 Tight: 0-4 **Gall: 1-3**
Aids: **Bl: 7-62** Vi: 0-0 Tstrap: 0-0
Best Rating: 68 5/01 Thsk 6f gd-fm

Decent sprint handicapper, out of form in 2001.

Williamshakespeare (IRE)

(88) (51)**74**

5-y-o b h Slip Anchor-Rostova (Blakeney)

H Soma Stall Zykloide

Placings:6/2302232/000-0 **(3991a)**

2001: 16^{0}SD

	Starts	1st	2nd	3rd	Win & Pl
Career Total (Turf)	10	0	4	2	6611
Career Total (AW)	2	0	0	0	

Going (Turf): Sf: 0-2 GS: 0-2 Gd: 0-2 GF: 0-4 Fm: 0-0
Distance: 5f/6f: 0-0 7f-8f: 0-1 9f-13f: 0-9 14f+: 0-2
Track : LH: 0-5 RH: 0-5 Tight: 0-2 Gall: 0-6
Aids: Bl: 0-1 Vi: 0-0 Tstrap: 0-0
Best Rating: 51 8/01 Jage 2m stand

Willie Conquer

104(112) (75)**75**

9-y-o ch g Master Willie-Maryland Cookie (USA) (Bold Hour)

P D Evans (Andrew Reid 21/9) Colin G R Booth

Placings:40/350/0021151/0320500/0030/150540/10010 11123**432-32155**102144111120 **(5225)**

2001: **12**^{3}SD, **10**^{2}SD, **10**^{1}SW, **12**^{5}SW, **10**^{5}SW, **10**^{1}SW, 9^{0}GF, 10^{2}GF, 9^{1}F, 10^{4}G, 10^{4}GF, 9^{1}GF, 10^{1}GS, 9^{1}G, 8^{1}GF, 9^{2}G, 10^{0}S

	Starts	1st	2nd	3rd	Win & Pl
Career Total (Turf)	50	14	5	4	73930
Career Total (AW)	9	2	2	2	16852

53	9/01	York	1m205y	E	G-F	£8775
49	8/01	Brig	1m1f209y	F(0-70)	GD	£2254
62	8/01	Yarm	1m2f21y	E	G-S	£3136
49	7/01	Sals	1m1f198y	F	G-F	£3192
53	7/01	Brig	1m1f209y	F	FRM	£2317
75	2/01	Ling	1m2f	D(0-85)H	SLW	£3737
73	1/01	Ling	1m2f	C(0-95)H	SLW	£8131
55	8/00	Brig	1m1f209y	F	FRM	£2310
55	8/00	Yarm	1m2f21y	E	GD	£2847
71	7/00	Sals	1m1f198y	F	FRM	£2478
61	7/00	Brig	1m1f209y	F	G-S	£2278
54	5/00	Brig	1m1f209y	G	FRM	£1967
85	6/99	Brig	1m3f196y	D(0-80)H	GD	£3675
92	10/96	NmkR	1m4f	B(0-100)H	G-F	£7995
82	9/96	Gdwd	1m4f	D(0-80)	G-F	£4308
80	8/96	Newb	1m4f5y	D(0-80)	GD	£6227

Total win prize-money £65630

Going (Turf): Sf: 0-2 GS: 2-4 **Gd: 4-16 GF: 4-24 Fm: 4-4**
Distance: 5f/6f: 0-0 7f-8f: 0-5 **9f-13f: 16-48** 14f+: 0-6
Track : **LH: 12-32** RH: 4-21 **Tight: 7-22** Gall: 3-21
Aids: Bl: 0-0 Vi: 0-0 Tstrap: 0-3
Best Rating: 75 2/01 Ling 1m2f slow

He has won seven times this year, five of them claimers and is a very useful tool at that level. Best at ten furlongs, he handles any ground and also goes well on Equitrack.

Willing

73 **28**

5-y-o b g Yaheeb (USA)-Droskin Vii (Damsire Unregistered)

T J Etherington Miss A H Sykes

Placings:60 **(4317)**

2001: 10^{6}GS, 12^{0}G

	Starts	1st	2nd	3rd	Win & Pl
Career Total (Turf)	2	0	0	0	0

Going (Turf): Sf: 0-0 GS: 0-1 Gd: 0-1 GF: 0-0 Fm: 0-0
Distance: 5f/6f: 0-0 7f-8f: 0-0 9f-13f: 0-2 14f+: 0-0
Track : LH: 0-1 RH: 0-1 Tight: 0-1 Gall: 0-0
Aids: Bl: 0-0 Vi: 0-0 Tstrap: 0-0
Best Rating: 28 8/01 Hayd 1m2f120y gd-sft

Willoughby's Boy (IRE)

106 **54**

4-y-o b g Night Shift (USA)-Andbell (Trojan Fen)

B Hanbury Mrs G E M Brown

Placings:0316162010-050203000400 **(5607)**

2001: 7^{0}GS, 7^{5}GF, 8^{0}GF, 7^{2}GF, 7^{0}F, 7^{3}GS, 7^{0}GF, 7^{0}G, 7^{0}GF, 8^{4}F, 8^{0}GS, 8^{0}GS

	Starts	1st	2nd	3rd	Win & Pl
Career Total (Turf)	22	3	2	2	23239

87	9/00	Sand	1m14y	C(0-85)	G-F	£6506
90	7/00	Yarm	7f3y	C(0-95)H	GD	£6922
82	5/00	Bevl	7f100y	D	GD	£4143

Total win prize-money £17574

Going (Turf): Sf: 0-0 GS: 0-5 **Gd: 2-6** GF: 1-9 Fm: 0-2
Distance: 5f/6f: 0-0 **7f-8f: 2-19** 9f-13f: 1-3 14f+: 0-0
Track : LH: 0-7 **RH: 2-6** Tight: 0-4 Gall: 0-0
Aids: Bl: 0-1 Vi: 0-0 Tstrap: 0-2
Best Rating: 88 6/01 Yarm 7f3y gd-fm

A useful handicapper over seven furlongs and a mile who excels on a fast surface. Running well earlier in the season without winning. Unsuccessfully tried in blinkers. Showed a return to form when fourth at Pontefract in September, but has since been disappointing at Newmarket in October, and looks too high in the handicap.

Willow Magic

(98) (46)**63**

4-y-o b f Petong-Love Street (Mummy's Pet)

S Dow Mrs Anne Malby

Placings:6002/**5**04303434450020-0 **(0091)**

2001: 7^{0}SD

	Starts	1st	2nd	3rd	Win & Pl
Career Total (Turf)	14	0	0	3	1564
Career Total (AW)	6	0	2	0	1507

Going (Turf): Sf: 0-3 GS: 0-1 Gd: 0-3 GF: 0-2 Fm: 0-5
Distance: 5f/6f: 0-17 7f-8f: 0-3 9f-13f: 0-0 14f+: 0-0
Track : LH: 0-16 RH: 0-1 Tight: 0-8 Gall: 0-1
Aids: Bl: 0-0 Vi: 0-0 Tstrap: 0-0
Best Rating: 34 1/01 Ling 7f stand

Willy Bang Bang

84 **26**
4-y-o b g Contract Law (USA)-Megan's Move (Move Off)
W Storey H S Hutchinson

Placings:000-00 **(1924)**
2001: 9^{0}F, 12^{0}GF

	Starts	1st	2nd	3rd	Win & Pl
Career Total (Turf)	5	0	0	0	

Going (Turf): Sf: 0-0 GS: 0-0 Gd: 0-2 GF: 0-2 Fm: 0-1
Distance: 5f/6f: 0-0 7f-8f: 0-1 9f-13f: 0-4 14f+: 0-0
Track : LH: 0-3 RH: 0-2 Tight: 0-4 Gall: 0-1
Aids: Bl: 0-0 Vi: 0-0 Tstrap: 0-0
Best Rating: 26 6/01 Newc 1m4f93y gd-fm

Willy Willy

79 **18**
8-y-o ch g Master Willie-Monsoon (Royal Palace)
G Brown (D L Williams 27/7) Berkshire Commercial Components Ltd

Placings:15040/0/60 **(3409)**
2001: 11^{6}G, 12^{0}GF

	Starts	1st	2nd	3rd	Win & Pl
Career Total (Turf)	8	1	0	0	4578

85 7/98 Ling 1m1f D G-F £3915
Total win prize-money £3915

Going (Turf): Sf: 0-1 GS: 0-1 Gd: 0-3 **GF: 1-3** Fm: 0-0
Distance: 5f/6f: 0-0 7f-8f: 0-0 **9f-13f: 1-8** 14f+: 0-0
Track : **LH: 1-6** RH: 0-0 **Tight: 1-4** Gall: 0-1
Aids: Bl: 0-0 Vi: 0-0 Tstrap: 0-0
Best Rating: 21 7/01 Brig 1m3f196y good

Wilming

77(77) (26)**46**
2-y-o ch f Komaite (USA)-Ming Blue (Primo Dominie)
J M Bradley R D Willis

Placings:000000 **(5079)**
2001: 5^{0}SD, 5^{0}SD, 5^{0}F, 5^{0}GF, 5^{0}G, 5^{0}S

	Starts	1st	2nd	3rd	Win & Pl
Career Total (Turf)	4	0	0	0	
Career Total (AW)	2	0	0	0	

Going (Turf): Sf: 0-1 GS: 0-0 Gd: 0-1 GF: 0-1 Fm: 0-1
Distance: 5f/6f: 0-6 7f-8f: 0-0 9f-13f: 0-0 14f+: 0-0
Track : LH: 0-3 RH: 0-0 Tight: 0-0 Gall: 0-2
Aids: Bl: 0-0 Vi: 0-0 Tstrap: 0-0
Best Rating: 46 6/01 Wwck 5f gd-fm

Wilson Bluebottle (IRE)

93 **64**
2-y-o ch g Priolo (USA)-Mauras Pride (IRE) (Cadeaux Genereux)
M W Easterby M W Easterby

Placings:60620000 **(5690)**
2001: 6^{6}G, 5^{0}GF, 5^{6}F, 7^{2}GF, 6^{0}HY, 6^{0}GS, 6^{0}S, 7^{0}S

	Starts	1st	2nd	3rd	Win & Pl
Career Total (Turf)	8	0	1	0	948

Going (Turf): Sf: 0-3 GS: 0-1 Gd: 0-1 GF: 0-2 Fm: 0-1
Distance: 5f/6f: 0-6 7f-8f: 0-2 9f-13f: 0-0 14f+: 0-0
Track : LH: 0-2 RH: 0-0 Tight: 0-1 Gall: 0-0
Aids: Bl: 0-0 Vi: 0-0 Tstrap: 0-0
Best Rating: 71 7/01 York 6f good

Front runner, suited by good ground or faster, below par on softer. Stays seven furlongs.

Wilson Blyth

101 **59**
3-y-o b g Puissance-Pearls (Mon Tresor)
A Berry Dennis Blyth & Owen Wilson

Placings:22143426-2605U053560000 **(5451)**
2001: 6^{2}S, 6^{6}S, 6^{0}GF, 6^{5}GF, 5^{U}GF, 5^{0}G, 5^{5}S, 5^{3}GF, 6^{5}GF, 6^{6}G, 5^{0}GF, 5^{0}G, 6^{0}S, 5^{0}HY

	Starts	1st	2nd	3rd	Win & Pl
Career Total (Turf)	22	1	4	2	10353

73 6/00 Haml 6f5y F G-F £2769
Total win prize-money £2769

Going (Turf): Sf: 0-6 GS: 0-2 Gd: 0-5 **GF: 1-9** Fm: 0-0
Distance: 5f/6f: 0-21 **7f-8f: 1-1** 9f-13f: 0-0 14f+: 0-0
Track : LH: 0-3 RH: 0-0 Tight: 0-1 Gall: 0-0
Aids: Bl: 0-0 Vi: 0-0 Tstrap: 0-0
Best Rating: 76 7/01 Newc 5f gd-fm

His only victory to date came in a four-runner event at Hamilton as a two-year-old. He has made the frame several times since, but looks held off his current mark. Six furlongs is probably his trip.

Win Alot

94(89) (42)**60**
3-y-o b c Aragon-Having Fun (Hard Fought)
J Hetherton Ruthven Urquhart

Placings:0060060 **(2643)**
2001: 7^{0}SD, 8^{0}SD, 7^{6}S, 9^{0}GF, 10^{0}GF, 7^{6}SD, 10^{0}GF

	Starts	1st	2nd	3rd	Win & Pl
Career Total (Turf)	4	0	0	0	0
Career Total (AW)	3	0	0	0	0

Going (Turf): Sf: 0-1 GS: 0-0 Gd: 0-0 GF: 0-3 Fm: 0-0
Distance: 5f/6f: 0-0 7f-8f: 0-4 9f-13f: 0-3 14f+: 0-0
Track : LH: 0-5 RH: 0-1 Tight: 0-0 Gall: 0-1
Aids: Bl: 0-0 Vi: 0-0 Tstrap: 0-0
Best Rating: 60 5/01 Rdcr 7f soft

Wind Chime (IRE)

104(98) (49)**67**
4-y-o ch c Arazi (USA)-Shamisen (Diesis)
A G Newcombe Chris Bradbury

Placings:24/200220**304**-**0043630216** **(2651)**
2001: 9^{0}SW, 7^{0}SD, 7^{4}SD, 8^{3}SD, 8^{6}SD, 8^{3}SD, 8^{0}G, 6^{2}GF, 7^{1}F, 8^{6}SD

	Starts	1st	2nd	3rd	Win & Pl
Career Total (Turf)	11	1	5	0	10277
Career Total (AW)	10	0	0	3	1238

61 6/01 Thsk 7f D(0-80)H FRM £4465
Total win prize-money £4466

Going (Turf): Sf: 0-1 GS: 0-2 Gd: 0-2 GF: 0-5 **Fm: 1-1**
Distance: 5f/6f: 0-2 **7f-8f: 1-14** 9f-13f: 0-5 14f+: 0-0
Track : **LH: 1-12** RH: 0-4 **Tight: 1-9** Gall: 0-3
Aids: Bl: 0-0 Vi: 0-0 Tstrap: 0-0
Best Rating: 61 6/01 Thsk 7f firm

Windchill

100 **50**
3-y-o ch f Handsome Sailor-Baroness Gymcrak (Pharly (FR))
T D Easterby Mrs Bridget Tranmer

Placings:00221134-0605003 **(4621)**
2001: 5^{0}GF, 6^{6}F, 7^{0}GF, 7^{5}GF, 6^{0}G, 7^{0}GF, 6^{3}F

	Starts	1st	2nd	3rd	Win & Pl
Career Total (Turf)	15	2	2	2	12155

57 6/00 Newc 6f E FRM £7280
52 6/00 Rdcr 7f G GD £1855
Total win prize-money £9135

Going (Turf): Sf: 0-2 GS: 0-1 **Gd: 1-3** GF: 0-5 **Fm: 1-4**
Distance: 5f/6f: 1-10 7f-8f: 1-5 9f-13f: 0-0 14f+: 0-0
Track : LH: 0-1 RH: 0-1 Tight: 0-1 Gall: 0-0
Aids: Bl: 0-0 Vi: 0-0 Tstrap: 0-0
Best Rating: 50 7/01 Newc 7f gd-fm

A small filly, won twice as a juvenile. Stays seven furlongs though may be best at shorter. Suited by fast ground and goes well at Newcastle.

Windmill Lane

84(95) (52d)**47d**
4-y-o b f Saddlers' Hall (IRE)-Alpi Dora (Valiyar)
B S Rothwell John H Price

Placings:05505/263021035050-000 **(0741)**
2001: 16^{0}SD, 16^{0}SW, 14^{0}GS

	Starts	1st	2nd	3rd	Win & Pl
Career Total (Turf)	15	1	1	1	5326
Career Total (AW)	5	0	1	1	957

58 6/00 Carl 2m1f52y F(0-60)H G-F £2320
Total win prize-money £2321

Going (Turf): Sf: 0-4 GS: 0-6 Gd: 0-2 **GF: 1-3** Fm: 0-0
Distance: 5f/6f: 0-0 7f-8f: 0-4 9f-13f: 0-8 **14f+: 1-8**
Track : LH: 0-12 **RH: 1-6** Tight: 0-6 **Gall: 1-2**
Aids: Bl: 0-0 Vi: 0-1 Tstrap: 0-0
Best Rating: 25 4/01 Muss 1m6f gd-sft

Windshift (IRE)

96(111) (71)**51**
5-y-o b g Forest Wind (USA)-Beautyofthepeace (IRE) (Exactly Sharp (USA))
D Shaw G E Griffiths

Placings:4001/521153150430/5316**00000004**-6140004206 **(5632)**
2001: 11^{6}SD, 9^{1}SW, 9^{4}SD, 9^{0}SW, 8^{0}SD, 8^{0}G, 8^{4}SD, 10^{2}GF, 9^{0}GF, 10^{6}G

	Starts	1st	2nd	3rd	Win & Pl
Career Total (Turf)	17	1	1	0	8619
Career Total (AW)	22	5	1	3	20513

71 1/01 Wolv 1m1f79y D(0-85)H SLW £3864
76 1/00 Wolv 1m100y D(0 85)H STD £3136
74 3/99 Wwck 1m C(0-95)H G-S £6970
78 3/99 Sthl 1m D(0-85)H STD £3766
69 2/99 Sthl 1m E(0-70)H STD £3023
57 12/98 Sthl 1m E H STD £2927
Total win prize-money £23688

Going (Turf): Sf: 0-7 **GS: 1-2** Gd: 0-5 GF: 0-3 Fm: 0-0
Distance: 5f/6f: 0-0 **7f-8f: 4-17** 9f-13f: 2-22 14f+: 0-0
Track : **LH: 6-32** RH: 0-1 **Tight: 2-13** Gall: 0-1
Aids: Bl: 1-8 **Vi: 4-23** Tstrap: 0-0
Best Rating: 71 1/01 Wolv 1m1f79y slow

Has chalked up victories on sand and one on turf at Warwick early on last season, as well as contesting some very tough handicaps. Returned to winning form back at Wolverhampton on his second start of this year and is obviously at his best on Fibresand.

Windsor Boy (IRE)

109 **83**
4-y-o b c Mtoto-Fragrant Belle (USA) (Al Nasr (FR))
P F I Cole Newgate Stud

Placings:165/22-050400 **(4697)**
2001: 12^{0}GS, 12^{5}GS, 12^{0}G, 11^{4}GF, 13^{0}G, 14^{0}GS

	Starts	1st	2nd	3rd	Win & Pl
Career Total (Turf)	11	1	2	0	138678

84 8/99 Bevl 1m100y E GD £3582
Total win prize-money £3583

Going (Turf): Sf: 0-2 GS: 0-3 **Gd: 1-4** GF: 0-2 Fm: 0-0
Distance: 5f/6f: 0-0 7f-8f: 0-1 **9f-13f: 1-8** 14f+: 0-2
Track : LH: 0-4 **RH: 1-5** Tight: 0-4 Gall: 0-5
Aids: Bl: 0-1 Vi: 0-0 Tstrap: 0-1
Best Rating: 95 7/01 NmkJ 1m4f gd-sft

Placed in the 2000 Chester Vase before running the useful German horse Kallisto close in the Italian Derby. Not at his best in 2001. Stays a mile and a half. Acts on a sound surface.

Wing Commander

98 **91**
2-y-o b c Royal Applause-Southern Psychic (USA) (Alwasmi (USA))
M L W Bell M B Hawtin

Placings:412 **(4832)**

2001: 6^{4}GF, 7^{1}G, 8^{2}GF

	Starts	1st	2nd	3rd	Win & Pl
Career Total (Turf)	3	1	1	0	6702

81 8/01 Ayr 7f50y E GD £3094

Total win prize-money £3094

Going (Turf): Sf: 0-0 GS: 0-0 **Gd: 1-1** GF: 0-2 Fm: 0-0
Distance: 5f/6f: 0-1 **7f-8f: 1-2** 9f-13f: 0-0 14f+: 0-0
Track : LH: 0-0 RH: 0-0 Tight: 0-0 Gall: 0-0
Aids: Bl: 0-0 Vi: 0-0 Tstrap: 0-0
Best Rating: 91 9/01 Newb 1m gd-fm

Well beaten at Ascot on his debut, but made no mistake at Ayr next time and ran a fine second in the Haynes, Hanson And Clark at Newbury. He should stay further than a mile.

Wingalong (IRE)

57

2-y-o ch f Flying Spur (AUS)-Dutch Queen (Ahonoora)
T D Easterby T H Bennett

Placings:6 **(0638)**
2001: 5^{6}S

	Starts	1st	2nd	3rd	Win & Pl
Career Total (Turf)	1	0	0	0	0

Going (Turf): Sf: 0-1 GS: 0-0 Gd: 0-0 GF: 0-0 Fm: 0-0
Distance: 5f/6f: 0-1 7f-8f: 0-0 9f-13f: 0-0 14f+: 0-0
Track : LH: 0-0 RH: 0-0 Tight: 0-0 Gall: 0-0
Aids: Bl: 0-0 Vi: 0-0 Tstrap: 0-0
Best Rating: 91 9/01 Newb 1m gd-fm

Winged Angel

101(82) (9)**54**

4-y-o ch g Prince Sabo-Silky Heights (IRE) (Head For Heights)
Miss J A Camacho Four Up One Down Partnership

Placings:400001500-6000 **(4258)**
2001: 9^{6}F, 8^{0}SD, 10^{0}G, 11^{0}GF

	Starts	1st	2nd	3rd	Win & Pl
Career Total (Turf)	11	1	0	0	7438
Career Total (AW)	2	0	0	0	

58 7/00 Rdcr 1m3f D(0-80)H G-F £7215

Total win prize-money £7215

Going (Turf): Sf: 0-2 GS: 0-0 Gd: 0-3 **GF: 1-4** Fm: 0-2
Distance: 5f/6f: 0-1 7f-8f: 0-5 **9f-13f: 1-7** 14f+: 0-0
Track : **LH: 1-11** RH: 0-1 **Tight: 1-6** Gall: 0-2
Aids: Bl: 0-0 Vi: 0-1 Tstrap: 0-0
Best Rating: 49 5/01 Rdcr 1m1f firm

Wings Of A Dove

88 **46**

3-y-o b f Hernando (FR)-Woodren (USA) (Woodman (USA))
G Wragg Miss K Rausing

Placings:5 (5113)
2001: 8^{5}HY

	Starts	1st	2nd	3rd	Win & Pl
Career Total (Turf)	1	0	0	0	0

Going (Turf): Sf: 0-1 GS: 0-0 Gd: 0-0 GF: 0-0 Fm: 0-0
Distance: 5f/6f: 0-0 7f-8f: 0-0 9f-13f: 0-1 14f+: 0-0
Track : LH: 0-1 RH: 0-0 Tight: 0-0 Gall: 0-0
Aids: Bl: 0-0 Vi: 0-0 Tstrap: 0-0
Best Rating: 46 10/01 Nott 1m54y heavy

Wings Of Soul (USA)

98 **64**

3-y-o b c Thunder Gulch (USA)-Party Cited (USA) (Alleged (USA))
P F I Cole Andy J Smith

Placings:3-5200000 **(5601)**
2001: 10^{5}S, 8^{2}GF, 10^{0}GF, 8^{0}GF, 8^{0}G, 9^{0}S, 8^{0}GS

	Starts	1st	2nd	3rd	Win & Pl
Career Total (Turf)	8	0	1	1	2700

Going (Turf): Sf: 0-3 GS: 0-1 Gd: 0-1 GF: 0-3 Fm: 0-0
Distance: 5f/6f: 0-0 7f-8f: 0-5 9f-13f: 0-3 14f+: 0-0
Track : LH: 0-2 RH: 0-2 Tight: 0-1 Gall: 0-1
Aids: Bl: 0-1 Vi: 0-0 Tstrap: 0-1
Best Rating: 83 5/01 Kemp 1m gd-fm

Bred to stay. Has posted creditable efforts over a mile and ten furlongs without scoring, but should get off the mark before long. Acts on fast ground.

Winning Pleasure (IRE)

103 (67)**72d**

3-y-o b g Ashkalani (IRE)-Karamana (Habitat)
A P Jarvis Mrs Barbara Ann Headon

Placings:000-53040205 **(4891)**
2001: 7^{5}GF, 8^{3}F, 6^{0}G, 7^{4}GF, 8^{0}GF, 6^{2}G, 7^{0}S, 8^{5}GF, 6^{1}SD

	Starts	1st	2nd	3rd	Win & Pl
Career Total (Turf)	11	0	1	1	2315

Going (Turf): Sf: 0-3 GS: 0-0 Gd: 0-3 GF: 0-4 Fm: 0-1
Distance: 5f/6f: 0-1 7f-8f: 0-10 9f-13f: 0-0 14f+: 0-0
Track : LH: 0-4 RH: 0-3 Tight: 0-2 Gall: 0-2
Aids: Bl: 0-1 Vi: 0-2 Tstrap: 0-0
Best Rating: 73 7/01 Newc 1m firm

He had three outings at two and has shown some ability in his starts this season. Probably needs at least a mile.

Winning Venture

111 **98**

4-y-o b c Owington-Push A Button (Bold Lad (IRE))
S P C Woods Seiichi Wada

Placings:231323/302300005-025220003310 **(5133)**
2001: 7^{0}S, 7^{2}S, 7^{5}GF, 7^{2}G, 7^{2}GF, 7^{0}G, 7^{0}G, 7^{0}G, 8^{3}G, 7^{3}G, 8^{1}GS, 7^{0}G

	Starts	1st	2nd	3rd	Win & Pl
Career Total (Turf)	27	2	6	7	73017

98 9/01 Gdwd 1m B(0-95) G-S £9355
79 8/99 Kemp 7f C SFT £5382

Total win prize-money £14738

Going (Turf): Sf: 1-5 GS: 1-5 Gd: 0-9 GF: 0-7 Fm: 0-1
Distance: 5f/6f: 0-6 **7f-8f: 2-21** 9f-13f: 0-0 14f+: 0-0
Track : LH: 0-4 **RH: 2-5** Tight: 0-2 **Gall: 1-1**
Aids: Bl: 0-1 Vi: 0-0 **Tstrap: 1-9**
Best Rating: 103 5/01 Hayd 7f30y soft

Out of his depth in Pattern company, he is too high in the handicap and winning opportunities are difficult to find, but he did find one in a four-runner classified event at Goodwood in September, his first win in over two years. He enjoys soft ground but also acts on faster. Usually held up and has a useful turn of foot.

Winsome Dolphin (IRE)

(85) (29)

4-y-o b g Dolphin Street (FR)-Wonder Bird (GER) (Days At Sea (USA))
P Howling Kentavr (uk) Ltd

Placings:060 **(1011)**
2001: 12^{0}SW, 9^{6}SD, 11^{0}SD

	Starts	1st	2nd	3rd	Win & Pl
Career Total (Turf)	0	0	0	0	
Career Total (AW)	3	0	0	0	0

Going (Turf): Sf: 0-0 GS: 0-0 Gd: 0-0 GF: 0-0 Fm: 0-0
Distance: 5f/6f: 0-0 7f-8f: 0-0 9f-13f: 0-3 14f+: 0-0
Track : LH: 0-3 RH: 0-0 Tight: 0-1 Gall: 0-0
Aids: Bl: 0-0 Vi: 0-0 Tstrap: 0-0
Best Rating: 29 2/01 Wolv 1m1f79y stand

Winter Dolphin (IRE)

90(95) (31)**51d**

3-y-o b f Dolphin Street (FR)-Winter Tern (USA) (Arctic Tern (USA))
I A Wood Neardown Stables

Placings:066040251-00640000 **(2324)**
2001: 7^{0}SD, 7^{0}SW, 7^{6}SD, 8^{4}S, 8^{0}HY, 6^{0}G, 7^{0}SD, 9^{0}SD

	Starts	1st	2nd	3rd	Win & Pl
Career Total (Turf)	7	0	0	0	0
Career Total (AW)	10	1	1	0	2309

59 12/00 Wolv 7f G STD £1813

Total win prize-money £1813

Going (Turf): Sf: 0-3 GS: 0-0 Gd: 0-3 GF: 0-1 Fm: 0-0
Distance: 5f/6f: 0-6 **7f-8f: 1-8** 9f-13f: 0-3 14f+: 0-0
Track : **LH: 1-13** RH: 0-0 **Tight: 1-5** Gall: 0-1
Aids: Bl: 0-0 Vi: 0-0 **Tstrap: 1-4**
Best Rating: 39 4/01 Nott 1m54y soft

Winter Jasmine

99 **69**

3-y-o b f Robellino (USA)-Wild Truffes (IRE) (Danehill (USA))
B J Meehan Mrs Susan Roy

Placings:040-664405 **(2617)**
2001: 6^{6}G, 7^{6}S, 7^{4}GF, 8^{4}F, 8^{0}GF, 8^{5}GF

	Starts	1st	2nd	3rd	Win & Pl
Career Total (Turf)	9	0	0	0	1006

Going (Turf): Sf: 0-1 GS: 0-0 Gd: 0-3 GF: 0-4 Fm: 0-1
Distance: 5f/6f: 0-4 7f-8f: 0-4 9f-13f: 0-1 14f+: 0-0
Track : LH: 0-1 RH: 0-3 Tight: 0-0 Gall: 0-3
Aids: Bl: 0-0 Vi: 0-1 Tstrap: 0-0
Best Rating: 69 6/01 Nott 1m54y firm

Wintertide

(103) (70)

5-y-o b g Mtoto-Winter Queen (Welsh Pageant)
R A Fahey Mark A Leatham

Placings:25 **(1011)**
2001: 12^{2}SD, 11^{5}SD

	Starts	1st	2nd	3rd	Win & Pl
Career Total (Turf)	0	0	0	0	
Career Total (AW)	2	0	1	0	836

Going (Turf): Sf: 0-0 GS: 0-0 Gd: 0-0 GF: 0-0 Fm: 0-0
Distance: 5f/6f: 0-0 7f-8f: 0-0 9f-13f: 0-2 14f+: 0-0
Track : LH: 0-2 RH: 0-0 Tight: 0-1 Gall: 0-0
Aids: Bl: 0-0 Vi: 0-0 Tstrap: 0-0
Best Rating: 70 3/01 Wolv 1m4f stand

Winner of bumpers at Catterick and Musselburgh so far, he looks as though he is suited by a strongly-run race.

Wintzig

73(100) (51)**56**

4-y-o b f Piccolo-Wrangbrook (Shirley Heights)
J M Bradley Alan Purvis

Placings:4561/05250330440-000 **(4906)**
2001: 8^{0}SD, 9^{0}SW, 9^{0}G

	Starts	1st	2nd	3rd	Win & Pl
Career Total (Turf)	14	1	1	1	5749
Career Total (AW)	4	0	0	1	314

65 9/99 Pont 1m4y E(0-85)H GD £3262

Total win prize-money £3262

Going (Turf): Sf: 0-0 GS: 0-3 **Gd: 1-6** GF: 0-5 Fm: 0-0
Distance: 5f/6f: 0-0 7f-8f: 0-6 **9f-13f: 1-12** 14f+: 0-0
Track : **LH: 1-12** RH: 0-2 Tight: 0-6 Gall: 0-1
Aids: Bl: 0-0 Vi: 0-0 Tstrap: 0-0
Best Rating: 47 1/01 Sthl 1m stand

She looked a real stayer when winning over a mile at Pontefract on her final start at two but has become disappointing. Best suited by slow ground. Lightly-raced in 2001.

Wiseman's Ferry (USA)

101 **99**

2-y-o ch c Hennessy (USA)-Emmaus (USA) (Silver Deputy (CAN))

A P O'Brien Mrs John Magnier

Placings:136244 **(4698)**

2001: 6^{1}F, 5^{3}GY, 5^{6}GF, 6^{2}GY, 6^{4}Y, 7^{4}GS

	Starts	1st	2nd	3rd	Win & Pl
Career Total (Turf)	6	1	1	1	41435

98	5/01	Cork	6f	FRM		£13000

Total win prize-money £13000

Going (Turf): Sf: 0-0 GS: 0-1 Gd: 0-0 GF: 0-1 **Fm: 1-1**

Distance: **5f/6f: 1-4** 7f-8f: 0-2 9f-13f: 0-0 14f+: 0-0

Track : LH: 0-0 RH: 0-0 Tight: 0-0 Gall: 0-0

Aids: Bl: 0-0 Vi: 0-0 Tstrap: 0-0

Best Rating: 99 9/01 Donc 7f gd-sft

Made a winning debut at Cork in May over six furlongs after running loose before the start. Ran a highly-respectable race in the Windsor Castle at Royal Ascot and has been taking on some of the top juveniles in Group races since. Effective at five to seven furlongs and handles any ground.

Wish

101 **92**

2-y-o b f Danehill (USA)-Dazzle (Gone West (USA))

Sir Michael Stoute Cheveley Park Stud

Placings:2010 **(5498)**

2001: 5^{2}GF, 5^{0}GF, 6^{1}G, 6^{0}HY

	Starts	1st	2nd	3rd	Win & Pl
Career Total (Turf)	4	1	1	0	4992

92	10/01	Rdcr	6f	D	GD	£3920

Total win prize-money £3920

Going (Turf): Sf: 0-1 GS: 0-0 **Gd: 1-1** GF: 0-2 Fm: 0-0

Distance: **5f/6f: 1-4** 7f-8f: 0-0 9f-13f: 0-0 14f+: 0-0

Track : LH: 0-0 RH: 0-0 Tight: 0-0 Gall: 0-0

Aids: Bl: 0-0 Vi: 0-0 Tstrap: 0-0

Best Rating: 92 10/01 Rdcr 6f good

A daughter of a Cherry Hinton winner, she ran well on her debut but disappointed when second favourite for the Windsor Castle. Returned from nearly four months off to take a better than average Redcar maiden.

Wishbone Alley (IRE)

69(105) (51)**39**

6-y-o b g Common Grounds-Dul Dul (USA) (Shadeed (USA))

R Wilman (M Dods 10/4) Century Racing

Placings:630050/2302625103006 0/005022102000030 3 0022/2132042030000030500000-206000 **(3702)**

2001: 6^{2}SD, 6^{0}SD, 6^{6}SW, 5^{0}SD, 6^{0}HY, 5^{0}G

	Starts	1st	2nd	3rd	Win & Pl
Career Total (Turf)	48	2	6	6	17799
Career Total (AW)	20	1	6	2	8143

47	1/00	Ling	5f	E(0-75)H	STD	£3412
53	6/99	Newc	6f	E(0-75)H	GD	£5719
63	8/98	Thsk	5f	D(0-80)H	G-F	£4597

Total win prize-money £13730

Going (Turf): Sf: 0-7 GS: 0-5 **Gd: 1-13 GF: 1-16** Fm: 0-6

Distance: **5f/6f: 3-54** 7f-8f: 0-13 9f-13f: 0-0 14f+: 0-0

Track : **LH: 1-24** RH: 0-9 **Tight: 1-18** Gall: 0-6

Aids: Bl: 1-10 Vi: 1-26 Tstrap: 0-0

Best Rating: 51 1/01 Ling 6f stand

Wishedhadgone-home (IRE)

(93) (30)**33**

4-y-o b f Archway (IRE)-Yavarro (Raga Navarro (ITY))

M Quinn Paul Green (Huyton)

Placings:540000500263/056004400500-0 **(0059)**

2001: 9^{0}SW

	Starts	1st	2nd	3rd	Win & Pl
Career Total (Turf)	12	0	0	0	585
Career Total (AW)	13	0	1	1	859

Going (Turf): Sf: 0-3 GS: 0-0 Gd: 0-3 GF: 0-5 Fm: 0-1

Distance: 5f/6f: 0-6 7f-8f: 0-11 9f-13f: 0-7 14f+: 0-1

Track : LH: 0-18 RH: 0-3 Tight: 0-15 Gall: 0-1

Aids: Bl: 0-1 Vi: 0-9 Tstrap: 0-0

Best Rating: 51 1/01 Ling 6f stand

Wishful Thinker

(76) (21)**55**

4-y-o b g Prince Sabo-Estonia (King's Lake (USA))

N Tinkler Mrs Marie Tinkler

Placings:320000/000301204-0 **(0172)**

2001: 12^{0}SD

	Starts	1st	2nd	3rd	Win & Pl
Career Total (Turf)	15	1	2	2	4972
Career Total (AW)	1	0	0	0	

40	7/00	Rdcr	1m3f	G	G-F	£1904

Total win prize-money £1904

Going (Turf): Sf: 0-1 GS: 0-3 Gd: 0-4 **GF: 1-7** Fm: 0-0

Distance: 5f/6f: 0-2 7f-8f: 0-5 **9f-13f: 1-9** 14f+: 0-0

Track : **LH: 1-7** RH: 0-5 **Tight: 1-5** Gall: 0-3

Aids: Bl: 0-0 Vi: 0-0 Tstrap: 0-0

Best Rating: 21 1/01 Sthl 1m4f stand

Wishingwell Lady (IRE)

56 **11**

2-y-o b f Desert King (IRE)-Friday Night (USA) (Trempolino (USA))

J S Wainwright Wishingwell Group

Placings:00 **(5401)**

2001: 8^{0}G, 8^{0}S

	Starts	1st	2nd	3rd	Win & Pl
Career Total (Turf)	2	0	0	0	

Going (Turf): Sf: 0-1 GS: 0-0 Gd: 0-1 GF: 0-0 Fm: 0-0

Distance: 5f/6f: 0-0 7f-8f: 0-1 9f-13f: 0-1 14f+: 0-0

Track : LH: 0-1 RH: 0-1 Tight: 0-0 Gall: 0-0

Aids: Bl: 0-0 Vi: 0-0 Tstrap: 0-0

Best Rating: 11 9/01 Kemp 1m good

With A Will

104 **65**

7-y-o b g Rambo Dancer (CAN)-Henceforth (Full Of Hope)

H Candy Henry Candy

Placings:405/0341000/0361140/046040/3314110-00043600 **(5465)**

2001: 8^{0}G, 9^{0}F, 8^{0}G, 8^{4}GF, 9^{3}G, 10^{6}GF, 10^{0}G, 10^{0}G

	Starts	1st	2nd	3rd	Win & Pl
Career Total (Turf)	38	6	0	5	22463

68	8/00	Sals	1m	E(0-70)H	G-F	£3224
62	8/00	Wind	1m67y	E(0-70)H	G-F	£3066
61	7/00	Wind	1m2f7y	E(0-65)	GD	£2912
62	6/98	Ling	1m1f	F(0-60)H	GD	£2973
59	5/98	Kemp	1m1f	E(0-80)H	GD	£3139
66	7/97	Chep	1m14y	D(0-80)H	G-F	£3852

Total win prize-money £19166

Going (Turf): Sf: 0-6 GS: 0-5 **Gd: 3-15 GF: 3-10** Fm: 0-2

Distance: 5f/6f: 0-2 7f-8f: 1-8 **9f-13f: 5-28** 14f+: 0-0

Track : LH: 1-11 **RH: 2-10 Tight: 3-14** Gall: 0-0

Aids: Bl: 0-0 Vi: 0-0 Tstrap: 0-0

Best Rating: 65 7/01 Kemp 1m1f good

With Panache

97 **35**

3-y-o b g Mtoto-Panache Arabelle (Nashwan (USA))

P Monteith (J Noseda 10/6) P Monteith

Placings:020000 **(5637)**

2001: 12^{0}GS, 10^{2}F, 9^{0}GF, 8^{0}G, 10^{0}HY, 11^{0}G

	Starts	1st	2nd	3rd	Win & Pl
Career Total (Turf)	6	0	1	0	876

Going (Turf): Sf: 0-1 GS: 0-1 Gd: 0-2 GF: 0-1 Fm: 0-1

Distance: 5f/6f: 0-0 7f-8f: 0-1 9f-13f: 0-5 14f+: 0-0

Track : LH: 0-3 RH: 0-2 Tight: 0-4 Gall: 0-0

Aids: Bl: 0-0 Vi: 0-0 Tstrap: 0-0

Best Rating: 35 6/01 Ripn 1m1f gd-fm

Without Words

99(88) (43)**40**

3-y-o ch f Lion Cavern (USA)-Sans Escale (USA) (Diesis)

M A Jarvis Mohammed Bin Hendi

Placings:544243300 **(5461)**

2001: 8^{5}S, 10^{4}S, 8^{4}G, 7^{2}GF, 7^{4}G, 6^{3}G, 8^{3}F, 7^{0}SD, 8^{0}G

	Starts	1st	2nd	3rd	Win & Pl
Career Total (Turf)	8	0	1	2	2980
Career Total (AW)	1	0	0	0	

Going (Turf): Sf: 0-2 GS: 0-0 Gd: 0-4 GF: 0-1 Fm: 0-1

Distance: 5f/6f: 0-0 7f-8f: 0-6 9f-13f: 0-3 14f+: 0-0

Track : LH: 0-5 RH: 0-3 Tight: 0-4 Gall: 0-1

Aids: Bl: 0-2 Vi: 0-0 Tstrap: 0-0

Best Rating: 75 4/01 NmkR 1m soft

Has had a number of chances in maidens at between seven and ten furlongs, including in blinkers. Appears best over an easy mile.

Witness

97 **66**

2-y-o b f Efisio-Actualite (Polish Precedent (USA))

B W Hills Mrs Belinda Harvey

Placings:603500 **(4894)**

2001: 6^{6}G, 6^{0}GF, 6^{3}GS, 5^{5}G, 6^{0}GF, 5^{0}GS

	Starts	1st	2nd	3rd	Win & Pl
Career Total (Turf)	6	0	0	1	578

Going (Turf): Sf: 0-0 GS: 0-2 Gd: 0-2 GF: 0-2 Fm: 0-0

Distance: 5f/6f: 0-6 7f-8f: 0-0 9f-13f: 0-0 14f+: 0-0

Track : LH: 0-0 RH: 0-0 Tight: 0-0 Gall: 0-0

Aids: Bl: 0-0 Vi: 0-0 Tstrap: 0-0

Best Rating: 78 7/01 NmkJ 6f good

Modest form in maiden company. Looks best suited by soft ground.

Witney Royale (IRE)

102 **63**

3-y-o ch g Royal Abjar (USA)-Collected (IRE) (Taufan (USA))

J S Moore Ernie Houghton

Placings:1400-0544560061220 **(5039)**

2001: 7^{0}G, 7^{5}G, 8^{4}GF, 8^{4}G, 10^{5}GF, 8^{6}GF, 8^{0}GY, 8^{0}GF, 9^{6}GF, 9^{1}GF, 10^{2}G, 15^{2}G, 17^{0}G

	Starts	1st	2nd	3rd	Win & Pl
Career Total (Turf)	17	2	2	0	10033

46	8/01	Brig	1m1f209yF		G-F	£2254
63	6/00	Donc	6f	E	G-F	£3136

Total win prize-money £5390

Going (Turf): Sf: 0-0 GS: 0-0 Gd: 0-7 **GF: 2-8** Fm: 0-0

Distance: 5f/6f: 1-2 7f-8f: 0-6 9f-13f: 1-7 14f+: 0-2

Track : **LH: 1-7** RH: 0-1 Tight: 0-2 Gall: 0-0

Aids: Bl: 0-1 Vi: 0-0 Tstrap: 0-0

Best Rating: 77 6/01 Newb 1m gd-fm

Won on juvenile debut at Doncaster over six furlongs, but faced some stiff tasks afterwards and needed a drop into selling grade to win again at Brighton in August. Suited by ten furlongs and acts on a sound surface.

Wittabourgh Blue(IRE)

(39)
2-y-o ch f Bluegrass Prince (IRE)-Sea Idol (IRE) (Astronef)
J S Moore Derek E Theobald

Placings:60 **(1474)**
2001: 5^{6}GF, 6^{0}SD

	Starts	1st	2nd	3rd	Win & Pl
Career Total (Turf)	1	0	0	0	0
Career Total (AW)	1	0	0	0	

Going (Turf): Sf: 0-0 GS: 0-0 Gd: 0-0 GF: 0-1 Fm: 0-0
Distance: 5f/6f: 0-2 7f-8f: 0-0 9f-13f: 0-0 14f+: 0-0
Track : LH: 0-2 RH: 0-0 Tight: 0-0 Gall: 0-0
Aids: Bl: 0-0 Vi: 0-0 Tstrap: 0-0

Grand daughter of a smart French juvenile sprinter, showed little promise on debut.

Wodhill Florin

90 **47**
3-y-o ch f Dancing Spree (USA)-Muarij (Star Appeal)
H J Collingridge Miss S Graham

Placings:0000 **(5601)**
2001: 10^{0}GF, 8^{0}GF, 9^{0}G, 8^{0}GS

	Starts	1st	2nd	3rd	Win & Pl
Career Total (Turf)	4	0	0	0	

Going (Turf): Sf: 0-0 GS: 0-1 Gd: 0-1 GF: 0-2 Fm: 0-0
Distance: 5f/6f: 0-0 7f-8f: 0-2 9f-13f: 0-2 14f+: 0-0
Track : LH: 0-0 RH: 0-3 Tight: 0-1 Gall: 0-2
Aids: Bl: 0-0 Vi: 0-0 Tstrap: 0-0
Best Rating: 47 7/01 Kemp 1m2f gd-fm

Wodhill Folly

99(96) (43)**68**
4-y-o ch f Faustus (USA)-Muarij (Star Appeal)
H J Collingridge Miss S Graham

Placings:60-460 **(5599)**
2001: 8^{4}GF, 8^{6}GF, 12^{0}GS, 12^{5}SD

	Starts	1st	2nd	3rd	Win & Pl
Career Total (Turf)	5	0	0	0	371

Going (Turf): Sf: 0-1 GS: 0-1 Gd: 0-0 GF: 0-3 Fm: 0-0
Distance: 5f/6f: 0-0 7f-8f: 0-2 9f-13f: 0-3 14f+: 0-0
Track : LH: 0-2 RH: 0-1 Tight: 0-1 Gall: 0-1
Aids: Bl: 0-0 Vi: 0-0 Tstrap: 0-0
Best Rating: 68 8/01 NmkJ 1m gd-fm

Wolf Venture

103(106) (81)**83**
3-y-o ch g Wolfhound (USA)-Relatively Sharp (Sharpen Up)
S P C Woods Steve Lambert

Placings:43500-11011 **(2485)**
2001: 7^{1}SD, 8^{1}SD, 7^{0}GF, 8^{1}G, 8^{1}HD

	Starts	1st	2nd	3rd	Win & Pl
Career Total (Turf)	7	2	0	1	11320
Career Total (AW)	3	2	0	0	7463

83	6/01	Bath	1m5y	D(0-85)H	HRD	£3835
79	6/01	Bath	1m5y	C(0-90)H	GD	£6825
81	5/01	Ling	1m	D(0-80)H	STD	£4004
59	4/01	Ling	7f	D	STD	£3244

Total win prize-money £17909

Going (Turf): Sf: 0-2 GS: 0-0 **Gd: 1-2** GF: 0-2 **Fm: 1-1**
Distance: 5f/6f: 0-3 7f-8f: 2-5 9f-13f: 2-2 14f+: 0-0
Track : **LH: 4-8** RH: 0-1 **Tight: 4-5** Gall: 0-0
Aids: Bl: 0-0 Vi: 0-0 Tstrap: 0-0
Best Rating: 83 6/01 Bath 1m5y hard

Suited by seven furlongs to a mile on a sharp track, handles Equitrack and fastish ground on turf, likes to make the running. Now in Hong Kong.

Wonderful Man

97(98) (48)**46**
5-y-o ch g Magical Wonder (USA)-Gleeful (Sayf El Arab (USA))
R D E Woodhouse M K Oldham

Placings:500/460/600-0100500 **(2515)**
2001: 11^{0}SD, 8^{1}SW, 7^{0}SD, 9^{0}F, 8^{5}GF, 7^{0}GF, 7^{0}F

	Starts	1st	2nd	3rd	Win & Pl
Career Total (Turf)	13	0	0	0	205
Career Total (AW)	3	1	0	0	2373

48	4/01	Sthl	1m	F(0-65)H	SLW	£2373

Total win prize-money £2373

Going (Turf): Sf: 0-2 GS: 0-2 Gd: 0-1 GF: 0-6 Fm: 0-2
Distance: 5f/6f: 0-3 **7f-8f: 1-8** 9f-13f: 0-5 14f+: 0-0
Track : **LH: 1-7** RH: 0-4 Tight: 0-4 Gall: 0-1
Aids: Bl: 0-0 Vi: 0-0 Tstrap: 0-0
Best Rating: 48 4/01 Sthl 1m slow

Wondergreen

101 **56**
3-y-o ch g Wolfhound (USA)-Tenderetta (Tender King)
T D Easterby Health Mail Ltd

Placings:600310-020012 **(2240)**
2001: 7^{0}S, 7^{2}S, 8^{0}F, 7^{0}GF, 7^{1}GF, 7^{2}G

	Starts	1st	2nd	3rd	Win & Pl
Career Total (Turf)	12	2	2	1	7852

56	6/01	Bevl	7f100y	F	G-F	£2474
53	9/00	Bevl	7f100y	E	G-F	£3051

Total win prize-money £5527

Going (Turf): Sf: 0-3 GS: 0-0 Gd: 0-3 **GF: 2-5** Fm: 0-1
Distance: 5f/6f: 0-3 **7f-8f: 2-9** 9f-13f: 0-0 14f+: 0-0
Track : LH: 0-5 **RH: 2-2** Tight: 0-0 Gall: 0-3
Aids: Bl: 0-0 Vi: 0-0 Tstrap: 0-0
Best Rating: 56 6/01 Bevl 7f100y gd-fm

Wontcostalotbut

102 (40)**40**
7-y-o b m Nicholas Bill-Brave Maiden (Three Legs)
M J Wilkinson Wontcostalot Partnership

Placings:00050/0/134/200-60054 **(5531)**
2001: 14^{6}HY, 16^{0}GF, 15^{0}S, 17^{5}GS, 16^{4}HY

	Starts	1st	2nd	3rd	Win & Pl
Career Total (Turf)	16	1	1	1	6228
Career Total (AW)	1	0	0	0	0

57	4/99	Folk	1m7f92y	E(0-70)H	HVY	£3150

Total win prize-money £3150

Going (Turf): Sf: 1-6 GS: 0-4 Gd: 0-3 GF: 0-2 Fm: 0-1
Distance: 5f/6f: 0-0 7f-8f: 0-2 9f-13f: 0-3 **14f+: 1-12**
Track : LH: 0-9 **RH: 1-8 Tight: 1-6** Gall: 0-2
Aids: Bl: 0-0 Vi: 0-0 Tstrap: 0-0
Best Rating: 43 3/01 Nott 1m6f15y heavy

Wood Be King

53 **27**
2-y-o b c Prince Sabo-Sylvan Dancer (IRE) (Dancing Dissident (USA))
A P James Anne & Mahendra Ramkaran

Placings:00 **(3202)**
2001: 5^{0}GF, 5^{0}G

	Starts	1st	2nd	3rd	Win & Pl
Career Total (Turf)	2	0	0	0	

Going (Turf): Sf: 0-0 GS: 0-0 Gd: 0-1 GF: 0-1 Fm: 0-0
Distance: 5f/6f: 0-2 7f-8f: 0-0 9f-13f: 0-0 14f+: 0-0
Track : LH: 0-1 RH: 0-0 Tight: 0-0 Gall: 0-0
Aids: Bl: 0-0 Vi: 0-0 Tstrap: 0-0
Best Rating: 27 7/01 Chep 5f16y good

Unplaced in two starts so far.

Wood Colony (USA)

94 **79**
3-y-o b g Woodman (USA)-Promenade Colony (USA) (Pleasant Colony (USA))
J L Dunlop Littleton Manor Racing

Placings:5040 **(3802)**
2001: 8^{5}S, 8^{0}F, 10^{4}S, 10^{0}G

	Starts	1st	2nd	3rd	Win & Pl
Career Total (Turf)	4	0	0	0	329

Going (Turf): Sf: 0-2 GS: 0-0 Gd: 0-1 GF: 0-0 Fm: 0-1
Distance: 5f/6f: 0-0 7f-8f: 0-1 9f-13f: 0-3 14f+: 0-0
Track : LH: 0-3 RH: 0-0 Tight: 0-0 Gall: 0-0
Aids: Bl: 0-0 Vi: 0-0 Tstrap: 0-0
Best Rating: 79 5/01 Newb 1m soft

Wood Dalling (USA)

104 **88**
3-y-o b c Woodman (USA)-Cloelia (USA) (Lyphard (USA))
H R A Cecil Wafic Said

Placings:04212 **(2630)**
2001: 8^{0}S, 8^{4}G, 8^{2}GF, 9^{1}GF, 9^{2}GF

	Starts	1st	2nd	3rd	Win & Pl
Career Total (Turf)	5	1	2	0	10181

79	6/01	Ripn	1m1f	D	G-F	£4371

Total win prize-money £4371

Going (Turf): Sf: 0-1 GS: 0-0 Gd: 0-1 **GF: 1-3** Fm: 0-0
Distance: 5f/6f: 0-0 7f-8f: 0-3 **9f-13f: 1-2** 14f+: 0-0
Track : LH: 0-0 **RH: 1-3 Tight: 1-2** Gall: 0-0
Aids: Bl: 0-0 Vi: 0-0 Tstrap: 0-0
Best Rating: 88 7/01 Gdwd 1m1f192y gd-fm

He gradually improved and got off the mark in a Ripon maiden in June, but was comfortably beaten when tried in handicap company. Carries his head high.

Wood Street (IRE)

86 **66**
2-y-o b c Eagle Eyed (USA)-San-Catrinia (IRE) (Knesset (USA))
Mrs A J Bowlby Robert Moore,Kelvin Jones,Amanda Bowlby

Placings:00500 **(5496)**
2001: 7^{0}G, 8^{0}HY, 7^{5}G, 7^{0}HY, 7^{0}HY

	Starts	1st	2nd	3rd	Win & Pl
Career Total (Turf)	5	0	0	0	0

Going (Turf): Sf: 0-3 GS: 0-0 Gd: 0-2 GF: 0-0 Fm: 0-0
Distance: 5f/6f: 0-0 7f-8f: 0-4 9f-13f: 0-1 14f+: 0-0
Track : LH: 0-1 RH: 0-1 Tight: 0-0 Gall: 0-0
Aids: Bl: 0-0 Vi: 0-0 Tstrap: 0-0
Best Rating: 66 9/01 Hayd 1m30y heavy

Woodbastwick Charm

(83) (21)**39**
4-y-o b g Charmer-Miss Mint (Music Maestro)
N P Littmoden The Wayfarers

Placings:0/0000056-005 **(0201)**
2001: 11^{0}SD, 9^{0}SW, 7^{5}SW

	Starts	1st	2nd	3rd	Win & Pl
Career Total (Turf)	8	0	0	0	0
Career Total (AW)	3	0	0	0	0

Going (Turf): Sf: 0-0 GS: 0-1 Gd: 0-3 GF: 0-3 Fm: 0-1
Distance: 5f/6f: 0-0 7f-8f: 0-3 9f-13f: 0-8 14f+: 0-0
Track : LH: 0-5 RH: 0-2 Tight: 0-6 Gall: 0-1
Aids: Bl: 0-0 Vi: 0-0 Tstrap: 0-0
Best Rating: 21 1/01 Ling 7f slow

Woodboro Kat (IRE)

87 **61**

2-y-o b c Woodborough (USA)-Kitty Kildare (USA) (Seattle Dancer (USA))

M Blanshard J M Beever

Placings:6 (3367)

2001: 7^{6}GF

	Starts	1st	2nd	3rd	Win & Pl
Career Total (Turf)	1	0	0	0	0

Going (Turf): Sf: 0-0 GS: 0-0 Gd: 0-0 GF: 0-1 Fm: 0-0
Distance: 5f/6f: 0-0 7f-8f: 0-1 9f-13f: 0-0 14f+: 0-0
Track : LH: 0-0 RH: 0-0 Tight: 0-0 Gall: 0-0
Aids: Bl: 0-0 Vi: 0-0 Tstrap: 0-0
Best Rating: 61 7/01 Ling 7f gd-fm

Woodboro Minstrel (IRE)

80 **44**

2-y-o ch c Woodborough (USA)-Quilting (Mummy's Pet)

Mrs A Duffield Sugarcube Racing

Placings:0 (5660)

2001: 5^{0}G

	Starts	1st	2nd	3rd	Win & Pl
Career Total (Turf)	1	0	0	0	

Going (Turf): Sf: 0-0 GS: 0-0 Gd: 0-1 GF: 0-0 Fm: 0-0
Distance: 5f/6f: 0-1 7f-8f: 0-0 9f-13f: 0-0 14f+: 0-0
Track : LH: 0-0 RH: 0-0 Tight: 0-0 Gall: 0-0
Aids: Bl: 0-0 Vi: 0-0 Tstrap: 0-0
Best Rating: 44 11/01 Muss 5f good

Woodbury

98 **72**

2-y-o b f Woodborough (USA)-Jeewan (Touching Wood (USA))

M D I Usher (Mrs P N Dutfield 25/8) P Sweeting

Placings:6202614500 (5690)

2001: 5^{6}GS, 5^{2}G, 6^{0}GF, 5^{2}HD, 6^{6}GF, 5^{1}GF, 6^{4}GF, 6^{5}GF, 7^{0}GS, 7^{0}S

	Starts	1st	2nd	3rd	Win & Pl
Career Total (Turf)	10	1	2	0	4939

72 8/01 Wind 5f10y F G-F £2411
Total win prize-money £2412

Going (Turf): Sf: 0-1 GS: 0-2 Gd: 0-1 **GF: 1-5** Fm: 0-1
Distance: 5f/6f: 1-8 7f-8f: 0-2 9f-13f: 0-0 14f+: 0-0
Track : LH: 0-5 **RH: 1-1** Tight: 0-2 **Gall: 1-3**
Aids: Bl: 0-0 Vi: 0-0 Tstrap: 0-0
Best Rating: 72 8/01 Wind 5f10y gd-fm

She hung her chance away at Bath on her second start, but faced some stiff tasks afterwards and had to be dropped into a seller at Windsor to gain her first win. She is better than a plater, as her performance in a good quality handicap at Doncaster demonstrates, athough she has disappointed since.

Woodfield

101 **64**

3-y-o b g Zafonic (USA)-Top Society (High Top)

J W Hills Wyck Hall Stud

Placings:0300-006544204 (5461)

2001: 8^{0}G, 9^{0}S, 7^{6}GF, 7^{5}GS, 7^{4}GS, 7^{4}GF, 7^{2}GF, 8^{0}G, 8^{4}G

	Starts	1st	2nd	3rd	Win & Pl
Career Total (Turf)	13	0	1	1	2824

Going (Turf): Sf: 0-1 GS: 0-4 Gd: 0-3 GF: 0-5 Fm: 0-0
Distance: 5f/6f: 0-0 7f-8f: 0-11 9f-13f: 0-2 14f+: 0-0
Track : LH: 0-1 RH: 0-1 Tight: 0-1 Gall: 0-0
Aids: Bl: 0-0 Vi: 0-0 Tstrap: 0-0
Best Rating: 65 8/01 NmkJ 7f gd-sft

A half-brother to two juvenile seven-furlong winners, shaped with promise at two over that trip. Made a pleasing reappearance at three, stepping up to a mile. Has raced over further and shorter since and does not seem to be progressing.

Woodland Blaze (IRE)

88 **74**

2-y-o b c Woodborough (USA)-Alpine Sunset (Auction Ring (USA))

C G Cox The Woodborough Partnership

Placings:000 (5038)

2001: 5^{0}GF, 6^{0}GY, 5^{0}G

	Starts	1st	2nd	3rd	Win & Pl
Career Total (Turf)	3	0	0	0	

Going (Turf): Sf: 0-0 GS: 0-0 Gd: 0-1 GF: 0-1 Fm: 0-0
Distance: 5f/6f: 0-3 7f-8f: 0-0 9f-13f: 0-0 14f+: 0-0
Track : LH: 0-1 RH: 0-0 Tight: 0-0 Gall: 0-1
Aids: Bl: 0-0 Vi: 0-0 Tstrap: 0-0
Best Rating: 74 8/01 Curr 6f gd-yld

Woodland Park (USA)

78 **46**

3-y-o b c Woodman (USA)-Yemanja (USA) (Alleged (USA))

J Noseda Robert Levitt

Placings:00 (0887)

2001: 9^{0}GS, 10^{0}GS

	Starts	1st	2nd	3rd	Win & Pl
Career Total (Turf)	2	0	0	0	

Going (Turf): Sf: 0-0 GS: 0-2 Gd: 0-0 GF: 0-0 Fm: 0-0
Distance: 5f/6f: 0-0 7f-8f: 0-0 9f-13f: 0-2 14f+: 0-0
Track : LH: 0-1 RH: 0-0 Tight: 0-1 Gall: 0-0
Aids: Bl: 0-0 Vi: 0-0 Tstrap: 0-0
Best Rating: 46 4/01 Brig 1m1f209y gd-sft

Woodland Princess (IRE)

87 **61**

2-y-o br f Woodborough (USA)-Lagta (Kris)

J L Eyre Pinnacle Woodborough Partnership

Placings:006 (4775)

2001: 6^{0}G, 7^{0}GF, 7^{6}G

	Starts	1st	2nd	3rd	Win & Pl
Career Total (Turf)	3	0	0	0	0

Going (Turf): Sf: 0-0 GS: 0-0 Gd: 0-2 GF: 0-1 Fm: 0-0
Distance: 5f/6f: 0-1 7f-8f: 0-2 9f-13f: 0-0 14f+: 0-0
Track : LH: 0-1 RH: 0-2 Tight: 0-0 Gall: 0-0
Aids: Bl: 0-0 Vi: 0-0 Tstrap: 0-0
Best Rating: 61 9/01 Bevl 7f100y good

Woodland River (USA)

108 **83**

4-y-o ch g Irish River (FR)-Wiener Wald (USA) (Woodman (USA))

J R Fanshawe Car Colston Hall Stud

Placings:00210-0020400 (5470)

2001: 8^{0}GF, 8^{0}GF, 8^{2}GF, 7^{0}GF, 8^{4}GF, 7^{0}G, 7^{0}S

	Starts	1st	2nd	3rd	Win & Pl
Career Total (Turf)	12	1	2	0	6044

78 7/00 Wwck 7f164y D GD £2990
Total win prize-money £2990

Going (Turf): Sf: 0-1 GS: 0-2 **Gd: 1-4** GF: 0-5 Fm: 0-0
Distance: 5f/6f: 0-0 **7f-8f: 1-9** 9f-13f: 0-3 14f+: 0-0
Track : LH: 1-4 RH: 0-3 Tight: 0-2 Gall: 0-0
Aids: Bl: 0-0 Vi: 0-0 Tstrap: 0-4
Best Rating: 83 8/01 Wind 1m67y gd-fm

Unraced at two, he appreciated the faster ground when runner-up on his third start last season over a mile and went one better when dropped to seven furlongs at Warwick. Made a pleasing reappearance at Haydock in May, but has suffered breathing problems and was just touched off at Nottingham in August when fitted with a tongue tie, although that has not had the same effect since. Acts on a sound surface.

Woodland Spirit

95 **84**

2-y-o b c Charnwood Forest (IRE)-Fantastic Charm (USA) (Seattle Dancer (USA))

D R C Elsworth The Rockbourne Partnership

Placings:0020 (5491)

2001: 6^{0}G, 6^{0}GF, 6^{2}HY, 6^{0}HY

	Starts	1st	2nd	3rd	Win & Pl
Career Total (Turf)	4	0	1	0	1255

Going (Turf): Sf: 0-2 GS: 0-0 Gd: 0-1 GF: 0-1 Fm: 0-0
Distance: 5f/6f: 0-2 7f-8f: 0-2 9f-13f: 0-0 14f+: 0-0
Track : LH: 0-0 RH: 0-0 Tight: 0-0 Gall: 0-0
Aids: Bl: 0-0 Vi: 0-0 Tstrap: 0-0
Best Rating: 84 10/01 Wind 6f heavy

A half-brother to a seven-furlong winner in Hong Kong, posted his best effort when runner-up in a six-furlong heavy ground Windsor maiden.

Woodlands

105 **46**

4-y-o b g Common Grounds-Forest Of Arden (Tap On Wood)

S Dow Epsom's Dream Team

Placings:030/3000-000431000000 (5027)

2001: 6^{0}GF, 7^{0}GF, 6^{0}F, 5^{4}F, 6^{3}GF, 5^{1}G, 5^{0}GF, 5^{0}G, 6^{0}F, 5^{0}G, 5^{0}GF, 5^{0}S

	Starts	1st	2nd	3rd	Win & Pl
Career Total (Turf)	19	1	0	3	6015

55 7/01 Bath 5f161y D(0-80)H GD £3922
Total win prize-money £3923

Going (Turf): Sf: 0-2 GS: 0-0 **Gd: 1-4** GF: 0-10 Fm: 0-3
Distance: 5f/6f: 1-14 7f-8f: 0-5 9f-13f: 0-0 14f+: 0-0
Track : LH: 1-6 RH: 0-2 Tight: 0-1 **Gall: 1-3**
Aids: Bl: 0-0 Vi: 0-0 Tstrap: 0-0
Best Rating: 55 7/01 Bath 5f161y good

Woodlands Energy

73(81) **6**

10-y-o b m Risk Me (FR)-Hallowed (Wolver Hollow)

P A Pritchard Woodlands (worcestershire) Ltd

Placings:50000/000/0/0000 (2424)

2001: 14^{0}SW, 16^{0}SD, 16^{0}SD, 16^{0}GF

	Starts	1st	2nd	3rd	Win & Pl
Career Total (Turf)	10	0	0	0	
Career Total (AW)	3	0	0	0	

Going (Turf): Sf: 0-1 GS: 0-1 Gd: 0-2 GF: 0-5 Fm: 0-1
Distance: 5f/6f: 0-0 7f-8f: 0-1 9f-13f: 0-7 14f+: 0-5
Track : LH: 0-11 RH: 0-2 Tight: 0-6 Gall: 0-0
Aids: Bl: 0-0 Vi: 0-0 Tstrap: 0-0
Best Rating: 55 7/01 Bath 5f161y good

Woodlark

95 **72**

2-y-o b c Zilzal (USA)-Prima Volta (Primo Dominie)

I A Balding Exors Of The Late Robert Hitchins

Placings:05306 (4587)

2001: 5^{0}GF, 6^{5}GF, 7^{3}G, 6^{0}G, 7^{6}HY

	Starts	1st	2nd	3rd	Win & Pl
Career Total (Turf)	5	0	0	1	642

Going (Turf): Sf: 0-1 GS: 0-0 Gd: 0-2 GF: 0-2 Fm: 0-0
Distance: 5f/6f: 0-3 7f-8f: 0-2 9f-13f: 0-0 14f+: 0-0
Track : LH: 0-2 RH: 0-0 Tight: 0-1 Gall: 0-0

Aids: Bl: 0-0 Vi: 0-0 Tstrap: 0-4
Best Rating: 72 7/01 Epsm 7f good

Woodsmoke (IRE)

97 **85**

2-y-o b c Woodborough (USA)-Ma Bella Luna (Jalmood (USA))
R Hannon T J Dale

Placings:01105036300 **(5102)**
2001: 5^0GS, 5^1GF, 5^1G, 5^0GF, 5^5GF, 5^0GF, 5^3GF, 5^6G, 5^3GF, 5^0G, 5^0GS

	Starts	1st	2nd	3rd	Win & Pl
Career Total (Turf)	11	2	0	2	8087

82	5/01	Bath	5f11y	D	GD	£3376
58	5/01	Brig	5f59y	D	G-F	£3244

Total win prize-money £6622

Going (Turf): Sf: 0-0 GS: 0-2 **Gd: 1-3 GF: 1-6** Fm: 0-0
Distance: **5f/6f: 2-11** 7f-8f: 0-0 9f-13f: 0-0 14f+: 0-0
Track : **LH: 2-3** RH: 0-1 Tight: 0-0 **Gall: 1-3**
Aids: Bl: 0-0 Vi: 0-0 Tstrap: 0-0
Best Rating: 85 8/01 Bath 5f161y gd-fm

7,000Irgns third foal of a mile three-year-old winner, he left his debut running behind when taking an average Brighton maiden and followed up in a Bath conditions event, though he may have been a fortunate winner. Finished eighth to Johannesburg in Norfolk Stakes at Royal Ascoy and has struggled to win a race since. Suited by the minimum trip and acts on good and good to firm.

Woodwind Down

89(95) (54)**50**

4-y-o b f Piccolo-Bint El Oumara (Al Nasr (FR))
M Todhunter Domino Racing

Placings:00/200003250-20 **(2787)**
2001: 9^2GF, 10^0GF

	Starts	1st	2nd	3rd	Win & Pl
Career Total (Turf)	11	0	2	1	2335
Career Total (AW)	2	0	1	0	864

Going (Turf): Sf: 0-1 GS: 0-0 Gd: 0-3 GF: 0-6 Fm: 0-1
Distance: 5f/6f: 0-0 7f-8f: 0-6 9f-13f: 0-7 14f+: 0-0
Track : LH: 0-5 RH: 0-4 Tight: 0-4 Gall: 0-0
Aids: Bl: 0-1 Vi: 0-0 Tstrap: 0-0
Best Rating: 45 6/01 Haml 1m1f36y gd-fm

Woody Bathwick (IRE)

91 **72**

2-y-o ch c Woodborough (USA)-Sheznice (IRE) (Try My Best (USA))
E J O'Neill (Dr J R J Naylor 22/7) W Clifford

Placings:56305300020 **(5458)**
2001: 5^5GS, 5^6S, 5^3GF, 6^0GF, 5^5F, 5^3GF, 5^0GF, 7^0G, 6^0GS, 5^2GF, 5^0G

	Starts	1st	2nd	3rd	Win & Pl
Career Total (Turf)	11	0	1	2	2529

Going (Turf): Sf: 0-1 GS: 0-2 Gd: 0-2 GF: 0-5 Fm: 0-1
Distance: 5f/6f: 0-10 7f-8f: 0-1 9f-13f: 0-0 14f+: 0-0
Track : LH: 0-2 RH: 0-1 Tight: 0-0 Gall: 0-2
Aids: Bl: 0-0 Vi: 0-0 Tstrap: 0-0
Best Rating: 72 9/01 Muss 5f gd-fm

A half-brother to three winners. He has run well enough to suggest that there is a race to be won with him. Has run over five to seven furlongs on a number of different types of ground.

Woodyates

107 **66**

4-y-o b f Naheez (USA)-Night Mission (IRE) (Night Shift (USA))
D R C Elsworth D Watson

Placings:0605001-003112402230 **(5008)**
2001: 11^0GS, 11^0GS, 9^3GF, 12^1S, 13^1GF, 10^2GF, 12^4GF, 12^0GF, 10^2GS, 12^2S, 16^3G, 16^0S

	Starts	1st	2nd	3rd	Win & Pl
Career Total (Turf)	19	3	3	2	14807

60	5/01	Newb	1m5f61y	E(0-75)H	G-F	£3598
50	5/01	Sals	1m4f	D(0-80)H	SFT	£4582
46	10/00	Wind	1m2f7y	G	HVY	£1907

Total win prize-money £10089

Going (Turf): Sf: 2-5 GS: 0-3 Gd: 0-4 GF: 1-7 Fm: 0-0
Distance: 5f/6f: 0-0 7f-8f: 0-2 **9f-13f: 2-14** 14f+: 1-3
Track : LH: 1-9 RH: 1-7 **Tight: 2-7** Gall: 1-5
Aids: Bl: 0-0 Vi: 0-0 Tstrap: 0-1
Best Rating: 66 9/01 Kemp 2m good

Woolfe

101(84) (30)**43**

4-y-o ch f Wolfhound (USA)-Brosna (USA) (Irish River (FR))
D A Nolan (I Semple 16/10) Mrs J McFadyen-Murray

Placings:33204-550004202000 **(5657)**
2001: 7^5SW, 9^5GF, 10^0GF, 8^0GF, 8^0GF, 9^4GS, 10^2G, 8^0S, 8^2F, 9^0G, 9^0HY, 8^0G

	Starts	1st	2nd	3rd	Win & Pl
Career Total (Turf)	16	0	3	2	4219
Career Total (AW)	1	0	0	0	0

Going (Turf): Sf: 0-3 GS: 0-2 Gd: 0-4 GF: 0-6 Fm: 0-1
Distance: 5f/6f: 0-0 7f-8f: 0-4 9f-13f: 0-13 14f+: 0-0
Track : LH: 0-7 RH: 0-8 Tight: 0-6 Gall: 0-3
Aids: Bl: 0-0 Vi: 0-4 Tstrap: 0-0
Best Rating: 63 5/01 Haml 1m1f36y gd-fm

Plating-class filly. Runner-up twice at Newcastle in the late summer. Stays ten furlongs, seems to act on any ground, has worn a visor.

Words And Deeds (USA)

93 **66**

2-y-o ch g Shadeed (USA)-Millfit (USA) (Blushing Groom (FR))
Mrs J R Ramsden Jonathan Ramsden

Placings:020 **(3877)**
2001: 5^0GF, 5^2F, 5^0GS

	Starts	1st	2nd	3rd	Win & Pl
Career Total (Turf)	3	0	1	0	1354

Going (Turf): Sf: 0-0 GS: 0-1 Gd: 0-0 GF: 0-1 Fm: 0-1
Distance: 5f/6f: 0-3 7f-8f: 0-0 9f-13f: 0-0 14f+: 0-0
Track : LH: 0-0 RH: 0-0 Tight: 0-0 Gall: 0-0
Aids: Bl: 0-0 Vi: 0-0 Tstrap: 0-0
Best Rating: 66 8/01 Thsk 5f firm

Good second in a Thirsk maiden, but little other form.

World Spinner

88 **59**

2-y-o b c Indian Ridge-Howaida (IRE) (Night Shift (USA))
E A L Dunlop Saeed Suhail

Placings:0 **(2612)**
2001: 7^0GF

	Starts	1st	2nd	3rd	Win & Pl
Career Total (Turf)	1	0	0	0	

Going (Turf): Sf: 0-0 GS: 0-0 Gd: 0-0 GF: 0-1 Fm: 0-0
Distance: 5f/6f: 0-0 7f-8f: 0-1 9f-13f: 0-0 14f+: 0-0
Track : LH: 0-0 RH: 0-0 Tight: 0-0 Gall: 0-0
Aids: Bl: 0-0 Vi: 0-0 Tstrap: 0-0
Best Rating: 59 6/01 NmkJ 7f gd-fm

Worldly Treasure (USA)

85 **80**

4-y-o b/br g Ghazi (USA)-Kitten's First (USA) (Lear Fan (USA))
D K Weld Kenneth L Ramsey

Placings:22110-0000055 **(3900a)**
2001: 7^0S, 10^0GF, 8^0GY, 9^0GY, 8^0GF, 8^5G, 8^5GY

	Starts	1st	2nd	3rd	Win & Pl
Career Total (Turf)	12	2	2	0	16980

95	8/00	Gway	1m100y	GD	£9750
85	6/00	Rosc	1m2f	GD	£4830

Total win prize-money £14580

Going (Turf): Sf: 0-2 GS: 0-0 **Gd: 2-3** GF: 0-2 Fm: 0-0
Distance: 5f/6f: 0-0 7f-8f: 0-5 **9f-13f: 2-7** 14f+: 0-0
Track : LH: 0-3 **RH: 2-2** Tight: 0-0 Gall: 0-0
Aids: Bl: 0-2 Vi: 0-0 Tstrap: 0-0
Best Rating: 80 7/01 Leop 1m good

Worth A Gamble

95 **48**

3-y-o ch g So Factual (USA)-The Strid (IRE) (Persian Bold)
H E Haynes Miss Sally R Haynes

Placings:000-0403 **(5670)**
2001: 9^0G, 8^4G, 7^0S, 8^3HY

	Starts	1st	2nd	3rd	Win & Pl
Career Total (Turf)	7	0	0	1	446

Going (Turf): Sf: 0-4 GS: 0-0 Gd: 0-2 GF: 0-1 Fm: 0-0
Distance: 5f/6f: 0-1 7f-8f: 0-3 9f-13f: 0-3 14f+: 0-0
Track : LH: 0-1 RH: 0-2 Tight: 0-2 Gall: 0-0
Aids: Bl: 0-0 Vi: 0-0 Tstrap: 0-0
Best Rating: 48 11/01 Wind 1m67y heavy

Worth A Ring

90(83) (32)**27**

3-y-o b f Chaddleworth (IRE)-Ring Of Pearl (Auction Ring (USA))
J Cullinan Turf 2000 Limited

Placings:0500-500 **(2343)**
2001: 8^5SD, 9^0F, 12^0SD

	Starts	1st	2nd	3rd	Win & Pl
Career Total (Turf)	2	0	0	0	
Career Total (AW)	5	0	0	0	0

Going (Turf): Sf: 0-1 GS: 0-0 Gd: 0-0 GF: 0-0 Fm: 0-1
Distance: 5f/6f: 0-2 7f-8f: 0-3 9f-13f: 0-2 14f+: 0-0
Track : LH: 0-5 RH: 0-0 Tight: 0-1 Gall: 0-0
Aids: Bl: 0-0 Vi: 0-0 Tstrap: 0-0
Best Rating: 26 6/01 Nott 1m1f213y firm

Worth The Risk

94(82) (3)**14**

4-y-o b f Chaddleworth (IRE)-Bay Risk (Risk Me (FR))
Don Enrico Incisa Don Enrico Incisa

Placings:60500050/350020-00000 **(3966)**
2001: 12^0SD, 11^0SD, 12^0G, 11^0G, 16^0GS

	Starts	1st	2nd	3rd	Win & Pl
Career Total (Turf)	16	0	1	1	1076
Career Total (AW)	3	0	0	0	0

Going (Turf): Sf: 0-3 GS: 0-2 Gd: 0-4 GF: 0-4 Fm: 0-3
Distance: 5f/6f: 0-5 7f-8f: 0-2 9f-13f: 0-9 14f+: 0-3
Track : LH: 0-10 RH: 0-6 Tight: 0-5 Gall: 0-5
Aids: Bl: 0-0 Vi: 0-0 Tstrap: 0-0
Best Rating: 14 8/01 Catt 1m3f214y good

Worthily (USA)

105 **100**

3-y-o b/br c Northern Spur (IRE)-Worth's Girl (USA) (Devil's Bag (USA))
M R Channon Salem Suhail

Placings:051211-3450002560 **(5261)**

2001: 11^{3}HY, 10^{4}HY, 11^{5}G, 16^{0}GF, 14^{0}G, 10^{0}G, 11^{2}GF, 12^{5}G, 10^{6}G, 10^{0}GS

	Starts	1st	2nd	3rd	Win & Pl
Career Total (Turf)	16	3	2	1	47041

100	10/00	NmkR	1m2f	A	SFT	£12528
95	10/00	Pont	1m4y	A	HVY	£12528
99	9/00	Kemp	1m	D	SFT	£3656

Total win prize-money £28712

Going (Turf): Sf: 3-7 GS: 0-1 Gd: 0-5 GF: 0-3 Fm: 0-0
Distance: 5f/6f: 0-0 7f-8f: 1-3 **9f-13f: 2-11** 14f+: 0-2
Track : LH: 1-6 RH: 1-7 Tight: 0-1 **Gall: 1-8**
Aids: Bl: 0-0 Vi: 0-0 Tstrap: 0-0
Best Rating: 101 9/01 York 1m3f195y gd-fm

Winner of two Listed races in the autumn of his two-year-old year, he ran well in France on his reappearance but has been found wanting since and is not up to Group level. Better effort when dropped into handicap company at York in September. Stays 12 furlongs.

Wotan (IRE)

77 **44**

3-y-o ch g Wolfhound (USA)-Triple Tricks (IRE) (Royal Academy (USA))
R Curtis A J J Racing

Placings:5660 **(5532)**
2001: 8^{5}GF, 7^{6}S, 7^{6}HY, 9^{0}HY

	Starts	1st	2nd	3rd	Win & Pl
Career Total (Turf)	4	0	0	0	0

Going (Turf): Sf: 0-3 GS: 0-0 Gd: 0-0 GF: 0-1 Fm: 0-0
Distance: 5f/6f: 0-0 7f-8f: 0-2 9f-13f: 0-2 14f+: 0-0
Track : LH: 0-2 RH: 0-0 Tight: 0-0 Gall: 0-0
Aids: Bl: 0-0 Vi: 0-0 Tstrap: 0-0
Best Rating: 44 7/01 Wwck 1m22y gd-fm

Wrangel (FR)

(93) (42)**47**

7-y-o ch g Tropular-Swedish Princess (Manado)
B J Llewellyn Miss Emily Jane Jones

Placings:0016-30 **(0539)**
2001: 12^{3}SW, 16^{0}SD

	Starts	1st	2nd	3rd	Win & Pl
Career Total (Turf)	3	1	0	0	2384
Career Total (AW)	3	0	0	1	420

47	8/00	Catt	1m3f214yF	G-F	£2383

Total win prize-money £2384

Going (Turf): Sf: 0-0 GS: 0-1 Gd: 0-1 **GF: 1-1** Fm: 0-0
Distance: 5f/6f: 0-0 7f-8f: 0-0 **9f-13f: 1-4** 14f+: 0-2
Track : LH: 1-5 RH: 0-1 **Tight: 1-3** Gall: 0-0
Aids: Bl: 0-0 Vi: 0-0 Tstrap: 0-0
Best Rating: 32 2/01 Sthl 1m4f slow

Xaloc Bay (IRE)

92(96) (76?)**44**

3-y-o br g Charnwood Forest (IRE)-Royal Jade (Last Tycoon)
K R Burke Mrs Melba Bryce

Placings:2200032-30060502006 **(5490)**
2001: 6^{3}S, 6^{0}S, 7^{0}GF, 6^{6}G, 6^{0}S, 7^{5}GF, 6^{0}G, 6^{2}G, 6^{0}HY, 6^{0}HY, 7^{0}HY, 7^{1}SD

	Starts	1st	2nd	3rd	Win & Pl
Career Total (Turf)	16	0	3	1	3648
Career Total (AW)	2	0	1	1	1101

Going (Turf): Sf: 0-8 GS: 0-0 Gd: 0-5 GF: 0-3 Fm: 0-0
Distance: 5f/6f: 0-12 7f-8f: 0-6 9f-13f: 0-0 14f+: 0-0
Track : LH: 0-1 RH: 0-0 Tight: 0-1 Gall: 0-0
Aids: Bl: 0-1 Vi: 0-4 Tstrap: 0-0
Best Rating: 66 4/01 Ripn 6f soft

He has shown ability on turf and sand, but he lacks acceleration. He has been tried in blinkers and a visor. Six furlongs or a sharp seven suit him best.

Xanadu

95 **59**

5-y-o ch g Casteddu-Bellatrix (Persian Bold)
Miss L A Perratt David Sutherland-Ian Hay

Placings:05/50100103/0011201012436020-000005160505000 **(5288)**
2001: 6^{0}S, 5^{0}S, 5^{0}GS, 6^{0}G, 5^{0}GF, 5^{5}G, 6^{1}GF, 5^{6}G, 6^{0}F, 5^{5}GF, 5^{0}GF, 5^{5}GF, 6^{0}G, 5^{0}G, 6^{0}HY

	Starts	1st	2nd	3rd	Win & Pl
Career Total (Turf)	41	7	3	2	46126

64	6/01	Haml	6f5y	E(0-70)	G-F	£3770
75	7/00	Hayd	5f	E(0-70)H	G-F	£3122
68	6/00	Muss	5f	C(0-95)H	FRM	£15210
65	5/00	Haml	6f5y	F(0-60)	FRM	£2912
64	5/00	Haml	6f5y	C(0-90)H	G-F	£8931
54	8/99	Carl	5f207y	F(0-60)H	FRM	£2850
43	7/99	Haml	6f5y	E	FRM	£3273

Total win prize-money £40069

Going (Turf): Sf: 0-5 GS: 0-3 Gd: 0-10 GF: 3-17 **Fm: 4-6**
Distance: 5f/6f: 3-32 **7f-8f: 4-9** 9f-13f: 0-0 14f+: 0-0
Track : LH: 0-3 **RH: 1-2** Tight: 0-0 **Gall: 1-2**
Aids: Bl: 0-0 Vi: 0-0 Tstrap: 0-0
Best Rating: 64 6/01 Haml 6f5y gd-fm

A winner four times in the 2000 season, he is very much suited to fast ground and had his ideal conditions when returning to winning form in a Hamilton amateurs' event in June. He goes particularly well on that track and is equally effective over five and six furlongs.

Xcel (IRE)

83 **62**

2-y-o b c Revoque (IRE)-Myran (IRE) (In The Wings)
L M Cumani M J Dawson

Placings:000 **(5015)**
2001: 7^{0}G, 7^{0}G, 7^{0}HY

	Starts	1st	2nd	3rd	Win & Pl
Career Total (Turf)	3	0	0	0	

Going (Turf): Sf: 0-1 GS: 0-0 Gd: 0-2 GF: 0-0 Fm: 0-0
Distance: 5f/6f: 0-0 7f-8f: 0-3 9f-13f: 0-0 14f+: 0-0
Track : LH: 0-1 RH: 0-0 Tight: 0-0 Gall: 0-0
Aids: Bl: 0-2 Vi: 0-0 Tstrap: 0-0
Best Rating: 62 9/01 Chep 7f16y good

Xellance (IRE)

106(101) (78)**75**

4-y-o b g Be My Guest (USA)-Excellent Alibi (USA) (Exceller (USA))
M Johnston T T Bloodstocks

Placings:000/151U0111221412314-0310 **(5692)**
2001: 13^{0}GS, 16^{3}HY, 16^{1}G, 16^{0}S, 16^{2}SD

	Starts	1st	2nd	3rd	Win & Pl
Career Total (Turf)	20	6	3	2	40146
Career Total (AW)	4	3	0	0	6738

72	11/01	Muss	2m	C(0-90)H	GD	£17485
74	8/00	Wwck	2m39y	D(0-80)H	GD	£3818
67	7/00	Rdcr	2m4y	E(0-75)H	G-F	£4654
65	7/00	Chep	2m2f	E(0-70)H	G-F	£2795
50	6/00	Rdcr	1m6f19y	F(0-60)H	FRM	£2884
48	6/00	Sthl	1m4f	F(0-65)H	STD	£2254
48	6/00	Muss	1m6f	F(0-60)H	FRM	£2268
46	5/00	Wolv	1m4f	F(0-65)H	STD	£2233
37	2/00	Sthl	1m3f	F(0-60)H	STD	£2251

Total win prize-money £40643

Going (Turf): Sf: 0-3 GS: 0-3 **Gd: 2-3 GF: 2-5 Fm: 2-5**
Distance: 5f/6f: 0-2 7f-8f: 0-1 9f-13f: 3-6 **14f+: 6-14**
Track : LH: 7-16 RH: 2-6 **Tight: 5-13** Gall: 0-2
Aids: Bl: 0-0 Vi: 0-0 Tstrap: 0-0
Best Rating: 73 10/01 Newb 2m heavy

Scored eight times in 2000 when he held his form very well, but was off the track for a year before reappearing at York in October. Fine effort at Newbury next time on ground that would have been much softer than ideal before winning at Musselburgh. Stays further than two miles and acts well on Fibresand and a sound surface on turf.

Xibalba

94 **48**

4-y-o b g Zafonic (USA)-Satanic Dance (FR) (Shareef Dancer (USA))
C E Brittain R Meredith

Placings:000/1400U-60500 **(5092)**
2001: 9^{6}GF, 10^{0}GF, 11^{5}GF, 9^{0}GF, 8^{0}GS

	Starts	1st	2nd	3rd	Win & Pl
Career Total (Turf)	13	1	0	0	2533

70	5/00	Nott	1m54y	G(0-70)H	GD	£2177

Total win prize-money £2177

Going (Turf): Sf: 0-1 GS: 0-2 **Gd: 1-4** GF: 0-6 Fm: 0-0
Distance: 5f/6f: 0-0 7f-8f: 0-2 **9f-13f: 1-11** 14f+: 0-0
Track : LH: 1-3 RH: 0-7 Tight: 0-2 Gall: 0-2
Aids: Bl: 0-0 Vi: 0-1 Tstrap: 0-0
Best Rating: 61 6/01 Bevl 1m1f207y gd-fm

Xipe Totec

103 **65**

3-y-o ch g Pivotal-Northern Bird (Interrex (CAN))
C E Brittain (R A Fahey 12/5) Mrs Brigitte Pollard

Placings:0136-0066030001 **(5292)**
2001: 6^{0}S, 6^{0}G, 8^{6}F, 8^{6}G, 8^{0}GF, 7^{3}G, 7^{0}G, 7^{0}G, 7^{0}S, 7^{1}S

	Starts	1st	2nd	3rd	Win & Pl
Career Total (Turf)	14	2	0	2	6829

63	10/01	Leic	7f9y	G(0-60)H	SFT	£2065
67	7/00	Hayd	6f	D	G-F	£3753

Total win prize-money £5819

Going (Turf): Sf: 1-3 GS: 0-0 Gd: 0-6 **GF: 1-3** Fm: 0-2
Distance: 5f/6f: 1-6 7f-8f: 1-6 9f-13f: 0-2 14f+: 0-0
Track : LH: 0-4 RH: 0-1 Tight: 0-0 Gall: 0-0
Aids: Bl: 0-0 Vi: 0-0 Tstrap: 0-0
Best Rating: 72 6/01 Nott 1m54y firm

Made most to score his first victory on fast ground over six furlongs at Haydock last summer, but did not show anything afterwards until landing a soft-ground seller at Leicester in October.

Xsynna

103(106) (60)**55**

5-y-o b g Cyrano De Bergerac-Rose Ciel (IRE) (Red Sunset)
M J Polglase (J A Gilbert 29/6) Mike Bromley

Placings:0020350001/3004354/260000-000000001500020060420 **(5449)**
2001: 6^{0}SD, 6^{0}SD, 5^{0}S, 6^{0}G, 5^{0}G, 5^{0}G, 5^{0}F, 6^{0}GF, 5^{0}G, 6^{1}SD, 6^{5}SD, 5^{0}G, 5^{0}GS, 8^{0}GF, 6^{2}G, 7^{0}GF, 6^{6}GF, 6^{0}SD, 7^{4}G, 5^{2}S, 6^{0}HY, 6^{0}SD

	Starts	1st	2nd	3rd	Win & Pl
Career Total (Turf)	30	0	3	2	4463
Career Total (AW)	14	2	1	1	6408

60	6/01	Sthl	6f	F(0-65)H	STD	£2450
64	12/98	Ling	6f	E H	STD	£2872

Total win prize-money £5322

Going (Turf): Sf: 0-6 GS: 0-2 Gd: 0-9 GF: 0-11 Fm: 0-2
Distance: 5f/6f: 2-35 7f-8f: 0-9 9f-13f: 0-0 14f+: 0-0
Track : LH: 2-21 RH: 0-4 **Tight: 1-10** Gall: 0-7
Aids: Bl: 0-7 Vi: 0-1 Tstrap: 0-0
Best Rating: 63 5/01 Bath 5f11y good

He was winning his first race since December 1998 when successful on the All-Weather at Southwell in June. Effective at five and six furlongs, yet to show he stays further. Has only won on sand, but has run some good races on turf.

Xtra

108 **111**

3-y-o b c Sadler's Wells (USA)-Oriental Mystique (Kris)
L M Cumani M J Dawson

Placings:03-4215 **(4114)**

2001: 11^{4}G, 12^{2}GF, 11^{1}S, 11^{5}G

	Starts	1st	2nd	3rd	Win & Pl
Career Total (Turf)	6	1	1	1	26671

102 7/01 Hayd 1m3f200yA SFT £17355
Total win prize-money £17355

Going (Turf): Sf: 1-3 GS: 0-0 Gd: 0-2 GF: 0-1 Fm: 0-0
Distance: 5f/6f: 0-0 7f-8f: 0-2 **9f-13f: 1-4** 14f+: 0-0
Track : **LH: 1-3** RH: 0-1 Tight: 0-1 Gall: 0-2
Aids: Bl: 0-0 Vi: 0-0 Tstrap: 0-0
Best Rating: 111 8/01 York 1m3f195y good

Fourth to Perfect Sunday in the Derby Trial at Lingfield in May and was beaten four lengths by the smart looking Year Two Thousand over 12 furlongs at Newmarket in June. Suited by the softer ground when getting off the mark in a Haydock Listed event in July and was not beaten far by eventual St Leger winner Milan at York. Should stay in excess of a mile and a half. Acts on soft ground but handles fast.

Xtrasensory

103 **85**
2-y-o b f Royal Applause-Song Of Hope (Chief Singer)
R Hannon The Waney Racing Group Inc

Placings:105 **(4191)**
2001: 6^{1}GF, 6^{0}GF, 6^{5}G

	Starts	1st	2nd	3rd	Win & Pl
Career Total (Turf)	3	1	0	0	6639

85 5/01 Gdwd 6f G-F £4514
Total win prize-money £4514

Going (Turf): Sf: 0-0 GS: 0-0 Gd: 0-1 **GF: 1-2** Fm: 0-0
Distance: **5f/6f: 1-3** 7f-8f: 0-0 9f-13f: 0-0 14f+: 0-0
Track : LH: 0-0 RH: 0-0 Tight: 0-0 Gall: 0-0
Aids: Bl: 0-0 Vi: 0-0 Tstrap: 0-0
Best Rating: 85 5/01 Gdwd 6f gd-fm

A May foal and a filly with potential, her dam won over five furlongs at two and she is a half-sister to several winners. She was always going like a winner herself when scoring over six furlongs on her debut at Goodwood. Reportedly pulled muscles in her back since then and probably needed her next run when well beaten in the Princess Margaret. Has won on good to firm.

Y To Kman (IRE)

104 **97d**
3-y-o b c Mujadil (USA)-Hazar (IRE) (Thatching)
R Hannon The Cayman 'A' Team

Placings:124061-30000 **(4590)**
2001: 6^{3}G, 6^{0}GF, 6^{0}GF, 6^{0}G, 6^{0}G

	Starts	1st	2nd	3rd	Win & Pl
Career Total (Turf)	11	2	1	1	14966

97 10/00 Yarm 5f43y D(0-85) SFT £3510
74 3/00 Kemp 5f D GD £4173
Total win prize-money £7683

Going (Turf): Sf: 1-3 GS: 0-0 **Gd: 1-6** GF: 0-2 Fm: 0-0
Distance: **5f/6f: 2-11** 7f-8f: 0-0 9f-13f: 0-0 14f+: 0-0
Track : LH: 0-1 RH: 0-0 Tight: 0-1 Gall: 0-0
Aids: Bl: 0-0 Vi: 0-0 Tstrap: 0-0
Best Rating: 97 5/01 Ling 6f good

He was an able sort over five furlongs. (DEAD)

Ya Habibi

99 **60**
3-y-o b c Selkirk (USA)-Rani (IRE) (Groom Dancer (USA))
T D Easterby (L M Cumani 19/5) G Shiel

Placings:004 **(5631)**
2001: 10^{0}GS, 10^{0}S, 10^{4}G

	Starts	1st	2nd	3rd	Win & Pl
Career Total (Turf)	3	0	0	0	0

Going (Turf): Sf: 0-1 GS: 0-1 Gd: 0-1 GF: 0-0 Fm: 0-0
Distance: 5f/6f: 0-0 7f-8f: 0-0 9f-13f: 0-3 14f+: 0-0
Track : LH: 0-3 RH: 0-0 Tight: 0-1 Gall: 0-1
Aids: Bl: 0-0 Vi: 0-0 Tstrap: 0-0
Best Rating: 60 5/01 Newb 1m2f6y soft

Showed little for Luca Cumani, but improved on his debut for Tim Easterby.

Ya Hajar

96 **97+**
2-y-o b f Lycius (USA)-Shy Lady (FR) (Kaldoun (FR))
M R Channon Jaber Abdullah

Placings:3116 **(5245a)**
2001: 6^{3}G, 6^{1}GF, 7^{1}GS, 8^{6}HO

	Starts	1st	2nd	3rd	Win & Pl
Career Total (Turf)	4	2	0	1	30251

97 8/01 Deau 7f G-S £21339
86 7/01 Asct 6f D G-F £8053
Total win prize-money £29393

Going (Turf): Sf: 0-0 **GS: 1-1** Gd: 0-1 **GF: 1-1** Fm: 0-0
Distance: 5f/6f: 1-2 7f-8f: 1-2 9f-13f: 0-0 14f+: 0-0
Track : LH: 0-0 RH: 0-1 Tight: 0-0 Gall: 0-0
Aids: Bl: 0-0 Vi: 0-0 Tstrap: 0-0
Best Rating: 97 8/01 Deau 7f gd-sft

Speedily-bred, she showed promise on her debut at the Newmarket July meeting and followed up in an Ascot maiden. She took a Group Three on easy ground at deauville, but was reported to have disliked the holding ground in the Marcel Boussac. Stays seven furlongs and should get a little further.

Yabint El Sham

(106) (56)**43**
5-y-o b m Sizzling Melody-Dalby Dancer (Bustiki)
B A McMahon G S D Imports Ltd

Placings:5106/00000001/52300000000000050206-11005 **(0534)**
2001: 6^{1}SW, 6^{1}SW, 5^{0}SD, 5^{0}SW, 6^{5}SD

	Starts	1st	2nd	3rd	Win & Pl
Career Total (Turf)	14	1	0	0	3496
Career Total (AW)	21	3	2	1	10353

56 1/01 Sthl 6f G SLW £1337
49 1/01 Wolv 6f F(0-60)H SLW £1736
63 12/99 Wolv 5f D(0-85)H STD £4045
85 8/98 Leic 5f2y D G-F £3496
Total win prize-money £10615

Going (Turf): Sf: 0-1 GS: 0-1 Gd: 0-4 **GF: 1-7** Fm: 0-1
Distance: **5f/6f: 4-28** 7f-8f: 0-5 9f-13f: 0-2 14f+: 0-0
Track : **LH: 3-22** RH: 0-1 **Tight: 2-18** Gall: 0-2
Aids: Bl: 0-0 Vi: 0-0 Tstrap: 0-7
Best Rating: 56 1/01 Sthl 6f slow

Yaheska (IRE)

90(89) (14)**28**
4-y-o b f Prince Of Birds (USA)-How Ya Been (IRE) (Last Tycoon)
J M Bradley N Savage

Placings:000/5000-00000 **(4292)**
2001: 12^{0}SD, 8^{0}SD, 11^{0}G, 7^{0}F, 10^{0}GF

	Starts	1st	2nd	3rd	Win & Pl
Career Total (Turf)	7	0	0	0	
Career Total (AW)	5	0	0	0	0

Going (Turf): Sf: 0-0 GS: 0-0 Gd: 0-2 GF: 0-3 Fm: 0-2
Distance: 5f/6f: 0-2 7f-8f: 0-4 9f-13f: 0-6 14f+: 0-0
Track : LH: 0-10 RH: 0-0 Tight: 0-4 Gall: 0-1
Aids: Bl: 0-2 Vi: 0-0 Tstrap: 0-0
Best Rating: 28 8/01 Chep 1m2f36y gd-fm

Yalail (IRE)

88(86) **23**
5-y-o b g Perugino (USA)-Cristalga (High Top)
Miss V Haigh (G Prodromou 8/6) Miss V Haigh

Placings:4060000/040-00500000 **(4552)**
2001: 12^{0}SD, 10^{0}SW, 11^{5}GS, 11^{0}F, 14^{0}SD, 11^{0}G, 11^{0}G, 14^{0}SW

	Starts	1st	2nd	3rd	Win & Pl
Career Total (Turf)	9	0	0	0	0
Career Total (AW)	9	0	0	0	0

Going (Turf): Sf: 0-0 GS: 0-1 Gd: 0-4 GF: 0-3 Fm: 0-1
Distance: 5f/6f: 0-1 7f-8f: 0-1 9f-13f: 0-13 14f+: 0-3
Track : LH: 0-16 RH: 0-0 Tight: 0-11 Gall: 0-0
Aids: Bl: 0-0 Vi: 0-1 Tstrap: 0-2
Best Rating: 24 5/01 Brig 1m3f196y gd-sft

Yalla Lara

82 **38**
2-y-o b f Marju (IRE)-Versami (USA) (Riverman (USA))
I A Balding Dubai Thoroughbred Racing

Placings:0 **(1148)**
2001: 5^{0}GS

	Starts	1st	2nd	3rd	Win & Pl
Career Total (Turf)	1	0	0	0	

Going (Turf): Sf: 0-0 GS: 0-1 Gd: 0-0 GF: 0-0 Fm: 0-0
Distance: 5f/6f: 0-1 7f-8f: 0-0 9f-13f: 0-0 14f+: 0-0
Track : LH: 0-0 RH: 0-0 Tight: 0-0 Gall: 0-0
Aids: Bl: 0-0 Vi: 0-0 Tstrap: 0-0
Best Rating: 38 5/01 Sals 5f gd-sft

Yanus

106 **42**
3-y-o b g Inchinor-Birsay (Bustino)
J S Goldie Mrs Janis Macpherson

Placings:000-20311000030 **(5400)**
2001: 10^{2}GF, 8^{0}GF, 14^{3}GF, 10^{1}GS, 10^{1}GS, 11^{0}GS, 10^{0}G, 11^{0}HY, 10^{0}G, 10^{3}HY, 10^{0}S

	Starts	1st	2nd	3rd	Win & Pl
Career Total (Turf)	14	2	1	2	9402

68 8/01 Ayr 1m2f192yE(0-70)H G-S £3307
55 7/01 Ayr 1m2f E(0-75)H G-S £4043
Total win prize-money £7351

Going (Turf): Sf: 0-4 **GS: 2-3** Gd: 0-3 GF: 0-4 Fm: 0-0
Distance: 5f/6f: 0-1 7f-8f: 0-2 **9f-13f: 2-10** 14f+: 0-1
Track : **LH: 2-10** RH: 0-1 Tight: 0-1 Gall: 0-1
Aids: Bl: 0-0 Vi: 0-0 Tstrap: 0-0
Best Rating: 68 8/01 Ayr 1m2f192y gd-sft

Showed a big improvement when stepped up in trip on his three-year-old reappearance. Likes to dominate, has two wins under his belt this term on an easy surface at around ten furlongs.

Yaounde (IRE)

96 **79**
2-y-o gr f Barathea (IRE)-Lost Dream (Niniski (USA))
E J O'Neill Dr Karen Sanderson

Placings:026 **(5662)**
2001: 8^{0}GF, 8^{2}HY, 8^{6}G

	Starts	1st	2nd	3rd	Win & Pl
Career Total (Turf)	3	0	1	0	1205

Going (Turf): Sf: 0-1 GS: 0-0 Gd: 0-1 GF: 0-1 Fm: 0-0
Distance: 5f/6f: 0-0 7f-8f: 0-1 9f-13f: 0-2 14f+: 0-0
Track : LH: 0-0 RH: 0-2 Tight: 0-2 Gall: 0-0
Aids: Bl: 0-0 Vi: 0-0 Tstrap: 0-0
Best Rating: 79 10/01 Wind 1m67y heavy

Yaqootah (USA)

102 **72**
3-y-o ch f Gone West (USA)-Sweet Roberta (USA) (Roberto (USA))
E A L Dunlop Hamdan Al Maktoum

Placings:0-03231 **(3489)**
2001: 7^{0}S, 6^{3}GF, 6^{2}GF, 6^{3}GS, 5^{1}GF

	Starts	1st	2nd	3rd	Win & Pl
Career Total (Turf)	6	1	1	2	5503

49 7/01 Newc 5f D G-F £2954
Total win prize-money £2954

Going (Turf): Sf: 0-1 GS: 0-1 Gd: 0-0 **GF: 1-4** Fm: 0-0
Distance: **5f/6f: 1-3** 7f-8f: 0-3 9f-13f: 0-0 14f+: 0-0
Track : LH: 0-0 RH: 0-0 Tight: 0-0 Gall: 0-0
Aids: Bl: 0-0 Vi: 0-0 Tstrap: 0-0
Best Rating: 72 7/01 NmkJ 6f gd-sft

Yarob (IRE)

108(85) (40) **80**

8-y-o ch g Unfuwain (USA)-Azyaa (Kris)
D Nicholls Lucayan Stud

Placings:120/040200/40/**420**/0501550505/0101026060 60-00203011026 **(3944)**
2001: 8^{0}SD, 9^{0}SD, 7^{2}G, 10^{0}G, 8^{3}GF, 10^{0}F, 10^{1}GF, 8^{1}GF, 8^{0}GF, 10^{2}GS, 8^{6}GF

	Starts	1st	2nd	3rd	Win & Pl
Career Total (Turf)	41	6	5	1	54065
Career Total (AW)	6	0	1	0	2323

60	7/01	Epsm	1m114y	E	G-F	£3493
68	6/01	Ches	1m2f75y	E	G-F	£3770
91	5/00	Donc	1m2f60y	C(0-90)H	G-S	£7345
82	4/00	Pont	1m4y	D(0-85)H	G-S	£7442
81	5/99	Donc	1m2f60y	C(0-90)H	G-F	£7067
82	7/95	Ling	6f	D	G-F	£4455

Total win prize-money £33575

Going (Turf): Sf: 0-2 GS: 2-6 Gd: 0-12 **GF: 4-19** Fm: 0-2
Distance: 5f/6f: 1-2 7f-8f: 0-15 **9f-13f: 5-30** 14f+: 0-0
Track : **LH: 5-33** RH: 0-6 Tight: 2-19 Gall: 2-11
Aids: Bl: 0-0 Vi: 0-0 Tstrap: 0-0
Best Rating: 88 5/01 Thsk 7f good

A useful handicapper in his prime, he is effective between seven and 10 furlongs. He has run some decent races in handicaps this season, but was just not able to win off his current mark and was dropped down successfully in grade to win claimers at Chester and Epsom. Best when able to dominate, but is far from an easy ride.

Yarrow Bridge

93 **80**

2-y-o b f Selkirk (USA)-Both Sides Now (USA) (Topsider (USA))
R Hannon Hassan Ahmadi

Placings:0041 **(4729)**
2001: 7^{0}GS, 6^{0}GS, 7^{4}GF, 6^{1}GF

	Starts	1st	2nd	3rd	Win & Pl
Career Total (Turf)	4	1	0	0	3314

80 9/01 Wwck 6f21y E G-F £2954
Total win prize-money £2954

Going (Turf): Sf: 0-0 GS: 0-2 Gd: 0-0 **GF: 1-2** Fm: 0-0
Distance: 5f/6f: 0-1 **7f-8f: 1-3** 9f-13f: 0-0 14f+: 0-0
Track : LH: 0-0 RH: 0-0 Tight: 0-0 Gall: 0-0
Aids: Bl: 0-0 Vi: 0-0 Tstrap: 0-0
Best Rating: 80 9/01 Wwck 6f21y gd-fm

Got off the mark at the fourth time of asking, in a maiden auction event at Warwick over six furlongs on good to firm, having shown promise in her three previous attempts.

Yaselda

99 **82+**

2-y-o b f Green Desert (USA)-Pripet (USA) (Alleged (USA))
C E Brittain Sheikh Marwan Al Maktoum

Placings:1 **(2722)**
2001: 6^{1}GF

	Starts	1st	2nd	3rd	Win & Pl
Career Total (Turf)	1	1	0	0	3346

82 7/01 Sthl 6f D G-F £3346
Total win prize-money £3346

Going (Turf): Sf: 0-0 GS: 0-0 Gd: 0-0 **GF: 1-1** Fm: 0-0
Distance: **5f/6f: 1-1** 7f-8f: 0-0 9f-13f: 0-0 14f+: 0-0
Track : **LH: 1-1** RH: 0-0 Tight: 0-0 Gall: 0-0
Aids: Bl: 0-0 Vi: 0-0 Tstrap: 0-0
Best Rating: 82 7/01 Sthl 6f gd-fm

A sister to the Prix Robert Papin winner Greenlander, she is bred for speed. Making her debut over six furlongs at Southwell in July, she finished well to beat the more experienced Lillies Bordello by a neck.

Yasey (JPN)

97 **89**

2-y-o bl c Sunday Silence (USA)-Millracer (USA) (Le Fabuleux)
D R Loder Sheikh Mohammed

Placings:22 **(5017)**
2001: 0^{2}GF, 7^{2}G

	Starts	1st	2nd	3rd	Win & Pl
Career Total (Turf)	2	0	2	0	6919

Going (Turf): Sf: 0-1 GS: 0-0 Gd: 0-0 GF: 0-1 Fm: 0-0
Distance: 5f/6f: 0-0 7f-8f: 0-2 9f-13f: 0-0 14f+: 0-0
Track : LH: 0-0 RH: 0-0 Tight: 0-0 Gall: 0-0
Aids: Bl: 0-0 Vi: 0-0 Tstrap: 0-0
Best Rating: 89 9/01 Asct 7f soft

He finished runner-up in his first two starts at Doncaster and Ascot, but will be much better as a three-year-old.

Yavana's Pace (IRE)

106 **117**

9-y-o ch g Accordion-Lady In Pace (Burslem)
M Johnston Mrs Joan Keaney

Placings:41351501/105025/30540355/31142223121/41 22011206/01043226522-4603110215 **(5585a)**
2001: 13^{4}GF, 15^{6}G, 20^{0}GF, 12^{3}S, 11^{1}HY, 15^{1}GS, 14^{0}GF, 12^{2}HY, 12^{1}HY, 15^{5}HY

	Starts	1st	2nd	3rd	Win & Pl
Career Total (Turf)	64	15	13	7	545187

117	10/01	Lonc	1m4f		HVY	£29098
113	9/01	Lonc	1m7f110y		G-S	£21339
103	8/01	Hayd	1m3f200yC		HVY	£6293
115	4/00	Hayd	1m3f200yA		SFT	£21000
114	9/99	Epsm	1m4f10y	A	G-F	£19650
115	8/99	Gdwd	1m6f	A	GD	£16014
115	6/99	Leic	1m3f183yA		G-S	£12821
114	11/98	Donc	1m4f	B H	SFT	£28235
98	9/98	Gway	1m4f		HVY	£12950
92	7/98	Sand	1m2f7y	B H	GD	£51650
87	5/98	Ayr	1m2f	C(0-90)H	SFT	£5507
75	6/96	Leop	7f	(0-90)H	GD	£4795
	11/95	Leop	1m1f	(0-100)H	YLD	£4110
	9/95	Gway	1m100y	(0-85)H	G-F	£3425
	5/95	Limk	7f		G-Y	£3425

Total win prize-money £240313

Going (Turf): Sf: 6-16 GS: 2-5 Gd: 3-17 GF: 1-13 Fm: 0-1
Distance: 5f/6f: 0-0 **7f-8f: 1-5** **9f-13f: 9-36** 14f+: 2-15
Track : LH: 6-22 RH: 6-30 **Tight: 2-6** Gall: 1-13
Aids: Bl: 0-0 Vi: 0-0 Tstrap: 0-0
Best Rating: 117 10/01 Lonc 1m4f heavy

An evergreen performer , she has been a grand servant to the Mark Johnston yard with a string of Group and Listed race wins over the years. Followed up a Haydock success with a win in a Group Three in France, but was outclassed in the Irish St Leger before an excellent second in Germany. Well ridden to take a Group Two at Longchamp in late October. Is best over 12 and 14 furlongs these days and needs a bit of cut in the ground.

Yazain (IRE)

80(70) (2) **18**

5-y-o b g Plps Pride-Trust Sally (Sallust)
P S McEntee (G Prodromou 30/7) Racing Thoroughbreds Plc

Placings:3000-0000 **(4872)**
2001: 8^{0}SD, 16^{0}GF, 8^{0}SD, 7^{0}G

	Starts	1st	2nd	3rd	Win & Pl
Career Total (Turf)	6	0	0	1	428
Career Total (AW)	2	0	0	0	

Going (Turf): Sf: 0-1 GS: 0-0 Gd: 0-2 GF: 0-2 Fm: 0-1
Distance: 5f/6f: 0-1 7f-8f: 0-5 9f-13f: 0-1 14f+: 0-1
Track : LH: 0-5 RH: 0-0 Tight: 0-2 Gall: 0-0
Aids: Bl: 0-1 Vi: 0-0 Tstrap: 0-1
Best Rating: 18 9/01 NmkR 7f good

Yazoo River Rebel

2-y-o b g Sabrehill (USA)-Bidweaya (USA) (Lear Fan (USA))
J R Norton Jeff Slaney

Placings:0 **(4598)**
2001: 8^{0}GF

	Starts	1st	2nd	3rd	Win & Pl
Career Total (Turf)	1	0	0	0	

Going (Turf): Sf: 0-0 GS: 0-0 Gd: 0-0 GF: 0-1 Fm: 0-0
Distance: 5f/6f: 0-0 7f-8f: 0-1 9f-13f: 0-0 14f+: 0-0
Track : LH: 0-1 RH: 0-0 Tight: 0-1 Gall: 0-0
Aids: Bl: 0-0 Vi: 0-0 Tstrap: 0-0
Best Rating: 18 9/01 NmkR 7f good

Year Two Thousand

108 **101**

3-y-o b c Darshaan-Vingt Et Une (FR) (Sadler's Wells (USA))
H R A Cecil Niarchos Family

Placings:2140 **(2943)**
2001: 12^{2}G, 12^{1}GF, 16^{4}GF, 14^{0}G

	Starts	1st	2nd	3rd	Win & Pl
Career Total (Turf)	4	1	1	0	9559

101 6/01 NmkR 1m4f D G-F £4823
Total win prize-money £4823

Going (Turf): Sf: 0-0 GS: 0-0 Gd: 0-2 **GF: 1-2** Fm: 0-0
Distance: 5f/6f: 0-0 7f-8f: 0-0 **9f-13f: 1-2** 14f+: 0-2
Track : LH: 0-0 **RH: 1-4** Tight: 0-0 **Gall: 1-4**
Aids: Bl: 0-0 Vi: 0-0 Tstrap: 0-0
Best Rating: 101 6/01 Asct 2m45y gd-fm

Improved significantly for his debut run at Newmarket and duly followed up there next time out. Stays a mile and a half. Acts on fast ground. Disappointed in Pattern class.

Yeast

92 **55d**

9-y-o b g Salse (USA)-Orient (Bay Express)
W J Haggas The Chosen Few Partnership

Placings:632/112101010/200/065404603/511020100/0 20112-00020600 **(4899)**
2001: 10^{0}G, 8^{0}GS, 8^{0}G, 7^{0}F, 8^{0}GF, 9^{6}GF, 8^{0}GF, 8^{0}GS

	Starts	1st	2nd	3rd	Win & Pl
Career Total (Turf)	47	10	7	2	139883

77	7/00	Leic	7f9y	E(0-70)	G-F	£3705
74	6/00	Ling	7f140y	E(0-70)	G-F	£2884
77	8/99	Ripn	1m	F	GD	£2822
84	6/99	Sals	1m	C(0-100)H	G-F	£6385
80	5/99	Chep	1m14y	D(0-75)	GD	£3753
108	10/96	NmkR	1m	A	G-F	£11464
107	7/96	Asct	1m	B(0-105)H	G-F	£14135
102	6/96	Asct	1m	B H	G-F	£55584
87	5/96	Asct	7f	B(0-110)H	G-F	£22665
83	3/96	Newc	1m	D	G-S	£3468

Total win prize-money £126869

Going (Turf): Sf: 0-1 GS: 1-6 Gd: 2-13 **GF: 7-25** Fm: 0-2
Distance: 5f/6f: 0-1 **7f-8f: 9-31** 9f-13f: 1-15 14f+: 0-0
Track : LH: 1-6 RH: 1-7 Tight: 1-3 Gall: 1-2
Aids: Bl: 0-1 Vi: 0-0 Tstrap: 0-0
Best Rating: 55 7/01 Nott 1m1f213y gd fm

A one-time very useful handicapper, winner of the 1996 Hunt Cup and a winner in Listed company, he is not the force of old.

Yellow Soil Star (IRE)

88(82) (29)**56**

2-y-o b f Perugino (USA)-Standing Ovation (Godswalk (USA))

P P Corrigan (Peter Corrigan 17/10) Edward O'Connor

Placings:60445000 **(5430a)**

2001: 5^{6}SD, 5^{0}G, 5^{4}SD, 6^{4}F, 5^{5}F, 7^{0}GF, 5^{0}SD, 8^{0}S

	Starts	1st	2nd	3rd	Win & Pl
Career Total (Turf)	**5**	**0**	**0**	**0**	**0**
Career Total (AW)	**3**	**0**	**0**	**0**	**0**

Going (Turf): Sf: 0-1 GS: 0-0 Gd: 0-1 GF: 0-1 Fm: 0-2
Distance: 5f/6f: 0-6 7f-8f: 0-2 9f-13f: 0-0 14f+: 0-0
Track : LH: 0-2 RH: 0-0 Tight: 0-1 Gall: 0-1
Aids: Bl: 0-1 Vi: 0-3 Tstrap: 0-0
Best Rating: 56 10/01 Navn 1m soft

Yellow Trumpet

79 **68**

3-y-o b f Petong-Daffodil Fields (Try My Best (USA))

M L W Bell Cheveley Park Stud

Placings:1-00 **(1527)**

2001: 6^{0}G, 6^{0}F

	Starts	1st	2nd	3rd	Win & Pl
Career Total (Turf)	**3**	**1**	**0**	**0**	**2880**
68 8/00 Carl 5f	F			GD	£2879

Total win prize-money £2880

Going (Turf): Sf: 0-0 GS: 0-0 **Gd: 1-2** GF: 0-0 Fm: 0-1
Distance: **5f/6f: 1-2** 7f-8f: 0-1 9f-13f: 0-0 14f+: 0-0
Track : LH: 0-1 **RH: 1-1** Tight: 0-0 **Gall: 1-1**
Aids: Bl: 0-0 Vi: 0-0 Tstrap: 0-0
Best Rating: 38 5/01 Thsk 6f good

Yenaled

104(103) (61)**65**

4-y-o gr g Rambo Dancer (CAN)-Fancy Flight (FR) (Arctic Tern (USA))

I Semple Martin Delaney

Placings:0046323563/316246225103-2000225253053331 **(5657)**

2001: 8^{2}GF, 8^{0}G, 7^{0}GF, 8^{0}GF, 9^{2}G, 9^{2}F, 10^{5}F, 10^{2}GF, 10^{5}GS, 10^{3}G, 9^{0}GF, 10^{5}F, **9**^{3}SD, **8**^{3}SD, **9**^{3}SD, 8^{1}G

	Starts	1st	2nd	3rd	Win & Pl
Career Total (Turf)	**35**	**3**	**8**	**6**	**22171**
Career Total (AW)	**3**	**0**	**0**	**3**	**1101**
63 11/01 Muss 1m	E(0-70)H			GD	£3108
63 9/00 Muss 7f30y	D(0-85)H			G-S	£4407
62 5/00 Muss 1m	F(0-65)H			FRM	£2814

Total win prize-money £10329

Going (Turf): Sf: 0-3 **GS: 1-5 Gd: 1-11** GF: 0-9 **Fm: 1-7**
Distance: 5f/6f: 0-2 **7f-8f: 3-20** 9f-13f: 0-16 14f+: 0-0
Track : LH: 0-16 **RH: 3-14 Tight: 3-21** Gall: 0-4
Aids: Bl: 0-0 Vi: 0-1 Tstrap: 0-0
Best Rating: 65 8/01 Newc 1m2f32y good

Suited by coming from behind in a strongly-run race. Best over a nine to ten furlongs on a sound surface. Runs well at Musselburgh. Acts on Fibresand.

Yertle (IRE)

108 **60**

4-y-o b g Turtle Island (IRE)-Minatina (IRE) (Ela-Mana-Mou)

J A R Toller Gerald Cooper

Placings:003600-203R611 **(4523)**

2001: 13^{2}GF, 14^{0}S, 14^{3}GF, 16^{R}GF, 14^{6}GF, 16^{1}G, 16^{1}GF

	Starts	1st	2nd	3rd	Win & Pl
Career Total (Turf)	**13**	**2**	**1**	**2**	**8829**
60 9/01 Ling 2m	E(0-70)H			G-F	£3360
54 8/01 Folk 2m93y	F(0-65)H			GD	£2590

Total win prize-money £5950

Going (Turf): Sf: 0-2 GS: 0-3 **Gd: 1-1 GF: 1-7** Fm: 0-0
Distance: 5f/6f: 0-0 7f-8f: 0-2 9f-13f: 0-4 **14f+: 2-7**
Track : LH: 1-4 RH: 1-6 **Tight: 2-5** Gall: 0-2
Aids: Bl: 0-0 Vi: 0-0 Tstrap: 0-0
Best Rating: 60 9/01 Ling 2m gd-fm

Has run better since being gelded and stepped up in trip to about 14 furlongs. Acts on fast ground. Dropped in grade to get off the mark at Folkestone in August 2001. Stays two miles. Has won on good ground.

Yetti

100 **70**

3-y-o ch f Aragon-Willyet (Nicholas Bill)

H Candy Henry Candy

Placings:225365-12000 **(3302)**

2001: 5^{1}S, 5^{2}GS, 5^{0}G, 5^{0}GF, 6^{0}GF

	Starts	1st	2nd	3rd	Win & Pl
Career Total (Turf)	**11**	**1**	**3**	**1**	**5283**
64 4/01 Nott 5f13y	F			SFT	£1897

Total win prize-money £1897

Going (Turf): Sf: 1-2 GS: 0-2 Gd: 0-1 GF: 0-5 Fm: 0-1
Distance: **5f/6f: 1-10** 7f-8f: 0-1 9f-13f: 0-0 14f+: 0-0
Track : LH: 0-1 RH: 0-2 Tight: 0-0 Gall: 0-3
Aids: Bl: 0-0 Vi: 0-0 Tstrap: 0-0
Best Rating: 70 5/01 Wind 5f10y gd-sft

She was knocking at the door with some fair efforts from poor draws in 2000 and was duly rewarded with a low-grade win at Nottingham on her debut the following season. She has been held since then.

Ynysmon

94 **48**

3-y-o b g Mind Games-Florentynna Bay (Aragon)

A Berry Chris & Antonia Deuters

Placings:504010-520600000 **(5503)**

2001: 5^{5}GF, 6^{2}G, 6^{0}S, 6^{6}GF, 6^{0}GF, 6^{0}G, 5^{0}GS, 6^{0}GS, 7^{0}HY

	Starts	1st	2nd	3rd	Win & Pl
Career Total (Turf)	**15**	**1**	**1**	**0**	**5425**
79 9/00 Muss 5f	D			G-S	£3672

Total win prize-money £3673

Going (Turf): Sf: 0-3 **GS: 1-3** Gd: 0-2 GF: 0-6 Fm: 0-1
Distance: **5f/6f: 1-12** 7f-8f: 0-3 9f-13f: 0-0 14f+: 0-0
Track : LH: 0-5 RH: 0-0 Tight: 0-1 Gall: 0-1
Aids: Bl: 0-0 Vi: 0-0 Tstrap: 0-0
Best Rating: 79 5/01 Wind 6f good

Has run well over five and six furlongs in the 2001 season. Should stay seven furlongs. Has won on good to soft but acts on a sound surface.

York Cliff

98 **84**

3-y-o b c Marju (IRE)-Azm (Unfuwain (USA))

J H M Gosden R Van Gelder

Placings:3-14 **(1743)**

2001: 8^{1}GS, 8^{4}GF

	Starts	1st	2nd	3rd	Win & Pl
Career Total (Turf)	**3**	**1**	**0**	**1**	**5877**
78 4/01 Newb 1m	D			G-S	£4615

Total win prize-money £4615

Going (Turf): Sf: 0-1 **GS: 1-1** Gd: 0-0 GF: 0-1 Fm: 0-0
Distance: 5f/6f: 0-0 **7f-8f: 1-2** 9f-13f: 0-1 14f+: 0-0
Track : LH: 0-1 RH: 0-0 Tight: 0-0 Gall: 0-0
Aids: Bl: 0-0 Vi: 0-0 Tstrap: 0-0
Best Rating: 78 4/01 Newb 1m gd-sft

A once-raced juvenile, he scored at the first attempt this season over a mile at Newbury on easy ground. Seemed unsuited by a fast surface next time.

York Whine (IRE)

97(96) (50)**48**

3-y-o ch f Tagula (IRE)-Cwm Deri (IRE) (Alzao (USA))

M J Polglase (W Jarvis 5/1) Paul J Dixon

Placings:012-2103004024P **(2034)**

2001: **7**^{2}SD, **7**^{1}SW, **7**^{0}SD, **8**^{3}SD, **8**^{0}SD, **8**^{0}SD, **11**^{4}SD, **8**^{0}SD, 8^{2}F, 7^{4}GF, 8^{P}F

	Starts	1st	2nd	3rd	Win & Pl
Career Total (Turf)	**4**	**0**	**1**	**0**	**712**
Career Total (AW)	**10**	**2**	**2**	**1**	**5373**
67 1/01 Wolv 7f	G(0-60)H			SLW	£1862
62 11/00 Sthl 7f	G			STD	£1904

Total win prize-money £3766

Going (Turf): Sf: 0-1 GS: 0-0 Gd: 0-0 GF: 0-1 Fm: 0-2
Distance: 5f/6f: 0-1 **7f-8f: 2-10** 9f-13f: 0-3 14f+: 0-0
Track : **LH: 2-11** RH: 0-1 **Tight: 1-1** Gall: 0-0
Aids: Bl: 0-2 Vi: 0-2 Tstrap: 0-0
Best Rating: 67 1/01 Wolv 7f slow

Yorker (USA)

97(105) (80)**80**

3-y-o b g Boundary (USA)-Shallows (USA) (Cox's Ridge (USA))

J M P Eustace Michael Scott

Placings:000-1203 **(2582)**

2001: 7^{1}SD, 6^{2}GS, 8^{0}GF, 7^{3}SD, 7^{0}SD

	Starts	1st	2nd	3rd	Win & Pl
Career Total (Turf)	**5**	**0**	**1**	**0**	**1201**
Career Total (AW)	**2**	**1**	**0**	**1**	**4762**
73 4/01 Sthl 7f	D(0-80)H			STD	£4163

Total win prize-money £4163

Going (Turf): Sf: 0-0 GS: 0-2 Gd: 0-0 GF: 0-3 Fm: 0-0
Distance: 5f/6f: 0-3 **7f-8f: 1-3** 9f-13f: 0-1 14f+: 0-0
Track : **LH: 1-4** RH: 0-1 Tight: 0-0 Gall: 0-0
Aids: Bl: 0-0 Vi: 0-0 Tstrap: 0-0
Best Rating: 80 6/01 Sthl 7f stand

Yorkie

87 **71**

2-y-o b g Aragon-Light The Way (Nicholas Bill)

I A Wood C H Stephenson & Partners

Placings:4406 **(4856)**

2001: 7^{4}GS, 6^{4}HY, 7^{0}GF, 7^{6}GF

	Starts	1st	2nd	3rd	Win & Pl
Career Total (Turf)	**4**	**0**	**0**	**0**	**677**

Going (Turf): Sf: 0-1 GS: 0-1 Gd: 0-0 GF: 0-2 Fm: 0-0
Distance: 5f/6f: 0-1 7f-8f: 0-3 9f-13f: 0-0 14f+: 0-0
Track : LH: 0-1 RH: 0-0 Tight: 0-1 Gall: 0-0
Aids: Bl: 0-0 Vi: 0-0 Tstrap: 0-0
Best Rating: 71 9/01 Leic 7f9y gd-fm

Yorkies Boy

110 **88**

6-y-o ro h Clantime-Slipperose (Persepolis (FR))

A Berry Mrs M Beddis

Placings:040214402454/1100002/205300000/0522041601040060-5610003406460300 **(5694)**

2001: 6^{5}S, 5^{6}G, 6^{1}GF, 6^{0}GF, 7^{0}GF, 6^{0}F, 6^{3}GF, 5^{4}G, 6^{0}G, 6^{6}G, 6^{4}G, 7^{6}GS, 6^{0}GF, 6^{3}GF, 6^{0}S, 6^{0}S

	Starts	1st	2nd	3rd	Win & Pl
Career Total (Turf)	**60**	**6**	**6**	**3**	**108233**
106 5/01 York 6f	B(0-105)H			G-F	£16254
96 8/00 Ches 6f18y	A			GD	£13572
99 7/00 Hayd 6f	C			G-F	£6177
113 5/98 NmkR 5f	A			G-S	£20000
109 4/98 NmkR 5f	A			SFT	£11002
76 6/97 Ches 5f16y	D			G-F	£3649

Total win prize-money £70655

Going (Turf): Sf: 1-15 GS: 1-5 Gd: 1-20 **GF: 3-18** Fm: 0-2
Distance: **5f/6f: 5-47** 7f-8f: 1-13 9f-13f: 0-0 14f+: 0-0
Track : **LH: 2-13** RH: 0-0 **Tight: 2-6** Gall: 0-5
Aids: Bl: 0-3 Vi: 0-0 Tstrap: 0-0

Best Rating: 106 5/01 York 6f gd-fm

Pacey sprinter who usually races prominently and acts on most surfaces. Caused a surprise when bouncing back to form in a York handicap in May, but has generally been below par since.

Yorkshire (IRE)

111 **105**

7-y-o ch g Generous (IRE)-Ausherra (USA) (Diesis)

P F I Cole Newgate Stud

Placings:1/023042/102655/5304-22110055 **(5691)**

2001: 12^{2}S, 14^{2}HY, 16^{1}G, 18^{1}G, 15^{0}G, 18^{0}G, 16^{5}GS, 12^{5}S

	Starts	1st	2nd	3rd	Win & Pl
Career Total (Turf)	25	4	5	2	98490

100	8/01	Ches	2m2f147y	B(0-105)H	GD	£15051
106	7/01	NmkJ	2m24y	B(0-105)H	GD	£10270
107	5/98	Newb	1m5f61y	A	G-F	£12185
97	10/96	Sals	1m	D	G-S	£3327

Total win prize-money £40833

Going (Turf): Sf: 0-6 GS: 1-4 **Gd: 2-11** GF: 1-4 Fm: 0-0
Distance: 5f/6f: 0-0 7f-8f: 1-2 9f-13f: 0-8 **14f+: 3-15**
Track : **LH: 2-16** RH: 1-8 Tight: 1-3 **Gall: 2-16**
Aids: Bl: 0-0 Vi: 0-0 Tstrap: 0-0
Best Rating: 106 7/01 NmkJ 2m24y good

A useful stayer, he recaptured his form this summer with pillar-to-post wins at Newmarket and Chester, but has been well beaten in Group and Listed company since. Goes well with cut in the ground.

Yorkshire Grey (IRE)

98(91) (57)**68**

3-y-o gr g Royal Abjar (USA)-Nirvavita (FR) (Highest Honor (FR))

A C Stewart A M Pickering

Placings:00360036400 **(5406)**

2001: 7^{0}S, 7^{0}GS, 7^{3}GF, 9^{6}GF, 6^{0}G, 7^{0}GS, 8^{3}GF, 9^{6}GF, 8^{4}SD, 7^{0}S, 8^{0}SD

	Starts	1st	2nd	3rd	Win & Pl
Career Total (Turf)	9	0	0	2	1079
Career Total (AW)	2	0	0	0	0

Going (Turf): **Sf: 0-2 GS: 0-2 Gd: 0-1 GF: 0-4 Fm: 0-0**
Distance: 5f/6f: 0-0 7f-8f: 0-7 9f-13f: 0-4 14f+: 0-0
Track : LH: 0-7 RH: 0-0 Tight: 0-3 Gall: 0-1
Aids: Bl: 0-1 Vi: 0-0 Tstrap: 0-0
Best Rating: 68 6/01 Yarm 7f3y gd-fm

He has ability, but does not look an easy ride and he may need more time.

You Da Man (IRE)

102(99) (73)**67**

4-y-o b g Alzao (USA)-Fabled Lifestyle (King's Lake (USA))

R Hannon Buddy Hackett

Placings:0600/**42241**251063-**0004**0004 **(3080)**

2001: 9^{0}SD, 10^{0}GS, 10^{0}G, 10^{4}G, 9^{0}F, 11^{0}GS, 11^{0}GF, 11^{4}GF

	Starts	1st	2nd	3rd	Win & Pl
Career Total (Turf)	17	1	1	1	7375
Career Total (AW)	6	1	2	0	4802

76	6/00	NmkJ	1m4f	D(0-80)H	G-F	£5564
73	3/00	Ling	1m2f	D	STD	£2769

Total win prize-money £8333

Going (Turf): Sf: 0-3 GS: 0-3 Gd: 0-5 **GF: 1-5** Fm: 0-1
Distance: 5f/6f: 0-0 7f-8f: 0-5 **9f-13f: 2-18** 14f+: 0-0
Track : LH: 1-10 RH: 1-6 Tight: 1-11 Gall: 1-3
Aids: Bl: 0-1 Vi: 0-0 Tstrap: 0-0
Best Rating: 67 5/01 Wind 1m2f7y good

A winner on Equitrack and turf last season, he has run better during the spring than his form figures would suggest and should find a race before long. Effective from ten to 12 furlongs.

You're An Angel

96 **72**

2-y-o b f Pursuit Of Love-Prima Cominna (Unfuwain (USA))

R Hannon William J Kelly

Placings:40420 **(5127)**

2001: 5^{4}G, 5^{0}G, 7^{4}GF, 7^{2}GS, 7^{0}HY

	Starts	1st	2nd	3rd	Win & Pl
Career Total (Turf)	5	0	1	0	1605

Going (Turf): **Sf: 0-1 GS: 0-1 Gd: 0-2 GF: 0-1 Fm: 0-0**
Distance: 5f/6f: 0-2 7f-8f: 0-3 9f-13f: 0-0 14f+: 0-0
Track : LH: 0-3 RH: 0-1 Tight: 0-1 Gall: 0-3
Aids: Bl: 0-0 Vi: 0-0 Tstrap: 0-0
Best Rating: 72 8/01 Epsm 7f gd-sft

She seems to be gradually getting her act together and ran her best race to date when runner-up in an Epsom maiden on her fourth start.

You're Special (USA)

106(103) (81+)**80**

4-y-o b g Northern Flagship (USA)-Pillow Mint (USA) (Stagedoor Johnny)

P C Haslam Les Buckley

Placings:55202/10006011112-6200040 **(5661)**

2001: 18^{6}S, 16^{2}S, 14^{0}HY, 17^{0}G, 13^{0}GS, 14^{4}GS, 16^{0}G

	Starts	1st	2nd	3rd	Win & Pl
Career Total (Turf)	18	3	2	0	23161
Career Total (AW)	5	2	2	0	6706

81	11/00	Sthl	1m6f	G(0-80)H	STD	£1991
78	11/00	Muss	2m	C(0-90)H	G-S	£13910
73	10/00	Nott	2m9y	F(0-60)H	SFT	£2878
64	10/00	Newc	2m19y	F(0-65)H	HVY	£2233
70	1/00	Wolv	1m1f79y	D	STD	£2795

Total win prize-money £23808

Going (Turf): **Sf: 2-6** GS: 1-6 Gd: 0-4 GF: 0-2 Fm: 0-0
Distance: 5f/6f: 0-2 7f-8f: 0-3 9f-13f: 1-6 **14f+: 4-12**
Track : **LH: 4-15** RH: 1-5 **Tight: 2-8** Gall: 1-5
Aids: Bl: 0-0 **Vi: 1-2** Tstrap: 0-0
Best Rating: 80 4/01 Kemp 2m soft

Improved for a step up in trip to two miles last autumn and ran up a sequence of four wins, including one on Fibresand. Suited by soft ground on turf, he avoided the fast ground of summer but has proved slightly disappointing after being brought back in the autumn.

Young Alex (IRE)

107(99) (89+)**79**

3-y-o ch g Midhish-Snipe Hunt (IRE) (Stalker)

K R Burke D G & D J Robinson

Placings:0114**541**-**124**425443 **(4251)**

2001: 7^{1}SW, 6^{2}SW, 7^{4}SD, 7^{4}G, 8^{2}GF, 8^{5}GF, 6^{4}G, 7^{4}GF, 7^{3}GF

	Starts	1st	2nd	3rd	Win & Pl
Career Total (Turf)	10	2	1	1	9017
Career Total (AW)	6	2	1	0	7926

81	2/01	Ling	7f	E(0-75)H	SLW	£2912
70	12/00	Ling	7f	E(0-75)	STD	£2842
69	7/00	Chep	6f16y	F	G-F	£2226
57	6/00	Brig	5f213y	F	FRM	£2247

Total win prize-money £10227

Going (Turf): Sf: 0-0 GS: 0-0 Gd: 0-3 **GF: 1-6 Fm: 1-1**
Distance: 5f/6f: 1-4 **7f-8f: 3-11** 9f-13f: 0-1 14f+: 0-0
Track : **LH: 3-11** RH: 0-1 **Tight: 2-7** Gall: 0-1
Aids: Bl: 0-0 Vi: 0-0 Tstrap: 0-0
Best Rating: 89 2/01 Ling 6f slow

Equally effective on turf or sand, he has yet to win beyond seven furlongs but does stay a mile judged on his good effort at Windsor in June. Needs fast ground on turf.

Young Annie

78(62)

3-y-o b f Young Ern-Snugfit Annie (Midyan (USA))

M J Ryan Mrs A M Byrne

Placings:00000000 **(5557)**

2001: 7^{0}GF, 7^{0}GF, 7^{0}GF, 7^{0}SD, 8^{0}SD, 9^{0}S, 9^{0}GS, 14^{0}S

	Starts	1st	2nd	3rd	Win & Pl
Career Total (Turf)	6	0	0	0	
Career Total (AW)	2	0	0	0	

Going (Turf): **Sf: 0-2 GS: 0-1 Gd: 0-0 GF: 0-3 Fm: 0-0**
Distance: 5f/6f: 0-0 7f-8f: 0-5 9f-13f: 0-2 14f+: 0-1
Track : LH: 0-4 RH: 0-1 Tight: 0-1 Gall: 0-0
Aids: Bl: 0-0 Vi: 0-0 Tstrap: 0-0
Best Rating: 26 5/01 Yarm 7f3y gd-fm

Young Bigwig (IRE)

104(100) (50)**59**

7-y-o b g Anita's Prince-Humble Mission (Shack (USA))

D W Chapman David W Chapman

Placings:41222153/5500000300/00100124503360000/20555300023005510560001012500/0603453340300 46003-210001232204000 **(5349)**

2001: 6^{2}SW, 7^{1}SD, 7^{0}SD, 7^{0}SD, 7^{0}SD, 6^{1}G, 6^{2}GF, 6^{3}GF, 6^{2}GF, 6^{2}SD, 6^{0}GF, 6^{4}G, 6^{0}F, 6^{0}HY, 5^{0}SD

	Starts	1st	2nd	3rd	Win & Pl
Career Total (Turf)	65	5	7	10	67002
Career Total (AW)	34	4	4	2	12883

51	5/01	Ripn	6f	E(0-70)H	GD	£3612
49	2/01	Wolv	7f	F(0-60)H	STD	£1764
67	10/99	Wolv	6f	E(0-70)H	STD	£3057
62	10/99	Wolv	6f	F(0-65)H	STD	£2472
64	6/99	Rdcr	6f	C(0-90)H	FRM	£7532
76	6/98	Haml	5f4y	E(0-75)H	SFT	£3533
75	5/98	Thsk	5f	D(0-80)H	GD	£4458
96	7/96	Gdwd	6f	C H	G-F	£8220
65	5/96	Wolv	5f	F	STD	£2381

Total win prize-money £37031

Going (Turf): Sf: 1-8 GS: 0-12 **Gd: 2-17** GF: 1-20 Fm: 1-8
Distance: **5f/6f: 8-85** 7f-8f: 1-14 9f-13f: 0-0 14f+: 0-0
Track : **LH: 4-38** RH: 0-2 **Tight: 4-21** Gall: 0-2
Aids: **Bl: 1-15** Vi: 0-0 Tstrap: 0-0
Best Rating: 59 6/01 Nott 6f15y gd-fm

A fair sprint handicapper, he ended a long losing run at Redcar in June, and twice won over six furlongs on the Wolverhampton Fibresand in October. Not altogether consistent.

Young Ibnr (IRE)

98(98) (48)**51d**

6-y-o b g Imperial Frontier (USA)-Zalatia (Music Boy)

B A McMahon Roy Penton

Placings:012564/**4002**20430503406060000/533/05601 44300150005-3040000 **(3612)**

2001: 5^{3}SD, 5^{0}GS, 5^{4}SD, 5^{0}SD, 5^{0}GS, 5^{0}G, 5^{0}G

	Starts	1st	2nd	3rd	Win & Pl
Career Total (Turf)	23	2	1	2	7416
Career Total (AW)	30	1	2	4	4318

51	8/00	Ripn	5f	F(0-60)H	GD	£2338
50	3/00	Wolv	5f	G	STD	£1877
82	4/97	Pont	5f	E	G-F	£2879

Total win prize-money £7094

Going (Turf): Sf: 0-3 GS: 0-7 **Gd: 1-5 GF: 1-8** Fm: 0-0
Distance: **5f/6f: 3-53** 7f-8f: 0-0 9f-13f: 0-0 14f+: 0-0
Track : **LH: 2-35** RH: 0-0 **Tight: 1-28** Gall: 0-3
Aids: Bl: 0-1 Vi: 0-3 Tstrap: 0-0
Best Rating: 48 3/01 Wolv 5f stand

Young Lion

101(86) (49)**89**

2-y-o b c Lion Cavern (USA)-Shimmer (Bustino)

C E Brittain C E Brittain

Placings:030113006 **(5521)**

2001: 6^{0}GF, 6^{3}G, 6^{0}GF, 5^{1}F, 6^{1}GF, 7^{3}GF, 7^{0}G, 6^{0}G, 6^{6}HY, 7^{0}SD

	Starts	1st	2nd	3rd	Win & Pl
Career Total (Turf)	9	2	0	2	10424

89 7/01 Pont 6f D G-F £3981
75 6/01 Ling 5f E FRM £3753
Total win prize-money £7735

Going (Turf): Sf: 0-1 GS: 0-0 Gd: 0-3 **GF: 1-4 Fm: 1-1**
Distance: **5f/6f: 2-6** 7f-8f: 0-3 9f-13f: 0-0 14f+: 0-0
Track : **LH: 1-2** RH: 0-0 Tight: 0-1 Gall: 0-0
Aids: Bl: 0-0 Vi: 0-0 Tstrap: 0-0
Best Rating: 89 7/01 Pont 6f gd-fm

Fairly useful performer who broke his maiden under a strong ride at Lingfield in June over five furlongs and followed up over six at Pontefract. Held in better races since.

Young Mazaad (IRE)

(83)
8-y-o b g Mazaad-Lucky Charm (IRE) (Pennine Walk)
D C O'Brien Mrs S Harris

Placings:00/**2444221**220/3006**0**/0600/**0-00** **(0178)**
2001: 8^{0}SD, 8^{0}SD

	Starts	1st	2nd	3rd	Win & Pl
Career Total (Turf)	17	1	3	1	5737
Career Total (AW)	8	0	3	0	2043

57 5/96 Folk 6f189y F GD £2381
Total win prize-money £2381

Going (Turf): Sf: 0-2 GS: 0-1 **Gd: 1-6** GF: 0-5 Fm: 0-3
Distance: 5f/6f: 0-5 **7f-8f: 1-15** 9f-13f: 0-5 14f+: 0-0
Track : LH: 0-14 **RH: 1-6 Tight: 1-15** Gall: 0-0
Aids: **Bl: 1-8** Vi: 0-1 Tstrap: 0-0

Young Monash (IRE)

90(78) (36)**33**
3-y-o b g General Monash (USA)-Sound Pet (Runnett)
B S Rothwell John H Price

Placings:4-00006 **(3427)**
2001: 6^{0}F, 6^{0}GF, 6^{0}SD, 5^{0}G, 6^{6}SD

	Starts	1st	2nd	3rd	Win & Pl
Career Total (Turf)	3	0	0	0	
Career Total (AW)	3	0	0	0	0

Going (Turf): Sf: 0-0 GS: 0-0 Gd: 0-1 GF: 0-1 Fm: 0-1
Distance: 5f/6f: 0-5 7f-8f: 0-1 9f-13f: 0-0 14f+: 0-0
Track : LH: 0-4 RH: 0-0 Tight: 0-1 Gall: 0-0
Aids: Bl: 0-0 Vi: 0-0 Tstrap: 0-0
Best Rating: 36 7/01 Sthl 6f stand

Young Rosein

106 **67**
5-y-o b m Distant Relative-Red Rosein (Red Sunset)
Mrs G S Rees J W Gittins

Placings:605/000541U20/003006113030-03313152030000 **(5688)**
2001: 8^{0}S, 8^{3}GF, 8^{3}F, 8^{1}GF, 8^{3}GF, 7^{1}GF, 7^{5}G, 8^{2}G, 7^{0}G, 6^{3}GF, 7^{0}G, 7^{0}S, 7^{0}S, 7^{0}S

	Starts	1st	2nd	3rd	Win & Pl
Career Total (Turf)	38	5	2	7	27013

68 7/01 Hayd 7f30y E(0-70)H G-F £3514
60 5/01 Ripn 1m D(0-85)H G-F £7202
58 8/00 Carl 7f214y E(0-70)H GD £2925
54 8/00 Hayd 1m30y E(0-70)H GD £3164
55 8/99 Muss 7f30y E(0-70)H G-F £2983
Total win prize-money £19788

Going (Turf): Sf: 0-9 GS: 0-4 Gd: 2-8 **GF: 3-13** Fm: 0-4
Distance: 5f/6f: 0-4 **7f-8f: 4-22** 9f-13f: 1-12 14f+: 0-0
Track : LH: 2-13 **RH: 3-11 Tight: 2-12** Gall: 0-3
Aids: Bl: 0-0 Vi: 0-0 Tstrap: 0-0
Best Rating: 68 7/01 Donc 1m good

A fair handicapper, she continues to run well despite rising in the handicap and has scored at Ripon and Haydock so far this season. Suited by seven furlongs or a mile on fast ground.

Young Tern

92(89) (56)**47**
3-y-o b g Young Ern-Turnaway (Runnett)
C G Cox P G Horrocks

Placings:00000-**6**006600 **(5681)**
2001: 8^{6}SD, 6^{0}GF, 10^{0}GF, 10^{6}GS, 8^{6}G, 8^{0}GS, 8^{0}S

	Starts	1st	2nd	3rd	Win & Pl
Career Total (Turf)	11	0	0	0	0
Career Total (AW)	1	0	0	0	0

Going (Turf): Sf: 0-3 GS: 0-3 Gd: 0-2 GF: 0-3 Fm: 0-0
Distance: 5f/6f: 0-4 7f-8f: 0-5 9f-13f: 0-3 14f+: 0-0
Track : LH: 0-3 RH: 0-1 Tight: 0-1 Gall: 0-2
Aids: Bl: 0-0 Vi: 0-0 Tstrap: 0-0
Best Rating: 63 6/01 NmkJ 1m2f gd-fm

He has yet to set the world alight and probably needs to come down the handicap some more.

Young-Un

93(109) (82)**57**
6-y-o b h Efisio-Stardyn (Star Appeal)
M J Ryan M F Kentish

Placings:0000500/00040300114340251/060020255000 3000**1122-33130** **(5657)**
2001: 8^{3}SD, 7^{3}SD, 9^{1}SW, 8^{3}SD, 8^{0}G, 8^{0}SD, 8^{5}SD

	Starts	1st	2nd	3rd	Win & Pl
Career Total (Turf)	41	3	3	3	18055
Career Total (AW)	8	3	2	3	22832

82 1/01 Wolv 1m1f79y C(0-100)H SLW £7995
71 11/00 Sthl 1m C(0-95)H STD £6922
64 11/00 Sthl 1m D(0-85)H STD £3165
62 11/99 Rdcr 1m2f E(0-75)H G-S £3270
53 8/99 Nott 1m1f213y E(0-75)H G-F £3643
48 8/99 Newc 1m1f9y E(0-70)H GD £3165
Total win prize-money £28162

Going (Turf): Sf: 0-5 **GS: 1-9 Gd: 1-12 GF: 1-13** Fm: 0-2
Distance: 5f/6f: 0-1 7f-8f: 2-16 **9f-13f: 4-32** 14f+: 0-0
Track : **LH: 6-30** RH: 0-12 **Tight: 2-17** Gall: 1-8
Aids: Bl: 0-1 Vi: 0-0 Tstrap: 0-5
Best Rating: 82 1/01 Wolv 1m1f79y slow

He improved a good deal on Fibresand over the winter of 2000, winning three times, and is currently rated some 14lb better on sand than on turf. Stays ten furlongs, but probably better over shorter.

Zaajel (IRE)

99 **72**
2-y-o b c Nashwan (USA)-Mehthaaf (USA) (Nureyev (USA))
J L Dunlop Hamdan Al Maktoum

Placings:2 **(5483)**
2001: 7^{2}HY

	Starts	1st	2nd	3rd	Win & Pl
Career Total (Turf)	1	0	1	0	1338

Going (Turf): Sf: 0-1 GS: 0-0 Gd: 0-0 GF: 0-0 Fm: 0-0
Distance: 5f/6f: 0-0 7f-8f: 0-1 9f-13f: 0-0 14f+: 0-0
Track : LH: 0-0 RH: 0-0 Tight: 0-0 Gall: 0-0
Aids: Bl: 0-0 Vi: 0-0 Tstrap: 0-0
Best Rating: 72 10/01 Donc 7f heavy

Zaajer (USA)

102 **88**
5-y-o ch g Silver Hawk (USA)-Crown Quest (USA) (Chief's Crown (USA))
J A B Old W E Sturt

Placings:21/10604/3315-505 **(1429)**
2001: 14^{5}HY, 12^{0}GS, 13^{5}S

	Starts	1st	2nd	3rd	Win & Pl
Career Total (Turf)	14	3	1	2	51826

112 8/00 Ches 1m5f89y A(0-110)H GD £19399
106 5/99 York 1m2f85y A SFT £13024
97 10/98 Asct 7f B SFT £7387
Total win prize-money £39811

Going (Turf): Sf: 2-7 GS: 0-3 Gd: 1-3 GF: 0-1 Fm: 0-0
Distance: 5f/6f: 0-0 7f-8f: 1-3 9f-13f: 1-7 14f+: 1-4
Track : **LH: 2-8** RH: 0-3 Tight: 1-2 Gall: 1-7
Aids: Bl: 0-0 Vi: 0-0 Tstrap: 0-0
Best Rating: 88 5/01 Newb 1m5f61y soft

Useful staying performer when trained by Ed Dunlop. He beat Lightning Arrow by a short head in Listed handicap at Chester in 2000, when he was also third twice in Listed company. Sold for 40,000 gns to join Jim Old, has run below form this season. Suited by soft conditions.

Zabat

82 **63**
2-y-o ch c Zamindar (USA)-Pluvial (Habat)
M Johnston Bep Partnership

Placings:0 **(1651)**
2001: 5^{0}F

	Starts	1st	2nd	3rd	Win & Pl
Career Total (Turf)	1	0	0	0	

Going (Turf): Sf: 0-0 GS: 0-0 Gd: 0-0 GF: 0-0 Fm: 0-1
Distance: 5f/6f: 0-1 7f-8f: 0-0 9f-13f: 0-0 14f+: 0-0
Track : LH: 0-0 RH: 0-0 Tight: 0-0 Gall: 0-0
Aids: Bl: 0-0 Vi: 0-0 Tstrap: 0-0
Best Rating: 63 5/01 Leic 5f218y firm

Zabionic (IRE)

(96) (58)**61**
4-y-o ch g Zafonic (USA)-Scene Galante (FR) (Sicyos (USA))
M Hill (M E Sowersby 12/5) Martin Hill

Placings:600/4000060-0 **(0691)**
2001: 16^{0}SD

	Starts	1st	2nd	3rd	Win & Pl
Career Total (Turf)	9	0	0	0	326
Career Total (AW)	2	0	0	0	

Going (Turf): Sf: 0-2 GS: 0-1 Gd: 0-3 GF: 0-2 Fm: 0-1
Distance: 5f/6f: 0-1 7f-8f: 0-4 9f-13f: 0-5 14f+: 0-1
Track : LH: 0-7 RH: 0-2 Tight: 0-1 Gall: 0-0
Aids: Bl: 0-3 Vi: 0-0 Tstrap: 0-0
Best Rating: 15 4/01 Sthl 2m stand

Zacchera

89 **79**
2-y-o ch f Zamindar (USA)-Palace Street (USA) (Secreto (USA))
G B Balding Miss B Swire

Placings:600 **(4573)**
2001: 6^{6}G, 6^{0}GF, 6^{0}G

	Starts	1st	2nd	3rd	Win & Pl
Career Total (Turf)	3	0	0	0	0

Going (Turf): Sf: 0-0 GS: 0-0 Gd: 0-2 GF: 0-1 Fm: 0-0
Distance: 5f/6f: 0-2 7f-8f: 0-1 9f-13f: 0-0 14f+: 0-0
Track : LH: 0-0 RH: 0-0 Tight: 0-0 Gall: 0-0
Aids: Bl: 0-0 Vi: 0-0 Tstrap: 0-0
Best Rating: 79 8/01 Newb 6f8y gd-fm

A half-sister to four winners including Duke of Modena and Palace Affair, has run well in maidens and is open to improvement.

Zaeema

94 **80+**
2-y-o br f Zafonic (USA)-Talented (Bustino)
D R Loder Maktoum Al Maktoum

Placings:1 **(2592)**
2001: 7^{1}GF

	Starts	1st	2nd	3rd	Win & Pl
Career Total (Turf)	1	1	0	0	4154

80 6/01 Donc 7f D G-F £4153
Total win prize-money £4154

Going (Turf): Sf: 0-0 GS: 0-0 Gd: 0-0 **GF: 1-1** Fm: 0-0
Distance: 5f/6f: 0-0 **7f-8f: 1-1** 9f-13f: 0-0 14f+: 0-0
Track : LH: 0-0 RH: 0-0 Tight: 0-0 Gall: 0-0
Aids: Bl: 0-0 Vi: 0-0 Tstrap: 0-0
Best Rating: 80 6/01 Donc 7f gd-fm

From a classy family, she confirmed her market support when winning a seven-furlong maiden at Doncaster on fast ground in June.

Zafair

92 **49**

3-y-o b/br f Zafonic (USA)-Danefair (Danehill (USA))
R Charlton K Abdulla

Placings:0 **(2934)**
2001: 10^{0}GF

	Starts	1st	2nd	3rd	Win & Pl
Career Total (Turf)	1	0	0	0	

Going (Turf): Sf: 0-0 GS: 0-0 Gd: 0-0 GF: 0-1 Fm: 0-0
Distance: 5f/6f: 0-0 7f-8f: 0-0 9f-13f: 0-1 14f+: 0-0
Track : LH: 0-0 RH: 0-1 Tight: 0-0 Gall: 0-1
Aids: Bl: 0-0 Vi: 0-0 Tstrap: 0-0
Best Rating: 49 7/01 Kemp 1m2f gd-fm

Zaffia

95 **76d**

4-y-o b f Zilzal (USA)-Zeffirella (Known Fact (USA))
P R Chamings Twenty Twenty Research

Placings:42/00-000 **(1715)**
2001: 8^{0}GS, 6^{0}S, 7^{0}GF

	Starts	1st	2nd	3rd	Win & Pl
Career Total (Turf)	7	0	1	0	786

Going (Turf): Sf: 0-2 GS: 0-1 Gd: 0-1 GF: 0-3 Fm: 0-0
Distance: 5f/6f: 0-0 7f-8f: 0-6 9f-13f: 0-1 14f+: 0-0
Track : LH: 0-2 RH: 0-1 Tight: 0-1 Gall: 0-0
Aids: Bl: 0-0 Vi: 0-0 Tstrap: 0-0
Best Rating: 56 5/01 Sals 6f212y soft

Zaffrani (IRE)

98 **93**

2-y-o b/br f Danehill (USA)-Zariysha (IRE) (Darshaan)
David Wachman Gigginstown House

Placings:32154455 **(5548a)**
2001: 6^{3}S, 7^{2}G, 7^{1}F, 6^{5}Y, 7^{4}S, 8^{4}G, 7^{5}S, 8^{5}YS

	Starts	1st	2nd	3rd	Win & Pl
Career Total (Turf)	8	1	1	1	17605

78 5/01 Dund 7f166y FRM £8625
Total win prize-money £8625

Going (Turf): Sf: 0-3 GS: 0-0 Gd: 0-2 GF: 0-0 **Fm: 1-1**
Distance: 5f/6f: 0-2 **7f-8f: 1-6** 9f-13f: 0-0 14f+: 0-0
Track : LH: 0-2 RH: 0-0 Tight: 0-0 Gall: 0-1
Aids: Bl: 0-1 Vi: 0-0 Tstrap: 0-0
Best Rating: 93 10/01 Leop 1m yld-sft

Won a fast ground maiden at Dundalk on her third start. Fourth in a Group Three over seven furlongs two outings later.

Zafilly

97(83) (44)**51**

3-y-o ch f Zafonic (USA)-Rifada (Ela-Mana-Mou)
G L Moore J B R Leisure Ltd

Placings:0005-0502600 **(3874)**
2001: 9^{0}GS, 11^{5}GS, 10^{0}GS, 11^{2}G, 10^{6}GF, 11^{0}G, 12^{0}G

	Starts	1st	2nd	3rd	Win & Pl
Career Total (Turf)	10	0	1	0	935
Career Total (AW)	1	0	0	0	0

Going (Turf): Sf: 0-2 GS: 0-3 Gd: 0-4 GF: 0-1 Fm: 0-0
Distance: 5f/6f: 0-0 7f-8f: 0-4 9f-13f: 0-7 14f+: 0-0
Track : LH: 0-4 RH: 0-3 Tight: 0-6 Gall: 0-1
Aids: Bl: 0-0 Vi: 0-0 Tstrap: 0-0
Best Rating: 51 5/01 Wind 1m3f135y good

Zafonium (USA)

102 **107**

4-y-o ch c Zafonic (USA)-Bint Pasha (USA) (Affirmed (USA))
P F I Cole Newgate Stud

Placings:31/24066-00 **(3600)**
2001: 10^{0}G, 12^{0}G

	Starts	1st	2nd	3rd	Win & Pl
Career Total (Turf)	9	1	1	1	41569

86 10/99 York 7f202y D SFT £7018
Total win prize-money £7018

Going (Turf): Sf: 1-1 GS: 0-1 Gd: 0-4 GF: 0-3 Fm: 0-0
Distance: 5f/6f: 0-0 **7f-8f: 1-2** 9f-13f: 0-7 14f+: 0-0
Track : **LH: 1-4** RH: 0-4 Tight: 0-1 **Gall: 1-5**
Aids: Bl: 0-2 Vi: 0-0 Tstrap: 0-0
Best Rating: 96 7/01 York 1m2f85y good

Winner of a York maiden at two, he ran well to finish runner-up in the King Edward VII Stakes at Royal Ascot on his belated return last season, but has not shown that level of form subsequently. He may be the sort that goes well fresh.

Zagaleta

104 **76**

4-y-o b f Sri Pekan (USA)-Persian Song (Persian Bold)
Andrew Turnell Dr John Hollowood

Placings:322/00021232-031001 **(3610)**
2001: 9^{0}HY, 8^{3}GS, 10^{1}F, 10^{0}GF, 10^{0}S, 9^{1}G

	Starts	1st	2nd	3rd	Win & Pl
Career Total (Turf)	17	3	5	3	17657

76 8/01 Nott 1m1f213yE(0-80)H GD £3220
71 5/01 Pont 1m2f6y E(0-70)H FRM £3802
65 8/00 Ayr 1m2f E(0-75)H GD £3984
Total win prize-money £11008

Going (Turf): Sf: 0-2 GS: 0-5 **Gd: 2-3** GF: 0-4 Fm: 1-3
Distance: 5f/6f: 0-4 7f-8f: 0-2 **9f-13f: 3-11** 14f+: 0-0
Track : **LH: 3-12** RH: 0-3 Tight: 0-5 Gall: 0-1
Aids: Bl: 0-0 Vi: 0-0 Tstrap: 0-1
Best Rating: 76 8/01 Nott 1m1f213y good

Fair ten-furlong handicapper. Acts on fast ground. Has got worked up beforehand in the past.

Zaha (IRE)

96(102) (57)**45**

6-y-o b h Lahib (USA)-Mayaasa (USA) (Lyphard (USA))
Mrs Lydia Pearce Exclusive Three Partnership

Placings:0003/**216**33655201050/6001400**06520**-000 **(5448)**
2001: 9^{0}G, 9^{0}G, 10^{0}HY

	Starts	1st	2nd	3rd	Win & Pl
Career Total (Turf)	25	2	1	3	9375
Career Total (AW)	9	1	2	0	3851

60 5/00 Nott 1m1f213yE(0-70)H G-S £3066
57 8/99 Yarm 1m2f21y F(0-60) GD £3028
64 2/99 Sthl 1m3f F STD £2191
Total win prize-money £8285

Going (Turf): Sf: 0-6 **GS: 1-5 Gd: 1-6** GF: 0-4 Fm: 0-4
Distance: 5f/6f: 0-0 7f-8f: 0-0 **9f-13f: 3-34** 14f+: 0-0
Track : **LH: 3-21** RH: 0-11 **Tight: 1-12** Gall: 0-4
Aids: Bl: 0-1 Vi: 0-3 Tstrap: 0-0
Best Rating: 45 8/01 Nott 1m1f213y good

Zahaalie (USA)

(61)

9-y-o ch g Zilzal (USA)-Bambee Tt (USA) (Better Bee)
J A Pickering Christian Wroe

Placings:23/50/0 **(0083)**
2001: 16^{0}SD

	Starts	1st	2nd	3rd	Win & Pl
Career Total (Turf)	3	0	1	1	1924
Career Total (AW)	2	0	0	0	0

Going (Turf): Sf: 0-0 GS: 0-0 Gd: 0-0 GF: 0-3 Fm: 0-0
Distance: 5f/6f: 0-0 7f-8f: 0-2 9f-13f: 0-2 14f+: 0-1
Track : LH: 0-2 RH: 0-0 Tight: 0-1 Gall: 0-0
Aids: Bl: 0-0 Vi: 0-0 Tstrap: 0-0

Zaheemah (USA)

106(104) (66+)**98**

3-y-o b f El Prado (IRE)-Port Of Silver (USA) (Silver Hawk (USA))
C E Brittain Saeed Manana

Placings:6452-312565 **(1972)**
2001: 10^{3}SD, 8^{1}SW, 7^{2}GS, 8^{5}G, 11^{6}GF, 8^{5}GF

	Starts	1st	2nd	3rd	Win & Pl
Career Total (Turf)	8	0	2	0	12289
Career Total (AW)	2	1	0	1	4153

66 2/01 Sthl 1m D SLW £3017
Total win prize-money £3017

Going (Turf): Sf: 0-0 GS: 0-2 Gd: 0-1 GF: 0-5 Fm: 0-0
Distance: 5f/6f: 0-3 **7f-8f: 1-3** 9f-13f: 0-4 14f+: 0-0
Track : **LH: 1-4** RH: 0-1 Tight: 0-3 Gall: 0-0
Aids: Bl: 0-0 Vi: 0-0 Tstrap: 0-0
Best Rating: 98 4/01 NmkR 7f gd-sft

She faced some stiff tasks on turf as a juvenile, but got off the mark with a comfortable victory in a Southwell maiden. Stepped up in class, she ran respectably, finishing fifth in Listed event at Epsom in June.

Zaidaan

(67) **68**

5-y-o b h Ezzoud (IRE)-River Maiden (USA) (Riverman (USA))
G M McCourt 'It Might Be Ten' Partnership

Placings:00/061/0-0 **(0323)**
2001: 12^{0}SD

	Starts	1st	2nd	3rd	Win & Pl
Career Total (Turf)	6	1	0	0	2750
Career Total (AW)	1	0	0	0	

68 7/99 Dund 1m1f (0-75)H FRM £2750
Total win prize-money £2750

Going (Turf): Sf: 0-0 GS: 0-0 Gd: 0-3 GF: 0-2 **Fm: 1-1**
Distance: 5f/6f: 0-1 7f-8f: 0-2 **9f-13f: 1-4** 14f+: 0-0
Track : **LH: 1-4** RH: 0-2 Tight: 0-1 Gall: 0-1
Aids: Bl: 0-0 Vi: 0-0 Tstrap: 0-0
Best Rating: 68 7/99 Dund 1m1f F

Zakat (FR)

81 **51**

2-y-o b g Zamindar (USA)-Rose Douceur (FR) (Polish Precedent (USA))
W R Muir Duncan J Wiltshire

Placings:00 **(4671)**
2001: 7^{0}G, 8^{0}G

	Starts	1st	2nd	3rd	Win & Pl
Career Total (Turf)	2	0	0	0	

Going (Turf): Sf: 0-0 GS: 0-0 Gd: 0-2 GF: 0-0 Fm: 0-0
Distance: 5f/6f: 0-0 7f-8f: 0-1 9f-13f: 0-1 14f+: 0-0
Track : LH: 0-0 RH: 0-1 Tight: 0-0 Gall: 0-0
Aids: Bl: 0-0 Vi: 0-0 Tstrap: 0-0
Best Rating: 51 9/01 Sand 7f16y good

Zamat

107 **44**

5-y-o b g Slip Anchor-Khandjar (Kris)
P Monteith I Bell

Placings:0/0400-23564452223 **(5032)**
2001: 11^{2}G, 12^{3}G, 12^{5}GF, 12^{6}GF, 11^{4}S, 15^{4}GS, 14^{5}G, 13^{2}GS,

14^{2}GF, 12^{2}G, 12^{3}GF

	Starts	1st	2nd	3rd	Win & Pl
Career Total (Turf)	16	0	4	2	5269

Going (Turf): Sf: 0-5 GS: 0-2 Gd: 0-5 GF: 0-4 Fm: 0-0
Distance: 5f/6f: 0-1 7f-8f: 0-1 9f-13f: 0-10 14f+: 0-4
Track : LH: 0-4 RH: 0-8 Tight: 0-7 Gall: 0-2
Aids: Bl: 0-0 Vi: 0-0 Tstrap: 0-0
Best Rating: 52 5/01 Haml 1m4f17y good

Maiden stayer. Effective at 12-14 furlongs, suited by cut in the ground.

Zaminstar (IRE)

92 **78**

2-y-o ch c Zamindar (USA)-Guanhumara (Caerleon (USA))
A P Jarvis Christopher Shankland

Placings:003200 **(4428)**
2001: 5^{0}GF, 6^{0}GF, 5^{3}G, 5^{2}GS, 6^{0}G, 7^{0}G

	Starts	1st	2nd	3rd	Win & Pl
Career Total (Turf)	6	0	1	1	1815

Going (Turf): Sf: 0-0 GS: 0-1 Gd: 0-3 GF: 0-2 Fm: 0-0
Distance: 5f/6f: 0-5 7f-8f: 0-1 9f-13f: 0-0 14f+: 0-0
Track : LH: 0-0 RH: 0-1 Tight: 0-0 Gall: 0-0
Aids: Bl: 0-0 Vi: 0-0 Tstrap: 0-0
Best Rating: 78 7/01 Yarm 5f43y good

Zamyatina (IRE)

96 **78**

2-y-o br f Danehill Dancer (IRE)-Miss Pickpocket (IRE) (Petorius)
R Hannon Salvatore Urso & Pietro Urso

Placings:221064 **(5621)**
2001: 5^{2}GF, 5^{2}S, 5^{1}G, 6^{0}GS, 5^{6}GS, 5^{4}GS

	Starts	1st	2nd	3rd	Win & Pl
Career Total (Turf)	6	1	2	0	4250

74	8/01	Brig	5f213y	F	GD	£2254

Total win prize-money £2254

Going (Turf): Sf: 0-1 GS: 0-3 **Gd: 1-1** GF: 0-1 Fm: 0-0
Distance: **5f/6f: 1-6** 7f-8f: 0-0 9f-13f: 0-0 14f+: 0-0
Track : **LH: 1-1** RH: 0-1 Tight: 0-0 Gall: 0-1
Aids: Bl: 0-0 Vi: 0-0 Tstrap: 0-0
Best Rating: 78 10/01 NmkR 5f gd-sft

A half-sister to a five-furlong juvenile winner, she progressed with racing, taking a six-furlong median auction at Brighton easily, but looked well held in a Doncaster sales race, and then in a nursery at Newmarket. Seems to handle most surfaces and is suited by six furlongs.

Zanana

90 **78**

2-y-o b f Zafonic (USA)-Divine Quest (Kris)
R Hannon Plantation Stud

Placings:2500 **(5372)**
2001: 5^{2}S, 6^{5}G, 7^{0}GS, 6^{0}G

	Starts	1st	2nd	3rd	Win & Pl
Career Total (Turf)	4	0	1	0	1070

Going (Turf): Sf: 0-1 GS: 0-1 Gd: 0-2 GF: 0-0 Fm: 0-0
Distance: 5f/6f: 0-3 7f-8f: 0-1 9f-13f: 0-0 14f+: 0-0
Track : LH: 0-0 RH: 0-0 Tight: 0-0 Gall: 0-0
Aids: Bl: 0-0 Vi: 0-0 Tstrap: 0-0
Best Rating: 78 7/01 NmkJ 6f good

Zanay

101(113) (119)**75**

5-y-o b h Forzando-Nineteenth Of May (Homing)
Miss Jacqueline S Doyle Tom Ford

Placings:422/310**41**/**111**040-05006 **(3220)**
2001: 10^{0}GF, 8^{5}GF, 9^{0}GF, 8^{0}GS, 7^{6}GF

	Starts	1st	2nd	3rd	Win & Pl
Career Total (Turf)	14	1	2	1	8846
Career Total (AW)	5	4	0	0	52327

106	3/00	Ling	1m2f	A	STD	£31900
96	2/00	Ling	1m2f	B	STD	£9309
119	2/00	Ling	1m2f	C(0-95)H	STD	£6792
97	12/99	Ling	1m2f	D	STD	£3820
81	10/99	Nott	1m54y	D	GD	£5117

Total win prize-money £56940

Going (Turf): Sf: 0-3 GS: 0-2 **Gd: 1-4** GF: 0-5 Fm: 0-0
Distance: 5f/6f: 0-0 7f-8f: 0-10 **9f-13f: 5-9** 14f+: 0-0
Track : **LH: 5-11** RH: 0-1 **Tight: 4-4** Gall: 0-2
Aids: Bl: 0-3 Vi: 0-0 Tstrap: 0-1
Best Rating: 75 6/01 Newb 1m gd-fm

He has really looked a serious talent on Equitrack, winning the Winter Derby in 2000. Not so good on turf, though he has won on the surface, and would be better off back on sand even if there are few opportunities for a horse of his class on that surface. He would have been interesting if taken to race in America.

Zandeed (IRE)

105(82) (42)**72**

3-y-o b g Inchinor-Persian Song (Persian Bold)
E A L Dunlop Ahmed Buhaleeba

Placings:50-00011110 **(5135)**
2001: 7^{0}SD, 7^{0}G, 10^{0}GF, 8^{1}G, 9^{1}G, 10^{1}GF, 10^{1}GF, 10^{0}G

	Starts	1st	2nd	3rd	Win & Pl
Career Total (Turf)	9	4	0	0	13738
Career Total (AW)	1	0	0	0	

72	7/01	Donc	1m2f60y	E(0-70)	G-F	£3493
72	7/01	Chep	1m2f36y	D(0-80)H	G-F	£3874
68	6/01	Nott	1m1f213yF(0-60)		GD	£2674
66	6/01	Hayd	1m30y	E(0-70)H	GD	£3696

Total win prize-money £13738

Going (Turf): Sf: 0-0 GS: 0-0 **Gd: 2-4 GF: 2-4** Fm: 0-1
Distance: 5f/6f: 0-2 7f-8f: 0-2 **9f-13f: 4-6** 14f+: 0-0
Track : **LH: 4-7** RH: 0-0 Tight: 0-2 **Gall: 1-1**
Aids: Bl: 0-0 **Vi: 4-5** Tstrap: 0-0
Best Rating: 72 7/01 Donc 1m2f60y gd-fm

Has been transformed since being fitted with a visor and completed a fine four-timer over distances from a mile to ten furlongs during the summer. Acts on a sound surface and is very effective when allowed an uncontested lead.

Zandicular

99 **92**

2-y-o b c Forzando-Perdicula (IRE) (Persian Heights)
R Hannon Nicholas R Hodges

Placings:62213 **(5363)**
2001: 6^{6}GF, 6^{2}GF, 6^{2}G, 6^{1}HY, 7^{3}GS

	Starts	1st	2nd	3rd	Win & Pl
Career Total (Turf)	5	1	2	1	8383

79	10/01	Ling	6f	D	HVY	£4956

Total win prize-money £4956

Going (Turf): Sf: 1-1 GS: 0-1 Gd: 0-1 GF: 0-2 Fm: 0-0
Distance: **5f/6f: 1-3** 7f-8f: 0-2 9f-13f: 0-0 14f+: 0-0
Track : LH: 0-0 RH: 0-0 Tight: 0-0 Gall: 0-0
Aids: Bl: 0-0 Vi: 0-0 Tstrap: 0-0
Best Rating: 92 10/01 NmkR 7f gd-sft

Fairly useful form as a juvenile. Bred to stay well. Proven on good to firm and heavy ground. Should stay a mile plus.

Zando's Charm

(60) **63**

3-y-o b f Forzando-Silver Charm (Dashing Blade)
J Akehurst The Plan Flow Leasing Partnership

Placings:501300-0 **(0055)**
2001: 8^{0}SD

	Starts	1st	2nd	3rd	Win & Pl
Career Total (Turf)	6	1	0	1	3337
Career Total (AW)	1	0	0	0	

62	8/00	Sals	6f212y	F	GD	£2247

Total win prize-money £2247

Going (Turf): Sf: 0-1 GS: 0-0 **Gd: 1-2** GF: 0-2 Fm: 0-1
Distance: 5f/6f: 0-2 **7f-8f: 1-5** 9f-13f: 0-0 14f+: 0-0
Track : LH: 0-3 RH: 0-1 Tight: 0-1 Gall: 0-2
Aids: Bl: 0-0 Vi: 0-0 Tstrap: 0-0
Best Rating: 62 8/00 Sals 6f212y G

Zandomeneghi (IRE)

91(83) (65)**66**

2-y-o ch g College Chapel-Fire Of London (Shirley Heights)
P F I Cole Richard Green (fine Paintings)

Placings:00500 **(5467)**
2001: 7^{0}GF, 7^{0}HY, 6^{5}SD, 6^{0}GS, 6^{0}S

	Starts	1st	2nd	3rd	Win & Pl
Career Total (Turf)	4	0	0	0	
Career Total (AW)	1	0	0	0	0

Going (Turf): Sf: 0-2 GS: 0-1 Gd: 0-0 GF: 0-1 Fm: 0-0
Distance: 5f/6f: 0-2 7f-8f: 0-3 9f-13f: 0-0 14f+: 0-0
Track : LH: 0-3 RH: 0-0 Tight: 0-1 Gall: 0-0
Aids: Bl: 0-1 Vi: 0-0 Tstrap: 0-0
Best Rating: 66 9/01 Newb 7f gd-fm

A brother to placed two-year-old Pudding Lane. Has yet to be placed but looks to be gradually getting the hang of things. Best effort came over six furlongs on the All-Weather at Wolverhampton in October.

Zanog

79 **55**

2-y-o b c Forzando-Logarithm (King Of Spain)
Miss Jacqueline S Doyle Blc Partnership

Placings:006 **(5125)**
2001: 7^{0}G, 5^{0}G, 5^{6}HY

	Starts	1st	2nd	3rd	Win & Pl
Career Total (Turf)	3	0	0	0	0

Going (Turf): Sf: 0-1 GS: 0-0 Gd: 0-2 GF: 0-0 Fm: 0-0
Distance: 5f/6f: 0-2 7f-8f: 0-1 9f-13f: 0-0 14f+: 0-0
Track : LH: 0-1 RH: 0-0 Tight: 0-0 Gall: 0-1
Aids: Bl: 0-0 Vi: 0-0 Tstrap: 0-0
Best Rating: 55 8/01 Bath 5f11y good

Zanzibar (IRE)

103 **112**

3-y-o b f In The Wings-Isle Of Spice (USA) (Diesis)
M L W Bell Mrs G Rowland Clark & Usk Valley Stud

Placings:523-1105650 **(5582a)**
2001: 11^{1}G, 11^{1}G, 12^{0}GF, 11^{5}G, 12^{6}G, 10^{5}HO, 10^{0}G

	Starts	1st	2nd	3rd	Win & Pl
Career Total (Turf)	10	2	1	1	140933

110	5/01	Siro	1m3f	GD	£125578
79	5/01	Leic	1m3f183yD(0-80)	GD	£3783

Total win prize-money £129361

Going (Turf): Sf: 0-0 GS: 0-0 **Gd: 2-8** GF: 0-1 Fm: 0-0
Distance: 5f/6f: 0-0 7f-8f: 0-2 **9f-13f: 2-8** 14f+: 0-0
Track : LH: 0-4 **RH: 1-5** Tight: 0-2 Gall: 0-2
Aids: Bl: 0-0 Vi: 0-0 Tstrap: 0-0
Best Rating: 112 9/01 Lonc 1m4f good

Improved a good deal from two to three, comfortably winning a Leicester classified event on her return before bolting up by seven lengths in the Italian Oaks. She ran no sort of a race in the Oaks and was reported to have returned jarred-up. Taking on the top fillies in the second half of the season, she at least confirmed her level of ability. Stays 12 furlongs and appreciates good ground.

Zaran

87 **63**

2-y-o gr f Inzar (USA)-African Light (Kalaglow)
N P Littmoden Turf 2000 Limited

Placings:650 **(3566)**
2001: 6^{6}GF, 7^{5}GF, 5^{0}GF

	Starts	1st	2nd	3rd	Win & Pl

	Starts	1st	2nd	3rd	Win & Pl
Career Total (Turf)	3	0	0	0	0

Going (Turf): Sf: 0-0 GS: 0-0 Gd: 0-0 GF: 0-3 Fm: 0-0
Distance: 5f/6f: 0-1 7f-8f: 0-2 9f-13f: 0-0 14f+: 0-0
Track : LH: 0-0 RH: 0-0 Tight: 0-0 Gall: 0-0
Aids: Bl: 0-0 Vi: 0-0 Tstrap: 0-0
Best Rating: 63 7/01 Ling 7f gd-fm

Zarconia (IRE)

78 **43**

2-y-o br f Inzar (USA)-Speedy Action (Horage)
Mrs P Sly David L Bayliss

Placings:60 **(5689)**
2001: 5^{6}S, 6^{0}S

	Starts	1st	2nd	3rd	Win & Pl
Career Total (Turf)	2	0	0	0	0

Going (Turf): Sf: 0-2 GS: 0-0 Gd: 0-0 GF: 0-0 Fm: 0-0
Distance: 5f/6f: 0-2 7f-8f: 0-0 9f-13f: 0-0 14f+: 0-0
Track : LH: 0-0 RH: 0-0 Tight: 0-0 Gall: 0-0
Aids: Bl: 0-0 Vi: 0-0 Tstrap: 0-0
Best Rating: 43 10/01 Nott 5f13y soft

Zargus

98 **92**

2-y-o b c Zamindar (USA)-My First Romance (Danehill (USA))
W R Muir Mrs Monique V Bruce Copp

Placings:221 **(5184)**
2001: 6^{2}GF, 5^{2}G, 5^{1}GS

	Starts	1st	2nd	3rd	Win & Pl
Career Total (Turf)	3	1	2	0	5973

73 10/01 Catt 5f D G-S £3430
Total win prize-money £3430

Going (Turf): Sf: 0-0 **GS: 1-1** Gd: 0-1 GF: 0-1 Fm: 0-0
Distance: 5f/6f: 1-3 7f-8f: 0-0 9f-13f: 0-0 14f+: 0-0
Track : LH: 0-1 RH: 0-0 Tight: 0-0 Gall: 0-1
Aids: Bl: 0-0 Vi: 0-0 Tstrap: 0-0
Best Rating: 92 9/01 Gdwd 6f gd-fm

Was an easy winner of a Catterick maiden having shown ability in previous runs, although the opposition looked ordinary.

Zarin (IRE)

104 **97**

3-y-o b c Inzar (USA)-Non Dimenticar Me (IRE) (Don't Forget Me)
J L Dunlop Littleton Manor Racing

Placings:210 **(1401a)**
2001: 7^{2}S, 7^{1}S, 8^{0}G

	Starts	1st	2nd	3rd	Win & Pl
Career Total (Turf)	3	1	1	0	5159

94 4/01 Kemp 7f D SFT £3802
Total win prize-money £3003

Going (Turf): Sf: 1-2 GS: 0-0 Gd: 0-1 GF: 0-0 Fm: 0-0
Distance: 5f/6f: 0-0 **7f-8f: 1-3** 9f-13f: 0-0 14f+: 0-0
Track : LH: 0-0 **RH: 1-1** Tight: 0-0 **Gall: 1-1**
Aids: Bl: 0-0 Vi: 0-0 Tstrap: 0-0
Best Rating: 94 4/01 Kemp 7f soft

Impressed in a Kempton maiden but was found wanting in the French Guineas.

Zarza Bay (IRE)

93(89) (61)**54**

2-y-o b c Hamas (IRE)-Frill (Henbit (USA))
K R Burke Mrs Melba Bryce

Placings:050505 **(5115)**
2001: 5^{0}GF, 6^{5}GF, 6^{0}GF, 7^{5}SD, 8^{0}GF, 9^{5}HY

	Starts	1st	2nd	3rd	Win & Pl
Career Total (Turf)	5	0	0	0	0
Career Total (AW)	1	0	0	0	0

Going (Turf): Sf: 0-1 GS: 0-0 Gd: 0-0 GF: 0-4 Fm: 0-0
Distance: 5f/6f: 0-3 7f-8f: 0-2 9f-13f: 0-1 14f+: 0-0
Track : LH: 0-2 RH: 0-1 Tight: 0-2 Gall: 0-0
Aids: Bl: 0-0 Vi: 0-0 Tstrap: 0-0
Best Rating: 81 6/01 Ayr 6f gd-fm

Zarzella

77 **43**

2-y-o b f Makbul-Zarzi (IRE) (Suave Dancer (USA))
M Wigham Perchance To Dream Partnership

Placings:5 **(3852)**
2001: 6^{5}G

	Starts	1st	2nd	3rd	Win & Pl
Career Total (Turf)	1	0	0	0	0

Going (Turf): Sf: 0-0 GS: 0-0 Gd: 0-1 GF: 0-0 Fm: 0-0
Distance: 5f/6f: 0-1 7f-8f: 0-0 9f-13f: 0-0 14f+: 0-0
Track : LH: 0-0 RH: 0-0 Tight: 0-0 Gall: 0-0
Aids: Bl: 0-0 Vi: 0-0 Tstrap: 0-0
Best Rating: 43 8/01 Asct 6f good

Zawrak (IRE)

85 **55**

2-y-o ch c Zafonic (USA)-Gharam (USA) (Green Dancer (USA))
A C Stewart Hamdan Al Maktoum

Placings:6 **(4895)**
2001: 7^{6}GS

	Starts	1st	2nd	3rd	Win & Pl
Career Total (Turf)	1	0	0	0	0

Going (Turf): Sf: 0-0 GS: 0-1 Gd: 0-0 GF: 0-0 Fm: 0-0
Distance: 5f/6f: 0-0 7f-8f: 0-1 9f-13f: 0-0 14f+: 0-0
Track : LH: 0-0 RH: 0-0 Tight: 0-0 Gall: 0-0
Aids: Bl: 0-0 Vi: 0-0 Tstrap: 0-0
Best Rating: 55 9/01 Leic 7f9y gd-sft

Zechariah

103(87) (19)**48**

5-y-o b g Kasakov-Runfawit Pet (Welsh Saint)
J L Eyre John R Ashcroft

Placings:5300525010**6**/236**0**05/4656400**400**-33031100 **(4802)**
2001: 8^{3}F, 8^{3}GF, 8^{0}F, 8^{3}GF, 8^{1}GF, 7^{1}GS, 8^{0}GS, 8^{0}F

	Starts	1st	2nd	3rd	Win & Pl
Career Total (Turf)	26	2	2	4	8980
Career Total (AW)	9	1	0	1	1740

48 8/01 Ayr 7f F(0-60)H G-S £2870
42 7/01 Muss 1m F(0-60)H G-F £2632
65 11/98 Wolv 1m100y G STD £1479
Total win prize-money £6982

Going (Turf): Sf: 0-5 **GS: 1-5** Gd: 0-4 **GF: 1-8** Fm: 0-4
Distance: 5f/6f: 0-4 **7f-8f: 2-24** 9f-13f: 1-7 14f+: 0-0
Track : LH: 2-24 RH: 1-6 **Tight: 2-14** Gall: 0-1
Aids: Bl: 0-0 Vi: 0-0 Tstrap: 0-0
Best Rating: 48 8/01 Ayr 7f gd-sft

Zeitlos

96 **63**

2-y-o b c Timeless Times (USA)-Petitesse (Petong)
G G Margarson Stableside Racing Partnership 4

Placings:040100604400 **(5458)**
2001: 5^{0}S, 5^{4}GF, 6^{0}GF, 5^{1}G, 5^{0}G, 5^{0}F, 5^{6}GF, 5^{0}F, 6^{4}G, 5^{4}S, 6^{0}GS, 5^{0}G

	Starts	1st	2nd	3rd	Win & Pl
Career Total (Turf)	12	1	0	0	3655

58 7/01 Leic 5f2y E GD £3052
Total win prize-money £3052

Going (Turf): Sf: 0-2 GS: 0-1 **Gd: 1-4** GF: 0-3 Fm: 0-2
Distance: 5f/6f: 1-11 7f-8f: 0-1 9f-13f: 0-0 14f+: 0-0
Track : LH: 0-3 RH: 0-0 Tight: 0-0 Gall: 0-1
Aids: Bl: 0-1 Vi: 0-0 Tstrap: 0-0
Best Rating: 63 9/01 Nott 6f15y good

A half-brother to a handful of juvenile winners, he scored over the minimum trip on his third start in a Leicester nursery. Unsuccessfully tried in blinkers, he has won on good ground, but has shown nothing since that run in July 2001.

Zelensky (IRE)

92(77) (44)**76**

2-y-o b c Danehill Dancer (IRE)-Malt Leaf (IRE) (Nearly A Nose (USA))
J A Osborne Mr & Mrs John Holmes

Placings:0625 **(4577)**
2001: 6^{0}SD, 6^{6}GS, 6^{2}G, 6^{5}G

	Starts	1st	2nd	3rd	Win & Pl
Career Total (Turf)	3	0	1	0	2385
Career Total (AW)	1	0	0	0	

Going (Turf): Sf: 0-0 GS: 0-1 Gd: 0-2 GF: 0-0 Fm: 0-0
Distance: 5f/6f: 0-3 7f-8f: 0-1 9f-13f: 0-0 14f+: 0-0
Track : LH: 0-1 RH: 0-0 Tight: 0-0 Gall: 0-0
Aids: Bl: 0-0 Vi: 0-0 Tstrap: 0-0
Best Rating: 76 8/01 Nott 6f15y good

A half-brother to Irish mile-winner Perugino's Malt. Is gradually getting the hang of things and should stay further.

Zeloso

104 **85d**

3-y-o b c Alzao (USA)-Silk Petal (Petorius)
R Charlton Tom Wilson

Placings:03021430-040046 **(4279)**
2001: 8^{0}GS, 9^{4}GF, 10^{0}G, 10^{0}GF, 8^{4}S, 7^{6}GF

	Starts	1st	2nd	3rd	Win & Pl
Career Total (Turf)	14	1	1	2	8644

79 8/00 Hayd 7f30y D GD £4101
Total win prize-money £4102

Going (Turf): Sf: 0-4 GS: 0-1 **Gd: 1-3** GF: 0-6 Fm: 0-0
Distance: 5f/6f: 0-1 **7f-8f: 1-7** 9f-13f: 0-6 14f+: 0-0
Track : LH: 1-5 RH: 0-3 Tight: 0-3 Gall: 0-1
Aids: Bl. 0-1 Vi: 0-2 Tstrap: 0-0
Best Rating: 85 6/01 Sals 1m1f198y gd-fm

Fairly useful nursery horse for John Dunlop when he showed his best form around seven furlongs. Did not show much for a new yard this season.

Zenda

96 **85**

2-y-o b f Zamindar (USA)-Hope (IRE) (Dancing Brave (USA))
J H M Gosden K Abdulla

Placings:23 **(5484)**
2001: 7^{2}G, 8^{3}HY

	Starts	1st	2nd	3rd	Win & Pl
Career Total (Turf)	2	0	1	1	3165

Going (Turf): Sf: 0-1 GS: 0-0 Gd: 0-1 GF: 0-0 Fm: 0-0
Distance: 5f/6f: 0-0 7f-8f: 0-2 9f-13f: 0-0 14f+: 0-0
Track : LH: 0-1 RH: 0-1 Tight: 0-0 Gall: 0-2
Aids: Bl: 0-0 Vi: 0-0 Tstrap: 0-0
Best Rating: 85 10/01 Donc 1m heavy

A half-sister to the useful Hopeful Light. Ran well on her Kempton debut behind Distant Valley and should have little difficulty winning races.

Zendium (IRE)

67(84) (26)**63**

3-y-o b g Earl Of Barking (IRE)-Speedy Action (Horage)
T D Easterby Mrs Jennifer E Pallister

Placings:0-000 **(1173)**

2001: 6^{0}SD, 8^{0}S, 7^{0}S

	Starts	1st	2nd	3rd	Win & Pl
Career Total (Turf)	3	0	0	0	
Career Total (AW)	1	0	0	0	

Going (Turf): Sf: 0-2 GS: 0-0 Gd: 0-1 GF: 0-0 Fm: 0-0
Distance: 5f/6f: 0-2 7f-8f: 0-2 9f-13f: 0-0 14f+: 0-0
Track : LH: 0-1 RH: 0-1 Tight: 0-1 Gall: 0-0
Aids: Bl: 0-0 Vi: 0-0 Tstrap: 0-0
Best Rating: 26 3/01 Sthl 6f stand

Zero Gravity

103 **41**
4-y-o b g Cosmonaut-Comfort (Chief Singer)
D J S Ffrench Davis Mrs Jenny Phillips

Placings:636-0063O000 **(4953)**
2001: 10^{0}GS, 10^{0}S, 9^{6}GF, 12^{3}GF, 14^{0}G, 13^{0}G, 13^{0}F, 16^{0}GS

	Starts	1st	2nd	3rd	Win & Pl
Career Total (Turf)	11	0	0	2	1738

Going (Turf): Sf: 0-1 GS: 0-2 Gd: 0-3 GF: 0-4 Fm: 0-1
Distance: 5f/6f: 0-0 7f-8f: 0-0 9f-13f: 0-7 14f+: 0-4
Track : LH: 0-5 RH: 0-5 Tight: 0-6 Gall: 0-3
Aids: Bl: 0-0 Vi: 0-0 Tstrap: 0-0
Best Rating: 63 4/01 Newb 1m2f6y gd-sft

Zetagalopon

90(91) (30)**37**
3-y-o b f Petong-Azola (IRE) (Alzao (USA))
C L Popham (J A Osborne 12/7) Miss Deborah Bullion

Placings:00-04440040 **(4210)**
2001: 7^{0}SD, 8^{4}SD, 10^{4}SW, 12^{4}SD, 11^{0}SD, 9^{0}F, 9^{4}SD, 11^{0}GF

	Starts	1st	2nd	3rd	Win & Pl
Career Total (Turf)	3	0	0	0	
Career Total (AW)	7	0	0	0	

Going (Turf): Sf: 0-0 GS: 0-0 Gd: 0-1 GF: 0-1 Fm: 0-1
Distance: 5f/6f: 0-1 7f-8f: 0-3 9f-13f: 0-6 14f+: 0-0
Track : LH: 0-9 RH: 0-0 Tight: 0-5 Gall: 0-0
Aids: Bl: 0-2 Vi: 0-0 Tstrap: 0-0
Best Rating: 35 1/01 Ling 1m stand

Zhitomir

107 **73**
3-y-o ch c Lion Cavern (USA)-Treasure Trove (USA) (The Minstrel (CAN))
S Dow M G Mackenzie

Placings:64061230-00500021410 **(5391)**
2001: 6^{0}GF, 7^{0}GF, 6^{5}GF, 6^{0}GF, 7^{0}GF, 6^{0}GF, 7^{2}S, 7^{1}G, 7^{4}GS, 7^{1}HY, 7^{0}GS

	Starts	1st	2nd	3rd	Win & Pl
Career Total (Turf)	19	3	2	1	20380

73	10/01	Ling	7f	E(0-70)H	HVY	£4077
70	9/01	Epsm	7f	D(0-80)H	GD	£7182
78	9/00	Epsm	6f	E	GD	£4290

Total win prize-money £15551

Going (Turf): Sf: 1-5 GS: 0-2 **Gd: 2-4** GF: 0-7 Fm: 0-0
Distance: 5f/6f: 1-8 **7f-8f: 2-10** 9f-13f: 0-0 14f+: 0-0
Track : **LH: 2-5** RH: 0-2 **Tight: 2-5** Gall: 0-0
Aids: Bl: 0-0 Vi: 0-0 Tstrap: 0-0
Best Rating: 79 6/01 Kemp 6f gd-fm

He is suited by undulating tracks and has won at Epsom and Lingfield this season. Suited by seven furlongs and the ground good or softer.

Zibeline (IRE)

106 **85**
4-y-o b g Cadeaux Genereux-Zia (USA) (Shareef Dancer (USA))
B R Millman Athole Still And Partners

Placings:5450/024415230-02052414000 **(5387)**
2001: 12^{0}S, 12^{2}F, 10^{0}GF, 11^{5}G, 12^{2}GF, 14^{4}GF, 13^{1}GF, 13^{4}GF, 13^{0}GF, 12^{0}HY, 18^{0}GS

	Starts	1st	2nd	3rd	Win & Pl
Career Total (Turf)	24	2	4	1	29726

83	8/01	Newb	1m5f61y	C(0-90)H	G-F	£7280
80	7/00	Chep	1m2f36y	D(0-80)H	G-F	£3900

Total win prize-money £11180

Going (Turf): Sf: 0-2 GS: 0-3 Gd: 0-7 **GF: 2-10** Fm: 0-2
Distance: 5f/6f: 0-0 7f-8f: 0-6 9f-13f: 1-13 14f+: 1-5
Track : **LH: 2-10** RH: 0-8 Tight: 0-1 **Gall: 1-13**
Aids: **Bl: 1-5** Vi: 0-0 Tstrap: 0-0
Best Rating: 85 9/01 York 1m5f194y gd-fm

Suited by a truly-run 12 furlongs plus and fast ground. Wore blinkers to winning effect at Newbury in August, but they did not have the same effect afterwards. Normally held up.

Zibet

105 **85**
3-y-o b f Kris-Zonda (Fabulous Dancer (USA))
E A L Dunlop Mohammed Al Nabouda

Placings:3-120 **(5005)**
2001: 7^{1}GS, 8^{2}S, 7^{0}S

	Starts	1st	2nd	3rd	Win & Pl
Career Total (Turf)	4	1	1	1	6959

84	7/01	NmkJ	7f	D	G-S	£4192

Total win prize-money £4193

Going (Turf): Sf: 0-3 **GS: 1-1** Gd: 0-0 GF: 0-0 Fm: 0-0
Distance: 5f/6f: 0-1 **7f-8f: 1-2** 9f-13f: 0-1 14f+: 0-0
Track : LH: 0-0 RH: 0-0 Tight: 0-0 Gall: 0-0
Aids: Bl: 0-0 Vi: 0-0 Tstrap: 0-0
Best Rating: 85 8/01 Chep 1m14y soft

She ran once at two and overcame a break of nine months to win a maiden at Newmarket over seven furlongs in July. Beaten in very soft ground next time, but she should continue to improve. Has a decent turn of foot. Has yet to encounter ground faster than good to soft.

Zidac

(91) (45)
9-y-o b/br g Statoblest-Sule Skerry (Scottish Rifle)
P J Makin Brian Brackpool

Placings:5/454400/2110/50204500350/003160/210016 013/0026225-0 **(0225)**
2001: 10^{0}SD

	Starts	1st	2nd	3rd	Win & Pl
Career Total (Turf)	37	5	4	3	19699
Career Total (AW)	8	1	2	0	3806

68	10/99	Brig	1m1f209yF(0-60)H		GD	£2389
63	6/99	Bath	1m2f46y	F	GD	£2514
62	2/99	Ling	1m2f	F(0-60)	STD	£2097
63	9/98	Wwck	1m2f169yF(0-60)H		G-F	£2910
74	5/96	Ling	1m2f	F(0-70)H	G-F	£2928
72	4/96	Leic	1m1f218yE(0-70)H		GD	£3616

Total win prize-money £16455

Going (Turf): Sf: 0-9 GS: 0-1 **Gd: 3-13** GF: 2-13 Fm: 0-1
Distance: 5f/6f: 0-0 7f-8f: 0-1 **9f-13f: 6-44** 14f+: 0-0
Track : **LH: 5-28** RH: 1-12 **Tight: 3-19** Gall: 0-3
Aids: Bl: 0-0 Vi: 0-0 Tstrap: 0-0
Best Rating: 35 2/01 Ling 1m2f stand

Zieting (IRE)

95(97) (50d)**37d**
3-y-o b g Zieten (USA)-Ball Cat (FR) (Cricket Ball (USA))
P W Hiatt (K R Burke 29/6) S C Clark

Placings:054400-006600603 **(4319)**
2001: 9^{0}SW, 8^{0}HY, 9^{6}GF, 10^{6}GF, 8^{0}G, 8^{0}GF, 11^{6}G, 15^{0}G, 10^{3}GF

	Starts	1st	2nd	3rd	Win & Pl
Career Total (Turf)	11	0	0	1	588
Career Total (AW)	4	0	0	0	0

Going (Turf): Sf: 0-2 GS: 0-0 Gd: 0-3 GF: 0-6 Fm: 0-0
Distance: 5f/6f: 0-4 7f-8f: 0-2 9f-13f: 0-8 14f+: 0-1
Track : LH: 0-7 RH: 0-2 Tight: 0-4 Gall: 0-1
Aids: Bl: 0-0 Vi: 0-0 Tstrap: 0-0
Best Rating: 42 6/01 Kemp 1m1f gd-fm

Zietunzeen (IRE)

106 **85**
3-y-o b f Zieten (USA)-Hawksbill Special (IRE) (Taufan (USA))
A Berry Chris & Antonia Deuters

Placings:233551521-000335003605 **(5189)**
2001: 7^{0}G, 6^{0}GF, 6^{0}GF, 7^{3}G, 6^{3}G, 6^{5}G, 7^{0}G, 6^{0}GF, 7^{3}S, 6^{6}HY, 6^{0}G, 5^{5}GS

	Starts	1st	2nd	3rd	Win & Pl
Career Total (Turf)	21	2	2	5	71366

71	10/00	Donc	6f	B	GD	£18910
70	8/00	Nott	6f15y	E	GD	£3770

Total win prize-money £22680

Going (Turf): Sf: 0-5 GS: 0-1 **Gd: 2-9** GF: 0-6 Fm: 0-0
Distance: 5f/6f: 1-14 7f-8f: 1-7 9f-13f: 0-0 14f+: 0-0
Track : LH: 0-2 RH: 0-1 Tight: 0-1 Gall: 0-0
Aids: Bl: 0-0 Vi: 0-0 Tstrap: 0-0
Best Rating: 85 9/01 Yarm 7f3y soft

She scored twice as a juvenile over six furlongs but has been unable to add to her tally this year. Acts on a sound surface. Sometimes loses ground at the start.

Zietzig (IRE)

106(84) (42)**69**
4-y-o b g Zieten (USA)-Missing You (Ahonoora)
K R Burke Nigel Shields

Placings:5051420/05500640100000-000204 **(4780)**
2001: 7^{0}G, 6^{0}S, 7^{0}GF, 6^{2}GF, 7^{0}GF, 6^{4}G

	Starts	1st	2nd	3rd	Win & Pl
Career Total (Turf)	25	2	2	0	53955
Career Total (AW)	2	0	0	0	

82	8/00	Gdwd	7f	C(0-100)H	GD	£29250
74	8/99	York	6f	E	GD	£11283

Total win prize-money £40534

Going (Turf): Sf: 0-3 GS: 0-5 **Gd: 2-9** GF: 0-8 Fm: 0-0
Distance: 5f/6f: 1-14 7f-8f: 1-13 9f-13f: 0-0 14f+: 0-0
Track : LH: 0-8 **RH: 1-2** Tight: 0-3 Gall: 0-3
Aids: Bl: 0-0 Vi: 0-0 Tstrap: 0-0
Best Rating: 69 9/01 Gdwd 6f good

Landed a valuable handicap at Glorious Goodwood in the summer of 2000, but has only shown that sort of form sparingly since and has looked a character at times.

Zig Zig (IRE)

99(95) (70)**62**
4-y-o b g Perugino (USA)-Queen Of Erin (IRE) (King Of Clubs)
Mrs A Duffield Miss Betty Duxbury

Placings:0/310-04000 **(3507)**
2001: 8^{0}GF, 10^{4}GF, 8^{0}SD, 7^{0}GF, 8^{0}GF

	Starts	1st	2nd	3rd	Win & Pl
Career Total (Turf)	7	0	0	1	599
Career Total (AW)	2	1	0	0	2821

70	6/00	Sthl	6f	D	STD	£2821

Total win prize-money £2821

Going (Turf): Sf: 0-1 GS: 0-0 Gd: 0-0 GF: 0-5 Fm: 0-1
Distance: **5f/6f: 1-2** 7f-8f: 0-5 9f-13f: 0-2 14f+: 0-0
Track : **LH: 1-3** RH: 0-4 Tight: 0-1 Gall: 0-1
Aids: Bl: 0-0 Vi: 0-0 Tstrap: 0-0
Best Rating: 65 6/01 Sthl 1m stand

Lightly raced. Gained his only success over six furlongs last term on the All-Weather. Did not appear to stay ten furlongs latest start. Best on a sound surface.

Zilarator (USA)

106 **94**
5-y-o b g Zilzal (USA)-Allegedly (USA) (Sir Ivor)
W J Haggas Wentworth Racing (pty) Ltd

Placings:012U0355/616152-660521 **(5226)**
2001: 12^{6}S, 18^{6}GF, 16^{0}F, 13^{5}G, 18^{2}G, 11^{1}S

	Starts	1st	2nd	3rd	Win & Pl
Career Total (Turf)	20	4	3	1	45019

81	10/01	York	1m3f195yC(0-85)		SFT	£7105

95	9/00	Kemp	1m4f	C(0-90)	SFT	£7058
91	4/00	Epsm	1m4f10y	C(0-95)H	HVY	£10773
72	4/99	Leic	1m1f218yD		HVY	£3541

Total win prize-money £28480

Going (Turf): **Sf: 4-9** GS: 0-3 Gd: 0-5 GF: 0-2 Fm: 0-1
Distance: 5f/6f: 0-0 7f-8f: 0-0 **9f-13f: 4-11** 14f+: 0-9
Track : LH: 2-12 RH: 2-8 Tight: 1-5 Gall: 1-10
Aids: Bl: 0-0 Vi: 0-0 Tstrap: 0-0
Best Rating: 94 5/01 Ches 2m2f147y gd-fm

A winner twice in 2000, including the Great Metropolitan at Epsom, soft ground is clearly a must. Looked well held all this season until a promising run when second at Chester in August, and scrambled home at York. Stays well.

Zilch

108 **109**

3-y-o ch c Zilzal (USA)-Bunty Boo (Noalto)
R Hannon Mary Mayall, Linda Corbett, Julie Martin

Placings:242341-105630 **(5004)**
2001: 6^{1}S, 7^{0}GF, 6^{5}Y, 6^{6}GY, 7^{3}GS, 6^{0}S

	Starts	1st	2nd	3rd	Win & Pl
Career Total (Turf)	**12**	**2**	**2**	**2**	**52567**

104	5/01	Newb	6f8y	B	SFT	£9581
95	11/00	Donc	6f	D	HVY	£3363

Total win prize-money £12946

Going (Turf): Sf: 2-4 GS: 0-1 Gd: 0-1 GF: 0-4 Fm: 0-0
Distance: 5f/6f: 1-9 7f-8f: 1-3 9f-13f: 0-0 14f+: 0-0
Track : LH: 0-0 RH: 0-1 Tight: 0-0 Gall: 0-0
Aids: Bl: 0-0 Vi: 0-0 Tstrap: 0-0
Best Rating: 109 8/01 Curr 6f gd-yld

Out of a good sprinting mare, he was a consistent sort as a juvenile, his best run being when a neck second in the Gimcrack, but his solitary win came on heavy. Usually held up off the pace, he has been known to sweat up on occasions. Won on his reappearance at three, looking likely to get seven furlongs, but ran badly on fast ground over that trip at Newmarket next time. Highly-tried since, he put in two good efforts in Ireland and ran quite well back over seven at Goodwood. Needs to drop in class to add to his total.

Zilkha

95 **33**

3-y-o gr f Petong-Peperonata (IRE) (Cyrano De Bergerac)
I A Balding Anthony & Valerie Hogarth

Placings:000-0604000 **(5174)**
2001: 6^{0}F, 6^{6}GF, 8^{0}GF, 8^{4}GF, 7^{0}F, 6^{0}GF, 8^{0}GS

	Starts	1st	2nd	3rd	Win & Pl
Career Total (Turf)	**10**	**0**	**0**	**0**	**0**

Going (Turf): Sf: 0-0 GS: 0-2 Gd: 0-1 GF: 0-5 Fm: 0-2
Distance: 5f/6f: 0-5 7f-8f: 0-4 9f-13f: 0-1 14f+: 0-0
Track : LH: 0-2 RH: 0-1 Tight: 0-1 Gall: 0-1
Aids: Bl: 0-1 Vi: 0-0 Tstrap: 0-0
Best Rating: 48 7/01 Sals 1m gd-fm

Zilmaid Dancer

87 **63**

2-y-o b f Zilzal (USA)-Briggsmaid (Elegant Air)
P W Harris April Connection

Placings:40 **(2056)**
2001: 6^{4}F, 6^{0}GF

	Starts	1st	2nd	3rd	Win & Pl
Career Total (Turf)	**2**	**0**	**0**	**0**	**0**

Going (Turf): Sf: 0-0 GS: 0-0 Gd: 0-0 GF: 0-1 Fm: 0-1
Distance: 5f/6f: 0-2 7f-8f: 0-0 9f-13f: 0-0 14f+: 0-0
Track : LH: 0-0 RH: 0-0 Tight: 0-0 Gall: 0-0
Aids: Bl: 0-0 Vi: 0-0 Tstrap: 0-0
Best Rating: 63 5/01 Rdcr 6f firm

Zincalo (USA)

101(101) (43)**43**

5-y-o gr g Zilzal (USA)-Silver Glitz (USA) (Grey Dawn Ii)
Mrs D Haine (C E Brittain 28/7) Mrs Diana Haine

Placings:0224600/**0**401336000-**443**040**0**000 **(3454)**
2001: 12^{4}SW, **16**^{4}SD, **16**^{3}SD, 15^{0}HY, 17^{4}GF, 11^{0}F, **12**^{0}SD, 11^{0}GF, 14^{0}GF

	Starts	1st	2nd	3rd	Win & Pl
Career Total (Turf)	**21**	**1**	**2**	**2**	**6424**
Career Total (AW)	**5**	**0**	**0**	**1**	**312**

57	6/00	Nott	1m6f15y	E(0-70)H	G-F	£2930

Total win prize-money £2930

Going (Turf): Sf: 0-5 GS: 0-1 Gd: 0-3 **GF: 1-9** Fm: 0-3
Distance: 5f/6f: 0-0 7f-8f: 0-0 9f-13f: 0-6 **14f+: 1-20**
Track : **LH: 1-20** RH: 0-5 Tight: 0-13 Gall: 0-3
Aids: Bl: 0-6 Vi: 0-1 **Tstrap: 1-13**
Best Rating: 43 5/01 Bath 2m1f34y gd-fm

He is very one-paced and looks as if he needs a severe test of stamina.

Zindabad (FR)

116 **116**

5-y-o b h Shirley Heights-Miznah (IRE) (Sadler's Wells (USA))
M Johnston Abdulla Buhaleeba

Placings:212/661115/33-141246 **(5124a)**
2001: 10^{1}G, 10^{4}GF, 11^{1}G, 12^{2}GF, 12^{4}GS, 12^{6}G

	Starts	1st	2nd	3rd	Win & Pl
Career Total (Turf)	**17**	**6**	**3**	**2**	**149149**

112	6/01	Loic	1m3f183y∧		GD	£13978
104	5/01	NmkR	1m2f	B	GD	£9210
112	8/99	Wind	1m2f7y	A	GD	£19650
112	7/99	Asct	1m2f	B(0-105)H	G-F	£13943
102	7/99	NmkJ	1m2f	B(0-105)H	G-F	£19250
97	9/98	Pont	1m4y	D	G-F	£3347

Total win prize-money £79378

Going (Turf): Sf: 0-1 GS: 0-2 **Gd: 4-6** GF: 2-8 Fm: 0-0
Distance: 5f/6f: 0-0 7f-8f: 0-2 **9f-13f: 6-15** 14f+: 0-0
Track : LH: 1-3 **RH: 3-12** Tight: 1-4 **Gall: 2-5**
Aids: Bl: 0-0 Vi: 0-0 Tstrap: 0-0
Best Rating: 116 9/01 Wood 1m4f good

He made great strides through 1999, winning two valuable handicaps and a Group Three, but raced only twice last year. He was favoured by the weights when just holding off Mubtaker by a short head in a conditions stakes at Newmarket in May and beat the same horse by the same margin in a Leicester Listed event in June. Beaten just a head by Sandmason in the Hardwicke at Royal Ascot, and ran well behind Mutamam on two occasions afterwards. Most of his wins have been over ten furlongs, but he stays 12 and is best on a sound surface.

Zinging

96 **76**

2-y-o b c Fraam-Hi Hoh (IRE) (Fayruz)
J J Bridger (M R Channon 25/8) Mrs Julie Jenner

Placings:451545004044 **(4730)**
2001: 5^{4}S, 5^{5}S, 5^{1}GS, 6^{5}GF, 6^{4}GF, 5^{5}GF, 5^{0}GF, 6^{0}G, 5^{4}G, 5^{0}S, 5^{4}GF, 5^{4}F

	Starts	1st	2nd	3rd	Win & Pl
Career Total (Turf)	**12**	**1**	**0**	**0**	**5752**

66	5/01	Haml	5f4y	D	G-S	£4231

Total win prize-money £4232

Going (Turf): Sf: 0-3 **GS: 1-1** Gd: 0-2 GF: 0-5 Fm: 0-1
Distance: **5f/6f: 1-11** 7f-8f: 0-1 9f-13f: 0-0 14f+: 0-0
Track : LH: 0-1 RH: 0-1 Tight: 0-1 Gall: 0-1
Aids: Bl: 0-0 Vi: 0-0 Tstrap: 0-0
Best Rating: 78 7/01 Kemp 5f gd-fm

Winner of a Hamilton maiden on softish ground, but he has been well held since including in a seller.

Zipping (IRE)

107 **111**

2-y-o b c Zafonic (USA)-Zelda (IRE) (Caerleon (USA))
Robert Collet R C Strauss

Placings:213122 **(5104)**
2001: 4^{2}GS, 5^{1}G, 5^{3}G, 5^{1}GS, 6^{2}GS, 6^{2}GS

	Starts	1st	2nd	3rd	Win & Pl
Career Total (Turf)	**6**	**2**	**3**	**1**	**112691**

100	7/01	MsnL	5f110y	G-S	£33948
	6/01	MsnL	5f	GD	£6984

Total win prize-money £40932

Going (Turf): Sf: 0-0 **GS: 1-4 Gd: 1-2** GF: 0-0 Fm: 0-0
Distance: **5f/6f: 2-5** 7f-8f: 0-0 9f-13f: 0-0 14f+: 0-0
Track : LH: 0-0 RH: 0-0 Tight: 0-0 Gall: 0-0
Aids: Bl: 0-0 Vi: 0-0 Tstrap: 0-0
Best Rating: 111 8/01 Deau 6f gd-sft

A high-class French colt, he just got up to win the Prix Robert Papin at Maisons Laffitte and only found Johannesburg too good in the Prix Morny, and again in the Middle Park. Suited by cut in the ground.

Ziria (IRE)

96 **95**

2-y-o b f Danehill Dancer (IRE)-Surprise Visitor (IRE) (Be My Guest (USA))
C Laffon-Parias L Marinopoulos

Placings:11500 **(5054)**
2001: 4^{1}G, 5^{1}G, 5^{5}GS, 5^{0}S, 6^{0}S

	Starts	1st	2nd	3rd	Win & Pl
Career Total (Turf)	**5**	**2**	**0**	**0**	**28032**

95	7/01	Chan	5f	GD	£21339
	5/01	StCl	4f110y	GD	£4753

Total win prize-money £26092

Going (Turf): Sf: 0-2 GS: 0-1 **Gd: 2-2** GF: 0-0 Fm: 0-0
Distance: **5f/6f: 1-4** 7f-8f: 0-0 9f-13f: 0-0 14f+: 0-0
Track : LH: 0-0 RH: 0-0 Tight: 0-0 Gall: 0-0
Aids: Bl: 0-0 Vi: 0-0 Tstrap: 0-0
Best Rating: 95 9/01 Chan 5f110y soft

Very free-running, speedy half-sister to winner Densim Blue. Won newcomers' event over 4.5 furlongs at Saint-Cloud in May, and followed up beating Dobby Road and Zipping in Group Three Prix du Bois at Chantilly in July. Has since disappointed behind those useful colts in the Robert Papin and Prix d'Arenberg and was well beaten in the Cheveley Park, but all of those races were on soft ground. Suited by five furlongs and good ground.

Zoe's Gold (USA)

(102) (73)

3-y-o b f St Jovite (USA)-Six Months Long (USA) (Northern Dancer)
J Noseda Mrs John M Weld

Placings:021 **(0232)**
2001: 8^{0}SD, 8^{2}SD, 9^{1}SD

	Starts	1st	2nd	3rd	Win & Pl
Career Total (Turf)	**0**	**0**	**0**	**0**	
Career Total (AW)	**3**	**1**	**1**	**0**	**3779**

73	2/01	Wolv	1m1f79y	D	STD	£2947

Total win prize-money £2947

Going (Turf): Sf: 0-0 GS: 0-0 Gd: 0-0 GF: 0-0 Fm: 0-0
Distance: 5f/6f: 0-0 7f-8f: 0-1 **9f-13f: 1-2** 14f+: 0-0
Track : **LH: 1-3** RH: 0-0 **Tight: 1-3** Gall: 0-0
Aids: Bl: 0-0 Vi: 0-0 Tstrap: 0-0
Best Rating: 73 2/01 Wolv 1m1f79y stand

Zoena

98(102) (62)**60**

4-y-o ch f Emarati (USA)-Exotic Forest (Dominion)
J G Portman Mrs R Pease

Placings:403040/0456305303165-150200 **(2961)**
2001: 6^{1}SD, 6^{5}SD, 6^{0}SW, 6^{2}GF, 6^{0}GF, 6^{0}GF

	Starts	1st	2nd	3rd	Win & Pl
Career Total (Turf)	**17**	**0**	**1**	**3**	**2824**
Career Total (AW)	**8**	**2**	**0**	**1**	**4826**

56	1/01	Ling	6f	E	STD	£2618
62	11/00	Ling	5f	F(0-60)H	STD	£1767

Total win prize-money £4386

Going (Turf): Sf: 0-1 GS: 0-0 Gd: 0-5 GF: 0-10 Fm: 0-1

Distance: **5f/6f: 2-25** 7f-8f: 0-0 9f-13f: 0-0 14f+: 0-0
Track : **LH: 2-13** RH: 0-1 **Tight: 2-10** Gall: 0-3
Aids: Bl: 0-0 Vi: 0-0 Tstrap: 0-0
Best Rating: 60 6/01 Sals 6f gd-fm

Bits and pieces of form in turf sprint handicaps, but both of her wins so far have come on the Lingfield Equitrack.

Zone

97 **91+**

2-y-o b c Zilzal (USA)-Thea (USA) (Marju (IRE))
P F I Cole Highclere Thoroughbred Racing Ltd

Placings:1 **(5684)**
2001: 8^{1}S

	Starts	1st	2nd	3rd	Win & Pl
Career Total (Turf)	1	1	0	0	4680

91	11/01	Donc	1m	E	SFT	£4680

Total win prize-money £4680

Going (Turf): Sf: 1-1 GS: 0-0 Gd: 0-0 GF: 0-0 Fm: 0-0
Distance: 5f/6f: 0-0 **7f-8f: 1-1** 9f-13f: 0-0 14f+: 0-0
Track : LH: 0-0 RH: 0-0 Tight: 0-0 Gall: 0-0
Aids: Bl: 0-0 Vi: 0-0 Tstrap: 0-0
Best Rating: 91 11/01 Donc 1m soft

His dam, a seven-furlong winner, is from the family of Group One-winning miler Fly To The Stars. He made an impressive debut at Doncaster and should make up into a smart colt at three.

Zonergem

103 **77**

3-y-o ch c Zafonic (USA)-Anasazi (IRE) (Sadler's Wells (USA))
Lady Herries Lady Herries

Placings:26 **(5182)**
2001: 9^{2}GS, 10^{6}HY

	Starts	1st	2nd	3rd	Win & Pl
Career Total (Turf)	2	0	1	0	1479

Going (Turf): Sf: 0-1 GS: 0-1 Gd: 0-0 GF: 0-0 Fm: 0-0
Distance: 5f/6f: 0-0 7f-8f: 0-0 9f-13f: 0-2 14f+: 0-0
Track : LH: 0-0 RH: 0-1 Tight: 0-2 Gall: 0-0
Aids: Bl: 0-0 Vi: 0-0 Tstrap: 0-0
Best Rating: 77 9/01 Gdwd 1m1f192y gd-sft

Zorro

58(95) (30)**56**

7-y-o gr g Touch Of Grey-Snow Huntress (Shirley Heights)
Jamie Poulton Mrs G M Temmerman

Placings:000/50160330/62224/51/10-0500 **(1074)**
2001: 13^{0}SD, 13^{5}SW, 13^{0}SD, 11^{0}GS

	Starts	1st	2nd	3rd	Win & Pl
Career Total (Turf)	12	2	0	2	6216
Career Total (AW)	12	1	3	0	4540

56	3/00	Wind	1m3f135y	E(0-70)H	G-F	£3010
53	12/99	Ling	1m5f	E(0-70)H	STD	£2353
57	6/97	Yarm	1m2f21y	G(0-70)H	FRM	£2168

Total win prize-money £7533

Going (Turf): Sf: 0-1 GS: 0-2 Gd: 0-2 **GF: 1-6 Fm: 1-1**
Distance: 5f/6f: 0-0 7f-8f: 0-3 **9f-13f: 3-21** 14f+: 0-0
Track : **LH: 2-17** RH: 0-4 **Tight: 3-18** Gall: 0-1
Aids: Bl: 0-2 Vi: 0-0 Tstrap: 0-0
Best Rating: 30 2/01 Ling 1m5f slow

Zoudie

99 **80**

3-y-o b f Ezzoud (IRE)-Patsy Western (Precocious)
J Noseda B McAllister

Placings:5-5202231 **(3891)**
2001: 10^{5}G, 11^{2}GF, 10^{0}GS, 10^{2}GF, 10^{2}GF, 9^{3}GF, 9^{1}F

	Starts	1st	2nd	3rd	Win & Pl
Career Total (Turf)	8	1	3	1	6665

66	8/01	Brig	1m1f209y	E	FRM	£2737

Total win prize-money £2737

Going (Turf): Sf: 0-1 GS: 0-1 Gd: 0-1 GF: 0-4 **Fm: 1-1**
Distance: 5f/6f: 0-0 7f-8f: 0-1 **9f-13f: 1-7** 14f+: 0-0
Track : **LH: 1-5** RH: 0-0 Tight: 0-1 Gall: 0-1
Aids: Bl: 0-0 Vi: 0-0 Tstrap: 0-0
Best Rating: 80 7/01 Pont 1m2f6y gd-fm

She had fluffed plenty of chances before finding a desperate maiden at Brighton in August.

Zozarharry (IRE)

106(108) (86+)**82**

3-y-o b c Nicolotte-Miss Butterfield (Cure The Blues (USA))
D J S Cosgrove (H R A Cecil 4/5) Colin Davey

Placings:005100-5100 **(4161)**
2001: 7^{5}G, 7^{1}SD, 7^{0}GS, 7^{0}GF

	Starts	1st	2nd	3rd	Win & Pl
Career Total (Turf)	6	0	0	0	0
Career Total (AW)	4	2	0	0	6169

86	6/01	Sthl	7f	D(0-85)H	STD	£3893
79	11/00	Sthl	6f	F	STD	£2275

Total win prize-money £6169

Going (Turf): Sf: 0-1 GS: 0-1 Gd: 0-1 GF: 0-3 Fm: 0-0
Distance: 5f/6f: 1-4 7f-8f: 1-6 9f-13f: 0-0 14f+: 0-0
Track : **LH: 2-4** RH: 0-0 Tight: 0-1 Gall: 0-0
Aids: Bl: 0-0 Vi: 0-0 Tstrap: 0-0
Best Rating: 86 6/01 Sthl 7f stand

Twice a winner on the Southwell All-Weather track for his current trainer, in between ran well in a Newmarket handicap for Henry Cecil. Stays seven furlongs.

Zsazsabella (IRE)

91 **78**

2-y-o b f Alzao (USA)-Zifta (USA) (Zilzal (USA))
J W Hills M Wauchope,Sir Simon Dunning,R Cottam

Placings:40 **(5277)**
2001: 7^{4}GF, 7^{0}GS

	Starts	1st	2nd	3rd	Win & Pl
Career Total (Turf)	2	0	0	0	347

Going (Turf): Sf: 0-0 GS: 0-1 Gd: 0-0 GF: 0-1 Fm: 0-0
Distance: 5f/6f: 0-0 7f-8f: 0-2 9f-13f: 0-0 14f+: 0-0
Track : LH: 0-0 RH: 0-1 Tight: 0-0 Gall: 0-1
Aids: Bl: 0-0 Vi: 0-0 Tstrap: 0-0
Best Rating: 78 9/01 Kemp 7f gd-fm

Zucchero

112 **91**

5-y-o br g Dilum (USA)-Legal Sound (Legal Eagle)
D W P Arbuthnot Philip Banfield

Placings:000/011126/61655436-23610 **(3443)**
2001: 7^{2}G, 7^{3}GF, 8^{6}GF, 8^{1}GF, 7^{0}GF

	Starts	1st	2nd	3rd	Win & Pl
Career Total (Turf)	22	5	2	2	54604

91	7/01	Newb	1m	B(0-105)H	G-F	£23200
80	7/00	Newb	7f64y	D(0-85)H	G-F	£4030
73	7/99	NmkJ	7f	D(0-80)H	G-F	£4776
66	7/99	Ling	7f	F(0-65)H	G-F	£2742
68	7/99	Chep	6f16y	E(0-70)H	G-F	£3165

Total win prize-money £37913

Going (Turf): Sf: 0-0 GS: 0-1 Gd: 0-2 **GF: 5-18** Fm: 0-1
Distance: 5f/6f: 0-3 **7f-8f: 5-18** 9f-13f: 0-1 14f+: 0-0
Track : **LH: 1-4** RH: 0-2 Tight: 0-1 **Gall: 1-2**
Aids: **Bl: 4-8** Vi: 0-1 Tstrap: 0-0
Best Rating: 91 7/01 Asct 7f gd-fm

A useful seven-furlong handicapper who is best on a sound surface and always capable of winning a decent prize or two. Was blinkered for his first four wins, but wore sheepskin cheek pieces on the bridle when scoring at Newbury.

Zuhair

109 (77)**81**

8-y-o ch g Mujtahid (USA)-Ghzaalh (USA) (Northern Dancer)
D Nicholls The Gardening Partnership

Placings:315/01036530200220/00640052000 4/00642 010411001000/0000000331505 0100-0000455033210000500 **(5381)**
2001: 5^{0}S, 6^{0}S, 5^{0}GS, 5^{0}GF, 6^{4}GF, 6^{5}GF, 5^{5}GF, 5^{0}G, 6^{3}GF, 5^{3}G, 6^{2}GF, 5^{1}GF, 6^{0}G, 6^{0}G, 6^{0}G, 6^{0}GF, 5^{5}G, 6^{0}G, 5^{0}S

	Starts	1st	2nd	3rd	Win & Pl
Career Total (Turf)	77	8	5	7	107056
Career Total (AW)	6	1	1	0	3566

83	8/01	Gdwd	5f	D(0-80)H	G-F	£9379
84	9/00	Gdwd	6f	C(0-95)H	GD	£14690
82	8/00	Gdwd	5f	D(0-80)H	G-F	£9555
88	8/99	York	6f	C(0-100)H	GD	£16960
83	7/99	Gdwd	6f	B H	G-F	£17320
74	7/99	Gdwd	5f	D(0-80)H	G-F	£9231
71	6/99	Ling	5f	E(0-70)H	G-F	£3223
66	5/97	Wolv	6f	G	STD	£1634
85	6/95	NmkJ	6f	D	G-F	£4230

Total win prize-money £86225

Going (Turf): Sf: 0-8 GS: 0-10 Gd: 2-33 **GF: 6-23** Fm: 0-2
Distance: **5f/6f: 9-77** 7f-8f: 0-5 9f-13f: 0-1 14f+: 0-0
Track : **LH: 1-11** RH: 0-0 **Tight: 1-8** Gall: 0-0
Aids: Bl: 0-2 Vi: 0-0 Tstrap: 0-0
Best Rating: 83 8/01 Gdwd 5f gd-fm

A useful sprint handicapper on his day, he is ideally suited by a sound surface. Goes particularly well at Goodwood where he has won five times including his only victories of both this and last season. What is expected from him in any given race is usually reflected in the market.

Zulfaa (USA)

104 **94**

3-y-o b f Bahri (USA)-Haniya (IRE) (Caerleon (USA))
J L Dunlop Hamdan Al Maktoum

Placings:412-55114 **(4275)**
2001: 10^{5}F, 10^{5}GS, 10^{1}GF, 9^{1}G, 9^{4}GS

	Starts	1st	2nd	3rd	Win & Pl
Career Total (Turf)	8	3	1	0	19637

94	8/01	Ripn	1m1f	C(0-90)H	GD	£6935
92	6/01	NmkJ	1m2f	C(0-90)H	G-F	£6171
82	8/00	Ling	7f140y	F	G-F	£2530

Total win prize-money £15638

Going (Turf): Sf: 0-1 GS: 0-2 Gd: 1-2 **GF: 2-2** Fm: 0-1
Distance: 5f/6f: 0-0 7f-8f: 1-3 **9f-13f: 2-5** 14f+: 0-0
Track : LH: 0-3 **RH: 2-3** Tight: 1-2 Gall: 1-3
Aids: Bl: 0-0 Vi: 0-0 Tstrap: 0-0
Best Rating: 94 8/01 Ripn 1m1f good

She shaped with considerable promise on her reappearance and won a ten-furlong handicap at Newmarket two runs later when making all. Did exactly the same thing when following up at Ripon and is an effective sort when able to dominate.

Zumtobel (IRE)

79 **43**

3-y-o b f Halling (USA)-Ziggy Belle (USA) (Danzig (USA))
J L Dunlop Stonethorn Stud Farms Limited

Placings:0 **(1146)**
2001: 8^{0}G

	Starts	1st	2nd	3rd	Win & Pl
Career Total (Turf)	1	0	0	0	

Going (Turf): Sf: 0-0 GS: 0-0 Gd: 0-1 GF: 0-0 Fm: 0-0
Distance: 5f/6f: 0-0 7f-8f: 0-1 9f-13f: 0-0 14f+: 0-0
Track : LH: 0-0 RH: 0-0 Tight: 0-0 Gall: 0-0
Aids: Bl: 0-0 Vi: 0-0 Tstrap: 0-0
Best Rating: 43 5/01 NmkR 1m good

FLAT JOCKEY STATISTICS 2001 (TURF ONLY)

	Since Wnr	£	1st	2nd	3rd	Unpl	Mts	cent	stake
K Fallon	1	1998522	159	119	106	560	944	16.8	-174.87
K Darley	5	1689680	156	117	109	567	949	16.4	**+ 5.47**
Pat Eddery	5	1004734	120	81	77	515	793	15.1	-108.55
T Quinn	9	939004	115	123	85	449	772	14.8	-100.69
D Holland	0	853159	95	57	68	358	578	16.4	**+35.51**
L Dettori	18	1823135	94	62	44	193	393	23.9	-11.49
R Hughes	1	742866	88	59	68	361	576	15.2	-14.84
J P Spencer	8	782452	80	69	41	352	542	14.7	**+53.06**
R Hills	9	1088019	79	73	55	235	442	17.8	-13.20
S Sanders	0	381866	77	65	49	423	614	12.5	- 3.64
W Supple	0	425481	71	65	60	447	643	11.0	-117.03
G Duffield	0	445360	67	53	62	482	664	10.0	-241.05
J Fortune	2	457390	66	72	70	454	662	9.9	-219.89
S Drowne	5	551271	64	79	69	557	769	8.3	-348.13
F Norton	34	469175	62	63	53	445	623	9.9	-89.03
J Fanning	8	308230	59	51	52	416	578	10.2	-61.16
M Hills	0	584894	57	51	48	324	480	11.8	-87.63
Dane O'Neill	21	495638	56	50	47	437	590	9.4	-168.19
R Winston	6	331184	55	67	83	530	735	7.4	-258.67
T E Durcan	0	294954	54	52	36	341	483	11.1	-54.60
F Lynch	22	235206	54	56	66	403	579	9.3	-203.13
K Dalgleish	7	303250	50	41	43	432	566	8.8	-64.18
B Doyle	7	228477	49	33	40	307	429	11.4	-31.89
J Carroll	16	204608	48	51	56	390	545	8.8	-200.31
P Robinson	8	505681	46	50	39	345	480	9.5	-188.48
G Carter	12	256856	45	22	46	264	377	11.9	-47.14
C Catlin	28	215904	43	39	37	401	520	8.2	**+ 3.19**
J Mackay	0	328193	40	31	37	300	408	9.8	-52.91
J Reid	15	196351	34	51	55	345	485	7.0	-246.17
M Fenton	17	242737	34	53	61	420	568	5.9	-302.53
W Ryan	7	210998	31	48	40	225	344	9.0	-138.72
P Dobbs	13	127845	30	27	35	196	288	10.4	-65.82
I Mongan	25	126607	29	33	25	308	395	7.3	-162.59
P Fitzsimons	19	159951	28	22	24	186	260	10.7	-85.36
Martin Dwyer	10	339788	28	33	49	394	504	5.5	-240.67
M J Kinane	33	2437927	26	17	18	101	162	16.0	- 3.67
P Hanagan	62	119286	26	28	30	310	394	6.5	-109.07
R Mullen	18	116506	25	26	35	315	401	6.2	-230.82
Darren Williams	13	110867	25	26	20	168	239	10.4	-99.73
Craig Williams	3	112823	25	31	38	203	297	8.4	-159.80
D Sweeney	57	137431	24	30	37	308	399	6.0	-149.30
M Roberts	31	315982	23	24	35	191	273	8.4	-118.28
C Rutter	32	99071	23	25	18	279	345	6.6	-131.01
Dean McKeown	33	202967	22	12	32	320	386	5.6	-181.92
S Whitworth	14	105369	22	17	21	296	356	6.1	-181.48
D Kinsella	0	127841	22	26	30	285	363	6.0	-69.25
P Doe	60	140928	21	25	24	331	401	5.2	-154.50
J Weaver	28	85189	21	26	26	252	325	6.4	-119.93
M Tebbutt	49	162777	21	28	26	213	288	7.2	-169.61
G Gibbons	49	72390	20	19	22	191	252	7.9	-15.00
Dale Gibson	24	107876	20	21	39	357	437	4.5	-215.25

WINNING TRAINERS 2001 (TURF ONLY)

	Races Won	Stakes £
1. A P O'Brien (IRE)	20	3,389,909
2. Sir Michael Stoute	75	2,135,925
3. Saeed Bin Suroor	24	1,932,735
4. M Johnston	112	1,782,070
5. B W Hills	103	1,675,670
6. R Hannon	103	1,399,146
7. J L Dunlop	107	1,355,681
8. M R Channon	67	975,766
9. M P Tregoning	53	975,611
10. E A L Dunlop	73	871,145
11. T D Easterby	73	783,923
12. H R A Cecil	48	773,275
13. G Wragg	29	741,666
14. J H M Gosden	54	729,464
15. M A Jarvis	53	693,910
16. J R Fanshawe	37	651,866
17. D R C Elsworth	35	641,949
18. P F I Cole	54	623,271
19. I A Balding	36	610,629
20. B J Meehan	64	562,024
21. D Nicholls	47	521,853
22. D R Loder	42	512,538
23. L M Cumani	25	492,317
24. G A Butler	41	492,279
25. P W Harris	36	486,886
26. A Berry	72	473,807
27. Sir Mark Prescott	52	450,232
28. Mrs A J Perrett	36	444,804
29. R Charlton	33	444,144
30. M L W Bell	44	433,682

WINNING OWNERS FLAT 2001 (TURF ONLY)

	Races Won	Stakes £
1. Godolphin	24	1,932,735
2. Hamdan Al Maktoum	108	1,779,558
3. Mrs John Magnier & Mr M Tabor	5	1,353,253
4. K Abdulla	71	1,096,772
5. M Tabor & Mrs John Magnier	11	1,019,201
6. Maktoum Al Maktoum	48	901,946
7. Cheveley Park Stud	38	805,816
8. Sheikh Mohammed	42	553,296
9. Lord Weinstock	5	493,160
10. Sheikh Ahmed Al Maktoum	28	424,052
11. J C Smith	13	372,757
12. Michael Tabor	2	276,523
13. Jaber Abdullah	9	261,133
14. P D Savill	9	249,717
15. Plantation Stud	8	230,800
16. Paul Dean	3	230,538
17. Mrs David Nagle & Mrs John Magnier	1	213,127
18. Lucayan Stud	15	208,066
19. Mr & Mrs G Middlebrook	9	207,070
20. Lael Stable & Mrs V Shelton	1	204,650
21. Mrs John Magnier	3	202,544
22. H H Aga Khan	12	200,682
23. M P Burke	9	198,629
24. M J Dawson	15	195,750
25. Saeed Suhail	7	191,975
26. Mollers Racing	8	190,794
27. Sir Alex Ferguson & Mrs John Magnier	2	188,500
28. Prince A A Faisal	11	182,379
29. Oremsa Partnership	4	177,843
30. Trevor C Stewart	2	176,400

Raceform Median Times 2001

ASCOT
5f 1m2
6f 1m16.2
7f 1m29.9
1m Round.................1m43.2
1m Straight..............1m41.9
1m2f 2m8.9
1m4f 2m34.1
2m45yds...................3m34.8
2m4f 4m23.9
2m6f34yds................4m57.7

AYR
5f 1m0.6
6f 1m13.7
7f 1m29.4
1m 1m43
1m1f.......................1m56.4
1m2f 2m12.2
1m2f192yds..............2m23.6
1m5f13yds................2m55.9
1m7f 3m23.7
2m1f105yds..............3m59.4

BATH
5f11yds....................1m2.5
5f161yds..................1m11.4
1m5yds....................1m41.2
1m2f46yds................2m11
1m3f144yds..............2m30.4
1m5f22yds................2m51.3
2m1f34yds................3m49.6

BEVERLEY
5f 1m4.2
7f100yds..................1m34.4
1m100yds.................2m7
1m3f216yds..............2m38.1
2m35yds...................3m39.4

BRIGHTON
5f59yds....................1m2.3
5f213yds..................1m10
6f209yds..................1m22.7
7f214yds..................1m34.9
1m1f209yds..............2m2.5
1m3f196yds..............2m31.9

CARLISLE
5f 1m1.6
5f207yds..................1m14.6
6f206yds..................1m27.6
7f214yds..................1m40.7
1m1f61yds................1m58.1
1m4f 2m34.8
1m6f32yds................3m7.3
2m1f52yds................3m49.7

CATTERICK
5f 1m0.8
5f212yds..................1m14.4
7f 1m27.7
1m3f214yds..............2m40.2
1m5f175yds..............3m4.9
1m7f177yds..............3m32.2

CHEPSTOW
5f16yds....................59.5
6f16yds....................1m12.2
7f16yds....................1m23.3
1m14yds...................1m35.9
1m2f36yds................2m9.2
1m4f23yds................2m38.3
2m49yds...................3m38.3
2m2f 4m

CHESTER
5f16yds....................1m2.3
6f18yds....................1m15.9
7f2yds......................1m28.7
7m122yds..................1m35.6
1m2f75yds................2m13.8
1m3f79yds................2m26.4
1m4f66yds................2m41
1m5f89yds................2m56.2
1m7f195yds..............3m33.9
2m2f147yds..............4m6.5

DONCASTER
5f 1m1.3
5f140yds..................1m7.9
6f 1m14.3
6f110yds..................1m20.7
7f 1m27.7
1m Round.................1m40.4
1m Straight..............1m41.3
1m2f60yds................2m11.8
1m4f 2m35.3
1m6f132yds..............3m9.7
2m110yds.................3m41.8
2m2f 3m57.7

EPSOM
5f 55.9
6f 1m10.6
7f 1m23.7
1m114yds.................1m45.5
1m2f18yds................2m8.7
1m4f10yds................2m38.5

FOLKESTONE
5f 1m0.8
6f 1m13.7
7f 1m28.1
1m1f149yds..............2m4.8
1m4f 2m39.8
1m7f92yds................3m27.2
2m93yds...................3m40.3

GOODWOOD
5f 59.1
6f 1m13
7f 1m28.2
1m 1m40.5
1m1f 1m57.1
1m1f192yds..............2m8.4
1m4f 2m39.1
1m6f 3m4.2
2m 3m30.8
2m4f 4m20.9

HAMILTON
5f4yds......................1m1.3
6f5yds......................1m13
1m65yds...................1m49.3
1m1f36yds................1m59
1m3f16yds................2m25.9
1m4f17yds................2m39.5
1m5f9yds..................2m52.6

HAYDOCK
5f 1m2.1
6f 1m14.7
7f30yds....................1m32.2

1m30yds..............1m45.6
1m2f120yds..........2m17.8
1m3f200yds..........2m35.6
1m6f 3m6.6
2m45yds..............3m38.7

KEMPTON

5f 1m1.6
6f 1m13.3
7f Jubilee..............1m27.1
7f 1m26.6
1m Jubilee...........1m40.5
1m 1m39.8
1m1f 1m54.8
1m2f Jubilee..........2m6.1
1m3f30yds............2m22.4
1m4f. 2m35
1m6f92yds............3m10.7
2m 3m30.4

LEICESTER

5f2yds..................1m1.1
5f218yds...............1m13.5
7f9yds...................1m26
1m8yds 1m39.2
1m1f218yds...........2m8.8
1m3f183yds...........2m35.3

LINGFIELD (Turf)

5f 59.1
6f 1m11.6
7f 1m24.3
7f140yds..............1m31.4
1m1f 1m55.6
1m2f 2m9.4
1m3f106yds...........2m29.2
1m6f 3m6.9
2m 3m33.1

LINGFIELD (AW)

5f 59.9
6f 1m13.3
7f 1m26.3
1m 1m39.8
1m2f 2m7.6
1m4f 2m34.2
1m5f 2m48.5
2m 3m34.8

MUSSELBURGH

5f 1m0.6
1m200yds.............1m54.2
1m4f31yds............2m39.6
1m6f 3m6.1
2m 3m34.7

NEWBURY

5f34yds.................1m2.9
6f8yds...................1m14.5
7f 1m27.9
7f64yds Round......1m31.3
1m 1m41.3
1m7yds Round.....1m38.7
1m1f 1m54.6
1m2f6yds..............2m8.7
1m3f5yds..............2m23.8
1m4f5yds..............2m36.7
1m5f61yds............2m51.8
2m 3m36.3

NEWCASTLE

5f 1m1.6
6f 1m15.2
7f 1m28
1m Round.............1m43.9
1m3yds.................1m41
1m1f9yds..............1m57.8
1m2f32yds............2m12
1m4f93yds............2m43.1
2m19yds...............3m35.2

NEWMARKET (Rowley)

5f 1m0.5
6f 1m13.1
7f 1m26.4
1m 1m39.4
1m1f 1m51.9
1m2f 2m5.6
1m4f 2m33.7
1m6f 3m1.1
2m 3m26.2
2m2f 3m52.6

NEWMARKET (July)

5f 59.8
6f 1m13.2
7f 1m26.7
1m 1m40.5
1m2f 2m6.4
1m4f 2m32.9
1m6f 3m11.6
2m 24y 3m27.0

NOTTINGHAM

5f13yds.................1m1.8
6f15yds.................1m14.8
1m54yds...............1m46.3
1m1f213yds...........2m9.5
1m6f15yds............3m7.1
2m9yds.................3m33.4

PONTEFRACT

5f 1m3.8
6f 1m17.4
1m4yds.................1m45.8
1m2f6yds..............2m14.1
1m4f8yds..............2m40.4
2m1f22y 3m52
2m1f216y 4m3
2m5f122y 5m0.8

REDCAR

5f 58.8
6f 1m11.8
7f 1m25
1m 1m37.9
1m1f 1m53.7
1m2f 2m7
1m3f 2m21
1m6f19yds............3m5
2m 3m32

RIPON

5f 1m0.2
6f 1m12.9
1m 1m41.1
1m1f 1m53.4
1m2f 2m8
1m4f60y 2m39.9
2m 3m32.8

SALISBURY

5f 1m1.6
6f 1m15.2
6f212yds..............1m29.2
1m 1m43.2
1m1f198yds..........2m8.5
1m4f 2m36.2
1m6f15yds............3m6.2

SANDOWN

5f6yds..................1m2.2
7f16yds................1m31.1
1m14yds...............1m43.9
1m1f 1m56.5

1m2f7yds..............2m10.2
1m3f91yds............2m28.2
1m6f 3m4.3
2m78yds...............3m38.3

SOUTHWELL (AW)

5f 1m0.4
6f 1m16.9
7f 1m30.9
1m 1m44.7
1m3f 2m29
1m4f 2m42
1m6f 3m10.1
2m 3m53.3

THIRSK

5f 1m0.1
6f 1m12.6
7f 1m27.3
1m 1m39.7
1m4f 2m35.2
2m 3m30.9

WARWICK

New distances introduced in 1999/2000.
No medians available.

WINDSOR

5f10yds.................1m1.2
6f 1m12.9
1m67yds.................1m45.4
1m2f7yds...............2m7.7
1m3f135yds...........2m29.8

WOLVERHAMPTON (AW)

5f 1m2.9
6f 1m15.8
7f 1m30.3
1m100yds..............1m51
1m1f79yds.............2m2.9
1m4f 2m41.9
1m6f166yds...........3m20.7
2m46yds................3m42.3

YARMOUTH

5f43yds.................1m2.7
6f3yds...................1m13.6
7f3yds...................1m26.6
1m3yds..................1m39.7
1m2f21yds.............2m7.9
1m3f101yds...........2m27.5
1m6f17yds.............3m5.4
2m 3m31.8
2m2f51yds.............4m6.9

YORK

5f 59.3
6f 1m12.7
6f214yds...............1m25.5
7f202yds...............1m39.6
1m205yds..............1m52.5
1m2f85yds.............2m12.1
1m3f195yds...........2m31.7
1m5f194yds...........2m58.9
1m7f195yds...........3m24.6

Winners of Principal Races

Group One Races

2000 GUINEAS

2001 Golan
2000 King's Best
1999 Island Sands
1998 King of Kings
1997 Entrepreneur
1996 Mark of Esteem
1995 Pennekamp
1994 Mister Baileys
1993 Zafonic
1992 Rodrigo de Triano

CORONATION CUP

2001 Mutafaweq
2000 Daliapour
1999 Daylami
1998 Silver Patriarch
1997 Singspiel
1996 Swain
1995 Sunshack
1994 Apple Tree
1993 Opera House
1992 Saddlers' Hall

1000 GUINEAS

2001 Ameerat
2000 Lahan
1999 Wince
1998 Cape Verdi
1997 Sleepytime
1996 Bosra Sham
1995 Harayir
1994 Las Meninas
1993 Sayyedati
1992 Hatoof

LOCKINGE STKS

2001 Medicean
2000 Aljabr
1999 Fly To the Stars
1998 Cape Cross
1997 First Island
1996 Soviet Line
1995 Soviet Line
1994 Emperor Jones
1993 Swing Low
1992 Selkirk

DERBY

2001 Galileo
2000 Sinndar
1999 Oath
1998 High-Rise
1997 Benny The Dip
1996 Shaamit
1995 Lammtarra
1994 Erhaab
1993 Commander in Chief
1992 Dr Devious

CORONATION STKS

2001 Banks Hill
2000 Crimplene
1999 Balisada
1998 Exclusive
1997 Rebecca Sharp
1996 Shake the Yoke
1995 Ridgewood Pearl
1994 Kissing Cousin
1993 Gold Splash
1992 Marling

OAKS

2001 Imagine
2000 Love Divine
1999 Ramruma
1998 Shahtoush
1997 Reams of Verse
1996 Lady Carla
1995 Moonshell
1994 Balanchine
1993 Intrepidity
1992 User Friendly

GOLD CUP

2001 Royal Rebel
2000 Kayf Tara
1999 Enzeli
1998 Kayf Tara
1997 Celeric
1996 Classic Cliche
1995 Double Trigger
1994 Arcadian Heights
1993 Drum Taps
1992 Drum Taps

ST JAMES'S PALACE STKS

2001 Black Minnaloushe
2000 Giant's Causeway
1999 Sendawar
1998 Dr Fong
1997 Starborough
1996 Bijou d'Inde
1995 Bahri
1994 Grand Lodge
1993 Kingmambo
1992 Brief Truce

PRINCE OF WALES'S STKS

2001 Fantastic Light
2000 Dubai Millennium
1999 Lear Spear
1998 Faithful Son
1997 Bosra Sham
1996 First Island
1995 Muhtarram
1994 Muhtarram
1993 Placerville
1992 Perpendicular

CORAL-ECLIPSE STKS

2001 Medicean
2000 Giant's Causeway
1999 Compton Admiral
1998 Daylami
1997 Pilsudski
1996 Halling
1995 Halling
1994 Ezzoud
1993 Opera House
1992 Kooyonga

JUDDMONTE INTERNATIONAL

2001 Sakhee
2000 Giant's Causeway
1999 Royal Anthem
1998 One So Wonderful
1997 Singspiel
1996 Halling
1995 Halling
1994 Ezzoud
1993 Ezzoud
1992 Rodrigo de Triano

JULY CUP

2001 Mozart
2000 Agnes World
1999 Stravinsky
1998 Elnadim
1997 Compton Place
1996 Anabaa
1995 Lake Coniston
1994 Owington
1993 Hamas
1992 Mr Brooks

YORKSHIRE OAKS

2001 Super Tassa
2000 Petrushka
1999 Ramruma
1998 Catchascatchcan
1997 My Emma
1996 Key Change
1995 Pure Grain
1994 Only Royale
1993 Only Royale
1992 User Friendly

KING GEORGE VI & QUEEN ELIZABETH DIAMOND STKS

2001 Galileo
2000 Montjeu
1999 Daylami
1998 Swain
1997 Swain
1996 Pentire
1995 Lammtarra
1994 King's Theatre
1993 Opera House
1992 St Jovite

NUNTHORPE STKS

2001 Mozart
2000 Nuclear Debate
1999 Stravinsky
1998 Lochangel
1997 Coastal Bluff & Ya Malak (d/heat)
1996 Pivotal
1995 So Factual
1994 Piccolo (Blue Siren disq.)
1993 Lochsong
1992 Lyric Fantasy

SUSSEX STKS

2001 Noverre
2000 Giant's Causeway
1999 Aljabr
1998 Among Men
1997 Ali-Royal
1996 First Island
1995 Sayyedati
1994 Distant View
1993 Bigstone
1992 Marling

NASSAU STKS

2001 Lailani
2000 Crimplene
1999 Zahrat Dubai
1998 Alborada
1997 Ryafan
1996 Last Second
1995 Caramba
1994 Hawajiss
1993 Lyphard's Delta
1992 Ruby Tiger

STANLEY LEISURE SPRINT CUP

2001 Nuclear Debate
2000 Pipalong
1999 Diktat
1998 Tamarisk
1997 Royal Applause
1996 Iktamal
1995 Cherokee Rose
1994 Lavinia Fontana
1993 Wolfhound
1992 Sheikh Albadou

QUEEN ELIZABETH II STKS

2001 Summoner
2000 Observatory
1999 Dubai Millennium
1998 Desert Prince
1997 Air Express
1996 Mark of Esteem
1995 Bahri
1994 Maroof
1993 Bigstone
1992 Lahib

DUBAI CHAMPION STKS

2001 Nayef
2000 Kalanisi
1999 Alborada
1998 Alborada
1997 Pilsudski
1996 Bosra Sham
1995 Spectrum
1994 Dernier Empereur
1993 Hatoof
1992 Rodrigo de Triano

ST LEGER

2001 Milan
2000 Millenary
1999 Mutafaweq
1998 Nedawi
1997 Silver Patriarch
1996 Shantou
1995 Classic Cliche
1994 Moonax
1993 Bob's Return
1992 User Friendly

Group Two Races

MASAI MILE

2001 Nicobar
2000 Indian Lodge
1999 Handsome Ridge
1998 Almushtarak
1997 Wixim
1996 Gabr
1995 Missed Flight
1994 Penny Drops
1993 Alhijaz
1992 Rudimentary

JOCKEY CLUB STKS

2001 Millenary
2000 Blueprint
1999 Silver Patriarch
1998 Romanov
1997 Time Allowed
1996 Riyadian
1995 Only Royale
1994 Silver Wisp
1993 Zinaad
1992 Sapience

TEMPLE STKS

2001 Cassandra Go
2000 Perryston View
1999 Tipsy Creek
1998 Bolshoi
1997 Croft Pool
1996 Mind Games
1995 Mind Games
1994 Lochsong
1993 Paris House
1992 Snaadee

DANTE STKS

2001 Dilshaan
2000 Sakhee
1999 Salford Express
1998 Saratoga Springs
1997 Benny The Dip
1996 Glory of Dancer
1995 Classic Cliche
1994 Erhaab
1993 Tenby
1992 Alnasr Alwasheek

YORKSHIRE CUP

2001 Marienbard
2000 Kayf Tara
1999 Churlish Charm
1998 Busy Flight
1997 Celeric
1996 Classic Cliche
1995 Moonax
1994 Key To My Heart
1993 Assessor
1992 Rock Hopper

QUEEN ANNE STKS

2001 Medicean
2000 Kalanisi
1999 Cape Cross
1998 Intikhab
1997 Allied Forces
1996 Charnwood Forest
1995 Nicolotte
1994 Barathea
1993 Alflora
1992 Lahib

RIBBLESDALE STKS

2001 Sahara Slew
2000 Miletrian
1999 Fairy Queen
1998 Bahr
1997 Yashmak
1996 Tulipa
1995 Phantom Gold
1994 Bolas
1993 Thawakib
1992 Armarama

HARDWICKE STKS

2001 Sandmason
2000 Fruits of Love
1999 Fruits of Love
1998 Posidonas
1997 Predappio
1996 Oscar Schindler
1995 Beauchamp Hero
1994 Bobzao
1993 Jeune
1992 Rock Hopper

KING'S STAND STKS

2001 Cassandra Go
2000 Nuclear Debate
1999 Mitcham
1998 Bolshoi
1997 Don't Worry Me
1996 Pivotal
1995 Piccolo
1994 Lochsong
1993 Elbio
1992 Sheikh Albadou

KING EDWARD VII STKS

2001 Storming Home
2000 Subtle Power
1999 Mutafaweq
1998 Royal Anthem
1997 Kingfisher Mill
1996 Amfortas
1995 Pentire
1994 Foyer
1993 Beneficial
1992 Beyton

CORK & ORRERY STKS

2001 Harmonic Way
2000 Superior Premium
1999 Bold Edge
1998 Tomba
1997 Royal Applause
1996 Atraf
1995 So Factual
1994 Owington
1993 College Chapel
1992 Shalford

PRINCESS OF WALES'S STKS

2001 Mutamam
2000 Little Rock
1999 Craigsteel
1998 Fruits of Love
1997 Shantou
1996 Posidonas
1995 Beauchamp Hero
1994 Wagon Master
1993 Desert Team
1992 Saddlers' Hall

GOODWOOD CUP

2001 Persian Punch
2000 Royal Rebel
1999 Kayf Tara
1998 Double Trigger
1997 Double Trigger
1996 Gey Shot
1995 Double Trigger
1994 Tioman Island
1993 Sonus
1992 Further Flight

GREAT VOLTIGEUR STKS

2001 Milan
2000 Air Marshall
1999 Fantastic Light
1998 Sea Wave
1997 Stowaway
1996 Dushyantor
1995 Pentire
1994 Sacrament
1993 Bob's Return
1992 Bonny Scot

CHALLENGE STKS

2001 Munir
2000 Last Resort
1999 Susu
1998 Decorated Hero
1997 Kahal
1996 Charnwood Forest
1995 Harayir
1994 Zieten
1993 Catrail
1992 Selkirk

FALMOUTH STKS

2001 Proudwings
2000 Alshakr
1999 Ronda
1998 Lovers Knot
1997 Ryafan
1996 Sensation
1995 Caramba
1994 Lemon Souffle
1993 Niche
1992 Gussy Marlowe

CELEBRATION MILE

2001 No Excuse Needed
2000 Medicean
1999 Cape Cross
1998 Muhtathir
1997 Among Men
1996 Mark of Esteem
1995 Harayir
1994 Mehthaaf
1993 Swing Low
1992 Selkirk

DIADEM STKS

2001 Nice One Clare
2000 Sampower Star
1999 Bold Edge
1998 Bianconi
1997 Elnadim
1996 Diffident
1995 Cool Jazz
1994 Lake Coniston
1993 Catrail
1992 Wolfhound

SUN CHARIOT STKS

2001 Independence
2000 Danceabout
1999 Lady In Waiting
1998 Kissogram
1997 One So Wonderful
1996 Last Second
1995 Warning Shadows
1994 La Confederation
1993 Talented
1992 Red Slippers

GEOFFREY FREER STKS

2001 Mr Combustible
2000 Murghem
1999 Silver Patriarch
1998 Multicoloured
1997 Dushyantor
1996 Phantom Gold
1995 Presenting
1994 Red Route
1993 Azzilfi
1992 Shambo

Top Two-Year-Old Races

MIDDLE PARK STKS

2001 Johannesburg
2000 Minardi
1999 Primo Valentino
1998 Lujain
1997 Hayil
1996 Bahamian Bounty
1995 Royal Applause
1994 Fard
1993 First Trump
1992 Zieten

DEWHURST STKS

2001 Rock of Gibraltar
2000 Tobougg
1999 Distant Music
1998 Mujahid
1997 Xaar
1996 In Command
1995 Alhaarth
1994 Pennekamp
1993 Grand Lodge
1992 Zafonic

MEON VALLEY STUD FILLIES'MILE

2001 Gossamer
2000 Crystal Music
1999 Teggiano
1998 Sunspangled
1997 Glorosia
1996 Reams of Verse
1995 Bosra Sham
1994 Aqaarid
1993 Fairy Heights
1992 Ivanka

RACING POST TROPHY

2001 High Chaparral
2000 Dilshaan
1999 Aristotle
1998 Commander Collins
1997 Saratoga Springs
1996 Medaaly
1995 Beauchamp King
1994 Celtic Swing
1993 King's Theatre
1992 Armiger

CHEVELEY PARK STKS

2001 Queen's Logic
2000 Regal Rose
1999 Seazun
1998 Wannabe Grand
1997 Embassy
1996 Pas De Reponse
1995 Blue Duster
1994 Gay Gallanta
1993 Prophecy
1992 Sayyedati

COVENTRY STKS

2001 Landseer
2000 Cd Europe
1999 Fasliyev
1998 Red Sea
1997 Harbour Master
1996 Verglas
1995 Royal Applause
1994 Sri Pekan
1993 Stonehatch
1992 Petardia

GIMCRACK STKS

2001 Rock of Gibraltar
2000 Bannister
1999 Mull Of Kintyre
1998 Josr Algarhoud
1997 Carrowkeel
1996 Abou Zouz
1995 Royal Applause
1994 Chilly Billy
1993 Turtle Island
1992 Splendent

SOLARIO STKS

2001 Redback
2000 King's Ironbridge
1999 Best of The Bests
1998 Raise A Grand
1997 Little Indian
1996 Brave Act
1995 Alhaarth
1994 Lovely Millie
1993 Island Magic
1992 White Crown

QUEEN MARY STKS

2001 Queen's Logic
2000 Romantic Myth
1999 Shining Hour
1998 Bint Allayl
1997 Nadwah
1996 Dance Parade
1995 Blue Duster
1994 Gay Gallanta
1993 Risky
1992 Lyric Fantasy

NORFOLK STKS

2001 Johannesburg
2000 Superstar Leo
1999 Warm Heart
1998 Rosselli
1997 Tippitt Boy
1996 Tipsy Creek
1995 Lucky Lionel
1994 Mind Games
1993 Turtle Island
1992 Niche

CHERRY HINTON STKS

2001 Silent Honour
2000 Dora Carrington
1999 Torgau
1998 Wannabe Grand
1997 Asfurah
1996 Dazzle
1995 Applaud
1994 Red Carnival
1993 Lemon Souffle
1992 Sayyedati

CHAMPAGNE VINTAGE STKS

2001 Naheef
2000 No Excuse Needed
1999 Ekraar
1998 Aljabr
1997 Central Park
1996 Putra
1995 Alhaarth
1994 Eltish
1993 Mister Baileys
1992 Maroof

ROYAL LODGE STKS

2001 Mutinyonthebounty
2000 Atlantis Prince
1999 Royal Kingdom
1998 Mutaahab
1997 Teapot Row
1996 Benny The Dip
1995 Mons
1994 Eltish
1993 Mister Baileys
1992 Desert Secret

LOWTHER STKS

2001 Queen's Logic
2000 Enthused
1999 Jemima
1998 Bint Allayl
1997 Cape Verdi
1996 Bianca Nera
1995 Dance Sequence
1994 Harayir
1993 Velvet Moon
1992 Niche

RICHMOND STKS

2001 Mister Cosmi
2000 Endless Summer
1999 Bachir
1998 Muqtarib
1997 Daggers Drawn
1996 Easycall
1995 Polaris Flight
1994 Sri Pekan
1993 First Trump
1992 Son Pardo

FLYING CHILDERS STKS

2001 Saddad
2000 Superstar Leo
1999 Mrs P
1998 Sheer Viking
1997 Land of Dreams
1996 Easycall
1995 Cayman Kai
1994 Raah Algharb
1993 Imperial Bailiwick
1992 Poker Chip

MILL REEF STKS

2001 Firebreak
2000 Bouncing Bowdler
1999 Primo Valentino
1998 Golden Silca
1997 Arkadian Hero
1996 Indian Rocket
1995 Kahir Almaydan
1994 Princely Hush
1993 Polish Laughter
1992 Forest Wind

CHAMPAGNE STKS

2001 Dubai Destination
2000 Noverre
1999 Distant Music
1998 Auction House
1997 Daggers Drawn
1996 Bahhare
1995 Alhaarth
1994 Sri Pekan
1993 Unblest
1992 Petardia

Major Handicaps

LINCOLN H'CAP

2001 Nimello
2000 John Ferneley
1999 Right Wing
1998 Hunters of Brora
1997 Kuala Lipis
1996 Stone Ridge
1995 Roving Minstrel
1994 Our Rita
1993 High Premium
1992 High Low

EBOR H'CAP

2001 Mediterranean
2000 Give The Slip
1999 Vicious Circle
1998 Tuning
1997 Far Ahead
1996 Clerkenwell
1995 Sanmartino
1994 Hasten to Add
1993 Sarawat
1992 Quick Ransom

AYR GOLD CUP

2001 Continent
2000 Bahamian Pirate
1999 Grangeville
1998 Always Alight
1997 Wildwood Flower
1996 Coastal Bluff
1995 Royale Figurine
1994 Daring Destiny
1993 Hard to Figure
1992 Lochsong

CAMBRIDGESHIRE H'CAP

2001 I Cried For You
2000 Katy Nowaitee
1999 She's Our Mare
1998 Lear Spear
1997 Pasternak
1996 Clifton Fox
1995 Cap Juluca
1994 Halling
1993 Penny Drops
1992 Rambo's Hall

CESAREWITCH H'CAP

2001 Distant Prospect
2000 Heros Fatal
1999 Top Cees
1998 Spirit of Love
1997 Turnpole
1996 Inchcailloch
1995 Old Red
1994 Captain's Guest
1993 Aahsaylad
1992 Vintage Crop

ROYAL HUNT CUP

2001 Surprise Encounter
2000 Caribbean Monarch
1999 Showboat
1998 Refuse To Lose
1997 Red Robbo
1996 Yeast
1995 Realities
1994 Face North
1993 Imperial Ballet
1992 Colour Sergeant

WOKINGHAM H'CAP	NORTHUMBERLAND PLATE
2001 Nice One Clare	2001 Archduke Ferdinand
2000 Harmonic Way	2000 Bay Of Islands
1999 Deep Space	1999 Far Cry
1998 Selhurstpark Flyer	1998 Cyrian
1997 Selhurstpark Flyer	1997 Windsor Castle
1996 Emerging Market	1996 Celeric
1995 Astrac	1995 Bold Gait
1994 Venture Capitalist	1994 Quick Ransom
1993 Nagida	1993 Highflying
1992 Red Rosein	1992 Witness Box

TOTE EXACTA H'CAP (formerly Hong Kong Trophy)	WILLIAM HILL MILE
2001 Ulundi	2001 Riberac
2000 Lady Angharad	2000 Persiano
1999 Moutahddee	1999 Lonesome Dude
1998 Yavana's Pace	1998 For Your Eyes Only
1997 Hawksley Hill	1997 Fly To The Stars
1996 Sheer Danzig	1996 Moscow Mist
1995 Yoush	1995 Khayrapour
1994 Knowth	1994 Fraam
1993 Smarginato	1993 Philidor
1992 Fire Top	1992 Little Bean

STEWARDS' CUP	JOHN SMITH'S CUP
2001 Guinea Hunter	2001 Foreign Affairs
2000 Tayseer	2000 Sobriety
1999 Harmonic Way	1999 Achilles
1998 Superior Premium	1998 Porto Foricos
1997 Danetime	1997 Pasternak
1996 Coastal Bluff	1996 Wilcuma
1995 Shikari's Son	1995 Naked Welcome
1994 For the Present	1994 Cezanne
1993 King's Signet	1993 Baron Ferdinand
1992 Lochsong	1992 Mr Confusion

Highest Raceform Speed Figures 2001

(figures recorded between November 6, 2000 and November 10, 2001)

Turf

A Bit Special 105 (7f,Thi,G,Jun 19)
A Touch Of Frost 111 (7f,Don,G,Sep 13)
Abajany 108 (8f,Goo,GF,Jun 22)
Abbajabba 107 (5f,Mus,S,Apr 7)
Able Millenium 106 (8f,Pon,GS,May 2)
Absent Friends 106 (5f,Bev,G,May 12)
Absolute Fantasy 106 (5f,Lin,F,Jun 24)
Abyssinian Wolf 107 (12f,Nmk,GF,Jun 29)
Ace Of Trumps 108 (8f,Mus,GS,Apr 12)
Achilles Wings 106 (12f,Chp,S,Aug 9)
Adelphi Theatre 105 (12f,Kem,G,Sep 7)
Adilabad 109 (10f,San,GF,May 29)
Adjawar 108 (12f,Sal,GF,Jun 27)
Admirals Place 109 (12½f,Ncs,GF,Jun 28)
Adobe 106 (8f,Kem,GF,Jly 22)
Adorara 106 (10f,Kem,GF,Jly 11)
Adweb 105 (6f,Kem,GF,Sep 24)
Aegean Dream 109 (11f,Nby,GF,Aug 17)
Afaan 109 (5f,Nby,GF,Aug 5)
Afkaar 105 (10f,Bat,G,Oct 1)
Ahraar 109 (12f,Don,G,Sep 15)
Air Mail 106 (5f,Don,S,Nov 9)
Akbar 111 (12f,Asc,G,Jun 19)
Al Azhar 105 (10f,Ayr,GS,Jly 24)
Al Ghabraa 105 (6f,Nmk,G,Aug 10)
Al Ihsas 107 (7f,Lei,GF,Jun 4)
Al Muallim 111 (7f,Eps,GF,Jly 5)
Alakananda 110 (12f,Bat,G,Oct 25)
Albarahin 119 (8f,San,S,Apr 27)
Albashoosh 107 (8f,Yor,GF,May 17)
Albuhera 110 (10½f,Yor,G,Aug 22)
Alcayde 105 (17f,Bat,G,Jun 16)
Alcazar 111 (14f,Nmk,G,Sep 22)
Aldebaran 113 (8f,Don,G,May 7)
Aldwych 111 (10f,Nby,GF,Jly 21)
Aldwych Arrow 105 (12f,Rip,G,Aug 6)
Alegranza 112 (5f,San,GF,Jly 7)
Alegria 107 (5f,Ncs,GF,Jun 29)
Alexius 114 (12f,Goo,GF,Jly 31)
All Grain 109 (12f,Hay,GS,Jly 7)
Alleluia 113 (18f,Don,G,Sep 13)
Allez Mousson 106 (17f,Pon,GS,Oct 8)
Almiddina 107 (7f,Sal,GF,Sep 6)
Alpen Wolf 109 (6f,Eps,GF,Jly 5)
Alphaeus 115 (10f,Nmk,G,Jly 11)
Alrisha 108 (16f,Nmk,G,Jly 11)
Alshadiyah 112 (7f,Don,G,Sep 13)
Alunissage 107 (14½f,Don,G,Sep 15)
Amaranth 108 (7f,Ncs,GS,Oct 3)
Amber Fort 107 (7f,Sal,S,May 17)
Ambitious 110 (5f,Ncs,GF,Jun 29)
Ameerat 111 (8f,Nmk,G,May 6)
America Calling 105 (6f,Kem,GF,Sep 24)
American Cousin 107 (5f,Mus,G,Jun 17)
Amicable 106 (7f,Nmk,GS,Oct 20)
Amoras 105 (7f,Kem,GF,Jun 27)
Amrak Ajeeb 105 (12f,Chp,S,Aug 9)
Anabaa Blue 109 (12f,Asc,GF,Jly 28)
Analyser 108 (8f,Nby,GF,Jly 21)
Analyze 106 (10f,Not,GF,Jly 14)
And Beyond 109 (16f,Asc,GF,Jun 19)
Angus-G 106 (10f,Rip,GF,Jun 10)
Annadawi 108 (12f,Rip,S,Apr 28)
Annette Vallon 107 (5f,Nby,GF,Aug 5)
Anniversary 105 (12f,Don,GF,Aug 4)
Another Victim 107 (6f,Sth,GF,May 30)
Antonio Canova 111 (6f,Ayr,GF,Sep 22)
Apache Point 105 (8f,Rip,GF,Jly 9)
April Stock 107 (12f,Nby,S,May 19)
Aquarius 108 (16f,Asc,GF,Jun 19)
Arabie 113 (12f,Asc,GF,Jun 21)
Arc 106 (9f,Ncs,G,Aug 24)
Archduke Ferdinand 109 (16f,Ncs,F,Jun 30)
Archirondel 105 (10f,Red,GF,Jun 12)
Aretino 113 (7f,Eps,GF,Jly 5)
Argamia 109 (14f,Not,S,Apr 23)
Arkadian Hero 109 (8f,Asc,G,Jun 19)
Armagnac 110 (6f,Yor,GS,Jun 16)
Arpeggio 106 (8f,Nmk,GS,Jly 10)
Arrive 114 (15f,Nmk,G,Jly 11)
Artifice 105 (6f,Kem,GF,Sep 24)
Ash Moon 105 (7f,Yar,S,Sep 4)
Ashleigh Baker 105 (10f,Ayr,HY,Oct 15)
Ashlinn 105 (7f,Nby,GS,Apr 21)
Asian Heights 107 (10f,San,HY,Apr 28)
Askham 113 (10f,Nmk,G,Jly 11)
Aspirant Dancer 105 (16f,Chs,S,Sep 26)
Astonished 116 (5f,Not,G,Aug 20)
Aswan 106 (8f,Ncs,GF,Aug 27)
Atavus 118 (7f,Nby,GF,Aug 18)
Atlantic Ace 111 (7f,Goo,GF,Jun 8)
Atlantic Rhapsody 111 (12f,Rip,S,Apr 28)
Atlantic Viking 109 (5f,Hay,HY,Sep 8)
Attache 106 (8f,Don,G,Sep 15)
Aunty Rose 105 (8f,Goo,GF,May 24)
Autumnal 109 (5f,Don,GS,Sep 13)
Avebury 105 (9f,Red,F,May 29)
Aveiro 106 (11½f,Yar,GF,May 30)

Baby Barry 109 (6f,Goo,G,Sep 19)
Baccura 108 (8f,Yor,GF,May 17)
Bach 117 (10f,Asc,GF,Jun 20)
Bahamian Pirate 115 (6f,Asc,S,Sep 29)
Bahrain 105 (8½f,Bev,GF,Jly 6)
Baileys Prize 105 (10f,Red,G,Oct 6)
Bakiri 107 (10f,Nmk,GS,Jly 20)
Bali Royal 107 (5f,Wdr,G,May 21)
Balladonia 109 (10f,Nby,GF,Jly 21)
Ballet Master 107 (10½f,Yor,G,Jly 14)
Bandanna 109 (6f,Asc,GF,Jly 27)
Bandbox 107 (6f,Goo,GF,Jly 1)
Banjo Bay 111 (8f,Nmk,G,Jly 12)
Bank On Him 106 (8f,San,G,Aug 8)
Banks Hill 113 (8f,Asc,GF,Jun 22)
Baratheastar 109 (7f,Goo,GS,Sep 27)
Basinet 105 (8f,Ncs,F,Jly 8)
Bawsian 108 (12f,Don,GS,Mar 22)
Bay Of Islands 106 (13½f,Chs,GF,May 10)
Beading 110 (7f,Sal,GF,Sep 6)
Beckett 106 (8f,Nmk,GS,Oct 4)
Beekeeper 115 (12f,Asc,GF,Jun 21)
Bel 106 (12f,Bat,G,Oct 25)
Benbyas 109 (11f,Red,S,May 3)
Bergamo 106 (12½f,Ncs,GF,Jun 28)
Bertolini 110 (6f,Yor,GF,May 17)
Best Of The Bests 106 (10f,Nmk,GS,Oct 20)
Best Port 108 (16f,Red,GF,Aug 12)
Beyond Calculation 105 (5f,Bev,GF,Aug 25)
Beyond The Clouds 109 (5f,Wdr,GF,Jun 2)
Bid For Fame 106 (12f,Asc,GF,Jly 14)
Big Future 107 (8f,Yor,G,Aug 23)
Big Moment 111 (12f,Don,GF,Jly 1)
Billaddie 105 (12f,Nmk,GS,Aug 3)
Billy Bathwick 105 (8f,Bat,G,May 21)
Bishops Court 111 (5f,Eps,GF,Jun 9)
Black Knight 108 (10½f,Chs,GF,May 10)
Black Minnaloushe 114 (10f,San,GF,Jly 7)
Blackheath 106 (5f,Lin,GS,May 11)
Blakeshall Boy 109 (5f,Wdr,G,May 21)
Blessingindisguise 105 (5f,Bev,GF,Aug 25)
Blue Away 106 (16f,Yar,GF,Jly 30)
Blue Gold 110 (10f,Kem,GF,Jun 27)
Blue Mountain 113 (8f,Yor,GF,May 16)
Blue Planet 107 (8f,Nby,GF,Sep 22)
Blue Street 108 (12f,Chp,S,Aug 9)
Blue Sugar 105 (12f,Thi,F,Jun 4)
Blue Velvet 108 (5f,Bev,G,May 12)
Blundell Lane 109 (6f,Nmk,G,Aug 17)
Boadicea The Red 105 (6f,Don,F,Jun 9)
Boanerges 107 (5f,Mus,GF,Jun 2)
Bocelli 108 (8f,Asc,S,Sep 29)
Bodfari Komaite 106 (5f,Rip,GF,Jun 10)
Bodfari Pride 107 (5f,Lin,GS,May 11)
Bogus Dreams 108 (10f,Eps,GF,Jun 9)
Boira 107 (8f,Yar,G,Jun 25)
Bold Effort 105 (6f,Bat,F,Jun 1)
Bold King 111 (8f,Kem,GS,May 7)
Bold Raider 107 (8f,Don,GF,Jly 1)
Bold State 106 (8½f,Bev,GF,Jly 31)
Boleyn Castle 109 (5f,Eps,G,Aug 27)
Bollin Nellie 108 (10f,Rip,G,Aug 18)
Bollin Thomas 109 (12f,Bev,GF,Aug 26)
Bon Ami 106 (6f,Goo,G,Aug 4)
Bonaguil 107 (10½f,Yor,GF,May 17)
Bond Boy 110 (5f,Don,S,Nov 9)
Bonnard 106 (8f,Goo,GF,Aug 25)
Border Arrow 117 (10f,Kem,S,Apr 16)
Border Subject 113 (7f,Lin,G,May 12)
Borders 113 (5f,Bev,G,May 12)
Borders Belle 107 (12f,Yor,G,Aug 21)
Boreas 114 (12f,Don,S,Nov 10)
Bosham Mill 111 (15f,Nmk,G,Jly 11)
Bouncing Bowdler 106 (7f,Eps,GS,Aug 31)
Bourgainville 107 (8f,Sal,GF,Jly 6)
Bow Strada 105 (14f,Yor,GS,Oct 13)
Brainwave 107 (5f,Chp,G,Jly 20)
Brave Burt 106 (5f,Nmk,GS,Jly 10)
Brecongill Lad 105 (5f,Rip,GF,Jun 10)
Brevity 114 (6f,Asc,GF,Jly 27)
Bright Spark 109 (8f,Mus,G,Jun 17)
Brilliant Red 108 (8f,Goo,GF,May 22)
Bring Sweets 106 (12f,Don,S,Mar 24)
Broadway Score 106 (9f,San,G,Sep 2)
Brother Joe 108 (16f,Hay,G,Jun 7)
Browning 105 (16f,Nby,GF,Sep 21)
Buddeliea 106 (8f,Kem,G,Sep 7)
Budelli 108 (6f,Don,GF,Jly 11)
Bullsefia 105 (7f,War,GF,May 26)
Burning Impulse 107 (8f,Nmk,GS,Oct 19)

Cadeaux Cher 110 (6f,Goo,G,Aug 4)
Calcavella 105 (7½f,Bev,GF,Jun 6)
Calcutta 112 (8f,Don,G,Sep 15)
Camberley 112 (7f,Asc,GF,Jly 28)
Canada 106 (10f,Ayr,GF,Jun 1)
Candice 105 (8f,San,G,Sep 1)
Candleriggs 111 (6f,Goo,G,Aug 4)
Canford 106 (10½f,Yor,G,Aug 22)
Canterloupe 106 (5f,Asc,GS,Oct 13)
Cantina 108 (7f,Asc,GF,Jly 28)
Capal Garmon 107 (16f,Asc,GF,Jun 19)
Cape Town 113 (8f,Asc,GF,Jly 14)
Capricho 111 (6f,Asc,GF,Jun 22)
Captain's Log 105 (10f,Not,G,May 11)
Caqui D'Or 108 (14f,Nmk,G,Oct 6)
Cardinal Venture 106 (7f,Don,GS,Sep 13)
Carens Hero 105 (8f,Bat,HD,Jun 27)
Cark 108 (5f,Ayr,HY,Oct 15)
Carlys Quest 110 (16f,Nby,GS,Apr 21)
Carnival Dancer 110 (10f,Ayr,GS,Jly 16)
Cashmere Lady 105 (10f,Not,HY,May 1)
Cassandra Go 119 (5f,San,GF,May 28)
Castleshane 108 (10f,Don,GF,Aug 4)

Catchy Word 108 (10½f,Yor,GF,May 17)
Caughnawaga 111 (9f,San,G,Aug 8)
Cauvery 109 (8f,Goo,GF,Jly 1)
Cayman Sunset 106 (9f,Nmk,G,May 4)
Cd Flyer 108 (6f,Goo,G,Aug 25)
Celebration Town 106 (8f,Yor,G,Jly 13)
Celtic Island 107 (10f,Don,GF,Sep 12)
Celtic Mill 107 (8f,Pon,GF,Aug 19)
Celtic Mission 109 (12f,Nmk,S,Oct 2)
Celtic Silence 110 (10½f,Yor,GF,May 16)
Celtic Venture 106 (7f,Goo,GF,Jun 29)
Ceralbi 105 (12½f,Ncs,GF,Jun 28)
Chafaya 107 (7f,Nmk,G,Aug 17)
Chakra 105 (6f,Goo,GF,May 31)
Champagne Rider 111 (10f,Kem,S,Apr 16)
Champion Lodge 105 (8f,Nmk,GS,Oct 19)
Chancellor 110 (11f,Nby,GF,Sep 22)
Charango 105 (5f,Rip,G,Aug 18)
Charlie Parkes 107 (5f,Bev,G,May 12)
Charming Lotte 105 (6f,Not,HY,May 1)
Chem's Truce 109 (10f,Kem,GF,May 26)
Chemicalattraction 108 (12f,Ham,G,Sep 3)
Chianti 109 (12f,Don,GS,Sep 14)
Chief Cashier 106 (10f,San,G,Jun 15)
Chief Wardance 105 (12f,Don,GS,Mar 22)
Chimes At Midnight 106 (12f,Asc,GF,Jly 28)
China Red 110 (8f,Pon,HY,Apr 10)
China Visit 116 (8f,Don,G,Sep 13)
Chispa 107 (5f,Eps,S,Apr 25)
Chookie Heiton 111 (5f,Nmk,GS,Oct 18)
Choto Mate 108 (7f,Lin,GF,Sep 5)
Churlish Charm 105 (16f,Nmk,G,May 5)
City Of London 105 (7f,Fol,GF,Jly 12)
Clearing 105 (7f,Nmk,S,Apr 18)
Clever Girl 105 (8f,Ncs,GF,Jun 28)
Coastal Bluff 109 (5f,Hay,GF,May 26)
Coco Loco 112 (16f,Nby,GS,Apr 21)
Cold Climate 105 (6f,Nby,GF,May 30)
College Maid 108 (6f,Ham,S,Jly 13)
Columbine 105 (5f,Bat,G,Oct 25)
Colway Ritz 106 (12½f,Ncs,GF,Jun 28)
Como 106 (6f,Lei,GS,Aug 12)
Companion 108 (8f,Kem,GF,Jly 22)
Compradore 106 (7f,Nby,GF,May 30)
Compton Arrow 107 (6f,Don,GF,Jly 11)
Compton Banker 107 (6f,Nmk,G,May 6)
Compton Bolter 114 (11f,Nby,GF,Sep 22)
Compton Commander 110 (12f,Asc,GF,Jun 21)
Conclude 112 (12f,Nmk,GS,Jly 20)
Coney Kitty 109 (7f,Asc,GF,Jun 20)
Connect 106 (5f,Yar,GF,Jun 1)
Conquestadora 107 (16½f,Don,S,Nov 10)
Continent 114 (6f,Ayr,GF,Sep 22)
Continuation 105 (12f,Asc,GF,Jun 21)
Contraband 105 (12f,Asc,GF,Jly 29)
Contrary Mary 106 (7f,Sal,GF,Jly 27)
Conwy Castle 105 (16f,Nmk,G,Jly 11)
Cork Harbour 110 (7f,Nmk,GS,Oct 20)
Cornelius 111 (8f,Nby,GS,Apr 21)
Corridor Creeper 106 (6f,Goo,GF,Jly 1)
Corsican Sunset 105 (10f,Sal,GS,May 17)
Corunna 105 (7f,Eps,GF,Jly 5)
Cosmic Case 108 (12½f,Ncs,GF,Jun 28)
Cosmic Song 106 (9f,Red,F,May 29)
Cotton House 116 (5f,San,GF,May 28)
Counsel's Opinion 107 (9f,San,G,Sep 1)
Court Express 106 (8f,Thi,G,May 5)
Court Of Appeal 107 (11½f,San,G,Jly 8)
Court Shareef 109 (16f,Nmk,G,Jly 11)
Courteous 111 (12f,Nmk,GF,Jun 30)
Covent Garden 105 (12f,Don,GF,Jly 11)
Cover Up 109 (18f,Don,G,Sep 13)
Coyote 107 (8f,Asc,G,Aug 12)
Cracow 110 (12f,Hay,GS,Jly 7)
Cream Tease 108 (7f,Lin,G,May 12)
Cretan Gift 106 (6f,Ncs,F,Jun 30)
Crimson Tide 115 (8f,Yor,GF,May 16)
Crosby Donjohn 107 (8f,Rip,GF,Jly 9)
Cruagh Express 107 (8f,Wdr,G,Aug 6)
Crystal Flite 106 (12f,Lei,G,Jly 25)
Crystal Music 111 (8f,Asc,GF,Jun 22)
Cubism 106 (6f,Goo,G,Aug 4)
Culzean 108 (10f,Kem,G,Jly 18)
Cumbrian Harmony 107 (7½f,Bev,GF,Aug 26)
Cupids Charm 106 (7f,Lin,GF,Sep 5)
Currency 106 (6f,Goo,GF,Jun 22)
Cyclone Connie 107 (5f,Nmk,GS,Oct 4)

D'Accord 106 (6f,Goo,GF,Jly 1)
Dakota Sioux 107 (8f,Goo,GF,Jly 1)
Dalampour 109 (12f,Nby,GS,Apr 20)
Damalis 107 (5f,Chs,GF,May 10)
Damask Rose 110 (14f,Nmk,G,Oct 6)
Dance In The Day 110 (12f,Bev,GF,Aug 26)
Dance On The Top 109 (12f,Asc,GF,Jun 21)
Dancing Bay 111 (13f,Ayr,HY,Oct 16)
Dancing Mystery 110 (5f,Asc,GS,Oct 13)
Dancing Phantom 109 (13f,Ayr,HY,Oct 16)
Dancing Ridge 108 (5f,Hay,S,Jly 15)
Dandoun 115 (8f,Don,G,May 7)
Danegold 106 (16½f,Fol,GF,Jun 7)
Danehurst 114 (6f,Nmk,GS,Oct 19)
Danielle's Lad 109 (6f,Chp,G,Jly 13)
Darandala 113 (12f,Nby,GF,Aug 5)
Daraaim 106 (14½f,Don,GS,Sep 14)
Dardanus 106 (12f,Nmk,GF,Jun 29)
Dare 109 (10f,Not,GS,Nov 5)
Dawari 105 (12f,Chs,GF,May 8)
Dayglow Dancer 108 (8f,Don,G,May 7)
Days Of Grace 106 (5f,San,G,Sep 2)
Dear Daughter 107 (8f,Bat,F,Jun 1)
Deep Space 107 (5f,Eps,GF,Jun 9)
Delegate 105 (6f,Nmk,G,Aug 17)
Dellus 113 (11½f,Wdr,GF,Aug 25)
Demophilos 113 (12f,Goo,GF,Jly 31)
Den'S-Joy 109 (8f,Wdr,G,Aug 6)
Denise Margaret 107 (10f,San,GF,Jly 7)
Dennis El Menace 109 (8f,Nby,GF,Sep 22)
Dennis Our Menace 107 (9f,San,S,Jun 16)
Desaru 106 (12f,Bev,GF,Aug 26)
Desert Deer 108 (8f,San,G,Jly 8)
Desert Fury 110 (7f,Goo,GF,Jun 8)
Dhuhook 110 (10f,Don,GF,Jly 12)
Diamond Max 107 (8f,Chp,S,Aug 9)
Dietrich 107 (5f,Asc,G,Jun 19)
Differential 110 (6f,Asc,GF,Jly 27)
Digital 105 (8f,Thi,G,May 5)
Dihatjum 106 (10f,Fol,GS,Sep 3)
Dilshaan 111 (10½f,Yor,GF,May 16)
Direct Deal 105 (12½f,War,GS,Jly 21)
Discerning 108 (11½f,Yar,G,Jly 3)
Dispol Rock 106 (12f,Rip,G,Aug 6)
Distant Music 111 (10½f,Yor,G,Aug 21)
Distant Prospect 107 (16f,Ncs,F,Jun 30)
Distinctive Dream 106 (6f,Goo,GF,Jly 1)
Divine Task 105 (7f,Lin,GF,Sep 11)
Doctor Dennis 106 (6f,Lin,F,Jun 13)
Doctor Spin 111 (6f,Asc,GF,Jun 22)
Don Fayruz 106 (8f,Bat,HD,Jun 27)
Don't Sioux Me 110 (12f,Nmk,GS,Aug 4)
Donna's Double 107 (10f,Rip,GF,Jun 10)
Dorchester 109 (5f,Don,S,Nov 9)
Double Fantasy 105 (6f,Don,GF,Jly 11)
Double Honour 113 (12f,Goo,GF,May 31)
Dower House 108 (10½f,Yor,GF,May 17)
Down To The Woods 105 (10½f,Hay,G,Aug 11)
Downland 115 (6f,Ncs,HY,Oct 24)
Dr Cool 105 (12f,Eps,G,Sep 15)
Dr Greenfield 111 (10½f,Chs,GF,May 10)
Dramatic Quest 113 (12f,Nmk,G,Oct 5)
Dream Magic 105 (8f,Hay,HY,Sep 7)
Dream With Me 106 (12f,Asc,HY,Sep 30)
Duck Row 109 (8f,Bat,G,Aug 19)
Duke Of Modena 113 (8f,Yor,G,Aug 23)
Dumaran 105 (7f,Chp,G,Jly 20)
Dunedin Rascal 105 (5f,Chs,GF,May 10)
Duraid 105 (8f,Yor,G,Jly 13)
Dusty Carpet 106 (10½f,Chs,G,Jly 13)

Early Morning Mist 112 (10f,Eps,GF,Jun 8)
Eastern Breeze 106 (10f,San,GF,Jly 7)
Eastern Purple 115 (5f,Not,G,Aug 20)
Eastern Trumpeter 106 (5f,Yor,G,Jly 13)
Eau Rouge 106 (5f,Not,GF,Jly 14)
Ecclesiastical 111 (8f,Hay,GF,May 26)
Ecstasy 105 (10f,Wdr,G,May 14)
Ecstatic 110 (9f,San,S,Jun 16)
Eighty Two 105 (10f,Nmk,GS,Aug 4)
Ekraar 116 (12f,Don,GS,Sep 14)
El Dolor 105 (5f,Ayr,GS,Jly 16)
El Hakma 107 (14½f,Don,GF,Sep 12)
Ela Athena 113 (11½f,Wdr,G,Jun 3)
Eljohar 111 (10f,San,GF,May 29)
Eljutan 105 (16f,Lin,GF,Sep 5)
Ellendune Girl 105 (6f,Not,G,Sep 21)
Ellens Academy 115 (6f,Asc,GF,Jun 22)
Ellens Lad 115 (5f,Not,S,Apr 3)
Elmhurst Boy 106 (10½f,Yor,GF,May 17)
Elmonjed 105 (8f,Rip,S,Apr 19)
Elsaamri 107 (12f,Nmk,S,Oct 2)
Elvington Boy 105 (5f,Mus,GF,Jun 2)
Emerald Peace 111 (5f,Kem,GF,May 26)
Encounter 107 (7f,Eps,S,Aug 31)
Endless Hall 117 (10f,Asc,GF,Jun 20)
Ennoblement 108 (10f,Don,GS,Sep 14)
Entail 109 (7½f,Bev,GF,Jun 6)
Enthused 108 (8f,Asc,GF,Jun 22)
Erebus 106 (8f,Rip,GF,Jly 9)
Escalado 111 (8f,Hay,HY,Sep 28)
Established 107 (16f,Lin,GF,Sep 5)
Establishment 107 (12f,Asc,GF,Jly 14)
Esyouelfcee 108 (10f,Ncs,GF,Aug 27)
Eternal Spring 111 (12f,Rip,S,Apr 28)
Euro Venture 106 (6f,Thi,F,Aug 3)
Everlasting Love 106 (10f,Ncs,GF,Aug 27)
Exalted 106 (13f,Ham,G,May 6)
Exeat 108 (7f,Thi,G,May 5)

Factual Lad 106 (7f,Goo,GS,Sep 27)
Fair Question 111 (15f,Nmk,G,Jly 11)
Fairy Prince 107 (6f,Nmk,GS,Aug 3)
Faithful Warrior 108 (8f,Pon,GF,Aug 19)
Falcon Goa 109 (6f,Don,GF,Jly 11)
Falconidae 105 (8f,Wdr,GF,Jun 11)
Fallen Star 106 (7f,Yar,S,Sep 4)
Fanaar 110 (8f,San,S,Apr 27)
Fantastic Light 124 (10f,Asc,GF,Jun 20)
Fantasy Believer 114 (5f,Don,HY,Oct 27)
Fantasy Ridge 105 (7f,Goo,GF,Aug 2)
Faraway Look 107 (10½f,Hay,G,Jun 7)
Fast Track 109 (7f,Goo,GF,Jun 8)
Fastina 106 (10f,Wdr,GF,Jly 23)
Fath 114 (5f,San,GF,May 28)
Father Juninho 109 (12f,Asc,G,Jun 19)
Father Thames 108 (8f,Yor,G,Aug 23)
Fatwa 109 (7f,Nby,GS,Apr 21)
Fearby Cross 108 (6f,Nmk,G,Aug 17)
Ferzao 110 (10½f,Yor,GF,May 17)
Ffynnon Gold 105 (7f,Sth,GF,May 30)
Field Of Vision 106 (13f,Ham,G,May 6)
Final Settlement 109 (15f,Nmk,GF,Aug 24)
Find The King 105 (14f,San,GF,Jly 26)
Finished Article 111 (9f,Goo,GF,Sep 12)
Fiori 105 (14f,Hay,G,Jun 8)
Fire Dome 107 (6f,Don,S,Mar 24)
Firework 108 (7f,Goo,GS,Sep 27)
First Ballot 109 (16f,Asc,G,Aug 11)
First Venture 105 (5f,Lin,GF,Jun 30)
Flak Jacket 111 (5f,Hay,S,Jly 15)
Flambe 108 (8f,Ncs,GF,Jun 6)
Flight Of Fancy 109 (10½f,Yor,F,May 15)

Flight Sequence 108 (10f,Wdr,G,May 14)
Flossy 109 (12f,Nmk,GS,Jly 21)
Fly With Me 105 (12f,Goo,GF,May 31)
Flying Lyric 108 (12f,Asc,GF,Jun 21)
Flying Millie 108 (6f,Asc,G,Aug 11)
Flying Tackle 108 (5f,Ayr,HY,Oct 15)
Flying Trapeze 105 (10f,Bat,HD,Jun 27)
Follow A Dream 105 (8f,Nby,GF,Jly 5)
Foodbroker Fancy 110 (10½f,Yor,G,Aug 21)
Foreign Affairs 115 (10f,Eps,GF,Jun 8)
Forest Dancer 107 (8f,Nby,GF,Jly 5)
Forest Heath 108 (10f,Lei,GS,Aug 12)
Forever Times 109 (7f,San,GF,Jly 7)
Forgotten Times 106 (5f,Eps,G,Sep 15)
Forwood 107 (8f,Don,G,May 7)
Forza Figlio 106 (10f,Not,GS,Nov 5)
Foundry Lane 106 (16f,Hay,G,Jun 7)
Francport 105 (6f,Ham,G,May 6)
Free Rider 112 (7f,Nmk,G,Oct 5)
French Lieutenant 105 (10f,Don,GF,Sep 12)
Frenchmans Bay 111 (8f,Nmk,G,May 5)
Freud 112 (6f,Asc,GF,Jun 21)
Fromsong 108 (5f,Not,S,Apr 23)
Fruhling Feuer 107 (8f,Not,G,May 11)
Fruit Punch 106 (10f,Pon,GS,May 2)
Fudge Brownie 107 (8f,Ham,G,May 18)
Fully Invested 105 (8f,Nmk,G,Oct 6)
Funny Valentine 111 (5f,Asc,G,Jun 19)
Further Outlook 111 (5f,Not,S,Apr 3)
Future Prospect 105 (7½f,Bev,GF,Jun 13)

Galileo 120 (12f,Asc,GF,Jly 28)
Gallant 105 (8f,Goo,GF,Jly 31)
Gallery God 111 (12f,Asc,G,Jun 19)
Galloway Boy 105 (5f,Ncs,GF,Jun 29)
Garden Society 106 (12f,Nby,GS,Apr 20)
Gay Heroine 108 (10f,San,GF,Jly 25)
Gdansk 110 (5f,Hay,HY,Sep 8)
Gem Bien 105 (8f,Wdr,GS,Apr 23)
General Hawk 108 (7f,Red,GF,Aug 12)
Genial Genie 105 (8f,Rip,GF,Jly 9)
Gentleman Venture 113 (10f,Kem,S,Apr 16)
Get Stuck In 111 (5f,Ncs,GF,Jun 29)
Ghazal 107 (6f,Asc,G,Aug 11)
Gilded Dancer 108 (8f,Hay,GF,May 26)
Gin Palace 109 (14f,Nmk,G,Oct 6)
Gingko 107 (10f,Don,G,May 7)
Give Back Calais 110 (7f,San,GF,Jly 7)
Give Me A Ring 107 (12f,Don,GF,May 26)
Give Notice 111 (15f,Nmk,GF,Aug 24)
Give The Slip 118 (10f,Asc,GF,Jun 20)
Gleaming Blade 106 (8f,Bat,G,Oct 1)
Glenrock 108 (7f,Hay,GF,Jly 6)
Glowing 110 (6f,Goo,GF,Jly 1)
Goggles 110 (8f,Don,G,Jly 18)
Golan 113 (8f,Nmk,G,May 5)
Golconda 107 (10½f,Yor,G,Jly 14)
Gold Academy 105 (10½f,Yor,G,Aug 22)
Gold Standard 106 (16f,Nby,GF,Sep 21)
Golden Dragon 109 (6f,Sth,GF,May 30)
Golden Snake 110 (12f,Asc,GF,Jly 28)
Golden Wells 105 (12f,Chs,GF,May 8)
Good Standing 107 (7f,Sal,GF,Sep 6)
Goretski 109 (5f,Don,S,Nov 9)
Got To Go 108 (8f,Asc,G,Aug 12)
Gracilis 108 (14f,Not,S,Apr 23)
Gralmano 107 (10f,Red,F,May 28)
Grampas 107 (10f,Asc,GF,Jun 23)
Grandera 118 (11f,Nby,GF,Sep 22)
Granny's Pet 108 (7f,Goo,GF,Aug 25)
Green Casket 106 (10f,Bev,GF,Jly 23)
Green Ideal 109 (10f,San,GF,Jly 25)
Greenaway Bay 108 (8f,Not,HY,Oct 30)
Greenhope 110 (12f,Goo,GF,May 31)
Greenwood 107 (6f,Yar,G,Jly 24)
Grey Cossack 105 (6f,Ayr,GS,Jly 23)
Greyfield 107 (10f,Lei,GS,Aug 12)
Gryffindor 107 (8f,Kem,S,Apr 14)
Guaranda 107 (10f,Sal,GF,Aug 15)
Guard Duty 107 (16f,Kem,S,Apr 14)
Gudlage 105 (10f,Red,F,May 28)
Guinea Hunter 115 (6f,Goo,G,Aug 4)

Hadleigh 108 (8f,Don,GF,Jly 1)
Hail The Chief 107 (8f,Goo,GF,Jly 1)
Halland 108 (7f,San,GF,Jly 7)
Halmahera 114 (6f,Hay,S,May 5)
Hamadeenah 106 (7f,Yor,F,May 15)
Hambleden 109 (12f,Hay,GS,Jly 7)
Hammer And Sickle 107 (6f,Eps,GF,Jly 5)
Hand Chime 110 (7f,Lin,G,May 12)
Hannibal Lad 112 (12f,Hay,GS,Jly 7)
Harewood End 107 (10f,Yar,G,May 29)
Harlequin 105 (12f,Bat,G,Jun 16)
Harlestone Grey 105 (12f,Bat,HD,Jun 27)
Harmonic Way 116 (6f,Asc,GF,Jun 21)
Harmony Hall 108 (8f,Yor,G,Jly 13)
Hata 109 (6f,Sal,GS,May 6)
Hatha Anna 114 (12f,Nmk,G,Oct 5)
Hawkeye 116 (8f,Asc,S,Sep 29)
Head In The Clouds 121 (12f,Nmk,GS,Nov 2)
Heathyardsblessing 105 (5f,Not,G,Aug 20)
Heavenly Whisper 109 (10½f,Yor,F,May 15)
Hello Sweety 108 (10f,Kem,GF,Jun 27)
Henry Hall 110 (5f,Nmk,G,Sep 22)
Henry Island 105 (16½f,Don,S,Nov 10)
Heretic 107 (8f,Kem,S,Apr 16)
Hernandita 105 (12f,Bat,G,Oct 25)
Herodotus 108 (8f,Kem,S,Apr 14)
Heros Fatal 108 (16f,Asc,G,Aug 11)
High Pitched 122 (12f,Nmk,GS,Nov 2)
High Policy 105 (17f,Pon,GS,Oct 8)
High Sun 105 (8f,Ham,GF,May 11)
Highland Reel 111 (8½f,Eps,GF,Jun 8)
Hightori 121 (10f,Asc,GF,Jun 20)
Hill Country 115 (12f,Nmk,GS,Jly 20)
Hilltop Warning 112 (7f,Eps,GF,Aug 16)
Hirapour 108 (16f,Nby,GF,Sep 21)
Ho Leng 107 (6f,Yor,GF,Sep 5)
Holding Court 116 (12f,Nmk,GS,Jly 10)
Holy Orders 108 (12f,Asc,G,Jun 19)
Honest Borderer 109 (7f,Lin,G,May 12)
Honest Warning 106 (7½f,Bev,GF,Jun 26)
Honesty Fair 112 (6f,Goo,G,Aug 4)
Hormuz 108 (8f,Yor,G,Jly 13)
Hot Tin Roof 112 (6f,Asc,S,Sep 29)
Hugs Dancer 108 (12½f,Ncs,GF,Jun 28)
Hugwity 106 (8f,Not,G,Aug 3)
Hunting Lion 111 (6f,Nmk,G,May 6)
Hureya 105 (8f,Yar,GF,May 30)
Hurricane Floyd 113 (7f,Asc,GF,Jly 28)

I Cried For You 110 (7f,Asc,S,Sep 29)
Ice 109 (8f,Yor,G,Jly 13)
Idle Power 108 (6f,Yar,G,Jly 24)
Iffah 106 (12f,Bri,F,May 25)
Il Cavaliere 105 (16f,Mus,G,Nov 7)
Ile Michel 107 (7f,Goo,GF,Jun 8)
Imagine 110 (12f,Eps,GF,Jun 8)
Imperial Beauty 107 (5f,Asc,G,Jun 19)
Imperial Dancer 105 (8f,Ayr,HY,Oct 15)
Inch Perfect 108 (9f,Yor,G,Jun 16)
Inchdura 110 (8f,Nby,GF,Sep 22)
Inchinnan 105 (9f,Kem,GF,Jly 4)
Indaba 108 (7f,Asc,GS,Oct 13)
Independence 111 (8f,Nmk,G,Oct 6)
Indian Bazaar 107 (5f,Lin,F,Jun 24)
Indian Blaze 105 (6f,Eps,GF,Jly 12)
Indian Creek 110 (10f,Nmk,GS,Oct 20)
Indian File 109 (12f,Hay,GS,Aug 9)
Indian Giver 105 (8f,Sal,GS,Jun 17)
Indian Plume 109 (8f,Hay,HY,Sep 28)
Indian Prince 113 (5f,Nmk,GS,Oct 4)
Indian Spark 114 (5f,Not,G,Aug 20)
Inglenook 109 (10f,Don,GS,Sep 14)
Inigo Jones 106 (12f,Asc,G,Aug 11)
Inspector General 109 (7f,San,GF,Jly 7)
Intrepidous 108 (8f,San,G,Sep 1)
Intricate Web 110 (7f,Thi,G,May 5)
Invader 108 (10f,San,GF,Jly 6)
Invermark 109 (14f,Hay,HY,Sep 28)
Invincible Spirit 110 (7f,Nmk,G,May 4)
Ionian Spring 107 (10½f,Yor,S,Oct 12)
Irish Distinction 106 (10f,Eps,GF,Jun 8)
Irish Sea 105 (15½f,Fol,HY,Apr 24)
Iron Mountain 106 (10f,Nmk,G,May 4)
Isadora 112 (12f,Asc,G,Sep 28)
Ishiguru 109 (6f,Nmk,G,Jly 12)
Island House 113 (12f,Nmk,G,Oct 5)
Island Queen 105 (8f,Wdr,GS,May 8)
Island Sands 121 (8f,San,S,Apr 27)
Island Sound 113 (12f,Nmk,GS,Jly 20)
Istihsaan 106 (7f,Ayr,GS,Jly 16)
It's A Secret 110 (10f,Ncs,GF,Aug 27)
Its Ecco Boy 107 (7f,Lin,GF,Sep 5)
Its Your Bid 105 (16f,Lin,GF,Sep 5)
Itsanothergirl 106 (10f,Ayr,HY,Oct 15)
Ivory's Joy 111 (5f,Nby,GF,Sep 22)

J R Stevenson 110 (8½f,Eps,GF,Jun 8)
Jack Dawson 108 (16f,Chs,GF,Jly 14)
Jahash 105 (16f,Chp,GF,Aug 27)
Jalindi 107 (7f,San,G,May 28)
Jalousie 111 (12f,Nmk,GS,Aug 4)
James Stark 105 (6f,Goo,GF,Jly 1)
Jardines Lookout 109 (18f,Don,G,Sep 13)
Jarn 107 (6f,Nmk,G,May 6)
Jasmick 109 (14f,Nmk,G,Oct 6)
Jawhari 106 (5f,Bri,GF,Sep 4)
Jedeydd 109 (7f,Hay,GF,Jly 6)
Jedi Knight 108 (10½f,Yor,GF,May 17)
Jentzen 109 (6f,Asc,G,Aug 11)
Jessica's Dream 111 (5f,Asc,S,Sep 30)
Jezebel 105 (5f,Nmk,G,May 5)
Jo Mell 109 (8f,Yor,GF,May 16)
Jodeeka 110 (5f,Rip,GF,Jun 10)
Joely Green 105 (11½f,Yar,GF,May 30)
Johannian 106 (12f,Nmk,GS,Aug 4)
John O'Groats 105 (6f,Hay,S,May 5)
Johnny Oscar 110 (15f,Nmk,GS,Jly 21)
Jokesmith 107 (10f,Sal,GF,Jun 12)
Jools 105 (8f,Nmk,GF,Jly 29)
Julius 107 (10f,Fol,GF,Jun 7)
Jumaireyah 107 (10½f,Hay,S,Jly 15)
Junikay 108 (10f,Kem,G,Sep 8)
Juniper 107 (5f,San,GF,Jly 7)
Just Murphy 105 (8f,Ncs,GF,Jun 6)
Just Nick 106 (9f,San,G,Sep 1)
Justafancy 105 (6f,Sth,GF,May 30)
Juwwi 106 (6f,Kem,GF,May 26)
Juyush 105 (16f,Nby,GF,Jly 20)

Kafezah 106 (8f,Bri,F,Jly 4)
Kagoshima 108 (17f,Pon,F,Jun 3)
Kahtan 105 (22f,Asc,GF,Jun 22)
Kai One 106 (7f,Hay,GF,Jun 7)
Kaiapoi 107 (12f,Hay,GS,Jly 7)
Kalanisi 122 (10f,Asc,GF,Jun 20)
Kaluana Court 105 (17f,Pon,GF,Aug 19)
Karameg 107 (7f,Nmk,G,Aug 11)
Kareeb 111 (8½f,Eps,GF,Jun 8)
Kass Alhawa 105 (8½f,Bev,GF,Jly 31)
Kathology 107 (7f,Hay,G,Jun 8)
Katy Nowaitee 109 (10f,Sal,GF,Aug 15)
Kayo 109 (6f,Nby,GF,Jly 5)
Kelburne 107 (8f,Goo,GF,Jly 31)
Keltos 107 (8f,Asc,G,Jun 19)
Kestral 107 (8f,Don,G,Jly 18)
Kez 105 (10f,Eps,GF,Jly 12)
Khazayin 105 (10f,Kem,GF,Jly 11)
Kier Park 110 (5f,Yor,G,Aug 23)
Kilkenny Castle 105 (7f,Nmk,G,Oct 6)
King Carew 105 (8f,Nby,GF,Sep 22)
King Flyer 110 (15f,Nmk,GF,Aug 24)

King Of Peru 105 (5f,Thi,GF,May 19)
King Priam 108 (10f,Red,G,Oct 6)
King's Ironbridge 106 (8f,Nmk,G,May 5)
King's Welcome 105 (10½f,Yor,F,May 15)
Kings Of Europe 105 (12½f,Ncs,GF,Jly 30)
Kingsclere 105 (8f,Goo,GF,Jly 1)
Kinsman 108 (8½f,Eps,GF,Jun 8)
Kirovski 107 (10f,Nby,GF,Sep 22)
Kissing Time 105 (5f,Bri,GF,Sep 4)
Knight's Emperor 105 (8f,Nmk,GF,Jun 22)
Knockholt 106 (16f,Hay,G,Jun 7)
Knocktopher Abbey 105 (8f,Don,GF,Jly 1)
Kuster 108 (8½f,Eps,GF,Jun 8)
Kuwait Rose 107 (8f,Rip,GF,Jly 9)
Kuwait Trooper 109 (11½f,Wdr,G,Jun 3)
Kyda 105 (10f,Kem,GF,Jun 27)
Kylkenny 107 (10f,Pon,F,Sep 20)
Kyllachy 113 (5f,Not,G,Aug 20)

L'Evangile 108 (12f,Asc,G,Sep 28)
La Notte 106 (8f,Hay,GF,May 26)
La Yolam 107 (8f,Yar,G,Jun 25)
Labasheeda 107 (10f,Kem,GF,Jun 27)
Labrett 110 (6f,Goo,G,Aug 4)
Lady Bear 108 (8f,Rip,S,Apr 19)
Lady Boxer 112 (6f,Hay,S,May 5)
Lady Jeannie 105 (8f,Wdr,GF,Jly 23)
Lady Jones 105 (14f,Sal,GS,Oct 3)
Lady Kinvarrah 105 (9f,Kem,GF,Jly 11)
Lady Lahar 107 (8f,Ham,G,Jun 27)
Lady Miletrian 108 (7f,Lin,G,May 12)
Lady Of Kildare 105 (7f,Goo,GF,Aug 2)
Lady Pahia 106 (7f,Goo,GF,Jun 22)
Laggan Minstrel 105 (8f,Wdr,GF,Jly 2)
Lago Di Varano 106 (6f,Yor,G,Jun 15)
Lagudin 112 (10f,Don,GS,Sep 14)
Lailani 116 (10f,Eps,GF,Jun 8)
Lancer 107 (12f,Don,GS,Mar 22)
Lapwing 110 (7f,Yor,F,May 15)
Late Night Out 114 (8f,Don,G,Sep 13)
Law Breaker 105 (5f,Wdr,G,May 21)
Le Fantasme 105 (8f,Kem,G,Sep 7)
Lear Spear 110 (12f,Nmk,GF,Jun 30)
Lennel 108 (8f,Mus,GF,May 4)
Lermontov 106 (9f,San,G,Sep 1)
Lethals Lady 110 (8f,Asc,GF,Jun 22)
Life Is Life 110 (18f,Don,G,Sep 13)
Lil's Jessy 107 (7f,Nmk,GS,Apr 17)
Lilium 116 (12f,Asc,G,Sep 28)
Lime Gardens 108 (12f,Asc,GF,Jun 21)
Lion's Domane 106 (7f,Thi,GF,May 12)
Little Amin 112 (8½f,Eps,GF,Jun 8)
Little Edward 108 (5f,San,GS,Aug 8)
Little Rock 117 (12f,Nmk,GS,Jly 10)
Litzinsky 105 (16½f,Don,S,Nov 10)
Livius 110 (12f,Hay,GS,Jly 7)
Locombe Hill 106 (8f,Nby,GS,Apr 21)
Lone Piper 105 (5f,Eps,G,Sep 15)
Looking For Love 105 (7f,Goo,GS,Sep 27)
Loop The Loup 105 (16f,Ncs,F,Jun 30)
Lord Alaska 110 (16f,Thi,GF,May 12)
Lord Eurolink 112 (10f,Bev,GS,Aug 16)
Lord Jim 105 (12f,Eps,GF,Jun 9)
Lord Joshua 106 (12f,Bat,G,Oct 25)
Lord Kintyre 111 (5f,Don,HY,Oct 27)
Lord Pacal 109 (6f,Nmk,GS,Aug 3)
Lord Protector 109 (7f,Yor,F,May 15)
Lordofenchantment 105 (7½f,Bev,GF,Jun 26)
Love Everlasting 115 (12f,Nby,GF,Aug 5)
Love You Too 108 (7f,Sal,GF,Jly 27)
Lucayan Chief 109 (15f,Nmk,G,Jly 11)
Lucido 113 (12f,Nby,GS,Apr 20)
Lucky Judge 107 (13f,Ham,G,May 6)
Lucky Rainbow 105 (10f,Wdr,HY,Oct 8)
Lunar Leo 113 (7f,San,GF,Jly 7)
Lunar Lord 108 (14f,Not,HY,Apr 3)
Lurina 105 (7f,Nmk,G,May 4)
Lycian 106 (10f,Lei,GF,Sep 11)
Lydia's Look 107 (6f,Thi,F,Jly 27)

Macaroon 111 (7f,Sal,GF,Sep 6)
Madame Jones 109 (8f,Not,G,Aug 3)
Madeline Bassett 106 (12f,Fol,GS,Sep 3)
Magic Flute 107 (8f,Bat,G,Jly 15)
Magic Of Love 109 (6f,Bat,G,Jly 15)
Mahfooth 108 (7f,Nmk,G,May 4)
Major Attraction 105 (12f,Pon,F,May 25)
Makarim 105 (12f,Kem,GF,Jly 22)
Maknaas 105 (16f,Yar,GF,Jly 30)
Malhub 112 (7f,Nmk,GF,Jun 2)
Mamzug 108 (8½f,Bev,GF,May 22)
Man O'Mystery 108 (10½f,Yor,G,Jly 14)
Mana D'Argent 106 (16f,Ncs,F,Jun 30)
Mana-Mou Bay 107 (10f,Fol,GF,Jun 7)
Maniatis 112 (12f,Goo,G,Aug 3)
Manzoni 106 (16f,Chs,G,Sep 1)
Marani 110 (12f,Asc,GF,Jun 21)
Marhoob 111 (10f,Eps,G,Aug 27)
Marienbard 112 (14f,Yor,GF,May 17)
Marika 110 (8f,Nmk,G,Jly 12)
Maromito 105 (5f,Eps,G,Aug 27)
Marrakech 107 (10½f,Hay,S,Jly 15)
Marsad 110 (6f,Goo,G,Aug 4)
Marshal Bond 105 (8f,Mus,S,Mar 29)
Martin's Sunset 107 (8f,Nby,GF,Sep 22)
Mary Jane 107 (5f,Thi,G,Aug 24)
Marzelle 105 (10f,Kem,GF,Jun 27)
Masilia 111 (14½f,Don,GF,Sep 12)
Master Cooper 107 (10f,Nmk,G,May 4)
Master Soden 108 (7f,Sal,GF,Jun 12)
Masterful 107 (10f,Goo,G,Aug 3)
Mastermind 115 (8f,Nby,GS,Apr 21)
Material Witness 105 (8f,Ham,G,Sep 3)
Matoaka 109 (7f,Fol,GF,Jun 29)
Mauri Moon 110 (7f,Goo,GF,Aug 2)
May Ball 106 (7f,Red,G,Oct 6)
Maycocks Bay 108 (10f,Not,GS,Nov 5)
Mayville Thunder 107 (8f,Nmk,G,May 5)
Mbele 107 (16½f,San,G,May 28)
Mcgillycuddy Reeks 108 (10f,Don,GF,Aug 4)
Medicean 115 (10f,San,GF,Jly 7)
Mediterranean 109 (14f,Yor,G,Aug 22)
Melanzana 106 (6f,Nmk,GS,Aug 3)
Melledgan 105 (11f,War,GF,Sep 17)
Melodian 109 (8f,Don,S,Mar 23)
Menaggio 106 (8f,Nmk,GF,Aug 25)
Mental Pressure 109 (16f,Thi,GF,May 12)
Merryvale Man 106 (10f,Ncs,HY,Oct 24)
Mersey Sound 109 (12f,Asc,GF,Jun 21)
Mesmeric 109 (12f,Chp,G,Sep 13)
Midnight Venture 110 (7f,Goo,GS,Sep 27)
Milan 115 (14½f,Don,G,Sep 15)
Miletrian 113 (11f,Nby,GF,Sep 22)
Millenary 116 (12f,Nmk,G,May 4)
Min Mirri 105 (7f,Lin,GF,Jun 30)
Minardi 108 (8f,Nmk,G,May 5)
Minivet 105 (10½f,Hay,S,Jly 15)
Mischief 107 (15½f,Fol,GF,Jly 30)
Misraah 115 (7f,Asc,GF,Jly 28)
Miss Fara 105 (14½f,Kem,G,Sep 8)
Miss George 107 (5f,Bev,GF,Jly 7)
Miss Lorilaw 107 (12f,Hay,GS,Jly 7)
Missouri 105 (15f,Ayr,G,Sep 20)
Mister Clinton 105 (6f,Fol,GF,Aug 23)
Mister Mal 109 (6f,Bri,GS,May 3)
Mister Rambo 107 (7f,Thi,G,May 5)
Misty Boy 105 (6f,Yar,GF,Jun 14)
Misty Eyed 115 (5f,Nby,GF,Sep 22)
Mitcham 112 (6f,Goo,G,Aug 4)
Mizhar 105 (6f,Ncs,F,Jun 30)
Modigliani 107 (6f,Asc,GF,Jun 21)
Modrik 111 (10f,Nmk,G,Jly 11)
Modus Operandi 106 (12f,Bev,GF,Aug 26)
Momentum 110 (9f,Yor,GF,Sep 5)
Monica Geller 107 (9f,Kem,GS,May 7)
Monkston Point 117 (6f,Hay,S,May 5)
Monnavanna 111 (7f,Chs,GF,May 9)
Mont Rocher 107 (10f,Goo,G,Sep 26)
Moojaz 105 (8f,Wdr,G,Aug 13)
Moon At Night 106 (8f,Wdr,G,Aug 6)
Moon Emperor 110 (16f,Asc,G,Aug 11)
Moon Goddess 111 (8f,Yar,G,Jun 25)
Moon Parade 108 (7f,Asc,GF,Jly 28)
Moon Solitaire 108 (12f,Goo,G,Aug 3)
Moonjaz 111 (12f,Pon,GF,Jly 10)
Moonlight Dancer 109 (8f,Wdr,GF,Jun 4)
Morgans Orchard 107 (12½f,Ncs,GF,Jun 28)
Mornings Minion 110 (8f,Nby,GS,Apr 21)
Morshdi 109 (12f,Asc,GF,Jly 28)
Morshid 106 (12f,Rip,S,Apr 19)
Mosayter 107 (9f,Goo,GF,Sep 12)
Moselle 111 (10f,Ncs,GF,Aug 27)
Mostarsil 106 (10f,Nmk,GS,Aug 4)
Mot Juste 107 (12f,Eps,GF,Jun 8)
Motto 109 (14½f,Don,GF,Sep 12)
Mount Abu 112 (6f,Asc,S,Sep 29)
Mousehole 106 (5f,Lin,F,Jun 24)
Mowaadah 108 (8f,Kem,G,Sep 7)
Mozart 118 (6f,Nmk,G,Jly 12)
Mr Combustible 110 (13f,Nby,GF,Aug 18)
Mr Fortywinks 106 (16f,Rip,S,Apr 28)
Mr Mahoose 105 (7f,Asc,S,Sep 29)
Mubtaker 118 (12f,Nmk,G,Oct 5)
Muchea 115 (8f,Yor,GF,May 16)
Mugharreb 106 (8f,Nmk,G,May 6)
Muja Farewell 105 (5f,Asc,GF,Jun 23)
Mujado 105 (6f,Yar,G,Jun 25)
Mull Of Kintyre 107 (7f,Goo,G,Aug 3)
Mumbling 107 (10f,Pon,GS,May 2)
Mungo Park 106 (5f,Nmk,G,Sep 22)
Munir 116 (7f,Nmk,GS,Oct 20)
Munjiz 112 (6f,Nmk,G,May 6)
Murghem 108 (14f,Hay,HY,Sep 28)
Murjana 105 (10f,Rip,GF,Sep 1)
Musha Merr 106 (10½f,Yor,GF,May 17)
Must Be Magic 107 (9f,Kem,GF,Jun 13)
Mutafaweq 113 (12f,Eps,GF,Jun 8)
Mutakarrim 109 (12f,Asc,G,Jun 19)
Mutamam 118 (12f,Nmk,GS,Jly 10)
Mutasawwar 107 (5f,Bev,GF,Jly 7)
Muthaaber 106 (8f,Nby,GF,Jly 21)
Muwakleh 110 (8f,Nmk,G,May 6)
Muyassir 110 (8f,Kem,GF,Jly 22)
My American Beauty 107 (5f,Not,GF,Jly 14)
My Legal Eagle 106 (16f,Chs,S,Sep 26)
My Lucy Locket 105 (8f,Nby,GF,Sep 22)
Mythical King 107 (12f,Lei,G,Jly 25)
Mytton's Again 108 (7f,Eps,GF,Jly 5)

Nadour Al Bahr 107 (10f,Asc,GF,Jly 28)
Nafisah 114 (12f,Nby,GF,Aug 5)
Najah 113 (10f,Bat,G,Oct 1)
Nashaab 110 (8½f,Eps,GF,Jun 8)
Nasmatt 109 (6f,Bat,G,Jly 15)
Nation 105 (10f,Eps,S,Aug 31)
Naughty Knight 107 (7½f,Bev,GF,Aug 26)
Navarre Samson 106 (16f,Chp,GF,Jly 27)
Nayef 114 (12f,Asc,S,Sep 30)
Needwood Blade 114 (7f,Asc,GF,Jly 28)
Niagara 109 (9f,Ham,G,Sep 2)
Nice One Clare 116 (6f,Asc,GF,Jun 22)
Nicobar 123 (8f,San,S,Apr 27)
Nigel's Lad 105 (16f,Thi,GF,May 12)
Night Flight 106 (6f,Yor,G,Jun 15)
Night Haven 110 (6f,Sal,GS,May 6)
Nigrasine 107 (8f,Pon,F,Sep 20)
Nimello 113 (8f,Kem,GS,May 7)
Nineacres 106 (5f,Nby,GF,Aug 5)
Nisr 107 (7f,Nmk,GS,Oct 20)
Niyabah 107 (10f,Red,G,Nov 5)
No Excuse Needed 113 (8f,Goo,GF,Aug 26)
Nobelist 109 (8f,Yor,GF,May 16)
Noble Pursuit 107 (8f,Goo,GF,Jly 1)

Nomore Mr Niceguy 105 (8f,Yor,G,Jly 13)
Noon Gun 110 (8f,Sal,GF,Aug 30)
Nooshman 114 (12f,Nmk,GS,Jly 20)
Norfolk Reed 107 (8f,Wdr,G,Jun 3)
Northgate 107 (8f,Rip,GF,Jly 9)
Norton 109 (7f,Asc,S,Sep 29)
Nose The Trade 111 (7f,Nmk,GS,Oct 20)
Notecard 105 (8f,Don,GF,Jly 12)
Nothing Daunted 105 (7f,Nmk,S,Apr 18)
Nouf 106 (8f,Red,GF,Aug 12)
Noukari 106 (12f,Don,GF,May 26)
Noverre 117 (8f,Asc,S,Sep 29)
Now Look Here 112 (6f,Don,S,Mar 24)
Nowell House 107 (12f,Nmk,S,Apr 18)
Nuclear Debate 118 (5f,San,GF,May 28)

Observatory 120 (10f,Asc,GF,Jun 20)
Ocean Tide 105 (13f,Ham,GS,Jun 20)
Olden Times 109 (8f,Asc,G,Jun 19)
Olivia Grace 108 (5f,Bat,G,Oct 25)
Olivo 107 (15½f,Fol,GF,Jly 30)
Omniheat 106 (10f,Red,S,Oct 30)
One Dinar 106 (8f,Rip,S,Apr 28)
Only For Gold 107 (7f,Ayr,GS,Jly 23)
Optimaite 108 (10f,Fol,GF,Jun 7)
Or Royal 105 (14f,Not,S,Apr 23)
Order 106 (14f,Hay,G,Jun 8)
Orientor 115 (6f,Asc,G,Aug 11)
Oscar Pepper 106 (7½f,Bev,GF,Jun 6)
Our Fred 106 (5f,San,GF,Jly 6)
Ovambo 105 (12f,Goo,GF,Aug 1)

Pagan Prince 107 (8f,San,G,Aug 8)
Pairumani Star 106 (13½f,Chs,GF,May 10)
Palace Affair 110 (7f,Lin,G,May 12)
Palanzo 109 (6f,Asc,G,Aug 11)
Palatial 105 (8f,Asc,G,Aug 12)
Palua 111 (16f,Nby,GS,Apr 21)
Pan Jammer 110 (6f,Ncs,F,Jun 30)
Pandjojoe 109 (6f,Ham,S,Jly 13)
Pantar 111 (10f,Red,F,May 28)
Para Glider 107 (10f,Wdr,HY,Oct 8)
Pardishar 110 (9f,San,G,Aug 8)
Parisien Star 109 (9f,Goo,GF,Sep 12)
Parker 112 (7f,Chs,GF,Jun 6)
Pasithea 109 (10f,Bev,GS,Aug 16)
Passion For Life 105 (6f,Sal,GS,Oct 3)
Patsy's Double 108 (6f,Lei,GS,Aug 12)
Pawn Broker 116 (10f,Kem,S,Apr 16)
Pays D'Amour 109 (7f,Nmk,G,Jly 12)
Peaceful Paradise 106 (8f,San,G,Sep 1)
Peacock Alley 113 (8f,Yor,GF,May 16)
Pearly Gates 111 (7f,Nmk,GS,Oct 20)
Peartree House 110 (8f,Yor,G,Jly 13)
Pension Fund 109 (9f,Yor,G,Jun 16)
Perfect Peach 113 (6f,Goo,G,Aug 4)
Perfect Pirouette 105 (10f,Kem,GF,Jly 11)
Perfect Sunday 109 (11½f,Lin,G,May 12)
Perpetuo 105 (12f,Rip,G,Aug 6)
Persian Pride 109 (10½f,Hay,S,Jly 15)
Persian Punch 112 (16f,Goo,G,Aug 2)
Persiano 110 (8f,Asc,G,Aug 11)
Peruvian Chief 105 (6f,Eps,GF,Jun 9)
Petit Marquis 110 (7f,Hay,GF,Jly 6)
Petrus 105 (7f,Bri,GF,May 8)
Petrushka 106 (12f,Eps,GF,Jun 8)
Pinchaninch 107 (12f,Chp,S,Aug 9)
Pinchincha 110 (10f,Don,GF,Aug 4)
Pipadash 112 (5f,Hay,HY,Sep 8)
Pipalong 115 (6f,Asc,S,Sep 29)
Pips Magic 109 (6f,Don,GF,Jly 11)
Pirro 106 (11½f,San,G,Jly 8)
Point Of Dispute 110 (7f,Nmk,G,Oct 5)
Polar Kingdom 110 (6f,Asc,G,Sep 28)
Polar Red 113 (12f,Nmk,G,Oct 5)
Pole Star 112 (10f,Nmk,G,Jly 11)
Polish Off 106 (8f,Pon,F,Sep 20)
Pomfret Lad 106 (6f,Goo,GF,May 22)
Porak 107 (10f,Fol,HY,Apr 24)
Port Moresby 110 (10f,Nmk,GS,Aug 4)
Port St Charles 107 (6f,Fol,GF,Aug 23)
Post Box 109 (14f,Nmk,G,Oct 6)
Potemkin 105 (10½f,Yor,GF,May 17)
Prairie Falcon 107 (14f,Yor,G,Jun 15)
Prairie Wolf 112 (9f,Goo,GF,Sep 12)
Premier Baron 109 (7f,Lin,G,May 12)
Premier Prize 111 (10f,Sal,GF,Aug 15)
Present 'n Correct 105 (5f,Bri,GF,Aug 29)
Presentation 107 (6f,Asc,GF,Jly 27)
Pride Of India 106 (17f,Pon,F,Jun 3)
Prime Recreation 105 (5f,Wdr,GF,Jun 2)
Primo Valentino 110 (6f,Nmk,GS,Apr 17)
Prince Of Blues 105 (5f,Thi,GF,May 19)
Princess Almora 107 (6f,Kem,GF,Sep 24)
Princess Chloe 106 (6f,Pon,G,Aug 8)
Princess Titania 107 (10½f,Hay,HY,Sep 8)
Priors Lodge 107 (7f,Goo,G,Aug 4)
Prix Star 107 (6f,Nmk,G,Aug 10)
Priya 105 (7f,Nby,GS,Apr 21)
Prize Dancer 107 (14f,Sal,GF,Jly 14)
Prize Winner 108 (12f,Asc,G,Jun 19)
Prizeman 107 (16f,Asc,GF,Jun 19)
Proceed With Care 111 (7f,Asc,GF,Jly 28)
Proper Squire 107 (15f,Nmk,GF,Aug 24)
Proud Chief 108 (6f,Eps,GF,Jly 12)
Proud Native 107 (5f,Eps,GF,Jun 9)
Proudwings 112 (8f,Asc,S,Sep 29)
Ptarmigan Ridge 107 (5f,Hay,G,Aug 11)
Pugin 107 (14½f,Don,G,Sep 15)
Pulau Tioman 113 (8f,Nby,GS,Apr 21)
Punishment 106 (10f,Kem,G,Sep 8)
Puppet Play 107 (7f,Red,GF,Aug 12)
Pure Coincidence 107 (5f,Don,GS,Mar 22)
Pure Elegancia 105 (5f,Lin,GS,May 11)
Putra Pekan 110 (8f,Yor,G,Aug 23)
Putra Sandhurst 107 (11½f,Lin,G,May 12)

Qaatef 112 (10f,San,GF,May 29)
Quebeck 107 (12f,Don,GF,Jly 1)
Quick To Please 106 (8f,Goo,GF,May 24)
Quitte La France 105 (12f,Hay,GS,Aug 9)

Racina 105 (5f,Nmk,G,May 5)
Rada's Daughter 107 (11½f,Wdr,G,Jun 3)
Rafiya 110 (14½f,Don,GF,Sep 12)
Rafters Music 107 (6f,Goo,G,Aug 25)
Ragamuffin 107 (5f,Ncs,GF,Jun 29)
Ragdale Hall 106 (10f,Kem,GF,May 26)
Raheibb 111 (7f,San,GF,Jly 7)
Railroader 106 (6f,Eps,GF,Jly 5)
Rainbow High 112 (18f,Don,G,Sep 13)
Rainbow River 106 (10f,Pon,GS,May 2)
Rajam 107 (12f,Kem,G,Sep 7)
Rampant 105 (12f,Lei,S,Oct 15)
Ranin 113 (14½f,Don,GF,Sep 12)
Ranville 108 (16f,Chs,S,Sep 26)
Rapparee 105 (10½f,Yor,G,Jun 15)
Rasoum 107 (6f,Lei,GS,Aug 12)
Ratio 109 (7f,Asc,GF,Jun 20)
Ravenswood 107 (16f,Ncs,F,Jun 30)
Ravishing 106 (5f,Bev,GF,Aug 25)
Reason 105 (16f,Asc,GF,Jun 19)
Reciprocal 107 (9f,Kem,GF,Jly 4)
Red Carnation 107 (10½f,Hay,HY,Sep 29)
Red Carpet 108 (8f,Nmk,G,May 5)
Red Millennium 108 (5f,Nby,GF,Sep 22)
Red N' Socks 110 (8f,Don,G,Sep 15)
Red Ramona 110 (15f,Nmk,GF,Aug 24)
Red Rosie 105 (10f,Bat,F,Jun 1)
Reef Diver 107 (8f,Kem,GF,May 26)
Reel Buddy 111 (7f,Nmk,GF,Jun 30)
Referendum 105 (5f,Ham,G,May 18)
Regal Song 108 (5f,Mus,S,Apr 7)
Regatta Point 110 (12f,Asc,GF,Jun 21)
Regent Court 105 (8f,Rip,G,May 10)
Relish The Thought 111 (12f,Nby,GF,Aug 5)
Renaissance Lady 107 (16½f,Fol,GF,Jun 7)
Repertory 110 (5f,Yor,G,Aug 23)
Return 105 (12f,Asc,G,Jun 19)
Rhythmicall 109 (15f,Nmk,GF,Aug 24)
Riberac 114 (8f,Asc,G,Aug 12)
Rich Gift 110 (6f,Asc,G,Sep 28)
Rigadoon 106 (17f,Pon,F,Jun 3)
Right Wing 119 (8f,San,S,Apr 27)
Ring Dancer 105 (5f,Yar,GF,Jun 1)
Ringside Jack 106 (10f,Don,G,May 7)
Risque Sermon 107 (6f,Eps,GF,Jly 5)
Rita's Rock Ape 106 (5f,Nby,GF,Aug 5)
Riverblue 106 (8f,Not,HY,Apr 3)
Riyadh 111 (14f,Nmk,G,Oct 6)
Roaring Twenties 105 (6f,Nmk,G,Aug 11)
Rob Leach 107 (10f,Wdr,G,May 14)
Robandela 107 (10f,Lei,GF,Sep 11)
Robzelda 108 (8f,Pon,HY,Apr 10)
Rockerlong 110 (12f,Nmk,GS,Jly 21)
Rolly Polly 110 (7f,Nby,GS,Apr 21)
Roman King 109 (10f,Eps,S,Apr 25)
Romantic Affair 108 (16f,Nmk,G,May 5)
Romantic Myth 107 (5f,Nmk,G,May 5)
Rose Gypsy 106 (8f,Asc,GF,Jun 22)
Rose Of America 106 (8f,Ncs,F,Jly 8)
Roses Of Spring 106 (6f,Thi,F,Jly 27)
Rosi's Boy 106 (8f,Goo,G,Aug 4)
Rosselli 107 (5f,Bev,G,May 12)
Royal Artist 106 (7f,Nmk,GF,Jun 22)
Royal Cavalier 108 (12f,Bev,GF,Aug 26)
Royal Measure 105 (14f,Not,S,Apr 16)
Royal Millennium 112 (7f,San,GF,Jly 7)
Royal Minstrel 109 (10f,Lei,GS,Aug 12)
Royal Rebel 107 (20f,Asc,GF,Jun 21)
Rozel 109 (5f,San,GF,Jly 7)
Rudi's Pet 110 (5f,Nmk,GF,Jly 27)
Rudik 105 (7f,Nmk,G,Oct 5)
Runaway Star 107 (12f,Rip,G,Aug 6)
Running Times 108 (16f,Bev,G,May 12)
Rushcutter Bay 116 (5f,Nmk,G,May 5)
Russian Rhapsody 108 (8f,Not,GS,Nov 5)
Ryan's Gold 108 (8f,Wdr,GF,Jun 4)
Rymer's Rascal 106 (7½f,Bev,GF,Aug 25)

Saabirr 106 (10f,San,GF,Jly 7)
Sabo Rose 108 (7f,Nmk,GF,Jun 10)
Sacred Song 113 (12f,Hay,GS,Jly 7)
Saddler's Quest 109 (12f,Nmk,GS,Nov 2)
Sagittarius 113 (12f,Asc,S,Sep 30)
Sahara Slew 112 (12f,Asc,GF,Jun 21)
Sailing Shoes 105 (5f,San,GF,Jly 25)
Sakhee 119 (10½f,Yor,G,Aug 21)
Salford Express 110 (12f,Nby,GS,Apr 20)
Salim Toto 105 (8f,Not,G,May 11)
Saltrio 105 (12f,Asc,HY,Sep 30)
Salty Jack 108 (8f,Goo,GF,Jly 1)
Salviati 108 (6f,Asc,GF,Jly 27)
Samsaam 111 (14f,Yor,GF,May 17)
San Sebastian 109 (16f,Nmk,G,May 5)
Sandmason 114 (12f,Nmk,G,May 4)
Santisima Trinidad 106 (8f,Thi,GF,Sep 8)
Saorsie 107 (8f,Wdr,GF,Jun 4)
Sarangani 109 (10f,Yar,G,May 29)
Saratov 106 (10½f,Yor,F,May 15)
Sarena Pride 107 (8f,Wdr,GS,May 8)
Sartorial 111 (6f,Yor,G,Jun 15)
Sauterne 111 (10f,Don,GF,Jly 12)
Sayedah 112 (12f,Nby,GF,Aug 5)
Scarpe Rosse 108 (10f,Bat,GS,May 1)
Scheming 110 (10f,Red,F,May 28)
Scorned 108 (12f,Nmk,GS,Oct 18)
Scotish Law 105 (7f,San,G,May 28)
Scottish Spice 107 (8f,San,S,Aug 19)
Scotty's Future 111 (10f,Don,GF,Aug 4)
Sea Mark 105 (10f,Don,GF,Sep 12)
Sea Star 105 (8f,Pon,GS,Oct 8)
Seagull 106 (10f,Nby,S,May 19)

Seattle Prince 107 (14f,Nmk,G,Oct 6)
Secret Conquest 105 (7f,Don,GF,Jun 30)
Seliana 113 (16f,Nby,GS,Apr 21)
Senator's Alibi 106 (8f,Hay,HY,Sep 7)
Senior Minister 109 (5f,Nby,GF,Sep 22)
Sequoyah 107 (8f,Asc,GF,Jun 22)
Serengeti Bride 105 (12f,Goo,G,Aug 26)
Serge Lifar 109 (14f,Nmk,G,Sep 22)
Serviceable 108 (8f,Rip,GF,Jly 9)
Seven No Trumps 112 (6f,Asc,GF,Jun 22)
Shaandar 111 (15f,Nmk,G,Jly 11)
Shadowblaster 105 (14f,Hay,GF,May 26)
Shamaiel 113 (11f,Nby,GF,Aug 17)
Shara 105 (12f,Chp,G,Sep 13)
Sharp Belline 108 (16f,Bev,G,May 12)
Sharp Hat 109 (5f,Don,HY,Oct 27)
Sharp Play 110 (10f,Red,F,May 28)
Shayadi 105 (10f,Pon,HY,Apr 10)
Sheppard's Watch 109 (7f,Goo,GF,Aug 2)
Shibboleth 113 (7f,Nmk,GF,Jun 30)
Shipton Wood 106 (14f,Sal,GF,Jly 14)
Shoeshine Boy 106 (5f,Thi,GF,May 19)
Shush 110 (10f,Eps,GF,Jun 8)
Sifat 105 (11½f,Yar,GF,May 30)
Sihafi 105 (5f,Ham,F,May 12)
Sikasso 108 (11f,Ham,G,May 6)
Silk St John 106 (8f,Don,GF,Jly 1)
Silky Dawn 109 (8f,Sal,GS,Jun 17)
Simply Sensational 105 (10f,Nby,S,May 18)
Sir Desmond 106 (5f,Asc,GS,Oct 13)
Sir Effendi 106 (7f,Hay,G,Jun 8)
Sir Ninja 109 (8f,Hay,HY,Sep 28)
Sir Sandrovitch 109 (5f,Pon,GF,Jly 20)
Sixty Seconds 108 (11f,Nby,GF,Aug 17)
Sky Dome 105 (9f,Kem,GF,Jun 13)
Skylarker 108 (11½f,Wdr,GF,Aug 25)
Slickly 114 (9f,San,G,Aug 8)
Sloane 105 (7f,Ncs,GF,Jly 28)
Slumbering 106 (7f,Yor,GS,Oct 13)
Smart Predator 113 (5f,Nmk,GS,Oct 18)
Smart Ridge 109 (8f,Asc,G,Aug 11)
Smirk 113 (8f,Yor,G,Aug 23)
Smokey From Caplaw 105 (7f,Don,GF,Jly 12)
Smokin Beau 112 (6f,Ayr,GF,Sep 22)
Smooth Sailing 106 (10f,Lei,GS,Aug 12)
Smyslov 106 (10f,Red,G,Oct 6)
Snowflake 110 (12f,Asc,GF,Jun 21)
Snowstorm 110 (12f,Goo,GF,Jly 31)
Soba Jones 109 (5f,Hay,S,Jly 15)
Social Contract 106 (7f,Lin,G,May 12)
Soft Breeze 107 (10f,Nby,GF,Sep 22)
Softly Tread 112 (7f,Don,G,Sep 13)
Soldier Point 106 (7f,Nmk,G,May 4)
Solitary 105 (16f,Rip,S,Apr 28)
Soller Bay 105 (8f,Nmk,GS,Nov 3)
Solo Flight 109 (12f,Asc,G,Jun 19)
Solo Mio 110 (16f,Nmk,G,May 5)
Sonatina 107 (8f,Goo,G,Aug 4)
Soviet Flash 118 (8f,Yor,GF,May 16)
Spa Lane 108 (16f,Bev,G,May 12)
Special 107 (12f,Pon,GF,Jly 10)
Spectina 110 (8f,Yar,G,Jun 25)
Speed Venture 107 (8f,Pon,HY,Apr 10)
Spencers Wood 107 (7f,Nmk,G,May 4)
Sporting Gesture 109 (12f,Don,G,Sep 15)
Spree Vision 105 (13f,Ham,G,May 6)
Spring Pursuit 106 (12f,Kem,GS,May 7)
St Expedit 113 (13½f,Chs,GF,May 10)
Stage Presence 105 (7f,Asc,GS,Oct 13)
Staging Post 109 (10f,Nmk,GS,Jly 20)
Stands To Reason 111 (9f,San,S,Jun 16)
Stanza 105 (8f,Mus,GF,May 21)
Staploy 105 (11½f,Yar,G,Jly 3)
Star Cast 106 (12f,Kem,G,Sep 7)
Stay Behind 105 (10f,Pon,GF,Jun 24)
Steel Band 111 (12f,Hay,GS,Jly 7)
Stitch In Time 105 (10f,Lin,GF,Jly 13)
Stoppes Brow 109 (8f,Goo,GF,Jun 22)
Storming Home 117 (12f,Asc,GF,Jly 28)

Stratton 111 (7f,Nmk,G,Oct 6)
Street Life 109 (10f,Wdr,HY,Oct 8)
Stretton 109 (8f,Yor,GF,May 17)
Stromsholm 106 (8f,Wdr,GF,Jly 2)
Style Dancer 109 (7f,Chs,GF,Jun 6)
Sugarfoot 111 (7f,Nmk,G,May 4)
Suggestive 109 (7f,Yar,G,May 29)
Summer View 108 (8f,Wdr,G,May 14)
Summoner 119 (8f,Asc,S,Sep 29)
Sunley Scent 106 (6f,Fol,G,Aug 13)
Sunley Sense 106 (5f,San,S,Aug 19)
Sunstone 107 (12f,Asc,GF,Jun 21)
Super Tassa 106 (12f,Yor,G,Aug 22)
Superior Premium 108 (6f,Asc,GF,Jun 21)
Superstar Leo 113 (5f,San,GF,May 28)
Sure Quest 105 (10½f,Hay,HY,Sep 29)
Surprise Encounter 108 (8f,Asc,GF,Jun 20)
Surprised 108 (6f,Goo,GF,Jly 1)
Sussex Lad 105 (5f,Bat,G,Oct 25)
Swallow Flight 122 (8f,San,S,Apr 27)
Sweet Angeline 105 (11½f,Yar,GF,May 30)
Swift Dispersal 108 (7f,San,G,May 28)
Swing Of The Tide 109 (8f,Ham,G,May 18)
Swino 106 (5f,Bri,GS,Apr 12)
Swynford Pleasure 109 (8f,Nmk,GF,Jun 22)
Swynford Welcome 109 (7f,Bri,S,Sep 30)
Sydenham 109 (10f,Don,GS,Sep 14)

Tadeo 107 (5f,Thi,GF,May 19)
Taffrail 108 (16f,Bev,G,Aug 15)
Taffs Well 107 (8f,Hay,GF,May 25)
Takamaka Bay 112 (12f,Asc,G,Jun 19)
Take Flite 106 (7f,Lin,GF,Sep 5)
Talaash 105 (12f,Nby,GS,Apr 20)
Tamarisk 110 (5f,Asc,G,Jun 19)
Tamburlaine 117 (7f,Nby,GF,Aug 18)
Tamiami Trail 110 (15f,Nmk,G,Jly 11)
Tapau 106 (7f,Bri,G,Aug 9)
Taranaki 106 (6f,Sal,GS,May 6)
Taras Emperor 109 (5f,Ayr,HY,Oct 15)
Tarboush 105 (8f,Wdr,G,Jun 3)
Tarfshi 108 (10f,Ncs,F,Jun 30)
Tayif 106 (6f,Ham,S,Jly 13)
Technician 107 (6f,Pon,F,Jun 3)
Tedburrow 111 (5f,Nmk,G,May 5)
Temple Way 109 (15f,Nmk,GF,Aug 24)
Tempting Fate 111 (8f,Asc,GF,Jun 22)
Tennessee Moon 106 (10f,Kem,GF,Jun 27)
Tensile 109 (16f,Nby,GS,Apr 21)
Terrestrial 107 (12f,Nmk,G,May 5)
Teyaar 106 (6f,Ham,G,May 6)
Thari 112 (11½f,Wdr,GF,Aug 25)
That Man Again 107 (5f,San,GF,Jly 6)
That's Jazz 105 (6f,Chp,GF,Jly 7)
Thats All Jazz 105 (7f,Chp,G,Jly 20)
The Butterwick Kid 107 (12f,Don,GS,Mar 22)
The Glen 109 (11f,Nby,GF,Aug 17)
The Tatling 107 (6f,Ayr,GF,Sep 22)
The Trader 117 (5f,Nby,GF,Sep 22)
The Whistling Teal 114 (8f,Pon,HY,Apr 10)
The Wife 105 (7½f,Bev,G,Sep 25)
Theatre Script 106 (12f,Asc,GF,Jun 22)
Thesis 108 (10f,Nmk,GF,Aug 25)
Thihn 111 (8½f,Eps,GF,Jun 8)
Three Lions 105 (16f,Nby,GF,Sep 21)
Three Points 114 (6f,Asc,GF,Jun 21)
Thunder Sky 105 (9f,Ham,GS,Jly 19)
Thundering Surf 110 (10f,San,GF,Jly 6)
Thundermill 105 (10f,Fol,GF,Aug 23)
Tick Tock 105 (5f,Ayr,G,Sep 20)
Tillerman 115 (7f,Asc,GF,Jly 28)
Time Away 111 (10½f,Yor,F,May 15)
Time For Music 105 (7f,Bri,F,Jun 1)

Time To Remember 109 (7f,Red,GF,Aug 12)
Time Vally 105 (8f,Don,G,Jly 18)
Tipperary Sunset 105 (8½f,Bev,G,May 12)
Tissifer 107 (10f,Asc,G,Sep 28)
Titian Angel 109 (15f,Nmk,GF,Aug 24)
Tiyoun 105 (12f,Rip,GF,Jun 10)
Tobougg 114 (10f,San,GF,Jly 7)
Toffee Nosed 110 (7f,Asc,GS,Oct 13)
Tom Tun 106 (6f,Don,S,Mar 23)
Tomasino 114 (12f,Asc,GF,Jun 21)
Tommy Smith 108 (5f,Bev,GF,Aug 25)
Tony Tie 107 (7f,Hay,GF,Jly 6)
Top Dirham 107 (7f,Eps,GF,Jun 8)
Topton 106 (7f,Nby,GF,May 30)
Torcello 109 (10½f,Chs,GF,May 10)
Toroca 113 (6f,Asc,S,Sep 29)
Torosay Spring 111 (6f,Asc,G,Sep 28)
Torrealta 106 (14½f,Don,GF,Sep 12)
Torrential Storm 106 (10½f,Yor,S,Oct 11)
Torrid Kentavr 108 (11½f,San,G,Jly 8)
Total Delight 106 (11½f,San,G,Jly 8)
Total Love 105 (5f,Bat,GS,May 1)
Totem Dancer 107 (16f,Red,GF,Aug 12)
Tough Speed 117 (8f,Don,G,Sep 13)
Trace Clip 112 (6f,Asc,GF,Jly 27)
Tramway 105 (12f,Hay,S,Jly 15)
Transatlantic 108 (9f,Kem,G,Jly 18)
Treasure Chest 106 (16f,Asc,GF,Jun 23)
Triphenia 105 (8½f,Bev,GF,May 22)
Triumphant Return 106 (5f,Nby,GF,Sep 22)
Trotter's Future 107 (10f,Lin,GF,Sep 5)
True Night 109 (7f,Asc,GF,Jly 28)
Tumbleweed Ridge 105 (7f,Chp,GF,Aug 27)
Turku 106 (8f,Hay,G,Aug 11)
Turn Of A Century 106 (10½f,Hay,S,Jly 15)
Turned Out Well 109 (16f,Bev,G,May 12)
Turnpole 109 (16f,Hay,G,Jun 7)
Turtle Valley 110 (14f,Not,HY,Apr 3)
Twilight Haze 105 (12f,Rip,S,Apr 19)
Twin Time 106 (8f,Bat,G,May 21)
Tycoon's Last 105 (10½f,Hay,HY,Sep 29)
Typhoon Ginger 107 (10f,Don,GF,Aug 4)

Ulundi 111 (10f,San,GF,Jly 6)
Umistim 109 (8f,Sal,F,Aug 16)
Undeniable 105 (16f,Yar,GF,Jly 30)
Undeterred 114 (6f,Goo,G,Aug 4)
Unshaken 109 (8f,Don,GF,Jly 1)
Up In Flames 105 (10½f,Yor,S,Oct 11)
Up Tempo 107 (8f,Hay,GF,May 26)

Vahorimix 113 (8f,Asc,S,Sep 29)
Valentine Band 107 (10½f,Yor,GF,May 16)
Valentino 111 (7f,Nmk,GF,Jun 30)
Valeureux 105 (8f,Not,HY,Mar 28)
Velvet Glade 107 (7f,Asc,GF,Jly 28)
Vicious Dancer 105 (6f,Lin,G,May 12)
Victoria Cross 107 (8f,Asc,G,Aug 12)
Vintage Premium 114 (8f,Yor,GF,May 16)
Virgin Soldier 105 (16f,Asc,G,Aug 11)
Vision Of Night 118 (5f,San,GF,May 28)
Vita Spericolata 114 (5f,Nby,GF,Sep 22)
Volata 112 (6f,Ncs,F,Jun 30)
Volontiers 110 (7f,Goo,GF,Jun 8)

Wahj 113 (7f,Chs,GS,Aug 31)
Waki Music 108 (8f,Don,G,Jly 18)
Wannabe Around 110 (8f,Sal,GF,Jly 6)
Warning Reef 109 (10f,Don,GF,Aug 4)
Warningford 116 (7f,Nby,GF,Aug 18)
Warrsan 107 (14f,San,GF,Jly 26)
Waseyla 107 (10f,Fol,GS,Sep 3)
Watching 107 (5f,Nmk,G,May 5)
Water Jump 114 (12f,Rip,S,Apr 28)

Wattno Eljohn 106 (8f,Kem,G,Sep 7)
Wave Of Optimism 106 (16f,Kem,S,Apr 14)
Waverley Road 106 (9f,Kem,GF,Jun 13)
Weecandoo 105 (9f,San,G,Sep 2)
Weet For Me 106 (14f,Yor,G,Jun 15)
Welcome Friend 111 (6f,Yar,GS,Aug 8)
Wellbeing 112 (12f,Eps,GF,Jun 8)
Welsh Wind 108 (7f,Yor,GS,Oct 13)
Westender 109 (12f,Hay,GS,Jly 7)
Western Flame 106 (5f,Chp,G,Jly 20)
Westfield Star 105 (7f,Thi,G,Jun 19)
Whale Beach 110 (7f,Eps,GF,Aug 16)
What-A-Dancer 107 (7f,Yor,GF,Sep 2)
When In Rome 110 (14½f,Don,G,Sep 15)
Where The Heart Is 108 (8f,Yor,GF,May 17)
Whisky Nine 106 (6f,Don,GF,Jly 11)
Whistler 105 (5f,Don,S,Nov 9)
White Emir 107 (7f,Eps,GF,Aug 16)
White Star Lady 108 (7½f,Bev,GF,Aug 26)
Whitefoot 105 (16f,Asc,G,Aug 11)
Willoughby's Boy 106 (7f,Yar,GF,Jun 1)
Windsor Boy 109 (12f,Nmk,GS,Jly 20)
Winning Venture 111 (7f,Hay,S,May 5)
Woodland River 108 (8f,Not,G,Aug 3)
Woodlands 105 (5f,Lin,F,Jun 24)
Woodyates 107 (12f,Chp,S,Aug 9)
Worthily 105 (16f,Asc,GF,Jun 19)

Xellance 106 (16f,Mus,G,Nov 7)
Xtra 108 (12f,Yor,G,Aug 21)

Yanus 106 (10f,Ayr,GS,Jly 24)
Yarob 108 (7f,Thi,G,May 5)
Yavana's Pace 106 (13½f,Chs,GF,May 10)
Year Two Thousand 108 (16f,Asc,GF,Jun 19)
Yertle 108 (16f,Lin,GF,Sep 5)
Yorkies Boy 110 (6f,Yor,GF,May 17)
Yorkshire 111 (16f,Nmk,G,Jly 11)
You'Re Special 106 (16f,Kem,S,Apr 14)
Young Alex 107 (8f,Wdr,GF,Jun 11)
Young Rosein 106 (8f,Yor,G,Jly 13)

Zaheemah 106 (7f,Nmk,GS,Apr 17)
Zamat 107 (12f,Ham,G,Sep 3)
Zandeed 105 (8f,Hay,G,Jun 8)
Zhitomir 107 (7f,Goo,GS,Sep 27)
Zibeline 106 (14f,Goo,GF,Jly 31)
Zibet 105 (8f,Chp,S,Aug 9)
Zietunzeen 106 (6f,Chp,G,Jly 13)
Zietzig 106 (6f,Goo,G,Sep 19)
Zilarator 106 (12f,Yor,S,Oct 11)
Zilch 108 (7f,Goo,GS,Sep 27)
Zindabad 116 (12f,Nmk,GS,Jly 10)
Zozarharry 106 (7f,Nmk,G,May 4)
Zucchero 112 (7f,Lin,G,May 12)
Zuhair 109 (6f,Goo,GF,Jly 1)

THREE YEAR-OLDS AND UPWARDS - Sand

Admirals Place 106 (12f,Lin,SD,Dec 13)
Afaan 112 (5f,Wol,SD,Feb 22)
Air Mail 112 (7f,Sth,SW,Jan 19)
Air Of Esteem 105 (8½f,Wol,SD,Nov 29)
Al's Alibi 106 (12f,Sth,SD,Dec 4)
Amaranth 108 (8½f,Wol,SD,Mar 10)
Amjad 106 (8f,Sth,SD,Jan 12)
Ansellad 106 (6f,Lin,SD,Jan 6)
Anstand 107 (7f,Wol,SD,Mar 24)
Arc 108 (9½f,Wol,SD,Mar 15)
Argamia 108 (12f,Wol,SD,Feb 20)
Arizona Lady 105 (9½f,Wol,SD,Nov 25)
Arpello 107 (14f,Sth,SW,Feb 23)

Balladeer 105 (12f,Wol,SD,Oct 6)
Ballet Master 105 (7f,Wol,SD,Nov 3)
Baron De Pichon 109 (12f,Wol,SD,Mar 15)
Battle Warning 109 (14f,Sth,SW,Feb 23)
Bawsian 111 (12f,Sth,SD,Dec 15)
Belinda 105 (11f,Sth,SD,Oct 1)
Blakeset 107 (6f,Wol,SW,Jan 11)
Bless 106 (12f,Lin,SW,Feb 14)
Blushing Prince 105 (9½f,Wol,SD,Oct 23)
Bold Ewar 108 (8½f,Wol,SD,Mar 10)
Border Glen 105 (6f,Lin,SD,Jan 17)
Branston Pickle 106 (6f,Wol,SW,Sep 6)
Browning 106 (12f,Lin,SW,Jan 31)
Buddeliea 105 (10f,Lin,SD,Mar 16)
Burgundy 111 (8f,Lin,SD,Dec 16)
Burning Truth 106 (11f,Sth,SW,Feb 12)

Caballe 107 (12f,Wol,SD,Jun 20)
Carrie Pooter 110 (6f,Wol,SD,Feb 15)
Champagne Rider 110 (8½f,Wol,SD,Mar 10)
Chief Of Justice 109 (12f,Sth,SD,Dec 15)
Chispa 106 (5f,Sth,SW,Jan 19)
Clarinch Claymore 110 (12f,Sth,SD,Feb 2)
Classy Cleo 106 (6f,Wol,SD,Jan 30)
Coccolona 106 (11f,Sth,SD,Oct 1)
Colonel Mustard 106 (9½f,Wol,SD,Nov 3)
Compton Bolter 113 (10f,Lin,SD,Nov 18)
Cookie Crumble 106 (6f,Wol,SD,Jan 30)
Cool Temper 107 (10f,Lin,SD,Apr 11)
Counsel's Opinion 111 (12f,Sth,SW,Apr 14)
Cretan Gift 105 (6f,Wol,SD,Mar 10)
Crimson Tide 113 (8f,Lin,SD,Dec 16)
Culzean 112 (9½f,Wol,SD,Dec 9)
Czar Wars 110 (6f,Sth,SW,Jan 22)

Dancing Mystery 111 (5f,Wol,SD,Feb 22)
Davis Rock 105 (8f,Sth,SD,Jan 29)
Diamond Geezer 110 (5f,Wol,SD,Dec 12)
Dil 106 (5f,Wol,SD,Dec 19)
Dixie Island 109 (10f,Lin,SW,Jan 31)
Doctor Dennis 105 (6f,Sth,SD,May 25)
Double Oscar 109 (5f,Wol,SD,Feb 22)
Dunedin Rascal 106 (5f,Wol,SD,Feb 22)

Eastern Trumpeter 111 (5f,Wol,SD,Dec 12)
Effervescent 111 (6f,Wol,SD,Jan 30)
Eighty Two 107 (9½f,Wol,SD,Dec 9)
Ellens Academy 105 (6f,Sth,SD,Apr 4)
Exclusion Zone 105 (12f,Lin,SD,Nov 9)

Fallachan 106 (8½f,Wol,SD,Mar 24)
Feast Of Romance 108 (6f,Wol,SD,Mar 14)
Fiennes 105 (5f,Sth,SD,Apr 10)
Fine Melody 106 (7f,Lin,SD,Nov 18)
Flapdoodle 106 (5f,Wol,SD,Jan 6)
Focused Attraction 109 (6f,Wol,SW,Jan 18)
Foreign Editor 109 (7f,Wol,SD,Dec 19)
Fraternity 105 (12f,Lin,SD,Jan 3)
Frilly Front 108 (5f,Wol,SD,Dec 19)
Funny Valentine 105 (6f,Lin,SD,Apr 2)
Fusul 105 (13f,Lin,SW,Feb 14)

Gaelic Foray 107 (7f,Lin,SD,Dec 13)
Garden Of Eden 107 (9½f,Wol,SD,Oct 23)
Golconda 107 (10f,Lin,SD,Nov 18)
Golden Rod 109 (11f,Sth,SD,Mar 26)
Gralmano 107 (8½f,Wol,SD,Feb 22)
Guilsborough 105 (8f,Sth,SD,Jan 1)

Hail The Chief 116 (8½f,Wol,SD,Nov 29)
Hannibal Lad 106 (9½f,Wol,SD,Dec 26)
Harewood End 105 (8f,Sth,SD,Apr 30)
Harik 105 (16f,Lin,SW,Feb 17)
Harvey Leader 106 (8f,Sth,SD,Jan 12)
Henry Tun 106 (5f,Sth,SD,Apr 10)
Hout Bay 105 (5f,Wol,SD,Jan 6)
Hugwity 109 (10f,Lin,SD,Apr 11)

Ice Prince 105 (8½f,Wol,SD,Mar 10)
If By Chance 106 (6f,Lin,SD,Jan 24)
Illusive 107 (6f,Wol,SD,Mar 10)
Imprevue 105 (12f,Lin,SW,Jan 31)
Indian Dance 106 (7f,Wol,SD,Dec 9)
Intricate Web 109 (7f,Wol,SW,Jan 11)
Invader 110 (8½f,Wol,SD,Mar 10)
Inver Gold 106 (9½f,Wol,SD,Aug 18)
Ionian Spring 110 (10f,Lin,SW,Feb 17)
Izzet Muzzy 109 (6f,Wol,SD,Sep 22)

Jack To A King 107 (5f,Wol,SD,Feb 8)
Jackerin 107 (5f,Lin,SD,Apr 3)
Jalousie 107 (12f,Sth,SD,Jun 8)
Jorrocks 115 (8f,Sth,SD,Jan 1)
Juwwi 110 (5f,Wol,SD,Feb 22)

Karpasiana 108 (12f,Wol,SD,Jun 20)
Kathakali 111 (9½f,Wol,SD,Dec 9)
Keen Hands 108 (7f,Wol,SW,Jan 18)
Kennet 110 (12f,Sth,SD,Feb 2)
Kentucky Bullet 108 (11f,Sth,SW,Jan 22)
Kinsman 109 (8f,Lin,SW,Feb 7)
Kirisnippa 108 (12f,Wol,SD,Jan 25)
Kumakawa 106 (7f,Sth,SD,Jun 29)
Kylkenny 111 (12f,Sth,SD,Feb 2)

Labrett 108 (6f,Lin,SD,Apr 11)
Lady Coldunell 107 (13f,Lin,SD,Apr 3)
Laurel Dawn 108 (5f,Lin,SD,Apr 2)
Lord Omni 105 (6f,Sth,SD,Feb 2)
Lost Spirit 109 (12f,Lin,SW,Feb 21)
Love's Design 109 (7f,Lin,SD,Apr 11)

Magelta 105 (8f,Lin,SD,Dec 16)
Magic Eagle 107 (7f,Sth,SD,Jan 8)
Makarim 109 (12f,Sth,SD,Mar 19)
Malaah 107 (8f,Lin,SD,Jan 17)
Mana D'Argent 106 (14f,Sth,SD,Apr 10)
Mangus 109 (5f,Wol,SD,Mar 15)
Manorbier 107 (5f,Wol,SD,Feb 22)
Maritun Lad 108 (5f,Wol,SD,Dec 12)
Marnie 108 (7f,Lin,SD,Feb 3)
Maromito 105 (5f,Sth,SD,Apr 17)
Marrel 105 (12f,Sth,SD,Jly 2)
Mayville Thunder 106 (10f,Lin,SD,Mar 16)
Mellow Jazz 112 (8½f,Wol,SD,Nov 29)
Mi Odds 114 (11f,Sth,SD,Jan 8)
Mice Ideas 109 (11f,Sth,SW,Jan 22)
Miss Hit 105 (5f,Wol,SD,Nov 15)
Mizhar 115 (5f,Wol,SD,Feb 22)
Moon Emperor 106 (10f,Lin,SD,Mar 17)
Moonlight Song 106 (7f,Lin,SD,Feb 3)
Morgans Orchard 109 (12f,Sth,SD,Mar 19)
Most-Saucy 108 (8f,Lin,SW,Feb 7)
Moyne Pleasure 107 (9½f,Wol,SD,Mar 10)
Mutasawwar 110 (5f,Wol,SD,Dec 12)
My Retreat 107 (9½f,Wol,SD,Nov 25)
My Tess 109 (8½f,Wol,SD,Nov 25)
Mytton's Again 105 (8f,Lin,SD,Mar 19)

Nadour Al Bahr 106 (10f,Lin,SD,Nov 18)
Naked Oat 109 (11f,Sth,SD,Apr 28)
Nashaab 105 (8½f,Wol,SD,Dec 26)
Night Sight 111 (12f,Sth,SD,Mar 19)
Nimello 113 (8½f,Wol,SD,Mar 10)
Nineacres 109 (5f,Wol,SD,Nov 15)
Nose The Trade 109 (8½f,Wol,SD,Feb 22)

Off Hire 106 (5f,Wol,SD,Feb 27)
On The Trail 108 (7f,Lin,SD,Feb 3)
Oscar Pepper 108 (7f,Sth,SD,Mar 16)
Our Fred 109 (5f,Wol,SW,Jan 23)

Paddywack 109 (6f,Wol,SD,Jan 30)
Paperweight 105 (12f,Sth,SD,Jun 8)
Parker 105 (8f,Lin,SD,Feb 3)
Pengamon 106 (7f,Lin,SD,Nov 22)
Pension Fund 108 (12f,Sth,SD,Feb 2)
Perigeux 107 (5f,Lin,SD,Apr 2)
Pretrail 110 (8½f,Wol,SW,Jan 20)
Pride Of Brixton 108 (5f,Wol,SD,Dec 12)
Prime Recreation 110 (5f,Wol,SD,Feb 8)
Prince Nico 109 (5f,Wol,SD,May 3)
Punishment 110 (12f,Wol,SD,Mar 15)
Pure Coincidence 105 (5f,Wol,SD,Dec 2)

Rainbow River 107 (12f,Sth,SW,Apr 14)
Rajah Eman 106 (11f,Sth,SD,Apr 28)
Rayik 107 (12f,Lin,SW,Feb 21)
Ready To Rock 105 (5f,Wol,SW,Feb 13)
Red Ryding Hood 105 (5f,Sth,SD,Mar 26)
Redoubtable 107 (6f,Lin,SD,Jan 6)
Resplendent Star 111 (10f,Lin,SW,Jan 31)
Risk Free 108 (8f,Lin,SD,Feb 3)
Risky Reef 106 (7f,Sth,SD,Jan 8)
Robandela 109 (12f,Sth,SD,Feb 2)
Roman Hideaway 108 (12f,Sth,SD,Jly 2)
Royal Insult 107 (7f,Lin,SD,Nov 18)

Sea Ya Maite 105 (7f,Sth,SD,Mar 13)
Secret Spring 105 (12f,Lin,SD,Nov 18)
Sergeant York 111 (10f,Lin,SD,Mar 17)
Shablam 107 (10f,Lin,SD,Nov 18)
Sharp Hat 112 (5f,Lin,SD,Apr 3)
Shotacross The Bow 105 (9½f,Wol,SD,Nov 3)
Silver Socks 111 (12f,Wol,SD,Feb 20)
Sir Ferbet 115 (8½f,Wol,SD,Nov 29)
Sir Sandrovitch 107 (5f,Wol,SD,Feb 8)
Smokin Beau 116 (5f,Wol,SD,Mar 15)
So Sober 106 (6f,Sth,SD,Mar 16)
Soaring Phoenix 106 (12f,Sth,SD,Jly 2)
Social Contract 110 (7f,Lin,SD,Feb 3)
Sofisio 106 (9½f,Wol,SD,Mar 15)
Sotonian 108 (5f,Wol,SD,Jan 6)
Spanish Star 107 (11f,Sth,SD,Jan 15)
Squirrel Nutkin 105 (6f,Wol,SD,Jan 30)
Stand By 107 (5f,Wol,SD,Nov 11)
Stitch In Time 106 (12f,Sth,SD,Dec 4)
Stratton 105 (7f,Lin,SD,Jan 27)
Summer Cherry 107 (10f,Lin,SD,Apr 11)
Sunset Glow 105 (12f,Sth,SW,Jan 22)
Supreme Angel 107 (6f,Wol,SW,Sep 6)

Tancred Times 107 (5f,Sth,SD,Apr 17)
Tapage 108 (7f,Lin,SW,Feb 21)
Temeraire 110 (10f,Lin,SW,Jan 31)
Teyaar 112 (5f,Wol,SD,Mar 15)
The Butterwick Kid 109 (14f,Sth,SD,Apr 10)
The Green Grey 110 (10f,Lin,SW,Feb 17)
The Prince 107 (8½f,Wol,SD,Mar 10)
Thunder Sky 107 (8½f,Wol,SD,Mar 10)
Tightrope 112 (8f,Lin,SD,Jan 10)
Tom Tun 114 (5f,Wol,SD,Feb 22)
Topton 105 (7f,Lin,SD,Nov 18)

Triphenia 108 (11f,Sth,SD,Apr 28)
Two Step 105 (7f,Lin,SD,Jan 27)

United Passion 105 (5f,Wol,SD,Nov 25)
Ursa Major 109 (9½f,Wol,SD,Dec 9)

Vasari 105 (8f,Lin,SD,Feb 3)
Vintage Premium 107 (8½f,Wol,SD,Mar 10)

Wahj 108 (8½f,Wol,SD,Mar 10)
Weet For Me 118 (11f,Sth,SD,Jan 8)
Westbound Road 108 (10f,Lin,SW,Mar 28)
Western Command 112 (11f,Sth,SD,Jan 8)
Westminster City 113 (11f,Sth,SD,Jan 8)
White Plains 115 (11f,Sth,SD,Jan 8)
Willie Conquer 112 (10f,Lin,SW,Jan 31)
Windshift 111 (11f,Sth,SD,Jan 8)
Wolf Venture 106 (8f,Lin,SD,May 11)

Xsynna 106 (6f,Sth,SD,Jun 29)

Yorker 105 (7f,Sth,SD,Jun 29)
Young-Un 109 (8f,Sth,SD,Jan 1)

Zozarharry 108 (7f,Sth,SD,Jun 29)

TWO YEAR-OLDS

Al Mohallab 109 (7f,Nby,GF,Sep 22)
Alexander Three D 106 (10f,Nmk,GS,Nov 3)
Asheer 108 (8f,Asc,S,Sep 29)

Bandari 114 (8f,Pon,S,Oct 22)
Berk The Jerk 106 (5f,Don,G,Sep 15)

Castle Gandolfo 108 (8f,Don,HY,Oct 27)
Comfy 105 (7f,Yor,G,Aug 21)
Continuously 105 (7f,Nmk,GF,Jly 29)
Coshocton 105 (8f,Asc,GS,Oct 13)

Distant Valley 110 (7f,Nmk,GS,Oct 20)
Dominica 105 (5f,Asc,GS,Oct 13)
Donegal Shore 108 (6f,Nmk,GS,Nov 2)
Dubai Destination 108 (7f,Don,GS,Sep 14)

Ellen Mooney 106 (7f,Chs,S,Sep 26)
Esligier 106 (5f,Don,GS,Sep 13)
Esloob 105 (8f,Asc,S,Sep 29)

Farqad 105 (6f,Nby,GF,Sep 21)
Fight Your Corner 110 (8f,Asc,GS,Oct 13)
Firebreak 106 (6f,Asc,GF,Jun 19)
Foreign Accent 105 (7f,Don,HY,Oct 26)

Good Girl 110 (5f,Nby,GF,Jly 21)
Gossamer 109 (8f,Asc,S,Sep 29)
Great View 107 (6f,Chp,GF,Jly 27)

Harry Jake 105 (7f,Don,GF,Aug 4)
Henri Lebasque 108 (8f,Goo,G,Sep 19)
High Chaparral 109 (8f,Don,HY,Oct 27)
High Sierra 106 (8f,Asc,S,Sep 29)

Infinite Spirit 105 (8f,Pon,S,Oct 22)
Islington 106 (7f,Nmk,G,Oct 6)

Johannesburg 111 (6f,Nmk,GS,Oct 4)

Kaieteur 107 (7f,Nby,GF,Sep 22)
King Of Happiness 109 (7f,Don,GF,Aug 4)
Kriskova 105 (8f,Goo,G,Sep 19)

Lady Links 106 (5f,Nby,GF,Jly 21)
Lahinch 109 (7f,Nmk,GS,Oct 20)
Landseer 108 (7f,Nmk,GS,Oct 20)
Leggy Lou 111 (6f,Asc,GF,Jly 28)
Love Regardless 111 (6f,Ncs,F,Sep 10)
Lupine 105 (5f,Hay,GF,Jun 9)

Mariinsky 105 (5f,Lin,GF,Aug 22)
Maryinsky 106 (8f,Asc,S,Sep 29)
Meshaheer 106 (6f,Asc,GF,Jun 19)
Misterah 108 (7f,Nmk,GS,Oct 20)
Mount Joy 107 (7f,Don,GF,Aug 4)
Mr Toad 105 (6f,Eps,GS,Aug 31)
Mubkera 106 (8f,Chp,GF,Aug 27)
Mutinyonthebounty 112 (8f,Asc,S,Sep 29)

Naheef 105 (7f,Goo,GF,Aug 1)
National Park 109 (7f,Chs,S,Sep 26)

Online Investor 108 (5f,Nby,GF,Jly 21)

Parasol 109 (8f,Asc,S,Sep 29)
Positive 105 (7f,Goo,G,Sep 26)
Prince Cyrano 106 (6f,Kem,G,Sep 7)
Protectress 107 (7f,Nmk,G,Oct 6)

Queen's Logic 114 (6f,Nmk,S,Oct 2)

Red Liason 109 (6f,Nmk,GS,Nov 2)
Red Rioja 105 (7f,Nmk,GS,Oct 20)
Redback 110 (7f,San,G,Sep 1)
Reefs Sis 107 (6f,Nmk,GS,Nov 2)
Rock Of Gibraltar 109 (7f,Nmk,GS,Oct 20)

Saddad 111 (5f,Don,G,Sep 15)
Silent Honor 107 (6f,Yor,G,Aug 23)
Snowfire 106 (7f,Nmk,G,Oct 6)
Sophisticat 109 (6f,Yor,G,Aug 23)
Sparkling Water 107 (8f,Goo,G,Sep 19)
Swiss Lake 108 (5f,Don,G,Sep 15)

Tendulkar 108 (7f,Nmk,GS,Oct 20)
Tholjanah 110 (8f,Asc,S,Sep 29)

Villa Del Sol 105 (6f,Lei,GS,Jly 19)

Where Or When 107 (7f,Nmk,GS,Oct 20)
Whitbarrow 105 (5f,Goo,GF,Aug 2)

Zipping 107 (6f,Nmk,GS,Oct 4)